P3 96
1207
1179

White Race come about
Because of a certain
incident

Pg 360 Addresses Doubt.

The Open Bible

Presented to

Rev. Alberta Basell

on this _12_ day of _October_
_1992_

May God add a blessing
to the reading of His words.

By _Myself_

Love You Much Always

The Open Bible, Expanded Edition
Copyright © 1985 by Thomas Nelson, Inc.

Holy Bible

Containing

The Old and New Testaments

in the

King James Version

The Open Bible®

EXPANDED
EDITION

with Read-along References™, Read-along Translations™
Biblical Cyclopedic Index
The Christian's Guide to the New Life
Book Introductions and Outlines
Visual Survey of the Bible
Special Study Aids.

WORDS OF CHRIST IN RED

THOMAS NELSON PUBLISHERS
Nashville

Welcome to . . .

The Open Bible®

EXPANDED
EDITION

The intent of this Study Bible is to make the Scriptures an open and rewarding book for the serious and committed Bible student, while at the same time presenting a meaningful Bible for the general reader. In combining scholarly commentary with the trusted *King James Version*, the publisher is pleased to present the labors of learned and reverent men who have sought to clarify the meaning of the Scriptures and bring the treasures of God's Holy Word into the possession of the reader. To that end, the following special features are provided.

The text is that of the *King James Version*, by far the best-selling English Bible translation of all time. Believing that the words of Scripture as originally penned in the Hebrew, Aramaic, and Greek were inspired by God, the translators gave to this version a beauty which affects the English language to this day. And since the Holy Scriptures are the eternal Word of God, the *King James Version* has spoken powerfully to generations, giving wisdom that leads to salvation, that men may serve Christ to the glory of God.

The helps and educational features found in this Bible have been prepared by eminent scholars under the supervision of Thomas Nelson Publishers. They are strictly non-sectarian. In this edition Read-along References™ and Read-along Translations™ are used to help you understand the text. The symbol "R" beside a word denotes a Read-along Reference™ which lists at the end of the verse other passages which have similar meanings or further bearing on the word or phrase indicated. This exciting cross-reference method of Bible study ties the magnificent truths of Scripture together.

The symbol "T" beside a word or phrase indicates a Read-along Translation™ and easy-to-understand equivalent, alternate, or literal translation at the end of the verse. When more than one reference or translation follows a verse, a center point "•" is used for division. When space does not allow the symbol letter (R or T) to precede the word or phrase referenced, then the symbol follows immediately at the end of the word or first word of the phrase referenced.

Immediately before each book of the Bible there is an introduction and outline of that book. These introductions are extensive and scholarly, and the outlines are designed to give the reader an overview of the book.

The period between the Old and the New Testament is treated fully and concisely in the definitive *Between the Testaments* section. This feature is designed to give the Bible student an understanding of this important period so he or she can properly relate history and the Holy Word.

The *Biblical Cyclopedic Index* is one of the major study aids in this edition. A marvel in itself, this distinctive section combines the most useful features of a concordance, reference system, and index, but it is better than any of them separately or all put together in some manner. With the *Biblical Cyclopedic Index*, the serious Bible student will find the riches of the Word unfolding in logical fashion. The busy pastor or speaker, searching the Scriptures for a message, will find the

Biblical Cyclopedic Index one of the most helpful tools to the explication of the Scriptures available in published form today.

An extremely important study feature is *The Christian's Guide to the New Life*. These twenty-eight outlines cover the major teachings of the Bible and literally help you open the Bible to the point-by-point development of each doctrine. With the study notes at the bottom of the pages, you actually cover the material of an advanced course in systematic theology, but in a much easier and clearer manner.

For convenience in Bible study, the reader is referred to the major classifications of *Bible Study Helps* found in **THE OPEN BIBLE** Expanded Edition. These helps provide a wealth of information normally found only in a complete library of books. Now they are yours in this new study Bible.

The *Bible Study Helps* section includes articles on *How to Study the Bible, Read Your Bible Through in a Year, Harmony of the Gospels,* and *Teachings and Illustrations of Jesus Christ.* Many other helps are included to make Bible study more meaningful.

The *Biblical Information* section features many items not commonly understood in the Scriptures plus countless bits of practical information in concise form. There is an extensive article, *The English Bible and Its Development,* and of special interest is the article, *The Greatest Archaeological Discoveries,* which includes scholarly discussion of the most recent archaeological finds.

Messianic Prophecies are indicated in **THE OPEN BIBLE** Expanded Edition by stars placed with the references in the appropriate passages. An *outline star* is used to indicate a prophecy later fulfilled in Jesus Christ. A *solid star* is used to indicate a prophecy that has been fulfilled in Jesus Christ.

This study edition of the Holy Bible is intended to make it an open Book to the reverent reader. It is hoped that this unique edition will truly make the Scriptures plain enough so all can have an *Open Bible.*

The Publisher

CONTRIBUTORS
to the Study Aids

KENNETH D. BOA, Ph.D.
Introductions and Outlines to the Books of the Bible and Visual Survey of the Bible, Author and Editor
Director of Publications, Search Ministries
Atlanta, Georgia

†WICK BROOMALL, A.M., Th.M.
Biblical Cyclopedic Index
Minister, Presbyterian Church
Augusta, Georgia

W. A. CRISWELL, D.D., Ph.D.
The Scarlet Thread of Redemption
Pastor, First Baptist Church
Dallas, Texas

ARTHUR L. FARSTAD, Th.D.
Consulting Editor
Bible Editor .
Dallas, Texas

PAUL R. FINK, Ed.S., Th.D.
Reader's Guide to Understanding the Bible, Contributing Editor
Professor of Pastoral Ministries,
Liberty Baptist College
Lynchburg, Virginia

BOB GREEN, Attorney
The Laws of the Bible

DONALD E. HOKE, D.D.
How to Study the Bible
Pastor, Cedar Springs Presbyterian Church
Knoxville, Tennessee

†R. G. LEE, D.D., LL.D., Ph.D.
A Guide to Christian Workers
Pastor-Evangelist
Memphis, Tennessee

MYLES LORENZEN, Th.M.
Visual Survey of the Bible, Contributor
Co-Pastor, Fellowship Bible Church
Roswell, Georgia

†Deceased

JIM BILL McINTEER, B.A.
Harmony of the Gospels
Minister, West End Church of Christ
Nashville, Tennessee

†CHARLES F. PFEIFFER, Ph.D.
Between the Testaments and Books of the Apocrypha
Professor, Central Michigan University
Mount Pleasant, Michigan

†WILBUR M. SMITH, D.D.
The English Bible and Its Development
Author and Lecturer

†MERRILL F. UNGER, Th.D., Ph.D.
The Greatest Archaeological Discoveries
Professor Emeritus, Dallas Theological
Seminary
Dallas, Texas

C. M. WARD, D.D.
A Guide to Christian Workers
Assemblies of God Radio Evangelist
Santa Cruz, California

WILLIAM WHITE, Ph.D.
The Greatest Archaeological Discoveries
Consulting Editor
Warrington, Pennsylvania

BRUCE H. WILKINSON, Th.M.
Introductions and Outlines to the Books of the Bible, Executive Editor
President, Walk Thru the Bible Ministries
Atlanta, Georgia

NEAL D. WILLIAMS, Th.D.
Reader's Guide to Understanding the Bible, Contributing Editor
Assistant Professor of Biblical Studies,
Liberty Baptist College
Lynchburg, Virginia

HAROLD L. WILLMINGTON, D.Min.
Reader's Guide to Understanding the Bible, Executive Editor
Vice President, Liberty Baptist College
Lynchburg, Virginia

CONTENTS
of the Open Bible

Books of the Old and New Testaments

EXPLANATION OF FORMAT

The format of this volume is designed to enhance the vividness and devotional quality of the Holy Scriptures and to assist the reader in personal study. To this end, special features have been incorporated both in the text of the Bible and in special study aids on each page.

Read-along™ Study Aids

Superior symbols of R or T usually precede the referenced word or phrase in the text (examples: ^Rglory, ^Tking of Israel). When space does not allow the superior symbol to precede the referenced word or phrase, the superior immediately follows the referenced word or the first word of the referenced phrase (examples: ^Rglory, ^Rking^T of Israel).

Superior R's indicate either cross-references or Messianic prophecies. These cross-references point out verses that will explain the referenced word or phrase in the text. A cross-reference in *square brackets* (example: [Deut. 12:5]) refers to a passage similar in theme or a conceptual reference to the passage in the text.

A superior R can also indicate a prophecy of the Messiah. The reference at the end of the verse will be followed by an outline or solid star. The outline star indicates a prophecy that at the time of the writing had yet to be fulfilled. The solid star indicates the fulfillment of a prophecy.

Superior T's indicate either translation notes or monies, weights, or measures. There are four kinds of *translation notes:*

— equivalent translations (in italic type with no introductory words; example: *mercy*), which are roughly similar in meaning to the translation in the text and help to clarify them;

— alternate translations (in italic type, preceded by "Or"; example: Or *mercy*), which are different from those in the text but are justified by the original languages;

— literal translations (in italic type, preceded by "Lit."; example: Lit. *mercy*); and

— notes that explain words or phrases in the text (in roman type; example: Mercy).

Words set in roman type in translation notes are explanatory only and are not translated from the original languages.

The monies, weights, or measures are conversions into modern measures of Bible terms. To further understand these calculations, turn to the article, "Monies, Weights, and Measures."

Subject headings, printed in *oblique type,* indicate the main subjects of the sections of text that follow them. These headings are not found in the original Hebrew, Aramaic, or Greek, but have been added to assist the reader in identifying topics and transitions in the biblical content. Whenever a parallel passage in Scripture exists, reference to that parallel is made with the subject heading.

The Text

Italic type in the text (example: God saw that *it was* good) indicates words that are not found in the original languages, but are needed for clarity in English.

Small Capitals in the New Testament text (example: BEHOLD, A VIRGIN SHALL CONCEIVE) indicate quotations from the Old Testament. The sources of the quotations are found in cross-references.

The covenant name of God in the Old Testament, represented by the Hebrew consonants, YHWH, is translated "Lord" or "God" (using capital letters as shown), as it has been throughout the history of the *King James Bible.*

An **OUTLINE STAR** or a **SOLID STAR** indicates a messianic reference. The outline star indicates the making of a prophecy. The solid star indicates the fulfillment of a prophecy.

SUBJECT HEADS and **PARALLEL PASSAGES** help the reader identify main subjects of the following text, and to locate parallel passages in Scripture.

ITALIC TYPE in the text indicates words not found in the original languages of Hebrew, Aramaic, or Greek, but needed for smooth English.

RED LETTER type is used in the New Testament to signify the words of Jesus Christ.

ACTS 1 — 1072

CHAPTER 1

Prologue to Acts

THE [R]former [T]treatise have I [T]made, O The-oph'-i-lus, of all that Jesus began both to do and teach,   *Luke 1:3 · book · written*

2 Until the day in which he [T]was taken up, after that he through the Holy Ghost had given commandments unto the apostles whom he had chosen: *ascended into heaven*

Appearances of the Resurrected Christ
Luke 24:44–49

3 [R]To whom also he shewed himself alive after his passion by many [T]infallible proofs, being seen of them forty days, and speaking of the things [T]pertaining to the kingdom of God: *Mark 16:14 · unmistakable · concerning*

4 And, [T]being assembled together with them, commanded them that they should not depart from Jerusalem, [R]but wait for the promise of the Father, which, *saith he,* ye have heard of me.   *when they came · Luke 24:49*

5 For John truly baptized with water; [R]but ye shall be baptized with the Holy Ghost not many days hence.   *2:4, 33; Matt. 3:11*

6 [R]When they therefore were come together, they asked of him, saying, Lord, wilt thou at this time [T]restore again the kingdom to Israel?   *Amos 9:11 · give back*

7 And he said unto them, It is not for you to know the times or the seasons, which the Father hath put in his own power.

8 [R]But ye shall receive power, after that the Holy Ghost is come upon you: and ye shall be witnesses unto me both in Jerusalem, and in all Ju-dae'-a, and in Sa-ma'-ri-a, and unto the uttermost part of the earth.

Ascension of Christ
Mark 16:19; Luke 24:50, 51

9 And when he had spoken these things, while they beheld, he was taken up; and a cloud received him out of their sight.

10 And while they looked stedfastly toward heaven as he went up, behold, two men stood by them in white apparel;

11 Which also said, Ye men of Galilee, why stand ye gazing up into heaven? this same Jesus, which is taken up from you into heaven, [R]shall so come in like manner as ye have seen him go into heaven.   *Rev. 1:7 ☆*

Anticipation of the Spirit—Luke 24:52

12 Then returned they unto Jerusalem from the mount called Olivet, which is from Jerusalem a sabbath day's journey.

13 [R]And when they were come in, they went up into an upper room, where abode both Peter, and James, and John, and Andrew, Philip, and Thomas, Bartholomew, and Matthew, James *the son of* Al-phae'-us, and Simon Ze-lo'-tes, and Judas *the brother* of James.   *Matt. 10:2–4; Luke 6:13–16*

14 These all continued [T]with one accord in prayer and supplication, with the women, and Mary the mother of Jesus, and with [R]his brethren.   *united · Matt. 13:55*

Appointment of Matthias—Matt. 27:7, 8

15 And in those days Peter [R]stood up in the midst of the disciples, and said, (the number of names together were about an hundred and twenty,)   *2:14; Luke 22:32*

16 Men *and* brethren, this scripture must needs have been fulfilled, [R]which the Holy Ghost by the mouth of David spake before concerning Judas, [R]which was guide to them that took Jesus.   *Ps. 41:9 · Luke 22:47*

17 For he was numbered with us, and had obtained part of [R]this ministry.   *v. 25*

18 [R]Now this man purchased a field with [R]the reward of iniquity; and falling headlong, he burst asunder in the midst, and all his bowels gushed out.   *Matt. 27:5 · Matt. 26:15*

19 And it was known unto all the [T]dwellers at Jerusalem; insomuch as that field is called in their proper tongue, A-cel'-da-ma, that is to say, The field of blood.   *people*

1:8 Empowered by God—One of the most common excuses for not becoming a Christian is the fear of failure to live the Christian life. Besides overlooking the fact that men cannot be saved on the basis of good works (Page 1207—Titus 3:5), this objection neglects the truth that God provides the power to live the Christian life. Before Christ was crucified He promised the coming of the Holy Spirit to help believers (Page 1061—John 16:13, 14). The subsequent events of the Book of Acts supply ample evidence of the fulfillment of this prophecy (Page 1075—Acts 4:7, 33; 6:8).

The power of the Holy Spirit was not designed solely for the first-century church. Rather, all Christians are indwelt by the Spirit and thus have His power available (Page 1129—1 Cor. 6:19). However, living the Christian life under the Spirit's power must not be thought of as simply allowing the Spirit to take control while the believer does nothing. The believer still must live the Christian life, though he does it through the Spirit's power. Romans 8:13 says, "If ye through the Spirit do mortify the deeds of the body, ye shall live." It is "ye" who are to put to death the sinful deeds of the body, but you are to do it through the Spirit's power.

The Christian who struggles in his own strength to live the Christian life will fail. He must by faith appropriate daily the power of the Holy Spirit (Page 1114—Rom. 8:4, 5). Described practically, this means that the believer trusts the Spirit to empower him in specific instances such as sharing his faith with others, resisting temptation, being faithful, etc. There is no *secret formula* that makes the Spirit's power available. It is simply a reliance on the Spirit to help.

Now turn to Page 1206—Titus 1:2: Promise of God.

THE CHRISTIAN'S GUIDE TO THE NEW LIFE is a point-by-point Bible study. The introduction leads you to the page of the first underlined verse. Detailed notes at the bottom of the page discuss the passage. Then they refer you to the next verses for study. You cover the material of an advanced course in systematic theology.

THE OPEN BIBLE

CROSS-REFERENCES, marked with a superior letter "R" in the text, point out verses using similar words of phrases.

20 For it is written in the book of Psalms, ^RLET HIS HABITATION BE DESOLATE, AND ^RLET NO MAN DWELL THEREIN: AND ^RHIS BISHOPRICK LET ANOTHER TAKE. *Ps. 69:25 • Ps. 109:8 •*

21 Wherefore of these men which have companied with us all the time that the Lord Jesus went in and out among us,

22 Beginning from the baptism of John, unto that same day that he was taken up from us, must one be ^Tordained to be a witness with us of his resurrection. *chosen*

23 And they ^Tappointed two, Joseph called ^RBar'-sa-bas, who was surnamed Justus, and Mat-thi'-as. *nominated • 15:22*

24 And they prayed, and said, Thou, Lord, which knowest the hearts of all *men,* shew whether of these two thou hast chosen,

25 ^RThat he may take ^Tpart of this ministry and apostleship, from which Judas by transgression fell, that he might go to his own ^Tplace. *v. 17 • the place in • reward*

26 And they gave forth their lots; and the lot fell upon Mat-thi'-as; and he was ^Tnumbered with the eleven apostles. *added to*

CHAPTER 2

Filling with the Holy Ghost

AND when ^Rthe day of Pentecost ^Twas fully come, ^Rthey were all with one accord in one place. *20:16 • had come • 1:14*

2 And suddenly there came a sound from heaven as of a rushing mighty wind, and it filled all the house where they were sitting.

3 And there appeared unto them ^Tcloven tongues ^Tlike as of fire, and it ^Tsat upon each of them. *divided • which looked like • rested*

4 And they were all filled with the Holy Ghost, and began to speak with other tongues, as the Spirit gave them utterance.

Speaking with Other Tongues

5 And there were dwelling at Jerusalem Jews, devout men, ^Rout of every ^Tnation under heaven. *[Zech. 2:11, 12] country • Lit. dialect*

6 Now when this was noised abroad, the multitude came together, and were ^Tconfounded, because that every man heard them speak in his own language. *disturbed*

7 And they were all amazed and marvelled, saying one to another, Behold, are not all these which ^Tspeak Gal-i-lae'-ans? *talk*

8 ^RAnd how hear we every man in our own ^Ttongue, wherein we were born? *v. 6 • Lit. dialect*

9 Par'-thi-ans, and Medes, and E'-lam-ites, and the ^Tdwellers in Mes-o-po-ta'-mi-a, and in Ju-dae'-a, and Cap-pa-do'-ci-a, in Pon'-tus, and Asia, *citizens of*

10 Phryg'-i-a, and Pam-phyl'-i-a, in Egypt, and in the parts of Lib'-y-a about Cy-re'-ne, and strangers of Rome, Jews and proselytes,

11 Cretes and A-ra'-bi-ans, we do hear them speak in our ^Ttongues the wonderful ^Tworks of God. *dialects • things God has done*

12 And they were all amazed, and were in ^Tdoubt, saying one to another, What meaneth this? *confused*

13 Others ^Tmocking said, These men are full of new wine. *made fun of the believers*

Peter Explains Pentecost

14 But Peter, standing up with the eleven, lifted up his voice, and said unto them, Ye men of Ju-dae'-a, and all *ye* that dwell at Jerusalem, be this known unto you, and ^Thearken to my words: *listen*

15 For these are not drunken, as ye suppose, ^Rseeing it is but ^Tthe third hour of the day. *1 Thess. 5:7 • 9 a.m.*

16 But this is ^Tthat which was spoken by the prophet Jo'-el; *Joel 2:28–32 • the Spirit*

17 AND IT SHALL COME TO PASS IN THE LAST DAYS, SAITH GOD, I WILL POUR OUT OF MY SPIRIT UPON ALL FLESH: AND YOUR SONS AND YOUR DAUGHTERS SHALL PROPHESY, AND YOUR YOUNG MEN SHALL SEE VISIONS, AND YOUR OLD MEN SHALL DREAM DREAMS:

18 AND ON MY SERVANTS AND ON MY HANDMAIDENS I WILL POUR OUT IN THOSE DAYS OF MY SPIRIT; AND THEY SHALL PROPHESY:

19 AND I WILL SHEW WONDERS IN HEAVEN ABOVE, AND SIGNS IN THE EARTH BENEATH; BLOOD, AND FIRE, AND VAPOUR OF SMOKE:

20 THE SUN SHALL BE TURNED INTO DARKNESS, AND THE MOON INTO BLOOD, BEFORE THAT GREAT AND NOTABLE DAY OF THE LORD COME:

21 AND IT SHALL COME TO PASS, THAT WHOSOEVER SHALL CALL ON THE NAME OF THE LORD SHALL BE SAVED.

22 Ye men of Israel, hear these words; Jesus of Nazareth, ^Ra man approved of God among you by miracles and wonders and signs, which God did by him in the midst of you, as ye yourselves also know: *Is. 50:5 •*

23 Him, ^Rbeing delivered by the determinate counsel and foreknowledge of God, ^Rye have taken, and by wicked hands have crucified and slain: *Matt. 26:24; Luke 22:22 • 5:30*

24 Whom God hath raised up, having loosed the pains of death: because it was not possible that he should be holden of it.

25 For David speaketh concerning him, ^RI FORESAW THE LORD ALWAYS BEFORE MY FACE; FOR HE IS ON MY RIGHT HAND, THAT I SHOULD NOT BE ^TMOVED: *Ps. 16:8–11 • • troubled*

26 THEREFORE DID MY HEART REJOICE, AND MY TONGUE WAS GLAD; MOREOVER ALSO MY FLESH SHALL REST IN HOPE:

27 BECAUSE THOU WILT NOT LEAVE MY SOUL IN HELL, NEITHER WILT THOU SUFFER THINE HOLY ONE TO SEE CORRUPTION.

28 THOU HAST MADE KNOWN TO ME THE WAYS OF LIFE; THOU SHALT MAKE ME FULL OF JOY WITH THY COUNTENANCE.

Type set in **SMALL CAPITALS** indicates text in the New Testament quoting the Old Testament.

The superior letter "T" in the text and italic type in the reference indicate an **EQUIVALENT TRANSLATION** which explains the text word.

CONCEPTUAL REFERENCES are cross-references in square brackets. They refer to passages similar in concept.

LITERAL TRANSLATION for a particular word or phrase is denoted with a superior letter "T" and the abbreviation "Lit." in the note.

ABBREVIATIONS

bu.	bushel, bushels	**in.**	inch, inches
c.	approximately	**lb.**	pound, pounds
cf.	compare	**lit.**	literally
ch., chs.	chapter, chapters	**ms., mss.**	manuscript, manuscripts
DSS	Dead Sea Scrolls	**masc.**	masculine
e.g.	for example	**mi.**	mile, miles
fem.	feminine	**oz.**	ounce, ounces
f., ff.	following verse, following verses	**pl.**	plural
		pt.	pint, pints
ft.	foot, feet	**qt.**	quart, quarts
gal.	gallon, gallons	**v., vv.**	verse, verses
Gr.	Greek	**vss.**	versions—ancient translations of the Bible
Heb.	Hebrew		
i.e.	that is		

HOW TO STUDY THE BIBLE

The Bible is the greatest book ever written. In it God Himself speaks to men. It is a book of divine instruction. It offers comfort in sorrow, guidance in perplexity, advice for our problems, rebuke for our sins, and daily inspiration for our every need.

The Bible is not simply one book. It is an entire library of books covering the whole range of literature. It includes history, poetry, drama, biography, prophecy, philosophy, science, and inspirational reading. Little wonder, then, that all or part of the Bible has been translated into more than 1,200 languages, and every year more copies of the Bible are sold than any other single book.

The Bible alone truly answers the greatest questions that men of all ages have asked: **"Where have I come from?" "Where am I going?" "Why am I here?" "How can I know the truth?"** For the Bible reveals the truth about God, explains the origin of man, points out the only way to salvation and eternal life, and explains the age-old problem of sin and suffering.

The great theme of the Bible is the Lord Jesus Christ and His work of redemption for mankind. The person and work of Jesus Christ are promised, prophesied, and pictured in the types and symbols of the Old Testament. In all of His truth and beauty, the Lord Jesus Christ is revealed in the Gospels; and the full meanings of His life, His death, and His resurrection are explained in the Epistles. His glorious coming again to earth in the future is unmistakably foretold in the Book of Revelation. The great purpose of the written Word of God, the Bible, is to reveal the living Word of God, the Lord Jesus Christ (read John 1:1–18).

Dr. Wilbur M. Smith relates seven great things that the study of the Bible will do for us:

1. The Bible discovers sin and convicts us.
2. The Bible helps cleanse us from the pollutions of sin.
3. The Bible imparts strength.
4. The Bible instructs us in what we are to do.
5. The Bible provides us with a sword for victory over sin.
6. The Bible makes our lives fruitful.
7. The Bible gives us power to pray.

You do not need a whole library of books to study the Bible. The Bible is its own best commentator and interpreter. With all of the instructive helps that you have in this new Bible, you have a whole lifetime of Bible study.

I. Personal Bible Study

A. Devotional Bible Study

The Bible is not an end in itself, but is a means to the end of knowing God and doing His will. The apostle Paul said, "Study to shew thyself approved unto God, a workman that needeth not to be ashamed, rightly dividing the word of truth" (**2 Tim. 2:15**). God has given us the Bible in order that we might know Him and that we might do His will here on earth.

Therefore, devotional Bible study is the most important kind of Bible study. Devotional Bible study means reading and studying the Word of God in order that we may hear God's voice and that we may know how to do His will and to live a better Christian life (see page 832).

A great scientist and medical doctor, Dr. Howard A. Kelly (Professor of Gynecology at Johns Hopkins University from 1889 through 1940), was also an avid student of the Bible. He once said: "The very best way to study the Bible is simply to read it daily with close attention and with prayer to see the light that shines from its pages, to meditate upon it, and to continue to read it until somehow it works itself, its words, its expressions, its teachings, its habits of thought, and its presentation of God and His Christ into the very warp and woof of one's being."

For your devotional reading and study of the Bible, here are several important, practical suggestions:

1. Begin your Bible reading with prayer (**Ps. 119:18; John 16:13,14,15**).

2. Take brief notes on what you read. Keep a small notebook for your Bible study (see number 4 below).

3. Read slowly through one chapter, or perhaps two or three chapters, or perhaps just one paragraph at a time. After reading, ask yourself what this passage means. Then reread it.

4. It is often very helpful in finding out the true meaning of a chapter or passage to ask yourself the following questions, then write the answers in your notebook:

  a. What is the main subject of this passage?

  b. Who are the persons revealed in this passage: Who is speaking? About whom is he speaking? Who is acting?

  c. What is the key verse of this passage?

  d. What does this passage teach me about the Lord Jesus Christ?

  e. Does this passage portray any sin for me to confess and forsake?

  f. Does this passage contain any command for me to obey?

  g. Is there any promise for me to claim?

  h. Is there any instruction for me to follow?

Not all of these questions may be answered in every passage.

5. Keep a spiritual diary. Either in your Bible study notebook mentioned above (number 2), or in a separate notebook entitled, "My Spiritual Diary," write down daily what God says to you

through the Bible. Write down the sins that you confess or the commands you should obey.

6. Memorize passages of the Word of God. No one is ever too old to memorize the Word of God. Write verses on cards with the reference on one side and the verse on the other. Carry these cards with you and review them while you're waiting for a train, standing in lunch line, etc.

Other persons prefer to memorize whole passages or chapters of the Bible. A small pocket Bible will help you to review these passages when you have spare moments. One of the best ways is to spend a few minutes every night before going to sleep, in order that your subconscious mind may help you fix these passages of God's Word in your mind while you're asleep (**Ps. 119:11**).

To meditate means "to reflect, to ponder, to consider, to dwell in thought." Through meditation the Word of God will become meaningful and real to you, and the Holy Spirit will use this time to apply the Word of God to your own life and its problems.

7. Obey the Word of God. As Paul said to Timothy in Second Timothy 3:16: "All scripture *is* given by inspiration of God, and *is* profitable for doctrine, for reproof, for correction, for instruction in righteousness." The Bible has been given to us that we may live a holy life, well-pleasing to God. Therefore God says, "But be ye doers of the word, and not hearers only" (**James 1:22**).

8. The Navigators, a group of men banded together just before World War II to encourage Bible study among Christian servicemen, developed a splendid plan for a personal, devotional study.

    a. After prayer, first read the Bible passage slowly and silently; then read it again aloud.

    b. In a large notebook divide the paper into columns and head each column as follows: Chapter title, Key verse, Significant truth, Cross-references, Difficulties in this passage (personal or possible), Application to me, and Summary or outline of the passage. In each of these columns, write the information desired.

Do not try to adopt all of these methods at once, but start out slowly, selecting those methods and suggestions which appeal to you. You will find, as millions of others have before you, that the more you read and study the Word of God, the more you'll want to read it. Therefore, the following suggestions of Bible study are made for those who wish to make a more intensive study of the Bible truths.

B. Study for Bible Knowledge

There are many valuable methods of Bible study. One may study the Bible, as if with a telescope, to see the great truths which stand out in every book. Or one may study the Bible as if with a microscope to find all of the marvelous details which are in this mine of spiritual riches. In this section there are several proven methods with which a person may conduct more intensive Bible study. The most important thing is to follow faithfully some systematic method of Bible study.

Bible Study by Chapters. In the Bible there are 1,189 chapters in the Old and New Testaments. In a little over three years, a person could make an intensive study of the whole Bible, taking a chapter a day. It is usually a good practice to start your Bible study in the New Testament.

1. Read through the chapter carefully, seeking to find its main subject or subjects.

2. As you read each chapter, give it a title which suggests its main content. If you are reading the Gospel of John, for example, you might give each chapter titles like this:

    ch. 1 "Jesus Christ, the Word of God"
    ch. 2 "The Wedding at Cana"
    ch. 3 "The New Birth"
    ch. 4 "The Woman at the Well"
    ch. 5 "The Healing of the Man at the Pool of Bethesda"

3. Reread the chapter again and make a simple outline which will include its main thoughts. For example in **John 1,** you might make an outline like this:

"Jesus Christ, the Word of God":

    a. Jesus Christ was the eternal Word of God, **1–9.**

    b. Jesus Christ came into the world, **10–18.**

    c. John witnesses that Christ is to come, **19–28.**

    d. John says that Jesus is the Lamb of God, **29–37.**

    e. Jesus Christ calls His first disciples, **38–51.**

4. Concerning each chapter, ask and answer the questions suggested in item number 4 of devotional Bible study hints above. Especially take note of any practical or theological problems in this chapter. Then, using your concordance, look up the key words in those verses and find out what other portions of the Bible say about this question or problem. Compare Scripture with Scripture to find its true meaning. Usually, to understand an important Bible chapter, you must study it together with the preceding or following chapters.

Bible Study by Paragraphs. A paragraph is several sentences of thought in writing. When an author changes the subject of emphasis in writing, he usually begins a new paragraph. (In this Bible, use the outline headings in the text as paragraph breaks, subdividing when appropriate.) Studying the Bible by paragraphs like this is often called analytic Bible study.

1. Read the paragraph carefully for its main thought or subject.

2. In order to find the relation of the important words and sentences in this paragraph, it is often helpful to rewrite the text. For example, if you were going to study the paragraph on prayer in

the Sermon on the Mount found in **Matthew 6:5–8,** you could rewrite this text:

"And when thou prayest, thou shalt not be as the hypocrites *are:* for they love to pray standing in the synagogues and in the corners of the streets, that they may be seen of men. Verily I say unto you, They have their reward.

"But thou, when thou prayest, enter into thy closet, and when thou hast shut thy door, pray to thy Father which is in secret; and thy Father which seeth in secret shall reward thee openly.

"But when ye pray, use not vain repetitions, as the heathen *do:* for they think that they shall be heard for their much speaking.

"Be not ye therefore like unto them: for your Father knoweth what things ye have need of, before ye ask him."

3. From the text which you've now rewritten so that you can see the relationship of the various parts of the paragraph, it is easy to make a simple outline. For example, using **Matthew 6:5–15,** your outline of this passage would be something like this:

"Jesus Teaches Us How to Pray"—**Matthew 6:5–15.**
   a. How not to pray: **Matthew 6:5–8**
      (1) Hypocritically in public, **6:5**
      (2) With useless repetition, **6:7, 8**
   b. How to pray: **Matthew 6:6, 9–13**
      (1) In private to your heavenly Father, **6:6**
      (2) Following the pattern of Jesus' model prayer, **6:9–13**

4. It is helpful also to look up in the concordance important words that occur in this paragraph. For example, the words "hypocrites," "heathen," etc. By comparing other passages of the Bible which teach about prayer, you'll be kept from making any mistakes concerning the true nature, conditions, and results of prayer according to the will of God.

Bible Study by Verses. In studying the historical passages of the Bible, such as most of the Old Testament or parts of the Gospels, each verse may have only one simple meaning.

But many verses in both the Old and New Testaments are rich with many great Bible truths which will demand more detailed study. There are many ways that you can study a single Bible verse.

1. Study it by the verbs in the verse. For example, if you were studying **John 3:16** you would find the following verbs: "loved . . . gave . . . should not perish . . . have . . ."

You could make a comparative list like this:
God loved   Man believes
God gave   Man shall not perish
             Man has everlasting life

Or simply take the nouns in this wonderful verse: "God . . . world . . . only begotten Son . . . whosoever . . . everlasting life."

2. Study a verse through the personalities re-

vealed. For example, once again taking **John 3:16,** these very simple but significant points are brought to light: "God . . . only begotten Son . . . whosoever . . . him."

3. Study a verse by looking for the great ideas revealed in it. Let us look again at **John 3:16** as our example. We might title this verse, "The greatest verse in the Bible." The following ideas are found in it:
   "God"—the greatest person
   "so loved"—the greatest devotion
   "the world"—the greatest number
   "he gave"—the greatest act
   "his only begotten Son"—the greatest gift
   "that whosoever believeth"—the greatest condition
   "should not perish"—the greatest mercy
   "have everlasting life"—the greatest result

4. Sometimes a combination of these various ideas applied to a verse will bring the richest results. For example, take **Romans 5:1:**
   "Therefore"—This verse depends on **4:25.** Our justification is based on and is guaranteed by Jesus' resurrection.
   "justified"—made righteous.
   "by faith"—method of our justification (see also **3:24; 4:9).**
   "have"—not future, but present tense—we have this *now.*
   "peace with God"—We were enemies, but now there is peace between us and God because of what Christ has done.
   "through our Lord Jesus Christ"—The way to peace with God is only through Jesus Christ.

Bible Study by Books. After you have begun to study the Bible by chapters or paragraphs or verses, you will be ready to study the Bible by books.

1. There are several methods of Bible book study.
   a. One is called the inductive method. This is a method of studying in detail the contents of a Bible book and then drawing from these details general conclusions or principles concerning the contents and purpose of the book.
   b. Another method of book study is called the synthetic method. By this method, one reads the Bible book over several times to receive the general impressions of the main ideas and purpose of the book without attention to the details. (It is sometimes hard to distinguish these two methods.)
   c. In some cases the study of a Bible book becomes a historical study, if that book relates the history of a nation or a man in a particular period of time. For example, the Book of Exodus tells the history of the children of Israel from the death of Joseph in Egypt until the erection of the tabernacle in

the wilderness in the time of Moses. This covers approximately 400 years.

2. Here are some methods for Bible study by books:

a. Read the book through to get the perspective and the general emphasis of the book.

b. Reread the book many times, each time asking yourself a relevant question and jotting down the answers you find as you read. Here are the most important questions to ask:

First reading: What is the central theme or emphasis of this book? What is the key verse?

Second reading: Remembering the theme of the book, see how it is emphasized and developed. Look for any special problems or applications.

Third reading: What does it tell me about the author and his circumstances when he wrote this book?

Fourth reading: What does the book tell me about the people to whom the book was written and their circumstances, need, or problems?

Fifth reading: What are the main divisions of the book? Is there any outline apparent in the logical organization and development of the book? During this reading, divide the text into the paragraphs as you see them and then give a title to each paragraph. Draw a line down the right side of the outline and on the other side write any problems, questions, words, or ideas that require further study by comparison with other passages in the Bible.

Sixth and successive readings: Look for other facts and/or information that your earlier readings have suggested. By now certain words will stand out in the book. See how often they recur. (For example, as you read the book of Philippians, you will soon find that the word "joy" occurs many times. This is one of the key words of the book, so note its occurrences and the circumstances surrounding it.)

As you read and reread a book, you'll find that you begin to see its structure and its outline very clearly. It is true, however, that there are other outlines for any given book. It depends on the principle of division that you select. For example, as you study the Book of Romans, you might adopt the outline that Dr. G. Allen Fleece, president of Columbia Bible College, has written:

The Book of Romans
Subject: "The Gospel" 1:16
  I. The Gospel for the lost sinner, 1—5
  II. The Gospel for the Christian, 6—8
  III. The Gospel for the whole world, 9—11

IV. The Gospel applied to daily living, 12—16

Of course, each of these great sections of this remarkable book can be divided into smaller subjects with great profit.

This method, applied to a book which is mainly historical, will also enable you to find a clear outline. In the case of a historical book, the outline will be largely chronological. The Book of Acts lends itself to this kind of study and outline.

The Book of Acts
Subject: "The Gospel Witness in the First Century"
Key verse: 1:8
Outline:
  I. Introduction: The apostles receive power, 1:1—2:4
  II. The witness in Jerusalem, 2:5—7:60
  III. The witness in Judaea and Samaria, 8:1—11:18
  IV. The beginning of the witness to the end of the earth, 11:19—28:31

Once again more careful study will give the details and further subdivisions of each of these great units of gospel history in this inspired record of the origin of the Christian church.

Bible Study by Words. There are two profitable and helpful ways of studying great words or subjects in the Word of God.

1. Word study by Bible books. Certain words have special significance in certain Bible books. For example, after studying the Gospel of John as a book and by chapters, you'll find it instructive and inspiring to trace the words "believe" and "belief." They occur almost 100 times. By reading the book hurriedly and underlining each passage where the words "believe" and "belief" occur, you'll understand why Bible scholars contend that the purpose of the Gospel of John is expressed by the author in John 20:31.

2. General word study. The fine index and concordance in this Bible will be a great help. Through the study of great Bible words, you can soon become familiar with the great doctrines of the Bible and understand the great theological principles which the Bible reveals.

With the concordance you might begin with the study of the word "grace." By tracing the occurrences of this word through the Old Testament and then into the New Testament, you will come to see that God has always dealt with His people in grace, and you will find in a concrete way the great truth of Ephesians 2:8.

Bible Study by Topics. Closely related to the method of study by words is the study according to great topics or subjects: Bible prayers, Bible promises, Bible sermons, Bible songs, Bible poems, etc.

Or one might study Bible geography by read-

ing rapidly through and looking for rivers, seas, and mountains highlighted in Scripture. For example, the mountain-top experiences in the life of Abraham are a thrilling study.

Another challenging study is to read rapidly through the Gospels and Epistles looking for the commands of the Lord to us. The list of Bible topics is unlimited.

First, for a topical study on prayer, look up the word "prayer" or "pray" in your concordance. Look up every form of these words and such related words as "ask," "intercession," etc. After you have looked up these verses, study them and bring together all the teaching on prayer that you find. You will find conditions of prayer, words to be used in prayer, results to expect from prayer, when to pray, and where to pray.

Bible Study Through Biography. The Bible is a record of God's revealing Himself to men and through men. The Old Testament as well as the New is rich in such biographical studies. Here are a few:

The life of Noah: Genesis 5:32—10:32
The life of Abraham: Genesis 12—25
The life of Joseph: Genesis 37—50
The life of Deborah: Judges 4; 5

Let us summarize various methods for studying the great Bible biographies:

1. Read the Bible book or passages in which this person's life is prominent, e.g., Abraham in **Genesis 12—25**, plus references to Abraham in **Hebrews 11** and **Romans 4.**

2. Trace a character with the Biblical Cyclopedic Index or a concordance.

3. Be careful to note indirect references to the person in other portions of Scripture.

Conclusion. There are many other methods of studying the Bible: the psychological method, the sociological method, the cultural method, the philosophical method, etc. Use all the Bible study methods suggested above. From time to time, change your method so that you'll not become too accustomed to any one method or tired from delving too deeply into one type of study.

II. Family Bible Study

Nothing is more important in a Christian home than the family altar. At a convenient time when all members of the family are home, father or mother should lead them in worship of God and in reading His Word. A simple program for family worship includes singing a hymn, an opening prayer by a family member, a brief Bible study, and a concluding period of prayer in which all members take part.

The family altar and Bible study will bind the family together, eliminate juvenile delinquency, foster deeper love, and enable each member to become a stronger, better Christian. Since family Bible study usually includes small children, it is wise to avoid deep, difficult topics and study

something of interest and help to all. Such subjects might be Bible biographies as outlined above, stories of miracles and deeds of Jesus as revealed in the Gospels, miracles in the Old Testament, and other narrative portions of the Bible. It is wise to keep the study brief and concentrate on a short passage of Scripture. For example, if the family is going to study the life of Moses, it could be divided into units like this:

First day: The birth of Moses: Exodus 2:1–10
Second day: Moses' great choice and great mistake: Hebrews 11:24–27; Exodus 2:11–15
Third day: Moses' wilderness training: Exodus 2:16–25
Fourth day: Moses' call to serve God: Exodus 3:1–22
Fifth day: Moses' argument with God: Exodus 4:1–17
Sixth day: Moses' return to Egypt: Exodus 4:18–31

Here are several practical hints on how to make your family Bible study interesting and profitable to all:

1. Keep your family Bible study reasonably short: one brief chapter or several paragraphs a day.

2. Have each member read a verse.

3. Appoint one family member to lead in worship each day and select the passage to read. This one may appoint others to help in the family worship.

4. Read through a Bible book, a chapter, or several paragraphs each day. As you read, together decide on a name or a title for each chapter and memorize this.

5. After reading the passage, have each member in the family explain one verse or one paragraph.

6. Let the leader (or the father or mother) prepare five or ten questions on the Bible passage and ask various members of the family to answer these questions after the passage has been read.

7. Study the beautiful maps in your Bible together and trace Paul's journeys or the wandering of the children of Israel in Egypt.

8. Study Bible topics together. Assign verses concerning a topic or great word to each member of the family. Let each read a verse and tell what the verse teaches about the topic or word.

9. After the Bible reading, have each member tell what this verse means or how it can be applied to personal life.

10. Make up Bible games by having each member make up questions to try to stump the others.

11. Study a Bible book together, using the hints given above. There are many wonderful ways to make the Bible the heart of your home.

III. Principles of Bible Interpretation

Since the Bible was written by many men over

a period covering 1,500 years, and since the last author of the Bible has been dead 1,900 years, there are definite problems in understanding the exact meaning of certain passages of the Bible.

There is a need to interpret clearly certain passages of the Bible because there is a gap between the way we think and the words we use today and the way of thinking and the words that these Bible writers used thousands of years ago. Bible scholars have pointed out that there are language gaps—differences in words that we use; there are cultural gaps—different customs were in vogue then. There are geographical gaps—certain rivers that are spoken of in the Bible have long since dried up. Some places that are spoken of frequently in the Bible are not on our modern maps. And then there are historical gaps—the Bible speaks of kings and empires which existed years ago.

Therefore, there is a need for Bible interpretation. This is a fascinating study in itself, but I want to give you just a few principles of interpretation of the Bible that will keep you from error and help you understand the difficult passages of the Word of God.

1. Always remember that the Bible is God's infallible, inerrantly inspired Word. There are no mistakes in the Bible. God has included everything in the Bible that He wants you to know and is necessary for you to know concerning salvation and your Christian life.

2. The second principle of interpretation is to interpret the Bible in the light of its historical background. There are three aspects of this:

   a. Study the personal circumstances of the writer. In studying the Book of the Revelation, it is important to understand where John was and what he was doing when God gave him this marvelous revelation. See **Revelation 1:1–10.**

   b. The second aspect of this principle is to study the culture and customs of the country at the time that the writing or story was taking place. For example, to understand the Book of Ruth, it is important to study the customs concerning widows, redemption of property, etc., as they are explained in **Leviticus 25** and **Deuteronomy 25.**

   c. A third aspect of this principle is to study and interpret the Bible in the light of the actual historical situation and events that were taking place at the time of the story. For example, in studying the Gospels it is important to realize that the entire land of

Palestine and all of the Jews were being governed and oppressed by the Roman Empire at that time.

3. Interpret the Bible according to the purpose and plan of each book.

Every Bible book has its specific purpose intended by the Holy Spirit to bring some special message to man. For example, it is important to remember that **First John** (see **1 John 5:13**) was written to Christians. Therefore the promise in **First John 1:9** is specifically applied to Christians.

4. One of the most important principles of interpretation is always to interpret according to the context of a verse.

The "context" includes the verses immediately preceding and immediately following the verse you are studying. If you do not take care to interpret the verse according to the context, you could make the Bible teach atheism. For the Bible itself says, "There is no God" (**Ps. 14:1**). But the context makes very clear what this verse means: The entire sentence says, "The fool hath said in his heart, There is no God."

Always study the passage immediately preceding and immediately following any verse, word, or topic to make sure that you see this truth in the setting which God intended.

5. Always interpret according to the correct meaning of words. You can find the correct meaning of a word in several ways. First of all, look up the usage of the word in other parts of the Bible to find how it was used in that generation. Another way is to look up its background or its root. You could do this with the use of a dictionary. Still another way is to look up the synonyms—words that are similar in meaning but slightly different: for example, "prayer," "intercession," "supplication."

6. Also interpret the Bible according to all of the parallel passages which deal with the subject and according to the message of the entire Bible.

The more you read the Bible, the more you will understand that in it God is revealing His way of salvation to men from beginning to end. And when you come to a difficult passage, think of it in the light of the overall purpose of the Bible. For example, the animal sacrifices of the Old Testament are meant to be a picture of the perfect sacrifice of Jesus Christ on the cross.

If you will follow these simple rules, you will be kept from error and extremes, and you will be helped to understand correctly the teachings of even the more difficult passages in God's Word.

THE CHRISTIAN'S GUIDE TO THE NEW LIFE

The Christian's Guide to the New Life offers a complete doctrinal overview of the Bible to assist you in a practical, simplified way to study your Bible. The six main areas of study, described below, are further amplified; these systematically cover all the important areas of biblical theology. This unique study feature places before the Bible student an exegesis of Scripture with hundreds of Scriptural references.

For the student just beginning Bible study, *The Christian's Guide to the New Life* covers in a fundamental way how to become a Christian, then steps the believer through the Christian life. The easy-to-use references and cross-references lead the reader toward a comprehensive, practical knowledge of God's Word.

The general organization of *The Christian's Guide to the New Life* includes six main areas of study:

Knowing God's Word
Understanding God's Being
Beginning the New Life
Growing in the New Life
Facing Problems in the New Life
Recognizing God's Institutions

These areas of study are subdivided into twenty-eight individual **Christian's Guides** with appropriate Bible references. All the material is organized in a simple format to assist you in more easily understanding the Bible, the inspired Word of God. Each numbered Christian's Guide has several discussions of Bible texts appearing on the page where the text occurs. For example, within the main area of study **Knowing God's Word** is Christian's Guide (1) **How God's Word Came to Us.** There are three discussions concerning how God's Word came to us: on page 207 is **Revelation of God's Word;** on page 699 is **Inspiration of God's Word;** and on page 618 is **Illumination of God's Word.**

This article, *The Christian's Guide to Understanding the Bible,* will serve as a general introduction, index, and guide to the various Christian's Guides. Each time you study one of the discussions in the Bible the last line will tell you where to turn for the next discussion. When you finish a main area of study, such as **Knowing God's Word,** the last line in the last discussion will tell you to turn to this article, *The Christian's Guide to the New Life.* Then, after reading the synopsis of the next main area of study, you will be ready to turn to the first discussion and follow the development of that area of study.

The Christian's Guide to the New Life can be used in three easy ways: for monthly study, daily study, and topical study.

- Monthly study—once a day for twenty-eight days study one of the numbered Christian's Guides. Read each of the discussions and look up the listed references.
- Daily study—once a day for 105 days study a single discussion in the Bible text. Read the complete discussion and look up the listed references.
- Topical study—using this article, *The Christian's Guide to Understanding the Bible,* as an index, study individual Christian's Guides and discussions as the need arises.

You are now ready to begin using *The Christian's Guide to the New Life.* For each of the six main areas of study a synopsis and an organization are provided. For each of the Christian's Guides page numbers and Scripture references are provided to help you find the various discussions in the Bible.

Knowing God's Word

Synopsis

Christians should know the Bible for many reasons, but the primary one is because God is its Author. All Bible students know that God is Creator (Gen. 1:1), Redeemer (Is. 60:16), and Judge (Gen. 18:25), but do we think of Him as the Author of the Bible? Human writers feel it vital that we read their books; it is much more important that we read God's book, the Bible.

About fourteen centuries before Christ, our Bible had its beginnings in the Sinai desert. In this arid place God spoke to Moses, who had once been a prince in Egypt and was nearly 120 years old at the time. At the Lord's command, Moses picked up his pen and began writing Scripture's first five books, Genesis through Deuteronomy. More than 1,500 years later, the divine manuscript was completed on a lonely, windswept island in the Mediterranean Sea by a former fisherman, John the apostle. From Genesis through Revelation, the final biblical book, there are sixty-six divinely inspired books. Over the centuries, approximately forty men and women—representing varied backgrounds and writing styles—served as channels for God's Word. Yet, in spite of these variations in time and talent, the completed work displays a marvelous historical, theological, geographical, topical, and biographical unity.

The Bible's practical benefits for us may well be summarized under two headings: knowing and growing. The Bible proclaims the good news of the gospel that we might know God; it explains

the will of God that all of us may grow spiritually before Him.

Scripture also reveals our place within God's program and answers crucial questions pertaining to our origin, purpose, and destiny. Because God has revealed His unchanging truths, the Christian faith provides real answers and guidance to every generation. Although we cannot grasp how individual events fit into God's program (Eccl. 11:5), we can understand God's basic plan in order to come to know and serve Him. Few joys can compare with realizing our places in God's program and working to fulfill our destinies.

Organization

Understanding God's Being

Synopsis

The Bible reveals the nature of God as spirit, unity, and trinity. He is a spirit—a personal, infinite being (John 4:24); He is one—one in substance or nature and incapable of being divided into separate parts (Deut. 6:4); and He is three—eternally existing in three coequal persons (Matt. 28:19). While great mystery surrounds God's nature, it is reassuring to know that our God is above us.

God's attributes are merely words we use to describe how God is and how He acts toward us. Among these attributes are love, holiness, constancy, justice, truth, eternality, omniscience (all-knowing), omnipresence (all-present), and omnipotence (all-powerful). The fact that we can grasp and understand this much about God is evidence of God's desire that all peoples may know Him.

The word *Father* is variously applied in the Bible. When God is spoken of as the Father of all men, it is as Creator; as the Father of Christ, it expresses an eternal, unique relationship; as the Father of believers, it denotes a relationship established by grace; and as Father of Israel, it means a bond established by covenant. However Father is used, it is a deliberately chosen word to communicate to men one of the primary ways God wants us to conceive of Him.

The title *Son of God* is one which Jesus never directly applied to Himself, but when others applied it to Him Jesus willingly accepted it as a claim to His own deity (John 10:24–38). Jesus often referred to Himself as "the Son," which was certainly an abbreviation for the Son of God. How significant is this term to the Christian? It is very important, because it helps establish some major truths without which we would be left with little evidence that the words of Jesus Christ were actually true. It can be said that as our relationship with the Son of God determines whether we will become Christians, our relationship with the Spirit of God determines what kind of believers we will be.

Organization

Beginning the New Life

Synopsis

Mankind is by nature sinful and needs the righteousness of God. We must be separated from sin and set apart to righteousness. If we are to approach God, we must do so on God's terms—we must have new lives in which our sins have been forgiven and obliterated.

It is one thing to be convinced of the need for the new life, but it is an entirely different thing to acquire the new life. When we are "saved" we are said to be new creatures (2 Cor. 5:17); to have passed from death to life (John 5:24); to have been transferred from the rule of darkness to the kingdom of God's Son (Col. 1:13); to have been born again (John 3:3); and to have been adopted by God (Gal. 4:4, 5). These wonderful results of having new life in Christ are offered freely to all who trust in Christ for salvation.

One of the most thrilling benefits of finding new life in Christ is "everlasting [eternal] life." We enter a new, personal relationship with God that gives us a fullness of spiritual vitality, and this new life is a gift which will never die. God can accomplish a life-changing transformation for all who truly believe in Christ.

Organization

Growing in the New Life

Synopsis

Knowing how to grow in the new life is essential. The old adage is ever true: "Sin will keep you from God's Word, and God's Word will keep you from sin."

No factor in Christian growth is more important than prayer. Prayer may be defined as talking with and listening to God. We talk to Him with our lips and heart, and He talks to us through His will. It involves a two-way conversation. Spiritual maturity is impossible without systematic prayer.

Worship is essential also to spiritual growth. Worship involves honor and respect toward God, the ceremony of private and public worship, and the joyful service of Christians to their Lord. Christians who submit to the lordship of Christ in reverence and service will grow in their spiritual lives.

The Bible describes Christian life as "[walking] in the Spirit" (Gal. 5:16). Walking best represents the step-by-step character of the spiritual life. Living by the Spirit's power is a moment-by-moment yielding to the Spirit's will and control. The evidence that we are walking in the Spirit is simply the display of the fruit of the Spirit (Gal. 5:22, 23). Walking in the Spirit involves confession of sin, yielding to God, and being filled with or controlled by the Spirit.

Organization

Confession
Page 1249—1 John 1:9
Petition
Page 276—1 Sam. 1:17
Thanksgiving
Page 1172—Phil. 4:6
Commitment
Page 625—Prov. 16:3

15. Stewardship
Using Spiritual Gifts
Page 1134—1 Cor. 12:1–10
Serving
Page 1157—Gal. 5:13
Giving
Page 1148—2 Cor. 9:6–8

16. Worship
The Meaning of Worship
Page 412—1 Chr. 16:29
The Expressions of Worship
Page 1224—Heb. 13:15
The Reasons for Worship
Page 444—2 Chr. 7:3

17. Participation in the Local Church
Definition of the Local Church
Page 1121—Rom. 16:5
Reasons for Participation in the Local
   Church
Page 1221—Heb. 10:25
Benefits of Participation in the Local
   Church
Page 1074—Acts 2:42–47

18. Sharing Our Faith
Sharing Our Faith: Why?
Page 974—Matt. 28:19
Sharing Our Faith: What?
Page 1137—1 Cor. 15:3, 4
Sharing Our Faith: How?
Page 1183—1 Thess. 1:5
Sharing Our Faith: When?
Page 1202—2 Tim. 4:2

19. Walking in the Spirit
Walking in the Spirit: Confession
Page 578—Ps. 73:1
Walking in the Spirit: Yielding
Page 1118—Rom. 12:1
Walking in the Spirit: Filling
Page 1158—Eph. 5:18

Facing Problems in the New Life

Synopsis

Just as we have problems in our physical lives, we also experience problems in our spiritual or new lives. Facing and conquering difficulties cause us to grow and be strengthened, whether those problems are physical or spiritual. As we grow in our new strength, we bring glory to God as He demonstrates His faithfulness and that His grace is sufficient for every need (2 Cor. 12:9).

Some of the problems that are common in the new life are sin, temptation, suffering, knowing the will of God, and doubt.

A believer must be especially wary of places, situations, and times in which he or she may be vulnerable to temptation. Certainly the best antidote to temptation is to be a growing Christian. The mind that is occupied with the things of the Lord cannot at the same time be susceptible to temptation.

Of all the possible sins against God, the most serious is that of self-will. This sin led to the fall of Satan (Is. 14:12–14), and it can be said to be the root of Adam's transgression (Gen. 3:1–7). It is, therefore, of utmost importance that the child of God find His will and perform it.

The dismissal of doubt and strengthening of faith are best accomplished by reading and understanding the Word of God (Rom. 10:17). The Holy Spirit will convict the willing heart of its power. Growing in the Word produces growth in faith; reading and understanding the Word are like planting seeds of faith in the heart. They will bear the mature fruit of faith.

Organization

20. Sin
What Sin Is
Page 569—Ps. 51:2
What Sin Does
Page 698—Is. 59:2
What Should Be Done About Sin
Page 560—Ps. 32:5

21. Temptation
Temptation by the World
Page 1250—1 John 2:15
Temptation by the Flesh
Page 996—Mark 14:38
Temptation by Satan
Page 424—1 Chr. 21:1

22. Suffering
Kinds of Suffering
Page 1238—1 Pet. 3:17
Purposes of Suffering
Page 519—Job 2:7
Response to Suffering
Page 519—Job 1:21
Examples of Suffering
Page 743—Jer. 37:15

23. Knowing the Will of God
Knowing the Will of God Through the
   Scriptures
Page 396—2 Kin. 23:3
Knowing the Will of God Through Prayer
   and Fasting
Page 832—Dan. 9:3, 4
Knowing the Will of God Through
   Submission to the Spirit
Page 662—Is. 6:8

Recognizing God's Institutions

Synopsis

God gave humanity four basic institutions: the family, human government, Israel, and the church. It may be observed that each of these institutions demonstrates a characteristic or attribute of God.

- The family illustrates the unity of God (Gen. 2:24; Deut. 6:4).
- Human government illustrates the judgment of God (Rom. 13:1, 2).
- Israel illustrates the election of God (Rom. 9:1–18; 11:1–5).
- The church illustrates the love of God (Eph. 5:22–27).

The family was the first human institution God created. Through the family God illustrates visibly the relationships which exist in the Godhead and the relationship which exists between Christ and His church. Through the family God sought to bring into proper relationship the world with Himself. He created all of the heavens and earth and the things in them that they might prepare the way for and sustain the crown of His creation—humanity.

God's purpose in human government is that it serve as both a custodian and an enforcer of His eternal law. It has been correctly noted that all the thousands of good and practical laws passed by hundreds of legislative bodies and rulers throughout history are in reality only amplifications of the Ten Commandments.

God's selection of Israel as a special nation may puzzle the Bible student, but His choice becomes obvious through study. When God promised Abraham that he would become the father of a great nation, He also promised that He would bless all peoples through that nation (Gen. 12:1–3). Israel was to be a channel of blessing as well as a recipient.

The church, illustrating God's love for us, is the fourth institution through which God works. The universal church—the Body of Christ (Col. 1:18)—comprises all believers since the institution of the church.

Organization

Read Your Bible Through In a Year

A systematic division of the books of the Bible, primarily for reading.

JANUARY

Date	MORNING MATT.	EVENING GEN.
1	1	1, 2, 3
2	2	4, 5, 6
3	3	7, 8, 9
4	4	10, 11, 12
5	5: 1–26	13, 14, 15
6	5:27–48	16, 17
7	6: 1–18	18, 19
8	6:19–34	20, 21, 22
9	7	23, 24
10	8: 1–17	25, 26
11	8:18–34	27, 28
12	9: 1–17	29, 30
13	9:18–38	31, 32
14	10: 1–20	33, 34, 35
15	10:21–42	36, 37, 38
16	11	39, 40
17	12: 1–23	41, 42
18	12:24–50	43, 44, 45
19	13: 1–30	46, 47, 48
20	13:31–58	49, 50
		EX.
21	14: 1–21	1, 2, 3
22	14:22–36	4, 5, 6
23	15: 1–20	7, 8
24	15:21–39	9, 10, 11
25	16	12, 13
26	17	14, 15
27	18: 1–20	16, 17, 18
28	18:21–35	19, 20
29	19	21, 22
30	20: 1–16	23, 24
31	20:17–34	25, 26

FEBRUARY

Date	MORNING MATT.	EVENING EX.
1	21: 1–22	27, 28
2	21:23–46	29, 30
3	22: 1–22	31, 32, 33
4	22:23–46	34, 35
5	23: 1–22	36, 37, 38
6	23:23–39	39, 40
		LEV.
7	24: 1–28	1, 2, 3
8	24:29–51	4, 5
9	25: 1–30	6, 7
10	25:31–46	8, 9, 10
11	26: 1–25	11, 12
12	26:26–50	13
13	26:51–75	14
14	27: 1–26	15, 16
15	27:27–50	17, 18
16	27:51–66	19, 20
17	28	21, 22
		MARK
18	1: 1–22	23, 24
19	1:23–45	25
20	2	26, 27
		NUM.
21	3: 1–19	1, 2
22	3:20–35	3, 4
23	4: 1–20	5, 6
24	4:21–41	7, 8
25	5: 1–20	9, 10, 11
26	5:21–43	12, 13, 14
27	6: 1–29	15, 16
28	6:30–56	17, 18, 19
29	7: 1–13	20, 21, 22

MARCH

Date	MORNING MARK	EVENING NUM.
1	7:14–37	23, 24, 25
2	8: 1–21	26, 27
3	8:22–38	28, 29, 30
4	9: 1–29	31, 32, 33
5	9:30–50	34, 35, 36
		DEUT.
6	10: 1–31	1, 2
7	10:32–52	3, 4
8	11: 1–18	5, 6, 7
9	11:19–33	8, 9, 10
10	12: 1–27	11, 12, 13
11	12:28–44	14, 15, 16
12	13: 1–20	17, 18, 19
13	13:21–37	20, 21, 22
14	14: 1–26	23, 24, 25
15	14:27–53	26, 27
16	14:54–72	28, 29
17	15: 1–25	30, 31
18	15:26–47	32, 33, 34
		JOSH.
19	16	1, 2, 3
	LUKE	
20	1: 1–20	4, 5, 6
21	1:21–38	7, 8, 9
22	1:39–56	10, 11, 12
23	1:57–80	13, 14, 15
24	2: 1–24	16, 17, 18
25	2:25–52	19, 20, 21
26	3	22, 23, 24
		JUDG.
27	4: 1–30	1, 2, 3
28	4:31–44	4, 5, 6
29	5: 1–16	7, 8
30	5:17–39	9, 10
31	6: 1–26	11, 12

APRIL

Date	MORNING LUKE	EVENING JUDG.
1	6:27–49	13, 14, 15
2	7: 1–30	16, 17, 18
3	7:31–50	19, 20, 21
		RUTH
4	8: 1–25	1, 2, 3, 4
		1 SAM.
5	8:26–56	1, 2, 3
6	9: 1–17	4, 5, 6
7	9:18–36	7, 8, 9
8	9:37–62	10, 11, 12
9	10: 1–24	13, 14
10	10:25–42	15, 16
11	11: 1–28	17, 18
12	11:29–54	19, 20, 21
13	12: 1–31	22, 23, 24
14	12:32–59	25, 26
15	13: 1–22	27, 28, 29
16	13:23–35	30, 31
		2 SAM.
17	14: 1–24	1, 2
18	14:25–35	3, 4, 5
19	15: 1–10	6, 7, 8
20	15:11–32	9, 10, 11
21	16	12, 13
22	17: 1–19	14, 15
23	17:20–37	16, 17, 18
24	18: 1–23	19, 20
25	18:24–43	21, 22
26	19: 1–27	23, 24
		1 KIN.
27	19:28–48	1, 2
28	20: 1–26	3, 4, 5
29	20:27–47	6, 7
30	21: 1–19	8, 9

MAY

Date	MORNING LUKE	EVENING 1 KIN.
1	21:20–38	10, 11
2	22: 1–20	12, 13
3	22:21–46	14, 15
4	22:47–71	16, 17, 18
5	23: 1–25	19, 20
6	23:26–56	21, 22
		2 KIN.
7	24: 1–35	1, 2, 3
8	24:36–53	4, 5, 6
	JOHN	
9	1: 1–28	7, 8, 9
10	1:29–51	10, 11, 12
11	2	13, 14
12	3: 1–18	15, 16
13	3:19–38	17, 18
14	4: 1–30	19, 20, 21
15	4:31–54	22, 23
16	5: 1–24	24, 25
		1 CHR.
17	5:25–47	1, 2, 3
18	6: 1–21	4, 5, 6
19	6:22–44	7, 8, 9
20	6:45–71	10, 11, 12
21	7: 1–27	13, 14, 15
22	7:28–53	16, 17, 18
23	8: 1–27	19, 20, 21
24	8:28–59	22, 23, 24
25	9: 1–23	25, 26, 27
26	9:24–41	28, 29
		2 CHR.
27	10: 1–23	1, 2, 3
28	10:24–42	4, 5, 6
29	11: 1–29	7, 8, 9
30	11:30–57	10, 11, 12
31	12: 1–26	13, 14

JUNE

Date	MORNING JOHN	EVENING 2 CHR.
1	12:27–50	15, 16
2	13: 1–20	17, 18
3	13:21–38	19, 20
4	14	21, 22
5	15	23, 24
6	16	25, 26, 27
7	17	28, 29
8	18: 1–18	30, 31
9	18:19–40	32, 33
10	19: 1–22	34, 35, 36
		EZRA
11	19:23–42	1, 2
12	20	3, 4, 5
13	21	6, 7, 8
	ACTS	
14	1	9, 10
		NEH.
15	2: 1–21	1, 2, 3
16	2:22–47	4, 5, 6
17	3	7, 8, 9
18	4: 1–22	10, 11
19	4:23–37	12, 13
		ESTH.
20	5: 1–21	1, 2
21	5:22–42	3, 4, 5
22	6	6, 7, 8
23	7: 1–21	9, 10
		JOB
24	7:22–43	1, 2
25	7:44–60	3, 4
26	8: 1–25	5, 6, 7
27	8:26–40	8, 9, 10
28	9: 1–21	11, 12, 13
29	9:22–43	14, 15, 16
30	10: 1–23	17, 18, 19

JULY

Date	MORNING ACTS	EVENING JOB
1	10:24-48	20, 21
2	11	22, 23, 24
3	12	25, 26, 27
4	13: 1-25	28, 29
5	13:26-52	30, 31
6	14	32, 33
7	15: 1-21	34, 35
8	15:22-41	36, 37
9	16: 1-21	38, 39, 40
10	16:22-40	41, 42
		PS.
11	17: 1-15	1, 2, 3
12	17:16-34	4, 5, 6
13	18	7, 8, 9
14	19: 1-20	10, 11, 12
15	19:21-41	13, 14, 15
16	20: 1-16	16, 17
17	20:17-38	18, 19
18	21: 1-17	20, 21, 22
19	21:18-40	23, 24, 25
20	22	26, 27, 28
21	23: 1-15	29, 30
22	23:16-35	31, 32
23	24	33, 34
24	25	35, 36
25	26	37, 38, 39
26	27: 1-26	40, 41, 42
27	27:27-44	43, 44, 45
28	28	46, 47, 48
	ROM.	
29	1	49, 50
30	2	51, 52, 53
31	3	54, 55, 56

AUGUST

Date	MORNING ROM.	EVENING PS.
1	4	57, 58, 59
2	5	60, 61, 62
3	6	63, 64, 65
4	7	66, 67
5	8: 1-21	68, 69
6	8:22-39	70, 71
7	9: 1-15	72, 73
8	9:16-33	74, 75, 76
9	10	77, 78
10	11: 1-18	79, 80
11	11:19-36	81, 82, 83
12	12	84, 85, 86
13	13	87, 88
14	14	89, 90
15	15: 1-13	91, 92, 93
16	15:14-33	94, 95, 96
17	16	97, 98, 99
	1 COR.	
18	1	100, 101, 102
19	2	103, 104
20	3	105, 106
21	4	107, 108, 109
22	5	110, 111, 112
23	6	113, 114, 115
24	7: 1-19	116, 117, 118
25	7:20-40	119: 1-88
26	8	119: 89-176
27	9	120, 121, 122
28	10: 1-18	123, 124, 125
29	10:19-33	126, 127, 128
30	11: 1-16	129, 130, 131
31	11:17-34	132, 133, 134

SEPTEMBER

Date	MORNING 1 COR.	EVENING PS.
1	12	135, 136
2	13	137, 138, 139
3	14: 1-20	140, 141, 142
4	14:21-40	143, 144, 145
5	15: 1-28	146, 147
6	15:29-58	148, 149, 150
		PROV.
7	16	1, 2
	2 COR.	
8	1	3, 4, 5
9	2	6, 7
10	3	8, 9
11	4	10, 11, 12
12	5	13, 14, 15
13	6	16, 17, 18
14	7	19, 20, 21
15	8	22, 23, 24
16	9	25, 26
17	10	27, 28, 29
18	11: 1-15	30, 31
		ECCL.
19	11:16-33	1, 2, 3
20	12	4, 5, 6
21	13	7, 8, 9
	GAL.	
22	1	10, 11, 12
		SONG
23	2	1, 2, 3
24	3	4, 5
25	4	6, 7, 8
		IS.
26	5	1, 2
27	6	3, 4
	EPH.	
28	1	5, 6
29	2	7, 8
30	3	9, 10

OCTOBER

Date	MORNING EPH.	EVENING IS.
1	4	11, 12, 13
2	5: 1-16	14, 15, 16
3	5:17-33	17, 18, 19
4	6	20, 21, 22
	PHIL.	
5	1	23, 24, 25
6	2	26, 27
7	3	28, 29
8	4	30, 31
	COL.	
9	1	32, 33
10	2	34, 35, 36
11	3	37, 38
12	4	39, 40
	1 THESS.	
13	1	41, 42
14	2	43, 44
15	3	45, 46
16	4	47, 48, 49
17	5	50, 51, 52
	2 THESS.	
18	1	53, 54, 55
19	2	56, 57, 58
20	3	59, 60, 61
	1 TIM.	
21	1	62, 63, 64
22	2	65, 66
		JER.
23	3	1, 2
24	4	3, 4, 5
25	5	6, 7, 8
26	6	9, 10, 11
	2 TIM.	
27	1	12, 13, 14
28	2	15, 16, 17
29	3	18, 19
30	4	20, 21
	TITUS	
31	1	22, 23

NOVEMBER

Date	MORNING TITUS	EVENING JER.
1	2	24, 25, 26
2	3	27, 28, 29
3	**PHILEM.**	30, 31
	HEB.	
4	1	32, 33
5	2	34, 35, 36
6	3	37, 38, 39
7	4	40, 41, 42
8	5	43, 44, 45
9	6	46, 47
10	7	48, 49
11	8	50
12	9	51, 52
		LAM.
13	10: 1-18	1, 2
14	10:19-39	3, 4, 5
		EZEK.
15	11: 1-19	1, 2
16	11:20-40	3, 4
17	12	5, 6, 7
18	13	8, 9, 10
	JAMES	
19	1	11, 12, 13
20	2	14, 15
21	3	16, 17
22	4	18, 19
23	5	20, 21
	1 PET.	
24	1	22, 23
25	2	24, 25, 26
26	3	27, 28, 29
27	4	30, 31, 32
28	5	33, 34
	2 PET.	
29	1	35, 36
30	2	37, 38, 39

DECEMBER

Date	MORNING 2 PET.	EVENING EZEK.
1	3	40, 41
	1 JOHN	
2	1	42, 43, 44
3	2	45, 46
4	3	47, 48
		DAN.
5	4	1, 2
6	5	3, 4
7	**2 JOHN**	5, 6, 7
8	**3 JOHN**	8, 9, 10
9	**JUDE**	11, 12
	REV.	**HOS.**
10	1	1, 2, 3, 4
11	2	5, 6, 7, 8
12	3	9, 10, 11
13	4	12, 13, 14
14	5	**JOEL**
		AMOS
15	6	1, 2, 3
16	7	4, 5, 6
17	8	7, 8, 9
18	9	**OBAD.**
19	10	**JON.**
		MIC.
20	11	1, 2, 3
21	12	4, 5
22	13	6, 7
23	14	**NAH.**
24	15	**HAB.**
25	16	**ZEPH.**
26	17	**HAG.**
		ZECH.
27	18	1, 2, 3, 4
28	19	5, 6, 7, 8
29	20	9, 10, 11, 12
30	21	13, 14
31	22	**MAL.**

Biblical
Cyclopedic
Index

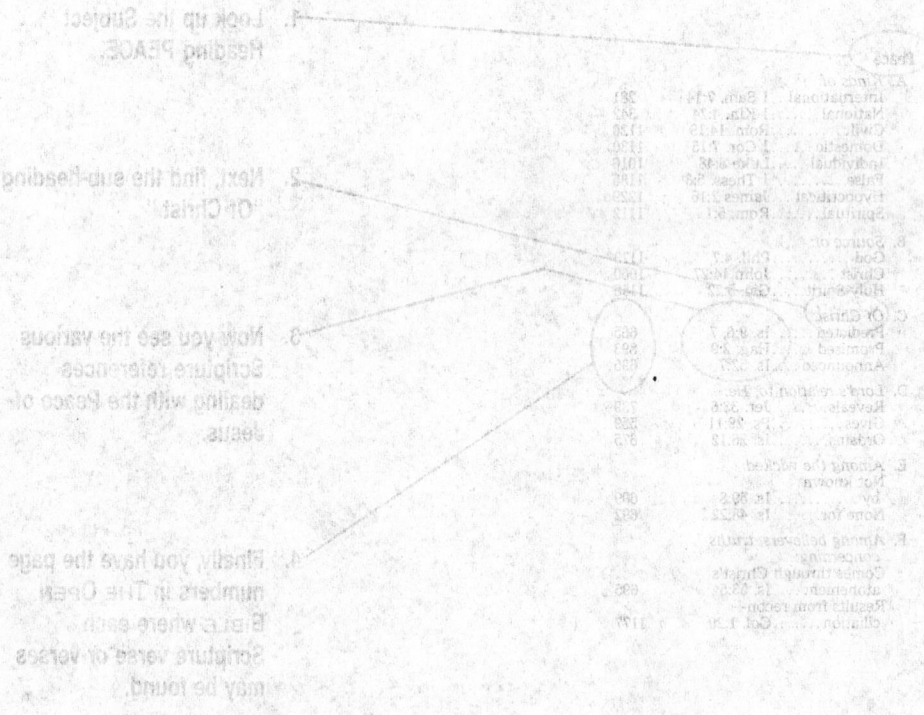

How to Use
The Biblical Cyclopedic Index

The Biblical Cyclopedic Index is a special kind of subject index that combines the best features of a concordance, a topical index, the usable study features of a syllabus, and other related study aids into one unique, quick, easy-to-use form. The Index offers advantages for personal Bible study that not even a combination of the above study helps would provide.

With over 8,000 subjects, names, places, things, concepts, events, and doctrines of the Bible, the Biblical Cyclopedic Index truly "opens" the Bible. It not only includes the Scripture references for the individual subjects (by appropriate sub-headings), it goes one convenient step further: it gives the actual page numbers in THE OPEN BIBLE where each Scripture verse or verses may be found.

An example will illustrate. Suppose you need to prepare or study a lesson on "The Peace of Jesus." Follow four easy steps.

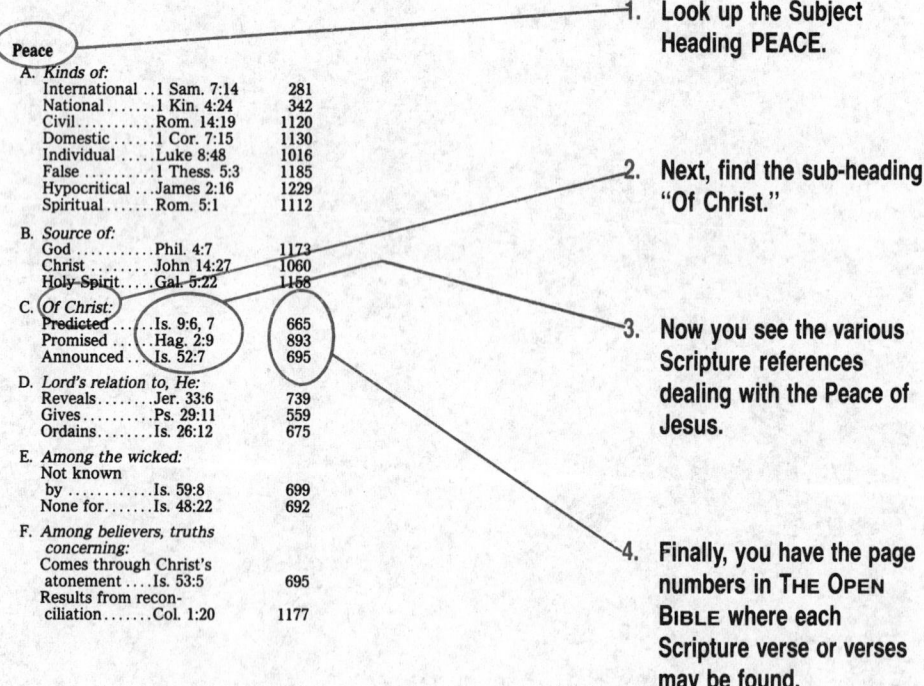

Peace

A. *Kinds of:*

International	1 Sam. 7:14	281
National	1 Kin. 4:24	342
Civil	Rom. 14:19	1120
Domestic	1 Cor. 7:15	1130
Individual	Luke 8:48	1016
False	1 Thess. 5:3	1185
Hypocritical	James 2:16	1229
Spiritual	Rom. 5:1	1112

B. *Source of:*

God	Phil. 4:7	1173
Christ	John 14:27	1060
Holy Spirit	Gal. 5:22	1158

C. *Of Christ:*

Predicted	Is. 9:6, 7	665
Promised	Hag. 2:9	893
Announced	Is. 52:7	695

D. *Lord's relation to, He:*

Reveals	Jer. 33:6	739
Gives	Ps. 29:11	559
Ordains	Is. 26:12	675

E. *Among the wicked:*

Not known		
by	Is. 59:8	699
None for	Is. 48:22	692

F. *Among believers, truths concerning:*

Comes through Christ's atonement	Is. 53:5	695
Results from reconciliation	Col. 1:20	1177

1. Look up the Subject Heading PEACE.

2. Next, find the sub-heading "Of Christ."

3. Now you see the various Scripture references dealing with the Peace of Jesus.

4. Finally, you have the page numbers in THE OPEN BIBLE where each Scripture verse or verses may be found.

The Biblical Cyclopedic Index has provided two important sources of information for you. First, you have the scriptural material needed to prepare or study your lesson. Second, you have this material in order as it appears in the Bible, so you have a ready-made outline for your personal use.

Biblical Cyclopedic Index

FROM GENESIS TO REVELATION

ARRANGED ALPHABETICALLY GIVING THE BOOK, CHAPTER, VERSE AND PAGE

WHERE EVERY REFERENCE IN THIS INDEX IS FOUND

29

SUBJECT	REFERENCE	PAGE	SUBJECT	REFERENCE	PAGE	SUBJECT	REFERENCE	PAGE

Abdeel—*servant of God*

The father of
Shelemiah........Jer. 36:26   742

Abdi—*servant of Yahweh*

1. The grandfather of
Ethan.........1 Chr. 6:44   410
2. A Levite.......2 Chr. 29:12   462
3. A Jew who divorced his foreign
wife..........Ezra 10:26   484

Abdiel—*servant of God*

A Gadite residing in
Gilead............1 Chr. 5:15, 16   409

Abdon—*servile*

1. A minor
judge.........Judg. 12:13-15   257
2. A Benjamite living in
Jerusalem.....1 Chr. 8:23, 28   413
3. A son of
Jeiel.........1 Chr. 8:30; 9:36   413
4. A courtier of King
Josiah.........2 Chr. 34:20   469
5. A Levitical   (Josh. 21:30   237
city.........(1 Chr. 6:74   411

Abed-nego—*servant of Nego*

Name given to Azariah, a Hebrew
captive...........Dan. 1:7   822
Appointed by Nebuchad-
nezzar............Dan. 2:49   825
Accused of
disobedience.....Dan. 3:12   825
Cast into furnace but
delivered......Dan. 3:13-27   825
Promoted by Nebuchad-
nezzar.......Dan. 3:28-30   826

Abel—*breath*

Adam's second
son..............Gen. 4:2   7
The first
shepherd........Gen. 4:2   7
Offering of,
accepted........Gen. 4:4   7
Hated and slain by
Cain............Gen. 4:8   8
Christ's blood superior
to..........Heb. 12:24   1223
Place of, filled by
Seth.............Gen. 4:25   8

Abel—*meadow*

1. A city involved in Sheba's
rebellion.....2 Sam. 20:14-18   329
2. Translated as "great stone of
Abel" in.....1 Sam. 6:18   281
First martyr...Matt. 23:35   966
Righteous.....Matt. 23:35   966
Sacrificed to God by
faith.........Heb. 11:4   1221
3. Elsewhere in place names (see
below)

Abel-beth-maachah—*meadow of the
house of oppression*

Captured by
Tiglath-pileser....2 Kin. 15:29   388
A town in North
Palestine....1 Kin. 15:20   329
Refuge of Sheba; saved from
destruction.......2 Sam. 20:14-22   329
Seized by
Ben-hadad........1 Kin. 15:20   357

Abel-maim—*meadow of waters*

Another name for Abel-beth-
maacah ....2 Chr. 16:4   451

Abel-meholah—*meadow of dancing*

Midianites
flee to............Judg. 7:22   251
A few miles east of
Jabesh-gilead...1 Kin. 4:12   342
Elisha's native
city..............1 Kin. 19:16   362

Abel-mizraim—*meadow of Egypt*

A place, east of Jordan, where
Israelites mourned for
Jacob............Gen. 50:10, 11   52

Abel-shittim—*meadow of acacias*

A place in Moab ..Num. 33:49   172

Abez—*whiteness*

A town of
Issachar..........Josh. 19:20   234

Abhor—*to detest; loathe; hate*

A. *Descriptive of:*
Disliking God's
laws ....Lev. 26:15   127
Prejudice toward non-
Israelites......Deut. 23:7   200
Right attitude toward
idolatry......Deut. 7:25, 26   186
Self-rejection ..Job 42:6   543
Israel abhorred by
Rezon.......1 Kin. 11:23-25   352
Israel's rejection by
God...........Ps. 89:38, 39   587
Rejection by former
friends........Job 19:19   529
Loss of
appetite......Job 33:20   537
Rejecting false
description....Prov. 24:24   632
B. *Expressive of God's loathing of:*
Israel's
idolatry ......Ps. 78:58, 59   582
Customs of other
nations........Lev. 20:23   120
Men of
bloodshed.....Ps. 5:6   549
C. *Expressive of Israel's rejection
of God's:*
Judgments.....Lev. 26:15   127
Statutes ......Lev. 26:43   128
Ceremonies ...1 Sam. 2:17   277
Promises.......Is. 7:16   663
D. *Expressive of the believer's
hatred of:*
Lying..........Ps. 119:163   603
Evil...........Rom. 12:9   1118

Abi—*an old form of "father of"*

King Hezekiah's
mother..........2 Kin. 18:2   390
Also called
Abijah...........2 Chr. 29:1   462

Abi-albon

An Arabathite.....2 Sam. 23:31   332

See Abiel

Abiasaph—*the father gathers*

A descendant of Levi through
Korah.............Ex. 6:24   61
Called Ebiasaph...1 Chr. 6:23, 37   410
Descendants of, act as
doorkeepers ......1 Chr. 9:19   414

Abiathar—*father of preeminence*

A priest who escapes Saul at
Nob.........1 Sam. 22:20-23   297
Becomes high priest under
David ....1 Sam. 23:6-12   298
Shares high priesthood with
Zadok.........2 Sam. 19:11   327
Remains faithful to
David ....2 Sam. 15:24-29   323
Informs David about
Ahithophel ....2 Sam. 15:34-36   323
Supports Adonijah's
usurpation ....1 Kin. 1:7, 9, 25   337
Deposed by   (1 Kin. 2:26, 27,
Solomon.......(35   340
Eli's line ends ...1 Sam. 2:31-35   278
Referred by
Christ ....Mark 2:26   980

Abib—*an ear of corn*

First month in Hebrew
year...........Ex. 12:1, 2   66
Commemorative of the
Passover ....Ex. 12:1-28   66
Called Nisan in postexilic
times...........Neh. 2:1   489

Abida, Abidah—*the father knows*

A son of Midian; grandson of
Abraham and
Keturah ....Gen. 25:4   26

Abidan—*the father is judge*

Represents tribe of
Benjamin.........Num. 1:11   133
Brings offering ....Num. 7:60, 65   143
Lead Benjamites ..Num. 10:24   146

Abide, abiding—*continuing in a
permanent state*

A. *Applied to:*
Earth's
existence......Ps. 119:90   601
Believer's
works.........1 Cor. 3:14   1127
Three graces...1 Cor. 13:13   1135
God's
faithfulness ...2 Tim. 2:13   1201
Christ's
priesthood ....Heb. 7:3   1218
God's Word....1 Pet. 1:23   1236
Believer's
eternity ......1 John 2:17   1250
B. *Sphere of, in the Christian's life:*
Christ ....John 15:4-6   1060
Christ's
words.........John 15:7   1060
Christ's love ..John 15:10   1060
Christ's
doctrine.......2 John 9   1256
The Holy
Spirit ....John 14:16   1059
God's Word....1 John 2:14, 24   1250
One's earthly
calling ....1 Cor. 7:20, 24   1130
The truth......2 John 2   1256
C. *Descriptive of the believer's:*
Protection .....Ps. 91:1   588
Satisfaction ...Prov. 19:23   627
Fruitfulness....John 15:4, 5   1060
Prayer life .....John 15:7   1060
Assurance .....1 John 2:28   1251

Abiel—*God is father*

1. The grandfather of Saul and
Abner...........1 Sam. 9:1, 2   282
2. David's mighty
man ....1 Chr. 11:32   416
Also called
Abi-albon .....2 Sam. 23:31   332

Abiezer—*the father is help*

1. A descendant of
Joseph.........Josh. 17:1, 2   232
Called Jeezer ..Num. 26:30   163
Family settles at
Ophrah ....Judg. 6:24   249
Gideon belongs
to.............Judg. 6:11, 12   249
Family rallies to Gideon's
call ....Judg. 6:34   250
2. A mighty man and commander
in David's
army.........2 Sam. 23:27   332

Abiezrite

A member of the family of
Abiezer...........Judg. 6:11   249
Judg. 6:24, 34   249

Abigail—*the father is joyful*

1. Nabal's beautiful and wise
wife..........1 Sam. 25:3   299
Appeases David's
anger ....1 Sam. 25:14-35   300
Becomes David's
wife..........1 Sam. 25:36-42   301

SUBJECT	REFERENCE	PAGE	SUBJECT	REFERENCE	PAGE	SUBJECT	REFERENCE	PAGE

Captured and
rescued ....1 Sam. 30:5, 18   304
Mother of
Chileab ....2 Sam. 3:3   311
2. A stepsister of
David........1 Chr. 2:16, 17   406

Abihail—*the father is might*
1. A Levite head of the house of
Merari ....Num. 3:35   137
2. Abishur's
wife.......1 Chr. 2:29   406
3. A Gadite chief in
Bashan.......1 Chr. 5:14   409
4. Wife of King
Rehoboam ....2 Chr. 11:18   448
5. Father of Queen
Esther ....Esth. 2:15   508

Abihu—*he is father*
Second of Aaron's four
sons.............Ex. 6:23   61
Ascends Mt.
Sinai ....Ex. 24:1, 9   78
Chosen as priest ..Ex. 28:1   82
Offers, with Nadab, strange
fire.............Lev. 10:1-7   108
Dies in the presence of the
Lord ....Num. 3:4   136
Dies without
heirs ....1 Chr. 24:2   428

Abihud—*the father is majesty*
A Benjamite ......1 Chr. 8:3   413

Abijah, Abia, Abiah—*Yahweh is Father*
1. Wife of
Hezron ....1 Chr. 2:24   406
2. Son of
Becher.......1 Chr. 7:8   412
3. Samuel's second son; follows
corrupt
ways.........1 Sam. 8:2, 3   282
4. Descendant of Aaron; head of
an office of
priests ......1 Chr. 24:3, 10   428
Zachariah belongs
to...........Luke 1:5   1004
5. Son of
Jeroboam I...1 Kin. 14:1-18   355
6. Another name for King
Abijam.......1 Kin. 11:20   448
Fathers 38 children by 14
wives ....2 Chr. 13:21   449
7. The mother of
Hezekiah......2 Chr. 29:1   462
Called Abi ...Esth. 18:2   390
8. A priest who signs the
document.....Neh. 10:7   499
9. A priest returning from Babylon
with Zerub-
babel.......Neh. 12:1, 4, 17   501

Abijam (another form of Abijah)
King of Judah...1 Kin. 14:31   356
Son and successor of King
Rehoboam......1 Kin. 15:1-7   356
Follows in his father's
sins ....1 Kin. 15:3, 4   356
Wars against King
Jeroboam ....1 Kin. 15:6, 7   357
Slays 500,000
Israelites.......2 Chr. 13:13-20   449
Fathers 38 children by 14
wives.........2 Chr. 13:21   449

Abilene—*grassy place*
A province or tetrarchy of
Syria.............Luke 3:1   1007

Ability—*power to perform*
A. Descriptive of:
Material
prosperity.....Deut. 16:17   194
Emotional
strength ......Num. 11:14   147
Military   (Num. 13:31   149
power........(1 Kin. 9:21   350
Physical
strength ....Ex. 18:18, 23   73

Mental
power........Gen. 15:5   17
Moral power...1 Cor. 3:2   1127
Spiritual
power........James 3:2   1229
Divine power ..Rom. 4:21   1111
B. Of God's power to:
Deliver ....1 Cor. 10:13   1132
Humble men...Dan. 4:37   827
Create life .....Matt. 3:9   943
Destroy.......Matt. 10:28   951
Preserve
believers ......John 10:28   1055
Keep His
promise.......Rom. 4:21   1111
Make us
stand ....Rom. 16:25   1122
Supply grace..2 Cor. 9:8   1148
Exceed our
petitions ......Eph. 3:20   1163
Service ....1 Pet. 4:11   1238
Comfort
others........2 Cor. 1:4   1143
Keep what we have
entrusted .....2 Tim. 1:12   1200
Save from
death ....Heb. 5:7   1217
Resurrect
men..........Heb. 11:19   1222
Keep from
falling.......Jude 24, 25   1263
C. Of Christ's power to:
Heal..........Matt. 9:28, 29   950
Subdue all
things.........Phil. 3:21   1172
Help His
own..........Heb. 2:18   1216
Have
compassion ...Heb. 4:15, 16   1217
Save
completely ...Heb. 7:25   1218
D. Of the Christian's power to:
Speak for the
Lord ....Luke 21:15   1032
Admonish .....Rom. 15:14   1120
Survive
testings ....1 Cor. 3:13-15   1127
Withstand
Satan ....Eph. 6:11, 13   1167
Convince
opposition.....Titus 1:9   1206
Bridle the whole
body.........James 3:2   1229

Abimael—*God is Father*
A son of Joktan ...Gen. 10:28   13

Abimelech—*the father is king*
1. A Philistine king of
Gerar ....Gen. 20:1-18   21
Makes treaty with
Abraham......Gen. 21:22-34   22
2. A second king of
Gerar ....Gen. 26:1-11   27
Tells Isaac to go
home ....Gen. 26:12-16   27
Makes a treaty with Isaac
concerning certain
wells.........Gen. 26:17-33   27
3. A son of Gideon by a
concubine.....Judg. 8:31   252
Conspires to become
king ....Judg. 9:1-4   252
Slays his 70
brothers.......Judg. 9:5   252
Made king of
Shechem......Judg. 9:6   252
Rebuked by Jotham, lone
survivor.......Judg. 9:7-21   253
Conspired against by
Gaal ....Judg. 9:22-29   253
Captures Shechem and
Thebez......Judg. 9:41-50   254
Death of .....Judg. 9:51-57   254
4. A son of Abiathar the
priest ....1 Chr. 18:16   423
Also called
Ahimelech ...1 Chr. 24:6   428

Abinadab—*the father is generous*
1. A man of Kirjath-jearim whose
house tabernacles
the ark of the
Lord ....1 Sam. 7:1, 2   281
2. The second of Jesse's eight
sons ....1 Sam. 16:8   290
A soldier in Saul's
army..........1 Sam. 17:13   291
3. A son of Saul slain at Mt.
Gilboa ....1 Sam. 31:1-8   305
Bones of, buried by men of
Jabesh ......1 Chr. 10:1-12   415
4. The father of one of Solomon's
sons-in-law....1 Kin. 4:11   342

Abinoam—*the father is pleasantness*
Father of Barak ...Judg. 4:6   247

Abiram—*the father is exalted*
1. Reubenite who conspired
against
Moses.......Num. 16:1-50   152
2. The firstborn   (1 Kin. 16:34   359
son of Hiel ...(Josh. 6:26   222

Abishag—*the father wanders*
A Shunammite employed as
David's nurse...1 Kin. 1:1-4, 15   337
Witnessed David's choice of
Solomon as
successor........1 Kin. 1:15-31   337
Adonijah slain for desiring to
marry her ....1 Kin. 2:13-25   339

Abishai—*father of a gift*
A son of Zeruiah, David's
sister..........2 Sam. 2:18   310
Brother of Joab and
Asahel ....1 Chr. 2:16   406
Rebuked by
David ....1 Sam. 26:5-9   301
Serves under Joab in David's
army ....2 Sam. 2:17, 18   310
Joins David in blood-revenge
against Abner ..2 Sam. 2:18-24   310
Co-commander of David's
army ....2 Sam. 10:9, 10   317
Loyal to David during Absalom's
uprising ....2 Sam. 16:9-12   324
Sternly rebuked by
David ....2 Sam. 19:21-23   328
Loyal to David during Sheba's
rebellion.......2 Sam. 20:1-6, 10   328
Slays 300
Philistines........2 Sam. 23:18   332
Slays 18,000
Edomites......1 Chr. 18:12, 13   423
Saves David by killing a
giant ....2 Sam. 21:16, 17   330

Abishalom—*father of peace*
A variant form of
Absalom.........1 Kin. 15:2, 10   356

Abishua—*the father is salvation*
1. A Benjamite ....1 Chr. 8:3, 4   413
2. Phinehas'
son ....1 Chr. 6:4, 5, 50   410

Abishur—*the father is a wall*
A Jerahmeelite ...1 Chr. 2:28, 29   406

Abital—*the father is dew*
Wife of David...2 Sam. 3:2, 4   311

Abitub—*the father is goodness*
A Benjamite ......1 Chr. 8:8-11   413

Abiud (Greek form of Abihud)
Ancestor of
Jesus............Matt. 1:13   941

Ablution—*ceremonial washing*
Of priests ....Ex. 30:18-21   86
Ex. 40:30, 31   96
Of ceremonially   (Lev. 14:7-9   113
unclean ....(Lev. 15:5-10   114
Of a house ....Lev. 14:52   114
By Pharisees ......Mark 7:1-5   985

SUBJECT	REFERENCE	PAGE	SUBJECT	REFERENCE	PAGE	SUBJECT	REFERENCE	PAGE
Abner—*the father is a lamp*			E. *Judgments upon, manifested in:*			A native of		
Commands Saul's			Stoning to			Ur .... Gen. 11:28, 31		14
army .... 1 Sam. 14:50, 51		288	death .... Deut. 17:2-5		195	Pagan		
Introduces David to			Destroying a			ancestors ..... Josh. 24:2		239
Saul .... 1 Sam. 17:55-58		292	city .... Deut. 13:13-17		191	Weds Sarai .... Gen. 11:29		14
Rebuked by {1 Sam. 26:5,			Forfeiting God's			B. *Wanderings of:*		
David 14-16		301	mercy .... Ezek. 5:11-13		775	Goes to		
Saul's cousin ..... 1 Sam. 14:50, 51		288	Experiencing God's			Haran .... Gen. 11:31		14
Supports Ish-bosheth as Saul's			fury .... Ezek. 20:7, 8		787	Receives {Gen. 12:1-3		14
successor .... 2 Sam. 2:8-10		310	F. *Things especially classed as:*			God's call .... {Acts 7:2-4		1078
Defeated by David's			Silver or gold from graven			Prompted by		
men .... 2 Sam. 2:12-17		310	images .... Deut. 7:25		186	faith .... Heb. 11:8		1221
Kills Asahel in			Perverse			Enters		
self-defense ..... 2 Sam. 2:18-23		310	man .... Prov. 3:32		617	Canaan .... Gen. 12:4-6		15
Pursued by Joab .. 2 Sam. 2:24-32		310	Seven sins ..... Prov. 6:16-19		618	Canaan promised to, by		
Slain by Joab ... 2 Sam. 3:8-27		311	False balance .. Prov. 11:1		621	God .... Gen. 12:1, 7		14
Death of, condemned by			Lying lips ..... Prov. 12:22		623	Pitched his tent near Beth-		
David .... 2 Sam. 3:28-39		311	Sacrifices of the			el .... Gen. 12:8		15
			wicked .... Prov. 15:8, 9		624	Famine sends him to		
Abolish—*to do away with*			Proud in			Egypt .... Gen. 12:10-20		15
A. *Of evil things:*			heart .... Prov. 16:5		625	Returns to Canaan		
Idolatry .... Is. 2:18		660	Justifying the			enriched ...... Gen. 13:1-5		15
Man-made			wicked .... Prov. 17:15		626	Chooses Hebron rather than		
ordinances .... Col. 2:20-22		1178	Scorner .... Prov. 24:9		631	strife .... Gen. 13:6-12		15
Death .... 1 Cor. 15:26		1137	Prayer of one who turns away			C. *Testing and victory of:*		
Evil works .... Ezek. 6:6		775	his ear .... Prov. 28:9		634	Separates from		
Enmity .... Eph. 2:15		1163	False			Lot .... Gen. 13:8-12		15
B. *Of things good for a while:*			worship .... Is. 1:13		659	Rescues captured		
Old covenant .. 2 Cor. 3:13		1144	Scant			Lot .... Gen. 14:14-16		16
Present			measures ..... Mic. 6:10		874	Receives Melchizedek's		
world .... Heb. 1:10-12		1215	Self-righteous-			blessing .... Gen. 14:18-20		16
Temporal			ness .... Luke 16:15		1026	Covenant renewed; a son		
rule .... 1 Cor. 15:24		1137				promised to .. Gen. 15:1-21		17
Partial things .. 1 Cor. 13:10		1135	**Abortion**—*accidental or planned*			Justified by {Gen. 15:6		17
C. *Of things not to be abolished:*			*miscarriage*			faith .... {Rom. 4:3		1111
God's righteous-			Laws			Takes Hagar as		
ness .... Is. 51:6		694	concerning ...... Ex. 21:22-25		76	concubine ..... Gen. 16:1-4		17
God's Word .... Matt. 5:18		945	Pronounced as a			Ishmael born .. Gen. 16:5-16		17
			judgment ...... Hos. 9:14		844	Covenant renewed; named		
Abomination of desolation			Sought to relieve			Abraham ...... Gen. 17:1-8		18
Predicted by {Dan. 9:27; 11:31;			misery .... Job 3:16		520	Household of,		
Daniel .... { 12:11		833	Of animals, by			circum- {Gen. 17:9-14, 23-		
Cited by Christ .. Matt. 24:15		967	thunder .... Ps. 29:9		559	cised .... { 27		18
			Figurative of abrupt			Promised a		
Abominations—*things utterly repulsive*			conversion .... 1 Cor. 15:8		1137	son .... Gen. 17:15-19		18
A. *Descriptive of:*						Covenant in		
Egyptians eating with			**Abound**—*to increase greatly*			Isaac, not {Gen. 17:20-22		18
Hebrews ...... Gen. 43:32		46	A. *Of good things:*			Ishmael ...... {Gal. 4:22-31		1157
Undesirable social			God's truth ..... Rom. 3:7		1110	Receives		
relations ..... Ex. 8:26		63	God's grace .... Rom. 5:15, 20		1112	messengers ... Gen. 18:1-15		18
Spiritist			Hope .... Rom. 15:13		1120	Intercedes concerning		
practices ..... Deut. 18:9-12		196	God's work .... 1 Cor. 15:58		1138	Sodom .... Gen. 18:16-33		19
Heathen			Suffering for			Witnesses Sodom's		
idolatry ...... Deut. 7:25, 26		186	Christ .... 2 Cor. 1:5		1143	doom .... Gen. 19:27, 28		20
Child-			Joy in			His faith saves		
sacrifice ..... Deut. 12:31		191	suffering ...... 2 Cor. 8:2		1147	Lot .... Gen. 19:29		20
Pagan gods .. 2 Kin. 23:13		397	Gracious			Sojourns at Gerar; deceives		
B. *Applied to perverse sexual*			works .... 2 Cor. 8:7		1147	Abimelech ... Gen. 20:1-18		21
relations:			Good works ... 2 Cor. 9:8		1148	Isaac born to, and		
Unnatural			Wisdom .... Eph. 1:8		1162	circumcised .. Gen. 21:1-8		21
acts .... Lev. 18:19-29		118	Love .... Phil. 1:9		1170	Sends Hagar and Ishmael		
Wrong			Fruitfulness ... Phil. 4:17, 18		1173	away .... Gen. 21:9-21		21
clothing ...... Deut. 22:5		199	Faith .... Col. 2:7		1178	Makes covenant with		
Prostitution and			Pleasing God .. 1 Thess. 4:1		1185	Abimelech ... Gen. 21:22-34		22
sodomy ...... Deut. 23:17, 18		200	Christian			Testing of, in offering		
Reclaiming a defiled			qualities .... 2 Pet. 1:5-8		1243	Isaac .... Gen. 22:1-19		22
woman .... Deut. 24:4		200	Blessings ...... Prov. 28:20		634	Receives news about		
Racial inter-			Charity .... 2 Thess. 1:3		1189	Nahor .... Gen. 22:20-24		23
marriage ..... Ezra 9:1-14		483	B. *Source of, in good things:*			Buys burial place for		
C. *In ceremonial matters, applied*			From God .... 2 Cor. 9:8		1148	Sarah .... Gen. 23:1-20		23
to:			From Christian			Obtains wife for		
Unclean {Lev. 11:10-23,			generosity ..... 2 Cor. 8:2, 3		1147	Isaac .... Gen. 24:1-67		24
animals ...... { 41-43		109	Faithfulness ... Prov. 28:20		634	Marries Keturah; fathers other		
Deformed			Generosity .... Phil. 4:14-18		1173	children;		
animals ...... Deut. 17:1		195	C. *Of evil things:*			dies; .... Gen. 25:1-10		26
Heathen practices in God's			Transgres-			D. *Characteristics of:*		
house .... 2 Chr. 36:14		471	sions .... Prov. 29:22		635	Friend of		
D. *Sinfulness of, seen in:*			Lawlessness ... Matt. 24:12		967	God .... 2 Chr. 20:7		454
Being			Increasing			Obedient ...... Gen. 22:1-18		22
enticed .... 1 Kin. 11:5, 7		351	sins .... Rom. 5:20		1112	Tither .... Gen. 14:20		16
Delighting in .. Is. 66:3		703				Heb. 7:1, 2, 4		1218
Rejecting admonitions			**Abraham**—*the father of a multitude*			Generous ..... Gen. 13:8, 9		15
against .... Jer. 44:4, 5		749	A. *Ancestry and family:*			Courageous .... Gen. 14:13-16		16
Polluting God's			Descendant of			Independent ... Gen. 14:21-23		16
house .... Jer. 7:30		715	Shem .... 1 Chr. 1:24-27		405	Man of		
Being {Ezek. 20:7,			Son of Terah .. Gen. 11:26		14	prayer .... Gen. 18:23-33		19
polluted ...... { 30-32		787	First named			Man of faith ... Gen. 15:6		17
			Abram .... Gen. 11:27		14	Rich man ...... Gen. 13:2		15

SUBJECT	REFERENCE	PAGE	SUBJECT	REFERENCE	PAGE	SUBJECT	REFERENCE	PAGE

Abuse—*application to a wrong purpose*

A. *Of physical things:*
Sexual perver- (Gen. 19:5-9,
sions.........{ 31-38   20
Immoral acts ..1 Cor. 6:9   1129
Torture........Judg. 16:21   260

B. *Of spiritual things:*
Misuse of (Num. 20:10-13   157
authority.....(1 Cor. 9:18   1132
Using the world
wrongly.......1 Cor. 7:31   1131
Perverting the
truth.........2 Pet. 2:10-22   1244
Corrupting God's
ordinances ....1 Sam. 2:12-17   277
1 Cor. 11:17-22   1133

C. *Manifested by:*
Unbelieving...Mark 15:29-32   998

Abyss

Translated:
"deep"...........Luke 8:31   1015
"bottomless (Rev. 9:1, 2, 11   1273
pit".........(Rev. 17:8   1279

Accad—*a city in the land of Shinar*

City in Shinar.....Gen. 10:10   13

Acceptance—*the reception of one's person or service*

A. *Objects of, before God:*
Righteousness and
justice ....Prov. 21:3   628
Our words and
meditations ..Ps. 19:14   555
Our
dedication....Rom. 12:1, 2   1118
Service ....Rom. 14:18   1120
Giving........Rom. 15:16, 27   1120
Offerings .....Phil. 4:18   1173
Intercession ..1 Tim. 2:1-3   1194
Helping
parents ......1 Tim. 5:4   1196
Spiritual
sacrifices....1 Pet. 2:5   1236
Suffering because of
Christ........1 Pet. 2:20   1237

B. *Qualifications of, seen in:*
Coming at (Is. 49:8   692
God's time ..(2 Cor. 6:2   1146
Meeting God's require-
ments........Job 42:8, 9   543
Receiving divine
sign.........Judg. 6:9-21   249
Noting God's (1 Sam. 7:8-10   281
response ....(John 12:28-30   1057
Responding to God's
renewal ......Ezek. 20:40-44   789
Manifesting spiritual
rectitude....Mic. 6:6-8   874

C. *Persons disqualified for, such as:*
The wicked ...Ps. 82:2   584
Blemished
sacrifices.....Mal. 1:8, 10, 13   907
Man's person ..Gal. 2:6   1155
Those who swear
deceitfully ....Ps. 24:3-6   556

Access to God

A. *By means of:*
Christ ....John 14:6   1059
Christ's
blood ....Eph. 2:13   1163
Holy Spirit.....Eph. 2:18   1163
Faith ....Rom. 5:2   1112
Clean hands ..Ps. 24:3-5   556
God's grace...Eph. 1:6   1162
Prayer.......Matt. 6:6   946

B. *Characteristics of:*
On God's
choosing......Ps. 65:4   574
Sinners
commanded (Is. 55:6, 7   696
to seek.......(James 4:8   1230

With
confidence ....Heb. 4:16   1217
Boldness.......Eph. 3:12   1163
Results from reconcili-
ation.........Col. 1:21, 22   1177
Open to
Gentiles.......Acts 14:27   1088
Experienced in Christ's
priesthood....Heb. 7:19-25   1218
Sought by God's
people ....Ps. 27:4   557
Bold in
prayer ....Heb. 4:16   1217
A blessing to be
chosen ....Ps. 65:4   574

Accho—*modern Acre (a seaport 8 miles north of Mt. Carmel)*

Assigned to
Asher ....Judg. 1:31   244
Called Ptolemais in the New
Testament.......Acts 21:7   1096

Accident—*event not foreseen*

A. *Caused by:*
An animal ....Num. 22:25   159
A fall ....2 Sam. 4:4   312

B. *Explanation of:*
Known to (Deut. 29:29   207
God..........(Prov. 16:9, 33   625
Misunderstood by
men...........Luke 13:4, 5   1023
Subject to God's
providence ....Rom. 8:28   1115

Accommodation—*adaptation caused by human limitations*

A. *Physically, caused by:*
Age and sex ...Gen. 33:13-15   35
Strength and
size ....1 Sam. 17:38-40   292
Inability to
repay ....Luke 7:41, 42   1014

B. *Spiritually, caused by:*
Man's
blindness......Matt. 13:10-14   954
Absence of the
Spirit ....John 16:12, 13   1061
Carnality ......1 Cor. 3:1, 2   1127
Spiritual
immaturity....Rom. 14:1-23   1119
Man's present
limitations ...1 Cor. 2:7-16   1127
Degrees of
light ....Heb. 9:7-15   1219

Accomplish—*to fulfill*

A. *Of God's Word concerning:*
Judah's
captivity .....Dan. 9:2   832
Judah's
return.........2 Chr. 36:22, 23   471
God's sovereign
plan...........Is. 55:11   696
The Messiah's
advent ....Dan. 9:24-27   833
Christ's
suffering ......Luke 18:31   1028
Christ's
death ....John 19:28-30   1064
Final events ..Dan. 12:7   837

B. *Of human things:*
Food ....1 Kin. 5:9   343
Purification
rites ....Esth. 2:12   508
Priestly
ministry......Luke 1:23   1004
Time of
pregnancy ....Luke 2:6   1006
Afflictions ....1 Pet. 5:9   1239

Accord—*united agreement*

A. *Descriptive of:*
A spontaneous
response ......Acts 12:10, 20   1085
Voluntary
action.........2 Cor. 8:17   1147

Single-
mindedness ...Josh. 9:2   224
Spiritual
unity..........Acts 1:14   1072

B. *Manifested in:*
Fellowship.....Acts 2:46   1074
Prayer........Acts 4:24   1076
Opposition.....Acts 7:57   1080
Response......Acts 8:6   1080
Decisions ......Acts 15:25   1089
Mind ....Phil. 2:2   1171

Accountability—*responsibility for own acts*

A. *Kinds of:*
Universal ......Rom. 14:12   1120
Personal ....2 Sam. 12:1-15   318
Personal and
family.........Josh. 7:1-26   222
Personal and
national......2 Sam. 24:1-17   333
Delayed but
exacted ......2 Sam. 21:1-14   329
Final ....Rom. 2:1-12   1109

B. *Determined by:*
Federal (Gen. 3:1-24   6
headship ...(Rom. 5:12-21   1112
Personal responsi-
bility ....Ezek. 18:1-32   786
Faithfulness ..Matt. 25:14-30   968
Knowledge ....Luke 12:47, 48   1022
Conscience ....Rom. 2:12-16   1109
Greater light...Rom. 2:17-29   1110
Maturity of
judgment .....1 Cor. 8:1-13   1131

Accursed—*under a curse*

A. *Caused by:*
Hanging on a
tree ....Deut. 21:23   198
Sin among God's
people ....Josh. 7:12   222
Possessing a banned
thing..........Josh. 6:18   222
Preaching contrary to the
Gospel ....Gal. 1:8, 9   1154
Blaspheming
Christ.........1 Cor. 12:3   1134

B. *Objects of being:*
A city ....Josh. 6:17   221
A forbidden
thing.........Josh. 22:20   238
An old sinner ..Is. 65:20   703
Christ haters or non-
believers ......1 Cor. 16:22   1139
Paul (for the sake of
Israel) ....Rom. 9:3   1115

Accusations—*charges*

A. *Kinds of:*
Pagan ....Dan. 3:8   825
Personal ....Dan. 6:24   830
Public ....John 18:29   1063
Perverted......1 Pet. 3:16   1238

B. *Sources of, in:*
The devil .....Job 1:6-12   518
Rev. 12:9, 10   1276
Enemies ......Ezra 4:6   478
Man's
conscience ....John 8:9   1051
God's Word ....John 5:45   1048
Hypocritical ...John 8:6, 10, 11   1051
The last days ..2 Tim. 3:1, 3   1201
Apostates......2 Pet. 2:10, 11   1244

C. *Forbidden:*
Against
servants.......Prov. 30:10   635
Falsely.........Luke 3:14   1008
Among
women........Titus 2:3   1206

D. *False, examples of, against:*
Jacob..........Gen. 31:26-30   33
Joseph.........Gen. 39:10-21   41
Ahimelech ...1 Sam. 22:11-16   297
David.........2 Sam. 10:3   317
Job............Job 2:3-5   519
Jeremiah......Jer. 26:8-11   731

SUBJECT	REFERENCE	PAGE	SUBJECT	REFERENCE	PAGE	SUBJECT	REFERENCE	PAGE

SUBJECT   REFERENCE   PAGE

Adultery—*sexual intercourse outside marriage*

A. *Defined:*

In God's Law . . Ex. 20:14	75
By Christ . . . . . Matt. 5:28, 32	945
By Paul . . . . Rom. 7:3	1113
In mental attitude . . . . . Matt. 5:28	945
As a work of the flesh . . . . Gal. 5:19	1158

B. *Sin of:*

Breaks God's Law . . . . Deut. 5:18	183
Punishable by death . . . . Lev. 20:10-12	120
Brings death . . . Prov. 2:18, 19	616
Makes one poor . . . . Prov. 29:3	634
Produces moral insensi- (Prov. 30:20	635
bility . . . . (2 Cor. 12:21	1151
Corrupts a land . . . . Hos. 4:1-3	842
Justifies divorce . . . . Matt. 19:7-9	961
Excludes from Christian fellowship . . . . . 1 Cor. 5:1-13	1128
Excludes from God's kingdom . . . . . . 1 Cor. 6:9, 10	1129
Merits God's judgments . . . . Heb. 13:4	1223
Ends in hell (Prov. 7:27	619
(Sheol) . . . . (Rev. 21:8	1282

C. *Forgiveness of, by:*

Man . . . . Judg. 19:1-4	262
Christ . . . . John 8:10, 11	1051
Repentance . . . . 2 Sam. 12:7-14	319
Regener- ation . . . . 1 Cor. 6:9-11	1129

D. *Examples of:*

Lot . . . . Gen. 19:31-38	20
Shechem . . . . . . Gen. 34:2	36
Judah . . . . Gen. 38:1-24	40
Eli's sons . . . . . . 1 Sam. 2:22	277
David . . . . 2 Sam. 11:1-5	317
Amnon . . . . 2 Sam. 13:1-20	320
The Samaritan woman . . . . John 4:17, 18	1045

Adultery, spiritual

Seen in Israel's idolatry . . . . Judg. 2:11, 17	245
Described graphically . . . . . . Ezek. 16	783
Symbolized in Hosea's marriage . . . . Hos. 1:1-3	840
Symbolized in final apostasy . . . . Rev. 17:1-5	1278
Figurative of friendship with the world . . . . James 4:4	1230
Figurative of (Rev. 2:14, 15, 20-	
false teaching . . (22	1269

Adummim—*red spots*

A hill between Jerusalem and Jericho . . . . Josh. 15:5, 7, 8	230
The probable site of Good Samaritan parable in . . . . Luke 10:30-37	1019

Advancement—*progression*

A. *Promotion to a higher office:*

Moses and Aaron, by the Lord . . . . 1 Sam. 12:6	285
Promised to Balaam . . . . . . Num. 22:16, 17	159
Joseph, by true interpre- tation . . . . Gen. 41:38-46	43
Levites, for loyalty . . . . Ex. 32:26-28	88
Phinehas, by decisive action . . . . . . Num. 25:7-13	162
Haman, by intrigue . . . . . . Esth. 3:1, 2	509
Mordecai, by ability . . . . Esth. 10:2	514
Daniel, by fidelity . . . . Dan. 2:48	824

Deacons, by faithfulness . . . 1 Tim. 3:10, 13	1195

B. *Conditions of, seen in:*

Humility . . . . . . Matt. 18:4	960
Faithfulness . . . Matt. 25:14-30	968
Skilled in (Prov. 22:29	630
work . . . . (Luke 22:24-30	1033
Service to others . . . . Luke 22:24-30	1033

C. *Hindrances to, occasioned by:*

Self-glory . . . . . Is. 14:12-15	669
1 Cor. 4:6-9	1128
Pride . . . . Ezek. 28:11-19	797
1 Pet. 5:5, 6	1239

Advantage—*superior circumstance or ability*

A. *In God's kingdom, none by:*

Birth . . . . Matt. 3:8, 9	943
Race . . . . Gal. 2:14-16	1155
Position . . . . . . John 3:1-6	1044
Works . . . . Matt. 5:20	945
Wealth . . . . Luke 9:25	1017

B. *In God's kingdom, some by:*

Industry . . . . . . 1 Cor. 15:10	1137
Faithfulness . . . Matt. 25:14-30	968
Kindred spirit . . . . Phil. 2:19-23	1171
Works . . . . 1 Cor. 3:11-15	1127
Dedication . . . . . Rev. 14:1-5	1277

Advent of Christ, the first

A. *Announced in the Old Testament by:*

Moses . . . . Deut. 18:18, 19	196
Samuel . . . . Acts 3:24	1075
David . . . . Ps. 40:6-8	564
Heb. 10:5-8	1220
Prophets . . . . . . Luke 24:26, 27	1037

B. *Prophecies fulfilled by his:*

Birth . . . . Is. 7:14	663
Matt. 1:23	942
Forerunner . . . . Mal. 3:1, 2	908
Matt. 3:1-3	943
Incarnation . . . . Is. 9:6	665
Time of (Dan. 9:24, 25	833
arrival . . . . . . (Mark 1:15	978
Rejection . . . . . Is. 53:1-4	695
Rom. 10:16-21	1116
Crucifixion . . . . Ps. 2:1, 2	548
Acts 4:24-28	1076
Atonement . . . . Is. 53:1-12	695
1 Pet. 1:18-21	1236
Resurrection . . . Ps. 16:8-11	552
Acts 2:25-31	1073
Priesthood . . . . Ps. 110:4, 5	597
Heb. 5:5, 6	1217

C. *His first coming:*

Introduces Gospel age . . . . Acts 3:24	1075
Consum- mates new (Jer. 31:31-34	736
covenant . . . . . (Heb. 8:6-13	1219
Fulfills prophecy . . . . . . Luke 24:44, 45	1037
Nullifies the ceremonial system . . . . Heb. 9	1219
Brings Gentiles in . . . . Acts 15:13-18	1089

Advent of Christ, the second (see Second coming of Christ)

Advents of Christ, compared

A. *First Advent:*

Prophesied . . . . . Deut. 18:18, 19	196
Is. 7:14	663
Came as man . . . . Phil. 2:5-8	1171
Announced . . . . Luke 2:10-14	1006
Time predicted . . . . . . Dan. 9:25	833
To save the lost . . . . Matt. 18:11	960
Subject to government . . . Matt. 17:24-27	959

B. *Second Advent:*

Prophesied . . . . . John 14:1-3	1059
1 Thess. 4:16	1185
Come as God . . 1 Thess. 4:16	1185
As a thief . . . . . . 1 Thess. 5:2	1185
At a time unknown . . . . . Matt. 24:36	967
To judge the (Matt. 25:31-33,	
lost . . . . (41-46	968
Source of govern- (Rev. 20:4-6	1281
ment . . . . (Rev. 22:3-5	1282

Adversaries—*those who actively oppose*

A. *Descriptive of:*

Satan . . . . 1 Pet. 5:8	1239
Gospel's enemies . . . . . . 1 Cor. 16:9	1138
Israel's enemies . . . . . . Josh. 5:13	221
An enemy . . . . . Esth. 7:6	511
A rival . . . . 1 Sam. 1:6	276
God's agent . . . 1 Kin. 11:14, 23	352
God's angel . . . . Num. 22:22	159

B. *Believer's attitude toward:*

Pray for . . . . . . Matt. 5:43, 44	946
Use God's weapons against . . . . Luke 21:15	1032
Not to be terrified by . . . . Phil. 1:28	1171
Not to give occasion to . . . 1 Tim. 5:14	1196
Remember God's judgment on . . . . Heb. 10:27	1221

Adversity—*adverse circumstances*

A. *Caused by:*

Man's sin . . . . . . Gen. 3:16-19	7
Disobedience to God's Law . . . . Lev. 26:14-20	127

B. *Purposes of, to:*

Punish for sin . . . . 2 Sam. 12:9-12	319
Humble us . . . . . 2 Chr. 33:12	467
Lead us to God's Word . . . . Deut. 8:2, 3	186
Chasten and correct . . . . Heb. 12:5-11	1223
Test our faith . . . . 1 Pet. 1:5-8	1235
Give us final rest . . . . Ps. 94:12, 13	589

C. *Reactions to:*

Rebellious . . . . . Ex. 14:4-8	69
Job 2:9	520
Distrustful . . . . . Ex. 6:8, 9	61
Complaining . . . Ruth 1:20, 21	269
Questioning . . . . Jer. 20:7-10	726
Fainting . . . . Prov. 24:10	631
Arrogant . . . . . . Ps. 10:6	551
Hopeful . . . . Lam. 3:31-40	764
Submissive . . . . Job 5:17-22	521
Joyful . . . . James 1:2-4	1228

D. *God's relation to, He:*

Troubles nations with . . . . 2 Chr. 15:5, 6	450
Knows the soul in . . . . Ps. 31:7	559
Saves us out of . . 1 Sam. 10:19	284
Redeems out of . . . . 2 Sam. 4:9	312

E. *Helps under:*

By prayer . . . . . . Jon. 2:1-7	867
By understanding God's (Lam. 3:31-39	764
purpose . . . . . (Rom. 5:3	1112

Advertise—*to make known publicly*

Messiah's advent . . . . Num. 24:14-19	161
A piece of property . . . . Ruth 4:4	271

Advice—*one's best judgment*

A. *Sought by:*

A king . . . . Esth. 1:13-15	507
Another ruler . . . . Acts 25:13-27	1100
A usurper . . . . . . 2 Sam. 16:20-23	324

SUBJECT	REFERENCE	PAGE	SUBJECT	REFERENCE	PAGE	SUBJECT	REFERENCE	PAGE

Five men ......2 Kin. 22:12-20 395

B. Sought from:
The ephod .....1 Sam. 23:9-12 298
A prophet .....Jer. 42:1-6 747
A dead
prophet ....1 Sam. 28:7-20 303
A council ......Acts 15:1-22 1088
A grieving
husband ......Judg. 20:4-7 264

C. Kinds of:
Helpful ....Ex. 18:12-25 73
Rejected........1 Kin. 12:6-8 353
Timely ....1 Sam. 25:32-34 300
Good ....2 Kin. 5:13, 14 376
God-
inspired ......2 Sam. 17:6-14 325
Foolish ....Job 2:9 520
Humiliating....Esth. 6:6-11 511
Fatal ....Esth. 5:14 510
Esth. 7:9, 10 511
Ominous........Matt. 27:19 972
Accepted ......Acts 5:34-41 1077

D. Sought from:
Congregation of
Israel ....Judg. 20:7 264

Advocate, Christ our

A. His interest in believers, by right of:
Election ......John 15:16 1060
Redemption....Eph. 1:7 1162
Regenera-
tion..........Col. 1:27 1177
Imputed
righteous-   {2 Cor. 5:21 1146
ness..........{Phil. 3:9 1172

B. His defense of believers by:
Prayer.........Luke 22:31-34 1033
Protection ....Heb. 13:6 1224
{Ps. 23:1 556
Provision .....{John 10:28 1055
Persever-
ance ....2 Tim. 4:17, 18 1202

C. His blessings upon believers:
Another
Comforter.....John 14:16, 17 1059
New command-
ment.........John 13:34, 35 1059
New nature...2 Cor. 5:17 1145
New name....Rev. 2:17 1269
New life ....John 4:14 1045
New
relationship ...John 15:15 1060

D. Our duties prescribed by Him:
Our mission—world evange-
lization ......Matt. 28:16-20 973
Our means—the Holy
Spirit ....Acts 1:8 1072
Our might—the
Gospel ....Rom. 1:16 1109
Our motivation—the love of
Christ.........2 Cor. 5:14, 15 1145

Aeneas—praise

A paralytic healed by
Peter............Acts 9:32-35 1082

Aenon—springs

A place near Salim where John the
Baptist baptized..John 3:22, 23 1044

Afar off—at a far distance

A. Applied physically to:
Distance.......Gen. 22:4 22
A journey .....Num. 9:10 145
Sound of joy...Ezra 3:13 478
Ostracism......Luke 17:12 1027

B. Applied spiritually to:
God's
knowledge ....Ps. 139:2 607
Unworthiness .. Luke 18:13 1028
Eternal
separation....Luke 16:23 1026
Backsliding ....Luke 22:54 1034
Gentiles ......Acts 2:39 1074
God's
promises ......Heb. 11:13 1222

Consignment to
doom ....Rev. 17:10-17 1279

Affability—a personality overflowing
with benign sociability

A. Manifested in:
Cordiality......Gen. 18:1-8 18
Compassion ...Luke 10:33-37 1019
Generosity.....Phil. 4:10, 14-18 1173
Unantagonizing
speech ....1 Sam. 25:23-31 300

B. Examples of:
Jonathan ......1 Sam. 18:1-4 293
Titus ....2 Cor. 8:16-18 1147
Timothy......Phil. 2:17-20 1171
Gaius..........3 John 1-6 1259
Demetrius .....3 John 12 1259

Affectation—a studied pretense

Parade of
egotism ....Esth. 6:6-9 511
Boast of the
power...........Dan. 4:28-30 827
Sign of
hypocrisy........Matt. 6:1, 2, 16 946
Outbreak of false
teachers..........2 Pet. 2:18, 19 1244
Sign of
antichrist........2 Thess. 2:4, 9 1189
Proof of spiritual
decay ....1 Cor. 4:6-8 1128

Affection—an inner feeling or emotion

A. Kinds of:
Natural.........Rom. 1:31 1109
Paternal ....Luke 15:20 1025
Maternal ......1 Kin. 3:16-27 341
Fraternal ......Gen. 43:30-34 46
Filial...........Gen. 49:29, 30 51
National ....Ps. 137:1-6 606
Racial ....Rom. 9:1-3 1115
For wife ......Eph. 5:25-33 1166
For husband ... Titus 2:4 1207
Christian ......Rom. 12:10 1118
Heavenly ......Col. 3:1, 2 1178

B. Good, characteristics of:
Loyal,
intense........Ruth 1:14-18 269
Memorable ....2 Sam. 1:17-27 309
Natural,
normal........2 Sam. 13:37-39 321
Tested, tried ...Gen. 22:1-19 22
Emotional .....John 11:33-36 1056
Grateful ......Luke 7:36-50 1014
Joyous.........Ps. 126:1-6 604
Christ-
centered ......Matt. 10:37-42 951

C. Evil, characteristics of:
Unnatural .....Rom. 1:18-32 1109
Pretended .....Matt. 26:47-49 970
Abnormal......2 Tim. 3:3 1201
Fleshly ....Rom. 13:13, 14 1119
Worldly........2 Tim. 4:10 1202
Defiling,
degrading......2 Pet. 2:10-12 1244
Agonizing, in
hell ....Luke 16:23-28 1026

Afflictions—hardships and trials

A. Visited upon:
Israel in
Egypt........Gen. 15:13 17
Samson by   {Judg. 16:5, 6,
Philistines....{ 19-21 259
David by
God...........Ps. 88:7 586
Judah by
God...........Lam. 3:33 765
Israel by the
world ....Ps. 129:1, 2 604
The just by   {Amos 5:12 858
the wicked....{Heb. 11:37 1222
Christians by the
world ....2 Cor. 1:6 1143

B. Design of, to:
Show God's
mercy..........Is. 63:9 702

Make us seek
God...........Hos. 5:15 843
Bring us back to
God...........Ps. 119:67 601
Humble us.....2 Chr. 33:12 467
Test us ....Is. 48:10 692

C. In the Christian's life:
A means of
testing ....Mark 4:17 982
A part of life...Matt. 24:9 967
To be
endured.......2 Tim. 4:5 1202
Part of
Gospel ....1 Thess. 1:6 1183
Must not be disturbed
by ....1 Thess. 3:3 1184
Commendable
examples of ...2 Tim. 3:11 1202
Momentary ....2 Cor. 4:17 1145
Sometimes
intense........2 Cor. 1:8-10 1143
Must be
shared ....Phil. 4:14 1173
Cannot separate from
God...........Rom. 8:35-39 1115
Deliverance from,
promised......Ps. 34:19 561
Need
prayer in.....James 5:13 1231
Terminated at Christ's
return........2 Thess. 1:4-7 1189

See also Trials

Afraid—overcome with fear

A. Caused by:
Nakedness.....Gen. 3:10 7
Unusual
dream........Gen. 28:16, 17 30
God's
presence ......Ex. 3:6 58
Moses'
approach......Ex. 34:30 90
A burning
mountain .....Deut. 5:5 183
Giant's   {1 Sam. 17:11,
raging........{ 24 291
A prophet's
words.........1 Sam. 28:20 303
Angel's
sword.........1 Chr. 21:30 426
God's
judgments ....Ps. 65:8 574
Gabriel's
presence ......Dan. 8:17 832
A terrifying
storm.........Jon. 1:5, 10 866
Peter's
sinking........Matt. 14:30 956
Changed
person ....Mark 5:15 983
Heavenly
hosts..........Luke 2:9 1006

B. Overcome by:
The Lord's
presence ......Ps. 3:5, 6 548
Trusting God ..Ps. 27:1-3 557
God's
protection.....Ps. 91:4, 5 588
Stability of
heart..........Ps. 112:7, 8 597
God's coming
judgment .....Is. 10:24-26 666
The Messiah's
advent........Is. 40:9-11 685
God's sovereign
power.........Is. 51:12, 13 694
Christ's comforting
words.........Matt. 14:27 956

Afternoon—part of the day following
noon

Called cool of the
day............Gen. 3:8 6

Afterthought—a later reflection

Of Esau........Heb. 12:16, 17 1223
Of the Israelites...Num. 14:40-45 151
Of one of two
sons..............Matt. 21:28-30 963

39

Removing
boundaries....Deut. 19:14   196
Roaming
cattle.........Ex. 22:5   76
Spreading
fire...........Ex. 22:6   76
Military
service.......Deut. 20:5, 6   197
Working on the
Sabbath......Ex. 34:21   90
Complete
harvest......Lev. 19:9, 10   119
E. God's part in:
Began in
Eden..........Gen. 2:15   5
Sin's penalty...Gen. 3:17   7
Providence of,
impartial.....Matt. 5:45   946
Goodness of,
recognized....Acts 14:16, 17   1088
Judgments against,
cited.........Hag. 1:10, 11   892
F. Figurative of:
Gospel seed....Matt. 13:1-9   954
Gospel
dispen-   {Matt. 13:24-30,
sation........{   36-43   954
God's
workers......John 4:36-38   1046
God's Word....Is. 55:10, 11   696
Spiritual
barrenness....Heb. 6:7, 8   1217
Spiritual bountiful-
ness..........2 Cor. 9:9, 10   1148
Final harvest..Mark 4:28, 29   982

Aground—stranded in shallow water

Ship carrying
Paul..............Acts 27:41   1103

Ague—a malarial fever; jaundice

A divine
punishment......Lev. 26:16   127

Agur—collector

Writer of
proverbs.........Prov. 30:1-33   635

Ahab—father's brother

1. A wicked king of
Israel.........1 Kin. 16:29   359
Marries
Jezebel........1 Kin. 16:31   359
Introduces Baal
worship.......1 Kin. 16:31-33   359
Denounced by
Elijah.........1 Kin. 17:1   359
Gathers prophets of
Baal..........1 Kin. 18:17-46   360
Wars against Ben-
hadad.........1 Kin. 20:1-43   363
Covets Naboth's
vineyard......1 Kin. 21:1-16   364
Death of,
predicted......1 Kin. 21:17-26   365
Repentance of, delays
judgment......1 Kin. 21:27-29   365
Joins Jehoshaphat against
Syrians......1 Kin. 22:1-4   365
Rejects Micaiah's
warning.......1 Kin. 22:5-33   365
Slain in
battle.........1 Kin. 22:34-37   367
Seventy sons of,
slain..........2 Kin. 10:1-11   381
Prophecies concerning,
fulfilled.......1 Kin. 22:38   367
2. Lying
prophet.......Jer. 29:21-23   734

Aharah—after his brother

Son of Benjamin..1 Chr. 8:1   413
Called Ahiram....Num. 26:38   163
Called Ehi.......Gen. 46:21   48

Aharhel—brother of Rachel

A descendant of
Judah............1 Chr. 4:8   408

Ahasai—Yahweh has grasped

A postexilic
priest.............Neh. 11:13   500
Also called
Jahzerah.........1 Chr. 9:12   414

Ahasbai—blooming, shining

The father of
Eliphelet.........2 Sam. 23:34   332

Ahasuerus—king

1. The father of Darius the
Mede.........Dan. 9:1   832
2. Persian king...Esth. 1:1   507
Makes Esther
queen.........Esth. 2:16, 17   508
Follows Haman's
intrigue.......Esth. 3:1, 8-12   509
Orders Jews
annihilated....Esth. 3:13-15   509
Responds to Esther's
plea.........Esth. 7:1-8   511
Orders Haman
hanged........Esth. 7:9, 10   511
Promotes
Mordecai......Esth. 8:1, 2   512
Reverses Haman's
plot.........Esth. 8:3-17   512
Exalts
Mordecai......Esth. 10:1-3   514
3. A king of Persia;
probably Xerxes,
486-465 B.C....Ezra 4:6   478

Ahava—a town in Babylonia

Jewish exiles gather
here.............Ezra 8:15-31   482

Ahaz—he has grasped

1. A king of Judah; son of
Jotham.......2 Kin. 16:1, 2   388
Pursues evil
ways.........2 Kin. 16:3, 4   388
Defends Jerusalem against
Rezin and
Pekah.........2 Kin. 16:5, 6   388
Refuses a divine
sign..........Is. 7:1-16   663
Defeated with great
loss.........2 Chr. 28:5-15   461
Becomes subject to
Assyria.......2 Kin. 16:7-9   388
Makes Damascus a pagan
city..........2 Kin. 16:10-18   388
Erects
sundial.......2 Kin. 20:11   393
Death of.......2 Kin. 16:19, 20   389
2. A descendant
of   {1 Chr. 8:35, 36   413
Jonathan....{1 Chr. 9:40-42   415
3. Ancestor of
Jesus.........Matt. 1:9   941

Ahaziah—Yahweh has grasped

1. A king of Israel; son of Ahab
and Jezebel...1 Kin. 22:40, 51   367
Worships
Baal.........1 Kin. 22:52, 53   367
Seeks alliance with Jehosh-
aphat........1 Kin. 22:48, 49   367
Falls through lattice; sends to
Baal-zebub, the god of Ekron
for help......2 Kin. 1:2-16   371
Dies according to Elijah's
word.........2 Kin. 1:17, 18   372
2. A king of Judah; son of
Jehoram and
Athaliah......2 Kin. 8:25, 26   380
Made king by Jerusalem
inhabitants....2 Chr. 22:1, 2   456
Taught evil by his
mother........2 Chr. 22:2, 3   456
Follows Ahab's
wickedness....2 Chr. 22:4   456
Joins Joram against the
Syrians.......2 Kin. 8:28   380
Visits wounded
Joram.........2 Kin. 9:16   381
Slain by
Jehu.........2 Kin. 9:27, 28   381

Called
Jehoahaz......2 Chr. 21:17   456
Called
Azariah.......2 Chr. 22:6   456

Ahban—brother of intelligence

A son of
Abishur..........1 Chr. 2:29   406

Aher—another

A Benjamite......1 Chr. 7:12   412

Ahi—brother

1. Gadite chief...1 Chr. 5:15   409
2. Asherite
chief..........1 Chr. 7:34   413

Ahiah—brother of Yahweh

1. A priest during Saul's
reign.........1 Sam. 14:3, 18   287
2. A secretary of
Solomon......1 Kin. 4:3   342
3. A Benjamite...1 Chr. 8:7   413

Ahiam—mother's brother

One of David's mighty
men.........2 Sam. 23:33   332

Ahian—fraternal

A Manassite......1 Chr. 7:19   412

Ahiezer—brother is help

1. Head of the tribe of
Dan..........Num. 1:12   134
2. Benjamite chief, joined David at
Ziklag........1 Chr. 12:3   417

Ahihud—brother is majesty

1. Asherite leader, helped Moses
divide
Canaan.......Num. 34:27   173
2. A Benjamite...1 Chr. 8:6, 7   413

Ahijah—brother of Yahweh

1. A great-grandson of
Judah..........1 Chr. 2:25   406
2. One of David's
warriors.......1 Chr. 11:36   416
3. A Levite treasurer in David's
reign.........1 Chr. 26:20   430
4. A prophet of Shiloh who
foretells division of Solomon's
kingdom......1 Kin. 11:29-39   352
Foretells elimination of
Jeroboam's
line..........1 Kin. 14:1-18   355
A writer of
prophecy.....2 Chr. 9:29   446
5. The father of
Baasha.......1 Kin. 15:27, 33   357
6. A Jew who seals Nehemiah's
covenant......Neh. 10:26   499
See Ahiah

Ahikam—my brother has arisen

A son of Shaphan the
scribe.........2 Kin. 22:12   395
Sent in Josiah's mission to
Huldah..........2 Kin. 22:12-14   395
Protects
Jeremiah......Jer. 26:24   732
The father of Gedaliah,
governor under
Nebuchad-   {2 Kin. 25:22   400
nezzar.......{Jer. 39:14   745

Ahilud—a child's brother

1. The father of Jehoshaphat, the
recorder under David and
Solomon......2 Sam. 8:16   316
2. The father of Baana, a
commissionary
official.........1 Kin. 4:7, 12   342

Ahimaaz—brother of anger

1. The father of Ahinoam, wife of
King Saul....1 Sam. 14:50   288
2. A son of Zadok the high
priest.........1 Chr. 6:8, 9   410

SUBJECT	REFERENCE	PAGE

Ahimaaz—continued
Warns David of Absalom's
plans.........2 Sam. 15:27, 36   323
Good man ....2 Sam. 18:27   326
First to tell David of Absalom's
defeat.......2 Sam. 18:19-30   326
3. Solomon's son-in-law and
commissioner in
Naphtali ......1 Kin. 4:15   342
May be the same as 2.

Ahiman—*my brother is a gift*
1. A giant son of Anak seen by
Israelite
spies.........Num. 13:22, 33   149
Driven out of Hebron by
Caleb.......Josh. 15:13, 14   231
Slain by tribe of
Judah........Judg. 1:10   244
2. A Levite
gatekeeper....1 Chr. 9:17   414

Ahimelech—*my brother is king*
1. The high priest at Nob during
Saul's reign...1 Sam. 21:1   296
Feeds David the
showbread...1 Sam. 21:2-6   296
Gives Goliath's sword to
David........1 Sam. 21:8, 9   296
Betrayed by
Doeg.........1 Sam. 22:9-16   297
Slain by Doeg at Saul's
command.....1 Sam. 22:17-19   297
Abiathar, son of,
escapes.....1 Sam. 22:20   297
David wrote
concerning....Ps. 52 (title)   570
2. Abiathar's
son ....2 Sam. 8:17   316
Co-priest with
Zadok ....1 Chr. 24:3, 6, 31   428
3. David's Hittite
warrior ......1 Sam. 26:6   301

Ahimoth—*my brother is death*
A Kohathite
Levite........1 Chr. 6:25   410

Ahinadab—*my brother is noble*
One of Solomon's
officers..........1 Kin. 4:14   342

Ahinoam—*my brother is delight*
1. Wife of Saul...1 Sam. 14:50   288
2. David's wife ...1 Sam. 25:43   301
Lived with David at
Gath.........1 Sam. 27:3   302
Captured by Amalekites at
Ziklag.....1 Sam. 30:5   304
Rescued by
David........1 Sam. 30:18   304
Lives with David in
Hebron ......2 Sam. 2:1, 2   309
Mother of
Amnon ......2 Sam. 3:2   311

Ahio—*brotherly*
1. Abinadab's
son ....2 Sam. 6:3   313
2. A Benjamite ...1 Chr. 8:14   413
3. A son of   {1 Chr. 8:31   413
Jehiel ....{1 Chr. 9:37   415

Ahira—*my brother is evil*
A tribal leader ....Num. 1:15   134

Ahisamach—*my brother supports*
A Danite........Ex. 31:6   86

Ahishahar—*brother of dawn*
A Benjamite ......1 Chr. 7:10   412

Ahishar—*my brother has sung*
A manager of Solomon's
household .....1 Kin. 4:6   342

Ahithophel—*brother of folly*
David's
counselor.....2 Sam. 15:12   323
Joins Absalom's
insurrection ......2 Sam. 15:31   323

Plans of, prepared against by
David ....2 Sam. 15:31-34   323
Counsels
Absalom.......2 Sam. 16:20-22   324
Reputed wise .....2 Sam. 16:23   324
Counsel of, rejected by
Absalom.......2 Sam. 17:1-22   324
Commits suicide ..2 Sam. 17:23   325

Ahitub—*my brother is goodness*
1. Phinehas'
son ....1 Sam. 14:3   287
2. The father of Zadok the
priest ....2 Sam. 8:17   316
3. The father of another
Zadok ....1 Chr. 6:11, 12   410

Ahlab—*fruitful*
A city of Asher....Judg. 1:31   244

Ahlai—*O would that!*
1. David's
warrior ....1 Chr. 11:41   417
2. Marries an Egyptian
servant ......1 Chr. 2:31-35   406

Ahoah—*brotherly*
A son of Bela .....1 Chr. 8:4   413

Ahohite—*a descendant of Ahoah*
Applied to Dodo,
Zalmon, and   {2 Sam. 23:9, 28   332
Ilai...............{1 Chr. 11:29   416

Aholah—*tent-woman*
Symbolic name of Samaria and
Israel.....Ezek. 23:4, 5, 36   791

Aholiab—*a father's tent*
Son of
Ahisamach .....Ex. 31:6   86

Ahumai—*heated by Yahweh*
A descendant of
Judah ....1 Chr. 4:2   407

Ahuzzam—*possessor*
A man of Judah...1 Chr. 4:6   408

Ahuzzath—*possession*
A friend of
Abimelech........Gen. 26:26   28

Ai—*ruin*
1. A city east of Beth-el in central
Palestine........Josh. 7:2   222
Abraham camps
near ....Gen. 12:8   15
A royal city of
Canaan ......Josh. 10:1   225
Israel
defeated at....Josh. 7:2-5   222
Israel destroys
completely ....Josh. 8:1-28   223
Occupied after
exile ....Ezra 2:28   476
2. An Ammonite city near
Heshbon ......Jer. 49:3   753

Aiah—*falcon*
1. A Horite......Gen. 36:24   38
2. The father of Rizpah, Saul's
concubine.....2 Sam. 3:7   311

Aijalon—*place of gazelles*
1. A town assigned to
Dan..........Josh. 19:42   235
Amorites not driven
from ....Judg. 1:35   245
Miracle there ..Josh. 10:12   226
Assigned to Kohathite
Levites......Josh. 21:24   236
City of
refuge......1 Chr. 6:66-69   411
Included in Benjamin's
territory ....1 Chr. 8:13   413
Fortified by
Rehoboam .....2 Chr. 11:5, 10   447
Captured by
Philistines....2 Chr. 28:18   462

2. The burial place of Elon, a
judge ....Judg. 12:12   257

Ain—*spring*
1. A town near
Riblah ....Num. 34:11   172
2. Town of
Judah........Josh. 15:32   231
Transferred to
Simeon ......Josh. 19:7   234
Later assigned to the
priests......Josh. 21:16   236
Called Ashan ..1 Chr. 6:59   411
3. Letter of the Hebrew
alphabet ....Ps. 119:121-128   602

Air—*the atmosphere around the earth*
Man given dominion
over..............Gen. 1:26-30   4
Man names
birds of..........Gen. 2:19, 20   5
God destroys
birds of........Gen. 6:7   9
Mystery of
eagle in ....Prov. 30:19   635
Satan, prince of ..Eph. 2:2   1162
Believers meet
Jesus in ....1 Thess. 4:17   1185
God's wrath poured
out in ....Rev. 9:2   1273
Figurative of
emptiness ....1 Cor. 9:26   1132

Akkub—*cunning*
1. Elioenai's
son ....1 Chr. 3:24   407
2. A Levite head of a family of
porters......1 Chr. 9:17   414
3. A family of
Nethinim......Ezra 2:45   476
4. A Levite
interpreter ....Neh. 8:7   496

Akrabbim—*scorpions*
An "ascent" on the south of the
Dead Sea.......Num. 34:4   172
One border of Judah—
Acrabbim ....Josh. 15:3   230

Alabaster—*a container for perfumes
and ointments*
Used by woman anointing
Jesus............Matt. 26:7   969

Alameth (see Alemeth)

Alammelech—*oak of a king*
Village of Asher...Josh. 19:26   235

Alamoth—*virgins*
A musical term probably indicating
a women's
choir ....1 Chr. 15:20   420

Alarm—*sudden and fearful surprise*
A. Caused physically by:
Sudden
attack........Judg. 7:20-23   251
Death plague ..Ex. 12:29-33   67
A mysterious manifesta-
tion..........1 Sam. 28:11-14   303
Prodigies of
nature ....Matt. 27:50-54   972
B. Caused spiritually by:
Sin ....1 Sam. 12:17-19   286
Remorse.......Gen. 27:34-40   29
Conscience ....Acts 24:24, 25   1100
Hopelessness in
hell ....Luke 16:22-31   1026
C. Shout of jubilee or warning:
Instruction to
Israel ....Num. 10:9   146
Causes
anguish.......Jer. 4:19   712
Prophecy of
judgment .....Jer. 49:2   753
See Agitation

SUBJECT	REFERENCE	PAGE	SUBJECT	REFERENCE	PAGE	SUBJECT	REFERENCE	PAGE

Almighty—continued

Applied to
Christ . . . . Rev. 1:8   1268

Almodad—*the beloved*

Eldest son of
Joktan . . . . Gen. 10:26   13

Almond—*a small tree bearing fruit*

Sent as a present to
Pharaoh . . . . Gen. 43:11   45
Used in the
tabernacle . . . . Ex. 25:33, 34   80
Aaron's rod
produces . . . . Num. 17:2, 3, 8   154
Used figuratively of old
age . . . . Eccl. 12:5   647
Translated "hazel"
in . . . . Gen. 30:37   32

Almon-diblathaim—*Almon of the double cake of figs*

An Israelite
encampment . . . . . Num. 33:46, 47   172

Alms, almsgiving—*gifts prompted by love to help the needy*

A. *Design of, to:*
Help the
poor . . . . Lev. 25:35   126
Receive a
blessing . . . . Deut. 15:10, 11   193

B. *Manner of bestowing with:*
A willing
spirit . . . . Deut. 15:7-11   193
Simplicity . . . . . Matt. 6:1-4   946
Cheerfulness . . . 2 Cor. 9:7   1148
True love . . . . . 1 Cor. 13:3   1135
Fairness to
all . . . . Acts 4:32-35   1076
Regularity . . . . . Acts 11:29, 30   1085
Law of
reciprocity . . . . Rom. 15:25-27   1121

C. *Cautions concerning:*
Not for man's
honor . . . . Matt. 6:1-4   946
Not for lazy . . . 2 Thess. 3:10   1190
Needful for the
rich . . . . 1 Tim. 6:17, 18   1197

D. *Rewarded:*
Now . . . . Deut. 14:28, 29   193
           2 Cor. 9:9, 10   1148
In heaven . . . . Matt. 19:21   961

E. *Examples of:*
Zaccheus . . . . . Luke 19:8   1029
Dorcas . . . . Acts 9:36   1082
Cornelius . . . . . Acts 10:2   1083
The early
Christians . . . . Acts 4:34-37   1076

Aloes—*a perfume-bearing tree*

A. *Used on:*
Beds . . . . Prov. 7:17   619
The dead . . . . . John 19:39   1065

B. *Figurative of:*
Israel . . . . Num. 24:5, 6   161
The Church . . . Ps. 45:8   567

Aloth—*ascents, steeps*

A town in Asher . . 1 Kin. 4:16   342

Alpha and Omega—*first and last letters of the Greek alphabet ("A to Z")*

Expressive of God's
and Christ's   (Rev. 1:8, 17, 18   1268
eternity . . . . (Rev. 21:6, 7   1282

Alphabet—*the letters of a language*

The Hebrew, seen
in . . . . Ps. 119   599

Alphaeus—*leader, chief*

1. The father of Levi
(Matthew) . . . . Mark 2:14   980
2. The father of
James . . . . Matt. 10:3   950

Altar—*an elevated structure*

A. *Uses of:*
Sacrifice . . . . . . Gen. 8:20   11
Incense . . . . . . (Ex. 30:1, 7, 8   85
         (Luke 1:10, 11   1004
National
unity . . . . Deut. 12:5, 6   190
A memorial . . . . Ex. 17:15, 16   72
Protection . . . . . Ex. 21:13, 14   76

B. *Made of:*
Earth . . . . Ex. 20:24   75
Unhewn
stone . . . . Ex. 20:25   75
Stones . . . . Deut. 27:5, 6   203
Natural rock . . . Judg. 6:19-21   249
Bronze . . . . Ex. 27:1-6   81

C. *Built worthily by:*
Noah . . . . Gen. 8:20   11
Abraham . . . . . Gen. 12:7, 8   15
Isaac . . . . Gen. 26:25   28
Jacob . . . . Gen. 33:18, 20   35
Moses . . . . Ex. 17:15   72
Joshua . . . . Deut. 27:4-7   203
Eastern
tribes . . . . Josh. 22:10, 34   237
Gideon . . . . Judg. 6:26, 27   249
Manoah . . . . . . Judg. 13:19, 20   258
Israelites . . . . . Judg. 21:4   265
Samuel . . . . 1 Sam. 7:17   282
Saul . . . . 1 Sam. 14:35   288
David . . . . 2 Sam. 24:18-25   333
Elijah . . . . 1 Kin. 18:31, 32   361

D. *Built unworthily (for idolatry) by:*
Gideon's
father . . . . Judg. 6:25-32   249
King
Jeroboam . . . . 1 Kin. 12:32, 33   354
King Ahab . . . . . 1 Kin. 18:30-32   361
King Ahaz . . . . . 2 Chr. 28:1, 3, 5   461
Israelite
people . . . . Is. 65:3   702
Athenians . . . . Acts 17:23   1092

E. *Pagan altars destroyed by:*
Gideon . . . . Judg. 6:25-29   249
King Asa . . . . . . 2 Chr. 14:2, 3   449
Jehoiada . . . . . . 2 Kin. 11:17, 18   383
King
Hezekiah . . . . . 2 Kin. 18:22   391
King Josiah . . . . 2 Kin. 23:12, 16,
                17   397

F. *Burnt offering:*
1. *Of the tabernacle, features concerning:*
Specifi-
cations . . . . . . Ex. 27:1-8   81
Bezaleel, builder
of . . . . Ex. 31:1-6, 9   86
Place of, outside
tabernacle . . . Ex. 40:6, 29   96
Only priests
allowed at . . . . Num. 18:3, 7   154
The defective not acceptable
on . . . . Lev. 22:22   122
The putting on of
blood . . . . Ex. 29:12   84
2. *Of Solomon's Temple:*
Described . . . . . 1 Kin. 8:63, 64   349
Renewed by
King Asa . . . . . . 2 Chr. 15:8   450
Cleansed by King
Hezekiah . . . . . 2 Chr. 29:18-24   463
Repaired by King
Manasseh . . . . 2 Chr. 33:16-18   467
Vessels of, carried to
Babylon . . . . . 2 Kin. 25:14   399
3. *Of the postexilic (Zerubbabel's) temple:*
Described . . . . . Ezra 3:1-6   477
Polluted . . . . . . Mal. 1:7, 8   907
4. *Of Ezekiel's vision:*
Described . . . . . Ezek. 43:13-27   812

G. *Incense:*
In the tabernacle,
described . . . . . Ex. 30:1-10   85

Location of . . . . Ex. 30:6   85
Anointed
with oil . . . . . . Ex. 30:26, 27   86
Annual atonement
made at . . . . . . Ex. 30:10   85
In Solomon's
Temple . . . . . . 1 Kin. 7:48   346
In John's
vision . . . . Rev. 8:3   1273

H. *New covenant:*
A place of spiritual
sacrifices . . . . Rom. 12:1, 2   1118
Christ, our
pattern . . . . . . Heb. 13:10-16   1224

Al-taschith—*destroy not*

A term found in the
title of . . . . Ps. 57; 59; 75   571

Altruism—*living for the good of others*

A. *Manifested in:*
Service . . . . Matt. 20:26-28   962
Doing good . . . . Acts 10:38   1084
Seeking the welfare of
others . . . . Gal. 6:1, 2, 10   1158
Helping the
weak . . . . Acts 20:35   1095

B. *Examples of:*
Moses . . . . Ex. 32:30-32   88
Samuel . . . . 1 Sam. 12:1-5   285
Jonathan . . . . . 1 Sam. 18:1-4   293
Christ . . . . John 13:4-17   1058
Paul . . . . 1 Cor. 9:19-22   1132

Alush—*wild place*

An Israelite
encampment . . . . . Num. 33:13, 14   171

Alvah—*high; tall*

An Edomite
chief . . . . Gen. 36:40   38
Also called Aliah . . 1 Chr. 1:51   405

Alvan—*tall*

A son of Shobal the
Horite . . . . Gen. 36:23   38
Also called Alian . . 1 Chr. 1:40   405

Always—*continually, forever*

A. *Of God's:*
Care . . . . Deut. 11:12   189
Covenant . . . . . 1 Chr. 16:15   420
Chide . . . . Ps. 103:9   591

B. *Of Christ's:*
Determi-
nation . . . . (Ps. 16:8-11   552
          (Acts 2:25-28   1073
Rejoicing . . . . . Prov. 8:30-31   620
Presence . . . . . Matt. 28:20   974
Obedience . . . . John 8:29   1052
Prayer . . . . John 11:42   1056

C. *Of the believer's:*
Prayer . . . . Luke 21:36   1033
Peace . . . . 2 Thess. 3:16   1190
Obedience . . . . Phil. 2:12   1171
Work . . . . 1 Cor. 15:58   1138
Defense . . . . . . 1 Pet. 3:15   1238
Rejoicing . . . . . Phil. 4:4   1172
Thanks-
giving . . . . 1 Thess. 1:2   1183
Victory . . . . 2 Cor. 2:14   1144
Conscience . . . Acts 24:16   1099
Confidence . . . 2 Cor. 5:6   1145
Sufficiency . . . . 2 Cor. 9:8   1148

D. *Of the unbeliever's:*
Probation . . . . . Gen. 6:3   9
Turmoil . . . . . . Mark 5:5   983
Rebellion . . . . . Acts 7:51   1080
Lying . . . . Titus 1:12   1206

Amad—*people of duration*

A city of Asher . . . . Josh. 19:26   235

Amal—*toil*

Asher's
descendant . . . . . . 1 Chr. 7:35   413

44

SUBJECT	REFERENCE	PAGE

Ashes—*the powdery residue of burned material*

A. *Used for:*
A miracle......Ex. 9:8-10 — 64
Purification....Num. 19:1-10 — 156
           Heb. 9:13 — 1219
A disguise.....1 Kin. 20:38, 41 — 364

B. *Symbolic of:*
Mourning......2 Sam. 13:19 — 320
           Esth. 4:1, 3 — 509
Dejection......Job 2:8 — 520
Repentance....Job 42:6 — 543
           Matt. 11:21 — 952
Fasting........Dan. 9:3 — 832

C. *Figurative of:*
Frailty........Gen. 18:27 — 19
Destruction....Ezek. 28:18 — 797
Victory........Mal. 4:3 — 909
Worthless-
   ness..........Job 13:12 — 526
Trans-
   formation....Is. 61:3 — 700
Deceit.........Is. 44:20 — 689
Afflictions....Ps. 102:9 — 591
Destruction....Jer. 6:26 — 714

Ashima—*heaven*

A god or idol worshiped by Assyrian colonists at Samaria.........2 Kin. 17:30 — 390

Ashkelon—*holm-oak*

One of five   { Josh. 13:3 — 229
Philistine cities . . {Jer. 47:5, 7 — 751
Captured by Judah...........Judg. 1:18 — 244
Men of, killed by Samson.........Judg. 14:19, 20 — 259
Repossessed by   { 1 Sam. 6:17 — 281
Philistines.......{2 Sam. 1:20 — 309
Doom of,   { Jer. 47:5, 7 — 751
pronounced   { Amos 1:8 — 855
by the   { Zeph. 2:4, 7 — 888
prophets.........{ Zech. 9:5 — 900

Ashkenaz

1. A descendant of Noah
through   { Gen. 10:3 — 13
Japheth......{1 Chr. 1:6 — 404
2. A nation (probably descendants of 1) associated with Ararat, Minni........Jer. 51:27 — 757

Ashnah—*hard, firm*

1. A village of Judah near Zorah........Josh. 15:33 — 231
2. Another village of Judah........Josh. 15:43 — 231

Ashpenaz

The chief of Nebuchadnezzar's eunuchs.........Dan. 1:3 — 822

Ashtaroth, Astaroth (plural of "Ashtoreth")

1. A city in Bashan;
residence of   { Deut. 1:4 — 178
King Og .....{Josh. 12:4 — 228
Captured by Israel.........Josh. 9:10 — 225
Assigned to Manasseh.....Josh. 13:31 — 229
Made a Levitical city ("Beeshterah")..Josh. 21:27 — 237
Uzzia, a native of......1 Chr. 11:44 — 417
2. A general designation of the Canaanite female   { 1 Sam. 7:3, 4 — 281
deities........{1 Sam. 31:10 — 305

Ashteroth-karnaim—*twin peaks near Ashtaroth*

A fortified city in Gilead occupied by the Rephaims........Gen. 14:5 — 16

Ashtoreth—*the name given by Hebrews to the goddess Ashtart (Astarte)*

A. *A mother goddess of love, fertility and war worshiped by:*
Philistines.....1 Sam. 31:10 — 305
Sidonians.....1 Kin. 11:5, 33 — 351
Hebrews (see below)

B. *Israel's relation to:*
Ensnared by...Judg. 2:13 — 245
           Judg. 10:6 — 254
Repent of, in Samuel's time..........1 Sam. 7:3, 4 — 281
Worship of, by Solomon.....1 Kin. 11:5, 33 — 351
Destroyed by Josiah.........2 Kin. 23:13 — 397
See Ashtaroth

Ashur—*blackness*

A descendant of { 1 Chr. 2:24 — 406
Judah ....{1 Chr. 4:5-7 — 408

Ashurites

A people belonging to Ish-bosheth's kingdom ....2 Sam. 2:8, 9 — 310

Ashvath—*made*

An Asherite......1 Chr. 7:33 — 413

Asia—*in New Testament times, the Roman province of proconsular Asia*

People from, at Pentecost........Acts 2:9, 10 — 1073
Paul forbidden to preach in.........Acts 16:6 — 1090
Paul's later ministry in.......Acts 19:1-26 — 1093
Paul plans to pass by..........Acts 20:16, 17 — 1095
Converts in, greeted by Paul...............Rom. 16:5 — 1121
Paul's great conflict in.........2 Cor. 1:8 — 1143
Peter writes to saints of..........1 Pet. 1:1 — 1235
Seven churches of......Rev. 1:4, 11 — 1268

Asiel—*God has made*

A Simeonite.......1 Chr. 4:35 — 408

Asking in prayer

A. *Based upon:*
God's fore-knowledge....Matt. 6:8 — 946
God's willingness....Luke 11:11-13 — 1020
God's love.....John 16:23-27 — 1061
Abiding in Christ..........John 15:7 — 1060

B. *Receiving of answer, based upon:*
Having faith...James 1:5, 6 — 1228
Keeping God's commands...1 John 3:22 — 1252
Regarding God's will..........1 John 5:14, 15 — 1253
Believing trust.........Matt. 21:22 — 963
Unselfish-ness.........James 4:2, 3 — 1230
In Christ's   { John 14:13, 14 — 1059
name ....{John 15:16 — 1060

Asnah—*thornbush*

The head of a family of Nethinims........Ezra 2:50 — 476

Asnapper—*probably the Aramaean name for "Ashurbanipal", an Assyrian king*

Called "the great and noble"...........Ezra 4:10 — 478

Asp—*a deadly snake*

Figurative of man's evil   { Deut. 32:33 — 211
nature...........{Rom. 3:13 — 1110
Figurative of man's changed nature............Is. 11:8 — 667

Aspatha—*horse-given*

A son of Haman ..Esth. 9:7 — 513

Aspiration—*exalted desire combined with holy zeal*

A. *Centered in:*
God Himself ...Ps. 42:1, 2 — 565
God's kingdom .....Matt. 6:33 — 947
The high calling ......Phil. 3:8-14 — 1172
Heaven........Col. 3:1, 2 — 1178
Acceptableness with Christ.........2 Tim. 2:4 — 1201

B. *Inspired by:*
Christ's love ...2 Cor. 5:14-16 — 1145
Work yet to   { Rom. 15:18-20 — 1120
be done......{2 Cor. 10:13-18 — 1149
Christ's grace ....2 Cor. 12:9-15 — 1150
The reward ....2 Tim. 4:7, 8 — 1202
The Lord's   { Matt. 24:42-47 — 967
return.........{1 John 3:1-3 — 1251
World's end....2 Pet. 3:11-14 — 1244

Asriel, Ashriel—*God has filled with joy*

A descendant of Manasseh and   { Num. 26:31 — 163
progenitor of the { Josh. 17:2 — 232
Asrielites ....{1 Chr. 7:14 — 412

Ass—*donkey*

A. *Used for:*
Riding.........Gen. 22:3 — 22
Carrying burdens.......Gen. 42:26 — 44
Food ....2 Kin. 6:25 — 378
Royalty.......Judg. 5:10 — 248

B. *Regulations concerning:*
Not to be yoked with an ox ....Deut. 22:10 — 199
To be rested { Ex. 23:12 — 78
on Sabbath...{Luke 13:15 — 1023
To be redeemed with a lamb.........Ex. 34:20 — 90

C. *Special features regarding:*
Spoke to Balaam.....Num. 22:28-31 — 159
Knowing his owner........Is. 1:3 — 658
Jawbone kills many ....Judg. 15:15-17 — 259
Jesus rides   { Zech. 9:9 — 901
upon one.....{Matt. 21:2, 5 — 963
All cared for by God..........Ps. 104:11 — 592

D. *Figurative of:*
Wildness (in Hebrew, "wild ass")........Gen. 16:12 — 17
Stubbornness..Hos. 8:9 — 844
Promiscuity....Jer. 2:24 — 710

Assassination—*killing by secret and sudden assault*

A. *Actual cases of:*
Eglon by Ehud.........Judg. 3:17, 20, 21 — 246
Sisera by Jael..........Judg. 4:17-21 — 247
Abner by Joab..........2 Sam. 3:27 — 311
Ish-bosheth by sons of Rimmon ......2 Sam. 4:5-8 — 312

Azrikam—*my help has arisen*

1. Son of
   Neariah.......1 Chr. 3:23   407
2. A son of
   Azel ....1 Chr. 8:38   413
3. A Merarite
   Levite........1 Chr. 9:14   414
4. Governor under King
   Ahaz.........2 Chr. 28:7   461

Azubah—*forsaken*

1. Wife of
   Caleb ....1 Chr. 2:18, 19   406
2. Mother of Jehosh-
   aphat ....1 Kin. 22:42   367

Azur, Azzur—*helpful*

1. Father of
   Hananiah .....Jer. 28:1   733
2. Father of
   Jaazaniah....Ezek. 11:1   779
3. A covenant
   signer........Neh. 10:17   499

Azzan—*strong*

Father of Paltiel...Num. 34:26   173

B

Baal—*lord, possessor, husband*

A. *The nature of:*
   The male god of the
   Phoenicians and Canaanites;
   the counterpart of the female
   Ashtaroth.....2 Kin. 23:5   397
   Connected
   with   {Num. 25:1, 3, 5   162
   immorality...{Hos. 9:10   844
   Incense
   burned in.....Jer. 7:9   715
   Kissing the   {1 Kin. 19:18   362
   image of .....{Hos. 13:1, 2   846
   Dervish rites by
   priests of......1 Kin. 18:26, 28   361
   Children burned in
   fire of.......Jer. 19:5   725
   Eating
   sacrifices......Ps. 106:28   594
B. *History of:*
   Among Moabites in Moses'
   time ....Num. 22:41   160
   Altars built to, during
   time of   {Judg. 2:11-14   245
   judges   {Judg. 6:28-32   249
   Jezebel introduces into
   Israel ....1 Kin. 16:31, 32   359
   Elijah's overthrow of, on Mt.
   Carmel.......1 Kin. 18:17-40   360
   Athaliah
   encourages
   worship in   {2 Kin. 11:14-20   383
   Judah.......{2 Chr. 22:2-4   456
   Revived again in
   Israel and   {Hos. 2:8   841
   Judah.......{Amos 5:26   858
   Ahaz makes
   images to ....2 Chr. 28:2-4   461
   Manasseh
   worships......2 Kin. 21:3   394
   Altars
   everywhere ..Jer. 11:13   718
   Overthrown by
   Josiah......2 Kin. 23:4, 5   396
   Denounced by {Jer. 19:4-6   725
   prophets .....{Ezek. 16:1, 2,
                   20, 21   783
   Historic
   retrospect....Rom. 11:4   1117

Baal—*master; possessor*

1. A Benjamite, from
   Gibeon........1 Chr. 8:30   413
2. A descendant of
   Reuben......1 Chr. 5:5, 6   409

3. A village of
   Simeon ....1 Chr. 4:33   408
   Also called Baalath-
   beer..........Josh. 19:8   234

Baalah—*mistress*

1. A town also known as Kirjath-
   jearim ....Josh. 15:9, 10   231
2. A hill in
   Judah.........Josh. 15:11   231
3. A town in South
   Judah.........Josh. 15:29   231
   Probably the same as
   Bilhah ....1 Chr. 4:29   408
   May be the same as
   Balah ....Josh. 19:3   234

Baaliath—*mistress*

A village of Dan ..Josh. 19:44   235
Fortified by
Solomon ....1 Kin. 9:18   350

Baalath-beer—*mistress of the well*

A border town of
Simeon.........Josh. 19:8   234
Called Ramath of the
south...........Josh. 19:8   234
Also called Baal ..1 Chr. 4:33   408

Baal-berith—*lord of covenant*

A god (Baal) of   {Judg. 8:33   252
Shechem ....{Judg. 9:4   252
Also called
El-berith ....Judg. 9:46   254

Baale—*Judah*

A town of Judah ..2 Sam. 6:2   313
Also called Baalah and
Kirjath-jearim ....Josh. 15:9, 10   231

Baal-gad—*lord of good fortune*

A place in the valley of
Lebanon..........Josh. 11:17   227

Baal-hamon—*lord of a multitude*

Site of Solomon's
vineyard.........Song 8:11   653

Baal-hanan—*lord of grace*

1. Edomite king ..Gen. 36:38   38
2. David's
   gardener ....1 Chr. 27:28   431

Baal-hazor—*lord of a village*

A place near
Ephraim.........2 Sam. 13:23   320

Baal-hermon—*lord of Hermon*

A mountain east of
Jordan ....Judg. 3:3   246

Baali—*my master (lord)*

A title rejected by
Yahweh..........Hos. 2:16   841

Baalim—*lords (plural of Baal)*

Deities of Canaanite
polytheism ......Judg. 10:10-14   255
Ensnared   {Judg. 2:11-14   245
Israelites ....{Judg. 3:7   246
Rejected in Samuel's
time............1 Sam. 7:4   281
Historic
reminder ......1 Sam. 12:10   285
Ahaz makes images
to ....2 Chr. 28:1-4   461

Baalis

An Ammonite
king.............Jer. 40:14   746

Baal-meon—*lord of Meon (habitation)*

An Amorite city on the Moabite
boundary......Ezek. 25:9   794
Rebuilt by   {Num. 32:38   170
Reubenites .....{Josh. 13:15, 17   229

Baal-peor, Baal of Peor—*lord of Peor*

A Moabite god ....Num. 25:1-5   162
Infected Israel; 24,000
died ....Num. 25:1-9   162

Vengeance
taken on ....Num. 31:1-18   168
Sin   {Deut. 4:3, 4   181
long   {Josh. 22:17   238
remembered.....{Ps. 106:28, 29   594
Historic
reminder ....1 Cor. 10:1-8   1132

Baal-perazim—*lord of breaking through*

Where David defeated the
Philistines........2 Sam. 5:18-20   313
Same as
Perazim..........Is. 28:21   677

Baal-shalisha—*lord of Shalisha*

A place from which Elisha received
food..............2 Kin. 4:42-44   375

Baal-tamar—*lord of the palm*

A place in
Benjamin........Judg. 20:33   265

Baal-zebub—*lord of flies*

A Philistine god at
Ekron ....2 Kin. 1:2   371
Ahaziah
inquired of ......2 Kin. 1:2, 6, 16   371
Also called   {Matt. 10:25   951
Beelzebub.......{Matt. 12:24   953

Baal-zephon—*lord of darkness*

Israelite camp   {Ex. 14:2, 9   69
site..............{Num. 33:7   171

Baana—*affliction*

1. Supply
   officer.........1 Kin. 4:12   342
2. Zadok's
   father..........Neh. 3:4   490

Baanah—*affliction*

1. A murderer of Ish-
   bosheth ......2 Sam. 4:1-12   312
2. Heled's
   father..........1 Chr. 11:30   416
3. A returning   {Ezra 2:2   475
   exile ....{Neh. 7:7   494
   Signs
   document.....Neh. 10:27   499
4. Supply
   officer..........1 Kin. 4:16   342

Baara—*foolish*

Shaharaim's
wife..............1 Chr. 8:8   413

Baaseiah—*work of Yahweh*

A Levite ancestor of
Asaph ....1 Chr. 6:40   410

Baasha—*boldness*

Gains throne by
murder...........1 Kin. 15:27, 28   357
Kills Jeroboam's
household........1 Kin. 15:29, 30   357
Wars against
Asa ....1 Kin. 15:16, 32   357
Restricts access to
Judah ....1 Kin. 15:17   357
Contravened by Asa's league with
Ben-hadad....1 Kin. 15:18-22   357
Evil reign......1 Kin. 15:33, 34   358

Babbler—*an inane talker*

The mumblings of
drunkards........Prov. 23:29-35   631
Like a serpent.....Eccl. 10:11   646
Paul called such...Acts 17:18   1092
Paul's warnings {1 Tim. 6:20   1197
against ....{2 Tim. 2:16   1201

Babe—*an infant child*

A. *Natural:*
   Moses..........Ex. 2:6   57
   John the
   Baptist.......Luke 1:41, 44   1005
   Christ ....Luke 2:12, 16   1006
   Timothy ....2 Tim. 3:15   1202
   Offspring ......Ps. 17:14   553

SUBJECT	REFERENCE	PAGE	SUBJECT	REFERENCE	PAGE	SUBJECT	REFERENCE	PAGE
B. *Figurative of:*			**Babylonish garment**—*a valuable robe worn in Babylon*			E. *Examples of, among believers:*		
Unenlight-						Lot ....Gen. 19:1-22		19
ened ....Rom. 2:20		1110	Coveted by			David..........2 Sam. 11:1-5		317
True	(Matt. 11:25	952	Achan............Josh. 7:21		223		Ps. 51:1-19	569
believers	Matt. 21:16	963				Peter ....Matt. 26:69-75		971
New			**Baca**—*weeping*				Luke 22:31, 32	1033
Christians.....1 Pet. 2:2		1236	Figurative of			Galatians ....Gal. 1:6		1154
Carnal	(1 Cor. 3:1	1127	sorrow ....Ps. 84:6		584		Gal. 4:9-11	1156
Christians....	Heb. 5:13	1217				Corinthians....1 Cor. 5:1-13		1128
			Bachelor—*unmarried man*			Churches of	(2 Tim. 1:15	1200
Babel—*confusion*			Described			Asia.........	Rev. 2, 3	1268
A city built by Nimrod in the plain			literally..........1 Cor. 7:26-33		1131	See Apostasy		
of Shinar........Gen. 10:8-10		13	Described	(Is. 56:3-5	696			
			figura-			**Badger**—*a species of dolphin or porpoise*		
Babel, Tower of			tively..........	Matt. 19:12	961			
A huge brick structure intended to				(Rev. 14:1-5	1277	Skins of, used in		
magnify man and preserve the			Not for elders .....Titus 1:5, 6		1206	tabernacle	(Ex. 26:14	80
unity of the						coverings....	Ex. 35:7	90
race..............Gen. 11:1-4		13	**Bachrites**			Used for sandals ..Ezek. 16:10		783
Objectives thwarted by			Family of					
God..............Gen. 11:5-9		13	Becher ....Num. 26:35		163	**Bag**—*a purse or pouch*		
						A. *Used for:*		
Babylon, city of			**Backbiting**—*reviling another in secret; slander*			Money..........2 Kin. 12:10		384
A. *History of:*							John 12:6	1057
Built by			A fruit of sin......Rom. 1:28-30		1109	Stones ....1 Sam. 17:40, 49		292
Nimrod ......Gen. 10:8-10		13	Expressed by the			Weights ....Deut. 25:13		201
Tower built			mouth..........Ps. 50:20		569		Prov. 16:11	625
there...........Gen. 11:1-9		13	An offspring of			Food		
Amraphel's			anger..........Prov. 25:23		632	("vessels") ....1 Sam. 9:7		283
capital ....Gen. 14:1		16	Merits			B. *Figurative of:*		
Occupied by Assyrians in			punishment ......Ps. 101:5		591	Forgiveness....Job 14:17		526
Manasseh's			Keeps from God...Ps. 15:1, 3		552	True righteous-		
time ....2 Chr. 33:11		467	To be laid aside ...1 Pet. 2:1		1236	ness..........Prov. 16:11		625
Greatest power under			Unworthy of			True riches ....Luke 12:33		1022
Nebuchad-			Christians ....2 Cor. 12:20		1151	Insecure		
nezzar ....Dan. 4:30		827				riches..........Hag. 1:6		892
A magnificent	(Is. 13:19	668	**Backsliding**—*to turn away from God after conversion*					
city	Is. 14:4	668				**Barhumite**—*a native of Baharum*		
Wide			A. *Described as:*			Applied to		
walls of ......Jer. 51:44		757	Turning from			Azmaveth ....2 Sam. 23:31		332
Gates of ......Is. 45:1, 2		689	God..........1 Kin. 11:9		351			
Bel, god of ....Is. 46:1		690	Turning to			**Bahurim**—*young men*		
Jews carried	(2 Kin. 25:1-21	399	evil ....Ps. 125:5		604	A village near		
captive to ...	2 Chr. 36:5-21	471	Turning to			Jerusalem ......2 Sam. 3:16		311
B. *Inhabitants, described as:*			Satan ....1 Tim. 5:15		1196	Where Shimei cursed		
Idolatrous .....Jer. 50:35, 38		755	Turning back to the			David ....2 Sam. 16:5		324
	Dan. 3:18	825	world ....2 Tim. 4:10		1202	Where two men hid in a		
Enslaved by			Tempting			well ....2 Sam. 17:17, 18		325
magic........Is. 47:1, 9-13		691	Christ..........1 Cor. 10:9		1132			
Sacrilegious...Dan. 5:1-3		827	Turning from first			**Bajith**—*house*		
C. *Prophecies concerning:*			love..........Rev. 2:4		1269	A derisive reference to the temple		
Babylon,	(Jer. 25:9	730	Turning from	(Gal. 1:6, 7	1154	of Moabite gods . Is. 15:2		669
God's agent .	Jer. 27:5-8	732	the Gospel ...	Gal. 3:1-5	1155			
God fights			B. *Prompted by:*			**Bakbakkar**—*investigator*		
with ....Jer. 21:1-7		726	Haughty			A Levite ....1 Chr. 9:15		414
Jews, 70 years	(Jer. 25:12	730	spirit..........Prov. 16:18		625			
in	Jer. 29:10	733	Spiritual	(2 Pet. 1:9	1243	**Bakbuk**—*a flask*		
First of great	(Dan. 2:31-38	824	blindness....	Rev. 3:17	1270	Head of postexilic		
empires	Dan. 7:2-4	830	Murmuring ....Ex. 17:3		72	family...........Ezra 2:51		476
Downfall of...Is. 13:1-22		668	Lusting after				Neh. 7:53	495
	Jer. 50:1-46	754	evil ....Ps. 106:14		594			
Cyrus, God's			Material	(Mark 4:18, 19	982	**Bakbukiah**—*Yahweh has poured out*		
agent ....Is. 45:1-4		689	things..........	1 Tim. 6:10	1197	1. A Levite of high		
Perpetual			Prosperity....Deut. 8:11-14		187	position ....Neh. 11:17		500
desolation	(Is. 13:19-22	668	Tribulation ....Matt. 13:20, 21		954	2. Levite porter...Neh. 12:25		501
of	Jer. 50:13, 39	755	C. *Results:*					
			Displeases			**Baker**—*one who cooks food* (bread)		
Babylon in the New Testament			God..........Ps. 78:56-59		582	A. *Kinds of:*		
A. *The city on the Euphrates*			Punishment ....Num. 14:43-45		151	Household .....Gen. 18:6		19
Listed as a point of				Jer. 8:5-13	716	Public ....Jer. 37:21		744
reference. .....Matt. 1:11, 12,			Blessings			Royal ....Gen. 40:1, 2		41
	17	941	withheld .....Is. 59:2		698	B. *Features of:*		
As the place of Israel's			Unworthi-			Usually a woman's		
exile ....Acts 7:43		1080	ness..........Luke 9:62		1018	job............Lev. 26:26		127
As the place of Peter's			D. *Examples of Israel's:*			Considered		
residence......1 Pet. 5:13		1239	At Meribah .....Ex. 17:1-7		72	menial ....1 Sam. 8:13		282
B. *The prophetic city*			At Sinai ......Ex. 32:1-35		87			
Fall			In wilderness . .Ps. 106:14-33		594	**Balaam**—*destroyer of the people*		
predicted......Rev. 14:8		1277	After Joshua's	(Judg. 2:8-23	245	A. *Information concerning:*		
Wrath taken			death	Ps. 106:34-43	594	A son of		
on ....Rev. 16:19		1278	In Solomon's	(1 Kin. 11:4-40	351	Beor ....Num. 22:5		159
Called "the Mother of			life..........	Neh. 13:26	503	From Mesopo-		
Harlots" ......Rev. 17:1-18		1278	During Asa's			tamia ....Deut. 23:4		199
Fall			reign..........2 Chr. 15:1-4		450	A soothsayer . Josh. 13:22		229
described......Rev. 18:1-24		1279	During Manasseh's			A prophet ....2 Pet. 2:15		1244
			reign..........2 Chr. 33:1-10		467	A Midianite...Num. 31:8		168
Babylonians—*sons of Babel*						Killed because		
Inhabitants of	(Ezra 4:9	478				of his sin......Num. 31:1-8		168
Babylonia	Ezek. 23:15-23	792						

SUBJECT	REFERENCE	PAGE	SUBJECT	REFERENCE	PAGE	SUBJECT	REFERENCE	PAGE

Balaam—continued

B. *Mission of:*

Balak sent to curse Israel .. { Num. 22:5-7 | 159
Josh. 24:9 | 240

Hindered by speaking ass .... { Num. 22:22-35 | 159
2 Pet. 2:16 | 1244

Curse becomes a blessing ...... { Deut. 23:4, 5 | 199
Josh. 24:10 | 240

C. *Prophecies of:*

Under divine control .. { Num. 22:18, 38 | 159
Num. 23:16, 20, 26 | 160

By the Spirit's prompting..... Num. 24:2 | 161

Blessed Israel three times ...... Num. 24:10 | 161

Spoke of the Messiah in final message...... Num. 24:14-19 | 161

D. *Nature of:*

"Unrighteousness"— greed ...... 2 Pet. 2:14, 15 | 1244

"Error"— rebellion ...... Jude 11 | 1262

Baladan—(Marduk) *has given a son*

Father of Merodach-baladan (*also spelled Berodach-baladan*).......... 2 Kin. 20:12 | 394

Balak, Balac—*empty*

A Moabite king .. Num. 22:4 | 159

Hired Balaam to curse Israel.......... Num. 22-24 | 134

Balances—*an instrument for weighing; scales*

A. *Used for weighing:*

Things........ Lev. 19:36 | 119
Money....... Jer. 32:10 | 737

B. *Laws concerning:*

Must be just... Lev. 19:36 | 119

False, an abomination ...... Prov. 11:1 | 621

Deceit, condemned ..... Amos 8:5 | 859

C. *Figurative of:*

God's justice... Job 31:6 | 536
Man's { Ps. 62:9 | 573
smallness .... Is. 40:12, 15 | 685

God's judgment ..... Dan. 5:27 | 829

Man's tribulation .... Rev. 6:5 | 1272

Bald Locust (see Locust)

A species of edible locust .... Lev. 11:22 | 109

Baldness—*a head without hair*

A. *Natural:*

Not a sign of leprosy...... Lev. 13:40, 41 | 112

Elisha mocked for .... 2 Kin. 2:23, 24 | 373

B. *Artificial:*

A sign of mourning ... Is. 22:12 | 673

An idolatrous practice...... { Lev. 21:5 | 121
Deut. 14:1 | 192

Inflicted upon captives...... Deut. 21:12 | 198

Forbidden to priests .... Ezek. 44:20 | 813

A part of Nazarite vow....... Num. 6:2, 9, 18 | 141

C. *Figurative of judgment, upon:*

Israel.......... { Is. 3:24 | 661
Amos 8:10 | 860

Moab......... Is. 15:2 | 669

Philistia........ Jer. 47:5 | 751

Tyre....... Ezek. 27:2, 31 | 795

Ball—*spherical object*

Prophetic .... Is. 22:18 | 673

Ballad singers

Rendered "they that speak proverbs" .... Num. 21:27 | 158

Balm—*an aromatic resin or gum*

A product of Gilead........... Jer. 8:22 | 716

Sent to Joseph .... Gen. 43:11 | 45

Exported to Tyre............. Ezek. 27:17 | 796

Healing qualities of ...... { Jer. 46:11 | 750
Jer. 51:8 | 756

Bamah—*high place*

A place of idolatry .... Ezek. 20:29 | 788

Bamoth—*high places*

Encampment site............. Num. 21:19, 20 | 158

Also called Bamoth-baal .... Josh. 13:17 | 229

Bamoth-baal—*high places of Baal*

Assigned to Reuben.......... Josh. 13:17 | 229

Ban (see Excommunication)

Bandage

Used as disguise ..1 Kin. 20:37-41 | 364

In prophecy against Egypt .... Ezek. 30:20-22 | 799

Bani—*built*

1. Gadite warrior ...... 2 Sam. 23:36 | 332

2. A Judahite... 1 Chr. 9:4 | 414

3. A postexilic family....... { Ezra 2:10 | 476
Neh. 10:14 | 499

4. A Merarite Levite....... 1 Chr. 6:46 | 410

5. A Levite; father of Rehum....... Neh. 3:17 | 491

6. Signed document ..... Neh. 10:13 | 499

7. Head of Levitical family........ Ezra 10:34 | 485

8. A postexilic Levite....... Ezra 10:38 | 485

9. A descendant of Asaph....... Neh. 11:22 | 500

Banishment—*forceful expulsion from one's place*

A. *Political, of:*

Absalom by David........ 2 Sam. 14:13, 14 | 321

The Jews into exile....... 2 Chr. 36:20, 21 | 471

The Jews from Rome......... Acts 18:2 | 1092

B. *Moral and spiritual, of:*

Adam from Eden....... Gen. 3:22-24 | 7

Cain from others........ Gen. 4:12, 14 | 8

Lawbreaker... Ezra 7:26 | 481

John to Patmos...... Rev. 1:9 | 1268

Satan from heaven........ Rev. 12:7-9 | 1275

The wicked to { Rev. 20:15 | 1281
lake of fire ... Rev. 21:8 | 1282

Bank

A. *A mound:*

Raised against a besieged city .... { 2 Sam. 20:15 | 329
Is. 37:33 | 684

B. *A place for money:*

Exchange charges ...... John 2:15 | 1044

Interest paid on deposits... { Matt. 25:27 | 968
Luke 19:23 | 1029

Bankruptcy—*inability to pay one's debts*

A. *Literal:*

Condition of David's men........... 1 Sam. 22:1, 2 | 297

Unjust steward ...... Matt. 18:23-27 | 960

B. *Moral and spiritual:*

Israel's condition ..... Hos. 4:1-5 | 842

Mankind's condition.. { Rom. 1:20-32 | 1109
Rom. 3:9-19 | 1110

Individual's condition.. { Phil. 3:4-8 | 1172
1 Tim. 1:13 | 1194

Banner—*a flag or standard*

A. *Literal:*

Used by armies .... Num. 2:2, 3 | 135

Signal for assembling.... Is. 18:3 | 671

Hosts.......... Num. 1:52 | 135

Enemy........ Ps. 74:4, 5 | 579

B. *Figurative of:*

Yahweh's name ("Yahweh is my banner") .. Ex. 17:15 | 72

God's salvation ... { Ps. 20:5 | 555
Ps. 60:4 | 572

God's protection..... Song 2:4 | 651

God's power ... Song 6:4, 10 | 653

Enemy force ... Is. 5:26 | 662

God's uplifted hand....... Is. 31:9 | 679

Christ .... Is. 11:10, 12 | 667

Banquet—*a sumptuous feast*

A. *Reasons for:*

Birthday....... Gen. 40:20 | 42

Marriage....... Gen. 29:22 | 31

Reunion ..Luke 15:22-25 | 1025

State affairs .. { Esth. 1:3, 5 | 507
Dan. 5:1 | 827

B. *Features of:*

Invitations sent.......... { Esth. 5:8, 9 | 510
Luke 14:16, 17 | 1024

Non-acceptance merits censure ... Luke 14:18-24 | 1024

Courtesies to guests...... Luke 7:34-46 | 1014

Special garment...... { Matt. 22:11 | 964
Rev. 3:4, 5 | 1270

A presiding governor..... John 2:8 | 1043

Protocol of seating...... { Gen. 43:33 | 46
Prov. 25:6, 7 | 632

Anointing oil .. Ps. 45:7 | 567

Honor guest noted .... 1 Sam. 9:22-24 | 283

Baptism, Christian

A. *Commanded by:*

Christ .... { Matt. 28:19, 20 | 974
Mark 16:15, 16 | 999

Peter .... Acts 10:46-48 | 1084

Christian ministers...... Acts 22:12-16 | 1097

B. *Administered by:*

The apostles ... Acts 2:1, 41 | 1073

Ananias ... Acts 9:17, 18 | 1082

Philip ...... Acts 8:12 | 1080
Acts 8:36-38 | 1081

Peter ..... Acts 10:44-48 | 1084

Paul ...... { Acts 18:8 | 1092
1 Cor. 1:14-17 | 1126

C. *Places:*

Jordan........ { Matt. 3:13-16 | 943
Mark 1:5-10 | 978

Jerusalem.... Acts 2:5, 41 | 1073

Samaria .... Acts 8:5, 12 | 1080

A house ...... Acts 10:44-48 | 1084

A jail......... Acts 16:25-33 | 1090

D. *Subjects of:*

Believing Jews......... Acts 2:14, 41 | 1073

Believing Gentiles...... { Acts 10:44-48 | 1084
Acts 18:8 | 1092

SUBJECT	REFERENCE	PAGE

Base—continued

Of humble
nature............2 Cor. 10:1   1149

Bashan—*smooth soil*

A vast highland east of
the Sea of Chinnereth
(Galilee)......Num. 21:33-35   158
Ruled by Og .....Deut. 29:7   206
Conquered by
Israel...........Neh. 9:22   498
Assigned to
Manasseh ....Deut. 3:13   181
Smitten by
Hazael ......2 Kin. 10:32, 33   383
Fine cattle ....Ezek. 39:18   807
Typical of   (Ps. 22:12   556
cruelty ....(Amos 4:1   857

Bashan Havoth-jair

A district named after
Jair ....Deut. 3:14   181

Bashemath—*fragrance*

1. Wife of Esau...Gen. 26:34   28
   Called Adah ...Gen. 36:2, 3   37
2. Wife of Esau...Gen. 36:3, 4, 13   37
   Called
   Mahalath ....Gen. 28:9   30
3. A daughter of
   Solomon ......1 Kin. 4:15   342

Basin—*cup or bowl for containing
liquids*

Moses used ......Ex. 24:6   78
Made for the
altar........Ex. 27:3; 38:3   81
Brought for
David ....2 Sam. 17:28, 29   325
Hiram made.....1 Kin. 7:40   346

Baskets—*something made to hold
objects*

A. *Used for carrying:*
   Produce ......Deut. 26:2   202
   Food ....Matt. 14:20   956
   Ceremonial
   offerings .....Ex. 29:3, 23   83
   Paul ....Acts 9:24, 25   1082
   Other objects
   (heads).......2 Kin. 10:7   382
B. *Symbolic of:*
   Approaching
   death ....Gen. 40:16-19   42
   Israel's
   judgment .....Amos 8:1-3   859
   Judah's
   judgment ....Jer. 24:1-10   729
   Hiding good
   works........Matt. 5:15   945

Bastard—*an illegitimate child*

A. *Penalty attached
   to*.............Deut. 23:2   199
B. *Examples of:*
   Ishmael.......Gen. 16:3, 15   17
            Gal. 4:22   1157
   Moab and
   Ammon.......Gen. 19:36-38   21
   Sons of Tamar by
   Judah........Gen. 38:12-30   40
   Jephthah ......Judg. 11:1   255
C. *Figurative of:*
   A mixed race ..Zech. 9:6   900
   The unregenerate
   state ....Heb. 12:8   1223

Bat—*a flying mammal*

Listed among   (Lev. 11:19   109
unclean kinds....(Deut. 14:18   192
Lives in dark
places ....Is. 2:19-21   660

Bath—*a liquid measure (about 9
gallons)*

A tenth of a
homer...........Ezek. 45:10, 11   814
For measuring oil (2 Chr. 2:10   439
and wine ....(Is. 5:10   661

Bathing

A. *For pleasure:*
   Pharaoh's
   daughter......Ex. 2:5   57
   Bath-sheba ....2 Sam. 11:2, 3   317
B. *For purification:*
   Cleansing the (Gen. 24:32   25
   feet ....(John 13:10   1058
   Ceremonial (Lev. 14:8   113
   cleansing.....(2 Kin. 5:10-14   376
   Before performing
   priestly   (Ex. 30:19-21   86
   duties........(Lev. 16:4, 24   116
   Jewish
   rituals........Mark 7:2   985

Bath-rabbim—*daughter of multitudes*

Gate of
Heshbon ....Song 7:4   653

Bath-sheba—*daughter of an oath*

Wife of Uriah .....2 Sam. 11:2, 3   317
Commits adultery with
David ....2 Sam. 11:4, 5   318
Husband's death contrived by
David ....2 Sam. 11:6-25   318
Mourns husband's
death............2 Sam. 11:26   318
Becomes David's
wife ....2 Sam. 11:27   318
Her first child
dies ....2 Sam. 12:14-19   319
Solomon's
mother.........2 Sam. 12:24   319
Secures throne for
Solomon ....1 Kin. 1:15-31   337
Deceived by
Adonijah........1 Kin. 2:13-25   339

Bath-shua—*daughter of prosperity*

Same as
Bath-sheba ....1 Chr. 3:5   407

Battering ram (see Armor)

Used in
destroying   (Ezek. 4:2   774
walls ....(Ezek. 21:22   790

Battle (see War)

Battle-axe—*an instrument of war*

Applied to Israel ..Jer. 51:19, 20   756

Battlement—*a lodge on roofs*

A protective ......Deut. 22:8   199
Figurative of partial
destruction ....Jer. 5:10   713

Bavai—*wisher*

Postexilic
worker ....Neh. 3:18   491

Bay—*inlet*

1. Dead Sea's cove at Jordan's
   mouth ....Josh. 15:5   230
   Used also of the
   Nile.........Is. 11:15   667
2. Color of a
   horse ....Zech. 6:2   898
3. Name of a tree; figurative of
   pride........Ps. 37:35   563

Bazluth—*stripping*

Head of a family ..Ezra 2:52   476
Called
Bazlith ....Neh. 7:54   495

Bdellium—*an oily gum, or a white pearl*

A valuable mineral of
Havilah ....Gen. 2:12   5
Manna colored
like..............Num. 11:7   147

Beach—*coast*

Place of:
Jesus' preaching ..Matt. 13:2   954
Fisherman's
task...........Matt. 13:48   955

Jesus' meal with
disciples.........John 21:8, 9   1066
A prayer
meeting ....Acts 21:5   1096
A notable
shipwreck ....Acts 27:39-44   1103
A miracle ....Acts 28:1-6   1103

Beacon—*a signal*

Figurative, a warning to
others ....Is. 30:17   678

Bealiah—*Yahweh is Lord*

A warrior ....1 Chr. 12:5   417

Bealoth—*mistresses*

Village of Judah...Josh. 15:24   231

Beam

A. *Physical:*
   Wood undergirding
   floors ....1 Kin. 7:2   345
   Part of weaver's
   frame ....1 Sam. 17:7   291
B. *Figurative of:*
   The cry for
   vengeance ....Hab. 2:11   883
   God's power ...Ps. 104:3   592
   Notorious
   faults ....Matt. 7:3-5   947

Bean—*a food*

Brought to David
by friends ......2 Sam. 17:27, 28   325
Mixed with grain for
bread...........Ezek. 4:9   774

Bear—*a wild animal*

A. *Natural:*
   Killed by
   David ....1 Sam. 17:34, 35   292
   Two tore up forty-two
   lads...........2 Kin. 2:23, 24   373
B. *Figurative of:*
   Fierce
   revenge.......2 Sam. 17:8   325
   Fool's folly....Prov. 17:12   626
   Wicked
   rulers ....Prov. 28:15   634
   World
   empire ....Dan. 7:5   830
   Final
   antichrist .....Rev. 13:2   1276
   Messianic
   times ....Is. 11:7   667
   A constel-
   lation ....Job 9:9   524

Bear—*to carry, yield*

A. *Used literally of:*
   Giving birth ...Gen. 17:19   18
   Carrying a (Josh. 3:13   219
   load..........(Jer. 17:21   724
   Cross.........Matt. 27:32   972
B. *Used figuratively of:*
   Excessive
   punishment ...Gen. 4:13   8
   Divine
   deliverance...Ex. 19:4   73
   Responsibility (Lev. 5:17   103
   for sin ....(Lev. 24:15   124
   Burden of
   leadership.....Deut. 1:9, 12   178
   Personal
   shame ....Ezek. 16:54   784
   Evangelism....Acts 9:15   1082
   Spiritual help ..Gal. 6:1, 2   1158
   Spiritual produc-
   tivity..........John 15:2, 4, 8   1060

Beard—*hair grown on the face*

A. *Long, worn by:*
   Aaron ....Ps. 133:2   605
   Samson.......Judg. 16:17   260
   David.........1 Sam. 21:12, 13   296
B. *In mourning:*
   Left
   untrimmed ....2 Sam. 19:24   328

SUBJECT	REFERENCE	PAGE	SUBJECT	REFERENCE	PAGE	SUBJECT	REFERENCE	PAGE
Plucked	Ezra 9:3	483	The apostles	Acts 5:40	1077	Iron, 13½ feet		
Clipped	Jer. 48:37, 38	752	Paul	Acts 16:18-24	1090	long	Deut. 3:11	181

C. Features regarding:

Beatitudes—*pronouncements of blessings*

Ivory — Amos 6:4 — 858

Leper's must be						Gold and		
shaven	Lev. 13:29-33	111	Jesus begins His	Matt. 5:3-12	945	silver	Esth. 1:6	507

sermon with.....Luke 6:20-22 — 1012

B. Used for:

Half-shaven, an						Sleep	Luke 11:7	1019
indignity	2 Sam. 10:4, 5	317	**Beautiful gate**—*gate at East of Temple area*			Rest	2 Sam. 4:5-7	312
Marring of,						Sickness	Gen. 49:33	51
forbidden	Lev. 19:27	119	Lame man healed			Meals	Amos 6:4	858
Shaven, by			there	Acts 3:1-10	1074	Prostitution	Prov. 7:16, 17	619
Egyptians	Gen. 41:14	42				Evil	Ps. 36:4	562
Spittle on, sign of			**Beauty, physical**			Marriage	Song 3:1	651
lunacy	1 Sam. 21:12, 13	296	**A. Temporal:**				Heb. 13:4	1223
Holding to, a token of			Seen in	Hos. 14:6	847	Singing	Ps. 149:5	611
respect	2 Sam. 20:9	329	nature	Matt. 6:28, 29	947	**C. Figurative of:**		

Beasts—*four-footed animals; mammals*

			Consumed in			The grave	Job 17:13-16	528
A. Characteristics of:			dissipation	Is. 28:1	676	Divine		
God-created	Gen. 1:21	4	Contest Abishag,			support	Ps. 41:3	565
Of their own			winner of	1 Kin. 1:1-4	337	Worldly		
order	1 Cor. 15:39	1138	Esther,			security	Is. 57:7	697
Named by			winner of	Esth. 2:1-17	507	**Bed**—*a garden plot*		
Adam	Gen. 2:20	6	Destroyed			Used literally	Song 6:2	652
Suffer in man's			by sin	Ps. 39:11	564	Used		
sin	Rom. 8:20-22	1114	Ends in			figuratively	Song 5:13	652
Perish at			grave	Ps. 49:14	568	**Bedad**—*separation*		
death	Ps. 49:12-15	568	**B. In Women:**			Father of Hadad	Gen. 36:35	38
Follow	Is. 1:3	658	Vain	Prov. 31:30	636	**Bedan**—*son of judgment*		
instincts	Jude 10	1262	Without					
Under God's			discretion	Prov. 11:22	622	1. Judge of		
control	1 Sam. 6:7-14	280	Enticements			Israel	1 Sam. 12:11	285
Wild	Mark 1:13	978	of	Prov. 6:25	619	2. Descendant of		
For man's	Gen. 9:3	11	Source of	Gen. 6:2	9	Manasseh	1 Chr. 7:17	412
food	Acts 10:12, 13	1083	temptation	2 Sam. 11:2-5	317	**Bedchamber**—*a bedroom*		
Eat people	1 Sam. 17:46	292	Leads to			A place of sleep	2 Sam. 4:7	312
	1 Cor. 15:32	1137	marriage	Deut. 21:10-13	198	Elijah's special	2 Kin. 4:8, 10	374
Used in			A bride's	Ps. 45:11	567	Secrets of	2 Kin. 6:12	377
sacrifices	Lev. 27:26-29	129	Sarah's	Gen. 12:11	15	Joash hidden in	2 Kin. 11:2	383
Spiritual			Rebekah's	Gen. 24:15, 16	24	**Bedeiah**—*servant of Yahweh*		
lessons	1 Kin. 4:30-33	342	Rachel's	Gen. 29:17	31	Son of Bani	Ezra 10:34, 35	485
from	Job 12:7	525	Daughters of			**Bedfellows**		
B. Treatment of:			Job	Job 42:15	543	Provide mutual		
No sexual relation			Abigail's	1 Sam. 25:3	300	warmth	Eccl. 4:11	642
with	Lev. 20:15, 16	120	Bath-sheba's	2 Sam. 11:2, 3	317	**Bee**—*insect*		
Proper care of, sign of a			Tamar's	2 Sam. 13:1	320	Abundant in		
righteous	Gen. 33:13, 14	35	Abishag's	1 Kin. 1:3, 4	337	Canaan	Judg. 14:8	258
man	Prov. 12:10	622	Vashti's	Esth. 1:11	507	Amorites		
Abuse of,			Esther's	Esth. 2:7	508	compared to	Deut. 1:44	179
rebuked	Num. 22:28-32	159	**C. In Men:**			David's enemies		
Extra food			Of Man	Is. 44:13	689	compared to	Ps. 118:12	599
for, while	Deut. 25:4	201	Of the aged	Prov. 20:29	628	Assyria		
working	1 Tim. 5:18	1196	Joseph's	Gen. 39:6	41	compared to	Is. 7:18	663
C. Typical of:			David's	1 Sam. 16:12, 13	290	See Honey		
Man's folly	Ps. 73:22	578	Absalom's	2 Sam. 14:25	322	**Beef, boiled**		
Unregenerate			**Beauty, spiritual**			Elisha gives		
men	Titus 1:12	1206	The Messiah	Ps. 110:3	597	people	1 Kin. 19:21	363
False				Is. 52:7	695	**Beeliada**—*the Lord knows*		
prophets	2 Pet. 2:12	1244	The true	Ps. 45:8-11	567	Son of David	1 Chr. 14:7	419
Antichrist	Rev. 13:1-4	1276	Israel	Song 1:8	650	Called Eliada	2 Sam. 5:14-16	313
See Animals			The meek	Ps. 149:4	611	**Beelzebub**		
Beaten gold—*gold shaped by hammering*			Spiritual			Prince of		
			worship	2 Chr. 20:21	454	demons	Matt. 12:24	953
Ornamental	1 Kin. 10:16, 17	351	Christian			Identified as		
shields	2 Chr. 9:15, 16	446	ministers	Rom. 10:15	1116	Satan	Matt. 12:26, 27	953
Beaten oil—*highest quality of olive oil*			Holy garments	Is. 52:1	694	Jesus thus called	Matt. 10:25	951
			Christ's rejection by			**Beer**—*a well*		
In sacrifices	Ex. 29:39, 40	85	Israel	Zech. 11:7-14	902	1. Moab station	Num. 21:16-18	158
In tent of meeting			**Bebai**—*fatherly*			2. Jotham's place of		
lamp	Lev. 24:2	124	1. Family head	Ezra 2:11	476	refuge	Judg. 9:21	253
Beaten silver—*silver shaped by hammering*			2. One who signs			**Beera**—*a well*		
			document	Neh. 10:15	499	An Asherite	1 Chr. 7:37	413
Overlaid idols	Is. 30:22	679	**Becher**—*young camel*			**Beerah**—*a well*		
	Hab. 2:19	883	1. Benjamin's			Reubenite		
In trade	Jer. 10:9	717	son	Gen. 46:21	48	prince	1 Chr. 5:6	409
Beatings—*striking the body with blows; floggings*			2. Son of					
			Ephraim	Num. 26:35	163			
A. Inflicted on:			Called Bered	1 Chr. 7:20	412			
The wicked	Deut. 25:3	201	**Bechorath**—*the first birth*					
The guilty	Lev. 19:20	119	Ancestor of Saul	1 Sam. 9:1	282			
Children	Prov. 22:15	629	**Bed**					
The disobe-	Prov. 26:3	633	**A. Made of:**					
dient	Luke 12:47, 48	1022	The ground	Gen. 28:11	30			
B. Victims of unjust beatings:								
A servant	Luke 20:10, 11	1031						
Christ	Is. 50:6	693						
	Mark 15:19	997						

SUBJECT	REFERENCE	PAGE

SUBJECT	REFERENCE	PAGE	SUBJECT	REFERENCE	PAGE	SUBJECT	REFERENCE	PAGE
Written by secretary	Jer. 36:4, 18	741	The Lord's judgment	Jer. 49:30-32	754	**Botch**—*a boil*		
B. *Contents of:*			B. *Division of:*			A punishment of disobedience	Deut. 28:27	204
Genealogies	Gen. 5:1	8	On percentage basis	Num. 31:26-47	168	**Bottle**—*a hollow thing* (vessel)		
Law of Moses	Deut. 31:9, 24, 26	208	Rear troops share in	1 Sam. 30:22-25	305	A. *Used for:*		
Geography	Josh. 18:9	233				Milk	Judg. 4:19	247
Wars	Num. 21:14	158	**Border**—*boundary*			Water	Gen. 21:14	21
Records	Ezra 4:15	478	A. *Marked by:*			Wine	Hab. 2:15	883
Miracles	Josh. 10:13	226	Natural landmarks	Josh. 18:16	234	B. *Made of:*		
Legislation	1 Sam. 10:25	284	Rivers	Josh. 18:19	234	Clay	Jer. 19:1, 10, 11	725
Lamenta- tions	2 Chr. 35:25	470	Neighbor's landmark	Deut. 19:14	196	Skins	Matt. 9:17	949
Proverbs	Prov. 25:1	632	B. *Enlargement of:*				Mark 2:22	980
Prophecies	Jer. 51:60-64	758	By God's power	Ex. 34:24	90	C. *Figurative of:*		
Symbols	Rev. 1:1	1268	A blessing	1 Chr. 4:10	408	God's remem- brance	Ps. 56:8	571
The Messiah	Luke 24:27, 44	1037				God's judgments	Jer. 13:12-14	720
	Heb. 10:7	1220	**Born again**—*new birth, regeneration*			Sorrow	Ps. 119:83	601
C. *Mentioned but not preserved:*			A. *Necessity of, because of:*			Impatience	Job 32:19	537
Book of wars	Num. 21:14	158	Inability	John 3:3, 5	1044	Clouds of rain	Job 38:37	541
Book of Jasher	Josh. 10:13	226	The flesh	John 3:6	1044	Old and new covenants	Matt. 9:17	949
Chronicles of David	1 Chr. 27:24	431	Deadness	Eph. 2:1	1162	**Bottomless pit**		
Book of Gad	1 Chr. 29:29	434	B. *Produced by:*			Apollyon, king of	Rev. 9:11	1274
Story of prophet Iddo	2 Chr. 13:22	449	The Holy Spirit	John 3:5, 8	1044	Beast comes from	Rev. 11:7	1275
Book of Nathan	1 Chr. 29:29	434		Titus 3:5	1207		Rev. 17:8	1279
Book of Jehu	2 Chr. 20:34	455	The Word of God	James 1:18	1228	Devil, cast into	Rev. 20:1-3	1281
				1 Pet. 1:23	1236	A prison	Rev. 20:7	1281
Book of God's judgment			Faith	1 John 5:1	1253	**Bough**—*branch of a tree*		
In visions of Daniel and	Dan. 7:10	830	C. *Results of:*			A. *Used:*		
John	Rev. 20:12	1281	New creature	2 Cor. 5:17	1145	To make ceremonial booths	Lev. 23:39-43	124
Book of the Law			Changed life	Rom. 6:4-11	1112	In siege of Shechem	Judg. 9:45-49	254
Called "the law of Moses"	Josh. 8:31, 32	224	Holy life	1 John 3:9	1251	B. *Figurative of:*		
Copied	Deut. 17:18	195	Righteous- ness	1 John 2:29	1251	Joseph's offspring	Gen. 49:22	51
Placed in the ark	Deut. 31:26	209	Love	1 John 3:10	1251	Judgment	Is. 17:1-11	670
Foundation of Israel's religion	Deut. 28:58	205	Victory	1 John 5:4	1253	Israel	Ps. 80:8-11	583
Lost and found	2 Kin. 22:8	395	**Borrow**—*to get by loan*			Nebuchadnezzar's kingdom	Dan. 4:10-12	826
Produces reformation	2 Kin. 23:2-14	396	A. *Regulations regarding:*			**Bow**—*an instrument for shooting arrows*		
Produces revival	Neh. 8:2, 8-18	496	From other nations, forbidden	Deut. 15:6	193	A. *Uses of:*		
Quoted	2 Kin. 14:6	383		Deut. 28:12	204	For hunting	Gen. 27:3	28
To be remembered	Josh. 1:7, 8	217	Obligation to repay	Ex. 22:14, 15	77	For war	Is. 7:24	664
	Mal. 4:4	909	Non-payment, wicked	Ps. 37:21	563	As a token of friendship	1 Sam. 18:4	293
Prophetic of Christ	Luke 24:27, 44	1037	Involves servitude	Prov. 22:7	629	As a commemorative song	2 Sam. 1:18	309
Book of Life			Evils of, corrected	Neh. 5:1-13	492	B. *Illustrative of:*		
A. *Contains:*			Christ's words on	Matt. 5:42	946	Strength	Job 29:20	535
The names of the saved	Phil. 4:3	1172	B. *Examples of:*			The tongue	Ps. 11:2	551
The deeds of the righteous	Mal. 3:16-18	909	Jewels	Ex. 11:2	66	Defeat	Hos. 1:5	840
B. *Excludes:*			A widow's vessels	2 Kin. 4:3	374	Peace	Hos. 2:18, 19	841
Renegades	Ex. 32:33	88	A woodsman's axe	2 Kin. 6:5	377	**Bowels**		
	Ps. 69:28	576	Christ's transpor- tation	Matt. 21:2, 3	963	A. *Used literally of:*		
Apostates	Rev. 13:8	1276				Intestines	Num. 5:22	140
	Rev. 17:8	1279	**Bosom**—*the breast as center of affections*			Source of offspring	Gen. 15:4	17
C. *Affords, basis of:*			A. *Expressive of:*			Source of descendants	Gen. 25:23	26
Joy	Luke 10:20	1018	Procreation	Gen. 16:5	17	Source of the Messiah	2 Sam. 7:12	315
Hope	Heb. 12:23	1223	Prostitution	Prov. 6:26, 27	619	Amasa's—shed out	2 Sam. 20:10	329
Judgment	Dan. 7:10	830	Anger	Eccl. 7:9	644	Jehoram's—fell out	2 Chr. 21:14-19	456
	Rev. 20:12-15	1281	Procras- tination	Prov. 19:24	627	Judas'—gushed out	Acts 1:16-18	1072
Booths—*stalls made of branches*			Protection	Is. 40:11	685	B. *Used figuratively of:*		
Used for cattle	Gen. 33:17	35	Iniquity	Job 31:33	536	Natural love	Gen. 43:30	46
Required in feast of tabernacle	Lev. 23:40-43	124	B. *Symbolic of:*			Deep emotion	Job 30:27	535
	Neh. 8:14-17	497	Man's impatience	Ps. 74:11	579	Intense suffering	Ps. 22:14	556
Booty—*spoils taken in war*			Christ's deity	John 1:18	1042	Great concern	Jer. 31:20	736
A. *Stipulations concerning:*			Eternal peace	Luke 16:22, 23	1026	Spiritual distress	Lam. 1:20	763
No Canaanites	Deut. 20:14-17	197	**Bosor**—*a lamp*					
No accursed thing	Josh. 6:17-19	221	Father of Balaam	2 Pet. 2:15	1244			
Destruction of Amalek	1 Sam. 15:2, 3	289	Same as Beor	Num. 22:5	159			
Destruction of Arad	Num. 21:1-3	157						

SUBJECT	REFERENCE	PAGE	SUBJECT	REFERENCE	PAGE	SUBJECT	REFERENCE	PAGE
Bruised—*continued*			Figurative of the Lord's			Rehoboam	1 Kin. 14:31	356
Satan's	Gen. 3:15	7	sacrifice	Is. 34:6, 7	681	Asa	1 Kin. 15:24	357
defeat	Rom. 16:20	1122	Figurative of			Manasseh	2 Kin. 21:18	395
Bucket—*container for water*			strength	Deut. 33:17	212	Amon	2 Kin. 21:23-26	395
Figurative of			**Bulrush**—*a reed*			Josiah	2 Chr. 35:23, 24	470
blessing	Num. 24:7	161	Used in Moses'			Jesus	Luke 23:50-53	1036
Pictures God's			ark	Ex. 2:3	57	Lazarus	John 11:14, 38	1055
magnitude	Is. 40:15	685	Found in river			**Buried alive**		
Buffet—*to strike with the fist*			banks	Job 8:11	523	Two rebellious		
Jesus	Matt. 26:67	971	Figurative of			families	Num. 16:27-34	153
subjected to	Mark 14:65	997	judgment	Is. 9:14	665	Desire of some	Rev. 6:15, 16	1272
Descriptive of			**Bulwark**—*defensive wall*			**Burning bush**		
Paul	2 Cor. 12:7	1150	Around			God speaks		
Figurative of self-			Jerusalem	Ps. 48:13	568	from	Ex. 3:2	58
discipline	1 Cor. 9:27	1132	Used in wars	Eccl. 9:14	645	**Bushel**—*a measurement*		
Build—*construct or erect*			Made of logs	Deut. 20:20	197	Mentioned by		
A. *Used literally, of:*			Foundation of			Christ	Matt. 5:15	945
City	Gen. 4:17	8	weapons	2 Chr. 26:15	460	**Business**—*one's work*		
Altar	Gen. 8:20	11	**Bunah**—*intelligence*			A. *Attitudes toward:*		
Tower	Gen. 11:4	13	A descendant of			See God's		
House	Gen. 33:17	35	Judah	1 Chr. 2:25	406	hand	James 4:13	1230
Sheepfolds	Num. 32:16	170	**Bunni**—*erected*			Be diligent	Prov. 22:29	630
Fortifica-	Deut. 20:20	197	1. A preexilic			Be		
tions	Ezek. 4:2	774	Levite	Neh. 11:15	500	industrious	Rom. 12:8, 11	1118
Temple	1 Kin. 6:1, 14	343	2. A postexilic			Be honest	2 Cor. 8:20-22	1148
	Ezra 4:1	478	Levite	Neh. 9:4	497	Put God's		
High place	1 Kin. 11:7	351	3. Signer of			first	Matt. 6:33, 34	947
Walls	Neh. 4:6	491	document	Neh. 10:15	499	Keep heaven in		
Tombs	Matt. 23:29	966	**Burden**—*load*			mind	Matt. 6:19-21	946
	Luke 11:47	1021	A. *Used physically of:*			Give portion	Mal. 3:8-12	909
Synagogue	Luke 7:2-5	1013	Load, cargo	Neh. 4:17	492	Avoid		
B. *Used figuratively, of:*			B. *Used figuratively of:*			anxiety	Luke 12:22-30	1022
Obeying			Care	Ps. 55:22	571	Remember the		
Christ	Matt. 7:24-27	948	Prophet's			fool	Luke 12:15-21	1021
Church	Matt. 16:18	958	message	Hab. 1:1	882	B. *Those diligent in:*		
Christ's res-	Matt. 26:61	971	Rules, rites	Luke 11:46	1021	Joseph	Gen. 39:11	41
urrection	John 2:19-21	1044	Sin	Ps. 38:4	563	Moses	Heb. 3:5	1216
Return to			Responsi-			Workers in		
legalism	Gal. 2:16-20	1155	bility	Gal. 6:2, 5	1158	Israel	2 Chr. 34:11, 12	468
Christian			Christ's law	Matt. 11:30	952	Daniel	Dan. 6:4	829
unity	Eph. 2:19-22	1163	**Burden-bearer**			Mordecai	Esth. 10:2, 3	514
	Acts 20:32	1095	Christ is the			Paul	Acts 20:17-35	1095
Spiritual	Col. 2:7	1178	believer's	Ps. 55:22	571	**Busybodies**—*meddlers*		
growth	1 Pet. 2:5	1236	**Burglarizing**—*stealing*			Women		
See Edification			Severe penalty			guilty of	1 Tim. 5:13	1196
Bukki			for	Ex. 21:16	76	Some	2 Thess. 3:11,	1190
1. Danite chief	Num. 34:22	173	See Stealing; Theft, thief			Christians	12	
2. A descendant of			**Burial**			Admonitions		
Aaron	1 Chr. 6:5, 51	410	A. *Features regarding:*			against	1 Pet. 4:15	1239
Bukkiah—*proved of Yahweh*			Body washed	Acts 9:37	1082	See Slander; Whisperer		
A Levite			Ointment			**Butler**—*an officer*		
musician	1 Chr. 25:4, 13	429	used	Matt. 26:12	969	Imprisonment of		
Bul—*growth*			Embalm			Pharaoh's	Gen. 40:1-13	41
Eighth Hebrew			sometimes	Gen. 50:26	52	Same as		
month	1 Kin. 6:38	345	Body			"cupbearer"	1 Kin. 10:5	350
Bull—*male of any bovine animal*			wrapped	John 11:44	1056	**Butter**—*curdled milk*		
Used in			Placed in			Article of diet	2 Sam. 17:29	325
sacrifices	Heb. 9:13	1219	coffin	Gen. 50:26	52	Set before		
Blood of,			Carried on a			visitors	Gen. 18:8	19
insufficient	Heb. 10:4	1220	bier	Luke 7:14	1013	Got by churning	Prov. 30:33	636
Wild, trapped	Is. 51:20	694	Mourners			Fed to infants	Is. 7:15, 22	663
Symbol of evil			attend	John 11:19	1056	Illustrative of		
men	Ps. 22:12	556	Graves			prosperity	Deut. 32:14	210
Symbol of mighty			provided	Gen. 23:5-20	23	Figurative of smooth		
men	Ps. 68:30	575	Tombs			words	Ps. 55:21	571
Restrictions on	Deut. 15:19, 20	194	erected	Matt. 23:27-29	966	**Buz**—*contempt*		
Sacrifices of,			B. *Places of:*			1. A Gadite	1 Chr. 5:14	409
inadequate	Ps. 69:30, 31	576	Abraham and			2. An Aramean tribe descending		
Blood of,			Sarah	Gen. 25:7-10	26	from Nahor	Gen. 22:20, 21	23
unacceptable	Is. 1:11	659	Deborah	Gen. 35:8	37	**Buzi**—*descendant of Buz*		
Figurative of the Lord's			Rachel	Gen. 35:19, 20	37	Father of		
sacrifice	Is. 34:6, 7	681	Miriam	Num. 20:1	156	Ezekiel	Ezek. 1:3	771
Figurative of			Moses	Deut. 34:5, 6	212	**Buzite**—*belonging to Buz*		
strength	Deut. 33:17	212	Gideon	Judg. 8:32	252	Of the tribe of		
Bullock—*young bull*			Samson and			Buz	Job 32:2	536
Used in			Manoah	Judg. 16:30, 31	260			
sacrifices	Ex. 29:1, 10-14	83	Saul and his	1 Sam. 31:12,	305			
Restrictions on	Deut. 15:19, 20	194	sons	13				
Sacrifices of,			David	1 Kin. 2:10	339			
inadequate	Ps. 69:30, 31	576	Joab	1 Kin. 2:33, 34	340			
Blood of,			Solomon	1 Kin. 11:43	353			
unacceptable	Is. 1:11	659						

SUBJECT	REFERENCE	PAGE	SUBJECT	REFERENCE	PAGE	SUBJECT	REFERENCE	PAGE

By and by (archaic expression meaning immediately or right away)
Quickly
offended.........Matt. 13:21   954
Rapid granting of a
wish.............Mark 6:25   984
Servant's duty ....Luke 7:7   1013
Signs of Christ's
return...........Luke 21:9   1032

Byway—*winding or secluded path*
Used by
travelers.........Judg. 5:6   248
Figurative of
error ....Jer. 18:15   724

Byword—*saying; remark*
Predicted as a
taunt.............Deut. 28:37   204
Job describes
himself..........Job 17:6   528

C

Cab
A measure for dry
things............2 Kin. 6:25   378

Cabbon—*surround*
Village of Judah...Josh. 15:40   231

Cabin—*a dungeon*
Jeremiah's imprisonment
in ....Jer. 37:16   743

Cabul—*unproductive*
1. Town of
Asher........Josh. 19:27   235
2. A district of Galilee offered to
Hiram.........1 Kin. 9:12, 13   349
Solomon placed people
in.............2 Chr. 8:2   445

Caesar—*a title of Roman emperors*
A. *Used in reference to:*
1. Augustus Caesar (31 B.C.–A.D. 14) Decree of brings Joseph
and Mary to
Bethlehem ....Luke 2:1   1006
2. Tiberius Caesar (A.D. 14–37)
Christ's ministry dated
by ....Luke 3:1-23   1007
Tribute paid
to............Matt. 22:17-21   964
Jews side
with ....John 19:12   1064
3. Claudius Caesar (A.D. 41–54)
Famine in time
of............Acts 11:28   1085
Banished Jews from
Rome.........Acts 18:2   1092
4. Nero Caesar (A.D. 54–68) Paul
appealed to ...Acts 25:8-12   1100
Converts in household
of............Phil. 4:22   1173
Paul before ....2 Tim. 4:16-18   1202
Called
Augustus .....Acts 25:21   1100
B. *Represented Roman authority*
Image   ⎰Matt. 22:19-21   964
on   ⎱Mark 12:15-16   992
coins.........Luke 20:24   1031
Received tax...Matt. 22:19, 21   964
            Mark 12:14, 17   992
            Luke 20:25   1031
Jesus called ⎰Luke 23:2   1035
threat to.....⎱John 19:12   1064
Pilate's loyalty to,
questioned....John 19:12   1064
Chosen over
Jesus.........John 19:12   1064

Caesar's household—*the imperial staff*
Greeted the
Philippians ......Phil. 4:22   1173

Caesarea—*pertaining to Caesar*
Roman capital of ⎰Acts 12:19   1085
Palestine ....⎱Acts 23:33   1099
Home of Philip....Acts 8:40   1081
                Acts 21:8   1096
Home of
Cornelius........Acts 10:1, 24, 25   1083
Peter
preached at ......Acts 10:34-43   1084
Paul preached   ⎰Acts 9:26-30   1082
here three   ⎱Acts 18:22   1093
times............⎱Acts 21:8   1096
Paul
escorted to ......Acts 23:23, 33   1099
Paul
imprisoned at....Acts 25:4   1100
Paul appealed to
Caesar at........Acts 25:8-13   1100

Caesarea Philippi
A city in north Palestine; scene of
Peter's great
confession........Matt. 16:13-20   958
Probable place of the
Transfiguration...Matt. 17:1-13   959

Cage—*an enclosure*
Judah
compared to......Jer. 5:27   713
Figurative of
captivity ....Ezek. 19:9   787
Babylon called ....Rev. 18:2   1279

Caiaphas—*depression*
Son-in-law of Annas; high
priest...........John 18:13   1063
Makes prophecy ..John 11:49-52   1056
Jesus before.....John 18:23, 24   1063
Apostles before ...Acts 4:1-22   1075

Cain—*smith, spear*
Adam's son ......Gen. 4:1   7
Offering   ⎰Gen. 4:2-7   7
rejected ....⎱Heb. 11:4   1221
Was of the wicked
one.............1 John 3:12   1251
Murders Abel .....Gen. 4:8   8
Becomes a
vagabond.........Gen. 4:9-15   8
Builds city ......Gen. 4:16, 17   8
A type of evil ....Jude 11   1262

Cainan—*fixed*
1. A son of
Arphaxad.....Luke 3:36   1008
2. A son of
Enosh.........Gen. 5:9-14   8
             1 Chr. 1:1, 2   404
             Luke 3:37, 38   1008

Cake—*a bread*
A. *Kinds of:*
Bread.........Ex. 29:23   84
Unleavened....Num. 6:19   141
Fig ....1 Sam. 30:12   304
Raisin ....1 Chr. 16:3   420
Barley ....Ezek. 4:12   774
Of fine flour ...Lev. 2:4   100
Leavened .....Lev. 7:13   105
Baked with   ⎰Ex. 29:23   84
oil ....⎱Num. 11:8   147
B. *Used literally of:*
Food ....2 Sam. 13:6   320
Idolatry......Jer. 44:19   749
Food prepared for
Elijah ....1 Kin. 17:13   359
C. *Used figuratively of:*
Defeat........Judg. 7:13   250
Weak
religion ......Hos. 7:8   843

Calah
A great city of Assyria built by
Nimrod..........Gen. 10:11, 12   13

Calamities—*disasters*
A. *Kinds of:*
Personal.....Job 6:2   522

Tribal.........Judg. 20:34-48   265
National.......Lam. 1:1-22   762
Punitive.......Num. 16:12-35   153
Judicial.......Deut. 32:35   211
Worldwide.....Luke 21:25-28   1032
Sudden ....Prov. 6:15   618
             1 Thess. 5:3   1185
B. *Attitudes toward:*
Unrepen-
tance ....Prov. 1:24-26   615
Repentance....Jer. 18:8   724
Hardness of
heart..........Ex. 14:8, 17   69
Bitterness......Ruth 1:20, 21   269
Defeat........1 Sam. 4:15-18   279
Submission ...Job 2:9, 10   520
Prayer-
fulness ......Ps. 141:5   608
Hopefulness ...Ps. 27:1-3   557

Calamus—*the sweet cane*
Used in holy oil ...Ex. 30:23   86
Figurative of
love..............Song 4:14   652
Rendered "sweet
cane" ....Jer. 6:20   714

Calcol, Chalcol
A son of Zerah....1 Chr. 2:6   406
Famous for
wisdom...........1 Kin. 4:31   343

Caldron—*a large kettle*
A. *Used literally of:*
Temple
vessels ....2 Chr. 35:13   470
B. *Used figuratively of:*
Leviathan's
smoke ....Job 41:20   543
Safety ....Ezek. 11:3, 7, 11   779
Oppression.....Mic. 3:3   872

Caleb—*dog; also bold*
1. Son of
Jephunneh....Josh. 15:13   231
Sent as spy ....Num. 13:2, 6   148
Gave good
report.........Num. 13:27, 30   149
His life saved ...Num. 14:5-12   149
Told to divide
Canaan ....Num. 34:17, 19   172
Entered
Canaan ....Num. 14:24-38   150
Eighty-five at end of
conquest......Josh. 14:6-13   230
Given   ⎰Josh. 14:14, 15   230
Hebron ......⎱Josh. 15:13-16   231
Gave daughter to
Othniel ....Judg. 1:12-15   244
Descendants
of.............1 Chr. 4:15   408
2. Son of
Hezron.......1 Chr. 2:18, 42   406
3. A son of Hur ..1 Chr. 2:50   407

Caleb-ephrath
Hezron died at ....1 Chr. 2:24   406

Calendar—*a system of dating*
Year divided ......1 Chr. 27:1-15   430
Determined by
moon.............Ps. 104:19   592
See Jewish calendar

Calf—*the young of a cow*
A. *Characteristics of:*
Playfulness
of..............Ps. 29:6   559
Used for
food ....Amos 6:4   858
A delicacy ....Luke 15:23, 27   1025
In sacrifice ....Lev. 9:2, 3   107
Redeemed, if
firstborn ....Num. 18:17   155
B. *Figurative of:*
Praise ....Hos. 14:2   846
Saints
sanctified .....Mal. 4:2   909

81

SUBJECT	REFERENCE	PAGE	SUBJECT	REFERENCE	PAGE	SUBJECT	REFERENCE	PAGE

Calf—continued

Patience .... Ezek. 1:7   772

Calf, Calves of Gold

A. *Making of:*

Inspired by Moses'
delay .... Ex. 32:1-4   87

Repeated by
Jeroboam ..... 1 Kin. 12:25-28   354

To represent
God........... Ex. 32:4, 5   87

To replace Temple
worship ...... 1 Kin. 12:26, 27   354

Priests appointed
for .... 1 Kin. 12:31   354

Sacrifices   (Ex. 32:6   87
offered to .... (1 Kin. 12:32, 33   354

B. *Sin of:*

Immorality ... 1 Cor. 10:6-8   1132

Great.......... Ex. 32:21, 30, 31   88

An apostasy .. Ex. 32:8   87

Wrathful ..... Deut. 9:14-20   187

Brings
punishment .. Ex. 32:26-29, 35   88

Repeated by   (Hos. 1:1   840
Jeroboam .... (Hos. 8:5, 6   844

Calker—*a sealer*

Used on Tyrian
vessels .... Ezek. 27:9, 27   795

Call

To:

Name............. Gen. 1:5   4

Pray .... Gen. 4:26   8

Be in reality.... Luke 1:35   1005

Set in office..... Ex. 31:2   86
  Is. 22:20   673

Give privileges .. Luke 14:16, 17   1024

Offer salvation .. Matt. 9:13   949

Engage in work.. 1 Cor. 7:20   1130

Calling—*one's vocation*

Faith and one's ... 1 Cor. 7:20-22   1130

Calling, the Christian

A. *Manifested through:*

Christ .... Matt. 9:13   949

Holy Spirit... Rev. 22:17   1283

Gospel........ 2 Thess. 2:14   1189

B. *Described as:*

Heavenly ..... Heb. 3:1   1216

Holy.......... 2 Tim. 1:9   1200

High.......... Phil. 3:14   1172

Irrevocable ... Rom. 11:29   1117

By grace...... Gal. 1:15   1154
  2 Tim. 1:9   1200

According to God's
purpose ..... 2 Tim. 1:9   1200

C. *Goals of:*

Fellowship with
Christ........ 1 Cor. 1:9   1126

Holiness .... 1 Thess. 4:7   1185

Liberty .... Gal. 5:13   1157

Peace.......... 1 Cor. 7:15   1130

Glory and
virtue....... 2 Pet. 1:3   1243

Eternal glory . 2 Thess. 2:14   1189

Eternal life ... 1 Tim. 6:12   1197

D. *Attitudes toward:*

Walk worthy
of............ Eph. 4:1   1164

Make it sure.. 2 Pet. 1:10   1243

Of Gentiles .. Eph. 4:17-19   1164

Calneh—*fort of Ana*

1. Nimrod's city . Gen. 10:9, 10   13

2. A city linked with Hamath and
Gath.......... Amos 6:2   858

Same as
Calno .... Is. 10:9   666

Calvary—*from the Latin "calvaria"*
(skull)

Christ was crucified
there.............. Luke 23:33   1035

Same as "Golgotha" in
Hebrew .... John 19:17   1064

Camel—*humpbacked animal*

A. *Used for:*

Riding .... Gen. 24:61, 64   26

Trade.......... Gen. 37:25   39

War .... Judg. 7:12   250

Hair of, for
clothing...... Matt. 3:4   943

Used for garment worn by John
the Baptist.... Matt. 3:4   943

Wealth .... Job 42:12   543

B. *Features of:*

Swift .... Jer. 2:23   710

Docile .... Gen. 24:11   24

Unclean ...... Lev. 11:4   109

Adorned...... Judg. 8:21, 26   252

Prize for
booty .... Job 1:17   519

Treated well .. Gen. 24:31, 32   25

Illustrative of the
impossible..... Matt. 19:24   961

Camon—*elevation*

Jair was buried
there .... Judg. 10:5   254

Camp—*to pitch a tent; take residence*

A. *The Lord's guidance of, by:*

An angel ..... Ex. 14:19   69
  Ex. 32:34   88

His presence... Ex. 33:14   89

A cloud........ Ps. 105:39   593

B. *Israel's:*

On leaving
Egypt........ Ex. 13:20   69

At Sinai ...... Ex. 18:5   73

Orderly....... Num. 2:2-34   135

Tabernacle in
center of...... Num. 2:17   135

Exclusion of:

Unclean .... Deut. 23:10-12   200

Lepers...... Lev. 13:46   112

Dead .... Lev. 10:4, 5   108

Executions
outside...... Lev. 24:23   124

Log kept of.... Num. 33:1-49   171

In battle....... Josh. 10:5, 31, 34   226

C. *Spiritual significance of:*

Christ's crucifixion
outside....... Heb. 13:12, 13   1224

God's people... Rev. 20:9   1281

Camphire—*henna, a fragrant shrub*

Illustrative of
beauty .... Song 1:14   651

Cana of Galilee

A village of upper Galilee; home of
Nathanael ...... John 21:2   1066

Christ's first
miracle at ...... John 2:1-11   1043

Healing at........ John 4:46-54   1046

Canaan—*low*

1. A son of
Ham.......... Gen. 10:6   13

Cursed by
Noah .... Gen. 9:20-25   12

2. Promised
land........... Gen. 12:5   15

Canaan, Land of

A. *Specifications regarding:*

Boundaries ... Gen. 10:19   13

Fertility........ Ex. 3:8, 17   58

Seven
nations....... Deut. 7:1   185

Language...... Is. 19:18   671

B. *God's promises concerning,*
given to:

Abraham ..... Gen. 12:1-3   14

Isaac .... Gen. 26:2, 3   27

Jacob......... Gen. 28:10-13   30

Israel......... Ex. 3:8   58

C. *Conquest of:*

Announced .... Gen. 15:7-21   17

Preceded by
spies .... Num. 13:1-33   148

Delayed by
unbelief....... Num. 14:1-35   149

Accomplished by the
Lord .... Josh. 23:1-16   239

Done only in   (Judg. 1:21,
part........... (27-36   244

Canaan, names of

Canaan .... Gen. 11:31   14

Land of
Hebrews......... Gen. 40:15   42

Palestina........ Ex. 15:14   70

Land of Israel.... 1 Sam. 13:19   287

Immanuel's land . Is. 8:8   664

Beulah........... Is. 62:4   701

Pleasant .... Dan. 8:9   831

The Lord's land .. Hos. 9:3   844

Holy land .... Zech. 2:12   897

Land of the
Jews .... Acts 10:39   1084

Land of promise... Heb. 11:9   1221

Canaanites—*original inhabitants of*
Palestine

A. *Described as:*

Descendants of
Ham.......... Gen. 10:5, 6   13

Under a
curse......... Gen. 9:25, 26   12

Amorites ...... Gen. 15:16   17

Seven
nations....... Deut. 7:1   185

Fortified...... Num. 13:28   149

Idolatrous .... Deut. 29:17   206

Defiled........ Lev. 18:24-27   118

B. *Destruction of:*

Commanded by
God........... Ex. 23:23, 28-33   78

Caused by
wickedness.... Deut. 9:4   187

In God's
time .... Gen. 15:13-16   17

Done in
degrees ...... Ex. 23:29, 30   78

C. *Commands prohibiting:*

Common league
with .... Deut. 7:1, 2   185

Intermarriage
with .... Deut. 7:1, 3   185

Idolatry of..... Ex. 23:24   78

Customs of .... Lev. 18:24-27   118

Canaanites—*a Jewish sect*

"Simon the
Canaanite"....... Matt. 10:4   950

Woman from that
region.......... Matt. 15:22   957

Called Zelotes..... Luke 6:15   1012

Candace—*dynastic title of Ethiopian*
queens

Conversion of
eunuch of .... Acts 8:27-39   1081

Candle—*a light*

A. *Used literally of:*

Household
lights .... Matt. 5:15   945

B. *Used figuratively of:*

Conscience ... Prov. 20:27   628

Prosperity ..... Job 29:3   534

Industry ...... Prov. 31:18   636

Death .... Job 18:6   528

God's justice.. Zeph. 1:12   887

Candlestick, the Golden

A. *Specifications regarding:*

Made of gold .. Ex. 25:31   80

After a divine
model........ Ex. 25:31-40   80

Set in holy
place.......... Heb. 9:2   1219

Continual burning
of............ Ex. 27:20, 21   82

Carried by
Kohathites.... Num. 4:4, 15   138

Temple's ten branches
of............. 1 Kin. 7:49, 50   346

SUBJECT	REFERENCE	PAGE	SUBJECT	REFERENCE	PAGE	SUBJECT	REFERENCE	PAGE
Taken to			False			**Carbuncle**—*a precious gem*		
Babylon.......Jer. 52:19		759	doctrines.....Deut. 13:1-10		191	In high priest's		
B. *Used figuratively of:*			**Cappadocia**—*a province of Asia Minor*			garment..........Ex. 28:17		82
Christ........Zech. 4:2, 11		898	Natives of, at			Figuratively of		
The church....Rev. 1:13, 20		1269	Pentecost ....Acts 2:1, 9		1073	glory..............Is. 54:12		696
Cane—*a tall sedgy grass*			Christians of, addressed by			Descriptive of Tyre's		
Used in {Is. 43:24		688	Peter............1 Pet. 1:1		1235	beauty ......Ezek. 28:12, 13		797
sacrifices.......{Jer. 6:20		714	Adnah ....2 Chr. 17:14		452			
Used in holy oil ...Ex. 30:23		86	**Captain**—*a civil or military officer*			**Carcas**—*severe*		
Trading city......Ezek. 27:23		796	A. *Applied literally to:*			Eunuch under		
Cankerworm—*a caterpillar-like insect*			Tribal heads ...Num. 2:3, 5		135	Ahasuerus........Esth. 1:10		507
Sent as			Military			**Carcase**—*a dead body, corpse*		
judgment.........Joel 1:4		850	leader........Judg. 4:2		247	A. *Used literally of:*		
Large appetite			King Saul....1 Sam. 9:15, 16		283	Sacrificial		
of ....Nah. 3:15		879	Arioch........Dan. 2:15		823	animals ......Gen. 15:9, 11		17
Canneh			Potiphar......Gen. 37:36		40	Unclean		
Trading city......Ezek. 27:23		796	David as			beasts........Lev. 5:2		103
Cannibalism—*using human flesh as*			leader.........1 Sam. 22:2		297	Lion..........Judg. 14:8		258
food			David as			Men......Deut. 28:25, 26		204
Predicted as a			king ....2 Sam. 5:2		312	Idols..........Jer. 16:18		723
judgment.........Deut. 28:53-57		205	Jehohanan....2 Chr. 17:15		452	B. *Used figuratively of:*		
Fulfilled in a			Temple police			Those in hell....Is. 66:24		704
siege ....2 Kin. 6:28, 29		378	head.........Luke 22:4		1033	Idolatrous		
Capacity—*ability to perform*			Roman			kings ....Ezek. 43:7, 9		812
Hindered by sin ...Gal. 5:17		1158	officer........Acts 21:31		1097	Attraction ...Matt. 24:28		967
Fulfilled in			B. *Applied spiritually to:*			C. *Laws regarding:*		
Christ...........Phil. 4:13		1173	Angel of the			Dwelling made unclean		
Capernaum—*village of Nahum*			Lord ....Josh. 5:14		221	by ....Num. 19:11-22		156
A. *Scene of Christ's healing of:*			**Captain, chief of the Temple**—*priest*			Contact with, makes		
Centurion's			*who kept order*			unclean ......Lev. 11:39		110
servant ......Matt. 8:5-13		948	Conspired with			Food made		
Nobleman's			Judas..........Luke 22:3, 4		1033	unclean ......Lev. 11:40		110
son ....John 4:46-54		1046	Arrested Jesus ...Luke 22:52-54		1034	**Carchemish**		
Peter's mother-in-			Arrested			Eastern capital of Hittites on the		
law ....Matt. 8:14-17		948	apostles ....Acts 5:24-26		1077	Euphrates........2 Chr. 35:20		470
The			**Captive**—*an enslaved person*			Conquered by		
demoniac ....Mark 1:21-28		979	A. *Good treatment of:*			Sargon II.........Is. 10:9		666
The paralytic ..Matt. 9:1-8		949	Compassion ...Ex. 6:4-8		61	Josiah wounded		
Various			Kindness ....2 Chr. 28:15		462	here..............2 Chr. 35:20-24		470
diseases......Matt. 8:16, 17		948	Mercy ....2 Kin. 6:21-23		377	**Care, carefulness**—*wise and provident*		
B. *Other events connected with:*			B. *Bad treatment of:*			*concern*		
Jesus' head-			Forced labor...2 Sam. 12:31		320	A. *Natural concern for:*		
quarters......Matt. 4:13-17		944	Blinded ....Judg. 16:21		260	Children ......Luke 2:44-49		1007
Simon Peter's			Maimed.......Judg. 1:6, 7		244	Duties ....Luke 10:40		1019
home ......Mark 1:21, 29		979	Ravished .....Lam. 5:11-13		766	Mate ......1 Cor. 7:32-34		1131
Jesus' sermon on the Bread of			Enslaved......2 Kin. 5:2		376	Health........Is. 38:1-22		684
Life........John 6:24-71		1048	Killed .....1 Sam. 15:32, 33		290	Life..........Mark 4:38		982
Other important			C. *Applied figuratively to those:*			Possessions ...Gen. 33:12-17		35
messages......Mark 9:33-50		989	Under Satan...2 Tim. 2:26		1201	B. *Spiritual concern for:*		
Judgment pronounced			Under sin.....2 Tim. 3:6		1201	Duties ....Phil. 2:20		1171
upon..........Matt. 11:23, 24		952	Liberated by			Office..........1 Tim. 3:1-8		1195
Caph			Christ........Luke 4:18		1009	A minister's		
Eleventh letter of Hebrew			**Captivity**—*a state of bondage;*			needs ....Phil. 4:10-12		1173
alphabet......Ps. 119:81-88		601	*enslavement*			The flock of {John 10:11		1054
Caphtor—*cup*			A. *Foretold regarding:*			God..........{1 Pet. 5:2, 3		1239
The place (probably Crete) from			Hebrews in			Churches ....2 Cor. 11:28		1150
which the Philistines came to			Egypt......Gen. 15:13, 14		17	Christians ....1 Cor. 12:25		1135
Palestine ....Jer. 47:4		751	Israelites .....Deut. 28:36-41		204	Spiritual		
Caphtorim			Ten tribes			things........Acts 18:12-17		1092
Those of			(Israel).......Amos 7:11		859	**Care, divine**—*God's concern for His*		
Caphtor ....Deut. 2:23		180	Judah.........Is. 39:6		685	*creatures*		
Descendants of			B. *Fulfilled:*			For the world .....Ps. 104:1-10		592
Mizraim........Gen. 10:13, 14		13	In Egypt.......Ex. 1:11-14		56	For animals ......Ps. 104:11-30		592
Conquerors of the			In many			For pagans ......Jon. 4:11		868
Avim............Deut. 2:23		180	captivities....Judg. 2:14-23		245	For Christians...Matt. 6:25-34		947
Capital punishment—*the death penalty*			In Assyria ....2 Kin. 17:6-24		389	Babylon..........Is. 47:1, 8-11		691
A. *Institution of:*			In Babylon ...2 Kin. 24:11-16		398	Ethiopians ......Ezek. 30:9		798
By God ....Gen. 9:5, 6		12	Under Rome...John 19:15		1064	Gallio ....Acts 18:17		1093
Ex. 21:12-17		76	C. *Causes of:*			Inhabitants of		
B. *Crimes punished by:*			Disobedi-			coastlands of		
Murder ....Gen. 9:5, 6		12	ence ....Deut. 28:36-68		204	coastlands ....Ezek. 39:6		807
Adultery.......Lev. 20:10		120	Idolatry......Amos 5:26, 27		858	Moab ....Jer. 48:10-17		752
Incest ....Lev. 20:11-14		120	Breaking Sabbatic			Nineveh.........Zeph. 2:10-15		888
Sodomy ......Lev. 20:13		120	law ....2 Chr. 36:20, 21		471	Those at ease in		
Rape ....Deut. 22:25		199				Zion............Amos 6:1		858
Witchcraft.....Ex. 22:18		77	**Caravan**—*a group traveling together*			Women of		
Disobedience to			Ishmaelite			Jerusalem ....Is. 32:9-11		680
parents ....Ex. 21:17		76	traders ....Gen. 37:25		39	**Careah**—*made bold*		
Blasphemy.....Lev. 24:11-16, 23		124	Jacob's family....Gen. 46:5, 6		48	Father of		
			Jacob's funeral...Gen. 50:7-14		52	Johanan.......2 Kin. 25:23		400
			Queen of Sheba...1 Kin. 10:1, 2		350	Same as Kareah...Jer. 40:8		746
			Returnees from					
			exile..............Ezra 8:31		482			

SUBJECT	REFERENCE	PAGE	SUBJECT	REFERENCE	PAGE	SUBJECT	REFERENCE	PAGE

Cares, worldly—*overmuch concern for earthly things, anxiety*

A. *Evils of:*
Chokes the
Word........Matt. 13:7, 22 — 954
Gluts the
soul..........Luke 21:34 — 1032
Obstructs the
Gospel.......Luke 14:18-20 — 1024
Hinders Christ's
work..........2 Tim. 2:4 — 1201
Manifests
unbelief.....Matt. 6:25-32 — 947

B. *Antidotes for God's:*
Protection....Ps. 37:5-11 — 562
Provision.....Matt. 6:25-34 — 947
Promises......Phil. 4:6, 7 — 1172

Carelessness—*lack of proper concern*
Babylon........Is. 47:1, 8-11 — 691
Ethiopians.......Ezek. 30:9 — 798
Inhabitants of
coastlands.......Ezek. 39:6 — 807
Nineveh..........Zeph. 2:15 — 888
Women of
Jerusalem.......Is. 32:9-11 — 680
Gallio............Acts 18:12-17 — 1092

Carmel—*field, park, garden*
1. Rendered as:
"Fruitful
field"..........Is. 10:18 — 666
"Plentiful
field"..........Is. 16:10 — 670
"Plentiful
country".....Jer. 2:7 — 709
2. City of
Judah.........Josh. 15:55 — 231
Site of Saul's
victory.......1 Sam. 15:12 — 289
Home of David's
wife..........1 Sam. 27:3 — 302
3. A mountain of
Palestine.......Josh. 19:26 — 235
Joshua defeated king
there..........Josh. 12:22 — 228
Scene of Elijah's
triumph.......1 Kin. 18:19-45 — 360
Elisha visits....2 Kin. 2:25 — 373
Place of
beauty.......Song 7:5 — 653
Figurative of
strength.....Jer. 46:18 — 751
Barrenness
foretold.......Amos 1:2 — 855

Carmelite, Carmelitess
Nabal.............1 Sam. 30:5 — 304
      2 Sam. 2:2 — 309
Hezrai.............2 Sam. 23:35 — 332
Abigail............1 Sam. 27:3 — 302

Carmi—*vinedresser*
1. Son of
Reuben.......Gen. 46:9 — 48
2. Father of
Achan........Josh. 7:1 — 222

Carnal—*fleshly, worldly*
Used literally of:
Sexual relations...Lev. 19:20 — 119
Paul calls
himself..........Rom. 7:14 — 1113
Gentiles ministered
in..............Rom. 15:27 — 1121
Paul calls brethren at
Corinth.......1 Cor. 3:1, 3 — 1127
Things not spiritual
called.........1 Cor. 9:11 — 1132

Carob pod—*seedcase of the carob, or locust tree*
Rendered "husk"; fed to
swine..........Luke 15:16 — 1025

Carpenter—*a skilled woodworker*
David's house
built by.........2 Sam. 5:11 — 313

Temple
repaired by.......2 Chr. 24:12 — 458
Idols made by.....Is. 44:13 — 689
Temple
restored by.......Ezra 3:7 — 477
Joseph
works as........Matt. 13:55 — 955

Carpenter tools—*implements for the carpenter trade*
Axe..............Deut. 19:5 — 196
Hammer.........Jer. 23:29 — 729
Line..............Zech. 2:1 — 897
Nail..............Jer. 10:4 — 717
Saw.............1 Kin. 7:9 — 345

Carpus—*fruit*
Paul's friend at
Troas............2 Tim. 4:13 — 1202

Carriage (outdated word for baggage)
Goods,
provisions......1 Sam. 17:22 — 291
An army's
baggage..........Is. 10:28 — 667
Heavy goods.....Judg. 18:21 — 262
A vehicle.........Is. 46:1 — 690

Carrion vulture
Unclean bird.....Lev. 11:18 — 109

Carshena—*plowman*
Prince of Persia...Esth. 1:14 — 507

Cart—*a wagon*
Used in moving...Gen. 45:19, 21 — 47
Made of wood.....1 Sam. 6:14 — 281
Sometimes
covered..........Num. 7:3 — 141
Drawn by cows...1 Sam. 6:7 — 280
Used in
threshing........Is. 28:28 — 677
Used for hauling..Amos 2:13 — 856
Ark carried by....2 Sam. 6:3 — 313
Figurative of sin..Is. 5:18 — 661

Carving—*cutting figures in wood or stone*
Used in worship...Ex. 31:1-7 — 86
Found in homes...1 Kin. 6:18 — 344
Employed by
idolators..........Judg. 18:18 — 262
Used in the
Temple..........1 Kin. 6:35 — 344

Casement—*lattice, criss-crossed strips of wood or metal*
Looked through...Prov. 7:6 — 619

Casiphia—*silvery*
Home of exiled
Levites..........Ezra 8:17 — 482

Casluhim
A tribe descended from
Mizraim..........Gen. 10:14 — 13
Descendant of
Ham.............1 Chr. 1:8, 12 — 404

Cassia—*amber*
An ingredient of holy
oil.............Ex. 30:24, 25 — 86
An article of
commerce.......Ezek. 27:19 — 796
Noted for
fragrance.........Ps. 45:8 — 567

Castaway—*worthless; reprobated*
The   {Matt. 25:30 — 968
rejected.........{2 Pet. 2:4 — 1243
Warning
concerning.....1 Cor. 9:27 — 1132

Caste—*divisions of society*
Some leaders of
low..............Judg. 11:1-11 — 255
David aware of...1 Sam. 18:18, 23 — 293
Jews and Samaritans
observe..........John 4:9 — 1045
Abolished.......Acts 10:28-35 — 1083

Castle—*fortress, tower*
A. *Used literally of:*
King's
residence......2 Kin. 15:25 — 388
An
encampment..Gen. 25:16 — 26
A tower for
guards........1 Chr. 6:54 — 411
Barracks for
soldiers.......Acts 21:34 — 1097
A fortress.......1 Chr. 11:7 — 416
David conquers
Jebusite.......1 Chr. 11:5, 7 — 416
B. *Used figuratively of:*
Offended
brother.......Prov. 18:19 — 627

Castor and Pollux—*sons of Jupiter*
Gods in Greek and Roman
mythology; figureheads on Paul's
ship to Rome.....Acts 28:11 — 1103

Castration—*removal of male testicles*
Disqualified for
congregation.....Deut. 23:1 — 199
Rights restored in new
covenant.........Is. 56:3-5 — 696
Figurative of absolute
devotion.........Matt. 19:12 — 961

Caterpillar—*an insect living on vegetation*
Works with
locust............Is. 33:4 — 680
Devours land.....Amos 4:9 — 857

Cattle—*animals (collectively)*
Created by God...Gen. 1:24 — 4
Adam named.....Gen. 2:20 — 6
Entered the ark...Gen. 7:13, 14 — 10
Struck by God...Ex. 12:29 — 67
Firstborn of, belong to
God...............Ex. 34:19 — 90
Can be unclean...Lev. 5:2 — 103
Taken as
plunder..........Josh. 8:2, 27 — 223
Belong to God....Ps. 50:10 — 569
Nebuchadnezzar eats
like.............Dan. 4:33 — 827
Pastureless.......Joel 1:18 — 850
East of Jordan good
for..............Num. 32:1, 4 — 169
Given as ransom..Num. 3:45 — 137

Caul
1. A lining surrounding the
stomach.......Ex. 29:13, 22 — 84
2. A hair net worn by
women..........Is. 3:18 — 660

Causeway—*a road or passage*
Steps leading into
temple..........1 Chr. 26:16, 18 — 430

Caution—*provident care; alertness*
For safety........Acts 23:10,
      16-24 — 1098
For defense.......Neh. 4:12-23 — 492
For attack.......1 Sam. 20:1-17 — 295
A principle.......Prov. 14:15, 16 — 624
Neglect of.......1 Sam. 26:4-16 — 301

Cave—*a cavern*
A. *Used for:*
Habitation.....Gen. 19:30 — 20
Refuge.......1 Kin. 18:4 — 360
Burial.........John 11:38 — 1056
Conceal-
ment..........1 Sam. 22:1 — 297
Protection.....Is. 2:19 — 660
      Rev. 6:15 — 1272
B. *Mentioned in Scripture:*
Machpelah.....Gen. 23:9 — 23
Makkedah.....Josh. 10:16, 17 — 226
Adullam.......1 Sam. 22:1 — 297
Engedi........1 Sam. 24:1, 3 — 298

SUBJECT	REFERENCE	PAGE	SUBJECT	REFERENCE	PAGE	SUBJECT	REFERENCE	PAGE

Character—continued

B. *Manifested by:*
Decisions
(Esau) ....Gen. 25:29-34   27
Destiny
(Judas).......John 6:70, 71   1050
Desires
(Demas) ....2 Tim. 4:10   1202
Deeds
(Saul)........1 Sam. 15:1-35   289

Character of God's people

A. *Their dedication:*
Hear Christ....John 10:3, 4   1054
Follow
Christ.........John 10:4, 5, 27   1054
Receive
Christ.........John 1:12   1042

B. *Their standing before God:*
Blameless......Phil. 2:15   1171
Faithful........Rev. 17:14   1279
Godly..........2 Pet. 2:9   1244
Holy...........Col. 3:12   1178

C. *Their graces:*
Humble.......1 Pet. 5:5   1239
Loving........1 Thess. 4:9   1185
Humility......Phil. 2:3, 4   1171
Meek.........Matt. 5:5   945
Merciful......Matt. 5:7   945
Obedient......Rom. 16:19   1122
Pure..........Matt. 5:8   945
Sincere ....2 Cor. 1:12   1143
Zealous.......Titus 2:14   1207
Courteous .....1 Pet. 3:8   1237
Unity of
mind.........Rom. 15:5-7   1120
Hospitable ....1 Pet. 4:9   1238
Generous.....2 Cor. 8:1-7   1147
Peaceable.....Heb. 12:14   1223
Patient ....James 5:7, 8   1230
Content ......Heb. 13:5   1223
Steadfast .....1 Cor. 15:58   1138

Character of the wicked

A. *Their attitude toward God:*
Hostile........Rom. 8:7   1114
Denial ....Ps. 14:1   552
Disobedi-
ence ....Titus 1:16   1206

B. *Their spiritual state:*
Blindness......2 Cor. 4:4   1144
Slavery to
sin............2 Pet. 2:14, 19   1244
Deadness.....Eph. 2:1   1162
Inability ......Rom. 8:8   1114

C. *Their works:*
Boastful......Ps. 10:3-6   551
Full of evil.....Rom. 1:29-32   1109
Haters of the
Gospel.......John 3:19, 20   1044
Sensual.......2 Pet. 2:12-22   1244

Charashim—*craftsmen*

Valley near
Jerusalem ....1 Chr. 4:14   408
Called the "valley of
craftsmen"......Neh. 11:35   501

Charchemish (see Carchemish)

Charger—*a dish or platter*

In tribal
offerings.........Num. 7:13   142
Translated
"dish"........Ex. 25:29   80
Used for a dead man's
head ....Matt. 14:8, 11   956
Used figuratively
("platter")........Luke 11:39   1020

Chariot—*a vehicle*

A. *Used for:*
Travel........Gen. 46:29   48
War ....1 Kin. 20:25   363

B. *Employed by:*
Kings..........1 Kin. 22:35   367
Persons of
distinction ....Gen. 41:43   43
God ....2 Kin. 2:11, 12   372

C. *Illustrative of:*
Clouds.........Ps. 104:3   592
God's
judgments ....Is. 66:15   704
Angels........2 Kin. 6:16, 17   377

Chariot, war machine

A. *Used by:*
Egyptians......Ex. 14:7   69
Canaanites ....Josh. 17:16   233
Philistines .....1 Sam. 13:5   286
Syrians ....2 Sam. 10:18   317
Assyrians......2 Kin. 19:20, 23   392
Jews...........2 Kin. 8:21   380

B. *Numbers employed by:*
Pharaoh—
600............Ex. 14:7   69
Jabin—
900............Judg. 4:3   247
Philistines—
30,000........1 Sam. 13:5   286

Chariot cities

Many in Solomon's
time..............1 Kin. 9:19   350

Chariot horses

Hamstrung........1 Chr. 18:4   423

Chariot of fire

Used in Elijah's exit from
earth ....2 Kin. 2:11   372

Chariots of the sun—*used in sun worship*

Destroyed........2 Kin. 23:11   397

Charitableness—*a generous spirit toward others*

Bearing burdens...Gal. 6:2-4   1158
Showing
forgiveness.......2 Cor. 2:1-10   1143
Seeking concord ..Phil. 4:1-3   1172
Helping the
tempted ....Gal. 6:1   1158
Encouraging the
weak.............Rom. 14:1-15   1119
Not finding fault ..Matt. 7:1-3   947
Descriptive of
Dorcas ....Acts 9:36   1082

Charity—*alms giving*

From within ......Luke 11:41   1020
Given freely......Luke 12:33   1022
Of Dorcas........Acts 9:36   1082

Charmers—*users of magic*

Falsified by God...Ps. 58:4, 5   572

Chastisement—*fatherly correction*

A. *Sign of:*
Sonship........Prov. 3:11, 12   616
God's love .....Deut. 8:5   186

B. *Design of, to:*
Correct........Jer. 24:5, 6   729
Prevent sin ....2 Cor. 12:7-9   1150
Bless ....Ps. 94:12, 13   589

C. *Response to:*
Penitence......2 Cor. 6:24-31   443
Submission ....2 Cor. 12:7-10   1150

Chastity—*sexual purity*

A. *Manifested in:*
Dress.........1 Pet. 3:1-6   1237
Looks ....Matt. 5:28, 29   945
Speech ....Eph. 5:4   1165
Intentions .....Gen. 39:7-12   41

B. *Aids to:*
Shun the
unchaste.....1 Cor. 5:11   1128
Consider your
sainthood .....Eph. 5:3, 4   1165
Dangers of
unchastity ....Prov. 6:24-35   619
Let marriage
suffice.........1 Cor. 7:1-7   1130
"Keep thyself
pure".........1 Tim. 5:22   1196

C. *Examples of:*
Job ....Job 31:1, 9-12   535
Joseph.........Gen. 39:7-20   41
Ruth ....Ruth 3:10, 11   271
Boaz...........Ruth 3:13, 14   271
Saints ....Rev. 14:4   1277

Cheating—*defrauding by deceitful means*

The Lord.........Mal. 3:8, 9   909
One's soul.......Matt. 16:26   958
The needy ....Amos 8:4, 5   859
Others ....1 Cor. 7:5   1130
See Dishonesty

Chebar—*joining*

River in
Babylonia ....Ezek. 1:3   771
Site of Ezekiel's visions and Jewish
captives........Ezek. 10:15, 20   778

Chedorlaomer—*servant of the god Lagamar*

A king of Elam; invaded
Canaan.........Gen. 14:1-16   16

Cheek—*side of face*

Micaiah struck
on...............1 Kin. 22:24   366
Struck on........Job 16:10   528
Messiah's
plucked ....Is. 50:6   693

Description of:
Beauty...........Song 5:13   652
Patience.........Matt. 5:39   946
Victory ....Ps. 3:7   549
Attack...........Mic. 5:1   873

Cheerfulness—*serene joyfulness*

A. *Caused by:*
A merry
heart.........Prov. 15:13   624
The Lord's
goodness......Zech. 9:16, 17   901
The Lord's
presence ......Mark 6:54, 55   985
Victory ....John 16:33   1062
Confidence ....Acts 24:10   1099

B. *Manifested in:*
Giving.........2 Cor. 9:7   1148
Christian
graces ....Rom. 12:8   1118
Times of
danger ....Acts 27:22-36   1102

Cheese—*a dairy product*

Used for food .....1 Sam. 17:18   291
Received by
David ....2 Sam. 17:29   325
Figurative of
trials ....Job 10:10   524

Chelal—*completeness; perfection*

A son of
Pahath-moab.....Ezra 10:30   485

Chelluh—*robust*

A son of Bani .....Ezra 10:35   485

Chelub—*basket; bird's cage*

1. A brother of
Shuah ....1 Chr. 4:11   408
2. Father of
Ezri...........1 Chr. 27:26   431

Chelubai

A son of Hezron ..1 Chr. 2:9   406
Another form of
Caleb............1 Chr. 2:18, 42   406

Chemarim—*servants, priests*

Denounced.......Zeph. 1:4   887
Translated "idolatrous
priests"........2 Kin. 23:5   397
Translated
"priests".........Hos. 10:5   845

SUBJECT	REFERENCE	PAGE	SUBJECT	REFERENCE	PAGE	SUBJECT	REFERENCE	PAGE

Children, natural—continued

G. *Examples of good:*
Isaac	Gen. 22:6-10	22
Joseph	Gen. 45:9, 10	47
Jephthah's daughter	Judg. 11:34-36	256
Samuel	1 Sam. 2:26	278
David	1 Sam. 17:20	291
Josiah	2 Chr. 34:1-3	468
Esther	Esth. 2:20	508
Daniel	Dan. 1:1-6	822
John the Baptist	Luke 1:80	1006
Jesus	Luke 2:51	1007
In the Temple	Matt. 21:15, 16	963
Timothy	2 Tim. 3:15	1202

H. *Examples of bad:*
Esau	Gen. 26:34, 35	28
Job's haters	Job 19:18	529
Sons of Eli	1 Sam. 2:12, 17	277
Sons of Samuel	1 Sam. 8:1-3	282
Absalom	2 Sam. 15:10	322
Adonijah	1 Kin. 1:5, 6	337
Elisha's mockers	2 Kin. 2:22-23	373
Adram-melech	2 Kin. 19:37	393

I. *Acts performed upon:*
Naming	Ruth 4:17	272
Blessing	Luke 1:67, 76-79	1005
Circum-cision	Luke 2:21	1006

J. *Murder of:*
By Pharaoh	Ex. 1:15, 16	57
By Herod the Great	Matt. 2:16-18	942
In war	Num. 31:12-17	168

Chileab—restraint of father
A son of David	2 Sam. 3:3	311
Also called Daniel	1 Chr. 3:1	407

Chilion—wasting away
Elimelech's son	Ruth 1:2	269
Orpah's deceased husband	Ruth 1:4, 5	269
Boaz redeems his estate	Ruth 4:9	271

Chilmad
A town or country trading with Tyre	Ezek. 27:23	796

Chimham—pining
A son of Barzillai	2 Sam. 19:37-40	328
Inn bearing his name	Jer. 41:17	747

Chinnereth, Cinneroth—lyre

1. A city of Naphtali ... Deut. 3:17 — 181
2. The region of Chinneroth ... 1 Kin. 15:20 — 357
   Same as plain of Gennesaret ... Matt. 14:34 — 956
3. The Old Testament name for Sea of Galilee ... Num. 34:11 — 172
   Also called Lake of Gennesaret and Sea of Galilee ... Luke 5:1 — 1010

Chios—snow
An island of the Aegean Sea; on Paul's voyage	Acts 20:15	1095

Chisleu
Ninth month of Hebrew year	Neh. 1:1	489

Chislon—trust, hope
Father of Elidad	Num. 34:21	173

Chisloth-tabor—the flanks of Tabor
A locality near Mt. Tabor	Josh. 19:12	234

Probably same as Chesulloth ... Josh. 19:18 — 234

Chittim, Kittim

The island of Cyprus; inhabited by descendants of Japheth (through Javan) ... Gen. 10:4 — 13

Ships of, in Balaam's prophecy ... Num. 24:24 — 162

A haven for Tyre's ships ... Is. 23:1-12 — 673

Mentioned in the prophets ... Jer. 2:10 — 710

Chiun—detestable thing

Pagan deity worshiped by Israel ... Amos 5:26 — 858

Chloe—verdure

Woman of Corinth ... 1 Cor. 1:11 — 1126

Choice, choose

A. *Of human things:*
Wives	Gen. 6:2	9
Land	Gen. 13:11	16
Soldiers	Ex. 17:9	72
King	1 Sam. 8:18	282
Apostles	Luke 6:13	1011
Church officers	Acts 6:5	1078
Missionaries	Acts 15:40	1089
Delegates	Acts 15:22, 25	1089

B. *Of God's choice:*
Moses as leader	Num. 16:28	153
Levites to priesthood	1 Sam. 2:28	278
Kings	1 Sam. 10:24	284
Jerusalem	Deut. 12:5	190
Israel as His people	Deut. 7:6-8	185
Cyrus as deliverer	Is. 45:1-4	689
The Servant (the Messiah)	Is. 42:1-7	687
The new Israel (the Church)	1 Pet. 2:9	1236
The weak as God's own	1 Cor. 1:27, 28	1126
The elect	Matt. 20:16	962

C. *Kind of:*
God and the Devil	Gen. 3:1-11	6
Life and death	Deut. 30:19, 20	208
God and idols	Josh. 24:15-28	240
Obedience and disobedi-ence	1 Sam. 15:1-35	289
God and Baal	1 Kin. 18:21-40	360
Wisdom and folly	Prov. 8:1-21	620
Obedience and sin	2 Pet. 2:4	1243
Christ and antichrist	1 John 2:18, 19	1250

D. *Factors determining choice, man's:*
First choice	Rom. 5:12	1112
Depraved nature	John 3:19-21	1044
Spiritual deadness	Eph. 4:17-19	1164
Blindness	John 9:39-41	1054
Inability	Rom. 8:7, 8	1114

E. *Bad choice made by:*
Disobeying God	Num. 14:1-45	149
Putting the flesh first	Gen. 25:29-34	27
Following a false prophet	Matt. 24:11, 24	967
Letting the world overcome	Matt. 19:16-22	961
Rejecting God's promises	Acts 13:44-48	1087

F. *Good choice made by:*
Using God's Word	Ps. 119:9-11	599
Believing God	Heb. 11:24-27	1222
Obedience	Acts 26:19-23	1101
Prayer	Eph. 1:16-19	1162
Faith	Heb. 11:8-10	1221

Choir—musicians trained to sing together

Appointed by Nehemiah ... Neh. 12:31 — 501
In house of God ... Neh. 12:40 — 502
Under instructor ... 1 Chr. 15:22, 27 — 420

Chor-ashan (see Ashan)

Chorazin

A city denounced for its unbelief ... Matt. 11:21 — 952

Chozeba

Town of Judah ... 1 Chr. 4:22 — 408

Christ—the Anointed One

A. *Pre-existence of:*
Affirmed in Old Testament	Ps. 2:7	548
Confirmed by Christ	John 8:58	1053
Proclaimed by apostles	Col. 1:15-19	1177

B. *Birth of:*
Predicted	Is. 7:14	663
Fulfilled	Matt. 1:18-25	942
In the fullness of time	Gal. 4:4	1156

C. *Deity of:*
Prophecy	Is. 9:6	665
Acknowledged by Christ	John 20:28, 29	1066
Acclaimed by witnesses	John 1:1, 14, 18	1042
Affirmed by apostles	Rom. 9:5	1115
	Heb. 1:8	1215

D. *Attributes of:*
All-powerful	Matt. 28:18	973
All-knowing	Col. 2:3	1177
Ever-present	Matt. 18:20	960
Eternal	John 1:1, 2, 15	1042

E. *Humanity of:*
Foretold	Gen. 3:15	7
	1 Cor. 15:45-47	1138
Took man's nature	John 1:14	1042
	Heb. 2:9-18	1215
Seed of woman	Gal. 4:4	1156
A son of man	Luke 3:38	1008
Of David's line	Matt. 22:45	965
A man	1 Tim. 2:5	1194
Four brothers	Mark 6:3	984

F. *Mission of:*
Do God's will	John 6:38	1049
Save sinners	Luke 19:10	1029
Bring in everlasting right-teousness	Dan. 9:24	833
Destroy Satan's works	Heb. 2:14	1215
	1 John 3:8	1251
Fulfill the Old Testament	Matt. 5:17	945
Give life	John 10:10, 28	1054
Abolish ceremo-nialism	Dan. 9:27	833
Complete revelation	Heb. 1:1	1215

G. *Worship of, by:*
Old Testament saints	Josh. 5:13-15	221
Demons	Mark 5:2, 6	983
Men	John 9:38	1054
Angels	Heb. 1:6	1215
Disciples	Luke 24:52	1037

SUBJECT   REFERENCE   PAGE | SUBJECT   REFERENCE   PAGE | SUBJECT   REFERENCE   PAGE

Colosse—continued

Paul writes against
errors of..........Col. 2:16-23   1178

Colossians, the epistle to the

Written by Paul...Col. 1:1   1176

Colt—*young beast of burden*

Descriptive of
Messiah..........Gen. 49:10, 11   51
Christ rides on...Matt. 21:2, 5, 7   963
Of camel, as gift..Gen. 32:13, 15   34

Come—*to approach; arrive*

Of invitation......Is. 1:18   659
Of salvation......Matt. 18:11   960
Of rest...........Matt. 11:28   952
Of promise.......John 14:3   1059
Of prayer........Heb. 4:16   1217
The final.........Rev. 22:17, 20   1283

Comfort—*to relieve distress; to console*

A. *Sources of:*
  God ....2 Cor. 1:3, 4   1143
  Christ ....Matt. 9:22   950
  Holy Spirit.....Acts 9:29-31   1082
  The
    Scriptures.....Rom. 15:4   1120
  Christian
    friends........2 Cor. 7:6   1147

B. *Those in need of:*
  Afflicted......Is. 40:1, 2   685
  Sorrowful......2 Cor. 2:6, 7   1143
  Weak.........1 Thess. 5:14   1185
  Discouraged ...2 Cor. 2:6, 7   1143
  Troubled......2 Cor. 7:5-7   1147
  One another ...1 Thess. 4:18   1185

Comforter—*the Holy Spirit*

Abides with
  believers.......John 14:16   1059
Teaches..........John 14:26   1060
Testifies of
  Christ.........John 15:26   1061
Convicts.........John 16:7-11   1061
Guides into
  truth..........John 16:13   1061
Glorifies Christ....John 16:14, 15   1061

Coming of Christ (see Second Coming of Christ)

Commander—*a leading official*

Names of:
Phichol ....Gen. 21:32   22
Sisera ....Judg. 4:7   247
Saul ....1 Sam. 9:15, 16   283
Abner............1 Sam. 17:55   292
Shobach ....2 Sam. 10:16   317
Joab ....2 Sam. 24:2   333
Amasa ....1 Kin. 2:32   340
Zimri............1 Kin. 16:9   358
Omri............1 Kin. 16:16   358
Shophach........1 Chr. 19:16   424
Adnah ....2 Chr. 17:14   452
Jehohanan.......2 Chr. 17:15   452
Rehum..........Ezra 4:8   478
Hananiah ....Neh. 7:2   494
Arioch ....Dan. 2:15   823
Lysias, ...Acts 24:7   1099

Commandment—*a rule imposed by authority*

A. *God's, described as:*
  Faithful........Ps. 119:86   601
  Broad..........Ps. 119:96   601
  A lamp ....Prov. 6:23   618
  Holy...........Rom. 7:12   1113
  Not burden-
    some.........1 John 5:3   1253

B. *Christ's, described as:*
  New...........John 13:34   1059
  Obligatory.....Matt. 5:19, 20   945
  Promissory ....John 15:10, 12   1060
  Eternal life ....John 12:49, 50   1058

Commandments, divine

Sought by men....Phil. 3:6-15   1172
Not material .....Rom. 14:1-23   1119

Lives an
  epistle of ....2 Cor. 3:1-3   1144
Revealed at
  judgment.........Matt. 25:20, 21   968

Commandment, the new

Given by Christ...John 13:34, 35   1059
Based on old......1 John 2:7-11   1250
                2 John 5   1256
Fulfills the Law ..Matt. 22:34-40   965

Commandments, the Ten

Divine origin......Ex. 20:1   75
Written by God ..Ex. 32:16   87
Described........Ex. 20:3-17   75
Christ sums up....Matt. 22:35-40   965
Spiritual nature ..Matt. 5:27, 28   945
Love fulfills ......Rom. 13:8-10   1119

Commerce—*trade on a large scale*

A. *Engaged in:*
  Locally ....Prov. 31:14-18   636
  Nationally .....2 Chr. 9:21   446
  Inter-
    nationally....Rev. 18:10-24   1279

B. *Abuses of:*
  Sabbath
    trading.......Neh. 13:15-22   502
  Temple
    business......John 2:13-16   1043
  Ignoring the
    Lord ....James 4:13-17   1230
    Pride ....Ezek. 28:2-18   796

Commission—*special assignment*

A. *Kinds of:*
  Christ's—to
    mankind .....John 3:16-18   1044
  Israel's—to the
    Gentiles.......Acts 13:45-47   1087
  The Church's—to the
    world ....Matt. 28:19, 20   974

B. *Requirements of:*
  Faithfulness ...2 Tim. 4:1-8   1202
  Diligence ......Rom. 15:15-32   1120
  Willingness ...1 Sam. 3:9, 10   278

Common—*public; general*

Normal, natural...1 Cor. 10:13   1132
Ceremonially
  unclean ....Acts 10:14   1083
Ordinary people...Jer. 26:23   732
Shared
  togetherness......Acts 2:44   1074
Things believed
  alike ....Titus 1:4   1206

Common people

Burial place of ....Jer. 26:23   732

Commonwealth—*a nation*

Descriptive of
  Israel...........Eph. 2:12   1163

Communion of the Lord's Supper (see Lord's Supper)

Communion of the Saints (see Fellowship)

Communion with Christ

A. *Based on:*
  Redemption....Heb. 2:10-13   1215
  Regener-
    ation..........1 Cor. 6:14-17   1129
  Resurrection
    (spiritual) .....Col. 3:1-3   1178

B. *Identifies Christians, in:*
  Name..........1 Pet. 4:12-16   1239
  Character......John 14:23   1060
  Hope ....1 John 3:1-3   1251

Communion with God

A. *Prerequisites of:*
  Reconcili-
    ation..........2 Cor. 5:18, 19   1146
  Acceptance of
    Christ........John 14:6   1059
  Obedience ....John 14:23   1060
  Holiness ......2 Cor. 6:14-18   1146

B. *Saints:*
  Desire such....Heb. 11:10   1221
  Seek it through
    prayer ....Matt. 6:6-15   946
  Realized fully in
    eternity.......Rev. 7:13-17   1273

Communism, Christian

A. *Supposedly found in:*
  Early church....Acts 2:44, 45   1074

B. *Differs from modern Communism:*
  In being
    voluntary .....Acts 5:4   1076
  Confined to
    Christians.....Acts 4:32   1076
  Not under government
    control.......Acts 4:34-37   1076

Companion—*a fellow worker*

Wife ....Mal. 2:14   908
Companion in
  tribulation......Rev. 1:9   1268
Co-worker ......Ezra 4:7, 9, 11   478
Fellow fool......Prov. 13:20   623
Fellow believer...Ps. 119:63   601
Fellow worker ...Phil. 2:23, 25   1171

Companions, evil

A. *Cause:*
  Rebellion......Num. 16:1-50   152
  Idolatry.......Ex. 32:1-8   87
  Violence,
    death ....Acts 23:12-22   1098
  Persecution....Acts 17:5-9   1091

B. *Warnings against:*
  Do not consent with
    them..........Prov. 1:10-19   615
  Avoid them....1 Cor. 5:9-11   1128
  Remember their
    end ....Rev. 22:11, 14,
                   15   1283

Comparison—*likeness; similarity*

A. *Worthy comparisons, between:*
  God's holiness
    and man's   (Is. 46:12, 13   691
    sinfulness ....{Is. 55:6-9   696
  Christ's glory and
    humiliation ...Phil. 2:5-11   1171
  Israel's call and responsi-
    bility..........Rom. 2:17-29   1110
  Gentile faith and Jewish
    unbelief......Matt. 12:41, 42   953
  Former and present
    unbelief......Matt. 11:20-24   952
  Old and new
    covenants.....2 Cor. 3:6-18   1144
  The believer's status now and
    hereafter......1 John 3:1-3   1251

B. *Unworthy comparisons, based on:*
  Position ....Num. 16:3   152
  Privileges......1 Cor. 3:1-9   1127
  Wealth ....James 2:1-9   1228

Compassion—*suffering with another, mercy*

A. *God's, described as:*
  Overabun-
    dant ....Ps. 86:13, 15   585
  New every
    morning.....Lam. 3:22, 23   764
    Great..........Is. 54:7   696
    Kindled.......Hos. 11:8   845

B. *God's, expressed:*
  Fully ....Ps. 78:38   582
  Sovereignly....Rom. 9:15   1115
  Unfailingly ....Lam. 3:22   764
  Willingly......Luke 15:18-20   1025

C. *Christ's, expressed toward the:*
  Weary ....Matt. 11:28-30   952
  Tempted......Heb. 2:17, 18   1216
  Helpless .....Mark 9:20-22   988
  Ignorant......Heb. 5:2   1217
  Sorrowful.....Luke 7:13, 14   1013
  Multitude.....Matt. 15:32   957

SUBJECT	REFERENCE	PAGE	SUBJECT	REFERENCE	PAGE	SUBJECT	REFERENCE	PAGE

D. *Examples of:*
David in
sorrow........Ps. 51:1-12 — 569
God to Israel ..Hos. 11:8 — 845
Christ to
sinners........Matt. 9:12, 13 — 949

E. *Christian's:*
Commanded...Zech. 7:9 — 899
Col. 3:12 — 1178
Jude 22 — 1263
Expressed......Heb. 10:34 — 1221
1 Pet. 3:8 — 1237
Illustrated .....Luke 10:30, 33 — 1019
Unified ....Phil. 2:1, 2 — 1171

Complete—*to finish*

Used of:
Purification rites ..Esth. 2:12 — 508
Priestly ministry ..Luke 1:23 — 1004
Time of
pregnancy.........Luke 2:6 — 1006

Complicity—*partnership in wrongdoing*

In Adam's sin .....Rom. 5:12 — 1112
In the sins of
others............Ps. 50:18 — 569
In national guilt...Matt. 27:24-26 — 972

Composure—*calmness; tranquility; self-possession*

Before enemies....Neh. 4:1-23 — 491
Under great
strain ....Acts 27:21-26 — 1102
Facing death......Acts 7:59, 60 — 1080
Lack of ....Dan. 6:18-20 — 829

Compromise—*agreement by concession*

A. *Forbidden with:*
Ungodly ....Ps. 1:1 — 548
Evil............Rom. 12:9 — 1118
Unbelievers...2 Cor. 6:14-18 — 1146
False ⎰Gal. 1:8-10 — 1154
teachers......⎱2 John 7-11 — 1256
Spiritual
darkness .....Eph. 5:11 — 1165

B. *Examples:*
Lot ....Gen. 13:12, 13 — 16
Gen. 19:1-29 — 19
Samson........Judg. 16:1-21 — 259
Solomon.......1 Kin. 11:1-14 — 351
Asa............2 Chr. 16:1-9 — 451
Jehoshaphat ...2 Chr. 18:1-3 — 452
2 Chr. 19:1, 2 — 453
2 Chr. 20:35-37 — 455

Concealment—*keeping something secret*

Of sin,
impossible........Is. 29:15 — 678
Of intrigue,
exposed ....Esth. 2:21-23 — 508
Of intentions,
revealed..........Acts 23:12-22 — 1098

Conceit—*self-flattery*

Of persons:
Goliath ....1 Sam. 17:42-44 — 292
Sanballat.........Neh. 4:1-3 — 491
Haman.............Esth. 6:6-9 — 511
The wicked ....Prov. 6:12-17 — 618
Christians,
deplored........Rom. 12:16 — 1118

Characteristic of:
False teachers.....1 Tim. 6:3, 4 — 1197
New convert ......1 Tim. 3:6 — 1195

Conceited—*a self-righteous spirit; haughty*

Christians warned
against..........Rom. 11:20 — 1117
Rich tempted to...1 Tim. 6:17 — 1197
To prevail in last
days.............2 Tim. 3:1-5 — 1201

Conception of children

In marriage ......Gen. 21:1-3 — 21
In adultery........2 Sam. 11:2-5 — 317
In virginity ....Matt. 1:18-21 — 942

Concision—*mutilation*

Used of legalistic
circumcision......Phil. 3:2 — 1171

Conclude—*to finish*

The main issue....Eccl. 12:13 — 647

Concubine—*a "wife" who is not legally a wife*

A. *Features regarding:*
Could be
divorced ......Gen. 21:10-14 — 22
Has certain
rights ....Deut. 21:10-14 — 198
Children of,
legitimate ....Gen. 22:24 — 23
Unfaithfulness
of.............Judg. 19:1, 2 — 262
Source of
trouble.......Gen. 21:9-14 — 22
Incompatible with
Christianity ...Matt. 19:5 — 961

B. *Men who had:*
Abraham ......Gen. 25:6 — 26
Nahor ....Gen. 22:23, 24 — 23
Jacob.........Gen. 30:1, 4 — 31
Eliphaz ....Gen. 36:12 — 38
Gideon ....Judg. 8:30, 31 — 252
Saul ....2 Sam. 3:7 — 311
David..........2 Sam. 5:13 — 313
Solomon......1 Kin. 11:1-3 — 351
Caleb.........1 Chr. 2:46 — 407
Manasseh.....1 Chr. 7:14 — 412
Rehoboam....2 Chr. 11:21 — 448
Abijah........2 Chr. 13:21 — 449
Belshazzar....Dan. 5:2 — 827

Concupiscence—*sinful desire*

A. *Causes of:*
Learning evil ..Rom. 16:19 — 1122
Making provision for
flesh ....Rom. 13:14 — 1119
Not fearing ⎰Prov. 8:13 — 620
God...........⎱Prov. 9:10 — 620
Not seeing
conse- ⎰Ex. 34:6, 7 — 89
quences of ⎰Rom. 6:23 — 1113
sin ....⎱Heb. 11:25 — 1222

B. *Fruits of:*
Evil
inclinations ...Rom. 7:7, 8 — 1113
Temptations ...James 1:14 — 1228
Unchastity.....1 Thess. 4:5 — 1185
Reprobation ...Rom. 1:21-32 — 1109

C. *Remedy for:*
Repentance....2 Cor. 7:9, 10 — 1147
James 4:9, 10 — 1230
Submitting to ⎰Rom. 12:1, 2 — 1118
God..........⎱James 4:7 — 1230
Resisting the
devil ....James 4:7 — 1230
Drawing near to
God...........James 4:8 — 1230
Walking in the
Spirit ....Rom. 8:1-8 — 1114

Condemnation—*the judicial act of declaring one guilty*

A. *Causes of:*
Adam's sin.....Rom. 5:12, 15-19 — 1112
Actual sin .....Matt. 27:3 — 971
Our words....Matt. 12:37 — 953
Self- ⎰Rom. 2:1 — 1109
judgment ....⎱Titus 3:10, 11 — 1207
Legal require-
ments........2 Cor. 3:9 — 1144
Rejection of
Christ........John 3:18, 19 — 1044

B. *Escape from:*
In Christ ......Rom. 8:1, 3 — 1114
By faith........John 3:18, 19 — 1044

Condescend—*to humble oneself to the level of others*

Christ's
example....John 13:3-5 — 1058
The believer's
practice.......Rom. 12:16 — 1118

The divine
model........Phil. 2:3-11 — 1171

Condolence—*an expression of sympathy*

A. *Received by:*
Job from
friends ....Job 2:11 — 520
Hanun from
David.........2 Sam. 10:2 — 317
Hezekiah from a
king ....2 Kin. 20:12 — 394
Mary from
Jesus.........John 11:23-35 — 1056

B. *Helps in expressing, assurance of:*
Trust ....Ps. 23:1-6 — 556
Hope ....John 14:1-4 — 1059
Resurrection...1 Thess. 4:13-18 — 1185
Help...........Is. 40:10, 11 — 685

Coney—*the Syrian rock hyrax*

Listed as
unclean ....Lev. 11:5 — 109
Lives among
rocks...........Ps. 104:18 — 592
Likened to
people..........Prov. 30:26 — 636

Confectionaries—*perfumers*

A female
occupation ....1 Sam. 8:13 — 282

Confederacy—*an alliance*

Denounced........Is. 8:12 — 664

Confessing Christ

A. *Necessity of:*
For salvation ..Rom. 10:9, 10 — 1116
A test of
faith ....1 John 2:23 — 1250
An evidence of spiritual
union ....1 John 4:15 — 1252
His confessing
us.............Matt. 10:32 — 951

B. *Content of:*
Christ's
incarnation ...1 John 4:2, 3 — 1252
Christ's
Lordship ......Phil. 2:11 — 1171

C. *Prompted by:*
Holy Spirit.....1 Cor. 12:3 — 1134
Faith ....Rom. 10:9 — 1116

D. *Hindrances to:*
Fear of men ...John 7:13 — 1050
Persecution....Mark 8:34, 35 — 987
False
teachers ......2 John 7 — 1256

Confession of sin

A. *Manifested by:*
Repentance....Ps. 51:1-19 — 569
Self-
abasement ....Jer. 3:25 — 711
Godly sorrow ..Ps. 38:18 — 563
Turning from
sin ....Prov. 28:13 — 634
Restitution ....Num. 5:6, 7 — 140

B. *Results in:*
Forgiveness....1 John 1:9, 10 — 1249
Pardon ....Ps. 32:1-5 — 560
Renewed
fellowship.....Ps. 51:12-19 — 569
Healing........James 5:16 — 1231

C. *Instances of:*
Aaron ....Num. 12:11 — 148
Israelites ......1 Sam. 12:19 — 286
David..........2 Sam. 24:10 — 333
Ezra...........Ezra 9:6 — 483
Nehemiah .....Neh. 1:6, 7 — 489
Daniel.........Dan. 9:4 — 832
Peter ....Luke 5:8 — 1010
Thief ....Luke 23:39-43 — 1036

Confidence—*assurance*

A. *True, based upon:*
God's Word....Acts 27:22-25 — 1102
Assurance ....2 Tim. 1:12 — 1200

SUBJECT	REFERENCE	PAGE	SUBJECT	REFERENCE	PAGE	SUBJECT	REFERENCE	PAGE

Contempt—*scorn compounded with disrespect*

A. *Forbidden toward:*
Parents........Prov. 23:22 630
Weak (Matt. 18:10 960
Christians....(Rom. 14:3 1119
Believing
masters......1 Tim. 6:2 1197
The poor .....James 2:1-3 1228

B. *Objects of:*
The
righteous .....Ps. 80:6 583
Spiritual
things........Matt. 22:2-6 964
Christ ....John 9:28, 29 1053

C. *Examples of:*
Nabal..........1 Sam. 25:10, 11 300
Michal........2 Sam. 6:16 314
Sanballat .....Neh. 2:19 490
Jews........Matt. 26:67, 68 971
False
teachers ......2 Cor. 10:10 1149
The wicked....Prov. 18:3 626

Contention—*a quarrelsome spirit*

A. *Caused by:*
Pride ....Prov. 13:10 623
Disagree-
ment..........Acts 15:36-41 1089
Divisions ......1 Cor. 1:11-13 1126
A quarrelsome
spirit..........Gal. 5:15 1158

B. *Antidotes:*
Avoid the
contentious ...Prov. 21:19 628
Avoid contro-
versies ......Titus 3:9 1207
Abandon the
quarrel........Prov. 17:14 626
Follow peace ..Rom. 12:18-21 1118

Contentious woman

Gets Samson's
secret ....Judg. 16:13-17 260
Called brawling ..Prov. 21:9, 19 628
Undesirable ......Prov. 25:24 632
Prov. 27:15 633

Contentment—*an uncomplaining acceptance of one's share*

A. *Opposed to:*
Worry ....Matt. 6:25, 34 947
Murmuring ....1 Cor. 10:10 1132
Greed........Heb. 13:5 1223
Envy ....James 3:16 1230

B. *Shown by our recognition of:*
Our unworthi-
ness..........Gen. 32:9, 10 34
Our trust .....Hab. 3:17-19 884
God's care ....Ps. 145:7-21 609
God's
provisions.....1 Tim. 6:6-8 1197
God's
promises ......Heb. 13:5 1223

Contracts—*covenants legally binding*

A. *Ratified by:*
Giving
presents.......Gen. 21:25-30 22
Public
witness ......Ruth 4:1-11 271
Oaths........Josh. 9:15, 20 225
Joining
hands........Prov. 17:18 626
Pierced ear ...Ex. 21:2-6 75

B. *Examples of:*
Abraham and
Abimelech ...Gen. 21:25-32 22
Solomon and
Hiram.........1 Kin. 5:8-12 343

Contrition—*a profound sense of one's sinfulness*

Of the heart......Ps. 51:17 569
The
publican.........Luke 18:13 1028
Peter's example ..Matt. 26:75 971

Controversy—*dispute between people*

Between men .....Deut. 25:1 201
Between God and
men.............Hos. 4:1 842
A public ....Acts 15:1-35 1088
A private........Gal. 2:11-15 1155

Conversion—*turning to God from sin*

A. *Produced by:*
God ....Acts 21:19 1096
Christ ....Acts 3:26 1075
Holy Spirit....1 Cor. 2:13 1127
The
Scriptures.....Ps. 19:7 555
Preaching......Rom. 10:14 1116

B. *Of Gentiles:*
Foretold ....Is. 60:1-5 699
Explained.....Rom. 15:8-18 1120
Acts 15:3 1088
Illustrated ....Acts 10:1-48 1083
Acts 16:25-34 1090
Confirmed ....Acts 15:1-31 1088
Defended ......Gal. 3:1-29 1155

C. *Results in:*
Repentance....Acts 26:20 1101
New creation ..2 Cor. 5:17 1145
Transfor-
mation........1 Thess. 1:9, 10 1183

D. *Fruits of:*
Faithfulness ...Matt. 24:45-47 967
Gentleness....1 Thess. 2:7 1184
Patience......Col. 1:10-12 1177
Love..........1 John 3:14 1251
Obedience ....Rom. 15:18 1120
Peacefulness ..James 3:17, 18 1230
Self-control ...2 Pet. 1:6 1243
Self-denial ...John 12:25 1057

Conviction—*making one conscious of his guilt*

A. *Produced by:*
Holy Spirit.....John 16:7-11 1061
The Gospel ....Acts 2:37 1074
Conscience ...John 8:9 1051
Rom. 2:15 1110
The Law......James 2:9 1229

B. *Instances of:*
Adam..........Gen. 3:8-10 6
Joseph's
brothers......Gen. 42:21, 22 44
Israel..........Ex. 33:2-4 88
David..........Ps. 51:1-17 569
Isaiah ....Is. 6:1-5 662
Men of
Nineveh......Matt. 12:41 953
Peter ....Luke 5:8 1010
Saul of
Tarsus ....Acts 9:4-18 1081
Philippian
jailer..........Acts 16:27-30 1090

Convocation—*a gathering for worship*

A. *Applied to:*
Sabbaths ......Lev. 23:2, 3 122
Passover......Ex. 12:16 67
Pentecost.....Lev. 23:16-21 123
Feast of
Trumpets ....Num. 29:1 166
Feast of
Weeks ......Num. 28:26 166
Feast of
Tabernacles ..Lev. 23:34-36 123
Day of
Atonement....Lev. 23:27 123

B. *Designed to:*
Gather the
people........Josh. 23:1-16 239
Worship God ..2 Kin. 23:21, 22 397

Cooking—*making food palatable*

Done by women ..Gen. 18:2-6 19
Carefully
performed.......Gen. 27:3-10 28
Savory dish .....Gen. 27:4 28
Vegetables .....Gen. 25:29 27
Forbidden on the
Sabbath ....Ex. 35:3 90
Fish..............Luke 24:42 1037

Cooperation—*working together*

A. *Kinds of:*
Man with
man ....Ex. 17:12 72
God with
man ....Phil. 2:12, 13 1171

B. *Needed to:*
Complete job ..Neh. 4:16, 17 492
Secure
results ....Matt. 18:19 960
Win converts ..John 1:40-51 1043
Maintain
peace ....Mark 9:50 989

C. *Basis:*
Obedience to
God..........Ps. 119:63 601
Faith ....Rom. 14:1-4 1119

Coos

An island between Rhodes and
Miletus..........Acts 21:1 1096

Coral—*a rocklike substance formed from skeletons of sea creatures*

Wisdom more valuable
than..............Job 28:18 534
Bought by
traders ....Ezek. 27:16 796

Corban—*an offering*

Money
dedicated........Mark 7:11 986

Cordiality—*sincere affection and kindness*

Abraham's ......Gen. 18:1-8 18
Seen in
Jonathan.........1 Sam. 20:11-23 295
Lacking in
Nabal ....1 Sam. 25:9-13 300

Coriander

A plant whose seed is compared to
manna ....Ex. 16:31 72

Corinth—*a city of Greece*

Paul labors at .....Acts 18:1-18 1092
Site of church.....1 Cor. 1:2 1126
Visited by
Apollos...........Acts 19:1 1093
Abode of
Erastus..........2 Tim. 4:20 1203

Corinthians, epistles to the—*two books of the New Testament*

Written by Paul...1 Cor. 1:1 1126
2 Cor. 1:1 1143

Cormorant

An unclean bird...Lev. 11:17 109

Corn—*the generic term for cereal grasses*

A. *Features regarding:*
Grown in
Palestine......2 Kin. 18:32 392
Chaff blown
from ....Matt. 3:12 943
Article of
food ....Gen. 42:1, 2, 19 44
Eaten, with
oil ....Lev. 2:14, 15 101
Parched ......Ruth 2:14 270

B. *Figurative of:*
Blessings .....Ezek. 36:29 805
Heavenly
food ....Ps. 78:24 581
Christ ....John 12:24 1057
Life's
maturity......Job 5:26 522

Cornelius—*a horn*

A religious
Gentile..........Acts 10:1-48 1083

Corner Stone—*a stone placed to bind two walls together*

Laid in Zion.......Is. 28:16 677

SUBJECT	REFERENCE	PAGE	SUBJECT	REFERENCE	PAGE	SUBJECT	REFERENCE	PAGE

Corner Stone—continued

Rejected	Ps. 118:22	599
Christ is	1 Pet. 2:6, 8	1236
Christ promised as	Zech. 4:7	898
Christ fulfills	Acts 4:11	1075
	1 Pet. 2:7	1236

Cornet—*a musical instrument*

Used on occasions	1 Chr. 15:28	420
A part of worship	2 Sam. 6:5	313
Used in Babylon	Dan. 3:7, 10	825

Corpse—*a dead body*

A. *Laws regarding:*

Dwelling made unclean by	Num. 19:11-22	156
Contact with, makes unclean	Lev. 11:39	110
Food made unclean	Lev. 11:40	110

B. *Used figuratively of:*

Those in hell	Is. 66:24	704
Idolatrous kings	Ezek. 43:7, 9	812
Attraction	Matt. 24:28	967

Correction—*punishment designed to restore*

A. *Means of:*

God's judgments	Jer. 46:28	751
The rod	Prov. 22:15	629
Wickedness	Jer. 2:19	710
Prayer	Jer. 10:24	718
Scriptures	2 Tim. 3:16	1202

B. *Benefits of:*

Needed for children	Prov. 23:13	630
Sign of sonship	Prov. 3:12	616
Brings rest	Prov. 29:17	635
Makes happy	Job 5:17	521

Corruption—*rottenness; depravity*

A. *Descriptive of:*

Physical blemishes	Mal. 1:14	907
Physical decay	Matt. 6:19, 20	946
Moral decay	Gen. 6:12	9
Eternal ruin	Gal. 6:8	1158

B. *Characteristics of:*

Unregenerate men	Luke 6:43-45	1012
Apostates	2 Cor. 2:6, 7	1143
	2 Pet. 2:12, 19	1244

C. *Deliverance from:*

By Christ	Acts 2:27, 31	1073
Promised	Rom. 8:21	1115
Through conversion	1 Pet. 1:18, 23	1236
Perfected in heaven	1 Cor. 15:42, 50	1138

Corruption, mount of

Site of pagan altars	1 Kin. 11:7	351
Altars of, destroyed	2 Kin. 23:13	397

Corruption of body

Results from Adam's sin	Rom. 8:21	1115
Begins in this life	2 Cor. 5:4	1145
Consummated by death	John 11:39	1056
Freedom from, promised	Rom. 8:21	1115
Freedom from, accomplished	1 Cor. 15:42	1138

Cosam—*a diviner*

Father of Addi	Luke 3:28	1008

Cosmetics

Used by Jezebel	2 Kin. 9:30	381
Futility of	Jer. 4:30	712

Cosmic conflagration—*to destroy by fire*

Day of judgment	2 Pet. 3:7-10	1244

Council—*Jewish Sanhedrin*

A judicial court	Matt. 5:22	945
Christ's trial	Matt. 26:57-59	970
Powers of, limited	John 18:31	1063
Apostles before	Acts 4:5-30	1075
Stephen before	Acts 6:12-15	1078
Paul before	Acts 23:1-5	1098

Counsel, God's

A. *Called:*

Immutable	Heb. 6:17	1218
Faithful	Is. 25:1	675
Wonderful	Is. 28:29	677
Great	Jer. 32:19	738
Sovereign	Dan. 4:35	827
Eternal	Eph. 3:11	1163

B. *Events determined by:*

History	Is. 46:10, 11	691
Christ's death	Acts 2:23	1073
Salvation	Rom. 8:28-30	1115
Union in Christ	Eph. 1:9, 10	1162

C. *Attitudes toward:*

Christians declare	Acts 20:27	1095
Proper reserve	Acts 1:7	1072
Wicked despise	Is. 5:19	661
They reject	Luke 7:30	1014

Counsel, man's

Jethro's accepted	Ex. 18:13-27	73
Hushai's followed	2 Sam. 17:14	325
Of a woman, brings peace	2 Sam. 20:16-20	329
David's dying	1 Kin. 2:1-10	339
Of old men, rejected	1 Kin. 12:8, 13	353
Of friends, avenged	{ Esth. 5:14	510
	{ Esth. 7:10	512

Counselor—*an advisor*

Christ is	Is. 9:6	665
Thy testimonies are	Ps. 119:24	600
Safety in many	Prov. 11:14	622
Brings security	Prov. 15:22	624
Jonathan, a	1 Chr. 27:32	431
Gamaliel	Acts 5:33-40	1077

Count—*to number*

Things counted:

Stars	Gen. 15:5	17
Days	Lev. 15:13	115
Years	Lev. 25:8	125
Booty	Num. 31:26	168
Weeks	Deut. 16:9	194
Money	2 Kin. 22:4	395
People	1 Chr. 21:17	425
Bones	Ps. 22:17	556
Towers	Ps. 48:12	568
Houses	Is. 22:10	673

Countenance—*facial expression*

A. *Kinds of:*

Unfriendly	Gen. 31:1, 2	32
Fierce	Deut. 28:50	205
Terrible	Judg. 13:6	257
Sad	Neh. 2:2, 3	489
Beautiful	1 Sam. 16:12	290
Cheerful	Prov. 15:13	624
Angry	Prov. 25:23	632
Hatred	Prov. 10:18	621

B. *Transfigured:*

Moses'	2 Cor. 3:7	1144
Christ's	Matt. 17:1, 2	959
The believer's	2 Cor. 3:18	1144

Counterfeit—*a spurious imitation of the real thing*

A. *Applied to persons:*

Christ	Matt. 24:4, 5, 24	966
Apostles	2 Cor. 11:13	1149
Ministers	2 Cor. 11:14, 15	1150
Christians	Gal. 2:3, 4	1155
Teachers	2 Pet. 2:1	1243
Prophets	1 John 4:1	1252
The antichrist	Rev. 19:20	1281

B. *Applied to things:*

Worship	Matt. 15:8, 9	957
Gospel	Gal. 1:6-12	1154
Miracles	2 Thess. 2:7-12	1189
Science	1 Tim. 6:20	1197
Commandments	Titus 1:13, 14	1206
Doctrines	Heb. 13:9	1224
Religion	James 1:26	1228
Prayers	James 4:3	1230

Country—*the land of a nation*

Commanded to leave	Gen. 12:1-4	14
Love of native	Gen. 30:25	32
Exiled from	Ps. 137:1-6	606
A prophet in his own	Luke 4:24	1009
A heavenly	Heb. 11:16	1222

Courage—*fearlessness in the face of danger*

A. *Manifested:*

Among enemies	Ezra 5:1-17	479
In battle	1 Sam. 17:46	292
Against great foes	Judg. 7:7-23	250
Against great odds	1 Sam. 17:32, 50	292
When threatened	Dan. 3:16-18	825
When intimidated	Dan. 6:7-13	829
When facing death	Judg. 16:28-30	260
In youth	1 Sam. 14:6-45	287
In old age	Josh. 14:10-12	230
Before a king	Esth. 4:8, 16	510
In moral crises	Neh. 13:1-31	502
In preaching Christ	Acts 3:12-26	1075
In rebuking	Gal. 2:11-15	1155

B. *Men encouraged to:*

Leaders	Deut. 31:7	208
Joshua	Josh. 1:5-7	217
Gideon	Judg. 7:7-11	250
Philistines	1 Sam. 4:9	279
Zerubbabel	Hag. 2:4	893
Solomon	1 Chr. 28:20	433

Course—*onward movement; advance*

A ship's direction	Acts 16:11	1090
A prescribed path	Judg. 5:20	248
One's life	2 Tim. 4:7	1202
The age	Eph. 2:2	1162
The cycle of life	James 3:6	1229
Orderly arrangement	1 Chr. 27:1-15	430

Courtesy—*visible signs of respect*

A. *Shown in:*

Manner of address	Gen. 18:3	19
Gestures of bowing	Gen. 19:1	19
Rising before superiors	Lev. 19:32	119
Well-wishing remarks	Gen. 43:29	46

SUBJECT	REFERENCE	PAGE	SUBJECT	REFERENCE	PAGE	SUBJECT	REFERENCE	PAGE
Curiosity—*seeking to know things forbidden or private*			Christians give	Rom. 13:6, 7	1119	**Dalmanutha**		
Into God's secrets, forbidden	John 21:21, 22	1067	B. *As a common practice:*			A place near the Sea of Galilee	Mark 8:10	987
Leads 50,070 to death	1 Sam. 6:19	281	Abominable	Lev. 18:30	118	**Dalmatia**—*deceitful*		
Curiosity seekers			Vain	Jer. 10:3	717	A region east of the Adriatic Sea; Titus departs to	2 Tim. 4:10	1202
Eve	Gen. 3:6	6	Worthy	Luke 4:16	1009	**Dalphon**—*crafty*		
Israelites	Ex. 19:21, 24	74	Traditional	Acts 21:21	1096	A son of Haman	Esth. 9:7-10	513
Babylonians	2 Kin. 20:12, 13	394	**Cuth, Cuthah**—*burning*			**Dam**—*mother*		
Herod	Matt. 2:3-8	942	People from, brought to Samaria	2 Kin. 17:24, 30	390	*Laws concerning:*		
Zacchaeus	Luke 19:1-6	1029	**Cymbal**—*hollow of a vessel*			Animals	Ex. 22:30	77
Certain Greeks	John 12:20, 21	1057	A musical instrument	{ 1 Chr. 13:8	418	Birds	Deut. 22:6, 7	199
Lazarus' visitors	John 12:9	1057		{ 1 Chr. 15:28	420	**Damages and Remuneration**		
Peter	Matt. 26:58	971	Figurative of pretense	1 Cor. 13:1	1135	A. *In law for:*		
At the crucifixion	Matt. 27:46-49	972	**Cypress**—*a hardwood tree*			Personal injury	Ex. 21:18, 19	76
Athenians	Acts 17:21	1092	Used by idol-makers	Is. 44:14-17	689	Causing miscarriage	Ex. 21:22	76
Curse, cursing—*a violent expression of evil upon others*			**Cyprus**—*fairness*			Injuries by animals	Ex. 21:28-32	76
A. *Pronounced upon:*			A large Mediterranean island; home of			Injuries to animals	Ex. 21:33-35	76
The earth	Gen. 3:17, 18	7	Barnabas	Acts 4:36	1076	Losses	Ex. 22:1-15	76
Cain	Gen. 4:9-11	8	Christians reach	Acts 11:19, 20	1084	Stealing	Lev. 6:1-7	104
Canaan	Gen. 9:25	12	Paul visits	Acts 13:4-13	1086	Defaming a wife	Deut. 22:13-19	199
Two sons	Gen. 49:5-7	51	Barnabas visits	Acts 15:39	1089	Rape	Deut. 22:28, 29	199
Disobedient	Deut. 28:15-45	204	Paul twice sails past	Acts 21:3	1096	B. *In practice:*		
Meroz	Judg. 5:23	248	**Cyrene**—*wall*			Jacob's	Gen. 31:38-42	33
Jericho's rebuilders	Josh. 6:26	222	A Greek colonial city in north Africa; home of			Samson's	Judg. 16:28-30	260
B. *Forbidden upon:*			Simon	Matt. 27:32	972	Tamar's	2 Sam. 13:22-32	320
Parents	Ex. 21:17	76	People from, at Pentecost	Acts 2:10	1073	Zacchaeus'	Luke 19:8	1029
Ruler	Ex. 22:28	77	Synagogue of	Acts 6:9	1078	Paul's	Acts 16:35-39	1091
Deaf	Lev. 19:14	119	Some from, become missionaries	Acts 11:20	1085	Philemon's	Philem. 10-18	1210
Enemies	Luke 6:28	1012	**Cyrenius**—*of Cyrene*			**Damaris**—*gentle*		
God	Job 2:9	520	Roman governor of Syria	Luke 2:1-4	1006	An Athenian woman converted by Paul	Acts 17:33, 34	1092
God's people	Gen. 12:3	15	**Cyrus**—*sun; throne*			**Damascus**—*chief city of Aram*		
C. *Instances of:*			A. *Prophecies concerning, God's:*			A. *In the Old Testament:*		
Goliath's	1 Sam. 17:43	292	"Anointed"	Is. 45:1	689	Abram passed through	Gen. 14:14, 15	16
Balaam's attempted	Num. 22:1-12	159	Liberator	Is. 45:1	689	Abram heir from	Gen. 15:2	17
The fig tree	Mark 11:21	992	Rebuilder	Is. 44:28	689	Captured by David	2 Sam. 8:5, 6	316
Peter's	Matt. 26:69-74	971				Rezon, king of	1 Kin. 11:23, 24	352
The crucified	Gal. 3:10, 13	1156				Ben-hadad, king of	1 Kin. 15:18	357
D. *Manifested by:*						Rivers of, mentioned	2 Kin. 5:12	376
Rebellious	2 Sam. 16:5-8	324	**D**			Elisha's prophecy in	2 Kin. 8:7-15	379
Curtains—*an awning-like screen*			**Dabbasheth**—*hump*			Taken by Assyrians	2 Kin. 16:9	388
Ten, in tabernacle	Ex. 26:1-13	80	Town of Zebulun	Josh. 19:10, 11	234	Prophecies concerning	Is. 8:3, 4	664
Figurative of the heavens	Ps. 104:2	592	**Daberath**—*pasture*			B. *In the New Testament; Paul:*		
Cush—*black*			Correct rendering of Dabareh	Josh. 21:28	237	Journeys to	Acts 9:1-9	1081
1. Ham's oldest son	1 Chr. 1:8-10	404	Assigned to Gershomites	1 Chr. 6:71, 72	411	Is converted near	Acts 9:3-19	1081
2. Means Ethiopia	Is. 18:1	671	**Dagon**—*fish*			First preaches at	Acts 9:20-22	1082
3. A Benjamite	Ps. 7 (Title)	549	The national god of the Philistines	Judg. 16:23	260	Escapes from	2 Cor. 11:32, 33	1150
Cushan—*blackness*			Falls before ark	1 Sam. 5:1-5	280	Revisits	Gal. 1:17	1154
Probably same as Cush	Hab. 3:7	883	**Dainties**—*savory food, delicacies*			**Damnation**—*condemnatory judgment*		
Cushan-rishathaim—*extra wicked*			Used as a warning	Prov. 23:3-6	630	A. *Described as:*		
Mesopotamian King			Unrighteous fellowship	Ps. 141:4	608	Having degrees	Matt. 23:14	965
Oppressed Israel	Judg. 3:8	246	**Dale, the King's**			Just	Rom. 3:8	1110
Othniel delivers Israel from	Judg. 3:9, 10	246	A valley near Jerusalem	Gen. 14:17-20	16	Justified	Rom. 13:2	1119
Cushi—*an Ethiopian*			Site of Absalom's monument	2 Sam. 18:18	326	Self-inflicted	1 Cor. 11:29	1134
1. Ancestor of Jehudi	Jer. 36:14	742	**Daleth**			Merited	1 Tim. 5:12	1196
2. Father of Zephaniah	Zeph. 1:1	887	The fourth letter in the Hebrew alphabet	Ps. 119:25-32	600	B. *Inflicted:*		
Cushite—*an Ethiopian*						Now	Rom. 14:23	1120
1. David's servant	2 Sam. 18:21-32	326				In eternity	Matt. 23:33	966
2. Moses' wife	Num. 12:1	148				**Damsel**—*a young woman*		
Custom—*tax; usage*						Rebekah	Gen. 24:57	25
A. *As a tax:*						Ruth	Ruth 2:5, 6	270
Matthew collected	Matt. 9:9	949						
Kings require	Matt. 17:25	959						

Elihoenai—continued

Korahite
gatekeeper ....1 Chr. 26:1-3   429

Elihoreph—*God of autumn*

One of Solomon's
scribes ....1 Kin. 4:3   342

Elihu—*He is my God*

1. Ancestor of
Samuel ....1 Sam. 1:1   276
Also called Eliab and
Eliel ....1 Chr. 6:27, 34   410
2. David's
brother ....1 Chr. 27:18   431
Called Eliab...1 Sam. 16:6   290
3. Manassite
captain.......1 Chr. 12:20   417
4. Temple
servant ....1 Chr. 26:1, 7   429
5. One who reproved Job and his
friends ....Job 32:2, 4-6   536

Elijah—*Yahweh is God*

1. Prophet
a. *Life of the prophet:*
Denounces
Ahab..........1 Kin. 17:1   359
Hides by the brook
Cherith ....1 Kin. 17:3   359
Fed by
ravens ....1 Kin. 17:4-7   359
Fed by
widow ....1 Kin. 17:8-16   359
Restores widow's
son ....1 Kin. 17:17-24   359
Sends message to
Ahab..........1 Kin. 18:1-16   360
Overthrows Baal
prophets ......1 Kin. 18:17-46   360
Flees from
Jezebel........1 Kin. 19:1-3   362
Fed by
angels........1 Kin. 19:4-8   362
Hears God.....1 Kin. 19:9-14   362
Sent on a
mission ....1 Kin. 19:15-21   362
Condemns
Ahab..........1 Kin. 21:15-29   365
Condemns
Ahaziah.......2 Kin. 1:1-16   371
Taken up to
heaven........2 Kin. 2:1-15   372
b. *Miracles of:*
Widow's oil....1 Kin. 17:14-16   359
Dead child
raised........1 Kin. 17:17-24   359
Causes rain....1 Kin. 18:41-45   362
Causes fire to consume
sacrifices.....1 Kin. 18:24-38   361
Causes fire to consume
soldiers ......2 Kin. 1:10-12   372
c. *Prophecies of:*
Drought ....1 Kin. 17:1   359
Ahab's
destruction....1 Kin. 21:17-29   365
Ahaziah's
death ....2 Kin. 1:2-17   371
Plague ....2 Chr. 21:12-15   455
d. *Significance of:*
Prophecy of his
coming........Mal. 4:5, 6   909
Appears with
Christ.........Matt. 17:1-4   959
Type of John the
Baptist........Luke 1:17   1004
2. Priest who divorced his foreign
wife..........Ezra 10:21   484

Elika—*God has spewed out*

David's warrior ...2 Sam. 23:25   332

Elim—*large trees*

Israel's
encampment .....Ex. 15:27   71
Place of palm
trees ....Num. 33:9, 10   171

Elimelech—*God is king*

Man of Judah .....Ruth 1:1, 2   269
Dies in Moab......Ruth 1:3   269
Kinsman of
Boaz ....Ruth 2:1, 3   270
Boaz buys his
land.............Ruth 4:3-9   271

Elioenai—*toward God are my eyes*

1. Descendant of
Benjamin .....1 Chr. 7:8   412
2. Simeonite
head..........1 Chr. 4:36   408
3. Son of
Neariah.......1 Chr. 3:23, 24   407
4. Postexilic
priest ....Neh. 12:41   502
Divorced his foreign
wife..........Ezra 10:19, 22   484
5. Son of Zattu; divorced his
foreign wife..Ezra 10:27   484

Eliphal—*God has judged*

David's warrior ...1 Chr. 11:26, 35   416
Called Eliphelet ...2 Sam. 23:34   332

Eliphaz—*God is fine gold*

1. Son of Esau ...Gen. 36:2, 4   37
2. One of Job's
friends ....Job 2:11   520
Rebukes Job ...Job 4:1, 5   521
Is forgiven.....Job 42:7-9   543

Elipheleh—*whom God makes distinguished*

Levite singer......1 Chr. 15:18, 21   419

Eliphelet—*God is deliverance*

1. Son of David ..1 Chr. 3:5, 6   407
2. Another son of
David.........2 Sam. 5:16   313
3. Descendant of
Jonathan......1 Chr. 8:33, 39   413
4. David's
warrior ....2 Sam. 23:34   332
5. Returnee from
Babylon.......Ezra 8:13   482
6. Son of Hashum; divorced his
foreign wife...Ezra 10:33   485

Elisabeth—*God is an oath*

Wife of
Zacharias ....Luke 1:5   1004
Barren ....Luke 1:7, 13   1004
Conceives a son...Luke 1:24, 25   1004
Cousin of Mary ...Luke 1:36   1005
Salutation to
Mary.............Luke 1:39-45   1005
Mother of John the
Baptist ....Luke 1:57-60   1005

Elisha—*God is salvation*

A. *Life of:*
Succeeds
Elijah..........1 Kin. 19:16   362
Follows
Elijah..........1 Kin. 19:19-21   362
Sees Elijah
translated......2 Kin. 2:1-12   372
Is recognized as a
prophet ....2 Kin. 2:13-22   373
Mocked........2 Kin. 2:23-25   373
Deals with
kings ....2 Kin. 3:11-20   373
Helps two
women.........2 Kin. 4:1-17   374
B. *Miracles of:*
Divides
Jordan ....2 Kin. 2:14   373
Purifies
water ....2 Kin. 2:19-22   373
Increases widow's
oil ....2 Kin. 4:1-7   374
Raises Shunammite's
son ....2 Kin. 4:18-37   375
Neutralizes
poison ....2 Kin. 4:38-41   375
Multiplies
bread ....2 Kin. 4:42-44   375

Heals Naaman the
leper..........2 Kin. 5:1-19   376
Inflicts Gehazi with
leprosy........2 Kin. 5:26, 27   377
Causes iron to
float ....2 Kin. 6:6   377
Reveals secret
counsels.......2 Kin. 6:8-12   377
Opens servant's
eyes ....2 Kin. 6:13-17   377
Strikes Syrian army with
blindness......2 Kin. 6:18-23   377
C. *Prophecies of:*
Birth of a
child ....2 Kin. 4:16   375
Abundance ....2 Kin. 7:1   378
King's death ...2 Kin. 7:2   378
Great famine ..2 Kin. 8:1-3   379
Hazael's
cruelty........2 Kin. 8:7-15   379
Joash's
victories ......2 Kin. 13:14-19   385

Elishah—*God is salvation*

Son of Javan......Gen. 10:4   13

Elishama—*God has heard*

1. Son of
Ammihud.....Num. 1:10   133
Ancestor of
Joshua.........1 Chr. 7:26   412
2. Man of
Judah.........1 Chr. 2:41   406
3. Son of David ..1 Chr. 3:1, 5, 6   407
Also called
Elishua........2 Sam. 5:15   313
4. Another son of
David.........2 Sam. 5:16   313
5. Teaching
priest ....2 Chr. 17:7, 8   451
6. Scribe ....Jer. 36:12, 20, 21   742

Elishaphat—*God has judged*

Captain...........2 Chr. 23:1   456

Elisheba—*God is an oath*

Wife of Aaron.....Ex. 6:23   61

Elishua—*God is salvation*

Son of David......2 Sam. 5:15   313
Called Elishama...1 Chr. 3:6   407

Eliud—*God is mighty*

Father of
Eleazar..........Matt. 1:14, 15   942

Elizaphan—*God has concealed*

1. Chief of
Kohathites....Num. 3:30   137
Heads family ..1 Chr. 15:5, 8   419
Family
consecrated ...2 Chr. 29:12-16   462
2. Son of
Parnach.......Num. 34:25   173

Elizur—*God is a rock*

Reubenite
warrior.........Num. 1:5   133

Elkanah—*God has possessed*

1. Father of
Samuel ....1 Sam. 1:1-23   276
2. Son of Korah ..Ex. 6:24   61
Escapes
judgment .....Num. 26:11   163
3. Levite ....1 Chr. 6:23-36   410
4. Descendant of
Korah.........1 Chr. 6:22, 23   410
5. Levite ....1 Chr. 9:16   414
6. Korahite
warrior ....1 Chr. 12:1, 6   417
7. Officer under
Ahaz.........2 Chr. 28:7   461
8. Doorkeeper of
the ark........1 Chr. 15:23   420

Elkoshite—*an inhabitant of Elkosh*

Descriptive of
Nahum..........Nah. 1:1   878

119

SUBJECT   REFERENCE   PAGE | SUBJECT   REFERENCE   PAGE | SUBJECT   REFERENCE   PAGE

Estrangement from God

Caused by:
Natural status.....Esth. 2:11, 12 — 508
Adam's sin.......Gen. 3:8-11, 24 — 6
Personal sin.......Ps. 51:9-12 — 569
National sin.......Jer. 2:14-17 — 710

Etam—*Wild beasts' lair*

1. Village of
   Simeon ....1 Chr. 4:32 — 408
2. Rock where Samson took
   refuge........Judg. 15:8-19 — 259
3. Town of
   Judah.........2 Chr. 11:6 — 447

Eternal, everlasting—*without end*

A. *Applied to Trinity:*
   God ....Ps. 90:2 — 587
   Christ ....Prov. 8:23 — 620
   Holy Spirit.....Heb. 9:14 — 1219

B. *Applied to God's attributes:*
   Home..........Eccl. 12:5 — 647
   Power ....Rom. 1:20 — 1109
   Covenant......Is. 55:3 — 696
   Gospel........Rev. 14:6 — 1277
   Counsels......Eph. 3:10, 11 — 1163
   Righteous-
   ness..........Ps. 119:142, 144 — 602
   Kingdom .....Ps. 145:13 — 610
   Truth.........Ps. 100:5 — 590
   Love.........Jer. 31:3 — 735
   Father........Is. 9:6 — 665

C. *Applied to the believer:*
   Comfort ......2 Thess. 2:16 — 1189
   Life...........John 3:15 — 1044
   Redemption...Heb. 9:12 — 1219
   Salvation .....Heb. 5:9 — 1217
   Inheritance...Heb. 9:15 — 1219
   Glory........1 Pet. 5:10 — 1239
   Kingdom .....2 Pet. 1:11 — 1243
   Reward.......John 4:36 — 1046
   Name.........Is. 56:5 — 697
   Glory........2 Tim. 2:10 — 1201
   Light ....Is. 60:19, 20 — 700
   Joy...........Is. 51:11 — 694
   Dwellings.....Luke 16:9 — 1026
   Purpose......Eph. 3:11 — 1163

D. *Applied to the wicked:*
   Damnation ....Mark 3:29 — 981
   Judgment.....Heb. 6:2 — 1217
   Punishment...Matt. 25:46 — 969
   Destruction...2 Thess. 1:9 — 1189
   Contempt.....Dan. 12:2 — 837
   Bonds ....Jude 6 — 1262
   Fire..........Matt. 25:41 — 969
   Sin ....Mark 3:29 — 981

Eternity—*time without end mentioned once*

God's habitation ..Is. 57:15 — 697

Etham—*sea bound*

Israel's
encampment .....Ex. 13:20 — 69

Ethan—*perpetuity*

1. One noted for
   wisdom.......1 Kin. 4:31 — 343
2. Levite ....1 Chr. 6:44 — 410
3. Ancestor of
   Asaph........1 Chr. 6:42, 43 — 410

Ethanim—*incessant rains*

Seventh month in the Hebrew
year..............1 Kin. 8:2 — 346

Ethbaal—*with Baal*

Father of
Jezebel..........1 Kin. 16:31 — 359

Ether—*plenty*

Town of Judah....Josh. 15:42 — 231

Ethics—*a system setting forth standards of right conduct*

Perversion of.....Rom. 1:19-32 — 1109
Law of..........Rom. 2:14-16 — 1109

Summary of
Christian ....Rom. 12:1-21 — 1118

Ethiopia (Cush)—*burnt face*

Country south of
Egypt ....Ezek. 29:10 — 797
Home of the Sons of
Ham ....Gen. 10:6 — 13
Famous for
minerals........Job 28:19 — 534
Merchandise of....Is. 45:14 — 690
Wealth of ......Is. 43:3 — 688
Militarily strong..2 Chr. 12:2, 3 — 448
Anguished
people.........Ezek. 30:4-9 — 798
Defeated by Asa ..2 Chr. 14:9-15 — 450
Subdued ....Dan. 11:43 — 836
Prophecies
against..........Is. 20:1-6 — 672
God's love for.....Amos 9:7 — 860
Hopeful promise ..Ps. 68:31 — 575

Ethiopians—*descendants of Cush*

Skin of,
unchangeable ....Jer. 13:23 — 720
Moses'
marriage to......Num. 12:1 — 148
Ebed-melech saves
Jeremiah ....Jer. 38:7 — 744
Eunuch
converted ....Acts 8:26-40 — 1081

Ethnan—*hire*

Judahite ....1 Chr. 4:5-7 — 408

Ethni—*liberal*

Levite.............1 Chr. 6:41 — 410

Eubulus—*prudent*

Christian at
Rome ....2 Tim. 4:21 — 1203

Eucharist (see Lord's Supper)

Eunice—*blessed with victory*

Mother of
Timothy..........2 Tim. 1:5 — 1200

Eunuch—*an officer or official, emasculated*

A. *Rules concerning:*
   Excluded from congre-
   gation.........Deut. 23:1 — 199
   Given
   promise.......Is. 56:3-5 — 696

B. *Duties of:*
   Guard ....Gen. 37:36 — 40
   Servant........Gen. 40:2, 7 — 41
   Attendant ....Dan. 1:3, 7, 10, 11 — 822
   Keeper of
   harem.........Esth. 2:3, 14 — 508
   Treasurer......Acts 8:27 — 1081

Euodias—*good journey*

Christian woman at
Philippi...........Phil. 4:2 — 1172

Euphrates—*that which makes fruitful*

River of Eden .....Gen. 2:14 — 5
Assyria bounded
by...............2 Kin. 23:29 — 398
Babylon on.......Jer. 51:13, 36 — 756
Boundary of {Gen. 15:18 — 17
God's promise..{1 Kin. 4:21, 24 — 342
Persian
boundary......Ezek. 4:10, 11 — 774
Scene of battle....Jer. 46:2, 6, 10 — 750
Exiled Jews weep
there ....Ps. 137:1 — 606
Angels bound
there ....Rev. 9:14 — 1274

Euroclydon—*east wind*

Violent wind......Acts 27:14 — 1102

Eutychus—*fortunate*

Sleeps during Paul's
sermon...........Acts 20:9 — 1095
Restored to life....Acts 20:12 — 1095

Evangelism—*declaring Gospel to the unregenerate*

A. *Scope:*
   To all {Matt. 28:19, 20 — 974
   nations.......{Mark 16:15 — 999
   House to
   house.........Acts 5:42 — 1078
   Always ....1 Pet. 3:15 — 1238
   As ambas-
   sadors.........2 Cor. 5:18-20 — 1146

B. *Source:*
   Jesus Christ ...Gal. 1:6-12 — 1154
   The Father ....John 6:44, 65 — 1049
   The Spirit......Acts 1:8 — 1072

Evangelist—*one who proclaims good news*

Distinct ministry ..Eph. 4:11 — 1164
Applied to Philip ..Acts 21:8 — 1096
Timothy
works as ....2 Tim. 4:5 — 1202

Eve—*life*

Made from
Adam's rib ......Gen. 2:18-22 — 5
Named by Adam ..Gen. 3:20 — 7
Deceived by
Satan ....Gen. 3:1-24 — 6
Leads Adam
to sin............1 Tim. 2:13, 14 — 1195

Evening—*last hours of sunlight*

Labor ceases......Judg. 19:16 — 263
Ruth 2:17 — 270
Workers paid .....Deut. 24:15 — 201
Ritual impurity {Lev. 11:24-28 — 109
ends.............{Num. 19:19 — 156
Meditation ....Gen. 24:63 — 26
Prayer ....Matt. 14:15, 23 — 956
Eating ....Luke 24:29, 30 — 1037
Sacrifice ....Ex. 29:38-42 — 85
Num. 28:3-8 — 165

Evening sacrifice—*part of Israelite worship*

Ritual described...Ex. 29:38-42 — 85
Part of continual
offering ....Num. 28:3-8 — 165

Events, Biblical, classified

A. *Originating, originating other events:*
   Creation.......Gen. 1 — 4
   Fall of man ....Rom. 5:12 — 1112

B. *Epochal, introducing new period:*
   Flood..........Gen. 6—8 — 9
   The death of {Matt. 27:50, 51 — 972
   Christ........{Heb. 9 — 1219

C. *Typical, foreshadowing some New Testament event:*
   The
   Passover.......{Ex. 12 — 66
   Christ as {John 1:35-37 — 1043
   Lamb........{1 Cor. 5:7, 8 — 1128
   Jonah and great fish—
   Christ's death and
   resurrec- {Jon. 1, 2 — 866
   tion.........{Matt. 12:38-41 — 953

D. *Prophetic, prophesying future events:*
   Return from {2 Chr. 36:22, 23 — 471
   exile ....{Jer. 29:10 — 733
   Destruction of {Luke 19:41-44 — 1030
   Jerusalem....{Luke 21:20-24 — 1032

E. *Redemptive, connected with man's salvation:*
   Advent of {Luke 2:11 — 1006
   Christ........{Gal. 4:4, 5 — 1156
   Death {Matt. 20:28 — 962
   of {Luke 24:44-47 — 1037
   Christ.......{1 Tim. 1:15 — 1194

F. *Unique, those without parallel:*
   Creation.......Gen. 1 — 4
   Virgin birth....Matt. 1:18-25 — 942
   Luke 1:30-37 — 1005

BIBLICAL CYCLOPEDIC INDEX

Face   **BIBLICAL CYCLOPEDIC INDEX**   *Faithfulness*

SUBJECT   REFERENCE   PAGE | SUBJECT   REFERENCE   PAGE | SUBJECT   REFERENCE   PAGE

B. *Form of fiction, contrary to:*
Edification.....1 Tim. 1:4   1194
Godliness......1 Tim. 4:6, 7   1196
Truth.........2 Tim. 4:4   1202
Facts.........2 Pet. 1:16   1243

Face—*front part of head*
A. *Acts performed on:*
Spitting on ....Deut. 25:9   201
Disfiguring
of............Matt. 6:16   946
Painting of ....2 Kin. 9:30   381
Hitting.......2 Cor. 11:20   1150
B. *Acts indicated by:*
Falling on—
worship......Gen. 17:3   18
Covering of—
mourning....2 Sam. 19:4   327
Hiding of—
disapproval ...Deut. 31:17, 18   209
Turning away of—
rejection......2 Chr. 30:9   464
Setting of—deter-
mination....2 Kin. 12:17   384

Face of the Lord
A. *Toward the righteous:*
Shine on......Num. 6:25   141
Do not hide....Ps. 102:2   591
Hide from our
sins.........Ps. 51:9   569
Shall see......Rev. 22:4   1282
B. *Toward the wicked:*
Is against......Ps. 34:16   561
Set against ....Jer. 21:10   726
They hide
from.........Rev. 6:16   1272

Failure
A. *Causes of:*
Contrary to God's
will.........Gen. 11:3-8   13
Disobe-
dience.......Num. 14:40-45   151
Sin...........Josh. 7:3-12   222
Lack of {Matt. 17:15-20   959
prayer {Mark 9:24-29   988
Not counting the
cost.........Luke 14:28-32   1025
Unbelief......Heb. 4:6   1216
B. *Examples of:*
Esau.........Gen. 25:29-34   27
Eli's sons .....1 Sam. 2:12-17   277
King Saul......1 Sam. 16:1   290
Absalom......2 Sam. 18:6-17   326
Hananiah......Jer. 28:1-17   733
Haman........Esth. 7:1-10   511

Fainting, faintheartedness—*a loss of
vital powers; weary*
A. *Causes of:*
Physical
fatigue.......Gen. 25:29, 30   27
Famine.......Gen. 47:13   49
Unbelief......Gen. 45:26   48
Fear.........Josh. 2:24   219
Sin...........Lev. 26:31   127
Sickness......Job 4:5   521
Human
weakness .....Is. 40:29-31   686
Ecstasy of
visions.......Dan. 8:27   832
Disappoint-
ment.........Jon. 4:8   868
God's
reproving ....Heb. 12:5   1223
B. *Antidotes against:*
Removal of the
fearful.......Deut. 20:8   197

Fair—(English rendering of numerous
Hebrew and Greek words)
Beautiful.......Gen. 6:2   9
    Song 1:15, 16   651
Unspotted......Zech. 3:5   897
Persuasive .....Prov. 7:21   619
    Gal. 6:12   1158
Good..........Matt. 16:2   958

Fair Havens
Harbor of Crete ...Acts 27:8   1102

Faith—*confidence in the testimony of
another*
A. *Nature of:*
Fruit of the
Spirit.......Gal. 5:22, 23   1158
Work of God ..John 6:29   1049
God's gift......Eph. 2:8   1162
Comes from the
heart.........Rom. 10:9, 10   1116
Substance of unseen
things........Heb. 11:1   1221
B. *Results from:*
Scriptures .....John 20:30, 31   1066
Preaching......John 17:20   1062
Gospel........Acts 15:7   1088
C. *Objects of:*
God..........John 14:1   1059
Christ........John 20:31   1066
Moses'
writings.......John 5:46   1048
Writings of the
prophets......Acts 26:27   1101
Gospel........Mark 1:15   978
God's
promises......Rom. 4:21   1111
D. *Kinds of:*
Saving........Rom. 10:9, 10   1116
Temporary.....Luke 8:13   1015
Intellectual ...James 2:19   1229
Dead.........James 2:17, 20   1229
E. *Described as:*
Boundless .....Luke 11:21-27   1056
Common ......Titus 1:4   1206
Great.........Matt. 8:10   948
Holy.........Jude 20   1263
Humble.......Luke 7:6, 7   1013
Little.........Matt. 8:26   949
Mutual.......Rom. 1:12   1108
Perfect.......James 2:22   1229
Precious.......2 Pet. 1:1   1243
Rootless.......Luke 8:13   1015
Small.........Matt. 17:20   959
Unfeigned.....1 Tim. 1:5   1194
United........Mark 2:5   980
Vain..........1 Cor. 15:14, 17   1137
Venturing .....Matt. 14:28, 29   956
F. *The fruits of:*
Remission of
sins..........Acts 10:43   1084
Justification ...Acts 13:39   1087
Freedom from condem-
nation.......John 3:18   1044
Salvation......Mark 16:16   999
Sanctifi-
cation........Acts 15:9   1088
Freedom from spiritual
death.........John 11:25, 26   1056
Spiritual
light.........John 12:36, 46   1058
Spiritual life ...John 20:31   1066
Eternal life ...John 3:15, 16   1044
Adoption .....John 1:12   1042
Access to
God..........Eph. 3:12   1163
Edification.....1 Tim. 1:4   1194
Preservation ...John 10:26-29   1055
Inheritance ....Acts 26:18   1101
Peace and
rest.........Rom. 5:1   1112
G. *Place of, in Christian life:*
Live by ....Rom. 1:17   1109
Walk by.......Rom. 4:12   1111
Pray by.......Matt. 21:22   963
Resist
evil by.......Eph. 6:16   1167
Overcome
world by......1 John 2:13-17   1250
Die in........Heb. 11:13   1222
H. *Growth of, in Christian life:*
Stand
fast in.......1 Cor. 16:13   1139
Continue in....Acts 14:22   1088
Be strong in ...Rom. 4:20-24   1111
Abound in.....2 Cor. 8:7   1147

Be grounded
in............Col. 1:23   1177
Hold fast ......1 Tim. 1:19   1194
Pray for
increase of....Luke 17:5   1027
Have assurance
of............2 Tim. 1:12   1200
I. *Examples of, in Old Testament:*
Abel..........Heb. 11:4   1221
Enoch........Heb. 11:5   1221
Noah.........Heb. 11:7   1221
Abraham .....Rom. 4:16-20   1111
Sarah.........Heb. 11:11   1221
Jacob.........Heb. 11:21   1222
Joseph........Heb. 11:22   1222
Moses........Heb. 11:23-29   1222
Caleb.........Josh. 14:6, 12   230
Rahab........Heb. 11:31   1222
Jonathan .....1 Sam. 14:6   287
David.........1 Sam. 17:37   292
Jehoshaphat ...2 Chr. 20:5, 12   454
Three Hebrew
captives......Dan. 3:16, 17   825
Job...........Job 19:25   529
Others........Heb. 11:32-39   1222
J. *Examples of, in New
Testament:*
Centurion .....Matt. 8:5-10   948
Jairus.........Mark 5:22, 23   983
Sick woman ...Mark 5:25-34   983
Syrophoenician
woman.......Mark 7:24-30   986
Bartimaeus ....Mark 10:46-52   990
Sinful
woman.......Luke 7:36-50   1014
Ten lepers .....Luke 17:11-19   1027
Certain
nobleman .....John 4:46-54   1046
Mary and
Martha.......John 11:1-32   1055
Thomas.......John 20:24-29   1066
Multitudes....Acts 5:14   1077
Stephen.......Acts 6:8   1078
Samaritans ...Acts 8:5-12   1080
Ethiopian
eunuch.......Acts 8:26-39   1081
Barnabas .....Acts 11:22-24   1085
Lydia.........Acts 16:14, 15   1090
Philippian
jailer.........Acts 16:25-34   1090
Paul..........Acts 27:23-25   1102

Faith as a body of belief
Priest
obedient to......Acts 6:7   1078
Churches
established in....Acts 16:5   1090
Stand fast in ....1 Cor. 16:13   1139
Paul preaches....Gal. 1:23   1155
Now revealed ....Gal. 3:23   1156
Household of....Gal. 6:10   1158
Contending for...Phil. 1:27   1171
Hold purely......1 Tim. 3:9   1195
Denial of.........1 Tim. 5:8   1196
Some erred from ..1 Tim. 6:10, 21   1197
Reprobate.......2 Tim. 3:8   1202
Paul keeps.......2 Tim. 4:7   1202
Chosen of God....Titus 1:1   1206
Common among
redeemed........Titus 1:4   1206
To be
sound in........Titus 1:13   1206

Faithfulness—*making faith a living
reality in one's life*
A. *Manifested in:*
God's service ..Matt. 24:45   967
Declaring God's
Word........Jer. 23:38   729
Bearing
witness.......Prov. 14:5   623
Keeping
secrets........Prov. 11:13   622
Helping
others........3 John 5   1259
Doing work....2 Chr. 34:12   468
Positions of
trust.........Neh. 13:13   502

125

SUBJECT	REFERENCE	PAGE

Faithfulness—continued

Reproving
others........Prov. 27:6 — 633
Conveying
messages......Prov. 25:13 — 632
Smallest
things........Luke 16:10-12 — 1026
B. *Illustrated in lives of:*
Abraham ......Gal. 3:9 — 1156
Abraham's
servant ......Gen. 24:32, 33 — 25
Joseph........Gen. 39:22, 23 — 41
Moses ....Num. 12:7 — 148
David.......2 Sam. 22:22-25 — 331
Elijah.........1 Kin. 19:10, 14 — 362
Josiah ......2 Kin. 22:1, 2 — 395
Abijah........2 Chr. 13:4-12 — 449
Micaiah.......2 Chr. 18:12, 13 — 452
Jehoshaphat ..2 Chr. 20:1-30 — 454
Azariah.......2 Chr. 26:16-20 — 460
Hanani and
Hananiah ....Neh. 7:1, 2 — 494
Isaiah ....Is. 39:1-8 — 685
Jeremiah ....Jer. 26:1-15 — 731
Daniel........Dan. 6:10 — 829
John the
Baptist.......Luke 3:7-19 — 1007
Jesus ....Heb. 3:1, 2 — 1216
Peter ....Acts 4:8-12 — 1075
Paul..........Acts 17:16, 17 — 1091

Faithfulness of God

A. *Described as:*
Everlasting ....Ps. 119:90 — 601
Established ...Ps. 89:2 — 586
Unfailing .....Ps. 89:33 — 587
Infinite ....Ps. 36:5 — 562
Great ....Lam. 3:23 — 764
Incompar-
able ....Ps. 89:8 — 586
B. *Manifested in:*
Counsels.......Is. 25:1 — 675
Covenant-
keeping ......Deut. 7:9 — 186
Forgiving
sins ....1 John 1:9 — 1249
Testimonies...Ps. 119:138 — 602
Judgments....Jer. 51:29 — 757
Promises......1 Kin. 8:20 — 347

Fall of man

A. *Occasion of:*
Satan's
temptation....Gen. 3:1-5 — 6
Eve's
yielding.......2 Cor. 11:3 — 1149
Adam's dis-
obedience....Rom. 5:12-19 — 1112
B. *Temporal consequences of:*
Driven from
Paradise .....Gen. 3:24 — 7
Condemned to hard
labor.........Gen. 3:16, 19 — 7
Condemned
to die........1 Cor. 15:22 — 1137
C. *Spiritual consequences of:*
Separated from
God..........Eph. 4:18 — 1164
Born in sin....John 3:6 — 1044
Evil in heart...Matt. 15:19 — 957
Corrupt and
perverse....Rom. 3:12-16 — 1110
In bondage
to sin ....Rom. 6:19 — 1113
In bondage to
Satan ...Heb. 2:14, 15 — 1215
Dead in sin ....Col. 2:13 — 1178
Spiritually
blind.........Eph. 4:18 — 1164
Utterly
depraved......Titus 1:15 — 1206
Change from, not in
man ....Jer. 2:22 — 710
Only God can
change........John 3:16 — 1044

Fallow deer—*roebuck*

Among clean
animals..........Deut. 14:5 — 192

In Solomon's
diet ....1 Kin. 4:22, 23 — 342

Fallow ground—*a field plowed and left for seeding*

Used (Jer. 4:3 — 711
figuratively.. (Hos. 10:12 — 845

False accusations

A. *Against men:*
Joseph.....Gen. 39:7-20 — 41
Moses ......Num. 16:1-3, 13 — 152
Ahimelech.....1 Sam. 22:10-16 — 297
David.........Ps. 41:5-9 — 565
Elijah........1 Kin. 18:17, 18 — 360
Naboth .....1 Kin. 21:1-14 — 364
Jeremiah .....Jer. 26:8-11 — 731
Amos........Amos 7:10, 11 — 859
Stephen ......Acts 6:11, 13 — 1078
Paul :........Acts 21:27-29 — 1096
B. *Against Christ:*
Gluttony......Matt. 11:19 — 952
Blasphemy....Matt. 26:64, 65 — 971
Insanity ......Mark 3:21 — 981
Demon
possession ....John 7:20 — 1050
Sabbath
desecration ...John 9:16 — 1053
Treason......John 19:12 — 1064

False apostles

Opposed Paul ....2 Cor. 11:1-15 — 1149

False Christs

Christ foretells their
coming..........Matt. 24:24 — 967
Christ warns
against..........Mark 13:21-23 — 994
See Antichrist

False confidence

A. *Characteristics of:*
Self-
righteous .....Rom. 2:3 — 1109
Spiritually
blind..........Is. 28:15, 19 — 677
Sensualist ....Gal. 6:7, 8 — 1158
Worldly
secure ......1 Thess. 5:3 — 1185
B. *Causes of trusting in:*
Riches.........1 Tim. 6:17 — 1197
Worldly
success ......Luke 12:19, 20 — 1021
Men ....Is. 30:1-5 — 678
Oneself ....Matt. 26:33-35 — 970
Ignoring God's
providence....James 4:13-15 — 1230
C. *Warnings against:*
Curse on ......Jer. 17:5 — 723
Do not glory in
men...........1 Cor. 3:21 — 1127
Man's
limitation ....2 Cor. 1:9 — 1143
Mighty will
fail...........Ps. 33:16, 17 — 560
Boasting.......1 Kin. 20:11 — 363
D. *Instances of:*
Babel's men....Gen. 11:4 — 13
Sennacherib ..2 Kin. 19:20-37 — 392
Asa ....2 Chr. 16:7-12 — 451
Peter ....Luke 22:33, 34 — 1034

Falsehood—*turning truth into a lie*

A. *Manifested by false:*
Witnesses......Ps. 27:12 — 558
Balances.......Prov. 11:1 — 621
Tongue........Ps. 120:3 — 603
Report........Ex. 23:1 — 77
Prophets......Jer. 5:2, 31 — 712
Science.......1 Tim. 6:20 — 1197
B. *God's people:*
Must avoid ....Ex. 23:7 — 77
Must hate .....Ps. 119:104, 128 — 601
Must endure...Acts 6:13 — 1078
Are falsely
charged (Jer. 37:14 — 743
with ....(Matt. 5:11 — 945

False professions

A. *Pretending to be:*
Harmless ......Josh. 9:3-16 — 224
Innocent ......Matt. 27:24 — 972
Divine........Acts 12:21-23 — 1086
Sincere.......Matt. 26:47-49 — 970
True
prophets......1 Kin. 22:6-12 — 365
B. *Exposed by:*
Prophets.......Jer. 28:1-17 — 733
Christ ....John 13:21-30 — 1058
Apostles......Acts 5:1-11 — 1076

False prophets

A. *Tests of:*
Doctrine.......Is. 8:20 — 664
Prophecies.....1 Kin. 13:1-32 — 354
Lives ....Matt. 7:15, 16 — 947
B. *Characteristics of:*
Prophesy
peace.........Jer. 23:17 — 728
Teach a lie.....Jer. 28:15 — 733
Pretend to be
true..........Matt. 7:22, 23 — 948
Teach
corruption ....2 Pet. 2:10-22 — 1244
C. *Examples of:*
Zedekiah ......1 Kin. 22:11, 12 — 366
Hananiah......Jer. 28:1-17 — 733
In the last
days ....Matt. 24:3, 11 — 966

False teachers

A. *Characteristics of:*
Grace-
perverters.....Gal. 1:6-8 — 1154
Money-lovers. .Luke 16:14 — 1026
Christ-
deniers........2 Pet. 2:1 — 1243
Truth-
resisters.......2 Tim. 3:8 — 1202
Fable-lovers ...2 Tim. 4:3, 4 — 1202
Destitute of the
truth..........1 Tim. 6:3-5 — 1197
Bound by
traditions ....Matt. 15:9 — 957
Unstable......1 Tim. 1:6, 7 — 1194
Deceitful .....Eph. 4:14 — 1164
Lustful ....2 Pet. 2:12-19 — 1244
B. *Prevalence of:*
In Paul's
time ....2 Tim. 1:14, 15 — 1200
During this
age ....1 Tim. 4:1-3 — 1195
At Christ's
return.........2 Tim. 4:3, 4 — 1202
C. *Examples of:*
Balaam ....Rev. 2:14 — 1269
Bar-jesus ......Acts 13:6 — 1086
Ephesian (Acts 20:30 — 1095
elders ....(Rev. 2:2 — 1269
Epicureans....Acts 17:18 — 1092
False (2 Cor. 11:5, 13 — 1149
apostles......(2 Cor. 12:11 — 1150
Herodians .....Mark 3:6 — 980
Mark 12:13 — 992
Hymenaeus....2 Tim. 2:17 — 1201
Libertines ....Acts 6:9 — 1078
Nicolaitanes ...Rev. 2:15 — 1269
Pharisees.....Matt. 23:26 — 966
Philetus ......2 Tim. 2:17 — 1201
Sadducees ....Matt. 16:12 — 958
Scribes ....Matt. 12:38, 39 — 953
Serpent
(Satan) ......Gen. 3:4 — 6
Stoic philo-
sophers ......Acts 17:18 — 1092

False weights

Prohibited......Deut. 25:13, 14 — 201

False witnesses

A. *Features regarding:*
Deceptive......Prov. 12:17 — 622
Cruel.........Prov. 25:18 — 632
Utter lies .....Prov. 6:19 — 618
Prov. 14:5 — 623
Shall perish....Prov. 21:28 — 629

SUBJECT	REFERENCE	PAGE

Firstlings—continued

Of unclean
beasts...........Num. 18:15   155
Ye shall bring, of your
herd...........Deut. 12:6   190
Males sanctify...Deut. 15:19   194
Glory is like......Deut. 33:17   212

Fish

A. *Features regarding:*
Created by
God........Gen. 1:20, 21   4
Worship of
forbidden.....Deut. 4:15-18   182
Caught by
net...........Matt. 4:18   944
Worshiped by
pagans........1 Sam. 5:4   280
Some disciples called as
fishermen....Matt. 4:18-21   944

B. *Miracles concerning:*
Jonah's
life in.........Jon. 1:17   867
Multiplied by
Christ.........Matt. 14:17-21   956
Bearing a
coin...........Matt. 17:27   959

C. *Figurative of:*
Men in the sea of
life.........Ezek. 47:9, 10   816
Ministers as
fishermen.....Matt. 4:19   944
Ignorant
men...........Eccl. 9:12   645

Fish Gate—*a gate of Jerusalem*

Manasseh built wall
there.......2 Chr. 33:13, 14   467
Built by sons of
Hassenaah....Neh. 3:3   490
Two choirs took their
stand...........Neh. 12:38-40   502
A cry there
prophesied.......Zeph. 1:10   887

Fish hook—*hook for catching fish*

Cannot catch
Leviathan.......Job 41:1   542
Fishing in the
brooks...........Is. 19:8   671

Fist fighting

Punishment of....Ex. 21:18, 19   76

Fitches—*vetches*

Annual plant for
forage...........Is. 28:25, 27   677
Same as rye in...Ezek. 4:9   774

Flag—*fluttering*

Name of many water
plants.............Ex. 2:3-5   57
Rendered as "weeds"
in...............Jon. 2:5   867

Flagellation—*punishment by whipping, flogging*

For immorality....Lev. 19:20   119
For defamation....Deut. 22:16-18   199
Forty blows....Deut. 25:3   201
Of Christ.........Matt. 27:26   972
Mark 15:15   997
Thirty-nine
lashes...........2 Cor. 11:24   1150
Of apostles.......Acts 5:40   1077

Flagon—*flask*

Small vessels for
liquids...........Is. 22:24   673

Flat nose

Disqualifies for
service...........Lev. 21:18   121

Flattery—*unjustified praise*

A. *Used by:*
False
prophets.....Rom. 16:18   1122
Hypocrites....Ps. 78:36   581
Wicked........Ps. 36:1-4   562

Prostitutes.....Prov. 2:16   616

B. *Attitude of saints toward:*
Should avoid
users of......Prov. 20:19   628
Pray against...Ps. 5:8, 9   549
Should not
use..........1 Thess. 2:5   1184

C. *Dangers of:*
Leads to ruin..Prov. 26:28   633
Brings
deception...Prov. 29:5   634
Corrupts......Dan. 11:21, 25,
27   835
Brings death...Acts 12:21-23   1086

Flax—*the flax plant*

Grown in Egypt and
Palestine......Ex. 9:31   65
Used for:
Cords...........Judg. 15:14   259
Weaving.........Is. 19:9   671
Garments
("linen")........Deut. 22:11   199

Flea—*a parasitic, blood-sucking insect*

Figurative of
insignificance.....1 Sam. 24:14   299

Fleece—*freshly sheared wool*

Given to priests...Deut. 18:3, 4   195
Sign to Gideon...Judg. 6:36-40   250
Warm...........Job 31:20   536

Flesh

A. *Used to designate:*
All created   (Gen. 6:13, 17,
life..........{ 19   9
Kinsmen (of same
nature).......Rom. 9:3, 5, 8   1115
The body......Job 33:25   537
Marriage.......Matt. 19:5   961
Human
nature.......John 1:14   1042
Christ's mys-   (John 6:51,
tical nature..{ 53-63   1049
Human
weakness.....Matt. 16:17   958
Outward
appearance....2 Cor. 5:16   1145
The evil principle in
man..........Rom. 7:18   1113
Food..........Ex. 16:12   71

B. *In a bad sense, described as:*
Having
passions......Gal. 5:24   1158
Producing evil
works.........Gal. 5:19-21   1158
Dominating the
mind..........Eph. 2:3   1162
Absorbing the
affections.....Rom. 13:14   1119
Seeking outward
display.......Gal. 6:12, 13   1158
Antagonizing the
Spirit.........Gal. 5:17   1158
Fighting against God's
Law...........Rom. 8:5-9   1114
Reaping
corruption....Gal. 6:8   1158
Producing
death.........Rom. 7:5   1113

C. *Christian's attitude toward:*
Still
confronts.....Rom. 7:18-23   1113
Source of
opposition.....Gal. 5:17   1158
Make no provision
for...........Rom. 13:14   1119
Do not love...1 John 2:15-17   1250
Do not
walk in.......Rom. 8:1, 4   1114
Do not
live in........Rom. 8:12, 13   1114
Crucified.....Gal. 5:24   1158

Fleshhook—*fork*

In tabernacle......Ex. 27:3   81
Num. 4:14   138

By priests.........1 Sam. 2:12-14   277
In Temple........1 Chr. 28:11, 17   432
2 Chr. 4:16   441

Flies—*small winged insects*

Cause of evil
odor...........Eccl. 10:1   646
Figurative of
Egypt..........Is. 7:18   663
Plague upon the (Ex. 8:21-31   63
Egyptians.......{Ps. 78:45   582

Flint—*a very hard stone*

Water from.......Deut. 8:15   187
Oil from.........Deut. 32:13   210
Turning into fountain of
water.........Ps. 114:8   598
Hoofs shall seem
like...........Is. 5:28   662
Figurative of a (Is. 50:7   693
fixed course...{Ezek. 3:9   773

Flock—*a group of domesticated animals*

Sheep and goats..Gen. 27:9   28
Nations........Jer. 51:23   757
National leaders..Jer. 25:34, 35   731
Jewish people....Jer. 13:17, 20   720
True church......Is. 40:11   685
Acts 20:28   1095

Flood—*overflowing of water*

A. *Used literally of:*
Earth's flood...Gen. 6:17   9

B. *Used figuratively of:*
Great trouble..Ps. 32:6   560
Hostile world
powers.......Ps. 93:3   588
An invading
army.........Jer. 46:7, 8   750
Great
destruction...Dan. 9:26   833
Testing.......Matt. 7:25, 27   948
Persecution....Rev. 12:15, 16   1276

Floodgates

Descriptive of
judgment.........Gen. 7:11   10

Floor

For threshing   (Judg. 6:37   250
wheat..........{1 Kin. 22:10   366
Of a building...1 Kin. 6:15   344

Flour—*finely ground wheat*

Offered in
sacrifices.....Lev. 5:11, 13   103

Flowers

A. *Described as:*
Wild..........Ps. 103:15, 16   592
Beautiful.....Matt. 6:28, 29   947
Sweet.........Song 5:13   652
Fading........Is. 40:7, 8   685

B. *Figurative of:*
Shortness of
life.........Job 14:2   526
Israel.........Is. 28:1   676
Man's glory....James 1:10, 11   1228

Flute—*a hollow musical instrument*

In Babylon.......Dan. 3:5   825
Used in God's
worship.........Ps. 150:4   611

Foal—*a colt, young donkey*

Given to Esau...Gen. 32:13-15   34
Ridden by   (Zech. 9:9   901
Christ..........{Matt. 21:5   963

Fodder—*food for domestic animals*

Given to oxen
and wild   (Job 6:5   522
asses.........{Is. 30:24   679

Following

A. *In Old Testament:*
Commanded...Deut. 8:6   186
Brought
reward.......Deut. 19:9   196

SUBJECT	REFERENCE	PAGE
"Remission"...Matt. 26:28		970
"Pardon"...Is. 55:7		696
"Remember no more"...Jer. 31:34		737
"Healed"...2 Chr. 30:18-20		464

B. Basis of:

SUBJECT	REFERENCE	PAGE
God's nature..Ps. 86:5		585
God's grace...Luke 7:42		1014
Shedding of blood...Heb. 9:22		1220
Christ's death...Col. 1:14		1177
Son's power...Luke 5:21-24		1010
Man's repentance...Acts 2:38		1074
Our forgiveness...Matt. 6:12-14		946
Faith in Christ...Acts 10:43		1084

C. Significance of:

SUBJECT	REFERENCE	PAGE
Shows God's righteousness...Rom. 3:25, 26		1111
Makes salvation real...Luke 1:77		1006
Must be preached...Luke 24:47		1037

Forgiving one another

A. The measure of:

SUBJECT	REFERENCE	PAGE
Seventy times seven...Matt. 18:21, 22		960
Unlimited...Luke 17:3, 4		1027
As God forgave us...Eph. 4:32		1165

B. Benefits of:

SUBJECT	REFERENCE	PAGE
Means of our forgiveness...Mark 11:25, 26		992
Restored Christian fellowship...2 Cor. 2:7-10		1143
Spiritual cleansing...James 5:15, 16		1231

C. Examples of:

SUBJECT	REFERENCE	PAGE
Esau and Jacob...Gen. 33:4-15		35
Joseph...Gen. 45:8-15		47
Moses...Num. 12:1-13		148
David...2 Sam. 19:18-23		327
Solomon...1 Kin. 1:52, 53		339
Jesus...Luke 23:34		1036
Stephen...Acts 7:59, 60		1080
Paul...2 Tim. 4:16		1202

Fork

Rendered:

SUBJECT	REFERENCE	PAGE
"Three-pronged fork"...1 Sam. 2:13, 14		277
"Fork"...Is. 30:24		679

Form—the outward appearance

A. Of physical things:

SUBJECT	REFERENCE	PAGE
Earth without...Gen. 1:2		4
Man in the womb...Is. 44:24		689
Sexes...1 Tim. 2:13		1195
Idols...Is. 44:10		689

B. Of spiritual realities:

SUBJECT	REFERENCE	PAGE
Incarnate Christ...{Is. 53:2		695
...{Rom. 9:20		1116
Molder...Rom. 9:20		1116
Christian truth...Rom. 6:17		1113
New birth...Gal. 4:19		1157
World passing away...1 Cor. 7:31		1131

Formalism—forms performed mechanically

A. Characterized by:

SUBJECT	REFERENCE	PAGE
Outward forms of religion...Is. 1:10-15		659
Lifelessness...Is. 58:1-14		698
Lukewarmness...Rev. 3:14-18		1270

B. Sign of:

SUBJECT	REFERENCE	PAGE
Hypocrisy...Luke 18:10-14		1028
Deadness...Phil. 3:4-8		1172
Last days...2 Tim. 3:1, 5		1201

Formula—a prescribed method

SUBJECT	REFERENCE	PAGE
Success...Prov. 22:29		630
Prosperity...Matt. 6:32, 33		947
Peace...Is. 26:3		675
Making friends...Prov. 18:24		627

Fornication—sexual relations among the unmarried

Evil of:

SUBJECT	REFERENCE	PAGE
Comes from evil heart...Matt. 15:19		957
Sins against the body...1 Cor. 6:18		1129
Excludes from God's kingdom...1 Cor. 6:9		1129
Disrupts Christian fellowship...1 Cor. 5:9-11		1128

Forsaken—left deserted

SUBJECT	REFERENCE	PAGE
God's house...Neh. 13:11		502
God's children...Ps. 37:25		563
Messiah...Is. 53:3		695
God's Son...Matt. 27:46		972

Forsaking Christ

SUBJECT	REFERENCE	PAGE
Disciples left...Matt. 26:56		970
Cause of separation...John 6:66-70		1050

Forsaking God

A. Manifested in:

SUBJECT	REFERENCE	PAGE
Going after idols...1 Kin. 11:33		352
Going backward...Jer. 15:6		721
Following human forms...Jer. 2:13		710

B. Evil of:

SUBJECT	REFERENCE	PAGE
Manifests ingratitude...Jer. 2:5-12		709
Brings confusion...Jer. 17:13		723
Merits God's wrath...Ezra 8:22		482

C. Examples of:

SUBJECT	REFERENCE	PAGE
Israel...2 Kin. 17:7-18		389
Judah...2 Chr. 12:1, 5		448

Fort—stronghold

SUBJECT	REFERENCE	PAGE
In Jerusalem...2 Sam. 5:9		313

Fortifications—walls or towers for protection

SUBJECT	REFERENCE	PAGE
Cities...1 Kin. 9:15		349
...2 Chr. 11:5-11		447
City of David...2 Sam. 5:7-9		313

Fortified cities

SUBJECT	REFERENCE	PAGE
Means of protection...2 Sam. 20:6		329
Mighty and strong...Deut. 9:1		187
Conquerable...Deut. 3:4, 5		180
Utterly destroyed...2 Kin. 3:19, 25		374
No substitute for God...Hos. 8:14		844

Fortress—center of military strength

SUBJECT	REFERENCE	PAGE
Nation's security...2 Chr. 26:9		460
Illustrative of God's protection...Ps. 18:2		553
Typical of Christ...Is. 33:16, 17		680
Applied to God's prophet...Jer. 6:27		714

Fortunatus—fortunate

SUBJECT	REFERENCE	PAGE
Christian at Corinth...1 Cor. 16:17		1139

Forty days

SUBJECT	REFERENCE	PAGE
Length of flood...Gen. 7:17		10
Israel's embalming...Gen. 50:2, 3		52
Moses on Mt. Sinai...Ex. 24:18		79

SUBJECT	REFERENCE	PAGE
Spies in Canaan...Num. 13:25		149
Moses' prayer...Deut. 9:25-29		188
The Philistine's arrogance...1 Sam. 17:16		291
Elijah's fast...1 Kin. 19:2, 8		362
Nineveh's probation...Jon. 3:4		867
Christ's temptation...Luke 4:1, 2		1008
Christ's ministry after His resurrection...Acts 1:3		1072

Forty stripes

SUBJECT	REFERENCE	PAGE
Limit for scourging...Deut. 25:3		201
Paul's, one less..2 Cor. 11:24		1150

Forty years

SUBJECT	REFERENCE	PAGE
Isaac's age at marriage...Gen. 25:20		26
Israel's diet...Ex. 16:35		72
Israel's wanderings...Num. 32:13		170
Same shoes for...Deut. 29:5		206
Period of rest...Judg. 3:11		246
Egypt's desolation...Ezek. 29:11-13		798
Saul's reign...Acts 13:21		1086
David's reign...1 Kin. 2:11		339
Solomon's reign...1 Kin. 11:42		353

Forwardness—haste; overboldness

SUBJECT	REFERENCE	PAGE
Peter's faltering...Matt. 14:28, 29		956
...Matt. 26:31-35		970
Paul's desire for the Corinthians...2 Cor. 8:8, 10		1147

Foundation

A. Used literally of:

SUBJECT	REFERENCE	PAGE
Cities...Josh. 6:26		222
Walls...Ezra 4:12		478
Houses...Luke 6:48		1012
Prison house...Acts 16:26		1090
House of the Lord...1 Kin. 6:37		344
Towers...Luke 14:28, 29		1025

B. Used figuratively of:

SUBJECT	REFERENCE	PAGE
Christ...Is. 28:16		677
...Matt. 16:18		958
Christian truth...Eph. 2:20		1163
God decrees...2 Tim. 2:19		1201
Security of parents...1 Tim. 6:19		1197
Eternal city...Heb. 11:10		1221

C. Importance of:

SUBJECT	REFERENCE	PAGE
Must be on a {Matt. 7:24		948
rock...{Matt. 16:18		958
Must be firm...Luke 6:48		1012
Must be Christ...1 Cor. 3:11		1127
Without, hopeless...Ps. 11:3		551

Foundation, Gate of the—a gate of Jerusalem

SUBJECT	REFERENCE	PAGE
Levites stationed there...2 Chr. 23:2-5		456
Possibly the {2 Kin. 11:16		383
Horse Gate...{2 Chr. 23:15		457

Fountain—a flow of water from the earth

Figurative of:

SUBJECT	REFERENCE	PAGE
Mouth of the righteous...Prov. 10:11		621
Understanding...Prov. 16:22		625
Rich blessings...Jer. 2:13		710

Fountain Gate—a gate of Jerusalem

SUBJECT	REFERENCE	PAGE
Viewed by Nehemiah...Neh. 2:13, 14		490
Repaired...Neh. 3:15		491

Foursquare

SUBJECT	REFERENCE	PAGE
Altar...Ex. 27:1		81
Breastplate...Ex. 39:8, 9		94
City of God...Rev. 21:16		1282

SUBJECT	REFERENCE	PAGE	SUBJECT	REFERENCE	PAGE	SUBJECT	REFERENCE	PAGE

Fruitless discussion—*self-conceited talk against God*

Characteristic of false
teachers..........1 Tim. 1:6, 7   1194

Fruit trees

Protected by
Law.............Lev. 19:23-25   119

Frying pan

Mentioned in......Lev. 2:7   101

Fulfill—*to bring to its designed end*

A. *Spoken of God's:*
Word..........Ps. 148:8   611
Prophecy ......1 Kin. 2:27   340
Threat.......2 Chr. 36:20, 21   471
Promise.......Acts 13:32, 33   1087
Righteous-
ness..........Matt. 3:15   943
Good
pleasure......2 Thess. 1:11   1189
Will ....Acts 13:22   1086

B. *Spoken of the believer's:*
Love..........Rom. 13:8   1119
Righ-
teousness .....Rom. 8:4   1114
Burden-
bearing ......Gal. 6:2   1158
Mission.......Col. 1:25   1177
Ministry ......Col. 4:17   1180

Full—*complete*

A. *Of natural things:*
Years..........Gen. 25:8   26
Breasts ....Job 21:24   531
Children ......Ps. 127:5   604
Cart ....Amos 2:13   856
Leprosy......Luke 5:12   1010

B. *Of miraculous things:*
Guidance .....Judg. 6:38   250
Supply.........2 Kin. 4:4, 6   374
Protection .....2 Kin. 6:17   377

C. *Of evil emotions:*
Evil...........Eccl. 9:3   645
Fury..........Dan. 3:19   825
Wrath ....Acts 19:28   1094
Envy ....Rom. 1:29   1109
Cursing.......Rom. 3:14   1110
Deadly
poison ....James 3:8   1229
Adultery......2 Pet. 2:14   1244

D. *Of good things:*
Power ....Mic. 3:8   872
Grace, truth ...John 1:14   1042
Joy...........John 15:11   1060
Faith ....Acts 6:5, 8   1078
Good works ...Acts 9:36   1082
Holy Spirit.....Acts 11:24   1085

Fuller—*one who treats or dyes cloth*

Outside city......2 Kin. 18:17   391
   Is. 7:3   663
God is like ....Mal. 3:2   908
Makes white .....Mark 9:3   988

Fullness—*completion*

A. *Of time:*
Christ's
advent ......Gal. 4:4   1156
Gentile age ....Rom. 11:25   1117
Age of grace..Eph. 1:10   1162

B. *Of Christ:*
Eternal
Christ........Col. 2:9   1178
Incarnate
Christ.......John 1:16   1042
Glorified
Christ........Eph. 1:22, 23   1162

Funeral—*burial rites*

Sad ....1 Kin. 13:29, 30   355
Joyful.............Luke 7:11-17   1013

Furlong—*a Greek measure of length*
(660 linear feet)

Measure on land or
sea ....Luke 24:13   1036

Furnace—*fire made very hot*

A. *Used literally of:*
Smelting
ovens ....Gen. 19:28   20
Baker's oven...Hos. 7:4   843

B. *Used figuratively of:*
Egyptian
bondage ......Deut. 4:20   182
Spiritual
refinement ....Ps. 12:6   552
Lust ....Hos. 7:4   843
Hell ....Matt. 13:42, 50   955
Punishment....Ezek. 22:18-22   791

Furnace, fiery

Deliverance
from ....Dan. 3:8-26   825

Furniture

Tabernacle........Ex. 31:7   86
Room.............2 Kin. 4:8-10   374

Future—*that which is beyond the present*

Only God knows ..Is. 41:21-23   687
Revealed by:
Christ............John 13:19   1058
The Spirit.......John 16:13   1061
Man's
ignorance of...Luke 19:41-44   1030
No provision for,
dangerous.......Luke 12:16-21   1021
Proper provision
for ....Matt. 6:19-34   946

G

Gaal—*loathing*

Son of Ebed; vilifies
Abimelech........Judg. 9:26-41   253

Gaash—*quaking*

Hill of Ephraim ...Judg. 2:9   245
Joshua's burial
near...........Josh. 24:30   240

Gaba—*a hill*

City of
Benjamin........Josh. 18:21, 24   234

Gabbai—*tax gatherer*

Postexilic
Benjamite ......Neh. 11:8   500

Gabbatha—*pavement*

Place of Pilate's
court............John 19:13   1064

Gabriel—*man of God*

Interprets Daniel's
vision ....Dan. 8:16-27   832
Reveals the prophecy of 70
weeks..........Dan. 9:21-27   833
Announces John's
birth ....Luke 1:11-22   1004
Announces Christ's
birth ....Luke 1:26-38   1004
Stands in God's
presence ....Luke 1:19   1004

Gad—*good fortune*

1. Son of Jacob by
Zilpah ....Gen. 30:10, 11   31
Father of seven sons who
founded tribal
families ....Gen. 46:16   48
2. Descendants of the tribe of
Gad.......Deut. 27:13   203
Census of......Num. 1:24, 25   134
Territory of......Num. 32:20-36   170
Captivity of....1 Chr. 5:26   409
Later references
to..............Rev. 7:5   1272

---

3. Seer of
David ....1 Sam. 22:5   297
Message of, to
David.........2 Sam. 24:10-16   333

Gadarenes, Gergesenes

People east of the Sea of
Galilee ....Mark 5:1   982
Healing of demon-possessed
here..............Matt. 8:28-34   949

Gaddi—*fortunate*

Manassite spy.....Num. 13:11   149

Gaddiel—*Gad (fortune) is God*

Zebulunite spy ....Num. 13:10   149

Gadi—*a Gadite*

Father of King
Menahem ....2 Kin. 15:14   387

Gaham—*burning*

Son of Nahor ......Gen. 22:23, 24   23

Gahar—*hiding place*

Head of a family of Temple
servants.........Ezra 2:47   476

Gain through loss

A. *Elements of:*
Death first.....John 12:24   1057
Servant
status.........Mark 9:35   989
Discount all temporal
gains.........Matt. 19:29   961
Loss of "life" ..Mark 8:35   987

B. *Examples of:*
Abraham ......Heb. 11:8-19   1221
Moses ....Heb. 11:24-27   1222
Ruth ....Ruth 1:16-18   269
Abigail ......1 Sam. 25:18-42   300
Esther ....Esth. 2:1-17   507
Christ ....Phil. 2:5-11   1171

Gains unjustly gotten

By:
Deceit ....Josh. 7:15-26   223
Violence ....Prov. 1:19   615
Oppression.......Prov. 22:16   629
Divination .....Acts 16:16, 19   1090
Unjust wages .....James 5:4   1230

Gaius—*commended*

1. Companion of
Paul ....Acts 19:29   1094
2. Convert at
Derbe........Acts 20:4   1094
3. Paul's host at
Corinth ......Rom. 16:23   1122
Corinthian
convert ......1 Cor. 1:14   1126
4. One addressed by
John..........3 John 1-5   1259

Galal—*a rolling*

1. Levite ....1 Chr. 9:15   414
2. Another
Levite.........1 Chr. 9:16   414

Galatia—*a province of Asia Minor*

Paul's first
visit to ....Acts 16:6   1090
Paul's second
visit to ....Acts 18:23   1093
Churches of......1 Cor. 16:1   1138
Peter writes to
Christians in ...1 Pet. 1:1   1235

Galatians—*people of Galatia*

Paul's:
Rebuke of their
instability......Gal. 1:6, 7   1154
Defense of the Gospel among
them ....Gal. 1:8-24   1154
Concern for
them ....Gal. 4:9-31   1156
Confidence in
them ....Gal. 5:7-13   1157

SUBJECT	REFERENCE	PAGE

SUBJECT	REFERENCE	PAGE	SUBJECT	REFERENCE	PAGE	SUBJECT	REFERENCE	PAGE
Deception			B. *Of man:*			David	(2 Sam. 17:26,	
discovered	Josh. 9:16-20	225	1. *Purposes of:*			takes	27	325
Made hewers of			Confirm			refuge in	2 Sam. 19:31	328
wood	Josh. 9:21-27	225	covenants	Gen. 21:27-32	22	In David's		
Rescued by			Appease			census	2 Sam. 24:1, 6	333
Joshua	Josh. 10:1-43	225	anger	1 Sam. 25:27-35	300	Elijah's		
Massacred by			Show respect	Judg. 6:18-21	249	birthplace	1 Kin. 17:1	359
Saul	2 Sam. 21:1	329	Manifest			Smitten by		
Avenged by			friendship	1 Sam. 30:26-31	305	Hazael	2 Kin. 10:32, 33	383
David	2 Sam. 21:2-9	329	Reward	2 Sam. 18:11, 12	326	Mentioned by		
			Memorialize an			Amos	Amos 1:3, 13	855
Giddalti—*I have made great*			event	Esth. 9:20-22	513			
Son of Heman	1 Chr. 25:4	429	Render			**Gilead, Balm of**—*an aromatic gum for*		
			worship	Matt. 2:11	942	*medicinal purposes*		
Giddel—*very great*			Give help	Phil. 4:10-18	1173	*Figurative of:*		
1. Head of family of Temple			Seal			National	(Jer. 8:22	716
servants	Ezra 2:47	476	friendship	1 Sam. 18:3, 4	293	healing	Jer. 51:8	756
2. Children of			2. *Times given:*					
Solomon's	(Ezra 2:56	476	Betrothals	Gen. 24:50-53	25	**Gilgal**—*a circle, a wheel*		
servants	Neh. 7:58	495	Weddings	Ps. 45:12	567	1. Memorial site between Jordan		
			Departures	Gen. 45:21-24	47	and Jericho	Josh. 4:19-24	220
Gideon—*cutter of trees*			Returns			Israel		
Son of Joash	Judg. 6:11	249	home	Luke 15:22, 23	1025	circumcised	Josh. 5:2-9	220
Called by an			Times of			Passover		
angel	Judg. 6:11-24	249	recovery	Job 42:10, 11	543	observed	Josh. 5:10	221
Destroys Baal's			Trials,			Site of Gibeonite		
altar	Judg. 6:25-32	249	forbidden	Ex. 23:8	77	covenant	Josh. 9:3-15	224
Fleece confirms call from			C. *Spiritual:*			On Samuel's		
God	Judg. 6:36-40	250	Listed as	(Rom. 12:6-8	1118	circuit	1 Sam. 7:15, 16	282
His army			explained	1 Cor. 12:4-30	1134	Saul made		
reduced	Judg. 7:2-8	250	Came from			king	1 Sam. 11:15	285
Encouraged by a			God	James 1:17	1228	Saul rejected	1 Sam. 13:4-15	286
dream	Judg. 7:9-15	250	Assigned			Denounced for		
Employs successful			sovereignty	1 Cor. 12:11, 28	1134	idolatry	Hos. 9:15	844
strategy	Judg. 7:16-25	251	Cannot be			2. Town near		
Soothes angry			bought	Acts 8:18-20	1081	Beth-el	2 Kin. 2:1	372
Ephraimites	Judg. 8:1-3	251	Always for			Home of		
Takes revenge on Succoth and			edification	Rom. 1:11	1108	Elisha	2 Kin. 4:38	375
Penuel	Judg. 8:4-22	251	Counterfeited by					
Refuses kingship	Judg. 8:22, 23	252	Satan	2 Cor. 11:13-15	1149	**Giloh**—*exile*		
Unwisely makes an			Spiritually			Town of Judah	Josh. 15:51	231
ephod	Judg. 8:24-27	252	discerned	1 Cor. 12:2, 3	1134			
Judgeship of forty			Love, the			**Gilonite**—*Giloh native*		
years	Judg. 8:28, 29	252	supreme	1 Cor. 13:1-13	1135	Ahithophel		
Father of 71						called	2 Sam. 15:12	323
sons	Judg. 8:30, 31	252	**Gihon**—*bursting forth*					
His death brings			1. River of			**Gimel**		
apostasy	Judg. 8:32-35	252	Eden	Gen. 2:13	5	Third letter in Hebrew		
Called Jerubbaal	Judg. 8:35	252	2. Spring outside			alphabet	Ps. 119:17-24	600
Man of faith	Heb. 11:32	1222	Jerusalem	1 Kin. 1:33-45	338	**Gimzo**—*producing sycamores*		
			3. Source of water			Village of Judah	2 Chr. 28:18	462
Gideoni—*a cutting down*			supply	2 Chr. 32:30	467			
Benjamite	Num. 1:11	133				**Gin**—*a trap*		
Father of			**Gilalai**—*weighty*			Used for catching beasts or		
Abidan	Num. 1:11	133	Levite musician	Neh. 12:36	501	birds	Amos 3:5	857
Brought offering for the tribe of						Used		
Benjamin	Num. 7:60-65	143	**Gilboa**—*bubbling fountain*			figuratively	Ps. 141:9	608
Over tribal army of			Range of limestone hills in					
Benjamin	Num. 10:24	146	Issachar	1 Sam. 28:4	302	**Ginath**—*protection*		
			Scene of Saul's			Father of Tibni	1 Kin. 16:21, 22	358
Gidom—*a cutting off*			death	1 Sam. 31:1-7	305			
Village of			Philistines desecrate Saul's			**Ginnetho**—*gardener*		
Benjamin	Judg. 20:45	265	body	1 Sam. 31:8, 9	305	Postexilic priest	Neh. 12:4	501
			Under David's					
Gier-eagle			curse	2 Sam. 1:17, 21	309	**Ginnethon**—*gardener*		
Unclean bird	Lev. 11:18	109				Family head and signer of		
			Gilead—*rocky or strong*			document	Neh. 10:6	499
Gifts			1. Grandson of			Probably same as Ginnethoi		
A. *Of God:*			Manasseh	Num. 26:29, 30	163	**Gird**—*to put on, as a belt*		
1. *Material:*			2. Father of			A. *Purposes of:*		
Food	Matt. 6:25, 26	947	Jephthah	Judg. 11:1	255	Strength-		
Rain	Matt. 5:45	946	3. Gadite	1 Chr. 5:14	409	ening	Prov. 31:17	636
Health	Phil. 2:25-30	1171	4. Condemned			Supporting		
Sleep	Prov. 3:23-25	617	city	Hos. 6:8	843	clothing	2 Kin. 4:29	375
Rest	Deut. 12:10	190	5. Mountain	Judg. 7:3	250	B. *Figurative of:*		
All things	1 Tim. 6:17	1197	6. Tableland east of the Jordan			Gladness	Ps. 30:11	559
All needs	Phil. 4:19	1173	between the Arnon and Jab-			Truth	Eph. 6:14	1167
2. *Spiritual:*			bok rivers	Judg. 20:1	263	Readiness	1 Pet. 1:13	1235
Christ	John 3:16	1044	Possessed by			C. *Those girding:*		
Holy Spirit	Luke 11:13	1020	Israel	Num. 21:21-31	158	Priests	Ex. 28:4, 39	82
Grace	James 4:6	1230	Assigned to Reuben, Gad, and			Warriors	1 Sam. 18:4	293
Wisdom	James 1:5	1228	Manasseh	Deut. 3:12-17	181	Jesus	John 13:3, 4	1058
Repentance	Acts 11:18	1084	Rebuked by					
Faith	Eph. 2:8	1162	Deborah	Judg. 5:17	248	**Girdle**—*waistcloth; sash; belt*		
New spirit	Ezek. 11:19	779	Hebrews			Priestly garment	Ex. 28:4, 39	82
Peace	Phil. 4:7	1173	flee to	1 Sam. 13:7	286	Worn by		
Rest	Heb. 4:1, 9	1216	Ish-bosheth's rule			warriors	1 Sam. 18:4	293
Glory	1 Pet. 5:10	1239	over	2 Sam. 2:8, 9	310			
Eternal life	John 10:28	1055						

SUBJECT	REFERENCE	PAGE
Girgashites—*an original tribe of Canaan*		
Descendants of		
Canaan..........	Gen. 10:15, 16	13
Land of, given to Abraham's		
descendants.....	Gen. 15:18, 21	17
Delivered to		
Israel..........	Josh. 24:11	240
Girl—*a female child*		
Sold for wine	Joel 3:3	852
Prophecy		
concerning......	Zech. 8:4, 5	900
Girzites—*inhabitants of Gezer*		
Raided by David ..	1 Sam. 27:8	302
Gispa—*fondle*		
Overseer..........	Neh. 11:21	500
Gittaim—*two winepresses*		
Village of		
Benjamin..........	Neh. 11:31, 33	501
Refuge of the		
Beerothites.......	2 Sam. 4:2, 3	312
Gittites—*natives of Gath*		
600 follow David ..	2 Sam. 15:18-23	323
Gittith—*belonging to Gath*		
Musical instrument or		
tune..............	Ps. 8; 81; 84	
	(Titles)	550
Giving to God		
A. *Manner of:*		
Without		
show.........	Matt. 6:1-4	946
According to		
ability.........	1 Cor. 16:1, 2	1138
Willingly........	1 Chr. 29:3-9	433
Liberally.......	2 Cor. 9:6-15	1148
Cheerfully.....	2 Cor. 9:7	1148
Propor-		
tionately.....	Mal. 3:10	909
B. *Examples of:*		
Israelites	Ex. 35:21-29	91
Princes of		
Israel	Num. 7:2-28	141
Poor widow....	Luke 21:1-4	1031
Macedonian		
churches.....	2 Cor. 8:1-5	1147
Gizonite		
Hashem thus		
described.........	1 Chr. 11:34	416
Gladness—*cheerfulness*		
A. *Causes of:*		
Forgiveness....	Ps. 51:8	569
Salvation	Is. 51:3, 11	694
	John 8:56	1053
Recovery of a		
son	Luke 15:32	1026
Restoration of		
hope..........	John 20:20	1065
Temporal		
blessings......	Acts 14:17	1088
Christ's		
coming........	1 Pet. 4:13	1239
B. *Wrong kinds of:*		
At an enemy's		
downfall	Prov. 24:17	631
At		
wickedness....	Hos. 7:3	843
Glass		
A. *Used literally of:*		
Crystal	Job 28:17, 18	534
B. *Used figuratively of:*		
Christ's glory ..	2 Cor. 3:18	1144
God's nature...	Rev. 4:6	1271
New		
Jerusalem.....	Rev. 21:18, 21	1282
Gleaning—*gathering grain left by reapers*		
Laws providing		
for	Lev. 19:9, 10	119

SUBJECT	REFERENCE	PAGE
Illustrated by		
Ruth	Ruth 2:2-23	270
Gideon's		
reference to	Judg. 8:2	251
Glede		
Unclean bird of		
prey.............	Deut. 14:12, 13	192
Glorification of Christ		
A. *Nature of:*		
Predicted	Is. 55:5	696
Prayed for.....	John 12:28	1057
Not of		
Himself	Heb. 5:5	1217
Prede-		
termined......	John 17:1	1062
B. *Accomplished by:*		
Father.........	John 13:31, 32	1059
Holy Spirit....	John 16:13, 14	1061
Miracles......	John 11:4	1055
His		
resurrection..	Acts 3:13	1075
Believers.......	Acts 21:20	1096
Glorifying God		
A. *By means of:*		
Praise	Ps. 50:23	569
Fruitfulness....	John 15:8	1060
Service	1 Pet. 4:11	1238
Suffering	1 Pet. 4:14, 16	1239
B. *Reason for:*		
Deliverance....	Ps. 50:15	569
Mercy shown..	Rom. 15:9	1120
Subjection.....	2 Cor. 9:13	1148
C. *Extent of:*		
Universal......	Ps. 86:9	585
In body and		
soul..........	1 Cor. 6:20	1130
Glory—*honor; renown*		
A. *Of temporal things:*		
Granted by		
God..........	Dan. 2:37	824
Used to		
entrap	Matt. 4:8	944
Not to be		
sought........	1 Thess. 2:6	1184
Quickly		
passes.........	1 Pet. 1:24	1236
B. *Of believers:*		
Given by		
God..........	John 17:22	1062
Transformed by the		
Spirit	2 Cor. 3:18	1144
Through Christ's		
death	Heb. 2:9, 10	1215
Follows		
salvation......	2 Tim. 2:10	1201
In suffering....	Rom. 5:3	1112
In the cross....	Gal. 6:14	1158
Greater than present		
suffering......	Rom. 8:18	1114
Hope of........	Col. 1:27	1177
At Christ's		
advent........	Col. 3:4	1178
Glory of Christ		
A. *Aspects of:*		
Manifested to		
men..........	John 2:11	1043
Not selfish.....	John 8:50	1052
Given by		
God...........	John 17:22	1062
Crowned		
with	Heb. 2:9	1215
Ascribed to		
forever.......	Heb. 13:21	1224
B. *Stages of:*		
Before		
creation.......	John 17:5	1062
Revealed in Old		
Testament	John 12:41	1058
In His		
incarnation...	John 1:14	1042
In His trans-		
figuration	Luke 9:28-36	1017

SUBJECT	REFERENCE	PAGE
In His		
resurrection..	Luke 24:26	1037
In His		
exaltation.....	1 Tim. 3:16	1195
At His return .	Matt. 25:31	968
In heaven	Rev. 5:12	1271
Glory of God		
A. *Manifested to:*		
Moses	Ex. 24:9-17	79
Stephen	Acts 7:55	1080
B. *Reflected in:*		
Christ	John 1:14	1042
Man...........	1 Cor. 11:7	1133
C. *Appearances of:*		
The		
tabernacle	Ex. 40:34	96
The Temple....	1 Kin. 8:11	347
At Jesus'		
birth..........	Luke 2:8-11	1006
D. *The believer's relation to:*		
Does all for ...	1 Cor. 10:31	1133
Illuminated		
by	2 Cor. 4:6	1144
Will stand in		
presence of ..	Jude 24	1263
E. *Man's relation to:*		
Corrupts.......	Rom. 1:23	1109
Falls short of ..	Rom. 3:23	1111
Refuse to give to		
God...........	Acts 12:23	1086
Glory of man		
Prefigured in		
creation	Heb. 2:6-8	1215
Lost by sin......	Rom. 3:23	1111
Soon passes		
away..........	1 Pet. 1:24	1236
Removed by		
death..........	Ps. 49:17	568
Restored by		
Christ	2 Cor. 5:17	1145
Gluttony—*excessive appetite*		
Sternly		
forbidden........	Prov. 23:1-3	630
Characteristic of the		
wicked	Phil. 3:19	1172
Leads to poverty ..	Prov. 23:21	630
Christ		
accused of.......	Matt. 11:19	952
Gnat—*small insect*		
Third plague on Egypt, produced		
from dust	Ex. 8:16-18	63
Used as		
illustration	Matt. 23:24	966
Gnosticism—*early heresy based on knowledge instead of faith*		
Warned against ...	Col. 2:8, 18	1178
Arrogant.........	1 Cor. 8:1	1131
False.............	1 Tim. 6:20	1197
Surpassed by		
Christ	Eph. 3:19	1163
Goad—*a pointed rod*		
Used as a		
weapon	Judg. 3:31	247
Figurative of pointed		
morals	Eccl. 12:11	647
Figurative of		
conscience	Acts 26:14	1101
Sharpened by		
files	1 Sam. 13:21	287
Goals, spiritual		
Provide		
motivation	Phil. 3:12-14	1172
Promise reward ...	1 Cor. 9:24, 25	1132
Goat—*a domesticated animal*		
A. *Literal uses of:*		
Clothing.......	Num. 31:20	168
	Heb. 11:37	1222
Milk of, food...	Prov. 27:27	634
Curtains.......	Ex. 26:7	80
Bottles.........	Josh. 9:4	225

SUBJECT	REFERENCE	PAGE	SUBJECT	REFERENCE	PAGE	SUBJECT	REFERENCE	PAGE

Be turned
from ....Gal. 5:3, 4   1157

Graces, Christian
Growth in,
commanded .....2 Pet. 1:5-8   1243

Grafting—*uniting a portion of one plant
to another*
Gentiles, on Israel's
stock.............Rom. 11:17, 24   1117

Grain—*the generic term for cereal
grasses*
A. *Features regarding:*
Grown in
Palestine.......2 Kin. 18:32   392
Article of
food ....Gen. 42:1, 2, 19   44
Offered mixed with
oil ....Lev. 2:14, 15   101
Roasted.......Ruth 2:14   270
B. *Figurative of:*
Blessings .....Ezek. 36:29   805
Christ ....John 12:24   1057
Life's
maturity .....Job 5:26   522

Grandchildren
Lot becomes father of, through
incest ....Gen. 19:30-38   20
Abdon's..........Judg. 12:13, 14   257
Widow's ....1 Tim. 5:4   1196
Iniquity visited
on................Ex. 34:7   89
Served idols......2 Kin. 17:41   390
Crown of old
men.............Prov. 17:6   626
Practice piety toward
family............1 Tim. 5:4   1196

Grandmother
Lois thus called ...2 Tim. 1:5   1200

Grapes
Grown in
Palestine ....Num. 13:23   149
Used for wine....Num. 6:3   141
"Sour grapes"....Ezek. 18:2   786
Figurative of
judgment.........Rev. 14:18   1277

See Vine, vineyard

Grass
A. *Features:*
Created by
God..........Gen. 1:11, 12   4
Produced by
rain...........Deut. 32:2   209
Adorns earth ..Matt. 6:30   947
Failure of, a
calamity .....Jer. 14:5, 6   721
Nebuchadnezzar
eats...........Dan. 4:1, 33   826
Disappears.....Prov. 27:25   634
Withered
away..........Is. 15:6   669
B. *Figurative of:*
Life's
shortness ....Ps. 90:5, 6   587
Prosperous
wicked.......Ps. 92:7   588
God's grace....Ps. 72:6   577

Grasshopper—*locust*
Used as food .....Lev. 11:22   109
Inferiority........Num. 13:33   149
Insignificance ...Is. 40:22   686
Burden............Eccl. 12:5   647
Destroys crops ...Ps. 78:46   582

See Locust

Gratitude (see Thankfulness)

Gratitude to man
A. *Reasons for:*
Deliverance from an
enemy ....Judg. 8:22, 23   252

Deliverance from
death ....1 Sam. 26:21-25   302
Interpretation of a
dream.........Dan. 2:46-48   824
Rescue from
murderers.....Esth. 6:1-6   511
B. *Examples of:*
Ruth to Boaz ..Ruth 2:8-17   270
Israelites to
Jonathan......1 Sam. 14:45   288
Abigail to
David.........1 Sam. 25:40-42   301
David to
Jonathan......2 Sam. 9:1   316
David to
Hanun........2 Sam. 10:1, 2   317
Pagans to
Paul..........Acts 28:1-10   1103

Grave—*a place of burial*
A. *Features regarding:*
Dug in
ground........Gen. 50:5   52
Some in
caves ....Gen. 23:9   23
Marker
set on.........Gen. 35:20   37
Touching of, makes
unclean ......Num. 19:16, 18   156
B. *Resurrection from:*
Symbolized ....Ezek. 37:1-14   805

Graveclothes—*clothes for the dead*
Lazarus attired
in ....John 11:43, 44   1056
Jesus lays His
aside ....Luke 24:12   1036

Gravel—*small pebbles*
Figurative of:
Distress..........Prov. 20:17   628
Numerous offspring; rendered
"grains"........Is. 48:19   692
Suffering.........Lam. 3:16   764

Graven image—*an idol*
Of Canaanites, to ⎧Deut. 7:1-5, 25   185
be destroyed....⎨Deut. 12:2, 3   190
Cause of God's ⎧Ps. 78:58   582
anger............⎨Jer. 8:19   716

See Idols, idolatry

Great
A. *Descriptive of:*
Sun and
moon ....Gen. 1:16   4
Euphrates .....Gen. 15:18   17
Mediter-
ranean........Josh. 1:4   217
Nineveh ....Jon. 3:2, 3   867
Babylon ....Rev. 14:8   1277
B. *Applied to God's:*
Nature.........Deut. 10:17   189
Signs and
miracles.......Deut. 29:3   206
Works ....Judg. 2:7   245
Victory ....2 Sam. 23:10, 12   332
Mercy ....2 Chr. 1:8   439
Wrath ....2 Chr. 34:21   469
Glory..........Ps. 21:5   555
Power ....Ps. 147:5   610
C. *Descriptive of Christ as:*
God ....Titus 2:13   1207
Prophet........Luke 7:16   1013
Priest.........Heb. 4:14   1217
King...........Luke 1:32, 33   1005
             Rev. 11:17   1275
Shepherd .....Heb. 13:20   1224
D. *Applied to the believer's:*
Reward........Matt. 5:12   945
Faith ....Matt. 15:28   957
Joy...........Acts 8:8   1080
Zeal ....Col. 4:13   1179
Affliction .....2 Cor. 8:2   1147
Boldness.......1 Tim. 3:13   1195
Promises.......2 Pet. 1:4   1243

E. *Applied to final things:*
Gulf fixed......Luke 16:26   1026
Wrath ....Rev. 6:17   1272
Tribulation ....Rev. 7:14   1273
White throne
judgment .....Rev. 20:11   1281

Great fish
Swallows Jonah...Jon. 1:17   867

Greatness, true
Hinges on:
God's gentleness ..Ps. 18:35   554
Great work ....Neh. 6:3   493
Unselfishness ....Jer. 45:5   750
Servanthood .....Matt. 23:11   965
God's estimate ....Matt. 5:19   945

Grecians
1. The people of
Greece........Joel 3:6   852
2. Greek-speaking
Jews ....Acts 6:1   1078
Hostile to
Paul ....Acts 9:29   1082
Gospel preached
unto ....Acts 11:20   1085

Greece—*the southern extremity of the
Balkan peninsula*
Prophecy
concerning ....Dan. 8:21   832
Paul preaches in ..Acts 17:16-31   1091
Called Javan ......Is. 66:19   704
Conflict with......Zech. 9:13   901

Greed—*excessive desire for things*
A. *Productive of:*
Defeat.........Josh. 7:11-26   222
Murder ....1 Kin. 21:1-16   364
Betrayal ....Luke 22:1-6   1033
B. *Examples of:*
Samuel's
sons ....1 Sam. 8:1, 3   282
False
prophets ......Is. 56:10, 11   697
False
teachers .....2 Pet. 2:14, 15   1244

See Avarice; Covetousness

Greek
1. Native of ⎧Joel 3:6   852
Greece........⎨Acts 16:1   1089
Spiritual
state of ....Rom. 10:12   1116
Some believe ...Acts 14:1   1087
2. Foreigners speaking
Greek.........John 12:20   1057
3. Language of
Greece........Acts 21:37   1097

Greyhound—*a tall, slender hound*
Poetically
described........Prov. 30:29, 31   636

Grief
A. *Causes of:*
Son's
marriage......Gen. 26:34, 35   28
Barrenness....1 Sam. 1:11, 16   276
Death ....2 Sam. 19:1, 2   327
Disease........Job 2:11-13   520
Sinners.......Ps. 119:158   602
Foolish son ....Prov. 17:25   626
B. *Descriptive of:*
Messiah ....Is. 53:3, 4, 10   695
God ....Ps. 95:10   589
Holy Spirit....Eph. 4:30   1165
God's saints ...Ps. 139:21   608

See Sorrow

Groves
1. Tamarisk ⎧Gen. 21:33   22
tree.........⎨1 Sam. 22:6   297
2. Idolatrous shrine
(Asherah).....Deut. 12:3   190
             2 Kin. 21:7   394
Destruction of, com-
manded........Ex. 34:13

SUBJECT	REFERENCE	PAGE	SUBJECT	REFERENCE	PAGE	SUBJECT	REFERENCE	PAGE

Groves—continued

Israel's fondness
for............Jer. 17:2 — 723
Punishment....Is. 27:9 — 676

Grow—*to increase*

A. *Of material things:*
Power.........2 Sam. 3:1 — 311
Age...........Josh. 23:1 — 239
Sound.........Ex. 19:19 — 74
B. *Of immaterial things:*
Spirituality ...Luke 2:40 — 1007
God's hand ....Num. 11:23 — 147
Old covenant ..Heb. 8:13 — 1219
God's
kingdom......Luke 13:18, 19 — 1023

Growth, spiritual

A. *Expressed by words indicating:*
Fruitfulness....John 15:2, 5 — 1060
Increase.......2 Cor. 9:10 — 1148
Addition.......2 Pet. 1:5-10 — 1243
Growth.........1 Pet. 2:2 — 1236
Building up ....Jude 20 — 1263
B. *Hindrances to:*
Lack of
knowledge ....Acts 18:24-28 — 1093
Carnality ......1 Cor. 3:1-3 — 1127
Instability ....Eph. 4:14, 15 — 1164
Dullness.......Heb. 5:11-14 — 1217

Grudge—*to harbor resentment*

Forbidden.........Lev. 19:18 — 119

Guard

A. *Aspects of:*
Called
mighty........2 Sam. 23:8-23 — 332
Often
foreigners.....2 Sam. 20:7 — 329
Respected .....Jer. 40:1-5 — 746
B. *Duties of:*
Run before
chariots.......2 Sam. 15:1 — 322
Form a military
guard.......1 Sam. 22:17 — 297
Keep watch....2 Kin. 11:5, 6 — 383
Carry out command-
ments.........Jer. 39:11-14 — 745
Execute
criminals......Dan. 2:14 — 823

Guardian—*a custodian*

Christ, of our
souls ....2 Tim. 1:12 — 1200

Guardian angels

Helpers ....Gen. 24:7 — 24
Heb. 1:1-14 — 1215
Protectors........Ps. 91:11 — 588
Matt. 18:10 — 960
Aided apostles ....Acts 5:17-19 — 1077
Acts 8:26 — 1081

Gudgodah—*cutting; cleft*

Israelite
encampment .....Deut. 10:7 — 188
Also called
Hor-hagidgad....Num. 33:32 — 171

Guest

Kinds of:
Terrified ....1 Kin. 1:41, 49 — 338
Dead..............Prov. 9:18 — 621
Unwelcomed......Prov. 25:17 — 632
Unprepared ......Matt. 22:11 — 964
Criticized ....Luke 7:39-50 — 1014
Congenial.........Acts 18:1-3 — 1092
Courteous........1 Cor. 10:27 — 1133
Angelic ....Heb. 13:2 — 1223

Guidance, divine

To meek..........Ps. 25:9 — 557
To wise ....Prov. 23:19 — 630
To good man......Ps. 112:5 — 597
In God's
strength..........Ex. 15:13 — 70
On every side .....2 Chr. 32:22 — 466
With God's eye ...Ps. 32:8 — 560

With counsel......Ps. 73:24 — 578
Like a flock ....Ps. 78:52 — 582
By skillfulness.....Ps. 78:72 — 582
Continually ....Is. 58:11 — 698

Guide—*a leader*

A. *Kinds of:*
Human ....Num. 10:29-32 — 146
Super-
natural.......Ex. 13:20-22 — 69
Blind ....Matt. 23:16, 24 — 966
B. *Goals of:*
Peace..........Luke 1:79 — 1006
Truth..........John 16:13 — 1061
God's Word....Acts 8:30, 31 — 1081

Guilt, universality of

Described as:
Filthy rags ....Is. 64:6 — 702
Fall short ....Rom. 3:23 — 1111
All declared......Rom. 5:12-14 — 1112
Gal. 3:22 — 1156

Guni—*colored*

1. One of Naphtali's
sons ....Gen. 46:24 — 48
1 Chr. 7:13 — 412
Descendants called
Gunites.......Num. 26:48 — 164
2. Gadite.........1 Chr. 5:15 — 409

Gur—*lion's cub*

Site of Ahaziah's
death.............2 Kin. 9:27 — 381

Gur-baal—*sojourn of Baal*

Place in Arabia....2 Chr. 26:7 — 460

H

Haahashtari—*runner*

Son of Ashur......1 Chr. 4:5, 6 — 408

Habaiah—*Jehovah has hidden*

Father of excommunicated Jewish
priests............Ezra 2:61, 62 — 477
Also spelled
Hobaiah..........Neh. 7:63, 64 — 495

Habakkuk—*embrace*

A. *Complaints of:*
God's silence ..Hab. 1:2-4 — 882
God's
response ......Hab. 1:5-11 — 882
Chaldean
cruelty........Hab. 1:12-17 — 882
God's
response ......Hab. 2:1-20 — 883
B. *Prayer of:*
Praise of
God...........Hab. 3:1-19 — 883

Habakkuk, the Book of—*a book of the
Old Testament*

Author...........Hab. 1:1 — 882
Setting...........Hab. 1:2-4 — 882
Historical
reference........Hab. 1:6 — 882
The life of the
just ....Hab. 2:4 — 883

Habaziniah

Grandfather of
Jaazaniah........Jer. 35:3 — 741

Habergeon—*a coat of mail*

Worn by priests...Ex. 28:32 — 83
Ex. 39:23 — 95

Habit—*a custom*

Kinds of:
Doing evil.........Jer. 13:23 — 720
Doing good ....Acts 10:38 — 1084
Of animals,
instinctive........2 Pet. 2:22 — 1244

Habitation—*a place of residence*

A. *Used literally of:*
Canaan........Num. 15:2 — 151
A tree ....Dan. 4:20, 21 — 827
Nation.........Acts 17:26 — 1092
B. *Used figuratively of:*
Eternity ....Is. 57:15 — 697
God's throne...Is. 63:15 — 702
Sky............Hab. 3:11 — 884
Heaven........Luke 16:9 — 1026
New
Jerusalem.....Is. 33:20 — 681

Habor—*joined together*

The river of
Gozan...........2 Kin. 17:6 — 389

Hachaliah—*darkness of Yahweh*

Father of
Nehemiah........Neh. 1:1 — 489

Hachilah—*dark; gloomy*

Hill in the wilderness of Ziph
where David
hid...............1 Sam. 23:19-26 — 298

Hachmoni

Tutor to king's
son...............1 Chr. 27:32 — 431

Hadad—*fierceness*

1. Ishmael's   ⎰Gen. 25:13, 15 — 26
son   ⎱1 Chr. 1:30 — 405
2. King of
Edom.........Gen. 36:35, 36 — 38
3. Another king of
Edom.........1 Chr. 1:50 — 405
Called Hadar ..Gen. 36:39 — 38
4. Edomite
leader.........1 Kin. 11:14-25 — 352

Hadadezer—*Hadad is a help*

King of Zobah ....2 Sam. 8:3-13 — 316
Defeated by
David ....2 Sam. 10:6-19 — 317

Hadadrimmon—*Hadad and Rimmon*

Name of the two Aramean deities;
a place in
Jezreel..........Zech. 12:11 — 902

Hadashah—*new*

Village of Judah...Josh. 15:37 — 231

Hadassah—*myrtle*

Esther's Jewish
name............Esth. 2:7 — 508

Hadattah—*new*

Town in south Judah; possibly
should be read as Hazor-
hadattah ....Josh. 15:25 — 231

Hadid—*sharp*

Town of
Benjamin.........Neh. 11:31, 34 — 501

Hadlai—*restful*

Ephraimite........2 Chr. 28:12 — 461

Hadoram—*Hadar is exalted*

1. Son of
Joktan.........Gen. 10:26, 27 — 13
2. Son of Tou ....1 Chr. 18:9, 10 — 423
3. Rehoboam's tribute
officer.........2 Chr. 10:18 — 447
Called
Adoram.......1 Kin. 12:18 — 353
Probably same as
Adoniram .....1 Kin. 4:6 — 342

Hadrach—*periodical return*

Place in Syria .....Zech. 9:1 — 900

Hagab—*locust*

Head of a family of Temple
servants..........Ezra 2:46 — 476

Harp—*a stringed musical instrument*

Used by:
The wicked ......Is. 5:11, 12		661
David............1 Sam. 16:16, 23		290
Prophets........1 Sam. 10:5		284

Temple
orchestra........1 Chr. 16:5   420
Temple
worshipers ......Ps. 33:2   560
Celebrators ......2 Chr. 20:27, 28   455
Jewish captives ...Ps. 137:2   606
Worshipers in
heaven..........Rev. 5:8   1271

Harpoon—*a barbed spear for hunting large fish*

Used against
Leviathan ....Job 41:7   542

Harrow

Instrument for breaking
clods.............Job 39:10   541
Figurative of
affliction ....Is. 28:24   677

Harsha—*enchanter*

Head of Temple   (Ezra 2:43, 52   476
servants.......... (Neh. 7:46, 54   495

Hart—*a male deer*

A. Described as:
Clean animal ..Deut. 12:15   190
Hunted
animal.......Lam. 1:6   762
B. Figurative of:
Christ ....Song 2:9, 17   651
Afflicted
saints ....Ps. 42:1-3   565
Converted
sinners........Is. 35:6   682

Harum—*exalted*

Judahite ....1 Chr. 4:8   408

Harumaph—*flat-nosed*

Father of
Jedaiah...........Neh. 3:10   490

Haruphite

Designation of
Shephatiah.......1 Chr. 12:5   417
Member of Hariph's
family...........Neh. 7:24   494

Haruz—*active*

Father-in-law of King
Manasseh ....2 Kin. 21:19   395

Harvest—*the time when the crops are ripe*

A. Occasion of:
Great joy......Is. 9:3   664
Bringing the first
fruits.........Lev. 23:10   123
Remembering the
poor ....Lev. 19:9, 10   119
B. Figuratively of:
Seasons of
grace ....Jer. 8:20   716
Judgment......Jer. 51:33   757
God's wrath ...Rev. 14:15   1277
Gospel oppor-
tunities ......Matt. 9:37, 38   950
World's end...Matt. 13:30, 39   954
Measure of
fruitfulness....2 Cor. 9:6   1148
C. Promises concerning:
To continue ...Gen. 8:22   11
Rain.........Jer. 5:24   713
Patience......James 5:7   1230
D. Failure caused by:
Drought.......Amos 4:7   857
Locusts.......Joel 1:4   850
Sin ....Is. 17:4-12   670

Hasadiah—*Yahweh has been gracious*

Son of
Zerubbabel.......1 Chr. 3:20   407

Hasenuah—*thorny*

Benjamite   (1 Chr. 9:7   414
family...... (Neh. 11:7-9   500

Hashabiah—*Yahweh has imputed*

1. Merarite
Levite.........1 Chr. 6:44, 45   410
Perhaps the same
as in..........1 Chr. 9:14   414
2. Levite
musician......1 Chr. 25:3, 19   429
3. Kohathite
Levite.........1 Chr. 26:30   430
4. Levite ruler...1 Chr. 27:17   431
5. Chief Levite during Josiah's
reign........2 Chr. 35:9   470
6. Postexilic
Levite.........Ezra 8:19, 24   482
Probably the
same in ....Neh. 10:11   499
7. Postexilic
ruler ....Neh. 3:17   491
8. Descendant of
Asaph.........Neh. 11:22   500
9. Priest in the time of
Joiakim ......Neh. 12:21   501

Hashabnah—*covenant sealer*

Signed covenant ..Neh. 10:25   499

Hashabniah—*Yahweh has regarded me*

1. Father of
Hattush.......Neh. 3:10   490
2. Postexilic
Levite.........Neh. 9:5   497
Probably the same as
Hashabiah 6

Hashbadana—*thoughtful judge*

Assistant to
Ezra.............Neh. 8:4   496

Hashem—*shining*

Father of David's
warriors..........1 Chr. 11:34   416
Also called
Jashen ....2 Sam. 23:32   332

Hashmonah—*fertility*

Israelite
encampment .....Num. 33:29   171

Hashub—*thoughtful*

1. Postexilic
workman .....Neh. 3:11   490
2. Signer of the
covenant.....Neh. 10:23   499
3. Levite chief.....Neh. 11:15   500

Hashubah—*esteemed*

Son of
Zerubbabel.......1 Chr. 3:19, 20   407

Hashum—*opulent*

Founder of postexilic
family...........Ezra 2:19   476
Assists Ezra and signs
document ....Neh. 8:4   496
Neh. 10:18   499

Hasrah—*want*

Grandfather of
Shallum ....2 Chr. 34:22   469
Called Harhas.....2 Kin. 22:14   396

Hassenaah—*thorny*

Father of postexilic
workmen........Neh. 3:3   490
Same as   (Ezra 2:35   476
Senaah...... (Neh. 7:38   494

Haste—*to do something quickly*

Prompted by   (2 Chr. 35:21   470
good .... (Luke 19:5, 6   1029
Prompted by   (Prov. 14:29   624
evil........... (Prov. 28:20   634

Hasupha—*naked*

Head of Temple
servants..........Ezra 2:43   476

Same as
Hashupha........Neh. 7:46   495

Hat

Better rendered as
"mantle" ....Dan. 3:21   825

Hate—*to dislike something with strong feeling*

A. Meanings of:
React as God
does ....Rev. 2:6   1269
Twist moral
judgments ....Prov. 8:36   620
Esteem of less
value........John 12:25   1057
Make a vital
distinction ....Luke 14:26   1025
Despise........Is. 1:14   659
B. Causes of:
Parental
favoritism.....Gen. 37:4, 5   39
Rape ....2 Sam. 13:14, 15, 22   320
Failure to
please.........1 Kin. 22:8   366
God's
purpose.......Ps. 105:25   593
Belonging to
Christ.........Matt. 24:9, 10   967
Evil nature ....John 3:20   1044
C. Objects of:
God's people...Gen. 26:27   28
God ....Ex. 20:5   75
Christ ....John 15:25   1061
Light ....John 3:20   1044
Evil men......Ps. 26:5   557
Wickedness.....Ps. 45:7   567
D. Toward Christians, sign of their:
Discipleship....Matt. 24:9   967
Election ......John 15:19   1060
Regen-
eration.....1 John 3:13-15   1251

Hatach—*chamberlain*

Esther's
attendant........Esth. 4:5-10   509

Hathath—*terror*

Son of Othniel ....1 Chr. 4:13   408

Hatipha—*captive*

Head of Temple
servants.........Ezra 2:43, 54   476

Hatita—*dug up*

Father of   (Ezra 2:42   476
porters.......... (Neh. 7:45   495

Hattil—*vacillating*

Ancestor of
Solomon's   (Ezra 2:55, 57   476
servants........ (Neh. 7:57-59   495

Hattush—*assembled*

1. Descendant of
David........Ezra 8:2   481
2. Man of
Judah.........1 Chr. 3:22   407
Probably the same as 1
3. Priest returning with
Zerubbabel....Neh. 12:1, 2   501
4. Postexilic
workman .....Neh. 3:10   490
5. Priest who signs
covenant......Neh. 10:1, 4   499

Haughtiness—*an arrogant spirit*

Precedes a fall ....Prov. 16:18   625
To be brought
low...........Is. 2:11, 17   660
Guilt of   (Ezek. 16:50   784
Jerusalem for... (Zeph. 3:11   888

Haunt—*to frequent a place*

Place of abode ....1 Sam. 23:22   298

151

Hearers—continued

Belief.........Rom. 10:14   1116
Conviction.....Acts 2:37   1074
Discrimi-
nation ....Luke 8:18   1015

B. *Reactions of:*
Responsive-
ness..........2 Sam. 7:17-29   315
Repentance ...2 Sam. 12:12, 13   319
Rebellion ......Ezek. 33:30-33   802
Retreat ....John 6:60-66   1049
Resistance.....Acts 7:51-54   1080
Rejoicing......Acts 13:48   1087
Rejection......Acts 28:23-29   1104
Research .....Acts 17:11   1091

Heart

A. *Seat of:*
Adultery.......Matt. 5:28   945
Desire ....Rom. 10:1   1116
Doubt ....Mark 11:23   992
Fear..........Is. 35:4   681
Hatred........Lev. 19:17   119
Glad..........Acts 2:26   1073
Love..........Mark 12:30, 33   993
Lust ....Rom. 1:24   1109
Meditation....Ps. 19:14   555
Mischief ......Ps. 28:3   558
Obedience ....Rom. 6:17   1113
Pride ....Prov. 16:5   625
Purpose.......2 Cor. 9:7   1148
Reason ....Mark 2:8   980
Rebellion .....Jer. 5:23   713
Rejoicing .....Acts 2:26   1073
Sorrow ....John 14:1   1059
Thought.......Matt. 9:4   949

B. *Of the wicked, described as:*
Blind ....Eph. 4:18   1164
Darkened.....Rom. 1:21   1109
Covetous .....2 Pet. 2:14   1244
Full of evil....Gen. 6:5   9
Unrepentant...Rom. 2:5   1109
Lustful ....Prov. 6:25   619
Proud.........Jer. 49:16   753
Rebellious ....Jer. 5:23   713
Uncir-
cumcised......Acts 7:51   1080

C. *God's action upon:*
Knows.........Ps. 44:21   566
Searches......1 Chr. 28:9   432
Enlightens ....2 Cor. 4:6   1144
Opens ....Acts 16:14   1090
Recreates.....Ezek. 11:19   779
Examines.....Jer. 12:3   719
Strengthens ...Ps. 27:14   558
Establishes....1 Thess. 3:13   1184

D. *Regenerate's, described as:*
Circumcised ...Rom. 2:29   1110
Clean.........Ps. 73:1   578
Contrite ......Ps. 51:17   569
Enlarged......Ps. 119:32   600
Enlightened...2 Cor. 4:6   1144
Fixed.........Ps. 57:7   571
Joyful in
God.........1 Sam. 2:1   277
Meditative....Ps. 4:4   549
Perfect ....Ps. 101:2   591
Prayerful .....1 Sam. 1:12, 13   276
Pure.........Matt. 5:8   945
Glad and
sincere......Acts 2:46   1074
Tender........2 Kin. 22:19   396
Treasury of
good.......Matt. 12:35   953
Wise.........Prov. 10:8   621

E. *Regenerate's, responses of:*
Believe with ...Rom. 10:10   1116
Keep with
diligence....Prov. 4:23   617
Love God
with all ....Matt. 22:37   965
Sanctify God
in..........1 Pet. 3:15   1238
Serve God
with all ......Deut. 26:16   202
Walk before God
with all ....1 Kin. 2:4   339
Trust the Lord
with all ......Prov. 3:5   616

Regard not iniquity
in............Ps. 66:18   574
Do God's will
from.........Eph. 6:6   1167

Hearth—a place for fire

Bed of live {Is. 30:14   678
coals ....{Ps. 102:3   591

Heartlessness—without moral feeling; cruelty

A. *Among unbelievers:*
Philistines, toward
Samson.......Judg. 16:21   260
Saul, toward
David........1 Sam. 18:25   293
Nabal, toward
David........1 Sam. 25:4-12   300
Haman, toward
Jews........Esth. 3:8-10   509
Levite, toward a certain
man ....Luke 10:30-32   1019

B. *Among professing believers:*
Laban, toward
Jacob........Gen. 31:7, 36-42   32
Jacob's sons, toward
Joseph.......Gen. 37:18-35   39
David, toward
Uriah........2 Sam. 11:9-27   318

Heath—a desert plant

Figurative of:
Self-sufficient
man...........Jer. 17:6   723
Devastation......Jer. 48:6   751

Heat, hot

Figurative of:
God's wrath....Deut. 9:19   188
Man's anger......Deut. 19:6   196
Determination ...Gen. 31:36   33
Zeal ....Ps. 39:3   564
Persecution .....Matt. 13:6, 21   954
Heavy toil.......Matt. 20:12   962
Real faith........Rev. 3:15   1270

Heathen (see Gentiles)

Heave offering

A. *Consited of:*
Firstfruits.....Num. 15:18-21   151
Tenth of all
tithes ....Num. 18:21-28   155

B. *Part of:*
All gifts........Num. 18:29   155
Spoils........Num. 31:26-47   168
Offerings ......Ex. 29:27   84
Lev. 7:14, 32   105

C. *Requirements concerning:*
To be the
best..........Num. 18:29   155
Brought to God's
house ....Deut. 12:5, 6   190
Given to
priests ....Ex. 29:27, 28   84
Sanctified the whole
offering......Num. 18:27-32   155
Eaten in a clean
place.........Lev. 10:12-15   108

Heaven—the place of everlasting bliss

A. *Inhabitants of:*
God ....1 Kin. 8:30   347
Christ ....Heb. 9:12, 24   1219
Holy Spirit......Ps. 139:7, 8   607
Angels........Matt. 18:10   960
Just men ......Heb. 12:22, 23   1223

B. *Things lacking in:*
Marriage......Matt. 22:30   965
Death ....Luke 20:36   1031
Flesh and
blood ....1 Cor. 15:50   1138
Imper-
ishable........1 Cor. 15:42, 50   1138
Sorrow ....Rev. 7:17   1273
Pain ....Rev. 21:4   1282
Curse.........Rev. 22:3   1282
Night.........Rev. 22:5   1282

Wicked
people ....Rev. 22:15   1283
End...........Matt. 25:46   969
Rev. 22:5   1282

C. *Positive characteristics of:*
Joy...........Luke 15:7, 10   1025
Rest ....Rev. 14:13   1277
Peace.........Luke 16:19-25   1026
Righ-
teousness .....2 Pet. 3:13   1244
Service ....Rev. 7:15   1273
Reward.......Matt. 5:11, 12   945
Inheritance....1 Pet. 1:4   1235
Glory.........Rom. 8:17, 18   1114

D. *Entrance into, for:*
Righteous .....Matt. 5:20   945
Changed......1 Cor. 15:51   1138
Saved.........John 3:5, 18, 21   1044
Called ....2 Pet. 1:10, 11   1243
Overcomers....Rev. 2:7, 10, 11   1269
Those
recorded .....Luke 10:20   1018
Obedient......Rev. 22:14   1283
Holy..........Rev. 19:8   1280

E. *Believer's present attitude toward:*
Given
foretaste of ...Acts 7:55, 56   1080
Earnestly
desires ....2 Cor. 5:2, 8   1145
Looks for......2 Pet. 3:12   1244
Considers "far better" than
now..........Phil. 1:23   1170
Puts treasure
there.........Luke 12:33   1022

F. *Described as:*
House ....John 14:2   1059
Kingdom ......Matt. 25:34   968
Abraham's
bosom ......Luke 16:22, 23   1026
Paradise ....2 Cor. 12:2, 4   1150
Better
country ......Heb. 11:10, 16   1221
Holy city ......Rev. 21:2, 10-27   1281
Rev. 22:1-5   1282

Heavens, natural

A. *Facts regarding:*
Created by
God..........Gen. 1:1   4
Stretched {Is. 42:5   687
out..........{Jer. 10:12   718
Will be {Heb. 1:10-12   1215
destroyed ...{2 Pet. 3:10   1244
New heavens {Is. 65:17   703
to follow.....{2 Pet. 3:13   1244

B. *Purposes of:*
To declare God's
glory..........Ps. 19:1   554
To declare God's righ-
teousness .....Ps. 50:6   568
To manifest God's
wisdom ......Prov. 8:27   620

Heaviness—a spirit of grief or anxiety

Unrelieved by
mirth.........Prov. 14:13   624
God's children
experience.......Phil. 2:26   1171
Needed
exchange........James 4:9   1230
Experienced by
Christ ....Ps. 69:20, 21   576
Remedy for ...Prov. 12:25   623

Heavy—oppressive

A. *Used literally of:*
Eli's weight....1 Sam. 4:18   279
Absalom's
hair ....2 Sam. 14:26   322
Stone.........Prov. 27:3   633

B. *Used figuratively of:*
Fatigue.......Matt. 26:43   970
Burdens ......2 Chr. 10:11, 14   447
Sins ....Is. 24:20   674
Sullenness ....1 Kin. 21:4   364
God's
judgments ....1 Sam. 5:6, 11   280

SUBJECT	REFERENCE	PAGE	SUBJECT	REFERENCE	PAGE	SUBJECT	REFERENCE	PAGE

Hermon—*sacred mountain*

Highest mountain (9,166 ft.) in
Syria; also called Sirion,
Shenir...........Deut. 3:8, 9 — 180
Northern limit of
conquest.......Josh. 11:3, 17 — 227
Joined with Tabor, Zion, and
Lebanon in Hebrew
poetry...........Ps. 89:12 — 586

Hero—*a person acclaimed for unusual deeds*

Caleb, a rejected ..Num. 13:30-33 — 149
Phinehas, a
rewarded........Num. 25:7-13 — 162
Deborah, a
militant ....Judg. 4:4-16 — 247
Jonathan, a   (1 Sam. 14:6-17,
rescued...........(38-45 — 287
David, a popular ..1 Sam. 18:5-8 — 293
Esther, a
hesitant ....Esth. 4:10-17 — 510

Herod—*family name of Idumaean rulers of Palestine*

1. Herod the Great,
procurator of Judaea
(37–4 B.C.)....Luke 1:5 — 1004
Inquires of Jesus'
birth ....Matt. 2:3-8 — 942
Slays Bethlehem
infants.......Matt. 2:12-18 — 942
2. Archelaus (4 B.C.–A.D. 6)
succeeds Herod the
Great ....Matt. 2:22 — 943
3. Herod Antipas, the tetrarch,
ruler of Galilee and Peraea (4
B.C.–A.D. 39)...Luke 3:1 — 1007
Imprisons John the
Baptist......Luke 3:18-21 — 1008
Has John the Baptist
beheaded ...Matt. 14:1-12 — 955
Disturbed about
Jesus.........Luke 9:7-9 — 1016
Jesus sent to
him ....Luke 23:7-11 — 1035
Becomes Pilate's
friend........Luke 23:12 — 1035
Opposes
Jesus.........Acts 4:27 — 1076
4. Philip, tetrarch of Ituraea
and
Trachonitis
(4 B.C.–A.D.   (Luke 3:1 — 1007
34)..........(Acts 13:1 — 1086
5. Herod Philip, disinherited
son of Herod
the Great .....Matt. 14:3 — 956
6. Herod Agrippa I
(A.D. 37–44) ..Acts 12:1, 19 — 1085
Kills James ....Acts 12:1, 2 — 1085
Imprisons
Peter.........Acts 12:3-11, 19 — 1085
Slain by an
angel........Acts 12:20-23 — 1085
7. Herod Agrippa II (A.D. 53–70)
Called Agrippa
and King   (Acts 25:22, 23 — 1100
Agrippa......(Acts 25:24, 26 — 1101
Festus tells him about
Paul ....Acts 25:13-27 — 1100
Paul makes a defense
before........Acts 26:1-23 — 1101
Rejects the
Gospel.......Acts 26:24-30 — 1101
Recognizes Paul's
innocency....Acts 26:31, 32 — 1102
8. Aristobulus; identified by some
as son of Herod the
Great ....Rom. 16:10 — 1121

Herodians—*an influential Jewish party*

Join Pharisees against
Jesus.............Mark 3:6 — 980
Seek to trap
Jesus.........Matt. 22:15-22 — 964
Jesus warns
against..........Mark 8:15 — 987

Herodias—*feminine form of Herod*

Granddaughter of Herod the Great;
plots John's
death...........Matt. 14:3-12 — 956
Married her
uncle............Mark 6:17, 18 — 984

Herodion

Christian at
Rome ....Rom. 16:11 — 1121

Heron

Unclean bird ..... (Lev. 11:19 — 109
              (Deut. 14:18 — 192

Hesed—*mercy*

Father of one of Solomon's
officers...........1 Kin. 4:7, 10 — 342

Heshbon—*intelligence*

Ancient Moabite city; taken by
Sihon, king of the
Amorites ....Num. 21:25-34 — 158
Taken by Moses...Num. 21:23-26 — 158
Assigned to
Reubenites ......Num. 32:1-37 — 169
Built by Reuben...Num. 32:37 — 170
On Gad's southern
boundary........Josh. 13:26 — 229
Levitical city.....Josh. 21:39 — 237
Later held by
Moabites ....Is. 15:1-4 — 669
Judgment of,
announced ....Is. 16:8-14 — 670
Fall of, predicted ..Jer. 48:2, 34, 35 — 751
Fishpools in ......Song 7:4 — 653

Heshmon—*fatness*

Town of Judah....Josh. 15:21, 27 — 231

Hesitation—*delay prompted by indecision*

Causes of:
Uncertain about God's
will.............1 Sam. 23:1-13 — 297
Fear of man.......John 9:18-23 — 1053
Selfish
unconcern......2 Cor. 8:10-14 — 1147
Unbelief ....John 20:24-28 — 1066

Heth—*terror*

Son of Canaan ....Gen. 10:15 — 13
Ancestor of the
Hittites.........Gen. 23:10 — 23
Abraham buys field from
sons of ....Gen. 23:3-20 — 23
Esau marries
daughters of.....Gen. 27:46 — 29
See Hittites

Hethlon—*hiding place*

Place indicating Israel's ideal
northern
boundary........Ezek. 47:15 — 816

Hewers of wood

A slave classification:
Gibeonites ....Josh. 9:17-27 — 225
Classed with "drawers of
water" ....Josh. 9:21, 23 — 225

Hezeki—*my strength*

Benjamite.........1 Chr. 8:17 — 413

Hezekiah—*Yahweh strengthens*

1. King of
Judah.........2 Chr. 29:1-3 — 462
Reforms Temple
services.......2 Chr. 29:3-36 — 462
Restores pure
worship.......2 Chr. 31:1-21 — 465
Military
exploits of ....2 Kin. 18:7-12 — 391
Defeated by Senna-
cherib.........2 Kin. 18:13 — 391
Sends messengers to
Isaiah.........2 Kin. 19:1-5 — 392
Rabshakeh's further
taunts.........2 Kin. 19:8-13 — 392

Prays
earnestly......2 Kin. 19:14-19 — 392
Encouraged by
Isaiah.........2 Kin. 19:20-37 — 392
Healed; his life prolonged 15
years.........2 Kin. 20:1-11 — 393
His thanks.....Is. 38:9-22 — 684
Rebuked for his
pride..........2 Kin. 20:12-19 — 394
Death of.......2 Kin. 20:20, 21 — 394
Ancestor of
Christ........Matt. 1:9 — 941
2. Ancestor of returning
exiles ....Ezra 2:1, 16 — 475
3. Ancestor of Zephaniah, spelled
Hizkiah ....Zeph. 1:1 — 887
4. Postexilic workman who
returned with
Zerubbabel....Ezra 2:16 — 476
5. Son of
Neariah.......1 Chr. 3:23 — 407

Hezion—*vision*

Grandfather of
Ben-hadad.......1 Kin. 15:18 — 357

Hezir—*swine*

1. Descendant of
Aaron.........1 Chr. 24:1, 15 — 428
2. One who signs
document.....Neh. 10:1, 20 — 499

Hezro

One of David's mighty
men.............1 Chr. 11:37 — 416

Hezron—*enclosure*

1. Place in south
Judah.........Josh. 15:1, 3 — 230
Same as
Hazaraddar ...Num. 34:4 — 172
2. Son of
Reuben ....Gen. 46:9 — 48
Founder of the
Hezronites ....Num. 26:6 — 162
3. Son of
Pharez ....Gen. 46:12 — 48
Head of tribal
family.........Num. 26:21 — 163
Ancestor of
David.........Ruth 4:18-22 — 272
Ancestor of
Christ........Matt. 1:3 — 941

Hiddai—*joyful*

One of David's
warriors.........2 Sam. 23:30 — 332
Same as Hurai ....1 Chr. 11:32 — 416

Hiddekel—*rapid*

Hebrew name of   (Gen. 2:14 — 5
the river Tigris ..(Dan. 10:4 — 834

Hide—*to conceal*

A. *Used literally of:*
Man in Eden ...Gen. 3:10 — 7
Baby Moses....Ex. 2:2, 3 — 57
Spies ....Josh. 6:17, 25 — 221
B. *Used figuratively of:*
God's face .....Deut. 31:17, 18 — 209
Protection ....Is. 49:2 — 692
Darkness .....Ps. 139:12 — 607
The Gospel ...2 Cor. 4:3 — 1144
Believer's life ..Col. 3:3 — 1178

Hiel—*God lives*

Native of Bethel; rebuilds
Jericho..........1 Kin. 16:34 — 359
Fulfills Joshua's
curse............Josh. 6:26 — 222

Hierapolis—*sacred city*

City of Asia Minor; center of
Christian
activity..........Col. 4:13 — 1179

Higgaion—*a deep sound*

Used as a musical
term ....Ps. 9:16 — 555

SUBJECT	REFERENCE	PAGE	SUBJECT	REFERENCE	PAGE	SUBJECT	REFERENCE	PAGE
Hurai—*free, noble*			**Hymenaeus**—*belonging to Hymen*			*Christ expressing, refers to:*		
One of David's mighty men	1 Chr. 11:32	416	False teacher excommunicated by Paul	1 Tim. 1:19, 20	1194	Bread of Life	John 6:35, 41, 48, 51	1049
Huram—*noble, free*			Teaches error	2 Tim. 2:17, 18	1201	Light of the world	John 8:12	1051
1. Son of Bela	1 Chr. 8:5	413	**Hymn**—*a spiritual song*				John 9:5	1053
2. King of Tyre	2 Chr. 2:11	439	A. *Occasions producing:*			Door of the sheep	John 10:7, 9	1054
Huri—*linen worker*			Great deliverance	Ex. 15:1-19	70	Good Shepherd	John 10:11, 14	1054
Gadite	1 Chr. 5:14	409	Great victory	Judg. 5:1-31	248	Resurrection and the Life	John 11:25	1056
Husband—*married man*			Prayer answered	1 Sam. 2:1-10	277	True and living Way	John 14:6	1059
A. *Regulations concerning:*			Mary's "Magnificat"	Luke 1:46-55	1005	True Vine	John 15:1, 5	1060
One flesh	Matt. 19:5, 6	961	Father's ecstasy	Luke 1:68-79	1005	**Ibleam**—*he destroys the people*		
Until death	Rom. 7:2, 3	1113	Angel's delight	Luke 2:14	1006	City assigned to Manasseh	Josh. 17:11, 12	233
Rights of	1 Cor. 7:1-5	1130	Old man's faith	Luke 2:29-32	1007	Canaanites remain in	Judg. 1:27	244
Sanctified by wife	1 Cor. 7:14-16	1130	Heaven's eternal praise	Rev. 5:9-14	1271	Called Bileam	1 Chr. 6:70	411
B. *Duties of, toward wife:*			B. *Purposes of:*			Ahaziah slain near	2 Kin. 9:27	381
Love	Eph. 5:25-33	1166	Worship God	2 Chr. 23:18	457	**Ibneiah**—*Yahweh builds up*		
Live with for life	Matt. 19:3-9	961	Express joy	Matt. 26:30	970	Head of a Benjamite family	1 Chr. 9:8	414
Be faithful to	Mal. 2:14, 15	908	Edify	1 Cor. 14:15	1136	**Ibnijah**—*Yahweh builds up*		
Be satisfied with	Prov. 5:18, 19	618	Testify to others	Acts 16:25	1090	Father of Reuel	1 Chr. 9:8	414
Instruct	1 Cor. 14:34, 35	1136	**Hypocrisy, hypocrite**—*showy, empty*			**Ibri**—*a Hebrew*		
Honor	1 Pet. 3:7	1237	*display of religion*			Son of Jaaziah	1 Chr. 24:27	428
Confer with	Gen. 31:4-16	32	A. *Kinds of:*			**Ibsam**—*fragrant*		
Provide for	1 Tim. 5:8	1196	Worldly	Matt. 23:5-7	965	Descendant of Issachar	1 Chr. 7:2	411
Rule over	Gen. 3:16	7	Legalistic	Rom. 10:3	1116	**Ibzan**—*active*		
C. *Kinds of:*			Evangelical	2 Pet. 2:10-22	1244	Judge of Israel	Judg. 12:8	257
Adam, blaming	Gen. 3:9-12	7	Satanic	2 Cor. 11:13-15	1149	Father of 60 children	Judg. 12:8, 9	257
Isaac, loving	Gen. 24:67	26	B. *Described as:*			**Ice**		
Elkanah, sympathetic	1 Sam. 1:8-23	276	Self-righteous	Luke 18:11, 12	1028	*Figurative of:*		
Nabal, evil	1 Sam. 25:3	299	"Holier than thou"	Is. 65:5	703	God casts forth	Ps. 147:17	610
Ahab, weak	1 Kin. 21:5-16	364	Blind	Matt. 23:17-26	966	By reason of	Job 6:16	522
David, ridiculed	2 Sam. 6:20	314	Covetous	2 Pet. 2:3	1243	**Ichabod**—*inglorious*		
Job, strong	Job 2:7-10	519	Showy	Matt. 6:2, 5, 16	946	Son of Phinehas	1 Sam. 4:19-22	279
Husbandman—*a man of the soil*			Highly critical	Matt. 7:3-5	947	**Iconium**—*image-like*		
Farmer	Gen. 9:20	12	Indignant	Luke 13:14-16	1023	City of Asia Minor; visited by Paul	Acts 13:51	1087
	2 Kin. 25:12	399	Bound by traditions	Matt. 15:1-9	956	Many converts in	Acts 14:1-6	1087
Tenant farmer	Matt. 21:33-42	964	Neglectful of major duties	Matt. 23:23, 24	966	Paul visits again	Acts 14:21	1088
Takes share of crops	2 Tim. 2:6	1201	Pretended but unpracticed	Ezek. 33:31, 32	802	Timothy's ministry	Acts 16:1, 2	1089
Hushah—*haste*			Interested in the externals	Luke 20:46, 47	1031	Paul persecuted	2 Tim. 3:11	1202
Judahite	1 Chr. 4:4	408	Fond of titles	Matt. 23:6, 7	965	**Iconoclast**—*a breaker of images*		
Hushai—*hasty*			Inwardly unregenerate	Luke 11:39	1020	Moses, an angry	Ex. 32:19, 20	88
Archite; David's friend	2 Sam. 15:32-37	323	C. *Examples of:*			Gideon, an inspired	Judg. 6:25-32	249
Feigns sympathy with Absalom	2 Sam. 16:16-19	324	Jacob	Gen. 27:6-35	28	Jehu, a subtle	2 Kin. 10:18-31	382
Defeats Ahithophel's advice	2 Sam. 17:5-23	324	Jacob's sons	Gen. 37:29-35	39	Josiah, a reforming	2 Kin. 23:12-25	397
Husham—*hastily*			Delilah	Judg. 16:4-20	259	**Idalah**—*memorial of God*		
Temanite king of Edom	Gen. 36:34, 35	38	Ishmael	Jer. 41:6, 7	747	Border town of Zebulun	Josh. 19:15	234
Hushathite			Herod	Matt. 2:7, 8	942	**Idbash**—*honey-sweet*		
Inhabitant of Hushah	2 Sam. 21:18	330	Pharisees	John 8:4-9	1051	Man of Judah	1 Chr. 4:3	407
Hushim—*hasters*			Judas	Matt. 26:25-49	970	**Iddo**—*festal*		
1. Head of a Danite family	Gen. 46:23	48	Ananias	Acts 5:1-10	1076	1. Chief officer under David	1 Chr. 27:21	431
Called Shuham	Num. 26:42	163	Peter	Gal. 2:11-14	1155	2. Father of Ahinadab	1 Kin. 4:14	342
2. Sons of Aher	1 Chr. 7:12	412	**Hyssop**—*a small plant*			3. Leader of Jews at Casiphia	Ezra 8:17-20	482
3. Wife of Shaharaim	1 Chr. 8:8, 11	413	Grows from walls	1 Kin. 4:33	343	4. Gershonite Levite	1 Chr. 6:20, 21	410
Huz			Used in sprinkling blood	Ex. 12:22	67	Called Adaiah	1 Chr. 6:41	410
Son of Nahor	Gen. 22:20, 21	23	Used to offer Jesus vinegar	John 19:28, 29	1064	5. Seer whose writings are cited	2 Chr. 9:29	446
Husks—*the pods of the carob or locust tree*			Typical of spiritual cleansing	Ps. 51:7	569			
Fed to swine	Luke 15:15, 16	1025						
Huzzab—*uncertain meaning*			**I**					
May refer to Assyrian queen or to Nineveh; or may be rendered "it is decreed"	Nah. 2:7	879	**I AM**—*a title indicating self-existence*					
			Revealed to Moses	Ex. 3:14	58			
			Said by Christ	John 8:57, 58	1053			

SUBJECT	REFERENCE	PAGE	SUBJECT	REFERENCE	PAGE	SUBJECT	REFERENCE	PAGE

Illumination, spiritual—continued

At conversion.....Heb. 6:4 — 1217
In Christian
truth............Eph. 1:18 — 1162
By Holy Spirit.....John 16:13-16 — 1061
By God ....1 Cor. 4:5 — 1128

Illustration—*something used to explain something else*

From:
Ancient history ...1 Cor. 10:1-14 — 1132
Current history ...Mark 12:1-11 — 992
Nature............Prov. 6:6-11 — 618

Illyricum—*a province of Europe*

Paul preaches.....Rom. 15:19 — 1120

Image (see Idols, idolatry)

Image of God

A. *In man:*
Created in .....Gen. 1:26, 27 — 4
Reason for sanctity of
life............Gen. 9:6 — 12
Reason for man's
headship......1 Cor. 11:7 — 1133
Restored by
grace.........Col. 3:10 — 1178
Transformed
of............2 Cor. 3:18 — 1144
B. *In Christ:*
In essential
nature........Col. 1:15 — 1177
Manifested on
earth.........John 1:14, 18 — 1042
Believers
conformed ....Rom. 8:29 — 1115

Imagination—*creating mental picture of*

A. *Described as:*
Evil............Gen. 6:5 — 9
Willful.........Jer. 18:12 — 724
Deceitful ......Prov. 12:20 — 623
Vain...........Rom. 1:21 — 1109
B. *Cleansing of:*
Promised ......Jer. 3:17 — 711
By the power of
God...........2 Cor. 10:5 — 1149

Imitation—*attempting to duplicate*

Of the good:
God..............Eph. 5:1 — 1165
Paul's conduct ....2 Thess. 3:7, 9 — 1190
Apostles ....1 Thess. 1:6 — 1183
Heroes of the
faith.............Heb. 6:12 — 1217
Good ....3 John 11 — 1259
Other churches ...1 Thess. 2:14 — 1184
See Example of Christ, the

Imla—*fullness*

Father of Micaiah the
prophet.......2 Chr. 18:7, 8 — 452
As Imlah.........1 Kin. 22:8, 9 — 366

Immanuel—*God (is) with us*

Name given to
the child born of (Is. 7:14 — 663
the virgin ....\Matt. 1:23 — 942
Emmanuel in.....Matt. 1:23 — 942

Immer—*eloquent*

1. Descendant of
Aaron.........1 Chr. 24:1-14 — 428
2. Father of
Pashur........Jer. 20:1 — 725
3. Founder of a postexilic
family........Ezra 2:37 — 476
The same as the father of
Meshille-
mith.........1 Chr. 9:12 — 414
Also the ancestor of priests
marrying
foreigners.....Ezra 10:19, 20 — 484
4. Person or place in
Babylonia .....Neh. 7:61 — 495
5. Zadok's
father.........Neh. 3:29 — 491

Immorality—*state of a wrongful act or relationship*

Attitude toward:
Consider sanctity of the
body ....1 Cor. 6:13-20 — 1129
Flee from it .....1 Cor. 6:18 — 1129
Get married......1 Cor. 7:2 — 1130
Abstain from it...1 Thess. 4:3 — 1185
Mention it not ....Eph. 5:3 — 1165
Corrupts the
earth..........Rev. 19:2 — 1280

Immortality—*eternal existence*

A. *Proof of, based upon:*
God's image in
man ....Gen. 1:26, 27 — 4
Translation of
Enoch and (Gen. 5:24 — 9
Elijah ....\2 Kin. 2:11, 12 — 372
Promises of (John 11:25, 26 — 1056
Christ........\John 14:2, 3 — 1059
Appearance of Moses and
Elijah ....Matt. 17:2-9 — 959
Eternal
rewards and
punish- (Matt. 25:31-46 — 968
ments........\Luke 16:19-31 — 1026
Resurrection (Rom. 8:11 — 1114
of Christ .....\1 Cor. 15:12-58 — 1137
Resurrection (Dan. 12:2, 3 — 837
of men.......\John 5:28, 29 — 1047
B. *Expression indicative of:*
"I am"........Matt. 22:32 — 965
"Today".......Luke 23:43 — 1036
"Shall never
die".........John 11:25, 26 — 1056
"The redemption of our
body"........Rom. 8:22, 23 — 1115
"Neither
death"......Rom. 8:38, 39 — 1115
"We know"...2 Cor. 5:1-10 — 1145
"A lively
hope".........1 Pet. 1:3-8 — 1235
"We shall be like
him".........1 John 3:2 — 1251

See Eternal, everlasting; Life, eternal

Immunity—*exemption from something*

From:
Egyptian
plagues..........Ex. 8:22, 23 — 63
Disease ....Deut. 7:15 — 186
Corruption ......Ps. 16:10, 11 — 552
Harm ....Luke 10:19 — 1018
Second death .....Rev. 20:6 — 1281

Immutability—*unchangeableness*

A. *Of God, expressed by:*
"I AM"........Ex. 3:14 — 58
"Thou art the
same"........Ps. 102:25-27 — 591
"I change
not".........Mal. 3:6 — 909
"Are without
repentance"...Rom. 11:29 — 1117
"Who cannot
lie"..........Titus 1:2 — 1206
"The immut-
ability".......Heb. 6:17, 18 — 1218
"No variable-
ness" ....James 1:17 — 1228
B. *Of Christ, expressed by:*
"I am".........John 8:58 — 1053
"Thou art the
same"........Heb. 1:12 — 1215
"Unchange-
able".........Heb. 7:22-24 — 1218
"The same"...Heb. 13:8 — 1224
"I am Alpha and
Omega".......Rev. 1:8-18 — 1268
C. *Of God, characteristics of:*
Unique ....Is. 43:10 — 688
Purposive......Ps. 138:8 — 607
Active ....Phil. 1:6 — 1170

Imna—*he keeps back*

Asherite chief....1 Chr. 7:35 — 413

Imnah—*prosperity*

1. Eldest
son of
Asher.........1 Chr. 7:30 — 412
Called Jimna (Num. 26:44 — 163
and Jimnah . .\Gen. 46:17 — 48
2. Levite in Hezekiah's
reign..........2 Chr. 31:14 — 465

Impartiality—*that which is equitable, just, and fair*

In God's:
Material
blessings ......Matt. 5:45 — 946
Spiritual
blessings ....Acts 10:34, 35 — 1084
Judgments ....Rom. 2:3-12 — 1109

Impatience—*inability to control one's desire for action*

A. *Causes of:*
Lust ....Gen. 19:4-9 — 20
Revenge ....Gen. 34:25-27 — 36
Irritability .....Num. 20:10 — 157
B. *Consequences of:*
Kept from promised
land..........Num. 20:10-12 — 157
Great sin .....Ex. 32:1, 21, 30 — 87
Foolish
statements ....Job 2:7-9 — 519
Loss of
birthright .....Gen. 25:29-34 — 27
Shipwreck .....Acts 27:29-34 — 1102

Impeccability (see Holiness of Christ)

Impediment—*something that hinders one's activity*

In speech, cured ..Mark 7:32-35 — 986
Avoided by
obedience ....Prov. 4:10, 12 — 617

Impenitence—*without a change of mind*

A. *Expressed by:*
Willful disobedi-
ence ....Jer. 44:15-19 — 749
Hardness of
heart..........John 12:37-40 — 1058
Refusing to
hear ....Luke 16:31 — 1027
Rebellion against the
truth..........1 Thess. 2:15, 16 — 1184
B. *Consequences of:*
Spiritual
bondage ......John 8:33-44 — 1052
Judicial
blindness......John 9:39-41 — 1054
Eternal
destruction....2 Thess. 1:8, 9 — 1189

Imperfection of man

A. *Manifested in:*
Falling short of God's
glory..........Rom. 3:23 — 1111
Total
corruption ....Is. 1:5, 6 — 658
B. *Remedy for:*
New
creature.......2 Cor. 5:17 — 1145
Conformity to
Christ.........1 John 3:2, 3 — 1251

Imperishable—*enduring, lasting forever*

Resurrected (1 Cor. 15:42, 52,
body ....\ 53 — 1138
Christian's
inheritance.......1 Pet. 1:4 — 1235
Seed of Christian
life..............1 Pet. 1:23 — 1236

Impertinence—*an action or remark inappropriate for the occasion*

Christ rebukes
Peter's ....Mark 8:31-33 — 987

SUBJECT	REFERENCE	PAGE	SUBJECT	REFERENCE	PAGE	SUBJECT	REFERENCE	PAGE

Impetuousness—*acting suddenly with little thought*

Characterized by:
Ill-considered
judgment........Esth. 1:10-22   507
Enraged
disposition.......Gen. 34:25-31   36
Hasty action .....Josh. 22:10-34   237

Import—*to receive from other countries*

Things imported:
Horses ....1 Kin. 10:28   351
Chariots ....2 Chr. 1:17   439
Fish..............Neh. 13:16   503

Importunity in prayer

Need involved.....Luke 11:5-13   1019
Christ's example ..Luke 22:44   1034
Great
intensity of.......Acts 12:5   1085
Results of........Mark 7:24-30   986

See Prayer

Impossibilities—*powerless, weak*

A. *Natural:*
Change one's
color.........Jer. 13:23   720
Hide from
God...........Ps. 139:7-12   607
Change one's
size ....Matt. 6:27   947
Control the
tongue........James 3:7, 8   1229
B. *Spiritual:*
God to sin .....Hab. 1:13   882
God to fail His
promises ......Titus 1:2   1206
Believers to be
lost ....John 10:27-29   1055

Imposter—*a pretender*

A. *Characteristics of:*
Not
believed as....Jer. 40:14-16   746
Speaks
falsely ....Josh. 9:3-14   224
Poses as real...2 Cor. 11:13-15   1149
Much like the
real ....Matt. 7:21-23   947
Deception of, revealed to
prophets .....Acts 13:8-12   1086
B. *Examples of:*
Jannes and
Jambres.......2 Tim. 3:8   1202
Judas..........John 13:18-30   1058
Antichrist......2 Thess. 2:1-4   1189

Impotent—*powerless*

Moab ....Is. 16:14   670

Imprecation—*pronouncing a curse*

God's enemies ....Ps. 55:5-15   570
One's enemies.....Ps. 35:4-8, 26   561
Heretics..........Gal. 1:9   1154
Persecutors ......Jer. 11:18-20   719
Forbidden........Luke 9:54-56   1018

See Curse, cursing

Imprisonment—*physical confinement in jail*

A. *Of Old Testament persons:*
Joseph.........Gen. 39:20   41
Simeon ....Gen. 42:19, 24   44
Samson........Judg. 16:21, 25   260
Jehoiachin....2 Kin. 25:27-29   400
Micaiah.......2 Chr. 18:25, 26   453
Jeremiah ......Jer. 32:2, 8, 12   737
B. *Of New Testament persons:*
John the
Baptist........Mark 6:17-27   984
Apostles......Acts 5:18   1077
Peter ....Acts 12:4   1085
Paul and
Silas ....Acts 16:24   1090
Paul ....Acts 23:10, 18   1098
John..........Rev. 1:9   1268

See Prisoners

Improvement—*a betterment*

Expressed by:
Growth ....1 Pet. 2:2   1236
Addition ....2 Pet. 1:5-11   1243
Press on ....Phil. 3:13-15   1172

Improvidence—*wasting present possession*

Material things....Luke 15:11-13   1025
Spiritual things...Luke 12:16-23   1021
Eternal things....Luke 16:19-31   1026

Impure—*ritually unclean; mixed with foreign elements*

Things impure:
Discharge........Lev. 15:30   115
Hands............Mark 7:2   985
Person...........Eph. 5:5   1165
Sons of Israel ....Lev. 16:16   116
Nations ....Ezra 6:21   480

Impurity (see Unclean)

Imputation—*counting or crediting something to another*

A. *Described as charging:*
Evil to an innocent
person ....Philem. 18   1210
Evil to an evil
person ....Lev. 17:4   117
Good to a good
person ....Ps. 106:30, 31   594
B. *Of Adam's sin to the race:*
Based on the
fall............Gen. 3:1-19   6
Explained
fully ....Rom. 5:12-21   1112
The wider implications
of.............Rom. 8:20-23   1114
C. *Of the believer's sin to Christ:*
Our iniquity laid on
Him...........Is. 53:5, 6   695
Made to be sin
for us........2 Cor. 5:21   1146
Became a curse
for us.........Gal. 3:13   1156
Takes away   (John 1:29   1042
our sins......(Heb. 9:28   1220
D. *Of Christ's righteousness to the believer:*
Negatively
stated........Rom. 4:6-8   1111
Positively
affirmed......Rom. 10:4-10   1116
Explained
graphically....Luke 15:22-24   1025
God justifies the
ungodly......Rom. 5:18, 19   1112
Christ becomes our righteous-
ness..........1 Cor. 1:30   1126
We become the righteousness
of God in
Him...........2 Cor. 5:21   1146
Illustrated by Abraham's
faith ....Rom. 4:3   1111

See Justification

Imrah—*He (God) resists*

Son of Zophah ...1 Chr. 7:36   413

Imri—*eloquent*

1. Son of Bani...1 Chr. 9:4   414
2. Father of
Zaccur......Neh. 3:2   490
3. May be Amariah
in.............Neh. 11:4   500

Inability (see Impossibilities)

Incarnation of Christ

A. *Foreshadowed by:*
Angel.........Josh. 5:13-15   221
Prophecies.....Is. 7:14   663
B. *Described as:*
Becoming
flesh ....John 1:14   1042
Born of
woman........Gal. 4:4   1156

Coming in
flesh ....1 John 4:2   1252
Appearing in
flesh ....1 Tim. 3:16   1195
Our likeness ...Rom. 8:3   1114
      Heb. 2:14   1215
Body ....Heb. 10:5, 10   1220
      1 John 1:1-3   1249
Dying in   (1 Pet. 3:18   1238
flesh ....(1 Pet. 4:1   1238
C. *Purposes of:*
Reveal the
Father ....John 14:8-11   1059
Do God's will ..Heb. 10:5-9   1220
Fulfill
prophecy......Luke 4:17-21   1009
Die for our
sins ....1 Pet. 3:18   1238
Fulfill all righteous-
ness..........Matt. 3:15   943
Reconcile the
world ....2 Cor. 5:18-21   1146
Become our high
priest ....Heb. 7:24-28   1218
Become our
example.......1 Pet. 2:21-23   1237
D. *Importance of:*
Evidence Christ's
deity..........Rom. 9:3-5   1115
Confirm Christ's
resurrection...Acts 2:24-32   1073
Mark of
believers .....1 John 4:1-6   1252

See Human nature of Christ

Incense—*sweet perfume*

A. *Offered:*
By priests.....Lev. 16:12, 13   116
On the altar ..Ex. 30:1-8   85
On day of
atonement ....Lev. 16:12, 13   116
According to strict
formula.......Ex. 30:34-36   86
B. *Illegal offering of:*
Forbidden .....Ex. 30:37, 38   86
Excluded from certain
offerings .....Lev. 5:11   103
Punished   (Lev. 10:1, 2   108
severely......(2 Chr. 26:16-21   460
Among
idolaters ......Is. 65:3   702
C. *Typical of:*
Worship ....Ps. 141:2   608
Prayer ....Rev. 5:8   1271
      Rev. 8:3, 4   1273
Praise ....Mal. 1:11   907
Approved
service........Eph. 5:2   1165
D. *Purposes of:*
Used in holy
oil ....Ex. 30:34-38   86
Used in meal
offerings .....Lev. 2:1, 2, 15   100
Excluded from certain
offerings .....Lev. 5:11   103
Used in the
showbread ....Lev. 24:7   124
Product of
Arabia ....Is. 60:6   700
Presented to
Jesus.........Matt. 2:11   942
Figurative of
worship ....Ps. 141:2   608

Incentives to good works

Reap kindness ....Hos. 10:12   845
Remain ....John 15:16   1060
Reap.............Gal. 6:7-10   1158

Incest—*sexual relations between persons related*

A. *Relations prohibited:*
Same family ...Lev. 18:6-12   118
Grand-
children.......Lev. 18:10   118
Aunts and
uncles.........Lev. 18:12-14   118
In-laws........Lev. 18:15, 16   118

SUBJECT	REFERENCE	PAGE	SUBJECT	REFERENCE	PAGE	SUBJECT	REFERENCE	PAGE

Ish-bosheth—*man of shame*

One of Saul's
sons..............2 Sam. 2:8   310
Made king........2 Sam. 2:8-10   310
Offends Abner ....2 Sam. 3:7-11   311
Slain; but assassins
executed ....2 Sam. 4:1-12   312

Ishhod—*man of majesty*

Manassite.........1 Chr. 7:18   412

Ishi, (I)—*salutary*

1. Son of
Appaim.......1 Chr. 2:31   406
2. Descendant of
Judah.........1 Chr. 4:20   408
3. Simeonite whose sons destroyed
Amalekites....1 Chr. 4:42   409
4. Manassite
leader.........1 Chr. 5:23, 24   409

Ishi, (II)—*my husband*

Symbolic name of
God..............Hos. 2:16, 17   841

Ishiah—*Yahweh will lend*

Son of Izrahiah ...1 Chr. 7:3   412
See Isshiah

Ishijah—*Yahweh will lend*

Son of Harim .....Ezra 10:31   485

Ishma—*desolate*

Man of Judah ....1 Chr. 4:1, 3   407

Ishmael—*God hears*

1. Abram's son by
Hagar........Gen. 16:3, 4, 15   17
Angel foretells his name and
character .....Gen. 16:11-16   17
Circumcised at
13.............Gen. 17:25   18
Mocks at Isaac's
feast.........Gen. 21:8, 9   22
Evidence of fleshly
origin........Gal. 4:22-31   1157
Becomes an
archer ....Gen. 21:20   22
Dwells in
wilderness ....Gen. 21:21   22
Marries an
Egyptian......Gen. 21:21   22
Buries his
father.........Gen. 25:9   26
Dies at age
137.............Gen. 25:17   26
His
generations ...Gen. 25:12-19   26
His descen-
dants ....1 Chr. 1:29-31   405
2. Descendant of
Jonathan......1 Chr. 8:38   413
3. Father of
Zebadiah......2 Chr. 19:11   453
4. Military officer under
Joash ....2 Chr. 23:1-3, 11   456
5. Son of Nethaniah; instigates
murder of
Gedaliah .....2 Kin. 25:22-25   400
6. Priest who divorced his foreign
wife.........Ezra 10:22   484

Ishmaelites—*descendants of Ishmael*

Settle at Havilah ..Gen. 25:17, 18   26
Joseph sold to.....Gen. 37:25-28   39
Sell Joseph to
Potiphar..........Gen. 39:1   41
Wear golden
earrings........Judg. 8:22, 24   252
Become known as
Arabians ....2 Chr. 17:11   452

Ishmaiah—*Yahweh hears*

1. Gibeonite......1 Chr. 12:4   417
2. Tribal chief in
Zebulun......1 Chr. 27:19   431

Ishmerai—*Yahweh keeps*
nite........1 Chr. 8:18   413

Ishod—*man of majesty*

Manassite.........1 Chr. 7:18   412

Ishpah—*firm, strong*

A Benjamite ......1 Chr. 8:16   413

Ishpan—*he will hide*

Son of Shashak ...1 Chr. 8:22, 25   413

Ish-tob—*man of Tob*

Small kingdom of
Aram............2 Sam. 10:6, 8   317
Jephthah seeks asylum
in ....Judg. 11:3, 5   255

Ishuah—*he is equal*

Son of Asher.....Gen. 46:17   48

Ishuai—*man of Yahweh*

1. Son of Asher and
chief..........1 Chr. 7:30   412
2. Son of Saul...1 Sam. 14:49   288

Island—*surrounded by water*

A. Descriptive of:
Coastal land of
Palestine......Is. 20:6   672
Land surrounded by
water.........Is. 23:2   673
Remote
regions........Is. 42:10   687

B. List of:
Caphtor
(Crete?)......Jer. 47:4   751
Clauda.........Acts 27:16   1102
Chios..........Acts 20:15   1095
Coos...........Acts 21:1   1096
Crete..........Acts 27:12   1102
Cyprus ....Acts 11:19   1084
Elishah ....Ezek. 27:7   795
Kittim
(Cyprus) ....Jer. 2:10   710
Melita ....Acts 28:1, 7, 9   1103
Patmos ....Rev. 1:9   1268
Rhodes ....Acts 21:1   1096
Samos ....Acts 20:15   1095
Samothrace.....Acts 16:11   1090
Syracuse.......Acts 28:12   1103
Tyre...........Is. 23:1, 2   673

Ismachiah—*Yahweh will sustain*

Temple overseer ..2 Chr. 31:13   465

Ispah—*to lay bear*

Benjamite.........1 Chr. 8:16   413

Israel—*God strives*

A. Used literally of:
Jacob..........Gen. 32:28   35
Descendants of
Jacob.........Gen. 49:16, 28   51
Ten northern tribes (in contrast
to Judah) .....1 Sam. 11:8   285
Restored nation after
exile ....Ezra 9:1   483

B. Used spiritually of:
Messiah ....Is. 49:3   692
God's redeemed
ones ....Rom. 9:6-13   1115
True church ....Gal. 6:16   1158

Israelites—*descendants of Israel (Jacob)*

A. Brief history of:
Begin as a nation in
Egypt.........Ex. 1:12, 20   56
Afflicted in
Egypt.........Ex. 1:12-22   56
Moses becomes their
leader.........Ex. 3:1-22   58
Saved from
plagues ....Ex. 9:4, 6, 26   64
Expelled from
Egypt.........Ex. 12:29-36   67
Pass through Red
Sea ....Ex. 14:1-31   69
Receive Law at
Sinai.........Ex. 19:1-25   73
Sin at Sinai....Ex. 32:1-35   87

Rebel at
Kadesh ....Num. 13:1-33   148
Wander 40
years.........Num. 14:26-39   150
Cross Jordan ..Josh. 4:1-24   219
Conquer
Canaan ....Josh. 12:1-24   228
Ruled by
judges ....Judg. 2:1-23   245
Samuel becomes
leader.........1 Sam. 7:1-17   281
Seek to have a
king ....1 Sam. 8:1-22   282
Saul chosen
king ....1 Sam. 10:18-27   284
David becomes
king ....2 Sam. 2:1-4   309
Solomon becomes
king ....1 Kin. 1:28-40   338
Kingdom
divided........1 Kin. 12:1-33   353
Israel (northern kingdom)
carried
captive.......2 Kin. 17:5-23   389
Judah (southern kingdom)
carried
captive.......2 Kin. 24:1-20   398
70 years in
exile ....2 Chr. 36:20, 21   471
Return after
exile ....Ezra 1:1-5   475
Nation rejects
Christ.........Matt. 27:20-27   972
Nation   {Luke 21:20-24   1032
destroyed ....{1 Thess. 2:14-16   1184

B. Blessed with:
Great leaders ..Heb. 11:8-40   1221
Inspired
prophets .....1 Pet. 1:10-12   1235
God's oracles ..Rom. 3:2   1110
Priesthood.....Rom. 9:3-5   1115
The Law.......Gal. 3:16-25   1156
Messianic
promises......Acts 3:18-26   1075
Tabernacle.....Heb. 9:1-10   1219
Messiah ......Dan. 9:24-27   833
God's
covenant......Jer. 31:31-33   736
Regathering ...Is. 27:12   676
Jer. 16:15, 16   723

C. Sins of:
Idolatry........Hos. 13:1-4   846
Hypocrisy .....Is. 1:11-14   659
Disobedi-
ence ....Jer. 7:22-28   715
Externalism....Matt. 23:1-33   965
Unbelief.......Rom. 11:1-31   1117
Works—right-
teousness ....Phil. 3:4-9   1172

D. Punishments upon:
Defeat.........Lev. 26:36-38   127
Curses upon....Deut. 28:15-46   204
Captivity .....Judg. 2:13-23   245
Destruction....Luke 19:42-44   1030
Dispersion ....Deut. 4:26-28   182
Blindness .....Rom. 11:25   1117
Forfeiture of
blessings......Acts 13:42-49   1087
Replaced by
Gentiles......Rom. 11:11-20   1117
See Jews

Israel, the religion of

A. History of:
Call of
Abraham......Gen. 12:1-3   14
Canaan
promised.....Gen. 15:18-21   17
Covenant at
Sinai.........Ex. 20   57
Covenant at
Shechem......Josh. 24:1-28   239
Ark brought to
Jerusalem.....2 Sam. 6   313
Dedication of the
Temple........1 Kin. 8:1-66   346
Reform move- {2 Kin. 23:4-14   396
ments........{2 Chr. 29:3-36   462

SUBJECT	REFERENCE	PAGE	SUBJECT	REFERENCE	PAGE	SUBJECT	REFERENCE	PAGE

Destruction of
Jerusalem.....Jer. 6 713
Restoration of the
Law..........Neh. 8; 9 495
B. *Beliefs about God:*
Creator........Gen. 1:1 4
  Ps. 104:24 592
Sustainer of
creation.......Ps. 104:27-30 592
Active in human
affairs........Deut. 26:5-15 202
Omniscient ....Ps. 139:1-6 607
Omnipresent...Jer. 23:23, 24 728
Everlasting ....Ps. 90:2 587
Moral.........Ex. 34:6, 7 89

Issachar—*man of hire*

1. Jacob's fifth
son ....Gen. 30:17, 18 31
2. Tribe of, descendants of Jacob's
fifth son ......Num. 26:23, 24 163
Prophecy
concerning....Gen. 49:14, 15 51
Census at
Sinai.........Num. 1:28, 29 134
On Gerizim ....Deut. 27:12 203
Inheritance
of............Josh. 19:17-23 234
Assists
Deborah ......Judg. 5:15 248
At David's
coronation....1 Chr. 12:32 418
Census in David's
time ....1 Chr. 7:1-5 411
Attended Hezekiah's
Passover......2 Chr. 30:18 464
Prominent person
of............Judg. 10:1 254
3. Doorkeeper....1 Chr. 26:1, 5 429

Isshiah—*Yahweh exists*

1. Descendant of
Issachar ......1 Chr. 7:1, 3 411
Son of
Izrahiah ......1 Chr. 7:3 412
2. Mighty man of
David........1 Chr. 12:1, 6 417
3. Kohathite (1 Chr. 23:20 427
Levite.......(1 Chr. 24:25 428
4. Levite and family
head..........1 Chr. 24:21 428

Italy—*a peninsula of southern Europe*

Soldiers of, in
Caesarea ....Acts 10:1 1083
Jews expelled
from ....Acts 18:2 1092
Paul sails for.....Acts 27:1, 6 1102
Christians in ......Acts 28:14 1103

Itching ears—*descriptive of desire for something exciting*

Characteristic of the last
days..............2 Tim. 4:2, 3 1202

Ithai—*with me (is Yahweh)*

Son of Ribai ......1 Chr. 11:31 416
Also called Ittai...2 Sam. 23:29 332

Ithamar—*island of palms*

Youngest son of
Aaron............Ex. 6:23 61
Consecrated as
priest............Ex. 28:1 82
Duty
entrusted to.....Ex. 38:21 94
Jurisdiction over Gershonites and
Merarites........Num. 4:21-33 138
Founder of Levitical
family............1 Chr. 24:4-6 428

Ithiel—*God is with me*

1. Man addressed by
Agur..........Prov. 30:1 635
2. Benjamite .....Neh. 11:7 500

Ithmah—*bereavement*

Moabite of David's mighty
men.............1 Chr. 11:46 417

Ithnan—*perennial*

Town in south
Judah ....Josh. 15:23 231

Ithra—*excellence*

Israelite (or Ishmaelite); father of
Amasa ....2 Sam. 17:25 325
Called Jether......1 Kin. 2:5, 32 339

Ithran—*excellent*

1. Son of
Dishon........Gen. 36:26 38
2. Son of
Zophah ....1 Chr. 7:37 413
Same as
Jether........1 Chr. 7:38 413

Ithream—*residue of the people*

Son of David.....2 Sam. 3:2-5 311

Ithrite—*pre-eminence*

Family dwelling at Kirjath-
jearim..........1 Chr. 2:53 407
One of David's
guard ....2 Sam. 23:38 333

Itinerary, Israelites in Wilderness

Leave Egypt ......Ex. 12:29-36 67
Cross Red Sea ....Ex. 14:1-31 69
Bitter water
sweetened.......Ex. 15:22-26 70
Manna in
wilderness.......Ex. 16:1-36 71
Water from a
rock............Ex. 17:1-7 72
Defeat of
Amalek.........Ex. 17:8-16 72
At Sinai.........Ex. 19:1-25 73
Depart Sinai ......Num. 10:33, 34 146
Lord sends
quails.........Num. 11:1-35 147
Twelve spies....Num. 13:1-33 148
Rebellion at
Kadesh.........Num. 14:1-45 149
Korah's
rebellion........Num. 16:1-34 152
Aaron's rod ......Num. 17:1-13 154
Moses' sin.......Num. 20:2-13 156
Fiery serpents....Num. 21:4-9 157
Balak and (Num. 22:1—
Balaam..........(24:25 159
Midianites
conquered.......Num. 31:1-24 168
Death of Moses ...Deut. 34:1-8 212
Accession of
Joshua ....Deut. 34:9 212

Ittah-kazin—*time of a judge*

On border of
Zebulun........Josh. 19:13, 16 234

Ittai—*with me (is Yahweh)*

1. One of David's
guard ....2 Sam. 23:23-29 332
2. Native of Gath; one of David's
com-
manders ......2 Sam. 15:18-22 323

Ituraea—*pertaining to Jetur*

Ruled by Philip....Luke 3:1 1007

Ivah—*sky*

City conquered by the
Assyrians.........Is. 37:13 683

Ivory—*the tusks of certain mammals*

Imported from
Tharshish ....1 Kin. 10:22 351
Imported from
Chittim..........Ezek. 27:6, 15 795
Ahab's palace
made of ....1 Kin. 22:39 367
Thrones
made of ....1 Kin. 10:18 351
Beds made of .....Amos 6:4 858
Sign of luxury.....Amos 3:15 857
Figuratively
used.............Song 5:14 652
Descriptive of
wealth ....Ps. 45:8 567

Among Babylon's
trade.............Rev. 18:12 1279

Izhar—*shining*

Son of Kohath ....Ex. 6:18, 21 61
  Num. 3:19 137
Ancestor of the (Num. 3:27 137
Izharites ....(1 Chr. 6:38 410

Izliah—*Yahweh delivers*

Son of Elpaal .....1 Chr. 8:18 413

Izrahiah—*Yahweh will shine*

Chief of
Issachar..........1 Chr. 7:1, 3 411

Izrahite—*descendant of Zerah*

Applied to
Shamhuth........1 Chr. 27:8 430

Izri—*fashioner*

Leader of Levitical
choir.............1 Chr. 25:11 429
Also called Zeri ...1 Chr. 25:3 429

Izziah—*Yahweh sprinkles*

One who divorced his foreign
wife..............Ezra 10:25 484

J

Jaakan, Jakan, Akan

Son of Ezer ....1 Chr. 1:42 405
Also called
Akan...........Gen. 36:27 38
Of Horite origin...Gen. 36:20-27 38
Tribe of, at
Beeroth ....Deut. 10:6 188
Dispossessed by
Edomites.........Deut. 2:12 179
Same as
Benejaakan ......Num. 33:31, 32 171

Jaakobah—*heel catcher*

Simeonite ....1 Chr. 4:36 408

Jaala, Jaalah—*wild she-goat*

Family head of exile
returnees........Ezra 2:56 476
Descendants of Solomon's
servants.........Neh. 7:57, 58 495

Jaalam

Son of Esau.....Gen. 36:5, 18 37

Jaanai—*answerer*

Gadite chief.......1 Chr. 5:12 409

Jaare-oregim—*forests of weavers*

Father of
Elhanan ....2 Sam. 21:19 330
Also called Jair...1 Chr. 20:5 424

Jaasiel—*God makes*

1. One of David's mighty
men...........1 Chr. 11:47 417
2. Son of Abner ...1 Chr. 27:21 431

Jaasu—*Yahweh makes*

Son of Bani; divorced foreign
wife..............Ezra 10:37 485

Jaazaniah—*Yahweh hearkens*

1. Military commander supporting
Gedaliah ......2 Kin. 25:23 400
2. Rechabite
leader.........Jer. 35:3 741
3. Idolatrous Israelite
elder..........Ezek. 8:11 777
4. Son of Azur; seen in Ezekiel's
vision.........Ezek. 11:1 779

Jaaziah—*Yahweh strengthens*

Merarite Levite ..1 Chr. 24:26, 27 428

Jaaziel—*God strengthens*

Levite musician ...1 Chr. 15:18, 20 419

173

SUBJECT	REFERENCE	PAGE	SUBJECT	REFERENCE	PAGE	SUBJECT	REFERENCE	PAGE

Jailor—*one who guards a prison*
At Philippi, converted by
Paul..............Acts 16:19-34   1090

Jair—*he enlightens*
1. Manassite ......(Num. 32:41   170
   warrior........(Deut. 3:14   181
   Conquers towns in
   Gilead ....Num. 32:41   170
2. Eighth judge of
   Israel ....Judg. 10:3-5   254
3. Father of Mordecai, Esther's
   uncle ....Esth. 2:5   508
4. Father of
   Elhanan......1 Chr. 20:5   424
   Called Jaare-
   oregim.......2 Sam. 21:19   330

Jairite
Descendant of Jair, the
Manassite.......2 Sam. 20:26   329

Jairus (Greek form of "*Jair*")
Ruler of the synagogue;
Jesus raises his   (Mark 5:22-24,
daughter ....(35-43   983

Jakeh—*pious*
Father of Agur....Prov. 30:1   635

Jakim—*He (God) raises up*
1. Descendant of
   Aaron.........1 Chr. 24:1, 12   428
2. Benjamite .....1 Chr. 8:19   413

Jalon—*passing the night*
Calebite, son of
Ezra..............1 Chr. 4:17   408

Jambres—*opposer*
Egyptian
magician ....2 Tim. 3:8   1202
See Jannes and Jambres

James—*a form of Jacob*
1. Son of
   Zebedee.......Matt. 4:21   946
   Fisherman.....Matt. 4:21   946
   One of the
   Twelve........Matt. 10:2   950
   In business with
   Peter..........Luke 5:10   1010
   Called
   Boanerges....Mark 3:17   981
   Of fiery
   disposition ....Luke 9:52-55   1018
   Makes a
   contention ....Mark 10:35-45   990
   One of inner
   circle ....Matt. 17:1   959
   Sees the risen
   Lord.........John 21:1, 2   1066
   Awaits the Holy
   Spirit ....Acts 1:13   1072
   Slain by Herod
   Agrippa.......Acts 12:2   1085
2. Son of Alphaeus; one of the
   Twelve.......Matt. 10:3, 4   950
   Identified usually as "the
   less" ....Mark 15:40   998
   Brother of
   Joses........Matt. 27:56   973
3. Son of Joseph and
   Mary.........Matt. 13:55, 56   955
   Lord's
   brother ....Gal. 1:19   1154
   Rejects Christ's
   claim ....Mark 3:21   981
   Becomes a
   believer.......Acts 1:13, 14   1072
   Sees the risen
   Lord ....1 Cor. 15:7   1137
   Becomes moderator of
   Jerusalem
   Council ......Acts 15:13-23   1089
   Paul confers with
   him ....Gal. 2:9, 12   1155
   Wrote an
   epistle ....James 1:1   1228

Brother of
Jude ....Jude 1   1262

James, the Epistle of—*a book of the New Testament*
Trials ....James 1:2-8   1228
Temptation ......James 1:12-18   1228
Doing the word ...James 1:19-25   1228
Faith and works ..James 2:14-26   1229
Patience ....James 5:7-11   1230
Converting the
sinner...........James 5:19, 20   1231

Jamin—*the right hand*
1. Son of
   Simeon ......Gen. 46:10   48
   Family head ...Ex. 6:14, 15   61
2. Man of
   Judah.........1 Chr. 2:27   406
3. Postexilic Levite; interprets the
   law ....Neh. 8:7, 8   496

Jaminites
Descendants of
Jamin ....Num. 26:12   163

Jamlech—*whom He (God) makes king*
Simeonite chief ...1 Chr. 4:34   408

Janai—*answerer*
Gadite chief.......1 Chr. 5:12   409

Jangling—*self-conceited talk against God*
Characteristic of false
teachers..........1 Tim. 1:6, 7   1194
Translated also
"babblings".......1 Tim. 6:20   1197

Jannai—*a form of John*
Ancestor of
Christ............Luke 3:23, 24   1008

Jannes and Jambres
Two Egyptian magicians; oppose
Moses..........2 Tim. 3:8   1202
Compare
account ....Ex. 7:11-22   62

Janoah—*rest; quiet*
1. Town of
   Naphtali ......2 Kin. 15:29   388
2. Border town of
   Ephraim ......Josh. 16:6, 7   232

Janum—*sleep*
Town near
Hebron..........Josh. 15:53   231

Japheth—*widespreading*
One of Noah's three
sons..............Gen. 5:32   9
Saved in the ark ..1 Pet. 3:20   1238
Receives Messianic
blessing ....Gen. 9:20-27   12
His descendants occupy Asia Minor
and Europe......Gen. 10:2-5   13

Japhia—*may He (God) cause to shine forth*
1. King of Lachish; slain by
   Joshua........Josh. 10:3-27   225
2. One of David's
   sons..........2 Sam. 5:13-15   313
3. Border town of
   Zebulun.......Josh. 19:10, 12   234

Japhlet—*He (God) will deliver*
Asherite family....1 Chr. 7:32, 33   412

Japhleti
Unidentified tribe on Joseph's
boundary.........Josh. 16:1, 3   232

Japho—*beautiful*
Hebrew form of
Joppa ....Josh. 19:46   235

Jarah—*honeycomb*
Descendant of King
Saul..............1 Chr. 9:42   415
Called
Jehoaddah.......1 Chr. 8:36   413

Jareb—*he will contend*
Figurative description of Assyrian
king..............Hos. 5:13   843

Jared—*descent*
Father of Enoch...Gen. 5:15-20   9
Ancestor of
Noah.............1 Chr. 1:2   404
Ancestor of
Christ...........Luke 3:37   1008

Jaresiah—*Yahweh nourishes*
Benjamite head ...1 Chr. 8:27   413

Jarha
Egyptian slave; marries master's
daughter.........1 Chr. 2:34-41   406

Jarib—*he contends*
1. Head of a Simeonite
   family.........1 Chr. 4:24   408
   Called Jachin ...Gen. 46:10   48
2. Man sent to search for
   Levites........Ezra 8:16, 17   482
3. Priest who divorced his foreign
   wife...........Ezra 10:18   484

Jarmuth—*height*
1. Royal city of
   Canaan ......Josh. 10:3   225
   King of, slain by
   Joshua.......Josh. 10:3-27   225
   Assigned to
   Judah.........Josh. 15:20, 35   231
   Inhabited after
   exile ....Neh. 11:29   500
2. Town in Issachar assigned to
   the Levites....Josh. 21:28, 29   237
   Called
   Ramoth.......1 Chr. 6:73   411
   Called
   Remeth.......Josh. 19:21   234

Jaroah—*new moon*
Gadite chief.......1 Chr. 5:14   409

Jashen—*sleeping*
Sons of, in David's
bodyguard.......2 Sam. 23:32   332
Called Hashem ...1 Chr. 11:34   416

Jasher—*upright*
Book of, quoted...Josh. 10:13   226

Jashobeam—*let the people return*
1. Chief of David's mighty
   men...........1 Chr. 11:11   416
   Becomes military
   captain........1 Chr. 27:2, 3   430
2. Benjamite
   warrior ....1 Chr. 12:1, 2, 6   417

Jashub—*he returns*
1. Issachar's
   son ....1 Chr. 7:1   411
   Head of
   family........Num. 26:24   163
   Called Job .....Gen. 46:13   48
2. Son of Bani; divorced his
   foreign wife...Ezra 10:29   484

Jashubi-lehem—*bread returns*
A man of Judah...1 Chr. 4:22   408

Jashubites
Descendants of
Jashub ....Num. 26:24   163

Jason (Greek equivalent for "*Joshua*" or "*Jesus*")
Welcomes Paul at
Thessalonica .....Acts 17:5-9   1091
Described as Paul's
kinsman.........Rom. 16:21   1122

SUBJECT   REFERENCE   PAGE | SUBJECT   REFERENCE   PAGE | SUBJECT   REFERENCE   PAGE

Jasper—a precious stone (quartz)

Set in high priest's
breastplate ......Ex. 28:20   83

Descriptive of:
Tyre's
adornments ......Ezek. 28:12, 13   797
Heavenly vision...Rev. 4:3   1271

Jathniel—God bestows

Korahite
porters ....1 Chr. 26:1, 2   429

Jattir—pre-eminence

Town of Judah....Josh. 15:48   231
Assigned to Aaron's
children ....Josh. 21:13, 14   236
David sends   (1 Sam. 30:26,
spoil to..........(27   305

Javan—Greece (Ionia)

Son of Japheth....Gen. 10:2, 4   13
Descendants of, to receive
good news........Is. 66:19, 20   704
Trade with Tyre...Ezek. 27:13, 19   795
King of, in Daniel's
visions ....Dan. 8:21   832
Conflict with......Zech. 9:13   901

Javelin—a light, short spear

Used by Saul......1 Sam. 18:10   293

Jaw—jawbone

Used figuratively of:
Power over the (Job 29:17   535
wicked ....(Prov. 30:14   635
God's
sovereignty.......Is. 30:28   679
Human trial......Hos. 11:4   845

Jawbone—cheekbone

Weapon used by
Samson ....Judg. 15:15-19   259

Jazer—helpful

Town east of Jordan near
Gilead............2 Sam. 24:5   333
Amorites driven
from ....Num. 21:32   158
Assigned to Gad ..Josh. 13:24, 25   229
Becomes Levitical
city ....Josh. 21:34, 39   237
Taken by
Moabites.........Is. 16:8, 9   670
Desired by sons of Reuben and
Gad ....Num. 32:1-5   169

Jaziz—shining

Shepherd over David's
flocks..........1 Chr. 27:31   431

Jealous, jealousy

A. Kinds of:
Divine.........Ex. 20:5   75
Marital ....Num. 5:12-31   140
Motherly ......Gen. 30:1   31
Brotherly ......Gen. 37:4-28   39
Sectional .....2 Sam. 19:41-43   328
National ......Judg. 8:1-3   251

B. Good causes of:
Zeal for the
Lord ....Num. 25:11   162
Concern over
Christians.....2 Cor. 11:2   1149

C. Evil causes of:
Favoritism.....Gen. 37:3-11   39
Regard for
names ....1 Cor. 3:3-5   1127
Carnality .....2 Cor. 12:20   1151
Amos 3:14-16   857

D. Described as:
Implacable.....Prov. 6:34, 35   619
Cruel..........Song 8:6   653
Burning ......Deut. 29:20   206
'ly........2 Cor. 11:2   1149

Jearim—forests

Mountain 10 miles west of
Jerusalem ....Josh. 15:10   231

Jeaterai—steadfast

Descendant of
Levi.............1 Chr. 6:21   410
Also called
Ethni.............1 Chr. 6:41   410

Jeberechiah—Yahweh blesses

Father of Zechariah (not the
prophet)..........Is. 8:2   664

Jebus—trodden under foot

Same as
Jerusalem ....1 Chr. 11:4   416
Entry denied to
David ....1 Chr. 11:5   416
Levite came
near.............Judg. 19:1, 11   262
See Zion; Sion

Jebusi, Jebusite—trodden under foot

Assigned to
Benjamin........Josh. 18:28   234
Same as
Jerusalem ....Josh. 18:28   234
On the border of
Judah ....Josh. 15:8   230

Jebusites

Descendants of
Canaan..........Gen. 10:15, 16   13
Mountain tribe....Num. 13:29   149
Land of, promised to
Israel............Gen. 15:18-21   17
Adoni-zedek, their king, raises
confederacy .....Josh. 10:1-5   225
Their king killed by
Joshua ....Josh. 10:23-26   226
Join fight against
Joshua ....Josh. 11:1-5   227
Assigned to
Benjamin........Josh. 18:28   234
Royal city not
taken ....Judg. 1:21   244
Taken by David ...2 Sam. 5:6-8   313
Old inhabitants
remain ....2 Sam. 24:16-25   333
Become slaves ...1 Kin. 9:20, 21   350

Jecoliah—Yahweh is able

Mother of King
Azariah ....2 Kin. 15:2   387
Called Jechiliah ..2 Chr. 26:3   460

Jeconiah—Yahweh establishes

Variant form of
Jehoiachin.......1 Chr. 3:16, 17   407
Abbreviated to
Coniah ....Jer. 22:24, 28   727
Son of Josiah .....Matt. 1:11   941
See Jehoiachin

Jedaiah—Yahweh has been kind

1. Priestly
family.........1 Chr. 24:7   428
2. Head of the
priests ....Neh. 12:6   501
3. Another head
priest ....Neh. 12:7, 21   501
4. Simeonite......1 Chr. 4:37   408
5. Postexilic
worker........Neh. 3:10   490
6. One who brings gifts for the
Temple........Zech. 6:10, 14   899

Jediael—known of God

1. Son of Benjamin and family
head ....1 Chr. 7:6, 10, 11   412
2. Manassite; joins
David...........1 Chr. 12:20   417
3. One of David's mighty
men ....1 Chr. 11:45   417
4. Korahite
porter..........1 Chr. 26:1, 2   429

Jedidah—beloved

Mother of King
Josiah............2 Kin. 22:1   395

Jedidiah—beloved of Yahweh

Name given to Solomon by
Nathan...........2 Sam. 12:24, 25   319

Jeduthun—praising

1. Levite musician appointed by
David...........1 Chr. 16:41, 42   421
Heads a family of
musicians.....2 Chr. 5:12   442
Name appears in Psalm
titles..........Ps. 39; 62; 77   564
Family officiates after
Exile...........Neh. 11:17   500
Possibly same as
Ethan..........1 Chr. 15:17, 19   419
2. Father of
Obed-edom....1 Chr. 16:38   421

Jegar-sahadutha—heap of testimony

Name given by Laban to memorial
stones...........Gen. 31:46, 47   34

Jehaleleel—God will flash light

1. Man of Judah and family
head ....1 Chr. 4:16   408
2. Merarite
Levite.........2 Chr. 29:12   462

Jehdeiah—Yahweh will make glad

1. Kohathite
Levite.........1 Chr. 24:20   428
2. Meronothite in charge of
David's
asses..........1 Chr. 27:30   431

Jehezekel—God will strengthen

Descendant of
Aaron............1 Chr. 24:1, 16   428

Jehiah—Yahweh lives

Doorkeeper ....1 Chr. 15:24   420

Jehiel—God lives

1. Levite
musician......1 Chr. 15:18, 20   419
2. Gershonite and family
head ....1 Chr. 23:8   427
3. Son of
Hachmoni....1 Chr. 27:32   431
4. Son of King Jehosh-
aphat ....2 Chr. 21:2, 4   455
5. Hemanite
Levite.........2 Chr. 29:14   463
6. Overseer in Hezekiah's
reign..........2 Chr. 31:13   465
7. Official of the
Temple.........2 Chr. 35:8   470
8. Father of Obadiah, a returned
exile...........Ezra 8:9   482
9. Father of
Shechaniah ...Ezra 10:2   483
10. Postexilic
priest ....Ezra 10:21   484
11. Postexilic
priest ....Ezra 10:26   484

Jehieli

A Levite family ...1 Chr. 26:21, 22   430

Jehizkiah—Yahweh strengthens

Ephraimite chief ..2 Chr. 28:12   461

Jehoadah—whom Yahweh adorns

Descendant of
Saul............1 Chr. 8:36   413
Also called
Jarah............1 Chr. 9:42   415

Jehoaddan—Yahweh delights

Mother of
Amaziah ....2 Kin. 14:2   386

Jehoahaz—Yahweh has taken hold of

1. Son and successor of Jehu, king
of Israel.......2 Kin. 10:35   383

SUBJECT   REFERENCE   PAGE | SUBJECT   REFERENCE   PAGE | SUBJECT   REFERENCE   PAGE

Seeks the Lord in
defeat........2 Kin. 13:2-9   385
2. Son and successor of Josiah,
king of
Judah.........2 Kin. 23:30-34 398
Called
Shallum.......1 Chr. 3:15   407
3. Another form of Ahaziah,
youngest son of King
Joram........2 Chr. 21:17   456

Jehoash (see Joash)

Jehohanan, Johanan—*Yahweh is gracious*
1. Korahite
Levite........1 Chr. 26:3   429
2. Captain under Jehosh-
aphat........2 Chr. 17:10, 15 452
3. Father of Ishmael, Jehoiada's
supporter.....2 Chr. 23:1   456
4. Priestly family
head.........Neh. 12:13   501
5. Priest who divorced his
wife..........Ezra 10:28   484
6. Son of Tobiah the
Ammonite....Neh. 6:17, 18   494
7. Postexilic
singer........Neh. 12:42   502

Jehoiachin—*Yahweh establishes*
Son of Jehoiakim; next to the last
king of Judah....2 Kin. 24:8 398
Deported to
Babylon......2 Kin. 24:8-16 398
Liberated by Evil-
merodach........Jer. 52:31-34 759
See Jeconiah

Jehoiada—*Yahweh knows*
1. Aaronite supporter of
David.........1 Chr. 12:27   418
2. Father of Benaiah, one of
David's
officers......2 Sam. 8:18   316
3. Son of Benaiah; one of David's
counselors....1 Chr. 27:34   431
4. High priest...2 Kin. 11:9 383
Proclaims Joash
king..........2 Kin. 11:4-16 383
Institutes a
covenant......2 Kin. 11:17-21 383
Instructs
Joash.........2 Kin. 12:2   384
Commanded to repair the
Temple........2 Kin. 12:3-16 384
Receives honorable
burial........2 Chr. 24:15, 16 458
5. Deposed
priest........Jer. 29:26   734
6. Postexilic
returnee.....Neh. 3:6   490

Jehoiakim—*Yahweh raises up*
Son of King
Josiah........2 Kin. 23:34, 35 398
Made Pharaoh's
official......2 Kin. 23:34, 36 398
Wicked king.....2 Chr. 36:5, 8 471
Burns Jeremiah's
roll.........Jer. 36:1-32   741
Becomes Nebuchadnezzar's
servant.......Dan. 24:1   398
Punished by the
Lord.........2 Kin. 24:2-4 398
Taken by Nebuchad-
nezzar.........2 Chr. 36:5, 6 471
Returns to
idolatry.......2 Chr. 36:5, 8 471
Treats Jeremiah with
contempt.......Jer. 36:21-28 742
Kills a true
prophet........Jer. 26:20-23 731
Bound in fetters..2 Chr. 36:6 471
Buried as an ass...Jer. 22:18, 19 727
Curse on.........Jer. 36:30, 31 742

Jehoiarib—*Yahweh contends*
Descendant of
Aaron...........1 Chr. 24:1, 6, 7 428

Founder of an order of
priests.........1 Chr. 9:10, 13 414

Jehonadab—*Yahweh is liberal*
A Rechabite......2 Kin. 10:15 382
See Jonadab

Jehonathan—*Yahweh has given*
1. Levite
teacher.......2 Chr. 17:8   451
2. Postexilic
priest........Neh. 12:1, 18 501

Jehoram—*Yahweh is high*
1. King of Judah; son and
successor of Jehosh-
aphat.........1 Kin. 22:50   367
Called Joram..2 Kin. 8:21, 23,
24   380
Reigns eight
years.........2 Kin. 8:16, 17 379
Marries Athaliah, who leads
him astray....2 Kin. 8:18, 19 379
Killed his
brothers......2 Chr. 21:2, 4, 13 455
Edom revolts
from.........2 Kin. 8:20-22 380
Elijah predicts his terrible
end..........2 Chr. 21:12-15 455
Nations fight
against.......2 Chr. 21:16, 17 456
Smitten by the Lord; dies in
disgrace......2 Chr. 21:18-20 456
2. King of Israel; son of
Ahab..........2 Kin. 1:17   372
Called Joram..2 Kin. 8:16, 25,
28   379
Reigns 12
years.........2 Kin. 3:1   373
Puts away
Baal..........2 Kin. 3:2   373
Joins Jehoshaphat against
Moabites......2 Kin. 3:1-27 373
Naaman sent to, for
cure..........2 Kin. 5:1-27 376
Informed by Elijah of Syria's
plans.........2 Kin. 6:8-23 377
Wounded in war with
Syria.........2 Kin. 8:28, 29 380
3. Levite
teacher.......2 Chr. 17:8   451

Jehoshabeath—*Yahweh is an oath*
Safeguards Joash from
Athaliah.......2 Chr. 22:11 456

Jehoshaphat—*Yahweh has judged*
1. King of Judah; son and
successor of
Asa...........1 Kin. 15:24   357
Reigns 25
years.........1 Kin. 22:42   367
Fortifies his
kingdom......2 Chr. 17:2   451
Institutes
reforms.......2 Chr. 17:3   451
Inaugurates public
instruction...2 Chr. 17:7-9 451
Honored and
respected.....2 Chr. 17:10-19 452
Joins Ahab against Ramoth-
gilead........1 Kin. 22:1-36 365
Rebuked by a
prophet.......2 Chr. 19:2, 3 453
Develops legal
system........2 Chr. 19:4-11 453
By faith defeats invading
forces........2 Chr. 20:1-30 454
Navy of,
destroyed.....2 Chr. 20:35-37 455
Provision for his
children......2 Chr. 21:2, 3 455
Death of......2 Chr. 21:1   455
Ancestor of
Christ........Matt. 1:8   941
2. Son of
Ahilud.......2 Sam. 8:16   316
Recorder under David and
Solomon......2 Sam. 20:24   329

3. Father of King
Jehu.........2 Kin. 9:2   380

Jehoshaphat, valley of
Described as a place of
judgment......Joel 3:2, 12   852

Jehosheba—*Yahweh is an oath*
King Joram's
daughter......2 Kin. 11:2   383

Jehovah—*title of God*
Defined........Ex. 6:3-5   61
Early known.....Gen. 4:26   8
Usually rendered LORD in
O.T..........Ex. 17:14   72
Used in certain
combinations...Gen. 22:14   23
Often found in names (e.g.,
Jehoshaphat,
Elijah).......1 Kin. 15:24   357
Applied to Christ {Is. 40:3   685
as Lord...... {Matt. 3:3   943

Jehovah-jireh—*Yahweh will provide*
Names used by
Abraham........Gen. 22:14   23

Jehovah-nissi—*Yahweh is my banner*
Name used by Moses for
memorial........Ex. 17:15, 16 72

Jehovah-shalom—*Yahweh is peace*
Name used by Gideon for
significant visit...Judg. 6:23, 24 249

Jehozabad—*Yahweh has bestowed*
1. Son of Obed-
edom.........1 Chr. 26:4   429
2. Son of a Moabitess; assassinates
Joash........2 Kin. 12:20, 21 384
Put to death..2 Chr. 25:3   459
3. Military captain under King
Jehosh-
aphat........2 Chr. 17:18   452

Jehozadak—*Yahweh has justified*
Son of Seraiah, the high
priest........1 Chr. 6:14   410
His father killed...2 Kin. 25:18-21 399
Carried captive to
Babylon.......1 Chr. 6:15   410
Father of Joshua the high
priest........Hag. 1:1, 12, 14 892

Jehu—*Yahweh is He*
1. Benjamite
warrior.......1 Chr. 12:3   417
2. Prophet and son of
Hanani.......1 Kin. 16:1   358
Denounces
Baasha.......1 Kin. 16:2-4, 7 358
Rebukes Jehosh-
aphat........2 Chr. 19:2, 3 453
Writes Jehoshaphat's
biography.....2 Chr. 20:34   455
3. Descendant of
Judah........1 Chr. 2:38   406
4. Simeonite......1 Chr. 4:35 408
5. Grandson of
Nimshi.......2 Kin. 9:2   380
Commander under
Ahab.........2 Kin. 9:25   381
Divinely commissioned to
destroy Ahab's
house........1 Kin. 19:16, 17 362
Carries out orders with
zeal.........2 Kin. 9:11-37 380
Killed Ahab's
sons.........2 Kin. 10:1-17 381
Destroys worshipers of
Baal.........2 Kin. 10:18-28 382
Serves the Lord
outwardly....2 Kin. 10:29-31 382

Jehubbah—*he hides*
Asherite.......1 Chr. 7:34   413

SUBJECT   REFERENCE   PAGE | SUBJECT   REFERENCE   PAGE | SUBJECT   REFERENCE   PAGE

Jehucal—*Yahweh is able*

Son of Shelemiah; sent by
Zedekiah to
Jeremiah ....Jer. 37:3   743
Also called Jucal ..Jer. 38:1   744

Jehud—*praise*

Town of Dan......Josh. 19:40, 45   235

Jehudi—*a man of Judah; a Jew*

Reads Jere-   (Jer. 36:14, 21,
miah's roll.......(23   742

Jehudijah—*a Jewess*

One of Mered's two wives; should
be rendered "the
Jewess" ....1 Chr. 4:18   408

Jeiel—*God snatches away*

1. Ancestor of
   Saul ....1 Chr. 9:35-39   415
2. One of David's mighty
   men...........1 Chr. 11:44   417
   Reubenite
   prince..........1 Chr. 5:6, 7   409
3. Levite
   musician.......1 Chr. 16:5   420
4. Porter ....1 Chr. 15:18, 21   419
   May be the same
   as 3...........1 Chr. 16:5   420
   Called Jehiah ..1 Chr. 15:24   420
5. Inspired
   Levite.........2 Chr. 20:14   454
6. Levite chief...2 Chr. 35:9   470
7. Scribe ....2 Chr. 26:11   460
8. Temple
   Levite.........2 Chr. 29:13   462
9. One who divorced his foreign
   wife..........Ezra 10:19, 43   484

Jekabzeel—*God will gather*

Town in Judah....Neh. 11:25   500
Called Kabzeel....Josh. 15:21   231
Home of Benaiah, David's
friend ....2 Sam. 23:20   332

Jekameam—*people will rise*

Kohathite Levite .1 Chr. 23:19   427

Jekamiah—*Yahweh will rise*

1. Son of
   Shallum.......1 Chr. 2:41   406
2. Son of
   Jeconiah ......1 Chr. 3:17, 18   407

Jekuthiel—*God will support*

Man of Judah .....1 Chr. 4:18   408

Jemima—*dove*

Job's daughter ....Job 42:14   543

Jemuel—*day of God*

Son of Simeon ...Gen. 46:10   48
Called Nemuel ....Num. 26:12   163

Jephthah—*he will open*

Gilead's son by a
harlot ....Judg. 11:1   255
Flees to Tob; becomes a
leader ....Judg. 11:2-11   255
Cites historical precedents against
invading
Ammonites......Judg. 11:12-27   255
Makes a vow before
battle ....Judg. 11:28-31   256
Defeats
Ammonites......Judg. 11:32, 33   256
Fulfills vow ....Judg. 11:34-40   256
Defeats quarrelsome
Ephraimites .....Judg. 12:1-7   256
Cited by Samuel .1 Sam. 12:11   285
In faith's
chapter..........Heb. 11:32   1222

Jephunneh—*it will be prepared*

1. Caleb's
   father.........Num. 13:6   149
   .....erite ....1 Chr. 7:38   413

Jerah—*moon*

Son of Joktan; probably an
Arabian tribe.....Gen. 10:26   13
                   1 Chr. 1:20   405

Jerahmeel—*may God have compassion*

1. Great-grandson of
   Judah..........1 Chr. 2:9, 25-41   406
2. Son of Kish, not Saul's
   father..........1 Chr. 24:29   428
3. King Jehoiakim's
   officer..........Jer. 36:26   742

Jerahmeelites

Raided by David ..1 Sam. 27:10   302

Jered—*descent*

A descendant of
Judah ....1 Chr. 4:18   408
See Jared

Jeremai—*high*

One who divorced his foreign
wife..............Ezra 10:19, 33   484

Jeremiah (I)—*Yahweh establishes*

A. *Life of:*
Son of Hilkiah; a
Benjamite.....Jer. 1:1   709
Native of
Anathoth .....Jer. 1:1   709
Called before
birth ....Jer. 1:4-10   709
Prophet under kings Josiah,
Jehoiakim, and
Zedekiah......Jer. 1:2, 3   709
Imprisoned by
Pashur........Jer. 20:1-6   725
Writes his prophecy; Jehoiakim
burns it ....Jer. 36:1-26   741
Prophecy
rewritten......Jer. 36:27-32   742
Accused of
desertion.......Jer. 37:1-16   743
Released by
Zedekiah......Jer. 37:17-21   743
Cast into a
dungeon ......Jer. 38:1-6   744
Saved by an
Ethiopian .....Jer. 38:7-28   744
Set free by Nebuchad-
nezzar ....Jer. 39:11-14   745
Given liberty of choice by
Nebuzar-
adan ....Jer. 40:1-6   746
Forced to flee to
Egypt ....Jer. 43:5-7   748
Last prophecies at Tahpanhes,
Egypt ....Jer. 43:8-13   748

B. *Characteristics of:*
Forbidden to
marry.........Jer. 16:1-13   722
Has internal
conflicts ......Jer. 20:7-18   726
Has incurable
pain...........Jer. 15:18   722
Motives misunder-
stood ....Jer. 37:12-14   743
Tells captives to build in
Babylon.......Jer. 29:4-9   733
Denounces false prophets in
Babylon.......Jer. 29:20-32   734
Rebukes
idolatry ....Jer. 7:9-21   715

C. *Prophecies of, foretell:*
Egypt's fall ....Jer. 43:8-13   748
70 years of
captivity ......2 Chr. 36:21   471
Restoration to
land...........Jer. 16:14-18   723
New
covenant.....Jer. 31:31-34   736
Herod's
massacre.....Jer. 31:15   736

D. *Teachings of:*
God's
sovereignty ...Jer. 18:5-10   724

God's
knowledge ....Jer. 17:5-10   723
Shame of
idolatry ....Jer. 10:14, 15   718
Spirituality of worship,
etc............Jer. 3:16, 17   711
Need of regen-
eration........Jer. 9:26   717
Man's sinful
nature ....Jer. 2:22   710
Gospel
salvation......Jer. 23:5, 6   728
Call of the
Gentiles.......Jer. 3:17-19   711

Jeremiah (II)

1. Benjamite
   warrior ....1 Chr. 12:4   417
2. Gadite
   warrior ....1 Chr. 12:10   417
3. Another Gadite
   warrior ....1 Chr. 12:13   417
4. Manassite
   head..........1 Chr. 5:23, 24   409
5. Father of Hamutal, a wife of
   Josiah........2 Kin. 23:31   398
6. Father of
   Jaazaniah.....Jer. 35:3   741
7. Postexilic
   priest ....Neh. 12:1, 7   501
   Head of a priestly
   line ....Neh. 12:12   501
8. Priest who signs the
   covenant......Neh. 10:2   499

Jeremiah, the Book of—*a book of the Old Testament*

Jeremiah's call ...Jer. 1:1-19   709
Jeremiah's life.....Jer. 26:1—45:5   731
Israel's sin against
God............Jer. 2:1—10:25   709
Against false
prophets.........Jer. 23:9-40   728
Against foreign
nations..........Jer. 46:1—51:64   750
The Messianic
king.............Jer. 23:1-8   728

Jeremoth—*elevation*

1. Son of
   Becher........1 Chr. 7:8   412
2. Benjamite ....1 Chr. 8:14   413
3. Merarite
   Levite.........1 Chr. 23:23   427
4. Musician of
   David.........1 Chr. 25:22   429
5. Ruler of
   Naphtali......1 Chr. 27:19   431
6. One who divorced his foreign
   wife...........Ezra 10:26   484
7. Another who divorced his
   foreign wife...Ezra 10:27   484
8. Spelled
   Jerimoth......1 Chr. 24:30   428

Jeriah, Jerijah—*Yahweh sees*

Kohathite Levite ..1 Chr. 23:19, 23   427
Hebronite chief ...1 Chr. 26:31   430

Jeribai—*Yahweh contends*

One of David's
warriors.........1 Chr. 11:46   417

Jericho—*place of fragrance*

City near the
Jordan..........Num. 22:1   159
Viewed by
Moses...........Deut. 34:1-3   212
Called the city of palm
trees ....Deut. 34:3   212
Viewed by spies...Josh. 2:1   218
Home of Rahab the
harlot ....Heb. 11:31   1222
Scene of Joshua's
vision...........Josh. 5:13-15   221
Destroyed by
Joshua ....Heb. 11:30   1222
Curse of
rebuilding of .....Josh. 6:26   222

SUBJECT	REFERENCE	PAGE
Assigned to		
Benjamin	Josh. 16:1, 7	232
Moabites retake	Judg. 3:12, 13	246
David's envoys tarry		
here	2 Sam. 10:4, 5	317
Rebuilt by Hiel	1 Kin. 16:34	359
Visited by Elijah and		
Elisha	2 Kin. 2:4-22	372
Zedekiah captured		
here	2 Kin. 25:5	399
Reinhabited after		
exile	Ezra 2:34	476
People of, help rebuild		
Jerusalem	Neh. 3:2	490
Blind men of, healed by		
Jesus	Matt. 20:29-34	962
Home of		
Zacchaeus	Luke 19:1-10	1029

Jeriel—*God sees*

Son of Tola	1 Chr. 7:2	411

Jerimoth

1. Son of Bela	1 Chr. 7:7	412
2. Warrior of		
David	1 Chr. 12:5	417
3. Musician of		
David	1 Chr. 25:4	429
4. Son of David	2 Chr. 11:18	448
5. Levite		
overseer	2 Chr. 31:13	465
6. Son of		
Becher	1 Chr. 7:8	412
7. Ruler of		
Naphtali	1 Chr. 27:19	431
8. Spelled		
Jeremoth	1 Chr. 23:23	427

See Jeremoth

Jerioth—*tent curtains*

One of Caleb's		
wives	1 Chr. 2:18	406

Jeroboam—*may the people increase*

1. Son of Nebat	1 Kin. 11:26	352
Rebels against		
Solomon	1 Kin. 11:26-28	352
Ahijah's prophecy		
concerning	1 Kin. 11:29-39	352
Flees to		
Egypt	1 Kin. 11:40	352
Recalled,	{ 1 Kin. 12:1-3, 12,	
made king	{ 20	353
Perverts the true		
religion	1 Kin. 12:25-33	354
Casts Levites		
out	2 Chr. 11:14	448
Rebuked by a man of		
God	1 Kin. 13:1-10	354
Leads people		
astray	1 Kin. 13:33, 34	355
His wife consults		
Ahijah	1 Kin. 14:1-18	355
War with		
Abijam	1 Kin. 15:7	357
Reigns 22		
years	1 Kin. 14:20	356
Struck by the		
Lord	2 Chr. 13:20	449
2. Jeroboam II; king of		
Israel	2 Kin. 13:13	385
Successor of Joash		
(Jehoash)	2 Kin. 14:16, 23	386
Conquers Hamath and		
Damascus	2 Kin. 14:25-28	386
Reigns wickedly 41		
years	2 Kin. 14:23, 24	386
Denounced by		
Amos	Amos 7:7-13	859
Death of	2 Kin. 14:29	387

Jeroham—*he is pitied*

1. Grandfather of		
Samuel	1 Sam. 1:1	276
2. Benjamite	1 Chr. 9:8	414
3. Father of Benjamite chief		
men	1 Chr. 8:27	413
4. Benjamite of		
Gedor	1 Chr. 12:7	417

SUBJECT	REFERENCE	PAGE
5. **Father of**		
Adaiah	1 Chr. 9:12	414
6. **Danite chief's**		
father	1 Chr. 27:22	431
7. **Military**		
captain	2 Chr. 23:1	456

Jerubbaal—*Baal contends*

Name given to Gideon for		
destroying Baal's		
altar	Judg. 6:32	250

Jerubbesheth—*let shame contend*

Father of		
Abimelech	2 Sam. 11:21	318

Jeruel—*founded by God*

Wilderness west of the Dead		
Sea	2 Chr. 20:16	454

Jerusalem—*possession of peace*

A. *Names applied to:*

City of God	Ps. 46:4	567
City of David	2 Sam. 5:6, 7	313
City of		
Judah	2 Chr. 25:28	460
Zion	Ps. 48:12	568
Jebusi	Josh. 18:28	234
Holy city	Matt. 4:5	944
Faithful city	Is. 1:21, 26	659
City of righteous-		
ness	Is. 1:26	659
City of truth	Zech. 8:3	899
City of the great		
King	Ps. 48:2	567
Salem	Gen. 14:18	16

B. *History of:*

Originally		
Salem	Gen. 14:18	16
Occupied by		
Jebusite	Josh. 15:8	230
King of, defeated by		
Joshua	Josh. 10:5-23	226
Assigned to		
Benjamin	Josh. 18:28	234
Attacked by		
Judah	Judg. 1:8	244
Jebusites		
remain in	Judg. 1:21	244
David brings Goliath's		
head to	1 Sam. 17:54	292
Conquered by		
David	2 Sam. 5:6-8	313
Name		
changed	2 Sam. 5:7-9	313
Ark		
brought to	2 Sam. 6:12-17	314
Saved from		
destruction	2 Sam. 24:16	333
Solomon builds Temple		
here	1 Kin. 5:5-8	343
Suffers in		
war	1 Kin. 14:25-27	356
Plundered by		
Israel	2 Kin. 14:13, 14	386
Besieged by		
Syrians	Is. 7:1	663
Earthquake		
damages	Amos 1:1	855
Miraculously		
saved	2 Kin. 19:31-36	393
Ruled by		
Egypt	2 Kin. 23:33-35	398
Besieged by		
Babylon	2 Kin. 24:10, 11	398
Captured by		
Babylon	Jer. 39:1-8	745
Desolate 70		
years	Jer. 25:11, 12	730
Temple		
rebuilt in	Ezra 1:1-4	475
Exiles		
return to	Ezra 2:1-70	475
Work on,		
hindered	Ezra 5:1-17	479
Walls of,		
dedicated	Neh. 12:27-47	501
Christ:		
Enters		
as king	Matt. 21:9, 10	963
Laments for	Matt. 23:37	966

SUBJECT	REFERENCE	PAGE
Crucified at	Luke 9:31	1017
Weeps over	Luke 19:41, 42	1030
Predicts destruc-		
tion	Luke 19:43, 44	1030
Gospel		
preached at	Luke 24:47	1037
Many miracles performed		
in	John 4:45	1046
Church begins		
here	Acts 2:1-47	1073
Christians of,		
persecuted	Acts 4:1-30	1075
Stephen		
martyred at	Acts 7:1-60	1078
First Christian council held		
here	Acts 15:1-29	1088
Paul:		
Visits	Acts 20:16	1095
Arrested in	Acts 21:30-36	1096
Taken from	Acts 23:12-33	1098

C. *Prophecies concerning:*

Destruction by		
Babylon	Jer. 20:5	725
Utter ruin	Jer. 26:18	731
Rebuilding by		
Cyrus	Is. 44:26-28	689
Christ's entry		
into	Zech. 9:9	901
Gospel proclaimed		
from	Is. 2:3	659
Perilous		
times	Matt. 24:1-22	966
Being under		
Gentiles	Luke 21:24	1032

D. *Described:*

Physically—	{ Ps. 48:12, 13	568
strong	{ Ps. 125:2	604
Morally—	{ Is. 1:1-16	658
corrupt	{ Jer. 5:1-5	712
Spiritually—the		
redeemed	Gal. 4:26-30	1157
Prophetically—New		
Jerusalem	Rev. 21:1-27	1281

See Zion; Sion

Jerusha—*possessed (married)*

Wife of King		
Uzziah	2 Kin. 15:33	388
Called Jerushah	2 Chr. 27:1	461

Jeshaiah—*Yahweh saves*

1. Musician of		
David	1 Chr. 25:3	429
2. Grandson of		
Zerubbabel	1 Chr. 3:21	407
3. Levite in David's		
reign	1 Chr. 26:25	430
4. Son of Athaliah; returns from		
Babylon	Ezra 8:7	482
5. Levite who returns with		
Ezra	Ezra 8:19	482
6. Benjamite	Neh. 11:7	500

Jeshanah—*old*

City of Ephraim taken by		
Abijah	2 Chr. 13:19	449

Jesharelah—*upright toward God*

Levite musician	1 Chr. 25:14	429
Called Asarelah	1 Chr. 25:2	429

Jeshebeab—*may the father tarry (live)*

Descendant of		
Aaron	1 Chr. 24:13	428

Jesher—*uprightness*

Caleb's son	1 Chr. 2:18	406

Jeshimon—*waste*

Wilderness west of the		
Dead Sea	1 Sam. 23:19, 24	298

Jeshishai—*aged*

Gadite	1 Chr. 5:14	409

Jeshohaiah—*humbled by Yahweh*

Leader in		
Simeon	1 Chr. 4:36	408

SUBJECT　REFERENCE　PAGE

Kedesh—continued
Home of
Barak........Judg. 4:6　247
People of, carried
captive.......2 Kin. 15:29　388

Keeper—*one who watches over, or guards*
Guardian of:
Sheep.............Gen. 4:2　7
Brother ....Gen. 4:9　8
Wardrobe........2 Kin. 22:14　396
Gate..............Neh. 3:29　491
Door.............1 Chr. 9:21　414
Women......Esth. 2:3, 8　508
Prison..........Acts 16:27　1090

Keeping—*holding or observing something firmly*
A. *Christian objects of:*
Christ's command-
ments........John 14:15-23　1059
God's com-
mandments ...1 John 5:2　1253
God's Word....Rev. 22:7, 9　1283
Unity of the
Spirit ....Eph. 4:3　1164
Faith ....2 Tim. 4:7　1202
Purity ....1 Tim. 5:22　1196
Oneself.....1 John 5:18　1253
In God's love ..Jude 21　1263
B. *Manner of, by God's:*
Power......John 10:28, 29　1055
Name........John 17:11, 12　1062
C. *Promises respecting:*
Provision......Ps. 121:3-8　603
Preservation...John 17:11, 12　1062
Power.........Rev. 2:26　1270
Purity ....Rev. 16:15　1278
See Heart

Kehelathah—*assembly*
Israelite camp.....Num. 33:22, 23　171

Keilah—*enclosed*
Town of Judah....Josh. 15:21, 44　231
Rescued from Philistines by
David ....1 Sam. 23:1-5　297
Betrays David.....1 Sam. 23:6-12　298
David escapes
from ....1 Sam. 23:13　298
Reoccupied after the
exile.............Neh. 3:17　491

Kelaiah—*Yahweh is light*
Levite who
divorced　{ Ezra 10:18, 19,
foreign wife .....{　23 　484
See Kelita

Kelita—*dwarf*
Levite who divorced foreign
wife..............Ezra 10:23　484
Explains the
Law..............Neh. 8:7　496
Called Kelaiah ...Ezra 10:23　484

Kemuel—*congregation of God*
1. Son of Nahor; father of six
sons ....Gen. 22:20, 21　23
2. Ephraimite
prince.........Num. 34:24　173
3. Levite in David's
time ....1 Chr. 27:17　431

Kenan—*fixed*
Descendant of
Adam ....1 Chr. 1:2　404
See Cainan

Kenath—*possession*
City of Gilead near Bozrah taken
by Nobah ...Num. 32:40, 42　170
Reconquered by Geshur and
Aram.............1 Chr. 2:23　406

Kenaz—*side, flank*
1. Descendant of
Esau......Gen. 36:10, 11　38

SUBJECT　REFERENCE　PAGE

2. Edomite
duke...........Gen. 36:42　38
3. Caleb's brother; father of
Othniel ....Josh. 15:17　231
Family called
Kenezites .....Num. 32:12　170
4. Grandson of
Caleb ....1 Chr. 4:15　408

Kenezite, Kenizzite
1. Canaanite tribe whose land is
promised to Abraham's
seed.........Gen. 15:19　17
2. Title applied to
Caleb ....Num. 32:12　170
Probably related to Kenaz, the
Edomite.......Gen. 36:11-42　38

Kenites—*pertaining to coppersmiths*
Canaanite tribe whose land is
promised to Abraham's
seed..............Gen. 15:19　17
Subjects of Balaam's
prophecy........Num. 24:20-22　161
Mix with
Midianites.......Num. 10:29　146
Member of, becomes Israel's
guide..........Num. 10:29-32　146
Settle with
Judahites........Judg. 1:16　244
Heber separates from
Kenites.........Judg. 4:11　247
Heber's wife (Jael) slays
Sisera ....Judg. 4:17-22　247
Spared by Saul in war with
Amalekites ......1 Sam. 15:6　289
David shows
friendship to.....1 Sam. 30:29　305
Recorded among Judahites;
ancestors of
Rechabites ......1 Chr. 2:55　407

Kerchief—*a covering for the head*
Worn by idolatrous women of
Israel.............Ezek. 13:18, 21　781

Keren-happuch—*horn of eye paint*
Daughter of Job...Job 42:14　543

Kerioth—*cities*
1. Town in south
Judah........Josh. 15:25　231
2. City of Moab ..Amos 2:2　856

Keros—*bent*
Head of a Nethinim family
returning
from exile ....Ezra 2:44　476

Kettle—*pot*
Large cooking
vessel ....1 Sam. 2:14　277
Same word rendered
"pots".........Ps. 81:6　583

Keturah—*incense*
Abraham's second
wife...........Gen. 25:1　26
Sons of:
Listed............Gen. 25:1, 2　26
Given gifts and sent
away.........Gen. 25:6　26

Key—*a small instrument for unlocking doors*
Used literally for:
Doors...........Judg. 3:25　246
Used figuratively of:
Prophetic authority of
Christ............Is. 22:22　673
Present authority of
Christ............Rev. 1:18　1269
Plenary authority of Christ's
apostles ....Matt. 16:19　958
Teachers ....Luke 11:52　1021

Kezia—*cassia*
Daughter of Job...Job 42:14　543

SUBJECT　REFERENCE　PAGE

Keziz—*cut off*
City of
Benjamin.......Josh. 18:21　234

Kibroth-hattaavah—*graves of lust*
Burial site of Israelites slain by
God ....Num. 11:33-35　148

Kibzaim—*double heap*
Ephraimite city assigned to
Kohathite
Levites..........Josh. 21:22　236
Called Jokmeam ..1 Chr. 6:68　411
See Jokmeam

Kid—*a young goat*
A. *Used for:*
Food ....Gen. 27:9　28
Payment.......Gen. 38:17-23　40
Sacrifices......Lev. 4:23　102
Offerings .....Judg. 13:15, 19　257
Festive
occasions ....Luke 15:29　1026
B. *Figurative of:*
Weakness ....Judg. 14:6　258
Peacefulness...Is. 11:6　667
See Goat

Kidnapping
A. *Punishment for:*
Death ....Ex. 21:16　76
B. *Examples of:*
Joseph.........Gen. 37:23-28　39
Daughters of
Shiloh........Judg. 21:20-23　266
Joash..........2 Kin. 11:1-12　383
Jeremiah .....Jer. 43:1-8　748

Kidneys
Select internal organs of an
animal ....Ex. 29:13, 22　84
Translated
"wheat".........Deut. 32:14　210

Kidron—*dark, turbid*
Valley (dry except for winter
torrents) near
Jerusalem ....John 18:1　1062
East boundary of
Jerusalem ....Jer. 31:40　737
Crossed by David and
Christ ....John 18:1　1062
Used for burials ..Jer. 26:23　732
Site of dumping of
idols..............2 Chr. 29:16　463

Killing—*causing life to cease*
A. *Reasons for:*
Take another's
wife..........Gen. 12:12　15
Take another's
property ......1 Kin. 21:19　365
Take
revenge......Gen. 27:42　29
Satisfy anger ..Num. 22:29　159
Hate..........John 5:18　1047
Execute God's { Num. 31:2,
wrath ...... {　16-19　168
Destroy
people ....Ex. 1:16　57
Seize a
throne ....2 Kin. 15:25　388
Put down
rebellion .....1 Kin. 12:27　354
Fulfill
prophecy......1 Kin. 16:1-11　358
Fear of
punishment ...Acts 16:27　1090
Get rid of an unwanted
person ....Matt. 21:38　964
B. *Reasons against:*
God's Law.....Ex. 20:13　75
Regard for
Life..........Gen. 37:21　39
One's 　　{ 1 Sam. 24:10　299
position ....{ 1 Sam. 11　276

SUBJECT	REFERENCE	PAGE	SUBJECT	REFERENCE	PAGE	SUBJECT	REFERENCE	PAGE
Friendly	Ex. 1:8	56	Under Hezekiah, help to cleanse Temple	2 Chr. 29:12, 15	462	Deceives Jacob in marriage arrangement	Gen. 29:15-30	30
Intuitive	1 Sam. 22:22	297				Agrees to Jacob's business arrangement	Gen. 30:25-43	32
Intellectual	John 7:15, 28	1050	C. *Sins of:*					
Saving	John 17:3	1062	Korah (of Izhar) leads rebellion	{Num. 16:1-35	152	Changes attitude toward Jacob	Gen. 31:1-9	32
Spiritual	1 Cor. 2:14	1127		{Jude 11	1262			
Revealed	Luke 10:22	1019				Pursues after fleeing Jacob	Gen. 31:21-25	33
B. *Sources of:*			**Kolaiah**—*voice of Yahweh*			Rebukes Jacob	Gen. 31:26-30	33
God	Ps. 94:10	589	1. Father of the false prophet Ahab	Jer. 29:21-23	734	Rebuked by Jacob	Gen. 31:31-42	33
Nature	Ps. 19:1, 2	554	2. Postexilic Benjamite family	Neh. 11:7	500	Makes covenant with Jacob	Gen. 31:43-55	34
Scriptures	2 Tim. 3:15	1202				2. City in the wilderness	Deut. 1:1	178
Doing God's will	John 7:17	1050	**Koph**					
C. *Believer's attitude toward:*			Letter of the Hebrew alphabet	Ps. 119:145-152	602	**Labor**—*physical or mental effort*		
Not to be puffed up	1 Cor. 8:1	1131	**Korah**—*baldness*			A. *Physical:*		
Should grow in	2 Pet. 3:18	1245	1. Son of Esau	Gen. 36:5, 14, 18	37	*Nature of:*		
Should add to	2 Pet. 1:5	1243	2. Son of Eliphaz and grandson of Esau	Gen. 36:16	38	As old as creation	Gen. 2:5, 15	5
Not to be forgetful of	2 Pet. 3:17	1245	3. Calebite	1 Chr. 2:42, 43	406	Ordained by God	Gen. 3:17-19	7
Accept our limitations of	1 Cor. 13:8-12	1135	4. Son of Izhar the Kohathite	Ex. 6:21, 24	61	One of the commandments	Ex. 20:9	75
Be filled with	Phil. 1:9	1170	Leads a rebellion against Moses and Aaron	Num. 16:1-3	152	From morning until night	Ps. 104:23	592
D. *Christ's, of:*			Warned by Moses	Num. 16:4-27	152	With the hands	1 Thess. 4:11	1185
God	Luke 10:22	1019	Supernaturally destroyed	Num. 16:28-35	153	To life's end	Ps. 90:10	587
Man's nature	John 2:24, 25	1044	Sons of, not destroyed	Num. 26:9-11	162	Without God, vanity	Eccl. 2:11	641
Man's thoughts	Matt. 9:4	949	Sons of, porters	1 Chr. 26:19	430	Shrinking from, denounced	2 Thess. 3:10	1190
Believers	John 10:14, 27	1054	**Korahites**			*Benefits of:*		
Things future	2 Pet. 1:14	1243	Descendants of Korah	Ex. 6:24	61	Profit	Prov. 14:23	624
All things	Col. 2:3	1177	Some become:			Happiness	Ps. 128:2	604
E. *Attitude of sinful men toward:*			David's warriors	1 Chr. 12:6	417	Proclaim gospel	1 Thess. 2:9	1184
Turn from	Rom. 1:21	1109	Servants	1 Chr. 9:19-31	414	Supply of other's	{Acts 20:35	1095
Ignorant of	1 Cor. 1:21	1126	Musicians	1 Chr. 6:22-32	410	needs	{Eph. 4:28	1165
Raised up against	2 Cor. 10:5	1149	A maschil for	Ps. 42 (Title)	565	Restful sleep	Eccl. 5:12	643
Did not acknowledge God	Rom. 1:28	1109	**Kore**—*a partridge*			Double honor	1 Tim. 5:17	1196
Never able to come to	2 Tim. 3:7	1201	1. Korahite Levite	1 Chr. 9:19	414	Eternal life	John 6:27	1049
F. *Value of:*			2. Porter of the eastern gate	2 Chr. 31:14	465	Not in vain	1 Cor. 15:58	1138
Superior to gold	Prov. 8:10	620	**Koz**—*thorn*				Phil. 2:16	1171
Increases strength	Prov. 24:5	631	Father of Anub	1 Chr. 4:8	408	B. *Spiritual:*		
Keeps from destruction	Is. 5:13	661	See Hakkoz			*Characteristics of:*		
Insures stability	Is. 33:6	680	**Kushaiah**—*bow of Yahweh (that is, rainbow)*			Commissioned by Christ	John 4:38	1046
Koa			Merarite Levite musician	1 Chr. 15:17	419	Accepted by few	Matt. 9:37, 38	950
People described as enemies of Jerusalem	Ezek. 23:23	792	Called Kishi	1 Chr. 6:44	410	Working with God	1 Cor. 3:9	1127
Kohath—*assembly*						By God's grace	1 Cor. 15:10	1137
Second son of Levi	Gen. 46:8, 11	48	**L**			Result of faith	1 Tim. 4:10	1196
Goes with Levi to Egypt	Gen. 46:11	48	**Laadah**—*festival*			Characterized by love	1 Thess. 1:3	1183
Brother of Jochebed, mother of Aaron and Moses	Ex. 6:16-20	61	Judahite	1 Chr. 4:21	408	Done in prayer	Col. 4:12	1179
Dies at age 133	Ex. 6:18	61	**Laadan**			Subject to discouragement	{Is. 49:4	692
Kohathites—*descendants of Kohath*			1. Son of Gershon, the son of Levi	1 Chr. 23:7-9	427		{Gal. 4:11	1156
A. *History of:*			Called Libni	1 Chr. 6:17	410	Interrupted by Satan	1 Thess. 3:5	1184
Originate in Levi's son (Kohath)	Gen. 46:11	48	2. Ephraimite	1 Chr. 7:26	412	See Work, the Christian's		
Divided into 4 groups (Amram, Izhar, Hebron, Uzziel)	Num. 3:19, 27	137	**Laban**—*white*			C. *Problems:*		
Numbering of	Num. 3:27, 28	137	1. Son of Bethuel	Gen. 24:24, 29	24	Inspired by opposition	Ezra 4:1-6	478
Duties assigned to	Num. 4:15-20	138	Brother of Rebekah	Gen. 24:15, 29	24	Complaint over wages	Matt. 20:1-16	962
Cities assigned to	Josh. 21:4-11	236	Father of Leah and Rachel	Gen. 29:16	30	Mistreatment of employees	Matt. 21:33-35	964
B. *Privileges of:*			Chooses Rebekah for Isaac	Gen. 24:29-60	25	Characteristics of last days	James 5:1-6	1230
Aaron and Moses	Ex. 6:20	61	Entertains Jacob	Gen. 29:1-14	30	**Labor** (childbirth)		
Special charge of sacred instruments	Num. 4:15-20	138				A. *Of a woman's, described as:*		
Temple music by Heman the Kohathite	1 Chr. 6:31-38	410				Fearful	Ps. 48:6	568
Under Jehoshaphat, lead in praise	2 Chr. 20:19	454				Painful	Is. 13:8	668
						Hazardous	Gen. 35:16-19	37

SUBJECT	REFERENCE	PAGE

Lo-ruhamah—*not pitied*

Symbolic name of Hosea's
daughter ....Hos. 1:6 — 840

Loss, spiritual

A. *Kinds of:*
One's self.....Luke 9:24, 25 — 1017
Reward.......1 Cor. 3:13-15 — 1127
Heaven.......Luke 16:19-31 — 1026

B. *Causes of:*
Love of this
life...........Luke 17:33 — 1027
Sin ....Ps. 107:17, 34 — 595

Lost—*not found*

Descriptive of men as:
Separated from
God............Luke 15:24, 32 — 1025
Unregenerated....Matt. 15:24 — 957
Objects of Christ's
mission........Luke 15:4-6 — 1025
Blinded by
Satan.........2 Cor. 4:3, 4 — 1144
Defiled...........Titus 1:15, 16 — 1206

Lot—*covering*

A. *Life of:*
Abraham's
nephew.......Gen. 11:27-31 — 14
Goes with Abraham to
Canaan......Gen. 12:5 — 15
Accompanies Abraham to
Egypt.....Gen. 13:1 — 15
Settles in
Sodom......Gen. 13:5-13 — 15
Rescued by
Abraham.....Gen. 14:12-16 — 16
Befriends
angels.......Gen. 19:1-14 — 19
Saved from Sodom's
destruction...Gen. 19:15, 22 — 20
His wife, disobedient,
becomes pillar of
salt ....Gen. 19:15, 17,
26 — 20
His daughters commit incest
with ....Gen. 19:30-38 — 20
Unwilling father of
Moabites and
Ammonites ...Gen. 19:37, 38 — 21

B. *Character of:*
Makes selfish
choice ....Gen. 13:5-13 — 15
Lacks moral
stability......Gen. 19:6-10 — 20
Loses moral
influence......Gen. 19:14, 20 — 20
Still "vexed" by
Sodomites....2 Pet. 2:7, 8 — 1243

Lotan—*a covering*

Tribe of Horites (Gen. 36:20, 29 — 38
in Mt. Seir......(1 Chr. 1:38, 39 — 405

Lot(s)—*a means of deciding doubtful
matters*

A. *Characteristic of:*
Preceded by
prayer ......Acts 1:23-26 — 1073
With divine
sanction .....Num. 26:55 — 164
Considered
final ....Num. 26:56 — 164
Used also by the
ungodly.......Matt. 27:35 — 972

B. *Used for:*
Selection of
scapegoat.....Lev. 16:8 — 116
Detection of a
criminal......Josh. 7:14-18 — 222
Selection of
warriors.......Judg. 20:9, 10 — 264
Choice of a
king ....1 Sam. 10:19-21 — 284
Deciding priestly
rotation.......Luke 1:9 — 1004

Lot's wife

Disobedient, becomes pillar of
salt.............Gen. 19:26 — 20
Event to be
remembered.....Luke 17:32 — 1027

Love, Christian

A. *Toward God:*
First command-
ment..........Matt. 22:37, 38 — 965
With all the
heart..........Matt. 22:37 — 965
More important than
ritual ....Mark 12:31-33 — 993
Gives
boldness ......1 John 4:17-19 — 1252

B. *Toward Christ:*
Sign of true
faith ....John 8:42 — 1052
Manifested in (John 14:15, 21,
obedience....(23 — 1059
Leads to
service........2 Cor. 5:14 — 1145

C. *Toward others:*
Second
command ....Matt. 22:37-39 — 965
Commanded by
Christ.........John 13:34 — 1059
Described in
detail ....1 Cor. 13:1-13 — 1135

Love of Christ, the

A. *Objects of:*
Father.........John 14:31 — 1060
Believers.......Gal. 2:20 — 1155
Church ....Eph. 5:2, 25 — 1165

B. *Described as:*
Knowing ......Eph. 3:19 — 1163
Personal......Gal. 2:20 — 1155
Conquering....Rom. 8:37 — 1115
Unbreakable...Rom. 8:35 — 1115
Intimate......John 14:21 — 1060
Imitative .....1 John 3:16 — 1251
Like the
Father's.....John 15:9 — 1060
Sacrificial......Gal. 2:20 — 1155

C. *Expressions of:*
In taking our
nature ......Heb. 2:16-18 — 1215
In dying for
us.............John 15:13 — 1060

Love of God, the

A. *Objects of:*
Christ ....John 3:35 — 1045
Christians .....2 Thess. 2:16 — 1189
Mankind.......Titus 3:4 — 1207
Cheerful
giver..........2 Cor. 9:7 — 1148

B. *Described as:*
Great..........Eph. 2:4 — 1162
Everlasting ...Jer. 31:3 — 735
Sacrificial......Rom. 5:8 — 1112

C. *As seen in believers':*
Hearts.........Rom. 5:5 — 1112
Regen-
eration........Eph. 2:4, 5 — 1162
Love...........1 John 4:7-12 — 1252
Faith ....1 John 4:16 — 1252
Security ....2 Thess. 3:5 — 1190
Daily life .....1 John 2:15-17 — 1250
Obedience .....1 John 2:5 — 1250
Without fear...1 John 4:17-19 — 1252
Glorification ...1 John 3:1, 2 — 1251

Love, physical

Isaac and
Rebekah ....Gen. 24:67 — 26
Jacob and
Rachel ....Gen. 29:11-30 — 30
Boaz and Ruth....Ruth 2:4-15 — 270
Samson and
Delilah ....Judg. 16:4, 15 — 259

Lovingkindness—*gentle and steadfast
mercy*

Attitude of believers, to:
Expect............Ps. 17:7 — 553
Ps. 36:10 — 562
Rejoice in........Ps. 63:3 — 573
Ps. 69:16 — 576

Loyalty—*fidelity to a person or cause*

A. *Kinds of:*
People.........Acts 25:7-11 — 1100
Relatives .....Esth. 2:21-23 — 508
King...........1 Sam. 24:6-10 — 299
Cause ....2 Sam. 11:9-11 — 318
Oath...........2 Sam. 21:7 — 330

B. *Signs of:*
General
obedience.....Rom. 13:1, 2 — 1119
Prayer for
rulers ....Ezra 6:10 — 480
Hatred of
disloyalty.....Josh. 22:9-20 — 237

Lucifer—*light-bearer*

Name applied to
Satan ....Is. 14:12 — 669
Allusion to
elsewhere ....Luke 10:18 — 1018

Lucius—*of light*

1. Prophet and teacher at
Antioch........Acts 13:1 — 1086
2. Paul's companion in
Corinth ......Rom. 16:21 — 1122

Lucre—*gain; money*

Priests guilty of ...1 Sam. 8:3 — 282
Elders must
avoid............1 Tim. 3:2, 3 — 1195
Deacons must
shun ....1 Tim. 3:8 — 1195
Sign of false
teachers.........Titus 1:11 — 1206

Lud, Ludim (plural)

1. Lud, a people descending from
Shem........1 Chr. 1:17 — 405
2. Ludim, a people descending
from Mizraim
(Egypt) ....Gen. 10:13 — 13
Mentioned as men of
war..........Ezek. 27:10 — 795

Luhith—*of tablets or planks*

Moabite town.....Is. 15:5 — 669

Luke—*another name for Lucius*

"The beloved
physician".......Col. 4:14 — 1179
Paul's last
companion ....2 Tim. 4:11 — 1202

Luke, the Gospel of—*a book of the
New Testament*

The
annunciation.....Luke 1:26-56 — 1004
John the Baptist ..Luke 3:1-22 — 1007
The temptation ...Luke 4:1-13 — 1008
Public ministry
begins..........Luke 4:15 — 1009
The disciples
chosen ....Luke 6:12-19 — 1011
The disciple's (Luke 10:25—
instructions ....(13:21 — 1019
The Jerusalem (Luke 19:28—
ministry.........(21:38 — 1030
The Last Supper ..Luke 22:1-38 — 1033
The (Luke 22:39—
Crucifixion ......(23:56 — 1034
The
Resurrection .....Luke 24:1-53 — 1036

Lukewarm—*neither hot nor cold*

Descriptive of
Laodicea ....Rev. 3:14-16 — 1270

Lunatic—*an insane person*

David acts as .....1 Sam. 21:13-15 — 297

200

SUBJECT	REFERENCE	PAGE	SUBJECT	REFERENCE	PAGE	SUBJECT	REFERENCE	PAGE

Nebuchadnezzar
inflicted as ......Dan. 4:31-36 — 827
Christ heals......Matt. 4:24 — 944
Christ declared....John 10:20 — 1055
Paul called.......Acts 26:24 — 1101

See Madness

Lust—*evil desire*
A. *Origin of, in:*
Satan.........1 John 3:8-12 — 1251
Heart.........Matt. 15:19 — 957
Flesh.......James 1:14, 15 — 1228
World ....2 Pet. 1:4 — 1243

B. *Described as:*
Deceitful ......Eph. 4:22 — 1165
Enticing....James 1:14, 15 — 1228
Hurtful .....1 Tim. 6:9 — 1197
Numerous ....2 Tim. 3:6 — 1201

C. *Among the unregenerate, they:*
Live and walk
in..........Eph. 2:3 — 1162
Are punished
with ....Rom. 1:24-32 — 1109

D. *Among false teachers, they:*
Walk after.....2 Pet. 2:10-22 — 1244
Will prevail in the last
days ....2 Pet. 3:3 — 1244
Are received because
of............2 Tim. 4:3, 4 — 1202

E. *Among Christians:*
Once lived in . .Eph. 2:3 — 1162
Consider it
dead ....Col. 3:5 — 1178
Deny ....Titus 2:12 — 1207
Flee from .....2 Tim. 2:22 — 1201
Not carry
out ....Gal. 5:16 — 1158

Luxuries
A. *Characteristic of:*
Egypt.........Heb. 11:24-27 — 1222
Tyre..........Ezek. 27:1-27 — 795
Ancient
Babylon......Dan. 4:30 — 827
Israel.........Amos 6:1-7 — 858
Persia ....Esth. 1:3-11 — 507
Harlot
Babylon......Rev. 18:10-13 — 1279

B. *Productive of:*
Temptation ....Josh. 7:20, 21 — 223
Physical
weakness .....Dan. 1:8, 10-16 — 822
Moral decay ...Nah. 3:1-19 — 879
Spiritual
decay ....Rev. 3:14-17 — 1270

Luz—*almond tree*
1. Ancient Canaanite
town..........Gen. 28:19 — 30
Called
Bethel.........Gen. 35:6 — 37
2. Hittite town ...Judg. 1:23-26 — 244

Lycaonia—*a rugged, inland district of Asia Minor*
Paul preaches in three of its
cities.............Acts 14:6, 11 — 1087

Lycia—*a province of Asia Minor*
Paul:
Visits Patara, a city
of ....Acts 21:1, 2 — 1096
Lands at Myra, a city
of ....Acts 27:5, 6 — 1102

Lydia—*from Lud*
1. Woman of Thyatira;
Paul's first
European {Acts 16:14, 15,
convert ......{ 40 — 1090
2. District of Asia Minor
containing Ephesus, Smyrna,
Thyatira, and
Sardis.........Rev. 1:11 — 1269

Lying (see Liars)

Lysanias—*ending sadness*
Tetrarch of
Abilene..........Luke 3:1 — 1007

Lysias, Claudius
Roman captain who rescues
Paul..............Acts 23:10 — 1098
Listens to Paul's
nephew ....Acts 23:16-22 — 1098
Sends Paul to
Felix...........Acts 23:23-31 — 1099
Felix awaits arrival
of ....Acts 24:22 — 1100

Lystra—*a city of Lycaonia*
Visited by Paul....Acts 14:6, 21 — 1087
Lame man healed
here..............Acts 14:8-10 — 1088
People of, attempt to worship Paul
and Barnabas.....Acts 14:11-18 — 1088
Paul stoned here ..2 Tim. 3:11 — 1202
Home of
Timothy.........Acts 16:1, 2 — 1089

M

Maacah, Maachah—*oppression*
1. Daughter of
Nahor.........Gen. 22:24 — 23
2. Small Syrian kingdom near Mt.
Hermon.......Deut. 3:14 — 181
Not possessed by
Israel ....Josh. 13:13 — 229
Called Syria-
maachah......1 Chr. 19:6, 7 — 423
3. Machir's wife ..1 Chr. 7:15, 16 — 412
4. One of Caleb's
concubines....1 Chr. 2:48 — 407
5. Father of
Shephatiah...1 Chr. 27:16 — 431
6. Ancestress of {1 Chr. 8:29 — 413
King Saul....{1 Chr. 9:35 — 415
7. One of David's
warriors......1 Chr. 11:43 — 417
8. Father of Achish, king of
Gath..........1 Kin. 2:39 — 340
9. David's wife and mother of
Absalom ......2 Sam. 3:3 — 311
10. Wife of Rehoboam; mother of
King Abijah..2 Chr. 11:18-21 — 448
Makes idol, is deposed as
queen-
mother........1 Kin. 15:13 — 357

Maachathites—*inhabitants of Maachah*
Not conquered by
Israel..........Josh. 13:13 — 229
Among Israel's
warriors.........2 Sam. 23:34 — 332
See Maacah

Maadai—*ornament of Yahweh*
Postexilic Jew; divorced his foreign
wife..............Ezra 10:34 — 485

Maadiah
Priest who returns from Babylon
with
Zerubbabel.......Neh. 12:5, 7 — 501
Same as Moadiah
in ....Neh. 12:17 — 501

Maai—*compassionate*
Postexilic
trumpeter ....Neh. 12:35, 36 — 501

Maaleh-acrabbim—*steep*
Ascent south of the Dead
Sea..............Josh. 15:3 — 230

Maarath—*barren place*
Town of Judah....Josh. 15:1, 59 — 230

Maaseiah—*work of Yahweh*
1. Levite musician during David's
reign............1 Chr. 15:16, 18 — 419
2. Levite captain under
Jehoiada......2 Chr. 23:1 — 456
3. Official during King Uzziah's
reign..........2 Chr. 26:11 — 460
4. Son of Ahaz, slain by
Zichri.........2 Chr. 28:7 — 461
5. Governor of Jerusalem during
King Josiah's
reign..........2 Chr. 34:1, 8 — 468
6. Ancestor of
Baruch........Jer. 32:12 — 737
7. Father of the false prophet
Zedekiah.....Jer. 29:21 — 734
8. Father of Zephaniah the
priest ....Jer. 21:1 — 726
9. Temple
doorkeeper....Jer. 35:4 — 741
10. Judahite postexilic
Jew...........Neh. 11:5 — 500
11. Benjamite ancestor of a
postexilic
Jew...........Neh. 11:7 — 500
12, 13, 14. Three
priests who
divorced
their foreign {Ezra 10:18, 21,
wives ....{ 22 — 484
15. Layman who divorced his
foreign wife...Ezra 10:30 — 485
16. Representative who signs the
covenant......Neh. 10:1, 25 — 499
17. One who stood by
Ezra ....Neh. 8:4 — 496
18. Levite who explains the
Law...........Neh. 8:7 — 496
19. Priest who takes part in
dedication
services.......Neh. 12:41 — 502
20. Another participating
priest ....Neh. 12:42 — 502
21. Father or ancestor of
Azariah.......Neh. 3:23 — 491

Maasiai—*work of Yahweh*
Priest of Immer's
family...........1 Chr. 9:12 — 414

Maath—*to be small*
Ancestor of
Christ...........Luke 3:26 — 1008

Maaz—*anger*
Judahite ....1 Chr. 2:27 — 406

Maaziah—*Yahweh is a refuge*
1. Descendant of Aaron; heads a
course of
priests ....1 Chr. 24:1-18 — 428
2. One who signs the
covenant......Neh. 10:1, 8 — 499

Macedonia—*Greece (northern)*
A. *In Old Testament prophecy:*
Called the kingdom of
Grecia ....Dan. 11:2 — 834
Brazen part of
Nebuchadnezzar's
image.........Dan. 2:32, 39 — 824
Described as a leopard with
four heads ....Dan. 7:6, 17 — 830
Described as a {Dan. 8:5, 21 — 831
"he" goat ....{Dan. 11:4 — 834

B. *In New Testament missions:*
Man of, appeals
to..............Acts 16:9, 10 — 1090
Paul preaches in,
at Philippi, {Acts 16:10—
etc...........{ 17:14 — 1090
Paul's troubles
in.............2 Cor. 7:5 — 1147
Churches of,
very {Rom. 15:26 — 1121
generous.....{2 Cor. 8:1-5 — 1147

Machbanai—*clad with a cloak*
One of David's mighty
men..............1 Chr. 12:13 — 417

SUBJECT   REFERENCE   PAGE | SUBJECT   REFERENCE   PAGE | SUBJECT   REFERENCE   PAGE

Machbenah—*lump*
Son of Sheva......1 Chr. 2:49   407

Machi
Father of the Gadite
spy...............Num. 13:15   149

Machir—*sold*
1. Manasseh's only
son ....Gen. 50:23   52
Founder of the family of
Machirites ....Num. 26:29   163
Conqueror of
Gilead ....Num. 32:39, 40   170
Name used of Manasseh
tribe ....Judg. 5:14   248
2. Son of
Ammiel .....2 Sam. 9:4, 5   316
Provides food for
David........2 Sam. 17:27-29   325

Machnadebai—*gift of the noble one*
Son of Bani; divorced foreign
wife..............Ezra 10:34, 40   485

Machpelah—*double*
Field containing a cave; bought by
Abraham.......Gen. 23:9-18   23
Sarah and Abraham buried
here...............Gen. 23:19; 25:9,
      10   24
Isaac, Rebekah, Leah, and Jacob
buried here.......Gen. 49:29-31   51

Madai—*middle*
Third son of Japheth; ancestor of
the Medes.......Gen. 10:2   13

Made—*something brought into being*
A. *Why Christ was made for us:*
Sin ....2 Cor. 5:21   1146
In our
likeness.......Phil. 2:7   1171
High priest ....Heb. 6:20   1218
B. *What Christians are made by
Him:*
Righteous .....2 Cor. 5:21   1146
Heirs ....Titus 3:7   1207

Madmannah—*dunghill*
Town in south
Judah ....Josh. 15:20, 31   231
Son of Shaaph ...1 Chr. 2:49   407

Madmen—*dunghill*
Moabite town.....Jer. 48:2   751

Madmenah—*dunghill or dungheap*
Town near
Jerusalem ....Is. 10:31   667

Madness—*emotional or mental
derangement*
A. *Kinds of:*
Extreme
jealousy.......1 Sam. 18:8-11   293
Extreme rage ..Luke 6:11   1011
B. *Causes of:*
Disobedience to God's
Laws.........Deut. 28:28   204
Judgment
sent by   {Dan. 4:31-34   827
God.........{Zech. 12:4   902
C. *Manifestations of:*
Irrational
behavior ......1 Sam. 21:12-15   296
Uncontrollable
emotions......Mark 5:1-5   982
Moral decay ...Jer. 50:38   755
See Insanity; Lunatic

Madon—*contention*
Canaanite town...Josh. 12:19   228
Joins confederacy against
Joshua..........Josh. 11:1-12   227

Magbish—*strong*
Town of Judah....Ezra 2:30   476

Magdala—*tower*
City of Galilee ....Matt. 15:39   957

Magdalene—*of Magdala*
Descriptive of one of the
Mary's ....Matt. 27:56   973
See Mary 3

Magdiel—*God is glory*
Edomite duke .....Gen. 36:43   38

Magi—*a priestly sect in Persia*
Brings gifts to the infant
Jesus.............Matt. 2:1, 2   942

Magic, magician—*the art of doing
superhuman things by "supernatural"
means*
A. *Special manifestations of:*
At the
exodus........Ex. 7:11   62
During apostolic
Christianity ...Acts 8:9, 18-24   1080
B. *Modified power of:*
Acknowledged in
history........Ex. 7:11, 22   62
Recognized in
prophecy......2 Thess. 2:9-12   1189
Fulfilled in
antichrist .....Rev. 13:13-18   1276
C. *Failure of, to:*
Perform
miracles.......Ex. 8:18, 19   63
Overcome
demons ....Acts 19:13-19   1093
D. *Condemnation of, by:*
Explicit Law ...Lev. 20:27   120
Their
inability.......Ex. 8:18   63
Final
judgment .....Rev. 21:8   1282
See Divination

Magistrates—*civil rulers*
A. *Descriptive of:*
Ruler ....Judg. 18:7   261
Authorities ....Luke 12:11   1021
B. *Office of:*
Ordained by
God...........Rom. 13:1, 2   1119
Due proper
respect........Acts 23:5   1098
C. *Duties of:*
To judge:
Impartially ...Deut. 1:17   178
Righteously...Deut. 25:1   201
D. *Christian's attitude toward:*
Pray for ....1 Tim. 2:1, 2   1194
Honor ....Ex. 22:28   77
Submit to.....1 Pet. 2:13, 14   1236

Magnanimity—*loftiness*
A. *Expressions of, toward men:*
Abram's offer to
Lot ....Gen. 13:7-12   15
Jacob's offer to
Esau..........Gen. 33:8-11   35
B. *Expression of, toward God:*
Moses' plea for
Israel ....Ex. 32:31-33   88
Paul's prayer for
Israel ....Rom. 9:1-3   1115

Magnificat—*he magnifies*
Poem of the Virgin
Mary..............Luke 1:46-55   1005

Magnify—*to make or declare great*
A. *Concerning God's:*
Name...........2 Sam. 7:26   315
Word..........Ps. 138:2   607
Law ....Is. 42:21   687
Christ's
name ....Acts 19:17   1094
B. *Duty of, toward God:*
With others......Ps. 34:3   561

With thanks-
giving.........Ps. 69:30   576
In the body....Phil. 1:20   1170

Magog—*region of Gog*
People among Japheth's
descendants......Gen. 10:2   13
Associated with
Gog..............Ezek. 38:2   806
Representatives of final
enemies ....Rev. 20:8   1281

Magor-missabib—*terror on every side*
Name indicating Pashur's
end...............Jer. 20:3   725

Magpiash—*collector of a cluster of stars*
Signer of the
covenant.........Neh. 10:20   499

Mahalah—*disease*
Manassite.........1 Chr. 7:14, 18   412

Mahalaleel—*praise of God*
1. Descendant of
Seth ....Gen. 5:12   8
2. Postexilic
Judahite ......Neh. 11:4   500

Mahalath—*sickness*
1. One of Esau's
wives ....Gen. 28:9   30
Called
Bashemath....Gen. 36:3, 4, 13   37
2. One of Rehoboam's
wives ....2 Chr. 11:18   448
3. Musical term ..Ps. 53 (Title)   570

Mahanaim—*two camps*
Name given by Jacob to a sacred
site.............Gen. 32:2   34
On boundary between Gad and
Manasseh ....Josh. 13:26, 30   229
Assigned to Merarite
Levites..........Josh. 21:38   237
Becomes Ish-bosheth's
capital..........2 Sam. 2:8-29   310
David flees to, during Absalom's
rebellion........2 Sam. 17:24, 27   325
Solomon places Ahinadab
over..............1 Kin. 4:14   342

Mahaneh-dan—*camp of Dan*
Place between Zorah and
Eshtaol..........Judg. 13:25   258

Maharai—*swift, hasty*
One of David's mighty
men..............2 Sam. 23:28   332
Becomes an army
captain..........1 Chr. 27:13   431

Mahath—*grasping*
1. Kohathite
Levite.........1 Chr. 6:35   410
2. Levite in Hezekiah's
reign..........2 Chr. 29:12   462
Appointed an overseer of
tithes ....2 Chr. 31:13   465

Mahavite
Applied to Eliel....1 Chr. 11:46   417

Mahazioth—*visions*
Levite musician ...1 Chr. 25:4, 30   429

Maher-shalal-hash-baz—*spoil speeds,
prey hastes*
Symbolic name of Isaiah's second
son; prophetic of the fall of
Damascus and
Samaria..........Is. 8:1-4   664

Mahlah—*disease*
1. Zelophehad's
daughter......Num. 26:33   163
2. Child of Ham-
moleketh......1 Chr. 7:18   412

Man—continued

D. *Final state of:*

Entered by new
birth..........John 3:1-12   1044

Continues
eternally......Matt. 25:46   969

Cannot be
changed .....Luke 16:26   1026

Determined
by faith or by {John 3:36   1045
unbelief......{2 Thess. 1:6-10   1189

E. *Christ's relation to:*

Gives light
to............John 1:9   1042

Knows nature
of............John 2:25   1044

Took nature
of............Heb. 2:14-16   1215

In the
likeness......Rom. 8:3   1114

Only Mediator
for...........1 Tim. 2:5   1194

Died for ......Heb. 9:26,28   1220
1 Pet. 1:18-21   1236

F. *Certain aspects of:*

First—Adam...1 Cor. 15:45, 47   1138
Last—Christ...1 Cor. 15:45   1138

Natural—unregen-
erate..........1 Cor. 2:14   1127

Outward—
physical.......2 Cor. 4:16   1145

Inner—
spiritual......Rom. 7:22   1114

New—
regenerate ....Eph. 2:15   1163

Man of sin (see Antichrist)

Manaen—*comforter*

Prophet and teacher in church at
Antioch ....Acts 13:1   1086

Manahath—*resting place*

1. Son of
Shobal........Gen. 36:23   38

2. City of exile for sons of
Ehud..........1 Chr. 8:6   413
Citizens of, called Manaheth-
ites ....1 Chr. 2:54   407

Manasseh—*making to forget*

1. Joseph's firstborn
son ....Gen. 41:50, 51   43
Adopted by
Jacob ....Gen. 48:5, 6   50
Loses his birthright to
Ephraim ......Gen. 48:13-20   50
Ancestor of a
tribe ....Num. 1:34, 35   134

2. Sons of ....Num. 26:28-34   163
Census of ......Num. 1:34, 35   134
One half of, desire region in
east Jordan ...Num. 32:33-42   170
Help Joshua against
Canaanites...Josh. 1:12-18   218
Division of, into eastern and
western......Josh. 22:7   237
Region assigned to eastern
half ....Deut. 3:12-15   181
Land assigned to western
half ....Josh. 17:1-13   232
Zelophehad's daughters
included in...Josh. 17:3, 4   232
Question concerning
altar ....Josh. 22:9-34   237
Joshua's challenge
to............Josh. 17:14-18   233
City (Golan) of refuge
in ....Josh. 20:8   236
Did not drive out
Canaanites...Judg. 1:27, 28   244
Gideon, a member
of............Judg. 6:15   249
Some of, help
David.........1 Chr. 12:19-31   417
Many support
Asa ....2 Chr. 15:9   450
Attend
Passovers .....2 Chr. 30:1-18   463

Idols destroyed
in.............2 Chr. 31:1   465

3. Intentional change of Moses'
name to.......Judg. 18:30   262

4. Son and successor of
Hezekiah, king of
Judah.........2 Kin. 21:1   394
Reigns wickedly;
restores {2 Kin. 21:1-16   394
idolatry......{2 Chr. 33:1-9   467
Captured and taken to
Babylon.......2 Chr. 33:10, 11   467
Repents and is
restored.......2 Chr. 33:12, 13   467
Removes idols and
altars ....2 Chr. 33:14-20   467

5, 6. Two men who divorce their
foreign
wives ....Ezra 10:30, 33   485

Mandrake—*a rhubarb-like herb, having
narcotic qualities*

Supposed to
induce human {Gen. 30:14-16   31
fertility.........{Song 7:13   653

Manger—*a feeding place for cattle*

Place of Jesus'
birth ....Luke 2:7, 12   1006
Called "crib".....Is. 1:3   658
Same as "stall"
in ....Luke 13:15   1023

Manifest—*to make something clear or
evident*

A. *Applied to God's:*
Nature.........Rom. 1:19   1109
Revelation.....Col. 1:26   1177
Knowledge ....2 Cor. 2:14   1144
Love...........1 John 4:9   1252

B. *Applied to Christ's:*
Nature.........1 Tim. 3:16   1195
Presence......John 1:31   1042
Life...........1 John 1:2   1249

C. *Applied to evil:*
Works of the
flesh ....Gal. 5:19   1158

Man's:
Deeds ....John 3:21   1044
Folly ....2 Tim. 3:9   1202

Manliness—*masculine characteristics at
their best*

A. *Qualities of:*
Self-control....1 Cor. 9:25-27   1132
Mature under-
standing ......1 Cor. 14:20   1136
Courage in {2 Sam. 10:11,
danger.......{ 12   317
Endure
hardship ......2 Tim. 2:3-5   1201

B. *Examples of:*
Caleb..........Num. 13:30   149
Joshua.........Josh. 1:1-11   217
Jonathan ......1 Sam. 14:1,
6-14   287
Daniel ....Dan. 6:1-28   829

Manna—*what is it?*

A. *Features regarding:*
Description
of.............Num. 11:7-9   147
Bread given {Ex. 16:4, 15   71
by God.......{John 6:30-32   1049
Previously
unknown .....Deut. 8:3, 16   186
Fell at
evening ......Num. 11:9   147
Despised by
people......Num. 11:4-6   147
Ceased at
conquest......Josh. 5:12   221

B. *Illustrative of:*
God's glory ....Ex. 16:7   71
Christ as the true
bread ....John 6:32-35   1049

Manners—*a way of life*

A. *Evil kinds:*
Sexual
immorality....Gen. 19:31-36   20
Customs of other
nations........Lev. 20:23   120
Careless
living ....Judg. 18:7   261

B. *Good kinds:*
Prayer.........Matt. 6:9   946
Faithfulness ...Acts 20:18   1095

Manoah—*rest, quiet*

Danite; father of
Samson ....Judg. 13:1-25   257

Mantle—*a garment*

Sheet or rug .....Judg. 4:18   247
Female garment...Is. 3:22   660
Upper garment
(coat) ....1 Sam. 15:27   290
Outer {1 Kin. 19:13, 19   362
garment (robe) ..{2 Kin. 2:8, 13, 14   372

Maoch—*oppression*

Father of Achish, king of
Gath ....1 Sam. 27:2   302

Maon—*abode*

1. Village in
Judah.........Josh. 15:55   231
David stayed {1 Sam. 23:24,
at............{ 25   298
House of
Nabal.........1 Sam. 25:2   299

2. Shammai's
son...........1 Chr. 2:45   406

3. People called Maonites among
Israel's
oppressors ....Judg. 10:12   255
Called
Mehunim .....2 Chr. 26:7   460
Listed among {Ezra 2:50   476
returnees.....{Neh. 7:52   495

Mara—*bitter*

Name chosen by
Naomi...........Ruth 1:20   269

Marah—*bitterness*

First Israelite camp after passing
through the Red
Sea..............Num. 33:8, 9   171

Maralah—*downward slope*

Village in
Zebulun.........Josh. 19:11   234

Maranatha—*our Lord, come*

Aramaic phrase expressive of
Christ's return...1 Cor. 16:22   1139
Compare the same thought
in ....Phil. 4:5   1171

Marble—*crystalline limestone*

In columns........Esth. 1:6   507
In Babylon's
trade.............Rev. 18:12   1279

Marduk—*bold*

Supreme deity of the
Babylonians......Jer. 50:2   754
Otherwise called
Bel ....Is. 46:1   690

Mareshah—*summit*

1. Father of
Hebron ....1 Chr. 2:42   406

2. Judahite ....1 Chr. 4:21   408

3. Town of
Judah.........Josh. 15:44   231
City built for defense by
Rehoboam .....2 Chr. 11:5, 8   447
Great battle here between Asa
and Zerah.....2 Chr. 14:9-12   450

Mariners—*sailors*

Skilled ....1 Kin. 9:27   350
Fearful............Jon. 1:5   866

SUBJECT   REFERENCE   PAGE

Matthan—*gift*

Ancestor of
Joseph ....Matt. 1:15, 16   942

Matthat—*gift*

1. Ancestor of
Christ.........Luke 3:24   1008
2. Another ancestor of
Christ.........Luke 3:29   1008

Matthew—*gift of Yahweh*

Tax gatherer......Matt. 9:9   949
Becomes Christ's
follower........Matt. 9:9   949
Appointed an
apostle ....Matt. 10:2, 3   950
Called Levi, the son of
Alphaeus ......Mark 2:14   980
Entertains Jesus with a great
feast ....Mark 2:14, 15   980
In the upper
room............Acts 1:13   1072
Author of the first
Gospel ....Matt. 1:1 (Title)   941

Matthew, the Gospel of—*a book of the New Testament*

Events of Jesus' (Matt. 1:18—
birth ....(2:23   942
John the Baptist ..Matt. 3:1-17   943
The temptation ...Matt. 4:1-11   943
Jesus begins His
ministry.........Matt. 4:12-17   944
The Great
Sermon ....Matt. 5:1—7:29   944
Christ, about John the
Baptist ....Matt. 11:1-19   951
Conflict with the Pharisees and
Sadducees.......Matt. 15:39—
       16:6   957
Peter's
confession.......Matt. 16:13-20   958
Prophecy of death and
resurrection....Matt. 20:17-19   962
Jerusalem entry...Matt. 21:1-11   963
Authority of (Matt. 21:23—
Jesus............(22:14   963
Woes to the
Pharisees........Matt. 23:1-36   965
Garden of
Gethsemane.....Matt. 26:36-56   970
Crucifixion and
burial ....Matt. 27:27-66   972
Resurrection of
Christ............Matt. 28:1-20   973

Matthias—*gift of Yahweh*

Chosen by lot to replace
Judas.............Acts 1:15-26   1072

Mattithiah—*gift of Yahweh*

1. Korahite
Levite.........1 Chr. 9:31   414
2. Levite, son of Jeduthun, and
Temple
musician......1 Chr. 15:18, 21   419
3. Jew who put away his foreign
wife..........Ezra 10:43   485
4. Levite attendant to
Ezra ....Neh. 8:4   496

Mattock—*an agricultural instrument for digging and hoeing*

Sharpened for
battle ....1 Sam. 13:20-22   287

Maturity, spiritual

Do away with childish
things......1 Cor. 13:11   1135
Be mature in your
thinking......1 Cor. 14:20   1136
Solid food is for ..Heb. 5:11-14   1217
Overcoming the evil
one............1 John 2:14   1250

Maul—*a stick or a club*

Used against
neighbor ....Prov. 25:18   632

Maw—*the fourth stomach of ruminants (divided-hoof animals)*

Given to the
priests............Deut. 18:3   195

Mazzaroth—*the signs of the Zodiac or a constellation*

Descriptive of God's
power............Job 38:32   541
Objects of idolatrous
worship ....2 Kin. 23:5   397

Meadow—*sown fields*

1. Reed grass or papyrus
thickets.......Is. 19:6, 7   671
Translated
"flag" in .....Job 8:11   523
2. Place near
Gibeah........Judg. 20:33   265

Meah, tower of the

Restored by
Eliashib ....Neh. 3:1   490

Meal—*ground grain used for food*

One-tenth of an ephah
of ....Num. 5:15   140
Used in
offerings..........1 Kin. 4:22   342
"Then bring".....2 Kin. 4:41   375
Millstones and
grind.............Is. 47:2   691
Three measures
of ....Matt. 13:33   955

Meals—*times of eating*

A. *Times of:*
Early
morning ......John 21:4-12   1066
At noon (for
laborers)......Ruth 2:14   270
In the
evening ......Gen. 19:1-3   19
B. *Extraordinary and festive:*
Guests
invited.......Matt. 22:3, 4   964
Received with a
kiss..........Luke 7:45   1014
Feet washed ..Luke 7:44   1014
Anointed with
ointment......Luke 7:38   1014
Proper dress ..Matt. 22:11, 12   964
Seated according to
rank..........Matt. 23:6   965
Special guest
honored......1 Sam. 9:22-24   283
Entertainment
provided .....Luke 15:25   1025
Temperate habits
taught ....Prov. 23:1-3   630
Intemperance
condemned ...Amos 6:4-6   858

See Entertainment; Feasts

Means of grace

A. *Agents of:*
Holy Spirit.....Gal. 5:16-26   1158
God's Word....1 Thess. 2:13   1184
Prayer.........Rom. 8:15-27   1114
Christian
fellowship.....Mal. 3:16-18   909
Public
worship.......1 Thess. 5:6   1185
Christian
witnessing ....Acts 8:4   1080
B. *Words expressive of:*
Stir up the
gift ....2 Tim. 1:6   1200
Neglect not the spiritual
gift ....1 Tim. 4:14   1196
Take heed to the
ministry.......Col. 4:17   1180
Grow in
grace ....2 Pet. 3:18   1245
C. *Use of, brings:*
Assurance .....2 Pet. 1:5-12   1243
Stability ....Eph. 4:11-16   1164

D. *Enemies of:*
Devil ....1 Thess. 3:5   1184
World ....1 John 2:15-17   1250
Coldness......Rev. 3:14-18   1270

Mearah—*cave*

Unconquered by
Joshua.........Josh. 13:1, 4   228

Measure—*a standard of size, quantity or values*

A. *Objectionable:*
Differing
(different).....Deut. 25:14, 15   201
Scant.........Mic. 6:10   874
Using themselves as a
gauge.........2 Cor. 10:12   1149
B. *As indicative of:*
Earth's
weight........Is. 40:12   685
Punishment
inflicted.......Matt. 7:2   947
C. *Figurative of:*
Great size .....Hos. 1:10   840
Sin's ripeness ..Matt. 23:32   966
The Spirit's
infilling........John 3:34   1045
Man's ability...2 Cor. 10:13   1149
Perfection of
faith ....Eph. 4:13, 16   1164

Measuring line—*a cord of specified length for measuring*

Signifies hope .....Jer. 31:38-40   737
           Zech. 2:1   897

Meat—*food in general (not just flesh)*

A. *Characteristics of:*
Given by
God...........Ps. 104:21, 27   592
Necessary for
man ....Gen. 1:29, 30   5
B. *Lack of:*
Testing of
faith ....Hab. 3:17   884
Provided by:
God ....Ps. 145:15   610
Christ ....John 21:5, 6   1066
C. *Prohibitions concerning:*
Not in itself com-
mendable .....1 Cor. 8:8   1131
Not to be a stumbling
block ....1 Cor. 8:13   1131
Life more important
than ....Matt. 6:25   947
D. *Figurative of:*
God's will......John 4:32, 34   1046
Christ ....John 6:27, 55   1049
Strong
doctrines......1 Cor. 3:2   1127

Mebunnai—*built*

One of David's mighty
men............2 Sam. 23:27   332
Called Sibbecai....1 Chr. 11:29   416

Mecherathite—*a dweller in Mecharah*

Descriptive of Hepher, one of
David's mighty
men............1 Chr. 11:36   416

Medad—*beloved*

One of the seventy elders receiving
the Spirit........Num. 11:26-29   147

Medan—*judgment*

Son of Abraham by
Keturah..........Gen. 25:1, 2   26

Meddling—*interfering with the affairs of others*

Brings a king's
death...........2 Chr. 35:21-24   470
Christians.........1 Pet. 4:15   1239
Such called
"busybodies" .....2 Thess. 3:11   1190

SUBJECT   REFERENCE   PAGE | SUBJECT   REFERENCE   PAGE | SUBJECT   REFERENCE   PAGE

Medeba—*full waters*

Old Moabite
town ....Num. 21:29, 30   158
Assigned to
Reuben..........Josh. 13:9, 16   229
Syrians defeated
here.............1 Chr. 19:6, 7   423
Reverts to Moab ..Is. 15:2   669

Medes, Media—*the people and country of the Medes*

A. *Characteristics of:*
Descendants of
Japheth.......Gen. 10:2   13
Part of Medo-Persian
empire ....Esth. 1:19   507
Inflexible laws
of............Dan. 6:8, 12, 15   829
Among those at
Pentecost.....Acts 2:9   1073

B. *Kings of, mentioned in the Bible:*
Cyrus..........Ezra 1:1   475
Ahasuerus....Ezra 4:6   478
Artaxerxes I ...Ezra 4:7   478
Darius........Ezra 6:1   479
Xerxes.......Dan. 11:2   834
Artaxerxes.....Ezra 6:14   480

C. *Place of, in Bible history:*
Israel deported
to.............2 Kin. 17:6   389
Babylon falls
to...........Dan. 5:30, 31   829
"Darius the Mede," new ruler of
Babylon.......Dan. 5:31   829
Daniel rises high in the
kingdom of ...Dan. 6:1-28   829
Cyrus, king of Persia, allows
Jews to
return........2 Chr. 36:22, 23   471
Esther and Mordecai live under
Ahasuerus, king
of.............Esth. 1:3, 19   507

D. *Prophecies concerning:*
Agents in Babylon's
fall............Is. 13:17-19   668
Cyrus, king of, God's
servant ....Is. 44:28   689
"Inferior"
kingdom ......Dan. 2:39   824
Compared to a
bear ....Dan. 7:5   830
Kings of ......Dan. 11:2   834
War with
Greece........Dan. 11:2   834

Mediation—*a friendly intervention designed to render assistance*

A. *Purposes of:*
Save a life .....Gen. 37:21, 22   39
Save a
people ....Ex. 32:11-13   87
Obtain a wife ..1 Kin. 2:13-25   339
Obtain
justice ....Job 9:33   524

B. *Motives prompting:*
People's fear ...Deut. 5:5   183
Regard for human
life...........Jer. 38:7-13   744
Sympathy for {2 Kin. 5:6-8   376
a sick man...{Matt. 17:15   959

C. *Methods used:*
Intense
prayer........Deut. 9:20-29   188
Flattery........1 Sam. 25:23-35   300
Appeal to self-preserva-
tion...........Esth. 4:12-17   510

Mediator, Christ our

A. *His qualifications:*
Bears God's
image, man's {Phil. 2:6-8   1171
likeness.....{Heb. 2:14-17   1215
Is both sinless
and sin- {Is. 53:6-10   695
bearer........{Eph. 2:13-18   1163

Endures God's wrath,
brings God's righ-
teousness .....Rom. 5:6-19   1112
Is sacrifice
and the {Heb. 7:27   1218
priest ....{Heb. 10:5-22   1220

B. *How He performs the function, by:*
Took our
nature ....1 John 1:1-3   1249
Died as our
substitute.....1 Pet. 1:18, 19   1236
Reconciled us to
God...........Eph. 2:16   1163

Medicine—*something prescribed to cure an illness*

A. *General prescriptions:*
Merry heart ...Prov. 15:13   624
Rest ....Ps. 37:7-11   562
Sleep ....John 11:12, 13   1055
Quarantine ....Lev. 12:1-4   110
Sanitation ....Deut. 23:10-14   200

B. *Specific prescriptions:*
Figs ....Is. 38:21   684
Roots and
leaves.........Ezek. 47:12   816
Wine ....1 Tim. 5:23   1197

C. *Used figuratively of:*
Salvation ......Jer. 8:22   716
Incurable-
ness...........Jer. 46:11   750
Spiritual stubborn-
ness...........Jer. 51:8, 9   756

See Diseases

Meditation—*quiet contemplation of spiritual truths*

A. *Objects of, God's:*
Word ....Ps. 119:148   602
Law ....Josh. 1:8   217
Instruction ....1 Tim. 4:15   1196

B. *Value of, for:*
Under-
standing ......Ps. 49:3   568
Spiritual
satisfaction ...Ps. 63:5, 6   573
Superior
knowledge ....Ps. 119:99   601

C. *Extent of:*
All the day ...Ps. 119:97   601
At evening.....Gen. 24:63   26
In night
watches.......Ps. 119:148   602

Mediterranean Sea

Described as:
Sea ....Gen. 49:13   51
Great {Josh. 1:4   217
Sea..............{Josh. 9:1   224
Sea of the
Philistines........Ex. 23:31   78
Uttermost Sea ....Deut. 11:24   190
Joel 2:20   851
Zech. 14:8   903

Mediums

A. *Described as:*
Source of
defilement ....Lev. 19:31   119
Abomination...Deut. 18:10-12   196
Whisperers ....Is. 8:19   664

B. *The practicers, to be:*
Cut off ....Lev. 20:6   120
Put to death ...Lev. 20:27   120

C. *Consulted by:*
Saul ....1 Sam. 28:3-25   302
Manasseh......2 Kin. 21:6   346

D. *Condemned by:*
Josiah ....2 Kin. 23:24   397

Meek

A. *Blessings upon:*
Gospel.........Is. 61:1   700
Spiritual
satisfaction ...Ps. 22:26   556

Guidance and
instruction ....Ps. 25:9   557
Salvation .....Ps. 76:9   580

B. *A Christian essential in:*
Living in the
Spirit ....Gal. 5:22, 23   1158
Receiving the
Word ....James 1:21   1228
Stating our
assurance.....James 3:13   1230

Megiddo—*place of troops*

City conquered by
Joshua ....Josh. 12:21   228
Assigned to
Manasseh ....Josh. 17:11   233
Inhabitants of, made
slaves ....Judg. 1:27, 28   244
Canaanites defeated
here ....Judg. 5:19-21   248
Site of Baana's
headquarters .....1 Kin. 4:12   342
Fortified by
Solomon ....1 Kin. 9:15-19   349
King Ahaziah dies
here ....2 Kin. 9:27   381
King Josiah killed
here ....2 Kin. 23:29, 30   398
Mentioned in
prophecy........Zech. 12:11   902
Site of
Armageddon .....Rev. 16:16   1278

Mehetabeel—*God benefits*

1. King Hadar's
wife.........Gen. 36:39   38
2. Father of
Delaiah ....Neh. 6:10   493

Mehida—*renowned*

Ancestor of a family of returning
Temple
servants.........Ezra 2:52   476

Mehir—*price*

Judahite ....1 Chr. 4:11   408

Meholathite—*a native of Meholah*

Descriptive of
Adriel ....1 Sam. 18:19   293

Mehujael—*smitten of God*

Cainite; father of
Methusael........Gen. 4:18   8

Mehuman—*faithful*

Eunuch under King
Ahasuerus........Esth. 1:10   507

Mehunim

Arabian tribe near Mt.
Seir ....2 Chr. 26:7   460
Smitten by
Simeonites ....1 Chr. 4:39-42   408
Descendants of, serve as
Nethinim.........Ezra 2:50   476

Me-jarkon—*waters of yellow color*

Territory of Dan near
Joppa ....Josh. 19:40, 46   235

Mekonah—*foundation*

Town of Judah....Neh. 11:25, 28   500

Melatiah—*Yahweh has set free*

Postexilic
workman.........Neh. 3:7   490

Melchi—*my king*

Two ancestors of
Jesus...........Luke 3:24, 28   1008

Melchizedek—*king of righteousness*

A. *Described as:*
King of
Salem.......Gen. 14:18   16
Priest of God ..Gen. 14:18   16
Receiver of a tenth of Abram's
goods.........Gen. 14:18-20   16

SUBJECT   REFERENCE   PAGE   SUBJECT   REFERENCE   PAGE   SUBJECT   REFERENCE   PAGE

Merchandise—*continued*
B. *Figurative of:*
Wisdom's
profit ....Prov. 3:13, 14   616
Gospel trans-
formation .....Is. 23:18   674

Merchants—*traders*
Characteristics of:
Crossed the sea ...Is. 23:2   673
Lamentation
over.............Ezek. 27:2-36   795
Some do not observe the
Sabbath ....Neh. 13:19-21   503
Burden people with
debts.............Neh. 5:1-13   492
Peddle goods......Neh. 13:16   503
Trade with
farmers..........Prov. 31:24   636
Form guilds.......Neh. 3:8-32   490
Destroyed with
Babylon ....Rev. 18:3-19   1279
Sailors, in Solomon's
service ....1 Kin. 9:27, 28   350
Bring gold to
Solomon ....2 Chr. 9:14   446
Bring horses to
Solomon ....2 Chr. 9:28   446

Mercurius
Paul acclaimed
as ....Acts 14:12   1088

Mercy
A. *Described as:*
Great..........Is. 54:7   696
Sure...........Is. 55:3   696
Abundant......1 Pet. 1:3   1235
Tender.........Ps. 25:6   557
New every
morning .....Lam. 3:22, 23   764
B. *Of God, seen in:*
Regener-
ation..........1 Pet. 1:3   1235
Salvation ......Titus 3:5   1207
Christ's
mission ......Luke 1:72, 78   1006
Forgiveness....Ps. 51:1   569
C. *In the Christian life:*
Received in
salvation......1 Cor. 7:25   1130
Taught as a principle of
life............Matt. 5:7   945
Practiced as a
gift ....Rom. 12:8   1118
Evidenced in God's
provinces .....Phil. 2:27   1171
Obtained in
prayer ....Heb. 4:16   1217
Reason of conse-
cration........Rom. 12:1   1118
Reason for
hope ....Jude 21   1263
D. *Special injunctions concerning:*
Put on........Col. 3:12   1178
E. *Examples of:*
David to
Saul ....1 Sam. 24:10-17   299
Christ to
sinners........Matt. 9:13   949
F. *Attitude of believers, to:*
Cast themselves
on ....2 Sam. 24:14   333
Look for......Jude 21   1263

Mercy seat—*the covering of the ark*
Made of pure
gold.............Ex. 25:17   79
Blood sprinkled
upon............Lev. 16:14, 15   116
God manifested
over............Lev. 16:2   115
Figurative of
Christ...........Heb. 9:5-12   1219

Mered—*rebellion*
Judahite........1 Chr. 4:17   408
Had two wives...1 Chr. 4:17, 18   408

Meremoth—*elevations*
1. Signer of the
covenant......Neh. 10:5   499

Called
Meraioth......Neh. 12:15   501
2. One who divorced his foreign
wife..........Ezra 10:34, 36   485
3. Priest, son of Uriah; weighs
silver and
gold...........Ezra 8:33   482
Repairs wall of
Jerusalem.....Neh. 3:4, 21   490

Meres—*the forgetful one*
Persian prince...Esth. 1:13, 14   507

Merib-baal—*Baal contends*
Another name for
Mephibosheth ....1 Chr. 8:34   413

Merit—*reward given for something
done additionally*
A. *Of man, impossible because:*
None is good ..Rom. 3:12   1110
None is
righteous .....Rom. 3:10   1110
We are all
sinful ....Is. 6:5   662
Our good comes from
God............1 Cor. 15:9, 10   1137
Our righteousness:
Is unavail-
ing...........Matt. 5:20   945
Is Christ's ....2 Cor. 5:21   1146
Cannot save ..Rom. 10:1-4   1116
B. *Of Christ:*
Secured by
obedience.....Rom. 5:17-21   1112
Secured by His
death ....Is. 53:10-12   695
Obtained by
faith ....Phil. 3:8, 9   1172

Merodach—*bold*
Supreme deity of the
Babylonians ......Jer. 50:2   754
Otherwise called
Bel ....Is. 46:1   690

Merodach-baladan—*Merodach has
given a son*
Sends ambassadors to
Hezekiah......Is. 39:1-8   685
Also called Berodach-
baladan ......2 Kin. 20:12   394

Merom—*high place*
Lake on Jordan north of the Sea of
Galilee ....Josh. 11:5, 7   227

Meronothite
Citizen of
Meronoth ......1 Chr. 27:30   431

Meroz—*refuge*
Town cursed for failing to help the
Lord ....Judg. 5:23   248

Merry—*a spirit of gaiety*
A. *Good, comes from:*
Heart..........Prov. 15:13, 15   624
Restoration ...Jer. 30:18, 19   735
Christian joy ..James 5:13   1231
B. *Evil, results from:*
Careless
unconcern ....Judg. 9:27   253
Drunkenness ..1 Sam. 25:36   301
False
optimism......1 Kin. 21:7   365
Sinful glee.....Rev. 11:10   1275

Mesha—*retreat*
1. Border of Joktan's descendants ....Gen. 10:30   13
2. Benjamite ....1 Chr. 8:8, 9   413
3. Son of Caleb...1 Chr. 2:42   406
4. King of
Moab ....2 Kin. 3:4   373

Meshach—*the shadow of the prince*
Name given to
Mishael ....Dan. 1:7   822

Advanced to high
position ....Dan. 2:49   825
Remains faithful in
testing ....Dan. 3:13-30   825

Meshech—*tall*
1. Son of
Japheth.......Gen. 10:2   12
Called
Mesech ....Ps. 120:5   603
Famous
traders........Ezek. 27:13   795
Confederates with
Gog...........Ezek. 38:2, 3   806
Inhabitants of the nether
world ....Ezek. 32:18, 26   800
2. Son of Shem...1 Chr. 1:17   405
Same as
Mash ....Gen. 10:23   13

Meshelemiah—*Yahweh repays*
Father of
Zechariah ....1 Chr. 9:21   414
Porter in the
Temple ....1 Chr. 26:1   429
Called
Shelemiah .....1 Chr. 26:14   430

Meshezabeel—*God delivers*
1. Postexilic wall
repairer ....Neh. 3:4   490
2. One who signs
covenant......Neh. 10:21   499
3. Judahite ....Neh. 11:24   500

Meshillemith—*recompense*
Postexilic priest ...1 Chr. 9:10-12   414
Called
Meshillemoth.....Neh. 11:13   500

Meshillemoth—*acts of recompense*
Ephraimite
leader ....2 Chr. 28:12   461

Meshobab—*restored*
Descendant of
Simeon..........1 Chr. 4:34-38   408

Meshullam—*recompensed; rewarded*
1, 2, 3. Three
Benjamites....1 Chr. 8:17   413
4. Gadite leader ..1 Chr. 5:11, 13   409
5. Shaphan's
grandfather ...2 Kin. 22:3   395
6. Hilkiah's
father.........1 Chr. 9:11   414
7. Son of
Zerubbabel...1 Chr. 3:19   407
8. Priest..........1 Chr. 9:10-12   414
9. Kohathite
overseer .....2 Chr. 34:12   468
10. Man commissioned to secure
Levites........Ezra 8:16   482
11. Levite who supports Ezra's
reforms ....Ezra 10:15   484
12. One who divorced his foreign
wife..........Ezra 10:29   484
13. Postexilic
workman .....Neh. 3:4, 30   490
His daughter married Tobiah's
son ....Neh. 6:18   494
14. Postexilic
workman .....Neh. 3:6   490
15. One of Ezra's
attendants ....Neh. 8:4   496
16, 17. Two priests who sign
covenant......Neh. 10:7, 20   499
18, 19. Two priests in Joiakim's
time ....Neh. 12:13, 16   501
20. Porter ....Neh. 12:25   501
21. Participant in dedication
services ......Neh. 12:33   501

Meshullemeth—*feminine form of
Meshullam*
Wife of King
Manasseh ....2 Kin. 21:18, 19   395

Mesobaite—*found of Yahweh*
Title given Jasiel ..1 Chr. 11:47   417

210

215

SUBJECT	REFERENCE	PAGE	SUBJECT	REFERENCE	PAGE	SUBJECT	REFERENCE	PAGE

Mischief—continued

Devise........Ps. 62:3	573
Prov. 6:14	618
Practice.......1 Sam. 23:9	298
Prov. 10:23	621
Run to........Prov. 6:18	618
Think to do....Neh. 6:2	493
Seek.........1 Kin. 20:7	363

Miser—*a covetous man*

A. *Characteristics of:*

Selfish........Eccl. 4:8	642
Covetous.....Luke 12:15	1021
Divided loyalty.......Matt. 6:24	947

B. *Punishment of:*

Dissatisfaction........Eccl. 5:10	643
Loss..........Matt. 6:19	946
Sorrows.......1 Tim. 6:10	1197
Destruction....Ps. 52:5, 7	570

C. *Examples of:*

Rich fool.....Luke 12:16-21	1021
Rich ruler.....Luke 18:18-23	1028
Ananias and Sapphira......Acts 5:1-11	1076

Miserable—*the wretched*

A. *State of:*

Wicked.......Rom. 3:12-16	1110
Trapped.......Rom. 7:24	1114
Lost..........Luke 13:25-28	1023

B. *Caused by:*

Forgetfulness of God..........Is. 22:12-14	673
Ignorance.....Luke 19:42-44	1030

Misfortune—*an unexpected adversity*

Explained by the nations..........Deut. 29:24-28	207
Misunderstood by Gideon.........Judg. 6:13	249
Understood by David........2 Sam. 16:5-13	324
Caused by sin.....Is. 59:1, 2	698

Misgab—*high place*

Moabite city......Jer. 48:1	751
Capital of Moab..Is. 15:1	669
Translated "high fort"...........Is. 25:12	675

Mishael—*who is like God?*

1. Kohathite
Levite.........Ex. 6:22	61
Removes dead bodies.........Lev. 10:4, 5	108
2. Hebrew name of
Meshach......Dan. 1:6-19	822
3. One of Ezra's
assistants.....Neh. 8:4	496

Mishal, Misheal

Town in Asher....Josh. 19:24, 26	235
Assigned to Levites........Josh. 21:30	237
Called Mashal.....1 Chr. 6:74	411

Misham—*swift*

Son of Elpaal.....1 Chr. 8:12	413

Mishma—*hearing*

1. Son of
{Gen. 25:13, 14	26
Ishmael....{1 Chr. 1:30	405
2. Descendant of
Simeon........1 Chr. 4:25	408

Mishmannah—*fatness*

One of David's Gadite warriors..........1 Chr. 12:10	417

Mishraites

Family living in Kirjath-jearim............1 Chr. 2:53	407

Mispar—*writing*

Exile returnee.....Ezra 2:2	475
Called Mispereth.......Neh. 7:7	494

Misrephoth-maim—*burning of waters*

Haven of fleeing Canaanites......Josh. 11:8	227
Near the Sidonians........Josh. 13:6	229

Missionaries—*those sent out to spread the Gospel*

Jonah........Jon. 3:2, 3	867
The early church.........Acts 8:4	1080
Philip............Acts 8:5	1080
Some from Cyrene become missionaries......Acts 11:20	1085
Paul and Barnabas........Acts 13:1-4	1086
Peter............Acts 15:7	1088
Apollos.........Acts 18:24	1093
Noah..........2 Pet. 2:5	1243

Mission of Christ

Do God's will.....John 6:38	1049
Save sinners.....Luke 19:10	1029
Bring in everlasting righteousness.....Dan. 9:24	833
Destroy Satan's {Heb. 2:14	1215
works..........{1 John 3:8	1251
Fulfill the Old Testament......Matt. 5:17	945
Give life.........John 10:10, 28	1054
Stop sacrifices....Dan. 9:27	833
Complete revelation........Heb. 1:1-3	1215

Missions

A. *Commands concerning:*

"Shall be".....Matt. 24:14	967
"Go".......Matt. 28:18-20	973
"Tarry".......Luke 24:49	1037
"Come".......Acts 16:9	1090

B. *Motives prompting:*

God's love.....John 3:16	1044
Christ's love..2 Cor. 5:14, 15	1145
Mankind's need.......Rom. 3:9-31	1110

C. *Equipment for:*

Word.........Rom. 10:14, 15	1116
Spirit.........Acts 1:8	1072
Prayer........Acts 13:1-4	1086

Mist—*a vapor (physical and spiritual)*

Physical (vapor)...Gen. 2:6	5
Spiritual (blindness).......Acts 13:11	1086
Eternal (darkness).......2 Pet. 2:17	1244

Mistake—*an error arising from human weakness*

Causes of:

Motives misunderstood....Josh. 22:9-29	237
Appearance misjudged........1 Sam. 1:13-15	276
Trust misplaced...Josh. 9:3-27	224

Mistress—*a married woman*

Over a maid......Gen. 16:4, 8, 9	17
Figurative of Nineveh........Nah. 3:4	879

Misunderstandings—*disagreements among*

Israelites........Josh. 22:9-29	237
Christ's disciples...Matt. 20:20-27	962
Apostles..........Gal. 2:11-15	1155
Christians........Acts 6:1	1078

Misused—*putting to a wrong use*

Guilt of, brings wrath...........2 Chr. 36:16	471

Mite—*Jews' smallest coin*

Widow's.........Mark 12:42	993

Mithcah—*sweetness*

Israelite encampment.....Num. 33:28, 29	171

Mithnite

Descriptive of Joshaphat, David's officer............1 Chr. 11:43	417

Mithredath—*consecrated to Mithra*

1. Treasurer of
Cyrus.........Ezra 1:8	475
2. Persian
official........Ezra 4:7	478

Mitre, miter—*headdress or turban*

Worn by the high priest..............Ex. 28:36-39	83
Inscription "Holiness to the Lord" worn on..........Ex. 39:28-31	95
Worn by Aaron for anointing and on Day of {Lev. 8:9	106
Atonement......{Lev. 16:4	116
Uncovering of upper lip a sign of uncleanness and mourning........Lev. 13:45	112
Uncovering of, forbidden........Lev. 21:10-12	121
Removal of, because of sin............Ezek. 21:26	790
Symbolic restoration of.................Zech. 3:5	897

Mitylene—*a city on the island of Lesbos*

Visited by Paul....Acts 20:13-15	1095

Mix (see Mingle; Miscegenation)

Mizar—*small*

Hill east of Jordan.............Ps. 42:6	565

Mizpah, Mizpeh—*watchtower*

1. Site of covenant between Jacob
and Laban....Gen. 31:44-53	34
2. Town in Gilead; probably same
as 1..........Judg. 10:17	255
Jephthah's {Judg. 11:11, 29,	
home........{ 34	255
Probably same as Ramath-mizpeh.......Josh. 13:26	229
3. Region near Mt.
Hermon......Josh. 11:3, 8	227
4. Town in
Judah......Josh. 15:1, 38	230
5. Place in Moab; David brings his
parents to....1 Sam. 22:3, 4	297
6. Town of
Benjamin......Josh. 18:21, 26	234
Outraged Israelites gather here..........Judg. 20:1, 3	263
Samuel gathers {1 Sam. 7:5-16	281
Israel......{1 Sam. 10:17-25	284
Built by Asa...1 Kin. 15:22	357
Residence of Gedaliah.......2 Kin. 25:23, 25	400
Home of exile returnees.....Neh. 3:7, 15, 19	490

Mizraim—*Egypt*

1. Son of Ham; ancestor of Ludim, Anamim,
etc..........1 Chr. 1:8, 11	404
2. Hebrew name for
Egypt........Gen. 50:11	52
Called the land of Ham..........Ps. 105:23, 27	593

Mizzah—*fear*

Grandson of Esau; a duke of Edom.............Gen. 36:13, 17	38

Mnason

Christian of Cyprus and Paul's host...............Acts 21:16	1096

Moab—*seed*

1. Son of Lot.....Gen. 19:33-37   21
2. Country of the
Moabites......Deut. 1:5	178

Morality—continued

B. *Of the regenerated:*
Based upon the new
birth . . . . 2 Cor. 5:17 — 1145
Prompted by the
Spirit . . . . Gal. 5:22, 23 — 1158
Comes from the
heart. . . . . Heb. 8:10 — 1219
No boasting
except in {1 Cor. 15:10 — 1137
Christ. . . . .{Phil. 3:7-10 — 1172

Morasthite—*a native of Moresheth*
Descriptive of
Micah . . . . Jer. 26:18 — 731

Mordecai—*dedicated to Mars*
1. Jew exiled in
Persia . . . . Esth. 2:5, 6 — 508
Brings up
Esther . . . . Esth. 2:7 — 508
Directs Esther's
movements . . . Esth. 2:10-20 — 508
Reveals plot to kill the
king . . . . Esth. 2:22, 23 — 508
Refuses homage to
Haman. . . . . . . Esth. 3:1-6 — 509
Gallows made
for . . . . Esth. 5:14 — 510
Honored by the
king . . . . Esth. 6:1-12 — 511
Is highly
exalted. . . . . . . Esth. 8:7, 15 — 512
Becomes
famous. . . . . . . Esth. 9:4 — 513
Writes to Jews about Feast of
Purim . . . . Esth. 9:20-31 — 513
2. Postexilic
returnee . . . . . Ezra 2:2 — 475

More—*something in addition*
A. *"More than" promises:*
Repentance . . . Matt. 18:13 — 960
Love. . . . . John 21:15 — 1066
B. *"Much more" promises:*
Grace. . . . . Rom. 5:9-17 — 1112
Witnessing . . . . Phil. 1:14 — 1170
Obedience . . . . Phil. 2:12 — 1171
C. *"No more" promises:*
Christ's
death . . . . Rom. 6:9 — 1112
Grace. . . . . Rom. 11:6 — 1117
Remember
sin . . . . Heb. 8:12 — 1219

Moreh—*teacher, soothsayer*
1. Place (oak tree or grove) near
Shechem . . . . . Gen. 12:6 — 15
Probably place of:
Idol-burying . . Gen. 35:4 — 37
Covenant-
stone . . . . Josh. 24:26 — 240
2. Hill in the valley of
Jezreel . . . . Judg. 7:1 — 250

Moresheth-gath—*possession of Gath*
Birthplace of Micah the
prophet . . . . Mic. 1:14 — 871

Moriah
God commands Abraham to
sacrifice Isaac
here . . . . Gen. 22:1-13 — 22
Site of Solomon's
Temple . . . . 2 Chr. 3:1 — 440

Morning—*the first part of the day*
A. *Early risers in:*
Do the LORD's
will . . . . Gen. 22:3 — 22
Worship . . . . . . Ex. 24:4 — 78
Do the LORD's
work. . . . . Josh. 6:12 — 221
Fight the LORD's
battles . . . . Josh. 8:10 — 223
Depart on a
journey . . . . . . Judg. 19:5, 8 — 262
Correct an
evil . . . . Dan. 6:19 — 829
Pray. . . . . Mark 1:35 — 979

Visit the
tomb . . . . Mark 16:2 — 998
Preach . . . . Acts 5:21 — 1077
B. *For the righteous, a time for:*
Joy . . . . Ps. 30:5 — 559
God's loving-
kindness . . . . . Ps. 92:2 — 588
God's
mercies . . . . . Lam. 3:22, 23 — 764
C. *For the unrighteous, a time of:*
Dread . . . . Deut. 28:67 — 205
Destruction . . . Is. 17:14 — 671
D. *Figurative of:*
Man's unrigh-
teousness . . . . Hos. 6:4 — 843
Judgment . . . . . Zeph. 3:5 — 888
God's light . . . . Amos 5:8 — 858
Christ's
return . . . . Rev. 2:28 — 1270

Morning sacrifice—*part of Israelite worship*
Ritual described . . . Ex. 29:38-42 — 85
Part of continual
offering . . . . . . Num. 28:3-8 — 165
Under Ahaz . . . . . 2 Kin. 16:15 — 389

Morning Star
Figurative of Christ:
To church at
Thyatira . . . . . . Rev. 2:24, 28 — 1270
Christ, of
Himself . . . . . . Rev. 22:16 — 1283
Applied to
Christ . . . . 2 Pet. 1:19 — 1243

Morsel—*a small piece of food*
Offered to
angels . . . . Gen. 18:5 — 19
Rejected by a doomed
man . . . . 1 Sam. 28:22 — 303
Asked of a dying
woman . . . . 1 Kin. 17:11, 12 — 359
Better than
strife . . . . Prov. 17:1 — 626
Exchanged for a
birthright . . . . . . Heb. 12:16 — 1223

Mortar (I)—*a vessel*
Vessel used for beating
grains . . . . Num. 11:8 — 147
Used
figuratively . . . . Prov. 27:22 — 634

Mortar (II)—*a building material*
Made of:
Clay . . . . Is. 41:25 — 687
Slime (bitumen) . . Gen. 11:3 — 13
Plaster . . . . Lev. 14:42, 45 — 114

Mortgage—*something given in security for debt*
Postexilic Jews burdened
with . . . . Neh. 5:3 — 492

Mortification—*a putting to death*
A. *Objects of:*
Law . . . . Rom. 7:4 — 1113
Sin . . . . Rom. 6:6, 11 — 1112
Flesh . . . . Rom. 13:14 — 1119
Members of earthly
body . . . . Col. 3:5 — 1178
B. *Agents of:*
Holy Spirit . . . . Rom. 8:13 — 1114
Our
obedience . . . . Rom. 6:17-19 — 1113

Mosera (sing.), **Moseroth** (pl.)—*bond*
Place of Aaron's death and
burial . . . . Deut. 10:6 — 188
Israelite
encampment . . . . Num. 33:30, 31 — 171

Moses—*drawn out*
A. *Early life of* (first 40 years):
Descendant of
Levi. . . . . Ex. 2:1 — 57

Son of Amram and
Jochebed . . . . . Ex. 6:16-20 — 61
Brother of Aaron and
Miriam . . . . Ex. 15:20 — 70
Born under
slavery . . . . Ex. 2:1-10 — 57
Hid by
mother . . . . Ex. 2:2, 3 — 57
Educated in Egyptian
wisdom . . . . . . Acts 7:22 — 1079
Refused Egyptian
sonship . . . . . . Heb. 11:23-27 — 1222
Defended his
people . . . . Ex. 2:11-14 — 57
Rejected, flees to
Midian . . . . Ex. 2:15 — 57
B. *In Midian* (second 40 years):
Married
Zipporah . . . . . Ex. 2:16-21 — 57
Father of two {Ex. 2:22 — 58
sons   {Acts 7:29 — 1079
Became Jethro's
shepherd . . . . . Ex. 3:1 — 58
C. *Leader of Israel* (last 40 years;
to the end of his life):
Heard God's
voice. . . . . Ex. 3:2-6 — 58
God's plan revealed to
him . . . . Ex. 3:7-10 — 58
Argued with
God . . . . Ex. 4:1-17 — 59
Met Aaron . . . . Ex. 4:14-28 — 59
Assembled elders of
Israelites . . . . . Ex. 4:29-31 — 60
Rejected by Pharaoh and
Israel . . . . Ex. 5:1-23 — 60
Conflict with Pharaoh; ten
plagues sent . . Ex. 7—12 — 62
Commanded to
institute the {Ex. 12:1-29 — 66
Passover   {Heb. 11:28 — 1222
D. *From Egypt to Sinai:*
Led people from
Egypt . . . . Ex. 12:30-38 — 67
Observed the
Passover . . . . . Ex. 12:39-51 — 67
Healed bitter
waters . . . . Ex. 15:22-27 — 70
People hunger; flesh
and manna {Ex. 16:1-36 — 71
supplied . . . . . {John 6:31, 32 — 1049
Came to
Sinai . . . . Ex. 19:1, 2 — 73
E. *At Sinai:*
Called to God's
presence . . . . . Acts 7:38 — 1079
Prepared Israel for the
Law . . . . Ex. 19:7-25 — 74
Received the
Law . . . . Ex. 20—23 — 75
Confirmed the covenant with
Israel . . . . Ex. 24:1-11 — 78
Stayed 40 days on
Sinai . . . . Ex. 24:12-16 — 79
Shown the pattern of the
tabernacle . . . . Ex. 25—31 — 79
Israel sins; Moses
interceded . . . . Ex. 32:1-35 — 87
Recommissioned and
encouraged . . . Ex. 33:1-23 — 88
Instructions received;
tabernacle
erected. . . . . . . Ex. 36—40 — 91
Consecrated
Aaron. . . . . Lev. 8:1-36 — 106
Numbered the
men. . . . . Num. 1:1-54 — 133
Observed the
Passover . . . . . Num. 9:1-5 — 145
F. *From Sinai to Kadesh-barnea:*
Resumed journey to
Canaan . . . . . . Num. 10:11-36 — 146
Complained; 70 elders
appointed . . . . Num. 11:1-35 — 147
Spoke against by Miriam and
Aaron . . . . Num. 12:1-6 — 148

SUBJECT	REFERENCE	PAGE

Mountain—continued

Mizar	Ps. 42:6	565
Moreh	Judg. 7:1	250
Moriah	Gen. 22:2	22
Nebo	Deut. 34:1	212
Olives or		
Olivet	Matt. 24:3	966
Pisgah	Num. 21:20	158
Sinai	Ex. 19:2-20	73
Sion or Zion	2 Sam. 5:7	313
Tabor	Judg. 4:6-14	247

B. *In Christ's life, place of:*

Temptation	Matt. 4:8	944
Sermon	Matt. 5:1	944
Prayer	Matt. 14:23	956
Transfigura-		
tion	Matt. 17:1, 2	959
Prophecy	Matt. 24:3	966
Agony	Matt. 26:30, 31	970
Ascension	Luke 24:50	1037

C. *Uses of:*

Boundaries	Num. 34:7, 8	172
Distant		
vision	Deut. 3:27	181
Hunting	1 Sam. 26:20	302
Warfare	1 Sam. 17:3	291
Protection	Amos 6:1	858
Refuge	Matt. 24:16	967
Idolatrous		
worship	Is. 65:7	703
Assembly		
sites	Josh. 8:30-33	224

D. *Significant Old Testament events on:*

Ark rested upon		
(Ararat)	Gen. 8:4	10
Abraham's testing		
(Moriah)	Gen. 22:1-19	22
Giving of the Law		
(Sinai)	Ex. 19:2-25	73
Moses' view of Canaan		
(Pisgah)	Deut. 34:1	212
Combat with Baalism		
(Carmel)	1 Kin. 18:19-42	360
David's city		
(Zion)	2 Sam. 5:7	313

E. *Figurative of:*

God's:		
Protection	Is. 31:4	679
Dwelling	Is. 8:18	664
Judgments	Jer. 13:16	720
Gospel age	Is. 27:13	676
Messiah's		
advent	Is. 40:9	685
Great joy	Is. 44:23	689
Great		
difficulties	Matt. 21:21	963
Pride of man	Luke 3:5	1007
Supposed		
faith	1 Cor. 13:2	1135

Mourning—*expression of sorrow*

A. *Caused by:*

Death	Gen. 50:10	52
Defection	1 Sam. 15:35	290
Disobedience	Ezra 9:4-7	483
Desolation	Joel 1:9, 10	850
Defeat	Rev. 18:11	1279
Discourage-		
ment	Ps. 42:9	566
Disease	Job 2:5-8	519

B. *Transformed into:*

Gladness	Is. 51:11	694
Hope	John 11:23-28	1056
Everlasting		
joy	Is. 35:10	682

C. *Signs of:*

Tearing of		
clothing	2 Sam. 3:31, 32	312
Ashes on		
head	2 Sam. 13:19	320
Sackcloth	Gen. 37:34	40
Neglect of		
appearance	2 Sam. 19:24	328
Presence of		
mourners	John 11:19, 31	1056
Apparel	2 Sam. 14:2	321
Shave head	Jer. 16:6, 7	722

Mouse, mice—*a small quadruped*

Accounted		
unclean	Lev. 11:29	109
Destructive of		
crops	1 Sam. 6:5	280
Eaten by idolatrous		
Israelites	Is. 66:17	704

Mouth

A. *Descriptive of:*

Top of a well	Gen. 29:2, 3, 8	30
Opening of a		
sack	Gen. 42:27, 28	44
Man's	Job 3:1	520

B. *Exhortations concerning:*

Make all		
acceptable	Ps. 19:14	555
Keep with a		
bridle	Ps. 39:1	564
Set a watch		
before	Ps. 141:3	608
Keep the corrupt		
from	Eph. 4:29	1165
Keep filthy language		
from	Col. 3:8	1178

C. *Of unregenerate, source of:*

Idolatry	1 Kin. 19:18	362
Lying	1 Kin. 22:13, 22, 23	366
Unfaith-		
fulness	Ps. 5:9	549
Cursing	Ps. 10:7	551
Pride	Ps. 17:10	553
Evil	Ps. 50:19	569
Lies	Ps. 63:11	573
Vanity	Ps. 144:8, 11	609
Foolishness	Prov. 15:2, 14	624

D. *Of regenerate, used for:*

Prayer	1 Sam. 1:12	276
God's Law	Josh. 1:8	217
Praise	Ps. 34:1	561
Wisdom	Ps. 37:30	563
Testimony	Eph. 6:9	1167
Confession	Rom. 10:8-10	1116
Righ-		
teousness	Ps. 71:15	577

Move—*to change the position*

A. *Of God's Spirit in:*

Creation	Gen. 1:2	4
Man	Judg. 13:25	258
Prophets	2 Pet. 1:21	1243

B. *Of things immovable:*

Righteous	Ps. 112:6	597
City of God	Ps. 46:4, 5	567
Eternal		
kingdom	Ps. 96:10	589

Mowing—*to cut grass*

First growth for		
taxes	Amos 7:1	859
Left on the		
ground	Ps. 72:6	577

Moza—*a going forth*

1. *Descendant of*

Judah	1 Chr. 2:46	407

2. *Descendant of*

Saul	1 Chr. 8:36, 37	413

Mozah—*drained*

A Benjamite		
town	Josh. 18:21, 26	234

Mufflers—*an elaborate veil*

Worn by women	Is. 3:16, 19	660

Mulberry tree

Referred to by		
Jesus	Luke 17:6	1027

Mule—*a hybrid between a horse and a donkey*

Breeding of,		
forbidden	Lev. 19:19	119
Sign of kingship	1 Kin. 1:33	338
Used in trade	Ezek. 27:14	795

Considered		
stubborn	Ps. 32:9	560

Multiply—*to increase in quantity or quality*

A. *Of good things:*

Holy seed	Jer. 30:19	735
Churches	Acts 9:31	1082
Word of God	Acts 12:24	1086
God's		
wonders	Ex. 7:3	62
Loaves and	Matt. 15:32-39	957
fish	John 6:1-15	1048

B. *Secret of:*

God's:		
Promise	Gen. 16:10	17
Oath	Gen. 26:3, 4	27
Man's		
obedience	Deut. 7:12, 13	186

Multitude—*a large number of people*

A. *Dangers of:*

Mixed, source of		
evil	Ex. 12:38	67
Follow after in doing		
evil	Ex. 23:2	77
Sacrifices,		
vain	Is. 1:11	659

B. *Christ's compassion upon:*

Teaching	Matt. 5:1	944
Healing	Matt. 12:15	952
Teaching parables		
to	Matt. 13:1-3, 34	954
Feeding	Matt. 14:15-21	956

C. *Their attitude toward Christ:*

Reaction to	Matt. 9:8, 33	949
Recognition	Matt. 14:5	956
of	Matt. 21:46	964
Reception of	Matt. 21:8-11	963
Running		
after	John 6:2	1048
Rejection of	Matt. 27:20	972

Munificence—*generous in giving*

Measure of, on:

God's part	Mal. 3:10	909
Israel's part	Ex. 36:3-7	91
Judah's part	1 Chr. 29:3-9	433
Christian's part	2 Cor. 8:1-5	1147

Munition

Kept for war	Nah. 2:1	878

Muppim—*obscurities*

Son of Benjamin	Gen. 46:21	48
Called Shupham	Num. 26:39	163
Shuppim and	1 Chr. 7:12, 15	412
Shephuphan	1 Chr. 8:5	413

Murder

A. *Defined as:*

Coming out of the		
heart	Matt. 15:19	957
Result from		
anger	Matt. 5:21, 22	945
Work of the		
flesh	Gal. 5:19-21	1158
Excluding from eternal		
life	1 John 3:15	1251

B. *Guilt of:*

Determined by		
witnesses	Num. 35:30	174
Not		
redeemable	Num. 35:30	174
Not forgiven by flight to the		
altar	Ex. 21:14	76

C. *Penalty of:*

Ordained by		
God	Gen. 9:6	12
Executed by avenger of		
blood	Deut. 19:6	196

See Homicide

Murmuring—*sullen dissatisfaction with things*

A. *Caused by:*

Thirst	Ex. 15:24	70

SUBJECT	REFERENCE	PAGE

Naarai—*pleasantness of Yahweh*

One of David's mighty
men..............1 Chr. 11:37   416

Nabal—*fool*

Wealthy sheep
owner...........1 Sam. 25:2, 3   299
Refuses David's
request.........1 Sam. 25:4-12   299
Abigail, wife of, appeases David's
wrath against ....1 Sam. 25:13-35   300
Drunk, dies of a
stroke............1 Sam. 25:36-39   301
Widow of, becomes David's
wife..............1 Sam. 25:39-42   301

Naboth—*sprout*

Owner of vineyard coveted by King
Ahab............1 Kin. 21:1-4   364
Accused falsely of blasphemy and
disloyalty.........1 Kin. 21:5-16   364
Murder of,
avenged..........1 Kin. 21:17-25   365

Nachon—*prepared*

Threshing floor, site of Uzzah's
death.............2 Sam. 6:6, 7   313

Called:
Perez-uzzah
("breach").......2 Sam. 6:8   314
Chidon...........1 Chr. 13:9   418

Nadab—*willing, liberal*

1. Eldest of Aaron's four
   sons ....Ex. 6:23   61
   Takes part in affirming
   covenant....Ex. 24:1, 9-12   78
   Becomes
   priest ....Ex. 28:1   82
   Consumed by
   fire...........Lev. 10:1-7   108
   Dies childless ..Num. 3:4   136
2. Judahite ....1 Chr. 2:28, 30   406
3. Benjamite .....1 Chr. 8:30   413
4. King of
   Israel.........1 Kin. 14:20   356
   Killed by
   Baasha........1 Kin. 15:25-31   357

Naggai

Ancestor of
Christ...........Luke 3:25   1008

Nagging woman

Gets Samson's
secret..........Judg. 16:13-17   260
Called brawling ...Prov. 21:9, 19   628
Undesirable ......Prov. 25:24   632
Prov. 27:15   633

Nahalal, Nahalol—*drinking place for flocks*

Village of
Zebulun..........Josh. 19:10, 15   234
Assigned to Merarite
Levites..........Josh. 21:35   237
Canaanites not driven
from ....Judg. 1:30   244

Nahaliel—*valley of God*

Israelite camp....Num. 21:19   158

Naham—*consolation*

Father of Keilah ..1 Chr. 4:19   408

Nahamani—*compassionate*

Returned after the
exile..............Neh. 7:7   494

Naharai—*snorting*

Armor-bearer of   (2 Sam. 23:37   332
Joab.............. (1 Chr. 11:39   417

Nahash—*serpent*

1. King of Ammon; makes
   impossible
   demands......1 Sam. 11:1-15   284
2. King of Ammon who treats
   David kindly ..2 Sam. 10:2   317

Son of, helps
David.........2 Sam. 17:27-29   325
3. Father of Abigail and Zeruiah,
   David's half
   sisters.........2 Sam. 17:25   325

Nahath—*descent*

1. Edomite
   chief..........Gen. 36:13   38
2. Kohathite
   Levite.........1 Chr. 6:26   410
   Called Tohu ...1 Sam. 1:1   276
3. Levite in Hezekiah's
   reign..........2 Chr. 31:13   465

Nahbi—*concealed*

Spy of Naphtali ...Num. 13:14   149

Nahor, Nachor—*snorting*

1. Grandfather of
   Abraham.......Gen. 11:24-26   14
2. Son of Terah, brother of
   Abraham.......Gen. 11:27   14
   Marries Milcah, begets eight
   sons by her and four by
   concubine.....Gen. 11:29   14
   City of
   Haran.........Gen. 24:10   24
   God of.........Gen. 31:53   34

Nahshon

Judahite leader....Num. 1:4, 7   133
Aaron's brother-in-
law.............Ex. 6:23   61
Ancestor of
David ....Ruth 4:20-22   272
Ancestor of
Christ...........Matt. 1:4   941

Nahum—*full of comfort*

Inspired prophet to Judah
concerning
Nineveh..........Nah. 1:1   878

Nahum, the Book of—*a book of the Old Testament*

The awesomeness of
God..............Nah. 1:1-15   878
The destruction of
Nineveh..........Nah. 2—3   878

Nail

A. *Significant uses of:*
   Killing a
   man ....Judg. 4:21, 25   247
   Holding idols in
   place..........Is. 41:7   686
   Fastening Christ to
   cross.........John 20:25   1066

B. *Figurative uses of:*
   Words fixed in the
   memory.......Eccl. 12:11   647
   Revived
   nation ....Ezra 9:8   483
   Messiah's
   kingdom ......Is. 22:23, 24   673
   Messiah's
   death ....Is. 22:25   673
   Atonement for man's
   sin ....Col. 2:14   1178

Nain—*pleasant*

Village south of Nazareth; Jesus
raises widow's son
here.............Luke 7:11-17   1013

Naioth—*habitations*

Prophets' school   (1 Sam. 19:18, 19,
in Ramah........ (22, 23   294

Naked, nakedness—*nude, nudity*

A. *Used of man's:*
   Original state ..Gen. 2:25   6
   Sinful state ....Gen. 3:7, 10, 11   6
   State of
   grace ....Rom. 8:35   1115
   Disembodied
   state..........2 Cor. 5:3   1145

B. *Evil of:*
   Strictly
   forbidden .....Lev. 18:6-20   118
   Brings a
   curse........Gen. 9:21-25   12
   Judged by
   God..........Ezek. 22:10   790
C. *Instances of:*
   Noah guilty
   of.............Gen. 9:21-23   12
   Forbidden, to
   priests ....Ex. 20:26   75
   Michal rebukes David
   for............2 Sam. 6:20-23   314
D. *Putting clothing on:*
   Indicates a changed
   life............Mark 5:15   983
   Promises a
   reward........Matt. 25:34-40   968
   Takes away
   shame.......Rev. 3:18   1270
   Sign of true
   faith ....James 2:15-17   1229
E. *Figurative of:*
   Separation from
   God...........Is. 20:3   672
   Israel's unworthi-
   ness..........Ezek. 16:7-22   783
   Judah's spiritual
   adultery......Ezek. 16:36-38   784
   God's
   judgment .....Ezek. 16:39   784
   Spiritual
   need ....Hos. 2:9   841
   Wickedness....Nah. 3:4, 5   879
   Needy ....Matt. 25:36, 38   969
   God's
   knowledge ....Heb. 4:13   1216
   Unprepared-
   ness..........Rev. 16:15   1278

Name—*a word used to identify a person, animal, or thing*

A. *Determined by:*
   Events of the
   time ....Gen. 30:8   31
   Prophetic
   position ......Gen. 25:26   27
   Fondness of
   hope..........Gen. 29:32-35   31
   Change of
   character .....John 1:42   1043
   Innate
   character ....1 Sam. 25:25   300
   Coming
   events ....Is. 8:1-4   664
   Divine
   mission ....Matt. 1:21   942
B. *Of God, described as:*
   Great.........Josh. 7:9   222
   Secret ....Judg. 13:18   258
   Glorious ....Is. 63:14   702
   Everlasting ....Ps. 135:13   606
   Excellent ......Ps. 148:13   611
   Holy..........Is. 57:15   697
C. *Of God, evil acts against:*
   Taken in
   vain...........Ex. 20:7   75
   Sworn falsely ..Lev. 19:12   119
   Lies spoken
   in.............Zech. 13:3   903
   Despised......Mal. 1:6   907
D. *Of God, proper attitude toward:*
   Exalt ....Ps. 34:3   561
   Praise ....Ps. 54:6   570
   Love..........Ps. 69:36   576
E. *Of Christ:*
   Given before
   birth..........Matt. 1:21, 23   942
   Hated by the
   world.........Matt. 10:22   951
   Deeds done in,
   rewarded......Matt. 10:42   951
   Believers baptized
   in.............Acts 2:38   1074
   Miracles performed
   by ....Acts 3:16   1075

SUBJECT	REFERENCE	PAGE	SUBJECT	REFERENCE	PAGE	SUBJECT	REFERENCE	PAGE

Figurative of something
impossible.......Matt. 19:24   961

Needlework—*embroidered work*
Of the
tabernacle.......Ex. 26:36; 28:39;
38:18   81

Needy—*the poor*

A. *Evil treatment of:*
Oppression.....Amos 4:1   857
Injustice
toward......Is. 10:2   666

B. *Promise toward:*
God's:
Remembrance
of.............Ps. 9:18   551
Deliverance...Ps. 35:10   561
Salvation of ..Ps. 72:4-13   577
Exaltation of..Ps. 113:7   597
Strength of ....Is. 25:4   675

C. *Right treatment of:*
Recom-
mended.......Deut. 24:14, 15   201
Remem-
bered.........Jer. 22:16   727
Rewarded......Matt. 25:34-40   968
See Poor, poverty

Negev—*dry, parched; denotes southern Palestine*
Hebron located
in.................Num. 13:22   149

Neglect—*to fail to respond to duties*

A. *Of material things:*
One's
appearance....2 Sam. 19:24   328
Needs of the
body.........Col. 2:23   1178

B. *Of spiritual things:*
Gospel.........Matt. 22:2-5   964
Salvation .....Heb. 2:1-3   1215

C. *Consequences of:*
Kept out.......Matt. 25:1-13   968
Sent to hell....Matt. 25:24-30   968
Reward lost....1 Cor. 3:10-15   1127

Nehelamite
Term applied to Shemaiah, a false
prophet ....Jer. 29:24-32   734

Nehemiah (I)—*Yahweh has comforted*
1. Leader in the postexilic
community....Ezra 2:2   475
2. Postexilic
workman .....Neh. 3:16   491

Nehemiah (II)—*Yahweh has comforted*

A. *Life of:*
Son of
Hachaliah.....Neh. 1:1   489
Cupbearer to the Persian
King Artaxerxes I
(465–424
B.C.) ....Neh. 1:11   489
Grieves over Jerusalem's
desolation...Neh. 1:4-11   489
Appointed
governor.....Neh. 5:14   493
Sent to rebuild
Jerusalem.....Neh. 2:1-8   489
Unwelcome by non-
Jews.........Neh. 2:9, 10   490
Views walls at
night.......Neh. 2:11-20   490
Gives list of
builders.......Neh. 3:1-32   490
Continues work in spite of
opposition....Neh. 4:1-23   491
Makes reforms among
Jews.......Neh. 5:1-19   492
Opposition continues, but work
completed....Neh. 6:1-19   493
Introduces law and
order.......Neh. 7:1-73   494

Participates with Ezra in
restored
worship......Neh. 8—10   495
Registers
inhabitants....Neh. 11:1-36   500
Registers priests and
Levites......Neh. 12:1-26   501
Returns to Artaxerxes; revisits
Jerusalem.....Neh. 13:6, 7   502
Institutes
reforms.......Neh. 13:1-31   502

B. *Character of:*
Patriotic......Neh. 1:1-4   489
Prayerful .....Neh. 1:5-11   489
Perceptive....Neh. 2:17-20   490
Persistent....Neh. 4:1-23   491
Persuasive....Neh. 5:1-13   492
Pure in
motives......Neh. 5:14-19   493
Persevering....Neh. 6:1-19   493
See the next article

Nehemiah, the Book of—*a book of the Old Testament*
Nehemiah's
prayer...........Neh. 1:4-11   489
Inspection of the
wall..............Neh. 2:11-16   490
Rebuilding the
wall..............Neh. 3:1-32   490
The enemies'
plot.............Neh. 6:1-14   493
The reading of the
Law..............Neh. 8:1-18   495
Confession of the
priests...........Neh. 9:4-38   497
Nehemiah's
reform ....Neh. 13:7-31   502

Nehum—*consolation*
Postexilic
returnee.......Neh. 7:7   494
Called Rehum.....Ezra 2:2   475

Nehushta—*of bronze*
Wife of King
Jehoiakim........2 Kin. 24:8   398

Nehushtan—*piece of brass*
Applied to brazen
serpent........2 Kin. 18:4   390

Neiel—*dwelling of God*
Town in Asher....Josh. 19:24, 27   235

Neigh—*to cry lustfully*
Used of:
Horses..........Jer. 8:16   716
Lustful desires ...Jer. 5:8   713
Rendered
"bellow"..........Jer. 50:11   755

Neighbor

A. *Sins against, forbidden:*
False witness ..Ex. 20:16   75
Coveting ......Ex. 20:17   75
Lying.........Lev. 6:2-5   104
Hating........Deut. 19:11-13   196
Despising....Prov. 14:21   624
Enticing ......Prov. 16:29   625
Deception ....Prov. 26:19   633
Flattery.......Prov. 29:5   634
Failure to
pay ....Jer. 22:13   727
Adultery.......Jer. 29:23   734

B. *Duties toward, encouraged:*
Love.........Rom. 13:9, 10   1119
Speak truth
to............Eph. 4:25   1165
Teach ....Jer. 31:34   737
Show mercy
to.............Luke 10:29, 37   1019

Nekeb—*a narrow pass*
Village in
Naphtali..........Josh. 19:33   235

Nekoda—*dotted*
Founder of a family of Temple
servants........Ezra 2:48   476
Genealogy of,
rejected.........Ezra 2:59, 60   476

Nemuel—*God is spreading*
1. Brother of Dathan and
Abiram ....Num. 26:9   162
2. Eldest son of
Simeon ....1 Chr. 4:24   408
Head of
Nemuelites....Num. 26:12   163
Called
Jemuel........Gen. 46:10   48

Nepheg—*sprout*
1. Izhar's son; Korah's
brother ......Ex. 6:21   61
2. David's son born in
Jerusalem.....2 Sam. 5:13-15   313

Nephew—*old English for grandson*
Applied to:
Abdon's.........Judg. 12:14   257
Widow's.........1 Tim. 5:4   1196
Used as a curse ...Is. 14:22   669

Nephtoah—*opening*
Border town between Judah and
Benjamin........Josh. 15:9   231

Nepotism—*putting relatives in public offices*
Joseph's..........Gen. 47:11, 12   49
Saul's...........1 Sam. 14:50   288
David's ....2 Sam. 8:16-18   316
Nehemiah's ....Neh. 7:2   494

Ner—*lamp*
Father of Abner;
grandfather of { 1 Sam. 14:50,
Saul.............{ 51   288

Nereus—*the name of a sea god*
Christian at
Rome ....Rom. 16:15   1121

Nergal—*a Babylonian god of war*
Worshiped by men of
Cuth ....2 Kin. 17:30   390

Nergal-sharezer—*Nergal preserve the king*
Babylonian prince during capture
of Jerusalem......Jer. 39:3, 13   745

Neri
Ancestor of
Christ............Luke 3:27   1008

Neriah—*Yahweh is a lamp*
Father of
Baruch..........Jer. 32:12   737

Nest

A. *Kinds of:*
Eagle's.........Job 39:27   541
Swallow's......Ps. 84:3   584
Great owl's ...Is. 34:15   681
Dove's........Jer. 48:28   752

B. *Figurative of:*
False
security......Num. 24:21, 22   161
Lord's resting
place.........Matt. 8:20   948
Full maturity ..Job 29:18   535
Something out of
place.........Prov. 27:8   633
Helplessness ...Is. 10:14   666

Net

A. *Kinds of:*
Design in a
structure......Ex. 27:4, 5   81
Trapping a bird or
animal........Prov. 1:17   615
Catching fish ..John 21:6-11   1066

SUBJECT	REFERENCE	PAGE	SUBJECT	REFERENCE	PAGE	SUBJECT	REFERENCE	PAGE
Begins at sunset	Gen. 28:11	30	Water of, turned to blood	Ex. 7:15, 20	62	**Noadiah**—*Jehovah has met by appointment*		
Established by God's covenant	Gen. 8:22	11	D. *Figurative of:* Judgment	Ezek. 30:12	798	1. Levite in Ezra's time	Ezra 8:33	482
Displays God's glory	Ps. 19:2	555		Amos 9:5	860	2. Prophetess who tries to frighten		
Designed for rest	Ps. 104:23	592	Army	Jer. 46:7-9	750	Nehemiah	Neh. 6:14	493
Wild beasts creep in	Ps. 104:20-22	592	**Nimrah**—*an abbreviation of Beth-nimrah*			**Noah (I)**—*rest*		
None in heaven	Zech. 14:7	903	Town in Gilead	Num. 32:3, 36	169	A. *Life of:* Son of Lamech	Gen. 5:28, 29	9
Divided into "watches" and hours	Mark 13:35	994	**Nimrim**—*wholesome waters*			Father of Shem, Ham and Japheth	Gen. 5:32	9
B. *Special events in:* Jacob's wrestling	Gen. 32:22-31	35	Place in south Moab	Is. 15:6	669	Finds favor with God	Gen. 6:8	9
Egypt's greatest plague	Ex. 12:12-31	66	**Nimrod**—*strong*			Lives in the midst of corruption	Gen. 6:1-13	9
Ordinance of the Passover	Ex. 12:42	68	Ham's grandson	Gen. 10:6-8	13	Instructed to build the ark	Gen. 6:13-22	9
King's sleeplessness	Esth. 6:1	511	Becomes a mighty hunter	Gen. 10:8, 9	13	Preacher of righteousness	2 Pet. 2:5	1243
Nehemiah's vigil	Neh. 2:11-16	490	Establishes cities	Gen. 10:10-12	13	Enters ark with family and animals	Gen. 7:1-24	10
Belshazzar slain	Dan. 5:30	829	Land of Assyria, thus described	Mic. 5:6	873	Preserved during flood	Gen. 8:1-17	10
Angelic revelation	Luke 2:8-15	1006	**Nimshi**—*Yahweh reveals*			Builds an altar	Gen. 8:18-22	11
Nicodemus' talk	John 3:2	1044	Grandfather of King Jehu	2 Kin. 9:2, 14	380	Covenant established with	Gen. 9:1-19	11
Release from prison	Acts 5:19	1077	Called Jehu's father	2 Kin. 9:20	381	Plants a vineyard; becomes drunk	Gen. 9:20, 21	12
Paul's escape	Acts 9:24, 25	1082	**Nineveh**—*the capital of ancient Assyria*			Pronounces curse and blessings	Gen. 9:22-27	12
Wonderful conversion	Acts 16:25-33	1090	A. *History of:* Built by Nimrod	Gen. 10:8-12	13	Dies at 950	Gen. 9:28, 29	12
Lord's return	Mark 13:35	994	Capital of Assyria	2 Kin. 19:36	393	B. *Character of:* Righteous	Gen. 6:9	9
C. *Good acts in:* Toil	Luke 5:5	1010	Jonah preaches to	Jon. 1:1, 2	866	Obedient	Heb. 11:7	1221
Prayer	1 Sam. 15:11	289	Citizens of repent	Jon. 3:5-9	867	In fellowship with God	Gen. 6:9	9
	Luke 6:12	1011	At the judgment seat	Matt. 12:41	953	Notable in history	Ezek. 14:14, 20	782
Song	Job 35:10	539	B. *Prophecies concerning its:*			**Noah (II)**—*trembling*		
	Ps. 42:8	566	Destruction by Babylon	Nah. 2:1-4	878	Daughter of Zelophehad	Num. 26:33	163
Flight from evil	{1 Sam. 19:10	294	Internal weakness	Nah. 3:11-17	879	**Nob**—*height*		
	Matt. 2:14	942	Utter desolation	Nah. 3:18, 19	879	City of priests; David flees to	1 Sam. 21:1-9	296
Dreams	Matt. 2:12, 13, 19	942	C. *Described as:* Great city	Jon. 3:2, 3	867	Priests of, killed by Saul	1 Sam. 22:9-23	297
D. *Evil acts in:* Drunkenness	Is. 5:11	661	Wealthy	Nah. 2:9	879	Near Jerusalem	Is. 10:32	667
Thievery	Obad. 5	863	Fortified	Nah. 3:8, 12	879	Reinhabited after the exile	Neh. 11:32	501
	Matt. 27:64	973	Wicked	Jon. 1:2	866	**Nobah**—*barking*		
Debauchery	1 Thess. 5:2-7	1185	Idolatrous	Nah. 1:14	878	1. Manassite leader	Num. 32:42	170
Betrayal	Matt. 26:31, 34, 46-50	970	Careless	Zeph. 2:15	888	2. Town in Gad	Judg. 8:11	251
Death	Luke 12:20	1021	Full of lies	Nah. 3:1	879	**Nobleman**—*one who belongs to the upper class*		
F. *Figurative of:* Present age	Rom. 13:11, 12	1119	**Ninth hour**—*3 P.M.*			*Jesus:* Heals son of	John 4:46-54	1046
Death	John 9:4	1053	Time of Christ's death	Matt. 27:46	972	Cites in parable	Luke 19:12-27	1029
Unregenerate state	1 Thess. 5:5, 7	1185	Customary hour of prayer	Acts 3:1	1074	**Nod**—*wandering exile*		
Judgment	Mic. 3:6	872	Time of Cornelius' vision	Acts 10:1, 3	1083	Place (east of Eden) of Cain's abode	Gen. 4:16, 17	8
Nighthawk			**Nisan**—*beginning*			**Nodab**—*nobility*		
Unclean bird	Lev. 11:16	109	Name of Abib (first month of Jewish year) after the exile	Neh. 2:1	489	Arabian tribe	1 Chr. 5:19	409
Night monster—*a nocturnal creature*			See Jewish calendar			**Nogah**—*brilliance*		
Dwells in ruins	Is. 34:14	681	**Nisroch**—*eagle, hawk*			One of David's sons	1 Chr. 3:1, 7	407
Nile—*Egypt's main river*			Sennacherib's god	2 Kin. 19:37	393	**Nohah**—*rest*		
A. *Called:* Sihor	Is. 23:3	673	**Nitre**—*carbonate of soda* (in the Bible)			Benjamin's fourth son	1 Chr. 8:1, 2	413
Stream of Egypt	Is. 27:12	676	Figurative of agitation	Prov. 25:20	632	**Noise**—*a sound of something*		
Sea	Nah. 3:8	879	As a cleansing agent	Jer. 2:22	710	A. *Kinds of:* Sea	Ps. 65:7	574
B. *Characteristics of:* Has seven streams	Is. 11:15	667	**No-amon**—*the Egyptian city Thebes*			Battle	Is. 13:4	668
Overflows annually	Jer. 46:8	750	Nineveh compared to	Nah. 3:8	879		Jer. 47:3	751
Source of Egyptian wealth	Is. 19:5-8	671				Sound of Songs	Ezek. 26:13	795
C. *Events connected with:* Drowning of male children	Ex. 1:22	57					Amos 5:23	858
Moses placed in	Ex. 2:3	57						

SUBJECT	REFERENCE	PAGE	SUBJECT	REFERENCE	PAGE	SUBJECT	REFERENCE	PAGE

Noise—continued

Mourners	Matt. 9:23	950
Crying	1 Sam. 4:13, 14	279
Revelry	Ex. 32:17, 18	87
Dog	Ps. 59:6	572
God's glory	Ezek. 43:2	811

B. *Figurative of:*

Strong opposition	Is. 31:4	679
Worthlessness	Jer. 46:17	751

Noisome—*something evil or deadly*

Hurtful beasts	Ezek. 14:15, 21	782
Deadly pestilence	Ps. 91:3	588
Foul sore	Rev. 16:2	1278

Nomad—*wanderer*

Life style of patriarchs	{Gen. 12:1-9	14
	{Gen. 13:1-18	15
Israel's history	Deut. 26:5	202

Noon—*midday*

A. *Time of:*

Eating	Gen. 43:16, 25	45
Resting	2 Sam. 4:5	312
Praying	Ps. 55:17	571
Crying aloud	Ps. 55:17	571
Drunkenness	1 Kin. 20:16	363
Destruction	Ps. 91:6	588
Death	2 Kin. 4:20	375

B. *Figurative of:*

Blindness	Deut. 28:29	204
Cleansing	Job 11:17	525

Nophah—*windy place*

Moabite town	Num. 21:29, 30	158

North

Refers to:

A geographical direction	{Gen. 28:14	30
	{Ps. 107:3	595
Invading forces	Is. 14:31	669
	Jer. 6:1	713

Nose, nostrils—*the organ of breathing*

A. *Used literally for:*

Breathing	Gen. 2:7	5
Smelling	Amos 4:10	857
Ornamentation	Is. 3:21	660
Bondage	Is. 37:29	684
Blood (forced)	Prov. 30:33	636
Behemoth	Job 40:15-24	542
Idols	Ps. 115:6	598
Nosebleeding produced by wringing	Prov. 30:33	636

B. *Used figuratively of:*

Man's life	Job 27:3	533
God's: Power	Ex. 15:8	70
Sovereign control	2 Kin. 19:28	393
Overindulgence	Num. 11:20	147
National hope (Zedekiah)	Lam. 4:20	766
Something very offensive	Is. 65:5	703

Nose jewels

Worn by women	Is. 3:21	660
Put in swine's snout	Prov. 11:22	622

Nothing—*not a thing*

Things classified as:
Service without:

Christ	John 15:5	1060
Love	1 Cor. 13:3	1135
Circumcision	1 Cor. 7:19	1130
Flesh	John 6:63	1049

Not my people, Not loved—*symbolic names of Hosea's children*

Lo-ammi	Hos. 1:9	840
Lo-ruhamah	Hos. 1:6	840

Nought

A. *Descriptive of:*
Something:

Fruitless	Is. 49:24	693
Without payment	Gen. 29:15	30
Vain	Mal. 1:10	907
Nothing	Is. 41:24	687

B. *Time of:*

Past	Neh. 4:15	492
Present	Amos 6:13	859
Future	Ps. 33:10	560

C. *Things that will come to:*

Wicked	Job 8:22	523
Wicked counsel	Is. 8:10	664
Babylon	Rev. 18:17	1280

Nourish—*provide means of growth to*

A. *Descriptive of the growth or care of:*

Children	Acts 7:20, 21	1079
Animals	2 Sam. 12:3	318
Plants	Is. 44:14	689
Family	Gen. 45:11	47
Country	Acts 12:20	1085

B. *Figurative of:*

Protection	Is. 1:2	658
Provision	Ruth 4:15	272
Pampering	James 5:5	1230
Preparedness	1 Tim. 4:6	1196

Novice—*one who is inexperienced; a recent Christian convert*

Bishops, not to be	1 Tim. 3:1, 6	1195

Now—*the present time*

A. *As contrasted with:*
Old

Testament	John 4:23	1045
Past	John 9:25	1053
Future	John 13:7, 19	1058

Two

conditions	Luke 16:25	1026

B. *In Christ's life, descriptive of His:*

Atonement	Rom. 5:11	1112
Humiliation	Heb. 2:8	1215
Resurrection	1 Cor. 15:20	1137
Glorification	John 13:31	1059
Intercession	Heb. 9:24	1220
Return	1 John 2:28	1251

C. *In the Christian's life, descriptive of:*

Salvation	Rom. 13:11	1119
Regeneration	John 5:25	1047
Reconciliation	Col. 1:21, 22	1177
Justification	Rom. 5:9	1112
Victory	Gal. 2:20	1155
Worship	John 4:23	1045
Suffering	1 Pet. 1:6-8	1235
Hope	Rev. 12:10	1276
Glorification	Rom. 8:21, 22	1115
	1 John 3:2	1251

D. *Descriptive of the present age as:*
Time of:

Opportunity	2 Cor. 6:2	1146
Evil	1 Thess. 2:6	1184
God's: Greater revelation	Eph. 3:5	1163
Completed redemption	Col. 1:26, 27	1177
Final dealing with mankind	Heb. 12:26	1223

Nuisance—*something very irritating*

Descriptive of:

Widow	Luke 18:2-5	1028

Numbers

Symbolic of:

One—unity	Deut. 6:4	184
	Matt. 19:6	961
Two—unity	Gen. 1:27	4
Two—division	1 Kin. 18:21	360
	Matt. 7:13, 14	947
Three—the Trinity	{Matt. 28:19	974
	{2 Cor. 13:14	1151
	{Hos. 6:1, 2	843
Three—resurrection	{Matt. 12:40	953
	{Luke 13:32	1024
Three—completion	1 Cor. 13:13	1135
Three—testing	Judg. 7:16	251
Four—completion	{Matt. 13:4-8	954
	{John 4:35	1046
Five—faithfulness	Matt. 25:15-20	968
Six—man's testing	{Gen. 1:27, 31	4
	{Rev. 13:18	1276
Seven—completion	Ex. 20:10	75
Seven—fulfillment	Josh. 6:4	221
Seven—perfection	Rev. 1:4	1268
Eighth—new beginning	{Ezek. 43:27	812
	{1 Pet. 3:20	1238
Ten—completion	Dan. 7:7	830
Tenth—God's part	{Gen. 14:20	16
	{Mal. 3:10	909
Twelve—God's purpose	{John 11:9	1055
	{Rev. 21:12-17	1282
Forty—testing	{Jon. 3:4	867
	{Matt. 4:2	943
Forty—judgment	{Num. 14:33	150
	{Ps. 95:10	589
Seventy—God's completed purpose	{Jer. 25:11	730
	{Dan. 9:24	833

Numbers, the Book of—*a book of the Old Testament*

The census	Num. 1:1—4:49	133
Cleansing of Levites	Num. 8:5-22	144
The cloud and the tabernacle	Num. 9:15-23	145
The provision of manna	Num. 11:4-9	147
The spies	Num. 13:1—14:45	148
The rebellion of Korah	Num. 16:1-35	152
The sin of Moses	Num. 20:1-13	156
Aaron's death	Num. 20:22-29	157
Balaam and Balak	{Num. 22:2—24:25	159
Offerings and feasts	{Num. 28:1—29:40	165
Settlements in Gilead	Num. 32:1-42	169
Preparation for Canaan	{Num. 33:50—35:34	172

Nun—*fish*

1. Father of Joshua, Israel's military leader

	Josh. 1:1	217
Called Non	1 Chr. 7:27	412

2. Letter in the Hebrew alphabet

	Ps. 119:105-112	601

Nurse—*nourishment and protection to the young*

A. *Duties of:*

Provide nourishment	Gen. 21:7	22
Protect	2 Kin. 11:2	383
Called "guardian"	2 Kin. 10:1, 5	381

SUBJECT	REFERENCE	PAGE	SUBJECT	REFERENCE	PAGE	SUBJECT	REFERENCE	PAGE

Omission, sins of—*continued*

Christians neglecting to
assemble.....Heb. 10:25   1221

B. *Concerning moral duties:*
Witnessing ...Ezek. 33:1-6   801
Warning......Jer. 42:1-22   747
Watch-
fulness....... { Matt. 24:42-51   967
        { Matt. 26:36-46   970

Omnipotence—*infinite power*

A. *Of God, expressed by His:*
Names ("Almighty,"
etc.) ....Gen. 17:1, 2   18
Creative
word..........Gen. 1:3   4
Control of:
Nature.......Amos 4:13   857
Nations.......Amos 1:1—2:3   855
All things.....Ps. 115:3   598
Power ....Rom. 4:17-24   1111
Unweariness..Is. 40:28   686

B. *Of Christ, expressed by His power over:*
Disease ....Matt. 8:3   948
Unclean
spirit........Mark 1:23-27   979
Devil ....Matt. 4:1-11   943
Death ....John 10:17, 18   1055
Destiny.......Matt. 25:31-33   968

C. *Of the Holy Spirit, expressed by:*
Christ's
anointing .....Is. 11:2   667
Confirmation of the
Gospel ....Rom. 15:19   1120

Omnipresence—*universal presence of*

God..............Jer. 23:23, 24   728
Christ............Matt. 18:20   960
Holy Spirit.......Ps. 139:7-12   607

Omniscience—*infinite knowledge of*

God..............Is. 40:14   685
Christ............Col. 2:2, 3   1177
Holy Spirit.....1 Cor. 2:10-13   1127

Omri—*Yahweh apportions*

1. Descendant of
Benjamin.....1 Chr. 7:8   412
2. Judahite.......1 Chr. 9:4   414
3. Chief officer of
Issachar ......1 Chr. 27:18   431
4. King of Israel; made king
by Israel's
army.........1 Kin. 16:15, 16   358
Prevails over Zimri and
Tibni.........1 Kin. 16:17-23   358
Builds
Samaria.......1 Kin. 16:24   358
Reigns
wickedly......1 Kin. 16:25-28   358

On—*stone*

1. Reubenite leader; joins Korah's
rebellion .....Num. 16:1   152
2. City of Lower Egypt; center of
sun-worship...Gen. 41:45, 50   43
Called Beth-
shemesh ......Jer. 43:13   748

See Heres

Onam—*vigorous*

1. Horite chief....Gen. 36:23   38
2. Man of
Judah.........1 Chr. 2:26, 28   406

Onan—*strong*

Second son of Judah; slain for
failure to consummate
union ....Gen. 38:8-10   40

Oneness—*unity*

A. *Of Christ, with:*
The Father ....John 10:30   1055
Christians .....Heb. 2:11   1215

B. *Among Christians of:*
Baptized......1 Cor. 12:13   1134
Union ....Ezek. 37:16-24   805
Headship .....Ezek. 34:23   803

Faith ....Eph. 4:4-6   1164
Mind ....Phil. 2:2   1171
Heart..........Acts 4:32   1076

See Unity of believers

Onesimus—*useful*

Slave of Philemon converted by
Paul in Rome.....Philem. 10-17   1210
With Tychicus, carries Paul's
letters to Colossae and to
Philemon.........Col. 4:7-9   1179

Onesiphorus—*profit-bearing*

Ephesian Christian commended for
his service......2 Tim. 1:16-18   1200

Onion—*a bulbous plant used for food*

Lusted after by
Israelites ....Num. 11:5   147

Only begotten

Of Christ's:
Incarnation ...John 1:14   1042
Godhead........John 1:18   1042
Mission ....{ John 3:16, 18   1044
           { 1 John 4:9   1252

Ono—*strong*

Town of Benjamin rebuilt by
Shamed ....1 Chr. 8:12   413
Reinhabited by
returnees........Ezra 2:1, 33   475

Onycha—*nail; claw; husk*

Ingredient of holy
incense...........Ex. 30:34   86

Onyx—*fingernail* (Greek)

Translation of a Hebrew word
indicating a   { Job 28:16   534
precious stone ...{ Ezek. 28:13   797
Found in
Havilah ....Gen. 2:11-12   5
Placed in high priest's
ephod ....Ex. 28:9-20   82
Gathered by
David ....1 Chr. 29:2   433

Open—*to unfasten; to unlock; to expose*

A. *Descriptive of miracles on:*
Earth..........Num. 16:30, 32   153
Eyes..........John 9:10-32   1053
Ears ....Mark 7:34, 35   986
Mouth........Luke 1:64   1005
Prison doors ..Acts 5:19, 23   1077
Death ....2 Kin. 4:35   375
Graves........Matt. 27:52   973

B. *Descriptive of spiritual things:*
God's
provision.....Ps. 104:28   592
God's bounty ..Mal. 3:10   909
Christ's
blood ....Zech. 13:1   902
Man's
corruption ....Rom. 3:13   1110
Spiritual
eyesight......Luke 24:31, 32   1037
Door of faith ..Acts 14:27   1088
Opportunity ...1 Cor. 16:9   1138

Ophel—*bulge, hill*

South extremity of Jerusalem's
eastern hill ......Neh. 3:15-27   491
Fortified by Jotham and
Manasseh .....2 Chr. 27:3   461
Residence of
Nethinim.........Neh. 3:26   491

Ophir—*rich*

1. Son of
Joktan........Gen. 10:26, 29   13
2. Land, probably in southeast
Arabia, inhabited by
descendants
of ....Gen. 10:29, 30   13
Famous for its
gold............1 Chr. 29:4   433

Ophni—*the high place*

Village of
Benjamin.........Josh. 18:24   234

Ophrah—*hind*

1. Judahite.......1 Chr. 4:14   408
2. Town in Benjamin near
Michmash.....Josh. 18:21, 23   234
3. Town in Manasseh; home of
Gideon.......Judg. 6:11, 15   249
Site of Gideon's
burial.........Judg. 8:32   252

Opportunity—*the best time for something*

A. *Kinds of:*
Rejected......Matt. 23:37   966
Spurned ......Luke 14:16-24   1024
Prepared......Acts 8:35-39   1081
Providential ..1 Cor. 16:9   1138
Good ....Gal. 6:10   1158

B. *Loss of, due to:*
Unbelief......Num. 14:40-43   151
Neglect.......Jer. 8:20   716
Unprepared-
ness..........Matt. 24:50, 51   968
Blindness .....Luke 19:41, 42   1030

Opposed—*stand against*

A. *Of evil things:*
Proud.........James 4:6   1230

B. *Of good things:*
Truth..........2 Tim. 3:8   1202

Oppression—*subjection to unjust hardships*

A. *Kinds of:*
Personal.......Is. 38:14   684
National......Ex. 3:9   58
Economic.....Mic. 2:1, 2   872
Messianic.....Is. 53:7   695
Spiritual ....Acts 10:38   1084

B. *Those subject to:*
Widows........Zech. 7:10   899
Hired
servant ....Deut. 24:14   201
Poor..........Ps. 12:5   552
People.........Is. 3:5   660
Soul..........Ps. 54:3   570

C. *Evils of, bring:*
Guilt ....Is. 59:12, 13   699
Reproach.....Prov. 14:31   624
Poverty.......Prov. 22:16   629
Judgment.....Ezek. 18:12, 13   786

D. *Punishment of:*
God's
judgment .....Is. 49:26   693
Captivity .....Is. 14:2, 4   668
Destruction
of.............Ps. 72:4   577

E. *Protection against:*
Sought in
prayer........Deut. 26:7   202
Given by the
LORD.........Ps. 103:6   591
Secured in
refuge........Ps. 9:9   550

F. *Agents of:*
Nations.......Judg. 10:12   255
Enemy........Ps. 42:9   566
            Ps. 106:42   594
Wicked.......Ps. 55:3   570
Man..........Ps. 119:134   602
Leaders.......Prov. 28:16   634
Sword ....Jer. 46:16   751
            Jer. 50:16   755
Devil ....Acts 10:38   1084
Rich..........James 2:6   1229

Oracle—*a revelation; a wise saying*

A. *Descriptive of the Holy of Holies:*
Place in
temple ....1 Kin. 6:16   344
Direction of
prayer ....Ps. 28:2   558

Mental
disturbance ...Ps. 55:4   570

B. Characteristics of:
Affects face....Joel 2:6   851
Means of
chastening...Job 15:20   527
Affects the whole
person ....Jer. 4:19   712
Common to all
men..........Rom. 8:22   1115

C. Remedies for:
Balm ....Jer. 51:8   756
Prayer.........Ps. 25:17, 18   557
God's
deliverance....Acts 2:24   1073
Heaven.......Rev. 21:4   1282

D. Figurative of:
Mental
anguish.......Ps. 48:6   568
Impending
trouble........Jer. 22:23   727
Distressing
news..........Is. 21:2, 3   672
Israel's
captivity .....Is. 26:17, 18   675

Paint—*to apply liquid colors*
Applied to a wide
house ....Jer. 22:14   727
Used by women ..2 Kin. 9:30   381
Used especially ⎰Jer. 4:30   712
by prostitutes ...⎱Ezek. 23:40   792

Paintings
Of Chaldeans (bas-
reliefs) ....Ezek. 23:14   792
Of animals and idols (on a
secret wall)......Ezek. 8:7-12   777

Pair—*two*
Sandals ....Amos 2:6   856
Turtledoves ....Luke 2:24   1006
Balances ....Rev. 6:5   1272

Palace—*a royal building*
A. Descriptive of:
King's
residence......2 Chr. 9:11   446
Foreign city ..Is. 25:2   675
Dwellings in
Zion ....Ps. 48:3   568
Heathen king's
residence......Ezra 6:2   479
Residence of the high
priest ....Matt. 26:3, 58   969
Fortified
place..........Neh. 7:2   494

B. Characteristics of:
Place of
luxury ....Luke 7:25   1013
Subject to
destruction...Is. 13:22   668

C. Figurative of:
Messiah's
temple ....Ps. 45:8, 15   567
Divine workman-
ship..........Ps. 144:12   609
Eternal city....Jer. 30:18   735

Palal—*judge*
Postexilic
laborer ....Neh. 3:25   491

Pale—*deficient in color*
Figurative of:
Shame............Is. 29:22   678

Palestine (see Canaan, Land of)

Palliation of sin—*excusing sin*
A. Manifested by:
Calling bad men
good..........Mal. 2:17   908
Describing sin as
good..........Is. 5:20   661
Justifying the
wicked..........Is. 5:23   662

Encouraging the
wicked..........Ezek. 13:22   781
Calling the proud
happy.........Mal. 3:13-15   909
Envying the
wicked........Ps. 73:3-15   578
Supposing God cannot
see sin ....Ps. 10:11-13   551
Ignoring
reproof........Job 34:5-36   538
Sinning
defiantly ......Is. 5:18, 19   661
Considering God indifferent
to evil.........Zeph. 1:12   887
Misjudging
people ....Matt. 11:18, 19   952
Questioning God's
Word ....Ezek. 20:49   789

B. Caused by:
Moral
darkness.....Matt. 6:23   947
Man-made
concepts .....Matt. 16:3-6   958
Hypocrisy .....Matt. 23:15-23   966
Evil heart......Luke 16:15   1026
False
teaching ......2 Pet. 2:1-19   1243

Pallu, Phallu—*distinguished*
Son of Reuben; ⎰Gen. 46:9   48
head of tribal ⎰Ex. 6:14   61
family...........⎱Num. 26:5, 8   162

Palm of the hand
Used literally of:
Priest's hand......Lev. 14:15, 26   113
Idol's hand.......1 Sam. 5:4   280
Daniel's hand .....Dan. 10:10   834
Soldier's hand.....Matt. 26:67   971

Palm tree
A. Uses of:
Fruit of, for
food ....Joel 1:12   850
Figures of, carved on
Temple........1 Kin. 6:29-35   344
Branches of, for
booths......Lev. 23:40-42   124
Places of, at Elim and
Jericho......Ex. 15:27   71
Site of, for
judgeship .....Judg. 4:5   247

B. Figurative of:
Righteous ...Ps. 92:12   588
Beauty........Song 7:7   653
Victory........John 12:13   1057

Palmerworm—*caterpillar*
Name probably designates the
locust ....Amos 4:9   857

Palms, city of
Moabites
conquer ....Judg. 3:12, 13   246

Palsy, paralysis—*loss of bodily motion*
Healed by:
Christ.............Matt. 4:24   944
Christians.........Acts 8:7   1080

Palti, Phalti—*abbreviation of Pelatiah*
1. Benjamite
spy ....Num. 13:9   149
2. Man to whom Saul gives
Michal, David's wife-to-be, in
marriage......1 Sam. 25:44   301

Paltiel, Phaltiel—*God has delivered*
1. Prince of
Issachar ......Num. 34:26   173
2. Same as
Palti 2 ....2 Sam. 3:15   311

Paltite, the
Native of Beth-
palet ....Josh. 15:27   231
Home of one of David's mighty
men..............2 Sam. 23:26   332

Same referred to as the
Pelonite ....1 Chr. 11:27   416

Pamphylia—*coastal region in South
Asia Minor*
People from, at
Pentecost ....Acts 2:10   1073
Paul visits........Acts 13:13   1086
John Mark
returns home ⎰Acts 13:13   1086
from ....⎱Acts 15:38   1089
Paul preaches in
cities of ....Acts 14:24, 25   1088
Paul sails past.....Acts 27:5   1102

Pan—*thin plate*
Offering in ....Lev. 2:5   101
Cooking ....Lev. 6:21   104
Pouring..........2 Sam. 13:9   320

Panic—*fright*
A. Among Israelites:
At the Red
Sea ....Ex. 14:10-12   69
Before the
Philistines.....1 Sam. 4:10   279
Of Judah before
Israel ....2 Kin. 14:12   386

B. Among nations:
Egyptians......Ex. 14:27   70
Philistines ....1 Sam. 14:22   288
Syrians ....2 Kin. 7:6, 7   378
Ammonites and
Moabites......2 Chr. 20:22-25   454

Pannag—*sweet*
Product of Palestine sold in
Tyre.............Ezek. 27:17   796

Paper—*sheet*
Writing material ..2 John 12   1256
See Papyrus

Paphos—*capital of Cyprus*
Paul blinds
Elymas...........Acts 13:6-13   1086

Paps—*the breasts of*
Prostitute ......Ezek. 23:21   792
Mary the virgin ...Luke 11:27   1020
Women ....Luke 23:29   1035
Son of man
(chest) ....Rev. 1:13   1269

Papyrus—*a tall marsh plant growing in
the Nile river region*
Referred to as
bulrush in ....Ex. 2:3   57
See Paper

Parables—*an earthly story with a
heavenly meaning*
A. Descriptive of:
Prophecy ......Num. 23:7-24   160
Discourse......Job 27:1-23   533
Wise saying...Prov. 26:7, 9   633
Prophetic
message.......Ezek. 17:1-10   785
Illustration (especially true of
Christ's) ......Matt. 13:18   954

B. Of Christ, characteristics of:
Numerous .....Mark 4:33, 34   982
Illustrative.....Luke 12:16-21   1021
Meaning of:
Self-evident....Mark 12:1-12   992
Unknown.....Matt. 13:36   955
Explained......Luke 8:9-15   1014
Prophetic......Luke 21:29-36   1032

C. Design of:
Bring under
conviction ....2 Sam. 12:1-6   318
Teach a spiritual
truth.........Is. 5:1-6   661
Illustrate a
point........Luke 10:25-37   1019
Fulfill
prophecy......Matt. 13:34, 35   955

SUBJECT   REFERENCE   PAGE | SUBJECT   REFERENCE   PAGE | SUBJECT   REFERENCE   PAGE

SUBJECT REFERENCE PAGE | SUBJECT REFERENCE PAGE | SUBJECT REFERENCE PAGE

Path—*a walk; manner of life*

A. *Of the wicked:*
Brought to
nothing......Job 6:18 522
Becomes
dark........Job 24:13 532
Is crooked.....Is. 59:8 699
Leads to
death........Prov. 2:18 616
Filled with
wickedness....Prov. 1:15, 16 615
Is destruc-
tive..........Is. 59:7 699
Followed by wicked
rulers........Is. 3:12 660
Made difficult by
God..........Hos. 2:6 841

B. *Of believers:*
Beset with
difficulties.....Job 19:8 529
Under God's
control.......Job 13:27 526
Hindered by the
wicked.......Job 30:13 535
Enriched by the
LORD..........Ps. 23:3 556
Upheld by
God..........Ps. 17:5 553
Provided with
light ....Ps. 119:105 601
Known by
God..........Ps. 139:3 607
Like a shining
light ....Prov. 4:18 617
Directed by
God..........Is. 26:7 675
To be
pondered....Prov. 4:26 617
No death at the
end..........Prov. 12:28 623
Sometimes
unknown.....Is. 42:16 687
Sometimes seems
crooked......Lam. 3:9 764
To be made
straight.....Heb. 12:13 1223

C. *Of righteousness:*
Taught by
father........Prov. 4:1, 11 617
Kept..........Prov. 2:20 616
Shown to   ⌠Ps. 16:11 552
Messiah......⌡Acts 2:28 1073
Taught to
believers.....Ps. 25:4, 5 557
Sought by   ⌠Ps. 119:35 600
believers.....⌡Is. 2:3 659
Rejected by
unbe-   ⌠Jer. 6:16 714
lieving ......⌡Jer. 18:15 724

D. *Of the Lord:*
True..........Ps. 25:10 557
Plain ....Ps. 27:11 558
Rich..........Ps. 65:11 574
Guarded......Prov. 2:8 616
Upright.......Prov. 2:13 616
Living ....Prov. 2:19 616
Peaceful......Prov. 3:17 616

Pathros—*the Southland*

Name applied to South (Upper)
Egypt ....Ezek. 29:10-14 797
Described as a lowly
kingdom ....Ezek. 29:14-16 798
Refuge for dispersed
Jews ....Jer. 44:1-15 748
Jews to be regathered
from ....Is. 11:11 667

Pathrusim—*the inhabitants of Pathros*

Hamitic people descending from
Mizraim and living in
Pathros..........Gen. 10:14 13

Patience—*the ability to bear trials
without grumbling*

A. *Of the Trinity:*
God, the author
of..........Rom. 15:5 1120

Christ, the example
of..............2 Thess. 3:5 1190
Spirit, the source
of............Gal. 5:22 1158

B. *Described as:*
Rewarded......Rom. 2:7 1109
Endured with
joy............Col. 1:11 1176

C. *Product of:*
Good heart ....Luke 8:15 1015
Tribulation ....Rom. 5:3, 4 1112
Testing of
faith ....James 1:3 1228
Hope ....Rom. 8:25 1115
Scriptures .....Rom. 15:4 1120

D. *Necessary grace, in:*
Times of
crises ....Luke 21:15-19 1032
Dealing with a
church........2 Cor. 12:12 1151
Opposing
evil ....Rev. 2:2 1269
Soundness of
faith ....Titus 2:2 1206
Waiting for Christ's
return.........James 5:7, 8 1230

Patmos—*an Aegan island off the
southwestern coast of Asia Minor*

John, banished here, receives the
Revelation.......Rev. 1:9 1268

Patriarchal age—*the time of Abraham,
Isaac, Jacob (between 1900 and 1600
B.C.)*

A. *Rulers of:*
Kings..........Gen. 12:15-20 15
Chiefs.........Gen. 26:1 27
Family heads
(fathers) ......Gen. 18:18, 19 19

B. *Business of:*
Cattle, etc.....Gen. 12:16 15
Caravans .....Gen. 37:28-36 39
Selling, etc....Gen. 23:1-20 23
Contracts.....Gen. 21:27-30 22
Business
agreements ..Gen. 30:28-34 32

C. *Customs of:*
Prevalence of
polygamy .....Gen. 16:4 17
Existence of
slavery........Gen. 12:16 15
Son's wife, selected by his
father..........Gen. 24:1-4 24
Children given significant
names ....Gen. 29:31-35 31

D. *Religion of:*
Existence of
idolatry ....Gen. 35:1, 2 36
Worship of God
Almighty......Gen. 14:19-22 16
God's covenant
recognized ....Gen. 12:1-3 14
Circumcision
observed......Gen. 17:10-14 18
Headship of
father.........Gen. 35:2 37
Obedience
primary.......Gen. 18:18, 19 19
Prayers and sacrifices
offered........Gen. 12:8 15
Blessings and curses
pronounced by
father.........Gen. 27:27-40 29
True faith   ⌠Matt. 15:28 957
believed......⌡Heb. 11:8-22 1221

Patriarchs—*ancient family, or tribal
heads*

Applied, in New Testament, to
Abraham, to Jacob's Sons, and to
David ....Heb. 7:4 1218

Patrimony—*inherited possessions*

Applied to Levites'
portion..........Deut. 18:8 196
Same idea found
in ....Luke 12:13 1021

See Inheritance, earthly

Patriotism—*love of one's country*

Manifested in:
Willingness to fight for one's
country ....1 Sam. 17:26-51 291
Concern for national
survival ....Esth. 4:13-17 510
Desire for national
revival ....Neh. 1:2-11 489
Loyalty to national
leader ....2 Sam. 2:10 310
Respect for national
leaders ....2 Sam. 1:18-27 309

Patrobas

Christian at
Rome ....Rom. 16:14 1121

Pattern—*a copy; an example*

A. *Of physical things:*
Tabernacle.....Heb. 8:5 1219
Temple ....1 Chr. 28:11-19 432

B. *Of spiritual things:*
Good works ...Titus 2:7 1207
Heavenly
originals ......Heb. 9:23 1220

See Example; Example of Christ, the

Pau, Pai—*groaning, bleating*

Edomite town, residence
of King Hadar ⌠Gen. 36:39 38
(Hadad).........⌡1 Chr. 1:50 405

Paul—*little*

A. *Life of:*

From birth to conversion:
Born at Tarsus in
Cilicia.........Acts 22:3 1097
Born a Roman
citizen ....Acts 22:25-28 1098
Called Saul until
changed to   ⌠Acts 9:11 1082
Paul ....⌡Acts 13:9 1086
Benjamite
Jew ....Phil. 3:5 1172
Citizen of
Tarsus ....Acts 21:39 1097
By trade a
tentmaker.....Acts 18:1, 3 1092
Zealot for   ⌠Gal. 1:14 1154
Judaism.......⌡Phil. 3:5 1172
Very strict   ⌠Acts 23:6 1098
Pharisee ......⌡Phil. 3:5, 6 1172
Educated under
Gamaliel ......Acts 22:3 1097
His sister in
Jerusalem .....Acts 23:16 1098
Apparently unmarried or a
widower ......1 Cor. 9:5 1132
Member of Jewish
council........Acts 26:10 1101
Zealous for the Mosaic
Law..........Acts 26:4, 5 1101
Consented to ⌠Acts 7:58 1080
Stephen's   ⌡Acts 8:1 1080
death ....⌡Acts 22:20 1097
Intensified   ⌠Acts 9:1-3 1081
persecution   ⌡Acts 22:3-5 1097
of   ⌠Acts 26:10, 11 1101
Christians....⌡Gal. 1:13 1154
Conscientious ⌠Acts 26:9 1101
persecutor ...⌡1 Tim. 1:13 1194

His conversion:
On road to
Damascus.....Acts 9:1-19 1081
At noon ....Acts 26:13 1101
Blinded by
supernatural ⌠Acts 9:3, 8 1081
vision........⌡2 Cor. 12:1-7 1150
Responded willingly to Jesus'
entreaty ......Acts 9:4-9 1081
Given a divine
commis-   ⌠Acts 9:6, 10-18 1081
sion-   ⌡Eph. 3:1-8 1163
Instructed and baptized by
Ananias.....Acts 9:6, 10-18 1081

SUBJECT	REFERENCE	PAGE

Pelonite

Descriptive of two of David's
mighty men ......1 Chr. 11:27, 36   416

Pen

Figurative of
tongue ....Ps. 45:1   566
Lying ....Jer. 8:8   716
Not preferred .....3 John 1:13   1259

Penalties—*punishment inflicted for wrongdoing*

A. *For sexual sins:*
Adultery—
death ....Lev. 20:10   120
Incest—
death ....Lev. 20:11-14   120
Sodomy— (Gen. 19:13, 17,
destruction...(24   20

B. *For bodily sins:*
Drunken-
ness— (1 Cor. 5:11   1128
exclusion.....(1 Cor. 6:9, 10   1129
Murder—
death ....Ex. 21:12-15   76
Persecution—God's
judgment .....Matt. 23:34-36   966

C. *For following heathen ways:*
Human sacrifice—
death ....Lev. 20:2-5   119
Witchcraft—
death ....Ex. 22:18   77
Idolatry—
death ....Ex. 22:20   77

D. *For internal sins:*
Ingratitude—
punished......Prov. 17:13   626
Pride—abomi-
nation ....Prov. 16:5   625
Unbelief—
exclusion .....Num. 20:12   157
Swearing— (Jer. 23:10   728
curse........(Zech. 5:3   898
Blasphemy— (Lev. 24:14-16,
death ....(23   124

Peniel—*the face of God*

Place east of Jordan; site of Jacob's
wrestling with
angel...........Gen. 32:24-31   35
See Penuel 1

Peninnah—*coral, pearl*

Elkanah's second
wife.............1 Sam. 1:2, 4   276

Penitence—*state of being sorry for one's sins*

A. *Results of:*
Forgiveness....Ps. 32:5, 6   560
Restoration....Job 22:23-29   531
Renewed
fellowship....Ps. 51:12, 13   569

B. *Examples of:*
Job ....Job 42:1-6   543
David.........Ps. 51:1-19   569
Josiah ....2 Kin. 22:1, 19   395
Publican......Luke 18:13   1028
Thief on the
cross........Luke 23:39-42   1036

C. *Elements:*
Acknowledg- (Job 33:27, 28   537
ment of sin..(Luke 15:18, 21   1025
Broken heart ..Ps. 34:18   561
Ps. 51:17   569
Plea for
mercy........Luke 18:13   1028
Confession.....1 John 1:9   1249

See Repentance

Penknife—*a scribe's knife*

Used by Jehoiakim on Jeremiah's
roll...............Jer. 36:23-28   742

Penny, pence—*the Roman denarius*

Debt of 100 ......Matt. 18:28   960

Day laborer's
pay............Matt. 20:2-13   962
Roman coin......Matt. 22:19-21   964
Two, the cost of
lodging..........Luke 10:35   1019
Ointment, worth
300............John 12:5   1057
Famine prices.....Rev. 6:6   1272

See Jewish measures

Pentecost—*fiftieth* (day)

A. *In the Old Testament:*
Called "the Feast of
Weeks".......Ex. 34:22, 23   90
Marks completion of barley
harvest .....Lev. 23:15, 16   123
Called "Feast of
Harvest".....Ex. 23:16   78
Work during,
prohibited.....Lev. 23:21   123
Two loaves
presented .....Lev. 23:17, 20   123
Other sacrifices
prescribed.....Lev. 23:18   123
Offerings given by
Levites.......Deut. 16:10-14   194
Time of conse-
cration.......Deut. 16:12, 13   194
Observed during Solomon's
time ....2 Chr. 8:12, 13   445

See Feasts, Hebrew

B. *In the New Testament:*
Day of the Spirit's coming; the
formation of the Christian
Church ....Acts 2:1-47   1073
Paul desires to
attend ....Acts 20:16   1095
Paul plans to stay in Ephesus
until ....1 Cor. 16:8   1138

Penuel—*the face of God*

1. Inhabitants of, slain by
Gideon........Judg. 8:8, 9, 17   251
Later refortified by
Jeroboam....1 Kin. 12:25   354
2. Judahite ......1 Chr. 4:4   408
3. Benjamite ....1 Chr. 8:25   413

Penury—*extreme poverty; destitution*

Widow's gift in,
commended .....Luke 21:1-4   1031

People

Found among
Israel............Deut. 7:6   185
Not limited to
Israel............Rom. 2:28, 29   1110
Called the
remnant.........Is. 11:10, 11, 16   667
(Is. 19:25   672
Gentiles included (Is. 65:1   702
in ....(Rom. 15:10, 11   1120
Became such by
covenant........Jer. 31:31-34   736
Secured through the
Messiah ....Ezek. 34:22-31   803
Accomplished by (Matt. 1:21   942
Christ's death ...(Luke 1:68, 77   1005
Separated from (2 Cor. 6:16-18   1146
others..........(Rev. 18:4   1279
God's true
Church..........1 Pet. 2:9, 10   1236
All nations (Rev. 5:9   1271
included in .....(Rev. 7:9   1273
God's eternal
people...........Rev. 21:3   1282

People of the land—*the conservative element of the population consisting mainly of landholders*

The influence of...2 Kin. 11:13-15   383
Taxed............2 Kin. 23:35   398

Peor—*opening*

1. Mountain of Moab opposite
Jericho........Num. 23:28   161
Israel's camp seen
from ....Num. 24:2   161

---

2. Moabite god
called Baal- (Num. 25:3, 5,
peor ....(18   162
Israelites punished for worship
of..............Num. 31:16   168

Perceive, perception—*knowledge derived through one of the senses*

Outward (2 Sam. 12:19   319
circumstances...(Acts 27:10   1102
Outward
intentions ......John 6:15   1048
Intuition..........1 Sam. 3:8   278
John 4:19   1045
(1 Sam. 12:17,
Unusual manifes-(18   286
tations ....(Acts 10:34   1084
Spiritual insight...Neh. 6:12   493
Acts 14:9   1088
God's blessings...2 Sam. 5:12   313
Neh. 6:16   493
Bitter (Eccl. 1:17   640
experience.......(Eccl. 3:22   642
Obvious (Matt. 21:45   964
implication ......(Luke 20:19   1031
God's (Gal. 2:9   1155
revelation ....(1 John 3:16   1251
Internal (Luke 8:46   1016
consciousness ...(Acts 8:23   1081

Perdition—*the state of the damned; destruction*

Judas Iscariot.....John 17:12   1062
Lost ....Phil. 1:28   1171
Antichrist........2 Thess. 2:3   1189
Rev. 17:8, 11   1279

Peres—*to split into pieces*

Sentence of
doom.............Dan. 5:28   829

Peresh—*dung*

Man of
Manasseh ....1 Chr. 7:16   412

Perez—*a breach*

One of Judah's twin sons by
Tamar............Gen. 38:24-30   40
Numbered among Judah's
sons..............Gen. 46:12   48
Founder of a tribal
family............Num. 26:20, 21   163
Descendants of, notable in later
times.............1 Chr. 27:3   430
Ancestor of David and
Christ............Ruth 4:12-18   272

Perezites

Descendants of
Perez.............Num. 26:20   163

Perfection—*the extreme degree of excellence*

A. *Applied to natural things:*
Day ....Prov. 4:18   617
Gold...........2 Chr. 4:21   441
Weights ......Deut. 25:15   201
Beauty.........Ezek. 28:12   797
Offering ......Lev. 22:21   122

B. *Applied to spiritual graces:*
Patience.......James 1:4   1228
Love...........Col. 3:14   1178
Holiness ......2 Cor. 7:1   1146
Praise ....Matt. 21:16   963
Faith ....1 Thess. 3:10   1184
Good works ...Heb. 13:21   1224
Unity..........John 17:23   1062
Strength.......2 Cor. 12:9   1150

C. *Means of:*
God ....1 Pet. 5:10   1239
Christ ....Heb. 10:14   1220
Holy Spirit....Gal. 3:3   1155
God's Word....2 Tim. 3:16, 17   1202
Ministry ......Eph. 4:11, 12   1164
Sufferings .....Heb. 2:10   1215

D. *Stages of:*
Eternally accom-
plished........Heb. 10:14   1220
Objective
goal...........Matt. 5:48   946

SUBJECT	REFERENCE	PAGE	SUBJECT	REFERENCE	PAGE	SUBJECT	REFERENCE	PAGE

Pervert—*to change something from its right use*

A. *Evil of, in dealing with:*
Man's
  judgment .....Deut. 24:17   201
God's:
  Judgment.....Job 8:3   523
  Word.........Jer. 23:36   729
  Ways........Acts 13:10   1086
  Gospel........Gal. 1:7   1154

B. *Caused by:*
  Drink.........Prov. 31:5   636
Worldly
  wisdom ....Is. 47:10   691
Spiritual
  blindness......Luke 23:2, 14   1035

Pestilence

Fifth Egyptian
  plague...........Ex. 9:1-16   64
Threatened by
  God.............Deut. 28:21   204
Sent because of David's
  sin ....2 Sam. 24:13, 15   333
Used for man's
  corrections ......Ezek. 38:22   807
Precedes the Lord's
  coming..........Hab. 3:5   883

Pestle—*instrument used for pulverizing material*

Figurative of severe
  discipline........Prov. 27:22   634

Peter

A. *Life of:*
Before his call:
  Simon   ⌠Matt. 16:17   958
  Barjona......⌡John 21:15   1066
Brother of
  Andrew......Matt. 4:18   944
Married   ⌠Mark 1:30   979
  man.........⌡1 Cor. 9:5   1132
Not highly
  educated.....Acts 4:13   1075
Fisherman .....Matt. 4:18   944

From his call to Pentecost:
Brought to Jesus by
  Andrew.......John 1:40-42   1043
Named Cephas by
  Christ.........John 1:42   1043
Called to discipleship by
  Christ.......Matt. 4:18-22   944
Mother-in-law
  healed ....Matt. 8:14, 15   948
Called as
  apostle........Matt. 10:2-4   950
Walks on
  water ....Matt. 14:28-33   956
Confessed Christ's
  deity.........Matt. 16:13-19   958
Rebuked by
  Jesus.........Matt. 16:21-23   958
Witnesses
  transfigura-   ⌠Matt. 17:1-8   959
  tion..........⌡2 Pet. 1:16-18   1243
Asked important
  questions .....Matt. 18:21   960
Refused Christ's menial
  service ......John 13:6-10   1058
Cuts off high priest's slave's
  ear...........John 18:10, 11   1063
Denied Christ three
  times ....Matt. 26:69-75   971
Wept bitterly . Matt. 26:75   971
Ran to Christ's
  sepulcher .....John 20:1-8   1065
Returned to
  fishing ....John 21:1-14   1066
Witnessed Christ's
  ascension ....Matt. 28:16-20   973
Returned to
  Jerusalem.....Acts 1:12-14   1072
Led disciples...Acts 1:15-26   1072

From Pentecost onward:
Explained Spirit's coming at
  Pentecost .....Acts 2:1-41   1073

Healed lame
  man ....Acts 3:1-11   1074
Pronounces
  judgment .....Acts 5:1-11   1076
Heals.........Acts 5:14-16   1077
Met Paul ......Acts 9:26   1082
           Gal. 1:17, 18   1154
Raises
  Dorcas........Acts 9:36-43   1082
Called to
  Gentiles......Acts 10:1-23   1083
Preached the Gospel to
  Gentiles......Acts 10:24-46   1083
Explained his action to
  apostles......Acts 11:1-18   1084
Imprisoned—
  delivered......Acts 12:3-19   1085
Attends Jerusalem
  Council ......Acts 15:7-14   1088
Rebuked by Paul for inconsis-
  tency ....Gal. 2:14   1155
Commended Paul's
  writings.......2 Pet. 3:15, 16   1244

B. *His life contrasted before and after Pentecost, once:*

Coward; now   ⌠Matt. 26:58,
  courageous...⌡ 69-74   971
Impulsive; now
  humble ......John 18:10   1063
Ignorant; now
  enlightened ...Matt. 16:21, 22   958
Deeply inquisitive; now
  submissive ...John 21:21, 22   1067
Boastful of self; now boastful of
  Christ.........Matt. 26:33, 34   970
Timid and afraid; now
  fearless ....Matt. 14:28-31   956

C. *Significance of:*
Often the representative for the
  others.........Matt. 17:24-27   959
Only disciple personally
  restored by the
  Lord ....John 21:15-19   1066
Leader in the early
  church........Acts 3:12-26   1075

Peter, the Epistles of—*books of the New Testament*

A. *First Peter*
God's
  salvation......1 Pet. 1:3-12   1235
Obedience and
  holiness.......1 Pet. 1:13-23   1235
Christ the corner
  stone ....1 Pet. 2:4-6   1236
A royal
  priesthood ....1 Pet. 2:9   1236
Christ's
  example.......1 Pet. 2:18-25   1237
Husbands and
  wives ....1 Pet. 3:1-7   1237
Partakers of His
  suffering ......1 Pet. 4:12-19   1239
Be humble before
  God...........1 Pet. 5:6-10   1239

B. *Second Peter*
Things pertaining to
  life............2 Pet. 1:1-4   1243
Diligent
  growth........2 Pet. 1:5-11   1243
False
  teachers ......2 Pet. 2:1-22   1243
The hope of the
  day ....2 Pet. 3:9, 10   1244

Pethahiah—*Yahweh opens* (the womb)

1. Priest of David's
  time ....1 Chr. 24:16   428
2. Judahite serving as a Persian
  official ....Neh. 11:24   500
3. Levite who divorced his foreign
  wife..........Ezra 10:19, 23   484
Prays with the other
  Levites........Neh. 9:4, 5   497

Pethor—*a town in North Mesopotamia*

Balaam's home....Num. 22:5, 7   159

Pethuel—*God delivers*

Father of Joel the
  prophet ....Joel 1:1   850

Petitions—*entreaties for favors*

A. *Offered to men:*
  Treacherous ...Dan. 6:7   829

B. *Offered to God:*
  Favored ....1 Sam. 1:17   276
  Granted ....1 Sam. 1:27   277

Peulthai—*reward of Yahweh*

Levite
  doorkeeper.......1 Chr. 26:5   429

Phaltiel—*deliverance of God*

Husband of
  Michal ....2 Sam. 3:14, 15   311

Phanuel—*face of God*

Father of Anna ...Luke 2:36   1007

Pharaoh—*great house*

A. *Unnamed ones, contemporary of:*
  Abraham ......Gen. 12:15-20   15
  Joseph.........Gen. 37:36   40
Moses (the
  oppression) ...Ex. 1:8-11   56
Moses (the
  exodus).......Ex. 5—14   60
  Solomon.......1 Kin. 3:1   341
             1 Kin. 11:17-20   352
  Hezekiah ......2 Kin. 18:21   391

B. *Named ones:*
  Shishak........1 Kin. 14:25, 26   356
  So.............2 Kin. 17:4   389
  Tirhakah ......2 Kin. 19:9   392
  Nechoh........2 Kin. 23:29   398
  Hophra........Jer. 44:30   750
Probably also referred
  to in ....Jer. 37:5, 7, 11   743

Pharisees—*separated ones*

A. *Characteristics of:*
  Jewish sect ....Acts 15:5   1088
Upholders of   ⌠Mark 7:3, 5-8   985
  traditions ....⌡Gal. 1:14   1154
Sticklers for
  Mosaic   ⌠Acts 26:5   1101
  Law..........⌡Phil. 3:5   1172
Very careful in
  outward   ⌠Matt. 23:23   966
  details ....⌡Luke 18:11   1028
Rigid in   ⌠Luke 5:33   1011
  fasting ......⌡Luke 18:12   1028
Zealous for
  Judaism.......Matt. 23:15   966
Lovers of
  display ....Matt. 23:5-7   965
  Covetous .....Luke 16:14   1026
Cruel perse-   ⌠Acts 9:1, 2   1081
  cutors........⌡Phil. 3:5, 6   1172

B. *Chief errors of, their:*
Outward righteous-
  ness..........Luke 7:36-50   1014
Blindness to spiritual
  things.........John 3:1-10   1044
Emphasis on the ceremonial
  Law..........Matt. 15:1-9   956
Perversion of
  Scripture......Matt. 15:1, 9   956
Self-justification before
  men..........Luke 16:14, 15   1026
Hindering potential
  believers......John 9:16, 22   1053
Refusal to accept
  Christ........Matt. 12:24-34   953

C. *Christ's description of:*
  Vipers ....Matt. 12:24, 34   953
  Blind ....Matt. 15:12-14   957
  Hypocrites.....Matt. 23:13-19   965
  Serpents......Matt. 23:33   966
Children of the
  devil ....John 8:13, 44   1051

D. *Attitude of, toward Christ, sought to:*
  Destroy Him...Matt. 12:14   952

SUBJECT	REFERENCE	PAGE	SUBJECT	REFERENCE	PAGE	SUBJECT	REFERENCE	PAGE

Pharisees—continued

Tempt Him ....Matt. 16:1 — 957
Matt. 19:3 — 961

Entangle
Him.........Matt. 22:15 — 964
Accuse Him ...Luke 11:53, 54 — 1021

Pharpar—*haste*

One of the two rivers of
Damascus.......2 Kin. 5:12 — 376

Pharzites

Descendants of Pharez
(Perez)...........Num. 26:20 — 163

Phebe—*pure, bright*

Deaconess of the church at
Cenchrea........Rom. 16:1, 2 — 1121

Phi-beseth—*the house of the goddess
Bast*

City of Lower Egypt 40 miles north
of Memphis .....Ezek. 30:17 — 798

Phichol

Captain of King Abimelech's
army ....Gen. 21:22, 32 — 22

Philadelphia—*brotherly love*

City of Lydia in Asia Minor;
church established
here..............Rev. 1:11 — 1269

Philanthropy

A. *Manifested by:*
Ethiopian......Jer. 38:6-13 — 744
Samaritan .....Luke 10:30, 33 — 1019
Roman
centurion....Luke 7:2-5 — 1013
Pagans ....Acts 28:2, 7, 10 — 1103
Christians .....Acts 4:34-37 — 1076

B. *Precepts concerning:*
"Do good unto
all" ....Gal. 6:10 — 1158
"Love your
enemies".....Matt. 5:43-48 — 946
"Follow that which is
good".........1 Thess. 5:15 — 1185

Philemon—*loving*

Christian at Colosse to whom Paul
writes ....Philem. 1 — 1210
Paul appeals to him to receive
Onesimus ....Philem. 9-21 — 1210

Philemon, the Epistle to—*a book of the
New Testament*

Thanksgiving ....Philem. 4-7 — 1210
Plea for
Onesimus ....Philem. 10-21 — 1210
Hope through
prayer..........Philem. 22 — 1210

Philetus—*worthy of love*

False teacher......2 Tim. 2:17, 18 — 1201

Philip—*lover of horses*

1. Son of Herod the
Great ....Matt. 14:3 — 956
2. One of the twelve
apostles........Matt. 10:3 — 950
Brought Nathanael to
Christ..........John 1:43-48 — 1043
Tested by
Christ..........John 6:5-7 — 1048
Introduced Greeks to
Christ.........John 12:20-22 — 1057
Gently rebuked by
Christ.........John 14:8-12 — 1059
In the upper
room.........Acts 1:13 — 1072
3. One of the seven
deacons.......Acts 6:5 — 1078
Called an
evangelist.....Acts 21:8 — 1096
Father of four prophet-
esses..........Acts 21:8, 9 — 1096
Preached in
Samaria......Acts 8:5-13 — 1080
Led the Ethiopian eunuch to
Christ........Acts 8:26-40 — 1081

Visited by
Paul ....Acts 21:8 — 1096

Philippi—*pertaining to Philip*

City of Macedonia (named after
Philip of Macedon); visited by
Paul...............Acts 16:12 — 1090
Acts 20:6 — 1095
Paul wrote letter to church
of ....Phil. 1:1 — 1170

Philippians, the Epistle to the—*a book
of the New Testament*

Thanksgiving .....Phil. 1:3-10 — 1170
Christ is
preached........Phil. 1:12-18 — 1170
To live is Christ...Phil. 1:21 — 1170
The humility of
Christ...........Phil. 2:5-11 — 1171
Lights in the
world ....Phil. 2:12-16 — 1171
Perseverance......Phil. 3 — 1171
Rejoicing in the
Lord ....Phil. 4:1-13 — 1172

Philistia—*the country of the Philistines*

"The land of the
Philistines".......Gen. 21:32, 34 — 22
"The borders of the
Philistines".....Josh. 13:2 — 228
Philistia..........Ps. 60:8 — 572

Philistim—*plural of Philistine*

Race of Canaanites inhabiting
Philistia ....Gen. 10:14 — 13

Philistines—*the people of Philistia*

A. *History of:*
Descendants of
Mizraim.......Gen. 10:13, 14 — 13
Originally on the island of
Caphtor.......Jer. 47:4 — 751
Israel commanded to
avoid ....Ex. 13:17 — 68
Not attacked by
Joshua........Josh. 13:1-3 — 228
Left to prove
Israel ....Judg. 3:1-4 — 246
Israel sold
into..........Judg. 10:6, 7 — 254
Delivered from, by
Samson......Judg. 13—16 — 257
Defeat Israel...1 Sam. 4:1-11 — 279
Take ark to house of
Dagon ....1 Sam. 4—5 — 279
Defeated at
Mizpeh........1 Sam. 7:7-14 — 281
Champion, Goliath,
killed ....1 Sam. 17:1-52 — 291
David seeks asylum
among ......1 Sam. 27:1-7 — 302
Gather at
Aphek; Saul
and sons   1 Sam. 29:1 — 303
slain by ......1 Sam. 31:1-13 — 305
Often defeated by
David ......2 Sam. 5:17-25 — 313
Besieged by
Nadab ......1 Kin. 15:27 — 357
War against
Jehoram ....2 Chr. 21:16, 17 — 456
Defeated by
Uzziah.......2 Chr. 26:6, 7 — 460
Defeated by
Hezekiah......2 Kin. 18:8 — 391

B. *Prophecies concerning:*
Union against
Israel ....Is. 9:11, 12 — 665
Punishment
pronounced ...Jer. 25:15, 20 — 730
Hatred against Israel
revenged......Ezek. 25:15-17 — 794
Destruction by
Pharaoh ......Jer. 47:1-7 — 751
Ultimate
decay ....Zeph. 2:4-6 — 888

Philologus—*lover of words*

Christian at
Rome ....Rom. 16:15 — 1121

Philosophy

Divisions of ......Acts 17:18 — 1092
Deception of ......Col. 2:8 — 1178

Phinehas—*oracle*

1. Eleazar's son; Aaron's
grandson......Ex. 6:25 — 61
Slays an Israelite and a
Midianite
woman........Num. 25:1-18 — 162
Wonderfully
rewarded......Ps. 106:30, 31 — 594
Fights against
Midianites.....Num. 31:6-12 — 168
Settles dispute over memorial
altar ....Josh. 22:11-32 — 238
Prays for
Israel ....Judg. 20:28 — 264
2. Younger son of
Eli ....1 Sam. 1:3 — 276
Worthless
man ....1 Sam. 2:12-25 — 277
Slain by
Philistines.....1 Sam. 4:11, 17 — 279
Wife of, dies in
childbirth .....1 Sam. 4:19-22 — 279
3. Father of a postexilic
priest ....Ezra 8:33 — 482

Phlegon—*scorching*

Christian at
Rome ....Rom. 16:14 — 1121

Phoebe—*pure, bright*

Deaconess of the church at
Cenchrea........Rom. 16:1, 2 — 1121

Phoenicia—*purple*

Mediterranean coastal region
including the cities of Ptolemais,
Tyre, Zarephath and Sidon;
evangelized by early
Christians ....Acts 11:19 — 1084
Jesus preaches
here ....Matt. 15:21 — 957

Phoenix—*harbor in southern Crete*

Paul was to winter
there ....Acts 27:12 — 1102

Phrygia—*a large province of Asia Minor*

Jews from, at
Pentecost ......Acts 2:1, 10 — 1073
Visited twice by
Paul............Acts 16:6 — 1090

Phurah—*branch*

Gideon's servant ..Judg. 7:10, 11 — 250

Phut, Put—*foreign bowman*

1. Third son of
Ham.........Gen. 10:6 — 13
2. Warriors (Libyans) allied with
Egypt.........Ezek. 27:10 — 795
Same as Libyans
in.............Jer. 46:9 — 750

Phuvah, Pua, Puah—*utterance*

1. Issachar's second
son ....Gen. 46:13 — 48
Descendants of
Punites ......Num. 26:23 — 163
2. Father of Tola, Israel's
judge ....Judg. 10:1 — 254

Phygellus—*fugitive*

Becomes an
apostate..........2 Tim. 1:15 — 1200

Phylactery—*charm*

Scripture verses placed on the
forehead; based upon a literal
interpretation
of ....Ex. 13:9-16 — 68
Condemned by
Christ ....Matt. 23:5 — 965

Physicians—*trained healers*

God the only
true ....Deut. 32:39 — 211

SUBJECT	REFERENCE	PAGE

Pirathonite—*inhabitant of Pirathon*

Descriptive of:
Abdon ....Judg. 12:13-15		257
Benaiah..........2 Sam. 23:30		332

Pisgah—*a mountain peak in the Abarim range in Moab*

Balaam offers sacrifice
upon ....Num. 23:14		160
Moses views promised land		
from ....Deut. 3:27		181
Site of Moses'		
death............Deut. 34:1-7		212
Summit of, called		
Nebo.............Deut. 32:49-52		211

See Nebo

Pisidia—*a mountainous district in Asia Minor*

Twice visited by ⎧Acts 13:13, 14		1086
Paul.............⎩Acts 14:24		1088

Pison—*freely flowing*

One of Eden's four
rivers.............Gen. 2:10, 11		5

Pispah—*dispersion*

Asherite ....1 Chr. 7:38		413

Pit—*a hole*

Figurative of:
Grave.............Ps. 30:9		559
Snare ....Ps. 35:7		561
Harlot ....Prov. 23:27		631
Mouth of strange		
woman..........Prov. 22:14		629
Destruction ....Ps. 55:23		571
Self-destruction ...Prov. 28:10		634
Hell...............Ps. 28:1		558
Devil's abode......Rev. 9:1, 2, 11		1273

See Abyss

Pitch

Ark covered
with..............Gen. 6:14		9
In Babel's tower...Gen. 11:3		13
In Moses' ark .....Ex. 2:3		57
Kings fall in......Gen. 14:10		16

Pitcher—*an earthenware vessel with handles*

A. Used for:
Water ....Gen. 24:16		24
Protection of a		
torch..........Judg. 7:16, 19		251

B. Figurative of:
Heart............Eccl. 12:6		647

Pithom—*mansion of the god Atum*

Egyptian city built by Hebrew
slaves ....Ex. 1:11		56

Pithon—*harmless*

Son of Micah .....1 Chr. 8:35		413

Pitilessness—*showing no mercy*

Examples of:
Rich man ....2 Sam. 12:1-6		318
Nebuchad-		
nezzar..........2 Kin. 25:6-21		399
Medes ....Is. 13:18		668
Edom ....Amos 1:11		855
Heartless		
creditor ....Matt. 18:29, 30		960
Strict		
religionists ......Luke 10:30-32		1019
Merciless		
murderers.......Acts 7:54-58		1080

Pity—*to show compassion*

A. Of God, upon:
Heathen ....Jon. 4:10, 11		868
Israel...........Is. 63:9		702
Faithful		
remnant ....Is. 54:8-10		696
Believer ....James 5:11		1230

B. Of men:
Pleaded........Job 19:21		529
Upon the		
poor ....Prov. 19:17		627
Upon		
children.......Ps. 103:13		592
Encouraged....1 Pet. 3:8		1237

See Compassion; Mercy

Plague—*a severe epidemic*

A. Descriptive of:
Divine		
judgment .....Ex. 9:14		64
Leprosy........Lev. 13:1-59		110
Disease........Mark 3:10		981
Final		
judgment ....Rev. 9:20		1274

B. Instances of:
In Egypt.......Ex. 11:1		66
At Kibroth-		
hattaavah....Num. 11:33, 34		148
At Kadesh.....Num. 14:37		150
At Peor........Josh. 22:17		238
Among:		
Philistines .....1 Sam. 5:7		280
Israelites .....2 Sam. 24:15		333
Sennacherib's		
soldiers ......Is. 37:36		684

C. Sent by God:
Because of		
sin ....Gen. 12:17		15
As final		
judgments ....Rev. 15:1, 8		1277

D. Remedy against, by:
Judgment......Ps. 106:29, 30		594
Prayer and		
confession ....1 Kin. 8:37, 38		348
Separation.....Rev. 18:4		1279
Promise........Ps. 91:10		588
Obedience ....Rev. 22:18		1283

Plain—*a geographically flat area; (usually refers to specific regional areas)*

Dry region ....Num. 22:1		159
	Deut. 3:17	181
	Deut. 34:3	212
Low regions......Jer. 17:26		724
	Obad. 19	863

Plait, plaiting—*to intertwine*

Of Christ's
crown...........Matt. 27:29		972
Of woman's hair ..1 Pet. 3:3		1237

Plaited hair

Contrasted to spiritual
adornment ....1 Pet. 3:3		1237

Plans—*methods of action*

Acknowledging God
in ....Prov. 3:6		616
Considering all		
possibilites ....Luke 14:31-33		1025
Leaving God out ..Luke 12:16-21		1021
Not trusting		
God ....Ps. 52:7		570

Plants

Created by God...Gen. 1:11, 12		4
Given as food .....Gen. 1:28, 29		5

Plants of the Bible

Anise ....Matt. 23:23		966
Bramble...........Judg. 9:14, 15		253
Brier.............Judg. 8:7, 16		251
Broom		
("juniper") ....Ps. 120:4		603
Calamus ....Song 4:14		652
Camphire		
(Henna)........Song 1:14		651
Cummin ....Is. 28:25, 27		677
Fitch............Ezek. 4:9		774
Garlic ....Num. 11:5		147
Gourd ....2 Kin. 4:39		375
Grass ....Ps. 103:15		592
Hyssop...........Ex. 12:22		67
Lily ....Song 5:13		652
Mallows..........Job 30:4		535

Mandrakes.......Gen. 30:14-16		31
Mint ....Matt. 23:23		966
Mustard..........Matt. 13:31		954
Myrtle ....Is. 55:13		696
Rose ....Is. 35:1		681
Rue..............Luke 11:42		1020
Saffron...........Song 4:14		652
Spikenard........Song 4:13, 14		652
Thorn............Judg. 8:7		251
Vine of Sodom ....Deut. 32:32		211
Wormwood.......Deut. 29:18		206

Plaster

A. Building material used on:
Infested		
walls.........Lev. 14:42, 48		114
Mt. Ebal.......Deut. 27:2, 4		202
Babylon's		
walls.........Dan. 5:5		828

See Lime; Mortar

B. Medicinal material:
Figs applied to Hezekiah's		
boil ....Is. 38:21		684

Platter

Deep dish or basin
("charger")......Matt. 14:8, 11		956
Side dish for		
food.............Matt. 23:25, 26		966
Used		
figuratively.....Matt. 23:25, 26		966

Play

Music............1 Sam. 16:16-23		290
Immoral acts......Ex. 32:6		87
Fighting ....2 Sam. 2:14		310
Dancing ....2 Sam. 6:5, 21		313
Fish..............Ps. 104:26		592
Children ....Is. 11:8		667

Plead—*to entreat intensely*

A. Asking for judgment against:
Idolatry........Judg. 6:31, 32		250
Evil king.......1 Sam. 24:15		299

B. Asking for protection of:
Poor............Prov. 22:23		630
Widows........Is. 1:17		659
Repentant .....Mic. 7:9		874

Please—*to satisfy*

A. Applied to God's:
Sovereignty....Ps. 115:3		598
Election ....1 Sam. 12:22		286
Method........1 Cor. 1:21		1126
Reactions to		
man ....1 Kin. 3:10		341
Purpose........Col. 1:19		1177
Creative acts ..1 Cor. 12:18		1135
Will ....Matt. 3:17		943

B. Applied to the unregenerate's:
Behavior.......Rom. 8:8		1114
Passions.......Matt. 14:6		956
Ways..........1 Thess. 2:15		1184
Prejudices .....Acts 12:3		1085

C. Applied to the regenerate's:
Faith ....Heb. 11:5, 6		1221
Calling ....2 Tim. 2:4		1201
Concern for		
others.........Rom. 15:26, 27		1121
Married life ...1 Cor. 7:12, 13		1130
Example,		
Christ.........John 8:29		1052

Pleasure—*satisfying the sensations*

A. Kinds of:
Physical ......Eccl. 2:1-10		640
Sexual........Gen. 18:12		19
Worldly.......Luke 8:14		1015
Immoral......Titus 3:3		1207
Spiritual......Ps. 36:8		562
Heavenly .....Ps. 16:11		552

B. God's, described as:
Sovereign.....Eph. 1:5, 9		1162
Creative ......Rev. 4:11		1271
In righteous-		
ness..........1 Chr. 29:17		433
Purpose.......Luke 12:32		1022
Not in evil....Ps. 5:4		549

SUBJECT	REFERENCE	PAGE	SUBJECT	REFERENCE	PAGE	SUBJECT	REFERENCE	PAGE

Not in the {Ezek. 18:23, 32   786
wicked........ Ezek. 33:11   801

C. *Christian's described as:*
Subject to God's
will .... 2 Cor. 12:10   1150
Inspired by
God........... Phil. 2:13   1171
Fulfilled by
God........... 2 Thess. 1:11   1189

D. *The unbeliever's, described as:*
Unsatisfying ... Eccl. 2:1   640
Enslaving...... Titus 3:3   1207
Deadening ... 1 Tim. 5:6   1196
Judged ...... 2 Thess. 2:12   1189
Defiant .... Rom. 1:32   1109

Pledge—*something given for security of a debt*

A. *Of material things:*
Garments...... Ex. 22:26   77
Regulations
concerning.... Deut. 24:10-17   201
Evil of .... Job 22:6   531
Restoration of, sign of
righteous-
ness.........Ezek. 18:7, 16   786
Unlawfully held
back.......... Ezek. 18:12   786

B. *Of spiritual things:*
The Holy Spirit in the
heart..........2 Cor. 1:22   1143
Given by
God...........2 Cor. 5:5   1145
Guarantee of future
redemption.... Eph. 1:13, 14   1162

See Borrow; Debt; Lending; Surety

Pleiades—*cluster of many stars*

Part of God's {Job 9:9   524
creation ......{Amos 5:8   858

Plenteous, plenty

A. *Of physical things:*
Food .... Gen. 41:29-47   43
Prosperity ..... Deut. 28:11   204
Productivity ... Jer. 2:7   709
Rain .... Ps. 68:9   575
Water .... Lev. 11:36   110

B. *Of spiritual things:*
God's loving
kindness ...... Ps. 86:5, 15   585
God's
redemption.... Ps. 130:7   605
Recom-
penses ...... Ps. 31:23   560
Souls in need .. Matt. 9:37   950

C. *How to obtain, by:*
Industry ...... Prov. 28:19   634
Putting God
first........... Prov. 3:9, 10   616
Lord's
blessing.......2 Chr. 31:10   465

See Abundance

Plottings

A. *Against:*
Poor.......... Ps. 10:7-11   551
Perfect .... Ps. 64:4-7   573
Prophets...... Jer. 18:18   724
Persecuted..... Matt. 5:11, 12   945

B. *Inspired by:*
Contempt...... Neh. 4:1-8   491
Hatred....... Gen. 37:8-20   39
Devil .... John 13:27   1059
Envy .... Matt. 27:18   972

C. *Examples of:*
Esau against
Jacob .... Gen. 27:41-45   29
Satan against
Job .... Job 1:8-22   518
Ahab against
Naboth .... 1 Kin. 21:1-16   364
Jews against
Jeremiah..... Jer. 26:8-15   731
Haman against the
Jews......... Esth. 7:3-6   511

Chaldeans against
Daniel .... Dan. 6:1-8   829
Jews against {Matt. 26:1-5   969
Christ........{John 11:47-53   1056
Jews against
Paul .... Acts 23:12-22   1098

Plow, plowing—*to dig up the earth for sowing seed*

A. *Used literally of:*
Elisha .... 1 Kin. 19:19   362
Forbidden with mixed
animals .... Deut. 22:10   199
Job's sons .... Job 1:14, 15   518

B. *Used figuratively of:*
Proper
learning....... Is. 28:24, 26   677
Wrongdoing ... Hos. 10:13   845
Punishment.... Hos. 10:11   845
Affliction ..... Ps. 129:3   604
Destruction ... Jer. 26:18   731
Persistent sin .. Job 4:8   521
Christian
labor.........1 Cor. 9:10   1132
Information from a
wife.........Judg. 14:18   258
Constancy in
decision....... Luke 9:62   1018
Perverse
action......... Amos 6:12   859

Plowman—*a farmer*

Used literally of:
Farming....... Is. 28:24   677

Used figuratively of:
Prosperity........ Amos 9:13   860
Christian
ministry....... 1 Cor. 9:10   1132

Plowshares—*the hard part of a plow*

Made into
swords .... Joel 3:10   852
Swords made
into .... Is. 2:4   659

Plumbline—*a cord with a weight (plummet)*

Figurative of:
Destruction ... 2 Kin. 21:13   394
God's judgment ... Amos 7:7, 8   859
God's building .... Zech. 4:10   898

Pochereth—*binder*

Descendants of, among Solomon's
servants.......... Ezra 2:57   476
Neh. 7:59   495

Poetry, Hebrew

A. *Classified according to form:*
Synonymous—repetition of
same
thoughts...... Ps. 19:2   555
Progressive—advance of
thought in second
line .... Job 3:17   520
Synthetic—second line adds
something
new.......... Ps. 104:19   592
Climactic—the thought climbs
to a climax ... Ps. 121:3, 4   603
Antithetic—the second line
contrasted with
first........... Prov. 14:1   623
Comparative—the "as"
compared with the
"so" .... Prov. 10:26   621
Acrostic—
alphabetic..... Ps. 119:1-176   599

B. *Classified according to function:*
Didactic {Deut. 32:1-43   209
(teaching)....{Job   518
Lyrics .... Ex. 15:1-19   70
Judg. 5:1-31   248
Elegies .... 2 Sam. 1:17-27   309
Psalms........ Ps.   548

Poison

Reptiles........... Deut. 32:24   210
Dragons .... Deut. 32:33   211
Adders........... Ps. 140:3   608
Gourd .... 2 Kin. 4:39, 40   375
Hemlock........ Hos. 10:4   845
Waters......... Jer. 8:14   716
Asps .... Rom. 3:13   1110
Job 20:16   530

Politeness—*refined manners*

A. *Manifested by:*
Kings......... Gen. 47:2-11   49
Hebrews....... Gen. 43:26-29   46
Romans .... Acts 27:3   1102
Pagans .... Acts 28:1, 2   1103
Christians .... Philem. 8-21   1210

B. *Counterfeited by:*
Trickery ..... 2 Sam. 20:9, 10   329
Deceit .... 2 Sam. 15:1-6   322
Hypocrisy .... Matt. 22:7, 8   964
Pride .... Luke 14:8-10   1024
Snobbery ..... James 2:1-4   1228
Selfishness ... 3 John 9, 10   1259

See Courtesy

Politicians—*governmental officials*

A. *Evils manifested by:*
Ambition ..... 2 Sam. 15:1-6   322
Flattery....... Dan. 6:4-15   829
Indifference.... Acts 18:12-16   1092
Avarice....... Acts 24:26   1100

B. *Good manifested by:*
Provision ...... Gen. 41:33-49   43
Protection .... Neh. 2:7-11   489
Piety .... 2 Chr. 34:1-33   468
Prayer........ 2 Chr. 20:6-12   454
Praise .... 2 Chr. 20:27-29   455

Poll

A. *Descriptive of a person:*
In a military {Num. 1:2, 18, 20   133
census ....{Num. 3:47   138

B. *Descriptive of cutting off the hair:*
Absalom ...... 2 Sam. 14:26   322
Priests........ Ezek. 44:20   813
Mourning
(figurative).... Mic. 1:16   871

Pollute—*to defile*

A. *Described as something unclean:*
Morally........ Num. 35:33, 34   174
Spiritually ..... Acts 15:20   1089

B. *Means of:*
Blood.......... Ps. 106:38   594
Idolatry....... Ezek. 20:30, 31   788
Abomina-
tions......... Jer. 7:30   715
Unregenerate
service....... Ezek. 44:7   813
Wickedness.... Jer. 3:1, 2   710
Contempt of the
Lord .... Mal. 1:7, 12   907
Captivity ...... Is. 47:6   691

See Unclean

Polygamy—*having more than one wife*

A. *Caused by:*
Barrenness of first
wife.......... Gen. 16:1-6   17
Desire for large
family........ Judg. 8:30   252
Political ties with other
countries...... 1 Kin. 3:1   341
Sexual desire .. 2 Chr. 11:23   448
Slavery........ Gen. 16:1, 3   17

B. *Contrary to:*
God's original
Law.......... Gen. 2:24   6
Ideal picture of
marriage...... Ps. 128:1-6   604
God's command-
ment........ Ex. 20:14   75

SUBJECT	REFERENCE	PAGE

Polygamy—continued

God's equal distribution
of the (Gen. 1:27 — 4
sexes........1 Cor. 7:2 — 1130
Relationship between Christ
and the
Church ....Eph. 5:22-33 — 1166

C. *Productive of:*
Dissension.....Gen. 16:1-6 — 17
Discord....1 Sam. 1:6 — 276
Degeneracy....1 Kin. 11:1-4 — 351

See Adultery; Family; Fornication;
Marriage

Pomegranate—*a small tree bearing an
apple-shaped fruit*

Grown in
Canaan......Num. 13:23 — 149
Ornaments of:
Worn by priests...Ex. 28:33 — 83
In temple ....1 Kin. 7:18 — 345
Sign of
fruitfulness......Hag. 2:19 — 893
Used
figuratively......Song 4:3 — 652

Pommel—*round; a bowl*

Round
ornament........2 Chr. 4:12, 13 — 441
Same as "bowl"...1 Kin. 7:41, 42 — 346

Pond, pool—*a reservoir of water*

A. *Used for:*
Washing......1 Kin. 22:38 — 367
Water supply ..2 Kin. 20:20 — 394
Irrigation......Eccl. 2:6 — 640
Healing......John 5:2-7 — 1046

B. *Famous ones:*
Gibeon ....2 Sam. 2:13 — 310
Hebron ......2 Sam. 4:12 — 312
Samaria ......1 Kin. 22:38 — 367
Bethesda ....John 5:2 — 1046
Siloam........John 9:7 — 1053
The upper ....Is. 7:3 — 663
The lower ....Is. 22:9, 11 — 673
The King's....Neh. 2:14 — 490

Pontus—*a coastal strip of north Asia
Minor*

Jews from, at
Pentecost ......Acts 2:5, 9 — 1073
Home of Aquila...Acts 18:2 — 1092
Christians of, addressed by
Peter............1 Pet. 1:1 — 1235

Poor, poverty

A. *Descriptive of:*
Needy ....Luke 21:2 — 1032
Lower
classes ......2 Kin. 24:14 — 399
Rebellious .....Jer. 5:3, 4 — 712
Holy
remnant ......Zeph. 3:12-14 — 889

B. *Causes of:*
God's
sovereignty ...1 Sam. 2:7 — 277
Sloth ....Prov. 6:10, 11 — 618
Lack of
industry......Prov. 24:30-34 — 632
Love of
pleasure......Prov. 21:17 — 628
Stubborn-
ness......Prov. 13:18 — 623
Empty
pursuits......Prov. 28:19 — 634
Drunkenness ..Prov. 23:21 — 630

C. *Wrong treatment of:*
Reproaches
God.........Prov. 14:31 — 624
Brings
punishment ...Prov. 21:13 — 628
Brings
poverty ......Prov. 22:16 — 629
Regarded by
God.........Eccl. 5:8 — 643
Judged by
God.........Is. 3:13-15 — 660

D. *Legislation designed for
protection of:*
Daily payment of
wages........Lev. 19:13 — 119
Sharing of tithes
with ....Deut. 14:28, 29 — 193
Loans to, without
interest ......Lev. 25:35, 37 — 126
Right to
glean ......Lev. 19:9, 10 — 119
Land of, restored in jubilee
year ......Lev. 25:25-30 — 125
Equal participation in
feasts........Lev. 16:11, 14 — 116
Permanent bondage of,
forbidden .....Deut. 15:12-15 — 193

See Needy; Poverty, spiritual

Poor in spirit—*humble, self-effacing*

Promised
blessing ....Matt. 5:3 — 945

Poplar tree

Used in deception of
Laban........Gen. 30:37 — 32
Pagan rites
among ....Hos. 4:13 — 842
Probably same as
"willows" in.....Lev. 23:40 — 124

Popularity—*one's esteem in the world*

Obtained by:
Heroic exploits....Judg. 8:21, 22 — 252
Unusual wisdom ..1 Kin. 4:29-34 — 342
Trickery ......2 Sam. 15:1-6 — 322
Outward display ..Matt. 6:2, 5, 16 — 946

Popularity of Jesus

A. *Factors producing His:*
Teaching ....Mark 1:22, 27 — 979
Healing......Mark 5:20 — 983
Miracles ....John 12:9-19 — 1057
Feeding the
people ......John 6:15-27 — 1048

B. *Factors causing decline of His:*
High ethical
standards ...Mark 8:34-38 — 987
Foretells His
death ....Matt. 16:21-28 — 958

Population—*the total inhabitants of a
place*

Israel's, increased in
Egypt ....Ex. 1:7, 8 — 56
Nineveh's, great...Jon. 4:11 — 868
Heaven's, vast ....Rev. 7:9 — 1273

Poratha

One of Haman's
sons........Esth. 9:8 — 513

Porch

Central court of a
house ....Matt. 26:71 — 971
Portico for
pedestrians......John 5:2 — 1046
Roofed
colonnade......John 10:23 — 1055
Court of the
temple ......1 Kin. 6:3, 6, 7 — 343

Porcius Festus—*successor to Felix*

Paul stands trial
before ......Acts 25:1-22 — 1100

Pork—*swine's flesh*

Classified as
unclean ......Lev. 11:7, 8 — 109

Port—*a harbor*

At Joppa..........Jon. 1:3 — 866
Fair Havens....Acts 27:8 — 1102
Phoenix......Acts 27:12 — 1102
Syracuse ......Acts 28:12 — 1103
Rhegium......Acts 28:13 — 1103
Puteoli......Acts 28:13 — 1103

Porter—*gatekeeper or doorkeeper*

Watchman of a
city ....2 Sam. 18:26 — 326

Watchman of a
house ....Mark 13:34 — 994
Shepherd's
attendant........John 10:3 — 1054
Official of the temple (see
below) ....1 Chr. 23:5 — 427
Origin of, in Moses'
time..........1 Chr. 9:17-26 — 414
Belongs to
Levites ......Neh. 12:47 — 502
Duties of, designed by
David ....1 Chr. 26:1-19 — 429
Office of,
important ....1 Chr. 9:26 — 414

Portico—*porch*

Solomon's........John 10:23 — 1055
Of Bethesda....John 5:2 — 1046

Portion—*a stipulated part*

A. *Of things material:*
Inheritance....Gen. 48:22 — 51

B. *Of good things:*
Spirit ....2 Kin. 2:9 — 372
Lord..........Ps. 119:57 — 600
Spiritual
riches.........Is. 61:7 — 700

C. *Of evil things:*
Things of the
world ....Ps. 17:14 — 553
Fellowship with the
wicked........Neh. 2:20 — 490

D. *Of things eternal:*
Punishment of the
wicked......Ps. 11:6 — 551

See Inheritance

Position—*place of influence*

Sought after by
Pharisees........Matt. 23:5-7 — 965
James and John
request........Mark 10:37 — 990
Seeking after,
denounced ......Luke 14:7-11 — 1024
Diotrephes, a seeker
after ....3 John 9 — 1259

Possess—*to acquire*

A. *Objects of:*
Promised
land.........Deut. 4:1, 5 — 181
Ruins........Is. 14:21 — 669
Spiritual
riches.........Is. 57:13 — 697
Christ ....Prov. 8:22 — 620
One's:
Soul ......Luke 21:19 — 1032
Body of
wife.........1 Thess. 4:4 — 1185
Sins........Job 13:26 — 526

B. *Of Canaan:*
Promised ......Gen. 17:8 — 18
Under oath ...Neh. 9:15 — 498
Israel challenged
to.............Num. 13:30 — 149

Possible—*that which can exist*

A. *Things possible:*
All, with God ..Matt. 19:26 — 961
All, to the
believer ......Mark 9:23 — 988
Peaceful
living ....Gal. 4:15 — 1157

B. *Things impossible:*
Deception of the
saints........Matt. 24:24 — 967
Removal of the
Cross ....Matt. 26:39 — 970
Christ's remaining in the
grave ....Acts 2:24 — 1073
Removal of sins by animal
sacrifice......Heb. 10:4 — 1220

Post

Private homes.....Ex. 12:7 — 66
Tabernacle........1 Sam. 1:9 — 276
Temple......1 Kin. 6:31, 33 — 344

SUBJECT   REFERENCE   PAGE | SUBJECT   REFERENCE   PAGE | SUBJECT   REFERENCE   PAGE

Pul—*strong*

King of Assyria; same as Tiglath-
pileser............2 Kin. 15:19   387

Pulpit—*a rostrum*

Ezra reads law
from ....Neh. 8:4-8   496

Pulse—*a vegetable diet*

Preferred by
Daniel............Dan. 1:12, 16   822

Punishment, everlasting (see Hell;
Eternal, everlasting)

Punishments—*penalties inflicted on
criminals*

A. *Agents of:*
State ....Rom. 13:1-4   1119
Nation........Josh. 7:25   223
Prophet........1 Sam. 15:33   290
Witnesses......John 8:3-7   1051
Soldiers.......Matt. 27:27-35   972

B. *Kinds of* (non-capital):
Imprison-
ment..........Matt. 5:25   945
Fine ....Ex. 21:22   76
Restitution ....Ex. 22:3-6   76
Retaliation....Deut. 19:21   197
Scourging .....Acts 22:25   1098
Bondage.......Matt. 18:25   960
Banishment....Rev. 1:9   1268
Torture.......Heb. 11:35   1222
Mutilation .....Judg. 1:5-7   244

C. *Kinds of* (capital):
Burning ......Gen. 38:24   40
Hanging.......Esth. 7:9, 10   511
Crucifying....Matt. 27:35   972
Beheading ....Mark 6:16, 27   984
Stoning........Lev. 24:14   124
Cutting in
pieces........Dan. 2:5   823
Exposing to
lions........Dan. 6:16, 24   829
Killing with the
sword........Acts 12:2   1085

See Capital punishment

Punites

Descendants of
Pua ....Num. 26:23   163

Punon

Israelite camp.....Num. 33:42, 43   171

Pur—*a lot*

Cast for Jews'
slaughter......Esth. 3:7   509
Origin of Purim ...Esth. 9:24-26   513

Purah—*branch*

Gideon's servant ..Judg. 7:10, 11   250

Purchase—*to buy*

A. *Used literally of:*
Cave ....Gen. 49:32   51
Field...........Jer. 32:9-16   737
Wife...........Ruth 4:10   271

B. *Used figuratively of:*
Israel's
redemption....Ex. 15:16   70
God's gifts.....Acts 8:20   1081
Church........Acts 20:28   1095

Pure, purity—*uncontaminated with
dross or evil*

A. *Descriptive of:*
Chastity.......1 Tim. 5:2   1196
Uncon-
taminated.....1 Kin. 5:11   343
Innocent ......Acts 20:26   1095
Regenerated...Titus 1:15   1206

B. *Applied figuratively to God's:*
Law ....Ps. 19:8   555
Word..........Ps. 119:140   602
Wisdom ....James 3:17   1230

C. *Applied figuratively to the
believer's:*
Heart ....Ps. 24:4   556
Mind ....2 Pet. 3:1   1244
Conscience ....1 Tim. 3:9   1195
Language.....Zeph. 3:9   888
Body ....Heb. 10:22   1220

D. *Applied to the Christian's life:*
Source.........Titus 1:15   1206
Command .....1 Tim. 4:12   1196
Means........Phil. 4:8   1173
Outward manifes-
tation ....James 1:27   1228
Inward
evidence ......1 Tim. 1:5   1194
Goal...........1 John 3:3   1251
Reward........Matt. 5:8   945
False ....Prov. 20:9   628

E. *Applied symbolically to:*
New
Jerusalem.....Rev. 21:18, 21   1282

Purge—*to cleanse thoroughly*

A. *Used, in the Old Testament,
ceremonially of:*
Cleansing......Ezek. 20:38   789
Separation from
idolatry ....2 Chr. 34:3, 8   468

B. *Used, in the Old Testament,
figuratively of:*
Reformation ..Ezek. 24:13   793
Regen-
eration........Is. 4:4   661
Sanctifica-
tion...........Is. 1:25   659
Forgiveness....Ps. 51:7   569
Consecration ..Is. 6:7   662
Atonement ....Mal. 3:3, 4   908
Judgment......Is. 22:14   673

Purification—*ceremonial or spiritual
cleansing*

A. *Objects of:*
Israelites at
Sinai..........Ex. 19:10   74
Priests at
ordination.....Ex. 29:4   84
Levites at
ordination.....Num. 8:6, 7   144
Offerings ......2 Chr. 4:6   441
High priest ....Lev. 16:4, 24   116
People
unclean.......Lev. 15:2-13   114
Nazarite after
vow..........Acts 21:24, 26   1096

B. *Accomplished by:*
Sprinkling .....Num. 19:13-18   156
Washing parts of the
body..........Ex. 30:18, 19   86
Washing the whole
body..........Lev. 8:6   106
Running
water ....Lev. 15:13   115

C. *Figurative of:*
Christ's
atonement ....Mal. 3:3   908
Regen-
eration........Acts 15:9   1088
Sanctifica-
tion...........James 4:8   1230
Obedience .....1 Pet. 1:22   1236

Purim—*lots*

Jewish festival celebrating being
rescued from Haman's
plot ....Esth. 9:26-28   513

Purloining—*stealing*

Forbidden........Titus 2:10   1207

Purple

Used in the
tabernacle.......Ex. 25:4   79
Sign of riches ....Luke 16:19   1026
Worn by royalty ..Judg. 8:26   252
Lydia, seller of ...Acts 16:14   1090

Purposes of God

Characteristics of:
Centered in
Christ............Eph. 3:11   1163
Irresistible ....Is. 14:26, 27   669
Unknown to the
wise..............Is. 19:11, 12   671
Made known......Jer. 50:45   756
Irreversible ......Jer. 4:28   712
Planned........Is. 23:9   674
Fulfilled..........Rom. 9:11   1115
Victorious........2 Chr. 32:2-22   466

Purposes of man

A. *Good:*
Hindered by evil
men..........Ezra 4:5   478
Known by
others.........2 Tim. 3:10   1202
Permitted.....Dan. 1:8-16   822
Accom-
plished........1 Kin. 5:5   343
Determine.....Ps. 17:3   553
Delayed ......Acts 19:21   1094
Not
vacillating.....2 Cor. 1:17   1143

B. *Evil:*
Known by
God...........Jer. 49:30   754
Designed against the
righteous ....Ps. 140:4   608
Hindered ....Dan. 6:17-23   829

Purse—*a bag*

One, forbidden ....Prov. 1:14   615
Disciples forbidden to
take..............Luke 10:4   1018

Pursue—*To go after*

"Enemy said, I
will"............Ex. 15:9   70
"Shall flee when
none" ....Lev. 26:17   127
"I will arise
and"............2 Sam. 17:1   324
"Seek peace,
and"...........Ps. 34:14   561
"Blood shall"......Ezek. 35:6   803

Put

Country and people in
Africa ....Is. 66:19   704

Puteoli—*little wells*

Seaport of Italy ...Acts 28:13   1103

Puthites

Descendants of
Caleb..........1 Chr. 2:50, 53   407

Putiel—*God enlightens*

Father-in-law of
Eleazar..........Ex. 6:25   61

Puah—*utterance*

Father of Tola ....Judg. 10:1   254

Pygarg—*a white-rumped antelope*

Clean animal......Deut. 14:5   192

Q

Quail—*a small bird*

Sent to satisfy
hunger...........Ex. 16:12, 13   71
Sent as a
judgment........Num. 11:31-34   148

Quarantine—*restricted in public
contacts*

Required of
lepers ....Lev. 13:45, 46   112
Miriam
consigned ....Num. 12:14-16   148

SUBJECT	REFERENCE	PAGE	SUBJECT	REFERENCE	PAGE	SUBJECT	REFERENCE	PAGE

Imposed under King
Azariah ....2 Kin. 15:1-5   387

Quarrel—*a dispute*

A. *Caused by:*
Flesh ....James 4:1, 2   1230
Hatred.........Mark 6:18, 19   984

B. *Productive of:*
Friction.......Matt. 20:20-24   962
Separation.....Acts 15:37-40   1089

C. *Cured by:*
Gentleness.....2 Tim. 2:24-26   1201
Forgiveness....Col. 3:13   1178
Unity of
mind.........Phil. 2:3, 4   1171

See Contention; Strife

Quarry—*a place for mining stone*

Israelites flee to
("Shebarim").....Josh. 7:5   222
Some near
Gilgal ....Judg. 3:19, 26   246
Same word translated "graven
images" in.......Deut. 7:5, 25   185

Quartus—*fourth*

Christian at
Corinth ....Rom. 16:23   1122

Quaternion—*a company of four soldiers*

Peter guarded by
four ....Acts 12:4   1085

Queen—*a king's wife*

A. *Applied to:*
Queen regent ..1 Kin. 10:1-13   350
Queen
mother........1 Kin. 15:13   357
Heathen
deity..........Jer. 44:15-30   749
Mystical
Babylon.......Rev. 18:7   1279

B. *Names of:*
Of Sheba ......1 Kin. 10:1   350
Vashti ....Esth. 1:9   507
Esther ....Esth. 5:3   510
Of Heaven.....Jer. 7:18   715
Of the South...Matt. 12:42   953

Quench—*to extinguish*

A. *Applied literally to:*
Fire...........Num. 11:2   147
Thirst.........Ps. 104:11   592

B. *Applied figuratively to:*
Love..........Song 8:7   653
God's wrath ..2 Kin. 22:17   396
Spirit ....1 Thess. 5:19   1185
Persecution....Heb. 11:34   1222

Question—*an inquiry*

Asked by:
Wicked ....Matt. 22:16-40   964
    John 18:33-38   1063
Sincere ....Matt. 18:1-6   959
    Acts 1:6   1072
Jesus.............Matt. 22:41-45   965

Quickening—*reviving again*

A. *Descriptive of:*
Spiritual
revival ....Ps. 71:20   577
Physical
resurrection...John 5:21   1047
Spiritual resurrection (regeneration) ...Eph. 2:5   1162

B. *Accomplished by:*
God ....1 Tim. 6:13   1197
Christ ....1 Cor. 15:45   1138
Holy Spirit....John 6:63   1049
God's Word...Ps. 119:25, 50   600
God's
precepts......Ps. 119:93   601

Quicksand—*sand which engulfs*

Endangers Paul's
ship ....Acts 27:17   1102

Quietness—*noiselessness*

A. *Descriptive of:*
Man...........Jer. 51:59   758
People........Judg. 18:7, 27   261
City ....2 Kin. 11:20   384
Nation........2 Chr. 14:1, 5   449
Earth.........Is. 14:7   668

B. *Realization of:*
Predicted .....Is. 32:17, 18   680
Comes from
God...........1 Chr. 22:9   426
Preferred .....Prov. 17:1   626
To be sought ..1 Thess. 4:11   1185
Undeniable ...Acts 19:36   1094
Commanded ..2 Thess. 3:12   1190
Obtainable.....Ps. 131:2   605
Very
valuable......1 Pet. 3:4   1237
Rewarded......Is. 30:15   678

Quitters, quitting

Unworthy........Luke 9:62   1018
Believers should (Gal. 6:9   1158
not...........(2 Thess. 3:13   1190
Press on ....Phil. 3:12-14   1172
Continue........2 Tim. 3:14   1202

Quiver—*a case for carrying arrows*

Used by:
Hunters ....Gen. 27:3   28
Soldiers.......Job 39:23   541
    Is. 22:6   673
Figurative of:
Children ......Ps. 127:5   604
Messiah ....Is. 49:2   692

Quotations

A. *Introduced by:*
"The Holy
Spirit" ....Acts 28:25   1104
"As it is
written" .....Rom. 15:9   1120
"The
Scripture".....Gal. 3:8   1156
Old Testament
writer.........Rom. 10:5-20   1116

B. *Purposes of:*
Cite
fulfillment.....Matt. 1:22, 23   942
Confirm a
truth..........Matt. 4:4   944
Prove a
doctrine.......Rom. 4:5-8   1111
Show the true
meaning .....Acts 2:25-36   1073

R

Raamah—*trembling*

Son of Cush.......Gen. 10:6, 7   13
Father of Sheba and
Dedan ....Gen. 10:7   13
Noted traders .....Ezek. 27:22   796

Raamiah—*Yahweh has thundered*

Postexilic chief....Neh. 7:7   494
Same as
Reelaiah.........Ezra 2:2   475

Raamses—*Ra (Egyptian sun god) created him*

Part of Egypt inhabited by
Jacob ....Gen. 47:11   49
Treasure city built by Hebrew
slaves ....Ex. 1:11   56

Rabbah, Rabbath—*great*

1. Town of
Judah ....Josh. 15:60   232
2. Capital of
Ammon........Amos 1:14   856
Bedstead of Og
here ....Deut. 3:11   181
On Gad's
boundary .....Josh. 13:25   229

Besieged by
Joab ....2 Sam. 12:26   319
Defeated and enslaved by
David.........2 Sam. 12:29-31   319
Destruction of,
foretold.......Jer. 49:2, 3   753

Rabbi, Rabboni—*my master*

A. *Applied to:*
John the
Baptist........John 3:26   1044
Jewish leader ..John 3:2   1044
Jesus Christ ...John 1:38, 49   1043

B. *Significance of:*
Coveted title...Matt. 23:6, 7   965
Forbidden by
Christ.........Matt. 23:8   965
Expressive of imperfect
faith ....Mark 14:45   996
    John 20:16   1065
Translated
"Master"......Mark 14:45   996

Rabbith—*multitude*

Frontier town of
Issachar..........Josh. 19:20   234

Rabble, the

Cause of discord ..Num. 11:4-6   147
Clamors for Jesus'
death............Matt. 26:47   970
Seeks Paul's life...Acts 17:1-8   1091

Rabboni—*Aramaic form of Rabbi*

Mary addresses Christ
as ....John 20:16   1065

Rab-mag—*head of the Magi*

Title applied to Nergal-
sharezer.........Jer. 39:3, 13   745

Rab-saris—*head chamberlain*

A. *Title applied to:*
Assyrian officials sent by
Sennach-
erib..........2 Kin. 18:17   391
Babylonian Nebu-
shasban....Jer. 39:13   745
Babylonian
prince........Jer. 39:3   745

B. *Office of:*
Considered
important.....Dan. 1:7   822

Rab-shakeh—*Head of the cupbearers*

Sent ....2 Kin. 18:17   391
King of Assyria
sent ....Is. 36:2   682
And told him the
words of ....Is. 36:22   682
Hear all the
words ....2 Kin. 19:4   392

Raca—*a term of insult*

Use of, forbidden by
Christ...........Matt. 5:21, 22   945

Race, Christian

Requirements of:
Discipline ......1 Cor. 9:24-27   1132
Patience ....Eccl. 9:11   645
Steadfastness .....Gal. 5:7   1157

Race, human

Unity of..........Gen. 3:20   7
Divisions of ......Gen. 10:1-32   13
Scattering of .....Gen. 11:1-9   13
Bounds of......Acts 17:26   1092
Depravity of ......Rom. 1:18-32   1109
Salvation of......John 3:16   1044

Rachal—*trader*

City in Judah .....1 Sam. 30:29   305

Rachel—*ewe*

Laban's younger daughter; Jacob's
favorite wife......Gen. 29:28-30   31
Supports her husband's
position ....Gen. 31:14-16   33

SUBJECT	REFERENCE	PAGE	SUBJECT	REFERENCE	PAGE	SUBJECT	REFERENCE	PAGE

Rape—*forced sexual relations*

A. *Features concerning:*
Death penalty
for...........Deut. 22:25-27 199
Captives subjected
to..............Is. 13:16 668

B. *Example of:*
Tamar by   ⌠2 Sam. 13:6-29,
Amnon.......⌡ 32, 33 320

Rapha, Raphah—*He (God) has healed*

1. Benjamin's fifth
son ....1 Chr. 8:1, 2 413
But not
listed..........Gen. 46:21 48
2. Descendant of
Jonathan......1 Chr. 8:37 413
Called Rephaiah
in............1 Chr. 9:43 415
3. Same word translated
"giant".......2 Sam. 21:16-20 330

Raphu—*cured*

Benjamite.........Num. 13:9 149

Rapture, the—*translation of saved at Christ's return*

Not all   ⌠1 Cor. 15:51 1138
will   ⎥1 Thess. 4:15,
sleep ....⎩ 17 1185
Dead in   ⌠1 Cor. 15:52 1138
Christ will   ⎥1 Thess. 4:13, 14,
rise.............⎩ 16 1185
Living to be
transformed......1 Cor. 15:51-53 1138
Saints caught
up...............1 Thess. 4:16, 17 1185

Rashness—*ill-advised and hasty action*

Examples of:
Moses' killing the
Egyptian ....Ex. 2:11, 12 57
Jephthah's vow ...Judg. 11:30-39 256
Israel's vow against the
Benjamites ....Judg. 21:1-6 265
Josiah's war against
Necho...........2 Chr. 35:20-24 470
Peter's cutting off the ear of
Malchus..........John 18:10 1063

Rationing—*limits prescribed for necessities*

By Joseph, to save
Egypt..........Gen. 41:35-57 43

Raven—*a flesh-eating bird*

A. *Characteristics of:*
Unclean for
food..........Lev. 11:15 109
Solitary in
habit.........Is. 34:11 681
Flesh-eating ...Prov. 30:17 635
Black..........Song 5:11 652

B. *Special features concerning:*
First creature sent from the
ark ....Gen. 8:7 11
Elijah fed by...1 Kin. 17:4-7 359
Fed by God...Luke 12:24 1022

Razor—*a sharp instrument used for cutting off hair*

Forbidden to:
Nazarites ....Num. 6:1-5 141
Samson..........Judg. 13:5 257
Mentioned in Hannah's
vow.............1 Sam. 1:11 276
Used by barbers...Ezek. 5:1 774

See Hair; Knife

Readiness—*being prepared for action*

A. *Descriptive of:*
Being
prepared......Matt. 22:4, 8 964
Being
responsive ....2 Cor. 8:11, 19 1147

B. *Objects of:*
Willing
people ....Luke 1:17 1004
Passover.......Luke 22:12, 13 1033
Lord's return ..Matt. 24:44 967
Preaching the
Gospel........Rom. 1:15 1108

Reading the Bible

A. *Blessings of:*
Brings
repentance....2 Kin. 22:8-20 395
Reminds us of
duties.........Neh. 8:12, 13 497
Produces
reformation ..Neh. 13:1-3 502
Gives knowledge of
prophecy....Rev. 1:3 1268

B. *Reactions to:*
Responsive-
ness...........Ex. 24:7 78
Rejection .....Jer. 36:21-28 742
Rebellion ....Luke 4:16-30 1009
Request for more
light ....Acts 8:29-35 1081
Research ......Acts 17:10, 11 1091

Reaiah—*Yahweh has provided for*

1. Reubenite .....1 Chr. 5:5 409
2. Founder of Nethinim
family.........Ezra 2:47 476
3. Calebite
family.........1 Chr. 4:2 407

Real property

A. *Characteristic features of:*
Property
desired........Gen. 23:4 23
Price
stipulated .....Gen. 33:19 35
Posts erected ..Deut. 19:14 196
Posterity remem-
bered ....Num. 33:54 172
Publicity
required........Ruth 4:1-4 271
Proof docu-
mented ......Jer. 32:10-17 737

B. *Unusual examples of:*
Monopoly of land
established....Gen. 47:20 49
Sale as a prophetic
proof.........Jer. 32:6-44 737
Mark of beast
required.......Rev. 13:16, 17 1276

Reaping

A. *Provisions concerning:*
Areas
restricted .....Lev. 19:9, 10 119
Times
restricted .....Lev. 25:1-11 125
Sin hinders ....Jer. 12:13 719

B. *Figurative of:*
Harvest of
souls..........John 4:35-38 1046
Trust in God...Matt. 6:26 947
Gospel age.....Amos 9:13-15 860
Injustice......Matt. 25:26 968
Payment for
services.......1 Cor. 9:11 1132
Blessings .....2 Cor. 9:6 1148
Reward for righteous-
ness..........Gal. 6:8, 9 1158
Punishment
for sin ....Hos. 10:13 845
Judgment on the
world ....Rev. 14:14-16 1277
Final
judgment .....Matt. 13:30-43 954

Reason—*the faculty by which we think*

A. *Faculty of:*
Makes men
sane ....Dan. 4:36 827
Prepares for
salvation....Is. 1:18 659
Makes men
guilty ....Mark 11:31-33 992

B. *Inadequacy of:*
Biased against the
truth..........Mark 2:6-8 980
Gospel not
explained ⌠1 Cor. 1:18-31 1126
by ....⎩1 Cor. 2:1-14 1127

Reba—*fourth part*

Midianite chief slain by
Israelites ....Num. 31:8 168
Josh. 13:21 229

Rebekah, Rebecca—*loops of a rope*

Daughter of
Bethuel..........Gen. 22:20-23 23
Becomes Isaac's
wife...........Gen. 24:15-67 24
Mother of Esau and
Jacob.........Gen. 25:21-28 26
Poses as Isaac's
sister.............Gen. 26:6-11 27
Disturbed by Esau's
marriages ....Gen. 26:34, 35 28
Causes Jacob to deceive
Isaac.........Gen. 27:1-29 28
Urges Jacob to leave
home............Gen. 27:42-46 29
Burial of, in
Machpelah ....Gen. 49:29-31 51
Mentioned by
Paul..............Rom. 9:10 1115

Rebellion—*active opposition to authority*

A. *Against:*
God ....Dan. 9:5, 9 832
God's word ....Num. 20:24 157
Davidic
kingship ....1 Kin. 12:19 353
Constituted
priesthood ....Num. 17:1-10 154
Spirit ....Is. 63:10 702

B. *Evil of:*
Keeps from
blessings ......Num. 20:24 157
Increases sin...Job 34:37 538
Needs to be
confessed .....Dan. 9:4-12 832
Characterizes a
people .....Is. 65:2 702

See Insurrection

Rebuilding Jerusalem

Permitted by
proclamation .....Ezra 1:1-4 475
Opposed ....Ezra 4:1-6 478
Neh. 4:1-3 491
Temple..........Ezra 5:1, 2 479
Ezra 6:14, 15 480
Walls ....Neh. 6:15, 16 493

Rebuke—*to reprimand sharply*

Jesus' power to restrain:
Sea ....Matt. 8:26 949
Demons..........Matt. 17:18 959
Fever ....Luke 4:39 1010
Peter............Mark 8:33 987

Rebuke for sin

A. *Manner of:*
Before all......1 Tim. 5:20 1196
With long-
suffering ......2 Tim. 4:2 1202
Sharply........Titus 2:15 1207
With all
authority......Titus 2:15 1207

B. *Examples of:*
Isaac by
Abimelech ....Gen. 26:6-11 27
Laban by
Jacob.........Gen. 31:36-42 33
Saul by
Samuel ....1 Sam. 13:13 286
Ahab by
Elijah..........1 Kin. 21:20 365
Judah by
Zechariah.....2 Chr. 24:20 458
Israel by
Ezra ....Ezra 10:10, 11 484

SUBJECT   REFERENCE   PAGE | SUBJECT   REFERENCE   PAGE | SUBJECT   REFERENCE   PAGE

Rebuke for sin—continued

David by

God...........Ps. 39:11   564

Peter by Paul . . Gal. 2:11-14   1155

Receive—to take into one's possession

A. Good things:

Word...........James 1:21   1228

Holy Spirit.....Acts 2:38   1074

Christ Jesus ...Col. 2:6   1177

Forgiveness...Acts 26:18   1101

Petitions.......1 John 3:22   1252

Reward.......1 Cor. 3:8, 14   1127

B. Evil things:

Punishment....Rom. 1:27   1109

Wrong.........Col. 3:25   1179

Beast's mark...Rev. 13:16   1276

Reward for unrighteous-

ness...........2 Pet. 2:13   1244

Rechab—rider

1. Assassin of Ish-

bosheth......2 Sam. 4:2, 6   312

2. Father of Jehonadab,

founder of the

Rechabites...2 Kin. 10:15-23   382

Related to the

Kenites ....1 Chr. 2:55   407

3. Postexilic

ruler..........Neh. 3:14   491

Rechabites—descendants of Rechab

Kenite clan fathered by Rechab

and believing in the simple

life...............Jer. 35:1-19   741

Rechah—softness

Place in Judah ...1 Chr. 4:12   408

Reciprocation—mutual interchange

Gentiles to Jews ..Rom. 15:27   1121

Students to

teachers..........Gal. 6:6   1158

Recompense—to pay back in kind

A. On the righteous:

Even now .....Prov. 11:31   622

According to one's righteous-

ness...........Ps. 18:20, 24   554

Eagerly

expected.....Heb. 10:35   1221

B. On the unrighteous:

Justly

deserved .....Rom. 1:27   1109

Belongs to God

only.........Heb. 10:30   1221

Will surely

come.........Jer. 51:56   758

To the next

generation ....Jer. 32:18   738

Fully at the second

advent........2 Thess. 1:6   1189

Reconciliation—making peace between enemies

A. Effected on men while:

Helpless ....Rom. 5:6   1112

Sinners ....Rom. 5:8   1112

Enemies of

God...........Rom. 5:10   1112

God-haters ....Col. 1:21   1177

B. Accomplished by:

God in

Christ.........2 Cor. 5:18   1146

Christ's

death ....Rom. 5:10   1112

Christ's

blood ....Eph. 2:13   1163

C. Productive of:

Peace with

God...........Rom. 5:1   1112

Access to

God...........Rom. 5:2   1112

Union of Jews and

Gentiles.......Eph. 2:14   1163

Recorder—high court official

Records events....2 Sam. 8:16   316

Represents the

king.............2 Kin. 18:18   391

Repairs the

Temple..........2 Chr. 34:8   468

Recover—to restore lost things

A. Of sickness:

By remedy.....2 Kin. 20:7   393

By a miracle...2 Kin. 5:3-14   376

Sought from

idols ....2 Kin. 1:2-17   371

Prayed for .....Is. 38:16   684

B. Of physical things:

Defeat in

war.........2 Chr. 13:19, 20   449

Conquered {2 Sam. 8:3   316

territory .....{2 Kin. 13:25   385

Captured

people ....Jer. 41:16   747

Recreation—relaxation and restoration

Among children,

natural........Zech. 8:5   900

Among adults, sometimes

boring.........Eccl. 2:1-11   640

Lord's place in ..Jer. 33:11   739

Of the wicked,

evil............Judg. 16:25   260

Rectitude—uprightness of life

True way of

living............Prov. 4:23-27   617

Red—being red or ruddy

Blood ....2 Kin. 3:22   374

Wine.............Prov. 23:31   631

Complexion......Lam. 4:7   765

Red dragon—another name for Satan

Seen in John's

vision...........Rev. 12:3-17   1275

Redemption—salvation by sacrifice

A. Defined as deliverance from:

Curse of the

Law...........Gal. 3:13   1156

Bondage of the

Law...........Gal. 4:5   1156

Iniquity.......Titus 2:14   1207

Enemies ....Ps. 136:24   606

Destruction...Ps. 103:4   591

Death ....Hos. 13:14   846

Grave ....Ps. 49:15   568

Vain

conversation ..1 Pet. 1:18   1236

Present evil

world.........Gal. 1:4   1154

B. Accomplished by:

God's power ...Deut. 7:8   186

Christ's

blood ....Eph. 1:7   1162

God's grace....Rom. 3:24, 25   1111

C. Benefits of:

Forgiveness....Col. 1:14   1177

Justification...Rom. 3:24   1111

Adoption ......Gal. 4:4, 5   1156

God's

possession ...1 Cor. 6:20   1130

God's people...Titus 2:14   1207

Purification...Titus 2:14   1207

Sealing ....Eph. 4:30   1165

Inheritance....Heb. 9:15   1219

Heaven's

glory.........Rev. 14:3, 4   1277

Red heifer (see Heifer)

Red horse—symbol of war

Seen in John's

vision ....Rev. 6:4   1272

Red Sea—sea of reeds

Locusts

destroyed........Ex. 10:19   64

Divided by God ..Ex. 14:21   69

Crossed by

Israel.............Ex. 14:22, 29   69

Egyptians

drowned.........Ex. 15:4, 21   70

Boundary of promised

land..............Ex. 23:31   78

Israelites camp

by.................Num. 33:10, 11   171

Ships built on .....1 Kin. 9:26   350

Reed—tall grass growing in marshes

Figurative of:

Weakness.........Is. 36:6   682

Instability........Matt. 11:7   951

God's measure ..Ezek. 40:3   808

Davidic line......Is. 42:3   687

Refining, spiritual

By afflictions......Is. 48:10   692

By fire ....Zech. 13:9   903

For a purpose.....John 15:2   1060

More precious than

gold..............1 Pet. 1:7   1235

Reflection—contemplation on

Past...............Mark 14:72   997

Present...........Luke 14:31-33   1025

Future............Acts 21:12-14   1096

Reformations, religious

Manifested by or in:

Recovery of the

Law..............2 Kin. 22:8-20   395

Resolving to follow the

Lord ....Ezra 10:1-17   483

Religious zeal for the

Lord ....Neh. 13:11-31   502

Restoration of

judges............2 Chr. 19:1-11   453

Refresh—to renew; to restore

Spiritual:

In the spirit.......1 Cor. 16:18   1139

In the heart.......Philem. 7, 20   1210

Often needed......2 Tim. 1:16   1200

Mutual............Rom. 15:32   1121

Special times....Acts 3:19   1075

Refused..........Is. 28:12   676

Refuge—a shelter against harm

Divine:

In the Lord ....Ps. 142:5   608

From storms ....Is. 4:5, 6   661

Time of trouble ...Ps. 9:9   550

Place of

protection ......Ps. 91:9, 10   588

Always ready .....Ps. 46:1   567

Refuge, cities of (see Cities, Levitical)

Refuse—to reject or decline

A. Of things, physical:

Marriage......Ex. 22:17   77

Passage......Num. 20:21   157

King..........1 Sam. 16:7   290

Display ......Esth. 1:12   507

Leader........Acts 7:35   1079

Martyrdom ...Acts 25:11   1100

Fables ....1 Tim. 4:7   1196

Adoption ......Heb. 11:24-26   1222

B. Of things, spiritual:

Hardness of

heart.........Ex. 7:14   62

Disobed-

ience........Ex. 16:28   72

Obedience ...1 Sam. 8:19   282

Messiah ......Ps. 118:22   599

Salvation ....Is. 8:6   664

Shame........Jer. 3:3   710

Repentance...Hos. 11:5   845

Healing ......Jer. 15:18   722

God ....Heb. 12:25   1223

Refuse Gate—a gate of Jerusalem

Nehemiah viewed city

from ....Neh. 2:13   490

Wall dedicated

near.............Neh. 12:31   501

Regard—to think highly of

Honors God.......Is. 17:7, 8   670

SUBJECT	REFERENCE	PAGE

Remorse—continued

Of a disciple......Luke 22:62   1034
In flame..........Luke 16:24   1026

Remphan—a name for Kiyyan

Worshiped by
  Israelites.........Acts 7:41-43   1079

Rend—to tear apart by force

A. Used literally of:
  Garments......Ezra 9:3, 5   483
  Clothing.......Esth. 4:1   509
  Rocks.........Matt. 27:51   972
  Veil...........Matt. 27:51   972
  Flesh.........Matt. 7:6   947
  Body.........Mark 9:26   988
B. Figuratively of:
  Repentance.....Joel 2:13   851
  Harlotry......Jer. 4:30   712
  Destruction....Hos. 13:8   846
  Dissolution of the old
    economy.....Mark 15:38   998
  Joy..........1 Kin. 1:40   338

Renewal of strength

A. Sources of:
  Holy Spirit.....Titus 3:5   1207
  Wait for the
    Lord..........Is. 40:31   686
  Cleansing from
    sin............Ps. 51:10   569
B. Objects of:
  Youth-
    fulness........Ps. 103:5   591
  Peoples......Is. 41:1-3   686
  Inward man..2 Cor. 4:16   1145
  New man.....Col. 3:10   1178
  Mind.........Rom. 12:2   1118

Renown—of great reputation

Man...........Gen. 6:4   9
City...........Ezek. 26:17   795
God...........Dan. 9:15   833
Plant..........Ezek. 34:29   803

Renunciation—giving up the right to do
something

Blessings of:
True discipleship..Luke 14:33   1025
True reward.....Mark 10:28-31   990
Future reward...Luke 18:28-30   1028

Repentance

A. Described as:
  "Turned".....Acts 9:35   1082
  "Repent"....Acts 8:22   1081
  "Return".....1 Sam. 7:3   281
  "Conver-
    sion".........Acts 15:3   1088
B. Kinds of:
  National......Joel 3:5-18   852
  Internal.......Ps. 51:10-13   569
  Unavailing....Heb. 12:16, 17   1223
  True.........Acts 9:1-20   1081
  Unreal.......Ex. 9:27-35   64
C. Derived from gift of:
  God..........Acts 11:18   1084
  Christ........Acts 5:31   1077
  Spirit.........Zech. 12:10   902
D. Things leading to:
  God's long-
    suffering......2 Pet. 3:9   1244
  God's
    goodness....Rom. 2:4   1109
  Conviction of
    sin...........Acts 2:37, 38   1074
E. Productive of:
  Life...........Acts 11:18   1084
  Remission of
    sins..........Mark 1:4   978
  New spirit....Ezek. 18:31   787
  New heart....Ezek. 18:31   787
  Joy..........Luke 15:7, 10   1025
F. Signs of:
  Reformation of
    life...........Matt. 3:8   943
  Restitution....Luke 19:8   1029
  Godly sorrow..2 Cor. 7:9, 10   1147

See Conversion

Rephael—God has healed

Levite porter......1 Chr. 26:7   429

Rephah—riches

Ancestor of
  Joshua.........1 Chr. 7:25-27   412

Rephaiah—Yahweh has healed

1. Man of
  Issachar......1 Chr. 7:2   411
2. Descendant of
  Jonathan......1 Chr. 9:43   415
  Called Rapha..1 Chr. 8:37   413
3. Simeonite
  prince.........1 Chr. 4:42, 43   409
4. Postexilic
  ruler..........Neh. 3:9   490
5. Descendant of
  David.........1 Chr. 3:21   407

Rephaim—giants

1. Early race of giants in
  Palestine......Gen. 14:5   16
  Among doomed
    nations........Gen. 15:20   17
  See Giants
2. Valley near {2 Sam. 23:13,
  Jerusalem...{   14   332
  Very fertile....Is. 17:5   670
  Scene of Philistine
    defeats........2 Sam. 5:18-22   313

Rephidim—rests

Israelite camp.....Num. 33:12-15   171
Moses struck
  rock..............Ex. 17:1-7   72
Amalek defeated..Ex. 17:8-16   72

Report—a transmitted account of
something

A. Kinds of:
  True..........1 Kin. 10:6   350
  Good.........Prov. 15:30   625
  False.........Ex. 23:1   77
  Defaming.....Jer. 20:10   726
  Slanderous...Rom. 3:8   1110
  Evil..........2 Cor. 6:8   1146
B. Good, obtained by:
  Fear..........Deut. 2:25   180
  Just life.......Acts 10:22   1083
  Devout life....Acts 22:12   1097
  Outsiders.....1 Tim. 3:7   1195
  Faith.........Heb. 11:2, 39   1221
  Friends.......3 John 12   1259

Reproach—something imputed to the
discredit of others

A. Objects of:
  God...........2 Kin. 19:4-23   392
  God's people..Neh. 6:13   493
  Messiah......Rom. 15:3   1120
  Christians....Luke 6:22   1012
B. Agents of:
  Enemies......Neh. 4:4   491
  Foolish.......Ps. 74:22   579
  Scorner.......Prov. 22:10   629
  Satan.........1 Tim. 3:7   1195
            1 Tim. 5:14, 15   1196
C. Evil causes of:
  Unbelief......Jer. 6:10   714
  Idolatry.......Ezek. 22:4   790
  Breaking God's
    Law..........Num. 15:30, 31   152
  Sin............Prov. 14:34   624
D. Good causes of:
  Faith in God's
    promises......Heb. 11:24-26   1222
  Living for
    Christ.........1 Pet. 4:14   1239
  Suffering for
    Christ.........Heb. 13:13   1224
E. Of God's people:
  Permitted by
    God..........Jer. 15:15   722

Reprobate—rejected after testing

A. Causes of:
  Not having
    Christ.........2 Cor. 13:3-5   1151
  Rejecting the
    faith..........2 Tim. 3:8   1202
  Spiritual
    barrenness....Heb. 6:7, 8   1217
  Lack of
    discipline......1 Cor. 9:24-27   1132
  Rejection by the
    Lord..........Jer. 6:30   714
B. Consequences of, given up to:
  Evil...........Rom. 1:24-32   1109
  Delusion......2 Thess. 2:11, 12   1189
  Blindness.....Matt. 13:13-15   954
  Destruction...2 Pet. 2:9-22   1244

Reproof—a cutting rebuke for
misconduct

A. Sources of:
  God...........Ps. 50:8, 21   568
  Backslidings...Jer. 2:19   710
  God's Word....2 Tim. 3:16   1202
  John the
    Baptist........Luke 3:16, 19   1008
B. Examples of:
  Samuel.......1 Sam. 13:13   286
  Daniel........Dan. 5:22, 23   828
  John the
    Baptist........Matt. 3:7-12   943
  Stephen......Acts 7:51   1080
  Paul.........Gal. 2:11   1155

Reprove—to express disapproval of

Designed for
  good.............Heb. 12:5   1223
Accomplished in
  love.............Rev. 3:19   1271

Reptiles of the Bible

A. Features concerning:
  Created by
    God...........Gen. 1:24, 25   4
  Made to praise
    God...........Ps. 148:7, 10   611
  Placed under man's
    power........Gen. 1:26   4
  Classified as
    unclean......Lev. 11:31-43   110
  Seen in a
    vision.........Acts 10:11-14   1083
  Worshiped by
    pagans........Rom. 1:23   1109
  Likeness of,
    forbidden.....Deut. 4:16, 18   182
  Portrayed on
    walls.........Ezek. 8:10   777
B. List of:
  Adder.........Prov. 23:32   631
  Asp...........Rom. 3:13   1110
  Chameleon...Lev. 11:30   110
  Cockatrice...Is. 11:8   667
  Dragon.......Deut. 32:33   211
  Ferret........Lev. 11:30   110
  Frog..........Rev. 16:13   1278
  Leviathan....Job 41:1, 2   542
  Lizard........Lev. 11:30   110
  Scorpion.....Deut. 8:15   187
  Serpents......Matt. 10:16   950
  Snake........Matt. 7:10   947
  Snail..........Ps. 58:8   572
  Tortoise......Lev. 11:29   109
  Viper.........Acts 28:3   1103

Reputation—public esteem; fame

A. Good:
  Wonderful
    asset.........Prov. 22:1   629
  Based on
    integrity......2 Cor. 8:18-24   1147
  Hated by
    wicked........Dan. 6:4-8   829
  Required of church
    officials.......Acts 6:3   1078
  Worthy of
    trust.........Acts 16:2   1090

SUBJECT	REFERENCE	PAGE	SUBJECT	REFERENCE	PAGE	SUBJECT	REFERENCE	PAGE

Resurrection of Christ—continued

LORD'S Day
(first day of / John 20:1, 19 — 1065
the week)....\ 1 Cor. 16:2 — 1138

D. *Purposes of:*
Fulfill
Scripture.....Luke 24:45, 46 — 1037
Forgive sins ...1 Cor. 15:17 — 1137
Justify the / Rom. 4:25 — 1111
sinner........\ Rom. 8:34 — 1115
Give hope ...1 Cor. 15:18, 19 — 1137
Make faith
real ....1 Cor. 15:14-17 — 1137
Prove His / Ps. 2:7 — 548
Sonship ...\ Rom. 1:4 — 1108
Set Him on David's
throne ....Acts 2:30-32 — 1074
Insure His / Acts 4:10, 11 — 1075
exaltation...\ Phil. 2:9, 10 — 1171
Guarantee the coming
judgment.....Acts 17:31 — 1092
Seal the believer's
resur- / Acts 26:23 — 1101
rection.......\ 1 Cor. 15:20, 23 — 1137

E. *Appearances of, to:*
Mary
Magdalene ....Mark 16:9 — 998
Other
women.......Matt. 28:9 — 973
Two disciples ..Luke 24:13-15 — 1036
Simon Peter ...Luke 24:34 — 1037
Ten apostles ...John 20:19, 24 — 1065
Eleven
apostles.......John 20:26 — 1066
Apostles at Sea of
Tiberias......John 21:1 — 1066
Apostles in
Galilee.......Matt. 28:16, 17 — 973
500 brethren ..1 Cor. 15:6 — 1137
All the / Luke 24:51 — 1037
apostles .....\ Acts 1:9 — 1072
Paul..........1 Cor. 15:8 — 1137
James ....1 Cor. 15:7 — 1137

Resurrections of the Bible

Widow's son ...1 Kin. 17:17-22 — 359
Shunammite's
son..........2 Kin. 4:32-35 — 375
Unnamed man ....2 Kin. 13:20, 21 — 385
Jairus's
daughter.....Matt. 9:23-25 — 950
Widow's only
son..........Luke 7:11-15 — 1013
Lazarus of
Bethany.......John 11:43, 44 — 1056
Many saints......Matt. 27:52, 53 — 973
Dorcas...........Acts 9:36-40 — 1082
In symbolism .....Rev. 11:8, 11 — 1275

Resurrection, spiritual

A. *Accomplished by power of:*
God ....Eph. 1:19 — 1162
Christ ....Eph. 5:14 — 1165
Holy Spirit.....Ezek. 11:19 — 779

B. *Features concerning:*
Takes place
now.........John 5:25 — 1047
Gives eternal
life.........John 5:24 — 1047
Delivers from spiritual
death ....Rom. 6:4, 13 — 1112
Changes life ...Is. 32:15 — 680
Issues in
immortality ...John 11:25, 26 — 1056
Delivers from Satan's
power........Acts 26:18 — 1101
Realized in new
life..........Phil. 3:10, 11 — 1172
Called "first" ...Rev. 20:5, 6 — 1281

Retaliation—*returning like for like*

Forbidden......Luke 9:54-56 — 1018
Return good, not
evil.............Prov. 25:21, 22 — 632
God's
responsibility ...Prov. 20:22 — 628
Christ's teaching
on...............Matt. 5:39-44 — 946

Retribution—*merited punishment for evil done*

A. *Expressed by:*
God's wrath ...Rom. 1:18 — 1109
Lamb's
wrath.........Rev. 6:16, 17 — 1272
Vengeance.....Jude 7 — 1262
Punishment.....2 Thess. 1:6-9 — 1189
Corruption.....2 Pet. 2:9-22 — 1244

B. *Due to the sinner's:*
Sin ....Rom. 2:1-9 — 1109
Evil works.....Ex. 32:34 — 88
Persecution of the
righteous .....2 Thess. 1:6 — 1189
Rejection of
Christ.........Heb. 10:29, 30 — 1221

C. *Deliverance from, by:*
Christ ....1 Thess. 1:10 — 1183
God's appoint-
ment.........1 Thess. 5:9 — 1185

Return

Descriptive of:
Going back
home.........Gen. 31:3, 13 — 32
Repentance ....2 Chr. 6:24, 38 — 443
Vengeance or
retribution ....1 Kin. 2:33, 44 — 340
Divine visitation ..Joel 2:14 — 851
Christ's advent....Acts 15:16 — 1089
Death.........Gen. 3:19 — 7

Reu—*friend*

Descendant of
Shem.............Gen. 11:10-21 — 14
Called Ragau......Luke 3:35 — 1008

Reuben—*behold a son*

Jacob's eldest
son.............Gen. 29:31, 32 — 31
Guilty of misconduct; loses preeminence.......Gen. 35:22 — 37
Proposes plan to save Joseph's
life............Gen. 37:21-29 — 39
Offers sons as
pledge............Gen. 42:37 — 45
Father of four
sons.............Gen. 46:8, 9 — 48
Pronounced
unstable.........Gen. 49:3, 4 — 51
Descendants of....Num. 26:5-11 — 162

Reubenites—*descendants of Reuben*

Divided into four tribal
families..........Num. 26:5-11 — 162
Elizur, warrior ....Num. 1:5 — 133
Census of, at
Sinai ....Num. 1:18-21 — 134
Census of, at
conquest........Num. 26:7 — 162
Place of, in
march...........Num. 2:10 — 135
Seek inheritance east of
Jordan ....Num. 32:1-42 — 169
Join in war against
Canaanites .....Josh. 1:12-18 — 218
Altar erected by,
misunderstood....Josh. 22:10-34 — 237
Criticized by
Deborah.........Judg. 5:15, 16 — 248
Enslaved by
Assyria..........2 Kin. 15:29 — 388

Reuel—*friend of God*

1. Son of Esau ...Gen. 36:2-4 — 37
2. Moses' father-in-
law ....Ex. 2:18 — 57
3. Benjamite ...1 Chr. 9:8 — 414
4. Gadite leader ..Num. 2:14 — 135
Called Deuel...Num. 7:42, 47 — 142

Reumah—*exalted*

Nahor's
concubine........Gen. 22:24 — 23

Revelation—*an uncovering of something hidden*

A. *Source of:*
God ....Dan. 2:28-47 — 824
Christ ....John 1:18 — 1042
The Spirit......1 Cor. 2:10 — 1127
Not in man ....Matt. 16:17 — 958

B. *Objects of:*
God ....Matt. 11:25, 27 — 952
Christ ....2 Thess. 1:7 — 1189
Man of sin ....2 Thess. 2:3, 6, 8 — 1189

C. *Instruments of:*
Prophets.......1 Pet. 1:10-12 — 1235
Daniel.........Dan. 10:1 — 833
Christ ....Heb. 1:1, 2 — 1215
Apostles ....1 Cor. 2:10 — 1127
Paul...........Gal. 1:16 — 1154

D. *Of the first advent:*
Predicted ......Is. 40:5 — 685
Revealed ......Is. 53:1 — 695
Rejected.......John 12:38-41 — 1058
Of God's righteous-
ness.........Is. 56:1 — 696
Of peace and / Jer. 33:6-8 — 739
truth........\ Eph. 2:11-17 — 1162

E. *Time of the second advent:*
Uncovering....Matt. 10:26 — 951
Judgment......Luke 17:26-30 — 1027
Victory........2 Thess. 2:3, 6, 8 — 1189
Glory.........1 Pet. 5:1 — 1239
Resurrection...Rom. 8:18, 19 — 1114
Reward........1 Cor. 3:13, 14 — 1127
Glorification ...1 John 3:2 — 1251
Grace.........1 Pet. 1:5, 13 — 1235
Joy...........1 Pet. 4:13 — 1239

F. *Of divine truth, characteristics of:*
God-
originated.....Dan. 2:47 — 824
Verbal........Heb. 1:1 — 1215
In the created
world ....Ps. 19:1, 2 — 554
Illuminative ...Eph. 1:17 — 1162
Now
revealed......Rom. 16:26 — 1122
Truth communi-
cating........Eph. 3:3, 4 — 1163

Revelation, the—*a book of the New Testament*

Vision of the Son of
Man.............Rev. 1:9-20 — 1268
Message to the seven
churches ....Rev. 2:1—3:22 — 1269
The book of seven
seals ....Rev. 4:1—6:17 — 1271
The judgment....Rev. 7:1—9:21 — 1272
The two beasts...Rev. 13 — 1276
Babylon / Rev. 17:1—
doomed ......\ 18:24 — 1278
The marriage
supper...........Rev. 19:6-10 — 1280
The judgment of the
wicked ....Rev. 20:11-15 — 1281
New heaven and new
earth...........Rev. 21:1-8 — 1281
The new
Jerusalem .....Rev. 21:9—22:5 — 1282
Christ's coming ...Rev. 22:6-21 — 1283

Revenge—*to take vengeance*

A. *Manifestation of:*
Belongs to
God............Rev. 18:20 — 1280
Performed by
rulers ....Rom. 13:4 — 1119
Righteously
allowed ....1 Kin. 20:42 — 364
Pleaded for ....Jer. 11:20 — 719
Disallowed among
men...........Prov. 20:22 — 628
Forbidden to
disciples......Luke 9:54, 55 — 1018

B. *Antidotes of:*
Overcome by
kindness....1 Sam. 25:30-34 — 300
Exhibit love....Luke 6:35 — 1012

SUBJECT	REFERENCE	PAGE	SUBJECT	REFERENCE	PAGE	SUBJECT	REFERENCE	PAGE
Bless	Rom. 12:14	1118	Sowing righteous-			Headquarters of:		
Forbear			ness	Prov. 11:18	622	Pharaoh		
wrath	Rom. 12:19	1119	Fearing God's command-			Nechoh	2 Kin. 23:31-35	398
Manifest			ments	Prov. 13:13	623	Nebuchad-	{ 2 Kin. 25:6, 20,	
forbearance	Matt. 5:38-41	946	Feeding an			nezzar	{ 21	399
Flee from	Gen. 27:41-45	29	enemy	Prov. 25:21, 22	632	Zedekiah blinded		
C. *Examples of:*			Simple			here	Jer. 39:5-7	745
Simeon and			service	Matt. 6:1	946			
Levi	Gen. 34:25	36	Grace through			**Rich**—*wealthy*		
Joseph	Gen. 42:9-24	44	faith	Rom. 4:4, 5, 16	1111	A. *Spiritual handicaps of:*		
Samson	Judg. 16:28-30	260	Faithful			Selfishly		
Joab	2 Sam. 3:27, 30	311	service	Col. 3:23, 24	1179	satisfied	Luke 6:24	1012
Jezebel	1 Kin. 19:2	362	Seeking God			Reluctant to leave		
Ahab	1 Kin. 22:26, 27	366	diligently	Heb. 11:6	1221	riches	Luke 18:22-25	1028
Haman	Esth. 3:8-15	509	C. *At Christ's return:*			Forgetful of		
Philistines	Ezek. 25:15-17	794	After the			God	Luke 12:15-21	1021
Herodias	Mark 6:19-24	984	resurrection	Rev. 11:18	1275	Indifferent to others'		
Jews	Acts 7:54, 59	1080	Tested by			needs	Luke 16:19-31	1026
			fire	1 Cor. 3:8-14	1127	Easily		
Reverence—*a feeling of deep respect,*			According to			tempted	1 Tim. 6:9	1197
love, awe and esteem			works	Rev. 22:12	1283	Hindered		
			See Crowns of Christians; Hire; Wages			spiritually	Matt. 19:23, 24	961
Manifested toward:						Misplaced		
God	Ps. 89:7	586	**Reward for the wicked**			trust	Prov. 11:28	622
God's house	Lev. 19:30	119	A. *Visited upon:*					
Christ	Matt. 21:37	964	Now	Ps. 91:8	588	B. *Applied, spiritually, to:*		
Kings	1 Kin. 1:31	338	At the			God	Eph. 2:4	1162
Parents	Heb. 12:9	1223	judgment	2 Tim. 4:14	1202	Christ	Rom. 10:12	1116
Husbands	Eph. 5:33	1166	B. *Measure of:*			Christians	James 2:5	1229
			By retri-			True riches	2 Cor. 8:9	1147
Reverend—*worthy of reverence*			bution	Rev. 18:6	1279	Good works	1 Tim. 6:18	1197
Applies only to God in the			According to the			Worldly		
Scriptures	Ps. 111:9	597	wickedness	2 Sam. 3:39	312	people	Jer. 5:27, 28	713
			Plentifully	Ps. 31:23	560	Self-		
Revile—*to speak of another abusively*						righteous	Hos. 12:8	846
Christ,			**Rezeph**—*glowing stone*			Synagogue of		
object of	Matt. 27:39	972	Place destroyed by the			Satan	Rev. 2:9	1269
Christ, submissive			Assyrians	2 Kin. 19:12	392			
under	1 Pet. 2:23	1237				**Riches, earthly**		
Christians,			**Rezia**—*delight*			A. *Described as:*		
objects of	Matt. 5:11	945	Asherite	1 Chr. 7:39	413	Spiritually		
Right attitude						valueless	Ps. 49:6, 7	568
toward	1 Cor. 4:12	1128	**Rezin**			Inferior	Heb. 11:26	1222
Punishment of	1 Cor. 6:10	1129	1. King of Damascus; joins Pekah			Fleeting	Prov. 23:5	630
False teachers	2 Pet. 2:10-12	1244	against			Unsatisfying	Eccl. 4:8	642
			Ahaz	2 Kin. 15:37	388	Hurtful	Eccl. 5:13, 14	643
Revival—*renewed zeal to obey God*			Confederacy of, inspires Isaiah's			Deceitful	Matt. 13:22	954
Conditions for:			great Messianic			Choking	Luke 8:14	1015
Humility	2 Chr. 7:14	444	prophecy	Is. 7:1—9:12	663	Uncertain	1 Tim. 6:17	1197
Prayer	2 Chr. 7:14	444	2. Head of a Nethinim			Corrupted	James 5:2	1230
	James 5:16	1231	family	Ezra 2:48	476			
Broken heart	Ps. 34:18	561				B. *Proper attitude toward:*		
Confession	Ps. 66:18	574	**Rezon**—*prince*			Not to:		
Repentance	2 Cor. 7:10	1147	Son of Eliadah; establishes Syrian			Put first	1 Kin. 3:11, 13	341
Turning from	{ 2 Chr. 7:14	444	kingdom	1 Kin. 11:23-25	352	Be trusted	Ps. 52:7	570
sin	{ 2 Tim. 2:19	1201				Set heart		
Complete	{ Acts 9:5, 6	1081	**Rhegium**—*a city of southern Italy*			upon	Prov. 30:8	573
surrender	{ Rom. 12:1, 2	1118	Paul's ship			Be desired	Prov. 30:8	635
			arrived at	Acts 28:13	1103	Not for ever	Prov. 27:24	634
Revive—*to live again more vigorously*						Use in giving	2 Cor. 8:2	1147
A. *Descriptive of:*			**Rhesa**			Remember God's		
Renewed			Ancestor of			supply	Phil. 4:19	1173
strength	Gen. 45:27	48	Christ	Luke 3:27	1008			
Refreshment	Judg. 15:19	259				**Riches, management of**		
Restoration	Neh. 4:2	491	**Rhoda**—*rose bush*			Reflects spiritual		
Resurrection	1 Kin. 17:22	360	Servant girl	Acts 12:13-16	1085	attitude	Luke 16:10-12	1026
Spiritual			**Rhodes**—*an island off the southwest*			Demands budget	Luke 14:28-30	1025
renewal	Ps. 71:20	577	*coast of Asia Minor*					
B. *Of the Spirit:*			Paul's ship			**Riches, spiritual**		
Given to the			passes by	Acts 21:1	1096	*Source of, in:*		
humble	Is. 57:15	697	**Rib**			God's Law	Ps. 119:14	600
Source of joy	Ps. 85:6	585	Eve formed of			Divine wisdom	Prov. 3:13, 14	616
Possible even in			Adam's	Gen. 2:22	6	Unselfish service	Prov. 13:7	623
trouble	Ps. 138:7	607				Reverential fear	Prov. 22:4	629
Source of	{ Hos. 6:2, 3	843	**Ribai**—*Yahweh strives*			Fulfillment	Rom. 11:12	1117
fruitfulness	{ Hos. 14:7	847	One of David's mighty			Christ	Col. 1:27	1177
			men	2 Sam. 23:29	332	Assurance	Col. 2:2	1177
Reward of the righteous						Christ's Word	Col. 3:16	1178
A. *Described as:*			**Ribband**—*a ribbon*					
Sure	Prov. 11:18	622	On the fringe of			**Riddle**—*a hidden saying solved by*		
Full	Ruth 2:12	270	garments	Num. 15:38	152	*guessing*		
Remem-			**Riblah**—*fertility*			Samson's		
bered	2 Chr. 15:7	450	1. Town on Israel's eastern			famous	Judg. 14:12-19	258
Great	Matt. 5:12	945	border	Num. 34:11	172	Classed as a		
Open	Matt. 6:4, 6, 18	946	2. Town in the land of			parable	Ezek. 17:2	785
B. *Obtained by:*			Hamath	2 Kin. 23:33	398	Avoided by God	Num. 12:8	148
Keeping God's command-								
ments	Ps. 19:11	555						

SUBJECT	REFERENCE	PAGE	SUBJECT	REFERENCE	PAGE	SUBJECT	REFERENCE	PAGE

Persecution....Dan. 7:21, 25   831

C. Their duty to:
Keep God's
Word ....Jude 3   1262
Grow
spiritually....Eph. 4:12   1164
Avoid evil .....Eph. 5:3   1165
Judge World...1 Cor. 6:1, 2   1129
Pray for
others.......Eph. 6:18   1167
Minister to
others........Heb. 6:10   1217

D. God's protection of, He:
Forsakes them
not ....Ps. 37:28   563
Gathers
them.........Ps. 50:5   568
Keeps them...1 Sam. 2:9   277
Counts them
precious.......Ps. 116:15   598
Intercedes for
them.........Rom. 8:27   1115
Will glorify
them........2 Thess. 1:10   1189

Salamis—*a town of Cyprus*
Paul preaches
here.............Acts 13:4, 5   1086

Salchah—*wandering*
City in Bashan ....Deut. 3:10   181

Salem—*peace*
Jerusalem's original
name.............Gen. 14:18   16
Used poetically....Ps. 76:2   580

Salim—*completeness*
Place near
Aenon...........John 3:23   1044

Sallai—*rejecter*
1. Benjamite
chief.........Neh. 11:8   500
2. Priestly
family.........Neh. 12:20   501
Called Sallu....Neh. 12:7   501

Sallu—*contempt*
Benjamite
family............1 Chr. 9:7   414
See Sallai 2

Salma—*clothing*
Son of Hur........1 Chr. 2:50, 51   407

Salmon
Father of Boaz ....Ruth 4:20, 21   272
Ancestor of
Christ............Matt. 1:4, 5   941

Salome—*feminine of Solomon*
1. Among ministering
women.......Mark 15:40, 41   998
Visits empty
tomb........Mark 16:1   998
2. Herodias' daughter (not
named in the
Bible)........Matt. 14:6-11   956

Salt
A. Uses of:
Seasoning:
Food ....Job 6:6   522
Sacrifice ......Lev. 2:13   101
Everlasting
covenant......Num. 18:19   155
Rubbed on infants at
birth ......Ezek. 16:4   783
Making land unpro-
ductive.......Judg. 9:45   254
B. Miracles connected with:
Lot's wife becomes pillar
of............Gen. 19:26   20
Elisha purified water
with ...2 Kin. 2:19-22   373

C. Figurative of:
God's everlasting
covenant......Num. 18:19   155
Barrenness and
desolation.....Deut. 29:23   207
Good
influence......Matt. 5:13   945
Peace in the
heart.......Mark 9:50   989
Wise speech ...Col. 4:6   1179
Final
judgment ....Mark 9:49   989
Reprobation ...Ezek. 47:9, 11   816

Salt, City of
City in the wilderness of
Judah ....Josh. 15:62   232

Salt Sea
Old Testament
name for the   {Gen. 14:3   16
Dead Sea......{Num. 34:3, 12   172

Salt, Valley of—*a valley south of the
Dead Sea*
Site of:
David's victory....2 Sam. 8:13   316
Amaziah's
victory......2 Kin. 14:7   386

Salu—*restored*
Simeonite prince ..Num. 25:14   162

Salutations—*greetings from one person
to another*
A. Normal:
Between:
Brothers......1 Sam. 17:22   291
Social ranks ..Gen. 47:7   49
Strangers.....1 Sam. 10:3, 4   283
Christians ....Judg. 18:15   262
On visits....Rom. 16:21-23   1122
B. Examples of forms used in:
"God be
gracious" .....Gen. 43:29   46
"Peace be with
thee" ......Judg. 19:20   263
"The Lord be with
you".......Ruth 2:4   270
"The Lord bless
thee" ....Ruth 2:4   270
"Blessed be
thou" ....Ruth 3:10   271
"Hail".......Luke 1:28   1004
"All hail" .....Matt. 28:9   973
See Benediction

Salvation
A. Descriptive of:
National
deliverance....Ex. 14:13   69
Deliverance from
enemies......2 Chr. 20:17   454
Messiah ......Matt. 1:21   942
B. Source of, in:
God's grace....Eph. 2:5, 8   1162
God's love....Rom. 5:8   1112
God's mercy...Titus 3:5   1207
Christ alone ...Acts 4:12   1075
Cross.........1 Cor. 1:18   1126
C. History of:
Promised to
Adam ....Gen. 3:15   7
Announced to
Abram ....Gen. 12:1-3   14
Revealed to the
prophets ......1 Pet. 1:10-12   1235
Longed for by the
saints ....Ps. 119:81, 174   601
Promised to
Gentiles.......Is. 45:21, 22   690
To be realized by the
Messiah.......Is. 59:16, 17   699
Seen in Christ's
birth........Luke 1:69, 77   1005
Christ, the
author ....Heb. 5:9   1217
Appeared to all
men..........Titus 2:11   1207

Proclaimed to
Israel ....Zech. 9:9   901
Accomplished on the
cross.........John 3:14, 15   1044
Preached through the
Gospel ....Eph. 1:13   1162
Rejected by
Israel ....Acts 13:26-46   1087
Extended to
Gentiles.......Acts 28:28   1104
This age, day
of.............2 Cor. 6:2   1146
God's long-suffering
in ....2 Pet. 3:9   1244
Final, nearer each
day ....Rom. 13:11   1119
Consummated in the second
advent ....Heb. 9:28   1220
Praise for, in
heaven........Rev. 7:10   1273
D. Requirements of:
Confession.....Acts 2:21   1073
Repentance....Mark 1:15   978
Faith ....John 3:14-18   1044
Regenera-
tion...........John 3:3-8   1044
Holy
scripture ......2 Tim. 3:15   1202
E. Negative blessings of,
deliverance from:
Sin ....Matt. 1:21   942
Satan's
power........Heb. 2:14, 15   1215
Wrath ....Rom. 5:9   1112
Eternal
death ....John 3:16, 17   1044
F. Positive blessings of:
Chosen to .....2 Thess. 2:13   1189
Appointed to ..1 Thess. 5:9   1185
Kept unto .....1 Pet. 1:5   1235
Rejoiced in ....1 Pet. 4:13   1239
To be worked
out ....Phil. 2:12   1171
G. Temporal aspects of:
Past ....Eph. 2:8   1162
Present ......1 Cor. 1:18   1126
Future........Heb. 9:28   1220

Samaria—*watch tower*
1. Capital of
Israel ....1 Kin. 16:24-29   358
Israel's "crown of
pride".......Is. 28:1   676
Besieged twice by
Ben-hadad ...1 Kin. 20:1-22   363
Miraculously
saved ....2 Kin. 6:8-23   377
Worshipers of Baal
destroyed .....2 Kin. 10:1-28   381
Threatened
with divine   {Is. 28:1-4   676
judgment ....{Amos 3:11, 12   857
Repopulated with
foreigners ....2 Kin. 17:24-41   390
2. Name of Northern
Kingdom......1 Kin. 21:1   364
3. District of Palestine in Christ's
time ....Luke 17:11-19   1027
Preaching in, forbidden by
Christ........Matt. 10:5   950
Gospel
preached......Acts 1:8   1072
Churches established
there..........Acts 9:31   1082
Paul preached
there.........Acts 15:3   1088

Samaritans—*inhabitants of Samaria*
Made of mixed
races..........2 Kin. 17:24-41   390
Seek alliance with
Jews ....Ezra 4:1-4   478
Help of, rejected by
Nehemiah .....Neh. 4:1, 2   491
Christ and the woman
of...........John 4:5-42   1045
Story of "the good
Samaritan".......Luke 10:30-37   1019

SUBJECT	REFERENCE	PAGE	SUBJECT	REFERENCE	PAGE	SUBJECT	REFERENCE	PAGE

Samaritans—continued

Beliefs of.........John 4:25 — 1045
Converts among ..Acts 8:5-25 — 1080

Samech

Letter of the Hebrew
alphabet.........Ps. 119:113-120 — 602

Samgar-nebo—*be gracious, Nebo*

Prince of Nebuchad-
nezzar............Jer. 39:3 — 745

Samlah—*a garment*

Edomite king ....Gen. 36:36, 37 — 38

Samos—*an island off the coast of Lydia*

Visited by Paul....Acts 20:15 — 1095

Samothracia—*an island in the Aegean Sea*

Visited by Paul....Acts 16:11 — 1090

Samson—*sunlike*

A. *Life of:*
Birth of,
predicted......Judg. 13:2-23 — 257
God's Spirit moves
him..........Judg. 13:24, 25 — 258
Desired a Philistine
wife..........Judg. 14:1-9 — 258
Propounded a
riddle........Judg. 14:10-14 — 258
Betrayed, kills 30
men.........Judg. 14:15-20 — 258
Enticed by Delilah, loses
strength ......Judg. 16:4-20 — 259
Blinded and
bound........Judg. 16:21 — 260
Destroyed
over 3,000 in {Judg. 16:22-31 — 260
his death.....{Heb. 11:32 — 1222

B. *Contrasts of his life:*
Parents' concern; his
unconcern ....Judg. 13:8 — 257
Obedient, victorious;
disobedient,
defeated .....Judg. 15:14 — 259
Seeks revenge; is
revenged......Judg. 15:1-8 — 259
Spirit-moved; animated by
lust ....Judg. 15:14 — 259
Physically strong; morally
weak.......Judg. 16:3, 12 — 259
Greater victory in
death than in {Judg. 16:29, 30 — 260
life...........{Heb. 11:32 — 1222

Samuel—*name of God* (a godly name)

A. *Life of:*
Born in answer to Hannah's
prayer .....1 Sam. 1:5-21 — 276
Dedicated to God before his
birth ....1 Sam. 1:11, 22 — 276
Brought to
Shiloh.........1 Sam. 1:24-28 — 277
His mother praised God
for ....1 Sam. 2:1-10 — 277
Received a revelation
concerning Eli's
house.........1 Sam. 3:1-19 — 278
Recognized as a
prophet .....1 Sam. 3:20, 21 — 279
Became a circuit
judge ....1 Sam. 7:15-17 — 282
Organized
porter   {1 Chr. 9:22 — 414
service....{1 Chr. 26:28 — 430
Called Israel to
repentance ..1 Sam. 7:3-6 — 281
Anointed Saul as
king ....1 Sam. 10:1 — 283
Lamented in
death ....1 Sam. 25:1 — 299

B. *Character of:*
Inspired as a
writer.......1 Chr. 29:29 — 434
Inspired as a
prophet ....Acts 3:24 — 1075
Diligent as a
judge ....1 Sam. 7:15-17 — 282

Faithful to
God..........Heb. 11:32-34 — 1222
Industrious in
service........1 Chr. 9:22 — 414
Devout in
life............Jer. 15:1 — 721
Powerful in
prayer ....Ps. 99:6 — 590
Remembered in
death ....1 Sam. 25:1 — 299

Samuel, the Books of—*books of the Old Testament*

A. *First Samuel:*
Birth of
Samuel ......1 Sam. 1:19-28 — 276
Hannah's
song ....1 Sam. 2:1-10 — 277
The ark
captured......1 Sam. 4:1-11 — 279
The ark
returned ......1 Sam. 6:1-21 — 280
Saul chosen as
king ....1 Sam. 9:1-27 — 282
Saul
anointed ......1 Sam. 10:1-27 — 283
Saul against the
Philistines...1 Sam. 13:1-4 — 286
Saul is
rejected.......1 Sam. 15:10-31 — 289
David is
anointed ......1 Sam. 16:1-13 — 290
David and
Goliath ....1 Sam. 17:23-58 — 291
Jonathan's
love..........1 Sam. 19:1-7 — 294
Saul against
David ....1 Sam. 23:6-29 — 298
David spares {1 Sam. 24:1-8 — 298
Saul.......{1 Sam. 26:1-16 — 301
The medium of En-
dor...........1 Sam. 28:7-25 — 303
David against the
Amalekites....1 Sam. 30:1-31 — 304
Death of
Saul ....1 Sam. 31:1-13 — 305

B. *Second Samuel:*
David's
lament........2 Sam. 1:17-27 — 309
David anointed as
king ....2 Sam. 2:1-7 — 309
The ark in
Zion ....2 Sam. 6:1-19 — 313
David plans the
Temple........2 Sam. 7:1-29 — 314
The kingdom
expands.......2 Sam. 8:1-18 — 315
David and Bath-
sheba ....2 Sam. 11:1-27 — 317
Nathan rebukes
David ....2 Sam. 12:1-12 — 318
David
repents........2 Sam. 12:13, 14 — 319
David's child
dies........2 Sam. 12:15-23 — 319
Amnon and
Tamar ....2 Sam. 13:1-19 — 320
The mighty
men.........2 Sam. 23:8-39 — 332
David takes a
census ....2 Sam. 24:1-25 — 333

Sanballat—*Sin* (the moon-god) *has given life*

Influential
Samaritan........Neh. 2:10 — 490
Opposes Nehemiah's
plans...........Neh. 4:7, 8 — 491
Seeks to assassinate
Nehemiah........Neh. 6:1-4 — 493
Fails in
intimidation ......Neh. 6:5-14 — 493
His daughter marries Eliashib, the
high priest........Neh. 13:4, 28 — 502

Sanctification—*growing in holiness*

Produced by:
God................1 Thess. 5:23 — 1186
Christ.............Heb. 2:11 — 1215

Holy Spirit........1 Pet. 1:2 — 1235
Truth ....John 17:17, 19 — 1062
Christ's blood.....Heb. 9:14 — 1219
Prayer ....1 Tim. 4:4, 5 — 1196

See Godliness; Holiness of Christians; Piety

Sanctimoniousness—*assumed and pretended holiness*

Condemned by
Christ............Matt. 6:5 — 946

Sanctuary (see Holy of Holies; Tabernacle)

Sand

Figurative uses of:
One's posterity....Gen. 22:17 — 23
Weight...........Job 6:3 — 522
Large number of
people..........Josh. 11:4 — 227
God's thoughts toward
us................Ps. 139:17, 18 — 608

Sandals, Shoe—*leather strapped to the feet*

A. *Characteristics of:*
Worn on the
feet............1 Kin. 2:5 — 339
Tied by a
latchet........Gen. 14:23 — 16
Some considered
worthless.....Amos 2:6 — 856
Used for dress
occasions .....Luke 15:22 — 1025
Worn as
adornment....Song 7:1 — 653
Worn out after a
journey......Josh. 9:5, 13 — 225
Preserved super-
naturally.....Deut. 29:5 — 206
Worn by Christ's
disciples......Mark 6:9 — 984

B. *Symbolism of:*
Taking on—readiness for a
journey.......Ex. 12:11 — 66
Putting off—
reverence   {Ex. 3:5 — 58
before God...{Josh. 5:15 — 221
Want of—
mourning ....2 Sam. 15:30 — 323
Giving to another—
manner of attestation
in Israel.....Ruth 4:7, 8 — 271
To unloose another's—act of
homage.......Luke 3:16 — 1008

C. *Figurative of:*
Protection and
provision.....Deut. 33:25 — 212
Preparation for
service.......Eph. 6:15 — 1167
Alertness....Is. 5:27 — 662

Sanitation and hygiene

A. *Laws relating to:*
Dead bodies ...Lev. 11:24-40 — 109
Contagion .....Num. 9:6, 10 — 145
Leprosy........Lev. 13:2-59 — 111
Menstrua-
tion..........Lev. 15:19-30 — 115
Women in
childbirth .....Lev. 12:2-8 — 110
Man's
discharge .....Lev. 15:2-18 — 114

B. *Provisions for health:*
Washing......Deut. 23:10, 11 — 200
Burning ....Num. 31:19-23 — 168
Isolation.....Lev. 13:2-5, 31-33 — 111
Destruction....Lev. 14:39-45 — 114
Covering
excrement ....Deut. 23:12, 13 — 200

Sanity, spiritual

Young men
urged to.........Titus 2:6 — 1207
Accomplished by
Christ ....Luke 8:35 — 1015

SUBJECT	REFERENCE	PAGE	SUBJECT	REFERENCE	PAGE	SUBJECT	REFERENCE	PAGE

Sephar—*numbering*

Place on Joktan's
boundary.........Gen. 10:30   13

Sepharad

Place inhabited by
exiles.............Obad. 20   863

Sepharvaim—*an Assyrian city*

People of, sent to
Samaria..........2 Kin. 17:24, 31   390

Sepulcher—*a place of burial*

A. *Used literally of:*
Place of
burial.........Gen. 23:6   23
Christ's
grave ....John 19:41, 42   1065

B. *Used figuratively of:*
Hypocrisy .....Matt. 23:27   966

Serah—*abundance*

Daughter of
Asher ...Gen. 46:17   48

Seraiah—*Yahweh has prevailed*

Called Sarah .....Num. 26:46   163

1. David's
secretary......2 Sam. 8:17   316
Called Sheva, ⎧2 Sam. 20:25   329
Shisha, and ⎨1 Kin. 4:3   342
Shavsha......⎩1 Chr. 18:16   423
2. Son of
Tanhumeth ..2 Kin. 25:23   400
3. Son of
Kenaz........1 Chr. 4:13, 14   408
4. Simeonite......1 Chr. 4:35   408
5. Chief priest...Jer. 52:24, 27   759
6. Postexilic
leader.......Neh. 12:1, 12   501
7. Signer of the
covenant......Neh. 10:2   499
8. Postexilic
priest ....Neh. 11:11   500
9. Officer of King
Jehoiakim....Jer. 36:26   742
10. Prince of Judah; carries
Jeremiah's prophecy to
Babylon......Jer. 51:59, 61   758

Seraphim—*burning ones*

Type of angels ....Is. 6:1, 2   662

Sered—*deliverance*

Son of Zebulun; founder of
Sardites ....Gen. 46:14   48

Sergius Paulus

Roman proconsul of Cyprus
converted by
Paul..............Acts 13:7-12   1086

Sermon—*a discourse on a Bible subject*

A prolonged
message.........Acts 20:7   1095

Sermon on the Mount

Preached by
Christ.............Matt. 5—7   944
Those blessed ....Matt. 5:3-12   945
Salt and light ...Matt. 5:13-16   945
The law fulfilled...Matt. 5:17-20   945
On anger.......Matt. 5:21-26   945
On adultery and
divorce..........Matt. 5:27-32   945
Oaths..............Matt. 5:33-37   945
Love your
enemies......Matt. 5:38-48   946
The religious ⎧Matt. 6:1-4   946
life...........⎨Matt. 6:5-15   946
How to pray .....Matt. 6:16-18   946
Undivided
devotion.........Matt. 6:19-34   946
Judging others ....Matt. 7:1-6   947
Encouragement to
pray.............Matt. 7:7-12   947
Entering the
kingdom ....Matt. 7:13-23   947

Two
foundations ......Matt. 7:24-27   948

Serpents

A. *Characteristics of:*
Created by
God..........Job 26:13   533
Subtle ....Gen. 3:1   6
Some
poisonous.....Num. 21:6   158
Live on rocks, walls,
etc. ....Prov. 30:19   635
Cursed by
God...........Gen. 3:14, 15   7

B. *Miracles connected with:*
Aaron's rod turned
into ....Ex. 7:9, 15   62
Israelites
cured by ⎧Num. 21:6-9   158
looking at....⎨John 3:14, 15   1044
Power over, given to
apostles......Mark 16:18   999
Healing from bite
of ....Acts 28:3-6   1103

C. *Figurative of:*
Intoxication ...Prov. 23:31, 32   631
Wisdom ....Matt. 10:16   950
Malice.........Ps. 58:3, 4   572
Unexpected
evil ....Eccl. 10:8   646
Enemies ....Is. 14:29   669
Christ ....John 3:14-16   1044
Satan.........Rev. 20:2   1281
Dan's
treachery .....Gen. 49:17   51
Sting of wine ..Prov. 23:31, 32   631
Wickedness of
sinners........Ps. 58:3, 4   572

Serug—*branch*

Descendant of
Shem...........Gen. 11:20-23   14
In Christ's
ancestry.........Luke 3:35   1008

Servant—*one who serves others*

A. *Descriptive of:*
Slave ....Gen. 9:25   12
Social
inferior...,...Gen. 19:2   20
Worshiper of
God...........1 Sam. 3:9   278
Messenger of
God...........Josh. 1:2   217
Messiah ....Is. 42:1   687
Follower of
Christ.........2 Tim. 2:24   1201

B. *Applied distinctively to:*
Prophets.......Zech. 1:6   896
Messiah ....Zech. 3:8   897
Moses ....Mal. 4:4   909
Christians ......Acts 2:18   1073
Glorified
saints ....Rev. 22:3   1282

See Slave

Service to God

A. *Requirements of:*
Fear ....Ps. 2:11   548
Upright
walking.......Ps. 101:6   591
Absolute
loyalty........Matt. 6:24   947
Regener-
ation..........Rom. 7:6   1113
Serve the
Lord..........Rom. 12:11   1118
Humility.......Acts 20:19   1095
Love...........Gal. 5:13   1157

B. *Rewards of:*
Divine honor ..John 12:26   1057
Acceptance before
God...........Rom. 14:18   1120
Inheritance ...Col. 3:24   1179
Eternal
blessed- ⎧Rev. 7:15   1273
ness..........⎨Rev. 22:3   1282

Seth—*appointed*

Third son of
Adam ....Gen. 4:25   8
In Christ's
ancestry.........Luke 3:38   1008

Sethur—*hidden*

Asherite spy .....Num. 13:2, 13   148

Setting—*woven together*

For precious stones worn by the
high priest......Ex. 28:11   82
Corded chains on
filigree ....Ex. 28:13, 14   82
Same Hebrew word translated
"interwoven".....Ps. 45:13   567

Seven

A. *Of social customs:*
Serving for a
wife...........Gen. 29:20, 27   31
Bowing........Gen. 33:3   35
Mourning......Gen. 50:10   52
Feast ....Judg. 14:12, 17   258
Fasting ....1 Sam. 31:13   305

B. *Of things:*
Days ....Gen. 2:3   5
Weeks.........Dan. 9:25   833
Months........Lev. 23:24-44   123
Years.........Gen. 41:1-57   42
Nations........Deut. 7:1   185
Ways..........Deut. 28:7   203
Women........Is. 4:1   661
Brethren......Mark 12:20-22   993
Spirits ....Matt. 12:45   953
Men ....Acts 6:3-5   1078
Churches......Rev. 1:4, 20   1268

C. *Of rituals:*
Victims of
sacrifices......Lev. 23:18   123
Sprinkling of
blood ....Lev. 4:6   102
Sprinkling of
oil ....Lev. 14:16   110
Passover......Ex. 12:15   67
Consecra-
tion...........Ex. 29:30, 35   84
Defilement....Lev. 12:2   110
Convocation...Lev. 23:24-44   123
Jubilee.........Lev. 25:8   125

D. *Miracles:*
Plagues........Ex. 7:25   62
Jericho's fall ..Josh. 6:4, 8, 13   221
Naaman's
baths ....2 Kin. 5:10   376
Loaves........Matt. 15:34   957
Baskets.......Matt. 15:37   957

E. *Of symbols:*
Purification ...Ps. 12:6   552
Worship ....Ps. 119:164   603
Gospel light...Is. 30:26   679
Spirits ....Rev. 1:4   1268
Seals ....Rev. 5:1   1271
Angels........Rev. 8:2   1273
Heads and
crowns.......Rev. 13:1   1276
Plagues.......Rev. 15:6   1277
Vials..........Rev. 15:7   1278
Kings.........Rev. 17:10   1279

Seven sayings from the cross

1. "Father, forgive
them"........Luke 23:34   1036
2. "To day shalt thou be with me
in paradise"...Luke 23:43   1036
3. "Woman, behold thy
son" ....John 19:26   1064
4. "My God, my
God"........Matt. 27:46   972
5. "I thirst" ......John 19:28   1064
6. "It is
finished"......John 19:30   1064
7. "Father, into thy
hands".......Luke 23:46   1036

Seventy

Elders appointed ..Ex. 24:1, 9   78

SUBJECT	REFERENCE	PAGE	SUBJECT	REFERENCE	PAGE	SUBJECT	REFERENCE	PAGE

Years in
Babylon..........Dan. 9:2   832
Weeks in prophetic
vision............Dan. 9:24   833
In forgiveness.....Matt. 18:22   960
Disciples sent
forth.............Luke 10:1   1018

Sexes—*male and female*
A. *Creation of:*
By God........Gen. 1:27   4
For:
  Union.......Gen. 2:23-25   6
  Helpfulness...Gen. 2:18   5
  Procreation...Gen. 4:1   7
  Sexual
  needs........Prov. 5:17-19   618
B. *Regulations concerning:*
Distinctive clothing
for...........Deut. 22:5   199
Marital relationships
of.............1 Cor. 11:3-16   1133
Equality in
Christ........Gal. 3:28   1156
Different functions
of.............1 Tim. 2:8-15   1194
Love
between.....Eph. 5:22-33   1166

Sexual love
Good and   {Gen. 1:27, 28   4
holy.........{Gen. 2:24, 25   6
For
procreation...Gen. 4:1   7
In marriage
only.........Prov. 5:15-20   618
Expression of {Song 1:12-15   651
love..........{Song 3:1-5   651
Mutual responsi-
bility.......1 Cor. 7:3-5   1130

Sexual perversion
A. *Types of:*
Adultery......Deut. 22:22-29   199
Prostitution...Deut. 23:17   200
Incest........Lev. 18:6-18   118
Homosex-
uality........Rom. 1:26, 27   1109
Mankind with
beasts......Deut. 27:21   203
B. *Judgment upon:*
Defilement....Lev. 18:22-28   118
Destruction...1 Cor. 5:1-5   1128
Death........Lev. 20:13-16   120

Shaalbim, Shaalabbin—*jackals*
Amorite city assigned to
Danites.......Josh. 19:42   235
Subdued by house of
Joseph.......Judg. 1:35   245

Shaalbonite—*an inhabitant of Shaalbim*
Eliahba called...2 Sam. 23:32   332

Shaaph—*friendship*
1. Descendant of
Caleb......1 Chr. 2:47   407
2. Son of Caleb...1 Chr. 2:49   407

Shaaraim—*double gate*
1. Village in
Judah........Josh. 15:36   231
2. City of
Simeon.......1 Chr. 4:31   408

Shaashgaz
Persian eunuch...Esth. 2:14   508

Shabbethai—*Sabbath-born*
Postexilic Levite..Ezra 10:15   484
Interprets the
law...............Neh. 8:7, 8   496

Shachia—*fame of Yahweh*
Benjamite.........1 Chr. 8:10   413

Shadow
A. *Used literally of:*
Man..........Acts 5:15   1077

Mountain......Judg. 9:36   253
Sundial.......2 Kin. 20:9-11   393
B. *Used figuartively of:*
Protection.....Ps. 91:1   588
Brevity......Ps. 102:11   591
Change.......James 1:17   1228
Death.........Matt. 4:16   944
Types..........Col. 2:17   1178
Old Testament
period.........Heb. 10:1   1220

Shadrach
Hananiah's Babylonian
name............Dan. 1:3, 7   822
Cast into the fiery
furnace......Dan. 3:1-28   825

Shage—*wandering*
Father of one of David's mighty
men..............1 Chr. 11:34   416

Shaharaim—*double dawn*
Benjamite.........1 Chr. 8:8-11   413

Shahazimah—*heights*
Town of
Issachar.........Josh. 19:17, 22   234

Shake—*to move violently*
A. *Descriptive of:*
Thunder.......Ps. 77:18   580
Earthquakes..Acts 4:31   1076
Fear..........Matt. 28:4   973
B. *Used figuratively of:*
Fear..........Is. 14:16   669
Second
advent........Heb. 12:26, 27   1223
Rejection.....Luke 9:5   1016
  Acts 18:6   1092

Shalem—*safe*
Town near Shechem; can mean "in
peace".........Gen. 33:18   35

Shalim—*district of foxes*
Mentioned in Saul's
pursuit...........1 Sam. 9:4   282

Shalisha—*a third part*
Mentioned in Saul's
pursuit...........1 Sam. 9:4   282

Shallecheth—*a casting out*
Gate of Solomon's
temple...........1 Chr. 26:16   430

Shallum—*recompense*
1. King of
Israel.........2 Kin. 15:10-15   387
2. Husband of
Huldah.......2 Kin. 22:14   396
3. Judahite......1 Chr. 2:40, 41   406
4. Simeonite....1 Chr. 4:25   408
5. Father of
Hilkiah......1 Chr. 6:12, 13   410
6. Naphtali's
son.............1 Chr. 7:13   412
7. Family of
porters........Ezra 2:42   476
8. Called
Shelemiah..1 Chr. 26:14   430
9. Father of
Jehizkiah.....2 Chr. 28:12   461
10. One who divorced his foreign
wife..........Ezra 10:24   484
11. Another who divorced his
foreign wife...Ezra 10:42   485
12. Son of
Hallohesh.....Neh. 3:12   491
13. Jeremiah's
uncle..........Jer. 32:7   737
14. Father of
Maaseiah.....Jer. 35:4   741

Shalmai—*Yahweh is recompenser*
Head of a family of
Nethinim........Ezra 2:46   476

Shalman
Contraction of
Shalmaneser.....Hos. 10:14   845

Shalmaneser—*Shulmanu (a god) is chief*
Assyrian king.....2 Kin. 17:3   389

Shama—*He (God) has heard*
Son of Hotham....1 Chr. 11:44   417

Shamariah—*Yahweh has kept*
Son of
Rehoboam........2 Chr. 11:18, 19   448

Shamble—*meat market*
Question concerning meat
bought in........1 Cor. 10:25   1133

Shame—*a feeling of guilt*
A. *Caused by:*
Rape..........2 Sam. 13:13   320
Defeat........2 Chr. 32:21   466
Folly.........Prov. 3:35   617
Idleness......Prov. 10:5   621
Pride.........Prov. 11:2   621
A wicked
wife.........Prov. 12:4   622
Lying.........Prov. 13:5   623
Stub-
bornness......Prov. 13:18   623
Haste in
speech.......Prov. 18:13   626
Mistreatment of
parents.......Prov. 19:26   627
Evil
companions...Prov. 28:7   634
Juvenile
delinquency...Prov. 29:15   635
Nakedness....Is. 47:3   691
Idolatry.......Jer. 2:26, 27   710
Impropriety...1 Cor. 11:6   1133
Lust..........Phil. 3:19   1172
B. *Of the unregenerate:*
Hardened in ..Jer. 8:12   716
Pleasure   {Rom. 1:26, 27,
in............{ 32   1109
Vessels of.....Rom. 9:21   1116
Glory in......Phil. 3:19   1172
Like foam.....Jude 13   1262
C. *In the Christian life, of:*
Unregenerate's
life...........Rom. 6:21   1113
Sinful things...Eph. 5:12   1165
Improper
behavior.....1 Cor. 11:14, 22   1133
Christ.........Rom. 1:16   1109

Shamed—*destruction*
Son of Elpaal.....1 Chr. 8:12   413

Shamer—*guard*
1. Levite.........1 Chr. 6:46   410
2. Asherite......1 Chr. 7:30, 34   412

Shamgar—*cupbearer*
Judge of Israel; struck down 600
Philistines........Judg. 3:31   247

Shamhuth—*desolation*
Commander in David's
army...........1 Chr. 27:8   430

Shamir—*a sharp point*
1. Town in
Judah........Josh. 15:1, 48   230
2. Town in
Ephraim......Judg. 10:1   254
3. Levite........1 Chr. 24:24   428

Shamma—*astonishment*
Asherite...........1 Chr. 7:36, 37   413

Shammah—*waste*
1. Son of Reuel...Gen. 36:13, 17   38
2. Son of Jesse...1 Sam. 16:9   290
Called
Shimea.......1 Chr. 2:13   406

SUBJECT	REFERENCE	PAGE	SUBJECT	REFERENCE	PAGE	SUBJECT	REFERENCE	PAGE

Shammah—continued
3. One of David's mighty
men...........2 Sam. 23:11 332
Also called Shammoth the
Harorite.......1 Chr. 11:27 416

Shammai—*celebrated*
1. Grandson of
Jerahmeel.....1 Chr. 2:28, 32 406
2. Descendant of
Caleb.........1 Chr. 2:44, 45 406
3. Descendant of
Judah.........1 Chr. 4:17 408

Shammoth—*waste*
One of David's mighty
men..............1 Chr. 11:27 416

Shammua—*renowned*
1. Reubenite
spy...........Num. 13:2-4 148
2. Son of David ..2 Sam. 5:13, 14 313
3. Levite........Neh. 11:17 500
4. Postexilic
priest.........Neh. 12:1, 18 501

Shamsherai—*sunlike*
Son of Jeroham ...1 Chr. 8:26 413

Shapham—*youthful*
Gadite............1 Chr. 5:12 409

Shaphan—*prudent, shy*
Scribe under
Josiah............2 Kin. 22:3 395
Takes book of the Law to
Josiah........2 Kin. 22:8-10 395
Is sent to Huldah for
interpretation ..2 Kin. 22:14 396
Assists in repairs of
temple ....2 Chr. 34:8 468
Father of notable (Jer. 36:10-12
son...............(25 742

Shaphat—*he has judged*
1. Simeonite
spy...........Num. 13:2-5 148
2. Son of
Shemaiah .....1 Chr. 3:22 407
3. Gadite chief ...1 Chr. 5:11, 12 409
4. One of David's
herdsmen ....1 Chr. 27:29 431
5. Father of the prophet
Elisha........1 Kin. 19:16, 19 362

Shapher—*beauty*
Israelite
encampment .....Num. 33:23 171

Sharai—*Yahweh is deliverer*
Divorced his foreign
wife..............Ezra 10:34, 40 485

Sharar—*firm*
Father of Ahiam ..2 Sam. 23:33 332

Sharers
A. Of physical things:
Sacrifices.....1 Cor. 10:18 1133
Suffering ......2 Cor. 1:7 1143
1 Pet. 4:13 1239
B. Of evil things:
Sins ....1 Tim. 5:22 1196
C. Of spiritual things:
Holiness.......Heb. 12:10 1223
Communion ...1 Cor. 10:16, 17 1133
Spiritual
things........Rom. 15:27 1121
Inheritance ....Col. 1:12 1177

Sharezer, Sherezer—*protect the king*
1. Son of Sennach-
erib...........Is. 37:38 684
2. Sent to Zechariah concerning
fasting........Zech. 7:1-3 899

Sharon—*plain*
1. Coastal plain between Joppa
and Mt.
Carmel........1 Chr. 27:29 431

Famed for
roses..........Song 2:1 651
2. Pasture east of the
Jordan........1 Chr. 5:16 409

Sharonite—*an inhabitant of Sharon*
Shitrai ....1 Chr. 27:29 431

Sharp—*having a keen edge; biting*
A. Descriptive of:
Stone..........Ex. 4:25 60
Knives.........Josh. 5:2, 3 220
Share.........1 Sam. 13:20, 21 287
Rocks ....1 Sam. 14:4 287
Arrows ....Is. 5:28 662
B. Used to compare a sword with:
Tongue ....Ps. 57:4 571
Adulteress....Prov. 5:4 617
Mouth.........Is. 49:2 692
God's Word....Heb. 4:12 1216
C. Figurative of:
Deceitfulness ..Ps. 52:2 570
Falsehood .....Prov. 25:18 632
Contention ....Acts 15:39 1089
Severe
rebuke......2 Cor. 13:10 1151
Christ's
conquest......Rev. 14:14-18 1277

Sharuhen—*abode of pleasure*
Town of Judah assigned to
Simeon...........Josh. 19:1, 6 234
Called (Josh. 15:36 231
Shaaraim.......(1 Chr. 4:31 408

Shashai—*whitish*
Divorced his foreign
wife............Ezra 10:34, 40 485

Shashak—*assaulter*
Benjamite.........1 Chr. 8:14, 25 413

Shaul—*asked (of God)*
1. King of
Edom.........Gen. 36:37 38
2. Son of
Simeon ......Gen. 46:10 48
Founder of a tribal
family........Num. 26:13 163
3. Kohathite
Levite........1 Chr. 6:24 410

Shave—*to cut off the hair*
A. Used worthily to express:
Accommo-
dation........Gen. 41:14 42
Cleansing......Lev. 14:8, 9 113
Commit-
ment.........Deut. 21:12 198
Mourning....Job 1:18-20 519
Sorrow ....Jer. 41:5 746
B. Used unworthily to express:
Defeat of a
Nazarite ......Judg. 16:19 260
Contempt....2 Sam. 10:4 317
Unnatural-
ness..........1 Cor. 11:5, 6 1133

Shaveh—*plain*
Valley near Salem; Abram meets
king of Sodom
here............Gen. 14:17, 18 16

Shaveh-kiriathaim—*plain of Kiriathaim*
Plain near Kiriathaim inhabited by
Emim ....Gen. 14:5 16

Shavsha, Shisha—*nobility*
David's
secretary.........1 Chr. 18:14, 16 423
Serves under Solomon
also ....1 Kin. 4:3 342

Sheal—*asking*
Divorced his foreign
wife..............Ezra 10:29 484

Shealtiel—*I have asked God*
Son of King Jeconiah and father of
Zerubbabel.......1 Chr. 3:17 407

Sheariah—*Yahweh has esteemed*
Descendant of
Saul..............1 Chr. 9:44 415

Shear-jashub—*a remnant shall return*
Symbolic name given to Isaiah's
son...............Is. 7:3 663

Sheba—*seven; an oath*
1. City in territory assigned to
Simeon.......Josh. 19:1, 2 234
2. Benjamite insur-
rectionist ....2 Sam. 20:1-22 328
3. Descendant of Cush through
Raamah.....Gen. 10:7 13
4. Descendant of
Shem ....Gen. 10:28 13
5. Grandson of Abraham and
Keturah......Gen. 25:3 26
6. Gadite chief ..1 Chr. 5:13 409
7. Land of, occupied by Sabeans,
famous (Job 1:15 519
traders......(Ps. 72:10 577
Queen of, visits Solomon;
marvels at his
wisdom ....1 Kin. 10:1-13 350
Mentioned by
Christ........Matt. 12:42 953

Shebah—*seven; an oath*
Name given to a well and town
(Beer-sheba)......Gen. 26:31-33 28

Shebaniah—*Yahweh has returned me*
1. Levite
trumpeter.....1 Chr. 15:24 420
2. Levite; offers prayer and signs
covenant......Neh. 9:4, 5 497
3. Levite who signs
covenant......Neh. 10:12 499
4. Priest who signs
covenant......Neh. 10:4 499

Shebarim—*breakings*
Place near Ai .....Josh. 7:5 222
See Quarry

Sheber—*breaking*
Son of Caleb ......1 Chr. 2:48 407

Shebna—*perhaps an abbreviation of Shebaniah*
Treasurer under
Hezekiah.........Is. 22:15 673
Demoted to position of
scribe ....2 Kin. 19:2 392
Man of pride and luxury; replaced
by Eliakim ....Is. 22:19-21 673

Shebuel—*God is renown*
1. Son of
Gershom......1 Chr. 23:16 427
2. Son of
Heman........1 Chr. 25:4 429

Shecaniah—*Yahweh has dwelt*
1. Descendant of
Zerubbabel....1 Chr. 3:21, 22 407
2. Postexilic
returnee ......Ezra 8:5 482
3. Descendant of
Aaron.........1 Chr. 24:11 428
4. Priest.........2 Chr. 31:15 465
5. Divorced his foreign
wife..........Ezra 10:2, 3 483
6. Father of
Shemaiah .....Neh. 3:29 491
Probably same as number 1
7. Postexilic
priest ....Neh. 12:3, 7 501
8. Father-in-law of
Tobiah........Neh. 6:18 494

278

SUBJECT	REFERENCE	PAGE	SUBJECT	REFERENCE	PAGE	SUBJECT	REFERENCE	PAGE

Shechem—*shoulder*

1. Son of Hamor; seduces Dinah, Jacob's daughter......Gen. 34:1-31　　36
2. Son of Gilead; founder of a tribal family...Num. 26:31　　163
3. Son of Shemida ......1 Chr. 7:19　　412
4. Ancient city of Ephraim ....Gen. 33:18　　35
Abram camps near ....Gen. 12:6　　15
Jacob buys ground here ....Gen. 33:18, 19　　35
Hivites, inhabit........Gen. 34:2　　36
Inhabitants of, slaughtered by Simeon and Levi..........Gen. 34:25-29　　36
Pastures near ....Gen. 37:12, 13　　39
Becomes city of refuge........Josh. 20:7　　236
Joseph buried here ....Josh. 24:32　　240
Joshua's farewell address here ......Josh. 24:1, 25　　239
Center of idol-worship.......Judg. 9:1, 4-7　　252
Town destroyed ....Judg. 9:23, 45　　253
Jeroboam made king here ......1 Kin. 12:1-19　　353
Name of, used poetically .....Ps. 108:7　　596

Shed—*to pour out*

A. *Descriptive of:*
Blood..........Gen. 9:6　　12
Bowels ....2 Sam. 20:10　　329
Holy Spirit.....Titus 3:6　　1207

B. *As applied to blood, indicative of:*
Justifiable execution .....Gen. 9:6　　12
Unjustifiable murder........Gen. 37:22　　39
Unacceptable sacrifice......Lev. 17:1-5　　117
Attempted vengeance ...{1 Sam. 25:31, 34}　　300
Unpardon-able..........2 Kin. 24:4　　398
Abomina-tion..........Prov. 6:16, 17　　618
Heinous crime ....Is. 59:7　　699
New covenant.....Matt. 26:28　　970

Shedeur—*shedder of light*

Reubenite leader ..Num. 1:5　　133

Sheep—*a domesticated animal*

A. *Characteristics of:*
Domesti-cated ....2 Sam. 12:3　　318
Gentle........Jer. 11:19　　719
Defenseless ..Mic. 5:8　　873
Needful of care..........Ezek. 34:5　　802

B. *Uses of, for:*
Food ....1 Sam. 25:18　　300
Milk..........1 Cor. 9:7　　1132
Clothing......Prov. 31:13　　636
Coverings ....Ex. 26:14　　80
Presents ......2 Sam. 17:29　　325
Tribute ....2 Kin. 3:4　　373
Sacrifice......Gen. 4:4　　7

C. *Uses of, in Levitical system as:*
Burnt offering ......Lev. 1:10　　100
Sin offering....Lev. 4:32　　103
Trespass offering ......Lev. 5:15　　103
Peace offering ......Lev. 22:21　　122

D. *Needs of, for:*
Protection .....Job 30:1　　535
Shepherd .....John 10:4, 27　　1054
Fold ....John 10:1　　1054
Pastures ......Ex. 3:1　　58
Water ....Gen. 29:8-10　　30
Rest ....Ps. 23:1, 2　　556
Shearing.......1 Sam. 25:2, 11　　300

E. *Figurative of:*
Innocent ......2 Sam. 24:17　　333
Wicked ....Ps. 49:14　　568
Jewish people ....Ps. 74:1　　579
Backsliders ...Jer. 50:6　　754
Lost sinners ...Matt. 9:36　　950
Christians .....John 10:1-16　　1054
Christ ....John 1:29　　1042
Saved ....Matt. 26:31-34　　970
Church ....Acts 20:28　　1095

See Lamb; Lamb of God

Sheepcote—*an enclosure for sheep*

David chosen ....2 Sam. 7:8　　315

Sheepfold—*shelter*

Enclosure for flocks ....Num. 32:16　　170
Entrance to, only by Christ ....John 10:1　　1054

Sheep Gate—*a gate of the restored Jerusalem*

Repaired ....Neh. 3:32　　491
Dedicated .....Neh. 12:38, 39　　502

Sheepmaster

Mesha, king of Moab............2 Kin. 3:4　　373

Sheepshearers

Employed by Judah ....Gen. 38:12　　40
Many employed by Nabal ....1 Sam. 25:7, 11　　300
Used figuratively.......Is. 53:7　　695

Sheets

Large piece of cloth ....Acts 11:5　　1084

Shehariah—*Yahweh is the dawn*

Benjamite......1 Chr. 8:26　　413

Shekel—*A Jewish measure (approximately .533 oz.)*

A. *As a weight:*
Standard of, defined.......Ex. 30:13　　85
Used in weighing......Josh. 7:21　　223
See Weights

B. *As money:*
Used in currency.....1 Sam. 9:8　　283
Fines paid in...Deut. 22:19, 29　　199
Revenues of the sanctuary paid in.............Neh. 10:32　　499

Shekinah—*a word expressing the glory and presence of God*

A. *As indicative of God's presence:*
In nature ......Ps. 18:7-15　　553
In the exodus from Egypt......Ex. 13:21, 22　　69
At Sinai ......Ex. 24:16-18　　79
In tabernacle ..Ex. 40:34-38　　96
Upon the mercy seat.......Ex. 25:22　　79
In the wilderness ...{Num. 9:15-23 / Num. 10:11-36}　　145 / 146
In the Temple.......2 Chr. 7:1-3　　443

B. *Illustrated by Christ in His:*
Divine nature ....Col. 2:9　　1178
Incarnation ...Luke 1:35　　1005
Nativity ......Luke 2:9　　1006

Manifestation {Hag. 2:9 / Zech. 2:5}　　893 / 897
to Israel......
Transfigur-ation..........2 Pet. 1:17　　1243
Ascension ....Acts 1:9　　1072
Transforming us by His {2 Cor. 3:18 / 2 Cor. 4:6}　　1144 / 1144
Spirit ....
Return........Matt. 24:44　　967
Eternal habitation with saints........Rev. 21:3　　1282

C. *Accompanied by:*
Angels.......Is. 6:1-4　　662
Cloud.........Num. 9:15-23　　145
Fire..........Heb. 12:18-21　　1223
Earthquake ...Hag. 2:21　　893

Shelah—*sprout; request*

1. Son of Arphaxad .....1 Chr. 1:18　　405
Called Salah ..Luke 3:35　　1008
2. Son of Judah ..Gen. 38:1-26　　40
Founder of the Shelanites.....Num. 26:20　　163

Shelemiah—*friend of Yahweh*

1. Father of Hananiah .....Neh. 3:30　　491
2. Postexilic priest ....Neh. 13:13　　502
3. Father of Irijah ....Jer. 37:13　　743
4. Porter ....1 Chr. 26:14　　430
Called Meshele-miah.......1 Chr. 9:21　　414
5. Ancestor of Jehudi ....Jer. 36:14　　742
6. Son of Abdeel.........Jer. 36:26　　742
7. Father of Jehucal ......Jer. 37:3　　743

Sheleph—*drawn out*

Son of Joktan; head of a tribe..............1 Chr. 1:20　　405

Shelesh—*might*

Asherite ......1 Chr. 7:35　　413

Shelomi—*at peace*

Father of an Asherite prince...........Num. 34:27　　173

Shelomith, Shelomoth—*peaceful*

1. Daughter of Dibri; her son executed......Lev. 24:10-23　　124
2. Chief Levite of Moses.........1 Chr. 23:18　　427
3. Gershonites in David's time ....1 Chr. 23:9　　427
4. Descendant of Moses, had charge of treasures......1 Chr. 26:25　　430
5. Son or daughter of King Rehoboam ....2 Chr. 11:20　　448
6. Daughter of Zerubbabel....1 Chr. 3:19　　407
7. Family who went with Ezra ....Ezra 8:10　　482

Shelumiel—*at peace with God*

Simeonite warrior........Num. 1:6　　133

Shem—*name; renown*

Oldest son of Noah.............Gen. 5:32　　9
Escapes the flood ....Gen. 7:13　　10
Receives a blessing.........Gen. 9:23, 26　　12
Ancestor of Semitic people...........Gen. 10:22-32　　13
Ancestor of:
Abram ....Gen. 11:10-26　　14
Jesus...........Luke 3:36　　1008

Shema—*report; rumor*

1. Reubenite .....1 Chr. 5:8　　409

SUBJECT | REFERENCE | PAGE | SUBJECT | REFERENCE | PAGE | SUBJECT | REFERENCE | PAGE

Shema—continued

2. Benjamite
   head..........1 Chr. 8:12, 13   413
3. Ezra's
   attendant.....Neh. 8:4   496
4. City of
   Judah.........Josh. 15:26   231
5. Son of
   Hebron.......1 Chr. 2:43   406

Shemaah—*fame*

Father of two of David's
warriors..........1 Chr. 12:3   417

Shemaiah—*Yahweh has heard*

1. Father of
   Shimri........1 Chr. 4:37   408
2. Reubenite.....1 Chr. 5:4   409
3. Levite who helped move the
   ark........1 Chr. 15:8, 12   419
4. Scribe in David's
   time.........1 Chr. 24:6   428
5. Son of
   Obed-edom....1 Chr. 26:4, 6, 7   429
6. Prophet of
   Judah.........1 Kin. 12:22-24   353
   Explains Shishak's invasion as
   divine
   punishment...2 Chr. 12:5-8   448
   Records Rehoboam's
   reign..........2 Chr. 12:15   448
7. Levite teacher under Jehoshaphat.......2 Chr. 17:8   451
8. Levite in Hezekiah's
   reign..........2 Chr. 29:14, 15   463
9. Levite
   treasurer......2 Chr. 31:14, 15   465
10. Officer of Levites in Josiah's
    reign..........2 Chr. 35:9   470
11. Father of
    Urijah.......Jer. 26:20   731
12. False
    prophet......Jer. 29:24-28   734
13. Father of
    Delaiah......Jer. 36:12   742
14. Descendant of
    David........1 Chr. 3:22   407
15. Keeper of the East Gate to
    Nehemiah.....Neh. 3:29   491
16. Merarite Levite living in
    Jerusalem.....1 Chr. 9:14   414
17. Son of
    Adonikam.....Ezra 8:13   482
18. Leading man under
    Ezra.........Ezra 8:16   482
19. Priest who divorced his foreign
    wife..........Ezra 10:21   484
20. Man who divorced his foreign
    wife..........Ezra 10:31   485
21. Prophet hired by
    Sanballat......Neh. 6:10-14   493
22. Priest who signs
    covenant......Neh. 10:1,8   499
23. Participant in dedication
    service........Neh. 12:34   501
24. Postexilic
    priest.........Neh. 12:35   501
25. Levite
    musician......Neh. 12:36   501

Shemariah—*Yahweh keeps*

1. Mighty man of
   Benjamin.....1 Chr. 12:5   417
2. Son of
   Rehoboam....2 Chr. 11:18, 19   448
3. Divorced his foreign
   wife......Ezra 10:31, 32   485

Shemeber—*splendor of heroism*

King of Zeboiim...Gen. 14:2   16

Shemed—*destruction*

Son of Elpaal.....1 Chr. 8:12   413

Shemer, Shamer—*guard*

1. Sells Omri hill on which
   Samaria is
   built..........1 Kin. 16:23, 24   358
2. Levite.........1 Chr. 6:46   410
3. Asherite......1 Chr. 7:30, 34   412

Shemida, Shemidah—*fame of knowing*

Descendant of Manasseh;
founder of the
Shemidaites......Num. 26:29, 32   163

Sheminith—*eighth*

Musical term......1 Chr. 15:21   420

Shemiramoth—*fame of the highest*

1. Levite musician in David's
   time.........1 Chr. 15:18, 20   419
2. Levite teacher under Jehoshaphat.......2 Chr. 17:8   451

Shemuel—*name of God*

1. Grandson of
   Issachar......1 Chr. 7:1, 2   411
2. Representative of
   Simeon.......Num. 34:20   173

Shen—*tooth; a pointed rock*

Rock west of
Jerusalem........1 Sam. 7:12   281

Shenir (see Senir)

Shenazar

Son of Jeconiah...1 Chr. 3:18   407

Shepham—*nakedness*

Place near the Sea of
Galilee.........Num. 34:11   172

Shephatiah—*Yahweh judges*

1. Benjamite
   warrior.......1 Chr. 12:5   417
2. Son of David..2 Sam. 3:4   311
3. Simeonite
   chief.........1 Chr. 27:16   431
4. Son of King Jeho-
   shaphat.......2 Chr. 21:2   455
5. Opponent of
   Jeremiah......Jer. 38:1   744
6. Descendant of
   Judah.........Neh. 11:4   500
7. Servant of Solomon whose
   descendants return from
   exile.........Ezra 2:57   476

Shepherd—*one who cares for the sheep*

A. *Duties of, toward his flock:*
   Defend.......1 Sam. 17:34-36   292
   Water........Gen. 29:2-10   30
   Give rest to...Jer. 33:12   739
   Know.........John 10:3-5   1054
   Number.......Jer. 33:13   739
   Secure pasture
   for............1 Chr. 4:39-41   408
   Search for the ⎰Ezek. 34:12-16   802
   lost..........⎱Luke 15:4, 5   1025
B. *Good, described as:*
   Faithful.......Gen. 31:38-40   33
   Fearless......1 Sam. 17:34-36   292
   Unselfish.....Luke 15:3-6   1025
   Considerate...Gen. 33:13, 14   35
   Believing.....Luke 2:8-20   1006
C. *Bad, described as:*
   Unfaithful.....Ezek. 34:1-10   802
   Cowardly.....John 10:12, 13   1054
   Selfish.........Is. 56:11, 12   697
   Ruthless......Ex. 2:17, 19   57
   Unbelieving...Jer. 50:6   754
D. *Descriptive of:*
   God...........Ps. 78:52, 53   582
   Christ........Heb. 13:20   1224
   Joshua........Num. 27:16-23   165
   David.........2 Sam. 5:2   312
   Judges........1 Chr. 17:6   422
   National
   leaders.......Jer. 49:19   753
   Cyrus........Is. 44:28   689
   Jewish
   leaders.......Matt. 9:36   950
   Church
   elders........1 Pet. 5:2   1239

Shepherd, Jesus the good

A. *Described prophetically in His:*
   Prophetic position
   (teaching).....Is. 40:10, 11   685
   Priestly
   position   ⎰Zech. 13:7   903
   (sacrifice)....⎱Matt. 26:31   970
   Kingly
   position   ⎰Ezek. 37:24   806
   (ruling)......⎱Matt. 2:6   942
B. *Described typically as:*
   Good.........John 10:11, 14   1054
   Chief.........1 Pet. 5:4   1239
   Great........Heb. 13:20   1224
   One..........John 10:16   1055
   Gentle.......Is. 40:11   685
   One who
   separates......Matt. 25:31-46   968

Shepho—*unconcern*

Son of Shobal.....Gen. 36:23   38

Sherah—*blood-relationship*

Daughter of Ephraim; builder of
cities.............1 Chr. 7:24   412

Sherebiah—*Yahweh has sent burning heat*

1. Levite family returning with
   Ezra.........Ezra 8:18   482
2. Levite who assists
   Ezra.........Neh. 8:7   496

Sheresh—*root*

Grandson of
Manasseh........1 Chr. 7:16   412

Sheriffs—*court officials*

Called by Nebuchad-
nezzar........Dan. 3:2, 3   825

Sheshach—*probably a cryptogram*

Symbolic of
Babylon.......Jer. 25:26   730

Sheshai—*whitish*

Descendant of
Anak...........Num. 13:22   149
Driven out by
Caleb..........Josh. 15:14   231
Destroyed by
Judah..........Judg. 1:10   244

Sheshan—*whitish*

Jerahmeelite......1 Chr. 2:31-35   406

Sheshbazzar—*sin (the moon god) protect the father*

Prince of Judah...Ezra 1:8, 11   475

Sheth (I)—*compensation*

Son of Adam (same as
Seth).............1 Chr. 1:1   404

Sheth (II)—*tumult*

Name descriptive of the
Moabites.......Num. 24:17   161

Shethar—*star*

Persian prince.....Esth. 1:14   507

Shethar-boznai—*starry splendor*

Official of Persia..Ezra 5:3, 6   479

Sheva—*self-satisfying*

1. Son of Caleb...1 Chr. 2:43, 49   406
2. David's
   scribe.........2 Sam. 20:25   329

Shibboleth—*stream or ear of corn*

Password.........Judg. 12:5, 6   257

Shicron—*drunkenness*

Town of Judah....Josh. 15:11   231

Shield—*a protective armor*

A. *Uses of:*
   Protection.....2 Chr. 14:8   450

SUBJECT	REFERENCE	PAGE	SUBJECT	REFERENCE	PAGE	SUBJECT	REFERENCE	PAGE

Shittim—continued

Reuben and Gad receive inheritance
here ....Num. 32:1-42   169

Scene of Moses' final addresses .....Deut. 1—34   178

Spies sent from ....Josh. 2:1   218

2. Valley blessed by the LORD.........Joel 3:18   852

Shittim wood—*wood of the shittah tree*

Used in:
Making the ark ...Ex. 25:10, 13   79

Table of showbread ....Ex. 37:10   93

Altar of incense ..Ex. 30:1   85

Altar of burnt offering ....Ex. 38:1, 6   93

Tabernacle boards............Ex. 26:15-37   80

Shiza—*splendor*

Reubenite.........1 Chr. 11:42   417

Shoa—*rich*

Race or tribe against Israel............Ezek. 23:23   792

Shobab—*returning*

1. Son of Caleb...1 Chr. 2:18   406
2. Son of David ..2 Sam. 5:14   313

Shobach—*expansion*

Commander of the Syrian army ....2 Sam. 10:16-18   317

Spelled Shophach ....1 Chr. 19:16, 18   424

Shobai—*glorious*

Head of a family of porters ....Ezra 2:42   476

Shobal—*flowing*

1. Son of Seir; a Horite chief ....Gen. 36:20-29   38
2. Judahite, son of Caleb and ancestor of the people of Kirjath-jearim ....1 Chr. 2:50, 52   407

Shobek—*forsaking*

Signer of Nehemiah's sealed covenant ......Neh. 10:24   499

Shobi—*Yahweh is glorious*

Ammonite who brings food to David ....{2 Sam. 17:27, 28}   325

Shoe—*footwear*

A. *Characteristics of:*
Worn on the feet ....1 Kin. 2:5   339

Tied by a latchet ....Gen. 14:23   16

Some considered worthless .....Amos 2:6   856

Used for dress occasions .....Luke 15:22   1025

Worn as adornment ....Song 7:1   653

Dirty after a trip ....Josh. 9:5, 13   225

Preserved supernaturally.. Deut. 29:5   206

B. *Symbolism of:*
Putting on—readiness for a journey ....Ex. 12:11   66

Putting off—reverence {Ex. 3:5 / Josh. 5:15}   58 / 221

Want of—mourning ....2 Sam. 15:30   323

Giving to another—renunciation of Mosaic marriage rights ....Ruth 4:7, 8   271

To loose another's—act of homage ......Luke 3:16   1008

C. *Figurative of:*
Preparation for service ....Eph. 6:15   1167

Protection and provision .....Deut. 33:25   212

Alertness ......Is. 5:27   662

See Sandals

Shoham—*beryl or onyx*

Merarite Levite ...1 Chr. 24:27   428

Shomer—*keeper, watchman*

Asherite ....1 Chr. 7:30, 32   412

Called Shamer ....1 Chr. 7:34   413

Shophan—*hidden*

Town in Gad......Num. 32:34, 35   170

Short—*not long; brief*

A. *Descriptive of:*
Life..........Ps. 89:47   587

Time of the devil on earth........Rev. 12:12   1276

Gospel age.....1 Cor. 7:29   1131

B. *Expressive of God's:*
Power ....Is. 50:2   693

Plan ....Rev. 22:6   1283

Provision .....Is. 59:1, 2   698

Tribulation ..Matt. 24:21, 22   967

Shoshannim—*lilies*

Musical term......Ps. 45 (Title)   566

Shoulder

A. *Of men, used for:*
Burdens ....Is. 46:7   691

Supporting clothes........Ex. 12:34   67

B. *Figurative of:*
Notable persons ......Ezek. 24:4, 5   793

Destruction....Ezek. 29:7   797

Servitude ......Is. 10:27   666

Rebellion ....Zech. 7:11   899

Messianic authority....Is. 9:6   665

Security ......Deut. 33:12   212

Twelve tribes ..Ex. 28:10-12   82

Shout, Shouted

A. *Occasions of, in:*
Conquest ....Josh. 6;5, 16, 20   217

Choosing a king ....1 Sam. 10:24   284

Sound of singing.......Ex. 32:17, 18   87

Laying foundation of the Temple.......Ezek. 3:11-13   773

B. *In spiritual things:*
At creation ....Job 38:7   540

In the Messiah's arrival ....Zech. 9:9   901

Shovel

1. Used for removing ashes ....Ex. 27:3   81
2. Winnowing tool............Is. 30:24   679

Showbread—*"bread of thy face"*

A. *Provisions concerning:*
Provided by the people ....Lev. 24:8   124

Prepared by the Levites........1 Chr. 9:32   414

Placed in two rows..........Ex. 25:30   80

Perennially supplied.........Num. 4:7   138

Presented to the Lord ....Lev. 24:7, 8   124

Provided for priests only ..{Lev. 24:9 / Matt. 12:4, 5}   124 / 952

B. *Table of:*
Placed in {Ex. 26:35 / Holy Place ...Heb. 9:2}   81 / 1219

Made of acacia.........Ex. 25:23-28   79

Carried by: Kohathite Levites........Num. 4:4, 7, 15   138

High priest ...Num. 4:7, 8, 16   138

C. *Symbolic of:*
Twelve tribes ..Ex. 28:10-12   82

Christ ....John 6:48   1049

Church ....1 Cor. 10:17   1133

Showers—*sudden outpourings*

A. *Used literally of rain:*
Withheld ......Jer. 3:3   710

Predicted ......Luke 12:54   1022

Requested .....Zech. 10:1   901

Blessing ....Ps. 65:10   574

B. *Used figuratively of:*
God's Word....Deut. 32:2   209

God's wrath ...Ezek. 13:11, 13   781

Messiah's advent ...Ps. 72:6   577

Gospel.........Ezek. 34:25, 26   803

Remnant .....Mic. 5:7   873

Shroud—*to cover or shelter*

Used figuratively......Ezek. 31:3   799

Shua, Shuah—*prosperity*

1. Son of Abraham by Keturah........Gen. 25:1, 2   26
2. Father of Judah's wife........Gen. 38:2, 12   40
3. Descendant of Judah.........1 Chr. 4:1, 11   407
4. Daughter of Heber.........1 Chr. 7:32   412

Shual—*jackal*

1. Asherite ....1 Chr. 7:30, 36   412
2. Region raided by a Philistine company......1 Sam. 13:17   287

Shubael, Shebuel

1. Levite, son of Amram ....1 Chr. 24:20   428
2. Levite, son of Heman........1 Chr. 25:4   429

Shuham—*depression*

Son of Dan ....Num. 26:42   163

Called Hushim ....Gen. 46:23   48

Head of the Shuhamites ......Num. 26:42, 43   163

Shuhite—*a descendant of Shua*

Bildad called; a descendant of Abraham {Gen. 38:2, 12 / by Keturah ...Job 2:11}   40 / 520

Shulamite—*a native of Shulam*

Shepherd's sweetheart ......Song 6:13   653

Shumathites

Family of Kirjath-jearim............1 Chr. 2:53   407

Shunammite—*a native of Shunem*

1. Abishag, David's nurse called ....1 Kin. 1:3, 15   337
2. Woman who cared for Elisha ....2 Kin. 4:8-12   374

Shunem—*uneven*

Border town of Issachar.........Josh. 19:18   234

Shuni—*fortunate*

Son of Gad.......Gen. 46:16   48

Shuppim—*serpent*

Levite porter ....1 Chr. 26:16   430

Shur—*fortification*

Wilderness in south Palestine ....Gen. 16:7   17

Israel went from Red Sea to ....Ex. 15:22   70

On Egypt's border............1 Sam. 15:7   289

SUBJECT	REFERENCE	PAGE	SUBJECT	REFERENCE	PAGE	SUBJECT	REFERENCE	PAGE

Hagar flees to.....Gen. 16:7   17

Shushan—*a city of Elam*
Residence of Persian
monarchs ....Esth. 1:2   507
Located on river
Ulai..............Dan. 8:2   831
Court of Ahasuerus
here.............Esth. 1:2, 5   507

Shut—*to close securely*
A. *Applied literally to:*
  Ark.............Gen. 7:16   10
  Door ....Gen. 19:6, 10   20
  Leper.........Lev. 13:4-44   111
  Animals ......Dan. 6:22   829
  Court.........Jer. 33:1   739
  Prison ....Acts 26:10   1101
B. *Applied figuratively to:*
  Womb.........1 Sam. 1:5, 6   276
  God's
  mercies ......Ps. 77:9   580
  Finality of
  salvation......Matt. 25:10   968
  Union with
  Christ........Song 4:12   652
  Spiritual
  blindness......Is. 6:10   663
  Awe...........Is. 52:15   695
  Heaven's
  glory.........Is. 60:11   700
  God's Word....Jer. 20:9   726
  Vision ....Dan. 12:4   837
  Secret prayer ..Matt. 6:6   946
  Christ's
  sovereignty ...Rev. 3:7, 8   1270

Shuthelah
1. Son of Ephraim; head of a
  family.......Num. 26:35, 36   163
2. Ephraimite.....1 Chr. 7:20, 21   412

Shuttle—*a weaving tool*
Our days swifter
than.............Job 7:6   523

Siaha, Sia—*assembly*
Family of
returning   {Ezra 2:43, 44   476
Nethinim.....{Neh. 7:47   495

Sibbecai, Sibbechai
One of David's mighty
men..............1 Chr. 11:29   416
Slays a Philistine
giant............2 Sam. 21:18   330
Commander of a
division ....1 Chr. 27:11   431

Sibmah, Shibmah—*balsam*
Town of Reuben ..Num. 32:3, 38   169
Famous for
wines ....Is. 16:8, 9   670

Sibraim—*double hope*
Place in north
Palestine......Ezek. 47:16   816

Sick, Sickness—*the state of being
unwell*
A. *Caused by:*
  Age............Gen. 48:1, 10   50
  Accident.......2 Kin. 1:2   371
  Wine ....Hos. 7:5   843
  Sins ....Mic. 6:13   874
  Despondency ..Prov. 13:12   623
  Prophetic
  visions ....Dan. 8:27   832
  Love..........Song 2:5   651
  God's
  judgment .....2 Chr. 21:14-19   456
  God's
  sovereignty ...John 11:4   1055
B. *Healing of, by:*
  Figs ....2 Kin. 20:7   393
  Miracle........1 Kin. 17:17-23   359
  Prayer.........James 5:14, 15   1231
  God's mercy ...Phil. 2:25-30   1171

See Diseases; Healing

Sickle—*an instrument for cutting grain*
Literally..........Deut. 16:9   194
Figuratively.......Mark 4:29   982
            Rev. 14:14-19   1277

Siddim, Vale of
Valley of bitumen pits near the
Dead Sea........Gen. 14:3, 8, 10   16

Sidon, Zidon—*fishery*
Canaanite city 20 miles north of
Tyre.............Gen. 10:15, 19   13
Israel's northern
boundary........Josh. 19:28   235
Canaanites not expelled
from ....Judg. 1:31   244
Israelites oppressed
by..............Judg. 10:12   255
Gods of, entice
Israelites ....1 Kin. 11:5, 33   351
Judgments pronounced
on...............Is. 23:12   674
Israelites sold as slaves
by..............Joel 3:4-6   852
People from, hear
Jesus............Luke 6:17   1012
Visited by Jesus...Matt. 15:21   957
Paul visits at......Acts 27:3   1102

Siege of a city—*a military blockade*
A. *Methods employed in:*
  Supplies cut
  off ....2 Kin. 19:24   393
  Ambushes
  laid ....Judg. 9:34   253
  Battering rams
  used ....Ezek. 4:2   774
  Arrows shot ...2 Kin. 19:32   393
B. *Suffering of:*
  Famine........2 Kin. 6:26-29   378
  Pestilence......Jer. 21:6   726
C. *Examples of:*
  Jericho ....Josh. 6:2-20   221
  Jerusalem......2 Kin. 24:10, 11   398
See War

Sieve, sift—*screen*
Used figuratively of:
God's judgment ...Amos 9:9   860
Satan's
temptation ....Luke 22:31   1033

Sign—*an outward token having
spiritual significance*
A. *Descriptive of:*
  Heavenly
  bodies.........Gen. 1:14   4
  Rainbow.......Gen. 9:12-17   12
  Circumcision ..Gen. 17:11   18
  Bloodshed ....Ex. 12:13   66
  God's
  wonders ......Ps. 65:8   574
  Covenant.....Rom. 4:11   1111
  Miracles ......Deut. 26:8   202
  Memorial......Num. 16:38   153
  Symbolic act...Is. 8:18   664
  Witness........Is. 19:19, 20   671
  Outward
  display.......John 4:48   1046
B. *Purposes of, to:*
  Authenticate {Deut. 13:1   191
  a prophecy...{1 Sam. 2:31, 34   278
  Strengthen {Judg. 6:17   249
  faith ....{Is. 7:11   663
  Recall God's
  blessings......Josh. 24:15-17   240
  Confirm God's {2 Kin. 19:28, 29   393
  Word ....{Heb. 2:4   1215
  Insure a {2 Kin. 20:5,
  promise......{ 9-11   393
  Confirm a
  prophecy......1 Kin. 13:3-5   354
C. *Concerning Christ in His:*
  Nativity ....Luke 2:12   1006
  Ministry ......John 20:30   1066
            Acts 2:22   1073
  Resurrection...Matt. 12:38-40   953

D. *Value of:*
  Discounted as
  such ....Matt. 16:1-4   957
  Demanded unneces-
  sarily ....John 6:30   1049
  Demonstrated by
  apostles.......Acts 5:12   1077
  Displayed by
  Paul ....Rom. 15:19   1120
E. *In prophecy, concerning:*
  Christ's first {Is. 7:11, 14   663
  advent.......{Matt. 1:21-23   942
  Second
  advent........Matt. 24:3, 30   966
  Antichrist.....2 Thess. 2:9   1189
  End...........Rev. 15:1   1277
F. *As assurance of:*
  Presence.......Ex. 3:12   58
  Judgment upon
  sin............Num. 17:10   154
  Goodness ......Ps. 86:17   585

Signify—*to make known by signs*
A. *Concerning men:*
  Peter's death...John 21:19   1066
  Ritual
  performed.....Acts 21:26   1096
  Jewish
  scheme ....Acts 23:15   1098
B. *Concerning predicted events:*
  New
  dispensation ..Heb. 9:8   1219
  Christ's:
  Death.........John 12:33   1057
  Sufferings ....1 Pet. 1:11   1235
  Gospel age.....Rev. 1:1   1268
  Famine........Acts 11:28   1085
  World's end....Heb. 12:27   1223

Sihon—*bold*
Amorite king residing at
Heshbon ....Num. 21:26-30   158
Victorious over
Moabites ....Num. 21:26-30   158
Ruler of five Midianite
princes ....Josh. 13:21   229
Refused Israel's request for
passage ....Deut. 2:26-28   180
Defeated by
Israel............Num. 21:21-32   158
Territory of, assigned to Reuben
and Gad.........Num. 32:1-38   169
Victory over, long
celebrated.......Deut. 31:4   208

Sihor—*black, turbid*
Name given to the
Nile ....Is. 23:3   673
Israel's southwestern
border...........Josh. 13:3   229

Silas, Silvanus—*wooded*
Leader in the Jerusalem
church ....Acts 15:22   1089
Christian
prophet ....Acts 15:32   1089
Sent on a
mission........Acts 15:22-35   1089
Became Paul's
companion ....Acts 15:36-41   1089
Roman citizen ....Acts 16:25-39   1090
Paul commended his work at
Corinth ....2 Cor. 1:19   1143
Called Silvanus....1 Thess. 1:1   1183
Associated in Paul's
writings.........2 Thess. 1:1   1189
Peter's helper ....1 Pet. 5:12   1239

Silence—*the lack of noise*
A. *Kinds of:*
  Will of {1 Pet. 2:15   1237
  God..........{Rev. 8:1   1273
  Troubled.......Jer. 20:9   726
B. *Virtue of:*
  Suitable time
  for............Eccl. 3:7   641
  Commanded...1 Cor. 14:34   1136

SUBJECT	REFERENCE	PAGE	SUBJECT	REFERENCE	PAGE	SUBJECT	REFERENCE	PAGE

Silence—continued

Sign of
prudence......Prov. 21:23   629

Sign of
wisdom ......Prov. 17:28   626

C. *Forbidden to God's:*
Watchmen...Is. 62:6   701
Messengers....Acts 5:27-42   1077
Praisers......Ps. 30:12   559

D. *Considered as:*
Blessing ......Zech. 2:13   897
Curse......1 Sam. 2:9   277
Judgment......Jer. 8:14   716
Punishment....Is. 15:1   669

E. *Of God:*
Broken in
judgment....Ps. 50:3   568
Misunderstood by
men......Ps. 50:21, 23   569

F. *Of Christ:*
Predicted ....Is. 53:7   695
Before:
Sinners......John 8:6   1051
High priest ...Matt. 26:62, 63   971
Pilate......Matt. 27:14   971
Herod ......Luke 23:9   1035

Silk—*a clothing material derived from the silkworm*

Sign of:
Luxury.........Ezek. 16:10, 13   783
Wantonness......Rev. 18:12   1279

Silla—*twig; basket*

Quarter of suburb of
Jerusalem .....2 Kin. 12:20   384

Silly women

Weighed down with
sin ....2 Tim. 3:6   1201

Siloam, Siloah—*sent*

Pool at
Jerusalem ......Neh. 3:15   491
Tower of, kills 18
people..........Luke 13:4   1023
Blind man washes
in ....John 9:1-11   1053

Silver—*a precious metal*

A. *Features concerning:*
Mined from the
earth.........Job 28:1   534
Melted by
fire........Ezek. 22:22   791
Sign of
wealth......Gen. 13:2   15
Used as
money......Gen. 23:15, 16   23
Article of
commerce....Ezek. 27:12   795
Given as
presents......1 Kin. 10:25   351
Used in:
Tabernacle..Ex. 38:19   94
Temple ......2 Kin. 12:13   384
Christ sold for {Zech. 11:12   902
30 pieces of ..{Matt. 26:15   969
Peter devoid
of............Acts 3:6   1074

B. *Figurative of:*
God's Word...Ps. 12:6   552
God's people..Zech. 13:9   903
Under-
standing ......Prov. 3:13, 14   616
Degen-
eration......Is. 1:22   659
Rejection......Jer. 6:30   714

Silversmith—*a worker in silver*

Demetrius, an
Ephesian......Acts 19:24-41   1094

Simeon—*hearing*

1. Son of Jacob by
Leah..........Gen. 29:32, 33   31
Joined Levi in massacre of
Shechemites...Gen. 34:25-31   36

Held as hostage by
Joseph ....Gen. 42:24, 36   44
Denounced by
Jacob ....Gen. 34:30   36
Sons of......Gen. 46:10   48

2. Tribe of, descendants of Jacob's
son ....Gen. 46:10   48
Number of, at first
census ....Num. 1:23   134
Number of, at second
census ......Num. 26:12-14   163
Position of, on Mt.
Gerizim ......Deut. 27:12   203
Inheritance of, within
Judah's .....Josh. 19:1-9   234
With Judah, fought
Canaanites..Judg. 1:1, 3, 17   243
Victory over Ham and
Amalekites...1 Chr. 4:24-43   408
Recognized in Ezekiel's
vision ....Ezek. 48:24-33   817

3. Ancestor of
Christ.........Luke 3:30   1008

4. Righteous man; blessed the
child Jesus ...Luke 2:25-35   1006

5. Christian prophet at
Antioch.......Acts 13:1   1086

6. Simon Peter ..Acts 15:14   1089

Similitude—*likeness of two things*

A. *Expressive of:*
Physical ....2 Chr. 4:3   441
Typical ....Rom. 5:14   1112
Literary
(simile) ......Ps. 144:12   609
Spiritual ......James 3:9   1229

B. *Expressed by:*
"Like" ....James 1:6   1228
"As"..........1 Pet. 2:5   1236
"Likeness"....Rom. 6:5   1112
"Liken"......Matt. 7:24, 26   948

Simon—*hearing*

1. Simon Peter ...Matt. 4:18   944
See Peter

2. One of the Twelve; called "the
Canaanite"....Matt. 10:4   950

3. One of Jesus'
brothers......Matt. 13:55   955

4. The leper ......Matt. 26:6   969

5. Pharisee ......Luke 7:36-40   1014

6. Man of
Cyrene......Matt. 27:32   972

7. Father of Judas
Iscariot ......John 6:71   1050

8. Sorcerer......Acts 8:9-24   1080

9. Tanner in
Joppa.........Acts 9:43   1083

Simple, the

Enlightened by {Ps. 19:7   555
God's Word ...{Ps. 119:105   601
Able to
understand......Prov. 1:4   615
Receptive of
correction ......Prov. 19:25   627
Void of
understanding....Prov. 7:7   619
Easily tempted ....Prov. 9:4, 16   620
Gullible ....Prov. 14:15   624
Inherit folly ......Prov. 14:18   624
Unmindful of
danger ....Prov. 22:3   629
The LORD
preserves.........Ps. 116:6   598

Simplicity—*that which is in its purest form*

A. *Necessary in:*
Prayer........Matt. 6:5-15   946
Dress........1 Pet. 3:3-5   1237
Conduct ......2 Cor. 1:12   1143
Giving........Rom. 12:8   1118
Preaching ....1 Thess. 2:3-7   1184

B. *Purposes of, to:*
Avoid outward
display.......Matt. 6:1-4   946
Defeat Satan ..2 Cor. 11:3, 4   1149

Remain pure in an evil
world ....Rom. 16:19   1122

Sin—*disobedience of God's Law*

A. *Defined as:*
Transgression.. 1 John 3:4   1251
Unrighteous-
ness........1 John 5:17   1253
Omission of known
duty ....James 4:17   1230
Not from
faith........Rom. 14:23   1120
Thought of
foolishness....Prov. 24:9   631

B. *Sources of, in:*
Satan.........John 8:44   1052
Man's heart....Matt. 15:19, 20   957
Lust ....James 1:15   1228
Adam's transgres-
sion ....Rom. 5:12, 16   1112
Natural birth ..Ps. 51:5   569

C. *Kinds of:*
National ......Prov. 14:34   624
Personal ......Josh. 7:20   223
Secret ....Ps. 90:8   587
Presump-
tuous ......Ps. 19:13   555
Open ....1 Tim. 5:24   1197
Shameless ....Is. 3:9   660
Youthful.......Ps. 25:7   557
Public ......2 Sam. 24:10, 17   333
Unforgive- {Matt. 12:21, 32   953
able........{John 8:24   1052
Of ignorance..Lev. 4:2   102
Willfully ......Heb. 10:26   1221

D. *Consequences of, among the unregenerate:*
Blindness ......John 9:41   1054
     2 Cor. 4:3, 4   1144
Servitude ......John 8:34   1052
Irreconcil-
able........1 Tim. 3:1-7   1195
Death ....Rom. 6:23   1113

E. *God's attitude toward:*
Withholds men
from ....Gen. 20:6   21
Punishes of ..Ex. 32:34   88
Provides a fountain
for ....Zech. 13:1   902
Blots out ...Is. 44:22   689
Casts away ..Mic. 7:19   875
Forgives ....Ex. 34:7   89
Remembers no
more........Jer. 31:34   737

F. *Christ's relationship to:*
Free of ....1 John 3:5   1251
Knew no ......2 Cor. 5:21   1146
Makes men conscious
of..........John 15:22, 24   1060
Died for our ..1 Cor. 15:3   1137
As an offering {Is. 53:10   695
for ....{Heb. 9:28   1220
Substitu- {Is. 53:5, 6   695
tionary.......{Matt. 26:28   970
Takes it
away.........John 1:29   1042
Saves His people
from ....Matt. 1:21   942
Has power to
forgive......Matt. 9:6   949
Makes reconciliation
for ....Heb. 2:17   1216
Purges our...Heb. 1:3   1215
Cleanses us
from ......1 John 1:7, 9   1249
Washes us
from ....Rev. 1:5   1268

G. *Regenerate must:*
Acknowl-
edge ....Ps. 32:5   560
Confess........Ps. 51:3, 4   569
Be sorry for...Ps. 38:18   563
Not serve......Rom. 6:6   1112
Not obey ......Rom. 6:6, 12   1112
Subdue ....Rom. 6:14-22   1113
Lay aside ......Heb. 12:1   1222
Resist........Heb. 12:4   1223
Keep from ....Ps. 19:13   555

SUBJECT	REFERENCE	PAGE

SUBJECT	REFERENCE	PAGE	SUBJECT	REFERENCE	PAGE	SUBJECT	REFERENCE	PAGE
Forbidden in Israel	Mic. 5:12	873	**Sosipater**—*saving a father*			To be punished	Rom. 2:9	1109
See Divination			Kinsman of Paul	Rom. 16:21	1122	**Soul winning**		
Sop—*a small portion of food*			**Sosthenes**—*of sound strength*			Importance of	James 5:20	1231
Christ gives to Judas	John 13:26-30	1059	1. Ruler of the synagogue at Corinth	Acts 18:17	1093	Christ's command	Matt. 4:19	944
			2. Paul's Christian brother	1 Cor. 1:1	1126	Our reward	Dan. 12:3	837
Sopater—*of sound parentage*						**Sound doctrine**		
One of Paul's companions	Acts 20:4	1094	**Sotai**—*Yahweh is turning aside*			A. *Manifested in:*		
Sophereth—*writer, scribe*			Head of a family of servants	Ezra 2:55	476	Heart's prayer	Ps. 119:80	601
Descendants of Solomon's servants	Neh. 7:57	495	**Sottish**—*thick-headed*			Speech	2 Tim. 1:13	1200
Sorcerers—*supposed possessors of supernatural powers*			Judah thus called	Jer. 4:22	712	Righteous living	1 Tim. 1:10	1194
A. *Prevalence of, in:*			**Soul**—*the immaterial part of man*			B. *Need of:*		
Assyria	Nah. 3:4, 5	879	A. *Descriptive of:*			For exhortation	Titus 1:9	1206
Egypt	Ex. 7:11	62	Man's life	1 Sam. 24:11	299	For the faith	Titus 1:13	1206
Babylon	Is. 47:9-13	691	People	Acts 2:41, 43	1074	Denied by some	2 Tim. 4:3	1202
Palestine	Acts 8:9-24	1080	Sinner	James 5:20	1231	**Sour grapes**—*not yet mature*		
Last days	Rev. 9:21	1274	Emotional life	1 Sam. 18:1, 3	293	Used proverbially	Jer. 31:29, 30	736
B. *Punishment of, described:*			Spiritual life	Ps. 42:1, 2, 4	565	**Sowing**—*scattering seed*		
Legally	Deut. 18:10-12	196	Disembodied	Rev. 6:9	1272	A. *Restrictions upon, regarding:*		
Prophetically	Mal. 3:5	908	state	Rev. 20:4	1281	Sabbath year	Lev. 25:3-22	125
Symbolically	Rev. 21:8	1282	B. *Characteristics of:*			Mingled seed	Lev. 19:19	119
See Divination; Magic, magician			Made by God	Gen. 2:7	5	Weather	Eccl. 11:4, 6	646
Sorcery—*the practice of magic*			Belongs to God	Ezek. 18:3, 4	786	B. *Figurative of evil things:*		
Forbidden in Israel	Deut. 18:10	196	Possesses immortality	Matt. 10:28	951	Iniquity	Job 4:8	521
Condemned by the prophets	Mic. 5:12	873	Most vital asset	Matt. 16:26	958	Wind	Hos. 8:7	844
Practiced by Manasseh	2 Chr. 33:6	467	Leaves body at death	Gen. 35:18	37	Discord	Prov. 6:14, 19	618
Work of the flesh	Gal. 5:20	1158	C. *Abilities of, able to:*			Strife	Prov. 16:28	625
Sore			Believe	Heb. 10:39	1221	False teaching	Matt. 13:25, 39	954
Intense feeling	2 Sam. 13:36	321	Love God	Luke 10:27	1019	Sin	Gal. 6:7, 8	1158
Crisis	Gen. 41:56, 57	44	Sin	Mic. 6:7	874	C. *Figurative of good things:*		
Plague	Lev. 13:42, 43	112	Prosper	3 John 2	1259	God's Word	Is. 55:10	696
Sorek—*a choice vine*			Survive death	Matt. 10:28	951	Reward	2 Cor. 9:6, 10	1148
Valley, home of Delilah	Judg. 16:4	259	D. *Duties of, to:*			Gospel	Matt. 13:3, 4, 37	954
Sorrow—*grief*			Keep itself	Deut. 4:9	182	Gospel messengers	John 4:36, 37	1046
A. *Kinds of:*			Seek the LORD	Deut. 4:29	182	Resurrection	1 Cor. 15:36-44	1138
Hypocritical	Matt. 14:9	956	Love the LORD	Deut. 6:5	184	Eternal life	Gal. 6:7-9	1158
Unfruitful	Matt. 19:22	961	Serve the LORD	Deut. 10:12	188	**Spain**—*a country in southwest Europe*		
Temporary	John 16:6, 20-22	1061	Store God's Word	Deut. 11:18	189	Paul desires to visit	Rom. 15:24, 28	1121
Continual	Rom. 9:2	1115	Keep God's Law	Deut. 26:16	202	**Sparrow**—*a small bird*		
Fruitful	2 Cor. 7:8-11	1147	Obey God	Deut. 30:2, 6, 10	207	Value of	Matt. 10:29, 31	951
Christian	1 Thess. 4:13	1185	Get wisdom	Prov. 19:8	627	**Spearmen**—*infantry men with spears*		
B. *Caused by:*			E. *Enemies of, seen in:*			One of, pierces Christ's side	John 19:34	1065
Sin	Gen. 3:16, 17	7	Fleshly lusts	1 Pet. 2:11	1236	Paul's military escort	Acts 23:23, 24	1099
Death	John 11:33-36	1056	Evil environment	2 Pet. 2:8	1243	**Speckled**		
Drunkenness	Prov. 23:29-35	631	Sin	Lev. 5:4, 15, 17	103	Spotted (of goats)	Gen. 30:32-39	32
Love of money	1 Tim. 6:10	1197	Adultery	Prov. 6:32	619	Colored (of birds)	Jer. 12:9	719
Apostasy	Ps. 16:4	552	Evil men	Prov. 22:24, 25	630	**Speech**—*the intelligible utterance of the mouth*		
Persecution	Esth. 9:22	513	Ignorance	Prov. 8:36	620	A. *Of the wicked, consisting of:*		
Hardship of life	Ps. 90:10	587	Hell	Prov. 23:14	630	Lies	Ps. 58:3	572
Knowledge	Eccl. 1:18	640	F. *Of the righteous:*			Cursing	Ps. 59:12	572
Distressing news	Acts 20:37, 38	1095	Kept by God	Ps. 121:7	603	Enticements	Prov. 7:21	619
C. *Of the righteous:*			Vexed by sin	2 Pet. 2:8	1243	Blasphemies	Dan. 7:25	831
Not like the world's	1 Thess. 4:13	1185	Subject to authorities	Rom. 13:1	1119	Earthly things	John 3:31	1045
Sometimes intense	Ps. 18:4, 5	553	Purified by obedience	1 Pet. 1:22	1236	Deception	Rom. 16:18	1122
Seen in the face	Neh. 2:2-4	489	Not allowed to famish	Prov. 10:3	621	B. *Of the righteous, consisting of:*		
None in God's blessings	Prov. 10:22	621	Restored	Ps. 23:1, 3	556	God's righteousness	Ps. 35:28	562
Shown in repentance	2 Cor. 7:10	1147	Enriched	Prov. 11:25	622	Wisdom	1 Cor. 2:6, 7	1127
To be removed	Is. 25:8	675	Satisfied	Prov. 13:25	623	God's Word	Ps. 119:172	603
None in heaven	Rev. 21:4	1282	Reign with Christ	Rev. 20:4	1281	Truth	Eph. 4:25	1165
Shall flee away	Is. 51:11	694	G. *Of the wicked:*			Mystery of Christ	Col. 4:3, 4	1179
See Grief			Desires evil	Prov. 21:10	628	Sound doctrine	Titus 2:1, 8	1206
			Delights in abominations	Is. 66:3	703			
			Has nothing	Prov. 13:4	623			
			Required	Luke 12:19, 20	1021			

SUBJECT	REFERENCE	PAGE	SUBJECT	REFERENCE	PAGE	SUBJECT	REFERENCE	PAGE

Speed—*to hasten*

"Let him make"...Is. 5:19 — 661
"They will come
with"............Is. 5:26 — 662

Spending—*paying out money or service for things*

A. *Wastefully, on:*
Harlots.......Luke 15:30 — 1026
Physicians.....Mark 5:26 — 983

B. *Wisely:*
In Christ's
service........2 Cor. 12:15 — 1151

Spices—*aromatic vegetable compounds*

A. *Uses of:*
Food.........Song 8:2 — 653
Incense.......Ex. 30:34-38 — 86
Fragrance.....Song 4:10 — 652

B. *Features concerning:*
Used as
presents.......Gen. 43:11 — 45
Objects of
commerce.....Gen. 37:25 — 39
Tokens of royal
favor..........1 Kin. 10:2 — 350
Stored in the
temple........1 Chr. 9:29 — 414
Sign of
wealth.......2 Kin. 20:13 — 394

Spider

Web of, figurative of:
Insecurity........Is. 59:5 — 698
Godless..........Job 8:14 — 523

Spies—*secret agents of a foreign government*

A. *Purpose of, to:*
Search out
Canaan.......Num. 13:1-33 — 148
Prepare for
invasion.....Josh. 2:1-21 — 218
Search out new
land..........Judg. 18:2-17 — 261
Make false
charges......Luke 20:20 — 1031

B. *Men accused of, falsely:*
Jacob's sons...Gen. 42:9-34 — 44
David's
servants......2 Sam. 10:3 — 317

Spikenard

Used as a
perfume..........Song 1:12 — 651
Mary uses it in
anointing   {Mark 14:3 — 995
Jesus............{John 12:3 — 1057

Spill—*to flow forth*

Water............2 Sam. 14:14 — 321
Wine............Luke 5:37 — 1011

Spinning—*twisting fibers together to form cloth*

Work done by
women........Ex. 35:25 — 91
Sign of industry...Prov. 31:19 — 636
As an
illustration......Matt. 6:28 — 947

Spirit—*an immaterial being*

A. *Descriptive of:*
Holy Spirit.....Gen. 1:2 — 4
Angels........Heb. 1:7, 14 — 1215
Man's immaterial
nature.......1 Cor. 2:11 — 1127
Evil...........1 Sam. 16:14-23 — 290
Believer's immaterial
nature.......1 Cor. 5:3, 5 — 1128
Controlling
influence......Is. 29:10 — 677
Inward
reality........Rom. 2:29 — 1110
Disembodied   {Heb. 12:23 — 1223
state.........{1 Pet. 3:19 — 1238

B. *Characteristics of, in man:*
Center of
emotions......1 Kin. 21:5 — 364
Source of
passions.......Ezek. 3:14 — 773
Cause of volitions
(will).........Prov. 16:32 — 626
Subject to
divine   {Deut. 2:30 — 180
influence.....{Is. 19:14 — 671
Leaves body   {Eccl. 12:7 — 647
at death......{James 2:26 — 1229
See Soul

Spirit, Holy (see Holy Spirit)

Spirit of Christ

A. *Descriptive of the Holy Spirit as:*
Dwelling in Old Testament
prophets......1 Pet. 1:10-11 — 1235
Sent by God...Gal. 4:6 — 1156
Given to
believers......Rom. 8:9 — 1114
Supplying
believers......Phil. 1:19 — 1170
Produces
boldness......Acts 4:29-31 — 1076
Commanded...Eph. 5:18 — 1165

B. *Christ's human spirit (consciousness), of His:*
Perception.....Mark 2:8 — 980
Emotions.....Mark 8:12 — 987
Life...........Luke 23:46 — 1036

Spirits, distinguishing of

A. *Described as:*
Spiritual gift...1 Cor. 12:10 — 1134
Necessary.....1 Thess. 5:19-21 — 1185

B. *Tests of:*
Christ's:
Deity.........1 Cor. 12:3 — 1134
Humanity.....1 John 4:1-6 — 1252
Christian
fellowship.....1 John 2:18, 19 — 1250

Spiritual—*the holy or immaterial*

A. *Applied to:*
Gifts...........1 Cor. 12:1 — 1134
Law...........Rom. 7:14 — 1113
Things.........Rom. 15:27 — 1121
Christians.....1 Cor. 3:1 — 1127
Resurrected
body..........1 Cor. 15:44-46 — 1138
Evil forces.....Eph. 6:12 — 1167

B. *Designating, Christians:*
Ideal state.....1 Cor. 3:1 — 1127
Discernment...1 Cor. 2:13-15 — 1127
Duty.........Gal. 6:1 — 1158
Manner of
life...........Col. 3:16 — 1178

Spiritual gifts (see Gifts, spiritual)

Spiritually—*a holy frame of mind*

Source of.........Gal. 5:22-26 — 1158
Expression of.....1 Cor. 13:1-13 — 1135
Growth in........2 Pet. 1:4-11 — 1243
Enemies of.....1 John 2:15-17 — 1250

Spite—*an injury prompted by contempt*

Of vexation of
grief..............Ps. 10:14 — 551
Described by
Christ...........Matt. 22:6 — 964

Spitting, spittle

A. *Symbolic of:*
Contempt.....Num. 12:14 — 148
Rejection.....Matt. 26:67 — 971
Uncleanness...Lev. 15:8 — 115

B. *Miraculous uses of, to heal:*
Dumb man....Mark 7:33-35 — 986
Blind man.....Mark 8:23-25 — 987
Man born
blind..........John 9:6, 7 — 1053

Spoil—*loot or plunder*

Clothing..........Ex. 3:22 — 59
Cattle.............Josh. 8:2 — 223

Sheep............Num. 31:32 — 169
House............Mark 3:27 — 981
Silver and gold....Nah. 2:9 — 879
Camp.............1 Sam. 17:53 — 292

Spokesman—*one who speaks for others*

Aaron deputed to
be................Ex. 4:14-16 — 59

Sponge—*a very absorbent sea fossil*

Full of vinegar, offered to
Christ...........Matt. 27:48 — 972

Spot, spotless

A. *Descriptive of:*
Blemish on the
face...........Job 11:15 — 525
Imperfection of the
body...........Song 4:7 — 652
Mixed colors...Gen. 30:32-39 — 32
Leopard's
spots..........Jer. 13:23 — 720

B. *Figuratively ("spotless") of:*
Sin.............Jude 23 — 1263
False
teachers.......2 Pet. 2:13 — 1244
Christ's
death.........1 Pet. 1:19 — 1236
Believer's
perfection.....2 Pet. 3:14 — 1244
Glorified
Church.......Eph. 5:27 — 1166
Perfect
offering......Num. 19:2 — 156
Obedience.....1 Tim. 6:14 — 1197

Springtime—*the season of nature's rebirth*

Symbolically
described........Song 2:11-13 — 651

Sprinkle

A. *Used literally of:*
Water.........Num. 8:7 — 144
Oil..............Lev. 14:16 — 113
Human blood..2 Kin. 9:33 — 381

B. *Of blood, used in:*
Passover.......Ex. 12:21, 22 — 67
Sinaitic   {Ex. 24:8 — 78
covenant.....{Heb. 9:19, 21 — 1220
Sin offering....Lev. 4:6 — 102
New
covenant......Heb. 12:24 — 1223

C. *Used figuratively of:*
Regener-
ation..........Heb. 10:22 — 1220
Purification....1 Pet. 1:2 — 1235

Square—*having four equal sides*

Altar..............Ex. 27:1 — 81
Breastplate.......Ex. 39:8, 9 — 94
City of God......Rev. 21:16 — 1282

Stab—*to pierce with a knife*

Asahel by Abner..2 Sam. 2:22, 23 — 310
Abner by Joab....2 Sam. 3:27 — 311
Amasa by Joab...2 Sam. 20:10 — 329

Stachys—*head of grain*

One whom Paul
loved...........Rom. 16:9 — 1121

Staff—*a long stick or rod*

A traveler's
support..........Gen. 32:10 — 34
Denotes food
support..........Lev. 26:26 — 127
A military
weapon..........Is. 10:24 — 666

Stairs, winding

Part of Solomon's
Temple...........1 Kin. 6:8 — 344

Stalls—*quarters for animals*

40,000 in Solomon's
time............1 Kin. 4:26 — 342

SUBJECT	REFERENCE	PAGE	SUBJECT	REFERENCE	PAGE	SUBJECT	REFERENCE	PAGE

Stammerer—*one who stutters*

Used of judicial
punishment ......Is. 28:11   676
Of the Gospel
age...............Is. 32:1, 4   679

Stars

A. *Features concerning:*
Created by
God...........Gen. 1:16   4
Ordained by
God...........Ps. 8:3   550
Set in the
expanse.......Gen. 1:17   4
Follow fixed
ordinances ....Jer. 31:35, 36   737
Named by
God........Ps. 147:4   610
Established
forever.......Ps. 148:3, 6   611
Of vast
numbers ......Gen. 15:5   17
Manifest God's
power.........Is. 40:26   686
Of different
proportions ...1 Cor. 15:41   1138
Very high......Job 22:12   531

B. *Worship of:*
Forbidden.....Deut. 4:19   182
Punished ......Deut. 17:3-7   195
Introduced by
Manasseh .....2 Kin. 21:3   394
Condemned
by the   (Jer. 8:2   715
prophets .....(Zeph. 1:4, 5   887

C. *List of, in Bible:*
Arcturus.......Job 9:9   524
Mazzaroth.....Job 38:32   541
Orion.........Job 9:9   524
Pleiades ......Job 9:9   524
Chambers of the
south ....Job 9:9   524
Of Beth-
lehem.........Matt. 2:2, 9, 10   942

D. *Figurative of:*
Christ's:
First advent ..Num. 24:17   161
Second
advent ......Rev. 22:16   1283
Angels........Rev. 1:16, 20   1269
Judgment.....Ezek. 32:7   800
False
security......Obad. 4   863
Glorified
saints ....Dan. 12:3   837
Apostates.....Jude 13   1262

State—*established government*

A. *Agents of:*
Under God's   (Dan. 4:17, 25   826
control.......(John 19:10, 11   1064
Sometimes
evil ....Mark 6:14-29   984
Sometimes
good.........Neh. 2:1-9   489
Protectors of the
Law..........Rom. 13:1-4   1119

B. *Duties of Christians to:*
Pray for ....1 Tim. 2:1, 2   1194
Pay taxes to ..Matt. 22:17-21   964
Be subject to ..Rom. 13:5, 6   1119
Resist (when
evil)..........Acts 4:17-21   1076

Stature—*the natural height of the body*

A. *Used physically of:*
Giants........Num. 13:32   149
Sabeans ......Is. 45:14   690

B. *Significance of:*
Normal, in human
growth........Luke 2:52   1007
Cannot be
changed ......Matt. 6:27   947
Not indicative of
greatness .....1 Sam. 16:7   290
In spiritual
things.........Eph. 4:13   1164

Statute of limitation

Recognized in the
Law.............Deut. 15:1-5, 9   193

Steadfastness—*firm, persistent and determined in one's endeavors*

A. *In human things, following:*
Person.........Ruth 1:18   269
Leader........Jer. 35:1-19   741
Principle......Dan. 1:8   822

B. *In spiritual things:*
Enduring chastise-
ment.........Heb. 12:7   1223
Bearing
persecution ...Rom. 8:35-37   1115
Maintaining perse-
verance ......Heb. 3:6, 14   1216
Stability of
faith..........Col. 2:5   1177
Persevering in
service........1 Cor. 15:58   1138
Resisting
Satan ....1 Pet. 5:9   1239
Defending Christian
liberty ....Gal. 5:1   1157

C. *Elements of, seen in:*
Having a
goal..........Phil. 3:12-14   1172
Discipline......1 Cor. 9:25-27   1132
Run the race ..Heb. 12:1, 2   1222
Never give
up ....Rev. 3:10, 21   1270

Stealing—*taking another's property*

Common on
earth............Matt. 6:19   946
Forbidden in:
Law.............Ex. 20:15   75
Gospel..........Rom. 13:9   1119
Christians not to
do..............Eph. 4:28   1165
Excludes from
heaven..........1 Cor. 6:9, 10   1129
None in heaven ...Matt. 6:20   946

Stephanas—*crowned*

Corinthian
Christian ....1 Cor. 1:16   1126
First convert of
Achaia...........1 Cor. 16:15   1139
Visits Paul ....1 Cor. 16:17   1139

Stephen—*wreath or crown*

One of the seven
deacons ....Acts 6:1-8   1078
Accused falsely by
Jews ....Acts 6:9-15   1078
Spoke before the Jewish
Sanhedrin......Acts 7:2-53   1078
Became first Christian
martyr ....Acts 7:54-60   1080
Saul (Paul) instigated in death
of ....Acts 7:58   1080

Steward, stewardship—*a trust granted for profitable use*

A. *Descriptive of:*
One over Joseph's
household.....Gen. 43:19   45
Curator or
guardian ......Matt. 20:8   962
Manager......Luke 16:2, 3   1026
Management of entrusted
duties.........1 Cor. 9:17   1132

B. *Duties of, to:*
Expend
monies.......Rom. 16:23   1122
Serve wisely ...Luke 12:42   1022

C. *Of spiritual things, based on:*
LORD's   (Ps. 24:1, 2   556
ownership....(Rom. 14:8   1120
Our
redemption...1 Cor. 6:20   1130
Gifts
bestowed   (Matt. 25:14, 15   968
upon us......(1 Pet. 4:10   1238
Offices given   (Eph. 3:2-10   1163
to us.........(Titus 1:7   1206

Faithful in responsi-
bilities ....Luke 16:1-3   1026

Stewardship, personal financial

Basic principles:
Settling
accounts ....Rom. 14:12   1120
God's   (Ps. 24:1   556
ownership.......(Rom. 14:7, 8   1120
Finances   (Matt. 19:16-22   961
and   (Luke 16:10-13   1026
spirituality   (1 Cor. 6:20   1130
inseparable ..(2 Cor. 8:3-8   1147
Needs will be   (Matt. 6:24-34   947
provided........(Phil. 4:19   1173
Content with   (Ps. 37:25   563
what God   (1 Tim. 6:6-10   1197
provides........(Heb. 13:5   1223
Righteousness...(Prov. 16:8   625
  (Rom. 12:17   1118
Avoid debt......(Prov. 22:7   629
  (Rom. 13:8   1119
Do not   (Prov. 6:1-5   618
co-sign ....(Prov. 22:26   630
Inheritance   (Prov. 17:2   626
uncertain.......(Prov. 20:21   628
Proper priority ....Matt. 6:19-21, 33   946
Prosperity   (Deut. 29:9   206
is from   (Ps. 1:1-3   548
God ....(3 John 2   1259
Saving ....Prov. 21:20   628
Laziness   (Prov. 24:30, 31   632
condemned......(Heb. 6:12   1217
Giving   (Prov. 3:9, 10   616
is   (Mal. 3:10-12   909
encouraged.....(2 Cor. 9:6-8   1148

Sticks—*pieces of wood*

Gathering on Sabbath
condemned......Num. 15:32-35   152
Necessary.........1 Kin. 17:10-12   359
Miracle
producing ....2 Kin. 6:6   377
Two become
one..............Ezek. 37:16-22   805
Viper in bundle
of ....Acts 28:3   1103

Stiff-necked—*rebellious; unteachable*

A. *Indicative of Israel's rebelliousness at:*
Sinai...........Ex. 32:9   87
Conquest ......Deut. 9:6, 13   187
Captivity ......2 Chr. 36:13   471
Christ's first
advent........Acts 7:51   1080

B. *Remedies of, seen in:*
Circumcision (regen-
eration).......Deut. 10:16   189
Yield to God...2 Chr. 30:8   464

Still

A. *Indicative of:*
God's voice....1 Kin. 19:12   362
God's
presence .....Ps. 139:18   608
Fright ....Ex. 15:16   70
Fixed
character .....Rev. 22:11   1283
Peace ....Jer. 47:6   751
Quietness .....Num. 13:30   149

B. *Accomplished by:*
God ....Ps. 107:29   595
Christ ....Mark 4:39   982
Submission ....Ps. 46:10   567
Communion ...Ps. 4:4   549

Stink—*a foul smell*

A. *Caused by:*
Dead fish ......Ex. 7:18, 21   62
Corpse........John 11:39   1056
Wounds ....Ps. 38:5   563

B. *Figurative of:*
Hostility toward
one ....Gen. 34:30   36
Hell ....Is. 34:3, 4   681

SUBJECT	REFERENCE	PAGE

SUBJECT	REFERENCE	PAGE	SUBJECT	REFERENCE	PAGE	SUBJECT	REFERENCE	PAGE

B. *Actual causes of, seen in:*
Self-seeking ...Luke 22:24   1033
Dispute between
men..........Gen. 13:7-11   15
Contentious
man ....Prov. 26:21   633
Being carnal...1 Cor. 3:3   1127
Disputes.......1 Tim. 6:4   1197

C. *Avoidance of, by:*
Being slow to
anger ....Prov. 15:18   624
Simplicity of
life..........Prov. 17:1   626
See Contention; Quarrel

Strike—*afflict; attack*

A. *Descriptive of:*
Smeared
blood ......Ex. 12:7, 22   66
Advance in
age ....Luke 1:7, 18   1004
Slapping.......John 18:22   1063
God's
judgment .....Ps. 39:10   564

B. *Of divine punishment, upon:*
Christ ....Is. 53:4, 8   695
Sinners ....Prov. 7:23   619
World ....Ps. 110:5   597
Rebellious ....Is. 14:6   668
Israel.........Is. 30:26   679

Striker—*a contentious person*
Disqualifies for church
office.............1 Tim. 3:3   1195

Stripes—*used in scourging*
Limit of........Deut. 25:1-4   201
Because of sin.....Ps. 89:32   587
Upon the
Messiah,   {Is. 53:5   695
healing...........{1 Pet. 2:24   1237
Uselessness of, on a
fool ....Prov. 17:10   626
Paul's experience {Acts 16:23, 33   1090
with...............{2 Cor. 11:23   1150

Striving, spiritual
To enter the strait
gate...............Luke 13:24   1023
Against sin........Heb. 12:4   1223
With divine help ..Col. 1:29   1177
In prayer ....Rom. 15:30   1121
For the faith of the
Gospel ....Phil. 1:27   1171

Stroke—*a blow*
With an ax........Deut. 19:5   196
With a sword .....Esth. 9:5   513

Strong drink (see Drunkenness)

Stronghold—*fortress*
David captured..2 Sam. 5:7, 9   313
The LORD is.......Nah. 1:7   878

Studs—*ornaments*
Of silver ....Song 1:11   650

Study—*intensive intellectual effort*
Of the   {Acts 17:10, 11   1091
Scriptures ....{2 Tim. 3:16, 17   1202

Stumble—*to trip on some obstacle*

A. *Occasions of, found in:*
Strong drink...Is. 28:7   676
God's Word....1 Pet. 2:8   1236
Christ ....Rom. 9:32, 33   1116
Christ
crucified ......1 Cor. 1:23   1126
Christian
liberty ....1 Cor. 8:9   1131

B. *Avoidance of, by:*
Following
wisdom ......Prov. 3:21, 23   616
See Offend, offense

Suah—*sweepings*
Asherite ....1 Chr. 7:36   413

Subjection—*the state of being under another's control*

A. *Of domestic and civil relationships:*
Servants to
masters to.....1 Pet. 2:18   1237
Citizens to
government...Rom. 13:1-6   1119
Children to
parents ....1 Tim. 3:4   1195
Wives to
husbands .....Eph. 5:24   1166
Younger to
elder..........1 Pet. 5:5   1239

B. *Of spiritual relationships:*
Creation to
sin ....Rom. 8:20, 21   1114
Demons to the
disciples.......Luke 10:17, 20   1018
Believers to the
Gospel ....2 Cor. 9:13   1148
Christians to one
another ......1 Pet. 5:5   1239
Christians to
God..........Heb. 12:9   1223
Creation to
Christ.........Heb. 2:5, 8   1215
Church to
Christ.........Eph. 5:24   1166
Christ to
God..........1 Cor. 15:28   1137

Subjugation—*the state of being subdued by force*
Physical
force.........1 Sam. 13:19-23   287
Spiritual
power........Mark 5:1-15   982

Submission—*humble obedience to another's will*
Each other.....Eph. 5:21   1166
Husbands......Eph. 5:22   1166
Rulers ....1 Pet. 2:13   1236
Elders ....1 Pet. 5:5   1239
Christian
leaders........Heb. 13:17   1224
God ....James 4:7   1230

Substitution—*replacing one person or thing for another*
Ram for the
man..............Gen. 22:13   23
Offering for the
offerer............Lev. 16:21, 22   116
Levites for the first-
born..............Num. 3:12-45   136
Christ for the   {Is. 53:4-6   695
sinner............{1 Pet. 2:24   1237

Subtlety—*craftiness of*
Satan ....Gen. 3:1   6
Wicked ....Acts 13:10   1086
Jewish leaders ..Matt. 26:3, 4   969
Jacob...........Gen. 27:35   29

Success—*accomplishment of goals in life*

A. *Rules of:*
Put God first...Matt. 6:32-34   947
Follow the
Book..........Josh. 1:7-9   217
Seek the
goal..........Phil. 3:13, 14   1172
Never give
up ....Gal. 6:9   1158
Do all for
Christ.........Phil. 1:20, 21   1170

B. *Hindrances of, seen in:*
Unbelief ....Heb. 4:6, 11   1216
Enemies ......Neh. 4:1-23   491
Sluggishness...Prov. 24:30-34   632
Love of the
world ....Matt. 16:26   958

Succoth—*booths*

1. Place east of the
Jordan ....Judg. 8:4, 5   251
Jacob's residence
here ....Gen. 33:17   35

2. Israel's first
camp ....Ex. 12:37   67

Succoth-benoth—*tabernacles of girls*
Idol set up in Samaria by
Babylonians......2 Kin. 17:30   390

Suchathites
Descendants of
Caleb............1 Chr. 2:42, 55   406

Suck—*to give milk to offspring*
Characteristics of:
True among
animals.........1 Sam. 7:9   281
Normal for human
mothers ....Job 3:12   520
Figurative of Israel's
restoration ....Is. 60:16   700
Figurative of
wicked ....Job 20:16   530

Suffering for Christ
Necessary in
Christian   {1 Cor. 12:26   1135
living...........{Phil. 1:29   1171
Blessed privilege ..Acts 5:41   1077
Never in vain .....Gal. 3:4   1155
After Christ's   {Phil. 3:10   1172
example.........{1 Pet. 2:20, 21   1237
Of short
duration..........1 Pet. 5:10   1239
Not comparable
to heaven's   {Rom. 8:18   1114
glory ....{1 Pet. 4:13   1239

Sufferings of Christ

A. *Features concerning:*
Predicted ......1 Pet. 1:11   1235
Announced ....Mark 9:12   988
Explained......Luke 24:26, 46   1037
Fulfilled ....Acts 3:18   1075
Witnessed ....1 Pet. 5:1   1239
Proclaimed ...Acts 17:2, 3   1091

B. *Benefits of, to Christ:*
Preparation for
priesthood ....Heb. 2:17, 18   1216
Learned
obedience.....Heb. 5:8   1217
Way to glory ..Heb. 2:9, 10   1215

C. *Benefits of, to Christians:*
Brought to
God...........1 Pet. 3:18   1238
Our:
Sins atoned...Heb. 9:26-28   1220
Example .....1 Pet. 2:21-23   1237
Fellowship....Phil. 3:10   1172
Consolation...2 Cor. 1:5-7   1143

Suicide—*self-murder*

A. *Thought of, induced by:*
Life's
weariness .....Job 3:20-23   520
Life's vanity ...Eccl. 2:17   641
Anger ....Jon. 4:3, 8, 9   867

B. *Brought on by:*
Hopeless-
ness..........Judg. 16:29, 30   260
Sin ....1 Kin. 16:18, 19   358
Disappoint-
ment..........2 Sam. 17:23   325
Betrayal of
Christ.........Matt. 27:3-5   971

C. *Other features concerning:*
Desired by
some..........Rev. 9:6   1274
Attempted but
prevented.....Acts 16:27, 28   1090
Imputed to
Christ.........John 8:22   1052
Satan tempts
Christ to......Luke 4:9   1009

D. *Principles prohibiting, found in:*
Body's
sacredness ....1 Cor. 6:19   1129
Prohibition against
murder........Ex. 20:13   75

Suicide—continued

Faith's
expectancy....2 Tim. 4:6-8, 18   1202

Sukkiim

African people in Shishak's
army.............2 Chr. 12:3   448

Summer

Made by God .....Ps. 74:17   579
Sign of God's
covenant........Gen. 8:22   11
Time of:
Fruit harvest.....2 Sam. 16:1, 2   324
Sowing and
harvest.........Prov. 6:6-8   618
Figurative of:
Industry..........Prov. 10:5   621
Opportunity......Jer. 8:20   716
Preceded by
spring...........Matt. 24:32   967

Sun

A. *Characteristics of:*
Created by
God..........Gen. 1:14, 16   4
Under God's   {Ps. 104:19   592
control......{Matt. 5:45   946
Made to rule...Gen. 1:16   4
Necessary for
fruit ....Deut. 33:14   212
Given for
light ....Jer. 31:35   737
Made for God's
glory...........Ps. 148:3   611
Causes:
Scorching.....Jon. 4:8   868
Sunstroke ....2 Kin. 4:18, 19   375

B. *Miracles connected with:*
Stands still.....Josh. 10:12, 13   226
Shadows of, turned
back..........2 Kin. 20:9-11   393
Darkening of, at
crucifixion ....Luke 23:44-49   1036
Going down at
noon.........Amos 8:9   860

C. *Worship of:*
Forbidden ....Deut. 4:19   182
By Manasseh ..2 Kin. 21:3, 5   394
By Jews ......Jer. 8:2   715

D. *Figurative of:*
God's
presence......Ps. 84:11   584
Earth's sphere of
action........Eccl. 1:3, 9, 14   640
God's Law .....Ps. 19:4-7   555
Future glory ...Matt. 13:43   955
Christ's glory ..Matt. 17:2   959

Sunday (see First day of week)

Sundial—*an instrument for telling time*
Miracle of.......Is. 38:8   684

Sundry—*in many parts*
Applied to God's
revelation ....Heb. 1:1   1215

Sunstroke—*stricken by sun's heat*
Child dies of ......2 Kin. 4:18-20   375

Superscription—*something inscribed on*
Roman coin......Mark 12:16   992
Cross of Christ....Luke 23:38   1036

Superstition—*gullible ideas based on fancy or fear*

A. *Causes of, in wrong views of:*
God ....1 Kin. 20:23   363
Holy objects ...1 Sam. 4:3   279
God's
providence....Jer. 44:15-19   749

B. *Manifestations of, in:*
Seeking illogical
causes ....Acts 28:4   1103
Ignorance of the true
God...........Acts 17:22   1092
Perverting true
religion ......Mark 7:1-16   985

Supper (see Lord's Supper)

Sur—*turning aside, entrance*
Name given to a
gate..............2 Kin. 11:6   383
Called "Gate of the
Foundation".....2 Chr. 23:5   457

Sure—*something trustworthy*

A. *Descriptive of divine things:*
God's law......Ps. 19:7   555
Messianic
line ....2 Sam. 23:5   332
Messiah ....Is. 22:23, 25   673
New
covenant......Acts 13:34   1087
God's:
Prophecies ...2 Pet. 1:19   1243
Promises......Rom. 4:16   1111
Purposes......2 Tim. 2:19   1201

B. *Applied to the believer's:*
Calling and
election ....2 Pet. 1:10   1243
Faith ....John 6:69   1050
Dedication.....Neh. 9:38   499
Life of faith....Is. 32:18   680
Confidence in God's
Word ....Luke 1:1   1004
Reward........Prov. 11:18   622

Surety—*one who guarantees another's debt*

A. *Descriptive of:*
Certainty......Gen. 15:13   17
Guarantee .....Gen. 43:9   45
Our Lord .....Heb. 7:22   1218

B. *Features concerning:*
Risks involved
in ....Prov. 11:15   622
Warning
against........Prov. 6:1-5   618

Surfeiting—*gluttonous indulgence*
Christ warns
against.........Luke 21:34   1032

Surname—*a family name*

A. *Descriptive of:*
Simon Peter ...Acts 10:5, 32   1083
John Mark.....Acts 12:12, 25   1085
Judas
Iscariot ......Luke 22:3   1033
Judas
Barsabas......Acts 15:22   1089
Joses
Barnabas......Acts 4:36   1076
James and John
Boanerges.....Mark 3:17   981

B. *Figurative of God's:*
Call of
Gentiles......Is. 44:5   689
Sovereignty over
kings ....Is. 45:4   690

Susanna—*lily*
Believing woman ministering to
Christ...........Luke 8:2, 3   1014

Susi—*horseman*
Mannassite spy ...Num. 13:11   149

Suspicion—*doubt of another's intent*

A. *Kinds of:*
Unjustified.....Josh. 22:9-31   237
Pretended .....Gen. 42:7-12   44
Unsuspected...John 13:21-28   1058

B. *Objects of:*
Esau by
Jacob ....Gen. 32:3-12   34
Jeremiah by
officials ....Jer. 37:12-15   743
Jews by
Haman.......Esth. 3:8, 9   509
Mary by
Joseph ....Matt. 1:18-25   942
Peter by a
damsel ......Matt. 26:69-74   971

Sustenance—*means of sustaining life*
Israel by the
Lord ....Neh. 9:21   498
Elijah by ravens and a
widow...........1 Kin. 17:1-9   359
Believer by the
Lord.............Ps. 3:5   548

Swaddling—*bandages, wrappings*
Figurative of
Jerusalem ....Ezek. 16:3, 4   783
Jesus wrapped
in ....Luke 2:7   1006

Swallow—*a long-winged, migratory bird*
Nesting in the
sanctuary ....Ps. 84:3   584
Noted for
chattering........Is. 38:14   684

Swallow—*to engulf; to overwhelm*

A. *Applied miraculously to:*
Aaron's rod....Ex. 7:12   62
Red Sea ....Ex. 15:12   70
Earth..........Num. 16:30-34   153
Great fish......Jon. 1:17   867

B. *Applied figuratively to:*
God's
judgments ....Ps. 21:9   555
Conquest .....Jer. 51:34, 44   757
Captivity ......Hos. 8:7, 8   844
Sorrow ....2 Cor. 2:7   1143
Resurrection...Is. 25:8   675

Swan
Should be translated "horned
owl".............Lev. 11:18   109

Swearing—*taking an oath*

A. *Kinds of:*
Proclama-
tory.........Ex. 17:16   72
Protective .....Gen. 21:23   22
Personal.......1 Sam. 20:17   295
Purificatory...Neh. 13:25-30   503
Promissory ...Luke 1:73   1006
Prohibited ....James 5:12   1230

B. *Of God, objects of:*
God's
purpose.......Is. 14:24, 25   669
God's
covenant......Is. 54:9, 10   696
Messianic
priesthood ....Heb. 7:21   1218
See Oaths

Sweat—*perspiration*
Penalty of man's
sin ....Gen. 3:18, 19   7
Cause of,
avoided ....Ezek. 44:18   813
Of Jesus, in
prayer...........Luke 22:44   1034

Sweet—*that which is pleasing to the taste*

A. *Descriptive, literally, of:*
Water ....Ex. 15:25   70
Honey.........Judg. 14:18   258
Incense........Ex. 25:6   79
Perfumes .....Esth. 2:12   508

B. *Descriptive, figuratively, of:*
God's Law.....Ps. 19:10   555
God's Word...Ps. 119:103   601
Spiritual
fellowship.....Ps. 55:14   571
Meditation.....Ps. 104:34   593
Pleasant
words........Prov. 16:24   625
Sleep ....Prov. 3:24   617
Christians .....2 Cor. 2:15   1144
Christian
service........Eph. 5:2   1165

Swim—*to propel oneself in water by natural means*
Miraculously, of
iron ....2 Kin. 6:6   377

SUBJECT	REFERENCE	PAGE

Taberah—*burning*

Israelite camp; fire destroys many
here..............Num. 11:1-3   147

Tabering—*drumming* (tabret)

Beating the breasts in
sorrow ....Nah. 2:7   879

Tabernacle

A. *Descriptive of:*
Moses' administrative
office.........Ex. 33:7-11   88
Structure erected at
Sinai.........Ex. 40:2, 35-38   96
Portable shrine containing an
idol ....Acts 7:43   1080
Tent prepared for the ark by
David.........1 Chr. 16:1-43   420
Lord's incarnate
Word ....John 1:14   1042
Heavenly   (Heb. 8:2, 5   1219
prototype ....(Heb. 9:11, 24   1219
Holy city .....Rev. 21:3   1282

B. *Sinaitic, constructed:*
By divine   (Ex. 25:8   79
revelation....(Heb. 8:5   1219
By craftsmen inspired by the
Spirit ....Ex. 31:1-11   86
Out of contributions willingly
supplied.......Ex. 25:1-9   79
For the manifestation
of God's   (Ex. 25:8   79
glory.........(Ex. 29:42, 43   85
In two parts—holy place
and   (Ex. 26:33, 34   81
Most Holy ...(Heb. 9:2-7   1219
With surrounding
court.........Ex. 40:8   96
Within a year's
time ....Ex. 40:2, 17   96

C. *History of:*
Set up at
Sinai.........Ex. 40:1-38   96
Sanctified and
dedicated ....Ex. 40:9-16   96
Moved by priests and
Levites.......Num. 4:1-49   138
Camped at
Gilgal.........Josh. 5:10, 11   221
Set up at
Shiloh.........Josh. 18:1   233
Israel's   (Judg. 18:31   262
center of   (1 Sam. 1:3, 9,
worship   (24   276
Ark of, taken by
Philistines.....1 Sam. 4:1-22   279
Worship not   (1 Sam. 7:1, 2,
confined to...(15-17   281
Located at Nob during Saul's
reign..........1 Sam. 21:1-6   296
Moved to
Gibeon........1 Kin. 3:4   341
Ark of, brought to Jerusalem by
David.........2 Sam. 6:17   314
Brought to the Temple by
Solomon ......1 Kin. 8:1, 4, 5   346

D. *Typology of, seen in:*
Christ ....John 1:14   1042
God's
household.....Eph. 2:19   1163
Believer.......1 Cor. 6:19   1129
Heaven........Heb. 9:23, 24   1220

E. *Typology of, seen in Christ:*
Candlestick—His enlightening
us...........Rev. 1:13   1269
Sacred bread—His sustaining
us...........John 6:27-59   1049
Altar of incense—His
intercession (John 17:1-26   1062
for us.........(Heb. 7:25   1218
Veil—His
flesh.........Heb. 10:20   1220
Ark (wood and gold)—His
humanity and
deity..........John 1:14   1042

Tabernacle, Feast of (see Feasts, Hebrew)

Table

A. *Descriptive of:*
Article of
furniture......Matt. 15:27   957
For
showbread ....Heb. 9:2   1219
Small writing
tablet ....Luke 1:63   1005
Tablet of wood or
stone ....Ex. 24:12   79

B. *Figurative of:*
Human heart ..Prov. 3:3   616
Christian's
heart.........2 Cor. 3:3   1144
God's
provision......Ps. 23:5   556
Intimate
fellowship.....Luke 22:30   1033
Lord's
Supper........1 Cor. 10:21   1133

Tabor—*mountain height*

1. Mountain on borders of
Zebulun and
Issachar .....Josh. 19:12, 22   234
Great among
mountains ....Jer. 46:18   751
Scene of rally
against   (Judg. 4:6, 12,
Sisera........(14   247
2. Town of
Zebulun.......1 Chr. 6:77   411
3. Oak of, near
Ramah.......1 Sam. 10:3   283

Tabret—*a musical instrument* (timbrel)

Used by:
Prophets ....1 Sam. 10:5   284
People ....Gen. 31:27   33

Tabrimmon—*Rimmon is good*

Father of
Ben-hadad.......1 Kin. 15:18   357

Taches—*hooks or clasps*

Couplings for
curtains ....Ex. 26:6, 11, 33   80

Tachmonite—*wise*

Descriptive of one of David's
heroes............2 Sam. 23:8   332
Same as Hachmonite
in ....1 Chr. 11:11   416

Tackling—*ropes, cord, line*

Ship's ropes.......Is. 33:23   681
All of a ship's removable
gear..............Acts 27:19   1102

Tactfulness—*the knack of knowing the right thing to do or say*

A. *Manifested in:*
Appeasing   (Gen. 32:4, 5,
hatred ....(13-21   34
Settling
disputes.......1 Kin. 3:24-28   341
Obtaining
one's   (Esth. 5:1-8   510
wishes ....(Esth. 7:1-6   511

B. *Illustrated by Christ, in:*
Rebuking a
Pharisee ......Luke 7:39-50   1014
Teaching
humility .....Mark 10:35-45   990
Forgiving a
sinner........John 8:1-11   1051
Rebuking His
disciples......John 21:15-23   1066

Tadmor—*palm tree*

Trading center near
Damascus........2 Chr. 8:4   445
A desert town....1 Kin. 9:18   350

Tahan—*encampment*

Ephraimite;
founder of the (Num. 26:35   163
Tahanites ......(1 Chr. 7:25   412

Tahath—*station*

1. Kohathite
Levite.........1 Chr. 6:24   410
2, 3. Two descendants of
Ephraim ......1 Chr. 7:20   412
4. Israelite
encampment ..Num. 33:26, 27   171

Tahpanhes, Tehaphnehes

City of Egypt;   (Jer. 2:16   710
refuge of fleeing (Jer. 44:1   748
Jews ....(Ezek. 30:18   798

Tahpenes—*royal wife*

Egyptian queen ...1 Kin. 11:19, 20   352

Tahrea—*flight*

Descendant of
Saul.............1 Chr. 9:41   415
Called Tarea .....1 Chr. 8:33, 35   413

Tahtim-hodshi

Place visited by census-taking
Joab..............2 Sam. 24:6   333

Tailoring—*the art of making clothes*

For Aaron's
garments.........Ex. 39:1   94

Tale

Stipulated
quantity..........Ex. 5:8, 18   60
Brief meditation...Ps. 90:9   587
Nonsensical talk ..Luke 24:11   1036

Talebearer—*one who gossips*

Reveals secrets....Prov. 11:13   622
Injures
character........Prov. 18:8   626
Creates strife......Prov. 26:20   633

Talent—*see Jewish measures*

Of gold ....Ex. 37:24   93
Of silver ....2 Kin. 5:5, 22, 23   376
Of bronze.........Ex. 38:29   94
Of iron...........1 Chr. 29:7   433
Parable of.........Matt. 25:14-30   968

Talitha, cumi—*"Damsel, arise"*

Jairus' daughter thus
addressed ....Mark 5:41   984

Talk—*verbal communication between persons*

A. *Described as:*
Divine ....Ex. 33:9   88
Deceitful ......Job 13:7   526
Proud..........1 Sam. 2:3   277
Mischievous ...Prov. 24:2   631
Vain...........Titus 1:10   1206
Foolish ....Eph. 5:4   1165

B. *Of good things, God's:*
Law ....Deut. 6:7   184
Judgment......Ps. 37:30, 31   563
Righ-
teousness .....Ps. 71:24   577
Power ....Ps. 145:11   610

Talmai—*plowman*

1. Son of Anak driven out by
Caleb ....Josh. 15:14   231
2. King of Geshur whose
daughter, Maacah, becomes
David's wife...2 Sam. 3:3   311

Talmon—*oppressor, violent*

Levite porter......1 Chr. 9:17   414
Descendants of, return from
exile..............Ezra 2:42   476
Members of, become temple
porters ....Neh. 11:19   500

SUBJECT   REFERENCE   PAGE | SUBJECT   REFERENCE   PAGE | SUBJECT   REFERENCE   PAGE

Thyine—*a small cone-bearing tree*
Wood of, used for
furniture ....Rev. 18:12   1279

Tibhath—*slaughter*
Town in the kingdom of
Zobah............1 Chr. 18:8   423

Tibni—*intelligent*
Son of Ginath.....1 Kin. 16:21, 22   358

Tidal—*splendor*
King allied with
Chedorlaomer ....Gen. 14:1, 9   16

Tidings
A. *Descriptive of:*
Joyful ....Gen. 29:13   30
Good..........1 Kin. 1:42   338
Bad............1 Sam. 11:4-6   285
Foreboding ...Jer. 37:5   743
Distressing.....2 Sam. 4:4   312
Fatal ....1 Sam. 4:19   279
B. *Of salvation:*
Out of Zion....Is. 40:9   685
By a person....Is. 41:27   687
Bringer of
peace.........Is. 52:7   695
By Christ......Is. 61:1-3   700

Tiglath-pileser—*my trust is in the god Ninib*
Powerful Assyrian king who
invades
Samaria.........2 Kin. 15:29   388

Tikvah—*hope*
1. Father-in-law of
Huldah........2 Kin. 22:14   396
Called
Tikvath.......2 Chr. 34:22   469
2. Father-in-law of
Jahaziah ......Ezra 10:15   484

Tile
Large brick of soft
clay.............Ezek. 4:1   774
Earthen roof.....Luke 5:19   1010

Tiller—*a farmer*
Man's first job ....Gen. 2:5   5
Sin's handicap
on..............Gen. 4:12   8
Industry in,
commended......Prov. 12:11   622

Tilon—*scorn*
Son of Shimon ...1 Chr. 4:20   408

Timaeus—*highly prized*
Father of
Bartimaeus......Mark 10:46   990

Timbrel—*a small hand drum*
Used in:
Entertainment ....Gen. 31:27   33
Worship ....Ps. 81:1-4   583

Time—*the period between two eternities*
A. *Computation of, by:*
Years..........Gen. 15:13   17
Months........1 Chr. 27:1   430
Weeks........Dan. 10:2   834
Days ....Gen. 8:3   10
Moments.......Ex. 33:5   88
Sundial........2 Kin. 20:9-11   393
B. *Events of, dated by:*
Succession of
families ....Gen. 5:1-32   8
Lives of great
men..........Gen. 7:6, 11   10
Succession of
kings ....1 Kin. 11:42, 43   353
Earthquakes...Amos 1:1   855
Important events (the
exodus).......1 Kin. 6:1   343

Important
emperors......Luke 3:1   1007
C. *Periods of, stated in years:*
Bondage in
Egypt.........Acts 7:6   1078
Wilderness
wanderings ...Deut. 1:3   178
Judges........Judg. 11:26   256
Captivity .....Dan. 9:2   832
Seventy weeks (490
years).........Dan. 9:24-27   833
D. *Sequence of prophetic events in, indicated by:*
"The time is fulfilled" (Christ's
advent) ......Mark 1:15   978
"The fullness of the time"
(Christ's
advent) ......Gal. 4:4   1156
"The times of the Gentiles" (the
Gospel age) ...Luke 21:24   1032
"The day of salvation" (the
Gospel age) ...2 Cor. 6:2   1146
"In the last days" (the Gospel
age)..........Acts 2:17   1073
"In the last days"
(the time before
Christ's   2 Tim. 3:1   1201
return).......2 Pet. 3:3   1244
"The last day"
(Christ's   John 6:39, 54   1049
return).......John 12:48   1058
"New heavens"
(eternity) .....2 Pet. 3:13   1244
E. *Importance of, indicated by:*
Shortness of
life...........Ps. 89:47   587
Making the most of
it ....Eph. 5:16   1165
Purpose of, for
salvation......2 Pet. 3:9, 15   1244
Uncertainty
of............Luke 12:16-23   1021
Our goal,   Heb. 11:10,
eternity......13-16   1221
God's plan in ..Acts 14:15-17   1088
F. *For everything:*
To give birth, to
die............Eccl. 3:1-8, 17   641

Timidity—*lack of courage*
Nicodemus........John 3:1, 2   1044
Joseph of
Arimathea.......John 19:38   1065
Certain people ....John 9:18-23   1053

Timna—*restraint*
1. Concubine of
Eliphaz ....Gen. 36:12, 22   38
2. Duke of
Edom ....Gen. 36:40   38

Timnah, Timnath, Thimnathah—
allotted portion
1. Town of
Judah.........Josh. 15:10   231
Assigned to
Dan...........Josh. 19:40, 43   235
Captured by
Philistines....2 Chr. 28:18   462
2. Town in Judah's hill
country ....Josh. 15:57   232

Timnath-serah—*extra portion*
Village in Ephraim's hill
country ....Josh. 19:50   235
Place of Joshua's
burial ....Josh. 24:29, 30   240
Called Timnath-
heres..........Judg. 2:9   245

Timnite—*an inhabitant of Timnah*
Samson thus
called ....Judg. 15:6   259

Timon—*deeming worthy*
One of the seven
deacons ....Acts 6:1-5   1078

Timothy, the Epistles to—*books of the New Testament*
A. *First Timothy:*
Toward true
doctrine.......1 Tim. 1:3-7   1194
Paul's
ministry.......1 Tim. 1:12-17   1194
Christ, the
Mediator......1 Tim. 2:5, 6   1194
Instructions to
women........1 Tim. 2:9-15   1194
Church
officials ....1 Tim. 3:1-13   1195
The good
minister.......1 Tim. 4:6-16   1196
Fight the good
fight ....1 Tim. 6:11-21   1197
B. *Second Timothy:*
Call to responsi-
bility..........2 Tim. 1:6-18   1200
Call for
strength ......2 Tim. 2:1-13   1201
Against
apostasy ......2 Tim. 3:1-9   1201
The Scriptures called
inspired.......2 Tim. 3:14-17   1202
Charge to
Timothy ......2 Tim. 4:1-8   1202
Paul's personal
concerns......2 Tim. 4:9-18   1202

Timothy—*revere God*
A. *Life of:*
Of mixed
parentage.....Acts 16:1, 3   1089
Faith of, from   2 Tim. 1:5   1200
childhood ....2 Tim. 3:15   1202
Becomes Paul's
companion...Acts 16:1-3   1089
Ordained by the
presbytery....1 Tim. 4:14   1196
Left behind at
Troas.........Acts 17:14   1091
Sent by Paul
to Thessa-   1 Thess. 3:1, 2,
lonica........6   1184
Rejoined Paul at
Corinth ....Acts 18:1-5   1092
Preached Christ to
Corinthians ...2 Cor. 1:19   1143
Sent by Paul into
Macedonia ....Acts 19:22   1094
Sent by Paul to
Corinth ......1 Cor. 4:17   1128
Returned with Paul to
Jerusalem.....Acts 20:1-5   1094
With Paul in   Phil. 1:1   1170
Rome........Phil. 2:19, 23   1171
Set free.......Heb. 13:23   1224
Left at Ephesus by
Paul ....1 Tim. 1:3   1194
Paul
summoned
him to   2 Tim. 4:9, 11,
Rome........21   1202
B. *Character of:*
Devout from
childhood ....2 Tim. 3:15   1202
Faithful in
service........Phil. 2:22   1171
Beloved by
Paul ....1 Tim. 1:2, 18   1194
Follows Paul's
way...........1 Cor. 4:17   1128
In need of
instruction....1 Tim. 4:12-16   1196
Of sickly
nature ....1 Tim. 5:23   1197
Urged to remain
faithful........1 Tim. 6:20, 21   1197
Emotional ....2 Tim. 1:4   1200

Tin—*a metal obtained by smelting*
Used in early
times............Num. 31:22   168
Brought from
Tarshish........Ezek. 27:12   795
Figurative of
degeneracy......Is. 1:25   659

SUBJECT	REFERENCE	PAGE	SUBJECT	REFERENCE	PAGE	SUBJECT	REFERENCE	PAGE

Tiphsah—*passage; crossing*

1. Place designating Solomon's northern boundary .....1 Kin. 4:24 — 342
2. Unidentified town attacked by Menahem .....2 Kin. 15:16 — 387

Tiras

Son of Japheth....Gen. 10:2 — 13

Tirathites

Family of scribes ....1 Chr. 2:55 — 407

Tire—*an ornamental headdress*

Worn by:
Ezekiel............Ezek. 24:17, 23 — 793
Daughters of Zion............Is. 3:18 — 660
Jezebel............2 Kin. 9:30 — 381

Tirhakah—*the king of Cush* (Nubia)

Opposes Sennacherib......2 Kin. 19:9 — 392

Tirhanah—*kindness*

Son of Caleb......1 Chr. 2:42, 48 — 406

Tiria—*foundation*

Son of Jehaleleel ..1 Chr. 4:16 — 408

Tirshatha—*governor*

Persian title used of Zerubbabel.......Ezra 2:63 — 477
Applied to Nehemiah........Neh. 8:9 — 496

Tirzah—*delight*

1. Zelophehad's youngest daughter......Num. 26:33 — 163
2. Town near Samaria......Josh. 12:24 — 228
Seat of Jeroboam's rule...........1 Kin. 14:17 — 356
Israel's kings rule here down to Omri........1 Kin. 16:6-23 — 358
Famous for its beauty......Song 6:4 — 653

Tishbite—*an inhabitant of Tishbeh*

Elijah thus called ....1 Kin. 17:1 — 359

Tithes—*the tenth of one's income*

Given by Abraham to Melchizedek......Heb. 7:1, 2, 6 — 1218
Promised by Jacob............Gen. 28:22 — 30
Belongs to the LORD............Lev. 27:30-33 — 129
Given to Levites ..Num. 18:21-24 — 155
Given by Levites to priests...........Num. 18:25-28 — 155
Taken to Temple..........Deut. 12:5-19 — 190
Rules regarding ...Deut. 14:22-29 — 193
Honesty in, required..........Deut. 26:13-15 — 202
Of animals, every tenth...........Lev. 27:32, 33 — 129
Recognition of, by Jews...........Neh. 13:5, 12 — 502
Promise regarding........Mal. 3:7-12 — 909
Pharisaic legalism on, condemned.......Luke 18:9-14 — 1028

Titles—*appellations of honor*

Condemned by Christ...........Matt. 23:1-10 — 965

Tittle—*a mark distinguishing similar letters*

Figurative of minute requirements ....Matt. 5:18 — 945

See Jot

Titus

Greek Christian and Paul's companion ......Titus 1:4 — 1206
Sent by Paul to Corinth ....2 Cor. 7:13, 14 — 1147
Organized Corinthian relief fund...........2 Cor. 8:6-23 — 1147
Met Paul in Macedonia ....2 Cor. 7:6, 7 — 1147
Accompanied Paul to Crete............Titus 1:5 — 1206
Sent by Paul to Dalmatia ....2 Tim. 4:10 — 1202

Titus, the Epistle to—*a book of the New Testament*

Qualifications of an elder ....Titus 1:5-9 — 1206
Against false teachings.......Titus 1:10-16 — 1206
Domestic life.....Titus 2:1-10 — 1206
Godly living......Titus 3:3-8 — 1207

Tizite

Description of Joha, David's mighty man ......1 Chr. 11:45 — 417

Tob—*good*

Jephthah's refuge east of the Jordan ....Judg. 11:3, 5 — 255

Tobadonijah—*good is Lord Yahweh*

Levite teacher.....2 Chr. 17:7, 8 — 451

Tobiah—*Yahweh is good*

1. Founder of a postexilic family........Ezra 2:60 — 477
2. Ammonite servant; ridiculed the Jews.........Neh. 2:10 — 490

Tobijah—*Yahweh is good*

1. Levite teacher ....2 Chr. 17:7, 8 — 451
2. Came from Babylon......Zech. 6:10, 14 — 899

Tochen—*a measure*

Town of Simeon ..1 Chr. 4:32 — 408

Toe—*the terminal part of the foot*

Aaron's, anointed ....Ex. 29:20 — 84
Of captives, amputated.......Judg. 1:6, 7 — 244
Of an image.......Dan. 2:41, 42 — 824

Togarmah

Northern country inhabited by decendants of Gomer ....Gen. 10:3 — 13

Toi

King of Hamath; sends embassy to salute David......2 Sam. 8:9-12 — 316

Token—*a visible sign*

A. Descriptive of:
Rainbow.......Gen. 9:12-17 — 12
Circumcision ..Gen. 17:11 — 18
Bloodshed .....Ex. 12:13 — 66
God's wonders ......Ps. 65:8 — 574
B. As assurance of:
God's: Presence.....Ex. 3:12 — 58
Judgment upon sin.........Num. 17:10 — 154
Goodness .....Ps. 86:17 — 585
Guarantee ....Josh. 2:12, 18, 21 — 218
Identification ..Mark 14:44 — 996
Genuineness ..2 Thess. 3:17 — 1190
Coming judgment ....2 Thess. 1:5 — 1189

Tola—*worm; scarlet*

1. Son of Issachar and family head......Gen. 46:13 — 48
2. Son of Puah; a judge of Israel ....Judg. 10:1 — 254

Tolad—*begetter*

Simeonite town ...1 Chr. 4:29 — 408
Called Eltolad.....Josh. 19:4 — 234

Tolerance—*an attitude of patience toward opposing views*

A. Approved in dealing with:
Disputes among brothers.......Mark 9:38-40 — 989
Weaker brother ....Rom. 14:1-23 — 1119
Repentant brother ....2 Cor. 2:4-11 — 1143
B. Condemned in dealing with:
Sin ....1 Cor. 5:1-13 — 1128
Evil.............2 Cor. 6:14-18 — 1146
Sin in ourselves......Mark 9:43-48 — 989
Error ....2 John 10, 11 — 1256

Toll—*taxes*

Imposed by Jews ....Ezra 4:20 — 478
Imposed upon Jews ....Ezra 4:13 — 478
Levites excluded from ....Ezra 7:24 — 481

Tomb—*a place of burial*

John's body placed in ....Mark 6:25-29 — 984
Christ's body placed in — Matt. 27:57-60 — 973
Joseph's — John 19:41, 42 — 1065

Tongue—*the organ of speech*

A. Descriptive of:
Language......Gen. 10:5, 20, 21 — 13
Speech ......Ex. 4:10 — 59
The physical organ ....Judg. 7:5 — 250
Externalism....1 John 3:18 — 1251
People or race........Is. 66:18 — 704
Spiritual gift...1 Cor. 12:10-30 — 1134
Submission ....Is. 45:23 — 690
B. Kinds of:
Backbiting.....Prov. 25:23 — 632
As of fire ......Acts 2:3 — 1073
Deceitful .....Mic. 6:12 — 874
Double ....1 Tim. 3:8 — 1195
False ....Ps. 120:3 — 603
Flattering.....Prov. 6:24 — 619
Just ....Prov. 10:20 — 621
Lying.........Prov. 21:6 — 628
Muttering .....Is. 59:3 — 698
New ....Mark 16:17 — 999
Perverse......Prov. 17:20 — 626
Sharpened....Ps. 140:3 — 608
Slow ....Ex. 4:10 — 59
Soft ....Prov. 25:15 — 632
Stammering ...Is. 33:19 — 681
Wholesome....Prov. 15:4 — 624
Wise.........Prov. 15:2 — 624
C. Characteristics of:
Small but important.....James 3:5 — 1229
Untameable...James 3:6-8 — 1229
Source of trouble........Prov. 21:23 — 629
Means of sin...Ps. 39:1 — 564
Known by God........Ps. 139:4 — 607
D. Proper employment of, in:
Speaking: God's righteous- ness.........Ps. 35:28 — 562
Wisdom......Ps. 37:30 — 563
God's Word...Ps. 119:172 — 603
Singing praises........Ps. 126:2 — 604
Kindness ....Prov. 31:26 — 636
Confessing Christ.........Phil. 2:11 — 1171

See Slander

SUBJECT	REFERENCE	PAGE	SUBJECT	REFERENCE	PAGE	SUBJECT	REFERENCE	PAGE

Uzzen-sherah—*top of Sherah*

Town built by Sherah, Ephraim's
daughter ....1 Chr. 7:24   412

Uzzi—*my strength*

1. Descendant of
   Aaron.........1 Chr. 6:5, 51   410
2. Descendant of
   Issachar ......1 Chr. 7:1-3   411
3. Son of Bela ....1 Chr. 7:7   412
4. Levite
   overseer ......Neh. 11:22   500
5. Postexilic
   priest ....Neh. 12:19, 42   501

Uzzia—*my strength is Yahweh*

One of David's mighty
men..............1 Chr. 11:44   417

Uzziah—*my strength is Yahweh*

1. Kohathite
   Levite.........1 Chr. 6:24   410
2. Father of
   Jehonathan ...1 Chr. 27:25   431
3. King of
   Judah, called ⎰2 Kin. 14:21   386
   Azariah ......⎱2 Kin. 15:1-7   387
   Reigned 52
   years..........2 Kin. 15:1, 2   387
   Reigned
   righteously....2 Chr. 26:4, 5   460
   Conquered the
   Philistines.....2 Chr. 26:6-8   460
   Strengthened
   Jerusalem.....2 Chr. 26:9   460
   Developed
   agriculture....2 Chr. 26:10   460
   Usurped priestly function;
   stricken with
   leprosy........2 Chr. 26:16-21   460
   Life of, written by
   Isaiah.........2 Chr. 26:22, 23   461
   Earthquake in the days
   of..............Amos 1:1   855
   Death of, time of Isaiah's
   vision.........Is. 6:1   662
4. Priest who divorced his foreign
   wife...........Ezra 10:19, 21   484
5. Judahite......Neh. 11:4   500

Uzziel—*God is my strength*

1. Levite, son of Kohath and
   family head ...Ex. 6:18, 22   61
2. Son of Bela ....1 Chr. 7:7   412
3. Simeonite
   captain........1 Chr. 4:41-43   408
4. Levite
   musician......1 Chr. 25:3, 4   429
5. Levite assisting in Hezekiah's
   reforms ....2 Chr. 29:14-19   463
6. Goldsmith working on
   Jerusalem's
   wall...........Neh. 3:8   490

V

Vagabond—*an aimless wanderer*

Curse on Cain ....Gen. 4:12, 14   8
Curse upon the
wicked ....Ps. 109:10   596
Professional exorcists thus
called ....Acts 19:13   1093

Vail (see Veil, the sacred; Veil,
woman's)

Vain—*empty; useless*

A. *Applied to physical things:*
  Beauty.........Prov. 31:30   636
  Life............Eccl. 6:12   643
  Customs.......Jer. 10:3   717
  Men............Job 11:12   525
  Adornment.....Jer. 4:30   712
  Healing........Jer. 46:11   750
  Sacrifice.......Is. 1:13   659
  Protection.....1 Sam. 25:21   300
  Safety ....Ps. 33:17   560

World's
creation.......Is. 45:18, 19   690
B. *Applied to spiritual things:*
  Obedience .....Deut. 32:46, 47   211
  Chastisement ..Jer. 2:30   710
  Visions ....Ezek. 13:7   781
  Serving God ...Mal. 3:14   909
  Faith ....1 Cor. 15:17   1137
  Words.........Eph. 5:6   1165
  Imaginations ..Rom. 1:21   1109
  Babblings......2 Tim. 2:16   1201
C. *Applied to possibilities:*
  God's grace....1 Cor. 15:10   1137
  Christ's
  death ....Gal. 2:21   1155
  Scriptures .....James 4:5   1230
  Faith ....1 Cor. 15:2-17   1136
  Religion ....James 1:26   1228
  Worship ....Is. 45:19   690
  Labor..........1 Thess. 3:5   1184
  Reception......1 Thess. 2:1, 2   1184
  Sufferings .....Gal. 3:4   1155

Vainglory—*conceit*

Very offensive in
the Christian's ⎰Gal. 5:26   1158
life..............⎱Phil. 2:3   1171

Vajezatha—*son of the atmosphere*

One of Haman's
sons..............Esth. 9:9   513

Valley Gate

Entrance into
Jerusalem ....Neh. 2:13   490

Valley of Dry Bones

Vision of
Ezekiel.........Ezek. 37:1-14   805

Vaniah—*Yahweh is praise*

Divorced his foreign
wife..............Ezra 10:36   485

Vanity—*emptiness, futility*

A. *Descriptive of:*
  Man's life......Ps. 144:4   609
  Sin's end ......Prov. 22:8   629
  Man's
  thoughts......Ps. 94:11   589
  Idolatry........Acts 14:15   1088
B. *Manifested in the wicked's:*
  Words.........Ps. 12:2   551
  Thoughts......Ps. 94:11   589
  Trust ....Is. 59:4   698
  Worship ....Jer. 51:17, 18   756
C. *Believer's attitude toward:*
  Request for removal
  from ....Prov. 30:8   635
  "Turn away mine
  eyes" ....Ps. 119:37   600
  Should not walk
  in..............Eph. 4:17   1164

Vashni—*weak*

Son of Samuel ....1 Chr. 6:28   410

Vashti—*beautiful woman*

Queen of Ahasuerus, deposed and
divorced..........Esth. 1:9-22   507

Vau

Letter in the Hebrew
alphabet..........Ps. 119:41-48   600

Veal

Prepared for King
Saul..............1 Sam. 28:21-25   303

Vegetables—*plants grown for food*

Part of God's
creation........Gen. 1:11, 12   4
Controversy
regarding.......Rom. 14:1-23   1119
Preferred by
Daniel...........Dan. 1:12, 16   822

Veil, the sacred

A. *Features regarding:*
  Made by divine
  command.....Ex. 26:31, 32   81
  Used to separate the holy and
  most holy....Ex. 26:33   81
  Means of concealing the divine
  person ......Ex. 40:3   96
  In the Temple
  also ....2 Chr. 3:14   440
  Rent at Christ's
  death ....Matt. 27:51   972
B. *Entrance through:*
  By the high priest
  alone ....Heb. 9:6, 7   1219
  On Day of Atonement
  only ....Heb. 9:7   1219
  Taking blood ..Heb. 9:7   1219
C. *Figurative of:*
  Old Testament dispensa-
  tion ....Heb. 9:8   1219
  Christ's flesh...Heb. 10:20   1220
  Access now into God's
  presence ......Heb. 10:19-22   1220

Veil, woman's

A. *Literal uses of:*
  For modesty ...Gen. 24:65   26
  For
  adornment....Is. 3:19   660
  To conceal
  identity ......Gen. 38:14   40
  To soften the divine glory
  of God........Ex. 34:33-35   90
B. *Figurative of:*
  Coming of the
  Lord ....Is. 25:7   675
  Turning to the
  Lord ....2 Cor. 3:14-16   1144

Vengeance—*retribution as a
punishment*

A. *Belonging to God, as:*
  Judgment upon
  sin ....Jer. 11:20-23   719
  Right not to
  be taken by ⎰Ezek. 25:12-17   794
  man.........⎱Heb. 10:30   1221
  Set time ......Jer. 46:9, 10   750
B. *Visitation of, by God, at:*
  Nation's fall ...Jer. 51:6, 11, 36   756
  Christ's first
  coming.......Is. 35:4-10   681
  Jerusalem's
  destruction...Luke 21:22   1032
  Sodom's
  destruction....Jude 7   1262
  Christ's
  return.........2 Thess. 1:8   1189

See Revenge

Venison—*the flesh of deer*

Isaac's favorite
dish..............Gen. 27:1-33   28

Ventriloquism—*appearing to speak
from another source*

From the dust.....Is. 29:4   677

Verdict—*a judicial decision*

Unjustly
rendered ....Luke 23:13-26   1035
Pronounced by
hypocrites.......John 8:1-11   1051

Verily, verily—*a strong affirmation*

A. *Concerning Christ's:*
  Glory.........John 1:51   1043
  Eternity ......John 8:58   1053
  Uniqueness ...John 10:1, 7   1054
  Mission ......John 6:32   1049
  Betrayal ......John 13:21   1058
  Death ....John 12:24   1057
B. *Concerning man's:*
  Spiritual
  bondage ......John 8:34   1052

SUBJECT	REFERENCE	PAGE	SUBJECT	REFERENCE	PAGE	SUBJECT	REFERENCE	PAGE

Visions—continued

Encourage-
ment.........Acts 18:9, 10   1092
Warning......Is. 21:2-6   672
Judgment....1 Sam. 3:15-18   279
Action for the
Lord........Acts 26:19, 20   1101

C. *Objects of, revealed in:*
Israel's
future........Gen. 15:1-21   17
Succession of world
empires......Dan. 7:1-8   830
Ram.........Dan. 8:1-7, 20   831
Expanding
river........Ezek. 47:1-12   815
Throne of
God.........Rev. 4:1-11   1271

Visit, visitation—*to go to see a person*

Descriptive of:
Going to a
person.........Acts 15:36   1089
God's care....Ps. 65:9   574
God's purposed
time............Luke 19:44   1030

Visitors

Moses and
Elijah ....Matt. 17:3   959

Vocation—*a calling*

We must walk worthy
of............Eph. 4:1   1164

Voice of God, the

A. *Importance of:*
Must be
obeyed.......Gen. 3:1-19   6
Disobedience to,
judged.......Jer. 42:5-22   747
Obedience to, the essence of
true religion..1 Sam. 15:19-24   289
Obedience to,
rewarded......Gen. 22:6-18   22
Sign of the
covenant......Josh. 24:24, 25   240

B. *Heard by:*
Adam.........Gen. 3:9, 10   7
Moses.........Ex. 19:19   74
Israel.........Deut. 5:22-26   184
Samuel......1 Sam. 3:1-14   278
Elijah.........1 Kin. 19:12, 13   362
Isaiah ....Is. 6:8-10   662
Ezekiel ....Ezek. 1:24, 25   772
         Ezek. 2:1   772
Christ ....Mark 1:11   978
Peter, James, and
John.........Matt. 17:1, 5   959
Paul..........Acts 9:4, 7   1081
John..........Rev. 1:10-15   1268

Vomit—*to throw up*

A. *Used literally of:*
Dog ....Prov. 26:11   633
One who eats in
excess ....Prov. 25:16   632
Drunken
man ....Is. 19:14   671
Great fish....Jon. 2:10   867

B. *Used figuratively of:*
False
teaching ......2 Pet. 2:22   1244
Judgment......Jer. 48:25, 26   752
Riches........Job 20:15   530

Vophsi—*rich*

Naphtalite spy ....Num. 13:14   149

Vow—*a voluntary pledge to fulfill an agreement*

A. *Objects of one's:*
Life...........Num. 6:1-21   141
Children ....1 Sam. 1:11-28   276
Possessions ....Gen. 28:22   30
Gifts..........Ps. 76:11   580

B. *Features concerning:*
Must be
voluntary .....Deut. 23:21, 22   200

Must be
uttered........Deut. 23:23   200
Once made,
binding ....Eccl. 5:4, 5   642
Benefits of, sometimes
included ......Gen. 28:20-22   30
Invalidity of,
specified .....Num. 30:1-16   167
Abuse of,
condemned ...Matt. 15:4-6   956
Rashness in,
condemned ...Prov. 20:25   628
Perfection in,
required......Lev. 22:18-25   122
Wickedness of
some.........Jer. 44:25   749

Voyage—*an extended trip*

Paul's to Rome....Acts 27:10   1102

Vulture—*a carrion-eating bird of prey*

Classed as
unclean ....Lev. 11:13, 14   109

W

Wafers—*thin cakes of flour*

Often made with
honey...........Ex. 16:31   72
Used in various   {Ex. 29:2   83
offerings........{Lev. 2:4   100

Wages, hire—*payments for work performed*

A. *Principles governing payment of:*
Must be paid
promptly.....Deut. 24:14, 15   201
Withholding of,
forbidden .....James 5:4   1230
Laborer worthy
of.............Matt. 10:10   950

B. *Paid to such classes as:*
Soldiers........2 Sam. 10:6   317
Fishermen .....Mark 1:20   979
Shepherds .....John 10:12, 13   1054
Masons and
carpenters ...2 Chr. 24:12   458
Farm
laborers.......Matt. 20:1-16   962
Male
prostitutes ....Deut. 23:18   200
Nurses.........Ex. 2:9   57
Ministers ......1 Cor. 9:4-14   1131
Teachers.....Gal. 6:6, 7   1158

C. *Figurative of:*
Spiritual
death ....Rom. 6:23   1113
Unrighteous-
ness.........2 Pet. 2:15   1244

Wagon—*a vehicle with wheels*

Used to move Jacob to
Egypt ....Gen. 45:19, 21   47
Used in moving
objects..........Num. 7:3-9   141

Wailing—*crying out in constant mourning*

A. *Caused by:*
King's decree ..Esth. 4:3   509
City's
destruction...Ezek. 27:31, 32   796
God's
judgment .....Amos 5:16, 17   858
Girl's death ....Mark 5:38-42   984
Christ's
return........Rev. 1:7   1268
Hell's
torments....Matt. 13:42, 50   955

B. *Performed by:*
Women........Jer. 9:17-20   717
Prophets......Mic. 1:8   871
Merchants ....Rev. 18:15, 19   1280

See Mourning

Waiting on the Lord

A. *Agents of:*
Creatures......Ps. 145:15   610
Creation.......Rom. 8:19, 23   1114
Gentiles ....Is. 51:5   694
Christians .....1 Cor. 1:7   1126

B. *Manner of:*
With the
soul..........Ps. 62:1, 5   573
With
quietness......Lam. 3:25, 26   764
With
patience ......Ps. 40:1   564
With
courage.......Ps. 27:14   558
All the day ....Ps. 25:5   557
Continually....Hos. 12:6   846
With great
hope..........Ps. 130:5, 6   605
With crying....Ps. 69:3   576

C. *Objects of God's:*
Salvation ......Is. 25:9   675
Law ....Is. 42:4   687
Protection .....Ps. 33:20   561
Pardon ....Ps. 39:7, 8   564
Food ....Ps. 104:27   592
Kingdom ......Mark 15:43   998
Holy Spirit.....Acts 1:4   1072
Son...........1 Thess. 1:10   1183

D. *Blessings attending, described as:*
Spiritual
renewal.......Is. 40:31   686
Not be
ashamed......Ps. 69:6   576
Inherit the
land..........Ps. 37:9, 34   562
Something
unusual.......Is. 64:4   702
Unusual
blessing.......Luke 12:36, 37   1022

Walk of believers

A. *Stated negatively, not:*
In darkness....John 8:12   1051
After the
flesh ....Rom. 8:1, 4   1114
As Gentiles ....Eph. 4:17   1164
In craftiness ...2 Cor. 4:2   1144
In sin..........Col. 3:5-7   1177
In disorder.....2 Thess. 3:6, 11   1190

B. *Stated positively:*
In the light ....1 John 1:7   1249
In the truth....3 John 3, 4   1259
In Christ ......Col. 2:6   1177
In the Spirit ...Gal. 5:16, 25   1158
In love ....Eph. 5:2   1165
As children of
light ....Eph. 5:8   1165
As Christ
walked........1 John 2:6   1250
After His command-
ments.........2 John 6   1256
By faith........2 Cor. 5:7   1145
In good
works.........Eph. 2:10   1162
Worthy.........Eph. 4:1   1164
Worthy of the
Lord..........Col. 1:10   1177
Worthy of
God...........1 Thess. 2:12   1184
Circum-
spectly........Eph. 5:15   1165
In wisdom......Col. 4:5   1179
Pleasing God ..1 Thess. 4:1   1185

Wall—*a rampart or partition*

A. *Used for:*
Shooting arrows
from ....2 Sam. 11:24   318
Observation ...2 Sam. 18:24   326

B. *Unusual events connected with:*
Woman lives
on ....Josh. 2:15   218
Jericho's, falls by
faith ....Josh. 6:5, 20   221
Saul's body   {1 Sam. 31:10,
fastened to...{   11   305

SUBJECT	REFERENCE	PAGE

Woman
throws stone 〔2 Sam. 11:20,
from .... 〔 21 ... 318
27,000 killed
by ....1 Kin. 20:30 ... 364
Son sacrificed
on ....2 Kin. 3:27 ... 374
Warning inscribed
on ....Dan. 5:5, 25-28 ... 828
Paul escapes
through.......Acts 9:25 ... 1082

C. *Figurative of:*
Defense........1 Sam. 25:16 ... 300
Protection .....Ezra 9:9 ... 483
Great power...Ps. 18:29 ... 554
Peacefulness..Ps. 122:7 ... 603
Self-
sufficiency ...Prov. 18:11 ... 626
Powerless.....Prov. 25:28 ... 632
Salvation ......Is. 26:1 ... 675
God's
kingdom ......Is. 56:5 ... 697
Heaven ......Is. 60:18-21 ... 700
Spiritual
leaders........Is. 62:6 ... 701
God's
messengers ...Jer. 1:18, 19 ... 709
Protection ....Zech. 2:5 ... 897
Hypocrisy .....Acts 23:3 ... 1098
Ceremonial
law ....Eph. 2:14 ... 1163
New
Jerusalem....Rev. 21:12-19 ... 1282

D. *Of Jerusalem:*
Built by
Solomon ......1 Kin. 3:1 ... 341
Broken down by
Jehoash.......2 Kin. 14:13 ... 386
Destroyed by Babylon-
ians..........2 Chr. 36:19 ... 471
Seen at night by
Nehemiah...Neh. 2:12-18 ... 490
Rebuilt by
returnees .....Neh. 6:1, 6, 15 ... 493
Dedication of .Neh. 12:27-47 ... 501

Wallow—*to roll about in an ungainly manner*

Blood ....2 Sam. 20:12 ... 329
Vomit............Jer. 48:26 ... 752
Ashes............Jer. 6:26 ... 714
On the ground ....Mark 9:20 ... 988
Mire ....2 Pet. 2:22 ... 1244

Wandering—*roaming about*

A. *Descriptive of:*
Hagar's
travels ....Gen. 21:14 ... 22
Israel's wilderness
travels ....Num. 32:13 ... 170
God's
pilgrims.......Heb. 11:37, 38 ... 1222
Captivity .....Hos. 9:17 ... 845
Joseph in the
field.........Gen. 37:15 ... 39
Syrian ....Deut. 26:5 ... 202
Early Saints ..Heb. 11:38 ... 1222

B. *Figurative of:*
Apostasy ......Ps. 119:10 ... 599
Dissatis-
faction........Prov. 27:8 ... 633
Hopelessness ..Jude 13 ... 1262

Wanderer—*one who moves about aimlessly*

Curse on Cain ....Gen. 4:12, 14 ... 8
Curse on the
wicked...........Ps. 109:10 ... 596
Professional exorcists
called ....Acts 19:13 ... 1093

Want—*to lack*

A. *Caused by:*
Hastiness .....Prov. 21:5 ... 628
Greed..........Prov. 22:16 ... 629
Sloth ....Prov. 24:30-34 ... 632
Debauchery...Dan. 5:27 ... 829
God's
judgments ....Amos 4:6 ... 857

Physical
need ....2 Cor. 8:14 ... 1147
B. *Provision against, by:*
Trusting the
LORD..........Ps. 23:1 ... 556
God's plan .....Jer. 33:17, 18 ... 739

Wantonness—*lustful behavior*

In suggestive
movements.......Is. 3:16 ... 660
Characteristic of doctrinal
laxity............2 Pet. 2:18 ... 1244
Unbecoming to a
Christian ....Rom. 13:13 ... 1119

War—*armed conflicts between nations*

A. *Caused by:*
Sin ....James 4:1, 2 ... 1230
God's
judgments ....2 Sam. 12:10 ... 319
God's decree...Ex. 17:16 ... 72

B. *Regulations concerning:*
Consultation of:
Urim ....1 Sam. 28:6 ... 303
Ephod ....1 Sam. 30:7, 8 ... 304
Prophets......1 Kin. 22:7-28 ... 366
Troops
mustered......Judg. 3:27 ... 246
Some
dismissed .....Deut. 20:5-8 ... 197
Spies
dispatched ....Num. 13:17 ... 149
Ark brought
in ....1 Sam. 4:4-6 ... 279
Sacrifice
offered ....1 Sam. 7:8, 9 ... 281
Speech
delivered .....2 Chr. 20:20-22 ... 454
Demand made for
surrender .....Deut. 20:10 ... 197
Trumpet
sounded.......Num. 10:9 ... 146

C. *Methods of attack, by:*
Ambush ....Josh. 8:3-26 ... 223
Surprise
attack........Judg. 7:16-22 ... 251
Personal combat of
champions ....1 Sam. 17:1-51 ... 291
Divided
tactics ....2 Sam. 10:9-14 ... 317
Massed
formation ....1 Kin. 22:31-33 ... 366
Battle cry.....Jer. 4:19 ... 712

D. *Captives of:*
Sometimes
eliminated ....Josh. 6:21 ... 222
Made
servants......2 Sam. 8:2 ... 316
Ruled over....2 Sam. 5:2 ... 312
Deported ......2 Kin. 17:6 ... 389

See Siege of a city

Wardrobe—*one's clothing*

Woman's..........Is. 3:18-23 ... 660
Directions
concerning ......1 Pet. 3:3-5 ... 1237
Keeper of ....2 Kin. 22:14 ... 396

Wares

Sold in Tyrus .....Ezek. 27:1-27 ... 795

Warfare, spiritual

A. *Enemies combatted:*
World ....James 4:1-4 ... 1230
Flesh ....1 Pet. 4:1-4 ... 1238
Devil ....1 Pet. 5:8 ... 1239
Invisible foes ..Eph. 6:12 ... 1167

B. *Conquest over, by:*
God's Word....Eph. 6:17 ... 1167
God's armor ..Eph. 6:10-17 ... 1167
Faith ....1 John 5:4, 5 ... 1253
Christ's
promise.......John 16:33 ... 1062

C. *Soldiers of, must:*
Avoid worldly entangle-
ments........2 Tim. 2:4 ... 1201
Pray...........Eph. 6:18 ... 1167

Deny self ......1 Cor. 9:25-27 ... 1132
Endure
hardness......2 Tim. 2:3, 10 ... 1201
Be self-
controlled.....1 Thess. 5:6 ... 1185
Be alert........1 Cor. 16:13 ... 1139
Wear armor ...Eph. 6:11 ... 1167

Warning—*to caution one concerning his action*

A. *Means of, by:*
God's Word....Ps. 19:9-11 ... 555
Prophet.......Ezek. 3:17-27 ... 773
Messenger.....Acts 20:31 ... 1095
Dream.........Matt. 2:12, 22 ... 942
Angel.........Acts 10:22 ... 1083
God ....Heb. 11:7 ... 1221

B. *Reactions to:*
Obeyed ....Jon. 3:1-10 ... 867
Accepted ......Heb. 11:7 ... 1221
Ignored........2 Sam. 2:20-23 ... 310
Rejected......Gen. 2:16, 17 ... 5
Scoffed at .....Gen. 19:14 ... 20
Disobeyed ...Num. 14:40-45 ... 151

C. *Disobedience to, brings:*
Judgment....Jude 6, 7 ... 1262
Torments....Luke 16:23-28 ... 1026
Destruction....Prov. 29:1 ... 634

Wash—*to cleanse something with a liquid*

A. *Kinds of:*
Ceremonial ....Ex. 30:18-20 ... 86
Miraculous ....John 9:7, 11, 15 ... 1053
Demonstra-
tive ....John 13:5-14 ... 1058
Symbolic .....Matt. 27:24 ... 972
Typical ....Ps. 51:2, 7 ... 569
Spiritual .....Acts 22:16 ... 1097
Regenerative ..Titus 3:5 ... 1207

B. *Materials used:*
Water ....Gen. 24:32 ... 25
Tears.........Luke 7:38, 44 ... 1014
Snow.........Job 9:30 ... 524
Wine ....Gen. 49:11 ... 51
Blood.........Ps. 58:10 ... 572

C. *Objects of:*
Hands ....Matt. 27:24 ... 972
Face..........Gen. 43:31 ... 46
Feet ....Gen. 18:4 ... 19
Body ....2 Sam. 11:2 ... 317
Clothes.......2 Sam. 19:24 ... 328

See Purification

Washpot

Moab described as
God's............Ps. 60:6-8 ... 572

Waste—*a state of ruin*

A. *Objects of:*
Cities..........Ezek. 19:7 ... 787
Nations........Nah. 3:7 ... 879
Captives.......Ps. 137:3 ... 606
Possessions ....Luke 15:13 ... 1025
Temple ....Is. 64:11 ... 702
Church ....Gal. 1:13 ... 1154
Parents........Prov. 19:26 ... 627
Body ....Job 14:10 ... 526

B. *Caused by:*
God's
judgments ....Amos 7:9 ... 859
Unbelief ....Num. 14:33 ... 150
Failure to serve
God...........Is. 60:12 ... 700
God's hatred..Mal. 1:3 ... 907
Squandering ...Luke 15:11-32 ... 1025

C. *State of:*
Lamented......Neh. 2:3, 17 ... 489
To be
corrected .....Is. 61:4 ... 700

Watch—*to attend to, guard*

The LORD........Gen. 31:49 ... 34
As guards.......2 Kin. 11:4-7 ... 383

SUBJECT	REFERENCE	PAGE	SUBJECT	REFERENCE	PAGE	SUBJECT	REFERENCE	PAGE

Watches of day, night—*period of time*
Jesus walks on
water..........Matt. 14:25 — 956
Time of coming...Matt. 24:43 — 967
Luke 12:37, 38 — 1022

Watchmen, spiritual
Set by God........Is. 62:6 — 701
Message to........Is. 21:11, 12 — 672
Responsibility of ..Ezek. 33:1-9 — 801
Some are
faithful...........Ezek. 3:17-21 — 773
Some are
faithless..........Is. 56:10 — 697
In vain without the
LORD.............Ps. 127:1 — 604
Leaders in the
church..........Heb. 13:17 — 1224

Water
A. *Described as:*
Living.........Jer. 2:13 — 710
Cold...........Jer. 18:14 — 724
Still............Ps. 23:2 — 556
Deep..........Ps. 69:2, 14 — 576
Standing.......Ps. 107:35 — 595
Mighty........Is. 28:2 — 676
B. *God's control over, He:*
Creates........Gen. 1:2, 6, 7 — 4
Gives.........Ps. 104:13 — 592
Blesses the earth
with ....Is. 55:10 — 696
Withholds .....Is. 50:2 — 693
Reveals His wonders
in............Ps. 107:23-32 — 595
Sets bounds
to.............Ps. 104:5-9 — 592
C. *Miracles connected with:*
Changed into
blood ......Ex. 7:17-25 — 62
Divided......Ex. 14:21-29 — 69
Bitter made
sweet........Ex. 15:22-25 — 70
From a rock...Ex. 17:1-7 — 72
Jordan
divided.......Josh. 3:14-17 — 219
From a
jawbone....Judg. 15:17-19 — 259
Consumed by
fire............1 Kin. 18:38 — 361
Valley, full of ..2 Kin. 3:16-24 — 374
Axe floats on..2 Kin. 6:5-7 — 377
Christ walks
on ....Mark 6:49-52 — 985
Changed into
wine.........John 2:1-11 — 1043
Healing of ....2 Kin. 2:19-22 — 373
D. *Normal uses of, for:*
Drinking......Gen. 24:43 — 25
Washing......Gen. 18:4 — 19
Animals ......Ps. 42:1 — 565
Vegetation....Deut. 11:10, 11 — 189
Sea creatures..Ps. 104:25, 26 — 592
E. *Special uses of, for:*
Ordination....Ex. 30:18-20 — 86
Cleansing....Ex. 40:7-32 — 96
Purification...Ex. 19:10 — 74
Baptism ......Acts 8:36-39 — 1081
Sanctifi-
cation........Eph. 5:26 — 1166
Business.....Ps. 107:23 — 595
F. *Figurative of:*
Instability ....Gen. 49:4 — 51
Cowardice....Josh. 7:5 — 222
Spiritual
growth.......Ps. 1:3 — 548
Peace.........Ps. 23:2 — 556
Afflictions ....Is. 43:2 — 688
Persecution...Ps. 124:4, 5 — 604
Adultery......Prov. 9:17 — 621
Universal
Gospel.......Is. 11:9 — 667
Salvation ......Is. 55:1 — 696
Gospel age....Is. 41:17-20 — 686
Holy Spirit..Ezek. 47:1-12 — 815
Eternal life ....Rev. 22:17 — 1283
Christ ....John 4:10-15 — 1045
Regeneration ..John 7:37, 38 — 1051

G. *Cure for:*
Doubting
captain........2 Kin. 5:1-15 — 376
Afflicted ......John 5:1-7 — 1046
Blind man ....John 9:6-11 — 1053
H. *Used for a test:*
By Gideon .....Judg. 7:4-7 — 250
I. *Conduit:*
Hezekiah
builds........2 Kin. 20:20 — 394

Water and blood
From Christ......John 19:34 — 1065

Water Gate—*a gate of Jerusalem*
Law is read ......Neh. 8:1, 2 — 495

Waterproofing—*making vessels watertight*
By means of:
Pitch.............Gen. 6:14 — 9
Slime and pitch ..Ex. 2:3 — 57

Wax (I)—*beeswax*
Figurative of
persecution......Ps. 22:14 — 556
Of the wicked before
God..........Ps. 68:2 — 575
Of the
mountains........Ps. 97:5 — 590

Wax (II)—*to grow, increase*
A. *Of material things:*
Power ....2 Sam. 3:1 — 311
Prestige.......Esth. 9:4 — 513
Age............Josh. 23:1 — 239
Sound ....Ex. 19:19 — 74
B. *Of immaterial things:*
Courage ....Heb. 11:34 — 1222
Spirituality ....Luke 2:40 — 1007
God's hand ....Num. 11:23 — 147
Old covenant ..Heb. 8:13 — 1219
God's
kingdom .....Luke 13:18, 19 — 1023

Way (see Highway; Path)

Way, Christ as
Leading to
Father...........John 14:6 — 1059

Way, God's
Right ....Hos. 14:9 — 847
Just.............Dan. 4:37 — 827
True ....Rev. 15:3 — 1277
Higher than
man's ....Is. 55:8, 9 — 696
Unsearchable .....Rom. 11:33 — 1118

Waymarks—*roadmarkings*
Give direction.....Jer. 31:21 — 736

Ways of God's people
A. *With reference to God's way, to:*
Understand....Ps. 119:27 — 600
Pray for direction
in..............Ex. 33:13 — 89
Walk in........Deut. 8:6 — 186
Remember....Deut. 8:2 — 186
Known........Ps. 67:2 — 575
Teach to trans-
gressors.......Ps. 51:13 — 569
Rejoice in .....Ps. 119:14 — 600
B. *God's attitude toward, He:*
Knows.........Ps. 1:6 — 548
Is acquainted
with ....Ps. 139:3 — 607
Delights in....Ps. 37:23 — 563
Leads us in...Ps. 139:24 — 608
Teaches ......Ps. 25:9, 12 — 557
Makes
known ......Ps. 103:7 — 591
Makes
perfect......Ps. 18:32 — 554
Blesses ....Prov. 8:32 — 620

C. *With reference to our way:*
Acknowledge Him
in..............Prov. 3:6 — 616
Commit to the
LORD..........Ps. 37:5 — 562
Makes
prosperous....Josh. 1:8 — 217
All before
God...........Ps. 119:168 — 603
Teach me......Ps. 143:8 — 609

Ways of man
Described as:
Perverse before
God ....Num. 22:32 — 160
Hard.............Prov. 13:15 — 623
Abomination....Prov. 15:9 — 624
Not good.........Prov. 16:29 — 625
Dark............Prov. 2:13 — 616

Weak, weakness
A. *Kinds of:*
Political ....2 Sam. 3:1 — 311
Physical ....Judg. 16:7, 17 — 260
2 Cor. 11:30 — 1150
Spiritual......Is. 35:3 — 681
Moral..........2 Sam. 3:39 — 312
Rom. 8:26 — 1115
B. *Caused by:*
Fasting ....Ps. 109:24 — 596
Discourage-
ment..........Neh. 6:9 — 493
Sin ....1 Cor. 11:26-30 — 1134
Discouraging
preaching .....Jer. 38:4 — 744
Conscientious
doubts........Rom. 14:1-23 — 1119
C. *Victory over, by:*
Christ ....2 Cor. 13:3, 4 — 1151
Grace.........2 Cor. 12:9, 10 — 1150
Faith ....Heb. 11:33, 34 — 1222
D. *Our duty toward, to:*
Bear...........Rom. 15:1 — 1120
Support........Acts 20:35 — 1095
1 Cor. 9:22 — 1132
Not become a stumbling
block ....1 Cor. 8:9 — 1131
E. *Our duties with reference to:*
Pleasure in ....2 Cor. 12:10 — 1150
Help those afflicted
with ....Rom. 15:1 — 1120

Wealth—*riches*
A. *Descriptive of:*
Material
possessions....Gen. 34:29 — 36
B. *Advantages of:*
Given by
God...........Deut. 8:18, 19 — 187
Source of
security ....Prov. 18:11 — 626
Adds friends ...Prov. 19:4 — 627
C. *Disadvantages of:*
Produces self-
sufficiency ....Deut. 8:17 — 187
Leads to
conceit........Job 31:25 — 536
Subject to
loss ....Prov. 13:11 — 623
Lost by
dissipation ....Prov. 5:8-10 — 618
Cannot save ...Ps. 49:6, 7 — 568
Must be left to
others.........Ps. 49:10 — 568
See Riches, earthly

Wean—*to accustom a child to independence from the mother's milk*
Celebrated ....Gen. 21:8 — 22
Figurative of spiritual
rest ....Ps. 131:2 — 605

Weapons, spiritual
Against:
World—faith......1 John 5:4 — 1253
Satan—armor of
God............Eph. 6:11-17 — 1167
Flesh—the Spirit ..Gal. 5:16-25 — 1158

SUBJECT　　REFERENCE　　PAGE | SUBJECT　　REFERENCE　　PAGE | SUBJECT　　REFERENCE　　PAGE

Wine—continued

F. *Intoxication from, falsely*
charged to:
Hannah........1 Sam. 1:12-16　276
Jesus ....Matt. 11:19　952
Apostles......Acts 2:13　1073

G. *Uses of, in:*
Offering ....Num. 15:4-10　151
Miracle ....John 2:1-10　1043
Lord's
Supper.......Matt. 26:27-29　970

H. *Figurative of:*
God's wrath ...Ps. 75:8　579
Wisdom's
blessings......Prov. 9:2, 5　620
Gospel.........Is. 55:1　696
Christ's
blood ....Matt. 26:27-29　970
Fornication....Rev. 17:2　1278

See Drunkenness; Temperance

Wings—*the locomotive appendages on*
flying creatures

A. *Used literally of:*
Flying
creatures......Gen. 1:21　4
Cherubim......Ex. 25:20　79

B. *Used figuratively of:*
God's mercy ...Ps. 57:1　571
Protection .....Luke 13:34　1024

Winking the eye

Hate..............Ps. 35:19　562
Evil..............Prov. 6:12, 13　618

Winnow—*to toss about*

A. *Used literally of:*
Fork for winnowing
grain..........Is. 30:24　679

B. *Used figuratively of judgments:*
God's..........Is. 30:24　679
Nation's ....Jer. 51:2　756
Christ's........Matt. 3:12　943

Winter—*the cold season of the year*

Made by God .....Ps. 74:17　579
Continuance of,
guaranteed.....Gen. 8:22　11
Time of snow .....2 Sam. 23:20　332
Hazards of travel
during...........2 Tim. 4:21　1203

Wipe—*to clean or dry*

A. *Used literally of:*
Dust removal ..Luke 10:11　1018
Feet dried .....John 13:5　1058

B. *Used figuratively of:*
Jerusalem's
destruction....2 Kin. 21:13　394
Tears
removed ......Rev. 7:17　1273

Wire—*threads*

Used in ephod.....Ex. 39:3　94

Wisdom—*knowledge guided by*
understanding

A. *Sources of, in:*
Spirit ....Ex. 31:3　86
Lord...........Ex. 36:1, 2　91
God's Law .....Deut. 4:6　181
Fear of the
LORD..........Prov. 9:10　620
Righteous .....Prov. 10:31　621

B. *Ascribed to:*
Workmen......Ex. 36:2　91
Women.......Prov. 31:26　636
Bezaleel.......Ex. 31:2-5　86
Joseph.........Acts 7:9, 10　1078
Moses ....Acts 7:22　1079
Joshua.........Deut. 34:9　212
Hiram ....1 Kin. 7:13, 14　345
Solomon......1 Kin. 3:12,
16-28　341
Children of
Issachar .....1 Chr. 12:32　418
Ezra ....Ezra 7:25　481
Daniel.........Dan. 1:17　823
Magi ....Matt. 2:1-12　942

Stephen ....Acts 6:3, 10　1078
Paul ....2 Pet. 3:15　1244

C. *Described as:*
Discreet ....Gen. 41:33　43
Technical
skill...........Ex. 28:3　82
Common
sense ....2 Sam. 20:14-22　329
Mechanical
skill..........1 Kin. 7:14　345
Understand-
ing............Prov. 10:13, 23　621
Military
ability.........Is. 10:13　666
Commercial
industry......Ezek. 28:3-5　796

D. *Value of:*
Gives
happiness .....Prov. 3:13　616
Benefits of,
many ....Prov. 4:5-10　617
Keeps from
evil...........Prov. 5:1-6　617
Better than
rubies.........Prov. 8:11　620
Above gold in
value ....Prov. 16:16　625
Should be
acquired .....Prov. 23:23　630
Excels folly ...Eccl. 2:13　641
Gives life .....Eccl. 7:12　644
Makes
strong ....Eccl. 7:19　644
Better than
weapons .....Eccl. 9:18　646
Insures
stability.......Is. 33:6　680
Produces good
fruit ....James 3:17　1230

E. *Limitations of:*
Cannot save
us.............1 Cor. 1:19-21　1126
Cause of self-
glory...........Jer. 9:23　717
Can pervert....Is. 47:10　691
Nothing, without
God...........Jer. 8:9　716
Can corrupt ...Ezek. 28:17　797
Of this world,
foolishness....1 Cor. 3:19　1127
Earthly,
sensual.......James 3:15　1230
Gospel not preached
in.............1 Cor. 2:1-5　1127

F. *Of believers:*
Given by
Christ.........Luke 21:15　1032
Gift of the
Spirit ....1 Cor. 12:8　1134
Given by
God...........Eph. 1:17　1162
Prayed for ....Col. 1:9　1176
Means of
instruction....Col. 1:28　1177
Lack of, ask
for............James 1:5　1228

Wisdom of Christ

Predicted ....Is. 11:1, 2　667
Incarnated ....1 Cor. 1:24　1126
Realized ....Luke 2:52　1007
Displayed ....Matt. 13:54　955
Perfected ....Col. 2:3　1177
Imputed ....1 Cor. 1:30　1126

Wisdom of God

A. *Described as:*
Universal ......Dan. 2:20　823
Infinite ....Ps. 147:5　610
Unsearchable ..Is. 40:28　686
Mighty ....Job 36:5　539
Perfect ....Job 37:16　540

B. *Manifested in:*
Creation.......Ps. 104:24　592
Nature........Job 38:34-41　541
Sovereignty...Dan. 2:20, 21　823
The Church....Eph. 3:10　1163

Wist, wit—*obsolete for "to know"*

Of things:
Unknown........Ex. 2:4　57
Known by
others.........Ex. 34:29　90
That should be
known ....Luke 2:49　1007

Witch—*one adept at magic*

Saul consults
one.............1 Sam. 28:7-25　303

Witchcraft—*the practice of sorcery*

Forbidden in
Israel..........Deut. 18:9-14　196
Used by Jezebel...2 Kin. 9:22　381
Condemned by the
prophets.......Mic. 5:12　873
Practiced by
Manasseh .....2 Chr. 33:6　467
Suppressed by
Saul...........1 Sam. 28:3, 9　302
Work of the
flesh.............Gal. 5:20　1158

See Divination

Wither—*to dry up*

A. *Caused by:*
God's
judgment .....Is. 40:7, 24　685
Christ's
judgment .....Matt. 21:19, 20　963
No root........Matt. 13:6　954
Heat...........James 1:11　1228

B. *Applied literally to:*
Ear of grain....Gen. 41:23　43
Gourd ....Jon. 4:7　867
Man's hand....Luke 6:6, 8　1011

Witnessing—*bearing testimony to*
something

A. *Elements of, seen in:*
Public
transaction....Ruth 4:1-11　271
Signing a
document.....Jer. 32:10-12　737
Calling
witnesses .....Lev. 5:1　103
Requiring two
witnesses .....1 Tim. 5:19　1196
Rejection of false
witnesses .....Prov. 24:28　632

B. *Material means of, by:*
Heap stones ...Gen. 31:44-52　34
Song ....Deut. 31:19-21　209
Altar ....Josh. 22:26-34　238
Works.........John 10:25　1055
Sign
(miracles).....Heb. 2:4　1215

C. *Spiritual means of, by:*
God's Law .....Deut. 31:26　209
Gospel.........Matt. 24:14　967
Father.........John 5:37　1048
Conscience ....Rom. 2:15　1110
Holy Spirit.....Rom. 8:16　1114

D. *To Christ as object, by:*
John the
Baptist........John 1:7, 8, 15　1042
His works .....John 5:36　1047
Father.........John 8:18　1051
Himself.......John 8:18　1051
Holy Spirit....John 15:26, 27　1061
His disciples ...John 15:27　1061
Prophets......Acts 10:43　1084

E. *Of Christians to Christ:*
Chosen ....Acts 10:41　1084
Commis-
sioned ....Acts 1:8　1072
Empowered....Acts 4:33　1076
Confirmed.....Heb. 2:3, 4　1215

F. *Objects of Christ's:*
Resurrection...Acts 2:32　1074
Saviourhood...Acts 5:31, 32　1077
Life............Acts 1:21, 22　1073
Mission........Acts 10:41-43　1084
Sufferings ....1 Pet. 5:1　1239

See Testimony

SUBJECT	REFERENCE	PAGE	SUBJECT	REFERENCE	PAGE	SUBJECT	REFERENCE	PAGE

SUBJECT   REFERENCE   PAGE | SUBJECT   REFERENCE   PAGE | SUBJECT   REFERENCE   PAGE

Works, Satan's (see Satan)

Works, the unbeliever's

A. *Described as:*
Wicked........Col. 1:21   1177
Done in
darkness.....Is. 29:15   678
Abominable...Ps. 14:1   552
Deceitful.....Prov. 11:18   622
Evil...........John 7:7   1050
Unfruitful....Eph. 5:11   1165

B. *God's attitude toward, will:*
Never forget..Amos 8:7   860
Reward.......Prov. 24:12   631
Bring to
judgment.....Rev. 20:12, 13   1281

C. *Believer's relation to:*
Cast off.......Rom. 13:12   1119
Have no fellowship
with..........Eph. 5:11   1165
Be delivered
from..........2 Tim. 4:18   1202

World

A. *God's relation to:*
Maker........Jer. 10:12   718
Possessor.....Ps. 24:1   556
Redeemer.....John 3:16   1044
Judge........Ps. 96:13   589

B. *Christ's relation to, as:*
Maker........John 1:10   1042
Sin-bearer....John 1:29   1042
Saviour......John 12:47   1058
Life..........John 6:33, 51   1049
Light........John 8:12   1051
Judge........Acts 17:31   1092
Overcomer....John 16:33   1062
Reconciler...2 Cor. 5:19   1146

C. *Christian's relation to:*
Light of......Matt. 5:14   945
Not of........John 17:14, 16   1062
Chosen out
of...........John 15:19   1060
Tribulation
in...........John 16:33   1062
Sent into by
Christ.......John 17:18   1062
Not conformed
to...........Rom. 12:2   1118
Crucified to....Gal. 6:14   1158
To live
soberly......Titus 2:12   1207
Unspotted
from.........James 1:27   1228
Overcomers
of...........1 John 5:4, 5   1253
Denying desires
of...........Titus 2:12   1207

D. *Dangers of, arising from:*
Wisdom......1 Cor. 3:19   1127
Love of......2 Tim. 4:10   1202
Friendship....James 4:4   1230
Corruptions..2 Pet. 1:4   1243
Lusts.........1 John 2:15-17   1250
False
prophets.....1 John 4:1   1252
Deceivers....2 John 7   1256

E. *In the plan of redemption:*
Elect chosen
before.......Eph. 1:4   1162
Revelation made
before.......Matt. 13:35   955
Sin's entrance
into..........Rom. 5:12   1112
Its guilt before
God..........Rom. 3:19   1110
Original revelation
to...........Rom. 1:20   1109
God's love
for..........John 3:16   1044
Christ's mission
to...........John 12:47   1058
Spirit's conviction
of...........John 16:8   1061
Gospel preached
in...........Matt. 24:14   967
Reconciliation
of...........2 Cor. 5:19   1146

Destruction
of.............2 Pet. 3:7   1244
Final judgment
of.............Acts 17:31   1092
Satan
deceives......Rev. 12:9   1276

Worm—*a soft-bodied, slender, creeping animal*

A. *Ravages of:*
On bread.....Ex. 16:15, 20   71
On plants....Jon. 4:7   867
On the body..Acts 12:23   1086
In the grave...Job 24:19, 20   532
In hell........Mark 9:44-48   989

B. *Figurative of:*
Insignifi-
cance........Job 25:6   533
Messiah......Ps. 22:6   556

Wormwood—*a bitter-tasting plant*

Figurative of
idolatry.........Deut. 29:18   206
Of adultery.......Prov. 5:4   617
Of God's
judgments......Jer. 9:15   717
Symbol of doom..Rev. 8:11   1273

Worry (see Cares, worldly)

Worship—*an act of reverence*

A. *Of God:*
Defined.......John 4:20-24   1045
Commanded...1 Chr. 16:29   421
Corrupted....Rom. 1:25   1109
Perverted.....2 Kin. 21:3, 21   394
Debated......1 Kin. 18:21-39   360

B. *Of Christ, by:*
Angels........Heb. 1:6   1215
Magi.........Matt. 2:1-2, 11   942
Men..........John 9:30-38   1053
Women.......Matt. 15:25   957
Disciples......Matt. 28:17   973
Heavenly
choir........Rev. 4:10, 11   1271

C. *Of wrong objects, such as:*
Heavenly
host.........Deut. 17:3   195
Other gods...Ex. 34:14   89
Demons......Deut. 32:17   210
Creatures....Rom. 1:25   1109
Images......Dan. 3:5-18   825
Man.........Acts 10:25, 26   1083
Antichrist....Rev. 13:4-13   1276

D. *Of wrong objects, by:*
Israel........2 Kin. 21:3, 21   394
Pagans......Rom. 1:25   1109
Professing
Christians....Col. 2:18   1178
World........2 Thess. 2:3-12   1189

Worthiness—*acceptableness for some benefit*

A. *Of Christ:*
For more
glory........Heb. 3:3   1216
To open the
book.........Rev. 5:2, 4   1271
To receive
worship......Rev. 5:9-14   1271

B. *Of believers, for:*
Provisions.....Matt. 10:10   950
Discipleship...Matt. 10:37   951
Their calling..Eph. 4:1   1164
Suffering.....Acts 5:41   1077
Their walk....Col. 1:10   1177
Honor........1 Tim. 6:1   1197
Kingdom.....2 Thess. 1:5   1189

Worthless—*useless, despicable*

Applied to Job's
friends..........Job 13:4   526
Sacrifice........Is. 1:13   659
Faith............1 Cor. 15:17   1137
Religion.........James 1:26   1228
Worship........Jer. 51:17, 18   756

Wound—*to injure*

A. *Of physical injury, by:*
God..........Deut. 32:39   211
Battle.........1 Sam. 31:3   305
Adultery......Prov. 6:32, 33   619
Robbers......Luke 10:30, 34   1019
Evil spirit......Acts 19:16   1094

B. *Of spiritual injury, by:*
Discourage-
ment.........Prov. 18:14   626
God's
punishment...Jer. 30:14   735
Drunkenness..Prov. 23:29, 30   631
Adultery......Prov. 6:32, 33   619
Sin...........Is. 1:6   658

Wrappings—*clothes for the dead*

Lazarus attired
in.................John 11:43, 44   1056
Jesus lays His
aside.............Luke 24:12   1036

Wrath of God

A. *Described as:*
Anger........Num. 32:10-13   170
Fury.........Ps. 90:9   587
Great........Zech. 7:12   899
Willing.......Rom. 9:22   1116
Revealed.....Rom. 1:18   1109
Stored up....Rom. 2:5-8   1109
Abiding......John 3:36   1045
Accom-
plished......Rev. 6:16, 17   1272

B. *Caused by:*
Apostasy.....2 Chr. 34:24, 25   469
Sympathy with
evil..........Lev. 10:1-6   108
Unfaithful-
ness.........Josh. 22:20   238
Provocations...2 Kin. 23:26   397
Fellowship with
evil..........2 Chr. 19:2   453
Mockery......2 Chr. 36:16   471
Idolatry......Ps. 78:58, 59   582
Inter-
marriage.....Ezra 10:10-14   484
Profaning the
Sabbath......Neh. 13:18   503
Speaking against
God..........Ps. 78:19-21   581

C. *Effects of, seen in:*
Egypt's
destruction....Ex. 15:4, 7   70
Great plague...Num. 11:33   148
Israel's
wanderings...Num. 32:10-13   170
Withholding of
rain.........Deut. 11:17   189
Destruction of a
people.......1 Sam. 28:18   303
Trouble.......Ps. 90:7   587
Man's death...Ps. 90:9   587
Jerusalem's
destruction....Luke 21:23, 24   1032
Punishments of
hell..........Rev. 14:10   1277
Final
judgments....Rev. 19:15   1280
Israel's
captivity......2 Chr. 36:16, 17   471

D. *Deliverance from, by:*
Atonement....Num. 16:46   154
Keeping an
oath.........Josh. 9:19, 20   225
Humbling
oneself......2 Chr. 32:26   466
Intercession...Ps. 106:23   594
Christ........Rom. 5:8, 9   1112
God's appoint-
ment.........1 Thess. 5:9   1185

Wrestling

Sisters..........Gen. 30:8   31
Jacob............Gen. 32:24-30   35
Christians........Eph. 6:12   1167

Write, writing, written

A. *Purposes of, to:*
Record God's
Word ....Ex. 24:4, 12　78
Record
history ....Luke 1:3　1004
Record
dictation ......Jer. 36:2, 27, 28　741
Make legal.....Deut. 24:1-4　200
Issue orders ...Esth. 8:5, 8, 10　512
Insure a
covenant......Neh. 9:38　499
Indicate
name ....Luke 1:63　1005
Indicate the
saved ....Rev. 20:15　1281
Establish
inspiration ....Rev. 22:18, 19　1283

B. *Unusual:*
By God's
finger ....Ex. 31:18　87
Destroyed and
restored......Jer. 36:21-32　742
On a wall.....Dan. 5:5-29　828
On the
ground.......John 8:6, 8　1051
On the cross...John 19:19-22　1064
In hearts ......Rom. 2:15　1110

C. *Of the Bible as written,*
involving its:
Authority......Acts 24:14　1099
Determination of
events ....Heb. 10:7-10　1220
Fulfillment.....Luke 21:22　1032
Messianic
character .....Luke 24:44, 46　1037
Saving
purpose......John 20:31　1066
Harmony ......Acts 15:15　1089
Spiritual aim...Rom. 15:4　1120
Finality........Rev. 22:18, 19　1283

D. *Figurative of:*
God's real
people ....Rev. 20:12, 15　1281
Indelible
character .....2 Cor. 3:2, 3　1144
Innate
knowledge ....Rom. 2:15　1110

Y

Yarn—*thread used in weaving*
Of linen...........1 Kin. 10:28　351

Years, thousand
In God's sight, one
day...........2 Pet. 3:8　1244
Time of Satan's
bondage..........Rev. 20:2-7　1281

Yield—*to produce; to surrender*

A. *Used literally of:*
Plants ....Gen. 1:11-29　4
Earth..........Ps. 67:6　575
Standing
grain..........Hos. 8:7　844
Death ....Acts 5:10　1077
Fountain ......James 3:12　1229
God's
servants.......Dan. 3:28　826

B. *Used figuratively of:*
Discipline......Heb. 12:11　1223
Spiritual
fruit ....Mark 4:8　982
Surrender......Rom. 6:13, 16　1112

Yoke—*a frame uniting animals for*
work

A. *Used literally on:*
Animals ....Deut. 21:3　198
Captives.......Jer. 28:10-14　733
Slaves ....1 Tim. 6:1　1197

B. *Used figuratively of:*
Oppression.....Deut. 28:48　205

Hard service ...1 Kin. 12:4-14　353
Submission ....Jer. 27:8　732
Bondage to
sin............Lam. 1:14　763
Discipleship....Matt. 11:29, 30　952
Legalistic
ordinances ....Gal. 5:1　1157
Marriage.......2 Cor. 6:14　1146

Young men

A. *Characteristics of, seen in:*
Unwise
counsel ....1 Kin. 12:8-14　353
Godly fervor...1 John 2:13, 14　1250
Passion........Prov. 7:7-23　619
Strength.......Prov. 20:29　628
Impatience ....Luke 15:12, 13　1025

B. *Special needs of:*
God's Word....Ps. 119:9　599
Knowledge and
discretion ....Prov. 1:4　615
Encourage-
ment..........Is. 40:30, 31　686
Full
surrender .....Matt. 19:20-22　961
Soberness......Titus 2:6　1207
Counsel ....1 John 2:13, 14　1250

Youth—*the early age of life*

A. *Evils of, seen in:*
Sin ....Ps. 25:7　557
Lusts ....2 Tim. 2:22　1201
Enticements ...Prov. 1:10-16　615
Self-will ......Luke 15:12, 13　1025

B. *Good of, seen in:*
Enthusiasm.....1 Sam. 17:26-51　291
Children.......Ps. 127:3, 4　604
Hardships......Lam. 3:27　764
Godly
example.......1 Tim. 4:12　1196

Z

Zaanan—*rich in flocks*
Town in west
Judah ....Mic. 1:11　871

Zaanannim
Border point of
Naphtali.........Josh. 19:32, 33　235

Zaavan—*unquiet*
Son of Ezer ....Gen. 36:27　38

Zabad—*gift*

1. Descendant of
Judah...........1 Chr. 2:3, 36　406
2. Ephraimite.....1 Chr. 7:20, 21　412
3. One of Joash's
murderers.....2 Chr. 24:26　458
Called
Jozachar.....2 Kin. 12:21　384
4. Son of Zattu..Ezra 10:27　484
5. Son of
Hashum......Ezra 10:33　485
6. Son of Nebo..Ezra 10:43　485

Zabbai—(God) *has given*

1. Man who divorced his foreign
wife..........Ezra 10:28　484
2. Father of
Baruch.......Neh. 3:20　491

Zabbud—*given* (by God)
Postexilic
returnee.........Ezra 8:14　482

Zabdi—(God) *has given*

1. Achan's
grandfather...Josh. 7:1, 17, 18　222
2. Benjamite .....1 Chr. 8:1, 19　413
3. One of David's
officers........1 Chr. 27:27　431

Zabdiel—*God has given*

1. Father of
Jashobeam....1 Chr. 27:2　430
2. Postexilic
official ....Neh. 11:14　500

Zabud—*bestowed*
Son of Nathan ...1 Kin. 4:5　342

Zaccai probably a contraction of
"Zechariah"
Head of a postexilic
family...........Ezra 2:9　476

Zacchaeus—*pure*
Wealthy tax-gatherer converted to
Christ............Luke 19:1-10　1029

Zaccur—*remembered*

1. Father of the Reubenite
spy ....Num. 13:2, 4　148
2. Simeonite......1 Chr. 4:24, 26　408
3. Merarite
Levite.........1 Chr. 24:27　428
4. Asaphite
Levite.........1 Chr. 25:2, 10　429
5. Signer of the
covenant......Neh. 10:1, 12　499
6. A treasurer under
Nehemiah.....Neh. 13:13　502

Zachariah—*Yahweh has remembered*

1. Son and successor
of King
Jeroboam { 2 Kin. 14:29　387
II { 2 Kin. 15:8-10　387
2. Grandfather of
Hezekiah......2 Kin. 18:1, 2　390

Zacharias
Father of John the
Baptist ....Luke 1:5-17　1004

Zacher—*memorial*
Benjamite........1 Chr. 8:31　413

Zadok—*righteous*

1. Descendant of
Aaron.........1 Chr. 24:1-3　428
Co-priest with
Abiathar ......2 Sam. 20:25　329
Loyal to
David ....2 Sam. 15:24-29　323
Gently rebuked by
David ....2 Sam. 19:11-14　327
Remained aloof from Adonijah's
usurpation ...1 Kin. 1:8-26　337
Commanded by David to anoint
Solomon ......1 Kin. 1:32-45　338
Replaces
Abiathar ......1 Kin. 2:35　340
Sons of,
faithful........Ezek. 48:11　817
2. Priest, the son or grandson of
Ahitub........1 Chr. 6:12　410
3. Jotham's maternal
grandfather ...2 Kin. 15:33　388
4. Postexilic workman, son of
Baana.........Neh. 3:4　490
5. Postexilic workman, son of
Immer.........Neh. 3:29　491
6. Ancestor of
Christ.........Matt. 1:14　942

Zaham—*foul*
Son of
Rehoboam........2 Chr. 11:18, 19　448

Zain
Letter of the Hebrew
alphabet........Ps. 119:49-56　600

Zair—*little*
Battle camp in
Edom ....2 Kin. 8:21　380

Zalaph—*caper-plant*
Father of
Hanum ....Neh. 3:30　491

MONIES, WEIGHTS, AND MEASURES

The Hebrews probably first used coins in the Persian period (500–350 B.C.). However, minting began around 700 B.C. in other nations. Prior to this, precious metals were weighed, not counted as money.

Some units appear as both measures of money and measures of weights. This comes from naming the coins after their weight. For example, the shekel was a weight long before it became the name of a coin.

It is helpful to relate biblical monies to current values. But we cannot make exact equivalents. The fluctuating value of money's purchasing power is difficult to determine in our own day. It is even harder to evaluate currencies used two- to three-thousand years ago.

Therefore, it is best to choose a value meaningful over time, such as a common laborer's daily wage. One day's wage corresponds to the ancient Jewish system (a silver shekel is four days' wages) as well as to the Greek and Roman systems (the drachma and the denarius were each coins representing a day's wage).

The monies chart below takes a current day's wage as thirty-two dollars. Though there are differences of economies and standards of living, this measure will help us apply meaningful values to the monetary units in the chart and in the biblical text.

Monies

Unit	Monetary Value	Equivalents	Translations
Jewish Weights			
Talent	gold—$5,760,000[1] silver—$384,000	3,000 shekels; 6,000 bekas	talent
Shekel	gold—$1,920 silver—$128	4 days' wages; 2 bekas; 20 gerahs	shekel
Beka	gold—$960 silver—$64	½ shekel; 10 gerahs	bekah
Gerah	gold—$96 silver—$6.40	¹⁄₂₀ shekel	gerah
Persian Coins			
Daric	gold—$1,280[2] silver—$64	2 days' wages; ½ Jewish silver shekel	dram
Greek Coins			
Tetradrachma (Stater)	$128	4 drachmas	piece of money
Didrachma	$64	2 drachmas	tribute
Drachma	$32	1 day's wage	piece of silver
Lepton	$.25	½ of a Roman kodrantes	mite
Roman Coins			
Aureus	$800	25 denarii	
Denarius	$32	1 day's wage	pence, penny
Assarius	$2	¹⁄₁₆ of a denarius	farthing
Kodrantes	$.50	¼ of an assarius	farthing

[1]Value of gold is fifteen times the value of silver.
[2]Value of gold is twenty times the value of silver.

Weights

Unit	Weight	Equivalents	Translations
Jewish Weights			
Talent	c. 75 pounds for common talent, c. 150 pounds for royal talent	60 minas; 3,000 shekels	talent
Mina	1.25 pounds	50 shekels	maneh, pound
Shekel	c. .4 ounce (11.4 grams) for common shekel c. .8 ounce for royal shekel	2 bekas; 20 gerahs	shekel
Beka	c. .2 ounce (5.7 grams)	½ shekel; 10 gerahs	half a shekel
Gerah	c. .02 ounce (.57 grams)	1/20 shekel	gerah
Roman Weight			
Litra	12 ounces		pound

Measures of Length

Unit	Length	Equivalents	Translations
Day's journey	c. 20 miles		day's journey
Roman mile	4,854 feet	8 stadia	mile
Sabbath day's journey	3,637 feet	6 stadia	sabbath day's journey
Stadion	606 feet	⅛ Roman mile	furlong
Rod	9 feet (10.5 feet in Ezekiel)	3 paces; 6 cubits	measuring reed, reed
Fathom	6 feet	4 cubits	fathom
Pace	3 feet	⅓ rod; 2 cubits	pace
Cubit	18 inches	½ pace; 2 spans	cubit
Span	9 inches	½ cubit; 3 handbreadths	span
Handbreadth	3 inches	⅓ span; 4 fingers	handbreadth
Finger	.75 inches	¼ handbreadth	finger

Dry Measures

Unit	Measure	Equivalents	Translations
Homer	6.52 bushels	10 ephahs	homer
Kor	6.52 bushels	1 homer; 10 ephahs	cor, measure
Lethech	3.26 bushels	½ kor	half homer
Ephah	.65 bushel, 20.8 quarts	1/10 homer	ephah

Dry Measures—Continued

Unit	Measure	Equivalents	Translations
Modius	7.68 quarts		bushel
Seah	7 quarts	⅓ ephah	measure
Omer	2.08 quarts	⅒ ephah; 1⅘ kab	omer
Kab	1.16 quarts	4 logs	cab
Choenix	1 quart		measure
Xestes	1⅙ pints		pot
Log	.58 pint	¼ kab	log

Liquid Measures

Unit	Measure	Equivalents	Translations
Kor	60 gallons	10 baths	cor
Metretes	10.2 gallons		firkin
Bath	6 gallons	6 hins	measure, bath
Hin	1 gallon	2 kabs	hin
Kab	2 quarts	4 logs	cab
Log	1 pint	¼ kab	log

The

Old Testament

of

The Open Bible®
EXPANDED EDITION

King James Version

GENESIS

THE BOOK OF GENESIS

The first part of Genesis focuses on the beginning and spread of sin in the world and culminates in the devastating flood in the days of Noah. The second part of the book focuses on God's dealings with one man, Abraham, through whom God promises to bring salvation and blessing to the world. Abraham and his descendants learn firsthand that it is always safe to trust the Lord in times of famine and feasting, blessing and bondage. From Abraham . . . to Isaac . . . to Jacob . . . to Joseph . . . God's promises begin to come to fruition in a great nation possessing a great land.

Genesis is a Greek word meaning "origin," "source," "generation," or "beginning." The original Hebrew title *Bereshith* means "In the Beginning."

The literary structure of Genesis is clear and is built around eleven separate units, each headed with the word *generations* in the phrase "These are the generations" or "The book of the generations": (1) Introduction to the Generations (1:1—2:3); (2) Heaven and Earth (2:4—4:26); (3) Adam (5:1—6:8); (4) Noah (6:9—9:29); (5) Sons of Noah (10:1—11:9); (6) Shem (11:10—26); (7) Terah (11:27—25:11); (8) Ishmael (25:12–18); (9) Isaac (25:19—35:29); (10) Esau (36:1—37:1); (11) Jacob (37:2—50:26).

THE AUTHOR OF GENESIS

Although Genesis does not directly name its author, and although Genesis ends some three centuries before Moses was born, the whole of Scripture and church history are unified in their adherence to the Mosaic authorship of Genesis.

The Old Testament is replete with both direct and indirect testimonies to the Mosaic authorship of the entire Pentateuch (Ex. 17:14; Lev. 1:1, 2; Num. 33:2; Deut. 1:1; Josh. 1:7; 1 Kin. 2:3; 2 Kin. 14:6; Ezra 6:18; Neh. 13:1; Dan. 9:11–13; Mal. 4:4). The New Testament also contains numerous testimonies (Matt. 8:4; Mark 12:26; Luke 16:29; John 7:19; Acts 26:22; Rom. 10:19; 1 Cor. 9:9; 2 Cor. 3:15).

The early church openly held to the Mosaic authorship, as does the first-century Jewish historian Josephus. As would be expected the Jerusalem Talmud supports Moses as author.

It would be difficult to find a man in all the range of Israel's life who was better prepared or qualified to write this history. Trained in the "wisdom of the Egyptians" (Acts 7:22), Moses had been providentially prepared to understand and integrate, under the inspiration of God, all the available records, manuscripts, and oral narratives.

THE TIME OF GENESIS

Genesis divides neatly into three geographical settings: (1) the Fertile Crescent (1—11); (2) Israel (12—36); (3) Egypt (37—50).

The setting of the first eleven chapters changes rapidly as it spans more than two thousand years and fifteen hundred miles, and paints the majestic acts of the Creation, the Garden of Eden, the Noahic Flood, and the towering citadel of Babel.

The middle section of Genesis rapidly funnels down from the broad brim of the two millennia spent in the Fertile Crescent to less than two hundred years in the little country of Canaan. Surrounded by the rampant immorality and idolatry of the Canaanites, the godliness of Abraham rapidly degenerates into gross immorality in some of his descendants.

In the last fourteen chapters, God dramatically saves the small Israelite nation from extinction by transferring the "seventy souls" to Egypt so that they may grow and multiply. Egypt is an unexpected womb for the growth of God's chosen nation Israel, to be sure, but one in which they are isolated from the maiming influence of Canaan.

Genesis spans more time than any other book in the Bible; in fact, it covers more than all sixty-five other books of the Bible put together.

Utilizing the same threefold division noted above, the following dates can be assigned:

A. 2,000 or more years, 4000–2090 B.C. (Gen. 1—11)
   1. Creation, 4000 B.C. or earlier (Gen. 1:1)
   2. Death of Terah, 2090 B.C. (Gen. 11:32)
B. 193 years, 2090–1897 B.C. (Gen. 12—36)
   1. Death of Terah, 2090 B.C. (Gen. 11:32)
   2. Joseph to Egypt, c. 1897 B.C. (Gen. 37:2)
C. 93 years, 1897–1804 B.C. (Gen. 37—50)
   1. Joseph to Egypt, c. 1897 B.C. (Gen. 37:2)
   2. Death of Joseph, 1804 B.C. (Gen. 50:26)

THE CHRIST OF GENESIS

Genesis moves from the general to the specific in its messianic predictions: Christ is the seed of the woman (3:15), from the line of Seth (4:25), the son of Shem (9:27), the descendant of Abraham (12:3), of Isaac (21:12), of Jacob (25:23), and of the tribe of Judah (49:10).

Christ is also seen in people and events that serve as figures. (A "figure" is a historical fact that illustrates a spiritual truth.) Adam is a "figure of

him that was to come" (Rom. 5:14). Both entered the world through a special act of God as sinless men. Adam is the head of the old creation; Christ is the Head of the new creation. Abel's acceptable offering of a blood sacrifice points to Christ, and there is a parallel in his murder by Cain. Melchizedek ("righteous king") is "made like unto the Son of God" (Heb. 7:3). He is the king of Salem ("peace") who brings forth bread and wine and is the priest of the Most High God. Joseph is also a type of Christ. Joseph and Christ are both objects of special love by their fathers, both are hated by their brethren, both are rejected as rulers over their brethren, both are conspired against and sold for silver, both are condemned though innocent, and both are raised from humiliation to glory by the power of God.

KEYS TO GENESIS

Key Word: Beginnings—Genesis gives the beginning of almost everything, including the beginning of the universe, life, man, sabbath, death, marriage, sin, redemption, family, literature, cities, art, language, and sacrifice.

Key Verses: Genesis 3:15; 12:3—"And I will put enmity between thee and the woman, and between thy seed and her seed; it shall bruise thy head, and thou shalt bruise his heel" (3:15).

"And I will bless them that bless thee, and curse him that curseth thee: and in thee shall all families of the earth be blessed" (12:3).

Key Chapter: Genesis 15—Central to all of Scripture is the Abrahamic Covenant, which is given in 12:1-3 and ratified in 15:1-21. Israel receives three specific promises: (1) the promise of a great land—"from the river of Egypt unto the great river, the river Euphrates" (15:18); (2) the promise of a great nation—"and I will make thy seed as the dust of the earth" (13:16); and (3) the promise of a great blessing—"and I will bless

thee, and make thy name great; and thou shalt be a blessing" (12:2).

SURVEY OF GENESIS

Genesis is not so much a history of man as it is the first chapter in the history of the *redemption* of man. As such, Genesis is a highly selective spiritual interpretation of history. Genesis is divided into four great events (1—11) and four great people (12—50).

The Four Great Events: Chapters 1—11 lay the foundation upon which the whole Bible is built and centers on four key events. (1) *Creation:* God is the sovereign Creator of matter, energy, space, and time. Man is the pinnacle of the Creation. (2) *Fall:* Creation is followed by corruption. In the first sin man is separated from God (Adam from God), and in the second sin, man is separated from man (Cain from Abel). In spite of the devastating curse of the Fall, God promises hope of redemption through the seed of the woman (3:15). (3) *Flood:* As man multiplies, sin also multiplies until God is compelled to destroy humanity with the exception of Noah and his family. (4) *Nations:* Genesis teaches the unity of the human race: we are all children of Adam through Noah, but because of rebellion at the Tower of Babel, God fragments the single culture and language of the post-flood world and scatters people over the face of the earth.

The Four Great People: Once the nations are scattered, God focuses on one man and his descendants through whom He will bless all nations (12—50). (1) *Abraham:* The calling of Abraham (12) is the pivotal point of the book. The three covenant promises God makes to Abraham (land, descendants, and blessing) are foundational to His program of bringing salvation upon the earth. (2) *Isaac:* God establishes His covenant with Isaac as the spiritual link with Abraham. (3)

FOCUS	FOUR EVENTS				FOUR PEOPLE			
REFERENCE	1:1——3:1——	—6:1——	—10:1—	—12:1—	—25:19—	—27:1—	—37:1——50:26	
DIVISION	CREATION	FALL	FLOOD	NATIONS	ABRAHAM	ISAAC	JACOB	JOSEPH
TOPIC	HUMAN RACE				HEBREW RACE			
	HISTORICAL				BIOGRAPHICAL			
LOCATION	FERTILE CRESCENT (Eden-Haran)				CANAAN (Haran-Canaan)			EGYPT (Canaan-Egypt)
TIME	c. 2000 YEARS (c. 4004-2090 B.C.)				193 YEARS (2090-1897 B.C.)			93 YEARS (1897-1804 B.C.)

Jacob: God transforms this man from selfishness to servanthood and changes his name to Israel, the father of the twelve tribes. (4) *Joseph:* Jacob's favorite son suffers at the hands of his brothers and becomes a slave in Egypt. After his dramatic rise to the rulership of Egypt, Joseph delivers his family from famine and brings them out of Canaan to Goshen.

Genesis ends on a note of impending bondage with the death of Joseph. There is great need for the redemption that is to follow in the Book of Exodus.

OUTLINE OF GENESIS

Part One: Primeval History (1:1—11:9)

Part Two: Patriarchal History (11:10—50:26)

CHAPTER 1

Creation of the World

IN the [R]beginning God created the heaven and the earth.   John 1:1, 2; Heb. 1:10

2 And the earth was without form, and void; and darkness *was* upon the face of the deep. [R]And the Spirit of God moved upon the face of the waters.   Ps. 33:6; Is. 40:13, 14

3 And God said, [R]Let there be [R]light: and there was light.   2 Cor. 4:6 · Heb. 11:3

4 And God saw the light, that *it was* good: and God divided the light from the darkness.

5 [R]And God called the light Day, and the darkness he called Night. And the evening and the morning were the first day.   Ps. 74:16

6 And God said, Let there be a [T]firmament in the midst of the waters, and let it divide the waters from the waters.   *expansion*

7 And God made the firmament, and divided the waters which *were* under the firmament from the waters which *were* above the firmament: and it was so.

8 And God called the firmament Heaven. And the evening and the morning were the second day.

9 And God said, [R]Let the waters under the heaven be gathered together unto one place, and let the dry *land* appear: and it was so.   Job 26:10; Prov. 8:29; Jer. 5:22; 2 Pet. 3:5

10 And God called the dry *land* Earth; and the [R]gathering together of the waters called he Seas: and God saw that *it was* good. Ps. 95:5

11 And God said, Let the earth bring forth grass, the herb yielding seed, *and* the fruit tree yielding fruit after his kind, whose seed *is* in itself, upon the earth: and it was so.

12 And the earth brought forth grass, *and* herb yielding seed after his kind, and the tree yielding fruit, whose seed *was* in itself, after his kind: and God saw that *it was* good.

13 And the evening and the morning were the third day.

14 And God said, Let there be lights in the firmament of the heaven to divide the day from the night; and let them be for signs, and for seasons, and for days, and years:

15 And let them be for [T]lights in the firmament of the heaven to give light upon the earth: and it was so.   *luminaries; lightbearers*

16 And God made two great lights; the greater light to rule the day, and the lesser light to rule the night: *he made* the stars also.

17 And God set them in the firmament of the heaven to give light upon the earth,

18 And to rule over the day and over the night, and to divide the light from the darkness: and God saw that *it was* good.

19 And the evening and the morning were the fourth day.

20 And God said, Let the waters bring forth abundantly the moving creature that hath [T]life, and fowl *that* may fly above the earth in the open firmament of heaven.   *soul*

21 [R]And God created great whales, and every living creature that moveth, which the waters brought forth abundantly, after their kind, and every winged fowl after his kind: and God saw that *it was* good.   6:20

22 And God blessed them, saying, Be fruitful, and multiply, and fill the waters in the seas, and let fowl multiply in the earth.

23 And the evening and the morning were the fifth day.

24 And God said, Let the earth bring forth the living creature after his kind, cattle, and [R]creeping thing, and beast of the earth after his kind: and it was so.   Rom. 1:23

25 And God made the beast of the earth after his kind, and cattle after their kind, and every thing that creepeth upon the earth after his kind: and God saw that *it was* good.

26 And God said, Let us make man in our image, after our likeness: and let them have dominion over the fish of the sea, and over the fowl of the air, and over the cattle, and over all the earth, and over every creeping thing that creepeth upon the earth.

27 So God created man in his *own* image,

in the image of God created he him; Rmale and female created he them.   5:2; Matt. 19:4

28 And God blessed them, and God said unto them, Be fruitful, and multiply, and replenish the earth, and subdue it: and have dominion over the fish of the sea, and over the fowl of the air, and over every living thing that moveth upon the earth.

29 And God said, Behold, I have given you every herb bearing seed, which is upon the face of all the earth, and every tree, in the which is the fruit of a tree yielding seed; to you it shall be for Tmeat.   food

30 And to every beast of the earth, and to every Rfowl of the air, and to every thing that creepeth upon the earth, wherein there is Tlife, I have given every green herb for meat: and it was so.   Job 38:41 · breath

31 And RGod saw every thing that he had made, and, behold, it was very good. And the evening and the morning were the sixth day.   Ps. 104:24; 119:68; 1 Tim. 4:4

CHAPTER 2

THUS the heavens and the earth were finished, and all the host of them.

2 RAnd on the seventh day God ended his work which he had made; and he rested on the seventh day from all his work which he had made.   Ex. 20:8-11; Ex. 31:17; Heb. 4:4

3 And God Rblessed the seventh day, and Tsanctified it: because that in it he had rested from all his work which God Tcreated and made.   [Is. 58:13] · set apart · in creating had made

Creation of Man

4 RThese are the generations of the heavens and of the earth when they were created, in the day that the LORD God made the earth and the heavens,   1:1; Ps. 90:1,2

5 And every Rplant of the field before it was in the earth, and every herb of the field before it grew: for the LORD God had not caused it to rain upon the earth, and there was not a man to till the ground.   1:12

6 But there went up a mist from the earth, and watered the whole face of the ground.

7 And the LORD God formed man Tof the dust of the ground, and breathed into his Rnostrils the breath of life; and man became a living soul.   of dust from the ground · 7:22

8 And the LORD God planted Ra garden eastward in REden; and there he put the man whom he had formed.   Is. 51:3 · 4:16

9 And out of the ground made the LORD God to grow every tree that is pleasant to the sight, and good for food; the tree of life also in the midst of the garden, and the tree of knowledge of good and Revil.   Rev. 22:2

10 And a Rriver Twent out of Eden to water the garden; and from thence it was parted, and became into four heads.   Ps. 46:4 · flowed

11 The name of the first is Pi'-son: that is it which compasseth Rthe whole land of Hav'-i-lah, where there is gold;   25:18

12 And the gold of that land is good: there is bdellium and the Tonyx stone.   beryl

13 And the name of the second river is Gi'-hon: the same is it that compasseth the Rwhole land of TE-thi-o'-pi-a.   Is. 18:1 · Cush

14 And the name of the third river is THid'-de-kel: that is it which goeth toward the east of TAssyria. RAnd the fourth river is Eu-phra'-tes.   Tigris · Asshur · 15:18

15 And the LORD God took Tthe man, and put him into the garden of REden to Tdress it and to keep it.   Adam · Is. 51:3 · cultivate

16 And the LORD God commanded the man, saying, ROf every tree of the garden thou mayest freely eat: 3:2, 3

17 RBut of the tree of the knowledge of good and evil, thou shalt not eat of it: for in the day that thou eatest thereof thou Tshalt surely die.   [Deut. 8:2] · dying thou shalt die

18 And the LORD God said, It is not good that the man should be alone; I will make him an help Tmeet for him.   fit

19 And out of the ground the LORD God formed every beast of the field, and every

---

2:15-17 The Edenic Covenant—The covenant in Eden is the first of the general or universal covenants. In it, Adam is charged to: (1) populate the earth (Gen. 1:28); (2) subdue the earth (Gen. 1:28); (3) exercise dominion over the animal creation (Gen. 1:28); (4) care for the Garden of Eden and enjoy its fruit (Gen. 1:29; 2:15); and (5) refrain from eating the fruit of the tree of the knowledge of good and evil, under penalty of death (Gen. 2:16, 17). The Edenic Covenant was terminated by man's disobedience, when Adam and Eve ate of the fruit of the tree of the knowledge of good and evil, resulting in their spiritual and physical deaths. This failure necessitated the establishment of the covenant with Adam (Page 7—Gen. 3:14-21).

Now turn to Page 7—Gen. 3:14-21: The Adamic Covenant.

2:18-25 How the Family Began—Genesis 2:18-25 fills in the details of the simple statement in Genesis 1:27: "male and female created he them." This account particularly amplifies the "and female" part of the statement and shows how woman was created. Three observations can be made on the passage that will help us to understand how the family began:

a. The need for woman (vv. 18-20). Woman is absolutely essential in God's plan. It was God who observed, "It is not good that the man should be alone" (v. 18), and determined to make a "help meet" for Adam. Woman's role in the will of God was to be a "help" who was suitable to man in

(continued on next page)

fowl of the air; and brought *them* unto ᵀAdam to see what he would call them: and whatsoever Adam called every living creature, that *was* the name thereof.   *the man*

20 And Adam ᵀgave names to all cattle, and to the fowl of the air, and to every beast of the field; but for Adam there was not found an help ᵀmeet for him.   *called • fit*

21 And the Lᴏʀᴅ God caused a ᴿdeep sleep to fall upon Adam, and he slept: and he took one of his ᵀribs, and closed up the flesh instead thereof;   15:12; 1 Sam. 26:12 • *sides*

22 ᴿAnd the rib, which the Lᴏʀᴅ God had taken from man, ᵀmade he a woman, and brought her unto the man.   3:20 • *builded*

23 And Adam said, This *is* ᵀnow ᴿbone of my bones, and flesh of my flesh: she shall be called Woman, because she was taken out of Man.   *at last this one* • Eph. 5:30

24 Therefore shall a man leave his father and his mother, and shall ᴿcleave unto his wife: and they shall be one flesh.   Mark 10:6–8

25 And they were both naked, the man and his wife, and were not ashamed.

CHAPTER 3

Temptation of Man

Nᴏᴡ the serpent was more subtil than any beast of the field which the Lᴏʀᴅ God had made. And he said unto the woman,

ᵀYea, hath God said, Ye shall not eat of every tree of the garden?   *Yea, because*

2 And the woman said unto the serpent, We may ᴿeat of the fruit of the trees of the garden: 2:16, 17

3 But of the fruit of the tree which *is* in the midst of the garden, God hath said, ᴿYe shall not eat of it, neither shall ye touch it, lest ye die.   2:17; Rev. 22:14

4 ᴿAnd the serpent said unto the woman, Ye shall not surely die: [2 Cor. 11:3]; 1 Tim. 2:14

5 For God doth know that in the day ye eat thereof, then ᴿyour eyes shall be opened, and ᴿye shall be as ᵀgods, knowing good and evil.   [v. 7] • [Is. 14:14; Acts 26:18] • *God*

Fall of Man

6 And when the woman saw that the tree *was* good for food, and that it *was* pleasant to the eyes, and a tree to be desired to make *one* wise, she took of the fruit thereof, and did eat, and gave also unto her husband with her; and he did eat.

7 ᴿAnd the eyes of them both were opened, and they knew that they *were* naked; and they sewed fig leaves together, and made themselves ᵀaprons.   vv. 5, 21 • *things to gird about*

Judgment on Man

8 And they heard the voice of the Lᴏʀᴅ God ᵀwalking in the garden in the ᵀcool of the day: and Adam and his wife hid them-

---

(continued from previous page)

every particular mental, spiritual, emotional, social, and physical need. God undertook an orientation program to show man the need that He alone had observed. He brought to man the birds and beasts He had created, so that man should exercise his dominion over them (v. 28) and name them (v. 19). However, in verse 20 it is noted that for Adam there was no "help" similar to himself.

b. The provision of woman for man (vv. 21–24). God caused Adam to go to sleep, and God removed one of his "ribs." Exactly what God removed is not known, but it was adequate for His purpose. He "made" (lit., *built*) a woman (v. 22) whom Adam recognized as being his equal, "bone of my bones, and flesh of my flesh." This resulted in what has become known as the universal law of marriage (v. 24), in which it can be seen that: (1) the responsibility for marriage is on the man's shoulders—he is to "leave his father and his mother"; (2) the responsibility for keeping the union together is on the man's shoulders—he is to "cleave unto" (i.e., stick to) his wife; and (3) the union is indissoluble—"they shall be one flesh."

c. The state of the first man and woman (v. 25). From the beginning the man and woman were "naked" in each other's presence and "were not ashamed." There is no shame in nudity when it occurs within the right context—the marital union. This passage clearly teaches that (1) sex was God's idea and is not sinful; (2) sex came before the Fall, and if the Fall had never taken place there still would be sexual relations between a man and his wife; and (3) propagation of the species is one, but not the exclusive, purpose for sex. The Bible gives two other reasons for sex: (1) to promote love between the husband and wife (Page 1223—Heb. 13:4), and (2) to prevent fornication—the unlawful satisfaction of the God-given sexual desire (Page 1130—1 Cor. 7:2).

Now turn to Page 184—Deut. 6:4–9: Three Essentials for a Christian Home.

3:6, 7 Adam's Sin—Adam's sin does not seem to be a very great sin from man's perspective. All he did was take a bite of some fruit. Adam's sin is serious in that the fruit was of the tree of the knowledge of good and evil, of which God said that he was not to eat under penalty of death (Page 5—Gen. 2:17). Up to this time Adam was morally innocent. When he sinned, he by nature became a sinner. As such he died. He died spiritually immediately and began to die physically. Adam was the first man ever to live upon the face of the earth. From Adam and Eve come every other human being who ever has lived upon the face of the earth. Thus Adam is the "federal head" from whom every other man came. Like begets like. Apples beget apples. Dogs beget dogs. Human beings beget human beings. Since Adam became a sinner before Eve conceived a child, every human being descended from him is a sinner just like him except Christ. Because of Adam's sin, death entered into the human race (Page 1112—Rom. 5:12–14); every human being needs to have the new life.

Now turn to Page 644—Eccl. 7:20: Individual Sin.

selves from the presence of the LORD God amongst the trees of the garden. *going · wind*

9 And the LORD God called unto Adam, and said unto him, ᴿWhere *art* thou?   4:9

10 And he said, I heard thy voice in the garden, ᴿand I was afraid, because I *was* naked; and I hid myself.   2:25; 1 John 3:20

11 And he said, Who told thee that thou *wast* naked? Hast thou eaten of the tree, ᴿwhereof I commanded thee that thou shouldest not eat?   [Rom. 5:12]

12 And the man said, ᴿThe woman whom thou gavest *to be* with me, she gave me of the tree, and I did eat.   [Prov. 28:13; Luke 14:18]

13 And the LORD God said unto the woman, What *is* this *that* thou hast done? And the woman said, ᴿThe serpent beguiled me, and I did eat.   *v.* 4; 2 Cor. 11:3; 1 Tim. 2:14

14 And the LORD God said unto the serpent, ᴿBecause thou hast done this, thou *art* cursed above all cattle, and above every beast of the field; upon thy belly shalt thou go, and ᴿdust shalt thou eat all the days of thy life: Deut. 28:15–20 · Is. 65:25; Mic. 7:17

15 ᴿAnd I will put enmity between thee and the woman, and between thy seed and her seed; ᵀit shall bruise thy head, and thou shalt bruise his heel.   Rom. 16:20; Gal. 4:4 ☆ · *He*

16 Unto the woman he said, I will greatly multiply thy sorrow and thy conception; in sorrow thou shalt bring forth children; and thy desire *shall be* ᵀto thy husband, and he shall ᴿrule over thee.   *for* · 1 Tim. 2:12

17 And unto Adam he said, Because thou hast hearkened unto the voice of thy wife, and hast eaten of the tree, of which I commanded thee, saying, Thou shalt not eat of it: cursed *is* the ground for thy sake; in sorrow shalt thou eat *of* it all the days of thy life;

18 Thorns also and thistles shall it bring forth to thee; and thou shalt eat the herb of the field;

19 In the sweat of thy face shalt thou eat bread, till thou return unto the ground; for out of it wast thou taken: for dust thou *art*, and unto dust shalt thou return.

20 And Adam called his wife's name ᵀEve; because she was the mother of all living. *life*

21 Unto Adam also and to his wife did the LORD God make coats of skins, and ᴿclothed them.   *v.* 7; Job 29:14; Zech. 3:4; Rev. 19:8

22 And the LORD God said, Behold, the man is become as one of us, to know ᴿgood and evil: and now, lest he put forth his hand, and take also of the tree of life, and eat, and live for ever: 2:9; Rev. 22:14

23 Therefore the LORD God sent him forth from the garden of Eden, ᴿto till the ground from whence he was taken.   4:2; 9:20

24 So he drove out the man; and he placed ᴿat the east of the garden of Eden Cher'-u-bims, and a flaming sword which turned every way, to keep the way of the tree of life.   2:8

CHAPTER 4

The Initial Conflict

AND Adam knew Eve his wife; and she conceived, and bare ᵀCain, and said, I have gotten a man from the LORD.   *to get*

2 And she again bare his brother Abel. And ᴿAbel was a keeper of sheep, but Cain was a tiller of the ground.   Luke 11:50, 51

3 And in process of time it came to pass, that Cain brought ᴿof the fruit of the ground an offering unto the LORD.   Num. 18:12

4 And Abel, he also brought of ᴿthe firstlings of his flock and of ᴿthe fat thereof. And

---

3:14–21 The Adamic Covenant—The covenant with Adam is the second general or universal covenant. It could be called the covenant with mankind, for it sets forth the conditions which will hold sway until the curse of sin is lifted (cf. Page 667—Is. 11:6–10; Page 1114—Rom. 8:18–23). According to the covenant, the conditions which will prevail are:

a. The serpent, the tool used by Satan to effect the fall of man, is cursed. The curse affects not only the instrument, the serpent, but also the indwelling energizer, Satan. Great physical changes took place in the serpent. Apparently it was upright; now it will go on its belly (v. 14). It was the most desirable animal of the animal creation; now it is the most loathsome. The sight or thought of a snake should be an effective reminder of the devastating effects of sin.

b. Satan is judged—he will enjoy limited success ("thou shalt bruise his heel," v. 15), but ultimately he will be judged ("it shall bruise thy head," v. 15).

c. The first prophecy of the coming of Messiah is given (v. 15).

d. There will be a multiplication of conception, necessitated by the introduction of death into the human race (v. 16).

e. There will be pain in childbirth (v. 16).

f. The woman is made subject to her husband (v. 16).

g. The ground is cursed and will bring forth weeds among the food which man must eat for his existence (vv. 17–19).

h. Physical change takes place in man; he will perspire when he works. He will have to work all his life long (v. 19).

i. In sinning, man dies spiritually, and ultimately will die physically. His flesh will decay until it returns to dust from which it was originally taken (v. 19).

Now turn to Page 11—Gen. 9:1–19: The Noahic Covenant.

the LORD had ^Rrespect unto Abel and to his offering: Num. 18:17 • Lev. 3:16 • Heb. 11:4

5 But unto Cain and to his offering he had not respect. And Cain was very ^Twroth, ^Rand his countenance fell. angry • 31:2

6 And the LORD said unto Cain, Why art thou ^Twroth? and why is thy ^Tcountenance^R fallen? angry • facial expression changed • Prov. 15:13

7 If thou doest well, shalt thou not be accepted? and if thou doest not well, sin lieth at the door. And unto thee *shall be* his desire, and thou shalt rule over him.

8 And Cain talked with Abel his brother: and it came to pass, when they were in the field, that Cain rose up against Abel his brother, and ^Tslew^R him. killed • Matt. 23:35

9 And the LORD said unto Cain, Where *is* Abel thy brother? And he said, I know not: *Am* I my brother's keeper?

10 And he said, What hast thou done? the voice of thy brother's blood ^Rcrieth unto me from the ground. Heb. 12:24; Rev. 6:10

11 And now *art* thou cursed from the earth, which hath opened her mouth to receive thy brother's blood from thy hand;

12 When thou ^Ttillest the ground, it shall ^Tnot henceforth yield unto thee her strength; a fugitive and a ^Tvagabond shalt thou be in the earth. cultivate • no longer • wanderer

13 And Cain said unto the LORD, My punishment *is* greater than I can bear.

14 Behold, thou hast driven me out this day from the face of the earth; and from thy face shall I be ^Rhid; and I shall be a fugitive and a vagabond in the earth; and it shall come to pass, ^R*that* every one that findeth me shall slay me. Is. 1:15 • 9:6

15 And the LORD said unto him, Therefore whosoever slayeth Cain, vengeance shall be taken on him ^Rsevenfold. And the LORD set a mark upon Cain, lest any finding him should kill him. Ps. 79:12; Ezek. 9:4, 6

The Ungodly Line of Cain

16 And Cain ^Rwent out from the presence of the LORD, and dwelt in the land of ^TNod, on the east of Eden. Jer. 23:39; 52:3 • wandering

17 And Cain knew his wife; and she conceived, and bare ^TE′-noch: and he builded a city, and called the name of the city, after the name of his son, E′-noch. teacher

18 And unto E′-noch was born I′-rad: and I′-rad begat Me-hu′-ja-el: and Me-hu′-ja-el begat Me-thu′-sa-el: and Me-thu′-sa-el begat ^TLa′-mech. Lemech

19 And La′-mech took unto him ^Rtwo wives: the name of the one *was* A′-dah, and the name of the other Zil′-lah. 1 Tim. 3:2

20 And A′-dah ^Tbare Ja′-bal: he was the father of such as dwell in tents, ^Rand *of such as have* ^Tcattle. gave birth to • 13:5 • livestock

21 And his brother's name *was* Ju′-bal: he

was the father of all such as handle the ^Tharp and ^Torgan. lyre • pipe

22 And Zil′-lah, she also bare Tu′-bal–cain, ^Tan instructer of every ^Tartificer in ^Tbrass and iron: and the sister of Tu′-bal–cain *was* Na′-a-mah. forger • craftsman • bronze

23 And La′-mech said unto his wives, A′-dah and Zil′-lah, Hear my voice; ye wives of La′-mech, hearken unto my speech: for I have slain a man to my wounding, and a young man to my hurt.

24 ^RIf Cain shall be avenged sevenfold, truly La′-mech seventy and sevenfold. v. 15

The Godly Line of Seth
1 Chr. 1:1–4; Luke 3:36–38

25 And Adam knew his wife again; and she bare a son, and called his name Seth: For God, *said she,* hath appointed me another seed instead of Abel, whom Cain slew.

26 And to Seth, to him also there was born a son; and he called his name E′-nos: then began men to call ^Tupon the name of the LORD. themselves by the name of the LORD

CHAPTER 5

THIS *is* the book of the generations of Adam. In the day that God created man, in the likeness of God made he him;

2 ^RMale and female created he them; and blessed them, and called their name Adam, in the day when they were created. 1:27

3 And Adam lived an hundred and thirty years, and begat *a son* in his own likeness, after his image; and called his name Seth:

4 And the days of Adam after he had begotten Seth were eight hundred years: ^Rand he begat sons and daughters: 1:28

5 And all the days that Adam lived were nine hundred and thirty years: and he died.

6 And Seth lived an hundred and five years, and ^Rbegat E′-nos: 4:26

7 And Seth lived after he ^Tbegat E′-nos eight hundred and seven years, and begat sons and daughters: became the father of

8 And all the days of Seth were nine hundred and twelve years: and he died.

9 And E′-nos lived ninety years, and begat ^TCa-i′-nan: Kenan

10 And E′-nos lived after he begat Ca-i′-nan eight hundred and fifteen years, and begat sons and daughters:

11 And all the days of E′-nos were nine hundred and five years: and he died.

12 And Ca-i′-nan lived seventy years, and begat ^TMa-ha′-la-le-el: Gr. Maleleel (praiser of God)

13 And Ca-i′-nan lived after he begat Ma-ha′-la-le-el eight hundred and forty years, and begat sons and daughters:

14 And all the days of Ca-i′-nan were nine hundred and ten years: and he died.

15 And Ma-ha'-la-le-el lived sixty and five years, and begat ^TJa'-red: *Jerded (Descending)*

16 And Ma-ha'-la-le-el lived after he begat Ja'-red eight hundred and thirty years, and begat sons and daughters:

17 And all the days of Ma-ha'-la-le-el were eight hundred ninety and five years: and he died.

18 And Ja'-red lived an hundred sixty and two years, and he begat ^RE'-noch: Jude 14, 15

19 And Ja'-red lived after he begat E'-noch eight hundred years, and begat sons and daughters:

20 And all the days of Ja'-red were nine hundred sixty and two years: and he died.

21 And E'-noch lived sixty and five years, and begat Me-thu'-se-lah:

22 And E'-noch walked with God after he begat Me-thu'-se-lah three hundred years, and begat sons and daughters:

23 And all the days of E'-noch were three hundred sixty and five years:

24 And ^RE'-noch walked with God: and he *was* not; for God took him.   2 Kin. 2:11

25 And Me-thu'-se-lah lived an hundred eighty and seven years, and begat La'-mech:

26 And Me-thu'-se-lah lived after he begat La'-mech seven hundred eighty and two years, and begat sons and daughters:

27 And all the days of Me-thu'-se-lah were nine hundred sixty and nine years: and he died.

28 And La'-mech lived an hundred eighty and two years, and begat a son:

29 And he called his name Noah, saying, This *same* shall comfort us concerning our work and toil of our hands, because of the ground ^Rwhich the LORD hath cursed.   3:17

30 And La'-mech lived after he begat Noah five hundred ninety and five years, and begat sons and daughters:

31 And all the days of La'-mech were seven hundred seventy and seven years: and he died.

32 And Noah was five hundred years old: and Noah begat Shem, Ham, and Ja'-pheth.

CHAPTER 6

The Ungodly Multiply

AND it came to pass, ^Rwhen men began to multiply on the face of the earth, and daughters were born unto them,   1:28

2 That the sons of God saw the daughters of men that they *were* fair; and they took them wives of all which they chose.

3 And the LORD said, ^RMy spirit shall not always ^Tstrive with man, ^Rfor that he also *is* flesh: yet his days shall be an hundred and twenty years.   [Gal. 5:16] · *rule in* · Ps. 78:39

4 There were giants in the earth in those ^Rdays; and also after that, when the sons of God came in unto the daughters of men, and they bare *children* to them, the same *became* mighty men which *were* of old, men of renown.   Num. 13:32, 33; Luke 17:27

The Ungodly Sin Continually

5 And God saw that the wickedness of man *was* great in the earth, and *that* every ^Rimagination of the thoughts of his heart *was* only evil ^Tcontinually.   8:21 · *all the day*

The Ungodly to Be Destroyed

6 And ^Rit repented the LORD that he had made man on the earth, and it ^Rgrieved him at his heart.   James 1:17 · Is. 63:10

7 ^RAnd the LORD said, I will destroy man whom I have created from the face of the earth; both man, and beast, and the creeping thing, and the fowls of the air; for it repenteth me that I have made them.   Ps. 7:11

The Godly to Be Saved

8 But Noah ^Rfound grace in the eyes of the LORD.   Ex. 33:12; Luke 1:30; Acts 7:46

9 These *are* the generations of Noah: Noah was a just man *and* perfect in his generations, *and* Noah walked with God.

10 And Noah begat three sons, ^RShem, Ham, and Ja'-pheth.   5:32

11 The earth also was corrupt before God, and the earth was filled with violence.

12 And God ^Rlooked upon the earth, and, behold, it was corrupt; for all flesh had corrupted his way upon the earth.   Ps. 14:2

13 And God said unto Noah, The end of all flesh is come before me; for the earth is filled with violence through them; and, behold, I will destroy them with the earth.

14 Make thee an ark of go'-pher wood; rooms shalt thou make in the ark, and shalt pitch it within and without with pitch.

15 And this *is the fashion* which thou shalt make it *of:* The length of the ark *shall be* three hundred cubits, the breadth of it fifty cubits, and the height of it thirty cubits.

16 A window shalt thou make to the ark, and in a ^Tcubit shalt thou finish it above; and the door of the ark shalt thou set in the side thereof; *with* lower, second, and third *stories* shalt thou make it.   *1.5 ft.*

17 ^RAnd, behold, I, even I, do bring a ^Rflood of waters upon the earth, to destroy all flesh, wherein *is* the breath of life, from under heaven; *and* every thing that *is* in the earth shall die.   7:4, 21–23 · 2 Pet. 3:6

18 But with thee will I establish my covenant; and ^Rthou shalt come into the ark, thou, and thy sons, and thy wife, and thy sons' wives with thee.   7:1, 7, 13; 2 Pet. 2:5

19 And of every living thing of all flesh, ^Rtwo of every *sort* shalt thou bring into the

ark, to keep *them* alive with thee; they shall be male and female.   7:8, 9, 15, 16

20 Of fowls after their kind, and of cattle after their kind, of every creeping thing of the earth after his kind, two of every *sort* shall come unto thee, to keep *them* alive.

21 And take thou unto thee of all food that is eaten, and thou shalt gather *it* to thee; and it shall be for food for thee, and for them.

22 Thus did Noah; ᴿaccording to all that God commanded him, so did he.   7:5, 9, 16

CHAPTER 7

The Ark Is Entered

AND the ᴿLᴏʀᴅ said unto Noah, Come thou and all thy house into the ark; for ᴿthee have I seen righteous before me in this generation.   Matt. 11:28; 2 Pet. 2:5 · 2 Pet. 2:9

2 Of every ᴿclean beast thou shalt take to thee by sevens, the male and his female: ᴿand of beasts that *are* not clean by two, the male and his female.   Lev. 11:1-31 · Lev. 10:10

3 Of fowls also of the air by sevens, the male and the female; to keep ᵀseed alive upon the face of all the earth.   *offspring*

4 For yet seven days, and I will cause it to rain upon the earth ᴿforty days and forty nights; and every living ᵀsubstance that I have made will I ᵀdestroy from off the face of the earth.   *vv.* 12, 17 · *thing* · *blot out*

5 ᴿAnd Noah did according unto all that the Lᴏʀᴅ commanded him.   6:22

6 And Noah *was* ᴿsix hundred years old when the flood of waters ᵀwas upon the earth.   5:32 · *came*

7 And Noah went in, and his sons, and his wife, and his sons' wives with him, into the ark, because of the waters of the flood.

8 Of ᴿclean beasts, and of beasts that *are* not clean, and of fowls, and of every thing that creepeth upon the earth,   *vv.* 2, 3

9 There went in two and two unto Noah into the ark, the male and the female, as God had commanded Noah.

10 And it came to pass ᵀafter seven days, that the waters of the flood ᵀwere upon the earth.   *on the seventh day* · *came*

The Earth Is Flooded

11 In the six hundredth year of Noah's life, in the second month, the seventeenth day of the month, the same day were all the fountains of the great deep broken up, and the windows of heaven were opened.

12 ᴿAnd the rain ᵀwas upon the earth forty days and forty nights.   *vv.* 4, 17 · *fell*

13 In the selfsame day entered ᴿNoah, and Shem, and Ham, and Ja'-pheth, the sons of Noah, and Noah's wife, and the three wives of his sons with them, into the ark;   *v.* 7

14 They, and every beast after his kind, and all the cattle after ᵀtheir kind, and every creeping thing that creepeth upon the earth after his kind, and every fowl after his kind, every bird of every ᵀsort.   *its* · *wing*

15 And they ᴿwent in unto Noah into the ark, ᴿtwo and two of all flesh, wherein *is* the breath of life.   6:20 · *v.* 9

16 And they that went in, went in male and female of all flesh, as God had commanded him: and the Lᴏʀᴅ shut him in.

17 And the flood was forty days upon the earth; and the waters increased, and bare up the ark, and it was lift up above the earth.

18 And the waters prevailed, and were increased greatly upon the earth; and the ark ᵀwent upon the face of the waters.   *floated*

19 And the waters prevailed exceedingly upon the earth; and all the high hills, that *were* under the whole heaven, were covered.

20 Fifteen cubits upward did the waters prevail; and the mountains were covered.

21 And all flesh died that moved upon the earth, both of fowl, and of cattle, and of beast, and of every creeping thing that creepeth upon the earth, and every man:

22 All in whose nostrils *was* the breath of life, of all that *was* in the dry *land*, died.

23 And every living substance was destroyed which was upon the face of the ground, both man, and cattle, and the creeping things, and the fowl of the heaven; and they were destroyed from the earth: and ᴿNoah only remained *alive*, and they that *were* with him in the ark.   2 Pet. 2:5

24 ᴿAnd the waters prevailed upon the earth an hundred and fifty days.   8:3, 4

CHAPTER 8

The Flood Recedes

AND God ᴿremembered Noah, and every living thing, and all the cattle that *was* with him in the ark: ᴿand God made a wind to pass over the earth, and the waters ᵀassuaged;   Ex. 2:24; Ps. 106:4 · Ex. 14:21 · *lowered*

2 The fountains also of the deep and the windows of heaven were stopped, and ᴿthe rain from heaven was restrained;   Job 38:37

3 And the waters ᵀreturned from off the earth continually: and after the end ᴿof the hundred and fifty days the waters were ᵀabated.   *receded* · 7:24 · *gone away*

4 And the ark rested in the seventh month, on the seventeenth day of the month, upon the mountains of Ar'-a-rat.

5 And the waters ᵀdecreased continually until the tenth month: in the tenth *month*, on the first *day* of the month, were the tops of the mountains seen.   *became less*

6 And it came to pass at the end of forty

days, that Noah opened ᴿthe window of the ark which he had made: 6:16

7 And he sent forth a raven, which ᵀwent forth to and fro, until the waters were dried up from off the earth.   *flew here and there*

8 Also he sent forth a ᴿdove from him, to see if the waters were abated from off the face of the ground;   Ps. 55:6

9 But the dove found no rest for the sole of her foot, and she returned unto him into the ark, for the waters *were* on the ᵀface of the whole earth: then he put forth his hand, and took her, and ᵀpulled her in unto him into the ark.   *surface · brought her*

10 And he ᵀstayed yet other seven days; and again he sent forth the dove out of the ark;   *held back*

11 And the dove came in to him in the evening; and, lo, in her mouth *was* an olive leaf pluckt off: so Noah knew that the waters were abated from off the earth.

12 And he stayed yet other seven days; and sent forth ᴿthe dove; which returned not again unto him any more.   Jer. 48:28

13 And it came to pass in the six hundredth and first year, in the first *month*, the first *day* of the month, the waters were dried up from off the earth: and Noah removed the covering of the ark, and looked, and, behold, the face of the ground was dry.

14 And in the second month, on the seven and twentieth day of the month, was the earth dried.

15 And God spake unto Noah, saying,

16 Go ᴿforth of the ark, ᴿthou, and thy wife, and thy sons, and thy sons' wives with thee.   Ps. 121:8 · 7:13

17 Bring forth with thee every living thing that *is* with thee, of all flesh, *both* of fowl, and of cattle, and of every creeping thing that creepeth upon the earth; that they may breed abundantly in the earth, and ᴿbe fruitful, and multiply upon the earth.   1:22, 28

18 And Noah went forth, and his sons, and his wife, and his sons' wives with him:

19 Every beast, every ᵀcreeping thing, and every fowl, *and* whatsoever creepeth upon the earth, after their ᵀkinds, went forth out of the ark.   *moving · families*

Noah Worships God

20 And Noah builded an altar unto the LORD; and took of ᴿevery clean beast, and of every clean fowl, and offered ᴿburnt offerings on the altar.   Lev. 11 · Ex. 10:25

21 And the LORD smelled a sweet savour; and the LORD said in his heart, I will not again curse the ground any more for man's sake; for the imagination of man's heart *is* evil from his youth; neither will I again smite any more every thing living, as I have done.

22 While the earth remaineth, seedtime and harvest, and cold and heat, and summer and winter, and day and night shall not cease.

CHAPTER 9

God's Covenant with Noah

AND God blessed Noah and his sons, and said unto them, ᴿBe fruitful, and multiply, and ᵀreplenish the earth.   1:28 · *fill up*

2 ᴿAnd the fear of you and the dread of you shall be upon every beast of the earth, and upon every fowl of the air, upon all that moveth *upon* the earth, and upon all the fishes of the sea; into your hand are they delivered.   1:26; Ps. 8:6; Hos. 2:18

3 ᴿEvery moving thing that liveth shall be ᵀmeat for you; even as the green herb have I given you all things.   1:29; [1 Tim. 4:3, 4] · *food*

4 But flesh with the life thereof, *which is* the ᴿblood thereof, shall ye not eat.   Lev. 17:10

9:1–19 The Noahic Covenant—The covenant with Noah is the third general or universal covenant. Noah has just passed through the universal flood in which all the world's population had been wiped out. Only Noah, his wife, his three sons, and their wives—eight people—constitute the world's population. Noah might have thought that the things provided by the covenant with Adam had now been changed. However, God gives the Noahic Covenant so that Noah and all the human race to follow might know that the provisions made in the Adamic Covenant remain in effect with one notable addition: the principle of human government which includes the responsibility of suppressing the outbreak of sin and violence, so that it will not be necessary to destroy the earth again by a flood. The provisions of the covenant are:

a. The responsibility to populate the earth is reaffirmed (v. 1).
b. The subjection of the animal kingdom to man is reaffirmed (v. 2).
c. Man is permitted to eat the flesh of animals. However, he is to refrain from eating blood (vv. 3, 4).
d. The sacredness of human life is established. Whatever sheds man's blood, whether man or beast, must be put to death (vv. 5, 6).
e. This covenant is confirmed to Noah, all mankind, and every living creature on the face of the earth (vv. 9, 10).
f. The promise is given never to destroy the earth again by a universal flood (v. 11). The next time God destroys the earth, the means will be fire (Page 1244—2 Pet. 3:10).
g. The rainbow is designated as a testimony of the existence of this covenant and the promise never to destroy the earth by flood. As long as we can see the rainbow we will know that the Noahic Covenant is in existence (vv. 12–17).

Now turn to Page 14—Gen. 12:1–3: The Abrahamic Covenant.

5 And surely your blood of your lives will ᵀI require; at the hand of every beast will I require it, and at the hand of man; at the hand of every man's brother will I require the life of man.   *I will hold you responsible*

6 ᴿWhoso sheddeth man's blood, by man shall his blood be shed: ᴿfor in the image of God made he man.   Matt. 26:52 · 1:27

7 And you, ᴿbe ye fruitful, and multiply; bring forth abundantly in the earth, and ᵀmultiply therein.   *vv.* 1, 19 · *became many*

8 And God spake unto Noah, and to his sons with him, saying,

9 And I, behold, I establish my covenant with you, and with your seed after you;

10 And with every living creature that *is* with you, of the fowl, of the cattle, and of every beast of the earth with you; from all that go out of the ark, to every beast of the earth.

11 And I will establish my covenant with you; neither shall all flesh be cut off any more by the waters of a flood; neither shall there any more be a flood to destroy the earth.

12 And God said, This *is* the ᴿtoken of the ᵀcovenant which I make between me and you and every living creature that *is* with you, for perpetual generations: *v.* 13 · *promise*

13 I do set ᴿmy bow in the cloud, and it shall be for a token of a covenant between me and the earth.   Ezek. 1:28; Rev. 4:3

14 And it shall come to pass, when I bring a cloud over the earth, that the ᵀbow shall be seen in the cloud: *rainbow*

15 And I will remember my covenant, which *is* between me and you and every living creature of all flesh; and the waters shall no more become a flood to destroy all flesh.

16 And the bow shall be in the cloud; and I will look upon it, that I may remember ᴿthe everlasting covenant between God and every living creature of all flesh that *is* upon the earth.   17:13, 19; Jer. 32:40; Heb. 13:20

17 And God said unto Noah, This *is* the ᵀtoken of the covenant, which I have established between me and all flesh that *is* upon the earth.   *sign*

The Sons of Noah

18 And the sons of Noah, that went forth of the ark, were Shem, and Ham, and Ja′-pheth: and Ham *is* the father of Canaan.

19 These *are* the three sons of Noah: and of them was the whole earth overspread.

Ham's Sin

20 And Noah began *to be* ᴿan husbandman, and he planted a vineyard: 3:19, 23

21 And he drank of the wine, ᴿand was drunken; and he was uncovered within his tent.   Prov. 20:1; Eph. 5:18

22 And Ham, the father of Canaan, saw the nakedness of his father, and told his two brethren ᵀwithout.   *outside*

23 And Shem and Ja′-pheth took a garment, and laid *it* upon both their shoulders, and ᵀwent backward, and covered the nakedness of their father; and their faces *were* ᵀbackward, and they saw not their father's nakedness.   *walked · turned away*

24 And Noah awoke from his wine, and knew what his ᵀyounger son had done unto him.   *youngest*

The Curse on Canaan

25 And he said, Cursed *be* Canaan; a servant of servants shall he be unto his brethren.

26 And he said, Blessed *be* the Lᴏʀᴅ God of Shem; and Canaan shall be his servant.

27 God shall enlarge Ja′-pheth, ᴿand he shall dwell in the tents of Shem; and Canaan shall be his servant.   Luke 3:36; John 1:14

Noah's Death

28 And Noah lived after the flood three hundred and fifty years.

29 And all the days of Noah were nine hundred and fifty years: and he died.

9:5 The Origin of Human Government—It has been assumed that human government was officially instituted after the great Flood in Genesis 9. However, some form of law and order undoubtedly existed prior to this period. This is strongly suggested by both Jesus and Jude. Jesus in Luke 17:26, 27 says that prior to the Flood in Noah's day people conducted their affairs in much the same manner as we do today. Jude gives us the text of a message Enoch preached to sinners prior to the Flood. (Page 1262—Jude 14, 15). We learn that one of the main factors which brought about the Flood was man's disobedience to the revealed law of God.

At any rate, there is certainly no doubt concerning the source of human government. God Himself is its divine author. Two individuals give testimony to this fact. Daniel reminds King Nebuchadnezzar that "the most High ruleth in the kingdom of men, and giveth it to whomsoever he will" (Page 827—Dan. 4:25). The apostle Paul exhorts Christians to be subject to the laws of human government because all earthly powers exist through God's divine permission (Page 1119—Rom. 13).

If one rightly understands the origin of human government, then the conclusion is reached that lawless anarchy is not only rebellion against human authority, but actual blasphemy against the divine Creator Himself.

Now turn to Page 1119—Rom. 13:1–4: The Function of Human Government.

CHAPTER 10

The Family of Japheth—1 Chr. 1:5–7

NOW these *are* the generations of the sons of Noah, Shem, Ham, and Ja'-pheth: ᴿand unto them were sons born after the flood.   9:1, 7, 19

2 The sons of Ja'-pheth; Go'-mer, and Ma'-gog, and Ma'-dai, and Ja'-van, and Tu'-bal, and Me'-shech, and Ti'-ras.

3 And the sons of Go'-mer; Ash'-ke-naz, and Ri'-phath, and To-gar'-mah.

4 And the sons of Ja'-van; E-li'-shah, and Tar'-shish, Kit'-tim, and ᵀDod'-a-nim. *Rodanim*

5 By these were the isles of the Gentiles divided in their lands; every one after his tongue, after their families, in their nations.

The Family of Ham—1 Chr. 1:8–12

6 ᴿAnd the sons of Ham; Cush, and Miz'-ra-im, and Phut, and Canaan.   1 Chr. 1:8

7 ᴿAnd the sons of Cush; Se'-ba, and Hav'-i-lah, and Sab'-tah, and Ra'-a-mah, and Sab'-te-chah: and the sons of Ra'-a-mah; She'-ba, and De'-dan.   1 Chr. 1:10

8 And Cush ᵀbegat Nimrod: he began to be a mighty one in the earth.   *fathered*

9 He was a mighty hunter before the LORD: wherefore it is said, Even as Nimrod the mighty hunter before the LORD.

10 And the beginning of his ᴿkingdom was Babel, and E'-rech, and Ac'-cad, and Cal'-neh, in the land of Shi'-nar.   Mic. 5:6

11 Out of that land ᵀwent forth Assh'-ur, and builded Nin'-e-veh, and the city Re-ho'-both, and Ca'-lah,   *he went forth into Assyria*

12 And Re'-sen between Nin'-e-veh and Ca'-lah: the same *is* a great city.

13 And Miz'-ra-im ᵀbegat Lu'-dim, and An'-a-mim, and Le'-ha-bim, and Naph'-tu-him,   *became the father of*

14 And Path-ru'-sim, and Cas'-lu-him, (ᴿout of whom came ᵀPhi-lis'-tim,) and Caph'-to-rim.   1 Chr. 1:12 • *Philistines*

The Family of Canaan—1 Chr. 1:13–16

15 ᴿAnd Canaan begat Si'-don his first-born, and ᴿHeth,   Jer. 47:4; 1 Chr. 1:13 • 23:3

16 And ᴿthe Jeb'-u-site, and the Am'-or-ite, ᴿand the Gir'-ga-site,   15:19–21 • Neh. 9:8

17 ᴿAnd the Hi'-vite, and the Ark'-ite, and the Si'-nite,   1 Chr. 1:15

18 ᴿAnd the Ar'-vad-ite, and the Zem'-a-rite, and the Ha'-math-ite: and afterward were the families of the Ca'-naan-ites spread abroad.   1 Chr. 1:16

19 ᴿAnd the border of the Ca'-naan-ites was from Si'-don, as thou comest to Ge'-rar, unto ᵀGa'-za; as thou goest, unto Sodom, and Go-mor'-rah, and Ad'-mah, and Ze-bo'-im, even unto La'-sha.   13:12, 14 • *Azzah*

20 These *are* the sons of Ham, ᵀafter their families, after their tongues, ᵀin their countries, *and* in their nations. *according to • by*

The Family of Shem—1 Chr. 1:17–23

21 Unto Shem also, the father of all the children of E'-ber, the brother of Ja'-pheth the elder, even to him were *children* born.

22 The children of Shem; E'-lam, and Assh'-ur, and Ar-phax'-ad, and Lud, and A'-ram.

23 And the children of A'-ram; ᴿUz, and Hul, and Ge'-ther, and Mash.   Job 1:1

24 And Ar-phax'-ad ᵀbegat ᴿSa'-lah;ᵀ and Sa'-lah begat E'-ber.   *fathered • 11:12 • Shelah*

25 ᴿAnd unto E'-ber were born two sons: the name of one *was* ᵀPe'-leg; for in his days was the earth divided; and his brother's name *was* Jok'-tan.   1 Chr. 1:19 • *division*

26 And Jok'-tan begat Al-mo'-dad, and She'-leph, and Ha'-zar-ma'-veth, and Je'-rah,

27 And Ha-do'-ram, and U'-zal, and Dik'-lah,

28 And ᴿO'-bal,ᵀ and A-bim'-a-el, and She'-ba,   1 Chr. 1:22 • *Ebal*

29 And O'-phir, and Hav'-i-lah, and Jo'-bab: all these *were* the sons of Jok'-tan.

30 And their ᵀdwelling ᵀwas from Me'-sha, as ᵀthou goest unto Se'-phar a mount of the east.   *community • extended • you go*

31 These *are* the sons of Shem, ᵀafter their families, after their tongues, ᵀin their lands, after their nations.   *according to • by*

32 These *are* the families of the sons of Noah, after their generations, in their nations: ᴿand by these were the nations divided in the earth after the flood.   9:19

CHAPTER 11

Construction of the Tower

AND the whole earth was of one language, and of one speech.

2 And it came to pass, as they journeyed from the east, that they found a plain in the land of Shi'-nar; and they dwelt there.

3 And they said one to another, Go to, let us make brick, and burn them throughly. And they had brick for stone, and slime had they for morter.

Rebellion at the Tower

4 And they said, Go to, let us build us a city and a tower, ᴿwhose top *may reach* unto heaven; and let us make us a name, lest we be scattered abroad upon the face of the whole earth.   Deut. 1:28

Judgment on All the Family Lines

5 ᴿAnd the LORD came down to see the city and the tower, which the children of men builded.   18:21; Ex. 3:8; 19:11, 18, 20; Ps. 53:2

6 And the LORD said, Behold, Rthe people Tis one, and they have all Rone language; and this they begin to do: and now nothing will be restrained from them, which they have Rimagined to do.   9:19 • are • v. 1 • Ps. 2:1

7 Go to, let us go down, and there Tconfound their language, that they may not understand one another's speech.   confuse

8 So Rthe LORD scattered them abroad from thence upon the face of all the earth: and they left off to build the city.   [Luke 1:51]

9 Therefore is the name of it called TBabel; because the LORD did there confound the language of all the earth: and from Tthence did the LORD scatter them abroad upon the face of all the earth.   confusion • there

Abram's Family Line
1 Chr. 1:24–27; Luke 3:34–36

10 These are the generations of Shem: Shem was an hundred years old, and begat Ar-phax'-ad two years after the flood:

11 And Shem lived after he Tbegat Ar-phax'-ad five hundred years, and begat sons and daughters.   became the father of

12 And Ar-phax'-ad lived five and thirty years, Rand begat Sa'-lah: Luke 3:35

13 And Ar-phax'-ad lived after he begat Sa'-lah four hundred and three years, and begat sons and daughters.

14 And Sa'-lah lived thirty years, and begat E'-ber:

15 And Sa'-lah lived after he begat E'-ber four hundred and three years, and begat sons and daughters.

16 RAnd E'-ber lived four and thirty years, and begat RPe'-leg: 1 Chr. 1:19 • Luke 3:35

17 And E'-ber lived after he begat Pe'-leg four hundred and thirty years, and begat sons and daughters.

18 And Pe'-leg lived thirty years, and begat Re'-u:

19 And Pe'-leg lived after he begat Re'-u two hundred and nine years, and begat sons and daughters.

20 And Re'-u lived two and thirty years, and begat RSe'-rug: Luke 3:35

21 And Re'-u lived after he begat Se'-rug two hundred and seven years, and begat sons and daughters.

22 And Se'-rug lived thirty years, and begat Na'-hor:

23 And Se'-rug lived after he begat Na'-hor two hundred years, and begat sons and daughters.

24 And Na'-hor lived nine and twenty years, and begat RTe'-rah: Josh. 24:2; Luke 3:34

25 And Na'-hor lived after he begat Te'-rah an hundred and nineteen years, and begat sons and daughters.

26 And Te'-rah lived seventy years, and Rbegat Abram, Na'-hor, and Ha'-ran. Josh. 24:2

Abram's Past

27 Now these are the generations of Te'-rah: Te'-rah begat Abram, Na'-hor, and Ha'-ran; and Ha'-ran begat Lot.

28 And Ha'-ran died Tbefore his father Te'-rah in the land of his nativity, in Ur of the RChal'-dees.   during his father's lifetime • Ezek. 11:24

29 And Abram and Na'-hor took them wives: the name of Abram's wife was Sa'-rai; and the name of Na'-hor's wife, Mil'-cah, the daughter of Ha'-ran, the father of Mil'-cah, and the father of Is'-cah.

30 But RSa'-rai was barren; she had no child.   16:1, 2; Luke 1:36

31 And Te'-rah Rtook Abram his son, and Lot the son of Ha'-ran his son's son, and Sa'-rai his daughter in law, his son Abram's wife; and they went forth with them from RUr of the Chal'-dees, to go into Rthe land of Ca-naan; and they came unto Ha'-ran, and dwelt there.   12:1 • Neh. 9:7 • 10:19

32 And the days of Te'-rah were two hundred and five years: and Te'-rah died in Ha'-ran.

CHAPTER 12

Initiation of the Covenant

NOW the RLORD had said unto Abram, Get thee out of thy country, and from thy kindred, and from thy father's house, unto a land that I will shew thee: [Heb. 11:8]

2 RAnd I will make of thee a great nation, and I will bless thee, and make thy name great; and thou shalt be a blessing: Gal. 3:8 ☆

12:1–3 The Abrahamic Covenant—The covenant with Abraham is the first of the theocratic covenants (pertaining to the rule of God). It is unconditional, depending solely upon God who obligates Himself in grace, indicated by the unconditional declaration, "I will," to bring to pass the promised blessings. The Abrahamic Covenant is the basis of all the other theocratic covenants and provides for blessings in three areas: (1) national—"I will make of thee a great nation," (2) personal—"I will bless thee, and make thy name great; and thou shalt be a blessing," and (3) universal—"in thee shall all families of the earth be blessed." This covenant was first given in broad outline and was later confirmed to Abraham in greater detail (cf. Page 16—Gen. 13:14–17; 15:1–7, 18–21; 17:1–8). The Abrahamic Covenant constitutes an important link in all that God began to do, has done throughout history, and will continue to do until the consummation of history. It is the one purpose of God for humans into which all of God's programs and works fit. The personal aspects of the Abrahamic Covenant are fourfold: (1) to be the father of a great nation, (2) to receive personal blessing, (3) to receive personal

3 And I will bless them that bless thee, and curse him that curseth thee: and in thee shall all families of the earth be blessed.

4 So Abram departed, as the LORD had spoken unto him; and Lot went with him: and Abram was seventy and five years old when he departed out of ᴿHa'-ran.   11:31

5 And Abram took Sa'-rai his wife, and Lot his brother's son, and all their substance that they had gathered, and the ᵀsouls that they had gotten ᴿin Ha'-ran; and they went forth to go into the land of Canaan; and into the land of Canaan they came.   persons • 11:31

6 And Abram ᴿpassed through the land unto the place of Si'-chem, ᴿunto the plain of Mo'-reh. ᴿAnd the Ca'-naan-ite was then in the land.   Heb. 11:9 • Deut. 11:30 • 10:18, 19

7 And the LORD appeared unto Abram, and said, Unto thy seed will I give this land: and there builded he an altar unto the LORD, who appeared unto him.

8 And he removed from thence unto a mountain on the east of Beth'-el, and pitched his tent, having Beth'-el on the west, and Ha'-i on the east: and there he builded an altar unto the LORD, and ᴿcalled ᵀupon the name of the LORD.   13:4 • prayed to

9 And Abram journeyed, going on still toward ᴿthe ᵀsouth.   13:1, 3, 14; Dan. 8:4, 9 • Negev

10 And there was ᴿa famine in the land: and Abram went down into Egypt to ᵀsojourn there; for the famine was ᴿgrievous in the land.   26:1 • to live there for a while • 43:1

11 And it came to pass, when he was come near to enter into Egypt, that he said unto Sa'-rai his wife, Behold now, I know that thou art ᴿa fair woman to look upon: 26:7

12 Therefore it shall come to pass, when the Egyptians shall see thee, that they shall say, This is his wife: and they ᴿwill kill me, but they will save thee alive.   20:11; 26:7

13 Say, I pray thee, thou art my sister: that it may be well with me for thy sake; and my soul shall live because of thee.

14 And it came to pass, that, when Abram was come into Egypt, the Egyptians ᵀbeheld the woman that she was very fair.   saw

15 The princes also of Pharaoh saw her, and commended her before Pharaoh: and the woman was taken into Pharaoh's house.

16 And ᵀhe entreated Abram well for her sake: and he ᵀhad sheep, and oxen, and he asses, and menservants, and maidservants, and she asses, and camels.   treated • gave him

17 And the LORD ᴿplagued Pharaoh and his house with great plagues because of Sa'-rai Abram's wife.   1 Chr. 16:21; [Ps. 105:14]

18 And Pharaoh called Abram, and said, ᴿWhat is this that thou hast done unto me? why ᵀdidst thou not tell me that she was thy wife?   20:9, 10; 26:10 • did you

19 Why ᵀsaidst thou, She is my sister? ᵀso I might have taken her to me to wife: now therefore behold thy wife, take her, and go thy way.   did you say • so I took her to be my wife

20 ᴿAnd Pharaoh commanded his men concerning him: and they sent him away, and his wife, and all that he had.   [Prov. 21:1]

CHAPTER 13

Abram's Separation from Lot

A ND Abram went up out of Egypt, he, and his wife, and all that he had, and Lot with him, ᴿinto the ᵀsouth.   12:9 • Negev

2 ᴿAnd Abram was very ᴿrich in cattle, in silver, and in gold.   Ps. 112:3; Prov. 10:22 • 24:35

3 And he went ᵀon his journeys ᴿfrom the ᵀsouth even to Beth'-el, unto the place where his tent had been at the beginning, between Beth'-el and Ha'-i;   by stages • 12:8, 9 • Negev

4 Unto the place of the altar, which he had made there at the first: and there Abram called on the name of the LORD.

5 And Lot also, ᵀwhich went with ᴿAbram, had flocks, and herds, and tents.   who • 12:5

6 And ᴿthe land was not able to ᵀbear them, that they might dwell together: for their ᵀsubstance was great, so that they could not dwell together.   36:7 • sustain • wealth

7 And there was a strife between the herdmen of Abram's cattle and the herdmen of Lot's cattle: and the Ca'-naan-ite and the Per'-iz-zite dwelled then in the land.

8 And Abram said unto Lot, ᴿLet there be no strife, I pray thee, between me and thee, and between my herdmen and thy herdmen; for we be ᵀbrethren.   [Phil. 2:14, 15] • relatives

9 Is not the whole land before thee? separate thyself, I pray thee, from me: ᴿif thou wilt take the left hand, then I will go to the right; or if thou depart to the right hand, then I will go to the left.   [Rom. 12:18]

10 And Lot lifted up his eyes, and beheld all the plain of Jordan, that it was well watered every where, before the LORD destroyed Sodom and Go-mor'-rah, ᴿeven as the

---

honor and reputation, and (4) to be the source of blessing to others. The universal aspects of the covenant are threefold: (1) blessings for those people and nations which bless Abraham and the nation which comes from him; (2) cursings upon those people and nations which curse Abraham and Israel; and (3) blessings upon all the families of the earth through the Messiah, who, according to the flesh, is Abraham's son and provides salvation for the entire world.

Now turn to Page 74—Ex. 19:5-8: The Mosaic Covenant.

garden of the LORD, like the land of Egypt, as thou comest unto Zo'-ar.   Is. 51:3

11 Then Lot chose him all the plain of Jordan; and Lot journeyed east: and they separated themselves the one from the other.

12 Abram dwelled in the land of Canaan, and Lot dwelled in the cities of the plain, and pitched *his* tent toward Sodom.

13 But the men of Sodom *were* wicked and sinners before the LORD exceedingly.

God's Promise to Abram

14 And the LORD said unto Abram, after that Lot ᴿwas separated from him, Lift up now thine eyes, and look from the place where thou art ᴿnorthward, and southward, and eastward, and westward: v. 11 • 28:14

15 For all the land which thou seest, to thee will I give it, and to thy seed for ever.

16 And I will make thy ᵀseedᴿ as the dust of the earth: so that if a man can number the dust of the earth, *then* shall thy seed also be numbered.   *descendants* • Num. 23:10

17 Arise, ᴿwalk through the land in the length of it and in the breadth of it; for ᴿI will give it unto thee.   Num. 13:17–24 • v. 15

18 Then Abram removed *his* tent, and came and dwelt ᵀin the plain of Mam'-re, ᴿwhich *is* in He'-bron, and built there ᴿan altar unto the LORD.   *by the oaks* • 35:27 • 8:20

CHAPTER 14

Abram Rescues Lot

AND it came to pass in the days of Am'-ra-phel king of Shi'-nar, A'-ri-och king of El'-la-sar, Ched-or-la'-o-mer king of E'-lam, and Ti'-dal king of nations;

2 *That these* made war with Be'-ra king of Sodom, and with Bir'-sha king of Go-mor'-rah, Shi'-nab king of ᴿAd'-mah, and Shem-e'-ber king of Ze-boi'-im, and the king of Be'-la, which is Zo'-ar.   Deut. 29:23

3 All these were joined together in the vale of Sid'-dim, which is the salt sea.

4 Twelve years they served Ched-or-la'-o-mer, and in the thirteenth year they rebelled.

5 And in the fourteenth year came Ched-or-la'-o-mer, and the kings that *were* with him, and smote the Reph'-a-ims in Ash'-te-roth Kar-na'-im, and the Zu'-zims in Ham, and the E'-mims in Sha'-veh Kir-i-a-tha'-im,

6 And the Ho'-rites in their mount Se'-ir, unto El-pa'-ran, which *is* by the wilderness.

7 And they returned, and came to En-mish'-pat, which *is* ᴿKa'-desh, and ᵀsmote all the country of the Am'-a-lek-ites, and also the Am'-or-ites, that dwelt ᴿin Haz'-e-zon-ta'-mar.   Num. 13:26 • *subdued* • 2 Chr. 20:2

8 And there went out the king of Sodom, and the king of Go-mor'-rah, and the king of Ad'-mah, and the king of Ze-boi'-im, and the

king of Be'-la (the same *is* Zo'-ar;) and they joined battle with them in the ᴿvaleᵀ of Sid'-dim;   v. 3 • *valley*

9 With Ched-or-la'-o-mer the king of E'-lam, and with Ti'-dal king of nations, and Am'-ra-phel king of Shi'-nar, and A'-ri-och king of El'-la-sar; four kings ᵀwith five. *against*

10 And the vale of Sid'-dim *was full of* ᴿslimepits; and the kings of Sodom and Go-mor'-rah fled, and fell there; and they that remained fled to the mountain.   11:3

11 And they took ᴿall the goods of Sodom and Go-mor'-rah, and all their ᵀvictuals, and went their way.   vv. 16, 21 • *food*

12 And they took Lot, Abram's ᴿbrother's son, ᴿwho dwelt in Sodom, and his goods, and departed.   11:27; 12:5 • 13:12

13 And there came one that had escaped, and told Abram the Hebrew; for he dwelt in the plain of Mam'-re the Am'-or-ite, brother of Esh'-col, and brother of A'-ner: and these *were* confederate with Abram.

14 And when Abram heard that his brother was taken captive, he ᵀarmed his ᵀtrained *servants,* ᴿborn in his own house, three hundred and eighteen, and pursued *them* unto Dan.   *led forth • instructed* • Eccl. 2:7

15 And he divided himself against them, he and his servants, by night, and smote them, and pursued them unto Ho'-bah, which *is* on the left hand of Damascus.

16 And he brought back all the goods, and also brought again his brother Lot, and his goods, and the women also, and the people.

Abram Refuses Reward

17 And the king of Sodom went out to meet him after his return from the slaughter of Ched-or-la'-o-mer, and of the kings that *were* with him, at the valley of Sha'-veh, which *is* the king's dale.

18 And Mel-chiz'-e-dek king of Sa'-lem brought forth bread and wine: and he *was* the priest of ᴿthe most high God.   Acts 16:17

19 And he blessed him, and said, Blessed *be* Abram of the most high God, ᴿpossessor of heaven and earth: v. 22

20 And blessed be the most high God, which hath delivered thine enemies into thy hand. ᴿAnd he gave him tithes of all. [Heb. 7:4]

21 And the king of Sodom said unto Abram, Give me the ᵀpersons, and take the goods to thyself.   *living people*

22 And Abram said to the king of Sodom, I ᴿhave ᵀlift up mine hand unto the LORD, the most high God, ᴿthe possessor of heaven and earth,   Dan. 12:7 • *solemnly promised* • v. 19

23 That I will not *take* from a thread even to a shoelatchet, and that I will not take any thing that *is* thine, lest thou shouldest say, I have made Abram rich:

24 Save only that which the young men have eaten, and the portion of the men which

went with me, ^RA'-ner, Esh'-col, and Mam'-re; let them take their portion.   v. 13

CHAPTER 15

God's Promise of Children

AFTER these things the word of the LORD came unto Abram ^Rin a vision, saying, Fear not, Abram: I *am* thy shield, *and* thy exceeding great reward.   Dan. 10:1

2 And Abram said, Lord GOD, what wilt thou give me, ^Rseeing I ^Tgo childless, and the steward of my house *is* this E-li-e'-zer of Damascus?   [17:18; Hab. 3:1; Acts 7:5] · *am*

3 And Abram said, Behold, to me thou hast given no seed: and, lo, ^Tone born in my house is mine heir.   *one of my servants*

4 And, behold, the word of the LORD *came* unto him, saying, This shall not be thine heir; but he that shall come forth out of thine own ^Tbowels shall be thine heir.   *body*

5 And he brought him forth abroad, and said, Look now toward heaven, and tell the stars, if thou be able to number them: and he said unto him, ^RSo shall thy seed be. Deut. 1:10

6 And he ^Rbelieved in the LORD; and he counted it to him for righteousness.   Gal. 3:6

7 And he said unto him, I *am* the LORD that brought thee out of Ur of the Chal'-dees, to give thee this land to inherit it.

8 And he said, Lord GOD, ^Rwhereby shall I know that I shall inherit it?   24:13, 14

9 And he said unto him, Take me an heifer of three years old, and a she goat of three years old, and a ram of three years old, and a turtledove, and a young pigeon.

10 And he took unto him all these, and ^Rdivided^T them in the midst, and laid each piece one against another: but ^Rthe birds divided he not. Jer. 34:18 · *cut them in twain* · Lev. 1:17

11 And when the fowls came down upon the carcases, Abram drove them away.

12 And when the sun was going down, a deep sleep fell upon Abram; and, lo, an horror of great darkness fell upon him.

13 And he said unto Abram, Know of a surety ^Rthat thy seed shall be a ^Tstranger in a land *that is* not their's, and shall serve them; and ^Rthey shall afflict them four hundred years;   Ex. 1:11 · *sojourner* · Ex. 12:40; Acts 7:6

14 And also that nation, whom they shall serve, ^Rwill I judge: and afterward shall they come out with great substance.   [Ex. 6:6]

15 And thou shalt go to thy fathers in peace; thou shalt be buried in a good old age.

16 But in the fourth generation they shall come hither again: ^Rfor the iniquity of the Am'-or-ites *is* not yet full.   [Matt. 23:31, 32]

17 And it came to pass, that, when the sun went down, and it was dark, behold a smoking furnace, and ^Ta burning lamp that passed between those pieces.   *flaming torch*

18 In the same day the LORD made a covenant with Abram, saying, Unto thy seed have I given this land, from the river of Egypt unto the great river, the river Eu-phra'-tes:

19 The ^RKen'-ites, and the Ken'-iz-zites, and the Kad'-mon-ites,   Josh. 21:43; Acts 13:19

20 And the ^RHit'-tites, and the Per'-iz-zites, and the Reph'-a-ims,   2 Kin. 7:6

21 And the Am'-or-ites, and the Ca'-naan-ites, and the Gir'-ga-shites, and the Jeb'-u-sites.

CHAPTER 16

A Carnal Plan for Children

NOW ^RSa'-rai Abram's wife bare him no children: and she had an handmaid, an Egyptian, whose name *was* Ha'-gar.   11:30

2 And Sa'-rai said unto Abram, Behold now, the LORD hath restrained me from bearing: I pray thee, ^Rgo in unto my maid; it may be that I may ^Tobtain children by her. And Abram ^Rhearkened to the voice of Sa'-rai.   30:3, 9 · *be builded by her* · 3:17

3 And Sa'-rai Abram's wife took ^RHa'-gar her maid the Egyptian, after Abram ^Rhad ^Tdwelt ten years in the land of Canaan, and gave her to her husband Abram to be his ^Twife.   [Gal. 4:24, 25] · 12:4, 5 · *lived* · *secondary*

4 And he went in unto Ha'-gar, and she conceived: and when she saw that she had conceived, her mistress was ^Rdespised^T in her eyes.   [Prov. 30:21, 23] · *she looked down on her*

5 And Sa'-rai said unto Abram, My wrong *be* upon thee: I have given my maid into thy ^Tbosom; and when she saw that she had conceived, I was despised in her eyes: the LORD judge between me and thee.   *arms*

6 But Abram said unto Sa'-rai, Behold, thy maid *is* in thy hand; do to her as it pleaseth thee. And when Sa'-rai dealt hardly with her, she fled from her face.

7 And the angel of the LORD found her by a fountain of water in the wilderness, by the fountain in the way to ^RShur.   Ex. 15:22

8 And he said, Ha'-gar, Sa'-rai's maid, ^Twhence camest thou? and whither wilt thou go? And she said, I flee from the face of my mistress Sa'-rai.   *where did you come from*

9 And the angel of the LORD said unto her, Return to thy mistress, and ^Rsubmit^T thyself under her hands.   [Titus 2:9] · *obey her*

10 And the angel of the LORD said unto her, I will multiply thy seed exceedingly, that it shall not be numbered for multitude.

11 And the angel of the LORD said unto her, Behold, thou *art* with child, and shalt bear a son, ^Rand shalt call his name ^TIsh'-ma-el; because ^Rthe LORD hath heard thy affliction.   Luke 1:13, 31 · *God hears* · Ex. 3:7, 9

12 And he will be a wild man; his hand *will be* against every man, and every man's hand

against him; and ᵀhe shall dwell in the presence of all his brethren.   *he shall prosper*

13 And she called the name of the LORD that spake unto her, Thou ᵀGod seest me: for she said, Have I also here looked after him that seeth me?   *El roi, that is, God is seeing*

14 Wherefore the well was called ᵀBe'-er–la–hai'–roi; behold, *it is* between Ka'-desh and Be'-red.   *the living one who sees me*

15 And ᴿHa'-gar bare Abram a son: and Abram called his son's name, which Ha'-gar bare, Ish'-ma-el.   Gal. 4:22

16 And Abram *was* ᴿfourscore and six years old, when Ha'-gar bare Ish'-ma-el to Abram.   v. 3; 12:4

CHAPTER 17

Institution of the Covenant: Circumcision

AND when Abram was ninety years old and nine, the LORD appeared to Abram, and said unto him, ᴿI *am* the Almighty God; walk before me, and be thou perfect.   Deut. 18:13

2 And I will make my ᴿcovenant between me and thee, and ᴿwill ᵀmultiply thee exceedingly.   [Gal. 3:17] · 12:2 · *give thee many heirs*

3 And Abram ᴿfell on his face: and God talked with him, saying,   v. 17; 18:2

4 As for me, behold, my covenant *is* with thee, and thou shalt be ᴿa father of ᵀmany nations.   [Rom. 4:11, 12, 16] · *multitude of nations*

5 ᴿNeither shall thy name any more be called Abram, but thy name shall be Abraham; for a father of many nations have I made thee.   1 Chr. 1:27; Neh. 9:7

6 And I will make thee ᵀexceeding fruitful, and I will make nations of thee, and kings shall come out of thee.   *many descendants*

7 And I ᵀwill ᴿestablish my covenant between me and thee and thy seed after thee in their generations for an everlasting covenant, to be a God unto thee, and to thy seed after thee.   *keep my promise* · Gal. 3:17 ☆

8 And ᴿI will give unto thee, and to thy seed after thee, the ᵀland ᴿwherein thou art a stranger, all the land of Canaan, for an everlasting possession; and I will be their God.   12:7 · *of thy sojournings* · 23:4; 28:4

9 And God said unto Abraham, Thou shalt keep my covenant therefore, thou, and thy seed after thee in their generations.

10 This *is* my covenant, which ye shall keep, between me and you and thy seed after thee; ᴿEvery man child among you shall be circumcised.   John 7:22; Acts 7:8

11 And ᴿye shall circumcise the flesh of your foreskin; and it shall be a token of the covenant betwixt me and you.   Ex. 12:48

12 And he that is eight days old ᴿshall be circumcised among you, every man child in your generations, he that is born in the house, or bought with money of any stranger, which *is* not of thy seed.   Lev. 12:3

13 He that is born in thy house, and he that is bought with thy money, must needs be circumcised: and my covenant shall be in your flesh for an everlasting covenant.

14 And the uncircumcised man child whose flesh of his foreskin is not circumcised, that soul shall be cut off from his people; he hath broken my covenant.

15 And God said unto Abraham, As for Sa'-rai thy wife, thou shalt not call her name Sa'-rai, but ᵀSarah *shall* her name *be*.   *princess*

16 And I will bless her, and give thee a son also of her: yea, I will bless her, and ᵀshe shall be *a mother* of nations; kings of people shall be of her.   *she shall become nations*

17 Then Abraham fell upon his face, and laughed, and said in his heart, Shall *a child* be born unto him that is an hundred years old? and shall Sarah, that is ninety years old, bear?

18 And Abraham ᵀsaid unto God, O that Ish'-ma-el might live before thee!   *prayed*

19 And God said, ᴿSarah thy wife shall bear thee a son indeed; and thou shalt call his name Isaac: and I will establish my covenant with him for an everlasting covenant, *and* with his seed after him.   [Gal. 4:28] ☆

20 And as for Ish'-ma-el, I have heard thee: Behold, I have blessed him, and will make him fruitful, and will multiply him exceedingly; ᴿtwelve princes shall he beget, and I will make him a great nation.   25:16

21 But my covenant will I establish with ᴿIsaac, ᴿwhich Sarah shall bear unto thee at this set time in the next year.   18:10 · 21:2

22 And he left off ᴿtalking with him, and God went up from Abraham.   18:33; 35:13

23 And Abraham took Ish'-ma-el his son, and all that were born in his house, and all that were bought with his money, every male among the men of Abraham's house; and circumcised the flesh of their foreskin in the selfsame day, as God had said unto him.

24 And Abraham *was* ninety years old and nine, when ᴿhe was circumcised in the flesh of his foreskin.   [Rom. 4:11]

25 And Ish'-ma-el ᴿhis son *was* thirteen years old, when he was circumcised in the flesh of his foreskin.   16:16

26 In the ᵀselfsame day was Abraham circumcised, and Ish'-ma-el his son.   *very same*

27 And all the men of his ᴿhouse, born in the house, and bought with money of the stranger, were circumcised with him.   18:19

CHAPTER 18

Sarah's Faith Is Tested

AND the LORD appeared unto him ᵀin the plains of Mam'-re: and he sat in the tent door in the heat of the day;   *by the oaks*

2 And he lift up his eyes and looked, and, lo, three men stood by him: and when he saw *them*, he ran to meet them from the tent door, and bowed himself toward the ground,

3 And said, My ᵀLord, if now I have found favour in thy sight, ᵀpass not away, I pray thee, from thy servant: *O Lord · do not pass by*

4 Let ᴿa little water, I pray you, be fetched, and wash your feet, and ᵀrest yourselves under the tree: 19:2; 24:32; 43:24 · *support*

5 And I will fetch a morsel of bread, and comfort ye your hearts; after that ye shall pass on: for therefore are ye come to your servant. And they said, So do, as thou hast said.

6 And Abraham hastened into the tent unto Sarah, and said, Make ready quickly ᵀthree measures of fine meal, knead *it*, and make cakes upon the hearth.   *6.524 bushels*

7 And Abraham ran unto the herd, and fetcht a calf tender and good, and gave *it* unto a young man; and he hasted to dress it.

8 And ᴿhe took butter, and milk, and the calf which he had dressed, and set *it* before them; and he ᵀstood by them under the tree, and they did eat.   19:3 · *like a waiter*

9 And they said unto him, Where *is* Sarah thy wife? And he said, Behold, in the tent.

10 And he said, ᴿI will certainly return unto thee ᴿaccording to the time of life; and, lo, ᴿSarah thy wife shall have a son. And Sarah heard *it* in the tent door, which *was* behind him.   Rom. 9:9 · 2 Kin. 4:16 · 17:19, 21

11 Now Abraham and Sarah *were* old *and* well stricken in age; *and* it ceased to be with Sarah after the manner of women.

12 Therefore Sarah laughed within herself, saying, After I am waxed old shall I have pleasure, my lord being old also?

13 And the LORD said unto Abraham, Wherefore did Sarah laugh, saying, Shall I of a surety bear a child, which am old?

14 ᴿIs any thing too hard for the LORD? ᴿAt the time appointed I will return unto thee, according to the time of life, and Sarah shall have a son.   [Num. 11:23] · 2 Kin. 4:16

15 Then Sarah denied, ᴿsaying, I laughed not; for she was afraid. And he said, ᴿNay; but thou didst laugh.   Ps. 63:11 · Matt. 12:25

Abraham's Faith Is Tested

16 And the men rose up from thence, and looked toward Sodom: and Abraham went with them to bring them on the way.

17 And the LORD said, ᴿShall I hide from Abraham that thing which I do;   [John 15:15]

18 Seeing that Abraham shall surely become a ᵀgreat and mighty nation, and all the nations of the earth shall be ᴿblessed in him?   *populous* · [12:3; 22:18; Acts 3:25; Gal. 3:8] ✸

19 For I know him, ᴿthat he will command his children and his ᵀhousehold after him, and they shall keep the way of the LORD, to do justice and judgment; that the LORD may bring upon Abraham that which he hath spoken of him.   [Deut. 4:9, 10; 6:7] · *family*

20 And the LORD said, Because ᴿthe cry of Sodom and Go-mor'-rah is great, and because their sin is very ᵀgrievous;   19:13 · *bad*

21 ᴿI will go down now, and see whether they have done altogether according to the cry of it, which is come unto me; and if not, ᴿI will know.   11:5 · Deut. 8:2; 13:3; 2 Cor. 11:11

22 And the men turned their faces from thence, ᴿand went toward Sodom: but Abraham stood yet before the LORD.   19:1

23 And Abraham ᴿdrew near, and said, ᴿWilt thou also ᴿdestroy the righteous with the wicked?   [Heb. 10:22] · Num. 16:22 · [Job 9:22]

24 ᵀPeradventure there be fifty righteous within the city: wilt thou also destroy and not ᵀspare the place for the ᴿfifty righteous that *are* therein?   *suppose · forgive* · [Matt. 7:13, 14]

25 That be far from thee to do after this manner, to slay the righteous with the wicked: and that the righteous should be as the wicked, that be far from thee: Shall not the Judge of all the earth do right?

26 And the LORD said, ᴿIf I find in Sodom fifty righteous within the city, then I will spare all the place for their sakes.   Jer. 5:1

27 And Abraham answered and said, Behold now, I have taken upon me to speak unto the Lord, ᵀwhich *am* ᴿbut dust and ashes: *I who* · [3:19; Job 4:19; 1 Cor. 15:47, 48]

28 Peradventure there shall lack five of the fifty righteous: wilt thou destroy all the city for *lack* of five? And he said, If I find there forty and five, I will not destroy *it*.

29 And he spake unto him ᴿyet again, and said, ᵀPeradventure there shall be forty found there. And he said, I will not do *it* for forty's sake.   1 Thess. 5:17 · *suppose*

30 And he said *unto him*, Oh let not the Lord be angry, and I will speak: Peradventure there shall thirty be found there. And he said, I will not do *it*, if I find thirty there.

31 And he said, Behold now, ᴿI have ᵀtaken upon me to speak unto the Lord: ᵀPeradventure there shall be twenty found there. And he said, I will not destroy *it* for twenty's sake.   Heb. 4:16 · *ventured · suppose*

32 And he said, Oh let not the Lord be angry, and I will speak yet but this once: Peradventure ten shall be found there. And he said, I will not destroy *it* for ten's sake.

33 And the LORD went his way, as soon as he had left communing with Abraham: and Abraham returned unto his place.

CHAPTER 19

Destruction of Sodom and Gomorrah

AND there ᴿcame two angels to Sodom at even; and Lot sat in the gate of Sodom:

and ᴿLot seeing *them* rose up to meet them; and he bowed himself with his face toward the ground;   18:22 · 18:1

2 And he said, Behold now, my lords, turn in,ᴿ I pray you, into your servant's house, and tarry all night, and wash your feet, and ye shall rise up early, and go on your ways. And they said, Nay; but we will abide in the street all night.   [Heb. 13:2]

3 And he pressed upon them greatly; and they turned in unto him, and entered into his house; and he made them a feast, and did bake unleavened bread, and they did eat.

4 But before they lay down, ᴿthe men of the city, *even* the men of Sodom, compassed the house round, both old and young, all the people from every quarter: 13:13

5 ᴿAnd they called unto Lot, and said unto him, Where *are* the men which came in to thee this night? bring them out unto us, that we ᴿmay know them.   Is. 3:9 · 4:1

6 And Lot went out at the door unto them, and shut the door after him,

7 And said, I pray you, brethren, ᴿdo not so wickedly.   [Judg. 19:23; Is. 5:20; Mal. 2:17]

8 Behold now, I have two daughters which have not known man; let me, I pray you, bring them out unto you, and do ye to them as *is* good in your eyes: only unto these men do nothing; for therefore came they under the shadow of my roof.

9 And they said, Stand back. And they said *again*, This one *fellow* ᴿcame in to sojourn, and he will needs be a judge: now will we deal worse with thee, than with them. And they pressed sore upon the man, *even* Lot, and came near to break the door.   2 Pet. 2:7, 8

10 But ᴿthe men put forth their hand, and pulled Lot into the house to them, and shut to the door.   *v.* 1

11 And they ᵀsmote the men that *were* at the door of the house with blindness, both small and great: so that they wearied themselves to find the door.   *made them unable to see*

12 And the men said unto Lot, Hast thou here any besides? son in law, and thy sons, and thy daughters, and whatsoever thou hast in the city, bring *them* out of this place:

13 For we will destroy this place, because the ᴿcry of them is ᵀwaxen great before the face of the LORD; and the LORD hath sent us to ᴿdestroy it.   18:20 · *grown loud* · Deut. 4:26

14 And Lot went out, and spake unto his sons in law, which married his daughters, and said, ᴿUp, get you out of this place; for the LORD will destroy this city. ᴿBut he seemed as one that mocked unto his sons in law.   Num. 16:21, 45 · Ex. 9:21; Luke 17:28; 24:11

15 And when the morning arose, then the ᵀangels hastened Lot, saying, Arise, take thy wife, and thy two daughters, which are here; lest thou be ᵀconsumed in the iniquity of the city.   *messengers* · *destroyed in the punishment*

16 And while he lingered, the men laid hold upon his hand, and upon the hand of his wife, and upon the hand of his two daughters; ᴿthe LORD being merciful unto him: ᴿand they brought him forth, and set him without the city.   Luke 18:13 · Ps. 34:22

17 And it came to pass, when they had brought them forth abroad, that he said, Escape for thy life; look not behind thee, neither stay thou in all the plain; escape to the mountain, lest thou be consumed.

18 And Lot said unto them, Oh, ᴿnot so, my Lord: Acts 10:14

19 Behold now, thy servant hath found grace in thy sight, and thou hast magnified thy mercy, which thou hast shewed unto me in saving my life; and I cannot escape to the mountain, lest some evil take me, and I die:

20 Behold now, this city *is* near to flee unto, and it *is* a little one: Oh, let me escape thither, (*is* it not a little one?) and ᵀmy soul shall live.   *my life will be saved*

21 And he said unto him, See, I have ᵀaccepted thee concerning this thing also, that I will not overthrow this city, for the which thou hast spoken.   *granted you this favour*

22 Haste thee, escape thither; for I cannot do any thing till thou be come thither. Therefore the name of the city was called Zo'-ar.

23 The ᵀsun was risen upon the earth when Lot entered into Zo'-ar.   *it was morning*

24 Then ᴿthe LORD rained upon Sodom and upon Go-mor'-rah brimstone and fire from the LORD out of heaven;   Deut. 29:23

25 And he overthrew those cities, and all the plain, and all the inhabitants of the cities, and that which grew upon the ground.

26 But his wife looked back from behind him, and she became a pillar of salt.

27 And Abraham ᵀgat up early in the morning to the place where ᴿhe stood before the LORD: *went* · 18:22

28 And he looked toward Sodom and Go-mor'-rah, and toward all the land of the plain, and beheld, and, lo, the smoke of the country went up as the smoke of a furnace.

29 And it came to pass, when God destroyed the cities of the plain, that God remembered Abraham, and sent Lot out of the midst of the overthrow, when he overthrew the cities in the which Lot dwelt.

The Sin of Lot

30 And Lot went up out of Zo'-ar, and ᴿdwelt in the mountain, and his two daughters with him; for he ᴿfeared to dwell in Zo'-ar: and he dwelt in a cave, he and his two daughters.   *vv.* 17, 19 · Matt. 14:30

31 And the firstborn said unto the younger, Our father *is* old, and *there is* not a man in the earth ᴿto come in unto us after the manner of all the earth: Deut. 25:5

32 Come, let us make our father drink wine, and we will lie with him, that we ᴿmay preserve seed of our father. [Mark 12:19]

33 And they made their father drink wine that night: and the firstborn went in, and lay with her father; and he perceived not when she lay down, nor when she arose.

34 And it came to pass on the morrow, that the firstborn said unto the younger, Behold, I lay ᵀyesternight with my father: let us make him drink wine this night also; and go thou in, *and* lie with him, that we may preserve seed of our father. *last night*

35 And they made their father drink wine that night also: and the younger arose, and lay with him; and he perceived not when she lay down, nor when she arose.

36 Thus were both the daughters of Lot with child by their father.

37 And the firstborn bare a son, and called his name Moab: the same *is* the father of the Mo′-ab-ites unto this day.

38 And the younger, she also bare a son, and called his name Ben–am′-mi: ᴿthe same *is* the father of the children of ᴿAmmon unto this day. Deut. 2:19 • Num. 21:24

CHAPTER 20

The Test of Abimelech

AND Abraham journeyed from ᴿthence toward the south country, and dwelled between ᴿKa′-desh and Shur, and ᴿsojourned in Ge′-rar. 18:1 • 16:7, 14 • 26:6

2 And Abraham said of Sarah his wife, ᴿShe *is* my sister: and A-bim′-e-lech king of Ge′-rar sent, and took Sarah. 12:13; 26:7

3 But ᴿGod came to A-bim′-e-lech in a dream by night, and said to him, ᴿBehold, thou *art but* a dead man, for the woman which thou hast taken; for she *is* ᵀa man's wife. Ps. 105:14 • *v.* 7 • *married to a husband*

4 But A-bim′-e-lech had not come near her: and he said, Lord, ᴿwilt thou slay also a righteous nation? 18:23; Deut. 32:4

5 Said he not unto me, She *is* my sister? and she, even she herself said, He *is* my brother: in the integrity of my heart and innocency of my hands have I done this.

6 And God said unto him in a dream, Yea, I know that thou didst this in the integrity of thy heart; for I also withheld thee from sinning ᴿagainst me: therefore ᵀsuffered I thee not to touch her. [Lev. 6:2] • *permitted*

7 Now therefore restore the man *his* wife; for he *is* a prophet, and he shall pray for thee, and thou shalt live: and if thou restore *her* not, know thou that thou shalt surely die, thou, and all that *are* thine.

8 Therefore A-bim′-e-lech rose early in the morning, and called all his servants, and told all these things in their ears: and the men were ᵀsore afraid. *badly frightened*

9 Then A-bim′-e-lech called Abraham, and said unto him, What hast thou done unto us? and what have I offended thee, that thou hast brought on me and on my kingdom a great sin? thou hast done deeds unto me ᴿthat ought not to be done. 34:7

10 And A-bim′-e-lech said unto Abraham, What ᵀsawest thou, that thou hast done this thing? *did you have in mind?*

11 And Abraham said, Because I thought, Surely the fear of God *is* not in this place; and they will slay me for my wife's sake.

12 And yet indeed *she is* my sister; she *is* the daughter of my father, but not the daughter of my mother; and she became my wife.

13 And it came to pass, when ᴿGod caused me to wander from my father's house, that I said unto her, This *is* thy kindness which thou shalt shew unto me; at every place whither we shall come, ᴿsay of me, He *is* my brother. [12:1, 9, 11; Heb. 11:8] • 12:13

14 And A-bim′-e-lech ᴿtook sheep, and oxen, and menservants, and womenservants, and gave *them* unto Abraham, and restored him Sarah his wife. 12:16

15 And A-bim′-e-lech said, Behold, ᴿmy land *is* before thee: dwell where it pleaseth thee. 13:9; 34:10

16 And unto Sarah he said, Behold, I have given ᴿthy brother ᵀa thousand *pieces* of silver: behold, he *is* to thee a covering of the eyes, unto all that *are* with thee, and with all *other*: thus she was reproved. 20:5 • *$128,000*

17 So Abraham prayed unto God: and God healed A-bim′-e-lech, and his wife, and his maidservants; and they bare *children*.

18 For the Lᴏʀᴅ ᴿhad fast closed up all the wombs of the house of A-bim′-e-lech, because of Sarah Abraham's wife. 12:17

CHAPTER 21

Birth of Isaac

AND the Lᴏʀᴅ ᴿvisited Sarah as he had said, and the Lᴏʀᴅ did unto Sarah ᴿas he had spoken. 1 Sam. 2:21 • [Gal. 4:23, 28]

2 For Sarah conceived, and bare Abraham a son in his old age, ᴿat the set time of which God had spoken to him. 17:21

3 And Abraham called the name of his son that was born unto him, whom Sarah bare to him, ᴿIsaac.ᵀ 17:19 • *laughter*

4 And Abraham ᴿcircumcised his son Isaac being eight days old, ᴿas God had commanded him. Acts 7:8 • 17:10, 12

5 And Abraham was an hundred years old, when his son Isaac was born unto him.

6 And Sarah said, God hath ᵀmade me to laugh, *so that* all that hear ᴿwill laugh with me. *prepared laughter for me* • Luke 1:58

7 And she said, Who would have said unto Abraham, that Sarah should have [T]given children suck? [R]for I have born *him* a son in his old age.   nursed children • 18:11, 12

8 And the child grew, and was weaned: and Abraham made a [R]great feast the *same* day that Isaac was weaned.   1 Kin. 8:65

9 And Sarah saw the son of Ha'-gar [R]the Egyptian, which she had born unto Abraham, [R]mocking.[T]   16:1 • [Gal. 4:29] • *making fun*

10 Wherefore she said unto Abraham, [R]Cast out this bondwoman and her son: for the son of this bondwoman shall not be heir with my son, *even* with Isaac.   Gal. 4:30

11 And the thing was very [T]grievous in Abraham's sight because of his son.   hard

12 And God said unto Abraham, Let it not be grievous in thy sight because of the lad, and because of thy bondwoman; in all that Sarah hath said unto thee, hearken unto her voice; for [R]in Isaac shall thy seed be called.   Matt. 1:2; [Rom. 9:7, 8; Heb. 11:18] ☆

13 And also of the son of the bondwoman will I make a nation, because he *is* thy seed.

14 And Abraham rose up early in the morning, and took bread, and a [T]bottle of water, and gave *it* unto Ha'-gar, putting *it* on her shoulder, and the child, and sent her away: and she departed, and wandered in the wilderness of Be'-er-she'-ba.   skin

15 And the water was [T]spent in the bottle, and she cast the child under one of the shrubs.   gone

16 And she went, and sat her down over against *him* a good way off, as it were a bowshot: for she said, Let me not see the death of the child. And she sat over against *him*, and lift up her voice, and wept.

17 And [R]God heard the voice of the lad; and the angel of God called to Ha'-gar out of heaven, and said unto her, What aileth thee, Ha'-gar? fear not; for God hath heard the voice of the lad where he *is*.   Ex. 3:7

18 Arise, lift up the lad, and [T]hold him in thine hand; for [R]I will make him a great nation.   take care of him • v. 13; 16:10; 25:12

19 And God opened her eyes, and she saw a well of water; and she went, and filled the bottle with water, and gave the lad drink.

20 And God [R]was with the lad; and he grew, and dwelt in the wilderness, [R]and became an archer.   28:15; 39:2, 3, 21 • 16:12

21 And he dwelt in the wilderness of Pa'-ran: and his mother [R]took him a wife out of the land of Egypt.   24:4; 25:18

22 And it came to pass at that time, that A-bim'-e-lech and Phi'-chol the chief captain of his host spake unto Abraham, saying, God *is* with thee in all that thou doest:

23 Now therefore [T]swear unto me here by God that thou wilt not deal falsely with me, nor with my son, nor with my son's son: *but* according to the kindness that I have done

unto thee, thou shalt do unto me, and to the land wherein thou hast sojourned.   promise

24 And Abraham said, I [T]will swear. promise

25 And Abraham reproved A-bim'-e-lech because of a well of water, which A-bim'-e-lech's servants had violently taken away.

26 And A-bim'-e-lech said, I wot not who hath done this thing: neither didst thou tell me, neither yet heard I *of it*, but to day.

27 And Abraham took sheep and oxen, and gave them unto A-bim'-e-lech; and both of them made [T]a covenant.   an agreement

28 And Abraham set seven ewe lambs of the flock by themselves.

29 And A-bim'-e-lech said unto Abraham, [R]What *mean* these seven ewe lambs which thou hast set by themselves?   33:8

30 And he said, For *these* seven ewe lambs shalt thou take of my hand, that [R]they may be [T]a [R]witness unto me, that I have digged this well.   31:48, 52 • *evidence* • 25:11

31 Wherefore he [R]called that place [T]Be'-er-she'-ba; because there they sware both of them.   22:19; 26:33 • *the well of the oath*

32 Thus they made a covenant at Be'-er-she'-ba: then [R]A-bim'-e-lech rose up, and Phi'-chol the chief captain of his host, and they returned into the land of the Phi-lis'-tines.   20:2

33 And *Abraham* planted a grove in Be'-er-she'-ba, and called there on the name of the LORD, the everlasting God.

34 And Abraham sojourned [R]in the Phi-lis'-tines' land many days.   22:19

CHAPTER 22

Offering of Isaac

A ND it came to pass after these things, that [R]God did tempt Abraham, and said unto him, Abraham: and he said, Behold, *here* I am.   [vv. 12, 16; James 1:12; 1 Pet. 1:7]

2 And he said, Take now thy son, thine only *son* Isaac, whom thou lovest, and get thee into the land of Mo-ri'-ah; and offer him there for a burnt offering upon one of the mountains which I will tell thee of.

3 And Abraham rose up early in the morning, and saddled his ass, and took two of his young men with him, and Isaac his son, and [T]clave the wood for the burnt offering, and rose up, and [R]went unto the place of which God had told him.   split • 6:22

4 Then on the third day Abraham lifted up his eyes, and saw the place afar off.

5 [R]And Abraham said unto his young men, Abide ye here with the ass; and I and the lad will go yonder and [R]worship, and come again to you.   [Heb. 11:19] • 24:26

6 And Abraham took the wood of the burnt offering, and [R]laid *it* upon Isaac his son;

and he took the fire in his hand, and a knife; and they went both of them together. John 19:17

7 And Isaac spake unto Abraham his father, and said, My father: and he said, Here *am* I, my son. And he said, Behold the fire and the wood: but where *is* the ᵀlambᴿ for a burnt offering? kid • Ex. 29:38–42

8 And Abraham said, My son, God will provide himself a lamb for a burnt offering: so they went both of them together.

9 And they came to the place which God had told him of; and Abraham built an altar there, and laid the wood in order, and bound Isaac his son, and ᴿlaid him on the altar upon the wood. [Heb. 11:17; James 2:21]

10 And Abraham stretched forth his hand, and took the knife to slay his son.

11 And the angel of the Lord called unto him out of heaven, and said, Abraham, Abraham: and he said, Here *am* I.

12 And he said, ᴿLay not thine hand upon the lad, neither do thou any thing unto him: for now I know that thou fearest God, seeing thou hast not withheld thy son, thine only *son* from me. 1 Sam. 15:22

13 And Abraham lifted up his eyes, and looked, and behold behind *him* a ram caught in a thicket by his horns: and Abraham went and took the ram, and offered him up for a burnt offering in the stead of his son.

14 And Abraham called the name of that place ᵀJe-ho'-vah-ji'-reh: as it is said *to* this day, In the mount of the Lord ᴿit shall be seen. the LORD will see, or, provide • v. 8

15 And the angel of the Lord called unto Abraham out of heaven the second time,

16 And said, ᴿBy myself have I sworn, saith the Lord, for because thou hast done this thing, and hast not withheld thy son, thine only *son:* Ps. 105:9; Luke 1:73; [Heb. 6:13, 14]

17 That in blessing I will bless thee, and in multiplying I will multiply thy seedᴿ as the stars of the heaven, and as the sand which *is* upon the sea shore; and thy seed shall possess the gate of his enemies; Deut. 1:10; 1 Kin. 4:20

18 ᴿAnd in thy seed shall ᴿall the nations of the earth be blessed; because thou hast obeyed my voice. [Acts 3:25] • Gal. 3:16 ☆

19 So Abraham returned unto his young men, and they rose up and went together to ᴿBe'-er-she'-ba; and Abraham dwelt at Be'-er-she'-ba. 21:31

20 And it came to pass after these things, that it was told Abraham, saying, Behold, ᴿMil'-cah, she hath also born children unto thy brother Na'-hor; 11:29

21 Huz his firstborn, and Buz his brother, and Kem'-u-el the father of Ar'-am,

22 And Che'-sed, and Ha'-zo, and Pil'-dash, and Jid'-laph, and Be-thu'-el.

23 And Be-thu'-el begat ᴿRebekahᵀ: these eight Mil'-cah did bear to Na'-hor, Abraham's brother. Rom. 9:10 • Rebecca

24 And his concubine, whose name *was* Reu'-mah, she bare also Te'-bah, and Ga'-ham, and Tha'-hash, and Ma'-a-chah.

CHAPTER 23

Death of Sarah

AND Sarah was an hundred and seven and twenty years old: *these were* the years of the life of Sarah.

2 And Sarah died in ᴿKir'-jath-ar'-ba; the same *is* ᴿHe'-bron in the land of Canaan: and Abraham came to mourn for Sarah, and to weep for her. Josh. 14:15 • v. 19; 13:18

3 And Abraham stood up from before his dead, and spake unto the ᴿsons of Heth, saying, 10:15

4 ᴿI *am* a stranger and a sojourner with you: ᴿgive me a possession of a buryingplace with you, that I may bury my dead out of my sight. [17:8; Heb. 11:9, 13] • Acts 7:5

5 And the children of Heth answered Abraham, saying unto him,

6 Hear us, my lord: thou *art* ᵀa mighty prince among us: in the choice of our sepulchres bury thy dead; none of us shall withhold from thee his sepulchre, but that thou mayest bury thy dead. a prince of God

7 And Abraham stood up, and bowed ᴿhimself to the people of the land, *even* to the children of Heth. [Rom. 13:7]

8 And he communed with them, saying, If it be ᴿyour mind that I should bury my dead out of my sight; hear me, and intreat for me to E'-phron the son of Zo'-har, 25:9

9 That he may give me the cave of Mach-pe'-lah, which he hath, which *is* in the end of his field; for ᵀas much money as it is worth he shall give it me for a possession of a buryingplace amongst you. full money

10 And E'-phron dwelt among the children of Heth: and E'-phron the Hit'-tite answered Abraham ᵀin the audience of the children of Heth, *even* of all that went in at the gate of his city, saying, in the presence

11 Nay, my lord, hear me: the field give I thee, and the cave that *is* therein, I give it thee; in the presence of the sons of my people give I it thee: bury thy dead.

12 And Abraham bowed down himself before the people of the land.

13 And he spake unto E'-phron in the audience of the people of the land, saying, But if thou *wilt give it,* I pray thee, hear me: I will give thee money for the field; take *it* of me, and I will bury my dead there.

14 And E'-phron answered Abraham, saying unto him,

15 My lord, hearken unto me: the land *is worth* ᵀfour hundred ᴿshek'-els of silver; what *is* that betwixt me and thee? bury therefore thy dead. $51,200 • Ex. 30:13; Ezek. 45:12

16 And Abraham hearkened unto E'-phron; and Abraham ^Rweighed to E'-phron the silver, which he had named in the audience of the sons of Heth, four hundred shek'-els of silver, current *money* with the merchant.   2 Sam. 14:26; Jer. 32:9; Zech. 11:12

17 And the field of E'-phron, which *was* in Mach-pe'-lah, which *was* before Mam'-re, the field, and the cave which *was* therein, and all the trees that *were* in the field, that *were* in all the borders round about, were made sure

18 Unto Abraham for a possession ^Rin the presence of the children of Heth, before all that went in at the gate of his city.   *v.* 10

19 And after this, ^RAbraham buried Sarah his wife in the cave of the field of Mach-pe'-lah before Mam'-re: the same *is* He'-bron in the land of Canaan.   35:29

20 And the field, and the cave that *is* therein, ^Twere ^Rmade sure unto Abraham for a possession of a buryingplace by the sons of Heth.   *was certified as the owner* • Jer. 32:10

CHAPTER 24

Isaac's Marriage

AND Abraham was old, *and* ^Twell stricken in age: and the LORD had blessed Abraham in all things.   *well advanced*

2 And Abraham said ^Runto his eldest servant of his house, that ^Rruled over all that he had, ^RPut, I pray thee, thy hand under my thigh: 15:2 • *v.* 10 • 1 Chr. 29:24

3 And I will make thee swear by the LORD, the God of heaven, and the God of the earth, that ^Rthou shalt not take a wife unto my son of the daughters of the Ca'-naan-ites, among whom I dwell: Deut. 7:3

4 ^RBut thou shalt go ^Runto my country, and to my kindred, and take a wife unto my son Isaac.   28:2 • 12:1; Heb. 11:15

5 And the servant said unto him, ^TPeradventure the woman will not be willing to follow me unto this land: must I needs bring thy son again unto the land from whence thou camest?   *Just in case*

6 And Abraham said unto him, ^RBeware thou that thou bring not my son thither again.   *v.* 8

7 The LORD God of heaven, which took me from my father's house, and from the land of my kindred, and which spake unto me, and that sware unto me, saying, Unto thy seed will I give this land; he shall send his angel before thee, and thou shalt take a wife unto my son from thence.

8 And if the woman will not be willing to follow thee, then ^Rthou shalt be clear from this my oath: ^Ronly bring not my son thither again.   Josh. 2:17, 20 • *v.* 6

9 And the servant ^Rput his hand under the

thigh of Abraham his master, and sware to him concerning that matter.   *v.* 2

10 And the servant took ten camels of the camels of his master, and departed; for all the ^Tgoods of his master *were* in his hand: and he arose, and went to Mes-o-po-ta'-mi-a, unto the city of Na'-hor.   *wealth*

11 And he made his camels to ^Tkneel down without the city by a well of water at the time of the evening, *even* the time that women go out to draw *water.*   *rest*

12 And he said, ^RO LORD God of my master Abraham, I pray thee, ^Tsend me good speed this day, and shew kindness unto my master Abraham.   *v.* 27 • *work things out favorably*

13 Behold, I stand *here* by the well of water; and ^Rthe daughters of the men of the city come out to draw water: Ex. 2:16

14 And let it come to pass, that the damsel to whom I shall say, Let down thy pitcher, I pray thee, that I may drink; and she shall say, Drink, and I will give thy camels drink also: *let the same be* she *that* thou hast appointed for thy servant Isaac; and ^Rthereby shall I know that thou hast shewed kindness unto my master.   [1 Sam. 16:7]

15 And it came to pass, before he had done speaking, that, behold, Rebekah came out, who was born to Be-thu'-el, son of Mil'-cah, the wife of Na'-hor, Abraham's brother, with her pitcher upon her shoulder.

16 And the damsel ^R*was* very fair to look upon, a virgin, neither had any man known her: and she went down to the well, and filled her pitcher, and came up.   26:7

17 And the servant ran to meet her, and said, Let me, I pray thee, ^Rdrink a little water of thy pitcher.   John 4:7

18 ^RAnd she said, Drink, my lord: and she hasted, and let down her pitcher upon her hand, and gave him drink.   *vv.* 14, 46; [1 Pet. 3:8]

19 And when she had done giving him drink, she said, I will draw *water* for thy camels also, until they have done drinking.

20 And she hasted, and emptied her pitcher into the trough, and ran again unto the well to draw *water,* and drew for all his camels.

21 And the man wondering at her held his peace, ^Tto wit whether the LORD had made his journey prosperous or not.   *as to*

22 And it came to pass, as the camels had done drinking, that the man took a golden ^Rearring^T of half a shek'-el weight, and two bracelets for her hands of ten *shek'-els* weight of gold;   Is. 3:19–21 • *jewel for the forehead*

23 And said, Whose daughter *art* thou? tell me, I pray thee: is there room *in* thy father's house for us to lodge in?

24 And she said unto him, ^RI *am* the daughter of Be-thu'-el the son of Mil'-cah, which she bare unto Na'-hor.   *v.* 15; 22:23

25 She said moreover unto him, We have both straw and ᵀprovender enough, and room to lodge in.   *food for the camels*

26 And the man ᴿbowed down his head, and worshipped the LORD.   *v. 52; Ex. 4:31*

27 And he said, Blessed *be* the LORD God of my master Abraham, who hath not left destitute my master of his mercy and his truth: I *being* in the way, the LORD led me to the house of my master's brethren.

28 And the ᵀdamsel ran, and told *them of* her mother's house these things.   *young girl*

29 And Rebekah had a brother, and his name *was* ᴿLaban: and Laban ran out unto the man, unto the well.   *29:5, 13*

30 And it came to pass, when he saw the ᵀearring and bracelets upon his sister's hands, and when he heard the words of Rebekah his sister, saying, Thus spake the man unto me; that he came unto the man; and, behold, he stood by the camels at the well.   *ring*

31 And he said, Come in, ᴿthou blessed of the LORD; wherefore standest thou without? for I have prepared the house, and room for the camels.   *Ruth 3:10; Ps. 115:15*

32 And the man came into the house: and he ungirded his camels, and ᴿgave straw and provender for the camels, and water to wash his feet, and the men's feet that *were* with him.   *43:24; Judg. 19:21*

33 And there was set *meat* before him to eat: but he said, I will not eat, until I have told mine errand. And he said, Speak on.

34 And he said, I *am* Abraham's servant.

35 And the LORD ᴿhath blessed my master greatly; and he is become great: and he hath given him flocks, and herds, and silver, and gold, and menservants, and maidservants, and camels, and asses.   *v. 1; 13:2*

36 And Sarah my master's wife bare a son to my master when she was old: and unto him hath he given all that he hath.

37 And my master ᴿmade me swear, saying, Thou shalt not take a wife to my son of the daughters of the Ca'-naan-ites, in whose land I dwell: *v. 3*

38 ᴿBut thou shalt go unto my father's house, and to my ᵀkindred, and take a wife unto my son.   *v. 4 • family*

39 And I said unto my master, Peradventure the woman will not follow me.

40 ᴿAnd he said unto me, The LORD, before whom I walk, will send his angel with thee, and ᵀprosper thy way; and thou shalt take a wife for my son of my kindred, and of my father's house: *v. 7 • make things work out*

41 Then shalt thou ᵀbe clear from *this* my oath, when thou comest to my kindred; and if they give not thee *one,* thou shalt be clear from my oath.   *have carried out your task*

42 And I came this day unto the well, and said, O LORD God of my master Abraham, if now thou do prosper my way which I go:

43 ᴿBehold, I stand by the well of water; and it shall come to pass, that when the virgin cometh forth to draw *water,* and I say to her, Give me, I pray thee, a little water of thy pitcher to drink;   *v. 13*

44 And she say to me, Both drink thou, and I will also draw for thy camels: *let* the same *be* the woman whom the LORD hath appointed out for my master's son.

45 And before I had done speaking in mine heart, behold, Rebekah came forth with her pitcher on her shoulder; and she went down unto the well, and drew *water:* and I said unto her, Let me drink, I pray thee.

46 And she made haste, and let down her pitcher from her *shoulder,* and said, Drink, and I will give thy camels drink also: so I drank, and she made the camels drink also.

47 And I asked her, and said, Whose daughter *art* thou? And she said, The daughter of Be-thu'-el, Na'-hor's son, whom Mil'-cah bare unto him: and I ᴿput the ᵀearring upon her face, and the bracelets upon her hands.   *Ezek. 16:11, 12 • ring in her nose*

48 And I bowed down my head, and worshipped the LORD, and blessed the LORD God of my master Abraham, which had led me in the right way to take ᴿmy master's brother's daughter unto his son.   *22:23*

49 And now if ye will deal kindly and truly with my master, tell me: and if not, tell me; ᵀthat I may turn to the right hand, or to the left.   *that I may go about my business*

50 Then Laban and Be-thu'-el answered and said, ᴿThe thing proceedeth from the LORD: we cannot ᴿspeak unto thee bad or good.   *Ps. 118:23; Matt. 21:42 • 31:24*

51 Behold, Rebekah ᴿis before thee, take *her,* and go, and let her be thy master's son's wife, as the LORD hath spoken.   *20:15*

52 And it came to pass, that, when Abraham's servant heard their words, he ᴿworshipped the LORD, *bowing himself* to the earth.   *vv. 26, 48*

53 And the servant brought forth jewels of silver, and jewels of gold, and raiment, and gave *them* to Rebekah: he gave also to her brother and to her mother precious things.

54 And they did eat and drink, he and the men that *were* with him, and tarried all night; and they rose up in the morning, and he said, Send me away unto my master.

55 And her brother and her mother said, Let the damsel abide with us *a few* days, at the least ten; after that she shall go.

56 And he said unto them, Hinder me not, seeing the LORD hath prospered my way; send me away that I may go to my master.

57 And they said, We will call the damsel, and ᵀenquire at her mouth.   *ask her*

58 And they called Rebekah, and said unto her, Wilt thou go with this man? And she said, I will go.

59 And they sent away Rebekah their sister, and ᴿher nurse, and Abraham's servant, and his men.   35:8

60 And they blessed Rebekah, and said unto her, Thou *art* our sister, be thou *the mother* of thousands of millions, and let thy ᵀseed ᵀpossess the gate of those which hate them.   *descendants • gain victory over*

61 And Rebekah arose, and her damsels, and they rode upon the ᴿcamels, and followed the man: and the servant took Rebekah, and went his way.   12:16

62 And Isaac came from the way of the ᴿwell La-hai′-roi; for he dwelt in the ᴿsouth country.   16:14; 25:11 • 20:1

63 And Isaac went out ᴿto meditate in the field at the eventide: and he lifted up his eyes, and saw, and, behold, the camels *were* coming.   Josh. 1:8; Ps. 1:2; 77:12; 119:15; 143:5

64 And Rebekah lifted up her eyes, and when she saw Isaac, ᴿshe lighted off the camel.   Josh. 15:18

65 For she *had* said unto the servant, What man *is* this that walketh in the field to meet us? And the servant *had* said, It *is* my master: therefore she took a vail, and covered herself.

66 And the servant told Isaac all things that he had done.

67 And Isaac brought her into his mother Sarah's tent, and took Rebekah, and she became his wife; and he loved her: and Isaac was comforted after his mother's *death.*

CHAPTER 25

Abraham Dies—1 Chr. 1:28–33

THEN again Abraham took a wife, and her name *was* Ke-tu′-rah.

2 And ᴿshe bare him Zim′-ran, and Jok′-shan, and Me′-dan, and Mid′-i-an, and Ish′-bak, and Shu′-ah.   1 Chr. 1:32

3 And Jok′-shan begat She′-ba, and De′-dan. And the sons of De′-dan were As-shu′-rim, and Le-tu′-shim, and Le-um′-mim.

4 And the sons of Mid′-i-an; E′-phah, and E′-pher, and Ha′-noch, and A-bi′-dah, and El-da′-ah. All these *were* the children of Ke-tu′-rah.

5 And ᴿAbraham gave all that he had unto Isaac.   24:36

6 But unto the sons of the concubines, which Abraham had, Abraham gave gifts, and ᴿsent them away from Isaac his son, while he yet lived, eastward, unto ᴿthe east country.   21:14 • Judg. 6:3

7 And these *are* the days of the years of Abraham's life which he lived, ᵀan hundred threescore and fifteen years.   *175 years old*

8 Then Abraham gave up the ghost, and died in a good old age, an old man, and full *of years;* and was gathered to his people.

9 And ᴿhis sons Isaac and Ish′-ma-el buried him in the cave of Mach-pe′-lah, in the field of E′-phron the son of Zo′-har the Hit′-tite, which *is* before Mam′-re;   35:29

10 ᴿThe field which Abraham purchased of the sons of Heth: ᴿthere was Abraham buried, and Sarah his wife.   23:16 • 49:31

11 And it came to pass after the death of Abraham, that God blessed his son Isaac; and Isaac dwelt by the well La-hai′-roi.

12 Now these *are* the generations of Ish′-ma-el, Abraham's son, ᴿwhom Ha′-gar the Egyptian, Sarah's handmaid, bare unto Abraham: 16:15

13 And ᴿthese *are* the names of the sons of Ish′-ma-el, by their names, according to their generations: the firstborn of Ish′-ma-el, Ne-ba′-joth; and Ke′-dar, and Ad′-be-el, and Mib′-sam,   1 Chr. 1:29

14 And Mish′-ma, and Du′-mah, and Mas′-sa,

15 Ha′-dar, and Te′-ma, Je′-tur, Na′-phish, and Ked′-e-mah:

16 These *are* the sons of Ish′-ma-el, and these *are* their names, by their towns, and by their ᵀcastles; ᴿtwelve princes according to their nations.   *encampments* • 17:20

17 And these *are* the years of the life of Ish′-ma-el, an hundred and thirty and seven years: and ᴿhe gave up the ghost and died; and was gathered unto his people.   v. 8

18 And they dwelt from Hav′-i-lah unto ᴿShur, that *is* before Egypt, as thou goest toward Assyria: *and* ᴿhe died in the presence of all his brethren.   20:1 • 16:12

The Family of Isaac

19 And these *are* the generations of Isaac, Abraham's son: Abraham begat Isaac:

20 And Isaac was forty years old when he took Rebekah to wife, the daughter of Be-thu′-el the Syrian of Pa′-dan-a′-ram, ᴿthe sister to Laban the Syrian.   24:29

21 And Isaac ᵀintreated the Lᴏʀᴅ for his wife, because she *was* barren: ᴿand the Lᴏʀᴅ was intreated of him, and ᴿRebekah his wife conceived.   *prayed to* • Ezra 8:23 • Rom. 9:10

22 And the children struggled together within her; and she said, If *it be* so, why *am* I thus? And she went to enquire of the Lᴏʀᴅ.

23 And the Lᴏʀᴅ said unto her, Two nations *are* in thy womb, and two manner of people shall be separated from thy bowels; and *the one* people shall be stronger than *the other* people; and the elder shall serve the younger.

24 And when her days to be delivered were fulfilled, behold, *there were* twins in her womb.

25 And the first came out red, ᴿall over like an hairy garment; and they called his name Esau.   v. 34; 27:11, 16, 23

26 And after that came his brother out, and his hand took hold on Esau's heel; and his name was called Jacob: and Isaac *was* threescore years old when she bare them.

27 And the boys grew: and Esau was a cunning hunter, a man of the field; and Jacob *was* a plain man, dwelling in tents.

28 And Isaac loved Esau, because he did ^Reat of *his* venison: ^Rbut Rebekah loved Jacob.　　　　　　　　　27:19, 25, 31 · 27:6

29 And Jacob ^Tsod pottage: and Esau came from the field, and he *was* faint:　*sod boiled stew*

30 And Esau said to Jacob, Feed me, I pray thee, with that same red *pottage;* for I *am* faint: therefore was his name called E'-dom.

31 And Jacob said, Sell me this day thy ^Rbirthright.　　　　Deut. 21:16, 17; 1 Chr. 5:1, 2

32 And Esau said, Behold, I *am* ^Tat the point to die: and what profit shall this birthright do to me?　　　　　　　*going to die*

33 And Jacob said, ^TSwear to me this day; and he sware unto him: and he sold his birthright unto Jacob.　　　*solemnly promise*

34 Then Jacob gave Esau bread and pottage of lentiles; and ^Rhe did eat and drink, and rose up, and went his way: thus Esau despised *his* ^Rbirthright.　Is. 22:13 · 1 Cor. 15:32

CHAPTER 26

The Failure of Isaac

AND there was a famine in the land, beside the first famine that was in the days of Abraham. And Isaac went unto A-bim'-e-lech king of the Phi-lis'-tines unto Ge'-rar.

2 And the LORD ^Rappeared unto him, and said, Go not down into Egypt; dwell in ^Rthe land which I shall tell thee of:　　12:7 · 12:1

3 ^RSojourn^T in this land, and I will be with thee, and will bless thee; for unto thee, and unto thy seed, I will give all these countries, and I will perform the oath which I sware unto Abraham thy father;　20:1 · *Stay for a while*

4 And I will make thy seed to multiply as the stars of heaven, and will give unto thy seed all these countries; and in thy seed ^Rshall all the nations of the earth be blessed; Gal. 3:8 ✫

5 ^RBecause that Abraham obeyed my voice, and kept my charge, my commandments, my statutes, and my laws.　22:16, 18

6 And Isaac dwelt in Ge'-rar:

7 And the men of the place asked *him* of his wife; and ^Rhe said, She *is* my sister: for ^Rhe feared to say, She *is* my wife; lest, *said* he, the men of the place should kill me for Rebekah; because she ^R*was* ^Tfair to look upon.　　12:13; 20:2 · Prov. 29:25 · 24:16 · *pretty*

8 And it came to pass, when he had been there a long time, that A-bim'-e-lech king of the Phi-lis'-tines looked out at a window, and saw, and, behold, Isaac *was* ^Tsporting with Rebekah his wife.　　　　　　　*playing*

9 And A-bim'-e-lech called Isaac, and said, Behold, of a surety she *is* thy wife: and how saidst thou, She *is* my sister? And Isaac said unto him, Because I said, Lest I die for her.

10 And A-bim'-e-lech said, What *is* this thou hast done unto us? one of the people might lightly have lien with thy wife, and ^Rthou shouldest have brought ^Rguiltiness upon us.　　　　　　　20:9 · Ex. 32:21

11 And A-bim'-e-lech charged all *his* people, saying, He that toucheth this man or his wife shall surely be put to death.

12 Then Isaac sowed in that land, and ^Treceived in the same year an hundredfold: and the LORD ^Rblessed him.　*reaped* · Job 42:12

13 And the man ^Rwaxed great, and ^Twent forward, and grew until he became very great:　　　　[Prov. 10:22; 24:35] · *made progress*

14 For he had possession of flocks, and possession of herds, and great store of servants: and the Phi-lis'-tines envied him.

15 For all the wells ^Rwhich his father's servants had digged in the days of Abraham his father, the Phi-lis'-tines had stopped them, and filled them with earth.　　21:30

16 And A-bim'-e-lech said unto Isaac, Go from us; for ^Rthou art much mightier than we.　　　　　　　　　　　Ex. 1:9

17 And Isaac departed thence, and ^Tpitched his tent in the valley of Ge'-rar, and dwelt there.　　　　　　*made his home*

18 And Isaac digged again the wells of water, which they had digged in the days of Abraham his father; for the Phi-lis'-tines had stopped them after the death of Abraham: and he called their names after the names by which his father had called them.

19 And Isaac's servants digged in the valley, and found there a well of ^Tspringing water.　　　　　　　　　　　*living*

20 And the herdmen of Ge'-rar did ^Tstrive with Isaac's herdmen, saying, The water *is* our's: and he called the name of the well E'-sek; because they strove with him.　*fight*

21 And they digged another well, and strove for that also: and he called the name of it ^TSit'-nah.　　　　　　*enmity*

22 And he removed from thence, and digged another well; and for that they strove not: and he called the name of it Re-ho'-both; and he said, For now the LORD ^Thath made room for us, and we shall be fruitful in the land.　　　　　*made it so we can stay*

23 And he went up from thence to ^RBe'-er-she'-ba.　　　　　　　22:19

24 And the LORD appeared unto him the same night, and said, I *am* the God of Abraham thy father: fear not, for I *am* with thee, and will bless thee, and multiply thy seed for my servant Abraham's sake.

25 And he builded ᵀan altar there, and called upon the name of the LORD, and pitched his tent there: and there Isaac's servants digged a well.   *a place to worship God*
26 Then A-bim′-e-lech went to him from Ge′-rar, and A-huz′-zath one of his friends, and Phi′-chol the chief captain of his army.
27 And Isaac said unto them, Wherefore come ye to me, seeing ye hate me, and have sent me away from you?
28 And they said, We saw certainly that the LORD was with thee: and we said, Let there be now an oath betwixt us, *even* betwixt us and thee, and let us make ᵀa covenant with thee;   *an agreement*
29 That thou wilt do us no ᵀhurt, as we have not touched thee, and as we have done unto thee nothing but good, and have sent thee away in peace: ᴿthou *art* now the blessed of the LORD.   harm • 24:31; Ps. 115:15
30 ᴿAnd he made them a feast, and they did eat and drink.   19:3
31 And they ᴿrose up betimes in the morning, and ᴿsware one to another: and Isaac sent them away, and they departed from him in peace.   19:27 • 21:31
32 And it came to pass the same day, that Isaac's servants came, and told him concerning the well which they had digged, and said unto him, We have found water.
33 And he called it ᵀShe′-bah: therefore the name of the city is ᵀBe′-er-she′-ba unto this day.   *an oath • the well of the oath*

The Failure of Esau

34 ᴿAnd Esau was forty years old when he took to wife Judith the daughter of Be-e′-ri the Hit′-tite, and Bash′-e-math the daughter of E′-lon the Hit′-tite: 36:2
35 Which ᴿwereᵀ a grief of mind unto Isaac and to Rebekah.   27:46 • *caused worry*

CHAPTER 27

Jacob Gains Esau's Blessing

AND it came to pass, that when Isaac was old, and his eyes were dim, so that he could not see, he called Esau his eldest son, and said unto him, My son: and he said unto him, Behold, *here am* I.
2 And he said, Behold now, I am old, I ᴿknow not the day of my death: Prov. 27:1
3 Now therefore take, I pray thee, thy weapons, thy quiver and thy bow, and go out to the field, and take me *some* venison;
4 And make me savoury meat, such as I love, and bring *it* to me, that I may eat; that my soul may bless thee before I die.
5 And Rebekah heard when Isaac spake to Esau his son. And Esau went to the field to hunt *for* venison, *and* to bring *it.*
6 And ᴿRebekah spake unto Jacob her son, saying, Behold, I heard thy father speak unto Esau thy brother, saying,   25:28

7 Bring me venison, and make me savoury meat, that I may eat, and bless thee before the LORD before my death.
8 Now therefore, my son, obey my voice according to that which I command thee.
9 Go now to the flock, and fetch me from thence two good kids of the goats; and I will make them ᴿsavoury meat for thy father, such as he loveth: *v. 4*
10 And thou shalt bring *it* to thy father, that he may eat, and that he ᴿmay bless thee before his death.   *v. 4; 48:16*
11 And Jacob said to Rebekah his mother, Behold, ᴿEsau my brother *is* a hairy man, and I *am* a smooth man: 25:25
12 My father ᵀperadventure will ᴿfeel me, and I shall seem to him as a deceiver; and I shall bring ᴿa curse upon me, and not a blessing.   *perhaps • v. 22 • 9:25; Deut. 27:18*
13 And his mother said unto him, Upon me *be* thy curse, my son: only obey my voice, and go fetch me *them.*
14 And he went, and fetched, and brought *them* to his mother: and his mother made savoury meat, such as his father loved.
15 And Rebekah took ᴿgoodlyᵀ raiment of her eldest son Esau, which *were* with her in the house, and put them upon Jacob her younger son: *v. 27 • good clothes from; 3:21*
16 And she put the skins of the kids of the goats upon his hands, and upon the smooth of his neck:
17 And she gave the savoury meat and the ᴿbread, which she had prepared, into the hand of her son Jacob.   18:8
18 And he came unto his father, and said, My father: and he said, Here *am* I; who *art* thou, my son?
19 And Jacob said unto his father, I *am* Esau thy firstborn; I have done according as thou badest me: arise, ᴿI pray thee, sit and eat of my venison, ᴿthat thy soul may bless me.   1 Kin. 13:18; Is. 28:15 • *v. 4*
20 And Isaac said unto his son, ᴿHow *is it* that thou hast found it so quickly, my son? And he said, ᴿBecause the LORD thy God brought *it* to me.   *v. 19 • 24:12*
21 And Isaac said unto Jacob, Come near, I pray thee, that I may feel thee, my son, whether thou *be* my very son Esau or not.
22 And Jacob went near unto Isaac his father; and he felt him, and said, The voice *is* Jacob's voice, but the hands *are* the hands of Esau.
23 And he discerned him not, because his hands were ᴿhairy, as his brother Esau's hands: so he blessed him.   *v. 16*
24 And he said, *Art* thou my very son Esau? And he said, ᴿI *am.*   Rom. 3:7, 8

25 And he said, Bring it near to me, and I will eat of my son's venison, Rthat my soul may bless thee. And he brought it near to him, and he did eat: and he brought him wine, and he drank.   vv. 4, 10, 19, 31

26 And his father Isaac said unto him, Come near now, and kiss me, my son.

27 And he came near, and kissed him: and he smelled the smell of his Traiment, and blessed him, and said, See, Rthe smell of my son is as the smell of a field which the LORD hath blessed: clothing • Song 4:11; Hos. 14:6

28 Therefore God give thee of the dew of heaven, and the fatness of the earth, and Rplenty of corn and wine: Deut. 33:28

29 Let people serve thee, and nations bow down to thee: be lord over thy brethren, and let thy mother's sons bow down to thee: Rcursed be every one that curseth thee, and blessed be he that blesseth thee.   Zeph. 2:8

30 And it came to pass, as soon as Isaac had made an Rend of blessing Jacob, and Jacob was yet scarce gone out from the presence of Isaac his father, that Esau his brother came in from his hunting.   25:25

31 And he also had made Tsavoury meat, and brought it unto his father, and said unto his father, Let my father arise, and Reat of his son's venison, that thy soul may bless me.   tasteful • v. 4

32 And Isaac his father said unto him, Who art thou? And he said, I am thy son, thy Rfirstborn Esau.   Ex. 13:2

33 And Isaac trembled very exceedingly, and said, Who? where is he that hath taken venison, and brought it me, and I have eaten of all before thou camest, and have blessed him? yea, Rand he shall be blessed.   28:3, 4

34 And when Esau heard the words of his father, Rhe cried with a great and exceeding bitter cry, and said unto his father, Bless me, even me also, O my father.   [Heb. 12:17]

35 And he said, Thy brother came with subtilty, and hath taken away thy blessing.

36 And he said, Is not he rightly named Jacob? for he hath Tsupplanted me these two times: he took away my birthright; and, behold, now he hath taken away my blessing. And he said, Hast thou not reserved a blessing for me?   gat ahead of me

37 And Isaac answered and said unto Esau, RBehold, I have made him thy lord, and all his brethren have I given to him for servants; and with corn and wine have I Tsustained him: and what shall I do now unto thee, my son?   2 Sam. 8:14 • provided for

38 And Esau said unto his father, Hast thou but one blessing, my father? bless me, even me also, O my father. And Esau lifted up his voice, Rand wept.   21:16; Heb. 12:17

39 And Isaac his father answered and said unto him, Behold, Rthy dwelling shall be the fatness of the earth, and of the dew of heaven from above;   v. 28

40 And by thy sword shalt thou live, and shalt serve thy brother; and it shall come to pass when thou shalt have the dominion, that thou shalt break his yoke from off thy neck.

41 And Esau Rhated Jacob because of the blessing wherewith his father blessed him: and Esau said in his heart, The days of mourning for my father are at hand; then will I slay my brother Jacob.   37:4, 8

42 And these words of Esau her elder son were told to Rebekah: and she sent and called Jacob her younger son, and said unto him, Behold, thy brother Esau, as touching thee, doth comfort himself, purposing to kill thee.

43 Now therefore, my son, Tobey my voice; and arise, flee thou to Laban my brother Rto Ha'-ran;   do as I tell you • 11:31

44 And Ttarry with him a few days, until thy brother's fury turn away;   stay

45 Until thy brother's anger turn away from thee, and he forget that which thou hast done to him: then I will send, and fetch thee from thence: why should I Tbe deprived also of you both in one day?   lose

46 And Rebekah said to Isaac, RI am weary of my life because of the daughters of Heth: Rif Jacob take a wife of the daughters of Heth, such as these which are of the daughters of the land, what good shall my life do me?   26:35; 28:8 • 24:3

CHAPTER 28

AND Isaac called Jacob, and blessed him, and Tcharged him, and said unto him, RThou shalt not take a wife of the daughters of Canaan.   instructed • 24:3

2 Arise, go to Pa'-dan-a'-ram, to the house of Be-thu'-el thy mother's father; and take thee a wife from thence of the daughters of Laban thy mother's brother.

3 And God Almighty bless thee, and make thee fruitful, and multiply thee, that thou mayest be a multitude of people;

4 And give thee the blessing of Abraham, to thee, and to thy seed with thee; that thou mayest inherit the land wherein thou art a stranger, which God gave unto Abraham.

5 And RIsaac sent away Jacob: and he went to Pa'-dan-a'-ram unto Laban, son of Be-thu'-el the Syrian, the brother of Rebekah, Jacob's and Esau's mother.   27:43

6 When Esau saw that Isaac had blessed Jacob, and sent him away to Pa'-dan-a'-ram, to take him a wife from thence; and that as he blessed him he gave him a charge, saying, RThou shalt not take a wife of the daughters of Canaan;   v. 1

7 And that Jacob obeyed his father and his mother, and was gone to Pa'-dan-a'-ram;

8 And Esau seeing that the daughters of Canaan pleased not Isaac his father;

9 Then went Esau unto Ish'-ma-el, and took unto the wives which he had Ma'-ha-lath the daughter of Ish'-ma-el Abraham's son, the sister of Ne-ba'-joth, to be his wife.

Jacob's Dream

10 And Jacob went out from Be'-er-she'-ba, and went toward ᴿHa'-ran.   12:4; Acts 7:2

11 And he lighted upon a certain place, and ᵀtarried there all night, because the sun was set; and he took of the stones of that place, and put *them for* his pillows, and lay down in that place to sleep.   *stayed*

12 And he dreamed, and behold a ᵀladder set up on the earth, and the top of it reached to heaven: and behold the angels of God ascending and descending on it.   *stairway*

13 And, behold, the LORD stood ᵀabove it, and said, ᴿI *am* the LORD God of Abraham thy father, and the God of Isaac: the land whereon thou liest, to thee will I give it, and to thy seed;   *beside him* • 26:24

14 And thy seed shall be as the dust of the earth, and thou shalt spread abroad to the west, and to the east, and to the north, and to the south: and in thee and in thy seed shall all the families of the earth be blessed.

15 And, behold, I *am* with thee, and will ᵀkeep thee in all *places* whither thou goest, and will bring thee again into this land; for I will not leave thee, until I have done *that* which I have spoken to thee of.   *protect*

16 And Jacob awaked out of his sleep, and he said, Surely the LORD is in ᴿthis place; and I knew *it* not.   Ex. 3:5; Josh. 5:15

17 And he was afraid, and said, ᴿHow ᵀdreadful *is* this place! this *is* none other but the house of God, and this *is* the gate of heaven.   [Ps. 68:35] • *awesome*

18 And Jacob rose up early in the morning, and took the stone that he had put *for* his pillows, and set it up *for* a pillar, ᴿand poured oil upon the top of it.   Lev. 8:10–12

19 And he called the name of that place ᵀBeth'-el: but the name of that city *was* called ᴿLuz at the first.   *house of God* • 35:6

20 And Jacob vowed a vow, saying, If God will be with me, and will keep me in this way that I go, and will give me ᴿbread to eat, and raiment to put on,   1 Tim. 6:8

21 So ᵀthat ᴿI come again to my father's house in peace; ᴿthen shall the LORD be my God: *I return with success* • Judg. 11:31 • Deut. 26:17

22 And this stone, which I have set *for* a pillar, ᴿshall be God's house: ᴿand of all that thou shalt give me I will surely give the tenth unto thee.   35:7, 14 • [Lev. 27:30]

CHAPTER 29

Jacob's Labours

THEN Jacob went on his journey, ᴿand came into the land of the ᴿpeople of the east.   Num. 23:7; Hos. 12:12 • Judg. 6:3, 33

2 And he looked, and behold a ᴿwell in the field, and, lo, there *were* three flocks of sheep lying by it; for out of that well they watered the flocks: and a great stone *was* upon the well's mouth.   24:10, 11; Ex. 2:15

3 And thither were all the flocks gathered: and they rolled the stone from the well's mouth, and watered the sheep, and put the stone again upon the well's mouth in his place.

4 And Jacob said unto them, My brethren, whence *be* ye? And they said, Of ᴿHa'-ran *are* we.   11:31

5 And he said unto them, Know ye ᴿLaban the son of Na'-hor? And they said, We know him.   24:29

6 And he said unto them, *Is* he well? And they said, *He is* well: and, behold, Ra'-chel his daughter cometh with the sheep.

7 And he said, Lo, *it is* yet ᵀhigh day, neither *is it* time that the cattle should be gathered together: water ye the sheep, and go and feed *them*.   *early in the day*

8 And they said, We cannot, until all the flocks be gathered together, and *till* they roll the stone from the well's mouth; then we water the sheep.

9 And while he yet spake with them, ᴿRa'-chel came with her father's ᴿsheep: for she kept them.   Ex. 2:16 • 4:2; 37:2

10 And it came to pass, when Jacob saw Ra'-chel the daughter of Laban his mother's brother, and the sheep of Laban his mother's brother, that Jacob went near, and ᴿrolled the stone from the well's mouth, and watered the flock of Laban his mother's brother.   Ex. 2:17

11 And Jacob ᴿkissed Ra'-chel, and lifted up his voice, and wept.   33:4; 45:14, 15

12 And Jacob told Ra'-chel that he *was* her father's brother, and that he *was* Rebekah's son: and she ran and told her father.

13 And it came to pass, when Laban heard the tidings of Jacob his sister's son, that he ran to meet him, and embraced him, and kissed him, and brought him to his house. And he told Laban all these things.

14 And Laban said to him, ᴿSurely thou *art* my bone and my flesh. And he abode with him the space of a month.   Judg. 9:2

15 And Laban said unto Jacob, Because thou *art* my brother, shouldest thou therefore ᵀserve me for nought? tell me, what *shall* thy ᴿwages *be*?   *work for nothing* • 31:41

16 And ᴿLaban had two daughters: the name of the elder *was* Leah, and the name of the younger *was* Ra'-chel.   24:29

17 Leah *was* tender eyed; but Ra'-chel was
ᴿbeautiful and well favoured.   12:11
18 And Jacob loved Ra'-chel; and said, ᴿI
will serve thee seven years for Ra'-chel thy
younger daughter.   31:41; 2 Sam. 3:14
19 And Laban said, *It is* better that I give
her to thee, than that I should give her to
another man: abide with me.
20 And Jacob served seven years for Ra'-
chel; and they seemed unto him *but* a few
days, for the love he had to her.
21 And Jacob said unto Laban, Give *me*
my wife, for my days are fulfilled, that I may
ᴿgo in unto her.   Judg. 15:1
22 And Laban gathered together all the
men of the place, and made a feast.
23 And it came to pass in the evening, that
he took Leah his daughter, and brought her
to him; and he went in unto her.
24 And Laban gave unto his daughter Leah
Zil'-pah his maid *for* an handmaid.
25 And it came to pass, that in the morning, behold, it *was* Leah: and he said to
Laban, What *is* this thou hast done unto me?
did not I serve with thee for Ra'-chel? wherefore then hast thou beguiled me?
26 And Laban said, ᵀIt must not be so done
in our ᵀcountry, to give the younger before
the firstborn.   *it is not our custom · land*
27 Fulfil her week, and we will give thee
this also for the service which thou shalt
serve with me yet seven other years.
28 And Jacob did so, and fulfilled her
week: and he gave him Ra'-chel his daughter
to wife also.
29 And Laban gave to Ra'-chel his daughter Bil'-hah his handmaid to be her maid.
30 And he went in also unto Ra'-chel, and
he loved also Ra'-chel more than Leah, and
served with him yet seven other years.
31 And when the Lᴏʀᴅ saw that Leah *was*
hated, he openedᵀ her womb: but Ra'-chel
was barren.   *enabled her to have children*
32 And Leah conceived, and bare a son,
and she called his name ᵀReuben: for she
said, Surely the Lᴏʀᴅ hath ᴿlooked upon my
affliction; now therefore my husband will
love me.   *a son* · [Ex. 4:31; Deut. 26:7]
33 And she conceived again, and bare a
son; and said, Because the ᴿLᴏʀᴅ hath heard
that I *was* hated, he hath therefore given me
this *son* also: and she called his name ᵀSim-
eon.   [1 Sam. 2:3] · *hearing*
34 And she conceived again, and bare a
son; and said, Now this time will my husband
be ᵀjoined unto me, because I have born him
three sons: therefore was his name called
ᴿLevi.   *attached to* · 35:23
35 And she conceived again, and bare a
son: and she said, Now will I praise the Lᴏʀᴅ:
therefore she called his name Judah; and ᵀleft
bearing.   *had no more children*

CHAPTER 30

AND when Ra'-chel saw that ᴿshe bare
Jacob no children, Ra'-chel ᴿenvied her
sister; and said unto Jacob, Give me children,
ᴿor else I die.   29:31 · 37:11 · [Job 5:2]
2 And Jacob's anger was kindled against
Ra'-chel: and he said, ᴿAmᵀ I in God's stead,
who hath withheld from thee the fruit of the
womb?   1 Sam. 1:5 · *Can I act as if I were God?*
3 And she said, Behold my maid Bil'-hah,
go in unto her; and she shall bear upon my
knees, that I may also have children by her.
4 And she gave him Bil'-hah her handmaid
to wife: and Jacob went in unto her.
5 And Bil'-hah ᴿconceived, and bare Jacob
a son.   21:2
6 And Ra'-chel said, God hath judged me,
and hath also heard my voice, and hath given
me a son: therefore called she his name Dan.
7 And Bil'-hah Ra'-chel's maid conceived
again, and bare Jacob a second son.
8 And Ra'-chel said, With ᵀgreat wrestlings
have I wrestled with my sister, and I have
prevailed: and she called his name Naph'-ta-
li.   *wrestlings of God*
9 When Leah saw that she had left bear-
ing, she took Zil'-pah her maid, and ᴿgave her
Jacob to wife.   v. 4
10 And Zil'-pah Leah's maid bare Jacob a
son.
11 And Leah said, A troop cometh: and she
called his name ᵀGad.ᴿ   *fortune* · 35:26
12 And Zil'-pah Leah's maid bare Jacob a
second son.
13 And Leah said, Happy am I, for the
daughters ᴿwill call me blessed: and she
called his name ᵀAsher.   Luke 1:48 · *happy*
14 And Reuben went in the days of wheat
harvest, and found mandrakes in the field,
and brought them unto his mother Leah.
Then Ra'-chel said to Leah, ᴿGive me, I pray
thee, of thy son's mandrakes.   25:30
15 And she said unto her, ᴿIs *it* a small
matter that thou hast taken my husband?
and wouldest thou take away my son's mandrakes also? And Ra'-chel said, Therefore he
shall lie with thee to night for thy son's
mandrakes.   [Num. 16:9, 13]
16 And Jacob came out of the field in the
evening, and Leah went out to meet him, and
said, Thou must come in unto me; for surely I
have hired thee with my son's mandrakes.
And he lay with her that night.
17 And God hearkened unto Leah, and she
conceived, and bare Jacob the fifth son.
18 And Leah said, God hath given me my
hire, because I have given my maiden to my
husband: and she called his name ᴿIs'-sa-
char.   35:23
19 And Leah conceived again, and bare
Jacob the sixth son.

20 And Leah said, God hath endued me *with* a good dowry; now will my husband dwell with me, because I have born him six sons: and she called his name Zeb'-u-lun.

21 And afterwards she bare a daughter, and called her name Dinah.

22 And God ᴿremembered Ra'-chel, and God hearkened to her, and ᴿopened her womb.   1 Sam. 1:19 • 29:31

23 And she conceived, and bare a son; and said, God hath taken away my reproach:

24 And she called his name Joseph; and said, The Lᴏʀᴅ shall add to me another son.

25 And it came to pass, when Ra'-chel had born Joseph, that Jacob said unto Laban, ᴿSend me away, that I may go unto mine own place, and to my country.   24:54, 56

26 Give *me* my wives and my children, for whom I have served thee, and let me go: for thou knowest my service which I have done thee.

27 And Laban said unto him, I pray thee, if I have found favour in thine eyes, *tarry: for* I have learned by experience that the Lᴏʀᴅ hath blessed me ᴿfor thy sake.   39:3, 5; 26:24

28 And he said, Appointᵀ me thy wages, and I will give *it.*   *tell me what you want for*

29 And he said unto him, ᴿThou knowest how I have served thee, and how thy cattle was with me.   31:6, 38–40; Matt. 24:45; Titus 2:10

30 For *it was* little which thou hadst before I *came,* and it is *now* increased unto a multitude; and the Lᴏʀᴅ hath blessed thee since my coming: and now when shall I ᴿprovide for mine own house also?   [1 Tim. 5:8]

31 And he said, What shall I give thee? And Jacob said, Thou shalt not give me any thing: if thou wilt do this thing for me, I will again feed *and* keep thy flock.

32 I will pass through all thy flock to day, removing from thence all the speckled and ᵀspotted cattle, and all the brown cattle among the sheep, and the spotted and speckled among the goats: and ᴿof *such* shall be my hire.   *dappled* • 31:8

33 So shall my righteousness answer for me ᵀin time to come, when it shall come for my hire before thy face: every one that *is* not speckled and spotted among the goats, and ᵀbrown among the sheep, that shall be counted stolen with me.   *later* • *black*

34 And Laban said, Behold, I would it might be ᴿaccording to thy word.   21:27

35 And he removed that day the he goats that were ringstraked and spotted, and all the she goats that were speckled and spotted, *and* every one that had *some* white in it, and all the brown among the sheep, and gave *them* into the hand of his sons.

36 And he set ᵀthree days' journey betwixt himself and Jacob: and Jacob fed the rest of ᴿLaban's flocks.   *60 mi.* • 31:9

37 And Jacob took him rods of green poplar, and of the hazel and chesnut tree; and pilled white ᵀstrakes in them, and made the white appear which *was* in the rods.   *stripes*

38 And he set the rods which he had ᵀpilled before the flocks in the gutters in the watering troughs when the flocks came to drink, that they should conceive when they came to drink.   *peeled*

39 And the flocks conceived before the rods, and brought forth cattle ringstraked, speckled, and spotted.

40 And Jacob did separate the lambs, and set the faces of the flocks toward the ringstraked, and all the brown in the flock of Laban; and he put his own flocks by themselves, and put them not unto Laban's cattle.

41 And it came to pass, whensoever the stronger cattle did conceive, that Jacob laid the rods before the eyes of the cattle in the gutters, that they might conceive among the rods.

42 But when the cattle were feeble, he put *them* not in: so the feebler were Laban's, and the stronger Jacob's.

43 And the man ᴿincreased exceedingly, and had much cattle, and maidservants, and menservants, and camels, and asses.   26:13, 14

CHAPTER 31

Jacob's Flight

AND he heard the words of Laban's sons, saying, Jacob hath taken away all that *was* our father's; and of *that* which *was* our father's hath he gotten all this ᵀglory.   *wealth*

2 And Jacob beheld ᴿthe countenance of Laban, and, behold, it *was* ᵀnot ᴿtoward him as before.   4:5 • *not friendly* • Deut. 28:54

3 And the Lᴏʀᴅ said unto Jacob, Return unto the land of thy fathers, and to thy kindred; and ᴿI will be with thee.   28:15

4 And Jacob sent and called Ra'-chel and ᴿLeah to the field unto his flock,   33:2

5 And said unto them, I see your father's countenance, that it *is* ᵀnot toward me as before; but the God of my father ᵀhath been with me.   *not in favour of me* • *has blessed me*

6 And ᴿye know that with all my ᵀpower I have served your father.   30:29 • *ability*

7 And your father hath deceived me, and changed my wages ᴿten times; but God suffered him not to hurt me.   Num. 14:22

8 If he said thus, The speckled shall be thy wages; then all the cattle bare speckled: and if he said thus, The ringstraked shall be thy hire; then bare all the cattle ringstraked.

9 ᴿThus God hath taken away the cattle of your father, and given *them* to me.   *v.* 16

10 And it came to pass at the time that the cattle conceived, that I lifted up mine eyes,

and saw in a dream, and, behold, the rams which leaped upon the cattle *were* ring-straked, speckled, and ᵀgrisled.   *spotted*

11 And the angel of God spake unto me in a dream, *saying*, Jacob: And I said, Here *am* I.

12 And he said, Lift up now thine eyes, and see, all the rams which leap upon the cattle *are* ringstraked, speckled, and grisled: for I have seen all that Laban doeth unto thee.

13 I *am* the God of Beth′-el, ᴿwhere thou anointedst the pillar, *and* where thou vowedst a vow unto me: now ᴿarise, get thee out from this land, and ᴿreturn unto the land of thy kindred.   28:18-20 · 32:9 · *v*. 3

14 And Ra′-chel and Leah answered and said unto him, *Is there* yet any portion or inheritance for us in our father's house?

15 Are we not counted of him strangers? for ᴿhe hath sold us, and hath quite devoured also our money.   29:15, 27; Neh. 5:8

16 For all the riches which God hath taken from our father, that *is* our's, and our children's: now then, whatsoever God hath said unto thee, do.

17 Then Jacob rose up, and set his sons and his wives upon camels;

18 And he carried away all his cattle, and all his goods which he had gotten, the cattle of his getting, which he had gotten in Pa′-dan-a′-ram, for ᴿto go to Isaac his father in the land of ᴿCanaan.   35:27-29 · 17:8

19 And Laban went to shear his sheep: and Ra′-chel had stolen the ᴿimagesᵀ that *were* her father's.   *vv*. 30, 34; 35:2 · *household gods*

20 And Jacob stole away unawares to Laban the Syrian, in that he told him not that he fled.

21 So he fled with all that he had; and he rose up, and passed over the river, and set his face *toward* the mount Gil′-e-ad.

22 And it was told Laban on the third day that Jacob was fled.

23 And he took ᴿhis brethren with him, and pursued after him seven days' journey; and they overtook him in the mount Gil′-e-ad.   13:8

24 And God ᴿcame to Laban the Syrian in a dream by night, and said unto him, Take heed that thou ᴿspeak not to Jacob either good or bad.   Job 33:15; Matt. 1:20 · 24:50

25 Then Laban overtook Jacob. Now Jacob had pitched his tent in the mount: and Laban with his brethren ᵀpitched in the mount of Gil′-e-ad.   *encamped*

26 And Laban said to Jacob, What hast thou done, that thou hast stolen away unawares to me, and carried away my daughters, as captives *taken* with the sword?

27 Wherefore didst thou flee away secretly, and ᵀsteal away from me; and didst not tell me, that I might have sent thee away with mirth, and with songs, with ᴿtabret, and with ᴿharp?   *cheat me* · Ex. 15:20 · 4:21

28 And hast not suffered me to ᴿkiss my sons and my daughters? ᴿthou hast now done foolishly in *so* doing.   *v*. 55 · 1 Sam. 13:13

29 It is in the power of my hand to do you hurt: but the God of your father spake unto me yesternight, saying, Take thou heed that thou speak not to Jacob either good or bad.

30 And now, *though* thou wouldest needs be gone, because thou ᵀsore longedst after thy father's house, *yet* wherefore hast thou stolen my gods?   *wanted very much to go home*

31 And Jacob answered and said to Laban, Because ᴿI was afraid: for I said, Peradventure thou wouldest take by force thy daughters from me.   26:7; 32:7, 11

32 With whomsoever thou findest thy gods, ᴿlet him not live: before our brethren ᵀdiscern thou what *is* thine with me, and take *it* to thee. For Jacob knew not that Ra′-chel had stolen them.   44:9 · *take note*

33 And Laban went into Jacob's tent, and into Leah's tent, and into the two maidservants' tents; but he found *them* not. Then went he out of Leah's tent, and entered into Ra′-chel's tent.

34 Now Ra′-chel had taken the images, and put them in the camel's ᵀfurniture, and sat upon them. And Laban ᵀsearched all the tent, but found *them* not.   *saddle* · *felt*

35 And she said to her father, Let it not displease my lord that I cannot ᴿrise up before thee; for the custom of women *is* upon me. And he searched, but found not the images.   Ex. 20:12; Lev. 19:32

36 And Jacob was wroth, and chode with Laban: and Jacob answered and said to Laban, What *is* my trespass? what *is* my sin, that thou hast so hotly pursued after me?

37 Whereas thou hast ᵀsearched all my ᵀstuff, what hast thou found of all thy household stuff? set *it* here before my brethren and thy brethren, that they may judge betwixt us both.   *felt* · *furniture*

38 ᵀThis twenty years *have* I *been* with thee; thy ewes and thy she goats have not cast their young, and the rams of thy flock have I not eaten.   *these*

39 That which was torn *of beasts* I brought not unto thee; I bare the loss of it; of my hand didst thou require it, *whether* stolen by day, or stolen by night.

40 *Thus* I was; in the day the drought consumed me, and the frost by night; and my sleep departed from mine eyes.

41 Thus have I been twenty years in thy house; I served thee fourteen years for thy two daughters, and six years for thy cattle: and thou hast changed my wages ten times.

42 Except the God of my father, the God of Abraham, and ᴿthe fear of Isaac, had ᵀbeen with me, surely thou hadst sent me away now empty. God hath seen mine affliction

and the labour of my hands, and rebuked *thee* yesternight.   *vv.* 5, 53 • *helped me*

43 And Laban answered and said unto Jacob, *These* daughters *are* my daughters, and *these* children *are* my children, and ^R*these* cattle *are* my cattle, and all that thou seest *is* mine: and what can I do this day unto these my daughters, or unto their children which they have born?   *v.* 1

44 Now therefore come thou, ^Rlet us make a covenant, I and thou; and let it be for a witness between me and thee.   26:28

45 And Jacob ^Rtook a stone, and set it up *for* a pillar.   35:14; 28:18; Josh. 24:26, 27

46 And Jacob said unto his brethren, Gather stones; and they took stones, and made an heap: and they did eat there upon the heap.

47 And Laban called it Je'-gar-sa-ha-du'-tha: but Jacob called it Gal'-e-ed.

48 And Laban said, This heap *is* a witness between me and thee this day. Therefore was the name of it called Gal'-e-ed;

49 And ^RMiz'-pah; for he said, The Lord watch between me and thee, when we are absent one from another.   Judg. 11:29

50 If thou shalt ^Tafflict my daughters, or if thou shalt take *other* wives beside my daughters, no man *is* with us; see, ^RGod *is* witness betwixt me and thee.   *harm* • Jer. 29:23

51 And Laban said to Jacob, Behold this heap, and behold *this* pillar, which I have cast betwixt me and thee;

52 This heap *be* witness, and *this* pillar *be* witness, that I will not pass over this heap to thee, and that thou shalt not pass over this heap and this pillar unto me, for harm.

53 The God of Abraham, and the God of Na'-hor, the God of their father, ^Rjudge betwixt us. And Jacob ^Tsware by the fear of his father Isaac.   16:5 • *promised solemnly*

54 ^RThen Jacob ^Toffered sacrifice upon the mount, and called his brethren to eat bread: and they did eat bread, and tarried all night in the mount.   Ex. 18:12 • *killed beasts*

55 And early in the morning Laban rose up, and kissed his sons and his daughters, and ^Rblessed them: and Laban departed, and ^Rreturned unto his place.   28:1 • 18:33

CHAPTER 32

Jacob Fights with the Angel

A ND Jacob went on his way, and the ^Tangels of God met him.   *messengers*

2 And when Jacob saw them, he said, This *is* God's host: and he called the name of that place ^TMa-ha-na'-im.   *twain camps*

3 And Jacob sent messengers before him to Esau his brother unto the land of Se'-ir, ^Rthe ^Tcountry of E'-dom.   *vv.* 7, 11 • *field*

4 And he commanded them, saying, Thus shall ye speak unto my lord Esau; Thy servant Jacob saith thus, I have sojourned with Laban, and ^Rstayed there until now: 31:41

5 And ^RI have oxen, and asses, flocks, and menservants, and womenservants: and I have sent to ^Ttell my lord, that ^RI may find grace in thy sight.   30:43 • *greet* • 33:8, 15

6 And the messengers returned to Jacob, saying, We came to thy brother Esau, and also ^Rhe cometh to meet thee, and four hundred men with him.   33:1

7 Then Jacob was ^Rgreatly afraid and ^Rdistressed: and he divided the people that *was* with him, and the flocks, and herds, and the camels, into two bands;   *v.* 11 • 35:3

8 And said, If Esau come to the one company, and ^Tsmite it, then the other company which is left shall escape.   *beat*

9 ^RAnd Jacob ^Tsaid, O God of my father Abraham, and God of my father Isaac, the Lord ^Rwhich saidst unto me, Return unto thy country, and to thy kindred, and I will deal well with thee: [Ps. 50:15] • *prayed* • 31:3, 13

10 I am not worthy of the least of all the mercies, and of all the truth, which thou hast shewed unto thy servant; for with ^Rmy staff I passed over this Jordan; and now I am become two ^Tbands.   Job 8:7 • *caravans*

11 Deliver me, I pray thee, from the hand of my brother, from the hand of Esau: for I fear him, lest he will come and smite me, *and* the mother with the children.

12 And ^Rthou saidst, I will surely do thee good, and ^Rmake thy seed as the sand of the sea, which cannot be numbered for multitude.   28:13–15 • 22:17

13 And he lodged there that same night; and took of that ^Twhich came to his hand a present for Esau his brother;   *which he had*

14 Two hundred she goats, and twenty he goats, two hundred ewes, and twenty rams,

15 Thirty ^Tmilch camels with their colts, forty ^Tkine, and ten bulls, twenty she asses, and ten foals.   *milk* • *cows*

16 And he delivered *them* into the hand of his servants, every drove by themselves; and said unto his servants, Pass over before me, and put a space betwixt drove and drove.

17 And he commanded the foremost, saying, When Esau my brother meeteth thee, and asketh thee, saying, Whose *art* thou? and whither goest thou? and whose *are* these before thee?

18 Then thou shalt say, *They be* thy servant Jacob's; it *is* a present sent unto my lord Esau: and, behold, also he *is* behind us.

19 And so commanded he the second, and the third, and all that followed the droves, saying, On this manner shall ye speak unto Esau, when ye find him.

20 And say ye moreover, Behold, thy servant Jacob is behind us. For he said, I will appease him with the present that goeth before me, and afterward I will see his face; peradventure he will accept of me.

21 So went the present over before him: and himself ᵀlodged that night in the ᵀcompany.   *spent* • *camp*

22 And he rose up that night, and took his two wives, and his two womenservants, and his eleven sons, ᴿand passed over the ford ᴿJab'-bok.   Deut. 3:16; Josh. 12:2 • Num. 21:24

23 And he took them, and sent them over the brook, and sent over that he had.

24 And ᴿJacob was left alone; and there ᴿwrestled a man with him until the ᵀbreaking of the day.   Josh. 5:13–15 • Hos. 12:3, 4 • *dawn*

25 And when he saw that he prevailed not against him, he touched the hollow of his thigh; and the hollow of Jacob's thigh was out of joint, as he wrestled with him.

26 And he said, Let me go, for the day breaketh. And he said, I will not let thee go, except thou bless me.

27 And he said unto him, What *is* thy name? And he said, Jacob.

28 And he said, Thy name shall be called no more Jacob, but ᵀIsrael: for as a prince hast thou power with God and with men, and hast ᵀprevailed.   *a prince of God* • *won success*

29 And Jacob asked *him*, and said, Tell *me*, I pray thee, thy name. And he said, Wherefore *is* it *that* thou dost ask after my name? And he blessed him there.

30 And Jacob called the name of the place ᵀPe-ni'-el: for ᴿI have seen God face to face, and my life is preserved.   *the face of God* • 16:13

31 ᴿAnd as he passed over ᴿPe-nu'-el the sun rose upon him, and he ᵀhalted upon his thigh.   2 Cor. 12:9 • *v.* 30; Judg. 8:8 • *limped*

32 Therefore the children of Israel eat not *of* the sinew which shrank, which *is* upon the hollow of the thigh, unto this day: because he ᵀtouched the hollow of Jacob's thigh in the sinew that shrank.   *Or struck*

CHAPTER 33

Jacob Makes Peace with Esau

AND Jacob lifted up his eyes, and looked, and, behold, ᴿEsau came, and with him four hundred men. And he divided the children unto Leah, and unto Ra'-chel, and unto the two handmaids.   32:6

2 And he put the handmaids and their children foremost, and ᴿLeah and her children after, and ᴿRa'-chel and Joseph ᵀhindermost.   35:23 • 35:19 • *last of all*

3 And he passed over before them, and bowed himself to the ground seven times, until he came near to his brother.

4 And Esau ran to meet him, and embraced him, ᴿand fell on his neck, and kissed him: and they wept.   45:14, 15

5 And he lifted up his eyes, and saw the women and the children; and said, Who *are* those with thee? And he said, The children ᴿwhich God hath graciously given thy servant.   [48:9; Ps. 127:3]; Is. 8:18

6 Then the handmaidens came near, they and their ᴿchildren, and they bowed themselves.   48:9

7 And Leah also with her children came near, and bowed themselves: and after came Joseph near and Ra'-chel, and they bowed themselves.

8 And he said, What *meanest* thou by all this drove which I met? And he said, *These are* to find grace in the sight of my lord.

9 And Esau said, I have enough, my brother; keep that thou hast unto thyself.

10 And Jacob said, Nay, I pray thee, ᵀif now I have found grace in thy sight, then receive my present at my hand: for therefore I ᴿhave seen thy face, as though I had seen the face of God, and thou wast pleased with me.   *if I seem nice to you* • 43:3; 2 Sam. 3:13

11 Take, I pray thee, my blessing that is brought to thee; because God hath dealt graciously with me, and because I have enough. And he urged him, and he took *it*.

12 And he said, Let us take our journey, and let us go, and I will go before thee.

13 And he said unto him, My lord knoweth that the children *are* ᵀtender, and the flocks and herds with young *are* with me: and if men should overdrive them one day, all the flock will die.   *young*

14 Let my lord, I pray thee, pass over before his servant: and I will lead on softly, according as the cattle that goeth before me and the children be able to endure, until I come unto my lord unto Se'-ir.

15 And Esau said, Let me now leave with thee *some* of the folk that *are* with me. And he said, What needeth it? ᴿlet me find grace in the sight of my lord.   34:11

16 So Esau returned that day on his way unto Se'-ir.

17 And Jacob journeyed to ᴿSuc'-coth, and built him an house, and made ᵀbooths for his cattle: therefore the name of the place is called Suc'-coth.   Josh. 13:27 • *shelters*

18 And Jacob came to ᴿSha'-lem, a city of She'-chem, which *is* in the land of Canaan, when he came from Pa'-dan-a'-ram; and pitched his tent before the city.   John 3:23

19 And he bought a parcel of a field, where he had spread his tent, at the hand of the children of Ha'-mor, She'-chem's father, for an hundred pieces of money.

20 And he erected there an altar, and ᴿcalled it El-e-lo'-he-Is'-ra-el.   35:7

CHAPTER 34

The Defilement of Dinah

AND ᴿDinah the daughter of Leah, which she bare unto Jacob, went out to see the daughters of the land.   30:21

2 And when She'-chem the son of Ha'-mor the ᴿHi'-vite, prince of the country, saw her, he ᴿtook her, and lay with her, and ᵀdefiled her.   v. 30 · 20:2 · humbled her

3 And his soul ᵀclave unto Dinah the daughter of Jacob, and he loved the damsel, and spake kindly unto the damsel.   clung

4 And She'-chem spake unto his father Ha'-mor, saying, Get me this damsel to wife.

5 And Jacob heard that he had ᴿdefiled Dinah his daughter: now his sons were with his cattle in the field: and Jacob held his peace until they were come.   2 Sam. 13:22

6 And Ha'-mor the father of She'-chem went out unto Jacob to commune with him.

7 And the sons of Jacob came out of the field when they heard it: and the men were ᵀgrieved, and they were very wroth, because he had ᵀwrought folly in Israel in lying with Jacob's daughter; which thing ought not to be done.   offended · done wrong

8 And Ha'-mor ᵀcommuned with them, saying, The soul of my son She'-chem longeth for your daughter: I pray you give her him to wife.   spoke

9 And ᴿmake ye ᴿmarriages with us, and give your daughters unto us, and take our daughters unto you.   Ex. 23:32 · 24:3

10 And ye shall dwell with us: and the land shall be before you; dwell and trade ye therein, and get you possessions therein.

11 And She'-chem said unto her father and unto her brethren, ᵀLet me find grace in your eyes, and what ye shall say unto me I will give.   treat me like a friend

12 Ask me never so much dowry and gift, and I will give according as ye shall say unto me: but give me the damsel to wife.

13 And the sons of Jacob answered She'-chem and Ha'-mor his father ᴿdeceitfully, and said, because he had defiled Dinah their sister: 31:7; Ex. 8:29

14 And they said unto them, We cannot do this thing, to give our sister to ᴿone that is ᴿuncircumcised; for ᴿthat were a reproach unto us: 17:14 · Ex. 12:48 · Josh. 5:9

15 But in this will we consent unto you: If ye will be as we be, that every male of you be circumcised;

16 Then will we give our daughters unto you, and we will take your daughters to us, and we will dwell with you, and we will become one people.

17 But if ye will not hearken unto us, to be circumcised; then will we take our daughter, and we will be gone.

18 And their words pleased Ha'-mor, and She'-chem Ha'-mor's son.

19 And the young man deferred not to do the thing, because he had delight in Jacob's daughter: and he was more honourable than all the house of his father.

20 And Ha'-mor and She'-chem his son came unto the gate of their city, and communed with the men of their city, saying,

21 These men are peaceable with us; therefore let them dwell in the land, and trade therein; for the land, behold, it is large enough for them; let us take their daughters to us for wives, and let us give them our daughters.

22 Only ᵀherein will the men consent unto us for to dwell with us, to be one people, if every male among us be circumcised, as they are circumcised.   on this condition

23 Shall not their cattle and their substance and every beast of their's be our's? only let us consent unto them, and they will dwell with us.

24 And unto Ha'-mor and unto She'-chem his son hearkened all that ᴿwent out of the gate of his city; and every male was circumcised, ᵀall that went out of the gate of his city.   23:10, 18 · the inhabitants

25 And it came to pass on the third day, when they were sore, that two of the sons of Jacob, Simeon and Levi, Dinah's brethren, took each man his sword, and came upon the city boldly, and slew all the males.

26 And they ᴿslew Ha'-mor and She'-chem his son with the edge of the sword, and took Dinah out of She'-chem's house, and went out.   49:5, 6

27 The sons of Jacob came upon the slain, and spoiled the city, because they had defiled their sister.

28 They took their sheep, and their oxen, and their asses, and that which was in the city, and that which was in the field,

29 And all their wealth, and all their little ones, and their wives took they captive, and spoiled even all that was in the house.

30 And Jacob said to Simeon and Levi, ᵀYe have troubled me to ᴿmake me to stink among the inhabitants of the land, among the Ca'-naan-ites and the Per'-iz-zites: and I being few in number, they shall gather themselves together against me, and slay me; and I shall be destroyed, I and my house.   caused me trouble · Ex. 5:21

31 And they said, ᴿShould he deal with our sister as with an ᴿharlot?   [Prov. 6:34] · Lev. 19:29

CHAPTER 35

The Devotion at Bethel

AND God said unto Jacob, Arise, go up to ᴿBeth'-el, and dwell there: and make

there an altar unto God, ^Rthat appeared unto thee ^Rwhen thou fleddest from the face of Esau thy brother.   28:19 · 28:13 · 27:43

2 Then Jacob said unto his household, and to all that *were* with him, Put away the strange gods that *are* among you, and be clean, and change your garments:

3 And let us arise, and go up to Beth'–el; and I will make there an altar unto God, who answered me in the day of my distress, and was with me in the way which I went.

4 And they gave unto Jacob all the ^Tstrange gods which *were* in their hand, and *all their* ^Rearrings which *were* in their ears; and Jacob hid them under ^Rthe oak which *was* by She'–chem.   idols · Hos. 2:13 · Josh. 24:26

5 And they journeyed: and ^Rthe terror of God was upon the cities that *were* round about them, and they did not pursue after the sons of Jacob.   [Deut. 11:25; 1 Sam. 14:15]

6 So Jacob came to ^RLuz, which *is* in the land of Canaan, that *is,* Beth'–el, he and all the people that *were* with him.   28:19, 22

7 And he built there an ^Raltar, and called the place ^TEl–beth'–el: because there God appeared unto him, when he fled from the face of his brother.   33:20 · *the God of Bethel*

8 But ^RDeb'–o–rah Rebekah's nurse died, and she was buried beneath Beth'–el under an oak: and the name of it was called ^TAl'–lon–bach'–uth.   24:59 · *The oak of weeping*

9 And ^RGod appeared unto Jacob again, when he came out of Pa'–dan–a'–ram, and ^Rblessed him.   Josh. 5:13; Dan. 10:5 · 32:29; Hos. 12:4

10 And ^RGod said unto him, Thy name *is* Jacob: ^Rthy name shall not be called any more Jacob, but Israel shall be thy name: and he called his name Israel.   32:28 · 17:5

11 And God said unto him, I *am* God Almighty: be fruitful and multiply; a nation and a company of nations shall be of thee, and kings shall come out of thy loins;

12 And the land ^Rwhich I gave Abraham and Isaac, to thee I will give it, and to thy seed after thee will I give the land.   12:7

13 And God ^Rwent up from him in the place where he talked with him.   17:22

14 And Jacob ^Rset up a pillar in the place where he talked with him, *even* a pillar of stone: and he poured a drink offering thereon, and he poured oil thereon.   28:18

15 And Jacob called the name of the place where God spake with him, Beth'–el.

The Deaths of Rachel and Isaac

16 And they journeyed from Beth'–el; and there was but ^Ta little way to come to ^REph'–rath: and Ra'–chel travailed, and she had hard labour.   *about 5 mi.* · v. 19; Ruth 4:11; Mic. 5:2, 3

17 And it came to pass, when she was in hard labour, that the midwife said unto her, Fear not; thou shalt have this son also.

18 And it came to pass, as her soul was in departing, (for she died) that she called his name Ben–o'–ni: but his father called him ^RBenjamin.^T   42:36 · *the son of the right hand*

19 And Ra'–chel died, and was buried in the way to Eph'–rath, which *is* Beth'–le–hem.

20 And Jacob set a ^Rpillar upon her grave: that *is* the pillar of Ra'–chel's grave ^Runto this day.   31:13, 45 · 1 Sam. 10:2

21 And Israel journeyed, and spread his tent beyond ^Rthe tower of E'–dar.   Mic. 4:8

22 And it came to pass, when Israel dwelt in that land, that Reuben went and lay with Bil'–hah his father's concubine: and Israel heard *it.* Now the sons of Jacob were twelve:

23 The sons of Leah; Reuben, Jacob's firstborn, and Simeon, and Levi, and Judah, and Is'–sa–char, and Zeb'–u–lun:

24 ^RThe sons of Ra'–chel; Joseph, and Benjamin: v. 18; 30:22–24

25 And ^Rthe sons of Bil'–hah, Ra'–chel's handmaid; Dan, and Naph'–ta–li: 30:5–8

26 And the ^Rsons of Zil'–pah, Leah's handmaid; ^RGad, and ^RAsher: these *are* the sons of Jacob, which were born to him in Pa'–dan–a'–ram.   30:10–13 · 49:19 · 49:20

27 And Jacob came unto Isaac his father unto ^RMam'–re, unto the ^Rcity of Ar'–bah, which *is* He'–bron, where Abraham and Isaac sojourned.   13:18 · Josh. 14:15

28 And the days of Isaac were an ^Rhundred and fourscore years.   25:26

29 And Isaac gave up the ^Tghost, and died, and was ^Rgathered unto his people, *being* old and ^Rfull of days: and his sons Esau and Jacob buried him.   spirit · 25:8 · 15:15

CHAPTER 36

The History of Esau—1 Chr. 1:35–42

NOW these *are* the generations of ^REsau, ^Rwho *is* E'–dom.   Rom. 9:13 · 25:30

2 Esau took ^Rhis wives of the daughters of Canaan; A'–dah the daughter of E'–lon the Hit'–tite, and ^RA–hol–i–ba'–mah^T the daughter of A'–nah the daughter of Zib'–e–on the Hi'–vite;   26:34 · v. 25 · *O-hol-i-ba'-mah*

3 And ^RBash'–e–math Ish'–ma–el's daughter, sister of Ne–ba'–joth.   28:9

4 And ^RA'–dah bare to Esau El'–i–phaz; and Bash'–e–math bare Reu'–el;   1 Chr. 1:35

5 And ^TA–hol–i–ba'–mah bare Je'–ush, and Ja–a'–lam, and Ko'–rah: these *are* the sons of Esau, which were born unto him in the land of Canaan.   O-hol-i-ba'-mah

6 And Esau took his wives, and his sons, and his daughters, and all the persons of his house, and his cattle, and all his beasts, and all his substance, which he had got in the land of Canaan; and went into the country from the face of his brother Jacob.

7 For their riches were more than that they might dwell together; and the land wherein they were strangers could not ᵀbear them because of their cattle.   support

8 Thus dwelt Esau in ᴿmount Se′-ir: ᴿEsau is E′-dom.   Deut. 2:5; Josh. 24:4 • vv. 1, 19

9 And these are the generations of Esau the father of the ᴿE′-dom-ites in mount Se′-ir: Num. 20:18

10 These are the names of Esau's sons; ᴿEl′-i-phaz the son of A′-dah the wife of Esau, Reu′-el the son of Bash′-e-math the wife of Esau.   1 Chr. 1:35

11 And the sons of El′-i-phaz were Te′-man, Omar, Ze′-pho, and Ga′-tam, and Ke′-naz.

12 And Tim′-na was concubine to El′-i-phaz Esau's son; and she bare to El′-i-phaz ᴿAm′-a-lek: these were the sons of A′-dah Esau's wife.   Ex. 17:8–14; Num. 24:20; 1 Sam. 15:2, 3

13 And these are the sons of Reu′-el; Na′-hath, and Ze′-rah, Sham′-mah, and Miz′-zah: these were the sons of Bash′-e-math Esau's wife.

14 And these were the sons of A-hol-i-ba′-mah, the daughter of A′-nah the daughter of Zib′-e-on, Esau's wife: and she bare to Esau Je′-ush, and Ja-a′-lam, and Ko′-rah.

15 These were ᵀdukes of the sons of Esau: the sons of El′-i-phaz the firstborn son of Esau; duke Te′-man, duke Omar, duke Ze′-pho, duke Ke′-naz,   chiefs

16 Duke Ko′-rah, duke Ga′-tam, and duke Am′-a-lek: these are the dukes that came of El′-i-phaz in the land of E′-dom; these were the sons of A′-dah.

17 And these are the sons of Reu′-el Esau's son; duke Na′-hath, duke Ze′-rah, duke Sham′-mah, duke Miz′-zah: these are the dukes that came of Reu′-el in the land of E′-dom; these are the sons of Bash′-e-math Esau's wife.

18 And these are the sons of ᵀA-hol-i-ba′-mah Esau's wife; duke Je′-ush, duke Ja-a′-lam, duke Ko′-rah: these were the dukes that came of A-hol-i-ba′-mah the daughter of A′-nah, Esau's wife.   O-hol-i-ba′-mah

19 These are the sons of Esau, who is E′-dom, and these are their ᵀdukes.   chiefs

20 These are the sons of Se′-ir the Ho′-rite, who inhabited the land; Lo′-tan, and Sho′-bal, and Zib′-e-on, and A′-nah,

21 And Di′-shon, and E′-zer, and Di′-shan: these are the dukes of the Ho′-rites, the children of Se′-ir in the land of E′-dom.

22 And the children of Lo′-tan were Ho′-ri and ᵀHe′-mam;ᴿ and Lo′-tan's sister was Tim′-na.   Homam • 1 Chr. 1:39

23 And the children of Sho′-bal were these; Al′-van, and Ma-na′-hath, and E′-bal, ᵀShe′-pho,ᴿ and O′-nam.   Shephi • 1 Chr. 1:40

24 And these are the children of Zib′-e-on; both A′-jah, and A′-nah: this was that A′-nah

that found the ᵀmules in the wilderness, as he fed the asses of Zib′-e-on his father.   hot springs

25 And the children of A′-nah were these; Di′-shon, and ᵀA-hol-i-ba′-mah the daughter of A′-nah.   O-hol-i-ba′-mah

26 And these are the children of ᴿDi′-shon; ᵀHem′-dan, and Esh′-ban, and Ith′-ran, and Che′-ran.   1 Chr. 1:41 • Am′-ram

27 The children of E′-zer are these; Bil′-han, and Za′-a-van, and ᵀA′-kan.   Ja′-kan

28 The children of Di′-shan are these; ᴿUz, and A′-ran.   Job 1:1

29 These are the ᵀdukes that came of the Ho′-rites; duke Lo′-tan, duke Sho′-bal, duke Zib′-e-on, duke A′-nah,   chiefs

30 Duke Di′-shon, ᵀduke E′-zer, duke Di′-shan: these are the dukes that came of Ho′-ri, among their dukes in the land of Se′-ir.   chief

31 And these are the kings that reigned in the land of E′-dom, before there reigned any ᴿking over the children of Israel.   17:6

32 And Be′-la the son of Be′-or reigned in E′-dom: and the name of his city was Din′-ha-bah.

33 And Be′-la died, and Jo′-bab the son of Ze′-rah of Boz′-rah reigned in his stead.

34 And Jo′-bab died, and Hu′-sham of the land of Tem′-a-ni reigned in his stead.

35 And Hu′-sham died, and Ha′-dad the son of Be′-dad, who smote Mid′-i-an in the field of Moab, reigned in his stead: and the name of his city was A′-vith.

36 And Ha′-dad died, and Sam′-lah of Mas-re′-kah reigned in his stead.

37 And Sam′-lah died, and Saul of Re-ho′-both by the river reigned in his stead.

38 And Saul died, and Ba′-al–ha′-nan the son of Ach′-bor reigned in his stead.

39 And Ba′-al–ha′-nan the son of Ach′-bor died, and ᴿHa′-dar reigned in his stead: and the name of his city was Pa′-u; and his wife's name was Me-het′-a-bel, the daughter of Ma′-tred, the daughter of Mez′-a-hab.   1 Chr. 1:50

40 And these are the names of the dukes that came of Esau, according to their families, after their places, by their names; duke Tim′-nah, duke Al′-vah, duke Je′-theth,

41 ᵀDuke ᵀA-hol-i-ba′-mah, duke E′-lah, duke Pi′-non,   chief • O-hol-i-ba′-mah

42 ᵀDuke Ke′-naz, duke Te′-man, duke Mib′-zar,   chief

43 Duke Mag′-di-el, duke I′-ram: these be the dukes of E′-dom, according to their habitations in the land of their possession: he is Esau the father of the E′-dom-ites.

CHAPTER 37

Joseph's Family Sins Against Him

AND Jacob dwelt in the land ᴿwherein his father was ᵀa stranger, in the land of Canaan.   17:8; 23:4; Heb. 11:9 • an immigrant

2 These *are* the generations of Jacob. Joseph, *being* ^Rseventeen years old, was feeding the flock with his brethren; and the lad *was* with the sons of Bil'-hah, and with the sons of Zil'-pah, his father's wives: and Joseph brought unto his father ^Rtheir ^Tevil report.   41:46 · 1 Sam. 2:22-24 · *unsatisfactory*

3 Now Israel loved Joseph more than all his children, because he *was* ^Rthe son of his old age: and he made him a coat of *many* ^Tcolours.^R   44:20; Judg. 5:30 · *pieces* · *vv.* 23, 32

4 And when his brethren saw that their father loved him more than all his brethren, they ^Rhated him, and could not speak ^Tpeaceably unto him.   27:41; 49:23 · *friendly*

5 And Joseph ^Rdreamed a dream, and he told *it* his brethren: and they hated him yet the more.   28:12; 31:10, 11, 24

6 And he said unto them, Hear, I pray you, this dream which I have dreamed:

7 For, behold, we *were* binding sheaves in the field, and, lo, my sheaf arose, and also stood upright; and, behold, your sheaves stood round about, and ^Tmade^R obeisance to my sheaf.   *bowed down in respect* · 42:6

8 And his brethren said to him, ^RShalt thou indeed reign over us? or shalt thou indeed have dominion over us? And they hated him yet the more for his dreams, and for his words.   49:26; Deut. 33:16

9 And he dreamed yet another dream, and told it his brethren, and said, Behold, I have dreamed a dream more; and, behold, ^Rthe sun and the moon and the eleven stars made obeisance to me.   46:29; 47:25

10 And he told *it* to his father, and to his brethren: and his father rebuked him, and said unto him, What *is* this dream that thou hast dreamed? Shall I and thy mother and thy brethren indeed come to bow down ourselves to thee to the earth?

11 And his brethren envied him; but his father ^Tobserved the saying.   *took notice of*

12 And his brethren went to feed their father's flock in ^RShe'-chem.   33:18-20

13 And Israel said unto Joseph, Do not thy brethren feed *the flock* in ^RShe'-chem? come, and I will send thee unto them. And he said to him, Here *am* I.   33:18-20

14 And he said to him, Go, I pray thee, see whether it be well with thy brethren, and well with the flocks; and bring me word again. So he sent him out of the vale of He'-bron, and he came to She'-chem.

15 And a certain man found him, and, behold, *he was* wandering in the field: and the man asked him, saying, What seekest thou?

16 And he said, I seek my brethren: tell me, I pray thee, where they feed *their flocks.*

17 And the man said, They are departed hence; for I heard them say, Let us go to Do'-than. And Joseph went after his brethren, and found them in ^RDo'-than.   2 Kin. 6:13

18 And when they saw him afar off, even before he came near unto them, ^Rthey conspired against him to slay him.   1 Sam. 19:1

19 And they said one to another, Behold, this ^Tdreamer cometh.   *master of dreams*

20 Come now therefore, and let us slay him, and cast him into some pit, and we will say, Some evil beast hath devoured him: and we shall see what will become of his dreams.

21 And ^RReuben heard *it*, and he delivered him out of their hands; and said, Let us not kill him.   42:22

22 And Reuben said unto them, Shed no blood, *but* cast him into this pit that *is* in the wilderness, and lay no hand upon him; that he might ^Trid him out of their hands, to deliver him to his father again.   *deliver*

23 And it came to pass, when Joseph was come unto his brethren, that they ^Rstript Joseph out of his coat, *his* coat of *many* colours that *was* on him;   Matt. 27:28

24 ^RAnd they took him, and cast him into a pit: and the pit *was* empty, *there was* no water in it.   Ex. 1:22; Jer. 38:6

25 And they sat down ^Tto eat bread: and they lifted up their eyes and looked, and, behold, a company of Ish'-me-el-ites came from Gil'-e-ad with their camels bearing spicery and ^Rbalm and myrrh, going to carry *it* down to Egypt.   *for a meal* · Jer. 8:22

26 And ^RJudah said unto his brethren, What profit *is it* if we slay our brother, and ^Rconceal his blood?   38:1 · *v.* 20

27 Come, and let us sell him to the Ish'-me-el-ites, and let not our hand be upon him; for he *is* our brother *and* our flesh. And his brethren were ^Tcontent.   *satisfied*

28 Then there passed by Mid'-i-an-ites merchantmen; and they drew and lifted up Joseph out of the pit, and sold Joseph to the Ish'-me-el-ites for ^Ttwenty *pieces* of silver: and they brought Joseph into Egypt. $2,560

29 And Reuben returned unto the pit; and, behold, Joseph *was* not in the pit; and he ^Rrent^T his clothes.   Job 1:20 · *tore in sorrow*

30 And he returned unto his brethren, and said, The ^Tchild ^R*is* not; and I, whither shall I go?   *youth* · 42:13, 26

31 ^RAnd they took ^RJoseph's coat, and killed a kid of the goats, and dipped the coat in the blood;   *v.* 3 · *v.* 23

32 And they sent the coat of *many* colours, and they brought *it* to their father; and said, This have we found: know now whether it *be* thy son's coat or ^Tno.   *not*

33 And he knew it, and said, *It is* my son's coat; an evil beast hath devoured him; Joseph is without doubt rent in pieces.

34 And Jacob ᴿrentᵀ his clothes, and put sackcloth upon his loins, and mourned for his son many days.   *v. 29 • tore his clothes in grief*

35 And all his sons and all his daughters rose up to comfort him; but he refused to be comforted; and he said, For ᴿI will go down into the grave unto my son mourning. Thus his father wept for him.   42:38

36 And ᴿthe Mid'-i-an-ites sold him into Egypt unto Pot'-i-phar, an officer of Pha-raoh's, *and* captain of the guard.   39:1

CHAPTER 38

Joseph's Family Sins with the Canaanites

A ND it came to pass at that time, that Judah went down from his brethren, and ᴿturned in to a certain ᴿA-dul'-lam-ite, whose name *was* Hi'-rah.   2 Kin. 4:8 • Josh. 15:35

2 And Judah saw there a daughter of a certain Ca'-naan-ite, whose name *was* Shu'-ah; and he took her, and went in unto her.

3 And she conceived, and bare a son; and he called his name ᴿEr.   46:12

4 And she conceived again, and bare a son; and she called his name O'-nan.

5 And she yet again conceived, and bare a son; and called his name She'-lah: and he was at Che'-zib, when she bare him.

6 And Judah took a wife for ᵀEr his firstborn, whose name *was* Ta'-mar.   *his oldest son*

7 And Er, Judah's firstborn, ᵀwas wicked in the sight of the Lᴏʀᴅ; ᴿand the Lᴏʀᴅ ᵀslew him.   *sinned • 1 Chr. 2:3 • destroyed*

8 And Judah said unto O'-nan, Go in unto ᴿthy brother's wife, and marry her, and raise up seed to thy brother.   Deut. 25:5

9 And O'-nan knew that the seed should not be ᴿhis; and it came to pass, when he went in unto his brother's wife, that he spilled *it* on the ground, lest that he should give seed to his brother.   Deut. 25:6

10 And the thing which he did displeased the Lᴏʀᴅ: wherefore he slew him also.

11 Then said Judah to Ta'-mar his daughter in law, Remain a widow at thy father's house, till She'-lah my son be grown: for he said, Lest peradventure he die also, as his brethren *did.* And Ta'-mar went and dwelt in her father's house.

12 And in process of time the daughter of Shu'-ah Judah's wife died; and Judah ᴿwas comforted, and went up unto his sheepshear-ers to Tim'-nath, he and his friend Hi'-rah the A-dul'-lam-ite.   2 Sam. 13:39

13 And it was told Ta'-mar, saying, Behold thy father in law goeth up ᴿto Tim'-nath to shear his sheep.   Josh. 15:10, 57

14 And she put her widow's garments off from her, and ᴿcovered her with a vail, and wrapped herself, and sat in an open place, which *is* by the way to Tim'-nath; for she saw that She'-lah was grown, and she was not given unto him to wife.   24:65

15 ᴿWhen Judah saw her, he thought her *to be* an harlot; because she had covered her face.   *vv.* 11, 26

16 And he turned unto her by the way, and said, ᵀGo to, I pray thee, let me come in unto thee; (for he knew not that she *was* his daughter in law.) And she said, What wilt thou give me, that thou mayest come in unto me?   *come*

17 And he said, I will send *thee* a ᴿkid from the flock. And she said, Wilt thou give me a pledge, till thou send *it?*   Judg. 15:1

18 And he said, What pledge shall I give thee? And she said, ᴿThy signet, and thy bracelets, and thy staff that *is* in thine hand. And he gave *it* her, and came in unto her, and she conceived by him.   *v.* 25; 41:42

19 And she arose, and went away, and ᴿlaid by her vail from her, and put on the garments of her widowhood.   *v.* 14

20 And Judah sent the kid by the hand of his friend the A-dul'-lam-ite, to receive *his* pledge from the woman's hand: but he found her not.

21 Then he asked the men of that place, saying, Where *is* the harlot, that *was* ᵀopenly by the way side? And they said, There was no harlot in this *place.*   *in public*

22 And he returned to Judah, and said, I cannot find her; and also the men of the place said, *that* there was no harlot in this *place.*

23 And Judah said, Let her take *it* to her, lest we be shamed: behold, I sent this kid, and thou hast not found her.

24 And it came to pass about three months after, that it was told Judah, saying, Ta'-mar thy daughter in law hath played the harlot; and also, behold, she *is* with child by whore-dom. And Judah said, Bring her forth, and let her be burnt.

25 When she *was* brought forth, she sent to her father in law, saying, By the man, whose these *are, am* I with child: and she said, ᴿDiscern, I pray thee, whose *are* these, the signet, and bracelets, and staff.   37:32

26 And Judah acknowledged *them,* and said, She hath been more righteous than I; because that I gave her not to She'-lah my son. And he knew her again no more.

27 And it came to pass in the time of her travail, that, behold, ᴿtwins *were* in her womb.   25:24–26

28 And it came to pass, when she travailed, that *the one* put out *his* hand: and the mid-wife took and bound upon his hand a scarlet thread, saying, This came out first.

29 And it came to pass, as he drew back his hand, that, behold, his brother came out: and she said, How hast thou broken forth? *this*

breach *be* upon thee: therefore his name was called [R]Pha'-rez.   Num. 26:20

30 And afterward came out his brother, that had the scarlet thread upon his hand: and his name was called [R]Zar'-ah.   Matt. 1:3

CHAPTER 39

Joseph's Test with the Egyptian Woman

AND Joseph was brought down to Egypt; and Pot'-i-phar, an officer of Pharaoh, captain of the guard, an Egyptian, bought him of the hands of the Ish'-me-el-ites, which had brought him down thither.

2 And the LORD was with Joseph, and he was [T]a prosperous man; and he was in the house of his master the Egyptian.   *successful*

3 And his master saw that the LORD *was* with him, and that the LORD made all that he did [T]to prosper in his hand.   *to be a success*

4 And Joseph [R]found[T] grace in his sight, and he served him: and he made him overseer over his house, and all *that* he had he put into his hand.   *v. 21 • was appreciated by him*

5 And it came to pass from the time *that* he had made him overseer in his house, and over all that he had, that [R]the LORD blessed the Egyptian's house for Joseph's sake; and the blessing of the LORD was upon all that he had in the house, and in the field.   30:27

6 And he left all that he had in Joseph's hand; and he knew not ought he had, save the bread which he did eat. And Joseph was *a* goodly *person*, and well favoured.

7 And it came to pass after these things, that his master's wife cast her eyes upon Joseph; and she said, [R]Lie with me.   *v. 10*

8 But he refused, and said unto his master's wife, Behold, my master wotteth not what *is* with me in the house, and he hath committed all that he hath to my hand;

9 [R]*There is* none greater in this house than I; neither hath he kept back any thing from me but thee, because thou *art* his wife: [R]how then can I do this great wickedness, and sin against God?   41:40 • Prov. 6:29

10 And it came to pass, as she spake to Joseph day by day, that he hearkened not unto her, to [R]lie by her, *or* to be with her.   *v. 7*

11 And it came to pass about this time, that *Joseph* went into the house to do his [T]business; and *there was* none of the men of the house there within.   *work*

12 And she caught him by his garment, saying, Lie with me: and he left his garment in her hand, and fled, and got him out.

13 And it came to pass, when she saw that he had left his [T]garment in her hand, and was fled forth,   *clothes*

14 That she called unto the men of her house, and spake unto them, saying, See, he

hath brought in an Hebrew unto us to mock us; he came in unto me to lie with me, and I cried with a loud voice:

15 And it came to pass, when he heard that I lifted up my voice and cried, that he left his garment with me, and fled, and got him out.

16 And she laid up his garment by her, until his lord came home.

17 And she [R]spake unto him according to these words, saying, The Hebrew servant, which thou hast brought unto us, came in unto me to mock me: Ex. 23:1; Ps. 120:3

18 And it came to pass, as I lifted up my voice and cried, that he left his garment with me, and fled out.

19 And it came to pass, when his master heard the words of his wife, which she spake unto him, saying, After this manner did thy servant to me; that his wrath was kindled.

20 And Joseph's master took him, and [R]put him into the [R]prison, a place where the king's prisoners *were* bound: and he was there in the prison.   Ps. 105:18 • 40:3, 15; 41:14

21 But the LORD was with Joseph, and shewed him mercy, and gave him favour in the sight of the keeper of the prison.

22 And the keeper of the prison [R]committed to Joseph's hand all the prisoners that *were* in the prison; and whatsoever they did there, he was [T]the doer *of it*.   *v. 4 • the director*

23 The keeper of the prison looked not to any thing *that was* under his hand; because [R]the LORD was with him, and *that* which he did, the LORD made *it* to prosper.   *vv. 2, 3*

CHAPTER 40

Joseph's Test with the Egyptian Society

AND it came to pass after these things, *that* the [R]butler of the king of Egypt and *his* baker had offended their [T]lord the king of Egypt.   *vv. 11, 13; Neh. 1:11 • master*

2 And Pharaoh was wroth against two *of* his officers, against the chief of the butlers, and against the chief of the bakers.

3 And he put them in ward in the house of the captain of the guard, into the prison, the place where Joseph *was* [T]bound.   *in jail*

4 And the captain of the guard charged Joseph with them, and he served them: and they continued a season in ward.

5 And they [R]dreamed a dream both of them, each man his dream in one night, each man according to the interpretation of his dream, the butler and the baker of the king of Egypt, which *were* bound in the prison.   41:1

6 And Joseph came in unto them in the morning, and looked upon them, and, behold, they *were* [T]sad.   *depressed*

7 And he asked Pharaoh's officers that *were* with him in [T]the ward of his lord's

house, saying, RWherefore look ye so Tsadly to day?   *prison* • Neh. 2:2 • *down-hearted*

8 And they said unto him, RWe have dreamed a dream, and *there is* no interpreter of it. And Joseph said unto them, RDo not interpretations *belong* to God? tell me *them*, I pray you.   41:15 • [41:16; Dan. 2:27, 28]

9 And the chief butler told his dream to Joseph, and said to him, In my dream, behold, a vine *was* before me;

10 And in the vine *were* three branches: and it *was* as though it budded, *and* her blossoms shot forth; and the clusters thereof brought forth ripe grapes:

11 And Pharaoh's Rcup *was* in my hand: and I took the grapes, and pressed them into Pharaoh's cup, and I gave the cup into Pharaoh's hand.   44:2

12 And Joseph said unto him, This *is* the Tinterpretation of it: The three branches Rare three days: *meaning* • 41:26

13 Yet within three days shall Pharaoh lift up thine head, and Trestore thee unto thy place: and thou shalt deliver Pharaoh's cup into his hand, after the former manner when thou wast his butler.   *give back your job*

14 But think on me when it shall be well with thee, and shew kindness, I pray thee, unto me, and make mention of me unto Pharaoh, and bring me out of this house:

15 For indeed RI was stolen away out of the land of the Hebrews: Rand here also have I done nothing that they should put me into the dungeon.   37:26–28 • 39:20

16 When the chief baker saw that the interpretation was good, he said unto Joseph, I also *was* in my dream, and, behold, *I had* three white Rbaskets on my head: Ex. 29:3

17 And in the uppermost basket *there was* of all manner of Tbakemeats for Pharaoh; and the birds did eat them out of the basket upon my head.   *baked foods*

18 And Joseph answered and said, RThis *is* the interpretation thereof: The three baskets *are* three days: *v.* 12

19 Yet within three days shall Pharaoh lift up thy head from off thee, and shall Rhang thee on a tree; and the birds shall eat thy flesh from off thee.   Deut. 21:22

20 And it came to pass the third day, *which was* Pharaoh's birthday, that he made a feast unto all his servants: and he lifted up the head of the chief butler and of the chief baker among his servants.

21 And he Rrestored the chief butler unto his butlership again; and Rhe gave the cup into Pharaoh's hand: *v.* 13 • Neh. 2:1

22 But he Rhanged the chief baker: as Joseph had interpreted to them.   Deut. 21:23

23 Yet did not the chief butler remember Joseph, but Rforgat him.   Eccl. 9:15, 16; Amos 6:6

CHAPTER 41

Joseph's Test with Pharaoh's Dreams

AND it came to pass at the end of two full years, that Pharaoh dreamed: and, behold, he stood by the Triver.   *Nile*

2 And, behold, there came up out of the river seven well favoured Tkine and fatfleshed; and they fed in a meadow.   *cows*

3 And, behold, seven other kine came up after them out of the river, Till favoured and leanfleshed; and stood by the *other* kine upon the brink of the river.   *scrawny*

4 And the ill favoured and leanfleshed Tkine did eat up the seven well favoured and fat kine. So Pharaoh awoke.   *cows*

5 And he slept and dreamed the second time: and, behold, seven ears of corn came up upon one stalk, Trank and good.   *fat*

6 And, behold, seven thin ears and blasted with the east wind sprung up after them.

7 And the seven thin ears devoured the seven Trank and full ears. And Pharaoh awoke, and, behold, *it was* a dream.   *fat*

8 And it came to pass in the morning that his spirit was troubled; and he sent and called for all the magicians of Egypt, and all the wise men thereof: and Pharaoh told them his dream; but *there was* none that could interpret them unto Pharaoh.

9 Then spake the chief butler unto Pharaoh, saying, TI do remember Rmy faults this day: *will make mention of* • 40:23

10 Pharaoh was wroth with his servants, and put me in ward in the captain of the guard's house, *both* me and the chief baker:

11 And Rwe dreamed a dream in one night, I and he; we dreamed each man according to the interpretation of his dream.   40:5; Judg. 7:13

12 And *there was* there with us a young man, an Hebrew, servant to the captain of the guard; and we told him, and he interpreted to us our dreams; to each man according to his dream he did interpret.

13 And it came to pass, Ras he interpreted to us, so it was; me he restored unto mine office, and him he hanged.   40:21, 22

14 RThen Pharaoh sent and called Joseph, and they Rbrought him hastily Rout of the dungeon: and he shaved *himself*, and changed his raiment, and came in unto Pharaoh.   Ps. 105:20 • Dan. 2:25 • [1 Sam. 2:8]

15 RAnd Pharaoh said unto Joseph, I have dreamed a dream, and Rthere is none that can interpret it: Rand I have heard say of thee, *that* thou canst understand a dream to interpret it.   *v.* 8 • Ps. 25:14 • *v.* 12; Dan. 5:16

16 And Joseph answered Pharaoh, saying, RIt *is* not in me: RGod shall give Pharaoh an answer of peace.   [2 Cor. 3:5] • 40:8

17 And Pharaoh said unto Joseph, RIn my dream, behold, I stood upon the bank of the river: *v.* 1

18 And, behold, there came up out of the river seven ᵀkine, fatfleshed and well favoured; and they fed in a meadow: *cows*

19 And, behold, seven other kine came up after them, poor and very ill favoured and leanfleshed, such as I never saw in all the land of Egypt for ᵀbadness: *poor condition*

20 And the lean and the ill favoured ᵀkine did eat up the first seven fat kine: *cows*

21 And when they had eaten them up, it could not be known that they had eaten them; but they *were* still ill favoured, as at the beginning. So I awoke.

22 ᴿAnd I saw in my dream, and, behold, seven ears came up in one stalk, full and good: *v. 6*

23 And, behold, seven ears, withered, thin, and ᵀblasted with the east wind, sprung up after them: *blighted*

24 And the thin ears devoured the seven good ears: and ᴿI told *this* unto the ᴿmagicians; but *there was* none that could declare it to me.   *v. 8; Dan. 4:7 • Ex. 7:11*

25 And Joseph said unto Pharaoh, The dream of Pharaoh *is* one: ᴿGod hath shewed Pharaoh what he *is* about to do.   *Rev. 4:1*

26 The seven good ᵀkine *are* seven years; and the seven good ears *are* seven years: the dream *is* one.   *cows*

27 And the seven thin and ill favoured ᵀkine that came up after them *are* seven years; and the seven empty ears ᵀblasted with the east wind shall be ᴿseven years of ᴿfamine.   *cows • blighted • 2 Kin. 8:1 • Hab. 3:17*

28 ᴿThis *is* the thing which I have spoken unto Pharaoh: What God *is* about to do he sheweth unto Pharaoh.   *vv. 25, 32; [Dan. 2:28]*

29 Behold, there come seven years of great plenty throughout all the land of Egypt:

30 And there shall arise after them seven years of famine; and all the plenty shall be forgotten in the land of Egypt; and the famine ᴿshall consume the land;   *47:13*

31 And the plenty shall not be known in the land by reason of that famine following; for it *shall be* very grievous.

32 ᴿAnd for that the dream was ᵀdoubled unto Pharaoh twice; *it is* because the thing *is* ᵀestablished by God, and God will shortly bring it to pass.   *vv. 25, 28 • repeated • prepared*

33 Now therefore let Pharaoh ᵀlook out a man ᴿdiscreetᵀ and wise, and set him over the land of Egypt.   *seek • v. 39 • cautious*

34 Let Pharaoh do *this*, and let him appoint ᵀofficers over the land, and ᴿtake up the fifth part of the land of Egypt in the seven plenteous years.   *overseers • Prov. 6:6–8*

35 And ᴿlet them gather all the food of those good years that come, and lay up corn under the hand of Pharaoh, and let them keep food in the cities.   *v. 48*

36 And that food shall be for store to the land against the seven years of famine, which shall be in the land of Egypt; that the land perish not through the famine.

Joseph's Exaltation over Egypt

37 And the thing was good in the eyes of Pharaoh, and in the eyes of all his servants.

38 And Pharaoh said unto his servants, Can we find *such a one* as this *is*, a man ᴿin whom the Spirit of God *is*?   *Num. 27:18*

39 And Pharaoh said unto Joseph, Forasmuch as God hath shewed thee all this, ᴿ*there is* none so ᴿdiscreet and wise as thou *art:*   *v. 33 • Prov. 2:11*

40 Thou shalt be ᵀover my house, and according unto ᵀthy word shall all my people be ruled: only in the throne will I be greater than thou.   *in charge of • your ideas*

41 And Pharaoh said unto Joseph, See, I have set thee over all the land of Egypt.

42 And Pharaoh took off his ring from his hand, and put it upon Joseph's hand, and arrayed him in vestures of fine linen, and put a gold chain about his neck;

43 And he made him to ride in the second chariot which he had; ᴿand they cried before him, Bow the knee: and he made him *ruler* over all the land of Egypt.   *Esth. 6:9*

44 And Pharaoh said unto Joseph, I *am* Pharaoh, and without thee shall no man lift up his hand or foot in all the land of Egypt.

45 And Pharaoh called Joseph's name Zaph'-nath–pa-a-ne'-ah; and he gave him to wife As'-e-nath the daughter of Pot-i-phe'-rah priest of ᴿOn. And Joseph went out over *all* the land of Egypt.   *Jer. 43:13*

46 And Joseph *was* thirty years old when he ᴿstoodᵀ before Pharaoh king of Egypt. And Joseph went out from the presence of Pharaoh, and went throughout all the land of Egypt.   *1 Sam. 16:21; 1 Kin. 12:6, 8 • took office*

47 ᴿAnd in the seven plenteous years the earth brought forth by handfuls.   *Lev. 26:4*

48 And he gathered up all the food of the seven years, which were in the land of Egypt, and laid up the food in the cities: the food of the field, which *was* round about every city, laid he up in the same.

49 And Joseph gathered corn ᴿas the sand of the sea, very much, until he left numbering; for *it was* without number.   *22:17*

50 And ᴿunto Joseph were born two sons before the years of famine came, which As'-e-nath the daughter of Pot-i-phe'-rah priest of On bare unto him.   *46:20; 48:5*

51 And Joseph called the name of the firstborn ᴿMa-nas'-sehᵀ: For God, *said he,* hath made me forget all my toil, and all my father's house.   *46:20 • forgetting*

52 And the name of the second called he E'-phra-im: For God hath caused me to be fruitful in the land of my affliction.

53 And the seven years of plenteousness, that was in the land of Egypt, were ended.

54 And the seven years of [T]dearth began to come, according as Joseph had said: and the dearth was in all lands; but in all the land of Egypt there was bread.   *famine*

55 And when all the land of Egypt was famished, the people cried to Pharaoh for bread: and Pharaoh said unto all the Egyptians, Go unto Joseph; [R]what he saith to you, do.   John 2:5

56 And the famine was over all the face of the earth: And Joseph opened all the storehouses, and sold unto the Egyptians; and the famine waxed sore in the land of Egypt.

57 [R]And all countries came into Egypt to Joseph for to [R]buy *corn;* because that the famine was *so* sore in all lands.   Deut. 9:28 • 42:3

CHAPTER 42

Joseph's Brothers Visit Egypt

NOW when Jacob saw that there was corn in Egypt, Jacob said unto his sons, Why do ye look one upon another?

2 And he said, Behold, I have heard that there is corn in Egypt: get you down thither, and buy for us from thence; that we may [R]live, and not die.   43:8; Is. 38:1

3 And Joseph's ten brethren went down to buy corn in Egypt.

4 But Benjamin, Joseph's brother, Jacob sent not with his brethren; for he said, Lest peradventure mischief befall him.

5 And the sons of Israel came to buy *corn* among those that came: for the famine was [R]in the land of Canaan.   41:57; Acts 7:11

6 And Joseph *was* the governor [R]over the land, *and he* it *was* that sold to all the people of the land: and Joseph's brethren came, and [R]bowed down themselves before him *with* their faces to the earth.   41:41 • 37:7

7 And Joseph saw his brethren, and he knew them, but made himself strange unto them, and spake roughly unto them; and he said unto them, Whence come ye? And they said, From the land of Canaan to buy food.

8 And Joseph knew his brethren, but [R]they knew not him.   37:2; 41:46, 53

9 And Joseph [R]remembered the dreams which he dreamed of them, and said unto them, Ye *are* spies; to see the [T]nakedness of the land ye are come.   37:5, 9 • *weakness*

10 And they said unto him, Nay, my lord, but to buy food are thy servants come.

11 We *are* all one man's sons; we *are* [R]true *men,* thy servants are no spies.   *vv.* 16, 19, 31, 34

12 And he said unto them, Nay, but to see the nakedness of the land ye are come.

13 And they said, Thy servants *are* twelve brethren, the sons of one man in the land of Canaan; and, behold, the youngest *is* this day with [R]our father, and one *is* not.   43:7

14 And Joseph said unto them, That *is it* that I spake unto you, saying, Ye *are* spies:

15 Hereby ye shall be proved: By the life of Pharaoh ye shall not go forth hence, except your youngest brother come hither.

16 Send one of you, and let him fetch your brother, and ye shall be [T]kept in prison, that your words may be proved, whether *there be any* truth in you: or else by the life of Pharaoh surely ye *are* spies.   *bound*

17 And he [T]put them [R]all together into [T]ward three days.   *gathered* • 40:4, 7 • *jail*

18 And Joseph said unto them the third day, This do, and live; *for* I fear God:

19 If ye *be* true *men,* let one of your brethren be bound in the house of your prison: go ye, carry corn for the famine of your houses:

20 But bring your youngest brother unto me; so shall your words be [T]verified, and ye shall not die. And they did so.   *proven true*

21 And they said one to another, We *are* verily guilty concerning our brother, in that we saw the anguish of his soul, when he besought us, and we would not hear; therefore is this distress come upon us.

22 And Reuben answered them, saying, Spake I not unto you, saying, Do not sin against the child; and ye would not hear? therefore, behold, also his blood is required.

23 And they knew not that Joseph understood *them;* for [T]he spake unto them by an interpreter.   *an interpreter was between them*

24 [R]And he turned himself about from them, and wept; and returned to them again, and [T]communed with them, and took from them Simeon, and bound him before their eyes.   43:14, 23, 30; 45:14, 15 • *spoke*

25 [R]Then Joseph commanded to fill their sacks with corn, and to restore every man's money into his sack, and to give them provision for the way: and [R]thus did he unto them.   44:1 • [Matt. 5:44; Rom. 12:17, 20, 21]

26 And they [T]laded their asses with the corn, and departed thence.   *loaded*

27 And as [R]one of them opened his sack to give his ass [T]provender in the inn, he [T]espied his money; for, behold, it *was* in his sack's mouth.   43:21 • *food* • *saw*

28 And he said unto his brethren, My money is restored; and, [T]lo, *it is* even in my sack: and their heart failed *them,* and they were afraid, saying one to another, [R]What *is* this *that* God hath done unto us?   *look* • 43:23

29 And they came unto Jacob their father unto the land of Canaan, and told him all that befell unto them; saying,

30 The man, *who is* the lord of the land, [R]spake [T]roughly to us, and took us for spies of the country.   *v.* 7 • *harshly*

31 And we said unto him, We *are* [R]true *men;* we are no spies: *v.* 11

32 We *be* twelve brethren, sons of our father; one *is* not, and the youngest *is* this day with our father in the land of Canaan.

33 And the man, ᵀthe lord of the country, said unto us, Hereby shall I know that ye *are* true *men;* leave one of your brethren *here* with me, and take *food for* the famine of your households, and be gone: *head man*

34 And bring your ᴿyoungest brother unto me: then shall I know that ye *are* no spies, but *that* ye *are* true *men:* so will I deliver you your brother, and ye shall ᴿtraffickᵀ in the land.   *v. 20; 43:3, 5 · 34:10 · do business*

35 And it came to pass as they emptied their sacks, that, behold, ᴿevery man's bundle of money *was* in his sack: and when *both* they and their father saw the bundles of money, they were afraid.   43:12, 15, 21

36 And Jacob their father said unto them, Me have ye ᴿbereaved *of my children:* Joseph *is* not, and Simeon *is* not, and ye will take ᴿBenjamin *away:* all these things are ᵀagainst me.   43:14 · [35:18; Rom. 8:28, 31] · *upon*

37 And Reuben spake unto his father, saying, Slay my two sons, if I bring him not to thee: deliver him into my hand, and I will bring him to thee again.

38 And he said, My son shall not go down with you; for his brother is dead, and he is left alone: if mischief befall him by the way in the which ye go, then shall ye bring down my gray hairs with sorrow to the grave.

CHAPTER 43

Joseph's Brothers' Second Journey to Egypt

AND the famine *was* sore in the land.
2 And it came to pass, when they had eaten up the corn which they had brought out of Egypt, their father said unto them, Go again, buy us a little food.

3 And Judah spake unto him, saying, The man did solemnly ᵀprotest unto us, saying, Ye shall not see my face, except your ᴿbrother *be* with you.   *warn · 42:20; 44:23*

4 If thou wilt send our brother with us, we will go down and buy thee food:

5 But if thou wilt not send *him,* we will not go down: for the man said unto us, Ye shall not see my face, except your brother *be* with you.

6 And Israel said, ᵀWherefore dealt ye *so* ill with me, *as* to tell the man whether ye had yet a brother?   *why did you do me such harm*

7 And they said, The man asked us straitly of our state, and of our kindred, saying, *Is* your father yet alive? have ye *another* brother? and we told him according to the tenor of these words: could we certainly know that he would say, Bring your brother down?

8 And Judah said unto Israel his father, Send the lad with me, and we will arise and go; ᴿthat we may live, and not die, both we, and thou, *and* also our little ones.   42:2

9 I will be ᵀsurety for him; of my hand shalt thou require him: if I bring him not unto thee, and set him before thee, then let me bear the blame for ever: *guarantee*

10 For except we had lingered, surely now we had returned this second time.

11 And their father Israel said unto them, If *it must be* so now, do this; take of the best fruits in the land in your vessels, and carry down the man a present, a little ᴿbalm, and a little honey, spices, and myrrh, ᵀnuts, and almonds: 37:25 · *pistachio nuts*

12 And take double money in your hand; and the money that was brought again in the mouth of your sacks, carry *it* again in your hand; peradventure it *was* an oversight:

13 Take also your brother, and arise, go again unto the man:

14 And God Almighty give you mercy before the man, that he may send away your other brother, and Benjamin. If I be bereaved *of my children,* I am bereaved.

15 And the men took ᴿthat present, and they took double money in their hand, and Benjamin; and rose up, and went down to Egypt, and stood before Joseph.   *v. 11*

16 And when Joseph saw Benjamin with them, he said to the ᴿruler of his house, Bring *these* men home, and ᵀslay, and make ready; for *these* men shall ᵀdine with me at noon.   44:1 · *kill the animals for our food · eat*

17 And the man did as Joseph bade; and the man brought the men into Joseph's house.

18 And the men were afraid, because they were brought into Joseph's house; and they said, Because of the money that was returned in our sacks at the first time are we brought in; that he may seek occasion against us, and fall upon us, and ᵀtake us for bondmen, and our asses.   *make us slaves*

19 And they came near to the steward of Joseph's house, and they communed with him at the door of the house,

20 And said, O sir, ᴿwe came indeed down at the first time to buy food: 42:3, 10

21 And ᴿit came to pass, when we came to the inn, that we opened our sacks, and, behold, *every* man's money *was* in the mouth of his sack, our money in full weight: and we have brought it again in our hand.   42:27, 35

22 And other money have we brought down in our hands to buy food: we cannot tell who put our money in our sacks.

23 And he said, Peace *be* to you, fear not: your God, and the God of your father, hath given you treasure in your sacks: ᵀI had your money. And ᴿhe brought Simeon out unto them.   *I received your money · 42:24, 28*

24 And the man brought the men into Joseph's house, and ^Rgave *them* water, and they washed their feet; and he gave their asses ^Tprovender.   18:4; 24:32 • *food*

25 And they made ready the present against Joseph came at noon: for they heard that they should eat bread there.

26 And when Joseph came home, they brought him the present which *was* in their hand into the house, and bowed^T themselves to him to the earth.   *humbled themselves*

27 And he asked them of *their* welfare, and said, ^R*Is* your father well, the old man of whom ye spake? *Is* he yet alive?   v. 7; 45:3

28 And they answered, Thy servant our father *is* in good health, he *is* yet alive. ^RAnd they bowed down their heads, and ^Tmade obeisance.   37:7, 10 • *acted with respect*

29 And he lifted up his eyes, and saw his brother Benjamin, ^Rhis mother's son, and said, Is this your younger brother, of whom ye spake unto me? And he said, God be gracious unto thee, my son.   35:17, 18

30 And Joseph made haste; for his ^Tbowels did yearn upon his brother: and he sought *where* to weep; and he entered into *his* chamber, and ^Rwept there.   *heart* • 42:24

31 And he washed his face, and went out, and refrained himself, and said, Set on ^Rbread.   45:1; v. 25

32 And they set on for him by himself, and for them by themselves, and for the Egyptians, which did eat with him, by themselves: because the Egyptians might not eat bread with the Hebrews; for that *is* ^Ran abomination unto the Egyptians.   46:34

33 ^RAnd they sat before him, the firstborn according to his ^Rbirthright, and the youngest according to his youth: and the men marvelled one at another.   42:7 • Deut. 21:16

34 And he took *and sent* messes unto them from before him: but Benjamin's mess was five times so much as any of their's. And they drank, and were merry with him.

CHAPTER 44

AND he commanded the steward of his house, saying, Fill the men's sacks *with* food, as much as they can carry, and put every man's money in his sack's mouth.

2 And put my ^Rcup, the silver cup, in the sack's mouth of the youngest, and his corn money. And he did according to the word that Joseph had spoken.   2 Sam. 12:3

3 As soon as the morning was light, the men were sent away, they and their asses.

4 *And* when they were gone out of the city, *and* not *yet* far off, Joseph said unto his steward, Up, follow after the men; and when thou dost overtake them, say unto them, Wherefore have ye rewarded evil for good?

5 *Is* not this *it* in which my lord drinketh, and whereby indeed he ^Tdivineth? ye have done evil in so doing.   *uses it to foretell the future*

6 And he overtook them, and he spake unto them these same words.

7 And they said unto him, Wherefore saith my lord these words? God forbid that thy servants should do according to this thing:

8 Behold, the money, which we found in our sacks' mouths, we brought again unto thee out of the land of Canaan: how then should we steal out of thy lord's house silver or gold?

9 With whomsoever of thy servants it be found, ^Rboth let him die, and we also will be my lord's ^Tbondmen.^R   31:32 • *slaves* • v. 16

10 And he said, Now also let it be according unto your words: he with whom it is found shall be my servant; and ye shall be blameless.

11 Then they speedily took down every man his sack to the ground, and opened every man his sack.

12 And he searched, *and* began at the eldest, and ^Tleft at the youngest: and the cup was found in Benjamin's sack.   *finished with*

13 Then they ^Rrent^T their clothes, and laded every man his ass, and returned to the city.   37:29, 34; Num. 14:6; 2 Sam. 1:11 • *tore*

14 And Judah and his brethren came to Joseph's house; for he *was* yet there: and they ^Rfell before him on the ground.   37:7

15 And Joseph said unto them, What deed *is* this that ye have done? wot ye not that such a man as I can certainly divine?

16 And Judah said, What shall we say unto my lord? what shall we speak? or how shall we clear ourselves? God hath ^Rfound out the iniquity of thy servants: behold, we *are* my lord's servants, both we, and *he* also with whom the cup is found.   [Num. 32:23]

17 And he said, God forbid that I should do so: *but* the man in whose hand the cup is found, he shall be my servant; and as for you, get you up in peace unto your father.

18 Then Judah came near unto him, and said, Oh my lord, let thy servant, I pray thee, speak a word in my lord's ears, and ^Rlet not thine anger burn against thy servant: for thou *art* even as Pharaoh.   Ex. 32:22

19 ^RMy lord asked his servants, saying, Have ye a father, or a brother?   43:7

20 And we said unto my lord, We have a father, an old man, and ^Ra child of his old age, a little one; and his brother is dead, and he alone is left of his mother, and his father loveth him.   37:3, 33; v. 30; 43:8

21 And thou saidst unto thy servants, ^RBring him down unto me, that I may set mine eyes upon him.   42:15, 20

22 And we said unto my lord, The lad cannot leave his father: for *if* he should leave his father, *his father* would die.

23 And thou saidst unto thy servants, Except your youngest brother come down with you, ye shall see my face no more.

24 And it came to pass when we came up unto thy servant my father, we told him the words of my lord.

25 And ^Rour father said, Go again, *and* buy us a little food.   43:2

26 ^RAnd we said, We cannot go down: if our youngest brother be with us, then will we go down: for we may not see the man's face, except our youngest brother *be* with us.   43:3

27 And thy servant my father said unto us, Ye know that my wife bare me two *sons:*

28 And the one went out from me, and I said, ^RSurely he is torn in pieces; and I saw him not since: 37:31-35

29 And if ye take this also from me, and mischief befall him, ye shall bring down my gray hairs with sorrow to the grave.

30 Now therefore when I come to thy servant my father, and the lad *be* not with us; seeing that ^Rhis life is bound up in the lad's life;   1 Sam. 18:1

31 It shall come to pass, when he seeth that the lad *is* not *with us,* that he will die: and thy servants shall ^Rbring down the gray hairs of thy servant our father with sorrow to the grave.   *v.* 29

32 For thy servant became ^Tsurety for the lad unto my father, saying, ^RIf I bring him not unto thee, then I shall bear the blame to my father for ever.   *guarantee* • 43:9

33 ^RNow therefore, I pray thee, let thy servant ^Tabide instead of the lad ^Ta bondman to my lord; and let the lad go up with his brethren.   1 Sam. 19:4 • *stay* • *a slave*

34 For how shall I go up to my father, and the lad *be* not with me? lest peradventure I see the evil that shall come on my father.

CHAPTER 45

THEN Joseph could not ^Rrefrain ^Thimself before all them that stood by him; and he cried, Cause every man to go out from me. ^RAnd there stood no man with him, while Joseph made himself known unto his brethren.   43:31 • *control* • Acts 7:13

2 And he ^Rwept aloud: and the Egyptians and the house of Pharaoh heard.   *vv.* 14, 15

3 And Joseph said unto his brethren, I *am* Joseph; ^Rdoth my father yet live? And his brethren could not answer him; for they were troubled at his presence.   43:27

4 ^RAnd Joseph said unto his brethren, Come near to me, I pray you. And they came near. And he said, I *am* Joseph your brother, whom ye sold into Egypt.   37:28

5 Now therefore be not ^Tgrieved, nor angry with yourselves, ^Rthat ye sold me hither: ^Rfor

God did send me before you to preserve life.   *sad* • 37:28 • 50:20; Ps. 105:16, 17

6 ^RFor these two years *hath* the famine *been* in the land: and yet *there are* five years, in the which *there shall* neither *be* earing nor harvest.   41:53

7 ^RAnd God sent me before you to preserve you a posterity in the earth, and to save your lives by a great deliverance.   *v.* 5

8 So now *it was* not you *that* sent me hither, but God: and he hath made me a father to Pharaoh, and lord of all his house, and a ruler throughout all the land of Egypt.

9 Haste ye, and go up to my father, and ^Rsay unto him, Thus saith thy son Joseph, God hath made me lord of all Egypt: come down unto me, ^Ttarry not: Acts 7:14 • *delay not*

10 And ^Rthou shalt dwell in the land of ^RGo'-shen, and thou shalt be near unto me, thou, and thy children, and thy children's children, and thy flocks, and thy herds, and all that thou hast: 47:1 • 46:28, 34

11 And there will I ^Rnourish thee; for yet *there are* five years of famine; lest thou, and thy household, and all that thou hast, come to poverty.   47:12

12 And, behold, your eyes see, and the eyes of my brother Benjamin, that *it is* ^Rmy mouth that speaketh unto you.   42:23

13 And ye shall tell my father of all my glory in Egypt, and of all that ye have seen; and ye shall haste and ^Rbring down my father hither.   46:6-28; Acts 7:14

14 And he fell upon his brother Benjamin's neck, and ^Rwept; and Benjamin wept upon his neck.   *v.* 2

15 Moreover he ^Rkissed all his brethren, and wept upon them: and after that his brethren talked with him.   48:10

16 And ^Rthe ^Tfame thereof was heard in Pharaoh's house, saying, Joseph's brethren are come: and it ^Tpleased Pharaoh well, and his servants.   Acts 7:13 • *news* • *was good news*

17 And Pharaoh said unto Joseph, Say unto thy brethren, This do ye; ^Tlade your beasts, and go, get you unto the land of Canaan;   *load*

18 And take your father and your households, and come unto me: and I will give you the good of the land of Egypt, and ye shall ^Teat the fat of the land.   *have the best*

19 Now thou art commanded, this do ye; take you ^Rwagons out of the land of Egypt for your little ones, and for your wives, and bring your father, and come.   *vv.* 21, 27; 46:5

20 Also regard not your stuff; for the good of all the land of Egypt *is* your's.

21 And the children of Israel did so: and Joseph gave them ^Rwagons, according to the commandment of Pharaoh, and gave them provision for the way.   *v.* 19; 46:5

22 To all of them he gave each man ^Rchanges of ^Traiment; but to Benjamin he

gave Tthree hundred *pieces* of silver, and five changes of raiment.   2 Kin. 5:5 • *new clothes* • *$38,400*

23 And to his father he sent after this *manner;* ten asses Tladen with the good things of Egypt, and ten she asses laden with corn and bread and meat for his father by the way.   *loaded*

24 So he sent his brethren away, and they departed: and he said unto them, TSee that ye fall not out by the way.   *be not angry*

25 And they went up out of Egypt, and came into the land of Canaan unto Jacob their father,

26 And told him, saying, Joseph *is* yet alive, and he *is* governor over all the land of Egypt. RAnd Jacob's heart fainted, for he believed them not.   Ps. 126:1; Luke 24:11, 41

27 And they told him all the words of Joseph, which he had said unto them: and when he saw the Rwagons which Joseph had sent to carry him, Tthe spirit of Jacob their father revived: *v. 19 • his confidence was restored*

28 And Israel said, *It is* enough; Joseph my son *is* yet alive: I will go and see him before I die.

CHAPTER 46

Jacob's Family Safe in Egypt

AND Israel took his journey with all that he had, and came to RBe'-er-she'-ba, and Toffered sacrifices Runto the God of his father Isaac.   21:31, 33 • *worshipped* • 26:24, 25

2 And God spake unto Israel Rin the visions of the night, and said, Jacob, Jacob. And he said, Here *am* I.   15:1; Job 33:14, 15

3 And he said, I *am* God, the God of thy father: fear not to go down into Egypt; for I will there make of theeR a great nation: Ex. 1:7

4 I will go down with thee into Egypt; and I will also surely bring thee up *again:* and Joseph shall put his hand upon thine eyes.

5 And RJacob rose up from Be'-er-she'-ba: and the sons of Israel carried Jacob their father, and their little ones, and their wives, in the wagons Rwhich Pharaoh had sent to carry him.   47:9; Acts 7:15 • 45:19, 21

6 And they took their cattle, and their goods, which they had gotten in the land of Canaan, and came into Egypt, RJacob, and all his Tseed with him: Deut. 26:5 • *children*

7 His sons, and his sons' sons with him, his daughters, and his sons' daughters, and all his seed brought he with him into Egypt.

8 And Rthese *are* the names of the children of Israel, which came into Egypt, Jacob and his sons: Reuben, Jacob's firstborn.   Ex. 1:1

9 And the Rsons of Reuben; Ha'-noch, and Phal'-lu, and Hez'-ron, and Car'-mi.   Ex. 6:14

10 And Rthe sons of Simeon; Jem'-u-el, and Ja'-min, and O'-had, and Ja'-chin, and Zo'-

har, and Sha'-ul the son of a Ca'-naan-i-tish woman.   Ex. 6:15; Num. 26:12

11 And the Rsons of RLevi; Ger'-shon, Ko'-hath, and Me-ra'-ri.   Ex. 6:16, 17 • 1 Chr. 6:1, 16

12 And the sons of Judah; Er, and O'-nan, and She'-lah, and Pha'-rez, and Za'-rah: but REr and O'-nan died in the land of Canaan. And Rthe sons of Pha'-rez were Hez'-ron and Ha'-mul.   38:3, 7, 10 • 38:29

13 And the sons of Is'-sa-char; To'-la, and Phu'-vah, and Job, and Shim'-ron.

14 And the Rsons of Zeb'-u-lun; Se'-red, and E'-lon, and Jah'-le-el.   Num. 26:26

15 These *be* the sons of Leah, which she bare unto Jacob in Pa'-dan-a'-ram, with his daughter Dinah: all the souls of his sons and his daughters *were* thirty and three.

16 And the sons of Gad; RZiph'-i-on, and Hag'-gi, Shu'-ni, and Ez'-bon, E'-ri, and Ar'-o-di, and A-re'-li.   Num. 26:15–17

17 RAnd the sons of Asher; Jim'-nah, and Ish'-u-ah, and Is'-u-i, and Be-ri'-ah, and Se'-rah their sister: and the sons of Be-ri'-ah; He'-ber, and Mal'-chi-el.   1 Chr. 7:30

18 These *are* the sons of Zil'-pah, whom Laban gave to Leah his daughter, and these she bare unto Jacob, *even* sixteen souls.

19 The Rsons of Ra'-chel RJacob's wife; Joseph, and Benjamin.   35:24 • 44:27

20 And unto Joseph in the land of Egypt were born Ma-nas'-seh and E'-phra-im, which As'-e-nath the daughter of Pot-i-phe'-rah priest of On bare unto him.

21 RAnd the sons of Benjamin *were* Be'-lah, and Be'-cher, and Ash'-bel, Ge'-ra, and Na'-a-man, E'-hi, and Rosh, Mup'-pim, and Hup'-pim, and Ard.   Num. 26:38; 1 Chr. 7:6

22 These *are* the sons of Ra'-chel, which were born to Jacob: all the souls *were* fourteen.

23 And the sons of Dan; Hu'-shim.

24 And the sons of Naph'-ta-li; Jah'-ze-el, and Gu'-ni, and Je'-zer, and Shil'-lem.

25 RThese *are* the sons of Bil'-hah, Rwhich Laban gave unto Ra'-chel his daughter, and she bare these unto Jacob: all the souls *were* seven.   30:5, 7 • 29:29

26 All the souls that came with Jacob into Egypt, Twhich came out of his loins, besides Jacob's sons' wives, all the souls *were* three-score and six;   *were his own offspring*

27 RAnd the sons of Joseph, which were born him in Egypt, *were* two souls: all the souls of the house of Jacob, which came into Egypt, *were* threescore and ten.   Ex. 1:5

28 And he sent Judah before him unto Joseph, to direct his face unto Go'-shen; and they came into the land of Go'-shen.

29 And Joseph Tmade ready his chariot, and went up to meet Israel his father, to Go'-shen, and presented himself unto him; and he Rfell on his neck, and wept on his neck a good while.   *prepared to travel* • 37:9; 45:14

30 And Israel said unto Joseph, ᴿNow let me die, since I have seen thy face, because thou *art* yet alive.   Luke 2:29, 30

31 And Joseph said unto his brethren, and unto his father's house, ᴿI will go up, and shew Pharaoh, and say unto him, My brethren, and my father's house, which *were* in the land of Canaan, are come unto me;   47:1

32 And the men *are* shepherds, for ᵀtheir trade hath been to feed cattle; and they have brought their flocks, and their herds, and all that they have.   *they were keepers of cattle*

33 And it shall come to pass, when Pharaoh shall call you, and shall say, ᴿWhat *is* your occupation?   47:2, 3

34 That ye shall say, Thy servants' trade hath been about cattle from our youth even until now, both we, *and* also our fathers: that ye may dwell in the land of Go'-shen; for every shepherd *is* ᴿan ᵀabomination unto the Egyptians.   43:32 • *taboo*

CHAPTER 47

THEN Joseph ᴿcame and told Pharaoh, and said, My father and my brethren, and their flocks, and their herds, and all that they have, are come out of the land of Canaan; and, behold, they *are* in ᴿthe land of Go'-shen.   46:31 • 45:10; 46:28

2 And he took some of his brethren, *even* five men, and presented them unto Pharaoh.

3 And Pharaoh said unto his brethren, ᴿWhat *is* your occupation? And they said unto Pharaoh, Thy servants *are* shepherds, both we, *and* also our fathers.   46:33, 34

4 They said moreover unto Pharaoh, ᴿFor to sojourn in the land are we come; for thy servants have no pasture for their flocks; for the famine *is* sore in the land of Canaan: now therefore, we pray thee, let thy servants ᴿdwell in the land of Go'-shen.   15:13 • 46:34

5 And Pharaoh spake unto Joseph, saying, Thy father and thy brethren are come unto thee:

6 The land of Egypt *is* before thee; in the best of the land make thy father and brethren to dwell; ᴿin the land of Go'-shen let them dwell: and if thou knowest *any* ᵀmen of activity among them, then make them rulers over my cattle.   *v.* 4 • *able men*

7 And Joseph brought in Jacob his father, and set him before Pharaoh: and Jacob ᴿblessed Pharaoh.   *v.* 10; 2 Sam. 14:22; 1 Kin. 8:66

8 And Pharaoh said unto Jacob, ᵀHow old *art* thou?   *how many years have you lived?*

9 And Jacob said unto Pharaoh, The days of the years of my ᵀpilgrimage *are* an hundred and thirty years: ᴿfew and evil have the days of the years of my life been, and have not ᴿattained unto the days of the years of

the life of my fathers in the days of their pilgrimage.   *life* • [Job 14:1] • 25:7

10 And Jacob ᴿblessed Pharaoh, and went out from before Pharaoh.   *v.* 7

11 And Joseph placed his father and his brethren, and gave them a possession in the land of Egypt, in the best of the land, in the land of ᴿRam'-e-ses, ᴿas Pharaoh had commanded.   Ex. 1:11; 12:37 • *v.* 6

12 And Joseph nourished his father, and his brethren, and all his father's household, with bread, according to *their* families.

13 And *there was* no bread in all the land; for the famine *was* very sore, ᴿso that the land of Egypt and *all* the land of Canaan fainted by reason of the famine.   Acts 7:11

14 ᴿAnd Joseph gathered up all the money that was found in the land of Egypt, and in the land of Canaan, for the corn which they bought: and Joseph brought the money into Pharaoh's house.   41:56

15 And when money failed in the land of Egypt, and in the land of Canaan, all the Egyptians came unto Joseph, and said, Give us bread: for ᴿwhy should we die in thy presence? for the money faileth.   *v.* 19

16 And Joseph said, Give your cattle; and I will give you for your cattle, if money fail.

17 ᴿAnd they brought their cattle unto Joseph: and Joseph gave them bread in *exchange* for horses, and for the flocks, and for the cattle of the herds, and for the asses: and he ᵀfed them with ᵀbread for all their cattle for that year.   1 Kin. 5:10 • *supplied* • *food*

18 When that year was ended, they came unto him the second year, and said unto him, We will not hide *it* from my lord, how that our money is spent; my lord also hath our ᴿherds of cattle; there is ᵀnot ought left in the sight of my lord, but our bodies, and our lands: Ex. 10:9 • *nothing*

19 Wherefore shall we die before thine eyes, both we and our land? ᴿbuy us and our land for bread, and we and our land will be servants unto Pharaoh: and give *us* seed, that we may ᴿlive, and not die, that the land be not desolate.   *v.* 23 • 43:8

20 And Joseph bought all the land of Egypt for Pharaoh; for the Egyptians sold every man his field, because the famine prevailed over them: so the land became Pharaoh's.

21 And as for the people, he removed them to cities from *one* end of the borders of Egypt even to the *other* end thereof.

22 ᴿOnly the land of the priests bought he not; for the priests had a portion *assigned them* of Pharaoh, and did eat their portion which Pharaoh gave them: wherefore they sold not their lands.   Lev. 25:34

23 Then Joseph said unto the people, Behold, I have ᴿbought you this day and your land for Pharaoh: lo, *here is* seed for you, and ye shall sow the land.   [*v.* 19; 1 Cor. 6:20]

24 ^RAnd it shall come to pass in the increase, that ye shall give the fifth *part* unto Pharaoh, and four parts shall be your own, for seed of the field, and for your food, and for them of your households, and for food for your little ones.   41:34

25 And they said, Thou hast saved our lives: let us find grace in the sight of my lord, and we will be Pharaoh's servants.

26 And Joseph made it a law over the land of Egypt unto this day, *that* Pharaoh should have the fifth *part;* except the land of the priests only, *which* became not Pharaoh's.

Jacob Blesses the Family in Egypt

27 And Israel dwelt in the land of Egypt, in the country of Go'-shen; and they had ^Rpossessions therein, and grew, and ^Tmultiplied exceedingly.   *v. 11 · increased in number*

28 And Jacob lived in the land of Egypt seventeen years: so the whole age of Jacob was an hundred forty and seven years.

29 And the time drew nigh that Israel must die: and he called his son Joseph, and said unto him, If now I have found grace in thy sight, put, I pray thee, thy hand under my thigh, and deal kindly and truly with me; bury me not, I pray thee, in Egypt:

30 But I will lie with my fathers, and thou shalt carry me out of Egypt, and ^Rbury me in their buryingplace. And he said, I will do as thou hast said.   49:29; 50:5, 13

31 And he said, ^TSwear unto me. And he sware unto him. And Israel bowed himself upon the bed's head.   *solemnly promise*

CHAPTER 48

A ND it came to pass after these things, that *one* told Joseph, Behold, thy father *is* sick: and he took with him his two sons, Ma-nas'-seh and E'-phra-im.

2 And *one* told Jacob, and said, Behold, thy son Joseph cometh unto thee: and Israel strengthened himself, and sat upon the bed.

3 And Jacob said unto Joseph, God Almighty appeared unto me at ^RLuz in the land of Canaan, and blessed me,   28:13, 19

4 And said unto me, Behold, I will make thee fruitful, and multiply thee, and I will make of thee a multitude of people; and will ^Rgive this land to thy seed after thee ^R*for* an everlasting possession.   [35:12; Ex. 6:8] · 17:8

5 And now thy ^Rtwo sons, E'-phra-im and Ma-nas'-seh, which were born unto thee in the land of Egypt before I came unto thee into Egypt, *are* mine; as Reuben and Simeon, they shall be mine.   41:50; 46:20

6 And thy issue, which thou begettest after them, shall be thine, *and* shall be called after the name of their brethren in their inheritance.

7 And as for me, when I came from Pa'-dan, ^RRa'-chel died ^Tby me in the land of Canaan in the way, when yet *there was* but ^Ta little way to come unto Eph'-rath: and I buried her there in the way of Eph'-rath; the same *is* Beth'-le-hem. 35:9 · *to my sorrow · about 5 mi.*

8 And Israel ^Rbeheld Joseph's sons, and said, Who *are* these?   *v. 10*

9 And Joseph said unto his father, ^RThey *are* my sons, whom God hath given me in this *place.* And he said, Bring them, I pray thee, unto me, and I will bless them.   33:5

10 Now ^Rthe eyes of Israel were ^Tdim for age, *so that* he could not see. And he brought them near unto him; and he kissed them, and embraced them.   27:1 · *heavy*

11 And Israel said unto Joseph, I had not thought to see thy face: and, lo, God hath shewed me also thy ^Tseed.   *children*

12 And Joseph brought them out from between his knees, and he bowed himself with ^Rhis face to the earth.   42:6

13 And Joseph took them both, E'-phra-im in his right hand toward Israel's left hand, and Ma-nas'-seh in his left hand toward Israel's right hand, and brought *them* near unto him.

14 And Israel stretched out his right hand, and laid *it* upon E'-phra-im's head, who *was* the younger, and his left hand upon Ma-nas'-seh's head, guiding his hands ^Twittingly; for Ma-nas'-seh *was* the firstborn.   *deliberately*

15 And ^Rhe blessed Joseph, and said, God, ^Rbefore whom my fathers Abraham and Isaac did walk, the God which fed me all my life long unto this day,   .49:24 · [Heb. 11:21]

16 The Angel which redeemed me from all evil, bless the lads; and let my name be named on them, and the name of my fathers Abraham and Isaac; and let them grow into a multitude in the midst of the earth.

17 And when Joseph saw that his father laid his right hand upon the head of E'-phra-im, it displeased him: and he held up his father's hand, to remove it from E'-phra-im's head unto Ma-nas'-seh's head.

18 And Joseph said unto his father, Not so, my father: for this *is* the firstborn; put thy right hand upon his head.

19 And his father refused, and said, I know *it,* my son, I know *it:* he also shall become a people, and he also shall be great: but truly ^Rhis younger brother shall be greater than he, and ^Rhis seed shall become a multitude of nations.   Deut. 33:17 · 28:14

20 And he blessed them that day, saying, In thee shall Israel bless, saying, God make thee as E'-phra-im and as Ma-nas'-seh: and he set E'-phra-im before Ma-nas'-seh.

21 And Israel said unto Joseph, Behold, I die: but God shall be with you, and bring you again unto the land of your fathers.

22 Moreover I have given to thee one Tportion above thy brethren, which I took out of the hand of the Am'-or-ite with my sword and with my bow. *mountain slope*

CHAPTER 49

AND Jacob called unto his sons, and said, Gather yourselves together, that I may Rtell you *that* which shall befall you Rin the last days. [Amos 3:7] • [Deut. 4:30, 31; Is. 39:6]

2 Gather yourselves together, and hear, ye sons of Jacob; and hearken unto Israel your father.

3 Reuben, thou *art* my firstborn, my might, and the Rbeginning T of my strength, the excellency of dignity, and the excellency of power: Deut. 21:17; Ps. 78:51 • *first fruits*

4 Unstable as water, thou shalt not excel; Rbecause thou wentest up to thy father's bed; then defiledst thou *it:* he went up to my couch. 35:22; Deut. 27:20

5 Simeon and Levi *are* brethren; instruments of cruelty *are in* their habitations.

6 O my soul, come not thou into their secret; unto their assembly, mine honour, be not thou united: for in their anger they slew a man, and in their selfwill they Tdigged down a wall. *brought disaster upon themselves*

7 Cursed *be* their anger, for *it was* fierce; and their wrath, for it was cruel: I will divide them in Jacob, and scatter them in Israel.

8 Judah, thou *art he* whom thy brethren shall praise: Rthy hand *shall be* in the neck of thine enemies; Rthy father's children shall bow down before thee. Ps. 18:40 • [Ps. 27:29]; 1 Chr. 5:2

9 Judah *is* a Rlion's whelp: from the prey, my son, thou art gone up: he stooped down, he couched as a lion, and as an old lion; who shall rouse him up? Ezek. 19:5–7

10 RThe sceptre shall not depart from Judah, nor a lawgiver from between his feet, until Shi'-loh come; and unto him *shall* the gathering of the people *be*. Ps. 60:7; Rev. 5:5 ✫

11 RBinding his foal unto the vine, and his ass's colt unto the choice vine; he washed his garments in wine, and his clothes in the blood of grapes: Deut. 8:7, 8

12 His eyes *shall be* red with wine, and his teeth white with milk.

13 Zeb'-u-lun shall dwell at the haven of the sea; and he *shall be* for an haven of ships; and his border *shall be* unto Zi'-don.

14 RIs'-sa-char *is* a strong ass couching down between two burdens: Ps. 68:13

15 And he saw that rest *was* good, and the land that *it was* pleasant; and bowed his shoulder to bear, and became a servant unto tribute.

16 RDan shall judge his people, as one of the tribes of Israel. Deut. 33:22

17 Dan shall be a serpent by the way, an adder in the path, that biteth the horse heels, so that his rider shall fall backward.

18 I have waited for thy salvation, O LORD.

19 RGad, a troop shall overcome him: but he shall overcome at the last. Deut. 33:20

20 ROut of Asher his bread *shall be* fat, and he shall yield royal dainties. Deut. 33:24

21 RNaph'-ta-li *is* a hind let loose: he giveth goodly words. Deut. 33:23

22 RJoseph *is* a fruitful bough, *even* a fruitful bough by a well; *whose* branches run over the wall: Deut. 33:13–17

23 The archers have Tsorely grieved him, and shot *at him,* and hated him: *harassed*

24 But his bow abode in strength, and the arms of his hands were made strong by the hands of the mighty God of Jacob; (from thence *is* the shepherd, the stone of Israel:)

25 *Even* by the God of thy father, who shall help thee; and by the Almighty, who shall bless thee with blessings of heaven above, blessings of the deep that lieth under, blessings of the breasts, and of the womb:

26 The blessings of thy father have prevailed above the blessings of my progenitors unto the utmost bound of Rthe everlasting hills: they shall be on the head of Joseph, and on the crown of the head of him that was separate from his brethren. Deut. 33:15

27 Benjamin shall ravin *as* a wolf: in the morning he shall devour the prey, and at night he shall divide the spoil.

28 All these *are* the twelve tribes of Israel: and this *is it* that their father spake unto them, and blessed them; every one according to his blessing he blessed them.

29 And he charged them, and said unto them, I am to be gathered unto my people: bury me with my fathers Rin the cave that *is* in the field of E'-phron the Hit'-tite, 50:13

30 In the cave that *is* in the field of Mach-pe'-lah, which *is* before Mam'-re, in the land of Canaan, Rwhich Abraham bought with the field of E'-phron the Hit'-tite for a possession of a buryingplace. 23:16

31 There they buried Abraham and Sarah his wife; there they buried Isaac and Rebekah his wife; and there I buried Leah.

32 The purchase of the field and of the cave that *is* therein *was* from the children of RHeth. 1 Chr. 1:13

Jacob Dies in Egypt

33 And when Jacob had made an end of commanding his sons, he gathered up his feet into the bed, and Tyielded up the ghost, and was gathered unto his people. *died*

CHAPTER 50

AND Joseph fell upon his father's face, and wept upon him, and kissed him.

2 And Joseph commanded his servants the physicians to Rembalm his father: and the physicians embalmed Israel.   Luke 24:1

3 And forty days were fulfilled for him; for so are fulfilled the days of those which are embalmed: and the Egyptians Rmourned[T] for him threescore and ten days.   v. 10 • wept

4 And when the days of his mourning were past, Joseph spake unto Rthe house of Pharaoh, saying, If now I have found grace in your eyes, speak, I pray you, in the ears of Pharaoh, saying,   [Esth. 4:2]

5 RMy father made me swear, saying, Lo, I die: in my grave Rwhich I have digged for me in the land of Canaan, there shalt thou bury me. Now therefore let me Tgo up, I pray thee, and bury my father, and I will come again.   47:29 • 2 Chr. 16:14; Is. 22:16 • travel

6 And Pharaoh said, Go up, and bury thy father, according as he made thee swear.

7 And Joseph went up to bury his father: and with him went up all the servants of Pharaoh, the elders of his house, and all the elders of the land of Egypt,

8 And all the house of Joseph, and his brethren, and his father's house: only their little ones, and their flocks, and their herds, they left in the land of Go'-shen.

9 And there went up with him both chariots and horsemen: and it was a very great company.

10 And they came to the threshingfloor of A'-tad, which is beyond Jordan, and there they mourned with a great and very sore lamentation: Rand he made a mourning for his father seven days.   1 Sam. 31:13

11 And when the inhabitants of the land, the Ca'-naan-ites, saw the mourning in the floor of A'-tad, they said, This is a Tgrievous mourning to the Egyptians: wherefore the name of it was called A'-bel-miz'-ra-im, which is beyond Jordan.   large funeral service

12 And his sons did unto him according as he commanded them:

13 For Rhis sons carried him into the land of Canaan, and buried him in the cave of the field of Mach-pe'-lah, which Abraham Rbought with the field for a possession of a

buryingplace of E'-phron the Hit'-tite, before Mam'-re.   49:29; Acts 7:16 • 23:16

14 And Joseph returned into Egypt, he, and his brethren, and all that went up with him to bury his father, after he had buried his father.

Joseph Dies in Egypt

15 And when Joseph's brethren saw that their father was dead, Rthey said, Joseph will Tperadventure hate us, and will certainly Trequite us all the evil which we did unto him.   [Job 15:21] • perhaps • retaliate for

16 And they sent a messenger unto Joseph, saying, Thy father did command before he died, saying,

17 So shall ye say unto Joseph, Forgive, I pray thee now, the trespass of thy brethren, and their sin; for they did unto thee evil: and now, we pray thee, forgive the trespass of the servants of the God of thy father. And Joseph wept when they spake unto him.

18 And his brethren also went and Rfell down before his face; and they said, Behold, we be thy servants.   37:7, 10; 41:43; 44:14

19 And Joseph said unto them, RFear not: for am I in the place of God?   45:5

20 RBut as for you, Rye thought evil against me; but RGod meant it unto good, to bring to pass, as it is this day, to save much people alive.   Ps. 56:5 • [Acts 3:13–15] • 37:26, 27; 45:5, 7

21 Now therefore fear ye not: I will nourish you, and your little ones. And he comforted them, and spake kindly unto them.

22 And Joseph dwelt in Egypt, he, and his father's house: and Joseph lived an hundred and ten years.

23 And Joseph saw E'-phra-im's children Rof the third generation: the children also of Ma'-chir the son of Ma-nas'-seh were brought up upon Joseph's knees.   Job 42:16

24 And Joseph said unto his brethren, I die: and RGod will surely visit you, and bring you out of this land unto the land Rwhich he sware to Abraham, to Isaac, and to Jacob.   48:21; Ex. 3:16, 17; Heb. 11:22 • 26:3

25 And RJoseph took an oath of the children of Israel, saying, God will surely Tvisit you, and ye shall carry up my bones from hence.   Ex. 13:19; Josh. 24:32; Acts 7:16 • come to help

26 So Joseph died, being an hundred and ten years old: and they Rembalmed him, and he was put in a coffin in Egypt.   v. 2

EXODUS

THE BOOK OF EXODUS

Exodus is the record of Israel's birth as a nation. Within the protective "womb" of Egypt, the Jewish family of seventy rapidly multiplies. At the right time, accompanied with severe "birth pains," an infant nation, numbering between two and three million people, is brought into the world where it is divinely protected, fed, and nurtured.

The Hebrew title, *We'elleh Shemoth*, "Now These *Are* the Names," comes from the first phrase in 1:1. Exodus begins with "Now" to show it as a continuation of Genesis. The Greek title is *Exodus*, a word meaning exit, departure, or going out. The Septuagint uses this word to describe the book by its key event (see 19:1, "gone forth"). In Luke 9:31 and in Second Peter 1:15, the word *exodus* speaks of physical death (Jesus and Peter). This embodies Exodus' theme of redemption, because redemption is accomplished only through death. The Latin title is *Liber Exodus*, "Book of Departure," taken from the Greek title.

THE AUTHOR OF EXODUS

Critics have challenged the Mosaic authorship of Exodus in favor of a series of oral and written documents that were woven together by editors late in Israel's history. Their arguments are generally weak and far from conclusive, especially in view of the strong external and internal evidence that points to Moses as the author.

External Evidence: Exodus has been attributed to Moses since the time of Joshua (cf. Ex. 20:25 with Josh. 8:30–32). Other biblical writers attribute Exodus to Moses: Malachi (Mal. 4:4), the disciples (John 1:45), and Paul (Rom. 10:5). This is also the testimony of Jesus (Mark 7:10; 12:26; Luke 20:37; John 5:46, 47; 7:19, 22, 23). Jewish and Samaritan traditions consistently hold to the Mosaic authorship of Exodus.

Internal Evidence: Portions of Exodus are directly attributed to Moses (Ex. 15; 17:8–14; 20:1–17; 24:4, 7, 12; 31:18; 34:1–27). Moses' usual procedure was to record events soon after they occurred in the form of historical annals. It is clear from Exodus that the author must have been an eyewitness of the Exodus and an educated man. He was acquainted with details about the customs and climate of Egypt and the plants, animals, and terrain of the wilderness. A consistency of style and development also points to a single author. Its antiquity is supported by the frequent use of ancient literary constructions, words, and expressions.

THE TIME OF EXODUS

If the early date for the Exodus (c. 1445 B.C.) is assumed, this book was composed during the forty-year wilderness journey, between 1445 B.C. and 1405 B.C. Moses probably kept an account of God's work, which he then edited in the plains of Moab shortly before his death. Exodus covers the period from the arrival of Jacob in Egypt (c. 1875 B.C.) to the erection of the tabernacle 431 years later in the wilderness (c. 1445 B.C.).

THE CHRIST OF EXODUS

Exodus contains no direct messianic prophecies, but it is full of figures and portraits of Christ. Here are seven: (1) *Moses:* In dozens of ways Moses is a figure of Christ (Deut. 18:15). Both Moses and Christ are prophets, priests, and kings (although Moses was never made King, he functioned as the ruler of Israel); both are kinsman-redeemers; both are endangered in infancy; both voluntarily renounce power and wealth; both are deliverers, lawgivers, and mediators. (2) *The Passover:* John 1:29, 36 and First Corinthians 5:7 make it clear that Christ is our slain God and the Passover Lamb. (3) *The seven feasts:* Each of these feasts portrays some aspect of the ministry of Christ. (4) *The Exodus:* Paul relates baptism to the Exodus event because baptism symbolizes death to the old and identification with the new (Rom. 6:2, 3; 1 Cor. 10:1, 2). (5) *The manna and water:* The New Testament applies both to Christ (John 6:31–35, 48–63; 1 Cor. 10:3, 4). (6) *The tabernacle:* In its materials, colors, furniture, and arrangement, the tabernacle clearly speaks of the person of Christ and the way of redemption. The development is progressive from suffering, blood, and death, to beauty, holiness, and the glory of God. The tabernacle is theology in a physical form. (7) *The High Priest:* In several ways the high priest foreshadows the ministry of Christ, our great High Priest (Heb. 4:14–16; 9:11, 12, 24–28).

KEYS TO EXODUS

Key Word: Redemption—Central to the Book of Exodus is the concept of redemption. Israel was redeemed *from* bondage in Egypt and *into* a covenant relationship with God. From the redemption of Moses in the Nile to the redeeming presence of God in the tabernacle, Exodus records God's overwhelming acts of deliverance, by which He demonstrates His right to be Israel's King.

Key Verses: Exodus 6:6; 19:5, 6—"Wherefore say unto the children of Israel, I *am* the LORD,

and I will bring you out from under the burdens of the Egyptians, and I will rid you out of their bondage, and I will redeem you with a stretched out arm, and with great judgments" (6:6).

"Now therefore, if ye will obey my voice indeed, and keep my covenant, then ye shall be a peculiar treasure unto me above all people: for all the earth *is* mine: And ye shall be unto me a kingdom of priests, and an holy nation" (19:5, 6).

Key Chapters: Exodus 12—14—The climax of the entire Old Testament is recorded in chapters 12—14: the salvation of Israel through blood (the Passover) and through power (the Red Sea). The Exodus is the central event of the Old Testament as the cross is of the New Testament.

SURVEY OF EXODUS

Exodus abounds with God's powerful redemptive acts on behalf of His oppressed people. It begins in pain and ends in liberation; it moves from the groaning of the people to the glory of God. It is the continuation of the story that begins in Genesis with the seventy descendants of Jacob who move from Canaan to Egypt. They have multiplied under adverse conditions to a multitude of over two million people. When the Israelites finally turn to God for deliverance from their bondage, God quickly responds by redeeming them "with a stretched out arm, and with great judgments" (6:6). God faithfully fulfills His promise made to Abraham centuries before (Gen. 15:13, 14).

The book falls into two parts: (1) redemption from Egypt (1—18); and (2) revelation from God (19—40).

Redemption from Egypt (1—18): After four centuries of slavery, the people of Israel cry to the God of Abraham, Isaac, and Jacob for deliverance. God has already prepared Moses for this purpose, and has commissioned him at the burning bush to stand before Pharaoh as the advocate for Israel. However, Pharaoh hardens his heart: "Who *is* the LORD, that I should obey his voice to let Israel go?" (5:2).

God soon reveals Himself to Pharaoh through a series of object lessons, the ten plagues. These plagues grow in severity until the tenth brings death to the firstborn of every household of Egypt. Israel is redeemed through this plague by means of the Passover lamb. The Israelites' faith in God at this point becomes the basis for their national redemption. As they leave Egypt, God guides them by a pillar of fire and smoke, and saves them from Egypt's pursuing army through the miraculous crossing of the sea. In the wilderness He protects and sustains them throughout their journeys.

Revelation from God (19—40): Now that the people have experienced God's deliverance, guidance, and protection, they are ready to be taught what God expects of them. The redeemed people must now be set apart to walk with God. This is why the emphasis moves from narration in chapters 1—18 to legislation in chapters 19—40. On Mount Sinai, Moses receives God's moral, civil, and ceremonial laws, as well as the pattern for the tabernacle to be built in the wilderness. After God judges the people for their worship of the golden calf, the tabernacle is constructed and consecrated. It is a building of beauty in a barren land and reveals much about the person of God and the way of redemption.

FOCUS	REDEMPTION FROM EGYPT				REVELATION FROM GOD	
REFERENCE	1:1———————2:1——————5:1———————— 15:22 ———————— 19:1 ————— 32:1 ———— 40:38					
DIVISION	THE NEED FOR REDEMPTION	THE PREPARATION FOR REDEMPTION	THE REDEMPTION OF ISRAEL	THE PRESERVATION OF ISRAEL	THE REVELATION OF THE COVENANT	THE RESPONSE OF ISRAEL TO THE COVENANT
TOPIC	NARRATION				LEGISLATION	
	SUBJECTION		REDEMPTION		INSTRUCTION	
LOCATION	EGYPT		WILDERNESS		MOUNT SINAI	
TIME	430 YEARS		2 MONTHS		10 MONTHS	

OUTLINE OF EXODUS

Part One: Redemption from Egypt (1:1—18:27)

Part Two: Revelation from God (19:1—40:38)

CHAPTER 1

Israel's Rapid Multiplication

NOW these *are* the names of the children of Israel, which came into Egypt; every man and his household came with Jacob.

2 Reuben, Simeon, Levi, and Judah,

3 Is'-sa-char, Zeb'-u-lun, and Benjamin,

4 Dan, and Naph'-ta-li, Gad, and Asher.

5 And all the souls that came out of the loins of Jacob were [R]seventy souls: for Joseph was in Egypt *already*.   [Deut. 10:22]

6 And [R]Joseph died, and all his brethren, and all that generation.   Gen. 50:26; Acts 7:15

7 [R]And the children of Israel were fruitful, and increased abundantly, and multiplied, and waxed exceeding mighty; and the land was filled with them.   [Gen. 12:2; 46:3]

Israel's Severe Affliction

8 Now there arose up a new [R]king over Egypt, which knew not Joseph.   Acts 7:18, 19

9 And he said unto his people, [R]Behold, the people of the children of Israel *are* more and [R]mightier than we: Ps. 105:24, 25 · Gen. 26:16

10 Come on, let us deal wisely with them; lest they multiply, and it come to pass, that, when there falleth out any war, they join also unto our enemies, and fight against us, and *so* get them up out of the land.

11 Therefore they did set over them taskmasters [R]to afflict them with their burdens. And they built for Pharaoh treasure cities, Pi'-thom [R]and Ra-am'-ses.   3:7 · Gen. 47:11

12 But the more they [R]afflicted them, [R]the more they multiplied and grew. And they

were ^Tgrieved because of the children of Israel. Job 5:17 • 1:7 • *worried*

13 And the Egyptians made the children of Israel to serve with ^Trigour: *hardship*

14 And they ^Rmade their lives bitter with hard bondage, ^Rin morter, and in brick, and in all manner of service in the field: all their service, wherein they made them serve, *was* with rigour. [Acts 7:19, 34] • Ps. 81:6

Israel's Planned Extinction

15 And the king of Egypt spake to the ^RHebrew midwives, of which the name of the one *was* Shiph'-rah, and the name of the other Pu'-ah: 2:6

16 And he said, ^RWhen ye do the office of a midwife to the Hebrew women, and see *them* upon the stools; ^Rif it *be* a son, then ye shall kill him: but if it *be* a daughter, then she shall live. Acts 7:19 • Matt. 2:16

17 But the midwives feared God, and did not as the king of Egypt commanded them, but saved the men children alive.

18 And the king of Egypt called for the midwives, and said unto them, Why have ye done this thing, and have saved the ^Tmen children alive? *male*

19 And ^Rthe midwives said unto Pharaoh, Because the Hebrew women *are* not as the Egyptian women; for they *are* lively, and are delivered ere the midwives come in unto them. 2 Sam. 17:19, 20

20 ^RTherefore God dealt well with the midwives: and the people multiplied, and ^Twaxed very mighty. [Is. 3:10] • *became very strong*

21 And it came to pass, because the midwives feared God, ^Rthat he ^Tmade them houses. 1 Kin. 11:38; Ps. 127:1 • *gave them families*

22 And Pharaoh ^Tcharged all his people, saying, ^REvery son that is born ye shall cast into ^Rthe river, and every daughter ye shall save alive. *commanded* • Acts 7:19 • Gen. 41:1

CHAPTER 2

Moses Is Redeemed from Murder

AND there went ^Ra man of the house of Levi, and took *to* wife a daughter of Levi. 6:20; Num. 26:59; 1 Chr. 23:14

2 And the woman conceived, and bare a son: and when she saw him that he *was a* goodly *child*, she hid him three months.

3 And when she could not longer hide him, she took for him an ^Rark of bulrushes, and daubed it with slime and with pitch, and put the child therein; and she laid *it* in the ^Tflags by the river's brink. Is. 18:2 • *reeds*

4 ^RAnd his sister stood afar off, to ^Twit what would be done to him. Num. 26:59 • *know*

5 And the daughter of Pharaoh came down to ^Rwash *herself* at the river; and her maidens walked along by the river's side; and when

she saw the ark among the flags, she sent her maid to fetch it. 7:15

6 And when she had opened *it*, she saw the child: and, behold, the babe wept. And she had compassion on him, and said, This *is one* of the ^RHebrews' children. *vv.* 1, 2

7 Then said his sister to Pharaoh's daughter, Shall I go and call to thee a ^Rnurse of the Hebrew women, that she may nurse the child for thee? Ruth 4:16

8 And Pharaoh's daughter said to her, Go. And the maid went and called the child's mother.

9 And Pharaoh's daughter said unto her, Take this child away, and nurse it for me, and I will give *thee* thy wages. And the woman took the child, and nursed it.

10 And the child grew, and she brought him unto Pharaoh's daughter, and ^Rhe became her son. And she called his name ^TMoses: and she said, Because I drew him out of the water. Acts 7:21 • *Mashah, to draw out*

Moses Tries to Redeem by Murder

11 And it came to pass in those days, when Moses was grown, that he went out unto his brethren, and looked on their burdens: and he spied an Egyptian ^Tsmiting an Hebrew, one of his brethren. *punishing*

12 And he looked this way and that way, and when he saw that *there was* no man, he slew the Egyptian, and hid him in the sand.

13 And when he went out the second day, behold, two men of the Hebrews strove together: and he said to him that did the wrong, Wherefore smitest thou thy fellow?

14 And he said, Who made thee a prince and a judge over us? intendest thou to kill me, as thou killedst the Egyptian? And Moses feared, and said, Surely this thing is known.

15 Now when Pharaoh heard this thing, he sought to slay Moses. But Moses fled from the face of Pharaoh, and dwelt in the land of Mid'-i-an: and he sat down by a well.

16 ^RNow the priest of Mid'-i-an had seven daughters: ^Rand they ^Rcame and drew *water*, and filled the troughs to water their father's flock. 3:1, 18 • Gen. 24:11; 1 Sam. 9:11 • Gen. 29:6–9

17 And the shepherds came and drove them away: but Moses stood up and helped them, and ^Rwatered their flock. Gen. 29:10

18 And when they came to ^RReu'-el^T their father, he said, How *is it that* ye are come so soon to day? 3:1; Num. 10:29 • *Jethro*

19 And they said, An Egyptian delivered us out of the hand of the shepherds, and also drew *water* enough for us, and watered the flock.

20 And he said unto his daughters, And where *is* he? why *is* it *that* ye have left the man? call him, that he may eat bread.

21 ^RAnd Moses was content to dwell with

the man: and he gave Moses ᴿZip-po′-rah his daughter.   Acts 7:29 • 4:25; 18:2

22 And she bare *him* a son, and he called his name ᴿGer′-shom: for he said, I have been a stranger in a strange land.   18:3

Israel Calls upon God

23 And it came to pass in process of time, that the king of Egypt died: and the children of Israel sighed by reason of the bondage, and they cried, and their cry came up unto God by reason of the bondage.

24 And God heard their groaning, and God remembered his ᴿcovenant with Abraham, with Isaac, and with Jacob.   [Gen. 15:14]

25 And God looked upon the children of Israel, and God had respect unto *them.*

CHAPTER 3

God Miraculously Appears

NOW Moses kept the flock of Je′-thro his father in law, ᴿthe priest of Mid′-i-an: and he led the flock to the backside of the desert, and came to ᴿthe mountain of God, *even* to Ho′-reb.   2:16 • 18:5; 1 Kin. 19:8

2 And ᴿthe angel of the Lord appeared unto him in a flame of fire out of the midst of a bush: and he looked, and, behold, the bush burned with fire, and the bush *was* not ᵀconsumed.   Deut. 33:16; Acts 7:30 • *burned up*

3 And Moses said, I will now turn aside, and see this ᴿgreat sight, why the bush is not burnt.   Acts 7:31

4 And when the Lord saw that he turned aside to see, God called ᴿunto him out of the midst of the bush, and said, Moses, Moses. And he said, Here *am* I.   Deut. 33:16

5 And he said, Draw not nigh hither: put off thy shoes from off thy feet, for the place whereon thou standest *is* holy ground.

6 Moreover he said, ᴿI *am* the God of thy father, the God of Abraham, the God of Isaac, and the God of Jacob. And Moses hid his face; for ᴿhe was afraid to look upon God.   Gen. 28:13; [Matt. 22:32]; Acts 7:32 • 1 Kin. 19:13

God Calls Moses to Leadership

7 And the Lord said, I have surely seen the affliction of my people which *are* in Egypt, and have heard their cry by reason of their taskmasters; for I know their sorrows;

8 And I am come down to deliver them out of the hand of the Egyptians, and to bring them up out of that land unto a good land and a large, unto a land flowing with milk and honey; unto the place of ᴿthe Ca′-naan-ites, and the Hit′-tites, and the Am′-or-ites, and the Per′-iz-zites, and the Hi′-vites, and the Jeb′-u-sites.   Gen. 15:21

9 Now therefore, behold, the cry of the children of Israel is come unto me: and I have also seen the ᴿoppression wherewith the Egyptians oppress them.   1:11, 13, 14

10 Come now therefore, ᴿand I will send thee unto Pharaoh, ᴿthat thou mayest bring forth my people the children of Israel out of Egypt.   [Mic. 6:4] • Gen. 15:13; Acts 7:6, 7

"Who Am I?"

11 And Moses said unto God, ᴿWho *am* I, that I should go unto Pharaoh, and that I should bring forth the children of Israel out of Egypt?   6:12; 1 Sam. 18:18

12 And he said, Certainly I will be with thee; and this *shall be* a ᵀtoken unto thee, that I have sent thee: When thou hast brought forth the people out of Egypt, ye shall serve God upon this mountain.   *sign*

"What Is His Name?"

13 And Moses said unto God, Behold, *when* I come unto the children of Israel, and shall say unto them, The God of your fathers hath sent me unto you; and they shall say to me, What *is* his name? what shall I say unto them?

14 And God said unto Moses, I AM THAT I AM: and he said, Thus shalt thou say unto the children of Israel, ᴿI AM hath sent me unto you.   [6:3; John 8:58; Heb. 13:8]

15 And God said moreover unto Moses, Thus shalt thou say unto the children of Israel, ᴿThe Lord God of your fathers, the God of Abraham, the God of Isaac, and the God of Jacob, hath sent me unto you: this *is* ᴿmy name for ever, and this *is* my memorial unto all generations.   [Hos. 12:5] • Ps. 135:13

16 Go, and gather the elders of Israel together, and say unto them, The Lord God of your fathers, the God of Abraham, of Isaac, and of Jacob, appeared unto me, saying, I have surely visited you, and *seen* that which is done to you in Egypt:

17 And I have said, I will bring you up out of ᵀthe affliction of Egypt unto the land of the Ca′-naan-ites, and the Hit′-tites, and the Am′-or-ites, and the Per′-iz-zites, and the Hi′-vites, and the Jeb′-u-sites, unto a land flowing with milk and honey.   *misery*

18 And ᴿthey shall ᵀhearken to thy voice: and ᴿthou shalt come, thou and the elders of Israel, unto the king of Egypt, and ye shall say unto him, The Lord God of the Hebrews hath met with us: and now let us go, we beseech thee, ᵀthree days' journey into the wilderness, that we may sacrifice to the Lord our God.   4:31 • *listen* • 5:1, 3 • *60 mi.*

19 And I am sure that the king of Egypt ᴿwill not let you go, no, ᴿnot by a mighty hand.   5:2 • 6:1

20 And I will stretch out my hand, and ᵀsmite Egypt with ᴿall my wonders which I will do in the midst thereof: and after that he will let you go.   *strike* • Deut. 6:22

21 And ᴿI will give this people favour in the sight of the Egyptians: and it shall come to pass, that, when ye go, ye shall not go empty: [11:3; 12:36; Prov. 16:7]

22 ᴿBut every woman shall borrow of her neighbour, and of her that sojourneth in her house, jewels of silver, and jewels of gold, and raiment: and ye shall put *them* upon your sons, and upon your daughters; and ye shall spoil the Egyptians.   11:2

CHAPTER 4
"They Will Not Believe Me"

AND Moses answered and said, But, behold, they will not believe me, nor hearken unto my voice: for they will say, The LORD hath not appeared unto thee.

2 ᴿAnd the LORD said unto him, What *is* that in thine hand? And he said, A rod.   *v.* 17

3 And he said, Cast it on the ground. And he cast it on the ground, and it became a serpent; and Moses fled from before it.

4 And the LORD said unto Moses, Put forth thine hand, and take it by the tail. And he put forth his hand, and caught it, and it became a rod in his hand:

5 That they may ᴿbelieve that ᴿthe LORD God of their fathers, the God of Abraham, the God of Isaac, and the God of Jacob, hath appeared unto thee.   19:9 • 3:15

6 And the LORD said furthermore unto him, Put now thine hand into thy bosom. And he put his hand into his bosom: and when he took it out, behold, his hand *was* leprous ᴿas snow.   Num. 12:10; 2 Kin. 5:27

7 And he said, Put thine hand into thy bosom again. And he put his hand into his bosom again; and plucked it out of his bosom, and, behold, ᴿit was turned again as his *other* flesh.   Num. 12:13, 14; Deut. 32:39

8 And it shall come to pass, if they will not believe thee, neither hearken to the voice of the ᴿfirst sign, that they will believe the voice of the latter sign.   7:6–13

9 And it shall come to pass, if they will not believe also these two signs, neither hearken unto thy voice, that thou shalt take of the water of the river, and pour *it* upon the dry *land:* and ᴿthe water which thou takest out of the river shall become blood upon the dry *land.*   7:19

"I Am Slow of Speech"

10 And Moses said unto the LORD, O my Lord, ᴿI *am* not eloquent, neither heretofore, nor since thou hast spoken unto thy servant:

but I *am* slow of speech, and ᵀof a slow tongue.   3:11 • *cannot talk very well*

11 And the LORD said unto him, ᴿWho hath made man's mouth? or who maketh the dumb, or deaf, or the seeing, or the blind? have not I the LORD?   Ps. 94:9

12 Now therefore go, and I will be ᴿwith thy mouth, and teach thee what thou shalt say.   [Matt. 10:19; Mark 13:11; Luke 12:11, 12; 21:14]

13 And he said, O my Lord, ᴿsend, I pray thee, ᵀby the hand *of him whom* thou wilt send.   [Jon. 1:3] • *some other person*

14 And the anger of the LORD was kindled against Moses, and he said, *Is* not Aaron the Levite thy brother? I know that he can speak well. And also, behold, ᴿhe cometh forth to meet thee: and when he seeth thee, he will be glad in his heart.   1 Sam. 10:2, 3, 5

15 And thou shalt speak unto him, and put words in his mouth: and I will be with thy mouth, and with his mouth, and ᴿwill teach you what ye shall do.   7:1, 2

16 And he shall be thy spokesman unto the people: and he shall be, *even* he shall be to thee instead of a mouth, and ᴿthou shalt be to him ᵀinstead of God.   7:1 • *as*

17 And thou shalt take ᴿthis rod in thine hand, wherewith thou shalt do signs.   *v.* 2

Moses Returns to Egypt

18 And Moses went and returned to Je'-thro his father in law, and said unto him, Let me go, I pray thee, and return unto my brethren which *are* in Egypt, and see whether they be yet alive. And Je'-thro said to Moses, Go in peace.

19 And the LORD said unto Moses in Mid'-i-an, Go, return into Egypt: for all the men are dead which sought thy life.

20 ᴿAnd Moses took his wife and his sons, and set them upon an ass, and he returned to the land of Egypt: and Moses took ᴿthe rod of God in his hand.   18:2–5 • Num. 20:8, 9

21 And the LORD said unto Moses, When thou goest to return into Egypt, see that thou do all those ᴿwondersᵀ before Pharaoh, which I have put in thine hand: but ᴿI will harden his heart, that he shall not let the people go.   3:20 • *miracles* • 7:3, 13; 9:12, 35

22 And thou shalt say unto Pharaoh, Thus saith the LORD, ᴿIsrael *is* my son, ᴿeven my firstborn: [2 Cor. 6:18] • Jer. 31:9

23 And I say unto thee, Let my son go, that he may serve me: and if thou refuse to let him go, behold, ᴿI will slay thy son, *even* thy firstborn.   11:5; 12:29

Moses Reinstitutes Circumcision

24 And it came to pass by ᴿthe way in the inn, that the LORD ᴿmet him, and sought to ᴿkill him.   Gen. 42:27 • Num. 22:22 • Gen. 17:14

25 Then Zip-po'-rah took ^Ra sharp stone, and cut off the foreskin of her son, and cast *it* at his feet, and said, Surely a bloody husband *art* thou to me.   Josh. 5:2, 3

26 So he let him go: then she said, ^TA bloody husband *thou art*, because of the circumcision.   *you are a bridegroom of blood*

Israel Accepts the Call of Moses as Deliverer

27 And the LORD said to Aaron, Go into the wilderness ^Rto meet Moses. And he went, and met him in ^Rthe mount of God, and kissed him.   *v. 14 • 3:1*

28 And Moses told Aaron all the words of the LORD who had sent him, and all the signs which he had commanded him.

29 And Moses and Aaron ^Rwent and gathered together all the elders of the children of Israel: 3:16; 12:21

30 ^RAnd Aaron spake all the words which the LORD had spoken unto Moses, and did the signs in the sight of the people.   *v. 16*

31 And the people ^Rbelieved: and when they heard that the LORD had visited the children of Israel, and that he had looked upon their affliction, then they bowed their heads and ^Tworshipped.   *vv. 8, 9 • thanked God*

CHAPTER 5

Pharaoh Rejects Moses

AND afterward Moses and Aaron went in, and told Pharaoh, ^RThus saith the LORD God of Israel, Let my people go, that they ^Tmay hold ^Ra feast unto me in the wilderness.   3:18 • *have a service of worship* • 10:9

2 And Pharaoh said, Who *is* the LORD, that I should obey his voice to let Israel go? I know not the LORD, neither will I let Israel go.

3 And they said, The God of the Hebrews hath met with us: let us go, we pray thee, three days' journey into the desert, and sacrifice unto the LORD our God; lest he fall upon us with pestilence, or with the sword.

4 And the king of Egypt said unto them, Wherefore do ye, Moses and Aaron, ^Tlet the people from their works? ^Tget you unto your ^Rburdens.   *loose • get to your work* • 1:11; 6:5-7

5 And Pharaoh said, Behold, the people of the land now *are* ^Rmany, and ye make them rest from their burdens.   1:7, 9

6 And Pharaoh commanded the same day the ^Rtaskmasters of the people, and their officers, saying,   *vv. 10, 13, 14; 1:11; 3:7*

7 Ye shall no more give the people straw to make ^Rbrick, as heretofore: let them go and gather straw for themselves.   1:14

8 And the ^Ttale of the bricks, which they did make heretofore, ye shall lay upon them;

ye shall not diminish *ought* thereof: for they *be* idle; therefore they cry, saying, Let us go *and* sacrifice to our God.   *quota*

9 Let there more work be laid upon the men, that they may labour therein; and let them not regard ^Tvain words.   *empty promises*

10 And the ^Rtaskmasters of the people went out, and their officers, and they spake to the people, saying, Thus saith Pharaoh, I will not give you straw.   *v. 6*

11 Go ye, get you straw where ye can find it: yet ^Rnot ^Tought of your work shall be diminished.   *v. 19 • any part*

12 So the people were scattered abroad throughout all the land of Egypt to gather stubble instead of straw.

13 And the taskmasters ^Thasted *them*, saying, Fulfil your works, *your* daily tasks, as when there was straw.   *urged*

14 And the ^Rofficers of the children of Israel, which Pharaoh's taskmasters had set over them, were beaten, *and* ^Rdemanded, Wherefore have ye not fulfilled your task in making brick both yesterday and to day, as heretofore?   *v. 6 • Is. 10:14, 24*

Israel Rejects Moses

15 Then the officers of the children of Israel came and cried unto Pharaoh, saying, Wherefore dealest thou thus with thy servants?

16 There is no straw given unto thy servants, and they say to us, Make brick: and, behold, thy servants *are* beaten; but the fault *is* in thine own people.

17 But he said, ^RYe *are* idle, *ye are* idle: therefore ye say, Let us go *and* do sacrifice to the LORD.   *v. 8*

18 Go therefore now, *and* work; for there shall no straw be given you, yet shall ye deliver the ^Ttale of bricks.   *number*

19 And the officers of the children of Israel did see *that* they *were* in evil *case*, after it was said, Ye shall not ^Tminish *ought* from your bricks of your daily task.   *reduce*

20 And they met Moses and ^RAaron, who stood in the way, as they came forth from Pharaoh: 6:20

21 ^RAnd they said unto them, The LORD look upon you, and judge; because ye have made our savour to be abhorred in the eyes of Pharaoh, and in the eyes of his servants, to put a sword in their hand to slay us.   6:9

Moses Questions God's Plan

22 And Moses returned unto the ^RLORD, and said, Lord, wherefore hast thou ^Tso evil entreated this people? why *is* it *that* thou hast sent me?   Num. 11:11; Jer. 4:10 • *done harm*

23 For since I came to Pharaoh to speak in thy name, he hath done evil to this people;

neither hast thou ᴿdelivered thy people at all.   3:8

CHAPTER 6

God Reassures Moses

THEN the Lᴏʀᴅ said unto Moses, Now shalt thou see what I will do to Pharaoh: for with a strong hand shall he let them go, and with a strong hand ᴿshall he drive them out of his land.   12:31, 33, 39

2 And God spake unto Moses, and said unto him, I *am* the ᴿLᴏʀᴅᵀ: 3:14, 15 • *Jehovah*

3 And I appeared unto Abraham, unto Isaac, and unto Jacob, by *the name of* God ᴿAlmighty, but by my name ᴿJᴇ-ʜᴏ'-ᴠᴀʜ was I not known to them.   [Is. 52:6] • 3:14

4 And I have also established my covenant with them, to give them the land of Canaan, the land of their pilgrimage, wherein they were ᵀstrangers.   *foreigners*

5 And ᴿI have also heard the groaning of the children of Israel, whom the Egyptians keep in bondage; and I have remembered my covenant.   2:24; [Job 34:28]; Acts 7:34

6 Wherefore say unto the children of Israel, I *am* the Lᴏʀᴅ, and ᴿI will bring you out from under the burdens of the Egyptians, and I will rid you out of their bondage, and I will redeem you with a stretched out arm, and with great judgments: [Deut. 26:8]

7 And I will take you to ᴿme for a people, and ᴿI will be to you a God: and ye shall know that I *am* the Lᴏʀᴅ your God, which bringeth you out from under the burdens of the Egyptians.   Deut. 4:20 • 16:12

8 And I will bring you in unto the land, concerning the which I did swear to give it to Abraham, to Isaac, and to Jacob; and I will give it you for an heritage: I *am* the Lᴏʀᴅ.

Moses Reassures Israel

9 And Moses spake so unto the children of Israel: but they hearkened not unto Moses for anguish of spirit, and for cruel bondage.

God Recommissions Moses

10 And the Lᴏʀᴅ spake unto Moses, saying,

11 ᴿGo in, speak unto Pharaoh king of Egypt, that he let the children of Israel go out of his land.   4:22, 23

12 And Moses spake before the Lᴏʀᴅ, saying, Behold, the children of Israel have not hearkened unto me; how then shall Pharaoh hear me, who *am* of uncircumcised lips?

13 And the Lᴏʀᴅ spake unto Moses and unto Aaron, and gave them a ᵀcharge unto the children of Israel, and unto Pharaoh king of Egypt, to bring the children of Israel out of the land of Egypt.   *command*

14 These *be* the heads of their fathers' houses. The sons of Reuben the firstborn of Israel; Ha'-noch, and Pal'-lu, Hez'-ron, and Car'-mi: these *be* the families of Reuben.

15 And the sons of Simeon; Jem'-u-el, and Ja'-min, and O'-had, and Ja'-chin, and Zo'-har, and Sha'-ul the son of a Ca'-naan-i-tish woman: these *are* the families of Simeon.

16 And these *are* the names of ᴿthe sons of Levi according to their generations; Ger'-shon, and Ko'-hath, and Me-ra'-ri: and the years of the life of Levi *were* an hundred thirty and seven years.   Gen. 46:11

17 The sons of Ger'-shon; Lib'-ni, and Shim'-i, according to their families.

18 And ᴿthe sons of Ko'-hath; Am'-ram, and Iz'-har, and He'-bron, and Uz-zi'-el: and the years of the life of Ko'-hath *were* an hundred thirty and three years.   1 Chr. 6:2, 18

19 And the sons of Me-ra'-ri; Ma'-ha-li and Mu'-shi: these *are* the families of Levi according to their ᵀgenerations.   *families*

20 And ᴿAm'-ram took him Joch'-e-bed his father's sister to wife; and she bare him Aaron and Moses: and the years of the life of Am'-ram *were* an hundred and thirty and seven years.   2:1, 2; Num. 3:19

21 And ᴿthe sons of Iz'-har; Ko'-rah, and Ne'-pheg, and Zich'-ri.   Num. 16:1; 1 Chr. 6:37, 38

22 And ᴿthe sons of Uz-zi'-el; Mish'-a-el, and El'-za-phan, and Zith'-ri.   Lev. 10:4

23 And Aaron took him E-lish'-e-ba, daughter of Am-min'-a-dab, sister of Na-ash'-on, to wife; and she bare him Na'-dab, and A-bi'-hu, E-le-a'-zar, and Ith'-a-mar.

24 And the ᴿsons of Ko'-rah; As'-sir, and El'-ka-nah, and A-bi'-a-saph: these *are* the families of the Kor'-hites.   Num. 26:11

25 And E-le-a'-zar Aaron's son took him one of the daughters of Pu'-ti-el to wife; and ᴿshe bare him Phin'-e-has: these *are* the heads of the fathers of the Levites according to their families.   Josh. 24:33

26 These *are* that Aaron and Moses, to whom the Lᴏʀᴅ said, ᴿBring out the children of Israel from the land of Egypt according to their ᴿarmies.   *v.* 13 • Num. 33:1

27 These *are* they which spake to Pharaoh king of Egypt, ᴿto bring out the children of Israel from Egypt: these *are* that ᴿMoses and Aaron.   5:1 • 32:7; 33:1; Ps. 77:20

Moses Objects

28 And it came to pass on the day *when* the Lᴏʀᴅ spake unto Moses in the land of Egypt,

29 That the Lᴏʀᴅ spake unto Moses, saying, I *am* the Lᴏʀᴅ: speak thou unto Pharaoh king of Egypt all that I say unto thee.

30 And Moses said before the Lᴏʀᴅ, Behold, ᴿI *am* of uncircumcised lips, and how shall Pharaoh hearken unto me?   4:10

CHAPTER 7

God Reassures Moses

AND the LORD said unto Moses, See, I have made thee a god to Pharaoh: and Aaron thy brother shall be thy prophet.

2 Thou ᴿshalt speak all that I command thee: and Aaron thy brother shall speak unto Pharaoh, that he send the children of Israel out of his land.   4:15; Deut. 18:18

3 And ᴿI will harden Pharaoh's heart, and ᴿmultiply my signs and my wonders in the land of Egypt.   4:21 • 11:9

4 But ᴿPharaoh shall not hearken unto you, that I may lay my hand upon Egypt, and bring forth mine armies, *and* my people the children of Israel, out of the land of Egypt ᴿby great judgments.   3:19 • 6:6

5 And ᴿthe Egyptians shall know that I *am* the LORD, when I ᴿstretch forth mine hand upon Egypt, and bring out the children of Israel from among them.   v. 17 • 3:20

6 And Moses and Aaron ᴿdid as the LORD commanded them, so did they.   Gen. 6:22; 7:5

7 And Moses *was* ᴿfourscore years old, and Aaron fourscore and three years old, when they spake unto Pharaoh.   Acts 7:23, 30

Aaron's Rod Swallows Pharaoh's Rods

8 And the LORD spake unto Moses and unto Aaron, saying,

9 When Pharaoh shall speak unto you, saying, ᴿShew a miracle for you: then thou shalt say unto Aaron, ᴿTake thy rod, and cast *it* before Pharaoh, *and* it shall become a serpent.   Is. 7:11; John 2:18; 6:30 • 4:2, 17

10 And Moses and Aaron went in unto Pharaoh, and they did so ᴿas the LORD had commanded: and Aaron cast down his rod before Pharaoh, and before his servants, and it ᴿbecame a serpent.   v. 9 • 4:3; 7:9

11 Then Pharaoh also called the wise men and the sorcerers: now the ᴿmagicians of Egypt, they also did in like manner with their enchantments.   Gen. 41:8

12 For they cast down every man his rod, and they became serpents: but Aaron's rod swallowed up their rods.

13 And he hardened Pharaoh's heart, that ᴿhe hearkened not unto them; as the LORD had said.   v. 4; 8:15

First Plague: Blood

14 And the LORD said unto Moses, ᴿPharaoh's heart *is* hardened, he refuseth to let the people go.   8:15; 10:1, 20, 27

15 Get thee unto Pharaoh in the morning; lo, he goeth out unto the ᴿwater; and thou shalt stand by the river's brink against he come; and the rod which was turned to a serpent shalt thou take in thine hand.   2:5

16 And thou shalt say unto him, The LORD God of the Hebrews hath sent me unto thee, saying, Let my people go, that they may serve me in the wilderness: and, behold, hitherto thou wouldest not hear.

17 Thus saith the LORD, In this thou shalt know that I *am* the LORD: behold, I will smite with the rod that *is* in mine hand upon the waters which *are* in the river, and they shall be turned ᴿto blood.   Rev. 16:4, 6

18 And the ᴿfish that *is* in the river shall die, and the river shall stink; and the Egyptians shall ᴿlotheᵀ to drink of the water of the river.   v. 21 • v. 24 • *not want*

19 And the LORD spake unto Moses, Say unto Aaron, Take thy rod, and ᴿstretch out thine hand upon the waters of Egypt, upon their streams, upon their rivers, and upon their ponds, and upon all their pools of water, that they may become blood; and *that* there may be blood throughout all the land of Egypt, both in *vessels of* wood, and in *vessels of* stone.   8:5, 6, 16; 9:22; 10:12, 21

20 And Moses and Aaron did so, as the LORD commanded; and he lifted up the rod, and smote the waters that *were* in the river, in the sight of Pharaoh, and in the sight of his servants; and all the waters that *were* in the river were turned to blood.

21 And the fish that *was* in the river died; and the river stank, and the Egyptians could not drink of the water of the river; and there was blood throughout all the land of Egypt.

22 And the magicians of Egypt did so with their ᵀenchantments: and Pharaoh's heart was hardened, neither did he hearken unto them; as the LORD had said.   *magic*

23 And Pharaoh turned and went into his house, ᵀneither did he set his heart to this also.   *and he did not lay even this to heart*

24 And all the Egyptians digged round about the river for water to drink; for they could not drink of the water of the river.

25 And seven days were fulfilled, after that the LORD had smitten the river.

CHAPTER 8

Second Plague: Frogs

AND the LORD spake unto Moses, Go unto Pharaoh, and say unto him, Thus saith the LORD, Let my people go, ᴿthat they may serve me.   3:12, 18; 4:23; 5:1, 3

2 And if thou refuse to let *them* go, behold, I will smite all thy borders with frogs:

3 And the river shall bring forth frogs abundantly, which shall go up and come into thine house, and into thy bedchamber, and upon thy bed, and into the house of thy servants, and upon thy people, and into thine ovens, and into thy kneadingtroughs:

4 And the frogs shall come up both on thee, and upon thy people, and upon all thy servants.

5 And the LORD spake unto Moses, Say unto Aaron, RStretch forth thine hand with thy rod over the streams, over the rivers, and over the ponds, and cause frogs to come up upon the land of Egypt.   7:19

6 And Aaron stretched out his hand over the waters of Egypt; and the Rfrogs came up, and covered the land of Egypt.   Ps. 78:45

7 RAnd the magicians did so with their Tenchantments, and brought up frogs upon the land of Egypt.   7:11, 22 · magic

8 Then Pharaoh called for Moses and Aaron, and said, Intreat the LORD, that he may take away the frogs from me, and from my people; and I will let the people go, that they may do sacrifice unto the LORD.

9 And Moses said unto Pharaoh, Glory over me: when shall I intreat for thee, and for thy servants, and for thy people, to destroy the frogs from thee and thy houses, that they may remain in the river only?

10 And he said, RTo morrow. And he said, Be it according to thy word: that thou mayest know that Rthere is none like unto the LORD our God.   Acts 24:25; 26:28 · [Jer. 10:6, 7]

11 And the Rfrogs shall depart from thee, and from thy houses, and from thy servants, and from thy people; they shall remain in the river only.   v. 13

12 And Moses and Aaron went out from Pharaoh: and Moses Rcried unto the LORD because of the frogs which he had brought against Pharaoh.   v. 30; 9:33; 10:18; 32:11

13 And the LORD did according to the word of Moses; and the frogs died out of the houses, out of the villages, and out of the fields.

14 And they gathered them together upon heaps: and the land stank.

15 But when Pharaoh saw that there was respite, he hardened his heart, and hearkened not unto them; as the LORD had said.

Third Plague: Lice

16 And the LORD said unto Moses, Say unto Aaron, Stretch out thy rod, and smite the dust of the land, that it may become lice throughout all the land of Egypt.

17 And they did so; for Aaron stretched out his hand with his rod, and smote the dust of the earth, and Rit became lice in man, and in beast; all the dust of the land became lice throughout all the land of Egypt.   Ps. 105:31

18 And the magicians did so with their Tenchantments to bring forth lice, but they Rcould not: so there were lice upon man, and upon beast.   magic · Acts 4:16; 2 Tim. 3:8, 9

19 Then the magicians said unto Pharaoh, This is the finger of God: and Pharaoh's Rheart was hardened, and he hearkened not unto them; as the LORD had said.   v. 15

Fourth Plague: Flies

20 And the LORD said unto Moses, Rise up early in the morning, and stand before Pharaoh; lo, he cometh forth to the water; and say unto him, Thus saith the LORD, Let my people go, that they may serve me.

21 Else, if thou wilt not let my people go, behold, I will send swarms of Rflies upon thee, and upon thy servants, and upon thy people, and into thy houses: and the houses of the Egyptians shall be full of swarms of flies, and also the ground whereon they are.   Ps. 78:45

22 And RI will Tsever in that day the land of Go'-shen, in which my people dwell, that no swarms of flies shall be there; to the end thou mayest know that I am the LORD in the midst of the earth.   9:4, 6, 26 · separate

23 And I will Rput Ta division between my people and thy people: to morrow shall this sign be.   [Ps. 111:9; 130:7] · sign of redemption

24 And the LORD did so; and there came a grievous swarm of flies into the house of Pharaoh, and into his servants' houses, and into all the land of Egypt: the land was corrupted by reason of the swarm of flies.

25 RAnd Pharaoh called for Moses and for Aaron, and said, Go ye, sacrifice to your God in the land.   vv. 8, 27, 28; 10:11, 24, 26

26 And Moses said, It is not meet so to do; for we shall sacrifice Rthe Tabomination of the Egyptians to the LORD our God: lo, shall we sacrifice the abomination of the Egyptians before their eyes, and will they not Tstone us?   [Deut. 7:25, 26; 12:31] · taboo · kill us

27 We will go Rthree T days' journey into the wilderness, and sacrifice to the LORD our God, as he shall command us.   3:18 · 60 mi.

28 And Pharaoh said, I will let you go, that ye may sacrifice to the LORD your God in the wilderness; only ye shall not go very far away: Rintreat T for me.   1 Kin. 13:6 · pray

29 And Moses said, Behold, I go out from thee, and I will intreat the LORD that the swarms of flies may depart from Pharaoh, from his servants, and from his people, to morrow: but let not Pharaoh Rdeal deceitfully any more in not letting the people go to sacrifice to the LORD.   vv. 8, 15

30 And Moses went out from Pharaoh, and Rintreated the LORD.   v. 12

31 And the LORD did according to the word of Moses; and he removed the swarms of flies from Pharaoh, from his servants, and from his people; there remained not one.

32 And Pharaoh Rhardened his heart at this time also, neither would he let the people go.   vv. 8, 15; 4:21

CHAPTER 9

Fifth Plague: Disease on Beasts

THEN the LORD said unto Moses, ^RGo in unto Pharaoh, and tell him, Thus saith the LORD God of the Hebrews, Let my people go, that they may serve me.   4:23; 8:1

2 For if thou ^Rrefuse to let *them* go, and wilt hold them still,   8:2

3 Behold, the hand of the LORD is upon thy cattle which *is* in the field, upon the horses, upon the asses, upon the camels, upon the oxen, and upon the sheep: *there shall be* a very ^Tgrievous murrain.   *bad sickness*

4 And ^Rthe LORD shall ^Tsever between the cattle of Israel and the cattle of Egypt: and there shall nothing die of all *that is* the children's of Israel.   8:22 · *make a difference*

5 And the LORD appointed a set time, saying, To morrow the LORD shall do this thing in the land.

6 And the LORD did that thing on the morrow, and ^Rall the cattle of Egypt died: but of the cattle of the children of Israel died not ^Rone.   Ps. 78:50 · *v.* 4

7 And Pharaoh sent, and, behold, there was not one of the cattle of the Israelites dead. And the heart of Pharaoh was hardened, and he did not let the people go.

Sixth Plague: Boils on Man and Beast

8 And the LORD said unto Moses and unto Aaron, Take to you handfuls of ashes of the furnace, and let Moses sprinkle it toward the heaven in the sight of Pharaoh.

9 And it shall become small dust in all the land of Egypt, and shall be a boil breaking forth *with* ^Tblains upon man, and upon beast, throughout all the land of Egypt.   *blisters*

10 And they took ashes of the furnace, and stood before Pharaoh; and Moses sprinkled it up toward heaven; and it became ^Ra boil breaking forth *with* blains upon man, and upon beast.   Deut. 28:27

11 And the ^Rmagicians could not stand before Moses because of the boils; for the boil was upon the magicians, and upon all the Egyptians.   [8:18, 19; 2 Tim. 3:9]

12 And the LORD hardened the heart of Pharaoh, and he hearkened not unto them; as the LORD had spoken unto Moses.

Seventh Plague: Hail

13 And the LORD said unto Moses, ^RRise up early in the morning, and stand before Pharaoh, and say unto him, Thus saith the LORD God of the Hebrews, Let my people go, that they may serve me.   8:20

14 For I will at this time send all my plagues upon thine heart, and upon thy servants, and upon thy people; ^Rthat thou mayest know that *there is* none like me in all the earth.   8:10

15 For now I will ^Rstretch out my hand, that I may smite thee and thy people with pestilence; and thou shalt be cut off from the earth.   3:20

16 And in very deed for ^Rthis *cause* have I raised thee up, for to shew *in* thee my power; and that my name may be declared throughout all the earth.   [Rom. 9:17; 1 Pet. 2:9]

17 As yet exaltest thou thyself against my people, that thou wilt not let them go?

18 Behold, to morrow about this time I will cause it to rain a very ^Tgrievous hail, such as hath not been in Egypt since the foundation thereof even until now.   *heavy*

19 ^RSend therefore now, *and* gather thy cattle, and all that thou hast in the field; *for* upon every man and beast which shall be found in the field, and shall not be brought home, the hail shall come down upon them, and they shall die.   vv. 6, 25

20 He that feared the word of the LORD among the servants of Pharaoh made his servants and his cattle flee into the houses:

21 And he that regarded not the word of the LORD left his servants and his cattle in the field.

22 And the LORD said unto Moses, Stretch forth thine hand toward heaven, that there may be hail in all the land of Egypt, upon man, and upon beast, and upon every herb of the field, throughout the land of Egypt.

23 And Moses stretched forth his rod toward heaven: and ^Rthe LORD sent thunder and hail, and the fire ran along upon the ground; and the LORD rained hail upon the land of Egypt.   Is. 30:30; Ezek. 38:22; Rev. 8:7

24 So there was hail, and fire ^Tmingled with the hail, very grievous, such as there was none like it in all the land of Egypt since it became a nation.   *flashing continually*

25 And the hail smote throughout all the land of Egypt all that *was* in the field, both man and beast; and the hail ^Rsmote every herb of the field, and brake every tree of the field.   Ps. 105:33

26 Only in the land of Go'-shen, where the children of Israel *were*, was there no hail.

27 And Pharaoh sent, and called for Moses and Aaron, and said unto them, I have sinned this time: the LORD *is* righteous, and I and my people *are* wicked.

28 ^TIntreat the LORD (for *it is* enough) that there be no *more* ^Tmighty thunderings and hail; and I will let you go, and ye shall stay no longer.   *pray to · voices of God*

29 And Moses said unto him, As soon as I am gone out of the city, I will ^Rspread abroad my hands unto the LORD; *and* the thunder shall cease, neither shall there be any more hail; that thou mayest know how that the ^Rearth *is* the LORD's.   Is. 1:15 · Ps. 24:1

30 But as for thee and thy servants, I know that ye will not yet fear the LORD God.

31 And the flax and the barley was smitten: Rfor the barley *was* in the ear, and the flax *was* Tbolled.   Ruth 1:22; 2:23 • *in bloom*

32 But the wheat and the Trie were not smitten: for they *were* not grown up.   *rye*

33 And Moses went out of the city from Pharaoh, and spread abroad his hands unto the LORD: and the thunders and hail ceased, and the rain was not poured upon the earth.

34 And when Pharaoh saw that the rain and the hail and the thunders were ceased, he sinned yet more, and hardened his heart, he and his servants.

35 And the heart of Pharaoh was hardened, neither would he let the children of Israel go; as the LORD had spoken by Moses.

CHAPTER 10

Eighth Plague: Locusts

AND the LORD said unto Moses, Go in unto Pharaoh: for I have hardened his heart, and the heart of his servants, that I might shew these my signs before him:

2 And that Rthou mayest tell in the ears of thy son, and of thy son's son, what things I have wrought in Egypt, and my signs which I have done among them; that ye may know how that I *am* the LORD.   Joel 1:3

3 And Moses and Aaron came in unto Pharaoh, and said unto him, Thus saith the LORD God of the Hebrews, How long wilt thou refuse to RhumbleT thyself before me? Rlet my people go, that they may serve me.   [1 Kin. 21:29; Job 42:6; James 4:10] • *bow down* • 4:23

4 Else, if thou refuse to let my people go, behold, to morrow will I bring the Rlocusts into thy Tcoast: Prov. 30:27; Rev. 9:3 • *country*

5 And they shall cover the face of the earth, that one cannot be able to see the earth: and they shall eat the residue of that which is escaped, which remaineth unto you from the hail, and shall eat every tree which groweth for you out of the field:

6 RAnd they shall fill thy houses, and the houses of all thy servants, and the houses of all the Egyptians; which neither thy fathers, nor thy fathers' fathers have seen, since the day that they were upon the earth unto this day. And he turned himself, and went out from Pharaoh.   8:3, 21

7 And Pharaoh's servants said unto him, How long shall this man Tbe Ra snare unto us? let the men go, that they may serve the LORD their God: knowest thou not yet that Egypt is destroyed?   *bring us trouble* • 23:33

8 And Moses and Aaron Rwere brought again unto Pharaoh: and he said unto them, Go, serve the LORD your God: Rbut who *are* they that shall go?   *v. 25* • *v. 26*

9 And Moses said, We will go with our young and with our old, with our sons and with our daughters, with our flocks and with our herds will we go; for we *must hold* a feast unto the LORD.

10 And he said unto them, Let the LORD be so with you, as I will let you go, and your little ones: look *to it;* for evil *is* before you.

11 RNot so: go now ye *that are* men, and serve the LORD; for that ye did desire. And they were Tdriven out from Pharaoh's presence.   *vv. 24, 26; 8:25, 27, 28* • *dismissed*

12 And the LORD said unto Moses, RStretch out thine hand over the land of Egypt for the locusts, that they may come up upon the land of Egypt, and Reat every herb of the land, *even* all that the hail hath left.   7:19 • *vv. 4, 5*

13 RAnd Moses stretched forth his rod over the land of Egypt, and the LORD brought an east wind upon the land all that day, and all *that* night; *and* when it was morning, the east wind brought the locusts.   14:16; Ps. 78:26; 105:34

14 And the locusts went up over all the land of Egypt, and rested in all the coasts of Egypt: very Tgrievous *were they;* before them there were no such locusts as they, neither after them shall be such.   *bad*

15 For they covered the face of the whole earth, so that the land was darkened; and they did eat every Therb of the land, and all the fruit of the trees which the hail had left: and there remained not any green thing in the trees, or in the herbs of the field, through all the land of Egypt.   *plant*

16 Then Pharaoh called for Moses and Aaron in haste; and he said, I have sinned against the LORD your God, and against you.

17 Now therefore forgive, I pray thee, my sin only this once, and Rintreat the LORD your God, that he may take away from me this death only.   8:8, 28; 1 Kin. 13:6

18 And he Rwent out from Pharaoh, and intreated the LORD.   8:30

19 And the LORD turned a mighty strong west wind, which took away the locusts, and cast them into the Red sea; there remained not one locust in all the coasts of Egypt.

20 But the LORD Rhardened Pharaoh's heart, so that he would not let the children of Israel go.   *v. 1; 4:21; 11:10*

Ninth Plague: Darkness

21 And the LORD said unto Moses, Stretch out thine hand toward heaven, that there may be darkness over the land of Egypt, even darkness *which* may be felt.

22 And Moses stretched forth his hand toward heaven; and there was a thick darkness in all the land of Egypt three days:

23 They saw not one another, neither rose any from his place for three days: Rbut all the children of Israel had Rlight in their dwellings.   8:22, 23 • Job 36:30

24 And Pharaoh called unto Moses, and

said, Go ye, serve the LORD; only let your flocks and your herds be Tstayed: let your little ones also go with you.   *left behind*

25 And Moses said, Thou must give us also sacrifices and burnt offerings, that we may sacrifice unto the LORD our God.

26 Our cattle also shall go with us; there shall not an hoof be left behind; for Rthereof must we take to serve the LORD our God; and we know not with what we must serve the LORD, until we come thither.   *vv. 11, 24*

27 But the LORD Rhardened Pharaoh's heart, and he would not let them go.   *v. 20*

28 RAnd Pharaoh said unto him, Get thee from me, take heed to thyself, see my face no more; for in *that* day thou seest my face thou shalt die.   *v. 11*

29 And Moses said, Thou hast spoken well, I will see thy face again no more.

CHAPTER 11

Tenth Plague: Death Announced

AND the LORD said unto Moses, Yet will I bring one plague *more* upon Pharaoh, and upon Egypt; afterwards he will let you go hence: when he shall let *you* go, he shall surely thrust you out hence altogether.

2 Speak now in the ears of the people, and let Revery man Tborrow of his neighbour, and every woman of her neighbour, jewels of silver, and jewels of gold.   *3:21; 12:35 • ask*

3 And the LORD gave the people favour in the sight of the Egyptians. Moreover the man Moses *was* very Tgreat in the land of Egypt, in the sight of Pharaoh's servants, and in the sight of the people.   *prominent*

4 And Moses said, Thus saith the LORD, RAbout Rmidnight will I go out into the midst of Egypt: *12:12, 23, 29 • Matt. 25:6*

5 And all the firstborn in the land of Egypt shall die, from the firstborn of Pharaoh that sitteth upon his throne, even unto the firstborn of the maidservant that *is* behind the mill; and all the firstborn of beasts.

6 And there shall be a great cry throughout all the land of Egypt, such as there was none like it, nor shall be like it any more.

7 RBut against any of the children of Israel shall not a dog move his tongue, against man or beast: that ye may know how that the LORD doth put a difference between the Egyptians and Israel.   *8:22*

8 And all these thy servants shall Rcome down unto me, and bow down themselves unto me, saying, Get thee out, and all the people that follow thee: and after that I will go out. RAnd he went out from Pharaoh in a great anger.   *12:31–33 • 2:11, 12*

9 And the LORD said unto Moses, Pharaoh shall not hearken unto you; that my wonders may be multiplied in the land of Egypt.

10 And Moses and Aaron did all these wonders before Pharaoh: Rand the LORD Rhardened Pharaoh's heart, so that he would not let the children of Israel go out of his land.   *10:20, 27; Rom. 2:5; 9:22 • 10:1*

CHAPTER 12

Instructions for the Passover

AND the LORD spake unto Moses and Aaron in the land of Egypt, saying,

2 RThis month *shall be* unto you the beginning of months: it *shall be* the first month of the year to you.   *13:4; Deut. 16:1*

3 Speak ye unto all the congregation of Israel, saying, In the Rtenth *day* of this month they shall take to them every man a lamb, according to the house of *their* fathers, a lamb for an house: *Josh. 4:19*

4 And if the household be too little for the lamb, let him and his neighbour next unto his house take *it* according to the number of the Tsouls; every man according to his eating shall make your count for the lamb.   *persons*

5 Your lamb shall be without blemish, a male of the first year: ye shall take *it* out from the sheep, or from the goats:

6 And ye shall keep it up until the Rfourteenth day of the same month: and the whole assembly of the congregation of Israel shall kill it in the evening.   *Lev. 23:5*

7 RAnd they shall take of the blood, and Rstrike *it* on the two side posts and on the Tupper door post of the houses, wherein they shall eat it.   *v. 22 • 24:8 • lintel*

8 And they shall eat the flesh in that night, roast with fire, and unleavened bread; *and* with Rbitter *herbs* they shall eat it.   *Deut. 16:3*

9 Eat not of it raw, nor sodden at all with water, but roast *with* fire; his head with his legs, and with the purtenance thereof.

10 And ye shall let nothing of it remain until the morning; and that which remaineth of it until the morning ye shall burn with fire.

11 And thus shall ye eat it; *with* your loins girded, your shoes on your feet, and your staff in your hand; and ye shall eat it in haste: it *is* the LORD's passover.

12 For I will pass through the land of Egypt this night, and will smite all the firstborn in the land of Egypt, both man and beast; and against all the gods of Egypt I will execute judgment: I *am* the LORD.

13 And the blood shall be to you for a token upon the houses where ye *are:* and when I see the blood, I will pass over you, and the plague shall not be upon you to destroy *you,* when I smite the land of Egypt.

14 And this day shall be unto you for a

memorial; and ye shall keep it a feast to the LORD throughout your generations; ye shall keep it a feast by an ordinance for ever.

15 Seven days shall ye eat unleavened bread; even the first day ye shall put away leaven out of your houses: for whosoever eateth leavened bread from the first day until the seventh day, ^Rthat ^Tsoul shall be ^Tcut off from Israel.   Num. 9:13 • *person • put away*

16 And in the first day *there shall be* ^Ran holy convocation, and in the seventh day there shall be an holy convocation to you; no manner of work shall be done in them, save *that* which every man must eat, that only may be done of you.   Lev. 23:7, 8

17 And ye shall observe *the feast of* unleavened bread; for in this selfsame day have I brought your armies out of the land of Egypt: therefore shall ye observe this day in your generations by an ordinance for ever.

18 ^RIn the first *month,* on the fourteenth day of the month at even, ye shall eat unleavened bread, until the one and twentieth day of the month at even.   Lev. 23:5

19 Seven days shall there be no leaven found in your houses: for whosoever eateth that which is leavened, even that soul shall be cut off from the congregation of Israel, whether he be a stranger, or born in the land.

20 Ye shall eat nothing leavened; in all your habitations shall ye eat unleavened bread.

Participation in the Passover

21 Then Moses called for all the elders of Israel, and said unto them, ^RDraw out and take you a lamb according to your families, and kill the passover.   Ezra 6:20; Mark 14:12–16

22 ^RAnd ye shall take a bunch of hyssop, and dip *it* in the blood that *is* in the bason, and ^Rstrike the lintel and the two side posts with the blood that *is* in the bason; and none of you shall go out at the door of his house until the morning.   Heb. 11:28 • *v.* 7

23 For the LORD will pass through to smite the Egyptians; and when he seeth the blood upon the lintel, and on the two side posts, the LORD will pass over the door, and ^Rwill not suffer the destroyer to come in unto your houses to smite you.   Ezek. 9:6

24 And ye shall observe this thing for an ordinance to thee and to thy sons for ever.

25 And it shall come to pass, when ye be come to the land which the LORD will give you, ^Raccording as he hath promised, that ye shall keep this service.   3:8, 17

26 ^RAnd it shall come to pass, when your children shall say unto you, What mean ye by this service?   Deut. 32:7; Josh. 4:6

27 That ye shall say, ^RIt *is* the ^Tsacrifice of the LORD'S passover, who passed over the houses of the children of Israel in Egypt,

when he smote the Egyptians, and delivered our houses. And the people ^Rbowed the head and worshipped.   *v.* 11 • *religious service* • 4:31

28 And the children of Israel went away, and ^Rdid as the LORD had commanded Moses and Aaron, so did they.   Heb. 11:28

Redemption Through the Passover

29 ^RAnd it came to pass, that at midnight the LORD smote all the firstborn in the land of Egypt, from the firstborn of Pharaoh that sat on his throne unto the firstborn of the captive that *was* in the dungeon; and all the firstborn of cattle.   11:4

30 And Pharaoh rose up in the night, he, and all his servants, and all the Egyptians; and there was a ^Rgreat cry in Egypt; ^Rfor *there was* not a house where *there was* not one dead.   11:6 • 2 Sam. 14:14

31 And he ^Rcalled for Moses and Aaron by night, and said, Rise up, *and* get you forth from among my people, ^Rboth ye and the children of Israel; and go, serve the LORD, as ye have said.   8:8 • 8:25; 10:9

32 ^RAlso take your flocks and your herds, as ye have said, and be gone; and ^Tbless me also.   10:26 • *pray for*

33 ^RAnd the Egyptians were urgent upon the people, that they might send them out of the land in haste; for they said, We *be* all dead *men.*   *v.* 39; 10:7; 11:8; Ps. 105:38

34 And the people took their ^Rdough before it was leavened, their ^Tkneadingtroughs being bound up in their ^Tclothes upon their shoulders.   *v.* 39; Num. 15:20 • *dough bowls • mantles*

35 ^RAnd the children of Israel did according to the word of Moses; and they borrowed of the Egyptians jewels of silver, and jewels of gold, and raiment: 3:21, 22

36 And the LORD gave the people favour in the sight of the Egyptians, so that they lent unto them *such things as they required.* And they spoiled the Egyptians.

Freedom Because of the Passover

37 And ^Rthe children of Israel journeyed from ^RRam'-e-ses to Suc'-coth, about ^Rsix hundred thousand on foot *that were* men, beside children.   Num. 33:3, 5 • Gen. 47:11 • Gen. 12:2

38 And a mixed multitude ^Rwent up also with them; and flocks, and herds, *even* ^Rvery much cattle.   17:3; Num. 11:4; 20:19 • Deut. 3:19

39 And they baked unleavened cakes of the dough which they brought forth out of Egypt, for it was not leavened; because ^Rthey were thrust out of Egypt, and could not tarry, neither had they prepared for themselves any ^Tvictual.   *v.* 33; 6:1; 11:1 • *food*

40 Now the ^Tsojourning of the children of Israel, who dwelt in Egypt, *was* four hundred and thirty years.   *time of their stay*

41 And it came to pass at the end of the four hundred and thirty years, even the

selfsame day it came to pass, that all ᴿthe hosts of the LORD went out from the land of Egypt.   *v.* 17; 3:8, 10; 6:6; 7:4

42 It *is* aᵀ night to be much observed unto the LORD for bringing them out from the land of Egypt: this *is* that night of the LORD to be observed of all the children of Israel in their generations.   *a night of watching*

43 And the LORD said unto Moses and Aaron, This *is* the ordinance of the passover: There shall no stranger eat thereof:

44 But every man's servant that is bought for money, when thou hast ᴿcircumcised him, then shall he eat thereof.   Gen. 17:12, 13

45 ᴿA foreigner and an hired servant shall not eat thereof.   Gen. 17:12, 13; Lev. 22:10, 11

46 In one house shall it be eaten; thou shalt not carry forth ought of the flesh abroad out of the house; ᴿneither shall ye break a bone thereof.   Num. 9:12; John 19:33, 36 ☆

47 ᴿAll the congregation of Israel shall ᵀkeep it.   *v.* 6; Num. 9:13, 14 · *do*

48 And when a stranger shall sojourn with thee, and will keep the passover to the LORD, let all his males be circumcised, and then let him come near and keep it; and he shall be as one that is born in the land: for no uncircumcised person shall eat thereof.

49 ᴿOne law shall be to him that is homeborn, and unto the stranger that sojourneth among you.   Num. 9:14; [Gal. 3:28]

50 Thus did all the children of Israel; as the LORD commanded Moses and Aaron, so did they.

51 ᴿAnd it came to pass the selfsame day, *that* the LORD did ᴿbring the children of Israel out of the land of Egypt ᴿby their armies.   *v.* 41 · 20:2 · 6:26

CHAPTER 13

Sanctification as a Result of the Passover

AND the LORD spake unto Moses, saying, 2 ᴿSanctifyᵀ unto me all the firstborn, whatsoever openeth the womb among the children of Israel, *both* of man and of beast: it *is* mine.   *v.* 12; Deut. 15:19; Luke 2:23 · *Set apart*

3 And Moses said unto the people, ᴿRemember this day, in which ye came out from Egypt, out of the house of ᵀbondage; for by strength of hand the LORD brought you out from this *place*: there shall no leavened bread be eaten.   Deut. 16:3 · *slavery*

4 ᴿThis day came ye out in the month A'-bib.   23:15; 34:18; Deut. 16:1

5 And it shall be when the LORD shall bring thee into the land of the Ca'-naan-ites, and the Hit'-tites, and the Am'-or-ites, and the Hi'-vites, and the Jeb'-u-sites, which he sware unto thy fathers to give thee, a land flowing

with milk and honey, that thou shalt keep this service in this month.

6 Seven days thou shalt eat unleavened bread, and in the seventh day *shall be* ᴿa feastᵀ to the LORD.   12:15-20 · *a religious ceremony*

7 Unleavened bread shall be eaten seven days; and there shall no leavened bread be seen with thee, neither shall there be leaven seen with thee in all thy quarters.

8 And thou shalt ᴿshew thy son in that day, saying, *This is done* because of that *which* the LORD did unto me when I came forth out of Egypt.   *v.* 14; 10:2; 12:26

9 And it shall be for a sign unto thee upon thine hand, and for a memorial between thine eyes, that the LORD'S law may be in thy mouth: for with a strong hand hath the LORD brought thee out of Egypt.

10 Thou shalt therefore keep this ᵀordinance in his season from year to year.   *rule*

11 And it shall be when the ᴿLORD shall bring thee into the land of the Ca'-naan-ites, as he sware unto thee and to thy fathers, and shall ᴿgive it thee,   *v.* 5 · Gen. 15:18; 17:8; 28:15

12 That thou shalt set apart unto the LORD all that openeth the matrix, and every firstling that cometh of a beast which thou hast; the males *shall be* the LORD'S.

13 And ᴿevery firstling of an ass thou shalt redeem with a lamb; and if thou wilt not redeem it, then thou shalt break his neck: and all the firstborn of man among thy children shalt thou redeem.   34:20

14 And it shall be when thy son asketh thee in time to come, saying, What *is* this? that thou shalt say unto him, By strength of hand the LORD brought us out from Egypt, from the house of ᵀbondage: *slaves*

15 And it came to pass, when Pharaoh would hardly let us go, that the LORD slew all the firstborn in the land of Egypt, both the firstborn of man, and the firstborn of beast: therefore I sacrifice to the LORD all that openeth the matrix, being males; but all the firstborn of my children I redeem.

16 And it shall be for ᴿa tokenᵀ upon thine hand, and for frontlets between thine eyes: for by strength of hand the LORD brought us forth out of Egypt.   *v.* 9 · *sign*

God Leads Israel

17 And it came to pass, when Pharaoh had let the people go, that God led them not *through* the way of the land of the Phi-lis'-tines, although that *was* near; for God said, Lest peradventure the people repent when they see war, and they return tó Egypt:

18 But God ᴿled the people about, *through* the way of the wilderness of the Red sea: and the children of Israel went up ᵀharnessed out of the land of Egypt.   14:2 · *armed*

19 And Moses took the bones of Joseph with him: for he had straitly ᵀsworn the

children of Israel, saying, God will surely
^Tvisit you; and ye shall carry up my bones
away hence with you.   *pledged • come to help*
20 And ^Rthey took their journey from Suc'-
coth, and encamped in E'-tham, in the edge
of the wilderness.   12:37; Num. 33:6
21 And ^Rthe LORD went before them by
day in a pillar of a cloud, to lead them the
way; and by night in a pillar of fire, to give
them light; to go by day and night: [Is. 4:5]
22 ^RHe took not away the pillar of the
cloud by day, nor the pillar of fire by night,
from before the people.   Gen. 28:15; Lev. 26:12

CHAPTER 14

AND the LORD spake unto Moses, saying,
2 Speak unto the children of Israel,
that they turn and encamp before ^RPi-ha-hi'-
roth, between ^RMig'-dol and the sea, over
against Ba'-al-ze'-phon: before it shall ye
encamp by the sea.   Num. 33:7 • Jer. 44:1

Pharaoh Follows Israel

3 For Pharaoh will say of the children of
Israel, ^RThey *are* entangled in the land, the
wilderness hath shut them in.   Ps. 71:10, 11
4 And I will harden Pharaoh's heart, that
he shall follow after them; and I will be
honoured upon Pharaoh, and upon all his
host; ^Rthat the Egyptians may know that I
am the LORD. And they did so.   7:5
5 And it was told the king of Egypt that
the people fled: and ^Rthe heart of Pharaoh
and of his servants was ^Tturned against the
people, and they said, Why have we done
this, that we have let Israel go from serving
us?   Ps. 105:25 • *changed toward*
6 And he ^Tmade ready his chariot, and
took his people with him: *prepared for war*
7 And he took ^Rsix hundred chosen chariots, and all the chariots of Egypt, and captains over every one of them.   15:4
8 And the LORD hardened the heart of
Pharaoh king of Egypt, and he pursued after
the children of Israel: and the children of
Israel went out with an high hand.
9 But the ^REgyptians pursued after them,
all the horses *and* chariots of Pharaoh, and
his horsemen, and his army, and overtook
them encamping by the sea, beside Pi-ha-hi'-
roth, before Ba'-al-ze'-phon.   Josh. 24:6

Israel Rebels Against God

10 And when Pharaoh drew nigh, the children of Israel lifted up their eyes, and, behold,
the Egyptians marched after them; and they
were sore afraid: and the children of Israel
cried out unto the LORD.
11 ^RAnd they said unto Moses, Because
there were no graves in Egypt, hast thou
taken us away to die in the wilderness?

wherefore hast thou dealt thus with us, to
carry us forth out of Egypt?   Ps. 106:7, 8
12 *Is* not this the word that we did tell thee
in Egypt, saying, Let us alone, that we may
serve the Egyptians? For *it had been* better
for us to serve the Egyptians, than that we
should die in the wilderness.

God Opens the Red Sea

13 And Moses said unto the people, Fear
ye not, stand still, and see the salvation of the
LORD, which he will shew to you to day: for
the Egyptians whom ye have seen to day, ye
shall see them again no more for ever.
14 ^RThe LORD shall fight for you, and ye
shall hold your peace.   [Is. 30:15; Acts 13:17]
15 And the LORD said unto Moses, Where-
fore criest thou unto me? speak unto the
children of Israel, that they go forward:
16 But lift thou up thy rod, and stretch out
thine hand over the sea, and divide it: and the
children of Israel shall go on dry *ground*
through the midst of the sea.
17 ^RAnd I, behold, I will harden the hearts
of the Egyptians, and they shall follow them:
and I will get me honour upon Pharaoh, and
upon all his host, upon his chariots, and upon
his horsemen.   *v.* 4
18 And the Egyptians shall ^Tknow that I
am the LORD, when I have gotten me honour
upon Pharaoh, upon his ^Rchariots, and upon
his horsemen.   *recognize • v.* 25
19 And the ^Tangel of God, ^Rwhich went before the camp of Israel, removed and went
behind them; and the pillar of the cloud went
from before their face, and stood behind
them: *messenger •* 13:21; Is. 63:9
20 And it came between the camp of the
Egyptians and the camp of Israel; and it was
a cloud and darkness *to them,* but it gave
light by night *to these:* so that the one came
not near the other all the night.
21 And Moses stretched out his hand over
the sea; and the LORD caused the sea to go
back by a strong east wind all that night, and
^Rmade the sea dry *land,* and the waters were
^Rdivided.   Ps. 66:6 • 15:8; Ps. 74:13
22 And ^Rthe children of Israel went into
the midst of the sea upon the dry *ground:* and
the waters *were* a wall unto them on their
right hand, and on their left.   15:19
23 ^RAnd the Egyptians pursued, and went
in after them to the midst of the sea, *even* all
Pharaoh's horses, his chariots, and his horsemen.   *vv.* 4, 17
24 And it came to pass, that in the morning
watch ^Rthe LORD looked unto the host of the
Egyptians through the pillar of fire and of the
cloud, and ^Ttroubled the host of the Egyptians,   13:21; Ps. 77:17 • *gave trouble to*
25 ^TAnd took off their chariot wheels, that
they drave them ^Theavily: so that the Egyptians said, Let us flee from the face of Israel;

for the LORD fighteth for them against the Egyptians.   *clogging • with difficulty*

26 And the LORD said unto Moses, Stretch out thine hand over the sea, that the waters may come again upon the Egyptians, upon their chariots, and upon their horsemen.

27 And Moses stretched forth his hand over the sea, and the sea ᵀreturned to his strength when the morning appeared; and the Egyptians fled against it; and the LORD ᵀoverthrew the Egyptians in the midst of the sea.   *flowed back as deep as before • defeated*

28 And ᴿthe waters returned, and ᴿcovered the chariots, and the horsemen, *and* all the host of Pharaoh that came into the sea after them; ᴿthere remained not so much as one of them.   Hab. 3:8, 13 • Ps. 106:11 • Ps. 78:53

29 But ᴿthe children of Israel walked upon dry *land* in the midst of the sea; and the waters *were* a wall unto them on their right hand, and on their left.   *v.* 22; Ps. 78:52, 53

30 Thus the LORD saved Israel that day out of the hand of the Egyptians; and Israel saw the Egyptians dead upon the sea shore.

31 And Israel saw that great ᵀwork which the LORD did upon the Egyptians: and the people ᵀfeared the LORD, and believed the LORD, and his servant Moses.   *hand • respected*

CHAPTER 15

Israel Praises God

THEN sang Moses and the children of Israel this song unto the LORD, and spake, saying, I will sing unto the LORD, for he hath triumphed gloriously: ᴿthe horse and his rider hath he thrown into the sea.   Jer. 51:21

2 The LORD *is* my strength and song, and he is become my salvation: ᴿhe *is* my God, and I will prepare him an habitation; my father's God, and I will exalt him.   [Ps. 48:14]

3 The LORD *is* a man of war: the LORD *is* his name.

4 ᴿPharaoh's chariots and his host hath he cast into the sea: ᴿhis chosen captains also are drowned in the Red sea.   14:28 • 14:7

5 The depths have covered them: they sank into the bottom as a stone.

6 ᴿThy right hand, O LORD, is become glorious in power: ᴿthy right hand, O LORD, hath dashed in pieces the enemy.   Ps. 118:15

7 And in the greatness of thine excellency thou hast overthrown them that rose up against thee: thou sentest forth thy wrath, *which* consumed them ᴿas stubble.   Is. 5:24

8 And with the blast of thy nostrils the waters were gathered together, the floods stood upright as an heap, *and* the depths were congealed in the heart of the sea.

9 ᴿThe enemy said, I will pursue, I will overtake, I will ᴿdivide the spoil; my lust shall

be satisfied upon them; I will draw my sword, my hand shall destroy them.   Judg. 5:30 • Is. 53:12

10 Thou didst blow with thy wind, the sea covered them: they sank as lead in the mighty waters.

11 Who *is* like unto thee, O LORD, among the gods? who *is* like thee, glorious in holiness, fearful *in* praises, doing wonders?

12 Thou stretchedst out thy right hand, the earth swallowed them.

13 ᴿThou in thy mercy hast led forth the people *which* thou hast redeemed: thou hast guided *them* in thy strength unto thy holy habitation.   [Ps. 77:15, 20]

14 ᴿThe people shall hear, *and* be afraid: ᴿsorrowᵀ shall take hold on the inhabitants of Pal-es-ti'-na.   Josh. 2:9 • Ps. 48:6 • *fear*

15 Then ᴿthe dukes of E'-dom shall be amazed; the mighty men of Moab, trembling shall take hold upon them; all the inhabitants of Canaan shall melt away.   Gen. 36:40

16 ᴿFear and dread shall fall upon them; by the greatness of thine arm they shall be *as* still ᴿas a stone; till thy people pass over, O LORD, till the people pass over, ᴿwhich thou hast purchased.   Josh. 2:9 • 1 Sam. 25:37 • Jer. 31:11

17 Thou shalt bring them in, and plant them in the mountain of thine inheritance, *in* the place, O LORD, *which* thou hast made for thee to dwell in, *in* the ᴿSanctuary, O Lord, *which* thy hands have established.   Ps. 78:54

18 The LORD shall reign for ever and ever.

19 For the horse of Pharaoh went in with his chariots and with his horsemen into the sea, and the LORD brought again the waters of the sea upon them; but the children of Israel went on dry *land* in the midst of the sea.

20 And Miriam ᴿthe prophetess, the sister of Aaron, took a timbrel in her hand; and all the women went out after her ᴿwith timbrels and with dances.   Judg. 4:4 • Ps. 150:4

21 And Miriam ᴿansweredᵀ them, ᴿSing ye to the LORD, for he hath triumphed gloriously; the horse and his rider hath he thrown into the sea.   1 Sam. 18:7 • *led them in a chorus • v. 1*

Preserved from Thirst

22 So Moses brought Israel from the Red sea, and they went out into the wilderness of ᴿShur; and they went three days in the wilderness, and found no water.   Gen. 25:18

23 And when they came to ᴿMa'-rah, they could not drink of the waters of Ma'-rah, for they *were* bitter: therefore the name of it was called ᵀMa'-rah.   Num. 33:8 • *bitterness*

24 And the people ᴿmurmured against Moses, saying, What shall we drink?   16:2

25 And he cried unto the LORD; and the LORD shewed him a tree, *which* when he had cast into the waters, the waters were made sweet: there he made for them a statute and an ordinance, and there he proved them,

26 And said, ^RIf thou wilt diligently hearken to the voice of the LORD thy God, and wilt do that which is right in his sight, and wilt give ear to his commandments, and keep all his statutes, I will put none of these diseases upon thee, which I have brought upon the Egyptians: for I *am* the LORD that healeth thee. Deut. 7:12, 15

27 ^RAnd they came to E'-lim, where *were* twelve wells of water, and threescore and ten palm trees: and they encamped there by the waters. Num. 33:9

CHAPTER 16

Preserved from Hunger

AND they took their journey from E'-lim, and all the congregation of the children of Israel came unto the wilderness of ^RSin, which *is* between E'-lim and Si'-nai, on the fifteenth day of the second month after their departing out of the land of Egypt. Ezek. 30:15

2 And the whole congregation of the children of Israel ^Tmurmured against Moses and Aaron in the wilderness: complained

3 And the children of Israel said unto them, Would to God we had died by the hand of the LORD in the land of Egypt, when we sat by the flesh pots, *and* when we did eat bread to the full; for ye have brought us forth into this wilderness, to kill this whole assembly with hunger.

4 Then said the LORD unto Moses, Behold, I will rain bread from heaven for you; and the people shall go out and gather a certain rate every day, that I may ^Tprove them, whether they will walk in my law, or no. test

5 And it shall come to pass, that on the sixth day they shall prepare *that* which they bring in; and ^Rit shall be twice as much as they gather daily. v. 22; Lev. 25:21

6 And Moses and Aaron said unto all the children of Israel, ^RAt even, then ye shall know that the LORD hath brought you out from the land of Egypt: vv. 12, 13; Num. 16:28–30

7 And in the morning, then ye shall see the glory of the LORD; for that he heareth your murmurings against the LORD: and what *are* we, that ye murmur against us?

8 And Moses said, *This shall be,* when the LORD shall give you in the evening flesh to eat, and in the morning bread to the full; for that the LORD heareth your murmurings which ye ^Tmurmur against him: and what *are* we? your murmurings *are* not against us, but ^Ragainst the LORD. complain • [Rom. 13:2]

9 And Moses spake unto Aaron, Say unto all the congregation of the children of Israel, Come near before the LORD: for he hath heard your ^Tmurmurings. complaints

10 And it came to pass, as Aaron spake unto the whole congregation of the children of Israel, that they looked toward the wilderness, and, behold, the glory of the LORD ^Rappeared in the cloud. Num. 16:19; 1 Kin. 8:10, 11

11 And the LORD spake unto Moses, saying,

12 I have heard the murmurings of the children of Israel: speak unto them, saying, At even ye shall eat flesh, and in the morning ye shall be filled with bread; and ye shall know that I *am* the LORD your God.

13 And it came to pass, that at even ^Rthe quails came up, and covered the camp: and in the morning the dew lay round about the host. Num. 11:31; Ps. 78:27, 28; 105:40

14 And when the dew that lay was gone up, behold, upon the face of the wilderness *there lay* ^Ra small round thing, *as* small as the hoar frost on the ground. Num. 11:7

15 And when the children of Israel saw *it,* they said one to another, ^TIt *is* man'-na: for they wist not what it *was.* And Moses said unto them, This *is* the bread which the LORD hath given you to eat. what is it?

16 This *is* the thing which the LORD hath commanded, Gather of it every man according to his eating, ^Ran^T o'-mer for every man, *according to* the number of your persons; take ye every man for *them* which *are* in his tents. v. 36 • 2.087 qt.

17 And the children of Israel did so, and gathered, some more, some less.

18 And when they did ^Tmete *it* with ^Tan o'-mer, ^Rhe that gathered much had nothing over, and he that gathered little had no lack; they gathered every man according to his eating. measure • 2.087 qt. • 2 Cor. 8:15

19 And Moses said, ^RLet no man leave of it till the morning. 23:18

20 Notwithstanding they hearkened not unto Moses; but some of them left of it until the morning, and it bred worms, and stank: and Moses was wroth with them.

21 And they gathered it every morning, every man according to his eating: and when the sun waxed hot, it melted.

22 And it came to pass, *that* on the sixth day they gathered twice as much bread, two o'-mers for one *man:* and all the rulers of the congregation came and told Moses.

23 ^RAnd he said unto them, This *is that* which the LORD hath said, To morrow *is* the rest of the ^Rholy sabbath unto the LORD: bake *that* which ye will bake *to day,* and ^Tseethe that ye will ^Tseethe; and that which remaineth over lay up for you to be kept until the morning. 23:12 • Neh. 9:14 • boil • cook

24 And they laid it up till the morning, as Moses bade: and it did not ^Rstink, neither was there any worm therein. v. 20

25 And Moses said, Eat that to day; for to day *is* a sabbath unto the LORD: to day ye shall not find it in the field.

26 ᴿSix days ye shall gather it; but on the seventh day, *which is* the sabbath, in it there shall be none.   20:9, 10

27 And it came to pass, *that* there went out *some* of the people on the seventh day for to gather, and they found none.

28 And the Lᴏʀᴅ said unto Moses, How long ᴿrefuseᵀ ye to keep my commandments and my laws?   Ps. 78:10, 22 • *will you disobey*

29 See, for that the Lᴏʀᴅ hath given you the sabbath, therefore he giveth you on the sixth day the bread of two days; abide ye every man in his place, let no man go out of his place on the seventh day.

30 So the people rested on the seventh day.

31 And the house of Israel called the name thereof Man'-na: and ᴿit *was* like coriander seed, white; and the taste of it *was* like wafers *made* with honey.   Num. 11:7

32 And Moses said, This *is* the thing which the Lᴏʀᴅ commandeth, Fill ᵀan o'-mer of it to be kept for your generations; that they may see the bread wherewith I have fed you in the wilderness, when I brought you forth from the land of Egypt.   *2.087 qt.*

33 And Moses said unto Aaron, ᴿTake a pot, and put an o'-mer full of man'-na therein, and lay it up before the Lᴏʀᴅ, to be kept for your generations.   Heb. 9:4; Rev. 2:17

34 As the Lᴏʀᴅ commanded Moses, so Aaron laid it up ᴿbefore the Testimony, to be kept.   25:16, 21; 40:20; Num. 17:10; Deut. 10:5

35 And the children of Israel did eat man'-na forty years, until they came to a land inhabited; they did eat man'-na, until they came unto the borders of the land of Canaan.

36 Now an o'-mer *is* the tenth *part* of an e'-phah.ᵀ   *20.87 qt.*

CHAPTER 17

Preserved from Thirst Again

AND all the congregation of the children of Israel journeyed from the wilderness of Sin, after their journeys, according to the commandment of the Lᴏʀᴅ, and ᵀpitched in Reph'-i-dim: and *there was* no water for the people to drink.   *made camp*

2 ᴿWherefore the people did ᵀchide with Moses, and said, Give us water that we may drink. And Moses said unto them, Why chide ye with me? wherefore do ye ᴿtemptᵀ the Lᴏʀᴅ?   Num. 20:3 • *argue* • [Deut. 6:16] • *provoke*

3 And the people thirsted there for water; and the people murmured against Moses, and said, Wherefore *is* this *that* thou hast brought us up out of Egypt, to kill us and our children and our cattle with thirst?

4 And Moses cried unto the Lᴏʀᴅ, saying, What shall I do unto this people? they be almost ready to stone me.

5 And the Lᴏʀᴅ said unto Moses, ᴿGo on before the people, and take with thee of the elders of Israel; and thy rod, wherewith ᴿthou ᵀsmotest the river, take in thine hand, and go.   Ezek. 2:6; 3:16, 18 • Num. 20:8 • *hit*

6 ᴿBehold, I will stand before thee there upon the rock in Ho'-reb; and ᴿthou shalt smite the rock, and there shall come water out of it, that the people may drink. And Moses did so in the sight of the elders of Israel.   3:1; Num. 20:10, 11 • Deut. 8:15

7 And he called the name of the place ᵀMas'-sah, and ᵀMer'-i-bah, because of the chiding of the children of Israel, and because they tempted the Lᴏʀᴅ, saying, Is the Lᴏʀᴅ among us, or not?   *proof • contention*

Preserved from Defeat

8 ᴿThen came Am'-a-lek, and fought with Israel in Reph'-i-dim.   Gen. 36:12; Deut. 25:17

9 And Moses said unto Joshua, Choose us out men, and go out, fight with Am'-a-lek: to morrow I will stand on the top of the hill with the rod of God in mine hand.

10 So Joshua did as Moses had said to him, and fought with Am'-a-lek: and Moses, Aaron, and Hur went up to the top ᴿof the hill.   24:14; 31:2

11 And it came to pass, when Moses held up his hand, that Israel prevailed: and when he let down his hand, Am'-a-lek prevailed.

12 But Moses' hands *were* heavy; and they took a stone, and put *it* under him, and he sat thereon; and Aaron and Hur stayed up his hands, the one on the one side, and the other on the other side; and his hands were steady until the going down of the sun.

13 And Joshua discomfited Am'-a-lek and his people with the edge of the sword.

14 And the Lᴏʀᴅ said unto Moses, ᴿWrite this *for* a memorial in a book, and rehearse *it* in the ears of Joshua: for ᴿI will utterly put out the remembrance of Am'-a-lek from under heaven.   34:27 • 1 Sam. 15:3, 7; 30:1, 17

15 ᴿAnd Moses built an altar, and called the name of it Je-ho'-vah–nis'-si: Gen. 22:14

16 For he said, Because the Lᴏʀᴅ hath sworn *that* the Lᴏʀᴅ *will have* war with Am'-a-lek from generation to generation.

CHAPTER 18

Preserved from Chaos—Deut. 1:12–17

WHEN ᴿJe'-thro, the priest of Mid'-i-an, Moses' father in law, heard of all that ᴿGod had done for Moses, and for Israel his people, *and* that the Lᴏʀᴅ had brought Israel out of Egypt;   2:16 • [Ps. 106:2, 8]

2 Then Je'-thro, Moses' father in law, took Zip-po'-rah, Moses' wife, ᴿafter he had sent her back,   4:26

3 And her two sons; of which the name of the one *was* Ger'-shom; for he said, I have been an alien in a strange land:

4 And the name of the other *was* ᵀE-li-e'-zer; ᴿfor the God of my father, *said he, was* mine help, and delivered me from the sword of Pharaoh: *my God is a help* • Gen. 49:25

5 And Je'-thro, Moses' father in law, came with his sons and his wife unto Moses into the wilderness, where he encamped at ᴿthe mount of God: 3:1, 12; 4:27

6 And he said unto Moses, I thy father in law Je'-thro am come unto thee, and thy wife, and her two sons with her.

7 And Moses went out to meet his father in law, and did obeisance, and ᴿkissed him; and they asked each other of *their* welfare; and they came into the tent.   Gen. 29:13

8 And Moses told his father in law all that the Lᴏʀᴅ had done unto Pharaoh and to the Egyptians for Israel's sake, *and* all the travail that had come upon them by the way, and *how* the Lᴏʀᴅ delivered them.

9 And Je'-thro rejoiced for all the ᴿgoodness which the Lᴏʀᴅ had done to Israel, whom he had delivered out of the hand of the Egyptians.   [Is. 63:7–14]

10 And Je'-thro said, Blessed *be* the Lᴏʀᴅ, who hath delivered you out of the hand of the Egyptians, and out of the hand of Pharaoh, who hath delivered the people from under the hand of the Egyptians.

11 Now I know that the Lᴏʀᴅ *is* greater than all gods: for in the thing wherein they dealt proudly *he was* above them.

12 ᴿAnd Je'-thro, Moses' father in law, took a burnt offering and sacrifices for God: and Aaron came, and all the elders of Israel, to ᵀeat bread with Moses' father in law ᴿbefore God.   Gen. 31:54 • *dine* • Deut. 12:7

13 And it came to pass on the morrow, that Moses sat to judge the people: and the people stood by Moses from the morning unto the evening.

14 And when Moses' father in law saw all that he did to the people, he said, What *is* this thing that thou doest to the people? why sittest thou thyself alone, and all the people stand by thee from morning unto even?

15 And Moses said unto his father in law, Because ᴿthe people come unto me to ᵀenquire ᴿof God: Lev. 24:12 • *ask* • Deut. 17:8–13

16 When they have a ᵀmatter, they come unto me; and I judge between one and another, and I do make *them* know the statutes of God, and his laws.   *problem*

17 And Moses' father in law said unto him, The thing that thou doest *is* not good.

18 Thou wilt surely wear away, both thou, and this people that *is* with thee: for this thing *is* too ᵀheavy for thee; thou art not able to perform it thyself alone.   *demanding*

19 Hearken now unto my voice, I will give thee counsel, and God shall be with thee: Be thou for the people to God-ward, that thou mayest ᴿbring the causes unto God: Num. 27:5

20 And thou shalt ᴿteach them ordinances and laws, and shalt shew them the way wherein they must walk, and ᴿthe work that they must do.   Deut. 5:1 • Deut. 1:18

21 Moreover thou shalt provide out of all the people able men, such as fear God, ᴿmen of truth, ᴿhating covetousness; and place *such* over them, *to be* rulers of thousands, *and* rulers of hundreds, rulers of fifties, and rulers of tens: Ezek. 18:8 • Deut. 16:19

22 And let them ᵀjudge the people at all seasons: and it shall be, *that* every great matter they shall bring unto thee, but every small matter they shall judge: so shall it be easier for thyself, and they shall bear *the* burden with thee.   *decide the problems*

23 If thou shalt do this thing, and God command thee *so*, then thou shalt be able to endure, and all this people shall also go to ᴿtheir place in peace.   2 Sam. 19:39

24 So Moses hearkened to the voice of his father in law, and did all that he had said.

25 And ᴿMoses chose able men out of all Israel, and made them heads over the people, rulers of thousands, rulers of hundreds, rulers of fifties, and rulers of tens.   Deut. 1:15

26 And they judged the people at all seasons: the ᴿhardᵀ causes they brought unto Moses, but every small matter they judged themselves.   Job. 29:16 • *difficult*

27 And Moses let his father in law depart; and he went his way into his own land.

CHAPTER 19

Location of the Giving of the Covenant

IN the ᴿthird month, when the children of Israel were gone forth out of the land of Egypt, the same day ᴿcame they *into* the wilderness of Si'-nai.   12:6 • Num. 33:15

2 For they were departed from Reph'-i-dim, and were come *to* the desert of Si'-nai, and had pitched in the wilderness; and there Israel camped before the mount.

Purpose of the Covenant

3 And Moses went up unto God, and the Lᴏʀᴅ ᴿcalled unto him out of the mountain, saying, Thus shalt thou say to the house of Jacob, and tell the children of Israel; 3:4

4 Ye have seen what I did unto the Egyptians, and *how* I bare you on eagles' wings, and brought you unto myself.

5 Now therefore, if ye will obey my voice indeed, and keep my covenant, then ye shall be a ᵀpeculiar treasure unto me above all people: for all the earth is mine: *special*

6 And ye shall be unto me a ᴿkingdom of priests, and an ᴿholy nation. These are the words which thou shalt speak unto the children of Israel.   Rev. 1:6 • [1 Cor. 3:17; 1 Pet. 2:5, 9]

Israel Accepts the Covenant

7 ᴿAnd Moses came and called for the elders of the people, and ᵀlaid before their faces all these words which the LORD commanded him.   4:29, 30 • *presented to them*

8 And ᴿall the people answered together, and said, All that the LORD hath spoken we will do. And Moses returned the words of the people unto the LORD.   24:3; Deut. 5:27

Israelites Sanctify Themselves

9 And the LORD said unto Moses, Lo, I come unto thee in a thick cloud, that the people may hear when I speak with thee, and believe thee for ever. And Moses told the words of the people unto the LORD.

10 And the LORD said unto Moses, Go unto the people, and sanctify them to day and to morrow, and let them wash their clothes,

11 And be ready against the third day: for the third day the LORD will come down in the sight of all the people upon mount Si'-nai.

12 And thou shalt set bounds unto the people round about, saying, Take heed to yourselves, that ye go not up into the mount, or touch the border of it: whosoever toucheth the mount shall be surely put to death:

13 There shall not an hand touch it, ᴿbut he shall surely be stoned, or shot through; whether it be beast or man, it shall not live: when the trumpet soundeth long, they shall come up to the mount.   Heb. 12:20

14 And Moses went down from the mount unto the people, and sanctified the people; and they washed their clothes.

15 And he said unto the people, Be ready against the third day: ᴿcome not ᵀat your wives.   [1 Cor. 7:5] • *near to*

16 And it came to pass on the third day in the morning, that there were thunders and lightnings, and a thick cloud upon the mount, and the voice of the trumpet exceeding loud; so that all the people that was in the camp ᴿtrembled.ᵀ   Heb. 12:21 • *were fearful*

17 And Moses brought forth the people out of the camp to meet with God; and they stood at the ᵀnether part of the mount.   *foot*

18 And mount Si'-nai was altogether on a smoke, because the LORD descended upon it in fire: and the smoke thereof ascended as the smoke of a furnace, and ᴿthe whole mount quaked greatly.   Jer. 4:24; [Heb. 12:26]

19 And when the voice of the trumpet sounded long, and waxed louder and louder, ᴿMoses spake, and ᴿGod answered him by a voice.   Heb. 12:21 • Neh. 9:13; Ps. 87:7

20 And the LORD came down upon mount Si'-nai, on the top of the mount: and the LORD called Moses up to the top of the mount; and Moses went up.

21 And the LORD said unto Moses, Go down, ᵀcharge the people, lest they break through unto the LORD ᴿto gaze, and many of them perish.   *command* • 3:5; 1 Sam. 6:19

22 And let the priests also, which come near to the LORD, ᴿsanctify themselves, lest the LORD break forth upon them.   Lev. 10:3

23 And Moses said unto the LORD, The people cannot come up to mount Si'-nai: for thou chargedst us, saying, ᴿSet bounds about the mount, and sanctify it.   v. 12

24 And the LORD said unto him, Away, get thee down, and thou shalt come up, thou, and Aaron with thee: but let not the priests and the people break through to come up unto the LORD, lest he break forth upon them.

25 So Moses went down unto the people, and spake unto them.

19:5–8 The Mosaic Covenant—The covenant with Moses is the second of the theocratic covenants (pertaining to the rule of God) and is conditional. It is introduced by the conditional formula, "If ye will obey my voice . . . then ye shall be a peculiar treasure." This covenant was given to the nation Israel so that those who believed God's promise given to Abraham in the Abrahamic Covenant (Page 14—Gen. 12:1–3) would know how they should conduct themselves. The Mosaic Covenant in its entirety governs three areas of their lives: (1) the commandments governed their personal lives particularly as they related to God (Page 75—Ex. 20:1–26); (2) the judgments governed their social lives particularly as they related to one another (Page 75—Ex. 21:1—24:11); and (3) the ordinances governed their religious lives so that the people would know how to approach God on the terms that He dictates (Page 79—Ex. 24:12—31:18). The Mosaic Covenant in no way replaced or set aside the Abrahamic Covenant. Its function is clearly set forth by Paul (Page 1156—Gal. 3:17–19), who points out that the law, the Mosaic Covenant, came 430 years after the Abrahamic Covenant. The Mosaic Covenant was added alongside the Abrahamic Covenant so that the people of Israel would know how to conduct their lives until "the seed," the Christ, comes and makes the complete and perfect sacrifice, toward which the sacrifices of the Mosaic Covenant only point. The Mosaic Covenant was never given so that by keeping it people could be saved, but so that they might realize that they cannot do what God wants them to do even when God writes it down on tables of stone. The Law was given that man might realize that he is helpless and hopeless when left to himself, and realize that his only hope is to receive the righteousness of God by faith in Jesus (Page 1156—Gal. 3:22–24).
    Now turn to Page 206—Deut. 29:10–15; 30:11–20: The Palestinian Covenant.

CHAPTER 20

Commandments Relating to God

AND God spake all these words, saying,
2 I *am* the LORD thy God, which have brought thee out of the land of Egypt, ^Rout of the house of ^Tbondage.   13:3 • *slavery*
3 Thou shalt have no other gods before me.
4 Thou shalt not make unto thee any graven image, or any likeness *of any thing* that *is* in heaven above, or that *is* in the earth beneath, or that *is* in the water under the earth:
5 Thou shalt not bow down thyself to them, nor serve them: for I the LORD thy God *am* a jealous God, visiting the iniquity of the fathers upon the children unto the third and fourth *generation* of them that hate me;
6 And shewing mercy unto thousands of them that love me, and keep my commandments.
7 ^RThou shalt not take the name of the LORD thy God in vain; for the LORD will not hold him guiltless that taketh his name in vain.   [Matt. 5:33]
8 Remember the sabbath day, to keep it holy.
9 ^RSix days shalt thou labour, and do all thy work: Ezek. 20:12; Luke 13:14
10 But the seventh day *is* the sabbath of the LORD thy God: *in it* thou shalt not do any work, thou, nor thy son, nor thy daughter, thy manservant, nor thy maidservant, nor thy cattle, ^Rnor thy stranger that *is* within thy gates: Gen. 2:2, 3
11 For *in* six days the LORD made heaven and earth, the sea, and all that in them *is,* and rested the seventh day: wherefore the LORD blessed the sabbath day, and hallowed it.

Commandments Relating to Man

12 ^RHonour thy father and thy mother: that thy days may be long upon the land which the LORD thy God giveth thee.   Eph. 6:2
13 ^RThou shalt not kill.   Rom. 13:9
14 Thou shalt not commit adultery.
15 ^RThou shalt not steal.   Lev. 19:11
16 ^RThou shalt not bear false witness against thy neighbour.   23:1; Deut. 5:20
17 Thou shalt not covet thy neighbour's house, thou shalt not covet thy neighbour's wife, nor his manservant, nor his maidservant, nor his ox, nor his ass, nor any thing that *is* thy neighbour's.

The Response of Israel

18 And ^Rall the people saw the thunderings, and the lightnings, and the noise of the trumpet, and the mountain smoking: and when the people saw *it,* they ^Tremoved, and stood afar off.   Heb. 12:18 • *moved away*

19 And they said unto Moses, Speak thou with us, and we will hear: but let not God speak with us, ^Tlest we die.   *for fear*
20 And Moses said unto the people, Fear not: ^Rfor God is come to ^Tprove you, and ^Rthat his fear may be before your faces, that ye sin not.   [Deut. 13:3] • *test* • Prov. 16:6; Is. 8:13
21 And the people stood afar off, and Moses drew near unto ^Rthe thick darkness where God *was.*   19:16

Provision for Approaching God

22 And the LORD said unto Moses, Thus thou shalt say unto the children of Israel, Ye have seen that I have talked with you ^Rfrom heaven.   Deut. 4:36
23 Ye shall not make ^Rwith me gods of silver, neither shall ye make unto you gods of gold.   32:1, 2, 4
24 An altar of earth thou shalt make unto me, and shalt sacrifice thereon thy burnt offerings, and thy peace offerings, ^Rthy sheep, and thine oxen: in all places where I ^Trecord my name I will come unto thee, and I will ^Rbless thee.   Lev. 1:2 • *put* • Gen. 12:2
25 And ^Rif thou wilt make me an altar of stone, thou shalt not build it of hewn stone: for if thou lift up thy tool upon it, thou hast ^Tpolluted it.   Deut. 27:5 • *made it unclean*
26 Neither shalt thou go up by steps unto mine altar, that thy nakedness be not discovered thereon.

CHAPTER 21

Rights of Persons

NOW these *are* the ^Tjudgments which thou shalt set before them.   *rulings*
2 ^RIf thou buy an Hebrew servant, six years he shall serve: and in the seventh he shall go out free for nothing.   Jer. 34:14
3 If he came in by himself, he shall go out by himself: if he were married, then his wife shall go out with him.
4 If his master have given him a wife, and she have born him sons or daughters; the wife and her children shall be her master's, and he shall go out by himself.
5 And if the servant shall plainly say, I love my master, my wife, and my children; I ^Twill not go out free: *do not want to*
6 Then his master shall bring him unto the ^Rjudges; he shall also bring him to the door, or unto the door post; and his master shall bore his ear through with an aul; and he shall serve him for ever.   12:12
7 And if a man ^Rsell his daughter to be a maidservant, she shall not go out as the menservants do.   Neh. 5:5
8 If she please not her master, who hath betrothed her to himself, then shall he let her

be redeemed: to sell her unto a ᵀstrange nation he shall have no power, seeing he hath dealt deceitfully with her.   *foreign*

9 And if he have betrothed her unto his son, he shall deal with her after the manner of daughters.

10 If he take him another *wife;* her food, her raiment, ᴿand her duty of marriage, shall he not diminish.   [1 Cor. 7:5]

11 And if he do not these three unto her, then shall she go out free without money.

12 ᴿHe that smiteth a man, so that he die, shall be surely put to death.   [Matt. 26:52]

13 And if a man lie not in wait, but God deliver *him* into his hand; then I will appoint thee a place whither he shall flee.

14 But if a man come ᴿpresumptuouslyᵀ upon his neighbour, to slay him with ᵀguile; thou shalt take him from mine altar, that he may die.   [Heb. 10:26] • *willfully* • *trickery*

15 And he that smiteth his father, or his mother, shall be surely put to death.

16 And he that ᵀstealeth a man, and selleth him, or if he be found in his hand, he shall surely be put to death.   *kidnaps*

17 And he that curseth his father, or his mother, shall surely be put to death.

18 And if men strive together, and one smite another with a stone, or with *his* fist, and he die not, but keepeth *his* bed:

19 If he rise again, and walk abroad ᴿupon his staff, then shall he that smote *him* be ᵀquit: only he shall pay *for* the loss of his time, and shall cause *him* to be thoroughly healed.   2 Sam. 3:29 • *free from responsibility*

20 And if a man smite his servant, or his maid, with a rod, and he die under his hand; he shall be surely punished.

21 Notwithstanding, if he continue a day or two, he shall not be punished: for he *is* his money.

22 If men strive, and hurt a woman with child, so that ᵀher fruit depart *from her,* and yet no mischief follow: he shall be surely punished, according as the woman's husband will lay upon him; and he shall pay as the judges *determine.*   *she has a miscarriage*

23 And if *any* ᵀmischief follow, then thou shalt give ᴿlife for life,   *harm* • Deut. 19:21

24 ᴿEye for eye, tooth for tooth, hand for hand, foot for foot,   Deut. 19:21; Matt. 5:38

25 Burning for burning, wound for wound, stripe for stripe.

26 And if a man smite the eye of his servant, or the eye of his maid, that it perish; he shall let him go free for his eye's sake.

27 And if he smite out his manservant's tooth, or his maidservant's tooth; he shall let him go free for his tooth's sake.

28 If an ox gore a man or a woman, that they die: then the ox shall be surely stoned, and his flesh shall not be eaten; but the owner of the ox *shall be* ᵀquit.   *free*

29 But if the ox were ᵀwont to push with his horn in time past, and it hath been testified to his owner, and he hath not kept him in, but that he hath killed a man or a woman; the ox shall be stoned, and his owner also shall be put to death.   *apt*

30 If there be laid on him a sum of money, then he shall give for ᴿthe ransom of his life whatsoever is laid upon him.   v. 22

31 Whether he have gored a son, or have gored a daughter, according to this judgment shall it be done unto him.

32 If the ox shall push a manservant or a maidservant; he shall give unto their master ᵀthirty shek′-els of silver, and the ox shall be stoned. $3,840

Rights of Property

33 And if a man shall open a pit, or if a man shall dig a pit, and not cover it, and an ox or an ass fall therein;

34 The owner of the pit shall make *it* good, *and* give money unto the owner of them; and the dead *beast* shall be his.

35 And if one man's ox hurt another's, that he die; then they shall sell the live ox, and divide the money of it; and the dead *ox* also they shall divide.

36 Or if it be known that the ox hath used to push in time past, and his owner hath not kept him in; he shall surely pay ox for ox; and the dead shall be his own.

CHAPTER 22

IF a man shall steal an ox, or a sheep, and kill it, or sell it; he shall restore five oxen for an ox, and four sheep for a sheep.

2 If a thief be found ᴿbreakingᵀ up, and be smitten that he die, *there shall* no blood *be* shed for him.   Matt. 24:43 • *entering the premises*

3 If the sun be risen upon him, *there shall be* blood *shed* for him; *for* he should make full restitution; if he have nothing, then he shall be ᵀsold for his theft.   *put into slavery*

4 If the theft be certainly ᴿfound in his hand alive, whether it be ox, or ass, or sheep; he shall restore double.   21:16

5 If a man shall cause a field or vineyard to be eaten, and shall put in his beast, and shall feed in another man's field; of the best of his own field, and of the best of his own vineyard, shall he make restitution.

6 If fire break out, and catch in thorns, so that the stacks of corn, or the standing corn, or the field, be consumed *therewith;* he that kindled the fire shall surely make restitution.

7 ᴿIf a man shall deliver unto his neighbour money or stuff to keep, and it be stolen

out of the man's house; ^Rif the thief be found, let him pay double.   Lev. 6:1-7 • v. 4

8 If the thief be not found, then the master of the house shall be brought unto the judges, *to see* whether ^The have put his hand unto his neighbour's goods.   *he has taken*

9 For all manner of trespass, *whether it be* for ox, for ass, for sheep, for raiment, *or* for any manner of lost thing, which *another* challengeth to be his, the ^Rcause of both parties shall come before the ^Tjudges; *and* whom the judges shall condemn, he shall pay double unto his neighbour.   Deut. 25:1 • *God*

10 If a man deliver unto his neighbour an ass, or an ox, or a sheep, or any beast, to keep; and it die, or be hurt, or driven away, no man seeing *it:*

11 *Then* shall an ^Roath of the Lord be between them both, that he hath not put his hand unto his neighbour's goods; and the owner of it shall accept *thereof*, and he shall not make *it* good.   Heb. 6:16

12 And if it be stolen from him, he shall make restitution unto the owner thereof.

13 If it be torn in pieces, *then* let him bring it *for* witness, *and* he shall not make good that which was torn.

14 And if a man borrow ^Tought of his neighbour, and it be hurt, or die, the owner thereof *being* not with it, he shall surely make *it* good.   *anything*

15 *But* if the owner thereof be with it, he shall not make *it* good: if it *be* an hired *thing*, it came for his hire.

Proper Conduct

16 And ^Rif a man entice a maid that is not betrothed, and lie with her, he shall surely endow her to be his wife.   Deut. 22:28

17 If her father utterly refuse to give her unto him, he shall pay money according to the ^Rdowry of virgins.   Gen. 34:12

18 Thou shalt not suffer a witch to live.

19 ^RWhosoever lieth with a beast shall surely be put to death.   Lev. 18:23; 20:15

20 ^RHe that sacrificeth unto *any* god, save unto the Lord only, he shall be utterly destroyed.   Lev. 17:7; Deut. 17:2, 3, 5

21 ^RThou shalt neither vex a ^Tstranger, nor oppress him: for ye were strangers in the land of Egypt.   Deut. 10:19 • *foreigner*

22 ^RYe shall not afflict any widow, or fatherless child.   Prov. 23:10, 11; Jer. 7:6; [James 1:27]

23 If thou afflict them in any wise, and they ^Rcry at all unto me, I will surely ^Rhear their cry;   [Deut. 15:9; Luke 18:7] • Ps. 18:6

24 And my wrath shall wax hot, and I will kill you with the sword; and your wives shall be widows, and your children fatherless.

25 If thou lend money to *any of* my people *that is* poor by thee, thou shalt not be to him as an ^Tusurer, neither shalt thou lay upon him ^Tusury.   *money lender • interest*

26 If thou at all take thy neighbour's raiment to pledge, thou shalt deliver it unto him by that the sun goeth down:

27 For that *is* his covering only, it *is* his raiment for his skin: wherein shall he sleep? and it shall come to pass, when he crieth unto me, that I will hear; for I *am* gracious.

28 ^RThou shalt not revile the ^Tgods, nor curse the ruler of thy people.   Acts 23:5 • *God*

29 Thou shalt not delay *to offer* the first of thy ripe fruits, and of thy liquors: the firstborn of thy sons shalt thou give unto me.

30 ^RLikewise shalt thou do with thine oxen, *and* with thy sheep: seven days it shall be with his ^Tdam; on the eighth day thou shalt give it me.   Deut. 15:19 • *mother*

31 And ye shall be holy men unto me: neither shall ye eat *any* flesh *that is* torn of beasts in the field; ye shall cast it to the dogs.

CHAPTER 23

Proper Justice

THOU shalt not raise a false report: put not thine hand with the wicked to be an ^Runrighteous witness.   Ps. 35:11; Acts 6:11

2 Thou shalt not follow a multitude to *do* evil; neither shalt thou speak in a cause to decline after many to wrest *judgment:*

3 Neither shalt thou ^Tcountenance a poor man in his ^Tcause.   *favour • lawsuit*

4 ^RIf thou meet thine enemy's ox or his ass going astray, thou shalt surely bring it back to him again.   Deut. 22:1-4; [Rom. 12:20]

5 ^RIf thou see the ass of him that hateth thee lying under his burden, ^Tand wouldest forbear to help him, thou shalt surely help with him.   Deut. 22:4 • *would you cease to help him*

6 ^RThou shalt not ^Twrest the judgment of thy poor in his cause.   Eccl. 5:8 • *thwart*

7 ^RKeep thee far from a false matter; and the innocent and righteous slay thou not: for I will not justify the wicked.   Eph. 4:25

8 And ^Rthou shalt take no ^Tgift: for the gift blindeth the wise, and perverteth the words of the righteous.   Prov. 15:27 • *bribe*

9 Also thou shalt not oppress a stranger: for ye know the heart of a stranger, seeing ye were strangers in the land of Egypt.

Sabbatical Year

10 And six years thou shalt sow thy land, and shalt gather in the fruits thereof:

11 But the seventh *year* thou shalt let it rest and lie still; that the poor of thy people may eat: and what they leave the beasts of the field shall eat. In like manner thou shalt deal with thy vineyard, *and* with thy ^Tolive-yard.   *olive trees*

12 ℞Six days thou shalt do thy work, and on the seventh day thou shalt rest: that thine ox and thine ass may rest, and the son of thy handmaid, and the stranger, may be refreshed.   20:8-11; Luke 13:14

13 And in all *things* that I have said unto you ᵀbe circumspect: and make no mention of the name of other gods, neither let it be heard out of thy mouth.   *take ye heed*

Three National Feasts

14 ℞Three times thou shalt keep a feast unto me in the year.   34:23; Deut. 16:16

15 Thou shalt keep the feast of unleavened bread: (thou shalt eat unleavened bread seven days, as I commanded thee, in the time appointed of the month A′-bib; for in it thou camest out from Egypt: and none shall appear before me empty:)

16 And the feast of harvest, the firstfruits of thy labours, which thou hast sown in the field: and the feast of ingathering, *which is* in the end of the year, when thou hast gathered in thy labours out of the field.

17 Three times in the year all thy males shall appear before the Lord GOD.

18 ℞Thou shalt not offer the blood of ᵀmy sacrifice with leavened bread; ℞neither shall the fat of my ᵀsacrifice remain until the morning.   Deut. 16:4 · *offering* · Deut. 14:21 · *feast*

19 ℞The first of the firstfruits of thy land thou shalt bring into the house of the LORD thy God. ℞Thou shalt not ᵀseethe a kid in his mother's milk.   Deut. 26:10 · Deut. 14:21 · *boil*

Conquest Regulations

20 Behold, I ℞send an Angel before thee, to keep thee in the way, and to bring thee into the place which I have prepared.   Josh. 5:14

21 Beware of him, and obey his voice, provoke him not; for he will not pardon your transgressions: for my name *is* in him.

22 But if thou shalt indeed obey his voice, and do all that I speak; then ℞I will be an enemy unto thine enemies, and an adversary unto thine adversaries.   Jer. 30:20

23 For mine Angel shall go before thee, and bring thee in unto the Am′-or-ites, and the Hit′-tites, and the Per′-iz-zites, and the Ca′-naan-ites, the Hi′-vites, and the Jeb′-u-sites: and I will ᵀcut them off.   *destroy them*

24 Thou shalt not bow down to their gods, nor serve them, nor do after their works: but thou shalt utterly overthrow them, and quite break down their images.

25 And ye shall ℞serve the LORD your God, and ℞he shall bless thy bread, and thy water; and I will take sickness away from the midst of thee.   [Matt. 4:10] · Deut. 28:5

26 ℞There shall nothing cast their young, nor be barren, in thy land: the number of thy days I will fulfil.   Deut. 7:14; 28:4

27 I will send ℞my fear before thee, and will destroy all the people to whom thou shalt come, and I will make all thine enemies turn their backs unto thee.   Deut. 2:25

28 And ℞I will send hornets before thee, which shall ℞drive out the Hi′-vite, the Ca′-naan-ite, and the Hit′-tite, from before thee.   Josh. 24:12 · 33:2; 34:11

29 ℞I will not drive them out from before thee in one year; lest the land become desolate, and the beast of the field multiply against thee.   Deut. 7:22

30 By little and little I will drive them out from before thee, until thou be increased, and inherit the land.

31 And ℞I will set thy ᵀbounds from the Red sea even unto the sea of the Phi-lis′-tines, and from the desert unto the river: for I will deliver the inhabitants of the land into your hand; and thou shalt drive them out before thee.   1 Kin. 4:21, 24 · *boundaries*

32 ℞Thou shalt make no ᵀcovenant with them, nor with their gods.   Deut. 7:2 · *agreement*

33 They shall not dwell in thy land, lest they make thee sin against me: for if thou serve their gods, ℞it will surely ᵀbe a snare unto thee.   1 Sam. 18:21; Ps. 106:36 · *lead thee astray*

CHAPTER 24

The Covenant Is Ratified Through Blood

AND he said unto Moses, ᵀCome up unto the LORD, thou, and Aaron, Na′-dab, and A-bi′-hu, and seventy of the elders of Israel; and worship ye afar off.   *come to worship*

2 And Moses alone shall come near the LORD: but they shall not come nigh; neither shall the people go up with him.

3 And Moses came and told the people all the words of the LORD, and all the ᵀjudgments: and all the people answered with one voice, and said, ℞All the words which the LORD hath said will we do.   *rulings · v. 7*

4 And Moses ℞wrote all the words of the LORD, and rose up early in the morning, and builded an altar under the hill, and twelve ℞pillars, according to the twelve tribes of Israel.   17:14; Deut. 31:9 · Gen. 28:18

5 And he sent young men of the children of Israel, which offered burnt offerings, ℞and sacrificed peace offerings of oxen unto the LORD.   18:12

6 And Moses ℞took half of the blood, and put *it* in basons; and half of the blood he sprinkled on the altar.   Heb. 9:18

7 And he ℞took the book of the covenant, and read in the audience of the people: and they said, All that the LORD hath said will we do, and be obedient.   Heb. 9:19

8 And Moses took the blood, and sprinkled *it* on the people, and said, Behold the blood of

the covenant, which the LORD hath made with you concerning all these words.

The God of the Covenant Is Revealed

9 Then went up Moses, and Aaron, Na'-dab, and A-bi'-hu, and seventy of the elders of Israel:

10 And they ^Rsaw the God of Israel: and *there was* under his feet as it were a paved work of a sapphire stone, and as it were the body of heaven in *his* clearness.   [John 1:18]

11 And upon the nobles of the children of Israel he laid not his hand: also they saw God, and did ^Reat and drink.   1 Cor. 10:18

The Revelation Is Given on Mount Sinai

12 And the LORD said unto Moses, Come up to me into the mount, and be there: and I will give thee ^Rtables of stone, and a law, and commandments which I have written; that thou mayest teach them.   [32:15]

13 And Moses rose up, and ^Rhis^T minister Joshua: and Moses went up into ^Rthe mount of God.   32:17 • *attendant* • 32:1

14 And he said unto the elders, Tarry ye here for us, until we come again unto you: and, behold, ^RAaron and Hur *are* with you: if any man have any matters to do, let him come unto them.   17:10, 12

15 And Moses went up into the mount, and ^Ra cloud covered the mount.   Matt. 17:5

16 And ^Rthe glory of the LORD abode upon mount Si'-nai, and the cloud covered it six days: and the seventh day he called unto Moses out of the midst of the cloud.   16:10

17 And the sight of the glory of the LORD *was* like devouring fire on the top of the mount in the eyes of the children of Israel.

18 And Moses went into the midst of the cloud, and ^Tgat him up into the mount: and ^RMoses was in the mount forty days and forty nights.   *got* • 34:28; Deut. 9:9

CHAPTER 25

The Offering for the Tabernacle

AND the LORD spake unto Moses, saying, 2 Speak unto the children of Israel, that they bring me an ^Toffering: of every man that giveth it ^Rwillingly with his heart ye shall take my offering.   *heave offering* • 2 Cor. 8:11

3 And this *is* the offering which ye shall take of them; gold, and silver, and brass,

4 And blue, and purple, and scarlet, and fine ^Tlinen, and goats' hair,   *cotton*

5 And rams' skins dyed red, and badgers' skins, and ^Tshit'-tim wood,   *acacia*

6 ^ROil for the light, spices for anointing oil, and for sweet incense,   27:20

7 Onyx stones, and stones to be set in the ^Re'-phod, and in the breastplate.   28:4, 6

The Purpose of the Tabernacle

8 And let them make me a ^Tsanctuary; that I may dwell among them.   *dwelling*

9 ^RAccording to all that I shew thee, *after* the pattern of the tabernacle, and the pattern of all the ^Tinstruments thereof, even so shall ye make *it*.   Acts 7:44; Heb. 8:2 • *furniture*

The Ark of the Covenant

10 ^RAnd they shall make an ark *of* shit'-tim wood: ^Ttwo cubits and a half *shall be* the length thereof, and a ^Tcubit and a half the breadth thereof, and a cubit and a half the height thereof.   37:1 • *45 in.* • *27 in.*

11 And thou shalt overlay it with pure gold, within and without shalt thou overlay it, ^Rand shalt make upon it a crown of ^Rgold round about.   Heb. 9:4 • 37:2

12 And thou shalt cast four rings of gold for it, and put *them* in the four ^Tcorners thereof; and two rings *shall be* in the one side of it, and two rings in the other side of it. *feet*

13 And thou shalt make staves *of* shit'-tim wood, and overlay them with gold.

14 And thou shalt put the staves into the rings by the sides of the ark, that the ark may be borne with them.

15 ^RThe staves shall be in the rings of the ark: they shall not be taken from it.   1 Kin. 8:8

16 And thou shalt put into the ark ^Rthe testimony which I shall give thee.   16:34

17 And thou shalt make a mercy seat *of* pure gold: two ^Tcubits and a half *shall be* the length thereof, and a ^Tcubit and a half the breadth thereof.   *45 in.* • *27 in.*

18 And thou shalt make two cher'-u-bims *of* gold, *of* beaten work shalt thou make them, in the two ends of the mercy seat.

19 And make one cherub on the one end, and the other cherub on the other end: *even* of the mercy seat shall ye make the cher'-u-bims on the two ends thereof.

20 And the cher'-u-bims shall stretch forth *their* wings on high, covering the mercy seat with their wings, and their faces *shall look* one to another; toward the mercy seat shall the faces of the cher'-u-bims be.

21 And thou shalt put the mercy seat above upon the ark; and in the ark thou shalt put the testimony that I shall give thee.

22 And there I will meet with thee, and I will commune with thee from above the mercy seat, from between the two cher'-u-bims which *are* upon the ark of the testimony, of all *things* which I will give thee in commandment unto the children of Israel.

The Table of Shewbread

23 Thou shalt also make a table *of* shit'-tim wood: two cubits *shall be* the length thereof,

and a cubit the breadth thereof, and a cubit and a half the height thereof.

24 And thou shalt overlay it with pure gold, and make thereto a ᵀcrown of gold round about.   *border*

25 And thou shalt make unto it a border of an ᵀhand breadth round about, and thou shalt make a golden crown to the border thereof round about.   *3 in.*

26 And thou shalt make for it four rings of gold, and put the rings in the four corners that *are* on the four feet thereof.

27 Over against the border shall the rings be for places of the staves to bear the table.

28 And thou shalt make the staves of shit'-tim wood, and overlay them with gold, that the table may be borne with them.

29 And thou shalt make the dishes thereof, and spoons thereof, and covers thereof, and bowls thereof, ᵀto cover withal: *of* pure gold shalt thou make them.   *to pour out*

30 And thou shalt set upon the table ᴿshewbread before me alway.   Lev. 24:5, 6

The Golden Candlestick

31 ᴿAnd thou shalt make a candlestick *of* pure gold: *of* beaten work shall the candlestick be made: his shaft, and his branches, his bowls, his knops, and his flowers, shall be of the same.   Zech. 4:2; Heb. 9:2; Rev. 1:12

32 And six branches shall come out of the sides of it; three branches of the candlestick out of the one side, and three branches of the candlestick out of the other side:

33 ᴿThree bowls made like unto almonds, *with* a ᵀknop and a flower in one branch; and three bowls made like almonds in the other branch, *with* a knop and a flower: so in the six branches that come out of the candlestick.   *37:19 · ornamental knob*

34 And ᴿin the candlestick *shall be* four bowls made like unto almonds, *with* their knops and their flowers.   *37:20-22*

35 And *there shall be* a knop under two branches of the same, and a knop under two branches of the same, and a knop under two branches of the same, according to the six branches that proceed out of the candlestick.

36 Their knops and their branches shall be of the same: all it *shall be* one beaten work *of* pure gold.

37 And thou shalt make the seven lamps thereof: and ᴿthey shall light the lamps thereof, that they may give light over against it.   Num. 8:2

38 And the ᵀtongs thereof, and the snuffdishes thereof, *shall be of* pure gold. *snuffers*

39 *Of* a ᵀtalent of pure gold shall he make it, with all these vessels.   *$5,760,000*

40 And ᴿlook that thou make *them* after their pattern, ᵀwhich was shewed thee in the mount.   [Heb. 8:5] · *which was shown to you*

CHAPTER 26

The Curtains of Linen

MOREOVER thou shalt make the tabernacle *with* ten curtains *of* fine twined linen, and blue, and purple, and scarlet: *with* cher'-u-bims of ᵀcunning work shalt thou make them.   *clever artistic work*

2 The length of one curtain *shall be* ᵀeight and twenty cubits, and the breadth of one curtain ᵀfour cubits: and every one of the curtains shall have one measure.   *42 ft. · 6 ft.*

3 The five curtains shall be coupled together one to another; and *other* five curtains *shall be* coupled one to another.

4 And thou shalt make loops of blue upon the edge of the one curtain from the selvedge in the coupling; and likewise shalt thou make in the uttermost edge of *another* curtain, in the coupling of the second.

5 Fifty loops shalt thou make in the one curtain, and fifty loops shalt thou make in the edge of the curtain that *is* in the coupling of the second; that the loops may take hold one of another.

6 And thou shalt make fifty taches of gold, and couple the curtains together with the taches: and it shall be one tabernacle.

7 And ᴿthou shalt make curtains *of* goats' hair to be a covering upon the tabernacle: eleven curtains shalt thou make.   *36:14*

8 The length of one curtain *shall be* ᵀthirty cubits, and the breadth of one curtain ᵀfour cubits: and the eleven curtains *shall be all* of one measure.   *45 ft. · 6 ft.*

9 And thou shalt couple five curtains by themselves, and six curtains by themselves, and shalt double the sixth curtain in the forefront of the tabernacle.

10 And thou shalt make fifty loops on the edge of the one curtain *that is* outmost in the coupling, and fifty loops in the edge of the curtain which coupleth the second.

11 And thou shalt make fifty taches of brass, and put the taches into the loops, and couple the tent together, that it may be one.

12 And the remnant that remaineth of the curtains of the tent, the half curtain that remaineth, shall hang over the backside of the tabernacle.

13 And a ᵀcubit on the one side, and a cubit on the other side of that which remaineth in the length of the curtains of the tent, it shall hang over the sides of the tabernacle on this side and on that side, to cover it.   *18 in.*

14 And ᴿthou shalt make a covering for the tent *of* rams' skins dyed red, and a covering above *of* ᵀbadgers' skins.   *36:19 · seal*

The Boards and Sockets

15 And thou shalt make boards for the tabernacle *of* shit'-tim wood standing up.

16 ᵀTen cubits *shall be* the length of a board, and a ᵀcubit and a half *shall be* the breadth of one board.   *15 ft. • 27 in.*

17 Two ᵀtenons *shall there be* in one board, set in order one against another: thus shalt thou make for all the boards of the tabernacle.   *clamps*

18 And thou shalt make the boards for the tabernacle, twenty boards on the south side southward.

19 And thou shalt make forty sockets of silver under the twenty boards; two sockets under one board for his two tenons, and two sockets under another board for his two tenons.

20 And for the second side of the tabernacle on the north side *there shall be* twenty boards:

21 And their forty sockets *of* silver; two sockets under one board, and two sockets under another board.

22 And for the sides of the tabernacle westward thou shalt make six boards.

23 And two boards shalt thou make for the corners of the tabernacle in the two sides.

24 And they shall be ᵀcoupled together beneath, and they shall be coupled together above the head of it unto one ring: thus shall it be for them both; they shall be for the two corners.   *twined*

25 And they shall be eight boards, and their sockets *of* silver, sixteen sockets; two sockets under one board, and two sockets under another board.

26 And thou shalt make bars of ᵀshit'-tim wood; five for the boards of the one side of the tabernacle,   *acacia*

27 And five bars for the boards of the other side of the tabernacle, and five bars for the boards of the side of the tabernacle, for the two sides westward.

28 And the middle bar in the midst of the boards shall reach from end to end.

29 And thou shalt overlay the boards with gold, and make their rings *of* gold for ᵀplaces for the bars: and thou shalt overlay the bars with gold.   *holders*

30 And thou shalt ᵀrear up the tabernacle ᴿaccording to the fashion thereof which was shewed thee in the mount.   *build • [Heb. 8:5]*

The Inner Vail

31 And ᴿthou shalt make a vail of blue, and purple, and scarlet, and fine twined linen of cunning work: with cher'-u-bims shall it be made: *Lev. 16:2; 2 Chr. 3:14; Matt. 27:51*

32 And thou shalt hang it upon four pillars of ᵀshit'-tim *wood* overlaid with gold: their hooks *shall be of* gold, upon the four sockets of silver.   *acacia*

33 And thou shalt hang up the vail under the taches, that thou mayest bring in thither within the vail the ark of the testimony: and

the vail shall divide unto you between the holy *place* and the most holy.

34 And ᴿthou shalt put the mercy seat upon the ark of the testimony in the most holy *place*.   *25:21; 40:20; Heb. 9:5*

35 And thou shalt set the table ᵀwithout the vail, and ᴿthe candlestick over against the table on the side of the tabernacle toward the south: and thou shalt put the table on the north side.   *outside • 40:24*

The Outer Vail

36 And ᴿthou shalt make an ᵀhanging for the door of the tent, *of* blue, and purple, and scarlet, and fine twined linen, wrought with needlework.   *36:37 • curtain*

37 And thou shalt make for the hanging ᴿfive pillars *of* shit'-tim *wood*, and overlay them with gold, *and* their hooks *shall be of* gold: and thou shalt cast five sockets of brass for them.   *36:38*

CHAPTER 27

The Brass Altar

AND thou shalt make an altar *of* shit'-tim wood, five cubits long, and five cubits broad; the altar shall be foursquare: and the height thereof *shall be* three cubits.

2 And thou shalt make the horns of it upon the four corners thereof: his horns shall be of the same: and ᴿthou shalt overlay it with brass.   *Num. 16:38*

3 And thou shalt make his pans to receive his ashes, and his shovels, and his basons, and his fleshhooks, and his firepans: all the vessels thereof thou shalt make *of* brass.

4 And thou shalt make for it a grate of network *of* brass; and upon the net shalt thou make four brasen rings in the four corners thereof.

5 And thou shalt put it under the ᵀcompass of the altar beneath, that the net may be even to the midst of the altar.   *ledge*

6 And thou shalt make ᵀstaves for the altar, ᵀstaves *of* shit'-tim wood, and overlay them with brass.   *poles • poles of acacia*

7 And the staves shall be put into the rings, and the staves shall be upon the two sides of the altar, to bear it.

8 Hollow with boards shalt thou make it: ᴿas it was shewed thee in the mount, so shall they make *it*.   *25:40; 26:30*

The Court of the Tabernacle

9 And ᴿthou shalt make the court of the tabernacle: for the south side southward *there shall be* hangings for the court of fine twined linen of an ᵀhundred cubits long for one side: *38:9-20 • 150 ft.*

10 And the twenty pillars thereof and their

twenty sockets *shall be of* brass; the hooks of the pillars and their fillets *shall be of* silver.

11 And likewise for the north side in length *there shall be* hangings of ^Tan hundred *cubits* long, and his twenty pillars and their twenty sockets *of* brass; the hooks of the pillars and their ^Tfillets *of* silver.   *150 ft. · bands*

12 And *for* the breadth of the court on the west side *shall be* hangings of ^Tfifty cubits: their pillars ten, and their sockets ten.   *75 ft.*

13 And the breadth of the court on the east side eastward *shall be* ^Tfifty cubits.   *75 ft.*

14 The hangings of one side *of the gate shall be* ^Tfifteen cubits: their pillars three, and their sockets three.   *22.5 ft.*

15 And on the other side *shall be* hangings ^Tfifteen *cubits:* their pillars three, and their sockets three.   *22.5 ft.*

16 And for the gate of the court *shall be* an hanging of ^Ttwenty cubits, *of* blue, and purple, and scarlet, and fine twined linen, wrought with needlework: *and* their pillars *shall be* four, and their sockets four.   *30 ft.*

17 All the pillars round about the court *shall be* filleted with silver; their hooks *shall be of* silver, and their sockets *of* brass.

18 The length of the court *shall be* an hundred cubits, and the breadth fifty every where, and the height five cubits *of* fine twined linen, and their sockets *of* brass.

19 All the vessels of the tabernacle in all the service thereof, and all the pins thereof, and all the pins of the court, *shall be of* brass.

The Oil for the Lamp

20 And ^Rthou shalt command the children of Israel, that they bring thee pure oil olive beaten for the light, to cause the lamp to burn always.   *35:8, 28; Lev. 24:2–4*

21 In the tabernacle of the congregation without the vail, which *is* before the testimony, Aaron and his sons shall order it from evening to morning before the LORD: *it shall be* a statute for ever unto their generations on the behalf of the children of Israel.

CHAPTER 28

The Command to Make the Priests' Garments

AND take thou unto thee ^RAaron thy brother, and his sons with him, from among the children of Israel, that he may minister unto me in the priest's office, *even* Aaron, Na′-dab and A-bi′-hu, E-le-a′-zar and Ith′-a-mar, Aaron's sons.   *Num. 18:7; Ps. 99:6*

2 And ^Rthou shalt make ^Tholy garments for Aaron thy brother for glory and for beauty.   *29:5, 29; 31:10 · specially for this use*

3 And thou shalt speak unto all *that are* wise hearted, whom I have filled with the spirit of wisdom, that they may make Aaron's

garments to consecrate him, that he may minister unto me in the priest's office.

4 And these *are* the garments which they shall make; a breastplate, and an e′-phod, and a robe, and a broidered coat, a mitre, and a girdle: and they shall make holy garments for Aaron thy brother, and his sons, that he may minister unto me in the priest's office.

5 ^RAnd they shall take gold, and blue, and purple, and scarlet, and fine linen.   *25:3*

The Ephod

6 And they shall make the e′-phod *of* gold, *of* blue, and *of* purple, *of* scarlet, and fine twined linen, with ^Tcunning work.   *artistic*

7 It shall have the two shoulderpieces thereof joined at the two edges thereof; and so it shall be ^Tjoined together.   *united*

8 And the curious girdle of the e′-phod, which *is* upon it, shall be of the same, according to the work thereof; *even of* gold, *of* blue, and purple, and scarlet, and fine twined linen.

9 And thou shalt take two onyx stones, and ^Tgrave on them the names of the children of Israel: *cut*

10 Six of their names on one stone, and *the* other six names of the rest on the other stone, according to their ^Rbirth.   *Gen. 29:31*

11 With the work of an engraver in stone, *like* the engravings of a signet, shalt thou engrave the two stones with the names of the children of Israel: thou shalt make them to be set in ^Touches of gold.   *settings*

12 And thou shalt put the two stones upon the shoulders of the e′-phod *for* stones of memorial unto the children of Israel: and ^RAaron shall bear their names before the LORD upon his two shoulders ^Rfor a ^Tmemorial.   *39:7 · Zech. 6:14 · remembrance*

13 And thou shalt make ouches *of* gold;

14 And two chains *of* pure gold at the ends; *of* ^Twreathen work shalt thou make them, and fasten the wreathen chains to the ^Touches.   *braided · settings*

The Breastplate

15 And thou shalt make the breastplate of judgment with cunning work; after the work of the e′-phod thou shalt make it; *of* gold, *of* blue, and *of* purple, and *of* scarlet, and *of* fine twined linen, shalt thou make it.

16 Foursquare it shall be *being* doubled; a ^Tspan *shall be* the length thereof, and a span *shall be* the breadth thereof.   *9 in.*

17 And thou shalt set in it settings of stones, *even* four rows of stones: *the first* row *shall be* a sardius, a topaz, and a ^Tcarbuncle: *this shall be* the first row.   *emerald*

18 And the second row *shall be* an emerald, a sapphire, and a diamond.

19 And the third row a ^Tligure, an agate, and an amethyst.   *jacinth; amber*

20 And the fourth row a beryl, and an onyx, and a jasper: they shall be set in gold in their ᵀinclosings.   *settings*

21 And the stones shall be with the names of the children of Israel, twelve, according to their names, *like* the engravings of a ᵀsignet; every one with his name shall they be according to the twelve tribes.   *seal*

22 And thou shalt make upon the breastplate chains at the ends *of* ᵀwreathen work *of* pure gold.   *braided*

23 And thou shalt make upon the breastplate two rings of gold, and shalt put the two rings on the two ends of the breastplate.

24 And thou shalt put the two wreathen *chains* of gold in the two rings *which are* on the ends of the breastplate.

25 And *the other* two ends of the two wreathen *chains* thou shalt fasten in the two ᵀouches, and put *them* on the shoulderpieces of the e'-phod before it.   *settings*

26 And thou shalt make two rings of gold, and thou shalt put them upon the two ends of the breastplate in the border thereof, which *is* in the side of the e'-phod inward.

27 And two *other* rings of gold thou shalt make, and shalt put them on the two sides of the e'-phod underneath, toward the forepart thereof, over against the *other* coupling thereof, above the ᵀcurious girdle of the e'-phod.   *embroidered*

28 And they shall bind the breastplate by the rings thereof unto the rings of the e'-phod with a lace of blue, that *it* may be above the curious girdle of the e'-phod, and that the breastplate be not loosed from the e'-phod.

29 And Aaron shall bear the names of the children of Israel in the breastplate of judgment upon his heart, when he goeth in unto the holy *place*, ᴿfor a memorial before the LORD continually.   *v. 12*

The Urim and Thummim

30 And thou shalt put in the breastplate of judgment the U'-rim and the Thum'-mim; and they shall be upon Aaron's heart, when he goeth in before the LORD: and Aaron shall bear the judgment of the children of Israel upon his heart before the LORD continually.

The Robe of the Ephod

31 And ᴿthou shalt make the robe of the e'-phod all *of* blue.   *39:22-26*

32 And there shall be an hole in the top of it, in the midst thereof: it shall have a binding of woven work round about the hole of it, as it were the hole of an ᵀhabergeon, that it be not rent.   *coat of mail*

33 And *beneath* upon the hem of it thou shalt make pomegranates *of* blue, and *of* purple, and *of* scarlet, round about the hem thereof; and bells of gold between them round about:

34 A golden bell and a pomegranate, a golden bell and a pomegranate, upon the hem of the robe round about.

35 And it shall be upon Aaron to minister: and his sound shall be heard when he goeth in unto the holy *place* before the LORD, and when he cometh out, that he die not.

The Holy Mitre

36 And ᴿthou shalt make a plate *of* pure gold, and grave upon it, *like* the engravings of a signet, HOLINESS TO THE LORD.   *39:30*

37 And thou shalt put it on a blue lace, that it may be upon the mitre; upon the forefront of the ᵀmitre it shall be.   *turban*

38 And it shall be upon Aaron's forehead, that Aaron may bear the iniquity of the holy things, which the children of Israel shall hallow in all their holy gifts; and it shall be always upon his forehead, that they may be accepted before the LORD.

The Priest's Coat

39 And thou shalt embroider the coat of fine linen, ᴿand thou shalt make the mitre *of* fine linen, and thou shalt make the girdle *of* needlework.   *39:27-29*

40 And for Aaron's sons thou shalt make coats, and thou shalt make for them ᴿgirdles, and ᵀbonnets shalt thou make for them, for glory and for beauty.   *29:9 · head pieces*

41 And thou shalt put them upon Aaron thy brother, and his sons with him; and shalt ᴿanoint them, and consecrate them, and sanctify them, that they may minister unto me in the priest's office.   *Lev. 10:7*

42 And thou shalt make them linen breeches to cover their nakedness; from the loins even unto the thighs they shall reach:

43 And they shall be upon Aaron, and upon his sons, when they come in unto the tabernacle of the congregation, or when they come near unto the altar to minister in the holy *place;* that they ᵀbear not iniquity, and die: *it shall be* a statute for ever unto him and his seed after him.   *have not sin*

CHAPTER 29

The Consecration of the Priests

AND this *is* the thing that thou shalt do unto them to hallow them, to minister unto me in the priest's office: ᴿTake one young bullock, and two rams without blemish,   *Lev. 8:1-34*

2 And ᴿunleavened bread, and cakes unleavened tempered with oil, and wafers unleavened anointed with oil: *of* wheaten flour shalt thou make them.   *Lev. 2:4; 6:20-22*

3 And thou shalt put them into one basket, and bring them in the basket, with the bullock and the two rams.

4 And Aaron and his sons thou shalt bring unto the door of the tabernacle of the congregation, and shalt wash them with water.

5 [R]And thou shalt take the garments, and put upon Aaron the coat, and the robe of the e'-phod, and the e'-phod, and the breastplate, and gird him with [R]the curious girdle of the e'-phod: 28:2; Lev. 8:7 · 28:8

6 [R]And thou shalt put the mitre upon his head, [R]and put the holy crown upon the [T]mitre. Lev. 8:9 · 28:36, 37 · turban

7 Then shalt thou take the anointing oil, and pour it upon his head, and anoint him.

8 And [R]thou shalt bring his sons, [R]and put coats upon them. Lev. 8:13 · 28:39, 40

9 And thou shalt gird them with girdles, Aaron and his sons, and put the bonnets on them: and the priest's office shall be their's for a perpetual statute: and thou shalt consecrate Aaron and his sons.

10 And thou shalt cause a bullock to be brought before the tabernacle of the congregation: and Aaron and his sons shall put their hands upon the head of the bullock.

11 And thou shalt kill the bullock before the LORD, by the door of the tabernacle of the congregation.

12 And thou shalt take of the blood of the bullock, and put it upon [R]the horns of the altar with thy finger, and pour all the blood beside the bottom of the altar. Lev. 8:15

13 And [R]thou shalt take all the fat that covereth the inwards, and the caul that is above the liver, and the two kidneys, and the fat that is upon them, and burn them upon the altar. Lev. 1:8; 3:3

14 But the flesh of the bullock, and his skin, and his dung, shalt thou burn with fire without the camp: it is a sin offering.

15 [R]Thou shalt also take one ram; and Aaron and his sons shall [R]put their hands upon the head of the ram. Lev. 8:18 · Lev. 1:4–9

16 And thou shalt slay the ram, and thou shalt take his blood, and sprinkle it round about upon the altar.

17 And thou shalt cut the ram in pieces, and wash the [T]inwards of him, and his legs, and put them unto his pieces, and [T]unto his head. entrails · upon

18 And thou shalt burn the whole ram upon the altar: it is a burnt offering unto the LORD: it is [T]a sweet savour, an offering made by fire unto the LORD. a pleasing thing

19 [R]And thou shalt take the other ram; and Aaron and his sons shall put their hands upon the head of the ram. Lev. 8:22

20 Then shalt thou kill the ram, and take of his blood, and put it upon the tip of the right ear of Aaron, and upon the tip of the right ear of his sons, and upon the thumb of their right hand, and upon the [T]great toe of

their right foot, and sprinkle the blood upon the altar round about. big

21 And thou shalt take of the blood that is upon the altar, and of the anointing oil, and sprinkle it upon Aaron, and upon his garments, and upon his sons, and upon the garments of his sons with him: and he shall be hallowed, and his garments, and his sons, and his sons' garments with him.

22 Also thou shalt take of the ram the fat and the rump, and the fat that covereth the inwards, and the [T]caul above the liver, and the two kidneys, and the fat that is upon them, and the right [T]shoulder; for it is a ram of consecration: fat · thigh

23 [R]And one loaf of bread, and one cake of oiled bread, and one wafer out of the basket of the unleavened bread that is before the LORD: Lev. 8:26

24 And thou shalt put all in the hands of Aaron, and in the hands of his sons; and shalt [R]wave[T] them for a wave offering before the LORD. Lev. 7:30; 10:14 · present

25 [R]And thou shalt receive them of their hands, and burn them upon the altar for a burnt offering, for a sweet savour before the LORD: it is an offering made by fire unto the LORD. Lev. 8:28

26 And thou shalt take [R]the breast of the ram of Aaron's consecration, and wave it for a wave offering before the LORD: and [R]it shall be thy part. Lev. 8:29 · Lev. 7:33

27 And thou shalt sanctify the breast of the wave offering, and the shoulder of the heave offering, which is waved, and which is [T]heaved up, of the ram of the consecration, even of that which is for Aaron, and of that which is for his sons: held up before the altar

28 And it shall be Aaron's and his sons' by a statute for ever from the children of Israel: for it is an heave offering: and [R]it shall be an heave offering from the children of Israel of the sacrifice of their peace offerings, even their heave offering unto the LORD. Lev. 10:15

29 And the holy garments of Aaron shall be his sons' after him, to be anointed therein, and to be consecrated in them.

30 And that son that is priest in his stead shall put them on seven days, when he cometh into the tabernacle of the congregation to minister in the holy place.

31 And thou shalt take the ram of the consecration, and [R]seethe[T] his flesh in the holy place. Lev. 8:31 · boil

32 And Aaron and his sons shall eat the flesh of the ram, and the [R]bread that is in the basket, [R]by the door of the tabernacle of the congregation. Matt. 12:4 · Lev. 6:16

33 And they shall eat those things wherewith the atonement was made, to consecrate and to sanctify them: but a stranger shall not eat thereof, because they are holy.

34 And if ᵀought of the flesh of the consecrations, or of the bread, remain unto the morning, then ᴿthou shalt burn the remainder with fire: it shall not be eaten, because it is holy.   any · Lev. 7:18; 8:32

35 And thus shalt thou do unto Aaron, and to his sons, according to all things which I have commanded thee: ᴿseven days shalt thou consecrate them.   Lev. 8:33–35

36 And thou shalt offer every day a bullock for a sin offering for atonement: and thou shalt cleanse the altar, when thou hast made ᵀan atonement for it, and thou shalt anoint it, to sanctify it.   special ceremony

37 Seven days thou shalt make an atonement for the altar, and sanctify it; and it shall be an altar most holy: ᴿwhatsoever toucheth the altar shall be holy.   Matt. 23:19

The Continual Offerings of the Priests

38 Now this is that which thou shalt offer upon the altar; two lambs of the first year ᴿday by day continually.   Dan. 12:11

39 The one lamb thou shalt offer in the morning; and the other lamb thou shalt offer ᵀat even: between the two evenings

40 And with the one lamb ᵀa tenth deal of flour mingled with ᵀthe fourth part of an hin of beaten oil; and the fourth part of an hin of wine for a drink offering.   2.087 qt. · 1 qt.

41 And the other lamb thou shalt ᴿoffer at ᵀeven, and shalt do thereto according to the ᵀmeat offering of the morning, and according to the drink offering thereof, for a sweet savour, an offering made by fire unto the LORD.   Ezra 9:4, 5; Ps. 141:2 · evening time · meal

42 This shall be ᴿa continual burnt offering throughout your generations at the door of the tabernacle of the congregation before the LORD: ᴿwhere I will meet you, to speak there unto thee.   30:8 · 25:22

43 And there I will meet with the children of Israel, and the tabernacle ᴿshall be sanctified by my glory.   Ezek. 43:5; Hag. 2:7, 9

44 And I will sanctify the tabernacle of the congregation, and the altar: I will ᴿsanctify also both Aaron and his sons, to minister to me in the priest's office.   Lev. 21:15

45 And ᴿI will dwell among the children of Israel, and will be their God.   25:8; Deut. 12:11

46 And they shall know that I am the LORD their God, that brought them forth out of the land of Egypt, that I may dwell among them: I am the LORD their God.

CHAPTER 30

The Altar of Incense

AND thou shalt make ᴿan altar to burn incense upon: of ᵀshit'-tim wood shalt thou make it.   37:25 · acacia

2 A ᵀcubit shall be the length thereof, and a cubit the breadth thereof; foursquare shall it be: and ᵀtwo cubits shall be the height thereof: the horns thereof shall be of the same.   18 in. · 3 ft.

3 And thou shalt overlay it with pure gold, the top thereof, and the sides thereof round about, and the horns thereof; and thou shalt make unto it a crown of gold round about.

4 And two golden rings shalt thou make to it under the crown of it, by the two corners thereof, upon the two sides of it shalt thou make it; and they shall be for places for the staves to bear it withal.

5 And thou shalt make the staves of shit'-tim wood, and overlay them with gold.

6 And thou shalt put it before the vail that is by the ark of the testimony, before the ᴿmercy seat that is over the testimony, where I will meet with thee.   25:21, 22

7 And Aaron shall burn thereon sweet incense every morning: when he dresseth the lamps, he shall burn incense upon it.

8 And when Aaron lighteth the lamps ᵀat even, he shall burn incense upon it, a perpetual incense before the LORD throughout your generations.   between the two evenings

9 Ye shall offer no strange incense thereon, nor burnt sacrifice, nor meat offering; neither shall ye pour drink offering thereon.

10 And ᴿAaron shall make an atonement ᵀupon the horns of it once in a year with the blood of the sin offering of atonements: once in the year shall he make atonement upon it throughout your generations: it is most holy unto the LORD.   Lev. 16:3–34 · for

The Ransom Money

11 And the LORD spake unto Moses, saying,

12 ᴿWhen thou takest the sum of the children of Israel after their number, then shall they give every man a ransom for his soul unto the LORD, when thou numberest them; that there be no plague among them, when thou numberest them.   Num. 26:2

13 This they shall give, every one that passeth among them that are numbered, half a shek'-el after the shek'-el of the sanctuary: (a shek'-el is twenty ge'-rahs:) an ᵀhalf shek'-el shall be the offering of the LORD. $64

14 Every one that passeth among them that are numbered, from twenty years old and above, shall give an ᵀoffering unto the LORD.   contribution

15 The rich shall not give more, and the poor shall not give less than ᵀhalf a shek'-el, when they give an offering unto the LORD, to make an atonement for your souls. $64

16 And thou shalt take the atonement money of the children of Israel, and shalt appoint it for the service of the tabernacle of

the congregation; that it may be a memorial unto the children of Israel before the LORD, to make an atonement for your souls.

The Laver of Brass

17 And the LORD spake unto Moses, saying,

18 RThou shalt also make a Tlaver of brass, and his foot also of brass, to wash withal: and thou shalt put it between the tabernacle of the congregation and the altar, and thou shalt put water therein.   38:8 · tub

19 For Aaron and his sons Rshall wash their hands and their feet thereat: Ps. 26:6

20 When they go into the tabernacle of the congregation, they shall wash with water, that they die not; or when they come near to the altar to minister, to burn offering made by fire unto the LORD:

21 So they shall wash their hands and their feet, that they die not: and it shall be a statute for ever to them, even to him and to his seed throughout their generations.

The Anointing Oil

22 Moreover the LORD spake unto Moses, saying,

23 Take thou also unto thee principal spices, of pure myrrh five hundred shek'-els, and of sweet cinnamon half so much, even two hundred and fifty shek'-els, and of sweet calamus two hundred and fifty shek'-els,

24 And of Rcassia Tfive hundred shek'-els, after the shek'-el of the sanctuary, and of oil olive an RhinT: Ps. 45:8 · 12.5 lb. · 29:40 · 1 gal.

25 And thou shalt make it an oil of holy ointment, an ointment compound after the art of the Tapothecary: it shall be Ran holy anointing oil.   perfumer · 37:29; Num. 35:25

26 RAnd thou shalt anoint the tabernacle of the congregation therewith, and the ark of the testimony,   40:9; Lev. 8:10; Num. 7:1

27 And the table and all his Tvessels, and the candlestick and his vessels, and the altar of incense,   utensils

28 And the altar of burnt offering with all his vessels, and the laver and his foot.

29 And thou shalt Tsanctify them, that they may be most holy: whatsoever toucheth them shall be holy.   set them apart

30 And thou shalt anoint Aaron and his sons, and consecrate them, that they may minister unto me in the priest's office.

31 And thou shalt speak unto the children of Israel, saying, This shall be an holy anointing oil unto me throughout your generations.

32 Upon Tman's flesh shall it not be poured, neither shall ye make any other like it, after the composition of it: Rit is holy, and it shall be holy unto you.   common · vv. 25, 37

33 Whosoever compoundeth any like it, or whosoever putteth any of it upon a stranger, shall even be cut off from his people.

The Incense

34 And the LORD said unto Moses, RTake unto thee sweet spices, stac'-te, and on'-y-cha, and gal'-ba-num; these sweet spices with pure frankincense: of each shall there be a Tlike weight: 25:6; 37:29 · equal part

35 And thou shalt make it a perfume, a confection after the art of the apothecary, tempered together, pure and holy:

36 And thou shalt beat some of it very small, and put of it before the testimony in the tabernacle of the congregation, Rwhere I will meet with thee: Rit shall be unto you most holy.   29:42; Lev. 16:2 · [v. 32; 29:37]

37 And as for the perfume which thou shalt make, ye shall not make to yourselves according to the composition thereof: it shall be unto thee holy for the LORD.

38 RWhosoever shall make like unto that, Tto smell thereto, Rshall even be cut off from his people.   v. 33 · to use as perfume · Lev. 7:20; 17:9

CHAPTER 31

Instructions for Building the Tabernacle

AND the LORD spake unto Moses, saying,

2 RSee, I have called by name Be-zal'-e-el the Rson of U'-ri, the son of Hur, of the tribe of Judah: 35:30; 36:1 · 1 Chr. 2:20

3 And I have Rfilled him with the spirit of God, in wisdom, and in understanding, and in knowledge, and in all manner of workmanship,   35:31; 1 Kin. 7:14; Zech. 12:10

4 To devise Tcunning works, to work in gold, and in silver, and in brass,   artful

5 And in Tcutting of stones, to set them, and in carving of timber, to work in all manner of workmanship.   engraving

6 And I, behold, I have given with him A-ho'-li-ab, the son of A-his'-a-mach, of the tribe of Dan: and in the hearts of all that are wise hearted I have put wisdom, that they may make all that I have commanded thee;

7 RThe tabernacle of the congregation, and the ark of the testimony, and Rthe mercy seat that is thereupon, and all the furniture of the tabernacle,   36:8 · 37:6

8 And Rthe table and his furniture, and Rthe pure candlestick with all his furniture, and the altar of incense,   37:10 · 37:17

9 And the altar of burnt offering with all his furniture, and the laver and his foot,

10 And Rthe cloths of service, and the holy garments for Aaron the priest, and the garments of his sons, to minister in the priest's office,   39:1, 41; Num. 4:5, 6

11 And the anointing oil, and sweet incense for the holy place: according to all that I have commanded thee shall they do.

Sign of the Covenant: The Sabbath

12 And the LORD spake unto Moses, saying,

13 Speak thou also unto the children of Israel, saying, RVerily my sabbaths ye shall Tkeep: for it is a sign between me and you throughout your generations; that ye may know that I am the LORD that doth Tsanctify you.   [Ezek. 20:12, 20] • observe • set you apart

14 Ye shall keep the sabbath therefore; for it is holy unto you: every one that defileth it shall surely be put to death: for whosoever doeth any work therein, that soul shall be cut off from among his people.

15 Six days may work be done; but in the seventh is the sabbath of rest, holy to the LORD: whosoever doeth any work in the sabbath day, he shall surely be put to death.

16 Wherefore the children of Israel shall keep the sabbath, to observe the sabbath throughout their generations, for a perpetual covenant.

17 It is a sign between me and the children of Israel for ever: for in six days the LORD made heaven and earth, and on the seventh day he rested, and was refreshed.

Two Tables Are Presented

18 And he gave unto Moses, when he had made an end of communing with him upon mount Si'-nai, Rtwo tables of testimony, tables of stone, written with the finger of God.   [32:15; 34:28; Deut. 4:13; 5:22; 2 Cor. 3:3]

CHAPTER 32

Israel Willfully Breaks the Covenant

AND when the people saw that Moses delayed to come down out of the mount, the people gathered themselves together unto Aaron, and said unto him, Up, Rmake us Tgods, which shall go before us; for as for this Moses, the man that brought us up out of the land of Egypt, we Twot not what is become of him.   v. 23 • a god • know

2 And Aaron said unto them, Break off the golden earrings, which are in the ears of your wives, of your sons, and of your daughters, and bring them unto me.

3 And all the people brake off the golden earrings which were in their ears, and brought them unto Aaron.

4 And he received them at their hand, and fashioned it with a graving tool, after he had made it a molten calf: and they said, These be thy gods, O Israel, which brought thee up out of the land of Egypt.

5 And when Aaron saw it, he built Tan altar before it; and Aaron made Rproclamation, and said, To morrow is a feast to the LORD.   place of worship • Lev. 23:2, 4, 21, 37; 2 Kin. 10:20

6 And they rose up early on the morrow, and offered burnt offerings, and brought peace offerings; and the people sat down to eat and to drink, and rose up to play.

God to Destroy Israel

7 And the LORD said unto Moses, RGo, get thee down; for thy people, which thou broughtest out of the land of Egypt, have Tcorrupted themselves: Dan. 9:14 • done wrong

8 They have turned aside quickly out of the way which RI commanded them: they have made them a molten calf, and have worshipped it, Rand have sacrificed thereunto, and said, RThese be thy gods, O Israel, which have brought thee up out of the land of Egypt.   20:3, 4, 23 • Deut. 32:17 • 1 Kin. 12:28

9 And the LORD said unto Moses, RI have seen this people, and, behold, it is a Tstiff-necked people: [Is. 48:4; Acts 7:51] • stubborn

10 Now therefore let me alone, that my wrath may wax hot against them, and that I may Tconsume them: and RI will make of thee a great nation.   destroy • Num. 14:12

Moses Intercedes for Israel

11 And Moses besought the LORD his God, and said, LORD, why doth thy wrath wax hot against thy people, which thou hast brought forth out of the land of Egypt with great power, and with a mighty hand?

12 Wherefore should the Egyptians speak, and say, For Tmischief did he bring them out, to slay them in the mountains, and to consume them from the face of the earth? Turn from thy fierce wrath, and repent of this evil against thy people.   harm

13 Remember Abraham, Isaac, and Jacob, thy servants, to whom thou RswarestT by thine own self, and saidst unto them, I will multiply your seed as the stars of heaven, and all this land that I have spoken of will I give unto your seed, and they shall inherit it for ever.   [Heb. 6:13] • didst promise

14 And the LORD repented of the evil which he thought to do unto his people.

Moses Disciplines Israel

15 And RMoses turned, and went down from the mount, and the two tables of the testimony were in his hand: the tables were written on both their sides; on the one side and on the other were they written.   Deut. 9:15

16 And the Rtables were the work of God, and the writing was the writing of God, graven upon the tables.   31:18

17 And when Joshua heard the noise of the people as they shouted, he said unto Moses, There is a noise of war in the camp.

18 And he said, It is not the voice of them that shout for mastery, neither is it the voice of them that cry for being overcome: but the noise of them that sing do I hear.

19 And it came to pass, as soon as he came nigh unto the camp, that he saw the calf, and the dancing: and Moses' anger waxed hot, and he cast the tables out of his hands, and brake them beneath the mount.

20 And he took the calf which they had made, and burnt *it* in the fire, and ground *it* to powder, and strawed *it* upon the water, and made the children of Israel drink *of it.*

21 And Moses said unto Aaron, ᴿWhat did this people unto thee, that thou hast brought so great a sin upon them?   Gen. 26:10

22 And Aaron said, Let not the anger of my lord wax hot: ᴿthou knowest the people, that they *are set* on mischief.   14:11

23 For they said unto me, ᴿMake us gods, which shall go before us: for *as for* this Moses, the man that brought us up out of the land of Egypt, we ᵀwot not what is become of him.   Acts 7:40; Phil. 1:22 • *know*

24 And I said unto them, Whosoever hath any gold, let them break *it* off. So they gave *it* me: then ᴿI cast it into the fire, and there came out this calf.   *v.* 4

25 And when Moses saw that the people *were* naked; (for Aaron ᴿhad made them naked unto *their* shame among their enemies:)   2 Chr. 28:19

26 Then Moses stood in the gate of the camp, and said, Who *is* on the LORD's side? *let him come* unto me. And all the sons of Levi gathered themselves together unto him.

27 And he said unto them, Thus saith the LORD God of Israel, Put every man his sword by his side, *and* go in and out from gate to gate throughout the camp, and slay every man his brother, and every man his companion, and every man his neighbour.

28 And the children of Levi did according to the word of Moses: and there fell of the people that day about three thousand men.

29 For Moses had said, Consecrate yourselves to day to the LORD, even every man upon his son, and upon his brother; that he may bestow upon you a blessing this day.

Moses Atones for Israel

30 And it came to pass on the morrow, that Moses said unto the people, Ye have sinned a great sin: and now I will go up unto the LORD; peradventure I shall ᴿmake an atonement for your sin.   Num. 25:13

31 And Moses returned unto the LORD, and said, Oh, this people have sinned a great sin, and have made them gods of gold.

32 Yet now, if thou wilt forgive their sin—; and if not, blot me, I pray thee, out of thy book which thou hast written.

33 And the LORD said unto Moses, ᴿWhosoever hath sinned against me, him will I blot out of my book.   [Ezek. 18:4; 33:2, 14]

God Sends His Angel

34 Therefore now go, lead the people unto *the place* of which I have spoken unto thee: behold, ᴿmine Angel shall go before thee: nevertheless in the day when I ᵀvisit I will visit their sin upon them.   Josh. 5:14 • *come to see*

35 ᴿAnd the LORD ᵀplagued the people, because they made the calf, which Aaron made.   3:17 • *smote*

CHAPTER 33

The Tabernacle Is Moved Outside the Camp

AND the LORD said unto Moses, Depart, *and* go up hence, thou ᴿand the people which thou hast brought up out of the land of Egypt, unto the land which I sware unto Abraham, to Isaac, and to Jacob, saying, Unto thy seed will I give it: 32:7

2 And I will send an angel before thee; and I will drive out the Ca'-naan-ite, the Am'-or-ite, and the Hit'-tite, and the Per'-iz-zite, the Hi'-vite, and the Jeb'-u-site:

3 Unto a land flowing with milk and honey: for I will not go up in the midst of thee; for thou *art* a ᵀstiffnecked people: lest I consume thee in the way.   *rebellious*

4 And when the people heard these evil tidings, they ᵀmourned: and no man did put on him his ornaments.   *were sorry*

5 For the LORD had said unto Moses, Say unto the children of Israel, Ye *are* a stiffnecked people: I will come up into the midst of thee in a moment, and consume thee: therefore now put off thy ornaments from thee, that I may know what to do unto thee.

6 And the children of Israel stripped themselves of their ornaments by the mount Ho'-reb.

7 And Moses took the tabernacle, and pitched it ᵀwithout the camp, afar off from the camp, and called it the Tabernacle of the congregation. And it came to pass, *that* every one which sought the LORD went out unto the tabernacle of the congregation, which *was* without the camp.   *outside*

Moses Talks to God

8 And it came to pass, when Moses went out unto the tabernacle, *that* all the people rose up, and stood every man ᴿat his tent door, and looked after Moses, until he was gone into the tabernacle.   Num. 16:27

9 And it came to pass, as Moses entered into the tabernacle, the cloudy pillar descended, and stood *at* the door of the tabernacle, and *the* LORD talked with Moses.

10 And all the people saw the cloudy pillar stand *at* the tabernacle door: and all the people rose up and ᴿworshipped, every man *in* his tent door.   4:31

11 And ^Rthe LORD spake unto Moses face to face, as a man speaketh unto his friend. And he turned again into the camp: but his servant Joshua, the son of Nun, a young man, departed not out of the tabernacle.   Num. 12:8

God Will Show Moses the Way

12 And Moses said unto the LORD, See, thou sayest unto me, Bring up this people: and thou hast not let me know ^Twhom thou wilt send with me. Yet thou hast said, I know thee by name, and thou hast also found grace in my sight.   *him whom*
13 Now therefore, I pray thee, if I have found grace in thy sight, shew me now thy way, that I may know thee, that I may find grace in thy sight: and ^Tconsider that this nation *is* thy people.   *have it in mind*
14 And he said, My presence shall go *with thee*, and I will give thee ^Trest.   *peace*
15 And he said unto him, If thy presence go not *with me*, carry us not up hence.
16 For wherein shall it be known here that I and thy people have found grace in thy sight? *is it* not in that thou goest with us? so ^Rshall we be separated, I and thy people, from all the people that *are* upon the face of the earth.   34:10
17 And the LORD said unto Moses, ^RI will do this thing also that thou hast spoken: for thou hast found grace in my sight, and I know thee by name.   *v. 12;* [James 5:16]

God Shows Moses His Glory

18 ^RAnd he said, I beseech thee, shew me ^Rthy glory.   *vv. 20–23* • [1 Tim. 6:16]
19 And he said, I will make all my goodness pass before thee, and I will proclaim the name of the LORD before thee; ^Rand will be ^Rgracious to whom I will be gracious, and will shew mercy on whom I will shew mercy.   [Rom. 9:15, 16, 18] • [Rom. 4:4, 16]
20 And he said, Thou canst not see my face: for there shall no man see me, and live.
21 ^RAnd the LORD said, Behold, *there is* a place by me, and thou shalt stand upon a rock: [Ps. 27:5; 61:2; 62:7]
22 And it shall come to pass, while my glory passeth by, that I will put thee in a ^Tclift of the rock, and will ^Rcover thee with my hand while I pass by: *cleft* • Ps. 91:1, 4
23 And I will take away mine hand, and thou shalt see my back parts: but my face shall ^Rnot be seen.   [John 1:18]

CHAPTER 34

Hewing of the Two Tables

AND the LORD said unto Moses, ^RHew^T thee two tables of stone like unto the first: and I will write upon *these* tables the words that were in the first tables, which thou brakest.   32:16, 19; 34:28 • *Cut out*
2 And be ready in the morning, and come up in the morning unto mount Si'-nai, and present thyself there to me ^Rin the top of the mount.   19:20
3 And no man shall ^Rcome up with thee, neither let any man be seen throughout all the mount; neither let the flocks nor herds feed before that mount.   19:12, 13
4 And he hewed two tables of stone like unto the first; and Moses rose up early in the morning, and went up unto mount Si'-nai, as the LORD had commanded him, and took in his hand the two tables of stone.

The Nature of God Is Revealed

5 And the LORD descended in the cloud, and stood with him there, and ^Rproclaimed^T the name of the LORD.   33:19 • *made known*
6 And the LORD passed by before him, and proclaimed, The LORD, The LORD God, merciful and gracious, longsuffering, and abundant in goodness and ^Rtruth,   [Ps. 108:4]
7 Keeping mercy for thousands, forgiving iniquity and transgression and sin, and that will by no means clear *the guilty;* visiting the iniquity of the fathers upon the children, and upon the children's children, unto the third and to the fourth *generation.*
8 And Moses made haste, and bowed his head toward the earth, and worshipped.
9 And he said, If now I have found grace in thy sight, O Lord, let my Lord, I pray thee, go among us; for it *is* a stiffnecked people; and pardon our iniquity and our sin, and take us for thine inheritance.

Renewal of the Covenant

10 And he said, Behold, I make a covenant: before all thy people I will do ^Rmarvels, such as have not been done in all the earth, nor in any nation: and all the people among which thou *art* shall see the work of the LORD: for it *is* a ^Tterrible thing that I will do with thee.   [Ps. 72:18] • *impressive*
11 ^RObserve thou that which I command thee this day: behold, I drive out before thee the Am'-or-ite, and the Ca'-naan-ite, and the Hit'-tite, and the Per'-iz-zite, and the Hi'-vite, and the Jeb'-u-site.   Deut. 6:25; Josh. 11:23
12 ^RTake heed to thyself, lest thou make a covenant with the inhabitants of the land whither thou goest, lest it be ^Tfor a snare in the midst of thee: 23:32 • *to lead you into evil*
13 But ye shall destroy their altars, break their images, and cut down their groves:
14 For thou shalt worship ^Rno other god: for the LORD, whose ^Rname *is* Jealous, *is* a ^Rjealous God: [20:3, 5] • [Is. 9:6; 57:15] • [20:5]
15 Lest thou make a covenant with the inhabitants of the land, and they go a ^Twhoring after their gods, and do sacrifice unto

their gods, and *one* call thee, and thou eat of his sacrifice;　　　　　*loving other gods*

16 And thou take of their daughters unto thy sons, and their daughters ᴿgo a whoring after their gods, and make thy sons go a whoring after their gods.　　　[Num. 25:1, 2]

17 Thou shalt make thee no molten gods.

18 The feast of unleavened bread shalt thou keep. Seven days thou shalt eat unleavened bread, as I commanded thee, in the time of the month A'-bib: for in the month A'-bib thou camest out from Egypt.

19 All that openeth the ᵀmatrix *is* mine; and every firstling among thy cattle, *whether* ox or sheep, *that is male.*　　　*womb*

20 But the firstling of an ass thou shalt redeem with a lamb: and if thou redeem *him* not, then shalt thou break his neck. All the firstborn of thy sons thou shalt redeem. And none shall appear before me empty.

21 ᴿSix days thou shalt work, but on the seventh day thou shalt rest: in earing time and in harvest thou shalt rest.　　　20:9

22 And thou shalt observe the feast of weeks, of the firstfruits of wheat harvest, and the feast of ingathering at the year's end.

23 ᴿThriceᵀ in the year shall all your men children appear before the Lord Goᴅ, the God of Israel.　　　23:14, 17 · *three times*

24 For I will ᴿcast out the nations before thee, and enlarge thy borders: neither shall any man desire thy land, when thou shalt go up to appear before the Lord thy God thrice in the year.　　　[33:2]; Ps. 78:55

25 ᴿThou shalt not offer the blood of my sacrifice with leaven; ᴿneither shall the sacrifice of the feast of the passover be left unto the morning.　　　23:18 · 12:10

26 The first of the firstfruits of thy land thou shalt bring unto the house of the Lord thy God. Thou shalt not ᵀseethe a kidᵀ in his mother's milk.　　　*boil · young goat*

27 And the Lord said unto Moses, Write thou these words: for ᵀafter the tenor of these words I have made a ᵀcovenant with thee and with Israel.　　　*according to · agreement*

28 And he was there with the Lord forty days and forty nights; he did neither eat bread, nor drink water. And ᴿhe wrote upon the tables the words of the covenant, the ten commandments.　　　*v.* 1; 31:18

Moses Returns from God

29 And it came to pass, when Moses came down from mount Si'-nai with the ᴿtwo tables of testimony in Moses' hand, when he came down from the mount, that Moses ᵀwist not that the skin of his face shone while he talked with him.　　　32:15 · *knew*

30 And when Aaron and all the children of Israel saw Moses, ᴿbehold, the skin of his face shone; and they were afraid to come nigh him.　　　2 Cor. 3:7

31 ᴿAnd Moses called unto them; and Aaron and all the rulers of the congregation returned unto him: and Moses talked with them.　　　16:22

32 And afterward all the children of Israel came nigh: ᴿand he gave them in commandment all that the Lord had spoken with him in mount Si'-nai.　　　24:3

33 And *till* Moses had done speaking with them, he put ᴿa vail on his face.　　　[2 Cor. 3:13]

34 But ᴿwhen Moses went in before the Lord to speak with him, he took the vail off, until he came out. And he came out, and spake unto the children of Israel *that* which he was commanded.　　　[2 Cor. 3:16]

35 And the children of Israel saw the face of Moses, that the skin of Moses' face shone: and Moses put the vail upon his face again, until he went in to speak with him.

CHAPTER 35

Israel Brings Offerings in Abundance

Aɴᴅ Moses gathered all the congregation of the children of Israel together, and said unto them, ᴿThese *are* the words which the Lord hath commanded, that *ye* should do them.　　　34:32

2 Six days shall work be done, but on the seventh day there shall be to you an holy day, a sabbath of rest to the Lord: whosoever doeth work therein shall be put to death.

3 ᴿYe shall kindle no fire throughout your habitations upon the sabbath day.　　　16:23

4 And Moses spake unto all the congregation of the children of Israel, saying, ᴿThis *is* the thing which the Lord commanded, saying,　　　25:1, 2

5 Take ye from among you an offering unto the Lord: ᴿwhosoever *is* of a willing heart, let him bring it, an offering of the Lord; gold, and silver, and brass,　　　25:2

6 ᴿAnd blue, and purple, and scarlet, and fine linen, and goats' *hair,*　　　36:8

7 And rams' skins dyed red, and ᵀbadgers' skins, and shit'-tim wood,　　　*seal*

8 And oil for the light, and spices for anointing oil, and for the sweet incense,

9 And onyx stones, and stones to be set for the e'-phod, and for the breastplate.

10 And every ᵀwise hearted among you shall come, and make all that the Lord hath commanded;　　　*man with good judgment*

11 ᴿThe tabernacle, his tent, and his covering, ᵀhis taches, and his boards, his bars, his pillars, and his sockets,　　　26:1, 2 · *its clasps*

12 The ark, and the staves thereof, *with* the mercy seat, and the vail of the covering,

13 The table, and his staves, and all his vessels, ᴿand the shewbread,　　　Lev. 24:5, 6

14 ᴿThe candlestick also for the light, and

ᵀhis furniture, and his lamps, with the oil for the light,   25:31 • *its vessels*

15 ᴿAnd the incense altar, and his staves, and the anointing oil, and the sweet incense, and the hanging for the door at the entering in of the tabernacle,   30:1

16 ᴿThe altar of burnt offering, with his brasen grate, his staves, and all his vessels, the laver and ᵀhis foot,   27:1 • *its stand*

17 ᴿThe hangings of the court, his pillars, and their sockets, and the hanging for the door of the court,   27:9

18 The ᵀpins of the tabernacle, and the pins of the court, and their cords,   *pegs*

19 The ᴿcloths of service, to do service in the holy *place*, the holy garments for Aaron the priest, and the garments of his sons, to minister in the priest's office.   31:10

20 And all the congregation of the children of Israel departed from the presence of Moses.

21 And they came, every one ᴿwhose heart stirred him up, and every one whom his spirit made willing, *and* they brought the LORD's offering to the work of the tabernacle of the congregation, and for all his service, and for the holy garments.   36:2

22 And they came, both men and women, as many as were willing hearted, *and* brought bracelets, and earrings, and rings, and tablets, all jewels of gold: and every man that offered *offered* an offering of gold unto the LORD.

23 And ᴿevery man, with whom was found blue, and purple, and scarlet, and fine linen, and goats' *hair*, and red skins of rams, and badgers' skins, brought *them*.   1 Chr. 29:8

24 Every one that did offer an offering of silver and brass brought the LORD's offering: and every man, with whom was found ᵀshit'-tim wood for any work of the service, brought *it*.   *acacia*

25 And all the women that were ᴿwise heartedᵀ did spin with their hands, and brought that which they had spun, *both* of blue, and of purple, and of scarlet, and of fine linen.   28:3; 31:6; 36:1 • *with good judgment*

26 And all the women whose heart stirred them up in wisdom spun goats' *hair*.

27 And ᴿthe rulers brought onyx stones, and stones to be set, for the e'-phod, and for the breastplate;   1 Chr. 29:6; Ezra 2:68

28 And spice, and oil for the light, and for the anointing oil, and for the sweet incense.

29 The children of Israel brought a ᴿwill-ingᵀ offering unto the LORD, every man and woman, whose heart made them willing to bring for all manner of work, which the LORD had commanded to be made by the hand of Moses.   *v.* 21; 1 Chr. 29:9 • *voluntary*

30 And Moses said unto the children of Israel, See, ᴿthe LORD hath called by name Be-zal'-e-el the son of U'-ri, the son of Hur, of the tribe of Judah;   31:1-6

31 ᴿAnd he hath filled him with the ᵀspirit of God, in wisdom, in understanding, and in knowledge, and in all manner of workmanship;   [Zech. 12:10] • *Spirit*

32 And to devise ᵀcurious works, to work in gold, and in silver, and in brass,   *artistic*

33 And in the cutting of stones, to set *them*, and in carving of wood, to make any manner of ᵀcunning work.   *cleverly done*

34 And he hath put in his heart that he may teach, *both* he, and A-ho'-li-ab, the son of A-his'-a-mach, of the tribe of Dan.

35 Them hath he filled with wisdom of heart, to work all manner of work, of the engraver, and of the cunning workman, and of the embroiderer, in blue, and in purple, in scarlet, and in fine linen, and of the weaver, *even* of them that do any work, and of those that devise cunning work.

CHAPTER 36

THEN wrought Be-zal'-e-el and A-ho'-li-ab, and every ᴿwise hearted man, in whom the LORD put wisdom and understanding to know how to work all manner of work for the service of the sanctuary, according to all that the LORD had commanded.   31:6; 35:10, 35

2 And Moses called Be-zal'-e-el and A-ho'-li-ab, and every wise hearted man, in whose heart the LORD had put wisdom, *even* every one ᵀwhose heart stirred him up to come unto the work to do it: *who was inwardly moved*

3 And they received of Moses all the offering, which the children of Israel had brought for the work of the service of the sanctuary, to make it *withal*. And they brought yet unto him free offerings every morning.

4 And all the wise men, that wrought all the work of the sanctuary, came every man from his work which they made;

5 And they spake unto Moses, saying, ᴿThe people bring much more than enough for the service of the work, which the LORD commanded to make.   2 Chr. 24:14; [2 Cor. 8:2, 3]

6 And Moses gave commandment, and they caused it to be proclaimed throughout the camp, saying, Let neither man nor woman make any more work for the offering of the sanctuary. ᴿSo the people were restrained from bringing.   [2 Cor. 8:2, 4]

7 For the stuff they had was sufficient for all the work to make it, and too much.

The Curtains

8 ᴿAnd every wise hearted man among them that wrought the work of the tabernacle made ten curtains *of* fine twined linen, and blue, and purple, and scarlet: *with* cher'-u-bims of cunning work made he them.   26:1

9 The length of one curtain *was* ᵀtwenty and eight cubits, and the breadth of one

curtain ᵀfour cubits: the curtains *were* all of one size.   *42 ft. · 6 ft.*

10 And he coupled the five curtains one unto another: and *the other* five curtains he coupled one unto another.

11 And he made loops of blue on the edge of one ᵀcurtain from the selvedge in the coupling: likewise he made in the uttermost side of *another* curtain, in the coupling of the second.   *outmost curtain in the first set*

12 ᴿFifty loops made he in one curtain, and fifty loops made he in the edge of the curtain which *was* in the coupling of the second: the loops held one *curtain* to another.   26:5

13 And he made fifty taches of gold, and coupled the curtains one unto another with the taches: so it became one tabernacle.

14 ᴿAnd he made curtains *of* goats' *hair* for the tent over the tabernacle: eleven curtains he made them.   26:7; 35:11; 40:19

15 The length of one curtain *was* ᵀthirty cubits, and ᵀfour cubits *was* the breadth of one curtain: the eleven curtains *were* of one size.   *45 ft. · 6 ft.*

16 And he coupled five curtains by themselves, and six curtains by themselves.

17 And he made fifty loops upon the uttermost edge of the curtain in the ᵀcoupling, and fifty loops made he upon the edge of the curtain which coupleth the second.   *first set*

18 And he made fifty taches *of* brass to couple the tent together, that it might be one.

19 And he made a covering for the tent *of* rams' skins dyed red, and a covering *of* ᵀbadgers' skins above *that.*   *seal skins*

The Boards

20 ᴿAnd he made boards for the tabernacle *of* shit'-tim wood, standing up.   26:15-29

21 The length of a board *was* ᵀten cubits, and the breadth of a board ᵀone cubit and a half.   *15 ft. · 27 in.*

22 One board had two ᵀtenons, equally distant one from another: thus did he make for all the boards of the tabernacle.   *pins*

23 And he made boards for the tabernacle; twenty boards for the south side southward:

24 And forty sockets of silver he made under the twenty boards; two sockets under one board for his two tenons, and two sockets under another board for his two tenons.

25 And for the other side of the tabernacle, *which is* toward the north corner, he made twenty boards,

26 And their forty sockets of silver; two sockets under one board, and two sockets under another board.

27 And for the sides of the tabernacle westward he made six boards.

28 And two boards made he for the corners of the tabernacle in the two sides.

29 And they were ᵀcoupled beneath, and coupled together at ᵀthe head thereof, to one

ring: thus he did to both of them in both the corners.   *joined · the top*

30 And there were eight boards; and their sockets *were* sixteen sockets of silver, under every board two sockets.

31 And he made ᴿbars of ᵀshit'-tim wood; five for the boards of the one side of the tabernacle,   26:26 · *acacia*

32 And five ᴿbars for the boards of the other side of the tabernacle, and five bars for the boards of the tabernacle for the sides westward.   26:26

33 And he made the middle bar to ᵀshoot through the boards from the one end to the other.   *pass*

34 And he overlaid the boards with gold, and made their rings *of* gold *to be* places for the bars, and overlaid the bars with gold.

The Vails

35 And he made a vail *of* blue, and purple, and scarlet, and fine twined linen: *with* cher'-u-bims made he it of cunning work.

36 And he made thereunto four pillars *of* shit'-tim *wood*, and overlaid them with gold: their hooks *were of* gold; and he cast for them four sockets of silver.

37 And he made an hanging for the tabernacle door *of* blue, and purple, and scarlet, and fine twined linen, of needlework;

38 And the five pillars of it with their hooks: and he overlaid their ᵀchapiters and their fillets with gold: but their five sockets *were of* brass.   *capitals*

CHAPTER 37

The Ark of the Covenant

AND Be-zal'-e-el made the ark *of* shit'-tim wood: ᵀtwo cubits and a half *was* the length of it, and a ᵀcubit and a half the breadth of it, and a cubit and a half the height of it: *45 in. · 27 in.*

2 And he overlaid it with pure gold within and without, and made a ᵀcrown of gold to it round about.   *rim; moulding*

3 And he cast for it four rings of gold, *to be* set by the four corners of it; even two rings upon the one side of it, and two rings upon the other side of it.

4 And he made ᵀstaves *of* ᵀshit'-tim wood, and overlaid them with gold.   *poles · acacia*

5 And he put the staves into the rings by the sides of the ark, to bear the ark.

6 And he made the ᴿmercy seat *of* pure gold: ᵀtwo cubits and a half *was* the length thereof, and ᵀone cubit and a half the breadth thereof.   25:17 · *45 in. · 27 in.*

7 And he made two ᴿcher'-u-bims *of* gold, beaten out of one piece made he them, on the two ends of the mercy seat;   1 Kin. 6:23

8 One cherub on the end on this side, and another cherub on the *other* end on that side: out of the mercy seat made he the cher'-u-bims on the two ends thereof.

9 And the cher'-u-bims spread out *their* wings on high, *and* covered with their wings over the mercy seat, with their faces one to another; *even* to the mercy seatward were the faces of the cher'-u-bims.

The Table of Shewbread

10 And he made ᴿthe table *of* shit'-tim wood: ᵀtwo cubits *was* the length thereof, and a cubit the breadth thereof, and a cubit and a half the height thereof: 25:23 · 3 ft.

11 And he overlaid it with pure gold, and made thereunto a crownᵀ of gold round about. *rim*

12 Also he made thereunto a ᵀborder of an ᵀhandbreadth round about; and made a ᵀcrown of gold for the border thereof round about. *frame · 3 in. · rim*

13 And he cast for it four rings of gold, and put the rings upon the four corners that *were* in the four feet thereof.

14 Over against the border were the rings, the places for the staves to bear the table.

15 And he made the staves *of* shit'-tim wood, and overlaid them with gold, to bear the table.

16 And he made the vessels which *were* upon the table, his ᴿdishes, and his spoons, and his bowls, and his covers to cover ᵀwithal, *of* pure gold. 25:29 · *everything*

The Gold Candlestick

17 And he made the candlestick *of* pure gold: *of* beaten work made he the candlestick; his shaft, and his branch, his bowls, his knops, and his flowers, were of the same:

18 And six branches going out of the sides thereof; three branches of the candlestick out of the one side thereof, and three branches of the candlestick out of the other side thereof:

19 Three bowls made after the fashion of almonds in one branch, a knop and a flower; and three bowls made like ᵀalmonds in ᵀanother branch, a knop and a flower: so throughout the six branches going out of the candlestick. *almond blossoms · one*

20 And in the candlestick *were* four bowls made like almonds, his knops, and his flowers:

21 And a knop under two branches of the same, and a knop under two branches of the same, and a knop under two branches of the same, according to the six branches going out of it.

22 Their knops and their branches were of the same: all of it *was* one beaten work *of* pure gold.

23 And he made his seven lamps, and his snuffers, and his snuffdishes, *of* pure gold.

24 *Of* a ᵀtalent of pure gold made he it, and all the vessels thereof. *$5,760,000*

The Altar of Incense

25 And he made the incense altar *of* shit'-tim wood: the length of it *was* ᵀa cubit, and the breadth of it a cubit; *it was* foursquare; and ᵀtwo cubits *was* the height of it; the horns thereof were of the same. *18 in. · 3 ft.*

26 And he overlaid it with pure gold, *both* the top of it, and the sides thereof round about, and the horns of it: also he made unto it a crown of gold round about.

27 And he made two rings of gold for it under the crown thereof, by the two corners of it, upon the two sides thereof, to be places for the staves to bear it withal.

28 And he made the staves *of* shit'-tim wood, and overlaid them with gold.

29 And he made the holy anointing oil, and the pure incense of sweet spices, according to the work of the apothecary.

CHAPTER 38

The Altar of Burnt Offerings

AND he made the altar of burnt offering *of* shit'-tim wood: ᵀfive cubits *was* the length thereof, and five cubits the breadth thereof; *it was* foursquare; and ᵀthree cubits the height thereof. *7.5 ft. · 4.5 ft.*

2 And he made the horns thereof on the four corners of it; the horns thereof were of the same: and he overlaid it with brass.

3 And he made all the vessels of the altar, the pots, and the shovels, and the basons, *and* the fleshhooks, and the firepans: all the vessels thereof made he *of* brass.

4 And he made for the altar a brasen grate of network under the ᵀcompass thereof beneath unto the midst of it. *ledge*

5 And he cast four rings for the four ends of the grate of brass, *to be* places for the staves.

6 And he made the staves *of* shit'-tim wood, and overlaid them with brass.

7 And he put the staves into the rings on the sides of the altar, to bear it withal; he made the altar hollow with boards.

The Brass Laver

8 ᴿAnd he made the laver *of* brass, and the foot of it *of* brass, of the ᵀlookingglasses of *the women* assembling, which assembled *at* the door of the tabernacle of the congregation. *30:18 · mirrors of the ministering women*

The Court

9 And he made the court: on the south side southward the hangings of the court *were of* fine twined linen, an hundred cubits:

10 Their pillars were twenty, and their brasen sockets twenty; the hooks of the pillars and their fillets were of silver.

11 And for the north side the hangings were an hundred cubits, their pillars were twenty, and their sockets of brass twenty; the hooks of the pillars and their fillets of silver.

12 And for the west side were hangings of Tfifty cubits, their pillars ten, and their sockets ten; the hooks of the pillars and their Tfillets of silver.   75 ft. · bands

13 And for the east side eastward Tfifty cubits.   75 ft.

14 The hangings of the one side of the gate were Tfifteen cubits; their pillars three, and their sockets three.   22.5 ft.

15 And for the other side of the court gate, on this hand and that hand, were hangings of Tfifteen cubits; their pillars three, and their sockets three.   22.5 ft.

16 All the hangings of the court round about were of fine twined linen.

17 And the sockets for the pillars were of brass; the hooks of the pillars and their fillets of silver; and the overlaying of their Tchapiters of silver; and all the pillars of the court were Tfilleted with silver.   capitals · banded

18 And the hanging for the gate of the court was needlework, of blue, and purple, and scarlet, and fine twined linen: and Ttwenty cubits was the length, and the height in the breadth was Tfive cubits, answerable to the hangings of the court.   30 ft. · 7.5 ft.

19 And their pillars were four, and their sockets of brass four; their hooks of silver, and the overlaying of their Tchapiters and their Tfillets of silver.   capitals · bands

20 And all the pins of the tabernacle, and of the court round about, were of brass.

The Sum of the Materials

21 This is the sum of the tabernacle, even of the tabernacle of testimony, as it was counted, according to the commandment of Moses, for the service of the Levites, by the hand of Ith'-a-mar, son to Aaron the priest.

22 And RBe-zal'-e-el the son of U'-ri, the son of Hur, of the tribe of Judah, made all that the LORD commanded Moses.   31:2, 6

23 And with him was A-ho'-li-ab, son of A-his'-a-mach, of the tribe of Dan, Tan engraver, and Ta cunning workman, and an embroiderer in blue, and in purple, and in scarlet, and fine linen.   a craftsman · skillful

24 All the gold that was occupied for the work in all the work of the holy place, even the gold of the offering, was twenty and nine talents, and seven hundred and thirty shek'-els, after the shek'-el of the sanctuary.

25 And the silver of them that were numbered of the congregation was an Thundred talents, and a thousand seven hundred and

threescore and fifteen shek'-els, after the shek'-el of the sanctuary: $38,627,200

26 A be'-kah for every man, that is, Thalf a shek'-el, after the shek'-el of the sanctuary, for every one that went to be numbered, from twenty years old and upward, for six hundred thousand and three thousand and five hundred and fifty men. $64

27 And of the hundred talents of silver were cast the sockets of the sanctuary, and the sockets of the vail; an hundred sockets of the hundred talents, a talent for a socket.

28 And of the thousand seven hundred seventy and five shek'-els he made hooks for the pillars, and overlaid their Tchapiters, and Tfilleted them.   capitals · banded

29 And the brass of the offering was Tseventy talents, and two thousand and four hundred shek'-els.   5,323 lb.

30 And therewith he made the sockets to the door of the tabernacle of the congregation, and the brasen altar, and the brasen grate for it, and all the vessels of the altar,

31 And the sockets of the court round about, and the sockets of the court gate, and all the pins of the tabernacle, and all the pins of the court round about.

CHAPTER 39

The Garments for the Priests

AND of the blue, and purple, and scarlet, they made cloths of service, to do service in the holy place, and made the holy garments for Aaron; as the LORD commanded Moses.

2 And he made the e'-phod of gold, blue, and purple, and scarlet, and fine twined linen.

3 And they did beat the gold into thin plates, and cut it into wires, to work it in the blue, and in the purple, and in the scarlet, and in the fine linen, with cunning work.

4 They made shoulderpieces for it, to couple it together: by the two edges was it coupled together.

5 And the curious girdle of his e'-phod, that was upon it, was of the same, according to the work thereof; of gold, blue, and purple, and scarlet, and fine twined linen; as the LORD commanded Moses.

6 RAnd they wrought onyx stones inclosed in Touches of gold, graven, as signets are graven, with the names of the children of Israel.   28:9 · settings

7 And he put them on the shoulders of the e'-phod, that they should be stones for a Rmemorial to the children of Israel; as the LORD commanded Moses.   28:12

8 RAnd he made the breastplate of cunning work, like the work of the e'-phod; of gold, blue, and purple, and scarlet, and fine twined linen.   28:15-28

9 It was foursquare; they made the breastplate double: a ᵀspan *was* the length thereof, and a span the breadth thereof, *being* doubled.   *9 in.*

10 And they set in it four rows of stones: *the first* row *was* a ᵀsardius, a topaz, and a carbuncle: this *was* the first row.   *ruby*

11 And the second row, an emerald, a sapphire, and a diamond.

12 And the third row, a ᵀligure, an agate, and an amethyst.   *jacinth*

13 And the fourth row, a beryl, an onyx, and a jasper: *they were* inclosed in ᵀouches of gold in their inclosings.   *settings*

14 And the stones *were* according to the names of the children of Israel, ᴿtwelve, according to their names, *like* the engravings of a signet, every one with his name, according to the twelve tribes.   *Rev. 21:12*

15 And they made upon the breastplate chains ᵀat the ends, *of* ᵀwreathen work *of* pure gold.   *twisted · like cords*

16 And they made two ᵀouches *of* gold, and two gold rings; and put the two rings in the two ends of the breastplate.   *settings*

17 And they put the two ᵀwreathen chains of gold in the two rings on the ends of the breastplate.   *braided*

18 And the two ends of the two wreathen chains they fastened in the two ᵀouches, and put them on the shoulderpieces of the e′-phod, before it.   *settings*

19 And they made two rings of gold, and put *them* on the two ends of the breastplate, upon the border of it, which *was* on the side of the e′-phod inward.

20 And they made two *other* golden rings, and put them on the two sides of the e′-phod underneath, toward the forepart of it, over against the *other* coupling thereof, above the curious girdle of the e′-phod.

21 And they did bind the breastplate by his rings unto the rings of the e′-phod with a lace of blue, that it might be above the curious girdle of the e′-phod, and that the breastplate might not be loosed from the e′-phod; as the LORD commanded Moses.

22 ᴿAnd he made the robe of the e′-phod *of* woven work, all *of* blue.   *28:31-34*

23 And *there was* an hole in the midst of the robe, as the hole of an habergeon, *with* a band round about the hole, that it should not rend.

24 And they made upon the hems of the robe pomegranates *of* blue, and purple, and scarlet, *and* twined *linen*.

25 And they made ᴿbells *of* pure gold, and put the bells between the pomegranates upon the hem of the robe, round about between the pomegranates;   *28:33*

26 A bell and a pomegranate, a bell and a pomegranate, round about the hem of the

robe to ᵀminister *in;* as the LORD commanded Moses.   *serve*

27 And they made coats *of* fine linen *of* woven work for Aaron, and for his sons,

28 ᴿAnd a mitre *of* fine linen, and goodly bonnets *of* fine linen, and ᴿlinen breeches *of* fine twined linen,   *Ezek. 44:18 · 28:42*

29 And a girdle *of* fine twined linen, and blue, and purple, and scarlet, *of* needlework; as the LORD commanded Moses.

30 ᴿAnd they made the plate of the holy crown *of* pure gold, and wrote upon it a writing, *like* to the engravings of a signet, HOLINESS TO THE LORD.   *28:36, 37*

31 And they tied unto it a lace of blue, to fasten *it* on high upon the mitre; as the LORD commanded Moses.

The Tabernacle Is Inspected by Moses

32 Thus was all the work of the tabernacle of the tent of the congregation finished: and the children of Israel did ᴿaccording to all that the LORD commanded Moses, so did they.   *vv. 42, 43; 25:40*

33 And they brought the tabernacle unto Moses, the tent, and all his furniture, ᵀhis taches, his boards, his bars, and his pillars, and his sockets,   *its clasps*

34 And the covering of rams' skins dyed red, and the covering of ᵀbadgers' skins, and the vail of the ᵀcovering,   *seals · screen*

35 The ark of the testimony, and the staves thereof, and the mercy seat,

36 The table, *and* all the vessels thereof, and the ᵀshewbread,   *bread of the presence*

37 The pure candlestick, *with* the lamps thereof, *even with* the lamps to be set in order, and all the vessels thereof, and the oil for light,

38 And the golden altar, and the anointing oil, and ᵀthe sweet incense, and the hanging for the tabernacle door,   *sweet spices*

39 The brasen altar, and his grate of brass, his staves, and all his vessels, the laver and ᵀhis foot,   *its stand*

40 The hangings of the court, his pillars, and his sockets, and the hanging for the court gate, his cords, and his pins, and all the vessels of the service of the tabernacle, for the tent of the congregation,

41 The cloths of service to do service in the holy *place*, and the holy garments for Aaron the priest, and his sons' garments, to ᵀminister in the priest's office.   *serve*

42 According to all that the LORD commanded Moses, so the children of Israel ᴿmade all the work.   *35:10*

43 And Moses did look upon all the work, and, behold, they had done it as the LORD had commanded, even so had they done it: and Moses ᴿblessed them.   *Lev. 9:22, 23*

CHAPTER 40

The Tabernacle Is Erected

A ND the LORD spake unto Moses, saying,
2 On the first day of the Rfirst month
shalt thou set up Rthe tabernacle of the tent
of the congregation.   12:2; 13:4 · 26:1, 30
3 And Rthou shalt put therein the ark of
the Ttestimony, and Tcover the ark with the
vail.   v. 21; 26:33 · tables of law · screen
4 And thou shalt bring in the table, and set
in order the things that are to be set in order
upon it; and thou shalt bring in the candlestick, and light the lamps thereof.
5 RAnd thou shalt set the altar of gold for
the incense before the ark of the testimony,
and put the Thanging of the door to the
tabernacle.   v. 26 · veil
6 And thou shalt set the altar of the burnt
offering before the door of the tabernacle of
the tent of the congregation.
7 And Rthou shalt set the laver between
the tent of the congregation and the altar,
and shalt put water therein.   v. 30; 30:18
8 And thou shalt set up the court round
about, and hang up the Thanging at the court
gate.   veil
9 And thou shalt take the anointing oil,
and Ranoint the tabernacle, and all that is
therein, and shalt hallow it, and all the vessels thereof: and it shall be holy.   30:26
10 And thou shalt anoint the altar of the
burnt offering, and all his vessels, and Tsanctify the altar: and it shall be an altar Tmost
holy.   set it apart · exclusively for God
11 And thou shalt anoint the laver and This
foot, and sanctify it.   its stand
12 And thou shalt bring Aaron and his
sons unto the door of the tabernacle of the
congregation, and wash them with water.
13 And thou shalt put upon Aaron the holy
garments, Rand anoint him, and sanctify him;
that he may minister unto me in the priest's
office.   28:41; 39:1, 41
14 And thou shalt bring his sons, and
clothe them with coats:
15 And thou shalt anoint them, as thou
didst anoint their father, that they may
minister unto me in the priest's office: for
their anointing shall surely be an everlasting
priesthood throughout their generations.
16 Thus did Moses: according to all that
the LORD commanded him, so did he.
17 And it came to pass in the first month in
the second year, on the first day of the
month, that the tabernacle was reared up.
18 And Moses reared up the tabernacle,
and fastened his sockets, and set up the
boards thereof, and put in the bars thereof,
and reared up his pillars.
19 And he spread abroad the tent over the
tabernacle, and put the covering of the tent

above upon it; as the LORD commanded Moses.
20 And he took and put the testimony into
the ark, and set the staves on the ark, and put
the mercy seat above upon the ark:
21 And he brought the ark into the tabernacle, and Rset up the vail of the covering,
and covered the ark of the testimony; as the
LORD commanded Moses.   26:33
22 RAnd he put the table in the tent of the
congregation, upon the side of the tabernacle
northward, without the vail.   26:35
23 RAnd he set the Rbread in order upon it
before the LORD; as the LORD had commanded Moses.   v. 4 · Lev. 24:5, 6
24 RAnd he put the candlestick in the tent
of the congregation, over against the table,
on the side of the tabernacle southward. 26:35
25 And he lighted the lamps before the
LORD; as the LORD commanded Moses.
26 And he put the golden altar in the tent
of the congregation before the vail:
27 RAnd he burnt sweet incense thereon;
as the LORD commanded Moses.   30:7
28 RAnd he set up the hanging at the door
of the tabernacle.   v. 5; 26:36
29 And he put the altar of burnt offering
by the door of the tabernacle of the tent of
the congregation, and Roffered upon it the
burnt offering and the meat offering; as the
LORD commanded Moses.   29:38
30 RAnd he set the laver between the tent
of the congregation and the altar, and put
water there, to wash withal.   v. 7; 30:18
31 And Moses and Aaron and his sons
washed their hands and their feet thereat:
32 When they went into the tent of the
congregation, and when they came near unto
the altar, they washed; Ras the LORD commanded Moses.   30:19
33 RAnd he reared up the court round
about the tabernacle and the altar, and set up
the hanging of the court gate. So Moses
finished the work.   v. 8; 27:9, 16

God Fills the Tabernacle with His Glory

34 Then Ra cloud covered the tent of the
congregation, and the glory of the LORD filled
the tabernacle.   Num. 9:15; 2 Chr. 5:13
35 And Moses Rwas not able to enter into
the tent of the congregation, because the
cloud abode thereon, and the glory of the
LORD filled the tabernacle. [Lev. 16:2]; 1 Kin. 8:11
36 And when the cloud was taken up from
over the tabernacle, the children of Israel
went onward in all their journeys:
37 But Rif the cloud were not taken up,
then they journeyed not till the day that it
was taken up.   Num. 9:19-22
38 For the cloud of the LORD was upon the
tabernacle by day, and Rfire was on it by
night, in the sight of all the house of Israel,
throughout all their journeys.   Neh. 9:12

THE THIRD BOOK OF MOSES, CALLED

LEVITICUS

📖 **THE BOOK OF LEVITICUS**
Leviticus is God's guidebook for His newly redeemed people, showing them how to worship, serve, and obey a holy God. Fellowship with God through sacrifice and obedience show the awesome holiness of the God of Israel. Indeed, "Ye shall be holy: for I the LORD your God am holy" (19:2).

Leviticus focuses on the worship and walk of the nation of God. In Exodus, Israel was redeemed and established as a kingdom of priests and a holy nation. Leviticus shows how God's people are to fulfill their priestly calling.

The Hebrew title is *Wayyiqra*, "And He Called." The Talmud refers to Leviticus as the "Law of the Priests," and the "Law of the Offerings." The Greek title appearing in the Septuagint is *Leuitikon*, "That Which Pertains to the Levites." From this word, the Latin Vulgate derived its name *Leviticus* which was adopted as the English title. This title is slightly misleading because the book does not deal with the Levites as a whole but more with the priests, a segment of the Levites.

✍️ **THE AUTHOR OF LEVITICUS**
The kind of arguments used to confirm the Mosaic authorship of Genesis and Exodus also apply to Leviticus because the Pentateuch is a literary unit. In addition to these arguments, others include the following:

External Evidence: (1) A uniform ancient testimony supports the Mosaic authorship of Leviticus. (2) Ancient parallels to the Levitical system of trespass offerings have been found in the Ras Shamra Tablets dating from about 1400 B.C. and discovered on the coast of northern Syria. (3) Christ ascribes the Pentateuch (which includes Leviticus) to Moses (cf. Matt. 8:2–4 and Lev. 14:1–4; Matt. 12:4 and Lev. 24:9; see also Luke 2:22).

Internal Evidence: (1) Fifty-six times in the twenty-seven chapters of Leviticus it is stated that God imparted these laws to Moses (see 1:1; 4:1; 6:1, 24; 8:1). (2) The Levitical Code fits the time of Moses. Economic, civil, moral, and religious considerations show it to be ancient. Many of the laws are also related to a migratory life-style.

⏳ **THE TIME OF LEVITICUS**
No geographical movement takes place in Leviticus: the children of Israel remain camped at the foot of Mount Sinai (25:1, 2; 26:46; 27:34). The new calendar of Israel begins with the first Passover (Ex. 12:2); and, according to

Exodus 40:17, the tabernacle is completed exactly one year later.

Leviticus picks up the story at this point and takes place in the first month of the second year. Numbers 1:1 opens at the beginning of the second month. Moses probably wrote much of Leviticus during that first month and may have put it in its final form shortly before his death in Moab, about 1405 B.C.

✝️ **THE CHRIST OF LEVITICUS**
The Book of Leviticus is replete with figures and allusions to the person and work of Jesus Christ. Some of the more important include: (1) *The five offerings:* The burnt offering pictures Christ's total offering in submission to His Father's will. The meat offering pictures Christ's sinless service. The peace offering is a figure of the fellowship believers have with God through the work of the cross. The sin offering pictures Christ as our guilt-bearer. The trespass offering pictures Christ's payment for the damage of sin. (2) *The high priest:* There are several comparisons and contrasts between Aaron, the first high priest, and Christ, our eternal high priest. (3) *The seven feasts:* Passover speaks of the substitutionary death of the Lamb of God. Christ died on the day of Passover. Unleavened Bread speaks of the holy walk of the believer (1 Cor. 5:6–8). Firstfruits speaks of Christ's resurrection as the firstfruits of the resurrection of all believers (1 Cor. 15:20–23). Christ rose on the day of Firstfruits. Pentecost speaks of the descent of the Holy Spirit after Christ's ascension. Trumpets, the Day of Atonement, and Tabernacles speak of events associated with the second advent of Christ. This may be why these three are separated by a long gap from the first four in Israel's annual cycle.

🔑 **KEYS TO LEVITICUS**
Key Word: Holiness—Leviticus centers around the concept of the holiness of God, and how an unholy people can acceptably approach Him and then remain in continued fellowship. The way to God is only through blood sacrifice, and the walk with God is only through obedience to His laws.

Key Verses: Leviticus 17:11; 20:7, 8—"For the life of the flesh *is* in the blood: and I have given it to you upon the altar to make an atonement for your souls: for it *is* the blood *that* maketh an atonement for the soul" (17:11).

"Sanctify yourselves therefore, and be ye holy: for I *am* the LORD your God. And ye shall keep

my statutes, and do them: I *am* the LORD which sanctify you" (20:7, 8).

Key Chapter: Leviticus 16—The Day of Atonement (*"Yom Kippur"*) was the most important single day in the Hebrew calendar as it was the only day the high priest entered into the Holy of Holies to "make an atonement for you, to cleanse you, *that* ye may be clean from all your sins before the LORD" (16:30).

SURVEY OF LEVITICUS

It has been said that it took God only one night to get Israel out of Egypt, but it took forty years to get Egypt out of Israel. In Exodus, Israel is redeemed and established as a kingdom of priests and a holy nation; and in Leviticus, Israel is taught how to fulfill their priestly call. They have been led out from the land of bondage in Exodus and into the sanctuary of God in Leviticus. They move from redemption to service, from deliverance to dedication. This book serves as a handbook for the Levitical priesthood, giving instructions and regulations for worship. Used to guide a newly redeemed people into worship, service, and obedience to God, Leviticus falls into two major sections: (1) sacrifice (1—17), and (2) sanctification (18—27).

Sacrifice (1—17): This section teaches that God must be approached by the sacrificial offerings (1—7), by the mediation of the priesthood (8—10), by the purification of the nation from uncleanness (11—15), and by the provision for national cleansing and fellowship (16 and 17). The blood sacrifices remind the worshipers that because of sin the holy God requires the costly gift of life (17:11). The blood of the innocent sacrificial animal becomes the substitute for the life of the guilty offerer: "without shedding of blood is no remission" (Heb. 9:22).

Sanctification (18—27): The Israelites serve a holy God who requires them to be holy as well. To be holy means to be "set apart" or "separated." They are to be separated *from* other nations *unto* God. In Leviticus the idea of holiness appears eighty-seven times, sometimes indicating ceremonial holiness (ritual requirements), and at other times moral holiness (purity of life). This sanctification extends to the people of Israel (18—20), the priesthood (21 and 22), their worship (23 and 24), their life in Canaan (25 and 26), and their special vows (27). It is necessary to remove the defilement that separates the people from God so that they can have a walk of fellowship with their Redeemer.

FOCUS	SACRIFICE				SANCTIFICATION				
REFERENCE	1:1——8:1————11:1———			16:1——18:1——21:1——		23:1————	25:1——		27:1——27:34
DIVISION	THE LAWS OF				THE LAWS OF SANCTIFICATION				
	THE OFFERINGS	CONSECRATION OF THE PRIESTS	CONSECRATION OF THE PEOPLE	NATIONAL ATONEMENT	FOR THE PEOPLE	FOR THE PRIESTS	IN WORSHIP	IN THE LAND OF CANAAN	THROUGH VOWS
TOPIC	THE WAY TO GOD				THE WALK WITH GOD				
	THE LAWS OF ACCEPTABLE APPROACH TO GOD				THE LAWS OF CONTINUED FELLOWSHIP WITH GOD				
LOCATION	MOUNT SINAI								
TIME	c. 1 MONTH								

OUTLINE OF LEVITICUS

Part One: The Laws of Acceptable Approach to God: Sacrifice (1:1—17:16)

Part Two: The Laws of Acceptable Walk with God: Sanctification (18:1—27:34)

CHAPTER 1

The Burnt Offering

AND the LORD ᴿcalled unto Moses, and spake unto him ᴿout of the tabernacle of the congregation, saying,   Ex. 19:3 · Ex. 40:34

2 Speak unto the children of Israel, and say unto them, ᴿIf any man of you bring an offering unto the LORD, ye shall bring your offering of the cattle, ᴿeven of the herd, and of the flock.   22:18, 19; Mark 7:11 · 22:19

3 If his offering be a burnt sacrifice of the herd, let him offer a male ᴿwithout blemish: he shall offer it of his own voluntary will at the door of the tabernacle of the congregation before the LORD.   Deut. 15:21

4 And he shall put his hand upon the head of the burnt offering; and it shall be accepted for him to make atonement for him.

5 And he shall kill the bullock before the LORD: and the priests, Aaron's sons, shall bring the blood, and sprinkle the blood round about upon the altar that is by the door of the tabernacle of the congregation.

6 ᴿAnd he shall ᵀflay the burnt offering, and cut it into his pieces.   7:8 · skin

7 ᴿAnd the sons of Aaron the priest shall put fire upon the altar, and ᴿlay the wood in order upon the fire: 6:8–13 · Gen. 22:9

8 ᴿAnd the priests, Aaron's sons, shall lay the parts, the head, and the fat, in order upon the wood that is on the fire which is upon the altar: 3:3, 4; 7:23, 24

9 But his inwards and his legs shall he wash in water: and the priest shall burn all on the altar, to be a burnt sacrifice, an offering made by fire, of a ᴿsweetᵀ savour unto the LORD.   [Ezek. 20:28, 41; 2 Cor. 2:15] · pleasing

10 And if his offering be of the flocks, namely, of the sheep, or of the goats, for a burnt sacrifice; he shall bring it a male ᴿwithout blemish.   v. 3

11 ᴿAnd he shall kill it on the side of the altar northward before the LORD: and the priests, Aaron's sons, shall sprinkle his blood round about upon the altar.   Ex. 40:22

12 And he shall cut it into his pieces, with his head and his fat: and the priest shall lay them in order on the wood that is on the fire which is upon the altar:

13 But he shall wash the inwards and the legs with water: and the priest shall bring it all, and burn it upon the altar: it is a burnt sacrifice, an offering made by fire, of a sweet savour unto the LORD.

14 And if the burnt sacrifice for his offering to the LORD be of fowls, then he shall bring his offering of ᴿturtledoves, or of young pigeons.   5:7; Gen. 15:9

15 And the priest shall bring it unto the altar, and wring off his head, and burn it on the altar; and the blood thereof shall be wrung out ᴿat the side of the altar: 5:9

16 And he shall pluck away his crop with his feathers, and cast it beside the altar on the east part, by the place of the ashes:

17 And he shall cleave it with the wings thereof, but ᴿshall not divide it asunder: and the priest shall burn it upon the altar, upon the wood that is upon the fire: it is a burnt sacrifice, an offering made by fire, of a sweet savour unto the LORD.   Gen. 15:10

CHAPTER 2

The Meat Offering

AND when any will offer a ᵀmeat ᴿoffering unto the LORD, his offering shall be of fine flour; and he shall pour oil upon it, and put frankincense thereon: meal · 6:14

2 And he shall bring it to Aaron's sons the priests: and he shall take thereout his handful of the flour thereof, and of the oil thereof, with all the frankincense thereof; and the priest shall burn ᴿthe memorial of it upon the altar, to be an offering made by fire, of a sweet savour unto the LORD: v. 9

3 And the remnant of the meat offering shall be Aaron's and his sons': ᴿit is a thing most ᵀholy of the offerings of the LORD made by fire.   Num. 18:9 · to be used only for this

4 And if thou bring an oblation of a meat offering baken in the oven, it shall be unleav-

ened cakes of fine flour mingled with oil, or unleavened wafers ᵀanointed with oil.   *spread*

5 And if thy oblation *be* a meat offering *baken* in a ᵀpan, it shall be *of* fine flour unleavened, mingled with oil.   *flat plate*

6 Thou shalt part it in pieces, and pour oil thereon: it *is* a meat offering.

7 And if thy oblation *be* a ᵀmeat offering *baken* in the ᴿfryingpan, it shall be made *of* fine flour with oil.   *meal • 7:9*

8 And thou shalt bring the meat offering that is made of these things unto the LORD: and when it is presented unto the priest, he shall bring it unto the altar.

9 And the priest shall take from the meat offering a memorial thereof, and shall burn *it* upon the altar: *it is* an ᴿoffering made by fire, of a sweet savour unto the LORD.   Ex. 29:18

10 And that which is left of the ᵀmeat offering *shall be* Aaron's and his sons': *it is* a thing most holy of the offerings of the LORD made by fire.   *meal*

11 No meat offering, which ye shall bring unto the LORD, shall be made with leaven: for ye shall burn no leaven, nor any honey, in any offering of the LORD made by fire.

12 ᴿAs for the ᵀoblation of the firstfruits, ye shall offer them unto the LORD: but they shall not be burnt on the altar for a sweet savour.   23:10, 11; Ex. 7:13; 22:29 • *offering*

13 And every oblation of thy meat offering shalt thou season with salt; neither shalt thou suffer the salt of the covenant of thy God to be lacking from thy meat offering: with all thine offerings thou shalt offer salt.

14 And if thou offer a meat offering of thy firstfruits unto the LORD, ᴿthou shalt offer for the meat offering of thy firstfruits green ears of corn dried by the fire, *even* corn beaten out of ᴿfull ears.   23:10, 14 • 2 Kin. 4:42

15 And ᴿthou shalt put oil upon it, and lay frankincense thereon: it *is* a meat offering. *v. 1*

16 And the priest shall burn ᴿthe ᵀmemorial of it, *part* of the beaten corn thereof, and *part* of the oil thereof, with all the frankincense thereof: *it is* an offering made by fire unto the LORD.   *v. 2 • token part*

CHAPTER 3

The Peace Offering

AND if his oblation *be* a sacrifice of peace offering, if he offer *it* of the herd; whether *it be* a male or female, he shall offer it without blemish before the LORD.

2 And ᴿhe shall lay his hand upon the head of his offering, and kill it *at* the door of the tabernacle of the congregation: and Aaron's sons the priests shall sprinkle the blood upon the altar round about.   Ex. 29:10

3 And he shall offer of the sacrifice of the peace offering an offering made by fire unto the LORD; ᴿthe ᵀfat that covereth the inwards, and all the fat that *is* upon the ᵀinwards,   4:8, 9; Ex. 29:13, 22 • *suet • entrails*

4 And the two kidneys, and the fat that *is* on them, which *is* by the ᵀflanks, and the ᵀcaul above the liver, with the kidneys, it shall he take away.   *loins • appendage of*

5 And Aaron's sons ᴿshall burn it on the altar upon the burnt sacrifice, which *is* upon the wood that *is* on the ᴿfire: *it is* an offering made by fire, ᴿof a sweet savour unto the LORD.   Ex. 29:13 • 6:12 • Num. 15:8–10

6 And if his offering for a sacrifice of peace offering unto the LORD *be* of the flock; male or female, he shall offer it without blemish.

7 If he offer ᴿa lamb for his offering, then shall he offer it before the LORD.   Num. 15:4, 5

8 ᴿAnd he shall lay his hand upon the head of his offering, ᴿand kill it before the tabernacle of the congregation: and Aaron's sons shall sprinkle the blood thereof round about upon the altar.   1:4 • *v. 2*

9 And he shall offer of the sacrifice of the peace offering an offering made by fire unto the LORD; the fat thereof, *and* the whole rump, it shall he take off ᵀhard by the backbone; and the fat that covereth the inwards, and all the fat that *is* upon the ᵀinwards,   *near • entrails*

10 And the two kidneys, and the fat that *is* upon them, which *is* by the flanks, and the caul above the liver, with the kidneys, it shall he take away.

11 And the priest shall burn it upon the altar: *it is* ᴿthe food of the offering made by fire unto the LORD.   [Ezek. 44:7; Mal. 1:7, 12]

12 And if his offering *be* a goat, then ᴿhe shall offer it before the LORD.   *vv. 1, 7*

13 And he shall lay his hand upon the head of it, and kill it before the tabernacle of the congregation: and the sons of Aaron shall sprinkle the blood thereof upon the altar round about.

14 And he shall offer thereof his offering, *even* an offering made by fire unto the LORD; the fat that covereth the inwards, and all the fat that *is* upon the inwards,

15 And the two kidneys, and the fat that *is* upon them, which *is* by the flanks, and the ᵀcaul above the liver, with the kidneys, it shall he take away.   *fat*

16 And the priest shall burn them upon the altar: *it is* the food of the offering made by fire for a sweet savour: ᴿall the fat *is* the LORD'S.   7:23, 25; 1 Sam. 2:15; 2 Chr. 7:7

17 *It shall be* a perpetual statute for your generations throughout all your dwellings, that ye eat neither fat nor blood.

CHAPTER 4

The Sin Offering

AND the LORD spake unto Moses, saying, 2 Speak unto the children of Israel, saying, If a soul shall sin through ignorance against any of the commandments of the LORD concerning things which ought not to be done, and shall do against any of them: 3 ᴿIf the priest that is ᵀanointed do sin according to the sin of the people; then let him bring for his sin, which he hath sinned, a young bullock without blemish unto the LORD for a sin offering.   8:12 · installed in office

4 And he shall bring the bullock ᴿunto the door of the tabernacle of the congregation ᵀbefore the LORD; and shall lay his hand upon the bullock's head, and kill the bullock before the LORD.   1:3, 4 · as unto the LORD

5 And the priest that is anointed ᴿshall take of the bullock's blood, and bring it to the tabernacle of the congregation: 16:14

6 And the priest shall dip his finger in the blood, and sprinkle of the blood seven times before the LORD, before the ᴿvail of the sanctuary.   Ex. 40:21, 26

7 And the priest shall ᴿput some of the blood upon the horns of the altar of sweet incense before the LORD, which is in the tabernacle of the congregation; and shall pour ᴿall the blood of the bullock at the bottom of the altar of the burnt offering, which is at the door of the tabernacle of the congregation.   8:15; 9:9; 16:18 · 5:9

8 ᴿAnd he shall take off from it all the fat of the bullock for the sin offering; the fat that covereth the inwards, and all the fat that is upon the inwards,   3:3, 4

9 And the two kidneys, and the fat that is upon them, which is by the ᵀflanks, and the ᵀcaul above the liver, with the kidneys, it shall he take away,   loins · fat

10 ᴿAs it was taken off from the bullock of the sacrifice of peace offerings: and the priest shall burn them upon the altar of the burnt offering.   3:3–5

11 ᴿAnd the skin of the bullock, and all his flesh, with his head, and with his legs, and his inwards, and his dung,   Ex. 29:14

12 Even the whole bullock shall he carry forth without the camp unto a clean place, where the ashes are poured out, and burn him on the wood with fire: where the ashes are poured out shall he be burnt.

13 And if the whole congregation of Israel sin through ignorance, and the thing be hid from the eyes of the assembly, and they have done somewhat against any of the commandments of the LORD concerning things which should not be done, and are guilty;

14 When the sin, which they have sinned against it, is ᵀknown, then the congregation shall offer a young bullock for the sin, and bring him before the tabernacle of the congregation.   when it is brought to their attention

15 And the elders of the congregation ᴿshall lay their hands upon the head of the bullock before the LORD: and the bullock shall be killed before the LORD.   1:4

16 ᴿAnd the priest that is anointed shall bring of the bullock's blood to the tabernacle of the congregation: [v. 5; Heb. 9:12–14]

17 And the priest shall dip his finger in some of the blood, and sprinkle it seven times before the LORD, even before the vail.

18 And he shall put some of the blood upon the horns of the altar which is before the LORD, that is in the tabernacle of the congregation, and shall pour out all the blood at the bottom of the altar of the burnt offering, which is at the door of the tabernacle of the congregation.

19 ᴿAnd he shall take all his fat from him, and burn it upon the altar.   v. 8

20 And he shall do with the bullock as he did with the bullock for a sin offering, so shall he do with this: ᴿand the priest shall make ᵀan atonement for them, and it shall be forgiven them.   Num. 9:5 · a reconciliation

21 And he shall carry forth the bullock ᵀwithout the camp, and burn him as he burned the first bullock: ᴿit is a sin offering for the congregation.   outside · Num. 15:24–26

22 When ᵀa ruler hath sinned, and ᴿdone somewhat through ignorance against any of the commandments of the LORD his God concerning things which should not be done, and is guilty;   any official · vv. 2, 13

23 Or ᴿif his sin, wherein he hath sinned, ᵀcome to his knowledge; he shall bring his offering, a kid of the goats, a male without blemish: 5:4 · is recognized by him to be wrong

24 And ᴿhe shall lay his hand upon the head of the goat, and kill it in the place where they kill the burnt offering before the LORD: it is a sin offering.   [v. 4; Is. 53:6]

25 ᴿAnd the priest shall take of the blood of the sin offering with his finger, and put it upon the horns of the altar of burnt offering, and shall pour out his blood at the bottom of the altar of burnt offering.   v. 30

26 ᴿAnd he shall burn all his fat upon the altar, as the fat of the sacrifice of peace offerings: ᴿand the priest shall make an atonement for him as concerning his sin, and it shall be forgiven him.   v. 19 · Num. 15:28

27 And ᴿif any one of the common people sin through ignorance, while he doeth somewhat against any of the commandments of the LORD concerning things which ought not to be done, and be guilty;   v. 2

28 Or ᴿif his sin, which he hath sinned, come to his knowledge: then he shall bring his offering, a kid of the goats, a female without blemish, for his sin which he hath sinned.   vv. 3, 14, 23, 32

29 And he shall lay his hand upon the head of the sin offering, and slay the sin offering in the place of the burnt offering.

30 And the priest shall take of the blood thereof with his finger, and put *it* upon the horns of the ᴿaltar of burnt offering, and shall pour out all the blood thereof at the bottom of the altar.   *vv.* 7, 18, 25, 34

31 And he shall take away all the fat thereof, ᴿas the fat is taken away from off the sacrifice of peace offerings; and the priest shall burn *it* upon the altar for a ᴿsweet savour unto the LORD; and ᴿthe priest shall make an atonement for him, and it shall be forgiven him.   3:3 • Gen. 8:21 • *v.* 26

32 And if he bring a lamb for a sin offering, he shall bring it a female without blemish.

33 ᴿAnd he shall lay his hand upon the head of the sin offering, and slay it for a sin offering in the place where they kill the burnt offering.   1:4

34 And the priest shall take of the blood of the sin offering with his finger, and put *it* upon the horns of the altar of burnt offering, and shall pour out all the blood thereof at the bottom of the altar:

35 And he shall take away all the fat thereof, as the fat of the lamb is taken away from the sacrifice of the peace offerings; and the priest shall burn them upon the altar, according to the offerings made by fire unto the LORD: and the priest shall make an atonement for his sin that he hath committed, and it shall be forgiven him.

CHAPTER 5

AND if a soul sin, and hear the voice of swearing, and *is* a witness, whether he hath seen or known *of it*; if he do not utter *it*, then he shall bear his iniquity.

2 Or ᴿif a soul touch any unclean thing, whether *it be* a carcase of an unclean beast, or a carcase of unclean cattle, or the carcase of unclean creeping things, and *if* it be hidden from him; he also shall be ᵀunclean, and ᴿguilty.   Num. 19:11, 13, 16 • *unfit • v.* 17

3 Or if he touch ᴿthe uncleanness of man, whatsoever uncleanness *it be* that a man shall be defiled withal, and ᵀit be hid from him; when he knoweth *of it*, then he shall be guilty.   chs. 12; 13; 15 • *unaware*

4 Or if a soul swear, pronouncing with *his* lips to do evil, or to do good, whatsoever *it be* that a man shall pronounce with an oath, and it be hid from him; when he knoweth *of it*, then he shall be guilty in one of these.

5 And it shall be, when he shall be guilty in one of these *things*, that he shall ᴿconfess that he hath sinned in that *thing*:   Num. 5:7

6 And he shall bring his ᵀtrespass offering

unto the LORD for his sin which he hath sinned, a ᴿfemale from the flock, a lamb or a kid of the goats, for a sin offering; and the priest shall make an atonement for him concerning his sin.   guilt • 4:28, 32

7 And if he be not able to bring a lamb, then he shall bring for his trespass, which he hath committed, two turtledoves, or two young pigeons, unto the LORD; one for a sin offering, and the other for a burnt offering.

8 And he shall bring them unto the priest, who shall offer *that* which *is* for the sin offering first, and wring off his head from his neck, but shall not divide *it* asunder:

9 And he shall sprinkle of the blood of the sin offering upon the side of the altar; and the rest of the blood shall be wrung out at the bottom of the altar: it *is* a sin offering.

10 And he shall offer the second *for* a burnt offering, according to the ᵀmanner: and ᴿthe priest shall make an atonement for him for his sin which he hath sinned, and it shall be forgiven him.   ordinance • 4:26

11 But if he be not able to bring two turtledoves, or two young pigeons, then he that sinned shall bring for his offering the ᵀtenth part of an e′-phah of fine flour for a sin offering; ᴿhe shall put no oil upon it, neither shall he put *any* frankincense thereon: for it *is* a sin offering.   2.087 qt. • Num. 5:15

12 Then shall he bring it to the priest, and the priest shall take his handful of it, *even* a memorial thereof, and burn *it* on the altar, according to the offerings made by fire unto the LORD: it *is* a sin offering.

13 ᴿAnd the priest shall make an atonement for him as touching his sin that he hath sinned in one of these, and it shall be forgiven him: and the remnant shall be the priest's, as a meat offering.   4:26

The Trespass Offering

14 And the LORD spake unto Moses, saying,

15 If a soul commit a trespass, and sin through ignorance, in the holy things of the LORD; then he shall bring for his trespass unto the LORD a ram without blemish out of the flocks, with thy estimation by shek′-els of silver, after ᴿthe shek′-el of the sanctuary, for a trespass offering: 27:25

16 And he shall make amends for the harm that he hath done in the holy thing, and shall add the fifth part thereto, and give it unto the priest: and the priest shall make an atonement for him with the ram of the trespass offering, and it shall be forgiven him.

17 And if a soul sin, and commit any of these things which are forbidden to be done by the commandments of the LORD; though he ᵀwist *it* not, yet is he guilty, and shall ᵀbear his iniquity.   *knew • responsibility*

18 [R]And he shall bring a ram without blemish out of the flock, with thy [T]estimation, for a trespass offering, unto the priest: and the priest shall make an atonement for him concerning his ignorance wherein he erred and [T]wist it not, and it shall be forgiven him.   *v. 15 • valuation • knew*

19 It is a trespass offering: he hath certainly trespassed against the LORD.

CHAPTER 6

AND the LORD spake unto Moses, saying, 2 If a soul sin, and commit a trespass against the LORD, and lie unto his neighbour in that which was delivered him to keep, or in fellowship, or in a thing taken away by violence, or hath deceived his neighbour;

3 Or [R]have found that which was lost, and lieth concerning it, and [R]sweareth falsely; in any of all these that a man doeth, sinning therein: *Deut. 22:1–3 • Jer. 7:9; Zech. 5:4*

4 Then it shall be, because he hath sinned, and is [T]guilty, that he shall [T]restore that which he took violently away, or the thing which he hath deceitfully gotten, or that which was delivered him to keep, or the lost thing which he found,   *responsible • pay for*

5 Or all that about which he hath sworn falsely; he shall even restore it in the principal, and shall add the fifth part more thereto, and give it unto him to whom it appertaineth, in the day of his trespass offering.

6 And he shall bring his trespass offering unto the LORD, [R]a ram without blemish out of the flock, with thy estimation, for a trespass offering, unto the priest: 5:15

7 [R]And the priest shall make an atonement for him before the LORD: and it shall be forgiven him for any thing of all that he hath done in trespassing therein.   4:26

The Burnt Offering

8 And the LORD spake unto Moses, saying, 9 Command Aaron and his sons, saying, This is the law of the burnt offering: It is the burnt offering, because of the burning upon the altar all night unto the morning, and the fire of the altar shall be burning in it.

10 [R]And the priest shall put on his linen garment, and his linen breeches shall he put upon his flesh, and take up the ashes which the fire hath consumed with the burnt offering on the altar, and he shall put them [R]beside the altar.   *Ezek. 44:17, 18 • 1:16*

11 And he shall put off his garments, and put on other garments, and carry forth the ashes without the camp unto a clean place.

12 And the fire upon the altar shall be burning in it; it shall not be put out: and the priest shall burn wood on it every morning, and lay the burnt offering in order upon it;

and he shall burn thereon [R]the fat of the peace offerings.   3:3, 9, 14

13 The fire shall ever be burning upon the altar; it shall never go out.

The Meat Offering

14 And this is the [T]law of the [T]meat offering: the sons of Aaron shall offer it before the LORD, before the altar.   *procedure • meal*

15 And he shall take of it his handful, of the flour of the meat offering, and of the oil thereof, and all the frankincense which is upon the meat offering, and shall burn it upon the altar for a sweet savour, even the [T]memorial of it, unto the LORD.   *token part*

16 [R]And the remainder thereof shall Aaron and his sons eat: with unleavened bread shall it be eaten in the holy place; in the court of the tabernacle of the congregation they shall eat it.   10:12–14

17 It shall not be baken with leaven. I have given it unto them for their portion of my offerings made by fire; it is most holy, as is the sin offering, and as the trespass offering.

18 All the males among the children of Aaron shall eat of it. It shall be a statute for ever in your generations concerning the offerings of the LORD made by fire: every one that toucheth them shall be holy.

19 And the LORD spake unto Moses, saying,

20 This is the offering of Aaron and of his sons, which they shall offer unto the LORD in the day when he is anointed; the tenth part of an e'-phah of fine flour for a meat offering perpetual, half of it in the morning, and half thereof at night.

21 In a pan it shall be made with oil; and when it is baken, thou shalt bring it in: and the baken pieces of the meat offering shalt thou offer for a sweet savour unto the LORD.

22 And the priest of his sons that is anointed in his stead shall offer it: it is a statute for ever unto the LORD; it shall be [T]wholly burnt.   *given over entirely to the LORD*

23 For every meat offering for the priest shall be wholly burnt: it shall not be eaten.

The Sin Offering

24 And the LORD spake unto Moses, saying,

25 Speak unto Aaron and to his sons, saying, This is the law of the sin offering: In the place where the burnt offering is killed shall the sin offering be killed before the LORD: it is [T]most holy.   *used only for this*

26 [R]The priest that offereth it for sin shall eat it: in the holy place shall it be eaten, in the court of the tabernacle of the congregation.   [10:17, 18; Num. 18:9, 10; Ezek. 44:28, 29]

27 [R]Whatsoever shall touch the flesh thereof shall be holy: and when there is sprinkled of the blood thereof upon any

garment, thou shalt wash that whereon it was sprinkled in the holy place.   Ex. 29:37

28 But the ᴿearthen vessel wherein it is ᵀsodden shall be broken: and if it be sodden in a brasen pot, it shall be both scoured, and rinsed in water.   11:3 • *cooked*

29 All the males ᴿamong the priests shall eat thereof: it *is* most holy.   *v.* 18

30 ᴿAnd no sin offering, whereof *any* of the blood is brought into the tabernacle of the congregation to reconcile *withal* in the holy *place,* shall be eaten: it shall be burnt in the fire.   4:7, 11, 12, 18, 21; 16:27; Heb. 13:11

CHAPTER 7

The Trespass Offering

LIKEWISE this *is* the law of the ᵀtrespass offering: it *is* most holy.   *guilt*

2 In ᴿthe place where they kill the burnt offering shall they kill the trespass offering: and the blood thereof shall he sprinkle round about upon the altar.   1:11

3 And he shall offer of it all the ᴿfat thereof; the rump, and the fat that covereth the inwards,   3:9

4 And the two kidneys, and the fat that *is* on them, which *is* by the flanks, and the ᵀcaul *that is* above the liver, ᴿwith the kidneys, it shall he take away: *fat* • 3:4

5 And the priest shall burn them upon the altar *for* an offering made by fire unto the Lᴏʀᴅ: it *is* a trespass offering.

6 ᴿEvery male among the priests shall eat thereof: it shall be eaten in the holy place: ᴿit *is* most holy.   6:16–18; Num. 18:9, 10 • 2:3

7 As the sin offering *is,* so *is* ᴿthe trespass offering: there is ᵀone law for them: the priest that maketh atonement therewith shall have it.   6:25, 26; 14:13 • *same procedure*

8 And the priest that offereth any man's burnt offering, *even* the priest shall have ᵀto himself the skin of the burnt offering which he hath offered.   *for his own use*

9 And all the ᵀmeat offering that is baken in the oven, and all that is dressed in the fryingpan, and ᵀin the pan, shall be the priest's that offereth it.   *meal* • *on the flat plate*

10 And every meat offering, mingled with oil, and dry, shall all the sons of Aaron have, one *as much* as another.

The Peace Offering

11 And ᴿthis *is* the ᵀlaw of the sacrifice of peace offerings, which he shall offer unto the Lᴏʀᴅ.   3:1; 22:18, 21; Ezek. 45:15 • *procedure*

12 If he offer it for a thanksgiving, then he shall offer with the sacrifice of thanksgiving unleavened cakes mingled with oil, and unleavened wafers anointed with oil, and cakes mingled with oil, of fine flour, fried.

13 Besides the cakes, he shall offer *for* his offering leavened bread with the sacrifice of thanksgiving of his peace offerings.

14 And of it he shall offer one out of the whole oblation *for* an heave offering unto the Lᴏʀᴅ, *and* it shall be the priest's that sprinkleth the blood of the peace offerings.

15 And the flesh of the sacrifice of his peace offerings for thanksgiving shall be eaten the same day that it is offered; he shall not leave any of it until the morning.

16 But if the sacrifice of his offering be ᵀa vow, or a voluntary offering, it shall be eaten the same day that he offereth his sacrifice: and on the morrow also the remainder of it shall be eaten: *something promised*

17 But ᴿthe remainder of the flesh of the sacrifice on the third day shall be burnt with fire.   Ex. 12:10

18 And if *any* of the flesh of the sacrifice of his peace offerings be eaten at all on the third day, it shall not be accepted, neither shall it be imputed unto him that offereth it: it shall be an abomination, and the soul that eateth of it shall bear his iniquity.

19 And the flesh that toucheth any unclean *thing* shall not be eaten; it shall be burnt with fire: and as for the flesh, all that be clean shall eat thereof.

20 But the soul that eateth *of* the flesh of the sacrifice of peace offerings, that *pertain* unto the Lᴏʀᴅ, ᴿhaving his uncleanness upon him, even that soul ᴿshall be cut off from his people.   [1 Cor. 11:28] • Gen. 17:14

21 Moreover the soul that ᵀshall touch any unclean *thing, as* the uncleanness of man, or *any* unclean beast, or any abominable unclean *thing,* and eat of the flesh of the sacrifice of peace offerings, which *pertain* unto the Lᴏʀᴅ, even that soul shall be cut off from his people.   *has anything to do with*

22 And the Lᴏʀᴅ spake unto Moses, saying,

23 Speak unto the children of Israel, saying, ᴿYe shall eat no manner of fat, of ox, or of sheep, or of goat.   *v.* 26; 3:17; Deut. 14:21

24 And the fat of the beast that dieth of itself, and the fat of that which is torn with beasts, may be used in any other use: but ye shall in no wise eat of it.

25 For whosoever eateth the fat of the beast, of which men offer an offering made by fire unto the Lᴏʀᴅ, even the soul that eateth *it* shall be cut off from his people.

26 ᴿMoreover ye shall eat no manner of blood, *whether it be* of fowl or of beast, in any of your dwellings.   Ezek. 33:25; [John 6:53]

27 Whatsoever ᵀsoul *it be* that eateth any manner of blood, even that soul shall be ᴿcut off from his people.   *person* • Ex. 12:15

28 And the Lᴏʀᴅ spake unto Moses, saying,

29 Speak unto the children of Israel, saying, [R]He that offereth the sacrifice of his peace offerings unto the LORD shall bring his [T]oblation unto the LORD of the sacrifice of his peace offerings.　　Ezek. 45:15 • *offering*

30 [R]His own hands shall bring the offerings of the LORD made by fire, the fat with the breast, it shall he bring, that [R]the breast may be waved *for* a wave offering before the LORD.　　3:3, 4, 9, 14 • 8:27; 9:21; Ex. 29:24, 27

31 [R]And the priest shall burn the fat upon the altar: but the [R]breast shall be Aaron's and his sons'.　　3:5, 11, 16 • Ex. 29:32

32 And [R]the right shoulder shall ye give unto the priest *for* an heave offering of the sacrifices of your peace offerings.　　*v. 34*

33 He among the sons of Aaron, that offereth the blood of the peace offerings, and the fat, shall have the right shoulder for *his* part.

34 For the wave breast and the heave shoulder have I taken of the children of Israel from off the sacrifices of their peace offerings, and have given them unto Aaron the priest and unto his sons by a statute for ever from among the children of Israel.

35 This *is the portion* of the anointing of Aaron, and of the anointing of his sons, out of the offerings of the LORD made by fire, in the day *when* he presented them to minister unto the LORD in the priest's office;

36 Which the LORD commanded to be given them of the children of Israel, in the day that he anointed them, *by* a statute for ever throughout their generations.

The Summary of the Offerings

37 This *is* the [T]law of the burnt offering, of the [T]meat offering, and of the sin offering, and of the trespass offering, and of the consecrations, and of the sacrifice of the peace offerings;　　*proper procedure • meal*

38 Which the LORD commanded [R]Moses in mount Si'-nai, in the day that [R]he commanded the children of Israel [R]to offer their oblations unto the LORD, in the wilderness of Si'-nai.　　Ex. 16:1 • Ex. 4:6 • 1:2

CHAPTER 8

Consecration Commanded by God

AND the LORD spake unto Moses, saying, 2 [R]Take Aaron and his sons with him, and the garments, and the anointing oil, and a bullock for the sin offering, and two rams, and a basket of unleavened bread;　　Ex. 29:1–3

3 And [R]gather thou all the congregation together [T]unto the door of the tabernacle of the congregation.　　Num. 1:18 • *in the front of*

4 And [R]Moses did as the LORD commanded him; and the assembly was gathered together unto the door of the tabernacle of the congregation.　　Gen. 6:22

5 And Moses said unto the congregation, This *is* the thing which the LORD commanded to be done.

Cleansing the Priests with Water

6 And Moses brought Aaron and his sons, and [R]washed them with water.　　Ex. 30:20

Special Garments

7 And he put upon him the coat, and girded him with the girdle, and clothed him with the robe, and put the e'-phod upon him, and he girded him with the curious girdle of the e'-phod, and bound *it* unto him therewith.

8 And he put the breastplate upon him: also he [R]put in the breastplate the [T]U'-rim and the [T]Thum'-mim.　　Ex. 28:30 • *lights • perfection*

9 And he put the mitre upon his head; also upon the mitre, *even* upon his forefront, did he put the golden plate, the holy crown; as the LORD commanded Moses.

Anointing with Oil

10 [R]And Moses took the anointing oil, and anointed the tabernacle and all that *was* therein, and sanctified them.　　Ex. 30:26–29

11 And he sprinkled thereof upon the altar seven times, and anointed the altar and all his vessels, both the laver and his foot, to [R]sanctify them.　　Ex. 29:36, 37; 30:29

12 And he [R]poured of the anointing oil upon Aaron's head, and anointed him, to sanctify him.　　21:10, 12; Ex. 29:7; 30:30; Ps. 133:2

13 And Moses brought Aaron's sons, and put coats upon them, and girded them with girdles, and put [T]bonnets upon them; as the LORD commanded Moses.　　*headpieces*

Consecrating with Blood

14 [R]And he brought the bullock for the sin offering: and Aaron and his sons laid their hands upon the head of the bullock for the sin offering.　　4:4; Ex. 29:10; Ezek. 43:19

15 And he slew *it;* and Moses took the blood, and put *it* upon the horns of the altar round about with his finger, and purified the altar, and poured the blood at the bottom of the altar, and sanctified it, to make [T]reconciliation upon it.　　*atonement*

16 [R]And he took all the fat that *was* upon the inwards, and the caul *above* the liver, and the two kidneys, and their fat, and Moses burned *it* upon the altar.　　Ex. 29:13

17 But the bullock, and his hide, his flesh, and his dung, he burnt with fire without the camp; as the LORD commanded Moses.

18 [R]And he brought the ram for the burnt offering: and Aaron and his sons laid their hands upon the head of the ram.　　Ex. 29:15

19 And he killed *it;* and Moses sprinkled the blood upon the altar round about.

20 And he cut the ram into pieces; and

Moses [R]burnt the head, and the pieces, and the fat.   1:8

21 And he washed the inwards and the legs in water; and Moses burnt the whole ram upon the altar: it was a burnt sacrifice for a [T]sweet savour, and an offering made by fire unto the LORD; [R]as the LORD commanded Moses.   pleasing • Ex. 29:18

22 And he brought the other ram, the ram of consecration: and Aaron and his sons laid their hands upon the head of the ram.

23 And he slew it; and Moses took of the [R]blood of it, and [R]put it upon the tip of Aaron's right ear, and upon the thumb of his right hand, and upon the great toe of his right foot.   14:14 • Ex. 29:20, 21

24 And he brought Aaron's sons, and Moses put of the blood upon the tip of their right ear, and upon the thumbs of their right hands, and upon the great toes of their right feet: and Moses sprinkled the blood upon the altar round about.

25 And he took the fat, and the rump, and all the fat that was upon the inwards, and the caul above the liver, and the two kidneys, and their fat, and the right shoulder:

26 [R]And out of the basket of unleavened bread, that was before the LORD, he took one unleavened cake, and a cake of oiled bread, and one wafer, and put them on the fat, and upon the right shoulder: Ex. 29:23

27 And he put all upon Aaron's hands, and upon his sons' hands, and waved them for a wave offering before the LORD.

28 [R]And Moses took them from off their hands, and burnt them on the altar upon the burnt offering: they were consecrations for a [R]sweet savour: it is an offering made by fire unto the LORD.   Ex. 29:25 • Gen. 8:21

29 And Moses took the breast, and waved it for a wave offering before the LORD: for of the ram of consecration it was Moses' part; as the LORD commanded Moses.

30 And [R]Moses took of the anointing oil, and of the blood which was upon the altar, and sprinkled it upon Aaron, and upon his garments, and upon his sons, and upon his sons' garments with him; and sanctified Aaron, and his garments, and his sons, and his sons' garments with him.   Ex. 29:21; 30:30

The Priests Are to Remain in the Tabernacle

31 And Moses said unto Aaron and to his sons, [R]Boil the flesh at the door of the tabernacle of the congregation: and there eat it with the bread that is in the basket of consecrations, as I commanded, saying, Aaron and his sons shall eat it.   Ex. 29:31, 32

32 And that which remaineth of the flesh and of the bread shall ye burn with fire.

33 And ye shall not go out of the door of the tabernacle of the congregation in seven days, until the days of your [T]consecration be at an end: for [R]seven days shall he consecrate you.   ceremony of dedication • Ezek. 43:25, 26

34 [R]As he hath done this day, so the LORD hath commanded to do, to make [T]an atonement for you.   [Heb. 7:16] • a reconciliation with God

35 Therefore shall ye abide at the door of the tabernacle of the congregation day and night seven days, and [R]keep[T] the charge of the LORD, that ye die not: for so I am commanded.   1 Kin. 2:3 • obey the regulations

36 So Aaron and his sons did all things which the [R]LORD commanded by the hand of Moses.   Gen. 6:22

CHAPTER 9

Offerings for the Priest

AND [R]it came to pass on the eighth day, that Moses called Aaron and his sons, and the elders of Israel;   Ezek. 43:27

2 And he said unto Aaron, Take thee a [T]young [R]calf for a sin offering, and a ram for a burnt offering, [R]without blemish, and offer them before the LORD.   bull • Ex. 29:21 • Ex. 12:5

3 And unto the children of Israel thou shalt speak, saying, [R]Take ye a kid of the goats for a sin offering; and a calf and a lamb, both of the first year, without blemish, for a burnt offering;   Ezra 6:17; 10:19

4 Also a bullock and a ram for peace offerings, to sacrifice before the LORD; and a [T]meat offering mingled with oil: for to day the LORD will appear unto you.   food

5 And they brought that which Moses commanded before the tabernacle of the congregation: and all the congregation drew near and stood before the LORD.

6 And Moses said, This is the thing which the LORD commanded that ye should do: and the glory of the LORD shall appear unto you.

7 And Moses said unto Aaron, Go unto the altar, and offer thy sin offering, and thy burnt offering, and make an atonement for thyself, and for the people: and offer the offering of the people, and make an atonement for them; as the LORD commanded.

8 Aaron therefore went unto the altar, and slew the calf of the sin offering, which was [T]for himself.   because of his own sins

9 And the sons of Aaron brought the blood unto him: and he dipped his [R]finger in the blood, and put it upon the horns of the altar, and poured out the blood at the bottom of the altar: 4:7

10 [R]But the fat, and the kidneys, and the caul above the liver of the sin offering, he burnt upon the altar; as the LORD commanded Moses.   8:16; Ex. 23:18

11 And the flesh and the hide he burnt with fire [T]without the camp.   outside

12 And he slew the [R]burnt offering; and

Aaron's sons presented unto him the blood, [R]which he sprinkled round about upon the altar.   Ex. 29:18 • 1:5; 8:19

13 And they presented the burnt offering unto him, with the pieces thereof, and the head: and he burnt *them* upon the altar.

14 [R]And he did wash the inwards and the legs, and burnt *them* upon the burnt offering on the altar.   8:21

Offerings for the People

15 [R]And he brought the people's offering, and took the goat, which *was* the sin offering for the people, and slew it, and offered it for sin, as the first.   [Is. 53:10; Heb. 2:17; 5:3]

16 And he brought the burnt offering, and offered it according to the manner.

17 And he brought the [T]meat offering, and took an handful thereof, and burnt *it* upon the altar, beside the burnt [T]sacrifice of the morning.   *food • offering*

18 He slew also the bullock and the ram for [R]a sacrifice of peace offerings, which *was* for the people: and Aaron's sons presented unto him the blood, which he sprinkled upon the altar round about,   3:1

19 And the fat of the bullock and of the ram, the rump, and that which [R]covereth *the inwards,* and the kidneys, and the caul *above* the liver: 3:9

20 And they put the fat upon the breasts, and he burnt the fat upon the altar:

21 And the breasts and the right shoulder Aaron waved [R]*for* a wave offering before the LORD; as Moses commanded.   Ex. 29:24

The Lord Accepts the Offerings

22 And Aaron lifted up his hand toward the people, and blessed them, and came down from offering of the sin offering, and the burnt offering, and peace offerings.

23 And Moses and Aaron went into the tabernacle of the congregation, and came out, and blessed the people: and the glory of the LORD appeared unto all the people.

24 And [R]there came a fire out from before the LORD, and consumed upon the altar the burnt offering and the fat: *which* when all the people saw, they shouted, and fell on their faces.   Gen. 4:4; 1 Kin. 18:38; 2 Chr. 7:1; Ps. 20:3

CHAPTER 10

The Sin of Nadab and Abihu

A ND Na'-dab and A-bi'-hu, the sons of Aaron, took either of them his censer, and put fire therein, and put incense thereon, and offered strange fire before the LORD, which he commanded them not.

2 And there [R]went out fire from the LORD, and devoured them, and they died before the LORD.   Num. 16:35

3 Then Moses said unto Aaron, This *is it* that the LORD spake, saying, I will be sanctified in them that come nigh me, and before all the people I will be [T]glorified. And Aaron held his peace.   *treated with honour*

4 And Moses called [R]Mish'-a-el and El'-za-phan, and the sons of Uz-zi'-el the uncle of Aaron, and said unto them, Come near, carry your brethren from [T]before the sanctuary out of the camp.   Ex. 6:18, 22 • *in front of*

5 So they went near, and carried them in their [R]coats out of the camp; as Moses had said.   8:13; Ex. 29:5

6 And Moses said unto Aaron, and unto E-le-a'-zar and unto Ith'-a-mar, his sons, Uncover not your heads, neither rend your clothes; lest ye die, and lest wrath come upon all the people: but let your brethren, the whole house of Israel, bewail the burning which the LORD hath kindled.

7 And [T]ye shall not go out from the door of the tabernacle of the congregation, lest ye die: [R]for the anointing oil of the LORD *is* upon you. And they did according to the word of Moses.   *you must tend to your office* • 21:12

8 And the LORD spake unto Aaron, saying,

9 [R]Do not drink wine nor strong drink, thou, nor thy sons with thee, when ye go into the tabernacle of the congregation, lest ye die: *it shall be* a statute for ever throughout your generations;   1 Tim. 3:3

10 And that ye may [R]put difference between holy and [T]unholy, and between unclean and clean;   20:25; Ezek. 44:23 • *common*

11 And that ye may teach the children of Israel all the statutes which the LORD hath spoken unto them by the hand of Moses.

The Sin of Eleazar and Ithamar

12 And Moses spake unto Aaron, and unto E-le-a'-zar and unto Ith'-a-mar, his sons that were left, Take the meat offering that remaineth of the offerings of the LORD made by fire, and eat it without leaven beside the altar: for it *is* [T]most holy: *to be used only for this*

13 And ye shall eat it in the holy place, because it *is* [T]thy due, and thy sons' due, of the sacrifices of the LORD made by fire: for so I am commanded.   *your share*

14 And [R]the wave breast and heave shoulder shall ye eat in a clean place; thou, and thy sons, and thy daughters with thee: for *they* be thy due, and thy sons' due, *which* are given out of the sacrifices of peace offerings of the children of Israel.   Num. 18:11

15 The heave shoulder and the wave breast shall they bring with the offerings made by fire of the fat, to wave *it for* a wave offering before the LORD; and it shall be thine, and thy sons' with thee, by a statute for ever; as the LORD hath commanded.

16 And Moses diligently sought [R]the goat of the sin offering, and, behold, it was burnt:

and he was angry with E-le-a'-zar and Ith'-a-mar, the sons of Aaron *which were* left *alive,* saying,   9:3, 15

17 Wherefore have ye not eaten the sin offering in the holy place, seeing it *is* most holy, and *God* hath given it you to bear the iniquity of the congregation, to make atonement for them before the LORD?

18 Behold, ᴿthe blood of it was not brought in within the holy *place:* ye should indeed have eaten it in the holy *place,* ᴿas I commanded.   6:30 · 6:26, 30

19 And Aaron said unto Moses, Behold, this day have they offered their sin offering and their burnt offering before the LORD; and such things have befallen me: and *if* I had eaten the sin offering to day, should it have been accepted in the sight of the LORD?

20 And when Moses heard *that,* he was content.

CHAPTER 11

Animals of the Earth

AND the LORD spake unto Moses and to Aaron, saying unto them,

2 Speak unto the children of Israel, saying, These *are* the beasts which ye shall eat among all the beasts that *are* on the earth.

3 Whatsoever parteth the hoof, and is ᵀclovenfooted, *and* cheweth the cud, among the beasts, that shall ye eat.   *split hoof*

4 Nevertheless these shall ye not eat of them that chew the cud, or of them that divide the hoof: *as* the camel, because he cheweth the cud, but divideth not the hoof; he *is* ᴿuncleanᵀ unto you.   Acts 10:14 · *unfit*

5 And the ᵀconey, because he cheweth the cud, but divideth not the hoof; he *is* ᵀunclean unto you.   *rock badger · unfit*

6 And the hare, because he cheweth the cud, but divideth not the hoof; he *is* unclean unto you.

7 And the swine, though he divide the hoof, and be clovenfooted, yet he cheweth not the cud; ᴿhe *is* unclean to you.   Is. 65:4

8 Of their flesh shall ye not eat, and their carcase shall ye not touch; ᴿthey *are* unclean to you.   [Mark 7:2, 15, 18; 1 Cor. 8:8; Heb. 9:10]

Living Things in the Waters

9 ᴿThese shall ye eat of all that *are* in the waters: whatsoever hath fins and scales in the waters, in the seas, and in the rivers, them shall ye eat.   Deut. 14:9

10 And all that have not fins and scales in the seas, and in the rivers, of all that move in the waters, and of any living thing which *is* in the waters, they *shall be* an ᴿabominationᵀ unto you: 7:21 · *unfit to use*

11 They shall be even an abomination unto you; ye shall not eat of their flesh, but ye shall have their carcases in abomination.

12 Whatsoever hath no fins nor scales in the waters, that *shall be* an abomination unto you.

Birds of the Air

13 And these *are they which* ye shall have in abomination among the fowls; they shall not be eaten, they *are* an abomination: the eagle, and the ossifrage, and the ospray,

14 And the vulture, and the ᵀkite after his kind;   *hawk*

15 Every raven after his kind;

16 And the owl, and the night hawk, and the cuckow, and the hawk after his kind,

17 And the little owl, and the cormorant, and the ᵀgreat owl,   *great horned owl*

18 And the swan, and the pelican, and the ᵀgier eagle,   *golden vulture*

19 And the stork, the heron after her kind, and the lapwing, and the bat.

Winged Insects

20 All fowls that creep, going upon *all* four, *shall be* an abomination unto you.

21 Yet these may ye eat of every flying creeping thing that goeth upon *all* four, which have legs above their feet, to leap withal upon the earth;

22 *Even* these of them ye may eat; ᴿthe locust after his kind, and the bald locust after his kind, and the beetle after his kind, and the grasshopper after his kind.   Matt. 3:4

23 But all *other* flying creeping things, which have ᴿfour feet, *shall be* an abomination unto you.   *vv. 20, 42*

The Carcases of the Unclean Animals

24 And ᴿfor these ye shall be unclean: whosoever toucheth the carcase of them shall be unclean until the even.   *v. 8*

25 And ᴿwhosoever beareth *ought* of the carcase of them ᴿshall wash his clothes, and be unclean until the even.   *v. 40 · 14:8; 15:5*

26 *The carcases* of every beast which divideth the hoof, and is not clovenfooted, nor cheweth the cud, *are* unclean unto you: every one that ᵀtoucheth them shall be unclean.   *has anything to do with*

27 And whatsoever goeth upon his paws, among all manner of beasts that go on *all* four, those *are* unclean unto you: whoso toucheth their carcase shall be unclean until the even.

28 And he that beareth the carcase of them shall wash his clothes, and be unclean until the even: they *are* unclean unto you.

Creeping Things

29 These also *shall be* unclean unto you among the creeping things that creep upon

the earth; the weasel, and ^Rthe mouse, and the ^Ttortoise after his kind,   Is. 66:17 · *great lizard*

30 And the ferret, and the chameleon, and the lizard, and the snail, and the mole.

31 These *are* unclean to you among all that creep: whosoever doth ^Rtouch them, when they be dead, shall be unclean until the even.   *v.* 8; Hag. 2:13

32 And upon whatsoever *any* of them, when they are dead, doth fall, it shall be unclean; whether *it be* any vessel of wood, or raiment, or skin, or sack, whatsoever vessel *it be*, wherein *any* work is done, it must be put into water, and it shall be unclean until the even; so it shall be cleansed.

33 And every earthen vessel, whereinto *any* of them falleth, whatsoever *is* in it shall be unclean; and ye shall break it.

34 Of all meat which may be eaten, *that* on which *such* water cometh shall be unclean: and all drink that may be drunk in every *such* vessel shall be unclean.

35 And every *thing* whereupon *any part* of their carcase falleth shall be unclean; *whether it be* oven, or ^Tranges for pots, they shall be broken down: *for* they *are* unclean, and shall be unclean unto you.   *hearth*

36 Nevertheless a ^Tfountain or ^Tpit, *wherein there is* plenty of water, shall be clean: but that which toucheth their carcase shall be unclean.   *spring · well*

37 And if *any part* of their carcase fall upon any sowing seed which is to be sown, it *shall be* clean.

38 But if *any* water be put upon the seed, and *any part* of their carcase fall thereon, it *shall be* unclean ^Tunto you.   *for food*

The Carcases of the Clean Animals

39 And if any beast, of which ye may eat, die; he that toucheth the carcase thereof shall be unclean until the even.

40 And ^Rhe that eateth of the carcase of it shall wash his clothes, and be unclean until the even: he also that beareth the carcase of it shall wash his clothes, and be unclean until the even.   17:15; 22:8; Deut. 14:21

The Purpose of Dietary Laws

41 ^RAnd every creeping thing that creepeth upon the earth *shall be* ^Tan abomination; it shall not be eaten.   *v.* 29 · *unfit for food*

42 Whatsoever goeth upon the belly, and whatsoever goeth upon *all* four, or whatsoever hath more feet among all creeping things that creep upon the earth, them ye shall not eat; for they *are* an abomination.

43 Ye shall not make your selves abominable with any creeping thing that creepeth, neither shall ye make yourselves unclean with them, that ye should be defiled thereby.

44 For I *am* the LORD your God: ye shall therefore sanctify yourselves, and ye shall be holy; for I *am* holy: neither shall ye defile yourselves with any manner of creeping thing that creepeth upon the earth.

45 For I *am* the LORD that bringeth you up out of the land of Egypt, to be your God: ye shall therefore be holy, for I *am* holy.

46 This *is* the ^Tlaw of the beasts, and of the fowl, and of every living creature that moveth in the waters, and of every creature that creepeth upon the earth: *regulation*

47 ^TTo make a difference between the unclean and the clean, and between the beast that may be eaten and the beast that may not be eaten.   *to show there is a difference*

CHAPTER 12

Laws Concerning Childbirth

AND the LORD spake unto Moses, saying, 2 Speak unto the children of Israel, saying, If a ^Rwoman have conceived seed, and born a man child: then ^Rshe shall be ^Tunclean seven days; ^Raccording to the days of the separation for her infirmity shall she be unclean.   [Ps. 51:5] · Luke 2:22 · *unfit* · 15:19

3 And in the ^Reighth day the flesh of his foreskin shall be circumcised.   Luke 1:59; 2:21

4 And she shall then continue in the blood of her purifying three and thirty days; she shall touch no hallowed thing, nor come into the sanctuary, until the days of her purifying be fulfilled.

5 But if she bear a maid child, then she shall be unclean two weeks, as in her separation: and she shall continue in the blood of her purifying threescore and six days.

6 And ^Rwhen the days of her purifying are fulfilled, for a son, or for a daughter, she shall bring a lamb of the first year for a burnt offering, and a young pigeon, or a turtledove, ^Rfor a sin offering, unto the door of the tabernacle of the congregation, unto the priest: Luke 2:22 · 5:7

7 Who shall offer it before the LORD, and make ^Tan atonement for her; and she shall be cleansed from the issue of her blood. This *is* the law for her that hath born a male or a female.   *a reconciliation*

8 ^RAnd if she be not able to bring a lamb, then she shall bring two turtles, or two young pigeons; the one for the burnt offering, and the other for a sin offering: ^Rand the priest shall make an atonement for her, and she shall be ^Tclean.   Luke 2:24 · 4:26 · *fit*

CHAPTER 13

Examination of People

AND the LORD spake unto Moses and Aaron, saying,

2 When a man shall have in the skin of his

flesh a rising, a scab, or bright spot, and it be in the skin of his flesh *like* the plague of leprosy; then he shall be brought unto Aaron the priest, or unto one of his sons the priests:

3 And the priest shall look on the plague in the skin of the flesh: and *when* the hair in the plague is turned white, and the plague in sight *be* deeper than the skin of his flesh, it *is* a plague of leprosy: and the priest shall look on him, and pronounce him unclean.

4 If the bright spot *be* white in the skin of his flesh, and in sight *be* not deeper than the skin, and the hair thereof be not turned white; then the priest shall ᵀshut up *him that hath* the plague seven days: *isolate*

5 And the priest shall look on him the seventh day: and, behold, *if* the plague in his sight ᵀbe at a stay, *and* the plague spread not in the skin; then the priest shall shut him up seven days more: *is not spreading*

6 And the priest shall look on him again the seventh day: and, behold, *if* the plague *be* ᵀsomewhat dark, *and* the plague spread not in the skin, the priest shall pronounce him clean: it *is but* a scab: and he ᴿshall wash his clothes, and be clean.   *dim • 11:25*

7 But if the scab ᴿspread much abroad in the skin, after that he hath been seen of the priest for his cleansing, he shall be seen of the priest again: *2 Chr. 26:19*

8 And *if* the priest see that, behold, the scab spreadeth in the skin, then the priest shall pronounce him unclean: it *is* a leprosy.

9 When the plague of leprosy is in a man, then he shall be brought unto the priest;

10 And the priest shall see *him*: and, behold, *if* the rising *be* white in the skin, and it have turned the hair white, and *there be* ᵀquick raw flesh in the rising;   *sensitive*

11 It *is* an ᵀold leprosy in the skin of his flesh, and the priest shall pronounce him ᵀunclean, and shall not ᵀshut him up: for he *is* unclean.   *chronic • unfit • isolate*

12 And if a leprosy break out abroad in the skin, and the leprosy cover all the skin of *him that hath* the plague from his head even to his foot, wheresoever the priest looketh;

13 Then the priest shall consider: and, behold, *if* the leprosy have covered all his flesh, he shall pronounce *him* clean *that hath* the plague: it is all turned white: he *is* clean.

14 But when raw flesh appeareth in him, he shall be unclean.

15 And the priest shall see the raw flesh, and pronounce him to be unclean: *for* the raw flesh *is* unclean: it *is* a leprosy.

16 Or if the raw flesh turn again, and be changed unto white, he shall come unto the priest;

17 And the priest shall see him: and, behold, *if* the plague be turned into white; then the priest shall pronounce *him* clean *that hath* the plague: he *is* clean.

18 The flesh also, in which, *even* in the skin thereof, was a boil, and is healed,

19 And in the place of the boil there be a ᵀwhite rising, or a bright spot, white, and somewhat reddish, and it be shewed to the priest;   *pimple; swelling*

20 And if, when the priest seeth it, behold, it *be* in sight lower than the skin, and the hair thereof be turned white; the priest shall pronounce him unclean: it *is* a plague of leprosy broken out of the boil.

21 But if the priest look on it, and, behold, *there be* no white hairs therein, and *if* it *be* not lower than the skin, but *be* somewhat dark; then the priest shall ᵀshut him up seven days: *isolate*

22 And if it spread much abroad in the skin, then the priest shall pronounce him unclean: it *is* ᵀa plague.   *an infection*

23 But if the bright spot ᵀstay in his place, *and* spread not, it *is* a burning boil; and the priest shall pronounce him clean.   *doesn't spread*

24 Or if there be *any* flesh, in the skin whereof *there is* a hot burning, and the quick *flesh* that burneth have a white bright spot, somewhat reddish, or white;

25 Then the priest shall look upon it: and, behold, *if* the hair in the bright spot be turned white, and it *be in* sight deeper than the skin; it *is* a leprosy broken out of the burning: wherefore the priest shall pronounce him unclean: it *is* the ᵀplague of leprosy.   *infection*

26 But if the priest look on it, and, behold, *there be* no white hair in the bright spot, and it *be* no ᵀlower than the *other* skin, but *be* somewhat dark; then the priest shall ᵀshut him up seven days: *deeper • isolate*

27 And the priest shall look upon him the seventh day: *and* if it be spread much abroad in the skin, then the priest shall pronounce him unclean: it *is* the plague of leprosy.

28 And if the bright spot stay in his place, *and* spread not in the skin, but it *be* somewhat dark; it *is* a rising of the burning, and the priest shall pronounce him clean: for it *is* an inflammation of the burning.

29 If a man or woman have a ᴿplague upon the head or the beard;   *vv. 29–46*

30 Then the priest shall see the plague: and, behold, if it *be* in sight deeper than the skin; *and there be* in it a yellow thin hair; then the priest shall pronounce him unclean: it *is* a dry scall, *even* a leprosy upon the head or beard.

31 And if the priest look on the plague of the scall, and, behold, it *be* not in sight deeper than the skin, and *that there is* no black hair in it; then the priest shall shut up *him that hath* the plague of the scall seven days:

32 And in the seventh day the priest shall look on the plague: and, behold, *if* the scall

spread not, and there be in it no yellow hair, and the scall be not in sight deeper than the skin;

33 He shall be shaven, but the scall shall he not shave; and the priest shall shut up him that hath the scall seven days more:

34 And in the seventh day the priest shall look on the scall: and, behold, if the [T]scall be not spread in the skin, nor be in sight deeper than the skin; then the priest shall [T]pronounce him clean: and he shall wash his clothes, and be clean.   eruption • declare

35 But if the [R]scall spread much in the skin after his cleansing;   vv. 7, 27

36 Then the priest shall look on him: and, behold, if the [T]scall be spread in the skin, the priest shall not seek for yellow hair; he is unclean.   eruption

37 But if the scall be in his sight at a stay, and that there is black hair grown up therein; the scall is healed, he is clean: and the priest shall pronounce him clean.

38 If a man also or a woman have in the skin of their flesh [T]bright spots, even white bright spots;   pimples

39 Then the priest shall look: and, behold, if the bright spots in the skin of their flesh be darkish white; it is a [T]freckled spot that groweth in the skin; he is clean.   eczema

40 And the man whose hair is fallen off his head, he is bald; yet is he clean.

41 And he that hath his hair fallen off from the part of his head toward his face, he is forehead bald: yet is he clean.

42 And if there be in the bald head, or bald [R]forehead, a white reddish sore; it is a leprosy sprung up in his bald head, or his bald forehead.   2 Chr. 26:19

43 Then the priest shall look upon it: and, behold, if the [T]rising of the sore be white reddish in his bald head, or in his bald forehead, as the leprosy appeareth in the skin of the flesh;   swelling

44 He is a leprous man, he is unclean: the priest shall pronounce him [T]utterly unclean; his plague is in his head.   altogether unfit

45 And the leper in whom the plague is, his clothes shall be rent, and his head bare, and he shall put a covering upon his upper lip, and shall cry, Unclean, unclean.

46 All the days wherein the plague shall be in him he shall be defiled; he is unclean: he shall [T]dwell alone; [T]without the camp shall his habitation be.   be in quarantine • outside

Examination of Garments

47 The garment also that the plague of leprosy is in, whether it be a woollen garment, or a linen garment;

48 Whether it be in the [T]warp, or woof; of linen, or of woollen; whether in a skin, or in any thing made of skin;   woven or knitted

49 And if the plague be greenish or reddish in the garment, or in the skin, either in the warp, or in the woof, or in any [T]thing of skin; it is a plague of leprosy, and shall be shewed unto the priest: vessel

50 And the priest shall look upon the plague, and [T]shut up it that hath the plague seven days: quarantine

51 And he shall look on the plague on the seventh day: if the plague be spread in the garment, either in the warp, or in the woof, or in a skin, or in any work that is made of skin; the plague is [R]a [T]fretting leprosy; it is unclean.   14:44 • spreading

52 He shall therefore burn that garment, whether warp or woof, in woollen or in linen, or any thing of skin, wherein the plague is: for it is a [T]fretting leprosy; it shall be burnt in the fire.   festering

53 And if the priest shall look, and, behold, the plague be not spread in the garment, either in the warp, or in the woof, or in any thing of skin;

54 Then the priest shall command that they wash the thing wherein the plague is, and he shall shut it up seven days more:

55 And the priest shall look on the plague, after that it is washed: and, behold, if the plague have not changed his colour, and the plague be not spread; it is unclean; thou shalt burn it in the fire; it is fret inward, whether it be bare within or without.

56 And if the priest look, and, behold, the plague be somewhat [T]dark after the washing of it; then he shall [T]rend it out of the garment, or out of the skin, or out of the warp, or out of the woof: faded • tear

57 And if it appear still in the garment, either in [T]the warp, or in the woof, or in any thing of skin; it is a spreading plague: thou shalt burn that wherein the plague is with fire.   woven or knitted stuff

58 And the garment, either warp, or woof, or whatsoever thing of skin it be, which thou shalt wash, if the plague be departed from them, then it shall be [R]washed the second time, and shall be clean.   Num. 31:24

59 This is the law of the plague of leprosy in a garment of woollen or linen, either in the warp, or woof, or any thing of skins, to pronounce it clean, or to pronounce it unclean.

CHAPTER 14

Cleansing of People

AND the LORD spake unto Moses, saying, 2 This shall be the law of the leper in the day of his cleansing: He [R]shall be brought unto the priest: Matt. 8:2, 4; Luke 5:12, 14; 17:14

3 And the priest shall go forth out of the

camp; and the priest shall look, and, behold, *if* the plague of leprosy be healed in the leper;

4 Then shall the priest command to take for him that is to be cleansed two ᵀbirds alive *and* clean, and ᴿcedar wood, and scarlet, and hyssop: *sparrows* • Num. 19:6

5 And the priest shall command that one of the birds be killed in an earthen vessel over running water:

6 As for the living bird, he shall take it, and the cedar wood, and the scarlet, and the ᴿhyssop, and shall dip them and the living bird in the blood of the bird *that was* killed over the running water: Ps. 51:7

7 And he shall sprinkle upon him that is to be cleansed from the leprosy seven times, and shall pronounce him clean, and shall let the living bird loose into the open field.

8 And he that is to be ᴿcleansed shall wash his clothes, and shave off all his hair, and wash himself in water, that he may be clean: and after that he shall come into the camp, and ᴿshall ᵀtarry abroad out of his tent seven days.   Num. 8:7 • Num. 12:15 • *stay outside*

9 But it shall be on the ᴿseventh day, that he shall shave all his hair off his head and his beard and his eyebrows, even all his hair he shall shave off: and he shall wash his clothes, also he shall wash his flesh in water, and he shall be clean.   Num. 19:19

10 And on the eighth day he shall take two he lambs without blemish, and one ewe lamb of the first year without blemish, and three tenth deals of fine flour *for* a meat offering, mingled with oil, and one log of oil.

11 And the priest that maketh *him* clean shall present the man that is to be made clean, and those things, before the LORD, *at* the door of the tabernacle of the congregation:

12 And the priest shall take one he lamb, and ᴿoffer him for a trespass offering, and the ᵀlog of oil, and ᴿwave them *for* a wave offering before the LORD: 5:2, 18 • *pint* • Ex. 29:24

13 And he shall slay the lamb ᴿin the place where he shall kill the sin offering and the burnt offering, in the holy place: for as the sin offering *is* the priest's, *so is* the trespass offering: it *is* most holy: Ex. 29:11

14 And the priest shall take *some* of the blood of the trespass offering, and the priest shall put *it* ᴿupon the tip of the right ear of him that is to be cleansed, and upon the thumb of his right hand, and upon the great toe of his right foot: 8:23; Ex. 29:20

15 And the priest shall take *some* of the ᵀlog of oil, and pour *it* into the palm of his own left hand: *pint*

16 And the priest shall dip his right finger in the oil that *is* in his left hand, and ᴿshall sprinkle of the oil with his finger seven times before the LORD: 4:6

17 And of the rest of the oil that *is* in his hand shall the priest put upon the tip of the right ear of him that is to be cleansed, and upon the thumb of his right hand, and upon the great toe of his right foot, upon the blood of the trespass offering:

18 And the remnant of the oil that *is* in the priest's hand he shall pour upon the head of him that is to be cleansed: ᴿand the priest shall make ᵀan atonement for him before the LORD.   4:26; 5:6 • *reconciliation*

19 And the priest shall offer the sin offering, and make an atonement for him that is to be cleansed from his uncleanness; and afterward he shall kill the burnt offering:

20 And the priest shall offer the burnt offering and the ᵀmeat offering upon the altar: and the priest shall make an atonement for him, and he shall be clean.   *meal*

21 And if he *be* poor, and cannot get so much; then he shall take one ᵀlamb *for* a ᵀtrespass offering to be waved, to make an atonement for him, and ᵀone tenth deal of fine flour mingled with oil for a meat offering, and a ᵀlog of oil;   *(he)* • *guilt* • 2.087 *qt.* • *pint*

22 ᴿAnd two turtledoves, or two young pigeons, such as he is able to get; and the one shall be a sin offering, and the other a burnt offering.   12:8; 15:14, 15

23 ᴿAnd he shall bring them on the eighth day for his cleansing unto the priest, ᵀunto the door of the tabernacle of the congregation, before the LORD.   vv. 10, 11 • *in front*

24 ᴿAnd the priest shall take the lamb of the trespass offering, and ᴿthe log of oil, and the priest shall wave them *for* a wave offering before the LORD: v. 12 • v. 10

25 And he shall kill the lamb of the trespass offering, ᴿand the priest shall take *some* of the blood of the trespass offering, and put *it* upon the ᴿtip of the right ear of him that is to be cleansed, and upon the thumb of his right hand, and upon the great toe of his right foot: vv. 14, 17 • v. 14

26 And the priest shall pour of the oil into the palm of his own left hand:

27 And the priest shall sprinkle with his right finger *some* of the oil that *is* in his left hand seven times before the LORD:

28 And the priest shall put of the oil that *is* in his hand upon the tip of the right ear of him that is to be cleansed, and upon the thumb of his right hand, and upon the great toe of his right foot, upon the place of the blood of the trespass offering:

29 And the rest of the oil that *is* in the priest's hand he shall put upon the head of him that is to be cleansed, to make an atonement for him before the LORD.

30 And he shall offer the one of ᴿthe turtledoves, or of the young pigeons, such as he can get;   v. 22; 15:14, 15

31 *Even* such as he is able to get, the one *for* a sin offering, and the other *for* a burnt offering, with the meat offering: and the priest shall make an atonement for him that is to be cleansed before the Lord.

32 This *is* the law *of him* in whom *is* the plague of leprosy, whose hand is not able to get *that which pertaineth* to his cleansing.

Cleansing of Houses

33 And the Lord spake unto Moses and unto Aaron, saying,

34 When ye be come into the land of Canaan, which I give to you for a possession, and I put the plague of leprosy in a house of the land of your possession;

35 And he that owneth the house shall come and tell the priest, saying, It seemeth to me *there is* as it were a plague in the house:

36 Then the priest shall command that they empty the house, before the priest go *into it* to see the plague, that all that *is* in the house be not made unclean: and afterward the priest shall go in to see the house:

37 And he shall look on the plague, and, behold, *if* the plague *be* in the walls of the house with hollow strakes, greenish or reddish, which in sight *are* lower than the wall;

38 Then the priest shall go out of the house to the door of the house, and Tshut up the house seven days: *quarantine*

39 And the priest shall come again the seventh day, and shall look: and, behold, *if* the plague be spread in the walls of the house;

40 Then the Rpriest shall command that they take away the stones in which the plague *is*, and they shall cast them into an unclean place without the city: [Jer. 15:19]

41 And he shall cause the house to be scraped within round about, and they shall pour out the dust that they scrape off without the city into an unclean place:

42 And they shall take other stones, and put *them* in the place of those stones; and he shall take other Rmorter, and shall plaister the house.   Ezek. 13:10

43 And if the plague come again, and break out in the house, after that he hath taken away the stones, and after he hath scraped the house, and after it is plaistered;

44 Then the priest shall come and look, and, behold, *if* the plague be spread in the house, it *is* Ra Tfretting leprosy in the house: it *is* unclean.   13:51; Zech. 5:4 · *spreading*

45 And he shall break down the house, the stones of it, and the timber thereof, and all the morter of the house; and he shall carry *them* forth out of the city into an Runclean place.   *v. 41*

46 Moreover he that goeth into the house all the while that it is shut up shall be Runclean until the even.   11:24; 15:5

47 And he that lieth in the house shall Rwash his clothes; and he that eateth in the house shall wash his clothes.   *v. 8*

48 And if the priest shall come in, and look *upon it*, and, behold, the plague hath not spread in the house, after the house was plaistered: then the priest shall pronounce the house clean, because the plague is healed.

49 And Rhe shall take to cleanse the house two birds, and cedar wood, and scarlet, and hyssop: *vv. 4–8*

50 And he shall kill the one of the birds in an earthen vessel over running water:

51 And he shall take the cedar wood, and the hyssop, and the scarlet, and the living bird, and dip them in the blood of the slain bird, and in the running water, and Rsprinkle the house seven times: Ex. 12:7

52 And he shall Tcleanse the house with the blood of the bird, and with the running water, and with the living bird, and with the cedar wood, and with the hyssop, and with the scarlet: *in a ceremonial way*

53 But he shall Rlet go the living bird out of the city into the open fields, and Rmake an atonement for the house: and it shall be clean.   16:21 · *v. 20; 4:20*

The Purpose of the Laws of Leprosy

54 This *is* the Tlaw for all manner of Rplague of leprosy, and scall,   *procedure · 26:21*

55 And for the Rleprosy of a garment, Rand of a house,   13:47 · *v. 34*

56 And Rfor a rising, and for a scab, and for a bright spot: 13:2

57 To teach when *it is* unclean, and when *it is* clean: this *is* the law of leprosy.

CHAPTER 15

Discharges of the Man

AND the Lord spake unto Moses and to Aaron, saying,

2 Speak unto the children of Israel, and say unto them, RWhen any man hath a running Tissue out of his flesh, *because of* his issue he *is* unclean.   Num. 5:2; 2 Sam. 3:29 · *sore*

3 And this shall be his uncleanness in his issue: whether his flesh run with his issue, or his flesh be stopped from his issue, it *is* his Runcleanness.   13:3

4 Every bed, whereon he lieth that hath the issue, is unclean: and every thing, whereon he sitteth, shall be unclean.

5 And whosoever Rtoucheth his bed shall wash his clothes, and bathe *himself* in water, and be unclean until the even.   5:2

6 And he that sitteth on *any* thing whereon he sat that hath the issue shall

Rwash his clothes, and bathe *himself* in water, and be unclean until the even.   6:27

7 And he that toucheth the flesh of him that hath the issue shall wash his clothes, and bathe *himself* in water, and be unclean until the even.

8 And if he that hath the issue Rspit upon him that is clean; then he shall wash his clothes, and bathe *himself* in water, and be unclean until the even.   Num. 12:14

9 And what saddle soever he rideth upon that hath the issue shall be unclean.

10 And whosoever toucheth any thing that was under him shall be unclean until the even: and he that beareth *any of* those things shall wash his clothes, and Rbathe *himself* in water, and be unclean until the even. Ex. 30:20

11 And whomsoever he toucheth that hath the Tissue, and hath not rinsed his hands in water, he shall wash his clothes, and bathe *himself* in water, and be unclean until the even.   *running sore*

12 And the Rvessel of earth, that he toucheth which hath the issue, shall be Tbroken: and every vessel of wood shall be rinsed in water.   6:28; 11:32, 33 · *destroyed*

13 And when he that hath an issue is cleansed of his issue; then Rhe shall number to himself seven days for his cleansing, and wash his clothes, and bathe his flesh in running water, and shall be clean.   v. 28; 14:8

14 And on the eighth day he shall take to him Rtwo turtledoves, or two young pigeons, and come before the LORD unto the door of the tabernacle of the congregation, and give them unto the priest: 14:22, 23

15 And the priest shall offer them, the one *for* a sin offering, and the other *for* a burnt offering; Rand the priest shall make Tan atonement for him before the LORD for his issue.   14:19, 31 · *reconciliation*

16 And if any man's seed of copulation go out from him, then he shall wash all his flesh in water, and be unclean until the even.

17 And every garment, and every skin, whereon is the seed of copulation, shall be washed with water, and be unclean until the even.

18 The woman also with whom man shall lie *with* seed of copulation, they shall *both* bathe *themselves* in water, and Rbe unclean until the even.   [Ex. 19:15; 1 Sam. 21:4; 1 Cor. 6:18]

Discharges of the Woman

19 And if a woman have an issue, *and* her issue in her flesh be blood, she shall be put apart seven days: and whosoever toucheth her shall be unclean until the even.

20 And every thing that she lieth upon in her separation shall be unclean: every thing also that she sitteth upon shall be unclean.

21 And whosoever toucheth her bed shall

wash his clothes, and bathe *himself* in water, and be unclean until the even.

22 And whosoever toucheth any thing that she sat upon shall wash his clothes, and bathe *himself* in water, and be unclean until the even.

23 And if it *be* on *her* bed, or on any thing whereon she sitteth, when he toucheth it, he shall be unclean until the even.

24 And Rif any man lie with her at all, and her Tflowers be upon him, he shall be unclean seven days; and all the bed whereon he lieth shall be unclean.   18:19 · *impurity*

25 And if a woman have an Rissue of her blood many days out of the time of her separation, or if it run beyond the time of her separation; all the days of the issue of her uncleanness shall be as the days of her separation: she *shall be* unclean. Matt. 9:20

26 Every bed whereon she lieth all the days of her issue shall be unto her as the bed of her separation: and whatsoever she sitteth upon shall be unclean, as the uncleanness of her separation.

27 And whosoever toucheth those things shall be unclean, and shall wash his clothes, and bathe *himself* in water, and be unclean until the even.

28 But Rif she be cleansed of her issue, then she shall number to herself seven days, and after that she shall be clean.   vv. 13–15

29 And on the eighth day she shall take unto her two turtles, or two young pigeons, and bring them unto the priest, to the door of the tabernacle of the congregation.

30 And the priest shall offer the Rone *for* a sin offering, and the other *for* a burnt offering; and the priest shall make an atonement for her before the LORD for the issue of her uncleanness.   5:7

The Purpose of the Laws of Discharges

31 Thus shall ye separate the children of Israel from their uncleanness; that they die not in their uncleanness, when they defile my tabernacle that *is* among them.

32 This *is* the Tlaw of him that hath an issue, and *of him* whose seed goeth from him, and is defiled therewith;   *regulation*

33 And of her that is sick of her Tflowers, and of him that hath an issue, of the man, Rand of the woman, and of him that lieth with her that is unclean.   *impurity · v. 25*

CHAPTER 16

Preparation of the High Priest

AND the LORD spake unto Moses after the death of the two sons of Aaron, when they offered before the LORD, and died;

2 And the LORD said unto Moses, Speak unto Aaron thy brother, that he come not at

all times into the holy *place* within the vail before the mercy seat, which *is* upon the ark; that he die not: for I will appear in the cloud upon the mercy seat.

3 Thus shall Aaron come into the holy *place:* Rwith a young bullock for a sin offering, and a ram for a burnt offering.   4:3

4 He shall put on the holy linen coat, and he shall have the linen breeches upon his flesh, and shall be girded with a linen girdle, and with the linen mitre shall he be attired: these *are* holy garments; therefore shall he wash his flesh in water, and *so* put them on.

5 And he shall take of Rthe congregation of the children of Israel two Tkids of the goats for a sin offering, and one ram for a burnt offering.   Ezra 6:17; Ezek. 45:22, 23 • *he-goats*

Identification of the Sacrifices

6 And Aaron shall offer his bullock of the sin offering, which *is* for himself, and make an atonement for himself, and for his house.

7 And he shall take the two goats, and present them before the LORD *at* the door of the tabernacle of the congregation.

8 And Aaron shall cast lots upon the two goats; one lot for the LORD, and the other lot for Tthe scapegoat.   *goat of removal; Azazel*

9 And Aaron shall bring the goat upon which the LORD's lot fell, and offer him *for* a sin offering.

10 But the goat, on which the lot fell to be the scapegoat, shall be presented alive before the LORD, to make Ran atonement with him, *and* to let him go for a scapegoat into the wilderness.   [1 John 2:2]

Atonement for the Priest

11 And Aaron shall bring the bullock of the sin offering, which *is* for himself, and shall make an atonement for himself, and for his house, and shall kill the bullock of the sin offering which *is* for himself:

12 And he shall take Ra censer full of burning coals of fire from off the altar before the LORD, and his hands full of Rsweet incense beaten small, and bring *it* within the vail: 10:1; Num. 16:18, 46; Rev. 8:5 • Ex. 30:34

13 And he shall put the incense upon the fire before the LORD, that the cloud of the incense may cover the mercy seat that *is* upon the testimony, that he die not:

14 And he shall take of the blood of the bullock, and Rsprinkle *it* with his finger upon the mercy seat eastward; and before the mercy seat shall he sprinkle of the blood with his finger seven times.   4:6

Atonement for the Tabernacle

15 RThen shall he kill the goat of the sin offering, that *is* for the people, and bring his blood within the vail, and do with that blood

as he did with the blood of the bullock, and sprinkle it upon the mercy seat, and before the mercy seat: [Heb. 2:17; 7:27]

16 And he shall Rmake an atonement for the holy *place,* because of the uncleanness of the children of Israel, and because of their transgressions in all their sins: and so shall he do for the tabernacle of the congregation, that remaineth among them in the midst of their uncleanness.   Ex. 29:36

17 And there shall be no man in the tabernacle of the congregation when he goeth in to make an atonement in the holy *place,* until he come out, and have made an atonement for himself, and for his household, and for all the congregation of Israel.

18 And he shall go out unto the altar that *is* before the LORD, and make an atonement for it; and shall take of the blood of the Tbullock, Rand of the blood of the goat, and Rput *it* upon the horns of the altar round about.   *bull* • Heb. 9:22, 23 • Ezek. 43:20, 22

19 And he shall sprinkle of the blood upon it with his finger seven times, and cleanse it, and Thallow it from the uncleanness of the children of Israel.   *present it as only for God*

Atonement for the People

20 And when he hath made an end of Treconciling the holy *place,* and the tabernacle of the congregation, and the altar, he shall bring the live goat: *atoning for*

21 And Aaron shall lay both his hands upon the head of the live goat, and confess over him all the Tiniquities of the children of Israel, and all their transgressions in all their sins, putting them upon the head of the goat, and shall send *him* away by the hand of a fit man into the wilderness: *sins*

22 And the goat shall bear upon him all their iniquities unto a land not inhabited: and he shall let go the goat in the wilderness.

23 And Aaron shall come into the tabernacle of the congregation, Rand shall put off the linen garments, which he put on when he went into the holy *place,* and shall leave them there: 6:11; Ezek. 42:14; 44:19

24 And he shall wash his flesh with water in the holy place, and put on his garments, and come forth, and Roffer his burnt offering, and the burnt offering of the people, and make Tan atonement for himself, and for the people.   Ex. 28:40, 41 • *ceremonial*

25 And Rthe fat of the sin offering shall he burn upon the altar.   4:10

26 And he that let go the goat for the scapegoat shall Rwash his clothes, Rand bathe his flesh in water, and afterward come into the camp.   11:25, 40 • 15:5

27 And the bullock *for* the sin offering, and the goat *for* the sin offering, whose blood was brought in to make atonement in the holy

place, shall one carry forth without the camp; and they shall burn in the fire their skins, and their flesh, and their dung.

28 And he that burneth them shall wash his clothes, and bathe his flesh in water and afterward he shall come into the camp.

Purpose of the Day of Atonement

29 And this shall be a statute for ever unto you: that in the seventh month, on the tenth day of the month, ye shall ᵀafflict your souls, and do no work at all, whether it be one of your own country, or a stranger that sojourneth among you: *afflict yourselves*

30 For on that day shall the priest make ᵀan atonement for you, to cleanse you, that ye may be clean from all your sins before the LORD. *ceremony of reconciliation*

31 ᴿIt shall be a ᵀsabbath of rest unto you, and ᴿye shall ᵀafflict your souls, by a statute for ever. *23:32 • resting period • Is. 58:3, 5 • humble*

32 And the priest, whom he shall anoint, and whom he shall consecrate to minister in the priest's office in his father's stead, shall make the atonement, and shall put on the linen clothes, even the holy garments:

33 And he shall make an ᴿatonement for the holy sanctuary, and he shall make an atonement for the tabernacle of the congregation, and for the altar, and he shall make an atonement for the priests, and for all the people of the congregation. *17:11*

34 ᴿAnd this shall be an everlasting statute unto you, to make an atonement for the children of Israel for all their sins ᴿonce a year. And he did as the LORD commanded Moses. *23:31; Num. 29:7 • Ex. 30:10*

CHAPTER 17

Laws Concerning the Location of Sacrifices

AND the LORD spake unto Moses, saying, 2 Speak unto Aaron, and unto his sons, and unto all the children of Israel, and say unto them; This is the thing which the LORD hath commanded, saying,

3 What man soever there be of the house of Israel, ᴿthat killeth an ox, or lamb, or goat, in the camp, or that killeth it ᵀout of the camp, *Deut. 12:5, 15, 21 • outside*

4 And bringeth it not unto the door of the tabernacle of the congregation, to offer an offering unto the LORD before the tabernacle of the LORD; blood shall be imputed unto that man; he hath shed blood; and that man shall be cut off from among his people:

5 To the end that the children of Israel may bring their sacrifices, ᴿwhich they offer in the open field, even that they may bring them unto the LORD, unto the door of the tabernacle of the congregation, unto the priest, and offer them for peace offerings unto the LORD. *Gen. 21:33; 22:2; 31:54*

6 And the priest shall sprinkle the blood upon the altar of the LORD at the door of the tabernacle of the congregation, and burn the fat for a sweet savour unto the LORD.

7 And they shall no more offer their sacrifices unto devils, after whom they have gone a whoring. This shall be a statute for ever unto them throughout their generations.

8 And thou shalt say unto them, Whatsoever man there be of the house of Israel, or of the strangers which sojourn among you, that offereth a burnt offering or sacrifice,

9 And bringeth it not unto the door of the tabernacle of the congregation, to offer it unto the LORD; even that man shall be ᵀcut off from among his people. *destroyed*

Laws Concerning the Use of Blood

10 And whatsoever man there be of the house of Israel, or of the strangers that sojourn among you, that eateth any manner of blood; I will even set my face against that soul that eateth blood, and ᵀwill cut him off from among his people. *destroy him*

11 For the life of the flesh is in the blood: and I have given it to you upon the altar to make an atonement for your souls: for ᴿit is ᵀthe blood that maketh an atonement for the soul. *[Heb. 9:22] • the death of the sacrifice*

12 Therefore I said unto the children of Israel, ᴿNo ᵀsoul of you shall eat blood, neither shall any stranger that sojourneth among you eat blood. *Deut. 12:16 • person*

13 And whatsoever man there be of the children of Israel, or of the strangers that sojourn among you, which ᴿhunteth and catcheth any beast or fowl that may be eaten; he shall even pour out the blood thereof, and cover it with dust. *7:26*

14 ᴿFor it is the life of all flesh; the blood of it is for the life thereof: therefore I said unto the children of Israel, Ye shall eat the blood of no manner of flesh: for the life of all flesh is the blood thereof: whosoever eateth it shall be cut off. *Gen. 9:4; Deut. 12:23*

15 And every soul that eateth that which died of itself, or that which was torn with beasts, whether it be one of your own country, or a stranger, he shall both wash his clothes, and bathe himself in water, and be unclean until the even: then shall he be clean.

16 But if he wash them not, nor bathe his flesh; then he shall bear his iniquity.

CHAPTER 18

Laws of Sexual Sin

AND the LORD spake unto Moses, saying, 2 Speak unto the children of Israel, and say unto them, I am the LORD your God.

3 After the doings of the land of Egypt, wherein ye dwelt, shall ye not do: and after the doings of the land of Canaan, whither I bring you, shall ye not do: neither shall ye walk in their ᵀordinances.   *ways*

4 ᴿYe shall do my ᵀjudgments, and keep mine ordinances, to walk therein: I *am* the LORD your God.   [Ezek. 20:19] • *ordinances*

5 Ye shall therefore keep my statutes, and my judgments: which if a man ᵀdo, he shall live in them: I *am* the LORD.   *practices*

6 None of you shall approach to any that is near of kin to him, to uncover *their* nakedness: I *am* the LORD.

7 ᴿThe nakedness of thy father, or the nakedness of thy mother, shalt thou not uncover: she *is* thy mother; thou shalt not uncover her nakedness.   20:11; Ezek. 22:10

8 ᴿThe nakedness of thy father's wife shalt thou not uncover: it *is* thy father's nakedness.   Gen. 35:22; 1 Cor. 5:1

9 The nakedness of thy sister, the daughter of thy father, or daughter of thy mother, *whether she be* born at home, or born abroad, *even* their nakedness thou shalt not uncover.

10 The nakedness of thy son's daughter, or of thy daughter's daughter, *even* their nakedness thou shalt not uncover: for their's *is* thine own nakedness.

11 The nakedness of thy father's wife's daughter, begotten of thy father, she *is* thy sister, thou shalt not uncover her nakedness.

12 ᴿThou shalt not uncover the nakedness of thy father's sister: she *is* thy father's near kinswoman.   20:19

13 Thou shalt not uncover the nakedness of thy mother's sister: for she *is* thy mother's near kinswoman.

14 Thou shalt not uncover the nakedness of thy father's brother, thou shalt not approach to his wife: she *is* thine aunt.

15 Thou shalt not uncover the nakedness of thy daughter in law: she *is* thy son's wife; thou shalt not uncover her nakedness.

16 ᴿThou shalt not uncover the nakedness of thy brother's wife: it *is* thy brother's nakedness.   20:21; Matt. 14:4

17 ᴿThou shalt not uncover the nakedness of a woman and her daughter, neither shalt thou take her son's daughter, or her daughter's daughter, to uncover her nakedness; *for* they *are* her near kinswomen: it *is* ᵀwickedness.   20:14 • *an evil thing to do*

18 Neither shalt thou take a wife to her sister, to ᵀvex *her*, to uncover her nakedness, beside the other in her life *time*.   *irritate*

19 Also thou shalt not approach unto a woman to uncover her nakedness, as long as she is put apart for her uncleanness.

20 ᴿMoreover thou shalt not ᵀlie carnally with thy neighbour's wife, to defile thyself with her.   [Prov. 6:25–33] • *have intercourse*

21 And thou shalt not let any of thy seed pass through *the fire* to ᴿMo'-lech,ᵀ neither shalt thou profane the name of thy God: I *am* the LORD.   Acts 7:43 • *Mo'-loch*

22 Thou shalt not lie with mankind, as with womankind: it *is* ᵀabomination.   *sin*

23 ᴿNeither shalt thou lie with any beast to defile thyself therewith: neither shall any woman stand before a beast to lie down thereto: it *is* ᵀconfusion.   Ex. 22:19 • *sin*

24 Defile not ye yourselves in any of these things: for in all these the nations are defiled which I cast out before you:

25 And the land is defiled: therefore I do visit the iniquity thereof upon it, and the land itself vomiteth out her inhabitants.

26 ᴿYe shall therefore ᵀkeep my statutes and my judgments, and shall not commit *any* of these ᵀabominations; *neither* any of your own nation, nor any stranger that sojourneth among you: vv. 5, 30 • *obey* • *sins*

27 (For all these abominations have the men of the land done, which *were* before you, and the land is defiled;)

28 That ᴿthe land spue not you out also, when ye defile it, as it spued out the nations that *were* before you.   Jer. 9:19

29 For whosoever shall commit any of these abominations, even the ᵀsouls that commit *them* shall be ᵀcut off from among their people.   *persons* • *destroyed*

30 Therefore shall ye keep mine ordinance, that ye commit not *any one* of these abominable customs, which were committed before you, and that ye defile not yourselves therein: I *am* the LORD your God.

CHAPTER 19

Laws of Social Order

AND the LORD spake unto Moses, saying, 2 Speak unto all the congregation of the children of Israel, and say unto them, ᴿYe shall be ᵀholy: for I the LORD your God *am* holy.   11:44 • *entirely committed in heart to God*

3 Ye shall ᵀfear every man his mother, and his father, and ᴿkeep my sabbaths: I *am* the LORD your God.   *respect* • Ex. 20:8

4 ᴿTurn ye not unto idols, ᴿnor make to yourselves ᵀmolten gods: I *am* the LORD your God.   Ex. 20:4; Ps. 96:5 • Ex. 34:17 • *images*

5 And ᴿif ye offer a sacrifice of peace offerings unto the LORD, ye shall offer it ᵀat your own will.   7:16 • *that ye may be accepted*

6 It shall be eaten the same day ye offer it, and on the morrow: and if ought remain until the third day, it shall be burnt in the fire.

7 And if it be eaten at all on the third day, it *is* abominable; it shall not be accepted.

8 Therefore *every one* that eateth it shall bear his iniquity, because he hath profaned

the hallowed thing of the LORD: and that soul shall be cut off from among his people.

9 And Rwhen ye reap the harvest of your land, thou shalt not wholly reap the corners of thy field, neither shalt thou gather the gleanings of thy harvest.   Deut. 24:19

10 And thou shalt not glean thy vineyard, neither shalt thou gather *every* grape of thy vineyard; thou shalt leave them for the poor and stranger: I *am* the LORD your God.

11 RYe shall not steal, neither deal falsely, Rneither lie one to another.   Ex. 20:15 • Eph. 4:25

12 And ye shall not swear by my name falsely, Rneither shalt thou profane the name of thy God: I *am* the LORD.   18:21

13 RThou shalt not defraud thy neighbour, neither rob *him:* Rthe wages of him that is hired shall not abide with thee all night until the morning.   Mark 10:19 • Mal. 3:5

14 Thou shalt not curse the deaf, nor put a stumblingblock before the blind, but shalt fear thy God: I *am* the LORD.

15 RYe shall do no unrighteousness in judgment: thou shalt not respect the person of the poor, nor honour the person of the mighty: *but* in righteousness shalt thou judge thy neighbour.   Ex. 23:3, 6; Ps. 82:2

16 Thou shalt not go up and down *as* a talebearer among thy people: neither shalt thou Tstand against the blood of thy neighbour: I *am* the LORD.   *do anything to harm*

17 Thou shalt not hate thy brother in thine heart: thou shalt in any wise rebuke thy neighbour, and not suffer sin upon him.

18 Thou shalt not Tavenge, nor bear any grudge against the children of thy people, but thou shalt love thy neighbour as thyself: I *am* the LORD.   *retaliate for any hurt*

19 Ye shall keep my statutes. Thou shalt not let thy cattle gender with a diverse kind: Rthou shalt not sow thy field with mingled seed: neither shall a garment mingled of linen and woollen come upon thee.   Deut. 22:9, 11

20 RAnd whosoever lieth carnally with a woman, that *is* a bondmaid, betrothed to an husband, and not at all redeemed, nor freedom given her; she shall be scourged; they shall not be put to death, because she was not free.   Deut. 22:23–27

21 And he shall bring his Rtrespass offering unto the LORD, unto the door of the tabernacle of the congregation, *even* a ram for a Ttrespass offering.   6:1–7 • *guilt*

22 And the priest shall make an atonement for him with the ram of the trespass offering before the LORD for his sin which he hath done: and the sin which he hath done shall be Rforgiven him.   Num. 15:25

23 And when ye shall come into the land, and shall have planted all manner of trees for food, then ye shall count the fruit thereof as Tuncircumcised: three years shall it be as

uncircumcised unto you: it shall not be eaten of.   *unfit*

24 But in the fourth year all the fruit thereof shall be Tholy to praise the LORD withal.   *holiness of praises to the LORD*

25 And in the fifth year shall ye eat of the fruit thereof, that it may yield unto you the increase thereof: I *am* the LORD your God.

26 Ye shall not eat *any thing* with the blood: Rneither shall ye use Tenchantment, nor Tobserve times.   Deut. 18:10 • *sorcery* • *astrology*

27 TYe shall not Tround the corners of your heads, neither shalt thou mar the corners of thy beard.   *like the pagans* • *shave*

28 Ye shall not Rmake any cuttings in your flesh for the dead, nor Tprint any marks upon you: I *am* the LORD.   Jer. 16:6 • *tattoo*

29 RDo not prostitute thy daughter, to cause her to be a whore; lest the land fall to whoredom, and the land become full of wickedness.   Deut. 23:17, 18

30 Ye shall keep my sabbaths, and reverence my sanctuary: I *am* the LORD.

31 Regard not them that have familiar spirits, neither seek after wizards, to be defiled by them: I *am* the LORD your God.

32 Thou shalt rise up before Tthe hoary head, and honour the face of the old man, and fear thy God: I *am* the LORD.   *the aged*

33 And Rif a stranger sojourn with thee in your land, ye shall not vex him.   Ex. 22:21

34 *But* the stranger that dwelleth with you shall be unto you as Tone born among you, and thou shalt love him as thyself; for ye were strangers in the land of Egypt: I *am* the LORD your God.   *one of your own family*

35 Ye shall Tdo no unrighteousness in judgment, in Tmeteyard, in weight, or in measure.   *not be dishonest* • *measures of length*

36 RJust balances, Tjust weights, a just Te'-phah, and a just Thin, shall ye have: I *am* the LORD your God, which brought you out of the land of Egypt.   Deut. 25:13, 15 • *fair* • *20.87 qt.* • *1 gal.*

37 RTherefore shall ye observe all my statutes, and all my judgments, and do them: I *am* the LORD.   Deut. 4:5, 6; 5:1; 6:25

CHAPTER 20

The Penalty for Worshipping Molech

AND the LORD spake unto Moses, saying, 2 RAgain, thou shalt say to the children of Israel, RWhosoever *he be* of the children of Israel, or of the strangers that Tsojourn in Israel, that giveth *any* of his seed unto Mo'-lech; he shall surely be put to death: the people of the land shall stone him with stones.   18:2 • Jer. 7:31 • *stay temporarily*

3 And I will set my face against that man, and will Tcut him off from among his people;

because he hath given of his seed unto ᴿMo′-lech, to defile my sanctuary, and to profane my holy name.   *destroy him* · 15:31

4 And if the people of the land do any ways ᵀhide their eyes from the man, when he giveth of his seed unto ᴿMo′-lech, and kill him not: *ignore his sin* · Deut. 17:2–5

5 Then I will set my face against that man, and against his family, and will cut him off, and all that go a whoring after him, to commit whoredom with Mo′-lech, from among their people.

The Penalty for Consulting Spirits

6 And the ᵀsoul that turneth after such as have familiar spirits, and after wizards, to go a whoring after them, I will even set my face against that soul, and will cut him off from among his people.   *the man that follows*

7 Sanctify yourselves therefore, and be ye holy: for I *am* the Lᴏʀᴅ your God.

8 And ye shall keep my statutes, and do them: I *am* the Lᴏʀᴅ which sanctify you.

The Penalty for Cursing Parents

9 ᴿFor every one that curseth his father or his mother shall be surely put to death: he hath cursed his father or his mother; his blood *shall be* upon him.   Deut. 27:16

The Penalty for Committing Sexual Sins

10 And ᴿthe man that committeth adultery with *another* man's wife, *even he* that committeth adultery with his neighbour's wife, the adulterer and the adulteress shall surely be put to death.   18:20; Deut. 22:22

11 And the man that lieth with his father's wife hath uncovered his father's nakedness: both of them shall surely be put to death; their blood *shall be* upon them.

12 And if a man lie with his daughter in law, both of them shall surely be put to death: they have ᵀwrought confusion; their blood *shall be* upon them.   *done evil*

13 If a man also lie with mankind, as he lieth with a woman, both of them have committed an abomination: they shall surely be put to death; their blood *shall be* upon them.

14 And if a man take a wife and her mother, it *is* wickedness: they shall be burnt with fire, both he and they; that there be no wickedness among you.

15 ᴿAnd if a man lie with a beast, he shall surely be put to death: and ye shall slay the beast.   18:23

16 And if a woman approach unto any beast, and lie down thereto, thou shalt kill the woman, and the beast: they shall surely be put to death; their blood *shall be* upon them.

17 And if a man shall take his sister, his father's daughter, or his mother's daughter,

and see her nakedness, and she see his nakedness; it *is* a wicked thing; and they shall be ᵀcut off in the sight of their people: he hath uncovered his sister's nakedness; he shall bear his iniquity.   *publicly destroyed*

18 And if a man shall lie with a woman having her sickness, and shall uncover her nakedness; he hath discovered her fountain, and she hath uncovered the fountain of her blood: and both of them shall be ᵀcut off from among their people.   *destroyed*

19 And thou shalt not uncover the nakedness of thy mother's sister, nor of thy father's sister: for he uncovereth his near kin: they shall bear their iniquity.

20 ᴿAnd if a man shall lie with his uncle's wife, he hath uncovered his uncle's nakedness: they shall bear their sin; they shall die childless.   18:14

21 ᴿAnd if a man shall take his brother's wife, it *is* ᵀan unclean thing: he hath uncovered his brother's nakedness; they shall be childless.   18:16 · *impurity*

The Purpose of the Laws of Sanctification of the People

22 Ye shall therefore keep all my statutes, and all my judgments, and do them: that the land, whither I bring you to dwell therein, ᴿspue you not out.   18:25; Rev. 3:16

23 ᴿAnd ye shall not walk in the manners of the nation, which I cast out before you: for they committed all these things, and therefore I abhorred them.   18:3, 24

24 But I have said unto you, Ye shall inherit their land, and I will give it unto you to possess it, a land that floweth with milk and honey: I *am* the Lᴏʀᴅ your God, which have separated you from *other* people.

25 Ye shall therefore put difference between clean beasts and unclean, and between unclean fowls and clean: and ye shall not make your souls abominable by beast, or by fowl, or by any manner of living thing that creepeth on the ground, which I have separated from you as unclean.

26 And ye shall be holy unto me: for I the Lᴏʀᴅ *am* holy, and have severed you from *other* people, that ye should be mine.

27 A man also or woman that hath a familiar spirit, or that is a wizard, shall surely be put to death: they shall stone them with stones: their blood *shall be* upon them.

CHAPTER 21

Laws Concerning Priests

Aᴺᴅ the Lᴏʀᴅ said unto Moses, Speak unto the priests the sons of Aaron, and say unto them, ᴿThere shall none be defiled for the dead among his people: Ezek. 44:25

2 ᵀBut for his kin, that is near unto him, *that is,* for his mother, and for his father, and for his son, and for his daughter, and for his brother,   *except*

3 And for his sister a virgin, that is nigh unto him, which hath had no husband; for her may he be defiled.

4 *But* ᴿhe shall not defile himself, *being* a chief man among his people, to profane himself.   Ezek. 24:16, 17

5 ᴿThey shall not make baldness upon their head, neither shall they shave off the corner of their beard, ᴿnor make any cuttings in their flesh.   19:27; Ezek. 44:20 • Deut. 14:1

6 They shall be ᴿholy unto their God, and not profane the name of their God: for the offerings of the Lᴏʀᴅ ᴿmade by fire, *and* the bread of their God, they do offer: therefore they shall be holy.   Ex. 22:31 • 3:11

7 ᴿTheyᵀ shall not take a wife *that is* a whore, or profane; neither shall they take a woman put away from her husband: for he *is* holy unto his God.   Ezek. 44:22 • *the priests*

8 Thou shalt ᵀsanctify him therefore; for he offereth the bread of thy God: he shall be holy unto thee: for I the Lᴏʀᴅ, which sanctify you, *am* holy.   *set apart from others*

9 ᴿAnd the daughter of any priest, if she profane herself by playing the whore, ᴿshe profaneth her father: she shall be burnt with fire.   19:29 • Gen. 38:24

Laws Concerning the High Priest

10 And *he that is* the high priest among his brethren, upon whose head the ᴿanointing oil was poured, and that is consecrated to put on the garments, shall not uncover his head, nor rend his clothes;   Num. 35:25

11 ᴿNeither shall he go in to any dead body, nor defile himself for his father, or for his mother;   Num. 19:14

12 Neither shall he go out of the sanctuary, nor profane the sanctuary of his God; for the crown of the anointing oil of his God *is* upon him: I *am* the Lᴏʀᴅ.

13 ᴿAnd he shall take a wife in her virginity.   *v.* 7

14 ᴿA widow, or a divorced woman, or profane, *or* an harlot, these shall he not take: but he shall take a virgin of his own people to wife.   Ezek. 44:22

15 Neither shall he profane his seed among his people: for I the Lᴏʀᴅ do sanctify him.

People Prohibited from the Priesthood

16 And the Lᴏʀᴅ spake unto Moses, saying,

17 Speak unto Aaron, saying, Whosoever *he be* of thy seed in their generations that hath *any* blemish, let him not approach to ᵀoffer the bread of his God.   *serve as a priest*

18 ᴿFor whatsoever man *he be* that hath a blemish, he shall not approach: a blind man, or a lame, or he that hath a flat nose, or any thing superfluous,   22:23

19 Or a man that is brokenfooted, or brokenhanded,

20 Or crookbackt, or a dwarf, or that hath a blemish in his eye, or be scurvy, or scabbed, ᴿor hath his stones broken;   Is. 56:3–5

21 No man that hath a blemish of the seed of Aaron the priest shall come nigh to offer the offerings of the Lᴏʀᴅ made by fire: he hath a blemish; he shall not come nigh to offer the bread of his God.

22 He shall eat the bread of his God, *both* of the most holy, and of the holy.

23 Only he shall not go in unto the vail, nor come nigh unto the altar, because he hath a blemish; that he profane not my sanctuaries: for I the Lᴏʀᴅ do sanctify them.

24 And Moses told *it* unto Aaron, and to his sons, and unto all the children of Israel.

CHAPTER 22

Things Prohibited of the Priesthood

Aɴᴅ the Lᴏʀᴅ spake unto Moses, saying, 2 Speak unto Aaron and to his sons, that they separate themselves from the holy things of the children of Israel, and that they profane not my holy name *in those things* which they hallow unto me: I *am* the Lᴏʀᴅ.

3 Say unto them, Whosoever *he be* of all your seed among your generations, that goeth unto the holy things, which the children of Israel hallow unto the Lᴏʀᴅ, having his uncleanness upon him, that soul shall be cut off from my presence: I *am* the Lᴏʀᴅ.

4 What man soever of the seed of Aaron *is* a leper, or hath a running issue; he shall not eat of the holy things, until he be clean. And ᴿwhoso toucheth any thing *that is* unclean *by* the dead, or ᴿa man whose seed goeth from him;   Num. 19:11 • 15:16

5 Or whosoever toucheth any creeping thing, whereby he may be made unclean, or a man of whom he may take uncleanness, whatsoever uncleanness he hath;

6 The soul which hath touched any such shall be unclean until even, and ᵀshall not eat of the holy things, unless he wash his flesh with water.   *shall not participate as a priest*

7 And when the sun is down, he shall be clean, and shall afterward eat of the holy things; because ᴿit *is* his food.   Num. 18:11, 13

8 ᴿThat which dieth of itself, or is torn *with beasts,* he shall not eat to defile himself therewith: I *am* the Lᴏʀᴅ.   Ezek. 44:31

9 They shall therefore ᵀkeep mine ᵀordinance, lest they bear sin for it, and die therefore, if they profane it: I the Lᴏʀᴅ do sanctify them.   *obey • regulation; charge*

10 There shall no stranger eat *of* the holy

thing: a sojourner of the priest, or an hired servant, shall not eat *of* the holy thing.

11 But if the priest buy *any* soul with his money, he shall eat of it, and he that is born in his house: they shall eat of his meat.

12 If the priest's daughter also be *married* unto a stranger, she may not eat of ᵀan offering of the holy things.   *the heave*

13 But if the priest's daughter be a widow, or divorced, and have no child, and is returned unto her father's house, as in her youth, she shall eat of her father's meat: but there shall no stranger eat thereof.

14 ᴿAnd if a man eat *of* the holy thing unwittingly, then he shall put the fifth *part* thereof unto it, and shall give *it* unto the priest with the holy thing.   5:15, 16

15 And they shall not ᵀprofane the holy things of the children of Israel, which they offer unto the LORD;   *treat as common*

16 Or ᵀsuffer them to bear the iniquity of trespass, when they eat their holy things: for I the LORD do sanctify them.   *allow*

Sacrifices Prohibited of the Priesthood

17 And the LORD spake unto Moses, saying,

18 Speak unto Aaron, and to his sons, and unto all the children of Israel, and say unto them, Whatsoever *he be* of the house of Israel, or of the strangers in Israel, that will offer his oblation for all his vows, and for all his freewill offerings, which they will offer unto the LORD for a burnt offering;

19 ᴿYe shall *offer* at your own will a male without blemish, of the beeves, of the sheep, or of the goats.   1:3; 21:18; Deut. 15:21

20 ᴿ*But* whatsoever hath a blemish, *that* shall ye not offer: for it shall not be acceptable for you.   [Eph. 5:27; Heb. 9:14; 1 Pet. 1:19]

21 And whosoever offereth a sacrifice of peace offerings unto the LORD to accomplish *his* vow, or a freewill offering in beeves or ᵀsheep, it shall be perfect to be accepted; there shall be no blemish therein.   *goats*

22 ᴿBlind, or broken, or maimed, or having ᵀa wen, or scurvy, or scabbed, ye shall not offer these unto the LORD, nor make ᴿan offering by fire of them upon the altar unto the LORD.   Mal. 1:8 • *sores* • 1:9, 13; 3:5

23 Either a bullock or a lamb that hath any thing superfluous or lacking in his parts, that mayest thou offer *for* a freewill offering; but for a vow it shall not be accepted.

24 Ye shall not offer unto the LORD ᴿthat which is bruised, or crushed, or broken, or cut; neither shall ye make *any offering thereof* in your land.   21:20

25 Neither from a stranger's hand shall ye offer ᴿthe bread of your God of any of these; because their ᴿcorruption *is* in them, *and* blemishes *be* in them: they shall not be accepted for you.   21:6, 17 • Mal. 1:14

26 And the LORD spake unto Moses, saying,

27 When a bullock, or a sheep, or a goat, is brought forth, then it shall be seven days under the ᵀdam; and from the eighth day and thenceforth it shall be accepted for an offering made by fire unto the LORD.   *mother*

28 And *whether it be* cow or ewe, ye shall not kill it and her young both in one day.

29 And when ye will ᴿoffer a sacrifice of thanksgiving unto the LORD, offer *it* ᵀat your own will.   Amos 4:5 • *as you feel you want to*

30 On the same day it shall be eaten up; ye shall leave ᴿnone of it until the morrow: I *am* the LORD.   7:15

The Purpose of the Laws of the Priesthood

31 ᴿTherefore shall ye keep my commandments, and do them: I *am* the LORD.   19:37

32 ᴿNeither shall ye profane my holy name; but ᴿI will be ᵀhallowed among the children of Israel: I *am* the LORD which hallow you,   18:21 • [Luke 11:2] • *treated as holy*

33 That brought you out of the land of Egypt, to be your God: I *am* the LORD.

CHAPTER 23

The Weekly Sabbath

AND the LORD spake unto Moses, saying, 2 Speak unto the children of Israel, and say unto them, *Concerning* the feasts of the LORD, which ye shall proclaim *to be* holy convocations, *even* these *are* my feasts.

3 ᴿSix days shall work be done: but the seventh day *is* the sabbath of rest, an holy convocation; ye shall do no work *therein*: it *is* the sabbath of the LORD in all your ᵀdwellings.   19:3; Deut. 5:13; Luke 13:14 • *homes*

Passover

4 ᴿThese *are* the feasts of the LORD, *even* holy convocations, which ye shall proclaim in their seasons.   *v.* 37; Ex. 23:2, 14

5 In the fourteenth *day* of the first month at even *is* the LORD'S passover.

Unleavened Bread

6 And on the fifteenth day of the same month *is* the feast of ᴿunleavened bread unto the LORD: seven days ye must eat unleavened bread.   *vv.* 6–17; Num. 6:15

7 ᴿIn the first day ye shall have an holy convocation: ye shall do no ᵀservile work therein.   Ex. 12:16; Num. 28:18, 25 • *menial task*

8 But ye shall offer an offering made by fire unto the LORD seven days: in the seventh day is an holy convocation: ye shall do no servile work *therein.*

Firstfruits

9 And the LORD spake unto Moses, saying,

10 Speak unto the children of Israel, and say unto them, When ye be come into the land which I give unto you, and shall ᴿreap the harvest thereof, then ye shall bring a ᵀsheaf of ᴿthe firstfruits of your harvest unto the priest: Ex. 23:19 · handful · [Rom. 11:16]

11 And he shall ᴿwaveᵀ the sheaf before the LORD, to be accepted for you: on the morrow after the sabbath the priest shall wave it. Ex. 29:24 · present in his hands

12 And ye shall offer that day when ye wave ᵀthe sheaf an he lamb without blemish of the first year for a burnt offering unto the LORD. 2.087 qt.

13 And the ᵀmeat offering thereof shall be ᵀtwo tenth deals of fine flour mingled with oil, an offering made by fire unto the LORD ᵀfor a sweet savour: and the drink offering thereof shall be of wine, the ᵀfourth part of an hin. meal · 4.174 qt. · pleasing to God · 1 qt.

14 And ᴿye shall eat neither bread, nor parched corn, nor green ears, until the selfsame day that ye have brought an offering unto your God: it shall be a statute for ever throughout your generations in all your dwellings. Ex. 34:26; Num. 15:20, 21

Pentecost

15 And ye shall count unto you from the morrow after the sabbath, from the day that ye brought ᵀthe sheaf of the wave offering; seven sabbaths shall be complete: 2.087 qt.

16 Even unto the morrow after the seventh sabbath shall ye number ᵀfifty days; and ye shall offer ᴿa new meat offering unto the LORD. Pentecost · Num. 28:26

17 Ye shall bring out of your habitations two ᵀwave loaves of two tenth deals: they shall be of fine flour; they shall be baken with leaven; they are ᴿthe firstfruits unto the LORD. to be offered to God · Num. 15:17-21

18 And ye shall offer with the bread seven lambs without blemish of the first year, and one young bullock, and two rams: they shall be for a burnt offering unto the LORD, with their ᵀmeat offering, and their drink offerings, even an offering made by fire, of sweet savour unto the LORD. meal

19 Then ye shall sacrifice ᴿone kid of the goats for a sin offering, and two lambs of the first year for a sacrifice of ᴿpeace offerings. 4:23, 28; Num. 28:30 · 3:1

20 And the priest shall wave them with the bread of the firstfruits for a wave offering before the LORD, with the two lambs: they shall be holy to the LORD for the priest.

21 And ye shall proclaim on the selfsame day, that it may be an holy convocation unto you: ye shall do no ᵀservile work therein: it shall be a ᵀstatute for ever in all your dwellings throughout your generations. laborious · law

22 And when ye reap the harvest of your land, thou shalt not make clean riddance of the corners of thy field when thou reapest, neither shalt thou gather any gleaning of thy harvest: thou shalt leave them unto the poor, and to the stranger: I am the LORD your God.

Trumpets

23 And the LORD spake unto Moses, saying,

24 Speak unto the children of Israel, saying, In the ᴿseventh month, in the first day of the month, shall ye have a sabbath, ᴿa memorial of blowing of trumpets, an holy ᵀconvocation. Num. 29:1 · 25:9 · gathering

25 Ye shall do no servile work therein: but ye shall offer an offering made by fire unto the LORD.

Day of Atonement

26 And the LORD spake unto Moses, saying,

27 Also on the tenth day of this seventh month there shall be a day of atonement: it shall be an holy convocation unto you; and ye shall afflict your souls, and offer an offering made by fire unto the LORD.

28 And ye shall do no work in that same day: for it is a day of atonement, ᴿto make an atonement for you before the LORD your God. 16:34

29 For whatsoever ᵀsoul it be that shall not be afflicted in that same day, he shall be cut off from among his people. person

30 And whatsoever soul it be that doeth any work in that same day, the same soul will I destroy from among my people.

31 Ye shall do no manner of work: it shall be a statute for ever throughout your generations in all your dwellings.

32 It shall be unto you a sabbath of rest, and ye shall afflict your souls: in the ninth day of the month at even, from even unto even, shall ye celebrate your sabbath.

Tabernacles

33 And the LORD spake unto Moses, saying,

34 Speak unto the children of Israel, saying, ᴿThe fifteenth day of this seventh month shall be the feast of tabernacles for seven days unto the LORD. Deut. 16:13

35 On the first day shall be an holy convocation: ye shall do no servile work therein.

36 Seven days ye shall offer an offering made by fire unto the LORD: on the eighth day shall be an holy convocation unto you; and ye shall offer an offering made by fire unto the LORD: it is a solemn assembly; and ye shall do no servile work therein.

37 ᴿThese *are* the feasts of the Lᴏʀᴅ, which ye shall proclaim *to be* holy convocations, to offer an offering made by fire unto the Lᴏʀᴅ, a burnt offering, and a meat offering, a sacrifice, and drink offerings, ᴿevery thing upon his day: *vv.* 2, 4 • Num. 28:1-29

38 ᴿBeside the sabbaths of the Lᴏʀᴅ, and beside your gifts, and beside all your vows, and beside all your freewill offerings, which ye give unto the Lᴏʀᴅ.   Num. 29:39

39 Also in the fifteenth day of the seventh month, when ye have ᴿgathered in the fruit of the land, ye shall keep a feast unto the Lᴏʀᴅ seven days: on the first day *shall be* a ᵀsabbath, and on the eighth day *shall be* a sabbath.   Ex. 23:16; Deut. 16:13 • *solemn rest*

40 And ye shall take you on the first day the boughs of goodly trees, branches of palm trees, and the boughs of thick trees, and willows of the brook; and ye shall rejoice before the Lᴏʀᴅ your God seven days.

41 And ye shall keep it a feast unto the Lᴏʀᴅ seven days in the year. *It shall be* a statute for ever in your generations: ye shall celebrate it in the seventh month.

42 ᴿYe shall dwell in ᵀbooths seven days; all that are Israelites born shall dwell in booths: Neh. 8:14-16; [Heb. 11:13, 16] • *tabernacles*

43 That your generations may know that I made the children of Israel to dwell in booths, when I brought them out of the land of Egypt: I *am* the Lᴏʀᴅ your God.

44 And Moses ᴿdeclared unto the children of Israel the feasts of the Lᴏʀᴅ.   *v.* 2

CHAPTER 24

Oil for the Lamps

Aɴᴅ the Lᴏʀᴅ spake unto Moses, saying, 2 ᴿCommand the children of Israel, that they bring unto thee pure oil olive beaten for the light, ᵀto cause the lamps to burn continually.   Ex. 27:20 • *to cause to ascend*

3 Without the vail of the testimony, in the tabernacle of the congregation, shall Aaron order it from the evening unto the morning before the Lᴏʀᴅ continually: *it shall be* a statute for ever in your generations.

4 He shall order the lamps upon the pure candlestick before the Lᴏʀᴅ continually.

The Shewbread

5 And thou shalt take fine flour, and bake twelve ᴿcakes thereof: ᵀtwo tenth deals shall be in one cake.   Ex. 25:30 • *4.174 qt.*

6 And thou shalt set them in two rows, six on a row, ᴿupon the ᵀpure table before the Lᴏʀᴅ.   2 Chr. 4:19; 13:11 • *table of pure gold*

7 ᴿAnd thou shalt put pure frankincense upon *each* row, that it may be on the bread for a memorial, *even* an offering made by fire unto the Lᴏʀᴅ.   2:2, 9, 16

8 ᴿEvery sabbath he shall set it in order before the Lᴏʀᴅ continually, *being taken* from the children of Israel by an everlasting ᵀcovenant.   1 Chr. 9:32; 2 Chr. 2:4 • *agreement*

9 And it shall be Aaron's and his sons'; and they shall eat it in the holy place: for it *is* most holy unto him of the offerings of the Lᴏʀᴅ made by fire by a perpetual statute.

Law of the Sanctified Name of God

10 And the son of an Israelitish woman, whose father *was* an Egyptian, went out among the children of Israel: and this son of the Israelitish *woman* and a man of Israel ᵀstrove together in the camp;   *fought*

11 And the Israelitish woman's son blasphemed the name *of the* Lᴏʀᴅ, and cursed. And they brought him unto Moses: (and his mother's name *was* Shel'-o-mith, the daughter of Dib'-ri, of the tribe of Dan:)

12 And they put him in ward, that the mind of the Lᴏʀᴅ might be shewed them.

13 And the Lᴏʀᴅ spake unto Moses, saying,

14 Bring forth him that hath cursed without the camp; and let all that heard *him* ᴿlay their hands upon his head, and let all the congregation stone him.   Deut. 13:9; 17:7

15 And thou shalt speak unto the children of Israel, saying, Whosoever curseth his God ᴿshall ᵀbear his sin.   20:17 • *be responsible*

16 And he that ᴿblasphemeth the name of the Lᴏʀᴅ, he shall surely be put to death, *and* all the congregation shall certainly stone him: as well the stranger, as he that is born in the land, when he blasphemeth the name *of the* Lᴏʀᴅ, shall be put to death.   [Matt. 12:31]

17 ᴿAnd he that killeth any man shall surely be put to death.   Ex. 21:12; Num. 35:31

18 ᴿAnd he that killeth a beast shall make it good; ᵀbeast for beast.   *v.* 21 • *life for life*

19 And if a man ᵀcause a blemish in his neighbour; as ᴿhe hath done, so shall it be done to him;   *harms* • Deut. 19:21; Matt. 5:38; 7:2

20 Breach for breach, eye for eye, tooth for tooth: as he hath caused a blemish in a man, so shall it be done to him *again.*

21 And he that killeth a beast, ᴿhe shall restore it: and he that killeth a man, he shall be put to death.   Ex. 21:33

22 Ye shall have one manner of law, as well for the stranger, as for one of your own country: for I *am* the Lᴏʀᴅ your God.

23 And Moses spake to the children of Israel, that they should bring forth him that had cursed out of the camp, and stone him with stones. And the children of Israel did as the Lᴏʀᴅ commanded Moses.

CHAPTER 25

Law of the Sabbath Year

AND the LORD spake unto Moses in mount Si'-nai, saying,

2 Speak unto the children of Israel, and say unto them, When ye come into the land which I give you, then shall the land ^Rkeep a sabbath unto the LORD.   26:34, 35

3 ^RSix years thou shalt sow thy field, and six years thou shalt prune thy vineyard, and gather in the fruit thereof;   Ex. 23:10, 11

4 But in the seventh year shall be a ^Tsabbath of rest unto the land, a sabbath for the LORD: thou shalt neither sow thy field, nor prune thy vineyard.   *the land shall lie fallow*

5 That which groweth of its own accord of thy harvest thou shalt not reap, neither gather the grapes of thy vine undressed: *for* it is a year of rest unto the land.

6 And the sabbath of the land shall be ^Tmeat for you; for thee, and for thy servant, and for thy maid, and for thy hired servant, and for thy stranger that sojourneth with thee,   *food*

7 And for thy cattle, and for the beast that *are* in thy land, shall all the increase thereof be ^Tmeat.   *food*

Law of the Year of Jubile

8 And thou shalt number seven sabbaths of years unto thee, seven times seven years; and the space of the seven sabbaths of years shall be unto thee forty and nine years.

9 Then shalt thou cause the trumpet of the jubile to sound on the tenth *day* of the seventh month, ^Rin the day of atonement shall ye make the trumpet sound throughout all your land.   23:24, 27

10 And ye shall hallow the fiftieth year, and proclaim liberty throughout *all* the land unto all the inhabitants thereof: it shall be a jubile unto you; and ye shall return every man unto his possession, and ye shall return every man unto his family.

11 A jubile shall that fiftieth year be unto you: ^Rye shall not sow, neither reap that which groweth of itself in it, nor gather *the* grapes in it of thy vine undressed.   *v.* 5

12 For it *is* the jubile; it shall be ^Tholy unto you: ^Rye shall eat the increase thereof out of the field.   *all for you alone* • *vv.* 6, 7

13 ^RIn the year of this jubile ye shall return every man unto his possession.   *v.* 10

14 And if thou sell ought unto thy neighbour, or buyest *ought* of thy neighbour's hand, ye shall not oppress one another:

15 According to the number of years after the jubile thou shalt buy of thy neighbour, *and* according unto the number of years of the fruits he shall sell unto thee:

16 ^RAccording to the multitude of years

thou shalt increase the price thereof, and according to the fewness of years thou shalt diminish the price of it: for *according* to the number *of the years* of the fruits doth he sell unto thee.   *vv.* 27, 51, 52

17 Ye shall not therefore ^Toppress one another; but thou shalt fear thy God: for I *am* the LORD your God.   *take advantage of*

18 Wherefore ye shall do my statutes, and keep my judgments, and do them; and ye shall dwell in the land in safety.

19 And the land shall yield her fruit, and ^Rye shall eat your fill, and dwell therein in safety.   26:5; Ezek. 34:25

20 And if ye shall say, ^RWhat shall we eat the seventh year? behold, we shall not sow, nor gather in our increase: Matt. 6:25

21 Then I will ^Rcommand my blessing upon you in the sixth year, and it shall bring forth fruit for three years.   Ex. 16:29

22 And ye shall sow the eighth year, and eat *yet* of old fruit until the ninth year; until her fruits come in ye shall eat *of* the old *store.*

23 The land shall not be sold ^Tfor ever: for the land *is* mine; for ye *are* ^Rstrangers and sojourners with me.   *in perpetuity* • Ps. 39:12

24 And in all the land of your possession ye shall grant a redemption for the land.

25 If thy brother be waxen poor, and hath sold away *some* of his possession, and if any of his kin come to redeem it, then shall he redeem that which his brother sold.

26 And if the man have none to redeem it, and himself be able to redeem it;

27 Then ^Rlet him count the years of the sale thereof, and restore the overplus unto the man to whom he sold it; that he may return unto his possession.   *vv.* 50–52

28 But if he be not able to restore *it* to him, then that which is sold shall remain in the hand of him that hath bought it until the year of jubile: and in the jubile it shall go out, and he shall return unto his possession.

29 And if a man sell a dwelling house in a walled city, then he may redeem it within a whole year after it is sold; *within* a full year may he redeem it.

30 And if it be not redeemed within the space of a full year, then the house that *is* in the walled city shall be established for ever to him that bought it throughout his generations: it shall not go out in the jubile.

31 But the houses of the villages which have no wall round about them shall be counted as the fields of the country: they may be redeemed, and they shall go out in the jubile.

32 Notwithstanding ^Rthe cities of the Levites, *and* the houses of the cities of their possession, may the Levites redeem at any time.   Num. 35:1–8

33 And if ^Ta man purchase of the Levites,

then the house that was sold, and the city of his possession, shall go out in *the year of* jubile: for the houses of the cities of the Levites *are* their possession among the children of Israel. *one of the Levites redeem them*

34 But ᴿthe field of the suburbs of their cities may not be sold; for it *is* their perpetual possession. Num. 35:2–5; Acts 4:36, 37

35 And if thy brother be waxen poor, and fallen in decay with thee; then thou shalt relieve him: *yea, though he be* a stranger, or a sojourner; that he may live with thee.

36 ᴿTake thou no ᵀusury of him, or increase: but fear thy God; that thy brother may live with thee. Ex. 22:25 · *interest on loans*

37 Thou shalt not give him thy money upon ᵀusury, nor lend him thy victuals for increase. *interest*

38 I *am* the Lᴏʀᴅ your God, which brought you forth out of the land of Egypt, to give you the land of Canaan, *and* to be your God.

39 ᴿAnd if thy brother *that dwelleth* by thee be waxen poor, and ᵀbe sold unto thee; thou shalt not compel him to serve as a bondservant: Deut. 15:12–18 · *in economic bondage*

40 *But* as an hired servant, ᴿ*and* as a sojourner, he shall be with thee, *and* shall serve thee unto the year of jubile: Ex. 21:2

41 And *then* shall he depart from thee, *both* he and his children with him, and shall return unto his own family, and unto the possession of his fathers shall he return.

42 For they *are* ᴿmy servants, which I brought forth out of the land of Egypt: they shall not be sold as bondmen. [1 Cor. 7:23]

43 Thou shalt not rule over him with ᵀrigour; but shalt fear thy God. *severity*

44 Both thy bondmen, and thy bondmaids, which thou shalt have, *shall be* of the ᵀheathen that are round about you; of them shall ye buy bondmen and bondmaids. *nations*

45 Moreover of the children of the strangers that do sojourn among you, of them shall ye buy, and of their families that *are* with you, which they begat in your land: and they shall be your possession.

46 And ᴿye shall take them as an inheritance for your children after you, to inherit *them for* a possession; they shall be your bondmen for ever: but over your brethren the children of Israel, ye shall not rule one over another with rigour. Is. 14:2

47 And if a sojourner or stranger wax rich by thee, and thy brother *that dwelleth* by him wax poor, and sell himself unto the stranger *or* sojourner by thee, or to the stock of the stranger's family:

48 After that he is sold he may be redeemed again; ᴿone of his brethren may redeem him: Neh. 5:5

49 Either his uncle, or his uncle's son, may redeem him, or *any* that is nigh of kin unto him of his family may redeem him; or if he be able, he may redeem himself.

50 And he shall reckon with him that bought him from the year that he was sold to him unto the year of jubile: and the price of his sale shall be according unto the number of years, ᴿaccording to the time of an hired servant shall it be with him. Is. 16:14

51 If *there* be yet many years *behind,* according unto them he shall give again the price of his redemption out of the money that he was bought for.

52 And if there remain but few years unto the year of jubile, then he shall count with him, *and* according unto his years shall he give him again the price of his redemption.

53 *And* as a yearly hired servant shall he be with him: *and the other* shall not rule with rigour over him in thy sight.

54 And if he be not redeemed in these *years,* then he shall go out in the year of jubile, *both* he, and his children with him.

55 For unto me the children of Israel *are* servants; they *are* my servants whom I brought forth out of the land of Egypt: I *am* the Lᴏʀᴅ your God.

CHAPTER 26

Basic Requirements of Obedience

YE shall make you no idols nor graven image, neither rear you up a ᵀstanding image, ᴿneither shall ye set up *any* image of stone in your land, to bow down unto it: for I *am* the Lᴏʀᴅ your God. *pillar* · Num. 33:52

2 Ye shall ᵀkeep my sabbaths, and reverence my sanctuary: I *am* the Lᴏʀᴅ. *respect*

Conditions and Results of Obedience

3 If ye walk in my statutes, and keep my commandments, and ᵀdo them; *practice*

4 Then I will give you rain in due season, and the land shall yield her increase, and the trees of the field shall yield their fruit.

5 And your threshing shall reach unto the vintage, and the vintage shall reach unto the sowing time: and ye shall eat your bread to the full, and dwell in your land safely.

6 And I will give peace in the land, and ᴿye shall lie down, and none shall make *you* afraid: and I will rid evil beasts out of the land, ᵀneither shall the sword go through your land. Ps. 4:8 · *there will be no war*

7 And ye shall chase your enemies, and they shall fall before you by the sword.

8 And ᴿfive of you shall chase an hundred, and an hundred of you shall put ten thousand to flight: and your enemies shall fall before you by the sword. Deut. 32:30

9 For I will ᴿhave respect unto you, and make you fruitful, and multiply you, and establish my covenant with you. Ex. 2:25

10 And ye shall eat old ᵀstore, and bring forth the old because of the new.   *supply*

11 And I will set my tabernacle among you: and my soul shall not abhor you.

12 And I will walk among you, and will be your God, and ye shall be my people.

13 I *am* the Lᴏʀᴅ your God, which brought you forth out of the land of Egypt, that ye should not be their ᵀbondmen; and I have broken ᴿthe bands of your yoke, and made you go ᵀupright.   *slaves* • Ezek. 34:27 • *free*

Conditions and Results of Disobedience

14 But if ye will not hearken unto me, and will not do all these commandments;

15 And if ye shall despise my statutes, or if ᵀyour soul abhor my judgments, so that ye will not do all my commandments, *but* that ye break my covenant: *your heart reject*

16 I also will do this unto you; I will even appoint over you terror, ᵀconsumption, and the ᵀburning ague, that shall consume the eyes, and cause sorrow of heart: and ye shall sow your seed ᵀin vain, for your enemies shall eat it.   *sickness* • *fever* • *to no profit*

17 And I will set my face against you, and ye shall be slain before your enemies: they that hate you shall reign over you; and ye shall flee when none pursueth.

18 And if ye will not yet for all this ᵀhearken unto me, then I will punish you seven times more for your sins.   *obey me*

19 And I will break the pride of your power; and I ᴿwill make your heaven as iron, and your earth as brass: Deut. 28:23

20 And your ᴿstrength shall be spent in vain: for ᴿyour land shall not yield her increase, neither shall the trees of the land yield their fruits.   Ps. 127:1 • Deut. 11:17

21 And if ye walk contrary unto me, and will not hearken unto me; I will bring seven times more plagues upon you according to your sins.

22 ᴿI will also send wild beasts among you, which shall rob you of your children, and destroy your cattle, and make you few in number; and ᴿyour *high* ways shall be desolate.   Deut. 32:24 • 2 Chr. 15:5; Zech. 7:14

23 And if ye ᴿwill not be reformed by me by these things, but will walk contrary unto me;   [Jer. 2:30; Amos 4:6–12]

24 ᴿThen will I also walk contrary unto you, and will punish you yet seven times for your sins.   Ps. 18:26

25 And ᴿI will bring a sword upon you, that shall avenge the quarrel of *my* covenant: and when ye are gathered together within your cities, I will send the pestilence among you; and ye shall be delivered into the hand of the enemy.   Ezek. 5:17

26 ᴿ*And* when I have broken the staff of your bread, ten women shall bake your bread in one oven, and they shall deliver *you* your bread again by weight: and ye shall eat, and not be satisfied.   Ps. 105:16

27 And if ye will not for all this hearken unto me, but walk contrary unto me;

28 Then I will walk contrary unto you also in fury; and I, even I, will chastise you seven times for your sins.

29 ᴿAnd ye shall ᵀeat the flesh of your sons, and the flesh of your daughters shall ye eat.   2 Kin. 6:29 • *be obliged to eat your own children*

30 And ᴿI will destroy your high places, and cut down your images, and cast your carcases upon the carcases of your idols, and my soul shall abhor you.   2 Chr. 34:3

31 And I will make your cities waste, and ᴿbring your sanctuaries unto desolation, and I ᵀwill not smell the savour of your sweet odours.   Ps. 74:7 • *will not accept your praise*

32 ᴿAnd I will bring the land into desolation: ᴿand your enemies which dwell therein shall be astonished at it.   Jer. 9:11 • Jer. 18:16

33 And ᴿI will scatter you among the heathen, and will draw out a sword after you: and your land shall be desolate, and your cities waste.   Ezek. 12:15; 20:23; 22:15

34 ᴿThen shall the land enjoy her sabbaths, as long as it lieth desolate, and ye *be* in your enemies' land; *even* then shall the land rest, and enjoy her sabbaths.   2 Chr. 36:21

35 As long as it lieth desolate it shall rest; because it did not rest in your ᴿsabbaths, when ye dwelt upon it.   25:2

36 And upon them that are left *alive* of you I will send a ᴿfaintness into their hearts in the lands of their enemies; and the sound of a shaken leaf shall chase them; and they shall flee, as fleeing from a sword; ᴿand they shall fall when none pursueth.   Is. 30:17 • Prov. 28:1

37 And they shall fall one upon another, as it were before a sword, when none pursueth: and ᴿye shall have no power to stand before your enemies.   Josh. 7:12, 13

38 ᴿAnd ye shall perish among the heathen, and the land of your enemies shall eat you up.   Deut. 4:26

39 And they that are left of you shall pine away in their iniquity in your enemies' lands; and also in the iniquities of their fathers shall they pine away with them.

The Promise of Restoration

40 If they shall confess their iniquity, and the iniquity of their fathers, with their trespass which they trespassed against me, and that also they have walked contrary unto me;

41 And *that* I also have walked contrary unto them, and have brought them into the land of their enemies; if then their uncircumcised hearts be humbled, and they then accept of the punishment of their iniquity:

42 Then will I remember my covenant with Jacob, and also my covenant with Isaac,

and also my covenant with Abraham will I remember; and I will remember the land.

43 The land also shall be left of them, and shall enjoy her sabbaths, while she lieth desolate without them: and they shall accept of the punishment of their iniquity: because, even because they despised my judgments, and because their soul abhorred my statutes.

44 And yet for all that, when they be in the land of their enemies, [R]I will not cast them away, neither will I abhor them, to destroy them utterly, and to break my covenant with them: for I *am* the LORD their God. [Rom. 11:2]

45 But I will [R]for their sakes remember the covenant of their ancestors, whom I brought forth out of the land of Egypt in the sight of the heathen, that I might be their God: I *am* the LORD.   [Rom. 11:28]

46 [R]These *are* the statutes and judgments and laws, which the LORD made between him and the children of Israel in mount Si'-nai by the hand of Moses.   27:34

CHAPTER 27

Consecration of Persons

A ND the LORD spake unto Moses, saying, 2 Speak unto the children of Israel, and say unto them, [R]When a man shall make a singular vow, the persons *shall be* for the LORD by thy [T]estimation.   Num. 6:2 • *valuation*

3 And thy [T]estimation shall be of the male from twenty years old even unto sixty years old, even thy estimation shall be [T]fifty shek'-els of silver, [R]after the shek'-el of the sanctuary.   *valuation* • *$6,400* • Ex. 30:13

4 And if it *be* a female, then thy estimation shall be [T]thirty shek'-els.   *$3,840*

5 And if *it be* from five years old even unto twenty years old, then thy estimation shall be of the male [T]twenty shek'-els, and for the female [T]ten shek'-els.   *$2,560* • *$1,280*

6 And if *it be* from a month old even unto five years old, then thy estimation shall be of the male [T]five shek'-els of silver, and for the female thy estimation *shall be* [T]three shek'-els of silver.   *$640* • *$384*

7 And if *it be* from sixty years old and above; if *it be* a male, then thy estimation shall be [T]fifteen shek'-els, and for the female [T]ten shek'-els.   *$1,920* • *$1,280*

8 But if he be poorer than thy estimation, then he shall present himself before the priest, and the priest shall value him; [R]according to his ability that vowed shall the priest value him.   5:11; 14:21-24

Consecration of Animals

9 And if *it be* a beast, whereof men bring an offering unto the LORD, all that *any man* giveth of such unto the LORD shall be holy.

10 He shall not alter it, nor change it, a good for a bad, or a bad for a good: and if he shall at all change beast for beast, then it and the exchange thereof shall be holy.

11 And if *it be* any unclean beast, of which they do not offer a sacrifice unto the LORD, then he shall present the beast before the priest:

12 And the priest shall value it, whether it be good or bad: as thou valuest it, *who art* the priest, so shall it be.

13 [R]But if he will at all redeem it, then he shall add a fifth *part* thereof unto thy estimation.   *vv.* 15, 19

Consecration of Houses

14 And when a man shall [T]sanctify his house *to be* [T]holy unto the LORD, then the priest shall estimate it, whether it be good or bad: as the priest shall estimate it, so shall it stand.   *set apart* • *only for the use of the LORD*

15 And if he that sanctified it will [T]redeem his house, then he shall add the fifth *part* of the money of thy estimation unto it, and it shall be his.   *buy back*

Consecration of Fields

16 And if a man shall sanctify unto the LORD *some part* of a field of his possession, then thy estimation shall be according to the seed thereof: an ho'-mer of barley seed *shall be valued* at [T]fifty shek'-els of silver.   *$6,400*

17 If he sanctify his field from the [R]year of jubile, according to thy [T]estimation it shall stand.   Num. 36:4 • *valuation*

18 But if he sanctify his field after the jubile, then the priest shall reckon unto him the money according to the years that remain, even unto the year of the jubile, and it shall be abated from thy estimation.

19 And if he that sanctified the field will in any wise redeem it, then he shall add the fifth *part* of the money of thy estimation unto it, and it shall be assured to him.

20 And if he will not redeem the field, or if he have sold the field to another man, it shall not be redeemed any more.

21 But the field, [R]when it goeth out in the jubile, shall be holy unto the LORD, as a field [R]devoted; [R]the possession thereof shall be the priest's.   v. 28 • Num. 18:14 • Ezek. 44:29

22 And if *a man* sanctify unto the LORD a field which he hath bought, which *is* not of the fields of [R]his possession;   25:10, 25

23 Then the priest shall reckon unto him the worth of thy estimation, *even* unto the year of the jubile: [R]and he shall give thine estimation in that day, *as* a holy thing unto the LORD.   v. 18

24 [R]In the year of the jubile the field shall return unto him of whom it was bought, *even* to him to whom the possession of the land *did belong*.   25:28

25 And all thy estimations shall be according to the ᵀshek'-el of the sanctuary: twenty ge'-rahs shall be the shek'-el.   *$128*

Firstborn Clean Animals

26 Only the ᴿfirstlingᵀ of the beasts, which should be the LORD's firstling, no man shall sanctify it; whether *it be* ox, or sheep: it is the LORD's.   Ex. 13:2, 12; 22:30 • *firstborn*
27 And if *it be* of an unclean beast, then he shall redeem *it* according to thine estimation, and shall add a fifth *part* of it thereto: or if it be not redeemed, then it shall be sold according to thy estimation.

Devoted Things

28 ᵀNotwithstanding no ᵀdevoted thing, that a man shall devote unto the LORD of all that he hath, *both* of man and beast, and of the field of his possession, shall be sold or redeemed: every devoted thing *is* most holy unto the LORD.   *but • dedicated to God*
29 ᴿNone devoted, which shall be devoted of men, shall be redeemed; *but* shall surely be put to death.   Num. 21:2

Tithes

30 And all the tithe of the land, *whether* of the seed of the land, *or* of the fruit of the tree, is the LORD's: *it is* holy unto the LORD.
31 ᴿAnd if a man will at all redeem ᵀought of his tithes, he shall add thereto the fifth *part* thereof.   *v.* 13 • *any*
32 And concerning the tithe of the herd, or of the flock, *even* of whatsoever ᴿpasseth under the rod, the tenth shall be holy unto the LORD.   Jer. 33:13; Ezek. 20:37; Mic. 7:14
33 He shall not search whether it be good or bad, ᴿneither shall he change it: and if he change it at all, then both it and the change thereof shall be holy; it shall not be redeemed.   *v.* 10

The Conclusion of Leviticus

34 ᴿThese *are* the commandments, which the LORD commanded Moses for the children of Israel in mount Si'-nai.   26:46

Weights

Unit	Weight	Equivalents	Translations
Jewish Weights Talent	c. 75 pounds for common talent, c. 150 pounds for royal talent	60 minas; 3,000 shekels	talent
Mina	1.25 pounds	50 shekels	maneh, pound
Shekel	c. .4 ounce (11.4 grams) for common shekel c. .8 ounce for royal shekel	2 bekas; 20 gerahs	shekel
Beka	c. .2 ounce (5.7 grams)	½ shekel; 10 gerahs	half a shekel
Gerah	c. .02 ounce (.57 grams)	¹⁄₂₀ shekel	gerah
Roman Weight Litra	12 ounces		pound

Liquid Measures

Unit	Measure	Equivalents	Translations
Kor	60 gallons	10 baths	cor
Metretes	10.2 gallons		firkin
Bath	6 gallons	6 hins	measure, bath
Hin	1 gallon	2 kabs	hin
Kab	2 quarts	4 logs	cab
Log	1 pint	¼ kab	log

NUMBERS

THE BOOK OF NUMBERS

Numbers is the book of wanderings. It takes its name from the two numberings of the Israelites—the first at Mount Sinai and the second on the Plains of Moab. Most of the book, however, describes Israel's experiences as they wander in the wilderness. The lesson of Numbers is clear. While it may be necessary to pass through wilderness experiences, one does not have to live there. For Israel, an eleven-day journey became a forty-year agony.

The title of Numbers comes from the first word in the Hebrew text, *Wayyedabber,* "And He Said." Jewish writings, however, usually refer to it by the fifth Hebrew word in 1:1, *Bemidbar,* "In the Wilderness," which more nearly indicates the content of the book. The Greek title in the Septuagint is *Arithmoi,* "Numbers." The Latin Vulgate followed this title and translated it *Liber Numeri,* "Book of Numbers." These titles are based on the two numberings: the generation of Exodus (Num. 1) and the generation that grew up in the wilderness and conquered Canaan (Num. 26). Numbers has also been called the "Book of the Journeyings," the "Book of the Murmurings," and the "Fourth Book of Moses."

THE AUTHOR OF NUMBERS

The evidence that points to Moses as the author of Numbers is similar to that for the previous books of the Pentateuch. These five books form such a literary unit that they rise or fall together on the matter of authorship.

External Evidence: The Jews, the Samaritans, and the early church give testimony to the Mosaic authorship of Numbers. Also a number of New Testament passages cite events from Numbers and associate them with Moses. These include John 3:14; Acts 7 and 13; First Corinthians 10:1-11; Hebrews 3 and 4; and Jude 11.

Internal Evidence: There are more than eighty claims that "the LORD spake unto Moses" (the first is 1:1). In addition, Numbers 33:2 makes this clear statement: "And Moses wrote their goings out according to their journeys by the command-ment of the LORD." Moses kept detailed records as an eyewitness of the events in this book. As the central character in Exodus through Deuteron-omy, he was better qualified than any other man to write these books.

Some scholars have claimed that the third-person references to Moses point to a different author. However, use of the third person was a common practice in the ancient world. Caesar, for example, did the same in his writings.

THE TIME OF NUMBERS

Leviticus covers only one month, but Numbers stretches over almost thirty-nine years (c. 1444-1405 B.C.). It records Israel's movement from the last twenty days at Mount Sinai (1:1; 10:11), the wandering around Kadesh-barnea, and finally the arrival in the plains of Moab in the fortieth year (22:1; 26:3; 33:50; Deut. 1:3). Their tents occupy several square miles whenever they camp since there are probably over two-and-a-half million people (based on the census figures in Numbers 1 and 26). God miraculously feeds and sustains them in the desert—He preserves their clothing and gives them manna, meat, water, leaders, and a promise (14:34).

THE CHRIST OF NUMBERS

Perhaps the clearest portrait of Christ in Numbers is the brass serpent on the stake, a picture of the Crucifixion (21:4-9): "And as Moses lifted up the serpent in the wilderness, even so must the Son of man be lifted up" (John 3:14). The rock that quenches the thirst of the multitudes is also a figure of Christ: "They drank of that spiritual Rock that followed them: and that Rock was Christ" (1 Cor. 10:4). The daily manna pictures the Bread of Life who later comes down from heaven (John 6:31-33).

Balaam foresees the rulership of Christ: "I shall see him, but not now: I shall behold him, but not nigh: there shall come a Star out of Jacob, and a Sceptre shall rise out of Israel" (24:17). The guidance and presence of Christ is seen in the pillar of cloud and fire, and the sinner's refuge in Christ may be seen in the six cities of refuge. The red heifer sacrifice (Num. 19) is also considered a figure of Christ.

KEYS TO NUMBERS

Key Word: Wanderings—Numbers re-cords the failure of Israel to believe in the promise of God and the resulting judgment of wandering in the wilderness for forty years.

Key Verses: Numbers 14:22, 23; 20:12— "Because all those men which have seen my glory, and my miracles, which I did in Egypt and in the wilderness, and have tempted me now these ten times, and have not hearkened to my voice; Surely they shall not see the land which I sware unto their fathers, neither shall any of them that provoked me see it" (14:22, 23).

"And the LORD spake unto Moses and Aaron, Because ye believed me not, to sanctify me in the eyes of the children of Israel, therefore ye shall

not bring this congregation into the land which I have given them" (20:12).

Key Chapter: Numbers 14—The critical turning point of Numbers may be seen in Numbers 14 when Israel rejects God by refusing to go up and conquer the Promised Land. God judges Israel "After the number of the days in which ye searched the land, *even* forty days, each day for a year, shall ye bear your iniquities, *even* forty years, and ye shall know my breach of promise" (14:34).

SURVEY OF NUMBERS

Israel as a nation is in its infancy at the outset of this book, only thirteen months after the Exodus from Egypt. In Numbers, the book of divine discipline, it becomes necessary for the nation to go through the painful process of testing and maturation. God must teach His people the consequences of irresponsible decisions. The forty years of wilderness experience transforms them from a rabble of ex-slaves into a nation ready to take the Promised Land. Numbers begins with the old generation (1:1—10:10), moves through a tragic transitional period (10:11—25:18), and ends with the new generation (26—36) at the doorway to the land of Canaan.

The Old Generation (1:1—10:10): The generation that witnessed God's miraculous acts of deliverance and preservation receives further direction from God while they are still at the foot of Mount Sinai (1:1—10:10). God's instructions are very explicit, reaching every aspect of their lives. He is the Author of order, not confusion; and this is seen in the way He organizes the people around the tabernacle. Turning from the outward conditions of the camp (1—4) to the

inward conditions (5—10), Numbers describes the spiritual preparation of the people.

The Tragic Transition (10:11—25:18): Israel follows God step by step until Canaan is in sight. Then in the crucial moment at Kadesh they draw back in unbelief. Their murmurings had already become incessant, "And *when* the people complained, it displeased the LORD: and the LORD heard *it*" (11:1). But their unbelief after sending out the twelve spies at Kadesh-barnea is something God will not tolerate. Their rebellion at Kadesh marks the pivotal point of the book. The generation of the Exodus will not be the generation of the conquest.

Unbelief brings discipline and hinders God's blessing. The old generation is doomed to literally kill time for forty years of wilderness wanderings—one year for every day spent by the twelve spies in inspecting the land. They are judged by disinheritance and death as their journey changes from one of anticipation to one of aimlessness. Only Joshua and Caleb, the two spies who believed God, enter Canaan. Almost nothing is recorded about these transitional years.

The New Generation (26—36): When the transition to the new generation is complete, the people move to the plains of Moab, directly east of the Promised Land (22:1). Before they can enter the land they must wait until all is ready. Here they receive new instructions, a new census is taken, Joshua is appointed as Moses' successor, and some of the people settle in the Transjordan.

Numbers records two generations (1—14 and 21—36), two numberings (1 and 26), two journeyings (10—14 and 21—27), and two sets of instructions (5—9 and 28—36). It illustrates both the kindness and severity of God (Rom. 11:22) and teaches that God's people can move forward only as they trust and depend on Him.

FOCUS	THE OLD GENERATION		THE TRAGIC TRANSITION				THE NEW GENERATION		
REFERENCE	1:1 —— 5:1	—— 10:11	— 13:1	— 15:1	— 20:1	— 26:1	— 28:1	— 31:1 — 36:13	
DIVISION	ORGANIZATION OF ISRAEL	SANCTIFICATION OF ISRAEL	TO KADESH	AT KADESH	IN WILDERNESS	TO MOAB	REORGANIZA-TION OF ISRAEL	REGULATIONS OF OFFERINGS AND VOWS	CONQUEST AND DIVISION OF ISRAEL
TOPIC	ORDER		DISORDER				REORDER		
	PREPARATION		POSTPONEMENT				PREPARATION		
LOCATION	MOUNT SINAI		WILDERNESS				PLAINS OF MOAB		
TIME	20 DAYS		38 YEARS 3 MONTHS AND 10 DAYS				c. 5 MONTHS		

OUTLINE OF NUMBERS

Part One: The Preparation of the Old Generation to Inherit the Promised Land (1:1—10:10)

Part Two: The Failure of the Old Generation to Inherit the Promised Land (10:11—25:18)

CHAPTER 1

The First Census of Israel

AND the LORD spake unto Moses in the wilderness of Si'-nai, in the tabernacle of the congregation, on the first day of the second month, in the second year after they were come out of the land of Egypt, saying,

2 ᴿTakeᵀ ye the sum of all the congregation of the children of Israel, after their families, by the house of their fathers, with the number of their names, every male by their polls;   2 Sam. 24:2; 1 Chr. 21:2 • take a census

3 From ᴿtwenty years old and upward, all that are able to go forth to war in Israel: thou and Aaron shall number them ᵀby their armies.   Ex. 30:14; 38:26 • company by company

4 And with you there shall be a man of every tribe; ᴿevery one head of the house of his fathers.   v. 16; Ex. 18:21, 24; Deut. 1:15

5 And these are the names of the men that shall stand with you: of the tribe of Reuben; E-li'-zur the son of Shed'-e-ur.

6 Of Simeon; She-lu'-mi-el the son of Zu-ri-shad'-dai.

7 Of Judah; Nah'-shon the son of Am-min'-a-dab.

8 Of Is'-sa-char; Ne-than'-e-el the son of Zu'-ar.

9 Of Zeb'-u-lun; E-li'-ab the son of He'-lon.

10 Of the children of Joseph: of E'-phra-im; E-lish'-a-ma the son of Am-mi'-hud: of Ma-nas'-seh; Ga-ma'-li-el the son of Pe-dah'-zur.

11 Of Benjamin; Ab'-i-dan the son of Gid-e-o'-ni.

12 Of Dan; A-hi-e′-zer the son of Am-mi-shad′-dai.

13 Of Asher; Pa′-gi-el the son of Oc′-ran.

14 Of Gad; E-li′-a-saph the son of Deu′-el.

15 Of Naph′-ta-li; A-hi′-ra the son of E′-nan.

16 These *were* the renowned of the congregation, princes of the tribes of their fathers, heads of ᵀthousands in Israel.   *clans*

17 And Moses and Aaron took these men which are expressed by *their* names:

18 And they assembled all the congregation together on the ᴿfirst *day* of the second month, and they declared their ᵀpedigreesᴿ after their families, by the house of their fathers, according to the number of the names, from twenty years old and upward, by their polls.   *v. 1 • lineages • Ezra 2:59*

19 As the LORD commanded Moses, so he numbered them in the wilderness of Si′-nai.

20 And the children of Reuben, Israel's eldest son, by their generations, after their families, by the house of their fathers, according to the number of the names, by their polls, every male from twenty years old and upward, all that were able to go forth to war;

21 Those that were numbered of them, *even* of the tribe of Reuben, *were* forty six thousand and five hundred.

22 ᴿOf the ᴿchildren of Simeon, by their generations, after their families, by the house of their fathers, those that were numbered of them, according to the number of the names, by their polls, every male from twenty years old and upward, all that were able to go forth to war;   *26:12-14 • 2:12, 13*

23 Those that were numbered of them, *even* of the tribe of Simeon, *were* fifty and nine thousand and three hundred.

24 Of the children of Gad, by their generations, after their families, by the house of their fathers, according to the number of the names, from twenty years old and upward, all that were able to go forth to war;

25 Those that were numbered of them, *even* of the tribe of Gad, *were* forty and five thousand six hundred and fifty.

26 Of the children of Judah, by their generations, after their families, by the house of their fathers, according to the number of the names, from twenty years old and upward, all that were able to go forth to war;

27 Those that were numbered of them, *even* of the tribe of Judah, *were* threescore and fourteen thousand and six hundred.

28 Of the children of Is′-sa-char, by their generations, after their families, by the house of their fathers, according to the number of the names, from twenty years old and upward, all that were able to go forth to war;

29 Those that were numbered of them,

even of the tribe of Is′-sa-char, *were* fifty and four thousand and four hundred.

30 Of the children of Zeb′-u-lun, by their generations, after their families, by the house of their fathers, according to the number of the names, from twenty years old and upward, all that were able to go forth to war;

31 Those that were numbered of them, *even* of the tribe of Zeb′-u-lun, *were* fifty and seven thousand and four hundred.

32 Of the children of ᴿJoseph, *namely*, of the children of E′-phra-im, by their generations, after their families, by the house of their fathers, according to the number of the names, from twenty years old and upward, all that were able to go forth to war;   Gen. 48:1-22

33 Those that were numbered of them, *even* of the tribe of ᴿE′-phra-im, *were* forty thousand and five hundred.   26:35-37

34 Of the children of Ma-nas′-seh, by their generations, after their families, by the house of their fathers, according to the number of the names, from twenty years old and upward, all that were able to go forth to war;

35 Those that were numbered of them, *even* of the tribe of Ma-nas′-seh, *were* thirty and two thousand and two hundred.

36 Of the children of Benjamin, by their generations, after their families, by the house of their fathers, according to the number of the names, from twenty years old and upward, all that were able to go forth to war;

37 Those that were numbered of them, *even* of the tribe of Benjamin, *were* thirty five thousand and four hundred.

38 Of the children of Dan, by their generations, after their families, by the house of their fathers, according to the number of the names, from twenty years old and upward, all that were able to go forth to war;

39 Those that were numbered of them, *even* of the tribe of Dan, *were* threescore and two thousand and seven hundred.

40 Of the children of Asher, by their generations, after their families, by the house of their fathers, according to the number of the names, from twenty years old and upward, all that were able to go forth to war;

41 Those that were numbered of them, *even* of the tribe of Asher, *were* forty and one thousand and five hundred.

42 ᴿOf the children of Naph′-ta-li, throughout their generations, after their families, by the house of their fathers, according to the number of the names, from twenty years old and upward, all that were able to go forth to war;   26:48-50

43 Those that were numbered of them, *even* of the tribe of Naph′-ta-li, *were* fifty three thousand and four hundred.

44 These *are* those that were numbered, which Moses and Aaron numbered, and the

[T]princes of Israel, *being* twelve men: each one was for the house of his fathers.   *leaders*

45 So were all those that were numbered of the children of Israel, by the house of their fathers, from twenty years old and upward, all that were able to go forth to war in Israel;

46 Even all they that were numbered were [R]six hundred thousand and three thousand and five hundred and fifty.   2:32; 26:51

47 But the Levites after the tribe of their fathers were not numbered among them.

48 For the LORD had spoken unto Moses, saying,

49 [R]Only thou shalt not number the tribe of Levi, neither take the sum of them among the children of Israel: 26:62

50 [R]But thou shalt appoint the Levites over the tabernacle of testimony, and over all the vessels thereof, and over all things that *belong* to it: they shall bear the tabernacle, and all the vessels thereof; and they shall minister unto it, and shall encamp round about the tabernacle.   3:25-37; Ex. 38:21

51 And when the tabernacle setteth forward, the Levites shall take it down: and when the tabernacle is to be pitched, the Levites shall set it up: and the stranger that cometh nigh shall be put to death.

52 And the children of Israel shall pitch their tents, [R]every man by his own camp, and every man by his own standard, throughout their hosts.   2:2, 34

53 But the Levites shall pitch round about the tabernacle of testimony, that there be no wrath upon the congregation of the children of Israel: and the Levites shall keep the charge of the tabernacle of testimony.

54 And the children of Israel did according to all that the LORD commanded Moses, so did they.

CHAPTER 2

On the East

AND the LORD spake unto Moses and unto Aaron, saying,

2 [R]Every man of the children of Israel shall pitch by his own standard, with the [T]ensign of their father's house: [T]far off about the tabernacle of the congregation shall they pitch.   1:52 • *banner* • *over against*

3 And on the east side toward the rising of the sun shall they of the standard of the camp of Judah pitch throughout their [T]armies: and Nah'-shon the son of Am-min'-a-dab *shall be* captain of the children of Judah.   *groups*

4 And his host, and those that were numbered of them, *were* threescore and fourteen thousand and six hundred.

5 And those that do [T]pitch next unto him *shall be* the tribe of Is'-sa-char: and Ne-than'-e-el the son of Zu'-ar *shall be* captain of the children of Is'-sa-char.   *encamp*

6 And his host, and those that were numbered thereof, *were* fifty and four thousand and four hundred.

7 *Then* the tribe of Zeb'-u-lun: and [R]E-li'-ab the son of He'-lon *shall be* captain of the children of Zeb'-u-lun.   1:9

8 And his host, and those that were numbered thereof, *were* fifty and seven thousand and four hundred.

9 All that were numbered in the camp of Judah *were* an hundred thousand and fourscore thousand and six thousand and four hundred, throughout their armies. These shall first [T]set forth.   *start on the march*

On the South

10 On the south side *shall be* the standard of the camp of Reuben according to their armies: and the captain of the children of Reuben *shall be* [R]E-li'-zur the son of Shed'-e-ur.   1:5

11 And his host, and those that were numbered thereof, *were* forty and six thousand and five hundred.

12 And those which pitch by him *shall be* the tribe of Simeon: and the captain of the children of Simeon *shall be* [R]She-lu'-mi-el the son of Zu-ri-shad'-dai.   1:6

13 And his host, and those that were numbered of them, *were* fifty and nine thousand and three hundred.

14 Then the tribe of Gad: and the captain of the sons of Gad *shall be* E-li'-a-saph the son of [R]Reu'-el.   1:14; 7:42, 47; 10:20

15 And his host, and those that were numbered of them, *were* forty and five thousand and six hundred and fifty.

16 All that were numbered in the camp of Reuben *were* an hundred thousand and fifty and one thousand and four hundred and fifty, throughout their armies. And they shall set forth in the second rank.

On the Middle

17 Then the tabernacle of the congregation shall set forward with the camp of the Levites in the midst of the camp: as they encamp, so shall they set forward, every man in his place by their standards.

On the West

18 On the west side *shall be* the standard of the camp of E'-phra-im according to their armies: and the captain of the sons of E'-phra-im *shall be* [R]E-lish'-a-ma the son of Am-mi'-hud.   1:10

19 And his host, and those that were numbered of them, *were* forty thousand and five hundred.

20 And by him *shall be* the tribe of Ma-nas'-seh: and the captain of the children of Ma-nas'-seh *shall be* [R]Ga-ma'-li-el the son of Pe-dah'-zur.   1:10

21 And his host, and those that were numbered of them, *were* thirty and two thousand and two hundred.

22 Then the tribe of Benjamin: and the captain of the sons of Benjamin *shall be* [R]Ab'-i-dan the son of Gid-e-o'-ni.   1:11

23 And his host, and those that were numbered of them, *were* thirty and five thousand and four hundred.

24 All that were numbered of the camp of E'-phra-im *were* an hundred thousand and eight thousand and an hundred, throughout their armies. [R]And they shall go forward in the third rank.   10:22

On the North

25 The [T]standard of the camp of Dan *shall be* on the north side by their armies: and the captain of the children of Dan *shall be* [R]A-hi-e'-zer the son of Am-mi-shad'-dai.   *banner* • 1:12

26 And his host, and those that were numbered of them, *were* threescore and two thousand and seven hundred.

27 And those that encamp by him *shall be* the tribe of Asher: and the captain of the children of Asher *shall be* [R]Pa'-gi-el the son of Oc'-ran.   1:13

28 And his host, and those that were numbered of them, *were* forty and one thousand and five hundred.

29 Then the tribe of Naph'-ta-li: and the captain of the children of Naph'-ta-li *shall be* [R]A-hi'-ra the son of E'-nan.   1:15

30 And his host, and those that were numbered of them, *were* fifty and three thousand and four hundred.

31 All they that were numbered in the camp of Dan *were* an hundred thousand and fifty and seven thousand and six hundred. [R]They shall go [T]hindmost with their [T]standards.   10:25 • *last in line* • *banners*

The Camp Is Arranged

32 These *are* those which were numbered of the children of Israel by the house of their fathers: [R]all those that were numbered of the camps throughout their hosts *were* six hundred thousand and three thousand and five hundred and fifty.   Ex. 38:26

33 But [R]the Levites were not numbered among the children of Israel; as the LORD commanded Moses.   1:47

34 And the children of Israel did according to all that the LORD commanded Moses: so they pitched by their standards, and so they set forward, every one after their families, according to the house of their fathers.

CHAPTER 3

The Family of Aaron

THESE also *are* the generations of Aaron and Moses in the day *that* the LORD spake with Moses in mount Si'-nai.

2 [R]And these *are* the names of the sons of Aaron; [R]Na'-dab the firstborn, and A-bi'-hu, E-le-a'-zar, and Ith'-a-mar.   26:60 • Ex. 6:23

3 These *are* the names of the sons of Aaron, [R]the priests which were anointed, whom he [T]consecrated to minister in the priest's office.   Ex. 28:41; Lev. 8 • *specially set aside*

4 And Na'-dab and A-bi'-hu died before the LORD, when they offered strange fire before the LORD, in the wilderness of Si'-nai, and they had no children: and E-le-a'-zar and Ith'-a-mar ministered in the priest's office in the sight of Aaron their father.

5 And the LORD spake unto Moses, saying,

The Ministry of the Levites

6 [R]Bring the tribe of Levi near, and present them before Aaron the priest, that they may [T]minister unto him.   8:6; *serve*

7 And they shall keep his charge, and the charge of the whole congregation before the tabernacle of the congregation, to do [R]the service of the tabernacle.   1:50

8 And they shall keep all the [T]instruments of the tabernacle of the congregation, and the charge of the children of Israel, to do the service of the tabernacle.   *furniture*

9 And thou shalt give the Levites unto Aaron and to his sons: they *are* wholly given unto him out of the children of Israel.

10 And thou shalt appoint Aaron and his sons, and they shall [T]wait on their priest's office: [R]and the stranger that cometh nigh shall be put to death.   *take care of* • v. 38

11 And the LORD spake unto Moses, saying,

12 And I, behold, I have taken the Levites from among the children of Israel instead of all the firstborn that openeth the [T]matrix among the children of Israel: therefore the Levites shall be mine;   *womb*

13 Because all the firstborn *are* mine; *for* on the day that I smote all the firstborn in the land of Egypt I hallowed unto me all the firstborn in Israel, both man and beast: mine shall they be: I *am* the LORD.

The Census Is Commanded

14 And the LORD spake unto Moses in the wilderness of Si'-nai, saying,

15 Number the children of Levi after the house of their fathers, by their families: [R]every male from a month old and upward shalt thou [T]number them.   v. 39 • *take a census*

16 And Moses numbered them according to the [T]word of the LORD, as he was commanded.   *mouth*

17 ᴿAnd these were the sons of Levi by their names; Ger'-shon, and Ko'-hath, and Me-ra'-ri.   26:57; Ex. 6:16; 1 Chr. 6:1, 16; 23:6

18 And these *are* the names of the sons of ᴿGer'-shon by their families; ᴿLib'-ni, and Shim'-e-i.   4:38-41 • Ex. 6:17

19 And the sons of Ko'-hath by their families; ᴿAm'-ram, and Iz'-e-har, He'-bron, and Uz-zi'-el.   4:34-37; Ex. 6:18

20 ᴿAnd the sons of Me-ra'-ri by their families; Mah'-li, and Mu'-shi. These *are* the families of the Levites according to the house of their fathers.   4:42-45; Ex. 6:19

The Census of Gershon

21 Of Ger'-shon *was* the family of the Lib'-nites, and the family of the Shim'-ites: these *are* the families of the Ger'-shon-ites.

22 Those that were numbered of them, according to the number of all the males, from a month old and upward, *even* those that were numbered of them *were* seven thousand and five hundred.

23 The families of the Ger'-shon-ites shall pitch behind the tabernacle westward.

24 And the ᵀchief of the house of the father of the Ger'-shon-ites *shall be* E-li'-a-saph the son of La'-el.   *head*

25 And the charge of the sons of Ger'-shon in the tabernacle of the congregation *shall be* the tabernacle, and the tent, the covering thereof, and the hanging for the door of the tabernacle of the congregation,

26 And ᴿthe hangings of the court, and ᴿthe curtain for the door of the court, which *is* by the tabernacle, and by the altar round about, and ᴿthe cords of it for all the service thereof.   Ex. 27:9 • Ex. 27:16 • Ex. 35:18

The Census of Kohath

27 And of Ko'-hath *was* the family of the Am'-ram-ites, and the family of the Iz'-e-har-ites, and the family of the He'-bron-ites, and the family of the Uz-zi'-el-ites: these *are* the families of the Ko'-hath-ites.

28 In the number of all the males, from a month old and upward, *were* eight thousand and six hundred, ᵀkeeping the charge of the sanctuary.   *taking care of*

29 ᴿThe families of the ᴿsons of Ko'-hath shall ᵀpitch on the side of the tabernacle southward.   1:53 • Ex. 6:18 • *encamp*

30 And the ᵀchief of the house of the father of the families of the Ko'-hath-ites *shall be* E-liz'-a-phan the son of Uz-zi'-el.   *head*

31 And their ᵀcharge *shall be* the ark, and the table, and the candlestick, and the altars, and the vessels of the sanctuary wherewith they minister, and the hanging, and all the service thereof.   *responsibility*

32 And E-le-a'-zar the son of Aaron the priest *shall be* chief over the chief of the Levites, *and have* the oversight of them that keep the charge of the sanctuary.

The Census of Merari

33 Of Me-ra'-ri *was* the family of the Mah'-lites, and the family of the Mu'-shites: these *are* the families of Me-ra'-ri.

34 And those that were numbered of them, according to the number of all the males, from a month old and upward, *were* six thousand and two hundred.

35 And the chief of the house of the father of the families of Me-ra'-ri *was* Zu'-ri-el the son of Ab-i-ha'-il: ᴿ*these* shall pitch on the side of the tabernacle northward.   1:53

36 And ᴿ*under* ᵀthe custody and charge of the sons of Me-ra'-ri *shall be* the boards of the tabernacle, and the bars thereof, and the pillars thereof, and the sockets thereof, and all the vessels thereof, and all that serveth thereto,   4:31, 32 • *the appointed charge*

37 And the pillars of the court round about, and their sockets, and their pins, and their cords.

The Summary of the Census

38 ᴿBut those that encamp before the tabernacle toward the east, *even* before the tabernacle of the congregation eastward, *shall be* Moses, and Aaron and his sons, keeping the charge of the sanctuary for the charge of the children of Israel; and ᴿthe stranger that ᵀcometh nigh shall be put to death.   1:53 • *v. 10* • *takes a hand in this*

39 All that were numbered of the Levites, which Moses and Aaron numbered at the commandment of the Lᴏʀᴅ, throughout their families, all the males from a month old and upward, *were* twenty and two thousand.

The Substitution of the Levites for the Firstborn

40 And the Lᴏʀᴅ said unto Moses, Number all the firstborn of the males of the children of Israel from a month old and upward, and take the number of their names.

41 ᴿAnd thou shalt take the Levites for me (I *am* the Lᴏʀᴅ) instead of all the firstborn among the children of Israel; and the cattle of the Levites instead of all the firstlings among the cattle of the children of Israel.   *vv. 12, 45*

42 And Moses numbered, as the Lᴏʀᴅ commanded him, all the firstborn among the children of Israel.

43 And all the firstborn males by the number of names, from a month old and upward, of those that were numbered of them, were twenty and two thousand two hundred and threescore and thirteen.

44 And the Lᴏʀᴅ spake unto Moses, saying,

45 Take the Levites instead of all the firstborn among the children of Israel, and

the cattle of the Levites instead of their cattle; and the Levites shall be mine: I *am* the LORD.

46 And for those that are to be redeemed of the two hundred and threescore and thirteen of the firstborn of the children of Israel, which are more than the Levites;

47 ᴿThou shalt even take ᵀfive shek'-els apiece by the poll, after the shek'-el of the sanctuary shalt thou take *them:* (the shek'-el *is* twenty ge'-rahs:)   Lev. 27:6 • $640

48 And thou shalt give the money, wherewith the odd number of them is to be redeemed, unto ᴿAaron and to his sons.   5:9

49 And Moses took the redemption money of them that were over and above them that were redeemed by the Levites:

50 Of the firstborn of the children of Israel took he the money; ᴿa ᵀthousand three hundred and threescore and five *shek'-els,* after the shek'-el of the sanctuary: *vv.* 46, 47 • $174,720

51 And Moses ᴿgave the money of them that were redeemed unto Aaron and to his sons, according to the word of the LORD, as the LORD commanded Moses.   *v.* 48

CHAPTER 4

The Ministry of Kohath

AND the LORD spake unto Moses and unto Aaron, saying,

2 Take the sum of the sons of Ko'-hath from among the sons of Levi, after their families, by the house of their fathers,

3 ᴿFrom thirty years old and upward even until fifty years old, all that enter into the host, to do the work in the tabernacle of the congregation.   1 Chr. 23:3, 24, 27

4 ᴿThis *shall be* the service of the sons of Ko'-hath in the tabernacle of the congregation, *about* the most holy things: *v.* 15

5 And when the camp setteth forward, Aaron shall come, and his sons, and they shall take down ᴿthe covering vail, and cover the ark of testimony with it: Ex. 26:31

6 And shall put thereon the covering of ᵀbadgers' skins, and shall spread over *it* a cloth wholly of ᴿblue, and shall put in ᴿthe staves thereof.   seal • Ex. 39:1 • Ex. 25:13; 1 Kin. 8:7, 8

7 ᴿAnd upon the table of shewbread they shall spread a cloth of blue, and put thereon the dishes, and the spoons, and the bowls, and covers to cover withal: and the continual bread shall be thereon: Ex. 25:30

8 And they shall spread upon them a cloth of ᴿscarlet, and cover the same with a covering of badgers' skins, and shall put in the staves thereof.   Josh. 2:18

9 And they shall take a cloth of blue, and cover the ᴿcandlestick of the light, ᴿand his lamps, and his tongs, and his snuffdishes, and

all the oil vessels thereof, wherewith they minister unto it: Ex. 25:31 • Ex. 25:37, 38

10 And they shall put it and all the vessels thereof within a covering of badgers' skins, and shall put *it* upon ᵀa bar.   *the frame*

11 And upon ᴿthe golden altar they shall spread a cloth of blue, and cover it with a covering of badgers' skins, and shall put to the staves thereof: Ex. 30:1, 3

12 And they shall take all the ᵀinstruments of ministry, wherewith they minister in the sanctuary, and put *them* in a cloth of blue, and cover them with a covering of badgers' skins, and shall put *them* on a bar: *vessels*

13 And they shall take away the ashes from the altar, and spread a purple cloth thereon:

14 And they shall put upon it all the vessels thereof, wherewith they minister about it, *even* the censers, the fleshhooks, and the shovels, and the basons, all the vessels of the altar; and they shall spread upon it a covering of badgers' skins, and put to the staves of it.

15 And when Aaron and his sons have made an end of covering the sanctuary, and all the vessels of the sanctuary, as the camp is to set forward; after that, the sons of Ko'-hath shall come to bear *it:* but they shall not touch *any* holy thing, lest they die. These things *are* the burden of the sons of Ko'-hath in the tabernacle of the congregation.

16 And to the office of E-le-a'-zar the son of Aaron the priest *pertaineth* the oil for the light, and the sweet incense, and ᴿthe daily meat offering, and the ᴿanointing oil, *and* the oversight of all the tabernacle, and of all that therein is, in the sanctuary, and in the vessels thereof.   Ex. 29:38 • Ex. 30:25

17 And the LORD spake unto Moses and unto Aaron, saying,

18 Cut ye not off the tribe of the families of the Ko'-hath-ites from among the Levites:

19 But thus do unto them, that they may live, and not die, when they approach unto the most holy things: Aaron and his sons shall go in, and ᵀappoint them every one to his service and to his burden: *assign*

20 But they shall not go in to see when the holy things are covered, lest they die.

The Ministry of Gershon

21 And the LORD spake unto Moses, saying,

22 Take also the sum of the sons of ᴿGer'-shon, throughout the houses of their fathers, by their families;   3:22

23 ᴿFrom thirty years old and upward until fifty years old shalt thou number them; all that enter in ᵀto perform the service, to do the work in the tabernacle of the congregation.   *v.* 3 • *serve in the tabernacle*

24 This *is* the service of the families of the Ger'-shon-ites, to serve, and for burdens:

25 And ᴿthey shall bear the curtains of the tabernacle, and the tabernacle of the congregation, his covering, and the ᴿcovering of the badgers' skins that is above upon it, and the hanging for the door of the tabernacle of the congregation,   3:25, 26 • Ex. 26:14

26 And the hangings of the court, and the hanging for the door of the gate of the court, which is by the tabernacle and by the altar round about, and their cords, and all the instruments of their service, and all that is made for them: so shall they serve.

27 At the appointment of Aaron and his sons shall be all the service of the sons of the Ger'-shon-ites, in all their burdens, and in all their service: and ye shall ᵀappoint unto them in charge all their burdens.   assign

28 This is the service of the families of the sons of Ger'-shon in the tabernacle of the congregation: and their ᵀcharge shall be ᴿunder the hand of Ith'-a-mar the son of Aaron the priest.   responsibility • v. 33

The Ministry of Merari

29 As for the sons of ᴿMe-ra'-ri, thou shalt number them after their families, by the house of their fathers;   v. 42

30 ᴿFrom thirty years old and upward even unto fifty years old shalt thou number them, every one that entereth into the ᵀservice, to do the work of the tabernacle of the congregation.   v. 3; Gen. 41:46 • ministration

31 And this is the charge of their burden, according to all their service in the tabernacle of the congregation; the boards of the tabernacle, and the bars thereof, and the pillars thereof, and sockets thereof,

32 And the pillars of the court round about, and their sockets, and their pins, and their cords, with all their instruments, and with all their ᵀservice: and by name ye shall ᴿreckon the instruments of the charge of their burden.   equipment • Ex. 38:21

33 This is the service of the families of the sons of Me-ra'-ri, according to all their service, in the tabernacle of the ᴿcongregation, under the hand of Ith'-a-mar the son of Aaron the priest.   v. 28

The Census of the Working Levites

34 ᴿAnd Moses and Aaron and the chief of the congregation numbered the sons of the Ko'-hath-ites after their families, and after the house of their fathers,   v. 2; 3:19, 27

35 From thirty ᴿyears old and upward even unto fifty years old, every one that entereth into the service, for the work in the tabernacle of the congregation: v. 47

36 And those that were numbered of them by their families were two thousand seven hundred and fifty.

37 These were they that were numbered of the families of the Ko'-hath-ites, all that might do service in the tabernacle of the congregation, which Moses and Aaron did number according to the commandment of the LORD by the hand of Moses.

38 And those that were numbered of the sons of Ger'-shon, throughout their families, and by the house of their fathers,

39 From thirty years old and upward even unto fifty years old, every one that entereth into the service, for the work in the tabernacle of the congregation,

40 Even those that were numbered of them, throughout their families, by the house of their fathers, were two thousand and six hundred and thirty.

41 ᴿThese are they that were numbered of the families of the sons of Ger'-shon, of all that might do service in the tabernacle of the congregation, whom Moses and Aaron did number according to the commandment of the LORD.   v. 22

42 And those that were numbered of the families of the sons of Me-ra'-ri, throughout their families, by the house of their fathers,

43 From thirty years old and upward even unto fifty years old, every one that entereth into the service, for the work in the tabernacle of the congregation,

44 Even those that were numbered of them after their families, were three thousand and two hundred.

45 These be those that were numbered of the families of the sons of Me-ra'-ri, whom Moses and Aaron numbered according to the word of the LORD by the hand of Moses.

46 All those that were numbered of the Levites, whom Moses and Aaron and the chief of Israel numbered, after their families, and after the house of their fathers,

47 ᴿFrom thirty years old and upward even unto fifty years old, every one that came to do the service of the ministry, and the service of the burden in the tabernacle of the congregation,   vv. 3, 23, 30; 1 Chr. 23:3

48 Even those that were numbered of them, were ᴿeight thousand and five hundred and ᵀfourscore.   3:39 • eighty

49 According to the commandment of the LORD they were numbered by the hand of Moses, ᴿevery one according to his service, and according to his ᵀburden: thus were they numbered of him, ᴿas the LORD commanded Moses.   vv. 15, 24 • responsibility • vv. 1, 21

CHAPTER 5

Separation of Unclean Persons

AND the LORD spake unto Moses, saying,
2 Command the children of Israel, that they put out of the camp every leper, and every one that hath ᵀan issue, and whosoever is defiled by the dead: a running sore

3 Both male and female shall ye put out, ^Twithout the camp shall ye put them; that they ^Tdefile not their camps, ^Rin the midst whereof I dwell.   *outside · contaminate* · [2 Cor. 6:17]

4 And the children of Israel did so, and put them out without the camp: as the LORD spake unto Moses, so did the children of Israel.

Separation in Restitution for Sin

5 And the LORD spake unto Moses, saying,

6 Speak unto the children of Israel, When a man or woman shall commit any sin that men commit, to do a trespass against the LORD, and that person be guilty;

7 ^RThen they shall confess their sin which they have done: and he shall recompense his trespass with the principal thereof, and add unto it the fifth *part* thereof, and give *it* unto *him* against whom he hath trespassed. Josh. 7:19

8 But if the man have no ^Rkinsman^T to recompense the trespass unto, let the trespass be recompensed unto the LORD, *even* to the priest; beside ^Rthe ram of the atonement, whereby an atonement shall be made for him.   [35:12; Is. 59:20] · *relative* · Lev. 6:6, 7; 7:7

9 And every ^Roffering of all the holy things of the children of Israel, which they bring unto the priest, shall be his.   Ex. 29:28

10 And every man's ^Thallowed things shall be his: whatsoever any man giveth the priest, it shall be his.   *set aside for God alone*

Separation from Suspected Infidelity

11 And the LORD spake unto Moses, saying,

12 Speak unto the children of Israel, and say unto them, If any man's wife go aside, and ^Tcommit a trespass against him,   *do wrong*

13 And a man ^Rlie with her carnally, and it be hid from the eyes of her husband, and be kept close, and she be defiled, and *there be no* witness against her, neither she be taken ^T*with the manner;*   Lev. 18:20 · *in the act*

14 And the spirit of ^Rjealousy come upon him, and he be jealous of his wife, and she be defiled: or if the spirit of jealousy come upon him, and he be jealous of his wife, and she be not defiled: Prov. 6:34

15 Then shall the man bring his wife unto the priest, and he shall bring her offering for her, ^Tthe tenth *part* of an e'-phah of barley meal; he shall pour no oil upon it, nor put frankincense thereon; for it *is* an offering of jealousy, an offering of memorial, bringing iniquity to remembrance.   *2.087 qt.*

16 And the priest shall bring her near, and set her before the LORD:

17 And the priest shall take holy water in an earthen vessel; and of the dust that is in the floor of the tabernacle the priest shall take, and put *it* into the water:

18 And the priest shall set the woman before the ^RLORD, and uncover the woman's head, and put the offering of memorial in her hands, which *is* the jealousy offering: and the priest shall have in his hand the bitter water that causeth the curse: [Heb. 13:4]

19 And the priest shall charge her by an oath, and say unto the woman, If no man have lain with thee, and if thou hast not ^Rgone aside to uncleanness *with another* instead of thy husband, be thou free from this bitter water that causeth the curse: *v.* 12

20 But if thou hast ^Rgone aside *to another* instead of thy husband, and if thou be defiled, and some man have lain with thee beside thine husband: *v.* 12

21 Then the priest shall charge the woman with an oath of cursing, and the priest shall say unto the woman, ^RThe LORD make thee a curse and an oath among thy people, when the LORD doth make thy thigh to rot, and thy belly to swell;   Jer. 29:22

22 And this water that causeth the curse shall go into thy bowels, to make *thy* belly to swell, and *thy* thigh to rot: ^RAnd the woman shall say, A'-men, a'-men.   Deut. 27:15

23 And the priest shall write these curses in a book, and he shall blot *them* out with the bitter water:

24 And he shall cause the woman to drink the bitter water that causeth the curse: and the water that causeth the curse shall enter into her, *and become* bitter.

25 Then the priest shall take the jealousy offering out of the woman's hand, and shall ^Rwave the offering before the LORD, and offer it upon the altar: Lev. 8:27

26 And the priest shall take an handful of the offering, *even* the memorial thereof, and burn *it* upon the altar, and afterward shall cause the woman to drink the water.

27 And when he hath made her to drink the water, then it shall come to pass, *that*, if she be defiled, and have done trespass against her husband, that the water that causeth the curse shall enter into her, *and become* bitter, and her belly shall swell, and her thigh shall rot: and the woman shall be ^Ta curse among her people.   *an outcast*

28 And if the woman be not defiled, but be clean; then she shall be free, and shall conceive seed.

29 This *is* the law of jealousies, when a wife goeth aside *to another* ^Rinstead of her husband, and is defiled;   *vv.* 12, 19

30 Or when the spirit of jealousy cometh upon him, and he be jealous over his wife, and shall set the woman before the LORD, and the priest shall execute upon her all this law.

31 Then shall the man be guiltless from iniquity, and this woman shall ^Tbear her iniquity.   *have responsibility for her wrong doing*

CHAPTER 6

Sanctification Through the Nazarite Vow

AND the LORD spake unto Moses, saying,
2 Speak unto the children of Israel,
and say unto them, When either man or
woman shall ᵀseparate *themselves* to ᵀvow a
vow of a ᴿNazarite, to separate *themselves*
unto the LORD: *set themselves aside · pledge ·* Judg. 13:5
3 ᴿHe shall separate *himself* from wine and
strong drink, and shall drink no vinegar of
wine, or vinegar of strong drink, neither shall
he drink any liquor of grapes, nor eat moist
grapes, or dried.   [Amos 2:12; Luke 1:15]
4 All the days of his separation shall he eat
nothing that is made of the ᵀvine tree, from
the kernels even to the husk.   *grapevine*
5 All the days of the vow of his separation
there shall no ᴿrazor come upon his head:
until the days be fulfilled, in the which he
separateth *himself* unto the LORD, he shall be
ᵀholy, *and* shall let the locks of the hair of his
head grow.   1 Sam. 1:11 · *for this service only*
6 All the days that he separateth *himself*
unto the LORD ᴿhe shall ᵀcome at no dead
body.   19:11–22; Lev. 21:11 · *not touch any*
7 He shall not make himself unclean for
his father, or for his mother, for his brother,
or for his sister, when they die: because the
consecration of his God is upon his head.
8 ᴿAll the days of his separation he *is* holy
unto the LORD.   [2 Cor. 6:17, 18]
9 And if any man die very suddenly by
him, and he hath defiled the head of his
consecration; then he shall ᴿshave his head in
the day of his cleansing, on the seventh day
shall he shave it.   Lev. 14:8, 9; Acts 18:18; 21:24
10 And ᴿon the eighth day he shall bring
two ᵀturtles, or two young pigeons, to the
priest, to the door of the tabernacle of the
congregation: Lev. 5:7; 14:22; 15:14, 29 · *doves*
11 And the priest shall offer the ᴿone for a
sin offering, and the other for a burnt offering, and make an atonement for him, for that
he sinned by the dead, and shall hallow his
head that same day.   Lev. 5:7
12 And he shall consecrate unto the LORD
the days of his separation, and shall bring a
lamb of the first year for a trespass offering:
but the days that were before shall be lost,
because his separation was defiled.
13 And this *is* the law of the Nazarite,
when the days of his separation are fulfilled:
he shall be brought unto the door of the
tabernacle of the congregation:
14 And he shall offer his offering unto the
LORD, one he lamb of the first year without
blemish for a burnt offering, and one ᵀewe
lamb of the first year without blemish ᴿfor a
sin offering, and one ram without blemish
ᴿfor peace offerings,   *she* · Lev. 4:2, 27, 32 · Lev. 3:6
15 ᴿAnd a basket of unleavened bread,
ᴿcakes of fine flour mingled with oil, and

wafers of unleavened bread ᴿanointed with
oil, and their meat offering, and their ᴿdrink
offerings.   Deut. 26:2 · Lev. 2:4 · Ex. 29:2 · 15:5, 7, 10
16 And the priest shall bring *them* before
the LORD, and shall offer his sin offering, and
his burnt offering:
17 And he shall offer the ram *for* a ᴿsacrifice of peace offerings unto the LORD, with
the basket of unleavened bread: the priest
shall offer also his ᵀmeat offering, and his
drink offering.   15:1–7 · *meal*
18 ᴿAnd the Nazarite shall shave the head
of his separation *at* the door of the tabernacle
of the congregation, and shall take the hair of
the head of his separation, and put *it* in the
fire which *is* under the sacrifice of the peace
offerings.   *v.* 9; Acts 21:24; [Rom. 6:6]
19 And the priest shall take the ᴿsoddenᵀ
shoulder of the ram, and one unleavened
cake out of the basket, and one unleavened
wafer, and ᴿshall put *them* upon the hands of
the Nazarite, after *the hair of* his separation
is shaven: 1 Sam. 2:15 · *sod* · Ex. 29:23, 24
20 And the priest shall ᵀwave them *for* a
wave offering before the LORD: this *is* holy for
the priest, with the wave breast and heave
shoulder: and ᴿafter that the Nazarite may
drink wine.   *present them to God · v.* 13
21 This *is* the law of the Nazarite who hath
vowed, *and of* his offering unto the LORD for
his separation, beside *that* that his hand shall
get: according to the vow which he vowed, so
he must do after the law of his separation.
22 And the LORD spake unto Moses, saying,
23 Speak unto Aaron and unto his sons,
saying, On this wise ye shall bless the children of Israel, saying unto them,
24 The LORD bless thee, and keep thee:
25 The LORD make his face shine upon
thee, and be gracious unto thee:
26 The LORD lift up his countenance upon
thee, and give thee peace.
27 And they shall put my name upon the
children of Israel; and I will bless them.

CHAPTER 7

Israel Gives Donations

AND it came to pass on ᴿthe day that Moses
had fully set up the tabernacle, and had
anointed it, and sanctified it, and all the
instruments thereof, both the altar and all the
vessels thereof, and had anointed them, and
sanctified them;   Ex. 40:17
2 That ᴿthe princes of Israel, heads of the
house of their fathers, who *were* the princes
of the tribes, ᵀand were over them that were
numbered, offered: 1:5–16 · *who stood*
3 And they brought their offering before
the LORD, six ᴿcovered wagons, and twelve
oxen; a wagon for two of the princes, and for

each one an ox: and they brought them before the tabernacle.   Is. 66:20

4 And the LORD spake unto Moses, saying,

5 Take it of them, that they ᵀmay be to do the service of the tabernacle of the congregation; and thou shalt give them unto the Levites, to every man according to his service.   may be used for the work

6 And Moses took the wagons and the oxen, and gave them unto the Levites.

7 Two wagons and four oxen ᴿhe gave unto the sons of Ger'-shon, according to their service: 4:23-28

8 ᴿAnd four wagons and eight oxen he gave unto the sons of Me-ra'-ri, according unto their service, under the hand of Ith'-a-mar the son of Aaron the priest.   4:33

9 But unto the sons of Ko'-hath he gave none: because ᴿthe service of the sanctuary belonging unto them was that they should bear upon their shoulders.   4:15

10 And the princes offered for dedicating of the altar in the day that ᴿit was anointed, even the princes offered their offering before the altar.   v. 1; 2 Chr. 7:9

11 And the LORD said unto Moses, They shall offer their offering, each prince on his day, for the dedicating of the altar.

12 And he that offered his offering the first day was ᴿNah'-shon the son of Am-min'-a-dab, of the tribe of Judah: 2:3

13 And his offering was one silver charger, the weight thereof was an ᵀhundred and thirty shek'-els, one silver bowl of ᵀseventy shek'-els, after the shek'-el of the sanctuary; both of them were full of fine flour mingled with oil for a meat offering: $16,640 · $8,960

14 One spoon of ᵀten shek'-els of gold, full of ᴿincense: $19,200 · Ex. 30:34

15 One young bullock, one ram, one lamb of the first year, for a burnt offering:

16 One kid of the goats for a sin offering:

17 And for a sacrifice of peace offerings, two oxen, five rams, five he goats, five lambs of the first year: this was the offering of Nah'-shon the son of Am-min'-a-dab.

18 On the second day Ne-than'-e-el the son of Zu'-ar, prince of Is'-sa-char, did offer:

19 He offered for his offering one silver ᵀcharger, the weight whereof was an hundred and thirty shek'-els, one silver bowl of seventy shek'-els, after the shek'-el of the sanctuary; both of them full of fine flour mingled with oil for a meat offering: platter

20 One spoon of gold of ᵀten shek'-els, full of incense: $19,200

21 One young ᵀbullock, one ram, one lamb of the first year, for a burnt offering: bull

22 One kid of the goats for a sin offering:

23 And for a sacrifice of peace offerings, two oxen, five rams, five he goats, five lambs

of the first year: this was the offering of Ne-than'-e-el the son of Zu'-ar.

24 On the third day E-li'-ab the son of He'-lon, prince of the children of Zeb'-u-lun, did offer:

25 His offering was one silver ᵀcharger, the weight whereof was an hundred and thirty shek'-els, one silver bowl of seventy shek'-els, after the shek'-el of the sanctuary; both of them full of fine flour ᵀmingled with oil for a ᵀmeat offering: platter · mixed · meal

26 One golden spoon of ᵀten shek'-els, full of incense: $19,200

27 One young bullock, one ram, one lamb of the first year, for a burnt offering:

28 One kid of the goats for a sin offering:

29 And for a sacrifice of peace offerings, two oxen, five rams, five he goats, five lambs of the first year: this was the offering of E-li'-ab the son of He'-lon.

30 On the fourth day ᴿE-li'-zur the son of Shed'-e-ur, prince of the children of Reuben, did offer: 1:5; 2:10

31 His offering was one silver ᵀcharger of the weight of an ᵀhundred and thirty shek'-els, one silver bowl of ᵀseventy shek'-els, after the shek'-el of the sanctuary; both of them full of fine flour mingled with oil for a ᵀmeat offering: platter · $16,640 · $8,960 · meal

32 One golden spoon of ᵀten shek'-els, full of incense: $19,200

33 One young bullock, one ram, one lamb of the first year, for a burnt offering:

34 One kid of the goats for a sin offering:

35 And for a sacrifice of peace offerings, two oxen, five rams, five he goats, five lambs of the first year: this was the offering of E-li'-zur the son of Shed'-e-ur.

36 On the fifth day ᴿShe-lu'-mi-el the son of Zu-ri-shad'-dai, prince of the children of Simeon, did offer: v. 41; 1:6; 2:12

37 His offering was one silver ᵀcharger, the weight whereof was an hundred and thirty shek'-els, one silver bowl of seventy shek'-els, after the shek'-el of the sanctuary; both of them full of fine flour mingled with oil for a ᵀmeat offering: platter · meal

38 One golden spoon of ᵀten shek'-els, full of incense: $19,200

39 One young bullock, one ram, one lamb of the first year, for a burnt offering:

40 One kid of the goats for a sin offering:

41 And for a sacrifice of peace offerings, two oxen, five rams, five he goats, five lambs of the first year: this was the offering of She-lu'-mi-el the son of Zu-ri-shad'-dai.

42 On the sixth day ᴿE-li'-a-saph the son of ᵀDeu'-el, prince of the children of Gad, offered: 1:14; 2:14 · Reuel

43 His offering was one silver charger of the weight of an hundred and thirty shek'-els, a silver bowl of seventy shek'-els, after the

shek'-el of the sanctuary; both of them full of fine flour mingled with ᴿoil for a meat offering: Lev. 2:5

44 One golden spoon of ᵀten shek'-els, full of incense: $19,200

45 One young bullock, one ram, one lamb of the first year, for a burnt offering:

46 One kid of the goats for a sin offering:

47 And for a sacrifice of peace offerings, two oxen, five rams, five he goats, five lambs of the first year: this was the offering of E-li'-a-saph the son of Deu'-el.

48 On the seventh day ᴿE-lish'-a-ma the son of Am-mi'-hud, prince of the children of E'-phra-im, offered: 1:10; 2:18

49 His offering was one silver charger, the weight whereof was ᵀan hundred and thirty shek'-els, one silver bowl of ᵀseventy shek'-els, after the shek'-el of the sanctuary; both of them full of fine flour mingled with oil for a meat offering: $16,640 · $8,960

50 One golden spoon of ᵀten shek'-els, full of incense: $19,200

51 One young bullock, one ram, one lamb of the first year, for a burnt offering:

52 One kid of the goats for a sin offering:

53 And for a sacrifice of peace offerings, two oxen, five rams, five he goats, five lambs of the first year: this was the offering of E-lish'-a-ma the son of Am-mi'-hud.

54 On the eighth day offered ᴿGa-ma'-li-el the son of Pe-dah'-zur, prince of the children of Ma-nas'-seh: 1:10; 2:20

55 His offering was one silver charger of the weight of an hundred and thirty shek'-els, one silver bowl of seventy shek'-els, after the shek'-el of the sanctuary; both of them full of fine flour mingled with oil for a meat offering:

56 One golden spoon of ᵀten shek'-els, full of ᴿincense: $19,200 · Ex. 30:7

57 One young bullock, one ram, one lamb of the first year, for a burnt offering:

58 One kid of the goats for a sin offering:

59 And for a ᴿsacrifice of peace offerings, two oxen, five rams, five he goats, five lambs of the first year: this was the offering of Ga-ma'-li-el the son of Pe-dah'-zur.   Lev. 3:1

60 On the ninth day ᴿAb'-i-dan the son of Gid-e-o'-ni, prince of the children of Benja-min, offered: 1:11; 2:22

61 His offering was one silver charger, the weight whereof was an hundred and thirty shek'-els, one silver bowl of seventy shek'-els, after the shek'-el of the sanctuary; both of them full of fine flour mingled with oil for a meat offering:

62 One golden spoon of ᵀten shek'-els, full of incense: $19,200

63 One young bullock, one ram, one lamb of the first year, for a burnt offering:

64 One kid of the goats for a sin offering:

65 And for a sacrifice of peace offerings, two oxen, five rams, five he goats, five lambs

of the first year: this was the offering of Ab'-i-dan the son of Gid-e-o'-ni.

66 On the tenth day ᴿA-hi-e'-zer the son of Am-mi-shad'-dai, prince of the children of Dan, offered: 1:12; 2:25

67 His offering was one silver charger, the weight whereof was an hundred and thirty shek'-els, one silver bowl of seventy shek'-els, after the shek'-el of the sanctuary; both of them full of fine flour mingled with oil for a meat offering:

68 One golden spoon of ᵀten shek'-els, full of incense: $19,200

69 One young bullock, one ram, one lamb of the first year, for a burnt offering:

70 One kid of the goats for a sin offering:

71 And for a sacrifice of peace offerings, two oxen, five rams, five he goats, five lambs of the first year: this was the offering of A-hi-e'-zer the son of Am-mi-shad'-dai.

72 On the eleventh day ᴿPa'-gi-el the son of Oc'-ran, prince of the children of Asher, offered: 1:13; 2:27

73 His offering was one silver ᵀcharger, the weight whereof was an ᵀhundred and thirty shek'-els, one silver bowl of ᵀseventy shek'-els, after the shek'-el of the sanctuary; both of them full of fine flour mingled with oil for a meat offering: platter · $16,640 · $8,960

74 One golden spoon of ᵀten shek'-els, full of incense: $19,200

75 One young bullock, one ram, one lamb of the first year, for a burnt offering:

76 One kid of the goats for a sin offering:

77 And for a sacrifice of peace offerings, two oxen, five rams, five he goats, five lambs of the first year: this was the offering of Pa'-gi-el the son of Oc'-ran.

78 On the twelfth day ᴿA-hi'-ra the son of E'-nan, prince of the children of Naph'-ta-li, offered: 1:15; 2:29

79 His offering was one ᴿsilver charger, the weight whereof was an hundred and thirty shek'-els, one silver bowl of seventy shek'-els, after the shek'-el of the sanctuary; both of them full of fine flour mingled with oil for a meat offering: Jer. 52:19

80 One golden spoon of ᵀten shek'-els, full of incense: $19,200

81 One young bullock, one ram, one lamb of the first year, for a burnt offering:

82 One kid of the goats for a sin offering:

83 And for a sacrifice of peace offerings, two oxen, five rams, five he goats, five lambs of the first year: this was the offering of A-hi'-ra the son of E'-nan.

84 This was the dedication of the altar, in the day when it was anointed, by the princes of Israel: twelve chargers of silver, twelve silver bowls, twelve spoons of gold:

85 Each charger of silver weighing ᵀan hundred and thirty shek'-els, each bowl ᵀseventy: all the silver vessels weighed two

thousand and four hundred *shek'-els*, after the shek'-el of the sanctuary: *$16,640 · $8,960*

86 The golden spoons *were* twelve, full of incense, *weighing* ^Tten *shek'-els* apiece, after the ^Rshek'-el of the sanctuary: all the gold of the spoons *was* an ^Thundred and twenty *shek'-els*.   *$19,200 · Ex. 30:13 · $230,400*

87 All the oxen for the burnt offering *were* twelve bullocks, the rams twelve, the lambs of the first year twelve, with their ^Rmeat offering: and the kids of the goats for sin offering twelve.   Lev. 2:1; 6:14–18

88 And all the oxen for the sacrifice of the peace offerings *were* twenty and four bullocks, the rams sixty, the he goats sixty, the lambs of the first year sixty. ^RThis^T *was* the dedication of the altar, after that it was ^Ranointed.   *vv.* 1, 10 · *each brought the same · v.* 1

89 And when Moses was gone into the tabernacle of the congregation ^Rto speak with ^Thim, then he heard ^Rthe voice of one speaking unto him from off the mercy seat that *was* upon the ark of testimony, from between the two cher'-u-bims: and he spake unto him.   [Ex. 33:9, 11] · *God* · Ex. 25:22; Lev. 1:1

CHAPTER 8

The Levites Are Consecrated

A ND the LORD spake unto Moses, saying, 2 Speak unto Aaron, and say unto him, When thou ^Tlightest^R the lamps, the seven lamps shall give light over against the candlestick.   *raise up* · Ex. 25:37; 40:25; Lev. 24:3, 4

3 And Aaron did so; he lighted the lamps thereof over against the candlestick, as the LORD commanded Moses.

4 And this work of the candlestick *was of* beaten gold, unto the shaft thereof, unto the flowers thereof, *was* beaten work: according unto the pattern which the LORD had shewed Moses, so he made the candlestick.

5 And the LORD spake unto Moses, saying, 6 Take the Levites from among the children of Israel, and cleanse them.

7 And thus shalt thou do unto them, to cleanse them: Sprinkle ^Rwater of purifying upon them, and let them ^Rshave all their flesh, and let them wash their clothes, and *so* make themselves clean.   19:9, 17 · Lev. 14:8

8 Then let them take a young bullock with his meat offering, *even* fine flour mingled with oil, and another young bullock shalt thou take for a sin offering.

9 And thou shalt bring the Levites before the tabernacle of the congregation: ^Rand thou shalt gather the whole assembly of the children of Israel together: Lev. 8:3

10 And thou shalt bring the Levites before the LORD: and the children of Israel shall put their hands upon the Levites:

11 And Aaron shall offer the Levites before the LORD *for* an ^Toffering of the children of Israel, that they may ^Texecute the service of the LORD.   *wave offering* · *do*

12 And the Levites shall lay their hands upon the heads of the bullocks: and thou shalt offer the one *for* a sin offering, and the other *for* a burnt offering, unto the LORD, to make an atonement for the Levites.

13 And thou shalt set the Levites before Aaron, and before his sons, and offer them *for* ^Tan offering unto the LORD.   *a wave*

14 Thus shalt thou separate the Levites from among the children of Israel: and the ^RLevites shall be ^Tmine.   3:12 · *for my service*

15 And after that shall the Levites go in to do the service of the tabernacle of the congregation: and thou shalt cleanse them, and ^Roffer them *for* an offering.   *vv.* 11, 13

16 For they *are* wholly given unto me from among the children of Israel; instead of ^Tsuch as open every womb, *even instead of* the firstborn of all the children of Israel, have I taken them unto me.   *the oldest children*

17 For all the firstborn of the children of Israel *are* mine, *both* man and beast: on the day that I smote every firstborn in the land of Egypt I sanctified them for myself.

18 And I have taken the Levites for all the firstborn of the children of Israel.

19 And ^RI have given the Levites *as* a gift to Aaron and to his sons from among the children of Israel, to do the service of the children of Israel in the tabernacle of the congregation, and to make an atonement for the children of Israel: that there be no ^Tplague among the children of Israel, when the children of Israel come nigh unto the sanctuary.   1:53; 3:9 · *judgment* or *punishment*

20 And Moses, and Aaron, and all the congregation of the children of Israel, did to the Levites according unto all that the LORD commanded Moses concerning the Levites, so did the children of Israel unto them.

21 ^RAnd the Levites were ^Tpurified, and they washed their clothes; and Aaron offered them *as* an offering before the LORD; and Aaron made an atonement for them to cleanse them.   *vv.* 7, 11 · *ceremonially cleansed*

22 ^RAnd after that went the Levites in to do their service in the tabernacle of the congregation before Aaron, and before his sons: ^Ras the LORD had commanded Moses concerning the Levites, so did they unto them.   *v.* 15 · *v.* 5

23 And the LORD spake unto Moses, saying,

24 This *is it* that *belongeth* unto the Levites: from twenty and five years old and upward they shall go in to wait upon the service of the tabernacle of the congregation:

25 And from the age of fifty years they

shall ᵀcease waiting upon the service *thereof*, and shall serve no more: *stop working*
26 ᴿBut shall minister with their brethren in the tabernacle of the congregation, to keep the charge, and shall do no service. Thus shalt thou do unto the Levites ᵀtouching their charge.   1:53 · *concerning their assignments*

CHAPTER 9

The Passover Is Celebrated

AND the Lord spake unto Moses in the wilderness of Si'-nai, in ᴿthe first month of the second year after they were come out of the land of Egypt, saying,   1:1
2 Let the children of Israel also keep ᴿthe passover at his appointed season.   Lev. 23:5
3 In the fourteenth day of this month, at even, ye shall keep it in his appointed season: according to all the rites of it, and according to all the ceremonies thereof, shall ye keep it.
4 And Moses spake unto the children of Israel, that they should keep the passover.
5 And ᴿthey kept the passover on the fourteenth day of the first month at even in the wilderness of Si'-nai: according to all that the Lord commanded Moses, so did the children of Israel.   Josh. 5:10
6 And there were certain men, who were ᵀdefiled by the dead body of a man, that they could not keep the passover on that day: ᴿand they came before Moses and before Aaron on that day: *unclean* · 27:2
7 ᴿAnd those men said unto him, We *are* defiled by the dead body of a man: wherefore are we kept back, that we may not offer an offering of the Lord in his appointed season among the children of Israel?   [1 Cor. 5:7, 8]
8 And Moses said unto them, ᴿStand ᵀstill, and ᴿI will hear what the Lord will command concerning you.   Ex. 18:15 · *Wait* · 27:5
9 And the Lord spake unto Moses, saying,
10 Speak unto the children of Israel, saying, If any man of you or of your ᵀposterity shall be unclean by reason of a dead body, or *be* in a journey afar off, yet he shall keep the passover unto the Lord.   *children*
11 The fourteenth day of the second month at even they shall keep it, *and* eat it with unleavened bread and bitter *herbs*.
12 ᴿThey shall leave none of it unto the morning, nor ᴿbreak any bone of it: according to all the ᵀordinances of the passover they shall keep it.   Ex. 12:10 · John 19:36 ☆ · *regulations*
13 But the man that *is* clean, and is not in a journey, and forbeareth to keep the passover, even the same soul shall be ᵀcut off from among his people: because he ᴿbrought not the offering of the Lord in his appointed season, that man shall bear his sin. *destroyed* · *v.* 7
14 And if a stranger shall ᵀsojourn among you, and will keep the passover unto the

Lord; according to the ordinance of the passover, and according to the manner thereof, so shall he do: ye shall have one ordinance, both for the stranger, and for him that was born in the land.   *stay for a while*

Guidance of the Cloud

15 And ᴿon the day that the tabernacle was reared up the cloud covered the tabernacle, *namely*, the tent of the testimony: and ᴿat even there was upon the tabernacle as it were the appearance of fire, until the morning.   Neh. 9:12, 19; Ps. 78:14 · Ex. 13:21; 40:38
16 So it was alway: the cloud covered it *by day*, and the appearance of fire by night.
17 And when the cloud was ᵀtaken up from the tabernacle, then after that the children of Israel journeyed: and in the place where the cloud abode, there the children of Israel pitched their tents.   *lifted up*
18 At the commandment of the Lord the children of Israel journeyed, and at the commandment of the Lord they ᵀpitched: as long as the cloud abode upon the tabernacle they rested in their tents.   *set up camp*
19 And when the cloud tarried long upon the tabernacle many days, then the children of Israel ᴿkept the charge of the Lord, and ᴿjourneyed not.   1:53; 3:8 · Gen. 49:18
20 And *so* it was, when the cloud was a few days upon the tabernacle; according to the commandment of the Lord they abode in their tents, and according to the commandment of the Lord they journeyed.
21 And *so* it was, when the cloud abode from even unto the morning, and *that* the cloud was taken up in the morning, then they journeyed: whether *it was* by day or by night that the cloud was taken up, they journeyed.
22 Or *whether it were* two days, or a month, or a year, that the cloud tarried upon the tabernacle, remaining thereon, the children of Israel ᴿabodeᵀ in their tents, and journeyed not: but when it was taken up, they journeyed.   Ex. 40:36, 37 · *stayed*
23 At the commandment of the Lord they rested in the tents, and at the commandment of the Lord they ᴿjourneyed: they ᴿkept the charge of the Lord, at the commandment of the Lord by the hand of Moses. Gen. 47:9 · *v.* 19

CHAPTER 10

Guidance of the Silver Trumpets

AND the Lord spake unto Moses, saying,
2 Make thee two trumpets of silver; of a whole piece shalt thou make them: that thou mayest use them for the ᴿcalling of the assembly, and for the journeying of the camps.   Is. 1:13
3 And when ᴿthey shall blow with them, all the assembly shall assemble themselves to

thee at the door of the tabernacle of the congregation. Jer. 4:5; Joel 2:15

4 And if they blow *but* with one *trumpet*, then the princes, *which are* ᴿheads of the thousands of Israel, shall gather themselves unto thee. 1:16; 7:2; Ex. 18:21

5 When ye blow an ᴿalarm, then ᴿthe camps that lie on the east parts shall go forward. Joel 2:1 • 2:3

6 When ye blow an alarm the second time, then the camps that lie on the south side shall ᵀtake their journey: they shall blow an alarm for their journeys. *start on their travels*

7 But when the congregation is to be gathered together, ᴿye shall blow, but ye shall not ᴿsound an alarm. *v.* 3 • Joel 2:1

8 And the sons of Aaron, the priests, shall blow with the trumpets; and they shall be to you for ᵀan ordinance for ever throughout your generations. *a rule to follow*

9 And ᴿif ye go to war in your land against the enemy that ᴿoppresseth you, then ye shall blow an alarm with the trumpets; and ye shall be ᴿremembered before the LORD your God, and ye shall be saved from your enemies. 31:6 • Judg. 2:18 • Gen. 8:1; Ps. 106:4

10 Also in the day of your gladness, and in your solemn days, and in the beginnings of your months, ye shall blow with the trumpets over your burnt offerings, and over the sacrifices of your peace offerings; that they may be to you for a memorial before your God: I *am* the LORD your God.

Israel Departs Mount Sinai

11 And it came to pass on the twentieth *day* of the second month, in the second year, that the cloud ᴿwas taken up from off the tabernacle of the testimony. 9:17

12 And the children of Israel took ᴿtheir journeys out of the ᴿwilderness of Si'-nai; and the cloud rested in the ᴿwilderness of Pa'-ran. Ex. 40:36 • Ex. 19:1 • Gen. 21:21; Deut. 1:1

13 And ᴿthey first took their journey ᴿaccording to the commandment of the LORD by the hand of Moses. Deut. 1:6 • vv. 5, 6

14 In the first *place* went the standard of the camp of the children of Judah according to their armies: and over his host *was* Nah'-shon the son of Am-min'-a-dab.

15 And over the host of the tribe of the children of ᴿIs'-sa-char *was* Ne-than'-e-el the son of Zu'-ar. Gen. 30:18

16 And over the host of the tribe of the children of ᴿZeb'-u-lun *was* E-li'-ab the son of He'-lon. Gen. 30:20

17 And the tabernacle was taken down; and the sons of Ger'-shon and the sons of Me-ra'-ri set forward, bearing the tabernacle.

18 And ᴿthe standard of the camp of Reu'ben set forward according to their

ᵀarmies: and over his host *was* E-li'-zur the son of Shed'-e-ur. 2:16 • *hosts*

19 And over the host of the tribe of the children of Simeon *was* She-lu'-mi-el the son of Zu-ri-shad'-dai.

20 And over the host of the tribe of the children of Gad *was* E-li'-a-saph the son of Deu'-el.

21 And the Ko'-hath-ites set forward, bearing the sanctuary: and *the other* did set up the tabernacle against they came.

22 And ᴿthe standard of the camp of the children of E'-phra-im set forward according to their armies: and over his host *was* E-lish'-a-ma the son of Am-mi'-hud. 2:24

23 And over the host of the tribe of the children of Ma-nas'-seh *was* Ga-ma'-li-el the son of Pe-dah'-zur.

24 And over the host of the tribe of the children of Benjamin *was* Ab'-i-dan the son of Gid-e-o'-ni.

25 And the standard of the camp of the children of Dan set forward, ᵀwhich *was* the rereward of all the camps throughout their hosts: and over his host *was* A-hi-e'-zer the son of Am-mi-shad'-dai. *acting as the rear guard*

26 And over the host of the tribe of the children of Asher *was* Pa'-gi-el the son of Oc'-ran.

27 And over the host of the tribe of the children of Naph'-ta-li *was* A-hi'-ra the son of E'-nan.

28 ᵀThus *were* the journeyings of the children of Israel according to their armies, when they set forward. *this is the way they travelled*

29 And Moses said unto Ho'-bab, the son of Ra-gu'-el the Mid'-i-an-ite, Moses' father in law, We are journeying unto the place of which the LORD said, I will give it you: come thou with us, and we will do thee good: for ᴿthe LORD hath ᵀspoken good concerning Israel. Ex. 3:8 • *promised to bring good*

30 And he said unto him, I will not go; but I will depart to mine own land, and to my kindred.

31 And he said, Leave us not, I pray thee; forasmuch as thou knowest how we are to encamp in the wilderness, and thou mayest be to us ᴿinstead of eyes. Job 29:15

32 And it shall be, if thou go with us, yea, it shall be, that ᴿwhat ᵀgoodness the LORD shall do unto us, the same will we do unto thee. [Ps. 22:27–31; 67:5–7]; Judg. 1:16 • *benefits*

33 ᴿAnd they departed from the mount of the LORD ᵀthree days' journey: and the ark of the covenant of the LORD ᴿwent before them in the three days' journey, to search out a resting place for them. *v.* 11 • 60 *mi.* • Deut. 1:33

34 And ᴿthe cloud of the LORD *was* upon them by day, when they went out of the camp. Ex. 13:21; Neh. 9:12, 19

35 And it came to pass, when the ark set forward, that Moses said, [R]Rise up, LORD, and let thine enemies be scattered; and let them that hate thee flee before thee.   Ps. 68:1
36 And when it rested, he said, Return, O LORD, unto the many thousands of Israel.

CHAPTER 11

Israel Complains About Circumstances

AND when the people complained, it displeased the LORD: and the LORD heard it; and [T]his anger was kindled; and the fire of the LORD burnt among them, and consumed them that were in the uttermost parts of the camp.   he was provoked
2 [R]And the people cried unto Moses; and when Moses [R]prayed unto the LORD, the fire was [T]quenched.   12:11, 13; 21:7 • [James 5:16] • stopped
3 And he called the name of the place [R]Tab'-e-rah[T]: because the fire of the LORD burnt among them.   Deut. 9:22 • a burning

Israel Complains About Food

4 And the mixt multitude that was among them [T]fell a lusting: and the children of Israel also wept again, and said, Who shall give us flesh to eat?   began to desire to have
5 [R]We remember the fish, which we did eat in Egypt [T]freely; the [R]cucumbers, and the melons, and the leeks, and the onions, and the garlick: Ex. 16:3 • for nothing • Is. 1:8
6 But now [T]our soul is dried away: there is nothing at all, beside this [R]man'-na, before our eyes.   we don't feel good any more • Josh. 5:12
7 And [R]the man'-na was as coriander seed, and the colour thereof as the colour of bdellium.   Ex. 16:14, 31
8 And the people went about, and gathered it, and ground it in [R]mills, or beat it in a mortar, and baked it in pans, and made cakes of it: and the taste of it was as the taste of fresh oil.   Matt. 24:41
9 And when the dew fell upon the camp in the night, the man'-na fell upon it.

Moses Complains About the People

10 Then Moses heard the people weep throughout their families, every man in the door of his tent: and [R]the anger of the LORD was [T]kindled greatly; Moses also was displeased.   Ps. 78:21 • provoked
11 And Moses said unto the LORD, Wherefore hast thou afflicted thy servant? and wherefore have I not found favour in thy sight, that thou layest the [T]burden of all this people upon me?   responsibility
12 Have I conceived all this people? have I begotten them, that thou shouldest say unto me, Carry them in thy bosom, as a nursing father beareth the sucking child, unto the land which thou swarest unto their fathers?

13 Whence should I have flesh to give unto all this people? for they weep unto me, saying, Give us flesh, that we may eat.

Moses Complains About His Own Life

14 I am not able to [T]bear all this people alone, because it is too heavy for me.   carry
15 And if thou [T]deal thus with me, kill me, I pray thee, [T]out of hand, if I have found favour in thy sight; and let me not see my wretchedness.   treat me this way • at once

God Provides for Moses

16 And the LORD said unto Moses, Gather unto me seventy men of the elders of Israel, whom thou knowest to be the elders of the people, and officers over them; and bring them unto the tabernacle of the congregation, that they may stand there with thee.
17 And I will come down and talk with thee there: and I will take of the spirit which is upon thee, and will put it upon them; and they shall bear the burden of the people with thee, that thou bear it not thyself alone.
18 And say thou unto the people, Sanctify yourselves against to morrow, and ye shall eat flesh: for ye have wept in the ears of the LORD, saying, Who shall give us flesh to eat? for it was well with us in Egypt: therefore the LORD will give you flesh, and ye shall eat.
19 Ye shall not eat one day, nor two days, nor five days, neither ten days, nor twenty days;
20 [R]But even a whole month, until it come out at your nostrils, and it be [T]loathsome unto you: because that ye have [T]despised the LORD which is among you, and have wept before him, saying, Why came we forth out of Egypt?   Ps. 78:29 • disgusting • belittled
21 And Moses said, The people, among whom I am, are six hundred thousand footmen; and thou hast said, I will give them flesh, that they may eat a whole month.
22 [R]Shall the flocks and the herds be slain for them, to [T]suffice them? or shall all the fish of the sea be gathered together for them, to suffice them?   2 Kin. 7:2 • be enough meat
23 And the LORD said unto Moses, [R]Is the LORD'S hand [T]waxed short? thou shalt see now whether my word shall come to pass unto thee or not.   Is. 50:2; 59:1 • become
24 And Moses went out, and told the people the words of the LORD, and gathered the seventy men of the elders of the people, and set them round about the tabernacle.
25 And the LORD came down in a cloud, and spake unto him, and took of the spirit that was upon him, and gave it unto the seventy elders: and it came to pass, that, when the [R]spirit rested upon them, [R]they prophesied, and did not cease.   24:2 • [Joel 2:28]
26 But there remained two of the men in

the camp, ^Rthe name of the one *was* El'-dad, and the name of the other Me'-dad: and the spirit rested upon them; and they *were* of them that were written, but ^Rwent not out unto the tabernacle: and they prophesied in the camp.   24:2 • Jer. 36:5

27 And there ran a young man, and told Moses, and said, El'-dad and Me'-dad do prophesy in the camp.

28 And ^RJoshua the son of Nun, the servant of Moses, *one* of his young men, answered and said, My lord Moses, ^Rforbid them.   Ex. 33:11; Josh. 1:1 • Mark 9:38; Luke 9:49

29 And Moses said unto him, Enviest thou for my sake? would God that all the LORD's people were prophets, *and* that the LORD would put his spirit upon them!

30 And Moses ^Tgat him into the camp, he and the elders of Israel.   *got*

God Provides Quail

31 And there went forth a ^Rwind from the LORD, and brought quails from the sea, and let *them* fall by the camp, as it were ^Ta day's journey on this side, and as it were a day's journey on the other side, round about the camp, and as it were ^Ttwo cubits high upon the face of the earth.   Ex. 16:13 • *20 mi.* • *3 ft.*

32 And the people stood up all that day, and all *that* night, and all the next day, and they gathered the quails: he that gathered least gathered ten ho'-mers: and they spread *them* all abroad for themselves round about the camp.

God Sends Plagues

33 And while the ^Rflesh^T *was* yet between their teeth, ere it was chewed, the wrath of the LORD was kindled against the people, and the LORD ^Tsmote the people with a very great plague.   Ps. 78:30, 31 • *meat* • *struck down*

34 And he called the name of that place Kib'-roth–hat-ta'-a-vah: because there they buried the people that lusted.

35 ^R*And* the people journeyed from Kib'-roth–hat-ta'-a-vah unto ^RHa-ze'-roth; and abode at Ha-ze'-roth.   33:17 • 12:16

CHAPTER 12

Miriam and Aaron Rebel

AND Miriam and Aaron spake against Mo-ses because of the ^TE-thi-o'-pi-an woman whom he had married: for he had married an E-thi-o'-pi-an woman.   *Cushite*

2 And they said, Hath the LORD indeed spoken only by Moses? hath he not spoken also by us? And the LORD heard *it*.

3 ^R(Now the man Moses *was* very ^Rmeek, above all the men which *were* upon the face of the earth.)   [Matt. 5:5; 11:29] • [20:10]

Miriam Is Punished

4 And the LORD spake suddenly unto Moses, and unto Aaron, and unto Miriam, Come out ye three unto the tabernacle of the congregation. And they three came out.

5 ^RAnd the LORD came down in the pillar of the cloud, and stood *in* the door of the tabernacle, and called Aaron and Miriam: and they both came forth.   11:25; 16:19; Ex. 19:9

6 And he said, Hear now my words: If there be a prophet among you, *I* the LORD will make myself known unto him in a vision, *and* will speak unto him in a dream.

7 ^RMy servant Moses *is* not so, who *is* faithful in all ^Rmine house.   [Josh. 1:1] • 1 Tim. 3:11

8 With him will I speak mouth to mouth, even ^Rapparently, and not in dark speeches; and the similitude of the LORD shall he behold: wherefore then were ye not afraid to speak against my servant Moses?   [1 Cor. 13:12]

9 And the anger of the LORD was kindled against them; and ^Rhe departed.   Gen. 17:22; 18:33

10 And the cloud departed from off the tabernacle; and, behold, Miriam *became* leprous, *white* as snow: and Aaron looked upon Miriam, and, behold, *she was* leprous.

Moses Intercedes

11 And Aaron said unto Moses, Alas, my lord, I beseech thee, ^Rlay not the sin upon us, wherein we have done foolishly, and wherein we have sinned.   2 Sam. 19:19; Prov. 30:32

12 Let her not be ^Ras one dead, of whom the flesh is half consumed when he cometh out of his mother's womb.   Ps. 88:4

13 And Moses cried unto the LORD, saying, Heal her now, O God, I beseech thee.

Miriam Is Restored

14 And the LORD said unto Moses, If her father had but spit in her face, should she not be ashamed seven days? let her be ^Tshut out from the camp seven days, and after that let her be received in *again*.   *exiled*

15 And Miriam was shut out from the camp seven days: and the people journeyed not till Miriam was brought in *again*.

16 And afterward the people removed from ^RHa-ze'-roth, and ^Tpitched in the wilderness of Pa'-ran.   11:35; 33:18 • *encamped*

CHAPTER 13

Investigation of the Promised Land
Deut. 1:22–40

AND the LORD spake unto Moses, saying, 2 ^RSend thou men, that they ^Tmay search the land of Canaan, which I give unto the children of Israel: of every tribe of their fathers shall ye send a man, every one a ruler among them.   32:8; Deut. 1:22 • *investigate*

3 And Moses by the commandment of the LORD sent them ᴿfrom the wilderness of Pa'-ran: all those men *were* heads of the children of Israel.   12:16; Deut. 1:19; 9:23

4 And these *were* their names: of the tribe of Reuben, Sham-mu'-a the son of Zac'-cur.

5 Of the tribe of Simeon, Sha'-phat the son of Ho'-ri.

6 ᴿOf the tribe of Judah, ᴿCaleb the son of Je-phun'-neh.   1 Chr. 4:15 • *v.* 30; Josh. 14:6, 7

7 Of the tribe of Is'-sa-char, I'-gal the son of Joseph.

8 Of the tribe of E'-phra-im, ᴿO-she'-a the son of Nun.   *v.* 16; Deut. 32:44

9 Of the tribe of Benjamin, Pal'-ti the son of Ra'-phu.

10 Of the tribe of Zeb'-u-lun, Gad'-di-el the son of So'-di.

11 Of the tribe of Joseph, *namely,* of the tribe of Ma-nas'-seh, Gad'-di the son of Su'-si.

12 Of the tribe of Dan, Am'-mi-el the son of Ge-mal'-li.

13 Of the tribe of Asher, Se'-thur the son of Mi'-cha-el.

14 Of the tribe of Naph'-ta-li, Nah'-bi the son of Voph'-si.

15 Of the tribe of Gad, Geu'-el the son of Ma'-chi.

16 These *are* the names of the men which Moses sent to spy out the land. And Moses called O-she'-a the son of Nun Je-hosh'-u-a.

17 And Moses sent them to spy out the land of Canaan, and said unto them, Get you up this *way* ᴿsouthward, and go up into ᴿthe mountain: Gen. 12:9; 13:1, 3 • Judg. 1:9

18 And ᵀsee the land, what it *is;* and the people that dwelleth therein, whether they *be* strong or weak, few or many;   *check on*

19 And what the land *is* that they dwell in, whether it *be* good or bad; and what cities they *be* that they dwell in, whether in ᵀtents, or in strong holds;   *camps*

20 And what the land *is,* whether it *be* fat or lean, whether there be wood therein, or not. And be ye of good courage, and bring of the fruit of the land. Now the time *was* the time of the firstripe grapes.

21 So they went up, and searched the land from the wilderness of Zin unto ᴿRe'-hob, as men come to Ha'-math.   Josh. 19:28

22 And they ascended by the ᵀsouth, and came unto He'-bron; where A-hi'-man, She'-shai, and Tal'-mai, the children of A'-nak, *were.* (Now He'-bron was built seven years before Zo'-an in Egypt.)   *Negev*

23 And they came unto the brook of Esh'-col, and cut down from thence a branch with one cluster of grapes, and they bare it between two upon a staff; and *they* brought of the pomegranates, and of the figs.

24 The place was called the brook Esh'-col, because of the cluster of grapes which the children of Israel cut down from thence.

25 And they returned from searching of the land after ᴿforty days.   Deut. 9:25

26 And they went and came to Moses, and to Aaron, and to all the congregation of the children of Israel, unto the wilderness of Pa'-ran, to Ka'-desh; and brought back word unto them, and unto all the congregation, and shewed them the fruit of the land.

27 And they told him, and said, We came unto the land whither thou sentest us, and surely it floweth with ᴿmilk and honey; ᴿand this *is* the fruit of it.   Ex. 3:8 • Deut. 1:25

28 Nevertheless the ᴿpeople *be* strong that dwell in the land, and the cities *are* walled, *and* very great: and moreover we saw the children of A'-nak there.   Deut. 1:28; 9:1, 2

29 The Am'-a-lek-ites dwell in the land of the south: and the Hit'-tites, and the Jeb'-u-sites, and the Am'-or-ites, dwell in the mountains: and the Ca'-naan-ites dwell by the sea, and by the coast of Jordan.

30 And ᴿCaleb stilled the people before Moses, and said, Let us go up at once, and ᵀpossess it; ᴿfor we are well able to overcome it.   14:6, 24 • *occupy* • [Mark 9:23]

31 But the men that went up with him said, We be not able to go up against the people; for they *are* stronger than we.

32 And they brought up an evil report of the land which they had searched unto the children of Israel, saying, The land, through which we have gone to search it, *is* a land that ᵀeateth up the inhabitants thereof; and ᴿall the people that we saw in it *are* men of a great stature.   *destroys* • Amos 2:9

33 And there we saw the giants, the sons of A'-nak, *which come* of the giants: and we were in our own sight as grasshoppers, and so we were in their sight.

CHAPTER 14

Israel Rebels Against God

AND all the congregation ᵀlifted up their voice, and cried; and the people ᴿwept that night.   *made loud lament* • 11:4; Deut. 1:45

2 ᴿAnd all the children of Israel ᴿmur-muredᵀ against Moses and against Aaron: and the whole congregation said unto them, Would God that we had died in the land of Egypt! or would God we had died in this wilderness!   Ex. 16:2 • 11:1 • *complained*

3 And wherefore hath the LORD brought us unto this land, to fall by the sword, that our wives and our children should be a prey? were it not better for us to return into Egypt?

4 And they said one to another, Let us make a captain, and let us return into Egypt.

5 Then Moses and Aaron fell on their faces before all the assembly of the congregation of the children of Israel.

6 And Joshua the son of Nun, and Caleb the son of Je-phun'-neh, *which were* of them that searched the land, rent their clothes:

7 And they spake unto all the company of the children of Israel, saying, ᴿThe land, which we passed through to search it, *is* an exceeding good land.   13:27; Deut. 1:25

8 If the LORD delight in us, then he will bring us into this land, and give it us; a land which floweth with milk and honey.

9 Only rebel not ye against the LORD, neither fear ye the people of the land; for they *are* bread for us: their ᵀdefence is departed from them, ᴿand the LORD *is* with us: fear them not.   *protection* • Gen. 48:21

10 But all the congregation bade stone them with stones. And the glory of the LORD appeared in the tabernacle of the congregation before all the children of Israel.

Moses Intercedes

11 And the LORD said unto Moses, How long will this people provoke me? and how long will it be ere they believe me, for all the signs which I have shewed among them?

12 I will smite them with the pestilence, and disinherit them, and will make of thee a greater nation and mightier than they.

13 ᴿAnd Moses said unto the LORD, Then the ᴿEgyptians shall hear *it,* (for thou broughtest up this people in thy might from among them;)   27:15; [Heb. 3:1] • Ex. 32:12; Ps. 106:23

14 And they will tell *it* to the inhabitants of this land: *for* they have heard that thou LORD *art* among this people, that thou LORD *art* seen face to face, and *that* thy cloud standeth over them, and *that* thou goest before them, by daytime in a pillar of a cloud, and in a pillar of fire by night.

15 Now *if* thou shalt kill *all* this people as one man, then the nations which have heard the fame of thee will speak, saying,

16 ᴿBecause the LORD was not ᴿable to bring this people into the land which he sware unto them, therefore he hath slain them in the wilderness.   Josh. 7:9 • Deut. 9:28

17 ᴿAnd now, I beseech thee, let the power of my LORD be ᵀgreat, according as thou hast spoken, saying,   Deut. 9:26 • *much recognized*

18 The LORD *is* ᴿlongsuffering,ᵀ and of great mercy, forgiving iniquity and transgression, and by no means clearing *the guilty,* ᴿvisiting the iniquity of the fathers upon the children unto the third and fourth *generation.*   Ex. 34:6, 7; Is. 48:9 • *slow to anger* • Ex. 20:5

19 Pardon, I beseech thee, the iniquity of this people according unto the greatness of thy mercy, and as thou hast forgiven this people, from Egypt even until now.

Israel to Wander and Die

20 And the LORD said, ᴿI have pardoned ᴿaccording to thy word: Mic. 7:18-20 • 1 John 5:14-16

21 But *as* truly *as* I live, all the earth shall be filled with the glory of the LORD.

22 Because all those men which have seen my glory, and my miracles, which I did in Egypt and in the wilderness, and have tempted me now these ten times, and have not hearkened to my voice;

23 Surely they shall not see the land which I sware unto their fathers, neither shall any of them that provoked me see it:

24 But my servant Caleb, because he had another spirit with him, and hath followed me fully, him will I bring into the land whereinto he went; and his seed shall possess it.

25 (Now the Am'-a-lek-ites and the Ca'-naan-ites dwelt in the valley.) To morrow turn you, ᴿand get you into the wilderness by the way of the Red sea.   Deut. 1:40

26 And the LORD spake unto Moses and unto Aaron, saying,

27 How long *shall I bear with* this evil congregation, which murmur against me? I have heard the murmurings of the children of Israel, which they murmur against me.

28 Say unto them, ᴿAs *truly as* I live, saith the LORD, as ye have spoken in mine ears, so will I do to you: Deut. 1:35; Heb. 3:17

29 ᴿYour carcases shall fall in this wilderness; and all that were numbered of you, according to your whole number, from twenty years old and upward, which have murmured against me,   Josh. 5:6

30 Doubtless ye shall not come into the land, *concerning* which I sware to make you dwell therein, save Caleb the son of Je-phun'-neh, and Joshua the son of Nun.

31 ᴿBut your little ones, which ye said should be a prey, them will I bring in, and they shall ᵀknow the land which ᴿye have ᵀdespised.   Deut. 1:39 • *appreciate* • Ps. 106:24 • *rejected*

32 But *as for* you, your ᵀcarcases, they ᵀshall fall in this wilderness.   *bodies* • *shall die*

33 And your children shall ᵀwander in the wilderness ᴿforty years, and ᴿbear your whoredoms, until your carcases be wasted in the wilderness.   *feed* • Deut. 2:7; 8:2 • Ezek. 23:35

34 After the number of the days in which ye searched the land, *even* forty days, each day for a year, shall ye bear your iniquities, *even* ᴿforty years, and ye shall know my ᵀbreach of promise.   13:25 • *alienation*

35 ᴿI the LORD have said, I will surely do it unto all ᴿthis ᵀevil congregation, that are gathered together against me: in this wilderness they shall be consumed, and there they shall die.   23:19 • 1 Cor. 10:5 • *sinful*

Spies Die Immediately

36 And the men, which Moses sent to search the land, who returned, and made all the congregation to murmur against him, by bringing up a slander upon the land,

37 Even those men that did bring up the

evil report upon the land, Rdied by the Rplague before the LORD.   [1 Cor. 10:10] • 16:49

38 But Joshua the son of Nun, and Caleb the son of Je-phun'-neh, *which were* of the men that went to search the land, lived *still*.

Moses Warns Israel—Deut. 1:41–44

39 And Moses told these sayings unto all the children of Israel: Rand the people mourned greatly.   *vv.* 28–35; Ex. 33:4

40 And they rose up early in the morning, and Tgat them up into the top of the mountain, saying, Lo, Rwe *be here*, and will go up unto the place which the LORD hath promised: for we have sinned.   *got* • Deut. 1:41

41 And Moses said, Wherefore now do ye transgress the commandment of the LORD? but Tit shall not prosper.   *you will not succeed*

42 RGo not up, for the LORD *is* not among you; that ye be not Tsmitten before your enemies.   1:42; Deut. 31:17 • *defeated*

43 For the Am'-a-lek-ites and the Ca'-naan-ites *are* there before you, and ye shall fall by the sword: Rbecause ye are turned away from the LORD, therefore the LORD will not be with you.   2 Chr. 15:2

44 RBut they presumed to go up unto the hill top: nevertheless the Rark of the covenant of the LORD, and Moses, departed not out of the camp.   Deut. 1:43; Josh. 7:1–8 • 3:6

Amalekites Defeat Israel

45 Then the Am'-a-lek-ites came down, and the Ca'-naan-ites which dwelt in that hill, and smote them, and Tdiscomfited them, *even* unto RHor'-mah.   *defeated* • 21:3

CHAPTER 15

Offerings to Thank the Lord

A ND the LORD spake unto Moses, saying, 2 RSpeak unto the children of Israel, and say unto them, When ye be come into the land of your habitations, which I give unto you,   Lev. 23:10; Deut. 7:1

3 And will make an offering by fire unto the LORD, a burnt offering, or a sacrifice in performing a vow, or in a freewill offering, or in your RsolemnT feasts, Tto make a sweet savour unto the LORD, of the herd, or of the flock: Lev. 23:1–44 • *set* • *to be pleasing*

4 Then Rshall he that offereth his offering unto the LORD bring a meat offering of a Ttenth deal of flour mingled with the Tfourth *part* of an hin of oil.   Lev. 2:1; 6:14 • 2.087 qt. • *1 qt.*

5 And the fourth *part* of an hin of wine for a drink offering shalt thou prepare with the burnt offering or sacrifice, for one lamb.

6 Or for a ram, thou shalt prepare *for* a meat offering two tenth deals of flour mingled with the third *part* of an hin of oil.

7 And for a drink offering thou shalt offer Tthe third *part* of an hin of wine, *for* a Rsweet savour unto the LORD.   42.7 oz. • Ezra 6:16

8 And when thou preparest a bullock *for* a burnt offering, or *for* a sacrifice in performing a vow, or peace offerings unto the LORD:

9 Then shall he bring with a bullock a meat offering of Tthree tenth deals of flour mingled with Thalf an hin of oil.   6.261 qt. • 2 qt.

10 And thou shalt bring for a drink offering Thalf an hin of wine, *for* an offering made by fire, of a sweet savour unto the LORD. 2 qt.

11 RThus shall it be done for one bullock, or for one ram, or for a lamb, or for a kid.   v. 28

12 According to the number that ye shall prepare, so shall ye do to every one according to their number.

13 All that are Tborn of the country shall do these things after this manner, in offering an offering made by fire, of a sweet savour unto the LORD.   *native*

14 And if a stranger Tsojourn with you, or whosoever *be* among you in your generations, and will offer an offering made by fire, of a sweet savour unto the LORD; as ye do, so he shall do.   *stays*

15 One ordinance *shall be both* for you of the congregation, and also for the stranger that sojourneth *with you*, an ordinance for ever in your generations: as ye *are*, so shall the stranger be before the LORD.

16 One law and one Tmanner shall be for you, and for the stranger that sojourneth with you.   *ordinance*

17 And the LORD spake unto Moses, saying,

18 RSpeak unto the children of Israel, and say unto them, When ye come into the land whither I bring you,   v. 2; Deut. 26:1

19 Then it shall be, that, when ye eat of Rthe bread of the land, ye shall offer up an heave offering unto the LORD.   Josh. 5:11, 12

20 RYe shall offer up a cake of the first of your dough *for* an heave offering: as ye *do* Rthe heave offering of the threshingfloor, so shall ye heave it.   Prov. 3:9, 10 • Lev. 2:14

21 Of the first of your dough ye shall give unto the LORD an heave offering in your generations.

Offerings for Unintentional Sins

22 And if ye have Terred, and not observed all these commandments, which the LORD hath spoken unto Moses,   *sinned*

23 *Even* all that the LORD hath commanded you by the hand of Moses, from the day that the LORD commanded *Moses*, and henceforward among your generations;

24 Then it shall be, Rif *ought* be committed by ignorance without the knowledge of the congregation, that all the congregation shall offer one young bullock for a burnt offering,

for a sweet savour unto the LORD, with his meat offering, and his drink offering, according to the ᵀmanner, and one kid of the goats for a sin offering.   Lev. 4:2 • *ordinance*

25 ᴿAnd the priest shall make an atonement for all the congregation of the children of Israel, and it shall be forgiven them; for it *is* ignorance: and they shall bring their offering, a sacrifice made by fire unto the LORD, and their sin offering before the LORD, for their ᵀignorance: Lev. 4:20 • *error*

26 And it shall be forgiven all the congregation of the children of Israel, and the stranger that sojourneth among them; seeing all the people *were* in ᴿignorance.   *v.* 24

27 And ᴿif any soul sin through ignorance, then he shall bring a she goat of the first year for a ᴿsin offering.   Lev. 4:27, 28 • Heb. 9:13

28 ᴿAnd the priest shall make an atonement for the soul that ᵀsinneth ignorantly, when he sinneth by ignorance before the LORD, to make an atonement for him; and it shall be forgiven him.   Lev. 4:35 • *errs*

29 Ye shall have one law for him that sinneth through ignorance, *both for* him that is born among the children of Israel, and for the stranger that sojourneth among them.

No Offering for Intentional Sins

30 But the soul that doeth *ought* ᵀpresumptuously, *whether he be* born in the land, or a stranger, the same reproacheth the LORD; and that soul shall be ᵀcut off from among his people.   *willfully • destroyed*

31 Because he hath despised the word of the LORD, and hath broken his commandment, that ᵀsoul shall utterly be cut off; his ᴿiniquity *shall be* upon him.   *person • 30:15*

32 And while the children of Israel were in the wilderness, they found a man that gathered sticks upon the sabbath day.

33 And they that found him gathering sticks brought him unto Moses and Aaron, and unto all the congregation.

34 And they put him ᴿinᵀ ward, ᴿbecause it was not ᵀdeclared what should be done to him.   Lev. 24:12 • *in prison* • 9:8 • *revealed*

35 And the LORD said unto Moses, ᴿThe man shall be surely put to death: ᴿall the congregation shall ᴿstone him with stones without the camp.   Ex. 31:14, 15 • Lev. 20:2 • Acts 7:58

36 And all the congregation brought him ᵀwithout the camp, and stoned him with stones, and he died; as the LORD commanded Moses.   *outside*

The Tassel on the Garment

37 And the LORD spake unto Moses, saying,

38 Speak unto the children of Israel, and bid them that they make them fringes in the borders of their garments throughout their generations, and that they put upon the fringe of the borders a ribband of blue:

39 And it shall be unto you for a fringe, that ye may look upon it, and remember all the commandments of the LORD, and do them; and that ye ᴿseek not after your own heart and your own eyes, after which ye use to go ᵀa whoring: Deut. 29:19 • *away from God*

40 That ye may remember, and do all my commandments, and be ᴿholy unto your God.   [Lev. 11:44, 45; Rom. 12:1; Col. 1:22; 1 Pet. 1:15, 16]

41 I *am* the LORD your God, which brought you out of the land of Egypt, to be your God: I *am* the LORD your God.

CHAPTER 16

Korah Rebels Against Moses and Aaron

NOW Ko'-rah, the son of Iz'-har, ᴿthe son of Ko'-hath, the son of Levi, and ᴿDa'-than and A-bi'-ram, the sons of E-li'-ab, and On, the son of Pe'-leth, sons of Reuben, took *men:*   Ex. 6:21; Jude 11 • 26:9

2 And they rose up before Moses, with certain of the children of Israel, two hundred and fifty princes of the assembly, famous in the congregation, men of renown:

3 And they gathered themselves together against Moses and against Aaron, and said unto them, Ye ᵀtake too much upon you, seeing all the congregation *are* holy, every one of them, and the LORD *is* among them: wherefore then lift ye up yourselves above the congregation of the LORD?   *assume too much*

4 And when Moses heard *it,* ᴿhe fell upon his face: 14:5; 20:6

5 And he spake unto Ko'-rah and unto all his company, saying, Even to morrow the LORD will shew who *are* his, and *who is* holy; and will cause *him* to come near unto him: even *him* whom he hath ᴿchosen will he cause to come near unto him.   17:5

6 This do; Take you ᵀcensers, Ko'-rah, and all his company;   *firepans*

7 And put fire therein, and put incense in them before the LORD to morrow: and it shall be *that* the man whom the LORD doth choose, he *shall be* ᵀholy: ye *take* too much upon you, ye sons of Levi.   *for this service only*

8 And Moses said unto Ko'-rah, Hear, I pray you, ye sons of Levi:

9 *Seemeth it but* a small thing unto you, that the God of Israel hath separated you from the congregation of Israel, to bring you near to himself to do the service of the tabernacle of the LORD, and to stand before the congregation to minister unto them?

10 And he hath brought thee near *to him,* and all thy brethren the sons of Levi with thee: and seek ye the priesthood also?

11 For which cause *both* thou and all thy company *are* gathered together against the

LORD: ^Rand what *is* Aaron, that ye ^Rmurmur^T against him?   Ex. 16:8 • [1 Cor. 10:10] • *complain*

12 And Moses sent to call ^RDa′-than and A-bi′-ram, the sons of E-li′-ab: which said, We will not come up: *v.* 27

13 *Is it* a small thing that thou hast brought us up out of a land that floweth with milk and honey, to kill us in the wilderness, except thou ^Rmake thyself altogether a prince over us?   Ex. 2:14; Acts 7:27, 35

14 Moreover thou hast not brought us into ^Ra land that floweth with milk and honey, or given us inheritance of fields and vineyards: wilt thou put out the eyes of these men? we will not come up.   Ex. 3:8

God Judges Korah

15 And Moses was very ^Twroth, and said unto the LORD, Respect not thou their offering: I have not taken one ass from them, neither have I hurt one of them.   *angry*

16 And Moses said unto Ko′-rah, Be thou and all thy company before the LORD, thou, and they, and Aaron, to morrow:

17 And take every man his censer, and put incense in them, and bring ye before the LORD every man his censer, two hundred and fifty censers; thou also, and Aaron, each *of you* his censer.

18 And they took every man his censer, and put fire in them, and laid incense thereon, and stood in the door of the tabernacle of the congregation with Moses and Aaron.

19 And Ko′-rah gathered all the congregation against them unto the door of the tabernacle of the congregation: and the glory of the LORD appeared unto all the congregation.

20 And the LORD spake unto Moses and unto Aaron, saying,

21 ^RSeparate yourselves from among this congregation, that I may ^Tconsume them in a moment.   *v.* 45; Gen. 19:17; Jer. 51:6 • *destroy*

22 And they ^Rfell upon their faces, and said, O God, the God of the spirits of all flesh, shall one man sin, and wilt thou be wroth with all the congregation?   14:5

23 And the LORD spake unto Moses, saying,

24 Speak unto the congregation, saying, ^RGet you up from about the tabernacle of Ko′-rah, Da′-than, and A-bi′-ram.   *v.* 45

25 And Moses rose up and went unto Da′-than and A-bi′-ram; and the elders of Israel followed him.

26 And he spake unto the congregation, saying, Depart, I pray you, from the tents of these wicked men, and touch nothing of their's, lest ye be consumed in all their sins.

27 So they gat up from the tabernacle of Ko′-rah, Da′-than, and A-bi′-ram, on every side: and Da′-than and A-bi′-ram came

out, and stood in the door of their tents, and their wives, and ^Rtheir sons, and their little children.   26:11; Ex. 20:5

28 And Moses said, Hereby ye shall know that ^Rthe LORD hath sent me to do all these works; for *I have* not *done them* of^T mine own mind.   Ex. 3:12–15 • *according to my own ideas*

29 If these men die ^Tthe common death of all men, or if they be ^Rvisited after the visitation of all men; *then* the LORD hath not sent me.   *as every man dieth* • Job 35:15; Is. 10:3

30 But if the LORD make a new thing, and the earth open her mouth, and swallow them up, with all that *appertain* unto them, and they go down ^Rquick^T into the pit; then ye shall understand that these men have ^Tprovoked the LORD.   [Ps. 55:15] • *alive* • *despised*

31 And it came to pass, as he had made an end of speaking all these words, that the ground clave asunder that *was* under them:

32 And the earth opened her mouth, and swallowed them up, and their houses, and ^Rall the men that *appertained* unto Ko′-rah, and all *their* goods.   26:11; 1 Chr. 6:22, 37; Ps. 106:17

33 They, and all that *appertained* to them, went down alive into the pit, and the earth closed upon them: and they perished from among the congregation.

34 And all Israel that *were* round about them fled at the cry of them: for they said, Lest the earth swallow us up *also*.

35 And there came out a fire from the LORD, and ^Tconsumed the two hundred and fifty men that offered incense.   *destroyed*

36 And the LORD spake unto Moses, saying,

37 Speak unto E-le-a′-zar the son of Aaron the priest, that he take up the censers out of the burning, and scatter thou the fire yonder; for they are hallowed.

38 The censers of these ^Rsinners against their own souls, let them make them broad plates *for* a covering of the altar: for they offered them before the LORD, therefore they are hallowed: and they shall be a sign unto the children of Israel.   Hab. 2:10

39 And E-le-a′-zar the priest took the brasen censers, wherewith they that were burnt had offered; and they were made broad plates *for* a covering of the altar:

40 *To be* a ^Tmemorial unto the children of Israel, ^Rthat no stranger, which *is* not of the seed of Aaron, come near to offer incense before the LORD; that he be not as Ko′-rah, and as his company: as the LORD said to him by the hand of Moses.   *reminder* • 3:10

Israel Rebels Against Moses and Aaron

41 But on the morrow all the congregation of the children of Israel ^Rmurmured against Moses and against Aaron, saying, Ye have killed the people of the LORD.   *v.* 3

God Judges Israel

42 And it came to pass, when the congregation was gathered against Moses and against Aaron, that they looked toward the tabernacle of the congregation: and, behold, Rthe cloud covered it, and Rthe glory of the LORD appeared.   Ex. 40:34 • v. 19

43 And Moses and Aaron came before the tabernacle of the congregation.

44 And the LORD spake unto Moses, saying,

45 Get you up from among this congregation, that I may consume them as in a moment. And they fell upon their faces.

46 And Moses said unto Aaron, Take a censer, and put fire therein from off the altar, and put on incense, and go quickly unto the congregation, and make an atonement for them: for there is wrath gone out from the LORD; the plague is begun.

47 And Aaron took as Moses commanded, and ran into the midst of the congregation; and, behold, the plague was begun among the people: and Rhe put on incense, and made an atonement for the people.   25:7, 8, 13

48 And he stood between the dead and the living; and the plague was Tstayed.   ceased

49 Now they that died in the plague were fourteen thousand and seven hundred, beside them that died about the matter of Ko'-rah.

50 And Aaron returned unto Moses unto the door of the tabernacle of the congregation: and the plague was stayed.

CHAPTER 17

Confirmation of the Divine Call

AND the LORD spake unto Moses, saying, 2 Speak unto the children of Israel, and take of every one of them a rod according to the house of *their* fathers, of all their princes according to the house of their fathers twelve rods: write thou every man's name upon his rod.

3 And thou shalt write Aaron's name upon the rod of Levi: for one rod *shall be* for the head of the house of their fathers.

4 And thou shalt lay them up in the tabernacle of the congregation before the testimony, Rwhere I will meet with you.   Ex. 25:22

5 And it shall come to pass, *that* the man's rod, whom I shall choose, shall blossom: and I will make to cease from me the murmurings of the children of Israel, whereby they murmur against you.

6 RAnd Moses spake unto the children of Israel, and every one of their princes gave him a rod Tapiece, for each prince one, according to their fathers' houses, *even* twelve rods: and the rod of Aaron *was* among their rods.   Josh. 9:15 • each

7 And Moses laid up the rods before the LORD in Rthe tabernacle of witness.   Ex. 38:21

8 And it came to pass, that on the morrow Moses went into the tabernacle of witness; and, behold, the rod of Aaron for the house of Levi was budded, and brought forth buds, and bloomed blossoms, and yielded almonds.

9 And Moses brought out all the rods from before the LORD unto all the children of Israel: and they looked, and took every man his rod.

10 And the LORD said unto Moses, Bring Aaron's rod again before the testimony, to be kept for a token against the rebels; Rand thou shalt quite take away their murmurings from me, that they die not.   v. 5

11 And Moses did *so:* as the LORD commanded him, so did he.

12 And the children of Israel spake unto Moses, saying, RBehold, we die, we perish, we all perish.   [Is. 6:5]

13 Whosoever cometh any thing near unto the tabernacle of the LORD shall die: shall we be Tconsumed with dying?   destroyed

CHAPTER 18

Remuneration of the Priesthood

AND the LORD said unto Aaron, Thou and thy sons and thy father's house with thee shall bear the iniquity of the sanctuary: and thou and thy sons with thee shall bear the iniquity of your priesthood.

2 And thy brethren also of the tribe of Levi, the tribe of thy father, bring thou with thee, that they may be joined unto thee, and minister unto thee: but Rthou and thy sons with thee *shall minister* before the tabernacle of Twitness.   3:10 • testimony

3 And they shall Tkeep thy charge, and the charge of all the tabernacle: only they shall not come nigh the vessels of the sanctuary and the altar, that neither they, nor ye also, die.   be responsible according to your word

4 And they shall be joined unto thee, and keep the charge of the tabernacle of the congregation, for all the service of the tabernacle: Rand a stranger shall not come Tnigh unto you.   3:10 • near

5 And ye shall keep Rthe charge of the sanctuary, and the charge of the altar: that there Tbe no wrath any more upon the children of Israel.   8:26 • be no further judgment

6 And I, behold, I have Rtaken your brethren the Levites from among the children of Israel: to you *they are* given *as* a gift for the LORD, to do the service of the tabernacle of the congregation.   3:12, 45

7 Therefore thou and thy sons with thee shall keep your priest's office for every thing

of the altar, and Rwithin the vail; and ye shall serve: I have given your priest's office *unto you as* a service of gift: and the stranger that cometh nigh shall be put to death.   Heb. 9:3, 6

8 And the Lord spake unto Aaron, Behold, RI also have given thee the Tcharge of mine heave offerings of all the hallowed things of the children of Israel; unto thee have I given them by reason of the anointing, and to thy sons, by an ordinance for ever.   5:9 • *ownership*

9 This shall be thine of the most holy things, *reserved* from the fire: every oblation of their's, every Tmeat offering of their's, and every sin offering of their's, and every trespass offering of their's, which they shall render unto me, *shall be* most holy for thee and for thy sons.   *meal*

10 RIn the most holy *place* shalt thou eat it; every male shall eat it: it shall be TholyR unto thee.   Lev. 6:16, 26 • *only for thy use* • 5:8-10

11 And this *is* thine; the heave offering of their gift, with all the wave offerings of the children of Israel: I have given them unto thee, and to thy sons and to thy daughters with thee, by a statute for ever: every one that is clean in thy house shall eat of it.

12 All the Tbest of the oil, and all the best of the wine, and of the wheat, the firstfruits of them which they shall offer unto the Lord, them have I given thee.   *fat*

13 *And* whatsoever is first ripe in the land, Rwhich they shall bring unto the Lord, shall be thine; every one that is clean in thine house shall eat *of* it.   Ex. 22:29; 23:19; 34:26

14 REvery thing Tdevoted in Israel shall be thine.   Lev. 27:1-33 • *given in worship*

15 Every thing that openeth Rthe matrix in all flesh, which they bring unto the Lord, *whether it be* of men or beasts, shall be thine: nevertheless the firstborn of man shalt thou surely redeem, and the firstling of unclean beasts shalt thou redeem.   Ex. 13:2

16 And those that are to be redeemed from a month old shalt thou redeem, Raccording to thine estimation, for the money of five shek'-els, after the shek'-el of the sanctuary, which *is* twenty ge'-rahs.   Lev. 27:6

17 RBut the firstling of a cow, or the first-ling of a sheep, or the firstling of a goat, thou shalt not redeem; they *are* holy: thou shalt sprinkle their blood upon the altar, and shalt burn their fat *for* an offering made by fire, for a sweet savour unto the Lord.   Deut. 15:19

18 And the flesh of them shall be thine, as the Rwave breast and as the right shoulder are thine.   Ex. 29:26, 28; Lev. 7:31-36

19 RAll the heave offerings of the holy things, which the children of Israel offer unto the Lord, have I given thee, and thy sons and thy daughters with thee, by a statute for ever: it *is* Ta covenant of salt for ever be-fore the Lord unto thee and to thy seed with thee.   v. 11 • *an unbreakable promise*

20 And the Lord spake unto Aaron, Thou shalt have no inheritance in their land, nei-ther shalt thou have any part among them: RI *am* thy part and thine inheritance among the children of Israel.   Ezek. 44:28

21 And, behold, I have given the children of Levi all Rthe tenth in Israel for Tan inheri-tance, for their service which they serve, *even* Rthe service of the tabernacle of the congregation.   Lev. 27:30-33 • *their share* • 3:7, 8

22 Neither must the children of Israel henceforth come nigh the tabernacle of the congregation, lest they bear sin, and die.

23 But the Levites shall Tdo the service of the tabernacle of the congregation, and they shall Rbear their iniquity: *it shall be* a statute for ever throughout your generations, that among the children of Israel Rthey have no inheritance.   *perform* • v. 1 • v. 20

24 But the tithes of the children of Israel, which they offer *as* an heave offering unto the Lord, I have given to the Levites to inherit: therefore I have said unto them, Among the children of Israel they shall have Tno inheritance.   *no share in the land*

25 And the Lord spake unto Moses, say-ing,

26 RThus speak unto the Levites, and say unto them, When ye take of the children of Israel the tithes which I have given you from them for your inheritance, then ye shall offer up an heave offering of it for the Lord, *even* a tenth *part* of the tithe.   Neh. 10:38

27 And *this* your heave offering shall be reckoned unto you, Ras though *it were* the Tcorn of the threshingfloor, and as the fulness of the winepress.   [2 Cor. 8:12] • *any small grain*

28 Thus ye also shall offer an heave offer-ing unto the Lord of all your tithes, which ye receive of the children of Israel; and ye shall give thereof the Lord's heave offering to Aaron the priest.

29 Out of all your gifts ye shall offer every heave offering of the Lord, Rof all the Tbest thereof, *even* the hallowed part thereof out of it.   v. 12 • *fat*

30 Therefore thou shalt say unto them, When ye have heaved the best thereof from it, then it shall be counted unto the Levites as the increase of the threshingfloor, and as the increase of the winepress.

31 And ye shall eat it in every place, ye and your households: for it *is* Ryour Treward for your service in the tabernacle of the congre-gation.   [1 Cor. 9:13; 1 Tim. 5:18] • *wages*

32 And ye shall bear no sin by reason of it, when ye have heaved from it the best of it: neither shall ye pollute the holy things of the children of Israel, lest ye die.

CHAPTER 19

Purification of the Red Heifer

AND the LORD spake unto Moses and unto Aaron, saying,

2 This *is* the ordinance of the law which the LORD hath commanded, saying, Speak unto the children of Israel, that they bring thee a red heifer without spot, wherein *is* no blemish, *and* upon which never came yoke:

3 And ye shall give her unto E-le-a'-zar the priest, that he may bring her ^Rforth without the camp, and *one* shall slay her before his face: 3:4

4 And E-le-a'-zar the priest shall take of her blood with his finger, and ^Rsprinkle of her blood directly before the tabernacle of the congregation seven times: Heb. 9:13

5 And *one* shall burn the heifer in his sight; ^Rher skin, and her flesh, and her blood, with her dung, shall he burn: Ex. 29:14

6 And the priest shall take cedar wood, and hyssop, and scarlet, and cast *it* into the midst of the burning of the heifer.

7 Then the priest shall wash his clothes, and he shall bathe his flesh in water, and afterward he shall come into the camp, and the priest shall be unclean until the even.

8 And he that burneth her shall wash his clothes in water, and bathe his flesh in water, and shall be unclean until the even.

9 And a man *that is* clean shall gather up the ashes of the heifer, and lay *them* up without the camp in a clean place, and it shall be kept for the congregation of the children of Israel for a water of separation: it *is* a ^Tpurification for sin.   *sin offering*

10 And he that gathereth the ashes of the heifer ^Rshall wash his clothes, and be unclean until the even: and it shall be unto the children of Israel, and unto the stranger that sojourneth among them, for a statute for ever.   *v. 7*

11 ^RHe that toucheth the dead body of any man shall be unclean seven days.   *v. 16*

12 ^RHe shall ^Rpurify himself with it on the third day, and on the seventh day he shall be clean: but if he purify not himself the third day, then the seventh day he shall not be clean.   31:19 • *v. 19*

13 Whosoever toucheth the dead body of any man that is dead, and purifieth not himself, defileth the tabernacle of the LORD; and that soul shall be cut off from Israel: because the water of separation was not sprinkled upon him, he shall be unclean; his uncleanness *is* yet upon him.

14 This *is* the law, when a man dieth in a tent: all that come into the tent, and all that *is* in the tent, shall be unclean seven days.

15 And every ^Ropen vessel, which hath no covering bound upon it, *is* unclean.   31:20

16 ^RAnd ^Rwhosoever toucheth one that is slain with a sword in the open fields, or a dead body, or a bone of a man, or a grave, shall be unclean seven days.   31:19 • *v. 11*

17 And ^Rfor an unclean *person* they shall take of the ^Rashes of the burnt heifer of purification for sin, and running water shall be put thereto in a vessel: *v. 2 • v. 9*

18 And a clean person shall take ^Rhyssop,^T and dip *it* in the water, and sprinkle *it* upon the tent, and upon all the vessels, and upon the persons that were there, and upon him that touched a bone, or one slain, or one dead, or a grave: Ps. 51:7 • *an aromatic plant*

19 And the clean *person* shall sprinkle upon the unclean on the third day, and on the seventh day: ^Rand on the seventh day he shall purify himself, and wash his clothes, and bathe himself in water, and shall be clean at ^Teven.   Lev. 14:9 • *evening*

20 But the man that shall be unclean, and shall not purify himself, that soul shall be cut off from among the congregation, because he hath defiled the sanctuary of the LORD: the water of separation hath not been sprinkled upon him; he *is* unclean.

21 And it shall be a perpetual statute unto them, that he ^Rthat sprinkleth the water of separation shall wash his clothes; and he that toucheth the water of separation shall be unclean until even.   *v. 7*

22 And whatsoever the unclean *person* toucheth shall be unclean; and the soul that toucheth *it* shall be unclean until even.

CHAPTER 20

Miriam Dies

THEN ^Rcame the children of Israel, *even* the whole congregation, into the desert of Zin in the first month: and the people abode in Ka'-desh; and ^RMiriam died there, and was buried there.   33:36 • 26:59

The Sin of Israel

2 And there was no water for the congregation: and they gathered themselves together against Moses and against Aaron.

3 And the people chode with Moses, and spake, saying, Would God that we had died when our brethren died before the LORD!

4 And why have ye brought up the congregation of the LORD into this wilderness, that we and our cattle should die there?

5 And wherefore have ye made us to come up out of Egypt, to bring us in unto this evil place? ^Rit *is* no place of seed, or of figs, or of vines, or of ^Rpomegranates; neither *is* there any water to drink.   16:14 • 1 Sam. 14:2

6 And Moses and Aaron went from the presence of the assembly unto the door of the

tabernacle of the congregation, and they fell upon their faces: and ᴿthe glory of the LORD appeared unto them.   14:10

The Command of God

7 And the LORD spake unto Moses, saying,

8 ᴿTake the rod, and gather thou the assembly together, thou, and Aaron thy brother, and speak ye unto the rock before their eyes; and it shall give forth his water, and thou shalt bring forth to them water out of the rock: so thou shalt give the congregation and their beasts drink.   Ex. 17:5

The Sin of Moses

9 And Moses took the rod ᴿfrom before the LORD, as he commanded him.   17:10

10 And Moses and Aaron gathered the congregation together before the rock, and he said unto them, Hear now, ye rebels; must we fetch you water out of this rock?

11 And Moses lifted up his hand, and with his rod he smote the rock twice: and ᴿthe water came out abundantly, and the congregation drank, and their beasts also.   Ex. 17:6

12 And the LORD spake unto Moses and Aaron, Because ye believed me not, to sanctify me in the eyes of the children of Israel, therefore ye shall not bring this congregation into the land which I have given them.

13 This is the water of Mer'-i-bah; because the children of Israel strove with the LORD, and he was sanctified in them.

Edom Refuses Passage

14 And Moses sent messengers from Ka'-desh unto the ᴿking of E'-dom, Thus saith thy brother Israel, Thou knowest all the ᵀtravel that hath befallen us: Gen. 36:31 · trouble

15 ᴿHow our fathers went down into Egypt, and we have dwelt in Egypt a long time; ᴿand the Egyptians ᵀvexed us, and our fathers: Gen. 46:6 · Acts 7:19 · abused

16 And when we cried unto the LORD, he heard our voice, and ᴿsent an angel, and hath brought us forth out of Egypt: and, behold, we are in Ka'-desh, a city in the uttermost of thy border: Ex. 3:2; 14:19

17 ᴿLet us pass, I pray thee, through thy country: we will not pass through the fields, or through the vineyards, neither will we drink of the water of the wells: we will go by the king's high way, we will not turn to the right hand nor to the left, until we have passed thy borders.   21:22

18 And E'-dom said unto him, Thou shalt not pass by me, lest I come out against thee with the sword.

19 And the children of Israel said unto him, We will go by the high way: and if I and my cattle drink of thy water, then I will pay for it: I will only, without doing any thing else, go through on my feet.

20 And he said, Thou shalt not go through. And E'-dom came out against him with much people, and with a strong hand.

21 Thus E'-dom refused to give Israel passage through his border: wherefore Israel ᴿturned away from him.   Deut. 2:8

Aaron Dies

22 And the children of Israel, even the whole congregation, journeyed from ᴿKa'-desh, and came unto mount Hor.   33:37

23 And the LORD spake unto Moses and Aaron in ᴿmount Hor, by the coast of the land of E'-dom, saying,   33:37

24 Aaron shall ᵀbe gathered unto his people: for he shall not enter into the land which I have given unto the children of Israel, because ye rebelled against my word at the water of Mer'-i-bah.   die and be buried

25 Take Aaron and E-le-a'-zar his son, and bring them up unto mount Hor:

26 And strip Aaron of his garments, and put them upon E-le-a'-zar his son: and Aaron shall be ᴿgathered unto his people, and shall die there.   v. 24

27 And Moses did as the LORD commanded: and they went up into mount Hor in the sight of all the congregation.

28 ᴿAnd Moses stripped Aaron of his garments, and put them upon E-le-a'-zar his son; and ᴿAaron died there in the top of the mount: and Moses and E-le-a'-zar came down from the mount.   Ex. 29:29, 30 · 33:38

29 And when all the congregation saw that Aaron was dead, they mourned for Aaron thirty days, even all the house of Israel.

CHAPTER 21

Israel's Victory over the Canaanites

AND when ᴿking A'-rad the Ca'-naan-ite, which dwelt in the south, heard tell that Israel came by the way of the spies; then he fought against Israel, and took some of them prisoners.   33:40; Judg. 1:16

2 And Israel ᵀvowed a vow unto the LORD, and said, If thou wilt indeed deliver this people into my hand, then I will utterly destroy their cities.   made a pledge

3 And the LORD hearkened to the voice of Israel, and delivered up the Ca'-naan-ites; and they utterly destroyed them and their cities: and he called the name of the place ᵀHor'-mah.ᴿ   utter destruction · 14:45

Israel Complains—Deut. 2:1

4 And they journeyed from mount Hor by the way of the Red sea, to compass the land of E'-dom: and the soul of the people was much discouraged because of the way.

5 And the people spake against God, and against Moses, Wherefore have ye brought us

up out of Egypt to die in the wilderness? for *there is* no bread, neither *is there any* water; and our soul loatheth this light bread.

God Judges with Serpents

6 And the LORD sent Rfiery serpents among the people, and they bit the people; and much people of Israel died.   Deut. 8:15

The Brass Serpent

7 RTherefore the people came to Moses, and said, We have sinned, for we have Tspoken against the LORD, and against thee; Rpray unto the LORD, that he take away the serpents from us. And Moses prayed for the people.   Ps. 78:34 • *objected to* • 1 Kin. 13:6; Acts 8:24

8 RAnd the LORD said unto Moses, Make thee a Rfiery serpent, and set it upon a pole: and it shall come to pass, that every one that is bitten, when he looketh upon it, shall live.   John 3:14, 15 • Is. 14:29; 30:6

9 And Moses made a serpent of brass, and put it upon a pole, and it came to pass, that if a serpent had bitten any man, when he beheld the serpent of brass, he lived.

Journey to Moab

10 And the children of Israel set forward, and Rpitched T in O'-both.   33:43 • *made camp*

11 And they journeyed from RO'-both, and pitched at TI'-je-ab'-a-rim, in the wilderness which *is* before Moab, toward the sunrising.   33:43, 44 • *heaps of Abarim*

12 RFrom thence they removed, and pitched in the valley of Za'-red.   Deut. 2:13

13 From thence they removed, and Tpitched on the other side of Arnon, which *is* in the wilderness that cometh out of the coasts of the Am'-or-ites: for RArnon *is* the border of Moab, between Moab and the Am'-or-ites.   *encamped* • 22:36; Judg. 11:18

14 Wherefore it is said in the book of the wars of the LORD, What he did in the Red sea, Rand in the brooks of Arnon,   Deut. 2:9

15 And at the stream of the brooks that goeth down to the dwelling of Ar, and lieth upon the border of Moab.

16 And from thence *they went* Rto Be'-er: that *is* the well whereof the LORD spake unto Moses, Gather the people together, and I will give them water.   Judg. 9:21

17 RThen Israel sang this song, Spring up, O well; sing ye unto it: Ps. 105:2; 106:12

18 The princes digged the well, the nobles of the people digged it, by *the direction of* the lawgiver, with their staves. And from the wilderness *they went* to Mat-ta'-nah:

19 And from Mat-ta'-nah to Na-ha'-li-el: and from Na-ha'-li-el to Ba'-moth:

20 And from Ba'-moth in the valley, that *is* in the country of Moab, to the top of Pis'-gah, which looketh toward Jesh'-i-mon.

Israel's Victory over the Amorites
Deut. 2:26–36

21 And RIsrael sent messengers unto Si'-hon king of the Am'-or-ites, saying, Judg. 11:19

22 RLet me pass through thy land: we will not turn into the fields, or into the vineyards; we will not drink *of* the waters of the well: *but* we will go along by the king's *high* way, until we be past thy borders.   20:16, 17

23 And Si'-hon would not suffer Israel to pass through his border: but Si'-hon gathered all his people together, and went out against Israel into the wilderness: and he came to Ja'-haz, and fought against Israel.

24 And RIsrael smote him with the edge of the sword, and Tpossessed his land from Arnon unto Jab'-bok, even unto the children of Ammon: for the border of the children of Ammon *was* strong.   Amos 2:9 • *seized*

25 And Israel took all these cities: and Israel Rdwelt in all the cities of the Am'-or-ites, in Hesh'-bon, and in all the villages thereof.   Amos 2:10

26 For Hesh'-bon *was* the city of Si'-hon the king of the Am'-or-ites, who had fought against the former king of Moab, and taken all his land out of his hand, even unto Arnon.

27 Wherefore Tthey that speak in proverbs say, Come into Hesh'-bon, let the city of Si'-hon be built and prepared: *the ballad singers*

28 For there is a fire gone out of Hesh'-bon, a flame from the city of Si'-hon: it hath consumed Ar of Moab, *and* the lords of the high places of Arnon.

29 Woe to thee, Moab! thou art undone, O people of Che'-mosh: he hath given his sons that escaped, and his daughters, into captivity unto Si'-hon king of the Am'-or-ites.

30 We have shot at them; Hesh'-bon is perished even unto Di'-bon, and we have laid them waste even unto No'-phah, which *reacheth* unto RMed'-e-ba.   Is. 15:2

31 Thus Israel dwelt in the land of the Am'-or-ites.

32 And Moses sent to spy out Ja-a'-zer, and they took the villages thereof, and drove out the Am'-or-ites that *were* there.

Israel's Victory over Bashan—Deut. 3:1–4

33 And they turned and went up by the way of Ba'-shan: and Og the king of Ba'-shan went out against them, he, and all his people, to the battle Rat Ed'-re-i.   Josh. 13:12

34 And the LORD said unto Moses, Fear him not: for I Thave delivered him into thy hand, and all his people, and his land; and thou shalt do to him as thou didst unto Si'-hon king of the Am'-or-ites, which dwelt at Hesh'-bon.   *will give you victory over him*

35 So they Tsmote him, and his sons, and all his people, until there was none left him alive: and they possessed his land.   *defeated*

CHAPTER 22

Balaam Is Sought by Balak

A ND the children of Israel set forward, and Tpitched in the plains of Moab on this side Jordan by Jericho.   set up their camp

2 And Ba'-lak the son of Zip'-por saw all that Israel had done to the Am'-or-ites.

3 And Moab was sore afraid of the people, because they were many: and Moab was distressed because of the children of Israel.

4 And Moab said unto the elders of Mid'-i-an, Now shall this company lick up all that are round about us, as the ox licketh up the grass of the field. And Ba'-lak the son of Zip'-por was king of the Mo'-ab-ites at that time.

5 RHe sent messengers therefore unto Ba'-laam the son of Be'-or to Pe'-thor, which is by the river of the land of the children of his people, to call him, saying, Behold, there is a people come out from Egypt: behold, they cover the face of the earth, and they abide Tover against me: Deut. 23:4 • opposite me

6 Come now therefore, I pray thee, curseT me this people; for they are too mighty for me: peradventure I shall prevail, that we may smite them, and that I may drive them out of the land: for I Twot that he whom thou blessest is blessed, and he whom thou cursest is cursed.   brought misfortune upon • know

7 And the elders of Moab and the elders of Mid'-i-an departed with the Trewards of divination in their hand; and they came unto Ba'-laam, and spake unto him the words of Ba'-lak.   payment for his fortune telling

8 And he said unto them, RLodge here this night, and I will bring you word again, as the LORD shall speak unto me: and the princes of Moab abode with Ba'-laam.   v. 19

9 RAnd God came unto Ba'-laam, and said, What men are these with thee?   v. 20

10 And Ba'-laam said unto God, Ba'-lak the son of Zip'-por, king of Moab, hath sent unto me, saying,

11 Behold, there is a people come out of Egypt, which covereth the face of the earth: come now, curse me them; Tperadventure I shall be able to overcome them, and drive them out.   perhaps

12 And God said unto Ba'-laam, Thou shalt not go with them; thou shalt not curse the people: for they are blessed.

13 And Ba'-laam rose up in the morning, and said unto the princes of Ba'-lak, Get you into your land: for the LORD refuseth to give me Tleave to go with you.   permission

14 And the princes of Moab rose up, and they went unto Ba'-lak, and said, Ba'-laam refuseth to come with us.

15 And Ba'-lak sent yet again princes, more, and more honourable than they.

16 And they came to Ba'-laam, and said to him, Thus saith Ba'-lak the son of Zip'-por,

Let nothing, I pray thee, hinder thee from coming unto me:

17 For I will promote thee unto very great honour, and I will do whatsoever thou sayest unto me: Rcome therefore, I pray thee, curse me this people.   v. 6

18 And Ba'-laam answered and said unto the servants of Ba'-lak, RIf Ba'-lak would give me his house full of silver and gold, RI cannot go beyond the word of the LORD my God, to do less or more.   24:13 • 1 Kin. 22:14

19 Now therefore, I pray you, Rtarry ye also here this night, that I may know what the LORD will say unto me more.   v. 8

20 RAnd God came unto Ba'-laam at night, and said unto him, If the men come to call thee, rise up, and go with them; but Ryet the word which I shall say unto thee, that shalt thou do.   v. 9 • v. 35; 23:12, 26

21 RAnd Ba'-laam rose up in the morning, and saddled his ass, and went with the princes of Moab.   2 Pet. 2:15

22 And God's anger was kindled because he went: and the angel of the LORD stood in the way Tfor an adversary against him. Now he was riding upon his ass, and his two servants were with him.   opposing him

23 And the ass saw the angel of the LORD standing in the way, and his sword drawn in his hand: and the ass turned aside out of the way, and went into the field: and Ba'-laam smote the ass, to turn her into the way.

24 But the angel of the LORD stood in a path of the vineyards, a wall being on this side, and a wall on that side.

25 And when the ass saw the angel of the LORD, she Tthrust herself unto the wall, and Tcrushed Ba'-laam's foot against the wall: and he smote her again.   pushed • pressed

26 And the angel of the LORD went further, and stood in a narrow place, where was no way to turn either to the right hand or to the left.

27 And when the ass saw the angel of the LORD, she fell down under Ba'-laam: and Ba'-laam's anger was kindled, and he smote the ass with a Tstaff.   his stick

28 And the LORD Ropened the mouth of the ass, and she said unto Ba'-laam, What have I done unto thee, that thou hast smitten me these three times?   2 Pet. 2:16

29 And Ba'-laam said unto the ass, Because thou hast Tmocked me: I would there were a sword in mine hand, Rfor now would I kill thee.   made a fool of • [Prov. 12:10]

30 And the ass said unto Ba'-laam, Am not I thine ass, upon which thou hast ridden ever since I was thine unto this day? was I ever wont to do so unto thee? And he said, Nay.

31 Then the LORD opened the eyes of Ba'-laam, and he saw the angel of the LORD standing in the way, and his sword drawn in

his hand: and he bowed down his head, and [T]fell flat on his face.   *in humble worship*

32 And the [T]angel of the LORD said unto him, Wherefore hast thou smitten thine ass these three times? behold, I went out to [T]withstand thee, because *thy* way is [T]perverse before me: *messenger • oppose • wrong*

33 And the ass saw me, and turned from me these three times: unless she had turned from me, surely now also I had slain thee, and saved her alive.

34 And Ba'-laam said unto the angel of the LORD, [R]I have sinned; for I knew not that thou stoodest in the way against me: now therefore, if it displease thee, I will get me back again.   Josh. 7:20; 2 Sam. 12:13

35 And the angel of the LORD said unto Ba'-laam, Go with the men: [R]but only the word that I shall speak unto thee, that thou shalt speak. So Ba'-laam went with the princes of Ba'-lak.   *v.* 20

36 And when Ba'-lak heard that Ba'-laam was come, he went out to meet him unto a city of Moab, [R]which *is* in the border of Arnon, which *is* in the utmost coast.   21:13

37 And Ba'-lak said unto Ba'-laam, Did I not earnestly send unto thee to call thee? wherefore camest thou not unto me? am I not able indeed to promote thee to honour?

38 And Ba'-laam said unto Ba'-lak, Lo, I am come unto thee: have I now any power at all to say any thing? the word that God putteth in my mouth, that shall I speak.

39 And Ba'-laam went with Ba'-lak, and they came unto Kir'-jath–hu'-zoth.

40 And Ba'-lak offered oxen and sheep, and sent to Ba'-laam, and to the princes that *were* with him.

The First Oracle of Balaam

41 And it came to pass on the morrow, that Ba'-lak took Ba'-laam, and brought him up into the high places of Ba'-al, that thence he might see the utmost *part* of the people.

CHAPTER 23

AND Ba'-laam said unto Ba'-lak, Build me here seven altars, and prepare me here seven oxen and seven rams.

2 And Ba'-lak did as Ba'-laam had spoken; and Ba'-lak and Ba'-laam [R]offered on *every* altar a bullock and a ram.   *vv.* 14, 30

3 And Ba'-laam said unto Ba'-lak, Stand by thy burnt offering, and I will go: [T]peradventure the LORD will come to meet me: and whatsoever he sheweth me I will tell thee. And he went to an high place.   *perhaps*

4 [R]And God met Ba'-laam: and he said unto him, I have prepared seven altars, and I have offered upon *every* altar a bullock and a ram.   *v.* 16

5 And the LORD [R]put a word in Ba'-laam's mouth, and said, Return unto Ba'-lak, and thus thou shalt speak.   Deut. 18:18; Jer. 1:9

6 And he returned unto him and, lo, he stood by his burnt sacrifice, he, and all the princes of Moab.

7 And he [T]took up his parable, and said, Ba'-lak the king of Moab hath brought me from A'-ram, out of the mountains of the east, *saying,* Come, curse me Jacob, and come, defy Israel.   *began his speech*

8 [R]How shall I curse, *whom* God hath not cursed? or how shall I defy, *whom* the LORD hath not defied?   [Is. 47:12]

9 For from the top of the rocks I see him, and from the hills I behold him: lo, [R]the people shall dwell alone, and shall not be reckoned among the nations.   Deut. 33:28

10 Who can count the dust of Jacob, and the number of the fourth *part* of Israel? Let me die the death of the righteous, [R]and let my last end be like his!   [Ps. 37:37]

11 And Ba'-lak said unto Ba'-laam, What hast thou done unto me? [R]I took thee to curse mine enemies, and, behold, thou hast blessed *them* altogether.   22:11

12 And he answered and said, [R]Must I not take heed to speak that which the LORD hath put in my mouth?   22:38

The Second Oracle of Balaam

13 And Ba'-lak said unto him, Come, I pray thee, with me unto another place, from whence thou mayest see them: thou shalt see but the utmost part of them, and shalt not see them all: and curse me them from thence.

14 And he brought him into the field of Zo'-phim, to the top of [T]Pis'-gah, [R]and built seven altars, and offered a bullock and a ram on *every* altar.   *the hill • vv.* 1, 2

15 And he said unto Ba'-lak, Stand here by thy burnt offering, while I meet *the* LORD yonder.

16 And the LORD met Ba'-laam, and [R]put a word in his mouth, and said, Go again unto Ba'-lak, and say thus.   *v.* 5; 22:35

17 And when he came to him, behold, he stood by his burnt offering, and the princes of Moab with him. And Ba'-lak said unto him, What hath the LORD spoken?

18 And he took up his parable, and said, Rise up, Ba'-lak, and hear; hearken unto me, thou son of Zip'-por:

19 God *is* not a man, that he should lie; neither the son of man, that he should repent: hath he said, and shall he not do *it*? or hath he spoken, and shall he not make it good?

20 Behold, I have received *commandment* to bless: and [R]he hath blessed; [R]and I cannot reverse it.   22:12; Gen. 12:2; 22:17 • [Is. 43:13]

21 [R]He hath not beheld iniquity in Jacob, neither hath he seen [T]perverseness in Israel:

the LORD his God *is* with him, and the shout of a king *is* among them.   [Ps. 32:2] • *wrong*

22 God brought them out of Egypt; he hath as it were the strength of an unicorn.

23 Surely *there is* no enchantment against Jacob, neither *is there* any divination against Israel: according to this time it shall be said of Jacob and of Israel, What hath God wrought!

24 Behold, the people shall rise up as a great lion, and lift up himself as a young lion: he shall not lie down until he eat *of* the prey, and drink the blood of the slain.

25 And Ba'-lak said unto Ba'-laam, Neither curse them at all, nor bless them at all.

26 But Ba'-laam answered and said unto Ba'-lak, Told not I thee, saying, RAll that the LORD speaketh, that I must do?   22:38

The Third Oracle of Balaam

27 And Ba'-lak said unto Ba'-laam, Come, I pray thee, I will bring thee unto another place; peradventure it will please God that thou mayest curse me them from thence.

28 And Ba'-lak brought Ba'-laam unto the top of Pe'-or, that looketh Rtoward Jesh'-i-mon.   21:20

29 And Ba'-laam said unto Ba'-lak, Build me here seven altars, and prepare me here seven bullocks and seven rams.

30 And Ba'-lak did as Ba'-laam had said, and offered a bullock and a ram on *every* altar.

CHAPTER 24

AND when Ba'-laam saw that it pleased the LORD to bless Israel, he went not, as at other times, to seek for enchantments, but he set his face toward the wilderness.

2 And Ba'-laam lifted up his eyes, and he saw Israel Rabiding *in his tents* according to their tribes; and Rthe spirit of God came upon him.   2:2 • 1 Sam. 10:10; 2 Chr. 15:1

3 And he took up his parable, and said, RBa'-laam the son of Be'-or hath said, and the man whose eyes are open hath said: vv. 15, 16

4 He hath said, which heard the words of God, which saw the vision of the Almighty, Rfalling *into a trance*, but having his eyes open: 1 Sam. 19:24; Ezek. 1:28

5 How goodly are thy tents, O Jacob, *and* thy tabernacles, O Israel!

6 As the valleys are they spread forth, as gardens by the river's side, as the trees of lign aloes which the LORD hath planted, *and* as cedar trees beside the waters.

7 He shall pour the water out of his buckets, and his seed *shall be* in many waters, and his king shall be higher than A'-gag, Rand his kingdom shall be exalted.   [Ps. 145:11]

8 God brought him forth out of Egypt; he hath as it were the strength of an unicorn: he shall eat up the nations his enemies, and shall break their bones, and pierce *them* through with his arrows.

9 RHe couched, he lay down as a lion, and as a great lion: who shall stir him up? Blessed *is* he that blesseth thee, and cursed *is* he that curseth thee.   Gen. 49:9

10 And Ba'-lak's anger was kindled against Ba'-laam, and he smote his hands together: and Ba'-lak said unto Ba'-laam, I called thee to curse mine enemies, and, behold, thou hast altogether blessed *them* these three times.

11 Therefore now flee thou to thy place: RI thought to promote thee unto great honour; but, lo, the LORD hath kept thee back from honour.   22:17, 37

12 And Ba'-laam said unto Ba'-lak, RSpake I not also to thy messengers which thou sentest unto me, saying,   22:18

13 If Ba'-lak would give me his house full of silver and gold, I cannot go beyond the commandment of the LORD, to do *either* good or bad of mine own mind; *but* what the LORD saith, that will I speak?

The Fourth Oracle of Balaam

14 And now, behold, I go unto my people: come *therefore, and* RI will advertise thee what this people shall do to thy people Rin the latter days.   [Mic. 6:5] • Gen. 49:1

15 And he took up his parable, and said, Ba'-laam the son of Be'-or hath said, and the man whose eyes are open hath said:

16 He hath said, which heard the words of God, and knew the knowledge of the most High, *which* saw the vision of the Almighty, falling *into a trance*, but having his eyes open:

17 I shall see him, but not now: I shall behold him, but not nigh: there shall come a RStar out of Jacob, and a Sceptre shall rise out of Israel, and shall smite the corners of Moab, and destroy all the children of Sheth.   Matt. 1:2 ☆

18 And E'-dom shall be a possession, Se'-ir also shall be a possession for his enemies; and Israel shall do Tvaliantly.   *triumphantly*

19 ROut of Jacob shall come he that Tshall have dominion, and shall destroy him that remaineth of the city.   Gen. 49:10 • *shall rule*

20 And when he looked on Am'-a-lek, he took up his parable, and said, Am'-a-lek *was* the first of the nations; but his latter end *shall be* that he perish for ever.

21 And he looked on the RKen'-ites, and took up his parable, and said, Strong is thy dwellingplace, and thou puttest thy nest in a rock.   Gen. 15:19

22 Nevertheless the Ken'-ite shall be wasted, until Assh'-ur shall carry thee away captive.

23 And he took up his parable, and said, Alas, who shall live when God doeth this!

24 And ships *shall come* from the coast of Chit'-tim, and shall afflict Assh'-ur, and shall afflict ᴿE'-ber, and he also shall perish for ever.   Gen. 10:21

25 And Ba'-laam rose up, and went and ᴿreturned to his place: and Ba'-lak also went his way.   31:8

CHAPTER 25

Israel Commits Harlotry

AND Israel abode in Shit'-tim, and the people began to ᵀcommit whoredom with the daughters of Moab.   *have illicit relations*

2 And ᴿthey called the people unto the sacrifices of their gods: and the people did eat, and bowed down to their gods.   Hos. 9:10

Phinehas Stays the Plague

3 And Israel joined himself unto Ba'-al-pe'-or: and ᴿthe anger of the LORD was kindled against Israel.   Ps. 106:29

4 And the LORD said unto Moses, ᴿTake all the heads of the people, and hang them up before the LORD against the sun, ᴿthat the fierce anger of the LORD may be turned away from Israel.   Deut. 4:3 • v. 11; Deut. 13:17

5 And Moses said unto ᴿthe judges of Israel, ᴿSlay ye every one his men that are joined unto Ba'-al-pe'-or.   Ex. 18:21 • Deut. 13:6, 9

6 And, behold, one of the children of Israel came and brought unto his brethren a ᴿMid'-i-an-i-tish woman in the sight of Moses, and in the sight of all the congregation of the children of Israel, ᴿwho *were* weeping *before* the door of the tabernacle of the congregation.   22:4 • Joel 2:17

7 And ᴿwhen Phin'-e-has, the son of E-le-a'-zar, the son of Aaron the priest, saw *it*, he rose up from among the congregation, and took a javelin in his hand;   Ps. 106:30

8 And he went after the man of Israel into the tent, and thrust both of them through, the man of Israel, and the woman through her belly. So the plague was stayed from the children of Israel.

9 And ᴿthose that died in the plague were twenty and four thousand.   Deut. 4:3; 1 Cor. 10:8

10 And the LORD spake unto Moses, saying,

11 Phin'-e-has, the son of E-le-a'-zar, the son of Aaron the priest, hath turned my wrath away from the children of Israel, while he was zealous for my sake among them, that I ᵀconsumed not the children of Israel in ᴿmy jealousy.   *destroyed* • [Ex. 20:5]

12 Wherefore say, ᴿBehold, I give unto him my covenant of peace: [Mal. 2:4, 5]

13 And he shall have it, and his seed after him, *even* the covenant of an everlasting priesthood; because he was zealous for his God, and ᵀmade an atonement for the children of Israel.   *effected reconciliation*

14 Now the name of the Israelite that was slain, *even* that was slain with the Mid'-i-an-i-tish woman, *was* Zim'-ri, the son of Sa'-lu, a prince of a chief house among the Simeon-ites.

15 And the name of the Mid'-i-an-i-tish woman that was slain *was* Coz'-bi, the daughter of ᴿZur; he *was* head over a people, *and* of a chief house in Mid'-i-an.   31:8

Israel to Destroy Moab

16 And the LORD spake unto Moses, saying,

17 ᴿVexᵀ the Mid'i-an-ites, and smite them: 31:2 • *fight against*

18 For they vex you with their ᵀwiles, wherewith they have ᵀbeguiled you in the matter of Pe'-or, and in the matter of Coz'-bi, the daughter of a prince of Mid'-i-an, their sister, which was slain in the day of the plague for Pe'-or's sake.   *tricky ways • deceived*

CHAPTER 26

The Second Census

AND it came to pass after the plague, that the LORD spake unto Moses and unto E-le-a'-zar the son of Aaron the priest, saying,

2 Take the sum of all the congregation of the children of Israel, from twenty years old and upward, throughout their fathers' house, all that are able to go to war in Israel.

3 And Moses and E-le-a'-zar the priest spake with them ᴿin the plains of Moab by Jordan *near* Jericho, saying,   v. 63; 22:1

4 *Take the sum of the people,* from twenty years old and upward; as the LORD commanded Moses and the children of Israel, which went forth out of the land of Egypt.

5 ᴿReuben, the eldest son of Israel: the children of Reuben; Ha'-noch, *of whom cometh* the family of the Ha'-noch-ites: of Pal'-lu, the family of the Pal'-lu-ites: Ex. 6:14

6 Of Hez'-ron, the family of the Hez'-ron-ites: of Car'-mi, the family of the Car'-mites.

7 These *are* the families of the Reu'-ben-ites: and they that were numbered of them were ᴿforty and three thousand and seven hundred and thirty.   1:21

8 And the sons of Pal'-lu; E-li'-ab.

9 And the sons of E-li'-ab; Nem'-u-el, and Da'-than, and A-bi'-ram. This *is that* Da'-than and A-bi'-ram, *which were* famous in the congregation, who strove against Moses and against Aaron in the company of Ko'-rah, when they strove against the LORD:

10 ᴿAnd the earth opened her mouth, and swallowed them up together with Ko'-rah,

when that company died, what time the fire devoured two hundred and fifty men: ^Rand they became a sign.   16:32, 35 • 16:38

11 Notwithstanding ^Rthe children of Ko'-rah died not.   16:27; Ex. 6:24; 1 Chr. 6:22

12 The sons of Simeon after their families: of Nem'-u-el, the family of the Nem'-u-el-ites: of Ja'-min, the family of the Ja'-min-ites: of Ja'-chin, the family of the Ja'-chin-ites:

13 Of Ze'-rah, the family of the Zar'-hites: of Sha'-ul, the family of the Sha'-u-lites.

14 These are the families of the Simeon-ites, ^Rtwenty and two thousand and two hundred.   1:23

15 The children of Gad after their families: of ^TZe'-phon, the family of the Ze'-phon-ites: of Hag'-gi, the family of the Hag'-gites: of Shu'-ni, the family of the Shu'-nites: Ziphion

16 Of ^TOz'-ni, the family of the Oz'-nites: of E'-ri, the family of the E'-rites: Ezbon

17 Of A'-rod, the family of the Ar'-o-dites: of A-re'-li, the family of the A-re'-lites.

18 These are the families of the children of Gad according to those that were numbered of them, forty thousand and five hundred.

19 The sons of Judah were Er and O'-nan: and Er and O'-nan died in the land of Canaan.

20 And ^Rthe sons of Judah after their families were; of She'-lah, the family of the She'-la-nites: of Pha'-rez, the family of the Phar'-zites: of Ze'-rah, the family of the Zar'-hites.   1 Chr. 2:3

21 And the sons of Pha'-rez were; of Hez'-ron, the family of the Hez'-ron-ites: of Ha'-mul, the family of the Ha'-mul-ites.

22 These are the families of Judah accord-ing to those that were numbered of them, ^Rthreescore and sixteen thousand and five hundred.   1:27

23 Of the sons of Is'-sa-char after their families: of To'-la, the family of the To'-la-ites: of Pu'-a, the family of the Pu'-nites:

24 ^ROf ^TJash'-ub, the family of the Jash'-ub-ites: of Shim'-ron, the family of the Shim'-ron-ites.   Gen. 46:13 • Job

25 These are the families of ^RIs'-sa-char according to those that were numbered of them, threescore and four thousand and three hundred.   1:29

26 Of the sons of Zeb'-u-lun after their families: of Se'-red, the family of the Sar'-dites: of E'-lon, the family of the E'-lon-ites: of Jah'-le-el, the family of the Jah'-le-el-ites.

27 These are the families of the Zeb'-u-lun-ites according to those that were numbered of them, ^Rthreescore thousand and five hun-dred.   1:31

28 The sons of Joseph after their families were Ma-nas'-seh and E'-phra-im.

29 Of the sons of Ma-nas'-seh: of ^RMa'-chir, the family of the Ma'-chir-ites: and Ma'-chir begat Gil'-e-ad: of Gil'-e-ad come the family of the Gil'-e-ad-ites.   Josh. 17:1

30 These are the sons of Gil'-e-ad: of Je-e'-zer, the family of the Je-e'-zer-ites: of He'-lek, the family of the He'-lek-ites:

31 And of As'-ri-el, the family of the As'-ri-el-ites: and of She'-chem, the family of the She'-chem-ites:

32 And of She-mi'-da, the family of the She-mi'-da-ites: and of He'-pher, the family of the He'-pher-ites.

33 And ^RZe-lo'-phe-had the son of He'-pher had no sons, but daughters: and the names of the daughters of ^RZe-lo'-phe-had were Mah'-lah, and Noah, Hog'-lah, Mil'-cah, and Tir'-zah.   27:1; 36:11 • 1 Chr. 7:15

34 These are the families of Ma-nas'-seh, and those that were numbered of them, fifty and two thousand and seven hundred.

35 These are the sons of E'-phra-im after their families: of Shu'-the-lah, the family of the Shu'-thal-hites: of ^RBe'-cher,^T the family of the Bach'-rites: of Ta'-han, the family of the Ta'-han-ites.   1 Chr. 7:20 • Bered

36 And these are the sons of Shu'-the-lah: of E'-ran, the family of the E'-ran-ites.

37 These are the families of the sons of E'-phra-im according to those that were num-bered of them, ^Rthirty and two thousand and five hundred. These are the sons of Joseph after their families.   1:33

38 The sons of Benjamin after their fam-ilies: of Be'-la, the family of the Be'-la-ites: of Ash'-bel, the family of the Ash'-bel-ites: of A-hi'-ram, the family of the A-hi'-ram-ites:

39 Of ^RShu'-pham, the family of the Shu'-pham-ites: of Hu'-pham, the family of the Hu'-pham-ites.   Gen. 46:21

40 And the sons of Be'-la were ^RArd^T and Na'-a-man: of Ard, the family of the Ard'-ites: and of Na'-a-man, the family of the Na'-a-mites.   1 Chr. 8:3 • Adda

41 These are the sons of Benjamin after their families: ^Rand they that were numbered of them were forty and five thousand and six hundred.   1:37

42 ^RThese are the sons of Dan after their families: of ^TShu'-ham, the family of the Shu'-ham-ites. These are the families of Dan after their families.   Gen. 46:23 • Hushim

43 All the families of the Shu'-ham-ites, according to those that were numbered of them, ^Rwere threescore and four thousand and four hundred.   1:39

44 Of the children of Asher after their families: of Jim'-na, the family of the Jim'-nites: of Jes'-u-i, the family of the Jes'-u-ites: of Be-ri'-ah, the family of the Be-ri'-ites.

45 Of the sons of Be-ri'-ah: of He'-ber, the family of the He'-ber-ites: of Mal'-chi-el, the family of the Mal'-chi-el-ites.

46 And the name of the daughter of Asher was ^TSarah.^R   Serah • 1 Chr. 7:30

47 These are the families of the sons of

Asher according to those that were numbered of them; who [R]were fifty and three thousand and four hundred.   1:41

48 [R]Of the sons of Naph'-ta-li after their families: of Jah'-ze-el, the family of the Jah'-ze-el-ites: of Gu'-ni, the family of the Gu'-nites: Gen. 46:24; 1 Chr. 7:13

49 Of Je'-zer, the family of the Je'-zer-ites: of Shil'-lem, the family of the Shil'-lem-ites.

50 These are the families of Naph'-ta-li according to their families: and they that were numbered of them were [R]forty and five thousand and four hundred.   1:43

51 [R]These were the numbered of the children of Israel, six hundred thousand and a thousand seven hundred and thirty.   Ex. 12:37

Method for Dividing the Land

52 And the LORD spake unto Moses, saying,

53 [R]Unto these the land shall be divided for an inheritance according to the number of names.   Josh. 11:23

54 [R]To many thou shalt give the [T]more inheritance, and to few thou shalt give the [T]less inheritance: to every one shall his inheritance be given according to those that were numbered of him.   33:54 • larger • smaller

55 Notwithstanding the land shall be divided by lot: according to the names of the tribes of their fathers they shall inherit.

56 According to the lot shall the possession thereof be divided between many and few.

The Levites Have No Inheritance

57 And these are they that were numbered of the Levites after their families: of Ger'-shon, the family of the Ger'-shon-ites: of Ko'-hath, the family of the Ko'-hath-ites: of Me-ra'-ri, the family of the Me-ra'-rites.

58 These are the families of the Levites: the family of the Lib'-nites, the family of the He'-bron-ites, the family of the Mah'-lites, the family of the Mu'-shites, the family of the Ko'-rath-ites. And Ko'-hath begat Am'-ram.

59 And the name of Am'-ram's wife was [R]Joch'-e-bed, the daughter of Levi, whom her mother bare to Levi in Egypt: and she bare unto Am'-ram Aaron and Moses, and Miriam their sister.   Ex. 2:1, 2; 6:20

60 [R]And unto Aaron was born Na'-dab, and A-bi'-hu, E-le-a'-zar, and Ith'-a-mar.   3:2

61 And Na'-dab and A-bi'-hu died, when they offered strange fire before the LORD.

62 And those that were numbered of them were twenty and three thousand, all males from a month old and upward: for they were not numbered among the children of Israel, because there was no inheritance given them among the children of Israel.

The Old Generation Has No Inheritance

63 These are they that were numbered by Moses and E-le-a'-zar the priest, who numbered the children of Israel [R]in the plains of Moab by Jordan near Jericho.   v. 3

64 But among these there was not a man of them whom Moses and Aaron the priest numbered, when they numbered the children of Israel in the wilderness of Si'-nai.

65 For the LORD had said of them, They [R]shall surely die in the wilderness. And there was not left a man of them, [R]save Caleb the son of Je-phun'-neh, and Joshua the son of Nun.   [1 Cor. 10:5, 6] • 14:30

CHAPTER 27

The Special Laws of Inheritance

THEN came the daughters of Ze-lo'-phe-had, the son of He'-pher, the son of Gil'-e-ad, the son of Ma'-chir, the son of Ma-nas'-seh, of the families of Ma-nas'-seh the son of Joseph: and these are the names of his daughters; Mah'-lah, Noah, and Hog'-lah, and Mil'-cah, and Tir'-zah.

2 And they stood before Moses, and before E-le-a'-zar the priest, and before the princes and all the congregation, by the door of the tabernacle of the congregation, saying,

3 Our father [R]died in the wilderness, and he was not in the company of them that gathered themselves together against the LORD in the company of Ko'-rah; but died in his own sin, and had no sons.   14:35

4 Why should the name of our father be done away from among his family, because he hath no son? Give unto us therefore a possession among the brethren of our father.

5 And Moses [R]brought their cause before the LORD.   9:8; Ex. 18:15, 19

6 And the LORD spake unto Moses, saying,

7 The daughters of Ze-lo'-phe-had speak right: thou shalt surely give them a possession of an inheritance among their father's brethren; and thou shalt cause the inheritance of their father to pass unto them.

8 And thou shalt speak unto the children of Israel, saying, [R]If a man die, and have no son, then ye shall cause his inheritance to pass unto his daughter.   36:9

9 And if he have no daughter, then ye shall give his inheritance unto his brethren.

10 And if he have no brethren, then ye shall give his inheritance unto his father's brethren.

11 And if his father have no brethren, then ye shall give his inheritance unto his kinsman that is next to him of his family, and he shall possess it: and it shall be unto the children of Israel a statute of judgment, as the LORD commanded Moses.

Moses Is Set Aside

12 And the LORD said unto Moses, ᴿGet thee up into this mount Ab'-a-rim, and see the land which I have given unto the children of Israel.   33:47; Deut. 3:27; 32:49

13 And when thou hast seen it, ᵀthou also shalt be gathered unto thy people, as Aaron thy brother was gathered.   *thou shalt die*

14 For ye rebelled against my commandment in the desert of Zin, in the strife of the congregation, to sanctify me at the water before their eyes: that is the water of Mer'-i-bah in Ka'-desh in the wilderness of Zin.

Joshua Is Appointed

15 And Moses spake unto the LORD, saying,

16 Let the LORD, the God of the spirits of all flesh, set a man over the congregation,

17 Which may go out before them, and which may go in before them, and which may lead them out, and which may bring them in; that the congregation of the LORD be not as sheep which have no shepherd.

18 And the LORD said unto Moses, Take thee Joshua the son of Nun, a man in whom is the spirit, and lay thine hand upon him;

19 And set him before E-le-a'-zar the priest, and before all the congregation; and give him ᵀa charge in their sight.   *instruction*

20 And thou shalt put some of thine honour upon him, that all the congregation of the children of Israel may be obedient.

21 ᴿAnd he shall stand before E-le-a'-zar the priest, who shall ask counsel for him after the judgment of U'-rim before the LORD: at his word shall they go out, and at his word they shall come in, both he, and all the children of Israel with him, even all the congregation.   Judg. 20:18, 23, 26

22 And Moses did as the LORD commanded him: and he took Joshua, and set him before E-le-a'-zar the priest, and before all the congregation:

23 And he laid his hands upon him, ᴿand gave him a charge, as the LORD commanded by the hand of Moses.   Deut. 3:28

CHAPTER 28

Daily Offering

A ND the LORD spake unto Moses, saying,
2 Command the children of Israel, and say unto them, My offering, and ᴿmy bread for my sacrifices made by fire, for a sweet savour unto me, shall ye observe to offer unto me in their due season.   [Mal. 1:7, 12]

3 And thou shalt say unto them, ᴿThis is the offering made by fire which ye shall offer unto the LORD; two lambs of the first year

without ᵀspot day by day, for a continual burnt offering.   Ex. 29:38 • *blemish*

4 The one lamb shalt thou offer in the morning, and the other lamb shalt thou offer at even;

5 And ᵀa tenth part of an e'-phah of flour for a ᴿmeat offering, mingled with the ᵀfourth part of an hin of beaten oil.   2.087 qt. • meal • 1 qt.

6 It is ᴿa continual burnt offering, which was ᵀordained in mount Si'-nai for a sweet savour, a sacrifice made by fire unto the LORD.   Ex. 29:42; Amos 5:25 • *ordered*

7 And the drink offering thereof shall be the fourth part of an ᵀhin for the one lamb: ᴿin the holy place shalt thou cause the strong wine to be poured unto the LORD for a drink offering.   1 qt. • Ex. 29:42

8 And the other lamb shalt thou offer at even: as the ᵀmeat offering of the morning, and as the drink offering thereof, thou shalt offer it, a sacrifice made by fire, of a ᵀsweet savour unto the LORD.   *meal • pleasing*

Weekly Offering

9 And on the sabbath day two lambs of the first year without spot, and two tenth deals of flour for a meat offering, mingled with oil, and the drink offering thereof:

10 This is ᴿthe burnt offering of every sabbath, beside the ᴿcontinual burnt offering, and his drink offering.   Ezek. 46:4 • v. 3

Monthly Offering

11 And in the beginnings of your months ye shall offer a burnt offering unto the LORD; two young bullocks, and one ram, seven lambs of the first year without spot;

12 And three tenth deals of flour for a meat offering, mingled with oil, for one bullock; and two tenth deals of flour for a meat offering, mingled with oil, for one ram;

13 And a several tenth deal of flour mingled with oil for a meat offering unto one lamb; for a burnt offering of a sweet ᵀsavour, a sacrifice made by fire unto the LORD.   *smell*

14 And their drink offerings shall be ᵀhalf an hin of wine unto a bullock, and the ᵀthird part of an hin unto a ram, and a ᵀfourth part of an hin unto a lamb: this is the burnt offering of every month throughout the months of the year.   2 qt. • 42.7 oz. • 1 qt.

15 And ᴿone kid of the goats for a sin offering unto the LORD shall be offered, beside the continual burnt offering, and his drink offering.   v. 22; 15:24

Passover

16 ᴿAnd in the fourteenth day of the first month is the passover of the LORD. Ezek. 45:21

Unleavened Bread

17 ᴿAnd in the fifteenth day of this month *is* the feast: seven days shall unleavened bread be eaten.   *Lev. 23:6*

18 In the first day *shall be* an holy convocation; ye shall do no manner of ᵀservile work *therein:*   *laborious*

19 But ye shall offer a sacrifice made by fire *for* a burnt offering unto the Lᴏʀᴅ; two young bullocks, and one ram, and seven lambs of the first year: ᴿthey shall be unto you without blemish: *v. 31; 29:8; Deut. 15:21*

20 And their meat offering *shall be of* flour mingled with oil: ᵀthree tenth deals shall ye offer for a bullock, and ᵀtwo tenth deals for a ram;   *6.261 qt. • 4.174 qt.*

21 A several tenth deal shalt thou offer for every lamb, throughout the seven lambs:

22 And one goat *for* a sin offering, to make ᵀan atonement for you.   *a reconciliation*

23 Ye shall offer these beside the burnt offering in the morning, which *is* for a continual burnt offering.

24 After this manner ye shall offer daily, throughout the seven days, the meat of the sacrifice made by fire, of a sweet savour unto the Lᴏʀᴅ: it shall be offered beside the continual burnt offering, and his drink offering.

25 And on the seventh day ye shall have an holy convocation; ye shall do no servile work.

Firstfruits

26 Also in the day of the firstfruits, when ye bring a new meat offering unto the Lᴏʀᴅ, after your weeks *be out,* ye shall have an holy convocation; ye shall do no servile work:

27 But ye shall offer the burnt offering for a sweet savour unto the Lᴏʀᴅ; ᴿtwo young bullocks, one ram, seven lambs of the first year;   *Lev. 23:18, 19*

28 And their meat offering of flour mingled with oil, three tenth deals unto one bullock, two tenth deals unto one ram,

29 A several ᵀtenth deal unto one lamb, throughout the seven lambs;   *2.087 qt.*

30 *And* one kid of the goats, to make ᵀan atonement for you.   *a reconciliation*

31 Ye shall offer *them* beside the continual burnt offering, and his meat offering, (they shall be unto you ᵀwithout blemish) and their drink offerings.   *nothing wrong*

CHAPTER 29

Trumpets

AND in the seventh month, on the first *day* of the month, ye shall have an holy convocation; ye shall do no servile work: it is a day of blowing the trumpets unto you.

2 And ye shall offer a burnt offering for a sweet savour unto the Lᴏʀᴅ; one young bullock, one ram, *and* seven lambs of the first year without blemish:

3 And their meat offering *shall be of* flour mingled with oil, three tenth deals for a bullock, *and* two tenth deals for a ram,

4 And one ᵀtenth deal for one lamb, throughout the seven lambs: *2.087 qt.*

5 And one kid of the goats *for* a sin offering, to make an atonement for you:

6 Beside the burnt offering of the ᵀmonth, and his meat offering, and ᴿthe daily burnt offering, and his meat offering, and their drink offerings, according unto their manner, for a sweet savour, a sacrifice made by fire unto the Lᴏʀᴅ.   *new moon • 15:11*

Atonement

7 And ᴿye shall have on the tenth *day* of this seventh month an holy convocation; and ye shall ᴿafflict your souls: ye shall not do any work *therein:*   *Lev. 16:29; 23:27 • Ps. 35:13*

8 But ye shall offer a burnt offering unto the Lᴏʀᴅ *for* a sweet savour; one young bullock, one ram, *and* seven lambs of the first year; ᴿthey shall be unto you without blemish: *28:19*

9 And their meat offering *shall be of* flour mingled with oil, three tenth deals to a bullock, *and* two tenth deals to one ram,

10 A several ᵀtenth deal for one lamb, throughout the seven lambs: *2.087 qt.*

11 One kid of the goats *for* a sin offering; beside the sin offering of atonement, and the continual burnt offering, and the meat offering of it, and their drink offerings.

Tabernacles

12 And on the fifteenth day of the seventh month ye shall have an holy convocation; ye shall do no servile work, and ye shall keep a feast unto the Lᴏʀᴅ seven days:

13 And ᴿye shall offer a burnt offering, a sacrifice made by fire, of a sweet savour unto the Lᴏʀᴅ; thirteen young bullocks, two rams, *and* fourteen lambs of the first year; they shall be without blemish: *Ezra 3:4*

14 And their meat offering *shall be of* flour mingled with oil, three tenth deals unto every bullock of the thirteen bullocks, two tenth deals to each ram of the two rams,

15 And a several ᵀtenth deal to each lamb of the fourteen lambs: *2.087 qt.*

16 And one kid of the goats *for* a sin offering; ᴿbeside the continual burnt offering, his meat offering, and his drink offering.   *28:3*

17 And on the second day *ye shall offer* twelve young bullocks, two rams, fourteen lambs of the first year without spot:

18 And their meat offering and their drink offerings for the bullocks, for the rams, and for the lambs, *shall be* according to their number, ᴿafter the manner: *15:12; 28:7, 14*

19 And one kid of the goats *for* a sin offering; ^Rbeside the continual burnt offering, and the meat offering thereof, and their drink offerings.   28:3

20 And on the third day eleven ^Tbullocks, two rams, fourteen lambs of the first year without blemish;   *bulls*

21 And their meat offering and their drink offerings for the bullocks, for the rams, and for the lambs, *shall be* according to their number, ^Rafter the manner: *v.* 18

22 And one goat *for* a sin offering; beside the continual burnt offering, and his meat offering, and his drink offering.

23 And on the fourth day ten bullocks, two rams, *and* fourteen lambs of the first year without blemish:

24 Their meat offering and their drink offerings for the bullocks, for the rams, and for the lambs, *shall be* according to their number, after the ^Tmanner: *ordinance*

25 And one kid of the goats *for* a sin offering; beside the continual burnt offering, his meat offering, and his drink offering.

26 And on the fifth day nine bullocks, two rams, *and* fourteen lambs of the first year without spot:

27 And their meat offering and their drink offerings for the bullocks, for the rams, and for the lambs, *shall be* according to their number, after the ^Tmanner: *ordinance*

28 And one goat *for* a sin offering; beside the continual burnt offering, and his meat offering, and his drink offering.

29 And on the sixth day eight bullocks, two rams, *and* fourteen lambs of the first year without blemish:

30 And their meat offering and their drink offerings for the bullocks, for the rams, and for the lambs, *shall be* according to their number, after the manner:

31 And one goat *for* a sin offering; beside the continual burnt offering, his meat offering, and his drink offering.

32 And on the seventh day seven bullocks, two rams, *and* fourteen lambs of the first year without blemish:

33 And their meat offering and their drink offerings for the bullocks, for the rams, and for the lambs, *shall be* according to their number, after the manner:

34 And one goat *for* a sin offering; beside the continual burnt offering, his meat offering, and his drink offering.

35 On the eighth day ye shall have a ^Rsolemn^T assembly: ye shall do no servile work *therein:*   Lev. 23:36 • *religious meeting to worship*

36 But ye shall offer a burnt offering, a sacrifice made by fire, of a sweet savour unto the LORD: one bullock, one ram, seven lambs of the first year without blemish:

37 Their meat offering and their drink offerings for the bullock, for the ram, and for

the lambs, *shall be* according to their number, after the ^Tmanner: *ordinance*

38 And one goat *for* a sin offering; beside the continual burnt offering, and his meat offering, ^Rand his drink offering.   Gen. 35:14

39 These *things* ye shall ^Tdo unto the LORD in your ^Rset^T feasts, beside your vows, and your freewill offerings, for your burnt offerings, and for your meat offerings, and for your drink offerings, and for your peace offerings.   *offer* • Neh. 10:33; Is. 1:14 • *scheduled*

40 And Moses told the children of Israel according to all that the LORD commanded Moses.

CHAPTER 30

The Regulations of Vows

A ND Moses spake unto ^Rthe heads of the tribes concerning the children of Israel, saying, This *is* the thing which the LORD hath commanded.   1:4, 16; 7:2

2 If a man ^Tvow a vow unto the LORD, or swear an oath to ^Tbind his soul with a bond; he shall not break his word, he shall do according to all that proceedeth out of his mouth.   *make a pledge* • *commit himself*

3 If a woman also vow a vow unto the LORD, and bind *herself* by a bond, *being* in her father's house in her youth;

4 And her father hear her vow, and her bond wherewith she hath bound her soul, and her father ^Tshall hold his peace at her: then all her vows shall stand, and every bond wherewith she hath bound her soul shall stand.   *shall not interfere*

5 But if her father disallow her in the day that he heareth; not any of her vows, or of her bonds wherewith she hath bound her soul, shall stand: and the LORD shall forgive her, because her father disallowed her.

6 And if she had at all an husband, when she vowed, or uttered ought out of her lips, wherewith she bound her soul;

7 And her husband heard *it,* and held his peace at her in the day that he heard *it:* then her vows shall stand, and her bonds wherewith she bound her soul shall stand.

8 But if her husband disallowed^T her on the day that he heard *it;* then he shall make her vow which she vowed, and that which she uttered with her lips, wherewith she bound her soul, of none effect: and the LORD shall forgive her.   *objected*

9 But every vow of a widow, and of her that is divorced, wherewith they have bound their souls, shall stand against her.

10 And if she vowed in her husband's house, or bound her soul by a bond with an oath;

11 And her husband heard *it,* and held his peace at her, *and* disallowed her not: then all

her vows shall stand, and every bond where-with she bound her soul shall stand.

12 But if her husband hath utterly made them void on the day he heard *them;* then whatsoever proceeded out of her lips concerning her vows, or concerning the bond of her soul, shall not stand: her husband hath made them void; ᴿand the LORD shall forgive her.   [Eph. 5:22; Col. 3:18; 1 Pet. 3:1]

13 Every vow, and every binding oath to afflict the soul, her husband may establish it, or her husband may make it void.

14 But if her husband altogether hold his peace at her from day to day; then he establisheth all her vows, or all her bonds, which *are* upon her: he confirmeth them, because he held his peace at her in the day that he heard *them.*

15 But if he shall any ways ᵀmake them void after that he hath heard *them;* then he shall bear her iniquity.   *make them null and*

16 These *are* the statutes, which the LORD commanded Moses, between a man and his wife, between the father and his daughter, *being yet* in her youth in her father's house.

CHAPTER 31
Destruction of the Midianites

AND the LORD spake unto Moses, saying, 2 ᵀAvenge the children of Israel ᵀof the Mid'-i-an-ites: afterward shalt thou be gathered unto thy people.   *retaliate • against*

3 And Moses spake unto the people, saying, Arm some of yourselves unto the war, and let them go against the Mid'-i-an-ites, and ᴿavenge the LORD of Mid'-i-an.   Lev. 26:25

4 Of every tribe a thousand, throughout all the tribes of Israel, shall ye send to the war.

5 So there were delivered out of the thousands of Israel, a thousand of *every* tribe, twelve thousand armed for war.

6 And Moses sent them to the war, a thousand of *every* tribe, them and Phin'-e-has the son of E-le-a'-zar the priest, to the war, with the holy instruments, and ᴿthe trumpets to blow in his hand.   10:9

7 And they warred against the Mid'-i-an-ites, as the LORD commanded Moses; and they slew all the ᴿmales.   Judg. 6:1, 2, 33

8 And they slew the kings of Mid'-i-an, beside the rest of them that were slain; *namely,* ᴿE'-vi, and Re'-kem, and Zur, and Hur, and Re'-ba, five kings of Mid'-i-an: ᴿBa'-laam also the son of Be'-or they slew with the sword.   Josh. 13:21, 22 • v. 16; 22:5

9 And the children of Israel took *all* the women of Mid'-i-an captives, and their little ones, and took the spoil of all their cattle, and all their flocks, and all their goods.

10 And they burnt all their cities wherein they dwelt, and all their goodly castles, with fire.

11 And ᴿthey took all the spoil, and all the prey, *both* of men and of beasts.   Deut. 20:14

12 And they brought the captives, and the prey, and the spoil, unto Moses, and ᴿE-le-a'-zar the priest, and unto the congregation of the children of Israel, unto the camp at the plains of Moab, which *are* by Jordan *near* Jericho.   Ex. 6:23

13 And Moses, and E-le-a'-zar the priest, and all the princes of the congregation, went forth to meet them without the camp.

14 And Moses was ᵀwroth with the officers of the host, *with* the captains over thousands, and captains over hundreds, which came from the ᵀbattle.   *angry • war*

15 And Moses said unto them, Have ye saved ᴿall the women alive?   Deut. 7:2; 20:16–18

16 Behold, these caused the children of Israel, through the counsel of Ba'-laam, to commit trespass against the LORD in the matter of Pe'-or, and there was a ᵀplague among the congregation of the LORD.   *sickness*

17 Now therefore ᴿkill every male among the little ones, and kill every woman that hath known man by lying with him.   Deut. 7:2

18 But all the women children, that ᴿhave not known a man by lying with him, keep alive for yourselves.   Deut. 21:10–14

Purification of Israel

19 And do ye abide without the camp seven days: whosoever hath killed any person, and whosoever hath touched any slain, purify *both* yourselves and your captives on the third day, and on the seventh day.

20 And purify all *your* raiment, and all that is made of skins, and all work of goats' *hair,* and all things made of wood.

21 And E-le-a'-zar the priest said unto the men of war which went to the battle, This *is* the ᵀordinance of the law which the LORD commanded Moses;   *rule*

22 Only the gold, and the silver, the brass, the iron, the tin, and the lead,

23 Every thing that may abide the fire, ye shall make *it* go through the fire, and it shall be clean: nevertheless it shall be ᵀpurified ᴿwith the water of separation: and all that abideth not the fire ye shall make go through the water.   *in a ceremony •* 19:9, 17

24 And ye shall wash your clothes on the seventh day, and ye shall be clean, and afterward ye shall come into the camp.

Distribution of the Spoils

25 And the LORD spake unto Moses, saying,

26 Take the sum of the ᵀprey that was taken, *both* of man and of beast, thou, and E-le-a'-zar the priest, and the chief fathers of the congregation: *captives*

27 And ᴿdivide the prey into two parts; between them that took the war upon them, who went out to battle, and between all the congregation: Josh. 22:8; 1 Sam. 30:24

28 ᴿAnd levy a tribute unto the LORD of the men of war which went out to battle: one soul of five hundred, *both* of the persons, and of the beeves, and of the asses, and of the sheep: 18:21-30

29 Take *it* of their half, and give *it* unto E-le-a′-zar the priest, ᵀ*for* an heave offering of the LORD.   *to be presented as a sacrifice*

30 And of the children of Israel's half, thou shalt take one portion of fifty, of the persons, of the beeves, of the asses, and of the flocks, of all manner of beasts, and give them unto the Levites, which keep the charge of the tabernacle of the LORD.

31 And Moses and E-le-a′-zar the priest did as the LORD commanded Moses.

32 And the booty, *being* the rest of the prey which the men of war had caught, was ᵀsix hundred thousand and seventy thousand and five thousand sheep,   *675,000*

33 And ᵀthreescore and twelve thousand ᵀbeeves,   *72,000 • cattle*

34 And ᵀthreescore and one thousand ᵀasses,   *61,000 • donkeys*

35 And thirty and two thousand persons in all, of women that had not known man by lying with him.

36 And the half, *which was* the portion of them that went out to war, was in number three hundred thousand and seven and thirty thousand and five hundred sheep:

37 And the LORD's tribute of the sheep was six hundred and threescore and fifteen.

38 And the ᵀbeeves *were* thirty and six thousand; of which the LORD's tribute *was* threescore and twelve.   *cattle*

39 And the asses *were* thirty thousand and five hundred; of which the LORD's ᵀtribute *was* threescore and one.   *levy*

40 And the persons *were* sixteen thousand; of which the LORD's tribute *was* thirty and two persons.

41 And Moses gave the tribute, *which was* the LORD's heave offering, unto E-le-a′-zar the priest, as the LORD commanded Moses.

42 And of the children of Israel's half, which Moses divided from the men that warred,

43 (Now the half *that pertained unto* the congregation was three hundred thousand and thirty thousand *and* seven thousand and five hundred sheep,

44 And thirty and six thousand beeves,

45 And thirty thousand asses and five hundred,

46 And sixteen thousand persons;)

47 Even of the children of Israel's half, Moses took one portion of fifty, *both* of man and of beast, and gave them unto the Levites,

which kept the charge of the tabernacle of the LORD; as the LORD commanded Moses.

48 And the officers which *were* over thousands of the host, the captains of thousands, and captains of hundreds, came near unto Moses:

49 And they said unto Moses, Thy servants have taken the sum of the men of war which *are* ᵀunder our charge, and there lacketh not one man of us.   *under our command*

50 We have therefore brought an oblation for the LORD, what every man hath gotten, of jewels of gold, chains, and bracelets, rings, earrings, and ᵀtablets, to make an atonement for our souls before the LORD.   *necklaces*

51 And Moses and E-le-a′-zar the priest took the gold of them, *even* all wrought jewels.

52 And all the gold of the ᵀoffering that they offered up to the LORD, of the captains of thousands, and of the captains of hundreds, was ᵀsixteen thousand seven hundred and fifty shek′-els.   *heave offering • $32,160,000*

53 (For ᴿthe men of war had taken spoil, every man for himself.)   *v. 32; Deut. 20:14*

54 And Moses and E-le-a′-zar the priest took the gold of the captains of thousands and of hundreds, and brought it into the tabernacle of the congregation, ᴿ*for*ᵀ a memorial for the children of Israel before the LORD.   *Ex. 30:16 • as a remembrance*

CHAPTER 32

Division of the Land
East of Jordan—Deut. 3:12-19

NOW the children of Reuben and the children of Gad had a very great multitude of cattle: and when they saw the land of Ja′-zer, and the land of Gil′-e-ad, that, behold, the place *was* a place for cattle;

2 The children of Gad and the children of Reuben came and spake unto Moses, and to E-le-a′-zar the priest, and unto the princes of the congregation, saying,

3 At′-a-roth, and Di′-bon, and Ja′-zer, and Nim′-rah, and Hesh′-bon, and E-le-a′-leh, and She′-bam, and Ne′-bo, and Be′-on,

4 *Even* the country which the LORD smote before the congregation of Israel, *is* a land for cattle, and thy servants have cattle:

5 Wherefore, said they, if we have found grace in thy sight, let this land be given unto thy servants for a possession, *and* bring us not over Jordan.

6 And Moses said unto the children of Gad and to the children of Reuben, Shall your brethren go to war, and shall ye sit here?

7 And wherefore discourage ye the heart of the children of Israel from going over into the land which the LORD hath given them?

8 Thus did your fathers, when I sent them from Ka'-desh-bar'-ne-a to see the land.

9 For ^Rwhen they went up unto the valley of Esh'-col, and saw the land, they discouraged the heart of the children of Israel, that they should not go into the land which the LORD had given them.   13:24, 31

10 And the LORD's anger was kindled the same time, and he sware, saying,

11 Surely none of the men that came up out of Egypt, from twenty years old and upward, shall see the land which I sware unto Abraham, unto Isaac, and unto Jacob; because they have not wholly followed me:

12 Save Caleb the son of Je-phun'-neh the Ken'-ez-ite, and Joshua the son of Nun: for they have wholly followed the LORD.

13 And the LORD's anger was ^Tkindled against Israel, and he made them wander in the wilderness forty years, until all the generation, that had done ^Tevil in the sight of the LORD, was consumed.   aroused · wrong

14 And, behold, ye are risen up in your fathers' stead, ^Tan increase of sinful men, to augment yet the ^Rfierce anger of the LORD toward Israel.   descendants · Deut. 1:34

15 For if ye turn away from after him, he will yet again leave them in the wilderness; and ye shall destroy all this people.

16 And they came near unto him, and said, We will build sheepfolds here for our cattle, and cities for our little ones:

17 But we ourselves will go ready armed before the children of Israel, until we have brought them unto their place: and our little ones shall dwell in the fenced cities because of the inhabitants of the land.

18 We will not return unto our houses, until the children of Israel have ^Tinherited every man his inheritance.   gained possession

19 For we will not inherit with them on yonder side Jordan, or ^Tforward; ^Rbecause our inheritance is fallen to us on this side Jordan eastward.   beyond · Josh. 12:1

20 And ^RMoses said unto them, If ye will do this thing, if ye will go armed before the LORD to war,   Deut. 3:18

21 And will go all of you armed over Jordan before the LORD, until he hath driven out his enemies from before him,

22 And the land be subdued before the LORD: then afterward ^Rye shall return, and be ^Tguiltless before the LORD, and before Israel; and this land shall be your possession before the LORD.   Josh. 22:4 · free of blame

23 But if ye will not do so, behold, ye have sinned against the LORD: and be sure ^Ryour sin will find you out.   Gen. 4:7; [Gal. 6:7]

24 Build you cities for your little ones, and folds for your sheep; and do that which hath proceeded out of your mouth.

25 And the children of Gad and the children of Reuben spake unto Moses, saying, Thy servants will do as my lord commandeth.

26 ^ROur little ones, our wives, our flocks, and all our cattle, shall be there in the cities of Gil'-e-ad: Josh. 1:14

27 ^RBut thy servants will pass over, every man armed for war, before the LORD to battle, as my lord saith.   Josh. 4:12

28 So ^Rconcerning them Moses commanded E-le-a'-zar the priest, and Joshua the son of Nun, and the chief fathers of the tribes of the children of Israel: Josh. 1:13

29 And Moses said unto them, If the children of Gad and the children of Reuben will pass with you over Jordan, every man armed to battle, before the LORD, and the land shall be subdued before you; then ye shall give them the land of Gil'-e-ad for a possession:

30 But if they will not pass over with you armed, they shall have possessions among you in the land of Canaan.

31 And the children of Gad and the children of Reuben answered, saying, As the LORD hath said unto thy servants, so will we do.

32 We will pass over armed before the LORD into the land of Canaan, that the possession of our inheritance on this side Jordan *may be* our's.

33 And Moses gave unto them, *even* to the children of Gad, and to the children of Reuben, and unto half the tribe of Ma-nas'-seh the son of Joseph, the kingdom of Si'-hon king of the Am'-or-ites, and the kingdom of Og king of Ba'-shan, the land, with the cities thereof in the coasts, *even* the cities of the country round about.

34 And the children of Gad built ^RDi'-bon, and At'-a-roth, and Ar'-o-er,   33:45, 46

35 And At'-roth, Sho'-phan, and ^RJa-a'-zer,^T and Jog'-be-hah,   vv. 1, 3 · Jazer

36 And Beth-nim'-rah, and Beth-ha'-ran, fenced cities: and folds for sheep.

37 And the children of Reuben built Hesh'-bon, and E-le-a'-leh, and Kir-ja-tha'-im,

38 And Ne'-bo, and Ba'-al-me'-on, (^Rtheir names being changed,) and Shib'-mah: and gave other names unto the cities which they builded.   v. 3

39 And the children of ^RMa'-chir the son of Ma-nas'-seh went to Gil'-e-ad, and took it, and ^Tdispossessed the Am'-or-ite which *was* in it.   Gen. 50:23 · drove out

40 And Moses ^Rgave Gil'-e-ad unto Ma'-chir the son of Ma-nas'-seh; and he dwelt therein.   Deut. 3:12, 13, 15; Josh. 13:31; 17:1

41 And Ja'-ir the son of Ma-nas'-seh went and took the small towns thereof, and called them ^RHa'-voth-ja'-ir.   Judg. 10:4

42 And No'-bah went and took Ke'-nath, and the villages thereof, and called it No'-bah, after his own name.

CHAPTER 33

From Egypt to Sinai

THESE *are* the journeys of the children of Israel, which went forth out of the land of Egypt with their armies ᴿunder the hand of Moses and Aaron.   Ps. 77:20; Mic. 6:4

2 And Moses wrote their goings out according to their journeys by the commandment of the LORD: and these *are* their journeys according to their goings out.

3 And they departed from Ram'-e-ses in the first month, on the fifteenth day of the first month; on the morrow after the passover the children of Israel went out with an high hand in the sight of all the Egyptians.

4 For the Egyptians buried all *their* firstborn, ᴿwhich the LORD had smitten among them: ᴿupon their gods also the LORD executed judgments.   Ex. 12:29 • [Ex. 12:12; 18:11]

5 And the children of Israel removed from Ram'-e-ses, and pitched in Suc'-coth.

6 And they departed from ᴿSuc'-coth, and ᵀpitched in E'-tham, which *is* in the edge of the wilderness.   Ex. 13:20 • *encamped*

7 And ᴿthey removed from E'-tham, and turned again unto Pi–ha–hi'-roth, which *is* before Ba'-al-ze'-phon: and they ᵀpitched before Mig'-dol.   Ex. 14:2, 9 • *made camp*

8 And they departed from before Pi–ha–hi'-roth, and ᴿpassed through the midst of the sea into the wilderness, and went ᵀthree days' journey in the wilderness of E'-tham, and pitched in Ma'-rah.   Ex. 14:22; 15:22, 23 • *60 mi.*

9 And they removed from Ma'-rah, and came unto E'-lim: and in E'-lim *were* twelve fountains of water, and threescore and ten palm trees; and they pitched there.

10 And they removed from E'-lim, and encamped by the Red sea.

11 And they removed from the Red sea, and encamped in the wilderness of Sin.

12 And they took their journey out of the wilderness of Sin, and encamped in Doph'-kah.

13 And they departed from Doph'-kah, and encamped in A'-lush.

14 And they removed from A'-lush, and encamped at ᴿReph'-i-dim, where was no water for the people to drink.   Ex. 17:1; 19:2

15 And they departed from Reph'-i-dim, and pitched in the wilderness of Si'-nai.

From Sinai to Kadesh

16 And they removed from the desert of Si'-nai, and pitched ᴿat ᵀKib'-roth-hat-ta'-a-vah.   11:34 • *the graves of lust*

17 And they departed from Kib'-roth-hat-ta'-a-vah, and encamped at Ha-ze'-roth.

The Wilderness Wanderings

18 And they departed from Ha-ze'-roth, and pitched in ᴿRith'-mah.   12:16

19 And they departed from Rith'-mah, and pitched at Rim'-mon-par'-ez.

20 And they departed from Rim'-mon-par'-ez, and pitched in Lib'-nah.

21 And they removed from Lib'-nah, and pitched at Ris'-sah.

22 And they journeyed from Ris'-sah, and ᵀpitched in Ke-hel'-a-thah.   *encamped*

23 And they went from Ke-hel'-a-thah, and pitched in mount Sha'-pher.

24 And they removed from mount Sha'-pher, and encamped in Har'-a-dah.

25 And they removed from Har'-a-dah, and pitched in Mak-he'-loth.

26 And they removed from Mak-he'-loth, and encamped at Ta'-hath.

27 And they departed from Ta'-hath, and pitched at Ta'-rah.

28 And they removed from Ta'-rah, and pitched in Mith'-cah.

29 And they went from Mith'-cah, and pitched in Hash-mo'-nah.

30 And they departed from Hash-mo'-nah, and encamped at Mo-se'-roth.

31 And they departed from ᴿMo-se'-roth, and pitched in Bene–ja'-a-kan.   Deut. 10:6

32 And they removed from Bene–ja'-a-kan, and encamped at Hor-ha-gid'-gad.

33 ᴿAnd they went from Hor-ha-gid'-gad, and pitched in Jot'-ba-thah.   Deut. 10:6, 7

34 And they removed from Jot'-ba-thah, and encamped at E-bro'-nah.

35 And they departed from E-bro'-nah, ᴿand encamped at E'-zi-on-ga'-ber.   Deut. 2:8

36 And they removed from E'-zi-on-ga'-ber, and pitched in the ᴿwilderness of Zin, which *is* Ka'-desh.   20:1; 27:14

From Kadesh to Moab

37 And they removed from ᴿKa'-desh, and pitched in mount Hor, in the edge of the land of E'-dom.   20:22, 23; 21:4

38 And ᴿAaron the priest went up into mount Hor at the commandment of the LORD, and died there, in the fortieth year after the children of Israel were come out of the land of Egypt, in the first *day* of the fifth month.   20:25, 28; Deut. 10:6; 32:50

39 And Aaron *was* an hundred and twenty and three years old when he died in mount Hor.

40 And ᴿking ᵀA'-rad the Ca'-naan-ite, which dwelt in the south in the land of Canaan, heard of the coming of the children of Israel.   21:1 • *the King of Arad*

41 And they departed from mount ᴿHor, and pitched in Zal-mo'-nah.   21:4

42 And they departed from Zal-mo'-nah, and pitched in Pu'-non.

43 And they departed from Pu'-non, and ᴿpitched in O'-both.   21:10

44 And ᴿthey departed from O'-both, and

pitched in ᵀI'-je–ab'-a-rim, in the border of Moab.   21:11 • *Heaps of Abarim*

45 And they departed from I'-im, and pitched ᴿin Di'-bon-gad.   32:34

46 And they removed from Di'-bon-gad, and encamped in Al'-mon–dib-la-tha'-im.

47 And they removed from Al'-mon–dib-la-tha'-im, ᴿand pitched in the mountains of Ab'-a-rim, before Ne'-bo.   21:20; Deut. 32:49

48 And they departed from the mountains of Ab'-a-rim, and ᴿpitched in the plains of Moab by Jordan *near* Jericho.   22:1

49 And they pitched by Jordan, from Beth-jes'-i-moth *even* unto ᴿA'-bel–shit'-tim in the plains of Moab.   25:1; Josh. 2:1

Instructions for Conquering Canaan

50 And the LORD spake unto Moses in the plains of Moab by Jordan, *near* Jericho, saying,

51 Speak unto the children of Israel, and say unto them, ᴿWhen ye are passed over Jordan into the land of Canaan;   Josh. 3:17

52 Then ye shall drive out all the inhabitants of the land from before you, and destroy all their ᵀpictures, and destroy all their molten images, and ᵀquite pluck down all their high places: *figured stones* • *demolish*

53 ᴿAnd ye shall dispossess *the inhabitants of* the land, and dwell therein: for I have given you the land to possess it.   Josh. 21:43

54 And ye shall divide the land by lot for an inheritance among your families: *and* to the more ye shall give the more inheritance, and to the fewer ye shall give the less inheritance: every man's *inheritance* shall be in the place where his lot falleth; according to the tribes of your fathers ye shall inherit.

55 ᴿBut if ye will not drive out the inhabitants of the land from before you; then it shall come to pass, that those which ye let remain of them *shall be* pricks in your eyes, and thorns in your sides, and shall vex you in the land wherein ye dwell.   Judg. 2:11–14

56 Moreover it shall come to pass, *that* I shall do unto you, as I thought to do unto them.

CHAPTER 34

The South

AND the LORD spake unto Moses, saying, 2 Command the children of Israel, and say unto them, When ye come into the land of Canaan; (this *is* the land that shall fall unto you for an inheritance, *even* the land of Canaan with the coasts thereof:)

3 Then your south quarter shall be from the wilderness of Zin along by the coast of E'-dom, and your south border shall be the outmost coast of the salt sea eastward:

4 And your border shall turn from the south ᴿto the ascent of A-krab'-bim, and pass on to Zin: and the going forth thereof shall be from the south ᴿto Ka'-desh–bar'-ne-a, and shall go on to Ha'-zar–ad'-dar, and pass on to Az'-mon: Josh. 15:3 • 13:26

5 And the border shall fetch a compass from Az'-mon unto the river of Egypt, and the goings out of it shall be at the sea.

The West

6 ᴿAnd *as for* the western border, ye shall even have the great sea for a border: this shall be your west border.   Ex. 23:31; Josh. 15:12

The North

7 And this shall be your ᴿnorth border: from the great sea ye shall point out for you ᴿmount Hor: Ezek. 47:15–17 • 33:37

8 From mount Hor ye shall point out *your* border ᴿunto the entrance of Ha'-math; and the goings forth of the border shall be to ᴿZe'-dad: 13:21 • Ezek. 47:15

9 And the border shall go on to Ziph'-ron, and the goings out of it shall be at Ha'-zar–e'-nan: this shall be your north border.

The East

10 And ye shall point out your east border from Ha'-zar–e'-nan to She'-pham:

11 And the coast shall go down from She'-pham to Rib'-lah, on the east side of A'-in; and the border shall descend, and shall reach unto the ᵀside of the sea ᴿof Chin'-ne-reth eastward: *shoulder* • Luke 5:1

12 And the border shall go down to Jordan, and the goings out of it shall be at ᴿthe ᵀsalt sea: this shall be your land with the coasts thereof round about.   v. 3 • *Dead*

13 And Moses commanded the children of Israel, saying, ᴿThis *is* the land which ye shall inherit by lot, which the LORD commanded to give unto the nine tribes, and to the half tribe: v. 2; Gen. 15:18; Josh. 14:1, 2

14 ᴿFor the tribe of the children of Reuben according to the house of their fathers, and the tribe of the children of Gad according to the house of their fathers, have received *their inheritance;* and half the tribe of Ma-nas'-seh have received their inheritance: 32:33; Josh. 14:2

15 The two tribes and the half tribe have received their inheritance on this side Jordan *near* Jericho eastward, toward the sunrising.

Officials for Dividing Canaan

16 And the LORD spake unto Moses, saying,

17 These *are* the names of the men which shall divide the land unto you: E-le-a'-zar the priest, and Joshua the son of Nun.

18 And ye shall take one prince of every tribe, to divide the land by inheritance.

19 And the names of the men *are* these: Of the tribe of Judah, Caleb the son of Je-phun'-neh.

20 And of the tribe of the children of Simeon, Shem'-u-el the son of Am-mi'-hud.

21 Of the tribe of Benjamin, E-li'-dad the son of Chis'-lon.

22 And the prince of the tribe of the children of Dan, Buk'-ki the son of Jog'-li.

23 The prince of the children of Joseph, for the tribe of the children of Ma-nas'-seh, Han'-ni-el the son of E'-phod.

24 And the prince of the tribe of the children of E'-phra-im, Kem'-u-el the son of Shiph'-tan.

25 And the prince of the tribe of the children of Zeb'-u-lun, E-liz'-a-phan the son of Par'-nach.

26 And the prince of the tribe of the children of Is'-sa-char, Pal'-ti-el the son of Az'-zan.

27 And the prince of the tribe of the children of Asher, A-hi'-hud the son of She-lo'-mi.

28 And the prince of the tribe of the children of Naph'-ta-li, Ped'-a-hel the son of Am-mi'-hud.

29 These *are they* whom the LORD commanded to divide the inheritance unto the children of Israel in the land of Canaan.

CHAPTER 35

Cities for the Levites

A ND[R] the LORD spake unto Moses in [R]the plains of Moab by Jordan *near* Jericho, saying,   Lev. 25:32–34 · 33:50

2 Command the children of Israel, that they give unto the Levites of the inheritance of their possession cities to dwell in; and ye shall give *also* unto the Levites suburbs for the cities round about them.

3 And the cities shall they have to dwell in; and the suburbs of them shall be for their cattle, and for their goods, and for all their beasts.

4 And the [T]suburbs of the cities, which ye shall give unto the Levites, *shall reach* from the wall of the city and outward a thousand cubits round about.   *pasture lands*

5 And ye shall measure from without the city on the east side two thousand cubits, and on the south side two thousand cubits, and on the west side two thousand cubits, and on the north side two thousand cubits; and the city *shall be* in the midst: this shall be to them the [T]suburbs of the cities.   *pasture lands*

6 And among the cities which ye shall give unto the Levites *there shall be* six cities for refuge, which ye shall appoint for the man-slayer, that he may flee thither: and to them ye shall add forty and two cities.

7 So all the cities which ye shall give to the Levites *shall be* forty and eight cities: them *shall ye give* with their suburbs.

8 And the cities which ye shall give *shall be* of the possession of the children of Israel: from *them that have* many ye shall give many; but from *them that have* few ye shall give few: every one shall give of his cities unto the Levites according to his inheritance which [T]he inheriteth.   *they inherit*

Cities of Refuge

9 And the LORD spake unto Moses, saying,

10 Speak unto the children of Israel, and say unto them, [R]When ye be come over Jordan into the land of Canaan;   Josh. 20:2

11 Then ye shall appoint you cities to be [T]cities of refuge for you; that the slayer may flee thither, which killeth any person [T]at unawares.   *places of safety · accidentally*

12 [R]And they shall be unto you cities for refuge from the avenger; that the manslayer die not, until he stand before the congregation in judgment.   Josh. 20:3, 5, 6

13 And of these cities which ye shall give [R]six cities shall ye have for refuge.   *v. 6*

14 [R]Ye shall give three cities on this side Jordan, and three cities shall ye give in the land of Canaan, *which* shall be cities of refuge.   Deut. 4:41; Josh. 20:8

15 These six cities shall be a refuge, *both* for the children of Israel, and for the stranger, and for the sojourner among [T]them: that every one that killeth any person [T]unawares may flee thither.   *unwittingly*

16 And if he smite him with an instrument of iron, so that he die, he *is* a murderer: the murderer shall surely be put to death.

17 And if he smite him with throwing a stone, wherewith he may die, and he die, he *is* a murderer: the murderer shall surely be put to [R]death.   *v.* 31; Gen. 9:6

18 Or *if* he smite him with an [T]hand weapon of wood, wherewith he may die, and he die, he *is* a murderer: the murderer shall surely be put to death.   *club*

19 [R]The revenger of blood himself shall slay the murderer: when he meeteth him, he shall slay him.   Deut. 19:6, 12; Josh. 20:3, 5

20 But if he thrust him of hatred, or hurl at him by laying of wait, that he die;

21 Or in enmity smite him with his hand, that he die: he that smote *him* shall surely be put to death; *for* he *is* a murderer: the revenger of blood shall slay the murderer, when he meeteth him.

22 But if he thrust him suddenly [R]without enmity, or have cast upon him any thing without laying of wait,   Ex. 21:13

23 Or with any stone, wherewith a man may die, seeing *him* not, and cast *it* upon him,

that he die, and *was* not his enemy, neither sought his harm:

24 Then [R]the congregation shall judge between the slayer and the revenger of blood according to these judgments: Josh. 20:6

25 And the congregation shall deliver the slayer out of the hand of the revenger of blood, and the congregation shall restore him to the city of his refuge, whither he was fled: and he shall abide in it unto the death of the high priest, [R]which was anointed with the holy oil.   Ex. 29:7; Lev. 4:3

26 But if the slayer shall at any time [T]come without the border of the city of his refuge, whither he was fled;   *travel outside*

27 And the revenger of blood find him without the borders of the city of his refuge, and the revenger of blood kill the slayer; he shall not be guilty of blood:

28 Because he should have remained in the city of his refuge until the death of the high priest: but after the death of the high priest the slayer shall return into the land of his possession.

29 So these *things* shall be for [R]a statute of judgment unto you throughout your generations in all your dwellings.   27:11

30 Whoso killeth any person, the murderer shall be put to death by the mouth of witnesses: but one witness shall not testify against any person *to cause him* to die.

31 Moreover ye shall take no satisfaction for the life of a murderer, which *is* guilty of death: but he shall be surely put to death.

32 And ye shall take no satisfaction for him that is fled to the city of his refuge, that he should come again to dwell in the land, until the death of the [T]priest.   *(high)*

33 So ye shall not pollute the land wherein ye *are:* for blood [R]it defileth the land: and the land cannot be cleansed of the blood that is shed therein, but [R]by the blood of him that shed it.   Ps. 106:38 • Gen. 9:6

34 Defile not therefore the land which ye shall inhabit, wherein I dwell: for I the LORD dwell among the children of Israel.

CHAPTER 36

Special Problems of Inheritance in Canaan

AND the chief fathers of the families of the children of Gil′-e-ad, the son of Ma′-chir, the son of Ma-nas′-seh, of the families of the sons of Joseph, came near, and spake before Moses, and before the princes, the chief fathers of the children of Israel:

2 And they said, The LORD commanded my lord to give the land for an inheritance by lot to the children of Israel: and [R]my lord was commanded by the LORD to give the inheritance of Ze-lo′-phe-had our brother unto his daughters.   27:1, 7

3 And if they be married to any of the sons of the *other* tribes of the children of Israel, then shall their inheritance be taken from the inheritance of our fathers, and shall be put to the inheritance of the tribe whereunto they are received: so shall it be taken from the lot of our inheritance.

4 And when the jubile of the children of Israel shall be, then shall their inheritance be put unto the inheritance of the tribe whereunto they are received: so shall their inheritance be taken away from the inheritance of the tribe of our fathers.

5 And Moses commanded the children of Israel according to the word of the LORD, saying, The tribe of the sons of Joseph [R]hath said well.   27:7

6 This *is* the thing which the LORD doth command concerning the daughters of Ze-lo′-phe-had, saying, Let them marry to whom they think best; only to the family of the tribe of their father shall they marry.

7 So shall not the inheritance of the children of Israel remove from tribe to tribe: for every one of the children of Israel shall [R]keep[T] himself to the inheritance of the tribe of his fathers.   1 Kin. 21:3 • *keep in the family*

8 And [R]every daughter, that possesseth an inheritance in any tribe of the children of Israel, shall be wife unto one of the family of the tribe of her father, that the children of Israel may enjoy every man the inheritance of his fathers.   1 Chr. 23:22

9 Neither shall the inheritance remove from *one* tribe to another tribe; but every one of the tribes of the children of Israel shall keep himself to his own inheritance.

10 Even as the LORD commanded Moses, so did the daughters of Ze-lo′-phe-had:

11 [R]For Mah′-lah, Tir′-zah, and Hog′-lah, and Mil′-cah, and Noah, the daughters of Ze-lo′-phe-had, were married unto their [T]father's brothers' sons: 27:1 • *first cousins*

12 *And* they were married into the families of the sons of Ma-nas′-seh the son of Joseph, and their inheritance remained in the tribe of the family of their father.

13 [R]These *are* the commandments and the judgments, which the LORD commanded by the hand of Moses unto the children of Israel [R]in the plains of Moab by Jordan *near* Jericho.   22:1; Lev. 26:46 • 26:3; 33:50

DEUTERONOMY

THE BOOK OF DEUTERONOMY

Deuteronomy, Moses' "Upper Desert Discourse," consists of a series of farewell messages by Israel's 120-year-old leader. It is addressed to the new generation destined to possess the land of promise—those who survived the forty years of wilderness wandering.

Like Leviticus, Deuteronomy contains a vast amount of legal detail, but its emphasis is on the laymen rather than the priests. Moses reminds the new generation of the importance of obedience if they are to learn from the sad example of their parents.

The Hebrew title of Deuteronomy is *Haddebharim*, "The Words," taken from the opening phrase in 1:1, "These *be* the words." The parting words of Moses to the new generation are given in oral and written form so that they will endure to all generations. Deuteronomy has been called "five-fifths of the Law" since it completes the five books of Moses. The Jewish people have also called it *Mishneh Hattorah*, "repetition of the Law," which is translated in the Septuagint as *To Deuteronomion Touto*, "This Second Law." Deuteronomy, however, is not a second law but an adaptation and expansion of much of the original law given on Mount Sinai. The English title comes from the Greek title *Deuteronomion*, "Second Law." Deuteronomy has also been appropriately called the "Book of Remembrance."

THE AUTHOR OF DEUTERONOMY

The Mosaic authorship of Deuteronomy has been vigorously attacked by critics who claim that Moses is only the originator of the tradition on which these laws are based. Some critics grant that part of Deuteronomy may have come from Mosaic times through oral tradition. The usual argument is that it was anonymously written not long before 621 B.C. and used by King Josiah to bring about his reform in that year (2 Kin. 22 and 23). There are several reasons why these arguments are not valid.

External Evidence: (1) The Old Testament attributes Deuteronomy and the rest of the Pentateuch to Moses (see Josh. 1:7; Judg. 3:4; 1 Kin. 2:3; 2 Kin. 14:6; Ezra 3:2; Neh. 1:7; Ps. 103:7; Dan. 9:11; Mal. 4:4). (2) Evidence from Joshua and First Samuel indicates that these laws existed in the form of codified written statutes and exerted an influence on the Israelites in Canaan. (3) Christ quotes it as God's Word in turning back Satan's three temptations (Matt. 4:4, 7, 10) and attributes it directly to Moses (Matt. 19:7–9; Mark 7:10; Luke 20:28; John 5:45–47).

(4) Deuteronomy is cited more than eighty times in seventeen of the twenty-seven New Testament books. These citations support the Mosaic authorship (see Acts 3:22; Rom. 10:19). (5) Jewish and Samaritan traditions point to Moses.

Internal Evidence: (1) Deuteronomy includes about forty claims that Moses wrote it. Read Deuteronomy 31: 24–26 (see also 1:1–5; 4:44–46; 29:1; 31:9). (2) Deuteronomy fits the time of Moses, not Josiah: Canaan is viewed from outside; the Canaanite religion is seen as a future menace; it assumes the hearers remember Egypt and the wilderness; Israel is described as living in tents; and there is no evidence of a divided kingdom. (3) A serious problem of misrepresentation and literary forgery would arise if this book were written in the seventh century B.C. (4) Geographical and historical details indicate a firsthand knowledge. (5) Deuteronomy follows the treaty form used in the fifteenth and fourteenth centuries B.C. (6) Moses' obituary in Chapter 34 was probably written by Joshua.

THE TIME OF DEUTERONOMY

Like Leviticus, Deuteronomy does not progress historically. It takes place entirely on the plains of Moab due east of Jericho and the Jordan River (1:1; 29:1; Josh. 1:2). It covers about one month: combine Deuteronomy 1:3 and 34:8 with Joshua 5:6–12. The book was written at the end of the forty-year period in the wilderness (c. 1405 B.C.) when the new generation was on the verge of entering Canaan. Moses wrote it to encourage the people to believe and obey God in order to receive God's blessings.

THE CHRIST OF DEUTERONOMY

The most obvious portrait of Christ is found in 18:15: "The LORD thy God will raise up unto thee a Prophet from the midst of thee, of thy brethren, like unto me; unto him ye shall hearken" (see also 18:16–19; Acts 7:37). Moses is a figure of Christ in many ways as he is the only biblical figure other than Christ to fill the three offices of prophet (34:10–12), priest (Ex. 32:31–35), and king (although Moses was not king, he functioned as ruler of Israel; 33:4, 5). Both are in danger of death during childhood; both are saviours, intercessors, and believers; and both are rejected by their brethren. Moses is one of the greatest men who ever lived, combining not just one or two memorable virtues but many.

KEYS TO DEUTERONOMY

Key Word: Covenant—The primary theme of the entire Book of Deuteronomy is the renewal of the covenant. Originally

established at Mount Sinai, the covenant is enlarged and renewed on the plains of Moab.

Key Verses: Deuteronomy 10:12, 13; 30:19, 20—"And now, Israel, what doth the LORD thy God require of thee, but to fear the LORD thy God, to walk in all his ways, and to love him, and to serve the LORD thy God with all thy heart and with all thy soul, To keep the commandments of the LORD, and his statutes, which I command thee this day for thy good?" (10:12, 13).

"I call heaven and earth to record this day against you, *that* I have set before you life and death, blessing and cursing: therefore choose life, that both thou and thy seed may live: That thou mayest love the LORD thy God, *and* that thou mayest obey his voice, and that thou mayest cleave unto him: for he *is* thy life, and the length of thy days: that thou mayest dwell in the land which the LORD sware unto thy fathers, to Abraham, to Isaac, and to Jacob, to give them" (30:19, 20).

Key Chapter: Deuteronomy 27—The formal ratification of the covenant occurs in Deuteronomy 27 as Moses, the priests, the Levites, and all of Israel "take heed, and hearken, O Israel; this day thou art become the people of the LORD thy God" (27:9).

SURVEY OF DEUTERONOMY

Deuteronomy, in its broadest outline, is the record of the renewal of the Old Covenant given at Mount Sinai. This covenant is reviewed, expanded, enlarged, and finally ratified in the plains of Moab. Moses accomplishes this primarily through three sermons that move from a retrospective, to an introspective, and finally to a prospective look at God's dealings with Israel.

Moses' First Sermon (1:1—4:43): Moses reaches into the past to remind the people of two undeniable facts in their history: (1) the moral judgment of God upon Israel's unbelief, and (2) the deliverance and provision of God during times of obedience. The simple lesson is that obedience brings blessing and disobedience brings punishment.

Moses' Second Sermon (4:44—26:19): This moral and legal section is the longest in the book because Israel's future as a nation in Canaan will depend upon a right relationship with God. These chapters review the three categories of the Law: (1) *The testimonies* (5—11). These are the moral duties—a restatement and expansion of the Ten Commandments plus an exhortation not to forget God's gracious deliverance. (2) *The statutes* (12:1—16:17). These are the ceremonial duties—sacrifices, tithes, and feasts. (3) *The ordinances* (16:18—26:19). These are the civil (16:18—20:20) and social (21—26) duties—the system of justice, criminal laws, laws of warfare, rules of property, personal and family morality, and social justice.

Moses' Third Sermon (27—34): In these chapters Moses writes history in advance. He predicts what will befall Israel in the near future (blessings and cursings) and in the distant future (dispersion among the nations and eventual return). Moses lists the terms of the covenant soon to be ratified by the people. Because Moses will not be allowed to enter the land, he appoints Joshua as his successor and delivers a farewell address to the multitude. God Himself buries Moses in an unknown place, perhaps to prevent idolatry. Moses finally enters the Promised Land when he appears with Christ on the Mount of Transfiguration (Matt. 17:3). The last three verses of the Pentateuch (34:10—12) are an appropriate epitaph for this great man.

FOCUS	FIRST SERMON	SECOND SERMON				THIRD SERMON		
REFERENCE	1:1————4:44————12:1————		16:18———21:1———		27:1———	29:1———31:1———34:12		
DIVISION	REVIEW OF GOD'S ACTS FOR ISRAEL	EXPOSITION OF THE DECALOGUE	CEREMONIAL LAWS	CIVIL LAWS	SOCIAL LAWS	RATIFICATION OF COVENANT	PALESTINIAN COVENANT	TRANSITION OF COVENANT MEDIATOR
TOPIC	WHAT GOD HAS DONE	WHAT GOD EXPECTED OF ISRAEL				WHAT GOD WILL DO		
	HISTORICAL	LEGAL				PROPHETICAL		
LOCATION	PLAINS OF MOAB							
TIME	c. 1 MONTH							

OUTLINE OF DEUTERONOMY

CHAPTER 1

The Preamble of the Covenant

THESE be the words which Moses spake unto all Israel on this side Jordan in the wilderness, in the plain over against ᵀthe Red sea, between Pa'-ran, and To'-phel, and Laban, and Ha-ze'-roth, and Diz'-a-hab. *Zuph*

2 (*There are* ᵀeleven days' *journey* from Ho'-reb by the way of mount ᴿSe'-ir unto Ka'-desh–bar'-ne-a.)   *220 mi.* • Gen. 32:3

3 And it came to pass in the fortieth year, in the eleventh month, on the first *day* of the month, *that* Moses spake unto the children of Israel, according unto all that the Lᴏʀᴅ had given him in commandment unto them;

4 ᴿAfter he had slain Si'-hon the king of the Am'-or-ites, which dwelt in Hesh'-bon, and Og the king of Ba'-shan, which dwelt at As'-ta-roth in Ed'-re-i: Num. 21:24, 33

5 On this side Jordan, in the land of Moab, began Moses to declare this law, saying,

From Mount Sinai to Kadesh—Ex. 18:18–26

6 The Lᴏʀᴅ our God spake unto us ᴿin Ho'-reb, saying, Ye have dwelt long ᴿenough in this mount: Ex. 3:1 • Ex. 19:1

7 Turn you, and take your journey, and go to the mount of the Am'-or-ites, and unto all *the places* nigh thereunto, in the plain, in the hills, and in the vale, and in the south, and by the sea side, to the land of the Ca'-naan-ites, and unto Leb'-a-non, unto the great river, the river Eu-phra'-tes.

8 Behold, I have set the land before you: go in and possess the land which the Lᴏʀᴅ ᵀsware unto your fathers, ᴿAbraham, Isaac, and Jacob, to give unto them and to their seed after them.   *promised* • Gen. 12:7; Ex. 33:1

9 And ᴿI spake unto you at that time, saying, I ᵀam not able to bear you myself alone: Ex. 18:18 • *cannot carry the whole responsibility*

10 The Lᴏʀᴅ your God hath multiplied you, and, behold, ᴿye *are* this day as the stars of heaven for multitude.   Gen. 15:5

11 (ᴿThe Lᴏʀᴅ God of your fathers make you a thousand times so many more as ye *are,* and bless you, ᴿas he hath promised you!)   2 Sam. 24:3 • Gen. 15:5

12 How can I myself alone bear your cumbrance, and your burden, and your strife?

13 Take you wise men, and understanding, and known among your tribes, and I will make them ᵀrulers over you.   *leaders*

14 And ye answered me, and said, The thing which thou ᵀhast spoken *is* good *for us* to do.   *has suggested*

15 So I took ᴿthe chief of your tribes, wise men, and known, and ᵀmade them heads over you, captains over thousands, and captains over hundreds, and captains over fifties, and captains over tens, and officers among your tribes.   Ex. 18:19–25 • *gave*

16 And I charged your judges at that time, saying, ᵀHear *the causes* between your brethren, and judge righteously between *every* man and his brother, and the stranger *that is* with him.   *listen to the problems*

17 ᴿYe shall not respect persons in judgment; *but* ye shall hear the small as well as the great; ye shall not be afraid of the face of man; for the judgment *is* God's: and the ᵀcause that is too hard for you, bring *it* unto me, and I will hear it.   16:19 • *problem*

18 And I ᴿcommanded you at that time all the things which ye should do.   Ex. 18:20

At Kadesh—Num. 13:1–14:45

19 And when we departed from Ho'-reb, ᴿwe went through all that great and terrible wilderness, which ye saw by the way of the mountain of the Am'-or-ites, as the Lᴏʀᴅ our God commanded us; and ᴿwe came to Ka'-desh–bar'-ne-a.   Jer. 2:6 • Num. 13:26

20 And I said unto you, Ye are come unto the mountain of the Am'-or-ites, which the Lᴏʀᴅ our God doth give unto us.

21 Behold, the Lᴏʀᴅ thy God hath set the land before thee: go up *and* possess *it,* as the Lᴏʀᴅ God of thy fathers hath said unto thee; fear not, neither be discouraged.

22 And ye came near unto me every one of you, and said, We will send men before us, and they shall ᵀsearch us out the land, and bring us word again by what way we must go up, and into what cities we shall come. *survey*

23 And the saying pleased me well: and I took twelve men of you, one of a tribe:

24 And they turned and went up into the mountain, and came unto the valley of ᴿEsh'-col, and searched it out.   Num. 13:21–25

25 And they took of the fruit of the land in their hands, and brought *it* down unto us, and brought us word again, and said, It *is* a good land which the Lᴏʀᴅ our God doth give us.

26 ᴿNotwithstanding ye would not go up, but rebelled against the commandment of the Lᴏʀᴅ your God: Num. 14:1–4

27 And ye ᵀmurmuredᴿ in your tents, and said, Because the Lᴏʀᴅ hated us, he hath brought us forth out of the land of Egypt, to deliver us into the hand of the Am'-or-ites, to destroy us.   *complained* • Ps. 106:25

28 Whither shall we go up? our brethren have discouraged our heart, saying, The people *is* ᴿgreater and taller than we; the cities *are* great and walled up to heaven; and moreover we have seen the sons of the An'-a-kims there.   Num. 13:28, 31–33

29 Then I said unto you, ᴿDread not, neither be afraid of them.   Num. 14:9

30 RThe LORD your God which goeth before you, he shall fight for you, according to all that he did for you in Egypt before your eyes;   3:22; Ex. 14:14; Neh. 4:20

31 And in the wilderness, where thou hast seen how that the LORD thy God bare thee, as a man doth bear his son, in all the way that ye went, until ye came into this place.

32 TYet in this thing ye did not believe the LORD your God,   *yet in spite of this word*

33 Who went in the way before you, to search you out a place to pitch your tents *in*, in fire by night, to shew you by what way ye should go, and in a cloud by day.

34 And the LORD heard the voice of your words, and was wroth, and sware, saying,

35 Surely there shall not one of these men of this evil generation see that good land, which I sware to give unto your fathers,

36 RSave Caleb the son of Je-phun'-neh; he shall see it, and to him will I give the land that he Thath trodden upon, and to his children, because he hath Twholly followed the LORD.   [Josh. 14:9] • *surveyed* • *obeyed fully*

37 RAlso the LORD was angry with me for your sakes, saying, Thou also shalt not go in thither.   3:26; Num. 20:12; 27:14; Ps. 106:32

38 *But* Joshua the son of Nun, Rwhich standeth before thee, he shall go in thither: Rencourage him: for he shall cause Israel to inherit it.   1 Sam. 16:22 • 3:28; 31:7, 23

39 Moreover your little ones, which ye said should be a prey, and your children, which in that day had no knowledge between good and evil, they shall go in thither, and unto them will I give it, and they shall possess it.

40 RBut *as for* you, turn you, and take your journey into the wilderness by the way of the Red sea.   Num. 14:25

41 Then ye answered and said unto me, We have sinned against the LORD, we will go up and fight, according to all that the LORD our God commanded us. And when ye had girded on every man his weapons of war, ye were ready to go up into the hill.

42 And the LORD said unto me, Say unto them, RGo not up, neither fight; for I *am* not among you; lest ye be Tsmitten before your enemies.   Num. 14:41-43 • *defeated*

43 So I spake unto you; and ye would not hear, but rebelled against the commandment of the LORD, and Rwent Tpresumptuously up into the hill.   Num. 14:44 • *willfully*

44 And the Am'-or-ites, which dwelt in that mountain, came out against you, and chased you, Ras bees do, and destroyed you in Se'-ir, *even* unto Hor'-mah.   Ps. 118:12

45 And ye returned and wept before the LORD; but the LORD would not hearken to your voice, nor give ear unto you.

46 So ye abode in Ka'-desh many days, according unto the days that ye abode *there*.

CHAPTER 2

"Meddle Not with Edom"—Num. 21:4

THEN we turned, and took our journey into the wilderness by the way of the Red sea, as the LORD spake unto me: and we compassed mount Se'-ir many days.

2 And the LORD spake unto me, saying,

3 Ye have compassed this mountain Rlong enough: turn you northward.   *vv.* 7, 14

4 And command thou the people, saying, Ye *are* to pass through the coast of your brethren the children of Esau, which dwell in Se'-ir; and they shall be afraid of you: take ye good heed unto yourselves therefore:

5 Meddle not with them; for I will not give you of their land, no, not so much as a footbreadth; Rbecause I have given mount Se'-ir unto Esau *for* a possession.   Josh. 24:4

6 Ye shall buy Tmeat of them for money, that ye may eat; and ye shall also buy water of them for money, that ye may drink.   *food*

7 For the LORD thy God hath blessed thee in all the works of thy hand: he knoweth thy walking through this great wilderness: these forty years the LORD thy God *hath been* with thee; thou hast lacked nothing.

8 And when we passed by from our brethren the children of Esau, which dwelt in Se'-ir, through the way of the plain from E'-lath, and from E'-zi-on-ga'-ber, we turned and passed by the way of the wilderness of Moab.

"Distress Not Moab"

9 And the LORD said unto me, Distress not the Mo'-ab-ites, neither contend with them in battle: for I will not give thee of their land *for* a possession; because I have given Ar unto the children of Lot *for* a possession.

10 RThe E'-mims dwelt therein in times past, a people great, and many, and tall, as Rthe An'-a-kims;   Gen. 14:5 • 9:2; Num. 13:22, 33

11 RWhich also were accounted giants, as the An'-a-kims; but the Mo'-ab-ites call them E'-mims.   *v.* 20; Gen. 14:5

12 The Ho'-rims also dwelt in Se'-ir beforetime; but the children of Esau succeeded them, when they had destroyed them from before them, and dwelt in their stead; as Israel did unto the land of his possession, which the LORD gave unto them.

13 Now rise up, *said I,* and get you over Rthe Tbrook Ze'-red. And we went over the brook Ze'-red.   Num. 21:12 • *valley,* Num. 13:23

14 And the space in which we came from Ka'-desh-bar'-ne-a, until we were come over the brook Ze'-red, *was* thirty and eight years; until all the generation of the men of war were wasted out from among the host, as the LORD sware unto them.

15 For indeed the hand of the LORD was against them, to destroy them from among the host, until they were consumed.

"Distress Not Ammon"

16 So it came to pass, when Rall the men of war were consumed and dead from among the people,   *v. 14*

17 That the LORD spake unto me, saying,

18 Thou art to pass over through Ar, the Tcoast of Moab, this day: *border*

19 And *when* thou comest nigh over against the children of Ammon, distress them not, nor meddle with them: for I will not give thee of the land of the children of Ammon *any* possession; because I have given it unto the children of Lot *for* a possession.

20 (That also was accounted a land of giants: giants dwelt therein in old time; and the Am'-mon-ites call them Zam-zum'-mims;

21 RA people great, and many, and tall, as the An'-a-kims; but the LORD destroyed them before them; and they succeeded them, and dwelt in their stead: *v. 10*

22 As he did to the children of Esau, Rwhich dwelt in Se'-ir, when he destroyed Rthe Ho'-rims from before them; and they succeeded them, and dwelt in their stead even unto this day: Gen. 36:8 · Gen. 14:6

23 And the A'-vims which dwelt in Ha-ze'-rim, *even* unto TAz'-zah, the Caph'-to-rims, which came forth out of Caph'-tor, destroyed them, and dwelt in their stead.)   *Ga'-za*

The Conquest of Sihon—Num. 21:21-25

24 Rise ye up, take your journey, and pass over the river Arnon: behold, I have given into thine hand Si'-hon the Am'-or-ite, king of Hesh'-bon, and his land: begin to possess *it*, and contend with him in battle.

25 This day will I begin to put the dread of thee and the fear of thee upon the nations *that are* under the whole heaven, who shall hear report of thee, and shall tremble, and be in anguish because of thee.

26 And I sent messengers out of the wilderness of Ked'-e-moth unto Si'-hon king of Hesh'-bon with words of peace, saying,

27 Let me pass through thy land: I will go along by the high way, I will neither turn unto the right hand nor to the left.

28 Thou shalt sell me meat for money, that I may eat; and give me water for money, that I may drink: Ronly I will pass through on my feet;   Num. 20:19

29 (RAs the children of Esau which dwell in Se'-ir, and the Mo'-ab-ites which dwell in Ar, did unto me;) until I shall pass over Jordan into the land which the LORD our God giveth us.   23:3, 4; Num. 20:18; Judg. 11:17

30 But Si'-hon king of Hesh'-bon would not let us pass by him: for the LORD thy God Rhardened his spirit, and made his heart obstinate, that he might deliver him into thy hand, as *appeareth* this day.   Ex. 4:21

31 And the LORD said unto me, Behold, I

have begun to give Si'-hon and his land before thee: Rbegin to possess, that thou mayest inherit his land.   [Josh. 1:3]

32 Then Si'-hon came out against us, he and all his people, to fight at Ja'-haz.

33 And the LORD our God Tdelivered him before us; and we smote him, and his sons, and all his people.   *gave us the victory over him*

34 And we took all his cities at that time, and utterly destroyed the men, and the women, and the little ones, of every city, we left none to remain:

35 Only the cattle we took Tfor a prey unto ourselves, Rand the spoil of the cities which we took.   *as a prize of war* · 3:7

36 RFrom Ar'-o-er, which *is* by the brink of the river of Arnon, and *from* the city that *is* by the river, even unto Gil'-e-ad, there was not one city too strong for us: the LORD our God delivered all unto us: 3:12; 4:48

37 Only unto the land of the children of Ammon thou camest not, *nor* unto any place of the river Jab'-bok, nor unto the cities in the mountains, nor unto whatsoever the LORD our God forbad us.

CHAPTER 3

The Conquest of Og—Num. 21:33-35

THEN we turned, and went up the way to Ba'-shan: and ROg the king of Ba'-shan came out against us, he and all his people, to battle at Ed'-re-i.   Num. 21:33

2 And the LORD said unto me, Fear him not: for I will deliver him, and all his people, and his land, into thy hand; and thou shalt do unto him as thou didst unto Si'-hon king of the Am'-or-ites, which dwelt at Hesh'-bon.

3 So the LORD our God delivered into our hands Og also, the king of Ba'-shan, and all his people: and we Tsmote him until none was left to him remaining.   *defeated*

4 And we took all his cities at that time, there was not a city which we took not from them, threescore cities, Rall the region of Ar'-gob, the kingdom of Og in Ba'-shan. 1 Kin. 4:13

5 All these cities *were* Tfenced with high walls, gates, and bars; beside Tunwalled towns a great many.   *fortified · rural*

6 And we utterly destroyed them, as we did unto Si'-hon king Rof Hesh'-bon, utterly destroying the men, women, and children, of every city.   2:24; Ps. 135:10-12

7 But all the cattle, and the spoil of the cities, we took for a prey to ourselves.

8 And we took at that time out of the hand of the two kings of the Am'-or-ites the land that *was* on this side Jordan, from the Triver of Arnon unto mount Hermon;   *valley*

9 (*Which* Hermon the Si-do'-ni-ans call Sir'-i-on; and the Am'-or-ites call it She'-nir;)

10 All the cities of the plain, and all Gil'-e-ad, and all Ba'-shan, unto Sal'-chah and Ed'-re-i, cities of the kingdom of Og in Ba'-shan.

11 ^RFor only Og king of Ba'-shan remained of the remnant of ^Rgiants; behold, his bedstead *was* a bedstead of iron; *is* it not in ^RRab'-bath of the children of Ammon? ^Tnine cubits *was* the length thereof, and ^Tfour cubits the breadth of it, after the cubit of a man.   Amos 2:9 • Gen. 14:5 • Jer. 49:2 • *13.5 ft.* • *6 ft.*

Land Is Granted to Two-and-a-Half Tribes
Num. 32:25-41

12 And this land, *which* we possessed at that time, from Ar'-o-er, which *is* by the river Arnon, and half mount Gil'-e-ad, and ^Rthe cities thereof, gave I unto the Reu'-ben-ites and to the Gad'-ites.   Num. 32:33

13 ^RAnd the rest of Gil'-e-ad, and all Ba'-shan, *being* the kingdom of Og, gave I unto the half tribe of Ma-nas'-seh; all the region of Ar'-gob, with all Ba'-shan, which was called the land of giants.   Josh. 13:29-31

14 ^RJa'-ir the son of Ma-nas'-seh took all the country of Ar'-gob unto the coasts of Gesh'-u-ri and Ma-ach'-a-thi; and called them after his own name, Ba'-shan-ha'-voth-ja'-ir, unto this day.   1 Chr. 2:22

15 And I gave Gil'-e-ad unto Ma'-chir.

16 And unto the Reu'-ben-ites and unto the Gad'-ites I gave from Gil'-e-ad even unto the river Arnon half the valley, and the border even unto the river Jab'-bok, *which is* the border of the children of Ammon;

17 The plain also, and Jordan, and the coast *thereof,* from Chin'-ne-reth ^Reven unto the sea of the plain, *even* the salt sea, under Ash'-doth-pis'-gah eastward.   4:49

18 And I commanded you at that time, saying, The LORD your God hath given you this land to possess it: ye shall pass over armed before your brethren the children of Israel, all *that are* ^Tmeet for the war.   *fit*

19 But your wives, and your little ones, and your ^Rcattle, *(for* I know that ye have much cattle,) shall abide in your cities which I have given you;   Ex. 12:38

20 Until the LORD have given rest unto your brethren, as well as unto you, and *until* they also possess the land which the LORD your God hath given them beyond Jordan: and *then* shall ye ^Rreturn every man unto his possession, which I have given you.   Josh. 22:4

Transition of Leadership

21 And ^RI commanded Joshua at that time, saying, Thine eyes have seen all that the LORD your God hath done unto these two kings: so shall the LORD do unto all the kingdoms whither thou passest.   [Num. 27:23]

22 Ye shall not fear them: for ^Rthe LORD your God he shall fight for you.   Ex. 14:14

23 And ^RI besought the LORD at that time, saying,   [2 Cor. 12:8, 9]

24 O Lord GOD, thou hast begun to shew thy servant ^Rthy greatness, and thy mighty hand: for what God *is there* in heaven or in earth, that can do according to thy works, and according to thy might?   11:2

25 I pray thee, let me go over, and see ^Rthe good land that *is* beyond Jordan, that goodly mountain, and Leb'-a-non.   Ex. 3:8

26 But the LORD was wroth with me for your sakes, and would not hear me: and the LORD said unto me, Let it suffice thee; speak no more unto me of this matter.

27 ^RGet thee up into the top of ^TPis'-gah, and lift up thine eyes westward, and northward, and southward, and eastward, and behold it with thine eyes: for thou shalt not go over this Jordan.   Num. 27:12 • *the hill*

28 But charge Joshua, and encourage him, and strengthen him: for he shall go over before this people, and he shall cause them to inherit the land which thou shalt see.

29 So we abode in ^Rthe valley over against ^RBeth-pe'-or.   34:6 • Num. 25:1-3

CHAPTER 4

Summary of the Covenant

NOW therefore hearken, O Israel, unto ^Rthe statutes and unto the judgments, which I teach you, for to do *them,* that ye may live, and go in and ^Tpossess the land which the LORD God of your fathers giveth you.   Lev. 19:37; Ezek. 20:11; [Rom. 10:5] • *live in*

2 ^RYe shall not add unto the word which I command you, neither shall ye ^Tdiminish *ought* from it, that ye may ^Tkeep the commandments of the LORD your God which I command you.   [Josh. 1:7] • *take away anything* • *obey*

3 Your eyes have seen what the LORD did because of Ba'-al-pe'-or: for all the men that followed Ba'-al-pe'-or, the LORD thy God hath destroyed them from among you.

4 But ye that did cleave unto the LORD your God *are* alive every one of you this day.

5 Behold, I have taught you statutes and judgments, even as the LORD my God commanded me, that ye should do so in the land whither ye go to possess it.

6 Keep therefore and do *them;* for this *is* your wisdom and your understanding in the sight of the nations, which shall hear all these statutes, and say, Surely this great nation *is* a wise and understanding people.

7 For ^Rwhat nation *is there* so great, who *hath* ^RGod^T so nigh unto them, as the LORD our God *is* in all *things that* we call upon him for?   [2 Sam. 7:23] • [Ps. 46:1; Is. 55:6] • *a god*

8 And what nation *is there* so great, that hath statutes and ^Tjudgments ^Rso righteous

as all this law, which I set before you this day?   *ordinances* • Ps. 89:14; 119:44

9 Only take heed to thyself, and keep thy soul diligently, lest thou forget the things which thine eyes have seen, and lest they depart from thy heart all the days of thy life: but teach them thy sons, and thy sons' sons;

10 *Specially* the day that thou stoodest before the LORD thy God in Ho'-reb, when the LORD said unto me, Gather me the people together, and I will make them hear my words, that they may learn to fear me all the days that they shall live upon the earth, and *that* they may teach their children.

11 And ye came near and stood under the mountain; and the mountain burned with fire unto the midst of heaven, with darkness, clouds, and thick darkness.

12 ^RAnd the LORD spake unto you out of the midst of the fire: ye heard the voice of the words, but saw no ^Tsimilitude; only *ye heard* a voice.   5:4, 22; Ex. 19:17–19 • *form*

13 And he declared unto you his ^Tcovenant, which he commanded you to perform, *even* ten commandments; and he wrote them upon two tables of stone.   *agreement*

14 And the LORD commanded me at that time to teach you statutes and judgments, that ye might ^Tdo them in the land whither ye go over to ^Tpossess it.   *practice* • *live in*

15 Take ye therefore good heed unto yourselves; for ye saw no manner of similitude on the day *that* the LORD spake unto you in Ho'-reb out of the midst of the fire:

16 Lest ye corrupt *yourselves*, and make you a graven image, the similitude of any figure, the likeness of male or female,

17 The likeness of any beast that *is* on the earth, the likeness of any winged fowl that flieth in the air,

18 The likeness of any thing that creepeth on the ground, the likeness of any fish that *is* in the waters beneath the earth:

19 And lest thou ^Rlift up thine eyes unto heaven, and when thou seest the sun, and the moon, and the stars, *even* all the host of heaven, shouldest be driven to ^Rworship them, and serve them, which the LORD thy God hath ^Tdivided unto all nations under the whole heaven.   17:3 • [Rom. 1:25] • *provided*

20 But the LORD hath taken you, and brought you forth out of the iron furnace, *even* out of Egypt, to be unto him a ^Rpeople of inheritance, as *ye are* this day.   27:9

21 Furthermore the LORD was angry with me for your sakes, and sware that I should not go over Jordan, and that I should not go in unto that good land, which the LORD thy God giveth thee *for* an inheritance:

22 But I must die in this land, ^RI must not go over Jordan: but ye shall go over, and ^Tpossess that good land.   3:27 • *live in*

23 Take heed unto yourselves, lest ye forget the covenant of the LORD your God, which he made with you, and make you a graven image, *or* the likeness of any *thing*, which the LORD thy God hath forbidden thee.

24 For the LORD thy God *is* a ^Tconsuming fire, *even* a jealous God.   *destroying*

25 When thou shalt beget children, and children's children, and ye shall have remained long in the land, and shall ^Tcorrupt *yourselves*, and make a graven image, *or* the likeness of any *thing*, and shall do evil in the sight of the LORD thy God, to provoke him to anger: *allow yourselves to do wrong*

26 I call heaven and earth to witness against you this day, that ^Rye shall soon utterly perish from off the land whereunto ye go over Jordan to possess it; ye shall not ^Tprolong *your* days upon it, but shall utterly be destroyed.   2 Chr. 36:14–20 • *continue to live in*

27 And the LORD ^Rshall scatter you among the nations, and ye shall be left few in number among the heathen, whither the LORD shall lead you.   Lev. 26:33; Neh. 1:8

28 And ^Rthere ye shall serve gods, the work of men's hands, wood and stone, ^Rwhich neither see, nor hear, nor eat, nor smell.   1 Sam. 26:19; Jer. 16:13 • Is. 44:9; 46:7

29 ^RBut if from thence thou shalt seek the LORD thy God, thou shalt find *him*, if thou seek him with all thy heart and with all thy soul.   [2 Chr. 15:4; Is. 55:6, 7]

30 When thou art in tribulation, and all these things are come upon thee, *even* in the latter days, if thou turn to the LORD thy God, and shalt be obedient unto his voice;

31 (For the LORD thy God *is* a merciful God;) he will not forsake thee, neither destroy thee, nor forget the covenant of thy fathers which he sware unto them.

32 For ask now of the days that are past, which were before thee, since the day that God created man upon the earth, and *ask* from the one side of heaven unto the other, whether there hath been *any such thing* as this great thing *is*, or hath been heard like it?

33 ^RDid *ever* people hear the voice of God speaking out of the midst of the fire, as thou hast heard, and live?   Ex. 24:11

34 Or hath God ^Tassayed to go *and* take him a nation from the midst of *another* nation, by ^Ttemptations, ^Rby signs, and by wonders, and by war, and by a mighty hand, and by a stretched out arm, and by great ^Tterrors, according to all that the LORD your God did for you in Egypt before your eyes?   *undertaken* • *trials* • Ex. 7:3 • *calamities*

35 Unto thee it was shewed, that thou mightest know that the LORD he *is* God; ^R*there is* none else beside him.   [32:39]

36 Out of heaven ^Rhe made thee to hear his voice, that he might instruct thee: and upon earth he shewed thee his great fire; and thou

heardest his words out of the midst of the fire. [v. 33; 8:5]; Neh. 9:13

37 And because he loved thy fathers, therefore he chose their seed after them, and brought thee out ᵀin his sight with his mighty power out of Egypt; *with his presence*

38 ᴿTo drive out nations from before thee greater and mightier than thou *art*, to bring thee in, to give thee their land *for* an inheritance, as *it is* this day. 7:1

39 Know therefore this day, and consider *it* in thine heart, that ᴿthe LORD he *is* God in heaven above, and upon the earth beneath: *there is* none else. Josh. 2:11

40 Thou shalt keep therefore his statutes, and his commandments, which I command thee this day, that it may go well with thee, and with thy children after thee, and that thou mayest ᵀprolong *thy* days upon the earth, which the LORD thy God giveth thee, for ever. *continue to live in the land*

41 Then Moses severed three cities on this side Jordan toward the sun rising;

42 That the slayer might flee thither, which should kill his neighbour unawares, and hated him not in times past; and that fleeing unto one of these cities he might live:

43 Namely, Be'-zer in the wilderness, in the plain country, of the Reu'-ben-ites; and Ra'-moth in Gil'-e-ad, of the Gad'-ites; and Go'-lan in Ba'-shan, of the Ma-nas'-sites.

The Introduction to the Law of God

44 And this *is* ᵀthe law which Moses set before the children of Israel: *the regulation*

45 These *are* the testimonies, and the statutes, and the ᵀjudgments, which Moses spake unto the children of Israel, after they came forth out of Egypt, *ordinances*

46 On this side Jordan, ᴿin the valley over against Beth-pe'-or, in the land of Si'-hon king of the Am'-or-ites, who dwelt at Hesh'-bon, whom Moses and the children of Israel ᴿsmote,ᵀ after they were come forth out of Egypt: 3:29 • 1:4; Num. 21:24 • *defeated*

47 And they possessed his land, and the land ᴿof Og king of Ba'-shan, two kings of the Am'-or-ites, which *were* on this side Jordan toward the ᵀsun rising; Num. 21:35 • *east*

48 From Ar'-o-er, which *is* by the bank of the river Arnon, even unto mount Si'-on, which is ᴿHermon, Ps. 133:3

49 And all the plain on this side Jordan eastward, even unto the sea of the plain, under the ᴿsprings of Pis'-gah. 3:17

CHAPTER 5

Setting of the Covenant

AND Moses called all Israel, and said unto them, Hear, O Israel, the statutes and judgments ᵀwhich I speak in your ears this day, that ye may learn them, and ᵀkeep, and do them. *which I announce • obey*

2 ᴿThe LORD our God made ᵀa covenant with us in Ho'-reb. Ex. 19:5 • *an agreement*

3 The LORD ᴿmade not this covenant with our fathers, but with us, *even* us, who *are* all of us here alive this day. Heb. 8:9

4 The LORD talked with you face to face in the mount out of the midst of the fire,

5 (I stood between the LORD and you at that time, to shew you the word of the LORD: for ye were afraid by reason of the fire, and went not up into the mount;) saying,

Commandments of the Covenant

6 ᴿI *am* the LORD thy God, which brought thee out of the land of Egypt, from the house of ᵀbondage. Ex. 20:2–17 • *slavery*

7 ᴿThou shalt have none other gods ᵀbefore me. Ex. 20:3 • *as more important to you than I am*

8 Thou shalt not make thee *any* graven image, *or* any likeness *of any thing* that *is* in heaven above, or that *is* in the earth beneath, or that *is* in the waters beneath the earth:

9 Thou shalt not bow down thyself unto them, nor serve them: for I the LORD thy God *am* a jealous God, visiting the iniquity of the fathers upon the children unto the third and fourth *generation* of them that hate me,

10 ᴿAnd shewing mercy unto thousands of them that love me and ᵀkeep my commandments. [Jer. 32:18]; Dan. 9:4 • *obey*

11 Thou shalt not take the name of the LORD thy God in vain: for the LORD will not hold *him* ᵀguiltless that taketh his name in vain. *innocent*

12 Keep the sabbath day to sanctify it, as the LORD thy God hath commanded thee.

13 ᴿSix days thou shalt labour, and do all thy work: Ex. 16:23; 23:12; Neh. 9:13, 14; Ezek. 20:12

14 But the seventh day *is* the ᴿsabbath of the LORD thy God: *in it* thou shalt not do any work, thou, nor thy son, nor thy daughter, nor thy manservant, nor thy maidservant, nor thine ox, nor thine ass, nor any of thy cattle, nor thy stranger that *is* within thy gates; that thy manservant and thy maidservant may rest as well as thou. Ex. 16:29; [Heb. 4:4]

15 And remember that thou wast a servant in the land of Egypt, and *that* the LORD thy God brought thee out thence through a mighty hand and by a stretched out arm: therefore the LORD thy God commanded thee to ᵀkeep the sabbath day. *treat it with respect*

16 ᴿHonour thy father and thy mother, as the LORD thy God hath commanded thee; ᴿthat thy days may be prolonged, and that it may go well with thee, in the land which the LORD thy God giveth thee. Lev. 19:3 • [Eph. 6:1–2]

17 ᴿThou shalt not kill. Ex. 20:13–16

18 Neither shalt thou commit adultery.

19 Neither shalt thou steal.

20 Neither shalt thou bear false witness against thy neighbour.

21 Neither shalt thou desire thy neighbour's wife, neither shalt thou covet thy neighbour's house, his field, or his manservant, or his maidservant, his ox, or his ass, or any *thing* that *is* thy neighbour's.

Response of Israel

22 These words the LORD spake unto all your assembly in the mount out of the midst of the fire, of the cloud, and of the thick darkness, with a great voice: and he added no more. And he wrote them in two tables of stone, and delivered them unto me.

23 ᴿAnd it came to pass, when ye heard the voice out of the midst of the darkness, (for the mountain did burn with fire,) that ye came near unto me, *even* all the heads of your tribes, and your elders;   Ex. 20:18, 19

24 And ye said, Behold, the LORD our God hath shewed us his glory and his greatness, and we have heard his voice out of the midst of the fire: we have seen this day that God doth talk with man, and he liveth.

25 Now therefore why should we die? for this great fire will ᵀconsume us: ᴿif we hear the voice of the LORD our God any more, then we shall die.   *destroy* • 18:16

26 ᴿFor who *is there of* all flesh, that hath heard the voice of the living God speaking out of the midst of the fire, as we *have,* and lived?   4:33

27 Go thou near, and hear all that the LORD our God shall say: and speak thou unto us all that the LORD our God shall speak unto thee; and we will hear *it,* and do *it.*

Response of God

28 And the LORD heard the voice of your words, when ye spake unto me; and the LORD said unto me, I have heard the voice of the words of this people, which they have spoken unto thee: ᴿthey have well said all that they have spoken.   18:17

29 ᴿO that there were such an heart in them, that they would fear me, and ᵀkeep all my commandments always, ᴿthat it might be well with them, and with their children for ever!   Ps. 81:13; Is. 48:18 • *obey* • 4:40

30 Go say to them, Get you into your tents again.

31 ᴿBut as for thee, stand thou here by me, ᴿand I will speak unto thee all the commandments, and the statutes, and the judgments, which thou shalt teach them, that they may do *them* in the land which I give them to possess it.   Ex. 24:12 • [Gal. 3:19]

32 Ye shall observe to do therefore as the LORD your God hath commanded you: ye shall ᵀnot turn aside to the right hand or to the left.   *not turn away from the line of obedience*

33 Ye shall walk in all the ways which the LORD your God hath commanded you, that ye may live, and *that it may be* well with you, and *that* ye may prolong *your* days in the land which ye shall possess.

CHAPTER 6

The Command to Teach the Law

NOW these *are* ᴿthe commandments, the statutes, and the judgments, which the LORD your God commanded to teach you, that ye might do *them* in the land whither ye go to possess it: 12:1; [Ps. 1:2]

2 That thou mightest fear the LORD thy God, to keep all his statutes and his commandments, which I command thee, thou, and thy son, and thy son's son, all the days of thy life; and that thy days may be prolonged.

3 Hear therefore, O Israel, and observe to do *it;* that it may be well with thee, and that ye may increase mightily, as the LORD God of thy fathers hath promised thee, in the land that floweth with milk and honey.

4 ᴿHear, O Israel: The LORD our God *is* one ᴿLORD: John 17:3; [1 Cor. 8:4, 6] • 4:35

5 And ᴿthou shalt love the LORD thy God ᴿwith all thine heart, and with all thy soul, and with all thy might.   Matt. 22:37 • 2 Kin. 23:25

6 And these words, which I command thee this day, shall be in thine heart:

7 And ᴿthou shalt teach them diligently unto thy children, and shalt talk of them when thou sittest in thine house, and when thou walkest by the way, and when thou liest down, and when thou risest up.   11:19

6:4–9 Three Essentials for a Christian Home—A new generation of Israel is gathered on the plains of Moab to hear Moses review the Law in preparation for their entrance to the Promised Land. The previous generation had died in unbelief in the wilderness. Moses begins his instruction by telling the people of Israel what a home is all about. He sets forth three components which must be true if the home is rightly related to God:
a. There must be a revelation of God (6:4). God revealed three things about Himself: (1) His eternality (LORD; Hebrew *Yahweh,* The Eternal); (2) His plurality (*Elohim,* Hebrew plural of God, there are three Persons in the Godhead); and (3) His unity—"one LORD"—the three Persons of the Godhead constitute one God; each is essential.
b. There must be a response to God's revelation (6:5). The response is to be a total response of love with all one's being, heart, soul, and mind. This is the only fitting response to the eternal God who has revealed Himself.

8 RAnd thou shalt bind them for a sign upon thine hand, and they shall be as frontlets between thine eyes.   Prov. 6:21; 7:3
9 RAnd thou shalt write them upon the posts of thy house, and on thy gates. [Is. 57:8]

10 And it shall be, when the LORD thy God shall have brought thee into the land which he sware unto thy fathers, to Abraham, to Isaac, and to Jacob, to give thee great and goodly cities, which thou buildedst not,
11 And houses full of all good *things*, which thou filledst not, and wells digged, which thou diggedst not, vineyards and olive trees, which thou plantedst not; when thou shalt have eaten and be full;
12 *Then* beware lest thou forget the LORD, Rwhich brought thee forth out of the land of Egypt, from the house of bondage.   8:11-18
13 Thou shalt Rfear the LORD thy God, and serve him, and Rshalt swear by his name.   Matt. 4:10; Luke 4:8 • [Is. 45:23; Jer. 4:2]
14 Ye shall not go after other gods, Rof the gods of the people which *are* round about you;   13:7
15 (For the LORD thy God *is* a jealous God among you) lest the anger of the LORD thy God be kindled against thee, and destroy thee from off the face of the earth.
16 Ye shall not Ttempt the LORD your God, as ye tempted *him* in Mas'-sah.   *provoke*
17 Ye shall Rdiligently Tkeep the commandments of the LORD your God, and his testimonies, and his statutes, which he hath commanded thee.   11:22; Ps. 119:4 • *obey*
18 And thou shalt do *that which is* right and good in the sight of the LORD: that it may be well with thee, and that thou mayest go in and possess the good land which the LORD sware unto thy fathers,
19 To cast out all thine enemies from before thee, as the LORD hath spoken.
20 *And* when thy son asketh thee in time to come, saying, What *mean* the testimonies, and the statutes, and the judgments, which the LORD our God hath commanded you?
21 Then thou shalt say unto thy son, We were Pharaoh's Tbondmen in Egypt; and the LORD brought us out of Egypt Rwith a Tmighty hand: *slaves* • Ex. 13:3 • *power*

22 And the LORD shewed signs and Rwonders, great and Tsore, upon Egypt, upon Pharaoh, and upon all his household, before our eyes: Ex. 4:21 • *grievous*
23 And he brought us out from thence, that he might bring us in, to give us the land which he sware unto our fathers.
24 And the LORD commanded us to do all these statutes, to fear the LORD our God, for our good always, Rthat he might preserve us alive, as *it is* at this day.   10:13
25 And Rit shall be our righteousness, if we Tobserve to do all these commandments before the LORD our God, as he hath commanded us.   [Lev. 18:5; Rom. 10:3, 5] • *are careful*

CHAPTER 7

The Command to Conquer Canaan

WHEN the LORD thy God shall bring thee into the land whither thou goest to possess it, and hath cast out many nations before thee, the Hit'-tites, and the Gir'-ga-shites, and the Am'-or-ites, and the Ca'naan-ites, and the Per'-iz-zites, and the Hi'-vites, and the Jeb'-u-sites, seven nations greater and mightier than thou;
2 And when the LORD thy God shall deliver them before thee; thou shalt smite them, *and* utterly destroy them; Rthou shalt make no Tcovenant with them, nor shew mercy unto them: Josh. 2:14 • *agreement*
3 RNeither shalt thou make marriages with them; thy daughter thou shalt not give unto his son, nor his daughter shalt thou take unto thy son.   Josh. 23:12-13; 1 Kin. 11:2
4 For they will Tturn away thy son from following me, that they may serve other gods: Rso will the anger of the LORD be kindled against you, and destroy thee suddenly.   *seduce* • 6:15
5 But thus shall ye deal with them; ye shall destroy their altars, and break down their images, and cut down their groves, and burn their graven images with fire.
6 For thou *art* an holy people unto the LORD thy God: the LORD thy God hath chosen thee to be a special people unto himself, above all people that *are* upon the face of the earth.

---

c. There must be a threefold responsibility (6:6-9). This threefold responsibility acts as a check upon the proper response. If the earthly father responds to God with love he will be fulfilling his threefold responsibility. If he fails in any particular, confession of sin is necessary because he does not love God with all his heart, soul, and mind. The threefold responsibility is: (1) to have God's truth govern his heart (6:6)—there must be heart reality, not mere external conformity or ceremony; (2) to have God's truth govern his home—this is evidenced by the fact that the father teaches the truths of God's revelation to his children by both formal (teach diligently) and informal (talk of them) instruction; and (3) to have God's truth govern his habits and conduct personally, privately, and publicly. In short, the home is to be a divine school in which the father is to be the teacher, under Christ.
Now turn to Page 1237—1 Pet. 3:1-6: The Role of the Wife.

7 The LORD did not set his love upon you, [R]nor choose you, because ye were more in number than any people; for ye *were* [R]the fewest of all people: 4:37 • 10:22

8 But because the LORD loved you, and because he would keep the oath which he had sworn unto your fathers, hath the LORD brought you out with a mighty hand, and redeemed you out of the house of bondmen, from the hand of Pharaoh king of Egypt.

9 Know therefore that the LORD thy God, he *is* God, [R]the faithful God, [R]which keepeth covenant and mercy with them that love him and keep his commandments to a thousand generations;   Heb. 11:11 • Neh. 1:5

10 And repayeth them that hate him to their face, to destroy them: he will not be [T]slack[R] to him that hateth him, he will repay him to his face.   *careless* • [2 Pet. 3:9, 10]

11 Thou shalt therefore keep the commandments, and the statutes, and the judgments, which I command thee this day, to do them.

12 Wherefore it shall come to pass, if ye hearken to these judgments, and keep, and do them, that the LORD thy God shall keep unto thee the covenant and the mercy which he sware unto thy fathers:

13 And he will love thee, and bless thee, and multiply thee: he will also bless [T]the fruit of thy womb, and the fruit of thy land, thy corn, and thy wine, and thine oil, the increase of thy [T]kine, and the flocks of thy sheep, in the land which he [T]sware unto thy fathers to give thee.   *your children • cattle • promised*

14 Thou shalt be blessed above all people: there shall not be male or female barren among you, or among your cattle.

15 And the [R]LORD will take away from thee all sickness, and will put none of the [T]evil diseases of Egypt, which thou knowest, upon thee; but will lay them upon all *them* that hate thee.   Ex. 15:26 • *harmful*

16 And thou shalt [T]consume all the people which the LORD thy God shall deliver thee; thine eye shall have no pity upon them: neither shalt thou serve their gods; for that *will* be a snare unto thee.   *destroy*

17 If thou shalt say in thine heart, These nations *are* [T]more than I; how can I [T]dispossess [R]them?   *stronger • put them out* • 1:17

18 Thou shalt not be afraid of them: *but* shalt well remember what the LORD thy God did unto Pharaoh, and unto all Egypt;

19 The great [T]temptations which thine eyes saw, and the signs, and the wonders, and the mighty hand, and the stretched out arm, whereby the LORD thy God brought thee out: so shall the LORD thy God do unto all the people of whom thou art afraid.   *plagues*

20 Moreover the LORD thy God [R]will [T]send the hornet among them, until they that

are left, and hide themselves from thee, be destroyed.   Josh. 24:12 • *cause them to be put to flight*

21 Thou shalt not be affrighted at them: for the LORD thy God *is* among you, a mighty God and [T]terrible.   *able to do wonders*

22 And the LORD thy God will put out those nations before thee by little and little: thou mayest not consume them at once, lest the beasts of the field increase upon thee.

23 [R]But the LORD thy God shall deliver them unto thee, and shall [T]destroy them with a [T]mighty destruction, until they be destroyed.   Josh. 10:10 • *discomfit • total destruction*

24 And he shall [T]deliver their kings into thine hand, and thou shalt destroy their name from under heaven: there shall no man be able to stand before thee, until thou have destroyed them.   *make prisoners*

25 The graven images of their gods shall ye burn with fire: thou shalt not desire the silver or gold *that is* on them, nor take *it* unto thee, lest thou be snared therein: for it *is* an abomination to the LORD thy God.

26 Neither shalt thou bring an abomination into thine house, lest thou be a cursed thing like it: *but* thou shalt utterly detest it, and thou shalt utterly abhor it; [R]for it *is* [T]a cursed thing.   Lev. 27:28 • *rejected by the LORD*

CHAPTER 8

The Command to Remember the Lord

ALL the commandments which I command thee this day shall ye [T]observe to do, that ye may live, and multiply, and go in and possess the land which the LORD [T]sware unto your fathers.   *be careful • promised*

2 And thou shalt remember all the way which the LORD thy God led thee these forty years in the wilderness, to humble thee, *and* to [T]prove thee, to [T]know what *was* in thine heart, whether thou wouldest keep his commandments, or [T]no.   *test • learn • not*

3 And he humbled thee, and suffered thee to hunger, and fed thee with man′-na, which thou knewest not, neither did thy fathers know; that he might make thee know that man doth not live by bread only, but by every *word* that proceedeth out of the mouth of the LORD doth man live.

4 Thy raiment waxed not old upon thee, neither did thy foot swell, these forty years.

5 Thou shalt also [T]consider in thine heart, that, as a man chasteneth his son, so the LORD thy God chasteneth thee.   *remember*

6 Therefore thou shalt keep the commandments of the LORD thy God, [R]to walk in his ways, and to fear him.   [5:33]

7 For the LORD thy God bringeth thee into a good land, [R]a land of brooks of water, of fountains and depths that spring out of valleys and hills;   11:10-12

8 A land of wheat, and barley, and vines, and fig trees, and pomegranates; a ᴿland of oil olive, and honey;   Ex. 3:8

9 A land wherein thou shalt eat bread without scarceness, thou shalt not lack any *thing* in it; a land whose stones *are* iron, and out of whose hills thou mayest dig brass.

10 When thou hast eaten and art full, then thou shalt bless the LORD thy God for the good land which he hath given thee.

11 ᴿBeware that thou forget not the LORD thy God, in not keeping his commandments, and his judgments, and his statutes, which I command thee this day: 4:9

12 ᴿLest *when* thou hast eaten and ᵀart full, and hast built ᵀgoodly houses, and dwelt *therein;*   Prov. 30:9 · satisfied · fine homes

13 And *when* thy herds and thy flocks multiply, and thy silver and thy gold is multiplied, and all that thou hast is multiplied;

14 Then ᵀthine heart be lifted up, and thou forget the LORD thy God, which brought thee forth out of the land of Egypt, from the house of bondage;   you get to be proud

15 Who led thee through that great and terrible wilderness, *wherein were* fiery serpents, and scorpions, and drought, where *there was* no water; who brought thee forth water out of the rock of flint;

16 Who fed thee in the wilderness with man'-na, which thy fathers knew not, that he might humble thee, and that he might prove thee, to do thee good at thy latter end;

17 And ᵀthou say in thine heart, My power and the might of *mine* hand hath gotten me this wealth.   think in your own mind

18 But thou shalt remember the LORD thy God: for *it is* he that giveth thee power to get wealth, ᴿthat he may ᵀestablish his covenant which he sware unto thy fathers, as *it is* this day.   7:8, 12 · bring to pass his promise

19 And it shall be, if thou do at all forget the LORD thy God, and walk after other gods, and serve them, and worship them, ᴿI testify against you this day that ᴿye shall surely perish.   4:26; 30:18 · 2 Chr. 36:14-20

20 As the nations which the LORD destroyeth before your face, ᴿso shall ye perish; because ye would not be obedient unto the voice of the LORD your God.   [Dan. 9:11, 12]

CHAPTER 9

Moses Rehearses Israel's Rebellion

HEAR, O Israel: Thou *art* to pass over Jordan this day, to go in to possess nations greater and mightier than thyself, cities great and fenced up to heaven,

2 A people great and tall, the ᴿchildren of the An'-a-kims, whom thou knowest, and *of whom* thou hast heard *say,* Who can stand before the children of A'-nak!   Num. 13:22

3 Understand therefore this day, that the LORD thy God *is* he which goeth over before thee; *as* a consuming fire he shall destroy them, and he shall bring them down ᵀbefore thy face: so shalt thou drive them out, and destroy them quickly, as the LORD hath said unto thee.   in front of your advance

4 Speak not thou in thine heart, after that the LORD thy God hath cast them out from before thee, saying, For my righteousness the LORD hath brought me in to possess this land: but ᴿforᵀ the wickedness of these nations the LORD doth drive them out from before thee.   Gen. 15:16 · because of their evil

5 Not for thy righteousness, or for the uprightness of thine heart, dost thou go to possess their land: but for the wickedness of these nations the LORD thy God doth drive them out from before thee, and that he may perform the word which the LORD sware unto thy fathers, Abraham, Isaac, and Jacob.

6 Understand therefore, that the LORD thy God giveth thee not this good land to possess it for thy righteousness; for thou *art* a ᵀstiffnecked people.   rebellious

7 Remember, *and* forget not, how thou ᵀprovokedst the LORD thy God to wrath in the wilderness: from the day that thou didst depart out of the land of Egypt, until ye came unto this place, ye have been ᵀrebellious against the LORD.   irritated · disobedient

8 Also ᴿin Ho'-reb ye provoked the LORD to ᵀwrath, so that the LORD was angry with you to have destroyed you.   Ex. 32:4 · anger

9 ᴿWhen I was gone up into the mount to receive the tables of stone, *even* the tables of the ᵀcovenant which the LORD made with you, then I ᵀabode in the mount forty days and forty nights, I neither did eat bread nor drink water: Ex. 24:12, 15 · agreement · stayed

10 ᴿAnd the LORD delivered unto me two tables of stone written with the finger of God; and on them *was written* according to all the words, which the LORD spake with you in the mount out of the midst of the fire in the day of the assembly.   Ex. 34:28

11 And it came to pass at the end of forty days and forty nights, *that* the LORD gave me the two tables of stone, *even* the tables of the covenant.

12 ᴿAnd the LORD said unto me, Arise, get thee down quickly from hence; for thy people which thou hast brought forth out of Egypt have ᵀcorrupted *themselves;* they are quickly turned aside out of the way which I commanded them; they have made them a molten image.   Ex. 32:10 · have done wrong

13 Furthermore the LORD spake unto me, saying, I have seen this people, and, behold, ᴿit is a ᵀstiffnecked people: v. 6 · rebellious

14 ᴿLet me alone, that I may destroy them, and blot out their name from under heaven:

and I will make of thee a nation mightier and greater than they. Ex. 32:10

15 RSo I turned and came down from the mount, and Rthe mount burned with fire: and the two tables of the covenant *were* in my two hands. Ex. 32:15 • Ex. 19:18

16 And RI looked, and, behold, ye had sinned against the LORD your God, *and* had made you a molten calf: ye had turned aside quickly out of the way which the LORD had commanded you. Ex. 32:19

17 And I took the two tables, and Rcast them out of my two hands, and brake them before your eyes. Ex. 32:19

18 And I Rfell down before the LORD, as at the first, forty days and forty nights: I Tdid neither eat bread, nor drink water, because of all your sins which ye sinned, in doing wickedly in the sight of the LORD, to provoke him to anger. Ex. 34:28 • *fasted*

19 For I was afraid of the anger and hot displeasure, wherewith the LORD was wroth against you to destroy you. But the LORD hearkened unto me at that time also.

20 And the LORD was very angry with Aaron to have destroyed him: and I prayed for Aaron also the same time.

21 And I took your sin, the calf which ye had made, Rand burnt it with fire, and stamped it, *and* ground *it* very small, *even* until it was as small as dust: and I cast the dust thereof into the brook that descended out of the mount. Ex. 32:20

22 And at Tab'-e-rah, and at RMas'-sah, and at Kib'-roth–hat-ta'-a-vah, ye Tprovoked the LORD to wrath. Ex. 17:7 • *irritated*

23 Likewise when the LORD sent you from Ka'-desh–bar'-ne-a, saying, Go up and possess the land which I have given you; then ye rebelled against the commandment of the LORD your God, and ye believed him not, nor Thearkened to his voice. *obeyed*

24 Ye have been rebellious against the LORD from the day that I knew you.

25 RThus I fell down before the LORD forty days and forty nights, as I fell down *at the first;* because the LORD had said he would destroy you. *v. 18*

26 I prayed therefore unto the LORD, and said, O Lord GOD, destroy not thy people and thine Tinheritance, which thou hast redeemed through thy Tgreatness, which thou hast brought forth out of Egypt with Ta mighty hand. *that belongs to you • power • strength*

27 Remember thy servants, Abraham, Isaac, and Jacob; look not unto the stubbornness of this people, nor to their wickedness, nor to their sin:

28 Lest Tthe land whence thou broughtest us out say, Because the LORD was not able to bring them into the land which he promised them, and because he hated them, he hath

brought them out to slay them in the wilderness. *the people*

29 Yet they *are* thy people and Rthine inheritance, which thou broughtest out by thy mighty power and by thy stretched out arm. Ps. 106:40

CHAPTER 10

Moses Rehearses God's Mercy

AT that time the LORD said unto me, Hew thee two tables of stone like unto the first, and come up unto me into the mount, and make thee an ark of wood.

2 And I will write on the tables the words that were in the first tables which thou brakest, and thou shalt put them in the ark.

3 And I made an ark *of* shit'-tim wood, and hewed two tables of stone like unto the first, Rand went up into the mount, having the two tables in mine hand. Ex. 34:4

4 And he wrote on the tables, according to the first writing, the ten Tcommandments, Rwhich the LORD spake unto you in the mount out of the midst of the fire in the day of the assembly: and the LORD gave them unto me. *words* • Ex. 34:28

5 And I turned myself and came down from the mount, and put the tables in the ark which I had made; Rand there they be, as the LORD commanded me. 1 Kin. 8:9

6 And the children of Israel took their journey from Be-e'-roth of the children of Ja'-a-kan to Mo-se'-ra: there Aaron died, and there he was buried; and E-le-a'-zar his son ministered in the priest's office in his stead.

7 RFrom thence they journeyed unto Gud'-go-dah; and from Gud'-go-dah to Jot'-bath, a land of rivers of waters. Num. 33:32, 33

8 At that time the LORD Tseparated the tribe of Levi, to bear the ark of the covenant of the LORD, to stand before the LORD to minister unto him, and to bless in his name, unto this day. *set apart for service*

9 RWherefore Levi hath no part nor inheritance with his brethren; the LORD *is* his inheritance, according as the LORD thy God promised him. 18:1, 2; Num. 18:20, 24

10 And RI stayed in the mount, according to the first time, forty days and forty nights; and Rthe LORD hearkened unto me at that time also, *and* the LORD would not destroy thee. 9:18; Ex. 34:28 • Ex. 32:14

11 And the LORD said unto me, Arise, take *thy* journey before the people, that they may go in and possess the land, which I sware unto their fathers to give unto them.

Love God

12 And now, Israel, what doth the LORD thy God require of thee, but to fear the LORD thy God, to walk in all his ways, and to love

him, and to serve the LORD thy God with all thy heart and with all thy soul,

13 To keep the commandments of the LORD, and his statutes, which I command thee this day ᵀfor thy good?   *for your benefit*

14 Behold, the heaven and the heaven of heavens *is* the LORD's ᴿthy God, the earth *also*, with all that therein *is*.   [Neh. 9:6]

15 Only the LORD ᵀhad a delight in thy fathers to love them, and he chose their ᵀseed after them, *even* you above all people, as *it is* this day.   *was pleased with · children*

16 Circumcise therefore the foreskin of your heart, and be no more stiffnecked.

17 For the LORD your God *is* God of gods, and Lord of lords, a great God, a mighty, and ᵀa terrible, which regardeth not persons, nor taketh reward: *able to do wonders*

18 ᴿHe doth execute the judgment of the fatherless and widow, and loveth the stranger, in giving him food and raiment.   Ps. 68:5

19 Love ye therefore the stranger: for ye were strangers in the land of Egypt.

20 Thou shalt fear the LORD thy God; him shalt thou serve, and to him shalt thou ᵀcleave, and swear by his name.   *cling closely*

21 He *is* thy praise, and he *is* thy God, that hath done for thee these great and terrible things, which thine eyes have seen.

22 Thy fathers went down into Egypt with threescore and ten persons; and now the LORD thy God hath made thee as the stars of heaven for multitude.

CHAPTER 11

Study and Obey the Commands

THEREFORE thou shalt love ᴿthe LORD thy God, and ᵀkeep his charge, and his statutes, and his judgments, and his commandments, alway.   6:5 · *obey his instructions*

2 And know ye this day: for *I speak* not with your children which have not known, and which have not seen the chastisement of the LORD your God, his greatness, his mighty hand, and his stretched out arm,

3 And his miracles, and his acts, which he did in the midst of Egypt unto Pharaoh the king of Egypt, and unto all his land;

4 And what he did unto the army of Egypt, unto their horses, and to their chariots; how he made the water of the Red sea to overflow them as they pursued after you, and *how* the LORD hath destroyed them unto this day;

5 And what he did unto you in the wilderness, until ye came into this place;

6 And what he did unto Da'-than and A-bi'-ram, the sons of E-li'-ab, the son of Reuben: how the earth ᵀopened her mouth, and swallowed them up, and their households, and their tents, and ᵀall the substance

that *was* in their possession, in the midst of all Israel: *split like a chasm · all they owned*

7 But your eyes have seen all the great acts of the LORD which he did.

8 Therefore shall ye keep all the commandments which I command you this day, that ye may be strong, and go in and possess the land, whither ye go to possess it;

9 And that ye may prolong *your* days in the land, which the LORD sware unto your fathers to give unto them and to their seed, a land that floweth with milk and honey.

10 For the land, whither thou goest in to possess it, *is* not as the land of Egypt, from whence ye came out, where thou sowedst thy seed, and ᵀwateredst *it* with thy foot, as a garden of herbs: *with a treadmill*

11 But the land, whither ye go to possess it, *is* a land of hills and valleys, *and* ᵀdrinketh water of the rain of heaven: *receives*

12 A land which the LORD thy God ᵀcareth for: the eyes of the LORD thy God *are* always upon it, from the beginning of the year even unto the end of the year.   *provides*

13 And it shall come to pass, if ye shall hearken diligently unto my commandments which I command you this day, to love the LORD your God, and to serve him with all your heart and with all your soul,

14 That I will give *you* the rain of your land in his due season, the first rain and the latter rain, that thou mayest gather in thy corn, and thy wine, and thine oil.

15 And I will send grass in thy fields for thy cattle, that thou mayest eat and be full.

16 Take heed to yourselves, that your heart be not deceived, and ye turn aside, and serve other gods, and worship them;

17 And *then* the LORD's wrath be kindled against you, and he shut up the heaven, that there be no rain, and that the land yield not her fruit; and *lest* ye perish quickly from off the good land which the LORD giveth you.

18 Therefore shall ye lay up these my words in your heart and in your soul, and bind them for a sign upon your hand, that they may be as frontlets between your eyes.

19 ᴿAnd ye shall teach them your children, speaking of them ᵀwhen thou sittest in thine house, and when thou walkest by the way, when thou liest down, and when thou risest up.   4:9, 10 · *at all routine times*

20 ᴿAnd thou shalt write them upon the door posts of thine house, and upon thy gates: 6:9

21 That your days may be multiplied, and the days of your children, in the land which the LORD sware unto your fathers to give them, as the days of heaven upon the earth.

Victory Depends upon Obedience

22 For if ye shall diligently keep all these commandments which I command you, to do

them, to love the LORD your God, to walk in all his ways, and to cleave unto him;

23 Then will the LORD ^Rdrive out all these nations from before you, and ye shall ^Rpossess greater nations and mightier than yourselves.   4:38 • 9:1

24 Every place whereon ^Tthe soles of your feet shall tread shall be your's: from the wilderness and Leb'-a-non, from the river, the river Eu-phra'-tes, even unto the uttermost sea shall your coast be.   *you walk*

25 There shall no man be able to ^Tstand before you: *for* the LORD your God shall lay the fear of you and the dread of you upon all the land that ye shall tread upon, as he hath said unto you.   *resist*

26 ^RBehold, I set before you this day a blessing and a curse;   30:1, 15, 19

27 ^RA blessing, if ye obey the commandments of the LORD your God, which I command you this day: 28:2; Ex. 20:6

28 And a curse, if ye will not obey the commandments of the LORD your God, but ^Tturn aside out of the way which I command you this day, to go after other gods, which ye have not known.   *go astray*

29 And it shall come to pass, when the LORD thy God hath brought thee in unto the land whither thou goest to possess it, that thou shalt put the blessing upon mount Ger'-i-zim, and the curse upon mount E'-bal.

30 *Are* they not on the other side Jordan, by the way where the sun goeth down, in the land of the Ca'-naan-ites, which dwell in the ^Tchampaign over against Gil'-gal, beside the ^Tplains of Mo'-reh?   *Arabah • oaks*

31 For ye shall pass over Jordan ^Tto go in to possess the land which the LORD your God giveth you, and ye shall ^Tpossess it, and dwell therein.   *to begin the conquest of • take charge of*

32 And ye shall observe to do all the statutes and ^Tjudgments which I set before you this day.   *decisions*

CHAPTER 12

Law of the Central Sanctuary

THESE *are* the statutes and judgments, which ye shall observe to do in the land, which the LORD God of thy fathers ^Tgiveth thee to possess it, ^Tall the days that ye live upon the earth.   *gives to you for your own • as long as*

2 ^RYe shall utterly destroy all the places, wherein the nations which ye shall ^Tpossess served their gods, ^Rupon the high mountains, and upon the hills, and under every green tree: Ex. 34:13 • *conquer* • 2 Kin. 16:4

3 And ye shall overthrow their altars, and break their pillars, and burn their groves with fire; and ye shall hew down the graven images of their gods, and destroy the names of them out of that place.

4 Ye shall not do ^Rso unto the LORD your God.   *v. 31*

5 But unto the place which the LORD your God shall choose out of all your tribes to put his name there, *even* unto his habitation shall ye seek, and thither thou shalt come:

6 And thither ye shall bring your burnt offerings, and your sacrifices, and your tithes, and heave offerings of your hand, and your vows, and your freewill offerings, and the firstlings of your herds and of your flocks:

7 And there ye shall eat before the LORD your God, and ye shall rejoice in all that ye put your hand unto, ye and your households, wherein the LORD thy God hath blessed thee.

8 Ye shall not do ^Tafter all *the things* that we do here this day, ^Revery man whatsoever *is* right in his own eyes.   *in the way that* • Judg. 17:6

9 For ye are not as yet come to ^Tthe rest and to the ^Tinheritance, which the LORD your God giveth you.   *victory • possessions*

10 But *when* ye go over Jordan, and dwell in the land which the LORD your God giveth you to inherit, and *when* ^Rhe giveth you rest from all your enemies round about, so that ye dwell in safety;   Josh. 11:23

11 Then there shall be a place which the LORD your God shall choose to cause his name to dwell there; thither shall ye bring all that I command you; your burnt offerings, and your sacrifices, your tithes, and the heave offering of your hand, and all your choice vows which ye vow unto the LORD:

12 And ye shall rejoice before the LORD your God, ye, and your sons, and your daughters, and your menservants, and your maidservants, and the Levite ^Rthat *is* within your gates; forasmuch as he hath no part nor inheritance with you.   14:27

13 Take heed to thyself that thou offer not thy burnt offerings in every place that thou seest:

14 But in the place which the LORD shall choose in one of thy tribes, there thou shalt offer thy burnt offerings, and there thou shalt do all that I command thee.

15 Notwithstanding thou mayest kill and eat flesh in all thy gates, whatsoever thy soul lusteth after, according to the blessing of the LORD thy God which he hath given thee: the unclean and the clean may eat thereof, as of the roebuck, and as of the hart.

16 ^ROnly ye shall not eat the blood; ye shall pour it upon the earth as water.   Lev. 7:26

17 Thou mayest not eat ^Twithin thy gates the tithe of thy corn, or of thy wine, or of thy oil, or the firstlings of thy herds or of thy flock, nor any of thy vows which thou vowest, nor thy freewill offerings, or heave offering of thine hand: *in your own homes*

18 But thou must eat them before the LORD thy God in the place which the LORD thy God shall choose, thou, and thy son, and

thy daughter, and thy manservant, and thy maidservant, and the Levite that is within thy gates: and thou shalt rejoice before the LORD thy God in ᵀall that thou puttest thine hands unto.   *all you undertake*

19 ᵀTake heed to thyself that thou forsake not the Levite as long as thou livest upon the earth.   *take personal precaution*

20 When the LORD thy God shall enlarge thy border, as he hath promised thee, and thou shalt say, I will eat flesh, because thy soul longeth to eat flesh; thou mayest eat flesh, whatsoever thy soul lusteth after.

21 If the place which the LORD thy God hath chosen to put his name there be too far from thee, then thou shalt kill of thy herd and of thy flock, which the LORD hath given thee, as I have commanded thee, and ᵀthou shalt eat in thy gates whatsoever thy soul lusteth after.   *you may eat this meat at home*

22 Even as the ᵀroebuck and the hart is eaten, so thou shalt eat them: the unclean and the clean shall eat of them alike.   *gazelle*

23 Only be sure that thou eat not the blood: for the blood is the life; and thou mayest not eat the life with the flesh.

24 ᴿThou shalt not eat it; thou shalt pour it upon the earth as water.   Lev. 17:10

25 Thou shalt not eat it; that ᵀit may go well with thee, and with thy children after thee, when thou shalt do that which is right in the sight of the LORD.   *you may prosper*

26 Only thy holy things which thou hast, and thy vows, thou shalt take, and go unto the place which the LORD shall choose:

27 ᴿAnd thou shalt offer thy burnt offerings, the flesh and the blood, upon the altar of the LORD thy God: and the blood of thy sacrifices shall be poured out upon the altar of the LORD thy God, and ᴿthou shalt eat the flesh.   Lev. 1:5, 9, 13, 17 • Lev. 3:1–17

28 Observe and hear all these words which I command thee, that it may go well with thee, and with thy children after thee for ever, when thou doest that which is good and right in the sight of the LORD thy God.

Law of Idolatry

29 When the LORD thy God shall ᵀcut off the nations from before thee, whither thou goest to possess them, and thou succeedest them, and dwellest in their land;   *destroy*

30 Take heed to thyself that thou be not snared by following them, after that they be destroyed from before thee; and that thou ᵀenquire not after their gods, saying, How did these nations serve their gods? even so will I do likewise.   *take any interest in*

31 Thou shalt not do so unto the LORD thy God: for every abomination to the LORD, which he hateth, have they done unto their gods; for even their sons and their daughters they have burnt in the fire to their gods.

32 What thing soever I command you, ᵀobserve to do it: thou shalt not add thereto, nor ᵀdiminish from it.   *be careful • take away*

CHAPTER 13

IF there arise among you a prophet, or a ᴿdreamer of dreams, ᴿand giveth thee a sign or a wonder,   Zech. 10:2 • Matt. 24:24

2 And the sign or the wonder come to pass, whereof he spake unto thee, saying, ᴿLet us go after other gods, which thou hast not known, and let us serve them;   vv. 6, 13

3 Thou shalt not hearken unto the words of that prophet, or that dreamer of dreams: for the LORD your God proveth you, to know whether ye love the LORD your God with all your heart and with all your soul.

4 Ye shall ᵀwalk after the LORD your God, and fear him, and keep his commandments, and obey his voice, and ye shall serve him, and cleave unto him.   *walk in the ways of*

5 And that prophet, or that dreamer of dreams, shall be put to death; because he hath spoken to turn you away from the LORD your God, which brought you out of the land of Egypt, and redeemed you out of the house of bondage, to ᵀthrust thee out of the way which the LORD thy God commanded thee to walk in. So shalt thou put the evil away from the midst of thee.   *mislead*

6 If thy brother, the son of thy mother, or thy son, or thy daughter, or the wife of thy bosom, or thy friend, which is as thine own soul, entice thee secretly, saying, Let us go and serve other gods, which thou hast not known, thou, nor thy fathers;

7 Namely, of the gods of the people which are round about you, nigh unto thee, or far off from thee, from the one end of the earth even unto the other end of the earth;

8 Thou shalt ᴿnot ᵀconsent unto him, nor hearken unto him; neither shall thine eye pity him, neither shalt thou spare, neither shalt thou conceal him: Prov. 1:10 • agree with

9 But thou shalt surely kill him; thine hand shall be first upon him to put him to death, and afterwards the hand of all the people.

10 And thou shalt stone him with stones, that he die; because he hath sought to thrust thee away from the LORD thy God, which brought thee out of the land of Egypt, from the house of bondage.

11 And all Israel shall hear, and ᴿfear, and shall do no more any such wickedness as this is among you.   17:13

12 If thou shalt hear say in one of thy cities, which the LORD thy God hath given thee to dwell there, saying,

13 Certain men, the ᵀchildren of Be′-li-al, are gone out from among you, and have ᵀwithdrawn the inhabitants of their city,

saying, Let us go and serve other gods, which ye have not known;   *base fellows · seduced*

14 Then shalt thou enquire, and make search, and ask diligently; and, behold, *if it be* truth, *and* the thing certain, *that* such abomination is wrought among you;

15 Thou shalt surely ᵀsmite the inhabitants of that city with the edge of the sword, destroying it utterly, and all that *is* therein, and the cattle thereof, with the edge of the sword.   *attack*

16 And thou shalt gather all ᵀthe spoil of it into the midst of the street thereof, and shalt burn with fire the city, and all the spoil thereof every whit, for the LORD thy God: and it shall be an heap for ever; it shall not be built again.   *property belonging to it*

17 And there shall cleave nought of the cursed thing to thine hand: that the LORD may turn from the fierceness of his anger, and shew thee mercy, and have compassion upon thee, and ᵀmultiply thee, as he hath sworn unto thy fathers;   *increase*

18 When thou shalt hearken to the voice of the LORD thy God, to keep all his commandments which I command thee this day, to do *that which is* right ᵀin the eyes of the LORD thy God.   *according to the will of God*

CHAPTER 14

Law of Food

YE *are* the children of the LORD your God: ye shall not cut yourselves, nor make any baldness between your eyes for the dead.

2 For thou *art* an holy people unto the LORD thy God, and the LORD hath chosen thee to be a peculiar people unto himself, above all the nations that *are* upon the earth.

3 ᴿThou shalt not eat any ᵀabominable thing.   *Ezek. 4:14 · evil*

4 ᴿThese *are* the beasts which ye shall eat: the ox, the sheep, and the goat,   *Lev. 11:1-45*

5 The hart, and the roebuck, and the fallow deer, and the wild goat, and the pygarg, and the wild ox, and the chamois.

6 And every beast that parteth the hoof, and cleaveth the cleft into two claws, *and* cheweth the cud among the beasts, that ye shall eat.

7 Nevertheless these ye shall not eat of them that chew the cud, or of them that divide the ᵀcloven hoof; *as* the camel, and the hare, and the coney: for they chew the cud, but divide not the hoof; *therefore* they *are* ᵀunclean unto you.   *split · unfit*

8 And the swine, because it divideth the hoof, yet cheweth not the cud, it *is* unclean unto you: ye shall not eat of their flesh, ᴿnor touch their dead carcase.   *Lev. 11:26, 27*

9 ᴿThese ye shall eat of all that *are* in the waters: all that have fins and scales shall ye eat: *Lev. 11:9*

10 And whatsoever hath not fins and scales ye may not eat; it *is* unclean unto you.

11 *Of* all ᵀclean birds ye shall eat.   *fit*

12 ᴿBut these *are* they of which ye shall not eat: the eagle, and the ᵀossifrage, and the ᵀospray,   *Lev. 11:13, 20 · vulture · buzzard*

13 And the ᵀglede, and the ᵀkite, and the ᵀvulture after his kind,   *red kite · falcon · kite*

14 And every raven after his kind,

15 And the owl, and the night hawk, and the cuckow, and the hawk after his kind,

16 The ᵀlittle owl, and the great owl, and the swan,   *screech owl*

17 And the ᵀpelican, and the ᵀgier eagle, and the ᵀcormorant,   *jacdaw · vulture · fisher owl*

18 And the stork, and the heron after her kind, and the ᵀlapwing, and the bat.   *hoopoe*

19 And every creeping thing that flieth *is* unclean unto you: they shall not be eaten.

20 *But of* all clean ᵀfowls ye may eat. *birds*

21 Ye shall not eat *of* any thing that dieth of itself: thou shalt give it unto the stranger that *is* in thy gates, that he may eat it; or thou mayest sell it unto an alien: for thou *art* an holy people unto the LORD thy God. Thou shalt not seethe a kid in his mother's milk.

14:2 Purpose of Israel—The modern-day student of the Bible may well ask why so much of Scripture is taken up with the history of a single nation. Certainly many Christians wonder why one nation should be called "God's chosen people." The answer to this question is bound up in God's purpose for Israel. When God promised Abraham that he would become the father of a great nation, He also promised that He would bless all peoples through that nation (Page 14—Gen. 12:1-3). Therefore Israel was to be a channel of blessing as well as a recipient. Even their deliverance from Egypt was partially designed to show other nations that Israel's God was the only true God (Page 62—Ex. 7:5; 14:18; Page 218—Josh. 2:9-11). It was further prophesied by Isaiah that the Messiah would bring salvation to the Gentiles (Page 692—Is. 49:6). Also in the Psalms there are many invitations to other nations to come and worship the Lord in Israel (Page 548—Ps. 2:10-12; 117:1). Ruth the Moabitess is an example of a foreigner who believed in Israel's God.

It is clear that God's promise to Abraham to bless the whole world through him is still being fulfilled. The life, ministry, and death of Jesus Christ, and the existence and influence of the church today, all came about through God's choice of Israel. All whom the church wins to Christ, whether Jew or Gentile, enter into those great blessings channeled through Israel.

Now turn to Page 432—1 Chr. 28:4-6: Government of Israel.

Law of the Tithes

22 ^RThou shalt truly tithe all the ^Tincrease of thy seed, that the field bringeth forth year by year.   Lev. 27:30 • *what you sow*

23 ^RAnd thou shalt eat before the LORD thy God, in the place which he shall choose to place his name there, the tithe of thy corn, of thy wine, and of thine oil, and ^Rthe firstlings of thy herds and of thy flocks; that thou mayest learn to ^Tfear the LORD thy God always.   12:5-7 • 15:19, 20 • *honour*

24 And if the way be too long for thee, so that thou art not able to carry it; *or* if the place be too far from thee, which the LORD thy God shall choose to set his name there, when the LORD thy God hath blessed thee:

25 Then shalt thou ^Tturn *it* into money, and bind up the money in thine hand, and shalt go unto the place which the LORD thy God shall choose: *exchange it for*

26 And thou shalt ^Tbestow that money for whatsoever thy soul lusteth after, for oxen, or for sheep, or for wine, or for strong drink, or for whatsoever thy soul desireth: and thou shalt eat there before the LORD thy God, and ^Tthou shalt rejoice, thou, and thine household,   *use • do this with gladness*

27 And the Levite that *is* within thy gates; thou shalt not forsake him; for he hath no part nor inheritance with thee.

28 At the end of three years thou shalt bring forth all the tithe of thine increase the same year, and shalt ^Tlay *it* up ^Twithin thy gates: *store it • in your house*

29 And the Levite, (because he hath no part nor inheritance with thee,) and the stranger, and the fatherless, and the widow, which *are* within thy gates, shall come, and shall eat ^Tand be satisfied; that the LORD thy God may bless thee in all the work of thine hand which thou doest.   *as much as they want*

CHAPTER 15

Law of the Debts

AT the end of *every* seven years thou shalt make a ^Trelease.   *cancellation of debts*

2 And this *is* the manner of the release: Every creditor that lendeth *ought* unto his neighbour shall ^Trelease *it;* he shall not exact *it* of his neighbour, or of his brother; because it is called the LORD's release.   *cancel the debt*

3 Of a foreigner thou mayest exact *it* again: ^Rbut *that* which is thine with thy brother thine hand shall release;   23:20

4 Save when there shall be no poor among you; for the LORD shall greatly bless thee in the land which the LORD thy God giveth thee *for* an inheritance to possess it:

5 Only if thou carefully ^Thearken unto the voice of the LORD thy God, to observe to do all these commandments which I command thee this day.   *listen*

6 For the LORD thy God blesseth thee, as he promised thee: and thou shalt lend unto many nations, but thou shalt not borrow; and thou shalt reign over many nations, but they shall not reign over thee.

7 If there be among you a poor man of one of thy brethren within any of thy gates in thy land which the LORD thy God giveth thee, thou shalt not harden thine heart, nor shut thine hand from thy poor brother:

8 But thou shalt open thine hand wide unto him, and shalt surely lend him sufficient for his need, *in that* which he wanteth.

9 Beware that there be not a thought in thy wicked heart, saying, The seventh year, the year of release, is at hand; and thine eye be evil against thy poor brother, and thou givest him nought; and he cry unto the LORD against thee, and it be sin unto thee.

10 Thou shalt surely give him, and ^Rthine heart shall not be ^Tgrieved when thou givest unto him: because that ^Rfor this thing the LORD thy God shall bless thee in all thy works, and in all that thou puttest thine hand unto.   2 Cor. 9:5, 7 • *hurt* • 14:29

11 For ^Rthe poor shall never cease out of the land: therefore I command thee, saying, Thou shalt ^Topen thine hand wide unto thy brother, to thy poor, and to thy needy, in thy land.   John 12:8 • *be liberal in giving unto*

Law of the Slaves

12 *And* ^Rif thy brother, an Hebrew man, or an Hebrew woman, be sold unto thee, and serve thee six years; then in the seventh year thou shalt let him go free from thee.   Ex. 21:2

13 And when thou ^Tsendest him out free from thee, thou shalt not let him go away ^Tempty: *let him go free • with nothing in his hand*

14 Thou shalt furnish him liberally out of thy flock, and out of thy ^Tfloor, and out of thy winepress: *of that* wherewith the LORD thy God hath ^Rblessed thee thou shalt give unto him.   *threshingfloor* • Prov. 10:22

15 And thou shalt remember that thou wast a ^Tbondman in the land of Egypt, and the LORD thy God redeemed thee: therefore I command thee this thing to day.   *slave*

16 And it shall be, ^Rif he say unto thee, I will not go away from thee; because he loveth thee and thine house, because he is ^Twell with thee;   Ex. 21:5, 6 • *fares well*

17 Then thou shalt take an aul, and thrust *it* through his ear unto the door, and he shall be thy servant for ever. And also unto thy maidservant thou shalt do likewise.

18 It shall not seem hard unto thee, when thou sendest him away free from thee; for he hath been worth a double hired servant *to* thee, in serving thee six years: and the LORD thy God shall bless thee in all that thou doest.

Law of Firstlings

19 All the firstling males that come of thy herd and of thy flock thou shalt ᵀsanctify unto the LORD thy God: thou shalt do no work with the firstling of thy bullock, nor shear the firstling of thy sheep.   *set apart*
20 Thou shalt eat *it* before the LORD thy God year by year in the place which the LORD shall choose, thou and thy household.
21 ᴿAnd if there be *any* blemish therein, *as if it be* lame, or blind, *or have* any ill blemish, thou shalt not ᵀsacrifice it unto the LORD thy God.   *Lev. 22:19–25 · offer it*
22 Thou shalt eat it within thy gates: the unclean and the clean *person shall eat it* alike, as the roebuck, and as the hart.
23 Only thou shalt not eat the blood thereof; thou shalt pour it upon the ground as water.

CHAPTER 16

Law of the Feasts

OBSERVE the month of A'-bib, and keep the passover unto the LORD thy God: for in the month of A'-bib the LORD thy God brought thee forth out of Egypt by night.
2 Thou shalt therefore ᵀsacrifice the passover unto the LORD thy God, of the flock and the herd, in the place which the LORD shall choose to place his name there.   *offer*
3 ᴿThou shalt eat no leavened bread with it; seven days shalt thou eat unleavened bread therewith, *even* the bread of affliction; for thou camest forth out of the land of Egypt in haste: that thou mayest remember the day when thou camest forth out of the land of Egypt all the days of thy life.   *Ex. 12:8, 15*
4 And there shall be no leavened bread seen with thee in all thy coast seven days; neither shall there *any* thing of the flesh, which thou sacrificedst the first day at even, remain all night until the morning.
5 Thou mayest not ᵀsacrifice the passover within any of thy ᵀgates, which the LORD thy God giveth thee: *offer · towns*
6 But at the place which the LORD thy God shall choose to place his name in, there thou shalt ᵀsacrifice the passover at even, at the going down of the sun, at the season that thou camest forth out of Egypt.   *offer*
7 And thou shalt roast and eat *it* in the place which the LORD thy God shall choose: and thou shalt ᵀturn in the morning, and go unto thy tents.   *return*
8 Six days thou shalt eat unleavened bread: and ᴿon the seventh day *shall be* a solemn assembly to the LORD thy God: thou shalt do no work *therein.*   *Ex. 12:16*
9 Seven weeks shalt thou number unto thee: begin to number the seven weeks from

such time as thou ᵀbeginnest *to put* the sickle to the corn.   *start to reap the grain*
10 And thou shalt keep the feast of weeks unto the LORD thy God with a tribute of a freewill offering of thine hand, which thou shalt give *unto the LORD thy God,* according as the LORD thy God hath blessed thee:
11 And ᴿthou shalt rejoice before the LORD thy God, thou, and thy son, and thy daughter, and thy manservant, and thy maidservant, and the Levite that *is* within thy gates, and the stranger, and the fatherless, and the widow, that *are* among you, in the place which the LORD thy God hath chosen to place his name there.   *v. 14*
12 And thou shalt remember that thou wast a bondman in Egypt: and thou shalt ᵀobserve and do these statutes.   *take care*
13 Thou shalt observe the feast of tabernacles seven days, after that thou hast gathered in thy ᵀcorn and thy wine: *grain*
14 And thou shalt rejoice in thy feast, thou, and thy son, and thy daughter, and thy manservant, and thy maidservant, and the Levite, the stranger, and the fatherless, and the widow, that *are* within thy gates.
15 Seven days shalt thou keep a solemn feast unto the LORD thy God in the place which the LORD shall choose: because the LORD thy God shall bless thee in all thine increase, and in all the works of thine hands, therefore thou shalt surely rejoice.
16 ᴿThree times in a year shall all thy males appear before the LORD thy God in the place which he shall choose; in the feast of unleavened bread, and in the feast of weeks, and in the feast of tabernacles: and they shall not appear before the LORD ᵀempty: *Ex. 23:14 · without some offering to give*
17 ᴿEvery man *shall give* as he is able, according to the blessing of the LORD thy God which he hath given thee.   *Lev. 14:30, 31*

Law of the Administration of the Judges

18 ᴿJudges and officers shalt thou make thee ᵀin all thy gates, which the LORD thy God giveth thee, throughout thy tribes: and they shall judge the people with just judgment.   *1:16; Ex. 23:1–8 · wherever you live*
19 Thou shalt not wrest judgment; thou shalt not respect persons, neither take ᵀa gift: for a gift doth blind the eyes of the wise, and pervert the words of the righteous.   *a bribe*
20 That which is altogether ᵀjust shalt thou follow, that thou mayest ᴿlive, and inherit the land which the LORD thy God giveth thee.   *fair · Ezek. 18:5*
21 Thou shalt not plant thee a grove of any trees near unto the altar of the LORD thy God, which thou shalt make thee.
22 Neither shalt thou set thee up *any* image; which the LORD thy God hateth.

CHAPTER 17

THOU shalt not sacrifice unto the LORD thy God *any* bullock, or sheep, wherein is blemish, *or* any evilfavouredness: for that *is* an abomination unto the LORD thy God.

2 If there be found among you, within any of thy gates which the LORD thy God giveth thee, man or woman, that hath wrought wickedness in the sight of the LORD thy God, in transgressing his covenant,

3 And hath gone and served other gods, and worshipped them, either Rthe sun, or moon, or any of the host of heaven, Rwhich I have not commanded;   4:19 · Jer. 7:22

4 And it be told thee, and thou hast heard *of it*, and enquired diligently, and, behold, *it be* true, *and* the thing certain, *that* such abomination is wrought in Israel:

5 Then shalt thou bring forth that man or that woman, which have committed that wicked thing, Tunto thy gates, *even* that man or that woman, and shalt Tstone them with stones, till they die.   in public · execute

6 At the mouth of two witnesses, or three witnesses, shall he that is worthy of death be put to death; *but* at the mouth of one witness he shall not be put to death.

7 The hands of the witnesses shall be first upon him to put him to death, and afterward the hands of all the people. So thou shalt put the evil away from among you.

8 If there arise a matter too hard for thee in judgment, between blood and blood, between plea and plea, and between stroke and stroke, *being* matters of Tcontroversy within thy gates: then shalt thou arise, and get thee up into the place which the LORD thy God shall choose;   argument

9 And thou shalt come unto the priests the Levites, and unto the judge that shall be in those days, and enquire; and they shall shew thee the sentence of judgment:

10 And thou shalt do according to the sentence, which they of that place which the LORD shall choose shall shew thee; and thou shalt observe to do according to all that they Tinform thee: advise

11 RAccording to the Tsentence of the law which they shall teach thee, and according to the judgment which they shall tell thee, thou shalt do: thou shalt not decline from the sentence which they shall shew thee, to the right hand, nor to the left.   25:1 · terms

12 And the man that will do Tpresumptuously, and will not Thearken unto the priest that standeth to minister there before the LORD thy God, or unto the judge, even that man shall die: and thou shalt put away the evil from Israel.   willfully · listen

13 And all the people shall hear, and fear, and do no more Tpresumptuously.   willfully

Law of the Administration of the King

14 When thou art come unto the land which the LORD thy God giveth thee, and shalt possess it, and shalt dwell therein, and shalt say, RI will set a king over me, like as all the nations that *are* about me;   1 Sam. 8:5

15 Thou shalt in any wise Tset *him* king over thee, Rwhom the LORD thy God shall choose: *one* Rfrom among thy brethren shalt thou set king over thee: thou mayest not set a Tstranger over thee, which *is* not thy brother.   install · 1 Sam. 10:24 · Jer. 30:21 · foreigner

16 But he shall not multiply horses to himself, nor Rcause the people to return to Egypt, to the end that he should multiply horses: forasmuch as the LORD hath said unto you, RYe shall henceforth return no more that way.   Is. 31:1 · 28:68

17 Neither shall he Tmultiply wives to himself, that his heart turn not away: neither shall he greatly Tmultiply to himself silver and gold.   take a harem · accumulate wealth

18 And it shall be, when he sitteth upon the throne of his kingdom, that he shall write him a copy of this law in a book out of *that which is* before the priests the Levites:

19 And Rit shall be with him, and he shall read therein all the days of his life: that he may learn to Tfear the LORD his God, to keep all the words of this law and these statutes, to do them: Ps. 119:97, 98 · honour

20 RThat his heart be not lifted up above his brethren, and that he Tturn not aside from the commandment, *to* the right hand, or *to* the left: to the end that he may prolong *his* days in his kingdom, he, and his children, in the midst of Israel.   John 1:45 ☆ · deviate

CHAPTER 18

Law of the Administration
of the Priest and Prophet

THE priests the Levites, *and* all the tribe of Levi, shall have no part nor inheritance with Israel: they shall eat the offerings of the LORD made by fire, and his inheritance.

2 Therefore shall they have no inheritance among their brethren: the LORD *is* their inheritance, as he hath said unto them.

3 And this shall be the priest's Tdue from the people, from them that offer a sacrifice, whether *it be* ox or sheep; and Rthey shall give unto the priest the shoulder, and the two cheeks, and the maw.   right · Lev. 7:30-34

4 The firstfruit *also* of thy corn, of thy wine, and of thine oil, and the first of the fleece of thy sheep, shalt thou give him.

5 For Rthe LORD thy God hath chosen him out of all thy tribes, Rto stand to minister in the name of the LORD, him and his sons for ever.   Ex. 28:1; 29:9 · 10:8

6 And if a Levite come from any of thy gates out of all Israel, where he sojourned, and come with all the desire of his mind unto the place which the LORD shall choose;

7 Then he shall minister in the name of the LORD his God, as all his brethren the Levites *do,* which stand there before the LORD.

8 They shall have ᵀlike portions to eat, beside that which cometh of the sale of his ᵀpatrimony. *the same for each • inheritance*

9 When thou art come into the land which the LORD thy God giveth thee, ᴿthou shalt not learn to do after the ᵀabominations of those nations. Lev. 18:26, 27, 30 • *evil practices*

10 There shall not be found among you *any* one that maketh his son or his daughter to ᵀpass through the fire, *or* that useth divination, *or* an observer of times, or an enchanter, or a witch, *a pagan religious rite*

11 ᴿOr a charmer, or a consulter with familiar spirits, or a wizard, or a ᴿnecromancer. Lev. 20:27 • 1 Sam. 28:7

12 For all that do these things *are* an abomination unto the LORD: and because of these abominations the LORD thy God doth drive them out from before thee.

13 Thou shalt be ᵀperfect with the LORD thy God. *entirely obedient*

14 For these nations, which thou shalt possess, hearkened unto observers of times, and unto diviners: but as for thee, the LORD thy God hath not suffered thee so *to do.*

15 ᴿThe LORD thy God will raise up unto thee a Prophet from the midst of thee, of thy brethren, like unto me; unto him ye shall hearken; John 1:45; Acts 3:22 ✶

16 According to all that thou desiredst of the LORD thy God in Ho′-reb in the day of the assembly, saying, Let me not hear again the voice of the LORD my God, neither let me see this great fire any more, that I die not.

17 And the LORD said unto me, ᴿThey have well *spoken that* which they have spoken. 5:28

18 ᴿI will raise them up a Prophet from among their brethren, like unto thee, and ᴿwill put my words in his mouth; ᴿand he shall speak unto them all that I shall command him. Acts 7:37 • Is. 51:16 • John 4:25; 6:14 ✶

19 ᴿAnd it shall come to pass, *that* whosoever will not hearken ᴿunto my words which he shall speak in my name, I will require *it* of him. Acts 3:23 ✶ • Matt. 17:5

20 But the prophet, which shall ᵀpresume to speak a word in my name, which I have not commanded him to speak, or ᴿthat shall speak in the name of other gods, even that prophet shall die. *dare to assume* • Jer. 2:8

21 And if thou say in thine heart, How shall we know the word which the LORD hath not spoken?

22 ᴿWhen a prophet speaketh in the name of the LORD, if the thing follow not, nor come to pass, that *is* the thing which the LORD hath

not spoken, *but* the prophet hath spoken it ᴿpresumptuously: thou shalt not be afraid of him. Jer. 28:9 • *v.* 20

CHAPTER 19

Cities of Refuge

WHEN the LORD thy God ᴿhath ᵀcut off the nations, whose land the LORD thy God giveth thee, and thou succeedest them, and dwellest in their cities, and in their houses; 12:29 • *destroyed*

2 Thou shalt separate three cities for thee in the midst of thy land, which the LORD thy God giveth thee to possess it.

3 Thou shalt prepare thee a way, and divide the coasts of thy land, which the LORD thy God giveth thee to inherit, into three parts, that every slayer may flee thither.

4 And ᴿthis *is* the case of the slayer, which shall flee thither, that he may live: Whoso killeth his neighbour ᵀignorantly, whom he hated not in time past; 4:42 • *unawares*

5 As when a man goeth into the wood with his neighbour to hew wood, and his hand fetcheth a stroke with the axe to cut down the tree, and the ᵀhead slippeth from the ᵀhelve, and ᵀlighteth upon his neighbour, that he die; he shall flee unto one of those cities, and live: *iron • handle • strikes*

6 Lest the avenger of the blood pursue the slayer, while his heart is hot, and overtake him, because the way is long, and slay him; whereas he *was* not worthy of death, inasmuch as he hated him not in time past.

7 Wherefore I command thee, saying, Thou shalt separate three cities for thee.

8 And if the LORD thy God ᴿenlarge thy coast, as he hath sworn unto thy fathers, and give thee all the land which he promised to give unto thy fathers; Gen. 15:18

9 If thou shalt keep all these commandments to do them, which I command thee this day, to love the LORD thy God, and to walk ever in his ways; then shalt thou add three cities more for thee, beside these three:

10 That innocent blood be not shed in thy land, which the LORD thy God giveth thee *for* an inheritance, and *so* blood be upon thee.

11 But if any man hate his neighbour, and ᵀlie in wait for him, and rise up against him, and smite him mortally that he die, and fleeth into one of these cities: *plan to kill*

12 Then the elders of his city shall send and fetch him thence, and deliver him into the hand of the avenger of blood, that he may die.

13 ᴿThine eye shall not pity him, but thou shalt put away *the guilt of* innocent blood from Israel, that it may go well with thee. 13:8

14 ᴿThou shalt not remove thy neighbour's landmark, which they of old time have set in

thine inheritance, which thou shalt inherit in the land that the LORD thy God giveth thee to possess it.   Hos. 5:10

Law of Witnesses

15 One witness shall not rise up against a man for any iniquity, or for any sin, in any sin that he sinneth: at the mouth of two witnesses, or at the mouth of three witnesses, shall the matter be established.

16 If a false witness ^Rrise up against any man to testify against him^R *that which is* wrong;   Ps. 27:12; 35:11 · Ex. 23:1

17 Then both the men, between whom the controversy *is*, shall stand before the LORD, ^Rbefore the priests and the judges, which shall be in those days;   17:9; 21:5

18 And the judges shall make diligent ^Tinquisition: and, behold, *if* the witness *be* a false witness, *and* hath testified falsely against his brother;   *enquiry, investigation*

19 Then shall ye do unto him, as he had thought to have done unto his brother: so shalt thou put the evil away from among you.

20 ^RAnd those which remain shall hear, and fear, and shall henceforth commit no more any such evil among you.   17:13

21 ^RAnd thine eye shall not pity; *but* ^Rlife *shall* go for life, eye for eye, tooth for tooth, hand for hand, foot for foot.   *v.* 13 · Matt. 5:38

CHAPTER 20

Law of Warfare

WHEN thou goest out to battle against thine enemies, and seest ^Rhorses, and chariots, *and* a people more than thou, ^Rbe not afraid of them: for the LORD thy God *is* with thee, which brought thee up out of the land of Egypt.   Ps. 20:7 · 7:18

2 And it shall be, when ye are come nigh unto the battle, that the priest shall approach and speak unto the people,

3 And shall say unto them, Hear, O Israel, ye approach this day unto battle against your enemies: let not your hearts faint, fear not, and do not tremble, ^Rneither be ye terrified because of them;   Josh. 23:10

4 For the LORD your God *is* he that goeth with you, ^Rto fight for you against your enemies, to save you.   1:30; 3:22; Josh. 23:10

5 And the officers shall speak unto the people, saying, What man *is there* that hath built a new house, and hath not dedicated it? let him go and return to his house, lest he die in the battle, and another man dedicate it.

6 And what man *is he* that hath planted a vineyard, and hath not *yet* eaten of it? let him *also* go and return unto his house, lest he die in the battle, and another man eat of it.

7 And what man *is there* that hath betrothed a wife, and hath not taken her? let him go and return unto his house, lest he die in the battle, and another man take her.

8 And the officers shall speak further unto the people, and they shall say, What man *is there that is* fearful and fainthearted? let him go and return unto his house, lest his brethren's heart faint as well as his heart.

9 And it shall be, when the officers have made an end of speaking unto the people, that they shall make captains of the armies to lead the people.

10 When thou comest nigh unto a city to fight against it, then proclaim peace unto it.

11 And it shall be, if it make thee answer of peace, and open unto thee, then it shall be, *that* all the people *that is* found therein shall be ^Ttributaries unto thee, ^Rand they shall serve thee.   *servants* · 1 Kin. 9:21

12 And if it will make no peace with thee, but will make war against thee, then thou shalt besiege it:

13 And when the LORD thy God hath delivered it into thine hands, ^Rthou shalt smite every male thereof with the edge of the sword: Num. 31:7

14 But the women, and the little ones, and the cattle, and all that is in the city, *even* all the spoil thereof, shalt thou take unto thyself; and thou shalt eat the spoil of thine enemies, which the LORD thy God hath given thee.

15 Thus shalt thou do unto all the cities which *are* very far off from thee, which *are* not of the cities of these nations.

16 But ^Rof the cities of these people, which the LORD thy God doth give thee *for* an inheritance, thou shalt save alive nothing that breatheth: 7:1, 2; Num. 21:2, 3, 35; 33:52

17 But thou shalt utterly destroy them; *namely*, the Hit'-tites, and the Am'-or-ites, the Ca'-naan-ites, and the Per'-iz-zites, the Hi'-vites, and the Jeb'-u-sites; as the LORD thy God hath commanded thee:

18 That they teach you not to do after all their ^Tabominations, which they have done unto their gods; so should ye sin against the LORD your God.   *evil ways*

19 When thou shalt besiege a city a long time, in making war against it to take it, thou shalt not destroy the trees thereof by forcing an ax against them: for thou mayest eat of them, and thou shalt not cut them down (for the tree of the field *is* man's *life*) to employ *them* in the siege:

20 Only the trees which thou knowest that they *be* not trees for meat, thou shalt destroy and cut them down; and thou shalt build bulwarks against the city that maketh war with thee, until it be subdued.

CHAPTER 21

Law of Unknown Murder

IF one be found slain in the land which the LORD thy God giveth thee to possess it, lying in the field, and it be not known who hath slain him:

2 Then thy elders and thy judges shall come forth, and they shall measure unto the cities which are round about him that is slain:

3 And it shall be, that the city which is next unto the slain man, even the elders of that city shall take an heifer, which Thath not been wrought with, and which hath not drawn in the yoke;   has not been harnessed for work

4 And the elders of that city shall bring down the heifer unto a rough valley, which is neither eared nor sown, and shall strike off the heifer's neck there in the valley:

5 And the priests the sons of Levi shall come near; for them the LORD thy God hath chosen to minister unto him, and to bless in the name of the LORD; and Rby their word shall every Tcontroversy and every Tstroke be tried: 17:8, 9 • argument • conflict

6 And all the elders of that city, that are next unto the slain man, Rshall wash their hands over the heifer that is beheaded in the valley: 26:6; Matt. 27:24

7 And they shall answer and say, Our hands have not shed this blood, neither have our eyes seen it.

8 Be merciful, O LORD, unto thy people Israel, whom thou hast redeemed, and lay not innocent blood unto thy people of Israel's charge. And the blood shall be forgiven them.

9 So Rshalt thou put away the guilt of innocent blood from among you, when thou shalt do that which is right in the sight of the LORD.   19:13

Law of Marriage

10 When thou goest forth to war against thine enemies, and the LORD thy God hath delivered them into thine hands, and thou hast taken them captive,

11 And seest among the captives a beautiful woman, and hast a desire unto her, that thou wouldest have her to thy wife;

12 Then thou shalt bring her home to thine house; Rand she shall shave her head, and Tpare her nails;   Lev. 14:8, 9; Num. 6:9 • cut

13 And she shall put the raiment of her captivity from off her, and shall remain in thine house, and Rbewail T her father and her mother a full month: and after that thou shalt go in unto her, and be her husband, and she shall be thy wife.   Ps. 45:10 • mourn

14 And it shall be, if thou have no delight in her, then thou shalt let her go whither she will; but thou shalt not sell her at all for money, thou shalt not make merchandise of her, because thou hast humbled her.

15 If a man have two wives, one beloved, and another hated, and they have born him children, both the beloved and the hated; and if the firstborn son be her's that was hated:

16 Then it shall be, Rwhen he maketh his sons to inherit that which he hath, that he may not make the son of the beloved firstborn before the son of the hated, which is indeed the firstborn: 1 Chr. 5:2; 26:10

17 But he shall acknowledge the son of the hated for the firstborn, by giving him a double portion of all that he hath: for he is Rthe beginning of his strength; Rthe right of the firstborn is his.   Gen. 49:3 • Gen. 25:31, 33

Law of the Rebellious Son

18 If a man have a Rstubborn and rebellious son, which will not obey the voice of his father, or the voice of his mother, and that, when they have chastened him, will not hearken unto them: Ps. 32:9

19 Then shall his father and his mother lay hold on him, and bring him out unto the elders of his city, and unto the gate of his place;

20 And they shall say unto the elders of his city, This our son is stubborn and rebellious, he will not obey our voice; he is a glutton, and a drunkard.

21 And all the men of his city shall stone him with stones, that he die: Rso shalt thou put evil away from among you; Rand all Israel shall hear, and fear.   13:5 • 13:11

22 And if a man have committed a sin Rworthy of death, and he be to be put to death, and thou hang him on a tree: 19:6

23 RHis body shall not remain all night upon the tree, but thou shalt in any wise bury him that day; (for he that is hanged is accursed of God;) that thy land be not defiled, which the LORD thy God giveth thee for an inheritance.   [John 19:31; Gal. 3:13]

CHAPTER 22

Law of the Brother's Property

THOU shalt not see thy brother's ox or his sheep go astray, and hide thyself from them: thou shalt in any case bring them again unto thy brother.

2 And if thy brother be not nigh unto thee, or if thou know him not, then thou shalt bring it unto thine own house, and it shall be with thee until thy brother seek after it, and thou shalt restore it to him again.

3 In like manner shalt thou do with his ass; and so shalt thou do with his raiment; and with all lost thing of thy brother's, which he hath lost, and thou hast found, shalt thou do likewise: thou mayest not hide thyself.

4 RThou shalt not see thy brother's ass or his ox fall down by Tthe way, and hide thyself

from them: thou shalt surely help him to lift *them* up again.   Ex. 23:5 • *roadside*

Law of Separation

5 The woman shall not wear that which pertaineth unto a man, neither shall a man put on a woman's garment: for all that do so *are* abomination unto the LORD thy God.

6 If a bird's nest chance to be before thee in the way in any tree, or on the ground, *whether they be* young ones, or eggs, and the ᵀdam sitting upon the young, or upon the eggs, ᴿthou shalt not take the dam with the young: *mother* • Lev. 22:28

7 *But* thou shalt in any wise let the dam go, and take the young to thee; that it may be well with thee, and *that* thou mayest ᵀprolong *thy* days.   *continue in blessedness*

8 When thou buildest a new house, then thou shalt make a ᵀbattlement for thy roof, that thou bring not blood upon thine house, if any man fall from thence.   *railing*

9 ᴿThou shalt not sow thy vineyard with ᵀdivers seeds: lest the fruit of thy seed which thou hast sown, and the fruit of thy vineyard, be defiled.   Lev. 19:19 • *different*

10 ᴿThou shalt not plow with an ox and an ass together.   [2 Cor. 6:14–16]

11 Thou shalt not wear a garment of divers sorts, *as* of woollen and linen together.

12 Thou shalt make thee fringes upon the four ᵀquarters of thy ᵀvesture, wherewith thou coverest *thyself*.   *sides* • *garment*

Law of Marriage

13 If any man take a wife, and go in unto her, ᴿand hate her,   24:1, 3

14 And give occasions of speech against her, and bring up an evil name upon her, and say, I took this woman, and when I came to her, I found her not a maid:

15 Then shall the father of the damsel, and her mother, take and bring forth *the tokens of* the damsel's virginity unto the elders of the city in the gate:

16 And the damsel's father shall say unto the elders, I gave my daughter unto this man ᵀto wife, and he hateth her;   *in marriage*

17 And, lo, he hath given occasions of speech against her, saying, I found notᵀ thy daughter a maid; and yet these *are the tokens of* my daughter's virginity. And they shall spread the cloth before the elders of the city.   *the tokens of virginity*

18 And the elders of that city shall take that man and chastise him;

19 And they shall ᵀamerce him in an ᵀhundred *shek'-els* of silver, and give *them* unto the father of the damsel, because he hath brought up an evil name upon a virgin of Israel: and she shall be his wife; he may not put her away all his days.   *fine* • *$728*

20 But if this thing be true, *and the tokens of* virginity be not found for the damsel:

21 Then they shall bring out the damsel to the door of her father's house, and the men of her city shall stone her with stones that she die: because she hath wrought folly in Israel, to play the whore in her father's house: so shalt thou put evil away from among you.

22 ᴿIf a man be found lying with a woman married to an husband, then they shall both of them die, *both* the man that lay with the woman, and the woman: so shalt thou put away evil from Israel.   John 8:5

23 If a damsel *that is* a virgin be ᴿbetrothed unto an husband, and a man find her in the city, and lie with her;   Matt. 1:18

24 Then ye shall bring them both out unto the gate of that city, and ye shall stone them with stones that they die; the damsel, because she cried not, *being* in the city; and the man, because he hath ᴿhumbled his neighbour's wife: ᴿso thou shalt put away evil from among you.   21:14 • *vv*. 21, 22

25 But if a man find a betrothed damsel in the field, and the man ᵀforce her, and lie with her: then the man only that lay with her shall die: *rape*

26 But unto the damsel thou shalt do nothing; *there is* in the damsel no sin *worthy* of death: for as when a man riseth against his neighbour, and slayeth him, even so *is* this matter:

27 For he found her in the field, *and* the betrothed damsel cried, and *there was* none to save her.

28 If a man find a damsel *that is* a virgin, which is not betrothed, and lay hold on her, and lie with her, and they be found;

29 Then the man that lay with her shall give unto the damsel's father ᴿfiftyᵀ *shek'-els* of silver, and she shall be his wife; ᴿbecause he hath humbled her, he may not put her away all his days.   *$88* • Ex. 22:16 • *v*. 24

30 ᴿA man shall not take his father's wife, nor discover his father's skirt.   1 Cor. 5:1

CHAPTER 23

Law of Acceptance into the Congregation

HE that is wounded in the stones, or hath his privy member cut off, shall not enter into the congregation of the LORD.

2 A bastard shall not enter into the congregation of the LORD; even to his tenth generation shall he not ᵀenter into the congregation of the LORD.   *serve as a priest*

3 An Am'-mon-ite or Mo'-ab-ite shall not enter into the congregation of the LORD; even to their tenth generation shall they not enter into the congregation of the LORD for ever:

4 Because they met you not with bread and with water in the way, when ye came

forth out of Egypt; and because they hired against thee Ba'-laam the son of Be'-or of Pe'-thor of Mes-o-po-ta'-mi-a, to curse thee.

5 Nevertheless the LORD thy God would not hearken unto Ba'-laam; but the LORD thy God turned the curse into a blessing unto thee, because the LORD thy God loved thee.

6 Thou shalt not seek their peace nor their prosperity all thy days for ever.

7 Thou shalt not abhor an E'-dom-ite; ᴿfor he *is* thy brother: thou shalt not abhor an Egyptian; because ᴿthou wast a stranger in his land.   Obad. 8-16 · 10:19; Lev. 19:34

8 The children that are begotten of them shall enter into the congregation of the LORD in their third generation.

9 When the host goeth forth against thine enemies, then keep thee from every wicked thing.

10 ᴿIf there be among you any man, that is not clean by reason of uncleanness that chanceth him by night, then shall he go abroad out of the camp, he shall not come within the camp: Lev. 15:16

11 But it shall be, when evening cometh on, ᴿhe shall wash *himself* with water: and when the sun is down, he shall come into the camp *again*.   Lev. 15:5

12 Thou shalt have a place also without the camp, whither thou shalt go forth abroad:

13 And thou shalt have a ᵀpaddle upon thy weapon; and it shall be, when thou wilt ease thyself abroad, thou shalt dig therewith, and shalt turn back and cover that which cometh from thee;   *shovel*

14 For the LORD thy God walketh in the midst of thy camp, to deliver thee, and to give up thine enemies before thee; therefore shall thy camp be holy: that he see no unclean thing in thee, and turn away from thee.

15 ᴿThou shalt not ᵀdeliver unto his master the servant which is escaped from his master unto thee: 1 Sam. 30:15 · *return to bondage*

16 He shall dwell with thee, *even* among you, in that place which he shall choose in one of thy gates, where it ᵀliketh him best: thou shalt not oppress him.   *pleases*

17 There shall be no whore ᴿof the daughters of Israel, nor ᴿa sodomite of the sons of Israel.   Prov. 2:16 · Gen. 19:5; 2 Kin. 23:7

18 Thou shalt not bring the hire of a whore,ᴿ or the price of a dog, into the house of the LORD thy God for any vow: for even both these *are* ᵀabomination unto the LORD thy God.   Lev. 18:22; 20:13 · *an evil thing*

19 Thou shalt not lend upon usury to thy brother; usury of money, usury of victuals, usury of any thing that is lent upon usury:

20 ᴿUnto a stranger thou mayest lend upon usury; but unto thy brother thou shalt not lend upon usury: ᴿthat the LORD thy God may bless thee in all that thou settest thine

hand to in the land whither thou goest to possess it.   15:3 · 15:10

21 When thou shalt vow a vow unto the LORD thy God, thou shalt not ᵀslack to pay it: for the LORD thy God will surely require it of thee; and it would be sin in thee.   *be slow*

22 But if thou shalt ᵀforbear to vow, it shall be no sin in thee.   *restrain from vowing*

23 ᴿThat which is gone out of thy lips thou shalt keep and perform; *even* a freewill offering, according as thou hast vowed unto the LORD thy God, which thou hast promised with thy mouth.   Ps. 66:13, 14

Laws for Harmony in the Nation

24 When thou comest into thy neighbour's vineyard, then thou mayest eat grapes thy fill at thine own pleasure; but thou shalt not put *any* in thy vessel.

25 When thou comest into the standing corn of thy neighbour, ᴿthen thou mayest pluck the ears with thine hand; but thou shalt not ᵀmove a sickle unto thy neighbour's standing corn.   Luke 6:1 · *begin to reap*

CHAPTER 24

WHEN a man hath taken a wife, and married her, and it come to pass that she find no favour in his eyes, because he hath found some uncleanness in her: then let him write her a bill of divorcement, and give *it* in her hand, and send her out of his house.

2 And when she is departed out of his house, she may go and be another man's *wife*.

3 And *if* the latter husband hate her, and write her a bill of divorcement, and giveth *it* in her hand, and sendeth her out of his house; or if the latter husband die, which took her *to be* his wife;

4 Her former husband, which sent her away, may not take her again to be his wife, after that she is defiled; for that *is* abomination before the LORD: and thou shalt not cause the land to sin, which the LORD thy God giveth thee *for* an inheritance.

5 When a man hath taken a new wife, he shall not go out to war, neither shall he be charged with any business: *but* he shall be free at home one year, and shall ᴿcheer up his wife which he hath taken.   Prov. 5:18

6 No man shall take the ᵀnether or the upper millstone to ᴿpledge: for he taketh *a man's* life to pledge.   *lower* · vv. 10–13; Ex. 22:26

7 If a man be found stealing any of his brethren of the children of Israel, and maketh merchandise of him, or selleth him; then that thief shall die; and thou shalt put evil away from among you.

8 Take heed in ᴿthe plague of leprosy, that thou ᵀobserve diligently, and do according to

all that the priests the Levites shall teach you: as I commanded them, *so* ye shall observe to do.   Lev. 13:2 • *be cautious*

9 Remember what the LORD thy God did unto [R]Miriam by the way, after that ye were come forth out of Egypt.   Num. 12:10

10 When thou dost [R]lend thy brother any thing, thou shalt not go into his house [T]to fetch his pledge.   [Matt. 5:42] • *secure some collateral*

11 Thou shalt stand abroad, and the man to whom thou dost lend shall bring out the pledge abroad unto thee.

12 And if the man *be* poor, thou shalt [T]not sleep with his pledge: *not keep it overnight*

13 [R]In any case thou shalt deliver him the pledge again when the sun goeth down, that he may sleep in his own raiment, and bless thee: and it shall be righteousness unto thee before the LORD thy God.   Ex. 22:26

14 Thou shalt not [R]oppress an hired servant *that is* poor and needy, *whether he be* of thy brethren, or of thy strangers that *are* in thy land within thy gates: [Mal. 3:5]

15 [T]At his day thou shalt give *him* his hire, neither shall the sun go down upon it; for he *is* poor, and setteth his heart upon it: lest he cry against thee unto the LORD, and it be sin unto thee.   *pay him wages each day*

16 The fathers shall not be put to death for the children, neither shall the children be put to death for the fathers: every man shall be put to death for his own sin.

17 [R]Thou shalt not pervert the judgment of the stranger, *nor* of the fatherless; nor take a widow's raiment to pledge: Prov. 22:22

18 But [R]thou shalt remember that thou wast a [T]bondman in Egypt, and the LORD thy God redeemed thee thence: therefore I command thee to do this thing.   *v. 22 • slave*

19 [R]When thou cuttest down thine harvest in thy field, and hast forgot [T]a sheaf in the field, thou shalt not go again to fetch it: it shall be for the stranger, [R]for the fatherless, and for the widow: that the LORD thy God may [R]bless thee in all the work of thine hands.   Lev. 19:9 • *2,087 qt.* • 15:10 • Ps. 41:1

20 [R]When thou beatest thine olive tree, thou shalt not go over the boughs again: it shall be for the stranger, for the fatherless, and for the widow.   Lev. 19:10

21 When thou gatherest the grapes of thy vineyard, thou shalt not glean *it* afterward: it shall be for the stranger, for the fatherless, and for the widow.

22 And thou shalt remember that thou wast a [R]bondman in the land of Egypt: therefore I command thee to do this thing.   *v. 18*

CHAPTER 25

IF there be a [T]controversy between men, and they come [T]unto judgment, that the *judges* may judge them; then they [R]shall justify the righteous, and condemn the wicked.   *conflict • to a judge* • Prov. 17:15

2 And it shall be, if the wicked man *be* [R]worthy to be beaten, that the judge shall cause him to lie down, [R]and to be beaten before his face, according to his fault, by a certain number.   Luke 12:48 • Matt. 10:17

3 Forty stripes he may give him, *and* not exceed: lest, *if* he should exceed, and beat him above these with many stripes, then thy brother should seem vile unto thee.

4 [R]Thou shalt not muzzle the ox when he [T]treadeth out *the corn*.   [Prov. 12:10] • *thresheth*

5 If brethren dwell together, and one of them die, and have no child, the wife of the dead shall not marry without unto a stranger: her husband's brother shall go in unto her, and take her to him to wife, and perform the duty of an husband's brother unto her.

6 And it shall be, *that* the firstborn which she beareth [R]shall succeed in the name of his brother *which is* dead, that [R]his name be not put out of Israel.   Gen. 38:9 • Ruth 4:10

7 And if the man like not to take his brother's wife, then let his brother's wife go up to the gate unto the elders, and say, My husband's brother refuseth to raise up unto his brother a name in Israel, he will not perform the duty of my husband's brother.

8 Then the elders of his city shall call him, and speak unto him: and *if* he stand *to it*, and say, [R]I like not to take her;   Ruth 4:6

9 Then shall his brother's wife come unto him in the presence of the elders, and [T]loose his shoe from off his foot, and spit in his face, and shall answer and say, So shall it be done unto that man that will not build up his brother's house.   *take off his shoe*

10 And his name shall be called in Israel, The house of him that hath his shoe loosed.

11 When men strive together one with another, and the wife of the one draweth near for to deliver her husband out of the hand of him that smiteth him, and putteth forth her hand, and taketh him by [T]the secrets: *the genitals*

12 Then thou shalt cut off her hand, [R]thine eye shall not pity *her*.   7:2; 19:13

13 Thou shalt not have in thy bag [T]divers weights, a great and a small.   *different*

14 Thou shalt not have in thine house divers measures, a great and a small.

15 *But* thou shalt have a perfect and just weight, [R]a perfect and just measure shalt thou have: [R]that thy days may be lengthened in the land which the LORD thy God giveth thee.   Prov. 11:1; [Rom. 12:17] • Ex. 20:12

16 For [R]all that do such things, *and* all that do unrighteously, *are* an [T]abomination unto the LORD thy God.   [1 Thess. 4:6] • *evil things*

17 [R]Remember what Am'-a-lek did unto

thee by the way, when ye were come forth out of Egypt;   Ex. 17:8; 1 Sam. 15:1–3

18 How he met thee by the way, and smote the hindmost of thee, *even* all *that were* feeble behind thee, when thou *wast* faint and weary; and he feared not God.

19 Therefore it shall be, when the LORD thy God hath given thee rest from all thine enemies round about, in the land which the LORD thy God giveth thee *for* an inheritance to possess it, *that* thou shalt ᴿblot out the remembrance of Am′-a-lek from under heaven; thou shalt not forget *it*.   Ex. 17:14

CHAPTER 26

Law of the Tithe

AND it shall be, when thou *art* come in unto the land which the LORD thy God giveth thee *for* an inheritance, and possessest it, and dwellest therein;

2 ᴿThat thou shalt take of the first of all the fruit of the earth, which thou shalt bring of thy land that the LORD thy God giveth thee, and shalt put *it* in a basket, and shalt go unto the place which the LORD thy God shall choose to place his name there.   Num. 18:13

3 And thou shalt go unto the priest that shall be in those days, and say unto him, I profess this day unto the LORD thy God, that I am come unto the country which the LORD sware unto our fathers for to give us.

4 And the priest shall take the basket out of thine hand, and set it down before the altar of the LORD thy God.

5 And thou shalt speak and say before the LORD thy God, A Syrian ready to perish *was* my father, and he went down into Egypt, and sojourned there with a few, and became there a nation, great, mighty, and populous:

6 And the ᴿEgyptians ᵀevil entreated us, and afflicted us, and laid upon us hard ᵀbondage: Ex. 1:11, 14 · *treated us harshly · slavery*

7 And ᴿwhen we cried unto the LORD God of our fathers, the LORD heard our voice, and looked on our affliction, and our labour, and our oppression: Ex. 2:22–25; 3:9; 4:31

8 And the LORD brought us forth out of Egypt with a mighty hand, and with an outstretched arm, and with great terribleness, and with signs, and with wonders:

9 And he hath brought us into this place, and hath given us this land, *even* ᴿa land that floweth with milk and honey.   Ex. 3:8

10 And now, behold, I have brought the firstfruits of the land, which thou, O LORD, hast given me. And thou shalt ᵀset it before the LORD thy God, and worship before the LORD thy God: *offer it as an offering*

11 And ᴿthou shalt rejoice in every good *thing* which the LORD thy God hath given unto thee, and unto thine house, thou, and the Levite, and the stranger that *is* among you.   12:7, 12, 18; 16:11

12 When thou hast made an end of tithing all the ᴿtithes of thine increase the third year, *which is* the year of tithing, and hast given *it* unto the Levite, the stranger, the fatherless, and the widow, that they may eat within thy gates, and be filled;   Lev. 27:30

13 Then thou shalt say before the LORD thy God, I have brought away the hallowed things out of *mine* house, and also have given them unto the Levite, and unto the stranger, to the fatherless, and to the widow, according to all thy commandments which thou hast commanded me: I have not transgressed thy commandments, ᴿneither have I forgotten *them*:   Ps. 119:141

14 I have not eaten thereof in ᵀmy mourning, neither have I taken away *ought* thereof for *any* ᵀunclean *use*, nor given *ought* thereof for the dead: *but* I have hearkened to the voice of the LORD my God, *and* have done according to all that thou hast commanded me.   *my own distress · unfit*

15 ᴿLook down from thy holy habitation, from heaven, and bless thy people Israel, and the land which thou hast given us, as thou swarest unto our fathers, a land that floweth with milk and honey.   Is. 63:15

Vow of Israel and of God

16 This day the LORD thy God hath commanded thee to do these statutes and ᵀjudgments: thou shalt therefore keep and do them with all thine heart, and with all thy soul.   *decisions*

17 Thou hast ᴿavouched ᵀthe LORD this day to be thy God, and to walk in his ways, and to keep his statutes, and his commandments, and his judgments, and to hearken unto his voice: Ex. 20:19 · *publicly claimed*

18 And ᴿthe LORD hath avouched thee this day to be his ᵀpeculiar people, as he hath promised thee, and that *thou* shouldest keep all his commandments;   Ex. 6:7 · *special*

19 And to ᵀmake thee high above all nations which he hath made, in praise, and in name, and in honour; and that thou mayest be an ᵀholy people unto the LORD thy God, as he hath spoken.   *lift you above · his use only*

CHAPTER 27

Erection of the Altar

AND Moses with the elders of Israel commanded the people, saying, ᵀKeep all the ᴿcommandments which I command you this day.   *obey · Josh. 22:5*

2 And it shall be on the day ᴿwhen ye shall pass over Jordan unto the land which the LORD thy God giveth thee, that ᴿthou shalt

set thee up great stones, and plaister them with plaister: Josh. 4:1 • Josh. 8:30-32

3 And thou shalt write upon them all the words of this law, when thou art passed over, that thou mayest go in unto the land which the LORD thy God giveth thee, a land that Rfloweth with milk and honey; as the LORD God of thy fathers hath promised thee. 26:9

4 Therefore it shall be when ye be gone over Jordan, that ye shall set up these stones, which I command you this day, Rin mount E'-bal, and thou shalt plaister them with plaister. 11:29; Josh. 8:30, 31

5 And there shalt thou build an altar unto the LORD thy God, an altar of stones: thou shalt not lift up any iron tool upon them.

6 Thou shalt build the altar of the LORD thy God of Twhole stones: and thou shalt offer burnt offerings thereon unto the LORD thy God: uncut

7 And thou shalt offer peace offerings, and shalt eat there, and Rrejoice before the LORD thy God. 26:11

8 And thou shalt write upon the stones all the words of this Rlaw very plainly. Josh. 8:32

Admonition to Obey the Law

9 And Moses and the priests the Levites spake unto all Israel, saying, Take heed, and hearken, O Israel; this day thou art become the people of the LORD thy God.

10 Thou shalt therefore obey the voice of the LORD thy God, and do his commandments and his statutes, which I command thee this day.

Proclamation of the Curses

11 And Moses charged the people the same day, saying,

12 These shall stand upon mount Ger'-i-zim to bless the people, when ye are come over Jordan; Simeon, and Levi, and Judah, and Is'-sa-char, and Joseph, and Benjamin:

13 And these shall stand upon mount E'-bal to curse; Reuben, Gad, and Asher, and Zeb'-u-lun, Dan, and Naph'-ta-li.

14 And the Levites shall speak, and say unto all the men of Israel with a loud voice,

15 Cursed be the man that maketh any graven or molten image, an Tabomination unto the LORD, the work of the hands of the craftsman, and putteth it in a Tsecret place. RAnd all the people shall answer and say, Amen. evil thing • hiding • Num. 5:22; Jer. 11:5

16 RCursed be he that setteth light by his father or his mother. And all the people shall say, Amen. 21:18; Ex. 20:12; Lev. 19:3

17 Cursed be he that Tremoveth his neighbour's landmark. And all the people shall say, Amen. schemes to get his property

18 RCursed be he that Tmaketh the blind to wander out of the way. And all the people shall say, Amen. Lev. 19:14 • is cruel to

19 Cursed be he that perverteth the judgment of the stranger, fatherless, and widow. And all the people shall say, Amen.

20 RCursed be he that lieth with his father's wife; because he uncovereth his father's skirt. And all the people shall say, Amen. 22:30; Lev. 18:8; 20:11

21 RCursed be he that lieth with any manner of beast. And all the people shall say, Amen. Lev. 18:23

22 RCursed be he that lieth with his sister, the daughter of his father, or the daughter of his mother. And all the people shall say, Amen. Ex. 22:19; Lev. 18:9

23 RCursed be he that lieth with his mother in law. And all the people shall say, Amen. Lev. 18:17; 20:14

24 RCursed be he that Tsmiteth his neighbour secretly. And all the people shall say, Amen. Lev. 24:17 • strikes with violence

25 RCursed be he that Ttaketh reward to slay an innocent person. And all the people shall say, Amen. Ex. 23:7, 8; Ezek. 22:12 • accepts pay

26 RCursed be he that confirmeth not all the words of this law to do them. And all the people shall say, Amen. Jer. 11:3; Gal. 3:10

CHAPTER 28

Promised Blessings for Obedience

AND it shall come to pass, if thou shalt hearken diligently unto the voice of the LORD thy God, to observe and to do all his commandments which I command thee this day, that the LORD thy God will set thee on high above all nations of the earth:

2 And all these blessings shall come on thee, and overtake thee, if thou shalt hearken unto the voice of the LORD thy God.

3 Blessed shalt thou be in the city, and blessed shalt thou be in the field.

4 Blessed shall be the Tfruit of thy body, and the fruit of thy ground, and the fruit of thy cattle, the increase of thy Tkine, and the flocks of thy sheep. children • cattle

5 Blessed shall be thy basket and thy store.

6 RBlessed shalt thou be Twhen thou comest in, and blessed shalt thou be when thou goest out. Ps. 121:8 • in all routine affairs

7 The LORD shall cause thine enemies that rise up against thee to be smitten before thy face: they shall come out against thee one way, and flee before thee seven ways.

8 The LORD shall Rcommand the blessing upon thee in thy storehouses, and in all that thou Rsettest thine hand unto; and he shall bless thee in the land which the LORD thy God giveth thee. Lev. 25:21 • 15:10

9 The LORD shall establish thee an holy people unto himself, as he hath sworn unto thee, if thou shalt keep the commandments of the LORD thy God, and walk in his ways.

10 And all people of the earth shall see that thou art called by the name of the Lord; and they shall be afraid of thee.

11 And the Lord shall make thee ᵀplenteous in goods, in the fruit of thy body, and in the fruit of thy cattle, and in the fruit of thy ground, in the land which the Lord sware unto thy fathers to give thee.   *rich*

12 The Lord shall open unto thee his ᵀgood treasure, the heaven ᴿto give the rain unto thy land in his season, and to bless all the work of thine hand: and thou shalt ᴿlend unto many nations, and thou shalt not borrow.   *benefits • Lev. 26:4 • 23:20*

13 And the Lord shall make thee the head, and not the tail; and thou shalt be above only, and thou shalt not be beneath; if that thou hearken unto the commandments of the Lord thy God, which I command thee this day, to observe and to do *them:*

14 ᴿAnd thou shalt not ᵀgo aside from any of the words which I command thee this day, *to* the right hand, or *to* the left, to go after other gods to serve them.   *5:32 • deviate*

Promised Curses for Disobedience

15 But it shall come to pass, if thou wilt not ᵀhearken unto the voice of the Lord thy God, to observe to do all his commandments and his statutes which I command thee this day; that all these curses shall come upon thee, and overtake thee: *listen*

16 Cursed *shalt* thou *be* in the city, and cursed *shalt* thou *be* in the field.

17 Cursed *shall be* thy basket and thy store.

18 Cursed *shall be* the ᵀfruit of thy body, and the fruit of thy land, the increase of thy ᵀkine, and the flocks of thy sheep.   *children • cattle*

19 Cursed *shalt* thou *be* when thou comest in, and cursed *shalt* thou *be* when thou goest out.

20 The Lord shall send upon thee cursing, vexation, and rebuke, in all that thou settest thine hand unto for to do, until thou be destroyed, and until thou perish quickly; because of the wickedness of thy doings, whereby thou hast forsaken me.

21 ᴿThe Lord shall make the ᵀpestilence cleave unto thee, until he have ᵀconsumed thee from off the land, whither thou goest to possess it.   *Lev. 26:25 • sickness • destroyed*

22 The Lord shall smite thee with a consumption, and with a fever, and with an inflammation, and with an extreme burning, and with the sword, and with ᵀblasting, and with mildew; and they shall pursue thee until thou perish.   *plant disease*

23 And thy heaven that *is* over thy head shall be brass, and the ᵀearth that *is* under thee *shall be* iron.   *unresponsive to cultivation*

24 ᴿThe Lord shall make the rain of thy land powder and dust: from heaven shall it come down upon thee, until thou be destroyed.   *11:17*

25 ᴿThe Lord shall cause thee to be ᵀsmitten before thine enemies: thou shalt go out one way against them, and flee seven ways before them: and shalt be removed into all the kingdoms of the earth.   *32:30 • defeated*

26 And thy carcase shall be meat unto all fowls of the air, and unto the beasts of the earth, and no man shall fray *them* away.

27 The Lord will smite thee with the ᵀbotch of Egypt, and with the ᵀemerods, and with the scab, and with the itch, whereof thou canst not be healed.   *boil • hemorrhoids*

28 The Lord shall smite thee with ᵀmadness, and blindness, and ᴿastonishmentᵀ of heart: *mental disorder • Jer. 4:9 • panic*

29 And thou shalt grope at noonday, as the blind gropeth in darkness, and thou shalt not prosper in thy ways: and thou shalt be only oppressed and ᵀspoiled evermore, and no man shall save *thee.*   *robbed*

30 ᴿThou shalt betroth a wife, and another man shall lie with her: thou shalt build an house, and thou shalt not dwell therein: thou shalt plant a vineyard, and shalt not gather the grapes thereof.   *Job 31:10*

31 Thine ox *shall be* slain before thine eyes, and thou shalt not eat thereof: thine ass *shall be* violently taken away from before thy face, and shall not be restored to thee: thy sheep *shall be* given unto thine enemies, and thou shalt have none to rescue *them.*

32 Thy sons and thy daughters *shall be* given unto another people, and thine eyes shall look, and ᴿfailᵀ *with longing* for them all the day long: and *there shall be* no might in thine hand.   *2 Chr. 29:9 • despair*

33 The fruit of thy land, and all thy labours, shall a nation which thou knowest not ᵀeat up; and thou shalt be only oppressed and crushed alway: *take away*

34 So that thou shalt be mad for the sight of thine eyes which thou shalt see.

35 The Lord shall smite thee in the knees, and in the legs, with a sore ᵀbotch that cannot be healed, ᴿfrom the sole of thy foot unto the top of thy head.   *boil • v. 27*

36 The Lord shall ᴿbring thee, and thy king which thou shalt set over thee, unto a nation which neither thou nor thy fathers have known; and there shalt thou serve other gods, wood and stone.   *2 Kin. 17:4, 6*

37 And thou shalt become an astonishment, a proverb, and a byword, among all nations whither the Lord shall lead thee.

38 Thou shalt carry much seed out into the field, and shalt gather *but* little in; for ᴿthe locust shall ᵀconsume it.   *Joel 1:4 • destroy*

39 ᴿThou shalt plant vineyards, and dress *them,* but shalt neither drink *of* the wine, nor gather *the grapes;* for the worms shall eat them.   *Is. 5:10; 17:10, 11; Zeph. 1:13*

40 Thou shalt have olive trees throughout all thy ᵀcoasts, but ᵀthou shalt not anoint *thyself* with the oil; for thine olive shall cast *his fruit*.   *borders • you won't have any oil*

41 Thou shalt beget sons and daughters, but thou shalt not enjoy them; for they shall ᵀgo into captivity.   *be taken away as slaves*

42 All thy trees and fruit of thy land shall the locust ᵀconsume.   *destroy*

43 The ᴿstranger that *is* within thee shall get up above thee very high; and thou shalt come down very low.   *v. 13*

44 He shall lend to thee, and thou shalt not lend to him: he shall be ᵀtheᴿ head, and thou shalt be the tail.   *the important one • vv. 12, 13*

45 Moreover all these curses shall come upon thee, and shall pursue thee, and overtake thee, till thou be destroyed; because thou hearkenedst not unto the voice of the LORD thy God, to keep his commandments and his statutes which he commanded thee:

46 ᴿAnd they shall be upon thee for a sign and for a ᵀwonder, and upon thy seed for ever.   *Is. 8:18; Ezek. 14:8 • miracle*

47 Because thou servedst not the LORD thy God with joyfulness, and with gladness of heart, for the abundance of all *things;*

48 Therefore shalt thou serve thine enemies which the LORD shall send against thee, in hunger, and in thirst, and in nakedness, and in want of all *things:* and he ᴿshall ᵀput a yoke of iron upon thy neck, until he have destroyed thee.   *Jer. 28:14 • oppress you*

49 The LORD shall bring a nation against thee from far, from the end of the earth, *as swift* as the eagle flieth; a nation whose ᵀtongue thou shalt not understand;   *language*

50 A nation of fierce countenance, which shall not ᵀregard the person of the old, nor shew favour to the young: *pay any respect to*

51 And he shall eat the fruit of thy cattle, and the fruit of thy land, until thou be destroyed: which *also* shall not leave thee *either* corn, wine, or oil, *or* the increase of thy ᵀkine, or flocks of thy sheep, until he have destroyed thee.   *cattle*

52 And he shall ᴿbesiege thee in all thy gates, until thy high and fenced walls come down, wherein thou trustedst, throughout all thy land: and he shall besiege thee in all thy gates throughout all thy land, which the LORD thy God hath given thee.   *2 Kin. 25:1*

53 And thou shalt eat the fruit of thine own body, the flesh of thy sons and of thy daughters, which the LORD thy God hath given thee, in the siege, and in the straitness, wherewith thine enemies shall distress thee:

54 *So that* the man *that is* tender among you, and very delicate, ᴿhis eye shall be evil toward his brother, and toward the wife of his bosom, and toward the remnant of his children which he shall leave: *15:9*

55 So that he will not give to any of them of the flesh of his children whom he shall eat: because he hath nothing left him in the siege, and in the straitness, wherewith thine enemies shall distress thee in all thy gates.

56 The tender and delicate woman among you, which would not adventure to set the sole of her foot upon the ground for delicateness and tenderness, her eye shall be evil toward the husband of her bosom, and toward her son, and toward her daughter,

57 And toward her young one that cometh out from between her feet, and toward her children which she shall bear: for she shall eat them for want of all *things* secretly in the siege and straitness, wherewith thine enemy shall distress thee in thy gates.

58 If thou wilt not observe to do all the words of this law that are written in this book, that thou mayest fear this glorious and fearful name, THE LORD THY GOD;

59 Then the LORD will make thy plagues wonderful, and the plagues of thy seed, *even* great plagues, and of long continuance, and sore sicknesses, and of long continuance.

60 Moreover he will bring upon thee all the diseases of Egypt, which thou wast afraid of; and they shall cleave unto thee.

61 Also every sickness, and every plague, which *is* not written in the book of this law, them will the LORD bring upon thee, ᴿuntil thou be destroyed.   *4:25, 26*

62 And ye ᴿshall be left few in number, whereas ye were ᴿas the stars of heaven for multitude; because thou wouldest not obey the voice of the LORD thy God.   *4:27 • Neh. 9:23*

63 And it shall come to pass, *that* as the LORD rejoiced over you to do you good, and to multiply you; so the LORD will rejoice over you to destroy you, and to bring you to nought; and ye shall be plucked from off the land whither thou goest to possess it.

64 And the LORD shall scatter thee among all people, from the one end of the earth even unto the other; and there thou shalt serve other gods, which neither thou nor thy fathers have known, *even* wood and stone.

65 And among these nations shalt thou find no ease, neither shall the sole of thy foot have rest: but the LORD shall give thee there a trembling heart, and failing of eyes, and ᵀsorrow of mind: *pining of soul*

66 And thy life shall hang in doubt before thee; and thou shalt fear day and night, and shalt have none assurance of thy life:

67 ᴿIn the morning thou shalt say, Would God it were ᵀeven! and at even thou shalt say, Would God it were morning! for the fear of thine heart wherewith thou shalt fear, and ᴿfor the sight of thine eyes which thou shalt see.   *Job 7:4 • night • v. 34*

68 And the LORD shall bring thee into Egypt again with ships, by the way whereof I

spake unto thee, Thou shalt see it no more again: and there ye shall be sold unto your enemies for ^Tbondmen and bondwomen, and no man shall buy you.   *slaves*

CHAPTER 29

The Covenant Is Based on the Power of God

THESE are the words of the covenant, which the LORD commanded Moses to make with the children of Israel in the land of Moab, beside ^Rthe covenant which he made with them in Ho'-reb.   5:2; Lev. 26:46

2 And Moses called unto all Israel, and said unto them, ^RYe have seen all that the LORD did before your eyes in the land of Egypt unto Pharaoh, and unto all his servants, and unto all his land;   Ex. 19:4

3 ^RThe great ^Ttemptations which thine eyes have seen, the signs, and those great miracles: 4:34 • *trials*

4 Yet ^Rthe LORD hath not given you an heart to ^Tperceive, and eyes to see, and ears to hear, unto this day.   [Eph. 4:18] • *understand*

5 ^RAnd I have led you forty years in the wilderness: ^Ryour clothes are not waxen old upon you, and thy shoe is not waxen old upon thy foot.   1:3; 8:2 • 8:4

6 Ye have not eaten bread, neither have ye drunk wine or strong drink: that ye might know that I am the LORD your God.

7 And when ye came unto this place, ^RSi'-hon the king of Hesh'-bon, and Og the king of Ba'-shan, came out against us unto battle, and we smote them: 2:32; Num. 21:23

8 And we took their land, and ^Rgave it for an inheritance unto the Reu'-ben-ites, and to the Gad'-ites, and to the half tribe of Ma-nas'-seh.   3:12, 13; Num. 32:32, 33

9 ^RKeep therefore the words of this ^Tcovenant, and do them, that ye may ^Rprosper in all that ye do.   4:6; 1 Kin. 2:3 • *agreement* • Josh. 1:7

Parties of the Covenant

10 Ye stand this day all of you before the LORD your God; your captains of your tribes, your elders, and your officers, with all the men of Israel,

11 Your little ones, your wives, and thy stranger that is in thy camp, from the hewer of thy wood unto the drawer of thy water:

12 That thou shouldest ^Tenter into covenant with the LORD thy God, and ^Rinto his oath, which the LORD thy God maketh with thee this day: *enter into this agreement* • Neh. 10:29

13 That he may ^Restablish thee to day for a people unto himself, and that he may be unto thee a God, as he hath said unto thee, and as he hath sworn unto thy fathers, to Abraham, to Isaac, and to Jacob.   28:9

14 Neither with you only ^Rdo I make this covenant and this oath;   [Jer. 31:31–33; Heb. 8:7–10]

15 But with him that standeth here with us this day before the LORD our God, ^Rand also with him that is not here with us this day: Acts 2:39

Scattering of Israel

16 (For ye know how we have dwelt in the land of Egypt; and how we came through the nations which ye passed by;

17 And ye have seen their ^Tabominations, and their idols, wood and stone, silver and gold, which were among them:)   *evil deeds*

18 Lest there should be among you man, or woman, or family, or tribe, whose heart turneth away this day from the LORD our God, to go and serve the gods of these nations; lest there should be among you a root that beareth gall and wormwood;

19 And it come to pass, when he heareth the words of this curse, that he bless himself in his heart, saying, I shall have peace, though I walk in the imagination of mine heart, ^Rto add drunkenness to thirst: Is. 30:1

20 The LORD will not spare him, but then the anger of the LORD and his jealousy shall ^Tsmoke against that man, and all the curses that are written in this book shall lie upon him, and the LORD shall blot out his name from under heaven.   *increase furiously*

21 And the LORD ^Rshall separate him unto evil out of all the tribes of Israel, according to all the curses of the covenant that are written in this book of the law: [Matt. 24:51]

22 So that the generation to come of your children that shall rise up after you, ^Rand the

---

29:10–15; 30:11–20 The Palestinian Covenant—The covenant concerning Palestine is the third of the theocratic covenants (pertaining to the rule of God). The Palestinian Covenant has two aspects: (1) the legal aspects which are immediate and conditional (Page 202—Deut. 27—29); and (2) the grace aspects which are future and unconditional (Page 207—Deut. 30:1–9). The enjoyment of the immediate blessings are introduced by the conditional formula: "if thou shalt hearken diligently unto the voice of the LORD thy God . . . the LORD thy God will set thee on high above all nations of the earth" (Page 203—Deut. 28:1). Sadly, Israel did not meet the condition of obedience, and is still experiencing God's curses and punishment for their disobedience (Page 204—Deut. 28:15–68). The unconditional grace aspects of the Palestinian Covenant have yet to be realized. God will regather the scattered people of Israel and establish them in the land He has promised unconditionally to give them. Deuteronomy concludes the Palestinian Covenant with a final warning and challenge for obedience (Page 207—Deut. 30:1–20).
Now turn to Page 314—2 Sam. 7:4–17: The Davidic Covenant.

[T]stranger that shall come from a far land, shall say, when they see the plagues of that land, and the sicknesses which the LORD hath laid upon it; Jer. 19:8; 49:17 • *foreigner*

23 *And that* the whole land thereof *is* brimstone, [R]and salt, *and* burning, *that* it is not sown, nor beareth, nor any grass groweth therein, [R]like the overthrow of Sodom, and Go-mor'-rah, Ad'-mah, and Ze-bo'-im, which the LORD overthrew in his anger, and in his wrath: Jer. 17:6 • Jer. 20:16

24 Even all nations shall say, Wherefore hath the LORD done thus unto this land? what *meaneth* the heat of this great anger?

25 Then men shall say, Because they have forsaken the covenant of the LORD God of their fathers, which he made with them when he brought them forth out of the land of Egypt:

26 For they went and served other gods, and worshipped them, gods whom they knew not, and *whom* he had not given unto them:

27 And the anger of the LORD was kindled against this land, [R]to bring upon it all the curses that are written in this book: Dan. 9:11

28 And the LORD [T]rooted them out of their land in anger, and in wrath, and in great indignation, and cast them into another land, as *it is* this day. *tore them away from*

29 The [T]secret *things belong* unto the LORD our God: but those *things which are* revealed *belong* unto us and to our children for ever, that *we* may do all the words of this law. *hidden realities*

CHAPTER 30

Restoration of Israel

AND it shall come to pass, when all these things are come upon thee, the blessing and the curse, which I have set before thee, and thou shalt [T]call *them* to mind among all the nations, whither the LORD thy God hath driven thee, *remember*

2 And shalt [R]return[T] unto the LORD thy God, and shalt obey his voice according to all that I command thee this day, thou and thy children, with all thine heart, and with all thy soul; Lam. 3:40; Joel 2:12 • *turn back again*

3 That then the LORD thy God will [T]turn thy captivity, and have compassion upon thee, and will return and gather thee from all the nations, whither the LORD thy God hath scattered thee. *reverse your status as slaves*

4 If *any* of thine be driven out [T]unto the outmost *parts* of heaven, from thence will the LORD thy God gather thee, and from thence will he fetch thee: *to the ends of the earth*

5 And the LORD thy God will bring thee into the land which thy fathers possessed, and thou shalt possess it; and he will do thee good, and multiply thee above thy fathers.

6 And the LORD thy God will circumcise thine heart, and the heart of thy seed, to love the LORD thy God with all thine heart, and with all thy soul, that thou mayest live.

7 [R]And the LORD thy God will put all these curses upon thine enemies, and on them that hate thee, which persecuted thee. 7:15

8 And thou shalt return and obey the voice of the LORD, and do all his commandments which I command thee this day.

9 And the LORD thy God will make thee plenteous in every work of thine hand, in the fruit of thy body, and in the fruit of thy cattle, and in the fruit of thy land, for good: for the LORD will again rejoice over thee for good, as he rejoiced over thy fathers:

10 If thou shalt hearken unto the voice of the LORD thy God, to keep his commandments and his statutes which [R]are written in this book of the law, *and* if thou turn unto the LORD thy God [R]with all thine heart, and with all thy soul. 29:21 • 4:29

29:29 Revelation of God's Word—Revelation may be defined as that process by which God imparted to man truths which he otherwise could not know. The details of creation in Genesis 1 and 2 are an example of revelation. As man was not created until the sixth day, we could not have possibly known the events occurring prior to this until God gave the facts to Moses.

We know God spoke to the human authors of our Bible; but just how did He speak? Was it in Hebrew? Greek? Angelic language? He spoke to them in their own language. God's call to young Samuel in the temple (Page 278—1 Sam. 3:1–10) proves this, for the boy at first mistook God's voice for that of the aged priest Eli. Sometimes God spoke through angels: Gabriel was sent from heaven to tell Mary she would give birth to the Messiah (Page 1004—Luke 1:26–37). On other occasions the Lord spoke directly to a man, as He did to Noah concerning the great Flood (Page 9—Gen. 6:13–21).

One of God's methods of communication in Scripture is to reveal His message through dreams and visions: The wise men (Page 942—Matt. 2:12) were warned in a dream not to return to Herod, while Peter was later instructed in a vision to minister to Cornelius (Page 1083—Acts 10:10–16). God has communicated in many different ways. He revealed Himself to Moses from a burning bush (Page 58—Ex. 3:4) and to Moses, Aaron, and Miriam out of a cloud (Page 148—Num. 12:4, 5).

One of the most important ways that divine truths were given in the Old Testament was through the Angel of the Lord. Most Bible students perceive this heavenly messenger to be the preincarnate Christ Himself. For example, it is the Angel of the Lord who reassured Joshua on the eve of a battle (Page 221—Josh. 5:13–15).

Now turn to Page 699—Is. 59:21: Inspiration of God's Word.

Ratification of the Palestinian Covenant

11 For this commandment which I command thee this day, ᴿit *is* not ᵀhidden from thee, neither *is* it far off.   Is. 45:19 • *too hard for*

12 ᴿIt *is* not in heaven, that thou shouldest say, Who shall go up for us to heaven, and bring it unto us, that we may hear it, and do it?   Prov. 30:4; Rom. 10:6

13 Neither *is* it beyond the sea, ᵀthat thou shouldest say, Who shall go over the sea for us, and bring it unto us, that we may hear it, and do it?   *to say*

14 But the word *is* very nigh unto thee, in thy ᴿmouth, and in thy heart, that thou mayest do it.   Rom. 10:8

15 See, ᴿI have set before thee this day life and good, and death and evil;   *vv.* 1, 19

16 In that I command thee this day ᴿto love the Lᴏʀᴅ thy God, to walk in his ways, and to keep his commandments and his statutes and his judgments, that thou ᴿmayest live and multiply: and the Lᴏʀᴅ thy God shall bless thee in the land whither thou goest to possess it.   6:5 • *v.* 19; 4:1

17 But if thine heart turn away, so that thou wilt not hear, but shalt be drawn away, and worship other gods, and serve them;

18 I denounce unto you this day, that ye shall surely perish, *and that* ye shall not prolong *your* days upon the land, whither thou passest over Jordan to go to possess it.

19 ᴿI call heaven and earth ᵀto record this day against you, *that* ᴿI have set before you life and death, blessing and cursing: therefore choose life, that both thou and thy seed may live: 4:26 • *to notice what I am saying* • *v.* 15

20 That thou mayest love the Lᴏʀᴅ thy God, *and* that thou mayest obey his voice, and that thou mayest cleave unto him: for he *is* thy life, and the length of thy days: that thou mayest dwell in the land which the Lᴏʀᴅ sware unto thy fathers, to Abraham, to Isaac, and to Jacob, to give them.

CHAPTER 31

Moses Charges Joshua and Israel

AND Moses went and spake these words unto all Israel.

2 And he said unto them, I *am* an hundred and twenty years old this day; I can no more go out and come in: also the Lᴏʀᴅ hath said unto me, Thou shalt not go over this Jordan.

3 The Lᴏʀᴅ thy God, he will go over before thee, *and* he will destroy these nations from before thee, ᴿand thou shalt possess them: *and* Joshua, he shall go over before thee, as the Lᴏʀᴅ hath said.   Josh. 11:23

4 ᴿAnd the Lᴏʀᴅ shall do unto them ᴿas he did to Sī′-hon and to Og, kings of the Am′-or-ites, and unto the land of them, whom he destroyed.   3:21 • Num. 21:24, 33

5 And ᴿthe Lᴏʀᴅ shall give them up before your face, that ye may do unto them according unto all the commandments which I have commanded you.   7:2; 20:10-20

6 Be strong and of a good courage, ᴿfear not, nor be afraid of them: for the Lᴏʀᴅ thy God, he *it is* that doth go with thee; he will not fail thee, nor forsake thee.   1:29

7 And Moses called unto Joshua, and said unto him in the sight of all Israel, Be strong and of a good courage: for thou must go with this people unto the land which the Lᴏʀᴅ hath sworn unto their fathers to give them; and thou shalt cause them to inherit it.

8 And the Lᴏʀᴅ, ᴿhe *it is* that doth go before thee; ᴿhe will be with thee, he will not fail thee, neither forsake thee: fear not, neither be dismayed.   Ex. 13:21 • Josh. 1:5, 9

9 And Moses wrote this law, and delivered it unto the priests the sons of Levi, which bare the ark of the covenant of the Lᴏʀᴅ, and unto all the elders of Israel.

10 And Moses commanded them, saying, At the end of *every* seven years, in the ᵀsolemnity of the ᴿyear of release, ᴿin the feast of tabernacles,   *set time* • 15:1 • Lev. 23:34

11 When all Israel is come to ᴿappear before the Lᴏʀᴅ thy God in the place which he shall choose, thou shalt read this law before all Israel in their hearing.   16:16

12 ᴿGather the people together, men, and women, and children, and ᵀthy stranger that *is* within thy gates, that they may hear, and that they may learn, and fear the Lᴏʀᴅ your God, and observe to do all the words of this law: 4:10 • *your alien*

31:12 Obedience to God's Word—Reading, memorizing, and meditating upon the Word of God are of no value without obedience to the Word of God. To obey the Word of God, you do what the Word of God indicates should be done in any situation. Obedience to the Word of God is the only way that the child of God can be pleasing to God in the new life. Obedience to God's Word results in: being treasured by God (Page 74—Ex. 19:5); blessedness (happiness) in life (Page 599—Ps. 119:2); not being ashamed (Page 599—Ps. 119:4-6); understanding (Page 601—Ps. 119:100); avoidance of evil (Page 601—Ps. 119:101); guidance for life (Page 601—Ps. 119:105); safety and freedom from anxiety (Page 616—Prov. 1:33); life (Page 627—Prov. 19:16; Page 786—Ezek. 18:19; Page 1052—John 8:51); God's blessing (Page 659—Is. 1:19); greatness in the kingdom of heaven (Page 945—Matt. 5:19); bearing fruit for God (Page 954—Matt. 13:23); manifesting love for God (Page 1060—John 14:23; Page 1250—1

13 And *that* their children, which have not known *any thing*, ^Rmay hear, and learn to fear the LORD your God, as long as ye live in the land whither ye go over Jordan to ^Tpossess it.   11:2; Ps. 78:6, 7 · *take it for your own*

God Charges Israel

14 And the LORD said unto Moses, Behold, thy days approach that thou must die: call Joshua, and present yourselves in the tabernacle of the congregation, that I may give him a ^Tcharge. And Moses and Joshua went, and presented themselves in the tabernacle of the congregation.   *commission*

15 And the LORD appeared in the tabernacle in a pillar of a cloud: and the pillar of the cloud stood over the door of the tabernacle.

16 And the LORD said unto Moses, Behold, thou shalt sleep with thy fathers; and this people will rise up, and ^Tgo a whoring after the gods of the strangers of the land, whither they go *to be* among them, and will forsake me, and break my covenant which I have made with them.   *play the harlot*

17 Then my anger shall be kindled against them in that day, and I will forsake them, and I will hide my face from them, and they shall be devoured, and many evils and troubles shall befall them; so that they will say in that day, Are not these evils come upon us, because our God *is* ^Rnot among us?   Num. 14:42

18 And ^RI will surely hide my face in that day for all the evils which they shall have wrought, in that they are turned unto other gods.   v. 17; [Is. 1:15, 16]

19 Now therefore write ye this song for you, and teach it the children of Israel: put it in their mouths, that this song may be a witness for me against the children of Israel.

20 For when I shall have brought them into the land which I sware unto their fathers, that floweth with milk and honey; and they shall have eaten and filled themselves, and waxen fat; ^Rthen will they turn unto other gods, and serve them, and provoke me, and break my covenant.   v. 16

21 And it shall come to pass, when many evils and troubles are befallen them, that this song shall testify against them as a witness; for it shall not be forgotten out of the mouths of their seed: for I know their imagination which they go about, even now, before I have brought them into the land which I sware.

The Book of the Law Is Deposited

22 Moses therefore wrote this song the same day, and taught it the children of Israel.

23 ^RAnd he gave Joshua the son of Nun a charge, and said, ^RBe strong and of a good courage: for thou shalt bring the children of Israel into the land which I sware unto them: and I will be with thee.   v. 14 · v. 7

24 And it came to pass, when Moses had made an end of writing the words of this law in a book, until they were finished,

25 That Moses commanded the Levites, which ^Rbare the ark of the covenant of the LORD, saying,   v. 9

26 Take this ^Rbook of the law, and put it in the side of the ark of the covenant of the LORD your God, that it may be there ^Rfor a witness against thee.   2 Kin. 22:8 · v. 19

27 For I know thy rebellion, and thy stiff neck: behold, while I am yet alive with you this day, ye have been rebellious against the LORD; and how much more after my death?

28 Gather unto me all the elders of your tribes, and your officers, that I may speak these words ^Tin their ears, and call heaven and earth to record against them.   *plainly*

29 For I know that ^Rafter my death ye will utterly corrupt *yourselves*, and turn aside from the way which I have commanded you; and evil will befall you in the latter days; because ye will do evil in the sight of the LORD, to provoke him to anger through the work of your hands.   [Acts 20:29]

30 And Moses spake in the ears of all the congregation of Israel the words of this song, until they were ended.

CHAPTER 32

The Song of Moses

G IVE ear, O ye heavens, and I will speak; and hear, O earth, the words of my mouth.

2 My ^Tdoctrine shall drop as the rain, my speech shall distil as the dew, as the small rain upon the tender herb, and as the showers upon the grass: *teaching*

3 Because I will publish the name of the LORD: ascribe ye greatness unto our God.

4 *He is* the Rock, his work *is* perfect: for all his ways *are* judgment: a God of truth and ^Rwithout iniquity, just and right *is* he.   Jer. 10:10

John 2:5); promise of God's presence (Page 1060—John 14:23; Page 1256—2 John 9); abiding in the love of God (Page 1060—John 15:10); evidence of the doctrine that has been taught (Page 1113—Rom. 6:17); assurance of salvation (Page 1250—1 John 2:3); eternal life (Page 1250—1 John 2:17); dwelling in God (Page 1252—1 John 3:24); love of God's children (Page 1253—1 John 5:2); and entrance into heaven (Page 1283—Rev. 22:7).
Now turn to Page 611—Ps. 150:1: Praise.

5 They have corrupted themselves, their spot *is* not *the spot* of his children: *they are* a perverse and crooked generation.

6 Do ye thus ᵀrequite the LORD, O foolish people and unwise? *is* not he ᴿthy father *that* hath bought thee? Hath he not ᴿmade thee, and established thee?   *repay* • Is. 63:16 • Ps. 74:2

7 Remember the days of old, consider the years of many generations: ᴿask thy father, and he will shew thee; thy elders, and they will tell thee.   Ex. 13:14

8 When the Most High ᴿdivided to the nations their inheritance, when he ᴿseparated the sons of Adam, he set the bounds of the people according to the number of the children of Israel.   Acts 17:26 • Gen. 11:8

9 For ᴿthe LORD's portion *is* his people; Jacob *is* the lot of his inheritance.   Ex. 19:5

10 He found him ᴿin a desert land, and in the waste howling wilderness; he led him about, he instructed him, he kept him as the apple of his eye.   Jer. 2:6

11 As an eagle stirreth up her nest, fluttereth over her young, spreadeth abroad her wings, taketh them, beareth them on her wings:

12 So the LORD alone did lead him, and *there was* no strange god with him.

13 He made him ride on the high places of the earth, that he might eat the increase of the fields; and he made him to suck honey out of the rock, and oil out of the flinty rock;

14 Butter of ᵀkine, and milk of sheep, with fat of lambs, and rams of the breed of Ba'-shan, and goats, ᴿwith the fat of kidneys ᵀof wheat; and thou didst drink the pure ᴿblood of the grape.   *cattle* • Ps. 81:16 • *finest* • Gen. 49:11

15 But Jesh'-u-run waxed fat, and kicked: thou art waxen fat, thou art grown thick, thou art covered *with fatness;* then he forsook God *which* made him, and lightly esteemed the ᴿRock of his salvation.   Ps. 95:1

16 ᴿThey provoked him to jealousy with strange *gods,* with ᵀabominations provoked they him to anger.   Ps. 78:58; 1 Cor. 10:22 • *evil actions*

17 They sacrificed unto devils, not to God; to gods whom they knew not, to new *gods that* came newly up, whom your fathers feared not.

18 Of the Rock *that* begat thee thou art unmindful, and hast forgotten God that formed thee.

19 And when the LORD saw *it,* he abhorred *them,* ᴿbecause of the provoking of his sons, and of his daughters.   Jer. 44:21-23

20 And he said, I will hide my face from them, I will see what their end *shall be:* for they *are* a very ᵀfroward generation, children in whom *is* no faith.   *perverse*

21 They have moved me to jealousy with *that which is* not God; they have provoked me to anger ᴿwith their ᵀvanities: and ᴿI will move them to jealousy with *those which are* not a people; I will provoke them to anger with a foolish nation.   Ps. 31:6 • *idols* • Rom. 10:19

22 For a fire is kindled in mine anger, and shall burn unto the lowest hell, and shall consume the earth with her increase, and set on fire the foundations of the mountains.

23 I will heap mischiefs upon them; I will spend mine arrows upon them.

24 *They shall be* burnt with hunger, and devoured with burning heat, and with bitter destruction: I will also send the teeth of beasts upon them, with the poison of serpents of the dust.

25 The sword without, and terror within, shall destroy both the young man and the virgin, the suckling *also* with the man of gray hairs.

26 ᴿI said, I would scatter them into corners, I would make the remembrance of them to cease from among men: Ezek. 20:23

27 Were it not that I feared the wrath of the enemy, lest their adversaries should behave themselves strangely, *and* lest they

---

32:7 God's Work in the Past—The Bible's revelation of God's work in the past provides an informative and exciting panorama of centuries of divine activity toward man.

First, it gives man an *education* in truths unknowable apart from divine revelation. For example, the creation of man described in Genesis 1 and 2 answers man's most basic questions: "Who am I?" and "Where did I come from?" Only God Himself could disclose these facts.

Second, the Bible sets forth a mass of historical *evidence* for the truthfulness of the Christian faith. The most outstanding of these evidences are fulfilled prophecy, the miracles of Christ, and Christ's death and resurrection. The believer's faith is thus grounded in historical events and is far removed from what some have called "a leap into the dark."

Third, the Bible records *examples* to help present-day Christians. Various failures of Israel and the resulting judgments of God are often cited in the New Testament as things to avoid, for example, their idolatry and grumbling in the wilderness (Page 1132—1 Cor. 10:11), and their unbelief at Kadesh (Page 1216—Heb. 4:11). Paul is said to be a living example for believers to follow (Page 1128—1 Cor. 4:16; 11:1), as is Jesus' humility in the midst of suffering (Page 1237—1 Pet. 2:21).

Fourth, the Bible provides *encouragement* for Christians in their life and witness. If God could use an adulterer and murderer like David, then God can certainly use a struggling Christian today if he possesses David's devotion to the Lord. Likewise, if God saved Saul of Tarsus, the chief enemy of the early church (Page 1081—Acts 9:1–31), then surely He can save the people with whom Christians share their Faith.

Now turn to Page 607—Ps. 139:14: God's Work in Our Lives.

should say, Our hand *is* high, and the LORD hath not done all this.

28 For they *are* a nation void of counsel, neither *is there any* understanding in them.

29 O that they were wise, *that* they understood this, *that* they would consider their latter end!

30 How should one chase a thousand, and two put ten thousand to flight, except their Rock R had sold them, and the LORD had shut them up?   Ps. 44:12

31 For their rock *is* not as our Rock, even our enemies themselves *being* judges.

32 For their vine *is* of the vine of Sodom, and of the fields of Go-mor'-rah: their grapes *are* grapes of gall, their clusters *are* bitter:

33 Their wine *is* R the poison of dragons, and the cruel venom of asps.   Ps. 58:4

34 *Is* not this laid up in store with me, *and* sealed up among my treasures?

35 To me *belongeth* vengeance, and recompence; their foot shall slide in *due* time: for the day of their calamity *is* at hand, and the things that shall come upon them T make haste.   *are going to happen soon*

36 For the LORD shall judge his people, and repent himself for his servants, when he seeth that *their* power is gone, and *there is* none shut up, or left.

37 And he shall say, R Where *are* their gods, *their* rock in whom they trusted,   Judg. 10:14

38 Which did eat the fat of their sacrifices, *and* drank the wine of their drink offerings? R Let them rise up and help you, *and* be your protection.   [Jer. 11:12]

39 See now that I, *even* I, *am* he, and *there* is no god with me: I kill, and I make alive; I wound, and I heal: neither *is there any* that can deliver out of my hand.

40 For I lift up my hand to heaven, and say, I live for ever.

41 If I whet my glittering sword, and mine hand take hold on judgment; I will render vengeance to mine enemies, and will reward them that hate me.

42 I will make mine arrows drunk with blood, and my sword shall devour flesh; *and that* with the blood of the slain and of the captives, from the beginning of revenges upon the enemy.

43 R Rejoice, O ye nations, *with* his people: for he will R avenge the blood of his servants, and will render vengeance to his adversaries, and R will be merciful unto his land, *and* to his people.   Rom. 15:10 · Rev. 19:2 · Ps. 85:1

44 And Moses came and spake all the words of this song in the ears of the people, he, and T Ho-she'-a the son of Nun.   *Joshua*

45 And Moses made an end of speaking all these words to all Israel:

46 And he said unto them, R Set your hearts unto all the words which I T testify among you this day, which ye shall command your children to observe to do, all the words of this law.   Ezek. 40:4; 44:5 · *certify*

47 For it *is* not a vain thing for you; because it *is* your life: and through this thing ye shall prolong *your* days in the land, whither ye go over Jordan to possess it.

Moses Is Ordered to Mount Nebo

48 And the LORD spake unto Moses that selfsame day, saying,

49 Get thee up into this mountain Ab'-a-rim, *unto* mount Ne'-bo, which *is* in the land of Moab, that *is* over against Jericho; and behold the land of Canaan, which I give unto the children of Israel for a possession:

50 And die in the mount whither thou goest up, and be gathered unto thy people; as R Aaron thy brother died in mount Hor, and was gathered unto his people: Num. 20:25

51 Because ye trespassed against me among the children of Israel at the waters of Mer'-i-bah-Ka'-desh, in the wilderness of Zin; because ye sanctified me not in the midst of the children of Israel.

52 Yet thou shalt see the land before *thee;* but thou shalt not go thither unto the land which I give the children of Israel.

CHAPTER 33

Moses Blesses the Tribes

A ND this *is* the blessing, wherewith Moses R the man of God blessed the children of Israel before his death.   Ps. 90: *Title*

2 And he said, The LORD came from Si'-nai, and rose up from Se'-ir unto them; he shined forth from mount Pa'-ran, and he came with R ten thousands of saints: from his right hand *went* a fiery law for them.   Dan. 7:10; Rev. 5:11

3 Yea, he loved the people; all his saints *are* in thy hand: and they sat down at thy feet; *every* one shall receive of thy words.

4 Moses commanded us a law, *even* the inheritance of the congregation of Jacob.

5 And he was king in R Jesh'-u-run, when the heads of the people *and* the tribes of Israel were gathered together.   32:15

6 R Let Reuben live, and not die; and let *not* his men be few.   Gen. 49:3, 4

7 And this *is the blessing* of Judah: and he said, Hear, LORD, the voice of Judah, and bring him unto his people: let his hands be sufficient for him; and be thou an help *to him* from his enemies.

8 And of Levi he said, *Let* thy Thum'-mim and thy U'-rim *be* with thy holy one, whom thou didst prove at Mas'-sah, *and with* whom thou didst strive at the waters of Mer'-i-bah;

9 Who said unto his father and to his mother, I have not seen him; neither did he

acknowledge his brethren, nor knew his own children: for they have Tobserved thy word, and kept thy covenant.   *carefully noted*

10 They shall teach Jacob thy judgments, and Israel thy law: they shall put incense before thee, and whole burnt sacrifice upon thine altar.

11 Bless, LORD, his substance, and accept the work of his hands: smite through the loins of them that rise against him, and of them that hate him, that they rise not again.

12 *And* of Benjamin he said, The beloved of the LORD shall dwell in safety by him; *and the* LORD shall cover him all the day long, and he shall dwell between his shoulders.

13 And of Joseph he said, Blessed of the LORD *be* his land, for the precious things of heaven, for the dew, and for the deep that coucheth beneath,

14 And for the precious fruits *brought forth* by the sun, and for the precious things put forth by the moon,

15 And for the chief things of Rthe ancient mountains, and for the precious things Rof the Tlasting hills,   Gen. 49:26 • Hab. 3:6 • *everlasting*

16 And for the precious things of the earth and fulness thereof, and *for* the good will of Rhim that dwelt in the bush: let *the blessing* come upon the head of Joseph, and upon the top of the head of him *that was* separated from his brethren.   Ex. 3:2, 4

17 His glory *is like* the firstling of his bullock, and his horns *are like* the horns of unicorns: with them he shall push the people together to the ends of the earth: and they *are* the ten thousands of E'-phra-im, and they *are* the thousands of Ma-nas'-seh.

18 And of Zeb'u-lun he said, RRejoice, Zeb'-u-lun, in thy going out; and, Is'-sa-char, in thy tents.   Gen. 49:13

19 They shall call the people unto the mountain; there they shall offer sacrifices of righteousness: for they shall suck *of* the abundance of the seas, and *of* treasures hid in the sand.

20 And of Gad he said, Blessed *be* he that enlargeth Gad: he dwelleth as a lion, and teareth the arm with the crown of the head.

21 And he provided the first part for himself, because there, *in* a portion of the lawgiver, *was he* seated; and he came with the heads of the people, he executed the justice of the LORD, and his judgments with Israel.

22 And of Dan he said, RDan *is* a lion's whelp: he shall leap from Ba'-shan.   Ezek. 19:2

23 And of Naph'-ta-li he said, O Naph'-ta-li, satisfied with favour, and full with the blessing of the LORD: possess thou the west and the south.

24 And of Asher he said, *Let* Asher *be* blessed with children; let him be acceptable to his brethren, and let him Rdip his foot in oil.   Job 29:6

25 Thy shoes *shall be* iron and brass; and as thy days, *so shall* thy strength *be.*

26 *There is* none like unto the God of Jesh'-u-run, *who* rideth upon the heaven in thy help, and in his excellency on the sky.

27 The eternal God *is thy* Rrefuge, and underneath *are* the everlasting arms: and he shall thrust out the enemy from before thee; and shall say, Destroy *them.*   [Ps. 90:1]

28 Israel then shall dwell in safety alone: the fountain of Jacob *shall be* upon a land of corn and wine; also his heavens shall drop down dew.

29 Happy *art* thou, O Israel: who *is* like unto thee, O people saved by the LORD, the shield of thy help, and who *is* the sword of thy excellency! And thine enemies shall be found liars unto thee; and thou shalt Ttread upon their high places.   *conquer their places of worship*

CHAPTER 34

Moses Views the Promised Land

AND Moses went up from the plains of Moab Runto the mountain of Ne'-bo, to the top of TPis'-gah, that *is* over against Jericho. And the LORD shewed him all the land of Gil'-e-ad, unto Dan,   Num. 27:12 • *the hill*

2 And all Naph'-ta-li, and the land of E'-phra-im, and Ma-nas'-seh, and all the land of Judah, unto the utmost sea,

3 And the Tsouth, and the plain of the valley of Jericho, Rthe city of palm trees, unto Zo'-ar.   *Negev* • 2 Chr. 28:15

4 And the LORD said unto him, RThis *is* the land which I sware unto Abraham, unto Isaac, and unto Jacob, saying, I will give it unto thy seed: RI have caused thee to see *it* with thine eyes, but thou shalt not go over thither.   Gen. 12:7; 26:3 • 3:27

Moses Dies and Is Mourned

5 RSo Moses the servant of the LORD died there in the land of Moab, according to the word of the LORD.   32:50; Num. 12:7

6 And he buried him in a valley in the land of Moab, over against Beth-pe'-or: but no man knoweth of his sepulchre unto this day.

7 And Moses *was* an hundred and twenty years old when he died: his eye was not dim, nor his natural force Tabated.   *gone down*

8 And the children of Israel wept for Moses in the plains of Moab Rthirty days: so the days of weeping *and* mourning for Moses were ended.   Gen. 50:3, 10; Josh. 4:19

Moses Is Replaced by Joshua

9 And Joshua the son of Nun was full of the Rspirit of wisdom; for RMoses had laid his hands upon him: and the children of Israel

hearkened unto him, and did as the LORD commanded Moses.   Is. 11:2 • Num. 27:18, 23

Moses Is Extolled in Israel

10 And there Rarose not a prophet since in Israel like unto Moses, Rwhom the LORD knew face to face,   18:15 • Ex. 33:11

11 In all Rthe signs and the wonders, which the LORD sent him to do in the land of Egypt to Pharaoh, and to all his servants, and to all his land,   7:19

12 And in all that mighty hand, and in all the great Tterror which Moses shewed in the sight of all Israel.   display of almighty power

Monies

Unit	Monetary Value	Equivalents	Translations
Jewish Weights			
Talent	gold—$5,760,000[1] silver—$384,000	3,000 shekels; 6,000 bekas	talent
Shekel	gold—$1,920 silver—$128	4 days' wages; 2 bekas; 20 gerahs	shekel
Beka	gold—$960 silver—$64	½ shekel; 10 gerahs	bekah
Gerah	gold—$96 silver—$6.40	¹⁄₂₀ shekel	gerah
Persian Coins			
Daric	gold—$1,280[2] silver—$64	2 days' wages; ½ Jewish silver shekel	dram
Greek Coins			
Tetradrachma (Stater)	$128	4 drachmas	piece of money
Didrachma	$64	2 drachmas	tribute
Drachma	$32	1 day's wage	piece of silver
Lepton	$.25	½ of a Roman kodrantes	mite
Roman Coins			
Aureus	$800	25 denarii	
Denarius	$32	1 day's wage	pence, penny
Assarius	$2	¹⁄₁₆ of a denarius	farthing
Kodrantes	$.50	¼ of an assarius	farthing

[1]Value of gold is fifteen times the value of silver.
[2]Value of gold is twenty times the value of silver.

THE BOOK OF

JOSHUA

THE BOOK OF JOSHUA

Joshua, the first of the twelve historical books (Joshua-Esther), forges a link between the Pentateuch and the remainder of Israel's history. Through three major military campaigns involving more than thirty enemy armies, the people of Israel learn a crucial lesson under Joshua's capable leadership: victory comes through faith in God and obedience to His word, rather than through military might or numerical superiority.

The title of this book is appropriately named after its central figure, Joshua. His original name is *Hoshea*, "salvation" (Num. 13:8); but Moses evidently changes it to *Yehoshua* (Num. 13:16), "Yahweh Is Salvation." He is also called *Yeshua*, a shortened form of *Yehoshua*. This is the Hebrew equivalent of the Greek name *Iesous* (Jesus). Thus, the Greek title given to the book in the Septuagint is *Iesous Naus*, "Joshua the Son of Nun." The Latin title is *Liber Josue*, the "Book of Joshua."

His name is symbolic of the fact that although he is the leader of the Israelite nation during the conquest, the Lord is the Conqueror.

THE AUTHOR OF JOSHUA

Although it cannot be proven, Jewish tradition seems correct in assigning the authorship of this book to Joshua himself. Joshua 24:26 makes this clear statement: "And Joshua wrote these words in the book of the law of God." This refers at least to Joshua's farewell charge, if not to the book as a whole (see also 18:9). Joshua, as Israel's leader and an eyewitness of most of the events, was the person best qualified to write the book. He even uses the first person in one place (5:6, "us"; "we" appears in some manuscripts of 5:1). The book was written soon after the events occurred: Rahab was still alive (6:25). Other evidences for early authorship are the detailed information about Israel's campaigns and use of the ancient names of Canaanite cities.

The unity of style and organization suggest a single authorship for the majority of the book. Three small portions, however, must have been added after Joshua's death. These are: (1) Othniel's capture of Kirjath-sepher (15:13–19; cf. Judg. 1:9–15), (2) Dan's migration to the north (19:47; cf. Judg. 18:27–29), and (3) Joshua's death and burial (24:29–33). These may have been inserted early in the time of the judges by Eleazer the priest and his son Phinehas (24:33).

Joshua, born a slave in Egypt, becomes a conqueror in Canaan. He serves as personal attendant to Moses, as one of the twelve spies (of whom only he and Caleb believed God), and as Moses' successor. His outstanding qualities are obedient faith, courage, and dedication to God and His Word.

THE TIME OF JOSHUA

Joshua divides neatly into three geographical settings: (1) the Jordan River (1—5); (2) Canaan (6—13:7); and (3) the twelve tribes situated on both sides of the Jordan (13:8—24:33).

The setting of the first five chapters begins east of the Jordan as Joshua replaces Moses, crosses the Jordan on dry land, and finally prepares for war west of the Jordan.

Like a wise general, Joshua utilizes the divide-and-conquer strategy; and his campaign leads him to central Canaan (6—8), southern Canaan (9 and 10), and finally to northern Canaan (11 and 12).

After listing those areas yet to be conquered (13:1–7), Joshua undertakes the long task of dividing the Promised Land to all the tribes. First, he settles those two-and-a-half tribes east of the Jordan (13:8–33) and then the nine-and-a-half tribes west of the Jordan (14:1–19, 51). Completing this, he is free to assign the six Cities of Refuge and the forty-eight Cities of Levites, which are scattered among all the tribes.

The book of Joshua cannot be dated precisely, but utilizing the same threefold division noted above, the following dates can be assigned:

A. One month, March-April, 1405 B.C. (Josh. 1—5)
   1. Death of Moses, March 1405 B.C. (Deut. 34:5–9)
   2. Crossing the Jordan, April 10, 1405 B.C. (Josh. 4:19)

B. Seven years, April 1405–1398 B.C. (Josh. 6:1—13:7)
   1. Caleb forty years old at Kadesh (Josh. 14:7)
   2. Caleb eighty-five years old at that time (Josh. 14:10)
   Note: forty-five years less thirty-eight years of wandering leaves seven years.

C. Eight years, 1398/7–1390 B.C. (Josh. 13:8–24)
   1. Division begun, 1398/7 B.C. (Josh. 14:7–10)
   2. Joshua dies at 110, c. 1390 B.C. (Josh. 24:39)

THE CHRIST OF JOSHUA

Although there are no direct messianic prophecies in the book, Joshua is clearly a figure of Christ. His name *Yeshua* ("Yahweh Is

Salvation") is the Hebrew equivalent of the name Jesus. In his role of triumphantly leading his people into their possessions, he foreshadows the One who will bring "many sons unto glory" (Heb. 2:10). "Now thanks be unto God, which always causeth us to triumph in Christ" (2 Cor. 2:14; see Rom. 8:37). Joshua succeeds Moses and wins the victory unreached by Moses. Christ will succeed the Mosaic Law and win the victory unreachable by the Law (John 1:17; Rom. 8:2–4; Gal. 3:23–25; Heb. 7:18, 19).

The "captain of the host of the LORD" (5:13–15) met by Joshua is evidently a preincarnate appearance of Christ (cf. Josh. 5:15 with Ex. 3:2).

Rahab's scarlet cord portrays safety through the blood (Heb. 9:19–22); and amazingly, this gentile woman is found in Christ's genealogy (Matt. 1:5).

KEYS TO JOSHUA
Key Word: Conquest—The entire Book of Joshua describes the entering, conquering, and occupying of the land of Canaan. The book begins with a statement of the promise of conquest, "Moses my servant is dead; now therefore arise, go over this Jordan . . . Every place that the sole of your foot shall tread upon, that have I given unto you" (1:2, 3) and ends with the completion of conquest "that not one thing hath failed of all the good things which the LORD your God spake concerning you; all are come to pass unto you, and not one thing hath failed thereof" (23:14).

Key Verses: Joshua 1:8; 11:23—"This book of the law shall not depart out of thy mouth; but thou shalt meditate therein day and night, that thou mayest observe to do according to all that is written therein: for then thou shalt make thy way prosperous, and then thou shalt have good success" (1:8).

"So Joshua took the whole land, according to all that the LORD said unto Moses; and Joshua gave it for an inheritance unto Israel according to their divisions by their tribes. And the land rested from war" (11:23).

Key Chapter: Joshua 24—Some of the most critical periods in Israel's. history are the transitions of leadership: Moses to Joshua; Joshua to the judges; the judges to the kings, and so on. Before his death and in preparation for a major transition of leadership by one man (Joshua) to many (the judges), Joshua reviews for the people God's fulfillment of His promises and then challenges them to review their commitment to the covenant (24:24, 25), which is the foundation for all successful national life.

SURVEY OF JOSHUA
Joshua resumes the narrative where Deuteronomy left off, and takes Israel from the wilderness to the Promised Land. Israel has now reached its climactic point of fulfilling the centuries-old promise in Genesis of a homeland. The first half of Joshua (1:1—13:7) describes the seven-year conquest of the land, and the second half (13:8—24:33) gives the details of the division and settlement of the land.

Conquest (1:1—13:7): The first five chapters record the spiritual, moral, physical, and military preparation of Joshua and the people for the impending conquest of Canaan. Joshua is given a charge by God to complete the task begun by Moses (1:2). After being encouraged by God, Joshua sends out two spies who come back with a favorable report (in contrast to the spies of the previous generation). Obedience and faith are united in the miraculous crossing of the Jordan River (3:1—4:24).

Joshua's campaign in central Canaan (6:1—8:35) places a strategic wedge between the northern and southern cities preventing a massive

FOCUS	CONQUEST OF CANAAN		SETTLEMENT IN CANAAN			
REFERENCE	1:1 ——— 6:1———	———13:8———	— 14:1———	— 20:1———	——— 22:1———	— 24:33
DIVISION	PREPARATION OF ISRAEL	CONQUEST OF CANAAN	SETTLEMENT OF EAST JORDAN	SETTLEMENT OF WEST JORDAN	SETTLEMENT OF RELIGIOUS COMMUNITY	CONDITIONS FOR CONTINUED SETTLEMENT
TOPIC	ENTERING CANAAN	CONQUERING CANAAN	DIVIDING CANAAN			
	PREPARATION	SUBJECTION	POSSESSION			
LOCATION	JORDAN RIVER	CANAAN	TWO AND A HALF TRIBES—EAST JORDAN NINE AND A HALF TRIBES—WEST JORDAN			
TIME	c. 1 MONTH	c. 7 YEARS	c. 8 YEARS			

Canaanite alliance against Israel. This divide-and-conquer strategy proves effective, but God's directions for taking the first city (Jericho) sound like foolishness from a military point of view. The Lord uses this to test the people and to teach them that Israel's success in battle will always be by His power and not their own might or cleverness. Sin must be dealt with at once because it brings severe consequences and defeat at Ai (7:1–26).

The southern and northern campaigns (9:1–13:7) are also successful, but an unwise oath made to the deceptive Gibeonites forces Israel to protect them and to disobey God's command to eliminate the Canaanites.

Settlement (13:8–24:33): Joshua is growing old, and God tells him to divide the land among the twelve tribes. Much remains to be won, and the tribes are to continue the conquest by faith after Joshua's death. Chapters 13:8–21:45 describe the allocation of the land to the various tribes as well as the inheritances of Caleb (14 and 15) and the Levites (21).

The last chapters (22:1–24:33) record the conditions for continued successful settlement in Canaan. Access to God, as well as His forgiveness, comes only through the divinely established sacrificial system; and civil war almost breaks out when the eastern tribes build an altar that is misinterpreted by the western tribes.

Realizing that blessing comes from God only as Israel obeys His covenant, Joshua preaches a moving sermon, climaxed by Israel's renewal of her allegiance to the covenant.

OUTLINE OF JOSHUA

Part One: The Conquest of Canaan (1:1—13:7)

Part Two: The Settlement in Canaan (13:8—24:33)

CHAPTER 1

Joshua Is Commissioned by God

NOW after the death of Moses the servant of the LORD it came to pass, that the LORD spake unto Joshua the son of Nun, [R]Moses' minister, saying,   Ex. 24:13

2 Moses my servant is dead; now therefore arise, go over this Jordan, thou, and all this people, unto the land which I do give to them, *even* to the children of Israel.

3 [R]Every place that [T]the sole of your foot shall tread upon, that have I given unto you, as I said unto Moses.   Deut. 11:24 • *walk*

4 From the wilderness and this Leb'-a-non even unto the great river, the river Eu-phra'-tes, all the land of the Hit'-tites, and unto the great sea toward the going down of the sun, shall be your [T]coast.   *border*

5 There shall not any man be able to stand before thee all the days of thy life: as I was with Moses, *so* I will be with thee: I will not fail thee, nor forsake thee.

6 [R]Be strong and of a good courage: for unto this people shalt thou divide for an inheritance the land, which I sware unto their fathers to give them.   Eph. 6:10

7 Only be thou strong and very courageous, that thou mayest observe to do according to all the law, which Moses my servant commanded thee: turn not from it *to* the right hand or *to* the left, that thou mayest prosper whithersoever thou goest.

8 [R]This book of the law [T]shall not depart out of thy mouth; but thou shalt meditate therein day and night, that thou mayest observe to do according to all that is written therein: for then thou shalt make thy way prosperous, and then thou shalt have good success.   Deut. 31:26 • *you shall not forget*

9 Have not I commanded thee? Be strong and of a good courage; be not afraid, neither be thou dismayed: for the LORD thy God *is* with thee whithersoever thou goest.

Joshua Commands the Tribes West of the Jordan

10 Then Joshua commanded the officers of the people, saying,

1:8 Meditating upon God's Word—Joshua had just succeeded Moses in the leadership of the nation Israel. Moses had led the nation for forty years and had the benefit that all the wisdom and culture of Egypt and the king's household could provide. Moses was a seasoned, multi-talented man who had walked closely with God. Joshua, by contrast, was relatively untried. He was assuming an awesome responsibility in taking command of two-and-a-half million people. If anyone needed a formula for success, Joshua did. Likely there were many well-meaning people with all kinds of advice and formulas to help Joshua in the seemingly impossible task that lay ahead. What comfort and assurance it must have been as the LORD (Yahweh) spoke directly to Joshua, assuring him of His presence with him as He had been with Moses (Josh. 1:5), and giving him the key to success—meditating upon God's Word.

Joshua is to meditate upon the Word of God day and night (i.e., at all times), and is promised (1) prosperity and (2) good success in the God-given task that lies ahead. Reading and memorizing God's Word provide the basis for meditating upon God's Word. You meditate upon the Word of God by rehearsing its thoughts over and over in order to understand its implications for the situations of life. Meditating upon the Word of God will guarantee prosperity and success in the new life.

Now turn to Page 208—Deut. 31:12: Obedience to God's Word.

11 Pass through the host, and command the people, saying, Prepare you victuals; for within three days ye shall pass over this Jordan, to go in to possess the land, which the LORD your God giveth you to possess it.

Joshua Commands the Tribes East of the Jordan

12 And to the Reu'-ben-ites, and to the Gad'-ites, and to half the tribe of Ma-nas'-seh, spake Joshua, saying,

13 Remember the word which Moses the servant of the LORD commanded you, saying, The LORD your God hath given you rest, and hath given you this land.

14 Your wives, your little ones, and your cattle, shall remain in the land which Moses gave you on this side Jordan; but ye shall pass before your brethren armed, all the mighty men of valour, and help them;

15 Until the LORD have given your brethren rest, as *he hath given* you, and they also have possessed the land which the LORD your God giveth them: then ye shall return unto the land of your possession, and enjoy it, which Moses the LORD's servant gave you on this side Jordan toward the sunrising.

Joshua Is Accepted by Israel

16 And they answered Joshua, saying, All that thou commandest us we will do, and whithersoever thou sendest us, we will go.

17 According as we hearkened unto Moses in all things, so will we hearken unto thee: only the LORD thy God ᴿbeᵀ with thee, as he was with Moses.   *vv. 5, 9; 1 Kin. 1:37 · bless you*

18 Whosoever *he be* that doth rebel against thy commandment, and will not hearken unto thy words in all that thou commandest him, he shall be put to death: only be strong and of a good courage.

CHAPTER 2

The Faith of Rahab

AND Joshua the son of Nun sent out of Shit'-tim two men to spy secretly, saying, Go view the land, even Jericho. And they went, and came into an harlot's house, named Ra'-hab, and lodged there.

2 ᴿAnd ᵀit was told the king of Jericho, saying, Behold, there came men ᵀin hither to night of the children of Israel to search out the country.   *[Ps. 127:1] · v. 22 · into our city*

3 And the king of Jericho sent unto Ra'-hab, saying, Bring forth the men that are come to thee, which are entered into thine house: for they be come to search out all the country.

4 And the woman took the two men, and hid them, and said thus, There came men unto me, but I wist not whence they *were:*

5 And it came to pass *about the time* of shutting of the gate, when it was dark, that the men went out: ᵀwhither the men went I ᵀwot not: pursue after them quickly; for ye shall overtake them.   *where · know*

6 But ᴿshe had brought them up to the roof of the house, and hid them with the stalks of flax, which she had ᵀlaid in order upon the roof.   *2 Sam. 17:19 · arranged evenly*

7 And the men pursued after them the way to Jordan unto the fords: and as soon as they which pursued after them were gone out, they shut the gate.

8 And before they were laid down, she came up unto them upon the roof;

9 And she said unto the men, I know that the LORD hath given you the land, and that your terror is fallen upon us, and that all the inhabitants of the land faint because of you.

10 For we have heard how the LORD ᴿdried up the water of the Red sea for you, when ye came out of Egypt; and what ye did unto the two kings of the Am'-or-ites, that *were* on the other side Jordan, Si'-hon and Og, whom ye utterly destroyed.   *Ex. 14:21*

11 And as soon as we had heard *these things,* our hearts did melt, neither did there remain any more courage in any man, because of you: for the LORD your God, he *is* God in heaven above, and in earth beneath.

12 Now therefore, I pray you, ᵀswear unto me by the LORD, since I have shewed you kindness, that ye will also shew kindness unto my father's house, and give me a true ᴿtoken: *promise · Ex. 12:13*

13 And *that* ye will save ᴿalive my father, and my mother, and my brethren, and my sisters, and all that they have, and deliver our lives from death.   *6:23-25*

14 And the men answered her, Our life for your's, if ye utter not this our business. And it shall be, when the LORD hath given us the land, that we will ᴿdeal kindly and truly with thee.   *Gen. 47:29*

15 Then she let them down by a cord through the window: for her house *was* upon the town wall, and she dwelt upon the wall.

16 And she said unto them, ᴿGet you to the mountain, lest the pursuers meet you; and hide yourselves there three days, until the pursuers be returned: and afterward may ye go your way.   *James 2:25*

17 And the men said unto her, We *will be* ᴿblamelessᵀ of this thine oath which thou hast made us swear.   *Ex. 20:7 · guiltless*

18 Behold, *when* we come into the land, thou shalt bind this line of scarlet thread in the window which thou didst let us down by: and thou shalt bring thy father, and thy mother, and thy brethren, and all thy father's household, home unto thee.

19 And it shall be, *that* whosoever shall go out of the doors of thy house into the street,

his blood *shall be* upon his head, and we *will be* guiltless: and whosoever shall be with thee in the house, his blood *shall be* on our head, if *any* hand be upon him.

20 And if thou utter this our business, then we will be ᵀquit of thine oath which thou hast made us to swear.   *guiltless*

21 And she said, According unto your words, so *be* it. And she sent them away, and they departed: and she bound the scarlet line in the window.

The Faith of the Spies

22 And they went, and came unto the mountain, and abode there three days, until the pursuers were returned: and the pursuers sought *them* throughout all the way, but found *them* not.

23 So the two men returned, and descended from the mountain, and passed over, and came to Joshua the son of Nun, and told him all *things* that befell them:

24 And they said unto Joshua, Truly ᴿthe LORD hath delivered into our hands all the land; for even all the inhabitants of the country do faint because of us. Ex. 23:31

CHAPTER 3

The Miraculous Crossing of the Jordan

AND Joshua rose early in the morning; and they removed from Shit'-tim, and came to Jordan, he and all the children of Israel, and lodged there before they passed over.

2 And it came to pass after three days, that the officers went through the host;

3 And they commanded the people, saying, When ye see the ark of the covenant of the LORD your God, and the priests the Levites ᵀbearing it, then ye shall remove from your place, and go after it.   *carrying*

4 Yet there shall be a space between you and it, about ᵀtwo thousand cubits by measure: come not near unto it, that ye may know the way by which ye must go: for ye have not passed *this* way heretofore.   *3,000 ft.*

5 And Joshua said unto the people, ᴿSanctify yourselves: for to morrow the LORD will do wonders among you.   Ex. 19:10, 14, 15

6 And Joshua spake unto the priests, saying, ᴿTake up the ark of the covenant, and pass over before the people. And they took up the ark of the covenant, and went before the people.   Num. 4:15

7 And the LORD said unto Joshua, This day will I begin to magnify thee in the sight of all Israel, that they may know that, as I was with Moses, *so* I will be with thee.

8 And thou shalt command the priests that bear the ark of the covenant, saying, When ye are come to the brink of the water of Jordan, ye shall stand still in Jordan.

9 And Joshua said unto the children of ᴿIsrael, Come hither, and hear the words of the LORD your God.   [Gen. 12:2; Rom. 11:26]

10 And Joshua said, Hereby ye shall ᵀknow that ᴿthe living God *is* among you, and *that* he will without fail ᴿdrive out from before you the Ca'-naan-ites, and the Hit'-tites, and the Hi'-vites, and the Per'-iz-zites, and the Gir'-ga-shites, and the Am'-or-ites, and the Jeb'-u-sites.   *realize* • Hos. 1:10 • Ex. 33:2

11 Behold, the ark of the covenant of ᴿthe Lord of all the earth passeth over before you into Jordan.   *v.* 13; Mic. 4:13

12 Now therefore ᴿtake you twelve men out of the tribes of Israel, out of every tribe a man.   4:2, 4

13 And it shall come to pass, as soon as the soles of the feet of the priests that bear the ark of the LORD, the Lord of all the earth, shall rest in the waters of Jordan, *that* the waters of Jordan shall be cut off *from* the waters that come down from above; and they shall stand upon an heap.

14 And it came to pass, when the people removed from their tents, to pass over Jordan, and the priests bearing the ᴿark of the covenant before the people;   Ps. 132:8; Acts 7:45

15 And as they that bare the ark were come unto Jordan, and the feet of the priests that bare the ark were dipped in the brim of the water, (for Jordan overfloweth all his banks ᴿall the time of harvest,)   4:18

16 That the waters which came down from above stood *and* rose up upon an heap very far from the city Adam, that *is* beside Zar'-e-tan: and those that came down toward the sea of the plain, *even* ᴿthe salt sea, failed, *and* were cut off: and the people passed over right against Jericho.   Gen. 14:3

17 And the priests that bare the ark of the covenant of the LORD stood firm on dry ground in the midst of Jordan, and all the Israelites passed over on dry ground, until all the people were passed clean over Jordan.

CHAPTER 4

The Memorial of the Crossing

AND it came to pass, when all the people were ᵀclean passed over Jordan, that the LORD spake unto Joshua, saying,   *entirely*

2 ᴿTake you twelve men out of the people, out of every tribe a man,   3:12

3 And command ye them, saying, Take you hence out of the midst of Jordan, out of the place where the priests' feet stood firm, twelve stones, and ye shall carry them over with you, and leave them in the lodging place, where ye shall lodge this night.

4 Then Joshua called the twelve men, whom he had prepared of the children of Israel, out of every tribe a man:

5 And Joshua said unto them, ᵀPass over before the ark of the LORD your God into the midst of Jordan, and take you up every man of you a stone upon his shoulder, according unto the number of the tribes of the children of Israel: *cross before the ark*

6 That this may be ᵀa sign among you, *that* when your children ask *their fathers* in time to come, saying, What ᵀmean ye by these stones?   *a memorial • do these stones signify?*

7 Then ye shall answer them, That the waters of Jordan were cut off before the ark of the covenant of the LORD; when it passed over Jordan, the waters of Jordan were cut off: and these stones shall be for a memorial unto the children of Israel for ever.

8 And the children of Israel did so as Joshua commanded, and took up twelve stones out of the midst of Jordan, as the LORD spake unto Joshua, according to the number of the tribes of the children of Israel, and carried them over with them unto the place where they lodged, and laid them down there.

9 And Joshua set up ᴿtwelve stones in the midst of Jordan, in the place where the feet of the priests which bare the ark of the covenant stood: and they are there ᵀunto this day.   Gen. 28:18 • *when this book was written*

10 For the priests which bare the ark stood in the midst of Jordan, until every thing was finished that the LORD commanded Joshua to speak unto the people, according to all that Moses commanded Joshua: and the people ᵀhasted and passed over.   *hurried*

11 And it came to pass, when all the people were ᵀclean passed over, that the ark of the LORD passed over, and the priests, in the presence of the people.   *altogether*

12 And the children of Reuben, and the children of Gad, and half the tribe of Ma-nas'-seh, passed over armed before the children of Israel, as Moses spake unto them:

13 About forty thousand ᵀprepared for war passed over before the LORD unto battle, to the plains of Jericho.   *with weapons*

14 On that day the LORD magnifiedᵀ Joshua in the sight of all Israel; and they ᵀfeared him, as they feared Moses, all the days of his life.   *increased his prestige • respected*

15 And the LORD spake unto Joshua, saying,

16 Command the priests that bear ᴿthe ark of the testimony, that they come up out of Jordan.   Ex. 25:16, 22

17 Joshua therefore commanded the priests, saying, Come ye up out of Jordan.

18 And it came to pass, when the priests that bare the ark of the covenant of the LORD were come up out of the midst of Jordan, *and* the soles of the priests' feet were lifted up unto the dry land, that the waters of Jordan returned unto their place, and flowed over all his banks, as *they did* before.

19 And the people came up out of Jordan on the ᴿtenth *day* of the first month, and encamped ᴿin Gil'-gal, in the east border of Jericho.   Ex. 12:1–3; Deut. 1:3 • 5:9

20 And ᴿthose twelve stones, which they took out of Jordan, did Joshua ᵀpitch in ᴿGil'-gal.   *v. 3 • set up •* 5:9, 10; Deut. 11:30

21 And he spake unto the children of Israel, saying, ᴿWhen your children shall ask their fathers in time to come, saying, What *mean* these stones?   *v. 6*

22 Then ᴿye shall let your children know, saying, ᴿIsrael came over this Jordan on dry land.   Ex. 12:26, 27 • 3:17

23 For the LORD your God dried up the waters of Jordan from before you, until ye were passed over, as the LORD your God did to the Red sea, ᴿwhich he dried up from before us, until we were gone over: Ex. 14:21

24 That all the people of the earth might know the ᴿhand of the LORD, that it *is* mighty: that ye might ᵀfear the LORD your God for ever.   Ps. 89:13 • *honour*

CHAPTER 5

The Canaanites Fear Israel

AND it came to pass, when all the kings of the Am'-or-ites, which *were* on the side of Jordan westward, and all the kings of the Ca'-naan-ites, which *were* by the sea, heard that the LORD had dried up the waters of Jordan from before the children of Israel, until we were passed over, that their heart melted, neither was there spirit in them any more, because of the children of Israel.

Circumcision Is Practiced

2 At that time the LORD said unto Joshua, Make thee sharp knives, and circumcise again the children of Israel the second time.

3 And Joshua made him sharp ᴿknives, and circumcised the children of Israel at the hill of the foreskins.   Ex. 4:25

4 And this *is* the cause why Joshua did circumcise: All the people that came out of Egypt, *that were* males, *even* all the men of war, died in the wilderness by the way, after they came out of Egypt.

5 Now all the people that came out were circumcised: but all the people *that were* born in the wilderness by the way as they came forth out of Egypt, *them* they had not circumcised.

6 For the children of Israel walked forty years in the wilderness, till all the people *that were* men of war, which came out of Egypt, were consumed, because they obeyed not the voice of the LORD: unto whom the LORD sware that he would not shew them the land, which the LORD sware unto their fathers that

he would give us, a land that floweth with milk and honey.

7 And their children, *whom* he raised up in their stead, them Joshua circumcised: for they were uncircumcised, because they had not circumcised them by the way.

8 And it came to pass, when they had done circumcising all the people, that they abode in their places in the camp, Rtill they were Twhole.   Gen. 34:25 · *healed*

9 And the LORD said unto Joshua, This day have I rolled away the reproach of Egypt from off you. Wherefore the name of the place is called Gil'-gal unto this day.

Passover Is Celebrated

10 And the children of Israel encamped in Gil'-gal, and kept the passover Ron the fourteenth day of the month at even in the plains of Jericho.   4:19; Ex. 12:6; Num. 9:5

11 And they did eat of the Told corn of the land on the Tmorrow after the passover, unleavened cakes, and Tparched *corn* in the selfsame day.   *ripe grain · next day · roasted grain*

From Manna to Corn

12 And the man'-na ceased on the morrow after they had eaten of the old corn of the land; neither had the children of Israel man'-na any more; but they did eat of the fruit of the land of Canaan that year.

The Captain of the Lord Appears

13 And it came to pass, when Joshua was by Jericho, that he lifted up his eyes and looked, and, behold, there stood a Rman Tover against him with his sword drawn in his hand: and Joshua went unto him, and said unto him, *Art* thou for us, or for our adversaries?   Ezek. 40:3 · *confronting*

14 And he said, Nay; but *as* captain of the host of the LORD am I now come. And Joshua Rfell on his face to the earth, and did worship, and said unto him, What saith my lord unto his servant?   Gen. 17:3; Num. 20:6

15 And the captain of the LORD's host said unto Joshua, RLoose thy shoe from off thy foot; for the place whereon thou standest *is* holy. And Joshua did so.   Ex. 3:5

CHAPTER 6

Victory at Jericho

NOW RJericho was Tstraitly shut up because of the children of Israel: none went out, and none came in.   2:1 · *securely*

2 And the LORD said unto Joshua, See, I have given into thine hand Jericho, and the king thereof, *and* the mighty men of valour.

3 And ye shall Tcompass the city, all *ye* men of war, *and* go round about the city once. Thus shalt thou do six days.   *go around*

4 And seven priests shall bear before the ark seven Rtrumpets of rams' horns: and the seventh day ye shall compass the city seven times, and Rthe priests shall blow with the trumpets.   Judg. 7:16, 22 · Num. 10:8

5 And it shall come to pass, that when they make a long *blast* with the ram's horn, *and* when ye hear the sound of the trumpet, all the people shall Rshout with a great shout; and the wall of the city shall fall down flat, and the people shall Tascend up every man straight before him.   *v. 20 · attack*

6 And Joshua the son of Nun called the priests, and said unto them, Take up the ark of the covenant, and let seven priests bear seven trumpets of rams' horns before the ark of the LORD.

7 And he said unto the people, Pass on, and compass the city, and let him that is armed pass on before the ark of the LORD.

8 RAnd it came to pass, when Joshua had spoken unto the people, that the seven priests bearing the seven trumpets of rams' horns passed on before the LORD, and blew with the trumpets: and the ark of the covenant of the LORD followed them.   4:13

9 And the armed men went before the priests that blew with the trumpets, and the rereward came after the ark, *the priests* going on, and blowing with the trumpets.

10 And Joshua had commanded the people, saying, Ye shall not shout, nor make any noise with your voice, neither shall *any* word proceed out of your mouth, until the day I bid you shout; then shall ye shout.

11 So the ark of the LORD compassed the city, going about *it* once: and they came into the camp, and lodged in the camp.

12 And Joshua rose early in the morning, and the priests took up the ark of the LORD.

13 RAnd seven priests bearing seven trumpets of rams' horns before the ark of the LORD went on continually, and blew with the trumpets: and the armed men went before them; Rbut the rereward came after the ark of the LORD, *the priests* going on, and blowing with the trumpets.   *v. 4 · v. 9*

14 And the second day they Tcompassed the city once, and returned into the camp: so they did six days.   *encircled*

15 And it came to pass on the seventh day, that they rose early about the dawning of the day, and compassed the city after the same manner seven times: only on that day they compassed the city seven times.

16 And it came to pass at the seventh time, when the priests blew with the trumpets, Joshua said unto the people, Shout; for the LORD hath given you the city.

17 And the city shall be Raccursed, *even* it, and all that *are* therein, to the LORD: only Ra'-hab the harlot shall live, she and all that

are with her in the house, because she hid the messengers that we sent.   Deut. 13:17

18 And ye, in any wise keep *yourselves* from the accursed thing, lest ye make *yourselves* [R]accursed, when ye take of the accursed thing, and make the camp of Israel a [T]curse, and trouble it.   7:12 • *accursed*

19 But all the [R]silver, and gold, and vessels of brass and iron, *are* [T]consecrated unto the LORD: they shall [T]come into the treasury of the LORD.   Num. 31:11, 12, 21–33 • *holy • be brought*

20 So the people shouted when *the priests* blew with the trumpets: and it came to pass, when the people heard the sound of the trumpet, and the people shouted with a great shout, that [R]the wall [R]fell down flat, so that the people went up into the city, every man straight before him, and they took the city.   Heb. 11:30 • 10:13

21 And they [R]utterly destroyed all that *was* in the city, both man and woman, young and old, and ox, and sheep, and ass, with the edge of the sword.   Deut. 7:2

22 But Joshua had said unto the two men that had spied out the country, Go into the harlot's house, and bring out thence the woman, and [R]all that she hath, [R]as ye sware unto her.   Gen. 19:12 • 2:14; Heb. 11:31

23 And the young men that were spies went in, and brought out Ra'-hab, [R]and her father, and her mother, and her brethren, and all that she had; and they brought out all her [T]kindred, and left them [T]without the camp of Israel.   2:13 • *families • outside*

24 And they [R]burnt the city with fire, [R]and all that *was* therein: only the silver, and the gold, and the vessels of brass and of iron, they put into the treasury of the house of the LORD.   Deut. 13:16 • Deut. 20:16–18

25 And Joshua saved Ra'-hab the harlot alive, and her father's household, and all that she had; and she dwelleth in Israel *even* unto this day; because she hid the messengers, which Joshua sent to spy out Jericho.

26 And Joshua [T]adjured *them* at that time, saying, [R]Cursed *be* the man before the LORD, that riseth up and buildeth this city Jericho: he shall lay the foundation thereof in his firstborn, and in his youngest *son* shall he set up the gates of it.   *gave strict orders* • 1 Kin. 16:34

27 So the LORD was with Joshua; and his fame was *noised* throughout all the country.

CHAPTER 7

Defeat at Ai

BUT the children of Israel committed a [R]trespass in the accursed thing: for A'-chan, the son of Car'-mi, [R]the son of Zab'-di, the son of Ze'-rah, of the tribe of Judah, took of the accursed thing: and the anger of the

LORD was [T]kindled against the children of Israel.   vv. 20, 21 • 1 Chr. 2:7 • *aroused*

2 And Joshua sent men from Jericho to A'-i, which *is* beside Beth–a'-ven, on the east side of Beth'–el, and spake unto them, saying, Go up and [T]view the country. And the men went up and viewed A'-i.   *survey*

3 And they returned to Joshua, and said unto him, Let not all the people go up; but let about two or three thousand men go up and smite A'-i; *and* make not all the people to labour thither; for they *are but* few.

4 So there went up thither of the people about three thousand men: [R]and they fled before the men of A'-i.   Lev. 26:17; Deut. 28:25

5 And the men of A'-i smote of them about thirty and six men: for they chased them *from* before the gate *even* unto Sheb'-a-rim, and smote them [T]in the going down: wherefore the hearts of the people melted, and became as water.   *on the hillside*

6 And Joshua rent his clothes, and fell to the earth upon his face before the ark of the LORD until the eventide, he and the elders of Israel, and put dust upon their heads.

7 And Joshua said, Alas, O Lord GOD, [R]wherefore hast thou at all brought this people over Jordan, to deliver us into the hand of the Am'-or-ites, to destroy us? would to God we had been content, and dwelt on the other side Jordan!   Ex. 17:3

8 O Lord, what shall I say, when Israel turneth their backs before their enemies!

9 For the Ca'-naan-ites and all the inhabitants of the land shall hear *of it*, and shall [T]environ us round, and [R]cut off our name from the earth: and what wilt thou do unto thy great name?   *encircle* • Deut. 32:26

10 And the LORD said unto Joshua, [T]Get thee up; [T]wherefore liest thou thus upon thy face?   *arise and do something • why*

11 Israel hath sinned, and they have also transgressed my covenant which I commanded them: for they have even taken of the accursed thing, and have also stolen, and dissembled[T] also, and they have put *it* even among their own stuff.   *lied*

12 Therefore the children of Israel could not stand before their enemies, *but* turned *their* backs before their enemies, because they were [T]accursed: neither will I be with you any more, except ye destroy the accursed from among you.   *unacceptable to God*

13 Up, [T]sanctify the people, and say, [R]Sanctify yourselves against to morrow: for thus saith the LORD God of Israel, *There is* an accursed thing in the midst of thee, O Israel: thou canst not stand before thine enemies, until ye take away the accursed thing from among you.   *consecrate* • 3:5

14 In the morning therefore ye shall be brought according to your tribes: and it shall

be, *that* the tribe which ᴿthe Lᴏʀᴅ taketh shall come according to the families *thereof;* and the family which the Lᴏʀᴅ shall take shall come by households; and the household which the Lᴏʀᴅ shall take shall come man by man.   1 Sam. 10:19

15 And it shall be, *that* he that is taken with the accursed thing shall be burnt with fire, he and all that he hath: because he hath transgressed the covenant of the Lᴏʀᴅ, and because he hath wrought folly in Israel.

16 So Joshua rose up early in the morning, and brought Israel by their tribes; and the tribe of Judah was ᵀtaken: *pointed out*

17 And he brought the family of Judah; and he took the family of the Zar'-hites: and he brought the family of the Zar'-hites man by man; and Zab'-di was taken:

18 And he brought his household man by man; and A'-chan, the son of Car'-mi, the son of Zab'-di, the son of Ze'-rah, of the tribe of Judah, ᴿwas taken.   1 Sam. 14:42

19 And Joshua said unto A'-chan, My son, ᴿgive, I pray thee, glory to the Lᴏʀᴅ God of Israel, and make confession unto him; and ᴿtell me now what thou hast done; hide *it* not from me.   1 Sam. 6:5 • 1 Sam. 14:43

20 And A'-chan answered Joshua, and said, Indeed ᴿI have sinned against the Lᴏʀᴅ God of Israel, and ᵀthus and thus have I done: Num. 22:34; 1 Sam. 15:24 • *it was like this*

21 When I saw among the spoils a goodly Bab-y-lo'-nish ᵀgarment, and ᵀtwo hundred shek'-els of silver, and a wedge of gold of ᵀfifty shek'-els weight, then I ᵀcoveted them, and took them; and, behold, they *are* hid in the earth in the midst of my tent, and the silver under it.   *mantle • $24,000 • $96,000 • wanted*

22 So Joshua sent messengers, and they ran unto the tent; and, behold, *it was* hid in his tent, and the silver under it.

23 And they took them out of the midst of the tent, and brought them unto Joshua, and unto ᴿall the children of Israel, and laid them out before the Lᴏʀᴅ.   3:5

24 And Joshua, and all Israel with him, took A'-chan the son of Ze'-rah, and the silver, and the garment, and the wedge of gold, and his sons, and his daughters, and his oxen, and his asses, and his sheep, and his tent, and all that he had: and they brought them unto the valley of A'-chor.

25 And Joshua said, Why hast thou troubled us? the Lᴏʀᴅ shall trouble thee this day. ᴿAnd all Israel stoned him with stones, and burned them with fire, after they had stoned them with stones.   Deut. 17:5

26 And they raised over him a great heap of stones unto this day. So the Lᴏʀᴅ turned from the fierceness of his anger. Wherefore the name of that place was called, The valley of ᵀA'-chor, unto this day.   *troubling*

CHAPTER 8

Victory at Ai

AND the Lᴏʀᴅ said unto Joshua, ᴿFear not, neither be thou dismayed: take all the people of war with thee, and arise, go up to A'-i: see, ᴿI have given into thy hand the king of A'-i, and his people, and his city, and his land: 1:9; Deut. 1:21 • 6:2

2 And thou shalt do to A'-i and her king as thou didst unto Jericho and her king: only the spoil thereof, and the cattle thereof, shall ye take for a prey unto yourselves: lay thee an ambush for the city behind it.

3 So Joshua arose, and all the people of war, to go up against A'-i: and Joshua chose out thirty thousand mighty men of valour, and sent them away by night.

4 And he commanded them, saying, Behold, ᴿye shall lie in wait against the city, *even* behind the city: go not very far from the city, but be ye all ready: Judg. 20:29

5 And I, and all the people that *are* with me, will approach unto the city: and it shall come to pass, when they come out against us, ᴿas at the first, that ᴿwe will flee before them,   7:5 • Judg. 20:32

6 (For they will come out after us) till we have drawn them from the city; for they will say, They flee before us, as at the first: therefore we will flee before them.

7 Then ye shall rise up from the ambush, and seize upon the city: for the Lᴏʀᴅ your God will deliver it into your hand.

8 And it shall be, when ye have taken the city, *that* ye shall set the city on fire: according to the commandment of the Lᴏʀᴅ shall ye do. See, I have commanded you.

9 Joshua therefore sent them forth: and they went to lie in ambush, and abode between Beth'–el and A'-i, on the west side of A'-i: but Joshua ᴿlodged that night among the people.   2 Sam. 17:8

10 And Joshua rose up early in the morning, and ᵀnumbered the people, and ᵀwent up, he and the elders of Israel, before the people to A'-i.   *called the roll • marched*

11 And all the people, *even the people* of war that *were* with him, went up, and drew nigh, and came before the city, and ᵀpitched on the north side of A'-i: now *there was* a valley between them and A'-i.   *made camp*

12 And he took about five thousand men, and set them to lie in ambush between Beth'–el and A'-i, on the west side of the city.

13 And when they had set the people, *even* all the host that *was* on the north of the city, and ᵀtheir liers in wait on the west of the city, Joshua went that night into the midst of the valley.   *as well as those*

14 And it came to pass, when the king of A'-i saw *it,* that they hasted and rose up early, and the men of the city went out against

Israel to battle, he and all his people, at a time appointed, before the plain; but he wist[T] not that *there were* liers in ambush against him behind the city.   *knew*

15 And Joshua and all Israel [R]made as if they were beaten before them, and fled by the way of the wilderness.   Judg. 20:36

16 And all the people that *were* in A'-i were called together to pursue after them: and they pursued after Joshua, and were drawn away from the city.

17 And there was not a man left in A'-i or Beth'-el, that went not out after Israel: and they left the city open, and pursued after Israel.

18 And the LORD said unto Joshua, Stretch out the spear that *is* in thy hand toward A'-i; for I will give it into thine hand. And Joshua stretched out the spear that *he had* in his hand toward the city.

19 And the ambush arose quickly out of their place, and they ran as soon as he had stretched out his hand: and they entered into the city, and took it, and [T]hasted and set the city on fire.   *hurried*

20 And when the men of A'-i looked behind them, they saw, and, behold, the smoke of the city ascended up to heaven, and they had no power to flee this way or that way: and the people that fled to the wilderness turned back upon the pursuers.

21 And when Joshua and all Israel saw that the ambush had taken the city, and that the smoke of the city ascended, then they turned again, and slew the men of A'-i.

22 And the other issued out of the city against them; so they were in the midst of Israel, some on this side, and some on that side: and they [T]smote them, so that they let none of them remain or escape.   *destroyed*

23 And the king of A'-i they took alive, and brought him to Joshua.

24 And it came to pass, when Israel had [T]made an end of slaying all the inhabitants of A'-i in the field, in the wilderness wherein they chased them, and when they were all [T]fallen on the edge of the sword, until they were consumed, that all the Israelites returned unto A'-i, and smote it with the edge of the sword.   *ceased • killed by the sword*

25 And *so* it was, *that* all that fell that day, both of men and women, *were* twelve thousand, *even* all the men of A'-i.

26 For Joshua [T]drew not his hand back, wherewith he [R]stretched out the spear, until he had [R]utterly destroyed all the inhabitants of A'-i.   *did not call a halt •* Ex. 17:11, 12 • 6:21

27 [R]Only the cattle and the spoil of that city Israel took for a prey unto themselves, according unto the word of the LORD which he [R]commanded Joshua.   Num. 31:22, 26 • v. 2

28 And Joshua burnt A'-i, and made it [R]an[T]

heap for ever, *even* a desolation unto this day.   Deut. 13:16 • *a ruin*

29 And the king of A'-i he hanged on a tree until eventide: and as soon as the sun was down, Joshua commanded that they should take his [T]carcase down from the tree, and cast it at the entering of the gate of the city, and raise thereon a great heap of stones, *that* remaineth unto this day.   *body*

Israel Worships the Lord

30 Then Joshua built an altar unto the LORD God of Israel in mount E'-bal,

31 As Moses the servant of the LORD commanded the children of Israel, as it is written in the [R]book of the law of Moses, an altar of whole stones, over which no man hath lift up *any* iron: and they offered thereon burnt offerings unto the LORD, and sacrificed peace offerings.   Deut. 27:5, 6

Israel Renews the Covenant

32 And he wrote there upon the stones a copy of the law of Moses, which he wrote in the presence of the children of Israel.

33 And all Israel, and their elders, and officers, and their judges, stood [T]on this side the ark and on that side before the priests the Levites, which bare the ark of the covenant of the LORD, as well [R]the [T]stranger, as he that was born among them; half of them over against mount Ger'-i-zim, and half of them over against mount E'-bal; as Moses the servant of the LORD had commanded before, that they should bless the people of Israel.   *on both sides of the ark •* Deut. 31:12 • *sojourner*

34 And afterward [R]he read all the words of the law, [R]the blessings and cursings, according to all that is written in the [R]book of the law.   Deut. 31:11; Neh. 8:3 • Deut. 28:2, 15 • 1:8

35 There was not a word of all that Moses commanded, which Joshua read not before all the congregation of Israel, with the women, and the little ones, and the strangers that were conversant among them.

CHAPTER 9

Failure with the Gibeonites

A ND it came to pass, when all the kings which *were* on this side Jordan, in the hills, and in the valleys, and in all the coasts of the [R]great sea over against Leb'-a-non, the Hit'-tite, and the Am'-or-ite, the Ca'-naan-ite, the Per'-iz-zite, the Hi'-vite, and the Jeb'-u-site, heard *thereof;*   Num. 34:6

2 That they [R]gathered themselves together, to fight with Joshua and with Israel, [T]with one accord.   Ps. 83:3, 5 • *united in purpose*

3 And when the inhabitants of [R]Gib'-e-on [R]heard what Joshua had done unto Jericho and to A'-i,   10:2; 2 Sam. 21:1, 2 • 6:27

4 They did work wilily, and went and made as if they had been ambassadors, and took old sacks upon their asses, and wine ᵀbottles, old, and rent, and bound up;   *skins*

5 And old shoes and clouted upon their feet, and old garments upon them; and all the bread of their provision was dry *and* mouldy.

6 And they went to Joshua unto the camp at Gil'-gal, and said unto him, and to the men of Israel, We be come from a far country: now therefore make ye a league with us.

7 And the men of Israel said unto the Hi'-vites, Peradventure ye dwell among us; and how shall we make a league with you?

8 And they said unto Joshua, We *are* thy servants. And Joshua said unto them, Who *are* ye? and from whence come ye?

9 And they said unto him, From a very far country thy servants are come because of the ᵀname of the LORD thy God: for we have ᴿheard the fame of him, and all that he did in Egypt,   *reputation* · 2:9, 10; Ex. 15:14

10 And all that he did to the two kings of the Am'-or-ites, that *were* beyond Jordan, to Si'-hon king of Hesh'-bon, and to Og king of Ba'-shan, which *was* at Ash'-ta-roth.

11 Wherefore our elders and all the inhabitants of our country spake to us, saying, Take victuals with you for the journey, and go to meet them, and say unto them, We *are* your servants: therefore now ᵀmake ye a league with us.   *sign a peace treaty*

12 This our bread we took hot *for* our provision out of our houses on the day we came forth to go unto you; but now, behold, it is dry, and it is mouldy:

13 And these ᵀbottles of wine, which we filled, *were* new; and, behold, they be ᵀrent: and these our garments and our shoes are become old by reason of the very long journey.   *wine-skins · torn*

14 And the men took of their ᵀvictuals, ᴿand ᵀasked not *counsel* at the mouth of the LORD.   *provisions · Num. 27:21 · did not seek guidance*

15 And Joshua ᴿmade peace with them, and made a ᴿleague with them, to let them live: and the princes of the congregation sware unto them.   2 Sam. 21:2 · Ex. 23:32

16 And it came to pass at the end of three days after they had made a league with them, that they heard that they *were* their neighbours, and *that* they dwelt among them.

17 And the children of Israel journeyed, and came unto their cities on the third day. Now their cities *were* ᴿGib'-e-on, and Che-phi'-rah, and Be-e'-roth, and ᴿKir'-jath-je'-a-rim.   18:25 · 15:9

18 And the children of Israel smote them not, because the princes of the congregation had sworn unto them by the LORD God of Israel. And all the congregation ᵀmurmured against the princes.   *complained*

19 But all the princes said unto all the congregation, We have ᴿsworn ᵀunto them by the LORD God of Israel: now therefore we may not touch them.   Mark 6:23 · *promised*

20 This we will do to them; we will even let them live, lest wrath be upon us, because of the oath which we sware unto them.

21 And the princes said unto them, Let them live; but let them be hewers of wood and drawers of water unto all the congregation; as the princes had promised them.

22 And Joshua called for them, and he spake unto them, saying, Wherefore have ye beguiled us, saying, We *are* very far from you; when ᴿye dwell among us?   *v. 16*

23 Now therefore ye *are* ᴿcursed, and there shall none of you be freed from being bond-men, and hewers of wood and drawers of water for the house of my God.   Gen. 9:25

24 And they answered Joshua, and said, Because it was ᵀcertainly told thy servants, how that the LORD thy God commanded his servant Moses to give you all the land, and to destroy all the inhabitants of the land from before you, therefore we were sore afraid of our lives because of you, and have done this thing.   *given as sure information*

25 And now, behold, we *are* ᴿin thine hand: as it seemeth good and right unto thee to do unto us, do.   Gen. 16:6

26 And so did he unto them, and delivered them out of the hand of the children of Israel, that they slew them not.

27 And Joshua made them that day ᴿhew-ers of wood and drawers of water for the congregation, and for the altar of the LORD, even unto this day, ᴿin the place which he should choose.   *vv. 21, 23 · Deut. 12:5*

CHAPTER 10

Victory over the Amorites

NOW it came to pass, when Ad-o'-ni-ze'-dek king of Jerusalem had heard how Joshua had taken A'-i, and had utterly destroyed it; ᴿas he had done to Jericho and her king, so he had done to ᴿA'-i and her king; and ᴿhow the inhabitants of Gib'-e-on had made peace with Israel, and were among them;   6:21 · 8:22, 26, 28 · 9:15

2 That they feared greatly, because Gib'-e-on *was* a great city, as one of the royal cities, and because it *was* greater than A'-i, and all the men thereof *were* mighty.

3 Wherefore Ad-o'-ni-ze'-dek king of Jerusalem sent unto Ho'-ham king of He'-bron, and unto Pi'-ram king of Jar'-muth, and unto Ja-phi'-a king of La'-chish, and unto De'-bir king of Eg'-lon, saying,

4 Come up unto me, and help me, that we may smite Gib'-e-on: for it hath made peace with Joshua and with the children of Israel.

5 Therefore the five kings of the ᴿAm'-or-ites, the king of Jerusalem, the king of He'-bron, the king of Jar'-muth, the king of La'-chish, the king of Eg'-lon, ᴿgathered them-selves together, and went up, they and all their hosts, and encamped before Gib'-e-on, and made war against it.   Num.13:29 • 9:2

6 And the men of Gib'-e-on sent unto Joshua to the camp to Gil'-gal, saying, Slack not thy hand from thy servants; come up to us quickly, and save us, and help us: for all the kings of the Am'-or-ites that dwell in the mountains are gathered together against us.

7 So Joshua ascended from Gil'-gal, he, and all the people of war with him, and all the ᵀmighty men of valour.   *brave soldiers*

8 And the LORD said unto Joshua, Fear them not: for I have delivered them into thine hand; there shall ᵀnot a man of them stand before thee.   *not one will escape being killed*

9 Joshua therefore came unto them sud-denly, *and* went up from Gil'-gal all night.

10 And the LORD discomfited them before Israel, and slew them with a great slaughter at Gib'-e-on, and chased them along the way that goeth up to Beth–ho'-ron, and smote them to A-ze'-kah, and unto Mak-ke'-dah.

11 And it came to pass, as they fled from before Israel, *and* were in the going down to Beth–ho'-ron, that the LORD cast down great stones from heaven upon them unto A-ze'-kah, and they died: *they were* more which died with hailstones than *they* whom the children of Israel slew with the sword.

12 Then spake Joshua to the LORD in the day when the LORD delivered up the Am'-or-ites before the children of Israel, and he said in the sight of Israel, Sun, stand thou still upon Gib'-e-on; and thou, Moon, in the valley of Aj'-a-lon.

13 And the sun stood still, and the moon stayed, until the people had avenged them-selves upon their enemies. *Is* not this written in the book of Ja'-sher? So the sun stood still in the midst of heaven, and hasted not to go down about a whole day.

14 And there was no day like that before it or after it, that the LORD ᵀhearkened unto the voice of a man: for ᴿthe LORD fought for Israel.   *obeyed • v. 42*

15 ᴿAnd Joshua returned, and all Israel with him, unto the camp to Gil'-gal.   *v. 43*

16 But these five kings fled, and hid them-selves in a cave at Mak-ke'-dah.

17 And it was told Joshua, saying, The five kings are found hid in a cave at Mak-ke'-dah.

18 And Joshua said, Roll great stones upon the mouth of the cave, and ᵀset men by it for to keep them: *place soldiers on guard*

19 And ᵀstay ye not, *but* pursue after your enemies, and smite the hindmost of them; ᵀsuffer them not to enter into their cities: for

the LORD your God hath delivered them into your hand.   *do not stop • do not allow*

20 And it came to pass, when Joshua and the children of Israel had made an end of slaying them with a very great slaughter, till they were consumed, that the rest *which* remained of them entered into fenced cities.

21 And all the people returned to the camp to Joshua at Mak-ke'-dah in peace: ᴿnone ᵀmoved his tongue against any of the chil-dren of Israel.   *Ex. 11:7 • nobody criticized*

22 Then said Joshua, Open the mouth of the cave, and bring out those five kings unto me out of the cave.

23 And they did so, and brought forth those five kings unto him out of the cave, the king of Jerusalem, the king of He'-bron, the king of Jar'-muth, the king of La'-chish, *and* the king of Eg'-lon.

24 And it came to pass, when they brought out those kings unto Joshua, that Joshua called for all the men of Israel, and said unto the captains of the men of war which went with him, Come near, put your feet upon the necks of these kings. And they came near, and put their feet upon the necks of them.

25 And Joshua said unto them, ᴿFear not, nor be dismayed, be strong and of good courage: for thus shall the LORD do to all your enemies against whom ye fight.   *1:9*

26 And afterward Joshua smote them, and slew them, and hanged them on five trees: and they ᴿwere hanging upon the trees until the evening.   *8:29; 2 Sam. 21:9*

27 And it came to pass at the time of the going down of the sun, *that* Joshua com-manded, and they ᴿtook them down off the trees, and cast them into the cave wherein they had been hid, and laid great stones in the cave's mouth, *which remain* until this very day.   *8:29; Deut. 21:23*

28 And that day Joshua took Mak-ke'-dah, and smote it with the edge of the sword, and the king thereof he utterly destroyed, them, and all the souls that *were* therein; he let none remain: and he did to the king of Mak-ke'-dah as he did unto the king of Jericho.

29 Then Joshua passed from Mak-ke'-dah, and all Israel with him, unto ᴿLib'-nah, and fought against Lib'-nah: *15:42; 21:13*

30 And the LORD delivered it also, and the king thereof, into the hand of Israel; and he smote it with the edge of the sword, and all the ᵀsouls that *were* therein; he let none remain in it; but did unto the king thereof as he did unto the king of Jericho.   *people*

31 And Joshua passed from Lib'-nah, and all Israel with him, unto La'-chish, and en-camped against it, and fought against it:

32 And the LORD delivered La'-chish into the hand of Israel, which took it on the second day, and smote it with the edge of the

sword, and all the souls that *were* therein, according to all that he had done to Lib'-nah.

33 RThen Ho'-ram king of Ge'-zer came up to help La'-chish; and Joshua smote him and his people, until he had left him none remaining.   11:5

34 And from La'-chish Joshua passed unto REg'-lon, and all Israel with him; and they encamped against it, and fought against it: *v.* 3

35 And they took it on that day, and smote it with the edge of the sword, and all the souls that *were* therein he utterly destroyed that day, according to all that he had done to La'-chish.

36 And Joshua went up from Eg'-lon, and all Israel with him, unto RHe'-bron; and they fought against it: 14:13; 15:13; Num. 13:22

37 RAnd they took it, and smote it with the edge of the sword, and the king thereof, and all the cities thereof, and all the souls that *were* therein; he left none remaining, according to all that he had done to Eg'-lon; but destroyed it utterly, and all the souls that *were* therein.   *v.* 28

38 And Joshua returned, and all Israel with him, to De'-bir; and fought against it:

39 RAnd he took it, and the king thereof, and all the cities thereof; and they smote them with the edge of the sword, and utterly destroyed all the souls that *were* therein; he left none remaining: as he had done to He'-bron, so he did to De'-bir, and to the king thereof; as he had done also to Lib'-nah, and to her king.   11:8

40 So Joshua Tsmote all the country of the hills, and of the south, and of the vale, and of the Tsprings, and all their kings: he left none remaining, but utterly destroyed all that breathed, as the LORD God of Israel Rcommanded.   *conquered · slopes · Deut.* 20:16, 17

41 And Joshua smote them from Ka'-desh-bar'-ne-a even unto Ga'-za, and all the country of Go'-shen, even unto Gib'-e-on.

42 RAnd all these kings and their land did Joshua take at one time, because the RLORD God of Israel fought for Israel.   11:18 · *v.* 14

43 And Joshua returned, and all Israel with him, unto the camp to Gil'-gal.

CHAPTER 11

Conquest of Northern Canaan

AND it came to pass, when Ja'-bin king of RHa'-zor had heard *those things*, that he Rsent to Jo'-bab king of Ma'-don, and to the king Rof Shim'-ron, and to the king of Ach'-shaph,   *v.* 10 · 10:3 · 19:15

2 And to the kings that *were* on the north of the mountains, and of the plains south of RChin'-ne-roth, and in the valley, and in the borders of Dor on the west,   Num. 34:11

3 *And to* the Ca'-naan-ite on the east and on the west, and *to* the Am'-or-ite, and the Hit'-tite, and the Per'-iz-zite, and the Jeb'-u-site in the mountains, and *to* the Hi'-vite under Hermon in the land of Miz'-peh.

4 And they went out, they and all their hosts with them, much people, even as the sand that *is* upon the sea shore in multitude, with horses and chariots very many.

5 And when all these kings were met together, they came and pitched together at the waters of Me'-rom, to fight against Israel.

6 And the LORD said unto Joshua, Be not afraid because of them: for to morrow about this time will I deliver them up all slain before Israel: thou shalt Though their horses, and burn their chariots with fire.   *hamstring*

7 So Joshua came, and all the people of war with him, against them by the waters of Me'-rom suddenly; and they fell upon them.

8 And the LORD delivered them into the hand of Israel, who smote them, and chased them unto great Zi'-don, and unto Mis'-re-photh-ma'-im, and unto the valley of Miz'-peh eastward; and they smote them, until they left them none remaining.

9 And Joshua did unto them as the LORD bade him: he Thoughed their horses, and burnt their chariots with fire.   *hamstrung*

10 And Joshua at that time turned back, and took Ha'-zor, and smote the king thereof with the sword: for Ha'-zor beforetime was the head of all those kingdoms.

11 And they Tsmote all the Tsouls that *were* therein with the edge of the sword, utterly destroying *them*: there was not any left to Rbreathe: Rand he burnt Ha'-zor with fire.   *struck · persons · 10:40 · Deut.* 20:16

12 And all the cities of those kings, and all the kings of them, did Joshua take, and smote them with the edge of the sword, *and* he utterly destroyed them, Ras Moses the servant of the LORD commanded.   Num. 33:52

13 But *as for* the cities that stood still in their strength, Israel burned none of them, save Ha'-zor only; *that* did Joshua burn.

14 And all the Rspoil of these cities, Rand the cattle, the children of Israel took for a prey unto themselves; but every man they smote with the edge of the sword, until they had destroyed them, neither left they any to breathe.   *Deut.* 20:14–18 · *Num.* 31:11, 12

15 As the LORD commanded Moses his servant, so did Moses command Joshua, and so did Joshua; he left nothing undone of all that the LORD commanded Moses.

The Summary of Conquered Territory

16 So Joshua took all that land, Rthe hills, and all the south country, Rand all the land of Go'-shen, and the valley, and the Tplain, and the mountain of Israel, and the valley of the same;   12:8 · 10:41 · *Arabah*

17 REven from the mount Ha'-lak, that

goeth up to Se′-ir, even unto Ba′-al–gad in the valley of Leb′-a-non under mount Hermon: and ᴿall their kings he took, and smote them, and slew them.   12:7 • Deut. 7:24

18 Joshua made war a long time with all those kings.

19 There was not a city that made peace with the children of Israel, save ᴿthe Hi′-vites the inhabitants of Gib′-e-on: all *other* they took in battle.   9:3, 7

20 For it was of the LORD to harden their hearts, ᴿthat they should come against Israel in battle, that he might destroy them utterly, *and* that they might have no ᵀfavour, but that he might destroy them, as the LORD commanded Moses.   Ex. 14:17 • *no mercy*

21 And at that time came Joshua, and cut off the An′-a-kims from the mountains, from He′-bron, from De′-bir, from A′-nab, and from all the mountains of Judah, and from all the mountains of Israel: Joshua destroyed them utterly with their cities.

22 There was none of the An′-a-kims left in the land of the children of Israel: only in Ga′-za, in ᴿGath, ᴿand in Ash′-dod, there remained.   1 Sam. 17:4 • 15:46

23 So Joshua took the whole land, according to all that the LORD said unto Moses; and Joshua gave it for an inheritance unto Israel according to their divisions by their tribes. And the land rested from war.

CHAPTER 12

Kings Conquered by Moses

NOW these *are* the kings of the ᴿland, which the children of Israel ᵀsmote, and possessed their land on the other side Jordan toward the rising of the sun, from the river Arnon unto mount Hermon, and all the plain on the east: Deut. 3:8 • *defeated*

2 ᴿSi′-hon king of the Am′-or-ites, who dwelt in Hesh′-bon, *and* ruled from Ar′-o-er, which *is* upon the bank of the river Arnon, and from the middle of the river, and from half Gil′-e-ad, even unto the river Jab′-bok, which *is* the border of the children of Ammon;   Num. 21:24; Deut. 2:24–27

3 And from the plain to the sea of Chin′-ne-roth on the east, and unto the sea of the plain, *even* the salt sea on the east, the way to Beth–jesh′-i-moth; and from ᵀthe south, under Ash′-doth–pis′-gah: Te′-man

4 And the coast of Og king of Ba′-shan, which *was* of the remnant of the giants, that dwelt at Ash′-ta-roth and at Ed′-re-i,

5 And reigned in ᴿmount Hermon, ᴿand in Sal′-cah, and in all Ba′-shan, unto the border of the Gesh′-u-rites and the Ma-ach′-a-thites, and half Gil′-e-ad, the border of Si′-hon king of Hesh′-bon.   Deut. 3:8 • Deut. 3:10

6 Them did Moses the servant of the LORD and the children of Israel smite: and Moses the servant of the LORD gave it *for* a possession unto the Reu′-ben-ites, and the Gad′-ites, and the half tribe of Ma-nas′-seh.

Kings Conquered by Joshua

7 And these *are* the kings of the country which Joshua and the children of Israel smote on this side Jordan on the west, from Ba′-al–gad in the valley of Leb′-a-non even unto the mount Ha′-lak, that goeth up to Se′-ir; which Joshua gave unto the tribes of Israel *for* a possession according to their divisions;

8 ᴿIn the mountains, and in the valleys, and in the plains, and in the springs, and in the wilderness, and in the south country; ᴿthe Hit′-tites, the Am′-or-ites, and the Ca′-naan-ites, the Per′-iz-zites, the Hi′-vites, and the Jeb′-u-sites: 10:40; 11:16 • 9:1

9 ᴿThe king of Jericho, one; the king of A′-i, which *is* beside Beth′-el, one;   6:2

10 ᴿThe king of Jerusalem, one; the king of He′-bron, one;   10:23

11 The king of Jar′-muth, one; the king of ᴿLa′-chish, one;   2 Kin. 14:19

12 The king of Eg′-lon, one; ᴿthe king of Ge′-zer, one;   10:33

13 ᴿThe king of De′-bir, one; the king of Ge′-der, one;   10:38, 39

14 The king of ᴿHor′-mah, one; ᴿthe king of A′-rad, one;   Judg. 1:17 • Num. 21:1

15 ᴿThe king of Lib′-nah, one; the king of A-dul′-lam, one;   10:29, 30

16 ᴿThe king of Mak-ke′-dah, one; ᴿthe king of Beth′-el, one;   10:28; 15:41 • Judg. 1:22

17 The king of Tap′-pu-ah, one; ᴿthe king of He′-pher, one;   1 Kin. 4:10

18 The king of A′-phek, one; the king of ᵀLa-shar′-on, one;   Shar′-on, Is. 33:9

19 The king of Ma′-don, one; ᴿthe king of Ha′-zor, one;   11:10

20 The king of ᴿShim′-ron-me′-ron, one; the king of Ach′-shaph, one;   11:1; 19:15

21 The king of ᴿTa′-a-nach, one; the king of Me-gid′-do, one;   21:25

22 ᴿThe king of Ke′-desh, one; the king of Jok′-ne-am of Carmel, one;   19:37

23 The king of Dor in the coast of Dor, one; the king of the nations of Gil′-gal, one;

24 The king of ᴿTir′-zah, one: all the kings thirty and one.   Deut. 7:24; 1 Kin. 14:17

CHAPTER 13

Unconquered Parts of Canaan

NOW Joshua ᴿwas old *and* stricken in years; and the LORD said unto him, Thou art old *and* stricken in years, and there remaineth yet very much land to be ᵀpossessed.   14:10; 23:1, 2 • *conquered*

2 ᴿThis *is* the land that yet remaineth: ᴿall the borders of the Phi-lis′-tines, and all ᴿGesh′-u-ri,   Judg. 3:1 • Joel 3:4 • v. 13; 2 Sam. 3:3

3 ᴿFrom Si'-hor, which is before Egypt, even unto the borders of Ek'-ron northward, which is counted to the Ca'-naan-ite: ᴿfive lords of the Phi-lis'-tines; the Ga'-zath-ites, and the Ash'-doth-ites, the Esh'-ka-lon-ites, the Git'-tites, and the Ek'-ron-ites; also ᴿthe A'-vites: Jer. 2:18 • Judg. 3:3 • Deut. 2:23

4 From the south, all the land of the Ca'-naan-ites, and Me-a'-rah that is beside the Si-do'-ni-ans, ᴿunto A'-phek, to the borders of ᴿthe Am'-or-ites: 19:30 • Judg. 1:34

5 And the land of ᴿthe Gib'-lites, and all Leb'-a-non, toward the sunrising, ᴿfrom Ba'-al-gad under mount Hermon unto the entering into Ha'-math. 1 Kin. 5:18 • 12:7

6 All the inhabitants of the hill country from Leb'-a-non unto Mis'-re-photh-ma'-im, and all the Si-do'-ni-ans, them will I drive out from before the children of Israel: only divide thou it by lot unto the Israelites for an inheritance, as I have commanded thee.

7 Now therefore divide this land for an inheritance unto the nine tribes, and the half tribe of Ma-nas'-seh,

Geographical Boundaries

8 With whom the Reu'-ben-ites and the Gad'-ites have received their inheritance, ᴿwhich ᴿMoses gave them, beyond Jordan eastward, even as Moses the servant of the LORD gave them; 22:4; Deut. 3:12, 13 • 12:1-6

9 From Ar'-o-er, that is upon the bank of the river Arnon, and the city that is in the midst of the river, ᴿand all the plain of Med'-e-ba unto Di'-bon; v. 16; Num. 21:30

10 And all the cities of Si'-hon king of the Am'-or-ites, which reigned in Hesh'-bon, unto the border of the children of Ammon;

11 ᴿAnd ᴿGil'-e-ad, and the border of the Gesh'-u-rites and Ma-ach'-a-thites, and all mount Hermon, and all Ba'-shan unto Sal'-cah; 12:5 • Num. 32:1

12 All the kingdom of Og in Ba'-shan, which reigned in Ash'-ta-roth and in ᴿEd'-re-i, who remained of ᴿthe remnant of the giants: for these did Moses ᵀsmite, and ᵀcast them out. 12:4 • Num. 21:34 • defeat • expelled

13 Nevertheless the children of Israel expelled ᴿnot the Gesh'-u-rites, nor the Ma-ach'-a-thites: but the Gesh'-u-rites and the Ma-ach'-a-thites dwell among the Israelites until this day. v. 11; 23:12, 13; Num. 33:55

Boundaries of Levi

14 Only unto the tribe of Levi he gave none inheritance; the ᵀsacrifices of the LORD God of Israel made by fire are their inheritance, as he said unto them. offerings

Boundaries of Reuben

15 ᴿAnd Moses gave unto the tribe of the children of Reuben inheritance ᵀaccording to their families. vv. 15-23 • divided to each family

16 And their coast was from Ar'-o-er, that is on the bank of the river Arnon, ᴿand the city that is in the midst of the river, and all the plain by Med'-e-ba; Num. 21:28

17 ᴿHesh'-bon, and all her cities that are in the plain; Di'-bon, and Ba'-moth-ba'-al, and Beth-ba'-al-me'-on, Num. 21:28, 30

18 ᴿAnd Ja'-ha-za, and Ked'-e-moth, and Meph'-a-ath, Num. 21:23

19 And Kir-ja-tha'-im, and Sib'-mah, and Za'-reth-sha'-har in the mount of the valley,

20 And Beth-pe'-or, and ᴿAsh'-doth-pis'-gah, and Beth-jesh'-i-moth, 12:3; Deut. 3:17

21 ᴿAnd all the cities of the plain, and all the kingdom of Si'-hon king of the Am'-or-ites, which reigned in Hesh'-bon, whom Moses smote ᴿwith the princes of Mid'-i-an, E'-vi, and Re'-kem, and Zur, and Hur, and Re'-ba, which were dukes of Si'-hon, dwelling in the country. Deut. 3:10 • Num. 31:8

22 ᴿBa'-laam also the son of Be'-or, the ᵀsoothsayer, did the children of Israel slay with the sword among them that were slain by them. Num. 22:5; 31:8 • fortune teller

23 And the border of the children of Reuben was Jordan, and the border thereof. This was the inheritance of the children of Reuben after their families, the cities and the villages thereof.

Boundaries of Gad

24 ᴿAnd Moses gave inheritance unto the tribe of Gad, even unto the children of Gad according to their families. Num. 34:14

25 And their ᵀcoast was Ja'-zer, and all the cities of Gil'-e-ad, and half the land of the children of Ammon, unto Ar'-o-er that is before ᴿRab'-bah; border • 2 Sam. 11:1; 12:26

26 And from Hesh'-bon unto Ra'-math-miz'-peh, and Bet'-o-nim; and from Ma-ha-na'-im unto the border of De'-bir;

27 And in the valley, Beth-a'-ram, and Beth-nim'-rah, and Suc'-coth, and Za'-phon, the rest of the kingdom of Si'-hon king of Hesh'-bon, Jordan and his border, even unto the edge of the sea of Chin'-ne-reth on the other side Jordan eastward.

28 This is the inheritance of the children of Gad after their families, the cities, and their villages.

Boundaries of the Half Tribe of Manasseh

29 ᴿAnd Moses gave inheritance unto the half tribe of Ma-nas'-seh: and this was the possession of the half tribe of the children of Ma-nas'-seh by their families. 1 Chr. 5:23

30 And their coast was from Ma-ha-na'-im, all Ba'-shan, all the kingdom of Og king of Ba'-shan, and all the towns of Ja'-ir, which are in Ba'-shan, threescore cities:

31 And half Gil'-e-ad, and ᴿAsh'-ta-roth, and Ed'-re-i, cities of the kingdom of Og in Ba'-shan, ᵀwere pertaining unto the children

of Ma'-chir the son of Ma-nas'-seh, *even* to the one half of the ᴿchildren of Ma'-chir by their families.   12:4 • *went to* • Num. 32:39, 40

32 These *are the countries* which Moses did ᵀdistribute for inheritance in the plains of Moab, on the other side Jordan, by Jericho, eastward.   *allocate*

33 But unto the tribe of Levi Moses gave not *any* inheritance: the LORD God of Israel *was* their inheritance, as he said unto them.

CHAPTER 14

Method of Setting Tribal Boundaries

A ND these *are the countries* which the children of Israel inherited in the land of Canaan, which E-le-a'-zar the priest, and Joshua the son of Nun, and the heads of the fathers of the tribes of the children of Israel, distributed for inheritance to them.

2 By ᴿlot *was* their inheritance, as the LORD commanded by the hand of Moses, for the nine tribes, and *for* the half tribe. Ps. 16:5

3 ᴿFor Moses had given the inheritance of two tribes and an half tribe on the other side Jordan: but unto the Levites he gave none inheritance among them.   13:8, 32, 33

4 For the children of Joseph were two tribes, Ma-nas'-seh and E'-phra-im: therefore they gave no part unto the Levites in the land, save cities to dwell *in*, with their suburbs for their cattle and for their substance.

5 ᴿAs the LORD commanded Moses, so the children of Israel did, and they divided the land.   21:2; Num. 35:2

Boundaries of Caleb

6 Then the children of Judah came unto Joshua in Gil'-gal: and Caleb the son of Jephun'-neh the Ken'-ez-ite said unto him, Thou knowest the thing that the LORD said unto Moses the man of God concerning me and thee in Ka'-desh-bar'-ne-a.

7 Forty years old *was* I when Moses the servant of the LORD ᴿsent me from Ka'-desh-bar'-ne-a to ᵀespy out the land; and I brought him word again as *it was* in mine heart.   Num. 13:6; 14:6 • *scout or spy*

8 Nevertheless my brethren that went up with me made the heart of the people melt: but I wholly followed the LORD my God.

9 And Moses ᵀsware on that day, saying, Surely the land whereon thy feet have trodden shall be thine inheritance, and thy children's for ever, because thou hast wholly followed the LORD my God.   *promised*

10 And now, behold, the LORD hath kept me alive, as he said, these forty and five years, even since the LORD spake this word unto Moses, while *the children of* Israel wandered in the wilderness: and now, lo, I *am* this day fourscore and five years old.

11 As yet I *am as* strong this day as I *was* in the day that Moses sent me: as my strength *was* then, even so *is* my strength now, for war, both to go out, and to come in.

12 Now therefore give me this mountain, whereof the LORD spake in that day; for thou heardest in that day how the An'-a-kims *were* there, and *that* the cities *were* great *and* fenced: ᴿif so be the LORD *will be* with me, then ᴿI shall be able to drive them out, as the LORD said.   Rom. 8:31 • Judg. 1:20

13 And Joshua ᴿblessed him, ᴿand gave unto Caleb the son of Je-phun'-neh He'-bron for an inheritance.   22:6 • 10:37

14 He'-bron therefore became the inheritance of Caleb the son of Je-phun'-neh the Ken'-ez-ite unto this day, because that he wholly followed the LORD God of Israel.

15 And ᴿthe name of He'-bron before *was* Kir'-jath-ar'-ba; *which Ar'-ba was* a great man among the An'-a-kims. ᴿAnd the land had ᵀrest from war.   15:13 • 11:23 • *peace*

CHAPTER 15

Boundaries of the Remainder of Judah

T HIS then was ᵀthe lot of the tribe of the children of Judah by their families; *even* to the border of E'-dom the wilderness of Zin southward *was* the uttermost part of the south ᵀcoast.   *the territory* • *border*

2 And their ᴿsouth border was from the shore of the salt sea, from the bay that looketh southward: Num. 34:4

3 And it went out to the south side ᴿto Ma-al'-eh-a-crab'-bim, and passed along to Zin, and ascended up on the south side unto Ka'-desh-bar'-ne-a, and passed along to Hez'-ron, and went up to A'-dar, and fetched a compass to Kar'-ka-a: Num. 34:3–4

4 *From thence* it passed ᴿtoward Az'-mon, and went out unto the river of Egypt; and the ᵀgoings out of that coast were at the sea: this shall be your south coast.   Num. 34:5 • *end*

5 And the east border *was* the salt sea, *even* unto the end of Jordan. And *their* border in the north quarter *was* from the bay of the sea at the uttermost part of Jordan:

6 And the border went up to Beth-hog'-la, and passed along by the north of Beth-ar'-a-bah; and the border went up to the ᴿstone of Bo'-han the son of Reuben: *marker*

7 And the border went up toward ᴿDe'-bir from ᴿthe valley of A'-chor, and so northward, looking toward Gil'-gal, that *is* before the going up to A-dum'-mim, which *is* on the south side of the river: and the border passed toward the waters of En-she'-mesh, and the goings out thereof were at ᴿEn-ro'-gel: 13:26 • 7:26 • 2 Sam. 17:17

8 And the border went up by the valley of the son of Hin'-nom unto the south side

of the Jeb'-u-site; the same is Jerusalem: and the border went up to the top of the mountain that lieth before the valley of Hin'-nom westward, which is at the end ᴿof the valley of the giants northward: 18:16

9 And the border was drawn from the top of the hill unto the fountain of the water of Neph'-to-ah, and went out to the cities of mount E'-phron; and the border was drawn to Ba'-al-ah, which is Kir'-jath-je'-a-rim:

10 And the border ᵀcompassed from Ba'-al-ah westward unto mount Se'-ir, and passed along unto the side of mount Je'-a-rim, which is Ches'-a-lon, on the north side, and went down to ᴿBeth-she'-mesh, and passed on to Tim'-nah: encircled · 19:22, 38

11 And the border went out unto the side of ᴿEk'-ron northward: and the border was ᵀdrawn to Shic'-ron, and passed along to mount Ba'-al-ah, and went out unto Jab'-neel; and the ᵀgoings out of the border were at the sea.   19:43 · extended · extreme limits

12 And the west border was ᴿto the great sea, and the coast thereof. This is the coast of the children of Judah round about according to their families.   v. 47; Num. 34:6, 7

13 And unto Caleb the son of Je-phun'-neh he gave a part among the children of Judah, according to the commandment of the LORD to Joshua, even the city of Ar'-ba the father of A'-nak, which city is He'-bron.

14 And Caleb drove thence the three sons of A'-nak, ᴿShe'-shai, and A-hi'-man, and Tal'-mai, the children of A'-nak.   Num. 13:22

15 And ᴿhe went up ᵀthence to the inhabitants of De'-bir: and the name of De'-bir before was Kir'-jath-se'-pher.   10:38 · then

16 And Caleb said, He that smiteth Kir'-jath-se'-pher, and taketh it, to him will I give Ach'-sah my daughter to wife.

17 And Oth'-ni-el the ᴿson of Ke'-naz, the brother of Caleb, took it: and he gave him Ach'-sah his daughter to wife.   Num. 32:12

18 And it came to pass, as she came unto him, that she moved him to ask of her father a field: and she lighted off her ass; and Caleb said unto her, What wouldest thou?

19 Who answered, Give me a blessing; for thou hast given me a south land; give me also springs of water. And he gave her the upper springs, and the ᵀnether springs.   lower

20 ᴿThis is the inheritance of the tribe of the children of Judah according to their families.   [Gen. 49:8-12]

21 And the uttermost cities of the tribe of the children of Judah toward the coast of E'-dom southward were Kab'-ze-el, and ᴿE'-der, and Ja'-gur,   Gen. 35:21

22 And Ki'-nah, and Di-mo'-nah, and A-da'-dah,

23 And Ke'-desh, and Ha'-zor, and Ith'-nan,

24 Ziph, and Te'-lem, and Be'-a-loth,

25 And Ha'-zor, Ha-dat'-tah, and Ke'-ri-oth, and Hez'-ron, which is Ha'-zor,

26 A'-mam, and She'-ma, and Mol'-a-dah,

27 And Ha'-zar-gad'-dah, and Hesh'-mon, and Beth-pa'-let,

28 And Ha'-zar-shu'-al, and ᴿBe'-er-she'-ba, and Biz-joth'-jah,   19:2; Gen. 21:31

29 Ba'-al-ah, and I'-im, and A'-zem,

30 And El-to'-lad, and Che'-sil, and ᴿHor'-mah,   19:4

31 And ᴿZik'-lag, and Mad-man'-nah, and San-san'-nah,   19:5; 1 Sam. 27:6; 30:1; 1 Chr. 12:1

32 And Leb'-a-oth, and Shil'-him, and A'-in, and Rim'-mon: all the cities are twenty and nine, with their villages:

33 And in the valley, ᴿEsh'-ta-ol, and Zo'-re-ah, and Ash'-nah,   Judg. 13:25

34 And Za-no'-ah, and En-gan'-nim, Tap'-pu-ah, and E'-nam,

35 Jar'-muth, and ᴿA-dul'-lam, So'-coh, and A-ze'-kah,   1 Sam. 22:1

36 And Sha-ra'-im, and Ad-i-tha'-im, and Ge-de'-rah, and Ged-e-ro-tha'-im; fourteen cities with their villages:

37 Ze'-nan, and Had'-a-shah, and Mig'-dal-gad,

38 And Dil'-e-an, and Miz'-peh, ᴿand Jok'-the-el,   2 Kin. 14:7

39 La'-chish, and Boz'-kath, and Eg'-lon,

40 And Cab'-bon, and Lah'-mam, and Kith'-lish,

41 And Ge-de'-roth, Beth-da'-gon, and Na'-a-mah, and Mak-ke'-dah; sixteen cities with their villages:

42 Lib'-nah, and E'-ther, and A'-shan,

43 And Jiph'-tah, and Ash'-nah, and Ne'-zib,

44 And Kei'-lah, and Ach'-zib, and Ma-re'-shah; nine cities with their villages:

45 Ek'-ron, with her towns and her villages:

46 From Ek'-ron even unto the sea, all that lay near Ash'-dod, with their villages:

47 Ash'-dod with her towns and her villages, Ga'-za with her towns and her villages, unto ᴿthe river of Egypt, and the great sea, and the border thereof: v. 4

48 And in the mountains, Sha'-mir, and Jat'-tir, and So'-coh,

49 And Dan'-nah, and ᴿKir'-jath-san'-nah, which is De'-bir,   vv. 15, 16

50 And A'-nab, and Esh'-te-moh, and A'-nim,

51 ᴿAnd Go'-shen, and Ho'-lon, and Gi'-loh; eleven cities with their villages: 10:41

52 Arab, and Du'-mah, and E'-she-an,

53 And ᵀJa'-num, and Beth-tap'-pu-ah, and A-phe'-kah,   Janus

54 And Hum'-tah, and ᴿKir'-jath-ar'-ba, which is He'-bron, and Zi'-or; nine cities with their villages: 14:15

55 ᴿMa-on, Carmel, and Ziph, and Jut'-tah,   1 Sam. 23:24, 25

56 And Jez'-re-el, and Jok'-de-am, and Za-no'-ah,

57 Cain, Gib'-e-ah, and Tim'-nah; ten cities with their villages:

58 Hal'-hul, Beth'-zur, and Ge'-dor,

59 And Ma'-a-rath, and Beth'-a-noth, and El'-te-kon; six cities with their villages:

60 ᴿKir'-jath-ba'-al, which is Kir'-jath-je'-a-rim, and Rab'-bah; two cities with their villages: 18:14; 1 Sam. 7:1, 2

61 In the wilderness, Beth-ar'-a-bah, Mid'-din, and Sec'-a-cah,

62 And Nib'-shan, and the city of Salt, and En-ge'-di; six cities with their villages.

63 As for the Jeb'-u-sites the inhabitants of Jerusalem, ᴿthe children of Judah could not drive them out: ᴿbut the Jeb'-u-sites dwell with the children of Judah at Jerusalem unto this day.   Judg. 1:8, 21 • 2 Sam. 5:6

CHAPTER 16

Boundaries of Joseph

A ND the lot of the children of Joseph ᵀfell from Jordan by Jericho, unto the water of Jericho on the east, to ᴿthe wilderness that goeth up from Jericho throughout mount Beth'-el,   went forth • 8:15

2 And goeth out from Beth'-el to ᴿLuz, and passeth along unto the borders of Ar'-chi to At'-a-roth,   18:13; Judg. 1:26

3 And goeth down westward to the coast of Japh-le'-ti, unto the coast of Beth-ho'-ron the ᵀnether, and to Ge'-zer: and the goings out thereof are at the sea.   lower

4 So the children of Joseph, Ma-nas'-seh and E'-phra-im, took their inheritance.

Boundaries of Ephraim

5 And the border of the children of E'-phra-im according to their families was thus: even the border of their inheritance on the east side was At'-a-roth-ad'-dar, ᴿunto Beth-ho'-ron the upper;   2 Chr. 8:5

6 And the border went out ᵀtoward the sea to ᴿMich'-me-thah on the north side; and the border went about eastward unto Ta'-a-nath-shi'-loh, and passed by it on the east to Ja-no'-hah;   westward at • 17:7

7 And it went down from Ja-no'-hah to At'-a-roth, ᴿand to Na'-a-rath, and came to Jericho, and went out at Jordan.   1 Chr. 7:28

8 The border went out from Tap'-pu-ah westward unto the river Ka'-nah; and the ᵀgoings out thereof were at the sea. This is the inheritance of the tribe of the children of E'-phra-im by their families.   extreme limits

9 And ᴿthe separate cities for the children of E'-phra-im were among the inheritance of the children of Ma-nas'-seh, all the cities with their villages.   17:9

10 And they drave not out the Ca'-naan-ites that dwelt in Ge'-zer: but the Ca'-naan-ites dwell among the E'-phra-im-ites unto this day, and serve under tribute.

CHAPTER 17

Boundaries of the Half Tribe of Manasseh

T HERE was also a lot for the tribe of Ma-nas'-seh; for he was the firstborn of Joseph; to wit, for Ma'-chir the firstborn of Ma-nas'-seh, the father of Gil'-e-ad: because he was ᵀa man of war, therefore he had Gil'-e-ad and Ba'-shan.   a great soldier

2 There was also a lot for the rest of the children of Ma-nas'-seh by their families; for the children of ᴿA'-bi-e'-zer,ᵀ and for the children of He'-lek, and for the children of As'-ri-el, and for the children of She'-chem, and for the children of He'-pher, and for the children of She-mi'-da: these were the male children of Ma-nas'-seh the son of Joseph by their families.   Num. 26:26–33 • Jeezer

3 But ᴿZe-lo'-phe-had, the son of He'-pher, the son of Gil'-e-ad, the son of Ma'-chir, the son of Ma-nas'-seh, had no sons, but daughters: and these are the names of his daughters, Mah'-lah, and Noah, Hog'-lah, Mil'-cah, and Tir'-zah.   Num. 26:33; 27:1

4 And they came near before ᴿE-le-a'-zar the priest, and before Joshua the son of Nun, and before the princes, saying, The Lᴏʀᴅ commanded Moses to give us ᵀan inheritance among our brethren. Therefore according to the commandment of the Lᴏʀᴅ he gave them an inheritance among the brethren of their father.   14:1 • a share

5 And there fell ten portions to Ma-nas'-seh, beside the land of Gil'-e-ad and Ba'-shan, which were on the other side Jordan;

6 Because the daughters of Ma-nas'-seh had an inheritance among his sons: and ᴿthe rest of ᴿMa-nas'-seh's sons had the land of Gil'-e-ad.   Num. 26:29 • 13:30, 31

7 And the coast of Ma-nas'-seh was from Asher to ᴿMich'-me-thah, that ᵀlieth before She'-chem; and the border went along on the right hand unto the inhabitants of En-tap'-pu-ah.   16:6 • was

8 Now Ma-nas'-seh had the ᵀland of Tap'-pu-ah: but ᴿTap'-pu-ah on the border of Ma-nas'-seh belonged to the children of E'-phra-im;   city of apples • 16:8

9 And the coast descended unto the river Ka'-nah, southward of the river: these cities of E'-phra-im are among the cities of Ma-nas'-seh: the coast of Ma-nas'-seh also was on the north side of the river, and the outgo-ings of it were at the sea:

10 Southward it was E'-phra-im's, and northward it was Ma-nas'-seh's, and the sea is ᵀhis ᵀborder; and they met together in

Asher on the north, and in Is′-sa-char on the east.   *its • boundary*

11 And Ma-nas′-seh had in Is′-sa-char and in Asher RBeth-she′-an and her towns, and Ib′-le-am and her towns, and the inhabitants of Dor and her towns, and the inhabitants of En′-dor and her towns, and the inhabitants of Ta′-a-nach and her towns, and the inhabitants of Me-gid′-do and her towns, *even* three countries.   1 Kin. 4:12

12 Yet Rthe children of Ma-nas′-seh could not drive out *the inhabitants of* those cities; but the Ca′-naan-ites would dwell in that land.   Judg. 1:27, 28

13 Yet it came to pass, when the children of Israel were waxen strong, that they put the Ca′-naan-ites to Rtribute;T but did not utterly drive them out.   16:10 • *taskwork*

14 And the children of Joseph spake unto Joshua, saying, Why hast thou given me *but* one Tlot and one portion to inherit, seeing I *am* a great people, forasmuch as the LORD hath blessed me hitherto?   *section*

15 And Joshua answered them, If thou *be* a great people, *then* get thee up to the wood country, and cut down for thyself there in Rthe land of the Per′-iz-zites and of the giants, if mount E′-phra-im be too Tnarrow for thee.   Gen. 15:20 • *limited*

16 And the children of Joseph said, The hill is not enough for us: and all the Ca′-naan-ites that dwell in the land of the valley have Rchariots of iron, *both they* who *are* of Beth-she′-an and her towns, and *they* who *are* of the valley of Jez′-re-el.   Judg. 1:19

17 And Joshua spake unto the house of Joseph, *even* to E′-phra-im and to Ma-nas′-seh, saying, Thou *art* a great people, and hast great power: thou shalt not have one Tlot only: *section*

18 But the mountain shall be thine; for it *is* a Twood, and thou shalt cut it down: and the Toutgoings of it shall be thine: for thou shalt drive out the Ca′-naan-ites, Rthough they have iron chariots, *and* though they *be* strong.   *forest • borders •* Deut. 20:1

CHAPTER 18

The Remaining Tribes Move to Shiloh

AND the whole congregation of the children of Israel assembled together at Shi′-loh, and set up the tabernacle of the congregation there. And the land was subdued before them.

New Method of Setting Tribal Boundaries

2 RAnd there remained among the children of Israel seven tribes, which had not yet received their inheritance.   Judg. 18:9

3 And Joshua said unto the children of Israel, How long *are* ye slack to go to possess

the land, which the LORD God of your fathers hath given you?

4 Give out from among you three men for *each* tribe: and I will send them, and they shall rise, and go through the land, and describe it according to the inheritance of them; and they shall come *again* to me.

5 And they shall divide it into seven parts: Judah shall abide in Ttheir coast on the south, and the house of Joseph shall abide in their coasts on the north.   *his border*

6 Ye shall therefore Tdescribe the land *into* seven parts, and bring *the description* hither to me, Rthat I may cast lots for you here before the LORD our God.   *diagram • v.* 10

7 But the Levites have no part among you; for the priesthood of the LORD *is* their inheritance: and Gad, and Reuben, and half the tribe of Ma-nas′-seh, have received their inheritance beyond Jordan on the east, which Moses the servant of the LORD gave them.

8 And the men arose, and went away: and Joshua charged them that went to describe the land, saying, Go and walk Rthrough the land, and describe it, and come again to me, that I may here cast lots for you before the LORD in Shi′-loh.   Gen. 13:17

9 And the men went and passed through the land, and described it by cities into seven Tparts in a Tbook, and came *again* to Joshua to the host at Shi′-loh.   *portions • scroll*

10 And Joshua cast lots for them in Shi′-loh before the LORD: and there Joshua divided the land unto the children of Israel according to their Tdivisions.   *family groups*

Boundaries of Benjamin

11 And the lot of the tribe of the children of Benjamin came up according to their families: and the Tcoast of their lot came forth between the children of Judah and the children of Joseph.   *area of their section*

12 RAnd their border on the north side was from Jordan; and the border went up to the side of Jericho on the north side, and went up through the mountains westward; and the Tgoings out thereof were at the wilderness of Beth-a′-ven.   16:1 • *end*

13 And the border went over from thence toward Luz, to the side of Luz, Rwhich *is* Beth′-el, southward: and the border descended to At′-a-roth-a′-dar, near the hill that *lieth* on the south side Rof the nether Beth-ho′-ron.   Gen. 28:19; Judg. 1:23 • 16:3

14 And the border was drawn *thence*, and compassed the corner of the sea southward, from the hill that *lieth* before Beth–ho′-ron southward; and the goings out thereof were at Kir′-jath-ba′-al, which *is* Kir′-jath-je′-a-rim, a city of the children of Judah: this *was* the west Tquarter.   *section*

15 And the south quarter *was* from the end Rof Kir′-jath-je′-a-rim, and the border went

out on the west, and went out to the well of waters of Neph'-to-ah: 1 Chr. 13:5, 6

16 And the border came down to the end of the mountain that *lieth* before ᴿthe valley of the son of Hin'-nom, *and* which *is* in the valley of the giants on the north, and descended to the valley of Hin'-nom, to the side of Jeb'-u-si on the south, and descended to ᴿEn-ro'-gel, 15:8 • 15:7

17 And was drawn from the north, and went forth to En-she'-mesh, and went forth toward Gel'-i-loth, which *is* over against the going up of A-dum'-mim, and descended to the stone of Bo'-han the son of Reuben,

18 And passed along toward the side over against ᴿAr'-a-bah northward, and went down unto Ar'-a-bah: 15:6

19 And the border passed along to the side of Beth-hog'-lah northward: and the ᵀoutgoings of the border were at the north bay of the salt sea at the south end of Jordan: this *was* the south coast. *extreme limits*

20 And Jordan was the border of it on the east side. This *was* the inheritance of the children of Benjamin, by the ᵀcoasts thereof round about, according to their families. *borders*

21 Now the cities of the tribe of the children of Benjamin according to their families were Jericho, and Beth-hog'-lah, and the valley of Ke'-ziz,

22 And Beth-ar'-a-bah, and Zem-a-ra'-im, and Beth'-el,

23 And A'-vim, and Pa'-rah, and Oph'-rah,

24 And Che'-phar-ha-am'-mo-nai, and Oph'-ni, and Ga'-ba; twelve cities with their villages:

25 Gib'-e-on, and Ra'-mah, and Be-e'-roth,

26 And Miz'-peh, and Che-phi'-rah, and Mo'-zah,

27 And Re'-kem, and Ir'-pe-el, and Tar'-a-lah,

28 And Ze'-lah, E'-leph, and Jeb'-u-si, which *is* Jerusalem, Gib'-e-ath, *and* Kir'-jath; fourteen cities with their villages. This *is* the inheritance of the children of Benjamin according to their families.

CHAPTER 19

Boundaries of Simeon

AND ᴿthe second lot came forth to Simeon, *even* for the tribe of the children of Simeon according to their families: and their inheritance was within the inheritance of the children of Judah. Judg. 1:3

2 And they had in their inheritance Be'-er-she'-ba, or She'-ba, and Mol'-a-dah,

3 And Ha'-zar-shu'-al, and Ba'-lah, and A'-zem,

4 And El-to'-lad, and Be'-thul, and Hor'-mah,

5 And Zik'-lag, and Beth-mar'-ca-both, and ᴿHa'-zar-su'-sah, 1 Chr. 4:31

6 And Beth-leb'-a-oth, and Sha-ru'-hen; thirteen cities and their villages:

7 A'-in, Rem'-mon, and E'-ther, and A'-shan; four cities and their villages:

8 And all the villages that *were* round about these cities to Ba'-al-ath-be'-er, ᴿRa'-math of the south. This *is* the inheritance of the tribe of the children of Simeon according to their families. 1 Sam. 30:27

9 Out of the portion of the children of Judah *was* the inheritance of the children of Simeon: for the part of the children of Judah was too much for them: therefore the children of Simeon had their inheritance within the inheritance of them.

Boundaries of Zebulun

10 ᴿAnd the third lot came up for the children of Zeb'-u-lun according to their families: and the ᵀborder of their ᵀinheritance was unto Sa'-rid: Gen. 49:13 • *boundary • land*

11 ᴿAnd their border went up toward the sea, and Mar'-a-lah, and reached to Dab'-ba-sheth, and reached to the river that *is* ᴿbefore Jok'-ne-am; Gen. 49:13 • 12:22; 21:34

12 And turned from Sa'-rid eastward toward the sunrising unto the border of Chis'-loth-ta'-bor, and then goeth out to Dab'-e-rath, and goeth up to Ja-phi'-a,

13 And from thence passeth on along on the east to ᴿGit'-tah-he'-pher, to It'-tah-ka'-zin, and goeth out to Rem'-mon-meth'-o-ar to Ne'-ah; 2 Kin. 14:25

14 And the border compasseth it on the north side to Han'-na-thon: and the ᵀoutgoings thereof are in the valley of Jiph'-thah-el: *extreme limits*

15 And Kat'-tath, and Na-hal'-lal, and Shim'-ron, and Id'-a-lah, and Beth'-le-hem: twelve cities with their villages.

16 This *is* the ᵀinheritance of the children of Zeb'-u-lun according to their families, these cities with their villages. *land*

Boundaries of Issachar

17 ᴿAnd the fourth ᵀlot came out to Is'-sa-char, for the children of Is'-sa-char according to their families. Gen. 49:14, 15 • *mess*

18 ᴿAnd their border was toward Jez'-re-el, and Che-sul'-loth, and Shu'-nem, 2 Kin. 4:8

19 And Haph-ra'-im, and Shi'-hon, and An-a-ha'-rath,

20 And Rab'-bith, and Kish'-i-on, and A'-bez,

21 ᴿAnd Re'-meth, and En-gan'-nim, and En-had'-dah, and Beth-paz'-zez; 21:29

22 And the ᵀcoast reacheth to Ta'-bor, and Sha-haz'-i-mah, and Beth-she'-mesh; and the outgoings of their border were at Jordan: sixteen cities with their villages. *border*

23 This *is* the inheritance of the tribe of the

children of Is'-sa-char according to their families, the cities and their villages.

Boundaries of Asher

24 ᴿAnd the fifth lot came out for the tribe of the children of Asher according to their families.   Judg. 1:31, 32

25 And their border was Hel'-kath, and Ha-li, and Be'-ten, and Ach'-shaph,

26 And A-lam'-me-lech, and A'-mad, and Mi'-she-al; and reacheth to ᴿCarmel westward, and to Shi'-hor–lib'-nath;   1 Sam. 15:12

27 And turneth toward the sunrising to Beth–da'-gon, and reacheth to Zeb'-u-lun, and to the valley of Jiph'-thah–el toward the north side of Beth–e'-mek, and Ne–i'-el, and goeth out to Ca'-bul on the left hand,

28 And He'-bron, and Re'-hob, and Ham'-mon, and Ka'-nah, *even* unto great Zi'-don;

29 And *then* the ᵀcoast turneth to Ra'-mah, and to the strong city Tyre; and the coast turneth to Ho'-sah; and the outgoings thereof are at the sea ᵀfrom the coast to ᴿAch'-zib: *border · by the regions of ·* Judg. 1:31

30 Um'-mah also, and A'-phek, and Re'-hob: twenty and two cities with their villages.

31 This *is* the inheritance of the tribe of the children of Asher according to their families, these cities with their villages.

Boundaries of Naphtali

32 The sixth lot came out to the children of Naph'-ta-li, *even* for the children of Naph'-ta-li according to their families.

33 And their coast was from He'-leph, from Al'-lon to Za-a-nan'-nim, and Ad'-a-mi, Ne'-keb, and Jab'neel, unto La'-kum; and the outgoings thereof were at Jordan:

34 And *then* the ᵀcoast turneth westward to Az'-noth–ta'-bor, and goeth out from thence to Huk'-kok, and reacheth to Zeb'-u-lun on the south side, and reacheth to Asher on the west side, and to Judah upon Jordan toward the ᵀsunrising.   *border · east*

35 And the ᵀfenced cities *are* Zid'-dim, Zer, and Ham'-math, Rak'-kath, and Chin'-ne-reth,   *fortified*

36 And Ad'-a-mah, and Ra'-mah, and Ha'-zor,

37 And ᴿKe'-desh, and Ed'-re-i, and En–ha'-zor,   20:7

38 And I'-ron, and Mig'-dal-el, Ho'-rem, and Beth-a'-nath, and Beth-she'-mesh; nineteen cities with their villages.

39 This *is* the inheritance of the tribe of the children of Naph'-ta-li according to their families, the cities and their villages.

Boundaries of Dan

40 ᴿ*And* the seventh lot came out for the tribe of the children of Dan according to their families.   Judg. 1:34–36

41 And the coast of their inheritance was Zo'-rah, and Esh'-ta-ol, and Ir–she'-mesh,

42 And ᴿSha-al-ab'-bin, and ᴿAj'-a-lon, and Jeth'-lah,   Judg. 1:35; 1 Kin. 4:9 · 10:12; 21:24

43 And E'-lon, and Thim'-na-thah, and ᴿEk'-ron,   15:11; Judg. 1:18

44 And El'-te-keh, and Gib'-be-thon, and Ba'-al-ath,

45 And Je'-hud, and Ben'-e-be'-rak, and Gath–rim'-mon,

46 And Me–jar'-kon, and Rak'-kon, with the border before ᵀJa'-pho.ᴿ   *Jop'-pa ·* Acts 9:36

47 And the coast of the children of Dan went out *too little* for them: therefore the children of Dan went up to fight against Le'-shem, and took it, and smote it with the edge of the sword, and possessed it, and dwelt therein, and called Le'-shem, Dan, after the name of Dan their father.

48 This *is* the inheritance of the tribe of the children of Dan according to their families, these cities with their villages.

Boundaries of Joshua

49 When they had made an end of dividing the land for inheritance by their coasts, the children of Israel gave an inheritance to Joshua the son of Nun among them:

50 According to the word of the LORD they gave him the city which he asked, *even* Tim'-nath–se'-rah in mount E'-phra-im: and he built the city, and dwelt therein.

51 ᴿThese *are* the inheritances, which E-le-a'-zar the priest, and Joshua the son of Nun, and the heads of the fathers of the tribes of the children of Israel, divided for an inheritance by lot ᴿin Shi'-loh before the LORD, at the door of the tabernacle of the congregation. So they made an end of dividing the country.   14:1 · 18:1, 10

CHAPTER 20

Six Cities of Refuge

THE LORD also spake unto Joshua, saying, 2 Speak to the children of Israel, saying, ᴿAppointᵀ out for you cities of refuge, whereof I spake unto you by the hand of Moses: Num. 35:6, 11, 14; Deut. 19:2, 9 · *set aside*

3 That the slayer that killeth *any* person ᵀunawares and ᵀunwittingly may flee thither: and they shall be your refuge from the avenger of blood.   *accidentally · unintentionally*

4 And when he that doth flee unto one of those cities shall stand at the entering of the gate of the city, and shall declare his cause in the ears of the elders of that city, they shall take him into the city unto them, and give him a place, that he may dwell among them.

5 ᴿAnd if the avenger of blood pursue after him, then they shall not deliver the slayer up

into his hand; because he smote his neighbour [T]unwittingly, and hated him not beforetime.   Num. 35:12 · *unintentionally*

6 And he shall dwell in that city, until he [T]stand before the congregation for judgment, *and* until the death of the high priest that shall be in those days: then shall the slayer return, and come unto his own city, and unto his own house, unto the city from whence he fled.   *comes before the people to be judged*

7 And they appointed Ke'-desh in Gali-lee in mount Naph'-ta-li, and She'-chem in mount E'-phra-im, and Kir'-jath-ar'-ba, which *is* He'-bron, in the mountain of Judah.

8 And on the other side Jordan by Jericho eastward, they assigned Be'-zer in the wilderness upon the plain out of the tribe of Reuben, and Ra'-moth in Gil'-e-ad out of the tribe of Gad, and Go'-lan in Ba'-shan out of the tribe of Ma-nas'-seh.

9 These were the cities appointed for all the children of Israel, and for the stranger that sojourneth among them, that whosoever killeth *any* person [T]at unawares might flee thither, and not die by the hand of the avenger of blood, [R]until he stood before the congregation.   *by accident · v. 6 · Josh. 20:6*

CHAPTER 21

The Families to Be Assigned Cities
1 Chr. 6:54–81

THEN came near the [T]heads of the fathers of the Levites unto E-le-a'-zar the priest, and unto Joshua the son of Nun, and unto the heads of the fathers of the tribes of the children of Israel;   *chief leaders*

2 And they spake unto them at [R]Shi'-loh in the land of Canaan, saying, [R]The LORD commanded by the hand of Moses to give us cities to dwell in, with the [T]suburbs thereof for our cattle.   18:1 · Num. 35:2 · *pasture*

3 And the children of Israel gave unto the Levites out of their inheritance, at the commandment of the LORD, these cities and their [T]suburbs.   *pasture lands*

4 And [T]the lot came out for the families of the Ko'-hath-ites: and the children of Aaron the priest, *which were* of the Levites, had by lot out of the tribe of Judah, and out of the tribe of Simeon, and out of the tribe of Benjamin, thirteen cities.   *the share*

5 And the rest of the children of Ko'-hath *had* by lot out of the families of the tribe of E'-phra-im, and out of the tribe of Dan, and out of the half tribe of Ma-nas'-seh, ten cities.

6 And the children of Ger'-shon *had* by lot out of the families of the tribe of Is'-sa-char, and out of the tribe of Asher, and out of the tribe of Naph'-ta-li, and out of the half tribe of Ma-nas'-seh in Ba'-shan, thirteen cities.

7 The children of Me-ra'-ri by their families

had out of the tribe of Reuben, and out of the tribe of Gad, and out of the tribe of Zeb'-u-lun, twelve cities.

Cities for the Kohathites

8 [R]And the children of Israel gave by lot unto the Levites these cities with their [T]suburbs, [R]as the LORD commanded by the hand of Moses.   *v. 3 · pasture lands · Num. 35:2*

9 And they gave out of the tribe of the children of Judah, and out of the tribe of the children of Simeon, these cities which are *here* [T]mentioned by name.   *called*

10 Which the children of Aaron, *being* of the families of the Ko'-hath-ites, *who were* of the children of Levi, had: for theirs was the first lot.

11 And they gave them the city of Ar'-ba the father of A'-nak, which *city is* He'-bron, [R]in the hill *country* of Judah, with the suburbs thereof round about it.   20:7

12 But the fields of the city, and the villages thereof, gave they to Caleb the son of Je-phun'-neh for his possession.

13 Thus they gave to the children of Aaron the priest He'-bron with her suburbs, *to be* a city of refuge for the slayer; [R]and Lib'-nah with her suburbs,   15:42

14 And Jat'-tir with her suburbs, [R]and Esh-te-mo'-a with her suburbs,   15:50

15 And [R]Ho'-lon[T] with her suburbs, and De'-bir with her suburbs,   1 Chr. 6:58 · *Hilen*

16 And [R]A'-in[T] with her suburbs, [R]and Jut'-tah with her suburbs, *and* Beth–she'-mesh with her suburbs; nine cities out of those two tribes.   1 Chr. 6:59 · *Ashan* · 15:55

17 And out of the tribe of Benjamin, [R]Gib'-e-on with her suburbs, [R]Ge'-ba[T] with her [T]suburbs,   18:25 · 18:24 · *Gaba · pasture*

18 An'-a-thoth [R]with her suburbs, and Al'-mon with her suburbs; four cities.   1 Chr. 6:60

19 All the cities of the children of Aaron, the priests, *were* thirteen cities with their [T]suburbs.   *pasture lands*

20 And the families of the children of Ko'-hath, the Levites which remained of the children of Ko'-hath, even they had the cities of their lot out of the tribe of E'-phra-im.

21 For they gave them [R]She'-chem with her [T]suburbs in mount E'-phra-im, *to be* a city of refuge for the slayer; and [R]Ge'-zer with her suburbs,   20:7 · Judg. 1:29 · *pasture lands*

22 And Kib'-za-im with her suburbs, and Beth–ho'-ron with her suburbs; four cities.

23 And out of the tribe of Dan, El'-te-keh with her [T]suburbs, Gib'-be-thon with her suburbs,   *pasture lands*

24 Ai'-ja-lon with her suburbs, Gath–rim'-mon with her suburbs; four cities.

25 And out of the half tribe of Ma-nas'-seh, Ta'-nach with her suburbs, and Gath–rim'-mon with her suburbs; two cities.

26 All the cities *were* ten with their Tsuburbs for the families of the children of Ko'-hath that remained.   *pasture lands*

Cities for the Gershonites

27 RAnd unto the children of Ger'-shon, of the families of the Levites, out of the *other* half tribe of Ma-nas'-seh *they gave* RGo'-lan in Ba'-shan with her suburbs, *to be* a city of refuge for the slayer; and Be-esh'-te-rah with her suburbs; two cities.   *v. 6 • 20:8*

28 And out of the tribe of Is'-sa-char, Ki'-shon with her suburbs, Dab'-a-reh with her Tsuburbs,   *pasture lands*

29 Jar'-muth with her suburbs, En-gan'-nim with her suburbs; four cities.

30 And out of the tribe of Asher, Mi'-shal with her suburbs, Ab'-don with her suburbs,

31 Hel'-kath with her suburbs, and Re'-hob with her suburbs; four cities.

32 And out of the tribe of Naph'-ta-li, Ke'-desh in Galilee with her suburbs, *to be* a city of Trefuge for the slayer; and Ham'-moth-dor with her suburbs, and Kar'-tan with her suburbs; three cities.   *protection*

33 All the cities of the Ger'-shon-ites according to their families *were* thirteen cities with their Tsuburbs.   *pasture lands*

Cities for the Merarites

34 And unto the families of the children of Me-ra'-ri, the rest of the Levites, out of the tribe of Zeb'-u-lun, Jok'-ne-am with her suburbs, and Kar'-tah with her suburbs,

35 Dim'-nah with her Tsuburbs, Na'-ha-lal with her suburbs; four cities.   *pasture lands*

36 And out of the tribe of Reuben, RBe'-zer with her suburbs, and Ja'-ha-zah with her Tsuburbs,   *20:8 • pasture lands*

37 Ked'-e-moth with her suburbs, and Meph'-a-ath with her suburbs; four cities.

38 And out of the tribe of Gad, RRa'-moth in Gil'-e-ad with her Tsuburbs, *to be* a city of refuge for the slayer; and Ma-ha-na'-im with her suburbs,   *20:8 • pasture lands*

39 Hesh'-bon with her suburbs, Ja'-zer with her suburbs; four cities in all.

40 So all the cities for the children of Me-ra'-ri by their families, which were remaining of the families of the Levites, were *by* their lot twelve cities.

41 All the cities of the Levites within the possession of the children of Israel *were* forty and eight cities with their suburbs.

42 These cities were every one with their Tsuburbs round about them: thus *were* all these cities.   *pasture lands*

The Settlement of Israel Is Completed

43 And the LORD gave unto Israel Rall the land which he sware to give unto their fathers; and they possessed it, and dwelt therein.   *Gen. 13:15; 15:18; 26:3; 28:4, 13*

44 And the LORD gave them rest round about, according to all that he sware unto their fathers: and there stood not a man of all their enemies before them; the LORD delivered all their enemies into their hand.

45 There failed Tnot ought of any good thing which the LORD had spoken unto the house of Israel; all came to pass.   *nothing*

CHAPTER 22

Joshua Challenges the Eastern Tribes

THEN Joshua called the Reu'-ben-ites, and the Gad'-ites, and the half tribe of Ma-nas'-seh,

2 And said unto them, Ye have Tkept all that Moses the servant of the LORD commanded you, Rand have obeyed my voice in all that I commanded you: *performed • 1:16, 17*

3 Ye have not left your brethren these many days unto this day, but have Tkept the charge of the commandment of the LORD your God.   *been faithful to your assigned task*

4 And now the LORD your God hath given rest unto your brethren, as he promised them: therefore now return ye, and get you unto your tents, *and* unto the land of your possession, which Moses the servant of the LORD gave you on the other side Jordan.

5 But take diligent heed to do the commandment and the law, which Moses the servant of the LORD charged you, to love the LORD your God, and to walk in all his ways, and to keep his commandments, and to cleave unto him, and to serve him with all your heart and with all your soul.

6 So Joshua blessed them, and sent them away: and they went unto their tents.

7 RNow to the *one* half of the tribe of Ma-nas'-seh Moses had given Tpossession in Ba'-shan: Rbut unto the *other* half thereof gave Joshua among their brethren on this side Jordan westward. And when Joshua sent them away also unto their tents, then he blessed them,   *Num. 32:33 • inheritance • 17:5*

8 And he spake unto them, saying, Return with much riches unto your tents, and with very much cattle, with silver, and with gold, and with brass, and with iron, and with very much Traiment: divide the spoil of your enemies with your brethren.   *clothing*

9 And the children of Reuben and the children of Gad and the half tribe of Ma-nas'-seh returned, and departed from the children of Israel out of Shi'-loh, which *is* in the land of Canaan, to go unto the country of Gil'-e-ad, to the land of their possession, whereof they were possessed, according to the word of the LORD by the hand of Moses.

Construction of the Altar

10 And when they came unto the borders of Jordan, that *are* in the land of Canaan, the

children of Reuben and the children of Gad and the half tribe of Ma-nas'-seh built there an altar by Jordan, a great altar to ᵀsee to.   *look upon*

Misunderstanding of the Altar

11 And the children of Israel heard ᴿsay, Behold, the children of Reuben and the children of Gad and the half tribe of Ma-nas'-seh have built an altar over against the land of Canaan, in the borders of Jordan, at the passage of the children of Israel.   Judg. 20:12

12 And when the children of Israel heard *of it*, the whole congregation of the children of Israel gathered themselves together at Shi'-loh, to go up to war against them.

13 And the children of Israel sent unto the children of Reuben, and to the children of Gad, and to the half tribe of Ma-nas'-seh, into the land of Gil'-e-ad, ᴿPhin'-e-has the son of E-le-a'-zar the priest,   Num. 25:7, 11

14 And with him ten princes, of each chief house a prince throughout all the tribes of Israel; and ᴿeach one *was* an head of the house of their fathers among the ᵀthousands of Israel.   Num. 1:4 · *families*

15 And they came unto the children of Reuben, and to the children of Gad, and to the half tribe of Ma-nas'-seh, unto the land of Gil'-e-ad, and they spake with them, saying,

16 Thus saith the whole congregation of the LORD, What trespass *is* this that ye have committed against the God of Israel, to turn away this day from following the LORD, in that ye have builded you an altar, that ye might rebel this day against the LORD?

17 *Is* the iniquity ᴿof Pe'-or too little for us, from which we are not cleansed until this day, although there was a plague in the congregation of the LORD,   Num. 25:1

18 But that ye must turn away this day from following the LORD? and it will be, *seeing* ye rebel to day against the LORD, that to morrow ᴿhe will be ᵀwroth with the whole congregation of Israel.   Num. 16:22 · *angry*

19 ᵀNotwithstanding, if the land of your possession *be* ᵀunclean, *then* pass ye over unto the land of the possession of the LORD, wherein the LORD's tabernacle dwelleth, and take possession among us: but rebel not against the LORD, nor rebel against us, in building you an altar ᵀbeside the altar of the LORD our God.   *however · unfit · in addition to*

20 Did not ᴿA'-chan the son of Ze'-rah commit a trespass in the ᵀaccursed thing, and wrath fell on all the congregation of Israel? and that man perished ᵀnot alone in his iniquity.   7:1 · *forbidden · others died with him*

Explanation of the Altar

21 ᴿThen the children of Reuben and the children of Gad and the half tribe of Ma-nas'-

seh answered, and said unto the heads of the thousands of Israel,   [Prov. 15:1; 24:26]

22 The LORD God of gods, the LORD God of gods, he knoweth, and Israel he shall know; if *it be* in rebellion, or if in transgression against the LORD, (save us not this day,)

23 That we have built us an altar to turn from following the LORD, or if to offer thereon burnt offering or meat offering, or if to offer peace offerings thereon, let the LORD himself requireᵀ *it;*   *bring us to account*

24 And if we have not *rather* done it for fear of *this* thing, saying, In time to come your children might speak unto our children, saying, What have ye to do with the LORD God of Israel?

25 For the LORD hath made Jordan a border between us and you, ye children of Reuben and children of Gad; ye have no part in the LORD: so shall your children make our children cease from fearing the LORD.

26 Therefore we said, Let us now prepare to build us an altar, not for burnt offering, nor for sacrifice:

27 But *that* it *may be* ᴿa witness between us, and you, and our generations after us, that we might do the service of the LORD before him with our burnt offerings, and with our sacrifices, and with our peace offerings; that your children may not say to our children in time to come, ᵀYe have no part in the LORD.   *v. 34 · you do not belong to*

28 Therefore said we, that it shall be, when they should so say to us or to our generations in time to come, that we may say *again*, Behold the pattern of the altar of the LORD, which our fathers made, not for burnt offerings, nor for sacrifices; but it *is* a ᴿwitness between us and you.   Gen. 31:44–49

29 God forbid that we should rebel against the LORD, and turn this day from following the LORD, to build an altar for burnt offerings, for ᵀmeat offerings, or for sacrifices, beside the altar of the LORD our God that *is* before his tabernacle.   *meal*

Celebration by the Western Tribes

30 And when Phin'-e-has the priest, and the princes of the congregation and heads of the thousands of Israel which *were* with him, heard the words that the children of Reuben and the children of Gad and the children of Ma-nas'-seh spake, it pleased them.

31 And Phin'-e-has the son of E-le-a'-zar the priest said unto the children of Reuben, and to the children of Gad, and to the children of Ma-nas'-seh, This day we perceive that the LORD *is* among us, because ye have not committed this trespass against the LORD: now ye have delivered the children of Israel out of the hand of the LORD.

32 And Phin'-e-has the son of E-le-a'-zar the priest, and the princes, returned from the

children of Reuben, and from the children of Gad, out of the land of Gil′-e-ad, unto the land of Canaan, to the children of Israel, and brought them word again.

33 And the thing pleased the children of Israel; and the children of Israel blessed God, and did not intend to go up against them in battle, to destroy the land wherein the children of Reuben and Gad dwelt.

34 And the children of Reuben and the children of Gad ᴿcalled the altar *Ed:* for it *shall be* a witness ᴿbetween us that the LORD *is* God.   Gen. 31:47–49 · 24:27

CHAPTER 23

A Reminder from History

AND it came to pass a long time after that the LORD had given rest unto Israel from all their enemies round about, that Joshua ᵀwaxed old *and* stricken in age.   *grew*

2 And Joshua called for all Israel, *and* for their elders, and for their heads, and for their judges, and for their officers, and said unto them, I am old *and* stricken in age:

3 And ye have seen all that the ᴿLORD your God hath done unto all these nations because of you; for the ᴿLORD your God *is* he that hath fought for you.   Ps. 44:3 · Ex. 14:14

4 Behold, ᴿI have divided unto you by lot these nations that remain, to be an inheritance for your tribes, from Jordan, with all the nations that I have ᵀcut off, even unto the great sea westward.   18:10 · *destroyed*

5 And the LORD your God, ᴿhe shall expel them from before you, and drive them from out of your sight; and ye shall possess their land, ᴿas the LORD your God hath promised unto you.   Ex. 23:30; 33:2 · Num. 33:53

6 Be ye therefore very courageous to keep and to do all that is written in the book of the law of Moses, that ye turn not aside therefrom *to* the right hand or *to* the left;

7 That ye come not among these nations, these that remain among you; neither make mention of the name of their gods, nor cause to swear *by them,* neither serve them, nor bow yourselves unto them:

8 But ᵀcleave unto the LORD your God, as ye have done unto this day.   *stay obediently*

9 For the LORD hath driven out from before you great nations and strong: but *as for* you, no man hath been able to ᵀstand before you unto this day.   *resist you in battle*

10 One man of you shall chase a thousand: for the LORD your God, he *it is* that fighteth for you, as he hath promised you.

11 Take good heed therefore unto yourselves, that ye love the LORD your God.

12 Else if ye do in any wise go back, and cleave unto the remnant of these nations, *even* these that remain among you, and shall

make marriages with them, and ᵀgo in unto them, and they to you: *fraternize with*

13 Know for a certainty that the LORD your God will no more drive out *any of* these nations from before you; but they shall be snares and traps unto you, and scourges in your sides, and thorns in your eyes, until ye perish from off this good land which the LORD your God hath given you.

14 And, behold, this day I ᵀ*am* going the way of all the earth: and ye know in all your hearts and in all your souls, that not one thing hath failed of all the good things which the LORD your God spake concerning you; all are come to pass unto you, *and* not one thing hath failed thereof.   *will die*

15 Therefore it shall come to pass, *that* as all good things are come upon you, which the LORD your God promised you; so shall the LORD bring upon you all evil things, until he have destroyed you from off this good land which the LORD your God hath given you.

16 When ye have transgressed the covenant of the LORD your God, which he commanded you, and have gone and served other gods, and bowed yourselves to them; then shall the anger of the LORD be kindled against you, and ye shall perish quickly from off the good land which he hath given unto you.

CHAPTER 24

Renewal of the Covenant

AND Joshua gathered all the tribes of Israel to She′-chem, and called for the elders of Israel, and for their heads, and for their judges, and for their officers; and they presented themselves before God.

2 And Joshua said unto all the people, Thus saith the LORD God of Israel, ᴿYour fathers dwelt on the other side of ᵀthe flood in old time, *even* Te′-rah, the father of Abraham, and the father of Na′-chor: and they served other gods.   Gen. 11:7–32 · *the river*

3 And I took your father Abraham from the other side of the flood, and led him throughout all the land of Canaan, and multiplied his seed, and gave him Isaac.

4 And I gave unto Isaac ᴿJacob and Esau: and I gave unto ᴿEsau mount Se′-ir, to possess it; ᴿbut Jacob and his children went down into Egypt.   Gen. 25:25 · Deut. 2:5 · Gen. 46:1, 6

5 I sent Moses also and Aaron, and I plagued Egypt, according to that which I did among them: and afterward I brought you out.

6 And I brought your fathers out of Egypt: and ᴿye came unto the sea; and the Egyptians pursued after your fathers with chariots and horsemen unto the Red sea.   Ex. 14:2–31

7 And when they cried unto the LORD, he put darkness between you and the Egyptians,

and brought the sea upon them, and ^Tcovered them; and your eyes have seen what I have done in Egypt: and ye dwelt in the wilderness a long season.   *drowned*

8 And I brought you into the land of the Am'-or-ites, which dwelt on the other side Jordan; ^Rand they fought with you: and I gave them into your hand, that ye might possess their land; and I destroyed them from before you.   Num. 21:21, 33

9 Then Ba'-lak the son of Zip'-por, king of Moab, arose and warred against ^RIsrael, and ^Rsent and called Ba'-laam the son of Be'-or to curse you: Judg. 11:25 • Num. 22:5

10 ^RBut I would not hearken unto Ba'-laam; therefore he blessed you still: so I delivered you out of his hand.   Deut. 23:5

11 And ^Rye went over Jordan, and came unto Jericho: and ^Rthe men of Jericho fought against you, the Am'-or-ites, and the Per'-iz-zites, and the Ca'-naan-ites, and the Hit'-tites, and the Gir'-ga-shites, the Hi'-vites, and the Jeb'-u-sites; and I delivered them into your hand.   3:14, 17 • 6:1; 10:1

12 And I sent the hornet before you, which drave them out from before you, *even* the two kings of the Am'-or-ites; *but* not with thy sword, nor with thy bow.

13 And I have given you a land for which ye did not labour, and ^Rcities which ye built not, and ye dwell in them; of the vineyards and ^Roliveyards which ye planted not do ye eat.   Deut. 6:10, 11 • 1 Sam. 8:14

14 Now therefore fear the LORD, and serve him in sincerity and in truth: and put away the gods which your fathers served on the other side of the ^Tflood, and in Egypt; and serve ye the LORD.   *great river*

15 And if it seem evil unto you to serve the LORD, ^Rchoose you this day whom ye will serve; whether the gods which your fathers served that *were* on the other side of the flood, or the gods of the Am'-or-ites, in whose land ye dwell: but as for me and my house, we will serve the LORD.   Ruth 1:15

16 And the people answered and said, God forbid that we should forsake the LORD, to serve other gods;

17 For the LORD our God, he *it is* that brought us up and our fathers out of the land of Egypt, from the house of bondage, and which did those great signs in our sight, and preserved us in all the way wherein we went, and among all the people through whom we passed:

18 And the LORD drave out from before us all the people, even the Am'-or-ites which dwelt in the land: ^Rtherefore will we also serve the LORD; for he *is* our God.   Ps. 116:16

19 And Joshua said unto the people, Ye cannot serve the LORD: for he *is* an holy God;

he *is* a jealous God; he will not forgive your transgressions nor your sins.

20 If ye forsake the LORD, and serve strange gods, then he will turn and ^Tdo you hurt, and ^Tconsume you, after that he hath done you good.   *bring calamity upon you • destroy*

21 And the people said unto Joshua, Nay; but we will serve the LORD.

22 And Joshua said unto the people, Ye *are* witnesses against yourselves that ^Rye have chosen you the LORD, to serve him. And they said, We *are* witnesses.   Ps. 119:173

23 Now therefore ^Rput away, *said he,* the ^Tstrange gods which *are* among you, and ^Tincline your heart unto the LORD God of Israel.   *v. 14; Gen. 35:2 • foreign • make up your minds*

24 And the people ^Rsaid unto Joshua, The LORD our God will serve, and his voice will we obey.   Deut. 5:24–27

25 So Joshua ^Rmade a covenant with the people that day, and set them a statute and an ordinance in She'-chem.   Ex. 15:25

26 And Joshua wrote these words in the book of the law of God, and took a great stone, and set it up there under an oak, that *was* by the sanctuary of the LORD.

27 And Joshua said unto all the people, Behold, ^Rthis stone shall be ^Ra witness unto us; for ^Rit hath heard all the words of the LORD which he spake unto us: it shall be therefore a witness unto you, lest ye deny your God.   22:27, 34 • Gen. 31:48 • Deut. 32:1

28 So ^RJoshua let the people depart, every man unto his inheritance.   Judg. 2:6

Joshua and Eleazar Die

29 ^RAnd it came to pass after these things, that Joshua the son of Nun, the servant of the LORD, died, *being* an hundred and ten years old.   Judg. 2:8

30 And they buried him in the border of his inheritance in ^RTim'-nath-se'-rah, which *is* in mount E'-phra-im, on the north side of the hill of Ga'-ash.   19:50; Judg. 2:9

31 And Israel served the LORD all the days of Joshua, and all the days of the elders that ^Toverlived Joshua, and which had ^Rknown all the works of the LORD, that he had done for Israel.   *outlived • Deut. 11:2*

32 ^RAnd the bones of Joseph, which the children of Israel brought up out of Egypt, buried they in She'-chem, in a parcel of ground which Jacob bought of the sons of Ha'-mor the father of She'-chem for an hundred pieces of silver: and it became the inheritance of the children of Joseph.   Gen. 50:25

33 And E-le-a'-zar the son of Aaron died; and they buried him in a hill *that* ^Tpertained to Phin'-e-has his son, which was given him in mount E'-phra-im.   *belonged*

THE BOOK OF

JUDGES

THE BOOK OF JUDGES
The Book of Judges stands in stark contrast to Joshua. In Joshua an obedient people conquered the land through trust in the power of God. In Judges, however, a disobedient and idolatrous people are defeated time and time again because of their rebellion against God.

In seven distinct cycles of sin to salvation, Judges shows how Israel had set aside God's law and in its place substituted *"that which was* right in his own eyes" (21:25). The recurring result of abandonment from God's law is corruption from within and oppression from without. During the nearly four centuries spanned by this book, God raises up military champions to throw off the yoke of bondage and to restore the nation to pure worship. But all too soon the "sin cycle" begins again as the nation's spiritual temperature grows steadily colder.

The Hebrew title is *Shophetim,* meaning "judges," "rulers," "deliverers," or "saviours." *Shophet* not only carries the idea of maintaining justice and settling disputes, but it is also used to mean liberating and delivering. First the judges deliver the people; then they rule and administer justice. The Septuagint used the Greek equivalent of this word, *Kritai* ("Judges"). The Latin Vulgate called it *Liber Judicum,* the "Book of Judges." This book could also appropriately be titled "The Book of Failure."

THE AUTHOR OF JUDGES
The author of Judges is anonymous, but Samuel or one of his prophetic students may have written it. Jewish tradition contained in the Talmud attributes Judges to Samuel, and certainly he was the crucial link between the period of the judges and the period of the kings.

It is clear from 18:31 and 20:27 that the book was written after the ark was removed from Shiloh (1 Sam. 4:3–11). The repeated phrase "In those days *there was* no king in Israel" (17:6; 18:1; 19:1; 21:25) shows that Judges was also written after the commencement of Saul's reign but before the divided kingdom. The fact that the Jebusites were dwelling in Jerusalem "unto this day" (1:21) means that it was written before 1004 B.C. when David dispossessed the Jebusites (2 Sam. 5:5–9). Thus, the book was written during the time of Samuel; and it is likely that Samuel compiled this book from oral and written source material. His prophetic ministry clearly fits the moral commentary of Judges, and the consistent style and orderly scheme of Judges point to a single compiler.

Judges 18:30 contains a phrase that poses a problem to this early date of composition: "until the day of the captivity of the land." If this refers to the 722 B.C. Assyrian captivity of Israel it could have been inserted by a later editor. It is more likely a reference to the Philistine captivity of the land during the time of the judges. This event is described as "captivity" in Psalm 78:61.

THE TIME OF JUDGES
If Judges was not written by Samuel it was at least written by one of his contemporaries between 1043 B.C. (the beginning of Saul's reign) and 1004 B.C. (David's capture of Jerusalem).

Joshua's seven-year conquest is general in nature; much of the land remains to be possessed (Josh. 13:1). There are still important Canaanite strongholds to be taken by the individual tribes. Some of the nations have been left "to prove Israel" (Judg. 3:1, 4). During this time, the Egyptians maintain strong control along the coastal routes, but they are not interested in the hill country where Israel is primarily established.

The events covered in Judges range from about 1380 B.C.–1045 B.C. (c. 335 years), but the period of the judges extends another thirty years since it includes the life of Samuel (1 Sam. 1:1—25:1). Evidently, the rulerships of some of the judges overlap because not all of them ruled over the entire land. Judges describes the cycles of apostasy, oppression, and deliverance in the southern region (3:7–31), the northern region (4:1—5:31), the central region (6:1—10:5), the eastern region (10:6—12:15), and the western region (13:1—16:31). The spread of apostasy covers the whole land.

THE CHRIST OF JUDGES
Each judge is a saviour and a ruler, a spiritual and political deliverer. Thus, the judges portray the role of Christ as the Saviour-King of His people. The Book of Judges also illustrates the need for a righteous king.

Including First Samuel, seventeen judges are mentioned altogether. Some are warrior-rulers (e.g., Othniel and Gideon), one is a priest (Eli), and one is a prophet (Samuel). This gives a cumulative picture of the three offices of Christ, who excelled all His predecessors in that He was the ultimate Prophet, Priest, and King.

KEYS TO JUDGES
Key Word: Cycles—The Book of Judges is written primarily on a thematic rather than a chronological basis (chs. 16—21 actually precede chs. 3—15). The author uses the accounts

of the various judges to prove the utter failure of living out the closing verse of Judges: "Every man did *that which was* right in his own eyes." To accomplish this, the author uses a five-point cycle to recount the repeated spiral of disobedience, destruction, and defeat. The five parts are: (1) sin, (2) servitude, (3) supplication, (4) salvation, and (5) silence.

Key Verses: Judges 2:20, 21; 21:25—"And the anger of the LORD was hot against Israel; and he said, Because that this people hath transgressed my covenant which I commanded their fathers, and have not hearkened unto my voice: I also will not henceforth drive out any from before them of the nations which Joshua left when he died" (2:20, 21).

"In those days *there was* no king in Israel: every man did *that which was* right in his own eyes" (21:25).

Key Chapter: Judges 2—The second chapter of Judges is a miniature of the whole book as it records the transition of the godly to the ungodly generation, the format of the cycles, and the purpose of God in not destroying the Canaanites.

SURVEY OF JUDGES

Following the death of Joshua, Israel plunges into a 350-year Dark Age. After Joshua and the generation of the conquest pass on, "there arose another generation after them, which knew not the LORD, nor yet the works which he had done for Israel" (2:10; see also 2:7-10; Josh. 24:31). Judges opens with a description of Israel's deterioration, continues with seven cycles of oppression and deliverance, and concludes with two illustrations of Israel's depravity.

Deterioration (1:1—3:4): Judges begins with short-lived military successes after Joshua's death, but quickly turns to the repeated failure of all the tribes to drive out their enemies. The people feel

the lack of a unified central leader, but the primary reasons for their failure are a lack of faith in God and a lack of obedience to Him (2:1-3). Compromise leads to conflict and chaos. Israel does not drive out the inhabitants (1:21, 27, 29, 30); instead of removing the moral cancer spread by the inhabitants of Canaan, they contract the disease. The Canaanite gods literally become a snare to them (2:3). Judges 2:11-23 is a microcosm of the pattern found in chapters 3—16 of Judges.

Deliverances (3:5—16:31): This section describes seven apostasies (fallings away from God), seven servitudes, and seven deliverances. Each of the seven cycles has five steps: sin, servitude, supplication, salvation, and silence. These also can be described by the words *rebellion, retribution, repentence, restoration,* and *rest.* The seven cycles connect together as a descending spiral of sin (2:19). Israel vacillates between obedience and apostasy as the people continually fail to learn from their mistakes. Apostasy grows, but the rebellion is not continual. The times of rest and peace are longer than the times of bondage. The monotony of Israel's sins can be contrasted with the creativity of God's methods of deliverance.

The judges are military and civil leaders during this period of loose confederacy. Thirteen are mentioned in this book, and four more are found in First Samuel (Eli, Samuel, Joel, and Abijah).

Depravity (17:1—21:25): These chapters illustrate (1) religious apostasy (17 and 18) and (2) social and moral depravity (19—21) during the period of the judges. Chapters 19—21 contain one of the worst tales of degradation in the Bible. Judges closes with a key to understanding the period: "Every man did *that which was* right in his own eyes" (21:25). The people are not doing what is wrong in their own eyes, but what is "evil in the sight of the LORD."

FOCUS	DETERIORATION		DELIVERANCE						DEPRAVITY		
REFERENCE	1:1———2:1	———3:5	———4:1	——6:1	——10:6	——12:8	——13:1	——17:1	——19:1	——20:1–21:25	
DIVISION	ISRAEL FAILS TO COMPLETE THE CONQUEST	GOD JUDGES ISRAEL	SOUTHERN CAMPAIGN	NORTHERN CAMPAIGN (1st)	CENTRAL CAMPAIGN	EASTERN CAMPAIGN	NORTHERN CAMPAIGN (2nd)	WESTERN CAMPAIGN	SIN OF IDOLATRY	SIN OF IMMORALITY	SIN OF CIVIL WAR
TOPIC	CAUSES OF THE CYCLES		CURSE OF THE CYCLES						CONDITIONS DURING THE CYCLES		
	LIVING WITH THE CANAANITES		WAR WITH THE CANAANITES						LIVING LIKE THE CANAANITES		
LOCATION	CANAAN										
TIME	c. 350 YEARS										

OUTLINE OF JUDGES

CHAPTER 1

Failure of Judah

NOW after the death of Joshua it came to
pass, that the children of Israel ᴿasked
the LORD, saying, ᵀWho shall go up for us
against the Ca'-naan-ites first, to fight
against them?   20:18 · who will lead
2 And the LORD said, ᴿJudah shall go up:

behold, I have delivered the land into his
hand.   Gen. 49:8
3 And Judah said unto Simeon his brother,
Come up with me into my ᵀlot, that we may
fight against the Ca'-naan-ites; and I likewise
will go with thee into thy lot. So Simeon went
with him.   land
4 And Judah went up; and the LORD delivered the Ca'-naan-ites and the Per'-iz-zites

into their hand: and they slew of them in Be'-zek ten thousand men.

5 And they found A-don'-i-be'-zek in Be'-zek: and they fought against him, and they slew the Ca'-naan-ites and the Per'-iz-zites.

6 But A-don'-i-be'-zek fled; and they pursued after him, and caught him, and cut off his thumbs and his [T]great toes.   big

7 And A-don'-i-be'-zek said, Threescore and ten kings, having their thumbs and their great toes cut off, gathered *their meat* under my table: [R]as I have done, so God hath requited me. And they brought him to Jerusalem, and there he died.   [James 2:13]

8 Now [R]the children of Judah had fought against Jerusalem, and had taken it, and smitten it with the edge of the sword, and set the city on fire.   Josh. 15:63

9 And afterward the children of Judah went down to fight against the Ca'-naan-ites, that dwelt in the mountain, and in the south, and in the valley.

10 And Judah [T]went against the Ca'-naan-ites that dwelt in He'-bron: (now the name of He'-bron before *was* [R]Kir'-jath-ar'-ba:) and they slew She'-shai, and A-hi'-man, and Tal'-mai.   *attacked* • Josh. 14:15

11 And from thence he went against the inhabitants of De'-bir: and the name of De'-bir before *was* Kir'-jath-se'-pher:

12 And Caleb said, He that smiteth Kir'-jath-se'-pher, and taketh it, to him will I give Ach'-sah my daughter to wife.

13 And Oth'-ni–el the son of Ke'-naz, Caleb's younger brother, took it: and he gave him Ach'-sah his daughter to wife.

14 And it came to pass, when she came *to him*, that she moved him to ask of her father a field: and she lighted from off *her* ass; and Caleb said unto her, What wilt thou?

15 And she said unto him, [R]Give me a blessing: for thou hast given me a south land; give me also springs of water. And Caleb gave her the upper springs and the nether springs.   Gen. 33:11

16 And the children of the Ken'-ite, Moses' father in law, went up out of the city of palm trees with the children of Judah into the wilderness of Judah, which *lieth* in the south of A'-rad; and they went and dwelt among the people.

17 [R]And Judah went with Simeon his brother, and they slew the Ca'-naan-ites that inhabited Ze'-phath, and utterly destroyed it. And the name of the city was called [R]Hor'-mah.   *v.* 3 • Num. 21:3; Josh. 19:4

18 Also Judah took Ga'-za with the coast thereof, and As'-ke-lon with the coast thereof, and Ek'-ron with the coast thereof.

19 And the LORD was with Judah; and he drave out *the inhabitants of* the mountain; but could not drive out the inhabitants of the valley, because they had chariots of iron.

20 And they gave He'-bron unto Caleb, as Moses said: and he [T]expelled thence the three sons of A'-nak.   *drove out from there*

Failure of Benjamin

21 [R]And the children of Benjamin did not drive out the Jeb'-u-sites that inhabited Jerusalem; but the Jeb'-u-sites dwell with the children of Benjamin in Jerusalem unto this day.   *v.* 8; Josh. 15:63

Failure of Tribes of Joseph

22 And the [T]house of Joseph, they also went up against Beth'-el: [R]and the LORD *was* with them.   *family* • *v.* 19

23 And the [T]house of Joseph [R]sent to [T]descry Beth'-el. (Now the name of the city before *was* Luz.)   *family* • Josh. 7:2 • *scout*

24 And the spies saw a man come forth out of the city, and they said unto him, Shew us, we pray thee, the entrance into the city, and we will shew thee mercy.

25 And when he shewed them the entrance into the city, they smote the city with the edge of the sword; [R]but they let go the man and all his family.   Josh. 6:25

26 And the man went into the land of the Hit'-tites, and built a city, and called the name thereof Luz: [T]which *is* the name thereof unto this day.   *it*

27 Neither did Ma-nas'-seh drive out *the inhabitants of* Beth-she'-an and her towns, nor Ta'-a-nach and her towns, nor the inhabitants of Dor and her towns, nor the inhabitants of Ib'-le-am and her towns, nor the inhabitants of Me-gid'-do and her towns: but the Ca'-naan-ites would dwell in that land.

28 And it came to pass, when Israel was strong, that they put the Ca'-naan-ites to tribute, and did not utterly drive them out.

29 Neither did E'-phra-im drive out the Ca'-naan-ites that dwelt in Ge'-zer; but the Ca'-naan-ites dwelt in Ge'-zer among them.

Failure of Zebulun

30 Neither did Zeb'-u-lun drive out the inhabitants of Kit'-ron, nor the inhabitants of Na'-ha-lol; but the Ca'-naan-ites dwelt among them, and became tributaries.

Failure of Asher

31 Neither did Asher drive out the inhabitants of Ac'-cho, nor the inhabitants of Zi'-don, nor of Ah'-lab, nor of Ach'-zib, nor of Hel'-bah, nor of A'-phik, nor of Re'-hob:

32 But the Asherites [R]dwelt among the Ca'-naan-ites, the inhabitants of the land: for they did not drive them out.   Ps. 106:34, 35

Failure of Naphtali

33 [R]Neither did Naph'-ta-li drive out the inhabitants of Beth-she'-mesh, nor the inhabitants of Beth–a'-nath; but he dwelt

among the Ca'-naan-ites, the inhabitants of the land: nevertheless the inhabitants of Beth–she'-mesh and of Beth–a'-nath became tributaries unto them.   Josh. 19:32–39

Failure of Dan

34 And the Am'-or-ites forced the children of Dan into the mountain: for they would not suffer them to come down to the valley:

35 But the Am'-or-ites would dwell in mount He'-res in Ai'-ja-lon, and in Sha-al'-bim: yet the hand of the house of Joseph prevailed, so that they became tributaries.

36 And the coast of the Am'-or-ites *was* Rfrom the going up to A-krab'-bim, from the rock, and upward.   Num. 34:4; Josh. 15:3

CHAPTER 2

Angel Announces Judgment

AND an angel of the Lord came up from Gil'-gal to RBo'-chim, and said, I made you to go up out of Egypt, and have brought you unto the land which I sware unto your fathers; and I said, I will never break my Tcovenant with you.   *v. 5 • agreement*

2 And ye shall make no league with the inhabitants of this land; ye shall Tthrow down their altars: but ye have not obeyed my voice: why have ye done this?   *destroy*

3 Wherefore I also said, I will not drive them out from before you; but they shall be *as thorns* in your sides, and their gods shall Tbe a snare unto you.   *lead you astray*

4 And it came to pass, when the angel of the Lord spake these words unto all the children of Israel, that the people Tlifted up their voice, and wept.   *cried out*

5 And they called the name of that place TBo'-chim: and they sacrificed there unto the Lord.   *weepers*

Godly Generation Dies

6 And when Joshua had let the people go, the children of Israel went every man unto his inheritance to possess the land.

7 RAnd the people served the Lord all the days of Joshua, and all the days of the elders that outlived Joshua, who had seen all the Rgreat works of the Lord, that he did for Israel.   Josh. 24:31 • [Ex. 4:21]

8 And RJoshua the son of Nun, the servant of the Lord, died, *being* an hundred and ten years old.   Josh. 24:29

9 And they buried him in the border of his inheritance in RTim'-nath-he'-res,T in the mount of E'-phra-im, on the north side of the hill Ga'-ash.   Josh. 19:50; 24:30 • *Timnath-serah*

10 And also all that generation Twere gathered unto their fathers: and there arose another generation after them, which knew

not the Lord, nor yet the works which he had done for Israel.   *died*

Judgment of God Is Described

11 And the children of Israel did evil in the sight of the Lord, and served Ba'-a-lim:

12 And they forsook the Lord God of their fathers, which brought them out of the land of Egypt, and followed other gods, of the gods of the people that *were* round about them, and bowed themselves unto them, and provoked the Lord to anger.

13 And they forsook the Lord, Rand served Ba'-al and Ash'-ta-roth.   10:6; Ps. 106:36

14 And the anger of the Lord was hot against Israel, and he delivered them into the hands of spoilers that spoiled them, and he sold them into the hands of their enemies round about, so that they could not any longer stand before their enemies.

15 Whithersoever they went out, Tthe hand of the Lord was against them for evil, as the Lord had said, and as the Lord had sworn unto them: and they were greatly distressed.   *the Lord worked against*

16 Nevertheless the Lord raised up judges, which delivered them out of the hand of those that Tspoiled them.   *mistreated*

17 And yet they would not hearken unto their judges, but they Twent a Rwhoring after other gods, and bowed themselves unto them: they turned quickly out of the way which their fathers walked in, obeying the commandments of the Lord; *but* they did not so.   *played the harlot with* • Ex. 34:15

18 And when the Lord raised them up judges, then Rthe Lord was with the judge, and delivered them out of the hand of their enemies all the days of the judge: Rfor it repented the Lord because of their groanings by reason of them that oppressed them and Tvexed them.   Josh. 1:5 • Gen. 6:6 • *troubled*

19 And it came to pass, when the judge was dead, *that* they returned, and corrupted *themselves* more than their fathers, in following other gods to serve them, and to bow down unto them; they ceased not from their own doings, nor from their stubborn way.

Enemy Is Left as a Test

20 And the anger of the Lord was hot against Israel; and he said, Because that this people hath Rtransgressed my covenant which I commanded their fathers, and have not hearkened unto my voice: [Josh. 23:16]

21 I also will not henceforth drive out any from before them of the Rnations which Joshua left when he died: Josh. 23:4, 13

22 RThat through them I may RproveT Israel, whether they will keep the way of the Lord to walk therein, as their fathers did keep *it*, or not.   3:1, 4 • Deut. 8:2, 16 • *test*

23 Therefore the Lord left those nations, without driving them out hastily; neither delivered he them into the hand of Joshua.

CHAPTER 3

NOW these *are* the nations which the Lord left, to ᵀprove Israel by them, *even* as many of Israel as ᵀhad not known all the wars of Canaan;   *test · had not experienced*

2 Only that the generations of the children of Israel might ᵀknow, to ᵀteach them war, at the least such as before knew nothing thereof;   *understand · prepare them for conflict*

3 *Namely,* ᴿfive lords of the Phi-lis'-tines, and all the Ca'-naan-ites, and the Si-do'-ni-ans, and the Hi'-vites that dwelt in mount Leb'-a-non, from mount Ba'-al-her'-mon unto the entering in of Ha'-math.   Josh. 13:3

4 And they were to ᴿproveᵀ Israel by them, to ᵀknow whether they would hearken unto the commandments of the Lord, which he commanded their fathers by the hand of Moses.   Josh. 9:3, 7; 11:19 · *test · find out*

The Judge Othniel

5 ᴿAnd the children of Israel dwelt among the Ca'-naan-ites, ᴿHit'-tites, and Am'-or-ites, and ᴿPer'-iz-zites, and Hi'-vites, and ᴿJeb'-u-sites: Ps. 106:35 · 1 Kin. 10:29 · Ezra 9:1 · 19:11

6 And ᴿthey took their daughters to be their wives, and gave their daughters to their sons, and served their gods.   Ex. 34:16

7 And the children of Israel did evil in the sight of the Lord, and forgat the Lord their God, and served Ba'-a-lim and the groves.

8 Therefore the anger of the Lord was hot against Israel, and he sold them into the hand of Chu'-shan-rish-a-tha'-im king of Mes-o-po-ta'-mi-a: and the children of Israel served Chu'-shan-rish-a-tha'-im eight years.

9 And when the children of Israel cried unto the Lord, the Lord raised up a ᵀdeliv-erer to the children of Israel, who delivered them, *even* Oth'-ni-el the son of Ke'-naz, Caleb's younger brother.   *saviour*

10 And ᴿthe spirit of the Lord came upon him, and he judged Israel, and went out to war: and the Lord delivered Chu'-shan-rish-a-tha'-im king of Mes-o-po-ta'-mi-a into his hand; and his hand prevailed against Chu'-shan-rish-a-tha'-im.   1 Sam. 11:6; 2 Chr. 15:1

11 And the land had rest forty years. And Oth'-ni-el the son of Ke'-naz died.

The Judge Ehud

12 ᴿAnd the children of Israel did evil again in the sight of the Lord: and the Lord strengthened Eg'-lon the king of Moab against Israel, because they had done evil in the sight of the Lord.   2:19

13 And he ᵀgathered unto him the children of Ammon and Am'-a-lek, and went and ᵀsmote Israel, and ᵀpossessed the city of palm trees.   *recruited to · attacked · captured*

14 So the children of Israel served Eg'-lon the king of Moab eighteen years.

15 But when the children of Israel ᴿcried unto the Lord, the Lord raised them up a deliverer, E'-hud the son of Ge'-ra, a Benja-mite, a man ᴿlefthanded: and by him the children of Israel sent a ᵀpresent unto Eg'-lon the king of Moab.   Ps. 78:34 · 20:16 · *tribute*

16 But E'-hud made him a ᵀdagger which had two edges, of a ᵀcubit length; and he did ᵀgird it under his raiment upon his right thigh.   *sword · 18 in. · fasten*

17 And he brought the ᴿpresentᵀ unto Eg'-lon king of Moab: and Eg'-lon *was* a very fat man.   Gen. 24:53; 1 Sam. 9:8; Job 42:11 · *tribute*

18 And when he had ᵀmade an end to offer the present, he sent away the people that ᵀbare the ᵀpresent.   *finished offering · carried · tribute*

19 But he himself turned again from the quarries that *were* ᵀby Gil'-gal, and said, I have a secret errand unto thee, O king: who said, ᵀKeep silence. And all that stood by him went out from him.   *back at · leave us alone*

20 And E'-hud came unto him; and he was sitting in a summer parlour, which he had for himself alone. And E'-hud said, I have a message from God unto thee. And he arose out of *his* seat.

21 And E'-hud put forth his left hand, and took the dagger from his right thigh, and ᴿthrust it into his belly: 2 Sam. 3:27

22 And the ᵀhaft also went in after the blade; and the fat closed upon the blade, so that he could not draw the dagger out of his belly; and the dirt came out.   *hilt*

23 Then E'-hud went forth through the ᴿporch, and shut the doors of the parlour upon him, and locked them.   1 Kin. 6:3

24 When he was gone out, his servants came; and when they saw that, behold, the doors of the parlour *were* locked, they said, Surely he ᴿcovereth ᵀhis feet in his summer chamber.   1 Sam. 24:3 · *is relieving himself*

25 And they tarried till they were ashamed: and, behold, he opened not the doors of the parlour; therefore they took a key, and opened *them:* and, behold, their lord *was* fallen down dead on the earth.

26 And E'-hud escaped while they tarried, and passed beyond the ᵀquarries, and escaped unto Se'-i-rath.   *graven images*

27 And it came to pass, when he was come, that he blew a trumpet in the ᴿmountain of E'-phra-im, and the children of Israel went down with him from the mount, and he ᵀbefore them.   Josh. 17:15 · *led*

28 And he said unto them, Follow after me: for ᴿthe Lord hath delivered your enemies

the Mo'-ab-ites into your hand. And they went down after him, and took ^Rthe fords of Jordan toward Moab, and suffered not a man to pass over.   7:9, 15 • Josh. 2:7

29 And they slew of Moab at that time about ten thousand men, all lusty, and all men of valour; and there escaped not a man.

30 So Moab was ^Tsubdued that day under the hand of Israel. And ^Rthe land had rest ^Tfourscore years.   defeated • v. 11 • eighty

The Judge Shamgar

31 And after him was ^RSham'-gar the son of A'-nath, which slew of the Phi-lis'-tines six hundred men with an ox goad: and he also delivered ^RIsrael.   5:6, 8 • 1 Sam. 4:1

CHAPTER 4

Deborah and Barak Are Called

AND ^Rthe children of Israel again did ^Revil in the sight of the LORD, when E'-hud was dead.   2:11; 6:1 • 2:19

2 And the LORD sold them into the hand of Ja'-bin king of Canaan, that reigned in Ha'-zor; the captain of whose host was Sis'-e-ra, which dwelt in Ha-ro'-sheth of the Gentiles.

3 And the children of Israel ^Tcried unto the LORD: for he had nine hundred chariots of iron; and twenty years he mightily oppressed the children of Israel.   prayed

4 And Deb'-o-rah, a prophetess, the wife of Lap'-i-doth, she judged Israel at that time.

5 And she dwelt under the palm tree of ^RDeb'-o-rah between Ra'-mah and Beth'-el in mount E'-phra-im: and the children of Israel came up to her for judgment.   Gen. 35:8

6 And she sent and called Ba'-rak the son of A-bin'-o-am out of Ke'-desh-naph'-ta-li, and said unto him, Hath not the LORD God of Israel commanded, saying, Go and draw toward mount Ta'bor, and take with thee ten thousand men of the children of Naph'-ta-li and of the children of Zeb'-u-lun?

7 And I will draw unto thee to the river Ki'-shon, Sis'-e-ra, the captain of Ja'-bin's army, with his chariots and his multitude; and I will deliver him into thine hand.

8 And Ba'-rak said unto her, If thou wilt go with me, then I will go: but if thou wilt not go with me, then I will not go.

9 And she said, I will surely go with thee: notwithstanding the journey that thou takest shall not be for thine honour; for the LORD shall ^Rsell Sis'-e-ra into the hand of a ^Rwoman. And Deb'-o-rah arose, and went with Ba'-rak to Ke'-desh.   2:14 • vv. 18, 21

10 And Ba'-rak called Zeb'-u-lun and Naph'-ta-li to Ke'-desh; and he went ^Tup with ten thousand men at his feet: and Deb'-o-rah went up with him.   into battle

11 Now He'-ber the Ken'-ite, which was of the children of Ho'-bab the father in law of Moses, had severed himself from the Ken'-ites, and pitched his tent unto the plain of Za-a-na'-im, which is by Ke'-desh.

Canaanites Are Defeated

12 And they shewed Sis'-e-ra that Ba'-rak the son of A-bin'-o-am ^Twas gone up to mount Ta'-bor.   had advanced

13 And Sis'-e-ra gathered together all his chariots, even nine hundred chariots of iron, and all ^Tthe people that were with him, from Ha-ro'-sheth of the ^TGentiles unto the river of Ki'-shon.   his soldiers • nations

14 And Deb'-o-rah said unto Ba'-rak, Up; for this is the day in which the LORD hath delivered Sis'-e-ra into thine hand: is not the LORD ^Tgone out before thee? So Ba'-rak went down from mount Ta'-bor, and ten thousand men after him.   advanced ahead of you

15 And the LORD ^Tdiscomfited Sis'-e-ra, and all his chariots, and all his host, with the edge of the sword before Ba'-rak; so that Sis'-e-ra lighted down off his chariot, and fled away on his feet.   defeated

16 But Ba'-rak pursued after the chariots, and after the host, unto Ha-ro'-sheth of the Gentiles: and all the ^Thost of Sis'-e-ra ^Tfell upon the edge of the sword; and there was not a man ^Rleft.   army • were killed in battle • Ex. 14:28

17 Howbeit Sis'-e-ra fled away on his feet to the tent of ^RJa'-el the wife of He'-ber the Ken'-ite: for there was peace between Ja'-bin the king of Ha'-zor and the house of He'-ber the Ken'-ite.   5:6

18 And Ja'-el went out to meet Sis'-e-ra, and said unto him, ^TTurn in, my lord, turn in to me; fear not. And when he had turned in unto her into the tent, she ^Tcovered him with a ^Tmantle.   come into my home • hid • blanket

19 And he said unto her, Give me, I pray thee, a little water to drink; for I am thirsty. And she opened a bottle of milk, and gave him drink, and ^Tcovered him.   hid

20 Again he said unto her, Stand in the door of the tent, and it shall be, when any man doth come and enquire of thee, and say, Is there any man here? that thou shalt say, ^RNo.   Gen. 12:13

21 Then Ja'-el He'-ber's wife ^Rtook a nail of the tent, and took an hammer in her hand, and went softly unto him, and smote the ^Tnail into his temples, and fastened it into the ground: for he was fast asleep and weary. So he ^Rdied.   5:26 • tent pin • 5:24–27

22 And, behold, as Ba'-rak pursued Sis'-e-ra, Ja'-el came out to meet him, and said unto him, Come, and I will shew thee the man whom thou seekest. And when he came into her tent, behold, Sis'-e-ra lay dead, and the nail was in his temples.

23 So God ᵀsubdued on that day Ja'-bin the king of Canaan before the children of Israel.   *brought down to defeat*

24 And the hand of the children of Israel prospered, and prevailed against Ja'-bin the king of Canaan, until they had destroyed Ja'-bin king of Canaan.

CHAPTER 5

Song of Deborah and Barak

THEN sang Deb'-o-rah and Ba'-rak the son of A-bin'-o-am on that day, saying,

2 Praise ye the LORD for the ᵀavenging of Israel, ᴿwhen the people ᵀwillingly offered themselves.   *bringing victory to* • 2 Chr. 17:16 • *dedicated*

3 Hear, O ye kings; give ear, O ye princes; I, *even* I, will sing unto the LORD; I will sing *praise* to the LORD God of Israel.

4 LORD, when thou wentest out of Se'-ir, when thou marchedst out of the field of E'-dom, the earth trembled, and the heavens dropped, the clouds also dropped water.

5 ᴿThe mountains ᵀmelted from before the LORD, *even* that Si'-nai from before the LORD God of Israel.   Ps. 97:5 • *disappeared*

6 In the days of ᴿSham'-gar the son of A'-nath, in the days of ᴿJa'-el, the highways were unoccupied, and the travellers walked through byways.   3:31 • 4:17

7 *The inhabitants of* the villages ceased, they ceased in Israel, until that I Deb'-o-rah arose, that I arose a mother in Israel.

8 They chose new gods; then *was* war in the gates: was there a shield or spear seen among forty thousand in Israel?

9 My heart *is* toward the governors of Israel, that offered themselves willingly among the people. Bless ye the LORD.

10 Speak, ye that ride on white asses, ye that sit in judgment, and walk by the way.

11 *They that are delivered* from the noise of archers in the places of drawing water, there shall they rehearse the righteous acts of the LORD, *even* the righteous acts *toward the inhabitants* of his villages in Israel: then shall the people of the LORD go down to the gates.

12 ᴿAwake, awake, Deb'-o-rah: awake, awake, utter a song: arise, Ba'-rak, and lead thy captivity captive, thou son of A-bin'-o-am.   Ps. 57:8

13 Then he made him ᵀthat remaineth have dominion over the nobles among the people: the LORD made me have dominion over the mighty.   *the only one left*

14 Out of E'-phra-im *was there* a root of them against Am'-a-lek; after thee, Benjamin, among thy people; out of Ma'-chir came down governors, and out of Zeb'-u-lun they that handle the pen of the writer.

15 And the princes of Is'-sa-char *were* with Deb'-o-rah; even Is'-sa-char, and also Ba'-rak: he was sent on foot into the valley. For the divisions of Reuben *there were* great thoughts of heart.

16 Why abodest thou among the sheepfolds, to hear the bleatings of the flocks? ᵀFor the divisions of Reuben *there were* great searchings of heart.   *In*

17 Gil'-e-ad abode beyond Jordan: and why did Dan remain in ships? Ash'-er continued on the sea shore, and abode in his breaches.

18 ᴿZeb'-u-lun and Naph'-ta-li *were* a people *that* ᵀjeoparded their lives unto the death in the high places of the field.   4:6, 10 • *risked*

19 The kings came *and* fought, then fought the kings of Canaan in Ta'-a-nach by the waters of Me-gid'-do; they took no gain of money.

20 They fought from heaven; the stars in their courses fought against Sis'-e-ra.

21 The river of Ki'-shon swept them away, that ancient river, the river Ki'-shon. O my soul, thou hast trodden down strength.

22 Then were the horsehoofs broken by the means of the pransings, the pransings of their mighty ones.

23 Curse ye Me'-roz, said the angel of the LORD, curse ye bitterly the inhabitants thereof; because they came not to the help of the LORD, to the help of the LORD against the mighty.

24 ᴿBlessed above women shall Ja'-el the wife of He'-ber the Ken'-ite be, blessed shall she be above women in the tent.   [Luke 1:28]

25 He asked water, *and* she gave him milk; she brought forth butter in a lordly dish.

26 She put her hand to the nail, and her right hand to the workmen's hammer; and with the hammer she smote Sis'-e-ra, she smote off his head, when she had pierced and stricken through his temples.

27 At her feet he bowed, he fell, he lay down: at her feet he bowed, he fell: where he bowed, there he fell down dead.

28 The mother of Sis'-e-ra looked out at a window, and cried through the lattice, Why is his chariot *so* long in coming? why tarry the wheels of his chariots?

29 Her wise ladies answered her, yea, she returned answer to herself,

30 Have they not sped? have they *not* divided the prey; to every man a damsel *or* two; to Sis'-e-ra a prey of divers colours, a prey of divers colours of needlework, of divers colours of needlework on both sides, *meet* for the necks of *them that take* the spoil?

31 So let all thine enemies perish, O LORD: but *let* them that love him *be* as the sun when he goeth forth in his might. And the land had rest forty years.

CHAPTER 6

Israel Sins

AND the children of Israel ^Rdid ^Tevil in the sight of the LORD: and the LORD delivered them ^Tinto the hand of Mid'-i-an seven years.   2:11 · sinned · under the control

2 And the hand of Mid'-i-an prevailed against Israel: and because of the Mid'-i-an-ites the children of Israel made them the dens which are in the mountains, and ^Rcaves, and strong holds.   1 Sam. 13:6

3 And so it was, when Israel had sown, that the Mid'-i-an-ites came up, and the Am'-a-lek-ites, and the children of the east, even they ^Tcame up against them;   attacked

4 And they encamped against them, and destroyed the increase of the earth, till thou come unto Ga'-za, and left no sustenance for Israel, neither sheep, nor ox, nor ass.

5 ^RFor they came up with their cattle and their tents, and they came as grasshoppers for multitude; for both they and their camels were without number: and they entered into the land to destroy it.   7:12; 8:10

6 And Israel was greatly impoverished because of the Mid'-i-an-ites; and the children of Israel ^Rcried unto the LORD.   prayed

7 And it came to pass, when the children of Israel ^Rcried unto the LORD because of the ^RMid'-i-an-ites,   1 Sam. 7:9 · 7:1

8 That the LORD sent a prophet unto the children of Israel, which said unto them, Thus saith the LORD God of Israel, I brought you up from Egypt, and brought you forth out of the house of bondage;

9 And I delivered you out of the hand of the Egyptians, and out of the hand of all that oppressed you, and drave them out from before you, and gave you their land;

10 And I said unto you, I am the LORD your God; ^Tfear not the gods of the Am'-or-ites, in whose land ye dwell: but ye have not obeyed my ^Rvoice.   pay no attention to · 2:1, 2

Gideon Called

11 And there came an angel of the LORD, and sat under an oak which was in Oph'-rah, that pertained unto Jo'-ash the A'-bi-ez'-rite: and his son Gideon threshed wheat by the winepress, to hide it from the Mid'-i-an-ites.

12 And the angel of the LORD appeared unto him, and said unto him, The LORD is with thee, thou mighty man of valour.

13 And Gideon said unto him, Oh my Lord, if the LORD be with us, why then is all this befallen us? and where be all his miracles which our fathers told us of, saying, Did not the LORD bring us up from Egypt? but now the LORD hath forsaken us, and delivered us into the hands of the Mid'-i-an-ites.

14 And the LORD looked upon him, and said, Go in this thy might, and thou shalt save Israel from the hand of the Mid'-i-an-ites: have not I sent thee?

15 And he said unto him, Oh my Lord, wherewith shall ^RI save Israel? behold, ^Rmy family is poor in Ma-nas'-seh, and I am the least in my father's house.   Ex. 3:11 · 1 Sam. 9:21

16 And the LORD said unto him, Surely I will be with thee, and thou shalt ^Tsmite the Mid'-i-an-ites as one man.   kill in battle

17 And he said unto him, If now I have found grace in thy sight, then ^Rshew me a sign that thou talkest with me.   vv. 36, 37

18 ^RDepart not hence, I pray thee, until I come unto thee, and bring forth my present, and set it before thee. And he said, I will tarry until thou come again.   Gen. 18:3, 5

19 ^RAnd Gideon went in, and made ready a kid, and unleavened cakes of an e'-phah of flour: the flesh he put in a basket, and he put the broth in a pot, and brought it out unto him under the oak, and presented it. Gen. 18:6–8

20 And the angel of God said unto him, Take the flesh and the unleavened cakes, and lay them upon this rock, and ^Rpour out the broth. And he did so.   1 Kin. 18:33, 34

21 Then the angel of the LORD put forth the end of the ^Rstaff that was in his hand, and touched the flesh and the unleavened cakes; and ^Rthere rose up fire out of the rock, and consumed the flesh and the unleavened cakes. Then the angel of the LORD departed out of his sight.   Mark 6:8 · Lev. 9:24

22 And when Gideon ^Tperceived that he was an angel of the LORD, Gideon said, Alas, O Lord GOD! for because I have seen an angel of the LORD face to face.   realized

23 And the LORD said unto him, Peace be unto thee; fear not: thou shalt not die.

24 Then Gideon built an altar there unto the LORD, and called it ^TJe-ho'-vah-sha'-lom: unto this day it is yet in Oph'-rah of the A'-bi-ez'-rites.   the LORD is peace

25 And it came to pass the same night, that the LORD said unto him, Take thy father's young bullock, even the second bullock of seven years old, and throw down the altar of Ba'-al that thy father hath, and cut down the grove that is by it:

26 And build an altar unto the LORD thy God upon the top of this rock, in the ordered place, and take the second bullock, and offer a burnt sacrifice with the wood of the grove which thou shalt cut down.

27 Then Gideon took ten men of his servants, and did as the LORD had said unto him: and so it was, because he feared his father's household, and the men of the city, that he could not do it by day, that he did it by night.

28 And when the men of the city arose early in the morning, behold, the altar of Ba'-al was cast down, and the grove was cut down that was by it, and the second bullock was offered upon the altar that was built.

29 And they said one to another, Who hath done this thing? And when they enquired and asked, they said, Gideon the son of Jo'-ash hath done this thing.

30 Then the men of the city said unto Jo'-ash, Bring out thy son, that he may ᴿdie: because he hath ᵀcast down the altar of Ba'-al, and because he hath cut down the grove that *was* by it.   [Deut. 13:6–9] • *torn apart*

31 And Jo'-ash said unto all that stood against him, Will ye plead for Ba'-al? will ye save him? he that will plead for him, let him be put to death whilst *it is yet* morning: if he *be* a god, let him plead for himself, because one hath cast down his altar.

32 Therefore on that day he called him ᴿJer-ub-ba'-al, saying, Let Ba'-al ᵀplead against him, because he hath thrown down his altar.   7:1 • *contend against*

33 Then all the Mid'-i-an-ites and the Am'-a-lek-ites and the children of the east were gathered together, and went over, and ᵀpitched in the valley of Jez'-re-el.   *made camp*

34 But the ᴿSpirit of the LORD came upon Gideon, and he blew a trumpet; and A'-bi-e'-zer was gathered after him.   1 Chr. 12:18

35 And he sent messengers throughout all Ma-nas'-seh; who also ᵀwas gathered after him: and he sent messengers unto Asher, and unto Zeb'-u-lun, and unto Naph'-ta-li; and they came up to meet them.   *mobilized*

36 And Gideon said unto God, If thou wilt save Israel by mine hand, as thou hast said,

37 Behold, I will put a fleece of wool in the floor; *and* if the dew be on the fleece only, and *it be* dry upon all the earth *beside*, then shall I know that thou wilt save Israel by mine hand, as thou hast said.

38 And it was so: for he rose up early on the ᵀmorrow, and thrust the fleece together, and wringed the dew out of the fleece, a bowl full of water.   *next day*

39 And Gideon said unto God, ᴿLet not thine anger be hot against me, and I will speak but this once: let me prove, I pray thee, but this once with the fleece; let it now be dry only upon the fleece, and upon all the ground let there be dew.   Gen. 18:32

40 And God did so that night: for it was dry upon the fleece only, and there was dew on all the ground.

CHAPTER 7

Midianites Defeated

THEN Jer-ub-ba'-al, who *is* Gideon, and all the people that *were* with him, rose up early, and ᵀpitched beside the well of Ha'-rod: so that the host of the Mid'-i-an-ites were on the north side of them, by the hill of Mo'-reh, in the valley.   *made camp*

2 And the LORD said unto Gideon, The people that *are* with thee *are* too many for me to give the Mid'-i-an-ites into their hands, lest Israel vaunt themselves against me, saying, Mine own hand hath saved me.

3 Now therefore go to, proclaim in the ears of the people, saying, Whosoever *is* fearful and afraid, let him return and depart early from mount Gil'-e-ad. And there returned of the people twenty and two thousand; and there remained ten thousand.

4 And the LORD said unto Gideon, The people *are* yet *too* many; bring them down unto the water, and I will ᵀtry them for thee there: and it shall be, *that* of whom I say unto thee, This shall go with thee, the same shall go with thee; and of whomsoever I say unto thee, This shall not go with thee, the same shall not go.   *put them to the test*

5 So he brought down the people unto the water: and the LORD said unto ᴿGideon, Every one that lappeth of the water with his tongue, as a dog lappeth, him shalt thou set by himself; likewise every one that boweth down upon his knees to drink.   *v. 19*

6 And the number of them that lapped, *putting* their hand to their mouth, were three hundred men: but all the rest of the people bowed down upon their knees to drink water.

7 And the LORD said unto Gideon, By the three hundred men that lapped will I save you, and deliver the Mid'-i-an-ites into thine hand: and let all the *other* people go every man ᵀunto his place.   *to his own home*

8 So the people took victuals in their hand, and their trumpets: and he sent all *the rest of* Israel every man unto his tent, and retained those three hundred men: and the ᵀhost of Mid'-i-an was beneath him in the valley. *army*

9 And it came to pass the ᴿsame ᴿnight, that the LORD said unto him, Arise, get thee down unto the host; ᴿfor I have delivered it into thine hand.   6:25 • Gen. 46:2, 3 • Josh. 2:24

10 But if thou fear to go down, go thou with Phu'-rah thy servant down to the host:

11 And thou shalt hear what they say; and afterward ᵀshall thine hands be strengthened to go down unto the host. Then went he down with Phu'-rah his servant unto the outside of the armed men that *were* in the ᵀhost.   *you will be encouraged* • *camp*

12 And the Mid'-i-an-ites and the Am'-a-lek-ites and ᴿall the children of the east lay along in the valley like ᵀgrasshoppers for multitude; and their camels *were* ᵀwithout number, ᴿas the sand by the sea side for multitude.   6:5, 33; 8:10 • *locusts* • *innumerable* • Josh. 11:4

13 And when Gideon was come, behold, *there was* a man that told a dream unto his fellow, and said, Behold, I dreamed a dream, and, lo, a cake of barley bread tumbled into the host of Mid'-i-an, and came unto a tent,

and smote it that it fell, and overturned it, that the tent lay along.

14 And his fellow answered and said, This *is* nothing else ^Tsave the sword of Gideon the son of Jo′-ash, a man of Israel: *for* into his hand hath ^RGod delivered Mid′-i-an, and all the host.   *except* • 6:14, 16

15 And it was *so*, when Gideon heard the telling of the dream, and the interpretation thereof, that he worshipped, and returned into the ^Thost of Israel, and said, Arise; for the LORD hath delivered into your hand the host of Mid′-i-an.   *army*

16 And he divided the three hundred men *into* three companies, and he put a trumpet in every man's hand, with empty pitchers, and ^Tlamps within the pitchers.   *torches*

17 And he said unto them, Look on me, and do ^Tlikewise: and, behold, when I come to the outside of the camp, it shall be *that,* as I do, so shall ye do.   *what you see me doing*

18 When I blow with a trumpet, I and all that *are* with me, then blow ye the trumpets also on every side of all the camp, and say, The sword of the LORD, and of Gideon.

19 So Gideon, and the hundred men that *were* with him, came unto the outside of the camp in the beginning of the middle watch; and they had but newly set the watch: and they blew the trumpets, and brake the pitchers that *were* in their hands.

20 And the three companies blew the trumpets, and brake the pitchers, and held the ^Tlamps in their left hands, and the trumpets in their right hands to blow *withal:* and they cried, The ^Rsword of ^Tthe LORD, and of Gideon.   *torches* • [1 Chr. 21:12] • *Jehovah*

21 And they stood every man in his place round about the camp: ^Rand all the ^Thost ran, and cried, and fled.   2 Kin. 7:7 • *army*

22 And the three hundred blew the trumpets, and the LORD ^Tset every man's sword against his fellow, even throughout all the host: and the host fled to Beth–shit′-tah in Zer′-e-rath, *and* to the border of A′-bel-me-ho′-lah, unto Tab′-bath.   *began to fight each other*

23 And the men of Israel ^Tgathered themselves together out of ^RNaph′-ta-li, and out of Asher, and out of all Ma-nas′-seh, and pursued after the Mid′-i-an-ites.   *rallied* • 6:35

24 And Gideon sent messengers throughout all mount E′-phra-im, saying, Come down against the Mid′-i-an-ites, and take before them the waters unto Beth–ba′-rah and Jordan. Then all the men of E′-phra-im gathered themselves together, and took the waters unto Beth–ba′-rah and Jordan.

25 And they took ^Rtwo princes of the Mid′-i-an-ites, O′-reb and Ze′-eb; and they slew O′-reb upon ^Rthe rock O′-reb, and Ze′-eb they slew at the winepress of Ze′-eb, and pursued Mid′-i-an, and brought the heads of O′-reb

and Ze′-eb to Gideon on the ^Rother side Jordan.   8:3; Ps. 83:11 • Is. 10:26 • 8:4

CHAPTER 8

AND the men of ^RE′-phra-im said unto him, Why hast thou served us thus, that thou calledst us not, when thou wentest to fight with the Mid′-i-an-ites? And they did ^Tchide with him sharply.   12:1 • *argue*

2 And he said unto them, What have I done now in comparison of you? *Is* not the ^Rgleaning of the grapes of E′-phra-im better than the vintage of A′-bi-e′-zer?   6:11

3 ^RGod hath delivered into your hands the princes of Mid′-i-an, O′-reb and Ze′-eb: and what was I able to do in comparison of you? Then their anger was ^Tabated toward him, when he had said that.   [Phil. 2:3] • *cooled off*

4 And Gideon came to Jordan, *and* passed over, he, and the three hundred men that *were* with him, faint, yet pursuing *them.*

5 And he said unto the men of ^RSuc′-coth, Give, I pray you, loaves of bread unto the people that follow me; for they *be* faint, and I am pursuing after Ze′-bah and Zal-mun′-na, kings of Mid′-i-an.   Gen. 33:17; Ps. 60:6

6 And the princes of Suc′-coth said, ^TAre the hands of Ze′-bah and Zal-mun′-na now in thine hand, that we should give bread unto thine army?   *have they already been captured?*

7 And ^RGideon said, Therefore when the LORD hath delivered Ze′-bah and Zal-mun′-na into mine hand, ^Rthen I will ^Ttear your flesh with the thorns of the wilderness and with briers.   7:15 • *v.* 16 • *thresh*

8 And he went up thence ^Rto Pe-nu′-el, and spake unto them likewise: and the men of Pe-nu′-el answered him as the men of Suc′-coth had answered *him.*   1 Kin. 12:25

9 And he spake also unto the men of Pe-nu′-el, saying, When I come again ^Tin peace, I will break down this tower.   *after the battle*

10 Now Ze′-bah and Zal-mun′-na *were* in Kar′-kor, and their hosts with them, about fifteen thousand *men*, all that were left of ^Rall the ^Thosts of the children of the east: for there fell an hundred and twenty thousand men that drew sword.   7:12 • *armies*

11 And Gideon went up by the way of them that dwelt in tents on the east of No′-bah and Jog′-be-hah, and ^Tsmote the host: for the host was secure.   *defeated*

12 And when Ze′-bah and Zal-mun′-na fled, he pursued after them, and took the two kings of Mid′-i-an, Ze′-bah and Zal-mun′-na, and discomfited all the host.

13 And Gideon the son of Jo′-ash returned from battle before the sun *was up,*

14 And caught a young man of the men of Suc′-coth, and enquired of him: and he ^Tdescribed unto him the princes of Suc′-coth,

and the elders thereof, *even* threescore and seventeen men.   *wrote down*

15 And he came unto the men of Suc'-coth, and said, Behold Ze'-bah and Zal-mun'-na, with whom ye did upbraid me, saying, *Are* the hands of Ze'-bah and Zal-mun'-na now in thine hand, that we should give bread unto thy men *that are* weary?

16 And he took the elders of the city, and thorns of the wilderness and briers, and with them he taught the men of Suc'-coth.

17 ᴿAnd he beat down the ᴿtower of Pe-nu'-el, and slew the men of the city. *v. 9 • 9:47*

18 Then said he unto Ze'-bah and Zal-mun'-na, What manner of men *were they* whom ye slew at ᴿTa'-bor? And they answered, As thou *art,* so *were* they; each one resembled the children of a king.   *Ps. 89:12*

19 And he said, They *were* my brethren, *even* the sons of my mother: *as* the Lᴏʀᴅ liveth, if ye had saved them alive, I would not slay you.

20 And he said unto Je'-ther his firstborn, Up, *and* slay them. But the youth drew not his sword: for he ᵀfeared, because he *was* yet a youth.   *hesitated*

21 Then Ze'-bah and Zal-mun'-na said, Rise thou, and fall upon us: for as the man *is,* so *is* his strength. And Gideon arose, and slew Ze'-bah and Zal-mun'-na, and took away the ornaments that *were* on their camels' necks.

Gideon Judges

22 Then the men of Israel said unto Gideon, Rule thou over us, both thou, and thy son, and thy son's son also: for thou hast delivered us from the hand of Mid'-i-an.

23 And Gideon said unto them, I will not rule over you, neither shall my son rule over you: the Lᴏʀᴅ shall rule over you.

24 And Gideon said unto them, I would desire a request of you, that ye would give me every man the earrings of his ᵀprey. (For they had golden earrings, because they *were* Ish'-ma-el-ites.)   *defeated enemy*

25 And they answered, We will ᴿwillingly give *them.* And they spread a garment, and did cast therein every man the ᴿearrings of his ᵀprey.   *Neh. 11:2 • Ex. 32:2, 3 • spoil*

26 And the weight of the golden earrings that he requested was a thousand and seven hundred *shek'-els* of gold; beside ornaments, and collars, and purple raiment that *was* on the kings of Mid'-i-an, and beside the chains that *were* about their camels' necks.

27 And Gideon ᴿmade an e'-phod thereof, and put it in his city, *even* in Oph'-rah: and all Israel went thither a whoring after it: which thing became ᴿa snare unto Gideon, and to his house.   *17:5 • Deut. 7:16*

28 Thus was Mid'-i-an subdued before the children of Israel, so that they lifted up their heads no more. And the country was in quietness forty years in the days of Gideon.

29 And ᴿJer-ub-ba'-al the son of Jo'-ash went and dwelt in his own house. *6:32; 7:1*

30 And Gideon had ᴿthreescore and ten sons of his body begotten: for he had many wives.   *9:2, 5*

31 ᴿAnd his concubine that *was* in She'-chem, she also bare him a son, whose name he called A-bim'-e-lech.   *9:1*

32 And Gideon the son of Jo'-ash died ᴿin a good old age, and was buried in the sepulchre of Jo'-ash his father, ᴿin Oph'-rah of the A'-bi-ez'-rites.   *Job 5:26 • v. 27*

Confusion After Gideon Dies

33 And it came to pass, ᴿas soon as Gideon was dead, that the children of Israel turned again, and went a whoring after Ba'-a-lim, and made Ba'-al-be'-rith their god.   *2:19*

34 And the children of Israel ᴿremembered not the Lᴏʀᴅ their God, who had delivered them out of the hands of all their enemies on every side: *Ps. 78:11, 42; 106:13, 21*

35 Neither shewed they kindness to the ᴿhouse of Jer-ub-ba'-al, *namely,* Gideon, according to all ᵀthe goodness which he had shewed unto Israel. *9:16, 18 • the constructive acts*

CHAPTER 9

Deception of Abimelech

A ND ᴿA-bim'-e-lech the son of Jer-ub-ba'-al went to She'-chem unto his mother's brethren, and ᵀcommuned with them, and with all the family of the house of his mother's father, saying,   *8:31 • conferred*

2 Speak, I pray you, in the ears of all the men of She'-chem, Whether *is* better for you, either that all the sons of Jer-ub-ba'-al, *which are* threescore and ten persons, reign over you, or that one reign over you? remember also that I *am* your bone and your flesh.

3 And his mother's brethren spake of him in the ears of all the men of She'-chem all these words: and ᵀtheir hearts inclined to follow A-bim'-e-lech; for they said, He *is* our ᴿbrother.   *they were inwardly led • Gen. 29:15*

4 And they gave him threescore and ten *pieces* of silver out of the house of Ba'-al-be'-rith, wherewith A-bim'-e-lech hired vain and light persons, which followed him.

5 And he went unto his father's house at Oph'-rah, and slew his brethren the sons of Jer-ub-ba'-al, *being* threescore and ten persons, ᵀupon one stone: notwithstanding yet Jo'-tham the youngest son of Jer-ub-ba'-al was left; for he hid himself.   *at one spot*

6 And all the men of She'-chem gathered together, and all the house of Mil'-lo, and went, and made A-bim'-e-lech king, by the plain of the pillar that *was* in She'-chem.

7 And when they told *it* to Jo'-tham, he went and stood in the top of mount Ger'-i-zim, and lifted up his voice, and cried, and said unto them, Hearken unto me, ye men of She'-chem, that God may hearken unto you.

8 The trees went forth *on a time* to anoint a king over them; and they said unto the olive tree, Reign thou over us.

9 But the ᴿolive tree said unto them, Should I leave my fatness, wherewith by me they honour God and man, and go to ᵀbe promoted over the trees? [Ps. 52:8] · *wave to and fro*

10 And the trees said to the ᴿfig tree, Come thou, *and* reign over us.   1 Kin. 4:25

11 But the fig tree said unto them, Should I forsake my sweetness, and my good fruit, and go to be promoted over the trees?

12 Then said the trees unto the vine, Come thou, *and* reign over us.

13 And the vine said unto them, Should I leave my wine, which cheereth God and man, and go to be promoted over the trees?

14 Then said all the trees unto the ᵀbramble, Come thou, *and* reign over us.   *thistle*

15 And the bramble said unto the trees, If in truth ye anoint me king over you, *then* come *and* put your trust in my shadow: and if not, let fire come out of the bramble, and devour the cedars of Leb'-a-non.

16 Now therefore, if ye have done truly and sincerely, in that ye have made A-bim'-e-lech king, and if ye have dealt well with Jer-ub-ba'-al and his house, and have done unto him ᴿaccording to ᵀthe deserving of his hands;   8:35 · *what his deeds deserved*

17 (For my father fought for you, and ᵀadventured his life far, and ᴿdelivered you out of the hand of Mid'-i-an: *ventured* · 8:22

18 And ye are risen up against my father's house this day, and have slain his sons, threescore and ten persons, upon one stone, and have made A-bim'-e-lech, the son of his maidservant, king over the men of She'-chem, because he *is* your brother;)

19 If ye then have dealt truly and sincerely with Jer-ub-ba'-al and with his house this day, *then* ᴿrejoice ye in A-bim'-e-lech, and let him also rejoice in you: Is. 8:6

20 But if not, ᴿlet ᵀfire come out from A-bim'-e-lech, and devour the men of She'-chem, and the house of Mil'-lo; and let fire come out from the men of She'-chem, and from the house of Mil'-lo, and devour A-bim'-e-lech.   *vv.* 15, 56, 57 · *destruction*

21 And Jo'-tham ran away, and fled, and went to ᴿBe'-er, and dwelt there, for fear of A-bim'-e-lech his brother.   2 Sam. 20:14

Destruction of Shechem

22 When A-bim'-e-lech had reigned three years over Israel,

23 Then God sent ᵀan evil spirit between A-bim'-e-lech and the men of She'-chem; and the men of She'-chem ᴿdealt treacherously with A-bim'-e-lech: *disaffection* · [Is. 33:1]

24 ᴿThat the cruelty *done* to the threescore and ten sons of Jer-ub-ba'-al might come, and their blood be laid upon A-bim'-e-lech their brother, which slew them; and upon the men of She'-chem, which aided him in the killing of his brethren.   1 Kin. 2:32

25 And the men of She'-chem set liers in wait for him in the top of the mountains, and they robbed all that came along that way by them: and it was told A-bim'-e-lech.

26 And Ga'-al the son of E'-bed came with his brethren, and went over to She'-chem: and the men of She'-chem put ᴿtheir confidence in him.   [Jer. 17:5]

27 And they went out into the fields, and gathered their vineyards, and trode *the grapes,* and ᵀmade merry, and went into the house of their god, and did eat and drink, and cursed A-bim'-e-lech.   *celebrated*

28 And Ga'-al the son of E'-bed said, ᴿWho *is* A-bim'-e-lech, and who *is* She'-chem, that we should serve him? *is* not *he* the son of Jer-ub-ba'-al? and Ze'-bul his officer? serve the men of ᴿHa'-mor the father of She'-chem: for why should we serve him?   1 Sam. 25:10 · Gen. 34:2

29 And ᴿwould to God this people were under my hand! then would I remove A-bim'-e-lech. And he said to A-bim'-e-lech, Increase thine army, and come out.   [Ps. 10:3]

30 And when Ze'-bul the ruler of the city heard the words ᴿof Ga'-al the son of E'-bed, his anger was ᵀkindled.   2 Sam. 15:4 · *aroused*

31 And he sent messengers unto A-bim'-e-lech ᵀprivily, saying, Behold, Ga'-al the son of E'-bed and his brethren be come to She'-chem; and, behold, they fortify the city against thee.   *craftily*

32 Now therefore ᵀup by night, thou and the people that *is* with thee, and ᵀlie in wait in the field: *march out at* · *set up an ambush*

33 And it shall be, *that* in the morning, as soon as the sun is up, thou shalt rise early, and set upon the city: and, behold, *when* he and the people that *is* with him come out against thee, ᴿthen mayest thou do to them as thou shalt find occasion.   1 Sam. 10:7

34 And A-bim'-e-lech rose up, and all the people that *were* with him, by night, and they laid wait against She'-chem in four companies.

35 And Ga'-al the son of E'-bed went out, and stood in the ᵀentering of the gate of the city: and A-bim'-e-lech rose up, and the people that *were* with him, from ᵀlying in wait.   *entrance* · *being in ambush*

36 And when Ga'-al saw the people, he said to Ze'-bul, Behold, there come people down from the top of the mountains. And

Ze'-bul said unto him, Thou seest the shadow of the mountains as *if they were* men.

37 And Ga'-al spake again and said, See there come people down by [R]the middle of the land, and another company come along by the [T]plain of Me-on'-e-nim.   Ezek. 38:12 · *oak*

38 Then said Ze'-bul unto him, [T]Where *is* now thy mouth, wherewith thou [R]saidst, Who *is* A-bim'-e-lech, that we should serve him? *is* not this the people that thou hast despised? go out, I pray now, and fight with them.   *what will you say now · vv. 28, 29*

39 And Ga'-al went out before the men of She'-chem, and fought with A-bim'-e-lech.

40 And A-bim'-e-lech chased him, and he fled before him, and many were overthrown *and* wounded, *even* unto the [T]entering of the gate.   *entrance*

41 And A-bim'-e-lech dwelt at A-ru'-mah: and Ze'-bul thrust out Ga'-al and his brethren, that they should not dwell in She'-chem.

42 And it came to pass on the [T]morrow, that the people went out into the field; and they told A-bim'-e-lech.   *next day*

43 And he took the people, and divided them into three companies, and laid wait in the field, and looked, and, behold, the people *were* come forth out of the city; and he rose up against them, and smote them.

44 And A-bim'-e-lech, and the company that *was* with him, rushed forward, and [T]stood in the entering of the gate of the city: and the two *other* companies ran upon all *the people* that *were* in the fields, and slew them.   *occupied the entrance*

45 And A-bim'-e-lech fought against the city all that day; and [R]he took the city, and slew the people that *was* therein, and beat down the city, and sowed it with salt.   *v. 20*

46 And when all the men of the tower of She'-chem heard *that*, they entered into an hold of the house of the god Be'-rith.

47 And it was told A-bim'-e-lech, that all the men of the [R]tower of She'-chem were gathered together.   2 Kin. 9:17

48 And A-bim'-e-lech gat him up to mount [R]Zal'-mon, he and all the people that *were* with him; and A-bim'-e-lech took an axe in his hand, and cut down a bough from the trees, and took it, and laid *it* on his shoulder, and said unto the people that *were* with him, What ye have seen me do, make haste, *and* do as I *have done*.   Ps. 68:14

49 And all the people likewise cut down every man his bough, and followed A-bim'-e-lech, and put *them* to the [T]hold, and set the hold on fire upon them; so that all the men of the tower of She'-chem died also, about a thousand men and women.   *stronghold*

Death of Abimelech

50 Then went A-bim'-e-lech to The'-bez, and encamped against The'-bez, and took it.

51 But there was a strong tower within the city, and thither fled all the men and women, and all they of the city, and shut *it* to them, and gat them up to the top of the tower.

52 And A-bim'-e-lech came unto the tower, and fought against it, and went hard unto the door of the tower to burn it with fire.

53 And a certain woman [R]cast a piece of a millstone upon A-bim'-e-lech's head, and all to brake his skull.   2 Sam. 11:21; Jer. 25:10

54 Then he called hastily unto the young man his armourbearer, and said unto him, Draw thy sword, and slay me, that men say not of me, A woman slew him. And his young man thrust him through, and he died.

55 And when the men of Israel saw that A-bim'-e-lech was dead, they departed every man [T]unto his place.   *went to his own home*

56 Thus God rendered the wickedness of A-bim'-e-lech, which he did unto his father, in slaying his seventy brethren:

57 And all the evil of the men of She'-chem did God [T]render upon their heads: and upon them came [R]the curse of Jo'-tham the son of Jer-ub-ba'-al.   *requite · Gen. 27:12*

CHAPTER 10

The Judge Tola

AND after A-bim'-e-lech there arose to defend Israel To'-la the son of Pu'-ah, the son of Dodo, a man of Is'-sa-char; and he dwelt in Sha'-mir in mount E'-phra-im.

2 And he judged Israel twenty and three years, and died, and was buried in Sha'-mir.

The Judge Jair

3 And after him arose Ja'-ir, a Gil'-e-ad-ite, and judged Israel twenty and two years.

4 And he had thirty sons that rode on thirty ass colts, and they had thirty cities, which are called Ha'-voth–ja'-ir unto this day, which *are* in the land of Gil'-e-ad.

5 And Ja'-ir died, and was buried in Ca'-mon.

Israel Sins

6 And the children of Israel did evil again in the sight of the LORD, and served Ba'-a-lim, and Ash'-ta-roth, and the gods of Syria, and the gods of Zi'-don, and the gods of Moab, and the gods of the children of Ammon, and the gods of the Phi-lis'-tines, and forsook the LORD, and served not him.

7 And the anger of the LORD was hot against Israel, and he [R]sold them into the hands of the Phi-lis'-tines, and into the hands of the children of Ammon.   2:14

8 And that year they [T]vexed and oppressed the children of Israel: eighteen years, all the children of Israel that *were* on the other side

Jordan in the land of the Am'-or-ites, which is
in Gil'-e-ad.   *troubled*

9 Moreover the children of Ammon passed
over Jordan to fight also against Judah, and
against Benjamin, and against the house
of E'-phra-im; so that Israel was ᵀsore distressed.   *badly*

10 ᴿAnd the children of Israel cried unto
the LORD, saying, We have sinned against
thee, both because we have forsaken our
God, and also served Ba'-a-lim.   1 Sam. 12:10

11 And the LORD said unto the children of
Israel, *Did* not *I deliver you* ᴿfrom the Egyptians, and ᴿfrom the Am'-or-ites, ᴿfrom the
children of Ammon, ᴿand from the Phi-lis'-
tines?   Ex. 14:30 • Num. 21:21 • 3:12, 13 • 3:31

12 ᴿThe Zi-do'-ni-ans also, ᴿand the Am'-a-
lek-ites, and the Ma'-on-ites, did oppress you;
and ye cried to me, and I delivered you out of
their hand.   1:31; 5:19 • 6:3

13 ᴿYet ye have forsaken me, and served
other gods: wherefore I will deliver you no
more.   [Deut. 32:15; Jer. 2:13]

14 Go and ᵀcry unto the gods which ye
have chosen; let them deliver you in the time
of your ᵀtribulation.   *call upon • trouble*

15 And the children of Israel said unto the
LORD, We have sinned: do thou unto us
whatsoever seemeth good unto thee; deliver
us only, we pray thee, this day.

16 And they put away the strange gods
from among them, and served the LORD: and
his soul was grieved for the misery of Israel.

17 Then the children of Ammon were
gathered together, and encamped in Gil'-e-ad.
And the children of Israel assembled themselves together, and encamped in Miz'-peh.

18 And the people *and* princes of Gil'-e-ad
said one to another, What man *is* he that will
begin to fight against the children of Ammon? he shall ᴿbe ᵀhead over all the inhabitants of Gil'-e-ad.   11:8, 11 • *leader of*

CHAPTER 11

Jephthah Is Called

NOW ᴿJeph'-thah the Gil'-e-ad-ite was ᴿa
mighty man of valour, and he *was* the
son of an harlot: and Gil'-e-ad begat Jeph'-
thah.   Heb. 11:32 called *Jephthae* • 6:12; 2 Kin. 5:1

2 And Gil'-e-ad's wife bare him sons; and
his wife's sons grew up, and they thrust out
Jeph'-thah, and said unto him, Thou shalt not
inherit in our father's house; for thou *art* the
son of a ᵀstrange woman.   *another*

3 Then Jeph'-thah fled from his brethren,
and dwelt in the land of Tob: and there were
gathered ᴿvainᵀ men to Jeph'-thah, and went
out with him.   1 Sam. 22:2 • *worthless*

4 And it came to pass ᵀin process of time,
that the children of Ammon ᴿmade war
against Israel.   *after days* • 10:9, 17

5 And it was so, that when the children of
Ammon made war against Israel, the elders
of Gil'-e-ad went to ᵀfetch Jeph'-thah out of
the land of Tob: *bring*

6 And they said unto Jeph'-thah, Come,
and be our captain, that we may fight with
the children of Ammon.

7 And Jeph'-thah said unto the elders of
Gil'-e-ad, Did not ye hate me, and expel me
out of my father's house? and why are ye
come unto me now when ye are in distress?

8 And the elders of Gil'-e-ad said unto
Jeph'-thah, Therefore we turn again to thee
now, that thou mayest go with us, and fight
against the children of Ammon, and be our
head over all the inhabitants of Gil'-e-ad.

9 And Jeph'-thah said unto the elders of
Gil'-e-ad, If ye bring me home again to fight
against the children of Ammon, and the LORD
deliver them before me, shall I be your head?

10 And the elders of Gil'-e-ad said unto
Jeph'-thah, The LORD be witness between us,
if we do not so according to thy words.

11 Then Jeph'-thah went with the elders of
Gil'-e-ad, and the people made him head and
captain over them: and Jeph'-thah ᵀuttered
all his words ᴿbefore the LORD in ᴿMiz'-
peh.   *worshipped and communed* • 10:17 • v. 29

Jephthah Judges

12 And Jeph'-thah sent messengers unto
the king of the children of Ammon, saying,
What hast thou to do with me, that thou art
come against me to fight in my land?

13 And the king of the children of Ammon
answered unto the messengers of Jeph'-thah,
Because Israel took away my land, when
they came up out of Egypt, from Arnon even
unto Jab'-bok, and unto Jordan: now therefore restore those *lands* again peaceably.

14 And Jeph'-thah sent messengers again
unto the king of the children of Ammon:

15 And said unto him, Thus saith Jeph'-
thah, ᴿIsrael ᵀtook not away the land
of Moab, nor the land of the children of
Ammon: Deut. 2:9, 19 • *did not seize*

16 But when Israel came up from Egypt,
and walked through the wilderness unto the
Red sea, and came to ᴿKa'-desh;   Num. 20:1

17 Then Israel sent messengers unto the
king of E'-dom, saying, Let me, I pray thee,
pass through thy land: but the king of E'-dom
would not ᵀhearken *thereto*. And in like
manner they sent unto the king of Moab: but
he would not *consent:* and Israel abode in
Ka'-desh.   *consider the request*

18 Then they went along through the wilderness, and ᵀcompassed the land of E'-dom,
and the land of Moab, and came by the east
side of the land of Moab, and pitched on the
other side of Arnon, but came not within the
border of Moab: for Arnon *was* the border of
Moab.   *went around*

19 And ᴿIsrael sent messengers unto Si'-hon king of the Am'-or-ites, the king of Hesh'-bon; and Israel said unto him, ᴿLet us pass, we pray thee, through thy land into my place. Deut. 2:26 • Num. 21:22; Deut. 2:27

20 But Si'-hon trusted not Israel to pass through his ᵀcoast: but Si'-hon gathered all his people together, and ᵀpitched in Ja'-haz, and fought against Israel. border • made camp

21 And the LORD God of Israel delivered Si'-hon and all his people into the hand of Israel, and they smote them: so Israel ᵀpossessed all the land of the Am'-or-ites, the inhabitants of that country. seized

22 And they possessed ᴿall the ᵀcoasts of the Am'-or-ites, from Arnon even unto Jab'-bok, and from the wilderness even unto Jordan. Deut. 2:36 • territories

23 So now the LORD God of Israel hath ᵀdispossessed the Am'-or-ites from before his people Israel, and shouldest thou ᵀpossess it? put out • take it for thine own?

24 Wilt not thou possess that which ᴿChe'-mosh thy god giveth thee to possess? So whomsoever ᴿthe LORD our God shall drive out from before us, them will we possess. 1 Kin. 11:7; Jer. 48:7 • [Deut. 9:4, 5; Josh. 3:10]

25 And now art thou any thing better than ᴿBa'-lak the son of Zip'-por, king of Moab? did he ever strive against Israel, or did he ever fight against them, Num. 22:2

26 While Israel dwelt in ᴿHesh'-bon and her towns, and in ᴿAr'-o-er and her towns, and in all the cities that be along by the coasts of Arnon, three hundred years? why therefore did ye not ᵀrecover them within that time? Num. 21:25 • Deut. 2:36 • recapture

27 Wherefore I have not sinned against thee, but thou doest me wrong to war against me: the LORD the Judge ᴿbe judge this day between the children of Israel and the children of Ammon. [1 Sam. 24:12, 15]

28 Howbeit the king of the children of Ammon hearkened not unto the words of Jeph'-thah which he sent him.

Jephthah Vows

29 Then ᴿthe Spirit of the LORD came upon Jeph'-thah, and he passed over Gil'-e-ad, and Ma-nas'-seh, and passed over Miz'-peh of Gil'-e-ad, and from Miz'-peh of Gil'-e-ad he passed over unto the children of Ammon. [3:10; 13:25; Gen. 1:2; Zech. 12:10]

30 And Jeph'-thah ᴿvowedᵀ a vow unto the LORD, and said, If thou shalt without fail deliver the children of Ammon into mine hands, Num. 30:2 • promised a promise

31 Then it shall be, that whatsoever cometh forth of the doors of my house to meet me, when I return in peace from the children of Ammon, shall surely be the LORD's, and I will offer it up for a burnt offering.

32 So Jeph'-thah passed over unto the children of Ammon to fight against them; and the LORD delivered them into his hands.

33 And he ᵀsmote them from Ar'-o-er, even till thou come to Min'-nith, even twenty cities, and unto the plain of the vineyards, with a very great slaughter. Thus the children of Ammon were subdued before the children of Israel. defeated

34 And Jeph'-thah came to Miz'-peh unto his house, and, behold, his daughter came out to meet him with timbrels and with dances: and she was his only child; beside her he had neither son nor daughter.

35 And it came to pass, when he saw her, that he ᵀrent his clothes, and said, Alas, my daughter! thou hast brought me very low, and thou art one of them that trouble me: for I have opened my mouth unto the LORD, and I cannot go back. tore in regret

36 And she said unto him, My father, if thou hast opened thy mouth unto the LORD, ᴿdo to me according to that which hath proceeded out of thy mouth; forasmuch as ᴿthe LORD hath taken vengeance for thee of thine enemies, even of the children of Ammon. Num. 30:2; Ruth 2:11 • 2 Sam. 18:19, 31

37 And she said unto her father, Let this thing be done for me: let me alone two months, that I may go up and down upon the mountains, and ᵀbewail my virginity, I and my ᵀfellows. lament • companions

38 And he said, Go. And he sent her away for two months: and she went with her companions, and bewailed her virginity upon the mountains.

39 And it came to pass at the end of two months, that she returned unto her father, who ᴿdid with her according to his vow which he had vowed: and she knew no man. And it was a custom in Israel, v. 31

40 That the daughters of Israel went yearly to lament the daughter of Jeph'-thah the Gil'-e-ad-ite four days in a year.

CHAPTER 12

Ephraim Is Conquered

AND the men of E'-phra-im ᵀgathered themselves together, and went northward, and said unto Jeph'-thah, Wherefore passedst thou over to fight against the ᴿchildren of Ammon, and didst not call us to go with thee? we will burn thine house upon thee with fire. were called • 8:1; 10:9

2 And Jeph'-thah said unto them, I and my people were at great strife with the children of Ammon; and when I called you, ye delivered me not out of their hands.

3 And when I saw that ye delivered me not, I put my life in my hands, and ᵀpassed over against the children of Ammon, and the

LORD delivered them into my hand: wherefore then are ye come up unto me this day, to fight against me?   *attacked*

4 Then Jeph'-thah gathered together all the men of Gil'-e-ad, and fought with E'-phraim: and the men of Gil'-e-ad smote E'-phraim, because they said, Ye Gil'-e-ad-ites *are* fugitives of E'-phra-im among the E'-phra-im-ites, *and* among the Ma-nas'-sites.

5 And the Gil'-e-ad-ites took the passages of Jordan before the E'-phra-im-ites: and it was so, that when those E'-phra-im-ites which were escaped said, Let me go over; that the men of Gil'-e-ad said unto him, *Art* thou an E'-phra-im-ite? If he said, Nay;

6 Then said they unto him, Say now Shib'-bo-leth: and he said Sib'-bo-leth: for he could not frame to pronounce *it* right. Then they took him, and slew him at the passages of Jordan: and there fell at that time of the E'-phra-im-ites forty and two thousand.

7 And Jeph'-thah judged Israel six years. Then died Jeph'-thah the Gil'-e-ad-ite, and was buried in *one of* the cities of Gil'-e-ad.

The Judge Ibzan

8 And after him ᴿIb'-zan of Beth'-le-hem judged Israel.   *v. 11*

9 And he had thirty sons, and thirty daughters, *whom* he sent abroad, and took in thirty daughters from abroad for his sons. And he judged Israel seven years.

10 Then died Ib'-zan, and was buried at Beth'-le-hem.

The Judge Elon

11 And after him ᵀE'-lon, a Zeb'-u-lon-ite, judged Israel; and ᴿhe judged Israel ten years.   *a civil judge in northeast Israel • v. 13*

12 And E'-lon the Zeb'-u-lon-ite died, and was buried in Ai'-ja-lon in the country of Zeb'-u-lun.

The Judge Abdon

13 And after him Ab'-don the son of Hil'-lel, a Pir'-a-thon-ite, ᴿjudged Israel.   *16:31*

14 And he had forty sons and thirty nephews, that rode on threescore and ten ass colts: and he judged Israel eight years.

15 And Ab'-don the son of Hil'-lel the Pir'-a-thon-ite died, and was buried in Pir'-a-thon in the land of E'-phra-im, ᴿin the mount of the Am'-a-lek-ites.   *3:13, 27*

CHAPTER 13

Miraculous Birth of Samson

AND the children of Israel ᴿdidᵀ evil again in the sight of the LORD; and the LORD delivered them into the hand of the Phi-lis'-tines forty years.   *2:11 • sinned again*

2 And there was a certain man of ᴿZo'-rah, of the family of the Danites, whose name *was* Ma-no'-ah; and his wife *was* barren, and bare not.   *16:31; Josh. 19:41*

3 And the angel of the LORD appeared unto the woman, and said unto her, Behold now, thou *art* barren, and bearest not: but thou shalt conceive, and bear a son.

4 Now therefore ᵀbeware, I pray thee, and ᴿdrink not wine nor strong drink, and eat not any unclean *thing*:   *take care • Num. 6:2, 3*

5 For, lo, thou shalt conceive, and bear a son; and no razor shall come on his head: for the child shall be a Nazarite unto God from the womb: and he shall begin to deliver Israel out of the hand of the Phi-lis'-tines.

6 Then the woman came and told her husband, saying, A man of God came unto me, and his countenance *was* like the countenance of an angel of God, very ᵀterrible: but I asked him not whence he *was*, neither told he me his name: *impressive*

7 ᴿBut he said unto me, Behold, thou shalt conceive, and bear a son; and now drink no wine nor strong drink, neither eat any unclean *thing*: for the child shall be a Nazarite to God from ᵀthe womb to the day of his death.   *Gen. 16:11; Luke 1:13-15 • the time he is born*

8 Then Ma-no'-ah ᴿintreated the LORD, and said, O my Lord, let the man of God which thou didst send come again unto us, and teach us what we shall do unto the child that shall be born.   *16:28; Hab. 3:1*

9 And God hearkened to the voice of Ma-no'-ah; and the angel of God came again unto the woman as she sat in the field: but Ma-no'-ah her husband *was* not with her.

10 And the woman made haste, and ran, and ᵀshewed her husband, and said unto him, Behold, the man hath appeared unto me, that came unto me the *other* day.   *told*

11 And Ma-no'-ah arose, and went after his wife, and came to the man, and said unto him, *Art* thou ᴿthe man that spakest unto the woman? And he said, I *am*.   *v. 8*

12 And Ma-no'-ah said, Now let thy words come to pass. How shall we order the child, and *how* shall we do unto him?

13 And the ᴿangel of the LORD said unto Ma-no'-ah, ᴿOf all that I said unto the woman let her beware.   *v. 11 • v. 4*

14 She may not eat of any *thing* that cometh of the ᴿvine, ᴿneither let her drink wine or strong drink, nor eat any unclean *thing*: all that I commanded her let her observe.   *Num. 6:4 • v. 4*

15 And Ma-no'-ah said unto the angel of the LORD, I pray thee, let us detain thee, until we shall have made ready a kid for thee.

16 And the angel of the LORD said unto Ma-no'-ah, Though thou detain me, I will not eat of thy ᵀbread: and if thou wilt offer a burnt offering, thou must offer it unto the

LORD. For Ma-no′-ah knew not that he *was* ᵀan angel of the LORD.   *food • a messenger*

17 And Ma-no′-ah said unto the angel of the LORD, ᴿWhat *is* thy name, that when thy sayings come to pass we may ᵀdo thee honour?   Gen. 32:29 • *give praise to thee*

18 And the angel of the LORD said unto him, ᴿWhy askest thou thus after my name, seeing it *is* ᴿsecret?ᵀ   Gen. 32:29 • [Is. 9:6] • *wonderful*

19 So Ma-no′-ah took a kid with a ᵀmeat offering, and offered *it* upon a rock unto the LORD: and *the angel* did wonderously; and Ma-no′-ah and his wife looked on.   *meal*

20 For it came to pass, when the flame went up toward heaven from off the altar, that the ᵀangel of the LORD ᵀascended in the flame of the altar. And Ma-no′-ah and his wife looked on *it*, and ᴿfell on their faces to the ground.   *messenger • went up • Lev. 9:24*

21 But the angel of the LORD did no more appear to ᴿMa-no′-ah and to his wife. ᴿThen Ma-no′-ah ᵀknew that he *was* an angel of the LORD.   *v. 16 • 6:22 • realized*

22 And Ma-no′-ah said unto his wife, We shall surely die, because we have seen God.

23 But his wife said unto him, If the LORD were pleased to kill us, he would not have received a burnt offering and a meat offering at our hands, neither would he have shewed us all these *things*, nor would as at this time have told us *such things* as these.

24 And the woman bare a son, and called his name Samson: and ᴿthe child grew, and the LORD blessed him.   1 Sam. 3:19; Luke 1:80

25 And the ᴿSpirit of the LORD began to ᵀmove him at times in the camp of Dan between Zo′-rah and Esh′-ta-ol.   14:19 • *inspire*

CHAPTER 14

Sinful Marriage of Samson

AND Samson went down ᴿto Tim′-nath, and saw a woman in Tim′-nath of the daughters of the Phi-lis′-tines.   Gen. 38:13

2 And he came up, and told his father and his mother, and said, I have seen a woman in Tim′-nath of the daughters of the Phi-lis′-tines: now therefore get her for me to wife.

3 Then his father and his mother said unto him, *Is there* never a woman among the daughters of ᴿthy brethren, or among all my people, that thou goest to take a wife of the uncircumcised Phi-lis′-tines? And Samson said unto his father, Get her for me; for she pleaseth me well.   Gen. 24:3, 4

4 But his father and his mother knew not that it *was* of the LORD, that he sought ᵀan occasion against the Phi-lis′-tines: for at that time the Phi-lis′-tines had dominion over Israel.   *a situation that could lead to war*

5 Then went Samson down, and his father and his mother, to Tim′-nath, and came to the vineyards of Tim′-nath: and, behold, a young ᴿlion roared against him. 1 Sam. 17:34, 35

6 And ᴿthe Spirit of the LORD came mightily upon him, and he ᵀrent him as he would have rent a kid, and *he had* nothing in his hand: but he told not his father or his mother what he had done.   3:10 • *tore apart*

7 And he went down, and talked with the woman; and she pleased Samson well.

8 And after a time he returned to take her, and he turned aside to see the carcase of the lion: and, behold, *there was* a swarm of bees and honey in the carcase of the lion.

9 And he took thereof in his hands, and went on eating, and came to his father and mother, and gave them, and they did eat: but he told not them that he had taken the honey out of the carcase of the lion.

10 So his father went down unto the woman: and Samson made there a ᴿfeast; for so used the young men to do.   Gen. 29:22

11 And it came to pass, when they saw him, that they brought thirty companions to be with him.

12 And Samson said unto them, I will now ᴿput forth a riddle unto you: if ye can certainly declare it me within the ᴿseven days of the feast, and find *it* out, then I will give you thirty ᵀsheets and thirty ᴿchange of garments: Luke 14:7 • Gen. 29:27 • *shirts* • 2 Kin. 5:22

13 But if ye cannot declare *it* me, then shall ye give me thirty sheets and thirty change of garments. And they said unto him, Put forth thy riddle, that we may hear it.

14 And he said unto them, Out of the eater came forth ᵀmeat, and out of the strong came forth sweetness. And they could not in three days expound the riddle.   *food*

15 And it came to pass on the seventh day, that they said unto Samson's wife, ᴿEntice thy husband, that he may declare unto us the riddle, lest we burn thee and thy father's house with fire: have ye called us to take that we have? *is it* not *so?*   16:5

16 And Samson's wife wept before him, and said, ᴿThou dost but hate me, and lovest me not: thou hast put forth a riddle unto the children of my people, and hast not told *it* me. And he said unto her, Behold, I have not told *it* my father nor my mother, and shall I tell *it* thee?   16:15

17 And she wept before him the seven days, while their feast lasted: and it came to pass on the seventh day, that he told her, because she lay sore upon him: and she told the riddle to the children of her people.

18 And the men of the city said unto him on the seventh day before the sun went down, What *is* sweeter than honey? And what *is* stronger than a lion? And he said unto them, If ye had not plowed with my heifer, ye had not found out my riddle.

19 And [R]the Spirit of the Lord came upon him, and he went down to Ash'-ke-lon, and slew thirty men of them, and took their spoil, and gave change of garments unto them which [T]expounded the riddle. And his anger was kindled, and he went up to his father's house.　　　　　　　　3:10; 13:25 · *explained*

20 But Samson's wife [R]was *given* to his companion, whom he had [T]used as [R]his friend.　　　15:2 · *been accustomed to have* · John 3:29

CHAPTER 15

Judgeship of Samson

BUT it came to pass within a while after, in the time of wheat harvest, that Samson visited his wife with a kid; and he said, I will go in to my wife into the chamber. But her father would not suffer him to go in.

2 And her father said, I verily thought that thou hadst utterly [R]hated her; therefore I gave her to thy companion: *is* not her younger sister fairer than she? take her, I pray thee, instead of her.　　　　　　　　　14:20

3 And Samson said concerning them, Now shall I be more blameless than the Phi-lis'-tines, though I do them a [T]displeasure.　*harm*

4 And Samson went and caught three hundred [T]foxes, and took [T]firebrands, and turned tail to tail, and put a firebrand in the midst between two tails.　　*jackals · torches*

5 And when he had set the [T]brands on fire, he let *them* go into the standing [T]corn of the Phi-lis'-tines, and burnt up both the shocks, and also the standing corn, with the vineyards *and* olives.　　*lighted the torches · grain*

6 Then the Phi-lis'-tines said, Who hath done this? And they answered, Samson, the son in law of the Tim'-nite, because he had taken his wife, and given her to his companion. [R]And the Phi-lis'-tines came up, and burnt her and her father with fire.　　14:15

7 And [R]Samson said unto them, Though ye have done this, yet will I be avenged of you, and after that I will cease.　　　　16:20

8 And he smote them hip and thigh with a great slaughter: and he went down and dwelt in the [T]top of the rock E'-tam.　　*cleft*

9 Then the Phi-lis'-tines went up, and [T]pitched in Judah, and spread themselves [R]in Le'-hi.　　　　　　　*made camp · v. 19*

10 And the men of Judah said, Why are ye come up against us? And they answered, To [T]bind Samson are we come up, to do to him as he hath done to us.　　　　*capture*

11 Then three thousand men of Judah went to the top of the rock E'-tam, and said to Samson, Knowest thou not that the Phi-lis'-tines *are* [R]rulers over us? what *is* this *that* thou hast done unto us? And he said unto them, As they did unto me, so have I done unto them.　　　　　　13:1; 14:4

12 And they said unto him, We are come down to bind thee, that we may deliver thee into the hand of the Phi-lis'-tines. And Samson said unto them, Swear unto me, that ye will not fall upon me yourselves.

13 And they spake unto him, saying, No; but we will bind thee fast, and deliver thee into their hand: but surely we will not kill thee. And they bound him with two new cords, and brought him up from the rock.

14 *And* when he came unto Le'-hi, the Phi-lis'-tines shouted against him: and the Spirit of the Lord came mightily upon him, and the cords that *were* upon his arms became as flax that was burnt with fire, and his bands loosed from off his hands.

15 And he found a [T]new jawbone of an ass, and put forth his hand, and took it, and slew a thousand men therewith.　　　　*fresh*

16 And Samson said, With the jawbone of an ass, heaps upon heaps, with the jaw of an ass have I slain a thousand men.

17 And it came to pass, when he had made an end of speaking, that he cast away the jawbone out of his hand, and called that place [T]Ra'-math-le'-hi.　*The lifting of the jawbone*

18 And he was sore athirst, and called on the Lord, and said, Thou hast given this great deliverance into the hand of thy servant: and now shall I die for thirst, and fall into the hand of the uncircumcised?

19 But God clave an hollow place that *was* in the jaw, and there came water thereout; and when he had drunk, his spirit came again, and he revived: wherefore he called the name thereof En-hak'-ko-re, which *is* in Le'-hi unto this day.

20 And he judged Israel [R]in the days of the Phi-lis'-tines twenty years.　　　　13:1

CHAPTER 16

Failure of Samson

THEN went Samson to Ga'-za, and saw there an harlot, and went in unto her.

2 *And it was told* the Ga'-zites, saying, Samson is come [T]thither. And they [R]compassed *him* in, and laid wait for him all night in the gate of the city, and were quiet all the night, saying, In the morning, when it is day, we shall kill him.　　　　　*here · Acts 9:24*

3 And Samson lay till midnight, and arose at midnight, and took the doors of the gate of the city, and the two posts, and went away with them, bar and all, and put *them* upon his shoulders, and carried them up to the top of an hill that *is* before He'-bron.

4 And it came to pass afterward, that he loved a [R]woman in the valley of So'-rek, whose name *was* De-li'-lah.　　　1 Kin. 11:1

5 And the lords of the Phi-lis'-tines came up unto her, and said unto her, Entice him,

and see wherein his great strength *lieth,* and by what *means* we may prevail against him, that we may bind him to ᵀafflict him: and we will give thee every one of us ᵀeleven hundred *pieces* of silver.   *do physical harm · $140,800*

6 ᴿAnd De-li'-lah said to Samson, Tell me, I pray thee, wherein thy great strength *lieth,* and wherewith thou mightest be bound to afflict thee.   1 Kin. 21:7

7 And Samson said unto her, If they bind me with seven ᵀgreen withs that were never dried, then shall I be ᵀweak, and be as another man.   *fresh cords · unable to get free*

8 Then the lords of the Phi-lis'-tines brought up to her seven green withs which had not been dried, and she bound him with them.

9 Now *there were* men lying in wait, abiding with her in the chamber. And she said unto him, The Phi-lis'-tines *be* upon thee, Samson. And he brake the withs, as a thread of tow is broken when it toucheth the fire. So his strength was not known.

10 And De-li'-lah said unto Samson, Behold, thou hast mocked me, and told me lies: now tell me, I pray thee, wherewith thou mightest be bound.

11 And he said unto her, If they bind me ᵀfast with new ropes that never were ᵀoccupied, then shall I be weak, and be as another man.   *securely · used for anything else*

12 De-li'-lah therefore took new ropes, and bound him therewith, and said unto him, The Phi-lis'-tines *be* upon thee, Samson. And *there were* ᵀliers in wait abiding in the chamber. And he brake them from off his arms like a thread.   *men in hiding*

13 And De-li'-lah said unto Samson, Hitherto thou hast mocked me, and told me lies: tell me wherewith thou mightest be bound. And he said unto her, If thou weavest the seven locks of my head with the web.

14 And she fastened *it* with the pin, and said unto him, The ᴿPhi-lis'-tines *be* upon thee, Samson. And he awaked out of his sleep, and went away with the pin of the beam, and with the web.   1 Sam. 4:1

15 And she said unto him, ᴿHow canst thou say, I love thee, when thine heart *is* not with me? thou hast mocked me these three times, and hast not told me wherein thy great strength *lieth.*   14:16

16 And it came to pass, when she pressed him daily with her words, and urged him, *so* that his soul was vexed unto death;

17 That he told her all his heart, and said unto her, There hath not come a razor upon mine head; for I *have been* a Nazarite unto God from my mother's womb: if I be shaven, then my strength will go from me, and I shall become weak, and be like any *other* man.

18 And when De-li'-lah saw that ᴿhe had told her all his heart, she sent and called for the lords of the Phi-lis'-tines, saying, Come up this once, for he hath shewed me all his heart. Then the lords of the Phi-lis'-tines came up unto her, and brought money in their hand.   [Ps. 41:9]

19 ᴿAnd she made him sleep upon her knees; and she called for a man, and she caused him to shave off the seven locks of his head; and she began to afflict him, and his strength went from him.   Prov. 7:26, 27

20 And she said, The Phi-lis'-tines *be* upon thee, Samson. And he awoke out of his sleep, and said, I will go out as at other times before, and shake myself. And he ᵀwist not that the LORD ᴿwas departed from him.   *knew* · 1 Sam. 16:14; 18:12; 28:15, 16; 2 Chr. 15:2

21 But the Phi-lis'-tines took him, and put out his eyes, and brought him down to Ga'-za, and bound him with fetters of brass; and he did grind in the prison house.

22 Howbeit the hair of his head began to grow again after he was shaven.

23 Then the lords of the Phi-lis'-tines gathered them together for to offer a great sacrifice unto ᴿDa'-gon their god, and to rejoice: for they said, Our god hath delivered Samson our enemy into our hand.   1 Sam. 5:2

24 And when the people saw him, they ᴿpraised their god: for they said, Our god hath delivered into our hands our enemy, and the destroyer of our country, which slew many of us.   Dan. 5:4

25 And it came to pass, when their hearts were merry, that they said, Call for Samson, that he may ᵀmake us sport. And they called for Samson out of the prison house; and he ᵀmade them sport: and they set him between the pillars.   *entertain us · entertained them*

26 And Samson said unto the lad that held him by the hand, ᵀSuffer me that I may feel the pillars whereupon the house standeth, that I may lean upon them.   *permit me to*

27 Now the house was full of men and women; and all the lords of the Phi-lis'-tines *were* there; and *there were* upon the ᴿroof about three thousand men and women, that beheld while Samson made sport.   Deut. 22:8

28 And Samson called unto the LORD, and said, O Lord GOD, remember me, I pray thee, and strengthen me, I pray thee, only this once, O God, that I may be at once avenged of the Phi-lis'-tines for my two eyes.

29 And Samson took hold of the two middle pillars upon which the house stood, and ᵀon which it was borne up, of the one with his right hand, and of the other with his left.   *he leaned on them*

30 And Samson said, Let me die with the Phi-lis'-tines. And he bowed himself with *all his* might; and the house fell upon the lords, and upon all the people that *were* therein. So the dead which he slew at his death were more than *they* which he slew in his life.

31 Then his brethren and all the house of his father came down, and took him, and brought *him* up, and ᴿburied him between Zo'-rah and Esh'-ta-ol in the buryingplace of Ma-no'-ah his father. And he judged Israel ᴿtwenty years.   13:25 · 15:20

CHAPTER 17

Example of Personal Idolatry

AND there was a man of mount E'-phra-im, whose name *was* ᴿMi'-cah.   18:2

2 And he said unto his mother, The eleven hundred *shek'-els* of silver that were taken from thee, about which thou cursedst, and spakest of also in mine ears, behold, the silver *is* with me; I took it. And his mother said, Blessed *be thou* of the LORD, my son.

3 And when he had restored the eleven hundred *shek'-els* of silver to his mother, his mother said, I had wholly dedicated the silver unto the LORD from my hand for my son, to make a graven image and a molten image: now therefore I will restore it unto thee.

4 Yet he restored the money unto his mother; and his mother took two hundred *shek'-els* of silver, and gave them to the ᵀfounder, who made thereof a graven image and a ᵀmolten image: and they were in the house of Mi'-cah.   *silversmith · melted*

5 And the man Mi'-cah had an house of gods, and made an ᴿe'-phod, and ter'-a-phim, and ᵀconsecrated one of his sons, who became his priest.   8:27 · *set apart to this office*

6 ᴿIn those days *there was* no king in Israel, ᴿ*but* every man did *that which was* right in his own eyes.   18:1; 19:1 · Deut. 12:8

7 And there was a young man out of Beth'-le-hem–ju'-dah of the family of Judah, who *was* a Levite, and he sojourned there.

8 And the man departed out of the city from Beth'-le-hem–ju'-dah to sojourn where he could find *a place:* and he came to ᴿmount E'-phra-im to the house of Mi'-cah, as he journeyed.   Josh. 24:33

9 And Mi'-cah said unto him, Whence comest thou? And he said unto him, I *am* a Levite of Beth'-le-hem–ju'-dah, and I go to sojourn where I may find *a place.*

10 And Mi'-cah said unto him, Dwell with me, and be unto me a father and a priest, and I will give thee ᵀten *shek'-els* of silver by the year, and a suit of apparel, and thy victuals. So the Levite went in. $72.80

11 And the Levite was content to dwell with the man; and the young man was unto him as one of his sons.

12 And Mi'-cah consecrated the Levite; and the young man ᴿbecame his priest, and was in the house of Mi'-cah.   18:30

13 Then said Mi'-cah, Now know I that the LORD will do me good, seeing I have a ᴿLevite to *my* priest.   Deut. 10:8, 9

CHAPTER 18

Example of Tribal Idolatry

IN those days *there was* no king in Israel: and in those days the tribe of the Danites sought them an inheritance to dwell in; for unto that day all *their* inheritance had not fallen unto them among the tribes of Israel.

2 And the children of Dan sent of their family five men from their coasts, men of valour, from Zo'-rah, and from Esh'-ta-ol, to spy out the land, and to search it; and they said unto them, Go, search the land: who when they came to mount E'-phra-im, to the house of Mi'-cah, they lodged there.

3 When they *were* by the house of ᴿMi'-cah, they knew the voice of the young man the Levite: and they turned in thither, and said unto him, Who brought thee hither? and what makest thou in this *place?* and what hast thou here?   17:1

4 And he said unto them, Thus and thus dealeth Mi'-cah with me, and hath ᴿhired me, and I am his priest.   17:10, 12

5 And they said unto him, ᴿAskᵀ counsel, we pray thee, of God, that we may know whether our way which we go shall be prosperous.   [Is. 30:1]; Hos. 4:12 · *seek the mind of God*

6 And the priest said unto them, ᴿGo in peace: ᵀbefore the LORD *is* your way wherein ye go.   1 Kin. 22:6 · *in the will of the LORD*

7 Then the five men departed, and came to ᴿLa'-ish, and saw the people that *were* therein, how they dwelt careless, after the manner of the Zi-do'-ni-ans, quiet and secure; and *there was* no magistrate in the land, that might put *them* to shame in *any* thing; and they *were* far from the Zi-do'-ni-ans, and had no business with *any* man.   *v.* 29

8 And they came unto their brethren to ᴿZo'-rah and Esh'-ta-ol: and their brethren said unto them, What *say* ye?   *v.* 2

9 And they said, ᴿArise, that we may go up against them: for we have seen the land, and, behold, it *is* very good: and ᵀare ye ᴿstill? be not slothful to go, *and* to enter to possess the land.   Josh. 2:23, 24 · *be* · 1 Kin. 22:3

10 When ye go, ye shall come unto a people ᴿsecure, and to a large land: for ᴿGod hath given it into your hands; ᴿa place where *there is* no want of any thing that *is* in the earth.   *vv.* 7, 27 · Josh. 2:23, 24 · Deut. 8:9

11 And there went from thence of the family of the Danites, out of Zo'-rah and out of Esh'-ta-ol, six hundred men ᵀappointed with weapons of war.   *armed*

12 And they went up, and pitched in Kir'-jath–je'-a-rim, in Judah: wherefore they

called that place Ma'-ha-neh–dan unto this day: behold, *it is* behind Kir'-jath-je'-a-rim.

13 And they passed thence unto mount E'-phra-im, and came unto ^Rthe house of Mi'-cah.   *v. 2*

14 Then answered the five men that went to spy out the country of La'-ish, and said unto their brethren, Do ye know that there is in these houses an e'-phod, and ter'-a-phim, and a graven image, and a molten image? now therefore consider what ye have to do.

15 And they turned ^Tthitherward, and came to the house of the young man the Levite, *even* unto the house of Mi'-cah, and ^Tsaluted him.   *toward that place · greeted*

16 And the ^Rsix hundred men appointed with their weapons of war, which *were* of the children of Dan, stood by the entering of the gate.   *v. 11*

17 And the five men that went to spy out the land went up, *and* came in thither, *and* took the graven image, and the e'-phod, and the ter'-a-phim, and the molten image: and the priest stood in the entering of the gate with the six hundred men *that were* appointed with weapons of war.

18 And these went into Mi'-cah's house, and fetched the carved image, the e'-phod, and the ter'-a-phim, and the molten image. Then said the priest unto them, What do ye?

19 And they said unto him, Hold thy peace, lay thine hand upon thy mouth, and go with us, and be to us a father and a priest: *is it* better for thee to be a priest unto the house of one man, or that thou be a priest unto a tribe and a family in Israel?

20 And the priest's heart was glad, and he took the e'-phod, and the ter'-a-phim, and the graven image, and went in the midst of the people.

21 So they turned and departed, and put the little ones and the cattle and the ^Tcarriage before them.   *goods*

22 *And* when they were a good way from the house of Mi'-cah, the men that ^Twere in the houses near to Mi'-cah's house were gathered together, and overtook the children of Dan.   *lived nearby*

23 And they cried unto the children of Dan. And they turned their faces, and said unto Mi'-cah, ^RWhat aileth thee, that thou comest with such a company?   *2 Kin. 6:28*

24 And he said, ^RYe have taken away my ^Tgods which I made, and the priest, and ye are gone away: and ^Twhat have I more? and what *is* this *that* ye say unto me, What aileth thee?   *17:5 · idols · what else do I own?*

25 And the children of Dan said unto him, Let not thy voice be heard among us, lest angry fellows run upon thee, and thou lose thy life, with the lives of thy household.

26 And the children of Dan went their way: and when Mi'-cah saw that they *were*

too strong for him, he turned and went back unto his house.

27 And they took *the things* which Mi'-cah had made, and the priest which he had, and came unto La'-ish, unto a people *that were* ^Tat quiet and secure: and they ^Tsmote them with the edge of the sword, and burnt the city with fire.   *at peace · destroyed them in battle*

28 And *there was* no deliverer, because it *was* ^Rfar from Zi'-don, and they had no business with *any* man; and it was in the valley that *lieth* by Beth–re'-hob. And they built a city, and dwelt therein.   *v. 7*

29 And they called the name of the city Dan, after the name of Dan their father, who was born unto Israel: howbeit the name of the city *was* La'-ish at the first.

30 And the children of Dan set up the graven image: and Jonathan, the son of Ger'-shom, the son of Ma-nas'-seh, he and his sons were priests to the tribe of Dan until the day of the captivity of the land.

31 And they set them up Mi'-cah's graven image, which he made, ^Rall the time that the house of God was in Shi'-loh.   *Josh. 18:1*

CHAPTER 19

Example of Personal Immorality

AND it came to pass in those days, when *there was* no king in Israel, that there was a certain Levite sojourning on the side of mount E'-phra-im, who took to him a concubine out of Beth–le-hem–ju'-dah.

2 And his concubine played the whore against him, and went away from him unto her father's house to Beth–le-hem–ju'-dah, and was there four whole months.

3 And her husband arose, and went after her, to speak friendly unto her, *and* to bring her again, having his servant with him, and a couple of asses: and she brought him into her father's house: and when the father of the damsel saw him, he rejoiced to meet him.

4 And his father in law, the damsel's father, ^Tretained him; and he abode with him three days: so they did eat and drink, and lodged there.   *detained*

5 And it came to pass on the fourth day, when they arose early in the morning, that he rose up to depart: and the damsel's father said unto his son in law, Comfort thine heart with a morsel of bread, and afterward go your way.

6 And they sat down, and did eat and drink both of them together: for the damsel's father had said unto the man, Be content, I pray thee, and tarry all night, and ^Tlet thine heart be merry.   *have a good time*

7 And when the man rose up to depart, his father in law urged him: therefore he lodged there again.

8 And he arose early in the morning on the fifth day to depart: and the damsel's father said, Comfort thine heart, I pray thee. And they tarried until afternoon, and they did eat both of them.

9 ᴿAnd when the man rose up to depart, he, and his concubine, and his servant, his father in law, the damsel's father, said unto him, Behold, now the day draweth toward evening, I pray you tarry all night: behold, the day groweth to an end, lodge here, that thine heart may be merry; and to morrow get you early on your way, that thou mayest go ᵀhome.   Luke 24:29 · *to thy tent*

10 But the man would not tarry that night, but he rose up and departed, and came over against Je'-bus, which is Jerusalem; and *there were* with him two asses saddled, his concubine also *was* with him.

Example of Tribal Immorality

11 *And* when they *were* by ᵀJe'-bus, the day was far spent; and the servant said unto his master, Come, I pray thee, and let us turn in into this city ᴿof the Jeb'-u-sites, and lodge in it.   *Jerusalem* · Josh. 15:8, 63

12 And his master said unto him, We will not turn aside hither into the city of a stranger, that is not of the children of Israel; we will pass over to Gib'-e-ah.

13 And he said unto his servant, Come, and let us draw near to one of these places to lodge all night, in Gib'-e-ah, or in Ra'-mah.

14 And they passed on and went their way; and the sun went down upon them *when they were* by Gib'-e-ah, which *belongeth* to Benjamin.

15 And they turned aside ᵀthither, to go in *and* to ᵀlodge in Gib'-e-ah: and when he went in, he sat him down in a street of the city: for *there was* no man that took them into his house to lodging.   *there · sleep*

16 And, behold, there came an old man from ᴿhis work out of the field at even, which *was* also of mount E'-phra-im; and he sojourned in Gib'-e-ah: but the men of the place *were* Benjamites.   Ps. 104:23

17 And when he had lifted up his eyes, he saw a ᵀwayfaring man in the street of the city: and the old man said, Whither goest thou? and whence comest thou?   *travelling*

18 And he said unto him, We *are* passing from Beth-le-hem-ju'-dah toward the side of mount E'-phra-im; from thence *am* I: and I went to Beth-le-hem-ju'-dah, but I *am now* going to the house of the LORD; and there *is* no man that receiveth me to house.

19 Yet there is both straw and ᵀprovender for our asses; and there is bread and wine also for me, and for thy handmaid, and for the young man *which is* with thy servants: *there* is no want of any thing.   *fodder*

20 And the old man said, Peace *be* with thee; howsoever *let* all thy wants *lie* upon me; ᴿonly lodge not in the street.   Gen. 19:2

21 So he brought him into his house, and gave provender unto the asses: and they washed their feet, and did eat and drink.

22 *Now* as they were making their hearts merry, behold, ᴿthe men of the city, certain sons of Be'-li-al, beset the house round about, *and* beat at the door, and spake to the master of the house, the old man, saying, Bring forth the man that came into thine house, that we may know him.   20:5

23 And the man, the master of the house, went out unto them, and said unto them, Nay, my brethren, *nay*, I pray you, do not *so* wickedly; seeing that this man is come into mine house, do not this folly.

24 Behold, *here is* my daughter a maiden, and his concubine; them I will bring out now, and humble ye them, and do with them what seemeth good unto you: but unto this man do not so vile a thing.

25 But the men would not hearken to him: so the man took his concubine, and brought her forth unto them; and they ᴿknew her, and abused her all the night until the morning: and when the day began to ᵀspring, they let her go.   Gen. 4:1 · *dawn*

26 Then came the woman in the dawning of the day, and fell down at the door of the man's house where her lord *was*, till it was light.

27 And her lord rose up in the morning, and opened the doors of the house, and went out to go his way: and, behold, the woman his ᵀconcubine was fallen down *at* the door of the house, and her hands *were* upon the threshold.   *secondary wife*

28 And he said unto her, Up, and let us be going. But ᴿnone answered. Then the man took her *up* upon an ass, and the man rose up, and gat him unto his place.   20:5

29 And when he was come into his house, he took a knife, and laid hold on his concubine, and ᵀdivided her, *together* with her bones, into twelve pieces, and sent her into all the coasts of Israel.   *cut her body into pieces*

30 And it was so, that all that saw it said, There was no such deed done nor seen from the day that the children of Israel came up out of the land of Egypt unto this day: consider of it, ᵀtake advice, and ᵀspeak *your* minds.   *confer · let us have your conclusions*

CHAPTER 20

War Between Israel and Dan

THEN ᴿall the children of Israel went out, and the congregation was gathered together as one man, from ᴿDan even to Be'-

er–she'-ba, with the land of Gil'-e-ad, unto the LORD in Miz'-peh. *v. 11 • 18:29*

2 And the chief of all the people, *even* of all the tribes of Israel, presented themselves in the assembly of the people of God, four hundred thousand footmen ᴿthat drew sword. 8:10

3 (Now the children of Benjamin heard that the children of Israel were gone up to Miz'-peh.) Then said the children of Israel, Tell *us*, how was this wickedness?

4 And the Levite, the husband of the woman that was slain, answered and said, I came into Gib'-e-ah that *belongeth* to Benjamin, I and my concubine, to lodge.

5 ᴿAnd the men of Gib'-e-ah rose against me, and beset the house round about upon me by night, *and* thought to have slain me: ᴿand my concubine have they ᵀforced, that she is dead. 19:22; Rom. 1:24–27 • 19:25, 26 • *raped*

6 And I took my concubine, and cut her in pieces, and sent her throughout all the country of the inheritance of Israel: for they have committed lewdness and folly in Israel.

7 Behold, ye *are* all children of Israel; ᴿgive here your advice and counsel. 19:30

8 And all the people arose as one man, saying, We will not any *of us* go to his tent, neither will we any *of us* turn into his house.

9 But now this *shall be* the thing which we will do to Gib'-e-ah; *we will go up* ᵀby lot against it; *in an orderly fashion*

10 And we will take ten men of an hundred throughout all the tribes of Israel, and an hundred of a thousand, and a thousand out of ten thousand, to fetch victual for the people, that they may do, when they come to Gib'-e-ah of Benjamin, according to all the folly that they have wrought in Israel.

11 So all the men of Israel were gathered against the city, knit together as one man.

12 ᴿAnd the tribes of Israel sent men through all the tribe of Benjamin, saying, What wickedness *is* this that is done among you? Deut. 13:14; Josh. 22:13, 16

13 Now therefore deliver *us* the men, the children of Be'-li-al, which *are* in Gib'-e-ah, that we may put them to death, and put away evil from Israel. But the children of Benjamin would not hearken to the voice of their brethren the children of Israel:

14 But the children of Benjamin gathered themselves together out of the cities unto Gib'-e-ah, to go out to battle against the children of Israel.

15 And the ᴿchildren of Benjamin were numbered at that time out of the cities twenty and six thousand men that drew sword, beside the inhabitants of Gib'-e-ah, which were numbered seven hundred chosen men. Num. 1:36, 37; 2:23; 26:41

16 Among all this people *there were* seven hundred chosen men ᴿlefthanded; every one

could sling stones at an hair *breadth*, and not miss. 3:15; 1 Chr. 12:2

17 And the men of Israel, beside Benjamin, were numbered four hundred thousand men that drew sword: all these *were* men of war.

18 And the children of Israel ῀arose, and ᴿwent up to the house of God, and ᴿasked ᵀcounsel of God, and said, Which of us shall go up first to the battle against the children of Benjamin? And the LORD said, Judah *shall go up* first. *vv. 23, 26 • 1:1 • advice*

19 And the children of Israel rose up in the morning, and encamped against Gib'-e-ah.

20 And the men of Israel went out to battle against Benjamin; and the men of Israel put themselves in array to fight against them at Gib'-e-ah.

21 And ᴿthe children of Benjamin came forth out of Gib'-e-ah, and destroyed down to the ground of the Israelites that day twenty and two thousand men. [Gen. 49:27]

22 And the people the men of Israel encouraged themselves, and set their battle again in array in the place where they put themselves in array the first day.

23 (ᴿAnd the children of Israel went up and wept before the LORD until even, and asked counsel of the LORD, saying, Shall I go up again to battle against the children of Benjamin my brother? And the LORD said, Go up against him.) *vv. 26, 27; Josh. 7:6*

24 And the children of Israel came near against the children of Benjamin the second day.

25 And ᴿBenjamin went forth against them out of Gib'-e-ah the second day, and destroyed down to the ground of the children of Israel again eighteen thousand men; all these drew the sword. *v. 21*

26 Then all the children of Israel, and all the people, ᴿwent up, and came unto ᵀthe house of God, and ᴿwept, and sat there before the LORD, and fasted that day until even, and offered burnt offerings and peace offerings before the LORD. *v. 18 • Bethel • 21:2*

27 And the children of Israel ᵀenquired of the LORD, (for the ark of the covenant of God *was* there in those days, *prayed to*

28 ᴿAnd Phin'-e-has, the son of E-le-a'-zar, the son of Aaron, stood before it in those days,) saying, Shall I yet again go out to battle against the children of Benjamin my brother, or shall I cease? And the LORD said, Go up; for to morrow I will deliver them into thine hand. Josh. 24:33

29 And Israel ᴿsetᵀ liers in wait round about Gib'-e-ah. Josh. 8:4 • *set an ambush*

30 And the children of Israel went up against the children of Benjamin on the third day, and put themselves in array against Gib'-e-ah, as at other times.

31 And the children of Benjamin went out against the people, *and* were drawn away

from the city; and they began to smite of the people, *and* kill, as at other times, in the highways, of which one goeth up to the house of God, and the other to Gib'-e-ah in the field, about thirty men of Israel.

32 And the children of Benjamin said, They *are* smitten down before us, as at the first. But the children of Israel said, [T]Let us flee, and draw them from the city unto the highways.   *let us make a strategic retreat*

33 And all the men of Israel rose up out of their place, and put themselves in array at Ba'-al-ta'-mar: and the [R]liers in wait of Israel came forth out of their places, *even* out of the meadows of Gib'-e-ah.   Josh. 8:9

34 And there came against Gib'-e-ah ten thousand chosen men out of all Israel, and the battle was [T]sore: but they [R]knew not that evil *was* near them.   *fierce* • Is. 47:11

35 And the LORD smote Benjamin before Israel: and the children of Israel destroyed of the Benjamites that day twenty and five thousand and an hundred men: all these [T]drew the sword.   *were experienced soldiers*

36 So the children of Benjamin saw that they were smitten: [R]for the men of Israel gave place to the Benjamites, because they trusted unto the liers in wait which they had set beside Gib'-e-ah.   Josh. 8:15

37 And the liers in wait hasted, and rushed upon Gib'-e-ah; and the liers in wait drew *themselves* along, and smote all the city with the edge of the sword.

38 Now there was an appointed [T]sign between the men of Israel and the liers in wait, that they should make a great flame with smoke rise up out of the city.   *signal*

39 And when the men of Israel retired in the battle, Benjamin began to smite *and* kill of the men of Israel about thirty persons: [R]for they said, Surely they are smitten down before us, as *in* the first battle.   *v. 22*

40 But when the flame began to arise up out of the city with a pillar of smoke, the Benjamites [R]looked behind them, and, behold, the [T]flame of the city [T]ascended up to heaven.   Josh. 8:20 • *whole* • *went up in smoke*

41 And when the men of Israel turned again, the men of Benjamin were amazed: for they saw that evil was come upon them.

42 Therefore they [T]turned *their backs* before the men of Israel unto the way of the wilderness; but the battle overtook them; and them which *came* out of the cities they destroyed in the midst of them.   *fled*

43 *Thus* they inclosed the Benjamites round about, *and* chased them, *and* [T]trode them down with ease over against Gib'-e-ah toward the [T]sunrising.   *defeated* • *east*

44 And there fell of Benjamin eighteen thousand men; all these *were* men of valour.

45 And they turned and fled toward the wilderness unto the rock of [R]Rim'-mon: and

they [T]gleaned of them in the highways five thousand men; and pursued hard after them unto Gi'-dom, and slew two thousand men of them.   1 Chr. 6:77 • *gathered*

46 So that all which [T]fell that day of Benjamin were twenty and five thousand men that drew the sword; all these *were* [T]men of valour.   *were killed* • *brave soldiers*

47 But six hundred men turned and fled to the wilderness unto the rock Rim'-mon, and abode in the rock Rim'-mon four months.

48 And the men of Israel turned again upon the children of Benjamin, and smote them with the edge of the sword, [T]as well the men of *every* city, [T]as the beast, and all that came to hand: also they set on fire all the cities that they came to.   *both* • *and*

CHAPTER 21

Israel's Foolish Vow

NOW the men of Israel had sworn in Miz'-peh, saying, There shall not any of us give his daughter unto Benjamin to wife.

2 And the people came to the house of God, and abode there till even before God, and lifted up their voices, and wept sore;

3 And said, O LORD God of Israel, why is this come to pass in Israel, that there should be to day one tribe lacking in Israel?

4 And it came to pass on the [T]morrow, that the people rose early, and [R]built there an altar, and offered burnt offerings and peace offerings.   *next day* • 2 Sam. 24:25

5 And the children of Israel said, Who *is* there among all the tribes of Israel that [T]came not up with the congregation unto the LORD? For they had made a great oath concerning him that came not up to the LORD to Miz'-peh, saying, He shall surely be put to death.   *did not join in the battle*

6 And the children of Israel repented them for Benjamin their brother, and said, There is one tribe cut off from Israel this day.

7 How shall we do for wives for them that remain, seeing we have [R]sworn by the LORD that we will not give them of our daughters [T]to wives?   *v. 1* • *in marriage*

Men at Jabesh-gilead Murdered

8 And they said, What one *is there* of the tribes of Israel that came not up to Miz'-peh to the LORD? And, behold, there came none to the camp from [R]Ja'-besh-gil'-e-ad to the assembly.   1 Sam. 11:1; 31:11

9 For the [T]people were numbered, and, behold, *there were* none of the inhabitants of Ja'-besh-gil'-e-ad there.   *census was taken*

10 And the congregation sent thither twelve thousand men of the [T]valiantest, and commanded them, saying, [R]Go and smite the inhabitants of Ja'-besh-gil'-e-ad with the

edge of the sword, with the women and the children. *bravest • v. 5; 5:23; 1 Sam. 11:7*

11 And this is the thing that ye shall do, Ye shall utterly destroy every male, and every woman that hath lain by man.

12 And they found among the inhabitants of Ja'-besh-gil'-e-ad four hundred young virgins, that had known no man by lying with any male: and they brought them unto the camp to ᴿShi'-loh, which is in the land of Canaan. *18:31*

13 And the whole congregation sent some to speak to the children of Benjamin ᴿthat were in the rock Rim'-mon, and to ᵀcall peaceably unto them. *20:47 • offer peace*

14 And Benjamin came again at that time; and they gave them wives which they had saved alive of the women of Ja'-besh-gil'-e-ad: and yet so they sufficed them not.

15 And the people ᵀrepented them for Benjamin, because that the LORD had made a breach in the tribes of Israel. *felt remorse*

Women of Shiloh Kidnapped

16 Then the ᴿelders of the congregation said, How shall we do for wives for them that remain, seeing the women are destroyed out of Benjamin? *Ruth 4:2*

17 And they said, There must be an inheritance for them that be escaped of Benjamin, that a tribe be not destroyed out of Israel.

18 Howbeit we may not give them wives of our daughters: ᴿfor the children of Israel have sworn, saying, Cursed be he that giveth a wife to Benjamin. *v. 1; 11:35*

19 Then they said, Behold, there is a ᴿfeast of the LORD in Shi'-loh ᵀyearly in a place which is on the north side of Beth'-el, on the east side of the highway that goeth up from Beth'-el to She'-chem, and on the south of Le-bo'-nah. *Lev. 23:2 • from year to year*

20 Therefore they commanded the children of Benjamin, saying, Go and ᵀlie in wait in the vineyards; *hide*

21 And see, and, behold, if the daughters of Shi'-loh come out to dance in dances, then come ye out of the vineyards, and catch you every man his wife of the daughters of Shi'-loh, and go to the land of Benjamin.

22 And it shall be, when their fathers or their brethren come unto us to complain, that we will say unto them, ᵀBe favourable unto them for our sakes: because we reserved not to each man his wife in the war: for ye did not ᴿgive unto them at this time, that ye should be guilty. *be gracious • vv. 1, 18*

23 And the children of Benjamin did so, and took them wives, according to their number, of them that danced, whom they caught: and they went and returned unto their inheritance, and ᴿrepairedᵀ the cities, and dwelt in them. *20:48 • rebuilt*

24 And the children of Israel departed thence at that time, every man to his tribe and to his family, and they went out from thence every man to his inheritance.

25 ᴿIn those days there was no king in Israel: ᴿevery man did that which was right in his own eyes. *17:6; 18:1; 19:1 • Deut. 12:8*

Jewish Feasts

Feast of	Month on Jewish Calendar	Day	Corresponding Month	References
*Passover (Unleavened Bread)	Nisan	14–21	Mar.–Apr.	Ex. 12:43—13:10; Matt. 26:17–20
*Pentecost (Firstfruits or Weeks)	Sivan	6 (50 days after Passover)	May–June	Deut. 16:9–12; Acts 2:1
Trumpets, Rosh Hashanah	Tishri	1, 2	Sept.–Oct.	Num. 29:1–6
Day of Atonement, Yom Kippur	Tishri	10	Sept.–Oct.	Lev. 23:26–32; Heb. 9:7
*Tabernacles (Booths or Ingathering)	Tishri	15–22	Sept.–Oct.	Neh. 8:13–18; John 7:2
Dedication (Lights), Hanukkah	Chislev	25 (8 days)	Nov.–Dec.	John 10:22
Purim (Lots)	Adar	14, 15	Feb.–Mar.	Esth. 9:18–32

*The three major feasts for which all males of Israel were required to travel to the Temple in Jerusalem (Ex. 23:14–19).

THE BOOK OF

RUTH

THE BOOK OF RUTH

Ruth is a cameo story of love, devotion, and redemption set in the black context of the days of the judges. It is the story of a Moabite woman who forsakes her pagan heritage in order to cling to the people of Israel and to the God of Israel. Because of her *faithfulness* in a time of national *faithlessness*, God rewards her by giving her a new husband (Boaz), a son (Obed), and a privileged position in the lineage of David and Christ (she is the great-grandmother of David).

Ruth is the Hebrew title of this book. This name may be a Moabite modification of the Hebrew word *reuit*, meaning friendship or association. The Septuagint entitles the book *Routh*, the Greek equivalent of the Hebrew name. The Latin title is *Ruth*, a transliteration of *Routh*.

THE AUTHOR OF RUTH

The author of Ruth is not given anywhere in the book, nor is he known from any other biblical passage. Talmudic tradition attributes it to Samuel but this is unlikely since David appears in Ruth 4:17, 22, and Samuel died before David's coronation (1 Sam. 25:1). Ruth was probably written during David's reign since Solomon's name is not included in the genealogy. The anonymity of the book, however, should not detract from its spiritual value or literary beauty.

THE TIME OF RUTH

Ruth divides neatly into four distinct settings: (1) the country of Moab (1:1–18); (2) a field in Beth-lehem (1:19—2:23); (3) a threshing floor in Beth-lehem (3:1–18); and (4) the city of Beth-lehem (4:1–22).

The setting of the first eighteen verses is Moab, a region northeast of the Dead Sea. The Moabites, descendants of Lot, worship Chemosh and other pagan gods. Scripture records two times when they fight against Israel (Judg. 3:12–30 and 1 Sam. 14:47). Ruth takes place about two centuries after the first war and about eighty years before the record.

Ruth 1:1 gives the setting of the remainder of the book: "Now it came to pass in the days when the judges ruled." This is a time of apostasy, warfare, decline, violence, moral decay, and anarchy. Ruth provides a cameo of the other side of the story—the godly remnant who remain true to the laws of God.

Because Ruth is written more to tell a beautiful story than to give all the historical facts of that period, the assignment of time is somewhat difficult. Utilizing the same fourfold division noted above, the following can be assigned:

A. Ruth 1:1–18 (note 1:4): The country of Moab (c. ten years)
B. Ruth 1:19—2:23 (note 1:22; 2:23): A field in Beth-lehem (months)
C. Ruth 3:1–18 (note 3:2, 8, 14, 18): A threshing floor in Beth-lehem (one day)
D. Ruth 4:1–22 (note 4:13–16): The city of Beth-lehem (c. one year)

THE CHRIST OF RUTH

The concept of the kinsman-redeemer or *goel* (3:9, "near kinsman") is an important portrayal of the work of Christ. The *goel* must (1) be related by blood to those he redeems (Deut. 25:5, 7–10; John 1:14; Rom. 1:3; Phil. 2:5–8; Heb. 2:14, 15); (2) be able to pay the price of redemption (2:1; 1 Pet. 1:18, 19); (3) be willing to redeem (3:11; Matt. 20:28; John 10:15, 18; Heb. 10:7); (4) be free himself (Christ was free from the curse of sin). The word *goel*, used thirteen times in this short book, presents a clear picture of the mediating work of Christ.

KEYS TO RUTH

Key Word: Kinsman-Redeemer—The Hebrew word for kinsman (*goel*) appears thirteen times in Ruth and basically means "one who redeems." By buying back the land of Naomi, as well as marrying Ruth and fathering a son to keep the family line alive, Boaz acts as a redeemer.

Key Verses: Ruth 1:16; 3:11—"And Ruth said, Intreat me not to leave thee, *or* to return from following after thee: for whither thou goest, I will go; and where thou lodgest, I will lodge: thy people *shall be* my people, and thy God my God" (1:16).

"And now, my daughter, fear not; I will do to thee all that thou requirest: for all the city of my people doth know that thou *art* a virtuous woman" (3:11).

Key Chapter: Ruth 4—In twenty-two short verses, Ruth moves from widowhood and poverty to marriage and wealth (2:1). In exercising the law regulating the redemption of property (Lev. 25:25–34) and the law concerning a brother's duty to raise up seed (children) in the name of the deceased (Deut. 25:5–10), Boaz brings a Moabite woman into the family line of David and eventually of Jesus Christ.

SURVEY OF RUTH

Ruth is the story of a virtuous woman who lives above the norm of her day. Although it was probably written during the time of David,

the events take place during the time of the judges. This period in Israel's history was generally a desert of rebellion and immorality, but the story of Ruth stands in contrast as an oasis of integrity and righteousness.

Ruth is "a virtuous woman" (3:11) who shows loyal love to her mother-in-law Naomi and her near-kinsman Boaz. In both relationships, goodness and love are clearly manifested. Her love is demonstrated in chapters 1 and 2 and rewarded in chapters 3 and 4.

Ruth's Love Is Demonstrated (1 and 2): The story begins with a famine in Israel, a sign of disobedience and apostasy (Deut. 28—30). An Israelite named Elimelech ("My God Is King") in a desperate act moves from Beth-lehem ("House of Bread"—note the irony) to Moab. Although he seeks life in that land, he and his two sons Mahlon ("Sick") and Chilion ("Pining") find only death. The deceased sons leave two Moabite widows, Orpah ("Stubborness") and Ruth ("Friendship"). Elimelech's widow, Naomi, hears that the famine in Israel is over and decides to return, no longer as Naomi ("Pleasant") but as Mara ("Bitter"). She tells her daughters-in-law to remain in Moab and remarry since there was no security for an unmarried woman in those days. Orpah chooses to leave Naomi and is never mentioned again. Ruth, on the other hand, resolves to cling to Naomi and follow Yahweh, the God of Israel. She therefore gives up her culture, people, and language because of her love.

Naomi's misfortune leads her to think that God is her enemy, but He has plans she does not yet realize. In her plight, she must let Ruth glean at the edge of a field. This is a humiliating and dangerous task because of the character of many of the reapers. However, God's providential care brings her to the field of Boaz, Naomi's kinsman. Boaz ("In Him Is Strength") begins to love, protect, and provide for her.

Ruth's Love Is Rewarded (3 and 4): Boaz takes no further steps toward marriage, so Naomi follows the accepted customs of the day and requests that Boaz exercise his right as kinsman-redeemer. In 3:10-13, Boaz reveals why he has taken no action: he is older than Ruth (perhaps twenty years her senior), and he is not the nearest kinsman. Nevertheless, God rewards Ruth's devotion by giving her Boaz as a husband and by providing her with a son, Obed, the grandfather of David.

FOCUS	RUTH'S LOVE DEMONSTRATED		RUTH'S LOVE REWARDED	
REFERENCE	1:1 ———————— 1:19		3:1 ———————— 4:1	———————— 4:22
DIVISION	RUTH'S DECISION TO STAY WITH NAOMI	RUTH'S DEVOTION TO CARE FOR NAOMI	RUTH'S REQUEST FOR REDEMPTION BY BOAZ	RUTH'S REWARD OF REDEMPTION BY BOAZ
TOPIC	RUTH AND NAOMI		RUTH AND BOAZ	
	DEATH OF FAMILY	RUTH CARES FOR NAOMI	BOAZ CARES FOR RUTH	BIRTH OF FAMILY
LOCATION	MOAB	FIELDS OF BETHLEHEM	THRESHING FLOOR OF BETHLEHEM	BETHLEHEM
TIME	c. 12 YEARS			

OUTLINE OF RUTH

Part One: Ruth's Love Is Demonstrated (1:1—2:23)

Part Two: Ruth's Love Is Rewarded (3:1—4:22)

CHAPTER 1

Ruth's Need to Remain with Naomi

NOW it came to pass in the days when the judges ruled, that there was a famine in the land. And a certain man of Beth–le-hem–ju′-dah went to sojourn in the country of Moab, he, and his wife, and his two sons.

2 And the name of the man was E-lim′-e-lech, and the name of his wife Na-o′-mi, and the name of his two sons Mah′-lon and Chil′-i-on, Eph′-rath-ites of Beth–le-hem–ju′-dah. And they came into the country of Moab, and ^Tcontinued there.   remained

3 And E-lim′-e-lech Na-o′-mi's husband died; and she was left, and her two sons.

4 And they took them wives of the women of Moab; the name of the one was Or′-pah, and the name of the other Ruth: and they dwelled there about ten years.

5 And Mah′-lon and Chil′-i-on died also both of them; and the woman was left of her two sons and her husband.

Ruth's Opportunity to Leave Naomi

6 Then she arose with her daughters in law, that she might return from the country of Moab: for she had heard in the country of Moab how that the LORD had visited his people in giving them bread.

7 Wherefore she went forth out of the place where she was, and her two daughters in law with her; and they went on the way to return unto the land of Judah.

8 And Na-o′-mi said unto her two daughters in law, Go, return each to her mother's house: the LORD deal kindly with you, as ye have dealt with the dead, and with me.

9 The LORD grant you that ye may find ^Rrest, each of you in the house of her husband. Then she kissed them; and they lifted up their voice, and wept.   3:1

10 And they said unto her, Surely we will return with thee unto thy people.

11 And Na-o′-mi said, Turn again, my daughters: why will ye go with me? are there yet any more sons in my womb, ^Rthat they may be your husbands?   Deut. 25:5

12 Turn again, my daughters, go your way; for I am too old to have an husband. If

I should say, I have hope, if I should have an husband also to night, and should also bear sons;

13 Would ye tarry for them till they were grown? would ye stay for them from having husbands? nay, my daughters; for it grieveth me much for your sakes that the hand of the LORD is gone out against me.

14 And they lifted up their voice, and wept again: and Or′-pah kissed her mother in law; but Ruth clave^T unto her.   clung

15 And she said, Behold, thy sister in law is gone back unto her people, and unto her gods: return thou after thy sister in law.

Ruth's Choice to Remain with Naomi

16 And Ruth said, Intreat me not to leave thee, or to return from following after thee: for whither thou goest, I will go; and where thou lodgest, I will lodge: thy people shall be my people, and thy God my God:

17 Where thou diest, will I die, and there will I be buried: the LORD do so to me, and more also, if ought but death part thee and me.

18 When she saw that she ^Twas stedfastly minded to go with her, then she left speaking unto her.   made up her mind

Ruth and Naomi Return to Bethlehem

19 So they two went until they came to Beth′-le-hem. And it came to pass, when they were come to Beth′-le-hem, that all the city was moved about them, and ^Tthey said, ^RIs this Na-o′-mi?   the women · Is. 23:7

20 And she said unto them, Call me not Na-o′-mi, call me Ma′-ra: for the Almighty hath dealt very bitterly with me.

21 I went out full, and the LORD hath brought me home again empty: why then call ye me Na-o′-mi, seeing the LORD hath ^Ttestified against me, and the Almighty hath afflicted me?   turned against me

22 So Na-o′-mi returned, and Ruth the Mo′-ab-i-tess, her daughter in law, with her, which returned out of the country of Moab: and they came to Beth′-le-hem ^Rin the beginning of barley harvest.   2:23; 2 Sam. 21:9

CHAPTER 2

Boaz Meets Ruth

AND Na-o'-mi had a ^Rkinsman of her husband's, a mighty man of wealth, of the family of ^RE-lim'-e-lech; and his name *was* ^RBo'-az.   3:2, 12 • 1:2 • 4:21

2 And Ruth the Mo'-ab-i-tess said unto Na-o'-mi, Let me now go to the field, and ^Rglean^T ears of corn after *him* in whose sight I shall find grace. And she said unto her, Go, my daughter.   Deut. 24:19 • *gather*

3 And she went, and came, and gleaned in the field after the reapers: and her ^Thap was to light on a part of the field *belonging* unto Bo'-az, who *was* of the kindred of E-lim'-e-lech.   *chanced upon,* or, *fortune*

4 And, behold, Bo'-az came from Beth'-lehem, and said unto the reapers, ^RThe LORD *be* with you. And they answered him, The LORD bless thee.   Luke 1:28; 2 Thess. 3:16

5 Then said Bo'-az unto his servant that was set over the reapers, Whose damsel *is* this?

6 And the servant that was set over the reapers answered and said, It *is* the Mo'-ab-i-tish damsel ^Rthat came back with Na-o'-mi out of the country of Moab: 1:22

7 And she said, I pray you, let me glean and gather after the reapers among the sheaves: so she came, and hath continued even from the morning until now, that she tarried a little in the house.

Boaz Protects Ruth

8 Then said Bo'-az unto Ruth, Hearest thou not, my daughter? Go not to glean in another field, neither go from hence, but abide here ^Tfast by my maidens: *close*

9 *Let* thine eyes *be* on the field that they do reap, and go thou after them: have I not charged the young men that they shall not ^Ttouch thee? and when thou art athirst, go unto the vessels, and drink of *that* which the young men have drawn.   *molest*

10 Then she ^Rfell on her face, and bowed herself to the ground, and said unto him, Why have I found grace in thine eyes, that thou shouldest ^Ttake knowledge of me, seeing I *am* a stranger?   1 Sam 25:23 • *pay attention to*

11 And Bo'-az answered and said unto her, It hath fully been shewed me, all that thou hast done unto thy mother in law since the death of thine husband: and *how* thou hast left thy father and thy mother, and the land of thy nativity, and art come unto a people which thou knewest not heretofore.

12 ^RThe LORD ^Trecompense thy work, and a full reward be given thee of the LORD God of Israel, ^Runder whose wings thou art come to trust.   1 Sam. 24:19; Ps. 58:11 • *repay* • Ps. 36:7

13 Then she said, Let me find favour in thy sight, my lord; for that thou hast comforted me, and for that thou hast spoken friendly unto thine handmaid, though I be not like unto one of thine handmaidens.

14 And Bo'-az said unto her, At mealtime ^Tcome thou hither, and eat of the bread, and dip thy morsel in the vinegar. And she sat beside the reapers: and he reached her parched *corn,* and she did eat, and ^Rwas sufficed, and left.   *draw near* • v. 18

15 And when she was risen up to ^Tglean, Bo'-az commanded his young men, saying, Let her glean even among the sheaves, and ^Treproach her not: *gather after the reapers* • *forbid*

16 And let fall also *some* of the handfuls of purpose for her, and leave *them,* that she may glean *them,* and rebuke her not.

Boaz Provides for Ruth

17 So she gleaned in the field until even, and beat out that she had gleaned: and it was about an ^Te'-phah of barley.   *.65 bu.*

18 And she took *it* up, and went into the city: and her mother in law saw what she had gleaned: and she brought forth, and gave to her ^Rthat she had reserved after she was sufficed.   v. 14

19 And her mother in law said unto her, Where hast thou gleaned to day? and where wroughtest thou? blessed be he that did take knowledge of thee. And she shewed her mother in law with whom she had wrought, and said, The man's name with whom I wrought to day *is* Bo'-az.

20 And Na-o'-mi said unto her daughter in law, ^RBlessed *be* he of the LORD, who hath not left off his kindness to the living and to the dead. And Na-o'-mi said unto her, The man *is* near of kin unto us, ^Rone of our next kinsmen.   3:10 • 3:9; 4:6

21 And Ruth the Mo'-ab-i-tess said, He said unto me also, Thou shalt ^Tkeep fast by my young men, until they have ended all my harvest.   *stay close*

22 And Na-o'-mi said unto Ruth her daughter in law, *It is* good, my daughter, that thou go out with his maidens, that they meet thee not in any other field.

23 So she kept fast by the maidens of Bo'-az to glean unto ^Rthe end of barley harvest and of wheat harvest; and dwelt with her mother in law.   Deut. 16:9

CHAPTER 3

Naomi Seeks Redemption for Ruth

THEN Na-o'-mi her mother in law said unto her, My daughter, shall I not seek rest for thee, that it may be well with thee?

2 And now *is* not Bo'-az of ^Rour ^Rkindred, ^Rwith whose maidens thou wast? Behold, he winnoweth barley to night in the threshingfloor.   Deut. 25:5–10 • 2:3 • 2:8

3 Wash thyself therefore, ^Rand anoint thee, and put thy raiment upon thee, and get thee down to the floor: *but* make not thyself known unto the man, until he shall have done eating and drinking.   2 Sam. 14:2

4 And it shall be, when he lieth down, that thou shalt ^Tmark the place where he shall lie, and thou shalt go in, and uncover his feet, and lay thee down; and he will tell thee what thou shalt do.   *know*

5 And she said unto her, All that thou sayest unto me I will do.

Ruth Obeys Naomi

6 And she went down unto the ^Tfloor, and did according to all that her mother in law bade her.   *threshingfloor*

7 And when Bo'-az had eaten and drunk, and ^Rhis^T heart was merry, he went to lie down at the end of the heap of corn: and she came softly, and uncovered his feet, and laid her down.   Esth. 1:10 • *felt very cheerful*

8 And it came to pass at midnight, that the man was afraid, and turned himself: and, behold, a woman lay at his feet.

9 And he said, Who *art* thou? And she answered, I *am* Ruth thine handmaid: spread therefore thy skirt over thine handmaid; for thou *art* ^Ra near kinsman.   *v. 12*

Boaz Desires to Redeem Ruth

10 And he said, Blessed *be* thou of the LORD, my daughter: *for* thou hast shewed more ^Tkindness in the latter end than at the beginning, inasmuch as thou followedst not young men, whether poor or rich.   *virtue*

11 And now, my daughter, fear not; I will do to thee all that thou requirest: for all the city of my people doth know that thou *art* ^Ra virtuous woman.   Prov. 12:4

12 And now it is true that I *am* thy ^Rnear kinsman: howbeit ^Rthere is a kinsman nearer than I.   *v. 9 • 4:1*

13 Tarry this night, and it shall be in the morning, *that* if he will perform unto thee the part of a kinsman, well; let him do the kinsman's part: but if he will not do the part of a kinsman to thee, then will I do the part of a kinsman to thee, *as* the LORD liveth: ^Tlie down until the morning.   *sleep*

14 And she lay at his feet until the morning: and she rose up before one could know another. And he said, ^RLet it not be known that a woman came into the floor.   [2 Cor. 8:21]

15 Also he said, Bring the vail that *thou hast* upon thee, and hold it. And when she held it, he measured six *measures* of barley, and laid *it* on her: and she went into the city.

16 And when she came to her mother in law, she said, ^TWho *art* thou, my daughter? And she told her all that the man had done to her.   *how did things work out for you?*

17 And she said, These six *measures* of barley gave he me; for he said to me, Go not empty unto thy mother in law.

18 Then said she, ^RSit still, my daughter, until thou know how the matter will fall: for the man will not be in rest, until he have finished the thing this day.   [Ps. 37:3, 5]

CHAPTER 4

Boaz Marries Ruth

THEN went Bo'-az up to the gate, and sat him down there: and, behold, ^Rthe kinsman of whom Bo'-az spake came by; unto whom he said, Ho, such a one! turn aside, sit down here. And he turned aside, and sat down.   3:12

2 And he took ten men of ^Rthe elders of the city, and said, Sit ye down here. And they sat down.   1 Kin. 21:8; Prov. 31:23

3 And he said unto the kinsman, Na-o'-mi, that is come again out of the country of Moab, selleth a ^Tparcel of land, which *was* our brother E-lim'-e-lech's: *plot*

4 And I thought to advertise thee, saying, Buy *it* before the inhabitants, and before the elders of my people. If thou wilt redeem *it*, redeem *it*: but if thou wilt not redeem *it*, *then* tell me, that I may know: for *there is* none to redeem *it* beside thee; and I *am* after thee. And he said, I will redeem *it*.

5 Then said Bo'-az, What day thou buyest the field ^Tof the hand of Na-o'-mi, thou must buy *it* also of Ruth the Mo'-ab-i-tess, the wife of the dead, to raise up the name of the dead upon his inheritance.   *from*

6 And the kinsman said, I cannot redeem *it* for myself, lest I ^Tmar mine own inheritance: ^Tredeem thou my right to thyself; for I cannot redeem *it*.   *forfeit • take my privileges*

7 Now this *was the manner* in former time in Israel concerning redeeming and concerning changing, for to confirm all things; a man plucked off his shoe, and gave *it* to his neighbour: and this *was* a testimony in Israel.

8 Therefore the kinsman said unto Bo'-az, Buy *it* for thee. So he drew off his shoe.

9 And Bo'-az said unto the elders, and *unto* all the people, Ye *are* witnesses this day, that I have bought all that *was* E-lim'-e-lech's, and all that *was* Chil'-i-on's and Mah'-lon's, of the hand of Na-o'-mi.

10 Moreover Ruth the Mo'-ab-i-tess, the wife of Mah'-lon, have I purchased to be my wife, to raise up the name of the dead upon his inheritance, ^Rthat the name of the dead be not cut off from among his brethren, and from the gate of his place: ye *are* witnesses this day.   Deut. 25:6

11 And all the people that *were* in the gate, and the elders, said, We *are* witnesses. The

LORD make the woman that is come into thine house like Ra'-chel and like Leah, which two did build the house of Israel: and do thou worthily in ᴿEph'-ra-tah, and be famous in Beth'-le-hem: Gen. 35:16

12 And let thy house be like the house of Pha'-rez, whom Ta'-mar bare unto Judah, of ᴿthe ᵀseed which the LORD shall give thee of this young woman. 1 Sam. 2:20 · children

Ruth Bears a Son, Obed

13 So Bo'-az ᴿtook Ruth, and she was his wife: and when he went in unto her, ᴿthe LORD gave her conception, and she bare a son. 3:11 · Gen. 29:31; Matt. 1:5

14 And the women said unto Na-o'-mi, Blessed be the LORD, which hath not left thee this day without a ᵀkinsman, that his name may be famous in Israel. redeemer

15 And he shall be unto thee a ᵀrestorer of thy life, and a ᵀnourisher of thine old age: for thy daughter in law, which loveth thee,

which is ᴿbetter to thee than seven sons, hath born him. renewer · supporter · 1 Sam. 1:8

Naomi Receives a New Family

16 And Na-o'-mi took the child, and laid it in her bosom, and became nurse unto it.

Ruth Is the Great-grandmother of David
Matt. 1:3–6

17 And the women her neighbours gave it a name, saying, There is a son born to Na-o'-mi; and they called his name O'-bed: he is the father of Jesse, the father of David.

18 Now these are the generations of Pha'-rez: Pha'-rez begat Hez'-ron,

19 And Hez'-ron begat Ram, and Ram begat Am-min'-a-dab,

20 And Am-min'-a-dab begat Nah'-shon, and Nah'-shon begat ᵀSal'-mon, Salmah

21 And Sal'-mon begat Bo'-az, and Bo'-az begat O'-bed,

22 And O'-bed begat Jesse, and Jesse begat ᴿDavid. 1 Sam. 16:13; 1 Chr. 2:15; Matt. 1:6

The Jewish Calendar

The Jews used two kinds of calendars:
Civil Calendar—official calendar of kings, childbirth, and contracts.
Sacred Calendar—from which festivals were computed.

NAMES OF MONTHS	CORRESPONDS WITH	NO. OF DAYS	MONTH OF CIVIL YEAR	MONTH OF SACRED YEAR	
TISHRI	Sept.–Oct.	30 days	1st	7th	The Jewish day was from sunset to sunset, in 8 equal parts:
HESHVAN	Oct.–Nov.	29 or 30	2nd	8th	
CHISLEV	Nov.–Dec.	29 or 30	3rd	9th	
TEBETH	Dec.–Jan.	29	4th	10th	FIRST WATCH . . . .SUNSET TO 9 P.M.
SHEBAT	Jan.–Feb.	30	5th	11th	SECOND WATCH . .9 P.M. TO MIDNIGHT
ADAR	Feb.–Mar.	29 or 30	6th	12th	THIRD WATCH . . . .MIDNIGHT TO 3 A.M.
NISAN	Mar.–Apr.	30	7th	1st	FOURTH WATCH . .3 A.M. TO SUNRISE
IYAR	Apr.–May	29	8th	2nd	
SIVAN	May–June	30	9th	3rd	FIRST HOUR . . . . .SUNRISE TO 9 A.M.
TAMMUZ	June–July	29	10th	4th	THIRD HOUR . . . . .9 A.M. TO NOON
AB	July–Aug.	30	11th	5th	SIXTH HOUR . . . . .NOON TO 3 P.M.
*ELUL	Aug.–Sept.	29	12th	6th	NINTH HOUR . . . . .3 P.M. TO SUNSET

*Hebrew months were alternately 30 and 29 days long. Their year, shorter than ours, had 354 days. Therefore, about every 3 years (7 times in 19 years) an extra 29-day-month, VEADAR, was added between ADAR and NISAN.

THE FIRST BOOK OF
SAMUEL

THE BOOK OF FIRST SAMUEL

The Book of First Samuel describes the transition of leadership in Israel from judges to kings. Three characters are prominent in the book: Samuel, the last judge and first prophet; Saul, the first king of Israel; and David, the king-elect, anointed but not yet recognized as Saul's successor.

The books of First and Second Samuel were originally one book in the Hebrew Bible, known as the "Book of Samuel" or simply "Samuel." This name has been variously translated "The Name of God," "His Name Is God," "Heard of God," and "Asked of God." The Septuagint divides Samuel into two books even though it is one continuous account. This division artificially breaks up the history of David. The Greek (Septuagint) title is *Bibloi Basileion,* "Books of Kingdoms," referring to the later kingdoms of Israel and Judah. First Samuel is called *Basileion Alpha,* "First Kingdoms." Second Samuel and First and Second Kings are called "Second, Third, and Fourth Kingdoms." The Latin Vulgate originally called the books of Samuel and Kings *Libri Regum,* "Books of the Kings." Later the Latin Bible combined the Hebrew and Greek titles for the first of these books, calling it *Liber I Samuelis,* the "First Book of Samuel," or simply "First Samuel."

THE AUTHOR OF FIRST SAMUEL

The author of First and Second Samuel is anonymous, but Jewish talmudic tradition says that it was written by Samuel. Samuel may have written the first portion of the book, but his death recorded in First Samuel 25:1 makes it clear that he did not write all of First and Second Samuel. Samuel did write a book (10:25), and written records were available. As the head of a company of prophets (10:5; 19:20), Samuel would be a logical candidate for biblical authorship.

First Chronicles 29:29 refers to "the Book of Samuel the Seer," "the Book of Nathan the Prophet," and "the Book of Gad the Seer." All three men evidently contributed to these books; and it is very possible that a single compiler, perhaps a member of the prophetic school, used these chronicles to put together the Book of Samuel. This is also suggested by the unity of plan and purpose and by the smooth transitions between sections.

THE TIME OF FIRST SAMUEL

If Samuel wrote the material in the first twenty-four chapters, he did so soon before his death (c. 1015 B.C.). He was born around 1105 B.C., and ministered as a judge and prophet in Israel between about 1067 and 1015 B.C. The books of Samuel end in the last days of David; so they must have been compiled after 971 B.C. The reference in First Samuel 27:6 to the divided monarchy in which Judah is separate from Israel indicates a compilation date after Solomon's death in 931 B.C. However, the silence regarding the Assyrian captivity of Israel in 722 B.C. probably means that First Samuel was written before this key event.

First Samuel covers the ninety-four-year period from the birth of Samuel to the death of Saul (c. 1105–1011 B.C.). The Philistines strongly oppress Israel from 1087 B.C. until the battle of Ebenezer in 1047 B.C. (7:10–14). However, even after this time the Philistines exercise military and economic control. They live in the coastal plains; and the hill country in which the Israelites dwell protects them from total conquest by the Philistines.

THE CHRIST OF FIRST SAMUEL

Samuel is a type of Christ in that he is a prophet, priest, and judge. Highly revered by the people, he brings in a new age.

David is one of the primary Old Testament portrayals of the person of Christ. He is born in Bethlehem, works as a shepherd, and rules as king of Israel. He is the anointed king who becomes the forerunner of the messianic King. His typical messianic psalms are born of his years of rejection and danger (see Ps. 22). God enables David, a man "after his own heart" (13:14), to become Israel's greatest king. The New Testament specifically calls Christ the "seed of David according to the flesh" (Rom. 1:3) and "the root and the offspring of David" (Rev. 22:16).

KEYS TO FIRST SAMUEL

Key Word: Transition—First Samuel records the critical transition in Israel from the rule of God through the judges to His rule through the kings.

This transition goes through three stages: Eli to Samuel, Samuel to Saul, and Saul to David.

Key Verses: First Samuel 13:14; 15:22—"But now thy kingdom shall not continue: the Lord hath sought him a man after his own heart, and the Lord hath commanded him *to be* captain over his people, because thou hast not kept *that* which the Lord commanded thee" (13:14).

"And Samuel said, Hath the Lord *as great* delight in burnt offerings and sacrifices, as in obeying the voice of the Lord? Behold, to obey *is*

better than sacrifice, *and* to hearken than the fat of rams" (15:22).

Key Chapter: First Samuel 15—First Samuel 15 records the tragic transition of kingship from Saul to David. As in all three changes recorded in First Samuel, God removes His blessing from one and gives it to another because of sin. "Because thou hast rejected the word of the LORD, he hath also rejected thee from *being* king" (15:23).

SURVEY OF FIRST SAMUEL
First Samuel records the crucial transition from the theocracy under the judges to the monarchy under the kings. The book is built around three key men: Samuel (1—7), Saul (8—31), and David (16—31).

Samuel (1—7): Samuel's story begins late in the turbulent time of the judges when Eli is the judge-priest of Israel. The birth of Samuel and his early call by Yahweh are found in chapters 1—3. Because of his responsiveness to God (3:19), he is confirmed as a prophet (3:20, 21) at a time when "the word of the LORD was precious in those days; *there was* no open vision" (3:1).

Corruption at Shiloh by Eli's notoriously wicked sons leads to Israel's defeat in the crucial battle with the Philistines (4:1-11). The ark of the covenant, God's "throne" among the people, is lost to the Philistines; the priesthood is disrupted by the deaths of Eli and his sons; and the glory of God departs from the tabernacle (Ichabod, "No Glory," 4:21). Samuel begins to function as the last of the judges and the first in the order of the prophets (Acts 3:24). His prophetic ministry (7:3-17) leads to a revival in Israel, the return of the ark, and the defeat of the Philistines. When Samuel is old and his sons prove to be unjust judges, the people wrongly cry out for a king. They want a visible military and judicial ruler so they can be "like all the nations" (8:5-20).

Saul (8—15): In their impatient demand for a king, Israel chooses less than God's best. Their motive (8:5) and criteria (9:2) are wrong. Saul begins well (9—11), but his good characteristics soon degenerate. In spite of Samuel's solemn prophetic warning (12), Saul and the people begin to act wickedly. Saul presumptuously assumes the role of a priest (cf. 2 Chr. 26:18) and offers up sacrifices (13). He makes a foolish vow (14) and disobeys God's command to destroy the Amalekites (15). Samuel's powerful words in 15:22, 23 evoke a pathetic response in 15:24-31.

Saul and David (16—31): When God rejects Saul, He commissions Samuel to anoint David as Israel's next king. God's king-elect serves in Saul's court (16:14—23:29) and defeats the Philistine Goliath (17). Jonathan's devotion to David leads him to sacrifice the throne (20:30, 31) in acknowledgment of David's divine right to it (18). David becomes a growing threat to the insanely jealous Saul; but he is protected from Saul's wrath by Jonathan, Michal, and Samuel (19).

Saul's open rebellion against God is manifested in his refusal to give up what God has said cannot be his. David is protected again by Jonathan from Saul's murderous intent (20), but Saul becomes more active in his pursuit of David. The future king flees to a Philistine city where he feigns insanity (21), and flees again to Adullam where a band of men forms around him (22).

David continues to escape from the hand of Saul, and on two occasions spares Saul's life when he has the opportunity to take it (24—26). David again seeks refuge among the Philistines, but is not allowed to fight on their side against Israel. Saul, afraid of impending battle against the Philistines, foolishly consults a medium at En-dor to hear the deceased Samuel's advice (28). The Lord rebukes Saul and pronounces his doom; he and his sons are killed by the Philistines on Mount Gilboa (31).

FOCUS	SAMUEL			SAUL		
REFERENCE	1:1————————4:1————8:1————————————13:1————15:10————31:13					
DIVISION	FIRST TRANSITION OF LEADERSHIP: ELI—SAMUEL	JUDGESHIP OF SAMUEL	SECOND TRANSITION OF LEADERSHIP: SAMUEL—SAUL	REIGN OF SAUL	THIRD TRANSITION OF LEADERSHIP: SAUL—DAVID
TOPIC	DECLINE OF JUDGES		RISE OF KINGS			
	ELI	SAMUEL	SAUL		DAVID	
LOCATION	CANAAN					
TIME	c. 94 YEARS					

OUTLINE OF FIRST SAMUEL

Part One: Samuel, the Last Judge (1:1—7:17)

Part Two: Saul, the First King (8:1—31:13)

CHAPTER 1

Hannah's Barrenness

NOW there was a certain man of Ra-math-a'-im-zo'-phim, of mount E'-phra-im, and his name *was* El'-ka-nah, the son of Jer'-o-ham, the son of E-li'-hu, the son of To'-hu, the son of Zuph, an Eph'-rath-ite:

2 And he had [R]two wives; the name of the one *was* Hannah, and the name of the other Pe-nin'-nah: and Pe-nin'-nah had children, but Hannah had no children.   Deut. 21:15-17

3 And this man went up out of his city [R]yearly to worship and to sacrifice unto the LORD of hosts in Shi'-loh. And the two sons of E'-li, Hoph'-ni and Phin'-e-has, the priests of the LORD, *were* there.   Luke 2:41

4 And when the time was that El'-ka-nah offered, he gave to Pe-nin'-nah his wife, and to all her sons and her daughters, portions:

5 But unto Hannah he gave a [T]worthy portion; for he loved Hannah: but the LORD had shut up her womb.   *double*

6 And her adversary also [T]provoked her sore, for to make her fret, because the LORD had shut up her womb.   *made her very unhappy*

7 And *as* he did so year by year, when she went up to the house of the LORD, so she provoked her; therefore she wept, and did not eat.

8 Then said El'-ka-nah her husband to her, Hannah, why weepest thou? and why eatest thou not? and why is thy heart grieved? *am* not I better to thee than ten sons?

9 So Hannah rose up after they had eaten in Shi'-loh, and after they had drunk. Now E'-li the priest sat upon a seat by a post of [R]the temple of the LORD.   3:3

10 And she *was* in bitterness of soul, and prayed unto the LORD, and wept [T]sore.   *much*

11 And she vowed a vow, and said, O LORD of hosts, if thou wilt indeed look on the affliction of thine handmaid, and [R]remember me, and not forget thine handmaid, but wilt give unto thine handmaid a man child, then I will give him unto the LORD all the days of his life, and [R]there shall no razor come upon his head.   Gen. 8:1 • Num. 6:5

12 And it came to pass, as she continued praying before the LORD, that E'-li marked her mouth.

13 Now Hannah, [R]she spake in her heart; only her lips moved, but her voice was not heard: therefore E'-li thought she had been drunken.   Gen. 24:45

14 And E'-li said unto her, [R]How long wilt thou be drunken? put away thy wine from thee.   Acts 2:4, 13

15 And Hannah answered and said, No, my lord, I *am* a woman of a sorrowful spirit: I have drunk neither wine nor strong drink, but have [R]poured[T] out my soul before the LORD.   Ps. 62:8 • *prayed earnestly*

16 Count not thine handmaid for a [T]daughter of Be'-li-al: for out of the abundance of my [T]complaint and grief have I spoken hitherto.   *wicked woman • provocation*

17 Then E'-li answered and said, Go in peace: and the God of Israel grant *thee* thy petition that thou hast asked of him.

18 And she said, Let thine handmaid find grace in thy sight. So the woman [R]went her way, and did eat, and her [R]countenance was no more *sad*.   Ruth 2:13 • Eccl. 9:7

Samuel's Birth

19 And they rose up in the morning early, and worshipped before the LORD, and returned, and came to their house to Ra'-mah: and El'-ka-nah [R]knew Hannah his wife; and the LORD remembered her.   Gen. 4:1

20 Wherefore it came to pass, when the time was come about after Hannah had conceived, that she bare a son, and called his name [T]Samuel, *saying*, Because I have asked him of the LORD.   *asked of God*

21 And the man El'-ka-nah, and all his house, [R]went up to offer unto the LORD the yearly sacrifice, and his vow.   *v. 3; Deut. 12:11*

1:17 Petition—One great difference between Christianity and all other religions is that the believer has a prayer-hearing and prayer-answering God. In the Old Testament during a contest with Elijah, the priests of Baal make desperate efforts to speak with their god by crying out and cutting themselves, but to no avail. "But *there was* no voice, nor any that answered" (Page 361—1 Kin. 18:26). How different from these words are those of the Psalmist: "*But* verily God hath heard *me;* he hath attended to the voice of my prayer" (Page 574—Ps. 66:19).
a. The nature of our petitions. First of all, God has commanded us to pray (Page 947—Matt. 7:7, 8; Page 1194—1 Tim. 2:8). When we pray, our petitions should be made by faith (Page 1228—James 1:6) in the name of Jesus (Page 1059—John 14:13). If these simple rules are followed, we can rest assured our prayers are being heard (Page 1252—1 John 3:22; 5:14, 15).
b. The objects of our prayers. For whom or what should we pray? First of all, we need to pray for ourselves, because unless we are in God's will, He cannot hear our petitions about other things. Thus we should begin by asking for cleansing (Page 1249—1 John 1:9) and wisdom (Page 1228—James 1:5). Other areas of our petitions concern spiritual leaders (Page 1179—Col. 4:3), sick believers (Page 1231—James 5:14, 15), rulers (Page 1194—1 Tim. 2:1–3), and even our enemies (Page 946—Matt. 5:44).
Now turn to Page 1172—Phil. 4:6: Thanksgiving.

22 But Hannah ᵀwent not up; for she said unto her husband, *I will not go up* until the child be weaned, and *then* I will ᴿbring him, that he may appear before the LORD, and there abide for ever.   *did not go along* • Luke 2:22

23 And El'-ka-nah her husband said unto her, Do what seemeth thee good; tarry until thou have weaned him; only the LORD establish his word. So the woman abode, and gave her son suck until she weaned him.

24 And when she had weaned him, she took him up with her, with three bullocks, and one e'-phah of flour, and a bottle of wine, and brought him unto the house of the LORD in Shi'-loh: and the child *was* young.

25 And ᴿthey slew a ᵀbullock, and ᴿbrought the child to E'-li. Lev. 1:5 • *bull* • Luke 2:22

26 And she said, Oh my lord, ᴿ*as* thy soul liveth, my lord, I *am* the woman that stood by thee here, praying unto the LORD. 2 Kin. 2:2

27 ᴿFor this child I prayed; and the LORD hath given me my petition which I asked of him: *vv.* 11–13; Matt. 7:7

28 ᴿTherefore also I have ᵀlent him to the LORD; as long as he liveth he shall be lent to the LORD. And he ᴿworshipped the LORD there.   *vv.* 11, 22 • *granted* • Gen. 24:26, 52

CHAPTER 2

Hannah's Prophetic Prayer

AND Hannah prayed, and said, My heart rejoiceth in the LORD, mine horn is exalted in the LORD: my mouth is enlarged over mine enemies; because I ᴿrejoice in thy salvation.   Ps. 9:14

2 *There is* none holy as the LORD: for *there is* none beside thee: neither *is there* any rock like our God.

3 Talk no more so exceeding proudly; let *not* arrogancy come out of your mouth: for the LORD *is* a God of knowledge, and by him actions are ᵀweighed.   *judged*

4 ᴿThe bows of the mighty men *are* broken, ᴿand they that stumbled are girded with strength.   Ps. 37:15 • [Heb. 11:32–34]

5 *They that were* full have hired out themselves for bread; and *they that were* hungry ceased: so that ᴿthe barren hath born seven; and ᴿshe that hath many children is waxed feeble.   Ps. 113:9 • Is. 54:1; Jer. 15:9

6 The LORD killeth, and maketh alive: he ᴿbringeth down to the ᵀgrave, and bringeth up.   [Is. 26:19] • *to the nether world*

7 The LORD maketh poor, and maketh rich: he bringeth low, and lifteth up.

8 He raiseth up the poor out of the dust, *and* lifteth up the beggar from the dunghill, to set *them* among princes, and to make them inherit the throne of glory: for the pillars of the earth *are* the LORD'S, and he hath set the world upon them.

9 He will keep the feet of his saints, and the wicked shall be silent in darkness; for by strength shall no man prevail.

10 The adversaries of the LORD shall be ᴿbroken to pieces; out of heaven shall he thunder upon them: the LORD shall judge the ends of the earth; and he shall give strength unto his king, and exalt the horn of his anointed.   Ex. 15:6; Ps. 2:9

11 And El'-ka-nah went to Ra'-mah to his house. And the child did ᵀminister unto the LORD before E'-li the priest.   *serve*

Sinfulness of Eli's Son

12 Now the sons of E'-li *were* sonsᵀ of Be'-li-al; they knew not the LORD.   *wicked men*

13 ᴿAnd the priest's custom with the people *was, that,* when any man offered sacrifice, the priest's servant came, while the flesh was ᵀin seething, with a fleshhook of three teeth in his hand;   Lev. 7:29–34 • *boiling*

14 And he struck *it* into the pan, or kettle, or caldron, or pot; all that the fleshhook brought up the priest took for ᴿhimself. So they did in ᴿShi'-loh unto all the Israelites that came thither.   Deut. 18:1–5 • 1:3

15 Also before they ᴿburnt the fat, the priest's servant came, and said to the man that sacrificed, Give flesh to roast for the priest; for he will not have ᵀsodden flesh of thee, but raw.   Lev. 3:3–5, 16 • *boiled*

16 And *if* any man said unto him, Let them not fail to burn the fat presently, and *then* take *as much* as thy soul desireth; then he would answer him, Nay; but thou shalt give *it me* now: and if not, I will take *it* by force.

17 Wherefore the sin of the young men was very great before the LORD: for men ᴿabhorred the offering of the LORD.   [Mal. 2:8]

18 ᴿBut Samuel ᴿministered before the LORD, *being* a child, girded with a linen e'-phod.   *v.* 11; 3:1 • 1:3, 21

19 Moreover his mother made him a little coat, and brought *it* to him from year to year, when she ᴿcame up with her husband to offer the yearly sacrifice.   1:3, 21

20 And E'-li ᴿblessed El'-ka-nah and his wife, and said, The LORD give thee seed of this woman for the ᵀloan which is ᴿlentᵀ to the LORD. And they went unto their own ᵀhome.   Gen. 14:19 • *petition* • 1:28 • *asked* • *place*

21 And the LORD visitedᵀ Hannah, so that she conceived, and bare three sons and two daughters. And the child Samuel ᴿgrew before the LORD.   *came to bless* • *v.* 26; Judg. 13:24

Compromise of Eli as Father

22 Now E'-li was very old, and heard all that his sons did unto all Israel; and how they lay with the women that assembled *at* the door of the tabernacle of the congregation.

23 And he said unto them, Why do ye such

things? for ᵀI hear of your evil dealings by all this people.   *I hear evil words of you*

24 Nay, my sons; for *it is* no good report ᴿthat I hear: ᵀye make the LORD's people to transgress.   1 Kin. 15:26 • *you lead them into sin*

25 If one man sin against another, the judge shall judge him: but if a man ᴿsin against the LORD, who shall intreat for him? Notwithstanding they hearkened not unto the voice of their father, ᴿbecause the LORD would slay them.   Num. 15:30 • Josh. 11:20

26 And the child Samuel grew on, and was ᴿin favour both with the LORD, and also with men.   Prov. 3:4

27 ᴿAnd there came a man of God unto E'-li, and said unto him, Thus saith the LORD, ᴿDid I plainly appear unto the house of thy father, when they were in Egypt in Pharaoh's house?   1 Kin. 13:1 • Ex. 4:14, 27

28 And did I choose him out of all the tribes of Israel *to be* my priest, to offer upon mine altar, to burn incense, to wear an e'-phod before me? and ᴿdid I give unto the house of thy father all the offerings made by fire of the children of Israel?   Num. 5:9

29 Wherefore kickᵀ ye at my sacrifice and at mine offering, which I have commanded *in my* ᴿhabitation; and honourest thy sons above me, to make yourselves fat with the ᵀchiefest of all the offerings of Israel my people?   *are you dissatisfied* • Deut. 12:5 • *best, first*

30 Wherefore the LORD God of Israel saith, ᴿI said indeed *that* thy house, and the house of thy father, should walk before me for ever: but now the LORD saith, Be it far from me; for them that honour me ᴿI will honour, and ᴿthey that despise me shall be lightly esteemed.   Ex. 29:9 • Ps. 91:14 • Mal. 2:9

31 Behold, the days come, that I will ᵀcut off thine arm, and the arm of thy father's house, that there shall not be an old man in thine house.   *reduce your strength*

32 And thou shalt see an enemy *in my* habitation, in all *the wealth* which God shall give Israel: and there shall not be ᴿan old man in thine house for ever.   Zech. 8:4

33 And the man of thine, *whom* I shall not cut off from mine altar, *shall be* to ᵀconsume thine eyes, and to grieve thine heart: and all the increase of thine house shall die in the ᵀflower of their age.   *blind* • *as men*

34 And this *shall be* ᴿa sign unto thee, that shall come upon thy two sons, on Hoph'-ni and Phin'-e-has; ᴿin one day they shall die both of them.   1 Kin. 13:3 • 4:11

35 ᴿAnd I will raise me up a faithful priest, *that* shall do according to *that* which is in mine heart and in my mind: and I will build him a sure house; and he shall walk before mine anointed for ever.   [Heb. 3:1]

36 And it shall come to pass, *that* every one that is left in thine house shall come *and* crouch to him for a piece of silver and a ᵀmorsel of bread, and shall say, ᵀPut me, I pray thee, into one of the priests' offices, that I may eat a piece of bread.   *loaf* • *assign*

CHAPTER 3

The Word of the Lord Does Not Come to Eli

AND the child Samuel ministered unto the LORD before E'-li. And the ᴿword of the LORD was ᵀprecious in those days; *there was* no open vision.   Ps. 74:9 • *rarely given*

The Word of the Lord Comes to Samuel

2 And it came to pass at that time, when E'-li *was* laid down in his place, and his eyes began to wax dim, *that* he could not see;

3 And ere the lamp of God went out in the temple of the LORD, where the ark of God *was,* and Samuel was laid down *to sleep;*

4 That the LORD called Samuel: and he answered, ᴿHere *am* I.   [Is. 6:8]

5 And he ran unto E'-li, and said, Here *am* I; for thou calledst me. And he said, I called not; lie down again. And he went and lay down.

6 And the LORD called yet again, Samuel. And Samuel arose and went to E'-li, and said, Here *am* I; for thou didst call me. And he answered, I called not, my son; lie down again.

7 Now Samuel ᴿdid not yet ᵀknow the LORD, neither was the word of the LORD yet revealed unto him.   1 Cor. 13:11 • *understand*

8 And the LORD called Samuel again the third time. And he arose and went to E'-li, and said, Here *am* I; for thou didst call me. And E'-li perceived that the LORD had called the child.

9 Therefore E'-li said unto Samuel, Go, lie down: and it shall be, if he call thee, that thou shalt say, ᴿSpeak, LORD; for thy servant heareth. So Samuel went and lay down in his place.   v. 10; Ps. 85:8

10 And the LORD came, and stood, and called as at other times, Samuel, Samuel. Then Samuel answered, Speak; for thy servant heareth.

11 And the LORD said to Samuel, Behold, I will do a thing in Israel, at which both the ears of every one that heareth it shall tingle.

12 In that day I will perform against E'-li ᴿall *things* which I have spoken concerning his house: when I begin, I will also make an end.   2:30–36; Ezek. 12:25; Luke 21:33

13 For I have told him that I will judge his house for ever for the iniquity which he knoweth; because his sons made themselves vile, and he restrained them not.

14 And therefore I have sworn unto the house of E'-li, that the iniquity of E'-li's house ᴿshall ᵀnot be purged with sacrifice nor offering for ever.   Is. 22:14 • *not be forgiven*

15 And Samuel lay until the morning, and opened the doors of the house of the LORD. And Samuel feared to shew E'-li the vision.

16 Then E'-li called Samuel, and said, Samuel, my son. And he answered, Here *am* I.

17 And he said, What *is* the thing that *the* LORD hath said unto thee? I pray thee hide *it* not from me: God do so to thee, and more also, if thou hide *any* thing from me of all the things that he said unto thee.

18 And Samuel told him every whit, and hid nothing from him. And he said, It *is* the LORD: let him do what seemeth him good.

Samuel Is Recognized as the New Leader of Israel

19 And Samuel grew, and the LORD was with him, and ᵀdid let none of his words fall to the ground.   *heard him when he prayed*

20 And all Israel from Dan even to Be'-er-she'-ba knew that Samuel *was* ᵀestablished *to be* a prophet of the LORD.   *ordained*

21 And the LORD appeared again in Shi'-loh: for the LORD revealed himself to Samuel in Shi'-loh by the word of the LORD.

CHAPTER 4

Conquest of Israel by Philistia

AND the ᴿword of Samuel came to all Israel. Now Israel went out against the Phi-lis'-tines to battle, and ᵀpitched beside ᴿEb'-en-e'-zer: and the Phi-lis'-tines pitched in A'-phek.   *3:21 • made camp • 7:12*

2 And the Phi-lis'-tines put themselves in array against Israel: and when they joined battle, Israel was ᵀsmitten before the Phi-lis'-tines: and they slew of the army in the field about four thousand men.   *defeated*

3 And when the people were come into the camp, the elders of Israel said, Wherefore hath the LORD smitten us to day before the Phi-lis'-tines? Let us fetch the ark of the covenant of the LORD out of Shi'-loh unto us, that, when it cometh among us, it may save us out of the hand of our enemies.

4 So the people sent to Shi'-loh, that they might bring from thence the ark of the covenant of the LORD of hosts, which dwelleth *between* the cher'-u-bims: and the two sons of E'-li, Hoph'-ni and Phin'-e-has, *were* there with the ark of the covenant of God.

5 And when the ark of the covenant of the LORD came into the camp, ᴿall Israel shouted with a great shout, so that the earth rang again.   [Ps. 5:11; Is. 12:6]

6 And when the Phi-lis'-tines heard the noise of the shout, they said, What *meaneth* the noise of this great shout in the camp of the Hebrews? And they understood that the ark of the LORD was come into the camp.

7 And the Phi-lis'-tines were afraid, for they said, God is come into the camp. And they said, ᴿWoe unto us! for there hath not been such a thing heretofore.   Ex. 15:14

8 Woe unto us! who shall deliver us out of the hand of these mighty Gods? these *are* the Gods that ᵀsmote the Egyptians with all the plagues in the wilderness.   *destroyed*

9 Be strong, and quit yourselves like men, O ye Phi-lis'-tines, that ye be not servants unto the Hebrews, as they have been to you: quit yourselves like men, and fight.

10 And the Phi-lis'-tines fought, and ᴿIsrael was ᵀsmitten, and they fled every man into his tent: and there was a very great slaughter; for there fell of Israel thirty thousand footmen.   *v. 2 • defeated*

Eli and His Sons Die

11 And ᴿthe ark of God was taken; and ᴿthe two sons of E'-li, Hoph'-ni and Phin'-e-has, were slain.   Ps. 78:61 • 2:34; Ps. 78:64

12 And there ran a man of Benjamin out of the army, and came to Shi'-loh the same day with his clothes ᵀrent, and ᴿwith ᵀearth upon his head.   *torn • Job 2:12 • sign of grief*

13 And when he came, lo, E'-li sat upon a seat by the wayside watching: for ᵀhis heart trembled for the ark of God. And when the man came into the city, and told *it*, all the city cried out.   *he was much concerned*

14 And when E'-li heard the noise of the crying, he said, What *meaneth* the noise of this tumult? And the man came in hastily, and told E'-li.

15 Now E'-li was ninety and eight years old; and ᴿhis eyes ᵀwere dim, that he could not see.   3:2; 1 Kin. 14:4 • *were weak*

16 And the man said unto E'-li, I *am* he that came out of the army, and I fled to day out of the army. And he said, What ᵀis there done, my son?   *happened there*

17 And the messenger answered and said, Israel is fled before the Phi-lis'-tines, and there hath been also a great slaughter among the people, and thy two sons also, Hoph'-ni and Phin'-e-has, are dead, and the ark of God is taken.

18 And it came to pass, when he made mention of the ark of God, that ᴿhe fell from off the seat backward by the side of the gate, and his neck brake, and he died: ᵀfor he was an old man, and heavy. And he had judged Israel forty years.   *v. 13 • the man*

19 And his daughter in law, Phin'-e-has' wife, was with child, *near* to be delivered: and when she heard the tidings that the ark of God was taken, and that her father in law and her husband were dead, she bowed herself and ᵀtravailed; for her pains came upon her.   *gave birth*

20 And about the time of her death the women that stood by her said unto her, Fear

not; for thou hast born a son. But she answered not, neither did she regard it.

21 And she named the child I'-cha-bod, saying, The glory is departed from Israel: because the ark of God was taken, and because of her father in law and her husband.

22 And she said, The glory is departed from Israel: for the ark of God is taken.

CHAPTER 5

The Philistines' Sin with the Ark

AND the Phi-lis'-tines took the ark of God, and brought it ᴿfrom Eb'-en-e'-zer unto ᴿAsh'-dod.   4:1; 7:12 • Josh. 13:3

2 When the Phi-lis'-tines took the ark of God, they brought it into the house of ᴿDa'-gon, and set it by Da'-gon.   Judg. 16:23

3 And when they of Ash'-dod arose early on the morrow, behold, Da'-gon was ᴿfallen upon his face to the earth before the ark of the Lᴏʀᴅ. And they took Da'-gon, and ᴿset him in his place again.   Is. 19:1; 46:1, 2 • Is. 46:7

4 And when they arose early on the morrow morning, behold, Da'-gon was fallen upon his face to the ground before the ark of the Lᴏʀᴅ; and ᴿthe head of Da'-gon and both the palms of his hands were cut off upon the threshold; only the stump of Da'-gon was left to him.   Ezek. 6:4, 6; Mic. 1:7

5 Therefore neither the priests of Da'-gon, nor any that come into Da'-gon's house, ᴿtreadᵀ on the threshold of Da'-gon in Ash'-dod unto this day.   Zeph. 1:9 • come into the temple

6 But the hand of the Lᴏʀᴅ was heavy upon them of Ash'-dod, and he destroyed them, and smote them with ᴿemerods, even Ash'-dod and the coasts thereof.   Deut. 28:27

7 And when the men of Ash'-dod saw that it was so, they said, The ark of the God of Israel shall not abide with us: for his hand is sore upon us, and upon Da'-gon our god.

8 They sent therefore and ᴿgathered all the lords of the Phi-lis'-tines unto them, and said, What shall we do with the ark of the God of Israel? And they answered, Let the ark of the God of Israel be carried about unto Gath. And they carried the ark of the God of Israel about thither.   v. 11; 29:6-11

9 And it was so, that, after they had carried it about, ᴿthe hand of the Lᴏʀᴅ was against the city with a very great destruction: and he smote the men of the city, both small and great, and they hadᵀ emerods in their secret parts.   7:13; Deut. 2:15 • tumors

10 Therefore they sent the ark of God to Ek'-ron. And it came to pass, as the ark of God came to Ek'-ron, that the Ek'-ron-ites cried out, saying, They have brought about the ark of the God of Israel to us, to ᵀslay ᵀus and ᵀour people.   destroy • me • my

11 So they ᴿsent and gathered together all the lords of the Phi-lis'-tines, and said, Send away the ark of the God of Israel, and let it go again to his own place, that it slay us not, and our people: for there was a deadly destruction throughout all the city; the hand of God was very heavy there.   v. 8

12 And the men that died not were ᵀsmitten with the ᵀemerods: and the cry of the city went up to heaven.   afflicted • tumors

CHAPTER 6

AND the ark of the Lᴏʀᴅ was in the country of the Phi-lis'-tines seven months.

2 And the Phi-lis'-tines called for the priests and the ᵀdiviners, saying, What shall we do to the ark of the Lᴏʀᴅ? tell us wherewith we shall send it to his place.   soothsayers

3 And they said, If ye send away the ark of the God of Israel, send it not empty; but in any wise return him a trespass offering: then ye shall be healed, and it shall be known to you why his hand is not removed from you.

4 Then said they, What shall be the trespass offering which we shall return to him? They answered, Five golden emerods, and five golden mice, according to the number of the lords of the Phi-lis'-tines: for one plague was on you all, and on your lords.

5 Wherefore ye shall make images of your emerods, and images of your mice that mar the land; and ye shall give glory unto the God of Israel: peradventure he will ᵀlighten his hand from off you, and from off your gods, and from off your land.   ease the calamities

6 Wherefore then do ye harden your hearts, as the Egyptians and Pharaoh hardened their hearts? when he had wrought wonderfully among them, ᴿdid they not let the people go, and they departed?   Ex. 12:31

7 Now therefore make a new cart, and take two milch ᵀkine, on which there hath come no yoke, and tie the kine to the cart, and bring their calves home from them: cows

8 And take the ark of the Lᴏʀᴅ, and lay it upon the cart; and put ᴿthe jewels of gold, which ye return him for a trespass offering, in a ᵀcoffer by the side thereof; and send it away, that it may go.   vv. 4, 5 • box

9 And see, if it goeth up by the way of his own coast to Beth–she'-mesh, then he hath done us this great evil: but if not, then we shall know that it is not his hand that smote us; it was a chance that happened to us.

The Israelites' Sin with the Ark

10 And the men did so; and took two milch ᵀkine, and tied them to the cart, and shut up their calves at home: cows

11 And they laid the ark of the Lᴏʀᴅ upon the cart, and the ᵀcoffer with the mice of gold and the images of their emerods.   chest

12 And the ᵀkine took the straight way to the way of Beth-she'-mesh, *and* went along the ᴿhighway, ᵀlowing as they went, and turned not aside *to* the right hand or *to* the left; and the lords of the Phi-lis'-tines went after them unto the border of Beth-she'-mesh.   *cows* • Num. 20:19 • *bellowing*

13 And *they of* Beth-she'-mesh *were* reaping their ᴿwheat harvest in the valley: and they lifted up their eyes, and saw the ark, and rejoiced to see *it*.   12:17

14 And the cart came into the field of Joshua, a Beth-she'-mite, and stood there, where *there was* a great stone: and they clave the wood of the cart, and offered the kine a burnt offering unto the LORD.

15 And ᴿthe Levites took down the ark of the LORD, and the ᵀcoffer that *was* with it, wherein the ᴿjewels of gold *were*, and put *them* on the great stone: and the men of Beth-she'-mesh offered burnt offerings and sacrificed sacrifices the same day unto the LORD.   Josh. 3:3 • *box* • Gen. 24:53

16 And when ᴿthe five lords of the Phi-lis'-tines had seen *it*, they returned to ᴿEk'-ron the same day.   Josh. 13:3 • 7:14

17 ᴿAnd these *are* the golden ᵀemerods which the Phi-lis'-tines returned *for* a trespass offering unto the LORD; for Ash'-dod one, for Ga'-za one, for As'-ke-lon one, for ᴿGath one, for Ek'-ron one;   *v*. 4 • *tumors* • 5:8

18 And the golden mice, *according to* the number of all the cities of the Phi-lis'-tines *belonging* to the five lords, *both* of ᵀfenced cities, and of country villages, even unto the great *stone of* Abel, whereon they set down the ark of the LORD: *which stone remaineth* unto this day in the field of Joshua, the Beth-she'-mite.   *fortified*

19 And ᴿhe ᵀsmote the men of Beth-she'-mesh, because they had looked into the ark of the LORD, even he smote of the people fifty thousand and threescore and ten men: and the people lamented, because the LORD had smitten *many* of the people with a great slaughter.   2 Sam. 6:7 • *caused harm to strike*

20 And the men of Beth-she'-mesh said, Who is able to stand before this holy LORD God? and to whom shall he go up from us?

21 And they sent messengers to the inhabitants of Kir'-jath-je'-a-rim, saying, The Phi-lis'-tines have brought again the ark of the LORD; come ye down, *and* fetch it up to you.

CHAPTER 7
The Acceptable Return of the Ark

AND the men of ᴿKir'-jath-je'-a-rim came, and fetched up the ark of the LORD, and brought it into the house of ᴿA-bin'-a-dab in the hill, and sanctified E-le-a'-zar his son to keep the ark of the LORD.   6:21 • 2 Sam. 6:4

2 And it came to pass, while the ark abode in Kir'-jath-je'-a-rim, that the time was long; for it was twenty years: and all the house of Israel lamented after the LORD.

Israel Returns to the Lord

3 And Samuel spake unto all the house of Israel, saying, If ye do return unto the LORD with all your hearts, *then* put away the strange gods and Ash'-ta-roth from among you, and prepare your hearts unto the LORD, and serve him only: and he will deliver you out of the hand of the Phi-lis'-tines.

4 Then the children of Israel did put away Ba'-a-limᵀ and Ash'-ta-roth, and served the LORD only.   *pagan worship and pleasure*

5 And Samuel said, ᴿGather all Israel to Miz'-peh, and ᴿI will pray for you unto the LORD.   10:17; Judg. 20:1 • Judg. 20:26; Neh. 9:1

6 And they gathered together to Miz'-peh, ᴿand drew water, and poured *it* out before the LORD, and ᴿfasted on that day, and said there, ᴿWe have sinned against the LORD. And Samuel judged the children of Israel in Miz'-peh.   2 Sam. 14:14 • Joel 2:12 • Judg. 10:10

Israel's Victory over Philistia

7 And when the Phi-lis'-tines heard that the children of Israel were gathered together to Miz'-peh, the lords of the Phi-lis'-tines went up against Israel. And when the children of Israel heard *it*, ᴿthey were afraid of the Phi-lis'-tines.   13:6; 17:11

8 And the children of Israel said to Samuel, Ceaseᵀ not to cry unto the LORD our God for us, that he will save us out of the hand of the Phi-lis'-tines.   *do not fail to pray*

9 And Samuel took a sucking lamb, and offered *it for* a burnt offering wholly unto the LORD: and Samuel cried unto the LORD for Israel; and the LORD heard him.

10 And as Samuel was offering up the burnt offering, the Phi-lis'-tines drew near to battle against Israel: but the LORD thundered with a great thunder on that day upon the Phi-lis'-tines, and discomfited them; and they were smitten before Israel.

11 And the men of Israel went out of Miz'-peh, and pursued the Phi-lis'-tines, and ᵀsmote them, until *they came* under Beth'-car.   *destroyed*

12 Then Samuel took a stone, and set *it* between Miz'-peh and Shen, and called the name of it ᵀEb'-en-e'-zer, saying, Hitherto hath the LORD helped us.   *the stone of help*

13 So the Phi-lis'-tines were subdued, and they came no more into the coast of Israel: and the hand of the LORD was against the Phi-lis'-tines all the days of Samuel.

14 And the cities which the Phi-lis'-tines had taken from Israel were restored to Israel, from Ek'-ron even unto Gath; and the coasts thereof did Israel deliver out of the hands of

the Phi-lis'-tines. And there was peace between Israel and the [R]Am'-or-ites.   Num. 13:29

15 And Samuel [R]judged Israel all the days of his life.   v. 6; 12:11

16 And he went from year to year in circuit to Beth'-el, and Gil'-gal, and Miz'-peh, and judged Israel in all those places.

17 And [R]his return was to [R]Ra'-mah; for there was his house; and there he judged Israel; and there he [R]built an altar unto the LORD.   8:4 • 1:1, 19; 2:11 • Judg. 21:4

CHAPTER 8

Israel Rejects Samuel's Sons as Leaders

AND it came to pass, when Samuel was old, that he [R]made his sons judges over Israel.   2 Sam. 7:8; 2 Chr. 19:5

2 Now the name of his firstborn was Jo'-el; and the name of his second, A-bi'-ah: they were judges in Be'-er-she'-ba.

3 And his sons walked not in his ways, but turned aside after [T]lucre, and took bribes, and perverted judgment.   money

4 Then all the elders of Israel gathered themselves together, and came to Samuel unto Ra'-mah,

5 And said unto him, Behold, thou art old, and thy sons walk not in thy ways: now [R]make us a king to judge us like all the nations.   v. 19; Deut. 17:14; Hos. 13:10; Acts 13:21

Israel Rejects God as King

6 But the thing [R]displeased Samuel, when they said, Give us a king to judge us. And Samuel prayed unto the LORD.   12:17

7 And the LORD said unto Samuel, Hearken unto the voice of the people in all that they say unto thee: for they have not rejected thee, but [R]they have rejected me, that I should not reign over them.   10:19

8 According to all the works which they have done since the day that I brought them up out of Egypt even unto this day, wherewith they have forsaken me, and served other gods, so do they also unto thee.

9 Now therefore [T]hearken unto their voice: howbeit yet protest solemnly unto them, and shew them the manner of the king that shall reign over them.   obey

Samuel Warns Israel

10 And Samuel told all the words of the LORD unto [R]the people that asked of him a king.   v. 4

11 And he said, This will be the manner of the king that shall reign over you: He will take your sons, and appoint them for himself, for his chariots, and to be his horsemen; and some shall run before his chariots.

12 And he will appoint him captains over thousands, and captains over fifties; and will

set them to [T]ear his ground, and to reap his harvest, and to make his instruments of war, and instruments of his chariots.   plow

13 And he will take your daughters to be [T]confectionaries, and to be cooks, and to be bakers.   perfumers

14 And he will take your fields, and your vineyards, and your oliveyards, even the best of them, and give them to his servants.

15 And he will take the tenth of your seed, and of your vineyards, and give to his officers, and to his servants.

16 And he will take your menservants, and your maidservants, and your [T]goodliest young men, and your asses, and put them to his work.   choicest

17 He will take the tenth of your [T]sheep: and ye shall be his [T]servants.   flocks • slaves

18 And ye shall cry out in that day because of your king which ye shall have chosen you; and the LORD will not hear you in that day.

19 Nevertheless the people refused to obey the voice of Samuel; and they said, Nay; but we will have a king over us;

20 That we also may be like all the nations; and that our king may judge us, and [T]go out before us, and fight our battles.   lead

21 And Samuel heard all the words of the people, and he [T]rehearsed them in the ears of the LORD.   talked them over with the LORD

22 And the LORD said to Samuel, [R]Hearken unto their voice, and make them a king. And Samuel said unto the men of Israel, Go ye every man unto his city.   Hos. 13:11

CHAPTER 9

God Chooses Saul

NOW there was a man of Benjamin, whose name was Kish, the son of A-bi'-el, the son of Ze'-ror, the son of Be-cho'-rath, the son of A-phi'-ah, a Benjamite, a mighty man of [T]power.   substance

2 And he had a son, whose name was Saul, a choice young man, and [T]a goodly: and there was not among the children of Israel a goodlier person than he: [R]from his shoulders and upward he was [T]higher than any of the people.   a superior person • 10:23 • taller

3 And the asses of Kish Saul's father were lost. And Kish said to Saul his son, Take now one of the servants with thee, and arise, go seek the [R]asses.   Matt. 21:2

4 And he passed through [T]mount E'-phra-im, and passed through the land of [R]Shal'-i-sha, but they found them not: then they passed through the land of Sha'-lim, and there they were not: and he passed through the land of the Benjamites, but they found them not.   the hill country of • 2 Kin. 4:42

5 And when they were come to the land of Zuph, Saul said to his servant that was with

him, Come, and let us return; lest my father Tleave *caring* for the asses, and take thought for us.   *stop being concerned*

6 And he said unto him, Behold now, *there is* in this city Ra man of God, and *he is* an honourable man; Rall that he saith cometh surely to pass: now let us go thither; peradventure he can shew us our way that we should go.   1 Kin. 13:1 • 3:19

7 Then said Saul to his servant, But, behold, *if* we go, what shall we bring the man? for the bread is Tspent in our vessels, and *there is* not a present to bring to the man of God: what have we?   *all used up*

8 And the servant answered Saul again, and said, Behold, I have here at hand the fourth part of a shek'-el of silver: *that* will I give to the man of God, to tell us our way.

9 (Beforetime in Israel, when a man went to enquire of God, thus he spake, Come, and let us go to the seer: for *he that is* now *called* a Prophet was beforetime called a Seer.)

10 Then said Saul to his servant, Well said; come, let us go. So they went unto the city where the man of God *was.*

11 *And* as they went up the hill to the city, Rthey found young maidens going out to draw water, and said unto them, Is the seer here?   Gen. 24:11; 29:9; Ex. 2:16

12 And they answered them, and said, He is; behold, *he is* before you: make haste now, for he came to day to the city; for Rthere is a Tsacrifice of the people to day in the Rhigh place: 16:2 • *service of worship* • 7:17

13 As soon as ye be come into the city, ye shall straightway find him, before he go up to the high place to eat: for the people will not eat until he come, because he doth bless the sacrifice; *and* afterwards they eat that be bidden. Now therefore get you up; for about Tthis time ye shall find him.   *today*

14 And they went up into the city: *and* when they were come into the city, behold, RSamuel came out Tagainst them, for to go up to the high place.   13:11 • *toward*

15 RNow the LORD had told Samuel in his ear a day before Saul came, saying,   15:1

16 To morrow about this time I will send thee a man out of the land of Benjamin, and thou shalt Tanoint him *to be* captain over my people Israel, that he may save my people out of the hand of the Phi-lis'-tines: for I have looked upon my people, because their Tcry is come unto me.   *appoint* • *prayer*

17 And when Samuel saw Saul, the LORD said unto him, RBehold the man whom I spake to thee of! this same shall reign over my people.   16:12; Hos. 13:11

18 Then Saul drew near to Samuel in the gate, and said, Tell me, I pray thee, where the Rseer's house *is.*   2 Sam. 15:27; 1 Chr. 25:5

19 And Samuel answered Saul, and said, I *am* the seer: go up before me unto the Rhigh

place; for ye shall eat with me to day, and to morrow I will let thee go, and will tell thee all that *is* in thine heart.   Gen. 22:2

20 And as for Rthine asses that were lost three days ago, set not thy mind on them; for they are found. And on whom Ris all the desire of Israel? *Is it* not on thee, and on all thy father's house?   *v. 3. • 8:5, 19*

21 And Saul answered and said, *Am* not I a Benjamite, of the smallest of the tribes of Israel? and my family the least of all the families of the tribe of Benjamin? wherefore then speakest thou so to me?

22 And Samuel took Saul and his servant, and brought them into the Tparlour, and made them sit in the chiefest place among them that were bidden, which *were* about thirty persons.   *guest-chamber*

23 And Samuel said unto the cook, Bring the portion which I gave thee, of which I said unto thee, Set it by thee.

24 And the cook took up the Tshoulder, and *that* which *was* upon it, and set *it* before Saul. And *Samuel* said, Behold that which is left! set *it* before thee, *and* eat: for unto this time hath it been kept for thee since I said, I have invited the people. So Saul did eat with Samuel that day.   *thigh*

25 And when they were come down from the high place into the city, *Samuel* communed with Saul upon the top of the house.

26 And they arose early: and it came to pass about the Tspring of the day, that Samuel called Saul to the top of the house, saying, Up, that I may send thee away. And Saul arose, and they went out both of them, he and Samuel, abroad.   *dawn*

27 *And* as they were going down to the end of the city, Samuel said to Saul, Bid the servant pass on before us, (and he passed on,) but stand thou still a while, that I may shew thee the word of God.

CHAPTER 10

THEN Samuel took a Tvial of oil, and poured *it* upon his head, Rand kissed him, and said, *Is it* not because Rthe LORD hath Tanointed thee *to be* captain over his inheritance?   *bottle* • Ps. 2:12 • Acts 13:21 • *chosen*

2 When thou art departed from me to day, then thou shalt find two men by Ra'-chel's sepulchre in the border of Benjamin at Zel'-zah; and they will say unto thee, The asses which thou wentest to seek are found: and, lo, thy father hath left the care of the asses, and sorroweth for Ryou, saying, What shall I do for my son?   9:5

3 Then shalt thou go on forward from Tthence, and thou shalt come to the Tplain of Ta'-bor, and there shall meet thee three men

going up ^{R}to God to Beth'-el, one carrying three kids, and another carrying three loaves of bread, and another carrying a bottle of wine: *there • oak* • Gen. 28:22; 35:1, 3, 7

4 And they will ^{T}salute thee, and give thee two *loaves* of bread; which thou shalt receive of their hands.   *greet*

5 After that thou shalt come to the hill of God, ^{R}where *is* the garrison of the Phi-lis'-tines: and it shall come to pass, when thou art come thither to the city, that thou shalt meet a company of prophets coming down from the high place with a psaltery, and a tabret, and a pipe, and a harp, before them; and they shall prophesy: 13:3

6 And the Spirit of the LORD will come upon thee, and thou shalt prophesy with them, and shalt be turned into another man.

7 And let it be, when these signs are come unto thee, *that* thou do as occasion serve thee; for ^{R}God *is* with thee.   Judg. 6:12

8 And thou shalt go down before me to Gil'-gal; and, behold, I will come down unto thee, to offer burnt offerings, *and* to sacrifice sacrifices of peace offerings: ^{R}seven days shalt thou tarry, till I come to thee, and shew thee what thou shalt do.   13:8

9 And it was so, that when he had turned his back to go from Samuel, ^{R}God ^{T}gave him another heart: and all those signs came to pass that day.   *v. 6 • changed his whole outlook*

10 And when they came thither to the hill, behold, ^{R}a company of prophets met him; and the Spirit of God came upon him, and he prophesied among them.   19:20

11 And it came to pass, when all that knew him beforetime saw that, behold, he prophesied among the ^{R}prophets, then the people said one to another, What *is* this *that* is come unto the son of Kish? ^{R}*Is* Saul also among the prophets?   19:24 • Matt. 13:54, 55

12 And one of the same place answered and said, But ^{R}who *is* their father? Therefore it became a proverb, *Is* Saul also among the prophets?   John 6:45

13 And when he had made an end of prophesying, he came to the high place.

14 And Saul's uncle said unto him and to his servant, Whither went ye? And he said, To seek the asses: and when we saw that *they were* no where, we came to Samuel.

15 And Saul's uncle said, Tell me, I pray thee, what Samuel said unto you.

16 And Saul said unto his uncle, ^{R}He told us plainly that the asses were found. But of the matter of the kingdom, whereof Samuel spake, he told him not.   9:20

Samuel Anoints Saul

17 And Samuel called the people together unto the LORD ^{R}to Miz'-peh;   7:5, 6

18 And said unto the children of Israel, ^{R}Thus saith the LORD God of Israel, I brought up Israel out of Egypt, and delivered you out of the hand of the Egyptians, and out of the hand of all kingdoms, *and* of them that oppressed you: Judg. 6:8, 9

19 And ye have this day rejected your God, who himself saved you out of all your adversities and your tribulations; and ye have said unto him, *Nay*, but set a king over us. Now therefore present yourselves before the LORD by your tribes, and by your thousands.

20 And when Samuel had caused all the tribes of Israel to come near, the tribe of Benjamin was taken.

21 When he had caused the tribe of Benjamin to come near by their families, the family of Ma'-tri was taken, and Saul the son of Kish was taken: and when they sought him, he could not be found.

22 Therefore they ^{R}enquired^T of the LORD further, if the man should yet come thither. And the LORD answered, Behold, he hath hid himself among the stuff.   23:2, 4 • *asked*

23 And they ran and ^{T}fetched him thence: and when he stood among the people, ^{R}he was ^{T}higher than any of the people from his shoulders and upward.   *brought* • 9:2 • *taller*

24 And Samuel said to all the people, See ye him ^{R}whom the LORD hath chosen, that *there is* none like him among all the people? And all the people shouted, and said, ^{T}God save the king.   2 Sam. 21:6 • *long live the king*

25 Then Samuel told the people the manner of the ^{R}kingdom, and wrote *it* in a book, and ^{R}laid *it* up before the LORD. And Samuel sent all the people away, every man to his house.   8:11 • Deut. 31:26

26 And Saul also went home ^{R}to Gib'-e-ah; and there went with him a band of men, whose hearts God had touched.   Judg. 20:14

27 ^{R}But the children^T of Be'-li-al said, How shall this man save us? And they despised him, and brought him no presents. But he held his peace.   11:12 • *wicked men*

CHAPTER 11

Israel Makes Saul King

THEN ^{R}Na'-hash the Am'-mon-ite came up, and ^{T}encamped against Ja'-besh-gil'-e-ad: and all the men of Ja'-besh said unto Na'-hash, Make ^{T}a covenant with us, and we will serve thee.   12:12 • *besieged • an agreement*

2 And Na'-hash the Am'-mon-ite answered them, On this *condition* will I make *a covenant* with you, that I may thrust out all your right eyes, and ^{T}lay it *for* ^{R}a reproach upon all Israel.   *thus put disgrace* • Gen. 34:14

3 And the elders of Ja'-besh said unto him, Give us seven days' respite, that we may send messengers unto all the ^{T}coasts of Israel: and then, if *there be* no man to ^{T}save us, we will come out to thee.   *borders • help*

4 Then came the messengers ᴿto Gib'-e-ah of Saul, and told the tidings in the ears of the people: and ᴿall the people lifted up their voices, and wept.   2 Sam. 21:6 • Judg. 2:4

5 And, behold, Saul came after the herd out of the field; and Saul said, What *aileth* the people that they weep? And they told him the tidings of the men of Ja'-besh.

6 ᴿAnd the Spirit of God came upon Saul when he heard those tidings, and his anger was kindled greatly.   Judg. 3:10

7 And he took a yoke of oxen, and hewed them in pieces, and sent *them* throughout all the ᵀcoasts of Israel by the hands of messengers, saying, Whosoever cometh not forth after Saul and after Samuel, so shall it be done unto his oxen. And the fear of the LORD fell on the people, and they came out ᵀwith one consent.   *borders • as one man,* Judg. 20:1

8 And when he numbered them in ᴿBe'-zek, the children ᴿof Israel were three hundred thousand, and the men of Judah thirty thousand.   Judg. 1:5 • 2 Sam. 24:9

9 And they said unto the messengers that came, Thus shall ye say unto the men of Ja'-besh-gil'-e-ad, To morrow, by *that time* the sun be hot, ye shall have ᵀhelp. And the messengers came and shewed *it* to the men of Ja'-besh; and they were glad.   *deliverance*

10 Therefore the men of Ja'-besh said, ᴿTo morrow we will come out unto you, and ye shall do with us all that seemeth good unto you.   v. 3

11 And it was *so* on the morrow, that Saul put the people in three companies; and they came into the midst of the host in the morning watch, and slew the Am'-mon-ites until the heat of the day: and it came to pass, that they which remained were scattered, so that two of them were not left together.

12 And the people said unto Samuel, ᴿWho *is* he that said, Shall Saul reign over us? ᴿbring the men, that we may put them to death.   10:27 • Luke 19:27

13 And Saul said, There shall not a man be put to death this day: for to day the LORD hath wrought salvation in Israel.

14 Then said Samuel to the people, Come, and let us go ᴿto Gil'-gal, and ᴿrenew the kingdom there.   10:8 • 10:25

15 And all the people went to Gil'-gal; and there they made Saul king ᴿbefore the LORD in Gil'-gal; and ᴿthere they sacrificed sacrifices of peace offerings before the LORD; and there Saul and all the men of Israel rejoiced greatly.   10:17 • 10:8

CHAPTER 12

Samuel Confirms Saul

AND Samuel said unto all Israel, Behold, I have ᵀhearkened unto your voice in all that ye said unto me, and ᴿhave made a king over you.   *granted your request* • 10:24

2 And now, behold, the king ᴿwalketh before you: ᴿand I am old and grayheaded; and, behold, my sons *are* with you: and I have walked before you from my childhood unto this day.   8:20; Num. 27:17 • 8:1, 5

3 Behold, here I *am:* witness against me before the LORD, and before his ᴿanointed: whose ox have I taken? or whose ass have I taken? or whom have I defrauded? whom have I oppressed? or of whose hand have I received *any* bribe to blind mine eyes therewith? and I will restore it you.   10:1

4 And they said, ᴿThou hast not defrauded us, nor oppressed us, neither hast thou taken ought of any man's hand.   Lev. 19:13

5 And he said unto them, The LORD *is* witness against you, and his anointed *is* witness this day, ᴿthat ye have not found ought ᴿin my hand. And they answered, He *is* witness.   John 18:38; Acts 23:9 • Ex. 22:4

6 And Samuel said unto the people, ᴿIt is the LORD ᴿthat ᵀadvanced Moses and Aaron, and that brought your fathers up out of the land of Egypt.   Mic. 6:4 • Ex. 6:26 • *appointed*

7 Now therefore ᵀstand still, that I may reason with you before the LORD of all the righteous acts of the LORD, which he did to you and to your fathers.   *pay attention*

8 When Jacob was come into Egypt, and your fathers cried unto the LORD, then the LORD ᴿsent Moses and Aaron, which brought forth your fathers out of Egypt, and made them dwell in this place.   Ex. 3:10

9 And when they ᴿforgat the LORD their God, he ᵀsold them into the hand of Sis'-e-ra, captain of the host of Ha'-zor, and into the hand of the Phi-lis'-tines, and into the hand of the king of Moab, and they fought against them.   Deut. 32:18 • *gave them to be slaves*

10 And they cried unto the LORD, and said, We have sinned, because we have forsaken the LORD, and have served Ba'-a-lim and Ash'-ta-roth: but now deliver us out of the hand of our enemies, and we will serve thee.

11 And the LORD sent Jer-ub-ba'-al, and Be'-dan, and Jeph'-thah, and Samuel, and delivered you out of the hand of your enemies on every side, and ye dwelled safe.

12 And when ye saw that ᴿNa'-hash the king of the children of Ammon came against you, ᴿye said unto me, Nay; but a king shall reign over us: when ᴿthe LORD your God *was* your king.   11:1 • 8:5, 19 • Judg. 8:23

13 Now therefore ᴿbehold the king ᴿwhom ye have chosen, *and* whom ye have desired! and, behold, ᴿthe LORD hath set a king over you.   10:24 • 8:5; vv. 17, 19; • Hos. 13:11

14 If ye will fear the LORD, and serve him, and obey his voice, and not rebel against the commandment of the LORD then shall both ye

and also the king that reigneth over you continue following the LORD your God:

15 But if ye will not obey the voice of the LORD, but rebel against the commandment of the LORD, then shall the hand of the LORD be against you, as *it was* against your fathers.

16 Now therefore Rstand and see this great thing, which the LORD will do before your eyes.   Ex. 14:13, 31

17 *Is it* not wheat harvest to day? RI will call unto the LORD, and he shall send thunder and rain; that ye may perceive and see that Ryour wickedness *is* great, which ye have done in the sight of the LORD, in asking you a king.   [James 5:16–18] • 8:7

18 So Samuel called unto the LORD; and the LORD sent Rthunder and rain that day: and Rall the people Tgreatly feared the LORD and Samuel.   Rev. 4:5 • Ex. 14:31 • *highly regarded*

19 And all the people said unto Samuel, Pray for thy servants unto the LORD thy God, that we die not: for we have added unto all our sins *this* evil, to ask us a king.

20 And Samuel said unto the people, Fear not: ye have done all this wickedness: yet turn not aside from following the LORD, but serve the LORD with all your heart;

21 And turn ye not aside: for *then should* ye go after vain *things*, which cannot profit nor deliver; for they *are* vain.

22 For Rthe LORD will not forsake his people Rfor his great name's sake: because Rit hath pleased the LORD to make you his people.   1 Kin. 6:13 • Josh. 7:9; Jer. 14:21 • Deut. 7:7, 8

23 Moreover as for me, God forbid that I should sin against the LORD in ceasing to pray for you: but RI will teach you the Rgood and the right way: Ps. 34:11 • 1 Kin. 8:36

24 Only fear the LORD, and serve him in truth with all your heart: for consider how great *things* he hath done for you.

25 But if ye shall still do wickedly, ye shall be consumed, both ye and your king.

CHAPTER 13

The Early Success of King Saul

SAUL reigned one year; and when he had reigned two years over Israel,

2 Saul chose him three thousand *men* of Israel; *whereof* two thousand were with Saul in Mich'-mash and in mount Beth'-el, and a thousand were with Jonathan in Gib'-e-ah of Benjamin: and the rest of the people he sent every man to his tent.

3 And Jonathan Tsmote the garrison of the Phi-lis'-tines that *was* in Ge'-ba, and the Phi-lis'-tines heard of it. And Saul blew the trumpet throughout all the land, saying, Let the Hebrews hear.   *attacked*

4 And all Israel heard say that Saul had smitten a garrison of the Phi-lis'-tines, and

that Israel also was Thad in abomination with the Phi-lis'-tines. And the people were called together after Saul to Gil'-gal.   *held*

Saul's Sinful Sacrifices

5 And the Phi-lis'-tines gathered themselves together to fight with Israel, thirty thousand chariots, and six thousand horsemen, and people as the sand which *is* on the sea shore in multitude: and they came up, and Tpitched in Mich'-mash, eastward from RBeth-a'-ven.   *encamped* • 14:23; Josh. 7:2

6 When the men of Israel saw that they were in a strait, (for the people were distressed,) then the people did hide themselves in caves, and in thickets, and in rocks, and in high places, and in pits.

7 And *some* of the Hebrews went over Jordan to the Rland of Gad and Gil'-e-ad. As for Saul, he *was* yet in Gil'-gal, and all the people followed him trembling.   Num. 32:1–42

8 RAnd he tarried seven days, according to the set time that Samuel *had appointed:* but Samuel came not to Gil'-gal; and the people were scattered from him.   10:8

9 And Saul said, Bring Thither a burnt offering to me, and peace offerings. And he offered the burnt offering.   *here*

10 And it came to pass, that as soon as he had made an end of offering the burnt offering, behold, Samuel came; and Saul went out to meet him, that he might salute him.

11 And Samuel said, What hast thou done? And Saul said, Because I saw that the people were scattered from me, and *that* thou camest not within the days appointed, and *that* the Phi-lis'-tines gathered themselves together at Mich'-mash;

12 Therefore said I, The Phi-lis'-tines will come down now upon me to Gil'-gal, and I have not Tmade supplication unto the LORD: I forced myself therefore, and offered a burnt offering.   *intreated the favour of*

13 And Samuel said to Saul, Thou hast done foolishly: Rthou hast Tnot kept the commandment of the LORD thy God, which he commanded thee: for now would the LORD have Testablished thy kingdom upon Israel for ever.   15:11 • *not obeyed* • *confirmed*

14 RBut now thy kingdom shall not continue: the LORD hath sought him a man after his own heart, and the LORD hath commanded him *to be* captain over his people, because thou hast not Tkept *that* which the LORD commanded thee.   15:28 • *obeyed*

15 And Samuel arose, and gat him up from Gil'-gal unto Gib'-e-ah of Benjamin. And Saul numbered the people *that were* present with him, about six hundred men.

16 And Saul, and Jonathan his son, and the people *that were* present with them, abode in Gib'-e-ah of Benjamin: but the Phi-lis'-tines encamped in Mich'-mash.

17 And the spoilers came out of the camp of the Phi-lis′-tines in three companies: one company turned unto the way *that leadeth to* Oph′-rah, unto the land of Shu′-al:

18 And another company turned the way *to* ᴿBeth-ho′-ron: and another company turned *to* the way of the border that looketh to the valley of ᴿZe-bo′-im toward the wilderness.   Josh. 16:3 • Gen. 14:2; Neh. 11:34

19 Now ᴿthere was no smith found throughout all the land of Israel: for the Phi-lis′-tines said, Lest the Hebrews make *them* swords or spears: 2 Kin. 24:14

20 But all the Israelites went down to the Phi-lis′-tines, to sharpen every man his ᵀshare, and his ᵀcoulter, and his ax, and his ᵀmattock.   *sickle • plow tool • hoe*

21 Yet they had a file for the mattocks, and for the coulters, and for the forks, and for the axes, and to sharpen the goads.

22 So it came to pass in the day of battle, that there was neither sword nor spear found in the hand of any of the people that *were* with Saul and Jonathan: but with Saul and with Jonathan his son was there found.

23 And the garrison of the Phi-lis′-tines went out to the passage of Mich′-mash.

CHAPTER 14

Saul's Selfish Curse

NOW it came to pass upon a day, that Jonathan the son of Saul said unto the young man that ᵀbare his armour, Come, and let us go over to the Phi-lis′-tines' garrison, that *is* on the other side. But he told not his father.   *carried his equipment*

2 And Saul tarried in the uttermost part of Gib′-e-ah under a pomegranate tree which *is* in Mig′-ron: and the people that *were* with him *were* about six hundred men;

3 And A-hi′-ah, the son of A-hi′-tub, I′-cha-bod's brother, the son of Phin′-e-has, the son of E′-li, the Lᴏʀᴅ's priest in Shi′-loh, wearing an e′-phod. And the people knew not that Jonathan was gone.

4 And between the passages, by which Jonathan sought to go over unto the Phi-lis′-tines' garrison, *there was* a sharp rock on the one side, and a sharp rock on the other side: and the name of the one *was* Bo′-zez, and the name of the other Se′-neh.

5 The forefront of the one *was* situate northward over against Mich′-mash, and the other southward over against Gib′-e-ah.

6 And Jonathan said to the young man that bare his armour, Come, and let us go over unto the garrison of these ᴿuncircumcised: it may be that the Lᴏʀᴅ will work for us: for *there is* no ᵀrestraint to the Lᴏʀᴅ to save by many or by few.   17:26 • *limitation*

7 And his armourbearer said unto him, Do all that *is* in thine heart: turn thee; behold, I *am* with thee according to thy heart.

8 Then said Jonathan, ᴿBehold, we will pass over unto *these* men, and we will ᵀdiscover ourselves unto them.   Judg. 7:9–14 • *reveal*

9 If they say thus unto us, Tarry until we come to you; then we will stand still in our place, and will not go up unto them.

10 ᴿBut if they say thus, Come up unto us; then we will go up: for the Lᴏʀᴅ hath delivered them into our hand: and this *shall be* a ᴿsign unto us.   Judg. 7:11 • 6:9

11 And both of them ᵀdiscovered themselves unto the garrison of the Phi-lis′-tines: and the Phi-lis′-tines said, Behold, the Hebrews come forth out of the holes where they had ᵀhid themselves.   *revealed • taken refuge*

12 And the men of the garrison answered Jonathan and his armourbearer, and said, Come up to us, and we will shew you a thing. And Jonathan said unto his armourbearer, Come up after me: for the Lᴏʀᴅ hath delivered them into the hand of Israel.

13 And Jonathan climbed up upon his hands and upon his feet, and his armourbearer after him: and they fell before Jonathan; and his armourbearer slew after him.

14 And that first slaughter, which Jonathan and his armourbearer made, was about twenty men, within as it were an half acre of land, *which* a yoke *of oxen might plow.*

15 And ᴿthere was ᵀtrembling in the host, in the field, and among all the people: the garrison, and the spoilers, they also trembled, and the earth quaked: so it was a very great trembling.   Job 18:11 • *panic*

16 And the watchmen of Saul in Gib′-e-ah of Benjamin looked; and, behold, the multitude melted away, and they ᴿwent on beating down *one another.*   v. 20; 17:51

17 Then said Saul unto the people that *were* with him, Number now, and see who is gone from us. And when they had numbered, behold, Jonathan and his armourbearer *were* not *there.*

18 And Saul said unto A-hi′-ah, Bring hither the ark of God. For the ark of God was at that time with the children of Israel.

19 And it came to pass, while Saul ᴿtalked unto the priest, that the ᵀnoise that *was* in the host of the Phi-lis′-tines went on and increased: and Saul said unto the priest, Withdraw thine hand.   Num. 27:21 • *tumult*

20 And Saul and all the people that *were* with him assembled themselves, and they came to the battle: and, behold, every man's sword was against his fellow, *and there was* a very great discomfiture.

21 Moreover the ᴿHebrews *that* were with the Phi-lis′-tines before that time, which went up with them into the camp *from the country* round about, even they also *turned* to be with

the Israelites that *were* with Saul and Jonathan.   29:4

22 Likewise all the men of Israel which ᴿhad ᵀhid themselves in mount E'-phra-im, *when* they heard that the Phi-lis'-tines fled, even they also followed hard after them in the battle.   13:6 · *taken refuge*

23 So the LORD saved Israel that day: and the battle passed over unto Beth-a'-ven.

24 And the men of Israel were distressed that day: for Saul had ᵀadjured the people, saying, Cursed *be* the man that eateth *any* food until evening, that I may be avenged on mine enemies. So none of the people tasted *any* food.   *solemnly commanded*

25 ᴿAnd all *they of* the land came to a wood; and there was ᴿhoney upon the ground.   Deut. 9:28; Matt. 3:5 · Num. 13:27; Matt. 3:4

26 And when the people were come into the ᵀwood, behold, ᴿthe honey dropped; but no man put his hand to his mouth: for the people feared the oath.   *forest* · Matt. 3:4

27 But Jonathan heard not when his father charged the people with the oath: wherefore he put forth the end of the rod that *was* in his hand, and dipped it in an honeycomb, and put his hand to his mouth; and his eyes were ᵀenlightened.   *became bright*

28 Then answered one of the people, and said, Thy father ᵀstraitly charged the people with an oath, saying, Cursed *be* the man that eateth *any* food this day. And the people were faint.   *strictly*

29 Then said Jonathan, My father hath troubled the land: see, I pray you, how mine eyes have ᵀbeen enlightened, because I tasted a little of this honey.   *become bright*

30 How much ᵀmore, if haply the people had eaten freely to day of the ᵀspoil of their enemies which they found? for had there not been now a much greater slaughter among the Phi-lis'-tines?   *better* · *plunder*

31 And they ᵀsmote the Phi-lis'-tines that day from Mich'-mash to Ai'-ja-lon: and the people were very faint.   *struck down*

32 And the people flew upon the spoil, and took sheep, and oxen, and calves, and slew *them* on the ground: and the people did eat *them* ᴿwith the blood.   Lev. 3:17

33 Then they told Saul, saying, Behold, the people sin against the LORD, in that they eat with the blood. And he said, Ye have transgressed: roll a great stone unto me this day.

34 And Saul said, Disperse yourselves among the people, and say unto them, Bring me hither every man his ox, and every man his sheep, and slay *them* here, and eat; and sin not against the LORD in eating with the blood. And all the people brought every man his ox with him that night, and slew *them* there.

35 And Saul ᴿbuilt an altar unto the LORD:

the same was the first altar that he built unto the LORD.   7:12, 17

36 And Saul said, Let us go down after the Phi-lis'-tines by night, and spoil them until the morning light, and let us not leave a man of them. And they said, Do whatsoever seemeth good unto thee. Then said the priest, Let us draw near hither unto God.

37 And Saul asked ᵀcounsel of God, Shall I go down after the Phi-lis'-tines? wilt thou deliver them into the hand of Israel? But ᴿhe answered him not that day.   *advice* · 28:6

38 And Saul said, Draw ye near hither, all the chief of the people: and know and see wherein this sin hath been this day.

39 For, *as* the LORD liveth, which saveth Israel, though it be in Jonathan my son, he shall surely die. But *there was* not a man among all the people *that* answered him.

40 Then said he unto all Israel, Be ye on one side, and I and Jonathan my son will be on the other side. And the people said unto Saul, Do what seemeth good unto thee.

41 Therefore Saul said unto the LORD God of Israel, Give a perfect *lot.* And Saul and Jonathan were taken: but the people escaped.

42 And Saul said, Cast *lots* between me and Jonathan my son. And Jonathan was taken.

43 Then Saul said to Jonathan, ᴿTell me what thou hast done. And Jonathan told him, and said, ᴿI did but taste a little honey with the end of the rod that *was* in mine hand, *and,* lo, I must die.   Josh. 7:19 · *v.* 27

44 And Saul answered, ᴿGod do so and more also: ᴿfor thou shalt surely die, Jonathan.   25:22; Ruth 1:17 · *v.* 39

45 And the people said unto Saul, Shall Jonathan die, who hath ᵀwrought this great salvation in Israel? God forbid: *as* the LORD liveth, there shall not one hair of his head fall to the ground; for he hath wrought with God this day. So the people rescued Jonathan, that he died not.   *achieved*

46 Then Saul went up ᵀfrom following the Phi-lis'-tines: and the Phi-lis'-tines went to their own place.   *after*

47 So Saul took the kingdom over Israel, and fought against all his enemies on every side, against Moab, and against the children of Ammon, and against E'-dom, and against the kings of Zo'-bah, and against the Phi-lis'-tines: and whithersoever he turned himself, he ᵀvexed *them.*   *fought with*

48 And he gathered an host, and ᴿsmote the Am'-a-lek-ites, and delivered Israel out of the hands of them that spoiled them. Ex. 17:14

49 Now ᴿthe sons of Saul were Jonathan, and Ish'-u-i, and Mel'-chi-shu'-a: and the names of his two daughters *were these;* the name of the firstborn Me'-rab, and the name of the younger Mi'-chal: 1 Chr. 8:33

50 And the name of Saul's wife *was* A-hin'-

o-am, the daughter of A-him′-a-az: and the name of the captain of his host *was* Abner, the son of Ner, Saul's uncle.

51 RAnd Kish *was* the father of Saul; and Ner the father of Abner *was* the son of A-bi′-el.   9:1, 21

52 And there was Tsore war against the Phi-lis′-tines all the days of Saul: and when Saul saw any strong man, or any valiant man, he took him unto him.   *hard fighting*

CHAPTER 15

Saul's Incomplete Obedience

SAMUEL also said unto Saul, RThe LORD sent me to anoint thee *to be* Rking over his people, over Israel: now therefore hearken thou unto the voice of the words of the LORD.   9:16 · 16:1

2 Thus saith the LORD of hosts, I remember *that* which Am′-a-lek did to Israel, Rhow he laid *wait* for him in the way, when he came up from Egypt.   Ex. 17:8; Deut. 25:17–19

3 Now go and Tsmite Am′-a-lek, and Rutterly destroy all that they have, and spare them not; but Rslay both man and woman, infant and suckling, ox and sheep, camel and ass.   *attack* · Lev. 27:28, 29; Josh. 6:17, 21 · 22:19

4 And Saul gathered the people together, and numbered them in Te-la′-im, two hundred thousand footmen, and ten thousand men of Judah.

5 And Saul came to a city of Am′-a-lek, and laid wait in the valley.

6 And Saul said unto Rthe Ken′-ites, Go, depart, get you down from among the Am′-a-lek-ites, lest I destroy you with them: for Rye shewed kindness to all the children of Israel, when they came up out of Egypt. So the Ken′-ites departed from among the Am′-a-lek-ites.   Num. 24:21 · Rev. 18:4

7 RAnd Saul smote the Am′-a-lek-ites from Hav′-i-lah *until* thou comest to RShur, that *is* over against Egypt.   14:48 · Gen. 16:7

8 And he took A′-gag the king of the Am′-a-lek-ites alive, and utterly destroyed all the people with the edge of the sword.

9 But Saul and the people spared A′-gag, and the best of the sheep, and of the oxen, and of the fatlings, and the lambs, and all *that was* good, and would not utterly destroy them: but every thing *that was* vile and refuse, that they destroyed utterly.

God Rejects Saul as King

10 Then came the word of the LORD unto Samuel, saying,

11 It repenteth me that I have set up Saul *to be* king: for he is turned back from following me, and hath not performed my commandments. And it grieved Samuel; and he cried unto the LORD all night.

12 And when Samuel rose early to meet Saul in the morning, it was told Samuel, saying, Saul came to Carmel, and, behold, he set him up a place, and is gone about, and passed on, and gone down to Gil′-gal.

13 And Samuel came to Saul: and Saul said unto him, RBlessed *be* thou of the LORD: I have Tperformed the commandment of the LORD.   Ruth 3:10 · *carried out*

14 And Samuel said, What *meaneth* then this bleating of the sheep in mine ears, and the lowing of the oxen which I hear?

15 And Saul said, They have brought them from the Am′-a-lek-ites: for the people spared the best of the sheep and of the oxen, to sacrifice unto the LORD thy God; and the rest we have utterly destroyed.

16 Then Samuel said unto Saul, Stay, and I will tell thee what the LORD hath said to me this night. And he said unto him, Say on.

17 And Samuel said, When thou *wast* little in thine own sight, *wast* thou not *made* the head of the tribes of Israel, and the LORD anointed thee king over Israel?

18 And the LORD sent thee on a journey, and said, Go and utterly destroy the sinners the Am′-a-lek-ites, and fight against them until they be Tconsumed.   *destroyed*

19 Wherefore then didst thou not obey the voice of the LORD, but didst fly upon the spoil, and didst evil in the sight of the LORD?

20 And Saul said unto Samuel, Yea, I have obeyed the voice of the LORD, and have gone the way which the LORD sent me, and have brought A′-gag the king of Am′-a-lek, and have utterly destroyed the Am′-a-lek-ites.

21 But the people took of the spoil, sheep and oxen, the chief of the things which should have been utterly destroyed, to sacrifice unto the LORD thy God in Gil′-gal.

22 And Samuel said, Hath the LORD *as great* delight in burnt offerings and sacrifices, as in obeying the voice of the LORD? Behold, Rto obey is better than sacrifice, *and* to hearken than the fat of rams.   [Hos. 6:6]

23 For rebellion *is as* the sin of Twitchcraft, and stubbornness *is as* iniquity and idolatry. Because thou hast rejected the word of the LORD, Rhe hath also rejected thee from *being* king.   *fortune telling* · 13:14

24 RAnd Saul said unto Samuel, I have sinned: for I have transgressed the commandment of the LORD, and thy words: because I Rfeared the people, and obeyed their voice.   26:21; 2 Sam. 12:13 · [Ex. 23:2; Is. 51:12, 13]

25 RNow therefore, I pray thee, Rpardon my sin, and turn again with me, that I may worship the LORD.   Ex. 10:17 · 2 Sam. 24:10

26 And Samuel said unto Saul, I will not return with thee: for thou hast rejected the word of the LORD, and the LORD hath rejected thee from being king over Israel.

27 And as Samuel turned about to go away, ^Rhe laid hold upon the skirt of his mantle, and it ^Trent.   1 Kin. 11:30 · *tore*

28 And Samuel said unto him, The LORD hath ^Trent the kingdom of Israel from thee this day, and hath given it to a neighbour of thine, *that is* better than thou.   *torn*

29 And also the Strength of Israel ^Rwill not lie nor ^Trepent: for he *is* not a man, that he should repent.   Titus 1:2 · *change his mind*

30 Then he said, I have sinned: *yet* ^Rhonour^T me now, I pray thee, before the elders of my people, and before Israel, and turn again with me, that I may worship the LORD thy God.   [John 5:44] · *treat me with honour*

31 So Samuel turned again after Saul; and Saul worshipped the LORD.

32 Then said Samuel, Bring ye ^Thither to me A'-gag the king of the Am'-a-lek-ites. And A'-gag came unto him ^Tdelicately. And A'-gag said, Surely the bitterness of death is past.   *here* · *cheerfully*

33 And Samuel said, ^RAs thy sword hath made women childless, so shall thy mother be childless among women. And Samuel hewed A'-gag in pieces before the LORD in Gil'-gal.   [Gen. 9:6]; Ex. 17:11; Num. 14:45; [Matt. 7:2]

34 Then Samuel went to ^RRa'-mah; and Saul went up to his house to ^RGib'-e-ah of Saul.   7:17 · 11:4

35 And ^RSamuel came no more to see Saul until the day of his death: nevertheless Samuel ^Rmourned for Saul: and the LORD ^Trepented that he had made Saul king over Israel.   19:24 · 16:1 · *changed his mind*

CHAPTER 16

God Anoints David as King

AND the LORD said unto Samuel, How long wilt thou mourn for Saul, seeing I have rejected him from reigning over Israel? fill thine horn with oil, and go, I will send thee to Jesse the Beth'-le-hem-ite: for I have provided me a king among his sons.

2 And Samuel said, How can I go? if Saul hear *it*, he will kill me. And the LORD said, Take an heifer with thee, and say, ^RI am come to sacrifice to the LORD.   9:12

3 And call Jesse to the sacrifice, ^Rand I will shew thee what thou shalt do: and thou shalt ^Ranoint^T unto me *him* whom I name unto thee.   Ex. 4:15; Acts 9:6 · 9:16 · *select*

4 And Samuel did that which the LORD spake, and came to Beth'-le-hem. And the elders of the town ^Rtrembled at his coming, and said, Comest thou peaceably?   21:1

5 And he said, Peaceably: I am come to sacrifice unto the LORD: ^Rsanctify^T yourselves, and come with me to the sacrifice. And he sanctified Jesse and his sons, and called them to the sacrifice.   Ex. 19:10 · *separate*

6 And it came to pass, when they were come, that he looked on E-li'-ab, and said, Surely the LORD's anointed *is* before him.

7 But the LORD said unto Samuel, Look not on his countenance, or on the height of his stature; because I have ^Trefused him: for *the* LORD *seeth* not as man seeth; for man looketh on the outward appearance, but the LORD looketh on the heart.   *rejected*

8 Then Jesse called ^RA-bin'-a-dab, and made him pass before Samuel. And he said, Neither hath the LORD chosen this.   17:13

9 Then Jesse made ^TSham'-mah^R to pass by. And he said, Neither hath the LORD chosen this.   *Shimma* · 1 Chr. 2:13

10 Again, Jesse made seven of his sons to pass before Samuel. And Samuel said unto Jesse, The LORD hath not chosen these.

11 And Samuel said unto Jesse, Are here all *thy* children? And he said, There remaineth yet the youngest, and, behold, he keepeth the sheep. And Samuel said unto Jesse, Send and ^Tfetch him: for we will not sit down till he come hither.   *bring*

12 And he sent, and brought him in. Now he *was* ruddy, *and* withal of a beautiful countenance, and goodly to look to. And the LORD said, Arise, anoint him: for this *is* he.

13 Then Samuel took the horn of oil, and anointed him in the midst of his brethren: and ^Rthe Spirit of the LORD came upon David from that day forward. So Samuel rose up, and went to Ra'-mah.   Num. 27:18

God Takes His Spirit from Saul

14 ^RBut the Spirit of the LORD departed from Saul, and ^Ran evil spirit from the LORD ^Ttroubled him.   Judg. 16:20 · Judg. 9:23 · *disturbed*

15 And Saul's servants said unto him, Behold now, an evil spirit from God troubleth thee.

16 Let our lord now command thy servants, *which are* before thee, to seek out a man, *who is* a cunning player on an harp: and it shall come to pass, when the evil spirit from God is upon thee, that he shall play with his hand, and thou shalt be well.

17 And Saul said unto his servants, ^TProvide me now a man that can play well, and bring *him* to me.   *find*

18 Then answered one of the servants, and said, Behold, I have seen a son of Jesse the Beth'-le-hem-ite, *that is* cunning in playing, and a mighty valiant man, and a man of war, and prudent in matters, and a comely person, and the LORD *is* with him.

19 Wherefore Saul sent messengers unto Jesse, and said, Send me David thy son, ^Rwhich *is* with the sheep.   17:15, 34

20 And Jesse took an ass *laden* with bread, and a bottle of wine, and a kid, and sent *them* by David his son unto Saul.

21 And David came to Saul, and ^Tstood before him: and he loved him greatly; and he became his armourbearer.   *reported for service*

22 And Saul sent to Jesse, saying, Let David, I pray thee, stand before me; for he hath found favour in my sight.

23 And it came to pass, when the ^Revil spirit from God was upon Saul, that David took an harp, and played with his hand: so Saul was refreshed, and was well, and the evil spirit departed from him.   *vv. 14, 16*

CHAPTER 17

David Defeats Goliath

NOW the Phi-lis'-tines gathered together their armies to battle, and were gathered together at Sho'-choh, which *belongeth* to Judah, and pitched between Sho'-choh and A-ze'-kah, in E'-phes-dam'-mim.

2 And Saul and the men of Israel were gathered together, and pitched by the ^Rvalley of E'-lah, and ^Tset the battle in array against the Phi-lis'-tines.   *21:9 · arranged to fight*

3 And the Phi-lis'-tines stood on a mountain on the one side, and Israel stood on a mountain on the other side: and *there was* a valley between them.

4 And there went out a champion out of the camp of the Phi-lis'-tines, named ^RGo-li'-ath, of Gath, whose height *was* ^Tsix cubits and a span.   *2 Sam. 21:19 · 9 ft. 9 in.*

5 And *he had* an helmet of ^Tbrass upon his head, and he *was* ^Tarmed with a coat of mail; and the weight of the coat *was* ^Tfive thousand shek'-els of brass.   *bronze · clothed · 125 lb.*

6 And *he had* ^Tgreaves of brass upon his legs, and a ^Rtarget^T of brass between his shoulders.   *shin armour of bronze · v. 45 · shield*

7 And the staff of his spear *was* like a weaver's beam; and his spear's head *weighed* ^Tsix hundred shek'-els of iron: and one bearing a shield went before him.   *15 lb.*

8 And he stood and cried unto the armies of Israel, and said unto them, Why are ye come out ^Tto set *your* battle in array? *am* not I a Phi-lis'-tine, and ye servants to Saul? choose you a man for you, and let him come down to me.   *to arrange for battle*

9 If he be able to fight with me, and to kill me, then will we be your servants: but if I prevail against him, and kill him, then shall ye be our servants, and serve us.

10 And the Phi-lis'-tine said, I ^Rdefy^T the armies of Israel this day; give me a man, that we may fight together.   *v. 26 · challenge*

11 When Saul and all Israel heard those words of the Phi-lis'-tine, they were dismayed, and greatly afraid.

12 Now David *was* ^Rthe son of that Eph'-rath-ite of Beth'-le-hem-ju'-dah, whose name *was* Jesse; and he had eight sons: and the

man ^Twent among men *for* an old man in the days of Saul.   *v. 58 · was considered to be*

13 And the three eldest sons of Jesse went *and* followed Saul to the battle: and the ^Rnames of his three sons that went to the battle *were* ^RE-li'-ab the first born, and next unto him A-bin'-a-dab, and the third Sham'-mah.   *16:6, 8, 9 · 1 Chr. 2:13*

14 And ^RDavid *was* the youngest: and the three eldest followed Saul.   *16:11*

15 ^RBut David went and returned from Saul ^Rto feed his father's sheep at Beth'-le-hem.   *16:19 · 2 Sam. 7:8*

16 And the Phi-lis'-tine drew near morning and evening, and presented himself forty days.

17 And Jesse said unto David his son, Take now for thy brethren ^Tan e'-phah of this parched *corn*, and these ten loaves, and run to the camp to thy brethren;   *.65 bu.*

18 And carry these ten cheeses unto the captain of *their* thousand, and look how thy brethren fare, and take their pledge.

19 Now Saul, and they, and all the men of Israel, *were* in the valley of E'-lah, fighting with the Phi-lis'-tines.

20 And David rose up early in the morning, and left the sheep with a keeper, and took, and went, as Jesse had commanded him; and he came to the trench, as the host was going forth to the fight, and shouted for the battle.

21 For Israel and the Phi-lis'-tines had put the battle in array, army against army.

22 And David left his carriage in the hand of the keeper of the carriage, and ran into the army, and came and saluted his brethren.

23 And as he talked with them, behold, there came up the champion, the Phi-lis'-tine of Gath, Go-li'-ath by name, out of the armies of the Phi-lis'-tines, and spake according to the same words: and David heard *them*.

24 And all the men of Israel, when they saw the man, ^Tfled from him, and were ^Tsore afraid.   *retreated · very much*

25 And the men of Israel said, Have ye seen this man that is come up? surely to defy Israel is he come up: and it shall be, *that* the man who killeth him, the king will enrich him with great riches, and ^Rwill give him his daughter, and make his father's house free in Israel.   *8:11; Josh. 15:16*

26 And David spake to the men that stood by him, saying, What shall be done to the man that killeth this Phi-lis'-tine, and taketh away the reproach from Israel? for who *is* this uncircumcised Phi-lis'-tine, that he should defy the armies of the living God?

27 And the people answered him after this manner, saying, ^RSo shall it be done to the man that killeth him.   *v. 25*

28 And E-li'-ab his eldest brother heard when he spake unto the men; and E-li'-ab's anger was kindled against David, and he said,

Why camest thou down hither? and with whom hast thou left those few sheep in the wilderness? I know thy pride, and the naughtiness of thine heart; for thou art come down that thou mightest see the battle.

29 And David said, What have I now done? ᴿ*Is there* not a cause?   *vv.* 17, 26, 27

30 And he turned from him toward another, and ᴿspake after the same manner: and the people answered him again ᵀafter the former manner.   *vv.* 26, 27 • *in the same way*

31 And when the words were heard which David spake, they ᵀrehearsed *them* before Saul: and he sent for him.   *reported*

32 And David said to Saul, Let no man's heart fail because of him; ᴿthy servant will go and fight with this Phi-lis'-tine.   16:18

33 And Saul said to David, ᴿThou art not able to go against this Phi-lis'-tine to fight with him: for thou *art but* a youth, and he a man of war from his youth.   Deut. 9:2

34 And David said unto Saul, Thy servant kept his father's sheep, and there came ᴿa lion, and a bear, and took a ᵀlamb out of the flock: Judg. 14:5 • *kid*

35 And I went out after him, and smote him, and delivered *it* out of his mouth: and when he arose against me, I caught *him* by his beard, and smote him, and slew him.

36 Thy servant slew both the lion and the bear: and this ᵀuncircumcised Phi-lis'-tine shall be as one of them, seeing he hath defied the armies of the living God.   *pagan*

37 David said moreover, The LORD that ᵀdelivered me out of the paw of the lion, and out of the paw of the bear, he will deliver me out of the hand of this Phi-lis'-tine. And Saul said unto David, Go, and ᴿthe LORD be with thee.   *saved* • 20:13

38 And Saul armed David with his armour, and he put an helmet of brass upon his head; also he armed him with a coat of mail.

39 And David girded his sword upon his armour, and he assayed to go; for he had not proved *it*. And David said unto Saul, I cannot go with these; for I have not proved *them*. And David put them off him.

40 And he took his staff in his hand, and chose him five smooth stones out of the ᵀbrook, and put them in a shepherd's bag which he had, even in a ᵀscrip; and ᴿhis sling *was* in his hand: and he drew near to the Phi-lis'-tine.   *valley* • *his wallet* • Judg. 20:16

41 And the Phi-lis'-tine came on and drew near unto David; and the man that bare the shield *went* before him.

42 And when the Phi-lis'-tine looked about, and saw David, he ᵀdisdained him: for he was *but* a youth, and ᴿruddy, and of a fair countenance.   *belittled* • 16:12

43 And the Phi-lis'-tine said unto David, ᴿ*Am* I a dog, that thou comest to me with

ᵀstaves? And the Phi-lis'-tine cursed David by his gods.   2 Sam. 3:8; 9:8; 16:9; 2 Kin. 8:13 • *sticks*

44 And the Phi-lis'-tine ᴿsaid to David, Come to me, and I will give thy flesh ᴿunto the fowls of the air, and to the beasts of the field.   1 Kin. 20:10, 11 • *v.* 46

45 Then said David to the Phi-lis'-tine, Thou comest to me with a sword, and with a spear, and with a shield: but I come to thee in the name of the LORD of hosts, the God of the armies of Israel, whom thou hast defied.

46 This day will the LORD deliver thee into mine hand; and I will smite thee, and take thine head from thee; and I will give the carcases of the host of the Phi-lis'-tines this day unto the fowls of the air, and to the wild beasts of the earth; ᴿthat all the earth may know that there is a God in Israel.   Is. 52:10

47 And all this assembly shall know that the LORD ᴿsaveth not with sword and spear: for ᴿthe battle *is* the LORD'S, and he will give you into our hands.   Hos. 1:7 • 2 Chr. 20:15

48 And it came to pass, when the Phi-lis'-tine arose, and came and drew nigh to meet David, that David ᵀhasted, and ran toward the army to meet the Phi-lis'-tine.   *hurried*

49 And David put his hand in his bag, and took thence a stone, and slang *it*, and smote the Phi-lis'-tine in his forehead, that the stone sunk into his forehead; and he fell upon his face to the earth.

50 So David prevailed over the Phi-lis'-tine with a sling and with a stone, and smote the Phi-lis'-tine, and slew him; but *there was* no sword in the hand of David.

51 Therefore David ran, and stood upon the Phi-lis'-tine, and ᴿtook his sword, and drew it out of the sheath thereof, and slew him, and cut off his head therewith. And when the Phi-lis'-tines saw their champion was dead, ᴿthey fled.   2 Sam. 23:21 • Heb. 11:34

52 And the men of Israel and of Judah arose, and shouted, and pursued the Phi-lis'-tines, ᵀuntil thou come to the valley, and to the gates of ᴿEk'-ron. And the wounded of the Phi-lis'-tines fell down by the way to ᴿSha-a-ra'-im, even unto Gath, and unto Ek'-ron.   *as far as* • Josh. 15:11 • Josh. 15:36

53 And the children of Israel returned from chasing after the Phi-lis'-tines, and they ᵀspoiled their tents.   *looted their camp*

54 And David took the head of the Phi-lis'-tine, and brought it to Jerusalem; but he put his armour in his tent.

55 And when Saul saw David go forth against the Phi-lis'-tine, he said unto Abner, the captain of the host, Abner, whose son *is* this youth? And Abner said, ᵀAs thy soul liveth, O king, I cannot tell.   *to tell the truth*

56 And the king said, Enquire thou whose son the ᵀstripling *is*.   *youth*

57 And as David returned from the slaughter of the Phi-lis'-tine, Abner took him, and

brought him before Saul ᴿwith the head of the Phi-lis'-tine in his hand. 　　　　　*v.* 54

58 And Saul said to him, Whose son *art* thou, *thou* young man? And David answered, ᴿI am the son of thy servant Jesse the Beth'-le-hem-ite. 　　　　　　　　　　　　*v.* 12

CHAPTER 18

Jonathan Loves David

AND it came to pass, when he had made an ᵀend of speaking unto Saul, that the soul of Jonathan ᵀwas knit with the soul of David, ᴿand Jonathan loved him as his own soul. 　　　*ceased • became fast friends • Deut.* 13:6

2 And Saul took him that day, ᴿand would let him go no more home to his father's house. 　　　　　　　　　　　　17:15

3 Then Jonathan and David made a covenant, because he loved him as his own soul.

4 And Jonathan ᵀstripped himself of the robe that *was* upon him, and gave it to David, and his garments, even to his sword, and to his bow, and to his girdle. 　　　*took off*

Israel Elevates David over Saul

5 And David went out whithersoever Saul sent him, *and* behaved himself wisely: and Saul set him over the men of war, and he was accepted in the sight of all the people, and also in the sight of Saul's servants.

6 And it came to pass as they came, when David was returned from the slaughter of the ᵀPhi-lis'-tine, that the women came out of all cities of Israel, singing and dancing, to meet king Saul, with tabrets, with joy, and with instruments of musick. 　　　　*Philistines*

7 And the women answered *one another* as they played, and said, Saul hath slain his thousands, and David his ten thousands.

8 And Saul was very wroth, and the saying displeased him; and he said, They have ascribed unto David ten thousands, and to me they have ascribed *but* thousands: and *what* can he have more but the kingdom?

9 And Saul ᵀeyed David from that day and forward. 　　　*viewed with suspicion and malice*

The Attempts of Saul to Slay David
By Throwing a Javelin at David

10 And it came to pass on the ᵀmorrow, that the evil spirit from God came upon Saul, ᴿand he prophesied in the midst of the house: and David played with his hand, as at other times: ᴿand *there was* a javelin in Saul's hand. 　　　*next day • Acts* 16:16 • 19:9

11 And Saul cast the javelin; for he said, I will smite David even to the wall *with it.* And David avoided out of his presence twice.

12 And Saul was ᴿafraid of David, because the LORD was with him, and was ᴿdeparted from Saul. 　　*vv.* 15, 29 • 16:14; 28:15

13 Therefore Saul ᵀremoved him from him, and made him his captain over a thousand; and ᴿhe went out and came in before the people. 　　*sent him out of his household • v.* 16

14 And David behaved himself wisely in all his ways; and the LORD *was* with him.

15 Wherefore when Saul saw that he behaved himself very wisely, he ᵀwas afraid of him. 　　　　　　　　　*stood in awe*

16 But ᴿall Israel and Judah loved David, ᴿbecause he went out and came in before them. 　　*vv.* 5, 13 • Num. 27:16, 17; 2 Sam. 5:2; 1 Kin. 3:7

By Tricking David to Fight the Philistines

17 And Saul said to David, Behold my elder daughter Me'-rab, her will I give thee to wife: only be thou valiant for me, and fight the LORD's battles. For Saul said, Let not mine hand be upon him, but let the hand of the Phi-lis'-tines be upon him.

18 And David said unto Saul, ᴿWho *am* I? and what *is* my life, *or* my father's family in Israel, that I should be son in law to the king? 　　*v.* 23; 9:21; 2 Sam. 7:18

19 But it came to pass at the time when Me'-rab Saul's daughter should have been given to David, that she was given unto A'-dri-el the Me-hol'-ath-ite to wife.

20 ᴿAnd Mi'-chal Saul's daughter loved David: and they told Saul, and the thing pleased him. 　　　　　　　　*v.* 28

21 And Saul said, I will give him her, that she may be a snare to him, and that ᴿthe hand of the Phi-lis'-tines may be against him. Wherefore Saul said to David, Thou shalt ᴿthis day be my son in law ᵀin the one of the ᵀtwain. 　　*v.* 17 • *v.* 26 • *a second time • two*

22 And Saul commanded his servants, *saying,* ᵀCommune with David secretly, and say, Behold, the king hath delight in thee, and all his servants love thee: now therefore be the king's son in law. 　　　　*Talk*

23 And Saul's servants spake those words in the ears of David. And David said, Seemeth it to you *a* light *thing* to be a king's son in law, seeing that I *am* a ᴿpoor man, and lightly esteemed? 　　　　　*Gen.* 34:11, 12

24 And the servants of Saul told him, saying, On this manner spake David.

25 And Saul said, Thus shall ye say to David, The king desireth not any dowry, but an hundred foreskins of the Phi-lis'-tines, to be avenged of the king's enemies. But Saul ᴿthought to make David ᵀfall by the hand of the Phi-lis'-tines. 　　　*v.* 17 • *be killed*

26 And when his servants told David these words, it pleased David well to be the king's son in law: and the days were not expired.

27 Wherefore David arose and went, he and ᴿhis men, and slew of the Phi-lis'-tines two hundred men; and ᴿDavid brought their foreskins, and they gave them in ᵀfull tale to

the king, that he might be the king's son in law. And Saul gave him Mi'-chal his daughter to wife. *v.* 13 · 2 Sam. 3:14 · *full count*

28 And Saul saw and knew that the LORD *was* with David, and *that* Mi'-chal Saul's daughter loved him.

29 And RSaul was yet the more afraid of David; and Saul became David's enemy Tcontinually. 2 Sam. 15:14 · *in everything*

30 Then the princes of the Phi-lis'-tines went forth: and it came to pass, after they went forth, *that* David behaved himself more Rwisely than all the servants of Saul; so that his name was much set by. *v.* 5

CHAPTER 19

By Commanding His Servants to Kill David

AND Saul spake to Jonathan his son, and to all his servants, that they should kill RDavid. 18:8, 9

2 But Jonathan Saul's son Rdelighted much in David: and Jonathan told David, saying, Saul my father seeketh to kill thee: now therefore, I pray thee, take heed to thyself until the morning, and abide in a secret *place*, and hide thyself: 18:1

3 And I will go out and stand beside my father in the field where thou *art*, and I will Tcommune with my father of thee; and what I see, that I will tell thee. *talk*

4 And Jonathan spake good of David unto Saul his father, and said unto him, Let not the king sin against his servant, against David; because he hath not sinned against thee, and because his works *have been* to Tthee-ward very good: *toward thee*

5 For he did put his life in his hand, and slew the Phi-lis'-tine, and the LORD wrought a great salvation for all Israel: thou sawest *it*, and didst rejoice: wherefore then wilt thou sin against innocent blood, to slay David without a cause?

6 And Saul hearkened unto the voice of Jonathan: and Saul sware, As the LORD liveth, he shall not be slain.

7 And Jonathan called David, and Jonathan shewed him all those things. And Jonathan brought David to Saul, and he was in his presence, as in times past.

By Throwing a Javelin at David Again

8 And there was war again: and David went out, and fought with the Phi-lis'-tines, and Rslew them with a great slaughter; and they fled from him. 18:27; 23:5

9 And Rthe evil spirit from the LORD was upon Saul, as he sat in his house with his javelin in his hand: and David played Twith *his* hand. 16:14; 18:10, 11 · *the harp*

10 And Saul sought to Tsmite· David even to the wall with the javelin; but he Tslipped away out of Saul's presence, and he smote the javelin into the wall: and David fled, and escaped that night. *strike · escaped*

By Sending His Messengers to Kill David

11 Saul also sent messengers unto David's house, to watch him, and to slay him in the morning: and Mi'-chal David's wife told him, saying, If thou save not thy life to night, to morrow thou shalt be slain.

12 So Mi'-chal let David down through a window: and he went, and fled, and escaped.

13 And Mi'-chal took an image, and laid *it* in the bed, and put a pillow of goats' *hair* for his bolster, and covered *it* with a cloth.

14 And when Saul sent messengers to take David, she said, He *is* sick.

15 And Saul sent the messengers *again* to see David, saying, Bring him up to me in the bed, that I may slay him.

16 And when the messengers were come in, behold, *there was* an image in the bed, with a pillow of goats' *hair* for his bolster.

17 And Saul said unto Mi'-chal, Why hast thou deceived me so, and sent away mine enemy, that he is escaped? And Mi'-chal answered Saul, He said unto me, Let me go; Rwhy should I kill thee? 2 Sam. 2:22

By Coming to Kill David at Samuel's House

18 So David fled, and escaped, and came to RSamuel to RRa'-mah, and told him all that Saul had done to him. And he and Samuel went and dwelt in Na'-ioth. 16:13 · 7:17

19 And it was told Saul, saying, Behold, David *is* at Na'-ioth in Ra'-mah.

20 And Saul sent messengers to take David: and when they saw the company of the prophets prophesying, and Samuel standing *as* appointed over them, the Spirit of God was upon the messengers of Saul, and they also Rprophesied. Num. 11:25; Joel 2:28

21 And when it was told Saul, he sent other messengers, and they prophesied likewise. And Saul sent messengers again the third time, and they prophesied also.

22 Then went he also to Ra'-mah, and came to a great well that *is* in Se'-chu: and he asked and said, Where *are* Samuel and David? And *one* said, Behold, *they be* at Na'-ioth in Ra'-mah.

23 And he went thither to Na'-ioth in Ra'-mah: and the Spirit of God was upon him also, and he went on, and prophesied, until he came to Na'-ioth in Ra'-mah.

24 RAnd he stripped off his clothes also, and prophesied before Samuel in like manner, and lay down naked all that day and all that night. Wherefore they say, RIs Saul also among the prophets? Is. 20:2 · 10:11

CHAPTER 20

By Commanding Jonathan to Bring David to Be Killed

AND David fled from Na'-ioth in Ra'-mah, and came and ᴿsaid before Jonathan, What have I done? what *is* mine iniquity? and what *is* my sin before thy father, that he seeketh my life? 24:9

2 And he said unto him, God forbid; thou shalt not die: behold, my father will do nothing either great or small, but that he will ᴿshew it me: and why should my father hide this thing from me? it *is* not so. 19:1

3 And David sware moreover, and said, Thy father certainly knoweth that I have found grace in thine eyes; and he saith, Let not Jonathan know this, lest he be ᵀgrieved: but ᴿtrulyᴿ *as* the Lᴏʀᴅ liveth, and *as* thy soul liveth, *there is* but a step between me and death. *unhappy* • Deut. 6:13 • 25:26; 2 Kin. 2:6

4 Then said ᴿJonathan unto David, Whatsoever thy soul ᵀdesireth, I will even do *it* for thee. 31:2 • *wishes to have done*

5 And David said unto Jonathan, Behold, to morrow *is* the new moon, and I should not fail to sit with the king ᵀat meat: but let me go, that I may hide myself in the field unto the third *day* at even. *at dinner*

6 If thy father at all miss me, then say, David earnestly asked *leave* of me that he might run to Beth'-le-hem his city: for *there is* a yearly sacrifice there for all the family.

7 If he say thus, *It is* well; thy servant shall have peace: but if he be very wroth, *then* be sure that evil is determined by him.

8 Therefore thou shalt deal kindly with thy servant; for thou hast brought thy servant into ᵀa covenant of the Lᴏʀᴅ with thee: notwithstanding, if there be in me iniquity, slay me thyself; for why shouldest thou bring me to thy father? *an agreement*

9 And Jonathan said, Far be it from thee: for if I knew certainly that evil were determined by my father to come upon thee, then would not I tell it thee?

10 Then said David to Jonathan, Who shall tell me? or what *if* thy father answer thee roughly?

11 And Jonathan said unto David, Come, and let us go out into the field. And they went out both of them into the field.

12 And Jonathan said unto David, O Lᴏʀᴅ God of Israel, when I have sounded my father about to morrow any time, *or* the third *day,* and, behold, *if there be* good toward David, and ᵀI then send not unto thee, and shew it thee; *if I do not send a report*

13 ᴿThe Lᴏʀᴅ do so and much more to Jonathan: but if it please my father *to do* thee evil, then I will shew it thee, and send thee away, that thou mayest go in peace: and ᴿthe

Lᴏʀᴅ be with thee, as he hath been with my father. Ruth 1:17 • 1 Chr. 22:11, 16

14 And thou shalt not only while yet I live shew me the kindness of the Lᴏʀᴅ, that I die not:

15 But *also* thou shalt not cut off thy kindness from my house for ever: no, not when the Lᴏʀᴅ hath cut off the enemies of David every one from the face of the earth.

16 So Jonathan made *a covenant* with the house of David, *saying,* Let the Lᴏʀᴅ even require *it* at the hand of David's enemies.

17 And Jonathan caused David to ᵀswear again, because he loved him: for he ᴿloved him as he loved his own soul. *promise* • 18:1

18 Then Jonathan said to David, To morrow *is* the new moon: and thou shalt be missed, because thy seat will be empty.

19 And *when* thou hast stayed three days, *then* thou shalt go down quickly, and come to the place where thou didst hide thyself when the business was *in hand,* and shalt remain by the ᵀstone E'-zel. *stone heap*

20 And I will shoot three arrows on the side *thereof,* as though I shot at a mark.

21 And, behold, I will send a lad, *saying,* Go, find out the ᴿarrows. If I expressly say unto the lad, Behold, the arrows *are* on this side of thee, take them; then come thou: for *there is* peace to thee, and no hurt; ᴿ*as* the Lᴏʀᴅ liveth. 2 Kin. 13:15 • Jer. 4:2

22 But if I say thus unto the young man, Behold, the arrows *are* beyond thee; go thy way: for the Lᴏʀᴅ hath sent thee away.

23 And *as touching* the matter which thou and I have spoken of, behold, the Lᴏʀᴅ *be* between thee and me for ever.

24 So David hid himself in the field: and when the ᴿnew moon was come, the king sat him down to eat meat. Ps. 81:3

25 And the king sat upon his seat, as at other times, *even* upon a seat by the wall: and Jonathan arose, and Abner sat by Saul's side, and David's place was empty.

26 Nevertheless Saul spake not any thing that day: for he thought, Something hath befallen him, he *is* ᴿnotᵀ clean; surely he *is* not clean. Lev. 7:21; 15:5 • *ceremonially unfit*

27 And it came to pass on the morrow, *which was* the second *day* of the month, that ᴿDavid's place was empty: and Saul said unto Jonathan his son, Wherefore cometh not the son of Jesse to ᵀmeat, neither yesterday, nor to day? *vv.* 18, 25 • *the table*

28 And Jonathan ᴿanswered Saul, David earnestly asked *leave* of me *to go* to Beth'-le-hem: *v.* 6

29 And he said, Let me go, I pray thee; for our family hath a sacrifice in the city; and my brother, he hath commanded me *to be there:* and now, ᵀif I have found favour in thine eyes, let me get away, I pray thee, and see my

brethren. Therefore he cometh not unto the king's table.   *if you think well of me*

30 Then Saul's anger was kindled against Jonathan, and he said unto him, Thou son of the perverse rebellious *woman,* do not I know that thou hast chosen the son of Jesse to thine own confusion, and unto the confusion of thy mother's nakedness?

31 For as long as the son of Jesse liveth upon the ground, thou shalt not be established, nor thy ᴿkingdom. Wherefore now send and fetch him unto ᴿme, for he ᵀshall surely die.   15:28 · 19:6–11 · *is the son of death*

32 And Jonathan answered Saul his father, and said unto him, ᴿWherefore shall he be slain? what hath he done?   Matt. 27:23

33 And Saul cast a javelin at him to smite him: whereby Jonathan knew that it was determined of his father to slay David.

34 So Jonathan arose from the table in fierce anger, ᴿand did eat no ᵀmeat the second day of the month: for he was ᵀgrieved for David, because his father had done him shame.   28:20 · *food · sorry*

35 And it came to pass in the morning, that Jonathan went out into the field at the time appointed with David, and a little lad with him.

36 And he said unto his lad, Run, find out now the arrows which I shoot. *And* as the lad ran, he shot an arrow beyond him.

37 And when the lad was come to the place of the arrow which Jonathan had shot, Jonathan cried after the lad, and said, *Is* not the arrow ᴿbeyond thee?   *vv. 21, 22*

38 And Jonathan cried after the lad, Make speed, ᴿhaste, ᵀstay not. And Jonathan's lad gathered up the arrows, and came to his master.   2 Sam. 15:14 · *do not delay*

39 But the lad knew not any thing: only Jonathan and David knew the matter.

40 And Jonathan gave his ᵀartillery unto his lad, and said unto him, Go, carry *them* to the city.   *weapons*

41 *And* as soon as the lad was gone, David arose out of *a place* toward the south, and fell on his face to the ground, and ᴿbowed himself three times: and they ᴿkissed one another, and wept one with another, until David ᵀexceeded.   Gen. 42:6 · 18:3 · *controlled himself*

42 And Jonathan said to David, ᴿGo in peace, forasmuch as we have sworn both of us in the name of the LORD, saying, ᴿThe LORD be between me and thee, and between my seed and thy seed for ever. And he arose and departed: and Jonathan went into the city.   *vv. 22, 23 · 20:15, 16, 23*

CHAPTER 21

David Is Protected by the Priest

THEN came David to Nob to A-him′-e-lech the priest: and A-him′-e-lech was afraid at the meeting of David, and said unto him, Why *art* thou alone, and no man with thee?

2 And David said unto A-him′-e-lech the priest, The king hath commanded me a business, and hath said unto me, Let no man know any thing of the business whereabout I send thee, and what I have commanded thee: and I have appointed *my* servants to such and such a place.

3 Now therefore what is under thine hand? give *me* five *loaves of* bread in mine hand, or what there is present.

4 And the priest answered David, and said, *There is* no common bread under mine hand, but there is ᵀhallowed bread; if the young men have kept themselves at least from women.   *bread set aside for worship use*

5 And David answered the priest, and said unto him, Of a truth women *have been* kept from us about these three days, since I came out, and the vessels of the young men are holy, and *the bread is* in a manner common, yea, though it were ᵀsanctified this day in the vessel.   *for this specific use*

6 So the priest gave him hallowed *bread:* for there was no bread there but the shewbread, ᴿthat was taken from before the LORD, to put ᵀhot bread in the day when it was taken away.   Lev. 24:8, 9 · *freshly baked*

7 Now a certain man of the servants of Saul *was* there that day, ᵀdetained before the LORD; and his name *was* Do′-eg, an E′-domite, the chiefest of the herdmen that *belonged* to Saul.   *taking time to worship*

8 And David said unto A-him′-e-lech, And is there not here under thine hand spear or sword? for I have neither brought my sword nor my weapons with me, because the king's business required ᵀhaste.   *speed*

9 And the priest said, The sword of Go-li′-ath the Phi-lis′-tine, whom thou slewest in the valley of E′-lah, behold, it *is here* wrapped in a cloth behind the e′-phod: if thou wilt take that, take *it:* for *there is* no other save that here. And David said, ᴿ*There is* none like that; give it me.   17:54

David Pretends to Be Mad

10 And David arose, and fled that day for fear of Saul, and went to ᵀA′-chish the king of ᴿGath.   *Abimelech,* Ps. 34, title · 27:2

11 And the servants of A′-chish said unto him, *Is* not this David the king of the land? did they not sing one to another of him in dances, saying, Saul hath slain his thousands, and David his ten thousands?

12 And David ᴿlaidᵀ up these words in his heart, and was sore afraid of A′-chish the king of Gath.   Luke 2:19 · *heard this with concern*

13 And he changed his behaviour before them, and feigned himself mad in their hands, and scrabbled on the doors of the gate, and let his spittle fall down upon his beard.

14 Then said A′-chish unto his servants, Lo, ye see the man is ᵀmad: ᵀwherefore *then* have ye brought him to me?   *demented • why*

15 Have I need of mad men, that ye have brought this *fellow* to play the mad man in my presence? shall this ᴿ*fellow* come into my house?   *2 Kin. 9:11*

CHAPTER 22

David Flees to Adullam—1 Chr. 12:16–18

DAVID therefore departed thence, and escaped to the cave A-dul′-lam: and when his brethren and all his father's house heard *it*, they went down thither to him.

2 ᴿAnd every one *that was* in distress, and every one that *was* in debt, and every one *that was* ᵀdiscontented, gathered themselves unto him; and he became a captain over them: and there were with him about four hundred men.   *Judg. 11:3 • bitter of soul*

3 And David went thence to Miz′-peh of Moab: and he said unto the king of Moab, Let my father and my mother, I pray thee, ᵀcome forth, *and be* with you, till I know what God will do for me.   *come to visit*

4 And he brought them before the king of Moab: and they dwelt with him all the while that David was in the ᵀhold.   *stronghold*

5 And the prophet Gad said unto David, Abide not in the hold; depart, and get thee into the land of Judah. Then David departed, and came into the forest of Ha′-reth.

Saul Slays the Priests of God

6 When Saul heard that David was discovered, and the men that *were* with him, (now Saul abode in Gib′-e-ah under a tree in Ra′-mah, having his spear in his hand, and all his servants *were* standing about him;)

7 Then Saul said unto his servants that stood about him, Hear now, ye Benjamites; will the son of Jesse give every one of you fields and vineyards, *and* make you all captains of thousands, and captains of hundreds;

8 That all of you have conspired against me, and *there is* none that sheweth me that ᴿmy son hath made a league with the son of Jesse, and *there is* none of you that is sorry for me, or sheweth unto me that my son hath stirred up my servant against me, to lie in wait, as at this day?   *v. 13; 18:3; 20:30*

9 Then answered Do′-eg the E′-dom-ite, which was set over the servants of Saul, and said, I saw the son of Jesse coming to Nob, to A-him′-e-lech the son of A-hi′-tub.

10 And he enquired of the LORD for him, and gave him ᵀvictuals, and gave him the sword of Go-li′-ath the Phi-lis′-tine.   *food*

11 Then the king sent to call A-him′-e-lech the priest, the son of A-hi′-tub, and all his father's house, the priests that *were* in Nob: and they came all of them to the king.

12 And Saul said, Hear now, thou son of A-hi′-tub. And he answered, Here I *am*, my lord.

13 And Saul said unto him, Why have ye conspired against me, thou and the son of Jesse, in that thou hast given him bread, and a sword, and ᵀhast enquired of God for him, that he should rise against me, ᴿto lie in wait, as at this day?   *prayed to God • v. 8*

14 Then A-him′-e-lech answered the king, and said, And who *is* so ᴿfaithful among all thy servants as David, which is the king's son in law, and goeth at thy bidding, and is ᵀhonourable in thine house?   *19:4, 5 • preferred*

15 Did I then begin to enquire of God for him? be it far from me: let not the king impute *any* thing unto his servant, *nor* to all the house of my father: for thy servant knew nothing of all this, less or more.

16 And the king said, Thou shalt surely die, ᴿA-him′-e-lech, thou, and all ᴿthy father's house.   *v. 9; 21:1 • Deut. 24:16*

17 And the king said unto the ᵀfootmen that stood about him, Turn, and ᴿslay the priests of the LORD; because their hand also *is* with David, and because they knew when he fled, and did not shew it to me. But the servants of the king ᴿwould not put forth their hand to fall upon the priests of the LORD.   *guard • 2 Kin. 10:25 • Ex. 1:17*

18 And the king said to Do′-eg, Turn thou, and fall upon the priests. And Do′-eg the E′-dom-ite turned, and he fell upon the priests, and slew on that day fourscore and five persons that did wear a linen e′-phod.

19 ᴿAnd Nob, the city of the priests, ᵀsmote he with the edge of the sword, both men and women, children and sucklings, and oxen, and asses, and sheep, with the edge of the sword.   *vv. 9, 11 • killed the population*

20 And one of the ᴿsons of A-him′-e-lech the son of A-hi′-tub, named A-bi′-a-thar, ᴿescaped, and fled after David.   *23:6 • 2:33*

21 And A-bi′-a-thar shewed David that Saul had slain the LORD's priests.

22 And David said unto A-bi′-a-thar, I knew *it* that day, when Do′-eg the E′-dom-ite *was* there, that he would surely tell Saul: I have occasioned *the death* of all the persons of thy father's ᵀhouse.   *family*

23 Abide thou with me, fear not: for he that seeketh my life seeketh thy life: but with me thou *shalt be* ᵀin safeguard.   *protected*

CHAPTER 23

David Smites the Philistines

THEN they told David, saying, Behold, the Phi-lis′-tines fight against ᴿKei′-lah, and they rob the threshingfloors.   *Josh. 15:44*

2 Therefore David enquired of the LORD, saying, Shall I go and smite these Phi-lis'-tines? And the LORD said unto David, Go, and smite the Phi-lis'-tines, and save Kei'-lah.

3 And David's men said unto him, Behold, Rwe be afraid here in Judah: how much more then if we come to Kei'-lah against the armies of the Phi-lis'-tines?   Prov. 29:25

4 Then David enquired of the LORD yet again. And the LORD answered him and said, Arise, go down to Kei'-lah; for I will deliver the Phi-lis'-tines into thine hand.

5 So David and his men went to Kei'-lah, and Rfought with the Phi-lis'-tines, and brought away their cattle, and smote them with a great slaughter. So David saved the inhabitants of Kei'-lah.   19:8; 2 Sam. 5:20

6 And it came to pass, when A-bi'-a-thar the son of A-him'-e-lech Rfled to David to Kei'-lah, that he came down with an e'-phod in his hand.   22:20

7 And it was told Saul that David was come to Kei'-lah. And Saul said, God hath delivered him into mine hand; for he is Tshut in, by entering into a town that Thath gates and bars.   surrounded • has a wall around it

8 And RSaul called all the people together to war, to go down to Kei'-lah, to besiege David and his men.   24:4

9 And David knew that Saul secretly Tpractised mischief against him; and Rhe said to A-bi'-a-thar the priest, Bring hither the e'-phod.   planned harm • 30:7

10 Then said David, RO LORD God of Israel, thy servant hath certainly heard that Saul seeketh to come to Kei'-lah, Rto destroy the city for my sake.   Ps. 5:3; 55:17 • 22:19

11 Will the men of Kei'-lah deliver me up into his hand? will Saul come down, as thy servant hath heard? O LORD God of Israel, I beseech thee, tell thy servant. And the LORD said, He will come down.

12 Then said David, Will the men of Kei'-lah Tdeliver me and my men into the hand of Saul? And the LORD said, They will deliver thee Rup.   surrender • Judg. 15:10–13

Saul Chases David

13 Then David and his men, Rwhich were about six hundred, arose and departed out of Kei'-lah, and went Twhithersoever Rthey could go. And it was told Saul that David was escaped from Kei'-lah; and he forbare to go forth.   22:2; 25:13 • wherever • 2 Sam. 15:20

14 And David Tabode in the wilderness in Tstrong holds, and remained in a mountain in the wilderness of Ziph. And Saul sought him every day, but God delivered him not into his hand.   lived • fortified places

15 And David saw that Saul was come out to seek his life: and David was in the wilderness of Ziph in a Twood.   the forest

16 And Jonathan Saul's son arose, and went to David into the wood, and strengthened his hand in God.

17 And he said unto him, Fear not: for the hand of Saul my father shall not find thee; and thou shalt be king over Israel, and I shall be next unto thee; and Rthat also Saul my father knoweth.   24:20

18 And they two made a covenant before the LORD: and David abode in the wood, and Jonathan went to his house.

19 Then Rcame up the Ziph'-ites to Saul to Gib'-e-ah, saying, Doth not David hide himself with us in strong holds in the wood, in the hill of Hach'-i-lah, which is on the south of TJesh'-i-mon?   26:1; Ps. 54: Title • desert

20 Now therefore, O king, come down according to all the desire of thy soul to come down; and Rour part shall be to deliver him into the king's hand.   v. 12; Ps. 54:3

21 And Saul said, Blessed be ye of the LORD; for ye have compassion on me.

22 Go, I pray you, prepare yet, and know and see his place where his Thaunt is, and who hath seen him there: for it is told me that he dealeth very Tsubtilly.   foot • cleverly

23 See therefore, and take knowledge of all the lurking places where he hideth himself, and come ye again to me with the certainty, and I will go with you: and it shall come to pass, if he be in the land, that I will Rsearch him out throughout all the thousands of Judah.   1 Kin. 18:10

24 And they arose, and went to Ziph before Saul: but David and his men were in the wilderness Rof Ma'-on, in the plain on the south of Jesh'-i-mon.   Josh. 15:55; 25:2

25 Saul also and his men went to seek him. And they told David: wherefore he came down Tinto a rock, and abode in the wilderness of Ma'-on. And when Saul heard that, he pursued after David in the wilderness of Ma'-on.   from the rock

26 And Saul went on this side of the mountain, and David and his men on that side of the mountain: and David made haste to get away for fear of Saul; for Saul and his men Tcompassed David and his men round about to take them.   encircled

27 But Rthere came a messenger unto Saul, saying, Haste thee, and come; for the Phi-lis'-tines have invaded the land.   Ps. 18

28 Wherefore Saul returned from pursuing after David, and went against the Phi-lis'-tines: therefore they called that place Se'-la–ham-mah-le'-koth.

29 And David went up from thence, and dwelt in strong holds at REn-ge'-di. 2 Chr. 20:2

CHAPTER 24

David Saves Saul's Life

AND it came to pass, when Saul was returned from following the Phi-lis'-tines,

that it was told him, saying, Behold, David *is* in the wilderness of En-ge'-di.

2 Then Saul took three thousand chosen men out of all Israel, and went to seek David and his men upon the rocks of the wild goats.

3 And he came to the sheepcotes by the way, where *was* a cave; and Saul went in ^Tto cover his feet: and David and his men remained in the sides of the cave.   *be relieved*

4 ^RAnd the men of David said unto him, Behold the day of which the LORD said unto thee, Behold, I will deliver thine enemy into thine hand, that thou mayest do to him as it shall seem good ^Tunto thee. Then David arose, and cut off the skirt of Saul's robe ^Tprivily.   26:8 • *in your sight* • *secretly*

5 And it came to pass afterward, that ^RDavid's heart smote him, because he had cut off Saul's skirt.   2 Sam. 24:10

6 And he said unto his men, ^RThe LORD forbid that I should do this thing unto my master, the LORD's anointed, to stretch forth mine hand against him, seeing he *is* the anointed of the LORD.   26:11; [Job 31:29, 30]

7 So David ^Rstayed^T his servants with these words, and suffered them not to rise against Saul. But Saul rose up out of the cave, and went on *his* way.   Ps. 7:4 • *restrained*

8 David also arose afterward, and went out of the cave, and cried after Saul, saying, My lord the king. And when Saul looked behind him, David stooped with his face to the earth, and bowed himself.

9 And David said to Saul, ^RWherefore hearest thou men's words, saying, Behold, David seeketh thy hurt?   [Prov. 16:28; 17:9]

10 Behold, this day thine eyes have seen how that the LORD had delivered thee to day into mine hand in the cave: and *some* bade *me* kill thee: but *mine eye* spared thee; and I said, ^RI will not put forth mine hand against my lord; for he *is* the LORD's anointed.   *v.* 4

11 Moreover, my father, see, yea, see the skirt of thy robe in my hand: for in that I cut off the skirt of thy robe, and killed thee not, know thou and see that *there is* neither evil nor transgression in mine hand, and I have not sinned against thee; yet thou huntest my soul to take it.

12 ^RThe LORD judge between me and thee, and the LORD avenge me of thee: but mine hand shall not be upon thee.   Job 5:8

13 As saith the proverb of the ancients, Wickedness proceedeth from the wicked: but mine hand shall not be upon thee.

14 After whom is the king of Israel come out? after whom dost thou pursue? ^Rafter a dead dog, after ^Ra flea.   2 Sam. 9:8 • 26:20

15 ^RThe LORD therefore be judge, and judge between me and thee, and ^Rsee, and ^Rplead my cause, and deliver me out of thine hand.   *v.* 12; Ps. 35:1 • 2 Chr. 24:22 • Mic. 7:9

16 And it came to pass, when David had made an end of speaking these words unto Saul, that Saul said, *Is* this thy voice, my son David? And Saul lifted up his voice, and wept.

17 And he said to David, Thou *art* more righteous than I: for thou hast rewarded me good, whereas I have rewarded thee evil.

18 And thou hast shewed this day how that thou hast dealt well with me: forasmuch as when the LORD had delivered me into thine hand, thou killedst me not.

19 For if a man ^Rfind his enemy, will he ^Tlet him go well away? wherefore the LORD reward thee good for that thou hast done unto me this day.   23:17 • *allow him to escape?*

20 And now, behold, I know well that thou shalt surely be king, and that the kingdom of Israel shall be established in thine hand.

21 Swear^T now therefore unto me by the LORD, that thou wilt not cut off my seed after me, and that thou wilt not destroy my name out of my father's house.   *promise*

22 And David sware unto Saul. And Saul went home; but David and his men gat them up unto the^T hold.   *the hiding place*

CHAPTER 25

Samuel the Judge Dies

AND ^RSamuel died; and all the Israelites were gathered together, and lamented him, and buried him in his house at Ra'-mah. And David arose, and went down to the wilderness of Pa'-ran.   28:3

David Marries Abigail

2 And *there was* a man in Ma'-on, whose ^Tpossessions *were* in Carmel; and the man *was* very great, and he had three thousand sheep, and a thousand goats: and he was shearing his sheep in Carmel.   *business was*

3 Now the name of the man *was* Na'-bal; and the name of his wife Ab'-i-gail: and *she was* a woman of good understanding, and of a beautiful countenance: but the man *was* ^Tchurlish and evil in his doings; and he *was* of the house ^Rof Caleb.   *surly* • 30:14

4 And David heard in the wilderness that Na'-bal did ^Rshear his sheep.   2 Sam. 13:23

5 And David sent out ten young men, and David said unto the young men, Get you up to Carmel, and go to Na'-bal, and greet him in my name:

6 And thus shall ye say to him that liveth *in prosperity*, ^RPeace *be* both to thee, and peace *be* to thine house, and peace *be* unto all that thou hast.   1 Chr. 12:18; Ps. 122:7; Luke 10:5

7 And now I have heard ^Rthat thou hast shearers: now thy shepherds which were with us, we hurt them not, ^Rneither was there ought missing unto them, all the while they were in Carmel.   2 Sam. 13:23 • *vv.* 15, 21

8 Ask thy young men, and they will shew thee. Wherefore ᵀlet the young men find favour in thine eyes: for we come in ᴿa good day: give, I pray thee, whatsoever cometh to thine hand unto thy servants, and to thy son David.   *be gracious to the young men* • Neh. 8:10

9 And when David's young men came, they spake to Na'-bal according to all those words in the name of David, and ceased.

10 And Na'-bal answered David's servants, and said, Who *is* David? and who *is* the son of Jesse? there be many servants now a days that break away every man from his master.

11 Shall I then take my bread, and my water, and my ᵀflesh that I have killed for my shearers, and give *it* unto men, whom I know not whence they *be*?   *slaughter*

12 So David's young men turned their way, and went again, and came and told him all those sayings.

13 And David said unto his men, Gird ye on every man his sword. And they girded on every man his sword; and David also girded on his sword: and there went up after David about four hundred men; and two hundred ᴿabode by the stuff.   30:24

14 But one of the young men told Ab'-i-gail, Na'-bal's wife, saying, Behold, David sent messengers out of the wilderness to salute our master; and he railed on them.

15 But the men *were* very good unto us, and we were not hurt, neither missed we any thing, as long as we were conversant with them, when we were in the fields:

16 They were ᴿa ᵀwall unto us both by night and day, all the while we were with them keeping the sheep.   Job 1:10 • *protection*

17 Now therefore know and consider what thou wilt do; for evil is determined against our master, and against all his household: for he is such a ᵀson of Be'-li-al, that *a man* cannot speak to him.   *wicked man*

18 Then Ab'-i-gail made haste, and took two hundred loaves, and two bottles of wine, and five sheep ready dressed, and ᵀfive measures of parched corn, and an hundred clusters of raisins, and two hundred cakes of figs, and laid *them* on asses.   10,873 bu.

19 And she said unto her servants, ᴿGo on before me; behold, I come after you. But she told not her husband Na'-bal.   Gen. 32:16

20 And it was so, as she rode on the ass, that she came down by the covert of the hill, and, behold, David and his men came down against her; and she met them.

21 Now David had said, Surely in vain have I kept all that this *fellow* hath in the wilderness, so that nothing was missed of all that *pertained* unto him: and he hath ᴿrequitedᵀ me evil for good.   Ps. 109:5 • *repaid*

22 So and more also do God unto the enemies of David, if I leave of all that *pertain*

to him by the morning light ᵀany that pisseth against the wall.   *one man child*

23 And when Ab'-i-gail saw David, she hasted, and ᴿlighted off the ass, and fell before David on her face, and ᴿbowed herself to the ground,   Josh. 15:18; Judg. 1:14 • 20:41

24 And fell at his feet, and said, Upon me, my lord, *upon* me *let this* iniquity *be:* and let thine handmaid, I pray thee, ᵀspeak in thine audience, and hear the words of thine handmaid.   *speak to you*

25 Let not my lord, I pray thee, ᵀregard this man of Be'-li-al, *even* Na'-bal: for as his name *is*, so *is* he; ᵀNa'-bal *is* his name, and folly *is* with him: but I thine handmaid saw not the young men of my lord, whom thou didst send.   *pay attention to* • *Fool*

26 Now therefore, my lord, *as* the Lᴏʀᴅ liveth, and *as* thy soul liveth, seeing the Lᴏʀᴅ hath withholden thee from coming to *shed* blood, and from avenging thyself with thine own hand, now let thine enemies, and they that seek evil to my lord, be as Na'-bal.

27 And now ᴿthis ᵀblessing which thine handmaid hath brought unto my lord, let it even be given unto the young men that follow my lord.   30:26; Gen. 33:11; 2 Kin. 5:15 • *gift*

28 I pray thee, forgive the trespass of thine handmaid: for the Lᴏʀᴅ will certainly make my lord a sure house; because my lord fighteth the battles of the Lᴏʀᴅ, and evil hath not been found in thee *all* thy days.

29 Yet a man is risen to pursue thee, and to seek thy soul: but the soul of my lord shall be ᵀbound in the bundle of life with the Lᴏʀᴅ thy God; and the souls of thine enemies, them shall he ᴿsling out, *as out* of the middle of a sling.   *protected to live* • Jer. 10:18

30 And it shall come to pass, when the Lᴏʀᴅ shall have done to my lord according to all the good that he hath spoken concerning thee, and ᴿshall have appointed thee ruler over Israel;   13:14

31 That this shall be no ᵀgrief unto thee, nor offence of heart unto my lord, either that thou hast shed blood causeless, or that my lord hath avenged himself: but when the Lᴏʀᴅ shall have dealt well with my lord, then remember thine handmaid.   *sadness*

32 And David said to Ab'-i-gail, ᴿBlessed *be* the Lᴏʀᴅ God of Israel, which sent thee this day to meet me: Ex. 18:10; Luke 1:68

33 And blessed *be* thy advice, and blessed *be* thou, which hast ᴿkept me this day from coming to *shed* blood, and from avenging myself with mine own hand.   v. 26

34 For in very deed, *as* the Lᴏʀᴅ God of Israel liveth, which hath kept me back from hurting thee, except thou hadst hasted and come to meet me, surely there had not been left unto Na'-bal by the morning light any that pisseth against the wall.

35 So David received of her hand *that* which she had brought him, and said unto her, Go up in peace to thine house; see, I have ^Thearkened to thy voice, and have accepted thy person.   *listened to your advice*

36 And Ab'-i-gail came to Na'-bal; and, behold, ^Rhe held a feast in his house, like the feast of a king; and Na'-bal's heart *was* merry within him, for he *was* very drunken: wherefore she told him nothing, less or more, until the morning light.   Dan. 5:1

37 But it came to pass in the morning, when the wine was gone out of Na'-bal, and his wife had told him these things, that ^This heart died within him, and he became *as* a stone.   *he lost all confidence*

38 And it came to pass about ten days *after*, that the LORD smote Na'-bal, that he died.

39 And when David heard that Na'-bal was dead, he said, Blessed *be* the LORD, that hath pleaded the cause of my reproach from the hand of Na'-bal, and hath kept his servant from evil: for the LORD hath returned the wickedness of Na'-bal upon his own head. And David sent and communed with Ab'-i-gail, to take her to him to wife.

40 And when the servants of David were come to Ab'-i-gail to Carmel, they spake unto her, saying, David sent us unto thee, to take thee to him to wife.

41 And she arose, and bowed herself on *her* face to the earth, and said, Behold, *let* thine handmaid *be* a servant to ^Rwash the feet of the servants of my lord.   Prov. 15:33

42 And Ab'-i-gail hasted, and arose, and rode upon an ass, with five damsels of her's that went after her; and she went after the messengers of David, and became his wife.

43 David also took A-hin'-o-am ^Rof Jez'-re-el; ^Rand they were also both of them his wives.   Josh. 15:56 · 27:3; 30:5

44 But Saul had given Mi'-chal his daughter, David's wife, to Phal'-ti the son of La'-ish, which *was* of ^RGal'-lim.   Is. 10:30

CHAPTER 26

David Saves Saul's Life Again

AND the Ziph'-ites came unto Saul to Gib'-e-ah, saying, ^RDoth not David hide himself in the hill of Hach'-i-lah, *which is* before Jesh'-i-mon?   23:19; Ps. 54: *Title*

2 Then Saul arose, and went down to the wilderness of Ziph, having ^Rthree thousand chosen men of Israel with him, to seek David in the wilderness of Ziph.   13:2

3 And Saul ^Tpitched in the hill of Hach'-i-lah, which *is* before Jesh'-i-mon, by the way. ^RBut David abode in the wilderness, and he saw that Saul came after him into the wilderness.   *encamped* · 23:15

4 David therefore sent out spies, and understood that Saul was come in very deed.

5 And David arose, and came to the place where Saul had ^Tpitched: and David beheld the place where Saul lay, and ^RAbner the son of Ner, the captain of his host: and Saul lay in the ^Ttrench, and the people pitched round about him.   *made camp* · 14:50 · *dug out*

6 Then answered David and said to A-him'-e-lech the Hit'-tite, and to A-bi'-shai ^Rthe son of Ze-ru'-iah, brother to Jo'-ab, saying, Who will ^Rgo down with me to Saul to the camp? And A-bi'-shai said, I will go down with thee.   1 Chr. 2:16 · Judg. 7:10, 11

7 So David and A-bi'-shai came to the people by night; and, behold, Saul lay sleeping within the trench, and his spear stuck in the ground at his bolster: but Abner and the people lay round about him.

8 Then said A-bi'-shai to David, God hath delivered thine enemy into thine hand this day: now therefore let me smite him, I pray thee, with the spear even to the earth at once, and I will not *smite* him the second time.

9 And David said to A-bi'-shai, Destroy him not: for who can stretch forth his hand against the LORD'S anointed, and be guiltless?

10 David said furthermore, *As* the LORD liveth, ^Rthe LORD shall smite him; or his day shall come to die; or he shall ^Rdescend into battle, and perish.   25:38 · 31:6

11 ^RThe LORD forbid that I should stretch forth mine hand against the LORD'S anointed: but, I pray thee, take thou now the spear that *is* at his ^Tbolster, and the cruse of water, and let us go.   24:6, 12 · *pillow*

12 So David took the spear and the cruse of water from Saul's ^Tbolster; and they ^Tgat them away, and no man saw *it*, nor knew *it*, neither awaked: for they *were* all asleep; because ^Ra deep sleep from the LORD was fallen upon them.   *pillow* · *got* · Gen. 2:21; 15:12

13 Then David went over to the other side, and stood on the top of an hill afar off; a great space *being* between them:

14 And David cried to the people, and to Abner the son of Ner, saying, Answerest thou not, ^RAbner? Then Abner answered and said, Who *art* thou *that* criest to the king?   14:50, 51

15 And David said to Abner, *Art* not thou a *valiant* man? and who *is* like to thee in Israel? wherefore then hast thou not kept thy lord the king? for there came one of the people in to destroy the king thy lord.

16 This thing *is* not good that thou hast done. *As* the LORD liveth, ye *are* worthy to die, because ye have not ^Tkept your master, the LORD'S anointed. And now see where the king's spear *is*, and the cruse of water that *was* at his ^Tbolster.   *guarded* · *pillow*

17 And Saul knew David's voice, and said,

Is this thy voice, my son David? And David said, *It is* my voice, my lord, O king.

18 And he said, Wherefore doth my lord thus pursue after his servant? for what have I done? or what evil *is* in mine hand?

19 Now therefore, I pray thee, let my lord the king hear the words of his servant. If the LORD have stirred thee up against me, let him accept an offering: but if *they be* the children of men, cursed *be* they before the LORD; for they have driven me out this day from abiding in the inheritance of the LORD, saying, Go, serve other gods.

20 Now therefore, let not my blood fall to the earth ᵀbefore the face of the LORD: for the king of Israel is come out to seek ᴿa flea, as when one doth hunt a partridge in the mountains.   *away from the presence* · 24:14

Saul Admits His Guilt

21 Then said Saul, I have sinned: return, my son David: for I will no more do thee harm, because my ᵀsoul was precious in thine eyes this day: behold, I have played the fool, and have erred exceedingly.   *life*

22 And David answered and said, Behold the king's spear! and let one of the young men come over and fetch it.

23 ᴿThe LORD render to every man his righteousness and his faithfulness: for the LORD delivered thee into *my* hand to day, but I would not stretch forth mine hand against the LORD's anointed.   *Ps. 7:8; 18:20*

24 And, behold, as thy life was much set by this day in mine eyes, so let my life be much set by in the eyes of the LORD, and let him deliver me out of all tribulation.

25 ᴿThen Saul said to David, Blessed *be* thou, my son David: thou shalt both do great things, and also shalt still ᴿprevail. So David went on his way, and Saul returned to his place.   24:19 · Gen. 32:28

CHAPTER 27

David Joins with the Philistines

AND ᴿ David said in his heart, I shall now perish one day by the hand of Saul: there is nothing better for me than that I should speedily escape into the land of the Phi-lis'-tines; and Saul shall despair of me, to seek me any more in any coast of Israel: so shall I escape out of his hand.   1 Chr. 29:28

2 And David arose, ᴿand he passed over with the six hundred men that *were* with him ᴿunto A'-chish, the son of Ma'-och, king of Gath.   25:13 · 21:10; 1 Kin. 2:39

3 And David dwelt with A'-chish at Gath, he and his men, every man with his household, *even* David ᴿwith his two wives, A-hin'-o-am the Jez'-re-el-i-tess, and Ab'-i-gail the Car'-mel-i-tess, Na'-bal's wife.   25:43

4 And it was told Saul that David was fled to Gath: and he sought no more again for him.

5 And David said unto A'-chish, If I have now found grace in thine eyes, let them give me a place in some town in the country, that I may dwell there: for why should thy servant dwell in the royal city with thee?

6 Then A'-chish gave him ᴿZik'-lag that day: wherefore Zik'-lag pertaineth unto the kings of Judah unto this day.   Josh. 15:31

7 And ᵀthe time that David dwelt in the country of the Phi-lis'-tines was a ᴿfull year and four months.   *the number of days* · 29:3

8 And David and his men went up, and invaded the Gesh'-u-rites, and the ᵀGez'-rites, and the Am'-a-lek-ites: for those *nations* were ᵀof old the inhabitants of the land, as thou goest to ᴿShur, even unto the land of Egypt.   *Girzites* · *in former times* · Ex. 15:22

9 And David ᵀsmote the land, and left neither man nor woman alive, and took away the sheep, and the oxen, and the asses, and the camels, and the apparel, and returned, and came to A'-chish.   *destroyed*

10 And A'-chish said, Whither have ye made a ᵀroad to day? And David said, Against the south of Judah, and against the south of the Je-rah'-me-el-ites, and against the south of the Ken'-ites.   *raid*

11 And David saved neither man nor woman alive, to bring *tidings* to Gath, saying, Lest they should tell on us, saying, So did David, and ᵀso *will be* his manner all the while he dwelleth in the country of the Phi-lis'-tines.   *this was his policy*

12 And A'-chish believed David, saying, He hath made his people Israel utterly to abhor him; therefore he shall be my servant for ever.

CHAPTER 28

AND ᴿit came to pass in those days, that the Phi-lis'-tines gathered their armies together for warfare, to fight with Israel. And A'-chish said unto David, Know thou assuredly, that thou shalt go out with me to battle, thou and thy men.   29:1

2 And David said to A'-chish, Surely thou shalt know what thy servant can do. And A'-chish said to David, Therefore will I make thee keeper of mine head for ever.

God Does Not Answer Saul

3 Now Samuel was dead, and all Israel had lamented him, and buried him in Ra'-mah, even in his own city. And Saul had put away ᵀthose that had familiar spirits, and the wizards, out of the land.   *mediums*

4 And the Phi-lis'-tines gathered themselves together, and came and pitched in

Shu'-nem: and Saul gathered all Israel together, and they pitched in Gil-bo'-a.

5 And when Saul saw the host of the Phi-lis'-tines, he was Rafraid, and his heart greatly trembled.   Job 18:11; Is. 57:20

6 And when Saul enquired of the LORD, the LORD answered him not, neither by dreams, nor by U'-rim, nor by prophets.

Saul Visits the Witch

7 Then said Saul unto his servants, Seek me a woman that hath a familiar spirit, that I may go to her, and enquire of her. And his servants said to him, Behold, Rthere is a woman that Thath a familiar spirit Rat En'-dor.   Acts 16:16 · is a sooth sayer · Josh. 17:1

8 And Saul disguised himself, and put on other raiment, and he went, and two men with him, and they came to the woman by night: and he said, I pray thee, divine unto me by the familiar spirit, and bring me him up, whom I shall name unto thee.

9 And the woman said unto him, Behold, thou knowest what Saul hath done, how he hath Rcut off those that have familiar spirits, and the wizards, out of the land: wherefore then layest thou a snare for my life, to cause me to die?   v. 3

10 And Saul sware to her by the LORD, saying, As the LORD liveth, there shall no punishment happen to thee for this thing.

11 Then said the woman, Whom shall I bring up unto thee? And he said, Bring me up Samuel.

12 And when the woman saw Samuel, she cried with a loud voice: and the woman spake to Saul, saying, Why hast thou deceived me? for thou art Saul.

13 And the king said unto her, Be not afraid: for what sawest thou? And the woman said unto Saul, I saw Rgods[T] ascending out of the earth.   Ex. 22:28 · spirits

14 And he said unto her, What form is he of? And she said, An old man cometh up; and he is covered with Ra mantle.[T] And Saul perceived that it was Samuel, and he stooped with his face to the ground, and bowed himself.   15:27; 24:8; 2 Kin. 2:8, 13 · robe

15 And Samuel said to Saul, Why hast thou disquieted me, to bring me up? And Saul answered, I am sore distressed; for the Phi-lis'-tines make war against me, and God is departed from me, and answereth me no more, neither by prophets, nor by dreams: therefore I have called thee, that thou mayest make known unto me what I shall do.

16 Then said Samuel, Wherefore then dost thou ask of me, seeing the LORD is departed from thee, and is become thine enemy?

17 And the LORD hath done to him, Ras he spake by me: for the LORD hath rent the kingdom out of thine hand, and given it to thy neighbour, even to David: 15:28

18 RBecause thou obeyedst not the voice of the LORD, nor executedst his fierce wrath upon Am'-a-lek, therefore hath the LORD done this thing unto thee this day.   Jer. 48:10

19 Moreover the LORD will also Tdeliver Israel with thee into the hand of the Phi-lis'-tines: and to morrow shalt Rthou and thy sons be with me: the LORD also shall deliver the host of Israel into the hand of the Phi-lis'-tines.   let Israel be defeated in battle · 31:2

20 Then Saul fell straightway Tall along on the earth, and was sore afraid, because of the words of Samuel: and there was no strength in him; for he had eaten no bread all the day, nor all the night.   flat on the ground

21 And the woman came unto Saul, and saw that he was sore troubled, and said unto him, Behold, thine handmaid hath obeyed thy voice, and I have Rput my life in my hand, and have hearkened unto thy words which thou spakest unto me.   19:5

22 Now therefore, I pray thee, hearken thou also unto the voice of thine handmaid, and let me set a Tmorsel of bread before thee; and eat, that thou mayest have strength, when thou goest on thy way.   piece

23 But he refused, and said, I will not eat. RBut his servants, together with the woman, Tcompelled him; and he hearkened unto their voice. So he arose from the earth, and sat upon the bed.   2 Kin. 5:13 · persuaded

24 And the woman had a fat calf in the house; and Rshe Thasted, and killed it, and took flour, and kneaded it, and did bake unleavened bread thereof: Gen. 18:6, 7 · hurried

25 And she brought it before Saul, and before his servants; and they did eat. Then they rose up, and went away that night.

CHAPTER 29

David Is Spared from Fighting Saul

NOW Rthe Phi-lis'-tines gathered together all their armies Rto A'-phek: and the Israelites Tpitched by a fountain which is in Jez'-re-el.   28:1 · 4:1 · made camp

2 And the lords of the Phi-lis'-tines passed on by hundreds, and by thousands: but David and his men passed on Tin the rereward Rwith A'-chish.   behind him · 28:1, 2

3 Then said the princes of the Phi-lis'-tines, What do these Hebrews here? And A'-chish said unto the princes of the Phi-lis'-tines, Is not this David, the servant of Saul the king of Israel, which hath been with me these days, or these years, and I have found no fault in him since he fell unto me unto this day?

4 And the princes of the Phi-lis'-tines were wroth with him; and the princes of the Phi-lis'-tines said unto him, RMake this fellow return, that he may go again to his place which thou hast appointed him, and let him

not go down with us to battle, lest in the battle he be an adversary to us: for wherewith should he reconcile himself unto his master? *should it* not *be* with the heads of these men?   1 Chr. 12:19

5 *Is* not this David, of whom they sang one to another in dances, saying, Saul slew his thousands, and David his ten thousands?

6 Then A'-chish called David, and said unto him, Surely, *as* the LORD liveth, thou hast been upright, and thy going out and thy coming in with me in the host *is* good in my sight: for I have not found evil in thee since the day of thy coming unto me unto this day: nevertheless the lords favour thee not.

7 Wherefore now return, and go in peace, that thou displease not the lords of the Phi-lis'-tines.

8 And David said unto A'-chish, But what have I done? and what hast thou found in thy servant so long as I have been with thee unto this day, that I may not go fight against the enemies of my lord the king?

9 And A'-chish answered and said to David, I know that thou *art* good in my sight, as an angel of God: notwithstanding the princes of the Phi-lis'-tines have said, He shall not go up with us to the battle.

10 Wherefore now rise up early in the morning with thy master's servants that are come with thee: and as soon as ye be up early in the morning, and have light, depart.

11 So David and his men rose up early to depart in the morning, to return into the land of the Phi-lis'-tines. RAnd the Phi-lis'-tines went up to Jez'-re-el.   2 Sam. 4:4

CHAPTER 30

God Answers David

AND it came to pass, when David and his men were come to Zik'-lag on the third day, that the RAm'-a-lek-ites had invaded the south, and Zik'-lag, and smitten Zik'-lag, and burned it with fire;   15:7

2 And had taken the women captives, that *were* therein: they slew not any, either great or small, Rbut carried *them* away, and went on their way.   27:11

3 So David and his men came to the city, and, behold, *it was* burned with fire; and their wives, and their sons, and their daughters, were taken captives.

4 Then David and the people that *were* with him lifted up their voice and wept, until they had no more power to weep.

5 And David's two wives were taken captives, A-hin'-o-am the Jez'-re-el-i-tess, and Ab'-i-gail the wife of Na'-bal the Car'-mel-ite.

6 And David was greatly distressed; for the people spake of stoning him, because the soul

of all the people was grieved, every man for his sons and for his daughters: but David encouraged himself in the LORD his God.

7 And David said to A-bi'-a-thar the priest, A-him'-e-lech's son, I pray thee, bring me hither the e'-phod. And A-bi'-a-thar brought thither the e'-phod to David.

8 RAnd David enquired at the LORD, saying, Shall I pursue after this troop? shall I overtake them? And he answered him, Pursue: for thou shalt surely overtake *them*, and without fail recover *all*.   23:2, 4, 9

David Kills the Enemy

9 So David went, Rhe and the six hundred men that *were* with him, and came to the brook Be'-sor, where those that were left behind stayed.   27:2

10 But David pursued, he and four hundred men: Rfor two hundred abode behind, which were so faint that they could not go over the brook Be'-sor.   vv. 9, 21

11 And they found an Egyptian in the field, and brought him to David, and gave him bread, and he did eat; and they made him drink water;

12 And they gave him a piece of a cake of figs, and two clusters of raisins: and when he had eaten, his spirit came again to him: for he had eaten no bread, nor drunk *any* water, three days and three nights.

13 And David said unto him, To whom *belongest* thou? and whence *art* thou? And he said, I *am* a young man of Egypt, servant to an Am'-a-lek-ite; and my master left me, because three days agone I fell sick.

14 We made an invasion *upon* the south of the Cher'-e-thites, and upon *the coast* which *belongeth* to Judah, and upon the south of Caleb; and we burned Zik'-lag with fire.

15 And David said to him, Canst thou bring me down to this company? And he said, TSwear unto me by God, that thou wilt neither kill me, nor deliver me into the hands of my master, and I will bring thee down to this company.   *promise*

16 And when he had brought him down, behold, *they were* spread abroad upon all the earth, eating and drinking, and dancing, because of all the great spoil that they had taken out of the land of the Phi-lis'-tines, and out of the land of Judah.

17 And David TRsmote them from the twilight even unto the evening of the next day: and there escaped not a man of them, save four hundred young men, Rwhich rode upon camels, and fled.   *beat down* • Ex. 17:14 • 11:11; 15:3

18 And David Rrecovered all that the Am'-a-lek-ites had carried away: and David rescued his two wives.   Gen. 14:16

19 And there was Rnothing lacking to

them, neither small nor great, neither sons nor daughters, neither spoil, nor any *thing* that they had taken to them: ᴿDavid recovered all. [1 Kin. 8:56] • *v. 8*

20 And David took all the flocks and the herds, *which* they drave before those *other* cattle, and said, This *is* David's spoil.

21 And David came to the two hundred men, which were so faint that they could not follow David, whom they had made also to abide at the brook Be'-sor: and they went forth to meet David, and to meet the people that *were* with him: and when David came near to the people, he saluted them.

22 Then answered all the wicked men and ᵀ*men* of Be'-li-al, of those that went with David, and said, Because they went not with us, we will not give them *ought* of the spoil that we have recovered, save to every man his wife and his children, that they may lead *them* away, and depart. *base fellows*

23 Then said David, Ye shall not do so, my brethren, with that which the LORD hath given us, ᴿwho hath preserved us, and delivered the company that came against us into our hand. Deut. 6:24

24 For who will hearken unto you in this matter? but as his part *is* that goeth down to the battle, so *shall* his part *be* that tarrieth by the stuff: they shall part alike.

25 And it was *so* from that day forward, that he made it a statute and an ordinance for Israel unto this day.

26 And when David came to Zik'-lag, he sent of the ᵀspoil unto the elders of Judah, *even* to his friends, saying, ᴿBehold a present for you of the spoil of the enemies of the LORD; *plunder* • 25:27, 28

27 To *them* which *were* in Beth'–el, and to *them* which *were* in south Ra'-moth, and to *them* which *were* in ᴿJat'-tir, Josh. 15:48

28 And to *them* which *were* in Ar'-o-er, and to *them* which *were* in Siph'-moth, and to *them* which *were* in Esh-te-mo'-a,

29 And to *them* which *were* in Ra'-chal, and to *them* which *were* in the cities of the Je-rah'-me-el-ites, and to *them* which *were* in the cities of the ᴿKen'-ites, Judg. 1:16

30 And to *them* which *were* in Hor'-mah, and to *them* which *were* in Chor-a'-shan, and to *them* which *were* in A'-thach,

31 And to *them* which *were* in ᴿHe'-bron, and to all the places where David himself and his men were wont to haunt. 2 Sam. 2:1

CHAPTER 31

The Enemy Kills Saul—1 Chr. 10:1–14

NOW the Phi-lis'-tines fought against Israel: and the men of Israel fled from before the Phi-lis'-tines, and fell down ᵀslain in mount ᴿGil-bo'-a. *wounded* • 28:4

2 And the Phi-lis'-tines followed hard upon Saul and upon his ᴿsons; and the Phi-lis'-tines slew Jonathan, and A-bin'-a-dab, and Mel'-chi-shu'-a, Saul's sons. 14:49

3 And ᴿthe battle went sore against Saul, and the archers hit him; and he was ᵀsore wounded of the archers. 2 Sam. 1:6 • *badly*

4 Then said Saul unto his armourbearer, Draw thy sword, and thrust me through therewith; lest these uncircumcised come and thrust me through, and ᵀabuse me. But his armourbearer would not; ᴿfor he was sore afraid. Therefore Saul took a sword, and fell upon it. *torture* • 2 Sam. 1:14

5 And when his armourbearer saw that Saul was dead, he fell likewise upon his sword, and died with him.

6 ᴿSo Saul died, and his three sons, and his armourbearer, and all his men, that same day together. 2 Sam. 1:6–10; 28:19

7 And when the men of Israel that *were* on the other side of the valley, and *they* that *were* on the other side Jordan, saw that the men of Israel fled, and that Saul and his sons were dead, they forsook the cities, and fled; and the Phi-lis'-tines came and dwelt in them.

8 And it came to pass on the ᵀmorrow, when the Phi-lis'-tines came to strip the slain, that they found Saul and his three sons fallen in mount Gil-bo'-a. *next day*

9 And they cut off his head, and stripped off his armour, and sent into the land of the Phi-lis'-tines round about, to publish *it* in the house of their idols, and among the people.

10 ᴿAnd they put his armour in the house of ᴿAsh'-ta-roth: and they fastened his body to the wall of Beth'-shan. 21:9 • 7:3

11 ᴿAnd when the inhabitants of Ja'-besh–gil'-e-ad heard of that which the Phi-lis'-tines had done to Saul; 11:3, 9, 11

12 ᴿAll the ᵀvaliant men arose, and went all night, and took the body of Saul and the bodies of his sons from the wall of Beth'-shan, and came to Ja'-besh, and burnt them there. 2 Sam. 2:4–7 • *able to fight*

13 And they took their bones, and ᴿburied *them* under ᴿa tree at Ja'-besh, ᴿand fasted seven days. 2 Sam. 21:12–14 • 22:6 • Gen. 50:10

THE SECOND BOOK OF

SAMUEL

THE BOOK OF SECOND SAMUEL

The Book of Second Samuel records the highlights of David's reign, first over the territory of Judah, and finally over the entire nation of Israel. It traces the ascension of David to the throne, his climactic sins of adultery and murder, and the shattering consequences of those sins upon his family and the nation.

See First Samuel for details on the titles of the books of Samuel. The Hebrew title for both books (originally one) is Samuel. The Greek title for Second Samuel is *Basileion Beta*, "Second Kingdoms." The Latin title is *Liber II Samuelis*, the "Second Book of Samuel," or simply "Second Samuel."

THE AUTHOR OF SECOND SAMUEL

Second Samuel was probably compiled by one man who combined the written chronicles of Nathan the prophet and Gad the seer (1 Chr. 29:29). In addition to these written sources, the compiler evidently used another source called "the book of Jasher" (1:18). See comments under First Samuel.

THE TIME OF SECOND SAMUEL

The date of the composition for First and Second Samuel was sometime after the death of Solomon (931 B.C.) but before the Assyrian captivity of the northern kingdom (722 B.C.). It is likely that Samuel was composed early in the divided kingdom, perhaps around 900 B.C.

The story of David begins in First Samuel 16 and ends in First Kings 2. Second Samuel records the major events of David's forty-year rule. His reign in Hebron begins in 1011 B.C. and ends in 1004 B.C. (5:5). His thirty-three-year reign over the united Judah and Israel lasts from 1004 B.C. to 971 B.C.

THE CHRIST OF SECOND SAMUEL

As seen in the introduction to First Samuel, David is one of the most important types of Christ in the Old Testament. In spite of his sins, he remains a man after God's own heart because of his responsive and faithful attitude toward God. He sometimes fails in his personal life, but he never flags in his relationship to the Lord. Unlike most of the kings who succeed him, he never allows idolatry to become a problem during his reign. He is a true servant of Yahweh, obedient to His Law, and an ideal king. His rule is usually characterized by justice, wisdom, integrity, courage, and compassion. Having conquered Jerusalem, he sits upon the throne of Melchizedek, the "righteous king"

(Gen. 14:18). David is the standard by which all subsequent kings are measured.

Of course, David's life as recorded in chapters 1—10 is a far better portrayal of the future Messiah than is his life as it is seen in 11—24. Sin mars potential. The closest way in which he foreshadows the coming King can be seen in the important covenant God makes with him (7:4—17). David wants to build a house for God; but instead, God makes a house for David. The same three promises of an eternal kingdom, throne, and seed are later given to Christ (Luke 1:32, 33). There are nine different dynasties in the northern kingdom of Israel, but there is only one dynasty in Judah. The promise of a permanent dynasty is fulfilled in Christ, the "son of David" (Matt. 21:9; 22:45), who will sit upon the throne of David (Is. 9:7; Luke 1:32).

KEYS TO SECOND SAMUEL

Key Word: David—The central character of Second Samuel is David, around whom the entire book is written. The key truth illustrated is the same as the theme of Deuteronomy: obedience brings blessing and disobedience brings judgment.

Key Verses: Second Samuel 7:12, 13; 22:21—"And when thy days be fulfilled, and thou shalt sleep with thy fathers, I will set up thy seed after thee, which shall proceed out of thy bowels, and I will establish his kingdom. He shall build an house for my name, and I will stablish the throne of his kingdom for ever" (7:12, 13).

"The LORD rewarded me according to my righteousness: according to the cleanness of my hands hath he recompensed me" (22:21).

Key Chapter: Second Samuel 11—The eleventh chapter of Second Samuel is pivotal for the entire book. This chapter records the tragic sins of David regarding Bath-sheba and her husband Uriah. All of the widespread blessings on David's family and his kingdom are quickly removed as God chastises His anointed one.

SURVEY OF SECOND SAMUEL

Second Samuel continues the account of the life of David at the point where First Samuel concludes. Soon after the death of Saul, the king-elect becomes the king enthroned, first over Judah when he reigns in Hebron for seven-and-a-half years and finally over all Israel when he reigns in Jerusalem for thirty-three years. This book reviews the key events in the forty-year reign of the man who is the halfway point between Abraham and Christ. It can be surveyed

in the three divisions: the triumphs of David (1—10), the transgressions of David (11), and the troubles of David (12—24).

The Triumphs of David (1—10): Chapters 1—4 record the seven-year reign of David over the territory of Judah. Even though Saul is David's murderous pursuer, David does not rejoice in his death because he recognizes that Saul has been divinely anointed as king. Saul's son Ish-bosheth is installed by Abner as a puppet king over the northern tribes of Israel. David's allies led by Joab defeat Abner and Israel (2:17; 3:1). Abner defects and arranges to unite Israel and Judah under David, but Joab kills Abner in revenge. The powerless Ish-bosheth is murdered by his own men, and David is made king of Israel (5:3). David soon captures and fortifies Jerusalem and makes it the civil and religious center of the now united kingdom. Under David's rule the nation prospers politically, spiritually, and militarily. David brings the ark to Jerusalem and seeks to build a house for God (7). His obedience in placing the Lord at the center of his rule leads to great national blessing (8—10). "And the LORD preserved David whithersoever he went" (8:14).

The Transgressions of David (11): David's crimes of adultery and murder mark the pivotal point of the book. Because of these transgressions, David's victories and successes are changed to the personal, family, and national troubles which are recorded throughout the rest of Second Samuel.

The Troubles of David (12—24): The disobedience of the king produces chastisement and confusion at every level. David's glory and fame fade, never to be the same again. Nevertheless, David confesses his guilt when confronted by Nathan the prophet and is restored by God. A sword remains in David's house as a consequence of the sin: the baby born to David and Bath-sheba dies, his son Amnon commits incest, and his son Absalom murders Amnon.

The consequences continue with Absalom's rebellion against his father. He shrewdly "stole the hearts of the men of Israel" (15:6). David is forced to flee from Jerusalem, and Absalom sets himself up as king. David would have been ruined, but God keeps Absalom from pursuing him until David has time to regroup his forces. Absalom's army is defeated by David's, and Joab kills Absalom in disobedience of David's orders to have him spared.

David seeks to amalgamate the kingdom, but conflict breaks out between the ten northern tribes of Israel and the two southern tribes of Judah and Benjamin. Israel decides to follow a man named Sheba in a revolt against David, but Judah remains faithful to him. This leads to war, and Joab defeats the rebels.

The closing chapters are actually an appendix to the book because they summarize David's words and deeds. They show how intimately the affairs of the people as a whole are tied to the spiritual and moral condition of the king. The nation enjoys God's blessing when David is obedient to the Lord, and suffers hardship when David disobeys God.

FOCUS	DAVID'S TRIUMPHS			DAVID'S TRANSGRESSIONS	DAVID'S TROUBLES	
REFERENCE	1:1——— 6:1———		8:1———	11:1——— 12:1———	13:37——— 24:25	
DIVISION	POLITICAL TRIUMPHS	SPIRITUAL TRIUMPHS	MILITARY TRIUMPHS	SINS OF ADULTERY AND MURDER	TROUBLES IN DAVID'S HOUSE	TROUBLES IN THE KINGDOM
TOPIC		SUCCESS		SIN	FAILURE	
		OBEDIENCE		DISOBEDIENCE	JUDGMENT	
LOCATION	DAVID IN HEBRON			DAVID IN JERUSALEM		
TIME	7½ YEARS			33 YEARS		

OUTLINE OF SECOND SAMUEL

Part One: The Triumphs of David (1:1—10:19)

Part Two: The Transgressions of David (11:1-27)

Part Three: The Troubles of David (12:1—24:25)

CHAPTER 1

King Saul Dies

NOW it came to pass after the [R]death of Saul, when David was returned from the slaughter of the Am′-a-lek-ites, and David had abode two days in Zik′-lag;   1 Sam. 31:6

2 It came even to pass on the third day, that, behold, [R]a man came out of the camp from Saul [R]with his clothes [T]rent, and earth upon his head: and so it was, when he came to David, that he fell to the earth, and did obeisance.   4:10 · 1 Sam. 4:12 · torn to show grief

3 And David said unto him, From whence comest thou? And he said unto him, Out of the camp of Israel am I [R]escaped.   1 Sam. 31:7

4 And David said unto him, [R]How went the matter? I pray thee, tell me. And he answered, That the people are fled from the battle, and many of the people also are fallen and dead; and Saul and Jonathan his son are dead also.   1 Sam. 4:16

5 And David said unto the young man that told him, How knowest thou that Saul and Jonathan his son be dead?

6 And the young man that told him said, As I [T]happened by chance upon mount Gil-bo′-a, behold, Saul leaned upon his spear; and, lo, the chariots and horsemen followed hard after him.   accidentally went by

7 And when he looked behind him, he saw me, and called unto me. And I answered, Here am I.

8 And he said unto me, Who art thou? And I answered him, I am an Am′-a-lek-ite.

9 He said unto me again, [T]Stand, I pray thee, upon me, and slay me: for [T]anguish is come upon me, because my life is yet whole in me.   move over with your sword · I am in trouble

10 So I stood upon him, and [R]slew him, because I was sure that he could not live after that he was fallen: and I took the crown that was upon his head, and the bracelet that was on his arm, and have brought them hither unto my lord.   Judg. 9:54

11 Then David took hold on his clothes, and [R]rent[T] them; and likewise all the men that were with him: 3:31; 13:31 · tore

12 And they mourned, and wept, and [R]fasted until even, for Saul, and for Jonathan his son, and for the people of the LORD, and for the house of Israel; because they were fallen by the sword.   3:35

13 And David said unto the young man that told him, Whence art thou? And he answered, I am the son of a stranger, an [R]Am′-a-lek-ite.   1 Sam. 15:3; 30:13

14 And David said unto him, How wast thou not afraid to stretch forth thine hand to destroy the LORD's anointed?

15 And [R]David called one of the young men, and said, Go near, and fall upon him. And he smote him that he died.   4:10, 12

16 And David said unto him, Thy blood be upon thy head; for [R]thy[T] mouth hath testified against thee, saying, I have slain the LORD's anointed.   v. 10 · you said yourself

17 And David lamented with this lamentation over Saul and over Jonathan his son:

18 (Also he bade them teach the children of Judah the [T]use of the bow: behold, it is written in the book of Ja′-sher.)   song

19 The beauty of Israel is slain upon thy high places: [R]how are the mighty fallen! v. 27

20 Tell it not in Gath, publish it not in the streets of As′-ke-lon; lest the daughters of the Phi-lis′-tines rejoice, lest the daughters of [R]the [T]uncircumcised triumph. 1 Sam. 31:4 · pagans

21 Ye mountains of Gil-bo′-a, let there be no dew, neither let there be rain, upon you, nor fields of offerings: for there the shield of the mighty is vilely cast away, the shield of Saul, as though he had not been [R]anointed with oil.   1 Sam. 10:1; Is. 21:5

22 From the blood of the slain, from the fat of the mighty, the bow of Jonathan turned not back, and the sword of Saul returned not empty.

23 Saul and Jonathan were lovely and pleasant in their lives, and in their death they were not divided: they were swifter than eagles, they were stronger than lions.

24 Ye daughters of Israel, weep over Saul, who clothed you in scarlet, with other delights, who put on ornaments of gold upon your apparel.

25 [R]How are the mighty fallen in the midst of the battle! O Jonathan, thou wast slain in thine high places.   vv. 19, 27

26 I am distressed for thee, my brother Jonathan: very pleasant hast thou been unto me: [R]thy love to me was wonderful, passing the love of women.   1 Sam. 18:1, 3; 19:2

27 How are the mighty fallen, and the weapons of war perished!

CHAPTER 2

David Is Anointed as King over Judah

AND it came to pass after this, that David [R]enquired of the LORD, saying, Shall I go up into any of the cities of Judah? And the LORD said unto him, Go up. And David said, Whither shall I go up? And he said, Unto He′-bron.   Judg. 1:1

2 So David went up thither, and his two wives also, A-hin′-o-am the Jez′-re-el-i-tess, and Ab′-i-gail Na′-bal's wife the Car′-mel-ite.

3 And his men that were with him did David bring up, every man with his household: and they dwelt in the cities of He′-bron.

4 [R]And the men of Judah came, and there they anointed David king over the house of

Judah. And they told David, saying, *That* Rthe men of Ja'-besh-gil'-e-ad *were they* that buried Saul.   *v. 11; 5:5 • 1 Sam. 31:11, 13*

5 And David sent messengers unto the men of Ja'-besh-gil'-e-ad, and said unto them, Blessed *be* ye of the Lord, that ye have shewed this kindness unto your lord, *even* unto Saul, and have buried him.

6 And now Rthe Lord Tshew kindness and truth unto you: and I also will Trequite you this kindness, because ye have done this thing.   *Ex. 34:6; 2 Tim. 1:16, 18 • do • repay*

7 Therefore now let your hands be strengthened, and be ye valiant: for your master Saul is dead, and also the house of Judah have anointed me king over them.

Ish-bosheth Is Made King over Israel

8 But Abner the son of Ner, captain of Saul's host, took Ish–bo'-sheth the son of Saul, and brought him over to Ma-ha-na'-im;

9 And made him king over RGil'-e-ad, and over the RAsh'-ur-ites, and over RJez'-re-el, and over E'-phra-im, and over Benjamin, and over all Israel.   *Josh. 22:9 • Judg. 1:32 • 1 Sam. 29:1*

10 Ish–bo'-sheth Saul's son *was* forty years old when he began to reign over Israel, and reigned two years. But the house of Judah followed David.

11 And the Ttime that David was king in He'-bron over the house of Judah was seven years and six months.   *number of days*

David's Victory over Ish-bosheth

12 And Abner the son of Ner, and the servants of Ish–bo'-sheth the son of Saul, went out from Ma-ha-na'-im to Gib'-e-on.

13 And Jo'-ab the son of Ze-ru'-iah, and the servants of David, went out, and met together by the pool of Gib'-e-on: and they sat down, the one on the one side of the pool, and the other on the other side of the pool.

14 And Abner said to Jo'-ab, Let the young men now arise, and Tplay before us. And Jo'-ab said, Let them arise.   *stage a contest*

15 Then there arose and went over by number twelve Tof Benjamin, which *pertained* to Ish–bo'-sheth the son of Saul, and twelve of the servants of David.   *for*

16 And they caught every one his fellow by the head, and *thrust* his sword in his fellow's side; so they fell down together: wherefore that place was called Hel'-kath-haz'-zu-rim, which *is* in Gib'-e-on.

17 And there was a very Tsore battle that day; and Abner was beaten, and the men of Israel, before the servants of David.   *severe*

18 And there were three sons of Ze-ru'-iah there, Jo'-ab, and A-bi'-shai, and A'-sa-hel: and A'-sa-hel *was* Ras light of foot Ras a wild Troe.   *1 Chr. 12:8; Hab. 3:19 • Ps. 18:33 • deer*

19 And A'-sa-hel pursued after Abner; and in going he turned not to the right hand nor to the left from following Abner.

20 Then Abner looked behind him, and said, *Art* thou A'-sa-hel? And he answered, I *am.*

21 And Abner said to him, Turn thee aside to thy right hand or to thy left, and lay thee hold on one of the young men, and take thee his armour. But A'-sa-hel would not turn aside from following of him.

22 And Abner said again to A'-sa-hel, Turn thee aside from following me: Twherefore should I Tsmite thee to the ground? Rhow then should I hold up my face to Jo'-ab thy brother?   *why • strike you • 3:27*

23 Howbeit he refused to turn aside: wherefore Abner with the hinder end of his spear smote him Runder the fifth Trib, that the spear came out behind him; and he fell down there, and died in the same place: and it came to pass, *that* as many as came to the place where A'-sa-hel fell down and died stood still.   *4:6; 20:10 • in the body*

24 Jo'-ab also and A-bi'-shai pursued after Abner: and the sun went down when they were come to the hill of Am'-mah, that *lieth* before Gi'-ah by the way of the wilderness of Gib'-e-on.

25 And the children of Benjamin gathered themselves together after Abner, and became one troop, and stood on the top of an hill.

26 Then Abner called to Jo'-ab, and said, TShall the sword devour for ever? knowest thou not that it will be bitterness in the latter end? how long shall it be then, ere thou bid the people return from following their brethren?   *shall we continue to kill each other?*

27 And Jo'-ab said, *As* God liveth, unless thou hadst spoken, surely then in the morning the people had Tgone up every one from following his brother.   *ceased pursuing*

28 So Jo'-ab blew a trumpet, and all the people stood still, and pursued after Israel no more, neither fought they any more.

29 And Abner and his men walked all that night through the plain, and passed over Jordan, and went through all Bith'-ron, and they came to RMa-ha-na'-im.   *v. 12*

30 And Jo'-ab returned from following Abner: and when he had gathered all the people together, there lacked of David's servants nineteen men and A'-sa-hel.

31 But the servants of David had smitten of Benjamin, and of Abner's men, *so that* three hundred and threescore men died.

32 And they took up A'-sa-hel, and buried him in the Tsepulchre of his father, which *was in* RBeth'-le-hem. And Jo'-ab and his men went all night, and they came to He'-bron at break of day.   *tomb • 1 Sam. 20:6*

CHAPTER 3

David's Growth over Ish-bosheth

NOW there was long war between the house of Saul and the house of David: but David waxed stronger and stronger, and the house of Saul waxed weaker and weaker.

2 And ᴿunto David were sons born in He'-bron: and his firstborn was Amnon, of A-hin'-o-am the Jez'-re-el-i-tess;   1 Chr. 3:1–4

3 And his second, Chil'-e-ab, of Ab'-i-gail the wife of Na'-bal the Car'-mel-ite; and the third, Ab'-sa-lom the son of Ma'-a-cah the daughter of Tal'-mai king of Ge'-shur;

4 And the fourth, ᴿAd-o-ni'-jah the son of Hag'-gith; and the fifth, Sheph-a-ti'-ah the son of Ab'-i-tal;   1 Kin. 1:5

5 And the sixth, Ith'-re-am, by Eg'-lah David's wife. These were born to David in He'-bron.

Abner's Murder

6 And it came to pass, while there was war between the house of Saul and the house of David, that Abner ᴿmade himself strong for the house of Saul.   2:8, 9

7 And Saul had a concubine, whose name *was* Riz'-pah, the daughter of A'-iah: and *Ish–bo'-sheth* said to Abner, Wherefore hast thou gone in unto my father's concubine?

8 Then was Abner very wroth for the words of Ish–bo'-sheth, and said, *Am* I a dog's head, which against Judah do shew kindness this day unto the house of Saul thy father, to his brethren, and to his friends, and have not delivered thee into the hand of David, that thou chargest me to day with a fault concerning this woman?

9 ᴿSo do God to ᴿAbner, and more also, except, as the LORD hath ᵀsworn to David, even so I do to him;   Ruth 1:17 • *vv.* 26, 27 • *promised*

10 To ᵀtranslate the kingdom from the house of Saul, and to set up the throne of David over Israel and over Judah, ᴿfrom Dan even to Be'-er-she'-ba.   *transfer* • 1 Sam. 3:20

11 And he could not answer Abner a word again, because he ᵀfeared him.   *was afraid of*

12 And Abner sent messengers to David on his behalf, saying, Whose *is* the land? saying *also*, Make thy ᵀleague with me, and, behold, my hand *shall be* with thee, to bring about all Israel unto thee.   *covenant*

13 And he said, Well; I will make a league with thee: but one thing I require of thee, that is, Thou shalt not see my face, except thou first bring Mi'-chal Saul's daughter, when thou comest to see my face.

14 And David sent messengers to Ish–bo'-sheth Saul's son, saying, Deliver *me* my wife Mi'-chal, which I espoused to me for an hundred foreskins of the Phi-lis'-tines.

15 And Ish-bo'-sheth sent, and took her from *her* husband, *even* from ᴿPhal'-ti-elᵀ the son of La'-ish.   1 Sam. 25:44 • *Phalti*

16 And her husband went with her along weeping behind her to Ba-hu'-rim. Then said Abner unto him, Go, return. And he returned.

17 And Abner had communication with the elders of Israel, saying, Ye sought for David in times past *to be* king over you:

18 Now then do *it:* for the LORD hath spoken of David, saying, By the hand of my servant David I will save my people Israel out of the hand of the Phi-lis'-tines, and out of the hand of all their enemies.

19 And Abner also spake in the ears of Benjamin: and Abner went also to speak in the ears of David in He'-bron all that seemed good to Israel, and that seemed good to the whole house of Benjamin.

20 So Abner came to David to He'-bron, and twenty men with him. And David made Abner and the men that *were* with him a feast.

21 And Abner said unto David, I will arise and go, and will gather all Israel unto my lord the king, that they may make a league with thee, and that thou mayest reign over all that thine heart desireth. And David sent Abner away; and he went in peace.

22 And, behold, the servants of David and Jo'-ab came from *pursuing* a troop, and brought in a great spoil with them: but Abner *was* not with David in He'-bron; for he had sent him away, and he was gone in peace.

23 When Jo'-ab and all the host that *was* with him were come, they told Jo'-ab, saying, Abner the son of Ner came to the king, and he hath sent him away, and he is gone in peace.

24 Then Jo'-ab came to the king, and said, What hast thou done? behold, Abner came unto thee; why *is* it *that* thou hast sent him away, and he is quite gone?

25 Thou knowest Abner the son of Ner, that he came to deceive thee, and to know ᴿthy going out and thy coming in, and to know all that thou doest.   1 Sam. 29:6; Is. 37:28

26 And when Jo'-ab was come out from David, he sent messengers after Abner, which brought him again from the well of Si'-rah: but David knew *it* not.

27 And when Abner was returned to He'-bron, Jo'-ab took him aside in the gate to speak with him ᵀquietly, and smote him there under the fifth *rib*, that he died, for the blood of A'-sa-hel his brother.   *secretly*

28 And afterward when David heard *it,* he said, I and my kingdom *are* ᵀguiltless before the LORD for ever from the blood of Abner the son of Ner: *innocent*

29 Let it rest on the head of Jo'-ab, and on all his father's house; and let there not fail ᵀfrom the house of Jo'-ab one that hath an issue, or that is a leper, or that leaneth on a

staff, or that falleth on the sword, or that lacketh bread.   *in the family*

30 So Jo'-ab and A-bi'-shai his brother slew Abner, because he had slain their brother A'-sa-hel at Gib'-e-on in the battle.

31 And David said to Jo'-ab, and to all the people that *were* with him, ᴿRendᵀ your clothes, and gird you with sackcloth, and mourn before Abner. And king David *himself* followed the ᵀbier.   Judg. 11:35 • *tear* • *litter*

32 And they buried Abner in He'-bron: and the king lifted up his voice, and wept at the grave of Abner; and all the people wept.

33 And the king lamented over Abner, and said, Died Abner as a fool dieth?

34 Thy hands *were* not bound, nor thy feet put into fetters: as a man falleth before wicked men, *so* fellest thou. And all the people wept again over him.

35 And when all the people came to cause David to eat meat while it was yet day, David sware, saying, ᴿSo do God to me, and more also, if I taste bread, or ought else, ᴿtill the sun be down.   Ruth 1:17 • 1:12

36 And all the people took notice *of it*, and it ᵀpleased them: as whatsoever the king did pleased all the people.   *good in their eyes*

37 For all the people and all Israel understood that day that it was not of the king to slay Abner the son of Ner.

38 And the king said unto his servants, Know ye not that there is a prince and a great man fallen this day in Israel?

39 And I *am* this day weak, though anointed king; and these men the sons of Ze-ru'-iah ᴿbe too ᵀhard for me: ᴿthe Lᴏʀᴅ shall reward the doer of evil according to his wickedness.   19:7 • *tough* • 2 Tim. 4:14

CHAPTER 4

Ish-bosheth's Murder

AND when Saul's son heard that Abner was dead in He'-bron, his hands were feeble, and all the Israelites were troubled.

2 And Saul's son had two men *that were* captains of bands: the name of the one *was* Ba'-a-nah, and the name of the other Re'-chab, the sons of Rim'-mon a Be-e'-roth-ite, of the children of Benjamin: (for Be-e'-roth also was reckoned to Benjamin:

3 And the Be-e'-roth-ites fled to Git'-ta-im, and were sojourners there until this day.)

4 And Jonathan, Saul's son, had a son *that was* lame of *his* feet. He was five years old when the tidings came of Saul and Jonathan out of Jez'-re-el, and his nurse took him up, and fled: and it came to pass, as she made haste to flee, that he fell, and became lame. And his name *was* Me-phib'-o-sheth.

5 And the sons of Rim'-mon the Be-e'-roth-ite, Re'-chab and Ba'-a-nah, went, and came about the heat of the day to the house of Ish-bo'-sheth, who lay on a bed at noon.

6 And they came thither into the midst of the house, *as though* they would have ᵀfetched wheat; and they ᴿsmote ᵀhim under the fifth *rib*: and Re'-chab and Ba'-a-nah his brother escaped.   *brought* • 20:10 • *struck*

7 For when they came into the house, he lay on his bed in his bedchamber, and they smote him, and slew him, and beheaded him, and took his head, and ᵀgat them away through the plain all night.   *escaped*

8 And they brought the head of Ish-bo'-sheth unto David to He'-bron, and said to the king, Behold the head of Ish-bo'-sheth the son of Saul thine enemy, which sought thy life; and the Lᴏʀᴅ hath avenged my lord the king this day of Saul, and of his seed.

Judgment on the Murder of Ish-bosheth

9 And David answered Re'-chab and Ba'-a-nah his brother, the sons of Rim'-mon the Be-e'-roth-ite, and said unto them, *As* the Lᴏʀᴅ liveth, ᴿwho hath redeemed my soul out of all adversity,   Gen. 48:16; 1 Kin. 1:29

10 When one told me, saying, Behold, ᴿSaul is dead, thinking to have brought good tidings, I took hold of him, and slew him in Zik'-lag, who *thought* that I would have given him a reward for his tidings: 1:2, 4, 15

11 How much more, when wicked men have slain a righteous person in his own house upon his bed? shall I not therefore now require his blood of your hand, and ᵀtake you away from the earth?   *destroy you*

12 And ᴿDavid commanded his young men, and they slew them, and cut off their hands and their feet, and hanged *them* up over the pool in He'-bron. But they took the head of Ish-bo'-sheth, and buried *it* in the sepulchre of Abner in He'-bron.   1:15

CHAPTER 5

David Is Anointed to Reign over Israel
1 Chr. 11:1-3

THEN came all the tribes of Israel to David unto He'-bron, and spake, saying, Behold, we *are* thy bone and thy flesh.

2 Also in time past, when Saul was king over us, thou wast he that leddest out and broughtest in Israel: and the Lᴏʀᴅ said to thee, Thou shalt feed my people Israel, and thou shalt be a captain over Israel.

3 ᴿSo all the elders of Israel came to the king to He'-bron; and king David made a league with them in He'-bron ᴿbefore the Lᴏʀᴅ: and they anointed David king over Israel.   3:21; 1 Chr. 11:3 • Judg. 11:11; 1 Sam. 23:18

4 David *was* thirty years old when he began to reign, *and* he reigned forty years.

5 In He'-bron he reigned over Judah ᴿseven years and six months: and in Jerusalem he reigned thirty and three years over all Israel and Judah.   2:11; 1 Chr. 3:4

Conquest of Jerusalem—1 Chr. 11:4–9

6 And the king and his men went to Jerusalem unto ᴿthe Jeb'-u-sites, the inhabitants of the land: which spake unto David, saying, Except thou take away the blind and the lame, thou shalt not come in hither: thinking, David cannot come in hither.   Josh. 15:63

7 Nevertheless David took the strong hold of Zion: the same is the city of David.

8 And David said on that day, Whosoever getteth up to the gutter, and smiteth the Jeb'-u-sites, and the lame and the blind, that are hated of David's soul, he shall be chief and captain. Wherefore they said, The blind and the lame shall not come into the house.

9 So David dwelt in the fort, and called it ᴿthe city of David. And David built round about from Mil'-lo and inward.   v. 7

10 And David went on, and grew great, and the Lᴏʀᴅ God of hosts was with him.

Alliance with Tyre—1 Chr. 14:1, 2

11 And Hiram king of Tyre sent messengers to David, and cedar trees, and carpenters, and ᵀmasons: ᴿand they built David an house.   hewers of the stone of the wall • 2 Kin. 12:11

12 And David ᴿperceivedᵀ that the Lᴏʀᴅ had established him king over Israel, and that he had exalted his kingdom for his people Israel's sake.   2 Kin. 4:9 • recognized

David's Family

13 And ᴿDavid took him more concubines and wives out of Jerusalem, after he was come from He'-bron: and there were yet sons and daughters born to David.   1 Chr. 3:9

14 And ᴿthese be the names of those that were born unto him in Jerusalem; ᵀShammu'-ah, and Sho'-bab, and Nathan, and Solomon,   1 Chr. 3:5–8 • Shimea, 1 Chr. 3:5

15 ᴿIb'-har also, and ᵀEl-i-shu'-a, and Ne'-pheg, and Ja-phi'-a,   1 Chr. 3:6 • Elishama

16 And E-lish'-a-ma, and ᵀE-li'-a-da,ᴿ and E-liph'-a-let.   Beeliada • 1 Chr. 14:7

Conquest of Philistia—1 Chr. 14:9–17

17 ᴿBut when the Phi-lis'-tines heard that they had anointed David king over Israel, all the Phi-lis'-tines came up to ᵀseek David; and David heard of it, ᴿand went down to the ᵀhold.   1 Chr. 11:16 • attack • 23:14 • fortress

18 The Phi-lis'-tines also came and spread themselves in the valley of Reph'-a-im.

19 And David ᴿenquired of the Lᴏʀᴅ, saying, Shall I go up to the Phi-lis'-tines? wilt thou deliver them into mine hand? And the Lᴏʀᴅ said unto David, Go up: for I will doubtless deliver the Phi-lis'-tines into thine hand.   1 Sam. 23:2, 4

20 And David came to ᴿBa'-al-per'-a-zim, and David smote them there, and said, The Lᴏʀᴅ hath ᵀbroken forth upon mine enemies before me, as the breach of waters. Therefore he called the name of that place Ba'-al-per'-a-zim.   Is. 28:21 • demonstrated his power

21 And there they left their images, and David and his men ᵀburned them.   took away

22 ᴿAnd the Phi-lis'-tines came up yet again, and spread themselves in the valley of Reph'-a-im.   1 Chr. 14:13

23 And when David enquired of the Lᴏʀᴅ, he said, Thou shalt not go up; but fetch a compass behind them, and come upon them over against the mulberry trees.

24 And let it be, when thou ᴿhearest the sound of a going in the tops of the mulberry trees, that then thou shalt bestir thyself: for then shall the Lᴏʀᴅ go out before thee, to smite the host of the Phi-lis'-tines.   2 Kin. 7:6

25 And David did so, as the Lᴏʀᴅ had commanded him; and smote the Phi-lis'-tines from Ge'-ba until thou come to Ga'-zer.

CHAPTER 6

Incorrect Transportation of the Ark
1 Chr. 13:1–14

AGAIN, David gathered together all the chosen men of Israel, thirty thousand.

2 And David arose, and went with all the people that were with him from Ba'-a-le of Judah, to bring up from thence the ark of God, whose name is called by the name of the Lᴏʀᴅ of hosts ᵀthat dwelleth between the cher'-u-bims.   who is to be met at the mercy seat

3 And they set the ark of God upon a new cart, and brought it out of the house of A-bin'-a-dab that was in ᵀGib'-e-ah: and Uz'-zah and A-hi'-o, the sons of A-bin'-a-dab, drave the new cart.   the hill

4 And they brought it out of ᴿthe house of A-bin'-a-dab which was at Gib'-e-ah, ᵀaccompanying the ark of God: and A-hi'-o went before the ark.   1 Sam. 7:1 • with

5 And David and all the house of Israel played ᴿbefore the Lᴏʀᴅ on all manner of instruments made of fir wood, even on harps, and on psalteries, and on timbrels, and on cornets, and on cymbals.   1 Sam. 18:6, 7

6 And when they came to ᴿNa'-chon's threshingfloor, Uz'-zah put forth his hand to the ark of God, and ᵀtook hold of it; for the oxen ᵀshook it.   1 Chr. 13:9 • held it • stumbled

7 And the anger of the Lᴏʀᴅ was kindled against Uz'-zah; and ᴿGod smote him there for his ᵀerror; and there he died by the ark of God.   1 Sam. 6:19 • rashness

8 And David was displeased, because the Lᴏʀᴅ had ᵀmade a breach upon Uz'-zah: and

he called the name of the place Pe'-rez-uz'-zah to this day.   *worked violence*

9 And [R]David was afraid of the LORD that day, and said, How shall the ark of the LORD come to me?   Ps. 119:120

10 So David would not remove the ark of the LORD unto him into the city of David: but David carried it aside into the house of O'-bed-e'-dom [R]the Git'-tite.   1 Chr. 13:13

11 And the ark of the LORD continued in the house of O'-bed-e'-dom the Git'-tite three months: and the LORD blessed O'-bed-e'-dom, and all his household.

Correct Transportation of the Ark
1 Chr. 15:25

12 And it was told king David, saying, The LORD hath blessed the house of O'-bed-e'-dom, and all that *pertaineth* unto him, because of the ark of God. [R]So David went and brought up the ark of God from the house of O'-bed-e'-dom into the city of David with gladness.   16:3; 1 Chr. 15:25

David Rejoices over the Ark—1 Chr. 15:26–28

13 And it was *so*, that when they that bare the ark of the LORD had gone [T]six paces, he sacrificed [R]oxen and fatlings.   *18 ft.* • 1 Kin. 8:5

14 And David danced[T] before the LORD with all *his* might; and David *was* girded with a linen e'-phod.   *engaged in ritual ceremonies*

15 So David and all the house of Israel brought up the ark of the LORD with shouting, and with the sound of the trumpet.

Michal Despises David—1 Chr. 15:29—16:3

16 And as the ark of the LORD came into the city of David, Mi'-chal Saul's daughter looked through a window, and saw king David leaping and dancing before the LORD; and she despised him in her heart.

17 And they brought in the ark of the LORD, and set it in his place, in the midst of the tabernacle that David had [T]pitched for it: and David offered burnt offerings and peace offerings before the LORD.   *set up*

18 And as soon as David had made an end of offering burnt offerings and peace offerings, [R]he blessed the people in the name of the LORD of hosts.   1 Kin. 8:14

19 [R]And he dealt among all the people, *even* among the whole multitude of Israel, as

well to the women as men, to every one a cake of bread, and a good piece *of flesh*, and a flagon *of wine*. So all the people departed every one to his house.   1 Chr. 16:3

20 Then David returned to bless his household. And Mi'-chal the daughter of Saul came out to meet David, and said, How glorious was the king of Israel to day, who uncovered himself to day in the eyes of the handmaids of his servants, as one of the vain fellows shamelessly uncovereth himself!

21 And David said unto Mi'-chal, It *was* before the LORD, which chose me before thy father, and before all his house, to appoint me ruler over the people of the LORD, over Israel: therefore will I play before the LORD.

22 And I will yet be more vile than thus, and will be base in mine own sight: and of the maidservants which thou hast spoken of, of them shall I be had in honour.

23 Therefore Mi'-chal the daughter of Saul had no child unto the day of her death.

CHAPTER 7

David Is Forbidden to Build God a House
1 Chr. 17:1, 2

AND it came to pass, when the king sat in his house, and the LORD had given him rest round about from all his enemies;

2 That the king said unto [R]Nathan the prophet, See now, I dwell in an house of cedar, [R]but the ark of God dwelleth [T]within [R]curtains.   5:11 • Acts 7:46 • *in a cloth tent* • Ex. 26:1

3 And Nathan said to the king, [R]Go, do all that *is* in thine heart; for the LORD *is* with thee.   1 Kin. 8:17, 18

God Promises David an Eternal House
1 Chr. 17:3–15

4 And it came to pass that night, that the word of the LORD came unto Nathan, saying,

5 Go and tell my servant David, Thus saith the LORD, [R]Shalt thou build me an house for me to dwell in?   1 Kin. 5:3, 4; 8:19, 33

6 Whereas I have not dwelt in *any* house since the time that I brought up the children of Israel out of Egypt, even to this day, but have walked in a tent and in a tabernacle.

7 In all *the places* wherein I have walked with all the children of Israel spake I a word

---

7:4–17 The Davidic Covenant—The covenant with David is the fourth of the theocratic covenants (pertaining to the rule of God). In this covenant David is promised three things: (1) a land forever (v. 10); (2) an unending dynasty (vv. 11, 16); and (3) an everlasting kingdom (vv. 13, 16). The birth of Solomon, David's son who is to succeed him, is predicted (v. 12). His particular role is to establish the throne of the Davidic Kingdom forever (v. 13). His throne continues, though his seed is cursed in the person of Jeconiah (Coniah), who was the king under whom the nation was carried captive to Babylon. Jeremiah prophesies that no one whose genealogical descent would be traced back to David through Jeconiah and Solomon would ever sit on David's throne (Page 727—Jer. 22:24–30). Joseph, the legal, but not physical, father of Jesus traces his lineage to David through Jeconiah (Page 941—Matt. 1:1–17). David, however, had another son, Nathan. His line was not cursed. Mary, the physical mother of Jesus, traces

with any of the tribes of Israel, whom I commanded to feed my people Israel, saying, Why build ye not me an house of cedar?

8 Now therefore so shalt thou say unto my servant David, Thus saith the Lord of hosts, RI took thee from the Tsheepcote, from following the sheep, to be ruler over my people, over Israel: *1 Sam. 16:11, 12 • pasture*

9 And I was with thee whithersoever thou wentest, and have Tcut off all thine enemies out of thy sight, and have made thee a great name, like unto the name of the great *men* that *are* in the earth.   *destroyed*

10 Moreover I will appoint a place for my people Israel, and will plant them, that they may dwell in a place of their own, and move no more; neither shall the children of wickedness afflict them any more, as beforetime,

11 And as since the time that I commanded judges *to be* over my people Israel, and have caused thee to rest from all thine enemies. Also the Lord telleth thee that he will Tmake thee an house.   *establish your family*

12 And when thy days be fulfilled, and thou Rshalt sleep with thy fathers, RI will set up thy seed after thee, which shall proceed out of thy bowels, and I will establish his kingdom.   *Deut. 31:16 • Ps. 132:11; Matt. 19:28 ☆*

13 RHe shall build an house for my name, and I will Rstablish the throne of his kingdom for ever.   *[1 Kin. 5:5; 8:19] • Matt. 19:28 ☆*

14 RI will be his father, and he shall be my son. If he commit iniquity, I will chasten him with the rod of men, and with the stripes of the children of men: *[Ps. 89:26; Heb. 1:5]*

15 But my mercy shall not depart away from him, Ras I took *it* from Saul, whom I put away before thee.   *1 Sam. 15:23, 28; 16:14*

16 And thine house and thy kingdom shall be established for ever before thee: thy throne shall be established for ever.

17 According to all these words, and according to all this vision, so did Nathan speak unto David.

David Praises God—1 Chr. 17:16–27

18 Then went king David in, and sat before the Lord, and he said, RWho *am* I, O Lord God? and what is Tmy house, that thou hast brought me hitherto?   *Ex. 3:11 • my family*

19 And this was yet a small thing in thy sight, O Lord God; but Rthou hast spoken also of thy servant's house for a great while

to come. And *is* this Tthe manner of man, O Lord God?   *vv. 11–16 • the way a man would do it?*

20 And what can David say more unto thee? for Rthou, Lord God, Rknowest thy servant.   *[1 Sam. 16:7] • Ps. 139:1*

21 For thy word's sake, and according to thine own heart, hast thou done all these great things, to make thy servant know *them.*

22 Wherefore Rthou art great, O Lord God: for *there is* none like thee, neither *is there* any God beside thee, according to all that we have heard with our ears.   *Jer. 10:6*

23 And what one nation in the earth *is* like thy people, *even* like Israel, whom God went to redeem for a people to himself, and to make him a name, and to do for you great things and terrible, for thy land, before thy people, which thou redeemedst to thee from Egypt, *from* the nations and their gods?

24 For thou hast confirmed to thyself thy people Israel *to be* a people unto thee for ever: and thou, Lord, art become their God.

25 RAnd now, O Lord God, the word that thou hast spoken concerning thy servant, and concerning his house, establish *it* for ever, and do as thou hast said.   *Matt. 19:28 ☆*

26 And let thy name be magnified for ever, saying, The Lord of hosts *is* the God over Israel: Rand let the house of thy servant David be established before thee.   *Matt. 25:31 ☆*

27 For thou, O Lord of hosts, God of Israel, hast Trevealed to thy servant, saying, RI will build thee an house: therefore hath thy servant found in his heart to pray this prayer unto thee.   *made known • v. 13*

28 And now, O Lord God, thou *art* that God, and thy words be true, and thou hast promised this goodness unto thy servant:

29 Therefore now let it please thee to Rbless the house of thy servant, that it may continue for ever before thee: for thou, O Lord God, hast spoken *it:* and with thy blessing let the house of thy servant be blessed Rfor ever.   *Num. 6:24–26; Ps. 3:8 • 22:51*

CHAPTER 8

David Defeats Philistia—1 Chr. 18:1

AND after this it came to pass, that David smote the Phi-lis'-tines, and subdued

her lineage back to David through Nathan (Page 1008—Luke 3:23–38). Notice the care and the extent to which God goes to keep His Word and to preserve its truthfulness. The virgin birth was absolutely essential not only to assure the sinless character of Jesus but also to fulfill the Davidic Covenant. Jesus receives His "blood right" to David's throne through his earthly mother, Mary, and His "legal right" to David's throne through his adoptive earthly father, Joseph. The virgin birth guarantees that one of David's line will sit on David's throne and rule forever, while at the same time preserving intact the curse and restriction on the line of descent through Jeconiah.
Now turn to Page 736—Jer. 31:31–34: The New Covenant.

them: and David took Me'-theg-am'-mah out of the hand of the Phi-lis'-tines.

David Defeats Moab—1 Chr. 18:2

2 And he smote Moab, and measured them with a line, casting them down to the ground; even with two lines measured he to put to death, and with one full line to keep alive. And *so* the Mo'-ab-ites became David's servants, *and* brought gifts.

David Defeats Zobah and Syria—1 Chr. 18:3–8

3 David smote also Had-ad-e'-zer, the son of Re'-hob, king of Zo'-bah, as he went to recover his border at the river Eu-phra'-tes.

4 And David took from him a thousand *chariots,* and seven hundred horsemen, and twenty thousand footmen: and David houghed all the chariot *horses,* but reserved of them *for* an hundred chariots.

5 ᴿAnd when the Syrians of Damascus came to succour Had-ad-e'-zer king of Zo'-bah, David slew of the Syrians two and twenty thousand men.   1 Kin. 11:23; 15:18

6 Then David put garrisons in Syria of Damascus: and the Syrians became servants to David, *and* brought gifts. And the LORD preserved David whithersoever he went.

7 And David took ᴿthe shields of gold that were on the servants of Had-ad-e'-zer, and brought them to Jerusalem.   1 Kin. 10:16

8 And from Be'-tah, and from ᵀBer'-o-thai, cities of Had-ad-e'-zer, king David took exceeding much brass.   *Chun,* 1 Chr. 18:8

David Receives Spoil from His Enemies
1 Chr. 18:9–12

9 When ᵀTo'-iᴿ king of ᴿHa'-math heard that David had smitten all the host of Had-ad-e'-zer,   *Tou* • 1 Chr. 18:9 • *v.* 4; 1 Kin. 8:65

10 Then To'-i sent ᴿJo'-ram his son unto king David, to salute him, and to bless him, because he had fought against Had-ad-e'-zer, and smitten him: for Had-ad-e'-zer had wars with To'-i. And Jo'-*ram* brought with him vessels of silver, and vessels of gold, and vessels of brass: 1 Chr. 18:10

11 ᴿWhich also king David ᴿdid dedicate unto the LORD, with the silver and gold that he had dedicated of all nations which he subdued;   1 Chr. 29:9 • 1 Kin. 7:51

12 Of Syria, and of Moab, and of the children of Ammon, and of the Phi-lis'-tines, and of Am'-a-lek, and of the spoil of Had-ad-e'-zer, son of Re'-hob, king of Zo'-bah.

David's Righteous Rule over Israel
1 Chr. 18:13–17

13 And David gat *him* a name when he returned from smiting of the Syrians in the valley of salt, *being* eighteen thousand *men.*

14 And he put garrisons in E'-dom; throughout all E'-dom put he garrisons, and

ᴿall they of E'-dom became David's servants. And the LORD ᵀpreserved David whithersoever he went.   Num. 24:18 • *gave victory to*

15 And David reigned over all Israel; and David executed judgment and ᴿjustice unto all his people.   1 Kin. 1:52

16 ᴿAnd Jo'-ab the son of Ze-ru'-iah *was* over the host; and ᴿJe-hosh'-a-phat the son of A-hi'-lud *was* recorder;   19:13 • 1 Kin. 4:3

17 And Za'-dok the son of A-hi'-tub, and A-him'-e-lech the son of A-bi'-a-thar, *were* the priests; and Se-ra'-iah *was* the scribe;

18 ᴿAnd Be-nai'-ah the son of Je-hoi'-a-da *was* over both the ᴿCher'-e-thites and the ᴿPel'-e-thites; and David's sons were ᵀchief rulers.   15:18 • 1 Chr. 18:17 • 1 Sam. 30:14 • *princes*

CHAPTER 9

David's Righteous Rule over Mephibosheth

AND David said, Is there yet any that is left of the house of Saul, that I may shew him kindness for Jonathan's sake?

2 And *there was* of the house of Saul a servant whose name *was* ᴿZi'-ba. And when they had called him unto David, the king said unto him, *Art* thou Zi'-ba? And he said, Thy servant *is* he.   16:1; 19:17, 29

3 And the king said, *Is* there not yet any of the house of Saul, that I may shew ᴿthe kindness of God unto him? And Zi'-ba said unto the king, Jonathan hath yet a son, *which is* ᴿlame on *his* feet.   1 Sam. 20:14 • 4:4

4 And the king said unto him, Where *is* he? And Zi'-ba said unto the king, Behold, he *is* in the house of ᴿMa'-chir, the son of Am'-mi-el, in Lo-de'-bar.   17:27–29

5 Then king David sent, and fetched him out of the house of Ma'-chir, the son of Am'-mi-el, from Lo-de'-bar.

6 Now when Me-phib'-o-sheth, the son of Jonathan, the son of Saul, was come unto David, he fell on his face, and did reverence. And David said, ᴿMe-phib'-o-sheth. And he answered, Behold thy servant!   16:4

7 And David said unto him, Fear not: for I will surely shew thee kindness for Jonathan thy father's sake, and will restore thee all the land of Saul thy father; and thou shalt eat bread at my table continually.

8 ᴿAnd he bowed himself, and said, What *is* thy servant, that thou shouldest look upon such ᴿa dead dog as I *am?*   1 Sam. 24:14 • 16:9

9 Then the king called to Zi'-ba, Saul's servant, and said unto him, ᴿI have given unto thy master's son all that ᵀpertained to Saul and to all his house.   • 16:4 • *belonged*

10 Thou therefore, and thy sons, and thy servants, shall ᵀtill the land for him, and thou shalt bring in *the fruits,* that thy master's son may have food to eat: but Me-phib'-o-sheth thy master's son shall eat bread alway at my

table. Now Zi'-ba had fifteen sons and twenty servants.   *cultivate*

11 Then said Zi'-ba unto the king, According to all that my lord the king hath commanded his servant, so shall thy servant do. RAs for Me-phib'-o-sheth, *said the king,* he shall eat at my table, as one of the king's sons.   Gen. 39:5

12 And Me-phib'-o-sheth had a young son, Rwhose name *was* Mi'-cha. And all that dwelt in the house of Zi'-ba *were* servants unto Me-phib'-o-sheth.   1 Chr. 8:34

13 So Me-phib'-o-sheth dwelt in Jerusalem: for he did eat continually at the king's table; and was lame on both his feet.

CHAPTER 10

Insult of Ammon—1 Chr. 19:1-5

AND it came to pass after this, that the king of the children of Ammon died, and Ha'-nun his son reigned in his stead.

2 Then said David, I will shew kindness unto Ha'-nun the son of Na'-hash, as his father shewed kindness unto me. And David sent to comfort him by the hand of his servants for his father. And David's servants came into the land of the children of Ammon.

3 And the princes of the children of Ammon said unto Ha'-nun their lord, Thinkest thou that David doth honour thy father, that he hath sent comforters unto thee? hath not RDavid *rather* sent his servants unto thee, to search the city, and to spy it out, and Rto overthrow it?   Gen. 42:9, 16 • Job 1:11

4 Wherefore Ha'-nun took David's servants, and shaved off the one half of Rtheir beards, and cut off their garments in the middle, Reven to their buttocks, and sent them away.   Is. 15:2; Jer. 41:5 • Is. 20:4; 47:2

5 When they told it unto David, he sent to meet them, because the men were greatly ashamed: and the king said, Tarry at Jericho until your beards be grown, and *then* return.

Ammon Is Defeated—1 Chr. 19:6-15

6 And when the children of Ammon saw thatR they stank before David, the children of Ammon sent and hired the Syrians of Beth-re'-hob, and the Syrians of Zo'-ba, twenty thousand footmen, and of king Ma'-a-cah a thousand men, and of TIsh'-tob twelve thousand men.   Gen. 34:30 • *the men of Tob*

7 And when David heard of *it,* he sent Jo'-ab, and all the host of the mighty men.

8 And the children of Ammon came out, and put the battle in array at the entering in of the gate: and Rthe Syrians of Zo'-ba, and of Re'-hob, and Ish'-tob, and Ma'-a-cah, *were* by themselves in the field.   *v.* 6

9 When Jo'-ab saw that the front of the battle was against him before and behind, he

chose of all the choice *men* of Israel, and put *them* in array against the Syrians:

10 And the rest of the people he delivered into the hand of RA-bi'-shai his brother, that he might put *them* in array against the children of Ammon.   16:9

11 And he said, If the Syrians be too strong for me, then thou shalt help me: but if the children of Ammon be too strong for thee, then I will come and help thee.

12 RBe of good courage, and let us play the men for our people, and for the cities of our God: and the LORD do Tthat which seemeth him good.   Deut. 31:6 • *according to his will*

13 And Jo'-ab drew nigh, and the people that *were* with him, unto the battle against the Syrians: and they fled before him.

14 And when the children of Ammon saw that the Syrians were fled, then fled they also before A-bi'-shai, and entered into the city. RSo Jo'-ab returned from the children of Ammon, and came to Jerusalem.   11:1

Syria Is Defeated—1 Chr. 19:16-19

15 And when the Syrians saw that they were smitten before Israel, they gathered themselves together.

16 And Had-ar-e'-zer sent, and brought out the Syrians that *were* beyond Tthe river: and they came to He'-lam; and RSho'-bach the captain of the host of Had-ar-e'-zer *went* before them.   Euphrates • 8:3-8; 1 Chr. 19:16

17 And when it was told David, he gathered all Israel together, and passed over Jordan, and came to He'-lam. And the Syrians set themselves in array against David, and fought with him.

18 And the Syrians fled before Israel; and David slew *the men of* seven hundred chariots of the Syrians, and forty thousand horsemen, and Tsmote Sho'-bach the captain of their host, who died there.   *destroyed*

19 And when all the kings *that were* servants to Had-ar-e'-zer saw that they were smitten before Israel, they made peace with Israel, and RservedT them. So the Syrians feared to help the children of Ammon any more.   8:6 • *payed tribute to*

CHAPTER 11

The Sin of Adultery

ANDR it came to pass, after the year was expired, at the time when kings go forth *to battle,* that RDavid sent Jo'-ab, and his servants with him, and all Israel; and they destroyed the children of Ammon, and besieged Rab'-bah. But David tarried still at Jerusalem.   1 Chr. 20:1 • 10:14; 1 Kin. 20:22, 26

2 And it came to pass in an eveningtide, that David arose from off his bed, Rand walked upon the roof of the king's house: and

from the roof he ᴿsaw a woman washing herself; and the woman *was* very beautiful to look upon.   Deut. 22:8 • [Matt. 5:28]

3 And David sent and enquired after the woman. And *one* said, Is not this Bath–she′-ba, the daughter of ᵀE-li′-am, the wife ᴿof U-ri′-ah the Hit′-tite?   *Ammiel* • 23:39

4 And David sent messengers, and took her; and she came in unto him, and he lay with her; for she was purified from her uncleanness: and she returned unto her house.

5 And the woman conceived, and sent and told David, and said, I *am* with child.

Uriah Does Not Sleep with Bath-sheba

6 And David sent to Jo′-ab, *saying*, Send me U-ri′-ah the Hit′-tite. And Jo′-ab sent ᴿU-ri′-ah to David.   12:9

7 And when U-ri′-ah was come unto him, David ᵀdemanded *of him* how Jo′-ab did, ᴿand how the people did, and how the war prospered.   *asked for a report* • Gen. 37:14; 1 Sam. 17:22

8 And David said to U-ri′-ah, Go down to thy house, and wash thy feet. And U-ri′-ah departed out of the king's house, and there followed him a mess *of meat* from the king.

9 But U-ri′-ah slept at the door of the king's house with all the servants of his lord, and went not down to his house.

10 And when they had told David, saying, U-ri′-ah went not down unto his house, David said unto U-ri′-ah, Camest thou not from *thy* journey? why *then* didst thou not go down unto thine house?

11 And U-ri′-ah said unto David, The ark, and Israel, and Judah, abide in tents; and my lord Jo′-ab, and the servants of my lord, are encamped in the open fields; shall I then go into mine house, to eat and to drink, and to lie with my wife? *as* thou livest, and *as* thy soul liveth, I will not do this thing.

12 And David said to U-ri′-ah, Tarry here to day also, and to morrow I will let thee depart. So U-ri′-ah abode in Jerusalem that day, and the morrow.

13 ᴿAnd when David had called him, he did eat and drink before him; and he made him drunk: and at even he went out to lie on his bed ᴿwith the servants of his lord, but went not down to his house.   [Hab. 2:13] • v. 9

David Commands Uriah's Murder

14 And it came to pass in the morning, that David ᴿwrote a letter to Jo′-ab, and sent *it* by the hand of U-ri′-ah.   1 Kin. 21:8, 9

15 And he wrote in the letter, saying, Set ye U-ri′-ah in the forefront of the hottest battle, and ᵀretire ye from him, ᴿthat he may be smitten, and die.   *withdraw your help* • 12:9

16 And it came to pass, when Jo′-ab observed the city, that he assigned U-ri′-ah unto a place where he knew that valiant men *were*.

17 And the men of the city went out, and fought with Jo′-ab: and there fell *some* of the people of the servants of David; and ᴿU-ri′-ah the Hit′-tite died also.   *v. 21*

18 Then Jo′-ab sent and told David all the things concerning the war;

19 And charged the messenger, saying, When thou hast made an end of telling the matters of the war unto the king,

20 And if so be that the king's wrath arise, and he say unto thee, Wherefore approached ye so nigh unto the city when ye did fight? knew ye not that they would shoot from the wall?

21 Who smote ᴿA-bim′-e-lech the son of Je-rub′-be-sheth? did not a woman cast a piece of a millstone upon him from the wall, that he died in The′-bez? why went ye nigh the wall? then say thou, Thy servant U-ri′-ah the Hit′-tite is dead also.   Judg. 9:50–54

22 So the messenger went, and came and shewed David all that Jo′-ab had sent him for.

23 And the messenger said unto David, Surely the men prevailed against us, and came out unto us into the field, and we were upon them even unto the entering of the gate.

24 And the shooters shot from off the wall upon thy servants; and *some* of the king's servants be dead, and thy servant U-ri′-ah the Hit′-tite is dead also.

25 Then David said unto the messenger, Thus shalt thou say unto Jo′-ab, Let not this thing displease thee, for the sword devoureth one as well as another: make thy battle more strong against the city, and overthrow it: and encourage thou him.

David and Bath-sheba Marry

26 And when the wife of U-ri′-ah heard that U-ri′-ah her husband was dead,ᴿ she mourned for her husband.   Gen. 50:10; Deut. 34:8

27 And when the mourning was past, David sent and fetched her to his house, and she ᴿbecame his wife, and bare him a son. But the thing that David had done ᵀdispleased the LORD.   12:9 • *was evil in the eyes of*

CHAPTER 12

Prophecy of the Sword

AND the LORD sent Nathan unto David. And ᴿhe came unto him, and said unto him, There were two men in one city; the one rich, and the other poor.   Ps. 51, title

2 The rich *man* had exceeding many flocks and herds:

3 But the poor *man* had nothing, save ᴿone little ewe lamb, which he had bought and nourished up: and it grew up together with him, and with his children; it did eat of his own ᵀmeat, and drank of his own ᴿcup, and

lay in his bosom, and was unto him as a daughter.   11:3 · *food* · 1 Chr. 28:17

4 And there came a ᴿtraveller unto the rich man, and he spared to take of his own flock and of his own herd, to dress for the wayfaring man that was come unto him; but took the poor man's lamb, and dressed it for the man that was come to him.   Jer. 14:8

5 ᴿAnd David's anger was greatly kindled against the man; and he said to Nathan, *As* the LORD liveth, the man that hath done this thing ᵀshall surely die: 1 Kin. 20:40 · *worthy to die*

6 And he shall restore the lamb ᴿfourfold, because he did this thing, and because he had no pity.   [Ex. 22:1]

7 And Nathan said to David, Thou *art* the man. Thus saith the LORD God of Israel, I anointed thee king over Israel, and I delivered thee out of the hand of Saul;

8 And I gave thee thy master's house, and thy master's wives into thy bosom, and gave thee the house of Israel and of Judah; and if *that had been* too little, I would moreover have given unto thee such and such things.

9 Wherefore hast thou despised the commandment of the LORD, to do evil in his sight? thou hast killed U-ri'-ah the Hit'-tite with the sword, and ᴿhast taken his wife *to be* thy wife, and hast slain him with the sword of the children of Ammon.   11:27

10 Now therefore ᴿthe sword shall never depart from thine house; because thou hast despised me, and hast taken the wife of U-ri'-ah the Hit'-tite to be thy wife.   13:28

11 Thus saith the LORD, Behold, I will raise up evil against thee out of thine own house, and I will ᴿtake thy wives before thine eyes, and give *them* unto thy neighbour, and he shall lie with thy wives in the sight of this sun.   16:21, 22; Deut. 28:30

12 For thou didst *it* secretly: ᴿbut I will do this thing before all Israel, and ᵀbefore the sun.   16:22 · *in front of the whole world*

David Repents for His Sin

13 ᴿAnd David said unto Nathan, I have sinned against the LORD. And Nathan said unto David, The LORD also hath put away thy sin; thou shalt not die.   1 Sam. 15:24; Job 7:20

14 Howbeit, because by this deed thou hast given great occasion to the enemies of the LORD ᴿto blaspheme, the child also *that is* born unto thee shall surely die.   Is. 52:5

God Takes Away the Son of Adultery

15 And Nathan departed unto his house. And the LORD struck the child that U-ri'-ah's wife bare unto David, and it was very sick.

16 David therefore ᵀbesought God for the child; and David fasted, and went in, and ᴿlay all night upon the earth.   *prayed* · 13:31

17 And the elders of his house arose, *and* went to him, to raise him up from the earth:

but he would not, neither did he eat bread with them.

18 And it came to pass on the seventh day, that the child died. And the servants of David feared to tell him that the child was dead: for they said, Behold, while the child was yet alive, we spake unto him, and he would not hearken unto our voice: how will he then ᵀvex himself, if we tell him that the child is dead?   *be upset*

19 But when David saw that his servants whispered, David perceived that the child was dead: therefore David said unto his servants, Is the child dead? And they said, He is dead.

20 Then David arose from the earth, and washed, and anointed *himself*, and changed his apparel, and came into the house of the LORD, and worshipped: then he came to his own house; and when he required, they set bread before him, and he did eat.

21 Then said his servants unto him, What thing *is* this that thou hast done? thou didst fast and weep for the child, *while it was* alive; but when the child was dead, thou didst rise and eat bread.

22 And he said, While the child was yet alive, I fasted and wept: ᴿfor I said, ᴿWho can tell *whether* GOD will be gracious to me, that the child may live?   Is. 38:1, 5 · Jon. 3:9

23 But now he is dead, wherefore should I fast? can I bring him back again? I shall go to him, but he shall not return to me.

God Gives Another Son

24 And David comforted Bath-she'-ba his wife, and went in unto her, and lay with her: and she bare a son, and he called his name Solomon: and the LORD loved him.

25 And he sent by the hand of Nathan the prophet; and he called his name ᴿJed-i-di'-ah, because of the LORD.   Neh. 13:26; Matt. 3:17

Joab's Loyalty to David—1 Chr. 20:1-3

26 And ᴿJo'-ab fought against ᴿRab'-bah of the ᴿchildren of Ammon, and took the royal city.   1 Chr. 20:1 · 11:1 · Deut. 3:11

27 ᴿAnd Jo'-ab sent messengers to David, and said, I have fought against Rab'-bah, and have taken the city of waters.   1 Chr. 20:1-3

28 Now therefore gather the rest of the people together, and encamp against the city, and take it: lest I take the city, and it be called after my name.

29 And David gathered all the people together, and went to Rab'-bah, and fought against it, and took it.

30 And he took their king's crown from off his head, the weight whereof *was* a ᵀtalent of gold with the precious stones: and it was *set* on David's head. And he brought forth the spoil of the city in great abundance.   *91 lb.*

31 And he brought forth the people that *were* therein, and put *them* under saws, and under harrows of iron, and under axes of iron, and made them pass through the brick-kiln: and thus did he unto all the cities of the children of Ammon. So David and all the people returned unto Jerusalem.

CHAPTER 13

Incest in David's House

AND it came to pass after this, that Ab'-sa-lom the son of David had a fair sister, whose name *was* Ta'-mar; and ᴿAmnon the son of David ᵀloved her.   2 Sam. 3:2 • *desired*

2 And Amnon was so ᵀvexed, that he fell sick for his sister Ta'-mar; for she *was* a virgin; and Amnon thought it ᵀhard for him to do any thing to her.   *upset • difficult*

3 But Amnon had a friend, whose name *was* Jon'-a-dab, ᴿthe son of Shim'-e-ah Da-vid's brother: and Jon'-a-dab *was* a very ᵀsubtil man.   1 Sam. 16:9 • *crafty*

4 And he said unto him, Why *art* thou, being the king's son, ᵀlean from day to day? wilt thou not tell me? And Amnon said unto him, I love Ta'-mar, my brother Ab'-sa-lom's sister.   *haggard*

5 And Jon'-a-dab said unto him, Lay thee down on thy bed, and make thyself sick: and when thy father cometh to see thee, say unto him, I pray thee, let my sister Ta'-mar come, and give me meat, and dress the meat in my sight, that I may see *it*, and eat *it* at her hand.

6 So Amnon lay down, and ᵀmade himself sick: and when the king was come to see him, Amnon said unto the king, I pray thee, let Ta'-mar my sister come, and ᴿmake me a couple of cakes in my sight, that I may eat at her hand.   *pretended • Gen. 18:6*

7 Then David sent home to Ta'-mar, say-ing, Go now to thy brother Amnon's house, and ᵀdress him meat.   *cook him some food*

8 So Ta'-mar went to her brother Amnon's house; and he was laid down. And she took flour, and kneaded *it*, and made cakes in his sight, and did bake the cakes.

9 And she took a pan, and poured *them* out before him; but he refused to eat. And Amnon said, Have out all men from me. And they went out every man from him.

10 And Amnon said unto Ta'-mar, Bring the meat into the chamber, that I may eat of thine hand. And Ta'-mar took the cakes which she had made, and brought *them* into the chamber to Amnon her brother.

11 And when she had brought *them* unto him to eat, he took hold of her, and said unto her, Come lie with me, my sister.

12 And she answered him, Nay, my brother, ᴿdo not ᵀforce me; for no such thing ought to be done in Israel: do not thou this ᵀfolly.   Gen. 34:2 • *humble me • sin*

13 And I, whither shall I cause my shame to go? and as for thee, thou shalt be as one of the fools in Israel. Now therefore, I pray thee, speak unto the king; for he will not ᵀwithhold me from thee.   *refuse*

14 Howbeit he would not hearken unto her voice: but, being stronger than she, ᴿforced her, and lay with her.   [Deut. 22:25]

15 Then Amnon hated her ᵀexceedingly; so that the hatred wherewith he hated her *was* greater than the love wherewith he had loved her. And Amnon said unto her, Arise, be gone.   *very much*

16 And she said unto him, *There is* no cause: this evil in sending me away *is* greater than the other that thou didst unto me. But he would not hearken unto her.

17 Then he called his servant that minis-tered unto him, and said, Put now this woman out from me, and bolt the door after her.

18 And *she had* ᴿa garment of divers col-ours upon her: for with such robes were the king's daughters *that were* virgins apparelled. Then his servant brought her out, and bolted the door after her.   Gen. 37:3; Judg. 5:30

19 And Ta'-mar put ᴿashes on her head, and ᵀrent her garment of divers colours that *was* on her, and ᴿlaid her hand on her head, and went on crying.   Job 2:12 • *tore • Jer. 2:37*

20 And Ab'-sa-lom her brother said unto her, Hath ᵀAmnon thy brother been with thee? but hold now thy peace, my sister: he *is* thy brother; regard not this thing. So Ta'-mar remained desolate in her brother Ab'-sa-lom's house.   *Aminon*

Amnon Is Murdered

21 But when king David heard of all these things, he was very ᵀwroth.   *angry*

22 And Ab'-sa-lom spake unto his brother Amnon ᴿneither good nor bad: for Ab'-sa-lom ᴿhated Amnon, because he had forced his sister Ta'-mar.   Gen. 24:50; 31:24 • [Lev. 19:17, 18]

23 And it came to pass after two full years, that Ab'-sa-lom had sheepshearers in Ba'-al-ha'-zor, which *is* beside E'-phra-im: and Ab'-sa-lom invited all the king's sons.

24 And Ab'-sa-lom came to the king, and said, Behold now, thy servant hath sheep-shearers; let the king, I beseech thee, and his servants go with thy servant.

25 And the king said to Ab'-sa-lom, Nay, my son, let us not all now go, lest we be chargeable unto thee. And he pressed him: howbeit he would not go, but blessed him.

26 Then said Ab'-sa-lom, If not, I pray thee, let my brother Amnon go with us. And the king said unto him, Why should he go with thee?

27 But Ab'-sa-lom pressed him, that he let Amnon and all the king's sons go with him.

28 Now Ab'-sa-lom had commanded his servants, saying, Mark ye now when Amnon's heart is merry with wine, and when I say unto you, Smite Amnon; then kill him, fear not: have not I commanded you? be courageous, and be ^Tvaliant.   *strong*

29 And the servants of Ab'-sa-lom did unto Amnon as Ab'-sa-lom had commanded. Then all the king's sons arose, and every man gat him up upon his mule, and fled.

30 And it came to pass, while they were in the way, that tidings came to David, saying, Ab'-sa-lom hath slain all the king's sons, and there is not one of them left.

31 Then the king arose, and tare his garments, and lay on the earth; and all his servants stood by with their clothes rent.

32 And Jon'-a-dab, the son of Shim'-e-ah David's brother, answered and said, Let not my lord suppose *that* they have slain all the young men the king's sons; for Amnon only is dead: for by the ^Tappointment of Ab'-sa-lom this hath been determined from the day that he forced his sister Ta'-mar.   *order*

33 Now therefore ^Rlet not my lord the king take the thing to his heart, to think that all the king's sons are dead: for Amnon only is dead.   19:19

34 But Ab'-sa-lom fled. And the young man that kept the watch lifted up his eyes, and looked, and, behold, there came much people by the way of the hill side behind him.

35 And Jon'-a-dab said unto the king, Behold, the king's sons come: as thy servant said, so it is.

36 And it came to pass, as soon as he had ^Tmade an end of speaking, that, behold, the king's sons came, and lifted up their voice and wept: and the king also and all his servants wept ^Tvery sore.   *ceased · a great deal*

Flight of Absalom

37 But ^RAb'-sa-lom fled, and went to ^RTal'-mai, the son of ^TAm-mi'-hud, king of ^RGe'-shur. And *David* mourned for his son every day.   *v. 34 · 3:3 · Ammihur · 14:23, 32*

38 So ^RAb'-sa-lom fled, and went to Ge'-shur, and was there three years.   *v. 34*

39 And *the soul of* king David longed to go forth unto Ab'-sa-lom: for ^Rhe was ^Rcomforted^T concerning Amnon, seeing he was dead.   *12:19-23 · Gen. 38:12 · relieved*

CHAPTER 14

Return of Absalom

NOW Jo'-ab the son of Ze-ru'-iah perceived that the king's heart ^T*was* ^Rtoward Ab'-sa-lom.   *yearned for · 13:39*

2 And Jo'-ab sent to Te-ko'-ah, and fetched thence a wise woman, and said unto her, I pray thee, feign thyself to be a mourner, and put on now mourning apparel, and anoint not thyself with oil, but be as a woman that had a long time mourned for the dead:

3 And come to the king, and speak on this manner unto him. So Jo'-ab ^Rput the words in her mouth.   *v. 19; Ex. 4:15*

4 And when the woman of Te-ko'-ah spake to the king, she fell on her face to the ground, and did obeisance, and said, Help, O king.

5 And the king said unto her, What aileth thee? And she answered, I *am* indeed a widow woman, and mine husband is dead.

6 And thy handmaid had two sons, and they two strove together in the field, and *there was* none to part them, but the one smote the other, and slew him.

7 And, behold, the whole family is risen against thine handmaid, and they said, Deliver him that smote his brother, that we may kill him, for the life of his brother whom he slew; and we will destroy the heir also: and so they shall quench my coal which is left, and shall not leave to my husband *neither* name nor remainder upon the earth.

8 And the king said unto the woman, Go to thine house, and I will give charge concerning thee.

9 And the woman of Te-ko'-ah said unto the king, My lord, O king, the iniquity *be* on me, and on my father's house: ^Rand the king and his throne *be* guiltless.   *1 Kin. 2:33*

10 And the king said, Whosoever saith *ought* unto thee, bring him to me, and he shall not touch thee any more.

11 Then said she, I pray thee, let the king remember the LORD thy God, that thou wouldest not suffer the revengers of blood to destroy any more, lest they destroy my son. And he said, *As* the LORD liveth, there shall not one hair of thy son fall to the earth.

12 Then the woman said, Let thine handmaid, I pray thee, speak *one* word unto my lord the king. And he said, Say on.

13 And the woman said, Wherefore then hast thou thought such a thing against the people of God? for the king doth speak this thing as one which is faulty, in that the king doth not fetch home again his banished.

14 For we must needs die, and *are* as water spilt on the ground, which cannot be gathered up again; neither doth God respect *any* person: yet doth he devise means, that his banished be not expelled from him.

15 Now therefore that I am come to speak of this thing unto my lord the king, *it is* because the people have made me afraid: and thy handmaid said, I will now speak unto the king; it may be that the king will perform the ^Trequest of his handmaid.   *word*

16 For the king will hear, to deliver his handmaid out of the ^Thand of the man *that*

would destroy me and my son together out of the Rinheritance of God.   *palm* • Deut. 32:9

17 Then thine handmaid said, The word of my lord the king shall now be comfortable: for Ras an angel of God, so is my lord the king to discern good and bad: therefore the LORD thy God will be with thee.   *v. 20*

18 Then the king answered and said unto the woman, Hide not from me, I pray thee, the thing that I shall ask thee. And the woman said, Let my lord the king now speak.

19 And the king said, *Is not* the hand of Jo'-ab with thee in all this? And the woman answered and said, *As* thy soul liveth, my lord the king, none can turn to the right hand or to the left from ought that my lord the king hath spoken: for thy servant Jo'-ab, he bade me, and he put all these words in the mouth of thine handmaid:

20 To fetch about this form of speech hath thy servant Jo'-ab done this thing: and my lord *is* wise, Raccording to the wisdom of an angel of God, to Rknow all *things* that *are* in the earth.   *v. 17; 19:27 • 18:13*

21 And the king said unto Jo'-ab, Behold now, I have done this thing: go therefore, bring the young man Ab'-sa-lom again.

22 And Jo'-ab fell to the ground on his face, and bowed himself, and thanked the king: and Jo'-ab said, To day thy servant knoweth that I have found grace in thy sight, my lord, O king, in that the king hath fulfilled the Trequest of This servant.   *word • your*

23 So Jo'-ab arose and went to RGe'-shur, and brought Ab'-sa-lom to Jerusalem. 13:37, 38

24 And the king said, Let him turn to his own house, and let him notT see my face. So Ab'-sa-lom returned to his own house, and saw not the king's face.   *not come to see me*

Deceit of Absalom

25 But in all Israel there was none to be so much praised as Ab'-sa-lom for his beauty: from the sole of his foot even to the crown of his head there was no blemish in him.

26 And when he Tpolled his head, (for it was at every year's end that he polled *it:* because *the hair* was heavy on him, therefore he polled it:) he weighed the hair of his head at Ttwo hundred shek'-els after the king's weight.   *cut his hair • 5 lb.*

27 And Runto Ab'-sa-lom there were born three sons, and one daughter, whose name *was* RTa'-mar: she was a woman of a Tfair countenance.   *18:18 • 13:1 • very beautiful*

28 So Ab'-sa-lom dwelt two full years in Jerusalem, and saw not the king's face.

29 Therefore Ab'-sa-lom sent for Jo'-ab, to have sent him to the king; but he would not come to him: and when he sent again the second time, he would not come.

30 Therefore he said unto his servants, See, Jo'-ab's field is near mine, and he hath barley there; go and set it on fire. And Ab'-sa-lom's servants set the field on fire.

31 Then Jo'-ab arose, and came to Ab'-sa-lom unto *his* house, and said unto him, Wherefore have thy servants set my field on fire?

32 And Ab'-sa-lom answered Jo'-ab, Behold, I sent unto thee, saying, Come hither, that I may send thee to the king, to say, Wherefore am I come from Ge'-shur? *it had been* good for me *to have been* there still: now therefore let me Tsee the king's face; Rand if there be *any* iniquity in me, let him kill me.   *come in to the king's court* • 1 Sam. 20:8

33 So Jo'-ab came to the king, and told him: and when he had called for Ab'-sa-lom, he came to the king, and bowed himself on his face to the ground before the king: and the king kissed Ab'-sa-lom.

CHAPTER 15

AND it came to pass after this, that Ab'-sa-lom prepared him chariots and horses, and fifty men to run before him.

2 And Ab'-sa-lom rose up early, Rand stood beside the way of the gate: and it was so, that when any man that had a controversy came to the king for judgment, then Ab'-sa-lom called unto him, and said, Of what city *art* thou? And he said, Thy servant *is* of one of the tribes of Israel.   *19:8; Ruth 4:1*

3 And Ab'-sa-lom said unto him, See, thy matters *are* good and right; but *there is* no man *deputed* of the king to hear thee.

4 Ab'-sa-lom said moreover, Oh that I were made judge in the land, that every man which hath any suit or cause might come unto me, and I would do him justice!

5 And it was so, that when any man came nigh *to him* to do him obeisance, he put forth his hand, and took him, and kissed him.

6 And on this manner did Ab'-sa-lom to all Israel that came to the king for judgment: Rso Ab'-sa-lom Tstole the hearts of the men of Israel.   [Rom. 16:18] • *won the favour*

Rebellion of Absalom

7 And it came to pass after forty years, that Ab'-sa-lom said unto the king, I pray thee, let me go and pay my vow, which I have vowed unto the LORD, in He'-bron.

8 For thy servant vowed a vow while I abode at Ge'-shur in Syria, saying, If the LORD shall bring me again indeed to Jerusalem, then I will Tserve the LORD.   *worship*

9 And the king said unto him, Go in peace. So he arose, and went to He'-bron.

10 But Ab'-sa-lom sent spies throughout all the tribes of Israel, saying, As soon as ye hear the sound of the trumpet, then ye shall say, Ab'-sa-lom reigneth in He'-bron.

11 And with Ab'-sa-lom went two hundred men out of Jerusalem, *that were* called; and they went in their ᵀsimplicity, and they knew not any thing.   *innocence*

12 And Ab'-sa-lom sent for A-hith'-o-phel the Gi'-lo-nite, David's counsellor, from his city, *even* from Gi'-loh, while he ᵀoffered sacrifices. And the conspiracy was strong; for the people ᴿincreased continually with Ab'-sa-lom.   *came to worship · Ps. 3:1*

Flight of David

13 And there came a messenger to David, saying, ᴿThe hearts of the men of Israel ᵀare after Ab'-sa-lom.   *v. 6; Judg. 9:3 · are committed to*

14 And David said unto all his servants that *were* with him at ᴿJerusalem, Arise, and let us ᴿflee; for we shall not *else* escape from Ab'-sa-lom: make speed to depart, lest he overtake us suddenly, and bring evil upon us, and ᵀsmite the city with the edge of the sword.   *12:11 · 19:9 · destroy*

15 And the king's servants said unto the king, Behold, thy servants *are ready to do* whatsoever my lord the king shall appoint.

16 And the king went forth, and all his household after him. And the king left ᴿten women, *which were* concubines, to keep the house.   *16:21, 22*

17 And the king went forth, and all the people after him, and ᵀtarried in a place that was far off.   *rested*

18 And all his servants passed on beside him; ᴿand all the Cher'-e-thites, and all the Pel'-e-thites, and all the Git'-tites, ᴿsix hundred men which came after him from Gath, passed on before the king.   *8:18 · 1 Sam. 23:13*

19 Then said the king to It'-tai the Git'-tite, Wherefore goest thou also with us? return to thy place, and abide with the king: for thou *art* a stranger, and also an exile.

20 Whereas thou camest *but* yesterday, should I this day make thee go up and down with us? seeing I go ᴿwhither I may, return thou, and take back thy brethren: mercy and truth *be* with thee.   *1 Sam. 23:13*

21 And It'-tai answered the king, and said,ᴿ As the LORD liveth, and *as* my lord the king liveth, surely in what place my lord the king shall be, whether in death or life, even there also will thy servant be.   *Ruth 1:16, 17*

22 And David said to It'-tai, Go and pass over. And It'-tai the Git'-tite passed over, and all his men, and all the little ones that *were* with him.

23 And all the country wept with a loud voice, and all the people ᵀpassed over: the king also himself passed over the brook Kid'-ron, and all the people passed over, toward ᴿthe way of the wilderness.   *fled · v. 28*

24 And lo Za'-dok also, and all the Levites *were* with him, bearing the ark of the cov-

enant of God: and they set down the ark of God; and A-bi'-a-thar went up, until all the people had done passing out of the city.

25 And the king said unto Za'-dok, Carry back the ark of God into the city: if I ᵀshall find favour in the eyes of the LORD, he ᴿwill bring me again, and shew me *both* it, and his habitation: *am favoured by Providence · [Ps. 43:3]*

26 But if he thus say, I have no delight in thee; behold, *here am* I, let him do to me ᵀas seemeth good unto him.   *according to his will*

27 The king said also unto Za'-dok the priest, *Art not* thou a ᴿseerᵀ? return into the city in peace, and ᴿyour two sons with you, A-him'-a-az thy son, and Jonathan the son of A-bi'-a-thar.   *1 Sam. 9:9 · prophet · 17:17*

28 See, ᴿI will tarry in the plain of the wilderness, until there come word from you to ᵀcertify me.   *17:16; Josh. 5:10 · assure*

29 Za'-dok therefore and A-bi'-a-thar carried the ark of God again to Jerusalem: and they tarried there.

30 And David ᵀwent up by the ascent of *mount* Olivet, and wept as he went up, and ᴿhad his head covered, and he went barefoot: and all the people that *was* with him covered every man his head, and they went up, weeping as they went up.   *travelled · Esth. 6:12*

31 And *one* told David, saying, ᴿA-hith'-o-phel *is* among the conspirators with Ab'-sa-lom. And David said, O LORD, I pray thee, ᴿturn the ᵀcounsel of A-hith'-o-phel into foolishness.   *Ps. 3:1, 2 · 16:23; 17:14, 23 · advice*

32 And it came to pass, that *when* David was come to the top *of the mount*, where he worshipped God, behold, Hu'-shai the ᴿAr'-chite came to meet him ᴿwith his coat rent, and earth upon his head: *Josh. 16:2 · 1:2*

33 Unto whom David said, If thou ᵀpassest on with me, then thou shalt be ᴿa burden unto me: *go · 19:35*

34 But if thou return to the city, and say unto ᴿAb'-sa-lom, I will be thy servant, O king; *as* I *have been* thy father's servant hitherto, so *will* I now also *be* thy servant: then mayest thou for me ᵀdefeat the counsel of A-hith'-o-phel.   *16:19 · block the advice*

35 And *hast thou* not there with thee Za'-dok and A-bi'-a-thar the priests? therefore it shall be, *that* what thing soever thou shalt hear out of the king's house, thou shalt tell *it* to Za'-dok and A-bi'-a-thar the priests.

36 Behold, *they have* there ᴿwith them their two sons, A-him'-a-az Za'-dok's *son*, and Jonathan A-bi'-a-thar's *son;* and ᴿby them ye shall send unto me every thing that ye can hear.   *v. 27 · 17:17*

37 So Hu'-shai ᴿDavid's ᴿfriend came into the city, ᴿand Ab'-sa-lom came into Jerusalem.   *16:16; 1 Chr. 27:33 · 1 Kin. 5:1 · 16:15*

CHAPTER 16

AND when David was a little past the top *of the hill*, behold, [R]Zi'-ba the servant of Me-phib'-o-sheth met him, with a couple of asses saddled, and upon them two hundred *loaves* of bread, and an hundred bunches of raisins, and an hundred of summer fruits, and a bottle of wine.   9:2–13

2 And the king said unto Zi'-ba, What meanest thou by these? And Zi'-ba said, The asses *be* for the king's household to ride on; and the bread and summer fruit for the young men to eat; and the wine, that such as be faint in the wilderness may drink.

3 And the king said, And where *is* [R]thy master's son? And Zi'-ba said unto the king, Behold, he abideth at Jerusalem: for he said, To day shall the house of Israel restore me the kingdom of my father.   9:9, 10

4 Then said the king to Zi'-ba, Behold, thine *are* all that *pertained* unto Me-phib'-o-sheth. And Zi'-ba said, I humbly beseech thee *that* I may [T]find grace in thy sight, my lord, O king.   *have your good will*

5 And when king David came to Ba-hu'-rim, behold, thence came out a man of the family of the house of Saul, whose name *was* [R]Shim'-e-i, the son of Ge'-ra: he came forth, and cursed still as he came.   19:16

6 And he cast stones at David, and at all the servants of king David: and [R]all the people and all the mighty men *were* on his right hand and on his left.   [Ex. 22:28]

7 [R]And thus said Shim'-e-i when he cursed, [T]Come out, come out, thou [T]bloody man, and thou man of Be'-li-al: 12:9 • *begone • murderer*

8 The LORD hath returned upon thee all the blood of the house of Saul, in whose stead thou hast reigned; and the LORD hath delivered the kingdom into the hand of Ab'-sa-lom thy son: and, behold, thou *art taken* in thy mischief, because thou *art* a bloody man.

9 Then said A-bi'-shai the son of Ze-ru'-iah unto the king, Why should this dead dog curse my lord the king? let me go over, I pray thee, and [T]take off his head.   *behead him*

10 And the king said, What have I to do with you, ye sons of Ze-ru'-iah? so let him curse, because the LORD hath said unto him, Curse David. [R]Who shall then say, Wherefore hast thou done so?   [Rom. 9:20]

11 And David said to A-bi'-shai, and to all his servants, Behold, my son, which came forth of my bowels, seeketh my life: how much more now *may this* Benjamite *do it*? let him alone, and let him curse; for [T]the LORD hath bidden him.   *he is doing as he is led*

12 It may be that the LORD will look on mine affliction, and that the LORD will requite me good for his cursing this day.

13 And as David and his men went by the way, Shim'-e-i went along on the hill's side over against him, and cursed as he went, and threw stones at him, and cast dust.

14 And the king, and all the people that *were* with him, came weary, and refreshed themselves there.

Reign of Absalom

15 And [R]Ab'-sa-lom, and all the people the men of Israel, came to Jerusalem, and A-hith'-o-phel with him.   15:12, 37

16 And it came to pass, when Hu'-shai the Ar'-chite, David's friend, was come unto Ab'-sa-lom, that Hu'-shai said unto Ab'-sa-lom, God save the king, God save the king.

17 And Ab'-sa-lom said to Hu'-shai, *Is* this thy kindness to thy friend? [R]why wentest thou not with thy friend?   [Prov. 17:17]

18 And Hu'-shai said unto Ab'-sa-lom, Nay; but whom the LORD, and this people, and all the men of Israel, choose, his will I be, and with him will I abide.

19 And again, [R]whom should I serve? *should I* not *serve* in the presence of his son? as I have served in thy father's presence, so will I be in thy presence.   15:34

20 Then said Ab'-sa-lom to A-hith'-o-phel, Give counsel among you what we shall do.

21 And A-hith'-o-phel said unto Ab'-sa-lom, Go in unto thy father's concubines, which he hath left to keep the house; and all Israel shall hear that thou art abhorred of thy father: then shall [R]the hands of all that *are* with thee be strong.   2:7; Zech. 8:13

22 So they spread Ab'-sa-lom a tent upon the top of the house; and [R]Ab'-sa-lom went in unto his father's concubines [R]in the sight of all Israel.   15:16; 20:3 • 12:11, 12

23 And the counsel of A-hith'-o-phel, which he counselled in those days, *was* as if a man had enquired at the oracle of God: so *was* all the counsel of A-hith'-o-phel both with David and with Ab'-sa-lom.

CHAPTER 17

MOREOVER [R]A-hith'-o-phel said unto Ab'-sa-lom, Let me now choose out twelve thousand men, and I will arise and pursue after David this night: *v.* 14

2 And I will come upon him while he *is* weary and weak handed, and will make him afraid: and all the people that *are* with him shall flee; and I will smite the king only:

3 And I will bring back all the people unto thee: the man whom thou seekest *is* as if all returned: *so* all the people shall be in peace.

4 And the saying pleased Ab'-sa-lom well, and all the elders of Israel.

5 Then said Ab'-sa-lom, [R]Call now Hu'-shai

the Ar'-chite also, and let us hear likewise what he saith.   15:32-34

6 And when Hu'-shai was come to Ab'-sa-lom, Ab'-sa-lom spake unto him, saying, A-hith'-o-phel hath spoken after this manner: shall we do *after* his saying? if not; speak thou.

7 And Hu'-shai said unto Ab'-sa-lom, The ^Tcounsel that A-hith'-o-phel hath given *is* not good at this time.   *advice*

8 For, said Hu'-shai, thou knowest thy father and his men, that they *be* mighty men, and they *be* ^Tchafed in their minds, as a bear robbed of her ^Twhelps in the field: and thy father *is* a man of war, and will not ^Tlodge with the people.   *angered • cubs • sleep*

9 Behold, he is hid now in some pit, or in some *other* place: and it will come to pass, when some of them be ^Toverthrown at the first, that whosoever heareth it will say, There is a slaughter among the people that follow Ab'-sa-lom.   *fallen*

10 And he also *that is* ^Tvaliant, whose heart *is* as the heart of a lion, shall utterly ^Rmelt: for all Israel knoweth that thy father *is* a mighty man, and *they* which *be* with him *are* valiant men.   *strong • Josh. 2:11*

11 Therefore I counsel that all Israel be generally gathered unto thee, from Dan even to Be'-er-she'-ba, ^Ras the sand that *is* by the sea for multitude; and that thou go to battle in thine own person.   Gen. 22:17

12 So shall we come upon him in some place where he shall be found, and we will light upon him ^Ras the dew falleth on the ground: and of him and of all the men that *are* with him there shall not be left so much as one.   Mic. 5:7

13 Moreover, if he be gotten into a city, then shall all Israel bring ropes to that city, and we will draw it into the river, until there be not one small stone found there.

14 And Ab'-sa-lom and all the men of Israel said, The counsel of Hu'-shai the Ar'-chite *is* better than the counsel of A-hith'-o-phel. For ^Rthe LORD had ^Tappointed to defeat the good counsel of A-hith'-o-phel, to the intent that the LORD might bring evil upon Ab'-sa-lom.   15:31, 34 • *arranged*

15 ^RThen said Hu'-shai unto Za'-dok and to A-bi'-a-thar the priests, Thus and thus did A-hith'-o-phel counsel Ab'-sa-lom and the elders of Israel; and thus and thus have I counselled.   15:35

16 Now therefore send quickly, and tell David, saying, ^TLodge not this night in the plains of the wilderness, but speedily pass over; lest the king be swallowed up, and all the people that *are* with him.   *do not settle down*

17 Now Jonathan and A-him'-a-az ^Rstayed by En-ro'-gel; for they might not be seen to come into the city: and a ^Twench went and

told them; and they went and told king David.   Josh. 2:4-7 • *maidservant*

18 Nevertheless a lad saw them, and told Ab'-sa-lom: but they went both of them away quickly, and came to a man's house ^Rin Ba-hu'-rim, which had a well in his court; whither they went down.   16:5

19 And ^Rthe woman took and spread a covering over the well's mouth, and spread ground corn thereon; and the thing was not known.   Josh. 2:4-6

20 And when Ab'-sa-lom's servants came to the woman to the house, they said, Where *is* A-him'-a-az and Jonathan? And ^Rthe woman said unto them, They be gone over the brook of water. And when they had sought and could not find *them*, they returned to Jerusalem.   Ex. 1:19; Josh. 2:4, 5

21 And it came to pass, after they were departed, that they came up out of the well, and went and told king David, and said unto David, Arise, and ^Tpass quickly over the water: for thus hath A-hith'-o-phel coun-selled against you.   *flee quickly away from*

22 Then David arose, and all the people that *were* with him, and they ^Tpassed over Jordan: by the ^Tmorning light there lacked not one of them that was not gone over Jordan.   *fled away from • dawn*

23 And when A-hith'-o-phel saw that his counsel was not followed, he saddled *his* ass, and arose, and ^Tgat him home to his house, to his city, and put his household in order, and hanged himself, and died, and was buried in the sepulchre of his father.   *got*

24 Then David came to ^RMa-ha-na'-im. And Ab'-sa-lom passed over Jordan, he and all the men of Israel with him.   Gen. 32:2

25 And Ab'-sa-lom made Am'-a-sa captain of the host instead of Jo'-ab: which Am'-a-sa *was* a man's son, whose name *was* ^TIth'-ra an Israelite, that went in to Ab'-i-gail the daugh-ter of Na'-hash, sister to Ze-ru'-iah Jo'-ab's mother.   *Jether an Ishmaelite*

26 So Israel and Ab'-sa-lom ^Tpitched in the land of Gil'-e-ad.   *made camp*

27 And it came to pass, when David was come to Ma-ha-na'-im, that Sho'-bi the son of Na'-hash of Rab'-bah of the children of Am-mon, and ^RMa'-chir the son of Am'-mi-el of Lo-de'-bar, and ^RBar-zil'-lai the Gil'-e-ad-ite of Ro-ge'-lim,   9:4 • 1 Kin. 2:7

28 Brought beds, and ^Tbasons, and earthen vessels, and wheat, and barley, and flour, and parched *corn*, and beans, and lentiles, and parched ^Tpulse,   *cups • seeds*

29 And honey, and butter, and sheep, and cheese of ^Tkine, for David, and for the people that *were* with him, to eat: for they said, The people ^Tis hungry, and weary, and thirsty, ^Rin the wilderness.   *cows • are •* 16:2

CHAPTER 18

Absalom's Murder

AND David ᵀnumbered the people that *were* with him, and ᴿset captains of thousands and captains of hundreds over them.   *organized* • Ex. 18:25; Num. 31:14; 1 Sam. 22:7

2 And David sent forth a third part of the people under the hand of Jo′-ab, and a third part under the hand of A-bi′-shai the son of Ze-ru′-iah, Jo′-ab's brother, ᴿand a third part under the hand of It′-tai the Git′-tite. And the king said unto the people, I will surely go forth with you myself also.   15:19

3 But the people answered, Thou shalt not go forth: for if we flee away, they will not care for us; neither if half of us die, will they care for us: but now *thou art* worth ten thousand of us: therefore now *it is* better that thou succour us out of the city.

4 And the king said unto them, What seemeth you best I will do. And the king stood by the gate side, and all the people came out by hundreds and by thousands.

5 And the king commanded Jo′-ab and A-bi′-shai and It′-tai, saying, *Deal* gently for my sake with the young man, *even* with Ab′-sa-lom. ᴿAnd all the people heard when the king gave all the captains charge concerning Ab′-sa-lom.   *v. 12*

6 So the people went out into the field against Israel: and the battle was in the ᴿwoodᵀ of E′-phra-im;   Josh. 17:15, 18 • *forest*

7 ᴿWhere the people of Israel were slain before the servants of David, and there was there a great slaughter that day of twenty thousand *men*.   [Prov. 11:21]

8 For the battle was there scattered over the face of all the country: and the ᵀwood ᵀdevoured more people that day than the sword devoured.   *forest* • *caused the death of*

9 And Ab′-sa-lom met the servants of David. And Ab′-sa-lom rode upon a mule, and the mule went under the thick boughs of a great oak, and ᴿhis head caught hold of the oak, and he was ᵀtaken up between the heaven and the earth; and the mule that *was* under him went away.   14:26 • *suspended*

10 And a certain man saw *it*, and told Jo′-ab, and said, Behold, I saw Ab′-sa-lom hanged in an oak.

11 And Jo′-ab said unto the man that told him, And, behold, thou sawest *him*, and why didst thou not smite him there to the ground? and I would have given thee ᵀten *shek′-els* of silver, and a girdle. $72.80

12 And the man said unto Jo′-ab, Though I should receive a thousand *shek′-els* of silver in mine hand, *yet* would I not put forth mine hand against the king's son: ᴿfor in our hearing the king charged thee and A-bi′-shai and It′-tai, saying, Beware that none *touch* the young man Ab′-sa-lom.   *v. 5*

13 Otherwise I should have wrought falsehood against mine own life: for there is no matter hid from the king, and thou thyself wouldest have set thyself against *me*.

14 Then said Jo′-ab, I may not ᵀtarry thus ᵀwith thee. ᴿAnd he took three darts in his hand, and thrust them through the heart of Ab′-sa-lom, while he *was* yet alive in the midst of the oak.   *delay* • *before thee* • 14:30

15 And ten young men that bare Jo′-ab's armour compassed about and ᵀsmote Ab′-sa-lom, and slew him.   *struck*

16 And ᴿJo′-ab blew the trumpet, and the people returned from pursuing after Israel: for Jo-ab held back the people.   2:28; 20:22

17 And they took Ab′-sa-lom, and cast him into a great pit in the wood, and ᴿlaid a very great heap of stones upon him: and all Israel fled every one to his tent.   Josh. 7:26

18 Now Ab′-sa-lom in his lifetime had taken and ᴿreared up for himself a ᵀpillar, which *is* in the king's dale: for he said, ᴿI have no son to keep my name in remembrance: and he called the pillar after his own name: and it is called unto this day, Ab′-sa-lom's place.   15:12 • *monument* • 14:27

19 Then saidᴿ A-him′-a-az the son of Za′-dok, Let me now run, and bear the king tidings, how ᴿthat the Lᴏʀᴅ hath avenged him of his enemies.   15:36 • *v. 31*

20 And Jo′-ab said unto him, Thou shalt not bear tidings this day, but thou shalt bear tidings another day: but this day thou shalt bear no tidings, because the king's son is dead.

21 Then said Jo′-ab to Cu′-shi, Go tell the king what thou hast seen. And Cu′-shi bowed himself unto Jo′-ab, and ran.

22 Then said A-him′-a-az the son of Za′-dok yet again to Jo′-ab, But howsoever, let me, I pray thee, also run after Cu′-shi. And Jo′-ab said, Wherefore wilt thou run, my son, seeing that thou hast no tidings ready?

23 But ᵀhowsoever, *said he*, let me run. And he said unto him, Run. Then A-him′-a-az ran by the way of the plain, and ᵀoverran Cu′-shi.   *come what may* • *outran*

24 And David sat between the two gates: and the watchman went up to the roof over the gate unto the wall, and lifted up his eyes, and looked, and behold a man running alone.

25 And the watchman cried, and told the king. And the king said, If he *be* alone, ᵀ*there is* tidings in his mouth. And he came apace, and drew near.   *he is bringing a message*

26 And the watchman saw another man running: and the watchman called unto the ᴿporter, and said, Behold *another* man running alone. And the king said, He also bringeth tidings.   1 Chr. 16:42

27 And the watchman said, Me thinketh the running of the foremost ᴿis like the running of A-him′-a-az the son of Za′-dok.

And the king said, ᴿHe *is* a good man, and cometh with good tidings. 2 Kin. 9:20 • 1 Kin. 1:42

28 And A-him'-a-az called, and said unto the king, All is well. And ᴿhe fell down to the earth upon his face before the king, and said, Blessed *be* the LORD thy God, which hath delivered up the men that lifted up their hand against my lord the king. 14:4

29 And the king said, ᴿIs the young man Ab'-sa-lom safe? And A-him'-a-az answered, When Jo'-ab sent the king's servant, and *me* thy servant, I saw a great tumult, but I knew not what *it was.* 20:9

30 And the king said *unto him,* Turn aside, *and* stand here. And he turned aside, and stood still.

31 And, behold, Cu'-shi came; and Cu'-shi said, Tidings, my lord the king: for the LORD hath ᴿavenged thee this day of all them that rose up against thee. v. 19; Judg. 5:31

32 And the king said unto Cu'-shi, ᴿIs the young man Ab'-sa-lom safe? And Cu'-shi answered, ᴿThe enemies of my lord the king, and all that rise against thee to do *thee* hurt, be as *that* young man *is.* v. 29 • 1 Sam. 25:26

33 And the king was much moved, and went up to the chamber over the gate, and wept: and as he went, thus he said, ᴿO my son Ab'-sa-lom, my son, my son Ab'-sa-lom! would God I had died for thee, O Ab'-sa-lom, my son, my son! 19:4; Ex. 32:32; Rom. 9:3

CHAPTER 19

Reproof of Joab

AND it was told Jo'-ab, Behold, the king weepeth and mourneth for Ab'-sa-lom.

2 And the victory that day was *turned* into mourning unto all the people: ᴿfor the people heard say that day how the king was grieved for his son. 18:5, 14

3 And the people gat them by stealth that day into the city, as people being ashamed steal away when they flee in battle.

4 But the king covered his face, and the king cried with a loud voice, O my son Ab'-sa-lom, O Ab'-sa-lom, my son, my son!

5 And Jo'-ab came into the house to the king, and said, Thou hast shamed this day the faces of all thy servants, which this day have saved thy life, and the lives of thy sons and of thy daughters, and the lives of thy wives, and the lives of thy concubines;

6 In that thou lovest thine enemies, and hatest thy friends. For thou hast declared this day, that thou regardest neither princes nor servants: for this day I perceive, that if Ab'-sa-lom had lived, and all we had died this day, then it had pleased thee well.

7 Now therefore arise, go forth, and speak comfortably unto thy servants: for I swear by the LORD, if thou go not forth, there will not

tarry one with thee this night: and that will be worse unto thee than all the evil that befell thee from thy youth until now.

Restoration of David

8 Then the king arose, and sat in the gate. And they told unto all the people, saying, Behold, the king doth ᴿsit in the gate. And all the people came before the king: for Israel had fled every man to his tent. 15:2

9 And all the people were at strife throughout all the tribes of Israel, saying, The king saved us out of the hand of our enemies, and ᴿhe delivered us out of the hand of the Phi-lis'-tines; and now he is ᴿfled out of the land for Ab'-sa-lom. 5:20 • 15:14

10 And Ab'-sa-lom, whomᴿ we anointed over us, is dead in battle. Now therefore why speak ye not a word of bringing the king back? 12:7

11 And ᴿking David sent to Za'-dok and to A-bi'-a-thar the priests, saying, Speak unto the elders of Judah, saying, Why are ye the last to bring the king back to his house? seeing the speech of all Israel is come to the king, ᵀeven to his house. 15:29 • *to bring him*

12 Ye *are* my brethren, ye *are* ᴿmy bones and my flesh: wherefore then are ye the last to bring back the king? 5:1

13 ᴿAnd say ye to Am'-a-sa, *Art* thou not of my bone, and of my flesh? God do so to me, and more also, if thou be not captain of the host before me ᵀcontinually in the ᵀroom of Jo'-ab. 17:25 • *permanently* • *place*

14 And he ᵀbowed the heart of all the men of Judah, even as *the heart of* one man; so that they sent *this word* unto the king, Return thou, and all thy servants. *moved the mind*

15 So the king returned, and came to Jordan. And Judah came to ᴿGil'-gal, to go to meet the king, to conduct the ᴿking over Jordan. Josh. 5:9; 1 Sam. 11:14, 15 • 17:22

16 And ᴿShim'-e-i the son of Ge'-ra, a Benjamite, which *was* of Ba-hu'-rim, hasted and came down with the men of Judah to meet king David. 16:5; 1 Kin. 2:8

17 And *there were* a thousand men of Benjamin with him, and ᴿZi'-ba the servant of the house of Saul, and his fifteen sons and his twenty servants with him; and they went over Jordan before the king. 9:2, 10

18 And there went over a ferry boat to carry over the king's household, and to do what he thought good. And Shim'-e-i the son of Ge'-ra fell down before the king, as he was come over Jordan;

19 And said unto the king, Letᵀ not my lord impute iniquity unto me, neither do thou remember that which thy servant did perversely the day that my lord the king went out of Jerusalem, that the king should take it to his heart. *do not hold me responsible*

20 For thy servant doth know that I have sinned: therefore, behold, I am come the first this day of all ᴿthe house of Joseph to go down to meet my lord the king.   16:5

21 But A-bi'-shai the son of Ze-ru'-iah answered and said, Shall not Shim'-e-i be put to death for this, because he ᴿcursed the Lᴏʀᴅ's anointed?   [Ex. 22:28; 1 Sam. 26:9]

22 And David said, What have I to do with you, ye sons of Ze-ru'-iah, that ye should this day be adversaries unto me? ᴿshall there any man be put to death this day in Israel? for do not I ᵀknow that I *am* this day king over Israel?   1 Sam. 11:13 • *realize*

23 Therefore ᴿthe king said unto Shim'-e-i, Thou shalt not die. And the king sware unto him.   1 Kin. 2:8, 9, 37, 46

24 And ᴿMe-phib'-o-sheth the son of Saul came down to meet the king, and had neither ᵀdressed his feet, nor trimmed his beard, nor washed his clothes, from the day the king departed until the day he came *again* in peace.   9:6 • *cared for*

25 And it came to pass, when he was come to Jerusalem to meet the king, that the king said unto him, ᴿWherefore wentest not thou with me, Me-phib'-o-sheth?   16:17

26 And he answered, My lord, O king, my servant deceived me: for thy servant said, I will saddle me an ass, that I may ride thereon, and go ᵀto the king; ᴿbecause thy servant *is* lame.   *with* • 9:3

27 And he hath ᵀslandered thy servant unto my lord the king; but my lord the king *is* as ᵀan angel of God: do therefore *what is* good in thine eyes.   *deceived* • *a messenger*

28 For all *of* my father's house were but dead men before my lord the king: yet didst thou set thy servant among them that did eat at thine own table. What right therefore have I yet to cry any more unto the king?

29 And the king said unto him, Why speakest thou any more of thy matters? I have said, Thou and Zi'-ba divide the land.

30 And Me-phib'-o-sheth said unto the king, Yea, let him take all, forasmuch as my lord the king is come again in peace unto his own house.

31 And Bar-zil'-lai the Gil'-e-ad-ite came down from Ro-ge'-lim, and went over Jordan with the king, to conduct him over Jordan.

32 Now Bar-zil'-lai was a very aged man, *even* fourscore years old: and he had provided the king of sustenance while he lay at Ma-ha-na'-im; for he *was* a very great man.

33 And the king said unto Bar-zil'-lai, Come thou over with me, and I will feed thee with me in Jerusalem.

34 And Bar-zil'-lai said unto the king, ᴿHow long have I to live, that I should go up with the king unto Jerusalem?   Gen. 47:8

35 I *am* this day ᴿfourscore years old: and can I discern between good and evil? can thy servant taste what I eat or what I drink? can I hear any more the voice of singing men and singing women? wherefore then should thy servant be yet a burden unto my lord the king?   Ps. 90:10

36 Thy servant will go a little way over Jordan with the king: and why should the king recompense it me with such a reward?

37 Let thy servant, I pray thee, turn back again, that I may die in mine own city, *and be buried* by the grave of my father and of my mother. But behold thy servant Chim'-ham; let him go over with my lord the king; and do to him what shall seem good unto thee.

38 And the king answered, Chim'-ham shall go over with me, and I will do to him that which shall seem good unto thee: and whatsoever thou shalt ᵀrequire of me, *that* will I do for thee.   *request*

39 And all the people went over Jordan. And when the king was come over, the king ᴿkissed Bar-zil'-lai, and blessed him; and he returned unto his own place.   Gen. 31:55

40 Then the king went on to Gil'-gal, and ᵀChim'-ham went on with him: and all the people of Judah ᵀconducted the king, and also half the people of Israel. *Chimham* • *went with*

41 And, behold, all the men of Israel came to the king, and said unto the king, ᴿWhy have our brethren the men of Judah stolen thee away, and ᴿhave brought the king, and his household, and all David's men with him, over Jordan?   *v.* 11; Judg. 8:1; 12:1 • *v.* 15

42 And all the men of Judah answered the men of Israel, Because the king *is* near of kin to us: wherefore then be ye angry for this matter? have we eaten at all of the king's cost? or hath he given us any gift?

43 And the men of Israel answered the men of Judah, and said, We have ten parts in the king, and we have also more *right* in David than ye: why then did ye despise us, that our advice should not be first had in bringing back our king? And the words of the men of Judah were ᵀfiercer than the words of the men of Israel.   *stronger in argument*

CHAPTER 20

AND there happened to be there a man of Be'-li-al, whose name *was* She'-ba, the son of Bich'-ri, a Benjamite: and he blew a trumpet, and said, We have no part in David, neither have we inheritance in the son of Jesse: every man to his tents, O Israel.

2 So every man of Israel went up from after David, *and* followed She'-ba the son of Bich'-ri: but the men of Judah clave unto their king, from Jordan even to Jerusalem.

3 And David came to his house at Jerusalem; and the king took the ten women *his* ᴿconcubines, whom he had left to keep the

house, and put them in ᵀward, and fed them, but went not in unto them. So they were shut up unto the day of their death, living in widowhood.   15:16; 16:21 · isolation

4 Then said the king to Am'-a-sa, ᵀAssemble me the men of Judah within three days, and be thou here present.   mobilize

5 So Am'-a-sa went to assemble the men of Judah: but he ᵀtarried longer than the set time which he had appointed him.   delayed

6 And David said to A-bi'-shai, Now shall She'-ba the son of Bich'-ri do us more harm than did Ab'-sa-lom: take thou ᴿthy lord's servants, and pursue after him, lest he get him fenced cities, and escape us.   11:11

7 And there went out after him Jo'-ab's men, and the ᴿCher'-e-thites, and the Pel'-e-thites, and all the mighty men: and they went out of Jerusalem, to pursue after She'-ba the son of Bich'-ri.   8:18; 1 Kin. 1:38

8 When they were at the great stone which is in ᴿGib'-e-on, Am'-a-sa ᵀwent before them. And Jo'-ab's garment that he had put on was girded unto him, and upon it a girdle with a sword fastened upon his loins in the sheath thereof; and as he ᵀwent forth it fell out.   2:13; 3:30 · came to meet · ran ahead

9 And Jo'-ab said to Am'-a-sa, Art thou in health, my brother? ᴿAnd Jo'-ab took Am'-a-sa by the beard with the right hand to kiss him.   Matt. 26:49; Luke 22:47

10 But Am'-a-sa took no heed to the sword that was in Jo'-ab's hand: so he smote him therewith ᴿin the fifth rib, and shed out his bowels to the ground, and struck him not again; and he died. So Jo'-ab and A-bi'-shai his brother pursued after She'-ba the son of Bich'-ri.   2:23

11 And one of Jo'-ab's men stood by him, and said, He that favoureth Jo'-ab, and he that is for David, let him go after Jo'-ab.

12 And Am'-a-sa wallowed in blood in the midst of the highway. And when the man saw that all the people stood still, he removed Am'-a-sa out of the highway into the field, and cast a cloth upon him, when he saw that every one that came by him stood still.

13 When he was removed out of the highway, all the people went on after Jo'-ab, to pursue after She'-ba the son of Bich'-ri.

14 And he went through all the tribes of Israel unto Abel, and to Beth–ma'-a-chah, and all the Be'-rites: and they were gathered together, and went also after him.

15 And they came and besieged him in Abel of Beth–ma'-a-chah, and they cast up a bank against the city, and it stood in the trench: and all the people that were with Jo'-ab battered the wall, to throw it down.

16 Then cried a wise woman out of the city, Hear, hear; say, I pray you, unto ᴿJo'-ab, Come near hither, that I may speak with thee.   14:2

17 And when he was come near unto her, the woman said, Art thou Jo'-ab? And he answered, I am he. Then she said unto him, Hear the words of thine handmaid. And he answered, I do hear.

18 Then she spake, saying, They were ᵀwont to speak in old time, saying, They shall surely ask counsel at Abel: and so they ended the matter.   accustomed

19 I am one of them that are peaceable and faithful in Israel: thou seekest to destroy a city and a mother in Israel: why wilt thou swallow up the inheritance of the LORD?

20 And Jo'-ab answered and said, Far be it, far be it from me, that I should swallow up or destroy.

21 The matter is not so: but a man of mount E'-phra-im, She'-ba the son of Bich'-ri by name, hath lifted up his hand against the king, even against David: deliver him only, and I will depart from the city. And the woman said unto Jo'-ab, Behold, his head shall be thrown to thee over the wall.

22 Then the woman went unto all the people ᴿin her wisdom. And they cut off the head of She'-ba the son of Bich'-ri, and cast it out to Jo'-ab. And he blew a trumpet, and they ᵀretired from the city, every man to his tent. And Jo'-ab returned to Jerusalem unto the king.   [Eccl. 9:13–16] · retreated

23 Now ᴿJo'-ab was over all the host of Israel: and Be-nai'-ah the son of Je-hoi'-a-da was over the Cher'-e-thites and over the Pel'-e-thites: 8:16, 18; 1 Kin. 4:3–6

24 And A-do'-ram was ᴿover the tribute: and ᴿJe-hosh'-a-phat the son of A-hi'-lud was recorder: 1 Kin. 4:6 · 8:16; 1 Kin. 4:3

25 And She'-va was scribe: and ᴿZa'-dok and A-bi'-a-thar were the priests: 1 Kin. 4:4

26 And I'-ra also the Ja'-ir-ite was ᵀa chief ruler about David.   David's priest

CHAPTER 21

Famine

THEN there was a famine in the days of David three years, year after year; and David enquired of the LORD. And the LORD answered, It is for Saul, and for his bloody house, because he slew the Gib'-e-on-ites.

2 And the king called the Gib'-e-on-ites, and said unto them; (now the Gib'-e-on-ites were not of the children of Israel, but ᴿof the remnant of the Am'-or-ites; and the children of Israel had sworn unto them: and Saul sought to slay them in his zeal to the children of Israel and Judah.)   Josh. 9:3, 15–17

3 Wherefore David said unto the Gib'-e-on-ites, What shall I do for you? and wherewith shall I make the atonement, that ye may bless the inheritance of the LORD?

4 And the Gib'-e-on-ites said unto him, RWe will have no silver nor gold of Saul, nor of his house; neither for us shalt thou kill any man in Israel. And he said, What ye shall say, that will I do for you.   Num. 35:31, 32

5 And they answered the king, The man that consumed us, and that devised against us that we should be destroyed from remaining in any of the coasts of Israel,

6 Let seven men of his sons be delivered unto us, and we will hang them up Runto the Lord in Gib'-e-ah of Saul, RwhomT the Lord did choose. And the king said, I will give them.   Num. 25:4 • 1 Sam. 10:24 • chosen of the LORD

7 But the king spared Me-phib'-o-sheth, the son of Jonathan the son of Saul, because of the Lord's oath that was between them, between David and Jonathan the son of Saul.

8 But the king took the two sons of Riz'-pah the daughter of A'-iah, whom she bare unto Saul, Ar-mo'-ni and Me-phib'-o-sheth; and the five sons of Mi'-chal the daughter of Saul, whom she brought up for A'-dri-el the son of Bar-zil'-lai the Me-hol'-ath-ite:

9 And he delivered them into the hands of the Gib'-e-on-ites, and they hanged them in the hill Rbefore the Lord: and they fell all seven together, and were put to death in the days of harvest, in Rthe first days, in the beginning of barley harvest.   6:17 • Ex. 9:31, 32

10 And RRiz'-pah the daughter of A'-iah took sackcloth, and spread it for her upon the rock, Rfrom the beginning of harvest until water dropped upon them out of heaven, and suffered neither the birds of the air to rest on them by day, nor the beasts of the field by night.   v. 8 • Deut. 21:23

11 And it was told David what Riz'-pah the daughter of A'-iah, the concubine of Saul, had done.

12 And David went and took the bones of Saul and the bones of Jonathan his son from the men of RJa'-besh-gil'-e-ad, which had stolen them from the street of RBeth'-shan, Rwhere the Phi-lis'-tines had hanged them, when the Phi-lis'-tines had slain Saul in Gilbo'-a: 1 Sam. 31:11-13 • Josh. 17:11 • 1 Sam. 31:8

13 And he brought up from thence the bones of Saul and the bones of Jonathan his son; and they gathered the bones of them that were hanged.

14 And the bones of Saul and Jonathan his son buried they in the country of Benjamin in Ze'-lah, in the sepulchre of Kish his father: and they performed all that the king commanded. And after that RGod Twas intreated for the land.   24:25 • heard the prayer

War with Philistia—1 Chr. 20:4-8

15 Moreover Rthe Phi-lis'-tines had yet war again with Israel; and David went down, and his servants with him, and fought against the Phi-lis'-tines: and David waxed faint.   5:17-25

16 And Ish'-bi-be'-nob, which was of the sons of Tthe giant, the weight of whose spear weighed three hundred shek'-els of brass in weight, he being girded with a new sword, thought to have slain David.   Rapha

17 But RA-bi'-shai the son of Ze-ru'-iah Tsuccoured him, and smote the Phi-lis'-tine, and killed him. Then the men of David sware unto him, saying, Thou shalt go no more out with us to battle, that thou quench not the light of Israel.   20:6-10 • rescued

18 And it came to pass after this, that there was again a battle with the Phi-lis'-tines at Gob: then RSib'-be-chai the Hu'-shath-ite slew TSaph, which was of the sons of Tthe giant.   1 Chr. 11: 29; 27:11 • Sippai • Rapha

19 And there was again a battle in Gob with the Phi-lis'-tines, where El-ha'-nan the son of TJa'-a-re-or'-e-gim, a Beth'-le-hem-ite, slew Rthe brother of Go-li'-ath the Git'-tite,R the staff of whose spear was like a weaver's beam.   Jair • 1 Chr. 20:5 • 1 Sam. 17:7

20 And there was yet a battle in Gath, where was a man of great stature, that had on every hand six fingers, and on every foot six toes, four and twenty in number; and he also was born Rto Tthe giant.   vv. 16, 18 • Rapha

21 And when he Tdefied Israel, Jonathan the son of RShim'-e-ah the brother of David slew him.   reproached • 1 Sam. 16:9

22 RThese four were born to the giant in RGath, and fell by the hand of David, and by the hand of his servants.   1 Chr. 20:8 • 2 Kin. 12:17

CHAPTER 22

Psalms of Thanksgiving

AND David Rspake unto the Lord the words of this song, in the day that the Lord had Rdelivered him out of the hand of all his enemies, and out of the hand of Saul: Ex. 15:1; Judg. 5:1 • Ps. 18, title; 34:19

2 And he said, The Lord is my rock, and my fortress, and my deliverer;

3 The God of my rock; in him will I trust: he is my shield, and the horn of my salvation, my high tower, and my refuge, my saviour; thou savest me from violence.

4 I will call on the Lord, who is worthy to be praised: so shall I be saved from mine enemies.

5 When the waves of death compassed me, the floods of ungodly men made me afraid;

6 The sorrows of hell compassed me about; the snares of death prevented me;

7 In my distress RI called upon the Lord, and cried to my God: and he did hear my voice out of his temple, and my cry did enter into his ears.   Ps. 116:4; 120:1

8 Then the earth shook and trembled; Rthe foundations of heaven moved and shook, because he was wroth.   Job 26:11

9 There went up a smoke Tout of his nostrils, and Rfire out of his mouth devoured: coals were kindled by it.   by · Ps. 97:3; Heb. 12:29

10 He bowed the heavens also, and came down; and darkness was under his feet.

11 And he rode upon a cherub, and did fly: and he was seen upon the wings of the wind.

12 RAnd he made darkness pavilions round about him, dark waters, and thick clouds of the skies.   Job 36:29

13 Through the brightness before him were Rcoals of fire kindled.   v. 9

14 The LORD thundered from heaven, and the most High uttered his voice.

15 And he sent out Rarrows, and scattered them; lightning, and discomfited them. Ps. 7:13

16 And the channels of the sea appeared, the foundations of the world were discovered, at the rebuking of the LORD, at the blast of the breath of his nostrils.

17 RHe sent from above, he took me; he drew me out of many waters;   Ps. 114:7

18 He delivered me from my strong enemy, and from them that hated me: for they were too strong for me.

19 They prevented me in the day of my calamity: but the LORD was my stay.

20 RHe brought me forth also into a large place: he delivered me, because he Rdelighted in me.   Ps. 31:8; 118:5 · 15:26

21 The LORD rewarded me according to my righteousness: according to the Rcleanness of my hands hath he recompensed me.   Ps. 24:4

22 For I have Rkept the ways of the LORD, and have not wickedly departed from my God.   Gen. 18:19; Ps. 119:3; 128:1

23 For all his Rjudgments were before me: and as for his statutes, I did not depart from them.   [Deut. 6:6–9; 7:12]

24 I was also upright before him, and have kept myself from mine iniquity.

25 Therefore the LORD hath recompensed me according to my righteousness; according to my cleanness in his eye sight.

26 With Rthe Tmerciful thou wilt shew thyself merciful, and with the upright man thou wilt shew thyself upright.   loyal · [Matt. 5:7]

27 With the pure thou wilt shew thyself pure; and Rwith the Tfroward thou wilt shew thyself unsavoury.   [Lev. 26: 23] · impudent

28 And the afflicted people thou wilt save: but thine eyes are upon Rthe haughty, that thou mayest bring them down.   Job 40:11

29 For thou art my Tlamp, O LORD: and the LORD will lighten my darkness.   candle

30 For by thee I have run through a troop: by my God have I leaped over a wall.

31 As for God, his way is perfect; the word of the LORD is tried: he is a buckler to all them that trust in him.

32 For Rwho is God, save the LORD? and who is a rock, save our God?   Is. 45:5, 6

33 God is my strength and power: and he maketh my way Tperfect.   complete

34 He maketh my feet Rlike hinds' feet: and setteth me upon my high places.   2:18

35 He teacheth my hands to war; so that a bow of steel is broken by mine arms.

36 Thou hast also given me the Rshield of thy salvation: and thy gentleness hath made me great.   [Eph. 6:16, 17]

37 Thou hast enlarged my steps under me; so that my feet did not slip.

38 I have pursued mine enemies, and Rdestroyed them; and turned not again until I had consumed them.   Ex. 15:9

39 And I have consumed them, and wounded them, that they could not arise: yea, they are fallen Runder my feet.   Mal. 4:3

40 For thou hast girded me with strength to battle: Rthem that rose up against me hast thou Tsubdued under me. [Ps. 44:5] · caused to bow

41 Thou hast also Rgiven me the necks of mine enemies, that I might destroy them that hate me.   Ex. 23:27; Josh. 10:24

42 They looked, but there was none to save; even Runto the LORD, but he Ranswered them not.   [Is. 17:7, 8] · 1 Sam. 28:6; Prov. 1:28

43 RThen did I beat them as small as the dust of the earth: I did stamp them as the mire of the street, and did Tspread them abroad.   Is. 10:6 · scatter

44 Thou also hast delivered me from the strivings of my people, Rthou hast kept me to be head of the heathen: a people which I knew not shall serve me.   8:1–14

45 RStrangers shall submit themselves unto me: as soon as they hear, they shall be obedient unto me.   Ps. 66:3; 81:15

46 Strangers shall fade away, and they shall be afraid out of their close places.

47 The LORD liveth; and blessed be my rock; and exalted be the God of the Rrock of my salvation.   v. 3; Ps. 89:26

48 It is God that avengeth me, and that Rbringeth down the people under me, Ps. 144:2

49 And that bringeth me forth from mine enemies: thou also hast lifted me up on high above them that rose up against me: thou hast delivered me from the violent man.

50 Therefore I will give thanks unto thee, O LORD, among the heathen, and I will sing praises unto thy name.

51 He is the tower of salvation for his king: and sheweth mercy to his anointed, unto David, and to his seed for evermore.

CHAPTER 23

NOW these be the last words of David. David the son of Jesse said, and the man who was raised up on high, the anointed of the God of Jacob, and the sweet Tpsalmist of Israel, said,   singer

2 ᴿThe Spirit of the LORD spake by me, and his word *was* in my tongue.   [2 Pet. 1:21]

3 The God of Israel said, the Rock of Israel spake to me, He that ruleth over men *must be* just, ruling in the fear of God.

4 And *he shall be* as the light of the morning, *when* the sun riseth, *even* a morning without clouds; *as* the tender grass *springing* out of the earth by clear shining after rain.

5 Although my house *be* not so with God; ᴿyet he hath made with me an everlasting covenant, ordered in all *things,* and sure: for *this is* all my salvation, and all *my* desire, although he make it not to grow.   Ps. 89:29

6 But *the sons* of Be'-li-al *shall be* all of them as thorns thrust away, because they cannot be taken with hands:

7 But the man *that* shall touch them must be ᵀfenced with iron and the staff of a spear; and ᴿthey shall be utterly burned with fire in the *same* place.   *armed* • [Matt. 3:10; 13:30; Heb. 6:8]

Deeds of David's Mighty Men—1 Chr. 11:10–41

8 These *be* the ᴿnames of the mighty men whom David had: The Tach'-mo-nite that sat in the seat, chief among the ᵀcaptains; the same *was* Ad'-i-no the Ez'-nite: *he lift up his spear* against eight hundred, whom he slew at one time.   1 Chr. 11:11–47 • *three*

9 And after him *was* E-le-a'-zar the son of Dodo the A-ho'-hite, *one* of the three mighty men with David, when they defied the Phi-lis'-tines *that* were there gathered together to battle, and the men of Israel were gone away:

10 He arose, and smote the Phi-lis'-tines until his hand was weary, and his hand clave unto the sword: and the LORD wrought a great victory that day; and the people returned after him only to spoil.

11 And after him *was* Sham'-mah the son of Ag'-e-e the Ha'-ra-rite. And the Phi-lis'-tines were gathered together into a troop, where was a piece of ground full of lentiles: and the people fled from the Phi-lis'-tines.

12 But he stood in the midst of the ᵀground, and defended it, and slew the Phi-lis'-tines: and the ᴿLORD wrought a great victory.   *plot* • *v.* 10

13 And ᵀthree of the thirty chief went down, and came to David in the harvest time unto the cave of A-dul'-lam: and the troop of the Phi-lis'-tines pitched in the valley of Reph'-a-im.   *the three captains over the thirty*

14 And David *was* then in ᴿan hold,ᵀ and the garrison of the Phi-lis'-tines *was* then in Beth'–le-hem.   1 Sam. 22:4, 5 • *the strong hold*

15 And David longed, and said, Oh that one would give me drink of the water of the well of Beth'–le-hem, which *is* by the gate!

16 And the three mighty men brake through the host of the Phi-lis'-tines, and drew water out of the well of Beth'–le-hem, that *was* by the gate, and took *it,* and

brought *it* to David: nevertheless he would not drink thereof, but poured it out unto the LORD.

17 And he said, Be it far from me, O LORD, that I should do this: *is not this* the blood of the men that went in jeopardy of their lives? therefore he would not drink it. These things did these three mighty men.

18 And ᴿA-bi'-shai, the brother of Jo'-ab, the son of Ze-ru'-iah, was chief among three. And he lifted up his spear against three hundred, *and* slew *them,* and had the name among three.   1 Chr. 11:20

19 Was he not most honourable of three? therefore he was their captain: howbeit he attained not unto the *first* three.

20 And Be-nai'-ah the son of Je-hoi'-a-da, the son of a valiant man, of Kab'-ze-el, who had done many acts, he slew two lionlike men of Moab: he went down also and slew a lion in the midst of a pit in time of snow:

21 And he slew an Egyptian, a goodly man: and the Egyptian had a spear in his hand; but he went down to him with a staff, and plucked the spear out of the Egyptian's hand, and slew him with his own spear.

22 These *things* did ᴿBe-nai'-ah the son of Je-hoi'-a-da, and had the name among three mighty men.   *v.* 20

23 He was more honourable than the thirty, but he attained not to the *first* three. And David set him ᴿover his guard.   8:18

24 ᴿA'-sa-hel the brother of Jo'-ab *was* one of the thirty; El-ha'-nan the son of Dodo of Beth'–le-hem,   2:18

25 ᴿSham'-mah the ᴿHa'-rod-ite, El'-i-ka the Ha'-rod-ite,   1 Chr. 11:27 • Judg. 7:1

26 ᴿHe'-lez the Pal'-tite, I'-ra the son of Ik'-kesh the Te-ko'-ite,   1 Chr. 11:27, 28; 27:10

27 A-bi-e'-zer the An'-e-tho-thite, Me-bun'-nai the Hu'-shath-ite,

28 Zal'-mon the A-ho'-hite, Ma'-ha-rai the ᴿNe-toph'-a-thite,   2 Kin. 25:23

29 He'-leb the son of Ba'-a-nah, a Ne-toph'-a-thite, It'-tai the son of Ri'-bai out of Gib'-e-ah of the children of Benjamin,

30 Be-nai'-ah the Pir'-a-thon-ite, Hid'-dai of the ᵀbrooks of Ga'-ash,   *valleys*

31 Ab'-i-al'-bon the Ar'-bath-ite, Az'-ma-veth the ᴿBar-hu'-mite,   3:16

32 E-li'-ah-ba the ᴿSha-al'-bo-nite, of the sons of Ja'-shen, Jonathan,   Josh. 19:42

33 ᴿSham'-mah the Ha'-ra-rite, A-hi'-am the son of Sha'-rar the Ha'-ra-rite,   *v.* 11

34 E-liph'-e-let the son of A-has'-bai, the son of the ᴿMa-ach'-a-thite, E-li'-am the son of A-hith'-o-phel the Gi'-lo-nite,   10:6

35 ᴿHez'-rai the ᴿCar'-mel-ite, Pa'-a-rai the Ar'-bite,   1 Chr. 11:37 • Josh. 15:55

36 I'-gal the son of Nathan of ᴿZo'-bah, Ba'-ni the Gad'-ite,   8:3

37 Ze'-lek the Am'-mon-ite, Na'-ha-ri the

RBe-e'-roth-ite, armourbearer to Jo'-ab the son of Ze-ru'-iah,   4:2

38 I'-ra an Ith'-rite, Ga'-reb an Ith'-rite,

39 RU-ri'-ah the Hit'-tite: thirty and seven in all.   11:3, 6

CHAPTER 24

The Census and the Plague—1 Chr. 29:26–30

AND Ragain the anger of the LORD was Tkindled against Israel, and he moved David against them to say, Go, Tnumber Israel and Judah.   21:1 • *aroused • take a census*

2 For the king said to Jo'-ab the captain of the host, which *was* with him, Go now through all the tribes of Israel, Rfrom Dan even to Be'-er-she'-ba, and number ye the people, that RI may know the number of the people.   3:10; Judg. 20:1 • [Jer. 17:5]

3 And Jo'-ab said unto the king, RNow the LORD thy God add unto the people, how many soever they be, an hundredfold, and that the eyes of my lord the king may see *it*: but why doth my lord the king Tdelight in this thing?   Deut. 1:11 • *want to do this*

4 Notwithstanding the king's word prevailed against Jo'-ab, and against the captains of the host. And Jo'-ab and the captains of the host went out from the presence of the king, to number the people of Israel.

5 And they passed over Jordan, and Tpitched in Ar'-o-er, on the right side of the city that *lieth* in the midst of the Triver of Gad, and toward Ja'-zer: *made camp • valley*

6 Then they came to Gil'-e-ad, and to the land of Tah'-tim-hod'-shi; and they came to Dan-ja'-an, and about to Zi'-don,

7 And came to the strong hold of Tyre, and to all the cities of the Hi'-vites, and of the Ca'-naan-ites: and they went out to the south of Judah, *even* to Be'-er-she'-ba.

8 So when they had gone through all the land, they came to Jerusalem at the end of nine months and twenty days.

9 And Jo'-ab gave up the Rsum of the number of the people unto the king: Rand there were in Israel eight hundred thousand Tvaliant men that drew the sword; and the men of Judah *were* five hundred thousand men.   Num. 1:44–46 • 1 Chr. 21:5 • *strong*

10 And David's heart smote him after that he had numbered the people. And David said unto the LORD, I have sinned greatly in that I have done: and now, I beseech thee, O LORD, take away the iniquity of thy servant; for I have done very foolishly.

11 For when David was up in the morning, the word of the LORD came unto the prophet Gad, David's seer, saying,

12 Go and say unto David, Thus saith the LORD, I offer thee three *things;* choose thee one of them, that I may *do it* unto thee.

13 So Gad came to David, and told him,

and said unto him, Shall Rseven years of famine come unto thee in thy land? or wilt thou flee three months before thine enemies, while they pursue thee? or that there be three days' pestilence in thy land? now Tadvise, and see what answer I shall return to him that sent me.   1 Chr. 21:12 • *consider*

14 And David said unto Gad, I am in a great strait: let us fall now into the hand of the LORD; for his mercies *are* great: and let me not fall into the hand of man.

15 So Rthe LORD sent a pestilence upon Israel from the morning even to the time appointed: and there died of the people Rfrom Dan even to Be'-er–she'-ba seventy thousand men.   1 Chr. 21:14; 27:24 • *v.* 2

16 And when the angel stretched out his hand upon Jerusalem to destroy it, the LORD repented him of the evil, and said to the angel that destroyed the people, It is enough: Tstay now thine hand. And the angel of the LORD was by the threshingplace of A-rau'-nah the Jeb'-u-site.   *hold back*

17 And David spake unto the LORD when he saw the angel that smote the people, and said, Lo, I have sinned, and I have done wickedly: but these sheep, what have they done? let thine hand, I pray thee, be against me, and against my father's house.

18 And Gad came that day to David, and said unto him, RGo up, rear an altar unto the LORD in the threshingfloor of TA-rau'-nah the Jeb'-u-site.   1 Chr. 21:18 • *Araniah*

19 And David, according to the saying of Gad, went up as the LORD commanded.

20 And A-rau'-nah looked, and saw the king and his servants coming on toward him: and A-rau'-nah went out, and bowed himself before the king on his face upon the ground.

21 And A-rau'-nah said, Wherefore is my lord the king come to his servant? And David said, To buy the threshingfloor of thee, to build an altar unto the LORD, that the plague may be stayed from the people.

22 And A-rau'-nah said unto David, Let my lord the king take and offer up what *seemeth* good unto him: behold, *here be* oxen for burnt sacrifice, and threshing instruments and *other* instruments of the oxen for wood.

23 All these *things* did A-rau'-nah, *as* a king, give unto the king. And A-rau'-nah said unto the king, The LORD thy God Raccept thee.   Ezek. 20:40, 41

24 And the king said unto A-rau'-nah, Nay; but I will surely buy *it* of thee at a price: neither will I offer burnt offerings unto the LORD my God of that which doth cost me nothing. So David bought the threshingfloor and the oxen for Tfifty shek'-els of silver. *$6,400*

25 And David built there an altar unto the LORD, and offered burnt offerings and peace offerings. So the LORD was intreated for the land, and the plague was stayed from Israel.

KINGS

THE BOOK OF FIRST KINGS

The first half of First Kings traces the life of Solomon. Under his leadership Israel rises to the peak of her size and glory. Solomon's great accomplishments, including the unsurpassed splendor of the temple which he constructs in Jerusalem, bring him worldwide fame and respect. However, Solomon's zeal for God diminishes in his later years as pagan wives turn his heart away from worship in the temple of God. As a result, the king with the divided heart leaves behind a divided kingdom. For the next century, the Book of First Kings traces the twin histories of two sets of kings and two nations of disobedient people who are growing indifferent to God's prophets and precepts.

Like the two books of Samuel, the two books of Kings were originally one in the Hebrew Bible. The original title was *Melechim,* "Kings," taken from the first word in 1:1, *Vehamelech,* "Now king." The Septuagint artificially divided the Book of Kings in the middle of the story of Ahaziah into two books. It called the books of Samuel "First and Second Kingdoms" and the books of Kings "Third and Fourth Kingdoms." The Septuagint may have divided Samuel, Kings, and Chronicles into two books each because the Greek required a greater amount of scroll space than did the Hebrew. The Latin title for these books is *Liber Regum Tertius et Quartus,* "Third and Fourth Book of Kings."

THE AUTHOR OF FIRST KINGS

The author of First and Second Kings is unknown, but evidence supports the talmudic tradition that Kings was written by the prophet Jeremiah. The author was clearly a prophet/historian as seen in the prophetic exposé of apostasy. Both First and Second Kings emphasize God's righteous judgment on idolatry and immorality. The style of these books is also similar to that found in Jeremiah. The phrase "unto this day" in First Kings 8:8 and 12:19 indicates a time of authorship prior to the Babylonian captivity (586 B.C.). However, the last two chapters of Second Kings were written after the captivity, probably by a Jewish captive in Babylon.

Evidently, the majority of First and Second Kings was written before 586 B.C. by a compiler who had access to several historical documents. Some of these are mentioned: "the book of the acts of Solomon" (11:41), "the book of the chronicles of the kings of Israel" (14:19), and "the book of the chronicles of the kings of Judah" (14:29; 15:7). These books may have been a part of the official court records (see 2 Kin. 18:18). In addition, Isaiah 36—39 was probably used as a source (cf. 2 Kin. 18—20).

THE TIME OF FIRST KINGS

The Book of Kings was written to the remaining kingdom of Judah before and after its Babylonian exile. The majority was compiled by a contemporary of Jeremiah, if not by Jeremiah himself (c. 646-570 B.C.). It is a record of disobedience, idolatry, and ungodliness which serves as an explanation for the Assyrian captivity of Israel (722 B.C.) and the Babylonian captivity of Judah (586 B.C.). First Kings covers the 120 years from the beginning of Solomon's reign in 971 B.C. through Ahaziah's reign ending in 851 B.C. The key date is 931 B.C., the year the kingdom was divided into the northern nation of Israel and the southern nation of Judah.

THE CHRIST OF FIRST KINGS

Solomon pictures Christ in a number of ways. His fabled wisdom points ahead to "Christ Jesus, who of God is made unto us wisdom" (1 Cor. 1:30). Solomon's fame, glory, wealth, and honor foreshadow Christ in His kingdom. Solomon's rulership brings knowledge, peace, and worship. However, despite Solomon's splendor, the Son of Man later says of His coming, "Behold, a greater than Solomon *is* here" (Matt. 12:42).

The prophet Elijah is more typical of John the Baptist than of Christ, but his prophetic ministry and miraculous works illustrate aspects of the life of Christ.

THE KEYS TO FIRST KINGS

Key Word: Division of the Kingdom—
The theme of First Kings centers around the fact that the welfare of Israel and Judah depends upon the faithfulness of the people and their king to the covenant. Historically, it was written to give an account of the reigns of the kings from Solomon to Jehoshaphat (Judah) and Ahaziah (Israel). The two books of Kings as a whole trace the monarchy from the point of its greatest prosperity under Solomon to its demise and destruction in the Assyrian and Babylonian captivities.

Theologically, First Kings provides a prophetically oriented evaluation of the spiritual and moral causes that led to the political and economic demise of the two kingdoms. The material is too selective to be considered a biography of the kings. For example, Omri was one of Israel's most important rulers from a

political point of view, but because of his moral corruption, his achievements are dismissed in a mere eight verses. The lives of these kings are used to teach that observance of God's law produces blessing, but apostasy is rewarded by judgment.

Key Verses: First Kings 9:4, 5; 11:11—"And if thou wilt walk before me, as David thy father walked, in integrity of heart, and in uprightness, to do according to all that I have commanded thee, *and* wilt keep my statutes and my judgments: Then I will establish the throne of thy kingdom upon Israel for ever, as I promised to David thy father, saying, There shall not fail thee a man upon the throne of Israel" (9:4, 5).

"Wherefore the LORD said unto Solomon, Forasmuch as this is done of thee, and thou hast not kept my covenant and my statutes, which I have commanded thee, I will surely rend the kingdom from thee, and will give it to thy servant" (11:11).

Key Chapter: First Kings 12—The critical turning point in First Kings occurs in chapter 12 when the united kingdom becomes the divided kingdom. Solomon dies, and his son Rehoboam becomes king and unwisely leads the nation into a civil war which tragically rips the nation into two separate, and at times conflicting, nations. Instead of unity, First Kings records the history of the two kings, two capitals, and two religions.

SURVEY OF FIRST KINGS

The first half of First Kings concerns the life of one of the most amazing men who ever lived. More than any man before or since, he knew how to amass and creatively use great wealth. With the sole exception of Jesus Christ, Solomon is the wisest man in human history. He brings Israel to the peak of its size and glory, and yet, the kingdom is disrupted soon after his death, torn in two by civil strife. This book divides

clearly into two sections: the united kingdom (1—11) and the divided kingdom (12—22).

United Kingdom (1—11): These chapters give an account of Solomon's attainment of the throne, wisdom, architectural achievements, fame, wealth, and tragic unfaithfulness. Solomon's half-brother Adonijah attempts to take the throne as David's death is nearing, but Nathan the prophet alerts David who quickly directs the coronation of Solomon as coregent (ch. 1). Solomon still has to consolidate his power and deal with those who oppose his rule. Only when this is done is the kingdom "established in the hand of Solomon" (2:46). Solomon's ungodly marriages (cf. 3:1) eventually turn his heart from the Lord, but he begins well with a genuine love for Yahweh and a desire for wisdom. This wisdom leads to the expansion of Israel to the zenith of her power. Solomon's empire stretches from the border of Egypt to the border of Babylonia, and peace prevails.

From a theocratic perspective, Solomon's greatest achievement is the building of the temple. The ark is placed in this exquisite building, which is filled with the glory of God. Solomon offers a magnificent prayer of dedication and binds the people with an oath to remain faithful to Yahweh.

Because the Lord is with him Solomon continues to grow in fame, power, and wealth. However, his wealth later becomes a source of trouble when he begins to purchase forbidden items. He acquires many foreign wives who lead him into idolatry. It is an irony of history that this wisest of men acts as a fool in his old age. God pronounces judgment and foretells that Solomon's son will rule only a fraction of the kingdom (Judah).

Divided Kingdom (12—22): Upon Solomon's death, God's words come to pass. Solomon's son Rehoboam chooses the foolish course of promis-

FOCUS	UNITED KINGDOM			DIVIDED KINGDOM		
REFERENCE	1:1————————3:1———————9:1—			——12:1————————15:1————	—16:29———22:53	
DIVISION	ESTABLISHMENT OF SOLOMON	RISE OF SOLOMON	DECLINE OF SOLOMON	DIVISION OF THE KINGDOM	REIGNS OF VARIOUS KINGS	REIGN OF AHAB WITH ELIJAH
TOPIC	SOLOMON			MANY KINGS		
	KINGDOM IN TRANQUILLITY			KINGDOMS IN TURMOIL		
LOCATION	JERUSALEM: CAPITAL OF UNITED KINGDOM			SAMARIA: CAPITAL OF ISRAEL JERUSALEM: CAPITAL OF JUDAH		
TIME	c. 40 YEARS			c. 90 YEARS		

ing more severe taxation. Jeroboam, an officer in Solomon's army, leads the ten northern tribes in revolt. They make him their king, leaving only Judah and Benjamin in the south under Rehoboam. This is the beginning of a chaotic period with two nations and two sets of kings. Continual enmity and strife exists between the northern and southern kingdoms. The north is plagued by apostasy (Jeroboam sets up a false system of worship) and the south by idolatry. Of all the northern and southern kings listed in this book, only Asa (15:9-24) and Jehoshaphat (22:41-50) do *"that which was* right in the eyes of the Lord" (15:11; 22:43). All of the others are idolaters, usurpers, and murderers.

Ahab brings a measure of cooperation between the northern and southern kingdoms, but he reaches new depths of wickedness as a king. He is the man who introduces Jezebel's Baal worship to Israel. The prophet Elijah ministers during this low period in Israel's history, providing a ray of light and witness of the word and power of God. But Ahab's encounter with Elijah never brings him to turn from his false gods to God. Ahab's treachery in the matter of Naboth's vineyard causes a prophetic rebuke from Elijah (21). Ahab repents (21:27-29) but later dies in battle because of his refusal to heed the words of Micaiah, another prophet of God.

OUTLINE OF FIRST KINGS

Part One: The United Kingdom (1:1—11:43)

Part Two: The Divided Kingdom (12:1—22:53)

CHAPTER 1

Decline of David

NOW king David was old *and* stricken in years; and they covered him with clothes, but he ᵀgat no heat.   *could not get warm*

2 Wherefore his servants said unto him, Let there be sought for my lord the king a young virgin: and let her stand before the king, and let her ᵀcherish him, and let her lie in thy bosom, that my lord the king may get heat.   *be a companion to him*

3 So they sought for a fair damsel throughout all the coasts of Israel, and found Ab'-i-shag a ᴿShu'-nam-mite, and brought her to the king.   Josh. 19:18

4 And the damsel *was* very fair, and cherished the king, and ministered to him: but the king knew her not.

Plot of Adonijah to Be King

5 Then ᴿAd-o-ni'-jah the son of Hag'-gith exalted himself, saying, I will be king: and he prepared him chariots and horsemen, and fifty men to run before him.   2 Sam. 3:4

6 And his father had not displeased him at any time in saying, Why hast thou done so? and he also *was a* very goodly *man*; and *his* mother bare him after Ab'-sa-lom.

7 And he conferred with Jo'-ab the son of Ze-ru'-iah, and with A-bi'-a-thar the priest: and they following Ad-o-ni'-jah helped him.

8 But Za'-dok the priest, and Be-na'-iah the son of Je-hoi'-a-da, and Nathan the prophet, and ᴿShim'-e-i, and Re'-i, and the mighty men which *belonged* to David, were not with Ad-o-ni'-jah.   4:18

9 And Ad-o-ni'-jah slew sheep and oxen and fat cattle by the stone of Zo'-he-leth,

which *is* by ᵀEn-ro'-gel, and called all his brethren the king's sons, and all the men of Judah the king's servants: *the well Rogel*

Anointing of Solomon

10 But Nathan the prophet, and Be-na'-iah, and the mighty men, and ᴿSolomon his brother, he called not.   2 Sam. 12:24

11 Wherefore Nathan spake unto Bath-she'-ba the mother of Solomon, saying, Hast thou not heard that Ad-o-ni'-jah the son of Hag'-gith ᵀdoth reign, and David our lord knoweth *it* not?   *does rule the throne*

12 Now therefore come, let me, I pray thee, ᵀgive thee counsel, that thou mayest save thine own life, and the life of thy son Solomon.   *give you advice*

13 Go and get thee in unto king David, and say unto him, Didst not thou, my lord, O king, swear unto thine handmaid, saying, ᴿAssuredly Solomon thy son shall reign after me, and he shall sit upon my throne? why then doth Ad-o-ni'-jah reign?   1 Chr. 22:9

14 Behold, while thou yet talkest there with the king, I also will come in after thee, and confirm thy words.

15 And Bath-she'-ba went in unto the king into the chamber: and ᴿthe king was very old; and Ab'-i-shag the Shu'-nam-mite ministered unto the king.   v. 1

16 And Bath-she'-ba bowed, and did obeisance unto the king. And the king said, What ᵀwouldest thou?   *do you wish?*

17 And she said unto him, My lord, ᴿthou swarest by the LORD thy God unto thine handmaid, *saying*, Assuredly Solomon thy son shall reign after me, and he shall sit upon my throne.   vv. 13, 30

18 And now, behold, Ad-o-ni'-jah reigneth; and now, my lord the king, thou knowest *it* not:

19 And he hath slain oxen and fat cattle and sheep in abundance, and hath called all the sons of the king, and A-bi'-a-thar the priest, and Jo'-ab the captain of the host: but Solomon thy servant hath he not called.

20 And thou, my lord, O king, the eyes of all Israel *are* upon thee, that thou shouldest tell them who shall sit on the throne of my lord the king after him.

21 Otherwise it shall come to pass, when my lord the king shall ᴿsleep with his fathers, that I and my son Solomon shall be counted ᵀoffenders.   2:10 • *criminals*

22 And, lo, while she yet talked with the king, Nathan the prophet also came in.

23 And they told the king, saying, Behold Nathan the prophet. And when he was come in before the king, he bowed himself before the king with his face to the ground.

24 And Nathan said, My lord, O king, hast thou said, Ad-o-ni'-jah shall reign after me, and he shall sit upon my throne?

25 For he is gone down this day, and hath slain oxen and fat cattle and sheep in abundance, and hath called all the king's sons, and the captains of the host, and A-bi'-a-thar the priest; and, behold, they eat and drink before him, and say, God save king Ad-o-ni'-jah.

26 ᴿBut me, *even* me thy servant, and Za'-dok the priest, and Be-na'-iah the son of Je-hoi'-a-da, and thy servant Solomon, hath he not called.   *vv. 8, 10*

27 Is this thing done by my lord the king, and thou hast not shewed *it* unto thy servant, who should sit on the throne of my lord the king after him?

28 Then king David answered and said, Call me Bath-she'-ba. And she came into the king's presence, and stood before the king.

29 And the king sware, and said, ᴿAs the LORD liveth, that hath redeemed my soul out of all distress,   2 Sam. 4:9; 12:5

30 ᴿEven as I sware unto thee by the LORD God of Israel, saying, Assuredly Solomon thy son shall reign after me, and he shall sit upon my throne in my stead; even so will I certainly do this day.   *vv. 13, 17*

31 Then Bath-she'-ba bowed with *her* face to the earth, and did ᵀreverence to the king, and said, ᴿLet my lord king David live for ever.   *obeisance* • Neh. 2:3; Dan. 2:4; 3:9

32 And king David said, Call me ᴿZa'-dok the priest, and ᴿNathan the prophet, and Be-na'-iah the son of Je-hoi'-a-da. And they came before the king.   v. 8 • 1 Chr. 29:29

33 The king also said unto them, Take with you the servants of your lord, and cause Solomon my son to ride upon mine own mule, and bring him down to Gi'-hon:

34 And let Za'-dok the priest and Nathan the prophet anoint him there king over Israel: and ᴿblow ye with the trumpet, and say, God save king Solomon.   2 Sam. 15:10

35 Then ye shall ᵀcome up after him, that he may come and sit upon my throne; for he shall be king in my stead: and I have appointed him to be ruler over Israel and over Judah.   *support him*

36 And Be-na'-iah the son of Je-hoi'-a-da answered the king, and said, A'-men: the LORD God of my lord the king say so *too*.

37 ᴿAs the LORD hath been with my lord the king, even so be he with Solomon, and ᴿmake his throne greater than the throne of my lord king David.   1 Sam. 20:13 • *v. 47*

38 So Za'-dok the priest, and Nathan the prophet, ᴿand Be-na'-iah the son of Je-hoi'-a-da, and the Cher'-e-thites, and the Pel'-e-thites, went down, and caused Solomon to ride upon king David's mule, and brought him to Gi'-hon.   *vv. 8, 33;* 2 Sam. 8:18; 23:20–23

39 And Za'-dok the priest took an horn of oil out of the tabernacle, and anointed Solomon. And they blew the trumpet; and all the people said, God save king Solomon.

40 And all the people came up after him, and the people piped with ᵀpipes, and rejoiced with great joy, so that the earth ᵀrent with the sound of them.   *flutes* • *was split*

Submission of Adonijah

41 And ᴿAd-o-ni'-jah and all the guests that *were* with him heard *it* as they had ᵀmade an end of eating. And when Jo'-ab heard the sound of the trumpet, he said, ᵀWherefore *is this* noise of the city being in an uproar?   v. 9 • *finished* • *why*

42 And while he yet spake, behold, Jonathan the son of A-bi'-a-thar the priest came: and Ad-o-ni'-jah said unto him, Come in; for thou *art* a ᵀvaliant man, and bringest good tidings.   *worthy*

43 And Jonathan answered and said to Ad-o-ni'-jah, Verily our lord king David hath made Solomon king.

44 ᴿAnd the king hath sent with him Za'-dok the priest, and Nathan the prophet, and Be-na'-iah the son of Je-hoi'-a-da, and the Cher'-e-thites, and the Pel'-e-thites, and they have caused him to ride upon the king's mule: v. 34

45 And Za'-dok the priest and Nathan the prophet have anointed him king in Gi'-hon: and they are come up from ᵀthence rejoicing, ᴿso that the city rang again. This *is* the noise that ye have heard.   *there* • *v. 40*

46 And also Solomon ᴿsitteth on the throne of the kingdom.   2:12; 1 Chr. 29:23

47 And moreover the king's servants came

to bless our lord king David, saying, RGod make the name of Solomon better than thy name, and make his throne greater than thy throne. RAnd the king Tbowed himself upon the bed.   v. 37 · Gen. 47:31 · *humbled*

48 And also thus said the king, Blessed *be* the LORD God of Israel, which hath Rgiven *one* to sit on my throne this day, mine eyes even seeing *it*.   3:6; Ps. 132:11, 12

49 And all the guests that *were* with Ad-o-ni'-jah were afraid, and rose up, and went every man his way.

50 And Ad-o-ni'-jah feared because of Solomon, and arose, and went, and Tcaught hold on the horns of the altar.   *took refuge*

51 RAnd it was told Solomon, saying, Behold, Ad-o-ni'-jah feareth king Solomon: for, lo, he hath caught hold on the horns of the altar, saying, Let king Solomon swear unto me to day that he will not slay his servant with the sword.   2:28

52 And Solomon said, If he will shew himself a worthy man, there shall not an hair of him fall to the earth: but if wickedness shall be found in him, he shall die.

53 So king Solomon sent, and they brought him down from the altar. And he came and Tbowed himself to king Solomon: and Solomon said unto him, Go to thine house.   *humbled*

CHAPTER 2

David's Charge to Solomon

NOW Rthe days of David drew nigh that he should die; and he Tcharged Solomon his son, saying,   Deut. 31:14 · *gave orders to*

2 I go the way of all the earth: be thou strong therefore, and shew thyself a man;

3 And keep the charge of the LORD thy God, to walk in his ways, to keep his statutes, and his commandments, and his judgments, and his testimonies, as it is written in the law of Moses, that thou mayest prosper in all that thou doest, and Twhithersoever thou turnest thyself;   *wherever you go*

4 That the LORD may continue his word which he spake concerning me, saying, If thy children take heed to their way, to walk before me in truth with all their heart and with all their soul, there shall not fail thee (said he) a man on the throne of Israel.

5 Moreover thou knowest also what Jo'-ab the son of Ze-ru'-iah did to me, *and* what he did to the two captains of the hosts of Israel, Runto Abner the son of Ner, and unto RAm'-a-sa the son of Je'-ther, whom he slew, and shed the blood of war in peace, and put the blood of war upon his girdle that *was* about his loins, and in his shoes that *were* on his feet.   2 Sam. 3:27 · 2 Sam. 20:10

6 Do therefore Raccording to thy wisdom, and let not his Thoar head go down to Tthe grave in peace.   *v. 9; Prov. 20:26 · gray · Sheol*

7 But shew kindness unto the sons of Bar-zil'-lai the Gil'-e-ad-ite, and let them be of those that eat at thy table: for so Rthey came to me when I fled Tbecause of Ab'-sa-lom thy brother.   2 Sam. 17:27 · *from*

8 And, behold, *thou hast* with thee Shim'-e-i the son of Ge'-ra, a Benjamite of Ba-hu'-rim, which cursed me with a grievous curse in the day when I went to Ma-ha-na'-im: but he came down to meet me at Jordan, and RI sware to him by the LORD, saying, I will not put thee to death with the sword.   2 Sam. 19:23

9 Now therefore Rhold him not guiltless: Rfor thou *art* a wise man, and knowest what thou oughtest to do unto him; Rbut his hoar head bring thou down to the grave with blood.   Ex. 20:7; Job 9:28 · v. 6 · vv. 36–46

David Dies—1 Chr. 3:4; 29:26–28

10 So David slept with his fathers, and was buried in Rthe city of David.   2 Sam. 5:7

11 And the days that David Rreigned over Israel *were* forty years: seven years reigned he in He'-bron, and thirty and three years reigned he in Jerusalem.   1 Chr. 29:26, 27

Solomon Is Established as King—1 Chr. 29:23

12 RThen sat Solomon upon the throne of David his father; and his kingdom was established Tgreatly.   1 Chr. 29:23; 2 Chr. 1:1 · *firmly*

Adonijah Is Executed

13 And Ad-o-ni'-jah the son of Hag'-gith came to Bath-she'-ba the mother of Solomon. And she said, RComest thou peaceably? And he said, Peaceably.   1 Sam. 16:4, 5

14 He said moreover, I have somewhat to say unto thee. And she said, Say on.

15 And he said, Thou knowest that the kingdom was mine, and *that* all Israel set their faces on me, that I should reign: howbeit the kingdom is turned about, and is become my brother's: for Rit was his Tfrom the LORD.   1 Chr. 22:9, 10; Dan. 2:21 · *in the will of God*

16 And now I ask one petition of thee, deny me not. And she said unto him, Say on.

17 And he said, Speak, I pray thee, unto Solomon the king, (for he will not say thee nay,) that he give me RAb'-i-shag the Shu'-nam-mite to wife.   1:3, 4; 2 Sam. 12:8

18 And Bath-she'-ba said, Well; I will speak for thee unto the king.

19 Bath-she'-ba therefore went unto king Solomon, to speak unto him for Ad-o-ni'-jah. And the king rose up to meet her, and Rbowed himself unto her, and sat down on his throne, and caused a Tseat to be set for the king's mother; Rand she sat on his right hand.   Ex. 20:12 · *showed honour · throne* · Ps. 45:9

20 Then she said, I desire one small

petition of thee; ᴿI pray thee, say me not nay. And the king said unto her, Ask on, my mother: for I will not say thee nay.   v. 16

21 And she said, Let Ab'-i-shag the Shu'-nam-mite be given to Ad-o-ni'-jah thy brother ᵀto wife.   in marriage

22 And king Solomon answered and said unto his mother, And why dost thou ask Ab'-i-shag the Shu-'nam-mite for ᴿAd-o-ni'-jah? ask for him the kingdom also; ᴿfor he is mine elder brother; even for him, and for ᴿA-bi'-a-thar the priest, and for Jo'-ab the son of Ze-ru'-iah.   2 Sam. 12:8 • v. 15 • 1:7

23 Then king Solomon sware by the LORD, saying, ᴿGod do so to me, and more also, if Ad-o-ni'-jah have not spoken this word against his own ᴿlife.   Ruth 1:17 • 1:52

24 Now therefore, as the LORD liveth, which hath established me, and set me on the throne of David my father, and who hath made me an house, as he promised, Ad-o-ni'-jah shall be put to death this day.

25 And king Solomon ᴿsent by the hand of Be-na'-iah the son of Je-hoi'-a-da; and he fell upon him that he died.   2 Sam. 8:18

Abiathar Is Removed

26 And unto A-bi'-a-thar the priest said the king, Get thee to ᴿAn'-a-thoth, unto thine own fields; for thou art worthy of death: but I will not at this time put thee to death, because thou barest the ark of the Lord GOD before David my father, and because thou hast been afflicted in all wherein my father was afflicted.   Josh. 21:18

27 So Solomon thrust out A-bi'-a-thar from being priest unto the LORD; that he might ᴿfulfil the word of the LORD, which he spake concerning the house of E'-li in Shi'-loh.   1 Sam. 2:31-35

Joab Is Executed

28 Then tidings came to Jo'-ab: for Jo'-ab had turned after Ad-o-ni'-jah, though he turned not after Ab'-sa-lom. And Jo'-ab fled unto the tabernacle of the LORD, and caught hold on the horns of the altar.

29 And it was told king Solomon that Jo'-ab was fled unto the tabernacle of the LORD; and, behold, he is by the altar. Then Solomon ᴿsent Be-na'-iah the son of Je-hoi'-a-da, saying, Go, fall upon him.   v. 25

30 And Be-na'-iah came to the tabernacle of the LORD, and said unto him, Thus saith the king, Come forth. And he said, Nay; but I will die here. And Be-na'-iah brought the king word again, saying, Thus said Jo'-ab, and thus he answered me.

31 And the king said unto him, ᴿDo as he hath said, and fall upon him, and bury him; that thou mayest take away the innocent

blood, which Jo'-ab shed, from me, and from the house of my father.   [Ex. 21:14]

32 And ᴿthe LORD shall return his blood upon his own head, who fell upon two men more righteous and better than he, and slew them with the sword, my father David not knowing thereof, to wit, ᴿAbner the son of Ner, captain of the host of Israel, and ᴿAm'-a-sa the son of Je'-ther, captain of the host of Judah.   [Gen. 9:6] • 2 Sam. 3:27 • 2 Sam. 20:10

33 Their blood shall therefore return upon the head of Jo'-ab, and ᴿupon the head of his seed for ever: ᴿbut upon David, and upon his seed, and upon his house, and upon his throne, shall there be peace for ever from the LORD.   2 Sam. 3:29 • [Prov. 25:5]

34 So ᴿBe-na'-iah the son of Je-hoi'-a-da went up, and fell upon him, and slew him: and he was buried in his own house in the wilderness.   v. 25

35 And the king put Be-na'-iah the son of Je-hoi'-a-da in his room over the host: and Za'-dok the priest did the king put in the room of A-bi'-a-thar.

Shimei Is Executed

36 And the king sent and called for ᴿShim'-e-i, and said unto him, Build thee an house in Jerusalem, and dwell there, and go not forth thence any whither.   v. 8

37 For it shall be, that on the day thou goest out, and passest over the brook Kid'-ron, thou shalt know for certain that thou shalt surely die: ᴿthy ᵀblood shall be upon thine own head.   Lev. 20:9 • it will be your own fault

38 And Shim'-e-i said unto the king, The saying is good: as my lord the king hath said, so will thy servant do. And Shim'-e-i dwelt in Jerusalem many days.

39 And it came to pass at the end of three years, that two of the servants of Shim'-e-i ran away unto A'-chish son of Ma'-a-chah king of Gath. And they told Shim'-e-i, saying, Behold, thy servants be in Gath.

40 And Shim'-e-i arose, and saddled his ass, and went to Gath to A'-chish to seek his servants: and Shim'-e-i went, and brought his servants from Gath.

41 And it was told Solomon that Shim'-e-i had gone from Jerusalem to Gath, and was come again.

42 And the king sent and called for Shim'-e-i, and said unto him, Did I not make thee to swear by the LORD, and protested unto thee, saying, Know for a certain, on the day thou goest out, and walkest abroad any whither, that thou shalt surely die? and thou saidst unto me, The word that I have heard is good.

43 Why then hast thou not kept the ᴿoath of the LORD, and the commandment that I have charged thee with?   Ezek. 17:19

44 The king said moreover to Shim'-e-i,

Thou knowest all the wickedness which thine heart is privy to, that thou didst to David my father: therefore the LORD shall return thy wickedness upon thine own head;

45 And king Solomon *shall be* blessed, and Rthe throne of David shall be established before the LORD for ever.   [Prov. 25:5]

46 So the king commanded Be-na'-iah the son of Je-hoi'-a-da; which went out, and fell upon him, that he died. And the kingdom was established in the hand of Solomon.

CHAPTER 3

Unwise Marriage of Solomon

AND Solomon made affinity with Pharaoh king of Egypt, and took Pharaoh's daughter, and brought her into the city of David, until he had made an end of building his own house, and the house of the LORD, and the wall of Jerusalem round about.

2 Only the people sacrificed in high places, because there was no house built unto the name of the LORD, until those days.

Request for Wisdom—2 Chr. 1:2–13

3 And Solomon loved the LORD, walking in the statutes of David his father: only he sacrificed and burnt incense in high places.

4 And the king went to Gib'-e-on to sacrifice there; Rfor that *was* the great high place: a thousand burnt offerings did Solomon offer upon that altar.   1 Chr. 16:39

5 RIn Gib'-e-on the LORD appeared to Solomon Rin a dream by night: and God said, Ask what I shall give thee.   9:2 • Matt. 1:20

6 RAnd Solomon said, Thou hast shewed unto thy servant David my father great mercy, according as he Rwalked before thee in truth, and in righteousness, and in uprightness of heart with thee; and thou hast kept for him this great kindness, that thou Rhast given him a son to sit on his throne, as *it is* this day.   2 Chr. 1:8 • 2 Kin. 20:3 • 1:48

7 And now, O LORD my God, thou hast made thy servant king instead of David my father: and I *am but* a little child: I know not how Rto go out or come in.   Num. 27:17

8 And thy servant *is* in the midst of thy people which thou Rhast chosen, a great people, Rthat cannot be numbered nor counted for multitude.   [Deut. 7:6] • Gen. 13:16

9 Give therefore thy servant an Tunderstanding heart Rto judge thy people, that I may Rdiscern between good and bad: for who is able to judge this thy so great a people?   *hearing* • Ps. 72:1, 2 • Is. 7:15; [Heb. 5:14]

10 And the speech pleased the LORD, that Solomon had asked this thing.

11 And God said unto him, Because thou hast asked this thing, and hast Rnot asked for thyself long life; neither hast asked riches for thyself, nor hast asked the life of thine enemies; but hast asked for thyself understanding to discern judgment;   [James 4:3]

12 Behold, I have done according to thy words: lo, I have given thee a wise and an understanding heart; so that there was none like thee before thee, neither after thee shall any arise like unto thee.

13 And RI have also given thee that which thou hast not asked, both riches, and honour: so that there shall not be any among the kings like unto thee all thy days.   1 Kin. 10:23

14 And if thou wilt walk in my ways, to Tkeep my statutes and my commandments, as thy father David did walk, then I will Tlengthen thy days.   *obey • prolong your life*

15 And Solomon Rawoke; and, behold, *it was* a dream. And he came to Jerusalem, and stood before the ark of the covenant of the LORD, and offered up burnt offerings, and offered peace offerings, and Rmade a feast to all his servants.   Gen. 41:7 • Mark 6:21

Display of Solomon's Wisdom

16 Then came there two women, *that were* harlots, unto the king, and Rstood before him.   Num. 27:2

17 And the one woman said, O my lord, I and this woman dwell in one house; and I was delivered of a child with her in the house.

18 And it came to pass the third day after that I was delivered, that this woman was delivered also: and we *were* together; *there was* no Tstranger with us in the house, Tsave we two in the house.   *other person • except*

19 And this woman's child died in the night; because she Toverlaid it.   *lay on*

20 And she arose at midnight, and took my son from beside me, while thine handmaid slept, and laid it in her bosom, and laid her dead child in my bosom.

21 And when I rose in the morning to give my child suck, behold, it was dead: but when I had Tconsidered it in the morning, behold, it was not my son, which I did bear.   *looked at*

22 And the other woman said, Nay; but the living *is* my son, and the dead *is* thy son. And this said, No; but the dead *is* thy son, and the living *is* my son. Thus they spake before the king.

23 Then said the king, The one saith, This *is* my son that liveth, and thy son *is* the dead: and the other saith, Nay; but thy son *is* the dead, and my son *is* the living.

24 And the king said, Bring me a sword. And they brought a sword before the king.

25 And the king said, Divide the living child in two, and give half to the one, and half to the other.

26 Then spake the woman whose the living child *was* unto the king, for her

[T]bowels yearned upon her son, and she said, O my lord, give her the living child, and in no wise slay it. But the other said, Let it be neither mine nor thine, *but* divide *it.*   *heart*

27 Then the king answered and said, Give her the living child, [T]and in no wise slay it: she *is* the mother thereof.   *by no means*

National Recognition of Solomon's Wisdom

28 And all Israel heard of the judgment which the king had judged; and they feared the king: for they saw that the [R]wisdom of God *was* in him, to do judgment.   *vv. 9, 11, 12*

CHAPTER 4

Eleven Princes

SO king Solomon was king over all Israel. 2 And these *were* the [R]princes which he had; [R]Az-a-ri'-ah the son of Za'-dok [T]the priest,   1 Chr. 27:22 • 1 Chr. 6:10 • *the chief officer*

3 El-i-ho'-reph and A-hi'-ah, the sons of Shi'-sha, scribes; Je-hosh'-a-phat the son of A-hi'-lud, the recorder.

4 And [R]Be-na'-iah the son of Je-hoi'-a-da *was* over the host: and Za'-dok and [R]A-bi'-a-thar *were* the priests: 2:35 • 2:27

5 And Az-a-ri'-ah the son of Nathan *was* over [R]the officers: and Za'-bud the son of Nathan *was* [R]principal officer, *and* [R]the king's friend: *v. 7* • 2 Sam. 8:18 • 1 Chr. 27:33

6 And A-hi'-shar *was* over the household: and [R]Ad-o-ni'-ram the son of Ab'-da *was* over the [T]tribute.   5:14 • *levy*

Twelve Officers

7 And Solomon had twelve officers over all Israel, which provided [T]victuals for the king and his household: each man his month in a year made provision.   *food*

8 And these *are* their names: [T]The son of Hur, [R]in mount E'-phra-im: *Ben-hur* • Josh. 24:33

9 [T]The son of De'-kar, in Ma'-kaz, and in [R]Sha-al'-bim, and Beth-she'-mesh, and E'-lon-beth-ha'-nan: *Ben-deker* • Judg. 1:35

10 [T]The son of He'-sed, in Ar'-u-both; to him *pertained* [R]So'-choh, and all the land of [R]He'-pher: *Ben-hesed* • Josh. 15:35 • Josh. 12:17

11 [R]The son of A-bin'-a-dab, in all the region of Dor; which had Ta'-phath the daughter of Solomon to wife: Josh. 11:1, 2

12 Ba'-a-na the son of A-hi'-lud; *to him pertained* [R]Ta'-a-nach and Me-gid'-do, and all [R]Beth-she'-an, which *is* by Zar'-ta-nah beneath Jez'-re-el, from Beth-she'-an to A'-bel-me-ho'-lah, *even* unto *the place that is* beyond Jok'-ne-am: Judg. 5:19 • Josh. 17:11

13 The son of Ge'-ber, in Ra'-moth-gil'-e-ad; to him *pertained* the towns of Ja'-ir the son of Ma-nas'-seh, which *are* in Gil'-e-ad; to him *also pertained* the region of Ar'-gob,

which *is* in Ba'-shan, threescore great cities with walls and brasen bars:

14 A-hin'-a-dab the son of Id'-do *had* [R]Ma-ha-na'-im: Josh. 13:26

15 [R]A-him'-a-az *was* in Naph'-ta-li; he also took Bas'-math the daughter of Solomon [T]to wife: 2 Sam. 15:27 • *as his wife*

16 Ba'-a-nah the son of [R]Hu'-shai *was* in Asher and in [T]A'-loth: 2 Sam. 15:32 • *Bealoth*

17 Je-hosh'-a-phat the son of Pa-ru'-ah, in Is'-sa-char:

18 [R]Shim'-e-i the son of E'-lah, in Ben-jamin: 1:8

19 Ge'-ber the son of U'-ri *was* in the country of Gil'-e-ad, *in* [R]the country of Si'-hon king of the Am'-or-ites, and of Og king of Ba'-shan; and *he was* the only officer which *was* in the land.   Deut. 3:8–10

Solomon Reigns in Wisdom

20 Judah and Israel *were* many, as the sand which *is* by the sea in multitude, eating and drinking, and making merry.

21 And [R]Solomon reigned over all kingdoms from the river unto the land of the Phi-lis'-tines, and unto the border of Egypt: [R]they brought presents, and served Solomon all the days of his life.   Ps. 72:8 • Ps. 68:29

22 And Solomon's provision for one day was [T]thirty measures of fine flour, and [T]threescore measures of meal,   *196 bushels* • *391 bushels*

23 Ten fat oxen, and twenty oxen out of the pastures, and an hundred sheep, beside harts, and roebucks, and fallowdeer, and fatted fowl.

24 For he had dominion over all *the region* on this side the river, from Tiph'-sah even to [T]Az'-zah, over [R]all the kings on this side the river: and he had peace on all sides round about him.   *Ga'-za* • Ps. 72:11

25 And Judah and Israel dwelt safely, every man [T]under his vine and under his fig tree, from Dan even to Be'-er-she'-ba, all the days of Solomon.   *with his own property*

26 And [R]Solomon had forty thousand stalls of [R]horses for his chariots, and twelve thousand horsemen.   10:26 • [Deut. 17:16]

27 And [R]those officers provided [T]victual for king Solomon, and for all that came unto king Solomon's table, every man in his month: they lacked nothing.   *v. 7* • *food supplies*

28 Barley also and straw for the horses and [T]dromedaries brought they unto the place where *the officers* were, every man according to his [T]charge.   *mules* • *responsibility*

29 And [R]God gave Solomon wisdom and understanding exceeding much, and [T]large-ness of heart, even as the sand that *is* on the sea shore.   3:12 • *generosity*

30 And Solomon's wisdom excelled the wisdom of all the children [R]of the east country, and all the wisdom of Egypt. Gen. 25:6

31 For he was wiser than all men; than E'-than the Ez'-ra-hite, and He'-man, and Chal'-col, and Dar'-da, the sons of Ma'-hol: and his fame was in all nations round about.

32 And ᴿhe spake three thousand proverbs: and his ᴿsongs were a thousand and five.   Prov. 1:1; Eccl. 12:9 · Song. 1:1

33 And he spake of trees, from the cedar tree that is in Leb'-a-non even unto the hyssop that springeth out of the wall: he spake also of beasts, and of fowl, and of creeping things, and of fishes.

34 And there came of all people to hear the wisdom of Solomon, from all kings of the earth, which had heard of his wisdom.

CHAPTER 5

Temple Materials—2 Chr. 2:3–12

AND Hiram king of Tyre sent his servants unto Solomon; for he had heard that they had ᵀanointed him king in the room of his father: ᴿfor Hiram was ever a lover of David.   *installed* · 2 Sam. 5:11; 1 Chr. 14:1

2 And Solomon sent to Hiram, saying,

3 Thou knowest how that David my father could not build an house unto the name of the LORD his God for the wars which were about him on every side, until the LORD put them under the soles of his feet.

4 But now the LORD my God hath given me rest on every side, so that there is neither adversary nor evil ᵀoccurrent.   *activity*

5 ᴿAnd, behold, ᴿI purpose to build an house unto the name of the LORD my God, ᴿas the LORD spake unto David my father, saying, Thy son, whom I will set upon thy throne in thy room, he shall build an house unto my name.   2 Chr. 2:4 · 1 Chr. 17:12 · 2 Sam. 7:13

6 Now therefore command thou that they hew me cedar trees out of Leb'-a-non; and my servants shall be with thy servants: and unto thee will I give hire for thy servants according to all that thou shalt ᵀappoint: for thou knowest that there is not among us any that ᵀcan skill to hew timber like unto the Si-do'-ni-ans.   *say · are skilled*

7 And it came to pass, when Hiram heard the words of Solomon, that he rejoiced greatly, and said, Blessed be the LORD this day, which hath given unto David a wise son over this great people.

8 And Hiram sent to Solomon, saying, I have considered the things which thou sentest to me for: and I will do all thy desire concerning timber of cedar, and concerning timber of fir.

9 My servants shall bring them down from Leb'-a-non unto the sea: and I will convey them by sea in floats unto the place that thou shalt appoint me, and will cause them to be

discharged there, and thou shalt receive them: and thou shalt accomplish my desire, ᴿin giving food for my household.   Acts 12:20

10 So Hiram gave Solomon cedar trees and fir trees *according to* all his desire.

11 And Solomon gave Hiram twenty thousand measures of wheat *for* food to his household, and twenty measures of pure oil: thus gave Solomon to Hiram year by year.

12 And the LORD gave Solomon wisdom, as he promised him: and there was peace between Hiram and ᴿSolomon; and they two ᵀmade a league together.   9:15 · *made a treaty*

Temple Labourers—2 Chr. 2:2, 17, 18

13 And king ᴿSolomon raised a ᵀlevy out of all Israel; and the levy was thirty thousand men.   4:6; 9:15 · *draft*

14 And he sent them to Leb'-a-non, ten thousand a month by courses: a month they were in Leb'-a-non, *and* two months at home: and Ad-o-ni'-ram *was* over the levy.

15 ᴿAnd Solomon had threescore and ten thousand that bare burdens, and fourscore thousand hewers in the mountains;   9:21

16 ᴿBeside the chief of Solomon's officers which *were* over the work, three thousand and three hundred, which ruled over the people that wrought in the work.   2 Chr. 2:2

17 And the king commanded, and they brought great stones, costly stones, *and* hewed stones, to lay the foundation of the house.

18 And Solomon's builders and Hiram's builders did ᵀhew *them*, and the ᵀstone-squarers: so they prepared timber and stones to build the house.   *fashion · Gebalites*

CHAPTER 6

The Temple Is Completed—2 Chr. 3:1–14

AND ᴿit came to pass in the four hundred and eightieth year after the children of Israel were come out of the land of Egypt, in the fourth year of Solomon's reign over Israel, in the month Zif, which *is* the second month, that ᴿhe began to build the house of the LORD.   2 Chr. 3:1, 2 · Acts 7:47

2 And ᴿthe house which king Solomon built for the LORD, the length thereof *was* ᵀthreescore cubits, and the breadth thereof ᵀtwenty *cubits*, and the height thereof ᵀthirty cubits.   Ezek. 41:1 · *90 ft.* · *30 ft.* · *45 ft.*

3 And the porch before the temple of the house, ᵀtwenty cubits *was* the length thereof, according to the breadth of the house; *and* ᵀten cubits *was* the breadth thereof before the house.   *30 ft.* · *15 ft.*

4 And for the house he made ᴿwindows of narrow ᵀlights.   Ezek. 40:16; 41:16 · *lattice-work*

5 And ᴿagainst the wall of the house he

built Tchambers round about, *against* the walls of the house round about, *both* of the temple and of the Toracle: and he made chambers round about: Ezek. 41:6 • *rooms* • *chapel*

6 The Tnethermost chamber *was* Tfive cubits broad, and the middle *was* Tsix cubits broad, and the third *was* Tseven cubits broad: for without *in the wall* of the house he made Tnarrowed rests round about, that *the beams* should not be fastened in the walls of the house.   *lowest story* • *7.5 ft.* • *9 ft.* • *10.5 ft.* • *offsets*

7 And the house, when it was in building, was built of stone made ready before it was brought thither: so that there was neither hammer nor axe *nor* any tool of iron heard in the house, while it was in building.

8 The door for the Tmiddle chamber *was* in the right side of the house: and they went up with winding stairs into the middle *chamber,* and out of the middle into the third.   *side*

9 RSo he built the house, and finished it; and covered the house with beams and boards of cedar.   *vv.* 14, 38

10 And *then* he built Tchambers against all the house, Tfive cubits high: and they rested on the house with timber of cedar.   *stories* • *7.5 ft.*

11 And the word of the LORD came to Solomon, saying,

12 *Concerning* this house which thou art in building, if thou wilt walk in my statutes, and execute my judgments, and keep all my commandments to walk in them; then will I perform my word with thee, which I spake unto David thy father:

13 And RI will dwell among the children of Israel, and will not Rforsake my people Israel.   Ex. 25:8; [2 Cor. 6:16; Rev. 21:3] • [Deut. 31:6]

14 RSo Solomon built the house, and finished it.   *vv.* 9, 38

15 And he built the walls of the house within with boards of Rcedar, Tboth the floor of the house, Tand the walls of the cieling: *and* he covered *them* on the inside with wood, and covered the floor of the house with planks of fir.   7:7 • *from* • *unto*

16 And he built Ttwenty cubits on the sides of the house, both the floor and the walls with boards of cedar: he even built *them* for it within, *even* for the oracle, *even* for the Rmost holy *place.*   *30 ft.* • 2 Chr. 3:8; Ezek. 45:3

17 And the house, that *is,* the temple Tbefore it, was Tforty cubits *long.*   *the oracle* • *60 ft.*

18 And the cedar of the house within *was* carved with Tknops and open flowers: all *was* cedar; there was no stone seen.   *gourds*

19 And the Toracle he prepared in the house within, to set there the ark of the covenant of the LORD.   *chapel*

20 And the oracle in the forepart *was* twenty cubits in length, and twenty cubits in breadth, and twenty cubits in the height

thereof: and he overlaid it with pure gold; and so covered the altar *which was of* cedar.

21 So Solomon overlaid the house Twithin with pure gold: and he made a partition by the chains of gold before the Toracle; and he overlaid it with gold.   *inside* • *inner sanctuary*

22 And the whole house he overlaid with gold, until he had finished all the house: also Rthe whole altar that *was* by the oracle he overlaid with gold.   Ex. 30:1, 3, 6

23 And within the oracle Rhe made two cher'-u-bims *of* olive tree, *each* Tten cubits high.   Ex. 37:7–9; 2 Chr. 3:10–12 • *15 ft.*

24 And Tfive cubits *was* the one wing of the cherub, and five cubits the other wing of the cherub: from the Tuttermost part of the one wing unto the uttermost part of the other *were* Tten cubits.   *7.5 ft.* • *outmost* • *15 ft.*

25 And the other cherub *was* Tten cubits: both the Rcher'-u-bims *were* of one measure and one size.   *15 ft.* • Ezek. 9:3

26 The height of the one cherub *was* ten cubits, and so *was it* of the other cherub.

27 And he set the cher'-u-bims within the inner house: and Rthey stretched forth the wings of the cher'-u-bims, so that the wing of the one touched the *one* wall, and the wing of the other cherub touched the other wall; and their wings touched one another in the midst of the house.   Ex. 25:20; 2 Chr. 5:8

28 And he overlaid the cher'-u-bims with gold.

29 And he carved all the walls of the house round about with carved Rfigures of cher'-u-bims and palm trees and open flowers, within and without.   Ex. 36:8, 35

30 And the floor of the house he overlaid with gold, within and without.

31 And for the Tentering of the oracle he made doors *of* olive tree: the lintel *and* side posts *were* a fifth part *of the wall.*   *entrance*

32 The two doors also *were of* olive tree; and he carved upon them carvings of cher'-u-bims and palm trees and open flowers, and overlaid *them* with gold, and spread gold upon the Rcher'-u-bims, and upon the palm trees.   Ex. 25:18

33 So also made he for the door of the temple posts *of* olive tree, Ta fourth part *of the wall.*   *in the form of a square*

34 And the two doors *were of* fir tree: the Rtwo Tleaves of the one door *were* folding, and the two leaves of the other door *were* folding.   Ezek. 41:23–25 • *panels*

35 And he carved *thereon* cher'-u-bims and palm trees and open flowers: and covered *them* with gold fitted upon the carved work.

36 And he built the Rinner court with three rows of hewed stone, and a row of cedar beams.   7:12

37 RIn the fourth year was the foundation

of the house of the LORD laid, in the month Zif: v. 1

38 And in the eleventh year, in the month Bul, which is the eighth month, was the house finished throughout all the parts thereof, and according to all the fashion of it. So was he seven years in building it.

CHAPTER 7

Construction of Solomon's House

BUT Solomon was building his own house ^Rthirteen years, and he finished all his house.   9:10; 2 Chr. 8:1

2 He built also the house of the forest of Leb'-a-non; the length thereof was an ^Thundred cubits, and the breadth thereof ^Tfifty cubits, and the height thereof ^Tthirty cubits, upon four rows of cedar pillars, with cedar beams upon the pillars.   150 ft. • 75 ft. • 45 ft.

3 And it was covered with cedar above upon the ^Tbeams, that lay on forty five pillars, fifteen in a row.   ribs

4 And there were windows in three rows, and light was against light in three ranks.

5 And all the doors and posts were square, with the windows: and light was against light in three ^Tranks.   tiers

6 And he made a porch of pillars; the length thereof was fifty cubits, and the breadth thereof thirty cubits: and the porch was before them: and the other pillars and the thick beam were before them.

7 Then he made a porch for the throne where he might judge, even the porch of judgment: and it was covered with cedar from one side of the floor to the other.

8 And his house where he dwelt had another court within the porch, which was of the like work. Solomon made also an house for Pharaoh's daughter, whom he had taken to wife, ^Tlike unto this porch.   similar to

9 All these were of costly stones, according to the measures of hewed stones, sawed with saws, within and without, even from the foundation unto the ^Tcoping, and so on the outside toward the great court.   top

10 And the foundation was of costly stones, even great stones, stones of ^Tten cubits, and stones of ^Teight cubits.   15 ft. • 12 ft.

11 And above were costly stones, after the measures of hewed stones, and cedars.

12 And the great court round about was with ^Rthree rows of hewed stones, and a row of cedar beams, both for the inner court of the house of the LORD, ^Rand for the porch of the house.   6:36 • John 10:23; Acts 3:11

Furnishings of the Temple
2 Chr. 3:15—5:1

13 And king Solomon sent and fetched ^RHiram^T out of Tyre.   2 Chr. 4:11 • Huram

14 He was a widow's son of the tribe of Naph'-ta-li, and his father was a man of Tyre, a worker in brass: and he was filled with wisdom, and understanding, and cunning to work all works in brass. And he came to king Solomon, and wrought all his work.

15 For he cast ^Rtwo pillars of brass, of ^Teighteen cubits high apiece: and a line of ^Ttwelve cubits did ^Tcompass either of them about.   2 Kin. 25:17; Jer. 52:21 • 27 ft. • 18 ft. • encircle

16 And he made two ^Tchapiters of ^Tmolten brass, to set upon the tops of the pillars: the height of the one chapiter was ^Tfive cubits, and the height of the other chapiter was five cubits: capitals • melted bronze • 7.5 ft.

17 And nets of checker work, and wreaths of chain work, for the chapiters which were upon the top of the pillars; seven for the one chapiter, and seven for the other chapiter.

18 And he made the pillars, and two rows round about upon the one network, to cover the ^Tchapiters that were upon the top, with pomegranates: and so did he for the other chapiter.   capitals

19 And the ^Tchapiters that were upon the top of the pillars were of lily work in the porch, ^Tfour cubits.   capitals • 6 ft.

20 And the chapiters upon the two pillars had pomegranates also above, over against the belly which was by the network: and the pomegranates were two hundred in rows round about upon the other chapiter.

21 ^RAnd he set up the pillars in the porch of the temple: and he set up the right pillar, and called the name thereof Ja'-chin: and he set up the left pillar, and called the name thereof Bo'-az.   2 Chr. 3:17

22 And upon the top of the pillars was lily work: so was the work of the pillars finished.

23 And he made a molten sea, ^Tten cubits from the one brim to the other: it was round all about, and his height was ^Tfive cubits: and a line of ^Tthirty cubits did compass it round about.   15 ft. • 7.5 ft. • 45 ft.

24 And under the brim of it round about there were ^Tknops compassing it, ten in ^Ta cubit, ^Rcompassing the sea round about: the knops were cast in two rows, when it was cast.   gourds • 18 in. • 2 Chr. 4:3

25 It stood upon twelve oxen, three looking toward the north, and three looking toward the west, and three looking toward the south, and three looking toward the east: and the sea was set above upon them, and all their hinder parts were inward.

26 And it was an ^Thand breadth thick, and the brim thereof was wrought like the brim of a cup, with flowers of lilies: it contained ^Ttwo thousand baths.   3 in. • 12,000 gal.

27 And he made ten ^Tbases of brass; ^Tfour cubits was the length of one base, and four

cubits the breadth thereof, and ᵀthree cubits the height of it. *supports · 6 ft. · 4.5 ft.*

28 And the work of the ᵀbases *was* on this manner: they had borders, and the borders *were* between the ᵀledges: *panels · frames*

29 And on the borders that *were* between the ledges *were* lions, oxen, and cher'-u-bims: and upon the ledges *there was* a base above: and beneath the lions and oxen *were* certain additions made of thin work.

30 And every base had four ᵀbrasen wheels, andᵀ plates of brass: and the fourᵀ corners thereof had undersetters: under the laver *were* undersetters molten, at the side of every addition. *bronze · axles · feet*

31 And the mouth of it within the chapiter and above *was* ᵀa cubit: but the mouth thereof *was* round *after* the work of the base, a ᵀcubit and an half: and also upon the mouth of it *were* gravings with their borders, foursquare, not round. *18 in. · 27 in.*

32 And under the ᵀborders *were* four wheels; and the axletrees of the wheels *were* joined to the base: and the height of a wheel *was* ᵀa cubit and half a cubit. *panels · 27 in.*

33 And the work of the wheels *was* like the work of a chariot wheel: their ᵀaxletrees, and their ᵀnaves, and their ᵀfelloes, and their spokes, *were* all ᵀmolten. *axles · hubs · rims · cast*

34 And *there were* four undersetters to the four corners of one base: *and* the undersetters *were* of the very base itself.

35 And in the top of the base *was there* a round compass of ᵀhalf a cubit high: and on the top of the base the ledges thereof and the borders thereof *were* of the same. *9 in.*

36 For on the plates of the ᵀledges thereof, and on the ᵀborders thereof, he ᵀgraved cher'-u-bims, lions, and palm trees, according to the ᵀproportion of every one, and additions round about. *frames · panels · carved · size*

37 ᴿAfter this *manner* he made the ten bases: all of them had ᵀone casting, one measure, *and* one size. *2 Chr. 4:14 · the same*

38 Then made he ten lavers of brass: one laver contained ᵀforty baths: *and* every laver was ᵀfour cubits: *and* upon every one of the ten bases one laver. *240 gallons · 6 ft.*

39 And he put five bases on the right side of the house, and five on the left side of the house: and he set the sea on the right side of the house eastward over against the south.

40 And Hiram made the lavers, and the shovels, and the basons. So Hiram ᵀmade an end of doing all the work that he made king Solomon for the house of the LORD: *finished*

41 The two pillars, and the *two* bowls of the chapiters that *were* on the top of the two pillars; and the two ᴿnetworks, to cover the two bowls of the chapiters which *were* upon the top of the pillars; *vv. 17, 18*

42 And ᴿfour hundred pomegranates for the two networks, *even* two rows of pomegranates for one network, to cover the two bowls of the chapiters that *were* ᵀupon the pillars; *v. 20 · upon the face of the pillars*

43 And the ten bases, and ten lavers on the bases;

44 And ᴿone sea, and twelve oxen under the sea; *vv. 23, 25*

45 ᴿAnd the pots, and the shovels, and the basons: and all these vessels, which Hiram made to king Solomon for the house of the LORD, *were of* bright brass. *Ex. 27:3*

46 In the plain of Jordan did the king cast them, in the clay ground between Suc'-coth and ᴿZar'-than. *Josh. 3:16*

47 And Solomon left all the vessels *unweighed,* because they were exceeding many: ᴿneither was the weight of the brass found out. *1 Chr. 22:3, 14*

48 And Solomon made all the vessels that *pertained* unto the house of the LORD: ᴿthe altar of gold, and the table of gold, whereupon the shewbread *was,* *2 Chr. 4:8*

49 And the ᴿcandlesticks of pure gold, five on the right *side,* and five on the left, before the oracle, with the flowers, and the lamps, and the tongs *of* gold, *Ex. 25:31–38*

50 And the bowls, and the snuffers, and the basons, and the spoons, and the ᴿcensersᵀ *of* pure gold; and the hinges *of* gold, *both* for the doors of the inner house, the most holy *place, and* for the doors of the house, ᵀto wit, of the temple. *Ex. 27:3 · firepans · namely*

51 ᴿSo was ended all the work that king Solomon made for the house of the LORD. And Solomon brought in the things ᴿwhich David his father had dedicated; *even* the silver, and the gold, and the vessels, did he put among the treasures of the house of the LORD. *2 Chr. 5:1 · 2 Sam. 8:11*

CHAPTER 8

The Ark Returns—2 Chr. 5:2–12

THEN Solomon assembled the elders of Israel, and all the heads of the tribes, the chief of the fathers of the children of Israel, unto king Solomon in Jerusalem, that they might bring up the ark of the covenant of the LORD out of the city of David, which *is* Zion.

2 And all the men of Israel assembled themselves unto king Solomon at the ᴿfeast in the month Eth'-a-nim, which *is* the seventh month. *v. 65; Lev. 23:34; 2 Chr. 7:8*

3 And all the elders of Israel came, ᴿand the priests took up the ark. *Num. 4:15; 7:9*

4 And they brought up the ark of the LORD, ᴿand the tabernacle of the congregation, and all the holy vessels that *were* in the

tabernacle, even those did the priests and the Levites bring up.   3:4; 2 Chr. 1:3

5 And king Solomon, and all the congregation of Israel, that were assembled unto him, *were* with him before the ark, Rsacrificing sheep and oxen, that could not be told nor numbered for multitude.   2 Sam. 6:13

6 And Rthe priests Rbrought in the ark of the covenant of the LORD unto Rhis place, into the oracle of the house, to the most holy *place, even* Runder the wings of the cher'-u-bims.   *v.* 3 • 2 Sam. 6:17 • 6:19 • 6:27

7 RFor the cher'-u-bims spread forth *their* two wings over the place of the ark, and the cher'-u-bims covered the ark and the staves thereof above.   6:27

8 And they drew out the staves, that the Tends of the staves were seen out in the holy *place* before the oracle, and they were not seen without: and there they are unto Tthis day.   *heads* • *when this record was written*

9 RThere *was* nothing in the ark save the two tables of stone, which Moses put there at Ho'-reb, when the LORD made *a covenant* with the children of Israel, when they came out of the land of Egypt.   Ex. 25:21

The Shechinah Returns—2 Chr. 5:13, 14

10 And it came to pass, when the priests were come out of the holy *place*, that the cloud Rfilled the house of the LORD,   Ex. 40:34

11 So that the priests could not stand to minister because of the cloud: for the Rglory of the LORD had filled the house of the LORD.   2 Chr. 7:1, 2; Ps. 8:1

Solomon's Sermon—2 Chr. 6:1–11

12 Then spake Solomon, The LORD said that he would dwell in the thick darkness.

13 RI have surely built thee an house to dwell in, Ra Tsettled place for thee to abide in for ever.   2 Sam. 7:13 • Ps. 132:14 • *permanent*

14 And the king turned his face about, and blessed all the congregation of Israel: (and all the congregation of Israel stood;)

15 And he said, RBlessed *be* the LORD God of Israel, which Rspake with his mouth unto David my father, and hath with his hand fulfilled *it*, saying,   Luke 1:68 • 2 Sam. 7:5, 25

16 Since the day that I brought forth my people Israel out of Egypt, I chose no city out of all the tribes of Israel to build an house, that my name might be therein; but I chose David to be over my people Israel.

17 And it Twas in the heart of David my father to build an house for the name of the LORD God of Israel.   *it was the intention of*

18 RAnd the LORD said unto David my father, Whereas it was in thine heart to build an house unto my name, thou didst well that it was in thine heart.   2 Chr. 6:8, 9

19 Nevertheless Rthou shalt not build the house; but thy son that shall come forth out of thy loins, Rhe shall build the house unto my name.   2 Sam. 7:5, 12, 13 • 5:3, 5

20 And the LORD hath performed his word that he spake, and I Tam risen up in the room of David my father, and sit on the throne of Israel, as the LORD Tpromised, and have built an house for the name of the LORD God of Israel.   *have taken the place* • *spoke*

21 And I have set there a place for the ark, wherein *is* the covenant of the LORD, which he made with our fathers, when he brought them out of the land of Egypt.

Solomon's Prayer—2 Chr. 6:12–39

22 And Solomon stood before the altar of the LORD in the presence of all the congregation of Israel, and Rspread forth his hands toward heaven: Ex. 9:33; Ezra 9:5

23 And he said, LORD God of Israel, *there is* no God like thee, in heaven above, or on earth beneath, who Tkeepest covenant and mercy with thy servants that walk before thee with all their heart: *keeps his word*

24 Who hast kept with thy servant David my father that thou promisedst him: thou spakest also with thy mouth, and hast fulfilled *it* with thine hand, as *it is* this day.

25 Therefore now, LORD God of Israel, keep with thy servant David my father that thou promisedst him, saying, There shall not fail thee a man in my sight to sit on the throne of Israel; so that thy children take heed to their way, that they walk before me as thou hast walked before me.

26 And now, O God of Israel, let thy word, I pray thee, be verified, which thou spakest unto thy servant David my father.

27 But Rwill God indeed dwell on the earth? behold, the heaven and heaven of heavens cannot contain thee; how much less this house that I have builded?   Is. 66:1

28 Yet Thave thou respect unto the prayer of thy servant, and to his supplication, O LORD my God, to hearken unto the cry and to the prayer, which thy servant prayeth before thee to day: *pay attention to*

29 That thine eyes may be open Ttoward this house night and day, *even* toward the place of which thou hast said, My name shall be there: that thou mayest hearken unto the prayer which thy servant shall make toward this place.   *to look with favour upon*

30 And hearken thou to the supplication of thy servant, and of thy people Israel, when they shall pray Ttoward this place: and hear thou in heaven thy dwelling place: and when thou hearest, forgive.   *in this place*

31 If any man trespass against his neighbour, and an oath be laid upon him to cause him to swear, and Tthe oath come before thine altar in this house: *he come and swear*

32 Then hear thou in heaven, and do, and judge thy servants, ᴿcondemning the wicked, to bring his way upon his head; and justifying the righteous, to give him according to his righteousness.   Deut. 25:1

33 When thy people Israel be smitten down before the enemy, because they have sinned against thee, and shall turn again to thee, and confess thy name, and pray, and make supplication unto thee in this house:

34 Then hear thou in heaven, and forgive the sin of thy people Israel, and bring them again unto the land which thou gavest unto their ᴿfathers.   [Deut. 30:1–3]

35 When heaven is shut up, and there is no rain, because they have sinned against thee; if they pray ᵀtoward this place, and confess thy name, and turn from their sin, when thou afflictest them: trusting thee in

36 Then hear thou in heaven, and forgive the sin of thy servants, and of thy people Israel, that thou ᴿteach them the good way wherein they should walk, and give rain upon thy land, which thou hast given to thy people for an inheritance.   Ps. 25:4

37 If there be in the land famine, if there be pestilence, blasting, mildew, locust, or if there be caterpiller; if their enemy besiege them in the land of their ᵀcities; whatsoever plague, whatsoever sickness there be;   gates

38 What prayer and supplication soever be made by any man, or by all thy people Israel, which shall know every man the plague of his own heart, and spread forth his ᵀhands toward this house: palms

39 Then hear thou in heaven thy dwelling place, and forgive, and do, and give to every man according to his ways, ᴿwhose heart thou knowest; (for thou, even thou only, ᴿknowest the hearts of all the children of men;)   [1 Sam. 2:3] • Ps. 11:4; [Jer. 17:10]

40 ᴿThat they may ᵀfear thee all the days that they live in the land which thou gavest unto our fathers.   [Ps. 130:4] • revere

41 Moreover concerning a stranger, that is not of thy people Israel, but cometh out of a far country for thy name's sake;

42 (For they shall hear of thy great name, and of thy ᴿstrong hand, and of thy stretched out arm;) when he shall come and pray toward this house;   Deut. 3:24

43 Hear thou in heaven thy dwelling place, and do according to all that the stranger calleth to thee for: that all people of the earth may know thy name, to ᴿfear thee, as do thy people Israel; and that they may know that this house, which I have builded, is called by thy name.   Ps. 102:15

44 If thy people go out to battle against their enemy, whithersoever thou shalt send them, and shall pray unto the Lᴏʀᴅ toward

the city which thou hast chosen, and toward the house that I have built for thy name:

45 Then hear thou in heaven their prayer and their supplication, and maintain their ᵀcause.   right

46 If they sin against thee, (for there is no man that sinneth not,) and thou be angry with them, and deliver them to the enemy, so that they carry them away captives unto the land of the enemy, far or near;

47 Yet if they shall bethink themselves in the land whither they were carried captives, and repent, and ᵀmake supplication unto thee in the land of them that carried them captives, ᴿsaying, We have sinned, and have done ᵀperversely, we have committed wickedness;   pray • Dan. 9:5 • wrong

48 And so return unto thee with all their heart, and with all their soul, in the land of their enemies, which led them away captive, and ᴿpray unto thee toward their land, which thou gavest unto their fathers, the city which thou hast chosen, and the house which I have built for thy name: Dan. 6:10

49 Then hear thou their prayer and their supplication in heaven thy dwelling place, and maintain their ᵀcause,   right

50 And forgive thy people that have sinned against thee, and all their transgressions wherein they have transgressed against thee, and give them compassion before them who carried them captive, that they may have compassion on them:

51 For ᴿthey be thy people, and thine inheritance, which thou broughtest forth out of Egypt, ᴿfrom the midst of the furnace of iron: Deut. 9:29; Neh. 1:10 • Deut. 4:20; Jer. 11:4

52 That thine eyes may be open unto the supplication of thy servant, and unto the supplication of thy people Israel, to hearken unto them in all that they call for unto thee.

53 For thou didst ᴿseparate them from among all the people of the earth, to be thine inheritance, as thou spakest by the hand of Moses thy servant, when thou broughtest our fathers out of Egypt, O Lord Gᴏᴅ.   Ezra 6:21

54 ᴿAnd it was so, that when Solomon had ᵀmade an end of praying all this prayer and supplication unto the Lᴏʀᴅ, he ᴿarose from before the altar of the Lᴏʀᴅ, from kneeling on his knees with his hands spread up to heaven.   2 Chr. 7:1 • finished • 2 Chr. 6:13

55 And he stood, and blessed all the congregation of Israel with a loud voice, saying,

56 Blessed be the Lᴏʀᴅ, that hath given rest unto his people Israel, according to all that he promised: there hath not failed one word of all his good promise, which he promised by the hand of Moses his servant.

57 The Lᴏʀᴅ our God be with us, as he was

with our fathers: Rlet him not leave us, nor forsake us: Deut. 31:6; Josh. 1:5; [Rom. 8:31-37]

58 That he may Rincline^T our hearts unto him, Rto walk in all his ways, and to keep his commandments, and his statutes, and his judgments, which he commanded our fathers. Ps. 119:36; Jer. 31:33 • lead • Gen. 5:22

59 And let these my words, wherewith I have made supplication before the LORD, be nigh unto the LORD our God day and night, that he maintain the cause of his servant, and the cause of his people Israel at all times, as Tthe matter shall require: every day

60 RThat all the people of the earth may Tknow that Rthe LORD is God, and that there is none else. 1 Sam. 17:46 • realize • Deut. 4:35, 39

61 Let your Rheart therefore be Tperfect with the LORD our God, to walk in his statutes, and to keep his commandments, as at this day. 11:4; 15:3, 14; 2 Kin. 20:3 • sincere

Israel Rejoices—2 Chr. 7:4-10

62 And the king, and all Israel with him, offered sacrifice before the LORD.

63 And Solomon offered a sacrifice of peace offerings, which he offered unto the LORD, two and twenty thousand oxen, and an hundred and twenty thousand sheep. RSo the king and all the children of Israel dedicated the house of the LORD. Ezra 6:15-18

64 The same day did the king hallow the middle of the court that was before the house of the LORD: for there he offered burnt offerings, and meat offerings, and the fat of the peace offerings: because the brasen altar that was before the LORD was too little to receive the burnt offerings, and meat offerings, and the fat of the peace offerings.

65 And at that time Solomon held a feast, and all Israel with him, a great congregation, from the entering in of Ha'-math unto Rthe river of Egypt, before the LORD our God, Rseven days and seven days, even fourteen days. Num. 34:5 • 2 Chr. 7:8

66 On the eighth day he sent the people away: and they blessed the king, and went unto their tents joyful and glad of heart for all the goodness that the LORD had done for David his servant, and for Israel his people.

CHAPTER 9

Reiteration of the Davidic Covenant
2 Chr. 7:11-22

A ND it came to pass, when Solomon had finished the building of the house of the LORD, and the king's house, and all Solomon's desire which he was pleased to do,

2 That Rthe LORD appeared to Solomon the second time, Ras he had appeared unto him at Gib'-e-on. Gen. 12:7; 2 Chr. 3:1 • 3:5; 11:9-13

3 And the LORD said unto him, I have heard thy prayer and thy supplication, that thou hast made before me: I have hallowed this house, which thou hast built, to put my name there for ever; and mine eyes and mine heart shall be there perpetually.

4 And if thou wilt walk before me, as David thy father walked, in integrity of heart, and in uprightness, to do according to all that I have commanded thee, and wilt keep my statutes and my judgments:

5 Then I will establish the throne of thy kingdom upon Israel for ever, as I promised to David thy father, saying, There shall not fail thee a man upon the throne of Israel.

6 But if ye shall at all Tturn from following me, ye or your children, and will not keep my commandments and my statutes which I have set before you, but go and serve other gods, and worship them: fall back

7 Then will I cut off Israel out of the land which I have given them; and this house, which I have hallowed for my name, will I cast out of my sight; and Israel shall be a proverb and a byword among all people:

8 And at this house, which is Thigh, every one that passeth by it shall be astonished, and shall hiss; and they shall say, RWhy hath the LORD done thus unto this land, and to this house? prominent • Jer. 22:8, 9

9 And they shall answer, RBecause they Rforsook the LORD their God, who brought forth their fathers out of the land of Egypt, and have taken hold upon other gods, and have worshipped them, and served them: therefore hath the LORD brought upon them all this evil. [Deut. 28:20; 29:25-28] • Jer. 2:10-13

Sale of Cities in Israel—2 Chr. 8:1, 2

10 And Rit came to pass at the end of twenty years, when Solomon had built the two houses, the house of the LORD, and the king's house, 6:37, 38; 7:1; 2 Chr. 8:1

11 (Now Hiram the king of Tyre had furnished Solomon with cedar trees and fir trees, and with gold, according to all his desire,) that then king Solomon gave Hiram twenty cities in the land of Galilee.

12 And Hiram came out from Tyre to see the cities which Solomon had given him; and they pleased him not.

13 And he said, What cities are these which thou hast given me, my brother? And he called them the land of RCa'-bul^T unto this day. Josh. 19:27 • displeasing, dirty

14 And Hiram sent to the king Tsixscore talents of gold. $691,200,000

Enslavement of the Canaanites
2 Chr. 8:4-18

15 And this is the reason of the Tlevy which king Solomon raised; for to build the

house of the LORD, and his own house, and Mil'-lo, and the wall of Jerusalem, and Ha'-zor, and Me-gid'-do, and Ge'-zer. *tax*

16 *For* Pharaoh king of Egypt had gone up, and taken Ge'-zer, and burnt it with fire, ᴿand slain the Ca'-naan-ites that dwelt in the city, and ᴿgiven it *for* a present unto his daughter, Solomon's wife. Josh. 16:10 • 3:1

17 And Solomon built ᴿGe'-zer, and ᴿBeth-ho'-ron the nether, Josh. 16:3 • 2 Chr. 8:5

18 And ᴿBa'-al-ath, and ᴿTad'-mor in the wilderness, in the land, Josh. 19:44 • 2 Chr. 8:4

19 And all the cities of store that Solomon had, and cities for his chariots, and cities for his horsemen, and that which Solomon desired to build in Jerusalem, and in Leb'-a-non, and in all the land of his dominion.

20 ᴿAnd all the people *that were* left of the ᴿAm'-or-ites, Hit'-tites, Per'-iz-zites, Hi'-vites, and Jeb'-u-sites, which *were* not of the children of Israel, 2 Chr. 8:7 • Gen. 10:16

21 Their children ᴿthat were left after them in the land, whom the children of Israel also were not able utterly to destroy, upon those did Solomon ᵀlevy a tribute of bondservice unto this day. Judg. 3:1 • *tax*

22 But of the children of Israel did Solomon ᴿmake no ᵀbondmen: but they *were* men of war, and his servants, and his princes, and his captains, and rulers of his chariots, and his horsemen. [Lev. 25:39] • *slaves*

23 These *were* the chief of the officers that *were* over Solomon's work, ᴿfive hundred and fifty, which bare rule over the ᴿpeople that wrought in the work. 2 Chr. 8:10 • 5:16

24 But ᴿPharaoh's daughter came up out of the city of David unto ᴿher house which *Solomon* had built for her: ᴿthen did he build Mil'-lo. 2 Chr. 8:11 • 7:8 • 2 Chr. 32:5

25 And three times in a year did Solomon offer burnt offerings and peace offerings upon the altar which he built unto the LORD, and he burnt incense upon the altar that *was* before the LORD. So he finished the house.

26 And ᴿking Solomon made a navy of ships in ᴿE'-zi-on-ge'-ber, which *is* beside E'-loth, on the shore of the Red sea, in the land of E'-dom. 2 Chr. 8:17, 18 • 22:48; Deut. 2:8

27 And Hiram sent in the navy his servants, shipmen that had knowledge of the sea, with the servants of Solomon.

28 And they came to O'-phir, and fetched from thence gold, four hundred and twenty talents, and brought *it* to king Solomon.

CHAPTER 10

Multiplication of Wealth—2 Chr. 9:1-24

AND when the ᴿqueen of She'-ba heard of the ᵀfame of Solomon concerning the name of the LORD, she came to prove him with hard questions. Matt. 12:42 • *reputation*

2 And she came to Jerusalem with a very great train, with camels that bare spices, and very much gold, and precious stones: and when she was come to Solomon, she communed with him of all that was in her heart.

3 And Solomon ᵀtold her all her questions: there was not *any* thing hid from the king, which he told her not. *answered*

4 And when the queen of She'-ba had seen all Solomon's wisdom, and the house that he had built,

5 And the ᵀmeat of his table, and the sitting of his servants, and the ᵀattendance of his ministers, and their apparel, and his cupbearers, and his ascent by which he went up unto the house of the LORD; there was no more spirit in her. *food • careful ministry*

6 And she said to the king, It was a true report that I heard in mine own land of thy ᵀacts and of thy wisdom. *sayings*

7 Howbeit I believed not the words, until I came, ᴿand mine eyes had seen *it:* and, behold, the half was not told me: thy wisdom and prosperity exceedeth the fame which I heard. [John 20:29]

8 Happy *are* thy men, happy *are* these thy servants, which stand continually before thee, *and* that hear thy wisdom.

9 Blessed be the LORD thy God, which delighted in thee, to set thee on the throne of Israel: because the LORD loved Israel for ever, therefore made he thee king, ᴿto ᵀdo judgment and justice. 2 Sam. 8:15 • *practise*

10 And she gave the king an ᵀhundred and twenty talents of gold, and of spices very great store, and precious stones: there came no more such abundance of spices as these which the queen of She'-ba gave to king Solomon. *$691,200,000*

11 And the navy also of Hiram, that brought gold from O'-phir, brought in from O'-phir great plenty ᴿof ᵀal'-mug trees, and precious stones. 2 Chr. 2:8; 9:10, 11 • *algum trees*

12 And the king made of the al'-mug trees pillars for the house of the LORD, and for the king's house, harps also and psalteries for singers: there came no such al'-mug trees, nor were seen unto this day.

13 And king Solomon gave unto the queen of She'-ba all her desire, whatsoever she asked, beside *that* which Solomon gave her of his royal bounty. So she turned and went to her own country, she and her servants.

14 Now the weight of gold that came to Solomon in one year was ᵀsix hundred threescore and six talents of gold, *$3.83 billion*

15 Beside *that he had* of the merchantmen, and of the traffick of the spice merchants,

and of all the kings of Arabia, and of the
Tgovernors of the country.   *captains*
16 And king Solomon made two hundred
targets *of* beaten gold: Tsix hundred *shek'-els*
of gold went to one target. $3,840,000
17 And *he made* Rthree hundred shields *of*
beaten gold; Tthree pound of gold went to one
shield: and the king put them in the house of
the forest of Leb'-a-non.   14:26 • $288,000
18 RMoreover the king made a great
throne of Rivory, and overlaid it with the best
gold.   2 Chr. 9:17 • v. 22; Ps. 45:8
19 The throne had six steps, and the top of
the throne *was* round behind: and *there were*
stays on either side on the place of the seat,
and two lions stood beside the stays.
20 And twelve lions stood there on the one
side and on the other upon the six steps:
there was not the like made in any kingdom.
21 RAnd all king Solomon's drinking
vessels *were of* gold, and all the vessels of the
house of the forest of Leb'-a-non *were of* pure
gold; none *were of* silver: it was nothing
accounted of in the days of Solomon. 2 Chr. 9:20
22 For the king had at sea a navy of
RThar'-shish with the navy of Hiram: once in
three years came the navy of Thar'-shish,
bringing gold, and silver, ivory, and apes, and
peacocks.   Gen. 10:4
23 So king Solomon exceeded all the kings
of the earth for riches and for wisdom.
24 And all the earth Tsought to Solomon,
Rto hear his wisdom, which God had put in
his heart.   *consulted* • 3:9, 12, 28
25 And they brought every man his present, vessels of silver, and vessels of gold, and
garments, and armour, and spices, horses,
and mules, a rate year by year.

Multiplication of Horses
2 Chr. 1:14–17; 9:25–28

26 RAnd Solomon Rgathered together
chariots and horsemen: and he had a
thousand and four hundred chariots, and
twelve thousand horsemen, whom he Tbestowed in the cities for chariots, and with the
king at Jerusalem.   4:26 • Deut. 17:16 • *assigned to*
27 RAnd the king Tmade silver to *be* in
Jerusalem as stones, and cedars made he to
be as the sycomore trees that *are* in the vale,
for abundance.   2 Chr. 1:15–17 • *gave*
28 And Solomon had horses brought out of
Egypt, and linen yarn: the king's merchants
received the linen yarn at a price.
29 And a chariot came up and went out of
Egypt for Tsix hundred *shek'-els* of silver, and
an horse for an Thundred and fifty: and so for
all the kings of the Hit'-tites, and for the
kings of Syria, did they bring *them* out Tby
their means. $76,800 • $19,200 • *at their expense*

CHAPTER 11

Intermarriage with Foreign Women

BUT Rking Solomon loved Rmany strange
women, together with theR daughter of
Pharaoh, women of the Mo'-ab-ites, Am'-
mon-ites, E'-dom-ites, Zi-do'-ni-ans, *and* Hit'-
tites;   [Neh. 13:26] • [Deut. 17:17] • 3:1
2 Of the nations *concerning* which the
LORD said unto the children of Israel, RYe
shall not go in to them, neither shall they
come in unto you: *for* surely they will turn
away your heart after their gods: Solomon
Tclave unto these in love.   Ex. 34:16 • *cherished*
3 And he had seven hundred wives,
princesses, and three hundred concubines:
and his wives turned away his heart.

Worship of Idols

4 For it came to pass, when Solomon was
old, *that* his wives turned away his heart
Tafter other gods: and his heart was not
Tperfect with the LORD his God, as *was* the
heart of David his father.   *to follow* • *sincere*
5 For Solomon Twent after RAsh'-to-reth
the goddess of the Zi-do'-ni-ans, and after
TMil'-com the abomination of the Am'-mon-
ites.   *followed* • v. 33; Judg. 2:13 • called *Molech, v. 7*
6 And Solomon did evil in the sight of the
LORD, and Twent not fully after the LORD, as
did David his father.   *did not fully obey*
7 RThen did Solomon build Tan high place
for Che'-mosh, the abomination of Moab, in
the hill that *is* before Jerusalem, and for Mo'-
lech, the abomination of the children of
Ammon.   Num. 33:52 • *a pagan shrine for worship*
8 And likewise did he for all his Tstrange
wives, which Tburnt incense and sacrificed
unto their gods.   *foreign* • *worshipped*

The Rebuke of God

9 And the RLORD was angry with Solomon,
Rbecause his heart was turned from the LORD
God of Israel, Rwhich had appeared unto him
twice.   Ex. 4:14 • vv. 2, 4 • 3:5; 9:2
10 And Rhad Tcommanded him concerning
this thing, that he should not go after other
gods: but he Tkept not that which the LORD
commanded.   6:12; 9:6 • *warned* • *did not obey*
11 Wherefore the LORD said unto Solomon,
Forasmuch as this is done of thee, and thou
hast not kept my covenant and my statutes,
which I have commanded thee, RI will surely
rend the kingdom from thee, and will give it
to thy servant.   v. 31
12 Notwithstanding in thy days I will not
do it for David thy father's sake: *but* I will
rend it out of the hand of thy son.
13 Howbeit I will not rend away all the
kingdom; *but* will give one tribe to thy son

for David my servant's sake, and ^Rfor Jerusalem's sake which I have chosen.   8:29

The Chastisement of God

14 And the LORD stirred^T up an adversary unto Solomon, Ha'-dad the E'-dom-ite: he *was* of the king's seed in E'-dom.   *inspired*

15 For it came to pass, when David was in E'-dom, and Jo'-ab the captain of the host was gone up to bury the slain, after he had smitten every male in E'-dom;

16 (For six months did Jo'-ab remain there with all Israel, until he had cut off every male in E'-dom:)

17 That Ha'-dad fled, he and certain E'-dom-ites of his father's servants with him, to go into Egypt; Ha'-dad *being* yet a little child.

18 And they arose out of Mid'-i-an, and came to Pa'-ran: and they took men with them out of Pa'-ran, and they came to Egypt, unto Pharaoh king of Egypt; which gave him an house, and ^Tappointed him victuals, and gave him land.   *provided him food*

19 And Ha'-dad found great favour in the sight of Pharaoh, so that he gave him ^Tto wife the sister of his own wife, the sister of Tah'-pe-nes the queen.   *in marriage*

20 And the sister of Tah'-pe-nes bare him Ge-nu'-bath his son, whom Tah'-pe-nes weaned in Pharaoh's house: and Ge-nu'-bath was in Pharaoh's household among the sons of Pharaoh.

21 And ^Rwhen Ha'-dad heard in Egypt that David slept with his fathers, and that Jo'-ab the captain of the host was dead, Ha'-dad said to Pharaoh, Let me depart, that I may go to mine own country.   2:10

22 Then Pharaoh said unto him, But what hast thou lacked with me, that, behold, thou seekest to go to thine own country? And he answered, Nothing: ^Thowbeit let me go in any ^Twise.   *only • case*

23 ^RAnd God ^Tstirred him up *another* adversary, Re'-zon the son of E-li'-a-dah, which fled from his lord ^RHad-ad-e'-zer king of Zo'-bah: *v. 14 • inspired • 2 Sam. 8:3; 10:16*

24 ^RAnd he gathered men unto him, and became captain over a band, when David slew them *of Zo'-bah:* and they went to Damascus, and dwelt therein, and reigned in ^RDamascus.   2 Sam. 8:3; 10:8, 18 • 15:18

25 And he was an adversary to Israel all the days of Solomon, beside the ^Tmischief that Ha'-dad *did:* and he ^Tabhorred Israel, and reigned over Syria.   *harm • was hostile to*

26 And Jer-o-bo'-am the son of Ne'-bat, an Eph'-rath-ite of Zer'-e-da, Solomon's servant, whose mother's name *was* Ze-ru'-ah, a widow woman, even he ^Rlifted^T up *his* hand against the king.   2 Sam. 20:21 • *rebelled*

27 And this *was* the cause that he lifted up his hand against the king: Solomon built ^RMil'-lo, *and* ^Trepaired the breaches of the city of David his father.   9:15, 24 • *closed*

28 And the man Jer-o-bo'-am *was* a mighty man of valour: and ^RSolomon seeing the young man that he was industrious, he made him ruler over all the ^Tcharge of the house of Joseph.   [Prov. 22:29] • *forced labour*

29 And it came to pass at that time when Jer-o-bo'-am went out of Jerusalem, that the prophet ^RA-hi'-jah the Shi'-lo-nite found him in the way; and he had clad himself with a new garment; and they two *were* alone in the field: 12:15; 14:2; 2 Chr. 9:29

30 And A-hi'-jah caught the new garment that *was* on him, and ^Rrent^T it *in* twelve pieces: 1 Sam. 15:27; 24:5 • *tore*

31 And he said to Jer-o-bo'-am, Take thee ten pieces: for ^Rthus saith the LORD, the God of Israel, Behold, I will ^Trend the kingdom out of ^Tthe hand of Solomon, and will give ten tribes to thee: *vv. 11, 13 • tear • the rule*

32 ^R(But he shall have one tribe for my servant David's sake, and for Jerusalem's sake, the city which I have chosen out of all the tribes of Israel:)   *v. 13; 12:21*

33 Because that they have forsaken me, and have worshipped Ash'-to-reth the goddess of the Zi-do'-ni-ans, Che'-mosh the god of the Mo'-ab-ites, and Mil'-com the god of the children of Ammon, and have not walked in my ways, to do *that which is* right in mine eyes, and *to keep* my statutes and my judgments, as *did* David his father.

34 Howbeit I will not take the whole kingdom out of his hand: but I will make him prince all the days of his life for David my servant's sake, whom I chose, because he kept my commandments and my statutes:

35 But ^RI will take the kingdom out of his son's hand, and will give it unto thee, *even* ten tribes.   *v. 12; 12:16, 17*

36 And unto his son will I give one tribe, that David my servant may have a light alway before me in Jerusalem, the city which I have chosen me to put my name there.

37 And I will take thee, and thou shalt reign according to all that thy soul desireth, and shalt be king over Israel.

38 And it shall be, if thou wilt hearken unto all that I command thee, and wilt walk in my ways, and do *that is* right in my sight, to keep my statutes and my commandments, as David my servant did; that I will be with thee, and build thee a sure house, as I built for David, and will give Israel unto thee.

39 And I will for this afflict^T the seed of David, but not for ever.   *punish*

40 Solomon sought therefore to kill Jer-o-bo'-am. And Jer-o-bo'-am arose, and fled into Egypt, unto Shi'-shak king of Egypt, and was in Egypt until the death of Solomon.

Death of Solomon—2 Chr. 9:29–31

41 And ᴿthe rest of the ᵀacts of Solomon, and all that he did, and his ᴿwisdom, *are* they not written in the book of the acts of Solomon?　　　　2 Chr. 9:29 • *words* • 4:31

42 And the time that Solomon reigned in Jerusalem over all Israel *was* forty years.

43 ᴿAnd Solomon ᴿsleptᵀ with his fathers, and was buried in the city of David his father: and ᴿRe-ho-bo'-am his son reigned in his stead.　　　　2 Chr. • 9:31 • 2:10 • died • 14:21

CHAPTER 12

Request of Israel to Rehoboam—2 Chr. 10:1–5

A ND ᴿRe-ho-bo'-am went to She'-chem: for all Israel were ᴿcome to She'-chem to make him king.　　　　2 Chr. 10:1 • Judg. 9:6

2 And it came to pass, when ᴿJer-o-bo'-am the son of Ne'-bat, who was yet in ᴿEgypt, heard *of it*, (for he was fled from the presence of king Solomon, and Jer-o-bo'-am dwelt in Egypt;)　　　　11:26 • 11:40; 14:21

3 That they sent and called him. And Jer-o-bo'-am and all the congregation of Israel came, and spake unto Re-ho-bo'-am, saying,

4 Thy father made our ᴿyoke ᵀgrievous: now therefore make thou the grievous service of thy father, and his heavy yoke which he put upon us, lighter, and we will serve thee.　　　4:7; 1 Sam. 8:11–18 • *hard to bear*

5 And he said unto them, ᴿDepartᵀ yet *for* three days, then come again to me. And the people departed.　　　　*v.* 12 • *give me time to think*

Foolish Response of Rehoboam—2 Chr. 10:6–15

6 And king Re-ho-bo'-am consulted with the old men, that stood before Solomon his father while he yet lived, and said, How do ye advise that I may answer this people?

7 And they spake unto him, saying, ᴿIf thou wilt be a servant unto this people this day, and wilt serve them, and answer them, and speak good words to them, then they will be thy servants for ever.　　　　[Prov. 15:1]

8 But he forsook the counsel of the old men, which they had given him, and consulted with the young men that were grown up with him, *and* which stood before him:

9 And he said unto them, What counsel give ye that we may answer this people, who have spoken to me, saying, Make the yoke which thy father did put upon us lighter?

10 And the young men that were grown up with him spake unto him, saying, Thus shalt thou speak unto this people that spake unto thee, saying, Thy father made our yoke heavy, but make thou *it* lighter unto us; thus shalt thou say unto them, My little *finger* shall be thicker than my father's loins.

11 And now whereas my father did lade you with a heavy yoke, I will add to your yoke: my father hath chastised you with whips, but I will chastise you with scorpions.

12 So ᴿJer-o-bo'-am and all the people came to Re-ho-bo'-am the third day, as the king had appointed, saying, ᴿCome to me again the third day.　　　*v.* 20; 11:28 • *v.* 5

13 And the king answered the people ᵀroughly, and ᵀforsook the old men's ᵀcounsel that they gave him;　　　*harshly • ignored • advice*

14 And spake to them after the counsel of the young men, saying, My father made your yoke heavy, and I will add to your yoke: my father *also* chastised you with whips, but I will chastise you with scorpions.

15 Wherefore the king hearkened not unto the people; for the cause was from the LORD, that he might perform his saying, which the LORD spake by A-hi'-jah the Shi'-lo-nite unto Jer-o-bo'-am the son of Ne'-bat.

Revolt of the Northern Tribes
2 Chr. 10:16–19; 11:1–4

16 So when all Israel saw that the king hearkened not unto them, the people answered the king, saying, What portion have we in David? neither *have we* inheritance in the son of Jesse: to your tents, O Israel: now see to thine own house, David. So Israel departed unto their tents.

17 But ᴿ*as for* the children of Israel which dwelt in the cities of Judah, Re-ho-bo'-am reigned over them.　　　　11:13, 36

18 Then king Re-ho-bo'-am sent A-do'-ram, who *was* over the tribute; and all Israel stoned him with stones, that he died. Therefore king Re-ho-bo'-am made speed to get him up to his chariot, to flee to Jerusalem.

19 So Israel rebelled against the ᵀhouse of David unto this day.　　　　*family of David*

20 And it came to pass, when all Israel heard that Jer-o-bo'-am was come again, that they sent and called him unto the congregation, and made him king over all ᴿIsrael: there was none that followed the house of David, but the tribe of Judah only.　　　11:13, 32

21 And when Re-ho-bo'-am was come to Jerusalem, he assembled all the house of Judah, with the tribe of Benjamin, an hundred and fourscore thousand chosen men, which were warriors, to fight against the house of Israel, to bring the kingdom again to Re-ho-bo'-am the son of Solomon.

22 But the word of God came unto She-ma'-iah the man of God, saying,

23 Speak unto Re-ho-bo'-am, the son of Solomon, king of Judah, and unto all the house of Judah and Benjamin, and to the ᴿremnant of the people, saying,　　　*v.* 17

24 Thus saith the LORD, Ye shall not ᵀgo up, nor fight against your brethren the

children of Israel: return every man to his house; for this thing is from me. They hearkened therefore to the word of the LORD, and ᵀreturned to depart, according to the word of the LORD.   *attack · turned to go home*

Sin of Jeroboam

25 Then Jer-o-bo'-am built She'-chem in mount E'-phra-im, and dwelt therein; and went out from thence, and built Pe-nu'-el.

26 And Jer-o-bo'-am said in his heart, Now shall the kingdom return to the house of David:

27 If this people go up to do sacrifice in the house of the LORD at Jerusalem, then shall the heart of this people turn again unto their lord, *even* unto Re-ho-bo'-am king of Judah, and they shall kill me, and go again to Re-ho-bo'-am king of Judah.

28 Whereupon the king took counsel, and made two calves *of* gold, and said unto them, It is too much for you to go up to Jerusalem: behold thy gods, O Israel, which brought thee up out of the land of Egypt.

29 And he set the one in Beth'-el, and the other put he in ᴿDan.   Judg. 18:29

30 And this ᵀthing became ᴿa sin: for the people went *to worship* before the one, *even* unto Dan.   13:34; 2 Kin. 17:21

31 And he made an ᴿhouse of high places, and made priests of the lowest of the people, which were not of the sons of Levi.   13:32

32 And Jer-o-bo'-am ᵀordained a feast in the eighth month, on the fifteenth day of the month, like unto the feast that *is* in Judah, and he offered upon the altar. So did he in Beth'-el, sacrificing unto the calves that he had made: and he placed in Beth'-el the priests of the ᵀhigh places which he had made.   *appointed · pagan shrines*

33 So he offered upon the altar which he had made in Beth'-el the fifteenth day of the eighth month, *even* in the month which he had devised of his own heart; and ordained a feast unto the children of Israel: and he offered upon the altar, and burnt incense.

CHAPTER 13

Warning of the Prophet

AND, behold, there came a man of God out of Judah ᵀby the word of the LORD unto Beth'-el: and Jer-o-bo'-am stood by the altar to burn incense.   *guided by the LORD*

2 And he cried against the altar in the word of the LORD, and said, O altar, altar, thus saith the LORD; ᴿBehold, a child shall be born unto the house of David, Jo-si'-ah by name; and upon thee shall he ᵀoffer the priests of the high places that burn incense

upon thee, and men's bones shall be burnt upon thee.   2 Kin. 23:15, 16 · *put to death*

3 And he gave ᴿa sign the same day, saying, This *is* the sign which the LORD hath spoken; Behold, the altar shall be ᵀrent, and the ashes that *are* upon it shall be poured out.   Is. 7:14; John 2:18; 1 Cor. 1:22 · *broken*

4 And it came to pass, when king Jer-o-bo'-am heard the saying of the man of God, which had cried against the altar in Beth'-el, that he put forth his hand from the altar, saying, Lay hold on him. And his hand, which he put forth against him, dried up, so that he could not pull it in again to him.

5 The altar also was ᵀrent, and the ashes poured out from the altar, according to the sign which the man of God had given by the word of the LORD.   *broken*

6 And the king answered and said unto the man of God, ᴿIntreatᵀ now the face of the LORD thy God, and pray for me, that my hand may be restored me again. And the man of God besought the LORD, and the king's hand was restored him again, and became as *it was* before.   Ex. 8:8 · *pray to*

Sin of the Prophet

7 And the king said unto the man of God, Come home with me, and refresh thyself, and ᴿI will give thee a ᵀreward.   1 Sam. 9:7 · *gift*

8 And the man of God said unto the king, ᴿIf thou wilt give me half thine house, I will not go in with thee, neither will I eat bread nor drink water in this place: Num. 22:18; 24:13

9 For so was it charged me by the word of the LORD, saying, ᴿEat no bread, nor drink water, nor turn again by the same way that thou camest.   [1 Cor. 5:11]

10 So he went another way, and returned not by the way that he came to Beth'-el.

11 Now there dwelt an old prophet in Beth'-el; and his sons came and told him all the works that the man of God had done that day in Beth'-el: the words which he had spoken unto the king, ᴿthem they told also to their father.   v. 25

12 And their father said unto them, What way went he? For his sons had seen what way the man of God went, which came from Judah.

13 And he said unto his sons, Saddle me the ass. So they saddled him the ass: and he rode thereon,

14 And went after the man of God, and found him sitting under an oak: and he said unto him, Art thou the man of God that camest from Judah? And he said, I *am*.

15 Then he said unto him, Come home with me, and ᵀeat bread.   *have dinner with me*

16 And he said, I may not return with thee, nor go in with thee: neither will I eat bread nor drink water with thee in this place:

17 For ᵀit was said to me ᴿby the word of the LORD, Thou shalt eat no bread nor drink water there, nor turn again to go by the way that thou camest.   *a word was* • 20:35

18 He said unto him, I *am* a prophet also as thou *art;* and an angel spake unto me by the word of the LORD, saying, Bring him back with thee into thine house, that he may eat bread and drink water. *But* he lied unto him.

19 So he went back with him, and did eat bread in his house, and drank water.

Judgment on the Prophet

20 And it came to pass, as they sat at the table, that the word of the LORD came unto the prophet that brought him back:

21 And he cried unto the man of God that came from Judah, saying, Thus saith the LORD, Forasmuch as thou hast disobeyed the mouth of the LORD, and hast not kept the commandment which the LORD thy God commanded thee,

22 But camest back, and hast eaten bread and drunk water in the place, of the which the LORD did say to thee, Eat no bread, and drink no water; thy carcase shall not come unto the sepulchre of thy fathers.

23 And it came to pass, after he had eaten bread, and after he had drunk, that he saddled for him the ass, *to wit,* for the prophet whom he had brought back.

24 And when he was gone, a lion met him by the way, and slew him: and his carcase was cast in the way, and the ass stood by it, the lion also stood by the carcase.

25 And, behold, men passed by, and saw the carcase cast in the way, and the lion standing by the carcase: and they came and told *it* in the city where the ᴿold prophet dwelt.   *v. 11*

26 And when the prophet that brought him back from the way heard *thereof,* he said, It *is* the man of God, who was disobedient unto the word of the LORD: therefore the LORD hath delivered him unto the lion, which hath torn him, and slain him, according to the word of the LORD, which he spake unto him.

27 And he spake to his sons, saying, Saddle me the ass. And they saddled *him.*

28 And he went and found his carcase cast in the way, and the ass and the lion standing by the carcase: the lion had not eaten the carcase, nor ᵀtorn the ass.   *broken*

29 And the prophet took up the carcase of the ᴿman of God, and laid it upon the ass, and brought it back: and the old prophet came to the city, to mourn and to bury him.   Deut. 33:1

30 And he laid his carcase in his own ᴿgrave; and they mourned over him, *saying,* ᴿAlas, my brother!   Deut. 10:6 • Gen. 50:10

31 And it came to pass, after he had buried him, that he spake to his sons, saying, When I am dead, then bury me in the sepulchre wherein the man of God *is* buried; lay my bones beside his bones:

32 For the saying which he ᵀcried by the word of the LORD against the altar in Beth′–el, and against all the houses of the high places which *are* in the cities of Sa-ma′-ri-a, shall surely come to pass.   *preached*

Continued Sin of Jeroboam

33 ᴿAfter this thing Jer-o-bo′-am returned not from his evil way, but made againᵀ of the lowest of the people priests of the high places: ᴿwhosoever would, he consecrated him, and he became *one* of the priests of the high places.   12:31, 32 • *from all* • Judg. 17:5

34 ᴿAnd this thing became sin unto the house of Jer-o-bo′-am, even ᴿto cut *it* off, and to destroy *it* from off the face of the earth.   12:30 • [14:10; 14:16]

CHAPTER 14

Judgment on Jeroboam

A T that time A-bi′-jah the son of Jer-o-bo′-am fell sick.

2 And Jer-o-bo′-am said to his wife, Arise, I pray thee, and disguise thyself, that thou be not known to be the wife of Jer-o-bo′-am; and get thee to Shi′-loh: behold, there *is* A-hi′-jah the prophet, which told me that ᴿI should be king over this people.   11:31

3 ᴿAnd take with thee ten loaves, and ᵀcracknels, and a ᵀcruse of honey, and go to him: he shall tell thee what shall become of the child.   1 Sam. 9:7, 8; 2 Kin. 4:42 • *cakes* • *jar*

4 And Jer-o-bo′-am's wife did so, and arose, ᴿand went to Shi′-loh, and came to the house of A-hi′-jah. But A-hi′-jah could not see; ᴿfor his eyes were ᵀset by reason of his age.   11:29 • 1 Sam. 3:2; 4:15 • *blind*

5 And the LORD said unto A-hi′-jah, Behold, the wife of Jer-o-bo′-am cometh to ask a thing of thee for her son; for he *is* sick: thus and thus shalt thou say unto her: for it shall be, when she cometh in, that she shall feign herself *to be* another *woman.*

6 And it was *so,* when A-hi′-jah heard the sound of her feet, as she came in at the door, that he said, Come in, thou wife of Jer-o-bo′-am; why feignest thou thyself *to be* another? for I *am* sent to thee *with* heavy *tidings.*

7 Go, tell Jer-o-bo′-am, Thus saith the LORD God of Israel, ᴿForasmuch as I exalted thee from among the people, and made thee prince over my people Israel,   2 Sam. 12:7, 8

8 And ᴿrentᵀ the kingdom away from the house of David, and gave it thee: and *yet* thou hast not been as my servant David, who kept my commandments, and who followed

me with all his heart, to do *that* only *which was* right in mine eyes;   11:31 • *tore*

9 But hast done evil above all that were before thee: ᴿfor thou hast gone and made thee other gods, and molten images, to provoke me to anger, and ᴿhast ᵀcast me behind thy back: 12:28 • Neh. 9:26 • *repudiated me*

10 Therefore, behold, I will bring evil upon the house of Jer-o-bo'-am, and will cut off from Jer-o-bo'-am him that pisseth against the wall, *and* him that is shut up and left in Israel, and will take away the remnant of the house of Jer-o-bo'-am, as a man taketh away dung, till it be all gone.

11 ᴿHim that dieth of Jer-o-bo'-am in the city shall the dogs eat; and him that dieth in the field shall the fowls of the air eat: for the LORD hath spoken *it*.   16:4; 21:24

12 Arise thou therefore, get thee to thine own house: *and* ᴿwhen thy feet enter into the city, the child shall die.   *v.* 17

13 And all Israel shall mourn for him, and bury him: for he only of Jer-o-bo'-am shall come to the grave, because in him there is found *some* good thing toward the LORD God of Israel in the house of Jer-o-bo'-am.

14 ᴿMoreover the LORD shall raise him up a king over Israel, who shall cut off the house of Jer-o-bo'-am that day: but what? even now.   15:27–29

15 For the LORD shall ᵀsmite Israel, as a reed is shaken in the water, and he shall ᴿroot up Israel out of this good land, which he gave to their fathers, and shall scatter them beyond the river, ᴿbecause they have made their ᵀgroves, provoking the LORD to anger.   *strike* • Ps. 52:5 • [Ex. 34:13] • *pagan shrines*

16 And he shall give Israel up because of the sins of Jer-o-bo'-am, ᴿwho did sin, and who made Israel to sin.   12:30; 13:34; 15:30

17 And Jer-o-bo'-am's wife arose, and departed, and came to ᴿTir'-zah: *and* ᴿwhen she came to the threshold of the door, the child died;   15:21, 33; 16:6, 8 • *v.* 12

18 And they buried him; and all Israel mourned for him, ᴿaccording to the word of the LORD, which he spake by the hand of his servant A-hi'-jah the prophet.   *v.* 13

19 And the rest of the acts of Jer-o-bo'-am, how he ᴿwarred, and how he reigned, behold, they *are* written in the book of the chronicles of the kings of Israel.   2 Chr. 13:2

20 And the days which Jer-o-bo'-am reigned *were* two and twenty years: and he slept with his fathers, and ᴿNa'-dab his son reigned in his stead.   15:25

Sin of Rehoboam

21 And Re-ho-bo'-am the son of Solomon reigned in Judah. Re-ho-bo'-am *was* forty and one years old when he began to reign, and he reigned seventeen years in Jerusalem,

the city ᴿwhich the LORD did choose out of all the tribes of Israel, to put his name there. ᴿAnd his mother's name *was* Na'-a-mah an Am'-mon-i-tess.   11:36 • *v.* 31

22 And Judah did evil in the sight of the LORD, and they provoked him to jealousy with their sins which they had committed, above all that their fathers had done.

23 For they also built them high places, and images, and ᴿgroves, on every high hill, and under every green tree.   [2 Kin. 17:9, 10]

24 And there were also sodomites in the land: *and* they did according to all the abominations of the nations which the LORD cast out before the children of Israel.

Judgment on Rehoboam—2 Chr. 12:2–16

25 ᴿAnd it came to pass in the fifth year of king Re-ho-bo'-am, *that* Shi'-shak king of Egypt came up against Jerusalem: 11:40

26 ᴿAnd he took away the treasures of the house of the LORD, and the treasures of the king's house; he even took away all: and he took away all the shields of gold ᴿwhich Solomon had made.   2 Chr. 12:9–11 • 10:17

27 And king Re-ho-bo'-am made in their stead brasen shields, and committed *them* unto the hands of the chief of the guard, which kept the door of the king's house.

28 And it was *so*, when the king went into the house of the LORD, that the guard ᵀbare them, and brought them back into the guard ᵀchamber.   *carried* • *room*

29 ᴿNow the rest of the acts of Re-ho-bo'-am, and all that he did, *are* they not written in the book of the chronicles of the kings of Judah?   *vv.* 29–31; 2 Chr. 12:15, 16

30 And there was war between Re-ho-bo'-am and Jer-o-bo'-am all *their* days.

31 And Re-ho-bo'-am ᵀslept with his fathers, and was buried with his fathers in the city of David. And his mother's name *was* Na'-a-mah an Am'-mon-i-tess. And A-bi'-jam his son reigned in his stead.   *died*

CHAPTER 15

Reign of Abijam in Judah—2 Chr. 13:1, 2; 14:1

NOW ᴿin the eighteenth year of king Jer-o-bo'-am the son of Ne'-bat reigned ᴿA-bi'-jam over Judah.   2 Chr. 13:1 • 2 Chr. 11:22

2 Three years reigned he in Jerusalem. And his mother's name *was* ᴿMa'-a-chah, the daughter of A-bish'-a-lom.   2 Chr. 13:2

3 And he walked in all the sins of his father, which he had done before him: and his heart was not perfect with the LORD his God, as the heart of David his father.

4 Nevertheless ᴿfor David's sake did the LORD his God give him a lamp in Jerusalem,

to set up his son after him, and to establish Jerusalem: 11:32, 36; 2 Chr. 21:7

5 Because David did *that which was* right in the eyes of the LORD, and turned not aside from any *thing* that he commanded him all the days of his life, save only in the matter of U-ri′-ah the Hit′-tite.

6 And there was war between Re-ho-bo′-am and Jer-o-bo′-am all the days of his life.

7 ᴿNow the rest of the acts of A-bi′-jam, and all that he did, *are* they not written in the book of the chronicles of the kings of Judah? And there was war between A-bi′-jam and Jer-o-bo′-am.   2 Chr. 13:2, 3, 22

8 And A-bi′-jam ᵀslept with his fathers; and they buried him in the city of David: and A′-sa his son reigned in his stead.   *died*

Obedience of Asa—2 Chr. 14:2; 15:16–18

9 And in the twentieth year of Jer-o-bo′-am king of Israel reigned A′-sa over Judah.

10 And forty and one years reigned he in Jerusalem. And his mother's name *was* Ma′-a-chah, the daughter of A-bish′-a-lom.

11 And A′-sa did *that which was* right in the eyes of the LORD, as *did* David his father.

12 ᴿAnd he took away the sodomites out of the land, and ᴿremoved all the idols that his fathers had made.   14:24; 22:46 • 2 Kin. 3:2

13 And also Ma′-a-chah his mother, even her he removed from *being* queen, because she had made an idol in a ᵀgrove; and A′-sa destroyed her idol, and ᴿburnt *it* by the brook Kid′-ron.   *pagan shrine* • Ex. 32:20

14 ᴿBut the high places were not removed: nevertheless A′-sa's heart was perfect with the LORD all his days.   22:43

15 And he brought in the things which his father had dedicated, and the things which himself had dedicated, into the house of the LORD, silver, and gold, and vessels.

Disobedience of Asa—2 Chr. 16:1–6

16 ᴿAnd there was war between A′-sa and Ba′-a-sha king of Israel all their days.   *v. 32*

17 And Ba′-a-sha king of Israel went up against Judah, and built Ra′-mah, ᴿthat he might not ᵀsuffer any to go out or come in to A′-sa king of Judah.   12:27 • *allow*

18 Then A′-sa took all the silver and the gold *that were* left in the treasures of the house of the LORD, and the treasures of the king's house, and delivered them into the hand of his servants: and king A′-sa sent them to ᴿBen-ha′-dad, the son of Tab′-ri-mon, the son of He′-zi-on, king of Syria, that dwelt at Damascus, saying,   2 Chr. 16:2

19 *There is* ᵀa league between me and thee, *and* between my father and thy father: behold, I have sent unto thee a present of silver and gold; come and break thy league with Ba′-a-sha king of Israel, that he may depart from me.   *an agreement*

20 So Ben-ha′-dad hearkened unto king A′-sa, and sent the captains of the hosts which he had against the cities of Israel, and smote I′-jon, and ᴿDan, and ᴿA′-bel–beth–ma′-a-chah, and all Cin′-ne-roth, with all the land of Naph′-ta-li.   12:29 • 2 Sam. 20:14

21 And it came to pass, when Ba′-a-sha heard *thereof,* that ᴿhe left off building of Ra′-mah, and dwelt in ᴿTir′-zah.   *v. 17* • 14:17

22 Then king A′-sa made a proclamation throughout all Judah; none *was* exempted: and they took away the stones of Ra′-mah, and the timber thereof, wherewith Ba′-a-sha had builded; and king A′-sa built with them Ge′-ba of Benjamin, and Miz′-pah.

Death of Asa—2 Chr. 16:12—17:1

23 The rest of all the acts of A′-sa, and all his might, and all that he did, and the cities which he built, *are* they not written in the book of the chronicles of the kings of Judah? Nevertheless in the time of his old age he was diseased in his feet.

24 And A′-sa ᵀslept with his fathers, and was buried with his fathers in the city of David his father: ᴿand Je-hosh′-a-phat his son reigned in his stead.   *died* • 2 Chr. 17:1

Reign of Nadab in Israel

25 And ᴿNa′-dab the son of ᴿJer-o-bo′-am began to reign over Israel in the second year of A′-sa king of Judah, and reigned over Israel two years.   14:20 • 11:28

26 And he did evil in the sight of the LORD, and walked in the way of his father, and in his sin wherewith he made Israel to sin.

27 ᴿAnd Ba′-a-sha the son of A-hi′-jah, of the house of Is′-sa-char, conspired against him; and Ba′-a-sha ᵀsmote him at ᴿGib′-be-thon, which *belonged* to the Phi-lis′-tines; for Na′-dab and all Israel laid siege to Gib′-be-thon.   14:14 • *defeated* • Josh. 19:44

28 Even in the third year of A′-sa king of Judah did Ba′-a-sha ᴿslay him, and reigned in his stead.   Judg. 3:21

29 And it came to pass, when he reigned, *that* he smote all the house of Jer-o-bo′-am; he left not to Jer-o-bo′-am any that breathed, until he had destroyed him, according unto the saying of the LORD, which he spake by his servant ᴿA-hi′-jah the Shi′-lo-nite: 11:29

30 Because of the sins of Jer-o-bo′-am which he sinned, and which he made Israel sin, by his provocation wherewith he provoked the LORD God of Israel to anger.

31 Now the rest of the acts of Na′-dab, and all that he did, *are* they not written in the book of the chronicles of the kings of Israel?

Reign of Baasha in Israel

32 ᴿAnd there was war between A′-sa and Ba′-a-sha king of Israel all their days. v. 16

33 In the third year of A′-sa king of Judah began Ba′-a-sha the son of A-hi′-jah to reign over all Israel in ᴿTir′-zah, twenty and four years. Josh. 12:24

34 And he did evil in the sight of the LORD, and walked in the way of Jer-o-bo′-am, and in his sin wherewith he made Israel to sin.

CHAPTER 16

THEN the ᴿword of the LORD came to ᴿJe′-hu the son of ᴿHa-na′-ni against Ba′-a-sha, saying, v. 7 • 2 Chr. 19:2; 20:34 • 2 Chr. 16:7-10

2 ᴿForasmuch as I ᵀexalted thee out of the dust, and made thee prince over my people Israel; and ᴿthou hast walked in the way of Jer-o-bo′-am, and hast made my people Israel to sin, to provoke me to anger with their sins; 14:7 • raised • 15:34

3 Behold, I will take away the posterity of Ba′-a-sha, and the posterity of his house; and will make thy house like the house of Jer-o-bo′-am the son of Ne′-bat.

4 Him that dieth of Ba′-a-sha in the city shall the dogs eat; and him that dieth of his in the fields shall the fowls of the air eat.

5 Now the rest of the acts of Ba′-a-sha, and what he did, and his might, ᴿare they not written in the book of the chronicles of the kings of Israel? 2 Chr. 16:11

6 So Ba′-a-sha ᵀslept with his fathers, and was buried in ᴿTir′-zah: and E′-lah his son reigned in his stead. died • 14:17; 15:21

7 And also by the hand of the prophet ᴿJe′-hu the son of Ha-na′-ni came the word of the LORD against Ba′-a-sha, and against his house, even for all the evil that he did in the sight of the LORD, in provoking him to anger with the work of his hands, in being like the house of Jer-o-bo′-am; and because ᴿhe killed him. v. 1 • 15:27, 29

Reign of Elah in Israel

8 In the twenty and sixth year of A′-sa king of Judah began E′-lah the son of Ba′-a-sha to reign over Israel in Tir′-zah, two years.

9 ᴿAnd his servant Zim′-ri, captain of half his chariots, conspired against him, as he was in Tir′-zah, drinking himself drunk in the house of Ar′-za ᴿstewardᵀ of his house in Tir′-zah. 2 Kin. 9:31 • Gen. 24:2; 39:4 • which was over

10 And Zim′-ri went in and ᵀsmote him, and killed him, in the twenty and seventh year of A′-sa king of Judah, and reigned in his stead. struck

11 And it came to pass, when he began to reign, as soon as he sat on his throne, that he slew all the house of Ba′-a-sha: he left him

not one that pisseth against a wall, neither of his kinsfolks, nor of his friends.

12 Thus did Zim′-ri destroy all the house of ᴿBa′-a-sha, ᴿaccording to the word of the LORD, which he spake against Ba′-a-sha ᴿby Je′-hu the prophet, v. 3 • 2 Chr. 19:2; 20:34 • v. 1

13 For all the sins of Ba′-a-sha, and the sins of E′-lah his son, by which they sinned, and by which they made Israel to sin, in provoking the LORD God of Israel to anger ᴿwith their ᵀvanities. 1 Sam. 12:21 • foolish ways

14 Now the rest of the acts of E′-lah, and all that he did, are they not written in the book of the chronicles of the kings of Israel?

Reign of Zimri in Israel

15 In the twenty and seventh year of A′-sa king of Judah did Zim′-ri reign seven days in Tir′-zah. And the people were ᵀencamped against Gib′-be-thon, which belonged to the Phi-lis′-tines. mobilized for battle

16 And the people that were encamped heard say, Zim′-ri hath conspired, and hath also slain the king: wherefore all Israel made Om′-ri, the captain of the host, king over Israel that day in the camp.

17 And Om′-ri went up from Gib′-be-thon, and all Israel with him, and they ᴿbesieged Tir′-zah. 20:1

18 And it came to pass, when Zim′-ri saw that the city was taken, that he went into the palace of the king's house, and burnt the king's house over him with fire, and died,

19 For his sins which he sinned in doing evil in the sight of the LORD, ᴿin walking in the way of Jer-o-bo′-am, and in his sin which he did, to make Israel to sin. 12:28

20 Now the rest of the acts of Zim′-ri, and his ᴿtreason that he wrought, ᴿare they not written in the book of the chronicles of the kings of Israel? 2 Kin. 11:14 • vv. 5, 14, 27

Reign of Omri in Israel

21 Then were the people of Israel divided into two parts: half of the people followed Tib′-ni the son of Gi′-nath, to make him king; and half followed Om′-ri.

22 But the people that followed ᴿOm′-ri ᵀprevailed against the people that followed Tib′-ni the son of Gi′-nath: so Tib′-ni died, and Om′-ri reigned. v. 28 • won the victory over

23 In the thirty and first year of ᴿA′-sa king of Judah began Om′-ri to reign over Israel, twelve years: six years reigned he in ᴿTir′-zah. v. 15 • 15:21; 2 Kin. 15:14

24 And he bought the hill Sa-ma′-ri-a of She′-mer for ᵀtwo talents of silver, and built on the hill, and called the name of the city which he built, after the name of She′-mer, owner of the hill, Sa-ma′-ri-a. $768,000

25 But ᴿOm′-ri ᵀwrought evil in the eyes of

the LORD, and ᴿdid worse than all that *were* before him.   Mic. 6:16 • *did wrong* • *vv.* 30-33

26 ᴿFor he ᴿwalked in all the way of Jer-o-bo′-am the son of Ne′-bat, and in his sin wherewith he made Israel to sin, to provoke the LORD God of Israel to anger with their ᴿvanities.ᵀ   12:28 • *v.* 19 • *v.* 13 • *foolish acts*

27 Now the rest of the acts of Om′-ri which he did, and his might that he shewed, *are* they not written in the book of the chronicles of the kings of Israel?

28 So ᴿOm′-ri slept with his fathers, and was buried in Sa-ma′-ri-a: and Ahab his son reigned in his stead.   Mic. 6:16

Sin of Ahab

29 And in the thirty and eighth year of A′-sa king of Judah began Ahab the son of Om′-ri to reign over Israel: and ᴿAhab the son of Om′-ri reigned over Israel in ᴿSa-ma′-ri-a twenty and two years.   17:1 • 20:1

30 And Ahab the son of Om′-ri did evil in the sight of the LORD ᵀabove all that *were* ᴿbefore him.   *more than all* • *v.* 25; 14:9

31 And it came to pass, as if it had been a light thing for him to walk in the sins of Jer-o-bo′-am the son of Ne′-bat, that he took to wife Jez′-e-bel the daughter of Eth′-ba-al king of the Zi-do′-ni-ans, and went and served Ba′-al, and worshipped him.

32 And he reared up an ᴿaltar for Ba′-al in ᴿthe house of Ba′-al, which he had built in Sa-ma′-ri-a.   18:19, 26 • 2 Kin. 10:21, 26, 27

33 And Ahab made a ᵀgrove; and Ahab did more to provoke the LORD God of Israel to anger than all the kings of Israel that were before him.   *pagan shrine for pleasure*

34 In his days did Hi′-el the Beth′-el-ite build Jericho: he laid the foundation thereof in A-bi′-ram his firstborn, and set up the gates thereof in his youngest *son* Se′-gub, according to the word of the LORD, which he spake by Joshua the son of Nun.

CHAPTER 17

Prophecy of the Drought

AND ᵀE-li′-jah the Tish′-bite, *who was* of the ᴿinhabitants of Gil′-e-ad, said unto Ahab, As the LORD God of Israel liveth, ᴿbefore whom ᵀI stand, there shall not be dew nor rain these years, but according to my word.   *Elijahu* • Judg. 12:4 • Deut. 10:8 • *I serve*

Miracle of Food

2 And the word of the LORD came unto him, saying,

3 Get thee ᵀhence, and turn thee eastward, and hide thyself by the brook Che′-rith, that *is* before Jordan.   *from here*

4 And it shall be, *that* thou shalt drink of the brook; and I have commanded the ᴿra-vens to feed thee there.   Job 38:41

5 So he went and did according unto the word of the LORD: for he went and dwelt by the brook Che′-rith, that *is* before Jordan.

6 And the ravens brought him bread and flesh in the morning, and bread and flesh in the evening; and he drank of the brook.

7 And it came to pass after a while, that the brook dried up, because there had been no rain in the land.

8 And the word of the LORD came unto him, saying,

9 Arise, get thee to ᴿZar′-e-phath, which *belongeth* to Zi′-don, and dwell there: behold, I have commanded a widow woman there to ᵀsustain thee.   Obad. 20; Luke 4:26 • *feed*

10 So he arose and went to Zar′-e-phath. And when he came to the gate of the city, behold, the widow woman *was* there gather-ing of sticks: and ᴿhe called to her, and said, Fetch me, I pray thee, a little water in a vessel, that I may drink.   Gen. 24:17; John 4:7

11 And as she was going to fetch *it*, he called to her, and said, Bring me, I pray thee, a morsel of bread in thine hand.

12 And she said, As the LORD thy God liveth, I have not a cake, but an handful of meal in a barrel, and a little oil in a cruse: and, behold, I *am* gathering two sticks, that I may go in and dress it for me and my son, that we may eat it, and die.

13 And E-li′-jah said unto her, Fear not; go *and* do as thou hast said: but make me thereof a little cake first, and bring *it* unto me, and after make for thee and for thy son.

14 For thus saith the LORD God of Israel, The barrel of meal shall not waste, neither shall the cruse of oil fail, until the day *that* the LORD sendeth rain upon the earth.

15 And she went and did according to the saying of E-li′-jah: and she, and he, and her house, did eat ᵀmany days.   *a full year*

16 *And* the barrel of meal ᵀwasted not, neither did the cruse of oil fail, ᴿaccording to the word of the LORD, which he spake by E-li′-jah.   *was not used up* • *v.* 18; Gen. 5:24

Miracle of the Resurrection of the Gentile Son

17 And it came to pass after these things, *that* the son of the woman, the mistress of the house, fell sick; and his sickness was so sore, that there was no breath left in him.

18 And she said unto E-li′-jah, What have I to do with thee, O thou man of God? art thou come unto me to call my sin to remembrance, and to slay my son?

19 And he said unto her, Give me thy son. And he took him out of her bosom, and carried him up into a loft, where he ᵀabode, and laid him upon his own bed.   *stayed*

20 And he ᴿcried unto the LORD, and said,

O Lord my God, hast thou also brought evil upon the widow with whom I sojourn, by slaying her son?   18:36; Gen. 15:2; Hab. 3:1

21 And he stretched himself upon the child three times, and cried unto the Lord, and said, O Lord my God, I pray thee, let this child's soul come into him again.

22 And the Lord heard the voice of E-li'-jah; and the soul of the child came into him again, and he revived.

23 And E-li'-jah took the child, and brought him down out of the chamber into the house, and delivered him unto his mother: and E-li'-jah said, See, thy son liveth.

24 And the woman said to E-li'-jah, Now by this RI know that thou art a Tman of God, and that the word of the Lord in thy mouth is truth.   John 3:2; 16:30 · prophet of God

CHAPTER 18

Challenge to Ahab

AND it came to pass Rafter many days, that the word of the Lord came to E-li'-jah in the third year, saying, Go, shew thyself unto Ahab; and RI will send rain upon the earth.   17:1 · Deut. 28:12

2 RAnd E-li'-jah went to shew himself unto Ahab. And there was a Tsore Rfamine in Sa-ma'-ri-a.   Gen. 6:22 · severe · Gen. 12:10

3 And Ahab called TO-ba-di'-ah, which was the governor of his house. (Now O-ba-di'-ah feared the Lord greatly: Obadiahu

4 For it was so, Rwhen TJez'-e-bel Tcut off the prophets of the Lord, that O-ba-di'-ah took an hundred prophets, and hid them by fifty in a cave, and fed them with bread and water.)   v. 13; 16:31; 19:1 · Izebel · killed

5 And Ahab said unto O-ba-di'-ah, Go into the land, unto all fountains of water, and unto all brooks: Tperadventure we may find grass to save the horses and mules alive, that we lose not all the beasts.   perhaps

6 So they divided the land between them to pass throughout it: Ahab went one way by himself, and O-ba-di'-ah went another way by himself.

7 And as O-ba-di'-ah was in the way, behold, E-li'-jah met him: and he knew him, and Tfell on his face, and said, TArt thou that my lord E-li'-jah?   bowed in respect · is it thou

8 And he answered him, I am: go, tell thy lord, Behold, E-li'-jah is here.

9 And he said, TWhat have I sinned, that thou wouldest deliver thy servant into the hand of Ahab, to slay me?   in what

10 RAs the Lord thy God liveth, there is no nation or kingdom, whither my lord hath not sent to seek thee: and when they said, He is not there; he took an oath of the kingdom and nation, that they found thee not.   17:1

11 And now thou sayest, Go, tell thy lord, Behold, E-li'-jah is here.

12 And it shall come to pass, as soon as I am gone from thee, that the Spirit of the Lord shall carry thee whither I know not; and so when I come and tell Ahab, and he cannot find thee, he shall slay me: but I thy servant fear the Lord from my youth.

13 RWas it not told my lord what I did when Jez'-e-bel Tslew the prophets of the Lord, how I hid an hundred men of the Lord's prophets by fifty in a cave, and fed them with bread and water?   v. 4 · killed

14 RAnd now thou sayest, Go, tell thy lord, Behold, E-li'-jah is here: and he shall slay me.   [Deut. 1:17]

15 And E-li'-jah said, As the Lord of hosts liveth, before whom I stand, I will surely Tshew myself unto him to day.   confront

16 So O-ba-di'-ah went to meet Ahab, and told him: and Ahab went to meet E-li'-jah.

17 And it came to pass, when Ahab saw E-li'-jah, that Ahab said unto him, Art thou he that Rtroubleth Israel?   Acts 16:20

18 And he answered, I have not troubled Israel; but thou, and thy father's house, in that ye have forsaken the commandments of the Lord, and thou hast followed Ba'-al-im.

19 Now therefore send, and gather to me all Israel unto mount Carmel, and the prophets of Ba'-al four hundred and fifty, Rand the prophets of the groves four hundred, which eat at Jez'-e-bel's table.   16:33

Victory on Mount Carmel

20 So Ahab sent unto all the children of Israel, and Rgathered the prophets together unto mount Carmel.   22:6

21 And E-li'-jah came unto all the people, and said, How long halt ye between two opinions? if the Lord be God, follow him: but if Ba'-al, then follow him. And the people answered him not a word.

18:21 **Cure for Doubt**—The cure for doubt depends to some extent on the thing doubted. However, the real problem is not in the object doubted but in the subject who doubts. Therefore, the following steps should be taken by the doubting Christian:

a. Confess the doubt to God as sin. Doubt is basically unbelief in God and His Word and is therefore sin (Page 1120—Rom. 14:23; Page 1221—Heb. 11:6). God has promised to hear our confession of even the darkest unbelief.

22 Then said E-li′-jah unto the people, ᴿI, even I only, remain a prophet of the LORD; ᴿbut Ba′-al's prophets are four hundred and fifty men.   19:10, 14 • v. 19

23 Let them therefore give us two bullocks; and let them choose one bullock for themselves, and cut it in pieces, and lay it on wood, and put no fire under: and I will ᵀdress the other ᵀbullock, and lay it on wood, and put no fire under: prepare • bull

24 And ᵀcall ye on the name of your gods, and I will call on the name of the LORD: and the God that ᴿanswereth by fire, let him be God. And all the people answered and said, It is well spoken.   pray you to • v. 38

25 And E-li′-jah said unto the prophets of Ba′-al, Choose you one bullock for yourselves, and ᵀdress it first; for ye are many; and call on the name of your gods, but put no fire under.   prepared

26 And they took the bullock which was given them, and they ᵀdressed it, and called on the name of Ba′-al from morning even until noon, saying, O Ba′-al, ᵀhear us. But there was no voice, nor any that answered. And they ᵀleaped upon the altar which was made.   prepared • answer • in pagan ritual

27 And it came to pass at noon, that E-li′-jah mocked them, and said, Cry aloud: for he is a god; either he is talking, or he is pursuing, or he is in a journey, or peradventure he sleepeth, and must be awaked.

28 And they cried aloud, and cut themselves after their manner with knives and lancets, till the blood gushed out upon them.

29 And it came to pass, when midday was past, and they prophesied until the time of the offering of the evening sacrifice, that there was ᴿneither voice, nor any to answer, ᵀnor any that regarded.   v. 26 • no one heeded

30 And E-li′-jah said unto all the people, Come near unto me. And all the people came

near unto him. And he repaired the altar of the LORD that was broken down.

31 And E-li′-jah took twelve stones, according to the number of the tribes of the sons of Jacob, unto whom the word of the LORD came, saying, Israel shall be thy name:

32 And with the ᴿstones he built an altar in the name of the LORD: and he made a trench about the altar, as great as would contain two measures of seed.   [Ex. 20:25]

33 And he ᴿput the wood in order, and cut the bullock in pieces, and laid him on the wood, and said, Fill four barrels with water, and ᴿpour it on the burnt sacrifice, and on the wood.   Lev. 1:6-8 • Judg. 6:20, 21

34 And he said, Do it the second time. And they did it the second time. And he said, Do it the third time. And they did it the third time.

35 And the water ran round about the altar; and he filled ᴿthe trench also with water.   vv. 32, 38

36 And it came to pass at the time of the offering of the evening sacrifice, that E-li′-jah the prophet came near, and said, LORD God of Abraham, Isaac, and of Israel, let it be known this day that thou art God in Israel, and that I am thy servant, and that I have done all these things at thy word.

37 Hear me, O LORD, hear me, that this people may know that thou art the LORD God, and that thou hast ᵀturned their heart back again.   changed their minds to believe in God

38 Then the fire of the LORD fell, and consumed the burnt sacrifice, and the wood, and the stones, and the dust, and licked up the water that was in the trench.

39 And when all the people saw it, they fell on their faces: and they said, ᴿThe LORD, he is the God; the LORD, he is the God.   v. 24

40 And E-li′-jah said unto them, ᴿTake the prophets of Ba′-al; let not one of them escape. And they took them: and E-li′-jah brought

---

b. Study the evidence for the Christian faith. Christians have nothing to fear by looking into the facts from any source of knowledge. The greatest evidence for the validity of Christianity, the resurrection of Christ, is attested by many proofs. Among these are the empty tomb, post-resurrection appearances, and transformed disciples. Since the Resurrection is true, it verifies everything the Bible says.

c. Make certain of your salvation. Paul exhorts Christians to examine themselves to make sure they are Christians (Page 1151—2 Cor. 13:5). So did the author of Hebrews (Page 1217—Heb. 6:1–9). Salvation from sin is by simple trust in Jesus Christ. Until you are assured of your salvation you will be troubled by enormous doubts.

d. Faithfully study the Word of God. "Faith cometh by hearing, and hearing by the word of God" (Page 1116—Rom. 10:17). Through study and application of the Bible, our faith is strengthened and matured. Most especially, we must master the doctrines or basic teachings of the Bible if we are to be stable, mature Christians (Page 1196—1 Tim. 4:13, 16; Page 1202—2 Tim. 3:16; Page 1206—Titus 2:1, 10).

e. Pray. The surest way to face doubts when they come is to have an extensive past history of answered prayer. The more a Christian prays with faith, the more that Christian sees God answer prayer; the more a person sees God answer prayer, the stronger that person's faith becomes while the doubt becomes less.

Now turn to Page 23—THE CHRISTIAN'S GUIDE: Recognizing God's Institutions.

them down to the brook Ki'-shon, and slew them there.   [Deut. 13:5]; 2 Kin. 10:25

Miracle of the Rain

41 And E-li'-jah said unto Ahab, Get thee up, eat and drink; for *there is* a sound of abundance of Rrain.   Ezra 10:9

42 So Ahab went up to eat and to drink. And E-li'-jah went up to the top of Carmel; and he cast himself down upon the earth, and put his face between his knees,

43 And said to his servant, Go up now, look toward the sea. And he went up, and looked, and said, *There is* nothing. And he said, Go again Rseven times.   2 Kin. 5:10

44 And it came to pass at the seventh time, that he said, Behold, Rthere ariseth a little cloud out of the sea, like a man's hand. And he said, Go up, say unto Ahab, Prepare *thy chariot*, and get thee down, that the rain stop thee not.   Luke 12:54

45 And it came to pass in the mean while, that the heaven was black with clouds and wind, and there was a great rain. And Ahab rode, and went to RJez'-re-el.   Josh. 17:16

46 And the hand of the LORD was on E-li'-jah; and he girded up his loins, and ran before Ahab to the entrance of Jez'-re-el.

CHAPTER 19

Elijah Flees from Jezebel

AND Ahab told Jez'-e-bel all that E'li'-jah had done, and withal how he had slain all the prophets with the sword.

2 Then Jez'-e-bel sent a messenger unto E-li'-jah, saying, So let the gods do *to me*, and more also, if I make not thy life as the life of one of them by to morrow about this time.

3 And when he saw *that*, he arose, and Twent for his life, and came to RBe'-er-she'-ba, which *belongeth* to Judah, and left his servant there.   *fled* • Gen. 21:31

Elijah Desires to Die

4 But he himself went a day's journey into the wilderness, and came and sat down under a juniper tree: and he Rrequested for himself that he might die; and said, It is enough; now, O LORD, take away my life; for I *am* not better than my fathers.   Jon. 4:3

5 And as he lay and slept under a juniper tree, behold, then Ran angel touched him, and said unto him, Arise *and* eat.   Gen. 28:11-15

6 And he looked, and, behold, *there was* a cake baken on the coals, and a cruse of water at his Thead. And he did eat and drink, and laid him down again.   *pillow*

7 And the Rangel of the LORD came again the second time, and touched him, and said, Arise *and* eat; because the journey *is* too great for thee.   Gen. 16:7; 2 Kin. 1:3

8 And he arose, and did eat and drink, and went in the strength of that meat Rforty days and forty nights unto RHo'-reb the mount of God.   Ex. 34:28; Matt. 4:2 • Ex. 3:1

Elijah Has Self-pity

9 And he came thither unto a Rcave, and lodged there; and, behold, the word of the LORD *came* to him, and he said unto him, What doest thou here, E-li'-jah?   1 Chr. 11:15

10 And he said, I have been very jealous for the LORD God of hosts: for the children of Israel have forsaken thy covenant, thrown down thine altars, and slain thy prophets with the sword; and I, *even* I only, am left; and they seek my life, to take it away.

11 And he said, Go forth, and stand upon the mount before the LORD. And, behold, the LORD passed by, and Ra great and strong wind Trent the mountains, and brake in pieces the rocks before the LORD; *but* the LORD *was* not in the wind: and after the wind an earthquake; *but* the LORD *was* not in the earthquake: Ezek. 1:4; 37:7 • *battered*

12 And after the earthquake a fire; *but* the LORD *was* not in the fire: and after the fire Ra still small voice.   Job 4:16; [Zech. 4:6]

13 And it was *so*, when E-li'-jah heard *it*, that Rhe Twrapped his face in his mantle, and went out, and stood in the entering in of the cave. RAnd, behold, *there came* a voice unto him, and said, What doest thou here, E-li'-jah?   Ex. 3:6; Is. 6:2 • *hid* • v. 9

14 RAnd he said, I have been very Tjealous for the LORD God of hosts: because the children of Israel have forsaken thy covenant, thrown down thine altars, Rand slain thy prophets with the sword; and I, *even* I only, am left; and they seek my life, to take it away.   v. 10 • *zealous* • Rom. 11:3

15 And the LORD said unto him, Go, return on thy way to the wilderness of Damascus: and when thou comest, Tanoint Haz'-a-el *to be* king over Syria: *appoint*

16 And Je'-hu the son of Nim'-shi shalt thou anoint *to be* king over Israel: and E-li'-sha the son of Sha'-phat of A'-bel-me-ho'-lah shalt thou anoint *to be* prophet in thy room.

17 And it shall come to pass, *that* him that escapeth the sword of Haz'-a-el shall Je'-hu slay: and him that escapeth from the sword of Je'-hu Rshall E-li'-sha slay.   [Hos. 6:5]

18 Yet TI have left *me* seven thousand in Israel, all the knees which have not bowed unto Ba'-al, and every mouth Twhich hath not kissed him.   *I will leave* • *which has not praised*

Call of Elisha

19 So he departed thence, and found E-li'-sha the son of Sha'-phat, who *was* plowing *with* twelve yoke *of* oxen before him, and he with the twelfth: and E-li'-jah passed by him, and cast his mantle upon him.

20 And he left the oxen, and ran after E-li′-jah, and said, Let me, I pray thee, kiss my father and my mother, and *then* I will follow thee. And he said unto him, Go back again: for what have I done to thee?

21 And he returned back from him, and took a yoke of oxen, and slew them, and boiled their flesh with the ᵀinstruments of the oxen, and gave unto the people, and they did eat. Then he arose, and went after E-li′-jah, and ministered unto him.   *yokes*

CHAPTER 20

First Victory over Syria

AND Ben-ha′-dad the king of Syria gathered all his host together: and *there were* thirty and two kings with him, and horses, and chariots: and he went up and besieged Sa-ma′-ri-a, and warred against it.

2 And he sent ᴿmessengers to ᴿAhab king of Israel into the city, and said unto him, Thus saith Ben-ha′-dad,   2 Kin. 14:8 • 21:25

3 Thy silver and thy gold *is* mine; thy wives also and thy children, *even* the ᵀgoodliest, *are* mine.   *fairest*

4 And the king of Israel answered and said, My lord, O king, according to thy saying, I *am* thine, and all that I have.

5 And the messengers came again, and said, Thus speaketh Ben-ha′-dad, saying, Although I have sent unto thee, saying, Thou shalt deliver me thy silver, and thy gold, and thy wives, and thy children;

6 Yet I will send my servants unto thee to morrow about this time, and they shall search thine house, and the houses of thy servants; and it shall be, *that* whatsoever is ᵀpleasant in thine eyes, they shall put *it* in their hand, and take *it* away.   *precious*

7 Then the king of Israel called all the elders of the land, and said, Mark, I pray you, and see how this *man* seeketh ᵀmischief: for he sent unto me for my wives, and for my children, and for my silver, and for my gold; and I denied him not.   *harm*

8 And all the elders and all the people said unto him, Hearken not *unto him*, nor consent.

9 Wherefore he said unto the messengers of Ben-ha′-dad, Tell my lord the king, All that thou didst send for to thy servant at the first I will do: but this thing I may not do. And the messengers departed, and brought him word again.

10 And Ben-ha′-dad sent unto him, and said, The gods do so unto me, and more also, if the dust of Sa-ma′-ri-a shall suffice for handfuls for all the people that follow me.

11 And the king of Israel answered and said, ᴿTell *him*, Let not him that girdeth on

his ᵀharness boast himself as he that putteth it off.   Prov. 27:1; [Eccl. 7:8] • *armour*

12 And it came to pass, when Ben-ha′-dad heard this message, as he *was* drinking, he and the kings in the pavilions, that he said unto his servants, ᵀSet *yourselves in array*. And they set *themselves in array* against the city.   *mobilize yourselves for battle*

13 And, behold, there came a prophet unto Ahab king of Israel, saying, Thus saith the LORD, Hast thou seen all this great multitude? behold, I will deliver it into thine hand this day; and thou shalt know that I *am* the LORD.

14 And Ahab said, By whom? And he said, Thus saith the LORD, *Even* by the young men of the princes of the provinces. Then he said, Who shall order the battle? And he answered, Thou.

15 Then he numbered the young men of the princes of the provinces, and they were two hundred and thirty two: and after them he numbered all the people, *even* all the children of Israel, *being* seven thousand.

16 And they went out at noon. But Ben-ha′-dad *was* ᴿdrinking himself drunk in the pavilions, he and the kings, the thirty and two kings that helped him.   *v. 12; 16:9*

17 And the young men of the princes of the provinces went out first; and Ben-ha′-dad sent out, and they told him, saying, There are men come out of Sa-ma′-ri-a.

18 And he said, Whether they be come out for peace, take them alive; or whether they be come out for war, take them alive.

19 So these young men of the princes of the provinces came out of the city, and the army which followed them.

20 And they slew every one his man: and the Syrians fled; and Israel pursued them: and Ben-ha′-dad the king of Syria escaped on an horse with the horsemen.

21 And the king of Israel went out, and ᵀsmote the horses and chariots, and slew the Syrians with a great slaughter.   *destroyed*

Second Victory over Syria

22 And the prophet came to the king of Israel, and said unto him, Go, strengthen thyself, and mark, and see what thou doest: ᴿfor at the return of the year the king of Syria will come up against thee.   2 Sam. 11:1

23 And the servants of the king of Syria said unto him, Their gods *are* gods of the hills; therefore they were stronger than we; but let us fight against them in the plain, and surely we shall be stronger than they.

24 And do this thing, Take the kings away, every man out of his place, and put captains in their ᵀrooms: *positions*

25 And ᵀnumber thee an army, like the army that thou hast lost, horse for horse, and chariot for chariot: and we will fight against

them in the plain, *and* surely we shall be stronger than they. And he hearkened unto their voice, and did so.   *muster*

26 And it came to pass ᴿat the return of the year, that Ben–ha'-dad numbered the Syrians, and went up to ᴿA'-phek, to fight against Israel.   *v. 22 • Josh. 13:4*

27 And the children of Israel were numbered, and were all present, and went against them: and the children of Israel pitched before them like two little flocks of kids; but the Syrians filled the country.

28 And there came a man of God, and spake unto the king of Israel, and said, Thus saith the LORD, Because the Syrians have said, The LORD *is* God of the hills, but he *is* not God of the valleys, therefore will I deliver all this great multitude into thine hand, and ye shall know that I *am* the LORD.

29 And they pitched one over against the other seven days. And *so* it was, that in the seventh day the battle was joined: and the children of Israel slew of the Syrians an hundred thousand footmen in one day.

30 But the rest fled to A'-phek, into the city; and *there* a wall fell upon twenty and seven thousand of the men *that were* left. And Ben–ha'-dad fled, ᴿand came into the city, into an inner chamber.   *2 Chr. 18:24*

31 And his servants said unto him, Behold now, we have heard that the kings of the house of Israel *are* merciful kings: let us, I pray thee, put sackcloth on our loins, and ropes upon our heads, and go out to the king of Israel: peradventure he will save thy life.

32 ᴿSo they girded sackcloth on their loins, and *put* ropes on their heads, and came to the king of Israel, and said, Thy servant Ben–ha'-dad saith, I pray thee, let me live. And he said, *Is* he yet alive? he *is* my brother.   *vv. 3-6, 31*

33 Now the men did diligently observe ᵀwhether *any thing would come* from him, and did hastily catch *it:* and they said, Thy brother Ben–ha'-dad. Then he said, Go ye, bring him. Then Ben–ha'-dad came forth to him; and he caused him to come up into the chariot.   *whether there would be any hopeful sign*

34 And *Ben–ha'-dad* said unto him, The cities, which my father took from thy father, I will restore; and thou shalt make streets for thee in Damascus, as my father made in Sama'-ri-a. Then *said Ahab,* I will send thee away with this covenant. So he made a covenant with him, and sent him away.

35 ᴿAnd a certain man of the sons of the prophets said unto his neighbour in the word of the LORD, Smite me, I pray thee. And the man refused to smite him.   *2 Kin. 2:3*

36 Then said he unto him, Because thou hast not obeyed the voice of the LORD, behold, as soon as thou art departed from me, a lion shall slay thee. And as soon as he was

departed from him, ᴿa lion found him, and slew him.   *13:24*

37 Then he found another man, and said, Smite me, I pray thee. And the man smote him, so that in smiting he wounded *him.*

38 So the prophet departed, and waited for the king by the way, and ᴿdisguised himself with ᵀashes upon his face.   *14:2 • dust*

39 And as the king passed by, he cried unto the king: and he said, Thy servant went out into the midst of the battle; and, behold, a man turned aside, and brought a man unto me, and said, Keep this man: if by any means he be missing, then shall thy life be for his life, or else thou shalt pay a talent of silver.

40 ᴿAnd as thy servant was busy here and there, he was gone. And the king of Israel said unto him, So *shall* thy judgment *be;* thyself hast decided *it.*   *[Job 15:6]; Luke 19:22*

41 And he hasted, and took the ashes away from his face; and the king of Israel discerned him that he *was* of the prophets.

42 And he said unto him, Thus saith the LORD, ᴿBecause thou hast let go out of *thy* hand a man whom I appointed to utter destruction, therefore thy life shall go for his life, and thy people for his people.   *22:31-37*

43 And the king of Israel ᴿwent to his house ᵀheavy and displeased, and came to Sa-ma'-ri-a.   *21:4 • downhearted*

CHAPTER 21

Murder of Naboth

AND it came to pass after these things, *that* Na'-both the Jez'-re-el-ite had a vineyard, which *was* in Jez'-re-el, hard by the palace of Ahab king of Sa-ma'-ri-a.

2 And Ahab spake unto Na'-both, saying, Give me thy vineyard, that I may have it for a garden of herbs, because it *is* near unto my house: and I will give thee for it a better vineyard than it; *or,* if it seem good to thee, I will give thee the worth of it in money.

3 And Na'-both said to Ahab, The LORD forbid it me, ᴿthat I should give the inheritance of my fathers unto thee.   *[Lev. 25:23]*

4 ᴿAnd Ahab came into his house ᵀheavy and displeased because of the word which Na'-both the Jez'-re-el-ite had spoken to him: for he had said, I will not give thee the inheritance of my fathers. And he laid him down upon his bed, and turned away his face, and would eat no bread.   *20:43 • unhappy*

5 But ᴿJez'-e-bel his wife came to him, and said unto him, Why is thy spirit so sad, that thou eatest no ᵀbread?   *19:1, 2 • food*

6 And he said unto her, Because I spake unto Na'-both the Jez'-re-el-ite, and said unto him, Give me thy vineyard for money; or else, if it please thee, I will give thee *another*

vineyard for it: and he answered, I will not give thee my vineyard.

7 And Jez'-e-bel his wife said unto him, ^RDost thou now govern the kingdom of Israel? arise, *and* eat bread, and let thine heart be merry: I will give thee the vineyard of Na'-both the Jez'-re-el-ite.   1 Sam. 8:14

8 So she wrote letters in Ahab's name, and sealed *them* with his seal, and sent the letters unto the elders and to the nobles that *were* in his city, dwelling with Na'-both.

9 And she wrote in the letters, saying, Proclaim a fast, and set Na'-both on high among the people:

10 And set two men, sons of Be'-li-al, before him, to bear witness against him, saying, ^RThou didst blaspheme God and the king. And *then* carry him out, and stone him, that he may die.   [Ex. 22:28]; Acts 6:11

11 And the men of his city, *even* the elders and the nobles who were the inhabitants in his city, did as Jez'-e-bel had sent unto them, *and* as it *was* written in the letters which she had sent unto them.

12 ^RThey proclaimed a fast, and set Na'-both on high among the people.   Is. 58:4

13 And there came in two men, ^Tchildren of Be'-li-al, and sat before him: and the men of Be'-li-al witnessed against him, *even* against Na'-both, in the presence of the people, saying, Na'-both did blaspheme God and the king. ^RThen they carried him forth out of the city, and stoned him with stones, that he died.   *worthless fellows* • 2 Kin. 9:26

14 Then they sent to Jez'-e-bel, saying, Na'-both is stoned, and is dead.

15 And it came to pass, when Jez'-e-bel heard that Na'-both was stoned, and was dead, that Jez'-e-bel said to Ahab, Arise, take possession of the vineyard of Na'-both the Jez'-re-el-ite, which he refused to give thee for money: for Na'-both is not alive, but dead.

16 And it came to pass, when Ahab heard that Na'-both was dead, that Ahab rose up to go down to the vineyard of Na'-both the Jez'-re-el-ite, to take possession of it.

Prediction of Ahab's Death

17 ^RAnd the word of the LORD came to E-li'-jah the Tish'-bite, saying,   [Ps. 9:12]

18 Arise, go down to meet Ahab king of Israel, ^Rwhich *is* in Sa-ma'-ri-a: behold, *he is* in the vineyard of Na'-both, whither he is gone down to possess it.   13:32; 2 Chr. 22:9

19 And thou shalt speak unto him, saying, Thus saith the LORD, Hast thou killed, and also taken possession? And thou shalt speak unto him, saying, Thus saith the LORD, In the place where dogs licked the blood of Na'-both shall dogs lick thy blood, even thine.

20 And Ahab said to E-li'-jah, Hast thou found me, O mine enemy? And he answered,

I have found *thee:* because ^Rthou^T hast sold thyself to work evil in the sight of the LORD.   [Rom. 7:14] • *you have given yourself over*

21 Behold, I will bring evil upon thee, and will take away thy posterity, ^Rand will cut off from Ahab him that pisseth against the wall, and him that is shut up and left in Israel,   14:10

22 And will make thine house like the house of ^RJer-o-bo'-am the son of Ne'-bat, and like the house of ^RBa'-a-sha the son of A-hi'-jah, for the provocation wherewith thou hast provoked *me* to anger, ^Rand made Israel to sin.   15:29 • 16:3, 11 • 12:30

23 And ^Rof Jez'-e-bel also spake the LORD, saying, The dogs shall eat Jez'-e-bel ^Rby the ^Twall of Jez'-re-el.   2 Kin. 9:36 • 2 Sam. 20:15 • *ditch*

24 ^RHim that dieth of Ahab in the city the dogs shall eat; and him that dieth in the field shall the fowls of the air eat.   14:11

25 But ^Rthere was none like unto Ahab, which did sell himself to work wickedness in the sight of the LORD, ^Rwhom Jez'-e-bel his wife ^Tstirred up.   16:30 • 16:31 • *inspired*

26 And ^Rhe did very abominably in following idols, according to all *things* as did the Am'-or-ites, whom the LORD cast out before the children of Israel.   15:12

27 And it came to pass, when Ahab heard those words, that he rent his clothes, and put sackcloth upon his flesh, and fasted, and lay in sackcloth, and went softly.

28 And the word of the LORD came to E-li'-jah the Tish'-bite, saying,

29 Seest thou how Ahab humbleth himself before me? because he humbleth himself before me, I will not bring the evil in his days: *but* ^Rin his son's days will I bring the evil upon his house.   *v.* 19; 2 Kin. 9:25; 10:11

CHAPTER 22

Promise of Victory by the False Prophets
2 Chr. 18:2–11

AND they continued three years without war between Syria and Israel.

2 And it came to pass in the third year, that ^RJe-hosh'-a-phat the king of Judah came down to the king of Israel.   2 Chr. 18:1, 2

3 And the king of Israel said unto his servants, Know ye that Ra'-moth in Gil'-e-ad *is* our's, and we *be* still, *and* take it not out of the hand of the king of Syria?

4 And he said unto Je-hosh'-a-phat, Wilt thou go with me to battle to Ra'-moth–gil'-e-ad? And Je-hosh'-a-phat said to the king of Israel, I *am* as thou *art*, my people as thy people, my horses as thy horses.

5 And Je-hosh'-a-phat said unto the king of Israel, ^REnquire, I pray thee, ^Tat the word of the LORD to day.   2 Kin. 3:11 • *for the will of God*

6 Then the king of Israel gathered the prophets together, about four hundred men,

and said unto them, Shall I go against Ra'-moth–gil'-e-ad to battle, or shall I forbear? And they said, Go up; for the Lord shall deliver *it* into the hand of the king.

7 And ᴿJe-hosh'-a-phat said, *Is there* not here a prophet of the Lᴏʀᴅ besides, that we might enquire of him?   2 Kin. 3:11

8 ᴿAnd the king of Israel said unto Je-hosh'-a-phat, *There is* yet one man, Mi-ca'-iah the son of Im'-lah, by whom we may enquire of the Lᴏʀᴅ: but I hate him; for he doth not prophesy good concerning me, but evil. And Je-hosh'-a-phat said, Let not the king say so.   19:10

9 Then the king of Israel called an ᵀofficer, and said, Hasten *hither* Mi-ca'-iah the son of Im'-lah.   *eunuch*

10 And the king of Israel and Je-hosh'-a-phat the king of Judah sat each on his throne, having put on their robes, in a void place in the entrance of the gate of Sa-ma'-ri-a; and all the prophets prophesied before them.

11 And Zed-e-ki'-ah the son of Che-na'-a-nah made him horns of ᴿiron: and he said, Thus saith the Lᴏʀᴅ, ᴿWith these shalt thou push the Syrians, until thou have consumed them.   1 Chr. 22:3 • Deut. 33:17; Zech. 1:18–21

12 And all the prophets prophesied so, saying, ᵀGo up to Ra'-moth–gil'-e-ad, and prosper: for the Lᴏʀᴅ shall deliver *it* into the king's hand.   *attack*

Promise of Defeat by Micaiah—2 Chr. 18:12–27

13 And the messenger that was gone to call Mi-ca'-iah spake unto him, saying, Behold now, the words of the prophets *declare* good unto the king with one mouth: let thy word, I pray thee, be like the word of one of them, and speak *that which is* good.

14 And Mi-ca'-iah said, ᴿAs the Lᴏʀᴅ liveth, ᴿwhat the Lᴏʀᴅ saith unto me, that will I speak.   18:10, 15 • Num. 22:38; 24:13

15 So he came to the king. And the king said unto him, Mi-ca'-iah, shall we go against Ra'-moth–gil'-e-ad to battle, or shall we ᵀforbear? And he answered him, Go, and prosper: for the Lᴏʀᴅ shall deliver *it* into the hand of the king.   *decide not to go*

16 And the king said unto him, How many times shall I ᴿadjure ᵀthee that thou tell me nothing but *that which is* true in the name of the Lᴏʀᴅ?   Matt. 26:63 • *command*

17 And he said, I saw all Israel ᴿscattered upon the hills, ᴿas sheep that have not a shepherd: and the Lᴏʀᴅ said, These have no master: let them return every man to his house in peace.   Matt. 9:36 • Num. 27:17

18 And the king of Israel said unto Je-hosh'-a-phat, ᴿDid I not tell thee that he would prophesy no good concerning me, but evil?   *v. 8*

19 And he said, Hear thou therefore the word of the Lᴏʀᴅ: ᴿI saw the Lᴏʀᴅ sitting on his throne, ᴿand all the host of heaven standing by him on his right hand and on his left.   Dan. 7:9 • [Matt. 18:10]

20 And the Lᴏʀᴅ said, Who shall persuade Ahab, that he may go up and fall at Ra'-moth–gil'-e-ad? And one said on this manner, and another said on that manner.

21 And there came forth a spirit, and stood before the Lᴏʀᴅ, and said, I will persuade him.

22 And the Lᴏʀᴅ said unto him, Wherewith? And he said, I will go forth, and I will be a lying spirit in the mouth of all his prophets. And he said, Thou shalt persuade *him*, and prevail also: go forth, and do so.

23 ᴿNow therefore, behold, the Lᴏʀᴅ hath put a lying spirit in the mouth of all these thy prophets, and the Lᴏʀᴅ hath spoken evil concerning thee.   [Ezek. 14:9]

24 But Zed-e-ki'-ah the son of Che-na'-nah went near, and smote Mi-ca'-iah on the cheek, and said, Which way went the Spirit of the Lᴏʀᴅ from me to speak unto thee?

25 And Mi-ca'-iah said, Behold, thou shalt see in that day, when thou shalt go into an inner chamber to hide thyself.

26 And the king of Israel said, Take Mi-ca'-iah, and carry him back unto Amon the governor of the city, and to Jo'-ash the king's son;

27 And say, Thus saith the king, ᴿPut this *fellow* in the prison, and feed him with bread of affliction and with water of affliction, until I come in peace.   2 Chr. 16:10

28 And Mi-ca'-iah said, If thou return at all in peace, ᴿthe Lᴏʀᴅ hath not spoken by me. And he said, Hearken, ᴿO people, every one of you.   Num. 16:29; Deut. 18:20–22 • Mic. 1:2

Defeat of Israel—2 Chr. 18:28–34

29 So ᴿthe king of Israel and Je-hosh'-a-phat the king of Judah went up to Ra'-moth–gil'-e-ad.   *vv. 3, 4*

30 And the king of Israel said unto Je-hosh'-a-phat, I will disguise myself, and enter into the battle; but put thou on thy robes. And the king of Israel disguised himself, and went into the battle.

31 But ᴿthe king of Syria commanded his thirty and two captains that had rule over his chariots, saying, ᴿFight neither with small nor great, save only with the king of Isra-el.   20:1, 16 • 20:24; 2 Chr. 18:30

32 And it came to pass, when the captains of the chariots saw Je-hosh'-a-phat, that they said, Surely it *is* the king of Israel. And they turned aside to fight against him: and Je-hosh'-a-phat cried out.

33 And it came to pass, when the captains of the chariots perceived that it *was* not the

king of Israel, that they turned back from pursuing him.

34 And a *certain* man drew a bow at a venture, and smote the king of Israel between the joints of the harness: wherefore he said unto the driver of his chariot, Turn thine hand, and carry me out of the host; ^Rfor I am wounded.   2 Chr. 35:23

35 And the battle increased that day: and the king was ^Tstayed up in his chariot against the Syrians, and died at even: and the blood ran out of the wound into the ^Tmidst of the chariot.   *propped · inside*

36 And there went a proclamation throughout the host about the ^Tgoing down of the sun, saying, Every man to his city, and every man to his own country.   *even*

Death of Ahab

37 So the king died, and was brought to Sa-ma′-ri-a; and they buried the king in Sa-ma′-ri-a.

38 And *one* washed the chariot in the pool of Sa-ma′-ri-a; and the ^Rdogs licked up his blood; and they washed his armour; ^Raccording ^Runto the word of the LORD which he spake.   Ps. 59:6 · Amos 3:15 · 21:19

39 Now the rest of the acts of Ahab, and all that he did, and ^Rthe ivory house which he made, and all the cities that he built, *are* they not written in the book of the chronicles of the kings of Israel?   Ezra 6:2; Ps. 45:8

40 So Ahab ^Tslept with his fathers; and A-ha-zi′-ah his son reigned in his stead.   *died*

The Reign of Jehoshaphat in Judah
2 Chr. 20:31—21:1

41 And ^RJe-hosh′-a-phat the son of A′-sa began to reign over Judah in the fourth year of Ahab king of Israel.   2 Chr. 20:31

42 Je-hosh′-a-phat *was* thirty and five years old when he began to reign; and he reigned twenty and five years in Jerusalem. And his mother's name *was* A-zu′-bah the daughter of Shil′-hi.

43 And he walked in all the ways of A′-sa his father; he turned not aside from it, doing *that which was* right in the eyes of the LORD: nevertheless the high places were not taken away; *for* the people offered and burnt incense yet in the high places.

44 And ^RJe-hosh′-a-phat made peace with the king of Israel.   *v.* 2; 2 Chr. 19:2

45 Now the rest of the acts of Je-hosh′-a-phat, and his might that he shewed, and how he warred, *are* they not written in the book of the chronicles of the kings of Judah?

46 ^RAnd the remnant of the sodomites, which remained in the days of his father A′-sa, he took out of the land.   14:24

47 ^R*There was* then no king in E′-dom: a deputy *was* king.   2 Sam. 8:14; 2 Kin. 3:9; 8:20

48 Je-hosh′-a-phat ^Rmade^T ships of Thar′-shish to go to O′-phir for gold: but they went not; for the ships were broken at ^RE′-zi-on-ge′-ber.   10:22 · *had ten ships* · 9:26

49 Then said A-ha-zi′-ah the son of Ahab unto Je-hosh′-a-phat, Let my servants go with thy ^Rservants in the ships. But Je-hosh′-a-phat would not.   Ps. 107:23

50 And Je-hosh′-a-phat ^Tslept with his fathers, and was buried with his fathers in the city of David his father: and Je-ho′-ram his son reigned in his stead.   *died*

The Reign of Ahaziah in Israel

51 A-ha-zi′-ah the son of Ahab began to reign over Israel in Sa-ma′-ri-a the seventeenth year of Je-hosh′-a-phat king of Judah, and reigned two years over Israel.

52 And he did evil in the sight of the LORD, and ^Rwalked in the way of his father, and in the way of his mother, and in the way of Jer-o-bo′-am the son of Ne′-bat, who made Israel to sin: 15:26; 21:25

53 For ^Rhe served Ba′-al, and worshipped him, and provoked to anger the LORD God of Israel, ^Taccording to all that his father had done.   16:31; Judg. 2:11 · *in the same way*

KINGS

THE BOOK OF SECOND KINGS

The Book of Second Kings continues the drama begun in First Kings—the tragic history of two nations on a collision course with captivity. The author systematically traces the reigning monarchs of Israel and Judah, first by carrying one nation's history forward, then retracing the same period for the other nation.

Nineteen consecutive evil kings rule in Israel, leading to the captivity by Assyria. The picture is somewhat brighter in Judah, where godly kings occasionally emerge to reform the evils of their predecessors. In the end, however, sin outweighs righteousness and Judah is marched off to Babylon. See "The Book of First Kings" for more detail concerning the title.

THE AUTHOR OF SECOND KINGS

See "The Author of First Kings" for a discussion of authorship. If this now divided book was not written by Jeremiah, it probably was written by a prophetic contemporary of his. The majority of Second Kings was written before the Babylonian captivity (see "unto this day" in 17:34, 41).

The literary style of Second Kings is similar to that of the Book of Jeremiah, and it has been observed that the omission of Jeremiah's ministry in the account of King Josiah and his successors may indicate that Jeremiah himself was the recorder of the events. However, the last two chapters were evidently added to the book after the Babylonian captivity and written by someone other than Jeremiah. The prophet Jeremiah was forced to flee to Egypt (Jer. 43:1–8), not to Babylon. It is interesting that Second Kings 24:18—25:30 is almost the same as Jeremiah 52.

THE TIME OF SECOND KINGS

The last recorded event in Second Kings is the release of Jehoiachin (25:27–30), which takes place in 560 B.C. Most of First and Second Kings probably was written just prior to 586 B.C., but chapters 24 and 25 were written after Jehoiachin's release, perhaps about 550 B.C.

Chapters 1—17 cover the 131 years from 853 B.C. (King Ahaziah of Israel) to 722 B.C. (the Assyrian captivity of Israel). Chapters 18—25 cover the 155 years from the beginning of Hezekiah's reign in 715 B.C. to the release of Jehoiachin in Babylon in 560 B.C. The united kingdom lasts for 112 years (1043–931 B.C.), the northern kingdom of Israel exists for another 209 years (931–722 B.C.), and the southern kingdom of Judah continues for an additional 136 years (722–586 B.C.). During this 457-year kingdom

period, there are great shifts of world power. Egyptian and Assyrian control over Palestine fluctuates; Assyria rises to preeminence, declines, and is finally conquered by Babylon.

The books of Kings show that judgment comes to the kingdoms of Israel and Judah because of their idolatry, immorality, and disunity. Judah lasts 136 years longer than Israel because of the relative goodness of eight of its twenty kings. Israel never breaks away from Jeroboam's idolatrous calf worship, but Judah experiences some periods of revival in the worship of Yahweh. During these years, God sends many of His prophets. Elijah, Elisha, Amos, and Hosea are in the northern kingdom, while in the southern kingdom Obadiah, Joel, Isaiah, Micah, Nahum, Zephaniah, Jeremiah, and Habakkuk are prophesying.

THE CHRIST OF SECOND KINGS

Unlike the nine different dynasties in the northern kingdom, the kings of Judah reign as one continuous dynasty. In spite of Queen Athaliah's attempt to destroy the house of David, God remains faithful to His covenant with David (2 Sam. 7) by preserving his lineage. Jesus the Messiah is his direct descendant.

While Elijah is a figure of John the Baptist (Matt. 11:14; 17:10–12; Luke 1:17), Elisha reminds us of Christ. Elijah generally lives apart from the people and stresses law, judgment, and repentance. Elisha lives among the people and emphasizes grace, life, and hope.

KEYS TO SECOND KINGS

Key Word: Captivities of the Kingdom— Second Kings records both the destruction and captivity of Israel by the Assyrians (2 Kin. 17), as well as the destruction and captivity of Judah by the Babylonians (2 Kin. 25).

The book was written selectively, not exhaustively, from a prophetic viewpoint to teach that the decline and collapse of the two kingdoms occurred because of failure on the part of the rulers and people to heed the warnings of God's messengers. The spiritual climate of the nation determined its political and economic conditions.

The prophets of Yahweh play a prominent role in First and Second Kings as God uses them to remind the kings of their covenant responsibilities as His theocratic administrators. When the king keeps the covenant, he and the nation are richly blessed. But judgment consistently falls upon those who refuse to obey God's law. God is seen in Kings as the controller of history who reveals His plan and purpose to His people. Unhappily,

the people are concerned more with their own plans, and their rejection of God's rule leads to exile at the hands of the Assyrians and Babylonians.

Key Verses: Second Kings 17:22, 23; 23:27— "For the children of Israel walked in all the sins of Jeroboam which he did; they departed not from them; Until the LORD removed Israel out of his sight, as he had said by all his servants the prophets. So was Israel carried away out of their own land to Assyria unto this day" (17:22, 23).

"And the LORD said, I will remove Judah also out of my sight, as I have removed Israel, and will cast off this city Jerusalem which I have chosen, and the house of which I said, My name shall be there" (23:27).

Key Chapter: Second Kings 25—The last chapter of Second Kings records the utter destruction of the city of Jerusalem and its glorious temple. Only the poor of Israel are left, and even some of them flee for their lives to Egypt. Hope is still alive, however, with the remnant in the Babylonian captivity as Evilmerodach frees Jehoiachin from prison and treats him kindly.

SURVEY OF SECOND KINGS

Without interruption Second Kings continues the narrative of First Kings. The twin kingdoms of Israel and Judah pursue a collision course with captivity as the glory of the once united kingdom becomes increasingly diminished. Division has led to decline and now ends in double deportation with Israel captured by Assyria and Judah by Babylon. This book traces the history of the divided kingdom in chapters 1—17 and the history of the surviving kingdom in chapters 18—25.

Divided Kingdom (1—17): These chapters record the story of Israel's corruption in a relentless succession of bad kings from Ahaziah to

Hoshea. The situation in Judah during this time (Jehoram to Ahaz) is somewhat better, but far from ideal. This dark period in the northern kingdom of Israel is interrupted only by the ministries of such godly prophets as Elijah and Elisha. At the end of Elijah's miraculous ministry, Elisha is installed and authenticated as his successor. He is a force for righteousness in a nation that never served the true God or worshiped at the temple in Jerusalem. Elisha's ministry is characterized by miraculous provisions of sustenance and life. Through him God demonstrates His gracious care for the nation and His concern for any person who desires to come to Him. However, like his forerunner Elijah, Elisha is basically rejected by Israel's leadership.

Elisha instructs one of his prophetic assistants to anoint Jehu king over Israel. Jehu fulfills the prophecies concerning Ahab's descendants by putting them to death. He kills Ahab's wife Jezebel, his sons, and also the priests of Baal. But he does not depart from the calf worship originally set up by Jeroboam. The loss of the house of Ahab means the alienation of Israel and Judah and the weakening of both. Israel's enemies begin to get the upper hand. Meanwhile, in Judah, Jezebel's daughter Athaliah kills all the descendants of David, except for Joash, and usurps the throne. However, Jehoiada the priest eventually removes her from the throne and places Joash in power. Joash restores the temple and serves God.

Syria gains virtual control over Israel, but there is no response to God's chastisement: the kings and people refuse to repent. Nevertheless, there is a period of restoration under Jeroboam II, but the continuing series of wicked kings in Israel leads to its overthrow by Assyria.

Surviving Kingdom (18—25): Of Israel's nineteen kings, not one is righteous in God's sight. All but one of its nine dynasties are created

FOCUS	DIVIDED KINGDOM			SURVIVING KINGDOM		
REFERENCE	1:1 —— 9:1	——	17:1 —— 18:1	—— 22:1	—— 25:1	—— 25:30
DIVISION	MINISTRY OF ELISHA UNDER AHAZIAH AND JEHORAM	REIGNS OF TEN KINGS OF ISRAEL AND EIGHT KINGS OF JUDAH	FALL OF ISRAEL	REIGNS OF HEZEKIAH AND TWO EVIL KINGS	REIGNS OF JOSIAH AND FOUR EVIL KINGS	FALL OF JUDAH
TOPIC	ISRAEL AND JUDAH			JUDAH		
	AHAZIAH TO HOSHEA			HEZEKIAH TO ZEDEKIAH		
LOCATION	ISRAEL DEPORTED TO ASSYRIA			JUDAH DEPORTED TO BABYLONIA		
TIME	131 YEARS (853–722 B.C.)			155 YEARS (715–560 B.C.)		

by murdering the previous king. In Judah, where there is only one dynasty, eight of its twenty rulers do what is right before God. Nevertheless, Judah's collapse finally comes, resulting in the Babylonian exile. Chapters 18—25 read more easily than chapters 1—17 because alternating the histories of the northern and southern kingdoms is no longer necessary. Only Judah remains.

Six years before the overthrow of Israel's capital of Samaria, Hezekiah becomes king of Judah. Because of his exemplary faith and reforms, God spares Jerusalem from Assyria and brings a measure of prosperity to Judah. However, Hezekiah's son Manasseh is so idolatrous that his long reign leads to the downfall of Judah. Even Josiah's later reforms cannot stem the tide of evil, and the four kings who succeed him are exceedingly wicked. Judgment comes with three deportations to Babylon. The third occurs in 586 B.C. when Nebuchadnezzar destroys Jerusalem and the temple. Still, the book ends on a note of hope with God preserving a remnant for Himself.

OUTLINE OF SECOND KINGS

Part One: The Divided Kingdom (1:1—17:41)

Part Two: The Surviving Kingdom of Judah (18:1—25:30)

CHAPTER 1

Political Situation Under Ahaziah—2 Kin. 3:5

THEN Moab ᴿrebelled against Israel ᴿafter the death of Ahab.   2 Sam. 8:2 · 3:5

Death of Ahaziah

2 And A-ha-zi′-ah fell down through a lattice in his upper chamber that *was* in Sa-ma′-ri-a, and was sick: and he sent messengers, and said unto them, Go, enquire of Ba′-al-ze′-bub the god of Ek′-ron whether I shall recover of this disease.

3 But the angel of the LORD said to E-li′-jah

the Tish′-bite, Arise, go up to meet the messengers of the king of Sa-ma′-ri-a, and say unto them, Is it not because *there is* not a God in Israel, *that* ye go to enquire of Ba′-al-ze′-bub the god of Ek′-ron?

4 Now therefore thus saith the LORD, ᴿThou shalt not come down from that bed on which thou art gone up, but shalt surely die. And E-li′-jah departed.   *vv. 6, 16*

5 And when the messengers turned back unto him, he said unto them, Why are ye now ᵀturned back?   *returned*

6 And they said unto him, There came a man up to meet us, and said unto us, Go,

Tturn again unto the king that sent you, and say unto him, Thus saith the LORD, RIs it not because there is not a God in Israel, that thou sendest to enquire of Ba'-al-ze'-bub the god of Ek'-ron? therefore thou shalt not come down from that bed on which thou art gone up, but shalt surely die. *return • v. 2*

7 And he said unto them, TWhat manner of man was he which came up to meet you, and told you these words? *what kind of man*

8 And they answered him, He was Ran hairy man, and girt with a girdle of leather about his loins. And he said, It is E-li'-jah the Tish'-bite. *Zech. 13:4; Matt. 3:4; Mark 1:6*

9 Then the king sent unto him a captain of fifty with his fifty. And he went up to him: and, behold, he sat on the top of an hill. And he spake unto him, Thou man of God, the king hath said, Come down.

10 And E-li'-jah answered and said to the captain of fifty, If I be a man of God, then Rlet fire come down from heaven, and Tconsume thee and thy fifty. And there came down fire from heaven, and consumed him and his fifty. *1 Kin. 18:36–38; Luke 9:54 • destroy*

11 Again also he sent unto him another captain of fifty with his fifty. And he answered and said unto him, O man of God, thus hath the king said, Come down quickly.

12 And E-li'-jah answered and said unto them, If I be a man of God, let fire come down from heaven, and consume thee and thy fifty. And the fire of God came down from heaven, and consumed him and his fifty.

13 And he sent again a captain of the third fifty with his fifty. And the third captain of fifty went up, and came and Tfell on his knees before E-li'-jah, and besought him, and said unto him, O man of God, I pray thee, let my life, and the life of these fifty thy servants, Rbe precious in thy sight. *bowed • Ps. 72:14*

14 Behold, there came fire down from heaven, and burnt up the two captains of the former fifties with their fifties: therefore let my life now be precious in thy sight.

15 And the Tangel of the LORD Rsaid unto E-li'-jah, Go down with him: be not afraid of him. And he arose, and went down with him unto the king. *messenger • v. 3*

16 And he said unto him, Thus saith the LORD, Forasmuch as thou hast sent messengers to enquire of Ba'-al-ze'-bub the god of Ek'-ron, is it not because there is no God in Israel to enquire of his word? therefore thou shalt not come down off that bed on which thou art gone up, but shalt surely die.

17 So he died according to the word of the LORD which E-li'-jah had spoken. And Je-ho'-ram reigned in his stead in the second year of Je-ho'-ram the son of Je-hosh'-a-phat king of Judah; because he had no son.

18 Now the rest of the acts of A-ha-zi'-ah which he did, are they not written in the book of the chronicles of the kings of Israel?

CHAPTER 2

A Chariot of Fire Takes Elijah

AND it came to pass, when the LORD would Rtake up E-li'-jah into heaven by a whirlwind, that E-li'-jah went with RE-li'-sha from Gil'-gal. *Gen. 5:24 • 1 Kin. 19:21*

2 And E-li'-jah said unto E-li'sha, RTarry here, I pray thee; for the LORD hath sent me to Beth'-el. And E-li'-sha said unto him, As the LORD liveth, and Ras thy soul liveth, I will not leave thee. So they went down to Beth'-el. *Ruth 1:15, 16 • 4:30; 1 Sam. 1:26*

3 And Rthe sons of the prophets that were at Beth'-el came forth to E-li'-sha, and said unto him, Knowest thou that the LORD will take away thy master Tfrom thy head to day? And he said, Yea, I know it; hold ye your peace. *1 Kin. 20:35 • from being your leader*

4 And E-li'-jah said unto him, E-li'-sha, tarry here, I pray thee; for the LORD hath sent me to Jericho. And he said, As the LORD liveth, and as thy soul liveth, I will not leave thee. So they came to Jericho.

5 And Rthe sons of the prophets that were at Jericho came to E-li'-sha, and said unto him, Knowest thou that the LORD will take away thy master from thy head to day? And he answered, Yea, I know it; Rhold T ye your peace. *v. 3 • Ex. 14:14 • say nothing about it*

6 And E-li'-jah said unto him, RTarry, I pray thee, here; for the LORD hath sent me Rto Jordan. And he said, As the LORD liveth, and as thy soul liveth, I will not leave thee. And they two went on. *v. 2 • Josh. 3:8, 15–17*

7 And Rfifty men of the sons of the prophets went, and stood to view afar off: and they two stood by Jordan. *vv. 15, 16*

8 And E-li'-jah took his mantle, and wrapped it together, and smote the waters, and they were divided hither and thither, so that they two went over on dry ground.

9 And it came to pass, when they were gone over, that E-li'-jah said unto E-li'-sha, Ask what I shall do for thee, before I be taken away from thee. And E-li'-sha said, I pray thee, let a Rdouble portion of thy spirit be upon me. *Deut. 21:17*

10 And he said, Thou hast asked a hard thing: nevertheless, if thou see me when I am taken from thee, it shall be so unto thee; but if not, it shall not be so.

11 And it came to pass, as they still went on, and talked, that, behold, there appeared Ra chariot of fire, and horses of fire, and

parted them both asunder; and E-li'-jah went up by a whirlwind into heaven.   6:17

Authority of Elijah Is Taken by Elisha

12 And E-li'-sha saw it, and he cried, RMy father, my father, the chariot of Israel, and the horsemen thereof. And he saw him no more: and he took hold of his own clothes, and Trent them in two pieces.   13:14 · tore

13 He took up also the Rmantle of E-li'-jah that fell from him, and went back, and stood by the bank of Jordan;   Ezra 9:3

14 And he took the mantle of E-li'-jah that fell from him, and smote the waters, and said, Where is the LORD God of E-li'-jah? and when he also had smitten the waters, they parted hither and thither: and E-li'-sha went over.

15 And when the sons of the prophets which were to view at Jericho saw him, they said, The spirit of E-li'-jah doth rest on E-li'-sha. And they came to meet him, and bowed themselves to the ground before him.

16 And they said unto him, Behold now, there be with thy servants fifty strong men; let them go, we pray thee, and seek thy master: Rlest peradventure the Spirit of the LORD hath taken him up, and cast him upon some mountain, or into some valley. And he said, Ye shall not send.   Acts 8:39

17 And when they urged him Rtill he was ashamed, he said, Send. They sent therefore fifty men; and they Tsought three days, but found him not.   8:11 · searched

18 And when they came again to him, (for he tarried at Jericho,) he said unto them, Did I not say unto you, Go not?

19 And the men of the city said unto E-li'-sha, Behold, I pray thee, the situation of this city is pleasant, as my lord seeth: but the water is naught, and the ground barren.

20 And he said, Bring me a new cruse, and put salt therein. And they brought it to him.

21 And he went forth unto the spring of the waters, and Rcast the salt in there, and said, Thus saith the LORD, I have healed these waters; there shall not be from thence any more death or barren land.   4:41; John 9:6

22 So the waters were Rhealed unto this day, according to the saying of E-li'-sha which he spake.   Ezek. 47:8, 9

23 And he went up from thence unto Beth'-el: and as he was going up by the way, there came forth little children out of the city, and mocked him, and said unto him, Go up, thou bald head; go up, thou bald head.

24 And he turned back, and looked on them, and Tcursed them in the name of the LORD. And there came forth two she bears out of the wood, and tare forty and two children of them.   called for judgment upon them

25 And he went from thence to Rmount Carmel, and from thence he returned to Sa-ma'-ri-a.   4:25; 19:23; 1 Kin. 18:19, 20

CHAPTER 3

Spiritual Evaluation of Jehoram

NOW RJe-ho'-ram the son of Ahab began to reign over Israel in Sa-ma'-ri-a the eighteenth year of Je-hosh'-a-phat king of Judah, and reigned twelve years.   1:17

2 And he wrought evil in the sight of the LORD; but not like his father, and like his mother: for Rhe put away the Timage of Ba'-al that his father made.   10:18 · idol

3 Nevertheless he Tcleaved unto Rthe sins of Jer-o-bo'-am the son of Ne'-bat, which made Israel to sin; he departed not therefrom.   followed closely · 1 Kin. 12:28, 31, 32

Political Situation Under Jehoram

4 And Me'-sha king of Moab was a sheepmaster, and rendered unto the king of Israel an hundred thousand lambs, and an hundred thousand rams, with the wool.

5 But it came to pass, when RAhab was dead, that the king of Moab Rrebelled against the king of Israel.   1:1 · 1 Kin. 12:16

6 And king Je-ho'-ram went out of Sa-ma'-ri-a the same time, and numbered all Israel.

7 And he went and sent to Je-hosh'-a-phat the king of Judah, saying, The king of Moab hath rebelled against me: wilt thou go with me against Moab to battle? And he said, I will go up: I am as thou art, my people as thy people, and my horses as thy horses.

8 And he said, Which way shall we go up? And he answered, The way through the wilderness of E'-dom.

9 So Rthe king of Israel went, and the king of Judah, and the king of E'-dom: and they fetched a compass of seven days' journey: and there was no water for the host, and for the cattle that followed them.   v. 1

10 RAnd the king of Israel said, Alas! that the LORD hath called these three kings together, to Tdeliver them into the hand of Moab!   Prov. 19:3; Is. 8:21 · give

11 But Je-hosh'-a-phat said, Is there not here a prophet of the LORD, that we may enquire of the LORD by him? And one of the king of Israel's servants answered and said, Here is E-li'-sha the son of Sha'-phat, which poured water on the hands of E-li'-jah.

12 And Je-hosh'-a-phat said, The word of the LORD is with him. So the king of Israel and Je-hosh'-a-phat and the king of E'-dom Rwent down to him.   2:25

13 And E-li'-sha said unto the king of Israel, What have I to do with thee? Rget thee to the prophets of thy father, and to the prophets of thy mother. And the king of Israel said unto him, Nay: for the LORD hath

called these three kings together, to deliver them into the hand of Moab.   Ruth 1:15

14 And E-li'-sha said, ᴿAs the LORD of hosts liveth, before whom I stand, surely, were it not that I regard the presence of Je-hosh'-a-phat the king of Judah, I would not look toward thee, nor see thee.   5:16

15 But now bring me a minstrel. And it came to pass, when the minstrel played, that the hand of the LORD came upon him.

16 And he said, Thus saith the LORD, Make this valley full of ditches.

17 ᴿFor thus saith the LORD, Ye shall not see wind, neither shall ye see rain; yet that valley shall be filled with water, that ye may drink, both ye, and your cattle, and your beasts.   Num. 11:25; 2 Chr. 20:37

18 ᴿAnd this is but a light thing in the sight of the LORD: he will deliver the Mo'-ab-ites also into your hand.   [Job 42:2]

19 And ye shall smite every fenced city, and every choice city, and shall fell every good tree, and stop all wells of water, and mar every good piece of land with stones.

20 And it came to pass in the morning, when the meat offering was offered, that, behold, there came water by the way of E'-dom, and the country was filled with water.

21 And when all the Mo'-ab-ites heard that the kings were come up to fight against them, they gathered all that were able to put on armour, and upward, and stood in the border.

22 And they rose up early in the morning, and the sun shone upon the water, and the Mo'-ab-ites saw the water on the other side as red as blood:

23 And they said, This is blood: the kings are surely slain, and they have smitten one another: now therefore, Moab, to the spoil.

24 And when they came to the camp of Israel, the Israelites rose up and smote the Mo'-ab-ites, so that they fled before them: but they went forward ᵀsmiting the Mo'-ab-ites, even in their country.   slaughtering

25 ᴿAnd they ᵀbeat down the cities, and on every good piece of land cast every man his stone, and filled it; and they stopped all the wells of water, and felled all the good trees: only in Kir-har'-a-seth left they the stones thereof; howbeit the slingers went about it, and smote it.   v. 19 • sacked

26 And when the king of Moab saw that the battle was too ᵀsore for him, he took with him seven hundred men that drew swords, to break through even unto the king of E'-dom: but they could not.   fierce

27 Then he took his eldest son that should have reigned in his stead, and offered him for a burnt offering upon the wall. And there was great indignation against Israel: ᴿand they departed from him, and returned to their own land.   8:20

CHAPTER 4

Miracle of the Increase of the Widow's Oil

NOW there cried a certain woman of the wives of ᴿthe sons of the prophets unto E-li'-sha, saying, Thy servant my husband is dead; and thou knowest that thy servant did fear the LORD: and the creditor is come ᴿto ᵀtake unto him my two sons to be ᵀbond-men.   2:3 • Matt. 18:25 • arrest • slaves

2 And E-li'-sha said unto her, What shall I do for thee? tell me, what hast thou in the house? And she said, Thine handmaid hath not any thing in the house, save a pot of oil.

3 Then he said, Go, borrow thee vessels abroad of all thy neighbours, even empty vessels; ᵀborrow not a few.   borrow many

4 And when thou art come in, thou shalt shut the door upon thee and upon thy sons, and shalt pour out into all those vessels, and thou shalt set aside that which is full.

5 So she went from him, and shut the door upon her and upon her sons, who brought the vessels to her; and she poured out.

6 And it came to pass, when the vessels were full, that she said unto her son, Bring me yet a vessel. And he said unto her, There is not a vessel more. And the oil stayed.

7 Then she came and told the man of God. And he said, Go, sell the oil, and pay thy debt, and live thou and thy children of the rest.

Miracle of the Shunammite's Son

8 And it fell on a day, that E-li'-sha passed to Shu'-nem, where was a great woman; and she constrained him ᵀto eat bread. And so it was, that as oft as he passed by, he turned in ᵀthither to eat bread.   to dine with her • to dine there

9 And she said unto her husband, Behold now, I perceive that this is an holy ᴿman of God, which passeth by us continually.   v. 7

10 Let us make a little chamber, I pray thee, on the wall; and let us set for him there a bed, and a table, and a stool, and a candlestick: and it shall be, when he cometh to us, that he shall turn in thither.

11 And it fell on a day, that he came ᵀthither, and he turned into the chamber, and lay there.   there

12 And he said to ᴿGe-ha'-zi his servant, Call this Shu'-nam-mite. And when he had called her, she stood before him.   vv. 29-31

13 And he said unto him, Say now unto her, Behold, thou hast ᵀbeen careful for us with all this care; what is to be done for thee? wouldest thou be spoken for to the king, or to the captain of the host? And she answered, I dwell among mine own people.   shown care

14 And he said, What then is to be done for her? And Ge-ha'-zi answered, Verily she hath no child, and her husband is old.

15 And he said, Call her. And when he had called her, she stood in the door.

16 And he said, About this season, according to the time of life, thou shalt embrace a son. And she said, Nay, my lord, *thou* man of God, ᴿdo not lie unto thine handmaid.   *v. 28*

17 And the woman conceived, and bare a son at that season that E-li'-sha had said unto her, according to the time of life.

18 And when the child was grown, it fell on a day, that he went out to his father to the ᴿreapers.   [Gen. 8:22]

19 And he said unto his father, My head, my head. And he said to ᵀa lad, Carry him to his mother.   *his servant*

20 ᴿAnd when he had taken him, and brought him to his mother, he sat on her knees till noon, and *then* died.   [Is. 49:15]

21 And she went up, and ᴿlaid him on ᴿthe bed of the man of God, and shut *the door* upon him, and went out.   *v. 32 • v. 7*

22 And she called unto her husband, and said, Send me, I pray thee, one of the young men, and one of the asses, that I may run to the man of God, and come again.

23 And he said, Wherefore wilt thou go to him to day? *it is* neither new moon, nor sabbath. And she said, *It shall be* well.

24 Then she saddled an ass, and said to her servant, Drive, and go forward; slack not *thy* riding for me, except I bid thee.

25 So she went and came unto the man of God to mount Carmel. And it came to pass, when the man of God saw her afar off, that he said to Ge-ha'-zi his servant, Behold, *yonder is* that Shu'-nam-mite:

26 Run now, I pray thee, to meet her, and say unto her, *Is it* well with thee? *is it* well with thy husband? *is it* well with the child? And she answered, *It is* well.

27 And when she came to the man of God to the hill, she caught him by the feet: but Ge-ha'-zi came near to thrust her away. And the man of God said, Let her alone; for her soul *is* ᴿvexed within her: and the Lᴏʀᴅ hath hid *it* from me, and hath not told me. 1 Sam. 1:10

28 Then she said, Did I desire a son of my lord? ᴿdid I not say, Do not deceive me? *v. 16*

29 Then he said to Ge-ha'-zi, ᴿGird up thy loins, and take my staff in thine hand, and go thy way: if thou meet any man, salute him not; and if any salute thee, answer him not again: and ᴿlay my staff upon the face of the child.   9:1 • Acts 19:12

30 And the mother of the child said, ᴿAs the Lᴏʀᴅ liveth, and *as* thy soul liveth, ᴿI will not leave thee. And he arose, and followed her.   2:2, 4 • Job 17:9

31 And ᴿGe-ha'-zi passed on before them, and laid the staff upon the face of the child; but *there was* neither voice, nor ᵀhearing. Wherefore he went again to meet

him, and told him, saying, The child is ᴿnot awaked.   5:20 • *attention* • John 11:11

32 And when E-li'-sha was come into the house, behold, the child was dead, *and* laid upon his bed.

33 He went in therefore, and ᴿshut the door upon them twain, and prayed unto the Lᴏʀᴅ.   *v. 4;* [Matt. 6:6]; Luke 8:51

34 And ᴿhe went up, and lay upon the child, and put his mouth upon his mouth, and his eyes upon his eyes, and his hands upon his hands: and ᴿhe stretched himself upon the child; and the flesh of the child ᵀwaxed warm.   1 Kin. 17:21–23 • Acts 20:10 • *became*

35 Then he returned, and walked in the house to and fro; and went up, ᴿand stretched himself upon him: and ᴿthe child sneezed seven times, and the child ᴿopened his eyes.   1 Kin. 17:21 • 8:1, 5 • 13:21

36 And he called Ge-ha'-zi, and said, Call this Shu'-nam-mite. So he called her. And when she was come in unto him, he said, Take up thy son.

37 Then she went in, and fell at his feet, and bowed herself to the ground, and ᴿtook up her son, and went out.   [Heb. 11:35]

Miracle of the Deadly Pottage

38 And E-li'-sha came again to Gil'-gal: and *there was* a ᴿdearthᵀ in the land; and the sons of the prophets *were* ᴿsitting before him: and he said unto his servant, Set on the great pot, and ᵀseethe pottage for the sons of the prophets.   8:1 • *drought* • 2:3 • *boil*

39 And one went out into the field to gather herbs, and found a wild vine, and gathered thereof wild ᴿgourds his lap full, and came and shred *them* into the pot of pottage: for they knew *them* not.   Jon. 4:6

40 So they poured out for the men to eat. And it came to pass, as they were eating of the pottage, that they cried out, and said, O thou man of God, *there is* ᴿdeath in the pot. And they could not eat *thereof*.   Ex. 10:17

41 But he said, Then bring meal. And he cast *it* into the pot; and he said, Pour out for the people, that they may eat. And there was no ᵀharm in the pot.   *evil thing*

Miracle of the Multiplication of the Loaves

42 And there came a man from Ba'-al-shal'-i-sha, ᴿand brought the man of God bread of the firstfruits, twenty loaves of barley, and full ears of ᵀcorn ᵀin the husk thereof. And he said, Give unto the people, that they may eat.   [Gal. 6:6] • *grain* • *in his sack*

43 And his ᵀservitor said, ᴿWhat, should I set this before an hundred men? He said again, Give the people, that they may eat: for thus saith the Lᴏʀᴅ, They shall eat, and shall leave *thereof*.   *servant* • John 6:9

44 So he set *it* before them, and they did

eat, ᴿand left ᵀthereof, according to the word of the LORD.   Matt. 14:20; 15:37; John 6:13 • some

CHAPTER 5

Miracle of the Healing of Naaman

NOW ᴿNa′-a-man, captain of the host of the king of Syria, was a great man with his master, and ᵀhonourable, because by him the LORD had given deliverance unto Syria: he was also a mighty man in valour, but he was a leper.   Luke 4:27 • respected

2 And the Syrians had gone out ᴿby companies, and had brought away captive out of the land of Israel a little maid; and she ᵀwaited on Na′-a-man's wife.   6:23 • served

3 And she said unto her mistress, Would God my lord were ᵀwith the prophet that is in Sa-ma′-ri-a! for he would ᵀrecover him of his leprosy.   before • heal

4 And one went in, and told his lord, saying, Thus and thus said the maid that is of the land of Israel.

5 And the king of Syria said, Go to, go, and I will send a letter unto the king of Israel. And he departed, and took with him ᵀten talents of silver, and six thousand pieces of gold, and ten changes of raiment. $3,840,000

6 And he brought the letter to the king of Israel, saying, Now when this letter is come unto thee, behold, I have therewith sent Na′-a-man my servant to thee, that thou mayest recover him of his leprosy.

7 And it came to pass, when the king of Israel had read the letter, that he ᵀrent his clothes, and said, Am I ᴿGod, to kill and to make alive, that this man doth send unto me to recover a man of his leprosy? wherefore consider, I pray you, and see how he seeketh a quarrel against me.   tore • [Gen. 30:2]

8 And it was so, when E-li′-sha the man of God had heard that the king of Israel had ᵀrent his clothes, that he sent to the king, saying, Wherefore hast thou rent thy clothes? let him come now to me, and he shall know that there is a prophet in Israel.   torn

9 So Na′-a-man came with his horses and with his chariot, and ᵀstood at the door of the house of E-li′-sha.   stopped in front

10 And E-li′-sha sent a messenger unto him, saying, ᴿGo and wash in Jordan seven times, and thy flesh shall come again to thee, and thou shalt be ᵀclean.   John 9:7 • healed

11 But Na′-a-man was wroth, and went away, and said, Behold, ᴿI thought, He will surely come out to me, and stand, and call on the name of the LORD his God, and ᵀstrike his hand over the place, and ᵀrecover the leper.   [Is. 55:8] • move up and down • heal the leprosy

12 Are not Ab′-a-na and Phar′-par, rivers of Damascus, better than all the waters of Israel? may I not wash in them, and be clean? So he turned and went away in a rage.

13 ᴿAnd his servants came near, and spake unto him, and said, My father, if the prophet had bid thee do some great thing, wouldest thou not have done it? how much rather then, when he saith to thee, ᴿWash, and be clean?   1 Sam. 28:23 • [John 3:5; Acts 22:16]

14 Then went he down, and dipped himself seven times in Jordan, according to the saying of the man of God: and his flesh came again like unto the flesh of a little child, and he was ᵀclean.   healthy

15 And he returned to the man of God, he and all his company, and came, and stood before him: and he said, Behold, now I know that there is no God in all the earth, but in Israel: now therefore, I pray thee, take a ᵀblessing of thy servant.   gift

16 But he said, As the LORD liveth, before whom I stand, I will receive none. And he urged him to take it; but he refused.

17 And Na′-a-man said, Shall there not then, I pray thee, be given to thy servant ᵀtwo mules' burden of earth? for thy servant will henceforth ᵀoffer neither burnt offering nor sacrifice unto other gods, but unto the LORD.   a little land • worship

18 In this thing the LORD pardon thy servant, that when my master goeth into the house of Rim′-mon to worship there, and ᴿhe leaneth on my hand, and I bow myself in the house of Rim′-mon: when I bow down myself in the house of Rim′-mon, the LORD pardon thy servant in this thing.   7:2, 17

19 And he said unto him, Go in peace. So he departed from him a little way.

20 But Ge-ha′-zi, the servant of E-li′-sha the man of God, said, Behold, my master hath spared Na′-a-man this Syrian, in not receiving at his hands that which he brought: but, as the LORD liveth, I will run after him, and take somewhat of him.

21 So Ge-ha′-zi followed after Na′-a-man. And when Na′-a-man saw him running after him, he ᵀlighted down from the chariot to meet him, and said, Is all well?   alighted

22 And he said, All is well. My master hath sent me, saying, Behold, even now there be come to me from mount E′-phra-im two young men of the sons of the prophets: give them, I pray thee, ᵀa talent of silver, and two changes of garments. $384,000

23 And Na′-a-man said, ᴿBe content, take ᵀtwo ᴿtalents. And he urged him, and bound two talents of silver in two bags, with two changes of garments, and laid them upon two of his servants; and they bare them before him.   6:3 • $768,000 • 15:19

24 And when he came to the ᵀtower, he took them from their hand, and ᴿbestowedᵀ

them in the house: and he let the men go, and they departed. *hill* • [Josh. 7:1, 11, 12, 21] • *hid*

25 But he went in, and stood before his master. And E-li′-sha said unto him, Whence *comest thou*, Ge-ha′-zi? And he said, ᴿThy servant went no whither. *v. 22*

26 And he said unto him, ᵀWent not mine heart *with thee*, when the man turned again from his chariot to meet thee? ᴿIs it a ᴿtime to receive money, and to receive garments, and oliveyards, and vineyards, and sheep, and oxen, and menservants, and maidservants? *was I not aware* • *v. 16* • [Eccl. 3:1]

27 The leprosy therefore of Na′-a-man ᴿshall cleave unto thee, and unto thy seed for ever. And he went out from his presence ᴿa leper *as white* as snow. [1 Tim. 6:10] • 15:5

CHAPTER 6

Miracle of the Floating Ax Head

AND the sons of the prophets said unto E-li′-sha, Behold now, the place where we dwell with thee is too strait for us.

2 Let us go, we pray thee, unto Jordan, and take ᵀthence every man a beam, and let us make us a place there, where we may dwell. And he answered, Go ye. *there*

3 And one said, Be ᴿcontent, I pray thee, and go with thy servants. And he answered, I will go. 5:23

4 So he went with them. And when they came to Jordan, they cut down wood.

5 But as one was felling a beam, the ax head fell into the water: and he cried, and said, Alas, master! for it was borrowed.

6 And the man of God said, Where fell it? And he shewed him the place. And ᴿhe cut down a stick, and cast *it* in ᵀthither; and the iron did swim. 2:21; 4:41; Ex. 15:25 • *there*

7 Therefore said he, Take *it* up to thee. And he put out his hand, and took it.

Syria's War Plan

8 Then the ᴿking of Syria warred against Israel, and took counsel with his servants, saying, In such and such a place *shall be* my camp. 8:28, 29

9 And ᴿthe man of God sent unto the king of Israel, saying, Beware that thou pass not such a place; for thither the Syrians are come down. *v. 12*; 4:1; ch. 7

10 And the king of Israel sent to the place which the ᴿman of God told him and warned him of, and ᴿsaved himself there, ᵀnot once nor twice. 7:2 • [Ps. 5:11] • *again and again*

11 Therefore the heart of the king of Syria was ᵀsore troubled for this thing; and he called his servants, and said unto them, Will ye not shew me which of us *is* ᵀfor the king of Israel? *very* • *supporting*

12 And one of his servants said, ᵀNone, my lord, O king: but E-li′-sha, the prophet that *is* in Israel, telleth the king of Israel the words that thou speakest in thy bedchamber. *no*

God's Chariots and Horses

13 And he said, Go and spy where he *is*, that I may send and fetch him. And it was told him, saying, Behold, *he is* in Do′-than.

14 Therefore sent he thither horses, and chariots, and a great host: and they came by night, and compassed the city about.

15 And when the servant of the man of God was risen early, and gone forth, behold, an host compassed the city both with horses and chariots. And his servant said unto him, Alas, my master! ᵀhow shall we do? *what*

16 And he answered, ᴿFear not: for ᴿthey that *be* with us *are* more than they that *be* with them. Ex. 14:13 • 2 Chr. 32:7; Ps. 55:18

17 And E-li′-sha prayed, and said, LORD, I pray thee, open his eyes, that he may see. And the LORD opened the eyes of the young man; and he saw: and, behold, the mountain *was* full of ᴿhorses and chariots of fire round about E-li′-sha. 2:11; Ps. 34:7; 68:17

Syria's Army Is Blinded

18 And when they came down to him, E-li′-sha prayed unto the LORD, and said, ᵀSmite this people, I pray thee, with blindness. And he smote them with blindness according to the word of E-li′-sha. *strike*

19 And E-li′-sha said unto them, This *is* not the way, neither *is* this the city: follow me, and I will bring you to the man whom ye seek. But he led them to Sa-ma′-ri-a.

20 And it came to pass, when they were come into Sa-ma′-ri-a, that E-li′-sha said, LORD, open the eyes of these *men*, that they may see. And the ᴿLORD opened their eyes, and they saw; and, behold, *they were* in the ᵀmidst of Sa-ma′-ri-a. *v. 17* • *center*

21 And the king of Israel said unto E-li′-sha, when he saw them, ᴿMy father, shall I smite *them*? shall I smite *them*? 2:12

22 And he answered, Thou shalt not smite *them*: wouldest thou smite those ᵀwhom thou hast taken captive with thy sword and with thy bow? set bread and water before them, that they may eat and drink, and go to their master. *prisoners of*

23 And he prepared great provision for them: and when they had eaten and drunk, he sent them away, and they went to their master. So ᴿthe bands of Syria came no more into the land of Israel. *vv.* 8, 9; 5:2

Siege of Samaria Causes Famine

24 And it came to pass after this, that Ben–ha′-dad king of Syria gathered all his host, and went up, and besieged Sa-ma′-ri-a.

25 And there was a great famine in Sa-ma'-ri-a: and, behold, they besieged it, until an ass's head was *sold* for fourscore *pieces* of silver, and the Tfourth part of a cab of dove's dung for Tfive *pieces* of silver.   *one pt. • $640*

26 And as the king of Israel was passing by upon the wall, there cried a woman unto him, saying, Help, my lord, O king.

27 And he said, If the LORD do not help thee, Twhence shall I help thee? out of the barnfloor, or out of the winepress?   *how*

28 And the king said unto her, TWhat aileth thee? And she answered, This woman said unto me, Give thy son, Rthat we may eat him to day, and we will eat my son to mor-row.   *what is wrong with you? • Jer. 19:9*

29 So Rwe boiled my son, and did eat him: and I said unto her on the next day, Give thy son, that we may eat him: and she hath hid her son.   Lev. 26:29; Deut. 28:53, 57

Elisha's Prophecies

30 And it came to pass, when the king heard the words of the woman, that he Rrent his clothes; and he passed by upon the wall, and the people looked, and, behold, *he had* sackcloth within upon his flesh.   1 Kin. 21:27

31 Then he said, God do so and more also to me, if the head of E-li'-sha the son of Sha'-phat shall stand on him this day.

32 But E-li'-sha sat in his house, and the elders sat with him; and *the king* sent a man from before him: but ere the messenger came to him, he said to the elders, See ye how this son of Ra murderer hath sent to take away mine head? look, when the messenger cometh, shut the door, and hold him fast at the door: *is* not the sound of his master's feet behind him?   1 Kin. 18:4

33 And while he yet talked with them, behold, the messenger came down unto him: and he said, RBehold, this evil *is* of the LORD; Rwhat T should I wait for the LORD any longer?   Is. 8:21; Jer. 2:25 • Job 2:9 • *why*

CHAPTER 7

THEN E-li'-sha said, Hear ye the word of the LORD; Thus saith the LORD, To morrow about this time shall a Tmeasure of fine flour *be sold* for a Tshek'-el, and Ttwo measures of barley for a shek'-el, in the gate of Sa-ma'-ri-a.   *2.2 bu. • $128 • 4.3 bu.*

2 RThen a lord on whose hand the king leaned answered the man of God, and said, Behold, *if* the LORD would make windows in heaven, might this thing be? And he said, Behold, thou shalt see *it* with thine eyes, but shalt not eat thereof.   *vv. 17, 19, 20*

3 And there were four leprous men at the entering in of the gate: and they said one to another, Why sit we here until we die?

4 If we say, We will enter into the city, then the famine *is* in the city, and we shall die there: and if we sit still here, we die also. Now therefore come, and let us fall unto the host of the Syrians: if they save us alive, we shall live; and if they kill us, we shall but die.

5 And they rose up in the twilight, to go unto the camp of the Syrians: and when they were come to the uttermost part of the camp of Syria, behold, *there was* no man there.

6 For the Lord had made the host of the Syrians Rto hear a noise of chariots, and a noise of horses, *even* the noise of a great host: and they said one to another, Lo, the king of Israel hath hired against us the kings of the Hit'-tites, and the kings of the Egyptians, to come upon us.   2 Sam. 5:24

7 RWherefore they Rarose and fled in the twilight, and left their tents, and their horses, and their asses, even the camp as it *was*, and fled for their life.   [Ps. 28:1] • Ps. 48:4–6

8 And when these lepers came to the uttermost part of the camp, they went into one tent, and did eat and drink, and Rcarried thence silver, and gold, and raiment, and went and hid *it;* and came again, and entered into another tent, and carried thence *also*, and went and hid *it.*   Josh. 7:21

9 Then they said one to another, We do not well: this day *is* a day of good tidings, and we hold our peace: if we tarry till the morning light, some mischief will come upon us: now therefore come, that we may go and tell the king's household.

10 So they came and called unto the porter of the city: and they told them, saying, We came to the camp of the Syrians, and, behold, *there was* no man there, neither voice of man, but horses tied, and asses tied, and the tents as they *were.*

11 And he called the porters; and they told *it* to the king's house within.

12 And the king arose in the night, and said unto his servants, I will now shew you what the Syrians have done to us. They know that we *be* hungry; therefore are they gone out of the camp Rto Thide themselves in the field, saying, When they come out of the city, we shall catch them alive, and get into the city.   Josh. 8:4–12 • *set up an ambush*

13 And one of his servants answered and said, Let *some* take, I pray thee, five of the horses that remain, which are left in the city, (behold, they *are* as all the multitude of Israel that are left in it: behold, *I say*, they *are* even as all the multitude of the Israelites that are consumed:) and let us send and see.

14 They took therefore two Tchariot horses; and the king sent after the host of the Syrians, saying, Go and see.   *chariots with*

15 And they went after them unto Jordan: and, lo, all the way *was* full of garments and

vessels, which the Syrians had cast away in their haste. And the messengers returned, and told the king.

16 And the people went out, and spoiled the tents of the Syrians. So a measure of fine flour was *sold* for [T]a shek'-el, and [T]two measures of barley for a shek'-el, [R]according to the word of the LORD.　　*$128 · 4.3 bu. · v. 1*

17 And the king appointed the lord on whose hand he leaned to have the charge of the gate: and the people [T]trode upon him in the gate, and he died, as the [T]man of God had said, who spake when the king came down to him.　　*trod him under foot · prophet*

18 And it came to pass as the man of God had spoken to the king, saying, Two measures of barley for a shek'-el, and a measure of fine flour for a shek'-el, shall be to morrow about this time in the gate of Sa-ma'-ri-a:

19 [R]And that lord answered the man of God, and said, Now, behold, [R]if the LORD should make windows in heaven, might such a thing be? And he said, Behold, thou shalt see it with thine eyes, but shalt not eat thereof.　　*Job 20:23; Jer. 17:6 · v. 2*

20 And so it fell out unto him: for the people trode upon him in the gate, and he died.

CHAPTER 8

Elisha's Ministry
with the Shunammite Woman

THEN spake E-li'-sha unto the woman, [R]whose son he had restored to life, saying, Arise, and go thou and thine household, and [T]sojourn wheresoever thou canst sojourn: for the LORD [R]hath called for a famine; and it shall also come upon the land seven years.　　*4:35 · dwell · Ps. 105:16*

2 And the woman arose, and did after the saying of the man of God: and she went with her household, and sojourned in the land of the Phi-lis'-tines seven years.

3 And it came to pass at the seven years' end, that the woman returned out of the land of the Phi-lis'-tines: and she went forth to [T]cry unto the king for her house and for her land.　　*appeal*

4 And the king talked with [R]Ge-ha'-zi the servant of the man of God, saying, Tell me, I pray thee, all the great things that E-li'-sha hath done.　　*4:12; 5:27*

5 And it came to pass, as he was telling the king how he had [R]restored a dead body to life, that, behold, the woman, whose son he had restored to life, cried to the king for her house and for her land. And Ge-ha'-zi said, My lord, O king, this *is* the woman, and this *is* her son, whom E-li'-sha restored to life.　　*4:35*

6 And when the king asked the woman, she told him. So the king appointed unto her

a certain officer, saying, Restore all that *was* her's, and all the fruits of the field since the day that she left the land, even until now.

Elisha's Ministry with the King of Syria

7 And E-li'-sha came to [R]Damascus; and [R]Ben-ha'-dad the king of Syria was sick; and it was told him, saying, [R]The man of God is come hither.　　*1 Kin. 11:24 · 6:24 · 5:20*

8 And the king said unto Haz'-a-el, Take a present in thine hand, and go, meet the man of God, and enquire of the LORD by him, saying, Shall I recover of this disease?

9 So Haz'-a-el went to meet him, and took a present with him, even of every good thing of Damascus, forty camels' burden, and came and stood before him, and said, Thy son Ben-ha'-dad king of Syria hath sent me to thee, saying, Shall I recover of this disease?

10 And E-li'-sha said unto him, [R]Go, say unto him, Thou mayest certainly recover: howbeit the LORD hath shewed me that [R]he shall surely die.　　*v. 14 · v. 15*

11 And he [T]settled his countenance stedfastly, [R]until he was ashamed: and the man of God [R]wept.　　*fixed his gaze · 2:17 · Luke 19:41*

12 And Haz'-a-el said, Why weepeth my lord? And he answered, Because I know [R]the evil that thou wilt do unto the children of Israel: their strong holds wilt thou set on fire, and their young men wilt thou slay with the sword, and [R]wilt dash their children, and rip up their women with child.　　*10:32; Amos 1:3 · 15:16*

13 And Haz'-a-el said, But what, [R]is thy servant a dog, that he should do this great thing? And E-li'-sha answered, [R]The LORD hath shewed me that thou *shalt be* king over Syria.　　*1 Sam. 17:43; 2 Sam. 9:8 · 1 Kin. 19:15*

14 So he departed from E-li'-sha, and came to his master; who said to him, What said E-li'-sha to thee? And he answered, He told me *that* thou shouldest surely recover.

15 And it came to pass on the morrow, that he took a thick cloth, and dipped *it* in water, and spread *it* on his face, so that he died: and Haz'-a-el reigned in his stead.

The Reign of Jehoram in Judah
2 Chr. 21:5-10, 20

16 And in the fifth year of Jo'-ram the son of Ahab king of Israel, Je-hosh'-a-phat *being* then king of Judah, Je-ho'-ram the son of Je-hosh'-a-phat king of Judah began to reign.

17 [R]Thirty and two years old was he when he began to reign; and he reigned eight years in Jerusalem.　　*2 Chr. 21:5*

18 And he walked in the way of the kings of Israel, as did the house of Ahab: for [R]the daughter of Ahab was his wife: and he did evil in the sight of the LORD.　　*vv. 26, 27*

19 Yet the LORD would not destroy Judah for David his servant's sake, [R]as he promised

him to give him alway a light, *and* to his children. 1 Kin. 11:36; 15:4; 2 Chr. 21:7

20 In his days ᴿE′-dom revolted from under the hand of Judah, ᴿand made a king over themselves. 2 Chr. 21:8–10 • 1 Kin. 22:47

21 So Jo′-ram went over to Za′-ir, and all the chariots with him: and he rose by night, and smote the E′-dom-ites which compassed him about, and the captains of the chariots: and the people fled into their tents.

22 Yet E′-dom revolted from under the hand of Judah unto this day. ᴿThen Lib′-nah revolted at the same time. 2 Chr. 21:10

23 And the rest of the acts of Jo′-ram, and all that he did, *are* they not written in the book of the chronicles of the kings of Judah?

24 And Jo′-ram slept with his fathers, and was buried with his fathers in the city of David: and ᴿA-ha-zi′-ahᵀ his son reigned in his stead. 2 Chr. 22:6; 21:17 • *Azariah,* and *Jehoahaz*

Spiritual Evaluation of Ahaziah
2 Kin. 9:29; 2 Chr. 22:1–4

25 In the twelfth year of Jo′-ram the son of Ahab king of Israel did A-ha-zi′-ah the son of Je-ho′-ram king of Judah begin to reign.

26 ᴿTwo and twenty years old *was* A-ha-zi′-ah when he began to reign; and he reigned one year in Jerusalem. And his mother's name *was* Ath-a-li′-ah, the daughter of Om′-ri king of Israel. 2 Chr. 22:2

27 And he walked in the way of the house of Ahab, and did evil in the sight of the LORD, as *did* the house of Ahab: for he *was* the son in law of the house of Ahab.

Battle Against Syria
2 Kin. 9:15, 16; 2 Chr. 22:5, 6

28 And he went ᴿwith Jo′-ram the son of Ahab to the war against Haz′-a-el king of Syria in ᴿRa′-moth–gil′-e-ad; and the Syrians wounded Jo′-ram. 2 Chr. 22:5 • 1 Kin. 22:3, 29

29 And ᴿking Jo′-ram went back to be healed in Jez′-re-el of the wounds which the Syrians had given him at Ra′-mah, when he fought against Haz′-a-el king of Syria. And A-ha-zi′-ah the son of Je-ho′-ram king of Judah went down to see Jo′-ram the son of Ahab in Jez′-re-el, because he was sick. 9:15

CHAPTER 9

Anointing of Jehu King over Israel

AND E-li′-sha the prophet called one of ᴿthe children of the prophets, and said unto him, ᴿGird up thy loins, and take this box of oil in thine hand, ᴿand go to Ra′-moth–gil′-e-ad: 1 Kin. 20:35 • 4:29 • 8:28, 29

2 And when thou comest thither, ᵀlook out there Je′-hu the son of Je-hosh′-a-phat the son of Nim′-shi, and go in, and make him arise up from among his brethren, and carry him to an inner chamber; *find*

3 Then take the box of oil, and pour *it* on his head, and say, Thus saith the LORD, I have anointed thee king over Israel. Then open the door, and flee, and tarry not.

4 So the young man, *even* the young man the prophet, went to Ra′-moth–gil′-e-ad.

5 And when he came, behold, the captains of the host *were* sitting; and he said, I have an errand to thee, O captain. And Je′-hu said, Unto which of all us? And he said, To thee, O captain.

6 And he arose, and went into the house; and he poured the oil on his head, and said unto him, Thus saith the LORD God of Israel, ᴿI have anointed thee king over the people of the LORD, *even* over Israel. *v. 3*

7 And thou shalt ᵀsmite the house of Ahab thy master, that I may avenge the blood of my servants the prophets, and the blood of all the servants of the LORD, ᴿat the hand of Jez′-e-bel. *destroy* • 1 Kin. 18:4; 21:15

8 For the whole house of Ahab shall perish: and I will cut off from Ahab ᵀhim that pisseth against the wall, and him that is shut up and left in Israel: *every male*

9 And I will make the house of Ahab like the house of ᴿJer-o-bo′-am the son of Ne′-bat, and like the house of ᴿBa′-a-sha the son of A-hi′-jah: 14:10 • 1 Kin. 16:3, 11, 12

10 ᴿAnd the dogs shall eat Jez′-e-bel in the portion of Jez′-re-el, and *there shall be* ᴿnone to bury *her.* And he opened the door, and fled. *vv.* 35, 36; 1 Kin. 21:23 • Deut. 28:26

11 Then Je′-hu came forth to the servants of his lord: and *one* said unto him, ᴿ*Is* all well? wherefore came this mad *fellow* to thee? And he said unto them, Ye know the man, and his ᵀcommunication. *v. 17 • message*

12 And they said, ᵀ*It is* false; tell us now. And he said, Thus and thus spake he to me, saying, Thus saith the LORD, I have anointed thee king over Israel. *that is not true*

13 Then ᴿthey hasted, and took every man his garment, and put *it* under him on the top of the stairs, and blew with trumpets, saying, Je′-hu is king. Matt. 21:7, 8

Execution of Joram

14 ᴿSo Je′-hu the son of Je-hosh′-a-phat the son of Nim′-shi ᵀconspired against Jo′-ram. (Now Jo′-ram had kept Ra′-moth–gil′-e-ad, he and all Israel, because of Haz′-a-el king of Syria. 8:28 • *plotted*

15 But ᴿking ᵀJo′-ram was returned to be healed in Jez′-re-el of the wounds which the Syrians had given him, when he fought with Haz′-a-el king of Syria.) And Je′-hu said, If it ᵀbe your minds, *then* let none go forth *nor* escape out of the city to go to tell *it* in Jez′-re-el. 8:29 • *Jehoram • suits your judgment*

16 So Je'-hu rode in a ᴿchariot, and went to Jez'-re-el; for Jo'-ram lay there. ᴿAnd A-ha-zi'-ah king of Judah was come down to see Jo'-ram. Acts 8:29 · 8:29

17 And there stood a watchman on the tower in Jez'-re-el, and he spied the company of Je'-hu as he came, and said, I see a company. And Jo'-ram said, Take an horseman, and send to meet them, and let him say, ᵀIs it peace? *are you coming in peace?*

18 So there went one on horseback to meet him, and said, Thus saith the king, Is it peace? And Je'-hu said, What hast thou to do with peace? turn thee behind me. And the watchman told, saying, The messenger came to them, but he cometh not again.

19 Then he sent out a second on horseback, which came to them, and said, Thus saith the king, ᴿIs it peace? And Je'-hu answered, What hast thou to do with peace? turn thee behind me. *vv. 18, 22*

20 And the watchman told, saying, He came even unto them, and cometh not again: and the driving is like the driving of Je'-hu the son of Nim'-shi; for he driveth furiously.

21 And Jo'-ram said, Make ready. And his chariot was made ready. And Jo'-ram king of Israel and A-ha-zi'-ah king of Judah went out, each in his chariot, and they went out against Je'-hu, and ᵀmet him in the ᴿportion of Na'-both the Jez'-re-el-ite. *found · v. 26*

22 And it came to pass, when Jo'-ram saw Je'-hu, that he said, ᴿIs it peace, Je'-hu? And he answered, What peace, so long as the whoredoms of thy mother Jez'-e-bel and her witchcrafts are so many? *vv. 18, 19*

23 And Jo'-ram turned his hands, and fled, and said to A-ha-zi'-ah, ᴿThere is ᵀtreachery, O A-ha-zi'-ah. *11:14 · treason*

24 And Je'-hu drew a bow with his full strength, and smote Je-ho'-ram between his arms, and the arrow went out at his heart, and he sunk down in his chariot.

25 Then said Je'-hu to Bid'-kar his captain, Take up, and cast him in the portion of the field of Na'-both the Jez'-re-el-ite: for remember how that, when I and thou rode together after Ahab his father, the Lᴏʀᴅ ᵀlaid this burden upon him; *passed this sentence*

26 Surely I have seen yesterday the blood of Na'-both, and the blood of his sons, saith the Lᴏʀᴅ; and I will requite thee in this ᵀplat, saith the Lᴏʀᴅ. Now therefore take and cast him into the plat of ground, according to the word of the Lᴏʀᴅ. *portion*

Death of Ahaziah—2 Kin. 8:25; 2 Chr. 22:9

27 ᴿBut when A-ha-zi'-ah the king of Judah saw this, he fled by the way of the garden house. And Je'-hu followed after him, and said, Smite him also in the chariot. And they did so at the going up to Gur, which is by ᴿIb'-le-am. And he fled to Me-gid'-do, and died there. 2 Chr. 22:9 · Josh. 17:11

28 ᴿAnd his servants carried him in a chariot to Jerusalem, and buried him in his ᴿsepulchreᵀ with his fathers in the city of David. 23:30 · 2 Chr. 16:14 · *grave*

29 And in the ᴿeleventh year of Jo'-ram the son of Ahab began A-ha-zi'-ah to reign over Judah. 8:25

Fulfillment of Elisha's Prophecy

30 And when Je'-hu was come to Jez'-re-el, Jez'-e-bel heard of it; ᴿand she painted her face, and ᵀtired her head, and looked out at a window. [Jer. 4:30]; Ezek. 23:40 · *dressed her hair*

31 And as Je'-hu entered in at the gate, she said, ᴿHad Zim'-ri peace, who slew his master? *vv. 18–22; 1 Kin. 16:9–20*

32 And he lifted up his face to the window, and said, Who is on my side? who? And there looked out to him two or three eunuchs.

33 And he said, Throw her down. So they threw her down: and some of her blood was sprinkled on the wall, and on the horses: and he trode her under foot.

34 And when he was come in, he did eat and drink, and said, Go, see now ᴿthis cursed woman, and bury her: for ᴿshe is a king's daughter. 1 Kin. 21:25 · [Ex. 22:28]

35 And they went to bury her: but they found no more of her than the skull, and the feet, and the palms of her hands.

36 Wherefore they came again, and told him. And he said, This is the word of the Lᴏʀᴅ, which he spake by his servant E-li'-jah the Tish'-bite, saying, In the portion of Jez'-re-el shall dogs eat the flesh of Jez'-e-bel:

37 And ᴿthe carcase of Jez'-e-bel shall be ᴿas dung upon the face of the field in the portion of Jez'-re-el; so that they shall not say, This is Jez'-e-bel. Jer. 8:1–3 · Ps. 83:10

CHAPTER 10

AND Ahab had seventy sons in Sa-mar'-i-a. And Je'-hu wrote letters, and sent to Sa-ma'-ri-a, unto the rulers of Jez'-re-el, to the elders, and to them that brought up Ahab's children, saying,

2 Now as soon as this letter cometh to you, seeing your master's sons are with you, and there are with you chariots and horses, a fenced city also, and armour;

3 ᴿLook ᵀeven out the best and ᵀmeetest of your master's sons, and set him on his father's throne, and fight for your master's house. [John 18:36] · *select · fittest*

4 But they were exceedingly afraid, and said, Behold, two kings stood not before him: how then shall we stand?

5 And he that was over the house, and he

that *was* over the city, the elders also, and the bringers up *of the children*, sent to Je'-hu, saying, RWe *are* thy servants, and will do all that thou shalt bid us; we will not make any king: do thou *that which is* good in thine eyes.   18:14; Josh. 9:8, 11; 1 Kin. 20:4, 32

6 Then he wrote a letter the second time to them, saying, If ye *be* Tmine, and *if* ye will hearken unto my voice, take ye the heads of the men your master's sons, and come to me to Jez'-re-el by to morrow this time. Now the king's sons, *being* seventy persons, *were* with the great men of the city, which brought them up.   *for me*

7 And it came to pass, when the letter came to them, that they took the king's sons, and Rslew seventy persons, and put their heads in baskets, and sent him *them* to Jez'-re-el.   11:1; Judg. 9:5; 1 Kin. 21:21

8 And there came a messenger, and told him, saying, They have brought the heads of the king's sons. And he said, Lay ye them in two heaps at the Tentering in of the gate until the morning.   *entrance*

9 And it came to pass in the morning, that he went out, and stood, and said to all the people, TYe *be* righteous: behold, I conspired against my master, and slew him: but who slew all these?   *you are innocent*

10 Know now that there shall fall unto the earth nothing of the word of the LORD, which the LORD spake concerning the house of Ahab: for the LORD hath done *that* which he spake by his servant E-li'-jah.

11 RSo Je'-hu slew all that remained of the house of Ahab in Jez'-re-el, and all his great men, and his kinsfolks, and his priests, until he left him none remaining.   1 Kin. 21:19, 29

12 And he arose and departed, and came to Sa-ma'-ri-a. *And* as he *was* at the shearing house in the way,

13 RJe'-hu met with the brethren of A-ha-zi'-ah king of Judah, and said, Who *are* ye? And they answered, We *are* the brethren of A-ha-zi'ah; and we go down Tto salute the children of the king and the children of the queen.   2 Chr. 22:8 • *greet*

14 And he said, Take them alive. And they took them alive, and slew them at the pit of the shearing house, *even* two and forty men; neither left he any of them.

15 And when he was departed thence, he lighted on Je-hon'-a-dab the son of Re'-chab *coming* to meet him: and he saluted him, and said to him, Is thine heart right, as my heart *is* with thy heart? And Je-hon'-a-dab answered, It is. If it be, give *me* thine hand. And he gave *him* his hand; and he took him up to him into the chariot.

16 And he said, Come with me, and see my Rzeal for the LORD. So they made him ride in his chariot.   1 Kin. 19:10

17 And when he came to Sa-ma'-ri-a, Rhe slew all that remained unto Ahab in Sa-ma'-ri-a, till he had destroyed him, according to the saying of the LORD, Rwhich he spake to E-li'-jah.   9:8; 2 Chr. 22:8 • 1 Kin. 21:21

18 And Je'-hu gathered all the people together, and said unto them, RAhab served Ba'-al a little; *but* Je'-hu shall serve him much.   1 Kin. 16:31, 32

19 Now therefore call unto me all the prophets of Ba'-al, all his servants, and all his priests; let none be wanting: for I have a great sacrifice *to do* to Ba'-al; whosoever shall be wanting, he shall not live. But Je'-hu did *it* in subtilty, to the intent that he might destroy the worshippers of Ba'-al.

20 And Je'-hu said, Proclaim a solemn assembly for Ba'-al. And they proclaimed *it*.

21 And Je'-hu sent through all Israel: and all the worshippers of Ba'-al came, so that there was not a man left that came not. And they came into the Rhouse of Ba'-al; and the house of Ba'-al was full from one end to another.   *vv.* 22–27; 11:18; 1 Kin. 16:32

22 And he said unto him that *was* over the vestry, Bring forth vestments for all the worshippers of Ba'-al. And he brought them forth vestments.

23 And Je'-hu went, and Je-hon'-a-dab the son of Re'-chab, into the house of Ba'-al, and said unto the worshippers of Ba'-al, Search, and Tlook that there be here with you none of the servants of the LORD, but the worshippers of Ba'-al only.   *see*

24 And when they went in to offer sacrifices and burnt offerings, Je'-hu appointed fourscore men without, and said, *If* any of the men whom I have brought into your hands escape, *he that letteth him go*, his life *shall be* Tfor the life of him.   *given up*

25 And it came to pass, as soon as he had made an end of offering the burnt offering, that Je'-hu said to the guard and to the captains, Go in, *and* slay them; let none come forth. And they Tsmote them with the edge of the sword; and the guard and the captains cast *them* out, and went to the city of the house of Ba'-al.   *killed*

26 And they brought forth the images out of the house of Ba'-al, and burned them.

27 And they brake down the image of Ba'-al, and brake down the house of Ba'-al, and made it a draught house unto this day.

28 RThus Je'-hu destroyed Ba'-al out of Israel.   21:3

Spiritual Evaluation of Jehu

29 Howbeit *from* the sins of Jer-o-bo'-am the son of Ne'-bat, who made Israel to sin, Je'-hu departed not from after them, *to wit*, Rthe golden calves that *were* in Beth'-el, and that *were* in Dan.   17:28; 1 Kin. 12:28, 29

30 And the LORD said unto Je'-hu, Because

thou hast done well in executing *that which is* right in mine eyes, *and* hast done unto the house of Ahab according to all that *was* in mine heart, thy children of the fourth *generation* shall sit on the throne of Israel.

31 But Je′-hu took no heed to walk in the law of the LORD God of Israel with all his heart: for he departed not from the sins of Jer-o-bo′-am, which made Israel to sin.

Political Situation Under Jehu

32 In those days the LORD began to ᵀcut Israel short: and Haz′-a-el smote them in all the coasts of Israel;   *bring calamity upon*

33 From Jordan eastward, all the land of Gil′-e-ad, the Gad′-ites, and the Reu′-ben-ites, and the Ma-nas′-sites, from ᴿAr′-o-er, which is by the ᵀriver Arnon, even ᴿGil′-e-ad and Ba′-shan.   Deut. 2:36 • *valley of the* • Amos 1:3

Death of Jehu

34 Now the rest of the acts of Je′-hu, and all that he did, and all his might, *are* they not written in the book of the chronicles of the kings of Israel?

35 And Je′-hu slept with his fathers: and they buried him in Sa-ma′-ri-a. And ᴿJe-ho′-a-haz his son reigned in his stead.   13:1

36 And the time that Je′-hu reigned over Israel in Sa-ma′-ri-a *was* twenty and eight years.

CHAPTER 11

Salvation of Joash—2 Chr. 22:10–12

AND when Ath-a-li′-ah the mother of A-ha-zi′-ah saw that her son was dead, she arose and destroyed all the seed royal.

2 But Je-hosh′-e-ba, the daughter of king Jo′-ram, sister of A-ha-zi′-ah, took ᵀJo′-ash the son of A-ha-zi′-ah, ᴿand ᵀstole him from among the king's sons *which were* slain; and they hid him, *even* him and his nurse, in the bedchamber from Ath-a-li′-ah, so that he was not slain.   *Jehoash • v. 21; 12:1 • took*

3 And he was with her hid in the house of the LORD six years. And Ath-a-li′-ah did reign over the land.

Overthrow of Athaliah by Jehoiada
2 Chr. 23:1–11

4 And the seventh year Je-hoi′-a-da sent and ᵀfetched the rulers over hundreds, with the captains and the guard, and brought them to him into the house of the LORD, and made a covenant with them, and took an oath of them in the house of the LORD, and shewed them the king's son.   *gathered*

5 And he commanded them, saying, This *is* the thing that ye shall do; A third part of you that enter in on the sabbath *shall even be* keepers of the watch of the king's house;

6 And a third part *shall be* at the gate of Sur; and a third part at the gate behind the guard: so shall ye keep the watch of the house, that it be not broken down.

7 And two ᵀparts of all you that go forth on the sabbath, even they shall ᵀkeep the watch of the house of the LORD ᵀabout the king.   *companies • guard • in the king's presence*

8 And ye shall ᵀcompass the king round about, every man with his weapons in his hand: and he that cometh within the ranges, let him be slain: and be ye with the king as he goeth out and as he cometh in.   *surround*

9 And the captains over the hundreds did according to all *things* that Je-hoi′-a-da the priest commanded: and they took every man his men that were to come in on the sabbath, with them that should go out on the sabbath, and came to Je-hoi′-a-da the priest.

10 And to the captains over hundreds did the priest give king David's spears and shields, that *were* in the temple of the LORD.

11 And the guard stood, every man with his weapons in his hand, round about the king, from the right corner of the temple to the left corner of the temple, *along* by the altar and the temple.

12 And he brought forth the king's son, and put the crown upon him, and gave *him* the testimony; and they made him king, and anointed him; and they clapped their hands, and said, God save the king.

Death of Athaliah—2 Chr. 23:12–15

13 And when Ath-a-li′-ah heard the noise of the guard *and* of the people, she came to the people into the temple of the LORD.

14 And when she looked, behold, the king stood by a pillar, as the manner *was*, and the princes and the trumpeters by the king, and all the people of the land rejoiced, and blew with trumpets: and Ath-a-li′-ah rent her clothes, and cried, Treason, Treason.

15 But Je-hoi′-a-da the priest commanded the captains of the hundreds, the officers of the host, and said unto them, Have her forth ᵀwithout the ranges: and him that followeth her kill with the sword. For the priest had said, Let her not be slain in the house of the LORD.   *outside the bounds of the temple*

16 And they laid hands on her; and she went by the ᵀway by the which the horses came into the king's house: and there was she slain.   *gate*

Renewal of the Covenant—2 Chr. 23:16–24:1

17 And Je-hoi′-a-da made a covenant between the LORD and the king and the people, that they should be the LORD's people; between the king also and the people.

18 And all the people of the land went into the house of Ba′-al, and brake it down; his altars and his images brake they in pieces

thoroughly, and slew Mat'-tan the priest of Ba'-al before the altars. And the priest appointed officers over the house of the LORD.

19 And he took the rulers over hundreds, and the ᴿcaptains, and the guard, and all the people of the land; and they brought down the king from the house of the LORD, and came by the way of the ᴿgate of the guard to the king's house. And he sat on the throne of the kings.   v. 4 • v. 6

20 And all the people of the land rejoiced, and the city was in quiet: and they slew Ath-a-li'-ah with the sword beside the king's house.

21 Seven years old was Je-ho'-ash when he began to reign.

CHAPTER 12

Spiritual Evaluation of Joash—2 Chr. 24:1, 2

IN the seventh year of Je'-hu ᴿJe-ho'-ash began to reign; and forty years reigned he in Jerusalem. And his mother's name was Zib'-i-ah of Be'-er-she'-ba.   2 Chr. 24:1

2 And Je-ho'-ash did that which was right in the sight of the LORD all his days wherein Je-hoi'-a-da the priest instructed him.

3 But ᴿthe high places were not taken away: the people still sacrificed and burnt incense in the high places.   1 Kin. 15:14; 22:43

Spiritual Situation Under Joash—2 Chr. 24:5–14

4 And Je-ho'-ash said to the priests, All the money of the ᵀdedicated things that is brought into the house of the LORD, even the money of every one that passeth the account, the money that every man is set at, and all the money that cometh into any man's heart to bring into the house of the LORD,   holy things

5 Let the priests take it to them, every man of his acquaintance: and let them repair the ᵀbreaches of the house, wheresoever any breach shall be found.   broken places

6 But it was so, that in the three and twentieth year of king Je-ho'-ash the priests had not repaired the breaches of the house.

7 Then king Je-ho'-ash called for Je-hoi'-a-da the priest, and the other priests, and said unto them, Why repair ye not the breaches of the house? now therefore receive no more money of your acquaintance, but deliver it for the breaches of the house.

8 And the priests consented to receive no more money of the people, neither to repair the breaches of the house.

9 But Je-hoi'-a-da the priest took ᴿa chest, and bored a hole in the lid of it, and set it beside the altar, on the right side as one cometh into the house of the LORD: and the priests that kept the door put therein all the money that was brought into the house of the LORD.   2 Chr. 24:8

10 And it was so, when they saw that there was much money in the chest, that ᴿthe king's ᵀscribe and the high priest came up, and they ᵀput up in bags, and ᵀtold the money that was found in the house of the LORD.   19:2; 22:3, 4, 12 • secretary • bound up • counted

11 And they gave the money, being ᵀtold, into the hands of them that did the work, that had the oversight of the house of the LORD: and they ᵀlaid it out to the ᴿcarpenters and builders, that wrought upon the house of the LORD,   counted • disbursed it • Is. 41:7

12 ᴿAnd to masons, and hewers of stone, and to buy timber and hewed stone to repair the breaches of the house of the LORD, and for all that was laid out for the house to repair it.   22:5, 6

13 Howbeit there were not made for the house of the LORD bowls of silver, snuffers, basons, trumpets, any vessels of gold, or vessels of silver, of the money that was brought into the house of the LORD:

14 But they gave that to the workmen, and repaired therewith the house of the LORD.

15 Moreover they ᵀreckoned not with the men, into whose hand they delivered the money to be bestowed on workmen: for they dealt faithfully.   did not watch

16 ᴿThe trespass money and sin money was not brought into the house of the LORD: ᴿit was the priests'.   [Lev. 5:15, 18] • [Lev. 7:7]

Political Situation Under Joash

17 Then Haz'-a-el king of Syria went up, and fought against Gath, and took it: and Haz'-a-el set his face to go up to Jerusalem.

18 And ᴿJe-ho'-ash king of Judah took all the hallowed things that Je-hosh'-a-phat, and Je-ho'-ram, and A-ha-zi'-ah, his fathers, kings of Judah, had dedicated, and his own hallowed things, and all the gold that was found in the treasures of the house of the LORD, and in the king's house, and sent it to Haz'-a-el king of Syria: and he ᵀwent away from Jerusalem.   16:8 • withdrew

Death of Joash—2 Chr. 24:25–27

19 And the rest of the acts of Jo'-ash, and all that he did, are they not written in the book of the chronicles of the kings of Judah?

20 And his servants arose, and made a conspiracy, and slew Jo'-ash in the house of Mil'-lo, which goeth down to Sil'-la.

21 For ᴿJoz'-a-char the son of Shim'-e-ath, and Je-hoz'-a-bad the son of ᵀSho'-mer, his servants, ᵀsmote him, and he died; and they buried him with his fathers in the city of David: and Am-a-zi'-ah his son reigned in his stead.   2 Chr. 24:26 • Shimrith • struck

CHAPTER 13

The Reign of Jehoahaz in Israel

IN the three and twentieth year of ᴿJo'-ash the son of A-ha-zi'-ah king of Judah ᴿJe-ho'-a-haz the son of Je'-hu ᴿbegan to reign over Israel in Sa-ma'-ri-a, *and reigned* seventeen years.   14:1 • 12:1 • 10:35

2 And he did *that which was* evil in the sight of the LORD, and followed the sins of Jer-o-bo'-am the son of Ne'-bat, which made Israel to sin; he departed not therefrom.

3 And the anger of the LORD was kindled against Israel, and he ᵀdelivered them into the hand of Haz'-a-el king of Syria, and into the hand of Ben–ha'-dad the son of Haz'-a-el, all *their* days.   *let them be defeated by*

4 And Je-ho'-a-haz besought the LORD, and the LORD hearkened unto him: for ᴿhe saw the oppression of Israel, because the king of Syria oppressed them.   14:26; [Ex. 3:7]

5 (And the LORD gave Israel a ᴿsaviour, so that they went out from under the hand of the Syrians: and the children of Israel dwelt in their tents, as beforetime.   *v. 25*

6 Nevertheless they departed not from the sins of the house of Jer-o-bo'-am, ᴿwho made Israel sin, *but* walked therein: and there remained the grove also in Sa-ma'-ri-a.)   *v. 2*

7 Neither did he leave of the people to Je-ho'-a-haz but fifty horsemen, and ten chariots, and ten thousand footmen; for the king of Syria had destroyed them, and had made them like the dust by threshing.

8 Now the rest of the acts of Je-ho'-a-haz, and all that he did, and his might, *are* they not written in the book of the chronicles of the kings of Israel?

9 And Je-ho'-a-haz ᵀslept with his fathers; and they buried him in Sa-ma'-ri-a: and Jo'-ash his son reigned in his stead.   *died*

Rule of Jehoash—2 Kin. 14:15, 16

10 In the thirty and seventh year of Jo'-ash king of Judah began Je-ho'-ash the son of Je-ho'-a-haz to reign over Israel in Sa-ma'-ri-a, *and reigned* sixteen years.

11 And he did *that which was* evil in the sight of the LORD; he departed not from all the sins of Jer-o-bo'-am the son of Ne'-bat, who made Israel sin: *but* he walked therein.

12 And the rest of the acts of Jo'-ash, and all that he did, and his might wherewith he fought against Am-a-zi'-ah king of Judah, *are* they not written in the book of the chronicles of the kings of Israel?

13 And Jo'-ash ᴿslept ᵀwith his fathers; and Jer-o-bo'-am sat upon his throne: and Jo'-ash was buried in Sa-ma'-ri-a with the kings of Israel.   14:16 • *died*

Prophecy of Israel's Victory

14 Now E-li'-sha was fallen sick of his sickness whereof he died. And Jo'-ash the king of Israel came down unto him, and wept over ᵀhis face, and said, O my father, my father, ᴿthe chariot of Israel, and the horsemen thereof.   *his death* • 2:12

15 And E-li'-sha said unto him, Take ᴿbow and arrows. And he took unto him bow and arrows.   1 Chr. 5:18

16 ᴿAnd he said to the king of Israel, Put thine hand upon the bow. And he put his hand *upon it:* and E-li'-sha put his hands upon the king's hands.   [Gen. 49:24]

17 And he said, Open the window eastward. And he opened *it.* Then E-li'-sha said, Shoot. And he shot. And he said, The arrow of the LORD's deliverance, and the arrow of deliverance from Syria: for thou shalt ᵀsmite the Syrians in A'-phek, till thou have consumed *them.*   *you shall defeat*

18 And he said, Take the arrows. And he took *them.* And he said unto the king of Israel, ᵀSmite upon the ground. And he smote thrice, and ᵀstayed.   *strike* • *stopped*

19 And the man of God was wroth with him, and said, Thou shouldest have smitten five or six times; then hadst thou smitten Syria till thou hadst consumed *it:* whereas now thou shalt smite Syria *but* thrice.

Death of Elisha

20 And E-li'-sha died, and they buried him. And the bands of the Mo'-ab-ites invaded the land at the coming in of the year.

Miracle of Resurrection at Elisha's Tomb

21 ᴿAnd it came to pass, as they were burying a man, that, behold, they spied a band *of men;* and they cast the man into the sepulchre of E-li'-sha: and when the man was let down, and touched the bones of E-li'-sha, he revived, and stood up on his feet.   19:35

Israel's Victory over Syria

22 But ᴿHaz'-a-el king of Syria oppressed Israel all the days of Je-ho'-a-haz.   8:12

23 And the LORD was gracious unto them, and had compassion on them, and had respect unto them, ᴿbecause of his covenant with Abraham, Isaac, and Jacob, and would not destroy them, neither cast he them from his presence as yet.   Ex. 32:13

24 So Haz'-a-el king of Syria died; and Ben–ha'-dad his son reigned in his stead.

25 And Je-ho'-ash the son of Je-ho'-a-haz took again out of the hand of Ben–ha'-dad the son of Haz'-a-el the cities, which he had taken out of the hand of Je-ho'-a-haz his father by war. Three times did Jo'-ash beat him, and recovered the cities of Israel.

CHAPTER 14

Spiritual Evaluation of Amaziah—2 Chr. 25:1–4

IN the second year of Jo'-ash son of Je-ho'-a-haz king of Israel reigned Am-a-zi'-ah the son of Jo'-ash king of Judah.

2 He was twenty and five years old when he began to reign, and reigned twenty and nine years in Jerusalem. And his mother's name *was* Je-ho-ad'-dan of Jerusalem.

3 And he did *that which was* right in the sight of the LORD, yet not like David his father: he did according to all things ᴿas Jo'-ash his father did.   12:2

4 Howbeit the high places were not taken away: as yet the people did sacrifice and burnt incense on the high places.

5 And it came to pass, as soon as the kingdom was ᵀconfirmed in his hand, that he ᵀslew his servants which had slain the king his father.   *firmly • killed*

6 But the children of the murderers he slew not: according unto that which is written in the book of the law of Moses, wherein the LORD commanded, saying, ᴿThe fathers shall not be put to death for the children, nor the children be put to death for the fathers; but every man shall be put to death for his own sin.   Deut. 24:16

Political Situation Under Amaziah
2 Chr. 25:11, 17–24

7 ᴿHe slew of E'-dom in the valley of salt ten thousand, and took ᵀSelah by war, ᴿand called the name of it Jok'-the-el unto this day.   2 Chr. 25:11 • *Petra, the rock* • Josh. 15:38

8 ᴿThen Am-a-zi'-ah sent messengers to Je-ho'-ash, the son of Je-ho'-a-haz son of Je'-hu, king of Israel, saying, Come, let us look one another in the face.   2 Chr. 25:17

9 And Je-ho'-ash the king of Israel sent to Am-a-zi'-ah king of Judah, saying, The thistle that *was* in Leb'-a-non sent to the ᴿcedar that *was* in Leb'-a-non, saying, Give thy daughter to my son to wife: and there passed by a wild beast that *was* in Leb'-a-non, and trode down the thistle.   1 Kin. 4:33

10 Thou hast indeed smitten E'-dom, and thine heart hath lifted thee up: glory *of this,* and tarry at home: for why shouldest thou meddle to *thy* hurt, that thou shouldest fall, *even* thou, and Judah with thee?

11 But Am-a-zi'-ah would not hear. Therefore Je-ho'-ash king of Israel went up; and he and Am-a-zi'-ah king of Judah looked one another in the face at Beth–she'-mesh, which *belongeth* to Judah.

12 And Judah was ᵀput to the worse before Israel; ᴿand they fled every man to their tents.   *defeated* • 2 Sam. 18:17

13 And Je-ho'-ash king of Israel took Am-a-zi'-ah king of Judah, the son of Je-ho'-ash the son of A-ha-zi'-ah, at Beth–she'-mesh, and came to Jerusalem, and brake down the wall of Jerusalem from ᴿthe gate of E'-phra-im unto ᴿthe corner gate, ᵀfour hundred cubits.   Neh. 8:16 • Jer. 31:38 • *600 ft.*

14 ᴿAnd he took all ᴿthe gold and silver, and all the vessels that were found in the house of the LORD, and in the treasures of the king's house, and hostages, and returned to Sa-ma'-ri-a.   12:18 • 1 Kin. 7:51

Death of Jehoash—2 Kin. 13:12, 13

15 ᴿNow the rest of the acts of Je-ho'-ash which he did, and his ᵀmight, and how he fought with Am-a-zi'-ah king of Judah, *are* they not written in the book of the chronicles of the kings of Israel?   13:12 • *strength*

16 And Je-ho'-ash ᵀslept with his fathers, and was buried in Sa-ma'-ri-a with the kings of Israel; and Jer-o-bo'-am his son reigned in his stead.   *died*

Death of Amaziah
2 Chr. 25:25—26:2

17 ᴿAnd Am-a-zi'-ah the son of Jo'-ash king of Judah lived after the death of Je-ho'-ash son of Je-ho'-a-haz king of Israel fifteen years.   2 Chr. 25:25

18 And the rest of the acts of Am-a-zi'-ah, *are* they not written in the book of the chronicles of the kings of Judah?

19 Now ᴿthey made a conspiracy against him in Jerusalem: and he fled to ᴿLa'-chish; but they sent after him to La'-chish, and slew him there.   2 Chr. 25:27 • Josh. 10:31

20 ᴿAnd they brought him on horses: and he was buried at Jerusalem with his fathers in the city of David.   2 Chr. 25:28

21 And all the people of Judah took ᴿAz-a-ri'-ah,ᵀ which *was* sixteen years old, and made him king instead of his father Am-a-zi'-ah.   15:13; 2 Chr. 26:1 • *he is called Uzziah*

22 He built ᴿE'-lath, and restored it to Judah, after that the king ᵀslept with his fathers.   2 Chr. 8:17; 16:6; 26:2 • *had died*

The Reign of Jeroboam II in Israel

23 In the fifteenth year of Am-a-zi'-ah the son of Jo'-ash king of Judah Jer-o-bo'-am the son of Jo'-ash king of Israel began to reign in Sa-ma'-ri-a, *and reigned* forty and one years.

24 And he did *that which was* evil in the sight of the LORD: he departed not from all the ᴿsins of Jer-o-bo'-am the son of Ne'-bat, who made Israel to sin.   1 Kin. 12:26–33

25 He restored the ᵀcoast of Israel from the entering of Ha'-math unto the sea of the plain, according to the word of the LORD God of Israel, which he spake by the hand of his servant Jonah, the son of A-mit'-tai, the prophet, which *was* of Gath–he'-pher.   *border*

26 For the LORD ᴿsaw the ᵀaffliction of

Israel, *that it was* very bitter: for ᴿthere *was* not any shut up, nor any left, nor any helper for Israel.   13:4 · *distress* · Deut. 32:36

27 ᴿAnd the Lᴏʀᴅ said not that he would blot out the name of Israel from under heaven: but he saved them by the hand of Jer-o-bo'-am the son of Jo'-ash.   [13:5]

28 Now the rest of the acts of Jer-o-bo'-am, and all that he did, and his might, how he warred, and how he recovered Damascus, and Ha'-math, *which belonged* to Judah, for Israel, *are* they not written in the book of the chronicles of the kings of Israel?

29 And Jer-o-bo'-am slept with his fathers, *even* with the kings of Israel; and Zach-a-ri'-ah his son reigned in his stead.

CHAPTER 15

The Reign of Azariah in Judah—2 Chr. 26:3–23

IN the twenty and seventh year of Jer-o-bo'-am king of Israel began Az-a-ri'-ah son of Am-a-zi'-ah king of Judah to reign.

2 ᴿSixteen years old was he when he began to reign, and he reigned two and fifty years in Jerusalem. And his mother's name *was* Jech-o-li'-ah of Jerusalem.   2 Chr. 26:3, 4

3 ᴿAnd he did *that which was* right in the sight of the Lᴏʀᴅ, according to all that his father Am-a-zi'-ah had done;   *v. 34*

4 ᵀSave that the high places were not removed: the people sacrificed and burnt incense still on the high places.   *except*

5 And the Lᴏʀᴅ smote the king, so that he was a leper unto the day of his death, and dwelt inᵀ a several house. And Jo'-tham the king's son *was* over the house, judging the people of the land.   *an infirmary*

6 And the rest of the acts of Az-a-ri'-ah, and all that he did, *are* they not written in the book of the ᵀchronicles of the kings of Judah?   *history*

7 So Az-a-ri'-ah ᵀslept with his fathers; and ᴿthey buried him with his fathers in the city of David: and Jo'-tham his son reigned in his stead.   *died* · 2 Chr. 26:23

The Reign of Zachariah in Israel

8 ᴿIn the thirty and eighth year of Az-a-ri'-ah king of Judah did ᴿZach-a-ri'-ah the son of Jer-o-bo'-am reign over Israel in Sa-ma'-ri-a six months.   *v.* 1 · 14:29

9 And he did *that which was* evil in the sight of the Lᴏʀᴅ, as his fathers had done: he departed not from the sins of Jer-o-bo'-am the son of Ne'-bat, who made Israel to sin.

10 And Shal'-lum the son of Ja'-besh conspired against him, and ᴿsmoteᵀ him ᵀbefore the people, and slew him, and reigned in his stead.   Amos 7:9 · *struck* · *in public*

11 And the rest of the acts of Zach-a-ri'-ah,

behold, they *are* written in the book of the chronicles of the kings of Israel.

12 This *was* the word of the Lᴏʀᴅ which he spake unto Je'-hu, saying, ᴿThy sons shall sit on the throne of Israel unto the fourth *generation.* And so it came to pass.   10:30

The Reign of Shallum in Israel

13 ᴿShal'-lum the son of Ja'-besh began to reign in the nine and thirtieth year of Uz-zi'-ah king of Judah; and he reigned a full month ᴿin Sa-ma'-ri-a.   *vv.* 1, 8 · 1 Kin. 16:24

14 For Men'-a-hem the son of Ga'-di went up from ᴿTir'-zah, and came to Sa-ma'-ri-a, and ᵀsmote Shal'-lum the son of Ja'-besh in Sa-ma'-ri-a, and slew him, and reigned in his stead.   1 Kin. 14:17; Song 6:4 · *struck*

15 And the rest of the acts of Shal'-lum, and his conspiracy which he made, behold, they *are* written in the book of the chronicles of the kings of Israel.

The Reign of Menahem in Israel

16 Then Men'-a-hem smote Tiph'-sah, and all that *were* therein, and the coasts thereof from Tir'-zah: because they ᵀopened not *to him,* therefore he smote *it; and* all ᴿthe women therein that were with child he ripped up.   *did not welcome him* · 8:12

17 In the nine and thirtieth year of Az-a-ri'-ah king of Judah began Men'-a-hem the son of Ga'-di to ᴿreign over Israel, *and* reigned ten years in Sa-ma'-ri-a.   *vv.* 1, 8, 13

18 And he did *that which was* evil in the sight of the Lᴏʀᴅ: he departed not all his days from the sins of Jer-o-bo'-am the son of Ne'-bat, who made Israel to sin.

19 *And* Pul the king of Assyria came against the land: and Men'-a-hem gave Pul a ᵀthousand talents of silver, that his hand might be with him to confirm the kingdom in his hand. $384,000,000

20 And Men'-a-hem ᴿexactedᵀ the money of Israel, *even* of all the mighty men of wealth, of each man ᵀfifty shek'-els of silver, to give to the king of Assyria. So the king of Assyria turned back, and stayed not there in the land.   23:35 · *took* · $6,400

21 And the rest of the acts of Men'-a-hem, and all that he did, *are* they not written in the book of the chronicles of the kings of Israel?

22 And Men'-a-hem slept with his fathers; and Pek-a-hi'-ah his son reigned in his stead.

The Reign of Pekahiah in Israel

23 In the ᴿfiftieth year of Az-a-ri'-ah king of Judah Pek-a-hi'-ah the son of Men'-a-hem began to reign over Israel in Sa-ma'-ri-a, *and* reigned two years.   *vv.* 1, 8, 13, 17

24 ᴿAnd he did *that which was* evil in the sight of the Lᴏʀᴅ: he departed not from the sins of Jer-o-bo'-am the son of Ne'-bat, who made Israel to sin.   *v.* 18

25 But Pe'-kah the son of Rem-a-li'-ah, a captain of his, conspired against him, and smote him in Sa-ma'-ri-a, in the palace of the king's house, with Ar'-gob and A-ri'-eh, and with him fifty men of the Gil'-e-ad-ites: and he killed him, and reigned in his room.

26 And the rest of the acts of Pek-a-hi'-ah, and all that he did, behold, they are written in the book of the chronicles of the kings of Israel.

The Reign of Pekah in Israel

27 In the two and fiftieth year of Az-a-ri'-ah king of Judah ᴿPe'-kah the son of Rem-a-li'-ah began to reign over Israel in Sa-ma'-ri-a, and reigned twenty years.   Is. 7:1

28 And he did that which was evil in the sight of the LORD: he departed not from the sins of Jer-o-bo'-am the son of Ne'-bat, who made Israel to sin.

29 In the days of Pe'-kah king of Israel came Tig'-lath–pi-le'-ser king of Assyria, and took I'-jon, and A'-bel-beth-ma'-a-chah, and Ja-no'-ah, and Ke'-desh, and Ha'-zor, and Gil'-e-ad, and Galilee, all the land of Naph'-ta-li, and carried them captive to Assyria.

30 And Ho-she'-a the son of E'-lah made a conspiracy against Pe'-kah the son of Rem-a-li'-ah, and ᵀsmote him, and slew him, and reigned in his stead, in the twentieth year of Jo'-tham the son of Uz-zi'-ah.   struck

31 And the rest of the acts of Pe'-kah, and all that he did, behold, they are written in the book of the chronicles of the kings of Israel.

The Reign of Jotham in Judah—2 Chr. 27:1-9

32 In the second year of Pe'-kah the son of Rem-a-li'-ah king of Israel began Jo'-tham the son of Uz-zi'-ah king of Judah to reign.

33 ᴿFive and twenty years old was he when he began to reign, and he reigned sixteen years in Jerusalem. And his mother's name was Je-ru'-sha, the daughter of Za'-dok.   2 Chr. 27:1

34 And he did that which was right in the sight of the LORD: he did ᴿaccording to all that his father Uz-zi'-ah had done.   v. 3

35 Howbeit the high places were not removed: the people sacrificed and burned incense still in the high places. He built the higher gate of the house of the LORD.

36 Now the rest of the acts of Jo'-tham, and all that he did, are they not written in the book of the chronicles of the kings of Judah?

37 In those days the LORD began to send against Judah Re'-zin the king of Syria, and ᴿPe'-kah the son of Rem-a-li'-ah.   v. 27

38 And Jo'-tham ᵀslept with his fathers, and was buried with his fathers in the city of David his father: and ᴿAhaz his son reigned in his ᵀstead.   died • 16:2 • place

CHAPTER 16

Spiritual Evaluation of Ahaz—2 Chr. 28:1-4

IN the seventeenth year of Pe'-kah the son of Rem-a-li'-ah Ahaz the son of Jo'-tham king of Judah began to reign.

2 ᴿTwenty years old was ᴿAhaz when he began to reign, and reigned sixteen years in Jerusalem, and did not that which was right in the sight of the LORD his God, like David his father.   2 Chr. 28:1-4 • v. 8

3 But he walked in the way of the kings of Israel, yea, and made his son to pass through the fire, according to the abominations of the heathen, whom the LORD cast out from before the children of Israel.

4 And he sacrificed and burnt incense in the high places, and ᴿon the hills, and under every green tree.   [Deut. 12:2]; 1 Kin. 14:23

Political Situation Under Ahaz
2 Chr. 28:5, 16, 21; Is. 7:1

5 Then Re'-zin king of Syria and Pe'-kah son of Rem-a-li'-ah king of Israel came up to Jerusalem to war: and they besieged Ahaz, but could not ᵀovercome him.   defeat

6 At that time Re'-zin king of Syria ᴿrecovered E'-lath to Syria, and drave the Jews from E'-lath: and the Syrians came to E'-lath, and dwelt there unto this day.   14:22

7 ᴿSo Ahaz sent messengers to Tig'-lath–pi-le'-ser king of Assyria, saying, I am thy servant and thy son: come up, and ᵀsave me out of the hand of the king of Syria, and out of the hand of the king of Israel, which rise up against me.   2 Chr. 28:16 • deliver

8 And Ahaz took the silver and gold that was found in the house of the LORD, and in the ᵀtreasures of the king's house, and sent it for a present to the king of Assyria.   treasuries

9 And the king of Assyria hearkened unto him: for the king of Assyria went up against Damascus, and took it, and carried the people of it captive to Kir, and slew Re'-zin.

10 And king Ahaz went to Damascus to meet Tig'-lath–pi-le'-ser king of Assyria, and saw an altar that was at Damascus: and king Ahaz sent to U-ri'-jah the priest the fashion of the altar, and the pattern of it, according to all the workmanship thereof.

11 And U-ri'-jah the priest built an altar according to all that king Ahaz had sent from Damascus: so U-ri'-jah the priest made it against king Ahaz came from Damascus.

12 And when the king was come from Damascus, the king saw the altar: and ᴿthe king approached to the altar, and ᵀoffered thereon.   2 Chr. 26:16, 19 • worshipped at it

13 And he burnt his burnt offering and his ᵀmeat offering, and poured his drink offering, and sprinkled the blood of his peace offerings, upon the altar.   meal

14 And he brought also the brasen altar,

which *was* Tbefore the LORD, from the forefront of the house, from between the altar and the house of the LORD, and put it on the north side of the altar. *dedicated to*

15 And king Ahaz commanded U-ri′-jah the priest, saying, Upon the great altar burn the morning burnt offering, and the evening meat offering, and the king's burnt sacrifice, and his meat offering, with the burnt offering of all the people of the land, and their meat offering, and their drink offerings; and sprinkle upon it all the blood of the burnt offering, and all the blood of the sacrifice: and the brasen altar shall be for me to enquire *by*.

16 Thus did U-ri′-jah the priest, according to all that king Ahaz commanded.

17 And king Ahaz cut off the borders of the bases, and removed the laver from off them; and took down the sea from off the brasen oxen that *were* under it, and put it upon a pavement of stones.

18 And the covert for the sabbath that they had built in the house, and the king's entry without, Tturned he from the house of the LORD for the king of Assyria. *removed*

Death of Ahaz—2 Chr. 28:26, 27

19 Now the rest of the acts of Ahaz which he did, *are* they not written in the book of the chronicles of the kings of Judah?

20 And Ahaz slept with his fathers, and Rwas buried with his fathers in the city of David: and RHez-e-ki′-ah his son reigned in his stead. 2 Chr. 28:27 • 18:9

CHAPTER 17

Spiritual Evaluation of Hoshea

IN the twelfth year of Ahaz king of Judah began Ho-she′-a the son of E′-lah to reign in Sa-ma′-ri-a over Israel nine years.

2 And he did *that which was* evil in the sight of the LORD, but not as the kings of Israel that were before him.

Imprisonment of Hoshea

3 Against him came up Shal-ma-ne′-ser king of Assyria; and Ho-she′-a became his servant, and gave him presents.

4 And the king of Assyria found conspiracy in Ho-she′-a: for he had sent messengers to So king of Egypt, and brought no Tpresent to the king of Assyria, as *he had done* year by year: therefore the king of Assyria shut him up, and bound him in Rprison. *tribute* • Is. 42:22

Captivity of Samaria—2 Kin. 18:9–12

5 Then the king of Assyria came up throughout all the land, and went up to Sa-ma′-ri-a, and besieged it three years.

6 In the ninth year of Ho-she′-a the king of Assyria took Sa-ma′-ri-a, and carried Israel away into Assyria, and placed them in Ha′-lah and in Ha′-bor *by* the river of Go′-zan, and in the cities of the Medes.

Causes of the Captivity

7 For *so* it was, that the children of Israel had sinned against the LORD their God, which had brought them up out of the land of Egypt, from under the hand of Pharaoh king of Egypt, and had feared other gods,

8 And walked in the statutes of the heathen, whom the LORD cast out from before the children of Israel, and of the kings of Israel, which they had made.

9 And the children of Israel did secretly *those* things that *were* not right against the LORD their God, and they built them high places in all their cities, from the tower of the watchmen to the fenced city.

10 And they set them up Timages and Tgroves in every high hill, and under every green tree: *idols • symbol of female deity*

11 And there they burnt incense in all the high places, as *did* the heathen whom the LORD carried away before them; and wrought wicked things to Rprovoke the LORD to anger:

12 For they served idols, Rwhereof the LORD had said unto them, RYe shall not do this thing. [Ex. 20:4; Lev. 26:1; Deut. 5:7, 8] • [Deut. 4:19]

13 Yet the LORD testified against Israel, and against Judah, by all the prophets, *and* by all Rthe seers, saying, Turn ye from your evil ways, and keep my commandments *and* my statutes, according to all the law which I commanded your fathers, and which I sent to you by my servants the prophets. 1 Sam. 9:9

14 TNotwithstanding they would not hear, but Thardened their necks, like to the neck of their fathers, that did not believe in the LORD their God. *however • became rebellious*

15 And they rejected his Tstatutes, and his covenant that he made with their fathers, and his testimonies which he testified against them; and they followed vanity, and became vain, and went after the heathen that *were* round about them, *concerning* whom the LORD had charged them, that they should not do like them. *laws*

16 And they left all the commandments of the LORD their God, and made them molten images, *even* two calves, and made a grove, and worshipped Tall the host of heaven, and served Ba′-al. *sun, moon, and stars*

17 RAnd they caused their sons and their daughters to pass through the fire, and used divination and enchantments, and sold themselves to do evil in the sight of the LORD, to provoke him to anger. 16:3

18 Therefore the LORD was very angry with Israel, and Rremoved them out of his sight: there was none left Rbut the tribe of Judah only. *v.* 6 • 1 Kin. 11:13, 32, 36

19 Also Judah kept not the command-ments of the LORD their God, but walked in the statutes of Israel which they made.

20 And the LORD rejected all the seed of Israel, and afflicted them, and delivered them into the hand of spoilers, until he had cast them out of his sight.

21 For ᴿhe ᵀrent Israel from the house of David; and they made Jer-o-bo'-am the son of Ne'-bat king: and Jer-o-bo'-am drave Israel from following the LORD, and made them sin a great sin.   1 Kin. 11:11 · tore away

22 For the children of Israel walked in all the sins of Jer-o-bo'-am which he did; they departed not from them;

23 Until the LORD removed Israel out of his sight, as he had said by all his servants the prophets. ᴿSo was Israel carried away out of their own land to Assyria unto this day.   v. 6

Sins of the Foreigners

24 And the king of Assyria brought men from Babylon, and from Cu'-thah, and from ᴿA'-va,ᵀ and from Ha'-math, and from Seph-ar-va'-im, and placed them in the cities of Sa-ma'-ri-a instead of the children of Israel: and they possessed Sa-ma'-ri-a, and dwelt in the cities thereof.   18:34 · Ivah

25 And so it was at the beginning of their dwelling there, that they ᵀfeared not the LORD: therefore the LORD sent lions among them, which slew some of them.   honoured

26 Wherefore they spake to the king of Assyria, saying, The nations which thou hast removed, and placed in the cities of Sa-ma'-ri-a, know not ᵀthe manner of the God of the land: therefore he hath sent lions among them, and, behold, they slay them, because they know not the manner of the God of the land.   the ways of God

27 Then the king of Assyria commanded, saying, Carry thither one of the priests whom ye brought from thence; and let them go and dwell there, and let him teach them the manner of the God of the land.

28 Then one of the priests whom they had carried away from Sa-ma'-ri-a came and dwelt in Beth'-el, and taught them how they should ᵀfear the LORD.   revere

29 Howbeit every nation made gods of their own, and put them ᴿin the houses of the high places which the Sa-mar'-i-tans had made, every nation in their cities wherein they dwelt.   1 Kin. 12:31; 13:32

30 And the men of ᴿBabylon made Suc'-coth-be'-noth, and the men of Cuth made Ner'-gal, and the men of Ha'-math made Ash'-i-ma,   v. 24

31 And the A'-vites made Nib'-haz and Tar'-tak, and the Se'-phar-vites burnt their children in fire to A-dram'-me-lech and A-nam'-me-lech, the gods of Seph-ar-va'-im.

32 So they feared the LORD, and made unto themselves of the lowest of them priests of the high places, which sacrificed for them in the houses of the high places.

33 They feared the LORD, and served their own gods, after the manner of the nations whom they carried away from ᵀthence.   there

34 Unto this day they do after the former manners: they fear not the LORD, neither do they after their statutes, or after their ordinances, or after the law and command-ment which the LORD commanded the children of Jacob, whom he named Israel;

35 With whom the LORD had made ᵀa covenant, and charged them, saying, ᴿYe shall not fear other gods, nor ᴿbow your-selves to them, nor serve them, nor sacrifice to them: an agreement · Judg. 6:10 · [Ex. 20:5]

36 But the LORD, who brought you up out of the land of Egypt with great power and a stretched out arm, him shall ye ᵀfear, and him shall ye worship, and to him shall ye ᵀdo sacrifice.   revere · offer ritual sacrifices

37 And the statutes, and the ordinances, and the law, and the commandment, which he wrote for you, ye shall observe to do for evermore; and ye shall not fear other gods.

38 And the covenant that I have made with you ᴿye shall not forget; neither shall ye ᵀfear other gods.   Deut. 4:23; 6:12 · revere

39 But the LORD your God ye shall ᵀfear; and he shall deliver you out of the hand of all your enemies.   revere

40 Howbeit they did not hearken, ᴿbut they did after their former manner.   [Matt. 6:24]

41 So these nations feared the LORD, and served their graven images, both their children, and their children's children: as did their fathers, so do they unto this day.

CHAPTER 18

Spiritual Evaluation of Hezekiah
2 Chr. 29:1, 2; 31:1

NOW it came to pass in the third year of Ho-she'-a son of E'-lah king of Israel, that ᴿHez-e-ki'-ah the son of Ahaz king of Judah began to reign.   2 Chr. 28:27

2 Twenty and five years old was he when he began to reign; and he reigned twenty and nine years in Jerusalem. His mother's name also was ᴿA'-bi,ᵀ the daughter of Zach-a-ri'-ah.   2 Chr. 29:1, 2 · Abijah

3 ᴿAnd he did that which was right in the sight of the LORD, according to all that David his father did.   20:3; 2 Chr. 31:20

4 He removed the high places, and brake the ᵀimages, and cut down the groves, and brake in pieces the brasen serpent that Moses had made: for unto those days the children of Israel did burn incense to it: and he called it ᵀNe-hush'-tan.   idols · only a piece of brass

5 He ^Rtrusted in the LORD God of Israel; ^Rso that after him was none like him among all the kings of Judah, nor *any* that were before him.   19:10; [Job 13:15; Ps. 13:5] • 23:25

6 For he ^Tclave to the LORD, *and* departed not from following him, but ^Tkept his commandments, which the LORD commanded Moses.   *walked closely with • obeyed*

7 And the LORD ^Rwas with him; *and* he prospered whithersoever he went forth: and he ^Rrebelled against the king of Assyria, and served him not.   [2 Chr. 15:2] • 16:7

8 He smote the Phi-lis'-tines, *even* unto Ga'-za, and the borders thereof, from the tower of the watchmen to the fenced city.

Invasion of Israel by Assyria—2 Kin. 17:5-7

9 And ^Rit came to pass in the fourth year of king Hez-e-ki'-ah, which *was* the seventh year of Ho-she'-a son of E'-lah king of Israel, *that* Shal-ma-ne'-ser king of Assyria came up against Sa-ma'-ri-a, and besieged it.   17:3-7

10 And at the end of three years they took it: *even* in the sixth year of Hez-e-ki'-ah, that is the ninth year of Ho-she'-a king of Israel, Sa-ma'-ri-a was taken.

11 And the king of Assyria did carry away Israel unto Assyria, and put them in Ha'-lah and in Ha'-bor *by* the river of Go'-zan, and in the cities of the Medes:

12 Because they obeyed ^Rnot the voice of the LORD their God, but transgressed his covenant, *and* all that Moses the servant of the LORD commanded, and would not hear *them,* nor do *them.*   17:7-18

First Invasion of Judah by Assyria—Is. 36:1

13 Now in the fourteenth year of king Hez-e-ki'-ah did Sen-nach'-e-rib king of Assyria come up against all the ^Tfenced cities of Judah, and took them.   *fortified*

14 And Hez-e-ki'-ah king of Judah sent to the king of Assyria to La'-chish, saying, I have offended; return from me: that which thou puttest on me will I bear. And the king of Assyria appointed unto Hez-e-ki'-ah king of Judah ^Tthree hundred talents of silver and ^Tthirty talents of gold. $115,200,000 • $172,800,000

15 And Hez-e-ki'-ah ^Rgave *him* all the silver that was found in the house of the LORD, and in the ^Ttreasures of the king's house.   12:18; 16:8; 1 Kin. 15:18, 19 • *treasures*

16 At that time did Hez-e-ki'-ah ^Tcut off *the* gold *from* the doors of the temple of the LORD, and *from* the pillars which Hez-e-ki'-ah king of Judah had overlaid, and gave ^Tit to the king of Assyria.   *strip • them*

Second Invasion of Judah by Assyria
2 Chr. 32:9-21; Is. 36:2—37:38

17 And the king of Assyria sent ^RTar'-tan and Rab'-sa-ris and Rab'-sha-keh from La'-chish to king Hez-e-ki'-ah with a great host

against Jerusalem. And they went up and came to Jerusalem. And when they were come up, they came and stood by the conduit of the upper pool, ^Rwhich *is* in the highway of the fuller's field.   Is. 20:1 • Is. 7:3

18 And when they had called to the king, there came out to them E-li'-a-kim the son of Hil-ki'-ah, which *was* over the household, and Sheb'-na the ^Tscribe, and Jo'-ah the son of A'-saph the recorder.   *secretary*

19 And Rab'-sha-keh said unto them, Speak ye now to Hez-e-ki'-ah, Thus saith the great king, the king of Assyria, What confidence *is* this wherein thou trustest?

20 Thou sayest, (but *they are but* ^Tvain words,) *I have* counsel and strength for the war. Now on whom dost thou trust, ^Rthat thou rebellest against me?   *empty words • v. 7*

21 Now, behold, thou trustest upon the staff of this bruised reed, *even* upon Egypt, on which if a man lean, it will go into his hand, and pierce it: ^Rso *is* Pharaoh king of Egypt unto all that trust on him.   [Jer. 2:13]

22 But if ye say unto me, We trust in the LORD our God: *is* not that he, ^Rwhose ^Thigh places and whose altars Hez-e-ki'-ah hath taken away, and hath said to Judah and Jerusalem, Ye shall worship before this altar in Jerusalem?   2 Chr. 31:1; 32:12 • *shrines*

23 Now therefore, I pray thee, give pledges to my lord the king of Assyria, and I will deliver thee two thousand horses, if thou be able on thy part to set riders upon them.

24 How then wilt thou turn away the face of one captain of the least of my master's servants, and put thy trust on Egypt for chariots and for horsemen?

25 Am I now come up without the LORD against this place to destroy it? The LORD said to me, Go up against this land, and destroy it.

26 Then said E-li'-a-kim the son of Hil-ki'-ah, and Sheb'-na, and Jo'-ah, unto Rab'-sha-keh, Speak, I pray thee, to thy servants in the Syrian language; for we understand *it:* and talk not with us in the Jews' language in the ears of the people that *are* on the wall.

27 But Rab'-sha-keh said unto them, Hath my master sent me to thy master, and to thee, to speak these words? *hath he* not *sent me* to the men which sit on the wall, that they may eat their own dung, and drink their own ^Tpiss with you?   *urine*

28 Then Rab'-sha-keh stood and cried with a loud voice in the Jews' language, and spake, saying, Hear the word of the great king, the king of Assyria:

29 Thus saith the king, Let not Hez-e-ki'-ah ^Tdeceive you: for he shall not be able to deliver you out of his hand: *mislead*

30 Neither let Hez-e-ki'-ah make you trust in the LORD, saying, The LORD will surely deliver us, and this city shall not be delivered into the hand of the king of Assyria.

31 Hearken not to Hez-e-ki'-ah: for thus saith the king of Assyria, Make *an agreement* with me by a present, and come out to me, and *then* eat ye every man of his own vine, and every one of his fig tree, and drink ye every one the waters of his cistern:

32 Until I come and take you away to a land like your own land, a land of corn and wine, a land of bread and vineyards, a land of oil olive and of honey, that ye may live, and not die: and hearken not unto Hez-e-ki'-ah, when he ᵀpersuadeth you, saying, The LORD will deliver us.   *deceiveth*

33 ᴿHath any of the gods of the nations delivered at all his land out of the hand of the king of Assyria?   2 Chr. 32:14; Is. 10:10, 11

34 Where *are* the gods of Ha'-math, and of Ar'-pad? where *are* the gods of Seph-ar-va'-im, He'-na, and I'-vah? have they delivered Sa-ma'-ri-a out of mine hand?

35 Who *are* they among all the gods of the countries, that have delivered their country out of mine hand, ᴿthat the LORD should deliver Jerusalem out of mine hand?   Dan. 3:15

36 ᴿBut the people held their peace, ᴿand answered him not a word: for the king's commandment was, saying, Answer him not.   Is. 42:2 • [Prov. 16:32]

37 Then came ᴿE-li'-a-kim the son of Hil-ki'-ah, which *was* over the household, and Sheb'-na the scribe, and Jo'-ah the son of A'-saph the recorder, to Hez-e-ki'-ah ᴿwith *their* clothes ᵀrent, and told him the words of Rab'-sha-keh.   *v. 26 • Is. 33:7 • torn for grief*

CHAPTER 19

A ND it came to pass, when king Hez-e-ki'-ah heard *it*, that he rent his clothes, and covered himself with sackcloth, and went into the house of the LORD.

2 And he sent E-li'-a-kim, which *was* over the household, and Sheb'-na the scribe, and the elders of the priests, covered with sackcloth, to Isaiah the prophet the son of Amoz.

3 And they said unto him, Thus saith Hez-e-ki'-ah, This day *is* a day of trouble, and of rebuke, and ᵀblasphemy: for the children are come to the birth, and *there is* not strength ᴿto bring forth.   *rejection • Is. 26:18*

4 It may be the LORD thy God will hear all the words of Rab'-sha-keh, ᴿwhom the king of Assyria his master hath sent to reproach the living God; and will ᴿreprove the words which the LORD thy God hath heard: wherefore lift up *thy* prayer for the remnant that are left.   18:35 • Ps. 50:21

5 ᴿSo the servants of king Hez-e-ki'-ah came to Isaiah.   Is. 37:5

6 And Isaiah said unto them, Thus shall ye say to your master, Thus saith the LORD, Be not afraid of the words which thou hast heard, with which the servants of the king of Assyria have blasphemed me.

7 Behold, I will send a ᵀblast upon him, and he shall hear a rumour, and shall return to his own land; and I will cause him to fall by the sword in his own land.   *hot wind*

8 ᴿSo Rab'-sha-keh returned, and found the king of Assyria warring against ᴿLib'-nah: for he had heard that he was departed from La'-chish.   Is. 37:8 • 18:14

9 ᴿAnd when he heard say of Tir'-ha-kah king of E-thi-o'-pi-a, Behold, he is come out to fight against thee: he sent messengers again unto Hez-e-ki'-ah, saying,   Is. 37:9

10 Thus shall ye speak to Hez-e-ki'-ah king of Judah, saying, Let not thy God ᴿin whom thou ᴿtrustest deceive thee, saying, Jerusalem shall not be delivered into the hand of the king of Assyria.   Is. 37:10 • 18:5

11 ᴿBehold, thou hast heard what the kings of Assyria have done to all lands, by destroying them ᵀutterly: and shalt thou be ᵀdelivered?   Is. 37:11 • *completely • saved*

12 Have the gods of the nations delivered them which my fathers have destroyed; *as* Go'-zan, and Ha'-ran, and Re'-zeph, and the children of Eden which *were* in The-la'-sar?

13 Where *is* the king of Ha'-math, and the king of Ar'-pad, and the king of the city of Seph-ar-va'-im, of He'-na, and I'-vah?

14 And Hez-e-ki'-ah received the letter of the hand of the messengers, and read it: and Hez-e-ki'-ah went up into the house of the LORD, and spread it before the LORD.

15 ᴿAnd Hez-e-ki'-ah prayed before the LORD, and said, O LORD God of Israel, ᴿwhich dwellest *between* the cher'-u-bims, ᴿthou art the God, *even* thou alone, of all the kingdoms of the earth; thou hast made heaven and earth.   Is. 37:15, 16 • Ps. 80:1 • [Is. 44:6]

16 LORD, bow down thine ear, and hear: open, LORD, thine eyes, and see: and hear the words of Sen-nach'-e-rib, which hath sent him to ᵀreproach the living God.   *belittle*

17 Of a truth, LORD, the kings of Assyria have destroyed the nations and their lands,

18 ᴿAnd have cast their gods into the fire: for they *were* no gods, but ᴿthe work of men's hands, wood and stone: therefore they have destroyed them.   Is. 37:19 • [Jer. 10:3–5]

19 Now therefore, O LORD our God, I beseech thee, save thou us out of his hand, that all the kingdoms of the earth may know that thou *art* the LORD God, *even* thou only.

20 Then Isaiah the son of Amoz sent to Hez-e-ki'-ah, saying, Thus saith the LORD God of Israel, ᴿ*That* which thou hast prayed to me against Sen-nach'-e-rib king of Assyria ᴿI have heard.   Is. 37:21 • Ps. 65:2

21 This *is* the word that the LORD hath spoken concerning him; The virgin the daughter of Zion hath despised thee, *and*

laughed thee to scorn; the daughter of Jerusalem hath shaken her head at thee.

22 Whom hast thou reproached and blasphemed? and against whom hast thou exalted *thy* voice, and lifted up thine eyes on high? *even* against the Holy One of Israel.

23 By thy messengers thou hast ᵀreproached the Lord, and hast said, With the multitude of my chariots I am come up to the height of the mountains, to the sides of Leb'-a-non, and will cut down the tall cedar trees thereof, *and* the choice fir trees thereof: and I will enter into the lodgings of his borders, *and into* the forest of his Carmel.   *belittled*

24 I have digged and drunk strange waters, and with the sole of my feet have I dried up all the rivers of besieged places.

25 Hast thou not heard long ago *how* I have done it, *and* of ancient times that I have formed it? now have I brought it to pass, that thou shouldest be to lay waste ᵀfenced cities *into* ruinous heaps.   *fortified*

26 Therefore their inhabitants were of ᵀsmall power, they were dismayed and confounded; they were *as* the grass of the field, and *as* the green herb, *as* ᴿthe grass on the house tops, and *as corn* blasted before it be grown up.   *little strength* · Ps. 129:6

27 But ᴿI know thy abode, and thy going out, and thy coming in, and thy rage against me.   Ps. 139:1; Is. 37:28

28 Because thy rage against me and thy tumult is come up into mine ears, therefore I will put my hook in thy nose, and my bridle in thy lips, and I will turn thee back by the way by which thou camest.

29 And this *shall be* a sign unto thee, Ye shall eat this year such things as grow of themselves, and in the second year that which springeth of the same; and in the third year sow ye, and reap, and plant vineyards, and eat the fruits thereof.

30 And the remnant that is escaped of the house of Judah shall yet again take root downward, and bear fruit upward.

31 ᴿFor out of Jerusalem shall go forth a remnant, and they that escape ᴿout of mount Zion: ᴿthe zeal of the LORD *of hosts* shall do this.   Is. 37:32 · Is. 10:20 · Is. 9:7

32 ᴿTherefore thus saith the LORD concerning the king of Assyria, ᴿHe shall not come into this city, nor shoot an arrow there, nor come before it with shield, nor cast a bank against it.   Is. 37:33 · Is. 8:7-10

33 ᴿBy the way that he came, by the same shall he return, ᴿand shall not come into this city, saith the LORD.   Is. 37:34 · v. 28

34 For ᴿI will defend this city, to save it, for mine own sake, and ᴿfor my servant David's sake.   20:6; Is. 37:35 · 1 Kin. 11:12

35 And ᴿit came to pass that night, that the angel of the LORD went out, and ᵀsmote in the camp of the Assyrians an hundred

fourscore and five thousand: and when they arose early in the morning, behold, they *were* all dead corpses.   Is. 37:36 · *struck*

36 So ᴿSen-nach'-e-rib king of Assyria departed, and went and returned, and dwelt at ᴿNin'-e-veh.   vv. 7, 28 · Gen. 10:11

37 And it came to pass, as he was worshipping in the house of Nis'-roch his god, that A-dram'-me-lech and Sha-re'-zer his sons smote him with the sword: and they escaped into the land of Ar-me'-ni-a. And E'-sar–had'-don his son reigned in his stead.

CHAPTER 20

Miraculous Recovery of Hezekiah
2 Chr. 32:24; Is. 38:1–8

IN those days was Hez-e-ki'-ah sick unto death. And the prophet Isaiah the son of Amoz came to him, and said unto him, Thus saith the LORD, Set thine house in order; for thou shalt die, and not live.

2 Then he turned his face to the wall, and prayed unto the LORD, saying,

3 I beseech thee, O LORD, ᴿremember now how I have walked before thee in truth and with a perfect heart, and have done *that which is* good in thy sight. And Hez-e-ki'-ah wept ᵀsore.   Neh. 5:9; 13:22 · *very much*

4 And it came to pass, afore Isaiah was gone out into the middle court, that the word of the LORD came to him, saying,

5 Turn again, and tell Hez-e-ki'-ah the captain of my people, Thus saith the LORD, the God of David thy father, ᴿI have heard thy prayer, I have seen thy tears: behold, I will heal thee: on the third day thou shalt go up unto the house of the LORD.   Ps. 65:2

6 And I will add unto thy days fifteen years; and I will deliver thee and this city out of the hand of the king of Assyria; and ᴿI will defend this city for mine own sake, and for my servant David's sake.   19:34

7 And ᴿIsaiah said, Take a lump of figs. And they took and laid *it* on the boil, and he recovered.   Is. 38:21

8 And Hez-e-ki'-ah said unto Isaiah, ᴿWhat *shall be* the sign that the LORD will heal me, and that I shall go up into the house of the LORD the third day?   Is. 7:11, 14

9 And Isaiah said, ᴿThis sign shalt thou have of the LORD, that the LORD will do the thing that he hath ᴿspoken: shall the shadow go forward ten degrees, or go back ten ᵀdegrees?   Is. 38:7, 8 · Num. 23:19 · *steps*

10 And Hez-e-ki'-ah answered, It is ᵀa light thing for the shadow to go down ten degrees: nay, but let the shadow return backward ten degrees.   *an easy*

11 And Isaiah the prophet cried unto the

LORD: and [R]he brought the shadow ten degrees backward, by which it had gone down in the dial of Ahaz.   Josh. 10:12–14; Is. 38:8

Judah's Wealth Is Exposed to Babylon
Is. 39:1, 2

12 At that time Be-ro'-dach–bal'-a-dan, the son of Bal'-a-dan, king of Babylon, sent letters and a present unto Hez-e-ki'-ah: for he had heard that Hez-e-ki'-ah had been sick.

13 And Hez-e-ki'-ah hearkened unto them, and shewed them all the house of his precious things, the silver, and the gold, and the spices, and the precious ointment, and all the house of his [T]armour, and all that was found in his treasures: there was nothing in his house, nor in all his dominion, that Hez-e-ki'-ah shewed them not.   jewels

Babylonian Exile Is Prophesied—Is. 39:3–8

14 Then came Isaiah the prophet unto king Hez-e-ki'-ah, and said unto him, What said these men? and from whence came they unto thee? And Hez-e-ki'-ah said, They are come from a far country, even from Babylon.

15 And he said, What have they seen in thine house? And Hez-e-ki'-ah answered, All the things that are in mine house have they seen: there is nothing among my treasures that I have not shewed them.

16 And Isaiah said unto Hez-e-ki'-ah, Hear the word of the LORD.

17 Behold, the days come, that all that is in thine house, and that which thy fathers have laid up in store unto this day, [R]shall be carried into Babylon: nothing shall be left, saith the LORD.   24:13; 25:13

18 And of thy sons that shall issue from thee, which thou shalt beget, [R]shall they take away; and they shall be eunuchs in the palace of the king of Babylon.   24:12

19 Then said Hez-e-ki'-ah unto Isaiah, Good is the word of the LORD which thou hast spoken. And he said, Is it not good, if peace and truth be in my days?

Death of Hezekiah—2 Chr. 32:32, 33

20 And the rest of the acts of Hez-e-ki'-ah, and all his might, and how he made a pool, and a conduit, and brought water into the city, are they not written in the book of the chronicles of the kings of Judah?

21 And [R]Hez-e-ki'-ah [T]slept with his fathers: and Ma-nas'-seh his son reigned in his stead.   2 Chr. 32:33 • died

CHAPTER 21

Spiritual Evaluation of Manasseh
2 Chr. 32:1–9

MA-NAS'-SEH [R]was twelve years old when he began to reign, and reigned

fifty and five years in Jerusalem. And his mother's name was Heph'-zi-bah.   2 Chr. 33:1

2 And he did that which was evil in the sight of the LORD, after the [T]abominations of the heathen, whom the LORD cast out before the children of Israel.   wicked practices

3 For he built up again the high places [R]which Hez-e-ki'-ah his father had destroyed; and he reared up altars for Ba'-al, and made a grove, [R]as did Ahab king of Israel; and worshipped all the host of heaven, and served them.   18:4 • 1 Kin. 16:32

4 And he built altars in the house of the LORD, of which the LORD said, In Jerusalem will I put my name.

5 And he built [T]altars for [R]all the host of heaven in the two courts of the house of the LORD.   worship centers • 23:4, 5, 12

6 And he made his son pass through the fire, and observed times, and used enchantments, and dealt with familiar spirits and wizards: he wrought much wickedness in the sight of the LORD, to provoke him to anger.

7 And he set a graven image of the grove that he had made in the house, of which the LORD said to David, and to Solomon his son, In this house, and in Jerusalem, which I have chosen out of all tribes of Israel, will I put my name for ever:

8 Neither will I make the feet of Israel move any more out of the land which I gave their fathers; only if they will observe to do according to all that I have commanded them, and according to all the law that my servant Moses commanded them.

9 But they hearkened not: and Ma-nas'-seh [R]seduced them to do more evil than did the nations whom the LORD destroyed before the children of Israel.   [Prov. 29:12]

10 And the LORD spake by his servants the prophets, saying,

11 Because Ma-nas'-seh king of Judah hath done these abominations, and hath done wickedly above all that the Am'-or-ites did, which were before him, and hath made Judah also to sin with his idols:

12 Therefore thus saith the LORD God of Israel, Behold, I am bringing such evil upon Jerusalem and Judah, that whosoever heareth of it, both [R]his ears shall tingle. Jer. 19:3

13 And I will stretch over Jerusalem the line of Sa-ma'-ri-a, and the plummet of the house of Ahab: and I will wipe Jerusalem as a man wipeth a dish, wiping it, and turning it upside down.

14 And I will forsake the remnant of mine inheritance, and deliver them into the hand of their enemies; and they shall become a prey and a spoil to all their enemies;

15 Because they have done that which was evil in my sight, and have provoked me to anger, since the day their fathers came forth out of Egypt, even unto this day.

Political Situation Under Manasseh

16 Moreover Ma-nas'-seh shed innocent blood very much, till he had filled Jerusalem from one end to another; beside his sin wherewith he made Judah to sin, in doing *that which was* evil in the sight of the LORD.

Death of Manasseh

17 Now the rest of the acts of Ma-nas'-seh, and all that he did, and his sin that he sinned, *are* they not written in the book of the chronicles of the kings of Judah?

18 And Ma-nas'-seh ᵀslept with his fathers, and was buried in the garden of his own house, in the garden of Uz'-za: and Amon his son reigned in his stead.   died

The Reign of Amon in Judah—2 Chr. 33:21-25

19 ᴿAmon *was* twenty and two years old when he began to reign, and he reigned two years in Jerusalem. And his mother's name *was* Me-shul'-le-meth, the daughter of Ha'-ruz of Jot'-bah.   *v.* 23; 2 Chr. 33:21-23

20 And he did *that which was* evil in the sight of the LORD, ᴿas his father Ma-nas'-seh did.   *vv.* 2, 6, 11, 16

21 And he walked in all the way that his father walked in, and served the idols that his father served, and worshipped them:

22 And he ᴿforsook the LORD God of his fathers, and walked not in the way of the LORD.   *v.* 17; 1 Kin. 11:33; 1 Chr. 28:9

23 ᴿAnd the servants of Amon conspired against him, and slew the king in his own house.   12:20; 14:19; 2 Chr. 33:24, 25

24 And the people of the land slew all them that had conspired against king Amon; and the people of the land made Jo-si'-ah his son king in his stead.

25 Now the rest of the acts of Amon which he did, *are* they not written in the book of the chronicles of the kings of Judah?

26 And he was buried in his sepulchre in the ᴿgarden of Uz'-za: and ᴿJo-si'-ah his son reigned in his stead.   *v.* 18 · Matt. 1:10

CHAPTER 22

Spiritual Evaluation of Josiah—2 Chr. 34:1, 2

ᴿJO-SI'-AH *was* eight years old when he began to reign, and he reigned thirty and one years in Jerusalem. And his mother's name *was* Je-di'-dah, the daughter of A-da'-iah of ᴿBos'-cath.   2 Chr. 34:1 · Josh. 15:39

2 And he did *that which was* right in the sight of the LORD, and walked in all the way of David his father, and turned not aside to the right hand or to the left.

The Temple Is Repaired—2 Chr. 34:8-13

3 ᴿAnd it came to pass in the eighteenth year of king Jo-si'-ah, *that* the king sent Sha'-phan the son of Az-a-li'-ah, the son of Me-shul'-lam, the scribe, to the house of the LORD, saying,   *vv.* 3-20; 2 Chr. 34:8

4 Go up to Hil-ki'-ah the high priest, that he may sum the silver which is brought into the house of the LORD, which the keepers of the door have gathered of the people:

5 And let them ᴿdeliver it into the hand of the doers of the work, that have the oversight of the house of the LORD: and let them give it to the doers of the work which is in the house of the LORD, to repair the breaches of the house,   12:11, 12, 14

6 Unto carpenters, and builders, and masons, and to buy timber and hewn stone to repair the house.

7 Howbeit ᴿthere was no reckoning made with them of the money that was delivered into their hand, because they dealt ᵀfaithfully.   12:15 · honestly

The Book of the Law Is Discovered 2 Chr. 34:15-18

8 And Hil-ki'-ah the high priest said unto Sha'-phan the scribe, ᴿI have found the book of the law in the house of the LORD. And Hil-ki'-ah gave the book to Sha'-phan, and he read it.   Deut. 31:24; 2 Chr. 34:14, 15

9 And Sha'-phan the scribe came to the king, and brought the king word again, and said, Thy servants have ᵀgathered the money that was found in the house, and have delivered it into the hand of them that do the work, that have the oversight of the house of the LORD.   melted

10 And ᴿSha'-phan the ᵀscribe shewed the king, saying, Hil-ki'-ah the priest hath delivered me a book. And Sha'-phan read it before the king.   2 Chr. 34:8 · secretary

Repentance of Josiah—2 Chr. 34:19-22

11 And it came to pass, when the king had heard the words of the book of the law, that he ᵀrent his clothes.   tore

12 And the king commanded Hil-ki'-ah the priest, and A-hi'-kam the son of Sha'-phan, and Ach'-bor the son of ᵀMi-cha'-iah, and Sha'-phan the scribe, and As-a-hi'-ah a servant of the king's, saying,   Micah

13 Go ye, ᵀenquire of the LORD for me, and for the people, and for all Judah, concerning the words of this book that is found: for great *is* ᴿthe wrath of the LORD that is kindled against us, because our fathers have not hearkened unto the words of this book, to do

according unto all that which is written concerning us.   *pray to* • [Deut. 29:27]

14 So Hil-ki'-ah the priest, and A-hi'-kam, and Ach'-bor, and Sha'-phan, and As-a-hi'-ah, went unto Hul'-dah the prophetess, the wife of Shal'-lum the son of Tik'-vah, the son of Har'-has, keeper of the wardrobe; (now she dwelt in Jerusalem ᵀin the college;) and they ᵀcommuned with her.   *in the second quarter* • *talked*

Prophecy of Blessing—2 Chr. 34:23-28

15 And she said unto them, Thus saith the LORD God of Israel, Tell the man that sent you to me,

16 Thus saith the LORD, Behold, I will bring evil upon this place, and upon the inhabitants thereof, *even* all the words of the book which the king of Judah hath read:

17 ᴿBecause they have forsaken me, and have burned incense unto other gods, that they might provoke me to anger with all the works of their hands; therefore my wrath shall be kindled against this place, and shall not be quenched.   21:22; Deut. 29:25

18 But to the king of Judah which sent you to enquire of the LORD, thus shall ye say to him, Thus saith the LORD God of Israel, *As touching* the words which thou has heard;

19 Because thine ᴿheart was ᵀtender, and thou hast humbled thyself before the LORD, when thou heardest what I spake against this place, and against the inhabitants thereof, that they should become a desolation and a curse, and hast rent thy clothes, and wept before me; I also have heard *thee*, saith the LORD.   [Is. 57:15] • *sensitive*

20 Behold therefore, I ᵀwill gather thee unto thy fathers, and thou shalt ᵀbe gathered into thy grave in peace; and thine eyes shall not see all the evil which I will bring upon

this place. And they brought the king word again.   *will take your life* • *die*

CHAPTER 23

Institution of the Covenant—2 Chr. 34:29-32

AND ᴿthe king sent, and they gathered unto him all the elders of Judah and of Jerusalem.   2 Chr. 34:29, 30

2 And the king went up into the house of the LORD, and all the men of Judah and all the inhabitants of Jerusalem with him, and the priests, and the prophets, and all the people, both small and great: and ᴿhe read in their ears all the words of the book of the covenant ᴿwhich was found in the house of the LORD.   Deut. 31:10-13 • 22:8

3 And the king stood by a pillar, and made ᵀa covenant before the LORD, to walk after the LORD, and to keep his commandments and his testimonies and his statutes with all *their* heart and all *their* soul, to perform the words of this covenant that were written in this book. And all the people stood to the covenant.   *an agreement*

Reforms Because of the Covenant
2 Chr. 34:33—35:19

4 And the king commanded Hil-ki'-ah the high priest, and the priests of the second order, and the keepers of the door, to bring forth out of the temple of the LORD all the vessels that were made for Ba'-al, and for ᴿthe grove, and for all the host of heaven: and he burned them ᵀwithout Jerusalem in the fields of Kid'-ron, and carried the ashes of them unto Beth'-el.   21:3, 7 • *outside*

23:3 Knowing the Will of God Through the Scriptures—The best way to study a subject often begins with a definition of that subject. What do we mean by the will of God? It is that holy and stated purpose of the Father to make His dear children as much like Christ as possible.

Without doubt the most important factor in finding God's will is the Bible itself. God speaks to us not in some loud voice, but through the Scriptures. *First,* the Scriptures declare He does have a definite will for my life. "The steps of a good man are ordered by the LORD" (Page 563—Ps. 37:23). "I will instruct thee and teach thee in the way which thou shalt go" (Page 560—Ps. 32:8). See also Ephesians 2:10; Hebrews 12:1. *Second,* God desires us to know this will for our lives. "Wherefore be ye not unwise, but understanding what the will of the Lord *is*" (Page 1165—Eph. 5:17). *Third,* this will is continuous. It does not begin when I am thirty years of age. God has a will for children, young people, adults, and senior citizens. See Isaiah 58:11. *Fourth,* God's will is specific. "And thine ears shall hear a word behind thee, saying, This *is* the way, walk ye in it" (Page 679—Is. 30:21). "The way of the righteous *is* made plain" (Page 624—Prov. 15:19). *Fifth,* God's will is profitable (Page 217—Josh. 1:8; Page 548—Ps. 1:1–3).

What is the will of God for us? As we have already noted, it differs from believer to believer. But here are four aspects in the will of God which apply to every Christian:
a. It is His will that we learn more about God (Page 1176—Col. 1:9).
b. It is His will that we grow in grace (Page 1185—1 Thess. 4:3).
c. It is His will that we study His Word (Page 1202—2 Tim. 3:14–17).
d. It is His will that we share our faith (Page 1072—Acts 1:8; Page 1194—1 Tim. 2:4; Page 1244—2 Pet. 3:9).

Now turn to Page 832—Dan. 9:3, 4: Knowing the Will of God Through Prayer and Fasting.

5 And he put down the idolatrous priests, whom the kings of Judah had ordained to burn incense in the high places in the cities of Judah, and in the places round about Jerusalem; them also that burned incense unto Ba'-al, to the sun, and to the moon, and to the planets, and to all the host of heaven.

6 And he brought out the ᴿgrove from the house of the LORD, without Jerusalem, unto the brook Kid'-ron, and burned it at the brook Kid'-ron, and stamped it small to powder, and cast the powder thereof upon the graves of the children of the people.   21:7

7 And he brake down the houses ᴿof the sodomites, that were by the house of the LORD, ᴿwhere the women wove hangings for the ᵀgrove.   1 Kin. 14:24 · Ezek. 16:16 · wooden idols

8 And he brought all the priests out of the cities of Judah, and defiled the high places where the priests had burned incense, from ᴿGe'-ba to Be'-er-she'-ba, and brake down the high places of the gates that were in the entering in of the gate of Joshua the governor of the city, which were on a man's left hand at the gate of the city.   1 Kin. 15:22

9 Nevertheless the priests of the high places came not up to the altar of the LORD in Jerusalem, but they did eat of the unleavened bread among their brethren.

10 And he defiled To'-pheth, which is in the valley of the children of Hin'-nom, that no man might make his son or his daughter to pass through the fire to Mo'-lech.

11 And he took away the horses that the kings of Judah had given to the sun, at the entering in of the house of the LORD, by the chamber of Na'-than-me'-lech the chamberlain, which was in the suburbs, and burned the chariots of the sun with fire.

12 And the altars that were on the top of the upper chamber of Ahaz, which the kings of Judah had made, and the altars which Ma-nas'-seh had made in the two courts of the house of the LORD, did the king beat down, and brake them down from thence, and cast the dust of them into the brook Kid'-ron.

13 And the high places that were before Jerusalem, which were on the right hand of the mount of ᵀcorruption, which Solomon the king of Israel had builded for Ash'-to-reth the abomination of the Zi-do'-ni-ans, and for Che'-mosh the abomination of the Mo'-ab-ites, and for Mil'-com the abomination of the children of Ammon, did the king defile.   evil

14 And he brake in pieces the images, and cut down the ᵀgroves, and filled their places with the bones of men.   female symbols

15 Moreover the altar that was at Beth'-el, and the ᴿhigh place which Jer-o-bo'-am the son of Ne'-bat, who made Israel to sin, had made, both that ᵀaltar and the high place he brake down, and burned the high place, and stamped it small to powder, and burned the grove.   1 Kin. 12:28-33; 13:2 · worship center

16 And as Jo-si'-ah turned himself, he spied the sepulchres that were there in the mount, and sent, and took the bones out of the sepulchres, and burned them upon the altar, and polluted it, according to the word of the LORD which the man of God proclaimed, who proclaimed these words.

17 Then he said, What ᵀtitle is that that I see? And the men of the city told him, It is ᴿthe sepulchre of the man of God, which came from Judah, and proclaimed these things that thou hast done against the altar of Beth'-el.   monument · 1 Kin. 13:1, 30, 31

18 And he said, Let him alone; let no man move his bones. So they let his bones alone, with the bones of ᴿthe prophet that came out of Sa-ma'-ri-a.   1 Kin. 13:11, 31

19 And all the houses also of the ᵀhigh places that were in the cities of Sa-ma'-ri-a, which the kings of Israel had made to provoke the LORD to anger, Jo-si'-ah took away, and did to them according to all the acts that he had done in Beth'-el.   pagan shrines

20 And ᴿhe slew all the priests of the high places that were there upon the altars, and burned men's bones upon them, and returned to Jerusalem.   1 Kin. 13:2

21 And the king commanded all the people, saying, ᴿKeep the passover unto the LORD your God, ᴿas it is written in the book of this covenant.   2 Chr. 35:1-17 · Ex. 12:3

22 Surely there was not holden such a passover from the days of the judges that judged Israel, nor in all the days of the kings of Israel, nor of the kings of Judah;

23 But in the eighteenth year of king Jo-si'-ah, wherein this passover was holden to the LORD in Jerusalem.

24 Moreover the workers with ᵀfamiliar spirits, and the wizards, and the ᵀimages, and the idols, and all the abominations that were spied in the land of Judah and in Jerusalem, did Jo-si'-ah put away, that he might perform the words of the law which were written in the book that Hil-ki'-ah the priest found in the house of the LORD.   mediums · carved symbols

25 And like unto him was there no king before him, that turned to the LORD with all his heart, and with all his soul, and with all his might, according to all the law of Moses; neither after him arose there any like him.

26 Notwithstanding the LORD turned not from the fierceness of his great wrath, wherewith his anger was kindled against Judah, because of all the provocations that Ma-nas'-seh had provoked him withal.

27 And the LORD said, I will remove Judah also out of my sight, as ᴿI have removed Israel, and will cast off this city Jerusalem which I have chosen, and the house of which I said, My name shall be there.   1 Kin. 8:29; 9:3

Political Situation Under Josiah
2 Chr. 35:20–23

28 Now the rest of the acts of Jo-si'-ah, and all that he did, *are* they not written in the book of the chronicles of the kings of Judah?

29 In his days Pha'-raoh–ne'-choh king of Egypt went up against the king of Assyria to the river Eu-phra'-tes: and king Jo-si'-ah went against him; and he slew him at Me-gid'-do, when he had seen him.

Death of Josiah
2 Chr. 35:24—36:1

30 ᴿAnd his servants carried him in a chariot dead from Me-gid'-do, and brought him to Jerusalem, and buried him in his own sepulchre. And ᴿthe people of the land took Je-ho'-a-haz the son of Jo-si'-ah, and anointed him, and made him king in his father's stead.   2 Chr. 35:24 • 2 Chr. 36:1

The Reign of Jehoahaz in Judah—2 Chr. 36:2–4

31 Je-ho'-a-haz *was* twenty and three years old when he began to reign; and he reigned three months in Jerusalem. And his mother's name *was* ᴿHa-mu'-tal, the daughter of Jer-e-mi'-ah of Lib'-nah.   24:18

32 ᴿAnd he did *that which was* evil in the sight of the LORD, according to all that his fathers had done.   21:2–7; Judg. 2:11

33 And Pha'-raoh–ne'-choh put him in bands at Rib'-lah in the land of Ha'-math, that he might not reign in Jerusalem; and put the land to a tribute of an ᵀhundred talents of silver, and a ᵀtalent of gold. $38,400,000 • $5,760,000

34 And Pha'-raoh–ne'-choh made E-li'-a-kim the son of Jo-si'-ah king in the room of Jo-si'-ah his father, and turned his name to Je-hoi'-a-kim, and took Je-ho'-a-haz away: and he came to Egypt, and died there.

The Reign of Jehoiakim in Judah
2 Chr. 36:5–8

35 And Je-hoi'-a-kim gave the silver and the gold to Pharaoh; but he taxed the land to give the money according to the commandment of Pharaoh: he exacted the silver and the gold of the people of the land, of every one according to his taxation, to give *it* unto Pha'-raoh–ne'-choh.

36 ᴿJe-hoi'-a-kim *was* twenty and five years old when he began to reign; and he reigned eleven years in Jerusalem. And his mother's name *was* Ze-bu'-dah, the daughter of Pe-da'-iah of Ru'-mah.   2 Chr. 36:5

37 And he did *that which was* evil in the

sight of the LORD, ᴿaccording to all that his fathers had done.   v. 32

CHAPTER 24

IN ᴿhis days Neb-u-chad-nez'-zar king of Babylon came up, and Je-hoi'-a-kim became his servant three years: then he turned and rebelled against him.   Dan. 1:1

2 ᴿAnd the LORD sent against him ᵀbands of the Chal'-dees, and bands of the Syrians, and bands of the Mo'-ab-ites, and bands of the children of Ammon, and sent them against Judah to destroy it, according to the word of the LORD, which he spake by his servants the prophets.   Ezek. 19:8 • *armies*

3 Surely at the commandment of the LORD came *this* upon Judah, to remove *them* out of his sight, for the sins of Ma-nas'-seh, according to all that he did;

4 ᴿAnd also for the innocent blood that he shed: for he filled Jerusalem with innocent blood; which the LORD would not pardon.   21:16

5 Now the rest of the acts of Je-hoi'-a-kim, and all that he did, *are* they not written in the book of the chronicles of the kings of Judah?

6 ᴿSo Je-hoi'-a-kim slept with his fathers: and Je-hoi'-a-chin his son reigned in his stead.   2 Chr. 36:6, 8; Jer. 22:18, 19

7 And the king of Egypt came not again any more out of his land: for ᴿthe king of Babylon had taken from the ᴿriver of Egypt unto the river Eu-phra'-tes all that pertained to the king of Egypt.   Jer. 46:2 • Gen. 15:18

The Reign of Jehoiachin in Judah
2 Chr. 36:9, 10

8 ᴿJe-hoi'-a-chin *was* eighteen years old when he began to reign, and he reigned in Jerusalem three months. And his mother's name *was* Ne-hush'-ta, the daughter of El-na'-than of Jerusalem.   1 Chr. 3:16; 2 Chr. 36:9

9 And he did *that which was* evil in the sight of the LORD, ᴿaccording to all that his father had done.   2 Kin. 21:2–7

10 At that time the servants of Neb-u-chad-nez'-zar king of Babylon came up against Jerusalem, and the city was besieged.

11 And Neb-u-chad-nez'-zar king of Babylon came ᴿagainst the city, and his servants did besiege it.   Dan. 1:1

12 And ᴿJe-hoi'-a-chin the king of Judah went out to the king of Babylon, he, and his mother, and his servants, and his princes, and his officers: and the king of Babylon took him in the eighth year of his reign.   Jer. 24:1

13 ᴿAnd he carried out thence all the treasures of the house of the LORD, and the treasures of the king's house, and cut in pieces all the vessels of gold which Solomon king of Israel had made in the temple of the LORD, as the LORD had said.   20:17

14 And ℛhe ᵀcarried away all Jerusalem, and all the princes, and all the mighty men of valour, *even* ten thousand captives, and all the craftsmen and smiths: none remained, save ℛthe poorest sort of the people of the land.   Jer. 24:1 • *took into captivity* • 25:12

15 And he carried away Je-hoi′-a-chin to Babylon, and the king's mother, and the king's wives, and his officers, and the mighty of the land, *those* carried he into captivity from Jerusalem to Babylon.

16 And ℛall the men of might, *even* seven thousand, and craftsmen and smiths a thousand, all *that were* strong *and* ᵀapt for war, even them the king of Babylon brought captive to Babylon.   Jer. 52:28 • *able*

Spiritual Evaluation of Zedekiah
2 Chr. 36:10–16; Jer. 52:1, 2

17 And ℛthe king of Babylon made Mat-ta-ni′-ah his father's brother king in his stead, and changed his name to Zed-e-ki′-ah. Jer. 37:1

18 ℛZed-e-ki′-ah *was* twenty and one years old when he began to reign, and he reigned eleven years in Jerusalem. And his mother's name *was* ℛHa-mu′-tal, the daughter of Jer-e-mi′-ah of Lib′-nah.   Jer. 52:1 • 23:31

19 ℛAnd he did *that which was* evil in the sight of the LORD, according to all that Je-hoi′-a-kim had done.   2 Chr. 36:12, 13

Political Situation Under Zedekiah
2 Chr. 36:17–20; Jer. 52:3–27

20 For through the anger of the LORD it came to pass in Jerusalem and Judah, until he had cast them out from his presence, ℛthat Zed-e-ki′-ah rebelled against the king of Babylon.   2 Chr. 36:13; Ezek. 17:15

CHAPTER 25

AND it came to pass in the ninth year of his reign, in the tenth month, in the tenth *day* of the month, *that* Neb-u-chad-nez′-zar king of Babylon came, he, and all his host, against Jerusalem, and pitched against it; and they built forts against it round about.

2 And the city was besieged unto the eleventh year of king Zed-e-ki′-ah.

3 And on the ninth *day* of the *fourth* month the famine prevailed in the city, and there was no bread for the people of the land.

4 And the city was broken up, and all the men of war *fled* by night by the way of the gate between two walls, which *is* by the king's garden: (now the Chal′-dees *were* against the city round about:) and *the king* went the way toward the plain.

5 And the army of the Chal′-dees pursued after the king, and overtook him in the plains of ℛJericho: and all his army were scattered from him.   Num. 22:1; 2 Chr. 28:15

6 So they took the king, and brought him up to the king of Babylon to Rib′-lah; and they gave judgment upon him.

7 And they slew the sons of Zed-e-ki′-ah before his eyes, and put out the eyes of Zed-e-ki′-ah, and bound him with fetters of brass, and carried him to Babylon.

8 And in the fifth month, on the seventh *day* of the month, which *is* the nineteenth year of king Neb-u-chad-nez′-zar king of Babylon, came Neb′-u-zar-a′-dan, ᵀcaptain of the guard, a servant of the king of Babylon, unto Jerusalem: *chief marshall*

9 ℛAnd he burnt the house of the LORD, ℛand the king's house, and all the houses of Jerusalem, and every great *man's* house burnt he with fire.   2 Chr. 36:19 • Jer. 39:8

10 And all the army of the Chal′-dees, that *were with* the captain of the guard, brake down the walls of Jerusalem round about.

11 Now the rest of the people *that were* left in the city, and the fugitives that fell away to the king of Babylon, with the remnant of the multitude, did Neb′-u-zar-a′-dan the captain of the guard carry away.

12 But the captain of the guard ℛleft of the poor of the land *to be* vinedressers and ᵀhusbandmen.   24:14; Jer. 40:7 • *farmers*

13 And the pillars of brass that *were* in the house of the LORD, and the bases, and the brasen sea that *was* in the house of the LORD, did the Chal′-dees break in pieces, and carried the brass of them to Babylon.

14 And ℛthe pots, and the shovels, and the snuffers, and the spoons, and all the vessels of brass wherewith they ministered, took they away.   Ex. 27:3; 1 Kin. 7:45

15 And the ℛfirepans, and the bowls, *and* such things as *were* of gold, *in* gold, and of silver, *in* silver, the captain of the guard took away.   Ex. 25:29

16 The two pillars, one sea, and the bases which Solomon had made for the house of the LORD; ℛthe brass of all these vessels was without weight.   1 Kin. 7:47

17 The height of the one pillar *was* ᵀeighteen cubits, and the ᵀchapiter upon it *was* brass: and the height of the chapiter *was* ᵀthree cubits; and the wreathen work, and pomegranates upon the chapiter round about, all of brass: and like unto these had the second pillar with wreathen work.   27 ft. • *capital* • 4.5 ft.

18 ℛAnd the captain of the guard took Se-ra′-iah the chief priest, and Zeph-a-ni′-ah the second priest, and the three keepers of the ᵀdoor: Jer. 52:24 • *threshold*

19 And out of the city he took an officer that was set over the men of war, and five men of them that were in the king's presence, which were found in the city, and the principal scribe of the host, which mustered the people of the land, and threescore men of

the people of the land *that were* found in the city:

20 And Neb'-u-zar-a'-dan captain of the guard took these, and brought them to the king of Babylon to ^RRib'-lah: 23:33

21 And the king of Babylon smote them, and slew them at Rib'-lah in the land of Ha'-math. ^RSo Judah was carried away out of their land.   Lev. 26:33; Deut. 28:36, 64

The Governorship of Gedaliah
Jer. 40:5—41:18

22 ^RAnd *as for* the people that remained in the land of Judah, whom Neb-u-chad-nez'-zar king of Babylon had left, even over them he made Ged-a-li'-ah the son of A-hi'-kam, the son of Sha'-phan, ruler.   Jer. 40:5

23 And when all the captains of the armies, they and their men, heard that the king of Babylon had made Ged-a-li'-ah governor, there came to Ged-a-li'-ah to ^RMiz'-pah, even Ish'-ma-el the son of Neth-a-ni'-ah, and Jo-ha'-nan the son of Ca-re'-ah, and Se-ra'-iah the son of Tan'-hu-meth the Ne-toph'-a-thite, and Ja-az-a-ni'-ah the son of a Ma-ach'-a-thite, they and their men.   Josh. 18:26

24 And Ged-a-li'-ah sware to them, and to their men, and said unto them, Fear not to be the servants of the Chal'-dees: dwell in the land, and serve the king of Babylon; and it shall be well with you.

25 But it came to pass in the seventh month, that Ish'-ma-el the son of Neth-a-ni'-ah, the son of E-lish'-a-ma, of the seed royal, came, and ten men with him, and ^Tsmote Ged-a-li'-ah, that he died, and the Jews and the Chal'-dees that were with him at Miz'-pah.   *struck and killed*

26 And all the people, both small and great, and the captains of the armies, arose, ^Rand came to Egypt: ^Rfor they were afraid of the Chal'-dees.   Jer. 43:4, 7 • Lev. 26:36

The Release of Jehoiachin in Babylon
Jer. 52:31—34

27 And it came to pass in the seven and thirtieth year of the captivity of Je-hoi'-a-chin king of Judah, in the twelfth month, on the seven and twentieth *day* of the month, *that* E'-vil-me-ro'-dach king of Babylon in the year that he began to reign did ^Tlift up the head of Je-hoi'-a-chin king of Judah out of prison;   *released*

28 And he spake kindly to him, and set his throne above the throne of the kings that *were* with him in Babylon;

29 And changed his prison garments: and he ^Tdid eat bread continually before him all the days of his life.   *ate with him always*

30 And his allowance *was* a continual allowance given him of the king, a daily rate for every day, all the days of his life.

Measures of Length

Unit	Length	Equivalents	Translations
Day's journey	c. 20 miles		day's journey
Roman mile	4,854 feet	8 stadia	mile
Sabbath day's journey	3,637 feet	6 stadia	sabbath day's journey
Stadion	606 feet	1/8 Roman mile	furlong
Rod	9 feet (10.5 feet in Ezekiel)	3 paces; 6 cubits	measuring reed, reed
Fathom	6 feet	4 cubits	fathom
Pace	3 feet	1/3 rod; 2 cubits	pace
Cubit	18 inches	1/2 pace; 2 spans	cubit
Span	9 inches	1/2 cubit; 3 hand-breadths	span
Handbreadth	3 inches	1/3 span; 4 fingers	handbreadth
Finger	.75 inches	1/4 handbreadth	finger

CHRONICLES

THE BOOK OF FIRST CHRONICLES

The books of First and Second Chronicles cover the same period of Jewish history described in Second Samuel through Second Kings, but the perspective is different. These books are no mere repetition of the same material, but rather form a divine editorial on the history of God's people. While Second Samuel and First and Second Kings give a political history of Israel and Judah, First and Second Chronicles present a religious history of the Davidic dynasty of Judah. The former are written from a prophetic and moral viewpoint, and the latter from a priestly and spiritual perspective. The Book of First Chronicles begins with the royal line of David and then traces the spiritual significance of David's righteous reign.

The books of First and Second Chronicles were originally one continuous work in the Hebrew. The title was *Dibere Hayyamim*, meaning "The Words [accounts, events] of the Days." The equivalent meaning today would be "The Events of the Times." Chronicles was divided into two parts in the third century B.C. Greek translation of the Hebrew Bible (the Septuagint). At that time it was given the name *Paraleipomenon*, "Of Things Omitted," referring to the things omitted from Samuel and Kings. Some copies add the phrase, *Basileon Iouda*, "Concerning the Kings of Judah." The first book of Chronicles was called *Paraleipomenon Primus*, "The First Book of Things Omitted." The name "Chronicles" comes from Jerome in his Latin Vulgate Bible (A.D. 385–405): *Chronicorum Liber*. He meant his title in the sense of "The Chronicles of the Whole of Sacred History."

THE AUTHOR OF FIRST CHRONICLES

Although the text does not identify the author, several facts seem to support the tradition in the Jewish Talmud that Ezra the priest was the author. The content points to a priestly authorship because of the emphasis on the temple, the priesthood, and the theocratic line of David in the southern kingdom of Judah. The narrative also indicates that Chronicles was at least written by a contemporary of Ezra. Chronicles is quite similar in style to the Book of Ezra, and both share a priestly perspective: genealogies, temple worship, ministry of the priesthood, and obedience to the law of God. In addition, the closing verses of Second Chronicles (36:22, 23) are repeated with minor changes as the opening verses of Ezra (1:1–3). Thus, Chronicles and Ezra may have been one consecutive history as were Luke and Acts.

Ezra was an educated scribe (Ezra 7:6), and according to the apocryphal Book of Second Maccabees 2:13–15, Nehemiah collected an extensive library which was available to Ezra for his use in compiling Chronicles. Many of these documents and sources are listed in the book (see "The Author of Second Chronicles"). Scholars of Israel accumulated and compared historical material, and the author of Chronicles was actually a compiler who drew from many sources under the guidance and inspiration of the Holy Spirit.

THE TIME OF FIRST CHRONICLES

The genealogies in chapters 1—9 cover the time from Adam to David, and chapters 10—29 focus on the thirty-three years of David's rule over the united kingdoms of Israel and Judah (1004–971 B.C.). However, the genealogies extend to about 500 B.C., as seen in the mention of Zerubbabel, grandson of King Jeconiah, who leads the first return of the Jews from exile in 538 B.C., and also Zerubbabel's two grandsons Pelatiah and Jesaiah (3:21).

Ezra probably completed Chronicles between 450 and 430 B.C. and addressed it to the returned remnant. Ezra leads some of the exiles to Jerusalem in 457 B.C. and ministers to the people as their spiritual leader. During Ezra's time, Nehemiah is the political leader and Malachi is the moral leader. Chronicles spends a disproportionate time on the reigns of David and Solomon because they bring the nation to its pinnacle. The book is written to the people of Israel's "Second Commonwealth" to encourage them and to remind them that they must remain the covenant people of God. This reminds the Jews of their spiritual heritage and identity during the difficult times they are facing.

THE CHRIST OF FIRST CHRONICLES

See the introductions to First and Second Samuel for descriptions of David as a figure of Christ. The Davidic Covenant of Second Samuel 7 is found again in First Chronicles 7:11–14. Solomon fulfilled part, but the promise of eternality of David's throne can only point to the coming of the Messiah.

The tribe of Judah is placed first in the national genealogy in First Chronicles because the monarchy, temple, and Messiah (Gen. 49:10) will come from this tribe. Since the books of Chronicles are the last books of the Hebrew

Bible, the genealogies in chapters 1—9 are a preamble to the genealogy of Christ in the first book of the New Testament.

KEYS TO FIRST CHRONICLES

Key Verses: First Chronicles 17:11-14; 29:11—"And it shall come to pass, when thy days be expired that thou must go to be with thy fathers, that I will raise up thy seed after thee, which shall be of thy sons; and I will establish his kingdom. He shall build me an house, and I will stablish his throne for ever. I will be his father, and he shall be my son: and I will not take my mercy away from him, as I took it from him that was before thee: But I will settle him in mine house and in my kingdom for ever: and his throne shall be established for evermore" (17:11-14).

"Thine, O LORD, is the greatness, and the power, and the glory, and the victory, and the majesty: for all that is in the heaven and in the earth is thine; thine is the kingdom, O LORD, and thou art exalted as head above all" (29:11).

Key Chapter· First Chronicles 17—Pivotal for the Book of First Chronicles as well as for the rest of the Scriptures is the Davidic Covenant recorded in Second Samuel 7 and First Chronicles 17. God promises David that He will "settle him [David's ultimate offspring, Jesus Christ] in mine house and in my kingdom for ever: and his throne shall be established for evermore" (1 Chr. 17:14).

SURVEY OF FIRST CHRONICLES

Chronicles retraces the whole story of Israel's history up to the return from captivity in order to give the returned remnant a divine perspective on the developments of their past. The whole Book of First Chronicles, like Second Samuel, is dedicated to the life of David. It begins with the royal line of David (1—9) before surveying key events of the reign of David (10—29).

Royal Line of David (1—9): These nine chapters are the most comprehensive genealogical tables in the Bible. They trace the family tree of David and Israel as a whole, but in a highly selective manner. The genealogies place a disproportionate emphasis on the tribes of Judah and Benjamin because Chronicles is not concerned with the northern kingdom but with the southern kingdom and the Davidic dynasty. They show God at work in selecting and preserving a people for Himself from the beginning of human history to the period after the Babylonian exile. The genealogies move from the patriarchal period (Adam to Jacob; 1:1—2:2) to the national period (Judah, Levi, and the other tribes of Israel; 2:3— 9:44). They demonstrate God's keeping of His covenant promises in maintaining the Davidic line through the centuries. The priestly perspective of Chronicles is evident in the special attention given to the tribe of Levi.

Reign of David (10—29): Compared with Second Samuel, David's life in First Chronicles is seen in an entirely different light. This is clear from both the omissions and the additions. Chronicles completely omits David's struggles with Saul, his seven-year reign in Hebron, his various wives, and Absalom's rebellion. It also omits the event in Second Samuel that hurt the rest of his life—his sin with Bath-sheba. Chronicles is written from a more positive perspective, emphasizing God's grace and forgiveness, in order to encourage the Jews who have just returned from captivity. Chronicles adds events not found in Second Samuel, such as David's preparations for the temple and its worship services.

Only one chapter is given to Saul's reign (10), because his heart was not right with God. David's story begins with his coronation over all Israel after he has already reigned for seven years as king over Judah. Chronicles stresses his deep

FOCUS	ROYAL LINE OF DAVID		REIGN OF DAVID				
REFERENCE	1:1	10:1 — 13:1	18:1	21:1		28:1 — 29:30	
DIVISION	GENEALOGIES OF DAVID AND ISRAEL	ACCESSION OF DAVID AS KING	ACQUISITION OF THE ARK	VICTORIES OF DAVID	PREPARATION FOR THE TEMPLE	LAST DAYS OF DAVID	
TOPIC	GENEALOGY			HISTORY			
	ANCESTRY			ACTIVITY			
LOCATION			ISRAEL				
TIME	THOUSANDS OF YEARS			c. 33 YEARS			

spiritual commitment, courage, and integrity. It emphasizes his concern for the things of the Lord, including his return of the ark and his desire to build a temple for God. God establishes His crucial covenant with David (17), and the kingdom is strengthened and expanded under his reign (18—20). His sin in numbering the people is recorded to teach the consequences of disobeying God's law. Most of the rest of the book (22—29) is concerned with David's preparations for the building of the temple and the worship associated with it. The priestly perspective of Chronicles can be seen in the disproportionate space given to the temple and the priests. David is not allowed to build the temple (28:3), but he designs the plans, gathers the materials, prepares the site, and arranges for the Levites, priests, choirs, porters, soldiers, and stewards. The book closes with his beautiful public prayer of praise and the accession of Solomon.

OUTLINE OF FIRST CHRONICLES

Part One: The Royal Line of David (1:1—9:44)

Part Two: The Reign of David (10:1—29:30)

CHAPTER 1

The Genealogy from Adam to Noah
Gen. 5:1–32; Luke 3:36–38

ADAM, ᴿSheth, E'-nosh, Gen. 4:25
2 Ke'-nan, Ma-ha'-la-le-el, Je'-red,
3 He'-noch, Me-thu'-se-lah, La'-mech,
4 Noah, Shem, Ham, and Ja'-pheth.

Sons of Japheth—Gen. 10:2–5

5 The sons of Ja'-pheth; Go'-mer, and Ma'-gog, and Ma'-dai, and Ja'-van, and Tu'-bal, and Me'-shech, and Ti'-ras.
6 And the sons of Go'-mer; Ash-che'-naz, and ᵀRi'-phath, and To-gar'-mah. Diphath
7 And the sons of Ja'-van; E-li'-shah, and Tar'-shish, Kit'-tim, and Dod'-a-nim.

Sons of Ham—Gen. 10:6–18

8 ᴿThe sons of Ham; Cush, and Miz'-ra-im, Put, and Canaan. Gen. 10:6
9 And the sons of Cush; Se'-ba, and Hav'-i-lah, and Sab'-ta, and Ra'-a-mah, and Sab'-te-cha. And the sons of Ra'-a-mah; She'-ba, and De'-dan.
10 And Cush begat Nimrod: he began to be ᵀmighty upon the earth. great
11 And Miz'-ra-im begat Lu'-dim, and An'-a-mim, and Le'-ha-bim, and Napth'-tu-him,
12 And Path-ru'-sim, and Cas'-lu-him, (of whom came the Phi-lis'-tines,) and ᴿCaph'-tho-rim. Deut. 2:23
13 And ᴿCanaan begat Zi'-don his first-born, and Heth, Gen. 10:15

14 The Jeb'-u-site also, and the Am'-or-ite, and the Gir'-ga-shite,

15 And the Hi'-vite, and the Ark'-ite, and the Si'-nite,

16 And the Ar'-vad-ite, and the Zem'-a-rite, and the Ha'-math-ite.

Sons of Shem
Gen. 10:21–29; 11:10–26; Luke 3:34–36

17 The sons of ᴿShem; E'-lam, and Assh'-ur, and Ar-phax'-ad, and Lud, and A'-ram, and Uz, and Hul, and Ge'-ther, and ᵀMe'-shech. *Gen. 10:22; 11:10 · Mash, Gen. 10:23*

18 And Ar-phax'-ad begat She'-lah, and She'-lah begat E'-ber.

19 And unto E'-ber were born two sons: the name of the one *was* Pe'-leg; because in his days the ᵀearth was divided: and his brother's name *was* Jok'-tan. *land*

20 And Jok'-tan begat Al-mo'-dad, and She'-leph, and Ha'-zar-ma'-veth, and Je'-rah,

21 Ha-do'-ram also, and U'-zal, and Dik'-lah,

22 And E'-bal, and A-bim'-a-el, and She'-ba,

23 And O'-phir, and Hav'-i-lah, and Jo'-bab. All these *were* the sons of Jok'-tan.

24 ᴿShem, Ar-phax'-ad, She'-lah, *Luke 3:36*

25 ᴿE'-ber, Pe'-leg, Re'-u, *Gen. 11:15*

26 Se'-rug, Na'-hor, Te'-rah,

27 ᴿAbram; the same is Abraham. *Gen. 17:5*

The Genealogy from Abraham to Isaac
Gen. 25:1–4, 12–16

28 The sons of Abraham; ᴿIsaac, and ᴿIsh'-ma-el. *Gen. 21:2 · Gen. 16:11, 15*

29 These *are* their generations: The firstborn of Ish'-ma-el, Ne-ba'-ioth; then Ke'-dar, and Ad'-be-el, and Mib'-sam,

30 Mish'-ma, and Du'-mah, Mas'-sa, ᵀHa'-dad,ᴿ and Te'-ma, *Hadar · Gen. 25:15*

31 Je'-tur, Na'-phish, and Ked'-e-mah. These are the sons of Ish'-ma-el.

32 Now the sons of Ke-tu'-rah, Abraham's concubine: she bare Zim'-ran, and Jok'-shan, and Me'-dan, and Mid'-i-an, and Ish'-bak, and Shu'-ah. And the sons of Jok'-shan; She'-ba, and De'-dan.

33 And the sons of Mid'-i-an; E'-phah, and E'-pher, and He'-noch, and A-bi'-da, and El-da'-ah. All these *are* the sons of Ke-tu'-rah.

34 And ᴿAbraham begat Isaac. The sons of Isaac; Esau and Israel. *Gen. 21:2*

Sons of Esau—Gen. 36:1–30

35 The sons of Esau; El'-i-phaz, Reu'el, and Je'-ush, and Ja-a'-lam, and Ko'-rah.

36 The sons of El'-i-phaz; ᴿTe'-man, and Omar, ᵀZe'-phi, and Ga'-tam, Ke'-naz, and Tim'-na, and Am'-a-lek. *Gen. 36:11 · Zepho*

37 The sons of Reu'-el; Na'-hath, Ze'-rah, Sham'-mah, and Miz'-zah.

38 And the sons of Se'-ir; Lo'-tan, and Sho'-bal, and Zib'-e-on, and A'-nah, and Di'-shon, and E'-zar, and Di'-shan.

39 And the sons of Lo'-tan; Ho'-ri, and Ho'-mam: and Tim'-na *was* Lo'-tan's sister.

40 The sons of Sho'-bal; A-li'-an, and Ma-na'-hath, and E'-bal, She'-phi, and O'-nam. And the sons of Zib'-e-on; A'-iah, and A'-nah.

41 The sons of A'-nah; Di'-shon. And the sons of Di'-shon; Am'-ram, and Esh'-ban, and Ith'-ran, and Che'-ran.

42 The sons of E'-zer; ᴿBil'-han, and Za'-van, and ᵀJa'-kan. The sons of Di'-shan; Uz, and A'-ran. *Gen. 36:27 · A'-kan*

Kings of Edom

43 Now these *are* the ᴿkings that reigned in the land of E'-dom before *any* king reigned over the children of Israel; Be'-la the son of Be'-or: and the name of his city *was* Din'-ha-bah. *Gen. 36:31–43*

44 And when Be'-la was dead, Jo'-bab the son of Ze'-rah of ᴿBoz'-rah reigned in his stead. *Is. 34:6*

45 And when Jo'-bab was dead, Hu'-sham of the land of the ᴿTe'-man-ites reigned in his ᵀstead. *Job 2:11 · place*

46 And when Hu'-sham was dead, Ha'-dad the son of Be'-dad, which ᵀsmote Mid'-i-an in the field of Moab, reigned in his stead: and the name of his city *was* A'-vith. *defeated*

47 And when Ha'-dad was dead, Sam'-lah of Mas-re'-kah reigned in his stead.

48 ᴿAnd when Sam'-lah was dead, Sha'-ul of Re-ho'-both by the river reigned in his stead. *Gen. 36:37*

49 And when Sha'-ul was dead, Ba'-al-ha'-nan the son of Ach'-bor reigned in his stead.

50 And when Ba'-al-ha'-nan was dead, Ha'-dad reigned in his stead: and the name of his city *was* Pa'-i; and his wife's name *was* Me-het'-a-bel, the daughter of Ma'-tred, the daughter of Mez'-a-hab.

Chiefs of Edom

51 Ha'-dad died also. And the ᴿdukes of E'-dom were; duke Tim'-nah, duke ᵀA-li'-ah, duke Je'-theth, *Gen. 36:40 · Alvah*

52 Duke A-hol-i-ba'-mah, duke E'-lah, duke Pi'-non,

53 Duke Ke'-naz, ᵀduke Te'-man, duke Mib'-zar, *chief*

54 Duke Mag'-di-el, duke I'-ram. These *are* the dukes of E'-dom.

CHAPTER 2

The Genealogy of the Sons of Jacob
Gen. 29:31–30:24; 35:16–18

THESE *are* the sons of ᵀIsrael; ᴿReuben, Simeon, Levi, and Judah, Is'-sa-char, and Zeb'-u-lun, *Jacob · Gen. 29:32; 35:22–26*

2 ᴿDan, Joseph, and Benjamin, Naph'-ta-li, Gad, and Asher.   Gen. 30:5

The Genealogy of the Sons of Judah
Gen. 46:12; Ruth 4:18–22; Matt. 1:3–6;
Luke 3:31–33

3 The sons of Judah; Er, and O'-nan, and She'-lah: which three were born unto him of the daughter of Shu'-a the Ca'-naan-i-tess. And Er, the firstborn of Judah, was evil in the sight of the LORD; and he slew him.

4 And ᴿTa'-mar his daughter in law ᴿbare him Pha'-rez and Ze'-rah. All the sons of Judah were five.   Gen. 38:6 • Matt. 1:3

5 The sons of ᴿPha'-rez; Hez'-ron, and Ha'-mul.   Gen. 46:12; Ruth 4:18

6 And the sons of Ze'-rah; ᵀZim'-ri, and E'-than, and He'-man, and Cal'-col, and ᵀDa'-ra: five of them in all.   Zabdi • Darda

7 And the sons of ᴿCar'-mi; ᵀA'-char, the troubler of Israel, who transgressed in the thing ᵀaccursed.   4:1 • Achan • devoted

8 And the sons of E'-than; Az-a-ri'-ah.

9 The sons also of Hez'-ron, that were born unto him; Je-rah'-me-el, and Ram, and Che-lu'-bai.

10 And Ram begat Am-min'-a-dab; and Am-min'-a-dab begat Nah'-shon, ᴿprince of the children of Judah;   Num. 1:7; 2:3

11 And Nah'-shon begat ᵀSal'-ma,ᴿ and Sal'-ma begat Bo'-az,   Sal'-mon • Ruth 4:21; Matt. 1:4

12 And ᴿBo'-az begat ᴿO'-bed, and O'-bed begat ᴿJesse,   Ruth 2:4; 4:13 • Luke 3:32 • Matt. 1:5

13 ᴿAnd Jesse begat his firstborn E-li'-ab, and A-bin'-a-dab the second, and ᵀShim'-maᴿ the third,   1 Sam. 16:6 • Shammah • 1 Sam. 16:9

14 Ne-than'-e-el the fourth, Rad'-dai the fifth,

15 O'-zem the sixth, David the seventh:

16 Whose sisters were Ze-ru'-iah, and Ab'-i-gail. And the sons of Ze-ru'-iah; A-bi'-shai, and Jo'-ab, and A'-sa-hel, three.

17 And Ab'-i-gail bare Am'-a-sa: and the father of Am'-a-sa was ᴿJe'-ther the Ish'-me-el-ite.   2 Sam. 17:25, Ithra an Israelite

18 And Caleb the son of Hez'-ron begat children of A-zu'-bah his wife, and of Je'-ri-oth: her sons are these; Je'-sher, and Sho'-bab, and Ar'-don.

19 And when A-zu'-bah was dead, Caleb ᵀtook unto him ᴿEph'-rath, which bare him Hur.   married • v. 50

20 And Hur begat U'-ri, and U'-ri begat ᴿBe-zal'-e-el.   Ex. 31:2; 38:22

21 And afterward Hez'-ron went in to the daughter of Ma'-chir the father of Gil'-e-ad, whom he married when he was threescore years old; and she bare him Se'-gub.

22 And Se'-gub begat ᴿJa'-ir, who had three and twenty cities in the land of Gil'-e-ad.   Judg. 10:3; 1 Kin. 4:13

23 And he took Ge'-shur, and A'-ram, with the towns of Ja'-ir, from them, with Ke'-nath,

and the towns thereof, even threescore cities. All these belonged to the sons of Ma'-chir the father of Gil'-e-ad.

24 And after that Hez'-ron was dead in Ca'-leb–eph'-ra-tah, then A-bi'-ah Hez'-ron's wife bare him Ashur the father of Te-ko'-a.

25 And the sons of Je-rah'-me-el the first-born of Hez'-ron were, Ram the firstborn, and Bu'-nah, and O'-ren, and O'-zem, and A-hi'-jah.

26 Je-rah'-me-el had also another wife, whose name was At'-a-rah; she was the mother of O'-nam.

27 And the sons of Ram the firstborn of Je-rah'-me-el were, Ma'-az, and Ja'-min, and E'-ker.

28 And the sons of O'-nam were, Sham'-mai, and Ja'-da. And the sons of Sham'-mai; Na'-dab, and A-bi'-shur.

29 And the name of the wife of A-bi'-shur was Ab-i-ha'-il, and she bare him Ah'-ban, and Mo'-lid.

30 And the sons of Na'-dab; Se'-led, and Ap'-pa-im: but Se'-led died without children.

31 And the sons of Ap'-pa-im; Ish'-i. And the sons of Ish'-i; She'-shan. And ᴿthe ᵀchildren of She'-shan; Ah'-lai.   vv. 34–41 • sons

32 And the sons of Ja'-da the brother of Sham'-mai; Je'-ther, and Jonathan: and Je'-ther died without ᵀchildren.   sons

33 And the sons of Jonathan; Pe'-leth, and Za'-za. These were the sons of Je-rah'-me-el.

34 Now She'-shan had no sons, but daughters. And She'-shan had a servant, an Egyptian, whose name was Jar'-ha.

35 And She'-shan gave his daughter to Jar'-ha his servant to ᵀwife; and she bare him At'-tai.   in marriage

36 And At'-tai begat Nathan, and Nathan begat ᴿZa'-bad,   11:41

37 And Za'-bad begat Eph'-lal, and Eph'-lal begat ᴿO'-bed,   2 Chr. 23:1

38 And O'-bed begat Je'-hu, and Je'-hu begat Az-a-ri'-ah,

39 And Az-a-ri'-ah begat He'-lez, and He'-lez begat E-le'-a-sah,

40 And E-le'-a-sah begat Sis'-a-mai, and Sis'-a-mai begat Shal'-lum,

41 And Shal'-lum begat Jek-a-mi'-ah, and Jek-a-mi'-ah begat E-lish'-a-ma.

42 Now the sons of Caleb the brother of Je-rah'-me-el were, Me'-sha his firstborn, which was the father of Ziph; and the sons of Ma-re'-shah the father of He'-bron.

43 And the sons of He'-bron; Ko'-rah, and Tap'-pu-ah, and Re'-kem, and She'-ma.

44 And She'-ma begat Ra'-ham, the father of Jor'-ko-am: and Re'-kem begat Sham'-mai.

45 And the son of Sham'-mai was Ma'-on: and Ma'-on was the father of Beth'-zur.

46 And E'-phah, Caleb's concubine, bare Ha'-ran, and Mo'-za, and Ga'-zez: and Ha'-ran begat Ga'-zez.

47 And the sons of Jah'-dai; Re'-gem, and Jo'-tham, and Ge'-sham, and Pe'-let, and E'-phah, and Sha'-aph.

48 Ma'-a-chah, Caleb's concubine, bare She'-ber, and Tir'-ha-nah.

49 She bare also Sha'-aph the father of Mad-man'-nah, She'-va the father of Mach-be'-nah, and the father of Gib'-e-a: and the daughter of Caleb was Ach'-sa.

50 These were the sons of Caleb the son of Hur, the firstborn of ᵀEph'-ra-tah; Sho'-bal the father of Kir'-jath–je'-a-rim,   *Ephrath*

51 Sal'-ma the father of Beth'-le-hem, Ha'-reph the father of Beth-ga'-der.

52 And Sho'-bal the father of Kir'-jath–je'-a-rim had sons; ᵀHar'-o-eh,ᴿ and half of the Ma-na'-heth-ites.   *Reaiah* · 4:2

53 And the families of Kir'-jath–je'-a-rim; the Ith'-rites, and the Pu'-hites, and the Shu'-math-ites, and the Mish'-ra-ites; of them came the Za'-re-ath-ites, and the Esh'-ta-ul-ites.

54 The sons of Sal'-ma; Beth'–le-hem, and the Ne-toph'-a-thites, ᵀAt'-a-roth, the house of Jo'-ab, and half of the Ma-na'-heth-ites, the Zo'-rites.   *Atroth-bethjoab*

55 And the families of the scribes which dwelt at Ja'-bez; the Ti'-rath-ites, the Shim'-e-ath-ites, and Su'-chath-ites. These are the Ken'-ites that came of He'-math, the father of the house of Re'-chab.

CHAPTER 3

The Genealogy of the Sons of David

NOW these were the sons of David, which were born unto him in He'-bron; the firstborn Amnon, of A-hin'-o-am the Jez'-re-el-i-tess; the second ᵀDaniel,ᴿ of Ab'-i-gail the Car'-mel-i-tess: *Chileab* · 2 Sam. 3:3

2 The third, ᴿAb'-sa-lom the son of Ma'-a-chah the daughter of Tal'-mai king of Ge'-shur: the fourth, Ad-o-ni'-jah the son of Hag'-gith: 2 Sam. 13:37; 15:1

3 The fifth, Sheph-a-ti'-ah of Ab'-i-tal: the sixth, Ith'-re-am by Eg'-lah his wife.

4 These six were born unto him in He'-bron; and there he reigned seven years and six months: and ᴿin Jerusalem he reigned thirty and three years.   2 Sam. 5:5

5 And these were born unto him in Jerusalem; Shim'-e-a, and Sho'-bab, and Na-than, and Solomon, four, of Bath'-shu-a the daughter of ᵀAm'-mi-el:ᴿ   *Eliam* · 2 Sam. 11:3

6 Ib'-har also, and ᵀE-lish'-a-ma,ᴿ and E-liph'-e-let,   *Elishua* · 2 Sam. 5:15

7 And No'-gah, and Ne'-pheg, and Ja-phi'-a,

8 And E-lish'-a-ma, and ᵀE-li'-a-da,ᴿ and E-liph'-e-let, nine.   *Beeliada* · 14:7

9 These were all the sons of David, beside the sons of the ᴿconcubines, and ᴿTa'-mar their sister.   1 Kin. 11:3 · 2 Sam. 13:1

The Genealogy of the Sons of Solomon
Matt. 1:7–12

10 And Solomon's son was Re-ho-bo'-am, ᵀA-bi'-aᴿ his son, A'-sa his son, Je-hosh'-a-phat his son,   *Abijam* · 1 Kin. 15:1

11 Jo'-ram his son, ᵀA-ha-zi'-ahᴿ his son, Jo'-ash his son,   *Jehoahaz* · 2 Chr. 21:17

12 Am-a-zi'-ah his son, ᵀAz-a-ri'-ahᴿ his son, Jo'-tham his son,   *Uzziah* · 2 Kin. 15:30

13 Ahaz his son, Hez-e-ki'-ah his son, Ma-nas'-seh his son,

14 Amon his son, Jo-si'-ah his son.

15 And the sons of Jo-si'-ah were, the first-born Jo-ha'-nan, the second Je-hoi'-a-kim, the third Zed-e-ki'-ah, the fourth Shal'-lum.

16 And the sons of Je-hoi'-a-kim: Jec-o-ni'-ah his son, Zed-e-ki'-ah his son.

17 And the sons of Jec-o-ni'-ah; ᵀAs'-sir, ᴿSa-la'-thi-el his son,   *the captive* · Matt. 1:12

18 Mal-chi'-ram also, and Pe-da'-iah, and She-na'-zar, Jec-a-mi'-ah, Hosh'-a-ma, and Ned-a-bi'-ah.

19 And the sons of Pe-da'-iah were, Ze-rub'-ba-bel, and Shim'-e-i: and the sons of Ze-rub'-ba-bel; Me-shul'-lam, and Han-a-ni'-ah, and Shel'-o-mith their sister:

20 And Ha-shu'-bah, and O'-hel, and Ber-e-chi'-ah, and Has-a-di'-ah, Ju'-shab-he'-sed, five.

21 And the sons of Han-a-ni'-ah; Pel-a-ti'-ah, and Je-sa'-iah: the sons of Re-pha'-iah, the sons of Arnan, the sons of O-ba-di'-ah, the sons of Shech-a-ni'-ah.

22 And the sons of Shech-a-ni'-ah; She-ma'-iah: and the sons of She-ma'-iah; ᴿHat'-tush, and I'-ge-al, and Ba-ri'-ah, and Ne-a-ri'-ah, and Sha'-phat, six.   Ezra 8:2

23 And the sons of Ne-a-ri'-ah; E-li-o-e'-nai, and Hez-e-ki'-ah, and Az'-ri-kam, three.

24 And the sons of E-li-o-e'-nai were, Ho-da'-iah, and E-li'-a-shib, and Pe-la'-iah, and Ak'-kub, and Jo-ha'-nan, and Da-la'-iah, and A-na'-ni, seven.

CHAPTER 4

The Genealogy of Judah

THE sons of Judah; Pha'-rez, Hez'-ron, and Car'-mi, and Hur, and Sho'-bal.

2 And ᵀRe-a'-iahᴿ the son of Sho'-bal begat Ja'-hath; and Ja'-hath begat A-hu'-mai, and La'-had. These are the families of the Zo'-rath-ites.   *Haroeh* · 2:52

3 And these were of the father of E'-tam; Jez'-re-el, and Ish'-ma, and Id'-bash: and the name of their sister was Haz-e-lel-po'-ni:

4 And Pe-nu'-el the father of Ge'-dor, and E'-zer the father of Hu'-shah. These are the sons of [R]Hur, the firstborn of Eph'-ra-tah, the father of Beth'-le-hem.   2:50; Ex. 31:2

5 And [R]Ashur the father of Te-ko'-a had two wives, He'-lah and Na'-a-rah.   2:24

6 And Na'-a-rah bare him A-hu'-zam, and He'-pher, and Tem'-e-ni, and Ha-a-hash'-ta-ri. These were the sons of Na'-a-rah.

7 And the sons of He'-lah were, Ze'-reth, and Jez'-o-ar, and Eth'-nan.

8 And Coz begat A'-nub, and Zo-be'-bah, and the families of A-har'-hel the son of Ha'-rum.

9 And Ja'-bez was [R]more [T]honourable than his brethren: and his mother called his name [T]Ja'-bez, saying, Because I bare him with sorrow.   Gen. 34:19 • famous • Sorrowful

10 And Ja'-bez called on the God of Israel, saying, Oh that thou wouldest bless me indeed, and enlarge my [T]coast, and that thine hand might be with me, and that thou wouldest keep me from evil, that it may not grieve me! And God granted him that which he requested.   border

11 And Che'-lub the brother of Shu'-ah begat Me'-hir, which was the father of Esh'-ton.

12 And Esh'-ton begat Beth-ra'-pha, and Pa-se'-ah, and Te-hin'-nah the father of Ir-na'-hash. These are the men of Re'-chah.

13 And the sons of Ke'-naz; Oth'-ni-el, and Se-ra'-iah: and the sons of Oth'-ni-el; [T]Ha'-thath.   Hathath and Meonothai who begat, etc.

14 And Me-on'-o-thai begat Oph'-rah: and Se-ra'-iah begat Jo'-ab, the father of the [R]valley [T]of Char'-a-shim; for they were craftsmen.   Neh. 11:35 • inhabitants of the valley

15 And the sons of Caleb the son of Je-phun'-neh; I'-ru, E'-lah, and Na'-am: and the sons of E'-lah, even [T]Ke'-naz.   Uknaz

16 And the sons of Je-ha-le'-le-el; Ziph, and Zi'-phah, Tir'-i-a, and A-sa'-re-el.

17 And the sons of Ezra were, Je'-ther, and Me'-red, and E'-pher, and Ja'-lon: and she bare Miriam, and Sham'-mai, and Ish'-bah the father of Esh-te-mo'-a.

18 And his wife Je-hu-di'-jah bare Je'-red the father of Ge'-dor, and He'-ber the father of So'-cho, and Je-ku'-thi-el the father of Za-no'-ah. And these are the sons of Bi-thi'-ah the daughter of Pharaoh, which Me'-red took.

19 [R]And the sons of his wife [T]Ho-di'-ah[R] the sister of Na'-ham, the father of Kei'-lah the Gar'-mite, and Esh-te-mo'-a the Ma-ach'-a-thite.   2 Kin. 25:23 • Jehudijah • v. 18

20 And the sons of Shi'-mon were, Am-non, and Rin'-nah, Ben–ha'-nan, and Ti'-lon. And the sons of Ish'-i were, Zo'-heth, and Ben-zo'-heth.

21 The sons of She'-lah the son of Judah

were, Er the father of Le'-cah, and La'-a-dah the father of Ma-re'-shah, and the families of the house of them that wrought fine linen, of the house of Ash-be'-a,

22 And Jo'-kim, and the men of Cho-ze'-ba, and Jo'-ash, and Sa'-raph, who had the dominion in Moab, and Jash'-u-bi-le'-hem. And these are [T]ancient things.   old-time

23 These were the potters, and those that dwelt among plants and hedges: there they dwelt with the king for his work.

The Genealogy of Simeon—Gen. 46:10

24 The sons of Simeon were, Nem'-u-el, and Ja'-min, Ja'-rib, Ze'-rah, and Sha'-ul:

25 Shal'-lum his son, Mib'-sam his son, Mish'-ma his son.

26 And the sons of Mish'-ma; Ham'-u-el his son, Zac'-chur his son, Shim'-e-i his son.

27 And Shim'-e-i had sixteen sons and six daughters; but his brethren had not many children, neither did all their family multiply, like to the children of Judah.

28 And they dwelt at [R]Be'-er-she'-ba, and Mol'-a-dah, and Ha'-zar-shu'-al,   Josh. 19:2

29 And at [T]Bil'-hah,[R] and at E'-zem, and at [T]To'-lad,[R]   Balah • Josh. 19:3 • Eltolad • Josh. 19:4

30 And at Be-thu'-el, and at Hor'-mah, and at Zik'-lag,

31 And at Beth-mar'-ca-both, and [T]Ha'-zar-su'-sim,[R] and at Beth-bir'-e-i, and at Sha-a-ra'-im. These were their cities unto the reign of David.   Hazarsusah • Josh. 19:5

32 And their villages were, [T]E'-tam,[R] and A'-in, Rim'-mon, and To'-chen, and A'-shan, five cities: Ether • Josh. 19:7

33 And all their villages that were round about the same cities, unto Ba'-al. These were their habitations, and their genealogy.

34 And Me-sho'-bab, and Jam'-lech, and Jo'-shah the son of Am-a-zi'-ah,

35 And Jo'-el, and Je'-hu the son of Jos-i-bi'-ah, the son of Se-ra'-iah, the son of A'-si-el,

36 And E-li-o-e'-nai, and Ja-a-ko'-bah, and Jesh-o-ha'-iah, and A-sa'-iah, and A'-di-el, and Je-sim'-i-el, and Be-na'-iah,

37 And Zi'-za the son of Shi'-phi, the son of Al'-lon, the son of Je-da'-iah, the son of Shim'-ri, the son of She-ma'-iah;

38 These mentioned by their names were [T]princes in their families: and the house of their fathers increased greatly.   leaders

39 And they went to the entrance of Ge'-dor, even unto the east side of the valley, to seek pasture for their flocks.

40 And [R]they found fat pasture and good, and the land was wide, and quiet, and peaceable; for they of [R]Ham had dwelt there of old.   Judg. 18:7-10 • Gen. 9:18

41 And these written by name came in the

days of Hez-e-ki'-ah king of Judah, and Rsmote[T] their tents, and the habitations that were found there, and destroyed them utterly unto this day, and dwelt in their rooms: because *there was* pasture there for their flocks.   2 Kin. 18:8 · *destroyed*

42 And *some* of them, *even* of the sons of Simeon, five hundred men, went to Rmount Se'-ir, having for their captains Pel-a-ti'-ah, and Ne-a-ri'-ah, and Re-pha'-iah, and Uz-zi'-el, the sons of Ish'-i.   Gen. 36:8, 9

43 And they Tsmote the rest of the Am'-a-lek-ites that were escaped, and dwelt there unto this day.   *defeated*

CHAPTER 5

The Genealogy of Reuben—Gen. 46:8, 9

NOW the sons of Reuben the firstborn of Israel, (for he *was* the firstborn; but, forasmuch as he defiled his father's bed, his birthright was given unto the sons of Joseph the son of Israel: and the genealogy is not to be reckoned after the birthright.

2 For Judah prevailed above his brethren, and of him *came* the chief ruler; but the Tbirthright *was* Joseph's:)   *blessing*

3 The sons, *I say,* of RReuben the firstborn of Israel *were,* Ha'-noch, and Pal'-lu, Hez'-ron, and Car'-mi.   Ex. 6:14; Num. 26:5

4 The sons of Jo'-el; She-ma'-iah his son, Gog his son, Shim'-e-i his son,

5 Mi'-cah his son, Re-a'-ia his son, Ba'-al his son,

6 Be-e'-rah his son, whom Til'-gath–pil-ne'-ser king of Assyria carried away *captive:* he *was* prince of the Reu'-ben-ites.

7 And his brethren by their families, Rwhen the genealogy of their generations was reckoned, *were* the chief, Je-i'-el, and Zech-a-ri'-ah,   *v.* 17

8 And Be'-la the son of A'-zaz, the son of She'-ma, the son of Jo'-el, who dwelt in Ar'-o-er, even unto Ne'-bo and Ba'-al-me'-on:

9 And eastward he inhabited unto the entering in of the wilderness from the river Eu-phra'-tes: because their cattle were Tmultiplied in the land of Gil'-e-ad.   *increased*

10 And in the days of Saul they made war with the Ha'-gar-ites, who fell by their hand: and they dwelt in their tents throughout all the east *land* of Gil'-e-ad.

The Genealogy of Gad

11 And the children of Gad dwelt over against them, in the land of RBa'-shan unto RSal'-chah: Josh. 13:11, 24 · Deut. 3:10

12 Jo'-el the chief, and Sha'-pham the next, and Ja'-a-nai, and Sha'-phat in Ba'-shan.

13 And their brethren of the house of their fathers *were,* Mi'-cha-el, and Me-shul'-lam, and She'-ba, and Jo'-rai, and Ja'-chan, and Zi'-a, and He'-ber, seven.

14 These *are* the children of Ab-i-ha'-il the son of Hu'-ri, the son of Ja-ro'-ah, the son of Gil'-e-ad, the son of Mi'-cha-el, the son of Je-shish'-ai, the son of Jah'-do, the son of Buz;

15 A'-hi the son of Ab'-di-el, the son of Gu'-ni, chief of the house of their fathers.

16 And they dwelt in Gil'-e-ad in Ba'-shan, and in her towns, and in all the suburbs of Shar'-on, upon their borders.

17 All these were reckoned by genealogies in the days of Jo'-tham king of Judah, and in the days of Jer-o-bo'-am king of Israel.

18 The sons of Reuben, and the Gad'-ites, and half the tribe of Ma-nas'-seh, of valiant men, men able to bear buckler and sword, and to shoot with bow, and skilful in war, *were* four and forty thousand seven hundred and threescore, that went out to the war.

19 And they made war with the RHa'-gar-ites, with RJe'-tur, and Ne'-phish, and No'-dab.   *v.* 10 · 1:31; Gen. 25:15

20 And they were helped against them, and the Ha'-gar-ites were delivered into their hand, and all that *were* with them: for they cried to God in the battle, and he Twas intreated of them; because they Rput their trust in him.   *heard their plea* · Ps. 22:4, 5

21 And they took away their cattle; of their camels fifty thousand, and of sheep two hundred and fifty thousand, and of asses two thousand, and of men an hundred thousand.

22 For there fell down many slain, because the war *was* of God. And they dwelt in their Tsteads until the captivity.   *places*

The Genealogy of Manasseh

23 And the children of the half tribe of Ma-nas'-seh dwelt in the land: they increased from Ba'-shan unto Ba'-al-her'-mon and RSe'-nir, and unto mount Hermon.   Deut. 3:9

24 And these *were* the heads of the house of their fathers, even E'-pher, and Ish'-i, and E-li'-el, and Az'-ri-el, and Jer-e-mi'-ah, and Hod-a-vi'-ah, and Jah'-di-el, Rmighty men of valour, famous men, *and* heads of the house of their fathers.   11:10

25 And they transgressed against the God of their fathers, and went a whoring after the gods of the people of the land, whom God destroyed before them.

26 And the God of Israel stirred up the spirit of RPul king of Assyria, and the spirit of Til'-gath–pil-ne'-ser king of Assyria, and he carried them away, even the Reu'-ben-ites, and the Gad'-ites, and the half tribe of Ma-nas'-seh, and brought them unto Ha'-lah, and Ha'-bor, and Ha'-ra, and to the river Go'-zan, unto this day.   2 Kin. 15:19

CHAPTER 6

The High Priestly Line
Gen. 46:11; 1 Chr. 6:50–53

THE sons of Levi; ᴿGer'-shon, ᵀKo'-hath, and Me-ra'-ri.   23:6 • *Gershom, v. 16*

2 And the sons of Ko'-hath; Am'-ram, Iz'-har, and He'-bron, and Uz-zi'-el.

3 And the children of Am'-ram; Aaron, and Moses, and Miriam. The sons also of Aaron; ᴿNa'-dab, and A-bi'-hu, E-le-a'-zar, and Ith'-a-mar.   Lev. 10:1

4 E-le-a'-zar begat Phin'-e-has, Phin'-e-has begat Ab-i-shu'-a,

5 And Ab-i-shu'-a begat Buk'-ki, and Buk'-ki begat Uz'-zi,

6 And Uz'-zi begat Zer-a-hi'-ah, and Zer-a-hi'-ah begat Me-ra'-ioth,

7 Me-ra'-ioth begat Am-a-ri'-ah, and Am-a-ri'-ah begat A-hi'-tub,

8 And ᴿA-hi'-tub begat Za'-dok, and Za'-dok begat A-him'-a-az,   2 Sam. 8:17

9 And A-him'-a-az begat Az-a-ri'-ah, and Az-a-ri'-ah begat Jo-ha'-nan,

10 And Jo-ha'-nan begat Az-a-ri'-ah, (he *it is* that executed the priest's office in the temple that Solomon built in Jerusalem:)

11 And ᴿAz-a-ri'-ah begat Am-a-ri'-ah, and Am-a-ri'-ah begat A-hi'-tub,   Ezra 7:3

12 And A-hi'-tub begat Za'-dok, and Za'-dok begat ᴿShal'-lum,   9:11

13 And Shal'-lum begat ᴿHil-ki'-ah, and Hil-ki'-ah begat Az-a-ri'-ah,   2 Kin. 22:4

14 And Az-a-ri'-ah begat ᴿSe-ra'-iah, and Se-ra'-iah begat Je-hoz'-a-dak,   Neh. 11:11

15 And ᴿJe-hoz'-a-dak went *into* captivity, ᴿwhen the LORD carried away Judah and Jerusalem by the hand of Neb-u-chad-nez'-zar.   Ezra 3:2 • 2 Kin. 25:18–21

The Levitical Line

16 The sons of Levi; ᴿGer'-shom, Ko'-hath, and Me-ra'-ri.   *v. 1*; Ex. 6:16

17 And these *be* the names of the sons of Ger'-shom; Lib'-ni, and Shim'-e-i.

18 And the sons of Ko'-hath *were*, Am'-ram, and Iz'-har, and He'-bron, and Uz-zi'-el.

19 The sons of ᴿMe-ra'-ri; Mah'-li, and Mu'-shi. And these *are* the families of the Levites according to their fathers.   Num. 3:36

20 Of Ger'-shom; Lib'-ni his son, Ja'-hath his son, ᴿZim'-mah his son,   *v. 42*

21 Jo'-ah his son, Id'-do his son, Ze'-rah his son, ᵀJe-at'-e-rai ᴿ his son.   *Ethni • v. 41*

22 The sons of Ko'-hath; Am-min'-a-dab his son, Ko'-rah his son, As'-sir his son,

23 El'-ka-nah his son, and E-bi'-a-saph his son, and As'-sir his son,

24 Ta'-hath his son, ᴿU-ri'-el his son, Uz-zi'-ah his son, and Sha'-ul his son.   *v. 36*

25 And the sons of El'-ka-nah; ᴿAm'-a-sai, and A-hi'-moth.   *vv. 35, 36*

26 *As for* El'-ka-nah: the sons of El'-ka-nah; ᵀZo'-phai ᴿ his son, and ᵀNa'-hath ᴿ his son,   *Zuph • v. 35; 1 Sam. 1:1 • Toah • v. 34*

27 ᴿE-li'-ab ᵀ his son, Jer'-o-ham his son, El'-ka-nah his son.   *v. 34 • Eliel*

28 And the sons of Samuel; the firstborn ᵀVash'-ni, ᴿ and A-bi'-ah.   *Called also Joel • v. 33*

29 The sons of Me-ra'-ri; Mah'-li, Lib'-ni his son, Shim'-e-i his son, Uz'-za his son,

30 Shim'-e-a his son, Hag-gi'-ah his son, A-sa'-iah his son.

The Musicians' Guild

31 And these *are they* whom David set over the service of song in the house of the LORD, after that the ᴿark had rest.   16:1

32 And they ministered before the dwelling place of the tabernacle of the congregation with singing, until Solomon had built the house of the LORD in Jerusalem: and *then* they ᵀwaited on their office according to their ᵀorder.   *served in • assignment*

33 And these *are* they that ᵀwaited with their children. Of the sons of the ᴿKo'-hath-ites: He'-man a singer, the son of Jo'-el, the son of Shem'-u-el,   *served • Num. 26:57*

34 The son of El'-ka-nah, the son of Jer'-o-ham, the son of E-li'-el, the son of To'-ah,

35 The son of ᵀZuph,ᴿ the son of El'-ka-nah, the son of Ma'-hath, the son of Am'-a-sai,   *Zophai • v. 26*

36 The son of El'-ka-nah, the son of ᴿJo'-el,ᵀ the son of Az-a-ri'-ah, the son of Zeph-a-ni'-ah,   *v. 24 • Shaul, Uzziah, Uriel*

37 The son of Ta'-hath, the son of As'-sir, the son of E-bi'-a-saph, the son of Ko'-rah,

38 The son of Iz'-har, the son of Ko'-hath, the son of Levi, the son of Israel.

39 And his brother ᴿA'-saph, who stood on his right hand, *even* A'-saph the son of Ber-a-chi'-ah, the son of Shim'-e-a,   15:17

40 The son of Mi'-cha-el, the son of Ba-a-se'-iah, the son of Mal-chi'-ah,

41 The son of ᴿEth'-ni, the son of Ze'-rah, the son of A-da'-iah,   *v. 21*

42 The son of E'-than, the son of Zim'-mah, the son of Shim'-e-i,

43 The son of Ja'-hath, the son of Ger'-shom, the son of Levi.

44 And their brethren the sons of Me-ra'-ri *stood* on the left hand: E'-than the son of Kish'-i, the son of Ab'-di, the son of Mal'-luch,

45 The son of Hash-a-bi'-ah, the son of Am-a-zi'-ah, the son of Hil-ki'-ah,

46 The son of Am'-zi, the son of Ba'-ni, the son of Sha'-mer,

47 The son of ᴿMah'-li, the son of Mu'-shi, the son of Me-ra'-ri, the son of Levi.   *v. 19*

48 Their brethren also the Levites *were* appointed unto all ᴿmanner of service of the tabernacle of the house of God.   9:14–34

The Generations of Aaron—1 Chr. 6:3–8

49 But Aaron and his sons offered upon the altar of the burnt offering, and on the altar of incense, *and were appointed* for all the work of the *place* most holy, and to make an atonement for Israel, according to all that Moses the servant of God had commanded.

50 And these *are* the ᴿsons of Aaron; E-le-a′-zar his son, Phin′-e-has his son, A-bi-shu′-a his son,   *vv. 4–8, 50–53*

51 Buk′-ki his son, Uz′-zi his son, Zer-a-hi′-ah his son,

52 Me-ra′-ioth his son, Am-a-ri′-ah his son, A-hi′-tub his son,

53 Za′-dok his son, A-him′-a-az his son.

Cities of the Priests and Levites—Josh. 21:1–42

54 Now these *are* their dwelling places throughout their castles in their ᵀcoasts, of the sons of Aaron, of the families of the Ko′-hath-ites: for their′s was the lot.   *regions*

55 ᴿAnd they gave them He′-bron in the land of Judah, and the suburbs thereof round about it.   Josh. 21:11, 12

56 ᴿBut the fields of the city, and the villages thereof, they gave to Caleb the son of Je-phun′-neh.   Josh. 14:13; 15:13

57 And to the sons of Aaron they gave the cities of Judah, *namely,* He′-bron, *the city of* refuge, and Lib′-nah with her suburbs, and Jat′-tir, and Esh-te-mo′-a, with their suburbs,

58 And ᵀHi′-lenᴿ with her suburbs, De′-bir with her suburbs,   *Holon* · Josh. 21:15

59 And ᵀA′-shan with her suburbs, and Beth-she′-mesh with her suburbs: *Ain*

60 And out of the tribe of Benjamin; Ge′-ba with her suburbs, and ᵀAl′-e-methᴿ with her suburbs, and An′-a-thoth with her suburbs. All their cities throughout their families *were* thirteen cities.   *Almon* · Josh. 21:18

61 And unto the sons of Ko′-hath, ᴿ*which were* left of the family of that tribe, *were cities given* out of the half tribe, *namely, out of the half tribe* of Ma-nas′-seh, ᴿby lot, ten cities.   *v. 66* · Josh. 21:5

62 And to the sons of Ger′-shom throughout their families out of the tribe of Is′-sa-char, and out of the tribe of Asher, and out of the tribe of Naph′-ta-li, and out of the tribe of Ma-nas′-seh in Ba′-shan, thirteen cities.

63 Unto the sons of ᴿMe-ra′-ri *were given* by lot, throughout their families, out of the tribe of Reuben, and out of the tribe of Gad, and out of the tribe of Zeb′-u-lun, ᴿtwelve cities.   Num. 3:36; 4:29, 42 · Josh. 21:7, 34

64 And the children of Israel gave to the Levites *these* cities with their suburbs.

65 And they gave by lot out of the tribe of the children of Judah, and out of the tribe of the children of Simeon, and out of the tribe of the children of Benjamin, ᴿthese cities, which are called by *their* names.   *vv. 57–60*

66 And ᴿ*the* ᵀresidue of the families of the sons of Ko′-hath had cities of their coasts out of the tribe of E′-phra-im.   *v. 61* · *some*

67 ᴿAnd they gave unto them, *of* the cities of refuge, She′-chem in mount E′-phra-im with her suburbs; *they* gave also Ge′-zer with her suburbs,   Josh. 21:21

68 And Jok′-me-am with her suburbs, and Beth-ho′-ron with her suburbs,

69 And Ai′-ja-lon with her suburbs, and Gath-rim′-mon with her suburbs:

70 And out of the half tribe of Ma-nas′-seh; A′-ner with her suburbs, and Bil′-e-am with her suburbs, for the family of the remnant of the sons of Ko′-hath.

71 Unto the sons of Ger′-shom *were given* out of the family of the half tribe of Ma-nas′-seh, Go′-lan in Ba′-shan with her suburbs, and Ash′-ta-roth with her suburbs:

72 And out of the tribe of ᴿIs′-sa-char; Ke′-desh with her suburbs, Dab′-e-rath with her suburbs,   Gen. 30:18; 35:23; 49:14

73 And Ra′-moth with her suburbs, and A′-nem with her suburbs:

74 And out of the tribe of ᴿAsher; Ma′-shal with her suburbs, and Ab′-don with her ᵀsuburbs,   Gen. 30:13; 2 Chr. 30:11 · *pasture lands*

75 And Hu′-kok with her suburbs, and Re′-hob with her suburbs:

76 And out of the tribe of Naph′-ta-li; ᴿKe′-desh in Galilee with her suburbs, and Ham′-mon with her suburbs, and Kir-ja-tha′-im with her suburbs.   Josh. 20:7; 21:32

77 Unto the rest of the children of ᴿMe-ra′-ri *were given* out of the tribe of Zeb′-u-lun, Rim′-mon with her suburbs, Ta′-bor with her suburbs: Num. 3:36; 4:29, 42

78 And on the other side Jordan by Jericho, on the east side of Jordan, *were given them* out of the tribe of ᴿReuben, Be′-zer in the wilderness with her suburbs, and Jah′-zah with her suburbs,   Gen. 29:32

79 Ked′-e-moth also with her suburbs, and Meph′-a-ath with her suburbs:

80 And out of the tribe of Gad; ᴿRa′-moth in Gil′-e-ad with her suburbs, and Ma-ha-na′-im with her suburbs,   2 Chr. 18:2

81 And ᴿHesh′-bon with her suburbs, and Ja′-zer with her suburbs.   Num. 21:26

CHAPTER 7

The Genealogy of Issachar—Gen. 46:13

NOW the sons of Is′-sa-char *were,* ᴿTo′-la, and ᵀPu′-ah, Jash′-ub, and Shim′-rom, four.   Gen. 46:13; Num. 26:23 · *Phuvah*

2 And the sons of To′-la; Uz′-zi, and Re-pha′-iah, and Je′-ri-el, and Jah′-mai, and Jib′-sam, and Shem′-u-el, heads of their father's house, to wit, of To′-la: *they were* valiant

men of might in their generations; whose number *was* in the days of David two and twenty thousand and six hundred.

3 And the sons of Uz'-zi; Iz-ra-hi'-ah: and the sons of Iz-ra-hi'-ah; Mi'-cha-el, and O-ba-di'-ah, and Jo'-el, Ish-i'-ah, five: all of them chief men.

4 And with them, by their generations, after the house of their fathers, *were* bands of soldiers for war, six and thirty thousand *men:* for they had many wives and sons.

5 And their brethren among all the families of Is'-sa-char *were* Rvaliant^T men of might, reckoned in all by their genealogies fourscore and seven thousand.   Gen. 10:8 · strong

The Genealogy of Benjamin—Gen. 46:21

6 *The sons* of RBenjamin; Be'-la, and Be'-cher, and Je-di'-a-el, three.   8:1-40; Gen. 46:21

7 And the sons of Be'-la; Ez'-bon, and Uz'-zi, and Uz-zi'-el, and Jer'-i-moth, and RI'-ri, five; heads of the house of *their* fathers, mighty men of valour; and were reckoned by their genealogies twenty and two thousand and thirty and four.   v. 12

8 And the sons of Be'-cher; Ze-mi'-ra, and Jo'-ash, and E-li-e'-zer, and E-li-o-e'-nai, and Om'-ri, and Jer'-i-moth, and A-bi'-ah, and An'-a-thoth, and A-la'-meth. All these *are* the sons of Be'-cher.

9 And the number of them, after their genealogy by their generations, heads of the house of their fathers, mighty men of valour, *was* twenty thousand and two hundred.

10 The sons also of Je-di'-a-el; Bil'-han: and the sons of Bil'-han; Je'-ush, and Benjamin, and E'-hud, and Che-na'-a-nah, and Ze'-than, and Thar'-shish, and A-hish'-a-har.

11 All these the sons of Je-di'-a-el, by the heads of their fathers, mighty men of valour, *were* seventeen thousand and two hundred *soldiers,* fit to go out for war *and* battle.

12 RShup'-pim also, and Hup'-pim, the children of TIr,R *and* Hu'-shim, the sons of TA'-her.R   Num. 26:38 · Iri · v. 7 · Ahiram · Num. 26:38

The Genealogy of Naphtali—Gen. 46:24

13 The sons of Naph'-ta-li; Jah'-zi-el, and Gu'-ni, and Je'-zer, and RShal'-lum,^T the sons of Bil'-hah.   Gen. 46:24; Num. 26:49 · Shillem

The Genealogy of Manasseh

14 The Rsons of Ma-nas'-seh; Ash'-ri-el, whom she bare: (*but* his concubine the A'-ram-i-tess bare RMa'-chir the father of Gil'-e-ad: Num. 26:29-34 · 2:21

15 And Ma'-chir took to wife *the sister* of Hup'-pim and Shup'-pim, whose sister's name *was* Ma'-a-chah;) and the name of the second

was Ze-lo'-phe-had: Rand Ze-lo'-phe-had had daughters.   Num. 26:33; 27:1

16 And Ma'-a-chah the wife of Ma'-chir bare a son, and she called his name Pe'-resh; and the name of his brother *was* She'-resh; and his sons *were* U'-lam and Ra'-kem.

17 And the sons of U'-lam; Be'-dan. These *were* the sons of Gil'-e-ad, the son of Ma'-chir, the son of Ma-nas'-seh.

18 And his sister Ham-mol'-e-keth bare I'-shod, and A-bi-e'-zer, and Ma-ha'-lah.

19 And the sons of She-mi'-dah were, A-hi'-an, and She'-chem, and Lik'-hi, and A'-ni-am.

The Genealogy of Ephraim

20 And the sons of E'-phra-im; Shu'-the-lah, and Be'-red his son, and Ta'-hath his son, and El'-a-dah his son, and Ta'-hath his son,

21 And Za'-bad his son, and Shu'-the-lah his son, and E'-zer, and E'-le-ad, whom the men of RGath *that were* born in *that* land slew, because they came down to Ttake away their cattle.   1 Sam. 5:8 · steal

22 And E'-phra-im their father Rmourned many days, and his brethren came to Rcomfort him.   Gen. 50:3 · Gen. 50:21; Job 2:11

23 And when he went in to his wife, she Rconceived, and bare a son, and he called his name Be-ri'-ah, because Tit went evil with his house.   Gen. 21:2 · there had been calamity

24 (And his daughter *was* She'-rah, Rwho built Beth–ho'-ron the Tnether, and the upper, and Uz'-zen-she'-rah.)   Josh. 16:3, 5 · lower

25 And Re'-phah *was* his son, also Re'-sheph, and Te'-lah his son, and Ta'-han his son,

26 La'-a-dan his son, Am-mi'-hud his son, E-lish'-a-ma his son,

27 TNon his son, Je-hosh'-u-ah his son. Num

28 And Rtheir possessions and habitations *were,* Beth'–el and the towns thereof, and eastward Na'-a-ran, and westward Ge'-zer, with the Ttowns thereof; She'-chem also and the towns thereof, unto Ga'-za and the towns thereof: Josh. 16:2 · daughters

29 And by the borders of the children of Ma-nas'-seh, Beth-she'-an and her towns, Ta'-a-nach and her towns, Me-gid'-do and her towns, Dor and her towns. In these dwelt the children of Joseph the son of Israel.

The Genealogy of Asher—Gen. 46:17

30 RThe sons of Asher; Im'-nah, and Is'-u-ah, and Ish'-u-ai, and Be-ri'-ah, and Se'-rah their sister.   Gen. 46:17; Num. 26:44, 46

31 And the sons of Be-ri'-ah; He'-ber, and Mal'-chi-el, who *is* the father of Bir'-za-vith.

32 And He'-ber begat Japh'-let, and Sho'-mer, and Ho'-tham, and Shu'-a their sister.

33 And the sons of Japh'-let; Pa'-sach, and Bim'-hal, and Ash'-vath. These *are* the children of Japh'-let.

34 And the sons of ᵀSha'-mer; A'-hi, and Roh'-gah, Je-hub'-bah, and A'-ram.   *Shomer*

35 And the sons of his brother He'-lem; Zo'-phah, and Im'-na, and She'-lesh, and A'-mal.

36 The sons of Zo'-phah; Su'-ah, and Har'-ne-pher, and Shu'-al, and Be'-ri, and Im'-rah,

37 Be'-zer, and Hod, and Sham'-ma, and Shil'-shah, and Ith'-ran, and Be-e'-ra.

38 And the sons of Je'-ther; Je-phun'-neh, and Pis'-pah, and A'-ra.

39 And the sons of Ul'-la; A'-rah, and Han'-i-el, and Re-zi'-a.

40 All these *were* the children of Asher, heads of *their* father's house, choice *and* mighty men of valour, chief of the princes. And the number throughout the genealogy of them that were apt to the war *and* to battle *was* twenty and six thousand men.

CHAPTER 8

The Genealogy of Benjamin—Gen. 46:21

NOW Benjamin begat ᴿBe'-la his first-born, Ash'-bel the second, and A-har'-ah the third,   7:6–12; Gen. 46:21; Num. 26:38

2 No'-hah the fourth, and Ra'-pha the fifth.

3 And the sons of Be'-la were, ᵀAd'-dar,ᴿ and Ge'-ra, and A-bi'-hud,   *Ard • Gen. 46:21*

4 And Ab-i-shu'-a, and Na'-a-man, and A-ho'-ah,

5 And Ge'-ra, and ᴿShe-phu'-phan,ᵀ and Hu'-ram.   Num. 26:39; 7:12 • *Shupham*

6 And these *are* the sons of E'-hud: these are the heads of the fathers of the inhabitants of Ge'-ba, and they ᵀremoved them to ᴿMa-na'-hath: *went into exile* • 2:52

7 And Na'-a-man, and A-hi'-ah, and Ge'-ra, he removed them, and begat Uz'-za, and A-hi'-hud.

8 And Sha-ha-ra'-im begat *children* in the country of Moab, after he had sent them away; Hu'-shim and Ba'-a-ra *were* his wives.

9 And he begat of Ho'-desh his wife, Jo'-bab, and Zib'-i-a, and Me'-sha, and Mal'-cham,

10 And Je'-uz, and Sha-chi'-a, and Mir'-ma. These *were* his sons, heads of the fathers.

11 And of Hu'-shim he begat Ab'-i-tub, and El-pa'-al.

12 The sons of El-pa'-al; E'-ber, and Mi'-sham, and Sha'-med, who built O'-no, and Lod, with the towns thereof:

13 Be-ri'-ah also, and ᴿShe'-ma, who *were* heads of the fathers of the inhabitants of Ai'-ja-lon, who drove away the inhabitants of Gath: *v. 21*

14 And A-hi'-o, Sha'-shak, and Jer'-e-moth,

15 And Zeb-a-di'-ah, and A'-rad, and A'-der,

16 And Mi'-cha-el, and Is'-pah, and Jo'-ha, the sons of Be-ri'-ah;

17 And Zeb-a-di'-ah, and Me-shul'-lam, and Hez'-e-ki, and He'-ber,

18 Ish'-me-rai also, and Jez-li'-ah, and Jo'-bab, the sons of El-pa'-al;

19 And Ja'-kim, and Zich'-ri, and Zab'-di,

20 And El-i-e'-nai, and Zil'-thai, and E-li'-el,

21 And A-da'-iah, and Be-ra'-iah, and Shim'-rath, the sons of ᵀShim'-hi;   *Shema*

22 And Ish'-pan, and He'-ber, and E'li'-el,

23 And Ab'-don, and Zich'-ri, and Ha'-nan,

24 And Han-a-ni'-ah, and E'-lam, and An-to-thi'-jah,

25 And Iph-e-de'-iah, and Pe-nu'-el, the sons of Sha'-shak;

26 And Sham'-she-rai, and She-ha-ri'-ah, and Ath-a-li'-ah,

27 And Jar-e-si'-ah, and E-li'-ah, and Zich'-ri, the sons of Jer'-o-ham.

28 These *were* heads of the fathers, by their generations, chief *men*. These ᵀdwelt in Jerusalem.   *lived*

29 And at Gib'-e-on dwelt the father of Gib'-e-on; whose ᴿwife's name *was* Ma'-a-chah: 9:35–38

30 And his firstborn son Ab'-don, and Zur, and Kish, and Ba'-al, and Na'-dab,

31 And Ge'-dor, and A-hi'-o, and ᵀZa'-cher.ᴿ   *Zechariah* • 9:37

32 And Mik'-loth begat Shim'-e-ah. And these also dwelt with their brethren in Jerusalem, ᵀover against them.   *opposite them*

33 And Ner begat Kish, and Kish begat Saul, and Saul begat Jonathan, and Mal'-chi–shu'-a, and ᴿA-bin'-a-dab, and ᵀEsh-ba'-al.   1 Sam. 14:49, *Ishui • Ish-bosheth*, 2 Sam. 2:8

34 And the son of Jonathan *was* Mer'-ib-ba'-al; and Mer'-ib-ba'-al begat Mi'-cah.

35 ᴿAnd the sons of Mi'-cah *were*, Pi'-thon, and Me'-lech, and Ta-re'-a, and Ahaz.   9:41

36 And Ahaz begat Je-ho'-a-dah; and Je-ho'-a-dah begat Al'-e-meth, and Az'-ma-veth, and Zim'-ri; and Zim'-ri begat Mo'-za,

37 And Mo'-za begat Bin'-e-a: ᴿRa'-phaᵀ *was* his son, E-le'-a-sah his son, A'-zel his son: 9:43 • *Rephaiah*

38 And A'-zel had six sons, whose names *are* these, Az'-ri-kam, Boch'-e-ru, and Ish'-ma-el, and She-a-ri'-ah, and O-ba-di'-ah, and Ha'-nan. All these *were* the sons of A'-zel.

39 And the sons of E'-shek his brother *were*, U'-lam his firstborn, Je'-hush the second, and E-liph'-e-let the third.

40 And the sons of U'-lam were mighty men of valour, archers, and had many sons, and sons' sons, an hundred and fifty. All these *are* of the sons of Benjamin.

CHAPTER 9

The Genealogy of the Twelve Tribes Who Returned

SO all Israel Twere reckoned by geneal-ogies; and, behold, they were written in the book of the kings of Israel and Judah, who were carried away to Babylon for their Ttransgression.   were registered · sins

2 RNow the first inhabitants that dwelt in their possessions in their cities were, the Israelites, the priests, Levites, and Rthe Neth'-i-nims.   Neh. 7:73 · Ezra 2:43; 8:20

3 And in RJerusalem dwelt the children of RJudah, and of the children of Benjamin, and of the children of E'-phra-im, and Ma-nas'-seh;   Neh. 11:1 · Gen. 29:35

4 U'-thai the son of Am-mi'-hud, the son of Om'-ri, the son of Im'-ri, the son of Ba'-ni, of the children of Pha'-rez the son of Judah.

5 And of the Shi'-lo-nites; A-sa'-iah the firstborn, and his sons.

6 And of the sons of Ze'-rah; Jeu'-el, and their brethren, six hundred and ninety.

7 And of the sons of RBenjamin; Sal'-lu the son of Me-shul'-lam, the son of Hod-a-vi'-ah, the son of Has-e-nu'-ah,   Gen. 35:18

8 And Ib-ne'-iah the son of Jer'-o-ham, and E'-lah the son of Uz'-zi, the son of Mich'-ri, and Me-shul'-lam the son of Sheph-a-thi'-ah, the son of Reu'-el, the son of Ib-ni'-jah;

9 And their brethren, according to their Tgenerations, nine hundred and fifty and six. All these men were chief of the fathers in the house of their fathers.   families

The Genealogy of the Priests Who Returned

10 RAnd of the priests; Je-da'-iah, and Je-hoi'-a-rib, and Ja'-chin,   Neh. 11:10

11 And TAz-a-ri'-ah the son of Hil-ki'-ah, the son of Me-shul'-lam, the son of Za'-dok, the son of Me-ra'-ioth, the son of A-hi'-tub, the ruler of the house of God;   Seraiah

12 And A-da'-iah the son of Jer'-o-ham, the son of Pash'-ur, the son of Mal-chi'-jah, and Ma-as'-i-ai the son of A'-di-el, the son of Jah'-ze-rah, the son of Me-shul'-lam, the son of Me-shil'-le-mith, the son of Im'-mer;

13 And their brethren, heads of the house of their fathers, a thousand and seven hundred and threescore; very able men for the work of the service of the house of God.

The Genealogy of the Levites Who Returned

14 And of the Levites; She-ma'-iah the son of Has'-shub, the son of Az'-ri-kam, the son of Hash-a-bi'-ah, of the sons of Me-ra'-ri;

15 And Bak-bak'-kar, He'-resh, and Ga'-lal, and Mat-ta-ni'-ah the son of Mi'-cah, the son of Zich'-ri, the son of A'-saph;

16 And RO-ba-di'-ah the son of She-ma'-iah, the son of Ga'-lal, the son of Je-du'-thun, and Ber-e-chi'-ah the son of A'-sa, the son of El'-ka-nah, that dwelt in the villages of the Ne-toph'-a-thites.   Neh. 11:17

17 And the porters were, Shal'-lum, and Ak'-kub, and Tal'-mon, and A-hi'-man, and their brethren: Shal'-lum was the chief;

18 Who hitherto waited in the Rking's gate eastward: they were porters in the companies of the children of Levi.   Ezek. 46:1, 2

19 And Shal'-lum the son of Ko'-re, the son of E-bi'-a-saph, the son of Ko'-rah, and his brethren, of the house of his father, the Ko'-rah-ites, were over the work of the service, keepers of the Tgates of the tabernacle: and their fathers, being over the host of the LORD, were keepers of the Tentry.   doors · entrance

20 And RPhin'-e-has the son of E-le-a'-zar was the ruler over them in time past, and the LORD was with him.   Num. 25:7–13; 31:6

21 And RZech-a-ri'-ah the son of Me-shel-e-mi'-ah was Tporter of the door of the tabernacle of the congregation.   26:2, 14 · keeper

22 All these which were chosen to be Tporters in the Tgates were two hundred and twelve. These were reckoned by their genealogy in their villages, whom David and Samuel the seer Tdid ordain in their Tset office.   keepers · doors · established them · assigned

23 So they and their children had the oversight of the Tgates of the house of the LORD, namely, the house of the tabernacle, by Twards.   doors · guards

24 In four quarters were the porters, toward the east, west, north, and south.

25 And their brethren, which were in their villages, were to come Rafter seven days from time to time with them.   2 Kin. 11:5

26 For these Levites, the four chief Tpor-ters, were in their Tset office, and were over the Tchambers and treasuries of the house of God.   keepers · assigned · rooms

27 And they lodged round about the house of God, because the Tcharge was upon them, and the opening thereof every morning pertained to them.   responsibility

28 And certain of them had the charge of the ministering vessels, that they should bring them in and out Tby tale.   by count

29 Some of them also were appointed to oversee the vessels, and all Tthe R instruments of the sanctuary, and the fine flour, and the wine, and the oil, and the frankincense, and the spices.   the holy utensils · 23:29

30 And some of the sons of the priests made Rthe ointment of the spices.   Ex. 30:23

31 And Mat-ti-thi'-ah, one of the Levites, who was the firstborn of Shal'-lum the Ko'-rah-ite, had the Tset office over the things that were made in the pans.   assigned

32 And other of their brethren, of the sons

of the Ko'-hath-ites, were over the shew-bread, to prepare it every sabbath.

33 And these are the singers, chief of the fathers of the Levites, who remaining in the chambers were free: for they were employed in that work day and night.

34 These chief fathers of the Levites were chief throughout their generations; these dwelt at RJerusalem.   Josh. 10:1

The Genealogy of Saul

35 And in Gib'-e-on dwelt the father of RGib'-e-on, Je-hi'-el, whose wife's name was RMa'-a-chah: vv. 35-44 • 8:29

36 And his firstborn son Ab'-don, then Zur, and Kish, and Ba'-al, and Ner, and Na'-dab,

37 And Ge'-dor, and A-hi'-o, and Zech-a-ri'-ah, and Mik'-loth.

38 And Mik'-loth begat Shim'-e-am. And they also dwelt with their brethren at Jerusalem, over against their brethren.

39 And Ner begat Kish; and Kish begat Saul; and Saul begat Jonathan, and Mal'-chi-shu'-a, and A-bin'-a-dab, and Esh-ba'-al.

40 And the son of Jonathan was Mer'-ib-ba'-al: and Mer'-ib-ba'-al begat Mi'-cah.

41 And the sons of Mi'-cah were, Pi'-thon, and Me'-lech, and Tah-re'-a, and Ahaz.

42 And Ahaz begat RJa'-rah; and Ja'-rah begat Al'-e-meth, and Az'-ma-veth, and Zim'-ri; and Zim'-ri begat Mo'-za;   8:36

43 And Mo'-za begat Bin'-e-a; and Re-pha'-iah his son, E-le'-a-sah his son, A'-zel his son.

44 And A'-zel had six sons, whose names are these, Az'-ri-kam, Boch'-e-ru, and Ish'-ma-el, and She-a-ri'-ah, and O-ba-di'-ah, and Ha'-nan: these were the sons of A'-zel.

CHAPTER 10

The House of Saul Dies in Battle
1 Sam. 31:1-7

NOW Rthe Phi-lis'-tines fought against Israel; and the men of Israel fled from before the Phi-lis'-tines, and Tfell down slain in mount Gil-bo'-a.   1 Sam. 31:1, 2 • were killed

2 And the Phi-lis'-tines followed hard after Saul, and after his sons; and the Phi-lis'-tines slew Jonathan, and TA-bin'-a-dab, and Mal-chi–shu'-a, the sons of Saul.   Ishui

3 And the battle went Tsore against Saul, and the archers hit him, and he was wounded of the archers.   heavily

4 Then said Saul to his armourbearer, Draw thy sword, and thrust me through therewith; lest these uncircumcised come and Tabuse me. But his armourbearer would not; for he was Tsore afraid. So Saul took a sword, and fell upon it.   torture • very much

5 And when his armourbearer saw that Saul was dead, he fell likewise on the sword, and died.

6 So Saul died, and his three sons, and all his house died together.

7 And when all the men of Israel that were in the valley saw that they fled, and that Saul and his sons were dead, then they forsook their cities, and fled: and the Phi-lis'-tines came and dwelt in them.

The Philistines Defile Saul
1 Sam. 31:8-13

8 And it came to pass on the morrow, when the Phi-lis'-tines came to Tstrip the slain, that they found Saul and his sons fallen in mount Gil-bo'-a.   rob

9 And when they had Tstripped him, they took his head, and his armour, and sent into the land of the Phi-lis'-tines round about, to carry tidings unto their idols, and to the people.   robbed

10 RAnd they put his armour in the house of their gods, and Rfastened his head in the temple of Da'-gon.   1 Sam. 5:2 • 1 Sam. 31:10

11 And when all Ja'-besh-gil'-e-ad heard all that the Phi-lis'-tines had done to Saul,

12 They arose, all the Rvaliant men, and took away the body of Saul, and the bodies of his sons, and brought them to Ja'-besh, and buried their bones under the oak in Ja'-besh, and fasted seven days.   1 Sam. 14:52

The Cause of Saul's Death

13 So Saul died for his transgression which he committed against the LORD, even against the word of the LORD, which he kept not, and also for asking counsel of one that had a familiar spirit, to enquire of it;

14 And enquired not of the LORD: therefore he slew him, and Rturned the kingdom unto David the son of Jesse.   1 Sam. 15:28

CHAPTER 11

Anointing of David as King—2 Sam. 5:1-3

THEN Rall Israel gathered themselves to David unto He'-bron, saying, Behold, we are thy bone and thy flesh.   2 Sam. 5:1

2 And moreover in time past, even when Saul was king, thou wast he that leddest out and broughtest in Israel: and the LORD thy RGod said unto thee, Thou shalt Rfeed my people Israel, and thou shalt be ruler over my people Israel.   1 Sam. 16:1-3 • Ps. 78:71

3 Therefore came all the elders of Israel to the king to He'-bron; and David made Ta covenant with them in He'-bron before the LORD; and they Tanointed David king over

Israel, according to the word of the Lord by Samuel. *an agreement · consecrated*

Conquest of Jerusalem—2 Sam. 5:6–10

4 And David and all Israel went to Jerusalem, which is Je′-bus; where the Jeb′-u-sites were, the inhabitants of the land.

5 And the inhabitants of Je′-bus said to David, Thou shalt not come hither. Nevertheless David took the castle of ᴿZion, which is the city of David. 2 Sam. 5:7

6 And David said, Whosoever ᵀsmiteth the Jeb′-u-sites first shall be ᵀchief and captain. So Jo′-ab the son of Ze-ru′-iah went first up, and was chief. *defeats · head*

7 And David dwelt in the castle; therefore they called it the city of David.

8 And he built the city round about, even from ᵀMil′-lo round about: and Jo′-ab repaired the rest of the city. *citadel*

9 So David ᵀwaxed greater and greater: for the Lord of hosts was with him. *grew*

The Chiefs—2 Sam. 23:8–12

10 These also are the chief of the mighty men whom David had, who strengthened themselves with him in his kingdom, and with all Israel, to make him king, according to the word of the Lord concerning Israel.

11 And this is the number of the mighty men whom David had; Ja-sho′-be-am, an Hach′-mo-nite, the chief of the captains: he lifted up his spear against three hundred slain by him at one time.

12 And after him was E-le-a′-zar the son of ᴿDodo, the A-ho′-hite, who was one of the three mighties. 27:4

13 He was with David at ᵀPas-dam′-mim, and there the Phi-lis′-tines were gathered together to battle, where was a parcel of ground full of barley; and the people fled from before the Phi-lis′-tines. *Ephes-dammim*

14 And they ᴿset themselves in the midst of that parcel, and delivered it, and slew the Phi-lis′-tines; and the Lord saved them by a great deliverance. [Eph. 6:13]

The Thirty Captains—2 Sam. 23:13–23

15 Now three of the thirty captains went down to the rock to David, into the cave of A-dul′-lam; and the host of the Phi-lis′-tines encamped ᴿin the valley of Reph′-a-im. 14:9

16 And David was then in the ᵀhold, and the Phi-lis′-tines′ ᴿgarrison was then at Beth′-le-hem. *fortress · 1 Sam. 10:5*

17 And David longed, and said, Oh that one would give me drink of the water of the well of Beth′-le-hem, that is at the gate!

18 And the three brake through the host of the Phi-lis′-tines, and drew water out of the well of Beth′-le-hem, that was by the gate, and took it, and brought it to David: but

David would not drink of it, but poured it out to the Lord,

19 And said, My God forbid it me, that I should do this thing: shall I drink the blood of these men that have put their lives in jeopardy? for with the jeopardy of their lives they brought it. Therefore he would not drink it. These things did these three mightiest.

20 And A-bi′-shai the brother of Jo′-ab, he was chief of the three: for lifting up his spear against three hundred, he slew them, and had a name among the three.

21 Of the three, he was more honourable than the two; for he was their captain: howbeit he attained not to the first three.

22 ᴿBe-na′-iah the son of Je-hoi′-a-da, the son of a ᵀvaliant man of Kab′-ze-el, who had done many acts; he slew two lionlike men of Moab: also he went down and slew a lion in a pit in a snowy day. 2 Sam. 8:18 · strong

23 And he slew an Egyptian, a man of great stature, five cubits high; and in the Egyptian's hand was a spear like a weaver's beam; and he went down to him with a staff, and plucked the spear out of the Egyptian's hand, and slew him with his own spear.

24 These things did Be-na′-iah the son of Je-hoi′-a-da, and had the name among the three mighties.

25 Behold, he was honourable among the thirty, but attained not to the first three: and David set him over his guard.

The Valiant Men—2 Sam. 23:24–39

26 Also the valiant men of the armies were, A′-sa-hel the brother of Jo′-ab, El-ha′-nan the son of Dodo of Beth′-le-hem,

27 ᵀSham′-moth the Ha′-ro-rite, ᴿHe′-lez the ᵀPel′-o-nite, *Shammah · 2 Sam. 23:26 · Paltite*

28 ᴿI′-ra the son of Ik′-kesh the Te-ko′-ite, A′-bi-e′-zer the An′-toth-ite, 27:9

29 ᵀSib′-be-cai ᴿ the Hu′-shath-ite, ᵀI′-lai the A-ho′-hite, *Mebunnai · 2 Sam. 23:27 · Zalmon*

30 Ma′-ha-rai the Ne-toph′-a-thite, He′-led the son of Ba′-a-nah the Ne-toph′-a-thite,

31 I′-thai the son of Ri′-bai of Gib′-e-ah, that pertained to the children of Benjamin, ᴿBe-na′-iah the Pir′-a-thon-ite, 27:14

32 ᵀHu′-rai of the brooks of Ga′-ash, ᵀA-bi′-el the Ar′-bath-ite, *Hiddai · Abialbon*

33 Az′-ma-veth the Ba-ha′-rum-ite, E-li′-ah-ba the Sha-al′-bo-nite,

34 The sons of Ha′-shem the Gi′-zo-nite, Jonathan the son of Sha′-ge the Ha′-ra-rite,

35 ᵀA-hi′-am the son of Sa′-car the Ha′-ra-rite, El′-i-phal the son of Ur, *Ahasbai*

36 He′-pher the Mech′-e-rath-ite, A-hi′-jah the Pel′-o-nite,

37 ᴿHez′-ro the Car′-mel-ite, Na′-a-rai the son of Ez′-bai, 2 Sam. 23:35

38 Jo′-el the brother of Nathan, Mib′-har ᵀthe son of Hag′-ge-ri, *the Haggerite*

39 Ze′-lek the Am′-mon-ite, Na′-ha-rai the Be′-roth-ite, the armourbearer of Jo′-ab the son of Ze-ru′-iah,

40 I′-ra the Ith′-rite, Ga′-reb the Ith′-rite,

41 ᴿU-ri′-ah the ᴿHit′-tite, Za′-bad the son of Ah′-lai,   2 Sam. 11:1–27 • 2 Kin. 7:6

42 Ad′-i-na the son of Shi′-za the Reu′-benite, a captain of the Reu′-ben-ites, and thirty with him,

43 Ha′-nan the son of Ma′-a-chah, and Josh′-a-phat the Mith′-nite,

44 Uz-zi′-a the Ash′-te-rath-ite, Sha′-ma and Je-hi′-el the sons of Ho′-than the Ar′-o-er-ite,

45 Je-di′-a-el the ᵀson of Shim′-ri, and Jo′-ha his brother, the Ti′-zite,   Shimrite

46 E-li′-el the Ma′-ha-vite, and Jer′-i-bai, and Josh-a-vi′-ah, the sons of El′-na-am, and Ith′-mah the Mo′-ab-ite,

47 E-li′-el, and O′-bed, and Ja′-si-el the Me-so′-ba-ite.

CHAPTER 12

The Mighty Men at Ziklag

NOW ᴿthese are they that came to David to Zik′-lag, while he yet kept himself ᵀclose because of Saul the son of Kish: and they were among the mighty men, helpers of the war.   1 Sam. 27:2 • in hiding

2 They were armed with bows, and could use both the right hand and the left in hurling stones and shooting arrows out of a bow, even of Saul's brethren of Benjamin.

3 The chief was A-hi-e′-zer, then Jo′-ash, the sons of ᵀShe-ma′-ah the Gib′-e-ath-ite; and Je′-zi-el, and Pe′-let, the sons of Az′-ma-veth; and Ber′-a-chah, and Je′-hu the An′-toth-ite,   Hasmaah

4 And Is-ma′-iah the Gib′-e-on-ite, a mighty man among the thirty, and over the thirty; and Jer-e-mi′-ah, and Ja-ha′-zi-el, and Jo-ha′-nan, and Jos′-a-bad the Ged′-e-rath-ite,

5 E-lu′-zai, and Jer′-i-moth, and Be-a-li′-ah, and Shem-a-ri′-ah, and Sheph-a-ti′-ah the Har′-u-phite,

6 El′-ka-nah, and Je-si′-ah, and A-zar′-e-el, and Jo-e′-zer, and Ja-sho′-be-am, the Kor′-hites,

7 And Jo-e′-lah, and Zeb-a-di′-ah, the sons of Jer′-o-ham of Ge′-dor.

8 And of the Gad′-ites there ᵀseparated themselves unto David into the hold to the wilderness men of might, and men of war fit for the battle, that could handle shield and buckler, whose faces were like the faces of lions, and were as swift as the roes upon the mountains;   came to support

9 E′-zer the first, O-ba-di′-ah the second, E-li′-ab the third,

10 Mish-man′-nah the fourth, Jer-e-mi′-ah the fifth,

11 At′-tai the sixth, E-li′-el the seventh,

12 Jo-ha′-nan the eighth, El′-za-bad the ninth,

13 Jer-e-mi′-ah the tenth, Mach′-ba-nai the eleventh.

14 These were of the sons of Gad, captains of the host: one of the least was over an hundred, and the greatest over a thousand.

15 These are they that went over Jordan in the first month, when it had overflown all his ᴿbanks; and they put to flight all them of the valleys, both toward the east, and toward the west.   Josh. 3:15; 4:18

16 And there came of the children of Benjamin and Judah to the hold unto David.

17 And David went out to meet them, and answered and said unto them, If ye be come peaceably unto me to help me, mine heart shall be knit unto you: but if ye be come to betray me to mine enemies, seeing there is no ᵀwrong in mine hands, the God of our fathers look thereon, and rebuke it.   violence

18 Then the spirit came upon ᴿAm′-a-sai, who was chief of the captains, and he said, Thine are we, David, and on thy side, thou son of Jesse: peace, peace be unto thee, and peace be to thine helpers; for thy God helpeth thee. Then David received them, and made them captains of the band.   2 Sam. 17:25

19 And there fell some of Ma-nas′-seh to David, when he came with the Phi-lis′-tines against Saul to battle: but they helped them not: for the lords of the Phi-lis′-tines upon ᵀadvisement sent him away, saying, He will ᵀfall to his master Saul to the jeopardy of our heads.   counsel • desert

20 As he went to Zik′-lag, there fell to him of Ma-nas′-seh, Ad′-nah, and Joz′-a-bad, and Je-di′-a-el, and Mi′-cha-el, and Joz′-a-bad, and E-li′-hu, and Zil′-thai, captains of the thousands that were of Ma-nas′-seh.

21 And they helped David against the band of the rovers: for they were all mighty men of valour, and were captains in the host.

22 For at that time day by day there came to David to help him, until it was a great ᵀhost, like the host of God.   army

The Mighty Men at Hebron

23 And these are the numbers of the ᵀbands that were ready armed to the war, and came to David to He′-bron, to turn the kingdom of Saul to him, ᴿaccording to the word of the LORD.   groups • 1 Sam. 16:1

24 The children of Judah that bare shield and spear were six thousand and eight hundred, ready armed to the war.

25 Of the children of Simeon, mighty men of valour for the war, seven thousand and one hundred.

26 Of the children of ᴿLevi four thousand and six hundred.   23:27; 2 Chr. 11:13
27 And Je-hoi'-a-da *was* the leader of the Aaronites, and with him *were* three thousand and seven hundred;
28 And ᴿZa'-dok, a young man mighty of valour, and of his father's house twenty and two captains.   6:8, 53; 2 Sam. 8:17
29 And of the children of Benjamin, the kindred of Saul, three thousand: for hitherto the greatest part of them had kept the ward of the house of Saul.
30 And of the children of E'-phra-im twenty thousand and eight hundred, mighty men of valour, ᵀfamous throughout the house of their fathers.   *men of names*
31 And of the half tribe of Ma-nas'-seh eighteen thousand, which were expressed by name, to come and make David king.
32 And of the children of Is'-sa-char, *which were men* that had understanding of the times, to know what Israel ought to do; the heads of them *were* two hundred; and all their brethren *were* at their commandment.
33 Of Zeb'-u-lun, such as went forth to battle, expert in war, with all instruments of war, fifty thousand, which could keep rank: *they were* not of double heart.
34 And of Naph'-ta-li a thousand captains, and with them with shield and spear thirty and seven thousand.
35 And of the Danites expert in war twenty and eight thousand and six hundred.
36 And of Asher, such as went forth to battle, expert in war, forty thousand.
37 And on the other side of Jordan, of the Reu'-ben-ites, and the Gad'-ites, and of the half tribe of Ma-nas'-seh, with all manner of instruments of war for the battle, an hundred and twenty thousand.
38 All these men of war, that could keep rank, came with a ᵀperfect heart to He'-bron, to make David king over all Israel: and all the rest also of Israel *were* of one heart to make David king.   *sincere purpose*
39 And there they were with David three days, eating and drinking: for their brethren had prepared for them.
40 Moreover they that were nigh them, *even* unto Is'-sa-char and Zeb'-u-lun and Naph'-ta-li, ᴿbrought bread on asses, and on camels, and on mules, and on oxen, *and* meat, meal, cakes of figs, and bunches of raisins, and wine, and oil, and oxen, and sheep abundantly: for *there was* joy in Israel.   1 Sam. 25:18

CHAPTER 13

Preparation to Move the Ark

AND David consulted with the ᴿcaptains of thousands and hundreds, *and* with every leader.   11:15; 12:34

2 And David said unto all the congregation of Israel, If *it seem* good unto you, and *that it be* of the Lᴏʀᴅ our God, let us send abroad unto our brethren every where, *that are* ᴿleftᵀ in all the land of Israel, and with them *also* to the priests and Levites *which are* in their cities *and* suburbs, that they may gather themselves unto us: 1 Sam. 31:1; Is. 37:4 • *remaining*
3 And let us bring again the ᴿark of our God to us: for we enquired not at it in the days of Saul.   1 Sam. 7:1
4 And all the congregation said that they would do so: for the thing was right in the eyes of all the people.
5 So ᴿDavid gathered all Israel together, from ᴿShi'-hor of Egypt even unto the entering of He'-math, to bring the ark of God from Kir'-jath-je'-a-rim.   1 Sam. 7:5 • Josh. 13:3

Uzza Dies for Touching the Ark
2 Sam. 6:1–11

6 And David went up, and all Israel, to ᴿBa'-al-ah, *that is,* to Kir'-jath-je'-a-rim, which *belonged* to Judah, to bring up thence the ark of God the Lᴏʀᴅ, ᴿthat dwelleth *between* the cher'-u-bims, whose name is called *on it.*   Josh. 15:9, 60 • 1 Sam. 4:4
7 And they carried the ark of God in a new cart out of the house of A-bin'-a-dab: and Uz'-za and A-hi'-o drave the cart.
8 ᴿAnd David and all Israel played before God with all *their* might, and with singing, and with harps, and with psalteries, and with timbrels, and with cymbals, and with trumpets.   2 Sam. 6:5
9 And when they came unto the threshingfloor of Chi'-don, Uz'-za put forth his hand to hold the ark; for the oxen stumbled.
10 And the anger of the Lᴏʀᴅ was kindled against Uz'-za, and he ᵀsmote him, because he put his hand to the ark: and there he ᴿdied before God.   *struck* • Lev. 10:2
11 And David was displeased, because the Lᴏʀᴅ had made a breach upon Uz'-za: wherefore that place is called ᵀPe'-rez-uz'-za to this day.   *the breach of Uzza*
12 And ᴿDavid was afraid of God that day, saying, How shall I bring the ark of God *home* to me?   Ps. 31:10; 32:3
13 So David brought not the ark *home* to himself to the city of David, but carried it aside into the ᴿhouse of O'-bed-e'-dom the Git'-tite.   26:4, 5
14 ᴿAnd the ark of God remained with the family of O'-bed-e'-dom in his house three months. And the Lᴏʀᴅ blessed the house of O'-bed-e'-dom, and all that he had.   2 Sam. 6:11

CHAPTER 14

David's House Is Constructed—2 Sam. 5:11, 12

NOW ᴿHiram king of Tyre sent messengers to David, and timber of cedars,

with masons and carpenters, to build him an house.   2 Sam. 5:11; 1 Kin. 5:1

2 And David perceived that the LORD had confirmed him king over Israel, for his kingdom ᵀwas lifted up on high, because of his people Israel.   *reached high prestige*

David's Children in Jerusalem

3 And David took ᵀmore wives at Jerusalem: and David begat more sons and daughters.   *yet*

4 Now these *are* the names of *his* children which he had in Jerusalem; Sham-mu'-a, and Sho'-bab, Nathan, and Solomon,

5 And Ib'-har, and El-i-shu'-a, and El'-pa-let,

6 And No'-gah, and Ne'-pheg, and Ja-phi'-a,

7 And E-lish'-a-ma, and ᵀBe-e-li'-a-da,ᴿ and E-liph'-a-let.   *Eliada • 2 Sam. 5:16*

David's Victory over the Philistines
2 Sam. 5:17–25

8 And when the Phi-lis'-tines heard that David was anointed king over all Israel, all the Phi-lis'-tines went up to seek David. And David heard *of it,* and went out against them.

9 And the Phi-lis'-tines came and spread themselves in the valley of Reph'-a-im.

10 And David enquired of God, saying, ᴿShall I go up against the Phi-lis'-tines? and wilt thou deliver them into mine hand? And the LORD said unto him, Go up; for I will deliver them into thine hand.   *v. 13*

11 So they came up to Ba'-al-per'-a-zim; and David smote them there. Then David said, God hath broken in upon mine enemies by mine hand like ᵀthe breaking forth of waters: therefore they called the name of that place Ba'-al-per'-a-zim.   *a flood*

12 And when they had left their ᵀgods there, David gave a commandment, and they were burned with fire.   *idols*

13 And the Phi-lis'-tines yet again ᵀspread themselves abroad in the valley.   *made a raid*

14 Therefore David ᵀenquired again of God; and God said unto him, Go not up after them; turn away from them, and come upon them over against the mulberry trees.   *prayed*

15 And it shall be, when thou shalt hear a sound of going in the tops of the mulberry trees, *that* then thou shalt go out to battle: for God is gone forth before thee to smite the host of the Phi-lis'-tines.

16 David therefore did as God commanded him: and they ᵀsmote the host of the Phi-lis'-tines from Gib'-e-on even to Ga'-zer.   *defeated*

17 And ᴿthe fame of David went out into all lands; and the LORD brought the ᵀfear of him upon all nations.   2 Chr. 26:8 • *respect*

CHAPTER 15

Spiritual Preparation to Move the Ark

AND *David* made him houses in the city of David, and prepared a place for the ark of God, ᴿand pitched for it a tent. *v.* 3; 16:1; 17:1-5

2 Then David said, None ought to carry the ark of God but the Levites: for them hath the LORD chosen to carry the ark of God, and to minister unto him for ever.

3 And David ᴿgathered all Israel together to Jerusalem, to bring up the ark of the LORD ᴿunto his place, which he had prepared for it.   13:5; 1 Kin. 8:1 • *vv.* 1, 12

4 And David assembled the children of Aaron, and the ᴿLevites: 6:16–30; 12:26–28

5 Of the sons of Ko'-hath; U-ri'-el the chief, and his brethren an hundred and twenty:

6 Of the sons of Me-ra'-ri; A-sa'-iah the chief, and his brethren two hundred and twenty:

7 Of the sons of Ger'-shom; Jo'-el the chief, and his brethren an hundred and thirty:

8 Of the sons of E-liz'-a-phan; She-ma'-iah the chief, and his brethren two hundred:

9 Of the sons of ᴿHe'-bron; E'-li'-el the chief, and his brethren fourscore: Ex. 6:18

10 Of the sons of Uz-zi'-el; Am-min'-a-dab the chief, and his brethren an hundred and twelve.

11 And David called for Za'-dok and A-bi'-a-thar the priests, and for the Levites, for U-ri'-el, A-sa'-iah, and Jo'-el, She-ma'-iah, and E-li'-el, and Am-min'-a-dab,

12 And said unto them, Ye *are* the chief of the fathers of the Levites: ᵀsanctify yourselves, *both* ye and your brethren, that ye may bring up the ark of the LORD God of Israel unto *the place that* I have prepared for it.   *set yourselves apart*

13 For because ye *did it* not at the first, the LORD our God made a breach upon us, for that we sought him not after the due order.

14 So the priests and the Levites ᵀsanctified themselves to bring up the ark of the LORD God of Israel.   *set themselves apart*

15 And the children of the Levites bare the ark of God upon their shoulders with the staves thereon, as ᴿMoses commanded according to the word of the LORD.   Ex. 25:14

16 And David spake to the chief of the Levites ᴿto appoint their brethren *to be* the singers with instruments of musick, psalteries and harps and cymbals, sounding, by ᵀlifting up the voice with joy.   13:8 • *singing*

17 So the Levites appointed ᴿHe'-man the son of Jo'-el; and of his brethren, A'-saph the son of Ber-e-chi'-ah; and of the sons of Me-ra'-ri their brethren, E'-than the son of Kush-a'-iah;   6:33

18 And with them their brethren of the second *degree,* Zech-a-ri'-ah, Ben, and Ja-a'-

zi-el, and She-mir'-a-moth, and Je-hi'-el, and Un'-ni, E-li'-ab, and Be-na'-iah, and Ma-a-se'-iah, and Mat-ti-thi'-ah, and E-liph'-e-leh, and Mik-ne'-iah, and O'-bed-e'-dom, and Je-i'-el, the porters.

19 So the ᴿsingers, He'-man, A'-saph, and E'-than, *were appointed* to sound with cymbals of brass;   Gen. 4:21

20 And Zech-a-ri'-ah, and A'-zi-el, and She-mir'-a-moth, and Je-hi'-el, and Un'-ni, and E-li'-ab, and Ma-a-se'-iah, and Be-na'-iah, with psalteries on Al'-a-moth;

21 And Mat-ti-thi'-ah, and E-liph'-e-leh, and Mik-ne'-iah, and O'-bed-e'-dom, and Je-i'-el, and Az-a-zi'-ah, with harps on the ᴿShem'-i-nith to excel.   Ps. 6 title

22 And Chen-a-ni'-ah, chief of the Levites, *was* for song: he instructed about the song, because he *was* ᵀskilful.   *trained*

23 And Ber-e-chi'-ah and El'-ka-nah *were* ᴿdoorkeepers for the ark.   2 Kin. 25:18

24 And Sheb-a-ni'-ah, and Je-hosh'-a-phat, and Ne-than'-e-el, and Am'-a-sai, and Zech-a-ri'-ah, and Be-na'-iah, and E-li-e'-zer, the priests, did blow with the trumpets before the ark of God: and O'-bed-e'-dom and Je-hi'-ah *were* doorkeepers for the ark.

Joyful Transportation of the Ark
2 Sam. 6:12–16

25 So David, and the elders of Israel, and the captains over thousands, went to bring up the ark of the covenant of the LORD out of the house of O'-bed-e'-dom with joy.

26 And it came to pass, when God helped the Levites that bare the ark of the covenant of the LORD, that they offered ᴿseven bullocks and seven rams.   Num. 23:1–4, 29

27 And David *was* clothed with a robe of fine linen, and all the Levites that bare the ark, and the singers, and Chen-a-ni'-ah the master of the song with the singers: David also *had* upon him an e'-phod of linen.

28 ᴿThus all Israel brought up the ark of the covenant of the LORD with shouting, and with sound of the cornet, and with trumpets, and with cymbals, making a noise with psalteries and harps.   13:8

29 And it came to pass, ᴿas the ark of the covenant of the LORD came to the city of David, that ᴿMi'-chal the daughter of Saul looking out at a window saw king David dancing and playing: and she ᵀdespised him in her heart.   2 Sam. 6:16 • 1 Sam. 18:20 • *hated*

CHAPTER 16

Offering of Sacrifices—2 Sam. 6:17–19

SO they brought the ark of God, and set it in the midst of the tent that David had pitched for it: and they offered burnt sacrifices and peace offerings before God.

2 And when David had ᵀmade an end of offering the burnt offerings and the peace offerings, he ᴿblessed the people in the name of the LORD.   *finished* • 1 Kin. 8:14

3 And he ᵀdealt to every one of Israel, both man and woman, to every one a loaf of bread, and a ᴿgood piece of flesh, and a flagon *of wine.*   *gave* • Gen. 18:8

Appointing Musicians

4 And he appointed *certain* of the Levites to minister before the ark of the LORD, and to ᴿrecord, and to thank and praise the LORD God of Israel: Ps. 38; 70, title

5 A'-saph the chief, and next to him Zech-a-ri'-ah, ᴿJe-i'-el, and She-mir'-a-moth, and Je-hi'-el, and Mat-ti-thi'-ah, and E-li'-ab, and Be-na'-iah, and O'-bed-e'-dom: and Je-i'-el with psalteries and with ᵀharps; but A'-saph made a sound with cymbals;   15:18 • *lyres*

6 Be-na'-iah also and Ja-ha'-zi-el the priests with trumpets continually before the ᴿark of the covenant of God.   Ex. 25:10

Praise Psalm of David

7 Then on that day David delivered first *this psalm* to thank the LORD into the hand of A'-saph and his brethren.

8 Give thanks unto the LORD, call upon his name, make known his deeds among the people.

9 Sing unto him, sing psalms unto him, talk ye of all his wondrous works.

10 Glory ye in his holy name: let the heart of them rejoice that seek the LORD.

11 ᴿSeek the LORD and his strength, seek his face continually.   Ps. 24:6

12 ᴿRemember his marvellous works that he hath done, his wonders, and the ᵀjudgments of his mouth;   Ps. 78:43–68; 103:2 • *wisdom*

13 O ye seed of Israel his servant, ye children of Jacob, his ᴿchosen ones.   Ps. 33:12

14 He *is* the LORD our God; ᴿhis judgments *are* in all the earth.   Ps. 48:10

15 Be ye mindful always of his ᵀcovenant; the word *which* he commanded to a thousand generations;   *agreement*

16 *Even of the covenant* which he made with Abraham, and of his oath unto Isaac;

17 And hath ᴿconfirmed the same to Jacob for a law, *and* to Israel *for* an everlasting covenant,   Gen. 35:11, 12

18 Saying, Unto thee will I give the land of Canaan, the ᵀlot of your inheritance;   *place*

19 When ye were but few, ᴿeven a few, and strangers in it.   Gen. 34:30

20 And *when* they went from nation to nation, and from *one* kingdom to another people;

21 He suffered no man to do them wrong: yea, he reproved kings for their sakes,

22 *Saying,* ᴿTouch not mine anointed, and do my prophets no harm.   Ps. 105:15

23 RSing unto the LORD, all the earth; shew forth from day to day his salvation.   Ps. 96

24 Declare his glory among the heathen; his marvellous works among all nations.

25 For Rgreat is the LORD, and Rgreatly to be praised: he also is to be feared above all gods.   Ps. 145:3 • Ps. 9:11

26 For all the gods Rof the people are idols: but the LORD made the heavens.   Lev. 19:4

27 Glory and honour are in his presence; strength and gladness are in his place.

28 RGive unto the LORD, ye kindreds of the people, give unto the LORD glory and strength.   Ps. 22:23

29 Give unto the LORD the Rglory due unto his name: bring an offering, and come before him: worship the LORD in the beauty of holiness.   Deut. 15:14

30 TFearR before him, all the earth: the world also shall be stable, that it be not moved.   Honour him • [Deut. 10:12]

31 RLet the heavens be glad, and let the earth rejoice: and let men say among the nations, The LORD reigneth.   Is. 44:23

32 Let the sea roar, and the fulness thereof: let the fields rejoice, and all that is therein.

33 Then shall the Rtrees of the wood sing out at the presence of the LORD, because he cometh to judge the earth.   Is. 55:12, 13

34 RO give thanks unto the LORD; for he is good; for his mercy endureth for ever.   Ps. 106:1

35 RAnd say ye, RSave us, O God of our salvation, and gather us together, and Rdeliver us from the heathen, that we may give thanks to thy holy name, and glory in thy praise.   Ps. 106:47 • Ps. 31:16 • Ps. 25:20

36 RBlessed be the LORD God of Israel for ever and ever. And all the people said, A'men, and praised the LORD.   2 Chr. 8:14; Ezra 3:4

Constant Ministry at the Ark

37 So he left there before the ark of the covenant of the LORD A'-saph and his brethren, to Tminister before the ark continually, as every day's work required: serve

38 And RO'-bed-e'-dom with their brethren, threescore and eight; O'-bed-e'-dom also the son of Je-du'-thun and Ho'-sah to be Tporters: 13:14 • doorkeepers

39 And Za'-dok the priest, and his brethren the priests, Rbefore the tabernacle of the LORD Rin the Thigh place that was at Gib'-e-on,   21:29 • 1 Kin. 3:4 • place of worship

40 To offer burnt offerings unto the LORD upon the altar of the burnt offering continually morning and evening, and to do according to all that is written in the law of the LORD, which he commanded Israel;

41 And with them He'-man and Je-du'-thun, and the rest that were chosen, who were Texpressed by name, to give thanks to the LORD, Rbecause his mercy endureth for ever;   designated • 2 Chr. 5:13; Ezra 3:11; Jer. 33:11

42 And with them He'-man and Je-du'-thun with trumpets and cymbals for those that should make a sound, and with musical instruments Tof God. And the sons of Je-du'-thun were porters.   for the songs

43 RAnd all the people departed every man to his house: and David returned to bless his house.   2 Sam. 6:19, 20

16:29 The Meaning of Worship—Worship refers to the supreme honor or veneration given either in thought or deed to a person or thing. The Bible teaches that God alone is worthy of worship (Page 558—Ps. 29:2), but it also sadly records accounts of those who worshiped other objects. Among those were people (Page 824—Dan. 2:46), false gods (Page 382—2 Kin. 10:19), images and idols (Page 659—Is. 2:8; Page 825—Dan. 3:5), heavenly bodies (Page 394—2 Kin. 21:3), Satan (Page 1276—Rev. 13:4), and demons (Page 1274—Rev. 9:20). It is indeed tragic that many worshiped gods they could carry and not the God who could carry them. God Almighty alone is worthy of worship (Page 1271—Rev. 4:11).

True worship involves at least three important elements:

a. Worship requires reverence. This includes the honor and respect directed toward the Lord in thought and feeling. It is one thing to obey a superior unwillingly; it is quite another to commit one's thoughts and emotions in that obedience. Jesus said that those who worship God must do so "in spirit and in truth" (Page 1045—John 4:24). The term spirit speaks of the personal nature of worship: It is from my person to God's person and involves the intellect, emotions, and will. The word truth speaks of the content of worship: God is pleased when we worship Him, understanding His true character.

b. Worship includes public expression. This was particularly prevalent in the Old Testament because of the sacrificial system. For example, when a believer received a particular blessing for which he wanted to thank God, it was not sufficient to say it privately; he expressed his thanks publicly with a thank-offering (Page 105—Lev. 7:12).

c. Worship means service. These two concepts are often linked together in Scripture (Page 187—Deut. 8:19). Furthermore, the words for worship in both Testaments originally referred to the labor of slaves for the master. Worship especially includes the joyful service which Christians render to Christ their Master. The concept of worship must not be restricted to church attendance, but should embrace an entire life of obedience to God.

Now turn to Page 1224—Heb. 13:15: The Expressions of Worship.

CHAPTER 17

Desire of David to Build God's House
2 Sam. 7:1-3

NOW it came to pass, as David sat in his house, that David said to Nathan the prophet, Lo, I dwell in an house of cedars, but the ark of the covenant of the LORD remaineth ᵀunder curtains.   *in a tent*

2 Then Nathan said unto David, Do all that *is* in thine heart; for God *is* with thee.

Covenant of God to Build David's House
2 Sam. 7:4-17

3 And it came to pass the same night, that the word of God came to Nathan, saying,

4 Go and tell David my servant, Thus saith the LORD, ᴿThou shalt not build me an house to dwell in: 28:2, 3

5 For I have not dwelt in an house since the day that I brought up Israel unto this day; but ᵀhave gone from tent to tent, and from *one* tabernacle *to another.*   *have been*

6 Wheresoever I have walked with all Israel, ᵀspake I a word to any of the judges of Israel, ᴿwhom I commanded to feed my people, saying, Why have ye not built me an house of cedars?   *did I ever say* · 2 Sam. 7:7

7 Now therefore thus shalt thou say unto my servant David, Thus saith the LORD of hosts, I took thee from the sheepcote, *even* from following the sheep, that thou shouldest be ruler over my people Israel:

8 And I have been with thee whithersoever thou hast walked, and have ᵀcut off all thine enemies from before thee, and have made thee a name like the name of the great men that *are* in the earth.   *destroyed*

9 Also I will ᵀordain a place for my people Israel, and will ᵀplant them, and they shall dwell in their place, and shall be moved no more; neither shall the children of wickedness ᵀwaste them any more, as at the beginning,   *prepare · establish · rob*

10 And since the time that I commanded judges *to be* over my people Israel. Moreover I will subdue all thine enemies. Furthermore I tell thee that the LORD will build thee an house.

11 And it shall come to pass, when thy days be ᵀexpired that thou must ᵀgo *to be* with thy fathers, that I will ᴿraise up thy seed after thee, which shall be of thy sons; and I will establish his kingdom.   *ended · die* · Matt. 1:6 ☆

12 He shall build me an house, and I will stablish his throne ᴿfor ever.   [Luke 1:33] ☆

13 ᴿI will be his father, and he shall be my son: and I will not take my mercy away from him, ᴿas I took *it* from *him* that was before thee: 2 Sam. 7:14, 15; Heb. 1:5 · 10:14 ☆

14 But I will settle him in mine house and

in my kingdom for ever: and his ᴿthrone shall be established for evermore.   Acts 2:30 ☆

15 According to all these words, and according to all this vision, so did Nathan speak unto David.

Praise Prayer of David—2 Sam. 7:18-29

16 And David the king came and sat before the LORD, and said, Who *am* I, O LORD God, and what *is* mine house, that thou hast brought me ᵀhitherto?   *to this point*

17 And *yet* this was a small thing in thine eyes, O God; for thou hast *also* spoken of thy servant's house for a great while to come, and hast regarded me according to the estate of a man of high degree, O LORD God.

18 What can David *speak* more to thee for the honour of thy servant? for thou knowest thy servant.

19 O LORD, ᴿfor thy servant's sake, and according to thine own heart, hast thou done all this greatness, in making known all *these* great things.   2 Sam. 7:21; Is. 37:35

20 O LORD, *there is* none like thee, neither *is there any* God beside thee, according to all that we have heard with our ears.

21 And what one nation in the earth *is* like thy people Israel, whom God went to redeem *to be* his own people, to make thee a name of greatness and terribleness, by driving out nations from before thy people, whom thou hast redeemed out of Egypt?

22 For thy people Israel didst thou ᴿmake thine own people for ever; and thou, LORD, becamest their God.   Ex. 19:5, 6

23 Therefore now, LORD, let the thing that thou hast spoken concerning thy servant and concerning his house be established for ever, and do as thou hast said.

24 Let it even be established, that thy name may be magnified for ever, saying, The LORD of hosts *is* the God of Israel, *even* a God to Israel: and *let* the house of David thy servant *be* established before thee.

25 For thou, O my God, hast told thy servant that thou wilt build him an house: therefore thy servant hath found *in his heart* to pray before thee.

26 And now, LORD, thou art God, and hast promised this goodness unto thy servant:

27 Now therefore let it please thee to bless the house of thy servant, that it may be before thee for ever: for thou blessest, O LORD, and *it shall be* blessed for ever.

CHAPTER 18

Victory over Philistia—2 Sam. 8:1

NOW after this it came to pass, that David ᵀsmote the Phi-lis'-tines, and subdued them, and took Gath and her towns out of the hand of the Phi-lis'-tines.   *defeated*

Victory over Moab—2 Sam. 8:2

2 And he ᵀsmote ᴿMoab; and the Mo'-ab-ites became David's servants, *and* brought gifts.   *defeated* • Zeph. 2:9

Victory over Zobah—2 Sam. 8:3, 4

3 And David ᵀsmote ᵀHad-ar-e'-zerᴿ king of Zo'-bah unto Ha'-math, as he went to stablish his dominion by the river Eu-phra'-tes.   *defeated* • *Hadadezer* • 2 Sam. 8:3
4 And David took from him a thousand chariots, and seven thousand horsemen, and twenty thousand footmen: David also ᵀhoughed all the chariot *horses,* but reserved of them an hundred chariots.   *crippled*

Victory over Syria—2 Sam. 8:5-13

5 And when the ᴿSyrians of ᵀDamascus came to help Had-ar-e'-zer king of Zo'-bah, David slew of the Syrians two and twenty thousand men.   1 Kin. 11:23-25 • *Darmesek*
6 Then David put *garrisons* in Syria-damascus; and the Syrians became David's servants, *and* brought gifts. Thus the LORD preserved David whithersoever he went.
7 And David took the shields of gold that were on the servants of Had-ar-e'-zer, and brought them to Jerusalem.
8 Likewise from Tib'-hath, and from Chun, cities of Had-ar-e'-zer, brought David very much brass, wherewith Solomon made the brasen sea, and the pillars, and the vessels of brass.
9 Now when ᵀTo'-u ᴿking of Ha'-math heard how David had smitten all the host of Had-ar-e'-zer king of Zo'-bah;   *Toi* • 2 Sam. 8:9
10 He sent ᵀHa-do'-ramᴿ his son to king David, to enquire of his welfare, and to congratulate him, because he had fought against Had-ar-e'-zer, and ᵀsmitten him; (for Had-ar-e'-zer had war with To'-u;) and *with* him all manner of vessels of gold and silver and brass.   *Jo'-ram* • 2 Sam. 8:10 • *defeated*
11 Them also king David dedicated unto the LORD, with the silver and the gold that he brought from all *these* nations; from E'-dom, and from Moab, and from the children of Ammon, and from the ᴿPhi-lis'-tines, and from ᴿAm'-a-lek.   2 Sam. 5:17-25 • 2 Sam. 1:1

Victory over Edom—2 Sam. 8:14-18

12 Moreover, A-bi'-shai the son Ze-ru'-iah slew of the E'-dom-ites in the valley of salt ᴿeighteen thousand.   2 Sam. 8:13
13 ᴿAnd he put garrisons in E'-dom; and all the E'-dom-ites became David's servants. Thus the LORD preserved David ᵀwhither-soever he went.   2 Sam. 8:14 • *wherever*
14 So David reigned over all Israel, and ᵀexecuted judgment and justice among all his people.   *administered*
15 And ᴿJo'-ab the son of Ze-ru'-iah *was*

over the host; and Je-hosh'-a-phat the son of A-hi'-lud, recorder.   11:6
16 And Za'-dok the son of A-hi'-tub, and A-bim'-e-lech the son of A-bi'-a-thar, *were* the priests; and Shav'-sha was scribe;
17 And Be-na'-iah the son of Je-hoi'-a-da *was* over the Cher'-e-thites and the Pel'-e-thites; and the sons of David *were* ᴿchief ᵀabout the king.   2 Sam. 8:18 • *at the hand of the king*

CHAPTER 19

Humiliation of David's Servants—2 Sam. 10:1-5

NOW it came to pass after this, that Na'-hash the king of the children of Ammon died, and his son reigned in his stead.
2 And David said, I will shew ᵀkindness unto Ha'-nun the son of Na'-hash, because his father shewed kindness to me. And David sent messengers to comfort him concerning his father. So the servants of David came into the land of the children of Ammon to Ha'-nun, to comfort him.   *courtesy*
3 But the princes of the children of Ammon said to Ha'-nun, Thinkest thou that David doth honour thy father, that he hath sent comforters unto thee? are not his servants come unto thee for to search, and to overthrow, and to spy out the land?
4 Wherefore Ha'-nun took David's servants, and ᴿshaved them, and cut off their garments in the midst ᵀhard by their but-tocks, and sent them away.   Is. 20:4 • *close to*
5 Then there went *certain,* and told David how the men were served. And he sent to meet them: for the men were greatly ashamed. And the king said, Tarry at Jericho until your beards be grown, and *then* return.

Victory over the Ammonites—2 Sam. 10:6-14

6 And when the children of Ammon saw that they had made themselves ᵀodious to David, Ha'-nun and the children of Ammon sent a ᵀthousand talents of silver to hire them chariots and horsemen out of Mes-o-po-ta'-mi-a, and out of Syr'-i-a-ma'-a-chah, and out of Zo'-bah.   *to stink* • *$384,000,000*
7 So they hired thirty and two thousand chariots, and the king of Ma'-a-chah and his people; who came and ᵀpitched before Med'-e-ba. And the children of Ammon gathered themselves together from their cities, and came to battle.   *made camp*
8 And when David heard *of it,* he sent Jo'-ab, and all the host of the mighty men.
9 And the children of Ammon came out, and put the battle in array before the gate of the city: and the kings that were come *were* by themselves in the field.
10 Now when Jo'-ab saw that the battle was set against him before and behind, he

chose out of all the choice of Israel, and put *them* in array against the Syrians.

11 And the rest of the people he delivered unto the hand of A-bi'-shai his brother, and they ᵀset *themselves* in array against the children of Ammon.   *organized themselves*

12 And he said, If the Syrians be too strong for me, then thou shalt help me: but if the children of Ammon be too strong for thee, then I will help thee.

13 Be of good courage, and let us behave ourselves ᵀvaliantly for our people, and for the cities of our God: and let the LORD do *that which is* good in his sight.   *with strength*

14 So Jo'-ab and the people that *were* with him drew ᵀnigh before the Syrians unto the battle; and they fled before him.   *near*

15 And when the children of Ammon saw that the Syrians were fled, they likewise fled before A-bi'-shai his brother, and entered into the city. Then Jo'-ab came to Jerusalem.

Victory over the Syrians—2 Sam. 10:15–19

16 And when the Syrians saw that they were ᵀput to the worse before Israel, they sent messengers, and drew forth the Syrians that *were* beyond the river: and Sho'-phach the captain of the host of Had-ar-e'-zer *went* before them.   *being defeated*

17 And it was told David; and he gathered all Israel, and passed over Jordan, and came upon them, and set *the battle* in array against them. So when David had ᵀput the battle in array against the Syrians, they fought with him.   *set up battle lines*

18 But the Syrians fled before Israel; and David slew of the Syrians ᴿseven thousand *men which fought* in chariots, and forty thousand footmen, and killed Sho'-phach the captain of the host.   2 Sam. 10:18

19 And when the servants of Had-ar-e'-zer saw that they were put to the worse before Israel, they made peace with David, and became his servants: neither would the Syrians help the children of Ammon any more.

CHAPTER 20

Victory over the Ammonites
2 Sam. 11:1; 12:26–31

AND it came to pass, that after the year was expired, at the time that kings go out to battle, Jo'-ab led forth the power of the army,

and wasted the country of the children of Ammon, and came and besieged Rab'-bah. But David ᵀtarried at Jerusalem. And Jo'-ab smote Rab'-bah, and destroyed it.   *delayed*

2 And David took the crown of their king from off his head, and found it to weigh a ᵀtalent of gold, and *there were* precious stones in it; and it was set upon David's head: and he brought also exceeding much ᵀspoil out of the city.   *91 pounds · loot*

3 And he brought out the people that *were* in it, and ᴿcut *them* with saws, and with harrows of iron, and with axes. Even so dealt David with all the cities of the children of Ammon. And David and all the people returned to Jerusalem.   2 Sam. 12:31

Victory over the Philistine Giants
2 Sam. 21:18–22

4 And it came to pass after this, that there arose war at Ge'-zer with the Phi-lis'-tines; at which time Sib'-be-chai the Hu'-shath-ite slew Sip'-pai, *that was* of the children of the giant: and they were subdued.

5 And there was war again with the Phi-lis'-tines; and El-ha'-nan the son of ᵀJa'-irᴿ slew Lah'-mi the brother of Go-li'-ath the Git'-tite, whose spear staff *was* like a weaver's beam.   *Jaareoregim · 2 Sam. 21:19*

6 And yet again there was war at Gath, where was a man of *great* stature, whose fingers and toes *were* four and twenty, six *on each hand,* and six *on each foot:* and he also was ᵀthe son of the giant.   *Rapha*

7 But when he defied Israel, Jonathan the son of Shim'-e-a David's brother slew him.

8 These were born unto the giant in Gath; and they fell by the hand of David, and by the hand of his servants.

CHAPTER 21

Temptation of David by Satan

AND Satan stood up against Israel, and provoked David to number Israel.

2 And David said to Jo'-ab and to the rulers of the people, Go, number Israel from Be'-er-she'-ba even to Dan; and bring the number of them to me, that I may know *it.*

3 And Jo'-ab answered, The LORD make his people an hundred times so many more as

---

21:1 Temptation by Satan—The role of Satan against the Christian is well summed up by the meaning of the name Satan—"adversary." He is also called "the devil," meaning "accuser." He can appear as a hideous dragon (Page 1275—Rev. 12:3, 4, 9) or as a beautifully deceptive "angel of light" (Page 1150—2 Cor. 11:14). He stands hatefully opposed to all the work of God and resourcefully promotes defiance among men (Page 982—Mark 4:15; Page 519—Job 2:4, 5).

When Satan sinned he was expelled from heaven (Page 1018—Luke 10:18), although apparently he still had some access to God (Page 518—Job 1:6). A multitude of angels cast in their lot with him in his

they *be:* but, my lord the king, *are* they not all my lord's servants? why then doth my lord require this thing? why will he be a cause of trespass to Israel?

4 Nevertheless the king's word prevailed against Jo'-ab. Wherefore Jo'-ab ^Rdeparted, and went throughout all Israel, and came to Jerusalem. 2 Sam. 24:4-9

Enumeration of Israel

5 And Jo'-ab gave the sum of the number of the people unto David. And all *they of* Israel were a thousand thousand and an hundred thousand men that drew sword: and Judah *was* four hundred threescore and ten thousand men that drew sword.

6 ^RBut Levi and Benjamin counted he not among them: for the king's word was abominable to Jo'-ab. 27:24

Prayer of David

7 And God was displeased with this thing; therefore he ^Tsmote Israel. *struck*

8 And David said unto God, I have sinned greatly, because I have done this thing: but now, I beseech thee, do away the iniquity of thy servant; for I have done very foolishly.

Three Choices of David

9 And the LORD spake unto ^RGad, David's ^Rseer, saying, 29:29; 2 Sam. 24:11 • 1 Sam. 9:9

10 Go and tell David, saying, Thus saith the LORD, I offer thee three *things:* choose thee one of them, that I may do *it* unto thee.

11 So Gad came to David, and said unto him, Thus saith the LORD, Choose thee

12 Either three years' famine; or three months to be destroyed before thy foes, while that the sword of thine enemies overtaketh *thee;* or else three days the sword of the LORD, even the pestilence, in the land, and the angel of the LORD destroying throughout all the ^Tcoasts of Israel. Now therefore advise

thyself what word I shall bring again to him that sent me. *borders*

13 And David said unto Gad, I am in a great strait: let me fall now into the hand of the LORD; for very great *are* his mercies: but let me not fall into the hand of man.

Judgment of Pestilence

14 So the LORD sent pestilence upon Israel: and there ^Rfell of Israel seventy thousand men. 27:24

15 And God sent an angel unto Jerusalem to destroy it: and as he was destroying, the LORD beheld, and he repented him of the evil, and said to the angel that destroyed, It is enough, stay now thine hand. And the angel of the LORD stood by the threshingfloor of ^TOr'-nan^R the Jeb'-u-site. *Araunah* • 2 Sam. 24:18

16 And David lifted up his eyes, and saw the angel of the LORD stand between the earth and the heaven, having a drawn sword in his hand stretched out over Jerusalem. Then David and the elders *of Israel, who were* clothed in sackcloth, fell upon their faces.

17 And David said unto God, *Is it* not I *that* commanded the people to be numbered? even I it is that have sinned and done evil indeed; ^Rbut *as for* these sheep, what have they done? let thine hand, I pray thee, O LORD my God, be on me, and on my father's house; but not on thy people, that they should be plagued. 2 Sam. 7:8

Withholding of Judgment by Sacrifices

18 Then the ^Rangel of the LORD commanded Gad to say to David, that David should go up, and set up an altar unto the LORD in the threshingfloor of Or'-nan the Jeb'-u-site. *vv.* 11, 12; 2 Chr. 3:1

19 And David went up at the saying of

---

fall and subsequently became the demons mentioned often in the Bible (Page 953—Matt. 12:24; Page 1275—Rev. 12:7). Although Satan's doom was secured by Jesus' death on the cross (Page 1061—John 16:11), he will continue to hinder God's program until he and his angels are cast into the lake of fire (Page 969—Matt. 25:41; Page 1281—Rev. 20:10).

The terrifying work of Satan in the unbeliever is described in Scripture as follows: he blinds their minds (Page 1144—2 Cor. 4:4); he takes the Word of God from their hearts (Page 1015—Luke 8:12); and he controls them (Page 1086—Acts 13:8). In regard to Christians, Satan may accuse them (Page 1276—Rev. 12:10), devour their testimony for Christ (Page 1239—1 Pet. 5:8), deceive them (Page 1150—2 Cor. 11:14), hinder their work (Page 1184—1 Thess. 2:18), tempt them to immorality (Page 1130—1 Cor. 7:5), and even be used by God to discipline Christians (Page 1128—1 Cor. 5:5; Page 1150—2 Cor. 12:7).

The Christian's response to Satan is to recognize his power and deception (Page 1144—2 Cor. 2:11; Page 1167—Eph. 6:11), to adhere steadfastly to the faith (Page 1239—1 Pet. 5:9), to resist him openly (Page 1230—James 4:7), and not to give him opportunities (Page 1165—Eph. 4:27). In practice, the best way to oppose him is to be a growing Christian. Also, in the light of his tremendous power to blind men to the gospel, Christians must always be aggressively and compassionately witnessing to the lost in order to snatch them from Satan's control (Page 1101—Acts 26:18). Believers can respond to temptation by Satan with confidence. We know that nothing can separate us from the love of God (Page 1115—Rom. 8:28–39).

Now turn to Page 1238—1 Pet. 3:17: Kinds of Suffering.

Gad, which he spake in the name of the LORD.

20 And Or'-nan turned back, and saw the angel; and his four sons with him hid themselves. Now Or'-nan was threshing wheat.

21 And as David came to Or'-nan, Or'-nan looked and saw David, and went out of the threshingfloor, and bowed himself to David with his face to the ground.

22 Then David said to Or'-nan, ᵀGrant me the place of this threshingfloor, that I may build an altar therein unto the LORD: thou shalt grant it me for the full price: that the plague may be stayed from the people.　give

23 And Or'-nan said unto David, Take it to thee, and let my lord the king do that which is good in his eyes: lo, I give thee the oxen also for burnt offerings, and the threshing instruments for wood, and the wheat for the meat offering; I give it all.

24 And king David said to Or'-nan, Nay; but I will verily buy it for the full price: for I will not take that which is thine for the LORD, nor offer burnt offerings without cost.

25 So David gave to Or'-nan for the place six hundred shek'-els of gold by weight.

26 And David built there an altar unto the LORD, and offered burnt offerings and peace offerings, and called upon the LORD; and ᴿhe answered him from heaven by fire upon the altar of burnt offering.　Lev. 9:24

27 And the LORD commanded the angel; and he ᵀput up his sword again into the sheath thereof.　ceased his affliction of the people

28 At that time when David saw that the LORD had answered him in the threshingfloor of Or'-nan the ᴿJeb'-u-site, then he ᵀsacrificed there.　Judg. 1:21; 3:5; 19:11 • worshipped

29 For the tabernacle of the LORD, which Moses made in the wilderness, and the altar of the burnt offering, were at that season in the high place at Gib'-e-on.

30 But David could not go before it to enquire of God: for he was afraid because of the sword of the angel of the LORD.

CHAPTER 22

Material Provisions for the Temple's Construction

THEN David said, ᴿThis is the house of the LORD God, and this is the altar of the burnt offering for Israel.　Deut. 12:5

2 And David commanded to gather together the strangers that were in the land of Israel; and he set masons to hew wrought stones to build the house of God.

3 And David prepared iron in abundance for the nails for the doors of the gates, and for the joinings; and brass in abundance ᴿwithoutᵀ weight;　v. 14 • beyond calculation

4 Also cedar trees in abundance: for the ᴿZi-do'-ni-ans and they of Tyre brought much cedar wood to David.　1 Kin. 5:6

5 And David said, ᴿSolomon my son is young and tender, and the house that is to be builded for the LORD must be exceeding magnifical, of fame and of glory throughout all countries: I will therefore now make preparation for it. So David prepared abundantly before his death.　29:1

David's Charge to Solomon

6 Then he called for ᴿSolomon his son, and charged him to build an house for the LORD God of Israel.　28:20; 29:23; 2 Chr. 1:1

7 And David said to Solomon, My son, as for me, it was in my mind to build an house unto the name of the LORD my God:

8 But the word of the LORD came to me, saying, ᴿThou hast shed blood abundantly, and hast made great wars: thou shalt not build an house unto my name, because thou hast shed much blood upon the earth in my sight.　28:3; 2 Sam. 7:5–13; 1 Kin. 5:3

9 Behold, a son shall be born to thee, who shall be a man of rest; and I will give him rest from all his enemies round about: for his name shall be Solomon, and I will give peace and quietness unto Israel in his days.

10 He shall build an house for my name; and ᴿhe shall be my son, and I will be his father; and I will establish the throne of his kingdom over Israel for ever.　Matt. 1:6; Heb. 1:5 ☆

11 Now, my son, the LORD be with thee; and prosper thou, and build the house of the LORD thy God, as he hath said of thee.

12 Only the LORD ᴿgive thee wisdom and understanding, and give thee charge concerning Israel, that thou mayest ᵀkeep the law of the LORD thy God.　1 Kin. 3:9, 12 • obey

13 Then shalt thou prosper, if thou takest heed to fulfil the statutes and judgments which the LORD charged Moses with concerning Israel: be strong, and of good courage; dread not, nor be dismayed.

14 Now, behold, in my trouble I have prepared for the house of the LORD an hundred thousand talents of gold, and a thousand thousand talents of silver; and of brass and iron without weight; for it is in abundance: timber also and stone have I prepared; and thou mayest add thereto.

15 Moreover there are workmen with thee in abundance, hewers and workers of stone and timber, and all manner of cunning men for every manner of work.

16 Of the ᴿgold, the silver, and the brass, and the iron, there is no number. Arise

therefore, and be doing, and ^Rthe LORD be with thee. Gen. 2:12 • v. 11

David's Charge to the Princes

17 David also commanded all the princes of Israel to help Solomon his son, *saying,*

18 *Is* not the LORD your God with you? ^Rand hath he *not* given you ^Trest on every side? for he hath given the inhabitants of the land ^Tinto mine hand; and the land is ^Tsubdued before the LORD, and before his people. Josh. 22:4 • *peace* • *under my control* • *conquered*

19 Now ^Rset your heart and your soul to seek the LORD your God; arise therefore, and build ye the sanctuary of the LORD God, to ^Rbring the ark of the covenant of the LORD, and the holy vessels of God, into the house that is to be built ^Rto the name of the LORD. 1 Chr. 28:9 • 2 Chr. 5:7 • 1 Kin. 5:3

CHAPTER 23

Enumeration of the Levites

SO when ^RDavid was old and full of days, he made ^RSolomon his son king over Israel. 29:28 • 28:5; 29:22; 1 Kin. 1:33

2 And he gathered together all the princes of Israel, with the priests and the Levites.

3 Now the Levites were numbered from the age of ^Rthirty years and upward: and their number by their polls, man by man, was thirty and eight thousand. Num. 4:3

4 Of which, twenty and four thousand *were* ^Tto ^Rset forward the work of the house of the LORD; and six thousand *were* ^Rofficers and judges: to oversee • Ezra 3:8, 9 • Deut. 16:18

5 Moreover four thousand *were* ^Tporters; and four thousand praised the LORD with the instruments ^Rwhich I made, said David, to praise therewith. doorkeepers • 2 Chr. 29:25, 26

6 And ^RDavid divided them into ^Tcourses among the sons of Levi, namely, Ger'-shon, Ko'-hath, and Me-ra'-ri. Num. 26:57 • *groups*

Organization of the Gershonites

7 Of the ^RGer'-shon-ites were, La'-a-dan, and Shim'-e-i. 26:21

8 The sons of La'-a-dan; the chief *was* Je-hi'-el, and Ze'-tham, and Jo'-el, three.

9 The sons of Shim'-e-i; Shel'-o-mith, and Ha'-zi-el, and Ha'-ran, three. These *were* the chief of the fathers of La'-a-dan.

10 And the sons of Shim'-e-i were, Ja'-hath, ^TZi'-na, and Je'-ush, and Be-ri'-ah. These four *were* the sons of Shim'-e-i. Zizah

11 And Ja'-hath was the chief, and Zi'-zah the second: but Je'-ush and Be-ri'-ah had not many sons; therefore they were in one ^Treckoning, according to *their* father's house. group

Organization of the Kohathites

12 ^RThe sons of Ko'-hath; Am'-ram, Iz'-har, He'-bron, and Uz-zi'-el, four. Ex. 6:18

13 The sons of Am'-ram; Aaron and Moses: and Aaron was separated, that he should sanctify the most holy things, he and his sons for ever, to burn incense before the LORD, to minister unto him, and ^Rto bless in his name for ever. Num. 6:23

14 Now *concerning* ^RMoses the man of God, ^Rhis sons were named of the tribe of Levi. Deut. 33:1 • 26:20-24

15 ^RThe sons of Moses were, Ger'-shom, and E-li-e'-zer. Ex. 18:3, 4

16 Of the sons of Ger'-shom, ^RSheb'-u-el^T *was* the chief. 26:24 • *Shubael*

17 And the sons of E-li-e'-zer were, ^RRe-ha-bi'-ah ^Tthe chief. And E-li-e'-zer had none other sons; but the sons of Re-ha-bi'-ah were very many. 26:25 • *the first*

18 Of the sons of Iz'-har; ^TShel'-o-mith^R the chief. Shelomoth • 24:22

19 Of the sons of He'-bron; Je-ri'-ah the first, Am-a-ri'-ah the second, Ja-ha'-zi-el the third, and Jek-a-me'-am the fourth.

20 Of the sons of Uz-zi'-el; Mi'-cah the first, and Je-si'-ah the second.

Organization of the Merarites

21 ^RThe sons of Me-ra'-ri; Mah'-li, and Mu'-shi. The sons of Mah'-li; E-le-a'-zar, and ^RKish. 24:26 • 24:29

22 And E-le-a'-zar died, and ^Rhad no sons, but daughters: and their ^Tbrethren the sons of Kish took them. 24:28 • *kinsmen*

23 ^RThe sons of Mu'-shi; Mah'-li, and E'-der, and Jer'-e-moth, three. 24:30

Duties of the Levites

24 These *were* the sons of Levi after the house of their fathers; *even* the chief of the fathers, as they were counted by number of names by their polls, that did the work for the service of the house of the LORD, from the age of twenty years and upward.

25 For David said, The LORD God of Israel hath given rest unto his people, that they may dwell in Jerusalem for ever:

26 And also unto the Levites; they shall no more ^Rcarry the tabernacle, nor any vessels of it for the service thereof. Num. 4:5

27 For by the ^Rlast words of ^RDavid the Levites *were* numbered from twenty years old and above: 2 Sam. 23:1 • Ex. 32:26

28 Because their office *was* to wait on the sons of Aaron for the service of the house of the LORD, in the courts, and in the chambers, and in the purifying of all holy things, and the work of the service of the house of God;

29 Both for the shewbread, and for the fine flour for meat offering, and for the unleav-

ened cakes, and for *that which is baked in* the pan, and for that which is fried, and for all manner of measure and size;

30 And to stand every morning to thank and praise the LORD, and likewise at even;

31 And to offer all burnt sacrifices unto the LORD in the sabbaths, in the new moons, and on the ᴿset feasts, by number, according to the order commanded unto them, continually before the LORD: Lev. 23:4

32 And that they should keep the charge of the tabernacle of the congregation, and the charge of the holy *place*, and the charge of the sons of Aaron their brethren, in the service of the house of the LORD.

CHAPTER 24

Divisions of the Sons of Aaron

NOW *these are* the divisions of the sons of Aaron. The sons of Aaron; Na'-dab, and A-bi'-hu, E-le-a'-zar, and Ith'-a-mar.

2 But ᴿNa'-dab and A-bi'-hu died before their father, and had no children: therefore E-le-a'-zar and Ith'-a-mar ᵀexecuted the priest's office.   Num. 3:4; 26:61 · *fulfilled*

3 And David distributed them, both ᴿZa'-dok of the sons of E-le-a'-zar, and A-him'-e-lech of the sons of Ith'-a-mar, according to their offices in their service.   6:8

4 And there were more chief men found of the sons of E-le-a'-zar than of the sons of Ith'-a-mar; and *thus* were they divided. Among the sons of E-le-a'-zar *there were* sixteen chief men of the house of *their* fathers, and eight among the sons of Ith'-a-mar according to the house of their fathers.

5 Thus were they ᵀdivided ᴿby lot, one sort with another; for the governors of the sanctuary, and governors *of the house* of God, were of the sons of E-le-a'-zar, and of the sons of Ith'-a-mar.   *organized* · *v.* 31; Lev. 16:8

6 And She-ma'-iah the son of Ne-than'-e-el the scribe, *one* of the Levites, wrote them before the king, and the princes, and Za'-dok the priest, and A-him'-e-lech the son of A-bi'-a-thar, and *before* the chief of the fathers of the priests and Levites: one principal household being taken for E-le-a'-zar, and *one* taken for Ith'-a-mar.

7 ᴿNow the first lot came forth to Je-hoi'-a-rib, the second to Je-da'-iah,   Ezra 2:36–39

8 The third to Ha'-rim, the fourth to Se-o'-rim,

9 The fifth to Mal-chi'-jah, the sixth to Mij'-a-min,

10 The seventh to Hak'-koz, the eighth to ᴿA-bi'-jah,   Neh. 12:4, 17; Luke 1:5

11 The ninth to Jesh'-u-a, the tenth to Shec-a-ni'-ah,

12 The eleventh to E-li'-a-shib, the twelfth to Ja'-kim,

13 The thirteenth to Hup'-pah, the fourteenth to Je-sheb'-e-ab,

14 The fifteenth to Bil'-gah, the sixteenth to Im'-mer,

15 The seventeenth to He'-zir, the eighteenth to Aph'-ses,

16 The nineteenth to Peth-a-hi'-ah, the twentieth to Je-hez'-e-kel,

17 The one and twentieth to Ja'-chin, the two and twentieth to Ga'-mul,

18 The three and twentieth to De-la'-iah, the four and twentieth to Ma-a-zi'-ah.

19 These *were* the ᵀorderingsᴿ of them in their service to come into the house of the LORD, according to their manner, under Aaron their father, as the LORD God of Israel had commanded him.   *assignments* · 9:25

Organization of the Kohathites

20 And the rest of the sons of Levi *were* these: Of the sons of Am'-ram; Shu'-ba-el: of the sons of Shu'-ba-el; Jeh-de'-iah.

21 Concerning Re-ha-bi'-ah: of the sons of Re-ha-bi'-ah, the first *was* Is-shi'-ah.

22 Of the Iz'-har-ites; Shel'-o-moth: of the sons of ᴿShel'-o-moth; Ja'-hath.   23:18

23 And the sons of He'-bron; Je-ri'-ah *the first*, Am-a-ri'-ah the second, Ja-ha'-zi-el the third, Jek-a-me'-am the fourth.

24 *Of* the sons of Uz-zi'-el; Mi'-chah: of the sons of Mi'-chah; Sha'-mir.

25 The brother of Mi'-chah *was* Is-shi'-ah: of the sons of Is-shi'-ah; Zech-a-ri'-ah.

Organization of the Merarites

26 The sons of Me-ra'-ri *were* Mah'-li and Mu'-shi: the sons of Ja-a-zi'-ah; Be'-no.

27 The sons of Me-ra'-ri by Ja-a-zi'-ah; Be'-no, and Sho'-ham, and Zac'-cur, and Ib'-ri.

28 Of Mah'-li *came* E-le-a'-zar, ᴿwho had no sons.   23:22

29 Concerning Kish: the son of Kish *was* Je-rah'-me-el.

30 The sons also of Mu'-shi; Mah'-li, and E'-der, and Jer'-i-moth. These *were* the sons of the Levites after the house of their fathers.

31 These likewise cast lots over against their brethren the sons of Aaron in the presence of David the king, and Za'-dok, and A-him'-e-lech, and the chief of the fathers of the priests and Levites, even the principal fathers over against their younger brethren.

CHAPTER 25

Organization of the Orders of the Musicians

MOREOVER David and the captains of the host ᵀseparated to the service of the sons of A'-saph, ᴿand of He'-man, and

of Je-du'-thun, who should prophesy with harps, with psalteries, and with cymbals: and the number of the workmen according to their service was: set aside • 6:33

2 Of the sons of A'-saph; Zac'-cur, and Joseph, and Neth-a-ni'-ah, and As-a-re'-lah, the sons of A'-saph under the hands of A'-saph, which Tprophesied according to the order of the king. interpreted God's word

3 Of Je-du'-thun: the sons of Je-du'-thun; Ged-a-li'-ah, and TZe'-ri, and Je-sha'-iah, Hash-a-bi'-ah, and Mat-ti-thi'-ah, six, under the hands of their father Je-du'-thun, who prophesied with a harp, to give thanks and to praise the LORD. Izri

4 Of He'-man: the sons of He'-man; Buk-ki'-ah, Mat-ta-ni'-ah, TUz-zi'-el,R Sheb'-u-el, and Jer'-i-moth, Han-a-ni'-ah, Ha-na'-ni, E-li'-a-thah, Gid-dal'-ti, and Ro-mam'-ti-e'-zer, Josh-bek'-a-shah, Mal'-lo-thi, Ho'-thir, and Ma-ha'-zi-oth: Azareel • v. 18

5 All these were the sons of He'-man the Rking's seer in the words of God, to lift up the horn. And God gave to He'-man fourteen sons and three daughters. 2 Sam. 24:11

6 All these were under the hands of their father for song in the house of the LORD, with Rcymbals, psalteries, and harps, for the service of the house of God, Raccording to the king's order to A'-saph, Je-du'-thun, and He'-man. 2 Sam. 6:5 • v. 2

7 So the number of them, with their brethren that were instructed in the songs of the LORD, even all that were cunning, was two hundred fourscore and eight.

8 And they Rcast lots, Tward against ward, as well the small as the great, the teacher as the scholar. Lev. 16:8 • for their duties

9 Now the first lot came forth for A'-saph to Joseph: the second to Ged-a-li'-ah, who with his brethren and sons were twelve:

10 The third to Zac'-cur, he, his sons, and his brethren, were twelve:

11 The fourth to Iz'-ri, he, his sons, and his brethren, were twelve:

12 The fifth to Neth-a-ni'-ah, he, his sons, and his brethren, were twelve:

13 The sixth to Buk-ki'-ah, he, his sons, and his brethren, were twelve:

14 The seventh to Je-shar'-e-lah, he, his sons, and his brethren, were twelve:

15 The eighth to Je-sha'-iah, he, his sons, and his brethren, were twelve:

16 The ninth to Mat-ta-ni'-ah, he, his sons, and his brethren, were twelve:

17 The tenth to Shim'-e-i, he, his sons, and his brethren, were twelve:

18 The eleventh to A-zar'-e-el, he, his sons, and his brethren, were twelve:

19 The twelfth to Hash-a-bi'-ah, he, his sons, and his brethren, were twelve:

20 The thirteenth to Shu'-ba-el, he, his sons, and his brethren, were twelve:

21 The fourteenth to Mat-ti-thi'-ah, he, his sons, and his brethren, were twelve:

22 The fifteenth to Jer'-e-moth, he, his sons, and his brethren, were twelve:

23 The sixteenth to Han-a-ni'-ah, he, his sons, and his brethren, were twelve:

24 The seventeenth to Josh-bek'-a-shah, he, his sons, and his brethren, were twelve:

25 The eighteenth to Ha-na'-ni, he, his sons, and his brethren, were twelve:

26 The nineteenth to Mal'-lo-thi, he, his sons, and his brethren, were twelve:

27 The twentieth to E-li'-a-thah, he, his sons, and his brethren, were twelve:

28 The one and twentieth to Ho'-thir, he, his sons, and his brethren, were twelve:

29 The two and twentieth to Gid-dal'-ti, he, his sons, and his brethren, were twelve:

30 The three and twentieth to Ma-ha'-zi-oth, he, his sons, and his brethren, were twelve:

31 The four and twentieth to Ro-mam'-ti-e'-zer, he, his sons, and his brethren, were twelve.

CHAPTER 26

Organization of the Gatekeepers

CONCERNING the divisions of the Tporters: Of the Kor'-hites was Me-shel-e-mi'-ah the son of Ko'-re, of the sons of TA'-saph.R doorkeepers • Ebiasaph • 6:37; 9:19

2 And the sons of Me-shel-e-mi'-ah were, RZech-a-ri'-ah the firstborn, Je-di'-a-el the second, Zeb-a-di'-ah the third, Jath'-ni-el the fourth, 9:21

3 E'-lam the fifth, Je-ho-ha'-nan the sixth, E-li-o-e'-nai the seventh.

4 Moreover the sons of O'-bed-e'-dom were, She-ma'-iah the firstborn, Je-hoz'-a-bad the second, Jo'-ah the third, and Sa'-car the fourth, and Ne-than'-e-el the fifth,

5 Am'-mi-el the sixth, Is'-sa-char the seventh, Pe-ul'-thai the eighth: Rfor God blessed Thim. 4:10; 13:14 • Obed-edom, as Ch. 13:14

6 Also unto She-ma'-iah his son were sons born, that ruled throughout the house of their father: for they were mighty men of valour.

7 The sons of She-ma'-iah; Oth'-ni, and Re'-pha-el, and O'-bed, El'-za-bad, whose brethren were strong men, E-li'-hu, and Sem-a-chi'-ah.

8 All these of the sons of O'-bed-e'-dom: they and their sons and their brethren, able men for strength for the service, were threescore and two of O'-bed-e'-dom.

9 And Me-shel-e-mi'-ah had sons and brethren, strong men, eighteen.

10 Also RHo'-sah, of the children of Me-ra'-ri, had sons; Sim'-ri the chief, (for though he

was not the firstborn, yet his father ᴿmade him the chief;)   16:38 • Gen. 48:19

11 Hil-ki'-ah the second, Teb-a-li'-ah the third, Zech-a-ri'-ah the fourth: all the sons and brethren of Ho'-sah were thirteen.

12 Among these were the divisions of the ᵀporters,ᴿ even among the chief men, having wards one against another, to minister in the house of the LORD.   doorkeepers • 2 Sam. 18:26

13 ᴿAnd they cast lots, as well the small as the great, according to the house of their fathers, for every gate.   24:5, 31; 25:8

14 And the lot eastward fell to ᵀShel-e-mi'-ah.ᴿ Then for Zech-a-ri'-ah his son, a wise counsellor, they cast lots; and his lot came out northward.   Meshelemiah • v. 1

15 To O'-bed-e'-dom southward; and to his sons the house of A-sup'-pim.

16 To Shup'-pim and Ho'-sah the lot came forth westward, with the gate Shal'-le-cheth, by the causeway of the going ᴿup, ward against ward.   1 Kin. 10:5; 2 Chr. 9:4

17 Eastward were six Levites, northward four a day, southward four a day, and toward A-sup'-pim two and two.

18 At ᴿPar'-bar westward, four at the causeway, and two at Par'-bar.   2 Kin. 23:11

19 These are the divisions of the ᵀportersᴿ among the sons of Ko'-re, and among the sons of Me-ra'-ri.   doorkeepers • 2 Sam. 18:26

Organization of the Treasures of the Temple

20 And of the Levites, A-hi'-jah was over the treasures of the house of God, and over the treasures of the dedicated things.

21 As concerning the sons of ᵀLa'-a-dan;ᴿ the sons of the Ger'-shon-ite La'-a-dan, chief fathers, even of La'-a-dan the Ger'-shon-ite, were Je-hi'-e-li.   Libni • 6:17

22 The sons of Je-hi'-e-li; Ze'-tham, and Jo'-el his brother, which were over the treasures of the house of the LORD.

23 Of the Am'-ram-ites, and the Iz'-har-ites, the He'-bron-ites, and the Uz-zi'-el-ites:

24 And Sheb'-u-el the son of Ger'-shom, the son of Moses, was ruler of the treasures.

25 And his brethren by E-li-e'-zer; Re-ha-bi'-ah his son, and Je-sha'-iah his son, and Jo'-ram his son, and Zich'-ri his son, and ᴿShel'-o-mith his son.   23:18

26 Which Shel'-o-mith and his brethren were over all the treasures of the ᴿdedicated things, which David the king, and the chief fathers, the captains over thousands and hundreds, and the captains of the host, had dedicated.   2 Sam. 8:11

27 Out of the ᵀspoilsᴿ won in battles did they dedicate to ᵀmaintain the house of the LORD.   loot • Gen. 34:28 • repair

28 And all that Samuel ᴿthe seer, and Saul the son of Kish, and Abner the son of Ner, and Jo'-ab the son of Ze-ru'-iah, had dedi-

cated; and whosoever had dedicated any thing, it was under the hand of Shel'-o-mith, and of his brethren.   1 Sam. 9:9

Organization of the Officers Outside of the Temple

29 Of the Iz'-har-ites, Chen-a-ni'-ah and his sons were for the outward business over Israel, for ᴿofficers and judges.   23:4

30 And of the He'-bron-ites, ᴿHash-a-bi'-ah and his brethren, men of valour, a thousand and seven hundred, were officers among them of Israel on this side Jordan westward in all the business of the LORD, and in the service of the king.   27:17

31 Among the He'-bron-ites was ᴿJe-ri'-jah the chief, even among the He'-bron-ites, according to the generations of his fathers. In the fortieth year of the reign of David they were sought for, and there were found among them mighty men of valour at Ja'-zer of Gil'-e-ad.   23:19

32 And his brethren, men of valour, were two thousand and seven hundred chief fathers, whom king David made rulers over the Reu'-ben-ites, the Gad'-ites, and the half tribe of Ma-nas'-seh, for every matter pertaining to God, and affairs of the king.

CHAPTER 27

The Twelve Captains of Israel

NOW the children of Israel after their number, to wit, the chief fathers and captains of thousands and hundreds, and their officers that served the king in any matter of the courses, which came in and went out month by month throughout all the months of the year, of every course were twenty and four thousand.

2 Over the first course for the first month was Ja-sho'-be-am the son of Zab'-di-el: and in his course were twenty and four thousand.

3 ᴿOf the children of Pe'-rez was the chief of all the captains of the host for the first month.   Gen. 38:29

4 And over the course of the second month was ᵀDo'-dai an A-ho'-hite, and of his course was Mik'-loth also the ruler: in his course likewise were twenty and four thousand.   Dodo

5 The third captain of the host for the third month was Be-na'-iah the son of Je-hoi'-a-da, a chief priest: and in his ᵀcourse were twenty and four thousand.   division

6 This is that Be-na'-iah, who was mighty among the thirty, and above the thirty: and in his course was Am-miz'-a-bad his son.

7 The fourth captain for the fourth month was A'-sa-hel the brother of Jo'-ab, and Zeb-a-di'-ah his son after him: and in his ᵀcourse were twenty and four thousand.   division

8 The fifth captain for the fifth month was

Sham'-huth the Iz'-ra-hite: and in his course *were* twenty and four thousand.

9 The sixth *captain* for the sixth month was ᴿI'-ra the son of Ik'-kesh the Te-ko'-ite: and in his course *were* twenty and four thousand. 11:28

10 The seventh *captain* for the seventh month was He'-lez the Pel'-o-nite, of the children of E'-phra-im: and in his ᵀcourse *were* twenty and four thousand. *division*

11 The eighth *captain* for the eighth month was ᴿSib'-be-cai the Hu'-shath-ite, of the Zar'-hites: and in his course *were* twenty and four thousand. 2 Sam. 21:18

12 The ninth *captain* for the ninth month was ᴿA-bi-e'-zer the An'-e-toth-ite, of the Benjamites: and in his ᵀcourse *were* twenty and four thousand. 11:28 · *division*

13 The tenth *captain* for the tenth month was ᴿMa'-ha-rai the Ne-toph'-a-thite, of the Zar'-hites: and in his course *were* twenty and four thousand. 2 Sam. 23:28

14 The eleventh *captain* for the eleventh month was Be-na'-iah the Pir'-a-thon-ite, of the children of E'-phra-im: and in his course *were* twenty and four thousand.

15 The twelfth *captain* for the twelfth month was ᵀHel'-dai ᴿthe Ne-toph'-a-thite, of Oth'-ni-el: and in his course *were* twenty and four thousand. *Heled* · 11:30

The Princes of the Twelve Tribes

16 Furthermore over the tribes of Israel: the ruler of the Reu'-ben-ites was E-li-e'-zer the son of Zich'-ri: of the Simeonites, Sheph-a-ti'-ah the son of Ma'-a-chah:

17 Of the Levites, Hash-a-bi'-ah the son of Kem'-u-el: of the Aaronites, Za'-dok:

18 Of ᴿJudah, ᴿE-li'-hu,ᵀ *one* of the brethren of David: of Is'-sa-char, Om'-ri the son of Mi'-cha-el: Deut. 33:7 · 1 Sam. 16:6 · *Eliab*

19 Of ᴿZeb'-u-lun, Ish-ma'-iah the son of O-ba-di'-ah: of Naph'-ta-li, Jer'-i-moth the son of Az'-ri-el: Judg. 1:30

20 Of the children of E'-phra-im, Ho-she'-a the son of Az-a-zi'-ah: of the half tribe of Ma-nas'-seh, Jo'-el the son of Pe-da'-iah:

21 Of the half *tribe* of Ma-nas'-seh in Gil'-e-ad, Id'-do the son of Zech-a-ri'-ah: of Benjamin, Ja-a'-si-el the son of Abner:

22 Of ᴿDan, A-zar'-e-el the son of Jer'-o-ham. These *were* the ᴿprinces of the tribes of Israel. Num. 1:39 · 28:1

23 But David took not the number of them from twenty years old and under: because ᴿthe Lᴏʀᴅ had said he would increase Israel like to the stars of the heavens. Gen. 15:5

24 Jo'-ab the son of Ze-ru'-iah began to number, but he finished not, because ᴿthere fell wrath for it against Israel; neither was the number ᵀput in the account of the Chronicles of king David. 21:7 · *recorded*

The Royal Officers of David

25 And over the king's treasures was Az'-ma-veth the son of A'-di-el: and over the ᴿstorehouses in the fields, in the cities, and in the villages, and in the castles, was Je-hon'-a-than the son of Uz-zi'-ah: 2 Chr. 32:28

26 And over them that did the ᴿwork of the field for tillage of the ground was Ez'-ri the son of Che'-lub: Gen. 2:15

27 And over the ᴿvineyards was Shim'-e-i the Ra'-math-ite: over the increase of the vineyards for the wine cellars was Zab'-di the Shiph'-mite: Ex. 22:5

28 And over the olive trees and the ᴿsycomore trees that *were* in the low plains was Ba'-al-ha'-nan the Ged'-e-rite: and over the cellars of oil was Jo'-ash: 1 Kin. 10:27

29 And over the herds that fed in ᴿShar'-on was Shit'-rai the Shar'-on-ite: and over the herds *that were* in the valleys was Sha'-phat the son of Ad'-lai: 5:16

30 Over the ᴿcamels also was O'-bil the Ish'-ma-el-ite: and over the asses was Jeh-de'-iah the Me-ron'-o-thite: Gen. 12:16

31 And over the flocks was Ja'-ziz the Ha'-ger-ite. All these *were* the rulers of the substance which was king David's.

The Counsellors of David

32 Also Jonathan David's uncle was a counsellor, a wise man, and a ᵀscribe: and Je-hi'-el the ᵀson of Hach'-mo-ni was with the king's sons: *secretary* · *Hachmonite*

33 And ᴿA-hith'-o-phel was the king's counsellor: and ᴿHu'-shai the Ar'-chite was the king's companion: 2 Sam. 15:12 · 2 Sam. 15:37

34 And after A-hith'-o-phel was Je-hoi'-a-da the son of ᴿBe-na'-iah, and ᴿA-bi'-a-thar: and the general of the king's army was ᴿJo'-ab. *v.* 5 · 1 Kin. 1:7 · 11:6

CHAPTER 28

Charge to Israel

AND ᴿDavid assembled all the princes of Israel, the princes of the tribes, and the captains of the companies that ministered to the king by ᵀcourse, and the captains over the thousands, and captains over the hundreds, and the stewards over all the substance and possession of the king, and of his sons, with the ᵀofficers, and with the mighty men, and with all the valiant *men*, unto Jerusalem. 23:2 · *division* · *eunuchs*

2 Then David the king stood up upon his feet, and said, Hear me, my brethren, and my people: As for me, ᴿI had in mine heart to build an house of rest for the ark of the ᵀcovenant of the Lᴏʀᴅ, and for ᴿthe footstool of our God, and had made ready for the building: 2 Sam. 7:2 · *agreement* · Ps. 99:5; 132:7

3 But God said unto me, Thou shalt not build an house for my name, because thou *hast been* a man of war, and hast shed blood.

4 Howbeit the LORD God of Israel chose me before all the house of my father to be king over Israel for ever: for he hath chosen Judah *to be* the ruler; and of the house of Judah, the house of my father; and among the sons of my father he ᵀliked me to make *me* king over all Israel: chose

5 And of all my sons, (for the LORD hath given me many sons,) ᴿhe hath chosen Solomon my son to sit upon the throne of the kingdom of the LORD over Israel.   22:9

6 And he said unto me, ᴿSolomon thy son, he shall build my house and my courts: for I have chosen him *to be* my son, and I will be his father.   22:9, 10; 2 Sam. 7:13, 14; 2 Chr. 1:9

7 Moreover ᴿI will establish his kingdom for ever, ᴿif he be ᵀconstant ᴿto do my commandments and my judgments, as at this day.   Matt. 1:6 ☆ · 22:13 · *faithful* · Josh. 23:8

8 Now therefore, in the sight of all Israel the congregation of the LORD, and in the audience of our God, keep and seek for all the ᴿcommandments of the LORD your God: that ye may possess this good land, and leave *it* for an inheritance for your children after you for ever.   Ex. 20:6

Charge to Solomon

9 And thou, Solomon my son, know thou the God of thy father, and serve him with a perfect heart and with a willing mind: for the LORD searcheth all hearts, and understandeth all the imaginations of the thoughts: if thou seek him, he will be found of thee; but if thou forsake him, he will cast thee off for ever.

10 Take heed now; ᴿfor the LORD hath chosen thee to build an house for the sanctuary: ᴿbe strong, and do *it*.   v. 6 · 22:13

Pattern for the Temple

11 Then David gave to Solomon his son ᴿthe ᵀpattern of the porch, and of the houses thereof, and of the treasuries thereof, and of the upper chambers thereof, and of the inner parlours thereof, and of the place of the mercy seat,   v. 19; Ex. 25:40 · *design*

12 And the pattern of all that he had by the spirit, of the courts of the house of the LORD, and of all the chambers round about, of the treasuries of the house of God, and of the treasuries of the dedicated things:

13 Also for the ᴿcourses of the priests and the ᴿLevites, and for all the work of the service of the house of the LORD, and for all the vessels of service in the house of the LORD.   24:1 · 23:6

14 *He gave* of gold by weight for *things* of gold, for all ᵀinstruments of all manner of service; ᴿsilver *also* for all instruments of silver by weight, for all instruments of every kind of service: vessels · Ex. 25:3

15 Even the weight for the candlesticks of gold, and for their lamps of gold, by weight for every candlestick, and for the lamps thereof: and for the ᴿcandlesticks of silver by

---

28:4–6 Government of Israel—The government of Israel may be considered under two important headings: the laws, and the leaders.

The laws:

a. The "commandments," especially the Ten Commandments, revealed God's holiness and set up a divine standard of righteousness for the people to follow (Page 75—Ex. 20:1–17).

b. The judgments governed the social life of the people and concerned masters and servants (Page 75—Ex. 21:1–11), physical injuries (Page 76—Ex. 21:12–36), protection of property rights (Page 76—Ex. 22:1–15), etc.

c. The ordinances included the sacrifices that showed that blood must be shed for sinners to be forgiven (Page 100—Lev. 1—17).

The leaders: At first Moses was the sole leader; then he was replaced by Joshua. After Joshua's death the nation was governed for many years by judges, who were usually raised up by God to oppose a specific enemy. Finally, at the people's request, God granted them a king, thus establishing the monarchy (Page 282—1 Sam. 8:5, 22). Under the monarchy there were four key leaders:

a. The *king* was the Lord's representative who ruled the people, but only as the Lord's servant. He led in war (Page 282—1 Sam. 8:20) and made judicial decisions (Page 322—2 Sam. 15:2); but he could not make law, since he himself was under the law (Page 195—Deut. 17:19). His relationship was so close to the Lord that he was adopted by the Lord (Page 315—2 Sam. 7:14; Page 548—Ps. 2:7).

b. The *priest* taught the Lord's laws and officiated at the offering of the sacrifices (Page 100—Lev. 1:5; Page 724—Jer. 18:18).

c. The *prophet* was the man of God who spoke for God and gave divine pronouncements for the present (forthtelling) or for the future (foretelling).

d. The *wise man* produced literary works stressing practical wisdom (Page 615—Prov. 1:1), taught discipline of character to the young (Page 629—Prov. 22:17), and gave counsel to the king (Page 324—2 Sam. 16:20). The choice of these men indicates an important biblical principle: God uses people to reach other people, a principle that is also evident in the Great Commission given to Christians (Page 974—Matt. 28: 19, 20).

Now turn to Page 558—Ps. 29:2: Worship by Israel.

weight, *both* for the candlestick, and *also* for the lamps thereof, according to the use of every candlestick. Ex. 25:31-39

16 And by weight *he gave* gold for the tables of shewbread, for every table; and *likewise* silver for the tables of silver:

17 Also pure gold for the fleshhooks, and the bowls, and the cups: and for the golden basons *he gave* gold by weight for every Rbason; and *likewise silver* by weight for every bason of silver: 2 Chr. 4:8

18 And for the altar of incense refined gold by weight; and gold for the pattern of the chariot of the Rcher′-u-bims, that spread out *their wings*, and covered the ark of the covenant of the LORD. 1 Sam. 4:4

19 All *this, said David*, the LORD made me understand in writing by *his* hand upon me, *even* all the works of this pattern.

20 And David said to Solomon his son, RBe strong and of good courage, and do *it:* fear not, nor be dismayed: for the LORD God, *even* my God, *will be* with thee; he will not fail thee, nor forsake thee, until thou hast finished all the work for the service of the house of the LORD. 22:13

21 And, behold, the courses of the priests and the Levites, *even they shall be with thee* for all the service of the house of God: and *there shall be* with thee for all manner of workmanship Revery willing skilful man, for any manner of service: also the princes and all the people *will be* wholly at thy command-ment. Ex. 35:25, 26

CHAPTER 29

Provisions of David for the Temple

FURTHERMORE David the king said unto all the congregation, Solomon my son, whom alone God hath chosen, *is yet* Ryoung and Ttender, and the work *is* great: for the palace *is* not for man, but for the LORD God. 22:5; 1 Kin. 3:7; Prov. 4:3 • *inexperienced*

2 Now I have prepared with all my might for the house of my God the gold for *things to be made* of gold, and the silver for *things* of silver, and the brass for *things* of brass, the iron for *things* of iron, and wood for *things* of wood; Ronyx stones, and *stones* to be set, glistering stones, and of divers colours, and all manner of precious stones, and marble stones in abundance. Rev. 21:18

3 Moreover, because RI have set my affection to the house of my God, I have of mine own Tproper good, of gold and silver, *which* I have given to the house of my God, over and above all that I have prepared for the holy house, Neh. 10:39 • *personal property*

4 *Even* Tthree thousand talents of gold, of the gold of RO′-phir, and seven thousand

talents of refined silver, to overlay the walls of the houses *withal:* $17.28 billion • 1 Kin. 9:28

5 The gold for *things* of gold, and the silver for *things* of silver, and for all manner of work *to be made* by the hands of artificers. And who *then* is willing to consecrate his service this day unto the LORD?

Provisions of Israel for the Temple

6 Then the chief of the fathers and princes of the tribes of Israel, and the captains of thousands and of hundreds, with the rulers of the king's work, offered willingly,

7 And gave for the service of the house of God of gold Tfive thousand talents and ten thousand drams, and of silver Tten thousand talents, and of brass Teighteen thousand talents, and Tone hundred thousand talents of iron. $28.8 billion • $3.84 billion • 675 tons • 3750 tons

8 And they with whom *precious* stones were found gave *them* to the treasure of the house of the LORD, by the hand of RJe-hi′-el the Ger′-shon-ite. 23:8; 26:21

9 Then the people rejoiced, for that they offered willingly, because with perfect heart they offered willingly to the LORD: and David the king also rejoiced with great joy.

David's Final Prayer of Thanksgiving

10 Wherefore David blessed the LORD before all the congregation: and RDavid said, Blessed *be* thou, LORD God of Israel Rour father, for ever and ever. Ps. 72:18 • Ps. 68:5

11 RThine, O LORD, *is* the greatness, and the power, and the glory, and the victory, and the majesty: for all *that is* in the heaven and in the earth *is thine;* thine *is* the kingdom, O LORD, and thou art exalted as head above all. Matt. 6:13; 1 Tim. 1:17; Rev. 5:13

12 Both riches and honour *come* of thee, and thou reignest over all; and in thine hand *is* power and might; and in thine hand *it is* to make great, and to give strength unto all.

13 Now therefore, our God, we thank thee, and praise thy glorious name.

14 But who *am* I, and what *is* my people, that we should be able to offer so willingly after this sort? for all things *come* of thee, and of thine own have we given thee.

15 For we *are* strangers before thee, and Tsojourners, as *were* all our fathers: our days on the earth *are* as a shadow, and *there is* Tnone abiding. *pilgrims • no expectation*

16 O LORD our God, all this Tstore that we have prepared to build thine an house for thine holy name *cometh* of thine hand, and *is* all thine own. *abundance*

17 I know also, my God, that thou triest the heart, and hast pleasure in uprightness. As for me, in the uprightness of mine heart I have willingly offered all these things: and

now have I seen with joy thy people, which are present here, to offer willingly unto thee.

18 O LORD God of Abraham, Isaac, and of Israel, our fathers, keep this for ever in the imagination of the thoughts of the heart of thy people, and ᵀprepare their heart unto thee: *establish*

19 And give unto Solomon my son a perfect heart, to keep thy commandments, thy testimonies, and thy statutes, and to do all *these things*, and to build the palace, *for* the which I have made provision.

Coronation of Solomon—1 Kin. 1:38–40; 2:12

20 And David said to all the congregation, Now bless the LORD your God. And all the congregation blessed the LORD God of their fathers, and bowed down their heads, and worshipped the LORD, and the king.

21 And they sacrificed sacrifices unto the LORD, and offered burnt offerings unto the LORD, on the morrow after that day, even a thousand ᵀbullocks, a thousand rams, *and* a thousand lambs, with their drink offerings, and sacrifices in abundance for all Israel: *bulls*

22 And did eat and drink before the LORD on that day with great gladness. And they made Solomon the son of David king the second time, and ᴿanointed *him* unto the LORD to be the ᵀchief governor, and Za'-dok to be priest.   23:1; 1 Kin. 1:35, 39 • *prince*

23 Then Solomon sat on the throne of the LORD as king instead of David his father, and prospered; and all Israel obeyed him.

24 And all the princes, and the mighty men, and all the sons likewise of king David, ᴿsubmitted themselves unto Solomon the king.   Eccl. 8:2

25 And the LORD magnified Solomon exceedingly in the sight of all Israel, and bestowed upon him *such* royal majesty as had not been on any king before him in Israel.

Death of King David

26 Thus David the son of Jesse ᴿreigned over all Israel.   18:14

27 ᴿAnd the time that he reigned over Israel *was* forty years; ᴿseven years reigned he in He'-bron, and thirty and three *years* reigned he in Jerusalem.   1 Kin. 2:11 • 2 Sam. 5:5

28 And he died in a good old age, ᴿfull of days, riches, and honour: and Solomon his son reigned in his ᵀstead.   23:1 • *place*

29 Now the acts of David the king, first and last, behold, they *are* written in the book of Samuel the ᴿseer, and in the book of ᴿNathan the prophet, and in the book of Gad the seer,   1 Sam. 9:9 • 2 Sam. 7:2–4

30 With all his reign and his might, and the times that went over him, and over Israel, and over all the kingdoms of the countries.

The Jewish Calendar

The Jews used two kinds of calendars:
Civil Calendar—official calendar of kings, childbirth, and contracts.
Sacred Calendar—from which festivals were computed.

NAMES OF MONTHS	CORRESPONDS WITH	NO. OF DAYS	MONTH OF CIVIL YEAR	MONTH OF SACRED YEAR		
TISHRI	Sept.–Oct.	30 days	1st	7th	The Jewish day was from sunset to sunset, in 8 equal parts:	
HESHVAN	Oct.–Nov.	29 or 30	2nd	8th		
CHISLEV	Nov.–Dec.	29 or 30	3rd	9th		
TEBETH	Dec.–Jan.	29	4th	10th	FIRST WATCH	..... SUNSET TO 9 P.M.
SHEBAT	Jan.–Feb.	30	5th	11th	SECOND WATCH	... 9 P.M. TO MIDNIGHT
ADAR	Feb.–Mar.	29 or 30	6th	12th	THIRD WATCH	..... MIDNIGHT TO 3 A.M.
NISAN	Mar.–Apr.	30	7th	1st	FOURTH WATCH	... 3 A.M. TO SUNRISE
IYAR	Apr.–May	29	8th	2nd		
SIVAN	May–June	30	9th	3rd	FIRST WATCH	..... SUNRISE TO 9 A.M.
TAMMUZ	June–July	29	10th	4th	SECOND WATCH	... 9 A.M. TO NOON
AB	July–Aug.	30	11th	5th	THIRD WATCH	..... NOON TO 3 P.M.
*ELUL	Aug.–Sept.	29	12th	6th	FOURTH WATCH	... 3 P.M. TO SUNSET

*Hebrew months were alternately 30 and 29 days long. Their year, shorter than ours, had 354 days. Therefore, about every 3 years (7 times in 19 years) an extra 29-day-month, VEADAR, was added between ADAR and NISAN.

CHRONICLES

📖 THE BOOK OF SECOND CHRONICLES

The Book of Second Chronicles parallels First and Second Kings but virtually ignores the northern kingdom of Israel because of its false worship and refusal to acknowledge the temple in Jerusalem. Chronicles focuses on those kings who pattern their lives and reigns after the life and reign of godly King David. It gives extended treatment to such zealous reformers as Asa, Jehoshaphat, Joash, Hezekiah, and Josiah.

The temple and temple worship, central throughout the book, befit a nation whose worship of God is central to its very survival. The book begins with Solomon's glorious temple and concludes with Cyrus's edict to rebuild the temple more than four hundred years later.

See "The Book of First Chronicles" for more detail on the title.

✍ THE AUTHOR OF SECOND CHRONICLES

For a discussion of the author of First and Second Chronicles, see "The Author of First Chronicles." The sources of First and Second Chronicles include official and prophetic records: (1) the book of the kings of Israel and Judah (or Judah and Israel) (1 Chr. 9:1; 2 Chr. 16:11; 20:34; 25:26; 27:7; 28:26; 32:32; 35:27; 36:8), (2) the story (or commentary) on the book of the kings (2 Chr. 24:27), (3) the book of Samuel the seer (1 Chr. 29:29), (4) the book of Nathan the prophet (1 Chr. 29:29; 2 Chr. 9:29), (5) the book of Gad the seer (1 Chr. 29:29), (6) the prophecy of Ahijah the Shilonite (2 Chr. 9:29), (7) the visions of Iddo the seer (2 Chr. 9:29; 12:15; 13:22), (8) the book of Shemaiah the prophet (2 Chr. 12:15), (9) the book of Iddo the prophet on genealogies (2 Chr. 12:15), (10) the story of the prophet Iddo (2 Chr. 13:22), (11) the book of Jehu the son of Hanani (2 Chr. 20:34), (12) the acts of Uzziah by Isaiah the prophet (2 Chr. 26:22), (13) the vision of Isaiah the prophet (2 Chr. 32:32), (14) the sayings of the seers (2 Chr. 33:19), (15) the account of the chronicles of king David (1 Chr. 27:24), (16) the writing of David and his son Solomon (2 Chr. 35:4). In addition to these, the author-compiler had access to genealogical lists and documents, such as the message and letters of Sennacherib (2 Chr. 32:10–17).

⏳ THE TIME OF SECOND CHRONICLES

See "The Time of First Chronicles" for the background of First and Second Chronicles. Chapters 1—9 cover the forty years from 971 B.C.

to 931 B.C., and chapters 10—36 cover the 393 years from 931 B.C. to 538 B.C. Jeremiah's prediction of a seventy-year captivity in Babylon (36:21; Jer. 29:10) is fulfilled in two ways: (1) a political captivity in which Jerusalem is overcome from 605 B.C. to 536 B.C., and (2) a religious captivity involving the destruction of the temple in 586 B.C. and the completion of the new temple in 516 or 515 B.C.

✝ THE CHRIST OF SECOND CHRONICLES

The throne of David has been destroyed, but the line of David remains. Murders, treachery, battles, and captivity all threaten the messianic line; but it remains clear and unbroken from Adam to Zerubbabel. The fulfillment in Christ can be seen in the genealogies of Matthew 1 and Luke 3.

The temple also prefigures Christ. Jesus says, "In this place is *one* greater than the temple" (Matt. 12:6). He also likens His body to the temple: "Destroy this temple, and in three days I will raise it up" (John 2:19). In Revelation 21:22 He replaces the temple: "And I saw no temple therein: for the Lord God Almighty and the Lamb are the temple of it."

🔑 KEYS TO SECOND CHRONICLES

Key Word: Priestly View of Judah—The Book of Second Chronicles provides topical histories of the end of the united kingdom (Solomon) and the kingdom of Judah. More than historical annals, Chronicles is a divine editorial on the spiritual characteristics of the Davidic dynasty. This is why it focuses on the southern rather than the northern kingdom. Most of the kings fail to realize that apart from the true mission as a covenant nation called to bring others to Yahweh, Judah has no calling, no destiny, and no hope of becoming great on her own. Only what is done in accordance with God's will has any lasting value. Chronicles concentrates on the kings who are concerned with maintaining the proper service of God and the times of spiritual reform. However, growing apostasy inevitably leads to judgment.

The temple in Jerusalem is the major unifying theme of First and Second Chronicles. Much of the material found in Second Samuel to Second Kings is omitted from Chronicles because it does not develop this theme. In First Chronicles 11—29, the central message is David's preparation for the construction and service of the temple. Most of Second Chronicles 1—9 is devoted to the building and consecration of the temple.

Chapters 10—36 omit the kings of Israel in the north because they have no ties with the temple. Prominence is given to the reigns of Judah's temple restorers (Asa, Jehoshaphat, Joash, Hezekiah, and Josiah). The temple symbolizes God's presence among His people and reminds them of their high calling. It provides the spiritual link between their past and future. Thus, Ezra wrote this book to encourage the people to accept the new temple raised on the site of the old and to remind them of their true calling and God's faithfulness despite their low circumstances. The Davidic line, temple, and priesthood are still theirs.

Key Verses: Second Chronicles 7:14; 16:9— "If my people, which are called by my name, shall humble themselves, and pray, and seek my face, and turn from their wicked ways; then will I hear from heaven, and will forgive their sin, and will heal their land" (7:14).

"For the eyes of the LORD run to and fro throughout the whole earth, to shew himself strong in the behalf of *them* whose heart *is* perfect toward him. Herein thou hast done foolishly: therefore from henceforth thou shalt have wars" (16:9).

Key Chapter: Second Chronicles 34—Second Chronicles records the reforms and revivals under such kings as Asa, Jehoshaphat, Joash, Hezekiah, and Josiah. Chapter 34 traces the dramatic revival that takes place under Josiah when the "book of the law" is found, read, and obeyed.

SURVEY OF SECOND CHRONICLES

This book repeatedly teaches that whenever God's people forsake Him, He withdraws His blessings, but trust in and obedience to the Lord bring victory. Since everything in Chronicles is related to the temple, it is not surprising that this concludes with Cyrus's edict to rebuild it. Solomon's glory is seen

in chapters 1—9, and Judah's decline and deportation in chapters 10—36.

Solomon's Reign (1—9): The reign of Solomon brings in Israel's golden age of peace, prosperity, and temple worship. The kingdom is united and its boundaries extend to their greatest point. Solomon's wealth, wisdom, palace, and temple become legendary. His mighty spiritual, political, and architectural feats raise Israel to her zenith. However, it is in keeping with the purpose of Chronicles that six of these nine chapters concern the construction and dedication of the temple.

The Reign of Judah's Kings (10—36): Unfortunately, Israel's glory is short-lived. Soon after Solomon's death the nation is divided, and both kingdoms begin a downward spiral that can only be delayed by the religious reforms. The nation generally forsakes the temple and the worship of Yahweh, and is soon torn by warfare and unrest. The reformation efforts on the part of some of Judah's kings are valiant, but never last beyond one generation. Nevertheless, about seventy percent of chapters 10—36 deals with the eight good kings, leaving only thirty percent to cover the twelve evil rulers. Each king is seen with respect to his relationship to the temple as the center of worship and spiritual strength. When the king serves Yahweh, Judah is blessed with political and economic prosperity.

Here is a brief survey of Judah's twenty rulers: (1) *Rehoboam*—Although he is not righteous, he humbles himself before God and averts His wrath (12:12). (2) *Abijah*—He enjoys a short and evil reign, but he conquers Israel because "the children of Judah . . . relied upon the LORD God" (13:18). (3) *Asa*—Although he destroys foreign altars and idols, conquers Ethiopia against great odds through his trust in God, and restores the altar of the Lord, yet he fails to trust God when threatened by Israel. (4) *Jehoshaphat*—He brings in a great revival; "His heart was lifted up in the

FOCUS	REIGN OF SOLOMON			REIGNS OF THE KINGS OF JUDAH		
REFERENCE	1:1	2:1	8:1	10:1	14:1	36:1 — 36:23
DIVISION	INAUGURATION OF SOLOMON	COMPLETION OF THE TEMPLE	THE GLORY OF SOLOMON'S REIGN	THE DIVISION OF THE KINGDOM	THE REFORMS UNDER ASA, JEHOSHAPHAT, JOASH, HEZEKIAH, AND JOSIAH	THE FALL OF JUDAH
TOPIC	THE TEMPLE IS CONSTRUCTED			THE TEMPLE IS DESTROYED		
	SPLENDOR			DISASTER		
LOCATION	JUDAH					
TIME	c. 40 YEARS			c. 393 YEARS		

ways of the LORD" (17:6). Jehoshaphat over-throws idols, teaches God's Word to the people, and trusts in God before battle. (5) *Jehoram*—A wicked king, he follows the ways of Ahab and marries his daughter. He leads Judah into idolatry and when he dies in pain, departs "without being desired" (21:20). (6 and 7) *Ahaziah* and *Athaliah*—Ahaziah is as wicked as his father, as is his mother Athaliah. Both are murdered. (8) *Joash*—Although he repairs the temple and restores the worship of God, when Jehoiada the priest dies, Joash allows the people to abandon the temple and return to idolatry. (9) *Amaziah*—Mixed in his relationship to God, he later forsakes the Lord for the gods of Edom. He is defeated by Israel and later murdered. (10) *Uzziah*—He begins well with the Lord and is blessed with military victories. However, when he becomes strong, he proudly and presumptuously plays the role of a priest by offering incense in the temple and therefore is struck with leprosy. (11) *Jotham*—Because he rebuilds the gate of the temple and reveres God, the Lord blesses him with prosperity and victory. (12) *Ahaz*—A wicked king and an idolator, he is oppressed by his enemies and forced to give tribute to the Assyrians from the temple treasures. (13)

Hezekiah—He repairs and reopens the temple and puts away the altars and idols set up by his father, Ahaz. Judah is spared destruction by Assyria because of his righteousness. His reforms are given only a few verses in Kings but three chapters in Chronicles. (14 and 15) *Manasseh* and *Amon*—Manasseh is Judah's most wicked king. He sets up idols and altars all over the land. However, he repents when he is carried away by Assyria. God brings him back to Judah and he makes a halfway reform, but it comes too late. Amon follows in his father's wickedness. Both kings are murdered. (16) *Josiah*—A leader in reforms and spiritual revival, he centers worship around the temple, finds the law and obeys it, and reinstitutes the Passover. (17, 18, and 19) *Jehoahaz, Jehoiakim, Jehoiachin*—Their relentless evil finally brings the downfall of Judah. The temple is ravaged in each of their reigns. (20) *Zedekiah*—Judah's last king is also wicked. Jerusalem and the temple are destroyed, and the captivity begins. Second Chronicles nevertheless ends on a note of hope at the end of the captivity, when Cyrus issues the decree for the restoration of Judah: "Who *is there* among you of all his people? The LORD his God *be* with him, and let him go up" (36:23).

OUTLINE OF SECOND CHRONICLES

Part One: The Reign of Solomon (1:1—9:31)

Part Two: The Reigns of the Kings of Judah (10:1—36:23)

CHAPTER 1

The Worship of Solomon—1 Kin. 3:4

AND Solomon the son of David was strengthened in his kingdom, and ᴿthe LORD his God was with him, and ᴿmagnified him exceedingly.   Gen. 39:2 • 1 Chr. 29:25

2 Then Solomon spake unto all Israel, to ᴿthe captains of thousands and of hundreds, and to the judges, and to every governor in all Israel, the chief of the fathers.   1 Chr. 27:1

3 So Solomon, and all the congregation with him, went to the ᵀhigh place that was at ᴿGib'-e-on; for there was the tabernacle of the congregation of God, which Moses the servant of the LORD had made in the wilderness.   *worship shrine* • 1 Kin. 3:4; 1 Chr. 16:39

4 But the ark of God had David brought up from Kir'-jath-je'-a-rim to the place which David had prepared for it: for he had pitched a tent for it at Jerusalem.

5 Moreover ᴿthe brasen altar, that ᴿBe-

zal'-e-el the son of U'-ri, the son of Hur, had made, he put before the tabernacle of the Lord: and Solomon and the congregation sought unto it.   Ex. 27:1, 2 • Ex. 31:2

6 And Solomon went up thither to the brasen altar before the Lord, which *was* at the tabernacle of the congregation, and offered a thousand burnt offerings upon it.

The Petition for Wisdom—1 Kin. 3:5–9

7 ᴿIn that night did God appear unto Solomon, and said unto him, Ask what I shall give thee.   1 Kin. 3:5–14; 9:2

8 And Solomon said unto God, Thou hast shewed great mercy unto David my father, and hast made me to reign in his stead.

9 Now, O Lord God, let thy promise unto David my father be established: ᴿfor thou hast made me king over a people like the dust of the earth in multitude.   1 Kin. 3:7, 8

10 ᴿGive me now wisdom and knowledge, that I may ᴿgo out and come in before this people: for who can judge this thy people, *that is so* great?   1 Kin. 3:9 • Num. 27:17; Deut. 31:2

The Provision of Wisdom—1 Kin. 3:10–14

11 And God said to Solomon, Because this was in thine heart, and thou hast not asked riches, wealth, or honour, nor the life of thine enemies, neither yet hast asked long life; but hast asked wisdom and knowledge for thyself, that thou mayest judge my people, over whom I have made thee king:

12 Wisdom and knowledge *is* granted unto thee; and I will give thee riches, and wealth, and honour, such as none of the kings have had that *have been* before thee, neither shall there any after thee have the like.

The Wealth of Solomon
1 Kin. 10:26–29; 2 Chr. 9:25–28

13 Then Solomon came *from his journey* to the high place that *was* at Gib'-e-on to Jerusalem, from before the tabernacle of the congregation, and reigned over Israel.

14 And Solomon gathered chariots and horsemen: and he had a thousand and four hundred chariots, and twelve thousand horsemen, which he placed in the chariot cities, and with the king at Jerusalem.

15 And the king ᵀmade silver and gold at Jerusalem *as plenteous* as stones, and cedar trees made he as the sycomore trees that *are* in the vale for abundance.   *gave*

16 And Solomon had horses brought out of Egypt, and linen yarn: the king's merchants received the linen yarn at a price.

17 And they fetched up, and brought forth out of Egypt a chariot for ᵀsix hundred *shek'-els* of silver, and an horse for ᵀan hundred and fifty: and so brought they out *horses* for all the kings of the Hit'-tites, and for the kings of Syria, by their means.   *$4,368 • $1,092*

CHAPTER 2

Selection of the Temple Builders
1 Kin. 5:15, 16

AND Solomon ᴿdetermined to build an house for the name of the Lord, and an house for his kingdom.   1 Kin. 5:5

2 And ᴿSolomon ᵀtold out threescore and ten thousand men to bear burdens, and fourscore thousand to ᵀhew in the mountain, and three thousand and six hundred to oversee them.   *v. 18 • counted • cut timber*

Selection of the Temple Materials

3 And Solomon sent to ᵀHu'-ram the king of Tyre, saying, As thou didst deal with David my father, and didst send him cedars to build him an house to dwell therein, *even so deal with me.*   *Hiram*

4 Behold, I build an house to the name of the Lord my God, to dedicate *it* to him, *and* to burn before him sweet incense, and for the continual shewbread, and for the burnt offerings morning and evening, on the sabbaths, and on the new moons, and on the solemn feasts of the Lord our God. This *is an ordinance* for ever to Israel.

5 And the house which I build *is* great: for great *is* our God above all gods.

6 ᴿBut who is able to build him an house, seeing the heaven and heaven of heavens cannot contain him? who *am* I then, that I should build him an house, save only to burn sacrifice before him?   1 Kin. 8:27; Is. 66:1

7 ᴿSend me now therefore a man ᵀcunning to work in gold, and in silver, and in brass, and in iron, and in purple, and crimson, and blue, and that ᵀcan skill to grave with the cunning men that *are* with me in Judah and in Jerusalem, whom David my father did provide.   *vv. 13, 14 • skilful • has skill to engrave*

8 Send me also cedar trees, fir trees, and al'-gum trees, out of Leb'-a-non: for I know that thy servants can skill to cut ᵀtimber in Leb'-a-non; and, behold, my servants *shall be* with thy servants,   *lumber*

9 Even to prepare me timber in abundance: for the house which I am about to build *shall be* wonderful great.

10 And, behold, I will give to thy servants, the hewers that cut timber, ᵀtwenty thousand measures of ᵀbeaten wheat, and twenty thousand measures of barley, and ᵀtwenty thousand baths of wine, and twenty thousand baths of oil.   *13,048 bu. • crushed • 120,000 gal.*

11 Then Hu'-ram the king of Tyre answered in writing, which he sent to Solomon, Because the Lord hath loved his people, he hath made thee king over them.

12 Hu'-ram said moreover, Blessed *be* the Lord God of Israel, that made heaven and

earth, who hath given to David the king a wise son, endued with prudence and understanding, that might build an house for the LORD, and an house for his kingdom.

13 And now I have sent a ᵀcunning ᴿman, endued with understanding, of Hu′-ram my father's,   *skilful* · 26:15

14 The son of a woman of the daughters of Dan, and his father *was* a man of Tyre, skilful to work in gold, and in silver, in brass, in iron, in stone, and in timber, in purple, in blue, and in fine linen, and in crimson; also to grave any manner of graving, and to ᵀfind out every device which shall be put to ᵀhim, with thy cunning men, and with the cunning men of my lord David thy father.   *solve every problem*

15 Now therefore the wheat, and the barley, the oil, and the wine, which ᴿmy lord hath spoken of, let him send unto his servants: *v. 10*

16 And we will cut wood out of Leb′-a-non, as much as thou shalt need: and we will bring it to thee in ᵀflotes by sea to Jop′-pa; and thou shalt carry it up to Jerusalem.   *rafts*

17 ᴿAnd Solomon numbered all the strangers that *were* in the land of Israel, after the numbering wherewith David his father had numbered them; and they were found an hundred and fifty thousand and three thousand and six hundred.   8:7, 8

18 And he set threescore and ten thousand of them *to be* bearers of burdens, and fourscore thousand *to be* hewers in the mountain, and three thousand and six hundred overseers to set the people a work.

CHAPTER 3

Construction of the Temple
1 Kin. 6:1—7:51

THEN ᴿSolomon began to build the house of the LORD at Jerusalem in mount Mo-ri′-ah, where *the LORD* appeared unto David his father, in the place that David had prepared in the threshingfloor of ᵀOr′-nan the Jeb′-u-site.   1 Kin. 6:1 · *Araunah*

2 And he began to build in the second *day* of the second month, in the fourth year of his reign.

3 Now these *are the things wherein* Solomon was instructed for the building of the house of God. The length by cubits after the first measure *was* ᵀthreescore cubits, and the breadth ᵀtwenty cubits.   *90 ft.* · *30 ft.*

4 And the porch that *was* in the front *of the house,* the length *of it was* according to the breadth of the house, twenty cubits, and the height *was* an hundred and twenty: and he overlaid it within with pure gold.

5 And the greater house he cieled with fir

tree, which he overlaid with fine gold, and set thereon palm trees and chains.

6 And he ᵀgarnished the house with precious stones for beauty: and the gold *was* gold of Par-va′-im.   *decorated*

7 ᴿHe overlaid also the house, the beams, the posts, and the walls thereof, and the doors thereof, with gold; and ᵀgraved cher′-u-bims on the walls.   1 Kin. 6:20–22 · *carved*

8 And he made the most holy house, the length whereof *was* according to the breadth of the house, twenty cubits, and the breadth thereof ᵀtwenty cubits: and he overlaid it with fine gold, *amounting* to ᵀsix hundred talents.   *30 ft.* · *$3,450,000,000*

9 And the weight of the nails *was* ᵀfifty shek′-els of gold. And he overlaid the upper chambers with gold.   *18.2 oz.*

10 And in the most holy house he made two cher′-u-bims ᵀof image work, and overlaid them with gold.   *of moveable work*

11 And the wings of the cher′-u-bims *were* ᵀtwenty cubits long: one wing *of the one cherub was* five cubits, reaching to the wall of the house: and the other wing *was likewise* ᵀfive cubits, reaching to the wing of the other cherub.   *30 ft.* · *7.5 ft.*

12 And *one* wing of the other cherub *was* five cubits, reaching to the wall of the house: and the other wing *was* five cubits *also,* joining to the wing of the other cherub.

13 The wings of these cher′-u-bims spread themselves forth ᵀtwenty cubits: and they stood on their feet, and their faces *were* ᵀinward.   *30 ft.* · *toward the inside*

14 And he made the ᴿvail *of* blue, and purple, and crimson, and fine linen, and wrought cher′-u-bims thereon.   Heb. 9:3

15 Also he made before the house ᴿtwo pillars of ᵀthirty and five cubits ᵀhigh, and the chapiter that *was* on the top of each of them *was* five cubits.   1 Kin. 7:15 · *52.5 ft.* · *long*

16 And he made chains, *as* in the oracle, and put *them* on the heads of the pillars; and made ᴿan hundred pomegranates, and put *them* on the chains.   1 Kin. 7:20

17 And he ᴿreared up the pillars before the temple, one on the right hand, and the other on the left; and called the name of that on the right hand Ja′-chin, and the name of that on the left Bo′-az.   1 Kin. 7:21

CHAPTER 4

MOREOVER he made an altar of brass, ᵀtwenty cubits the length thereof, and twenty cubits the breadth thereof, and ᵀten cubits the height thereof.   *30 ft.* · *15 ft.*

2 Also he made a molten sea of ten cubits from brim to brim, round in compass, and five

cubits the height thereof; and a line of thirty cubits did compass it round about.

3 RAnd under it *was* the Tsimilitude of oxen, which did compass it round about: ten in Ta cubit, compassing the sea round about. Two rows of oxen *were* cast, when it was cast.   1 Kin. 7:24-26 · *images like oxen* · *18 in.*

4 It stood upon twelve oxen, three looking toward the north, and three looking toward the west, and three looking toward the south, and three looking toward the east: and the Tsea *was set* above upon them, and all their hinder parts *were* inward.   *large basin*

5 And the thickness of it *was* an handbreadth, and the brim of it like the work of the brim of a cup, with flowers of lilies; *and* it received and held three thousand baths.

6 He made also ten lavers, and put five on the right hand, and five on the left, to wash in them: such things as they offered for the burnt offering they washed in them; but the sea *was* for the priests to wash in.

7 RAnd he made ten candlesticks of gold Raccording to their form, and set *them* in the temple, five on the right hand, and five on the left.   1 Kin. 7:49 · Ex. 25:31

8 RHe made also ten tables, and placed *them* in the temple, five on the right side, and five on the left. And he made an hundred Tbasons of gold.   1 Kin. 7:48 · *bowls*

9 Furthermore Rhe made the court of the priests, Rand the great court, and doors for the court, and overlaid the doors of them with brass.   1 Kin. 6:36 · 2 Kin. 21:5

10 And he set the sea on the right side of the east end, over against the south.

11 And Hu'-ram made the pots, and the shovels, and the Tbasons. And Hu'-ram finished the work that he was to make for king Solomon for the house of God;   *bowls*

12 To wit, the two pillars, and the pommels, and the chapiters *which were* on the top of the two pillars, and the two wreaths to cover the two pommels of the chapiters which *were* on the top of the pillars;

13 And Rfour hundred pomegranates on the two wreaths; two rows of pomegranates on each wreath, to cover the two Tpommels of the Tchapiters which *were* upon the pillars.   1 Kin. 7:20 · *bowls* · *heads of the pillars*

14 He made also Rbases, and Tlavers made he upon the bases;   1 Kin. 7:27, 43 · *caldrons*

15 One sea, and twelve oxen under it.

16 The pots also, and the shovels, and the fleshhooks, and all their instruments, did Hu'-ram his father make to king Solomon for the house of the LORD of bright brass.

17 RIn the plain of Jordan did the king cast them, in the clay ground between Suc'-coth and Ze-red'-a-thah.   1 Kin. 7:46

18 RThus Solomon made all these vessels in great abundance: for the weight of the brass could not be found out.   1 Kin. 7:47

19 And RSolomon made all the vessels that *were for* the house of God, the golden altar also, and the tables whereon Rthe shewbread *was set;*   1 Kin. 7:48-50 · Ex. 25:30

20 Moreover the candlesticks with their lamps, that they should burn after the manner before the oracle, of pure gold;

21 And Rthe flowers, and the lamps, and the tongs, *made he of* Rgold, *and* that Tperfect gold;   Ex. 25:31 · Gen. 2:12 · *perfections of gold*

22 And the snuffers, and the basons, and the spoons, and the censers, *of* pure gold: and the entry of the house, the inner doors thereof for the most holy *place*, and the doors of the house of the temple, *were of* gold.

CHAPTER 5

THUS all the work that Solomon made for the house of the LORD was finished: and Solomon brought in *all* the things that David his father had dedicated; and the silver, and the gold, and all the instruments, put he among the treasures of the house of God.

The Installation of the Ark—1 Kin. 8:1-9

2 RThen Solomon assembled the elders of Israel, and all the heads of the tribes, the chief of the fathers of the children of Israel, unto Jerusalem, to bring up the ark of the covenant of the LORD Rout of the city of David, which is Zion.   1 Kin. 8:1 · 2 Sam. 6:12

3 Wherefore all the men of Israel assembled themselves unto the king in the feast which *was* in the seventh month.

4 And all the elders of Israel came; and the RLevites took up the ark.   1 Chr. 15:2, 15

5 And they brought up the Rark, and the Rtabernacle of the congregation, and all the holy vessels that *were* in the tabernacle, these did the priests *and* the Levites bring up.   35:3; Ex. 25:10 · 24:6; Ex. 25:8

6 Also king Solomon, and all the congregation of Israel that were assembled unto him before the ark, sacrificed sheep and oxen, which Tcould not be told nor numbered for multitude.   *was beyond estimate*

7 And the priests brought in the ark of the covenant of the LORD unto his place, to the Roracle of the house, into the most Rholy *place, even* under the wings of the Rcher'-u-bims: 4:20 · Ex. 26:33 · Ex. 25:18

8 For the cher'-u-bims spread forth *their* wings over the place of the ark, and the cher'-u-bims covered the ark and the staves thereof above.

9 And they drew out the staves *of the ark*, that the ends of the staves were seen from

the ark before the oracle; but they were not seen without. And there it is unto this day.

10 *There was* nothing in the ark save the two tables which Moses [R]put *therein* at Ho'-reb, [T]when the LORD made *a covenant* with the children of Israel, when they came out of Egypt.   6:11; Deut. 10:2, 5 · *where*

11 And it came to pass, when the priests were come out of the holy *place:* (for all the priests *that were* present were sanctified, *and* did not *then* wait by course:

12 Also the Levites *which were* the singers, all of them of A'-saph, of He'-man, of Je-du'-thun, with their sons and their brethren, *being* arrayed in white linen, having cymbals and psalteries and harps, stood at the east end of the altar, and with them an hundred and twenty priests sounding with trumpets:)

The Glory of the Lord Fills the Temple
1 Kin. 8:10, 11

13 It came even to pass, as the trumpeters and singers *were* as one, to make one sound to be heard in praising and thanking the LORD; and when they lifted up *their* voice with the trumpets and cymbals and instruments of musick, and praised the LORD, *saying,* For *he is* good; for his mercy *endureth* for ever: that *then* the house was filled with a cloud, *even* the house of the LORD;

14 So that the priests could not stand to minister by reason of the cloud: for the glory of the LORD had filled the house of God.

CHAPTER 6

The Sermon of Solomon—1 Kin. 8:12-21

THEN [R]said Solomon, The LORD hath said that he would dwell in [T]the [R]thick darkness.   1 Kin. 8:12-21 · *an invisible place* · Lev. 16:2

2 [R]But I have built an house of habitation for thee, and a [R]place for thy dwelling for ever.   2 Sam. 7:13 · 7:12

3 And the king turned his face, and blessed the whole congregation of Israel: and all the congregation of Israel stood.

4 And he said, Blessed *be* the LORD God of Israel, who hath with his hands fulfilled *that* which he spake with his mouth to my father David, [R]saying,   1 Chr. 17:5

5 Since the day that I brought forth my people out of the land of Egypt I chose no city among all the tribes of Israel to build an house in, that my name might be there; neither chose I any man to be a ruler over my people Israel:

6 [R]But I have chosen Jerusalem, that my name might be there; and have chosen David to be over my people Israel.   Zech. 2:12

7 Now it was in the heart of David my

father to build an house for [T]the name of the LORD God of Israel.   *the public worship*

8 But the LORD said to David my father, Forasmuch as it was in thine heart to build an house [R]for my name, thou didst well in that it was in thine heart: Mark 14:6

9 Notwithstanding thou shalt not build the house; but thy son which shall come forth out of thy loins, he shall build the house for my [R]name.   1 Chr. 28:3-6

10 The LORD therefore hath performed his word that he hath spoken: for I am risen up in the room of David my father, and am set on the throne of Israel, as the LORD promised, and have built the house for the name of the LORD God of Israel.

11 And in it have I put the ark, wherein *is* the [T]covenant[R] of the LORD, that he made with the children of Israel.   *agreement* · 5:7, 10

The Prayer of Solomon—1 Kin. 8:22-53

12 And he stood before the altar of the LORD in the presence of all the congregation of Israel, and spread forth his hands:

13 For Solomon had made a brasen scaffold, of [T]five cubits long, and five cubits broad, and three cubits high, and had set it in the midst of the court: and upon it he stood, and kneeled down upon his knees before all the congregation of Israel, and spread forth his hands toward heaven,   7.5 ft.

14 And said, O LORD God of Israel, *there is* no God like thee in the heaven, nor in the earth; which keepest covenant, and *shewest* mercy unto thy servants, that walk before thee with all their hearts:

15 [R]Thou which hast kept with thy servant David my father that which thou hast promised him; and spakest with thy mouth, and hast fulfilled *it* with thine hand, as *it is* this day.   1 Chr. 22:9, 10

16 Now therefore, O LORD God of Israel, keep with thy servant David my father that which thou hast promised him, saying, There shall not fail thee a man in my sight to sit upon the throne of Israel; yet so that thy children take heed to their way to walk in my law, as thou hast walked before me.

17 Now then, O LORD God of Israel, let thy word be [R]verified, which thou hast spoken unto thy servant David.   1 Kin. 8:56

18 But will God in very deed dwell with men on the earth? behold, heaven and the heaven of heavens cannot contain thee; how much less this house which I have built!

19 Have respect therefore to the prayer of thy servant, and to his supplication, O LORD my God, to hearken [R]unto the cry and the prayer which thy servant prayeth before thee: Job 34:28

20 That thine eyes may be [R]open upon this house day and night, upon the place whereof

thou hast said that thou wouldest put thy name there; to hearken unto the prayer which thy servant prayeth ᵀtoward^R this place.   7:15 · *in this place* · Ps. 5:7; Dan. 6:10

21 Hearken therefore unto the supplications of thy servant, and of thy people Israel, which they shall make toward this place: hear thou from thy dwelling place, *even* from heaven; and when thou hearest, forgive.

22 If a man sin against his neighbour, and an oath be laid upon him to make him ᵀswear, and the oath come before thine altar in this house;   *testify as to his part*

23 Then hear thou from heaven, and do, and judge thy servants, by requiting the wicked, by recompensing his way upon his own head; and by justifying the righteous, by giving him according to his righteousness.

24 And if thy people Israel be put to the worse before the enemy, because they have sinned against thee; and shall return and confess thy name, and pray and make supplication before thee in this house;

25 Then hear thou from the heavens, and forgive the sin of thy people Israel, and bring them again unto the land which thou gavest to them and to their fathers.

26 When the heaven is shut up, and there is no rain, because they have sinned against thee; *yet* if they pray toward this place, and confess thy name, and turn from their sin, when thou dost afflict them;

27 Then hear thou from heaven, and forgive the sin of thy servants, and of thy people Israel, when thou hast taught them the good way, wherein they should walk; and send rain upon thy land, which thou hast given unto thy people for an inheritance.

28 If there be dearth in the land, if there be pestilence, if there be blasting, or mildew, locusts, or caterpillers; if their enemies besiege them in the cities of their land; whatsoever sore or whatsoever sickness *there be*:

29 *Then* what prayer *or* what supplication soever shall be made of any man, or of all thy people Israel, when every one shall know his own sore and his own grief, and shall spread forth his hands ᵀin this house: *toward this house*

30 Then hear thou from heaven thy dwelling place, and forgive, and render unto every man according unto all his ways, whose heart thou knowest; (for thou only knowest the hearts of the children of men:)

31 That they may fear thee, to walk in thy ways, so long as they live in the land which thou gavest unto our fathers.

32 Moreover concerning the stranger, which is not of thy people Israel, but is come from a far country for thy great name's sake, and thy mighty hand, and thy stretched out arm; if they come and pray in this house;

33 Then hear thou from the heavens, *even* from thy dwelling place, and do according to all that the stranger calleth to thee for; that all people of the earth may know thy name, and fear thee, as *doth* thy people Israel, and may know that this ᵀhouse which I have built is called by thy name.   *temple*

34 If thy people go out to war against their enemies by the way that thou shalt send them, and they pray unto thee toward this city which thou hast chosen, and the house which I have built for thy name;

35 Then hear thou from the heavens their prayer and their supplication, and ᵀmaintain their cause.   *help them in their conflict*

36 If they sin against thee, (for *there is* no man which sinneth not,) and thou be angry with them, and deliver them over before *their* enemies, and they carry them away captives unto a land far off or near;

37 Yet *if* they bethink themselves in the land whither they are carried captive, and turn and pray unto thee in the land of their captivity, saying, We have sinned, we have done amiss, and have dealt wickedly;

38 If they return to thee with all their heart and with all their soul in the land of their captivity, whither they have carried them captives, and pray toward their land, which thou gavest unto their fathers, and *toward* the city which thou hast chosen, and toward the house which I have built for thy name:

39 Then hear thou from the heavens, *even* from thy dwelling place, their prayer and their supplications, and maintain their cause, and forgive thy people which have sinned against thee.

40 Now, my God, let, I beseech thee, thine eyes be open, and *let* thine ears *be* attent unto the prayer *that is made* in this place.

41 Now therefore arise, O LORD God, into thy resting place, thou, and the ark of thy strength: let thy priests, O LORD God, be clothed with salvation, and let thy saints ^Rrejoice in goodness.   Neh. 9:25

42 O LORD God, ᵀturn not away the face of thine anointed: ^Rremember the mercies of David thy servant.   *do not shut out* · Is. 55:3

CHAPTER 7

The Fire of the Lord Consumes the Sacrifices

NOW ^Rwhen Solomon had made an end of praying, the fire came down from heaven, and consumed the burnt offering and the sacrifices; and ^Rthe glory of the LORD filled the house.   1 Kin. 8:54 · 1 Kin. 8:10, 11

2 And the priests could not enter into the house of the LORD, because the glory of the LORD had filled the LORD's house.

3 And when all the children of Israel saw how the fire came down, and the glory of the LORD upon the house, they bowed themselves with their faces to the ground upon the pavement, and worshipped, and praised the LORD, *saying*, For *he is* good; Rfor his mercy *endureth* for ever.   20:21

The Nation Offers Sacrifices—1 Kin. 8:62–64

4 Then the king and all the people offered sacrifices before the LORD.

5 And king Solomon offered a sacrifice of twenty and two thousand oxen, and an hundred and twenty thousand sheep: so the king and all the people dedicated the house of God.

6 And the priests waited on their offices: the Levites also with instruments of musick of the LORD, which David the king had made to praise the LORD, because his mercy *endureth* for ever, when David praised by their ministry; and the priests sounded trumpets before them, and all Israel stood.

7 Moreover Solomon hallowed the middle of the court that *was* before the house of the LORD: for there he offered burnt offerings, and the fat of the peace offerings, because the brasen altar which Solomon had made was Tnot able to receive the burnt offerings, and the meat offerings, and the fat.   *not large enough*

The Nation Celebrates the Feasts of Tabernacles 1 Kin. 8:65—9:1

8 Also at the same time Solomon kept the feast seven days, and all Israel with him, a very great congregation, from the entering in of Ha'-math unto the river of Egypt.

9 And in the eighth day they made a Rsolemn assembly: for they kept the dedication of the altar seven days, and the feast seven days.   Lev. 23:36

10 And Ron the three and twentieth day of the seventh month he sent the people away into their tents, glad and merry in heart for the goodness that the LORD had shewed unto David, and to Solomon, and to Israel his people.   1 Kin. 8:66

11 Thus RSolomon finished the house of the LORD, and the king's house: and all that came into Solomon's heart to make in the house of the LORD, and in his own house, he prosperously effected.   1 Kin. 9:1

The Lord Confirms the Covenant—1 Kin. 9:2–9

12 And the LORD appeared to Solomon by night, and said unto him, I have heard thy prayer, Rand have chosen this place to myself for an house of sacrifice.   Deut. 12:5

13 RIf I shut up heaven that there be no rain, or if I command the locusts to devour the land, or if I send pestilence among my people;   6:26, 28; Deut. 28:23, 24; 1 Kin. 17:1

14 If my people, which are called by my name, shall Rhumble themselves, and pray, and seek my face, and turn from their wicked ways; Rthen will I Rhear from heaven, and will forgive their sin, and will heal their land.   [Deut. 28:10] · James 4:10 · 6:27, 30

15 Now Rmine eyes shall be open, and mine ears Tattent unto the prayer *that is made* in this place.   6:20, 40 · *attentive*

16 For now have I chosen and sanctified this house, that my name may be there for ever: and mine eyes and Tmine heart shall be there perpetually.   *my concern*

17 RAnd as for thee, if thou wilt walk before me, as David thy father walked, and do according to all that I have commanded thee, and shalt observe my statutes and my Tjudgments;   1 Kin. 9:4 · *ordinances*

18 Then will I stablish the throne of thy kingdom, according as I have covenanted with David thy father, saying, There shall not fail thee a man *to be* ruler in Israel.

7:3 The Reasons for Worship—The first reason for worship is simply that God commands it (Page 421—1 Chr. 16:29; Page 944—Matt. 4:10). The first four of the Ten Commandments, which are also the longest, clearly charge men to worship the one true God and Him alone (Page 75—Ex. 20:3–10). To allow any person or thing to usurp the position of lordship over us constitutes gross disobedience to the will of God and incurs His terrible wrath (Page 75—Ex. 20:5; Page 203—Deut. 27:15). All people are destined to pay homage to God anyway, even if unwillingly (Page 1171—Phil. 2:10).

An equally important reason for worship is that God deserves our worship. He alone possesses the attributes that merit our worship and service. Among these are goodness (Page 590—Ps. 100:4, 5), mercy (Page 60—Ex. 4:31), holiness (Page 590—Ps. 99:5, 9), and creative power (Page 1271—Rev. 4:11). When men of biblical times clearly saw the unveiled glory of God, they could not help but fall prostrate in worship. Examples of this response can be seen in the actions of Moses (Page 89—Ex. 34:5–8), Paul (Page 1081—Acts 9:3–6), and John (Page 1268—Rev. 1:9–17).

A final reason for worship is that men need to give it. People cannot find personal fulfillment apart from the glad submission of themselves in worshipful obedience to God. He is the Creator and they are the creatures (Page 1271—Rev. 4:11). People who adopt as their master anything less than God are building their lives on quicksand. They will be no stronger than the object they worship (Page 598—Ps. 115:4–8). One who worships God, however, not only participates in the occupation of heaven (Page 1273—Rev. 7:9–12), but finds joyful satisfaction for the present (Page 1118—Rom. 12:2; Page 1179—Col. 3:24).

Now turn to Page 1121—Rom. 16:5: Definition of the Local Church.

19 But if ye turn away, and forsake my statutes and my commandments, which I have set before you, and shall go and serve other gods, and worship them;

20 Then will I pluck Tthem up by the roots out of my land which I have given them; and this house, which I have Tsanctified for my name, will I cast out of my sight, and will make it to be a proverb and a byword among all nations.   Israel · set apart

21 And this Thouse, which is Thigh, shall be an astonishment to every one that passeth by it; so that he shall say, Why hath the LORD done thus unto this land, and unto this Thouse?   temple · notable · temple

22 RAnd it shall be answered, Because they forsook the LORD God of their fathers, which brought them forth out of the land of Egypt, and laid hold on other gods, and worshipped them, and served them: therefore hath he brought all this evil upon them.   Judg. 2:13

CHAPTER 8

Enlargement of Solomon's Territory
1 Kin. 9:10-19

AND it came to pass at the end of twenty years, wherein Solomon had built the house of the LORD, and his own house,

2 That the cities which Hu′-ram had restored to Solomon, Solomon built them, and caused the children of Israel to dwell there.

3 And Solomon went to Ha′-math-zo′-bah, and prevailed against it.

4 RAnd he built Tad′-mor in the wilderness, and all the Tstore cities, which he built in Ha′-math.   1 Kin. 9:17, 18 · supply depots

5 Also he built Beth-ho′-ron the upper, and Beth-ho′-ron the Tnether, fenced cities, with walls, gates, and bars;   lower

6 And Ba′-al-ath, and all the Tstore cities that Solomon had, and all the chariot cities, and the cities of the horsemen, and all that Solomon desired to build in Jerusalem, and in Leb′-a-non, and throughout all the land of his dominion.   storage

Subjugation of the Enemies of Solomon
1 Kin. 9:20-23

7 As for all the people that were left of the Hit′-tites, and the Am′-or-ites, and the Per′-iz-zites, and the Hi′-vites, and the Jeb′-u-sites, which were not of Israel,

8 But of their children, who were left after them in the land, whom the children of Israel consumed not, them did Solomon make to pay tribute until this day.

9 RBut of the children of Israel did Solomon make no Tservants for his work; but they were men of war, and chief of his captains, and captains of his chariots and horsemen.   [Ex. 19:5; Lev. 25:39] · slaves

10 And these were the chief of king Solomon's officers, even Rtwo hundred and fifty, that bare rule over the people. 1 Kin. 9:23

Religious Practices of Solomon—1 Kin. 9:24, 25

11 And Solomon brought up the daughter of Pharaoh out of the city of David unto the house that he had built for her: for he said, My wife shall not dwell in the house of David king of Israel, because the places are holy, whereunto the ark of the LORD hath come.

12 Then Solomon offered burnt offerings unto the LORD on the altar of the LORD, which he had built before the porch,

13 Even after a certain rate every day, offering according to the commandment of Moses, on the sabbaths, and on the new moons, and on the solemn feasts, Rthree times in the year, even in the feast of unleavened bread, and in the feast of weeks, and in the feast of tabernacles.   Ex. 23:14-17

14 And he appointed, according to the order of David his father, the courses of the priests to their service, Tand the Levites to their charges, to praise and minister before the priests, as the duty of every day required: the porters also by their courses at every gate: for so had David the man of God commanded.   assignment

15 And they Tdeparted not from the commandment of the king unto the priests and Levites concerning any matter, or concerning the treasures.   did not deviate

16 Now all the work of Solomon was prepared unto the day of the foundation of the house of the LORD, and until it was finished. So the house of the LORD was perfected.

Economic Operations of Solomon
1 Kin. 9:26-28

17 Then went Solomon to RE′-zi-on-ge′-ber, and to TE′-loth,R at the sea side in the land of E′-dom.   20:36; 1 Kin. 9:26 · Elath · Deut. 2:8

18 And Hu′-ram sent him by the hands of his servants ships, and servants that had knowledge of the sea; and they went with the servants of Solomon to O′-phir, and took thence four hundred and fifty talents of gold, and brought them to king Solomon.

CHAPTER 9

The Queen of Sheba Visits—1 Kin. 10:1-13

AND when the queen of She′-ba heard of the fame of Solomon, she came to Tprove Solomon with hard questions at Jerusalem, with a very great company, and camels that bare spices, and gold in abundance, and precious stones: and when she

was come to Solomon, she communed with him of all that was in her heart.   *test*

2 And Solomon ᵀtold her all her questions: and there was nothing hid from Solomon which he told her not.   *answered*

3 And when the queen of She′-ba had seen the wisdom of Solomon, and the house that he had built,

4 And the meat of his table, and the sitting of his servants, and the attendance of his ministers, and their apparel; his ᴿcupbearers also, and their apparel; and his ascent by which he went up into the house of the LORD; there was no more spirit in her.   Neh. 1:11

5 And she said to the king, It was a true report which I heard in mine own land of ᵀthine acts, and of thy wisdom: *thy sayings*

6 Howbeit I believed not their words, until I came, and mine eyes had seen it: and, behold, the one half of the greatness of thy wisdom was not told me: for thou exceedest the fame that I heard.

7 Happy are thy men, and happy are these thy servants, which stand continually before thee, and hear thy wisdom.

8 Blessed be the LORD thy God, which delighted in thee to ᴿset thee on his throne, to be king for the LORD thy God: because thy God loved Israel, to establish them for ever, therefore made he thee king over them, to do judgment and justice.   1 Chr. 28:5

9 And she gave the king an ᵀhundred and twenty talents of gold, and of spices great abundance, and precious stones: neither was there any such spice as the queen of She′-ba gave king Solomon.   *$691,200,000*

10 And the servants also of ᵀHu′-ram, and the servants of Solomon, which brought gold from O′-phir, brought ᴿal′-gumᵀ trees and precious stones.   Hiram · 1 Kin. 10:11 · almug

11 And the king made of the al′-gum trees terraces to the house of the LORD, and to the king's palace, and harps and psalteries for singers: and there were none such seen before in the land of Judah.

12 And king Solomon gave to the queen of She′-ba all ᵀher desire, whatsoever she asked, beside that which she had brought unto the king. So she turned, and went away to her own land, she and her servants.   *she requested*

Solomon's Wealth
1 Kin. 10:14–29; 2 Chr. 1:14–17

13 Now the weight of gold that came to Solomon in one year was ᵀsix hundred and threescore and six talents of gold; *$3,836,160,000*

14 Beside that which chapmen and merchants brought. And all the kings of Arabia and governors of the country brought gold and silver to Solomon.

15 And king Solomon made two hundred targets of beaten gold: ᵀsix hundred shek′-els of beaten gold went to one target.   *$218,400*

16 And three hundred shields made he of beaten gold: ᵀthree hundred shek′-els of gold went to one shield. And the king put them in the house of the forest of Leb′-a-non. *$109,200*

17 Moreover the king made a great throne of ivory, and overlaid it with pure gold.

18 And there were six steps to the throne, with a footstool of gold, which were fastened to the throne, and ᵀstays on each side of the sitting place, and two lions standing by the stays: *arm rests*

19 And twelve lions stood there on the one side and on the other upon the six steps. There was not the like made in any kingdom.

20 And all the drinking vessels of king Solomon were of gold, and all the vessels of the house of the forest of Leb′-a-non were of pure gold: none were of silver; it was not any thing accounted of in the days of Solomon.

21 For the king's ᴿships went to Tar′-shish with the servants of Hu′-ram: every three years once came the ships of Tar′-shish bringing gold, and silver, ᵀivory, and apes, and peacocks.   20:36, 37 · elephants' tusks

22 And king Solomon passed all the kings of the earth in riches and wisdom.

23 And all the kings of the earth sought the presence of Solomon, to hear his wisdom, that God had put in his heart.

24 And they brought every man his present, vessels of silver, and vessels of gold, and raiment, harness, and spices, horses, and mules, a rate year by year.

25 And Solomon had four thousand stalls for horses and chariots, and twelve thousand horsemen; whom he bestowed in the chariot cities, and with the king at Jerusalem.

26 And he reigned over all the kings from the river even unto the land of the Phi-lis′-tines, and to the border of Egypt.

27 ᴿAnd the king ᵀmade silver in Jerusalem as stones, and cedar trees made he as the sycomore trees that are in the low plains in abundance.   1:15–17; 1 Kin. 10:27 · gave

28 And they brought unto Solomon horses out of Egypt, and out of all lands.

The Death of Solomon—1 Kin. 11:41–43

29 Now the rest of the acts of Solomon, first and last, are they not written in the book of Nathan the prophet, and in the prophecy of A-hi′-jah the Shi′-lo-nite, and in the visions of Id′-do the ᵀseer against Jer-o-bo′-am the son of Ne′-bat?   *prophet*

30 ᴿAnd Solomon reigned in Jerusalem over all Israel forty years.   1 Kin. 11:42, 43

31 And Solomon slept with his fathers, and he was buried in the city of David his father: and Re-ho-bo′-am his son reigned in his stead.

CHAPTER 10

Division of the Kingdom—1 Kin. 12:1–19

AND ᴿRe-ho-bo'-am went to She'-chem: for to She'-chem were all Israel come to ᵀmake him king.   1 Kin. 12:1 · *crown him as king*

2 And it came to pass, when Jer-o-bo'-am the son of Ne'-bat, who *was* in Egypt, ᴿwhither he had fled from the presence of Solomon the king, heard *it*, that Jer-o-bo'-am returned out of Egypt.   1 Kin. 11:40

3 And they sent and called him. So Jer-o-bo'-am and all Israel came and spake to Re-ho-bo'-am, saying,

4 ᴿThy father made our yoke grievous: now therefore ease thou somewhat the grievous ᵀservitude of thy father, and his heavy yoke that he put upon us, and we will serve thee.   Ex. 1:14 · *service*

5 And he said unto them, Come again unto me after three days. And the people departed.

6 And king ᴿRe-ho-bo'-am ᵀtook counsel with the old men that had stood before Solomon his father while he yet lived, saying, What counsel give ye *me* to return answer to this people?   11:5 · *asked for advice*

7 And they spake unto him, saying, If thou be kind to this people, and please them, and speak ᵀgood words to them, they will be thy servants for ever.   *pleasantly*

8 ᴿBut he forsook the counsel which the old men gave him, and took counsel with the young men that were brought up with him, that stood before him.   1 Kin. 12:8–11

9 And he said unto them, What advice give ye that we may return answer to this people, which have spoken to me, saying, Ease somewhat the yoke that thy father did put upon us?

10 And the young men that were brought up with him spake unto him, saying, Thus shalt thou answer the people that spake unto thee, saying, Thy father made our yoke heavy, but make thou *it* somewhat lighter for us; thus shalt thou say unto them, My little *finger* shall be thicker than my father's loins.

11 For whereas my father put a heavy yoke upon you, I will put more to your yoke: my father chastised you with whips, but I *will chastise you* with scorpions.

12 So ᴿJer-o-bo'-am and all the people came to Re-ho-bo'-am on the third day, as the king ᵀbade, saying, Come again to me on the third day.   1 Kin. 12:12–14 · *appointed*

13 ᴿAnd the king answered them roughly; and king Re-ho-bo'-am forsook the ᵀcounsel of the old men,   Ps. 34:13 · *advice*

14 And answered them after the advice of the young men, saying, My father made your yoke heavy, but I will add thereto: my father chastised you with whips, but I *will chastise you* with scorpions.

15 So the king hearkened not unto the people: ᴿfor the cause was of God, that the Lord might perform his word, which he spake by the hand of A-hi'-jah the Shi'-lo-nite to Jer-o-bo'-am the son of Ne'-bat. 1 Kin. 12:15,24

16 And when all Israel *saw* that the king would not hearken unto them, the people answered the king, saying, What portion have we in David? and *we have* none inheritance in the son of Jesse: every man to your tents, O Israel, *and* now, David, see to thine own house. So all Israel went to their tents.

17 But *as for* the children of Israel that dwelt in the cities of Judah, Re-ho-bo'-am reigned over them.

18 Then king Re-ho-bo'-am sent ᴿHa-do'-ram that *was* over the ᵀtribute; and the children of Israel stoned him with stones, that he died. But king Re-ho-bo'-am ᵀmade speed to get him up to *his* chariot, to flee to Jerusalem.   1 Kin. 4:6; 5:14 · *taskwork · hastened*

19 ᴿAnd Israel rebelled against the house of David unto this day.   1 Kin. 12:19

CHAPTER 11

*Kingdom of Judah Is Strengthened
1 Kin. 12:21–24*

AND when Re-ho-bo'-am was come to Jerusalem, he gathered of the house of Judah and Benjamin an hundred and fourscore thousand chosen *men*, which were warriors, to fight against Israel, that he might bring the kingdom again to Re-ho-bo'-am.

2 But the word of the Lord came to She-ma'-iah the man of God, saying,

3 Speak unto Re-ho-bo'-am the son of Solomon, king of Judah, and to all Israel in Judah and Benjamin, saying,

4 Thus saith the Lord, Ye shall not go up, nor fight against your brethren: return every man to his house: for this thing is ᵀdone of me. And they obeyed the words of the Lord, and returned from going against Jer-o-bo'-am.   *according to my will*

5 And Re-ho-bo'-am dwelt in Jerusalem, and built cities for defence in Judah.

6 He built even Beth'-le-hem, and E'-tam, and Te-ko'-a,

7 And Beth'-zur, and Sho'-co, and A-dul'-lam,

8 And Gath, and Ma-re'-shah, and Ziph,

9 And Ad-o-ra'-im, and La'-chish, and A-ze'-kah,

10 And Zo'-rah, and Ai'-ja-lon, and He'-bron, which *are* in Judah and in Benjamin ᵀfenced cities.   *fortified*

11 And he fortified the strong holds, and put captains in them, and store of ᵀvictual, and of oil and wine.   *food*

12 And in every several city *he put* shields and spears, and made them exceeding strong, having Judah and Benjamin on his side.

13 And the priests and the Levites that *were* in all Israel ᵀresorted to him out of all their ᵀcoasts.   *came · territories*

14 For the Levites left their suburbs and their possession, and came to Judah and Jerusalem: for Jer-o-bo′-am and his sons had ᴿcast them off from ᵀexecuting the priest's office unto the LORD: *13:9 · performing*

15 And he ordained him priests for the high places, and for the ᵀdevils, and for the calves which he had made.   *he-goats*

16 And after them out of all the tribes of Israel such as set their hearts to seek the LORD God of Israel came to Jerusalem, to sacrifice unto the LORD God of their fathers.

17 So they ᴿstrengthened the kingdom of Judah, and made Re-ho-bo′-am the son of Solomon strong, three years: for three years they walked in the way of David and Solomon.   *12:1*

18 And Re-ho-bo′-am took him Ma′-ha-lath the daughter of Jer′-i-moth the son of David to wife, *and* Ab-i-ha′-il the daughter of ᴿE-li′-ab the son of Jesse;   *1 Sam. 16:6*

19 Which bare him ᵀchildren; Je′-ush, and Sham-a-ri′-ah, and Za′-ham.   *sons*

20 And after her he took ᴿMa′-a-chah the daughter of Ab′-sa-lom; ᴿwhich bare him A-bi′-jah, and At′-tai, and Zi′-za, and Shel′-o-mith.   *1 Kin. 15:2 · 1 Kin. 14:31*

21 And Re-ho-bo′-am loved Ma′-a-chah the daughter of Ab′-sa-lom above all his wives and his concubines: ᴿ(for he took eighteen wives, and threescore concubines; and begat twenty and eight sons, and threescore daughters.)   *Deut. 17:17*

22 And Re-ho-bo′-am ᴿmade A-bi′-jah the son of Ma′-a-chah the chief, *to be* ruler among his brethren: for *he* thought to make him king.   *Deut. 21:15-17*

23 And he dealt wisely, and dispersed of all his ᵀchildren throughout all the countries of Judah and Benjamin, unto every fenced city: and he gave them victual in abundance. And he ᵀdesired many wives.   *sons · sought for them*

CHAPTER 12

Kingdom of Judah Is Weakened
1 Kin. 14:25-28

AND ᴿit came to pass, when Re-ho-bo′-am had established the kingdom, and had strengthened himself, he forsook the law of the LORD, and all Israel with him.   *11:17*

2 And it came to pass, *that* in the fifth year of king Re-ho-bo′-am Shi′-shak king of Egypt came up against Jerusalem, because they had transgressed against the LORD,

3 With twelve hundred chariots, and

threescore thousand horsemen: and the people *were* without number that came with him out of Egypt; ᴿthe Lu′-bims, the Suk′-ki-ims, and the E-thi-o′-pi-ans.   *16:8*

4 And he took the fenced cities which *pertained* to Judah, and came to Jerusalem.

5 Then came ᴿShe-ma′-iah the prophet to Re-ho-bo′-am, and *to* the princes of Judah, that were gathered together to Jerusalem because of Shi′-shak, and said unto them, Thus saith the LORD, ᴿYe have forsaken me, and therefore have I also left you in the hand of Shi′-shak.   *11:2 · Deut. 28:15*

6 Whereupon the princes of Israel and the king humbled themselves; and they said, ᴿThe LORD *is* righteous.   *Ex. 9:27*

7 And when the LORD saw that they humbled themselves, the word of the LORD came to She-ma′-iah, saying, They have humbled themselves; *therefore* I will not destroy them, but I will grant them some deliverance; and my wrath shall not be poured out upon Jerusalem by the hand of Shi′-shak.

8 Nevertheless they shall be his servants; that they may know my service, and the service of the kingdoms of the countries.

9 So Shi′-shak king of Egypt came up against Jerusalem, and took away the treasures of the house of the LORD, and the treasures of the king's house; he took all: he carried away also the shields of gold which Solomon had ᴿmade.   *9:15, 16*

10 Instead of which king Re-ho-bo′-am made shields of brass, and committed *them* to the hands of the ᵀchief of the guard, that kept the entrance of the king's house.   *captain*

11 And when the king entered into the house of the LORD, the guard came and fetched them, and brought them again into the guard chamber.

12 And when he humbled himself, the wrath of the LORD turned from him, that he would not destroy *him* altogether: ᴿand also in Judah things went well.   *19:3*

Death of Rehoboam—1 Kin. 14:21, 22, 29-31

13 So king Re-ho-bo′-am strengthened himself in Jerusalem, and reigned: for Re-ho-bo′-am *was* one and forty years old when he began to reign, and he reigned seventeen years in Jerusalem, the city which the LORD had chosen out of all the tribes of Israel, to put his name there. And his mother's name *was* Na′-a-mah an Am′-mon-i-tess.

14 And he did evil, ᴿbecause he prepared not his heart to seek the LORD.   *1 Sam. 7:3*

15 Now the acts of Re-ho-bo′-am, first and last, *are* they not written in the book of She-ma′-iah the prophet, ᴿand of Id′-do the seer concerning genealogies? ᴿAnd *there were* wars between Re-ho-bo′-am and Jer-o-bo′-am continually.   *9:29 · 1 Kin. 14:30*

16 And Re-ho-bo'-am slept with his fathers, and was buried in the city of David: and A-bi'-jah his son reigned in his stead.

CHAPTER 13

War of Abijah and Jeroboam—1 Kin. 15:1, 2, 7

NOW ᴿin the eighteenth year of king Jer-o-bo'-am began A-bi'-jah to reign over Judah.   1 Kin. 15:1, 2

2 He reigned three years in Jerusalem. His mother's name also *was* Mi-cha'-iah the daughter of U-ri'-el of Gib'-e-ah. And there was war between A-bi'-jah and Je-ro-bo'-am.

3 And A-bi'-jah set the battle in array with an army of valiant men of war, *even* four hundred thousand chosen men: Je-ro-bo'-am also set the battle in array against him with eight hundred thousand chosen men, *being* mighty men of valour.

4 And A-bi'-jah stood up upon mount ᴿZem-a-ra'-im, which *is* in ᵀmount E'-phra-im, and said, Hear me, thou Jer-o-bo'-am, and all Israel;   Josh. 18:22 • *the hill country of*

5 Ought ye not to know that the Lᴏʀᴅ God of Israel gave the kingdom over Israel to David for ever, *even* to him and to his sons ᴿby a covenant of salt?   Num. 18:19

6 Yet Jer-o-bo'-am the son of Ne'-bat, the servant of Solomon the son of David, is risen up, and hath rebelled against his lord.

7 And there are gathered unto him ᵀvain men, the children of Be'-li-al, and have strengthened themselves against Re-ho-bo'-am the son of Solomon, when Re-ho-bo'-am was young and tenderhearted, and could not withstand them.   *foolish, wicked men*

8 And now ye think to withstand the kingdom of the Lᴏʀᴅ in the hand of the sons of David; and ye *be* a great multitude, and *there are* with you golden calves, which Jer-o-bo'-am made you for gods.

9 Have ye not cast out the priests of the Lᴏʀᴅ, the sons of Aaron, and the Levites, and have made you priests after the manner of the nations of *other* lands? so that whosoever cometh to consecrate himself with a young bullock and seven rams, *the same* may be a priest of *them that are* no gods.

10 But as for us, the Lᴏʀᴅ *is* our God, and we have not forsaken him; and the priests, which minister unto the Lᴏʀᴅ, *are* the sons of Aaron, and the Levites ᵀwait upon *their* business: *attend to their responsibility*

11 And they burn unto the Lᴏʀᴅ every morning and every evening burnt sacrifices and sweet incense: the shewbread also *set they in order* upon the pure table; and the candlestick of gold with the lamps thereof, to burn every evening: for we keep the charge of the Lᴏʀᴅ our God; but ye have forsaken him.

12 And, behold, God himself *is* with us for *our* captain, and his priests with sounding trumpets to cry alarm against you. O children of Israel, fight ye not against the Lᴏʀᴅ God of your fathers; for ye shall not prosper.

13 ᴿBut Jer-o-bo'-am ᵀcaused an ambushment to come about behind them: so they were before Judah, and the ambushment *was* behind them.   Josh. 8:4–9 • *planned*

14 And when Judah looked back, behold, the battle *was* before and behind: ᴿand they cried unto the Lᴏʀᴅ, and the priests sounded with the trumpets.   14:11

15 Then the men of Judah gave a shout: and as the men of Judah shouted, it came to pass, that God smote Jer-o-bo'-am and all Israel before A-bi'-jah and Judah.

16 And the children of Israel fled before Judah: ᴿand God delivered them into their hand.   16:8

17 And A-bi'-jah and his people slew them with a great slaughter: so there fell down slain of Israel five hundred thousand chosen men.

18 Thus the children of Israel were brought under at that time, and the children of Judah prevailed, because they relied upon the Lᴏʀᴅ God of their fathers.

19 And A-bi'-jah pursued after Jer-o-bo'-am, and took cities from him, Beth'-el with the towns thereof, and Jesh'-a-nah with the towns thereof, and ᴿE'-phra-in with the towns thereof.   Josh. 15:9

20 Neither did Jer-o-bo'-am recover strength again in the days of A-bi'-jah: and the Lᴏʀᴅ struck him, and he died.

Death of Abijah

21 But A-bi'-jah ᵀwaxed mighty, and married fourteen wives, and begat twenty and two sons, and sixteen daughters.   *became*

22 And the rest of the acts of A-bi'-jah, and his ways, and his sayings, *are* written in the story of the ᴿprophet Id'-do.   9:29

CHAPTER 14

Evaluation of Asa—1 Kin. 15:8–12

SO A-bi'-jah slept with his fathers, and they buried him in the city of David: and A'-sa his son reigned in his stead. In his days the land was quiet ten years.

2 And A'-sa did *that which was* good and right in the eyes of the Lᴏʀᴅ his God:

3 For he took away the altars of the strange *gods*, and the high places, and brake down the images, and cut down the groves:

4 And commanded Judah ᴿto seek the Lᴏʀᴅ God of their fathers, and to do the law and the commandment.   [7:14]

5 Also he took away out of all the cities of

Judah the high places and the images: and the kingdom was quiet before him.

6 And he built ᵀfenced cities in Judah: for the land had ᵀrest, and he had no war in those years; ᴿbecause the LORD had given him rest.   *fortified • peace • 15:15*

7 Therefore he said unto Judah, ᴿLet us build these cities, and make about *them* walls, and towers, gates, and bars, *while* the land *is* yet before us; because we have sought the LORD our God, we have sought *him,* and he hath given us rest on every side. So they built and prospered.   8:5

8 And A'-sa had an army *of men* that bare ᵀtargets and spears, out of Judah three hundred thousand; and out of Benjamin, that bare shields and drew bows, two hundred and fourscore thousand: all these *were* mighty men of valour.   *large shields*

Victory over the Ethiopians

9 And there came out against them Ze'-rah the E-thi-o'pi-an with an host of a thousand thousand, and three hundred chariots; and came unto Ma-re'-shah.

10 Then A'-sa went out against him, and they set the battle in array in the valley of Zeph'-a-thah at Ma-re'-shah.

11 And A'-sa ᴿcried unto the LORD his God, and said, LORD, *it is* nothing with thee to help, whether with many, or with them that have no power: help us, O LORD our God; for we rest on thee, and in thy name we go against this multitude. O LORD, thou *art* our God; let not man prevail against thee.   Ps. 22:5

12 So the LORD ᴿsmote ᵀthe E-thi-o'-pi-ans before A'-sa, and before Judah; and the E-thi-o'-pi-ans fled.   13:15 • *defeated*

13 And A'-sa and the people that *were* with him pursued them unto Ge'-rar: and the E-thi-o'pi-ans were overthrown, that they could not recover themselves; for they were destroyed before the LORD, and before his host; and they carried away very much spoil.

14 And they smote all the cities round about Ge'-rar; for the fear of the LORD came upon them: and they spoiled all the cities; for there was exceeding much spoil in them.

15 They smote also the tents of cattle, and carried away sheep and camels in abundance, and returned to Jerusalem.

CHAPTER 15

Exhortation of Azariah

AND ᴿthe Spirit of God came upon Az-a-ri'-ah the son of O'-ded: 20:14; Judg. 3:10

2 And he went out to meet A'-sa, and said unto him, Hear ye me, A'-sa, and all Judah and Benjamin; The LORD *is* with you, while ye be with him; and if ye seek him, he will be found of you; but ᴿif ye forsake him, he will forsake you.   24:20

3 Now ᴿfor a long season Israel *hath been* without the true God, and without a teaching priest, and without law.   Hos. 3:4

4 But when they in their trouble did turn unto the LORD God of Israel, and sought him, he was found of them.

5 And in those times *there was* no peace to him that went out, nor to him that came in, but great ᵀvexations *were* upon all the inhabitants of the countries.   *troubles*

6 And nation was ᵀdestroyed of nation, and city of city: for God did ᵀvex them with all adversity.   *beaten in pieces • trouble*

7 ᴿBe ye strong therefore, and let not your hands be ᵀweak: for your work shall be rewarded.   Josh. 1:7, 9 • *slack*

Reforms of Asa—1 Kin. 15:13–15

8 And when A'-sa heard these words, and the prophecy of O'-ded the prophet, he took courage, and put away the ᵀabominable idols out of all the land of Judah and Benjamin, and out of the cities which he had taken from mount E'-phra-im, and ᵀrenewed the altar of the LORD, that *was* before the porch of the LORD.   *evil • rebuilt*

9 And he gathered all Judah and Benjamin, and ᴿthe strangers with them out of E'-phra-im and Ma-nas'-seh, and out of Simeon: for they fell to him out of Israel in abundance, when they saw that the LORD his God *was* with him.   11:16

10 So they gathered themselves together at Jerusalem in the third month, in the fifteenth year of the reign of A'-sa.

11 And they offered unto the LORD ᵀthe same time, of ᴿthe ᵀspoil *which* they had brought, seven hundred oxen and seven thousand sheep.   *in that day • 14:13 • loot*

12 And they entered into a covenant to seek the LORD God of their fathers with all their heart and with all their soul;

13 ᴿThat whosoever would not seek the LORD God of Israel ᴿshould be put to death, whether small or great, whether man or woman.   Ex. 22:20 • Deut. 13:5, 9, 15

14 And they sware unto the LORD with a loud voice, and with shouting, and with trumpets, and with cornets.

15 And all Judah rejoiced at the oath: for they had sworn with all their heart, and ᴿsought him with their whole desire; and he was found of them: and the LORD gave them ᵀrest round about.   *v. 2 • peace*

16 And also *concerning* Ma'-a-chah the ᵀmother of A'-sa the king, he removed her from *being* queen, because she had made an idol in a grove: and A'-sa cut down her idol, and ᵀstamped *it,* and burnt *it* at the brook Kid'-ron.   *grandmother • crushed*

17 But ᴿthe high places were not taken away out of Israel: nevertheless the heart of A′-sa was perfect all his days.   14:3, 5

18 ᴿAnd he brought into the house of God the things that his father had dedicated, and that he himself had dedicated, silver, and gold, and vessels.   Ezra 8:28

19 And there was no more war unto the five and thirtieth year of the reign of A′-sa.

CHAPTER 16

Victory over the Syrians—1 Kin. 15:16–22

IN the six and thirtieth year of the reign of A′-sa Ba′-a-sha king of Israel came up against Judah, and built Ra′-mah, ᴿto the intent that he might let none go out or come in to A′-sa king of Judah.   15:9

2 Then A′-sa brought out silver and gold out of the treasures of the house of the Lord and of the king's house, and sent to Ben-ha′-dad king of Syria, that dwelt at ᵀDamascus, saying,   Darmesek

3 There is a league between me and thee, as there was between my father and thy father: behold, I have sent thee silver and gold; go, break thy league with Ba′-a-sha king of Israel, that he may depart from me.

4 And Ben-ha′-dad hearkened unto king A′-sa, and sent the captains of his armies against the cities of Israel; and they smote I′-jon, and Dan, and A′-bel-ma′-im, and all the ᴿstore cities of Naph′-ta-li.   Ex. 1:11

5 And it came to pass, when Ba′-a-sha heard it, that he left off building of Ra′-mah, and let his work cease.

6 Then A′-sa the king took all Judah; and they carried away the stones of Ra′-mah, and the timber thereof, wherewith Ba′-a-sha ᵀwas building; and he built therewith Ge′-ba and Miz-pah.   had builded

Rebuke of Hanani

7 And at that time ᴿHa-na′-ni the seer came to A′-sa king of Judah, and said unto him, Because thou hast relied on the king of Syria, and not relied on the Lord thy God, therefore is the host of the king of Syria escaped out of thine hand.   1 Kin. 16:1

8 Were not ᴿthe E-thi-o′-pi-ans and ᴿthe Lu′-bims a huge host, with very many chariots and horsemen? yet, ᴿbecause thou didst rely on the Lord, he delivered them into thine hand.   14:9 • 12:3 • 13:16, 18

9 ᴿFor the eyes of the Lord run to and fro throughout the whole earth, to shew himself strong in the behalf of them whose heart is perfect toward him. Herein thou hast done foolishly: therefore from henceforth thou shalt have wars.   Job 34:21

10 Then A′-sa was wroth with the seer, and ᴿput him in a prison house; for he was in a rage with him because of this thing. And A′-sa ᵀoppressed some of the people the same time.   Jer. 20:2; Matt. 14:3 • crushed

Death of Asa—1 Kin. 15:23, 24

11 ᴿAnd, behold, the acts of A′-sa, first and last, lo, they are written in the book of the kings of Judah and Israel.   1 Kin. 15:23

12 And A′-sa in the thirty and ninth year of his reign was diseased in his feet, until his disease was exceeding great: yet in his disease he ᴿsoughtᵀ not to the Lord, but to the physicians.   Jer. 17:5 • did not seek help from

13 And A′-sa slept with his fathers, and died in the one and fortieth year of his reign.

14 And they buried him in his own sepulchres, which he had made for himself in the city of David, and laid him in the bed which was filled with sweet odours and divers kinds of spices prepared by the apothecaries′ art: and they made a very great burning for him.

CHAPTER 17

Evaluation of Jehoshaphat

AND ᴿJe-hosh′-a-phat his son reigned in his stead, and strengthened himself against Israel.   20:31; 1 Kin. 15:24

2 And he placed ᵀforces in all the fenced cities of Judah, and set garrisons in the land of Judah, and in the cities of E′-phra-im, which A′-sa his father had taken.   soldiers

3 And the Lord was with Je-hosh′-a-phat, because he walked in the first ways of his father David, and sought not unto Ba′-al-im;

4 But sought to the Lord God of his father, and walked in his commandments, and not after the ᵀdoings of Israel.   customs

5 Therefore the Lord stablished the kingdom in his hand; and all Judah broughtᵀ to Je-hosh′-a-phat presents; ᴿand he had riches and honour in abundance.   gave • 18:1

6 And his heart was lifted up in the ways of the Lord: moreover he took away the high places and groves out of Judah.

Instruction by the Priests and Levites

7 Also in the third year of his reign he sent to his princes, even to Ben-ha′-il, and to O-ba-di′-ah, and to Zech-a-ri′-ah, and to Ne-than′-e-el, and to Mi-cha′-iah, ᴿto teach in the cities of Judah.   15:3

8 And with them he sent ᴿLevites, even She-ma′-iah, and Neth-a-ni′-ah, and Zeb-a-di′-ah, and A′-sa-hel, and She-mir′-a-moth, and Je-hon′-a-than, and Ad-o-ni′-jah, and To-bi′-jah, and Tob-ad-o-ni′-jah, Levites; and with them E-lish′-a-ma and Je-ho′-ram, priests.   19:8

9 ᴿAnd they taught in Judah, and had the book of the law of the Lord with them, and

went about throughout all the cities of Judah, and taught the people. Neh. 8:7

Expansion of the Kingdom

10 And ᴿthe fear of the LORD fell upon all the kingdoms of the lands that *were* round about Judah, so that they made no war against Je-hosh′-a-phat. Gen. 35:5

11 Also *some* of the Phi-lis′-tines brought Je-hosh′-a-phat presents, and tribute silver; and the A-ra′-bi-ans brought him flocks, seven thousand and seven hundred rams, and seven thousand and seven hundred he goats.

12 And Je-hosh′-a-phat ᵀwaxed great exceedingly; and he built in Judah ᵀcastles, and cities of store. *prospered · strong holds*

13 And he had much business in the cities of Judah: and the men of war, mighty men of valour, *were* in Jerusalem.

14 And these *are* the numbers of them according to the house of their fathers: Of Judah, the captains of thousands; Ad′-nah the chief, and with him mighty men of valour three hundred thousand.

15 And next to him *was* Je-ho-ha′-nan the captain, and with him two hundred and fourscore thousand.

16 And next ᵀhim *was* Am-a-si′-ah the son of Zich′-ri, ᴿwho willingly offered himself unto the LORD; and with him two hundred thousand mighty men of valour. *(to)* · Judg. 5:2, 9

17 And of Benjamin; E-li′-a-da a mighty man of valour, and with him armed men with bow and shield two hundred thousand.

18 And next ᵀhim *was* Je-hoz′-a-bad, and with him an hundred and fourscore thousand ready prepared for the war. *(to)*

19 These waited on the king, beside ᴿ*those* whom the king put in the ᵀfenced cities throughout all Judah. *v. 2 · fortified*

CHAPTER 18

Alliance with Ahab—1 Kin. 22:2–35

NOW Je-hosh′-a-phat had riches and honour in abundance, and ᵀjoined affinity with Ahab. *entered into a mutual agreement*

2 ᴿAnd after *certain* years he went down to Ahab to Sa-ma′-ri-a. And Ahab killed sheep and oxen for him in abundance, and for the people that *he had* with him, and persuaded him to ᵀgo up *with him* to Ra′-moth-gil′-e-ad. 1 Kin. 22:2 · *join in an attack upon*

3 And Ahab king of Israel said unto Je-hosh′-a-phat king of Judah, Wilt thou go with me to Ra′-moth-gil′-e-ad? And he answered him, I *am* as thou *art*, and my people as thy people; and *we will be* with thee in the war.

4 And Je-hosh′-a-phat said unto the king of Israel, ᵀEnquire, I pray thee, at the word of the LORD to day. *pray for guidance*

5 ᴿTherefore the king of Israel gathered together of prophets four hundred men, and said unto them, Shall we go to Ra′-moth-gil′-e-ad to battle, or shall I forbear? And they said, Go up; for God will deliver *it* into the king's hand. 1 Kin. 18:19

6 But Je-hosh′-a-phat said, *Is there* not here a prophet of the LORD ᵀbesides, that we might enquire of him? *yet; or, more*

7 And the king of Israel said unto Je-hosh′-a-phat, *There is* yet one man, by whom we may enquire of the LORD: but I hate him; for he never prophesied good unto me, but always evil: the same *is* Mi-ca′-iah the son of Im′-la. And Je-hosh′-a-phat said, Let not the king say so.

8 And the king of Israel called for one *of his* ᵀofficers, and said, Fetch quickly Mi-ca′-iah the son of Im′-la. *eunuchs*

9 And the king of Israel and Je-hosh′-a-phat king of Judah sat either of them on his throne, clothed in *their* robes, and they sat in ᵀa void place at the entering in of the gate of Sa-ma′-ri-a; and all the prophets prophesied before them. *an open space*

10 And Zed-e-ki′-ah the son of Che-na′-a-nah had made him horns of iron, and said, Thus saith the LORD, With these thou shalt push Syria until they be consumed.

11 And all the prophets prophesied so, saying, Go up to Ra′-moth-gil′-e-ad, and prosper: for the LORD shall deliver *it* into the hand of the king.

12 And the messenger that went to call Mi-ca′-iah spake to him, saying, Behold, the words of the prophets *declare* good to the king ᵀwith one assent; let thy word therefore, I pray thee, be like one of their's, and speak thou good. *with unanimous voice*

13 And Mi-ca′-iah said, As the LORD liveth, even what my God saith, that will I speak.

14 And when he was come to the king, the king said unto him, Mi-ca′-iah, shall we go to Ra′-moth-gil′-e-ad to battle, or shall I forbear? And he said, Go ye up, and prosper, and they shall be delivered into your hand.

15 And the king said to him, ᴿHow many times shall I ᵀadjure thee that thou say nothing but the truth to me in the name of the LORD? 1 Kin. 22:16 · *command*

16 Then he said, I did see all Israel scattered upon the mountains, as sheep that have no shepherd: and the LORD said, ᴿThese have no master; let them return *therefore* every man to his house in peace. 1 Kin. 22:36

17 And the king of Israel said to Je-hosh′-a-phat, Did I not tell thee *that* he would not prophesy good unto me, but evil?

18 Again he said, Therefore hear the word of the LORD; I saw the LORD sitting upon his throne, and all the host of heaven standing on his right hand and *on* his left.

19 And the LORD said, Who shall entice

Ahab king of Israel, that he may go up and ᵀfall at Ra'-moth–gil'-e-ad? And one spake saying after this manner, and another saying after that manner. *be killed*

20 Then there came out a ᴿspirit, and stood before the Lᴏʀᴅ, and said, I will entice him. And the Lᴏʀᴅ said unto him, ᵀWherewith? *Job 1:6 • by what means*

21 And he said, I will go out, and be a lying spirit in the mouth of all his prophets. And *the* Lᴏʀᴅ said, Thou shalt entice *him,* and thou shalt also prevail: go out, and do *even* so.

22 Now therefore, behold, ᴿthe Lᴏʀᴅ hath put a lying spirit in the mouth of these thy prophets, and the Lᴏʀᴅ hath spoken evil against thee. *Job 12:16; Is. 19:14; Ezek. 14:9*

23 Then Zed-e-ki'-ah the son of Che-na'-a-nah came near, and ᴿsmoteᵀ Mi-ca'-iah upon the cheek, and said, Which way went the Spirit of the Lᴏʀᴅ from me to speak unto thee? *Jer. 20:2; Mark 14:65; Acts 23:2 • struck*

24 And Mi-ca'-iah said, Behold, thou shalt see on that day when thou shalt go into an inner chamber to hide thyself.

25 Then the king of Israel said, Take ye Mi-ca'-iah, and carry him back to Amon the governor of the city, and to Jo'-ash the king's son;

26 And say, Thus saith the king, ᴿPut this *fellow* in the prison, and feed him with bread of affliction and with water of affliction, until I return in peace. *16:10*

27 And Mi-ca'-iah said, If thou certainly return in peace, *then* hath not the Lᴏʀᴅ spoken by ᴿme. And he said, ᵀHearken, all ye people. *Deut. 18:22 • listen*

28 So the king of Israel and Je-hosh'-a-phat the king of Judah ᴿwent up to Ra'-moth–gil'-e-ad. *Deut. 1:43*

29 And the king of Israel said unto Je-hosh'-a-phat, I will ᴿdisguise myself, and will go to the battle; but put thou on thy robes. So the king of Israel disguised himself; and they went to the battle. *35:22*

30 Now the king of Syria had commanded the captains of the chariots that *were* with him, saying, Fight ye not with small or great, ᵀsave only with the king of Israel. *except*

31 And it came to pass, when the captains of the chariots saw Je-hosh'-a-phat, that they said, It *is* the king of Israel. Therefore they compassed about him to fight: but Je-hosh'-a-phat cried out, and the Lᴏʀᴅ helped him; and God moved them *to depart* from him.

32 For it came to pass, that, when the captains of the chariots ᵀperceived that it was not the king of Israel, they turned back again from pursuing him. *saw*

33 And a *certain* man drew a bow at a venture, and smote the king of Israel between the joints of the ᵀharness: therefore he said to his chariot man, Turn thine hand,

that thou mayest carry me out of the host; for I am ᵀwounded. *armour • made sick*

34 And the battle increased that day: ᵀhowbeit the king of Israel stayed *himself* up in *his* chariot against the Syrians until the even: and about the time of the sun going down he ᴿdied. *and • [Ps. 37:35–38]*

CHAPTER 19

AND Je-hosh'-a-phat the king of Judah returned to his house in peace to Jerusalem.

2 And Je'-hu the son of Ha-na'-ni ᴿthe seer went out to meet him, and said to king Je-hosh'-a-phat, Shouldest thou help the ungodly, and ᴿlove them that hate the Lᴏʀᴅ? therefore *is* ᴿwrath upon thee from before the Lᴏʀᴅ. *1 Sam. 9:9 • Ps. 139:21 • 32:25*

3 Nevertheless there are good things found in thee, in that thou hast taken away the groves out of the land, and hast ᴿprepared thine heart to seek God. *30:19*

4 And Je-hosh'-a-phat dwelt at Jerusalem: and he went out again through the people from Be'-er-she'-ba to mount E'-phra-im, ᴿand brought them back unto the Lᴏʀᴅ God of their fathers. *15:8–13*

Organization of the Kingdom

5 ᴿAnd he set judges in the land throughout all the ᵀfenced cities of Judah, city by city, *Deut. 16:18–20 • fortified*

6 And said to the judges, Take heed what ye do: for ye judge not for man, but for the Lᴏʀᴅ, who *is* with you in the judgment.

7 Wherefore now let the fear of the Lᴏʀᴅ be upon you; take heed and do *it:* for *there is* no iniquity with the Lᴏʀᴅ our God, nor respect of persons, nor taking of gifts.

8 Moreover in Jerusalem did Je-hosh'-a-phat set of the Levites, and *of* the priests, and of the ᵀchief of the fathers of Israel, for the judgment of the Lᴏʀᴅ, and for controversies, when they returned to Jerusalem. *heads*

9 And he charged them, saying, Thus shall ye do in the fear of the Lᴏʀᴅ, faithfully, and with a ᵀperfect heart. *sincere*

10 And what cause soever shall come to you of your brethren that dwell in their cities, between blood and blood, between law and commandment, statutes and judgments, ye shall even warn them that they trespass not against the Lᴏʀᴅ, and so wrath come upon you, and upon your brethren: this do, and ye shall not trespass.

11 And, behold, Am-a-ri'-ah the chief priest *is* over you ᴿin all matters of the Lᴏʀᴅ; and Zeb-a-di'-ah the son of Ish'-ma-el, the ruler of the house of Judah, for all the king's matters: also the Levites *shall be* officers

before you. Deal courageously, and the LORD shall be with the good. 1 Chr. 26:30

CHAPTER 20

Victory over Moab and Ammon

IT came to pass after this also, *that* the children of RMoab, and the children of Ammon, and with them *other* Rbeside the Am'-mon-ites, came against Je-hosh'-a-phat to battle. 19:5; 1 Chr. 18:2 · 26:7

2 Then there came some that told Je-hosh'-a-phat, saying, There cometh a great multitude against thee from beyond the sea on this side Syria; and, behold, they *be* in Haz'-a-zon-ta'-mar, which *is* En-ge'-di.

3 And Je-hosh'-a-phat feared, and set Thimself to seek the LORD, and Rproclaimed a fast throughout all Judah. *his face* · Ezra 8:21

4 And Judah gathered themselves together, to ask Rhelp of the LORD: even out of all the cities of Judah they came to seek the LORD. 14:11

5 And Je-hosh'-a-phat stood in the congregation of Judah and Jerusalem, in the house of the LORD, before the new court,

6 And said, O LORD God of our fathers, *art* not thou RGod in heaven? and Rrulest *not* thou over all the kingdoms of the heathen? and Rin thine hand *is there not* power and might, so that none is able to withstand thee? Matt. 6:9 · Dan. 4:17 · Matt. 6:13

7 *Art* not thou our God, *who* didst drive out the inhabitants of this land before thy people Israel, and gavest it to the seed of Abraham Rthy friend for ever? Is. 41:8

8 And they dwelt therein, and have built thee a sanctuary therein for thy name, saying,

9 RIf, *when* evil cometh upon us, *as* the sword, judgment, or pestilence, or famine, we stand before this house, and in thy presence, (for thy Rname *is* in this house,) and cry unto thee in our affliction, then thou wilt hear and help. 6:28–30 · 6:20

10 And now, behold, the children of Ammon and Moab and mount Se'-ir, whom thou Rwouldest not let Israel invade, when they came out of the land of Egypt, but Rthey turned from them, and destroyed them not; Deut. 2:4, 9, 19 · Num. 20:21

11 Behold, *I say, how* they reward us, to come to Tcast us out of thy possession, which thou hast given us to inherit. *drive*

12 O our God, wilt thou not judge them? for we have no might against this great company that cometh against us; neither know we what to do: but our eyes *are* upon thee.

13 And all Judah stood before the LORD, with Rtheir little ones, their wives, and their children. Ezra 8:21

14 Then upon Ja-ha'-zi-el the son of Zech-a-ri'-ah, the son of Be-na'-iah, the son of Je-i'-el, the son of Mat-ta-ni'-ah, a Levite of the sons of A'-saph, came the Spirit of the LORD in the Tmidst of the congregation; *presence*

15 And he said, Hearken ye, all Judah, and ye inhabitants of Jerusalem, and thou king Je-hosh'-a-phat, Thus saith the LORD unto you, RBe not afraid nor dismayed by reason of this great multitude; for the battle *is* not your's, but God's. Ex. 14:13, 14

16 To morrow go ye down against them: behold, they come up by the cliff of Ziz; and ye shall find them at the end of the brook, before the wilderness of Je-ru'-el.

17 RYe shall not *need* to fight in this *battle:* set yourselves, stand ye *still,* and see the salvation of the LORD with you, O Judah and Jerusalem: fear not, nor be dismayed; to morrow go out against them: for the LORD *will be* with you. Ex. 14:13, 14

18 And Je-hosh'-a-phat Rbowed his head with *his* face to the ground: and all Judah and the inhabitants of Jerusalem fell before the LORD, worshipping the LORD. Ex. 4:31

19 And the Levites, of the children of the Ko'-hath-ites, and of the children of the Kor'-hites, stood up to praise the LORD God of Israel with a loud voice on high.

20 And they rose early in the morning, and went forth into the wilderness of Te-ko'-a: and as they went forth, Je-hosh'-a-phat stood and said, Hear me, O Judah, and ye inhabitants of Jerusalem; RBelieve in the LORD your God, so shall ye be Testablished; believe his prophets, so shall ye prosper. Is. 7:9 · *kept safe*

21 And when he had consulted with the people, he appointed singers unto the LORD, and that should praise the beauty of holiness, as they went out before the army, and to say, Praise the LORD; Rfor his mercy *endureth* for ever. 1 Chr. 16:41

22 And when they began to sing and to praise, Rthe LORD set ambushments against the children of Ammon, Moab, and mount Se'-ir, which were come against Judah; and they were Tsmitten. 1 Sam. 14:20 · *defeated*

23 For the children of Ammon and Moab stood up against the inhabitants of mount Se'-ir, utterly to slay and destroy *them:* and when they Thad made an end of the inhabitants of Se'-ir, Revery one helped to destroy another. *had destroyed all* · Judg. 7:22

24 And when Judah came toward the watch tower in the wilderness, they looked unto the multitude, and, behold, they *were* dead bodies fallen to the earth, and none escaped.

25 And when Je-hosh'-a-phat and his people came to take away the spoil of them, they found among them in abundance both riches with the dead bodies, and precious

jewels, which they stripped off for themselves, more than they could carry away: and they were three days in gathering of the spoil, it was so much.

26 And on the fourth day they assembled themselves in the valley of Ber'-a-chah; for there they blessed the LORD: therefore the name of the same place was called, The valley of Ber'-a-chah, unto this day.

27 Then they returned, every man of Judah and Jerusalem, and Je-hosh'-a-phat in the forefront of them, to go again to Jerusalem with joy; for the LORD had made them to rejoice over their enemies.

28 And they came to Jerusalem with psalteries and Tharps and trumpets unto the house of the LORD.   *lyres*

29 And theT fear of God was on all the kingdoms of *those* countries, when they had heard that the LORD fought against the enemies of Israel.   *respect and reverence*

30 So the realm of Je-hosh'-a-phat was quiet: for his RGod gave him Trest round about.   15:15; 1 Kin. 22:41–43; Job 34:29 • *peace*

Summary of the Reign of Jehoshaphat
1 Kin. 22:41–45

31 And Je-hosh'-a-phat reigned over Judah: he *was* thirty and five years old when he began to reign, and he reigned twenty and five years in Jerusalem. And his mother's name *was* A-zu'-bah the daughter of Shil'-hi.

32 RAnd he walked in the way of A'-sa his father, and departed not from it, doing *that which was* right in the sight of the LORD. 14:2

33 Howbeit the Thigh places were not taken away: for as yet the people had not Rprepared their hearts unto the God of their fathers.   *pagan shrines for worship* • 12:14

34 Now the rest of the acts of Je-hosh'-a-phat, first and last, behold, they *are* written in the book of Je'-hu the son of Ha-na'-ni, Rwho is Tmentioned in the book of the kings of Israel.   1 Kin. 16:1, 7 • *inserted*

The Sin and Death of Jehoshaphat
1 Kin. 22:48

35 And after this did Je-hosh'-a-phat king of Judah join himself with A-ha-zi'-ah king of Israel, who did very wickedly:

36 And he joined himself with him to make ships to go to Tar'-shish: and they made the ships in E'-zi-on-ga'-ber.

37 Then E-li-e'-zer the son of Dod'-a-vah of Ma-re'-shah prophesied against Je-hosh'-a-phat, saying, Because thou hast joined thyself with A-ha-zi'-ah, the LORD hath broken thy works. And the ships were broken, that they were not able to go to Tar'-shish.

CHAPTER 21

Evaluation of Jehoram
1 Kin. 22:50; 2 Kin. 8:17–19

NOW Je-hosh'-a-phat slept with his fathers, and was buried with his fathers in the city of David. And Je-ho'-ram his son reigned in his stead.

2 And he had brethren the sons of Je-hosh'-a-phat, Az-a-ri'-ah, and Je-hi'-el, and Zech-a-ri'-ah, and Az-a-ri'-ah, and Mi'-cha-el, and Sheph-a-ti'-ah: all these *were* the sons of Je-hosh'-a-phat king of RIsrael.   12:6

3 And their father gave them great gifts of silver, and of gold, and of precious things, Rwith Tfenced cities in Judah: but the kingdom gave he to Je-ho'-ram; because he *was* the firstborn.   11:5 • *fortified*

4 Now when Je-ho'-ram was risen up to the kingdom of his father, he Tstrengthened himself, and slew all his brethren with the sword, and Tdivers also of the princes of Israel.   *increased his power* • *several*

5 RJe-ho'-ram *was* thirty and two years old when he began to reign, and he reigned eight years in Jerusalem.   2 Kin. 8:17–22

6 RAnd he walked in the way of the kings of Israel, like as did the house of Ahab: for he had the daughter of Ahab to wife: and he wrought *that which was* evil in the eyes of the LORD.   1 Kin. 12:28–30

7 Howbeit the LORD would not destroy the house of David, because of the covenant that he had made with David, and as he promised to give a Tlight to him and to his sons for ever.   *sign of the blessing of God*

Revolt by Edom and Libnah—2 Kin. 8:20–22

8 RIn his days the E'-dom-ites revolted from under the Tdominion of Judah, and made themselves a king.   2 Kin. 8:20 • *rule*

9 Then Je-ho'-ram went forth with his princes, and all his chariots with him: and he rose up by night, and smote the E'-dom-ites which Tcompassed him in, and the captains of the chariots.   *surrounded*

10 So the E'-dom-ites revolted from under the hand of Judah unto this day. The same time *also* did Lib'-nah revolt from under his hand; because he had forsaken the LORD God of his fathers.

11 Moreover he made high places in the mountains of Judah, and caused the inhabitants of Jerusalem to commit fornication, and Tcompelled Judah *thereto*.   *led*

Warning of Elijah

12 And there came a writing to him from E-li'-jah the prophet, saying, Thus saith the LORD God of David thy father, Because thou hast not walked in the ways of Je-hosh'-a-phat thy father, Rnor in the ways of A'-sa king of Judah,   14:2–5

13 But hast walked in the way of the kings of Israel, and hast made Judah and the inhabitants of Jerusalem to go a whoring, like to the whoredoms of the house of Ahab, and also hast slain thy brethren of thy father's house, *which were* better than thyself:

14 Behold, with a great plague will the LORD smite thy people, and thy children, and thy wives, and all thy goods:

15 And thou *shalt have* great sickness by disease of thy bowels, until thy bowels fall out by reason of the sickness day by day.

Invasion by Philistia and Arabia

16 Moreover the LORD Rstirred up against Je-ho'-ram the spirit of the Phi-lis'-tines, and of the RA-ra'-bi-ans, that *were* near the E-thi-o'-pi-ans: 1 Kin. 11:14, 23 • 17:11

17 And they came up into Judah, and brake into it, and carried away all the substance that was found in the king's house, and his sons also, and his wives; so that there was never a son left him, save TJe-ho'-a-haz, the youngest of his sons. *Ahaziah,* 22:1; *Azariah,* 22:6

Death of Jehoram

18 And after all this the LORD smote him in his bowels with an incurable disease.

19 And it came to pass, that in process of time, after the end of two years, his bowels fell out by reason of his sickness: so he died Tof sore diseases. And his people made Tno burning for him, like the burning of his fathers.   *in great agony • no public mourning*

20 Thirty and two years old was he when he began to reign, and he reigned in Jerusalem eight years, and Rdeparted Twithout being desired. Howbeit they buried him in the city of David, but not in the sepulchres of the kings.   Jer. 22:18, 28 • *having been unpopular*

CHAPTER 22

The Reign of Ahaziah
2 Kin. 8:27–29; 9:15, 16, 27, 28; 10:12–14

AND the inhabitants of Jerusalem made A-ha-zi'-ah his youngest son king in his stead: for the band of men that came with the A-ra'-bi-ans to the camp had slain all the Reldest. So A-ha-zi'-ah the son of Je-ho'-ram king of Judah reigned.   21:17

2 Forty and two years old *was* A-ha-zi'-ah when he began to reign, and he reigned one year in Jerusalem. His mother's name also *was* Ath-a-li'-ah the daughter of Om'-ri.

3 He also walked in the ways of the house of Ahab: for his mother was his Tcounsellor to do wickedly.   *advisor*

4 Wherefore he did evil in the sight of the LORD like the house of Ahab: for they were his counsellors after the death of his father to his destruction.

5 He walked also after their Tcounsel, and Rwent with Je-ho'-ram the son of Ahab king of Israel to war against Haz'-a-el king of Syria at Ra'-moth-gil'-e-ad: and the Syrians smote Jo'-ram.   *advice* • 2 Kin. 8:28

6 RAnd he returned to be healed in Jez'-re-el because of the wounds which were given him at Ra'-mah, when he fought with Haz'-a-el king of Syria. And Az-a-ri'-ah the son of Je-ho'-ram king of Judah went down to see Je-ho'-ram the son of Ahab at Jez'-re-el, because he was sick.   2 Kin. 9:15

7 And the Tdestruction of A-ha-zi'-ah was of God by coming to Jo'-ram: for when he was come, he went out with Je-ho'-ram against Je'-hu the son of Nim'-shi, Rwhom the LORD had anointed to Tcut off the house of Ahab.   *treading down* • 2 Kin. 9:6, 7 • *destroy*

8 And it came to pass, that, when Je'-hu was executing judgment upon the house of Ahab, and found the princes of Judah, and the sons of the brethren of A-ha-zi'-ah, that ministered to A-ha-zi'-ah, he slew them.

9 And he sought A-ha-zi'-ah: and they caught him, (for he was hid in Sa-ma'-ri-a,) and brought him to Je'-hu: and when they had slain him, they buried him: Because, said they, he *is* the son of Je-hosh'-a-phat, who sought the LORD with all his heart. So the house of A-ha-zi'-ah had no power to Tkeep still the kingdom.   *maintain order in*

The Reign of Athaliah—2 Kin. 11:1–16

10 But when Ath-a-li'-ah the mother of A-ha-zi'-ah saw that her son was dead, she arose and destroyed all the Tseed royal of the house of Judah.   *children of the king*

11 But Je-ho-shab'-e-ath, the daughter of the king, took Jo'-ash the son of A-ha-zi'-ah, and stole him from among the king's sons that were slain, and put him and his nurse in a bedchamber. So Je-ho-shab'-e-ath, the daughter of king Je-ho'-ram, the wife of Je-hoi'-a-da the priest, (for she was the sister of A-ha-zi'-ah,) hid him from Ath-a-li'-ah, so that she slew him not.

12 And he was with them hid in the house of God six years: and Ath-a-li'-ah reigned over the land.

CHAPTER 23

AND Rin the seventh year Je-hoi'-a-da strengthened himself, and took the captains of hundreds, Az-a-ri'-ah the son of Jer'-o-ham, and Ish'-ma-el the son of Je-ho-ha'-nan, and Az-a-ri'-ah the son of O'-bed, and Ma-a-se'-iah the son of A-da'-iah, and E-lish'-a-phat the son of Zich'-ri, into Tcovenant with him.   2 Kin. 11:4 • *agreement*

2 And they went about in Judah, and gathered the Levites out of all the cities of

Judah, and the chief of the fathers of Israel, and they came to Jerusalem.

3 And all the congregation made ᵀa covenant with the king in the house of God. And he said unto them, Behold, the king's son shall reign, as the LORD hath ᴿsaid of the sons of David. *an agreement* • 2 Sam. 7:12

4 This *is* the thing that ye shall do; A third part of you entering on the sabbath, of the priests and of the Levites, *shall be* ᵀporters of the ᵀdoors; *keepers • thresholds*

5 And a third part *shall be* at the king's house; and a third part at the gate of the foundation: and all the people *shall be* in the courts of the house of the LORD.

6 But let none come into the house of the LORD, save the priests, and they that minister of the Levites; they shall go in, for they *are* holy: but all the people shall ᵀkeep the watch of the LORD. *be on guard for*

7 And the Levites shall compass the king round about, every man with his weapons in his hand; and whosoever *else* cometh into the house, he shall be put to death: but be ye with the king when he cometh in, and when he goeth out.

8 So the Levites and all Judah did according to all things that Je-hoi'-a-da the priest had commanded, and took every man his men that were to come in on the sabbath, with them that were to go *out* on the sabbath: for Je-hoi'-a-da the priest dismissed not ᴿthe courses. 1 Chr. 24, 25

9 Moreover Je-hoi'-a-da the priest delivered to the captains of hundreds spears, and bucklers, and shields, that *had been* king David's, which *were* in the house of God.

10 And he set all the people, every man having his weapon in his hand, from the right side of the temple to the left side of the temple, along by the altar and the temple, by the king round about.

11 Then they brought out the king's son, and put upon him the crown, and *gave him* the testimony, and made him king. And Je-hoi'-a-da and his sons anointed him, and said, ᵀGod save the king. *long live*

12 Now when ᴿAth-a-li'-ah heard the noise of the people running and praising the king, she came to the people into the house of the LORD: 22:10

13 And she looked, and, behold, the king stood at his pillar at the entering in, and the princes and the trumpets by the king: and all the people of the land rejoiced, and sounded with trumpets, also the singers with instruments of musick, and ᴿsuch as taught to sing praise. Then Ath-a-li'-ah ᵀrent her clothes, and said, Treason, Treason. 1 Chr. 25:8 • *tore*

14 Then Je-hoi'-a-da the priest brought out the captains of hundreds that were set over the host, and said unto them, Have her forth of the ranges: and whoso followeth her, let

him be slain with the sword. For the priest said, Slay her not in the house of the LORD.

15 So they laid hands on her; and when she was come to the entering of the horse gate by the king's house, they slew her there.

Revival of Jehoiada—2 Kin. 11:17–20

16 And Je-hoi'-a-da made ᵀa covenant between him, and between all the people, and between the king, that they should be the LORD's people. *an agreement*

17 Then all the people went to the house of Ba'-al, and brake it down, and brake his altars and his images in pieces, and slew Mat'-tan the priest of Ba'-al before the altars.

18 Also Je-hoi'-a-da appointed the offices of the house of the LORD by the hand of the priests the Levites, whom David had distributed in the house of the LORD, to offer the burnt offerings of the LORD, as *it is* written in the law of Moses, with rejoicing and with singing, *as it was ordained* by David.

19 And he set the porters at the gates of the house of the LORD, that none *which was* unclean in any thing should enter in.

20 ᴿAnd he took the captains of hundreds, and the nobles, and the governors of the people, and all the people of the land, and brought down the king from the house of the LORD: and they came through the high gate into the king's house, and set the king upon the throne of the kingdom. 1 Kin. 9:22; 2 Kin. 11:19

21 And all the people of the land rejoiced: and the city was quiet, after that they had slain Ath-a-li'-ah with the sword.

CHAPTER 24

Evaluation of Joash
2 Kin. 11:21—12:2

JO'-ASH ᴿwas seven years old when he began to reign, and he reigned forty years in Jerusalem. His mother's name also *was* Zib'-i-ah of Be'-er-she'-ba. 2 Kin. 11:21

2 And Jo'-ash ᴿdid *that which was* right in the sight of the LORD all the days of Je-hoi'-a-da the priest. 26:5

3 And Je-hoi'-a-da took for him two wives; and he begat sons and daughters.

Repair of the Temple—2 Kin. 12:4–16

4 And it came to pass after this, *that* Jo'-ash was minded ᵀto repair the house of the LORD. *to renew*

5 And he gathered together the priests and the Levites, and said to them, Go out unto the cities of Judah, and gather of all Israel money to repair the house of your God from year to year, and see that ye hasten the matter. Howbeit the Levites hastened *it* not.

6 And the king called for Je-hoi'-a-da the chief, and said unto him, Why hast thou not

required of the Levites to bring in out of Judah and out of Jerusalem the collection, *according to the commandment* of Moses the servant of the Lord, and of the congregation of Israel, for the tabernacle of witness?

7 For the 'sons of Ath-a-li'-ah, that wicked woman, had ^Tbroken up the house of God; and also all the ^Rdedicated things of the house of the Lord did they ^Tbestow upon Ba'-al-im.   *damaged* • 2 Kin. 12:4 • *give to*

8 And at the king's commandment they made a chest, and set it ^Twithout at the gate of the house of the Lord.   *outside*

9 ^RAnd they made a proclamation through Judah and Jerusalem, to bring in to the Lord ^Rthe collection *that* Moses the servant of God *laid* upon Israel in the wilderness.   36:22 • *v.* 6

10 And all the princes and all the people rejoiced, and brought in, and cast into the chest, until they had made an end.

11 Now it came to pass, that at what time the chest was brought unto the king's office by the hand of the Levites, and ^Rwhen they saw that *there was* much money, the king's scribe and the high priest's officer came and emptied the chest, and took it, and carried it to his place again. Thus they did day by day, and gathered money in abundance. 2 Kin. 12:10

12 And the king and Je-hoi'-a-da gave it to such as did the work of the service of the house of the Lord, and hired masons and carpenters to repair the house of the Lord, and also such as wrought iron and brass to mend the house of the Lord.

13 So the workmen wrought, and the work was ^Tperfected by them, and they set the house of God ^Tin his state, and strengthened it.   *completed* • *in its original design*

14 And when they had finished *it,* they brought the rest of the money before the king and Je-hoi'-a-da, whereof were made vessels for the house of the Lord, *even* vessels to minister, and to offer *withal,* and spoons, and vessels of gold and silver. And they offered burnt offerings in the house of the Lord continually all the days of Je-hoi'-a-da.

Death of Jehoiada

15 But Je-hoi'-a-da waxed old, and was full of days when he died; an hundred and thirty years old *was he* when he died.

16 And they buried him in the city of David among the kings, ^Rbecause he had done good in Israel, both toward God, and toward his house.   21:20

Murder of Jehoiada's Son

17 Now after the death of Je-hoi'-a-da came the princes of Judah, and ^Tmade obeisance to the king. Then the king hearkened unto them.   *submitted themselves*

18 And they left the house of the Lord God of their fathers, and served groves and idols: and wrath came upon Judah and Jerusalem for this their trespass.

19 Yet he sent prophets to them, to bring them again unto the Lord; and they testified against them: but they would not give ear.

20 And the Spirit of God came ^Rupon Zech-a-ri'-ah the son of Je-hoi'-a-da the priest, which stood above the people, and said unto them, Thus saith God, Why transgress ye the commandments of the Lord, that ye cannot prosper? because ye have forsaken the Lord, he hath also forsaken you. Judg. 6:34

21 And they conspired against him, and ^Rstoned him with stones at the commandment of the king in the court of the house of the Lord.   Matt. 23:35; Acts 7:58, 59

22 Thus Jo'-ash the king remembered not the kindness which Je-hoi'-a-da his ^Tfather had done to him, but slew his son. And when he died, he said, ^RThe Lord look upon *it,* and require *it.*   *foster father* • Neh. 9:26

Destruction of Judah by Syria

23 And it came to pass at the end of the year, *that* the host of Syria came up against him: and they came to Judah and Jerusalem, and destroyed all the princes of the people from among the people, and sent all the spoil of them unto the king of ^TDamascus. *Darmesek*

24 For the army of the Syrians ^Rcame with a small company of men, and the Lord delivered a very great host into their hand, because they had forsaken the Lord God of their fathers. So they executed judgment against Jo'-ash.   Lev. 26:8

Death of Joash—2 Kin. 12:20, 21

25 And when they were departed from him, (for they left him in great diseases,) his own servants conspired against him for the blood of the sons of Je-hoi'-a-da the priest, and slew him on his bed, and he died: and they buried him in the city of David, but they buried him not in the sepulchres of the kings.

26 And these are they that conspired against him; Za'-bad the son of Shim'-e-ath an Am'-mon-i-tess, and Je-ho'-za-bad the son of ^TShim'-rith a Mo'-ab-i-tess.   *Shomer*

27 Now *concerning* his sons, and the greatness of the burdens *laid* upon him, and the repairing of the house of God, behold, they *are* written in the ^Tstory of the book of the kings. And Am-a-zi'-ah his son reigned in his stead.   *commentary*

CHAPTER 25

Evaluation of Amaziah—2 Kin. 14:1-6

AM-A-ZI'-AH ^R*was* twenty and five years old *when* he began to reign, and he reigned twenty and nine years in Jerusalem.

And his mother's name *was* Je-ho-ad'-dan of Jerusalem.   2 Kin. 14:1-6

2 And he did *that which was* right in the sight of the LORD, Rbut not with a Tperfect heart.   *v. 14; 2 Kin. 14:4 · sincere*

3 Now it came to pass, when the kingdom was established to him, that he slew his servants that had killed the king his father.

4 But he slew not their children, but *did* as *it is* written in the law in the book of Moses, where the LORD commanded, saying, The fathers shall not die for the children, neither shall the children die for the fathers, but every man shall die for his own sin.

Victory over Edom

5 Moreover Am-a-zi'-ah gathered Judah together, and made them captains over thousands, and captains over hundreds, according to the houses of *their* fathers, throughout all Judah and Benjamin: and he numbered them from twenty years old and above, and found them three hundred thousand choice *men, able* to go forth to war, that could handle spear and shield.

6 He hired also an hundred thousand mighty men of valour out of Israel for an Thundred talents of silver.   *$38,400,000*

7 But there came a man of God to him, saying, O king, let not the army of Israel go with thee; for the LORD *is* not with Israel, *to wit, with* all the children of E'-phra-im.

8 But if thou wilt go, do Tit, be strong for the battle: God shall make thee fall before the enemy: for God hath Rpower to help, and to cast down.   *valiantly · 20:6*

9 And Am-a-zi'-ah said to the man of God, But what shall we do for the hundred talents which I have given to the army of Israel? And the man of God answered, The LORD is able to give thee much more than this.

10 Then Am-a-zi'-ah separated them, *to wit,* the army that was come to him out of E'-phra-im, to go home again: wherefore their anger was greatly kindled against Judah, and they returned home in great anger.

11 And Am-a-zi'-ah Tstrengthened himself, and led forth his people, and went to the valley of salt, and smote of the children of Se'-ir ten thousand.   *took courage*

12 And *other* ten thousand *left* alive did the children of Judah carry away captive, and brought them unto the top of the rock, and cast them down from the top of the rock, that they all were broken in pieces.

13 But the soldiers of the army which Am-a-zi'-ah sent back, that they should not go with him to battle, fell upon the cities of Judah, from Sa-ma'-ri-a even unto Beth-ho'-ron, and smote three thousand of them, and took much Tspoil.   *loot*

Idolatry of Amaziah

14 Now it came to pass, after that Am-a-zi'-ah was come from the slaughter of the E'-dom-ites, that he brought the gods of the children of Se'-ir, and set them up *to be* his gods, and bowed down himself before them, and burned incense unto them.

15 Wherefore the anger of the LORD was kindled against Am-a-zi'-ah, and he sent unto him a prophet, which said unto him, Why hast thou sought after the gods of the people, which Rcould not deliver their own people out of thine hand?   *v. 11*

16 And it came to pass, as he talked with him, that *the king* said unto him, Art thou made of the king's counsel? forbear; why shouldest thou be smitten? Then the prophet forbare, and said, I know that God hath determinedT to destroy thee, because thou hast done this, and hast not hearkened unto my Tcounsel.   *counseled · advice*

Defeat of Judah by Israel—2 Kin. 14:8-14

17 Then Am-a-zi'-ah king of Judah took advice, and sent to Jo'-ash, the son of Je-ho'-a-haz, the son of Je'-hu, king of Israel, saying, Come, let us see one another in the face.

18 And Jo'-ash king of Israel sent to Am-a-zi'-ah king of Judah, saying, The thistle that *was* in Leb'-a-non sent to the cedar that *was* in Leb'-a-non, saying, Give thy daughter to my son to wife: and there passed by a wild beast that *was* in Leb'-a-non, and trode down the thistle.

19 Thou sayest, Lo, thou hast smitten the E'-dom-ites; and thine heart lifteth thee up to boast: abide now at home; why shouldest thou meddle to *thine* hurt, that thou shouldest fall, *even* thou, and Judah with thee?

20 But Am-a-zi'-ah would not hear; for it *came* of God, that he might deliver them into the hand *of their enemies,* because they Rsought after the gods of E'-dom.   *v. 14*

21 So Jo'-ash the king of Israel went up; and they saw one another in the face, *both* he and Am-a-zi'-ah king of Judah, at Beth-she'-mesh, which *belongeth* to Judah.

22 And Judah was put to the worse before Israel, and they fled every man to his tent.

23 And Jo'-ash the king of Israel took Am-a-zi'-ah king of Judah, the son of Jo'-ash, the son of Je-ho'-a-haz, at Beth-she'-mesh, and brought him to Jerusalem, and brake down the wall of Jerusalem from the gate of E'-phra-im to the corner gate, four hundred cubits.

24 And *he took* all the gold and the silver, and all the vessels that were found in the house of God with RO'-bed-e'-dom, and the treasures of the king's house, the hostages also, and returned to Sa-ma'-ri-a.   *1 Chr. 26:15*

Death of Amaziah—2 Kin. 14:17–20

25 ᴿAnd Am-a-zi'-ah the son of Jo'-ash king of Judah lived after the death of Jo'-ash son of Je-ho'-a-haz king of Israel fifteen years.   2 Kin. 14:17-22

26 Now the rest of the acts of ᴿAm-a-zi'-ah, first and last, behold, *are* they not written in the book of the kings of Judah and Israel?   2 Kin. 14:1, 5, 8

27 Now after the time that Am-a-zi'-ah did turn away from following the Lᴏʀᴅ they made a conspiracy against him in Jerusalem; and he fled to La'-chish: but they sent to La'-chish after him, and slew him there.

28 And they brought him upon horses, and buried him with his fathers in the city of ᵀJudah.ᴿ   *David as it is* · 2 Kin. 14:20

CHAPTER 26

Evaluation of Uzziah—2 Kin. 14:21, 22; 15:1–3

THEN all the people of Judah took ᴿUz-zi'-ah,ᵀ who *was* sixteen years old, and made him king in the room of his father Am-a-zi'-ah.   2 Kin. 14:21, 22 · *Azariah*

2 He built E'-loth, and restored it to Judah, after that the king slept with his fathers.

3 Sixteen years old *was* Uz-zi'-ah when he began to reign, and he reigned fifty and two years in Jerusalem. His mother's name also *was* Jec-o-li'-ah of Jerusalem.

4 ᴿAnd he did *that which was* right in the sight of the Lᴏʀᴅ, according to all that his father Am-a-zi'-ah did.   2 Kin. 14:21; 15:3

5 And he sought God in the days of Zech-a-ri'-ah, who had understanding in the visions of God: and as long as he sought the Lᴏʀᴅ, God made him to prosper.

Victories of Uzziah

6 And he went forth and warred against the Phi-lis'-tines, and brake down the wall of Gath, and the wall of Jab'-neh, and the wall of Ash'-dod, and built cities about Ash'-dod, and among the Phi-lis'-tines.

7 And God helped him against the Phi-lis'-tines, and against the A-ra'-bi-ans that dwelt in Gur-ba'-al, and the Me-hu'-nims.

8 And the Am'-mon-ites ᴿgave gifts to Uz-zi'-ah: and his name spread abroad *even* to the entering in of Egypt; for he strengthened *himself* exceedingly.   17:11

9 Moreover Uz-zi'-ah built towers in Jerusalem at the ᴿcorner gate, and at the valley gate, and at the turning *of the wall,* and fortified them.   Neh. 3:13, 19, 32; Zech. 14:10

10 Also he built towers in the desert, and digged many ᵀwells: for he had much cattle, both in the low country, and in the plains: husbandmen *also,* and vine dressers in the

mountains, and in ᵀCarmel: for he loved ᵀhusbandry.   *cisterns · fruitful fields · agriculture*

11 Moreover Uz-zi'-ah had an host of fighting men, that went out to war by bands, according to the number of their account by the hand of Je-i'-el the scribe and Ma-a-se'-iah the ruler, under the hand of Han-a-ni'-ah, *one* of the king's captains.

12 The whole number of the chief of the fathers of the mighty men of valour *were* two thousand and six hundred.

13 And under their hand *was* an army, three hundred thousand and seven thousand and five hundred, that made war with mighty power, to help the king against the enemy.

14 And Uz-zi'-ah prepared for them throughout all the host shields, and spears, and helmets, and ᵀhabergeons, and bows, and slings *to cast* stones.   *coats of mail*

15 And he made in Jerusalem engines, invented by ᵀcunning men, to be on the towers and upon the bulwarks, to shoot arrows and great stones withal. And his name spread far abroad; for he was marvellously helped, till he was strong.   *clever*

Sinful Offering of Uzziah

16 But when he was strong, his heart was ᴿlifted up to *his* destruction: for he transgressed against the Lᴏʀᴅ his God, and went into the temple of the Lᴏʀᴅ to burn incense upon the altar of incense.   25:19

17 And Az-a-ri'-ah the priest went in after him, and with him fourscore priests of the Lᴏʀᴅ, *that were* ᵀvaliant men: *great*

18 And they withstood Uz-zi'-ah the king, and said unto him, It *appertaineth* not unto thee, Uz-zi'-ah, to burn incense unto the Lᴏʀᴅ, but to the ᴿpriests the sons of Aaron, that are consecrated to burn incense: go out of the sanctuary; for thou hast trespassed; neither *shall it be* for thine honour from the Lᴏʀᴅ God.   Ex. 30:7, 8

19 Then Uz-zi'-ah was wroth, and *had* a censer in his hand to burn incense: and while he was wroth with the priests, ᴿthe leprosy even rose up in his forehead before the priests in the house of the Lᴏʀᴅ, from beside the incense altar.   Num. 12:10; 2 Kin. 5:27

20 And Az-a-ri'-ah the chief priest, and all the priests, looked upon him, and, behold, he *was* leprous in his forehead, and they thrust him out from thence; yea, himself hastedᵀ also to go out, because the Lᴏʀᴅ had ᵀsmitten him.   *hurried · struck*

21 ᴿAnd Uz-zi'-ah the king was a leper unto the day of his death, and dwelt in a several house, *being* a leper; for he was cut off from the house of the Lᴏʀᴅ: and Jo'-tham his son *was* over the king's house, judging the people of the land.   2 Kin. 15:5

Death of Uzziah—2 Kin. 15:7

22 ᴿNow the rest of the acts of Uz-zi′-ah, first and last, did ᴿIsaiah the prophet, the son of Amoz, write.   2 Kin. 20:1 • Is. 1:1

23 ᴿSo Uz-zi′-ah slept with his fathers, and they buried him with his fathers in the field of the burial which *belonged* to the kings; for they said, He *is* a leper: and Jo′-tham his son reigned in his stead.   Is. 6:1

CHAPTER 27

The Reign of Jotham—2 Kin. 15:33-38

JO′-THAM ᴿ*was* twenty and five years old when he began to reign, and he reigned sixteen years in Jerusalem. His mother's name also *was* Je-ru′-shah, the daughter of Za′-dok.   2 Kin. 15:32-35

2 And he did *that which was* right in the sight of the Lᴏʀᴅ, according to all that his father Uz-zi′-ah did: howbeit he entered not into the temple of the Lᴏʀᴅ. And ᴿthe people did yet ᵀcorruptly.   2 Kin. 15:35 • *evilly*

3 He built the high gate of the house of the Lᴏʀᴅ, and on the wall of ᵀO′-phelᴿ he built much.   *the tower* • 33:14; Neh. 3:26

4 Moreover he built ᴿcities in the ᵀmountains of Judah, and in the forests he built castles and towers.   11:5 • *hill country*

5 He fought also with the king of the Am′-mon-ites, and prevailed against them. And the children of Ammon gave him the same year an ᵀhundred talents of silver, and ᵀten thousand measures of wheat, and ten thousand of barley. So much did the children of Ammon pay unto him, both the second year, and the third. $38,400,000 • 6,524 bu.

6 So Jo′-tham became mighty, because he prepared his ways before the Lᴏʀᴅ his God.

7 ᴿNow the rest of the acts of Jo′-tham, and all his wars, and his ways, lo, they *are* written in the book of the kings of Israel and Judah.   2 Kin. 15:36

8 ᴿHe was five and twenty years old when he began to reign, and reigned sixteen years in Jerusalem.   2 Kin. 15:5

9 And Jo′-tham slept with his fathers, and they buried him in the city of David: and Ahaz his son reigned in his stead.

CHAPTER 28

Evaluation of Ahaz—2 Kin. 16:1-4

AHAZ ᴿ*was* twenty years old when he began to reign, and he reigned sixteen years in Jerusalem: but he did not *that which was* right in the sight of the Lᴏʀᴅ, like David his father: 2 Kin. 16:2-4

2 For he walked in the ways of the kings of Israel, and made also ᴿmoltenᵀ images for Ba′-al-im.   Ex. 34:17; Lev. 19:4 • *idols*

3 Moreover he burnt incense in the valley of the son of Hin′-nom, and burnt his children in the fire, after the abominations of the heathen whom the Lᴏʀᴅ had cast out before the children of Israel.

4 He sacrificed also and burnt incense in the ᵀhigh places, and on the hills, and under every green tree.   *pagan shrines for worship*

Defeat of Judah—2 Kin. 16:5-8; Is. 7:1

5 Wherefore the Lᴏʀᴅ his God delivered him into the hand of the king of Syria; and they ᴿsmoteᵀ him, and carried away a great multitude of them captives, and brought *them* to Damascus. And he was also delivered into the hand of the king of Israel, who smote him with a great slaughter.   2 Kin. 16:5, 6 • *defeated*

6 For ᴿPe′-kah the son of Rem-a-li′-ah slew in Judah an hundred and twenty thousand in one day, *which were* all ᵀvaliant men; because they had forsaken the Lᴏʀᴅ God of their fathers.   2 Kin. 15:27 • *great*

7 And Zich′-ri, a mighty man of E′-phra-im, slew Ma-a-se′-iah the king's son, and Az′-ri-kam the governor of the house, and El′-ka-nah *that was* next to the king.

8 And the children of Israel carried away captive of their brethren two hundred thousand, women, sons, and daughters, and took also away much ᵀspoil from them, and brought the spoil to Sa-ma′-ri-a.   *loot*

9 But a prophet of the Lᴏʀᴅ was there, whose name *was* O′-ded: and he went out before the host that came to Sa-ma′-ri-a, and said unto them, Behold, ᴿbecause the Lᴏʀᴅ God of your fathers was wroth with Judah, he hath delivered them into your hand, and ye have slain them in a rage *that* reacheth up unto heaven.   [Is. 10:5]

10 And now ye purpose to keep under the children of Judah and Jerusalem for ᵀbondmen and bondwomen unto you: *but are there* not with you, even with you, sins against the Lᴏʀᴅ your God?   *men slaves*

11 Now hear me therefore, and deliver the captives again, which ye have taken captive of your brethren: ᴿfor the fierce wrath of the Lᴏʀᴅ *is* upon you.   James 2:13

12 Then certain of the heads of the children of E′-phra-im, Az-a-ri′-ah the son of Jo-ha′-nan, Ber-e-chi′-ah the son of Me-shil′-le-moth, and Je-hiz-ki′-ah the son of Shal′-lum, and Am′-a-sa the son of Had′-lai, stood up against them that came from the war,

13 And said unto them, Ye shall not bring in the captives hither: for whereas we have offended against the Lᴏʀᴅ *already,* ye intend to add *more* to our sins and to our trespass: for our trespass is great, and *there is* ᴿfierce wrath against Israel.   Ps. 78:49

14 So the armed men left the captives and the ᵀspoil before the princes and all the congregation.   *loot*

15 And the men which were expressed by name rose up, and took the captives, and with the spoil clothed all that were naked among them, and arrayed them, and shod them, and gave them to eat and to drink, and anointed them, and carried all the feeble of them upon asses, and brought them to Jericho, the city of palm trees, to their brethren: then they returned to Sa-ma′-ri-a.

16 ᴿAt that time did king Ahaz send unto the kings of Assyria to help him.   2 Kin. 16:7

17 ᴿFor again the E′-dom-ites had come and ᵀsmitten Judah, and carried away captives.   Obad. 10–14 • *defeated*

18 The Phi-lis′-tines also had invaded the cities of the low country, and of the south of Judah, and had taken Beth–she′-mesh, and Aj′-a-lon, and Ge-de′-roth, and Sho′-cho with the villages thereof, and Tim′-nah with the villages thereof, Gim′-zo also and the villages thereof: and they dwelt there.

19 For the Lᴏʀᴅ brought Judah low because of Ahaz king of Israel; for he ᵀmade Judah naked, and transgressed ᵀsore against the Lᴏʀᴅ.   *dealt wantonly in Judah • much*

20 And Til′-gath–pil-ne′-ser king of Assyria came unto him, and distressed him, but ᵀstrengthened him not.   *would not help him*

21 ᴿFor Ahaz took away a portion *out* of the house of the Lᴏʀᴅ, and *out* of the house of the king, and of the princes, and gave *it* unto the king of Assyria: ᴿbut ᵀhe helped him not.   2 Kin. 16:8, 9 • 1 Sam. 7:12 • *it*

Idolatry of Ahaz—2 Kin. 16:12

22 And in the time of his distress did he trespass yet more against the Lᴏʀᴅ: this *is that* king ᴿAhaz.   2 Kin. 16:8, 11–18

23 For he sacrificed unto the gods of Damascus, which smote him: and he said, Because the gods of the kings of Syria help them, *therefore* will I sacrifice to them, that they may help me. But they were the ruin of him, and of all Israel.

24 And Ahaz gathered together the vessels of the house of God, and cut in pieces the vessels of the house of God, and shut up the doors of the house of the Lᴏʀᴅ, and he made him altars in every corner of Jerusalem.

25 And ᵀin every several city of Judah he made high places to burn incense unto other gods, and provoked to anger the Lᴏʀᴅ God of his fathers.   *in every city of Judah*

Death of Ahaz—2 Kin. 16:20

26 Now the rest of his acts and of all his ways, first and last, behold, they *are* written in the book of the kings of Judah and Israel.

27 And Ahaz slept with his fathers, and they buried him in the city, *even* in Jerusa-

lem: but they brought him not into the sepulchres of the kings of Israel: and Hez-e-ki′-ah his son reigned in his stead.

CHAPTER 29

Evaluation of Hezekiah—2 Kin. 18:2, 3

HEZ-E-KI′-AH began to reign *when he was* five and twenty years old, and he reigned nine and twenty years in Jerusalem. And his mother's name *was* A-bi′-jah, the daughter ᴿof Zech-a-ri′-ah.   26:5

2 ᴿAnd he did *that which was* right in the sight of the Lᴏʀᴅ, according to all that David his father had done.   28:1; 34:2

Purification of the Temple

3 He in the first year of his reign, in the first month, ᴿopened the doors of the house of the Lᴏʀᴅ, and repaired them.   *v. 7*

4 And he brought in the priests and the Levites, and gathered them together into the ᵀeast street,   *broad place on the east*

5 And said unto them, Hear me, ye Levites, ᴿsanctify now yourselves, and sanctify the house of the Lᴏʀᴅ God of your fathers, and carry forth the ᵀfilthiness out of the holy place.   35:6; 1 Chr. 15:12 • *debris*

6 For our fathers have trespassed, and done *that which was* evil in the eyes of the Lᴏʀᴅ our God, and have forsaken him, and have turned away their faces from the habitation of the Lᴏʀᴅ, and turned *their* backs.

7 ᴿAlso they have shut up the doors of the porch, and put out the lamps, and have not burned incense nor offered burnt offerings in the holy place unto the God of Israel.   28:24

8 Wherefore the wrath of the Lᴏʀᴅ was upon Judah and Jerusalem, and he hath delivered them to trouble, to astonishment, and to hissing, as ye see with your eyes.

9 For, lo, our fathers have fallen by the sword, and our sons and our daughters and our wives *are* in captivity for this.

10 Now *it is* in mine heart to make a covenant with the Lᴏʀᴅ God of Israel, that his fierce wrath may turn away from us.

11 My sons, be not now negligent: for the Lᴏʀᴅ hath chosen you to stand before him, to serve him, and that ye should minister unto him, and burn incense.

12 Then the Levites arose, Ma′-hath the son of Am′-a-sai, and Jo′-el the son of Az-a-ri′-ah, of the sons of the Ko′-hath-ites: and of the sons of Me-ra′-ri, Kish the son of Ab′-di, and Az-a-ri′-ah the son of Je-hal′-e-lel: and of the Ger′-shon-ites; Jo′-ah the son of Zim′-mah, and Eden the son of Jo′-ah:

13 And of the sons of E-liz′-a-phan; Shim′-ri, and Je-i′-el: and of the sons of A′-saph; Zech-a-ri′-ah, and Mat-ta-ni′-ah:

14 And of the sons of He'-man; ^RJe-hi'-el, and Shim'-e-i: and of the sons of Je-du'-thun; She-ma'-iah, and Uz-zi'-el.   1 Chr. 15:18

15 And they gathered their brethren, and ^Rsanctified themselves, and came, according to the commandment of the king, by the words of the LORD, ^Rto cleanse the house of the LORD.   v. 5 • 1 Chr. 23:28

16 And the priests went into the inner part of the house of the LORD, to cleanse it, and brought out all the ^Tuncleanness that they found in the temple of the LORD into the court of the house of the LORD. And the Levites took it, to carry it out abroad into the brook Kid'-ron.   debris

17 Now they began on the first day of the first month to sanctify, and on the eighth day of the month came they to the porch of the LORD: so they sanctified the house of the LORD in eight days; and in the sixteenth day of the first month they made an end.

18 Then they went in to Hez-e-ki'-ah the king, and said, We have cleansed all the house of the LORD, and the altar of burnt offering, with all the vessels thereof, and the shewbread table, with all the vessels thereof.

19 Moreover all the vessels, which king Ahaz in his reign did ^Rcast^T away in his transgression, have we prepared and ^Tsanctified, and, behold, they are before the altar of the LORD.   28:24 • throw away • set apart

Restoration of Temple Worship

20 Then Hez-e-ki'-ah the king rose early, and gathered the rulers of the city, and went up to the house of the LORD.

21 And they brought seven bullocks, and seven rams, and seven lambs, and seven he goats, for a ^Rsin offering for the kingdom, and for the sanctuary, and for Judah. And he commanded the priests the sons of Aaron to offer them on the altar of the LORD. Lev. 4:3–14

22 So they killed the bullocks, and the priests received the blood, and sprinkled it on the altar: likewise, when they had killed the rams, they sprinkled the blood upon the altar: they killed also the lambs, and they sprinkled the blood upon the altar.

23 And they brought ^Tforth the he goats for the sin offering before the king and the congregation; and they laid their ^Rhands upon them: near • Lev. 4:15, 24

24 And the priests killed them, and they made ^Treconciliation with their blood upon the altar, ^Rto make an atonement for all Israel: for the king commanded that the burnt offering and the sin offering should be made for all Israel.   sin offering • Lev. 14:20

25 And he set the Levites in the house of the LORD with cymbals, with psalteries, and with harps, according to the commandment of David, and of Gad the king's seer, and

Nathan the prophet: for so was the commandment of the LORD by his prophets.

26 And the Levites stood with the instruments ^Rof David, and the priests with ^Rthe trumpets.   Amos 6:5 • 1 Chr. 15:24; 16:6

27 And Hez-e-ki'-ah commanded to offer the burnt offering upon the altar. And when the burnt offering began, ^Rthe song of the LORD began also with the trumpets, and with the instruments ordained by David king of Israel.   23:18

28 And all the congregation worshipped, and the singers sang, and the trumpeters sounded: and all this continued until the burnt offering was finished.

29 And when they had made an end of offering, the king and all that were present with him bowed themselves, and worshipped.

30 Moreover Hez-e-ki'-ah the king and the princes commanded the Levites to sing praise unto the LORD with the words of David, and of A'-saph the seer. And they sang praises with ^Rgladness, and they bowed their heads and worshipped.   Neh. 8:17

31 Then Hez-e-ki'-ah answered and said, Now ye have consecrated yourselves unto the LORD, come near and bring sacrifices and thank offerings into the house of the LORD. And the congregation brought in sacrifices and thank offerings; and as many as were of a free heart burnt offerings.

32 And the number of the burnt offerings, which the congregation brought, was threescore and ten bullocks, an hundred rams, and two hundred lambs: all these were for a burnt offering to the LORD.

33 And the consecrated things were six hundred oxen and three thousand sheep.

34 But the priests were too few, so that they could not ^Tflay all the burnt offerings: wherefore their brethren the Levites did help them, till the work was ended, and until the other priests had sanctified themselves: ^Rfor the Levites were more upright in heart to sanctify themselves than the priests. skin • 30:3

35 And also the burnt offerings were in abundance, with the fat of the peace offerings, and the drink offerings for every burnt offering. So the ^Tservice of the house of the LORD was set in order.   worship program

36 And Hez-e-ki'-ah rejoiced, and all the people, that God had prepared the people: for the thing was done suddenly.

CHAPTER 30

Celebration of the Passover

AND Hez-e-ki'-ah sent to all Israel and Judah, and wrote letters also to E'-phraim and Ma-nas'-seh, that they should come to the house of the LORD at Jerusalem, to keep the passover unto the LORD God of Israel.

2 For the king had taken counsel, and his princes, and all the congregation in Jerusalem, to keep the passover in the second ᴿmonth.   Num. 9:10, 11

3 For they could not keep it at that time, because the priests had not sanctified themselves sufficiently, neither had the people gathered themselves together to Jerusalem.

4 And the thing pleased the king and all the congregation.

5 So they established a decree to make proclamation throughout all Israel, ᴿfrom Be'-er-she'-ba even to Dan, that they should come to keep the passover unto the LORD God of Israel at Jerusalem: for they had not ᵀdone it of a long time in such sort as it was written.   Judg. 20:1 • kept it in great numbers

6 So the posts went with the letters from the king and his princes throughout all Israel and Judah, and according to the commandment of the king, saying, Ye children of Israel, turn again unto the LORD God of Abraham, Isaac, and Israel, and he will return to the remnant of you, that are escaped out of the hand of the kings of Assyria.

7 And be not ye like your fathers, and like your brethren, which trespassed against the LORD God of their fathers, who therefore gave them up to desolation, as ye see.

8 Now be ye not stiffnecked, as your fathers were, but yield yourselves unto the LORD, and enter into his sanctuary, which he hath ᵀsanctified for ever: and serve the LORD your God, that the fierceness of his wrath may turn away from you.   set apart

9 For if ye turn again unto the LORD, your brethren and your children shall find compassion before them that lead them captive, so that they shall come again into this land: for the LORD your God is gracious and merciful, and will not turn away his face from you, if ye return unto him.

10 So the posts passed from city to city through the country of E'-phra-im and Ma-nas'-seh even unto Zeb'-u-lun: but they laughed them to scorn, and mocked them.

11 Nevertheless ᴿdivers of Asher and Ma-nas'-seh and of Zeb'-u-lun humbled themselves, and came to Jerusalem.   11:16

12 Also in Judah the hand of God was to give them ᵀone heart to do the commandment of the king and of the princes, ᴿby the word of the LORD.   unity • 29:25

13 And there assembled at Jerusalem much people to keep the feast of unleavened bread in the second month, a very great congregation.

14 And they arose and took away the ᴿaltars that were in Jerusalem, and all the altars for incense took they away, and cast them into the brook Kid'-ron.   28:24

15 Then they killed the passover on the fourteenth day of the second month: and the priests and the Levites were ashamed, and sanctified themselves, and brought in the burnt offerings into the house of the LORD.

16 And they stood in their place ᵀafter their manner, according to the law of Moses the man of God: the priests sprinkled the blood, which they received of the hand of the Levites.   in their proper order

17 For there were many in the congregation that were not ᵀsanctified: ᴿtherefore the Levites had the charge of the killing of the passovers for every one that was not clean, to sanctify them unto the LORD.   set apart • 29:34

18 For a multitude of the people, even ᴿmany of E'-phra-im, and Ma-nas'-seh, Is'-sa-char, and Zeb'-u-lun, had not cleansed themselves, yet did they eat the passover otherwise than it was written. But Hez-e-ki'-ah prayed for them, saying, The good LORD pardon every one   vv. 1, 11

19 That ᴿprepareth his heart to seek God, the LORD God of his fathers, though he be not cleansed according to the purification of the sanctuary.   19:3; Ex. 12:15; 13:6

20 And the LORD hearkened to Hez-e-ki'-ah, and healed the people.

21 And the children of Israel that were present at Jerusalem kept ᴿthe feast of unleavened bread seven days with great gladness: and the Levites and the priests praised the LORD day by day, singing with loud instruments unto the LORD.   Ex. 12:15

22 And Hez-e-ki'-ah spake ᵀcomfortably unto all the Levites that taught the good knowledge of the LORD: and they did eat throughout the feast seven days, offering peace offerings, and making confession to the LORD God of their fathers.   encouragingly

Extra Feast Days

23 And the whole assembly took counsel to keep ᴿother seven days: and they kept other seven days with gladness.   1 Kin. 8:65

24 For Hez-e-ki'-ah king of Judah did give to the congregation a thousand bullocks and seven thousand sheep; and the princes gave to the congregation a thousand bullocks and ten thousand sheep: and a great number of priests ᴿsanctified themselves.   29:34

25 And all the congregation of Judah, with the priests and the Levites, and all the congregation that came out of Israel, and the strangers that came out of the land of Israel, and that dwelt in Judah, rejoiced.

26 So there was great joy in Jerusalem: for ᴿsince the time of Solomon the son of David king of Israel there was not the like in Jerusalem.   7:8–10

27 Then the priests the Levites arose and blessed the people: and their voice was heard, and their prayer came *up* to his holy dwelling place, *even* unto heaven.

CHAPTER 31

Destruction of the Idols—2 Kin. 18:4

NOW when all this was finished, all Israel that were present went out to the cities of Judah, and brake the images in pieces, and cut down the ᵀgroves, and threw down the high places and the altars out of all Judah and Benjamin, in E'-phra-im also and Ma-nas'-seh, until they had utterly destroyed them all. Then all the children of Israel returned, every man to his possession, into their own cities.   *idols*

Contribution for the Priests and Levites

2 And Hez-e-ki'-ah appointed the courses of the priests and the Levites after their courses, every man according to his service, the priests and Levites for burnt offerings and for peace offerings, to minister, and to give thanks, and to praise in the gates of the ᵀtents of the LORD.   *camp*

3 *He appointed* also the king's ᵀportion of his substance for the burnt offerings, *to wit,* for the morning and evening burnt offerings, and the burnt offerings for the sabbaths, and for the new moons, and for the set feasts, as *it is* written in the law of the LORD.   *share*

4 Moreover he commanded the people that dwelt in Jerusalem to give the portion of the priests and the Levites, that they might be encouraged in ᴿthe law of the LORD.   Mal. 2:7

5 And as soon as the commandment came abroad, the children of Israel brought in abundance ᴿthe firstfruits of corn, wine, and oil, and ᵀhoney, and of all the increase of the field; and the tithe of all *things* brought they in abundantly.   Ex. 22:29 • *dates*

6 And *concerning* the children of Israel and Judah, that dwelt in the cities of Judah, they also brought in the tithe of oxen and sheep, and the tithe of holy things which were consecrated unto the LORD their God, and laid *them* by heaps.

7 In the third month they began to lay the foundation of the heaps, and finished *them* in the seventh month.

8 And when Hez-e-ki'-ah and the princes came and saw the heaps, they blessed the LORD, and his people Israel.

9 Then Hez-e-ki'-ah questioned with the priests and the Levites concerning the heaps.

10 And Az-a-ri'-ah the chief priest of the house of Za'-dok answered him, and said, ᴿSince *the people* began to bring the offerings into the house of the LORD, we have had enough to eat, and have left plenty: for the LORD hath blessed his people; and that which is left *is* this great store.   [Mal. 3:10]

Reorganization of the Priests and Levites

11 Then Hez-e-ki'-ah ᴿcommanded to prepare ᵀchambers in the house of the LORD; and they prepared *them,*   1 Kin. 6:5, 8 • *storehouses*

12 And brought in the offerings and the tithes and the dedicated *things* faithfully: ᴿover which Con-o-ni'-ah the Levite *was* ruler, and ᴿShim'-e-i his brother *was* the next.   Neh. 13:13 • 35:9

13 And Je-hi'-el, and Az-a-zi'-ah, and Na'-hath, and A'-sa-hel, and Jer'-i-moth, and Joz'-a-bad, and E-li'-el, and Is-ma-chi'-ah, and Ma'-hath, and Be-na'-iah, *were* overseers under the hand of Con-o-ni'-ah and Shim'-e-i his brother, at the commandment of Hez-e-ki'-ah the king, and Az-a-ri'-ah the ruler of the house of God.

14 And Ko'-re the son of Im'-nah the Levite, the ᵀporter toward the east, *was* over the freewill offerings of God, to distribute the ᵀoblations of the LORD, and the most holy things.   *keeper* • *offerings*

15 And next him *were* Eden, and Mi-ni'-a-min, and Jesh'-u-a, and She-ma'-iah, Am-a-ri'-ah, and Shec-a-ni'-ah, in ᴿthe cities of the priests, in *their* ᵀset office, to give to their brethren by courses, as well to the great as to the small: Josh. 21:9 • *assigned*

16 Beside their genealogy of males, from three years old and upward, *even* unto every one that entereth into the house of the LORD, his daily portion for their service in their charges according to their courses;

17 Both to the genealogy of the priests by the house of their fathers, and the Levites ᴿfrom twenty years old and upward, in their charges by their courses;   1 Chr. 23:24

18 And to the genealogy of all their little ones, their wives, and their sons, and their daughters, through all the congregation: for in their set office they sanctified themselves in ᵀholiness: *solemn service to the Lord*

19 Also of the sons of Aaron the priests, which were in ᴿthe fields of the suburbs of their cities, in every several city, the men that were ᴿexpressed by name, to give portions to all the males among the priests, and to all that were reckoned by genealogies among the Levites.   Num. 35:2 • *vv.* 12–15

20 And thus did Hez-e-ki'-ah throughout all Judah, and ᴿwrought *that which was* good and right and ᵀtruth before the LORD his God.   2 Kin. 20:3; 22:2 • *faithful*

21 And in every work that he began in the service of the house of God, and in the law, and in the commandments, to seek his God, he did *it* with all his heart, and prospered.

CHAPTER 32

Invasion by Assyria
2 Kin. 18:17—19:37; Is. 36:2—37:38

AFTER ᴿthese things, and the establishment thereof, Sen-nach'-e-rib king of Assyria came, and entered into Judah, and encamped against the fenced cities, and thought to win them for himself.   Is. 36:1

2 And when Hez-e-ki'-ah saw that Sennach'-e-rib was come, and that he was purposed to fight against Jerusalem,

3 He took counsel with his princes and his mighty men to stop the waters of the fountains which *were* without the city: and they did help him.

4 So there was gathered much people together, who stopped all the fountains, and the brook that ran through the midst of the land, saying, Why should the kings of Assyria come, and find much water?

5 Also he strengthened himself, ᴿand built up all the wall that was broken, and raised *it* up to the towers, and another wall without, and repaired Mil'-lo *in* the city of David, and made darts and shields in abundance.   25:23

6 And he set captains of war over the people, and gathered them together to him in the street of the gate of the city, and spake comfortably to them, saying,

7 Be strong and courageous, be not afraid nor dismayed for the king of Assyria, nor for all the multitude that *is* with him: for *there be* more with us than with him:

8 With him *is* an ᴿarm of flesh; but ᴿwith us *is* the LORD our God to help us, and to fight our battles. And the people ᵀrested themselves upon the words of Hez-e-ki'-ah king of Judah.   [1 John 4:4] • [Rom. 8:31] • *trusted*

9 After this did Sen-nach'-e-rib king of Assyria send his servants to Jerusalem, (but he *himself laid siege* against La'-chish, and all his power with him,) unto Hez-e-ki'-ah king of Judah, and unto all Judah that *were* at Jerusalem, saying,

10 ᴿThus saith Sen-nach'-e-rib king of Assyria, Whereon do ye trust, that ye abide in the siege in Jerusalem?   2 Kin. 18:19

11 Doth not Hez-e-ki'-ah persuade you to give over yourselves to die by famine and by thirst, saying, ᴿThe LORD our God shall deliver us out of the hand of the king of Assyria?   2 Kin. 18:30

12 ᴿHath not the same Hez-e-ki'-ah taken away his ᵀhigh places and his altars, and commanded Judah and Jerusalem, saying, Ye shall worship before one altar, and burn incense upon it?   2 Kin. 18:22 • *shrines*

13 Know ye not what I and my fathers have done unto all the people of *other* lands? ᴿwere the gods of the nations of those lands any ways able to deliver their lands out of mine hand?   2 Kin. 18:33-35

14 ᴿWho *was there* among all the gods of those nations that my fathers utterly destroyed, that could deliver his people out of mine hand, that your God should be able to deliver you out of mine hand?   Is. 10:9

15 Now therefore ᴿlet not Hez-e-ki'-ah deceive you, nor persuade you on this manner, neither yet believe him: for no god of any nation or kingdom was able to deliver his people out of mine hand, and out of the hand of my fathers: how much less shall your God deliver you out of mine hand?   2 Kin. 18:29

16 And his servants spake yet *more* against the LORD God, and against his servant Hez-e-ki'-ah.

17 He wrote also letters to rail on the LORD God of Israel, and to speak against him, saying, As the gods of the nations of *other* lands have not delivered their people out of mine hand, so shall not the God of Hez-e-ki'-ah deliver his people out of mine hand.

18 ᴿThen they cried with a loud voice in the Jews' speech unto the people of Jerusalem that *were* on the wall, to affright them, and to ᵀtrouble them; that they might take the city.   2 Kin. 18:28 • *disturb*

19 And they spake against the God of Jerusalem, as against the gods of the people of the earth, *which were* ᴿthe work of the hands of ᴿman.   2 Kin. 19:18 • Ps. 96:5

20 And for this *cause* ᴿHez-e-ki'-ah the king, and the prophet Isaiah the son of Amoz, prayed and cried to heaven.   2 Kin. 16:20

21 ᴿAnd the LORD sent an angel, which cut off all the mighty men of valour, and the leaders and captains in the camp of the king of Assyria. So he returned with shame of face to his own land. And when he was come into the house of his god, they that came forth of his own bowels slew him there with the sword.   2 Kin. 19:35

22 Thus the LORD saved Hez-e-ki'-ah and the inhabitants of Jerusalem from the hand of Sen-nach'-e-rib the king of Assyria, and from the hand of all ᵀother, and guided them on every side.   *his enemies*

Restoration of Hezekiah
2 Kin. 20:1-11; Is. 38:1-8

23 And many brought gifts unto the LORD to Jerusalem, and presents to Hez-e-ki'-ah king of Judah: so that he was magnified in the sight of all nations from thenceforth.

24 In those days Hez-e-ki'-ah was sick to the death, and prayed unto the LORD: and he spake unto him, and he gave him a sign.

25 But Hez-e-ki'-ah rendered not again according to the benefit *done* unto him; ᵀfor his heart was lifted up: therefore there was wrath upon him, and upon Judah and Jerusalem.   *for he became proud*

26 Notwithstanding Hez-e-ki'-ah humbled himself for the pride of his heart, *both* he and

the inhabitants of Jerusalem, so that the wrath of the LORD came not upon them Rin the days of Hez-e-ki'-ah.　　2 Kin. 20:19

Wealth of Hezekiah

27 And Hez-e-ki'-ah had exceeding much riches and honour: and he made himself treasuries for silver, and for gold, and for precious stones, and for spices, and for shields, and for all manner of Tpleasant jewels;　　*costly vessels*
28 Storehouses also for the increase of corn, and wine, and oil; and stalls for all manner of beasts, and cotes for flocks.
29 Moreover he provided him cities, and possessions of flocks and herds in abundance: for RGod had given him Tsubstance very much.　　1 Chr. 29:12 • *property*
30 RThis same Hez-e-ki'-ah also stopped the upper watercourse of Gi'-hon, and brought it straight down to the west side of the city of David. And Hez-e-ki'-ah prospered in all his works.　　Is. 22:9, 11

Sin of Hezekiah—2 Kin. 20:12–19; Is. 39:1–8

31 Howbeit in *the business of* the ambassadors of the princes of Babylon, who sent unto him to enquire of the wonder that was *done* in the land, God left him, to try him, that he might know all *that* was in his heart.

Death of Hezekiah—2 Kin. 20:20, 21

32 Now the rest of the acts of Hez-e-ki'-ah, and his goodness, behold, they *are* written in the vision of Isaiah the prophet, the son of Amoz, *and* in the Rbook of the kings of Judah and Israel.　　2 Kin. 18, 19, 20
33 And Hez-e-ki'-ah slept with his fathers, and they buried him in the chiefest of the sepulchres of the sons of David: and all Judah and the inhabitants of Jerusalem did him honour at his death. And Ma-nas'-seh his son reigned in his stead.

CHAPTER 33

The Reign of Manasseh—2 Kin. 21:1–9, 17, 18

MA-NAS'-SEH *was* twelve years old when he began to reign, and he reigned fifty and five years in Jerusalem:
2 But did *that which was* evil in the sight of the LORD, like unto the abominationsT of the heathen, whom the LORD had cast out before the children of Israel.　　*evil doings*
3 For he built again the high places which Hez-e-ki'-ah his father had broken down, and he reared up altars for Ba'-al-im, and made groves, and worshipped all the host of heaven, and served them.
4 Also he built altars in the house of the LORD, whereof the LORD had said, In Jerusalem shall my name be for ever.

5 And he built altars for all the host of heaven Rin the two courts of the house of the LORD.　　4:9
6 And he caused his children to pass through the fire in the valley of the son of Hin'-nom: also he observed times, and used enchantments, and used witchcraft, and dealt with a familiar spirit, and with wizards: he wrought much evil in the sight of the LORD, to provoke him to anger.
7 And he set a carved image, the idol which he had made, in the Thouse of God, of which God had said to David and to Solomon his son, In this house, and in Jerusalem, which I have chosen before all the tribes of Israel, will I put my name for ever:　　*temple*
8 RNeither will I any more remove the foot of Israel from out of the land which I have appointed for your fathers; so that they will take heed to do all that I have commanded them, according to the whole law and the statutes and the ordinances by the hand of Moses.　　2 Sam. 7:10
9 So Ma-nas'-seh made Judah and the inhabitants of Jerusalem to err, *and* to do worse than the heathen, whom the LORD had destroyed before the children of Israel.
10 And the LORD spake to Ma-nas'-seh, and to his people: Rbut they would not Thearken.　　1 Kin. 11:9–11 • *obey*
11 Wherefore the LORD brought upon them the captains of the host of the king of Assyria, which took Ma-nas'-seh Tamong the thorns, and Rbound him with fetters, and carried him to Babylon.　　*in chains* • Job 36:8
12 And when he was Tin affliction, he besought the LORD his God, and Rhumbled himself greatly before the God of his fathers,　　*troubled* • 32:26; [1 Pet. 5:6]
13 And prayed unto him: and he was Rintreated of him, and heard his supplication, and brought him again to Jerusalem into his kingdom. Then Ma-nas'-seh Rknew that the LORD he *was* God.　　Ezra 8:23 • Dan. 4:25
14 Now after this he built a wall without the city of David, on the west side of Gi'-hon, in the valley, even to the entering in at the fish gate, and compassed about TO'-phel, and raised it up a very great height, and put captains of war in all the fenced cities of Judah.　　*the tower*
15 And he took away the strange gods, and the idol out of the house of the LORD, and all the altars that he had built in the mount of the house of the LORD, and in Jerusalem, and cast *them* out of the city.
16 And he repaired the altar of the LORD, and sacrificed thereon peace offerings and Rthank offerings, and commanded Judah to serve the LORD God of Israel.　　Lev. 7:12
17 RNevertheless the people did sacrifice still in Tthe high places, *yet* unto the LORD their God only.　　32:12 • *pagan shrines*

18 Now the rest of the acts of Ma-nas'-seh, and his prayer unto his God, and the words of the seers that spake to him in the name of the LORD God of Israel, behold, they *are written* in the book of the kings of Israel.

19 His prayer also, and *how God was* intreated of him, and all his sin, and his trespass, and the places wherein he built high places, and set up groves and graven images, before he was humbled: behold, they *are* written among the sayings of the seers.

20 So Ma-nas'-seh slept with his fathers, and they buried him in his own house: and Amon his son reigned in his stead.

The Reign of Amon—2 Kin. 21:19–26

21 RAmon *was* two and twenty years old when he began to reign, and reigned two years in Jerusalem.   2 Kin. 21:19; 1 Chr. 3:14

22 But he did *that which was* evil in the sight of the LORD, as did Ma-nas'-seh his father: for Amon sacrificed unto all the Tcarved images which Ma-nas'-seh his father had made, and served them;   *idols*

23 And humbled not himself before the LORD, Ras Ma-nas'-seh his father had humbled himself; but Amon Ttrespassed more and more.   *v. 12 • sinned*

24 And his servants Rconspired against him, and slew him in his own house.   24:25

25 But the people of the land slew all them that had conspired against king Amon; and the people of the land made Jo-si'-ah his son king in his stead.

CHAPTER 34

Evaluation of Josiah—2 Kin. 22:1, 2

JO-SI'-AH Rwas eight years old when he began to reign, and he reigned in Jerusalem one and thirty years.   2 Kin. 22:1

2 And he did *that which was* right in the sight of the LORD, and walked in the ways of David his father, and Tdeclined *neither* to the right hand, nor to the left.   *turned*

Early Reforms of Josiah

3 For in the eighth year of his reign, while he was yet young, he began to seek after the God of David his father: and in the twelfth year he began to purge Judah and Jerusalem from the high places, and the groves, and the carved images, and the molten images.

4 And they brake down the altars of Ba'-al-im in his presence; and the Timages, that *were* on high above them, he cut down; and the groves, and the carved images, and the molten images, he brake in pieces, and made dust *of them,* and strowed *it* upon the graves of them that had sacrificed unto them.   *idols*

5 And he Rburnt the bones of the priests

upon their Raltars, and cleansed Judah and Jerusalem.   1 Kin. 13:2 • 2 Kin. 23:20

6 And *so* Rdid he in the cities of Ma-nas'-seh, and E'-phra-im, and Simeon, even unto Naph'-ta-li, with their Tmattocks round about.   2 Kin. 23:15, 19 • *mauls*

7 And when he had broken down the altars and the groves, and had beaten the Tgraven images into powder, and cut down all the idols throughout all the land of Israel, he returned to Jerusalem.   *idols*

Repair of the Temple—2 Kin. 22:3–7

8 Now in the eighteenth year of his reign, when he had purged the land, and the house, he sent Sha'-phan the son of Az-a-li'-ah, and Ma-a-se'-iah the Rgovernor of the city, and Jo'-ah the son of Jo'-a-haz the recorder, to repair the house of the LORD his God.   18:25

9 And when they came to Hil-ki'-ah the high priest, they delivered Rthe money that was brought into the house of God, which the Levites that kept the doors had gathered of the hand of Ma-nas'-seh and E'-phra-im, and of all the remnant of Israel, and of all Judah and Benjamin; and they returned to Jerusalem.   2 Kin. 12:4

10 And they put *it* in the hand of the workmen that had the oversight of the house of the LORD, and they gave it to the workmen that wrought in the house of the LORD, to repair and amend the house:

11 Even to the artificers and builders gave they *it,* to buy hewn stone, and timber for couplings, and to floor the houses which the kings of Judah had destroyed.

12 And the men did the work faithfully: and the overseers of them *were* Ja'-hath and O-ba-di'-ah, the Levites, of the sons of Me-ra'-ri; and Zech-a-ri'-ah and Me-shul'-lam, of the sons of the Ko'-hath-ites, to set *it* forward; and *other of* the Levites, all that could skill of instruments of musick.

13 Also *they were* over Rthe bearers of burdens, and *were* overseers of all that wrought the work in any manner of service: Rand of the Levites *there were* scribes, and officers, and porters.   8:10 • 1 Chr. 23:4, 5

Discovery of the Law
2 Kin. 22:8—23:20

14 And when they brought out the money that was brought into the house of the LORD, RHil-ki'-ah the priest Rfound a book of the law of the LORD *given* by Moses.   *v. 9 • 2 Kin. 22:8*

15 And Hil-ki'-ah answered and said to Sha'-phan the scribe, I have found the book of the law in the house of the LORD. And Hil-ki'-ah delivered the book to Sha'-phan.

16 And Sha'-phan carried the book to the king, and brought the king word back again, saying, All that was committed to thy servants, they do *it*.

17 And they have gathered together the money that was found in the house of the LORD, and have delivered it into the hand of the overseers, and to the hand of the workmen.

18 Then Sha′-phan the scribe told the king, saying, Hil-ki′-ah the priest hath given me a book. And Sha′-phan read it before the king.

19 And it came to pass, when the king had Rheard the words of the law, Rthat he Trent his clothes.   Neh. 8:9 • Josh. 7:6 • *tore*

20 And the king commanded Hil-ki′-ah, and RA-hi′-kam the son of Sha′-phan, and TAb′-donR the son of Mi′-cah, and Sha′-phan the scribe, and A-sa′-iah a servant of the king's, saying,   Jer. 26:24 • *Achbor* • 2 Kin. 22:12

21 Go, enquire of the LORD for me, and for them that are left in Israel and in Judah, concerning the words of the book that is found: for great is the wrath of the LORD that is poured out upon us, because our fathers have not kept the word of the LORD, to do after all that is written in this book.

22 And Hil-ki′-ah, and *they* that the king *had appointed,* went to Hul′-dah the prophetess, the wife of Shal′-lum the son of RTik′-vath, the son of THas′-rah, keeper of the wardrobe; (now she dwelt in Jerusalem in the college:) and they spake to her to that *effect.*   2 Kin. 22:14 • *Harhas*

23 And she answered them, Thus saith the LORD God of Israel, Tell ye the man that sent you to me,

24 Thus saith the LORD, Behold, I will bring evil upon this place, and upon the inhabitants thereof, *even* all the curses that are written in the book which they have read before the king of Judah:

25 Because they have forsaken me, and have Tburned incense unto other gods, that they might provoke me to anger with all the works of their hands; therefore my wrath shall be poured out upon this place, and shall not be quenched.   *worshipped*

26 And as for the king of Judah, who sent you to enquire of the LORD, so shall ye say unto him, Thus saith the LORD God of Israel *concerning* the words which thou hast heard;

27 Because thine heart was tender, and thou didst humble thyself before God, when thou heardest his words against this place, and against the inhabitants thereof, and humbledst thyself before me, and didst rend thy clothes, and weep before me; I have even heard *thee* also, saith the LORD.

28 RBehold, I will gather thee to thy fathers, and thou shalt be gathered to thy grave in peace, neither shall thine eyes see all the evil that I will bring upon this place, and upon the inhabitants of the same. So they brought the king word again.   Num. 23:10

29 Then the king sent and gathered together all the elders of Judah and Jerusalem.

30 And the king went up into the house of the LORD, and all the men of Judah, and the inhabitants of Jerusalem, and the priests, and the Levites, and all the people, great and small: and he read in their ears all the words of the book of the covenant that was found in the house of the LORD.

31 And the king stood in his place, and made a covenant before the LORD, to walk after the LORD, and to keep his commandments, and his testimonies, and his statutes, with all his heart, and Twith all his soul, to perform the words of the covenant which are written in this book.   *earnestly*

32 And he caused all that were present in Jerusalem and Benjamin to Tstand *to it.* RAnd the inhabitants of Jerusalem did according to the covenant of God, the God of their fathers.   *subscribe to it* • Ex. 19:5

33 And Jo-si′-ah took away all the Rabominations out of all the countries that *pertained* to the children of Israel, and made all that were present in Israel to serve, *even* to serve the LORD their God. RAnd all his days they departed not from following the LORD, the God of their fathers.   *vv.* 3–7; 1 Kin. 11:5 • Jer. 3:10

CHAPTER 35

Celebration of the Passover—2 Kin. 23:21–23

MOREOVER RJo-si′-ah kept a passover unto the LORD in Jerusalem: and they killed the passover on the Rfourteenth *day* of the first month.   2 Kin. 23:21, 22 • Ezra 6:19

2 And he set the priests in their Tcharges, and encouraged them to the service of the house of the LORD,   *tasks*

3 And said unto the Levites that taught all Israel, which were holy unto the LORD, Put the holy ark in the house which Solomon the son of David king of Israel did build; *it shall* not *be* a Tburden upon *your* shoulders: serve now the LORD your God, and his people Israel,   *responsibility*

4 And prepare *yourselves* by the houses of your fathers, after your courses, according to the writing of David king of Israel, and according to the writing of Solomon his son.

5 And stand in the holy *place* according to the divisions of the families of the fathers of your brethren the people, and *after* the division of the families of the Levites.

6 So Rkill the passover, and Rsanctify yourselves, and prepare your brethren, that *they* may do according to the word of the LORD by the hand of Moses.   *v.* 1 • 29:5

7 And Jo-si′-ah Rgave to the people, of the flock, lambs and kids, all for the passover offerings, for all that were present, to the number of thirty thousand, and three

thousand ᵀbullocks: these *were* of the king's ᵀsubstance.   30:24 · *bulls · property*

8 And his ᴿprinces gave willingly unto the people, to the priests, and to the Levites: Hil-ki'-ah and Zech-a-ri'-ah and Je-hi'-el, rulers of the house of God, ᴿgave unto the priests for the passover offerings two thousand and six hundred ᵀ*small cattle*, and three hundred oxen.   Num. 7:2 · 31:13 · *sheep*

9 ᴿCon-a-ni'-ah also, and She-ma'-iah and Ne-than'-e-el, his brethren, and Hash-a-bi'-ah and Je-i'-el and Joz'-a-bad, chief of the Levites, gave unto the Levites for passover offerings five thousand *small cattle*, and five hundred oxen.   31:12

10 So the service was prepared, and the priests ᴿstood in their place, and the Levites in their ᵀcourses, according to the king's commandment.   Ezra 6:18 · *assigned tasks*

11 And they killed the passover, and the priests sprinkled *the blood* from their hands, and the Levites ᵀflayed *them*.   *skinned*

12 And they removed the burnt offerings, that they might give according to the divisions of the families of the people, to offer unto the Lord, as *it is* written ᴿin the book of Moses. And so *did they* with the oxen. Lev. 3:3

13 And they roasted the passover with fire according to the ᵀordinance: but the *other* holy *offerings* sodᵀ they in pots, and in caldrons, and in pans, and divided *them* speedily among all the people.   *law · cooked*

14 And afterward they made ready for themselves, and for the priests: because the priests the sons of Aaron *were busied* in offering of burnt offerings and the fat until night; therefore the Levites prepared for themselves, and for the priests the sons of Aaron.

15 And the singers the sons of A'-saph *were* in their place, according to the commandment of David, and A'-saph, and He'-man, and Je-du'-thun the king's seer; and the porters *waited* at every gate; they might not depart from their service; for their brethren the Levites prepared for them.

16 So all the service of the Lord was prepared the same day, to keep the passover, and to offer burnt offerings upon the altar of the Lord, according to the commandment of king Jo-si'-ah.

17 And the children of Israel that were present kept the passover at that time, and the feast of unleavened bread seven days.

18 ᴿAnd there was no passover like to that kept in Israel from the days of Samuel the prophet; neither did all the kings of Israel keep such a passover as Jo-si'-ah kept, and the priests, and the Levites, and all Judah and Israel that were present, and the inhabitants of Jerusalem.   2 Kin. 23:21, 22

19 In the eighteenth year of the reign of Jo-si'-ah was this passover kept.

Death of Josiah—2 Kin. 23:28–30

20 After all this, when Jo-si'-ah had prepared the temple, Ne'-cho king of Egypt came up to fight against Char'-che-mish by Eu-phra'-tes: and Jo-si'-ah went out against him.

21 ᴿBut he sent ambassadors to him, saying, What have I to do with thee, thou king of Judah? *I come* not against thee this day, but against the house wherewith I have war: for God commanded me to make haste: forbear thee from *meddling with* God, who *is* with me, that he destroy thee not.   25:19

22 Nevertheless Jo-si'-ah would not turn his face from him, but ᴿdisguised himself, that he might fight with him, and hearkened not unto the words of Ne'-cho from the mouth of God, and came to fight in the valley of ᴿMe-gid'-do.   1 Kin. 22:30 · Judg. 5:19

23 And the archers shot at king Jo-si'-ah; and the king said to his servants, Have me away; for I am ᵀsore wounded.   *badly*

24 His servants therefore took him out of that chariot, and put him in the second chariot that he had; and they brought him to Jerusalem, and he died, and was buried in *one of* the sepulchres of his fathers. And all Judah and Jerusalem mourned for Jo-si'-ah.

25 And Jer-e-mi'-ah lamented for Jo-si'-ah: and all the singing men and the singing women spake of Jo-si'-ah in their lamentations to this day, ᴿand made them an ordinance in Israel: and, behold, they *are* written in the lamentations.   Jer. 22:20

26 Now the rest of the acts of Jo-si'-ah, and his goodness, according to *that which was* written in the law of the Lord,

27 And his deeds, first and last, behold, they *are* written in the book of the kings of Israel and Judah.

CHAPTER 36

The Reign of Jehoahaz—2 Kin. 23:30–33

THEN the people of the land took Je-ho'-a-haz the son of Jo-si'-ah, and made him king in his father's stead in Jerusalem.

2 Je-ho'-a-haz *was* twenty and three years old when he began to reign, and he reigned three months in Jerusalem.

3 And the king of Egypt ᵀput him down at Jerusalem, and ᵀcondemned the land in an ᵀhundred talents of silver and a ᵀtalent of gold.   *subdued him · assessed · $38,400,000 · $5,760,000*

The Reign of Jehoiakim
2 Kin. 23:24—24:6

4 And the king of Egypt made E-li'-a-kim his brother king over Judah and Jerusalem, and turned his name to Je-hoi'-a-kim. And

Ne'-cho took Je-ho'-a-haz his brother, and carried him to Egypt.

5 ᴿJe-hoi'-a-kim was twenty and five years old when he began to reign, and he reigned eleven years in Jerusalem: and he did that which was ᴿevil in the sight of the LORD his God.   2 Kin. 23:36, 37 • Jer. 22:13-19

6 Against him came up Neb-u-chad-nez'-zar king of Babylon, and bound him in fetters, to carry him to Babylon.

7 Neb-u-chad-nez'-zar also carried of the vessels of the house of the LORD to Babylon, and put them in his temple at Babylon.

8 Now the rest of the acts of Je-hoi'-a-kim, and his abominations which he did, and that which was found in him, behold, they are written in the book of the kings of Israel and Judah: and ᴿJe-hoi'-a-chin his son reigned in his stead.   1 Chr. 3:16

The Reign of Jehoiachin
2 Kin. 24:8-17; Jer. 37:1

9 Je-hoi'-a-chin was eight years old when he began to reign, and he reigned three months and ten days in Jerusalem: and he did that which was evil in the sight of the LORD.

10 And when the year was expired, king Neb-u-chad-nez'-zar sent, and brought him to Babylon, with the goodly vessels of the house of the LORD, and made Zed-e-ki'-ah his brother king over Judah and Jerusalem.

Evaluation of Zedekiah
2 Kin. 24:18, 19; Jer. 52:1, 2

11 ᴿZed-e-ki'-ah was one and twenty years old when he began to reign, and reigned eleven years in Jerusalem.   Jer. 52:1

12 And he did that which was evil in the sight of the LORD his God, and humbled not himself before Jer-e-mi'-ah the prophet speaking from the mouth of the LORD.

Destruction of Jerusalem
2 Kin. 24:20—25:21; Jer. 52:3-27

13 And ᴿhe also rebelled against king Neb-u-chad-nez'-zar, who had made him swear by God: but he stiffened his neck, and hardened his heart from turning unto the LORD God of Israel.   Jer. 52:3

14 Moreover all the chief of the priests, and the people, transgressed very much after all the ᵀabominations of the heathen; and

polluted the house of the LORD which he had hallowed in Jerusalem.   evil deeds

15 And the LORD God of their fathers sent to them by his messengers, rising up betimes, and sending; because he had compassion on his people, and on his dwelling place:

16 But they mocked the messengers of God, and ᵀdespised his words, and ᴿmisused his prophets, until the ᴿwrath of the LORD arose against his people, till there was no ᵀremedy.   scoffed at • Matt. 23:34 • Ps. 79:5 • healing

17 ᴿTherefore he brought upon them the king of the Chal'-dees, who ᴿslew their young men with the sword in the house of their sanctuary, and had no compassion upon young man or maiden, old man, or him that stooped for age: he gave them all into his hand.   2 Kin. 25:1; Ezra 9:7 • Ps. 74:20

18 ᴿAnd all the vessels of the house of God, great and small, and the treasures of the house of the LORD, and the treasures of the king, and of his princes; all these he brought to Babylon.   vv. 7, 10; 2 Kin. 25:13

19 And they burnt the house of God, and brake down the wall of Jerusalem, and burnt all the palaces thereof with fire, and destroyed all the ᵀgoodly vessels thereof. precious

20 And them that had escaped from the sword carried he away to Babylon; where they were servants to him and his sons until the reign of the kingdom of Persia:

21 To fulfil the word of the LORD by the mouth of Jer-e-mi'-ah, until the land ᴿhad enjoyed her sabbaths: for as long as she lay desolate ᴿshe kept sabbath, to fulfil threescore and ten years.   Dan. 9:2 • Lev. 25:4, 5

The Proclamation by Cyrus
to Return to Jerusalem—Ezra 1:1-3

22 Now in the first year of Cyrus king of Persia, that the word of the LORD spoken by the mouth of Jer-e-mi'-ah might be accomplished, the LORD ᵀstirred up the spirit of Cyrus king of Persia, that he made a proclamation throughout all his kingdom, and put it also in writing, saying,   inspired

23 Thus saith Cyrus king of Persia, All the kingdoms of the earth hath the LORD God of heaven given me; and he hath charged me to build him an house in Jerusalem, which is in Judah. Who is there among you of all his people? The LORD his God be with him, and let him go up.

THE BOOK OF

EZRA

THE BOOK OF EZRA

Ezra continues the Old Testament narrative of Second Chronicles by showing how God fulfills His promise to return His people to the land of promise after seventy years of exile. Israel's "second Exodus," this one from Babylon, is less impressive than the return from Egypt because only a remnant chooses to leave Babylon.

Ezra relates the story of two returns from Babylon—the first led by Zerubbabel to rebuild the temple (1—6), and the second under the leadership of Ezra to rebuild the spiritual condition of the people (7—10). Sandwiched between these two accounts is a gap of nearly six decades, during which Esther lives and rules as queen in Persia.

Ezra is the Aramaic form of the Hebrew word *ezer*, "help," and perhaps means "Yahweh helps." Ezra and Nehemiah were originally bound together as one book because Chronicles, Ezra, and Nehemiah were viewed as one continuous history. The Septuagint, a Greek-language version of the Old Testament translated in the third century B.C., calls Ezra-Nehemiah, *Esdras Deuteron*, "Second Esdras." First Esdras is the name of the apocryphal Book of Esdras. The Latin title is *Liber Primus Esdrae*, "First Book of Ezra." In the Latin Bible, Ezra is called First Ezra and Nehemiah is called Second Ezra.

THE AUTHOR OF EZRA

Although Ezra is not specifically mentioned as the author, he is certainly the best candidate. Jewish tradition (the Talmud) attributes the book to Ezra, and portions of the book (7:28—9:15) are written in the first person, from Ezra's point of view. The vividness of the details and descriptions favors an author who was an eyewitness of the later events of the book. As in Chronicles, there is a strong priestly emphasis, and Ezra was a direct priestly descendant of Aaron through Eleazar, Phineas, and Zadok (7:1–5). He studied, practiced, and taught the Law of the Lord as an educated scribe (7:1–12). Also according to Second Maccabees 2:13–15, he had access to the library of written documents gathered by Nehemiah. Ezra no doubt used this material in writing Ezra 1—6 as he did in writing Chronicles. Some think that Ezra composed Nehemiah as well by making use of Nehemiah's personal diary.

Ezra was a godly man marked by strong trust in the Lord, moral integrity, and grief over sin. He was a contemporary of Nehemiah (Neh. 8:1–9; 12:36) who arrived in Jerusalem in 444 B.C.

Tradition holds that Ezra was the founder of the Great Synagogue where the canon of Old Testament Scripture was settled. Another tradition says that he collected the biblical books into a unit and that he originated the synagogue form of worship.

Ezra wrote this book probably between 457 B.C. (the events of Ezra 7—10) and 444 B.C. (Nehemiah's arrival in Jerusalem). During the period covered by the Book of Ezra, Gautama Buddha (c. 560–480 B.C.) is in India, Confucius (551–479 B.C.) is in China, and Socrates (470–399 B.C.) is in Greece.

THE TIME OF EZRA

The following table shows the chronological relationship of the books of Ezra, Nehemiah, and Esther:

538–515 B.C.	483–473 B.C.
Zerubbabel	Esther
Ezra 1—6	Book of Esther
First Return	–

457 B.C.	444–c. 425 B.C.
Ezra	Nehemiah
Ezra 7—10	Book of Nehemiah
Second Return	Third Return

These books fit against the background of these Persian kings:

Cyrus	(559–530 B.C.)
Cambyses	(530–522 B.C.)
Smerdis	(522 B.C.)
Darius I	(521–486 B.C.)
Ahasuerus	(486–464 B.C.)
Artaxerxes I	(464–423 B.C.)
Darius II	(423–404 B.C.)

Cyrus the Persian overthrows Babylon in October 539 B.C. and issues his decree allowing the Jews to return in 538 B.C. The temple is begun in 536 B.C. The exile lasts only fifty years after 586 B.C., but the seventy-year figure for the captivity is taken from a beginning date of 606 B.C. when the first deportation to Babylon takes place. The rebuilding of the temple is discontinued in 534 B.C., resumed in 520 B.C., and completed in 515 B.C. It is begun under Cyrus and finished under Darius I. The two intervening kings, Cambyses and Smerdis, are not mentioned in any of these books. The prophets Haggai and Zechariah minister during Zerubbabel's time, about 520 B.C.

and following years. Esther's story fits entirely in the reign of Xerxes, and Ezra ministers during the reign of Artaxerxes I, as does Nehemiah. There were three waves of deportation to Babylon (606, 597, and 586 B.C.) and three returns from Babylon: 538 B.C. (Zerubbabel), 457 B.C. (Ezra), and 444 B.C. (Nehemiah).

✝ THE CHRIST OF EZRA

Ezra reveals God's continued fulfillment of His promise to keep David's descendants alive. Zerubbabel himself is part of the messianic line as the grandson of Jeconiah (Jehoiachin, 1 Chr. 3:17-19; see Matt. 1:12, 13). There is a positive note of hope in Ezra and Nehemiah because the remnant has returned to the land of promise. In this land the messianic promises will be fulfilled, because they are connected with such places as Beth-lehem, Jerusalem, and Zion. Christ will be born in Bethlehem (Mic. 5:2), not in Babylon.

The Book of Ezra as a whole also typifies Christ's work of forgiveness and restoration.

🔑 KEYS TO EZRA

Key Word: Temple—The basic theme of Ezra is the restoration of the temple and the spiritual, moral, and social restoration of the returned remnant in Jerusalem under the leadership of Zerubbabel and Ezra. Israel's worship is revitalized and the people are purified. God's faithfulness is seen in the way He sovereignly protects His people through a powerful empire while they are in captivity. They prosper in their exile, and God raises up pagan kings who are sympathetic to their cause and encourage them to rebuild their homeland. God also provides zealous and capable spiritual leaders who direct the return and the rebuilding. He keeps His promise: "And I will be found of you, saith the LORD: and I will turn away your captivity, and I will gather you from all the nations, and from all the places whither I have driven you, saith the LORD; and I will bring you again into the place whence I caused you to be carried away captive" (Jer. 29:14).

Key Verses: Ezra 1:3; 7:10—"Who *is there* among you of all his people? his God be with him, and let him go up to Jerusalem, which *is* in Judah, and build the house of the LORD God of Israel, (he *is* the God,) which *is* in Jerusalem" (1:3).

"For Ezra had prepared his heart to seek the law of the LORD, and to do *it*, and to teach in Israel statutes and judgments" (7:10).

Key Chapter: Ezra 6—Ezra 6 records the completion and dedication of the temple which stimulates the obedience of the remnant to keep the Passover and separate themselves from the "filthiness of the heathen of the land" (6:21).

🅰 SURVEY OF EZRA

Ezra continues the story exactly where Second Chronicles ends and shows how God's promise to bring His people back to their land is fulfilled (Jer. 29:10-14). God is with these people; and although their days of glory seem over, their spiritual heritage still remains and God's rich promises will be fulfilled. Ezra relates the story of the first two returns from Babylon, the first led by Zerubbabel and the second led decades later by Ezra. Its two divisions are the restoration of the temple (1—6) and the reformation of the people (7—10), and they are separated by a fifty-eight year gap during which the story of Esther takes place.

The Restoration of the Temple (1—6): King Cyrus of Persia overthrows Babylon in 539 B.C. and issues a decree in 538 B.C. that allows the exiled Jews to return to their homeland. Isaiah prophesied two centuries before that the temple would be rebuilt and actually named Cyrus as the one who would bring it about (Is. 44:28—45:4). Cyrus may have read and responded to this passage.

FOCUS	RESTORATION OF THE TEMPLE		REFORMATION OF THE PEOPLE	
REFERENCE	1:1————————3:1————		——7:1————————9:1————10:44	
DIVISION	FIRST RETURN TO JERUSALEM	CONSTRUCTION OF THE TEMPLE	SECOND RETURN TO JERUSALEM	RESTORATION OF THE PEOPLE
TOPIC	ZERUBBABEL		EZRA	
	FIRST RETURN OF 49,897		SECOND RETURN OF 1,754	
LOCATION	PERSIA TO JERUSALEM		PERSIA TO JERUSALEM	
TIME	22 YEARS (538—516 B.C.)		1 YEAR (458—457 B.C.)	

Out of a total Jewish population of perhaps 2 or 3 million, only 49,897 choose to take advantage of this offer. Only the most committed are willing to leave a life of relative comfort in Babylon, endure a trek of nine hundred miles, and face further hardship by rebuilding a destroyed temple and city. Zerubbabel, a "prince" of Judah (a direct descendant of king David), leads the faithful remnant back to Jerusalem. Those who return are from the tribes of Judah, Benjamin, and Levi; but it is evident that representatives from the other ten tribes eventually return as well. The ten "lost tribes" are not entirely lost.

Zerubbabel's priorities are in the right place: he first restores the altar and the religious feasts before beginning work on the temple itself. The foundation of the temple is laid in 536 B.C., but opposition arises and the work ceases from 534 to 520 B.C. While Ezra 4:1-5, 24 concerns Zerubbabel, 4:6-23 concerns opposition to the building of the wall of Jerusalem some time between 464 and 444 B.C. These verses may have been placed here to illustrate the antagonism to the work of rebuilding. The prophets Haggai and Zechariah exhort the people to get back to building the temple (5:1, 2), and the work begins again under Zerubbabel and Joshua the high priest. Tatnai, a Persian governor, protests to King Darius I about

the temple building and challenges their authority to continue. King Darius finds the decree of Cyrus and confirms it, even forcing Tatnai to provide whatever is needed to complete the work. It is finished in 515 B.C.

The Reformation of the People (7—10): A smaller return under Ezra takes place in 457 B.C., eighty-one years after the first return under Zerubbabel. Ezra the priest is given authority by King Artaxerxes I to bring people and contributions for the temple in Jerusalem. God protects this band of less than two thousand men and they safely reach Jerusalem with their valuable gifts from Persia. Many priests but few Levites return with Zerubbabel and Ezra (2:36-42; 8:15-19). God uses Ezra to rebuild the people spiritually and morally. When Ezra discovers that the people and the priests have intermarried with foreign women, he identifies with the sin of his people and offers a great intercessory prayer on their behalf. During the gap of fifty-eight years between Ezra 6 and 7, the people fall into a confused spiritual state and Ezra is alarmed. They quickly respond to Ezra's confession and weeping by making a covenant to put away their foreign wives and to live in accordance with God's law. This confession and response to the Word of God brings about a great revival and changes lives.

OUTLINE OF EZRA

Part One: The Restoration of the Temple of God (1:1—6:22)

Part Two: The Reformation of the People of God (7:1—10:44)

CHAPTER 1

Decree of Cyrus—2 Chr. 36:22, 23

NOW in the first year of Cyrus king of Persia, that the word of the LORD by the mouth of Jer-e-mi'-ah might be fulfilled, the LORD ᵀstirred up the spirit of Cyrus king of Persia, ᴿthat he made a proclamation throughout all his kingdom, and put it also in writing, saying,   *inspired* · 5:13, 14

2 Thus saith Cyrus king of Persia, The LORD God of heaven hath given me all the kingdoms of the earth; and he hath ᴿcharged me to build him an house at Jerusalem, which is in Judah.   Is. 44:28; 45:1, 13

3 Who is there among you of all his people? his God be with him, and let him go up to Jerusalem, which is in Judah, and build the house of the LORD God of Israel, (he is the God,) which is in Jerusalem.

4 And whosoever remaineth in any place where he sojourneth, let the men ᵀof his place help him with silver, and with gold, and with goods, and with beasts, beside the ᴿfree-will offering for the house of God that is in Jerusalem.   *of his community* · Num. 15:3

Gifts from Israel and Cyrus

5 Then rose up the chief of the fathers of Judah and Benjamin, and the priests, and the Levites, with all them whose spirit God had raised, to go up to build the house of the LORD which is in Jerusalem.

6 And all they that were about them ᵀstrengthened their hands with vessels of silver, with gold, with goods, and with beasts, and with precious things, beside all that was willingly offered.   *increased their power*

7 Also Cyrus the king ᴿbrought forth the vessels of the house of the LORD, ᴿwhich Neb-u-chad-nez'-zar had brought forth out of Jerusalem, and had put them in the ᵀhouse of his gods;   2 Kin. 24:13 · 2 Chr. 36:7 · *temple*

8 Even those did Cyrus king of Persia bring forth by the hand of Mith'-re-dath the treasurer, and ᵀnumbered them unto Shesh-baz'-zar, the prince of Judah.   *assigned*

9 And this is the number of them: thirty ᵀchargers of gold, a thousand chargers of silver, nine and twenty knives,   *chests*

10 Thirty ᴿbasons of gold, silver basons of a second sort four hundred and ten, and other vessels a thousand.   1 Kin. 7:50

11 All the vessels of gold and of silver were five thousand and four hundred. All these did Shesh-baz'-zar bring up with them of the captivity that were brought up from Babylon unto Jerusalem.

CHAPTER 2

The Leaders

NOW ᴿthese are the children of the province that went up out of the captivity, of those which had been carried away, whom Neb-u-chad-nez'-zar the king of Babylon had carried away unto Babylon, and came again unto Jerusalem and Judah, every one unto his city;   Neh. 7:6

2 Which came with Ze-rub'-ba-bel: Jesh'-u-a, Ne-he-mi'-ah, Se-ra'-iah, ᵀRe-el-a'-iah, Mor'-de-cai, Bil'-shan, Miz'-par, Big'-vai, Re'-hum, Ba'-a-nah. The number of the men of the people of Israel: *Raamiah*

The People

3 The children of Pa'-rosh, two thousand an hundred seventy and two.

4 The children of Sheph-a-ti'-ah, three hundred seventy and two.

5 The children of A'-rah, ᴿseven hundred seventy and five.   Neh. 7:10

6 The children of ᴿPa'-hath–mo'-ab, of the children of Jesh'-u-a and Jo'-ab, two thousand eight hundred and twelve.   Neh. 7:11

7 The children of E'-lam, a thousand two hundred fifty and four.

8 The children of Zat'-tu, nine hundred forty and five.

9 The children of Zac'-cai, seven hundred and threescore.

10 The children of [T]Ba'-ni,[R] six hundred forty and two.   Binnui • Neh. 7:15

11 The children of Be'-bai, six hundred twenty and three.

12 The children of Az'-gad, a thousand two hundred twenty and two.

13 The children of A-don'-i-kam, six hundred sixty and six.

14 The children of Big'-vai, two thousand fifty and six.

15 The children of A'-din, four hundred fifty and four.

16 The children of A'-ter of Hez-e-ki'-ah, ninety and eight.

17 The children of Be'-zai, three hundred twenty and three.

18 The children of [T]Jo'-rah,[R] an hundred and twelve.   Hariph • Neh. 7:24

19 The children of Ha'-shum, two hundred twenty and three.

20 The children of [T]Gib'-bar,[R] ninety and five.   Gib'-e-on • Neh. 7:25

21 The children of [R]Beth'-le-hem, an hundred twenty and three.   Gen. 48:7

22 The men of Ne-to'-phah, fifty and six.

23 The men of An'-a-thoth, an hundred twenty and eight.

24 The children of [T]Az'-ma-veth,[R] forty and two.   Bethazmaveth • Neh. 7:28

25 The children of [R]Kir'-jath-a'-rim, Che-phi'-rah, and Be-e'-roth, seven hundred and forty and three.   Neh. 7:29

26 The children of [R]Ra'-mah and Ga'-ba, six hundred twenty and one.   Josh. 18:25

27 The men of Mich'-mas, an hundred twenty and two.

28 The men of [R]Beth'-el and [R]A'-i, two hundred twenty and three.   Gen. 28:19 • Gen. 12:8

29 The children of Ne'-bo, fifty and two.

30 The children of Mag'-bish, an hundred fifty and six.

31 The children of the other E'-lam, a thousand two hundred fifty and four.

32 The children of Ha'-rim, three hundred and twenty.

33 The children of Lod, Ha'-did, and O'-no, seven hundred twenty and five.

34 The children of [R]Jericho, three hundred forty and five.   Num. 22:1

35 The children of Se-na'-ah, three thousand and six hundred and thirty.

The Priests

36 The priests: the children of [R]Je-da'-iah, of the house of Jesh'-u-a, nine hundred seventy and three.   1 Chr. 24:7

37 The children of [R]Im'-mer, a thousand fifty and two.   1 Chr. 24:14

38 The children of [R]Pash'-ur, a thousand two hundred forty and seven.   1 Chr. 9:12

39 The children of [R]Ha'-rim, a thousand and seventeen.   1 Chr. 24:8

The Levites

40 The Levites: the children of [R]Jesh'-u-a and Kad'-mi-el, of the children of [T]Hod-a-vi'-ah, seventy and four.   3:9 • Judah

41 The singers: the children of [R]A'-saph, an hundred twenty and eight.   1 Chr. 15:17

42 The children of the porters: the children of Shal'-lum, the children of A'-ter, the children of Tal'-mon, the children of Ak'-kub, the children of Hat'-i-ta, the children of Sho'-bai, in all an hundred thirty and nine.

The Servants

43 [R]The Neth'-i-nims: the children of Zi'-ha, the children of Ha-su'-pha, the children of Tab'-ba-oth,   7:7; 1 Chr. 9:2

44 The children of Ke'-ros, the children of [T]Si'-a-ha, the children of Pa'-don,   Sia

45 The children of Leb'-a-nah, the children of Hag'-a-bah, the children of Ak'-kub,

46 The children of Ha'-gab, the children of Shal'-mai, the children of Ha'-nan,

47 The children of Gid'-del, the children of Ga'-har, the children of Re-a'-iah,

48 The children of Re'-zin, the children of Ne-ko'-da, the children of Gaz'-zam,

49 The children of Uz'-za, the children of Pa-se'-ah, the children of Be'-sai,

50 The children of As'-nah, the children of Me-hu'-nim, the children of Ne-phu'-sim,

51 The children of Bak'-buk, the children of Ha-ku'-pha, the children of Har'-hur,

52 The children of Baz'-luth, the children of Me-hi'-da, the children of Har'-sha,

53 The children of Bar'-kos, the children of Sis'-e-ra, the children of Tha'-mah,

54 The children of Ne-zi'-ah, the children of Hat'-i-pha.

55 The children of Solomon's servants: the children of So'-tai, the children of Soph'-e-reth, the children of Pe-ru'-da,

56 The children of Ja-a'-lah, the children of Dar'-kon, the children of Gid'-del,

57 The children of Sheph-a-ti'-ah, the children of Hat'-til, the children of Poch'-e-reth of Ze-ba'-im, the children of A'-mi.

58 All the [R]Neth'-i-nims, and the children of [R]Solomon's servants, were three hundred ninety and two.   Josh. 9:21, 27; 1 Chr. 9:2 • 1 Kin. 9:21

The People

59 And these were they which went up from Tel-me'-lah, Tel-har'-sa, Cherub, Ad'-dan, and Im'-mer: but they could not shew

their father's house, and their ᵀseed, whether they *were* of Israel: *pedigree*

60 The children of De-la'-iah, the children of To-bi'-ah, the children of Ne-ko'-da, six hundred fifty and two.

The Priests

61 And of the children of the priests: the children of Ha-ba'-iah, the children of Koz, the children of Bar-zil'-lai; which took a wife of the daughters of Bar-zil'-lai the Gil'-e-ad-ite, and was called after their name:

62 These sought their register *among* those that were reckoned by genealogy, but they were not found: ᴿtherefore were they, as polluted, put from the priesthood.   Num. 3:10

63 And the ᵀTir-sha'-tha said unto them, that they should not eat of the most holy things, till there stood up a priest with U'-rim and with Thum'-mim.   *governor*

The People Who Returned

64 ᴿThe whole congregation together *was* forty and two thousand three hundred *and* threescore,   Neh. 7:66; Is. 10:22

65 Beside their servants and their maids, of whom *there were* seven thousand three hundred thirty and seven: and *there were* among them two hundred ᴿsinging men and singing women.   2 Chr. 35:25; Neh. 12:42

66 Their horses *were* seven hundred thirty and six; their mules, two hundred forty and five;

67 Their camels, four hundred thirty and five; *their* asses, six thousand seven hundred and twenty.

The Gifts the People Gave

68 And *some* of the chief of the fathers, when they came to the house of the LORD which *is* at Jerusalem, offered freely for the house of God to set it up in his place:

69 They gave after their ability unto the ᴿtreasure of the work threescore and ᵀone thousand drams of gold, and ᵀfive thousand pound of silver, and one hundred priests' garments.   1 Chr. 26:20 · $86,985,495 · $32,000,000

70 So the priests, and the Levites, and *some* of the people, and the singers, and the porters, and the Neth'-i-nims, dwelt in their cities, and all Israel in their cities.

CHAPTER 3

Spiritual Preparation of the People

AND when the seventh month was come, and the children of Israel *were* in the cities, the people gathered themselves together ᵀas one man to Jerusalem.   *in unity*

2 Then stood up ᵀJesh'-u-a ᴿthe son of Joz'-a-dak, and his brethren the priests, and Ze-rub'-ba-bel the son of She-al'-ti-el, and his brethren, and builded the altar of the God of Israel, to offer burnt offerings thereon, as *it is* written in the law of Moses the man of God.   Joshua · Hag. 1:1; 2:2

3 And they set the altar upon his bases; for fear *was* upon them because of the people of those countries: and they offered burnt offerings thereon unto the LORD, *even* burnt offerings morning and evening.

4 They kept also the feast of tabernacles, as *it is* written, and *offered* the daily burnt offerings by number, according to the custom, as the duty of every day required;

5 And afterward *offered* the continual burnt offering, both of the new moons, and of all the set feasts of the LORD that were consecrated, and of every one that willingly offered a freewill offering unto the LORD.

6 From the first day of the seventh month began they to offer burnt offerings unto the LORD. But the foundation of the temple of the LORD was not *yet* laid.

Completion of the Temple Foundation

7 They gave money also unto the masons, and to the carpenters; and meat, and drink, and oil, unto them of Zi'-don, and to them of Tyre, to bring cedar trees from Leb'-a-non to the sea of Jop'-pa, according to the grant that they had of Cyrus king of Persia.

8 Now in the second year of their coming unto the house of God at Jerusalem, in the second month, began Ze-rub'-ba-bel the son of She-al'-ti-el, and Jesh'-u-a the son of Joz'-a-dak, and the remnant of their brethren the priests and the Levites, and all they that were come out of the captivity unto Jerusalem; and appointed the Levites, from twenty years old and upward, to set forward the work of the house of the LORD.

9 Then stood ᴿJesh'-u-a *with* his sons and his brethren, Kad'-mi-el and his sons, the sons of Judah, ᵀtogether, to set forward the workmen in the house of God: the sons of Hen'-a-dad, *with* their sons and their brethren the Levites.   2:40 · *as one*

10 And when the builders laid the foundation of the temple of the LORD, they ᵀset the priests in their apparel with trumpets, and the Levites the sons of A'-saph with cymbals, to praise the LORD, after the ordinance of David king of Israel.   *assigned*

11 ᴿAnd they sang together by course in praising and giving thanks unto the LORD; because *he is* good, for his mercy *endureth* for ever toward Israel. And all the people shouted with a great shout, when they praised the LORD, because the foundation of the house of the LORD was laid.   Ex. 15:21

12 But many of the priests and Levites and chief of the fathers, ^Rwho were ancient men, that had seen the first house, when the foundation of this house was laid before their eyes, wept with a loud voice; and many shouted aloud for joy: Hag. 2:3

13 So that the people could not discern the noise of the ^Rshout of joy from the noise of the weeping of the people: for the people shouted with a loud shout, and the noise was heard afar off.   6:22

CHAPTER 4

Present Opposition Under Darius

NOW when ^Rthe ^Tadversaries of Judah and Benjamin heard that the children of the captivity builded the temple unto the LORD God of Israel;   vv. 7-9 · enemies

2 Then they came to Ze-rub'-ba-bel, and to the chief of the fathers, and said unto them, Let us build with you: for we seek your God, as ye do; and we do ^Tsacrifice unto him since the days of E'-sar-had'-don king of As'-sur, which brought us up hither.   worship

3 But Ze-rub'-ba-bel, and Jesh'-u-a, and the rest of the chief of the fathers of Israel, said unto them, Ye have nothing to do with us to build an house unto our God; but we ourselves together will build unto the LORD ^TGod of Israel, as king Cyrus the king of Persia hath commanded us.   (the)

4 Then ^Rthe people of the land ^Tweakened the hands of the people of Judah, and troubled them in building,   3:3 · hindered

5 And hired counsellors against them, to frustrate their purpose, all the days of Cyrus king of Persia, even until the reign of ^RDa-ri'-us king of Persia.   5:5; 6:1

Later Opposition Under Ahasuerus

6 And in the reign of ^TA-has-u-e'-rus, in the beginning of his reign, wrote they unto him an accusation against the inhabitants of Judah and Jerusalem.   Ahashverosh

Later Opposition Under Artaxerxes

7 And in the days of Ar-tax-erx'-es wrote Bish'-lam, Mith'-re-dath, Ta'-be-el, and the rest of their companions, unto Ar-tax-erx'-es king of Persia; and the writing of the letter was written in the Syrian tongue, and interpreted in the Syrian tongue.

8 Re'-hum the chancellor and Shim'-shai the ^Tscribe wrote a letter against Jerusalem to Ar-tax-erx'-es the king in this sort: secretary

9 Then wrote Re'-hum the chancellor, and Shim'-shai the scribe, and the rest of their companions; ^Rthe Di'-na-ites, the A-phar'-sath-chites, the Tar'-pel-ites, the A-phar'-sites, the Ar'-che-vites, the Babylonians, the

Su'-san-chites, the De-ha'-vites, and the E'-lam-ites,   2 Kin. 17:30, 31

10 ^RAnd the rest of the nations whom the great and noble As-nap'-per brought over, and ^Tset in the cities of Sa-ma'-ri-a, and the rest that are on this side the river, ^Rand at such a time.   v. 1 · assigned · 7:12

11 This is the copy of the ^Rletter that they sent unto him, even unto Ar-tax-erx'-es the king; Thy servants the men on this side the river, and at such a time.   2 Sam. 11:14

12 Be it known unto the king, that the Jews which came up from thee to us are come unto Jerusalem, building the rebellious and the bad city, and have set up the walls thereof, and joined the foundations.

13 Be it known now unto the king, that, if this city be builded, and the walls set up again, then will they not pay ^Rtoll, tribute, and custom, and so thou shalt endamage the revenue of the kings.   7:24

14 Now because we have maintenance from the king's palace, and it was not ^Tmeet for us to see the king's dishonour, therefore have we sent and certified the king;   fitting

15 That search may be made in the book of the records of thy fathers: so shalt thou find in the book of the records, and know that this city is a rebellious city, and hurtful unto kings and provinces, and that they have moved sedition within the same of old time: for which cause was this city destroyed.

16 We certify the king that, if this city be builded again, and the walls thereof set up, by this means thou shalt have ^Tno portion on this side the river.   no territory

17 Then sent the king an answer unto Re'-hum the chancellor, and to Shim'-shai the scribe, and to the rest of their companions that dwell in Sa-ma'-ri-a, and unto the rest beyond the river, Peace, and at such a time.

18 The letter which ye sent unto us hath been ^Rplainly read before me.   Neh. 8:8

19 And ^TI commanded, and search hath been made, and it is found that this city of old time hath made insurrection against kings, and that rebellion and sedition have been made therein.   by me a decree is set

20 There have been mighty kings also over Jerusalem, which have ruled over all countries beyond the river; and toll, tribute, and custom, was paid unto them.

21 ^TGive ye now commandment to cause these men to cease, and that this city be not builded, until another commandment shall be given from me.   make a decree

22 Take heed now that ye fail not to do this: why should damage grow to the hurt of the kings?

23 Now when the copy of king Ar-tax-erx'-es' letter was read before ^RRe'-hum, and Shim'-shai the scribe, and their companions,

they went up in haste to Jerusalem unto the Jews, and made them to cease by force and power.   Prov. 4:16

Present Interruption
of Construction Under Darius

24 Then ceased the work of the ᴿhouse of God which *is* at Jerusalem. So it ceased unto the second year of the reign of Da-ri′-us king of Persia.   2:68

CHAPTER 5

Resumption of the Temple Construction
Hab. 1:1; Zech. 1:1

THEN the prophets, Hag′-gai the prophet, and Zech-a-ri′-ah the son of Id′-do, prophesied unto the Jews that *were* in Judah and Jerusalem in the name of the God of Israel, *even* unto them.

2 Then rose up ᴿZe-rub′-ba-bel the son of She-al′-ti-el, and Jesh′-u-a the son of Joz′-a-dak, and began to build the house of God which *is* at Jerusalem: and with them *were* the prophets of God helping them.   3:2

Opposition by Tatnai

3 At the same time came to them Tat′-nai, governor on this side the river, and She′-thar–boz′-nai, and their companions, and said thus unto them, Who hath commanded you to build this house, and to make up this wall?

4 ᴿThen said we unto them after this manner, What are the names of the men that make this building?   *v.* 10

5 But the eye of their God was upon the elders of the Jews, that they could not cause them to cease, till the matter came to Da-ri′-us: and then they returned answer by letter concerning this *matter.*

The Letter to Darius

6 The copy of the letter that Tat′-nai, governor on this side the river, and She′-thar–boz′-nai, and his companions the A-phar′-sach-ites, which *were* on this side the river, sent unto Da-ri′-us the king:

7 They sent a letter unto him, wherein was written thus; Unto Da-ri′-us the king, all peace.

8 Be it known unto the king, that we went into the province of Ju-de′-a, to the ᵀhouse of the great God, which is builded with ᵀgreat stones, and timber is laid in the walls, and this work goeth fast on, and prospereth in their hands.   *temple · huge*

9 Then asked we those elders, *and* said unto them thus, Who commanded you to build this house, and to make up these walls?

10 We asked their names also, to ᵀcertify thee, that we might write the names of the men that *were* the chief of them.   *notify*

11 And thus they returned us answer, saying, We are the servants of the God of heaven and earth, and build the house that was builded these many years ago, which a great king of Israel builded and set up.

12 But after that our fathers had provoked the God of heaven unto wrath, he gave them into the hand of ᴿNeb-u-chad-nez′-zar the king of Babylon, the Chal-de′-an, who destroyed this house, and carried the people away into Babylon.   2 Kin. 24:2

13 But in the first year of Cyrus the king of Babylon *the same* king Cyrus made a decree to build this ᵀhouse of God.   *temple*

14 And ᴿthe vessels also of gold and silver of the house of God, which Neb-u-chad-nez′-zar took out of the temple that *was* in Jerusalem, and brought them into the temple of Babylon, those did Cyrus the king take out of the temple of Babylon, and they were delivered unto *one,* whose name *was* Shesh-baz′-zar, whom he had made governor;   1:7, 8

15 And said unto him, Take these vessels, go, carry them into the temple that *is* in Jerusalem, and let the house of God be builded in his place.

16 Then came the same Shesh-baz′-zar, *and* laid the foundation of the ᵀhouse of God which *is* in Jerusalem: and since that time even until now hath it been in building, and *yet* it is not finished.   *temple*

17 Now therefore, if *it seem* good to the king, ᴿlet there be search made in the king's treasure house, which is there at Babylon, whether it be *so,* that a decree was made of Cyrus the king to build this house of God at Jerusalem, and let the king send his pleasure to us concerning this matter.   6:1, 2

CHAPTER 6

Confirmation of the Temple Construction

THEN Da-ri′-us the king made a decree, ᴿand search was made in the house of the ᵀrolls, where the ᵀtreasures were laid up in Babylon.   5:17 · *archives · documents*

2 And there was found at ᵀAch′-me-tha, in the palace that is ᴿin the province of the Medes, a roll, and therein *was* a record thus written: *Ecbatana* · 2 Kin. 17:6

3 ᴿIn the first year of Cyrus the king *the same* Cyrus the king made a decree *concerning* the house of God at Jerusalem, Let the house be builded, the place where they offered sacrifices, and let the foundations thereof be strongly laid; the height thereof ᵀthreescore cubits, *and* the breadth thereof ᵀthreescore cubits;   1:1; 5:13 · *90 ft.* · *90 ft.*

4 *With* three rows of great stones, and a row of new timber: and let the expences be given out of the king's ᵀhouse: *treasury*

5 And also let the golden and silver vessels of the house of God, which Neb-u-chad-nez'-zar took forth out of the temple which *is* at Jerusalem, and brought unto Babylon, be restored, and ᵀbrought again unto the temple which *is* at Jerusalem, *every* one to his place, and place *them* in the house of God.   *go*

6 ᴿNow *therefore*, Tat'-nai, governor beyond the river, She'-thar–boz'-nai, and your companions ᴿthe A-phar'-sach-ites, which *are* beyond the river, be ye far from thence: 5:3 • 4:9

7 Let the work of this house of God alone; let the governor of the Jews and the elders of the Jews ᴿbuild this house of God in his place.   Is. 44:28

8 Moreover I make a decree what ye shall do to the elders of these Jews for the building of this house of God: that of the king's goods, *even* of the tribute beyond the river, forth-with expences be given unto these men, that they be not hindered.

9 And that which they have need of, both young bullocks, and rams, and lambs, for the burnt offerings of the God of heaven, wheat, salt, wine, and oil, according to the appoint-ment of the priests which *are* at Jerusalem, let it be given them day by day without fail:

10 That they may offer sacrifices of sweet savours unto the God of heaven, and pray for the life of the king, and of his sons.

11 Also I have made a decree, that whosoever shall alter this word, let timber be pulled down from his house, and being set up, let him be hanged thereon; and let his house be made a dunghill for this.

12 And the God that hath caused his name to dwell there destroy all kings and people, that shall put to their hand to alter *and* to destroy this house of God which *is* at Jerusalem. I Da-ri'-us have made a decree; let it be done with speed.

Completion of the Temple

13 Then Tat'-nai, ᴿgovernor on this side the river, She'-thar–boz'-nai, and their companions, according to that which Da-ri'-us the king had sent, so they did speedily. *v. 6*

14 And the elders of the Jews builded, and they prospered through the prophesying of Hag'-gai the prophet and Zech-a-ri'-ah the son of Id'-do. And they builded, and finished *it*, according to the commandment of the God of Israel, and according to the commandment of Cyrus, and Da-ri'-us, and Ar-tax-erx'-es king of Persia.

15 And this house was finished on the third day of the month A'-dar, which was in the sixth year of the reign of Da-ri'-us the king.

Dedication of the Temple

16 And the children of Israel, the priests, and the Levites, and the rest of the children of the captivity, kept ᴿthe dedication of this house of God with joy,   2 Chr. 7:5

17 And offered at the dedication of this house of God an hundred bullocks, two hundred rams, four hundred lambs; and for a sin offering for all Israel, twelve he goats, according to the number of the tribes of Israel.

18 And they set the priests in their divisions, and the Levites in their courses, for the service of God, which *is* at Jerusalem; as ᴿit is written in the book of Moses.   Num. 3:6

Celebration of the Passover

19 And the ᴿchildren of the captivity kept the passover ᴿupon the fourteenth *day* of the first month.   1:11 • Ex. 12:6

20 For the priests and the Levites were purified together, all of them *were* pure, and ᴿkilled the passover for all the children of the captivity, and for their brethren the priests, and for themselves.   2 Chr. 35:11

21 And the children of Israel, which were come again out of captivity, and all such as had separated themselves unto them from the filthiness of the heathen of the land, to seek the LORD God of Israel, did eat,

22 And kept the feast of unleavened bread seven days with joy: for the LORD had made them joyful, and turned the heart ᴿof the king of Assyria unto them, to strengthen their hands in the work of the house of God, the God of Israel.   1:1

CHAPTER 7

Ezra's Qualifications

NOW after these things, in the reign of ᴿAr-tax-erx'-es king of Persia, Ezra ᴿthe son of Se-ra'-iah, the son of Az-a-ri'-ah, the son of Hil-ki'-ah,   Neh. 2:1 • 1 Chr. 6:14

2 The son of Shal'-lum, the son of Za'-dok, the son of A-hi'-tub,

3 The son of Am-a-ri'-ah, the son of Az-a-ri'-ah, the son of Me-ra'-ioth,

4 The son of Zer-a-hi'-ah, the son of Uz'-zi, the son of Buk'-ki,

5 The son of A-bish'-u-a, the son of Phin'-e-has, the son of E-le-a'-zar, the son of Aaron the chief priest:

6 This Ezra went up from Babylon; and he *was* ᴿa ᵀready scribe in the law of Moses, which the LORD God of Israel had given: and the king granted him all his request, ᴿaccord-ing to the hand of the LORD his God upon him.   *vv*. 11, 12 • *an able scholar* • 8:22

7 And there went up *some* of the children of Israel, and of the priests, and the Levites,

and the singers, and the porters, and the Neth'-i-nims, unto Jerusalem, in the seventh year of Ar-tax-erx'-es the king.

8 And he came to Jerusalem in the fifth month, which *was* in the seventh year of the king.

9 For upon the first *day* of the first month began he to go up from Babylon, and on the first *day* of the fifth month came he to Jerusalem, Raccording to the good hand of his God upon him.   Neh. 2:8, 18

10 For Ezra had prepared his heart to seek the law of the LORD, and to do *it*, and to teach in Israel statutes and judgments.

Artaxerxes' Letter

11 Now this *is* the copy of the letter that the king Ar-tax-erx'-es gave unto Ezra the priest, the scribe, *even* a scribe of the words of the commandments of the LORD, and of his statutes to Israel.

12 Ar-tax-erx'-es, king of kings, unto Ezra the priest, a scribe of the law of the God of heaven, perfect *peace*, and at such a time.

13 I make a Rdecree, that all they of the people of Israel, and *of* his priests and Levites, in my realm, which are minded of their own freewill to go up to Jerusalem, go with thee.   6:1

14 Forasmuch as thou art sent of the king, and of his seven counsellors, to enquire concerning Judah and Jerusalem, according to the law of thy God which *is* in thine hand;

15 And to carry the silver and gold, which the king and his counsellors have freely offered unto the God of Israel, Rwhose habitation *is* in Jerusalem,   2 Chr. 6:2

16 RAnd all the silver and gold that thou canst find in all the province of Babylon, with the freewill offering of the people, and of the priests, offering willingly for the Thouse of their God which *is* in Jerusalem: 8:25 • temple

17 That thou mayest buy speedily with this money bullocks, rams, lambs, with their meat offerings and their drink offerings, and Roffer them upon the altar of the house of your God which *is* in Jerusalem.   Deut. 12:5, 11

18 And whatsoever shall seem good to thee, and to thy brethren, to do with the rest of the silver and the gold, that do after the will of your God.

19 The vessels also that are given thee for the service of the house of thy God, *those* deliver thou before the God of Jerusalem.

20 And whatsoever more shall be needful for the house of thy God, which thou shalt have occasion to Rbestow, bestow *it* out of the king's treasure house.   vv. 21-23; 6:4

21 And I, *even* I Ar-tax-erx'-es the king, do make a decree to all the treasurers which *are* beyond the Triver, that whatsoever Ezra the priest, Rthe scribe of the law of the God of

heaven, shall require of you, it be done speedily,   *Euphrates River • v.* 6

22 Unto an Thundred talents of silver, and to an Thundred measures of wheat, and to an Thundred baths of wine, and to an hundred baths of oil, and salt without prescribing *how much*.   *$2,184,000 • 65 bu. • 600 gal.*

23 Whatsoever is commanded by the God of heaven, let it be Tdiligently done for the Thouse of the God of heaven: for why should there be wrath against the realm of the king and his sons?   *exactly • temple*

24 Also we certify you, that touching any of the priests and Levites, singers, Tporters, Neth'-i-nims, or ministers of this house of God, it shall not be lawful to impose toll, tribute, or custom, upon them.   *doorkeepers*

25 And thou, Ezra, after the wisdom of thy God, that *is* in thine hand, set magistrates and judges, which may judge all the people that *are* beyond the river, all such as know the laws of thy God; and Rteach ye them that know *them* not.   *v.* 10

26 And whosoever will not do the law of thy God, and the law of the king, let judgment be executed speedily upon him, Rwhether *it be* unto death, or Tto banishment, or to confiscation of goods, or to imprisonment.   *6:11, 12 • to rooting out*

Ezra's Response

27 Blessed *be* the LORD God of our fathers, which hath put *such a thing* as this in the king's heart, to beautify the house of the LORD which *is* in Jerusalem:

28 And Rhath extended mercy unto me before the king, and his counsellors, and before all the king's mighty princes. RAnd I was strengthened as Rthe hand of the LORD my God *was* upon me, and I gathered together out of Israel chief men to go up with me.   *[9:9] • [Ps. 28:8] • vv. 6, 9; 5:5; 8:18*

CHAPTER 8

Census of the Returning Israelites

THESE *are* now the chief of their fathers, and *this is* the genealogy of them that went up with me from Babylon, in the reign of Ar-tax-erx'-es the king.

2 Of the sons of Phin'-e-has; Ger'-shom: of the sons of Ith'-a-mar; Daniel: of the sons of David; RHat'-tush.   1 Chr. 3:22

3 Of the sons of Shech-a-ni'-ah, of the sons of RPha'-rosh; Zech-a-ri'-ah: and with him were reckoned by genealogy of the males an hundred and fifty.   2:3

4 Of the sons of RPa'-hath-mo'-ab; El-i-ho-e'-nai the son of Zer-a-hi'-ah, and with him two hundred males.   10:30

5 Of the sons of Shech-a-ni'-ah; the son of Ja-ha'-zi-el, and with him three hundred males.

6 Of the sons also of A'-din; E'-bed the son of Jonathan, and with him fifty males.

7 And of the sons of E'-lam; Je-sha'-iah the son of Ath-a-li'-ah, and with him seventy males.

8 And of the sons of Sheph-a-ti'-ah; Zeb-a-di'-ah the son of Mi'-cha-el, and with him fourscore males.

9 Of the sons of Jo'-ab; O-ba-di'-ah the son of Je-hi'-el, and with him two hundred and eighteen males.

10 And of the sons of Shel'-o-mith; the son of Jos-i-phi'-ah, and with him an hundred and threescore males.

11 And of the sons of ^RBe'-bai; Zech-a-ri'-ah the son of Be'-bai, and with him twenty and eight males.   10:28

12 And of the sons of Az'-gad; Jo-ha'-nan ^Tthe son of Hak'-ka-tan, and with him an hundred and ten males.   *the youngest son*

13 And of the last sons of A-don'-i-kam, whose names *are* these, E-liph'-e-let, Je-i'-el, and She-ma'-iah, and with them threescore males.

14 Of the sons also of Big'-vai; U'-thai, and Zab'-bud, and with them seventy males.

Acquisition of Temple Leadership

15 And I gathered them together to the river that runneth to A-ha'-va; and there abode we in tents three days: and I viewed the people, and the priests, and found there none of the sons of Levi.

16 Then sent I for E-li-e'-zer, for A'-ri-el, for She-ma'-iah, and for El-na'-than, and for Ja'-rib, and for El-na'-than, and for Nathan, and for Zech-a-ri'-ah, and for Me-shul'-lam, chief men; also for Joi'-a-rib, and for El-na'-than, men of understanding.

17 And I sent them with commandment unto Id'-do the chief at the place Ca-siph'-i-a, and ^TI told them what they should say unto Id'-do, *and* to his brethren the Neth'-i-nims, at the place Ca-siph'-i-a, that they should bring unto us ministers for the house of our God.   *I put words in their mouth*

18 And by the good hand of our God upon us they brought us a man of understanding, of the sons of Mah'-li, the son of Levi, the son of Israel; and Sher-e-bi'-ah, with his sons and his brethren, eighteen;

19 And ^RHash-a-bi'-ah, and with him Je-sha'-iah of the sons of Me-ra'-ri, his brethren and their sons, twenty;   Neh. 12:24

20 ^RAlso of the Neth'-i-nims, whom David and the princes had appointed for the service of the Levites, two hundred and twenty Neth'-i-nims: all of them were ^Texpressed by name.   2:43 • *registered*

Proclamation of a Fast

21 Then I proclaimed a fast there, at the river of A-ha'-va, that we might ^Tafflict ourselves before our God, to seek of him a ^Rright way for us, and for our little ones, and for all our substance.   *humble* • Ps. 5:8

22 For ^RI was ashamed to require of the king a band of soldiers and horsemen to help us against the enemy in the way: because we had spoken unto the king, saying, The hand of our God *is* upon all them for good that seek him; but his power and his wrath *is* against all them that forsake him.   1 Cor. 9:15

23 So we fasted and besought our God for this: and he was intreated of us.

The Return Is Completed

24 Then I separated twelve of the chief of the priests, Sher-e-bi'-ah, Hash-a-bi'-ah, and ten of their brethren with them,

25 And weighed unto them the silver, and the gold, and the vessels, *even* the offering of the house of our God, which the king, and his counsellors, and his lords, and all Israel *there* present, had offered:

26 I even weighed unto their hand six hundred and fifty talents of silver, and silver vessels an ^Thundred talents, *and* of gold an ^Thundred talents; $38,400,000 • $576,000,000

27 Also twenty basons of gold, of a ^Tthousand drams; and two vessels of ^Tfine copper, precious as gold. $1,424,176 • *brass*

28 And I said unto them, Ye *are* ^Rholy unto the LORD; the vessels *are* holy also; and the silver and the gold *are* a freewill offering unto the LORD God of your fathers.   Deut. 33:8

29 Watch ye, and keep *them,* ^Runtil ye weigh *them* before the chief of the priests and the Levites, and chief of the fathers of Israel, at Jerusalem, in the chambers of the house of the LORD.   vv. 33, 34

30 So took the priests and the Levites the weight of the silver, and the gold, and the vessels, to bring *them* to Jerusalem unto the house of our God.

31 Then we departed from the river of A-ha'-va on the twelfth *day* of the first month, to go unto Jerusalem: and the hand of our God was upon us, and he delivered us from the hand of the enemy, and of such as lay in wait by the way.

32 And we ^Rcame to Jerusalem, and abode there three days.   Neh. 2:11

33 Now on the fourth day was the silver and the gold and the vessels ^Rweighed in the house of our God by the hand of ^RMer'-e-moth the son of U-ri'-ah the priest; and with him *was* E-le-a'-zar the son of Phin'-e-has; and with them *was* Joz'-a-bad the son of Jesh'-u-a, and No-a-di'-ah the son of Bin'-nu-i, Levites;   vv. 26, 30 • Neh. 3:4, 21

34 By number *and* by weight of every one: and all the weight was written at that time.

35 *Also* the children of those that had been carried away, which were come out of the captivity, offered burnt offerings unto the God of Israel, twelve bullocks for all Israel, ninety and six rams, seventy and seven lambs, twelve he goats *for* a sin offering: all *this was* a burnt offering unto the LORD.

36 And they delivered the king's commissions unto the king's lieutenants, and to the governors on this side the river: and they furthered the people, and the house of God.

CHAPTER 9

Israel Intermarries

NOW when these things were done, the princes came to me, saying, The people of Israel, and the priests, and the Levites, have not separated themselves from the people of the lands, *doing* according to their abominations, *even* of the Ca'-naan-ites, the Hit'-tites, the Per'-iz-zites, the Jeb'-u-sites, the Am'-mon-ites, the Mo'-ab-ites, the Egyptians, and the Am'-or-ites.

2 For they have ᴿtaken of their daughters for themselves, and for their sons: so that the holy seed have mingled themselves with the people of *those* lands: yea, the hand of the princes and rulers hath been chief in this ᵀtrespass.   Ex. 34:16 • *wrong doing*

Lamentation of Ezra

3 And when I heard this thing, I rent my garment and my mantle, and plucked off the hair of my head and of my beard, and sat down ᵀastonied.   *confounded*

4 Then were assembled unto me every one that trembled at the words of the God of Israel, because of the transgression of those that had been carried away; and I sat astonied until the evening sacrifice.

God's Faithfulness

5 And at the evening sacrifice I arose up from my ᵀheaviness; and having ᵀrent my garment and my mantle, I fell upon my knees, and ᴿspread out my hands unto the LORD my God,   *humiliation • torn •* Ex. 9:29

6 And said, O my God, I am ashamed and blush to lift up my face to thee, my God: for ᴿour iniquities are increased over *our* head, and our ᵀtrespass is grown up unto the heavens.   Ps. 38:4 • *wrong doing; vv.* 13, 15

7 Since the days of our fathers *have* ᴿwe *been* in a great trespass unto this day; and for our iniquities have we, our kings, *and* our priests, been delivered into the hand of the kings of the lands, to the sword, to captivity,

and to a spoil, and to ᵀconfusion of face, as *it is* this day.   Ps. 106:6 • *embarrassment*

8 And now for a little space grace hath been *shewed* from the LORD our God, to leave us a remnant to escape, and to give us ᵀa nail in his holy place, that our God may lighten our eyes, and give us a little reviving in our bondage.   *a place in God's plan*

9 For we *were* bondmen; yet our God hath not forsaken us in our bondage, but hath extended mercy unto us in the sight of the kings of Persia, to give us a reviving, to set up the house of our God, and to repair the desolations thereof, and to give us a wall in Judah and in Jerusalem.

Israel's Unfaithfulness

10 And now, ᴿO our God, what shall we say after this? for we have ᴿforsaken thy commandments,   *v.* 6 • Deut. 28:20

11 Which thou hast commanded by thy servants the prophets, saying, The land, unto which ye go to possess it, is an unclean land with the filthiness of the people of the lands, with their ᵀabominations, which have filled it from one end to another with their uncleanness.   *evil customs*

12 Now therefore give not your daughters unto their sons, neither take their daughters unto your sons, nor seek their peace or their wealth for ever: that ye may be strong, and eat the good of the land, and leave *it* for an inheritance to your children for ever.

13 And after all that is come upon us for our evil deeds, and for our great trespass, seeing that thou our God hast punished us less than our iniquities *deserve*, and hast given us *such* deliverance as this;

14 ᵀShould we again break thy commandments, and join in ᵀaffinity with the people of these abominations? wouldest not thou be angry with us till thou hadst ᵀconsumed *us*, so that *there should be* no remnant nor escaping?   *shall • fellowship • destroyed*

15 O LORD God of Israel, thou *art* righteous: for we remain yet escaped, as *it is* this day: behold, we *are* before thee ᴿin our trespasses: for we cannot stand before thee because of this.   1 Cor. 15:17

CHAPTER 10

Israel Laments

NOW when Ezra had prayed, and when he had confessed, weeping and casting himself down before the house of God, there assembled unto him out of Israel a very great congregation of men and women and children: for the people wept very sore.

2 And Shech-a-ni'-ah the son of Je-hi'-el, *one* of the sons of E'-lam, answered and said

unto Ezra, We have ᴿtrespassed against our God, and have taken strange wives of the people of the land: yet now there is hope in Israel concerning this thing.   Neh. 13:23-27

The Covenant Is Instituted

3 Now therefore let us make a covenant with our God to put away all the wives, and such as are born of them, according to the ᵀcounsel of my lord, and of those that tremble at the commandment of our God; and let it be done according to the law.   *advice*

4 Arise; for *this* matter *belongeth* unto thee: we also *will be* with thee: ᴿbe of good courage, and do *it*.   1 Chr. 28:10

5 Then arose Ezra, and made the chief priests, the Levites, and all Israel, ᴿto ᵀswear that they should do according to this word. And they sware.   Neh. 5:12 • *promise*

Separation Is Accepted

6 Then Ezra rose up from before the house of God, and went into the chamber of Jo-ha′-nan the son of E-li′-a-shib: and *when* he came thither, he ᴿdid eat no bread, nor drink water: for he mourned because of the transgression of them that had been carried away. Deut. 9:18

7 And they made proclamation throughout Judah and Jerusalem unto all the children of the captivity, that they should gather themselves together unto Jerusalem;

8 And that whosoever would not come within three days, according to the counsel of the princes and the elders, all his substance should be ᵀforfeited, and himself separated from the congregation of those that had been carried away.   *confiscated*

9 Then all the men of Judah and Benjamin gathered themselves together unto Jerusalem within three days. It *was* the ninth month, on the twentieth *day* of the month; and ᴿall the people sat in the street of the house of God, ᵀtrembling because of *this* matter, and for the great rain.   1 Sam. 12:18 • *deeply concerned*

10 And Ezra the priest stood up, and said unto them, Ye have transgressed, and ᵀhave taken strange wives, to increase the trespass of Israel.   *have caused to dwell*

11 Now therefore ᴿmake confession unto the LORD God of your fathers, and do his ᵀpleasure: and ᴿseparate yourselves from the people of the land, and from the strange wives.   Josh. 7:19; [Prov. 28:13] • *will* • *v. 3*

12 Then all the congregation answered and said with a loud voice, As thou hast said, so must we do.

13 But the people *are* many, and *it is* a time of much rain, and we are not able to stand ᵀwithout, neither *is this* a work of one day or two: for we are many that have ᵀtransgressed in this thing.   *outside* • *done wrong*

14 Let now our ᵀrulers of all the congregation stand, and let all them which have taken strange wives in our cities come at appointed times, and with them the elders of every city, and the judges thereof, until ᴿthe fierce wrath of our God for this matter be turned from us.   *princes* • 2 Chr. 30:8

15 Only Jonathan the son of A′-sa-hel and Ja-ha-zi′-ah the son of Tik′-vah were employed about this *matter:* and Me-shul′-lam and Shab′-be-thai the Levite helped them.

16 And the children of the captivity did so. And Ezra the priest, *with* certain chief of the fathers, after the house of their fathers, and all of them by *their* names, were separated, and sat down in the first day of the tenth month to examine the matter.

17 And they ᵀmade an end with all the men that had taken strange wives by the first day of the first month.   *finished*

Separation of Priests

18 And among the sons of the priests there were found that had taken strange wives: *namely,* of the sons of Jesh′-u-a the son of Joz′-a-dak, and his brethren; Ma-a-se′-iah, and E-li-e′-zer, and Ja′-rib, and Ged-a-li′-ah.

19 And they ᵀgave their hands that they would put away their wives; and *being* ᴿguilty, *they offered* a ram of the flock for their ᵀtrespass.   *solemnly promised* • Lev. 6:4, 6 • *guilt*

20 And of the sons of Im′-mer; Ha-na′-ni, and Zeb-a-di′-ah.

21 And of the sons of Ha′-rim; Ma-a-se′-iah, and E-li′-jah, and She-ma′-iah, and Je-hi′-el, and Uz-zi′-ah.

22 And of the sons of Pash′-ur; E-li-o-e′-nai, Ma-a-se′-iah, Ish′-ma-el, Ne-than′-e-el, Joz′-a-bad, and El′-a-sah.

Separation of Levites

23 Also of the Levites; Joz′-a-bad, and Shim′-e-i, and Ke-la-iah, (the same *is* Kel′-i-ta,) Peth-a-hi′-ah, Judah, and E-li-e′-zer.

24 Of the singers also; E-li′-a-shib: and of the ᵀporters; Shal′-lum, and Te′-lem, and U′-ri.   *gatekeepers*

Separation of People

25 Moreover of Israel: of the sons of Pa′-rosh; Ra-mi′-ah, and Je-zi′-ah, and Mal-chi′-ah, and Mi′-a-min, and E-le-a′-zar, and Mal-chi′-jah, and Be-na′-iah.

26 And of the sons of E′-lam; Mat-ta-ni′-ah, Zech-a-ri′-ah, and Je-hi′-el, and Ab′-di, and Jer′-e-moth, and E-li′-ah.

27 And of the sons of Zat′-tu; E-li-o-e′-nai, E-li′-a-shib, Mat-ta-ni′-ah, and Jer′-e-moth, and Za′-bad, and A-zi′-za.

28 Of the sons also of Be′-bai; Je-ho-ha′-nan, Han-a-ni′-ah, Zab′-bai, *and* Ath′-lai.

29 And of the sons of Ba′-ni; Me-shul′-lam,

Mal'-luch, and A-da'-iah, Jash'-ub, and She'-al, and Ra'-moth.

30 And of the sons of Pa'-hath-mo'-ab; Ad'-na, and Che'-lal, Be-nai'-ah, Ma-a-se'-iah, Mat-ta-ni'-ah, Be-zal'-e-el, and Bin'-nu-i, and Ma-nas'-seh.

31 And of the sons of Ha'-rim; E-li-e'-zer, Ish-i'-jah, Mal-chi'-ah, She-ma'-iah, Shim'-e-on,

32 Benjamin, Mal'-luch, and Shem-a-ri'-ah.

33 Of the sons of Ha'-shum; Mat-te'-nai, Mat'-ta-thah, Za'-bad, E-liph'-e-let, Jer'-e-mai, Ma-nas'-seh, and Shim'-e-i.

34 Of the sons of Ba'-ni; Ma'-a-dai, Am'-ram, and U'-el,

35 Be-na'-iah, Be-de'-iah, Chel'-luh,

36 Va-ni'-ah, Mer'-e-moth, E-li'-a-shib,

37 Mat-ta-ni'-ah, Mat-te'-nai, and Ja'-a-sau,

38 And Ba'-ni, and Bin'-nu-i, Shim'-e-i,

39 And Shel-e-mi'-ah, and Nathan, and A-da'-iah,

40 Mach-na-de'-bai, Sha'-shai, Sha'-rai,

41 A-zar'-e-el, and Shel-e-mi'-ah, Shem-a-ri'-ah,

42 Shal'-lum, Am-a-ri'-ah, and Joseph.

43 Of the sons of Ne'-bo; Je-i'-el, Mat-ti-thi'-ah, Za'-bad, Ze-bi'-na, Ja'-dau, and Jo'-el, Be-na'-iah.

44 All these had taken Tstrange wives: and Rsome of them had wives by whom they had children.

foreign • 10:3

Monies

Unit	Monetary Value	Equivalents	Translations
Jewish Weights			
Talent	gold—$5,760,000[1] silver—$384,000	3,000 shekels; 6,000 bekas	talent
Shekel	gold—$1,920 silver—$128	4 days' wages; 2 bekas; 20 gerahs	shekel
Beka	gold—$960 silver—$64	½ shekel; 10 gerahs	bekah
Gerah	gold—$96 silver—$6.40	¹⁄₂₀ shekel	gerah
Persian Coins			
Daric	gold—$1,280[2] silver—$64	2 days' wages; ½ Jewish silver shekel	dram
Greek Coins			
Tetradrachma (Stater)	$128	4 drachmas	piece of money
Didrachma	$64	2 drachmas	tribute
Drachma	$32	1 day's wage	piece of silver
Lepton	$.25	½ of a Roman kodrantes	mite
Roman Coins			
Aureus	$800	25 denarii	
Denarius	$32	1 day's wage	pence, penny
Assarius	$2	¹⁄₁₆ of a denarius	farthing
Kodrantes	$.50	¼ of an assarius	farthing

[1]Value of gold is fifteen times the value of silver.
[2]Value of gold is twenty times the value of silver.

THE BOOK OF
NEHEMIAH

📖 **THE BOOK OF NEHEMIAH**
Nehemiah, contemporary of Ezra and cupbearer to the king in the Persian palace, leads the third and last return to Jerusalem after the Babylonian exile. His concern for the welfare of Jerusalem and its inhabitants prompts him to take bold action. Granted permission to return to his homeland, Nehemiah challenges his countrymen to arise and rebuild the shattered wall of Jerusalem. In spite of opposition from without and abuse from within, the task is completed in only fifty-two days, a feat even the enemies of Israel must attribute to God's enabling. By contrast, the task of reviving and reforming the people of God within the rebuilt wall demands years of Nehemiah's godly life and leadership.

The Hebrew for Nehemiah is *Nehemyah*, "Comfort of Yahweh." The book is named after its chief character, whose name appears in the opening verse. The combined book of Ezra-Nehemiah is given the Greek title *Esdras Deuteron*, "Second Esdras" (see "The Book of Ezra") in the Septuagint, a third-century B.C. Greek-language translation of the Hebrew Old Testament. The Latin title of Nehemiah is *Liber Secundus Esdrae*, "Second Book of Ezra" (Ezra was the first). At this point, it is considered a separate book from Ezra, and is later called *Liber Nehemiae*, "Book of Nehemiah."

✒ **THE AUTHOR OF NEHEMIAH**
Clearly, much of this book came from Nehemiah's personal memoirs. The reporting is remarkably candid and vivid. Certainly 1:1—7:5; 12:27–43; and 13:4–31 are the "words of Nehemiah" (1:1). Some scholars think that Nehemiah composed those portions and compiled the rest. Others think that Ezra wrote 7:6—12:26 and 12:44—13:3, and that he compiled the rest making use of Nehemiah's diary. A third view that neither wrote it seems least likely from the evidence. Nehemiah 7:5–73 is almost the same as Ezra 2:1–70, and both lists may have been taken from another record of the same period.

As cupbearer to Artaxerxes I, Nehemiah holds a position of great responsibility. His role of tasting the king's wine to prevent him from being poisoned places Nehemiah in a position of trust and confidence as one of the king's advisers. As governor of Jerusalem from 444 to 432 B.C. (5:14; 8:9; 10:1; 13:6), Nehemiah demonstrates courage, compassion for the oppressed, integrity, godliness, and selflessness. He is willing to give up the luxury and ease of the palace to help his people.

He is a dedicated layman who has the right priorities and is concerned for God's work, who is able to encourage and rebuke at the right times, who is strong in prayer, and who gives all glory and credit to God.

⧖ **THE TIME OF NEHEMIAH**
See "The Time of Ezra," because both Ezra and Nehemiah share the same historical background. The Book of Nehemiah fits within the reign of Artaxerxes I of Persia (464–423 B.C.). Esther is Artaxerxes' stepmother, and it is possible that she is instrumental in Nehemiah's appointment as the king's cupbearer. Nehemiah leaves Persia in the twentieth year of Artaxerxes (2:1), returns to Persia in the thirty-second year of Artaxerxes (13:6), and leaves again for Jerusalem "after certain days" (13:6), perhaps about 425 B.C. This book could not have been completed until after his second visit to Jerusalem.

The historical reliability of this book is supported by the Elephantine papyri. These ancient documents mention Sanballat (2:19) and Jehohanan (6:18; 12:23), and indicate that Bigvai replaces Nehemiah as governor of Judah by 410 B.C.

Malachi lives and ministers during Nehemiah's time, and a comparison of the books shows that many of the evils encountered by Nehemiah are specifically denounced by Malachi. The cold-hearted indifference toward God described in both books remains a problem in Israel during the four hundred years before Christ, during which there is no revelation from God.

✝ **THE CHRIST OF NEHEMIAH**
Like Ezra, Nehemiah portrays Christ in His ministry of restoration. Nehemiah illustrates Christ in that he gives up a high position in order to identify with the plight of his people; he comes with a specific mission and fulfills it; and his life is characterized by prayerful dependence upon God.

In this book, everything is restored except the king. The temple is rebuilt, Jerusalem is reconstructed, the covenant is renewed, and the people are reformed. The messianic line is intact, but the King is yet to come. The decree of Artaxerxes in his twentieth year (2:2) marks the beginning point of Daniel's prophecy of the seventy weeks (see Dan. 9:25–27). "Know therefore and understand, *that* from the going forth of the commandment to restore and to build Jerusalem unto the Messiah the Prince *shall be* seven weeks, and threescore and two weeks: the

street shall be built again, and the wall, even in troublous times" (Dan. 9:25). The Messiah will come at the end of the sixty-nine weeks, and this is exactly fulfilled in A.D. 33 (see "The Christ of Daniel").

KEYS TO NEHEMIAH

Key Word: Jerusalem Walls—While Ezra deals with the religious restoration of Judah, Nehemiah is primarily concerned with Judah's political and geographical restoration. The first seven chapters are devoted to the rebuilding of Jerusalem's walls, because Jerusalem was the spiritual and political center of Judah. Without walls, Jerusalem could hardly be considered a city at all. As governor, Nehemiah also establishes firm civil authority. Ezra and Nehemiah work together to build the people spiritually and morally so that the restoration will be complete.

Key Verses: Nehemiah 6:15, 16; 8:8—"So the wall was finished in the twenty and fifth *day* of *the month* Elul, in fifty and two days. And it came to pass, that when all our enemies heard *thereof*, and all the heathen that *were* about us saw *these things*, they were much cast down in their own eyes: for they perceived that this work was wrought of our God" (6:15, 16).

"So they read in the book in the law of God distinctly, and gave the sense, and caused *them* to understand the reading" (8:8).

Key Chapter: Nehemiah 9—The key to the Old Testament is the covenant, which is its theme and unifying factor. Israel's history can be divided according to the nation's obedience or disobedience to God's conditional covenant: blessings from obedience and destruction from disobedience. Nehemiah 9 records that upon completion of the Jerusalem wall the nation reaffirmed its loyalty to the covenant.

SURVEY OF NEHEMIAH

Nehemiah is closely associated with the ministry of his contemporary, Ezra. Ezra is a priest who brings spiritual revival; Nehemiah is a governor who brings physical and political reconstruction and leads the people in moral reform. They combine to make an effective team in rebuilding the postexilic remnant. Malachi, the last Old Testament prophet, also ministers during this time to provide additional moral and spiritual direction. The Book of Nehemiah takes us to the end of the historical account in the Old Testament, about four hundred years before the birth of the promised Messiah. Its two divisions are: the reconstruction of the wall (1—7), and the restoration of the people (8—13).

The Reconstruction of the Wall (1—7): Nehemiah's great concern for his people and the welfare of Jerusalem leads him to take bold action. The walls of Jerusalem, destroyed by Nebuchadnezzar in 586 B.C., evidently have been almost rebuilt after 464 B.C. when Artaxerxes I took the throne of Persia (see Ezra 3:6–23). When he hears that opposition led to their second destruction, Nehemiah prays on behalf of his people and then secures Artaxerxes' permission, provision, and protection for the massive project of rebuilding the walls.

The return under Nehemiah in 444 B.C. takes place thirteen years after the return led by Ezra, and ninety-four years after the return led by Zerubbabel. Nehemiah inspects the walls and challenges the people to "rise up and build" (2:18). Work begins immediately on the wall and its gates, with people building portions corresponding to where they are living.

However, opposition quickly arises, first in the form of mockery, then in the form of conspiracy when the work is progressing at an alarming rate. Nehemiah overcomes threats of force by setting

FOCUS	RECONSTRUCTION OF THE WALL		RESTORATION OF THE PEOPLE	
REFERENCE	1:1————————3:1————————		8:1———————————11:1—————————13:31	
DIVISION	PREPARATION TO RECONSTRUCT THE WALL	RECONSTRUCTION OF THE WALL	RENEWAL OF THE COVENANT	OBEDIENCE TO THE COVENANT
TOPIC	POLITICAL		SPIRITUAL	
	CONSTRUCTION		INSTRUCTION	
LOCATION	JERUSALEM			
TIME	19 YEARS (444–425 B.C.)			

half of the people on military watch and half on construction. While the external opposition continues to mount, internal opposition also surfaces. The wealthier Jews are abusing and oppressing the people, forcing them to mortgage their property and sell their children into slavery. Nehemiah again deals with the problem by the twin means of prayer and action. He also leads by example when he sacrifices his governor's salary. In spite of deceit, slander, and treachery, Nehemiah continues to trust in God and to press on with singleness of mind until the work is completed. The task is accomplished in an incredible fifty-two days, and even the enemies recognize that it can only have been accomplished with the help of God (6:16).

The Restoration of the People (8—13): The construction of the walls is followed by consecration and consolidation of the people. Ezra the priest is the leader of the spiritual revival (8—10), reminiscent of the reforms he led thirteen years earlier (Ezra 9 and 10). Ezra stands on a special wooden podium after the completion of the walls and gives the people a marathon reading of the law, translating from the Hebrew into Aramaic so they can understand. They respond with weeping, confession, obedience, and rejoicing. The Levites and priests lead them in a great prayer that surveys God's past work of deliverance and loyalty on behalf of His people, and magnifies God's attributes of holiness, justice, mercy, and love. The covenant is then renewed with God as the people commit themselves to separate from the Gentiles in marriage and to obey God's commandments.

Lots are drawn to determine who will remain in Jerusalem and who will return to the cities of their inheritance. One-tenth are required to stay in Jerusalem, and the rest of the land is resettled by the people and priests. The walls of Jerusalem are dedicated to the Lord in a joyful ceremony accompanied by instrumental and vocal music.

Unfortunately, Ezra's revival is short-lived, and Nehemiah, who returned to Persia in 432 B.C. (13:6), makes a second trip to Jerusalem about 425 B.C. to reform the people. He cleanses the temple, enforces the Sabbath, and requires the people to put away all foreign wives.

OUTLINE OF NEHEMIAH

Part One: The Reconstruction of the Wall (1:1—7:73)

Part Two: The Restoration of the People (8:1—13:31)

CHAPTER 1

Discovery of the Broken Wall

THE words of ᴿNe-he-mi′-ah the son of Hach-a-li′-ah. And it came to pass in the month Chis′-leu, in the twentieth year, as I was in Shu′-shan the palace,   10:1

2 That Ha-na′-ni, ᴷone of my brethren, came, he and *certain* men of Judah; and I asked them concerning the Jews that had escaped, which were left of the captivity, and concerning Jerusalem.   7:2

3 And they said unto me, The remnant that are left of the captivity there in the province *are* in great affliction and reproach: the wall of Jerusalem also *is* broken down, and the gates thereof are burned with fire.

Nehemiah Intercedes with God

4 And it came to pass, when I heard these words, that I sat down and wept, and mourned *certain* days, and fasted, and prayed before the God of heaven,

5 And said, I beseech thee, O Lᴏʀᴅ God of heaven, the great and terrible God, that keepeth covenant and mercy for them that love him and observe his commandments:

6 Let thine ear now be attentive, and thine eyes open, that thou mayest hear the prayer of thy servant, which I pray before thee now, day and night, for the children of Israel thy servants, and confess the sins of the children of Israel, which we have sinned against thee: both I and my father's house have sinned.

7 We have dealt very corruptly against thee, and have not kept the commandments, nor the statutes, nor the judgments, which thou commandedst thy servant Moses.

8 Remember, I beseech thee, the word that thou commandedst thy servant Moses, saying, ᴿIf ye transgress, I will scatter you abroad among the nations: Lev. 26:33

9 But *if* ye turn unto me, and keep my commandments, and do them; though there were of you cast out unto the uttermost part of the heaven, *yet* will I gather them from thence, and will bring them unto the place that I have chosen to set my name there.

10 Now these *are* thy servants and thy people, whom thou hast redeemed by thy great power, and by thy strong hand.

11 O Lᴏʀᴅ, I beseech thee, let now thine ear be attentive to the prayer of thy servant, and to the prayer of thy servants, who ᴿdesire to fear thy name: and prosper, I pray thee, thy servant this day, and grant him mercy in the sight of this man. For I was the king's ᴿcupbearer.   Is. 26:8 • 2:1

CHAPTER 2

Nehemiah Intercedes with Artaxerxes

AND it came to pass in the month Ni′-san, in the twentieth year of ᴿAr-tax-erx′-es the king, *that* wine *was* before him: and ᴿI took up the wine, and gave *it* unto the king. Now I had not been *beforetime* sad in his presence.   Ezra 7:1 • 1:11

2 Wherefore the king said unto me, Why *is* thy countenance sad, seeing thou *art* not sick? this *is* nothing *else* but sorrow of heart. Then I was very sore afraid,

3 And said unto the king, Let the king live for ever: why should not my countenance be sad, when the city, the place of my fathers' sepulchres, *lieth* waste, and the gates thereof are consumed with fire?

4 Then the king said unto me, For what dost thou make request? ᴿSo I prayed to the God of heaven.   1:4

5 And I said unto the king, If it please the king, and if thy servant have found favour in thy sight, that thou wouldest send me unto Judah, unto the city of my fathers' sepulchres, that I may build it.

6 And the king said unto me, (the ᵀqueen also sitting by him,) For how long shall thy journey be? and when wilt thou return? So it pleased the king to send me; and I set him ᴿa time.   wife • 5:14; 13:6

7 Moreover I said unto the king, If it please the king, let letters be given me to the governors beyond the river, that they may convey me over till I come into Judah:

8 And a letter unto A′-saph the keeper of the king's forest, that he may give me timber to make beams for the gates of the palace

which *appertained* ᴿto the house, and for the wall of the city, and for the house that I shall enter into. And the king granted me, ᴿaccording to the good hand of my God upon me.   3:7 • Ezra 5:5; 7:6, 9, 28

Arrival of Nehemiah in Jerusalem

9 Then I came to the ᴿgovernors beyond the river, and gave them the king's letters. Now the ᴿking had sent captains of the army and horsemen with me.   v. 7 • Ezra 8:22

10 When ᴿSan-bal'-lat the Hor'-o-nite, and To-bi'-ah the servant, the Am'-mon-ite, heard *of it*, it grieved them exceedingly that there was come a man to seek the welfare of the children of Israel.   v. 19; 4:1

11 So I ᴿcame to Jerusalem, and was there three days.   Ezra 8:32

Nehemiah Inspects the Broken Walls

12 And I arose in the night, I and some few men with me; neither told I *any* man what my God had put in my heart to do at Jerusalem: neither *was there any* beast with me, save the beast that I rode upon.

13 And I went out by night ᴿby the gate of the valley, even before the dragon well, and to the dung port, and ᵀviewed the walls of Jerusalem, which were ᴿbrokenᵀ down, and the gates thereof were ᵀconsumed with fire.   3:13 • surveyed • v. 17 • dilapidated • destroyed

14 Then I went on to the ᴿgate of the ᴿfountain, and to the king's pool: but *there was* no place for the beast *that was* under me to pass.   3:15 • 2 Kin. 20:20

15 Then went I up in the night by the ᴿbrook, and ᵀviewed the wall, and turned back, and entered by the gate of the valley, and *so* returned.   2 Sam. 15:23; Jer. 31:40 • surveyed

16 And the rulers knew not ᵀwhither I went, or what I did; neither had I as yet told *it* to the Jews, nor to the priests, nor to the nobles, nor to the rulers, nor to the rest that did the work.   where

Nehemiah Exhorts the People

17 Then said I unto them, Ye see the distress that we *are* in, how Jerusalem *lieth* waste, and the gates thereof are burned with fire: come, and let us build up the wall of Jerusalem, that we be no more a reproach.

18 Then I told them of ᴿthe hand of my God which was good upon me; as also the king's words that he had spoken unto me. And they said, Let us rise up and build. So they ᴿstrengthenedᵀ their hands for *this* good work.   v. 8 • 2 Sam. 2:7 • encouraged themselves

Nehemiah Answers the Enemies

19 But when San-bal'-lat the Hor'-o-nite, and To-bi'-ah the servant, the Am'-mon-ite, and Ge'-shem the A-ra'-bi-an, heard *it*, ᴿthey laughed us to scorn, and despised us, and said, What *is* this thing that ye do? ᴿwill ye rebel against the king?   4:1 • 6:6

20 Then answered I them, and said unto them, ᴿThe God of heaven, he will prosper us; therefore we his servants will arise and build: ᴿbut ye have no portion, nor right, nor memorial, in Jerusalem.   v. 4 • Ezra 4:3

CHAPTER 3

Record of the Builders

THEN ᴿE-li'-a-shib the high priest rose up with his brethren the priests, and they builded the sheep gate; they sanctified it, and set up the doors of it; even unto the tower of Me'-ah they sanctified it, unto the tower of Ha-nan'-e-el.   12:10

2 And next unto him builded ᴿthe men of Jericho. And next to them builded Zac'-cur the son of Im'-ri.   7:36; Ezra 2:34

3 ᴿBut the fish gate did the sons of Has-se-na'-ah build, who *also* laid the beams thereof, and set up the doors thereof, the locks thereof, and the bars thereof.   12:39

4 And next unto them repaired Mer'-e-moth the son of U-ri'-jah, the son of Koz. And next unto them repaired Me-shul'-lam the son of Ber-e-chi'-ah, the son of Me-shez'-a-beel. And next unto them repaired Za'-dok the son of Ba'-a-na.

5 And next unto them the Te-ko'-ites repaired; but their nobles put not their necks to the work of their ᵀLord.   lord

6 Moreover ᴿthe old gate repaired Je-hoi'-a-da the son of Pa-se'-ah, and Me-shul'-lam the son of Bes-o-de'-iah; they laid the beams thereof, and set up the doors thereof, and the locks thereof, and the bars thereof.   12:39

7 And next unto them repaired Mel-a-ti'-ah the Gib'-e-on-ite, and Ja'-don the Me-ron'-o-thite, ᴿthe men of Gib'-e-on, and of Miz'-pah, unto the ᴿthrone of the governor on this side the river.   7:25 • 2:8

8 Next unto him repaired Uz-zi'-el the son of Har-ha'-iah, of the goldsmiths. Next unto him also repaired Han-a-ni'-ah the son of *one of* the apothecaries, and they fortified Jerusalem unto the broad wall.

9 And next unto them repaired Re-pha'-iah the son of Hur, the ᴿruler of the half part of Jerusalem.   vv. 12, 17

10 And next unto them repaired Je-da'-iah the son of Ha-ru'-maph, even over against his house. And next unto him repaired Hat'-tush the son of Hash-ab-ni'-ah.

11 Mal-chi'-jah the son of Ha'-rim, and Ha'-shub the son of Pa'-hath–mo'-ab, repaired the other ᵀpiece, ᴿand the tower of the furnaces.   section • 12:38

12 And next unto him repaired Shal'-lum the son of Ha-lo'-hesh, the ruler of the half part of Jerusalem, he and his daughters.

13 The valley gate repaired Ha'-nun, and the inhabitants of Za-no'-ah; they built it, and set up the doors thereof, the locks thereof, and the bars thereof, and a thousand cubits on the wall unto the dung gate.

14 But the dung gate repaired Mal-chi'-ah the son of Re'-chab, the ruler of part of ^RBeth–hac'-ce-rem; he build it, and set up the doors thereof, the ^Tlocks thereof, and the bars thereof.   Jer. 6:1 • bolts

15 But ^Rthe gate of the fountain repaired Shal'-lun the son of Col-ho'-zeh, the ruler of part of Miz'-pah; he built it, and covered it, and set up the doors thereof, the locks thereof, and the bars thereof, and the wall of the pool of ^RSi-lo'-ah by the king's garden, and unto the stairs that go down from the city of David.   2:14 • John 9:7

16 After him repaired Ne-he-mi'-ah the son of Az'-buk, the ruler of the half part of Beth'-zur, unto the place over against the sepulchres of David, and to the pool that was made, and unto the house of the mighty.

17 After him repaired the Levites, Re'-hum the son of Ba'-ni. Next unto him repaired Hash-a-bi'-ah, the ruler of the half part of Kei'-lah, in his part.

18 After him repaired their brethren, Ba'-vai the son of Hen'-a-dad, the ruler of the half part of Kei'-lah.

19 And next to him repaired E'-zer the son of Jesh'-u-a, ^Rthe ruler of Miz'-pah, another piece over against the going up to the armoury at the turning of the wall.   v. 15

20 After him Ba'-ruch the son of Zab'-bai earnestly repaired the other piece, from the turning of the wall unto the door of the house of E-li'-a-shib the high priest.

21 After him repaired Mer'-e-moth the son of U-ri'-jah the son of Koz another piece, from the door of the house of E-li'-a-shib even to the end of the house of E-li'-a-shib.

22 And after him repaired the priests, the men of the ^Tplain.^R   circuit • 12:28

23 After him repaired Benjamin and Ha'-shub over against their house. After him repaired Az-a-ri'-ah the son of Ma-a-se'-iah the son of An-a-ni'-ah by his house.

24 After him repaired Bin'-nu-i the son of Hen'-a-dad another piece, from the house of Az-a-ri'-ah unto ^Rthe turning of the wall, even unto the corner.   v. 19

25 Pa'-lal the son of U'-zai, over against the turning of the wall, and the tower which lieth out from the king's high house, that was by the ^Rcourt of the prison. After him Pe-da'-iah the son of Pa'-rosh.   Jer. 32:2

26 Moreover the Neth'-i-nims ^Tdwelt in O'-phel, unto the place over against the water gate toward the east, and the tower that lieth out.   which dwelt in Ophel, repaired unto

27 After them the ^RTe-ko'-ites repaired another piece, over against the great tower that ^Tlieth out, even unto the wall of ^RO'-phel.   v. 5 • projects • 2 Chr. 27:3; 33:14

28 From above the horse gate repaired the priests, every one over against his house.

29 After them repaired Za'-dok the son of Im'-mer over against his house. After him repaired also She-ma'-iah the son of Shech-a-ni'-ah, the keeper of the east gate.

30 After him repaired Han-a-ni'-ah the son of Shel-e-mi'-ah, and Ha'-nun the sixth son of Za'-laph, another piece. After him repaired Me-shul'-lam the son of Ber-e-chi'-ah over against his ^Tchamber.   room

31 After him repaired Mal-chi'-ah the ^Rgoldsmith's son unto the place of the Neth'-i-nims, and of the merchants, over against the gate Miph'-kad, and to the going up of the corner.   vv. 8, 32

32 And between the going up of the corner unto the ^Rsheep gate repaired the goldsmiths and the merchants.   v. 1

CHAPTER 4

Opposition Through Ridicule

BUT it came to pass, ^Rthat when San-bal'-lat heard that we builded the wall, he was ^Twroth, and took great indignation, and mocked the Jews.   2:10, 19 • angry

2 And he spake before his brethren and the army of Sa-ma'-ri-a, and said, What do these feeble Jews? will they fortify themselves? will they sacrifice? will they make an end in a day? will they revive the stones out of the heaps of the rubbish which are burned?

3 Now ^RTo-bi'-ah the Am'-mon-ite was by him, and he said, Even that which they build, if a ^Tfox go up, he shall even break down their stone wall.   2:10, 19 • jackal

4 ^RHear, O our God; for we are despised: and ^Rturn their ^Treproach upon their own head, and give them for a prey in the land of captivity: Ps. 123:3, 4 • Prov. 3:34 • criticism

5 And ^Rcover not their iniquity, and let not their sin be blotted out from before thee: for they have provoked thee to anger before the builders.   Ps. 69:27, 28; Jer. 18:23

6 So built we the wall; and all the wall was joined together unto the half thereof: for the people had a mind to work.

Opposition Through Threat of Attack

7 But it came to pass, that ^Rwhen San-bal'-lat, and To-bi'-ah, and the A-ra'-bi-ans, and the Am'-mon-ites, and the Ash'-dod-ites, heard that the walls of Jerusalem were made up, and that the breaches began to be stopped, then they were very wroth,   v. 1

8 And ᴿconspired all of them together to come *and* to fight against Jerusalem, and to hinder it.   Ps. 83:3–5

9 Nevertheless ᴿwe made our prayer unto our God, and set a watch against them day and night, because of them.   [Ps. 50:15]

Opposition Through Discouragement

10 And Judah said, The strength of the bearers of burdens is ᵀdecayed, and *there is* much ᵀrubbish; so that we are not able to build the wall.   worn out • debris

11 And our adversaries said, They shall not know, neither see, till we come in the midst among them, and slay them, and cause the work to cease.

12 And it came to pass, that when the Jews which dwelt by them came, they said unto us ten times, From all places whence ye shall return unto us *they will be upon you.*

13 Therefore set I in the lower places behind the wall, *and* on the higher places, I even set the people after their families with their swords, their spears, and their bows.

14 And I looked, and rose up, and said unto the nobles, and to the rulers, and to the rest of the people, Be not ye afraid of them: remember the Lord, *which is* great and ᵀterrible, and fight for your brethren, your sons, and your daughters, your wives, and your houses.   majestic

15 And it came to pass, when our enemies heard that it was known unto us, ᴿand God had brought their ᵀcounselᴿ to nought, that we returned all of us to the wall, every one unto his work.   Job 5:12 • *plans* • 2 Sam. 17:14

16 And it came to pass from that time forth, *that* the half of my servants wrought in the work, and the other half of them held both the spears, the shields, and the bows, and the habergeons; and the rulers *were* behind all the house of Judah.

17 They which builded on the wall, and they that bare burdens, with those that laded, *every one* with one of his hands wrought in the work, and with the other *hand* held a weapon.

18 For the builders, every one had his sword girded by his side, and so builded. And he that sounded the trumpet *was* by me.

19 And I said unto the nobles, and to the rulers, and to the rest of the people, The work is great and large, and we are separated upon the wall, one far from another.

20 In what place *therefore* ye hear the sound of the trumpet, resort ye thither unto us: ᴿour God shall fight for us.   Ex. 14:14

21 So we laboured in the work: and half of them held the spears from the rising of the morning till the stars appeared.

22 Likewise at the same time said I unto the people, Let every one with his servant lodge within Jerusalem, that in the night they may be a guard to us, and labour on the day.

23 So neither I, nor my brethren, nor my servants, nor the men of the guard which followed me, none of us put off our clothes, *saving that* every one ᵀput them off for washing.   went with his weapon to the water

CHAPTER 5

Opposition Through Extortion

AND there was a great cry of the people and of their wives against their ᴿbrethren the Jews.   Deut. 15:7

2 For there were that said, We, our sons, and our daughters, *are* many: therefore we take up ᵀcorn *for them*, that we may eat, and live.   grain

3 *Some* also there were that said, We have mortgaged our lands, vineyards, and houses, that we might buy corn, because of the ᵀdearth.   famine

4 There were also that said, We have borrowed money ᴿfor the king's tribute, *and that* upon our lands and vineyards.   Ezra 4:13

5 Yet now our flesh *is* as the flesh of our brethren, our children as their children: and, lo, we bring into bondage our sons and our daughters to be servants, and *some* of our daughters are brought unto bondage *already:* neither *is it* in our power *to redeem them;* for other men have our lands and vineyards.

6 And I was very angry when I heard their cry and these words.

7 Then I consulted with myself, and I rebuked the nobles, and the rulers, and said unto them, Ye exact usury, every one of his brother. And I ᵀset a great assembly against them.   called a solemn meeting

8 And I said unto them, We after our ability have redeemed our brethren the Jews, which were sold unto the heathen; and will ye even sell your brethren? or shall they be sold unto us? Then held they their peace, and found nothing *to answer.*

9 Also I said, It *is* not good that ye do: ought ye not to walk in the fear of our God ᴿbecause of the ᵀreproach of the heathen our enemies?   [1 Pet. 2:12] • *criticism*

10 I likewise, *and* my brethren, and my servants, might exact of them money and corn: I pray you, let us leave off this usury.

11 Restore, I pray you, to them, even this day, their lands, their vineyards, their oliveyards, and their houses, also the hundredth *part* of the money, and of the corn, the wine, and the oil, that ye exact of them.

12 Then said they, We will restore *them,* and will require nothing of them; so will we do as thou sayest. Then I called the priests,

and took an oath of them, that they should do according to this promise.

13 Also [R]I shook my lap, and said, So God shake out every man from his house, and from his labour, that performeth not this promise, even thus be he shaken out, and emptied. And all the congregation said, A'-men, and praised the LORD. And the people did according to this promise.   Acts 18:6

Nehemiah's Unselfish Example

14 Moreover from the time that I was appointed to be their governor in the land of Judah, from the twentieth year even unto the two and thirtieth year of Ar-tax-erx'-es the king, that is, twelve years, I and my brethren have not eaten the bread of the governor.

15 But the former governors that had been before me were chargeable unto the people, and had taken of them bread and wine, beside [T]forty shek'-els of silver; yea, even their servants bare rule over the people: but so did not I, because of the fear of God. $5,120

16 Yea, also I continued in the [R]work of this wall, neither bought we any land: and all my servants were gathered thither unto the work.   4:1; 6:1

17 Moreover there were [R]at my table an hundred and fifty of the Jews and rulers, beside those that came unto us from among the heathen that are about us.   1 Kin. 18:19

18 Now that [R]which was prepared for me daily was one ox and six choice sheep; also fowls were prepared for me, and once in ten days store of all sorts of wine: yet for all this [R]required not I the bread of the governor, because the [T]bondage was heavy upon this people.   1 Kin. 4:22 • vv. 14, 15 • taxation

19 [R]Think upon me, my God, for good, according to all that I have done for this people.   13:22; 2 Kin. 20:3

CHAPTER 6

Opposition Through Compromise

NOW it came to pass, when San-bal'-lat, and To-bi'-ah, and Ge'-shem the A-ra'-bi-an, and the rest of our enemies, heard that I had builded the wall, and that there was no [T]breach left therein; (though at that time I had not set up the doors upon the gates;)   gap

2 That San-bal'-lat and Ge'-shem sent unto me, saying, Come, let us meet together in some one of the villages in the plain of O'-no. But they thought to do me mischief.

3 And I sent messengers unto them, saying, I am doing a great work, so that I cannot come down: why should the work cease, whilst I leave it, and come down to you?

4 Yet they sent unto me four times after this sort; and I answered them after the same manner.

Opposition Through Slander

5 Then sent San-bal'-lat his servant unto me in like manner the fifth time with an open letter in his hand;

6 Wherein was written, It is reported among the [T]heathen, and [T]Gash'-mu saith it, [R]that thou and the Jews think to rebel: for which cause thou buildest the wall, that thou mayest be their king, according to these words.   nations • Geshem, v. 1 • 2:19

7 And thou hast also appointed prophets to preach of thee at Jerusalem, saying, There is a king in Judah: and now shall it be reported to the king according to these words. Come now therefore, and let us take counsel together.

8 Then I sent unto him, saying, There are no such things done as thou sayest, but thou [T]feignest them out of thine own heart.   pretend

9 For they all made us afraid, saying, Their hands shall be weakened from the work, that it be not done. Now therefore, O God, strengthen my hands.

Opposition Through Treachery

10 Afterward I came unto the house of She-ma'-iah the son of De-la'-iah the son of Me-het'-a-beel, who was shut up; and he said, Let us meet together in the house of God, within the temple, and let us [R]shut the doors of the temple: for they will come to slay thee; yea, in the night will they come to slay thee.   Jer. 36:5

11 And I said, Should such a man as I flee? and who is there, that, being as I am, would go into the temple to save his life? I will not go in.

12 And, lo, I perceived that God had not sent him; but that [R]he pronounced this prophecy against me: for To-bi'-ah and San-bal'-lat had hired him.   Ezek. 13:22

13 Therefore was he hired, that I should be [R]afraid, and do so, and sin, and that they might have matter for an evil report, that they might [T]reproach me.   2 Cor. 11:26 • criticize

14 [R]My God, think thou upon To-bi'-ah and San-bal'-lat according to these their works, and on the [R]prophetess No-a-di'-ah, and the rest of the prophets, that would have put me in fear.   13:29 • Ezek. 13:17

Completion of the Reconstruction

15 So the [R]wall was finished in the twenty and fifth day of the month E'-lul, in fifty and two days.   4:1, 2

16 And it came to pass, that when all our enemies heard thereof, and all the heathen that were about us saw these things, they

were much cast down in their own eyes: for they perceived that this work was Twrought of our God. *accomplished*

17 Moreover in those days the nobles of Judah sent many letters unto To-bi'-ah, and *the letters* of RTo-bi'-ah came unto them. 2:10

18 For *there were* many in Judah sworn unto him, because he *was* the son in law of Shech-a-ni'-ah the son of A'-rah; and his son Jo-ha'-nan had taken the daughter of Me-shul'-lam the son of Ber-e-chi'-ah.

19 Also they reported his good deeds before me, and uttered my words to him. *And* To-bi'-ah sent letters to put me in fear.

CHAPTER 7

Organization of Jerusalem

NOW it came to pass, when the wall was built, and I had Rset up the doors, and the Tporters and the singers and the Levites were appointed, 6:1 · *gatekeepers*

2 That I gave my brother Ha-na'-ni, and Han-a-ni'-ah the ruler of the palace, charge over Jerusalem: for he *was* a faithful man, and feared God above many.

3 And I said unto them, Let not the gates of Jerusalem be opened until the sun be hot; and while they stand Tby, let them shut the doors, and bar *them:* and appoint watches of the inhabitants of Jerusalem, every one in his watch, and every one *to be* over against his house. *on guard*

4 Now the city *was* Tlarge and great: but the people *were* few therein, and the houses *were* not builded. *broad in spaces*

The Plan

5 And my God put into mine heart to gather together the nobles, and the rulers, and the people, that they might be reckoned by genealogy. And I found a register of the genealogy of them which came up at the first, and found written therein,

6 These *are* the children of the province, that went up out of the captivity, of those that had been carried away, whom Neb-u-chad-nez'-zar the king of Babylon had carried away, and came again to Jerusalem and to Judah, every one unto his city;

The Leaders

7 Who came with Ze-rub'-ba-bel, Jesh'-u-a, Ne-he-mi'-ah, TAz-a-ri'-ah, RRa-a-mi'-ah, Na-ham'-a-ni, Mor'-de-cai, Bil'-shan, Mis'-pe-reth, Big'-vai, Ne'-hum, Ba'-a-nah. The number, *I say,* of the men of the people of Israel *was* this; *Seraiah · Ezra 2:2*

The Men of Israel

8 The children of Pa'-rosh, two thousand an hundred seventy and two.

9 The children of Sheph-a-ti'-ah, three hundred seventy and two.

10 The children of A'-rah, six hundred fifty and two.

11 The children of Pa'-hath–mo'-ab, of the children of Jesh'-u-a and Jo'-ab, two thousand and eight hundred *and* eighteen.

12 The children of E'-lam, a thousand two hundred fifty and four.

13 The children of Zat'-tu, eight hundred forty and five.

14 The children of Zac'-cai, seven hundred and threescore.

15 The children of TBin'-nu-i,R six hundred forty and eight. *Bani · Ezra 2:10*

16 The children of Be'-bai, six hundred twenty and eight.

17 The children of Az'-gad, two thousand three hundred twenty and two.

18 The children of A-don'-i-kam, six hundred threescore and seven.

19 The children of Big'-vai, two thousand threescore and seven.

20 The children of A'-din, six hundred fifty and five.

21 The children of A'-ter of Hez-e-ki'-ah, ninety and eight.

22 The children of Ha'-shum, three hundred twenty and eight.

23 The children of Be'-zai, three hundred twenty and four.

24 The children of THa'-riph, Ran hundred and twelve. *Jora · Ezra 2:18*

25 The children of TGib'-e-on, Rninety and five. *Gibbar · Ezra 2:20*

26 The men of Beth'-le-hem and Ne-to'-phah, an hundred fourscore and eight.

27 The men of An'-a-thoth, an hundred twenty and eight.

28 The men of TBeth–az'-ma-veth,R forty and two. *Azmaveth · Ezra 2:24*

29 RThe men of TKir'-jath–je'-a-rim, Che-phi'-rah, and Be-e'-roth, seven hundred forty and three. *Ezra 2:25 · Kirjatharim*

30 The men of Ra'-mah and Ga'-ba, six hundred twenty and one.

31 The men of Mich'-mas, an hundred and twenty and two.

32 The men of RBeth'-el and RA'-i, an hundred twenty and three. *Gen. 28:19 · Gen. 12:8*

33 The men of the other Ne'-bo, fifty and two.

34 The children of the other E'-lam, a thousand two hundred fifty and four.

35 The children of Ha'-rim, three hundred and twenty.

36 The children of Jericho, three hundred forty and five.

37 The children of Lod, Ha'-did, and O'-no, seven hundred twenty and one.

38 The children of Se-na'-ah, three thousand nine hundred and thirty.

The Priests

39 The priests: the children of ^RJe-da′-iah, of the house of ^RJesh′-u-a, nine hundred seventy and three. 1 Chr. 24:7 • Ezra 2:2

40 The children of ^RIm′-mer, a thousand fifty and two. 1 Chr. 24:14

41 The children of ^RPash′-ur, a thousand two hundred forty and seven. 1 Chr. 9:12

42 The children of ^RHa′-rim, a thousand and seventeen. 1 Chr. 24:8

The Levites

43 The Levites: the children of Jesh′-u-a, of Kad′-mi-el, and of the children of ^THo-de′-vah,^R seventy and four. Hodaviah • Ezra 2:40

44 The singers: the children of ^RA′-saph, an hundred forty and eight. 1 Chr. 15:17

45 The ^Rporters: the children of Shal′-lum, the children of A′-ter, the children of Tal′-mon, the children of Ak′-kub, the children of Hat′-i-ta, the children of Sho′-bai, an hundred thirty and eight. doorkeepers

The Servants

46 The ^RNeth′-i-nims: the children of Zi′-ha, the children of Ha-shu′-pha, the children of Tab′-ba-oth, 1 Chr. 9:2

47 The children of Ke′-ros, the children of ^TSi′-a, the children of Pa′-don, Siaha

48 The children of Leb′-a-na, the children of Hag′-a-ba, the children of Shal′-mai,

49 The children of Ha′-nan, the children of Gid′-del, the children of Ga′-har,

50 The children of Re-a′-iah, the children of Re′-zin, the children of Ne-ko′-da,

51 The children of Gaz′-zam, the children of Uz′-za, the children of Pha-se′-ah,

52 The children of Be′-sai, the children of Me-u′-nim, the children of Ne-phish′-e-sim,

53 The children of Bak′-buk, the children of Ha-ku′-pha, the children of Har′-hur,

54 The children of Baz′-lith, the children of Me-hi′-da, the children of Har′-sha,

55 The children of Bar′-kos, the children of Sis′-e-ra, the children of Ta′-mah,

56 The children of Ne-zi′-ah, the children of Hat′-i-pha.

57 The children of Solomon's servants: the children of So′-tai, the children of Soph′-e-reth, the children of ^TPe-ri′-da, Perudu

58 The children of Ja-a′-la, the children of Dar′-kon, the children of Gid′-del,

59 The children of Sheph-a-ti′-ah, the children of Hat′-til, the children of Poch′-e-reth of Ze-ba′-im, the children of Amon.

60 All the ^RNeth′-i-nims, and the children of Solomon's servants, were three hundred ninety and two. 1 Chr. 9:2

The Men of Israel

61 And these were they which went up also from Tel-me′-lah, Tel-har′-e-sha, Cherub, Ad′-don, and Im′-mer: but they could not shew their father's house, nor their seed, whether they were of Israel.

62 The children of De-la′-iah, the children of To-bi′-ah, the children of Ne-ko′-da, six hundred forty and two.

The Priests

63 And of the priests: the children of Ha-ba′-iah, the children of Koz, the children of Bar-zil′-lai, which took one of the daughters of Bar-zil′-lai the Gil′-e-ad-ite to wife, and was called after their name.

64 These sought their register among those that were reckoned by genealogy, but it was not found: therefore were they, as polluted, put from the priesthood.

65 And ^Tthe Tir-sha′-tha^R said unto them, that they should not eat of the most holy things, till there stood up a priest with U′-rim and Thum′-mim. the governor • 8:9

The Total of the Remnant

66 The whole congregation together was forty and two thousand three hundred and threescore,

67 Beside their manservants and their maidservants, of whom there were seven thousand three hundred thirty and seven: and they had two hundred forty and five singing men and singing women.

68 Their horses, seven hundred thirty and six: their mules, two hundred forty and five:

69 Their camels, four hundred thirty and five: six thousand seven hundred and twenty asses.

The Gifts of the Remnant for the Temple

70 And ^Tsome of the chief of the fathers gave unto the work. ^RThe ^TTir-sha′-tha gave to the treasure a ^Tthousand drams of gold, fifty basons, five hundred and thirty priests' garments. part • 8:9 • governor • $1,424,176

71 And some of the chief of the fathers gave to the treasure of the work twenty thousand drams of gold, and ^Ttwo thousand and two hundred pounds of silver. $14,080,000

72 And that which the rest of the people gave was twenty thousand drams of gold, and two thousand pounds of silver, and threescore and seven priests' garments.

73 So the priests, and the Levites, and the ^Tporters, and the singers, and some of the people, and the Neth′-i-nims, and all Israel, dwelt in their cities; ^Rand when the seventh month came, the children of Israel were in their cities. keepers • Ezra 3:1

CHAPTER 8

Reading of the Law

AND all the people gathered themselves together as one man into the ^Tstreet that was before the water gate; and they

spake unto Ezra the ᴿscribe to bring the book of the law of Moses, which the LORD had commanded to Israel. *broad place • Ezra 7:6*

2 And ᴿEzra the priest brought the law before the congregation both of men and women, and all ᵀthat could hear with understanding, upon the first day of the seventh month. *v. 9 • that understood in hearing*

3 And he read therein before the street that *was* before the water gate from the morning until midday, before the men and the women, and those that could understand; and the ears of all the people *were attentive* unto the book of the law.

4 And Ezra the scribe stood upon a ᵀpulpit of wood, which they had made for the purpose; and beside him stood Mat-ti-thi'-ah, and She'-ma, and A-na'-iah, and U-ri'-jah, and Hil-ki'-ah, and Ma-a-se'-iah, on his right hand; and on his left hand, Pe-da'-iah, and Mish'-a-el, and Mal-chi'-ah, and Ha'-shum, and Hash-bad'-a-na, Zech-a-ri'-ah, *and* Me-shul'-lam. *tower of wood*

5 And Ezra opened the book in the ᵀsight of all people; (for he was above all the people;) and when he opened it, all the people ᴿstood up: *eyes • Judg. 3:20*

6 And Ezra blessed the LORD, the great God. And all the people answered, A'-men, A'-men, with lifting up their hands: and they bowed their heads, and worshipped the LORD with *their* faces to the ground.

7 Also Jesh'-u-a, and Ba'-ni, and Sher-e-bi'-ah, Ja'-min, Ak'-kub, Shab'-be-thai, Ho-di'-jah, Ma-a-se'-iah, Kel'-i-ta, Az-a-ri'-ah, Joz'-a-bad, Ha'-nan, Pe-la'-iah, and the Levites, caused the people to understand the law: and the people *stood* in their place.

8 So they read in the book in the law of God distinctly, and gave the sense, and caused *them* to understand the reading.

*Israel Celebrates
Her Understanding of the Law*

9 And Ne-he-mi'-ah, which *is* ᵀthe Tir-sha'-tha, and Ezra the priest the scribe, and the Levites that taught the people, said unto all the people, This day *is* holy unto the LORD your God; mourn not, nor weep. For all the people wept, when they heard the words of the law. *the governor*

10 Then he said unto them, Go your way, eat the fat, and drink the sweet, ᴿand send portions unto them for whom nothing is prepared: for *this* day *is* holy unto our Lord: neither be ye sorry; for the joy of the LORD is your strength. *Esth. 9:19; Rev. 11:10*

8:3 Reading God's Word—The person who can read well has a much better opportunity of knowing and understanding God's Word than the person who has to rely upon what others tell him about the Word of God. Reading the Word of God is a very important part of communicating God's Word to God's people. Public Scripture reading was a regular part of the worship services in Israel and in the early church. Today we are blessed above all people in history, for not only does nearly everyone know how to read, but there also are enough copies of the Bible available so that everyone may have a personal copy. Here are some suggestions to aid you in receiving the greatest benefit from reading the Bible:

a. Read the Bible prayerfully. Ask the Spirit of God to meet your heart's need as you read (Page 600—Ps. 119:18).

b. Read the Bible thoughtfully. Think about the meaning and implications of what you are reading.

c. Read the Bible carefully. Take careful note not only of the words that are used but also of how they relate to one another.

d. Read the Bible repeatedly. It may be of great help to read the same portion over daily for a month's time. This is a good way for its words to take root in your heart. If you are reading a short book, read it every day. Divide longer books into manageable portions of two or three chapters and read that portion through every day.

e. Read the Bible extensively. Sometimes it is of great help to read large portions of the Word of God through at one sitting. If you do this, do it at a time when you are alert and not likely to be disturbed during your reading.

f. Read the Bible regularly. It is good to have a particular time every day when you habitually give yourself to the reading of the Word of God.

g. Read the Bible faithfully. Inevitably there will be days when you will fail to read the Bible. Do not let your momentary lapse discourage you. Faithfully resume your practice of reading God's Word.

h. Read the Bible obediently. Because the Bible is God's Word written to you, it is essential to obey it (Page 78—Ex. 24:3).

Now turn to Page 531—Job 22:22: Memorizing God's Word.

8:9 God's Word Convicts—One of the great proofs that the Bible is really God's inspired Word is its unique ability to convict men and women of their sins. Let us consider but a few Old and New Testament examples which demonstrate the lifesaving power of the Scriptures.

Old Testament examples:

a. Josiah, a young and godly Judean king who ruled the Lord's people more than six centuries before Christ, succeeds a wicked ruler who hated righteousness. At the beginning of Josiah's rule a copy of God's Word is found in the temple. When it is read to the king, both he and his people are convicted of their sins in not keeping God's law. A great revival takes place (see Page 469—2 Chr. 34:18-21).

11 So the Levites stilled all the people, saying, Hold your peace, for the day is holy; neither be ye [T]grieved. *depressed*

12 And all the people went their way to eat, and to drink, and to [R]send portions, and to make great mirth, because they had [R]understood the words that were declared unto them. *v. 10 • vv. 7, 8*

Israel Obeys the Law

13 And on the second day were gathered together the chief of the fathers of all the people, the priests, and the Levites, unto Ezra the scribe, even to understand the words of the law.

14 And they found written in the law which the LORD had commanded by Moses, that the children of Israel should dwell in booths in the feast of the seventh month:

15 And that they should publish and proclaim in all their cities, and in Jerusalem, saying, Go forth unto the mount, and fetch olive branches, and pine branches, and myrtle branches, and palm branches, and branches of thick trees, to make booths, as it is written.

16 So the people went forth, and brought them, and made themselves booths, every one upon the roof of his house, and in their courts, and in the courts of the house of God, and in the street of the water gate, and in the street of the gate of E'-phra-im.

17 And all the congregation of them that were come again out of the captivity made booths, and sat under the booths: for since the days of Jesh'-u-a the son of Nun unto that day had not the children of Israel done so. And there was very great gladness.

18 Also day by day, from the first day unto the last day, he read in the book of the law of God. And they kept the feast seven days; and on the eighth day was a solemn assembly, according unto the manner.

CHAPTER 9

Spiritual Preparation of Israel

NOW in the twenty and fourth day of this month the children of Israel were assembled with fasting, and with sackclothes, [R]and earth upon them. *Job 2:12*

2 And [R]the seed of Israel separated themselves from all strangers, and stood and confessed their sins, and the iniquities of their fathers. *13:3, 30; Gen. 12:1; Ezra 10:11*

3 And they stood up in their place, and [R]read in the book of the law of the LORD their God one fourth part of the day; and another fourth part they confessed, and worshipped the LORD their God. *8:7, 8*

The Great Deliverances of God

4 Then stood up upon the [T]stairs, [R]of the Levites, Jesh'-u-a, and Ba'-ni, Kad'-mi-el, Sheb-a-ni'-ah, Bun'-ni, Sher-e-bi'-ah, Ba'-ni, and Chen'-a-ni, and cried with a loud voice unto the LORD their God. *scaffold • 8:7*

5 Then the Levites, Jesh'-u-a, and Kad'-mi-el, Ba'-ni, Hash-ab-ni'-ah, Sher-e-bi'-ah, Ho-di'-jah, Sheb-a-ni'-ah, and Peth-a-hi'-ah, said, Stand up and bless the LORD your God for ever and ever: and blessed be [R]thy glorious name, which is exalted above all blessing and praise. *1 Chr. 29:13*

6 Thou, even thou, art LORD alone; thou hast made heaven, the heaven of heavens, with all their host, the earth, and all things that are therein, the seas, and all that is therein, and thou preservest them all; and the host of heaven worshippeth thee.

7 Thou art the LORD the God, who didst choose [R]Abram, and broughtest him forth out of Ur of the Chal'-dees, and gavest him the name of [R]Abraham; *Gen. 11:31 • Gen. 17:5*

8 And foundest his heart faithful before thee, and madest a covenant with him to give the land of the Ca'-naan-ites, the Hit'-tites, the Am'-o-rites, and the Per'-iz-zites, and the Jeb'-u-sites, and the Gir'-ga-shites, to give it, I say, to his seed, and hast performed thy words; for thou art righteous:

9 [R]And didst see the [T]affliction of our fathers in Egypt, and [R]heardest their cry by the Red sea; *Ex. 2:25 • distress • Ex. 14:10*

10 And shewedst signs and wonders upon Pharaoh, and on all his servants, and on all the people of his land: for thou knewest that they dealt proudly against them. So didst thou get thee a name, as it is this day.

---

b. Nehemiah returns to help the returning Jews rebuild the gates in the Jerusalem wall. This great wall builder thinks the Word of God to be so important that he assembles the people and has the Scriptures read to them for three hours per day. This soon causes them to confess their sins (Page 497—Neh. 9:3).

New Testament examples: Before Jesus left this earth He promised that the Holy Spirit would soon come upon the apostles. "And when he is come, he will reprove the world of sin, and of righteousness, and of judgment" (Page 1061—John 16:8). There are many instances in the New Testament where we see the Holy Spirit using God's Word to convict people of their sin. At Pentecost, Peter uses the Scriptures to rebuke Israel for crucifying its Messiah. This sermon results in three thousand souls being convicted and accepting Christ (Page 1074—Acts 2:37, 41).

Now turn to Page 553—Ps. 17:4: God's Word Corrects.

11 And thou didst divide the sea before them, so that they went through the midst of the sea on the dry land; and their persecutors thou threwest into the deeps, ^{R}as a stone into the mighty waters.   Ex. 15:5

12 Moreover thou ^{R}leddest them in the day by a cloudy pillar; and in the night by a pillar of fire, to give them light in the way wherein they should go.   Ex. 13:21

13 Thou camest down also upon mount Si'-nai, and spakest with them from heaven, and gavest them right judgments, and true laws, good statutes and commandments:

14 And madest known unto them thy ^{R}holy sabbath, and commandedst them precepts, statutes, and laws, by the hand of Moses thy servant: Ex. 16:23; 20:8; 23:12

15 And ^{R}gavest them bread from heaven for their hunger, and broughtest forth water for them out of the rock for their thirst, and promisedst them that they should go in to possess the land which thou hadst sworn to give them.   Ex. 16:14

The Great Sins of Israel

16 But they and our fathers dealt proudly, and hardened their necks, and hearkened not to thy commandments,

17 And refused to obey, neither were mindful of thy wonders that thou didst among them; but hardened their necks, and in their rebellion appointed ^{R}a captain to return to their bondage: but thou *art* a God ready to pardon, ^{R}gracious and merciful, slow to anger, and of great kindness, and forsookest them not.   Num. 14:4 · Joel 2:13

18 Yea, ^{R}when they had made them a molten calf, and said, This *is* thy God that brought thee up out of Egypt, and had ^{T}wrought great provocations;   Ex. 32:4 · *worked*

19 Yet thou in thy manifold mercies forsookest them not in the wilderness: the pillar of the cloud departed not from them by day, to lead them in the way; neither the pillar of fire by night, to shew them light, and the way wherein they should go.

20 Thou gavest also thy good spirit to instruct them, and withheldest not thy ^{R}man'-na from their mouth, and gavest them ^{R}water for their thirst.   Ex. 16:15 · Ex. 17:6

21 Yea, ^{R}forty years didst thou sustain them in the wilderness, *so that* they lacked nothing; their ^{R}clothes waxed not old, and their feet swelled not.   Deut. 2:7 · Deut. 8:4

22 Moreover thou gavest them kingdoms and nations, and didst divide them into corners: so they possessed the land of Si'-hon, and the land of the king of Hesh'-bon, and the land of Og king of Ba'-shan.

23 ^{R}Their children also multipliedst thou as the stars of heaven, and broughtest them into the land, concerning which thou hadst

promised to their fathers, that they should go in to possess *it*.   Gen. 15:5; 22:17

24 So the children went in and possessed the land, and thou subduedst before them the inhabitants of the land, the Ca'-naan-ites, and gavest them into their hands, with their kings, and the people of the land, that they might do with them as they would.

25 And they took strong cities, and a fat land, and possessed houses full of all goods, ^{T}wells digged, vineyards, and oliveyards, and fruit trees in abundance: so they did eat, and were filled, and became fat, and delighted themselves in thy great goodness.   *cisterns*

26 Nevertheless they were disobedient, and rebelled against thee, and cast thy law behind their backs, and slew thy prophets which testified against them to turn them to thee, and they wrought great provocations.

27 Therefore thou deliveredst them into the hand of their enemies, who vexed them: and in the time of their trouble, when they cried unto thee, thou heardest *them* from heaven; and according to thy manifold mercies thou gavest them saviours, who saved them out of the hand of their enemies.

28 But after they had rest, they did evil again before thee: therefore leftest thou them in the hand of their enemies, so that they had the dominion over them: yet when they returned, and cried unto thee, thou heardest *them* from heaven; and many times didst thou deliver them according to thy mercies;

29 And testifiedst against them, that thou mightest bring them again unto thy law: yet they dealt proudly, and hearkened not unto thy commandments, but sinned against thy judgments, (which if a man do, he shall live in them;) and withdrew the shoulder, and hardened their neck, and would not hear.

30 Yet many years didst thou forbear them, and testifiedst against them by thy spirit in thy prophets: yet would they not give ear: therefore gavest thou them into the hand of the people of the lands.

31 Nevertheless for thy great mercies' sake ^{R}thou didst not utterly consume them, nor forsake them; for thou ^{R}art a gracious and merciful God.   Jer. 4:27 · *v.* 17

Renewal of the Covenant

32 Now therefore, our God, the great, the mighty, and the terrible God, who keepest covenant and mercy, let not all the trouble seem little before thee, that hath come upon us, on our kings, on our princes, and on our priests, and on our prophets, and on our fathers, and on all thy people, since the time of the kings of Assyria unto this day.

33 Howbeit ^{R}thou *art* just in all that is brought upon us; for thou hast done right, but we have done wickedly: Ps. 119:137

34 Neither have our kings, our princes, our

priests, nor our fathers, kept thy law, nor hearkened unto thy commandments and thy testimonies, wherewith thou didst ᵀtestify against them.   *witnessed*

35 For they have not served thee in their kingdom, and in thy great goodness that thou gavest them, and in the large and fat land which thou gavest before them, neither turned they from their wicked works.

36 Behold, we *are* servants this day, and *for* the land that thou gavest unto our fathers to eat the fruit thereof and the good thereof, behold, we *are* servants in it:

37 And ᴿit yieldeth much increase unto the kings whom thou hast set over us because of our sins: also they have dominion over our bodies, and over our cattle, at their pleasure, and we *are* in great distress.   Deut. 28:33, 51

38 And ᵀbecause of all this ᴿwe make a sure *covenant*, and write *it;* and our princes, Levites, *and* priests, seal *unto* it.   *yet for* • 10:29

CHAPTER 10

Ratifiers of the Covenant

NOW those that sealed *were*, Ne-he-mi′-ah, the ᵀTir-sha′-tha, ᴿthe son of Hach-a-li′-ah, and Zid-ki′-jah,   *governor* • 1:1

2 Se-ra′-iah, Az-a-ri′-ah, Jer-e-mi′-ah,
3 Pash′-ur, Am-a-ri′-ah, Mal-chi′-jah,
4 Hat′-tush, Sheb-a-ni′-ah, Mal′-luch,
5 Ha′-rim, Mer′-e-moth, O-ba-di′-ah,
6 Daniel, Gin′-ne-thon, Ba′-ruch,
7 Me-shul′-lam, A-bi′-jah, Mij′-a-min,
8 Ma-a-zi′-ah, Bil′-gai, She-ma′-iah: these *were* the priests.
9 And the Levites: both Jesh′-u-a the son of Az-a-ni′-ah, Bin′-nu-i of the sons of Hen′-a-dad, Kad′-mi-el;
10 And their brethren, Sheb-a-ni′-ah, Ho-di′-jah, Kel′-i-ta, Pe-la′-iah, Ha′-nan,
11 Mi′-cha, Re′-hob, Hash-a-bi′-ah,
12 Zac′-cur, Sher-e-bi′-ah, Sheb-a-ni′-ah,
13 Ho-di′-jah, Ba′-ni, Ben′-i-nu.
14 The chief of the people; Pa′-rosh, Pa′-hath-mo′-ab, E′-lam, Zat′-thu, Ba′-ni,
15 Bun′-ni, Az′-gad, Be′-bai,
16 Ad-o-ni′-jah, Big′-vai, A′-din,
17 A′-ter, Hiz-ki′-jah, Az′-zur,
18 Ho-di′-jah, Ha′-shum, Be′-zai,
19 Ha′-riph, An′-a-thoth, Ne′-bai,
20 Mag′-pi-ash, Me-shul′-lam, He′-zir,
21 Me-shez′-a-beel, Za′-dok, Jad-du′-a,
22 Pel-a-ti′-ah, Ha′-nan, A-na′-iah,
23 Ho-she′-a, Han-a-ni′-ah, Ha′-shub,
24 Hal-lo′-hesh, Pil′-e-ha, Sho′-bek,
25 Re′-hum, Ha-shab′-nah, Ma-a-se′-iah,
26 And A-hi′-jah, Ha′-nan, A′-nan,
27 Mal′-luch, Ha′-rim, Ba′-a-nah.

Stipulations of the Covenant

28 And the rest of the people, the priests, the Levites, the porters, the singers, the Neth′-i-nims, ᴿand all they that had separated themselves from the people of the lands unto the law of God, their wives, their sons, and their daughters, every one having knowledge, and having understanding;   13:3; Ezra 9:1

29 They clave to their brethren, their nobles, and entered into a curse, and into an oath, to walk in God's law, which was given by Moses the servant of God, and to observe and do all the commandments of the LORD our Lord, and his judgments and his statutes;

30 And that we would not give ᴿour daughters unto the people of the land, nor take their daughters for our sons: Ex. 34:16

31 And *if* the people of the land bring ware or any victuals on the sabbath day to sell, *that* we would not buy it of them on the sabbath, or on ᵀthe holy day: and *that* we would ᵀleave the seventh year, and the exaction of every debt.   *a* • *forego*

32 Also we made ᵀordinances for us, to charge ourselves yearly with the ᵀthird part of a shek′-el ᴿfor the service of the house of our God;   *laws* • *$45* • Matt. 17:24

33 For the shewbread, and for the ᴿcontinual meat offering, and for the continual burnt offering, of the sabbaths, of the new moons, for the set feasts, and for the holy *things*, and for the sin offerings to make an atonement for Israel, and *for* all the work of the house of our God.   Num. 28:28, 29

34 And we cast the lots among the priests, the Levites, and the people, ᴿfor the wood offering, to bring *it* into the house of our God, after the houses of our fathers, at times appointed year by year, to burn upon the altar of the LORD our God, as *it is* written in the law: 13:31

35 And ᴿto bring the firstfruits of our ground, and the firstfruits of all fruit of all trees, year by year, unto the house of the LORD: Ex. 23:19; 34:26; Lev. 19:23; Num. 18:12

36 ᴿAlso the firstborn of our sons, and of our cattle, as *it is* written in the law, and the firstlings of our herds and of our flocks, to bring to the house of our God, unto the priests that minister in the house of our God: Ex. 13:2, 12, 13; Lev. 27:26, 27; Num. 18:15, 16

37 And *that* we should bring the firstfruits of our dough, and our offerings, and the fruit of all manner of trees, of wine and of oil, unto the priests, to the chambers of the ᵀhouse of our God; and the tithes of our ground unto the Levites, that the same Levites might have the tithes in all the cities of our tillage.   *temple*

38 And the priest the son of Aaron shall be with the Levites, when the Levites take tithes: and the Levites shall bring up the tithe of the tithes unto the house of our God, to the chambers, into the treasure house.

39 For the children of Israel and the children of Levi shall bring the offering of the

corn, of the new wine, and the oil, unto the chambers, where *are* the vessels of the sanctuary, and the priests that minister, and the porters, and the singers: and we will not forsake the house of our God.

CHAPTER 11

Plan for the Resettlement

AND the ᴿrulers of the people dwelt at Jerusalem: the rest of the people also cast lots, to bring one of ten to dwell in Jerusalem ᴿthe holy city, and nine parts *to dwell* in *other* cities.   7:4 • Matt. 4:5; 27:53

2 And the people blessed all the men, that ᴿwillingly offered themselves to dwell at Jerusalem.   Judg. 5:9; 2 Chr. 17:16

Resettlement Within Jerusalem

3 Now these *are* the chief of the province that dwelt in Jerusalem: but in the cities of Judah dwelt every one in his possession in their cities, *to wit*, Israel, the priests, and the Levites, and ᴿthe Neth′-i-nims, and the children of Solomon's servants.   Ezra 2:43

4 And at Jerusalem dwelt *certain* of the children of Judah, and of the children of Benjamin. Of the children of Judah; Ath-a-i′-ah the son of Uz-zi′-ah, the son of Zech-a-ri′-ah, the son of Am-a-ri′-ah, the son of Sheph-a-ti′-ah, the son of Ma-ha′-la-le-el, of the children of ᵀPe′-rez;   *Pharez*

5 And Ma-a-se′-iah the son of Ba′-ruch, the son of Col-ho′-zeh, the son of Ha-za′-iah, the son of A-da′-iah, the son of Joi′-a-rib, the son of Zech-a-ri′-ah, the son of Shi-lo′-ni.

6 All the sons of Pe′-rez that dwelt at Jerusalem *were* four hundred threescore and eight ᵀvaliant men.   *strong*

7 And these *are* the sons of Benjamin; Sal′-lu the son of Me-shul′-lam, the son of Jo′-ed, the son of Pe-da′-iah, the son of Ko-la′-iah, the son of Ma-a-se′-iah, the son of Ith′-i-el, the son of Je-sa′-iah.

8 And after him Gab′-bai, Sal′-lai, nine hundred twenty and eight.

9 And Jo′-el the son of Zich′-ri *was* their overseer: and Judah the son of Sen-u′-ah *was* second over the city.

10 ᴿOf the priests: Je-da′-iah the son of Joi′-a-rib, Ja′-chin.   1 Chr. 9:10

11 Se-ra′-iah the son of Hil-ki′-ah, the son of Me-shul′-lam, the son of Za′-dok, the son of Me-ra′-ioth, the son of A-hi′-tub, *was* the ruler of the house of God.

12 And their brethren that did the work of the house *were* eight hundred twenty and two: and A-da′-iah the son of Jer′-o-ham, the son of Pel-a-li′-ah, the son of Am′-zi, the son of Zech-a-ri′-ah, the son of Pash′-ur, the son of Mal-chi′-ah,

13 And his brethren, ᴿchief of the fathers,

two hundred forty and two: and Am′-a-shai the son of A-zar′-e-el, the son of A′-ha-sai, the son of Me-shil′-le-moth, the son of Im′-mer,   7:70, 71

14 And their brethren, mighty men of valour, an hundred twenty and eight: and their overseer *was* Zab′-di-el, the son of ᵀone of the great men.   *Haggedolim*

15 Also of the Levites: She-ma′-iah the son of Ha′-shub, the son of Az-ri′-kam, the son of Hash-a-bi′-ah, the son of Bun′-ni;

16 And Shab′-be-thai and Joz′-a-bad, of the chief of the Levites, *had* the oversight of the outward business of the house of God.

17 And Mat-ta-ni′-ah the son of Mi′-cha, the son of ᴿZab′-di, the son of A′-saph, *was* the ᵀprincipal to begin the thanksgiving in prayer: and Bak-bu-ki′-ah the second among his brethren, and Ab′-da the son of Sham-mu′-a, the son of Ga′-lal, the son of Je-du′-thun.   1 Chr. 9:15 • *head*

18 All the Levites in ᴿthe holy city *were* two hundred fourscore and four.   *v. 1*

19 Moreover the porters, Ak′-kub, Tal′-mon, and their brethren that kept the gates, *were* an hundred seventy and two.

20 And the ᵀresidue of Israel, of the priests, *and* the Levites, *were* in all the cities of Judah, ᴿevery one in his inheritance.   *rest • v. 3*

21 ᴿBut the Neth′-i-nims dwelt in ᵀO′-phel: and Zi-ha and Gis′-pa *were* over the Neth′-i-nims.   3:26; 2 Chr. 27:3 • *the tower*

22 The ᴿoverseer also of the Levites at Jerusalem *was* Uz′-zi the son of Ba′-ni, the son of Hash-a-bi′-ah, the son of Mat-ta-ni′-ah, the son of Mi′-cha. Of the sons of A′-saph, the singers *were* over the ᵀbusiness of the ᵀhouse of God.   *vv. 9, 14 • activities • temple*

23 For *it was* the king's commandment concerning them, that a certain portion should be for the singers, due for every day.

24 And Peth-a-hi′-ah the son of Me-shez′-a-beel, of the children of ᵀZe′-rah the son of Judah, *was* at the king's hand in all matters concerning the people.   *Zarah*

Resettlement Outside of Jerusalem

25 And for the villages, with their fields, *some* of the children of Judah dwelt at Kir′-jath-ar′-ba, and *in* the villages thereof, and at Di′-bon, and *in* the villages thereof, and at Je-kab′-ze-el, and *in* the villages thereof,

26 And at Jesh′-u-a, and at Mol′-a-dah, and at Beth-phe′-let,

27 And at Ha′-zar-shu′-al, and at Be′-er-she′-ba, and *in* the villages thereof,

28 And at ᴿZik′-lag, and at Me-ko′-nah, and in the villages thereof,   Josh. 15:31

29 And at En-rim′-mon, and at Za′-re-ah, and at Jar′-muth,

30 Za-no′-ah, A-dul′-lam, and *in* their villages, at ᴿLa′-chish, and the fields thereof, at ᴿA-ze′-kah, and *in* the villages thereof. And

they dwelt from Be'-er-she'-ba unto the valley of Hin'-nom.   Josh. 10:31 • Josh. 10:10

31 The children also of Benjamin ^Tfrom Ge'-ba *dwelt* at Mich'-mash, and Ai'-ja, and Beth'-el, and *in* their villages,   *of Geba*

32 *And* at An'-a-thoth, Nob, An-a-ni'-ah,

33 Ha'-zor, Ra'-mah, Git'-ta-im,

34 Ha'-did, Ze-bo'-im, Ne-bal'-lat,

35 Lod, and O'-no, ^Rthe valley of craftsmen.   1 Chr. 4:14

36 And of the Levites *were* divisions *in* Judah, *and* in Benjamin.

CHAPTER 12

Register of the Priests and the Levites

NOW these *are* the ^Rpriests and the Levites that went up with Ze-rub'-babel the son of She-al'-ti-el, and Jesh'-u-a: ^RSe-ra'-iah, Jer-e-mi'-ah, Ezra,   Ezra 2:1, 2 • 10:2-8

2 Am-a-ri'-ah, ^TMal'-luch, Hat'-tush,   *Melicu*

3 ^RShech-a-ni'-ah,^T ^RRe'-hum,^T ^TMer'-e-moth,^R   *v. 14 • Shebaniah • v. 15 • Harims • Meraioth • v. 15*

4 Id'-do, ^TGin'-ne-tho, A-bi'-jah,   *Ginnethon*

5 Mi'-a-min, Ma-a-di'-ah, Bil'-gah,

6 She-ma'-iah, and Joi'-a-rib, Je-da'-iah,

7 Sal'-lu, A'-mok, Hil-ki'-ah, Je-da'-iah. These *were* the chief of the priests and of their brethren in the days of Jesh'-u-a.

8 Moreover the Levites: Jesh'-u-a, Bin'-nu-i, Kad'-mi-el, Sher-e-bi'-ah, Judah, *and* Mat-ta-ni'-ah, ^Rwhich *was* over the thanksgiving, he and his brethren.   11:17

9 Also Bak-bu-ki'-ah and Un'-ni, their brethren, *were* ^Tover against them in the ^Twatches.   *stood opposite • service*

10 And Jesh'-u-a begat Joi'-a-kim, Joi'-a-kim also begat E-li'-a-shib, and E-li'-a-shib begat Joi'-a-da,

11 And Joi'-a-da begat Jonathan, and Jonathan begat Jad-du'-a.

12 And in the days of Joi'-a-kim were priests, the chief of the fathers: of Se-ra'-iah, Me-ra'-iah; of Jer-e-mi'-ah, Han-a-ni'-ah;

13 Of Ezra, Me-shul'-lam; of Am-a-ri'-ah, Je-ho-ha'-nan;

14 Of ^RMel'-i-cu, Jonathan; of Sheb-a-ni'-ah, Joseph;   *v. 2*

15 Of Ha'-rim, Ad'-na; of Me-ra'-ioth, Hel'-kai;

16 Of Id'-do, Zech-a-ri'-ah; of Gin'-ne-thon, Me-shul'-lam;

17 Of A-bi'-jah, Zich'-ri; of Mi-ni'-a-min, of Mo-a-di'-ah, Pil'-tai;

18 Of Bil'-gah, Sham-mu'-a; of She-ma'-iah, Je-hon'-a-than;

19 And of Joi'-a-rib, Mat-te'-nai; of Je-da'-iah, Uz'-zi;

20 Of Sal'-lai, Kal'-lai; of A'-mok, E'-ber;

21 Of Hil-ki'-ah, Hash-a-bi'-ah; of Je-da'-iah, Ne-than'-e-el.

22 The Levites in the days of E-li'-a-shib,

Joi'-a-da, and Jo-ha'-nan, and Jad-du'-a, *were* recorded chief of the fathers: also the priests, to the reign of Da-ri'-us the Persian.

23 The sons of Levi, the chief of the fathers, *were* written in the book of the ^Rchronicles, even until the days of Jo-ha'-nan the son of E-li'-a-shib.   1 Chr. 9:14

24 And the chief of the Levites: Hash-a-bi'-ah, Sher-e-bi'-ah, and Jesh'-u-a the son of Kad'-mi-el, with their brethren over against them, to praise *and* to give thanks, according to the commandment of David the man of God, ward over against ward.

25 Mat-ta-ni'-ah, and Bak-bu-ki'-ah, O-ba-di'-ah, Me-shul'-lam, Tal'-mon, Ak'-kub, *were* porters keeping the ward at the ^Tthresholds of the gates.   *storehouses*

26 These *were* in the days of Joi'-a-kim the son of Jesh'-u-a, the son of Joz'-a-dak, and in the days of Ne-he-mi'-ah the governor, and of Ezra the priest, the scribe.

Dedication of the Jerusalem Wall

27 And at ^Rthe dedication of the wall of Jerusalem they sought the Levites out of all their places, to bring them to Jerusalem, to keep the dedication with gladness, both with thanksgivings, and with singing, *with* cymbals, psalteries, and with harps. Ps. 30, title

28 And the sons of the singers gathered themselves together, both out of the plain country round about Jerusalem, and from the ^Rvillages of Ne-toph'-a-thi;   1 Chr. 9:16

29 Also from the house of Gil'-gal, and out of the fields of Ge'-ba and Az'-ma-veth: for the singers had builded them villages round about Jerusalem.

30 And the priests and the Levites purified themselves, and ^Rpurified the people, and the gates, and the wall.   Ezra 6:20

31 Then I brought up the princes of Judah upon the wall, and appointed two great *companies of them that gave* thanks, *whereof* ^Rone went on the right hand upon the wall toward the ^Rdung gate: *v. 38 • 2:13*

32 And after them went Ho-sha'-iah, and half of the princes of Judah,

33 And Az-a-ri'-ah, Ezra, and Me-shul'-lam,

34 Judah, and Benjamin, and She-ma'-iah, and Jer-e-mi'-ah,

35 And *certain* of the priests' sons with trumpets; *namely,* Zech-a-ri'-ah the son of Jonathan, the son of She-ma'-iah, the son of Mat-ta-ni'-ah, the son of Mi-cha'-iah, the son of Zac'-cur, the son of A'-saph:

36 And his brethren, She-ma'-iah, and A-zar'-a-el, Mil'-a-lai, Gil'-a-lai, Ma'-ai, Ne-than'-e-el, and Judah, Ha-na'-ni, with the musical instruments of David the man of God, and Ezra the scribe before them.

37 ^RAnd at the fountain gate, which was

over against them, they went up by the stairs of the city of David, at the going up of the wall, above the house of David, even unto the water gate eastward.   2:14; 3:15

38 And the other *company of them that gave* thanks went over against *them*, and I after them, and the half of the people upon the wall, from beyond Rthe tower of the furnaces even unto the broad wall;   3:11

39 And from above the gate of E'-phra-im, and above the old gate, and above the fish gate, and the tower of Ha-nan'-e-el, and the tower of Me'-ah, even unto the sheep gate: and they stood still in the prison gate.

40 So stood the two *companies of them that gave* thanks in the house of God, and I, and the half of the rulers with me:

41 And the priests; E-li'-a-kim, Ma-a-sei'-ah, Mi-ni'-a-min, Mi-cha'-iah, E-li-o-e'-nai, Zech-a-ri'-ah, *and* Han-a-ni'-ah, with trumpets;

42 And Ma-a-se'-iah, and She-ma'-iah, and E-le-a'-zar, and Uz'-zi, and Je-ho-ha'-nan, and Mal-chi'-jah, and E'-lam, and E'-zer. And the singers sang loud, with Jez-ra-hi'-ah *their* overseer.

43 Also that day they offered great sacrifices, and rejoiced: for God had made them rejoice with great joy: the wives also and the children rejoiced: so that the joy of Jerusalem was heard even afar off.

44 And at that time were some appointed over the chambers for the treasures, for the offerings, for the firstfruits, and for the tithes, to gather into them out of the fields of the cities the portions of the law for the priests and Levites: for Judah rejoiced for the priests and for the Levites that waited.

45 And both the singers and the porters kept the ward of their God, and the ward of the purification, according to the commandment of David, *and* of Solomon his son.

46 For in the days of David and A'-saph of old *there were* chief of the singers, and songs of praise and thanksgiving unto God.

47 And all Israel in the days of Ze-rub'-babel, and in the days of Ne-he-mi'-ah, gave the portions of the singers and the porters, every day his portion: and they sanctified *holy things* unto the Levites; and the Levites sanctified *them* unto the children of Aaron.

CHAPTER 13

Separation from the Heathen

ON that day they read in the book of Moses in the audience of the people; and therein was found written, that the Am'-mon-ite and the Mo'-ab-ite should not come into the congregation of God for ever;

2 Because they met not the children of Israel with bread and with water, but Rhired Ba'-laam against them, that he should curse

them: Rhowbeit our God turned the curse into a blessing.   Josh. 24:9, 10 • Deut. 23:5

3 Now it came to pass, when they had heard the law, Rthat they separated from Israel all the mixed multitude.   9:2; 10:28

4 And before this, E-li'-a-shib the priest, having the oversight of the chamber of the house of our God, *was* allied unto To-bi'-ah:

5 And he had prepared for him a great chamber, where aforetime they laid the meat offerings, the frankincense, and the vessels, and the tithes of the corn, the new wine, and the oil, which was commanded *to be given* to the Levites, and the singers, and the porters; and the offerings of the priests.

6 But in all this *time* was not I at Jerusalem: Rfor in the two and thirtieth year of Ar-tax-erx'-es king of Babylon came I unto the king, and after certain days Tobtained I leave of the king: 5:14 • *I earnestly requested*

7 And I came to Jerusalem, and understood of the evil that E-li'-a-shib did for To-bi'-ah, in Rpreparing him a chamber in the courts of the Thouse of God.   v. 5 • *temple*

8 And it grieved me sore: therefore I cast forth all the household stuff of To-bi'-ah out of the chamber.

9 Then I commanded, and they cleansed the chambers: and thither brought I again the vessels of the house of God, with the meat offering and the frankincense.

Restoration of Levitical Support

10 And I perceived that the portions of the Levites had not been given *them:* for the Levites and the singers, that did the work, were fled every one to his field.

11 Then contended I with the rulers, and said, RWhy is the house of God forsaken? And I gathered them together, and set them in their Tplace.   10:39 • *rank*

12 RThen brought all Judah the tithe of the corn and the new wine and the oil unto the Ttreasuries.   10:38; 12:44 • *storehouses*

13 And I made treasurers over the treasuries, Shel-e-mi'-ah the priest, and Za'-dok the scribe, and of the Levites, Pe-da'-iah: and next to them *was* Ha'-nan the son of Zac'-cur, the son of Mat-ta-ni'-ah: for they were counted Rfaithful, and their office *was* to distribute unto their brethren.   1 Cor. 4:2

14 RRemember me, O my God, concerning this, and wipe not out my good deeds that I have done for the house of my God, and for the Toffices thereof.   5:19 • *services*

Restoration of the Sabbath

15 In those days saw I in Judah *some* treading winepresses on the sabbath, and bringing in sheaves, and lading asses; as also wine, grapes, and figs, and all *manner of* burdens, which they brought into Jerusalem on the sabbath day: and I testified *against them* in the day wherein they sold victuals.

16 There dwelt men of Tyre also therein, which brought fish, and all manner of Tware, and sold on the sabbath unto the children of Judah, and in Jerusalem.   *wares*

17 Then I contended with the nobles of Judah, and said unto them, What evil thing *is* this that ye do, and profane the sabbath day?

18 RDid not your fathers thus, and did not our God bring all this evil upon us, and upon this city? yet ye bring more wrath upon Israel by profaning the sabbath.   [Ezra 9:13]; Jer. 17:21

19 And it came to pass, that when the gates of Jerusalem began to be dark before the sabbath, I commanded that the gates should be shut, and charged that they should not be opened till after the sabbath: and *some* of my servants set I at the gates, *that* there should no burden be brought in on the sabbath day.

20 So the merchants and sellers of all kind of Tware Tlodged Twithout Jerusalem once or twice.   *merchandise · spent the night · outside*

21 Then I Ttestified against them, and said unto them, Why Tlodge ye about the wall? if ye do *so* again, I will lay hands on you. From that time forth came they no *more* on the sabbath.   *warned · spend the night*

22 And I commanded the Levites that Rthey should cleanse themselves, and *that* they should come *and* keep the gates, to sanctify the sabbath day. Remember me, O my God, *concerning* this also, and spare me according to the greatness of thy mercy.   12:30

Restoration from Mixed Marriages

23 In those days also saw I Jews *that* Rhad married wives of RAsh'-dod, of RAm'-mon, *and* of Moab: Ezra 9:2 · 4:7 · v. 1

24 And their children spake half in the speech of Ash'-dod, and could not speak in the Jews' language, but according to the language of each people.

25 And I contended with them, and cursed them, and smote certain of them, and plucked off their hair, and made them swear by God, *saying*, Ye shall not give your daughters unto their sons, nor take their daughters unto your sons, or for yourselves.

26 RDid not Solomon king of Israel sin by these things? yet among many nations was there no king like him, who was beloved of his God, and God made him king over all Israel: nevertheless even him did outlandish women cause to sin.   1 Kin. 11:1

27 Shall we then hearken unto you to do all this great evil, to Rtransgress against our God in marrying strange wives?   [Ezra 10:2]

28 And *one* of the sons Rof Joi'-a-da, the son of E-li'-a-shib the high priest, *was* son in law to San-bal'-lat the Hor'-o-nite: therefore I chased him from me.   12:10, 22

29 RRemember them, O my God, because they have defiled the priesthood, and Rthe Tcovenant of the priesthood, and of the Levites.   6:14 · Mal. 2:4, 11, 12 · *agreement*

Restoration in Summary

30 Thus cleansed I them from all strangers, and appointed the wards of the priests and the Levites, every one in his business;

31 And for Rthe wood offering, at times appointed, and for the firstfruits. Remember me, O my God, for good.   10:34

Measures of Length

Unit	Length	Equivalents	Translations
Day's journey	c. 20 miles		day's journey
Roman mile	4,854 feet	8 stadia	mile
Sabbath day's journey	3,637 feet	6 stadia	sabbath day's journey
Stadion	606 feet	⅛ Roman mile	furlong
Rod	9 feet (10.5 feet in Ezekiel)	3 paces; 6 cubits	measuring reed, reed
Fathom	6 feet	4 cubits	fathom
Pace	3 feet	⅓ rod; 2 cubits	pace
Cubit	18 inches	½ pace; 2 spans	cubit
Span	9 inches	½ cubit; 3 hand-breadths	span
Handbreadth	3 inches	⅓ span; 4 fingers	handbreadth
Finger	.75 inches	¼ handbreadth	finger

THE BOOK OF

ESTHER

📖 THE BOOK OF ESTHER

God's hand of providence and protection on behalf of His people is evident throughout the Book of Esther, though His name does not appear once. Haman's plot brings grave danger to the Jews and is countered by the courage of beautiful Esther and the counsel of her wise cousin Mordecai, resulting in a great deliverance. The Feast of Purim becomes an annual reminder of God's faithfulness on behalf of His people.

Esther's Hebrew name was *Hadassah*, "Myrtle" (2:7), but her Persian name *Ester* was derived from the Persian word for "star" (*stara*). The Greek title for this book is *Esther*, and the Latin title is *Hester*.

✍ THE AUTHOR OF ESTHER

While the author's identity is not indicated in the text, the evident knowledge of Persian etiquette and customs, the palace in Shushan, and details of the events in the reign of Ahasuerus indicate that the author lived in Persia during this period. The obvious Jewish nationalism and knowledge of Jewish customs further suggest that the author was Jewish. If this Persian Jew was not an eyewitness, he probably knew people who were. The book must have been written soon after the death of King Ahasuerus (464 B.C.), because 10:2, 3 speaks of his reign in the past tense. Some writers suggest that Mordecai himself wrote the book; this seems unlikely, for although Mordecai did keep records (9:20), 10:2, 3 implies that his career was already over. Nevertheless, the author certainly made use of Mordecai's records and may have had access to the book of the chronicles of the kings of Media and Persia (2:23; 10:2). Ezra and Nehemiah have also been suggested for authorship, but the vocabulary and style of Esther is dissimilar to that found in their books. It seems likely that a younger contemporary of Mordecai composed the book.

⏳ THE TIME OF ESTHER

Ahasuerus is the Hebrew name and Xerxes the Greek name of Khshayarsh, king of Persia in 486–464 B.C. According to 1:3, the feast of Xerxes took place in his third year, or 483 B.C. The historian Herodotus refers to this banquet as the occasion of Xerxes' planning for a military campaign against Greece. But in 479 B.C. he was defeated by the Greeks at Salamis, and Herodotus tells us that he sought consolation in his harem. This corresponds to the time when he held a "contest" and crowned Esther queen of

Persia (2:16, 17). Since the events of the rest of the book took place in 473 B.C. (3:7–12), the chronological span is ten years (483–473 B.C.). The probable time of authorship was between 464 B.C. (the end of Xerxes' reign; see 10:2, 3) and about 435 B.C. (the palace at Shushan was destroyed by fire during that period, and such an event would probably have been mentioned). The historical and linguistic features of Esther do not support a date later than 400 B.C., as there is no trace of Greek influence.

Xerxes was a boisterous man of emotional extremes, whose actions were often strange and contradictory. This fact sheds light on his ability to sign a decree for the annihilation of the Jews, and two months later to sign a second decree allowing them to overthrow their enemies.

Esther was addressed to the many Jews who did not return to their homeland. Not all the godly people left—some did not return for legitimate reasons. Most were disobedient in staying in Persia. Nevertheless, God continued to care for His people in voluntary exile.

✝ THE CHRIST OF ESTHER

Esther, like Christ, puts herself in the place of death for her people but receives the approval of the king. She also portrays Christ's work as Advocate on our behalf. This book reveals another satanic threat to destroy the Jewish people and thus, the messianic line. God continues to preserve His people in spite of opposition and danger, and nothing can prevent the coming of the Messiah.

🔑 KEYS TO ESTHER

Key Word: Providence—The Book of Esther was written to show how the Jewish people were protected and preserved by the gracious hand of God from the threat of annihilation. Although God disciplines His covenant people, He never abandons them. The God of Israel is the sovereign controller of history, and His providential care can be seen throughout this book: He raises a Jewish girl out of obscurity to become the queen of the most powerful empire in the world; He ensures that Mordecai's loyal deed is recorded in the palace records; He guides Esther's admission to the king's court; He superintends the timing of Esther's two feasts; He is involved in Ahasuerus's insomnia and the cure he uses for it; He sees that Haman's gallows will be utilized in an unexpected way; He gives Esther great favor in the sight of the king; and He brings about the new decree and the eventual victory of the Jews.

Key Verses: Esther 4:14; 8:17—"For if thou altogether holdest thy peace at this time, *then* shall there enlargement and deliverance arise to the Jews from another place; but thou and thy father's house shall be destroyed: and who knoweth whether thou art come to the kingdom for *such* a time as this?" (4:14).

"And in every province, and in every city, whithersoever the king's commandment and his decree came, the Jews had joy and gladness, a feast and a good day. And many of the people of the land became Jews; for the fear of the Jews fell upon them" (8:17).

Key Chapter: Esther 8—According to the Book of Esther, the salvation of the Jews is accomplished through the revised decree of King Ahasuerus, allowing the Jews to defend themselves against their enemies. Chapter 8 records this pivotal event with the accompanying result that "many of the people of the land became Jews" (8:17).

SURVEY OF ESTHER

The story of Esther fits between chapters 6 and 7 of Ezra, between the first return led by Zerubbabel and the second return led by Ezra. It provides the only biblical portrait of the vast majority of Jews who choose to remain in Persia rather than return to Palestine. God's guiding and protective hand on behalf of His people is evident throughout this book, even though His name does not appear in it. The clearly emerging message is that God uses ordinary men and women to overcome impossible circumstances to accomplish His gracious purposes. Chapters 1—4 describe the threat to the Jews, and chapters 5—10 describe the triumph of the Jews.

The Threat to the Jews (1—4): The story begins in Ahasuerus' winter palace at Susa. The king provides a lavish banquet and display of royal glory for the people of Susa, and proudly seeks to make Queen Vashti's beauty a part of the program. When she refuses to appear, the king is counseled to depose her and seek another queen, because it is feared that the other women will become insolent if Vashti goes unpunished. Esther later finds favor in the eyes of Ahasuerus and wins the royal "beauty pageant." At her cousin Mordecai's instruction, she does not reveal that she is Jewish. With her help, Mordecai is able to warn the king of an assassination plot, and his deed is recorded in the palace records. Meanwhile, Haman becomes captain of the princes, but Mordecai refuses to bow to him. When he learns that Mordecai is Jewish, Haman plots for a year to eliminate all Jews, as his rage and hatred grow. He casts lots (purim) daily during this period until he determines the best day to have them massacred. Through bribery and lies he convinces Ahasuerus to issue an edict that all Jews in the empire will be slain eleven months hence in a single day. Haman conceives his plot in envy and a vengeful spirit, and he executes it with malicious craft. The decree creates a state of confusion, and Mordecai asks Esther to appeal to the king to spare the Jews. At the peril of her life, Esther decides to see the king and reveal her nationality in a desperate attempt to dissuade Ahasuerus. Mordecai convinces her that she has been called to her high position for this purpose.

The Triumph of the Jews (5—10): After fasting, Esther appears before the king and wisely invites him to a banquet along with Haman. At the banquet she requests that they attend a second banquet, as she seeks the right moment to divulge her request. Haman is flattered but later enraged when he sees Mordecai. He takes his wife's suggestion to build a large gallows for Mordecai (he cannot wait the eleven months for Mordecai to be slain). That night Ahasuerus

FOCUS	THREAT TO THE JEWS		TRIUMPH OF THE JEWS	
REFERENCE	1:1 ——————— 2:21 ———————		5:1 ——————— 8:4 ——————— 10:3	
DIVISION	SELECTION OF ESTHER AS QUEEN	FORMULATION OF THE PLOT BY HAMAN	TRIUMPH OF MORDECAI OVER HAMAN	TRIUMPH OF ISRAEL OVER HER ENEMIES
TOPIC	FEASTS OF AHASUERUS		FEASTS OF ESTHER AND PURIM	
	GRAVE DANGER		GREAT DELIVERANCE	
LOCATION	PERSIA			
TIME	10 YEARS (483 – 473 B.C.)			

decides to treat his insomnia by reading the palace records. Reading about Mordecai's deed, he wants him to be honored. Haman, mistakenly thinking the king wants to honor him, tells the king how the honor should be bestowed, only to find out that the reward is for Mordecai. He is humbled and infuriated by being forced to honor the man he loathes. At Esther's second banquet Ahasuerus offers her as much as half of his kingdom for the third time. She then makes her plea for her people and accuses Haman of his treachery. The infuriated king has Haman hanged on the gallows that Haman intended for Mordecai. The gallows, seventy-five feet high, was designed to make Mordecai's downfall a city-wide spectacle, but it ironically provides Haman with unexpected public attention—posthumously.

Persian law sealed with the king's ring (3:12)

cannot be revoked, but at Esther's request the king issues a new decree to all the provinces that the Jews may assemble and defend themselves on the day when they are attacked by their enemies. This decree changes the outcome intended by the first order and produces great joy. Mordecai is also elevated and set over the house of Haman. When the fateful day of the two decrees arrives, the Jews defeat their enemies in their cities throughout the Persian provinces, but do not take the plunder. The next day becomes a day of celebration and an annual Jewish holiday called the Feast of Purim. The word is derived from the Assyrian *puru*, meaning "lot," referring to the lots cast by Haman to determine the day decreed for the Jewish annihilation. The narrative closes with the advancement of Mordecai to a position second only to the king.

OUTLINE OF ESTHER

Part One: The Threat to the Jews (1:1—4:17)

Part Two: The Triumph of the Jews (5:1—10:3)

CHAPTER 1

The Feasts of Ahasuerus

NOW it came to pass in the days of A-has-u-e'-rus, (this *is* A-has-u-e'-rus which reigned, ^Rfrom India even unto E-thi-o'-pi-a, ^Rover an hundred and seven and twenty provinces:)   8:9 • Dan. 6:1

2 *That* in those days, when the king A-has-u-e'-rus sat on the throne of his kingdom, which *was* in Shu'-shan the palace,

3 In the third year of his reign, he made a feast unto all his princes and his servants; the power of Persia and Me'-di-a, the nobles and princes of the provinces, *being* before him:

4 When he shewed the riches of his glorious kingdom and the honour of his excellent majesty many days, *even* an hundred and fourscore days.

5 And when these days were expired, the king made a feast unto all the people that were present in Shu'-shan the palace, both unto great and small, seven days, in the court of the garden of the king's palace;

6 *Where were* white, green, and blue, *hangings,* fastened with cords of fine linen and purple to silver rings and pillars of marble: ^Rthe beds *were of* gold and silver, upon a pavement of red, and blue, and white, and black, marble.   7:8; Amos 2:8; 6:4

7 And they gave *them* drink in vessels of gold, (the vessels being diverse one from another,) and royal wine in abundance, according to the ^Tstate of the king.   *bounty*

8 And the drinking *was* according to the law; none ^Tdid compel: for so the king had appointed to all the officers of his house, that they should do according to every man's pleasure.   *could*

Refusal of Queen Vashti

9 Also Vash'-ti the queen made a feast for the women *in* the royal house which *be-longed* to king A-has-u-e'-rus.

10 On the seventh day, when the heart of the king was merry with wine, he commanded Me-hu'-man, Biz'-tha, ^RHar-bo'-na, Big'-tha, and A-bag'-tha, Ze'-thar, and Car'-cas, the seven chamberlains that served in the presence of A-has-u-e'-rus the king,   7:9

11 To bring Vash'-ti the queen before the king with the crown royal, to shew the people and the princes her beauty: for she *was* fair to look on.

12 But the queen Vash'-ti refused to come at the king's commandment by *his* chamberlains: therefore was the king very ^Twroth, and his anger burned in him.   *angry*

Counsel to King Ahasuerus

13 Then the king said to the ^Rwise men, ^Rwhich knew the times, (for so *was* the king's

manner toward all that knew law and judgment: Dan. 2:12; Matt. 2:1 • 1 Chr. 12:32

14 And the next unto him *was* Car-she'-na, She'-thar, Ad-ma'-tha, Tar'-shish, Me'-res, Mar'-se-na, *and* Me-mu'-can, the ^Rseven princes of Persia and Me'-di-a, ^Rwhich saw the king's face, *and* which sat the first in the kingdom;)   Ezra 7:14 • 2 Kin. 25:19

15 What shall we do unto the queen Vash'-ti according to law, because she hath not performed the commandment of the king A-has-u-e'-rus by the chamberlains?

16 And Me-mu'-can answered before the king and the princes, Vash'-ti the queen hath not done wrong to the king only, but also to all the princes, and to all the people that *are* in all the provinces of the king A-has-u-e'-rus.

17 For *this* deed of the queen shall come abroad unto all women, so that they shall despise their husbands in their eyes, when it shall be reported, The king A-has-u-e'-rus commanded Vash'-ti the queen to be brought in before him, but she came not.

18 *Likewise* shall the ^Tladies of Persia and Me'-di-a say this day unto all the king's princes, which have heard of the deed of the queen. Thus *shall there arise* ^Ttoo much contempt and wrath.   *princesses • enough*

Commandment of King Ahasuerus

19 If it please the king, let there go a royal commandment from him, and let it be written among the laws of the Persians and the Medes, that ^Rit be not altered, That Vash'-ti come no more before king A-has-u-e'-rus; and let the king give her royal ^Testate unto another that is better than she.   8:8 • *position*

20 And when the king's decree which he shall make shall be published throughout all his empire, (for it is great,) all the wives shall ^Rgive to their husbands honour, both to great and small.   [Col. 3:18; 1 Pet. 3:1]

21 And the saying pleased the king and the princes; and the king did according to the word of Me-mu'-can:

22 For he sent letters into all the king's provinces, ^Rinto every province according to the writing thereof, and to every people after their language, that every man should ^Rbear rule in his own house, and that it should be published according to the language of every people.   8:9 • [1 Tim. 2:12]

CHAPTER 2

Decree to Search for Vashti's Replacement

AFTER these things, when the wrath of king A-has-u-e'-rus was appeased, he remembered Vash'-ti, and what she had done, and what was decreed against her.

2 Then said the king's servants that ministered unto him, ^RLet there be fair young virgins sought for the king: 1 Kin. 1:2

3 And let the king appoint officers in all the provinces of his kingdom, that they may gather together all the fair young virgins unto Shu'-shan the palace, to the house of the women, unto the custody of ^THe'-ge^R the king's ^Tchamberlain, keeper of the women; and let their things for purification be given *them:*   *Hegai • v. 8 • official*

4 And let the maiden which pleaseth the king be queen instead of Vash'-ti. And the thing pleased the king; and he did so.

Preparation of Esther

5 *Now* in Shu'-shan the palace there was a certain Jew, whose name *was* ^RMor'-de-cai, the son of Ja'-ir, the son of Shim'-e-i, the son of Kish, a Benjamite;   *v. 21*

6 Who had been carried away from Jerusalem with the captivity which had been carried away with ^TJec-o-ni'-ah king of Judah, whom Neb-u-chad-nez'-zar the king of Babylon had carried away.   *Jehoiachin*

7 And he ^Tbrought up Ha-das'-sah, that *is,* Esther, his uncle's daughter: for she had neither father nor mother, and the maid *was* fair and beautiful; whom Mor'-de-cai, when her father and mother were dead, took for his own daughter.   *reared*

8 So it came to pass, when the king's commandment and his decree was heard, and when many maidens were gathered together unto Shu'-shan the palace, to the custody of He'-gai, that Esther was brought also unto the king's house, to the custody of He'-gai, keeper of the women.

9 And the maiden pleased him, and she obtained kindness of him; and he speedily gave her her things for purification, with such things as belonged to her, and seven maidens, *which were* ^Tmeet to be given her, out of the king's house: and he preferred her and her maids unto the best *place* of the house of the women.   *proper*

10 Esther had not shewed her people nor her kindred: for Mor'-de-cai had charged her that she should not shew *it.*

11 And Mor'-de-cai walked every day before the court of the women's house, to know how Esther did, and what should become of her.

12 Now when every maid's turn was come ^Rto go in to king A-has-u-e'-rus, after that she had been twelve months, according to the manner of the women, (for so were the days of their purifications accomplished, *to wit,* six months with oil of myrrh, and six months with sweet odours, and with *other* things for the purifying of the women;)   [1 Thess. 4:4, 5]

13 Then thus came *every* maiden unto the king; whatsoever she desired was given her to go with her out of the house of the women unto the king's house.

14 In the evening she went, and on the morrow she returned into the second house of the women, to the custody of Sha-ash'-gaz, the king's ^Tchamberlain, which kept the concubines: she came in unto the king no more, except the king delighted in her, and that she were called by name.   *official*

Selection of Queen Esther

15 Now when the turn of Esther, ^Rthe daughter of Ab-i-ha'-il the uncle of Mor'-de-cai, who had taken her for his daughter, was come to go in unto the king, she required nothing but what He'-gai the king's chamberlain, the keeper of the women, ^Tappointed. And Esther ^Robtained favour in the sight of all them that looked upon her.   *v. 7 • said • 5:2, 8*

16 So Esther was taken unto king A-has-u-e'-rus into his house royal in the tenth month, which *is* the month Te'-beth, in the seventh year of his reign.

17 And the king loved Esther above all the women, and she obtained grace and favour in his sight more than all the virgins; ^Rso that he set the royal crown upon her head, and made her queen instead of Vash'-ti.   1:11

18 Then the king ^Rmade a great feast unto all his princes and his servants, *even* Esther's feast; and he made ^Ta release to the provinces, and gave gifts, ^Raccording to the state of the king.   1:3 • *a royal order* • 1:7

19 And ^Rwhen the virgins were gathered together the second time, then Mor'-de-cai sat ^Rin the king's gate.   *vv. 3, 4 • v. 21; 3:2*

20 ^REsther had not *yet* shewed her kindred nor her people; as Mor'-de-cai had charged her: for Esther did ^Tthe commandment of Mor'-de-cai, like as when she was brought up with him.   *v. 10 • the word of Mordecai*

Mordecai Reveals the Plot to Murder the King

21 In those days, while Mor'-de-cai sat in the king's gate, two of the king's ^Tchamberlains, Big'-than and Te'-resh, of those which kept the door, were ^Twroth, and sought to lay hand on the king A-has-u-e'-rus.   *officials • angry*

22 And the ^Tthing was known to Mor'-de-cai, ^Rwho told *it* unto Esther the queen; and Esther certified the king *thereof* in Mor'-de-cai's name.   *matter • 6:2*

23 And when inquisition was made of the matter, it was found out; therefore they were both hanged on a tree: and it was written in the book of the chronicles before the king.

CHAPTER 3

Haman Is Promoted

AFTER these things did king A-has-u-e'-rus promote Ha'-man the son of Ham-med'-a-tha the ᴿA'-gag-ite, and advanced him, and ᵀset his seat above all the princes that were with him.   1 Sam. 15:8 • assigned his office

The Reason for Haman's Plot

2 And all the king's servants, that were ᴿin the king's gate, bowed, and reverenced Ha'-man: for the king had so commanded concerning him. But Mor'-de-cai ᴿbowed not, nor did him reverence.   2:19 • Ps. 15:4

3 Then the king's servants, which were in ᴿthe king's gate, said unto Mor'-de-cai, Why transgressest thou the ᴿking's commandment?   2:19 • v. 2

4 Now it came to pass, when they spake daily unto him, and he hearkened not unto them, that they told Ha'-man, to see whether Mor'-de-cai's matters would stand: for he had told them that he was a Jew.

5 And when Ha'-man saw that Mor'-de-cai bowed not, nor did him reverence, then was Ha'-man ᴿfull of wrath.   Dan. 3:19

6 And he thought scorn to lay hands on Mor'-de-cai alone; for they had shewed him the people of Mor'-de-cai: wherefore Ha'-man sought to destroy all the Jews that were throughout the whole kingdom of A-has-u-e'-rus, even the people of Mor'-de-cai.

Presentation of the Plot

7 In the first month, that is, the month Ni'-san, in the twelfth year of king A-has-u-e'-rus, ᴿthey cast Pur, that is, the lot, before Ha'-man from day to day, and from month to month, to the twelfth month, that is, ᴿthe month A'-dar.   9:24-26 • Ezra 6:15

8 And Ha'-man said unto king A-has-u-e'-rus, There is a certain people scattered abroad and dispersed among the people in all the provinces of thy kingdom; and ᴿtheir laws are diverse from all people; neither keep they the king's laws: therefore it is not for the king's profit to suffer them.   Ezra 4:13; Acts 16:20

9 If it please the king, let it be written that they may be destroyed: and I will pay ᵀten thousand talents of silver to the hands of those that have the charge of the business, to bring it into the king's treasuries. $3,840,000,000

Publication of the Decree

10 And the king took ᴿhis ring from his hand, and gave it unto Ha'-man the son of Ham-med'-a-tha the A'-gag-ite, the Jews' ᵀenemy.ᴿ   8:2, 8 • oppressor • 7:6

11 And the king said unto Ha'-man, The silver is given to thee, the people also, to do with them as it seemeth good to thee.

12 ᴿThen were the king's ᵀscribes called on the thirteenth day of the first month, and there was written according to all that Ha'-man had commanded unto the king's lieutenants, and to the governors that were over every province, and to the rulers of every people of every province ᴿaccording to the writing thereof, and to every people after their language; in the name of king A-has-u-e'-rus was it written, and sealed with the king's ring.   8:9 • secretaries • 1:22

13 And the letters were sent by posts into all the king's provinces, to destroy, to kill, and to cause to perish, all Jews, both young and old, little children and women, in one day, even upon the thirteenth day of the twelfth month, which is the month A'-dar, and to take the spoil of them for a prey.

14 The copy of the writing for ᵀa commandment to be given in every province was published unto all people, that they should be ready against that day.   court order

15 The ᵀposts went out, being hastened by the king's commandment, and the decree was given in Shu'-shan the palace. And the king and Ha'-man sat down to drink; but the city Shu'-shan was ᵀperplexed.   messengers • disturbed

CHAPTER 4

Lamentation of the Jews

WHEN Mor'-de-cai perceived all that was done, Mor'-de-cai rent his clothes, and put on sackcloth with ashes, and went out into the midst of the city, and cried with a loud and a bitter cry;

2 And came even before the king's gate: for none might enter into the king's gate clothed with sackcloth.

3 And in every province, whithersoever the king's commandment and his decree came, there was great mourning among the Jews, and fasting, and weeping, and wailing; and many lay in sackcloth and ashes.

The Plan of Mordecai

4 So Esther's maids and her chamberlains came and told it her. Then was the queen exceedingly grieved; and she sent raiment to clothe Mor'-de-cai, and to take away his sackcloth from him: but he received it not.

5 Then called Esther for Ha'-tach, one of the king's ᵀchamberlains, whom he had appointed to attend upon her, and gave him a commandment to Mor'-de-cai, to know what it was, and why it was.   officials

6 So Ha'-tach went forth to Mor'-de-cai unto the ᵀstreet of the city, which was before the king's gate.   broad place

7 And Mor'-de-cai told him of all that had happened unto him, and of ᴿthe sum of the

money that Ha'-man had promised to pay to the king's treasuries for the Jews, to destroy them.   3:9

8 Also he gave him the copy of the writing of the decree that was given at Shu'-shan to destroy them, to shew it unto Esther, and to declare it unto her, and to charge her that she should go in unto the king, to make supplication unto him, and to make request before him for her people.

9 And Ha'-tach came and told Esther the words of Mor'-de-cai.

10 Again Esther spake unto Ha'-tach, and gave him commandment unto Mor'-de-cai;

11 All the king's servants, and the people of the king's provinces, do know, that whosoever, whether man or woman, shall come unto the king into the inner court, who is not called, there is one law of his to put him to death, except such to whom the king shall hold out the golden sceptre, that he may live: but I have not been called to come in unto the king these thirty days.

12 And they told to Mor'-de-cai Esther's words.

13 Then Mor'-de-cai commanded to answer Esther, Think not with thyself that thou shalt escape in the king's house, more than all the Jews.

14 For if thou altogether holdest thy peace at this time, then shall there [T]enlargement and deliverance arise to the Jews from another place; but thou and thy father's house shall be destroyed: and who knoweth whether thou art come to the kingdom for such a time as this?   help

The Promise of Queen Esther

15 Then Esther bade them return Mor'-de-cai this answer,

16 Go, gather together all the Jews that are present in Shu'-shan, and [R]fast ye for me, and neither eat nor drink three days, night or day: I also and my maidens will fast likewise; and so will I go in unto the king, which is not according to the law: [R]and if I perish, I perish.   2 Chr. 20:3 • Gen. 43:14

17 So Mor'-de-cai went his way, and did according to all that Esther had commanded him.

CHAPTER 5

Esther's First Feast

NOW it came to pass on the third day, that Esther put on her royal apparel, and stood in the inner court of the king's house, over against the king's house: and the king sat upon his royal throne in the royal house, over against the gate of the house.

2 And it was so, when the king saw Esther the queen standing in the court, that she obtained favour in his sight: and the king held out to Esther the golden sceptre that was in his hand. So Esther drew near, and touched the top of the sceptre.

3 Then said the king unto her, What wilt thou, queen Esther? and what is thy request? [R]it shall be even given thee to the half of the kingdom.   7:2; Mark 6:23

4 And Esther answered, If it seem good unto the king, let the king and Ha'-man come this day unto the banquet that I have prepared for him.

5 Then the king said, Cause Ha'-man to make haste, that he may do as Esther hath said. So the king and Ha'-man came to the banquet that Esther had prepared.

6 [R]And the king said unto Esther at the banquet of wine, What is thy petition? and it shall be granted thee: and what is thy request? even to the half of the kingdom it shall be performed.   7:2

7 Then answered Esther, and said, My petition and my request is;

8 If I have found favour in the sight of the king, and if it please the king to grant my petition, and to perform my request, let the king and Ha'-man come to the banquet that I shall prepare for them, and I will do to morrow as the king hath said.

Haman Plots to Kill Mordecai

9 Then went Ha'-man forth that day joyful and with a glad heart: but when Ha'-man saw Mor'-de-cai [R]in the king's gate, [R]that he stood not up, nor moved for him, he was full of indignation against Mor'-de-cai.   2:19 • 3:5

10 Nevertheless Ha'-man refrained himself: and when he came home, he sent and called for his friends, and Ze'-resh his wife.

11 And Ha'-man told them of the glory of his riches, and [R]the multitude of his children, and all the things wherein the king had [R]promoted him, and how he had advanced him above the princes and servants of the king.   9:7-10 • 3:1

12 Ha'-man said moreover, Yea, Esther the queen did let no man come in with the king unto the banquet that she had prepared but myself; and [R]to morrow am I invited unto her also with the king.   v. 8

13 Yet all this availeth me nothing, so long as I see Mor'-de-cai the Jew sitting at the [R]king's gate.   v. 9

14 Then said Ze'-resh his wife and all his friends unto him, Let a [T]gallows be made of [T]fifty cubits high, and to morrow [R]speak thou unto the king that Mor'-de-cai may be hanged thereon: then go thou in merrily with the king unto the banquet. And the thing pleased Ha'-man; and he caused [R]the gallows to be made.   tree • 75 ft. • 6:4 • 7:10

CHAPTER 6

King Ahasuerus' Plan to Honour Mordecai

ON that night ᵀcould not the king sleep, and he commanded to bring the book of records of the chronicles; and they were read before the king.   *the king's sleep fled away*

2 And it was found written, that Mor'-de-cai had told of ᵀBig'-tha-naᴿ and Te'-resh, two of the king's chamberlains, the keepers of the door, who sought to lay hand on the king A-has-u-e'-rus.   *Bigthan • 2:21*

3 And the king said, What honour and dignity hath been done to Mor'-de-cai for this? Then said the king's servants that ministered unto him, There is nothing done for him.

Haman's Plan to Honour Himself

4 And the king said, Who *is* in the court? Now Ha'-man was come into the outward court of the king's house, ᴿto speak unto the king to hang Mor'-de-cai on the gallows that he had prepared for him.   5:14

5 And the king's servants said unto him, Behold, Ha'-man standeth in the court. And the king said, Let him come in.

6 So Ha'-man came in. And the king said unto him, ᴿWhat shall be done unto the man whom the king delighteth to honour? Now Ha'-man thought in his heart, To whom would the king delight to do honour more than to myself?   7:2; 9:6

7 And Ha'-man answered the king, For the man whom the king delighteth to honour,

8 Let the royal apparel be brought which the king *useth* to wear, and ᴿthe horse that the king rideth upon, and the ᴿcrown royal which is set upon his head: 1 Kin. 1:33 • 1:11

9 And let this apparel and horse be delivered to the hand of one of the king's most noble princes, that they may array the man *withal* whom the king delighteth to honour, and bring him on horseback through the street of the city, ᴿand proclaim before him, Thus shall it be done to the man whom the king delighteth to honour.   Gen. 41:43

Haman Is Forced to Honour Mordecai

10 Then the king said to Ha'-man, ᴿMake haste, *and* take the apparel and the horse, as thou hast said, and do even so to Mor'-de-cai the Jew, that sitteth at the king's gate: let nothing fail of all that thou hast spoken.   5:5

11 Then took Ha'-man the apparel and the horse, and arrayed Mor'-de-cai, and brought him on horseback through the street of the city, and proclaimed before him, Thus shall it be done unto the man whom the king delighteth to honour.

12 And Mor'-de-cai came again to the king's gate. But Ha'-man hasted to his house mourning, and having his head covered.

13 ᴿAnd Ha'-man told Ze'-resh his wife and all his friends every *thing* that had befallen him. Then said his wise men and Ze'-resh his wife unto him, If Mor'-de-cai *be* of the seed of the Jews, before whom thou hast begun to fall, thou shalt not prevail against ᴿhim, but shalt surely fall before him.   5:10 • Zech. 2:8

14 And while they *were* yet talking with him, came the king's ᵀchamberlains, and hasted to bring Ha'-man unto ᴿthe banquet that Esther had prepared.   *officials* • 5:8

CHAPTER 7

Esther's Second Feast

SO the king and Ha'-man came to ᵀbanquet with Esther the queen.   *drink*

2 And the king said again unto Esther on the second day ᴿat the banquet of wine, What *is* thy petition, queen Esther? and it shall be granted thee: ᴿand what *is* thy request? and it shall be performed, *even* to the half of the kingdom.   5:6 • 9:12

3 Then Esther the queen answered and said, ᴿIf I have found favour in thy sight, O king, and if it please the king, let my life be given me at my petition, and my people at my request: 5:8; 8:5

4 For we are sold, I and my people, to be destroyed, to be slain, and to perish. But if we had been sold for bondmen and bondwomen, I had held my tongue, although the enemy could not countervail the king's damage.

Haman Is Indicted

5 Then the king A-has-u-e'-rus answered and said unto Esther the queen, Who is he, and where is he, that ᵀdurst presume in his heart to do so?   *dares*

6 And Esther said, The adversary and enemy *is* this wicked Ha'-man. Then Ha'-man was afraid before the king and the queen.

7 ᴿAnd the king arising from the banquet of wine in his wrath *went* into the palace garden: and Ha'-man stood up to make request for his life to Esther the queen; for he saw that there was evil determined against him by the king.   1:5, 12

8 Then the king returned out of the palace garden into the place of the banquet of wine; and Ha'-man was fallen upon the bed whereon Esther *was*. Then said the king, Will he force the queen also before me in the house? As the word went out of the king's mouth, they ᴿcovered Ha'-man's face.   Job 9:24

Haman Is Hanged

9 And ᴿHar-bo'-nah, one of the ᵀchamberlains, said before the king, Behold also, ᴿthe ᵀgallows ᵀfifty cubits high, which Ha'-man had made for Mor'-de-cai, who had spoken

good for the king, standeth in the house of Ha'-man. Then the king said, Hang him thereon.   1:10 • *officials* • [Prov. 11:5, 6] • *tree* • 75 ft.

10 So they hanged Ha'-man on the gallows that he had prepared for Mor'-de-cai. Then was the king's wrath pacified.

CHAPTER 8

Mordecai Is Given Haman's House

O N that day did the king A-has-u-e'-rus give the house of Ha'-man the Jews' enemy unto Esther the queen. And Mor'-de-cai came before the king; for Esther had told Rwhat he was unto her.   2:7

2 And the king took off Rhis ring, which he had taken from Ha'-man, and gave it unto Mor'-de-cai. And Esther set Mor'-de-cai over the house of Ha'-man.   3:10

3 And Esther spake yet again before the king, and fell down at his feet, and besought him with tears to put away the mischief of Ha'-man the A'-gag-ite, and his device that he had devised against the Jews.

Esther's Petition to King Ahasuerus

4 Then Rthe king held out the golden sceptre toward Esther. So Esther arose, and stood before the king,   4:11; 5:2

5 And said, RIf it please the king, and if I have found favour in his sight, and the thing seem right before the king, and I be pleasing in his eyes, let it be written to reverse the letters devised by Ha'-man the son of Hammed'-a-tha the A'-gag-ite, which he wrote to destroy the Jews which are in all the king's provinces: 5:8; 7:3

6 For how can I endure to see Rthe evil that shall come unto my people? or how can I endure to see the destruction of my kindred?   7:4; 9:1; Neh. 2:3

King Ahasuerus' Counter-Decree

7 Then the king A-has-u-e'-rus said unto Esther the queen and to Mor'-de-cai the Jew, Behold, RI have given Esther the house of Ha'-man, and him they have hanged upon the gallows, because he laid his hand upon the Jews.   v. 1; Prov. 13:22

8 Write ye also for the Jews, as it Tliketh you, in the king's name, and seal it with the king's ring: for the writing which is written in the king's name, and sealed with the king's ring, may no man reverse.   *pleases*

9 Then were the king's scribes called at that time in the third month, that is, the month Si'-van, on the three and twentieth day thereof; and it was written according to all that Mor'-de-cai commanded unto the Jews, and to the lieutenants, and the deputies and rulers of the provinces which are from

India unto E-thi-o'-pi-a, an hundred twenty and seven provinces, unto every province Raccording to the writing thereof, and unto every people after their language, and to the Jews according to their writing, and according to their language.   3:12

10 RAnd he wrote in the king A-has-u-e'-rus' name, and sealed it with the king's ring, and sent letters by Tposts on horseback, and riders on mules, camels, and young dromedaries: 3:12, 13 • *messengers*

11 Wherein the king granted the Jews which were in every city to gather themselves together, and to stand for their life, to destroy, to slay, and to cause to perish, all the power of the people and province that would assault them, both little ones and women, and to take the spoil of them for a prey,

12 RUpon one day in all the provinces of king A-has-u-e'-rus, namely, upon the thirteenth day of the twelfth month, which is the month A'-dar.   3:13; 9:1

13 The copy of the writing for a commandment to be given in every province was published unto all people, and that the Jews should be ready against that day to avenge themselves on their enemies.

14 So the posts that rode upon mules and camels went out, being hastened and pressed on by the king's commandment. And the decree was given at Shu'-shan the palace.

Many Gentiles Are Converted

15 And Mor'-de-cai went out from the presence of the king in royal apparel of Tblue and white, and with a great crown of gold, and with a garment of fine linen and purple: and Rthe city of Shu'-shan rejoiced and was glad.   *violet* • Prov. 29:2

16 The Jews had Rlight, and gladness, and joy, and honour.   Ps. 97:11

17 And in every province, and in every city, whithersoever the king's commandment and his decree came, the Jews had joy and gladness, a feast and a good day. And many of the people of the land Rbecame Jews; for the fear of the Jews fell upon them.   Ps. 18:43

CHAPTER 9

Victories on the First Day

N OW in the twelfth month, that is, the month A'-dar, on the thirteenth day of the same, when the king's commandment and his decree drew near to be put in execution, in the day that the enemies of the Jews hoped to have power over them, (though it was turned to the contrary, that the Jews had rule over them that hated them;)

2 The Jews ᴿgathered themselves together in their cities throughout all the provinces of the king A-has-u-e'-rus, to lay hand on such as sought their hurt: and no man could withstand them; for ᴿthe fear of them fell upon all people.   *v. 16 • 8:17*

3 And all the rulers of the provinces, and the lieutenants, and the deputies, and officers of the king, helped the Jews; because the fear of Mor'-de-cai fell upon them.

4 For Mor'-de-cai *was* great in the king's house, and his fame went out throughout all the provinces: for this man Mor'-de-cai ᴿwaxed greater and greater.   *2 Sam. 3:1*

5 Thus the Jews smote all their enemies with the stroke of the sword, and slaughter, and destruction, and did what they would unto those that hated them.

6 And in Shu'-shan the palace the Jews slew and destroyed five hundred men.

7 And Par-shan'-da-tha, and Dal'-phon, and As-pa'-tha,

8 And Por'-a-tha, and A-da'-li-a, and A-rid'-a-tha,

9 And Par-mash'-ta, and A-ri'-sai, and A-ri'-dai, and Va-jez'-a-tha,

10 ᴿThe ten sons of Ha'-man the son of Ham-med'-a-tha, ᴿthe enemy of the Jews, slew they; ᴿbut on the ᵀspoil laid they not their hand.   *5:11 • Ps. 21:10 • 8:11 • property*

11 On that day the number of those that were slain in ᴿShu'-shan the palace ᵀwas brought before the king.   *Neh. 1:1 • came*

Victories on the Second Day

12 And the king said unto Esther the queen, The Jews have slain and destroyed five hundred men in Shu'-shan the palace, and the ten sons of Ha'-man; what have they done in the rest of the king's provinces? now ᴿwhat *is* thy petition? and it shall be granted thee: or what *is* thy request further? and it shall be done.   *5:6*

13 Then said Esther, If it please the king, let it be granted to the Jews which *are* in Shu'-shan to do to morrow also ᴿaccording unto this day's decree, and let Ha'-man's ten sons be hanged upon the gallows.   *8:11*

14 And the king commanded it so to be done: and the decree was given at Shu'-shan; and they hanged Ha'-man's ten sons.

15 For the Jews that *were* in Shu'-shan gathered themselves together on the fourteenth day also of the month A'-dar, and slew three hundred men at Shu'-shan; but on the ᵀprey they laid not their hand.   *loot*

16 But the other Jews that *were* in the king's provinces ᴿgathered themselves together, and stood for their lives, and had rest from their enemies, and slew of their foes seventy and five thousand, but they laid not their hands on the ᵀprey,   *v. 2 • loot*

The Feast of Purim

17 On ᴿthe thirteenth day of the month A'-dar; and on the fourteenth day of the same rested they, and made it a day of feasting and gladness.   *vv. 1, 21*

18 But the Jews that *were* at Shu'-shan assembled together on the thirteenth *day* thereof, and on the fourteenth thereof; and on the fifteenth *day* of the same they rested, and made it a day of feasting and gladness.

19 Therefore the Jews of the villages, that dwelt in the unwalled towns, made the fourteenth day of the month A'-dar *a day of* gladness and feasting, ᴿand a good day, and of sending portions one to another.   *8:17*

20 And Mor'-de-cai wrote these things, and sent letters unto all the Jews that *were* in all the provinces of the king A-has-u-e'-rus, *both* nigh and far,

21 To stablish *this* among them, that they should keep the fourteenth day of the month A'-dar, and the fifteenth day of the same, yearly,

22 As the days wherein the Jews rested from their enemies, and the month which was turned unto them from sorrow to joy, and from mourning into a good day: that they should make them days of feasting and joy, and of ᴿsending ᵀportions one to another, and gifts to the poor.   *v. 19 • gifts*

23 And the Jews undertook to do as they had begun, and as Mor'-de-cai had written unto them;

24 Because Ha'-man the son of Ham-med'-a-tha, the A'-gag-ite, the enemy of all the Jews, had devised against the Jews to destroy them, and had cast Pur, that *is*, the lot, to consume them, and to destroy them;

25 But ᴿwhen ᵀEsther came before the king, he commanded by letters that his wicked device, which he devised against the Jews, should return upon his own head, and that he and his sons should be hanged on the gallows.   *7:5 • the matter*

26 Wherefore they called these days Pu'-rim after the name of ᵀPur. Therefore for all the words of this letter, and *of that* which they had seen concerning this matter, and which had come unto them,   *Lot*

27 The Jews ordained, and took upon them, and upon their seed, and upon all such as joined themselves unto them, so as it should not fail, that they would keep these two days according to their writing, and according to their *appointed* time every year;

28 And *that* these days *should be* remembered and kept throughout every generation, every family, every province, and every city; and *that* these days of Pu'-rim should not fail from among the Jews, nor the memorial of them perish from their seed.

29 Then Esther the queen, ^Rthe daughter of Ab-i-ha'-il, and Mor'-de-cai the Jew, wrote with all authority, to confirm this ^Rsecond letter of Pu'-rim.   2:15 · 8:10

30 And he sent the letters unto all the Jews, to ^Rthe hundred twenty and seven provinces of the kingdom of A-has-u-e'-rus, *with* words of peace and truth,   1:1

31 To confirm these days of Pu'-rim in their times *appointed*, according as Mor'-de-cai the Jew and Esther the queen had enjoined them, and as they had decreed for themselves and for their seed, the matters of ^Rthe fastings and their cry.   4:3, 16

32 And the decree of Esther confirmed these matters of ^RPu'-rim; and it was written in the book.   *v.* 26

CHAPTER 10

The Fame of Mordecai

AND the king A-has-u-e'-rus laid a tribute upon the land, and *upon* ^Rthe isles of the sea.   Gen. 10:5; Ps. 72:10; Is. 24:15

2 And all the acts of his power and of his might, and the declaration of the greatness of Mor'-de-cai, whereunto the king ^Tadvanced him, *are* they not written in the book of the chronicles of the kings of Me'-di-a and Persia?   *made him great;* 8:15

3 For Mor'-de-cai the Jew *was* next unto king A-has-u-e'-rus, and great among the Jews, and accepted of the multitude of his brethren, seeking the ^Twealth of his people, and speaking peace to all his seed.   *good*

Jewish Feasts

Feast of	Month on Jewish Calendar	Day	Corresponding Month	References
*Passover (Unleavened Bread)	Nisan	14–21	Mar.–Apr.	Ex. 12:43—13:10; Matt. 26:17–20
*Pentecost (Firstfruits or Weeks)	Sivan	6 (50 days after Passover)	May–June	Deut. 16:9–12; Acts 2:1
Trumpets, *Rosh Hashanah*	Tishri	1, 2	Sept.–Oct.	Num. 29:1–6
Day of Atonement, *Yom Kippur*	Tishri	10	Sept.–Oct.	Lev. 23:26–32; Heb. 9:7
*Tabernacles (Booths or Ingathering)	Tishri	15–22	Sept.–Oct.	Neh. 8:13–18; John 7:2
Dedication (Lights), *Hanukkah*	Chislev	25 (8 days)	Nov.–Dec.	John 10:22
Purim (Lots)	Adar	14, 15	Feb.–Mar.	Esth. 9:18–32

*The three major feasts for which all males of Israel were required to travel to the Temple in Jerusalem (Ex. 23:14–19).

THE BOOK OF

JOB

THE BOOK OF JOB
Job is perhaps the earliest book of the Bible. Set in the period of the patriarchs (Abraham, Isaac, Jacob, and Joseph), it tells the story of a man who loses everything—his wealth, his family, his health—and wrestles with the question, Why?

The book begins with a heavenly debate between God and Satan, moves through three cycles of earthly debates between Job and his friends, and concludes with a dramatic "divine diagnosis" of Job's problem. In the end, Job acknowledges the sovereignty of God in his life and receives back more than he had before his trials.

Iyyōb is the Hebrew title for this book, and the name has two possible meanings. If derived from the Hebrew word for persecution, it means "Persecuted One." It is more likely that it comes from the Arabic word meaning "To Come Back" or "Repent." If so, it may be defined "Repentant One." Both meanings apply to the book. The Greek title is *Iob*, and the Latin title is *Iob*.

THE AUTHOR OF JOB
The author of Job is unknown, and there are no textual hints as to his identity. Commentators, however, have been generous with suggestions: Job, Elihu, Moses, Solomon, Isaiah, Hezekiah, Jeremiah, Baruch, and Ezra have all been nominated. The non-Hebraic cultural background of this book may point to gentile authorship. The rabbinic traditions are inconsistent, but one talmudic tradition suggests that Moses wrote the book. The land of Uz (1:1) is adjacent to Midian, where Moses lived for forty years, and it is conceivable that Moses obtained a record of the dialogue left by Job or Elihu.

THE TIME OF JOB
Lamentations 4:21 locates Uz in the area of Edom, southeast of the Dead Sea. This is also in the region of northern Arabia, and Job's friends come from nearby countries.

It is important to distinguish the date of the events in Job from the date of its writing. Accurate dating of the events is difficult because there are no references to contemporary historical occurrences. However, a number of facts indicate a patriarchal date for Job, perhaps between Genesis 11 and 12 or not long after the time of Abraham: (1) Job lived 140 years *after* the events in the book (42:16); his lifespan must have been close to 200 years. This fits the patriarchal period (Abraham lived 175 years, Gen. 24:7). (2) Job's wealth is measured in terms of livestock (1:3;

42:12) rather than gold and silver. (3) Like Abraham, Isaac, and Jacob, Job is the priest of his family and offers sacrifices. (4) There are no references to Israel, the Exodus, the Mosaic law, or the tabernacle. (5) Fitting Abraham's time, the social unit in Job is the patriarchal family-clan. (6) The Chaldeans who murder Job's servants (1:17) are nomads and have not yet become city-dwellers. (7) Job uses the characteristic patriarchal name for God, *Shaddai* ("the Almighty"), thirty-one times. This early term is found only seventeen times in the rest of the Old Testament. The rare use of Yahweh, "the LORD," also suggests a pre-Mosaic date. Ezekiel 14:14, 20 and James 5:11 show that Job was a historical person.

Several theories have been advanced for the date of writing: (1) It was written shortly after the events occurred, perhaps by Job or Elihu. (2) It was written by Moses in Midian (1485–1445 B.C.). (3) It was written in the time of Solomon (c. 950 B.C.). (Job is similar to other wisdom literature of this time; compare the praises of wisdom in Job 28 and Proverbs 8. The problem here is the great time lag of about a thousand years). (4) It was written during or after the Babylonian captivity.

THE CHRIST OF JOB
Job acknowledges a Redeemer (see 19:25–27) and cries out for a Mediator (9:33; 25:4; 33:23). The book raises problems and questions which are answered perfectly in Christ who identifies with our sufferings (Heb. 4:15). Christ is the believer's Life, Redeemer, Mediator, and Advocate.

KEYS TO JOB
Key Word: Sovereignty—The basic question of the book is, Why do the righteous suffer if God is loving and all-powerful? Suffering itself is not the central theme; rather, the focus is on what Job *learns* from his suffering—the sovereignty of God over all creation. The debate in chapters 3—37 regards whether God would allow this suffering to happen to a person who is innocent. The oversimplified solutions offered by Job's three friends are simply inadequate. Elihu's claim that God can use suffering to purify the righteous is closer to the mark. The conclusion at the whirlwind is that God is sovereign and worthy of worship in *whatever* He chooses to do. Job must learn to trust in the goodness and power of God in adversity by enlarging his concept of God. Even this "perfect" man (1:1) needs to repent when he becomes proud and self-righteous. He has to come to the end of his own resources, humble himself,

and acknowledge the greatness and majesty of the Lord. Job teaches that God is Lord "of *things* in heaven, and *things* in earth, and *things* under the earth" (Phil. 2:10). He is omniscient, omnipotent, and good. As such, His ways are sometimes incomprehensible to men and women, but He can always be trusted. Without the divine perspective in chapters 1 and 2 and in 38—42, chapters 3—37 are a mystery. Job does not have access to chapters 1 and 2, but he is responsible to trust God when all appearances are contrary. Suffering is not always associated with sin; God often sovereignly uses it to test and teach.

Key Verses: Job 13:15; 37:23, 24—"Though he slay me, yet will I trust in him: but I will maintain mine own ways before him" (13:15).

"*Touching* the Almighty, we cannot find him out: *he is* excellent in power, and in judgment, and in plenty of justice: he will not afflict. Men do therefore fear him: he respecteth not any *that are* wise of heart" (37:23, 24).

Key Chapter: Job 42—The last chapter of the book records the climax of the long and difficult struggle Job has with himself, his wife, his friends, and even his God. Upon Job's full recognition of the utter majesty and sovereignty of the Lord, he repents and no longer demands an answer as to the "why" of his plight.

SURVEY OF JOB

The Book of Job concerns the transforming crisis in the life of a great man who lived perhaps four thousand years ago. Job's trust in God (1 and 2) changes to complaining and growing self-righteousness (3—31; see 32:1 and 40:8), but his repentance (42:1-6) leads to his restoration (42:7-17). The trials bring about an important transformation: The man after the process is different from the man before the process. The Book of Job divides into three parts:

the dilemma of Job (1 and 2), the debates of Job (3—37), and the deliverance of Job (38—42).

The Dilemma of Job (1 and 2): Job is not a logical candidate for disaster (see 1:1, 8). His moral integrity and his selfless service to God heighten the dilemma. Behind the scene, Satan ("accuser") charges that no one loves God from pure motives, but only for material blessings (1:10). To refute Satan's accusations, God allows him to strike Job with two series of assaults. In his sorrow Job laments the day of his birth but does not deny God (1:21; 2:10).

The Debates of Job (3—37): Although Job's "comforters" reach wrong conclusions, they are his friends: of all who know Job, they are the only ones who come; they mourn with him in seven days of silent sympathy; they confront Job without talking behind his back. However, after Job breaks the silence, a three-round debate follows in which his friends say Job must be suffering because of his sin. Job's responses to their simplistic assumptions make the debate cycles increase in emotional fervor. He first accuses his friends of judging him, and later appeals to the Lord as his judge and refuge.

Job makes three basic complaints: (1) God does not hear me (13:3, 24; 19:7; 23:3-5; 30:20); (2) God is punishing me (6:4; 7:20; 9:17); and (3) God allows the wicked to prosper (21:7). His defenses are much longer than his friends' accusations; in the process of defending his innocence, he becomes guilty of self-righteousness.

After Job's five-chapter closing monologue (27—31), Elihu freshens the air with a more perceptive and accurate view than those offered by Eliphaz, Bildad, or Zophar (32—37). He tells Job that he needs to humble himself before God and submit to God's process of purifying his life through trials.

The Deliverance of Job (38—42): After Elihu's

FOCUS	DILEMMA OF JOB	DEBATES OF JOB					DELIVERANCE OF JOB
REFERENCE	1:1————————3:1———	15:1———	22:1———	27:1———		32:1———	38:1——42:17
DIVISION	CONTROVERSY OF GOD AND SATAN	FIRST CYCLE OF DEBATE	SECOND CYCLE OF DEBATE	THIRD CYCLE OF DEBATE	FINAL DEFENSE OF JOB	SOLUTION OF ELIHU	CONTROVERSY OF GOD WITH JOB
TOPIC	CONFLICT	DEBATE					REPENTANCE
	PROSE	POETRY					PROSE
LOCATION	LAND OF UZ (NORTH ARABIA)						
TIME	PATRIARCHAL PERIOD (c. 2000 B.C.)						

preparatory discourse, God Himself ends the debate by speaking to Job from the whirlwind. In His first speech God reveals His power and wisdom as Creator and Preserver of the physical and animal world. Job responds by acknowledging his own ignorance and insignificance; he can offer no rebuttal (40:3-5). In His second speech God reveals His sovereign authority and challenges Job with two illustrations of His power to control the uncontrollable. This time Job responds by acknowledging his error with a repentant heart (42:1-6). If Job cannot understand God's ways in the realm of nature, how then can he understand God's ways in the spiritual realm? God makes no reference to Job's personal sufferings, and hardly touches on the real issue of the debate. However, Job catches a glimpse of the divine perspective; and when he acknowledges God's sovereignty over his life, his worldly goods are restored twofold. Job prays for his three friends who have cut him so deeply, but Elihu's speech is never rebuked. Thus, Satan's challenge becomes God's opportunity to build up Job's life. "Behold, we count them happy which endured. Ye have heard of the patience of Job, and have seen the end of the Lord; that the Lord is very pitiful, and of tender mercy" (James 5:11; see James 1:12).

OUTLINE OF JOB

Part One: The Dilemma of Job (1:1—2:13)

Part Two: The Debates of Job (3:1—37:24)

Part Three: The Deliverance of Job (38:1—42:17)

CHAPTER 1

The Circumstances of Job

THERE was a man in the land of Uz, whose name *was* Job; and that man was ᵀperfect and upright, and one that feared God, and ᵀeschewed evil.   *good · avoided*

2 ᴿAnd there were born unto him seven sons and three daughters.   42:13; [Gen. 33:5]

3 His ᵀsubstanceᴿ also was seven thousand sheep, and three thousand camels, and five hundred yoke of oxen, and five hundred she asses, and a very great household; so that this man was ᴿthe greatest of all the men of the east.   *property* · 42:12 · 29:25; 31:37

4 ᴿAnd his sons went and feasted *in their* houses, every one his day; and sent and called for their three sisters to eat and to drink with them.   Eccl. 2:10

5 And it was so, when the days of *their* feasting were gone about, that Job sent and sanctified them, and rose up early in the morning, and offered burnt offerings *according* to the number of them all: for Job said, It may be that my sons have sinned, and ᵀcursed God in their hearts. Thus did Job continually.   *renounced*

The First Assault of Satan

6 Now there was a day when the sons of God came to present themselves before the LORD, and Satan came also among them.

7 And the LORD said unto Satan, Whence comest thou? Then Satan answered the LORD, and said, From ᴿgoing to and fro in the earth, and from walking up and down in it.   [1 Pet. 5:8]

8 And the LORD said unto ᴿSatan, Hast thou considered my servant Job, that *there is* none like him in the earth, a ᵀperfect and upright man, one that feareth God, and ᵀescheweth evil?   [Rev. 12:9, 10] · *good · avoids*

9 Then Satan answered the LORD, and said, Doth Job fear God for ᵀnought?   *nothing*

10 Hast not thou made an hedge about him, and about his house, and about all that he hath on every side? thou hast blessed the work of his hands, and his ᵀsubstance is increased in the land.   *property*

11 ᴿBut put forth thine hand now, and touch all that he hath, and he will ᴿcurse thee to thy face.   2:5; 19:21 · Is. 8:21

12 And the LORD said unto Satan, ᴿBehold, all that he hath *is* in thy power; only upon himself put not forth thine hand. So Satan went forth from the presence of the LORD.   [Luke 4:6]

13 And there was a day when his sons and his daughters *were* eating and drinking wine in their eldest brother's house:

14 And there came a messenger unto Job,

and said, The oxen were plowing, and the asses feeding beside them:

15 And the Sa-be′-ans fell *upon them,* and took them away; yea, they have slain the servants with the edge of the sword; and I only am escaped alone to tell thee.

16 While he *was* yet speaking, there came also another, and said, ᵀThe fire of God is fallen from heaven, and hath burned up the sheep, and the servants, and ᵀconsumed them; and I only am escaped alone to tell thee.   *a great fire · destroyed*

17 While he *was* yet speaking, there came also another, and said, The Chal-de′-ans made out three bands, and fell upon the camels, and have carried them away, yea, and slain the servants with the edge of the sword; and I only am escaped alone to tell thee.

18 While he *was* yet speaking, there came also another, and said, Thy sons and thy daughters *were* eating and drinking wine in their eldest brother's house:

19 And, behold, there came a great wind from the wilderness, and ᵀsmote the four corners of the house, and it fell upon the young men, and they are dead; and I only am escaped alone to tell thee.   *struck*

20 Then Job arose, and ᵀrent his ᵀmantle, and shaved his head, and fell down upon the ground, and worshipped,   *tore · robe*

21 And said, ᴿNaked came I out of my mother's womb, and naked shall I return thither: the Lᴏʀᴅ ᴿgave, and the Lᴏʀᴅ hath ᴿtaken away; ᴿblessed be the name of the Lᴏʀᴅ.   1 Tim. 6:7 · [James 1:17] · Gen. 31:16 · Eph. 5:20

22 ᴿIn all this Job sinned not, nor ᵀcharged God foolishly.   *2:10 · accused*

CHAPTER 2

The Second Assault of Satan

AGAIN there was a day when the sons of God came to present themselves before the Lᴏʀᴅ, and Satan came also among them to present himself before the Lᴏʀᴅ.

2 And the Lᴏʀᴅ said unto Satan, From whence comest thou? And ᴿSatan answered the Lᴏʀᴅ, and said, From going to and fro in the earth, and from walking up and down in it.   *1:7*

3 And the Lᴏʀᴅ said unto Satan, Hast thou considered my servant Job, that *there is* none like him in the earth, ᴿa perfect and an upright man, one that feareth God, and escheweth evil? and still he holdeth fast his integrity, although thou movedst me against him, ᴿto destroy him without cause. *1:1, 8 · 9:17*

4 And Satan answered the Lᴏʀᴅ, and said, Skin for skin, yea, all that a man hath will he give for his life.

5 ᴿBut put forth thine hand now, and touch his ᴿbone and his flesh, and he will curse thee to thy face.   *1:11 · 19:20*

6 And the Lᴏʀᴅ said unto Satan, Behold, he *is* in thine hand; but save his life.

7 So went Satan forth from the presence of the Lᴏʀᴅ, and smote Job with sore boils from the sole of his foot unto his crown.

1:21 Response to Suffering—In the hour of suffering the Christian should attempt to determine first of all just why he may be suffering. One can suffer because of his position or his disposition. Peter brings this truth out in his first epistle: "Servants, *be* subject to *your* masters with all fear; not only to the good and gentle, but also to the froward. For this *is* thankworthy, if a man for conscience toward God endure grief, suffering wrongfully" (Page 1237—1 Pet. 2:18, 19).

Suffering is often a two-sided coin. On the one side suffering may be viewed as coming from God to bring out the best in us. See Genesis 22:1, 2, 15–18; Hebrews 11:17. On the other side Satan attempts to use the same temptation and suffering to bring out the worst in us (Page 1228—James 1:13, 14). Finally, the believer can react to suffering in three different ways:

a. Despise it, that is, treat it too lightly, as did Esau his birthright (Page 1223—Heb. 12:5, 16).

b. Faint under it, that is, treat it too seriously (Page 1223—Heb. 12:5).

c. Be exercised by it, that is, receive instruction from it. This is the reaction desired by God (Page 1223—Heb. 12:1–13).

During this time both Peter and Paul advise us to commit our pain and suffering to God, realizing He is faithful to work all things out for our good and God's glory (Page 1115—Rom. 8:28; Page 1239—1 Pet. 4:19). James tells us to count it all joy when we experience these dark hours (Page 1228—James 1:2).

Now turn to Page 743—Jer. 37:15: Examples of Suffering.

2:7 Purposes of Suffering—Perhaps the most painful question confronting the believer is the problem of suffering. Why does a loving and wise God permit His children to suffer? The Scriptures offer a number of reasons for this.

a. To produce fruit. If we allow suffering to accomplish its purpose, it can bring forth patience (Page 1221—Heb. 10:36; Page 1228—James 1:3), joy (Page 559—Ps. 30:5; 126:6), knowledge (Page 589—Ps. 94:12), and maturity (Page 1239—1 Pet. 5:10).

b. To silence the devil. Satan once accused Job of merely serving God for the material blessings involved. But the Lord allowed the devil to torment Job to demonstrate that His servant loved God because of who He was, and not for what he could get from Him (Page 518—Job 1:9–12; 2:3–7).

c. To glorify God (Page 1053—John 9:1–3; 11:1–4).

(continued on next page)

8 And he took him a potsherd to scrape himself withal; ^Rand he sat down among the ashes.   Ezek. 27:30; Matt. 11:21

9 Then said his wife unto him, Dost thou still retain thine integrity? ^Tcurse God, and die.   renounce

10 But he said unto her, Thou speakest as one of the foolish women speaketh. What? shall we receive good at the hand of God, and shall we not receive evil? In all this did not Job sin with his lips.

The Arrival of Job's Friends

11 Now when Job's three friends heard of all this evil that was come upon him, they came every one from his own place; El'-i-phaz the ^RTe'-man-ite, and Bil'-dad the ^RShu'-hite, and Zo'-phar the Na'-a-ma-thite: for they had made an appointment together to come ^Rto mourn with him and to comfort him.   Jer. 49:7 · Gen. 25:2 · 42:11

12 And when they lifted up their eyes afar off, and ^Tknew him not, they lifted up their voice, and wept; and they ^Trent every one his mantle, and sprinkled dust upon their heads toward heaven.   recognized · tore

13 So they sat down with him upon the ground ^Rseven days and seven nights, and none spake a word unto him: for they saw that *his* grief was very great.   Gen. 50:10

CHAPTER 3

Job's First Speech

AFTER this opened Job his mouth, and cursed his day.

2 And Job ^Tspake, and said,   answered

3 ^RLet the day perish wherein I was born, and the night in which it was said, There is a man child conceived.   Jer. 20:14-18

4 Let that day be darkness; let not God regard it from above, neither let the light shine upon it.

5 Let darkness and ^Rthe shadow of death stain it; let a cloud dwell upon it; let the blackness of the day terrify it.   10:21

6 As for that night, let darkness seize upon it; ^Tlet it not be joined unto the days of the year, let it not come into the number of the months.   let it not rejoice among the days

7 Lo, let that night be ^Tsolitary, let no joyful voice come therein.   isolation

8 Let them curse it that curse the day, who are ready to raise up their mourning.

9 Let the stars of the twilight thereof be dark; let it look for light, but *have* none; neither let it see the dawning of the day:

10 Because it shut not up the doors of my *mother's* womb, nor hid sorrow from mine eyes.

11 ^RWhy died I not from the womb? *why* did I *not* ^Tgive up the ghost when I came out of the belly?   10:18 · give up my life

12 Why did the knees prevent me? or why the breasts that I should suck?

13 For now should I have ^Rlain still and been quiet, I should have slept: then had I been at rest,   14:10-15

14 With kings and counsellors of the earth, which built desolate places for themselves;

15 Or with princes that had gold, who filled their houses with silver:

16 Or as an hidden untimely birth I had not been; as infants *which* never saw light.

17 There the wicked cease *from* troubling; and there the weary be at rest.

18 *There* the prisoners rest together; they hear not the voice of the oppressor.

19 The small and great are there; and the servant *is* free from his master.

20 Wherefore is light given to him that is in misery, and life unto the bitter *in* soul;

21 Which ^Rlong for death, but it *cometh* not; and dig for it more than for ^Thid treasures;   Rev. 9:6 · hidden

22 Which rejoice exceedingly, *and* are glad, when they can find the grave?

23 *Why is light given* to a man ^Rwhose way is hid, and whom God hath hedged in?   [9:28]

24 For my ^Rsighing cometh before I eat, and my ^Rroarings ^Tare poured out like the waters.   6:7 · Ps. 42:4 · cries

25 For the thing ^Rwhich I greatly feared is come upon me, and that which I was afraid of is come unto me.   [9:28]

(continued from previous page)

d. To make us like Jesus. "That I may know him, and the power of his resurrection, and the fellowship of his sufferings, being made conformable unto his death" (Page 1172—Phil. 3:10).

e. To teach us dependence. This is brought out by both Christ (Page 1060—John 15:1–5) and the apostle Paul (Page 1150—2 Cor. 12:1–10).

f. To refine our lives (Page 574—Ps. 66:10–12; Page 626—Prov. 17:3; Page 1235—1 Pet. 1:6, 7).

g. To rebuke our sin (Page 1237—1 Pet. 2:20; 3:17; 4:15). As a faithful earthly father must in love punish his erring child, so does our heavenly Father (Page 1223—Heb. 12:5–9).

h. To enlarge our ministry towards others (Page 1143—2 Cor. 1:3–7). It has been observed that he who has suffered much speaks many languages (understands others).

Now turn to Page 519—Job 1:21: Response to Suffering.

26 I was not in safety, neither had I rest, neither was I quiet; yet trouble came.

CHAPTER 4

Eliphaz Believes the Innocent Do Not Suffer

THEN El'-i-phaz the Te'-man-ite answered and said,

2 If we ᵀassay to commune with thee, wilt thou be grieved? but who can withhold himself from speaking?   undertake

3 Behold, thou hast instructed many, and thou hast strengthened the weak hands.

4 Thy words have upholden him that was falling, and thou ᴿhast strengthened ᵀthe feeble knees.   Is. 35:3 · *bowing knees*

5 But now it is come upon thee, and thou faintest; it ᴿtoucheth thee, and thou art troubled.   19:21

6 Is not *this* ᴿthy fear, thy confidence, thy hope, and the uprightness of thy ways?   1:1

7 Remember, I pray thee, ᴿwho *ever* perished, being innocent? or where were the righteous cut off?   [36:6; Ps. 37:25]

8 Even as I have seen, they that plow iniquity, and sow wickedness, reap the same.

9 By the blast of God they perish, and ᵀby the ᴿbreath of his nostrils are they consumed.   by His anger · Is. 30:33

10 The roaring of the lion, and the voice of the fierce lion, and ᴿthe teeth of the young lions, are broken.   Ps. 58:6

11 ᴿThe old lion perisheth for lack of prey, and the stout lion's whelps are scattered abroad.   29:17; Ps. 34:10

12 Now a thing was secretly brought to me, and mine ear received a little thereof.

13 In thoughts from the visions of the night, when deep sleep falleth on men,

14 Fear came upon me, and ᴿtrembling, which made all my bones to shake.   Hab. 3:16

15 Then a spirit passed before my face; the hair of my flesh stood up:

16 It stood still, but I could not discern the form thereof: an image *was* before mine eyes, ᵀ*there was* silence, and I heard a voice, *saying*,   I heard a still voice

17 Shall mortal man be more just than God? shall a man be more pure than ᴿhis maker?   31:15; 32:22; 35:10

18 Behold, he ᴿput no trust in his servants; and his angels he charged with folly: 15:15

19 How much less *in* them that dwell in houses of clay, whose foundation *is* in the dust, *which* are crushed before the moth?

20 ᴿThey are ᵀdestroyed from morning to evening: they perish for ever without any regarding *it*.   Ps. 90:5 · *beaten in pieces*

21 Doth not their ᴿexcellency *which is* in them go away? they die, even ᴿwithout wisdom.   8:22 · 18:21

CHAPTER 5

Eliphaz Calls Job Foolish

CALL now, if there be any that will answer thee; and ᴿto which of the saints wilt thou turn?   15:15

2 For ᴿwrath killeth the foolish man, and envy slayeth the silly one.   Prov. 12:16

3 I have seen the foolish taking root: but suddenly I cursed his habitation.

4 His ᴿchildren are far from ᴿsafety, and they are crushed in the gate, neither is *there* any to deliver *them*.   4:11 · Ps. 119:155

5 Whose harvest the hungry eateth up, and taketh it even out of the thorns, and the ᴿrobber swalloweth up their substance.   18:8-10

6 Although ᴿaffliction cometh not forth of the dust, neither doth trouble spring out of the ground;   15:35

7 Yet ᴿman is born unto trouble, as the sparks fly upward.   14:1

Eliphaz Encourages Job to Appeal to God

8 I would ᴿseek unto God, and unto God would I commit my cause: 13:2, 3

9 Which ᴿdoeth great things and unsearchable; marvellous things without number: 9:10; 37:14, 16

10 Who ᴿgiveth rain upon the earth, and sendeth waters upon the fields: [36:27-29]

11 ᴿTo set up on high those that be low; that those which mourn may be exalted to safety.   Ps. 113:7

12 ᴿHe disappointeth the devices of the crafty, so that their hands cannot perform *their* ᵀenterprise.   Neh. 4:15 · *intention*

13 ᴿHe taketh the wise in their own craftiness: and the counsel of the ᵀfroward is carried headlong.   1 Cor. 3:19 · *bold*

14 They ᴿmeet with darkness in the daytime, and grope in the noonday as in the night.   12:25; 15:30

15 But ᴿhe saveth the poor from the sword, from their mouth, and from the hand of the mighty.   Ps. 35:10

16 ᴿSo the poor hath hope, and ᴿiniquity stoppeth her mouth.   1 Sam. 2:8 · Ps. 107:41, 42

*Eliphaz Encourages Job
Not to Despise God's Discipline*

17 ᴿBehold, happy *is* the man whom God correcteth: therefore despise not thou the chastening of the Almighty: Ps. 94:12

18 For he maketh sore, and bindeth up: he woundeth, and his hands make whole.

19 He shall deliver thee in six troubles: yea, in seven there shall no evil touch thee.

20 ᴿIn famine he shall redeem thee from death: ᴿand in war from the power of the sword.   Ps. 33:19; 37:19 · Ps. 144:10

21 RThou shalt be hid from the scourge of the tongue: neither shalt thou be afraid of destruction when it cometh.   Ps. 31:20

22 At destruction and famine thou shalt laugh: Rneither shalt thou be afraid of the beasts of the earth.   Ps. 91:13; Is. 11:8, 9

23 RFor thou shalt be in league with the stones of the field: and the beasts of the field shall be at peace with thee.   Ps. 91:12

24 And thou shalt know that thy tabernacle shall be in peace; and thou shalt visit thy habitation, and shalt not sin.

25 Thou shalt know also that Rthy seed shall be great, and thine offspring Ras the grass of the earth.   Ps. 112:2 • Ps. 72:16

26 RThou shalt come to thy grave in a full age, like as a shock of corn cometh in in his season.   [Prov. 10:27]

27 Lo this, we have searched it, so it is; hear it, and know thou it for thy good.

CHAPTER 6

Job's Deep Anguish

B UT Job answered and said,
2 O that my grief were Tthroughly weighed, and my calamity laid in the balances together!   actually appreciated

3 For now it would be Rheavier than the sand of the sea: therefore my words Tare swallowed up.   23:2 • rash

4 RFor the arrows of the Almighty are within me, the poison whereof drinketh up my spirit: the terrors of God do set themselves in array against me.   Ps. 38:2

5 Doth the wild ass bray when he hath grass? or loweth the ox over his fodder?

6 Can that which is Tunsavoury be eaten without salt? or is there any taste in the white of an egg?   tasteless

7 RThe things that my soul refused to touch are as my sorrowful meat.   33:20

8 Oh that I might have my request; and that God would grant me the thing that I long for!

9 Even that it would Rplease God to destroy me; that he would let loose his hand, and cut me off!   10:1; Num. 11:15

10 Then should I yet have comfort; yea, I would harden myself in sorrow: let him not spare; for RI have not concealed the words of the Holy One.   Acts 20:20

11 What is my strength, that I should hope? and what is mine end, that I should prolong my life?

12 Is my strength the strength of stones? or is my flesh of brass?

13 Is not my Rhelp in me? and is wisdom driven quite from me?   26:2

Job Seeks His Friends' Sympathy

14 To him that is afflicted pity should be shewed from his friend; but he forsaketh the fear of the Almighty.

15 RMy brethren have dealt deceitfully as a brook, and Ras the stream of brooks they pass away;   Ps. 38:11 • Jer. 15:18

16 Which are blackish by reason of the ice, and wherein the snow is hid:

17 RWhat time they wax warm, they vanish: when it is hot, they are consumed out of their place.   24:19

18 The paths of their way are turned aside; they go to nothing, and perish.

19 The troops of RTe′-ma looked, the companies of She′-ba waited for them. Is. 21:14

20 They were Rconfounded T because they had hoped; they came thither, and were ashamed.   Jer. 14:3 • confused

21 For now ye are no thing; ye see my casting down, and are afraid.

22 Did I say, Bring unto me? or, Give a reward for me of your substance?

23 Or, Deliver me from the enemy's hand? or, Redeem me from the hand of the mighty?

24 Teach me, and I will hold my tongue: and cause me to understand wherein I have erred.

25 How forcible are right words! but what doth your arguing Treprove?   establish

26 Do ye imagine to reprove words, and the Rspeeches of one that is desperate, which are as wind?   15:2; 16:3

27 Yea, ye overwhelm the fatherless, and ye Rdig a pit for your friend.   Ps. 57:6

28 Now therefore be content, look upon me; for it is evident unto you if I lie.

29 Return, I pray you, Tlet it not be iniquity; yea, return again, my righteousness is Tin it.   not be unfair • in this manner

30 Is there iniquity in my tongue? cannot my taste discern perverse things?

CHAPTER 7

Job Questions God's Continuing Trials

I S there not Ran appointed time to man upon earth? are not his days also like the days of an hireling?   14:5

2 As a servant Tearnestly desireth the shadow, and as an hireling looketh for the reward of his work;   longs for shade

3 So am I made to possess months of vanity, and Rwearisome nights are appointed to me.   16:7

4 RWhen I lie down, I say, When shall I arise, and the night be gone? and I am full of tossings to and fro unto the dawning of the day.   Deut. 28:67

5 My flesh is ᴿclothed with worms and clods of dust; my skin is broken, and become loathsome.   2:7

6 My days are swifter than a weaver's shuttle, and are spent without hope.

7 O remember that ᴿmy life is wind: mine eye shall no more see good.   7:16; Ps. 78:39

8 ᴿThe eye of him that hath seen me shall see me no more: thine eyes are upon me, and ᵀI am not.   20:9 · no more

9 As the cloud is consumed and vanisheth away; so ᴿhe that goeth down to the grave shall come up no more.   2 Sam. 12:23

10 He shall return no more to his house, neither shall his place know him any more.

11 Therefore I will not refrain my mouth; I will speak in the anguish of my spirit; I will complain in the bitterness of my soul.

12 Am I a sea, or a ᴿwhale, that thou settest a watch over me?   Ezek. 32:2, 3

13 When I say, My bed shall comfort me, my couch shall ease my complaint;

14 Then thou scarest me with dreams, and terrifiest me through visions:

15 So that my soul chooseth strangling, and death rather ᵀthan my life.   than my bones

16 I loathe it; I would not live alway: let me alone; for my days are vanity.

17 ᴿWhat is man, that thou shouldest magnify him? and that thou shouldest set thine heart upon him?   Ps. 8:4; 144:3

18 And that thou shouldest visit him every morning, and try him every moment?

19 ᴿHow long wilt thou not depart from me, nor let me alone till I swallow down my spittle?   10:20; 14:6

20 I have sinned; what shall I do unto thee, ᴿO thou preserver of men? why hast thou set me as a mark against thee, so that I am a burden to myself?   35:3, 6

21 And why dost thou not pardon my transgression, and take away mine iniquity? for now shall I ᵀsleep in the dust; and thou shalt seek me in the morning, but I shall not be.   be dead in the grave

CHAPTER 8

Bildad's First Speech

THEN answered Bil'-dad the Shu'-hite, and said,

2 How long wilt thou speak these things? and how long shall the ᴿwords of thy mouth be like a strong wind?   6:26

3 Doth God ᵀpervert judgment? or doth the Almighty pervert justice?   twist

4 If ᴿthy children have sinned against him, and he have cast them away for their transgression;   1:5, 18, 19

5 ᴿIf thou wouldest seek unto God be-

times, and make thy supplication to the Almighty;   [5:17-27]

6 If thou wert pure and upright; surely now he would awake for thee, and make the habitation of thy righteousness prosperous.

7 Though thy beginning was small, yet thy latter end should greatly increase.

8 ᴿFor ᵀenquire, I pray thee, of the former age, and prepare thyself to the search of their fathers: Deut. 4:32 · ask

9 (For ᴿwe are but of yesterday, and know nothing, because our days upon earth are a shadow:)   14:2

10 Shall not they teach thee, and tell thee, and utter words out of their heart?

11 Can the rush grow up without mire? can the flag grow without water?

12 ᴿWhilst it is yet in his greenness, and not cut down, it withereth before any other herb.   Ps. 129:6

13 So are the paths of all that ᴿforget God; and the hypocrite's hope shall perish: Ps. 9:17

14 Whose hope shall be cut off, and whose trust shall be a ᴿspider's web.   Is. 59:5, 6

15 ᴿHe shall lean upon his house, but it shall not stand: he shall hold it fast, but it shall not endure.   Ps. 49:11

16 He is green before the sun, and his branch shooteth forth in his garden.

17 His roots are wrapped about the heap, and seeth the place of stones.

18 ᴿIf he destroy him from his place, then ᵀit shall deny him, saying, I have not seen thee.   7:10 · seem God had no part in it

19 Behold, this is the joy of his way, and out of the earth shall others grow.

20 Behold, God will not cast away a perfect man, neither will he help the evil doers:

21 Till he fill thy ᴿmouth with laughing, and thy lips with rejoicing.   Ps. 126:1, 2

22 They that hate thee shall be clothed with shame; and the dwelling place of the wicked ᵀshall come to nought.   shall not be

CHAPTER 9

Job Argues His Case

THEN Job answered and said,
2 I know it is so of a truth: but how should ᴿman be just with God?   25:4

3 If he will ᵀcontend with him, he cannot answer him one of a thousand.   dispute

4 ᴿHe is wise in heart, and mighty in strength: who hath hardened himself against him, and hath prospered?   36:5

5 ᴿWhich removeth the mountains, and they know not; which overturneth them in his anger.   [26:6-14]

6 Which shaketh the earth out of her place, and the pillars thereof tremble.

7 Which commandeth the sun, and it riseth not; and sealeth up the stars.

8 Which alone spreadeth out the heavens, and treadeth upon the waves of the sea.

9 Which maketh Arc-tu'-rus, O-ri'-on, and Ple'-ia-des, and the chambers of the south.

10 Which doeth great things past finding out; yea, and wonders without number.

11 Lo, he goeth by me, and I see *him* not: he passeth on also, but I perceive him not.

12 ᴿBehold, he taketh away, who can hinder him? who will say unto him, ᴿWhat doest thou?   11:10 • [Is. 45:9]

13 *If* God will not withdraw his anger, the proud helpers do stoop under him.

14 How much less shall I answer him, *and* choose out my words *to reason* with him?

15 ᴿWhom, though I were righteous, *yet* would I not answer, *but* I would make supplication to my judge.   [vv. 20, 21]

16 If I had called, and he had answered me; *yet* would I not believe that he had hearkened unto my voice.

17 For he breaketh me with a tempest, and multiplieth my wounds without cause.

18 He will not suffer me to take my breath, but filleth me with bitterness.

19 If *I speak* of strength, lo, *he is* strong: and if of ᵀjudgment, who shall set me a time to plead?   *justice*

20 If I justify myself, mine own mouth shall condemn me: *if I say,* I *am* perfect, it shall also prove me ᵀperverse.   *guilty*

21 *Though* I *were* perfect, *yet* would I not know my soul: I would despise my life.

22 This *is* one *thing,* therefore I said *it,* He destroyeth the perfect and the wicked.

23 If the scourge slay suddenly, he will laugh at the trial of the innocent.

24 The earth is given into the ᴿhand of the wicked: he covereth the faces of the judges thereof; if not, where, *and* who *is* he? 12:6; 16:11

25 Now my days are swifter than a post: they flee away, they see no good.

26 They are passed away as the swift ships: as the eagle *that* hasteth to the prey.

27 ᴿIf I say, I will forget my complaint, I will leave off my ᵀheaviness, and comfort *myself;*   7:13 • *depression*

28 I am afraid of all my sorrows, I know that thou wilt not hold me innocent.

29 *If* I be ᴿwicked, why then labour I in vain?   [Ps. 37:32, 33]

30 ᴿIf I wash myself with snow water, and make my hands never so clean;   [Jer. 2:22]

31 Yet shalt thou plunge me in the ditch, and mine own clothes shall abhor me.

32 For ᴿhe *is* not a man, as I *am, that* I should answer him, *and* we should come together in ᵀjudgment.   *v. 3 • court*

33 Neither is there any daysman betwixt us, *that* might lay his hand upon us both.

34 Let him take his ᵀrod away from me, and let not his fear terrify me: *chastisement*

35 Then ᴿwould I speak, and not fear him; but *it is* not so with me.   13:22

CHAPTER 10

Job Questions His Oppression

MY soul is weary of my life; I will leave my complaint upon myself; I will speak in the bitterness of my soul.

2 I will say unto God, ᴿDo not condemn me; shew me wherefore thou contendest with me.   9:29

3 *Is it* good unto thee that thou shouldest oppress, that thou shouldest despise the work of thine hands, and shine upon the ᴿcounsel of the wicked?   21:16

4 Hast thou eyes of flesh? or ᴿseest thou as man seeth?   [1 Sam. 16:7]

5 *Are* thy days as the days of man? *are* thy ᴿyears as man's days,   [36:26]

6 That thou enquirest after mine iniquity, and searchest after my sin?

7 ᴿThou knowest that I am not wicked; and *there is* none that can deliver out of thine hand.   13:18

8 Thine hands ᵀhave made me and fashioned me together round about; yet thou dost destroy me.   *took pains*

9 Remember, I beseech thee, that ᴿthou hast made me as the clay; and wilt thou bring me into dust again?   33:6

10 ᴿHast thou not poured me out as milk, and curdled me like cheese?   [Ps. 139:14–16]

11 Thou hast clothed me with skin and flesh, and hast ᵀfenced me with bones and sinews.   *knit*

12 Thou hast granted me life and favour, and thy visitation hath preserved my spirit.

13 And these *things* hast thou hid in thine heart: I know that this *is* with thee.

14 If I sin, then thou markest me, and thou wilt not acquit me from mine iniquity.

15 If I be wicked, ᴿwoe unto me; and *if* I be righteous, *yet* will I not lift up my head. I *am* full of confusion; therefore ᴿsee thou mine affliction;   Is. 3:11 • Ps. 25:18

16 For it increaseth. ᴿThou huntest me as a fierce lion: and again thou shewest thyself marvellous upon me.   Is. 38:13

17 Thou renewest thy witnesses against me, and increasest thine indignation upon me; changes and war *are* against me.

18 ᴿWherefore then hast thou brought me forth out of the womb? Oh that I had given up the ghost, and no eye had seen me! 3:11–13

19 I should have been as though I had not been; I should have been carried from the womb to the grave.

20 ᴿ*Are* not my days few? cease *then, and* ᴿlet me alone, that I may take comfort a little,   Ps. 39:5 • 7:16, 19

21 Before I go *whence* I shall not return,
Reven to the land of darkness Rand the
shadow of death;   Ps. 88:12 • Ps. 23:4
22 A land of darkness, as darkness *itself;*
and of the shadow of death, without any
order, and *where* the light *is* as darkness.

CHAPTER 11

Zophar's First Speech

THEN answered Zo'-phar the Na'-a-ma-
thite, and said,
2 Should not the multitude of words be
answered? Rand should a man Tfull of talk be
justified?   15:2; 18:2 • *talkative*
3 Should thy lies make men Thold their
peace? and when thou mockest, shall no man
make thee ashamed?   *refrain from*
4 For Rthou hast said, My doctrine *is* pure,
and I am clean in thine eyes.   6:30
5 But oh that God would speak, and open
his lips against thee;
6 And that he would shew thee the secrets
of wisdom, that *they are* double to that which
is! Know therefore that RGod exacteth of
thee *less* than thine iniquity *deserveth.*   15:5
7 RCanst thou by searching find out God?
canst thou find out the Almighty unto
perfection?   33:12, 13; 36: 26; [Eccl. 3:11]
8 *It is* as high as heaven; what canst thou
do? deeper than hell; what canst thou know?
9 The measure thereof *is* longer than the
earth, and broader than the sea.
10 RIf he cut off, and shut up, or gather
together, then who can hinder him?   9:12
11 For he knoweth vain men: he seeth
wickedness also; will he not then consider *it?*
12 For Rvain man would be wise, though
man be born *like* a wild ass's colt.   [Ps. 39:5]
13 If thou Rprepare thine heart, and stretch
out thine hands toward him;   [Ps. 78:8]
14 If iniquity *be* in thine hand, put it far
away, and Rlet not wickedness dwell in thy
tabernacles.   Ps. 101:3
15 RFor then shalt thou lift up thy face
without spot; yea, thou shalt be stedfast, and
shalt not fear: 22:26; Ps. 118:6
16 Because thou shalt forget *thy* misery,
and remember *it* as waters *that* pass away:
17 And *thine* Tage Rshall be clearer than
the noonday; thou shalt shine forth, thou
shalt be as the morning.   *life* • Prov. 4:18
18 And thou shalt be secure, because there
is hope; yea, thou shalt dig *about thee, and*
thou shalt take thy rest in safety.
19 Also thou shalt lie down, and none shall
make *thee* afraid; yea, many Rshall make suit
unto thee.   Lev. 26:6; Is. 17:2
20 But the eyes of the wicked shall fail, and
they shall not escape, and their hope *shall be
as* the giving up of the ghost.

CHAPTER 12

Job Tells His Friends Only God Knows

AND Job answered and said,
2 No doubt but Rye *are* the people, and
wisdom shall die with you.   16:1, 2
3 But I have understanding as well as you;
I *am* not inferior to you: yea, who knoweth
not such things as these?
4 I am *as* one mocked of his neighbour,
who calleth upon God, and he answereth
him: the just upright *man is* laughed to scorn.
5 RHe that is ready to slip with *his* feet *is as*
a lamp despised in the thought of him that is
at ease.   Prov. 14:2
6 The Ttabernacles of robbers prosper, and
they that provoke God are secure; into whose
hand God bringeth *abundantly.*   *tents*
7 But ask now the beasts, and they shall
teach thee; and the fowls of the air, and they
shall tell thee:
8 Or speak to the earth, and it shall teach
thee; and the fishes of the sea shall declare
unto thee:
9 Who knoweth not in all these that the
hand of the LORD hath wrought this?
10 In whose hand *is* the soul of every
living thing, and the breath of all mankind.
11 RDoth not the ear Ttry words? and the
mouth taste his meat?   34:3 • *test*
12 With the ancient *is* wisdom; and in
Tlength of days understanding.   *age*
13 With Thim *is* wisdom and strength, he
hath counsel and understanding.   God
14 Behold, Rhe breaketh down, and it
cannot be built again: he shutteth up a man,
and there can be no opening.   Is. 25:2
15 Behold, he Rwithholdeth the waters, and
they dry up: also he sendeth them out, and
they overturn the earth.   [1 Kin. 8:35, 36]
16 With him *is* strength and wisdom: the
deceived and the deceiver *are* his.
17 He leadeth counsellors away Tspoiled,
and maketh the judges fools.   *robbed*
18 He Rlooseth the bond of kings, and
girdeth their loins with a girdle.   Ps. 116:16
19 He leadeth princes away Tspoiled, and
overthroweth the mighty.   *robbed*
20 RHe removeth away the speech of the
trusty, and taketh away the understanding of
the aged.   32:9
21 He poureth contempt upon princes, and
weakeneth the strength of the mighty.
22 He Rdiscovereth deep things out of
darkness, and bringeth out to light the
shadow of death.   Dan. 2:22; [1 Cor. 4:5]
23 He increaseth the nations, and destroyeth them: he enlargeth the nations, and
straiteneth them *again.*
24 He taketh away the heart of the chief of
the people of the earth, and Rcauseth them to

wander in a wilderness *where there is* no way.   Ps. 107:4

25 ^RThey grope in the dark without light, and he maketh them to ^Rstagger like *a* drunken *man.*   5:14 • Ps. 107:27

CHAPTER 13

Job Begs God to Speak to Him

LO, mine eye hath seen all *this,* mine ear hath heard and understood it.

2 ^RWhat ye know, *the same* do I know also: I *am* not inferior unto you.   12:3

3 ^RSurely I would speak to the Almighty, and I desire to reason with God.   23:3

4 But ye *are* forgers of lies, ^Rye *are* all physicians of no value.   6:21; [Jer. 23:32]

5 O that ye would altogether hold your peace! and it should be your wisdom.

6 Hear now my reasoning, and hearken to the pleadings of my lips.

7 ^RWill ye speak ^Twickedly for God? and talk deceitfully for him?   36:4 • *foolishly*

8 Will ye ^Taccept his person? will ye contend for God?   *consider him great*

9 Is it good that he should search you out? or as one man mocketh another, do ye *so* mock him?

10 He will surely ^Treprove you, if ye do secretly accept persons.   *criticize*

11 Shall not his excellency make you afraid? and his dread fall upon you?

12 Your remembrances *are* like unto ashes, your bodies to bodies of clay.

13 Hold your peace, let me alone, that I may speak, and let come on me what *will.*

14 Wherefore do I take my flesh in my teeth, and put my life in mine hand?

15 ^RThough he slay me, yet will I trust in him: ^Rbut I will maintain mine own ways before him.   Ps. 23:4 • 27:5

16 He also *shall be* my salvation: for an hypocrite shall not come before him.

17 Hear diligently my speech, and my declaration with your ears.

18 Behold now, I have ordered *my* cause; I know that I shall be justified.

19 ^RWho *is* he *that* will plead with me? for now, if I hold my tongue, I shall ^Tgive up the ghost.   Is. 50:8 • *die*

20 Only do not two *things* unto me: then I will not hide myself from thee.

21 Withdraw thine hand far from me: and let not thy dread make me afraid.

22 Then call thou, and I will answer: or let me speak, and answer thou me.

23 ^RHow many *are* mine iniquities and sins? make me to know my transgression and my sin.   7:21

24 ^RWherefore hidest thou thy face, and holdest me for thine enemy?   Ps. 13:1

25 Wilt thou break a leaf driven to and fro? and wilt thou pursue the dry stubble?

26 For thou writest bitter things against me, and ^Rmakest me to possess the iniquities of my youth.   9:18; 20:11

27 ^RThou puttest my feet also in the stocks, and lookest ^Tnarrowly unto all my paths; thou settest a print upon the heels of my feet.   33:11 • *critically*

28 And he, as a rotten thing, consumeth, as a garment that is moth eaten.

CHAPTER 14

Job Mourns That Man Has Only One Life

MAN that *is* born of a woman *is* of ^Tfew days, and full of trouble.   *short life*

2 ^RHe cometh forth like a flower, and is cut down: he fleeth also as a shadow, and continueth not.   8:9; Ps. 90:5, 6; Is. 40:6

3 And ^Rdost thou open thine eyes upon such an one, and bringest me into judgment with thee?   Ps. 8:4; 144:3

4 Who ^Rcan bring a clean *thing* out of an unclean? not one.   [Ps. 51:2, 5, 10; John 3:6]

5 ^RSeeing his days *are* ^Tdetermined, the number of his months *are* with thee, thou hast appointed his bounds that he cannot pass;   7:1 • *decreed*

6 Turn from him, that he may rest, till he shall accomplish, as an hireling, his day.

7 For there is hope of a tree, if it be cut down, that it will sprout again, and that the tender branch thereof will not cease.

8 Though the root thereof ^Twax old in the earth, and the stock thereof die in the ground;   *grow*

9 *Yet* through the scent of water it will bud, and bring forth boughs like a plant.

10 But man dieth, and wasteth away: yea, man giveth up the ghost, and where *is* he?

11 ^R*As* the waters fail from the sea, and the flood decayeth and drieth up: Is. 19:5

12 So man lieth down, and riseth not: till the heavens *be* no more, they shall not awake, nor be raised out of their sleep.

13 O that thou wouldest hide me in the grave, that thou wouldest keep me secret, until thy wrath be past, that thou wouldest appoint me a set time, and remember me!

14 If a man die, shall he live *again?* all the days of my appointed time ^Rwill I wait, till my change come.   13:15

15 ^RThou shalt call, and I will answer thee: thou wilt have a desire to the work of thine hands.   13:22

16 ^RFor now thou numberest my steps: dost thou not watch over my sin?   31:4

17 My transgression *is* sealed up in a bag, and thou sewest up mine iniquity.

18 And surely the mountain ^Tfalling

cometh to nought, and the rock is removed out of his place.   *crumbles away*

19 The waters wear the stones: thou washest away the things which grow *out* of the dust of the earth; and thou ᴿdestroyest the hope of man.   7:6

20 Thou prevailest for ever against him, and he ᴿpasseth: thou changest his countenance, and sendest him away.   20:7

21 His sons come to honour, and ᴿhe knoweth *it* not; and they are brought low, but he perceiveth *it* not of them.   Eccl. 9:5

22 But his flesh upon him shall have pain, and his soul within him shall mourn.

CHAPTER 15

Job's Mouth Condemns Him

THEN answered El'-i-phaz the Te'-man-ite, and said,

2 Should a wise man utter vain knowledge, and fill his belly with the east wind?

3 Should he reason with unprofitable talk? or with speeches wherewith he can do no good?

4 Yea, thou castest off fear, and ᵀrestrainest prayer before God.   *hinders*

5 For thy mouth uttereth thine iniquity, and thou choosest the tongue of the crafty.

6 ᴿThine own mouth condemneth thee, and not I: yea, thine own lips testify against thee.   18:7; [Luke 19:22]

7 *Art* thou the first man *that* was born? or wast thou made before the hills?

8 Hast thou heard the secret of God? and dost thou ᵀrestrain wisdom to thyself?   *limit*

9 What knowest thou, that we know not? *what* understandest thou, which *is* not in us?

10 With us *are* both the grayheaded and very aged men, much elder than thy father.

11 *Are* the consolations of God small with thee? is there any secret thing with thee?

12 Why doth thine heart carry thee away? and what do thy eyes wink at,

13 That thou turnest thy spirit against God, and lettest *such* words go out of thy mouth?

The Wicked Suffer

14 ᴿWhat *is* man, that he should be clean? and *he* which is born of a woman, that he should be righteous?   Prov. 20:9

15 ᴿBehold, he putteth no trust in his saints; yea, the ᴿheavens are not clean in his sight.   5:1 • 25:5

16 How much more abominable and filthy *is* man, which drinketh iniquity like water?

17 I will shew thee, hear me; and that *which* I have seen I will declare;

18 Which wise men have told ᴿfrom their fathers, and have not hid *it*:   8:8

19 Unto whom alone the earth was given, and no stranger passed among them.

20 The wicked man travaileth with pain all *his* days, ᴿand the number of years is hidden to the oppressor.   Ps. 90:12

21 A ᴿdreadful sound *is* in his ears: ᴿin prosperity the destroyer shall come upon him.   18:11 • 1 Thess. 5:3

22 ᴿHe believeth not that he shall return out of darkness, and he is waited for of the sword.   [20:23–29]

23 He ᴿwandereth abroad for bread, *saying,* Where *is it?* he knoweth that the day of darkness is ready at his hand.   Ps. 59:15

24 Trouble and anguish shall make him afraid; they shall prevail against him, as a king ready to the battle.

25 For he stretcheth out his hand against God, and ᵀstrengtheneth himself against the Almighty.   *conducts arrogantly*

26 He runneth upon him, *even* on *his* neck, upon the thick bosses of his bucklers:

27 ᴿBecause he covereth his face with his fatness, and maketh collops of fat on *his* flanks.   Ps. 17:10; 73:7; 119:70

28 And he dwelleth in desolate cities, *and* in houses which no man inhabiteth, which are ready to become heaps.

29 He shall not be rich, neither shall his ᵀsubstance continue, neither shall he prolong the perfection thereof upon the earth. *property*

30 He shall not depart out of darkness; the flame shall dry up his branches, and by the breath of his mouth shall he go away.

31 Let not him that is deceived trust in vanity: for vanity shall be his recompence.

32 It shall be accomplished before his time, and his branch shall not be green.

33 He shall shake off his unripe grape as the vine, and shall ᴿcast off his flower as the olive.   14:2

34 For the congregation of hypocrites *shall be* desolate, and fire shall consume the tabernacles of ᵀbribery.   *corrupt*

35 ᴿThey conceive mischief, and bring forth ᵀvanity, and their belly prepareth deceit.   Ps. 7:14; Is. 59:4 • *iniquity*

CHAPTER 16

Job Calls His Friends Miserable Comforters

THEN Job answered and said,

2 I have heard many such things: ᴿmiserable comforters *are* ye all.   21:34

3 Shall ᵀvain words have an end? or what emboldeneth thee that thou answerest? *empty*

4 I also could speak as ye *do:* if your soul were in my soul's stead, I could heap up words against you, and ᴿshake mine head at you.   Ps. 22:7; Lam. 2:15

5 *But* I would ᵀstrengthen you with my

mouth, and the moving of my lips should ᵀassuage *your* grief.   encourage · relieve

Job Laments His Situation

6 Though I speak, ᴿmy grief is not ᵀassuaged: and *though* I forbear, what am I eased?   [9:27, 28] · *eased*
7 But now he hath made me weary: thou hast made desolate all my company.
8 ᴿAnd thou hast filled me with wrinkles, *which* is a witness *against me:* ᴿand my leanness rising up in me beareth witness to my face.   10:17 · Ps. 109:24
9 He teareth *me* in his wrath, who hateth me: he gnasheth upon me with his teeth; mine enemy sharpeneth his eyes upon me.
10 They have ᴿgaped upon me with their mouth; they have smitten me upon the cheek reproachfully; they have gathered themselves together against me.   Ps. 22:13
11 God ᴿhath delivered me to the ungodly, and turned me over into the hands of the wicked.   1:15, 17
12 I was at ease, but he hath broken me asunder: he hath also taken *me* by my neck, and shaken me to pieces, and ᴿset me up for his ᵀmark.   7:20 · *target*
13 ᴿHis archers ᵀcompass me round about, he cleaveth my reins asunder, and doth not spare; he poureth out my gall upon the ground.   6:4; 19:12 · *surround*
14 He breaketh me with breach upon breach, he runneth upon me like a giant.

Job Defends His Innocence

15 I have sewed sackcloth upon my skin, and ᴿdefiled my horn in the dust.   30:19
16 My face is foul with weeping, and on my eyelids *is* ᴿthe shadow of death;   24:17
17 Not for *any* ᴿinjustice in mine hands: also my prayer *is* pure.   Is. 59:6
18 O earth, cover not thou my blood, and ᴿlet my cry have no place.   27:9; [Ps. 66:18]
19 Also now, behold, ᴿmy witness *is* in heaven, and my record *is* on high.   Rom. 1:9
20 My friends scorn me: ᴿ*but* mine eye poureth out *tears* unto God.   17:7
21 O that one might plead for a man with God, as a man *pleadeth* for his neighbour!
22 When a few years are come, then I shall go the way *whence* I shall not return.

CHAPTER 17

God Makes Job a Byword

MY breath is corrupt, my days are extinct, the graves *are* ready for me.
2 *Are there* not mockers with me? and doth not mine eye continue in their ᴿprovocation?   1 Sam. 1:6

3 Lay down now, put me in a surety with thee; who *is* he *that* ᴿwill strike hands with me?   Prov. 6:1; 17:18; 22:26
4 For thou hast ᴿhid their heart from understanding: therefore shalt thou not exalt *them.*   12:20; 32:9
5 He that speaketh flattery to *his* friends, even the eyes of his children shall fail.
6 He hath made me also ᴿa byword of the people; and aforetime I was as a tabret.   30:9
7 Mine eye also is dim by reason of sorrow, and all my members *are* as a shadow.
8 Upright *men* shall be astonied at this, and the ᴿinnocent shall stir up himself against the hypocrite.   22:19
9 The righteous also shall hold on his way, and he that hath ᴿclean hands shall be stronger and stronger.   Ps. 24:4
10 But as for you all, do ye return, and come now: ᴿfor I cannot find *one* wise *man* among you.   12:2
11 My days are past, my purposes are broken off, *even* the thoughts of my heart.
12 They change the night into day: the light *is* short because of darkness.
13 If I wait, the grave *is* mine house: I have made my bed in the darkness.
14 I have said to ᵀcorruption, Thou *art* my father: to the worm, *Thou art* my mother, and my sister.   *decay*
15 And where *is* now my ᴿhope? as for my hope, who shall see it?   7:6
16 They shall go down to the bars of the pit, when *our* rest together *is* in the dust.

CHAPTER 18

Bildad's Second Speech

THEN answered Bil'-dad the Shu'-hite, and said,
2 How long *will it be ere* ye make an end of words? mark, and afterwards we will speak.
3 Wherefore are we counted ᴿas beasts, *and* reputed vile in your sight?   Ps. 73:22
4 He teareth himself in his anger: shall the earth be forsaken for thee? and shall the rock be removed out of his place?
5 Yea, ᴿthe light of the wicked shall be put out, and the spark of his fire shall not shine.   Prov. 13:9; 20:20; 24:20
6 The light shall be dark in his tabernacle, and his candle shall be put out with him.
7 The steps of his strength shall be straitened, and ᴿhis own counsel shall cast him down.   15:6
8 For ᴿhe is cast into a net by his own feet, and he walketh upon a snare.   Ps. 9:15
9 The gin shall take *him* by the heel, *and* the robber shall prevail against him.
10 The snare *is* laid for him in the ground, and a trap for him in the way.

11 Terrors shall make him afraid on every side, ^Rand shall drive him to his feet.   20:8

12 His strength shall be hungerbitten, and destruction *shall be* ready at his side.

13 It shall devour the strength of his skin: *even* the firstborn of death^R shall devour his strength.   Zech. 14:12

14 ^RHis confidence shall be rooted out of his tabernacle, and it shall bring him to the king of terrors.   18:6; 27:18

15 It shall dwell in his tabernacle, because *it is* none of his: ^Rbrimstone shall be scattered upon his habitation.   Ps. 11:6

16 His roots shall be dried up beneath, and above shall his branch be cut off.

17 ^RHis remembrance shall perish from the earth, and he shall have no name in the street.   24:20; [Ps. 34:16]; Prov. 10:7

18 He shall be driven from light into darkness, and chased out of the world.

19 ^RHe shall neither have son nor nephew among his people, nor any remaining in his dwellings.   Is. 14:22

20 They that come after *him* shall be astonied^R at his ^Tday, as they that went before were affrighted.   Ps. 37:13 • *fate*

21 Surely such *are* the dwellings of the wicked, and this *is* the place *of him that* ^Rknoweth not God.   Jer. 9:3; 1 Thess. 4:5

CHAPTER 19

Job's Response to Bildad

THEN Job answered and said,
2 How long will ye vex my soul, and break me in pieces with words?

3 These ten times have ye ^Treproached me: ye are not ashamed *that* ye make yourselves ^Tstrange to me.   *criticized • alien*

4 And be it indeed *that* I have erred, mine error remaineth with myself.

5 If indeed ye will ^Rmagnify *yourselves* against me, and plead against me mine ^Treproach: Ps. 35:26; 38:16 • *fault*

6 Know now that God hath overthrown me, and hath compassed me with his net.

7 Behold, ^RI cry out of ^Twrong, but I am not heard: I cry aloud, but *there is* no ^Tjudgment.   Hab. 1:2 • *violence • justice*

8 He hath ^Tfenced up my way that I cannot pass, and he hath set darkness in my paths.   *shut up*

9 He hath stripped me of my glory, and taken the crown *from* my head.

10 He hath destroyed me on every side, and I am gone: and mine ^Rhope hath he removed like a tree.   17:15, 16

11 He hath also kindled his wrath against me, and ^Rhe counteth me unto him as *one of* his enemies.   13:24

12 His troops come together, and raise up their way against me, and encamp round about my ^Ttabernacle.   *tent*

13 ^RHe hath put my brethren far from me, and mine acquaintance are verily estranged from me.   Ps. 31:11; 69:8; 88:8

14 My kinsfolk have failed, and my ^Tfamiliar friends have forgotten me.   *intimate*

15 They that dwell in mine house, and my maids, count me for a stranger: I am an alien in their sight.

16 I called my servant, and he gave *me* no answer; I intreated him with my mouth.

17 My breath is ^Tstrange to my wife, though I intreated for the children's *sake* of mine own body.   *repulsive*

18 Yea, young^T children despised me; I arose, and they spake against me.   *wicked*

19 ^RAll my ^Tinward friends abhorred me: and they whom I loved are turned against me.   Ps. 55:13 • *close*

20 ^RMy bone cleaveth to my skin and to my flesh, and I am escaped with the skin of my teeth.   16:8; Ps. 102:5; Lam. 4:8

21 Have pity upon me, have pity upon me, O ye my friends; ^Rfor the hand of God hath touched me.   Ps. 38:2

22 Why do ye ^Rpersecute me as God, and are not satisfied with my flesh?   Ps. 69:26

23 Oh that my words were now written! oh that they were printed in a book!

24 That they were graven with an iron pen and lead in the rock for ever!

25 For I know *that* my ^Rredeemer liveth, and *that* he shall stand at the latter *day* upon the earth: Ps. 78:35; Prov. 23:11

26 ^TAnd *though* after my skin *worms* destroy this *body*, yet ^Rin my flesh shall I see God: *my skin is flayed • 1 Cor. 13:12*

27 Whom I shall see for myself, and mine eyes shall behold, and not another; *though* my reins be consumed within me.

28 But ye should say, Why persecute we him, seeing the root of the matter is found in me?

29 Be ye afraid of the sword: for wrath *bringeth* the punishments of the sword, that ye may know *there is* a judgment.

CHAPTER 20

Zophar's Second Speech

THEN answered Zo'phar the Na'-a-ma-thite, and said,
2 Therefore do my thoughts cause me to answer, and for *this* I make haste.

3 I have ^Theard the check of my reproach, and the spirit of my understanding causeth me to answer.   *become aware of*

4 Knowest thou *not* this ^Rof old, since man was placed upon earth,   8:8

5 RThat the triumphing of the wicked *is* short, and the Rjoy of the hypocrite *but* for a moment?   Ps. 37:35 • 8:13

6 Though his excellency mount up to the heavens, and his head reach unto the clouds;

7 *Yet* he shall Rperish for ever like his own dung: they which have seen him shall say, Where *is* he?   4:20; 14:10

8 He shall fly away Ras a dream, and shall not be found: yea, he shall be chased away as a vision of the night.   Ps. 73:20

9 RThe eye also *which* saw him shall *see him* no more; neither shall his place any more behold him.   7:8; 8:18

10 His children shall seek to please the poor, and his hands shall restore their goods.

11 His bones are full of Rthe sin of his youth, which shall lie down with him in the dust.   21:23, 24

12 Though wickedness be sweet in his mouth, *though* he hide it under his tongue;

13 *Though* he spare it, and forsake it not; but keep it still within his mouth:

14 *Yet* his meat in his bowels is Tturned, *it is* the gall of asps within him.   soured

15 He hath swallowed down riches, and he shall vomit them up again: God shall cast them out of his belly.

16 He shall suck the Rpoison of asps: the viper's tongue shall slay him.   Deut. 32:24

17 He shall not see the rivers, the floods, the brooks of honey and butter.

18 That which he laboured for shall he restore, and shall not swallow *it* down: according to *his* substance *shall* the restitution *be,* and he shall not rejoice *therein.*

19 Because he hath oppressed *and* hath forsaken the poor; *because* he hath violently taken away an house which he builded not;

20 Surely he shall not feel quietness in his belly, Rhe shall not save of that which he desired.   Eccl. 5:13-15

21 There shall none of his meat be left; therefore shall no man look for his goods.

22 In the fulness of his sufficiency he shall be in Tstraits: every hand of the wicked shall come upon him.   need

23 *When* he is about to fill his belly, *God* shall cast the fury of his wrath upon him, and shall rain *it* upon him while he is eating.

24 He shall flee from the iron weapon, *and* the bow of steel shall strike him through.

25 It is drawn, and cometh out of the body; yea, the glittering sword cometh out of his gall: terrors *are* upon him.

26 All darkness *shall be* hid in his secret places: aT fire not blown shall consume him; it shall go ill with him that is left in his tabernacle.   unfanned fire

27 The heaven shall reveal his iniquity; and the earth shall rise up against him.

28 The Rincrease of his house shall depart, *and his goods* shall flow away in the day of his wrath.   Deut. 28:31

29 RThis *is* the portion of a wicked man from God, and the heritage Tappointed unto him by God.   27:13 • assigned

CHAPTER 21

Job's Response to Zophar

BUT Job answered and said,
2 Hear diligently my speech, and let this be your Tconsolations.   comfort

3 TSuffer me that I may speak; and after that I have spoken, mock on.   allow me

4 As for me, *is* my complaint to man? and if *it were so,* Rwhy should not my spirit be troubled?   6:11

5 Mark me, and be astonished, Rand lay *your* hand upon *your* mouth.   40:4

6 Even when I remember I am afraid, and trembling taketh hold on my flesh.

7 RWherefore do the wicked live, become old, yea, are mighty in power?   Jer. 12:1

8 RTheir Tseed is established in their sight with them, and their offspring before their eyes.   Ps. 17:14 • children

9 Their houses *are* safe from fear, neither *is* the rod of God upon them.

10 Their bull gendereth, and faileth not; their cow calveth, and casteth not her calf.

11 They send forth their little ones like a flock, and their children dance.

12 They take the timbrel and harp, and rejoice at the sound of the organ.

13 They spend their days in wealth, and in a moment go down to the grave.

14 RTherefore they say unto God, Depart from us; for we desire not the knowledge of thy ways.   22:17

15 RWhat *is* the Almighty, that we should serve him? and what profit should we have, if we pray unto him?   Ex. 5:2

16 Lo, their good *is* not in their hand: the counsel of the wicked is far from me.

17 How oft is the Rcandle of the wicked put out! and *how oft* cometh their destruction upon them! *God* Rdistributeth sorrows in his anger.   18:5 • [31:2, 3]

18 They are as stubble before the wind, and as chaff that the storm carrieth away.

19 GodR layeth up his iniquity for his children: he rewardeth him, and he shall know *it.*   [Ex. 20:5]; Jer. 31:29; Ezek. 18:2

20 His eyes shall see his destruction, and he shall drink of the wrath of the Almighty.

21 For what pleasure *hath* he in his house after him, when the number of his months is cut off in the midst?

22 Shall *any* teach God knowledge? seeing he judgeth those that are high.

23 One dieth in his full strength, being wholly at ease and quiet.

24 His breasts are full of milk, and his bones are moistened with Rmarrow.   Prov. 3:8

25 And another dieth in the bitterness of his soul, and never eateth with pleasure.

26 They shall Rlie down alike in the dust, and the worms shall cover them.   Eccl. 9:2

27 Behold, I know your thoughts, and the Tdevices *which* ye wrongfully imagine against me.   *ideas*

28 For ye say, Where *is* the Rhouse of the prince? and where *are* the Rdwelling places of the wicked?   31:37 • 8:22

29 Have ye not asked them that go by the way?

30 RThat the wicked is reserved to the day of destruction? they shall be brought forth to the day of wrath.   [Prov. 16:4]

31 Who shall declare his way to his face? and who shall repay him *what* he hath done?

32 Yet shall he be brought to the grave, and shall remain in the tomb.

33 The clods of the valley shall be sweet unto him, and every man shall draw after him, as *there are* innumerable before him.

34 How then comfort ye me in vain, seeing in your answers there remaineth falsehood?

CHAPTER 22

Eliphaz's Third Speech

THEN El'-i-phaz the Te'-man-ite answered and said,

2 RCan a man be profitable unto God, as he that is wise may be profitable unto himself?   [Ps. 16:2; Luke 17:10]

3 *Is it* any pleasure to the Almighty, that thou art righteous? or *is it* gain *to him*, that thou makest thy ways perfect?

4 Will he reprove thee for fear of thee? will he enter with thee into judgment?

5 RIs not thy wickedness great? and thine iniquities infinite?   15:5

6 For thou hast Rtaken a pledge from thy brother for nought, and stripped the naked of their clothing.   Deut. 24:6, 17

7 Thou hast not given water to the weary to drink, and thou Rhast withholden bread from the hungry.   31:31

8 But *as for* the mighty man, he had the earth; and the honourable man dwelt in it.

9 Thou hast sent Rwidows away empty, and the arms of the fatherless have been broken.   24:3, 21; 29:13; 31:16

10 Therefore snares *are* round about thee, and sudden fear troubleth thee;

11 Or darkness, *that* thou canst not see; and abundance of waters cover thee.

12 *Is* not RGod in the height of heaven? and behold the height of the stars, how high they are!   [11:7-9]

13 And thou sayest, How doth God know? can he judge through the dark cloud?

14 RThick clouds *are* a covering to him, that he seeth not; and he walketh in the circuit of heaven.   26:9

15 Hast thou marked the old way which Rwicked men have trodden?   34:36

16 Which Rwere cut down out of time, whose foundation was Toverflown with a flood: 15:32 • *washed away*

17 Which said unto God, Depart from us: and what can the Almighty do for them?

18 Yet he filled their houses with good *things:* but the Tcounsel of the wicked is far from me.   *advice*

19 The righteous see *it*, and are glad: and the innocent laugh them to scorn.

20 Whereas our Tsubstance is not cut down, but the remnant of them the fire Tconsumeth.   *property • destroys*

21 Acquaint now thyself with him, and Rbe at peace: thereby good shall come unto thee.   [Ps. 34:10]; Is. 27:5

22 Receive, I pray thee, the law from his mouth, and lay up his words in thine heart.

23 If thou return to the Almighty, thou shalt be Tbuilt up, thou shalt put away iniquity far from thy tabernacles.   *helped*

24 Then shalt thou Rlay up gold Tas dust, and the *gold* of O'-phir as the stones of the brooks.   2 Chr. 1:15 • *on the dust*

25 Yea, the Almighty shall be thy defence, and thou shalt have plenty of silver.

26 For then shalt thou have thy Rdelight in the Almighty, and shalt lift up thy face unto God.   27:10

22:22 Memorizing God's Word—You are not always able to study the Bible by reading it. If you have memorized a portion of the Word of God, you are able to gain insights into its meaning at times when a Bible is not readily available. The Bible recognizes the importance of Scripture memorization. The following benefits can be cited:
  a. It keeps the child of God from sinning (Page 600—Ps. 119:11).
  b. It provides comfort in times of trouble (Page 600—Ps. 119:52, 92).
  c. It stays your mind upon God (Page 566—Ps. 43:3).
  d. It provides daily sustenance for the spiritual life (Page 186—Deut. 8:3).
  e. It provides continual and ready guidance in all the situations of life (Page 618—Prov. 6:20-23).
  f. It provides the basis for formal and informal instruction of your children (Page 184—Deut. 6:6, 7).
      Now turn to Page 217—Josh. 1:8: Meditating upon God's Word.

27 ᴿThou shalt make thy prayer unto him, and he shall hear thee, and thou shalt pay thy vows.   [Is. 58:9–11]

28 Thou shalt also decree a thing, and it shall be established unto thee: ᴿand the light shall shine upon thy ways.   Ps. 112:4

29 When *men* are cast down, then thou shalt say, *There is* lifting up; and ᴿhe shall save the humble person.   [James 4:6]

30 He shall deliver the island of the innocent: ᴿand it is delivered by the pureness of thine hands.   [Ps. 18:20; 24:3, 4]

CHAPTER 23

Job Will Come Forth as Gold

THEN Job answered and said,

2 Even to day *is* my complaint bitter: my stroke is heavier than my groaning.

3 Oh that I knew where I might find him! *that* I might come *even* to his seat!

4 I would order *my* cause before him, and fill my mouth with arguments.

5 I would know the words *which* he would answer me, and understand what he would say unto me.

6 Will he plead against me with *his* great power? No; but he would put *strength* in me.

7 There the righteous might ᵀdispute with him; so should I be delivered for ever from my judge.   *debate*

8 Behold, I go forward, but he *is* not *there;* and backward, but I cannot perceive him:

9 On the left hand, where he doth work, but I cannot behold *him:* he hideth himself on the right hand, that I cannot see *him:*

10 But he ᴿknoweth the way that I take: *when* ᴿhe hath tried me, I shall come forth as gold.   [Ps. 139:1–3] • [Ps. 17:3; James 1:12]

11 ᴿMy foot hath held his steps, his way have I kept, and not declined.   Ps. 17:5

12 Neither have I gone back from the commandment of his lips; ᴿI have esteemed the words of his mouth more than my necessary *food.*   6:10; 22:22

13 But he *is* in one *mind,* and who can turn him? and *what* ᴿhis soul desireth, even *that* he doeth.   Ps. 115:3

14 For he performeth the *thing that is* ᴿappointed for me: and many such *things are* with him.   [1 Thess. 3:2–4]

15 Therefore am I troubled at his presence: when I consider, I am afraid of him.

16 For God ᴿmaketh my heart soft, and the Almighty troubleth me: Ps. 22:14

17 Because I was not cut off before the darkness, *neither* ᴿhath he covered the darkness from my face.   19:8

CHAPTER 24

God Seems Indifferent to the Wicked

WHY, seeing times are not hidden from the Almighty, do they that know him not ᴿsee his days?   [Is. 2:12; Obad. 15]

2 *Some* remove the landmarks; they violently take away flocks, and feed *thereof.*

3 They drive away the ass of the fatherless, they take the widow's ox for a pledge.

4 They turn the needy out of the way: the poor of the earth hide themselves together.

5 Behold, *as* wild asses in the desert, go they ᴿforth to their work; rising betimes for a prey: the wilderness *yieldeth* food for them and for *their* children.   Ps. 104:23

6 They reap *every* one his ᵀcorn in his field: and they gather the vintage of the wicked.   *grain*

7 They cause the naked to lodge without clothing, that *they have* no covering in the ᴿcold.   Ex. 22:26, 27

8 They are wet with the showers of the mountains, and ᴿembrace the rock for want of a shelter.   Lam. 4:5

9 They pluck the fatherless from the breast, and take a pledge of the poor.

10 They cause *him* to go naked ᴿwithout clothing, and they take away the sheaf *from* the hungry;   31:19

11 *Which* make oil within their walls, *and* tread *their* winepresses, and suffer thirst.

12 Men groan from out of the city, and the soul of the wounded crieth out: yet God ᴿlayeth not folly *to* them.   9:23, 24

13 They are of those that rebel against the light; they know not the ways thereof, nor abide in the paths thereof.

14 ᴿThe murderer rising with the light killeth ᴿthe poor and needy, and in the night is as a thief.   Mic. 2:1 • Ps. 10:8

15 ᴿThe eye also of the adulterer waiteth for the twilight, saying, No eye shall see me: and disguiseth *his* face.   Prov. 7:7–10

16 In the dark they dig through houses, *which* they had marked for themselves in the daytime: they know not the light.

17 For the morning *is* to them even as the shadow of death: if *one* know *them, they are* in the ᴿterrors of the shadow of death.   15:21

18 He *is* swift as the waters; their portion is cursed in the earth: he beholdeth not the way of the ᴿvineyards.   vv. 6, 11

19 ᴿDrought and heat consume the snow waters: *so doth* the grave *those which* have sinned.   6:16, 17

20 ᴿThe womb shall forget him; the worm shall feed sweetly on him; ᴿhe shall be no more remembered; and wickedness shall be broken as a tree.   [Is. 49:15] • Prov. 10:7

21 He ᵀevil entreateth the barren *that* beareth not: and doeth not good to the widow.   *preys upon*
22 He draweth also the mighty with ᴿhis power: he riseth up, ᴿand no *man* is sure of life.   9:4 · 18:20
23 *Though* it be given him *to be* in safety, whereon he resteth; yet ᴿhis eyes *are* upon their ways.   [Prov. 15:3]
24 They are ᵀexalted for a little while, but are gone and brought low; they are taken out of the way as all *other*, and cut off as the tops of the ears of corn.   *prosperous*
25 And if *it be* not so now, ᴿwho will make me a liar, and make my speech nothing worth?   27:4

CHAPTER 25

Bildad's Third Speech

THEN answered Bil′-dad the Shu′-hite, and said,
2 Dominion and fear *are* with him; he maketh peace in his high places.
3 Is there any number of his armies? and upon whom doth not his light arise?
4 ᴿHow then can man be justified with God? or how can he be clean *that is* born of a woman?   4:17; 9:2
5 Behold even to the moon, and it shineth not; yea, the stars are not pure in his sight.
6 How much less man, *that is* a worm? and the son of man, *which is* a worm?

CHAPTER 26

Job's Response to Bildad

BUT Job answered and said,
2 How hast thou helped *him that is* without power? *how* savest thou the arm *that hath* no strength?
3 How hast thou counseled *him that hath* no wisdom? and *how* hast thou plentifully declared the thing as it is?
4 To whom hast thou uttered words? and whose spirit came from thee?
5 Dead *things* are formed from under the waters, and the inhabitants thereof.
6 ᴿHell *is* naked before him, and destruction hath no covering.   [Ps. 139:8]
7 He stretcheth out the north over the empty place, *and* hangeth the earth upon nothing.
8 He bindeth up the waters in his thick clouds; and the cloud is not rent under them.
9 He holdeth back the face of his throne, *and* spreadeth his cloud upon it.
10 ᴿHe hath compassed the waters with bounds, until the day and night come to an end.   [38:1–11]; Prov. 8:29

11 The pillars of heaven tremble and are ᵀastonished at his reproof.   *amazed*
12 ᴿHe divideth the sea with his power, and by his understanding he smiteth through the proud.   Is. 51:15; Jer. 31:35
13 ᴿBy his spirit he hath garnished the heavens; his hand hath formed ᴿthe ᵀcrooked serpent.   9:8 · Is. 27:1 · *fleeing*
14 Lo, these *are* parts of his ways: but how little a portion is heard of him? but the thunder of his power who can understand?

CHAPTER 27

Job Affirms His Righteousness

MOREOVER Job continued his parable, and said,
2 *As* God liveth, ᴿ*who* hath taken away my judgment; and the Almighty, *who* hath vexed my soul;   34:5
3 All the while my breath *is* in me,ᴿ and the spirit of God *is* in my nostrils;   [33:4]
4 My lips shall not speak wickedness, nor ᴿmy tongue utter deceit.   6:28
5 God forbid that I should justify you: till I die ᴿI will not ᵀremove mine integrity from me.   2:9; 13:15 · *forsake*
6 My righteousness I ᴿhold fast, and will not let it go: ᴿmy heart shall not reproach *me* so long as I live.   2:3 · Acts 24:16
7 Let mine enemy be as the wicked, and he that riseth up against me as the unrighteous.
8 ᴿFor what *is* the hope of the hypocrite, though he hath gained, when God taketh away his soul?   Luke 12:20
9 ᴿWill God hear his cry when trouble cometh upon him?   [John 9:31; James 4:3]
10 Will he delight himself in the Almighty? will he always call upon God?
11 I will teach you by the hand of God: *that* which *is* with the Almighty will I not conceal.
12 Behold, all ye yourselves have seen *it;* why then are ye thus altogether vain?
13 This *is* the portion of a wicked man with God, and the heritage of oppressors, *which* they shall receive of the Almighty.
14 ᴿIf his children be multiplied, *it is* for the sword: and his offspring shall not be satisfied with bread.   Esth. 9:10; Hos. 9:13
15 Those that remain of him shall be buried in death: and his widows shall not weep.
16 Though he heap up silver as the dust, and prepare raiment as the clay;
17 He may prepare *it,* but ᴿthe just shall put *it* on, and the innocent shall divide the silver.   20:18–21; Prov. 28:8
18 He buildeth his house as a moth, and ᴿas a booth *that* the keeper maketh.   18:14

19 The rich man shall lie down, but he shall not be gathered: he openeth his eyes, and he *is* ^Rnot.   20:7

20 Terrors take hold on him as waters, a tempest stealeth him away in the night.

21 The east wind carrieth him away, and he departeth: ^Rand as a storm hurleth him out of his place.   7:10

22 For *God* shall cast upon him, and not spare: he would fain flee out of his hand.

23 *Men* shall clap their hands at him, and shall hiss him out of his place.

CHAPTER 28

Job Observes That Man Cannot Discover Wisdom

SURELY there is ^Ta vein for the silver, and a place for gold *where* they fine *it*.   *mine*

2 Iron is taken out of the earth, and brass *is* molten *out of* the stone.

3 He setteth an end to darkness, and searcheth out all perfection: the stones of darkness, and the shadow of death.

4 The flood breaketh out from the inhabitant; *even the waters* ^Tforgotten of the foot: they are dried up, they are gone away from men.   *no irrigation*

5 *As for* the earth, out of it cometh bread: and under it is turned up as it were fire.

6 The stones of it *are* the place of sapphires: and it hath ^Tdust of gold.   *gold ore*

7 *There is* a path which no fowl knoweth, and which the vulture's eye hath not seen:

8 The lion's whelps have not trodden it, nor the fierce lion passed by it.

9 He putteth forth his hand upon the rock; he overturneth the mountains by the roots.

10 He cutteth out rivers among the rocks; and his eye seeth every precious thing.

11 He bindeth the floods from overflowing; and *the thing that is* hid bringeth he forth to light.

12 But where shall wisdom be found? and where *is* the place of understanding?

13 Man knoweth not the price thereof; neither is it found in the land of the living.

14 ^RThe depth saith, It *is* not in me: and the sea saith, *It is* not with me.   *v. 22*

15 It cannot be gotten for gold, neither shall silver be weighed *for* the price thereof.

16 It cannot be valued with the gold of O'-phir, with the precious onyx, or the sapphire.

17 ^RThe gold and the crystal cannot equal it: and the exchange of it *shall not be for* jewels of fine gold.   Prov. 8:10; 16:16

18 No mention shall be made of coral, or of pearls: for the price of ^Rwisdom *is* above rubies.   Prov. 8:11

19 The topaz of E-thi-o'-pi-a shall not equal it, neither shall it be valued with ^Rpure gold.   Prov. 8:19

20 Whence then cometh wisdom? and where *is* the place of understanding?

21 Seeing it is hid from the eyes of all living, and kept close from the fowls of the air.

22 Destruction and death say, We have heard the fame thereof with our ears.

23 God understandeth the way thereof, and he knoweth the place thereof.

24 For he looketh to the ends of the earth, *and* seeth under the whole heaven;

25 To make the weight for the winds; and he weigheth the waters by measure.

26 When he made a decree for the rain, and a way for the lightning of the thunder;

27 Then did he see it, and declare it; he prepared it, yea, and searched it out.

28 And unto man he said, Behold, ^Rthe fear of the LORD, that *is* wisdom; and to depart from evil *is* understanding.   Ps. 111:10

CHAPTER 29

Job Remembers His Happy Past

MOREOVER Job continued his parable, and said,

2 Oh that I were as *in* months past, as *in* the days *when* God preserved me;

3 ^RWhen his candle shined upon my head, *and when* by his light I walked *through* darkness;   18:6

4 As I was in the days of my youth, when the secret of God *was* upon my tabernacle;

5 When the Almighty *was* yet with me, *when* my children *were* about me;

6 When I washed my steps with butter, and the rock poured me out rivers of oil;

7 When I went out to the ^Rgate through the city, *when* I prepared my seat in the street!   31:21

8 The young men saw me, and hid themselves: and the aged arose, *and* stood up.

9 The princes refrained talking, and ^Rlaid *their* hand on their mouth.   21:5

10 The nobles held their peace, and their tongue cleaved to the roof of their mouth.

11 When the ^Rear heard *me*, then it blessed me; and when the eye saw *me*, it gave witness to me: 4:3, 4

12 Because ^RI delivered the poor that cried, and the fatherless, and *him that had* none to help him.   [Ps. 72:12; Prov. 21:13]

13 The blessing of him that was ready to perish came upon me: and I caused the widow's heart to sing for joy.

14 ^RI put on righteousness, and it clothed me: my judgment *was* as a robe and a diadem.   Ps. 132:9; [Is. 59:17; Eph. 6:14]

15 I was ᴿeyes to the blind, and feet *was* I to the lame.   Num. 10:31

16 I *was* a father to the poor: and the cause *which* I knew not I searched out.

17 And I brake the jaws of the wicked, and plucked the spoil out of his teeth.

18 Then I said, I shall die in my nest, and I shall multiply *my* days as the sand.

19 ᴿMy root *was* spread out ᴿby the waters, and the dew lay all night upon my branch.   [Jer. 17:7, 8] • Hos. 14:5

20 My glory *was* ᵀfresh in me, and my bow was renewed in my hand.   *new*

21 Unto me *men* gave ear, and waited, and kept silence at my counsel.

22 After my words they spake not again; and my speech dropped upon them.

23 And they waited for me as for the rain; and they opened their mouth wide *as* for ᴿthe latter rain.   Zech. 10:1

24 *If* I laughed on them, they believed *it* not; and the light of my countenance they ᵀcast not down.   *did not despise*

25 I chose out their way, and sat ᴿchief, and dwelt as a king in the army, as one *that* comforteth the mourners.   31:37

CHAPTER 30

Job Describes His Present Humiliation

BUT now *they that are* younger than I have me in ᴿderision, whose fathers I would have disdained to have set with the dogs of my flock.   12:4

2 Yea, whereto *might* the strength of their hands *profit* me, in whom old age was perished?

3 For want and famine *they were* ᵀsolitary; fleeing into the wilderness in former time desolate and waste.   *not common*

4 Who cut up mallows by the bushes, and juniper roots *for* their ᵀmeat.   *food*

5 They were driven forth from among men, (they cried after them as *after* a thief;)

6 To dwell in the cliffs of the valleys, *in* caves of the earth, and *in* the rocks.

7 Among the bushes they brayed; under the nettles they were gathered together.

8 *They were* children of fools, yea, children of base men: they were viler than the earth.

9 ᴿAnd now am I their song, yea, I am their byword.   17:6; Lam. 3:14

10 They abhor me, they flee far from me, and ᵀspare not to spit in my face.   *hesitate*

11 Because he ᴿhath loosed my cord, and afflicted me, they have also let loose ᵀthe bridle before me.   12:18 • *restraint*

12 Upon *my* right *hand* rise the youth; they push away my feet, and ᴿthey raise up against me the ways of their destruction. 19:12

13 They ᴿmar my path, they set forward my calamity, they have no helper.   Is. 3:12

14 They came *upon me* as a ᵀwide breaking in *of waters:* in the desolation they rolled themselves *upon me.*   *flood*

15 Terrors are turned upon me: they pursue my soul as the wind: and my welfare passeth away ᴿas a cloud.   Hos. 13:3

16 ᴿAnd now my soul is poured out upon me; the days of affliction have taken hold upon me.   Ps. 42:4

17 My bones are pierced in me in the night season: and my sinews take no rest.

18 By the great force *of my disease* is my garment ᵀchanged: it bindeth me about as the collar of my coat.   *distorted*

19 He hath cast me into the ᴿmire, and I am become like dust and ashes.   Ps. 69:2, 14

20 I cry unto thee, and thou dost not hear me: I stand up, and thou regardest me *not.*

21 Thou art ᵀbecome cruel to me: with thy strong hand thou ᵀopposest thyself against me.   *turned to be • persecute*

22 Thou liftest me up to the wind; thou causest me to ride *upon it,* and ᵀdissolvest my substance.   *destroys property*

23 For I know *that* thou wilt bring me *to* death, and *to* the ᴿhouse appointed for all living.   Eccl. 12:5

24 Howbeit he will not stretch out *his* hand to the grave, though they ᴿcry in his destruction.   19:7

25 ᴿDid not I weep for him that was in trouble? was *not* my soul grieved for the poor?   Ps. 35:13; Rom. 12:15

26 ᴿWhen I looked for good, then evil came *unto me:* and when I waited for light, there came darkness.   Jer. 8:15

27 My bowels boiled, and rested not: the days of affliction ᵀprevented me.   *beset*

28 I went mourning without the sun: I stood up, *and* I cried in the congregation.

29 ᴿI am a brother to dragons, and a companion to ᵀowls.   Mic. 1:8 • *ostriches*

30 ᴿMy skin is black upon me, and my bones are burned with heat.   Ps. 119:83

31 My ᴿharp also is *turned* to mourning, and my organ into the voice of them that weep.   Is. 24:8

CHAPTER 31

Innocent of Sensual Sins

I MADE a covenant with mine eyes; why then should I think upon a maid?

2 For what ᴿportion of God *is there* from above? and *what* inheritance of the Almighty from on high?   20:29

3 *Is* not destruction to the wicked? and a strange *punishment* to the workers of iniquity?

4 ^RDoth not he see my ways, and count all my steps? Prov. 5:21; [Jer. 32:19]

5 If I have ^Rwalked with vanity, or if my foot hath hasted to deceit; Mic. 2:11

6 Let me be weighed in an even balance, that God may know mine integrity.

7 If my step hath turned out of the way, and ^Rmine heart walked after mine eyes, and if any blot hath cleaved to mine hands; 23:11

8 *Then* let me sow, and let another eat; yea, let my offspring be rooted out.

9 If mine heart have been ^Tdeceived by a woman, or *if* I have laid wait at my neighbour's door; enticed

10 *Then* let my wife ^Tgrind unto another, and let others bow down upon her. serve

11 For this *is* an heinous crime; yea, it *is* an iniquity *to be punished by* the judges.

12 For it *is* a ^Rfire *that* consumeth to destruction, and would root out all mine increase. 15:30

Innocent of Abusing His Power

13 If I ^Rdid despise the cause of my manservant or of my maidservant, when they contended with me; [Deut. 24:14, 15]

14 What then shall I do when God riseth up? and when he visiteth, what shall I answer him?

15 ^RDid not he that made me in the womb make him? and ^Tdid not one fashion us in the womb? 10:3 • *did not same one*

16 ^RIf I have withheld the poor from *their* desire, or have caused the eyes of the widow to fail; [Ex. 22:22–24]

17 Or have ^Reaten my morsel myself alone, and the fatherless hath not eaten thereof; 22:7

18 (For from my youth he was brought up with me, as *with* a father, and I have guided her from my mother's womb;)

19 If I have seen any perish for want of clothing, or any poor without covering;

20 If his loins have not ^Rblessed me, and *if* he were *not* warmed with the fleece of my sheep; Deut. 24:13

21 If I have lifted up my hand against the fatherless, when I saw my help in the gate:

22 *Then* let mine arm fall from my shoulder blade, ^Rand mine arm be broken from the bone. 38:15

23 For ^Rdestruction *from* God *was* a terror to me, and by reason of his ^Thighness I could not endure. Is. 13:6 • *majesty*

Innocent of Trusting in His Wealth

24 ^RIf I have made gold my hope, or have said to the fine gold, *Thou art* my confidence; [Mark 10:24]

25 ^RIf I rejoiced because my wealth *was* great, and because mine hand had gotten much; Ps. 62:10

26 If I beheld the sun when it shined, or the moon walking *in* brightness;

27 And my heart hath been secretly enticed, or my mouth hath kissed my hand:

28 This also *were* an iniquity *to be punished by* the judge: for I should have ^Rdenied the God *that is* above. Josh. 24:27; Is. 59:13

Innocent of Not Caring for His Enemies

29 ^RIf I rejoiced at the destruction of him that hated me, or lifted up myself when evil found him; [Prov. 17:5; 24:17]; Obad. 12

30 Neither have I suffered my mouth to sin by wishing a curse to his soul.

31 If the men of my tabernacle said not, Oh that we had of his flesh! we ^Rcannot be satisfied. 22:7

32 The stranger did not lodge in the street: *but* I opened my doors to the traveller.

33 If I covered my transgressions ^Ras Adam, by hiding mine iniquity in my bosom: Gen. 3:10; [Prov. 28:13]

34 Did I fear a great multitude, or did the contempt of families terrify me, that I kept silence, *and* went not out of the door?

Job Pleads to Meet God and Defend Himself

35 Oh that one would hear me! behold, my desire *is*, ^Rthat the Almighty would answer me, and *that* mine adversary had written a book. 19:7; 30:20

36 Surely I would take it upon my shoulder, *and* bind it *as* a crown to me.

37 ^RI would declare unto him the number of my steps; as a prince would I go near unto him. [v. 4]

38 If my land cry against me, or that the furrows likewise thereof complain;

39 If ^RI have eaten the fruits thereof without money, or have caused the owners thereof to lose their life: [James 5:4]

40 Let thistles grow instead of wheat, and ^Tcockle instead of barley. The words of Job are ended. weeds

CHAPTER 32

Elihu Intervenes in the Debate

SO these three men ceased to answer Job, because he *was* righteous in his own eyes.

2 Then was kindled the wrath of E-li'-hu the son of Bar'-a-chel the Buz'-ite, of the kindred of Ram: against Job was his wrath kindled, because he justified himself rather than God.

3 Also against his three friends was his wrath kindled, because they had found no answer, and *yet* had condemned Job.

4 Now E-li'-hu had waited till Job had spoken, because they *were* elder than he.

5 When E-li'-hu saw that *there was* no answer in the mouth of *these* three men, then his wrath was kindled.

6 And E-li'-hu the son of Bar'-a-chel the Buz'-ite answered and said, I *am* young, and ye *are* very old; wherefore I was afraid, and durst not shew you mine opinion.

7 I said, Days should speak, and multitude of years should teach wisdom.

8 But *there is* a spirit in man: and ᴿthe inspiration of the Almighty ᴿgiveth them understanding.   Prov. 2:6 · 38:36

9 Great men are not *always* wise: neither do the aged understand judgment.

10 Therefore I said, Hearken to me; I also will shew mine opinion.

11 Behold, I waited for your words; I gave ear to your reasons, whilst ye ᵀsearched out what to say.   considered

12 Yea, I attended unto you, and, behold, *there was* none of you that convinced Job, *or* that answered his ᵀwords: argument

13 Lest ye should say, We have found out wisdom: God thrusteth him down, not man.

14 Now he hath not directed *his* words against me: neither will I answer him with your speeches.

15 They were amazed, they answered no more: they left off speaking.

16 When I had waited, (for they spake not, but stood still, *and* answered no more;)

17 *I said*, I will answer also my part, I also will shew mine opinion.

18 For I am full of matter, the spirit within me constraineth me.

19 Behold, my belly *is* as wine *which* hath no vent; it is ready to burst like new bottles.

20 I will speak, that I may be refreshed: I will open my lips and answer.

21 Let me not, I pray you, ᵀaccept any man's person, neither let me give flattering titles unto man.   be impressed

22 For I know not to give flattering titles; *in so doing* my maker would soon take me away.

CHAPTER 33

Elihu Challenges Job to Debate

WHEREFORE, Job, I pray thee, hear my speeches, and hearken to all my words.

2 Behold, now I have opened my mouth, my tongue hath spoken in my mouth.

3 My words *shall be of* the uprightness of my heart: ᴿand my lips shall utter knowledge clearly.   6:28; 27:4

4 The spirit of God hath made me, and the breath of the Almighty hath given me life.

5 If thou canst answer me, set *thy words* in order before me, stand up.

6 Behold, I *am* according to thy wish in God's stead: I also am formed out of the clay.

7 Behold, my ᵀterror shall not make thee afraid, neither shall my hand be heavy upon thee.   fear

Elihu Quotes Job's Complaints

8 Surely thou hast spoken ᵀin mine hearing, and I have heard the voice of *thy* words, *saying*,   in my ears

9 I am clean without transgression, I *am* innocent; neither *is there* iniquity in me.

10 Behold, he findeth occasions against me, ᴿhe counteth me for his enemy,   16:9

11 ᴿHe putteth my feet in the stocks, he marketh all my paths.   13:27

Elihu Answers Job's Complaints

12 Behold, *in* this thou art not just: I will answer thee, that God is greater than man.

13 Why dost thou strive against him? for he giveth not account of any of his matters.

14 ᴿFor God speaketh once, yea twice, *yet* man perceiveth it not.   Ps. 62:11

15 ᴿIn a dream, in a vision of the night, when deep sleep falleth upon men, in slumberings upon the bed;   [Num. 12:6]

16 ᴿThen he openeth the ears of men, and sealeth their instruction,   [36:10, 15]

17 That he may withdraw man *from his* ᵀpurpose, and hide pride from man.   work

18 He keepeth back his soul from the pit, and his life from perishing by the sword.

19 He is chastened also with pain upon his bed, and the multitude of his ᴿbones with strong *pain:*   30:17

20 ᴿSo that his life abhorreth bread, and his soul dainty meat.   Ps. 107:18

21 His flesh is consumed away, that it cannot be seen; and his ᴿbones *that* were not seen stick out.   Ps. 22:17

22 Yea, his soul draweth near unto the grave, and his life to the destroyers.

23 If there be a ᴿmessenger with him, an interpreter, one among a thousand, to shew unto man his uprightness;   Gen. 40:8

24 Then he is gracious unto him, and saith, Deliver him from going down to the pit: I have found ᵀa ransom.   atonement

25 His flesh shall be fresher than a child's: he shall return to the days of his youth:

26 He shall ᴿpray unto God, and he will be favourable unto him: and he shall see his face with joy: for he will render unto man his righteousness.   22:27; 34:28

27 He looketh upon men, and *if any* say, I have sinned, and perverted *that which was* right, and it profited me not;

28 He will deliver his soul from going into the pit, and his life shall see the light.

29 Lo, all ᴿthese *things* worketh God oftentimes with man,   [Eph. 1:11; Phil. 2:13]

30 To bring back his soul from the pit, to be enlightened with the light of the living.

31 Mark well, O Job, hearken unto me: hold thy peace, and I will speak.

32 If thou hast any thing to say, answer me: speak, for I desire to justify thee.

33 If not, hearken unto me: hold thy peace, and I shall teach thee wisdom.

CHAPTER 34

Elihu Challenges Job to Debate Again

FURTHERMORE E-li'-hu answered and said,

2 Hear my words, O ye wise *men;* and give ear unto me, ye that have knowledge.

3 ᴿFor the ear ᵀtrieth words, as the mouth tasteth meat.   6:30; 12:11 • *tests*

4 Let us choose to us judgment: let us know among ourselves what *is* good.

Elihu Quotes Job's Complaints

5 For Job hath said, I am righteous: and God hath taken away my judgment.

6 Should I lie against my right? my wound *is* incurable without transgression.

7 What man *is* like Job, ᴿ*who* drinketh up ᵀscorning like water?   15:16 • *sarcasm*

8 Which goeth in ᴿcompany with the workers of iniquity, and walketh with wicked men.   22:15

9 For he hath said, ᴿIt profiteth a man nothing that he should delight himself with God.   35:3; Ps. 50:18

Elihu Answers Job's Complaints

10 Therefore hearken unto me, ye men of understanding: far be it from God, *that he should do* wickedness; and *from* the Almighty, *that he should commit* iniquity.

11 ᴿFor the work of a man shall he render unto him, and cause every man to find according to *his* ways.   Ps. 62:12; [Matt. 16:27]

12 Yea, surely God will not do wickedly, neither will the Almighty ᴿpervertᵀ judgment.   8:3 • *distort justice*

13 ᴿWho hath given him a charge over the earth? or who hath disposed the whole world?   [38:4]

14 If he set his heart upon man, *if he* gather unto himself his spirit and his breath;

15 ᴿAll flesh shall perish together, and man shall turn again unto dust.   [Gen. 3:19]

16 If now *thou hast* understanding, hear this: hearken to the voice of my words.

17 ᴿShall even he that hateth right govern? and wilt thou condemn him that is most just?   2 Sam. 23:3

18 *Is it fit* to say to a king, *Thou art* wicked? *and* to princes, *Ye are* ungodly?

19 *How much less to him* that ᴿaccepteth not the persons of princes, nor regardeth the rich more than the poor? for they all *are* the work of his hands.   Acts 10:34

20 In a moment shall they die, and the people shall be troubled ᴿat midnight, and pass away: and the mighty shall be taken away without hand.   Ex. 12:29

21 ᴿFor his eyes *are* upon the ways of man, and he seeth all his goings.   31:4

22 ᴿ*There is* no darkness, nor shadow of death, where the workers of iniquity may hide themselves.   [Ps. 139:12; Amos 9:2, 3]

23 For he will not lay upon man more *than right;* that he should ᵀenter into judgment with God.   *start an argument*

24 ᴿHe shall break in pieces mighty men ᵀwithout number, and set others in their stead.   12:19 • *without searching out*

25 Therefore he knoweth their works, and he overturneth *them* in the night, so that they are destroyed.

26 ᴿHe striketh them as wicked men in the open sight of others;   Ps. 9:5; 11:5

27 Because they turned back from him, and would not consider any of his ways:

28 So that they cause the cry of the poor to come unto him, and he ᴿheareth the cry of the ᵀafflicted.   Ex. 22:23 • *troubled*

29 When he giveth quietness, who then can make trouble? and when he hideth *his* face, who then can behold him? whether *it be done* against a nation, or against a man only:

30 That the hypocrite reign not, lest ᴿthe people be ensnared.   1 Kin. 12:28, 30

31 Surely it is meet to be said unto God, I have ᴿborne *chastisement,* I will not offend *any more:*   33:27

32 *That which* I see not teach thou me: if I have done iniquity, I will do no more.

33 *Should it be* according to thy mind? he will recompense it, whether thou refuse, or whether thou choose; and not I: therefore speak what thou knowest.

34 Let men of understanding tell me, and let a wise man hearken unto me.

35 Job hath spoken without knowledge, and his words *were* without wisdom.

36 My desire *is that* Job may be tried unto the end ᴿbecause of *his* answers ᵀfor wicked men.   22:15 • *like*

37 For he addeth rebellion unto his sin, he ᴿclappeth *his* hands among us, and multiplieth his words against God.   27:23

CHAPTER 35

Elihu's Third Rebuttal

E-LI'-HU spake moreover, and said,
2 Thinkest thou this to be ᵀright, *that* thou saidst, My righteousness *is* more than God's?   *justice*

3 For thou saidst, What advantage will it be unto thee? *and,* What profit shall I have, *if I be cleansed* from my sin?

4 I will answer thee, and ᴿthy companions with thee.   34:8

5 ᴿLook unto the heavens, and see; and behold the clouds *which* are higher than thou.   22:12; Gen. 15:5; Ps. 8:3

6 If thou sinnest, what doest thou against him? or *if* thy transgressions be multiplied, what doest thou unto him?

7 If thou be righteous, what givest thou him? or what receiveth he of thine hand?

8 Thy wickedness *may hurt* a man as thou *art;* and thy righteousness *may profit* the son of man.

9 By reason of the multitude of oppressions they make *the oppressed* to cry: they cry out by reason of the arm of the mighty.

10 But none saith, Where *is* God my maker, who giveth songs in the night;

11 Who ᴿteacheth us more than the beasts of the earth, and maketh us wiser than the fowls of heaven?   Ps. 94:12

12 There they cry, but none giveth answer, because of the pride of evil men.

13 ᴿSurely God will not hear vanity, neither will the Almighty regard it.   Is. 1:15

14 ᴿAlthough thou sayest thou shalt not see him, *yet* judgment *is* before him; therefore ᴿtrust thou in him.   9:11 · Ps. 37:5

15 But now, because *it is* not *so,* he hath visited in his anger; yet he knoweth *it* not in great extremity:

16 ᴿTherefore doth Job open his mouth in vain; he multiplieth words without knowledge.   34:35

CHAPTER 36

Elihu Believes That God Is Disciplining Job

E-LI′-HU also proceeded, and said,
2 Suffer me a little, and I will shew thee ᵀthat *I have* yet to speak on God's behalf.   *that there is more to be said*

3 I will fetch my knowledge from afar, and will ascribe righteousness to my Maker.

4 For truly ᴿmy words *shall* not *be* false: he that is ᴿperfect in knowledge *is* with thee.   33:3 · 37:16

5 Behold, God *is* mighty, ᴿand despiseth not *any:* ᴿhe *is* mighty in strength *and* wisdom.   [Ps. 22:24; 69:33] · 12:13

6 He preserveth not the life of the wicked: but giveth right to the poor.

7 ᴿHe withdraweth not his eyes from the righteous: but with kings *are they* on the throne; yea, he doth establish them for ever, and they are exalted.   [Ps. 33:18]

8 And if *they be* bound in fetters, *and* be holden in ᵀcords of affliction;   *bonds*

9 Then he sheweth them their work, and their transgressions that they have ᴿexceeded.   15:25

10 ᴿHe openeth also their ear to discipline, ᴿand commandeth that they return from iniquity.   33:16 · [2 Kin. 17:13]

11 If they obey and serve *him,* they shall ᴿspend their days in prosperity, and their years in pleasures.   21:13; [Is. 1:19, 20]

12 But if they obey not, they shall perish by ᴿthe sword, and they shall die without knowledge.   15:22

13 But the hypocrites in heart heap up wrath: they cry not when he bindeth them.

14 They die in youth, and their life *is* among the ᴿunclean.   Deut. 23:17

15 He delivereth the poor in his affliction, and openeth their ears in oppression.

16 Even so would he have removed thee out of the strait *into* a broad place, where *there is* no straitness; and that which should be set on thy table *should be* full of fatness.

17 But thou hast fulfilled the ᴿjudgment of the wicked: judgment and justice take hold *on thee.*   22:5, 10, 11

18 Because *there is* wrath, *beware* lest he take thee away with *his* stroke: then a great ransom cannot deliver thee.

19 ᴿWill he esteem thy riches? *no,* not gold, nor all the forces of strength.   [Prov. 11:4]

20 Desire not the ᴿnight, when people are cut off in their place.   34:20, 25

21 Take heed, regard not iniquity: for this hast thou chosen rather than affliction.

Elihu Reminds Job of the Greatness of God

22 Behold, God exalteth by his power: who ᴿteacheth like him?   35:11

23 Who hath enjoined him his way? or who can say, Thou hast wrought iniquity?

24 Remember that thou ᴿmagnify his work, which men behold.   Ps. 92:5; Rev. 15:3

25 Every man may see it; man may behold *it* afar off.

26 Behold, God *is* great, and we ᵀknow *him* not, ᴿneither can the number of his years be searched out.   *comprehend* · [Ps. 90:2]

27 For he ᴿmaketh small the drops of water: they pour down rain according to the vapour thereof;   Ps. 147:8

28 ᴿWhich the clouds do drop *and* distil upon man abundantly.   Prov. 3:20

29 Also can *any* understand the spreadings of the clouds, *or* the noise of his tabernacle?

30 Behold, he spreadeth his light upon it, and covereth the bottom of the sea.

31 For by them judgeth he the people; he ᴿgiveth meat in abundance.   [Acts 14:17]

32 ᴿWith clouds he covereth the light; and commandeth it *not to shine* by *the cloud* that cometh betwixt.   Ps. 147:8

33 ᴿThe noise thereof sheweth concerning it, the cattle also concerning the vapour. 37:2

CHAPTER 37

A^T this also my heart trembleth, and is moved out of his place.

2 Hear attentively the noise of his voice, and the sound *that* goeth out of his mouth.

3 He directeth it under the whole heaven, and his lightning unto the ends of the earth.

4 After it a voice roareth: he thundereth with the voice of his excellency; and he will not stay them when his voice is heard.

5 God thundereth marvellously with his voice; ^Rgreat things doeth he, which we cannot comprehend.　　　　　5:9

6 For ^Rhe saith to the snow, Be thou *on* the earth; likewise to the small rain, and to the great rain of his strength.　　Ps. 147:16

7 He ^Tsealeth up the hand of every man; that all men may know his work.　*controls*

8 Then the beasts ^Rgo into dens, and remain in their places.　　Ps. 104:22

9 Out of the ^Rsouth cometh the whirlwind: and cold out of the north.　　9:9

10 By the breath of God frost is given: and the breadth of the waters is ^Tstraitened. *frozen*

11 Also by watering he wearieth the thick cloud: ^Rhe scattereth his bright cloud:　36:29

12 And it is turned round about by his counsels: that they may ^Rdo whatsoever he commandeth them upon the ^Rface of the world in the earth.　　Ps. 148:8 • Is. 14:21

13 He causeth it to come, whether for correction, or for his land, or for mercy.

14 Hearken unto this, O Job: stand still, and consider the wondrous works of God.

15 Dost thou know when God disposed them, and caused the light of his cloud to shine?

16 ^RDost thou know the balancings of the clouds, the wondrous works of him which is perfect in knowledge?　　　　36:29

17 How thy garments *are* warm, when he quieteth the earth by the south *wind*?

18 Hast thou with him ^Rspread out the sky, *which is* strong, *and* as a molten looking glass?　　　　　Gen. 1:6; [Is. 44:24]

19 Teach us what we shall say unto him; *for* we cannot order *our speech* by reason of ^Tdarkness.　　*lack of understanding*

20 Shall it be told him that I speak? If a man speak, surely he shall be swallowed up.

21 And now *men* see not the bright light which *is* in the clouds: but the wind passeth, and cleanseth them.

22 Fair weather cometh out of the north: with God *is* ^Tterrible majesty.　　*wonderful*

23 *Touching* the Almighty, we cannot find him out: ^Rhe *is* excellent in power, and in judgment, and in plenty of justice: he will not afflict.　　　　　　[9:4]

24 Men do therefore fear him: he respecteth not any *that are* wise of heart.

CHAPTER 38

God Questions Job from the Realm of Creation

T^{HEN} the L<small>ORD</small> answered Job ^Rout of the whirlwind, and said,　　Ex. 19:16

2 ^RWho *is* this that darkeneth counsel by words without knowledge?　　34:35

3 Gird up now thy loins like a man; for I will demand of thee, and answer thou me.

4 ^RWhere wast thou when I laid the foundations of the earth? declare, if thou hast understanding.　　　　　Ps. 104:5

5 ^RWho hath laid the measures thereof, if thou knowest? or who hath stretched the line upon it?　　　　Prov. 8:29; Is. 40:12

6 Whereupon are the foundations thereof fastened? or who laid the corner stone thereof;

7 When the morning stars sang together, and all ^Rthe sons of God shouted for joy?　1:6

8 ^ROr *who* shut up the sea with doors, when it brake forth, *as if* it had issued out of the womb?　　　　Gen. 1:9; Ps. 33:7

9 When I made the cloud the garment thereof, and thick darkness a swaddlingband for it,

10 And ^Rbrake up for it my decreed *place*, and set bars and doors,　　26:10

11 And said, Hitherto shalt thou come, but no further: and here shall thy proud waves ^Rbe stayed?　　　　Ps. 89:9; 93:4

12 Hast thou ^Rcommanded the morning since thy days; *and* caused the ^Tdayspring to know his place;　　[Ps. 148:5] • *dawn*

13 That it might take hold of the ends of the earth, that ^Rthe wicked might be shaken out of it?　　　　34:25

14 It is turned as clay *to* the seal; and they stand as a garment.

15 And from the wicked their ^Rlight is withholden, and ^Rthe high arm shall be broken.　　18:5 • [Num. 15:30]; Ps. 10:15

16 Hast thou ^Rentered into the springs of the sea? or hast thou walked in the search of the depth?　　[Ps. 77:19]; Prov. 8:24

17 Have ^Rthe gates of death been opened unto thee? or hast thou seen the doors of the shadow of death?　　　Ps. 9:13

18 Hast thou perceived the breadth of the earth? declare if thou knowest it all.

19 Where *is* the way *where* light dwelleth? and *as for* darkness, where *is* the place thereof,

20 That thou shouldest take it to the bound thereof, and that thou shouldest know the paths *to* the house thereof?

21 Knowest thou *it*, ^Rbecause thou wast then born? or *because* the number of thy days *is* great?　　　　15:7

22 Hast thou entered into ^Rthe treasures of the snow? or hast thou seen the treasures of the ^Rhail,　　[Ps. 147:16] • Ex. 9:18

23 ᴿWhich I have reserved against the time of trouble, against the day of battle and war?   Josh. 10:11; Is. 30:30

24 By what way is the ᴿlight parted, *which* scattereth the east wind upon the earth? 26:10

25 Who hath divided a watercourse for the overflowing of waters, or a way for the lightning of thunder;

26 To cause it to rain on the earth, *where* no man *is; on* the wilderness, wherein *there is* no man;

27 ᴿTo satisfy the desolate and waste *ground;* and to cause the bud of the tender herb to spring forth?   Ps. 107:35

28 ᴿHath the rain a father? or who hath begotten the drops of dew?   [Ps. 147:8; Jer. 14:22]

29 Out of whose womb came the ice? and the ᴿhoary frost of heaven, who hath ᵀgendered it?   Ps. 147:16 · been the father

30 The waters are hid as *with* a stone, and the face of the deep is ᴿfrozen.   [37:10]

31 Canst thou bind the sweet influences of Ple′-ia-des, or loose the bands of O-ri′-on?

32 Canst thou bring forth ᵀMaz′-za-roth in his season? or canst thou guide Arc-tu′-rus with his sons?   *twelve signs*

33 Knowest thou ᴿthe ᵀordinances of heaven? canst thou set the dominion thereof in the earth?   Jer. 31:35 · laws

34 Canst thou lift up thy voice to the clouds, that ᴿabundance of waters may cover thee?   22:11; 36:27, 28

35 Canst thou send lightnings, that they may go, and say unto thee, Here we *are?*

36 ᴿWho hath put wisdom in the inward parts? or who hath given understanding to the heart?   [32:8; Ps. 51:6; Eccl. 2:26]

37 Who can number the clouds in wisdom? or who can stay the bottles of heaven,

38 When the dust groweth into hardness, and the clods cleave fast together?

God Questions Job from the Realm of Animals

39 Wilt thou hunt the prey for the lion? or fill the appetite of the young lions,

40 When they ᵀcouch in *their* dens, *and* abide in the covert to lie in wait?   *crouch*

41 ᴿWho provideth for the raven his food? when his young ones cry unto God, they wander for lack of meat.   [Matt. 6:26]

CHAPTER 39

K NOWEST thou the time when the wild goats of the rock bring forth? *or* canst thou mark when ᴿthe hinds do calve? Ps. 29:9

2 Canst thou number the months *that* they fulfil? or knowest thou the time when they bring forth?

3 They bow themselves, they bring forth their young ones, they cast out their sorrows.

4 Their young ones are in good liking, they grow up with ᵀcorn; they go forth, and return not unto them.   *in the open field*

5 Who hath sent out the wild ass free? or who hath loosed the bands of the wild ass?

6 Whose house I have made the wilderness, and the barren land his dwellings.

7 He scorneth the multitude of the city, neither regardeth he the crying of the driver.

8 The range of the mountains *is* his pasture, and he searcheth after ᴿevery green thing.   Gen. 1:29

9 Will the ᴿunicorn be willing to serve thee, or abide by thy crib?   Deut. 33:17

10 Canst thou bind the ᵀunicorn with his band in the furrow? or will he harrow the valleys after thee?   *wild ox*

11 Wilt thou trust him, because his strength *is* great? or wilt thou leave thy labour to him?

12 Wilt thou believe him, that he will bring home thy seed, and gather *it into* thy barn?

13 *Gavest thou* the goodly wings unto the peacocks? or wings and feathers unto the ostrich?

14 Which leaveth her eggs in the earth, and warmeth them in dust,

15 And forgetteth that the foot may crush them, or that the wild beast may break them.

16 She is ᴿhardened against her young ones, as though *they were* not her's: her labour is in vain without fear;   Lam. 4:3

17 Because God hath deprived her of wisdom, neither hath he ᴿimparted to her understanding.   35:11

18 What time she lifteth up herself on high, she scorneth the horse and his rider.

19 Hast thou given the horse strength? hast thou clothed his neck with thunder?

20 Canst thou make him afraid as a grasshopper? the glory of his nostrils *is* terrible.

21 He paweth in the valley, and rejoiceth in *his* strength: ᴿhe goeth on to meet the armed men.   Jer. 8:6

22 He mocketh at fear, and is not ᵀaffrighted; neither turneth he back from the sword.   *dismayed*

23 The quiver rattleth against him, the glittering spear and the shield.

24 He swalloweth the ground with fierceness and rage: neither believeth he that *it is* the sound of the trumpet.

25 He saith among the trumpets, Ha, ha; and he smelleth the battle afar off, the thunder of the captains, and the shouting.

26 Doth the hawk fly by thy wisdom, *and* stretch her wings toward the south?

27 Doth the eagle mount up at thy command, and make her nest on high?

28 She dwelleth and abideth on the rock,

upon the crag of the rock, and the strong place.

29 From thence she ^Rseeketh^T the prey, *and* her eyes behold afar off.   9:26 • *spies*

30 Her young ones also suck up blood: and where the slain *are*, there *is* she.

CHAPTER 40

God Demands an Answer to His Questions

MOREOVER the LORD answered Job, and said,

2 Shall he that ^Rcontendeth with the Almighty instruct *him*? he that reproveth God, let him answer it.   9:3

Job's First Answer to God

3 Then Job answered the LORD, and said,

4 Behold, I am vile; what shall I answer thee? I will lay mine hand upon my mouth.

5 Once have I spoken; but ^RI will not answer: yea, twice; but I will proceed no further.   9:3, 15

God Tells Job to Save Himself

6 ^RThen answered the LORD unto Job out of the whirlwind, and said,   38:1

7 ^RGird up thy loins now like a man: ^RI will demand of thee, and declare thou unto me.   38:3 • 42:4

8 ^RWilt thou also disannul my judgment? wilt thou condemn me, that thou mayest be righteous?   [Ps. 51:4; Rom. 3:4]

9 Hast thou an arm like God? or canst thou thunder with a voice like him?

10 Deck thyself now *with* majesty and excellency; and array thyself with glory and beauty.

11 Cast abroad the ^Rrage of thy wrath: and behold every one *that is* proud, and abase him.   Is. 42:25; [Nah. 1:6, 8]

12 ^RLook on every one *that is* proud, *and* bring him low; and tread down the wicked in their place.   1 Sam. 2:7; [Is. 13:11]

13 ^RHide them in the dust together; *and* bind their faces in secret.   [Is. 2:10–12]

14 Then will I also confess unto thee that thine own right hand can save thee.

God Compares the Power of Job with That of the Behemoth

15 Behold now behemoth, which I made with thee; he eateth grass as an ox.

16 Lo now, his strength *is* in his loins, and his force *is* in the navel of his belly.

17 He moveth his tail like a cedar: the sinews of his stones are wrapped together.

18 His bones *are as* strong pieces of brass; his bones *are* like bars of iron.

19 He *is* the ^Rchief of the ways of God: he that made him can make his sword to approach *unto* him.   41:33

20 Surely the mountains bring him forth food, where all the beasts of the field play.

21 He lieth under the shady trees, in the covert of the reed, and fens.

22 The shady trees cover him *with* their shadow; the willows of the brook compass him about.

23 Behold, he drinketh up a river, *and* hasteth not: he ^Ttrusteth that he can draw up Jordan into his mouth.   *is confident*

24 He taketh it with his eyes: *his* nose pierceth through ^Tsnares.   *barbs*

CHAPTER 41

God Compares the Power of Job with That of the Leviathan

CANST thou draw out ^Rleviathan with an hook? or his tongue with a cord *which* thou lettest down?   Is. 27:1

2 Canst thou put an hook into his nose? or bore his jaw through with a thorn?

3 Will he make many supplications unto thee? will he speak soft *words* unto thee?

4 Will he make a covenant with thee? wilt thou take him for a servant for ever?

5 Wilt thou play with him as *with* a bird? or wilt thou bind him for thy maidens?

6 Shall the companions make a banquet of him? shall they part him among the merchants?

7 Canst thou fill his skin with barbed irons? or his head with fish spears?

8 Lay thine hand upon him, remember the battle, do no more.

9 Behold, the hope of him is ^Tin vain: shall not *one* be cast down even at the sight of him?   *is false*

10 None *is* so fierce that dare stir him up: who then is able to stand before me?

11 ^RWho hath ^Tprevented me, that I should repay *him*? *whatsoever is* under the whole heaven is mine.   [Rom. 11:35] • *hindered*

12 I will not conceal his parts, nor his power, nor his comely proportion.

13 Who can ^Tdiscover the face of his garment? *or* who can come *to him* with his double bridle?   *uncover*

14 Who can open the doors of his face? his teeth *are* terrible round about.

15 *His* scales *are his* pride, shut up together *as with* a close seal.

16 One is so near to another, that no air can come between them.

17 They are joined one to another, they stick together, that they cannot be ^Tsundered.   *separated*

18 By his neesings a light doth shine, and his eyes *are* like the eyelids of the morning.

19 Out of his mouth go burning lamps, *and* sparks of fire leap out.

20 Out of his nostrils goeth smoke, as *out of a* ᵀseething pot or caldron.   *boiling*
21 His breath kindleth coals, and a flame goeth out of his mouth.
22 In his neck remaineth strength, and sorrow is turned into joy before him.
23 The ᵀflakes of his flesh are joined together: they are firm in themselves; they cannot be moved.   *folds*
24 His heart is as firm as a stone; yea, as hard as a piece of the nether *millstone.*
25 When he raiseth up himself, the mighty are afraid: by reason of breakingsᵀ they purify themselves.   *consternation*
26 The sword of him that layeth at him cannot hold: the spear, the dart, nor the ᵀhabergeon.   *javelin*
27 He esteemeth iron as straw, *and* brass as rotten wood.
28 The arrow cannot make him flee: slingstones are turned with him into stubble.
29 Darts are counted as stubble: he laugheth at the shaking of a spear.
30 Sharp stones *are* under him: he spreadeth sharp pointed things upon the mire.
31 He maketh the deep to boil like a pot: he maketh the sea like a pot of ointment.
32 He maketh a path to shine after him; *one* would think the deep *to be* hoary.
33 ᴿUpon earth there is not his like, who is made without fear.   40:19
34 He beholdeth all high *things:* he *is* a king over all the children of pride.

CHAPTER 42

Job Confesses Lack of Understanding

THEN Job answered the LORD, and said,
2 I know that thou ᴿcanst do every *thing,* and *that* no thought can be withholden from thee.   Gen. 18:14
3 Who *is* he that hideth counsel without knowledge? therefore have I uttered that I understood not; ᴿthings too wonderful for me, which I knew not.   [Ps. 40:5]

Job Repents of His Rebellion

4 Hear, I beseech thee, and I will speak: ᴿI will demand of thee, and declare thou unto me.   38:3; 40:7
5 I have heard of thee by the hearing of the ear: but now mine eye seeth thee.

6 Wherefore I ᴿabhorᵀ *myself,* and repent in dust and ashes.   40:4 · *despise*

The Deliverance of Job and His Friends

7 And it was *so,* that after the LORD had spoken these words unto Job, the LORD said to El′-i-phaz the Te′-man-ite, My wrath is kindled against thee, and against thy two friends: for ye have not spoken of me *the thing that is* right, as my servant Job *hath.*
8 Therefore take unto you now seven bullocks and seven rams, and go to my servant Job, and offer up for yourselves a burnt offering; and my servant Job shall pray for you: ᴿfor him will I accept: lest I deal with you *after your* folly, in that ye have not spoken of me *the thing which is* right, like my servant Job.   1 Sam. 25:35
9 So El′-i-phaz the Te′-man-ite and Bil′-dad the Shu′-hite *and* Zo′-phar the Na′-a-math-ite went, and did according as the LORD commanded them: the LORD also accepted Job.
10 And the LORD ᵀturned the captivity of Job, when he prayed for his friends: also the LORD gave Job ᴿtwice as much as he had before.   *reversed the fortunes* · Is. 40:2
11 Then came there unto him ᴿall his brethren, and all his sisters, and all they that had been of his acquaintance before, and did eat bread with him in his house: and they bemoaned him, and comforted him over all the evil that the LORD had brought upon him: every man also gave him a piece of money, and every one an earring of gold.   19:13
12 So the LORD blessed ᴿthe latter end of Job more than his beginning: for he had ᴿfourteen thousand sheep, and six thousand camels, and a thousand yoke of oxen, and a thousand she asses.   8:7 · 1:3
13 ᴿHe had also seven sons and three daughters.   1:2
14 And he called the name of the first, Je-mi′-ma; and the name of the second, Ke-zi′-a; and the name of the third, Ker′-en-hap′-puch.
15 And in all the land were no women found *so* fair as the daughters of Job: and their father gave them inheritance among their brethren.
16 After this ᴿlived Job an hundred and forty years, and saw his sons, and his sons′ sons, *even* four generations.   5:26; Prov. 3:16
17 So Job died, *being* old and full of days.

THE BOOK OF

PSALMS

📖 **THE BOOK OF PSALMS**

The Book of Psalms is the largest and perhaps most widely used book in the Bible. It explores the full range of human experience in a very personal and practical way. Its 150 "songs" run from the Creation through the patriarchal, theocratic, monarchical, exilic, and postexilic periods. The tremendous breadth of subject matter in the Psalms includes diverse topics, such as jubilation, war, peace, worship, judgment, messianic prophecy, praise, and lament. The Psalms were set to the accompaniment of stringed instruments and served as the temple hymnbook and devotional guide for the Jewish people.

The Book of Psalms was gradually collected and originally unnamed, perhaps due to the great variety of material. It came to be known as *Sepher Tehillim*—"Book of Praises"—because almost every psalm contains some note of praise to God. The Septuagint uses the Greek word *Psalmoi* as its title for this book, meaning poems sung to the accompaniment of musical instruments. It also calls it the *Psalterium* ("a collection of songs"), and this word is the basis for the term "Psalter." The Latin title is *Liber Psalmorum*, "Book of Psalms."

✍️ **THE AUTHOR OF PSALMS**

Although critics have challenged the historical accuracy of the superscriptions regarding authorship, the evidence is strongly in their favor. Almost half (seventy-three) of the psalms are designated as Davidic: 3—9; 11—32; 34—41; 51—65; 68—70; 86; 101; 103; 108—110; 122; 124; 131; 133; and 138—145. David's wide experience as shepherd, musician, warrior, and king (1011—971 B.C.) is reflected in these psalms. The New Testament reveals that the anonymous psalms 2 and 95 were also written by this king whose name means "Beloved of Yahweh" (Acts 4:25; Heb. 4:7). In addition to the seventy-five by David, twelve were by Asaph, "Collector," a priest who headed the service of music (50; 73—83; Ezra 2:41); ten were by the sons of Korah, "Bald," a guild of singers and composers (42; 44—49; 84; 85; 87; Num. 26:9—11); two were by Solomon, "Peaceful," Israel's most powerful king (72; 127); one was by Moses, "Son of the Water," a prince, herdsman, and deliverer (90); one was by Heman, "Faithful," a wise man (88; 1 Kin. 4:31; 1 Chr. 15:19); and one was by Ethan, "Enduring," a wise man (89; 1 Kin. 4:31; 1 Chr. 15:19). The remaining fifty psalms are anonymous: 1; 2; 10; 33; 43; 66; 67; 71; 91—100; 102; 104—107; 111—121; 123; 125; 126; 128—130;

132; 134—137; and 146—150. Some of the anonymous psalms are traditionally attributed to Ezra.

⌛ **THE TIME OF PSALMS**

The psalms cover a wide time span from Moses (c. 1410 B.C.) to the postexilic community under Ezra and Nehemiah (c. 430 B.C.). Because of their broad chronological and thematic range, the psalms were written to different audiences under many conditions. They therefore reflect a multitude of moods and as such are relevant to every reader.

The five books were compiled over several centuries. As individual psalms were written, some were used in Israel's worship. A number of small collections were independently made, like the pilgrimage songs and groups of Davidic psalms (1—41, 51—70, 138—145). These smaller anthologies were gradually collected into the five books. The last stage was the uniting and editing of the five books themselves. David (1 Chr. 15:16), Hezekiah (2 Chr. 29:30; Prov. 25:1), and Ezra (Neh. 8) were involved in various stages of collecting the psalms. David was the originator of the temple liturgy of which his psalms were a part. The superscriptions of thirteen psalms specify key events in his life: First Samuel 19:11 (Ps. 59); 21:11 (Ps. 56); 21:13 (Ps. 34); 22:1 (Ps. 142); 22:9 (Ps. 52); 23:19 (Ps. 54); 24:3 (Ps. 57); Second Samuel 8:13 (Ps. 60); 12:13 (Ps. 51); 15:16 (Ps. 3); 15:23 (Ps. 63); 16:5 (Ps. 7); 22:2—51 (Ps. 18).

Here are four things to remember when interpreting the psalms: (1) When the superscription gives the historical event, the psalm should be interpreted in that light. When it is not given, there is little hope in reconstructing the historical occasion. Assuming occasions will probably hurt more than help the interpretive process. (2) Some of the psalms are associated with definite aspects of Israel's worship (e.g., 5:7; 66:13; 68:24, 25), and this can help in understanding those psalms. (3) Many of the psalms use definite structure and motifs. (4) Many psalms anticipate Israel's Messiah and are fulfilled in Christ. However, care must be taken not to allegorize them and forget the grammatical-historical method of interpretation.

✝️ **THE CHRIST OF PSALMS**

Many of the psalms specifically anticipated the life and ministry of Jesus Christ, the One who came centuries later as the promised Messiah ("Anointed One").

There are five different kinds of messianic

psalms: (1) *Typical Messianic.* The subject of the psalm is in some respects a type, or figure, of Christ (see 34:20; 69:4, 9). (2) *Typical Prophetic.* The psalmist uses language to describe his present experience, which points beyond his own life and becomes historically true only in Christ (see 22). (3) *Indirectly Messianic.* At the time of composition the psalm refers to a king or the house of David in general, but awaits final fulfillment in Christ (see 2; 45; 72). (4) *Purely Prophetic.* Refers solely to Christ without reference to any other son of David (see 110). (5) *Enthronement.* Anticipates the coming of Yahweh and the consummation of His kingdom, which will be fulfilled in the person of Christ (see 96—99).

Some of the specific messianic prophecies in the Book of Psalms include:

Prophecy		Fulfillment
2:7	God will declare Him to be His Son.	Matthew 3:17
8:6	All things will be put under His feet.	Hebrews 2:8
16:10	He will be resurrected from the dead.	Mark 16:6, 7
22:1	God will forsake Him in His hour of need.	Matthew 27:46
22:7, 8	He will be scorned and mocked.	Luke 23:35
22:16	His hands and feet will be pierced.	John 20:25, 27
22:18	Others will gamble for His clothes.	Matthew 27:35, 36
34:20	Not one of His bones will be broken.	John 19:32, 33, 36
35:11	He will be accused by false witnesses.	Mark 14:57
35:19	He will be hated without a cause.	John 15:25
40:7, 8	He will come to do God's will.	Hebrews 10:7
41:9	He will be betrayed by a friend.	Luke 22:47
45:6	His throne will be forever.	Hebrews 1:8
68:18	He will ascend to God's right hand.	Mark 16:19
69:9	Zeal for God's house will consume Him.	John 2:17
69:21	He will be given vinegar and gall to drink.	Matthew 27:34
109:4	He will pray for His enemies.	Luke 23:34
109:8	His betrayer's office will be fulfilled by another.	Acts 1:20
110:1	His enemies will be made subject to Him.	Matthew 22:44
110:4	He will be a priest like Melchizedek.	Hebrews 5:6
118:22	He will be the chief cornerstone.	Matthew 21:42
118:26	He will come in the name of the Lord.	Matthew 21:9

KEYS TO PSALMS

Key Word: Worship—The central theme of the Book of Psalms is worship—God is worthy of all praise because of who He is, what He has done, and what He will do. His goodness extends through all time and eternity. The psalms present personal responses to God as they reflect on His program for His people. There is a keen desire to see His program fulfilled and His name extolled. Many of the psalms survey the Word of God and the attributes of God, especially during difficult times. This kind of faith produces confidence in His power in spite of circumstances.

The psalms were used in the two temples and some were part of the liturgical service. They also served as an individual and communal devotional guide.

Key Verses: Psalm 19:14; 145:21—"Let the words of my mouth, and the meditation of my heart, be acceptable in thy sight, O LORD, my strength, and my redeemer" (19:14).

"My mouth shall speak the praise of the LORD: and let all flesh bless his holy name for ever and ever" (145:21).

Key Chapter: Psalm 100—So many of the favorite chapters of the Bible are contained in the Book of Psalms that it is difficult to select the key chapter among such psalms as Psalms 1; 22; 23; 24; 37; 72; 100; 101; 119; 121; and 150. The two central themes of worship and praise are beautifully wed in Psalm 100.

SURVEY OF PSALMS

The Psalter is really five books in one, and each book ends with a doxology (see Chart). The last psalm is the closing doxology for Book 5 and for the Psalter as a whole. After the psalms were written, editorial superscriptions or instructions were added to 116 of them. These superscriptions are historically accurate and are even numbered as the first verses in the Hebrew text. They designate fifty-seven psalms as *mizmor,* "psalm"—a song accompanied by a stringed instrument. Another twenty-nine are called *shir,* "song" and thirteen are called *maskil,* "contemplative poem." Six are called *miktam,* perhaps meaning "epigram" or "inscription poem." Five are termed *tepillah,* "prayer" (see Hab. 3), and only one is called *tehillah,* "praise" (145). In addition to these technical terms, the psalms can be classified according to certain themes: Creation psalms (8 and 19), Exodus psalms (78), penitence psalms (6), pilgrimage psalms (120—134), and messianic psalms (see Christ in Psalms). There are even nine acrostic psalms in which the first verse or line begins with the first letter of the Hebrew alphabet, the next begins with the second, and so on (9; 10; 25; 34; 37; 111; 112; 119; 145).

First Chronicles 16:4 supports another approach to classification: "to invoke, to thank, and to praise the LORD, the God of Israel" (RSV). This leads to three basic types—lament, thanksgiving, and praise psalms. The following classification further divides the psalms into ten types: (1) *Individual Lament Psalms:* Directly addressed to God, these psalms petition Him to rescue and defend an individual. They have these elements: (a) an introduction (usually a cry to God), (b) the lament, (c) a confession of trust in God, (d) the petition, (e) a declaration or vow of praise. Most psalms are of this type (e.g., 3—7; 12; 13; 22; 25—28; 35; 38—40; 42; 43; 51; 54—57; 59; 61; 63; 64; 69—71; 86; 88; 102; 109; 120; 130; 140—143). (2) *Communal Lament Psalms:* The only difference is that the nation rather than an individual makes the lament (e.g., 44; 60; 74; 79; 80; 83; 85; 90; and 123). (3) *Individual Thanksgiving Psalms:* The psalmist publicly acknowledges God's activity on his behalf. These psalms thank God for something He has already done or express confidence in what He will yet do. They have these elements: (a) a proclamation to praise God, (b) a summary statement, (c) a report of deliverance, and (d) a renewed vow of praise (e.g., 18; 30; 32; 34; 40; 41; 66; 106; 116; and 138). (4) *Communal Thanksgiving Psalms:* In these psalms the acknowledgement is made by the nation rather than an individual (see 124 and 129). (5) *General Praise Psalms:* These psalms are more general than the thanksgiving psalms. The psalmist attempts to magnify the name of God and boast about His greatness (see 8; 19; 29; 103; 104; 139; 148; 150). The joyous exclamation "hallelujah" ("praise the LORD!") is found in several of these psalms. (6) *Descriptive Praise Psalms:* These psalms praise God for His attributes and acts (e.g., 33; 36; 105; 111; 113;

117; 135; 136; 146; 147). (7) *Enthronement Psalms:* These psalms describe Yahweh's sovereign reign over all (see 47; 93; 96—99). Some anticipate the kingdom rule of Christ. (8) *Pilgrimage Songs:* Also known as Songs of Zion, these psalms were sung by pilgrims traveling up to Jerusalem for the three annual religious feasts of Passover, Pentecost, and Tabernacles (see 43; 46; 48; 76; 84; 87; 120—134). (9) *Royal Psalms:* The reigns of the earthly King and the heavenly King are portrayed in most of these psalms (e.g., 2; 18; 20; 21; 45; 72; 89; 101; 110; 132; and 144). (10) *Wisdom and Didactic Psalms:* The reader is exhorted and instructed in the way of righteousness (see 1; 37; 119).

There is a problem with the so-called imprecatory ("to call down a curse") psalms. These psalms invoke divine judgment on one's enemies (see 7; 35; 40; 55; 58; 59; 69; 79; 109; 137; 139; and 144). Although some of them seem unreasonably harsh, a few things should be kept in mind: (1) they call for divine justice rather than human vengeance; (2) they ask for God to punish the wicked and thus vindicate His righteousness; (3) they condemn sin (in Hebrew thinking no sharp distinction exists between a sinner and his sin); and (4) even Jesus calls down a curse on several cities and tells His disciples to curse cities that do not receive the gospel (Matt. 10:14, 15).

A number of special musical terms (some obscure) are used in the superscriptions of the psalms. "To the chief Musician" appears in fifty-five psalms indicating that there is a collection of psalms used by the conductor of music in the temple, perhaps for special occasions. "Selah" is used seventy-one times in the psalms and three times in Habakkuk 3. This word may mark a pause, a musical interlude, or a crescendo.

BOOK	BOOK I (1-41)	BOOK II (42-72)	BOOK III (73-89)	BOOK IV (90-106)	BOOK V (107-150)
CHIEF AUTHOR	DAVID	DAVID AND KORAH	ASAPH	ANONYMOUS	DAVID AND ANONYMOUS
NUMBER OF PSALMS	41	31	17	17	44
BASIC CONTENT	SONGS OF WORSHIP	HYMNS OF NATIONAL INTEREST		ANTHEMS OF PRAISE	
TOPICAL LIKENESS TO PENTATEUCH	GENESIS: MAN AND CREATION	EXODUS: DELIVERANCE AND REDEMPTION	LEVITICUS: WORSHIP AND SANCTUARY	NUMBERS: WILDERNESS AND WANDERING	DEUTERONOMY: SCRIPTURE AND PRAISE
CLOSING DOXOLOGY	41:13	72:18, 19	89:52	106:48	150:1-6
POSSIBLE COMPILER	DAVID	HEZEKIAH OR JOSIAH		EZRA OR NEHEMIAH	
POSSIBLE DATES OF COMPILATION	c. 1020-970 B.C.	c. 970-610 B.C.		UNTIL c. 430 B.C.	
SPAN OF AUTHORSHIP	ABOUT 1,000 YEARS (c. 1410-430 B.C.)				

OUTLINE OF PSALMS

Book One: Psalms 1—41

1. Two Ways of Life Contrasted
2. Coronation of the Lord's Anointed
3. Victory in the Face of Defeat
4. Evening Prayer for Deliverance
5. Morning Prayer for Guidance
6. Prayer for God's Mercy
7. Wickedness Justly Rewarded
8. God's Glory and Man's Dominion
9. Praise for Victory over Enemies
10. Petition for God's Judgment
11. God Tests the Children of Men
12. The Pure Words of the Lord
13. The Prayer for God's Answer—Now
14. The Characteristics of the Godless
15. The Characteristics of the Godly
16. Eternal Life for One Who Trusts
17. "Hide Me Under the Shadow of Thy Wings"
18. Thanksgiving for Deliverance by God
19. The Works and Words of God
20. Trust Not in Chariots and Horses but in God
21. Triumph of the King
22. Psalm of the Cross
23. Psalm of the Divine Shepherd
24. Psalm of the King of Glory
25. Acrostic Prayer for Instruction
26. "Examine Me, O Lord, and Prove Me"
27. Trust in the Lord and Be Not Afraid
28. Rejoice Because of Answered Prayer
29. The Powerful Voice of God
30. Praise for Dramatic Deliverance
31. "Be of Good Courage"
32. The Blessedness of Forgiveness
33. God Considers All Man's Works
34. Seek the Lord
35. Petition for God's Intervention
36. The Excellent Lovingkindness of God
37. "Rest in the Lord"
38. The Heavy Burden of Sin
39. Know the Measure of Man's Days
40. Delight to Do God's Will
41. The Blessedness of Helping the Poor

Book Two: Psalms 42—72

42. Seek After the Lord
43. "Hope in God"
44. Prayer for Deliverance by God
45. The Psalm of the Great King
46. "God Is Our Refuge and Strength"
47. The Lord Shall Subdue All Nations
48. The Praise of Mount Zion
49. Riches Cannot Redeem
50. The Lord Shall Judge All People
51. Confession and Forgiveness of Sin
52. The Lord Shall Judge the Deceitful
53. A Portrait of the Godless
54. The Lord Is Our Helper
55. "Cast Thy Burden upon the Lord"
56. Fears in the Midst of Trials
57. Prayers in the Midst of Perils
58. Wicked Judges Will Be Judged
59. Petition for Deliverance from Violent Men

60. A Prayer for Deliverance of the Nation
61. A Prayer When Overwhelmed
62. Wait upon God
63. Thirst for God
64. A Prayer for God's Protection
65. God's Provision Through Nature
66. Remember What God Has Done
67. God Shall Govern the Earth
68. God Is the Father of the Fatherless
69. Petition for God to Draw Near
70. Prayer for the Poor and Needy
71. Prayer for the Aged
72. The Reign of the Messiah

Book Three: Psalms 73—89

73. The Perspective of Eternity
74. Request for God to Remember His Covenant
75. "God Is the Judge"
76. The Glorious Might of God
77. When Overwhelmed, Remember God's Greatness
78. God's Continued Guidance in Spite of Unbelief
79. Avenge the Defilement of Jerusalem
80. Israel's Plea for God's Mercy
81. God's Plea for Israel's Obedience
82. Rebuke of Israel's Urgent Judges
83. Plea for God to Destroy Israel's Enemies
84. The Joy of Dwelling with God
85. Prayer for Revival
86. "Teach Me Thy Way, O Lord"
87. Glorious Zion, City of God
88. Crying from Deepest Affliction
89. Claiming God's Promises in Affliction

Book Four: Psalms 90—106

90. "Teach Us to Number Our Days"
91. Abiding in "the Shadow of the Almighty"
92. It Is Good to Praise the Lord
93. The Majesty of God
94. Vengeance Belongs Only to God
95. Call to Worship the Lord
96. Declare the Glory of God
97. Rejoice! The Lord Reigns!
98. Sing a New Song to the Lord
99. "Exalt Ye the Lord Our God"
100. "Serve the Lord with Gladness"
101. Commitments of a Holy Life
102. Prayer of an Overwhelmed Saint
103. Bless the Lord, All Ye People!
104. Psalm Rehearsing Creation
105. Remember, God Keeps His Promises
106. "We Have Sinned"

Book Five: Psalms 107—150

107. God Satisfies the Longing Soul
108. Awake Early and Praise the Lord
109. Song of the Slandered
110. The Coming of the Priest-King-Judge
111. Praise for God's Tender Care
112. The Blessings of Those Who Fear God

BOOK I

PSALM 1

Two Ways of Life Contrasted

BLESSED ᴿis the man that walketh not in the counsel of the ungodly, nor standeth in the way of sinners, ᴿnor sitteth in the seat of the scornful.   Prov. 4:14 • Jer. 15:17

2 But ᴿhis delight is in the law of the Lord; ᴿand in his law doth he meditate day and night.   119:35 • [Josh. 1:8]

3 And he shall be like a tree ᴿplanted by the rivers of water, that bringeth forth his fruit in his season; his leaf also shall not ᵀwither; and whatsoever he doeth shall ᴿprosper.   [92:12-14] • fade • 128:2

4 The ungodly are not so: but are like the chaff which the wind driveth away.

5 Therefore the ungodly shall not ᵀstand in the judgment, nor sinners in the ᵀcongregation of the righteous.   rise • assembly

6 For ᴿthe Lord knoweth the way of the righteous: but the way of the ungodly shall perish.   [Nah. 1:7; John 10:14]

PSALM 2

Coronation of the Lord's Anointed

WHYᴿ do the heathen rage, and the people imagine a vain thing?   [Acts 4:25-28] ☆

2 The kings of the earth set themselves, and the rulers take counsel together, against the Lord, and against his anointed, saying,

3 Let us break their bands asunder, and cast away their cords from us.

4 He that sitteth in the heavens ᴿshall laugh: the Lord shall have them in ᴿderision.   37:13 • 59:8

5 Then shall he speak unto them in his wrath, and vex them in his sore displeasure.

6 Yet have I ᵀset my king upon my holy hill of Zi′-on.   founded

7 I will declare the decree: the Lord hath said unto me, ᴿThou art my Son; this day have I ᴿbegotten thee.   Matt. 3:17 • [Luke 1:35] ☆

8 Ask of me, and I shall give thee the heathen for thine ᴿinheritance, ᴿand the uttermost parts of the earth for thy possession.   22:27 • 65:2

9 ᴿThou shalt break them with a rod of iron; thou shalt dash them in pieces like a potter's vessel.   110:5, 6; [Rev. 2:27] ☆

10 Be wise now therefore, O ye kings: be instructed, ye judges of the earth.

11 ᴿServe the Lord with fear, ᴿand rejoice with trembling.   5:7 • 119:120

12 Kiss the Son, lest he be angry, and ye perish from the way, when his wrath is kindled but a little. ᴿBlessed are all they that put their trust in him.   34:8

PSALM 3

Victory in the Face of Defeat

A Psalm of David, when he fled from Ab′-sa-lom his son.

LORD, how are they ᴿincreased that trouble me! many are they that rise up against me.   69:4; 2 Sam. 15:12

2 Many there be which say of my soul, There is no help for him in God.   Selah.

3 But thou, O Lord, art a shield for me; my glory, and the lifter up of mine head.

4 I cried unto the Lord with my voice, and he heard me out of his holy hill.   Selah.

5 ᴿI laid me down and slept; I awaked; for the Lord sustained me.   Lev. 26:6

6 ᴿI will not be afraid of ten thousands of

people, that have ^Rset *themselves* against me round about.　　　　　27:3 • 118:10–13

7 ^RArise, O Lᴏʀᴅ; save me, O my God: ^Rfor thou hast smitten all mine enemies *upon* the cheek bone; thou hast broken the teeth of the ungodly.　　　　　7:6 • Job 16:10

8 Salvation *belongeth* unto the Lᴏʀᴅ: thy blessing *is* upon thy people.　Selah.

PSALM 4

Evening Prayer for Deliverance

To the chief Musician on Neg′-i-noth, A Psalm of David.

HEAR me when I call, O God of my righteousness: thou hast ^Tenlarged me *when I was* in distress; have mercy upon me, and hear my prayer.　　　　　*relieved*

2 O ye sons of men, how long *will ye turn* my glory into shame? *how long* will ye love vanity, *and* seek after leasing?　Selah.

3 But know that ^Rthe Lᴏʀᴅ hath set apart him that is godly for himself: the Lᴏʀᴅ will hear when I call unto him.　　　　　[135:4]

4 ^RStand in awe, and sin not: ^Rcommune with your own heart upon your bed, and be still.　Selah.　　　　　99:1 • 77:6

5 Offer ^Rthe sacrifices of righteousness, and put your trust in the Lᴏʀᴅ.　　　51:19

6 *There be* many that say, Who will shew us *any* good? Lᴏʀᴅ, lift thou up the light of thy countenance upon us.

7 Thou hast put ^Rgladness in my heart, more than in the time ^R*that* their corn and their wine increased.　　　97:11 • 119:14

8 ^RI will both lay me down in peace, and sleep: ^Rfor thou, Lᴏʀᴅ, only makest me dwell in safety.　　　Job 11:19 • Deut. 12:10

PSALM 5

Morning Prayer for Guidance

To the chief Musician upon Ne′-hi-loth, A Psalm of David.

GIVE ear to my words, O Lᴏʀᴅ, consider my ^Tmeditation.　　　　*thoughts*

2 Hearken unto the voice of my cry, my King, and my God: for unto thee will I pray.

3 My voice shalt thou hear in the morning, O Lᴏʀᴅ; in the morning will I direct *my prayer* unto thee, and will look up.

4 For thou *art* not a God that ^Rhath pleasure in wickedness: neither shall evil dwell with thee.　　　　　[11:5; 34:16]

5 The foolish shall not stand in thy sight: thou hatest all workers of iniquity.

6 ^RThou shalt destroy them that speak ^Tleasing: the Lᴏʀᴅ will abhor the bloody and deceitful man.　　　　52:4 • *falsehood*

7 But as for me, I will come *into* thy house

in the multitude of thy mercy: *and* in thy fear will I worship toward thy holy temple.

8 ^RLead me, O Lᴏʀᴅ, in thy righteousness because ^Rof mine enemies; make thy way straight before my face.　　　31:3 • 27:11

9 For *there is* no ^Rfaithfulness in their mouth; their inward part *is* very wickedness; their throat *is* an open sepulchre; they flatter with their tongue.　　　　　52:3

10 Destroy thou them, O God; let them fall by their own ^Rcounsels; cast them out in the multitude of their transgressions; for they have rebelled against thee.　　　　9:16

11 But let all those that put their trust in thee rejoice: let them ever shout for joy, because thou defendest them: let them also that love thy name be joyful in thee.

12 For thou, Lᴏʀᴅ, ^Rwilt bless the righteous; with favour wilt thou ^Tcompass him as *with* a shield.　　　[29:11] • *surround*

PSALM 6

Prayer for God's Mercy

To the chief Musician on Neg′-i-noth upon Shem′-i-nith, A Psalm of David.

O LORD, ^Rrebuke me not in thine anger, neither chasten me in thy hot displeasure.　　　　　38:1; 118:18

2 Have mercy upon me, O Lᴏʀᴅ; ^Rfor I *am* weak: O Lᴏʀᴅ, ^Rheal me; for my bones are ^Tvexed.　　　102:4 • 41:4 • *troubled*

3 My soul is also ^Tsore vexed: but thou, O Lᴏʀᴅ, how long?　　　　*very troubled*

4 Return, O Lᴏʀᴅ, ^Rdeliver my soul: oh save me for thy mercies' sake.　　　17:13

5 For in death *there is* no remembrance of thee: in the grave who shall give thee thanks?

6 I am weary with my groaning; ^Tall the night make I my bed to swim; I water my couch with my ^Rtears.　　*every night* • 42:3

7 Mine eye is consumed because of grief; it waxeth old because of all mine enemies.

8 ^RDepart from me, all ye workers of iniquity; for the Lᴏʀᴅ hath ^Rheard the voice of my weeping.　　　[Matt. 25:41] • 3:4

9 ^RThe Lᴏʀᴅ hath heard my supplication; the Lᴏʀᴅ will receive my prayer.　　116:1

10 ^RLet all mine enemies be ashamed and ^Tsore vexed: let them return *and* be ashamed suddenly.　　　　71:24 • *troubled*

PSALM 7

Wickedness Justly Rewarded

Shig-ga′-ion of David, which he sang unto the Lᴏʀᴅ, concerning the words of Cush the Benjamite.

O LORD my God, in thee do I put my trust: ^Rsave me from all them that persecute me, and deliver me:　　　31:15

2 RLest he tear my soul like a lion, Rrend-ingT it in pieces, while there is none to deliver.   Is. 38:13 • 50:22 • tearing

3 O LORD my God, Rif I have done this; if there be iniquity in my hands;   2 Sam. 16:7

4 If I have rewarded evil unto him that was at peace with me; (yea, I have delivered him that without cause is mine enemy:)

5 Let the enemy persecute my soul, and take it; yea, let him tread down my life upon the earth, and lay mine honour in the dust. Selah.

6 Arise, O LORD, in thine anger, Rlift up thyself because of the rage of mine enemies: and Rawake for me to the judgment that thou hast commanded.   94:2 • 44:23

7 So shall the congregation of the people Tcompass thee about: for their sakes therefore return thou on high.   surround

8 RThe LORD shall judge the people: judge me, O LORD, Raccording to my righteousness, and according to mine integrity that is in me.   [96:13; 98:9] • [18:20]

9 Oh let the wickedness of the wicked come to an end; but Testablish the just: Rfor the righteous God trieth the hearts and Treins.   sustain • [1 Sam. 16:7] • kidneys

10 My defence is of God, which saveth the Rupright in heart.   125:4

11 God judgeth the righteous, and God is angry with the wicked every day.

12 If he turn not, he will whet his sword; he hath bent his bow, and made it ready.

13 He hath also prepared for him the instruments of death; he Rordaineth his arrows against the persecutors.   18:14

14 RBehold, he travaileth with iniquity, and hath Rconceived mischief, and brought forth falsehood.   Job 15:35 • Is. 59:4

15 He made a pit, and digged it, and is fallen into the ditch which he made.

16 His mischief shall return upon his own head, and his violent dealing shall come down upon his own Tpate.   head

17 I will praise the LORD Raccording to his righteousness: and will sing praise to the name of the LORD most high.   [71:15, 16]

PSALM 8

God's Glory and Man's Dominion

To the chief Musician upon Git'-tith, A Psalm of David.

O LORD our Lord, how excellent is thy name in all the earth! who hast set thy glory above the heavens.

2 ROut of the mouth of babes and sucklings hast thou ordained strength because of thine enemies, that thou mightest still the enemy and the avenger.   Matt. 21:15, 16 ☆

3 When I Rconsider thy heavens, the work of thy fingers, the moon and the stars, which thou hast ordained;   [89:11]

4 RWhat is man, that thou art mindful of him? and the son of man, that thou visitest him?   144:3; Job 7:17

5 RFor thou hast made him a little lower than the angels, and hast crowned him with glory and honour.   [82:6; Gen. 1:26]

6 Thou madest him to have dominion over the works of thy hands; thou Rhast put all things under his feet: [Gen. 1:26]

7 RAll sheep and oxen, yea, and the beasts of the field;   Gen. 1:28

8 The fowl of the air, and the fish of the sea, and whatsoever passeth through the paths of the seas.

9 O LORD our Lord, how Texcellent is thy Rname in all the earth!   majestic • 138:2

PSALM 9

Praise for Victory over Enemies

To the chief Musician upon Muth–lab'-ben, A Psalm of David.

I WILL praise thee, O LORD, with Rmy whole heart; I will RshewT forth all thy marvellous works.   86:12 • 26:7 • tell

2 I will be glad and Rrejoice in thee: I will Rsing praise to thy name, O Rthou most High.   5:11 • 66:2 • [83:18]

3 When mine enemies are turned back, they shall fall and perish at thy presence.

4 RFor thou hast maintained my right and my cause; thou Tsatest in the throne judging right.   140:12 • did sit

5 Thou hast rebuked the heathen, thou hast destroyed the wicked, thou hast Rput out their name for ever and ever.   Prov. 10:7

6 O thou enemy, destructions are come to a perpetual end: and thou hast destroyed cities; their memorial is perished with them.

7 But the LORD shall endure for ever: he hath prepared his throne for judgment.

8 And Rhe shall judge the world in righteousness, he shall minister judgment to the people in uprightness.   [96:13]

9 The LORD also will be a refuge for the oppressed, a refuge in times of trouble.

10 And they that know thy name will put their trust in thee: for thou, LORD, hast not forsaken them that seek thee.

11 Sing praises to the LORD, which Rdwelleth in Zion: Rdeclare among the people his doings.   76:2 • 105:1

12 RWhen he maketh inquisition for blood, he remembereth them: he forgetteth not the cry of the humble.   Gen. 9:5

13 Have mercy upon me, O LORD; consider my trouble which I suffer of them that Rhate me, thou that Rliftest me up from the gates of death: 38:19 • 20:5

14 That I may shew forth all thy praise in ^Tthe gates of the daughter of Zion: I will rejoice in thy salvation.   *public presence*

15 ^RThe heathen are sunk down in the pit *that* they made: in the net which they hid is their own foot taken.   7:15, 16

16 The LORD is ^Rknown *by* the judgment *which* he executeth: the wicked is snared in the work of his own hands. Hig-ga'-ion. Selah.   [9:4]

17 The wicked shall be turned into hell, *and* all the nations that forget God.

18 ^RFor the needy shall not alway be forgotten: ^Rthe expectation of the poor shall *not* perish for ever.   12:5 · Prov. 23:18

19 Arise, O LORD; let not man prevail: let the heathen be judged in thy sight.

20 Put them in fear, O LORD: *that* the nations may know themselves *to be but* men. Selah.

PSALM 10

Petition for God's Judgment

WHY ^Rstandest thou afar off, O LORD? *why* ^Rhidest thou *thyself* in times of trouble?   22:1 · 13:1

2 ^RThe wicked in *his* pride doth persecute the poor: ^Rlet them be taken in the devices that they have imagined.   73:6 · 7:16

3 For the wicked ^Rboasteth of his heart's desire, and ^Rblesseth the covetous, *whom* the LORD abhorreth.   94:4 · Prov. 28:4

4 The wicked, through the pride of his countenance, will not seek *after God:* God *is* not in all his ^Rthoughts.   14:1

5 His ways are always grievous; thy judgments *are* far above out of his sight: *as for* all his enemies, he puffeth at them.

6 He hath said in his heart, I shall not be moved: for *I shall* never *be* in adversity.

7 ^RHis mouth is full of cursing and deceit and fraud: ^Runder his tongue *is* mischief and vanity.   Rom. 3:14 · Job 20:12

8 ^RHe sitteth in the lurking places of the villages: in the secret places doth he murder the ^Rinnocent: his eyes are privily set against the poor.   11:2 · [2 Kin. 24:4]

9 He lieth in wait secretly as a lion in his den: ^Rhe lieth in wait to catch the poor: he doth catch the poor, when he draweth him into his ^Rnet.   Mic. 7:2 · 140:5

10 He croucheth, *and* humbleth himself, that the poor may fall by his strong ones.

11 He hath ^Rsaid in his heart, God hath forgotten: he hideth his face; he will never see *it.*   10:4

12 Arise, O LORD; O God, ^Rlift up thine hand: forget not the humble.   Mic. 5:9

13 Wherefore doth the wicked ^Tcontemn God? he hath said in his heart, Thou wilt not ^Trequire *it.*   *despise · investigate*

14 Thou hast seen *it;* for thou beholdest mischief and spite, to requite *it* with thy hand: the poor committeth himself unto thee; thou art the helper of the fatherless.

15 ^RBreak thou the arm of the wicked and the evil *man:* ^Rseek out his wickedness *till* thou find none.   37:17 · 140:11

16 The LORD *is* King for ever and ever: the heathen are perished out of his land.

17 LORD, thou hast heard the ^Tdesire of the humble: thou wilt prepare their heart, thou wilt cause thine ear to hear: *petition*

18 To ^Rjudge the fatherless and the oppressed, that the man of the earth may ^Rno more oppress.   [146:9] · Is. 29:20

PSALM 11

God Tests the Children of Men

To the chief Musician, *A Psalm* of David.

IN ^Rthe LORD put I my ^Ttrust: how say ye to my soul, Flee *as* a bird to your mountain?   56:11 · *faith*

2 For, lo, ^Rthe wicked bend *their* bow, they make ready their arrow upon the string, that they may ^Tprivily shoot at the upright in heart.   64:3, 4 · *in the darkness*

3 ^RIf the ^Tfoundations be destroyed, what can the righteous do?   82:5 · *truth*

4 The LORD *is* in his holy temple, the LORD's throne *is* in heaven: his eyes behold, his eyelids ^Ttry, the children of men.   *evaluate*

5 The LORD ^Rtrieth^T the righteous: but the wicked and him that loveth violence his soul hateth.   Gen. 22:1 · *tests*

6 Upon the wicked he shall rain snares, fire and brimstone, and an horrible tempest: *this shall be* the portion of their cup.

7 For the righteous LORD ^Rloveth righteousness; his countenance doth ^Rbehold the upright.   33:5 · 16:11; 17:15

PSALM 12

The Pure Words of the Lord

To the chief Musician upon Shem'-i-nith, A Psalm of David.

HELP, LORD; for the ^Rgodly man ceaseth; for the faithful fail from among the children of men.   [Is. 57:1]

2 ^RThey speak ^Tvanity every one with his neighbour: *with* flattering lips *and* with a double heart do they speak.   41:6 · *foolishly*

3 The LORD shall cut off all flattering lips, *and* the tongue that speaketh proud things:

4 ^RWho have said, With our ^Rtongue will we prevail; our lips *are* our own: who *is* lord over us?   73:8, 9 · James 3:5

5 For the oppression of the poor, for the sighing of the needy, ^Rnow will I arise, saith the LORD; I will set *him* in ^Rsafety *from him that* puffeth at him. Is. 33:10 • 34:6

6 The words of the LORD *are* ^Rpure words: *as* silver ^Ttried in a furnace of earth, purified seven times. 119:38; Prov. 30:5 • *tested*

7 Thou shalt keep ^Tthem, O LORD, thou shalt ^Rpreserve them from this generation for ever. *the godly* • [37:28; 97:10]

8 The ^Rwicked walk on every side, when the vilest men are exalted. 55:10

PSALM 13

The Prayer for God's Answer—Now

To the chief Musician, A Psalm of David.

HOW long wilt thou ^Rforget me, O LORD? for ever? ^Rhow long wilt thou hide thy face from me? 44:24 • 89:46

2 How long shall I take counsel in my soul, *having* sorrow in my heart daily? how long shall mine enemy be exalted over me?

3 Consider *and* hear me, O LORD my God: ^Rlighten^T mine eyes, ^Rlest I sleep the *sleep of* death; 1 Sam. 14:29 • *cheer me* • Jer. 51:39

4 Lest mine enemy say, I have prevailed against him; *and* those that ^Rtrouble me rejoice when I am moved. 25:2; 38:16

5 But I have ^Rtrusted in thy mercy; my heart shall rejoice in thy salvation. 52:8

6 I will ^Rsing unto the LORD, because he hath dealt bountifully with me. 96:1

PSALM 14

The Characteristics of the Godless

To the chief Musician, *A Psalm* of David.

THE ^Rfool hath said in his heart, *There is* no God. They are corrupt, they have done abominable works, ^R*there is* none that doeth good. 10:4; 53:1 • [Rom. 3:10–12]

2 The LORD looked down from heaven upon the children of men, to see if there were any that did ^Runderstand, *and* seek God. 92:6

3 They are all gone aside, they are *all* together become ^Tfilthy: *there is* none that doeth good, no, not one. *corrupt*

4 Have all the workers of iniquity no knowledge? who eat up my people *as* they eat bread, and call not upon the LORD.

5 There were they in great fear: for God *is* in the generation of the righteous.

6 Ye have shamed the counsel of the poor, because the LORD *is* his refuge.

7 Oh that the salvation of Israel *were come* out of Zion! when the LORD bringeth back the captivity of his people, Jacob shall rejoice, *and* Israel shall be glad.

PSALM 15

The Characteristics of the Godly

A Psalm of David.

LORD, ^Rwho shall abide in thy tabernacle? who shall dwell in thy holy hill? 24:3

2 ^RHe that walketh uprightly, and worketh righteousness, and ^Rspeaketh the truth in his heart. Is. 33:15 • Zech. 8:16

3 *He that* backbiteth not with his tongue, nor doeth evil to his neighbour, ^Rnor taketh up a reproach against his neighbour. Ex. 23:1

4 ^RIn whose eyes a vile person is contemned; but he honoureth them that fear the LORD. *He that* sweareth to *his own* hurt, and changeth not. Esth. 3:2

5 *He that* putteth not out his money to usury, ^Rnor taketh reward against the innocent. He that doeth these *things* shall never be moved. Ex. 23:8; Deut. 16:19

PSALM 16

Eternal Life for One Who Trusts

Mich'-tam of David.

PRESERVE^R me, O God: for in thee do I put my trust. 17:8

2 O *my soul,* thou hast said unto the LORD, Thou *art* my Lord: ^Rmy goodness *extendeth* not to thee: Job 35:7

3 ^RBut to the saints that *are* in the earth, and to the excellent, ^Rin whom *is* all my delight. 101:6 • 119:63

4 Their sorrows shall be multiplied *that* hasten *after* another *god:* their drink offerings of blood will I not offer, ^Rnor take up their names into my lips. Josh. 23:7

5 The LORD *is* ^Rthe portion of mine inheritance and of my cup: thou maintainest my lot. 73:26; Lam. 3:24

6 The lines are fallen unto me in pleasant *places;* yea, I have a goodly heritage.

7 I will bless the LORD, who hath given me ^Tcounsel: my ^Treins also instruct me in the night seasons. *guidance* • *mind*

8 ^RI have set the LORD always before me: because *he is* at my right hand, ^RI shall not be moved. [Acts 2:25–28] • [112:6]

9 Therefore my ^Rheart is glad, and my glory rejoiceth: my flesh also shall ^Rrest in hope. 13:5 • 4:8

10 ^RFor thou wilt not leave my soul in hell; ^Rneither wilt thou suffer thine Holy One to see corruption. [49:15; Acts 2:31, 32] ✩ • Acts 13:35

11 Thou wilt shew me the path of life: in thy presence *is* fulness of joy; at thy right hand *there are* pleasures for evermore.

PSALM 17

"Hide Me Under the Shadow of Thy Wings"

A Prayer of David.

HEAR the right, O LORD, attend unto my cry, give ear unto my prayer, *that goeth* not out of ᵀfeigned lips.   *deceitful*

2 ᴿLet my ᵀsentence come forth from thy presence; let thine eyes behold the things that are ᴿequal.   [103:6] · *fate* · [98:9]

3 Thou hast proved mine heart; thou hast visited *me* in the night; thou hast tried me, *and* shalt find ᵀnothing; I am purposed *that* my mouth shall not transgress.   *no evil*

4 Concerning the works of men, ᴿby the word of thy lips I have kept *me from the* paths of the ᵀdestroyer.   [119:9] · *violent one*

5 ᴿHold up my goings in thy paths, *that* my footsteps slip not.   119:133

6 ᴿI have called upon thee, for thou wilt hear me, O God: incline thine ear unto me, *and hear* my speech.   116:2

7 ᴿShew thy marvellous lovingkindness, O thou that savest by thy right hand them which put their trust *in thee* from those that rise up *against them.*   31:21

8 Keep me as the apple of the eye, hide me under the shadow of thy wings,

9 From the wicked that oppress me, *from* my ᴿdeadly enemies, *who* ᵀcompass me about.   27:12 · *surround*

10 They are inclosed in their own fat: with their mouth they speak proudly.

11 ᴿThey have now compassed us in our steps: they have set their eyes ᴿbowing down to the earth;   88:17 · 37:14

12 Like as a ᴿlion *that* is greedy of his prey, and as it were a young lion lurking in secret places.   7:2

13 Arise, O LORD, ᵀdisappoint him, cast him down: deliver my soul from the wicked, *which is* thy sword: *anticipate*

14 From men *which are* thy hand, O LORD, from men of the world, *which have* their ᴿportion in *this* life, and whose belly thou fillest with thy hid *treasure:* they are full of children, and leave the rest of their *substance* to their babes.   [Luke 16:25]

15 As for me, ᴿI will behold thy face in righteousness: I shall be satisfied, when I awake, with thy likeness.   [1 John 3:2]

PSALM 18

Thanksgiving for Deliverance by God

To the chief Musician, *A Psalm* of David, the servant of the LORD, who spake unto the LORD the words of this song in the day *that* the LORD delivered him from the hand of all his enemies, and from the hand of Saul: And he said,

I WILL love thee, O LORD, my strength.

2 The LORD *is* my rock, and my fortress, and my deliverer; my God, my strength, ᴿin whom I will trust; my buckler, and the horn of my salvation, *and* my high tower.   Heb. 2:13

3 I will call upon the LORD, ᴿ*who is worthy* to be praised: so shall I be saved from mine enemies.   76:4; 96:4

4 ᴿThe sorrows of death ᵀcompassed me, and the floods of ungodly men made me afraid.   116:3 · *engulfed*

5 The sorrows of hell compassed me about: the snares of death prevented me.

6 ᴿIn my distress I called upon the LORD, and cried unto my God: he heard my voice out ᴿof his temple, and my cry came before him, *even* into his ears.   50:15 · 3:4

7 Then the earth shook and trembled; the foundations also of the hills moved and were shaken, because he was wroth.

8 There went up a smoke out of his nostrils, ᴿand fire out of his mouth devoured: coals were kindled by it.   50:3

9 He bowed the heavens also, and came down: and darkness *was* under his feet.

10 And he rode upon a ᴿcherub, and did

17:4 God's Word Corrects—There are many symbols for God's Word that can be found in the Bible itself. It can be thought of as a mirror (Page 1228—James 1:23-25), a seed (Page 1236—1 Pet. 1:23), a lamp (Page 601—Ps. 119:105), a sword (Page 1167—Eph. 6:17), and even as food (Page 1217—Heb. 5:12-14). But the Bible also serves as a measuring rod or ruler. Many teachers have used wooden rulers in their classes not only to give the right measurement but, on occasion, to correct a misbehaving pupil. God's Word likewise can do both of these things. It should be used as a standard against which to measure our beliefs. What about certain religious groups which claim Christ was not God, or that the Bible is filled with silly tales? Immediately we can reject such claims by using our divine written ruler to discover that such arguments simply do not measure up.

Sometimes our heavenly teacher uses His written ruler to correct us when we are in the wrong. Israel's great king, David, once experienced this. "Thou hast dealt well with thy servant, O LORD, according unto thy word. . . . Before I was afflicted I went astray: but now have I kept thy word" (Page 601—Ps. 119:65, 67).

There are times when God's Word can correct believers when they are in honest and unintentional error. Aquila and Priscilla, a godly Christian couple, use the Scriptures to help a powerful young preacher named Apollos (Page 1093—Acts 18:24-26). Paul does the same thing for some former disciples of John the Baptist he meets in the city of Ephesus (Page 1093—Acts 19:1-7).

Now turn to Page 599—Ps. 119:9: God's Word Cleanses.

fly: yea, ᴿhe did fly upon the wings of the wind. [80:1] • 104:3

11 He made darkness his secret place; his pavilion round about him *were* dark waters *and* thick clouds of the skies.

12 ᴿAt the brightness *that was* before him his thick clouds passed, hail *stones* and ᴿcoals of fire. 104:2 • Hab. 3:5

13 The Lᴏʀᴅ also thundered in the heavens, and the Highest gave ᴿhis voice; hail *stones* and coals of fire. 29:3

14 ᴿYea, he sent out his arrows, and scattered them; and he shot out lightnings, and discomfited them. 144:6

15 Then the channels of waters were seen, and the foundations of the world were discovered at thy rebuke, O Lᴏʀᴅ, at the blast of the breath of thy nostrils.

16 ᴿHe sent from above, he took me, he drew me out of many waters. 144:7

17 He ᴿdelivered me from my strong enemy, and from them which hated me: for they were too strong for me. 59:1

18 They prevented me in the day of my calamity: but the Lᴏʀᴅ was my stay.

19 ᴿHe brought me forth also into ᵀa large place; he delivered me, because he delighted in me. 31:8 • *broad*

20 ᴿThe Lᴏʀᴅ rewarded me according to my righteousness; according to ᴿthe cleanness of my hands hath he recompensed me. [Job 33:26] • [Job 22:30]

21 ᴿFor I have kept the ways of the Lᴏʀᴅ, and have not ᴿwickedly departed from my God. [37:34] • 2 Chr. 34:33

22 ᴿFor all his ᵀjudgments *were* before me, and I did not put away his statutes from me. 119:30 • *ordinances*

23 I was also upright before him, and I kept ᴿmyself from mine iniquity. 19:12

24 Therefore hath the Lᴏʀᴅ recompensed me according to my righteousness, according to the cleanness of my hands in his eyesight.

25 ᴿWith the merciful thou wilt shew thyself merciful; with an upright man thou wilt shew thyself upright; 1 Kin. 8:32

26 With the pure thou wilt shew thyself pure; and with the ᵀfroward thou wilt shew thyself ᵀfroward. *perverse* • *opposed*

27 For thou wilt save the afflicted people; but wilt bring down high looks.

28 For thou wilt light my candle: the Lᴏʀᴅ my God will enlighten my darkness.

29 For by thee I have ᴿrun through a troop; and by my God have I ᴿleaped over a wall. 118:10–12 • 40:2

30 *As for* God, ᴿhis way *is* perfect: the word of the Lᴏʀᴅ is tried: he *is* a buckler to all those that trust in him. [19:7]

31 ᴿFor who *is* God save the Lᴏʀᴅ? or who *is* a rock save our God? 1 Sam. 2:2

32 *It is* God that girdeth me with strength, and maketh my way perfect.

33 He maketh my feet like hinds' *feet*, and setteth me upon my high places.

34 He teacheth my hands to war, so that a bow of steel is broken by mine arms.

35 Thou hast also given me the ᴿshield of thy salvation: and ᴿthy right hand hath holden me up, and ᴿthy gentleness hath made me great. 33:20 • 63:8 • [138:6]

36 Thou hast ᵀenlarged my steps under me, that my feet did not slip. *supported*

37 ᴿI have pursued mine enemies, and overtaken them: neither did I turn again till they were consumed. [44:5]

38 I have wounded them that they were not ᴿable to rise: they are fallen ᴿunder my feet. 36:12 • 47:3

39 ᴿFor thou hast girded me with strength unto the battle: thou hast subdued under me those that rose up against me. *v.* 32

40 Thou hast also given me the necks of mine enemies; that ᴿI might destroy them that hate me. [94:23]

41 They cried, but *there was* none to save *them:* ᴿeven unto the Lᴏʀᴅ, but he answered them not. Job 27:9

42 Then did I beat them small as the dust before the wind: I did ᴿcast them out as the dirt in the streets. Zech. 10:5

43 Thou hast delivered me from the strivings of the people; *and* thou hast made me the head of the heathen: ᴿa people *whom* I have not known shall serve me. [Is. 52:15]

44 As soon as they hear of me, they shall obey me: ᴿthe strangers shall ᵀsubmit themselves unto me. [66:3] • *yield*

45 The strangers shall fade away, and be afraid out of their ᵀclose places. *hiding*

46 ᴿThe Lᴏʀᴅ liveth; and blessed *be* my rock; and let the ᴿGod of my salvation be exalted. [Job 19:25] • 51:14

47 *It is* God that ᴿavengeth me, and subdueth the people under me. [94:1]

48 He ᴿdelivereth me from mine enemies: yea, ᴿthou liftest me up above those that rise up against me: thou hast delivered me from the violent man. 3:7 • 59:1

49 Therefore will I ᵀgive thanks unto thee, O Lᴏʀᴅ, among the heathen, and sing praises unto thy name. *confess*

50 Great deliverance giveth he to his king; and sheweth mercy to his anointed, to David, and to his seed for evermore.

PSALM 19

The Works and Words of God

To the chief Musician, A Psalm of David.

THE ᴿheavens ᵀdeclare the glory of God; and the firmament sheweth his handywork. [Rom. 1:19] • *tell of*

2 Day unto day uttereth speech, and night unto night sheweth knowledge.

3 *There is* no ᵀspeech nor language, *where* their voice is not heard.   *words*

4 ᴿTheir line is gone out through all the earth, and their words to the end of the world. In them hath he ᴿset a tabernacle for the sun,   Rom. 10:18 · 104:2

5 Which *is* as a bridegroom coming out of his chamber, *and* rejoiceth as a strong man to run a race.

6 ᴿHis going forth *is* from the end of the heaven, and his circuit unto the ends of it: and there is nothing hid from the heat thereof.   113:3

7 The law of the Lᴏʀᴅ *is* perfect, converting the soul: the testimony of the Lᴏʀᴅ *is* sure, making wise the simple.

8 The statutes of the Lᴏʀᴅ *are* right, rejoicing the heart: the commandment of the Lᴏʀᴅ *is* pure, enlightening the eyes.

9 The fear of the Lᴏʀᴅ *is* clean, enduring for ever: ᴿthe judgments of the Lᴏʀᴅ *are* true *and* righteous altogether.   [119:142]

10 More to be desired *are they* than ᴿgold, yea, than much fine gold: sweeter also than honey and the honeycomb.   119:72

11 Moreover by them is ᴿthy servant warned: *and* in keeping of them *there is* great ᴿreward.   [17:4] · [Prov. 29:18]

12 Who can understand *his* errors? cleanse thou me from secret *faults.*

13 Keep back thy servant also from presumptuous *sins;* let them not have dominion over me: then shall I be upright, and I shall be innocent from the great transgression.

14 Let the words of my mouth, ᴿand the meditation of my heart, be acceptable in thy sight, O Lᴏʀᴅ, my ᵀstrength, and my redeemer.   104:34 · *rock*

PSALM 20

Trust Not in Chariots and Horses but in God

To the chief Musician, A Psalm of David.

THE Lᴏʀᴅ ᵀhear thee ᴿin the day of trouble; the name of the God of Jacob defend thee;   *answer* · 50:15

2 Send thee help from the sanctuary, and ᴿstrengthen thee out of Zion;   110:2

3 ᴿRemember all thy offerings, and accept thy burnt sacrifice;   Selah.   Acts 10:4

4 Grant thee according to thine own heart, and fulfil all thy ᵀcounsel.   *purpose*

5 We will rejoice in thy salvation, and in the name of our God we will set up *our* banners: the Lᴏʀᴅ fulfil all thy petitions.

6 Now know I that the Lᴏʀᴅ saveth his anointed; he ᴿwill hear him from his holy heaven with the ᴿsaving strength of his right hand.   Is. 58:9 · 28:8

7 Some ᵀ*trust* in chariots, and some in horses: but ᴿwe will remember the name of the Lᴏʀᴅ our God.   *boast* · [2 Chr. 32:8]

8 They are brought down and fallen: but we are risen, and stand upright.

9 ᴿSave, Lᴏʀᴅ: let the ᴿking hear us when we call.   3:7 · 17:6

PSALM 21

Triumph of the King

To the chief Musician, A Psalm of David.

THE king shall ᴿjoy in thy strength, O Lᴏʀᴅ; and in thy salvation how greatly shall he rejoice!   [59:16, 17]

2 Thou hast ᴿgiven him his heart's desire, and hast not withholden the request of his lips.   Selah.   [37:4]

3 For thou ᵀpreventest him with the blessings of goodness: thou settest a crown of pure gold on his head.   *do meet*

4 He asked life of thee, *and* thou gavest *it* him, *even* length of days for ever and ever.

5 ᴿHis glory *is* great in thy salvation: honour ᴿand majesty hast thou laid upon him.   9:14 · [8:5; 96:6]

6 For thou hast made him most blessed for ever: thou hast made him exceeding glad with ᵀthy countenance.   *your favour*

7 For the king ᵀtrusteth in the Lᴏʀᴅ, and through the mercy of the most High he shall ᵀnot be moved.   *confides* · *be kept safely*

8 Thine hand shall ᴿfind out all thine enemies: thy right hand shall find out those that hate thee.   [Is. 10:10, 11]

9 Thou shalt make them ᴿas a fiery oven in the time of thine anger: the Lᴏʀᴅ shall swallow them up in his wrath, and the fire shall devour them.   [Mal. 4:1]

10 Their ᵀfruit shalt thou destroy from the earth, and their seed from among the children of men.   *offspring*

11 For they intended evil against thee: they imagined a mischievous device, *which* they are not able *to perform.*

12 ᴿTherefore shalt thou make them turn their back, *when* thou shalt make ready *thine arrows* upon thy strings against the face of them.   18:40

13 Be thou exalted, Lᴏʀᴅ, in thine own strength: ᴿso will we sing and praise thy power.   59:16; 81:1

PSALM 22

Psalm of the Cross

To the chief Musician upon Ai′-je-leth Sha′-har, A Psalm of David.

MY ᴿGod, my God, why hast thou forsaken me? *why art thou so* far from

helping me, *and from* the words of my
^Troaring? [Mark 15:34] ☆ • *lamentations*

2 O my God, I ^Rcry in the daytime, but
thou hearest not; and in the night season, and
am not silent. 42:3; 88:1

3 But ^Rthou *art* holy, O *thou* that inhabit-
est the praises of Israel. [99:9]

4 Our fathers trusted in thee: they trusted,
and thou didst deliver them.

5 They cried unto thee, and were delivered: ^Rthey trusted in thee, and were not
^Tconfounded. Is. 49:23 • *shamed*

6 But I *am* a worm, and no man; a reproach of men, and despised of the people.

7 ^RAll they that see me laugh me to scorn:
they ^Tshoot out the lip, they shake the head,
saying, Matt. 27:39; Mark 15:29; Luke 23:35 ☆ • *ridicule*

8 He ^Ttrusted on the LORD *that* he would
deliver him: ^Rlet him deliver him, seeing he
delighted in him. *relied on* • Matt. 27:43 ☆

9 ^RBut thou *art* he that took me out of the
womb: thou didst make me hope *when I was*
upon my mother's breasts. [71:6]

10 I was cast upon thee from the womb:
thou *art* my God from my mother's belly.

11 Be not far from me; for trouble *is* near;
for *there is* ^Rnone to help. 2 Kin. 14:26

12 Many bulls have compassed me: strong
bulls of Ba'-shan have beset me round.

13 They gaped upon me *with* their mouths,
as a ravening and a roaring lion.

14 I am poured out like water, and all my
bones are out of joint: my heart is like wax; it
is melted in the midst of my bowels.

15 My strength is dried up like a potsherd;
and my tongue cleaveth to my jaws; and
thou hast brought me into the dust of death.

16 For dogs have compassed me: the assembly of the wicked have inclosed me: they
pierced ^Rmy hands and my feet. John 20:27 ☆

17 I may tell all my bones: they look *and*
^Rstare upon me. Matt. 27:36, 39; John 19:37 ☆

18 ^RThey part my garments among them,
and cast lots upon my vesture. Luke 23:34 ☆

19 But be not thou far from me, O LORD: O
my strength, haste thee to help me.

20 Deliver my soul from the sword; ^Rmy
darling from the power of the dog. 35:17

21 ^RSave me from the lion's mouth: ^Rfor
thou hast heard me from the horns of the
^Tunicorns. 2 Tim. 4:17 • Is. 34:7 • *wild oxen*

22 ^RI will declare thy name unto ^Rmy
brethren: in the midst of the congregation
will I praise thee. Mark 1:21, 39 ☆ • [Rom. 8:29]

23 Ye that fear the LORD, praise him; all ye
the seed of Jacob, glorify him; and fear him,
all ye the seed of Israel.

24 For he hath not despised nor abhorred
the affliction of the afflicted; neither hath he
hid his face from him; but ^Rwhen he cried
unto him, he heard. 31:22; Heb. 5:7

25 ^RMy praise *shall be* of thee in the great

congregation: ^RI will pay my vows before
them that fear him. 35:18 • Eccl. 5:4

26 The meek shall eat and be ^Rsatisfied:
they shall praise the LORD that seek him:
your heart shall live for ever. [107:9]

27 ^RAll the ends of the world shall remember and turn unto the LORD: and all the
^Rkindreds of the nations shall worship before
thee. [82:8] • [86:9]

28 For the kingdom *is* the LORD's: and he *is*
the governor among the nations.

29 All *they* ^T*that be* fat upon earth shall
eat and worship: all they that go down to the
dust shall bow before him: and none can keep
alive his own soul. *prosperous*

30 A seed shall serve him; it shall be accounted to the Lord for a generation.

31 They shall come, and shall declare his
righteousness unto a people that shall be
born, that he hath done *this.*

PSALM 23

Psalm of the Divine Shepherd

A Psalm of David.

THE LORD *is* ^Rmy shepherd; ^RI shall not
^Twant. [Is. 40:11] • [Phil. 4:19] • *be in need*

2 ^RHe maketh me to lie down in green
pastures: he leadeth me beside the still waters. Ezek. 34:14; [Rev. 7:17]

3 He ^Trestoreth my soul: ^Rhe leadeth me in
the paths of righteousness for his name's
sake. *brings back* • 5:8

4 Yea, though I walk through the valley of
^Rthe shadow of death, ^RI will fear no evil: for
thou *art* with me; thy rod and thy staff they
comfort me. 3:6 • [Is. 43:2]

5 Thou preparest a table before me in the
presence of mine enemies: thou anointest my
head with oil; my cup runneth over.

6 Surely goodness and mercy shall follow
me all the days of my life: and I will dwell in
the house of the LORD for ever.

PSALM 24

Psalm of the King of Glory

A Psalm of David.

THE ^Rearth *is* the LORD's, and the fulness
thereof; the ^Rworld, and they that dwell
therein. 1 Cor. 10:26 • [Ps. 89:11]

2 For he hath founded it upon the seas,
and established it upon the floods.

3 Who shall ascend into the hill of the
LORD? or who shall stand in his holy place?

4 He that hath clean hands, and a pure
heart; who hath not lifted up his soul unto
vanity, nor sworn deceitfully.

5 He shall receive the ^Rblessing from the
LORD, and righteousness from the God of his
salvation. [115:13]

6 This *is* the generation of them that seek him, that seek thy face, O Jacob.　Selah.

7 ᴿLift up your heads, O ye gates; and be ye lift up, ye everlasting doors; and the King of glory shall come in.　　　　　　Is. 26:2

8 Who *is* this King of glory? The Lᴏʀᴅ ᴿstrong and mighty, the Lᴏʀᴅ ᴿmighty in battle.　　　　　Deut. 4:34 · [Ex. 15:3, 6]

9 Lift up your heads, O ye gates; even lift *them* up, ye everlasting doors; ᴿand the King of glory shall come in.　　　　　　57:11

10 Who is this King of glory? The Lᴏʀᴅ of hosts, he *is* the King of glory.　Selah.

PSALM 25

Acrostic Prayer for Instruction

A *Psalm* of David.

UNTO thee, O Lᴏʀᴅ, do I lift up my soul. 2 O my God, I ᴿtrust in thee: let me not be ashamed, ᴿlet not mine enemies triumph over me.　　　　　　　31:1 · 41:11

3 Yea, let none that wait on thee be ashamed: ᴿlet them be ashamed which transgress without cause.　　　　　[Hab. 1:13]

4 ᴿShew me thy ways, O Lᴏʀᴅ; teach me thy paths.　　　　　　Ex. 33:13

5 ᴿLead me in thy truth, and teach me: for thou *art* the God of my salvation; on thee do I ᴿwait all the day.　　　　　43:3 · 40:1

6 Remember, O Lᴏʀᴅ, ᴿthy tender mercies and thy lovingkindnesses; for they *have been* ᴿever of old.　　　　　98:3 · 103:17

7 Remember not ᴿthe sins of my youth, nor my transgressions: ᴿaccording to thy mercy remember thou me for thy goodness' sake, O Lᴏʀᴅ.　　　　　Job 13:26 · 51:1

8 Good and upright *is* the Lᴏʀᴅ: therefore will he teach sinners in the way.

9 The meek will he guide in judgment: and the meek will he teach his way.

10 All the paths of the Lᴏʀᴅ *are* mercy and truth unto such as ᵀkeep his ᵀcovenant and his testimonies.　　　　*obey · agreement*

11 ᴿFor thy name's sake, O Lᴏʀᴅ, pardon mine iniquity; for it *is* great.　　31:3

12 What man *is* he that ᴿfeareth the Lᴏʀᴅ? ᴿhim shall he teach in the way *that* he shall choose.　　　　　[31:19] · [37:23]

13 ᴿHis soul shall dwell at ease; and his seed shall inherit the earth.　　[Prov. 19:23]

14 ᴿThe secret of the Lᴏʀᴅ *is* with them that fear him; and he will shew them his covenant.　　　　Job 29:4; [Prov. 3:32]

15 Mine eyes *are* ever toward the Lᴏʀᴅ; for he shall pluck my feet out of the net.

16 Turn thee unto me, and have mercy upon me; for I *am* desolate and afflicted.

17 The troubles of my heart are enlarged: O bring thou me out of my distresses.

18 ᴿLook upon mine affliction and my pain; and forgive all my sins.　2 Sam. 16:12

19 Consider mine enemies; for they are many; and they hate me with cruel hatred.

20 ᴿO keep my soul, and deliver me: let me ᴿnot be ashamed; for I put my trust in thee.　　　　　86:2 · 25:2

21 Let integrity and uprightness preserve me; for I ᵀwait on thee.　　　　*trust*

22 ᴿRedeemᵀ Israel, O God, out of all his troubles.　　　　　[130:8] · *deliver*

PSALM 26

"Examine Me, O Lᴏʀᴅ, and Prove Me"

A *Psalm* of David.

JUDGE me, O Lᴏʀᴅ; for I have walked in mine integrity: I have trusted also in the Lᴏʀᴅ; *therefore* I shall not ᴿslide.　Heb. 10:23

2 ᴿExamine me, O Lᴏʀᴅ, and prove me: try my reins and my heart.　　　　139:23

3 For thy lovingkindness *is* before mine eyes: and I have walked in thy truth.

4 I have not sat with vain persons, neither will I go in with dissemblers.

5 I have hated the congregation of evildoers; and will not sit with the wicked.

6 I will wash mine hands in innocency: so will I compass thine altar, O Lᴏʀᴅ:

7 That I may ᵀpublish with the ᴿvoice of thanksgiving, and tell of all thy wondrous works.　　　　　　*make known* · 9:1

8 Lᴏʀᴅ, ᴿI have loved the habitation of thy house, and the place where ᴿthine honour dwelleth.　　　　　27:4 · 24:7

9 Gather not my soul with sinners, nor my life with ᴿbloody men:　　　[139:19]

10 In whose hands *is* mischief, and their right hand is full of ᴿbribes.　　　15:5

11 But as for me, I ᴿwill walk in mine integrity: ᴿredeem me, and be merciful to me.　　　　v. 1 · 44:26; 69:18

12 My foot standeth in an even place: in the congregations will I bless the Lᴏʀᴅ.

PSALM 27

Trust in the Lord and Be Not Afraid

A *Psalm* of David.

THE Lᴏʀᴅ *is* my ᴿlight and my salvation; whom shall I fear? the Lᴏʀᴅ *is* the strength of my life; of whom shall I be afraid?　　　　　[Is. 60:20; Mic. 7:8]

2 When the wicked, *even* mine enemies and my foes, came upon me to ᴿeat up my flesh, ᴿthey stumbled and fell.　14:4 · John 18:6 ☆

3 ᴿThough an host should encamp against me, my heart shall not fear: though war should rise against me, ᵀin this *will* I ᴿbe confident.　3:6 · *in spite of this* · Job 4:6

4 ᴿOne *thing* have I desired of the Lᴏʀᴅ, that will I seek after; that I may ᴿdwell in the house of the Lᴏʀᴅ all the days of my life, to

behold the beauty of the LORD, and to enquire in his temple.   26:8 · 23:6

5 For ᴿin the time of trouble he shall hide me in his pavilion: in the secret of his tabernacle shall he hide me; he shall ᴿset me up upon a rock.   50:15 · 40:2

6 And now shall ᴿmine head be lifted up above mine enemies round about me: therefore will I offer in his tabernacle ᴿsacrifices of joy; I will sing, yea, I will sing praises unto the LORD.   3:3 · 107:22

7 ᴿHear, O LORD, when I cry with my voice: ᵀhave mercy also upon me, and ᴿanswer me.   [4:3] · show favour · 13:3

8 When thou saidst, ᴿSeek ye my face; my heart said unto thee, Thy face, LORD, will I ᴿseek.   [Amos 5:6] · 34:4

9 ᴿHide not thy face far from me; put not thy servant away in anger: thou hast been my help; leave me not, neither forsake me, O God of my salvation.   69:17

10 When my father and my mother forsake me, then the LORD will take me up.

11 Teach me thy way, O LORD, and lead me in a plain path, because of mine enemies.

12 Deliver me not over unto the will of mine enemies: ᴿfor false witnesses are risen up against me, and such as breathe out cruelty.   Matt. 26:60, 61 ☆

13 I had fainted, unless I had believed to see the goodness of the LORD ᴿin the land of the living.   Job 28:13; Ezek. 26:20

14 ᵀWaitᴿ on the LORD: be of good courage, and he shall strengthen thine heart: wait, I say, on the LORD.   trust · Prov. 20:22

PSALM 28

Rejoice Because of Answered Prayer

A Psalm of David.

UNTO thee will I cry, O LORD my rock; ᴿbe not silent to me: ᴿlest, if thou be silent to me, I become like them that go down into the pit.   83:1 · 88:4

2 Hear the voice of my supplications, when I cry unto thee, ᴿwhen I lift up my hands toward thy holy oracle.   5:7

3 Draw me not away with the wicked, and with the workers of iniquity, ᴿwhich speak peace to their neighbours, but ᵀmischief is in their hearts.   12:2 · evil

4 Give them according to their deeds, and according to the wickedness of their endeavours: give them after the work of their hands; render to them their desert.

5 Because ᴿthey ᵀregard not the works of the LORD, nor the operation of his hands, he shall destroy them, and not build them up.   Is. 5:12 · pay no attention

6 Blessed be the LORD, because he hath heard the voice of my supplications.

7 The LORD is ᴿmy strength and my shield; my heart ᴿtrusted in him, and I am helped: therefore my heart greatly rejoiceth; and with my song will I praise him.   18:2 · 13:5; 112:7

8 The LORD is their strength, and he is the saving strength of his anointed.

9 Save thy people, and bless ᴿthine inheritance: feed them also, ᴿand lift them up for ever.   [33:12; Deut. 9:29] · [Is. 40:11]

PSALM 29

The Powerful Voice of God

A Psalm of David.

GIVE unto the LORD, O ye mighty, give unto the LORD glory and strength.

2 Give unto the LORD the glory due unto his name; worship the LORD in ᴿthe beautyᵀ of holiness.   2 Chr. 20:21 · glorious sanctuary

3 The voice of the LORD is upon the waters: ᴿthe God of glory thundereth: the LORD is upon many waters.   [Job 37:4, 5]

4 The voice of the LORD is powerful; the voice of the LORD is full of majesty.

5 The voice of the LORD ᵀbreaketh the cedars; yea, the LORD breaketh ᴿthe cedars of Leb'-a-non.   is in command · Is. 2:13

29:2 Worship by Israel—The central aspect of Israel's worship was the object of their worship, the Lord. While other nations paid homage to many gods (Page 206—Deut. 29:18), only Israel worshiped the one true God (Page 75—Ex. 20:3). This worship could be private (Page 89—Ex. 34:8), as a family (Page 22—Gen. 22:5), or corporate (Page 434—1 Chr. 29:20), as a congregation.

Since so much of the Bible is devoted to Israel's public worship, it deserves special notice. It included offering sacrifices (Page 276—1 Sam. 1:3), adopting a reverent posture (Page 444—2 Chr. 7:6), verbal praise—either spoken (Page 421—1 Chr. 16:36) or sung (Page 571—Ps. 57:7), instrumental praise (Page 611—Ps. 150:3–5), prayer (Page 442—2 Chr. 6:14–42), and the great feasts (Page 123—Lev. 23; 25). One need only read the Psalms to see the excellent form and spirit in which the godly of Israel worshiped.

The first place of worship for the people of Israel was the tabernacle constructed by Moses (Page 79—Ex. 25—27; 30; 31; 35—40) and later the magnificent temple constructed by Solomon (Page 426—1 Chr. 22:5). These structures served to localize the worship of the entire nation. This geographic limitation stands in bold contrast to the privilege of immediate and direct access to God now available to the New Testament believer who himself is the temple of God (Page 1217—Heb. 4:16; Page 1129—1 Cor. 6:19).

Now turn to Page 1079—Acts 7:38: The Meaning of the Word *Church.*

6 ᴿHe maketh them also to ᵀskip like a calf; Leb'-a-non and Sir'-i-on like a young unicorn. 　　　　　　　114:4 · *obey promptly*

7 The voice of the LORD ᵀdivideth the flames of fire. 　　　　　　　　　*controls*

8 The voice of the LORD shaketh the wilderness; the LORD shaketh the wilderness of ᴿKa'-desh. 　　　　　　　Num. 13:26

9 The voice of the LORD ᴿmaketh the ᵀhinds to calve, and discovereth the forests: and in his temple doth every one speak of *his* glory. 　　　　　　　Job 39:1 · *deer*

10 The LORD sitteth upon the flood; yea, the LORD sitteth King for ever.

11 ᴿThe LORD will give strength unto his people; the LORD will bless his people with ᴿpeace. 　　　　　[Is. 40:29] · [37:11]

PSALM 30

Praise for Dramatic Deliverance

A Psalm *and* Song *at* the dedication of the house of David.

I WILL ᵀextol thee, O LORD; for thou hast ᴿlifted me up, and hast not made my foes to rejoice over me. 　　　　　*praise* · 28:9

2 O LORD my God, I ᴿcried unto thee, and thou hast healed me. 　　　　　88:13

3 O LORD, thou hast brought up my soul from the grave: thou hast kept me alive, that I should not go down to the pit.

4 Sing unto the LORD, O ye saints of his, and give thanks at the remembrance of his ᴿholiness. 　　　　　Ex. 3:15; Hos. 12:5

5 For his anger *endureth but* a moment; in his favour *is* life: weeping may endure for a night, but joy *cometh* in the morning.

6 And in my prosperity I said, I shall never ᴿbe moved. 　　　　　[62:2, 6]

7 LORD, by thy favour thou hast made my mountain to stand strong: thou didst hide thy face, *and* I was troubled.

8 I cried to thee, O LORD; and unto the LORD I made supplication.

9 What profit *is there* in my blood, when I ᴿgo down to the pit? Shall the dust praise thee? shall it declare thy truth? 　　　[28:1]

10 Hear, O LORD, and have mercy upon me: LORD, ᴿbe thou my helper. 　　　54:4

11 Thou hast turned for me my mourning into dancing: thou hast put off my sackcloth, and girded me with gladness;

12 To the end that *my* glory may sing praise to thee, and not be silent. O LORD my God, I will give thanks unto thee for ever.

PSALM 31

"Be of Good Courage"

To the chief Musician, A Psalm of David.

IN ᴿthee, O LORD, do I put my trust; let me never be ᴿashamed: deliver me in thy righteousness. 　　　　　25:2 · 25:11

2 ᴿBow down thine ear to me; deliver me speedily: be thou my strong rock, for an house of defence to save me. 　　　71:2

3 ᴿFor thou *art* my rock and my fortress; therefore ᴿfor thy name's sake lead me, and guide me. 　　　　　[18:2] · 23:3

4 Pull me out of the net that they have laid privily for me: for thou *art* my strength.

5 Into thine hand I commit my spirit: thou hast redeemed me, O LORD God of truth.

6 I have hated them ᴿthat regard lying vanities: but I trust in the LORD. 　Jon. 2:8

7 I will be glad and rejoice in thy mercy: for thou hast considered my trouble; thou hast known my soul in adversities;

8 And hast not ᴿshutᵀ me up into the hand of the enemy: thou hast set my feet in a large room. 　　　[Deut. 32:30] · *given over*

9 Have mercy upon me, O LORD, for I am in trouble: mine eye is consumed with grief, *yea*, my soul and my belly.

10 For my life is spent with ᴿgrief, and my years with sighing: my strength faileth because of mine iniquity, and my bones are consumed. 　　　　　13:2

11 I was a reproach among all mine enemies, but ᴿespecially among my neighbours, and a fear to mine acquaintance: they that did see me without fled from me. 　38:11; 88:8

12 ᴿI am forgotten as a dead man out of mind: I am like a broken vessel. 　88:4, 5

13 ᴿFor I have heard the slander of many: fear *was* on every side: while they took counsel together against me, they devised to take away my life. 　　　　　Jer. 20:10

14 But I trusted in thee, O LORD: I said, Thou ᴿart my God. 　　　　　140:6

15 ᴿMy times *are* in thy hand: deliver me from the hand of mine enemies, and from them that persecute me. 　[Job 14:5; 24:1]

16 Make thy face to shine upon thy servant: save me for thy mercies' sake.

17 ᴿLet me not be ashamed, O LORD; for I have called upon thee: let the wicked be ashamed, *and* ᴿlet them be silent in the ᵀgrave. 　　　25:20 · 25:3 · *sheol*

18 Let the lying lips be put to silence; which ᴿspeak grievous things proudly and contemptuously against the righteous. 　94:4

19 *Oh* how great *is* thy goodness, which thou hast laid up for them that fear thee; *which* thou hast wrought for them that trust in thee before the sons of men!

20 ᴿThou shalt hide them in the secret of thy presence from the pride of man: thou shalt keep them secretly in a pavilion from the strife of tongues. 　　　　　[27:5]

21 Blessed *be* the LORD: for ᴿhe hath shewed me his marvellous kindness in a ᵀstrong city. 　　　　　17:7 · *fortified*

22 For I said in my haste, ᴿI am cut off from before thine eyes: nevertheless thou

heardest the voice of my supplications when I cried unto thee.   Lam. 3:54

23 O love the LORD, all ye his saints: *for* the LORD preserveth the faithful, and plentifully rewardeth the proud doer.

24 [R]Be of good courage, and he shall strengthen your heart, all ye that hope in the LORD.   [27:14]

PSALM 32

The Blessedness of Forgiveness

A Psalm of David, Mas'-chil.

BLESSED *is he whose* transgression *is* forgiven, *whose* sin *is* covered.

2 Blessed *is* the man unto whom the LORD imputeth not [T]iniquity, and in whose spirit *there is* no [T]guile.   *sin · deceit*

3 When I kept silence, my bones waxed old through my roaring all the day long.

4 For day and night thy hand was heavy upon me: my moisture is turned into the drought of summer.   Selah.

5 I acknowledged my sin unto thee, and mine iniquity have I not hid. I[R] said, I will confess my transgressions unto the LORD; and thou forgavest the iniquity of my sin. Selah.   [Prov. 28:13; 1 John 1:9]

6 For this shall every one that is godly pray unto thee in a time when thou mayest be found: [R]surely in the floods of great waters they shall not come nigh unto him.   Is. 43:2

7 [R]Thou *art* my hiding place; thou shalt preserve me from trouble; thou shalt compass me about with [R]songs of deliverance. Selah.   91:1 · Ex. 15:1; Judg. 5:1

8 I will instruct thee and teach thee in the way which thou shalt go: [T]I will guide thee [R]with mine eye.   *counsel* · [33:18]

9 Be ye not as the horse, *or* as the mule, *which* have no understanding: whose mouth must be held in with bit and bridle, lest they come near unto thee.

10 [R]Many sorrows *shall be* to the wicked: but he that trusteth in the LORD, mercy shall compass him about.   [Rom. 2:9]

11 [R]Be glad in the LORD, and rejoice, ye righteous: and shout for joy, all *ye that are* upright in heart.   64:10

PSALM 33

God Considers All Man's Works

REJOICE in the LORD, O ye righteous: *for* praise is comely for the upright.

2 Praise the LORD with [R]harp: sing unto him with the psaltery *and* an instrument of ten strings.   71:22

3 [R]Sing unto him a new song; play skilfully with a loud noise.   40:3; Rev. 5:9

4 [R]For the word of the LORD *is* right; and all his works *are done* in truth.   [19:8]

5 He loveth righteousness and judgment: the earth is full of the goodness of the LORD.

6 [R]By the word of the LORD were the heavens made; and all the host of them by the breath of his mouth.   [Heb. 11:3]

7 [R]He gathereth the waters of the sea together as an heap: he layeth up the depth in storehouses.   78:13; Ex. 15:8

8 Let all the [R]earth fear the LORD: let all the inhabitants of the world [R]stand in awe of him.   67:7 · 96:9

9 For [R]he spake, and it was *done;* he commanded, and it stood fast.   Gen. 1:3

10 [R]The LORD bringeth the counsel of the heathen to nought: he maketh the devices of the people of none effect.   Is. 8:10

11 [R]The counsel of the LORD standeth for ever, the thoughts of his heart to all generations.   [Job 23:13; Prov. 19:21]

12 Blessed *is* the nation whose God *is* the LORD; *and* the people *whom* he hath [R]chosen for his own inheritance.   [Ex. 19:5]

13 [R]The LORD looketh from heaven; he beholdeth all the sons of men.   Job 28:24

14 From the place of his habitation he looketh upon all the inhabitants of the earth.

15 He fashioneth their hearts alike; [R]he considereth all their works.   [Jer. 32:19]

16 [R]There is no king saved by the multitude of an host: a mighty man is not delivered by much strength.   44:6

17 [R]An horse *is* a [T]vain thing for safety:

32:5 What Should Be Done About Sin—The believer should never condone or attempt to excuse his sin. There are only two things that should be done about sin: confess it and forsake it. The Old and New Testaments are agreed on this. David confessed his sin and experienced the Lord's forgiveness. John agrees as he points out: "If we confess our sins, he is faithful and just to forgive us *our* sins, and to cleanse us from all unrighteousness" (Page 1249—1 John 1:9). To "confess" means *to acknowledge* or *to say the same thing as.* The believer is instructed that he is to say the same thing as God says about his sin, "It is sin." When the believer confesses his sin he has the assurance that God "is faithful" (He can be counted upon to keep His Word) and "just" (He is just in dealing with our sins because He paid the price for them) "to forgive us *our* sins and to cleanse us from all unrighteousness." There is no sin too great and no sin too small—God is able to cleanse us completely from anything that is inconsistent with His own moral character. Having received forgiveness and cleansing, the believer is to forsake his sin and yield himself completely to God. In doing this the believer is restored to full fellowship with God.

Now turn to Page 1250—1 John 2:15: Temptation by the World.

neither shall he deliver *any* by his great strength.   [20:7] • *useless*

18 RBehold, the eye of the LORD *is* upon them that fear him, upon them that hope in his mercy;   [Job 36:7; 1 Pet. 3:12]

19 To deliver their soul from death, and Rto keep them alive in famine.   Job 5:20

20 Our soul Rwaiteth for the LORD: he *is* our help and our shield.   Is. 8:17

21 For our heart shall rejoice in him, because we have trusted in his holy name.

22 Let thy mercy, O LORD, be upon us, according as we hope in thee.

PSALM 34

Seek the Lord

A Psalm of David, when he changed his behaviour before A-bim'-e-lech; who drove him away, and he departed.

I WILL bless the LORD at all times: his praise *shall* continually *be* in my mouth.

2 My soul shall Rmake her boast in the LORD: the humble shall hear *thereof*, and be glad.   44:8; [Jer. 9:24]

3 O Rmagnify the LORD with me, and let us exalt his name together.   35:27

4 I sought the LORD, and he heard me, and delivered me from all my fears.

5 They looked unto him, and were lightened: and their faces were not ashamed.

6 This poor man cried, Rand the LORD heard *him*, and saved him out of all his troubles.   *v. 4*

7 RThe angel of the LORD encampeth round about them that fear him, and delivereth them.   [91:11]; Dan. 6:22

8 O taste and see that the LORD *is* good: blessed *is* the man *that* trusteth in him.

9 O fear the LORD, ye his saints: for *there is* no want to them that fear him.

10 The young lions do lack, and suffer hunger: Rbut they that seek the LORD shall not want any good *thing*.   [84:11]

11 Come, ye children, hearken unto me: I will teach you the fear of the LORD.

12 What man *is* he *that* desireth life, *and* loveth *many* days, that he may see good?

13 RKeep thy tongue from evil, and thy lips from speaking guile.   Prov. 13:3

14 RDepart from evil, and do good; seek peace, and pursue it.   Is. 1:16, 17

15 RThe eyes of the LORD *are* upon the righteous, and his ears *are* open unto their cry.   [33:18]

16 RThe face of the LORD *is* against them that do evil, to cut off the remembrance of them from the earth.   Jer. 44:11

17 *The righteous* Rcry, and the LORD Theareth, and Tdelivereth them out of all their troubles.   *v. 6 • has heard • has rescued*

18 RThe LORD *is* nigh Runto them that are

of a broken heart; and saveth such as be of a contrite spirit.   [145:18] • Is. 61:1

19 RMany *are* the afflictions of the righteous: but the LORD delivereth him out of them all.   71:20; [2 Tim. 3:11, 12]

20 RHe keepeth all his bones: not one of them is broken.   John 19:33, 36 ✶

21 Evil shall slay the wicked: and they that hate the righteous shall be desolate.

22 The LORD Rredeemeth the soul of his servants: and none of them that trust in him shall be desolate.   71:23

PSALM 35

Petition for God's Intervention

A Psalm of David.

PLEADT *my cause*, O LORD, with them that strive with me: fight against them that fight against me.   *defend*

2 TTake hold of shield and buckler, and stand up for mine help.   *put armour on*

3 Draw out also the spear, and stop *the* way against them that persecute me: say unto my soul, I Ram thy salvation.   [62:2]

4 RLet them be Tconfounded and put to shame that seek after my soul: let them be turned back and brought to confusion that devise my hurt.   70:2 • *ashamed*

5 Let them be as chaff before the wind: and let the angel of the LORD chase *them*.

6 Let their way be dark and slippery: and let the angel of the LORD persecute them.

7 For without cause have they Rhid for me their net *in* a pit, *which* without cause they have digged for my soul.   69:4

8 Let Rdestruction come upon him at unawares; and let his net that he hath hid catch himself: into that very destruction let him fall.   [55:23]; Is. 47:11

9 And my soul shall be joyful in the LORD: it shall rejoice in his salvation.

10 All my bones shall say, LORD, Rwho *is* like unto thee, which deliverest the poor from him that is too strong for him, yea, the poor and the needy from him that spoileth him?   [Ex. 15:11; Mic. 7:18]

11 RFalse witnesses did rise up; they laid to my charge *things* that I knew not. Mark 14:57 ✶

12 RThey rewarded me evil for good *to* the Tspoiling of my soul.   John 10:32 • *bereaving*

13 But as for me, Rwhen they were sick, my clothing *was* sackcloth: I humbled my soul with fasting; and my prayer returned into mine own bosom.   Job 30:25

14 I behaved myself as though *he had been* my friend *or* brother: I Rbowed down heavily, as one that mourneth *for his* mother.   38:6

15 But in mine Tadversity they rejoiced, and gathered themselves together: *yea*, the Tabjects gathered themselves together

against me, and I knew *it* not; they did tear *me*, and ceased not: *halting · outcasts*

16 With hypocritical mockers in feasts, they gnashed upon me with their teeth.

17 Lord, how long wilt thou ᴿlook on? rescue my soul from their destructions, my darling from the lions.   [Hab. 1:13]

18 ᴿI will give thee thanks in the great congregation: I will praise thee among much people.   22:22

19 Let not them that are mine enemies wrongfully rejoice over me: *neither* let them ᴿwink with the eye that ᴿhate me without a cause.   Prov. 6:13; 10:10 · John 15:24, 25 ✶

20 For they speak not peace: but they ᴿdevise deceitful matters against *them that are* quiet in the land.   Jer. 9:8; Mic. 6:12

21 Yea, they opened their mouth wide against me, *and* said, ᴿAha, aha, our eye hath seen it.   40:15; 70:3

22 *This* thou hast seen, O Lᴏʀᴅ: keep not silence: O Lord, be not far from me.

23 ᴿStir up thyself, and awake to my judgment, *even* unto my cause, my God and my Lord.   7:6; 44:23

24 ᴿJudge me, O Lᴏʀᴅ my God, according to thy righteousness; and let them not rejoice over me.   9:4; 26:1

25 Let them not say in their hearts, Ah, so would we have it: let them not say, We have ᵀswallowed him up.   *put an end to*

26 Let them be ashamed and brought to confusion together that rejoice at mine hurt: let them be clothed with shame and dishonour that magnify *themselves* against me.

27 ᴿLet them shout for joy, and be glad, that favour my righteous cause: yea, let them say continually, Let the Lᴏʀᴅ be magnified, which hath pleasure in the prosperity of his servant.   Rom. 12:15

28 And my ᴿtongue shall speak of thy righteousness *and* of thy praise all the day long.   51:14; 71:15, 24

PSALM 36

The Excellent Lovingkindness of God

To the chief Musician, *A Psalm* of David, the servant of the Lᴏʀᴅ.

THE transgression of the wicked saith within my heart, *that* ᴿthere is no fear of God before his eyes.   Rom. 3:18

2 For he ᴿflattereth himself in his own eyes, until his iniquity be found to be hateful.   Deut. 29:19

3 ᴿThe words of his mouth *are* iniquity and deceit: ᴿhe hath left off to be wise, *and* to do good.   10:7 · 94:8; Jer. 4:22

4 ᴿHe deviseth mischief upon his bed; he setteth himself in a way *that is* not good; he abhorreth not evil.   Prov. 4:16

5 Thy ᴿmercy, O Lᴏʀᴅ, *is* in the heavens;

and thy faithfulness *reacheth* unto the clouds.   57:10; 103:11; 108:4

6 Thy righteousness *is* like the great mountains; thy judgments *are* a great deep: O Lᴏʀᴅ, thou preservest man and beast.

7 How ᵀexcellent *is* thy lovingkindness, O God! therefore the children of men put their trust under the shadow of thy wings. *precious*

8 They shall be abundantly satisfied with the fatness of thy house; and thou shalt make them drink of the river of thy pleasures.

9 ᴿFor with thee *is* the fountain of life: in thy light shall we see light.   [Jer. 2:13]

10 O continue thy lovingkindness unto them ᴿthat know thee; and thy righteousness to the upright in heart.   [Jer. 22:16]

11 Let not the foot of pride come against me, and let not the hand of the wicked ᵀremove me.   *drive me away*

12 There are the workers of iniquity fallen: they are cast down, ᴿand shall not be able to rise.   140:10; Is. 26:14

PSALM 37

"Rest in the Lᴏʀᴅ"

A Psalm of David.

FRET ᴿnot thyself because of evildoers, neither be thou envious against the workers of iniquity.   73:3; Prov. 3:31

2 For they shall soon be cut down like the grass, and wither as the green herb.

3 ᴿTrust in the Lᴏʀᴅ, and do good; *so* shalt thou ᴿdwell in the land, and verily thou shalt be fed.   [62:8] · [Deut. 30:20]

4 Delight thyself also in the Lᴏʀᴅ; and he shall give thee the desires of thine heart.

5 Commit thy way unto the Lᴏʀᴅ; trust also in him; and he shall bring *it* to pass.

6 ᴿAnd he shall bring forth thy righteousness as the light, and thy judgment as the noonday.   Job 11:17; [Is. 58:8, 10]

7 Rest in the Lᴏʀᴅ, and wait patiently for him: fret not thyself because of him who prospereth in his way, because of the man who bringeth wicked devices to pass.

8 Cease from anger, and forsake wrath: fret not thyself in any wise to do evil.

9 For evildoers shall be ᵀcut off: but those that wait upon the Lᴏʀᴅ, they shall ᴿinherit the earth.   *destroyed* · [Is. 57:13]

10 For yet a little while, and the wicked *shall* not *be:* yea, thou shalt diligently consider his place, and it *shall* not *be.*

11 ᴿBut the meek shall inherit the earth; and shall delight themselves in the ᴿabundance of peace.   Matt. 5:5 · 72:7

12 The wicked plotteth against the just, and gnasheth upon him with his teeth.

13 The Lᴏʀᴅ shall laugh at him: for he seeth that ᴿhis day is coming.   Job 18:20

14 The wicked have drawn out the sword,

and have bent their bow, to cast down the poor and needy, *and* to slay such as be of upright conversation.

15 Their sword shall enter into their own heart, and their bows shall be broken.

16 A little that a righteous man hath *is* better than the riches of many wicked.

17 For the ^Rarms of the wicked shall be broken: but the LORD upholdeth the righteous.   10:15; Job 38:15; Ezek. 30:21

18 The LORD ^Rknoweth the days of the upright: and their inheritance shall be for ever.   [1:6; 31:7]

19 They shall not be ashamed in the evil time: and in the ^Rdays of famine they shall be satisfied.   33:19

20 But the wicked shall perish, and the enemies of the LORD *shall be* ^Ras the fat of lambs: they shall consume; into smoke shall they consume away.   Lev. 3:11

21 The wicked borroweth, and payeth not again: but ^Rthe righteous ^Tsheweth mercy, and giveth.   112:5, 9 • *is gracious*

22 ^RFor *such as be* blessed of him shall inherit the earth; and *they that be* ^Rcursed of him shall be cut off.   [Prov. 3:33] • Job 5:3

23 The steps of a *good* man are ordered by the LORD: and he delighteth in his way.

24 ^RThough he fall, he shall not be utterly cast down: for the LORD upholdeth *him with* his hand.   [145:14]; Prov. 24:16

25 I have been young, and *now* am old; yet have ^RI not seen the righteous forsaken, nor his seed begging bread.   [Heb. 13:5]

26 ^RHe is ever merciful, and lendeth; and his ^Tseed *is* blessed.   v. 21 • *descendants*

27 ^RDepart from evil, and do good; and dwell for evermore.   34:14

28 ^RFor the LORD loveth ^Tjudgment, and forsaketh not his saints; they are preserved for ever: ^Rbut the seed of the wicked shall be cut off.   11:7 • *justice* • Is. 14:20

29 ^RThe righteous shall inherit the land, and dwell therein for ever.   Prov. 2:21

30 The mouth of the righteous speaketh wisdom, and his tongue talketh of judgment.

31 ^RThe law of his God *is* in his heart; none of his steps shall slide.   [Jer. 31:33]

32 The wicked ^Rwatcheth the righteous, and seeketh to slay him.   10:8

33 The LORD will not leave him in his hand, nor condemn him when he is judged.

34 ^RWait on the LORD, and keep his way, and he shall exalt thee to inherit the land: when the ^Rwicked are cut off, thou shalt see it.   [27:14] • 52:5

35 I have seen the wicked in great power, and spreading himself like a green bay tree.

36 Yet he passed away, and, lo, ^Rhe *was* not: yea, I sought him, but he could not be found.   Job 20:5

37 Mark the perfect *man*, and behold the upright: for the end of *that* man *is* peace.

38 ^RBut the transgressors shall be destroyed together: ^Rthe end of the wicked shall be cut off.   [1:4] • 73:17

39 But the ^Rsalvation of the righteous *is* of the LORD: *he is* their strength ^Rin the time of trouble.   [26:1] • [9:9]

40 And ^Rthe LORD shall help them, and deliver them: he shall deliver them from the wicked, and save them, because they trust in him.   Is. 31:5

PSALM 38

The Heavy Burden of Sin

A Psalm of David, to bring to remembrance.

O LORD, ^Rrebuke me not in thy wrath: neither chasten me in thy hot displeasure.   6:1

2 For thine arrows ^Tstick fast in me, and thy hand presseth me sore.   *sunk deep*

3 *There is* no soundness in my flesh because of thine anger; neither *is there any* rest in my bones because of my sin.

4 ^RFor mine iniquities are gone over mine head: as an heavy burden they are too heavy for me.   40:12; Ezra 9:6

5 My ^Twounds stink *and* are corrupt because of my foolishness.   *stripes*

6 I am troubled; I am bowed down greatly; I go mourning all the day long.

7 For my loins are filled with a ^Rloathsome ^T*disease:* and *there is* no soundness in my flesh.   102:3 • *burning*

8 ^RI am feeble and sore broken: I have ^Troared by reason of the disquietness of my heart.   Lam. 1:13; 5:17 • *groan*

9 Lord, ^Rall my desire *is* before thee; and my groaning is not hid from thee.   [10:17]

10 My heart panteth, ^Rmy strength faileth me: as for the light of mine eyes, it also is gone from me.   31:10

11 ^RMy lovers and my friends stand aloof from my sore; and ^Rmy kinsmen stand afar off.   88:18 • Luke 23:49

12 They also that seek after my life lay snares *for me:* ^Rand they that seek my hurt speak mischievous things, and imagine deceits all the day long.   Eccl. 10:13

13 ^RBut I, as a deaf *man*, ^Theard not; and *I was* as a dumb man *that* openeth not his mouth.   Matt. 26:62, 63; 27:12-14 ☆ • *hear not*

14 Thus I was as a man that heareth not, and in whose mouth *are* no reproofs.

15 For in thee, O LORD, ^Rdo I hope: thou wilt hear, O Lord my God.   39:7

16 For I said, *Hear me, lest otherwise* they should rejoice over me: when my foot slippeth, they magnify *themselves* against me.

17 For I *am* ready ^Tto halt, and my sorrow *is* continually before me.   *fall*

18 For I will declare mine iniquity; I will be ^Rsorry for my sin.   [2 Cor. 7:9, 10]

19 But mine enemies *are* [T]lively, *and* they are strong: and they that hate me wrongfully are multiplied.   *vigorous*

20 They also [R]that render evil for good are mine adversaries; because I follow *the thing that* good *is*.   35:12

21 Forsake me not, O LORD: O my God, be [R]not far from me.   22:19

22 Make [R]haste to help me, O Lord my salvation.   40:13

PSALM 39

Know the Measure of Man's Days

To the chief Musician, *even* to Je-du'-thun, A Psalm of David.

I SAID, [R]I will take heed to my ways, that I sin not with my tongue: I will keep my mouth with a bridle, while the wicked is before me.   1 Kin. 2:4; [James 3:2]

2 [R]I was dumb with silence, I held my peace, *even* from good; and my sorrow was [T]stirred.   38:13 · *grew worse*

3 [R]My heart was hot within me, while I was musing the fire burned: *then* spake I with my tongue,   32:4; Jer. 20:9

4 LORD, make me to know [R]mine end, and the measure of my days, what it *is; that* I may know how frail I *am*.   Job 6:11

5 Behold, thou hast made my days *as* an handbreadth; and mine age *is* as nothing before thee: verily every man at his best state *is* altogether vanity.   Selah.

6 Surely every man [R]walketh in a vain shew: surely they are disquieted in vain: he heapeth up *riches,* and knoweth not who shall gather them.   [1 Cor. 7:31]; James 1:10

7 And now, Lord, what wait I for? [R]my hope *is* in thee.   38:15

8 Deliver me from all my transgressions: make me not the reproach of the foolish.

9 [R]I was dumb, I opened not my mouth; because [R]thou didst *it*.   *v*. 2 · 2 Sam. 16:10

10 Remove thy stroke away from me: I am consumed by the blow of thine hand.

11 When thou with rebukes dost correct man for iniquity, thou makest his beauty [R]to consume away like a moth: surely every man *is* vanity.   Selah.   Job 13:28

12 Hear my prayer, O LORD, and give ear unto my cry; hold not thy peace at my tears: for I *am* a stranger with thee, *and* a sojourner, as all my fathers *were*.

13 O spare me, that I may recover strength, before I go hence, and be no more.

PSALM 40

Delight to Do God's Will

To the chief Musician, A Psalm of David.

I WAITED patiently for the LORD; and he inclined unto me, and heard my cry.

2 He brought me up also out of an horrible pit, out of the miry clay, and set my feet upon a rock, *and* established my goings.

3 And he hath put a new song in my mouth, *even* praise unto our God: many shall see *it,* and fear, and shall trust in the LORD.

4 [T]Blessed *is* that man that maketh the LORD his trust, and respecteth not the proud, nor such as turn aside to lies.   *happy*

5 [R]Many, O LORD my God, *are* thy wonderful works *which* thou hast done, and thy thoughts *which are* to us-ward: they cannot be reckoned up in order unto thee: *if* I would declare and speak *of them,* they are more than can be numbered.   [Job 5:8, 9]

6 [R]Sacrifice and offering thou didst not desire; mine ears hast thou opened: burnt offering and sin offering hast thou not required.   [1 Sam. 15:22]; Is. 1:11; Heb. 10:5, 6

7 Then said I, Lo, I come: in the volume of the book *it is* written of me,

8 I delight to do thy will, O my God: yea, thy law *is* [R]within my heart.   [2 Cor. 3:3]

9 I have preached righteousness in the

40:8 We Know God's Will Through His Word—Knowing the will of God must not be thought of merely as finding a certain vocation in life. That aspect represents only a small part of God's will. Rather, the will of God is for everyone to live in conformity to His revealed will in His Word.

a. First of all, and most important, the will of God means believing in Christ (Page 1049—John 6:40). If we do not take this first step in doing God's will, we will not be saved from judgment (Page 947—Matt. 7:21; 12:50); if we do, we will live forever (Page 1250—1 John 2:17).

b. Second, there are clear statements of Scripture which teach that God's will for every Christian includes sanctification (Page 1185—1 Thess. 4:3), giving thanks to God (Page 1185—1 Thess. 5:18), doing good (Page 1237—1 Pet. 2:15), and suffering for doing the right thing (Page 1238—1 Pet. 3:17).

c. Third, the Bible is God's will and must be applied to our lives (Page 207—Deut. 29:29). This fact involves commands to be obeyed, principles to be followed, prohibitions of things to be avoided, and living examples to be imitated or shunned. An attitude of delightful desire should fill all attempts to do God's will (Ps. 40:8). God takes great joy in those who cheerfully do His will.

Although the Bible is a complete revelation of God's will, there are always decisions we must make that are not covered by specific statements of Scripture. In order to know God's will in such instances we must be in fellowship with the Lord (Page 1249—1 John 1:6, 7), seek principles from the Word (Page

great congregation: lo, I have not refrained my lips, O LORD, thou knowest.

10 I have not hid thy righteousness within my heart; I have declared thy faithfulness and thy salvation: I have not concealed thy lovingkindness and thy truth from the great congregation.

11 Withhold not thou thy tender mercies from me, O LORD: let thy lovingkindness and thy truth continually preserve me.

12 For innumerable evils have compassed me about: Rmine iniquities have taken hold upon me, so that I am not able to look up; they are more than the hairs of mine head: therefore my heart Rfaileth me. [65:3] • [73:26]

13 Be pleased, O LORD, to deliver me: O LORD, make Rhaste to help me. 71:12

14 RLet them be ashamed and confounded together that seek after my soul to destroy it; let them be driven backward and put to shame that wish me evil. 70:2

15 Let them be desolate for a reward of their shame that say unto me, Aha, aha.

16 Let all those that seek thee rejoice and be glad in thee: let such as love thy salvation Rsay continually, The LORD be magnified. 35:27

17 But I am poor and needy; yet the Lord thinketh upon me: thou art my help and my deliverer; make no tarrying, O my God.

PSALM 41

The Blessedness of Helping the Poor

To the chief Musician, A Psalm of David.

BLESSED is he that Rconsidereth the poor: the LORD will deliver him Rin time of trouble. [Prov. 14:21] • 27:5

2 The LORD will Tpreserve him, and keep him alive; and he shall be blessed upon the earth: and thou wilt not deliver him unto the will of his enemies. *protect*

3 The LORD will strengthen him upon the bed of Tlanguishing: thou wilt Tmake all his bed in his sickness. *sickness • restore*

4 I said, LORD, be merciful unto me: heal Rmy soul; for I have sinned against thee. 103:3

5 Mine enemies speak evil of me, When shall he die, and his name perish?

6 And if he come to see me, he speaketh vanity: his heart gathereth iniquity to itself; when he goeth abroad, he telleth it.

7 All that hate me whisper together against me: against me do they Rdevise my hurt. 56:5

8 TAn evil disease, say they, cleaveth fast unto him: and now that he lieth he Rshall rise up no more. *a thing of Belial* • 71:10, 11

9 RYea, mine own familiar friend, in whom I trusted, which did eat of my bread, hath lifted up his heel against me. John 13:18; 17:12 ✩

10 But thou, O LORD, be merciful unto me, and raise me up, that I may requite them.

11 By this I know that Rthou favourest me, because mine enemy doth not triumph over me. [147:11]

12 And as for me, thou upholdest me in mine integrity, and Rsettest me before thy face for ever. [Job 36:7]

13 RBlessed be the LORD God of Israel from everlasting, and to everlasting. A-men', and A-men'. 72:18, 19

BOOK II

PSALM 42

Seek After the Lord

To the chief Musician, Mas'-chil, for the sons of Ko'-rah.

AS the hart panteth after the water brooks, so panteth my soul after thee, O God.

2 RMy soul thirsteth for God, for the living God: when shall I come and appear before God? Josh. 3:10; [Jer. 10:10]

3 RMy tears have been my meat day and night, while they continually say unto me, Where is thy God? 80:5

4 When I remember these things, I pour out my soul in me: for I had gone with the multitude, I went with them to the house of God, with the voice of joy and praise, with a multitude that kept holyday.

5 RWhy art thou cast down, O my soul? and why art thou disquieted in me? hope thou in God: for I shall yet praise him for the help of his countenance. 38:6

6 O my God, my soul is cast down within me: therefore will I remember thee from the Rland of Jordan, and of the Her'-mon-ites, from the hill Mi'-zar. 2 Sam. 17:22

7 Deep calleth unto deep at the noise of thy waterspouts: Rall thy waves and thy billows are gone over me. 69:1, 2

1132—1 Cor. 10:6), obtain advice from godly counselors (Page 622—Prov. 11:14; 15:22; 24:6), use common sense, and remember that God works through our own minds and desires to do His will (Page 1171—Phil. 2:13). When none of these principles seem to work, we must simply make the best possible decision, realizing that God will shut the door if it is not His will. Paul, for example, planned to go and see the Roman Christians, although not knowing if God would actually permit it in His will (Page 1121—Rom. 15:22–32). In most cases, however, the believer who thoroughly searches the Word will find the basis for an intelligent decision.
 Now turn to Page 210—Deut. 32:7: God's Work in the Past.

8 *Yet* the LORD will command his loving-kindness in the daytime, and ᴿin the night his song *shall be* with me, *and* my prayer unto the God of my life.　　149:5; Job 35:10

9 I will say unto God my rock, Why hast thou forgotten me? why go I mourning because of the oppression of the enemy?

10 *As* with a sword in my bones, mine enemies reproach me; ᴿwhile they say daily unto me, Where *is* thy God?　　*v.* 3

11 ᴿWhy art thou cast down, O my soul? and why art thou disquieted within me? hope thou in God: for I shall yet praise him, *who is* the ᵀhealth of my countenance, and my God.　　43:5 • *salvation*

PSALM 43

"Hope in God"

JUDGE me, O God, and plead my cause against an ungodly nation: O deliver me from the deceitful and unjust man.

2 For thou *art* the God of my strength: why dost thou cast me off? why go I mourning because of the oppression of the enemy?

3 O send out thy light and thy truth: let them lead me; let them bring me unto thy holy hill, and to thy tabernacles.

4 Then will I go unto the altar of God, unto God my exceeding joy: yea, upon the harp will I praise thee, O God my God.

5 ᴿWhy art thou cast down, O my soul? and why art thou disquieted within me? hope in God: for I shall yet praise him, *who is* ᵀthe health of my countenance, and my God.　　42:11 • *salvation*

PSALM 44

Prayer for Deliverance by God

To the chief Musician for the sons of Ko'-rah, Mas'-chil.

WE have heard with our ears, O God, our fathers have told us, *what* work thou didst in their days, in the times of old.

2 *How* thou didst drive out the heathen with thy hand, and plantedst them; *how* thou didst afflict the people, and cast them out.

3 For they got not the land in possession by their own sword, neither did their own arm save them: but thy right hand, and thine arm, and the light of thy countenance, because thou hadst a favour unto them.

4 ᴿThou art my King, O God: command deliverances for Jacob.　　[74:12]

5 Through thee will we push down our enemies: through thy name will we tread them under that rise up against us.

6 For ᴿI will not trust in my bow, neither shall my sword save me.　　33:16

7 ᴿBut thou hast saved us from our enemies, and hast put them to shame that hated us.　　[136:24]

8 ᴿIn God we boast all the day long, and praise thy name for ever.　　Selah.　　34:2

9 But thou hast cast off, and put us to shame; and goest not forth with our armies.

10 Thou makest us to ᴿturn back from the enemy: and they which hate us spoil for themselves.　　Lev. 26:17; Josh. 7:8

11 ᴿThou hast given us like sheep *appointed* for ᵀmeat; and hast ᴿscattered us among the heathen.　　*v.* 22 • *food* • Deut. 4:27

12 Thou sellest thy people for nought, and dost not increase *thy wealth* by their price.

13 ᴿThou makest us a reproach to our neighbours, a scorn and a derision to them that are round about us.　　Deut. 28:37

14 ᴿThou makest us a byword among the heathen, a shaking of the head among the people.　　Job 17:6; Jer. 24:9

15 My confusion *is* continually before me, and ᴿthe shame of my face hath covered me,　　69:7; 2 Chr. 32:21

16 For the voice of him that reproacheth and blasphemeth; ᴿby reason of the enemy and avenger.　　8:2

17 ᴿAll this is come upon us; yet have we not forgotten thee, neither have we dealt falsely in thy covenant.　　Dan. 9:13

18 Our heart is not turned back, neither have our steps declined from thy way;

19 Though thou hast sore broken us in ᴿthe place of dragons, and covered us ᴿwith the shadow of death.　　Job 30:29 • Job 3:5

20 If we have forgotten the name of our God, or ᴿstretchedᵀ out our hands to ᴿa strange god;　　Deut. 6:14 • *worshipped* • 81:9

21 ᴿShall not God search this out? for he knoweth the secrets of the heart.　　[139:1, 2]

22 ᴿYea, for thy sake are we killed all the day long; we are counted as ᴿsheep for the slaughter.　　Rom. 8:36 • [Is. 53:7]; Jer. 12:3

23 Awake, ᴿwhy sleepest thou, O Lord? arise, cast *us* not off for ever.　　78:65

24 Wherefore hidest thou thy face, *and* forgettest our affliction and our oppression?

25 For our soul is bowed down to the dust: our belly cleaveth unto the earth.

26 Arise ᵀfor our help, and ᴿredeem us for thy mercies' sake.　　*a help for us* • 6:4; 25:22

PSALM 45

The Psalm of the Great King

To the chief Musician upon Sho-shan'-nim, for the sons of Ko'-rah, Mas'-chil, A Song of loves.

MY heart is ᵀinditing a good matter: I speak of the things which I have made touching the king: my tongue *is* the pen of a ready writer.　　*overflowing with*

2 Thou art fairer than the children of men: ^Rgrace is poured into thy lips: therefore God hath blessed thee for ever.   21:6

3 Gird thy sword upon *thy* thigh, O *most* mighty, with thy glory and thy majesty.

4 And in thy majesty ride prosperously because of truth and meekness *and* righteousness; and thy right hand shall teach thee ^Tterrible things.   *wonderful*

5 Thine ^Rarrows *are* sharp ^Rin the heart of the king's enemies; *whereby* the people fall under thee.   18:14; 120:4 • 2 Sam. 18:14

6 Thy throne,^R O God, *is* for ever and ever: the sceptre of thy kingdom *is* a ^Tright ^Rsceptre.   [93:2]; Heb. 1:8, 9 • *true* • [98:9]

7 Thou ^Rlovest righteousness, and hatest wickedness: therefore God, thy God, hath ^Ranointed thee with the oil of gladness above thy fellows.   [11:7; 33:5] • 2:2

8 All thy garments *smell* of myrrh, and aloes, *and* cassia, out of the ivory palaces, whereby they have made thee glad.

9 Kings' daughters *were* among thy honourable women: upon thy right hand did stand the queen in gold of O'-phir.

10 Hearken, O daughter, and consider, and ^Tincline thine ear; forget also thine own people, and thy father's house;   *listen*

11 So shall the king greatly desire thy beauty: for he *is* thy ^RLord; and ^Rworship thou him.   Gen. 18:12; 1 Pet. 3:6 • Eph. 5:33

12 And the daughter of Tyre *shall be there* with a gift; *even* ^Rthe rich among the people shall intreat thy favour.   Is. 49:23

13 The king's daughter *is* all glorious within: her clothing *is* of wrought gold.

14 She shall be ^Rbrought unto the king in ^Rraiment of needlework: the virgins her companions that follow her shall be brought unto thee.   Song 1:4 • Judg. 5:30

15 With ^Rgladness and rejoicing shall they be brought: they shall enter into the king's palace.   Acts 2:46

16 Instead of thy fathers shall be thy children, ^Rwhom thou mayest make princes in all the earth.   [1 Pet. 2:9; Rev. 1:6]

17 I will make thy name to be remembered in all generations: therefore shall the people praise thee for ever and ever.

PSALM 46

"God Is Our Refuge and Strength"

To the chief Musician for the sons
of Ko'-rah, A Song upon Al'-a-moth.

GOD is our refuge and strength, ^Ra very present help in trouble.   [Deut. 4:7]

2 Therefore will not we fear, though the earth be removed, and though the mountains be carried into the midst of the sea;

3 ^RThough the waters thereof roar *and* be

troubled, *though* the mountains shake with the swelling thereof.   Selah.   93:3, 4

4 *There is* a river, the streams whereof shall make glad the city of God, the holy *place* of the tabernacles of the most High.

5 God *is* ^Rin the midst of her; she shall not be moved: God shall help her, *and that* right early.   [Deut. 23:14; Is. 12:6]

6 ^RThe heathen raged, the kingdoms were moved: ^Rhe uttered his voice, the earth ^Rmelted.   2:1, 2 • 18:13; Joel 2:11 • Amos 9:5

7 The LORD of hosts ^R*is* with us; the God of Jacob *is* our refuge.   Selah.   Num. 14:9

8 Come, behold the works of the LORD, what desolations he hath made in the earth.

9 ^RHe maketh wars to cease unto the end of the earth; he breaketh the bow, and cutteth the spear in sunder; he burneth the chariot in the fire.   Ezek. 39:9

10 Be still, and ^Rknow that I *am* God: ^RI will be exalted among the heathen, I will be exalted in the earth.   [100:3] • [Is. 2:11, 17]

11 ^RThe LORD of hosts *is* with us; the God of Jacob *is* our refuge.   Selah.   [Deut. 23:14]

PSALM 47

The Lord Shall Subdue All Nations

To the chief Musician,
A Psalm for the sons of Ko'-rah.

O CLAP your hands, all ye people; shout unto God with the voice of triumph.

2 For the LORD most high *is* terrible; *he is* a great King over all the earth.

3 ^RHe shall subdue the people under us, and the nations under our feet.   18:47

4 He shall choose our ^Rinheritance for us, the ^Rexcellency of Jacob whom he loved. Selah.   [1 Pet. 1:4] • Amos 6:8; 8:7; Nah. 2:2

5 God is ^Rgone up with a shout, the LORD with the sound of a trumpet.   68:18, 25

6 ^RSing praises to God, sing praises: sing praises unto our King, sing praises.   68:4

7 For God *is* the King of all the earth: sing ye praises with understanding.

8 God reigneth over the heathen: God sitteth upon the throne of his holiness.

9 The princes of the people are gathered together, *even* the people of the God of Abraham: for the shields of the earth *belong* unto God: he is greatly exalted.

PSALM 48

The Praise of Mount Zion

A Song *and* Psalm for the sons of Ko'-rah.

GREAT *is* the LORD, and greatly to be praised in the ^Rcity of our God, ^R*in* the mountain of his holiness.   46:4 • 2:6

2 Beautiful for situation, the joy of the

whole earth, *is* mount Zion, *on* the sides of the north, the city of the great King.

3 God Tis known in her palaces for a Rrefuge.   *has made himself known* • 46:7

4 For, lo, Rthe kings were assembled, they passed by together.   2 Sam. 10:6–19

5 They saw *it, and* so they marvelled; they were troubled, *and* hasted away.

6 Fear Rtook hold upon them there, *and* pain, as of a woman in travail.   Ex. 15:15

7 Thou breakest the Rships of Tar'-shish with an east wind.   1 Kin. 10:22

8 As we have heard, so have we seen in the Rcity of the LORD of hosts, in the city of our God: God will Restablish it for ever. Selah.   46:4; 87:3; Matt. 5:35 • 87:5; [Is. 2:2]

9 We have thought of thy lovingkindness, O God, in the midst of thy temple.

10 According to thy name, O God, so *is* thy praise unto the ends of the earth: thy right hand is full of righteousness.

11 Let mount RZion rejoice, let the Tdaughters of Judah be glad, because of thy judgments.   97:8 • *cities*

12 Walk about Zion, and go round about her: Ttell the towers thereof.   *number*

13 TMark ye well her bulwarks, consider her palaces; that ye may tell *it* to the generation following.   *set your heart to*

14 For this God *is* our God for ever and ever: he will be our guide *even* unto death.

PSALM 49

Riches Cannot Redeem

To the chief Musician,
A Psalm for the sons of Ko'-rah.

HEAR Rthis, all *ye* people; give ear, all *ye* inhabitants of the world: 78:1

2 Both Rlow and high, rich and Tpoor, Ttogether.   62:9 • *helpless* • *alike*

3 My mouth shall speak of Rwisdom; and the meditation of my heart *shall be* of Runderstanding.   37:30 • [119:130]

4 I will incline mine ear to a parable: I will open my dark saying upon the harp.

5 Wherefore should I Rfear in the days of evil, *when* the iniquity of my heels shall Tcompass me about?   23:4; 27:1 • *surround*

6 They that Rtrust in their wealth, and boast themselves in the multitude of their riches;   Job 31:24; [Prov. 11:28; Mark 10:24]

7 TNone *of them* can by any means Rredeem his brother, nor Rgive to God a ransom for him: *no man* • Matt. 25:8, 9 • Job 36:18, 19

8 (For the redemption of their soul *is* Tprecious, and it ceaseth for ever:)   *costly*

9 That he should still live for ever, *and* Rnot T see corruption.   89:48 • *be destroyed*

10 For he seeth *that* wise men die, likewise the fool and the brutish person perish, and leave their wealth to others.

11 Their inward thought *is, that* their houses *shall continue* for ever, *and* their dwelling places to all generations; they call *their* lands after their own names.

12 Nevertheless man *being* in honour abideth not: he is like the beasts *that* perish.

13 This their way *is* their folly: yet their posterity approve their sayings.   Selah.

14 Like sheep they are laid in the grave; death shall feed on them; and the upright shall have dominion over them in the morning; and their beauty shall consume in the grave from their dwelling.

15 RBut God Rwill redeem my soul from the power of the grave: for he shall receive me. Selah.   Acts 2:31, 32 ✶ • [16:10]; 56:13; [Hos. 13:14]

16 Be not thou afraid when one is made rich, when the glory of his house is increased;

17 RFor when he dieth he shall carry nothing away: Rhis glory shall not descend after him.   17:14; 1 Tim. 6:7 • Is. 5:14

18 TThough while he lived he blessed This soul: and *men* will praise thee, when thou doest well to thyself.   *for* • *himself*

19 He shall go to the generation of his fathers; they shall never see light.

20 Man *that is* in honour, and understandeth not, is like the beasts *that* perish.

PSALM 50

The Lord Shall Judge All People

A Psalm of A'-saph.

THE Rmighty God, *even* the LORD, hath spoken, and called the earth Tfrom the rising of the sun unto the going down thereof.   Is. 9:6 • *throughout the whole day*

2 Out of Zion, the perfection of beauty, RGod hath shined.   80:1; 94:1; Deut. 33:2

3 Our God shall Rcome, and shall not keep silence: Ra fire shall Tdevour before him, and it shall be very tempestuous round about him.   [96:13] • [97:3] • *destroy*

4 RHe shall call to the heavens from above, and to the earth, that he may judge his people.   Deut. 4:26; 31:28; 32:1; Is. 1:2

5 Gather Rmy saints together unto me; Rthose that have made a covenant with me by Rsacrifice.   Deut. 33:3 • Ex. 24:7 • 50:8

6 And Rthe heavens shall declare his righteousness: for God *is* judge himself. Selah.   89:5; 97:6

7 RHear, O my people, and I will speak; O Israel, and I will testify against thee: RI *am* God, *even* thy God.   49:1 • Ex. 20:2

8 RI will not Treprove thee for thy sacrifices or thy burnt offerings, *to have been* continually before me.   Jer. 7:22 • *rebuke*

9 I will take no bullock out of thy house, *nor* he goats out of thy folds.

10 For every beast of the forest *is* mine, *and* the cattle upon a thousand hills.

11 I know all the fowls of the mountains: and the wild beasts of the field *are* mine.

12 If I were hungry, I would not tell thee: for the ᴿworld *is* mine, and the fulness thereof.   [Deut. 10:14; Job 41:11]; 1 Cor. 10:26

13 Will I eat the flesh of ᴿbulls, or drink the blood of goats?   *v. 9*

14 ᴿOffer unto God thanksgiving; and pay thy vows unto the most High: 27:6

15 And ᴿcall upon me in the day of trouble: I will ᴿdeliver thee, and thou shalt glorify me.   91:15; 107:6; [Zech. 13:9] • 81:7

16 But unto the wicked God saith, What hast thou to do to ᵀdeclare my statutes, or *that* thou shouldest take my ᵀcovenant in thy mouth?   *profess to obey • agreement*

17 ᴿSeeing thou hatest instruction, and castest my words behind thee.   Rom. 2:21

18 When thou sawest a thief, then thou consentedst with him, and hast been ᴿpartaker with adulterers.   1 Tim. 5:22

19 Thou givest thy mouth to evil, and ᴿthy tongue frameth deceit.   36:3; 52:2

20 Thou sittest *and* ᴿspeakest against thy brother; thou ᴿslanderest thine own mother's son.   Job 19:18; Matt. 10:21 • Amos 7:10

21 These *things* hast thou done, and I kept silence; thou thoughtest that I was altogether *such an one* as thyself: *but* I ᴿwill ᵀreprove thee, and set *them* ᵀin order before thine eyes.   [90:8] • *rebuke • in detail*

22 Now consider this, ye that ᴿforget God, lest I ᴿtear *you* in pieces, and *there be* none to deliver.   [9:17; Job 8:13] • 7:2

23 Whoso offereth praise glorifieth me: and to him that ordereth *his* conversation *aright* will I shew the salvation of God.

PSALM 51

Confession and Forgiveness of Sin

To the chief Musician, A Psalm of David, when Nathan the prophet came unto him, after he had gone in to Bath-she′-ba.

HAVE mercy upon me, O God, according to thy lovingkindness: according unto the multitude of thy tender mercies ᴿblot out my transgressions.   [Is. 43:25]

2 Wash me throughly from mine iniquity, and cleanse me from my sin.

3 For I ᴿacknowledge my transgressions: and my sin *is* ever before me.   Is. 59:12

4 Against thee, thee only, have I sinned, and done *this* evil in thy sight: that thou mightest be justified when thou speakest, *and* be ᵀclear when thou judgest.   *pure*

5 Behold, I was ᴿshapen in iniquity; and in sin did my mother conceive me.   [58:3]

6 Behold, thou desirest ᴿtruth in the inward parts: and in the hidden *part* thou shalt make me to know wisdom.   Job 38:36

7 ᴿPurge me with hyssop, and I shall be clean: wash me, and I shall be ᴿwhiter than snow.   Num. 19:18; Heb. 9:19 • [Is. 1:18]

8 Make me to hear ᴿjoy and gladness; *that* the bones *which* thou hast broken ᴿmay rejoice.   Is. 35:10; Joel 1:16 • [Matt. 5:4]

9 ᴿHide thy face from my sins, and blot out all mine iniquities.   [Is. 38:17; Jer. 16:17]

10 Create in me a clean heart, O God; and renew a right spirit within me.

11 Cast me not away from thy presence; and take not thy holy spirit from me.

12 Restore unto me the joy of thy salvation; and uphold me *with thy* ᴿfreeᵀ spirit.   110:3 • *willing*

13 *Then* will I ᴿteach transgressors thy ways; and sinners shall be ᴿconverted unto thee.   [Prov. 11:30]; Acts 9:21, 22 • [22:27]

14 Deliver me from bloodguiltiness, O God, thou God of my salvation: *and* my tongue shall sing aloud of thy righteousness.

15 O Lord, ᴿopen thou my lips; and my mouth shall shew forth thy praise.   Ex. 4:15

16 For ᴿthou desirest not ᴿsacrifice; else would I give *it*: thou delightest not in burnt offering.   40:6 • 50:8; [1 Sam. 15:22]

17 ᴿThe sacrifices of God *are* a broken spirit: a broken and a contrite heart, O God, thou wilt not despise.   [Is. 57:15]

18 Do good in thy good pleasure unto Zion: build thou the walls of Jerusalem.

19 Then shalt thou be pleased with ᴿthe sacrifices of righteousness, with burnt offering and whole burnt offering: then shall they offer bullocks upon thine altar.   4:5

51:2 What Sin Is—In dealing with sin it is important to know what sin is. If asked to define sin, people will come up with many different definitions as to what sin is—usually the things that the individual does not like. One of the most common definitions of sin is *missing the mark*—a failure to live up to an expected standard. The problem with this definition is that it fails to take into account that when the mark is missed, something is hit. Another definition of sin is found in First John 3:4, "Sin is the transgression of the law." Put simply according to this verse, sin is anything that is contrary to what the Word of God commands or forbids. This definition, however, does not take into account those things about which the Word of God is silent. The best definition for sin is found in First John 5:17, "All unrighteousness is sin."

Now turn to Page 698—Is. 59:2: What Sin Does.

PSALM 52

The Lord Shall Judge the Deceitful

To the chief Musician, Mas'-chil,
A *Psalm* of David, when Do'-eg the
E'-dom-ite came and told Saul, and said
unto him, David is come to the house of
A-him'-e-lech.

W HY boastest thou thyself in mischief, O
mighty man? the goodness of God
endureth continually.

2 Thy tongue Rdeviseth mischiefs; like a
sharp rasor, working deceitfully.   5:9

3 Thou Rlovest evil more than good; *and*
Rlying rather than to speak righteousness.
Selah.   36:4; 64:3 • [58:3]; Jer. 9:5

4 Thou lovest all devouring words, TO *thou*
deceitful tongue.   *and the*

5 God shall likewise destroy thee for ever,
he shall take thee away, and pluck thee out
of *thy* dwelling place, and root thee out of the
land of the living.   Selah.

6 The righteous also shall Rsee, and fear,
and shall laugh at him: [37:34]; 40:3

7 Lo, *this is* the man *that* made not God his
strength; but Rtrusted in the abundance of his
riches, *and* Rstrengthened himself in his wickedness.   49:6 • 10:6

8 But I *am* Rlike a green olive tree in the
house of God: I trust in the mercy of God for
ever and ever.   92:12; 128:3; Jer. 11:16

9 RI will praise thee for ever, because thou
hast done *it*: and I will wait on thy name; for
it is good before thy saints.   30:12

PSALM 53

A Portrait of the Godless

To the chief Musician upon Ma'-ha-lath,
Mas'-chil, *A Psalm* of David.

T HE Rfool hath said in his heart, *There is*
no God. Corrupt are they, and have done
abominable iniquity: *there is* none that doeth
good.   14:1-7; Rom. 3:10

2 God looked down from heaven upon the
children of men, to see if there were *any* that
did understand, that did seek God.

3 REvery one of them is gone back: they
are altogether become filthy; *there is* none
that doeth good, no, not one.   [130:3]

4 Have the workers of iniquity no knowledge? who eat up my people *as* they eat
bread: they have not called upon God.

5 There were they in great fear, Rwhere no
fear was: for God hath scattered the bones of
him that encampeth *against* thee: thou hast
put *them* to shame, because God hath despised them.   Lev. 26:17

6 Oh that the salvation of Israel *were come*
out of Zion! When God bringeth back the
captivity of his people, Jacob shall rejoice,
and Israel shall be glad.

PSALM 54

The Lord Is Our Helper

To the chief Musician on Neg'-i-noth,
Mas'-chil, *A Psalm* of David, when the
Ziph'-ims came and said to Saul, Doth not
David hide himself with us?

S AVE me, O God, by thy name, and judge
me by Rthy strength.   [2 Chr. 20:6]

2 RHear my prayer, O God; Rgive ear to the
words of my mouth.   17:6; 55:1 • 5:1

3 For strangers are risen up against me,
and oppressors seek after my soul: they have
not set God before them.   Selah.

4 Behold, God *is* mine helper: the Lord *is*
with them that uphold my soul.

5 He shall reward evil unto mine enemies:
Tcut them off in thy truth.   *destroy*

6 I will freely sacrifice unto thee: I will
praise thy name, O LORD; for *it is* good.

7 For he hath delivered me out of all
trouble: and mine eye hath seen This *desire*
upon mine enemies.   *judgment*

PSALM 55

"Cast Thy Burden upon the LORD"

To the chief Musician on Neg'-i-noth,
Mas'-chil, *A Psalm* of David.

G IVE ear to my prayer, O God; and Rhide
not thyself from my supplication.   27:9

2 Attend unto me, and hear me: I mourn in
my complaint, and make a noise;

3 Because of the voice of the enemy, because of the oppression of the wicked: Rfor
they cast iniquity upon me, and Rin wrath
they hate me.   2 Sam. 16:7, 8 • 71:11

4 My heart is sore pained within me: and
the terrors of death are fallen upon me.

5 Fearfulness and trembling are come
upon me, and horror hath overwhelmed me.

6 And I said, Oh that I had wings like a
dove! *for then* would I fly away, and Rbe at
rest.   116:7; Job 3:13

7 Lo, *then* would I wander far off, *and*
remain in the wilderness.   Selah.

8 I would hasten my escape from the
Rwindy storm *and* tempest.   Is. 4:6; 25:4; 29:6

9 Destroy, O Lord, *and* Tdivide their
tongues: for I have seen Rviolence and strife
in the city.   *bring confusion among them* • Jer. 6:7

10 Day and night they go about it upon the
walls thereof: Tmischief Ralso and sorrow *are*
in the midst of it.   *evil* • Prov. 1:16

11 Wickedness *is* in the midst thereof:
deceit and guile depart not from her streets.

12 For *it was* not an enemy *that* reproached me; then I could have borne *it*:
neither *was* it he that hated me *that* did
Rmagnify *himself* against me; then I would
have hid myself from him: 35:26

13 But *it was* thou, a man mine equal, my guide, and mine acquaintance.

14 We took sweet counsel together, *and* walked unto the house of God in company.

15 Let death seize upon them, *and* let them go down quick into hell: for wickedness *is* in their dwellings, *and* among them.

16 As for me, I will call upon God; and the LORD shall save me.

17 [R]Evening, and morning, and at noon, will I pray, and cry aloud: and he shall hear my voice.   141:4; Dan. 6:10; Acts 3:1

18 He hath delivered my soul in peace from the battle *that was* against me: for [R]there were many with me.   2 Chr. 32:7, 8

19 God shall hear, and afflict them, [R]even he that abideth of old.   Selah.   Because they have [T]no changes, therefore they fear not God.   [90:2] • *do not change*

20 He hath put forth his hands against such as [R]be at peace with him: he hath broken his [T]covenant.   7:4 • *agreement*

21 *The words* of his mouth were smoother than butter, but war *was* in his heart: his words were softer than oil, yet *were* they [T]drawn swords.   *ready to wound*

22 [R]Cast thy burden upon the LORD, and he shall sustain thee: he shall never suffer the righteous to be moved.   [37:5]

23 But thou, O God, shalt bring them down into the pit of destruction: bloody and deceitful men shall not live out half their days; but I will trust in thee.

PSALM 56

Fears in the Midst of Trials

To the chief Musician upon Jo'-nath-e'-lem-re-cho'-kim, Mich'-tam of David, when the Phi-lis'-tines took him in Gath.

B E merciful unto me, O God: for man would [R]swallow me up; he fighting daily [R]oppresseth me.   57:3 • 17:9

2 Mine enemies would daily [R]swallow *me* up: for *they* be many that fight against me, O thou most High.   57:3; 124:3

3 [T]What time I am [R]afraid, I will [R]trust in thee.   *when* • 55:4, 5 • 11:1; 57:1; Luke 17:5

4 In God I will praise his word, in God I have put my trust; [R]I will not fear what flesh can do unto me.   118:6; [Heb. 13:6]

5 Every day they [T]wrest my words: all their thoughts *are* against me for evil.   *twist*

6 They gather themselves together, they hide themselves, they [T]mark my steps, when they wait for my soul.   *watch*

7 Shall they escape by iniquity? in *thine* anger cast down the people, O God.

8 Thou [T]tellest my wanderings: put thou my tears [R]into thy bottle: *are they* not in thy book?   *records* • 39:12

9 [R]When I cry *unto thee*, [R]then shall mine enemies turn back: this I know; for [R]God *is* for me.   102:2 • 9:3 • [41:11; Rom. 8:31]

10 In God will I praise *his* word: in the LORD will I praise *his* word.

11 In God have I put my trust: I will not be afraid what man can do unto me.

12 Thy [R]vows[T] *are* upon me, O God: I will render praises unto thee.   50:14 • *promises*

13 For thou hast [R]delivered my soul from death: *wilt* not *thou deliver* my feet from falling, that I may walk before God in the light of the living?   33:19; 49:15; 86:13

PSALM 57

Prayers in the Midst of Perils

To the chief Musician, Al-tas'-chith, Mich'-tam of David, when he fled from Saul in the cave.

B E merciful unto me, O God, be merciful unto me: for my soul trusteth in thee: yea, in the shadow of thy wings will I make my refuge, until *these* calamities be overpast.

2 I will cry unto God most high; unto God that performeth *all things* for me.

3 He shall send from heaven, and save me *from* the reproach of him that would [T]swallow me up.   Selah.   God shall send forth his mercy and his truth.   *completely destroy*

4 My soul *is* among lions: *and* I lie *even* among them that are set on fire, *even* the sons of men, whose teeth *are* spears and arrows, and their tongue a sharp sword.

5 Be thou exalted, O God, above the heavens; *let* thy glory *be* above all the earth.

6 [R]They have prepared a net for my steps; my soul is bowed down: they have digged a pit before me, into the midst whereof they are fallen *themselves*.   Selah.   10:9

7 [R]My heart is fixed, O God, my heart is fixed: I will sing and give praise.   108:1

8 Awake up, my glory; awake, psaltery and harp: I *myself* will awake early.

9 I will praise thee, O Lord, among the people: I will [T]sing unto thee among the nations.   *sing praise*

10 For thy mercy *is* great unto the heavens, and thy truth unto the clouds.

11 Be thou exalted, O God, above the heavens: *let* thy glory *be* above all the earth.

PSALM 58

Wicked Judges Will Be Judged

To the chief Musician, Al-tas'-chith, Mich'-tam of David.

D O ye indeed speak righteousness, O congregation? do ye [R]judge uprightly, O ye sons of men?   82:2; [Deut. 16:20]

2 Yea, in heart ye [R]work wickedness; ye

[T]weigh[R] the violence of your hands in the earth.   Mal. 3:15 • *dispense* • 94:20

3 [R]The wicked are estranged from [T]the womb: they [R]go astray as soon as they be born, speaking lies.   [Is. 48:8] • *birth* • [53:3]

4 [R]Their poison *is* like the [R]poison of a serpent: *they are* like the deaf adder *that* stoppeth her ear;   Eccl. 10:11 • 140:3

5 Which will not hearken to the voice of charmers, charming never so wisely.

6 [R]Break[T] their teeth, O God, in their mouth: break out the great teeth of the young lions, O LORD.   Job 4:10 • *oppose them*

7 Let them melt away as waters *which* run continually: *when* he bendeth *his bow to shoot* his arrows, let them be as cut in pieces.

8 As a snail *which* melteth, let *every one of them* pass away: *like* the untimely birth of a woman, *that* they may not see the sun.

9 Before your pots can feel the thorns, he shall take them away as with a whirlwind, both living, and in *his* wrath.

10 The righteous shall rejoice when he seeth the vengeance: [R]he shall wash his feet in the blood of the wicked.   68:23

11 [R]So that a man shall say, Verily *there is* a reward for the righteous: verily he is a God that judgeth in the earth.   [18:20]

PSALM 59

Petition for Deliverance from Violent Men

To the chief Musician, Al-tas'-chith, Mich'-tam of David; when Saul sent, and they watched the house to kill him.

D ELIVER[R] me from mine enemies, O my God: [R]defend me from them that rise up against me.   143:9 • 20:1; 69:29; 71:4

2 Deliver me from the workers of iniquity, and save me from bloody men.

3 For, lo, they lie in wait for my soul: the mighty are gathered against me; not *for* my transgression, nor *for* my sin, O LORD.

4 They run and prepare themselves without *my* fault: awake to help me, and behold.

5 Thou therefore, [R]O LORD God of hosts, the God of Israel, awake to visit all the heathen: be not merciful to any wicked transgressors.   Selah.   69:6; 80:4; 84:8

6 [R]They return at evening: they [T]make a noise like a [R]dog, and go round about the city.   22:16 • *create disturbance* • Prov. 26:17

7 Behold, they belch out with their mouth: [R]swords *are* in their lips: for [R]who, *say they,* doth hear?   57:4 • 10:11

8 But thou, O LORD, shalt laugh at them; thou shalt have all the heathen in derision.

9 *Because of* his strength will I wait upon thee: [R]for God *is* my defence.   [62:2]

10 The God of my mercy shall [R]prevent[T] me: God shall let [R]me see *my desire* upon mine enemies.   21:3 • *anticipate* • 54:7

11 Slay them not, [R]lest my people forget: scatter them by thy power; and bring them down, O Lord our shield.   Deut. 4:9

12 [R]For the sin of their mouth and the words of their lips let them even be [R]taken in their pride: and for cursing and lying *which* they speak.   Prov. 12:13 • Zeph. 3:11

13 Consume *them* in wrath, consume *them,* that they *may* not *be:* and let them know that God ruleth in Jacob unto the ends of the earth.   Selah.

14 And [R]at evening let them return; *and* let them make a noise like a dog, and go round about the city.   *v.* 6

15 Let them wander up and down for meat, and grudge if they be not satisfied.

16 But I will [R]sing of thy power; yea, I will sing aloud of thy mercy in the morning: for thou hast been my defence and refuge in the day of my trouble.   21:13

17 Unto thee, [R]O my strength, will I sing: for God *is* my [R]defence, *and* the God of my mercy.   *v.* 9; 18:1 • *v.* 10

PSALM 60

A Prayer for Deliverance of the Nation

To the chief Musician upon Shu'-shan-e'-duth, Mich'-tam of David, to teach; when he strove with A'-ram-na-ha-ra'-im and with A'-ram-zo'-bah, when Jo'-ab returned, and smote of E'-dom in the valley of salt twelve thousand.

O GOD, [R]thou hast cast us off, thou hast scattered us, thou hast been displeased; O turn thyself to us again.   44:9

2 Thou hast made the [R]earth to tremble; thou hast broken it: [R]heal the breaches thereof; for it shaketh.   18:7 • [2 Chr. 7:14]

3 [R]Thou hast shewed thy people hard things: [R]thou hast made us to drink the wine of astonishment.   71:20 • Jer. 25:15

4 [R]Thou hast given a banner to them that fear thee, that it may be displayed because of the truth.   Selah.   20:5; Is. 5:26

5 That thy beloved may be delivered; save *with* thy right hand, and hear me.

6 God hath spoken in his holiness; I will rejoice, I will divide [R]She'-chem, and mete out the valley of Suc'-coth.   Gen. 12:6; 33:18

7 Gil'-e-ad *is* mine, and Ma-nas'-seh *is* mine; E'-phra-im also *is* the strength of mine head; Judah *is* my lawgiver;

8 [R]Moab *is* my washpot; over [R]E'-dom will I cast out my shoe: Phi-lis'-ti-a, triumph thou because of me.   2 Sam. 8:2 • 2 Sam. 8:14

9 Who will bring me *into* the strong city? who will lead me into E'-dom?

10 *Wilt* not thou, O God, *which* hadst cast us off? and *thou,* O God, *which* didst [R]not go out with our armies?   Josh. 7:12

11 Give us help from trouble: ^Rfor ^Tvain *is* the help of man.   [118:9]; 146:3 • *of no real help*

12 Through God we shall do valiantly: for he *it is that* shall tread down our enemies.

PSALM 61

A Prayer When Overwhelmed

To the chief Musician upon Neg′-i-nah,
A Psalm of David.

HEAR^R my cry, O God; ^Rattend unto my prayer.   64:1 • 86:6

2 From the end of the earth will I cry unto thee, when my heart is overwhelmed: lead me to the rock *that* is higher than I.

3 For thou hast been a shelter for me, *and* a strong tower from the enemy.

4 I will abide in thy ^Rtabernacle for ever: ^RI will trust in the covert of thy wings. Selah.   23:6; 27:4; 1 Chr. 29:3 • 17:8; 91:4

5 For thou, O God, hast heard my vows: thou hast given *me* the heritage of those that ^Rfear^T thy name.   86:11 • *revere*

6 Thou wilt ^Rprolong the king's life: *and* his years as many generations.   21:4

7 He shall ^Tabide^R before God for ever: O prepare mercy ^Rand truth, *which* may ^Tpreserve him.   *remain* • 41:12 • 40:11 • *save*

8 So will I sing praise unto thy name for ever, that I may daily perform my vows.

PSALM 62

Wait upon God

To the chief Musician, to Je-du′-thun,
A Psalm of David.

TRULY my soul waiteth upon God: from him *cometh* my salvation.

2 He only *is* my rock and my salvation; *he is* my defence; I shall not be greatly moved.

3 How long will ye imagine mischief against a man? ye shall be slain all of you: ^Ras^T a bowing wall *shall ye be, and as* a tottering fence.   Is. 30:13 • *are soon to collapse*

4 They only consult to cast *him* down from his excellency: ^Rthey delight in lies: they ^Rbless with their mouth, but they curse inwardly.   Selah.   4:2 • 28:3; 55:21

5 My soul, ^Twait thou only upon God; for my expectation *is* from him.   *look for help*

6 He only *is* my rock and my salvation: *he is* my defence; I shall not be moved.

7 ^RIn God *is* my salvation and my glory: the rock of my strength, *and* my ^Rrefuge, *is* in God.   [85:9; Jer. 3:23] • [46:1]

8 ^RTrust in him at all times; ye people, ^Rpour out your heart before him: God *is* a refuge for us.   Selah.   [37:3, 5] • 42:4

9 ^RSurely men of low degree *are* ^Rvanity, *and* men of high degree *are* a lie: to be ^Tlaid in the balance, they *are* altogether *lighter* than vanity.   49:2 • 39:5 • *useless*

10 Trust not in oppression, and become not vain in robbery: if riches increase, set not your heart *upon them*.

11 God hath spoken once; twice have I heard this; that power *belongeth* unto God.

12 Also unto thee, O Lord, *belongeth* mercy: for ^Rthou ^Trenderest to every man according to his work.   [Matt. 16:27] • *gives*

PSALM 63

Thirst for God

A Psalm of David, when he was
in the wilderness of Judah.

O GOD, thou *art* my God; early will I seek thee: my soul thirsteth for thee, my flesh longeth for thee in a dry and thirsty land, where no water is;

2 To see ^Rthy power and thy glory, so *as* I have seen thee in the sanctuary.   27:4

3 Because thy ^Rlovingkindness *is* better than life, my lips shall praise thee.   [69:16]

4 Thus will I ^Tbless thee while I live: I will lift up my hands in thy name.   *praise*

5 My soul shall be satisfied as ^Twith marrow and fatness; and my mouth shall praise thee with joyful lips: *the very best*

6 When I remember thee upon my bed, *and* meditate on thee in the *night* watches.

7 Because thou hast been my help, therefore ^Tin the ^Rshadow of thy wings will I rejoice.   *in your protecting presence* • 17:8

8 My soul ^Tfolloweth hard after thee: thy right hand upholdeth me.   *obey carefully*

9 But those *that* seek my soul, to destroy *it*, shall go into the lower parts of the earth.

10 They shall fall by the sword: they shall be ^Ta portion for foxes.   *in ruins*

11 But the king shall rejoice in God; ^Revery one that sweareth by him shall glory: but the mouth of them that speak lies ^Rshall be stopped.   Deut. 6:13 • Prov. 19:5

PSALM 64

A Prayer for God's Protection

To the chief Musician, A Psalm of David.

HEAR my voice, O God, ^Rin my prayer: ^Rpreserve my life from fear of the enemy.   55:2 • 140:1

2 Hide me from the ^Tsecret counsel of the wicked; from the ^Tinsurrection of the ^Rworkers of iniquity: *conspiracy* • *violence* • 59:2

3 Who ^Twhet their tongue like a sword, ^Rand bend *their bows to shoot* their arrows, *even* bitter words: *sharpen* • 58:7

4 That they may ^Rshoot in secret at the perfect: suddenly do they shoot at him, and ^Rfear not.   10:8; 11:2 • [55:19]

5 They encourage themselves *in* an evil matter: they commune of laying snares privily; they say, Who shall see them?

6 They ^Tsearch out iniquities; they accomplish a diligent search: both the inward *thought* of every one *of them,* and the heart, *is* deep.   *scheme to do evil*

7 But God shall shoot at them *with* an arrow; suddenly shall they be wounded.

8 So they shall ^Tmake their own tongue to fall upon themselves: ^Rall that see them shall flee away.   *put the blame* • 22:7

9 And all men shall ^Rfear, and shall declare the work of God; for they shall wisely consider of his doing.   40:3

10 The righteous shall be ^Rglad in the LORD, and shall trust in him; and all the upright in heart shall glory.   Job 22:19

PSALM 65

God's Provision Through Nature

To the chief Musician,
A Psalm *and* Song of David.

PRAISE waiteth for thee, O God in Si'-on: and unto thee shall the ^Rvow be performed.   116:18

2 O thou that hearest prayer, ^Runto thee shall all flesh come.   [86:9]; 145:21; [Is. 66:23]

3 ^RIniquities prevail against me: *as for* our transgressions, thou shalt ^Rpurge them away.   38:4; 40:12 • [79:9; Heb. 9:14]

4 ^TBlessed *is the man whom* thou choosest, and causest to approach *unto thee, that* he may dwell in thy courts: we shall be satisfied with the goodness of thy house, *even* of thy holy temple.   *happy*

5 *By* ^Rterrible things in righteousness wilt thou answer us, O ^RGod of our salvation; *who art* the confidence of all the ^Rends of the earth, and of them that are afar off *upon* the sea: 45:4 • 85:4 • 22:27

6 Which by his strength setteth fast the mountains; *being* girded with power:

7 ^RWhich ^Tstilleth the noise of the seas, the noise of their waves, ^Rand the tumult of the people.   Matt. 8:26 • *quiets* • Is. 17:13

8 They also that dwell in the ^Ruttermost parts are afraid at thy ^Ttokens: thou makest the outgoings of the morning and evening to rejoice.   2:8; 139:9; Is. 24:16 • *signs*

9 Thou ^Tvisitest the earth, and ^Rwaterest it: thou greatly enrichest it with the river of God, *which* is full of water: thou preparest them corn, when thou hast so provided for it.   *come to bless* • 68:9; 104:13

10 Thou waterest the ridges thereof abundantly: thou settlest the furrows thereof: thou makest it soft ^Rwith showers: thou blessest the springing thereof.   72:6

11 Thou crownest the year with thy goodness; and thy paths drop fatness.

12 ^RThey drop *upon* the pastures of the wilderness: and the little ^Rhills rejoice on every side.   Job 38:26, 27; Joel 2:22 • 98:8

13 The pastures are clothed with flocks; the valleys also are covered over with corn; they shout for joy, they also sing.

PSALM 66

Remember What God Has Done

To the chief Musician, A Song *or* Psalm.

MAKE^R a joyful noise unto God, all ye lands: 81:1; 95:1; 98:4; 100:1

2 ^RSing forth the honour of his name: make his ^Rpraise glorious.   79:9; [Is. 42:8] • Is. 42:12

3 Say unto God, How ^Rterrible^T *art thou in* thy works! through the greatness of thy power shall thine enemies submit themselves unto thee.   65:5 • *impressive*

4 ^RAll the earth shall worship thee, and shall sing unto thee; they shall sing *to* thy name.   Selah.   22:27; 67:7; [86:9]

5 ^RCome and see the works of God: *he is* ^Tterrible^R *in his* doing toward the children of men.   46:8 • *awesome* • 106:22

6 ^RHe turned the sea into dry *land:* they went through ^Rthe flood on foot: there did we rejoice in him.   106:9 • 114:3

7 He ^Rruleth by his power for ever; his eyes behold the nations: let not the rebellious exalt themselves.   Selah.   145:13

8 O bless our God, ye people, and make the ^Rvoice of his praise to be heard: 98:4

9 Which ^Rholdeth our soul in life, and suffereth not our feet to be moved.   30:3

10 For thou, O God, hast ^Tproved us: thou hast tried us, as silver is tried.   *tested*

11 Thou broughtest us into the net; thou laidst affliction upon our loins.

12 ^RThou hast caused men to ride over our heads; ^Rwe went through fire and through water: but thou broughtest us out into a wealthy *place.*   Is. 51:23 • Is. 43:2

13 I will go into thy house with burnt offerings: I will pay thee my vows,

14 Which my lips have uttered, and my mouth hath spoken, when I was in trouble.

15 I will offer unto thee burnt sacrifices of fatlings, with the incense of ^Rrams: I will offer bullocks with goats.   Selah.   Num. 6:14

16 ^RCome *and* hear, all ye that fear God, and I will ^Rdeclare what he hath done for my soul.   34:11 • [71:15, 24]

17 I cried unto him with my mouth, and he was extolled with my tongue.

18 ^RIf I regard iniquity in my heart, the Lord will not hear *me:*   [John 9:31; James 4:3]

19 *But* verily God hath heard *me;* he hath attended to the voice of my prayer.

20 ^RBlessed *be* God, which ^Rhath not turned away my prayer, nor his mercy from me.   68:35 • 22:24

PSALM 67

God Shall Govern the Earth

To the chief Musician on Neg'-i-noth,
A Psalm or Song.

GOD be merciful unto us, and ᴿbless us; and ᴿcause his face to shine upon us; Selah.   Num. 6:25 • 4:6; 31:16; [80:3, 7, 19]

2 That thy way may be known upon earth, thy saving health among all nations.

3 Let the ᴿpeople praise thee, O God; let all the people praise thee.   66:4

4 O let the ᴿnations be glad and sing for joy: for ᴿthou shalt judge the people righteously, and govern the nations upon earth. Selah.   100:1, 2 • 9:8; [96:10, 13]

5 Let the ᴿpeople praise thee, O God; let all the people praise thee.   v. 3

6 Then shall the earth yield her increase; and God, even our own God, shall bless us.

7 God shall bless us; and ᴿall the ends of the earth shall fear him.   22:27; 33:8

PSALM 68

God Is the Father of the Fatherless

To the chief Musician,
A Psalm or Song of David.

LET ᴿGod arise, let his enemies be ᵀscattered: let them also that hate him flee ᵀbefore him.   Num. 10:35 • defeated • in defeat

2 As smoke is driven away, so drive them away: as wax melteth before the fire, so let the wicked perish at the presence of God.

3 But ᴿlet the righteous be glad; let them rejoice before God: yea, let them exceedingly rejoice.   32:11; 64:10; 97:12

4 Sing unto God, sing praises to his name: extol him that rideth upon the heavens by his name JAH, and rejoice before him.

5 ᴿA father of the fatherless, and a ᴿjudge of the widows, is God in his ᴿholy habitation.   [10:14; 146:9] • Deut. 10:18 • Deut. 26:15

6 God setteth the solitary in families: he bringeth out those which are bound with chains: but the rebellious dwell in a dry land.

7 O God, ᴿwhen thou wentest forth before thy people, when thou didst march through the wilderness;   Selah: Ex. 13:21

8 The earth shook, the heavens also dropped at the presence of God: even Si'-nai itself was moved at the presence of God, the God of Israel.

9 ᴿThou, O God, didst send a plentiful rain, whereby thou didst confirm thine inheritance, when it was weary.   Deut. 11:11

10 Thy congregation hath dwelt therein: ᴿthou, O God, hast prepared of thy goodness for the poor.   74:19; 78:20; Deut. 26:5

11 The Lord gave the word: great was the company of those that published it.

12 Kings of armies did flee apace: and she that tarried at home divided the spoil.

13 Though ye have lien among the pots, yet shall ye be as the wings of a dove covered with silver, and her feathers with yellow gold.

14 When the Almighty scattered kings in it, it was white as snow in Sal'-mon.

15 The hill of God is as the hill of Ba'-shan; an high hill as the hill of Ba'-shan.

16 Why leap ye, ye high hills? this is the hill which God desireth to dwell in; yea, the Lᴏʀᴅ will dwell in it for ever.

17 The chariots of God are twenty thousand, even thousands of angels: the Lord is among them, as in Si'-nai, in the holy place.

18 Thou hast ascended on high, thou hast led captivity captive: thou hast received gifts for men; yea, for the rebellious also, that the Lᴏʀᴅ God might dwell among them.

19 Blessed be the Lord, who daily ᴿloadeth us with benefits, even ᴿthe God of our salvation.   Selah.   [55:22; Is. 46:4] • 65:5

20 He that is our God is the God of salvation; and ᴿunto Gᴏᴅ the Lord belong the issues from death.   [49:15; 56:13; Deut. 32:39]

21 But God shall wound the head of his enemies, and the hairy scalp of such an one as goeth on still in his trespasses.

22 The Lord said, I will bring again from Ba'-shan, I will bring my people again from the depths of the sea:

23 ᴿThat thy foot may be dipped in the blood of thine enemies, ᴿand the tongue of thy dogs in the same.   58:10 • 1 Kin. 21:19

24 They have seen ᴿthy ᵀgoings, O God; even the goings of my God, my King, ᴿin the sanctuary.   77:13 • procedures • 63:2

25 The singers went before, the players on instruments followed after; among them were the damsels playing with timbrels.

26 Bless ye God in the congregations, even the Lord, from the fountain of Israel.

27 There is ᴿlittle Benjamin with their ruler, the princes of Judah and their ᵀcouncil, the princes of Zeb'-u-lun, and the princes of Naph'-ta-li.   1 Sam. 9:21 • company

28 Thy God hath ᴿcommanded thy strength: strengthen, O God, that which thou hast wrought for us.   42:8; 44:4

29 Because of thy temple at Jerusalem shall kings bring presents unto thee.

30 Rebuke the company of spearmen, ᴿthe multitude of the bulls, with the calves of the people, till every one submit himself with pieces of silver: scatter thou the people that delight in war.   22:12

31 ᴿPrinces shall come out of Egypt; ᴿE-thi-o'-pi-a shall soon ᴿstretch out her hands unto God.   Is. 19:21 • Is. 45:14 • 44:20

32 Sing unto God, ye ᴿkingdoms of the earth; O ᴿsing praises unto the Lord. Selah: 102:22 • [67:4]

33 To him that rideth upon the heavens of heavens, *which were* of old; lo, he doth send out his voice, *and that* a mighty voice.

34 ᴿAscribe ye strength unto God: his excellency *is* over Israel, and ᴿhis strength *is* in the ᵀclouds.   29:1 · 150:1 · *heavens*

35 O God, ᴿ*thou art* terrible out of thy holy places: the God of Israel *is* he that ᴿgiveth strength and power unto *his* people. Blessed *be* God.   76:12 · 29:11

PSALM 69

Petition for God to Draw Near

To the chief Musician upon Sho-shan'-nim, *A Psalm* of David.

SAVE me, O God; for ᴿthe waters are come in unto *my* soul.   *vv.* 14, 15; 32:6

2 ᴿI sink in deep mire, where *there is* no standing: I am come into deep waters, where the floods overflow me.   40:2

3 ᴿI am weary of my crying: my throat is dried: ᴿmine eyes fail while I wait for my God.   6:6 · 38:10; 119:82; Deut. 28:32

4 ᴿThey that hate me without a cause are more than the hairs of mine head: they that would destroy me, *being* mine enemies wrongfully, are mighty: then I restored *that* which I took not away.   John 15:25 ☆

5 O God, thou knowest ᴿmy foolishness; and my sins are not hid from thee.   38:5

6 Let not them that wait on thee, O Lord GOD of hosts, be ashamed for my sake: let not those that seek thee be confounded for my sake, O God of Israel.

7 Because for thy sake I have borne reproach; shame hath covered my face.

8 ᴿI am become a ᴿstranger unto my brethren, and an alien unto my mother's children.   Mark 3:21 ☆ · 31:11; 38:11; Job 19:13–15

9 For the zeal of thine house hath eaten me up; and the reproaches of them that reproached thee are fallen upon me.

10 When I wept, *and chastened* my soul with fasting, that was to my reproach.

11 I made ᴿsackcloth also my garment; and I became a proverb to them.   35:13

12 They that sit in the gate speak against me; and I *was* the song of the drunkards.

13 But as for me, my prayer *is* unto thee, O LORD, ᴿ*in* an acceptable time: O God, in the multitude of thy mercy hear me, in the truth of thy salvation.   32:6; Is. 49:8

14 Deliver me out of the mire, and let me not sink: let me be delivered from them that hate me, and out of the deep waters.

15 Let not the waterflood overflow me, neither let the deep swallow me up, and let not the pit shut her mouth upon me.

16 Hear me, O LORD; for thy lovingkindness *is* good: turn unto me according to the multitude of thy tender mercies.

17 And hide not thy face from thy servant; for I am in trouble: hear me speedily.

18 Draw nigh unto my soul, *and* redeem it: deliver me because of mine enemies.

19 Thou hast known ᴿmy reproach, and my shame, and my dishonour: mine adversaries *are* all before thee.   22:6

20 ᴿReproach hath broken my heart; and I am full of heaviness: and I looked *for some* to take pity, but *there was* none; and for comforters, but I found none.   Rom. 15:3 ☆

21 They gave me also ᴿgall for my meat; ᴿand in my thirst they gave me vinegar to drink.   Deut. 29:18 · Matt. 27:34, 48 ☆

22 ᴿLet their table become a snare before them: and *that which should have been* for *their* welfare, *let it become* a trap. Rom. 11:9–12

23 ᴿLet their eyes be darkened, that they see not; and make their ᴿloins continually to shake.   Is. 6:10 · Dan. 5:6

24 Pour out thine indignation upon them, and let thy wrathful anger take hold of them.

25 ᴿLet their habitation be desolate; *and* let none dwell in their tents.   Matt. 23:38

26 For they persecute ᴿhim whom thou hast smitten; and they talk to the grief of those whom thou hast wounded.   [Is. 53:4]

27 Add iniquity unto their iniquity: and let them not come into thy righteousness.

28 Let them ᴿbe blotted out of the ᴿbook of the living, and not be written with the righteous.   [Ex. 32:33; Rev. 3:5] · Phil. 4:3

29 But I *am* poor and sorrowful: let thy salvation, O God, set me up on high.

30 ᴿI will praise the name of God with a song, and will ᴿmagnify him with ᴿthanksgiving.   [28:7] · 34:3 · 50:14

31 ᴿ*This* also shall please the LORD better than an ox *or* bullock that hath horns and ᵀhoofs.   50:13, 14; 51:16 · *divided hoofs*

32 The humble shall see *this, and* be glad: and your heart shall live that seek God.

33 For the LORD heareth the poor, and despiseth not ᴿhis prisoners.   Eph. 3:1

34 ᴿLet the heaven and earth praise him, the seas, ᴿand every thing that ᵀmoveth therein.   96:11 · Is. 55:12 · *creepeth*

35 For God will save Zion, and will build the cities of Judah: that they may dwell there, and have it in possession.

36 ᴿThe seed also of his servants shall inherit it: and they that love his name ᴿshall dwell therein.   102:28 · [37:29]

PSALM 70

Prayer for the Poor and Needy

To the chief Musician, *A Psalm* of David, to bring to remembrance.

MAKE haste, O God, to deliver me; make haste to help me, O LORD.

2 Let them be ashamed and confounded

that seek after ᵀmy soul: let them be turned backward, and put to confusion, that desire my hurt. *me*

3 ᴿLet them be turned back for a reward of their shame that say, Aha, aha. 40:15

4 Let all those that seek thee rejoice and be glad in thee: and let such as love thy salvation say continually, Let God be magnified.

5 But I *am* poor and needy: make haste unto me, O God: thou *art* my help and my deliverer; O Lᴏʀᴅ, make no tarrying.

PSALM 71

Prayer for the Aged

IN thee, O Lᴏʀᴅ, do I put my trust: let me never be put to confusion.

2 ᴿDeliver me in thy righteousness, and cause me to escape: ᴿincline thine ear unto me, and save me. 31:1 · 17:6

3 ᴿBe thou my strong habitation, whereunto I may continually resort: thou hast given commandment to save me, for thou *art* my rock and my fortress. 44:4

4 ᴿDeliver me, O my God, out of the hand of the wicked, out of the hand of the unrighteous and cruel man. 140:1, 4

5 For thou *art* ᴿmy hope, O Lord Gᴏᴅ: *thou art* my trust from my youth. [Jer. 17:7]

6 ᴿBy thee have I been holden up from the womb: thou art he that ᴿtook me out of my mother's bowels: my praise *shall be* continually of thee. 22:10; Is. 46:3 · [22:9]

7 ᴿI am as a wonder unto many; but thou *art* ᴿmy strong refuge. 1 Cor. 4:9 · 61:3

8 Let my mouth be filled *with* thy praise *and with* thy honour all the day.

9 Cast me not off in the time of old age; forsake me not when my strength faileth.

10 For mine enemies speak against me; and they that ᵀlay wait for my soul ᵀtake counsel together, *plan to do me harm · confer*

11 Saying, ᴿGod hath forsaken him: persecute and take him; ᴿfor *there is* none to deliver *him*. 3:2 · 7:2

12 O God, be not far from me: O my God, ᴿmake haste for my help. 70:1

13 Let them be ᴿconfounded *and* consumed that are adversaries to my soul; let them be covered *with* reproach and dishonour that seek my hurt. 35:4, 26

14 But I will ᴿhope continually, and will yet praise thee more and more. [130:7]

15 My mouth shall shew forth thy righteousness *and* thy salvation all the day; for I know not the numbers *thereof*.

16 I will ᴿgo in the strength of the Lord Gᴏᴅ: I will ᴿmake mention of thy righteousness, *even* of thine only. 106:2 · 51:14

17 O God, thou ᴿhast taught me from my youth: and hitherto have I ᴿdeclared thy wondrous works. Deut. 4:5; 6:7 · 26:7; [40:5]

18 Now also when I am old and greyheaded, O God, forsake me not; until I have shewed thy strength unto *this* generation, *and* thy power to every one *that* is to come.

19 Thy righteousness also, O God, *is* very high, who hast done great things: ᴿO God, who *is* like unto thee! 35:10

20 ᴿThou, which hast shewed me great and sore troubles, ᴿshalt quicken me again, and shalt bring me up again from the depths of the earth. 60:3 · Hos. 6:1, 2

21 ᴿThou shalt increase my greatness, and comfort me on every side. [23:4]

22 I will also praise thee ᴿwith the psaltery, *even* thy truth, O my God: unto thee will I sing with the ᴿharp, O thou ᴿHoly One of Israel. 2 Kin. 19:22 · 33:2 · 78:41

23 My lips shall ᴿgreatly rejoice when I sing unto thee; and ᴿmy soul, which thou hast redeemed. 5:11; 32:11 · [34:22]; 55:18

24 My tongue also shall talk of thy righteousness all the day long: for they are ᵀconfounded, for they are brought unto shame, that seek my hurt. *frustrated*

PSALM 72

The Reign of the Messiah

A Psalm for Solomon.

GIVE the king ᴿthy judgments, O God, and thy righteousness unto the king's son. 24:5; 1 Kin. 3:9; 1 Chr. 22:13

2 He shall ᴿjudge thy people with righteousness, and thy poor with judgment. [Is. 9:7] ☆

3 ᴿThe mountains shall bring ᴿpeace to the people, and the little hills, by righteousness. 85:10 · [Is. 2:3, 4; 9:5, 6; Mic. 4:3, 4]

4 He shall ᴿjudge the poor of the people, he shall save the children of the needy, and shall break in pieces the oppressor. Is. 11:4 ☆

5 They shall fear thee ᴿas long as the sun and moon endure, throughout all generations. vv. 7, 17; [89:36, 37; Is. 9:7] ☆

6 ᴿHe shall come down ᴿlike rain upon the mown grass: as showers *that* water the earth. Hos. 6:3 · Deut. 32:2; 2 Sam. 23:4

7 In his days shall the righteous ᵀflourish; and ᴿabundance of peace so long as the moon endureth. *prosper* · Is. 2:4 ☆

8 ᴿHe shall have dominion also from sea to sea, and from the river unto the ends of the earth. Ex. 23:31; [Is. 9:6; Zech. 9:10]

9 ᴿThey that dwell in the wilderness shall ᴿbow before him; and his enemies shall ᴿlick the dust. 74:14 · 22:29 · Is. 49:23 ☆

10 ᴿThe kings of Tar'-shish and of the isles shall bring presents: the kings of She'-ba and Se'-ba shall offer gifts. 2 Chr. 9:21

11 ^RYea, all kings shall fall down before him: all nations shall serve him.   Is. 49:23 ☆

12 For he ^Rshall deliver the needy when he crieth; the ^Rpoor also, and *him* that hath no helper.   [v. 4]; Job 29:12 • [72:4] ☆

13 He shall spare the poor and needy, and shall save the souls of the needy.

14 He shall ^Rredeem their soul from deceit and violence: and ^Rprecious shall their blood be in his sight.   69:18 • [116:15] ☆

15 And he shall live, and to him shall be given of the ^Rgold of She′-ba: prayer also shall be made for him continually; *and* daily shall he be praised.   Is. 60:6 ☆

16 There shall be ^Tan handful of corn in the earth upon the top of the mountains; the fruit thereof shall shake like Leb′-a-non: and *they* of the city shall flourish like grass of the earth.   *fruitful*

17 His name shall endure for ever: his name shall be continued ^Ras long as the sun: and *men* shall be blessed in him: all nations shall call him blessed.   [89:36] ☆

18 Blessed *be* the LORD God, the God of Israel, who only doeth wondrous things.

19 And ^Rblessed *be* his glorious name for ever: and let the whole earth be filled *with* his glory; A-men′, and A-men′.   [Neh. 9:5]

20 The prayers of David the son of Jesse are ended.

BOOK III

PSALM 73

The Perspective of Eternity

A Psalm of A′-saph.

TRULY God *is* ^Rgood to Israel, *even* to such as are of a clean heart.   [86:5]

2 But as for me, my feet were almost gone; my steps had well nigh slipped.

3 ^RFor I was envious at the foolish, *when* I saw the prosperity of the wicked.   37:1

4 For *there are* no bands ^Tin their death: but their strength *is* firm.   *at*

5 They *are* not in trouble *as other* men; neither are they plagued like *other* men.

6 Therefore pride ^Tcompasseth them about as a chain; violence covereth them ^R*as* a garment.   *surrounds* • 109:18

7 Their eyes stand out with fatness: they have more than heart could wish.

8 They are corrupt, and speak wickedly *concerning* oppression: they speak loftily.

9 ^RThey set their mouth against the heavens, and their tongue walketh through the earth.   1 Sam. 17:44

10 Therefore his people return hither: and waters of a full *cup* are wrung out to them.

11 And they say, How doth God know? and is there knowledge in the most High?

12 Behold, these *are* the ungodly, who prosper in the world; they increase *in* riches.

13 Verily I have cleansed my heart *in* vain, and washed my hands in innocency.

14 For all the day long have I been plagued, and chastened every morning.

15 If I say, I will speak thus; behold, I should offend *against* the ^Rgeneration of thy children.   [14:5]

16 ^RWhen I thought to know this, it *was* too ^Tpainful for me;   [Eccl. 8:17] • *difficult*

17 Until I went into the sanctuary of God; *then* understood I their ^Tend.   *hereafter*

18 Surely thou didst set them in ^Rslippery places: thou castedst them down into ^Rdestruction.   35:6 • 35:8; 36:12

19 How are they *brought* into ^Rdesolation, as in a moment! they are utterly ^Rconsumed with terrors.   Is. 47:11 • Job 18:11

20 As a ^Rdream when *one* awaketh; *so,* O Lord, when thou ^Rawakest, thou shalt despise their image.   Job 20:8 • 78:65

21 Thus my heart was grieved, and I was ^Rpricked in my reins.   Acts 2:37

22 ^RSo foolish *was* I, and ignorant: I was as a ^Rbeast before thee.   92:6 • 49:20

23 Nevertheless I *am* continually with thee: thou hast holden *me* by my right hand.

24 Thou shalt guide me with thy counsel, and afterward receive me *to* glory.

25 ^RWhom have I in heaven *but thee?* and

73:1 Walking in the Spirit: Confession—An important prerequisite to walking in the Spirit is the confession of sin. Sin must be confessed in order to restore fellowship and to continue receiving God's power (Page 1249—1 John 1:5-10). Confession means that we agree with God about our sin. This involves much more than simply acknowledging the sin. Confession requires an attitude of sorrow for the sin and a willingness to turn from it. It does not mean that we will never commit the same sin again, but it does mean that the attitude of repentance is present.

Confession should be made at the moment the Christian becomes aware of sin. Apart from this rule, moreover, the Scriptures mention two specific times for confession: before the close of the day (Page 1165—Eph. 4:26) and before the Lord's Supper is observed (Page 1134—1 Cor. 11:27-32). Failure to do the latter is a special cause for discipline from the Lord.

Confession of sin should normally involve only those who have knowledge of the sin. This means that private sins should be confessed privately (Page 1249—1 John 1:9); sins between individuals confessed between those involved (Page 945—Matt. 5:23, 24); and public sins confessed publicly (Page 960—Matt. 18:17). Public confession normally is made for the edification of the church (Page 1136—1 Cor. 14:26).

Now turn to Page 1118—Rom. 12:1: Walking in the Spirit: Yielding.

there is none upon earth *that* I desire beside thee. [16:2; Phil. 3:8]
26 ᴿMy flesh and my heart ᵀfaileth: *but* God *is* the strength of my heart, and my portion for ever.   84:2 · *falter in weakness*
27 For, lo, they that are far from thee shall perish: thou hast destroyed all them that go ᴿa whoring from thee.   106:39
28 But *it is* good for me to ᴿdraw near to God: I have put my trust in the Lord Gᴏᴅ, that I may declare all thy works.   [Heb. 10:22]

PSALM 74

Request for God to Remember His Covenant

Mas'-chil of A'-saph.

O GOD, why hast thou ᴿcast *us* off for ever? *why* doth thine anger smoke against the sheep of thy pasture?   44:9
2 Remember thy congregation, *which* thou hast purchased of old; the rod of thine inheritance, *which* thou hast ᴿredeemed; this mount Zion, wherein thou hast dwelt.   77:15
3 Lift up thy feet unto the ᴿperpetual desolations; *even* all *that* the enemy hath done wickedly in the sanctuary.   Is. 61:4
4 Thine enemies ᵀroarᴿ in the midst of thy congregations; ᴿthey set up their ensigns *for* signs.   *threaten* · Lam. 2:7 · Num. 2:2
5 *A man* was famous according as he had lifted up axes upon the thick trees.
6 But now they break down the carved work thereof at once with axes and hammers.
7 They have cast fire into thy ᵀsanctuary, they have defiled *by casting down* the dwelling place of thy name to the ground.   *temple*
8 They said in their hearts, Let us destroy them together: they have burned up all the synagogues of God in the land.
9 We see not our signs: ᴿthere *is* no more any prophet: neither *is there* among us any that knoweth how long.   1 Sam. 3:1
10 O God, how long shall the adversary ᵀreproach? shall the enemy blaspheme thy name for ever?   *belittle us for our weakness*
11 ᴿWhy withdrawest thou thy ᴿhand, even thy right hand? ᴿpluck *it* out of thy bosom.   Lam. 2:3 · [Ex. 7:5 · 59:13]
12 For ᴿGod *is* my King of old, working salvation in the midst of the earth.   44:4
13 ᴿThou didst divide the sea by thy strength: thou brakest the heads of the ᵀdragons in the waters.   Ex. 14:21 · *crocodiles*
14 Thou brakest the heads of ᴿleviathan in pieces, *and* gavest him *to be* meat to the people inhabiting the wilderness.   104:26
15 Thou didst cleave the fountain and the flood: thou driedst up mighty rivers.
16 ᴿThe day *is* thine, the night also *is* thine: thou hast prepared the light and the sun.   104:19; 136:7, 8; Gen. 1:14–18

17 Thou hast set all the borders of the earth: thou hast made summer and winter.
18 Remember this, *that* the enemy hath reproached, O Lᴏʀᴅ, and *that* the foolish people have blasphemed thy name.
19 O deliver not the soul of thy turtledove unto the multitude *of the wicked:* forget not the congregation of thy poor for ever.
20 Have respect unto the covenant: for the dark places of the earth are full of the habitations of cruelty.
21 O let not the ᴿoppressed return ashamed: ᴿlet the poor and needy praise thy name.   [103:6 · 35:10; Is. 41:17]
22 Arise, O God, ᴿplead thine own cause: remember how the ᴿfoolish man ᵀreproacheth thee daily.   43:1 · 14:1; 53:1 · *belittles*
23 Forget not the voice of thine ᴿenemies: the ᴿtumult of those that rise up against thee increaseth continually.   *v.* 10 · 65:7

PSALM 75

"God Is the Judge"

To the chief Musician, Al-tas'-chith, A Psalm *or* Song of A'-saph.

U NTO thee, O God, do we give thanks, *unto* thee do we give thanks: for *that* ᵀthy name is near thy wondrous works declare.   *you are nearby to help us*
2 When I shall receive the congregation ᵀI will judge uprightly.   *I, even I*
3 The ᴿearth and all the inhabitants thereof are dissolved: I bear up the ᴿpillars of it.   Selah.   46:6; Is. 24:19 · [1 Sam. 2:8]
4 I said unto the fools, Deal not foolishly: and to the wicked, Lift not up the horn:
5 Lift not up your horn on high: ᴿspeak *not* ᵀwith a stiff neck.   1 Sam. 2:3 · *in rebellion*
6 For promotion *cometh* neither from the east, nor from the west, nor from the south.
7 But ᴿGod *is* the judge: he putteth down one, and setteth up another.   50:6
8 For in the hand of the Lᴏʀᴅ *there is* a cup, and the wine is red; it is full of mixture; and he poureth out of the same: but the dregs thereof, all the wicked of the earth shall wring *them* out, *and* drink *them*.
9 But I will ᴿdeclare for ever; I will sing praises to the God of Jacob.   22:22; 40:10
10 All the ᵀhorns of the wicked also will I cut off; *but* ᴿthe horns of the righteous shall be exalted.   *strength* · 89:17; 92:10

PSALM 76

The Glorious Might of God

To the chief Musician on Neg'-i-noth, A Psalm *or* Song of A'-saph.

I N Judah *is* God ᴿknown: his name *is* ᴿgreat in Israel.   48:3 · [99:3]

2 In Sa'-lem also is his ᴿtabernacle, and his dwelling place in Zion.   27:5

3 There ᴿbrakeᵀ he the arrows of the bow, the shield, and the sword, and the battle. Selah.   46:9; Ezek. 39:9 · *broke in pieces*

4 Thou *art* more glorious *and* excellent than the mountains of prey.

5 The stouthearted are spoiled, they have slept their sleep: and none of the men of might have found their hands.

6 ᴿAt thy rebuke, O God of Jacob, both the chariot and horse are ᵀcast into a dead sleep.   78:53; 80:16; Ex. 15:1, 21 · *stunned*

7 Thou, *even* thou, *art* to be feared: and ᴿwho may stand in thy sight when once thou art angry?   [Nah. 1:6; Mal. 3:2; Rev. 6:17]

8 Thou didst cause judgment to be heard from heaven; the earth feared, and was still,

9 When God ᴿarose to judgment, to save all the meek of the earth.   Selah.   74:22

10 ᴿSurely the wrath of man shall praise thee: the remainder of wrath shalt thou restrain.   [Ex. 9:16; Rom. 9:17]

11 Vow, and pay unto the Lᴏʀᴅ your God: let all that be round about him bring presents unto him that ought to be feared.

12 He shall cut off the spirit of princes: *he is* terrible to the kings of the earth.

PSALM 77

*When Overwhelmed,
Remember God's Greatness*

To the chief Musician, to Je-du'-thun,
A Psalm of A'-saph.

I CRIED unto God with my voice, ᴿ*even* unto God with my voice; and he ᵀgave ear unto me.   3:4; 142:1 · *listened*

2 In the day of my trouble I sought the Lord: my ᴿsore ran in the night, and ceased not: my soul refused to be comforted.   88:9

3 I remembered God, and was ᴿtroubled: I ᴿcomplained, and my spirit was overwhelmed.   Selah.   42:5, 11; 43:5 · 55:2

4 Thou holdest mine eyes waking: I am so troubled that I ᴿcannot speak.   39:9

5 I have considered the ᴿdays of old, the years of ancient times.   Deut. 32:7; Is. 51:9

6 I call to remembrance my song in the night: I commune with mine own heart: and my spirit made diligent search.

7 Will the Lord ᴿcast off for ever? and will he be favourable no more?   44:9

8 Is his mercy clean gone for ever? doth *his* promise fail for evermore?

9 Hath God ᴿforgotten to be gracious? hath he in anger shut up his ᴿtender mercies? Selah.   [Is. 49:15 · 25:6; 40:11; 51:1]

10 And I said, This *is* my ᵀinfirmity: *but I will remember* the years of the ᴿright hand of the most High.   *weakness* · 44:2, 3

11 I will remember the ᴿworks of the Lᴏʀᴅ: surely I will remember thy wonders of old.   44:1; 105:5; 143:5

12 I will ᴿmeditate also of all thy work, and talk of thy doings.   104:34; 145:5

13 Thy way, O God, *is* in the ᴿsanctuary: who *is* so great a God as our God?   63:2

14 Thou *art* the ᴿGod that doest ᴿwonders: thou hast ᴿdeclared thy strength among the people.   [Dan. 4:3 · 72:18] · 106:8

15 Thou hast with *thine* arm ᴿredeemed thy people, the sons of Jacob and ᴿJoseph. Selah.   74:2; Ex. 6:6; Deut. 9:29 · 80:1

16 The waters saw thee, O God, the waters saw thee; they were afraid: the depths also were ᵀtroubled.   *deeply stirred*

17 The ᴿclouds poured out water: the skies ᴿsent out a sound: thine ᴿarrows also went abroad.   Judg. 5:4 · 68:33 · 18:14

18 The voice of thy thunder *was* in the heaven: the lightnings lightened the world: the earth trembled and shook.

19 ᴿThy way *is* in the sea, and thy path in the great waters, and thy footsteps are not known.   Is. 51:10; Hab. 3:15

20 ᴿThou leddest thy people like a flock by the hand of Moses and Aaron.   78:52

PSALM 78

God's Continued Guidance in Spite of Unbelief

Mas'-chil of A'-saph.

GIVEᴿ ear, O my people, *to* my law: ᴿin- clineᵀ your ears to the words of my mouth.   Is. 51:4 · Is. 55:3 · *listen*

2 I ᴿwill open my mouth in a parable: I will utter dark sayings of old: Matt. 13:34, 35

3 Which we have heard and ᵀknown, and ᴿour fathers have told us.   *come to know* · 44:1

4 We will not hide *them* from their children, shewing to the generation to come the praises of the Lᴏʀᴅ, and his strength, and his wonderful works that he hath done.

5 For he established a testimony in Jacob, and appointed a law in Israel, which he commanded our fathers, that they should make them known to their children:

6 ᴿThat the generation to come might

78:4 History of Israel—The biblical history of Israel covers 1,800 years and represents a marvelous panorama of God's gracious working through promise, miracle, blessing, and judgment. Israel begins as only a promise to Abraham (Page 14—Gen. 12:2). For over four hundred years the people of Israel rely on that promise, especially during the period of bondage to Egypt. Finally, in God's perfect timing,

know *them, even* the children *which* should be born; *who* should arise and declare *them* to their children: 102:18

7 That they might set their hope in God, and ᴿnot forget the works of God, but ᴿkeep his commandments: Deut. 4:9; 6:12 • [Deut. 4:2]

8 And might not be as their fathers, a stubborn and rebellious generation; a generation *that* set not their heart aright, and whose spirit was not stedfast with God.

9 The children of E'-phra-im, ᴿ*being* armed, *and* carrying bows, ᴿturned back in the day of battle.   1 Chr. 12:2 • 78:57

10 ᴿThey kept not the covenant of God, and refused to walk in his law;   2 Kin. 17:15

11 And ᴿforgat his works, and his wonders that he had shewed them.   106:13

12 ᴿMarvellous things did he in the sight of their fathers, in the land of Egypt, ᴿ*in* the field of Zo'-an.   Ex. 7:12 • v. 3; Num. 13:22

13 ᴿHe divided the sea, and caused them to pass through; and ᴿhe made the waters to stand as an heap.   74:13; 136:13 • 33:7

14 In the daytime also he led them with a cloud, and all the night with a light of fire.

15 ᴿHe ᵀclave the rocks in the wilderness, and gave *them* drink as out of the great depths.   Num. 20:11; [1 Cor. 10:4] • *split*

16 He brought ᴿstreams also out of the rock, and caused waters to run down like rivers.   Num. 20:8, 10, 11

17 And they sinned yet more against him by ᴿprovoking the most High in the wilderness.   Deut. 9:22; Is. 63:10; Heb. 3:16

18 And ᴿthey tempted God in their heart by asking meat for their lust.   Ex. 16:2

19 ᴿYea, they ᵀspake against God; they said, Can God ᵀfurnish a table in the wilderness?   Num. 11:4 • *criticized • order*

20 ᴿBehold, he smote the rock, that the waters gushed out, and the streams overflowed; can he give bread also? can he provide flesh for his people?   Num. 20:11

21 Therefore the Lᴏʀᴅ heard *this*, and was wroth: so a fire was kindled against Jacob, and anger also came up against Israel;

22 Because they ᴿbelieved not in God, and trusted not in his salvation: [Heb. 3:18]

23 Though he had commanded the ᵀclouds from above, ᴿand opened the doors of heaven,   *skies* • Gen. 7:11; [Mal. 3:10]

24 ᴿAnd had rained down manna upon them to eat, and had given them of ᴿthe corn of heaven.   Ex. 16:4 • 105:40; John 6:31

25 Man did eat angels' food: he sent them ᵀmeat to ᴿthe full.   *food* • Ex. 16:3, 4

26 ᴿHe caused an east wind to blow in the heaven: and by his power he brought in the south wind.   Num. 11:31

27 He rained flesh also upon them as dust, and ᴿfeathered fowls like as the sand of the sea: 105:40; Ex. 16:13

28 And he let *it* fall in the midst of their camp, round about their habitations.

29 So they did eat, and were well filled: for he gave them their own desire;

30 They were not ᵀestranged from their ᵀlust. But ᴿwhile their meat *was* yet in their mouths,   *separated • desire* • Num. 11:33

31 The ᴿwrath of God came upon them, and slew the fattest of them, and smote down the chosen *men* of Israel.   Job 20:23

32 For all this they sinned still, and believed not for his wondrous works.

33 Therefore their days did he consume in vanity, and their years in trouble.

34 ᴿWhen he slew them, then they sought him: and they returned and ᴿenquired early after God.   Hos. 5:15 • 63:1

35 And they remembered that ᴿGod *was* their rock, and the high God ᴿtheir redeemer.   [Is. 41:14 • 74:2; Ex. 15:13; Deut. 9:26]

36 Nevertheless they did ᴿflatter him with their mouth, and they lied unto him with their tongues.   Ex. 32:7, 8; Ezek. 33:31

He brings the nation out of Egypt with the greatest series of miracles known in the entire Old Testament (Page 62—Ex. 7—15). This event is called the Exodus, meaning *a going out*. Since it constitutes the miraculous birth of the nation, it is to this great act of redemption that the nation always looks back as the foremost example of God's care for His people (Page 580—Ps. 77:14-20; 78:12-55; Page 845—Hos. 11:1).

Once God has redeemed Israel He establishes His covenant with them at Mount Sinai (Page 74—Ex. 19:5-8). From that point forward the nation is truly the Lord's possession, and He is their God. The covenant foretells gracious blessings for obedience and severe judgments for disobedience. The rest of Israel's history demonstrates the certainty of that prophecy. Through the periods of conquest, judges, monarchy, exile, restoration, and gentile domination, Israel is blessed when she obeys and judged when she disobeys. The nation is finally destroyed in A.D. 70, although this event is not described in the New Testament. Many prophecies, however, promise a future redemption for Israel (Page 1117—Rom. 11:26).

The practical value of studying Israel's history is threefold:

a. It sets forth examples to be followed or avoided (Page 1132—1 Cor. 10:6).

b. It shows God's control of all historical events, in that He was able to deal with Israel as He chose (Page 580—Ps. 78).

c. It serves as a model for all ages of God's kindness and mercy toward His people (Page 592—Ps. 103:14).

Now turn to Page 192—Deut. 14:2: Purpose of Israel.

37 For their heart was not right with him, neither were they stedfast in his covenant.

38 But he, *being* full of compassion, forgave *their* iniquity, and destroyed *them* not: yea, many a time [R]turned he his anger away, and did not stir up all his wrath.   Num. 14:20

39 For [R]he remembered [R]that they *were but* flesh; a wind that passeth away, and cometh not again.   [103:14 • John 3:6]

40 How oft did they provoke him in the wilderness, *and* grieve him in the desert!

41 Yea, they turned back and tempted God, and limited the Holy One of Israel.

42 They [R]remembered not [R]his hand, *nor* the day when he [R]delivered them from the enemy.   Judg. 8:34 • [44:3] • 106:10

43 How he had wrought his signs in Egypt, and his wonders in the field of Zo'-an:

44 And had turned their rivers into blood; and their floods, that they could not drink.

45 [R]He sent divers sorts of flies among them, which devoured them; and [R]frogs, which destroyed them.   Ex. 8:4 • Ex. 8:6

46 He gave also their increase unto the caterpiller, and their labour unto the locust.

47 He destroyed their vines with hail, and their sycomore trees with frost.

48 He gave up their cattle also to the hail, and their flocks to hot thunderbolts.

49 He cast upon them the fierceness of his anger, wrath, and indignation, and trouble, by sending evil angels *among them.*

50 He made a way to his anger; he spared not their soul from death, but gave [R]their life over to the pestilence;   Ex. 12:29, 30

51 And [R]smote all the firstborn in Egypt; the chief of *their* strength in the tabernacles of Ham: 105:36; 135:8; 136:10

52 But [R]made his own people to go forth like sheep, and guided them in the wilderness like a flock.   77:20; Ex. 15:22

53 And he [R]led them on safely, so that they feared not: but the sea [R]overwhelmed their enemies.   Ex. 14:19, 20 • 106:11

54 And he brought them to the border of his sanctuary, *even to* this mountain, *which* his right hand had purchased.

55 [R]He cast out the heathen also before them, and [R]divided them an inheritance by line, and made the tribes of Israel to dwell in their tents.   44:2 • Josh. 13:7

56 Yet they tempted and provoked the most high God, and kept not his testimonies:

57 But [R]turned back, and dealt unfaithfully like their fathers: they were turned aside like a deceitful bow.   Ezek. 20:27

58 For they provoked him to anger with their high places, and moved him to jealousy with their [T]graven images.   *carved*

59 When God heard *this,* he was [T]wroth, and greatly abhorred Israel: *angry*

60 So that he [R]forsook the tabernacle of Shi'-loh, the tent *which* he placed among men;   78:67; 1 Sam. 4:11; Jer. 7:12, 14; 26:6

61 And delivered his strength into captivity, and his glory into the enemy's hand.

62 He gave his people over also unto the sword; and was wroth with his inheritance.

63 The [T]fire consumed their young men; and [R]their maidens were not given to marriage.   *calamity destroyed* • Jer. 7:34

64 Their priests fell by the sword; and their widows made no lamentation.

65 Then the Lord [R]awaked as one out of sleep, *and* like a mighty man that shouteth by reason of wine.   44:23; 73:20

66 And [R]he smote his enemies in the [T]hinder parts: he put them to a perpetual reproach.   1 Sam. 5:6 • *rear*

67 Moreover he refused the tabernacle of Joseph, and chose not the tribe of E'-phra-im:

68 But chose the tribe of Judah, the mount Zion [R]which he loved.   [87:2; 132:13]

69 And he [R]built his sanctuary like high *palaces,* like the earth which he hath established for ever.   [2 Sam. 7:13]; 1 Kin. 6:1–38

70 [R]He chose David also his servant, and took him from the sheepfolds: 1 Sam. 16:11

71 From following [R]the ewes great with young he brought him to feed Jacob his people, and Israel his inheritance.   [Is. 40:11]

72 So he fed them according to the [R]integrity of his heart; and guided them by the skilfulness of his hands.   1 Kin. 9:4

PSALM 79

Avenge the Defilement of Jerusalem

A Psalm of A'-saph.

O GOD, the heathen are come into thine inheritance; thy holy temple have they defiled; they have laid Jerusalem on heaps.

2 [R]The dead bodies of thy servants have they given *to be* meat unto the fowls of the heaven, the flesh of thy saints unto the beasts of the earth.   Jer. 7:33; 16:4; 19:7

3 Their blood have they shed like water round about Jerusalem; and [R]*there was* none to bury *them.*   Jer. 14:16; 16:4

4 We are become a [R]reproach to our neighbours, a scorn and derision to them that are round about us.   44:13; 80:6

5 How long, Lord? wilt thou be angry for ever? shall thy jealousy [R]burn like fire?   89:46

6 [R]Pour out thy wrath upon the heathen that have [R]not known thee, and upon the kingdoms that have [R]not called upon thy name.   Jer. 10:25 • Is. 45:4; 1 Thess. 4:5 • 53:4

7 For they have [T]devoured Jacob, and laid waste his dwelling place.   *destroyed*

8 O remember not against us former iniq-

uities: let thy tender mercies speedily prevent us: for we are brought very low.

9 Help us, O God of our salvation, for the glory of thy name: and deliver us, and purge away our sins, for thy name's sake.

10 ^RWherefore^T should the ^Theathen say, Where *is* their God? let him be known among the heathen ^Tin our sight *by* the revenging of the blood of thy servants *which is* shed.   42:10 · *why · nations · in our time*

11 Let ^Rthe sighing of the prisoner come before thee; according to the greatness of ^Tthy power ^Tpreserve thou those that are appointed to die;   102:20 · *thine arm · save*

12 And ^Trender unto our neighbours sevenfold into their bosom ^Rtheir reproach, wherewith they have reproached thee, O Lord.   *pay back* · 74:10, 18, 22

13 So we thy people and sheep of thy pasture will give thee thanks for ever: we will shew forth thy praise to all generations.

PSALM 80

Israel's Plea for God's Mercy

To the chief Musician upon Sho-shan'-nim–E'-duth, A Psalm of A'-saph.

G IVE ear, O Shepherd of Israel, thou that leadest Joseph like a flock; thou that dwellest *between* the cherubims, shine forth.

2 Before E'-phra-im and Benjamin and Ma-nas'-seh stir up thy strength, and ^Tcome *and* save us.   *come for salvation to us*

3 Turn us again, O God, and cause thy face to shine; and we shall be saved.

4 O ^RLORD God of hosts, ^Rhow long wilt thou be angry against the prayer of thy people?   59:5; 84:8 · 79:5; 85:5

5 ^RThou feedest them ^Twith the bread of tears; and givest them tears to drink in great measure.   42:3; Is. 30:20 · *in sorrow*

6 Thou makest us a strife ^Runto our neighbours: and ^Rour enemies laugh among themselves.   44:13; 79:4 · Job 30:1

7 ^RTurn^T us again, O God of hosts, and cause thy face to shine; and we shall be saved.   Is. 1:26 · *restore us*

8 Thou hast brought ^Ra vine out of Egypt: thou hast cast out the heathen, and planted it.   [Is. 5:1, 7]; Jer. 2:21; Ezek. 15:6

9 Thou ^Rpreparedst *room* before it, and ^Rdidst cause it to take deep root, and it filled the land.   Josh. 24:12; Is. 5:2 · Hos. 14:5

10 The hills were covered with the shadow of it, and the boughs thereof *were like* ^Tthe goodly cedars.   *mighty cedars*

11 She sent out her boughs ^Runto the sea, and her branches unto the river.   72:8

12 Why hast thou *then* ^Rbroken down her hedges, so that all they which pass by the way do pluck her?   Is. 5:5; Nah. 2:2

13 The boar out of the ^Twood doth ^Rwaste^T it, and the wild beast of the field doth devour it.   *forest* · Jer. 5:6 · *eat*

14 Return, we beseech thee, O God of hosts: ^Rlook down from heaven, and behold, and visit this vine;   102:19; Is. 63:15

15 And the ^Rvineyard which thy right hand hath planted, and the branch *that* thou madest strong for thyself.   *v. 8*

16 *It is* burned with fire, *it is* cut down: ^Rthey perish at the rebuke of thy countenance.   [39:11]

17 ^RLet thy hand be upon the man of thy right hand, upon the son of man *whom* thou madest strong for thyself.   89:21

18 So will not we go back from thee: quicken us, and we will call upon thy name.

19 ^TTurn^R us again, O LORD God of hosts, cause thy face to shine; and we shall be saved.   *restore us* · v. 3, Is. 1:26

PSALM 81

God's Plea for Israel's Obedience

To the chief Musician upon Git'-tith, A *Psalm* of A'-saph.

S ING aloud unto God our strength: make a joyful noise unto the God of Jacob.

2 Take a psalm, and bring hither the timbrel, the pleasant harp with the psaltery.

3 Blow up the trumpet in the ^Rnew moon, in the time appointed, on our solemn ^Rfeast day.   Num. 10:10; Is. 1:14 · Lev. 23:24

4 For ^Rthis *was* a statute for Israel, *and* a law of the God of Jacob.   Num. 10:10

5 This he ordained in Joseph *for* a testimony, when he went out through the land of Egypt: ^R*where* I heard a language *that* I understood not.   Deut. 28:49; Jer. 5:15

6 I removed his shoulder from the burden: his hands were delivered from the pots.

7 Thou calledst in trouble, and I delivered thee; ^RI answered thee in the secret place of thunder: I proved thee at the ^Rwaters of Mer'-i-bah.   Selah.   Ex. 19:19 · 95:8

8 ^RHear, O my people, and I will testify unto thee: O Israel, if ^Rthou wilt ^Rhearken unto me;   [50:7 · 95:7] · Deut. 4:1

9 There shall no strange god be in thee; neither shalt thou worship any strange god.

10 I *am* the LORD thy God, which brought thee out of the land of Egypt: open thy mouth wide, and I will fill it.

11 But my people would not hearken to my voice; and Israel would none of me.

12 ^RSo I gave them up unto their own hearts' lust: *and* they walked in their own counsels.   [Job 8:4; Acts 7:42; Rom. 1:24, 26]

13 Oh that my people had hearkened unto me, *and* Israel had walked in my ways!

14 I should soon have ^Rsubdued their en-

emies, and ᴿturned my hand against their adversaries.   18:47; 47:3 · Amos 1:8

15 The haters of the LORD should have submitted themselves unto him: but their time should have endured for ever.

16 He should have fed them also with the finest of the wheat: and with honey out of the rock should I have satisfied thee.

PSALM 82

Rebuke of Israel's Urgent Judges

A Psalm of A'-saph.

GOD standeth in the congregation of the mighty; he judgeth among the gods.

2 How long will ye judge unjustly, and accept the persons of the wicked?   Selah.

3 ᵀDefend the poor and fatherless: do justice to the afflicted and needy.   *judge*

4 ᴿDeliver the poor and needy: rid *them* out of the hand of the wicked.   Job 29:12

5 They know not, neither will they understand; they walk on in darkness: all the foundations of the earth are out of course.

6 I have ᴿsaid, Ye *are* gods; and all of you *are* children of the most High.   John 10:34

7 But ᴿye shall die like men, and fall like one of the princes.   Job 21:32; Ezek. 31:14

8 ᴿArise, O God, ᴿjudge the earth: for thou shalt inherit all nations.   [12:5 · 58:11]

PSALM 83

Plea for God to Destroy Israel's Enemies

A Song *or* Psalm of A'-saph.

KEEP not thou silence, O God: hold not thy peace, and be not still, O God.

2 For, lo, ᴿthine enemies ᵀmake a tumult: and they that hate thee have ᵀlifted up the head.   81:15 · *riot · becomes proud*

3 ᴿThey have taken crafty counsel against thy people, and consulted ᴿagainst thy hidden ones.   64:2; [Is. 29:15 · 27:5; 31:20]

4 They have said, Come, and let us cut them off from *being* a nation; that the name of Israel may be no more in remembrance.

5 For they have ᴿconsulted together with one ᵀconsent: they are ᵀconfederate against thee: 2:2; Dan. 6:7 · *heart · united*

6 ᴿThe ᵀtabernacles of E'-dom, and the Ish'-ma-el-ites; of Moab, and the Ha-gar-enes';   137:7; 2 Chr. 20:1, 10, 11 · *tents*

7 Ge'-bal, and Ammon, and Am'-a-lek; the Phi-lis'-tines with the inhabitants of Tyre;

8 As'-sur also is joined with them: they have holpen the children of Lot.   Selah.

9 Do unto them ᴿas *unto* the Mid'-i-an-ites; as *to* ᴿSis'-e-ra, as *to* Jabin, at the brook of Ki'-son: Judg. 7:22 · Judg. 4:14, 22, 23

10 *Which* perished at En'-dor: they became *as* ᵀdung for the earth.   *refuse*

11 Make their nobles like ᴿO'-reb, and like Ze'-eb: yea, all their princes as ᴿZe'-bah, and as Zal-mun'-na: Judg. 7:25 · Judg. 8:12, 21

12 Who said, ᴿLet us take to ourselves the houses of God in possession.   2 Chr. 20:11

13 ᴿO my God, make them like a wheel; as the stubble before the wind.   35:5

14 As the fire burneth a wood, and as the flame setteth the mountains on fire;

15 So persecute them with thy tempest, and make them afraid with thy storm.

16 ᴿFill their faces with shame; that they may seek thy name, O LORD.   Job 10:15

17 Let them be ᴿconfounded and troubled for ever; yea, ᴿlet them be put to shame, and perish: 35:4; 70:2 · 25:3

18 ᴿThat *men* may know that thou, whose name alone *is* ᵀJEHOVAH, *art* the most high over all the earth.   [92:8] · *the LORD*

PSALM 84

The Joy of Dwelling with God

To the chief Musician upon Git'-tith, A Psalm for the sons of Ko'-rah.

HOW ᴿamiable *are* thy ᴿtabernacles, O LORD of hosts!   27:4 · 43:3; 132:5

2 My soul longeth, yea, even fainteth for the courts of the LORD: my heart and my flesh crieth out for the living God.

3 Yea, the sparrow hath found an house, and the swallow a nest for herself, where she may lay her young, *even* thine altars, O LORD of hosts, my King, and my God.

4 ᴿBlessed *are* they that dwell in thy house: they will be still ᴿpraising thee. Selah.   [65:4 · 42:5, 11]

5 Blessed *is* the man whose strength *is* in thee; in whose heart *are* the ways *of them.*

6 *Who* passing through the valley of Ba'-ca make it a well; ᴿthe rain also filleth the pools.   [107:35; Joel 2:23]

7 They go ᴿfromᵀ strength to strength, *every one of them* in Zion appeareth before God.   Prov. 4:18 · *from company to company*

8 ᴿO LORD God of hosts, hear my prayer: give ear, O God of Jacob.   Selah.   59:5

9 Behold, O God our ᴿshield, and look upon the face of thine anointed.   3:3

10 For a ᴿday in thy courts *is* better than a thousand. I had rather be a ᴿdoorkeeper in the house of my God, than to dwell in the tents of wickedness.   27:4 · 1 Chr. 23:5

11 For the LORD God *is* a sun and ᴿshield: the LORD will give grace and glory: ᴿno good *thing* will he withhold from them that walk uprightly.   Gen. 15:1 · [34:9]

12 O LORD of hosts, ᴿblessed *is* the man that trusteth in thee.   [2:12; 40:4]

PSALM 85

Prayer for Revival

To the chief Musician,
A Psalm for the sons of Ko'-rah.

LORD, thou hast been Tfavourable unto thy land: thou hast Rbrought back the captivity of Jacob. *gracious* • Ezra 1:11

2 Thou hast Rforgiven the iniquity of thy people; thou hast Rcovered all their sin. Selah. [103:3; Num. 14:19; Jer. 31:34 • 32:1]

3 Thou hast taken away all thy wrath: thou hast Rturned *thyself* from the fierceness of thine anger. 106:23

4 Turn us, O God of our salvation, and cause thine anger toward us to cease.

5 RWilt thou be angry with us for ever? wilt thou Tdraw out thine anger to all generations? 79:5; 80:4 • *prolong*

6 Wilt thou not Rrevive us again: that thy people may rejoice in thee? Hab. 3:2

7 Shew us thy mercy, O LORD, and Rgrant us thy salvation. 106:4

8 I will hear what God the LORD will Rspeak: for he will speak peace unto his people, and to his saints: but Rlet them not turn again to Tfolly. Hag. 2:9 • 78:57 • *sin*

9 Surely his salvation *is* nigh them that fear him; that glory may dwell in our land.

10 RMercy and truth are met together; Rrighteousness and peace have kissed *each other.* [89:14]; Prov. 3:3 • 72:3; [Is. 32:17]

11 Truth shall Rspring out of the Tearth; and righteousness shall look down from heaven. [Is. 45:8] • *land*

12 Yea, the LORD shall give *that which is* good; and our land shall yield her increase.

13 Righteousness shall go before him; and shall set *us* in the way of his steps.

PSALM 86

"Teach Me Thy Way, O LORD"

A Prayer of David.

BOW down thine ear, O LORD, hear me: for I *am* Rpoor and needy. 40:17

2 TPreserve my soul; for I *am* Tholy: O thou my God, save thy servant that Ttrusteth in thee. *save* • *one whom God favours* • *confides*

3 Be Rmerciful unto me, O Lord: Rfor I cry unto thee daily. 4:1; 57:1 • 25:5

4 Rejoice the soul of thy servant: for unto thee, O Lord, do I lift up my soul.

5 For thou, Lord, *art* good, and Rready to forgive; and plenteous in mercy unto all them that call upon thee. 130:4

6 RGive ear, O LORD, unto my prayer; and attend to the voice of my supplications. 55:1

7 In the day of my trouble I will call upon thee: for thou wilt answer me.

8 Among the gods *there is* Rnone like unto thee, O LORD; neither *are there any works* like unto thy works. [Ex. 15:11]

9 RAll nations whom thou hast made shall come and worship before thee, O Lord; and shall glorify thy name. 22:27

10 For thou *art* great, and Rdoest wondrous things: thou *art* God alone. Ex. 15:11

11 RTeach me thy way, O LORD; I will walk in thy truth: Runite my heart to Tfear thy name. 25:5 • Jer. 32:39 • *revere*

12 I will Rpraise thee, O Lord my God, with Rall my heart: and I will glorify thy name for evermore. 111:1 • [Deut. 6:5]

13 For great *is* thy mercy toward me: and thou hast Rdelivered my soul from the Tlowest hell. 30:3 • *sheol*

14 O God, the proud are Rrisen against me, and the assemblies of Rviolent *men* have sought after my soul; and have not set thee before them. 54:3 • 71:10; 94:21

15 But thou, O Lord, *art* a God full of Rcompassion, and gracious, longsuffering, and plenteous in mercy and truth. [86:5]

16 O turn unto me, and have mercy upon me; give thy strength unto thy servant, and save the Rson of thine handmaid. 116:16

17 Shew me Ta token for good; that they which hate me may see *it,* and be ashamed: because thou, LORD, hast holpen me, and comforted me. *evidence of good*

PSALM 87

Glorious Zion, City of God

A Psalm *or* Song for the sons of Ko'-rah.

HIS foundation *is* in the holy mountains. 2 The LORD loveth the gates of Zion more than all the dwellings of Jacob.

3 Glorious things are spoken of thee, O Rcity of God. Selah. 46:4; 48:8

4 I will make mention of RRa'-hab and Babylon to them that know me: behold Philis'-ti-a, and RTyre, with E-thi-o'-pi-a; this *man* was born there. Job 9:13 • 45:12

5 And of Zion it shall be said, This and that man was born in her: and the highest himself shall Restablish her. 48:8

6 The LORD shall count, when he Rwriteth up the people, *that* this *man* was born there. Selah. 69:28; Is. 4:3

7 As well the Rsingers as the Rplayers on instruments *shall be there:* all my Rsprings *are* in thee. 68:25 • 149:3 • [36:9]

PSALM 88

Crying from Deepest Affliction

A Song *or* Psalm for the sons of Ko'-rah, to the chief Musician upon Ma'-ha-lath Le-an'-noth, Mas'-chil of He'-man the Ez'-ra-hite.

O LORD God of my salvation, I have cried day *and* night before thee:

2 Let my prayer come before thee: ᵀincline ᴿthine ear unto my cry;   *listen* • 31:2

3 For my soul is full of troubles: and my life draweth nigh unto the ᵀgrave.   *sheol*

4 I ᵀam counted with them that ᵀgo ᴿdown into the pit: I am as a man *that hath* ᴿno strength: *have been • are dying* • [28:1] • 22:11

5 ᵀFree ᴿamong the dead, like the slain that lie in the grave, whom thou rememberest no more: and they are ᴿcut off from thy hand.·   *set free* • 31:12 • 31:22; [Is. 53:8]

6 Thou hast ᴿlaid me in the lowest pit, in darkness, in the deeps.   Lam. 3:55

7 Thy ᴿwrath lieth ᵀhard upon me, and thou hast afflicted *me* with ᴿall thy waves. Selah.   32:4; 39:10 • *heavy* • 42:7

8 Thou hast put away ᴿmine acquaintance far from me; thou hast made me an abomination unto them: *I am* shut up, and I cannot come forth.   31:11; 142:4

9 Mine eye mourneth by reason of affliction: LORD, I have called daily upon thee, I have stretched out my hands unto thee.

10 Wilt thou shew wonders to the dead? ᴿshall the dead arise *and* praise thee? Selah.   6:5; 30:9

11 Shall thy ᴿlovingkindness be declared in the grave? *or* thy faithfulness in destruction?   [17:7; Deut. 7:9]

12 Shall thy wonders be known in the ᴿdark? and thy righteousness in the land of forgetfulness?   88:6; Job 10:21

13 But unto ᴿthee have I cried, O LORD; and ᴿin the morning shall my prayer ᵀprevent thee.   30:2 • 5:3 • *come before*

14 LORD, why ᴿcastest thou off my soul? *why* hidest thou thy face from me?   43:2

15 I *am* afflicted and ᴿready to die from *my* youth up: *while* I suffer ᴿthy terrors I am distracted.   Prov. 24:11 • Job 6:4; 31:23

16 Thy ᴿfierce wrath goeth over me; thy terrors have cut me off.   2 Chr. 28:11; [Is. 13:13]

17 They came round about me daily like water; they compassed me about together.

18 ᴿLover and friend hast thou put far from me, *and* mine acquaintance into darkness.   31:11; 38:11; 88:8; Job 19:13

PSALM 89

Claiming God's Promises in Affliction

Mas'-chil of E'-than the Ez'-ra-hite.

I WILL sing of the mercies of the LORD for ever: with my mouth will I make known thy faithfulness to all generations.

2 For I have said, Mercy shall be built up for ever: ᴿthy faithfulness shalt thou establish in the very heavens.   [119:89]

3 I have made a covenant with my chosen, I have sworn unto David my servant,

4 Thy ᴿseed will I establish for ever, and build up thy throne ᴿto all generations. Selah.   [2 Sam. 7:16 • Is. 9:7; Luke 1:33]

5 And ᴿthe heavens shall praise thy wonders, O LORD: thy faithfulness also in the congregation of the saints.   [19:1]

6 For who in the heaven can be compared unto the LORD? *who* among the sons of the mighty can be likened unto the LORD?

7 God is greatly to be feared in the assembly of the saints, and to be had in reverence of all *them that are* about him.

8 O LORD God of hosts, ᴿwho *is* a strong LORD like unto thee? or to thy faithfulness round about thee?   35:10; 71:5

9 Thou rulest the raging of the sea: when the waves thereof arise, thou stillest them.

10 Thou hast broken Ra'-hab in pieces, as one that is slain; thou hast scattered thine enemies with thy strong arm.

11 The heavens *are* thine, the earth also *is* thine: *as for* the world and the fulness thereof, thou hast founded them.

12 The north and the south thou hast created them: ᴿTa'-bor and ᴿHermon shall rejoice in thy name.   Josh. 19:22 • Josh. 12:1

13 Thou hast a mighty arm: strong is thy hand, *and* high is thy right hand.

14 ᴿJustice and judgment *are* the ᵀhabitation of thy throne: ᴿmercy and truth shall go before thy face.   97:2 • *foundation* • 85:13

15 Blessed *is* the people that know the ᴿjoyful sound: they shall walk, O LORD, in the light of thy countenance.   98:6

16 In ᴿthy name shall they ᴿrejoice all the day: and in thy righteousness shall ᴿthey be exalted.   105:3 • [Deut. 12:7 • 91:14]

17 For thou *art* the glory of ᴿtheir strength: and in thy favour ᴿour horn shall be exalted.   [28:8] • 75:10; 92:10; 148:14

18 For the LORD *is* ᴿour defence; and the Holy One of Israel *is* our king.   [47:9]

19 Then thou spakest in vision to thy holy one, and saidst, I have laid help upon *one that is* mighty; I have exalted *one* ᴿchosen out of the people.   1 Kin. 11:34

20 ᴿI have found David my servant; with my holy oil have I anointed him: Acts 13:22

21 With whom my hand shall be established: mine arm also shall strengthen him.

22 The enemy shall not exact upon him; nor the son of wickedness afflict him.

23 And I will beat down his foes before his face, and plague them that hate him.

24 But my faithfulness and my mercy *shall be* with him: and in my name shall his horn be exalted.ᴿ   v. 1; 132:17

25 I will set his hand also ᴿin the sea, and his right hand in the rivers.   72:8

26 He shall cry unto me, Thou *art* ᴿmy

father, my God, and Rthe Trock of my salvation. [1 Chr. 22:10] • 95:1 • *strength*

27 Also I will make him *my* Rfirstborn, higher than the kings of the earth. Rev. 1:5 ✭

28 RMy mercy will I keep for him for evermore, and my Rcovenant shall stand fast with him. *v.* 33; [Ex. 34:7] • *vv.* 3, 34

29 His seed also will I make *to endure* for ever, and his throne as the days of heaven.

30 If his children Rforsake my law, and walk not in my judgments; [2 Sam. 7:14]

31 If they break my statutes, and Tkeep^R not my commandments; *obey* • Deut. 11:28

32 Then will I visit their transgression with the rod, and their iniquity with stripes.

33 Nevertheless my lovingkindness will I not Tutterly take from him, nor suffer my faithfulness to fail. *completely*

34 My covenant will I not break, nor alter the thing that is gone out of my lips.

35 Once have I sworn Rby my holiness that I will not lie unto David. Amos 4:2

36 His seed shall endure for ever, and his throne Ras the sun before me. 72:5

37 It shall be established for ever Ras the moon, and *as* a faithful Rwitness in heaven. Selah. 72:5 • Job 16:19

38 But thou hast cast off and abhorred, thou hast been wroth with thine anointed.

39 Thou hast made void the covenant of thy servant: Rthou hast profaned his crown *by casting it* to the ground. Lam. 5:16

40 Thou hast broken down all his hedges; thou hast brought his strong holds to ruin.

41 All that pass by the way Tspoil him: he is a reproach to his neighbours. *rob*

42 RThou hast set up the right hand of his adversaries; Rthou hast made all his enemies to rejoice. 13:2 • 80:6

43 Thou hast also turned the edge of his sword, and Thast Rnot made him to stand in the battle. *has not helped him* • 44:10

44 Thou hast made his glory to cease, and cast his throne down to the ground.

45 The days of his youth hast thou Rshortened: thou hast Rcovered him with shame. Selah. 102:23 • 44:15; 71:13; 109:29

46 How long, LORD? wilt thou hide thyself for ever? shall thy wrath burn like fire?

47 Remember how short my time is: wherefore hast thou made all men in vain?

48 What man *is he that* liveth, and shall not Rsee death? shall he deliver his soul from the hand of the grave? Selah. [22:29]

49 Lord, where *are* thy former lovingkindnesses, *which* thou Rswarest unto David Rin thy truth? 2 Sam. 7:15 • 54:5

50 Remember, Lord, the reproach of thy servants; *how* I do bear in my bosom *the reproach of* all the mighty people;

51 Wherewith thine enemies have reproached, O LORD; wherewith they have reproached the footsteps of thine anointed.

52 RBlessed *be* the LORD for evermore. A-men', and A-men'. 41:13; 72:19; 106:48

BOOK IV

PSALM 90

"Teach Us to Number Our Days"

A Prayer of Moses the man of God.

LORD, Rthou hast been our dwelling place in all generations. [Ezek. 11:16]

2 RBefore the mountains were brought forth, or ever thou hadst Tformed the earth and the world, even from everlasting to everlasting, thou *art* God. Prov. 8:25 • *created*

3 Thou turnest man to destruction; and sayest, Return, ye children of men.

4 RFor a thousand years in thy sight *are but* as yesterday when it is past, and *as* a Rwatch in the night. [39:5] • Matt. 14:25

5 Thou carriest them away as with a flood; they are *as* a sleep: in the morning *they are* like grass *which* groweth up.

6 In the morning it Rflourisheth, and groweth up; in the evening it is Rcut down, and withereth. Job 14:2 • [92:7; Matt. 6:30]

7 For we are Tconsumed by thine anger, and by thy wrath are we troubled. *destroyed*

8 RThou hast set our iniquities before thee, our Rsecret *sins* in the light of thy countenance. [Jer. 16:17] • 19:12; [Eccl. 12:14]

9 For Rall our days are passed away in thy wrath: we spend our years as a tale *that is told.* 78:33

10 The days of our years *are* threescore years and ten; and if by reason of strength *they be* fourscore years, yet *is* their Tstrength Rlabour and sorrow; for it is soon cut off, and we fly away. *violence* • [Eccl. 12:2–7]

11 Who knoweth the Rpower of thine anger? even according to thy Rfear, *so is* thy wrath. [76:7] • Neh. 5:9

12 So teach *us* to number our days, that we may apply *our* hearts unto wisdom.

13 Return, O LORD, how long? and let it repent thee concerning thy servants.

14 O Rsatisfy us early with thy mercy; Rthat we may rejoice and be glad all our days. [36:8; 65:4; 103:5; Jer. 31:14] • 85:6

15 RMake us glad according to the days *wherein* thou hast afflicted us, *and* the years *wherein* we have seen evil. 86:4

16 Let thy work appear unto thy servants, and thy glory unto their children.

17 And let the beauty of the LORD our God be upon us: and Restablish thou the work of our hands upon us; yea, the work of our hands establish thou it. [37:23]

PSALM 91

Abiding in "the Shadow of the Almighty"

HE that dwelleth in the secret place of the most High shall abide ᴿunder the shadow of the Almighty.   17:8

2 ᴿI will say of the Lᴏʀᴅ, *He is* my ᴿrefuge and my ᴿfortress: my God; in him will I ᴿtrust.ᵀ   142:5 · v. 9 · 18:2 · 25:2 · *confide*

3 Surely he shall deliver thee from the snare of the fowler, *and* from the ᵀnoisome pestilence.   *raging epidemic*

4 He shall cover thee with his feathers, and under his wings shalt thou trust: his truth *shall be thy* shield and buckler.

5 ᴿThou shalt not be afraid for the ᴿterror by night; *nor* for the ᴿarrow *that* flieth by day;   [Job 5:19–23] · Song 3:8 · 64:4

6 *Nor* for the ᵀpestilence *that* walketh in darkness; *nor* for the destruction *that* ᵀwasteth at noonday.   *epidemic · destroys*

7 A thousand shall fall at thy side, and ten thousand at thy right hand; ᴿ*but* it shall not come nigh thee.   Josh. 14:10

8 Only with thine eyes shalt thou behold and see the reward of the wicked.

9 Because thou hast made the Lᴏʀᴅ, *which is* ᴿmy refuge, *even* the most High, thy habitation;   90:1

10 There shall no evil befall thee, neither shall any plague come nigh thy dwelling.

11 For he shall give his angels charge over thee, to keep thee in all thy ways.

12 They shall ᵀbear thee up in *their* hands, lest thou dash thy foot against a stone.   *hold*

13 Thou shalt ᴿtread upon the lion and adder: the young lion and the dragon shalt thou trample under feet.   Dan. 6:22

14 Because he hath set his love upon me, therefore will I deliver him: I will set him on high, because he hath known my name.

15 He shall ᴿcall upon me, and I will answer him: I *will be* with him in trouble; I will deliver him, and honour him.   Job 12:4

16 With ᴿlong life will I satisfy him, and shew him my salvation.   Prov. 3:2

PSALM 92

It Is Good to Praise the Lord

A Psalm *or* Song for the sabbath day.

IT is a ᴿgood *thing* to give thanks unto the Lᴏʀᴅ, and to ᴿsing praises unto thy name, O most High: 147:1 · [135:3]

2 To ᴿshewᵀ forth thy lovingkindness in the morning, and thy ᴿfaithfulness ᵀevery night,   59:16 · *talk about* · 89:1 · *in the*

3 ᴿUpon an instrument of ten strings, and upon the psaltery; upon the harp with a ᵀsolemn sound.   33:2; 1 Sam. 10:5 · *deep tone*

4 For thou, Lᴏʀᴅ, hast made me glad

ᴿthrough thy work: I will ᴿtriumph in the ᴿworks of thy hands.   [40:5] · 106:47 · 8:6

5 ᴿO Lᴏʀᴅ, how great are thy works! *and* thy thoughts are very deep.   [Is. 28:29]

6 A ᵀbrutish man knoweth not; neither doth a fool understand this.   *unthinking*

7 When the wicked ᴿspring as the grass, and when all the ᴿworkers of iniquity do flourish; *it is* that they shall be ᴿdestroyed for ever: 90:5 · 94:4 · [37:38]

8 ᴿBut thou, Lᴏʀᴅ, *art* ᵀmostᴿ high for evermore.   [83:18] · *in control* · [93:4; 113:5]

9 For, lo, thine enemies, O Lᴏʀᴅ, for, lo, thine enemies shall perish; all the workers of iniquity shall be scattered.

10 But ᴿmyᵀ horn shalt thou exalt like *the horn of* an ᵀunicorn: I shall be ᴿanointed with fresh oil.   75:10 · *my strength · wild ox* · 23:5

11 Mine eye also shall see *my desire* on mine enemies, *and* mine ears shall hear *my desire* of the wicked that rise up against me.

12 ᴿThe righteous shall ᵀflourish like the palm tree: he shall grow like a ᴿcedar in Leb'-a-non.   [Ps. 1:3] · *prosper* · 104:16; Ezek. 31:3

13 Those that be ᴿplanted in the house of the Lᴏʀᴅ shall flourish ᴿin the courts of our God.   80:15; [Is. 60:21] · 100:4; 116:19

14 They shall still bring forth fruit in old age; they shall be fat and flourishing;

15 ᵀTo shew that the Lᴏʀᴅ *is* upright: ᴿhe is my rock, and ᴿ*there is* no unrighteousness in him.   *to prove* · [Deut. 32:4] · [Rom. 9:14]

PSALM 93

The Majesty of God

THE Lᴏʀᴅ reigneth, he is ᵀclothed with majesty; the Lᴏʀᴅ is clothed with strength, ᴿwherewith he hath girded himself: the world also is stablished, that it cannot be ᵀmoved.   *covered · 65:6 · shaken*

2 ᴿThy throne *is* established of old: thou ᴿ*art* from everlasting.   45:6; [Lam. 5:19] · [90:2]

3 The ᴿfloods have ᵀlifted up, O Lᴏʀᴅ, the floods have lifted up their voice; the floods lift up their waves.   96:11; 98:7, 8 · *raised up*

4 ᴿThe Lᴏʀᴅ on high *is* mightier than the noise of many waters, *yea, than* the mighty waves of the sea.   65:7; 89:6, 9; 92:8

5 Thy ᴿtestimonies are very ᵀsure: ᴿholiness ᵀbecometh thine house, O Lᴏʀᴅ, for ever.   [19:7] · *certain* · 29:2 · *will appear in*

PSALM 94

Vengeance Belongs Only to God

O LORD God, to whom vengeance belongeth; O God, to whom vengeance belongeth, ᵀshew thyself.   *let yourself be seen*

2 Lift up thyself, thou judge of the earth: render a reward to the proud.

3 LORD, Rhow long shall the wicked, how long shall the wicked triumph?   [Job 20:5]

4 *How long* shall they Rutter *and* speak Thard things? *and* all the workers of iniquity boast themselves?   31:18 · *willful*

5 They Rbreak in pieces thy people, O LORD, and afflict thine heritage.   Is. 3:15

6 They Rslay the widow and the stranger, and murder the fatherless.   Ex. 22:22; Is. 10:2

7 Yet they say, The LORD shall not see, neither shall the God of Jacob regard *it*.

8 Understand, ye brutish among the people: and ye fools, when will ye be wise?

9 He that Rplanted the ear, shall he not hear? he that formed the eye, Rshall he not see?   [Ex. 4:11; Prov. 20:12] · Gen. 6:5

10 He that Tchastiseth the heathen, shall not he correct? he that teacheth man knowledge, *shall not he know?*   *punishes*

11 The LORD knoweth the thoughts of man, that they *are* Tvanity.   *empty*

12 Blessed *is* the man whom thou Tchastenest, RO LORD, and Rteachest him out of thy law;   *corrects* · [119:71; Deut. 8:5] · 119:171

13 That thou mayest give him Trest Rfrom the days of adversity, until Rthe pit be digged for the wicked.   *relief* · Job 49:5 · 9:15

14 For Rthe LORD will not cast off his people, neither will he forsake his inheritance.   [1 Sam. 12:22]; Lam. 3:31; Rom. 11:2

15 But Rjudgment shall return unto righteousness: and all the upright in heart shall follow it.   97:2; [Is. 42:3]; Mic. 7:9

16 Who will Rrise up for me against the evildoers? or who will stand up for me against the workers of iniquity?   Num. 10:35

17 Unless the LORD *had been* my help, my soul had almost dwelt in silence.

18 When I said, RMy foot slippeth; thy mercy, O LORD, held me up.   38:16; 73:2

19 In the multitude of my thoughts within me thy comforts delight my soul.

20 Shall Rthe throne of iniquity Thave fellowship with thee, which Rframeth mischief by a law?   Amos 6:3 · *be friendly* · 50:16

21 They Rgather themselves together against the soul of the righteous, and Rcondemn the innocent blood.   56:6 · [Prov. 17:15]

22 But the LORD is my Rdefence; and my God *is* the Rrock of my refuge.   [18:2]; 71:7 · [9:9]

23 And he shall Rbring upon them their own iniquity, and shall Rcut them off in their own wickedness; *yea,* the LORD our God shall cut them off.   7:16 · Gen. 19:15

PSALM 95

Call to Worship the Lord

O COME, let us Rsing unto the LORD: let us make a joyful noise to Rthe rock of our salvation.   66:1; 81:1 · [89:26]

2 Let us Rcome before his Tpresence with thanksgiving, and make a joyful noise unto him with psalms.   Mic. 6:6 · *face*

3 For Rthe LORD *is* a great God, and a great King above all Tgods.   96:4; 97:9 · *rulers*

4 In his hand *are* the deep places of the earth: the strength of the hills *is* his also.

5 RThe sea *is* his, and he made it: and his hands formed the dry *land*.   Gen. 1:9, 10

6 O come, let us worship and bow down: let us kneel before the LORD our maker.

7 For he *is* our God; and we *are* the people of his pasture, and the sheep of his hand. To day if ye will hear his voice,

8 Harden not your heart, Ras in the provocation, *and* as in the day of temptation in the wilderness: Ex. 17:2, 7; Num. 20:13

9 When Ryour fathers Ttempted me, proved me, and saw my work.   78:18 · *tested*

10 RForty years long was I grieved with *this* generation, and said, It *is* a people that do err in their heart, and they have not known my ways: Acts 7:36; Heb. 3:10

11 Unto whom I sware in my wrath that they should not enter into my rest.

PSALM 96

Declare the Glory of God

O SING unto the LORD a new song: sing unto the LORD, all the earth.

2 Sing unto the LORD, bless his name; shew forth his salvation from day to day.

3 Declare his Rglory among the heathen, his wonders among all people.   145:12

4 For the LORD *is* great, and greatly to be praised: he *is* to be feared above all gods.

5 For all the gods of the nations *are* idols: but the LORD made the heavens.

6 Honour and majesty *are* before him: strength and beauty *are* in his sanctuary.

7 TGive unto the LORD, O ye Rkindreds of the people, Rgive unto the LORD glory and strength.   *ascribe* · 22:27 · 45:12

8 Give unto the LORD the Rglory *due unto* his name: bring an Roffering, and come into his courts.   79:9; 115:1 · 45:12

9 O worship the LORD in the beauty of holiness: fear before him, all the earth.

10 Say among the heathen *that* the LORD reigneth: the world also shall be established that it shall not be Tmoved: he shall judge the people righteously.   *shaken*

11 RLet the heavens rejoice, and Rlet the earth be glad; Rlet the sea roar, and the fulness thereof.   Is. 49:13 · 97:1 · 98:7

12 Let the Rfield be joyful, and all that *is* therein: then shall all the Rtrees of the wood rejoice   65:13; Is. 35:1 · Is. 44:23

13 Before the LORD: for Rhe cometh, for he cometh to judge the earth: Rhe shall judge the world with righteousness, and the people with his truth.   98:9 · [Rev. 19:11]

PSALM 97

Rejoice! The Lord Reigns!

THE LORD Rreigneth; let the Rearth rejoice; let the multitude of RislesT be glad thereof.   [96:10] • 96:11 • Is. 42:10, 12 • coast lands

2 RClouds and darkness are round about him: Rrighteousness and judgment are the habitation of his throne.   18:11 • [89:14]

3 RA fire goeth before him, and burneth up his enemies round about.   18:8; Heb. 12:29

4 RHis lightnings enlightened the world: the earth saw, and trembled.   Ex. 19:18

5 RThe hills melted like wax at the presence of the LORD, at the presence of the Lord of the whole earth.   Mic. 1:4; Nah. 1:5

6 RThe heavens declare his righteousness, and all the people see his glory.   [19:1]

7 Confounded be all they that serve graven images, that boast themselves of idols: Rworship him, all ye gods.   [Heb. 1:6]

8 Zion heard, and Rwas glad; and the daughters of Judah rejoiced because of thy judgments, O LORD.   48:11; Zeph. 3:14

9 For thou, LORD, art high above all the earth: thou art exalted far above all gods.

10 Ye that love the LORD, hate evil: he preserveth the souls of his saints; he delivereth them out of the hand of the wicked.

11 RLight is sown for the righteous, and gladness for the upright in heart.   Job 22:28

12 RRejoice in the LORD, ye righteous; Rand give thanks Tat the remembrance of his holiness.   33:1 • 30:4 • to the memorial

PSALM 98

Sing a New Song to the Lord

A Psalm.

O SING unto the LORD a Rnew song; for he hath done Rmarvellous things: his Rright hand, and his Rholy arm, hath gotten him the victory.   33:3 • [40:5] • Ex. 15:6 • [Is. 52:10]

2 The LORD hath made known his salvation: Rhis righteousness hath he openly shewed in the sight of the heathen.   Is. 62:2

3 He hath Rremembered his mercy and his truth toward the house of Israel: Rall the ends of the earth have seen the salvation of our God.   [Luke 1:54, 72] • 22:27

4 RMake a joyful noise unto the LORD, all the earth: Rmake a loud noise, and Rrejoice, and sing praise.   100:1 • Is. 44:23 • Deut. 12:7

5 Sing unto the LORD with the harp; with the harp, and the voice of a psalm.

6 With Rtrumpets and sound of cornet Rmake a joyful noise before Rthe LORD, the King.   Num. 10:10; 2 Chr. 15:14 • 66:1 • 47:7

7 Let the Rsea roar, and the fulness thereof; the Rworld, and they that dwell therein.   96:11 • [24:1]

8 Let the floods Tclap their hands: let the hills be joyful together   give applause

9 Before the LORD; Rfor he cometh to judge the earth: with righteousness shall he judge the world, and the people with equity.   [96:10]

PSALM 99

"Exalt Ye the LORD Our God"

THE LORD reigneth; let the people Ttremble: he sitteth between the cherubims; let the earth be moved.   be impressed

2 The LORD is Rgreat in Zion; and he is Rhigh above all the people.   48:1; Is. 12:6 • [97:9]

3 Let them praise thy Rgreat and terrible name; for it is Rholy.   76:1; Deut. 28:58 • 22:3

4 The king's strength also loveth Tjudgment; thou dost Testablish equity, Rthou executest judgment and righteousness in Jacob.   justice • make fairness the rule • [Jer. 23:5]

5 TExalt ye the LORD our God, and worship at his footstool; for he is holy.   praise

6 Moses and Aaron among his priests, and Samuel among them that Tcall upon his name; they Rcalled upon the LORD, and he answered them.   pray unto him • Ex. 15:25

7 He Rspake unto them in the cloudy pillar: they kept his testimonies, and the Tordinance that he gave them.   Ex. 33:9 • law

8 RThou answeredst them, O LORD our God: thou wast a God that Rforgavest them, though thou Ttookest vengeance of their inventions.   106:44 • [78:38] • dealt in judgment

9 Exalt the LORD our God, and worship at his holy hill; for the LORD our God is holy.

PSALM 100

"Serve the LORD with Gladness"

A Psalm of praise.

MAKE Ra joyful noise unto the LORD, Tall ye lands.   95:1 • all the earth

2 Serve the LORD with gladness: come before his presence with singing.

3 Know ye that the LORD he is God: Rit is he that hath made us, Tand not we ourselves; we are his people, and the sheep of his pasture.   [Eph. 2:10] • and His we are

4 Enter into his gates with thanksgiving, and into his courts with praise: be thankful unto him, and bless his name.

5 For Rthe LORD is good; his mercy is everlasting; and his Rtruth endureth to all generations.   [25:8; Jer. 33:11] • 119:90

PSALM 101

Commitments of a Holy Life

A Psalm of David.

I WILL Rsing of mercy and judgment: unto thee, O LORD, will I sing.   51:14

2 I will behave myself wisely in a perfect way. O when wilt thou come unto me? I will walk within my house with a perfect heart.

3 I will set no wicked thing before mine eyes: I hate the work of them ᴿthat turn aside; *it* shall not cleave to me.   Josh. 23:6

4 A froward heart shall depart from me: I will not ᵀknow a wicked *person.*   *esteem*

5 Whoso privily slandereth his neighbour, him will I cut off: him that hath an high look and a proud heart will not I suffer.

6 Mine eyes *shall be* upon the faithful of the land, that they may dwell with me: he that walketh ᵀinᴿ a perfect way, he shall serve me.   *perfect in the way* • [119:1]

7 He that worketh deceit shall not dwell within my house: he that telleth lies ᵀshall not tarry in my sight.   *shall not be established*

8 I will ᴿearly destroy all the wicked of the land; that I may cut off all wicked doers from the city of the LORD.   [75:10]

PSALM 102

Prayer of an Overwhelmed Saint

A Prayer of the afflicted, when he is overwhelmed, and poureth out his complaint before the LORD.

HEARᴿ my prayer, O LORD, and let my ᴿcry come unto thee.   39:12 • Ex. 2:23

2 ᴿHide not thy face from me in the day *when* I am in trouble; ᴿincline thine ear unto me: in the day *when* I call ᴿanswer me speedily.   69:17 • 31:2 • 69:17

3 For my days are consumed like smoke, and my bones are burned as an hearth.

4 My heart is smitten, and withered like grass; so that I forget to eat my bread.

5 By reason of the voice of my groaning ᴿmy bones cleave to my skin.   Job 19:20

6 I am like a ᴿpelican of the wilderness: I am like an owl of the desert.   Zeph. 2:14

7 I ᴿwatch, and am as a sparrow ᴿalone upon the house top.   77:4 • 38:11; John 16:32

8 Mine enemies ᴿreproach me all the day; *and* they that are ᴿmad against me are ᴿsworn against me.   31:11 • Acts 26:11 • Is. 65:15

9 For I have eaten ashes like bread, and ᴿmingled my drink with weeping,   42:3; 80:5

10 Because of thine indignation and thy wrath: for thou hast ᵀliftedᴿ me up, and cast me down.   *given me prosperity* • Job 27:21

11 My days *are* like a shadow that declineth; and I am withered like grass.

12 But thou, O LORD, shalt ᴿendure for ever; and thy ᴿremembrance unto all generations.   9:7; 10:16; Lam. 5:19 • [135:13]; Ex. 3:15

13 Thou shalt ᴿarise, *and* have ᴿmercy upon Zion: for ᴿthe time to favour her, yea, the set time, is come.   [12:5] • Is. 60:10 • 119:126

14 For thy servants take pleasure in her stones, and favour the dust thereof.

15 So the ᴿheathenᵀ shall fear the name of the LORD, and ᴿall the kings of the earth thy glory.   67:7; 1 Kin. 8:43 • *nations* • 138:4

16 When the LORD shall ᴿbuild up Zion, ᴿhe shall appear in his glory.   147:2 • [Is. 60:1, 2]

17 He will regard the prayer of the destitute, and not despise their prayer.

18 This shall be ᴿwritten for the generation to come: and the people which shall be created shall praise the LORD.   Deut. 31:19

19 For he hath ᴿlooked down from the height of his sanctuary; from heaven did the LORD behold the earth;   14:2; 53:2

20 To hear the groaning of the prisoner; to loose those that are appointed to death;

21 To ᴿdeclare the name of the LORD in Zion, and his praise in Jerusalem;   22:22

22 When the people are gathered together, and the kingdoms, to serve the LORD.

23 He weakened my strength in the way; he ᴿshortened my days.   39:5

24 ᴿI said, O my God, take me not away in the midst of my days: ᴿthy years *are* throughout all generations.   [39:13 • 90:2]

25 Of old hast ᴿthou laid the foundation of the earth: and ᴿthe heavens *are* the work of thy hands.   [Gen. 1:1; Neh. 9:6 • 96:5]

26 ᴿThey shall perish, but thou shalt endure: yea, all of them shall wax old like a garment; as a vesture shalt thou change them, and they shall be changed: Is. 34:4

27 But ᴿthou *art* the same, and thy years shall have no end.   [Is. 41:4; 43:10]; Mal. 3:6

28 ᴿThe children of thy servants ᵀshall continue, and their ᴿseed shall be established before thee.   69:36 • *shall dwell* • 89:4

PSALM 103

Bless the Lord, All Ye People!

A *Psalm* of David.

BLESS the LORD, O my soul: and all that is within me, *bless* his holy name.

2 Bless the LORD, O my soul, and ᴿforget not ᵀall his benefits: Deut. 6:12; 8:11 • *any of*

3 Who forgiveth all thine iniquities; who ᴿhealeth all thy diseases;   [Ex. 15:26]

4 Who redeemeth thy life from destruction; ᴿwho crowneth thee with lovingkindness and tender mercies;   [5:12]

5 Who ᴿsatisfieth thy mouth with good *things; so that* ᴿthy youth is renewed like the eagle's.   107:9; 145:16 • [Is. 40:31]

6 The LORD ᴿexecuteth righteousness and judgment for all that are oppressed.   99:4

7 ᴿHe made known his ways unto Moses, his acts unto the children of Israel.   147:19

8 The LORD *is* merciful and gracious, slow to anger, and plenteous in mercy.

9 ᴿHe will not always chide: neither will he keep *his anger* for ever.   [30:5; Is. 57:16]

10 ᴿHe hath not dealt with us after our

sins; nor rewarded us according to our iniquities. [Deut. 9:5; Ezra 9:13; Lam. 3:22]

11 For ᴿas the heaven is high above the earth, so ᵀgreat is ᴿhis mercy toward them that fear him. 36:5; 57:10 • *mighty* • Gen. 18:26

12 As far as the east is from the west, so far hath he ᴿremoved our transgressions from us. [2 Sam. 12:13; Is. 43:25; Zech. 3:9]

13 Like as a father pitieth *his* children, so the Lᴏʀᴅ pitieth them that fear him.

14 For he knoweth our frame; he remembereth that we *are* ᴿdust. Gen. 3:19

15 *As for* man, his days *are* as grass: as a flower of the field, so he flourisheth.

16 ᴿFor the wind passeth over it, and it is gone; and ᴿthe place thereof shall ᵀknow it no more. Is. 40:7 • Job 7:10; 8:18 • *remember*

17 But the ᴿmercy of the Lᴏʀᴅ *is* from everlasting to everlasting upon them that fear him, and his ᴿrighteousness unto children's children; 25:6 • [105:8; Ex. 20:6]

18 ᴿTo such as keep his ᵀcovenant, and to those that remember his commandments to do them. [Deut. 7:9] • *agreement*

19 The Lᴏʀᴅ hath prepared his ᴿthrone in the heavens; and ᴿhis kingdom ruleth over all. 11:4 • [47:2, 8; Dan. 4:25]

20 ᴿBless the Lᴏʀᴅ, ye his angels, that ᴿexcel in strength, that ᴿdo his commandments, ᴿhearkening unto the voice of his word. 148:2 • 29:1 • [Matt. 6:10] • [Heb. 1:14]

21 Bless ye the Lᴏʀᴅ, all ye his hosts; *ye* ministers of his, that do his pleasure.

22 Bless the Lᴏʀᴅ, ᴿall his works in all places of his ᵀdominion: bless the Lᴏʀᴅ, O my soul. 145:10 • *sovereignty*

PSALM 104

Psalm Rehearsing Creation

BLESSᴿ the Lᴏʀᴅ, O my soul. O Lᴏʀᴅ my God, thou art very great; thou art clothed with honour and majesty. 103:22

2 Who coverest *thyself* with ᴿlight as *with* a garment: who ᴿstretchest out the heavens like a curtain: [Dan. 7:9] • [Is. 40:22]

3 ᴿWho layeth the beams of his chambers in the waters: who maketh the ᵀclouds ᴿ his chariot: who walketh upon the ᴿwings of the wind: [Amos 9:6] • *thick clouds* • Is. 19:1 • 18:10

4 Who maketh his ᵀangels spirits; his ᵀministers a flaming fire: *messengers* • *servants*

5 *Who* laid the foundations of the earth, *that* it should not be removed for ever.

6 Thou ᴿcoveredst it with the ᵀdeep as *with* a garment: the waters stood above the mountains. Gen. 1:2 • *ocean*

7 At thy ᴿrebuke they fled; at the voice of thy thunder they hasted away. 18:15; 106:9

8 They go up by the mountains; they go down by the valleys unto the ᴿplace which thou hast founded for them. 33:7

9 Thou hast set a ᴿbound that they may not pass over; that they turn not again to cover the earth. Job 38:10, 11; [Jer. 5:22]

10 He sendeth the ᴿsprings into the valleys, *which* run among the hills. 107:35

11 They give drink to every beast of the field: the wild asses quench their thirst.

12 By them shall the fowls of the heaven have their ᴿhabitation, *which* ᵀsing among the branches. [Matt. 8:20] • *give a voice*

13 ᴿHe watereth the hills from his ᵀchambers: the earth is satisfied with ᴿthe fruit of thy works. 147:8 • *dwelling place* • Jer. 10:13

14 He causeth the grass to grow for the cattle, and herb for the service of man: that he may bring forth food out of the earth;

15 And wine *that* maketh glad the heart of man, *and* oil to make *his* face to shine, and bread *which* strengtheneth man's heart.

16 ᴿThe trees of the Lᴏʀᴅ are full *of sap;* the cedars of Leb'-a-non, which he hath planted; Num. 24:6; 1 Kin. 4:33; Is. 2:13

17 Where the birds make their nests: *as for* the stork, the fir trees *are* her house.

18 The high hills *are* a refuge for the wild goats; *and* the rocks for the conies.

19 ᴿHe appointed the moon for seasons: the sun knoweth his going down. Gen. 1:14

20 ᴿThou makest darkness, and it is night: wherein ᴿall the beasts of the forest do creep forth. [74:16; Is. 45:7] • [50:10]

21 ᴿThe young lions roar after their prey, and seek their meat from God. Job 38:39

22 The sun ariseth, they gather themselves together, and lay them down in their dens.

23 Man goeth forth unto ᴿhis work and to his labour until the evening. Gen. 3:19

24 ᴿO Lᴏʀᴅ, how manifold are thy works! in wisdom hast thou made them all: the earth is full of thy riches. [Jer. 10:12]

25 *So is* this great and wide ᴿsea, wherein *are* things creeping innumerable, both small and great beasts. 8:8; 69:34

26 There go the ships: *there is* that leviathan, *whom* thou hast made to play therein.

27 ᴿThese wait all upon thee; that thou mayest ᴿgive *them* their ᵀmeatᴿ in due season. [136:25] • 147:9 • *food* • Job 36:31; 38:41

28 *That* thou ᴿgivest them they gather: thou openest ᴿthine hand, they are filled with good. [145:16] • 2 Chr. 30:12; [John 10:28]

29 Thou hidest thy face, they are troubled: ᴿthou takest away their breath, they die, and return to their dust. Job 34:15

30 ᴿThou sendest forth thy spirit, they are ᴿcreated: and thou renewest the face of the earth. [Job 33:4]; Ezek. 37:9 • [Gen. 1:1]

31 The glory of the Lᴏʀᴅ shall endure for ever: the Lᴏʀᴅ shall rejoice in his works.

32 He looketh on the earth, and it ᴿtrembleth:ᵀ ᴿhe toucheth the hills, and they smoke. 97:4, 5 • *is shaken* • 144:5

33 ᴿI will sing unto the Lᴏʀᴅ as long as I

live: I will ^Rsing praise to my God while I have my being.   63:4 · 146:2

34 My ^Rmeditation of him shall be sweet: I will be ^Rglad in the LORD.   19:14 · 9:2

35 Let ^Rthe sinners be ^Tconsumed out of the earth, and let the ^Rwicked be no more. ^RBless thou the LORD, O my soul. Praise ye the LORD.   37:38 · *destroyed* · 37:10 · *v.* 1

PSALM 105

Remember, God Keeps His Promises

O GIVE^R thanks unto the LORD; call upon his name: ^Rmake known his deeds among the people.   106:1 · 145:12

2 Sing unto him, sing psalms unto him: ^Rtalk ye of all his wondrous works.   119:27

3 Glory ye in his holy name: let the heart of them rejoice that seek the LORD.

4 Seek the LORD, and ^Rhis strength: ^Rseek his face ^Tevermore.   63:2 · 27:8 · *continually*

5 ^RRemember his marvellous works ^Tthat he hath done; his wonders, and the ^Rjudgments of his mouth;   77:11 · *which* · 119:13

6 O ye seed of ^RAbraham his servant, ye children of ^RJacob his chosen.   *v.* 42 · [135:4]

7 He *is* the LORD our God: ^Rhis judgments *are* in all the earth.   Gen. 28:21; [Is. 26:9]

8 He hath ^Rremembered his ^Tcovenant for ever, the word which he commanded to a thousand generations.   Luke 1:72 · *agreement*

9 Which covenant he made with Abraham, and his oath unto Isaac;

10 And ^Rconfirmed the same unto Jacob for a law, *and* to Israel for an ^Reverlasting covenant: [Gen. 28:13–15] · Gen. 9:16; Is. 24:5

11 Saying, Unto thee will I give the land of Canaan, the lot of your inheritance:

12 When they were *but* a few men in number; yea, very few, and strangers in it.

13 ^RWhen they went from one nation to another, from *one* kingdom to another people;   *v.* 23

14 He suffered no man to do them wrong: yea, he reproved kings for their sakes;

15 ^RSaying, Touch not mine anointed, and do my prophets no harm.   Gen. 26:11

16 Moreover he called for a famine upon the land: he brake the whole staff of bread.

17 He sent a man before them, *even* Joseph, *who* was sold for a servant:

18 Whose feet they hurt with fetters: ^The was laid in iron: *his neck in an iron collar*

19 Until the time that his word came: ^Rthe word of the LORD tried him.   Gen. 41:25

20 The king sent and loosed him; *even* the ruler of the people, and let him go free.

21 He made him lord of his house, and ruler of all his ^Tsubstance: *property*

22 To bind his princes at his pleasure; and teach his ^Tsenators wisdom.   *elders*

23 Israel also came into Egypt; and Jacob sojourned in the land of Ham.

24 And he increased his people greatly; and made them stronger than their enemies.

25 He turned their heart to hate his people, to deal subtilly with his servants.

26 He ^Rsent Moses his servant; *and* ^RAaron whom he had chosen.   Ex. 3:10; 4:12 · Ex. 4:14

27 They shewed his signs among them, and ^Twonders in the land of Ham.   *miracles*

28 He sent darkness, and made it dark; and they rebelled not against his word.

29 ^RHe turned their waters into blood, and slew their fish.   Ex. 7:20, 21

30 Their land brought forth frogs in abundance, in the chambers of their kings.

31 He spake, and there came divers sorts of flies, *and* lice in all their coasts.

32 ^RHe gave them hail for rain, *and* flaming fire in their land.   Ex. 9:23–25

33 He smote their vines also and their fig trees; and brake the trees of their coasts.

34 He spake, and the locusts came, and caterpillers, and that without number,

35 And did eat up all the herbs in their land, and devoured the fruit of their ground.

36 He smote also all the firstborn in their land, the chief of all their strength.

37 ^RHe brought them forth also with silver and gold: and *there was* not one feeble *person* among their tribes.   Ex. 12:35

38 Egypt was glad when they departed: for the fear of them fell upon them.

39 ^RHe spread a cloud for a covering; and fire to give light in the night.   Ex. 13:21

40 ^R*The* people asked, and he brought ^Rquails, and ^Rsatisifed them with the bread of heaven.   78:18 · 78:27 · 78:24; Ex. 16:15

41 ^RHe opened the rock, and the waters gushed out; they ran in the dry places *like* a river.   Ex. 17:6; Num. 20:11; Is. 48:21

42 For he remembered ^Rhis holy promise, *and* Abraham his servant.   Gen. 15:14

43 And he brought forth his people with joy, *and* his chosen with ^Tgladness: *singing*

44 ^RAnd gave them the lands of the heathen: and they ^Rinherited the labour of the people;   78:55; Josh. 13:7 · Deut. 6:10, 11

45 That they might observe his statutes, and keep his laws. Praise ye the LORD.

PSALM 106

"We Have Sinned"

P RAISE ye the LORD. ^RO give thanks unto the LORD; for *he is* good: for his mercy endureth for ever.   105:1

2 Who can utter the mighty acts of the LORD? *who* can shew forth all his praise?

3 RBlessed *are* they that keep Rjudgment, *and* he that Rdoeth righteousness at Rall times.   [1:1] • Deut. 6:20 • 15:2 • [Gal. 6:9]

4 Remember me, O LORD, with the favour *that thou bearest unto* thy people: O Tvisit me with thy salvation;   *come to*

5 That I may see the good of thy chosen, that I may Rrejoice in the gladness of thy nation, that I may Rglory with thine inheritance.   118:15 • 105:3

6 RWe have sinned Rwith our fathers, we have committed iniquity, we have done wickedly.   1 Kin. 8:47 • 78:8, 57; Neh. 9:2; Zech. 1:4

7 Our fathers understood not thy wonders in Egypt; they remembered not the multitude of thy mercies; but provoked *him* at the sea, *even* at the Red sea.

8 Nevertheless he saved them for his name's sake, Rthat he might make his mighty power to be known.   Ex. 9:16

9 He rebuked the Red sea also, and it was dried up: so he led them through the depths, as through the wilderness.

10 And he Rsaved them from the hand of him that hated *them*, and redeemed them from the hand of the enemy.   Ex. 14:30

11 And the waters covered their enemies: there was not one of them left.

12 RThen believed they his words; they Rsang his praise.   Ex. 14:31 • 105:43; [Ex. 15:1–21]

13 They soon forgat his works; they Twaited not for his counsel: *did not depend on*

14 But lusted exceedingly in the wilderness, and tempted God in the desert.

15 And he gave them their request; but sent leanness into their soul.

16 RThey envied Moses also in the camp, *and* Aaron the saint of the LORD.   Num. 16:1–4

17 RThe earth opened and swallowed up Dathan, and covered the company of A-bi'-ram.   37:38; Num. 16:32

18 And a fire was kindled in their company; the flame burned up the wicked.

19 RThey made a calf in Ho'-reb, and worshipped the molten image.   Ex. 32:4

20 Thus they changed their glory into the similitude of an ox that eateth grass.

21 They Rforgat God their saviour, which had done great things in Egypt;   78:11

22 RWondrous works in the land of Ham, *and* terrible things by the Red sea.   105:27

23 Therefore he said that he would destroy them, had not Moses his chosen Rstood before him in the breach, to turn away his wrath, lest he should destroy *them*.   Ezek. 22:30

24 Yea, they despised the pleasant land, they believed not his word:

25 But murmured in their tents, *and* hearkened not unto the voice of the LORD.

26 Therefore he lifted up his hand against them, to overthrow them in the wilderness:

27 To overthrow their seed also among the nations, and to scatter them in the lands.

28 They joined themselves also unto Ba'-al-pe'-or, and ate the sacrifices of the dead.

29 Thus they Rprovoked *him* to anger with their Tinventions: and the Rplague brake in upon them.   Num. 25:4 • *doings* • Lev. 26:21

30 RThen stood up RPhin'-e-has, and executed judgment: and *so* the Rplague was Tstayed.   Num. 25:7 • Ex. 6:25 • Num. 25:8 • *checked*

31 And that was counted unto him Rfor righteousness unto all generations for evermore.   Num. 25:11

32 RThey angered *him* also at the waters of strife, so that it Rwent ill with Moses for their sakes: 81:7; 95:9; Num. 20:2–13 • Num. 20:12

33 Because they provoked his spirit, so that he spake unadvisedly with his lips.

34 They did not destroy the nations, concerning whom the LORD commanded them:

35 But were mingled among the Theathen, and learned their works.   *nations*

36 And Rthey served their idols: which were a snare unto them.   Deut. 7:16; Judg. 2:12

37 Yea, they sacrificed their sons and their daughters unto Tdevils,   *evil spirits*

38 And shed Rinnocent blood, *even* the blood of their sons and of their daughters, whom they sacrificed unto the idols of Canaan: and Rthe land was polluted with blood.   94:21 • [Num. 35:33; Is. 24:5]

39 Thus were they Tdefiled with their own works, and went a whoring with their Town inventions.   *unclean* • *own ideas*

40 Therefore was the wrath of the LORD kindled against his people, insomuch that he abhorred his own inheritance.

41 And Rhe gave them into the hand of the heathen; and they that hated them ruled over them.   [Judg. 2:14; Neh. 9:27]

42 Their enemies also Roppressed them, and they were brought into subjection under their hand.   Ex. 1:14; Judg. 4:3; 10:12

43 Many times did he deliver them; but they provoked *him* with their counsel, and were Rbrought low for their iniquity.   Judg. 6:6

44 Nevertheless he regarded their affliction, when Rhe heard their cry: Judg. 10:10

45 RAnd he remembered for them his covenant, and Rrepented according to the multitude of his mercies.   105:8 • Judg. 2:18

46 He made them also to be pitied of all those that carried them captives.

47 RSave us, O LORD our God, and Rgather us from among the heathen, to give thanks unto thy holy name, *and* Rto triumph in thy praise.   1 Chr. 16:35 • 147:2 • 47:1

48 Blessed *be* the LORD God of Israel from everlasting to everlasting: and let all the people say, A-men'. Praise ye the LORD.

BOOK V

PSALM 107

God Satisfies the Longing Soul

O GIVE thanks unto the LORD, for *he is* good: for his mercy *endureth* for ever.
2 Let ᴿthe redeemed of the LORD say *so,* whom he hath ᴿredeemed from the hand of the enemy;   Is. 35:9, 10; 62:12 • 78:42; 106:10
3 And ᴿgathered them out of the lands, from the east, and from the west, from the north, and from the south.   106:47; Deut. 30:3
4 They wandered in the wilderness in a solitary way; they found no city to dwell in.
5 ᴿHungry and thirsty, their soul fainted in them.   77:3; Num. 21:4; Deut. 28:48
6 ᴿThen they cried unto the LORD in their trouble, *and* he delivered them out of their distresses.   vv. 13, 19, 28; 50:15
7 And he led them forth by the right way, that they might go to a city of habitation.
8 ᴿOh that *men* would praise the LORD *for* his goodness, and *for* his wonderful works to the children of men!   vv. 15, 21, 31
9 For he satisfieth the longing soul, and filleth the hungry soul with goodness.
10 Such as ᴿsit in darkness and in the shadow of death, *being* ᴿboundᵀ in affliction and iron;   143:3; [Is. 42:7] • [102:20] • *prisoners*
11 Because they ᴿrebelled against the words of God, and contemned ᴿthe counsel of the most High: Lam. 3:42 • [73:24]
12 Therefore he brought down their heart with labour; they fell down, and *there was* ᴿnone to help.   22:11; [72:12]; Is. 41:28
13 Then they ᴿcried unto the LORD in their trouble, *and* he ᴿsaved them out of their distresses.   v. 6; Ex. 2:23 • [27:1]
14 He brought them out of darkness and the shadow of death, and ᵀbrake their bands in sunder.   *set them free*
15 Oh that *men* would ᴿpraise the LORD ᴿ*for* his goodness, and *for* his wonderful works to the children of men!   9:11 • [25:8]
16 For he hath broken the gates of brass, and cut the bars of iron in sunder.
17 Fools because of their transgression, and because of their iniquities, are afflicted.
18 ᴿTheir soul abhorreth all manner of meat; and they ᴿdraw near unto the ᴿgates of death.   102:4; Job 33:20 • 88:3 • 9:13; Job 38:17
19 Then they ᴿcry unto the LORD in their trouble, *and* ᴿhe saveth them out of their distresses.   Ex. 2:23 • Ex. 3:7
20 He sent his word, and healed them, and delivered *them* from their destructions.
21 Oh that *men* would ᴿpraise the LORD ᴿ*for* his goodness, and *for* his wonderful works to the children of men!   9:11 • [25:8]
22 And ᴿlet them sacrifice the sacrifices of thanksgiving, and ᴿdeclare his works with ᵀrejoicing.   50:14; 116:17 • 9:11 • *singing*

23 They that go ᴿdown to the sea in ships, that do business in great waters;   Is. 42:10
24 These see the ᴿworks of the LORD, and his wonders in the ᵀdeep.   8:3 • *ocean*
25 For he ᴿcommandeth, and ᴿraiseth the stormy wind, which ᴿlifteth up the waves thereof.   105:31 • Jon. 1:4 • [93:3, 4]
26 They mount up to the heaven, they go down again to the depths: ᴿtheir soul is melted because of trouble.   22:14; 119:28
27 They reel to and fro, and stagger like a drunken man, and are at their wit's end.
28 ᴿThen they cry unto the LORD in their trouble, and he bringeth them out of their distresses.   Jon. 1:14
29 He ᴿmaketh the storm a calm, so that the waves thereof are still.   65:7; 89:9
30 Then are they glad because they be quiet; so ᴿhe bringeth them unto their desired haven.   Acts 27:44
31 ᴿOh that *men* would praise the LORD *for* his goodness, and *for* his wonderful works to the children of men!   vv. 8, 15, 21
32 ᴿLet them exalt him also ᴿin the congregation of the people, and praise him in the assembly of the elders.   [29:2] • [145:5]
33 He turneth rivers into a wilderness, and the watersprings into dry ground;
34 A fruitful land into barrenness, for the wickedness of them that dwell therein.
35 He turneth the wilderness into a standing water, and dry ground into watersprings.
36 And there he maketh the hungry to dwell, that they may prepare a ᴿcity for habitation;   vv. 4, 7
37 And sow the fields, and plant vineyards, which may yield fruits of increase.
38 He blesseth them also, so that they are multiplied greatly; and ᴿsuffereth not their cattle to decrease.   Deut. 7:14
39 Again, they are ᴿminished and ᴿbrought low through oppression, affliction, and sorrow.   Ezek. 5:11; 29:15 • 38:6
40 He poureth contempt upon princes, and causeth them to wander in the ᵀwilderness, *where there is* no way.   *void place*
41 ᴿYet setteth he the poor on high from affliction, and ᴿmaketh *him* families like a flock.   [113:7, 8] • [113:9; Job 21:11]
42 The righteous shall see *it,* and rejoice: and all iniquity shall stop her mouth.
43 Whoso *is* wise, and will observe these *things,* even they shall understand the lovingkindness of the LORD.

PSALM 108

Awake Early and Praise the Lord

A Song *or* Psalm of David.

O GOD, my heart is fixed; I will sing and give praise, even with my glory.

2 ᴿAwake,ᵀ psaltery and harp: I *myself* will awake early. 57:8-11 • *be alert*

3 I will ᴿpraise thee, O Lᴏʀᴅ, among the people: and I will sing praises unto thee among the nations. 2 Chr. 5:13

4 For thy mercy *is* great above the heavens: and thy truth *reacheth* unto the clouds.

5 Be thou exalted, O God, above the heavens: and thy glory above all the earth;

6 That thy beloved may be delivered: save *with* thy right hand, and answer me.

7 God hath spoken in his holiness; I will rejoice, I will divide She'-chem, and ᵀmete out the valley of Suc'-coth. *measure*

8 Gil'-e-ad *is* mine; Ma-nas'-seh *is* mine; E'-phra-im also *is* the strength of mine head; ᴿJudah *is* my lawgiver; [Gen. 49:10]

9 ᴿMoab *is* my washpot; over E'-dom will I cast out my shoe; over Phi-lis'-ti-a ᴿwill I triumph. Num. 26:3 • [59:13]

10 ᴿWho will bring me into the strong city? who will lead me into E'-dom? 60:9

11 ᴿ*Wilt* not *thou*, O God, *who* hast cast us off? and wilt not thou, O God, go forth with our hosts? 44:9; Deut. 8:2

12 ᴿGive us help from trouble: for vain *is* the help of man. 118:9; Deut. 33:29

13 Through God we shall do valiantly: for he *it is that* shall tread down our enemies.

PSALM 109

Song of the Slandered

To the chief Musician, A Psalm of David.

HOLD not thy peace, O God of my praise;
2 For the mouth of the wicked and the mouth of the ᵀdeceitful are opened against me: they have spoken against me with a lying tongue. *lawless one*

3 They compassed me about also with ᴿwords of hatred; and fought against me ᴿwithout a cause. 69:4 • John 15:23-25 ☆

4 For my love they are my ᴿadversaries: but ᴿI *give myself unto* prayer. 38:20 • 69:13

5 And ᴿthey have rewarded me evil for good, and hatred for my love. 35:7, 12; 38:20

6 Set thou a wicked man over him: and let Satan stand at his right hand.

7 When he shall be judged, let him be condemned: and let his prayer become sin.

8 Let ᴿhis days be few; *and* ᴿlet another take his ᵀoffice. [55:23] • Acts 1:20 • *goods*

9 ᴿLet his children be fatherless, and his ᴿwife a widow. Ex. 22:24 • Jer. 18:21

10 Let his children be continually ᵀvagabonds, and beg: let them seek *their* bread also out of their desolate places. *wanderers*

11 Let the extortioner catch all that he hath; and let the strangers spoil his labour.

12 Let there be none to ᴿextend mercy unto him: ᴿneither let there be any to favour his fatherless children. Ezra 7:28 • Job 5:4

13 ᴿLet his ᵀposterity be cut off; *and* in the generation following let their ᴿname be blotted out. 21:10 • *descendants* • Prov. 10:7

14 ᴿLet the iniquity of his fathers be remembered with the Lᴏʀᴅ; and let not the sin of his mother be blotted out. [Ex. 20:5]

15 Let them be before the Lᴏʀᴅ continually, that he may ᴿcut off the memory of them from the earth. [34:16]; Job 18:17

16 Because that he remembered not to shew mercy, but persecuted the poor and needy man, that he might even slay the ᴿbrokenᵀ in heart. [34:18] • *contrite*

17 ᴿAs he loved cursing, so let it come unto him: as he delighted not in blessing, so let it be far from him. Prov. 14:14

18 As he ᴿclothed himself with cursing like as with his garment, so let it ᴿcome into his bowels like water, and like oil into his bones. *v. 29; 73:6; [Ezek. 7:27] • Num. 5:22*

19 Let it be unto him as the ᴿgarment *which* covereth him, and for a girdle wherewith he is girded continually. *v. 29*

20 *Let* this *be* the reward of mine adversaries from the Lᴏʀᴅ, and of them that ᵀspeak evil against my soul. *think harm*

21 But do thou for me, O Gᴏᴅ the Lord, ᴿfor thy name's sake: because thy ᴿmercy *is* good, deliver thou me. [23:3; Ezek. 36:22] • 69:16

22 For ᴿI *am* poor and needy, and my heart is ᴿwounded within me. 40:17 • 147:4

23 I am gone ᴿlike the shadow when it declineth: I am tossed up and down ᴿas the locust. 102:11 • Ex. 10:19; Job 39:20

24 My ᴿknees are weak through fasting; and my flesh faileth of fatness. Heb. 12:12

25 I became also a ᵀreproach unto them: *when* they looked upon me they shaked their heads. *an example of distress*

26 ᴿHelp me, O Lᴏʀᴅ my God: O save me according to thy mercy: 119:86

27 That they may know that this *is* thy hand; *that* thou, Lᴏʀᴅ, hast done it.

28 Let them curse, but bless thou: when they arise, let them be ᵀashamed; but let ᴿthy servant rejoice. *defeated* • Is. 65:14

29 Let mine adversaries be clothed with ᵀshame, and let them cover themselves with their own confusion, as with a mantle. *defeat*

30 I will greatly praise the Lᴏʀᴅ with my mouth; yea, ᴿI will praise him among the multitude. 22:22; [2 Chr. 5:13]

31 For ᴿhe shall stand at the right hand of the poor, to save *him* from ᵀthose that condemn his soul. [16:8] • *the judges of his soul*

PSALM 110

The Coming of the Priest-King-Judge

A Psalm of David.

THE ᴿLᴏʀᴅ said unto my Lord, Sit thou at my right hand, until I ᴿmake thine enemies thy footstool. Matt. 22:44 • [Eph. 1:22]

2 The LORD shall send Rthe rod of thy strength out of Zion: Rrule thou in the midst of thine enemies.   [45:6]; Jer. 48:17 • [2:9]

3 RThy people *shall be* Twilling in the day of thy power, Rin the beauties of holiness from the womb of the morning: thou hast the dew of thy youth.   Judg. 5:2 • *beginning* • 96:9

4 The LORD hath sworn, and will not repent, Thou *art* a Rpriest for ever after the order of Mel-chiz'-e-dek.   [Heb. 5:6, 10] ☆

5 The Lord at thy right hand shall strike through kings in the day of his wrath.

6 He shall judge among the heathen, he shall fill *the places* with the dead bodies; he shall wound the heads over many countries.

7 He shall drink of the brook in the way: Rtherefore shall he lift up the head.   [Is. 53:12]

PSALM 111

Praise for God's Tender Care

PRAISET ye the LORD. RI will praise the LORD with *my* whole heart, Rin the assembly of the upright, and *in* the congregation.   *hallelujah* • 35:18 • 89:7; 149:1

2 RThe works of the LORD *are* great, Rsought out of all them that have pleasure therein.   92:5 • 143:5

3 His work *is* honourable and glorious: and his righteousness endureth for ever.

4 He hath made his wonderful works to be remembered: Rthe LORD *is* gracious and full of compassion.   [86:5; 103:8; 145:8]

5 He hath Rgiven Tmeat unto them that fear him: he Rwill ever be mindful of his covenant.   [Matt. 6:31–33] • *food* • [105:8]

6 He hath shewed his people the power of his works, that he may give them the Theritage R of the heathen.   *property* • [37:11]

7 The works of his hands *are* verity and judgment; all his commandments *are* sure.

8 They stand fast for ever and ever, *and* are done in truth and uprightness.

9 He sent redemption unto his people: he hath commanded his covenant for ever: holy and reverend *is* his name.

10 The fear of the LORD *is* the beginning of wisdom: a good understanding have all they that do *his commandments:* his praise endureth for ever.

PSALM 112

The Blessings of Those Who Fear God

PRAISE ye the LORD. Blessed *is* the man that feareth the LORD, *that* delighteth greatly in his commandments.

2 His seed shall be mighty upon earth: the generation of the upright shall be blessed.

3 Wealth and riches *shall be* in his house: and his righteousness endureth for ever.

4 RUnto the upright there ariseth light in the darkness: *he is* gracious, and full of compassion, and righteous.   Job 11:17

5 RA good man sheweth favour, and Rlendeth: he will guide his affairs with discretion.   [37:21; Rom. 12:10] • [Deut. 15:8; Matt. 5:42]

6 RSurely he shall not be Tmoved for ever: Rthe righteous shall be in everlasting remembrance.   [15:5]; 55:20 • *shaken* • Prov. 10:7

7 He shall not be afraid of evil tidings: his heart is fixed, trusting in the LORD.

8 His Rheart *is* established, Rhe shall not be afraid, until he Rsee *his desire* upon his enemies.   Heb. 13:9 • [27:1]; Prov. 3:24 • 54:7

9 He hath dispersed, he hath given to the poor; his righteousness endureth for ever; his horn shall be exalted with honour.

10 The wicked shall see *it,* and be grieved; he shall gnash with his teeth, and melt away: the desire of the wicked shall perish.

PSALM 113

The Condescending Grace of God

PRAISE ye the LORD. RPraise, O ye Rservants of the LORD, praise the name of the LORD.   135:1 • [34:22]; 69:36; 79:10

2 RBlessed be the name of the LORD from this time forth and for evermore.   145:21

3 RFrom the rising of the sun unto the going down of the same the LORD'S Rname *is* to be praised.   Mal. 1:11; 50:1 • [18:3; 48:1, 10]

4 The LORD *is* high above all nations, *and* Rhis glory above the heavens.   [8:1]

5 Who *is* like unto the LORD our God, who dwelleth on high,

6 Who humbleth *himself* to behold *the things that are* in heaven, and in the earth!

7 He raiseth up the poor out of the dust, *and* lifteth the needy out of the dunghill;

8 That he may Rset *him* with princes, *even* with the princes of his people.   [Job 36:7]

9 RHe maketh the barren woman to keep house, *and to be* a joyful mother of children. Praise ye the LORD.   1 Sam. 2:5

PSALM 114

In Praise for the Exodus

WHEN RIsrael went out of Egypt, the house of Jacob Rfrom a people of Tstrange language;   Ex. 13:3 • 81:5 • *foreign*

2 RJudah was his sanctuary, *and* Israel his Rdominion.   Ex. 6:7; 15:17; 29:45, 46 • [Ex. 19:6]

3 RThe sea saw *it,* and fled: RJordan was driven back.   77:16; Ex. 14:21 • Josh. 3:13, 16

4 RThe mountains skipped like rams, *and* the little hills like lambs.   29:6

5 RWhat *ailed* thee, O thou sea, that thou fleddest? thou Jordan, *that* thou wast driven back?   Hab. 3:8

6 Ye mountains, *that* ye skipped like rams; *and* ye little hills, like lambs?

7 ᴿTremble, thou earth, at the presence of the Lord,ᴿ at the presence of the God of Jacob;   96:9; Ex. 19:18 • [1 Chr. 29:11]

8 Which turned the rock *into* a standing water, the flint into a fountain of waters.

PSALM 115

To God Alone Be the Glory

NOT unto us, O Lᴏʀᴅ, not unto us, but unto thy name give glory, for thy mercy, *and* for thy truth's sake.

2 ᴿWherefore should the heathen say, ᴿWhere *is* now their God?   79:10 • 42:3, 10

3 But our God *is* in the heavens: he hath done whatsoever he hath pleased.

4 Theirᴿ idols *are* silver and gold, the work of men's hands.   135:15; Jer. 10:3

5 They have mouths, but they speak not: eyes have they, but they see not:

6 They have ears, but they hear not: noses have they, but they smell not:

7 They have hands, but they handle not: feet have they, but they walk not: neither speak they through their throat.

8 They that make them are like unto them; *so is* every one that trusteth in them.

9 ᴿO Israel, trust thou in the Lᴏʀᴅ: he *is* their help and their shield.   118:2, 3

10 O house of ᴿAaron, trust in the Lᴏʀᴅ: he *is* their help and their shield.   135:19

11 Ye that fear the Lᴏʀᴅ, trust in the Lᴏʀᴅ: he *is* their help and their shield.

12 The Lᴏʀᴅ hath been mindful of us: he will bless *us;* he will bless the house of Israel; he will bless the house of Aaron.

13 ᴿHe will bless them that fear the Lᴏʀᴅ, *both* small and great.   128:1

14 ᴿThe Lᴏʀᴅ shall increase you more and more, you and your children.   Deut. 1:11

15 Ye *are* ᴿblessed of the Lᴏʀᴅ ᴿwhich made heaven and earth.   [Gen. 14:19 • Neh. 9:6]

16 The heaven, *even* the ᴿheavens, *are* the Lᴏʀᴅ's: but the ᴿearth hath he given to the children of men.   [89:11] • 8:6

17 ᴿThe dead praise not the Lᴏʀᴅ, neither any that go down into silence.   6:5

18 But we will bless the Lᴏʀᴅ from this time forth and for evermore. Praise the Lᴏʀᴅ.

PSALM 116

Love the Lord for What He Has Done

I ᴿLOVE the Lᴏʀᴅ, because he hath heard my voice *and* my supplications.   18:1

2 Because he ᵀhath inclined ᴿhis ear unto me, therefore will I call upon *him* as long as I live.   *is ready to hear* • 17:6

3 ᴿThe sorrows of death compassed me, and the pains of ᵀhell gat hold upon me: I found trouble and sorrow.   18:4 • *sheol*

4 Then ᴿcalled I upon the name of the Lᴏʀᴅ; O Lᴏʀᴅ, I beseech thee, ᴿdeliver my soul.   18:6 • 17:13; 22:20

5 ᴿGracious *is* the Lᴏʀᴅ, and ᴿrighteous; yea, our God *is* merciful.   103:8 • [Neh. 9:8]

6 ᴿThe Lᴏʀᴅ preserveth the simple: I was brought low, and he helped me.   Prov. 1:4

7 Return unto thy rest, O my soul; for the Lᴏʀᴅ hath dealt bountifully with thee.

8 ᴿFor thou hast delivered my soul from death, mine eyes from tears, *and* my feet from falling.   56:13; 86:13

9 I will walk before the Lᴏʀᴅ ᴿin the land of the living.   27:13

10 ᴿI believed, therefore have I spoken: I was greatly ᴿafflicted: 2 Cor. 4:13 • 88:7

11 I said in my haste, All men *are* liars.

12 What shall I ᴿrender unto the Lᴏʀᴅ *for* all his benefits toward me?   2 Chr. 32:25

13 I will take the ᴿcup of salvation, and call upon the name of the Lᴏʀᴅ.   16:5

14 I will pay my vows unto the Lᴏʀᴅ now in the presence of all his people.

15 ᴿPrecious in the sight of the Lᴏʀᴅ *is* the death of his saints.   72:14

16 O Lᴏʀᴅ, truly I *am* thy servant; I *am* thy servant, *and* the son of thine handmaid: thou hast loosed my bonds.

17 I will offer to thee ᴿthe sacrifice of thanksgiving, and will ᴿcall upon the name of the Lᴏʀᴅ.   50:14 • *v.* 13

18 I will pay my vows unto the Lᴏʀᴅ now in the presence of all his people,

19 In the ᴿcourtsᵀ of the Lᴏʀᴅ's house, in the midst of thee, O Jerusalem. Praise ye the Lᴏʀᴅ.   96:8 • *house*

PSALM 117

The Praise of All Nations

O ᴿPRAISE the Lᴏʀᴅ, all ye nations: praise him, all ye people.   Rom. 15:11

2 For his merciful kindness is great toward us: and ᴿthe truth of the Lᴏʀᴅ *endureth* for ever. Praise ye the Lᴏʀᴅ.   100:5

PSALM 118

Better to Trust God than Man

O ᴿGIVE thanks unto the Lᴏʀᴅ; for *he is* good: ᴿbecause his mercy *endureth* for ever.   1 Chr. 16:8 • [136:1–26]

2 ᴿLet Israel now say, that his mercy *endureth* for ever.   115:9

3 Let the ᴿhouse of Aaron now say, that his mercy *endureth* for ever.   115.10

4 Let them now that fear the Lᴏʀᴅ say, that his mercy *endureth* for ever.

5 ᴿI called upon the Lᴏʀᴅ in distress: the Lᴏʀᴅ answered me, *and set me* in ᵀa large place.   120:1 • *prosperity*

6 ᴿThe LORD is on my side; I will not fear: what can man do unto me?   [27:1]
7 ᴿThe LORD taketh my part with them that help me: therefore shall I see my desire upon them that hate me.   54:4
8 ᴿIt is better to trust in the LORD than to put confidence in man.   40:4
9 ᴿIt is better to trust in the LORD than to put confidence in princes.   146:3
10 All nations compassed me about: but in the name of the LORD will I destroy them.
11 They ᴿcompassed me about; yea, they compassed me about: but in the name of the LORD I will destroy them.   88:17
12 They compassed me about like bees; they are quenched as the fire of thorns: for in the name of the LORD I will destroy them.
13 Thou hast thrust ᵀsore at me that I might fall: but the LORD helped me.   hard
14 ᴿThe LORD is my strength and song, and is become my salvation.   Ex. 15:2; Is. 12:2
15 The voice of rejoicing and salvation is in the ᵀtabernacles of the righteous: the right hand of the LORD doeth valiantly.   tents
16 The right hand of the LORD is exalted: the right hand of the LORD doeth valiantly.
17 ᴿI shall not die, but live, and ᴿdeclare the works of the LORD.   Hab. 1:12 · 73:28
18 The LORD hath chastened me sore: but he hath not given me over unto death.
19 Open to me the gates of righteousness: I will go into them, and I will praise the LORD:
20 ᴿThis gate of the LORD, ᴿinto which the righteous shall enter.   Is. 35:8 · 140:13
21 I will praise thee: for thou hast heard me, and art become my salvation.
22 The stone which the builders refused is become the head stone of the corner.
23 ᵀThis is the LORD'S doing; it is marvellous in our eyes.   this is from the Lord
24 This is the day which the LORD hath made; we will rejoice and be glad in it.

25 Save now, I beseech thee, O LORD: O LORD, I beseech thee, send now prosperity.
26 ᴿBlessed be he that cometh in the name of the LORD: we have blessed you out of the house of the LORD.   Matt. 21:9; Luke 19:38 ☆
27 God is the LORD, which hath shewed us ᵀlight: bind the sacrifice with cords, even unto the horns of the altar.   relief
28 Thou art my God, and I will praise thee: thou art my God, I will exalt thee.
29 O give thanks unto the LORD; for he is good: for his mercy endureth for ever.

PSALM 119

An Acrostic in Praise of the Scriptures

א ALEPH

BLESSED are the undefiled in the way, who walk in the law of the LORD.
2 Blessed are they that ᵀkeep his testimonies, and that ᴿseek him ᴿwith the whole heart.   obey · [Deut. 4:29] · [Deut. 6:5]
3 ᴿThey also do no ᵀiniquity: they walk in his ways.   [1 John 3:9; 5:18] · perversity
4 ᴿThou hast commanded us to keep thy precepts diligently.   Deut. 4:13; Neh. 9:13
5 ᴿO that my ways were directed to ᴿkeep thy statutes!   Prov. 4:26 · Deut. 12:1
6 Then shall I not be ashamed, when I have respect unto all thy commandments.
7 I will praise thee with ᵀuprightness of heart, when I shall have learned thy righteous judgments.   genuine intention
8 I will keep thy statutes: ᴿO forsake me not utterly.   38:21; 71:9

ב BETH

9 Wherewithal shall a young man cleanse his way? by ᴿtaking heed thereto according to thy word.   1 Kin. 2:4; 8:25

10 With my whole heart have I ᴿsought

119:9 God's Word Cleanses—One of the pieces of furniture in the Old Testament tabernacle was called the brass laver (Page 93—Ex. 38:8). It consisted of a huge upright brass bowl filled with water, resting upon a pedestal. The priests would often stop at this laver and wash. The Word of God may be thought of in terms of that laver, for it too has the power to cleanse. The Old Testament laver could only remove the physical dirt from human hands, but the Scriptures possess the ability to take away our moral filth (Page 1236—1 Pet. 1:22).

"If we confess our sins, he is faithful and just to forgive us our sins, and to cleanse us from all unrighteousness" (Page 1249—1 John 1:9). What areas of my life can the Bible cleanse?

It can cleanse me from wrong thoughts. Sometimes we are tempted to think critically of others; God's Word can prevent this (Page 548—Ps. 1:2). On other occasions fearful thoughts may race through our minds; the Scriptures will prevent this also (Page 217—Josh. 1:8). In fact, the Bible will establish our total thought-life if we but allow it to do so (Page 1173—Phil. 4:8, 9; Page 1243—2 Pet. 1:5–10).

It can cleanse me from wrong words. Of all the Bible authors, James seems to be God's expert on the sins of the human tongue. In the first chapter of his book, he deals with this very thing and shows the absolute necessity of dependence upon the Scriptures to keep our words true (Page 1228—James 1:22–26). See also Psalm 119:172.

It can cleanse me from wrong actions. Jesus promised us this would be the case: "Now ye are clean through the word which I have spoken unto you" (Page 1060—John 15:3).

Finally, God's Word will keep us from wrong thoughts, words, and actions; or else wrong thoughts, words, and actions will keep us from God's Word.

Now turn to Page 1052—John 8:31: God's Word Confirms.

thee: O let me not ᴿwander from thy commandments.   2 Chr. 15:15 · v. 21

11 ᴿThy word have I hid in mine heart, that I might not sin against thee.   Luke 2:19

12 Blessed art thou, O LORD: teach me thy ᵀstatutes.   laws

13 With my lips have I ᴿdeclared all the ᵀjudgments of thy mouth.   40:9 · ordinances

14 ᴿI have rejoiced in the way of thy testimonies, as much as in all riches.   34:11

15 I will meditate in thy precepts, and ᵀhave respect unto thy ways.   regard

16 I will ᴿdelight myself in thy statutes: I will not forget thy word.   1:2

‎ג GIMEL

17 Deal bountifully with thy servant, that I may live, and ᵀkeep thy word.   obey

18 Open thou mine eyes, that I may behold wondrous things out of thy law.

19 ᴿI am a stranger in the earth: hide not thy commandments from me.   Gen. 47:9

20 My soul breaketh for the longing that it hath unto thy judgments at all times.

21 Thou hast ᴿrebuked the proud that are ᴿcursed, which do err from thy commandments.   68:30 · Deut. 27:26

22 Remove from me reproach and contempt; for I have kept thy testimonies.

23 ᴿPrinces also did sit and speak against me: but thy servant did meditate in thy statutes.   v. 161

24 Thy testimonies also are my delight and my ᵀcounsellors.   advisors

‎ד DALETH

25 My soul cleaveth unto the dust: quicken thou me according to thy word.

26 I have declared my ways, and thou heardest me: teach me thy statutes.

27 Make me to understand the way of thy precepts: so ᴿshall I ᵀtalk of thy wondrous works.   105:2 · meditate on

28 My soul melteth for heaviness: strengthen thou me according unto thy word.

29 Remove from me the way of lying: and grant me thy law graciously.

30 I have chosen the way of truth: thy judgments have I laid before me.

31 I have ᴿstuck unto thy testimonies: O LORD, put me not to shame.   Deut. 11:22

32 I will run the way of thy commandments, when thou shalt enlarge my heart.

‎ה HE

33 Teach me, O LORD, the way of thy statutes; and I shall keep it unto the end.

34 Give me understanding, ᴿand I shall keep thy law; yea, I shall observe it with my whole heart.   1 Chr. 22:12; Ezek. 44:24

35 Make me to go in the path of thy commandments; for therein do I delight.

36 ᴿIncline my heart unto thy testimonies, and not to covetousness.   1 Kin. 8:58

37 Turn away mine eyes from beholding vanity; and quicken thou me in thy way.

38 ᴿStablish thy word unto thy servant, who is devoted to thy fear.   2 Sam. 7:25

39 Turn away my ᴿreproach which I fear: for thy judgments are good.   v. 22

40 Behold, I have longed after thy precepts: quicken me in thy righteousness.

‎ו VAU

41 Let thy ᴿmercies come also unto me, O LORD, even thy salvation, ᴿaccording to thy word.   v. 77 · vv. 58, 76, 116

42 So shall I have ᴿwherewithᵀ to answer him that ᴿreproacheth me: for I trust in thy word.   Prov. 27:11 · a word · 102:8

43 And take not the word of truth utterly out of my mouth; for I have hoped in thy ᵀjudgments.   ordinances

44 So shall I ᴿkeep thy law continually for ever and ever.   v. 33

45 ᴿAnd I will walk at liberty: for I seek thy precepts.   Prov. 4:12

46 I will speak of thy testimonies also before kings, and will not be ashamed.

47 And I will delight myself in thy commandments, which I have loved.

48 My hands also will I lift up unto thy commandments, ᴿwhich I have loved; and I will meditate in thy statutes.   v. 97

‎ז ZAIN

49 Remember the word unto thy servant, upon which thou hast caused me to hope.

50 This is my ᴿcomfort in my affliction: for thy word hath quickened me.   Job 6:10

51 ᴿThe ᵀproud have had me greatly in derision: yet have I not ᴿdeclined from thy law.   Job 30:1; Jer. 20:7 · insolent · Job 23:11

52 I remembered thy judgments of old, O LORD; and have comforted myself.

53 Horror hath taken hold upon me because of the wicked that forsake thy law.

54 Thy statutes have been my songs in the house of my ᴿpilgrimage.   Gen. 47:9

55 I have remembered thy name, O LORD, in the night, and have kept thy law.

56 This I had, because I kept thy precepts.

‎ח CHETH

57 ᴿThou art my portion, O LORD: I have said that I would keep thy words.   16:5

58 ᴿI entreated thy favour with my whole heart: ᴿbe merciful unto me according to thy word.   1 Kin. 13:6 · 41:4; 56:1

59 I ᴿthought on my ways, and turned my feet unto thy testimonies.   Mark 14:72

60 I made haste, and delayed not to ᵀkeep thy commandments.   obey

61 The bands of the wicked have robbed me: but I have not forgotten thy law.

62 ᴿAt midnight I will rise to give thanks

unto thee because of thy ᴿrighteous judg-
ments.   Acts 16:25 · v. 7
63 I *am* a companion of all *them* that fear
thee, and of them that keep thy precepts.
64 ᴿThe earth, O Lᴏʀᴅ, is full of thy
ᵀmercy: teach me thy statutes.   33:5 · *grace*

ɴ TETH

65 Thou hast dealt well with thy servant, O
Lᴏʀᴅ, according unto thy word.
66 Teach me good judgment and knowledge: for I have believed thy commandments.
67 ᴿBefore I was afflicted I went astray:
but now have I kept thy word.   Jer. 31:18, 19
68 Thou *art* ᴿgood, and doest good; teach
me thy statutes.   86:5; Deut. 8:16
69 The proud have ᴿforgedᵀ a lie against
me: *but* I will keep thy precepts with *my*
whole heart.   Job 13:4 · *prepared*
70 ᴿTheir heart is as fat as grease; *but* I
delight in thy law.   Acts 28:27
71 *It is* good for me that I have been
afflicted; that I might learn thy statutes.
72 The law of thy mouth *is* better unto me
than thousands of gold and silver.

ꞌ JOD

73 ᴿThy hands have made me and fashioned me: give me understanding, that I may
learn thy commandments.   Job 10:8
74 ᴿThey that fear thee will be glad when
they see me; because I have hoped in thy
word.   34:2; 35:27; 107:42
75 I know, O Lᴏʀᴅ, that thy judgments *are*
right, and ᴿ*that* thou in faithfulness hast
afflicted me.   [Heb. 12:10]
76 Let, I pray thee, thy merciful kindness
be for my comfort, according to thy word
unto thy servant.
77 Let thy tender mercies come unto me,
that I may live: for thy law *is* my delight.
78 Let the proud be ashamed; for they
dealt perversely with me without a cause: *but*
I will meditate in thy precepts.
79 Let those that fear thee turn unto me,
and those that have known thy testimonies.
80 Let my heart be ᵀsound in thy statutes;
that I be not ashamed.   *blameless*

ɔ CAPH

81 ᴿMy soul fainteth for thy salvation: *but*
I hope in thy word.   [73:26]; 84:2
82 Mine ᴿeyes fail for thy word, saying,
When wilt thou comfort me?   Is. 38:14
83 For I am become like a bottle in the
smoke; *yet* do I not forget thy statutes.
84 How many *are* the days of thy servant?
ᴿwhen wilt thou execute judgment on them
that persecute me?   Rev. 6:10
85 ᴿThe proud have digged pits for me,
which *are* not after thy law.   35:7
86 All thy commandments *are* faithful:
they persecute me wrongfully; help thou me.

87 They had almost consumed me upon
earth; but I forsook not thy precepts.
88 Quicken me after thy lovingkindness;
so shall I keep the testimony of thy mouth.

ה LAMED

89 ᴿFor ever, O Lᴏʀᴅ, thy word is settled in
heaven.   Matt. 24:34; [1 Pet. 1:25]
90 Thy faithfulness *is* unto all generations:
thou hast established the earth, and it ᵀabid-
eth.ᴿ   *stands* · Eccl. 1:4
91 They continue this day according to
thine ordinances: for all *are* thy servants.
92 Unless thy law *had been* my delights, I
should then have perished in mine affliction.
93 I will never forget thy precepts: for with
them thou hast quickened me.
94 I *am* thine, save me; for I have ᴿsought
thy precepts.   *v.* 45
95 The wicked have ᴿwaited for me to
destroy me: *but* I will consider thy testimonies.   40:14; Is. 32:7
96 I have seen an end of all perfection: *but*
thy commandment *is* exceeding broad.

ɔ MEM

97 O how love I thy law! ᴿit *is* my
meditation all the day.   1:2
98 Thou through thy commandments hast
made me ᴿwiser than mine enemies: for they
are ever with me.   Deut. 4:6
99 I have more understanding than all my
teachers: ᴿfor thy testimonies *are* my meditation.   *v.* 15
100 I understand more than the ancients,
because I keep thy precepts.
101 I have refrained my feet from every
evil way, that I might keep thy word.
102 I have not ᴿdeparted from thy judgments: for thou hast taught me.   Deut. 17:20
103 How sweet are thy words unto my
taste! *yea, sweeter* than honey to my mouth.
104 Through thy precepts I get understanding: therefore I hate every false way.

ɔ NUN

105 ᴿThy word *is* a lamp unto my feet, and
a light unto my path.   Prov. 6:23
106 I have sworn, and I will perform *it,*
that I will keep thy righteous judgments.
107 I am afflicted very much: quicken me,
O Lᴏʀᴅ, according unto thy word.
108 Accept, I beseech thee, ᴿthe freewill
offerings of my mouth, O Lᴏʀᴅ, and teach me
thy judgments.   Hos. 14:2; Heb. 13:15
109 ᴿMy soul *is* continually in my hand:
yet do I not forget thy law.   Job 13:14
110 The wicked have laid a snare for me:
yet I erred not from thy precepts.
111 ᴿThy testimonies have I taken as an
heritage for ever: for they *are* the rejoicing of
my heart.   Deut. 33:4
112 I have inclined mine heart to perform
thy statutes alway, *even* ᴿunto the end.   *v.* 33

ס SAMECH

113 I hate ᴿvain thoughts: but thy law do I love.   1 Kin. 18:21; James 1:8; 4:8

114 ᴿThou art my hiding place and my shield: I hope in thy word.   [32:7]

115 Depart from me, ye evildoers: for I will keep the commandments of my God.

116 Uphold me according unto thy word, that I may live: and let me not ᴿbe ashamed of my hope.   [Rom. 5:5; 9:33]

117 ᵀHold thou me up, and I shall be safe: and I will have ᵀrespect unto thy statutes continually.   strengthen · regard

118 Thou hast ᵀtrodden down all them that ᴿerr from thy statutes: for their deceit is falsehood.   rejected · vv. 10, 21

119 Thou puttest away all the wicked of the earth ᴿlike ᵀdross: therefore I love thy testimonies.   Is. 1:22, 25 · refuse

120 ᴿMy flesh trembleth for fear of thee; and I am afraid of thy judgments.   Hab. 3:16

ע AIN

121 ᴿI have done judgment and justice: leave me not to mine oppressors.   Job 29:14

122 Be ᴿsurety for thy servant for good: let not the proud oppress me.   Heb. 7:22

123 Mine ᴿeyes fail for thy salvation, and for the word of thy righteousness.   v. 82

124 Deal with thy servant according unto thy mercy, and teach me thy statutes.

125 I am thy servant; give me understanding, that I may know thy testimonies.

126 It is time for thee, LORD, ᴿto work: for they have made void thy law.   Jer. 18:23

127 Therefore I love thy commandments above gold; yea, above fine gold.

128 Therefore I esteem all thy ᴿprecepts concerning all things to be right; and I hate every false way.   [19:8]

פ PE

129 Thy testimonies are wonderful: therefore doth my soul ᵀkeep them.   obey

130 ᴿThe entrance of thy words giveth light; ᴿit giveth understanding unto the simple.   Prov. 6:23 · [19:7]

131 I opened my mouth, and panted: for I longed for thy commandments.

132 ᴿLook thou upon me, and be merciful unto me, ᴿas thou usest to do unto those that love thy name.   106:4 · [2 Thess. 1:6]

133 Order my steps in thy word: and let not any iniquity have dominion over me.

134 ᴿDeliver me from the oppression of man: so will I keep thy precepts.   Luke 1:74

135 ᴿMake thy face to shine upon thy servant; and teach me thy statutes.   4:6

136 Rivers of waters run down mine eyes, because they keep not thy law.

צ TZADDI

137 ᴿRighteous art thou, O LORD, and upright are thy judgments.   [Neh. 9:31]

138 Thy testimonies that thou hast commanded are righteous and very faithful.

139 My zeal hath consumed me, because mine enemies have forgotten thy words.

140 ᴿThy word is very pure: therefore thy servant loveth it.   [12:6; 19:8]

141 I am small and ᴿdespised: yet do not I ᴿforget thy precepts.   22:6 · v. 61

142 Thy righteousness is an everlasting righteousness, and thy law is the truth.

143 Trouble and anguish have taken hold on me: yet thy commandments are my ᴿdelights.   v. 24

144 ᴿThe righteousness of thy testimonies is everlasting: give me understanding, and I shall live.   [19:9]

ק KOPH

145 I cried with my whole heart; hear me, O LORD: I will keep thy statutes.

146 I cried unto thee; ᴿsave me, and I shall keep thy testimonies.   3:7

147 I prevented the dawning of the morning, and cried: I hoped in thy word.

148 Mine eyes prevent the night watches, that I might meditate in thy word.

149 Hear my voice according unto thy lovingkindness: O LORD, ᵀquicken me according to thy judgment.   revive

150 They draw nigh that follow after mischief: they are far from thy law.

151 Thou art ᴿnear, O LORD; and all thy commandments are truth.   [145:18]

152 Concerning thy testimonies, I have known of old that thou hast founded them ᴿfor ever.   Prov. 3:1

ר RESH

153 Consider mine affliction, and deliver me: for I do not forget thy law.

154 ᴿPlead my cause, and deliver me: quicken me according to thy word.   35:1

155 Salvation is ᴿfar from the wicked: for they seek not thy statutes.   Job 5:4

156 Great are thy tender mercies, O LORD: quicken me according to thy judgments.

157 Many are my persecutors and mine enemies; yet do I not ᴿdeclineᵀ from thy testimonies.   v. 51 · turn aside from

158 I beheld the transgressors, and was grieved; because they kept not thy word.

159 Consider how I ᴿlove thy ᵀprecepts: quicken me, O LORD, according to thy lovingkindness.   v. 47 · laws

160 ᴿThy word is true from the beginning: and every one of thy righteous judgments endureth for ever.   139:17

ש SCHIN

161 ᴿPrincesᵀ have persecuted me without a cause: but my heart standeth in awe of thy word.   1 Sam. 24:11; 26:18 · rulers

162 I rejoice at thy word, as one that
Rfindeth great spoil.   1 Sam. 30:16; Is. 9:3
163 I hate and abhor Tlying: *but* thy law do
I love.   *falsehood*
164 Seven times a day do I praise thee
because of thy Rrighteous judgments.   *v. 7*
165 Great peace have they which love thy
law: and nothing shall offend them.
166 RLORD, I have hoped for thy salvation,
and done thy commandments.   *v. 81*
167 My soul hath Rkept thy testimonies;
and I love them exceedingly.   *v. 129*
168 I have kept thy precepts and thy testimonies: for all my ways *are* before thee.

ת TAU

169 Let my Rcry come near before thee, O
LORD: Rgive me understanding according to
thy word.   Job 16:18 · *v. 27*
170 Let my supplication come before thee:
deliver me according to thy word.
171 My lips shall utter praise, when thou
Rhast taught me thy statutes.   [Mic. 4:2]
172 My tongue shall speak of thy word: for
all thy commandments *are* righteousness.
173 Let thine hand help me; for RI have
chosen thy precepts.   Josh. 24:22
174 RI have longed for thy salvation, O
LORD; and thy law *is* my delight.   *v. 166*
175 Let my soul live, and it shall praise
thee; and let thy judgments help me.
176 RI have gone astray like a lost sheep;
seek thy servant; for I do not forget thy
commandments.   [Is. 53:6]; Jer. 50:6

PSALM 120

A Cry in Distress

A Song of degrees.

IN Rmy distress I Tcried unto the LORD, and
he heard me.   Jon. 2:2 · *prayed*
2 Deliver my soul, O LORD, from lying lips,
and from a Rdeceitful tongue.   Zeph. 3:13
3 What shall be given unto thee? or what
shall be done unto thee, thou false tongue?
4 RSharp arrows of the mighty, with coals
of juniper.   45:5; Prov. 25:18
5 Woe is me, that I sojourn in Me'-sech,
that I dwell in the tents of Ke'-dar!
6 My soul hath long dwelt with him that
Thateth peace.   *is opposed to*
7 I *am for* peace: but when I speak, they
are Rfor war.   55:21

PSALM 121

God Is Our Keeper

A Song of degrees.

I RWILL lift up mine eyes unto the hills,
from whence cometh my help.   [Jer. 3:23]

2 RMy help *cometh* from the LORD, which
made heaven and earth.   [124:8]
3 He will not suffer thy foot to be moved:
he that keepeth thee will not slumber.
4 Behold, he that keepeth Israel shall neither slumber nor sleep.
5 The LORD *is* thy keeper: the LORD *is* Rthy
shade upon thy right hand.   Is. 25:4
6 RThe sun shall not smite thee by day, nor
the moon by night.   91:5; Is. 49:10
7 The LORD shall preserve thee from all
evil: he shall Rpreserve thy soul.   41:2
8 The LORD shall Rpreserve thy going out
and thy coming in from this time forth, and
even for evermore.   Deut. 28:6

PSALM 122

"Pray for the Peace of Jerusalem"

A Song of degrees of David.

I WAS glad when they said unto me, Let us
go into the house of the LORD.
2 Our feet shall stand Twithin thy Rgates, O
Jerusalem.   *in your house* · Jer. 7:2
3 Jerusalem is builded as a city that is
Rcompact together: 2 Sam. 5:9
4 Whither the tribes go up, the tribes of
the LORD, unto the testimony of Israel, to
give thanks unto the name of the LORD.
5 RFor there are set thrones of judgment,
the thrones of the house of David.   Deut. 17:8
6 RPray for the peace of Jerusalem: they
shall prosper that love thee.   51:18
7 Peace be within thy walls, *and* prosperity
within thy Rpalaces.   Jer. 17:27
8 For my brethren and companions' sakes,
I will now say, Peace *be* within thee.
9 Because of the house of the LORD our
God I will Rseek thy good.   Neh. 2:10

PSALM 123

Plea for the Mercy of God

A Song of degrees.

UNTO thee Rlift I up mine eyes, O thou
that dwellest in the heavens.   121:1
2 Behold, as the eyes of servants *look* unto
the hand of their masters, *and* as the eyes of a
maiden unto the hand of her mistress; so our
eyes Twait upon the LORD our God, until that
he have mercy upon us.   *look*
3 Have mercy upon us, O LORD, have
mercy upon us: for we are Rexceedingly filled
with contempt.   Neh. 4:4
4 Our soul is exceedingly filled with the
Rscorning of those that are at ease, *and* with
the contempt of the proud.   Neh. 2:19

PSALM 124

God Is on Our Side

A Song of degrees of David.

IF it had not been the LORD who was on our side, Rnow may Israel say;   129:1
2 If it had not been the LORD who was on our side, when men rose up against us:
3 Then they had swallowed us up quick, when their wrath was kindled against us:
4 Then the Rwaters had overwhelmed us, the stream had gone over our soul: 18:16
5 Then the RproudT waters had Tgone over our soul.   Job 38:11 · raging · swept
6 Blessed be the LORD, who hath not given us as a Rprey to their teeth.   Prov. 30:14
7 Our soul is escaped Ras a bird out of the snare of the fowlers: the snare is broken, and we are escaped.   2 Cor. 11:33
8 ROur help is in the name of the LORD, who made heaven and earth.   [121:2]

PSALM 125

Trust in the Lord and Abide for Ever

A Song of degrees.

THEY that trust in the LORD shall be as mount Zion, which cannot be removed, Rbut abideth for ever.   Eccl. 1:4
2 As the mountains are round about Jerusalem, so the LORD is round about his people from henceforth even for ever.
3 For the rod of the wicked shall not rest upon the lot of the righteous; lest the righteous put forth their hands unto iniquity.
4 RDo good, O LORD, unto those that be good, and to them that are Rupright in their hearts.   [119:68] · [7:10]
5 As for such as turn aside unto their crooked Rways, the LORD shall lead them forth with the workers of iniquity: but peace shall be upon Israel.   Job 23:11

PSALM 126

"Sow in Tears . . . Reap in Joy"

A Song of degrees.

WHEN the LORD Tturned Ragain the captivity of Zion, we were like them that dream.   reversed · Jer. 29:14
2 Then was our mouth filled with laughter, and our tongue with singing: then said they among the heathen, The LORD hath done great things for them.
3 The LORD hath done great things for us; whereof we are Rglad.   Is. 25:9
4 TTurn again our captivity, O LORD, as the Rstreams in the south.   reverse · Is. 35:6
5 They that sow in tears shall reap in joy.
6 He that goeth forth and weepeth, bearing precious seed, shall doubtless come again with rejoicing, bringing his sheaves with him.

PSALM 127

Children Are God's Heritage

A Song of degrees for Solomon.

EXCEPT the LORD build the house, they labour in vain that build it: except Rthe LORD keep the city, the watchman waketh but in vain.   [121:3–5]
2 It is vain for you to rise up early, to sit up late, to Reat the bread of sorrows: for so he giveth his beloved sleep.   [Gen. 3:17]
3 Lo, children are an heritage of the LORD: and the fruit of the womb is his reward.
4 As arrows are in the hand of a Rmighty man; so are children of the youth.   112:2
5 Happy is the man that hath his quiver full of them: they shall not be ashamed, but they shall Tspeak with the enemies in the gate.   meet

PSALM 128

Blessing on the House of the God-fearing

A Song of degrees.

BLESSED is every one that feareth the LORD; that walketh in his ways.
2 RFor thou shalt eat the labour of thine hands: happy shalt thou be, Rand it shall be well with thee.   Is. 3:10 · Eph. 6:3
3 Thy wife shall be as a fruitful vine by the sides of thine house: thy children like olive plants round about thy table.
4 Behold, that thus shall the Tman be blessed that feareth the LORD.   strong man
5 RThe LORD shall bless thee out of Zion: and thou shalt see the good of Jerusalem all the days of thy life.   134:3
6 Yea, thou shalt Rsee thy children's children, and peace upon Israel.   Job 42:16

PSALM 129

Plea of the Persecuted

A Song of degrees.

MANY a time have they Rafflicted me from Rmy youth, Rmay Israel now say;   [Jer. 1:19] · Hos. 2:15 · 124:1
2 Many a time have they Tafflicted me from my youth: Tyet they have not prevailed against me.   persecuted · nevertheless
3 The plowers plowed upon my back: they made long their furrows.
4 The LORD is Rrighteous: he hath cut asunder the cords of the wicked.   119:137
5 Let them all be confounded and turned back that Rhate Zion.   Mic. 4:11
6 Let them be as Rthe grass upon the housetops, which withereth afore it groweth up: 37:2; 2 Kin. 19:26
7 Wherewith the mower filleth not his

hand; nor he that bindeth sheaves his ᴿbosom. 79:12

8 Neither do they which go by say, ᴿThe blessing of the LORD be upon you: we bless you in the name of the LORD. Ruth 2:4

PSALM 130

"My Soul Waiteth for the Lord"

A Song of degrees.

OUT ᴿof the depths have I cried unto thee, O LORD. Lam. 3:55

2 Lord, hear my voice: let thine ears be attentive to the voice of my supplications.

3 ᴿIf thou, LORD, shouldest mark iniquities, O Lord, who shall stand? [143:2]

4 But there is ᴿforgiveness with thee, that thou mayest be feared. [Ex. 34:7; Is. 55:7]

5 ᴿI wait for the LORD, my soul doth wait, and in his word do I hope. [27:14]

6 My soul waiteth for the Lord more than they that watch for the morning: I say, more than they that watch for the morning.

7 Let Israel ᴿhope in the LORD: for with the LORD there is ᵀmercy, and with him is plenteous redemption. 131:3 • grace

8 And ᴿhe shall redeem Israel from all his iniquities. [103:3, 4]; Rom. 3:24

PSALM 131

A Childlike Faith

A Song of degrees of David.

LORD, my heart is not ᵀhaughty, nor mine eyes lofty: neither do I ᵀexercise myself in great matters, or in things too ᵀhigh for me. arrogant • engage • difficult

2 Surely I have behaved and quieted myself, as a child that is weaned of his mother: my soul is even as a weaned child.

3 ᴿLet Israel hope in the LORD from henceforth and for ever. [130:7]

PSALM 132

Trust in the God of David

A Song of degrees.

LORD, remember David, and all ᴿhis afflictions: 2 Sam. 16:12; 1 Chr. 22:14

2 How he sware unto the LORD, and vowed unto the mighty God of Jacob;

3 Surely I will not come into the tabernacle of my house, nor go up into my bed;

4 I will ᴿnot give sleep to mine eyes, or slumber to mine eyelids, Prov. 6:4

5 Until I find out a place for the LORD, an habitation for the mighty God of Jacob.

6 Lo, we heard of it at Eph'-ra-tah: ᴿwe found it in the fields of the wood. 1 Sam. 7:1

7 We will go into his tabernacles: ᴿwe will worship at his footstool. 5:7; 99:5

8 Arise, O LORD, into thy rest; thou, and ᴿthe ark of thy strength. 78:61

9 Let thy priests be clothed with righteousness; and let thy saints shout for joy.

10 For thy servant David's sake turn not away the face of thine anointed.

11 The LORD hath sworn in truth unto David; he will not turn from it; Of the fruit of thy body will I set upon thy throne.

12 If thy children will keep my covenant and my testimony that I shall teach them, their children shall also ᴿsit upon thy throne for evermore. [Luke 1:32; Acts 2:30]

13 ᴿFor the LORD hath chosen Zion; he hath desired it for his habitation. [48:1, 2]

14 This is my rest for ever: ᴿhere will I dwell; for I have desired it. Matt. 23:21

15 I will abundantly bless her provision: I will satisfy her poor with bread.

16 ᴿI will also clothe her priests with salvation: ᴿand her saints shall shout aloud for joy. 2 Chr. 6:41 • 1 Sam. 4:5

17 There will I make the ᴿhorn of David to bud: I have ordained a lamp for mine anointed. Ezek. 29:21; Luke 1:69

18 His enemies will I clothe with shame: but upon himself shall his crown flourish.

PSALM 133

Beauty of the Unity of the Brethren

A Song of degrees of David.

BEHOLD, how good and how pleasant it is for brethren to dwell together in unity!

2 It is like the precious ᴿointment upon the head, that ran down upon the beard, even Aaron's beard: that went down to the skirts of his garments; Ex. 29:7

3 As the ᴿdew of Hermon, and as the dew that descended upon the mountains of Zion: for there the LORD commanded the blessing, even life for evermore. Prov. 19:12

PSALM 134

Praise the Lord in the Evening

A Song of degrees.

BEHOLD, bless ye the LORD, all ye servants of the LORD, which by ᴿnight stand in the house of the LORD. 1 Chr. 9:33

2 ᴿLift up your hands in the ᴿsanctuary, and bless the LORD. [1 Tim. 2:8] • 63:2

3 The LORD that ᴿmade heaven and earth bless thee out of Zion. 124:8

PSALM 135

God Has Done Great Things!

PRAISEᴿ ye the LORD. Praise ye the name of the LORD; ᴿpraise him, O ye servants of the LORD. 113:1 • 134:1

2 Ye that stand in the house of the LORD, in the courts of the house of our God,

3 Praise the LORD; for ^Rthe LORD is good: sing praises unto his name; ^Rfor it is pleasant.   [119:68] • 147:1

4 For the LORD hath chosen Jacob unto himself, and Israel for his peculiar treasure.

5 For I know that the LORD is great, and that our Lord is above all gods.

6 ^RWhatsoever the LORD pleased, that did he in heaven, and in earth, in the seas, and all deep places.   115:3

7 ^RHe causeth the vapours to ascend from the ends of the earth; he maketh lightnings for the rain; he bringeth the wind out of his treasuries.   Jer. 10:13; 51:16

8 ^RWho smote the firstborn of Egypt, both of man and beast.   78:51; Ex. 12:12

9 ^RWho sent tokens and wonders into the midst of thee, O Egypt, upon Pharaoh, and upon all his servants.   78:43

10 ^RWho smote great nations, and slew mighty kings;   136:17

11 ^RSi'-hon king of the Am'-o-rites, and Og king of Ba'-shan, and ^Rall the kingdoms of Canaan: Deut. 29:7 • Josh. 12:7

12 ^RAnd gave their land for an heritage, an heritage unto Israel his people.   78:55

13 ^RThy name, O LORD, endureth for ever; and thy memorial, O LORD, throughout all generations.   102:12; [Ex. 3:15]

14 ^RFor the LORD will judge his people, and he will ^Trepent himself concerning his servants.   Deut. 32:36 • change his ways

15 The idols of the heathen are silver and gold, the work of men's hands.

16 They have mouths, but they speak not; eyes have they, but they see not;

17 They have ears, but they hear not; neither is there any breath in their mouths.

18 They that make them are like unto them: so is every one that trusteth in them.

19 ^RBless the LORD, O house of Israel: bless the LORD, O house of Aaron: 115:9, 10

20 Bless the LORD, O house of Levi: ye that ^Rfear the LORD, bless the LORD.   118:4

21 Blessed be the LORD out of Zion, which dwelleth at Jerusalem. Praise ye the LORD.

PSALM 136

God's Mercy Endures for Ever

O GIVE thanks unto the LORD; for he is good: for his mercy endureth for ever.

2 O give thanks unto ^Rthe God of gods: for his mercy endureth for ever.   Deut. 10:17

3 O give thanks to the ^RLord of lords: for his mercy endureth for ever.   Deut. 10:17

4 To him who alone doeth great wonders: for his mercy endureth for ever.

5 To him that by wisdom made the heavens: for his mercy endureth for ever.

6 ^RTo him that stretched out the earth above the waters: for his mercy endureth for ever.   24:2; Gen. 1:9; [Is. 42:5]

7 ^RTo him that made great lights: for his mercy endureth for ever: Gen. 1:14

8 ^RThe sun to rule by day: for his mercy endureth for ever: Gen. 1:16

9 The moon and stars to rule by night: for his mercy endureth for ever.

10 To him that smote Egypt in their firstborn: for his mercy endureth for ever:

11 And brought out Israel from among them: for his mercy endureth for ever:

12 ^RWith a strong hand, and with a stretched out arm: for his mercy endureth for ever.   Ex. 6:1; 13:9; 1 Kin. 8:42

13 To him which divided the Red sea into parts: for his mercy endureth for ever:

14 And made Israel to pass through the midst of it: for his mercy endureth for ever:

15 But overthrew Pharaoh and his host in the Red sea: for his mercy endureth for ever.

16 ^RTo him which led his people through the wilderness: for his mercy endureth for ever.   Ex. 13:18; 15:22; Deut. 8:15

17 ^RTo him which smote great kings: for his mercy endureth for ever: 135:10

18 ^RAnd slew famous kings: for his mercy endureth for ever: Deut. 29:7

19 ^RSi'-hon king of the Am'-o-rites: for his mercy endureth for ever: Num. 21:21

20 ^RAnd Og the king of Ba'-shan: for his mercy endureth for ever: Num. 21:33

21 ^RAnd gave their land for an heritage: for his mercy endureth for ever: Josh. 12:1

22 Even an heritage unto Israel his servant: for his mercy endureth for ever.

23 Who remembered us in our low estate: for his mercy endureth for ever:

24 And hath redeemed us from our enemies: for his mercy endureth for ever.

25 ^RWho giveth food to all flesh: for his mercy endureth for ever.   [104:27]

26 O give thanks unto the God of heaven: for his mercy endureth for ever.

PSALM 137

Tears in Exile

B Y ^Rthe rivers of Babylon, there we sat down, yea, we ^Rwept, when we remembered Zion.   Ezek. 1:1, 3 • Neh. 1:4

2 We hanged our harps upon the ^Rwillows in the midst thereof.   Lev. 23:40

3 For there they that carried us away captive required of us a song; and they that wasted us required of us mirth, saying, Sing us one of the songs of Zion.

4 How shall we sing the ^RLORD's song in a strange land?   2 Chr. 29:27; Neh. 12:46

5 ^RIf I forget thee, O Jerusalem, let my right hand forget her cunning.   Is. 65:11

6 If I do not remember thee, let my tongue cleave to the roof of my mouth; if I prefer not Jerusalem above my chief joy.

7 Remember, O LORD, Rthe children of E′-dom in the day of Jerusalem; who said, TRase *it*, rase *it*, *even* to the Rfoundation thereof.   Is. 34:5, 6; Lam. 4:21 • *destroy* • [Hab. 3:13]

8 O daughter of Babylon, who art to be destroyed; happy *shall he be*, that rewardeth thee as thou hast served us.

9 Happy *shall he be*, that taketh and dasheth thy little ones against the stones.

PSALM 138

God Answered My Prayer

A Psalm of David.

I WILLR praise thee with my whole heart: Rbefore the gods will I sing praise unto thee.   111:1 • [95:3; 96:4]

2 I will worship Rtoward thy holy temple, and praise thy name for thy lovingkindness and for thy truth: for thou hast Rmagnified thy word above all thy name.   28:2 • Is. 42:21

3 In the day when I Rcried thou answeredst me, *and* strengthenedst me *with* strength in my soul.   118:5

4 RAll the kings of the earth shall praise thee, O LORD, when they hear the words of thy mouth.   72:11; 102:15

5 Yea, they shall sing in the ways of the LORD: for great *is* the glory of the LORD.

6 RThough the LORD *be* high, yet Rhath he Trespect unto the lowly: but the proud he knoweth afar off.   [113:4-7] • [James 4:6] • *regard*

7 RThough I walk in the midst of trouble, thou wilt revive me: thou shalt stretch forth thine hand against the wrath of mine enemies, and thy right hand shall save me. [23:3, 4]

8 RThe LORD will Tperfect *that which* concerneth me: thy mercy, O LORD, *endureth* for ever: forsake not the works of thine own hands.   [Phil. 1:6] • *accomplish*

PSALM 139

"Search Me, O God"

To the chief Musician, A Psalm of David.

O LORD, Rthou hast searched me, and known *me*.   17:3; Jer. 12:3

2 RThou knowest my downsitting and mine uprising, thou Runderstandest my thought afar off.   2 Kin. 19:27 • Is. 66:18

3 RThou compassest my path and my Tlying down, and art acquainted *with* all my ways.   [Job 31:4] • *bed*

4 For *there is* not a word in my tongue, *but*, lo, O LORD, thou knowest it altogether.

5 Thou hast beset me behind and before, Rand laid thine hand upon me.   Job 9:33

6 *Such* knowledge *is* too wonderful for me; it is high, I cannot *attain* unto it.

7 Whither shall I go from thy spirit? or whither shall I flee from thy presence?

8 RIf I ascend up into heaven, thou *art* there: Rif I make my bed in hell, behold, thou *art there*.   Amos 9:2 • [Prov. 15:11]

9 *If* I take the wings of the morning, *and* dwell in the uttermost parts of the sea;

10 Even there shall thy hand Rlead me, and thy right hand shall hold me.   [23:2, 3]

11 If I say, Surely the Rdarkness shall cover me; even the night shall be light about me.   Job 22:13

12 Yea, the darkness hideth not from thee; but the night shineth as the day: the darkness and the light *are* both alike *to thee*.

13 For thou hast possessed my reins: thou hast covered me in my mother's womb.

14 I will praise thee; for I am fearfully *and* wonderfully made: marvellous *are* thy works; and *that* my soul knoweth right well.

15 My substance was not hid from thee, when I was made in secret, *and* curiously wrought in the lowest parts of the earth.

16 Thine Reyes did see my substance, yet being unperfect; and in thy book all *my* members were written, *which* in continuance

---

139:14 God's Work in Our Lives—All people possess an inward desire that their work should have meaning and permanence (Page 587—Ps. 90:16, 17). If man's work is not to be lost in the vastness of eternity, however, it must conform to the work God has designed for man. This work for the present day can be known only from God's Word.

According to the Word of God, the initial work of God is for us to believe in Jesus Christ (Page 1049— John 6:29; Page 1113—Rom. 6:17, 18). Apart from entering into this vital relationship with God, man cannot even begin to work for God. After coming to know Christ, the new Christian discovers God's program for the present from the Scriptures. It is, first of all, His work in the Christian himself. Regeneration is only the beginning of God's work in the believer. It actually introduces a process of becoming like Christ which God promises ultimately to bring to perfection (Page 1170—Phil. 1:6). The Christian's cheerful obedience to God's will as revealed in His Word helps speed this work along.

Second, no Christian can overlook God's work in the world. Jesus' command to spread the good news of the Gospel to all men appears near the end of all four Gospels and at the beginning of the Book of Acts. God's method is that men proclaim the gospel and that the Holy Spirit convict (Page 1061— John 16:8–11).

Finally, God's work is in and through the church, the organism ordained by Christ for this age (Page 958—Matt. 16:18). God works in the church through the Spirit and through spiritually gifted people to strengthen and bless it (Page 1164—Eph. 4:11–13).

Now turn to Page 5—Gen. 2:15–17: The Edenic Covenant.

were fashioned, when *as yet there was* none of them.   [Job 10:8–10]

17 RHow precious also are thy thoughts unto me, O God! how great is the sum of them!   [40:5; 92:5]

18 *If* I should count them, they are more in number than the sand: when I Rawake, I am still with thee.   3:5

19 Surely thou wilt Rslay the wicked, O God: Rdepart from me therefore, ye bloody men.   [Is. 11:4] • 6:8; 119:115

20 For they speak against thee wickedly, *and* thine enemies take *thy name* in vain.

21 RDo not I hate them, O LORD, that hate thee? and am not I grieved with those that rise up against thee?   2 Chr. 19:2

22 I hate them with Tperfect hatred: I count them mine enemies.   utmost

23 Search me, O God, and know my heart: try me, and know my thoughts:

24 And see if *there be any* wicked way in me, and lead me in the way everlasting.

PSALM 140

Preserve Me from Violence

To the chief Musician, A Psalm of David.

DELIVERR me, O LORD, from the Revil man: preserve me from the violent man;   17:13 • 36:4

2 TWhich Timagine mischiefs in *their* heart; Rcontinually are they gathered together *for* war.   who • plan evil • 56:6

3 They have Rsharpened their tongues like a serpent; adders' Rpoison *is* under their lips. Selah.   57:4 • James 3:8

4 Keep me, O LORD, from the hands of the wicked; preserve me from the violent man; who have purposed to overthrow my goings.

5 The proud have hid a snare for me, and cords; they have spread a net by the wayside; they have set Tgins for me.   Selah.   snares

6 I said unto the LORD, Thou *art* my God: hear the voice of my supplications, O LORD.

7 RO GOD the Lord, the strength of my salvation, thou hast Rcovered my head in the day of battle.   [28:8] • 144:10

8 Grant not, O LORD, the desires of the wicked: further not Rhis wicked device; *lest* they exalt themselves.   Selah.   Esth. 9:25

9 *As for* the head of those that compass me about, let the Rmischief of their own lips cover them.   7:16; Prov. 18:7

10 RLet burning coals fall upon them: let them be cast into the fire; into deep pits, that they rise not up again.   11:6

11 Let not an evil speaker be established in the earth: Revil shall Thunt the violent man to overthrow *him*.   34:21 • follow

12 I know that the LORD will Rmaintain the cause of the afflicted, *and* the right of the poor.   9:4; 18:27; 1 Kin. 8:45

13 RSurely the righteous shall give thanks unto thy name: the upright shall dwell in thy presence.   97:12

PSALM 141

"Set a Watch, O LORD, Before My Mouth"

A Psalm of David.

LORD, I cry unto thee: make Rhaste unto me; give ear unto my voice, when I cry unto thee.   22:19; 38:22

2 Let my prayer be set forth before thee *as* incense; *and* the lifting up of my hands *as* Rthe evening sacrifice.   Ex. 29:41

3 RSet a watch, O LORD, before my mouth; Rkeep the door of my lips. 34:13 • Mic. 7:5

4 RIncline not my heart to *any* evil thing, to practise Rwicked works with men that work iniquity: Rand let me not eat of their dainties.   119:36 • Is. 32:6 • Prov. 23:6

5 RLet the righteous smite me; *it shall be* a kindness: and let him reprove me; *it shall be* an excellent oil, *which* shall not break my head: for yet my prayer also *shall be* in their calamities.   Prov. 9:8

6 When their Tjudges are Roverthrown in stony places, they shall hear my words; for they are sweet.   rulers • 2 Chr. 25:12

7 ROur bones are scattered at the grave's mouth, as when one cutteth and cleaveth *wood* upon the earth.   53:5

8 But Rmine eyes *are* unto thee, O GOD the Lord: in thee is my trust; leave not my soul destitute.   25:15

9 Keep me from Rthe snares *which* they have laid for me, and the Tgins of the workers of iniquity.   38:12 • traps

10 RLet the wicked fall into their own nets, whilst that I withal escape.   7:15

PSALM 142

"No Man Cared for My Soul"

Mas'-chil of David;
A Prayer when he was in the cave.

I CRIEDR unto the LORD with my voice; with my voice unto the LORD did I make my supplication.   77:1

2 RI poured out my complaint before him; I shewed before him my trouble.   102:1–11

3 When my spirit was overwhelmed within me, then thou knewest my path. In the way wherein I walked have they Tprivily laid a snare for me.   secretly

4 I looked on *my* right hand, and beheld, but *there was* no man that would know me: refuge failed me; no man cared for my soul.

5 I cried unto thee, O LORD: I said, Thou *art* Rmy refuge *and* my Rportion in the land of the living.   91:2 • 16:5

6 TAttend unto my cry; for I am brought

very low: deliver me from my persecutors; for they are stronger than I.   *give heed*

7 ᴿBring my soul out of prison, that I may praise thy name: the righteous shall compass me about; for thou shalt deal bountifully with me.   143:11

PSALM 143

"Teach Me to Do Thy Will"

A Psalm of David.

HEAR my prayer, O Lᴏʀᴅ, give ear to my supplications: in thy faithfulness answer me, *and* in thy righteousness.

2 And ᴿenter not into judgment with thy servant: for in thy sight shall no man living be justified.   Job 14:3; 22:4

3 For the enemy hath ᴿpersecuted my soul; he hath smitten my life down to the ground; he ᴿhath made me to dwell in darkness, as those that have been long dead.   44:25 • Lam. 3:6

4 Therefore is my spirit overwhelmed within me; my heart within me is desolate.

5 ᴿI remember the days of old; I ᴿmeditate on all thy works; I muse on the work of thy hands.   77:5, 10, 11 • 105:2

6 I ᴿstretch forth my hands unto thee: ᴿmy soul *thirsteth* after thee, as a thirsty land. Selah.   Job 11:13 • 42:2

7 Hear me speedily, O Lᴏʀᴅ: my spirit faileth: hide not thy face from me, lest I be like unto them that go down into the pit.

8 Cause me to hear thy lovingkindness in the morning; for in thee do I trust: cause me to know the way wherein I should walk; for I lift up my soul unto thee.

9 ᴿDeliver me, O Lᴏʀᴅ, from mine enemies: I flee unto thee to hide me.   31:15

10 ᴿTeach me to do thy will; for thou *art* my God: thy spirit *is* good; lead me into the land of uprightness.   25:4

11 Quicken me, O Lᴏʀᴅ, ᴿfor thy name's sake: for thy righteousness' sake bring my soul out of trouble.   25:11

12 And of thy mercy ᴿcut off mine enemies, and destroy all them that afflict my soul: for I *am* thy servant.   54:5

PSALM 144

"What Is Man?"

A Psalm of David.

BLESSED *be* the Lᴏʀᴅ my strength, ᴿwhich teacheth my hands to war, *and* my fingers to fight: 2 Sam. 22:35

2 My ᵀgoodness, and my ᴿfortress; my high tower, and my ᵀdeliverer; my shield, and *he* in whom I trust; who subdueth my people under me.   *mercy* • 18:2 • *liberator*

3 Lᴏʀᴅ, what *is* ᴿman, that thou takest

knowledge of him! *or* the son of man, that thou makest account of him!   8:4

4 ᴿMan is like to vanity: his days *are* as a shadow that passeth away.   [39:11]

5 ᴿBow thy heavens, O Lᴏʀᴅ, ᴿand come down: ᴿtouch the mountains, and they shall smoke.   18:9 • Is. 64:1 • 104:32

6 Cast forth lightning, and scatter them: shoot out thine arrows, and destroy them.

7 Send thine hand ᴿfrom above; rid me, and deliver me out of great waters, from the hand of strange children;   18:16

8 Whose mouth ᴿspeaketh vanity, and their right ᴿhand *is* a right hand of falsehood.   12:2 • Deut. 32:40

9 I will sing a new song unto thee, O God: upon a psaltery *and* an instrument of ten strings will I sing praises unto thee.

10 ᴿ*It is he* that giveth ᵀsalvation unto kings: who delivereth David his servant from the hurtful sword.   18:50 • *victory*

11 Rid me, and deliver me from the hand of strange children, whose mouth speaketh vanity, and their ᴿright hand *is* a right hand of falsehood: Is. 44:20

12 That our sons *may be* ᴿas plants grown up in their youth; *that* our daughters *may be* as corner stones, polished *after* the similitude of a palace: [92:12–14]

13 *That* our ᴿgarners *may be* full, affording all manner of store: *that* our sheep may bring forth thousands and ten thousands in our streets: [Prov. 3:9, 10]

14 ᴿ*That* our oxen *may be* strong to labour; *that there be* no breaking in, nor going out; that *there be* no complaining in our streets.   Prov. 14:4

15 ᴿHappy *is that* people, that is in such a case: *yea,* happy *is that* people, whose God *is* the Lᴏʀᴅ.   [33:12]

PSALM 145

Testify to God's Great Acts

David's *Psalm* of praise.

I WILL extol thee, my God, O king; and I will bless thy name for ever and ever.

2 Every day will I bless thee; ᴿand I will praise thy name for ever and ever.   71:6

3 Great *is* the Lᴏʀᴅ, and greatly to be praised; and his greatness *is* unsearchable.

4 One generation shall praise thy works to another, and shall declare thy mighty acts.

5 I will speak of the glorious honour of thy majesty, and of thy wondrous works.

6 And *men* shall speak of the might of thy ᵀterribleᴿ acts: and I will declare thy greatness.   *glorious* • Deut. 10:21

7 They shall ᵀabundantly utter the memory of thy great goodness, and shall sing of thy righteousness.   *eagerly*

8 The Lord is gracious, and full of compassion; slow to anger, and of great mercy.

9 ᴿThe Lord is good to all: and his tender mercies are over all his works.   Nah. 1:7

10 All thy works shall praise thee, O Lord; and thy saints shall bless thee.

11 They shall speak of the ᴿglory of thy kingdom, and talk of thy power;   Jer. 14:21

12 ᴿTo make known to the sons of men his mighty acts, and the ᴿglorious majesty of his kingdom.   105:1 • [Is. 2:10, 19]

13 ᴿThy kingdom is an everlasting kingdom, and thy dominion endureth throughout all generations.   [1 Tim. 1:17]

14 The Lord upholdeth all that fall, and raiseth up all those that be bowed down.

15 The eyes of all wait upon thee; and thou givest them their meat in due season.

16 Thou openest thine hand, and satisfiest the desire of every living thing.

17 The Lord is righteous in all his ways, and ᵀholy in all his works.   merciful

18 ᴿThe Lord is nigh unto all them that call upon him, to all that call upon him ᴿin truth.   [Deut. 4:7] • [John 4:24]

19 He will ᴿfulfil the desire of them that fear him: ᴿhe also will hear their cry, and will save them.   21:2 • [Prov. 15:29]

20 The Lord preserveth all them that love him: but all the wicked will he destroy.

21 My ᴿmouth shall speak the praise of the Lord: and let all flesh bless his holy name for ever and ever.   71:8

PSALM 146

"Put Not Your Trust in Princes"

PRAISE ye the Lord. ᴿPraise the Lord, O my soul.   103:1

2 ᴿWhile I live will I praise the Lord: I will sing praises unto my God while I have any being.   63:4

3 Put not your trust in princes, nor in the son of man, in whom there is no help.

4 ᴿHis breath goeth forth, ᴿhe returneth to his earth; in that very day ᴿhis thoughts perish.   104:29 • [Eccl. 12:7] • [33:10]

5 ᴿHappy is he that hath the God of Jacob for his help, whose hope is in the Lord his God: Jer. 17:7

6 ᴿWhich made heaven, and earth, ᴿthe sea, and all that therein is: which keepeth truth for ever: Rev. 14:7 • Acts 14:15

7 Which executeth judgment for the oppressed: which giveth food to the hungry. ᴿThe Lord looseth the prisoners: 107:10

8 The Lord openeth the eyes of the blind: the Lord raiseth them that are bowed down: the Lord loveth the righteous:

9 The Lord preserveth the strangers; he relieveth the fatherless and widow: but the way of the wicked he turneth upside down.

10 ᴿThe Lord shall reign for ever, even thy God, O Zion, unto all generations. Praise ye the Lord.   Ex. 15:18

PSALM 147

God Heals the Brokenhearted

PRAISE ye the Lord: for it is good to sing praises unto our God; for it is pleasant; and praise is ᵀcomely.   appropriate

2 The Lord doth build up Jerusalem: he gathereth together the outcasts of Israel.

3 He healeth the ᴿbroken in heart, and bindeth up their wounds.   [51:17]

4 He ᵀtelleth the number of the stars; he calleth them all by their names.   counts

5 Great is our Lord, and of great power: his understanding is infinite.

6 The Lord lifteth up the meek: he casteth the wicked down to the ground.

7 Sing unto the Lord with thanksgiving; sing praise upon the harp unto our God:

8 Who covereth the heaven with clouds, who prepareth rain for the earth, who maketh grass to grow upon the mountains.

9 ᴿHe giveth to the beast his food, and to the young ravens which cry.   Job 38:41

10 He delighteth not in the strength of the ᴿhorse: he taketh not pleasure in the ᴿlegs of a man.   33:17 • [1 Sam. 16:7]

11 The Lord taketh pleasure in them that fear him, in those that hope in his mercy.

12 Praise the Lord, O Jerusalem; praise thy God, O Zion.

13 For he hath strengthened ᴿthe bars of thy gates; he hath ᴿblessed thy children within thee.   Neh. 3:3; 7:3 • 37:26

14 He maketh peace in thy borders, and filleth thee with the finest of the wheat.

15 He sendeth forth his commandment upon earth: his word runneth very swiftly.

16 ᴿHe giveth snow like wool: he scattereth the hoarfrost like ashes.   Job 37:6

17 He casteth forth his ᴿice like morsels: who can stand before his cold?   Job 37:10

18 ᴿHe sendeth out his word, and melteth them: he causeth his wind to blow, and the waters flow.   33:9; 107:20

19 He sheweth his word unto Jacob, his statutes and his judgments unto Israel.

20 He hath not dealt so with any nation: and as for his judgments, they have not known them. Praise ye the Lord.

PSALM 148

All Creation Praises the Lord

PRAISE ye the Lord. Praise ye the Lord ᴿfrom the heavens: praise him ᴿin the heights.   69:34 • Job 16:19

2 ᴿPraise ye him, all his angels: praise ye him, all his hosts.   103:20

3 Praise ye him, sun and moon: praise him, all ye stars of light.

4 Praise him, ye heavens of heavens, and ye waters that *be* above the heavens.

5 Let them praise the name of the LORD: for he commanded, and they were created.

6 ^RHe hath also stablished them for ever and ever: he hath made a decree which shall not pass.   [Jer. 31:35, 36]

7 Praise the LORD from the earth, ^Rye ^Tdragons, and all deeps: 74:13 · *sea monsters*

8 Fire, and hail; snow, and vapours; stormy wind ^Rfulfilling his word: Job 37:12

9 ^RMountains, and all hills; fruitful trees, and all cedars: Is. 44:23; 49:13

10 Beasts, and all cattle; ^Rcreeping things, and flying fowl: Hos. 2:18

11 Kings of the earth, and all people; princes, and all judges of the earth:

12 Both young men, and maidens; old men, and children:

13 Let them praise the name of the LORD: for ^Rhis name alone is excellent; his glory *is* above the earth and heaven.   Is. 12:4

14 ^RHe also exalteth the horn of his people, the praise of all his saints; *even* of the children of Israel, a people near unto him. Praise ye the LORD.   1 Sam. 2:1

PSALM 149

"The LORD Taketh Pleasure in His People"

PRAISE ye the LORD. ^RSing unto the LORD a new song, *and* his praise in the congregation of saints.   33:3

2 Let Israel rejoice in him that ^Rmade him: let the children of Zion be joyful in their ^RKing.   95:6 · Judg. 8:23

3 ^RLet them praise his name in the dance: let them sing praises unto him with the timbrel and harp.   2 Sam. 6:14

4 For ^Rthe LORD taketh pleasure in his people: ^Rhe will beautify the meek with salvation.   35:27 · Is. 61:3

5 Let the saints be joyful in glory: ^Rlet them sing aloud upon their beds.   Job 35:10

6 *Let* the high *praises* of God *be* in their mouth, and a twoedged sword in their hand;

7 To execute vengeance upon the heathen, *and* punishments upon the people;

8 To bind their kings with chains, and their ^Rnobles with fetters of iron;   Nah. 3:10

9 ^RTo execute upon them the judgment written: this honour have all his saints. Praise ye the LORD.   Ezek. 28:26

PSALM 150

"Praise Ye the LORD"

PRAISE ye the LORD. Praise God in his ^Rsanctuary: praise him in the ^Rfirmament of his power.   73:17 · 19:1

2 Praise him for his mighty acts: praise him according to his excellent greatness.

3 Praise him with the sound of the ^Rtrumpet: praise him with the psaltery and harp. 98:6

4 Praise him with the ^Rtimbrel and dance: praise him with stringed instruments and organs.   149:3

5 Praise him upon the loud cymbals: praise him upon the high sounding cymbals.

6 Let every thing that ^Rhath breath praise the LORD. Praise ye the LORD.   145:21

150:1 Praise—To praise God is to acknowledge the glories of His excellent person. It differs somewhat from thanksgiving, which describes what God has done rather than what He is. Here are some facts about praise.

a. God alone is worthy of our praise (Page 553—Ps. 18:3; 113:3).

b. It is His will for us that we praise Him (Page 569—Ps. 50:23; Page 688—Is. 43:21).

c. This praise should be continuous (Page 561—Ps. 34:1; 71:6) and also public (Page 556—Ps. 22:25).

d. We are to praise God for His holiness (Page 454—2 Chr. 20:21), grace (Page 1162—Eph. 1:6), goodness (Page 606—Ps. 135:3), and kindness (Page 607—Ps. 138:2).

e. All nature praises God (Page 611—Ps. 148:7-10).

f. The sun, moon, and stars praise Him (Page 554—Ps. 19:1; 143:3).

g. The angels praise Him (Page 610—Ps. 148:2).

In fact, we are told that on occasion God uses even the wrath of men to praise Him (Page 580—Ps. 76:10). An example of this is seen in the selling of Joseph by his brothers into slavery (Page 39—Gen. 37:28). God later uses this cruel act to promote Joseph as second ruler over all Egypt. As Joseph would remind his brothers: "But as for you, ye thought evil against me; *but* God meant it unto good, to bring to pass, as *it is* this day, to save much people alive" (Page 52—Gen. 50:20).

Now turn to Page 1249—1 John 1:9: Confession.

THE
PROVERBS

📖 THE BOOK OF PROVERBS

The key word in Proverbs is *wisdom*, "the ability to live life skillfully." A godly life in an ungodly world, however, is no simple assignment. Proverbs provides God's detailed instructions for His people to deal successfully with the practical affairs of everyday life: how to relate to God, parents, children, neighbors, and government. Solomon, the principal author, uses a combination of poetry, parables, pithy questions, short stories, and wise maxims to give in strikingly memorable form the common sense and divine perspective necessary to handle life's issues.

Because Solomon, the pinnacle of Israel's wise men, was the principal contributor, the Hebrew title of this book is *Mishle Shelomoh*, "Proverbs of Solomon" (1:1). The Greek title is *Paroimiai Salomontos*, "Proverbs of Solomon." The Latin title *Liber Proverbiorum*, "Book of Proverbs," combines the words *pro* "for" and *verba* "words" to describe the way the proverbs concentrate many words into a few. The Rabbinical writings called Proverbs *Sepher Hokhmah*, "Book of Wisdom."

✍️ THE AUTHOR OF PROVERBS

Solomon's name appears at the beginning of the three sections he wrote: 1:1 for chapters 1—9, 10:1 for chapters 10:1—22:16, and 25:1 for chapters 25—29. According to First Kings 4:32, he spoke 3,000 proverbs and 1,005 songs. Only about 800 of his 3,000 proverbs are included in the two Solomonic collections in this book. No man was better qualified than Solomon to be the principal contributor. He asked for wisdom (1 Kin. 3:5–9) and God granted it to him (1 Kin. 4:29–31) to such a degree that people from foreign lands came to hear him speak (1 Kin. 4:34; 10:1–13, 24). His breadth of knowledge, aptitude, skill, and perception were extraordinary. In every area Solomon brought prosperity and glory to Israel until his latter years (cf. 1 Kin. 11:4).

It is likely that Solomon collected and edited proverbs other than his own. According to Ecclesiastes 12:9, "he gave good heed, and sought out, *and* set in order many proverbs." The second collection of Solomonic proverbs in 25—29 was assembled by the scribes of King Hezekiah because of his interest in spiritually benefitting his subjects with the Word of God. The prophets Isaiah and Micah ministered during Hezekiah's time, and it has been suggested that they also might have been involved in this collection.

Proverbs 22:17—24:34 consists of "the words of the wise" (22:17; 24:23). Some of these sayings are quite similar to those found in The Wisdom of Amenemope, a document of teachings on civil service by an Egyptian who probably lived between 1000 b.c. and 600 b.c. Wise men of this period went to hear one another, and it is probable that Amenemope borrowed certain aphorisms from Hebrew literature. If the *hakhamim* ("wise men") lived before Solomon's time, he may have been the collector and editor of this series of wise sayings.

There is no biblical information about Agur (30) or Lemuel (31). Agur ben Jakeh (30:1) is simply called an oracle, and Lemuel is called a king and an oracle (31:1). Both have been identified with Solomon, but there is no basis for this suggestion.

⏳ THE TIME OF PROVERBS

Proverbs is a collection of topical maxims and is not a historical book. It is a product of the wisdom school in Israel. According to Jeremiah 18:18 and Ezekiel 7:26, three groups communicated to the people on behalf of God: the priests imparted the Law; the prophets communicated the divine word and visions; and the sages, or elders, gave counsel to the people. The sages provided the practical application of godly wisdom to specific problems and decisions. The "Preacher" of Ecclesiastes is a good example of the wisdom school (Eccl. 1:1, 12; 7:27; 12:8–10). *Qoheleth*, or "Preacher," meant "one who addresses an assembly": he presided over a "school" of wise men and "taught the people knowledge" (Eccl. 12:9). "My son" in Proverbs and Ecclesiastes evidently refers to the pupil. This was parallel to Samuel's role of heading Israel's school of prophets.

Wisdom literature is also found in other countries of the ancient Near East. In Egypt, written examples can be found as early as 2700 b.c. Although the style was similar to Israel's wisdom literature, the proverbs and sayings of these countries differed from those of Israel in content because they lacked the character of the righteous standards of the Lord.

Solomon's proverbs were written by 931 b.c., and his proverbs in chapters 25—29 were collected by Hezekiah about 230 years later (Hezekiah reigned from 715 to 686 b.c.). Under Solomon, Israel was at its spiritual, political, and economic summit. Solomon probably wrote his proverbs in his middle years, before his character began to decline into carnality, materialism, and idolatry.

✝️ THE CHRIST OF PROVERBS

In Proverbs 8, wisdom is personified and seen in its perfection. It is divine (8:22–31), it is the source of biological and

spiritual life (8:35, 36; 3:18), it is righteous and moral (8:8, 9), and it is available to all who will receive it (8:1–6, 32–35). This wisdom became incarnate in Christ "in whom are hid all the treasures of wisdom and knowledge" (Col. 2:3). "But of him are ye in Christ Jesus, who of God is made unto us wisdom, and righteousness, and sanctification, and redemption" (1 Cor. 1:30; cf. 1 Cor. 1:22–24).

KEYS TO PROVERBS

Key Word: Wisdom—Proverbs is one of the few biblical books that clearly spells out its purpose. The purpose statement in 1:2–6 is twofold: (1) to impart moral discernment and discretion (1:3–5), and (2) to develop mental clarity and perception (1:2, 6). The words "wisdom and instruction" in 1:2 complement each other because *wisdom (hokhmah)* means "skill," and *instruction (musar)* means "discipline." No skill is perfected without discipline, and when a person has skill he has freedom to create something beautiful. Proverbs deals with the most fundamental skill of all: practical righteousness before God in every area of life. This requires knowledge, experience, and a willingness to put God first (see 3:5–7). Chapters 1—9 are designed to create a felt need for wisdom, and Proverbs as a whole is designed both to prevent and to remedy ungodly life-styles. The book served as a manual to impart the legacy of wisdom, prudence, understanding, discretion, knowledge, guidance, competence, correction, counsel, and truth—from generation to generation.

Key Verses: Proverbs 1:5–7 and 3:5, 6—"A wise *man* will hear, and will increase learning; and a man of understanding shall attain unto wise counsels: To understand a proverb, and the interpretation; the words of the wise, and their dark sayings. The fear of the Lord *is* the beginning of knowledge: *but* fools despise wisdom and instruction" (1:5–7).

"Trust in the Lord with all thine heart; and lean not unto thine own understanding. In all thy ways acknowledge him, and he shall direct thy paths" (3:5, 6).

Key Chapter: Proverbs 31—The last chapter of Proverbs is unique in ancient literature, as it reveals a very high and noble view of women. The woman in these verses is: (1) a good woman (31:13, 15, 16, 19, 25), (2) a good wife (31:11, 12, 23, 24), (3) a good mother (31:14, 15, 18, 21, 27), and (4) a good neighbor (31:20–26). Her conduct, concern, speech, and life stand in sharp contrast to the woman pictured in Proverbs 7.

SURVEY OF PROVERBS

Proverbs is the most intensely practical book in the Old Testament because it teaches skillful living in the multiple aspects of everyday life. Its specific precepts include instruction on wisdom and folly, the righteous and the wicked, the tongue, pride and humility, justice and vengeance, the family, laziness and work, poverty and wealth, friends and neighbors, love and lust, anger and strife, masters and servants, life and death. Proverbs touches upon every facet of human relationships, and its principles transcend the bounds of time and culture.

The Hebrew word for "proverb" *(mashal)* means "comparison, similar, parallel." A proverb uses a comparison or figure of speech to make a pithy but poignant observation. Proverbs have been defined as simple illustrations that expose fundamental realities of life. These maxims are not theoretical but practical; they are easily memorized, based on real-life experience, and designed for use in the mainstream of life. The proverbs are general statements and illustrations of timeless truth, which allow for, but do not condone, exceptions to the rule. The key word is *hokhmah*, "wisdom": it literally means "skill" (in living). Wisdom is more than shrewdness or intelligence. Instead, it relates to practical

FOCUS	PURPOSE OF PROVERBS	PROVERBS TO YOUTH	PROVERBS OF SOLOMON	PROVERBS OF SOLOMON (HEZEKIAH)	WORDS OF AGUR	WORDS OF LEMUEL
REFERENCE	1:1————1:8————10:1————			25:1————————30:1————		31:1————31:31
DIVISION	PURPOSE AND THEME	FATHER'S EXHORTATIONS	FIRST COLLECTION OF SOLOMON	SECOND COLLECTION OF SOLOMON	NUMERICAL PROVERBS	VIRTUOUS WIFE
TOPIC	PROLOGUE	PRINCIPLES OF WISDOM			EPILOGUE	
	COMMENDATION OF WISDOM	COUNSEL OF WISDOM			COMPARISONS OF WISDOM	
LOCATION	JUDAH					
TIME	c. 950 – 700 B.C.					

righteousness and moral acumen. The Book of Proverbs may be divided into six segments: the purpose of Proverbs (1:1-7), the proverbs to the youth (1:8—9:18), the proverbs of Solomon (10:1—24:34), the proverbs of Solomon copied by Hezekiah's men (25:1—29:27), the words of Agur (30:1-33), and the words of King Lemuel (31:1-31).

The Purpose of Proverbs (1:1-7): The brief prologue states the author, theme, and purpose of the book.

The Proverbs to the Youth (1:8—9:18): Following the introduction, there is a series of ten exhortations, each beginning with "My son" (1:8—9:18). These messages introduce the concept of wisdom in the format of a father's efforts to persuade his son to pursue the path of wisdom in order to achieve godly success in life. Wisdom rejects the invitation of crime and foolishness, rewards seekers of wisdom on every level, and wisdom's discipline provides freedom and safety (1—4). Wisdom protects one from illicit sensuality and its consequences, from foolish practices and laziness, and from adultery and the lure of the harlot (5—7). Wisdom is to be preferred to folly because of its divine origin and rich benefits (8 and 9). There are four kinds of fools, ranging from those who are naive and uncommitted to scoffers who arrogantly despise the way of God. The fool is not mentally deficient; he is self-sufficient, ordering his life as if there were no God.

The Proverbs of Solomon (10:1—24:34): There is a minimal amount of topical arrangement in these chapters. There are some thematic clusters (e.g., 26:1-12, 13-16, 20-22), but the usual units are one-verse maxims. It is helpful to assemble and organize these proverbs according to such specific themes as money and speech. This Solomonic collection consists of 375 proverbs of Solomon. Chapters 10—15 contrast right and wrong in practice, and all but nineteen proverbs use antithetic parallelism, that is, parallels of paired opposite principles. Chapters 16:1—22:16 offer a series of self-evident moral truths and all but eighteen proverbs use synonymous parallelism, that is, parallels of paired identical or similar principles. The words of wise men (22:17—24:34) are given in two groups. The first group includes thirty distinct sayings (22:17—24:22), and six more are found in the second group (24:23-34).

The Proverbs of Solomon Copied by Hezekiah's Men (25:1—29:27): This second Solomonic collection was copied and arranged by "the men of Hezekiah" (25:1). These proverbs in chapters 25—29 further develop the themes in the first Solomonic collection.

The Words of Agur (30:1-33): The last two chapters of Proverbs form an appendix of sayings by two otherwise unknown sages, Agur and Lemuel. Most of Agur's material is given in clusters of numerical proverbs.

The Words of King Lemuel (31:1-31): The last chapter includes an acrostic of twenty-two verses (the first letter of each verse consecutively follows the complete Hebrew alphabet) portraying a virtuous wife (31:10-31).

OUTLINE OF PROVERBS

CHAPTER 1

The Purpose of Proverbs

THE ᴿProverbs of Solomon the son of
David, king of Israel;   1 Kin. 4:32
2 To know wisdom and instruction; to
perceive the words of understanding;
3 To ᴿreceive the instruction of wisdom,
justice, and judgment, and equity;   [19:20]
4 To give subtilty to the simple, to the
young man knowledge and discretion.
5 ᴿA wise *man* will hear, and will increase
learning; and a man of understanding shall
attain unto wise counsels: 9:9
6 To understand a proverb, and ᵀthe
interpretation; the words of the wise, and
their ᴿdark sayings.   *meaning* • Ps. 78:2
7 ᴿThe fear of the Lᴏʀᴅ *is* the beginning of
knowledge: *but* fools despise wisdom and
instruction.   15:33; Job 28:28

Obey Parents

8 ᴿMy son, hear the instruction of thy
father, ᴿand forsake not the law of thy
mother: 4:1 • 6:20

9 For they *shall be* an ornament of grace
unto thy head, and chains about thy neck.

Avoid Bad Company

10 My son, if sinners entice thee, ᴿconsent
thou not.   Gen. 39:7, 8; Deut. 13:8
11 If they say, Come with us, let us ᴿlay
wait for blood, let us lurk privily for the
innocent without cause: Jer. 5:26
12 Let us ᴿswallow them up alive as the
grave; and whole, ᴿas those that go down
into the pit: Ps. 124:3 • Ps. 28:1
13 We shall find all precious substance, we
shall fill our houses with spoil:
14 Cast in thy lot among us; let us all have
one purse:

15 My son, walk not thou in the way with
them; refrain thy foot from their path:
16 ᴿFor their feet run to evil, and make
haste to shed blood.   [Is. 59:7]
17 Surely in ᵀvain the net is spread in the
sight of any bird.   *useless*
18 And they ᴿlay wait for their *own* blood;
they lurk privily for their *own* lives. [11:19]
19 ᴿSo *are* the ways of every one that is
greedy of gain; *which* taketh away the life of
the owners thereof.   [1 Tim. 6:10]

Seek Wisdom

20 ᴿWisdom crieth without; she uttereth
her voice in the streets: [John 7:37]
21 She crieth in the chief place of ᵀcon-
course, in the openings of the gates: in the
city she uttereth her words, *saying*,   *streets*
22 How long, ye ᵀsimple ones, will ye love
simplicity? and the ᴿscorners delight in their
scorning, and fools hate knowledge? *naive* • 5:12
23 Turn you at my reproof: behold, ᴿI will
pour out my spirit unto you, I will make
known my words unto you.   Joel 2:28
24 ᴿBecause I have called, and ye refused;
I have stretched out my hand, and no man
regarded;   Is. 66:4; Jer. 7:13
25 But ye have set at nought all my
counsel, and would none of my reproof:
26 ᴿI also will laugh at your calamity; I will
mock when your fear cometh;   Ps. 2:4
27 When your fear cometh as desolation,
and your destruction cometh ᴿas a whirlwind; when distress and anguish cometh
upon you.   [10:25]
28 ᴿThen shall they call upon me, but I will
not answer; they shall seek me early, but
they shall not find me: 1 Sam. 8:18
29 For that they hated knowledge, and did
not choose the fear of the Lᴏʀᴅ:
30 ᴿThey would none of my counsel: they
despised all my reproof.   Ps. 81:11

1:8 The Role of Children—Both the Old and New Testaments agree that children have only one responsibility in the family—to obey their parents. The admonition of Solomon is more fully explained by Paul in Ephesians 6:1–3: "Children, obey your parents in the Lord: for this is right. Honour thy father and mother; which is the first commandment with promise; That it may be well with thee, and thou mayest live long on the earth." *Children* is an inclusive term. It is not a matter of either sex or age that is involved.

Twice in Scripture God has intervened and directly stated what He would have children do. The last time was nearly two thousand years ago when He gave a revelation to Paul for the church. The first time was nearly thirty-four hundred years ago when He gave a revelation to Moses and Israel in which He commanded, "Honour thy father and thy mother." God's will for children is that they are to obey their parents. The expression *in the Lord* does not limit the responsibility only to the circumstances where the parents are believers. Colossians 3:20 clearly points out that children are to obey their parents "in all things," not just in those things pertaining to Christian living. *In the Lord* more properly is understood to mean by the Lord or because it is the Lord's directive (this is what God says children are to do). *For this is right* indicates that for children to obey their parents is righteous or godlike. Such obedience is perfectly illustrated by God the Son who was completely obedient to God the Father, even though that obedience resulted in His death (Page 1171—Phil. 2:6–8).

Two things are promised to children who obey their parents: it will be well with them—they will have a happy life; and they will have a long life. These are the two things that children want most, and obedience to parents is the only way to assure them. That is why this is the first commandment with promise; from it springs all the other important issues of life. The child who has not learned to obey his parents, who are God's representatives in the family, will not learn to obey God.

Now turn to Page 1166—Eph. 6:4: The Role of the Parents.

31 Therefore ᴿshall they eat of the fruit of their own way, and be filled with their own devices.   Job. 4:8; Jer. 6:19

32 For ᵀthe turning away of the simple shall slay them, and the prosperity of fools shall destroy them.   *refusal to listen*

33 But ᴿwhoso hearkeneth unto me shall dwell safely, and shall be quiet from fear of evil.   3:24–26; Ps. 25:12, 13

CHAPTER 2

M Y son, ᴿif thou wilt receive my words, and ᴿhideᵀ my commandments with thee;   [4:10] • [3:1] • *lay up*

2 ᴿSo that thou incline thine ear unto wisdom, *and* apply thine heart to understanding;   22:17

3 Yea, if thou criest after knowledge, *and* liftest up thy voice for understanding;

4 ᴿIf thou seekest her as silver, and searchest for her as *for* hid treasures;   [3:14]

5 Then shalt thou understand the fear of the LORD, and find the knowledge of God.

6 ᴿFor the LORD giveth wisdom: out of his mouth *cometh* knowledge and understanding.   [James 1:5]

7 He layeth up sound wisdom for the righteous: ᴿ*he is* a ᵀbuckler to them that walk uprightly.   [Ps. 84:11] • *shield*

8 He keepeth the paths of judgment, and ᴿpreserveth the way of his saints.   [1 Sam. 2:9]

9 ᴿThen shalt thou understand righteousness, and judgment, and equity; *yea*, every good path.   8:20

10 ᴿWhen wisdom entereth into thine heart, and ᴿknowledge is pleasant unto thy soul;   [14:33] • [22:18]

11 Discretion shall preserve thee, ᴿunderstanding shall keep thee: 6:22

12 To ᴿdeliver thee from the way of the evil *man*, from the man that speaketh ᵀfroward things;   [28:26] • *perverse*

13 Who leave the paths of uprightness, to ᴿwalk in the ways of darkness;   [John 3:19]

14 Who rejoice to do evil, *and* ᴿdelight in the frowardness of the wicked;   [Rom. 1:32]

15 ᴿWhose ways *are* crooked, and *they* ᵀfroward in their paths: [21:8] • *perverse*

16 To deliver thee from ᴿthe strange woman, *even* from the stranger *which* flattereth with her words;   5:20

17 Which forsaketh the ᴿguide of her youth, and forgetteth the ᵀcovenant of her God.   Mal. 2:14, 15 • *agreement*

18 For ᴿher house ᵀinclineth unto death, and her paths unto the dead.   7:27 • *sinks*

19 None that go unto her return again, neither take they hold of the paths of life.

20 That thou mayest walk in the way of good *men*, and keep the ᴿpaths of the righteous.   [4:18]

21 For the upright shall dwell in the land, and the perfect shall remain in it.

22 But the wicked shall be cut off from the earth, ᴿand the transgressors shall be rooted out of it.   Deut. 28:63

CHAPTER 3

Benefits of Wisdom

M Y son, forget not my law; but let thine heart keep my commandments:

2 For length of days, and long life, and ᴿpeace, shall they add to thee.   Ps. 119:165

3 Let not mercy and truth forsake thee: ᴿbind them about thy neck; write them upon the table of thine heart: Deut. 6:8

4 So shalt thou find favour and good understanding in the sight of God and man.

5 ᴿTrust in the LORD with all thine heart; ᴿand lean not unto thine own understanding.   [Ps. 37:3, 5] • Jer. 9:23

6 ᴿIn all thy ways acknowledge him, and he shall direct thy paths.   [1 Chr. 28:9]

7 ᴿBe not wise in thine own eyes: fear the LORD, and depart from evil.   Rom. 12:16

8 It shall be health to thy navel, and ᴿmarrowᵀ to thy bones.   Job 21:24 • *refreshment*

9 Honour the LORD with thy substance, and with the firstfruits of all thine increase:

10 ᴿSo shall thy barns be filled with plenty, and thy ᵀpresses shall burst out with new wine.   Deut. 28:8 • *vats*

11 My ᴿson, despise not the chastening of the LORD; neither be weary of his correction: [Job 5:17; Heb. 12:5, 6]

12 For whom the LORD loveth he correcteth; ᴿeven as a father the son *in whom* he ᵀdelighteth.   Deut. 8:5 • *satisfied*

13 Happy *is* the man *that* findeth wisdom, and the man *that* getteth ᴿunderstanding. 4:5

14 ᴿFor the merchandise of it *is* better than the merchandise of silver, and the gain thereof than fine gold.   Job 28:13

15 She *is* more precious than rubies: and all the things thou canst desire are not to be compared unto her.

16 Length of days *is* in her right hand; *and* in her left hand riches and honour.

17 ᴿHer ways *are* ways of pleasantness, and all her paths *are* peace.   Matt. 11:29

18 She *is* ᴿa tree of life to them that lay hold upon her: and happy *is* every one that retaineth her.   11:30; Gen. 2:9

19 ᴿThe LORD by wisdom hath founded the earth; by understanding hath he established the heavens.   Ps. 104:24

20 By his knowledge the depths are broken up, and the clouds drop down the dew.

21 My son, ᴿlet not them depart from thine eyes: keep sound wisdom and discretion: 4:21

22 So shall they be ᴿlife unto thy soul, and grace to thy neck.   4:22; Deut. 32:47

23 Then shalt thou walk in thy way safely, and thy foot shall not stumble.

24 When thou Rliest down, thou shalt not be afraid: yea, thou shalt lie down, and thy sleep shall be sweet. Job 11:19

25 RBe not afraid of sudden fear, neither of the Rdesolation of the wicked, when it cometh. Ps. 91:5; 1 Pet. 3:14 · Job 5:21

26 For the LORD shall be thy confidence, and shall keep thy foot from being taken.

Be Kind to Others

27 RWithhold not good from Tthem to whom it is due, when it is in the power of thine hand to do it. Rom. 13:7 · owners

28 RSay not unto thy neighbour, Go, and come again, and to morrow I will give; when thou hast it by thee. Lev. 19:13

29 Devise not evil against thy neighbour, seeing he dwelleth securely by thee.

30 Strive not with a man without cause, if he have done thee no harm.

31 REnvy thou not the oppressor, and choose none of his ways. Ps. 37:1

32 For the froward is abomination to the LORD: but his secret is with the righteous.

33 RThe curse of the LORD is in the house of the wicked: but Rhe blesseth the habitation of the just. Deut. 11:28 · Job 8:6

34 RSurely he scorneth the scorners: but he giveth grace unto the lowly. James 4:6

35 The wise shall inherit glory: but shame shall be the promotion of fools.

CHAPTER 4

Father Says Get Wisdom

HEAR, Rye children, the instruction of a father, and attend to know understanding. Ps. 34:11

2 For I give you good Rdoctrine, Rforsake ye not my law. Deut. 32:2 · Ps. 89:30

3 For I was my father's son, tender and only beloved in the sight of my mother.

4 He taught me also, and said unto me, Let thine heart retain my words: Rkeep my commandments, and live. 7:2

5 RGet wisdom, get understanding: forget it not; neither Tdecline from the words of my mouth. 2:2, 3 · turn away

6 Forsake her not, and she shall preserve thee: love her, and she shall keep thee.

7 RWisdom is the principal thing; therefore get wisdom: and with all thy getting get understanding. 8:23

8 RExalt her, and she shall promote thee: she shall bring thee to honour, when thou dost embrace her. [1 Sam. 2:30]

9 She shall give to thine head Ran ornament of grace: a crown of glory shall she deliver to thee. 1:9

10 Hear, O my son, and receive my

sayings; and the years of thy life shall be many.

11 I have taught thee in the way of wisdom; I have led thee in right paths.

12 When thou goest, Rthy steps shall not Tbe straitened; and when thou runnest, thou shalt not stumble. Ps. 18:36 · hindered

13 Take fast hold of instruction; let her not go: keep her; for she is thy life.

Avoid the Wicked

14 REnter not into the path of the wicked, and go not in the way of evil men. [Ps. 1:1]

15 Avoid it, pass not by it, turn from it, and pass away.

16 For they sleep not, except they have done mischief; and their sleep is taken away, unless they cause some to fall.

17 RFor they eat the bread of wickedness, and drink the wine of violence. [13:2]

18 But the path of the just is Ras the shining light, that shineth more and more unto the perfect day. Matt. 5:14, 45; 2 Sam. 23:4

19 The way of the wicked is as darkness: they know not at what they stumble.

20 My son, Rattend to my words; incline thine ear unto my sayings. 5:1

21 Let them not depart from thine eyes; keep them in the midst of thine heart.

22 For they are life unto those that find them, and Rhealth to all their flesh. 3:8

Keep Your Heart

23 Keep thy heart with all diligence; for out of it Rare the issues of life. Matt. 12:34

24 Put away from thee Ta froward mouth, and perverse lips put far from thee. deceitful

25 Let thine eyes look right on, and let thine eyelids look straight before thee.

26 RPonder the path of thy feet, and let all thy ways be established. Heb. 12:13

27 RTurn not to the right hand nor to the left: remove thy foot from evil. Deut. 5:32

CHAPTER 5

Do Not Commit Adultery

MY son, attend unto my wisdom, and bow thine ear to my understanding:

2 That thou mayest regard discretion, and that thy lips may keep knowledge.

3 RFor the lips of a strange woman drop as an honeycomb, and her mouth is Rsmoother than oil: 2:16 · [Ps. 55:21]

4 But her end is Rbitter as wormwood, sharp as a twoedged sword. [Eccl. 7:26]

5 RHer feet go down to death; her steps take hold on Thell. 7:27 · Sheol

6 Lest thou shouldest Tponder the path of life, her ways are Tmoveable, that thou canst not know them. reflect · unstable

7 Hear me now therefore, O ye children, and depart not from the words of my mouth.

8 Remove thy way far from her, and come not ᵀnigh the door of her house: *near*

9 Lest thou give thine honour unto others, and thy years unto the cruel:

10 Lest strangers be filled with thy wealth; and thy labours *be* in the house of ᵀa stranger;   *an alien*

11 And thou mourn at the last, when thy flesh and thy body are consumed,

12 And say, How have I hated instruction, and my heart despised reproof;

13 And have not obeyed the voice of ᴿmy teachers, nor inclined mine ear to them that instructed me!   1:8

14 I was almost in all evil in the midst of the congregation and assembly.

Do Be Faithful to Your Spouse

15 Drink waters out of thine own cistern, and running waters out of thine own well.

16 Let thy fountains be dispersed abroad, *and* rivers of waters in the streets.

17 Let them be only thine own, and not strangers' with thee.

18 Let thy fountain be blessed: and rejoice with ᴿthe wife of thy youth.   Mal. 2:14

19 ᴿ*Let her be as* the loving hind and pleasant roe; let her breasts satisfy thee at all times; and be thou ᵀravished always with her love.   Song 2:9, 17 • *exhilarated*

20 And why wilt thou, my son, be ravished with ᴿa strange woman, and embrace the bosom of a stranger?   2:16

21 ᴿFor the ways of man *are* before the eyes of the LORD, and he pondereth all his goings.   Job 14:16; Jer. 16:17

22 ᴿHis own iniquities shall take the wicked himself, and he shall be holden with the cords of his sins.   Ps. 9:15; 40:12

23 ᴿHe shall die without instruction; and in the greatness of his folly he shall go astray.   [Job 36:12]

CHAPTER 6

Avoid Surety

MY son, ᴿif thou be ᵀsurety for thy friend, *if* thou hast stricken thy hand with a stranger,   11:15 • *guarantee*

2 Thou art snared with the words of thy mouth, thou art taken with the words of thy mouth.

3 Do this now, my son, and deliver thyself,

when thou art come into the hand of thy ᵀfriend; go, humble thyself, and make sure thy friend.   *neighbour*

4 ᴿGive not sleep to thine eyes, nor slumber to thine eyelids.   Ps. 132:4

5 Deliver thyself as a roe from the hand *of the hunter*, and as a ᴿbird from the hand of the fowler.   Ps. 91:3; 124:7

Do Not Be Lazy

6 ᴿGo to the ant, thou sluggard; consider her ways, and be wise: Job 12:7

7 Which having no ᴿguide, overseer, or ruler,   30:27

8 Provideth her meat in the summer, *and* gathereth her food in the harvest.

9 How long wilt thou sleep, O sluggard? when wilt thou arise out of thy sleep?

10 *Yet* a little sleep, a little slumber, a little folding of the hands to sleep:

11 So shall thy poverty come as one that travelleth, and thy want as an armed man.

12 A naughty person, a wicked man, walketh with a froward mouth.

13 He winketh with his eyes, he speaketh with his feet, he teacheth with his fingers;

14 Frowardness *is* in his heart, he deviseth mischief continually; he soweth discord.

15 Therefore shall his calamity come suddenly; suddenly shall he ᴿbe broken ᴿwithout remedy.   Jer. 19:11 • 2 Chr. 36:16

16 These six *things* doth the LORD hate; yea, seven *are* an abomination unto him:

17 ᴿA proud look, a lying tongue, and hands that shed innocent blood,   Ps. 101:5

18 ᴿAn heart that deviseth wicked imaginations, ᴿfeet that be swift in running to mischief,   24:2; Gen. 6:5 • 1:16

19 A false witness *that* speaketh lies, and he that soweth discord among brethren.

Do Not Commit Adultery

20 My son, keep thy father's commandment, and forsake not the law of thy mother:

21 ᴿBind them continually upon thine heart, *and* tie them about thy neck.   3:3

22 When thou goest, it shall lead thee; when thou sleepest, it shall keep thee; and *when* thou awakest, it shall talk with thee.

23 ᴿFor the commandment *is* a lamp; and the law *is* light; and reproofs of instruction *are* the way of life: Ps. 19:8

6:23 Illumination of God's Word—Illumination is the last of three important steps taken by God in communicating His Word to us. The first step was revelation which occurred when God spoke to the Bible authors. The second step was inspiration, that process whereby God guided them in correctly writing or uttering His message. But now a third step is needed to provide understanding for men and women as they hear God's revealed and inspired message. This vital step is illumination, that divine process whereby God causes the written revelation to be understood by the human heart.

This third step is needed because unsaved man is blinded both by his fallen, fleshly nature (Page 1127—1 Cor. 2:14) and by Satan himself (Page 1144—2 Cor. 4:3, 4).

24 ^RTo keep thee from the evil woman, from the flattery of the tongue of a ^Tstrange woman.   2:16; 7:5 • *foreign*

25 ^RLust not after her beauty in thine heart; ^Rneither let her take thee with her eyelids.   [Matt. 5:28] • 2 Kin. 9:30

26 For by means of a whorish woman *a man is brought* to a piece of bread: and the adulteress will hunt for the precious life.

27 Can a man take fire in his bosom, and his clothes not be burned?

28 Can one go upon hot coals, and his feet not be burned?

29 So he that ^Rgoeth in to his neighbour's wife; whosoever toucheth her ^Rshall not be innocent.   Ezek. 18:6; 33:26 • 16:5

30 *Men* do not despise a thief, if he steal to satisfy his soul when he is hungry;

31 But *if* he be found, ^Rhe shall restore sevenfold; he shall give all the substance of his house.   Ex. 22:1–4

32 *But* whoso committeth adultery with a woman ^Rlacketh understanding: he *that* doeth it destroyeth his own soul.   7:7

33 A wound and dishonour shall he get; and his reproach shall not be wiped away.

34 ^RFor jealousy *is* the rage of a man: therefore he will not spare in the day of vengeance.   27:4; Song 8:6

35 ^THe will not regard any ransom; neither will he rest content, though thou givest many gifts.   *not accept*

CHAPTER 7

M Y son, keep my words, and ^Rlay up my commandments with thee.   6:20

2 Keep my commandments, and live; and my law as the apple of thine eye.

3 ^RBind them upon thy fingers, write them upon the table of thine heart.   3:3

4 Say unto wisdom, Thou *art* my sister; and call understanding *thy* kinswoman:

5 ^RThat they may keep thee from the strange woman, from the stranger *which* flattereth with her words.   2:16; 5:3

6 ^RFor at the window of my house I looked through my casement,   Judg. 5:28

7 And beheld among the simple ones, I

discerned among the youths, a young man ^Rvoid of understanding,   [6:32]

8 Passing through the street near her corner; and he went the way to her house,

9 ^RIn the twilight, in the evening, in the black and dark night: Job 24:15

10 And, behold, there met him a woman *with* the ^Rattire of an harlot, and subtil of heart.   Gen. 38:14, 15

11 (^RShe *is* loud and stubborn; ^Rher feet abide not in her house: 9:13 • Titus 2:5

12 Now *is* she without, now in the streets, and lieth in wait at every corner.)

13 So she caught him, and kissed him, *and* with an ^Timpudent face said unto him,   *brasen*

14 ^R*I have* peace offerings with me; this day have I payed my vows.   Lev. 7:11

15 Therefore came I forth to meet thee, diligently to seek thy face, and I have found thee.

16 I have decked my bed with ^Rcoverings of tapestry, with carved *works,* with ^Rfine linen of Egypt.   31:22 • Is. 19:9

17 I have perfumed my bed with myrrh, aloes, and ^Rcinnamon.   Ex. 30:23

18 Come, let us take our fill of love until the morning: let us ^Tsolace ourselves with ^Tloves.   *delight • caresses*

19 For ^Tthe goodman *is* not at home, he is gone a long journey: *husband*

20 He hath taken a ^Rbag of money with him, *and* will come home at the day appointed.   Gen. 42:35

21 With ^Rher much fair speech she caused him to yield, ^Rwith the flattering of her lips she forced him.   5:3 • Ps. 12:2

22 He goeth after her straightway, as an ox goeth to the slaughter, or as a fool to the correction of the stocks;

23 Till a dart strike through his liver; ^Ras a bird hasteth to the snare, and knoweth not that it *is* for his life.   Eccl. 9:12

24 ^RHearken unto me now therefore, O ye children, and attend to the words of my mouth.   5:7

25 Let not thine ^Rheart decline to her ways, go not astray in her paths.   5:8

26 For she hath cast down many wounded: yea, ^Rmany strong *men* have been slain by her.   Neh. 13:26

27 ^RHer house *is* the way to ^Thell, going down to the chambers of death.   2:18 • *Sheol*

The Person behind this illumination is the Holy Spirit. Just prior to His crucifixion, Christ promised to send the Holy Spirit, who would illuminate both unsaved people (Page 1061—John 16:8–11) and Christians (Page 1060—John 14:26; 16:13, 14).

An important example of the Holy Spirit's using God's Word to illuminate sinners is seen at Pentecost, where three thousand people are saved after hearing Simon Peter preach about Christ and the Cross (Page 1074—Acts 2:36–41).

But Christians also need this illumination to help them fully grasp the marvelous message in God's Word. Paul tells us that the Holy Spirit will show these tremendous truths to us as we read the Scriptures (Page 1127—1 Cor. 2:10; Page 1144—2 Cor. 4:6).

Now turn to Page 496—Neh. 8:9: God's Word Convicts.

CHAPTER 8

Praise of Wisdom

DOTH not ᴿwisdom cry? and understanding put forth her voice? 1:20
2 She standeth in the top of high places, by the way in the places of the paths.
3 She crieth at the gates, at the entry of the city, at the coming in at the doors.
4 Unto you, O men, I call; and my voice *is* to the sons of man.
5 O ye simple, understand wisdom: and, ye fools, be ye of an understanding heart.
6 Hear; for I will speak of ᴿexcellent things; and the opening of my lips *shall be* right things. 22:20
7 For my mouth shall speak truth; and wickedness *is* an abomination to my lips.
8 All the words of my mouth *are* in righteousness; *there* is nothing ᴿfroward or perverse in them. Deut. 32:5; Phil. 2:15
9 They *are* all ᴿplain to him that understandeth, and right to them that ᴿfind knowledge. [14:6] • 3:13
10 Receive my instruction, and not silver; and knowledge rather than choice gold.
11 ᴿFor wisdom *is* better than rubies; and all the things that may be desired are not to be compared to it. Job 28:15; Ps. 19:10
12 I wisdom dwell with prudence, and find out knowledge of witty inventions.
13 ᴿThe fear of the LORD *is* to hate evil: pride, and arrogancy, and the evil way, and the froward mouth, do I hate. 16:6
14 Counsel *is* mine, and sound wisdom: I *am* understanding; I have strength.
15 ᴿBy me kings reign, and princes decree justice. [Rom. 13:1]
16 By me princes rule, and nobles, *even* all the judges of the earth.
17 ᴿI love them that love me; and those that seek me early shall find me. [1 Sam. 2:30]
18 ᴿRiches and honour *are* with me; *yea,* durable riches and righteousness. 3:16
19 My fruit *is* ᴿbetter than gold, yea, than fine gold; and my revenue ᴿthan choice silver. 3:14 • [10:20]
20 I lead in the way of righteousness, in the midst of the paths of judgment:
21 That I may cause those that love me to inherit ᵀsubstance; and I will ᴿfill their treasures. *property* • 24:4
22 The LORD possessed me in the beginning of his way, before his works of old.
23 I was set up from everlasting, from the beginning, or ever the earth was.
24 When *there* were no ᴿdepths, I was brought forth; when *there* were no fountains abounding with water. Ex. 15:5
25 Before the mountains were settled, before the hills was I brought forth:
26 While as yet he had not made the earth,

nor the fields, nor the highest part of the dust of the world.
27 When he prepared the heavens, I *was* there: when he ᴿset a compass upon the face of the depth: Job 26:10
28 When he established the clouds above: when he strengthened the fountains of the deep:
29 ᴿWhen he gave to the sea his decree, that the waters should not pass his commandment: when he appointed the foundations of the earth: Gen. 1:9, 10
30 ᴿThen I was by him, *as* one brought up *with him:* and I was daily *his* delight, rejoicing always before him; [John 1:1, 2]
31 Rejoicing in the habitable part of his earth; and ᴿmy delights *were* with the sons of men. Ps. 16:3
32 Now therefore ᴿhearken unto me, O ye children: for ᴿblessed *are they that* keep my ways. 5:7 • Luke 11:28
33 ᴿHear instruction, and be wise, and refuse it not. 4:1
34 ᴿBlessed *is* the man that heareth me, watching daily at my gates, waiting at the posts of my doors. 3:18
35 For whoso findeth me findeth life, and shall ᴿobtain favour of the LORD. [12:2]
36 But he that sinneth against me ᴿwrongeth his own soul: all they that hate me ᴿlove death. 1:31, 32 • 21:6

CHAPTER 9

WISDOM hath builded her house, she hath hewn out her seven pillars:
2 ᴿShe hath killed her beasts; ᴿshe hath mingled her wine; she hath also furnished her table. Matt. 22:4 • Song 8:2
3 She hath sent forth her maidens: she crieth upon the highest places of the city,
4 ᴿWhoso *is* simple, let him turn in hither: *as for* him that ᵀwanteth understanding, she saith to him, 8:5 • *lacks*
5 ᴿCome, eat of my bread, and drink of the wine *which* I have mingled. Is. 55:1
6 Forsake the foolish, and live; ᴿand go in the way of understanding. [Ezek. 11:20]
7 He that ᴿreproveth a scorner getteth to himself shame: and he that rebuketh a wicked *man getteth* himself a blot. 23:9
8 ᴿReprove not a ᵀscorner, lest he hate thee: ᴿrebuke a wise man, and he will love thee. Matt. 7:6 • *scoffer* • [10:8]
9 Give *instruction* to a wise *man,* and he will be yet wiser: teach a just *man,* and ᴿhe will increase in learning. [Matt. 13:12]
10 ᴿThe fear of the LORD *is* the beginning of wisdom: and the knowledge of the holy *is* understanding. Job 28:28
11 For by me thy days shall be multiplied, and the years of thy life shall be increased.
12 ᴿIf thou be wise, thou shalt be wise for

thyself: but *if* thou scornest, thou alone shalt bear *it*.   Job 22:2

Foolish Woman

13 ^RA foolish woman *is* clamorous: *she is* simple, and knoweth nothing.   7:11

14 For she sitteth at the door of her house, on a seat ^Rin the high places of the city,   *v.* 3

15 To call ^Tpassengers who go right on their ways: *those passing by*

16 ^RWhoso *is* ^Tsimple, let him turn in hither: and *as for* him that wanteth understanding, she saith to him,   *v.* 4 · *naive*

17 ^RStolen waters are sweet, and bread *eaten* in secret is pleasant.   5:15

18 But he knoweth not that the dead *are* there; *and that* her guests *are* ^Rin the depths of ^Thell.   7:27 · *Sheol*

CHAPTER 10

Proverbs Contrasting the Godly and the Wicked

THE proverbs of Solomon. ^RA wise son maketh a glad father: but a foolish son *is* the heaviness of his mother.   15:20

2 Treasures of wickedness profit nothing: but righteousness delivereth from death.

3 ^RThe Lord will not suffer the soul of the righteous to famish: but he casteth away the substance of the wicked.   28:25

4 He becometh poor that dealeth *with* a slack hand: but ^Rthe hand of the diligent maketh rich.   12:24

5 He that gathereth in summer *is* a wise son: *but* he that sleepeth in harvest *is* ^Ra son that causeth shame.   19:26

6 Blessings *are* upon the head of the just: but ^Rviolence covereth the mouth of the wicked.   *v.* 11; Esth. 7:8; Obad. 10

7 The memory of the just *is* blessed: but the name of the wicked shall rot.

8 The wise in heart will receive commandments: but a prating fool shall fall.

9 ^RHe that walketh uprightly walketh ^Tsurely: but he that perverteth his ways shall be known.   [Ps. 23:4] · *safely*

10 He that ^Rwinketh with the eye causeth sorrow: but a prating fool shall fall.   6:13

11 ^RThe mouth of a righteous *man is* a well of life: but violence covereth the mouth of the wicked.   13:14; 18:4

12 Hatred stirreth up strifes: but ^Rlove covereth all sins.   [1 Cor. 13:7]

13 In the ^Rlips of him that hath understanding wisdom is found: but ^Ra rod *is* for the back of him that is^T void of understanding.   [v. 31] · 19:29 · *lacks*

14 Wise *men* lay up knowledge: but the mouth of the foolish *is* near destruction.

15 The ^Rrich man's wealth *is* his strong city: the destruction of the poor *is* their poverty.   Job 31:24; Ps. 52:7

16 The ^Rlabour of the righteous *tendeth* to life: the fruit of the wicked to sin.   11:18

17 He ^R*is in* the way of life that ^Tkeepeth instruction: but he that refuseth reproof erreth.   6:23 · *heedeth*

18 He that hideth hatred *with* lying lips, and he that uttereth a slander, *is* a fool.

19 ^RIn the multitude of words there wanteth not sin: but he that refraineth his lips *is* wise.   [18:21]

20 The tongue of the just *is as* choice silver: the heart of the wicked *is* little worth.

21 The lips of the righteous feed many: but ^Rfools die for want of wisdom.   Hos. 4:6

22 The blessing of the Lord, it maketh rich, and he addeth no sorrow with it.

23 *It is* as sport to a fool to do mischief: but a man of understanding hath wisdom.

24 ^RThe fear of the wicked, it shall come upon him: but ^Rthe desire of the righteous shall be granted.   Job 15:21 · Ps. 145:19

25 As the whirlwind passeth, ^Rso *is* the wicked no *more*: but ^Rthe righteous *is* an everlasting foundation.   [Ps. 37:9, 10] · Ps. 15:5

26 As vinegar to the teeth, and as smoke to the eyes, so *is* the ^Rsluggard to them that send him.   26:6

27 ^RThe fear of the Lord ^Tprolongeth days: but ^Rthe years of the wicked shall be shortened.   9:11 · *addeth* · Job 15:32

28 The hope of the righteous *shall be* gladness: but the ^Rexpectation of the wicked shall perish.   Job 8:13

29 ^RThe way of the Lord *is* strength to the upright: but ^Rdestruction *shall be* to the workers of iniquity.   13:6 · Ps. 1:6

30 The righteous shall never be removed: but the wicked shall not inhabit the earth.

31 ^RThe mouth of the just bringeth forth wisdom: but the ^Tfroward tongue shall be cut out.   [10:13; Ps. 37:30] · *perverse*

32 The lips of the righteous know ^Rwhat is acceptable: but the mouth of the wicked *speaketh* frowardness.   Eccl. 12:10

CHAPTER 11

A FALSE balance *is* abomination to the Lord: but a just weight *is* his delight.

2 *When* pride cometh, then cometh shame: but with the lowly *is* wisdom.

3 The ^Rintegrity of the upright shall guide them: but the perverseness of transgressors shall destroy them.   13:6

4 Riches profit not in the day of wrath: but righteousness delivereth from death.

5 ^RThe righteousness of the perfect shall direct his way: but the ^Rwicked shall fall by his own wickedness.   3:6 · 5:22

6 The righteousness of the upright shall deliver them: but transgressors shall be taken in *their* own naughtiness.

7 ᴿWhen a wicked man dieth, *his* expectation shall perish: ᴿand the hope of unjust *men* perisheth.   [10:28] • Job 8:13

8 The righteous is delivered out of trouble, and the wicked cometh in his stead.

9 An hypocrite with ᴿ*his* mouth destroyeth his neighbour: but through knowledge shall the just be delivered.   16:29

10 ᴿWhen it goeth well with the righteous, the city rejoiceth: and when the wicked perish, *there is* shouting.   Esth. 8:15

11 By the blessing of the upright the city is ᴿexalted: but it is overthrown by the mouth of the wicked.   [14:34]

12 He that is ᵀvoid of wisdom despiseth his neighbour: but a man of understanding holdeth his peace.   *lacks*

13 ᴿA ᵀtalebearer revealeth secrets: but he that is of a faithful spirit concealeth the matter.   Lev. 19:16 • *gossiping person*

14 ᴿWhere no ᵀcounsel *is*, the people fall: but in the multitude of counsellors *there is* safety.   1 Kin. 12:1 • *good advice*

15 He that is ᵀsurety for a stranger shall smart *for it*: and he that hateth suretiship is sure.   *guarantee*

16 A ᴿgracious woman retaineth honour: and strong *men* retain riches.   31:28, 30

17 ᴿThe merciful man doeth good to his own soul: but *he that is* cruel troubleth his own flesh.   [Matt. 5:7; 25:34–36]

18 The wicked worketh a deceitful work: but ᴿto him that soweth righteousness *shall be* a sure reward.   Hos. 10:12

19 As righteousness *tendeth* to life: so he ᴿthat pursueth evil *pursueth it* to his own death.   [Rom. 6:23]

20 They that are of a froward heart *are* abomination to the LORD: but *such as are* upright in *their* way *are* his delight.

21 *Though* hand *join* in hand, the wicked shall not be unpunished: but the seed of the righteous shall be delivered.

22 ᴿ*As* a jewel of gold in a swine's snout, *so is* a fair woman which is without discretion.   Gen. 24:47

23 The desire of the righteous *is* only good: *but* the expectation of the wicked *is* wrath.

24 There is that scattereth, and yet increaseth; and *there is* that withholdeth more than is meet, but *it tendeth* to poverty.

25 ᴿThe liberal soul shall be made fat: ᴿand he that watereth shall be watered also himself.   [2 Cor. 9:6] • Matt. 5:7

26 He that withholdeth corn, the people shall curse him: but blessing *shall be* upon the head of him that selleth *it*.

27 He that diligently seeketh good procureth favour: but ᴿhe that seeketh mischief, it shall come unto him.   Esth. 7:10

28 He that trusteth in his riches shall fall: but the righteous shall flourish as a branch.

29 He that troubleth his own house ᴿshall inherit the wind: and the fool *shall be* servant to the wise of heart.   Eccl. 5:16

30 The fruit of the righteous *is* a tree of life; and he that winneth souls *is* wise.

31 ᴿBehold, the righteous shall be ᵀrecompensed in the earth: much more the wicked and the sinner.   2 Sam. 22:21 • *rewarded*

CHAPTER 12

Wᴴᴼᔆᴼ loveth instruction loveth knowledge: but he that hateth reproof *is* ᵀbrutish.   *stupid*

2 A ᴿgood *man* obtaineth favour of the LORD: but a man of wicked devices will he condemn.   3:4; 8:35

3 ᴿA man shall not be established by wickedness: but the ᴿroot of the righteous shall not be moved.   [11:5] • [10:25]

4 ᴿA virtuous woman *is* a crown to her husband: but she that maketh ashamed *is* as rottenness in his bones.   1 Cor. 11:7

5 The thoughts of the righteous *are* right: *but* the counsels of the wicked *are* deceit.

6 ᴿThe words of the wicked *are* to lie in wait for blood: but the mouth of the upright shall deliver them.   1:11, 16

7 ᴿThe wicked are overthrown, and *are* not: but the ᴿhouse of the righteous shall stand.   Job 34:25 • [Matt. 7:24–27]

8 A man shall be commended according to his wisdom: but he that is of a perverse ᵀheart shall be ᴿdespised.   *mind* • 18:3

9 ᴿ*He that is* despised, and hath a servant, *is* better than he that honoureth himself, and lacketh bread.   13:7

10 ᴿA righteous *man* regardeth the life of his beast: but the tender mercies of the wicked *are* cruel.   Deut. 25:4

11 He that tilleth his land shall be satisfied with bread: but he that followeth vain persons *is* void of understanding.

12 ᴿThe wicked desireth the net of evil *men:* but the root of the righteous ᴿyieldeth *fruit.*   21:10 • 11:30

13 ᴿThe wicked is snared by the transgression of *his* lips: ᴿbut the just shall come out of trouble.   11:8 • 2 Pet. 2:9

14 A man shall be satisfied with good by the fruit of *his* mouth: and the recompense of a man's hands shall be rendered unto him.

15 ᴿThe way of a fool *is* right in his own eyes: but he that hearkeneth unto counsel *is* wise.   [14:12; 16:2]

16 A fool's wrath is presently known: but a prudent *man* covereth shame.

17 ᴿ*He that* speaketh truth sheweth forth righteousness: but a false witness deceit.   14:5

18 ᴿThere is that speaketh like the piercings of a sword: but the ᴿtongue of the wise *is* health.   Ps. 57:4 • 4:22

19 The lip of truth shall be established for ever: but a lying tongue *is* but for a moment.

20 Deceit *is* in the heart of them that imagine evil: but to the counsellors of peace *is* joy.

21 There shall no evil happen to the just: but the wicked shall be filled with mischief.

22 Lying lips *are* abomination to the LORD: but they that deal truly *are* his delight.

23 ᴿA prudent man concealeth knowledge: but the heart of fools proclaimeth foolishness.   13:16; 15:2

24 The hand of the diligent shall bear rule: but the slothful shall be under tribute.

25 Heaviness in the heart of man maketh it stoop: but a good word maketh it glad.

26 The righteous *is* more excellent than his neighbour: but the way of the wicked seduceth them.

27 The slothful *man* roasteth not that which he took in hunting: but the substance of a diligent man *is* precious.

28 In the way of righteousness *is* life; and in the pathway *thereof there is* no death.

CHAPTER 13

A WISE son *heareth* his father's instruction: but a scorner heareth not rebuke.

2 ᴿA man shall eat good by the fruit of *his* mouth: but the soul of the transgressors *shall eat* violence.   12:14

3 ᴿHe that keepeth his mouth keepeth his life: *but* he that ᴿopeneth wide his lips shall have destruction.   Ps. 39:1 • 18:7

4 ᴿThe soul of the sluggard desireth, and *hath* nothing: but the soul of the diligent shall be made fat.   10:4

5 A righteous *man* hateth lying: but a wicked *man* ᵀis loathsome, and cometh to shame.   *acts disgustingly*

6 ᴿRighteousness keepeth *him that is* upright in the way: but wickedness overthroweth the sinner.   11:3–6

7 There is that maketh himself rich, yet *hath* nothing: *there is* that maketh himself poor, yet *hath* great riches.

8 The ransom of a man's life *are* his riches: but the poor heareth not rebuke.

9 The light of the righteous rejoiceth: but the lamp of the wicked shall be put out.

10 Only by pride cometh contention: but with the well advised *is* wisdom.

11 ᴿWealth *gotten* by ᵀvanity shall be diminished: but he that gathereth by labour shall increase.   20:21 • *fraud*

12 Hope deferred maketh the heart sick, but ᴿwhen the desire cometh, *it is* a tree of life.   *v.* 19

13 Whoso ᴿdespiseth the word shall be destroyed: but he that feareth the commandment shall be rewarded.   Num. 15:31

14 The law of the wise *is* a fountain of life, to depart from the snares of death.

15 Good understanding giveth favour: but the way of transgressors *is* hard.

16 Every prudent *man* dealeth with knowledge: but a fool ᵀlayeth open *his* folly. *displays*

17 A wicked messenger falleth into mischief: but a faithful ambassador *is* health.

18 Poverty and shame *shall be to* him that refuseth instruction: but he that regardeth reproof shall be honoured.

19 The desire accomplished is sweet to the soul: but *it is* abomination to fools to depart from evil.

20 ᴿHe that walketh with wise *men* shall be wise: but a companion of fools shall be destroyed.   2:20; 15:31

21 ᴿEvil pursueth sinners: but to the righteous good shall be repaid.   Ps. 32:10

22 A good *man* leaveth an inheritance to his children's children: and the wealth of the sinner *is* laid up for the just.

23 ᴿMuch food *is in* the ᵀtillage of the poor: but there is *that is* destroyed for want of judgment.   12:11 • *fallow ground*

24 ᴿHe that spareth his rod hateth his son: but he that loveth him chasteneth him ᵀbetimes.   19:18 • *early*

25 ᴿThe righteous eateth to the satisfying of his soul: but the belly of the ᴿwicked shall want.   Ps. 34:10 • Luke 15:14

CHAPTER 14

E VERY wise woman buildeth her house: but the foolish ᵀplucketh it down with her hands.   *tears down*

2 He that walketh in his uprightness feareth the LORD: ᴿbut *he that is* perverse in his ways despiseth him.   2:15

3 In the mouth of the foolish *is* a rod of pride: but the lips of the wise shall preserve them.

4 Where no oxen *are*, the crib *is* clean: but much increase *is* by the strength of the ox.

5 ᴿA faithful witness will not lie: but a false witness will utter lies.   Rev. 1:5; 3:14

6 ᴿA scorner seeketh wisdom, and *findeth it* not: but knowledge *is* easy unto him that understandeth.   8:9; 17:24

7 ᴿGo from the presence of a foolish man, when thou perceivest not *in him* the ᵀlips of knowledge.   23:9 • *words*

8 The wisdom of the prudent *is* to understand his way: but the folly of fools *is* deceit.

9 ᴿFools make a mock at sin: but among the righteous *there is* favour.   Is. 1:11

10 The heart knoweth ᴿhis own bitterness; and a stranger doth not intermeddle with his joy.   1 Sam. 1:10; Job 21:25

11 ᴿThe house of the wicked shall be overthrown: but the tabernacle of the upright shall flourish.   Job 8:15

12 ᴿThere is a way which seemeth right

unto a man, but [R]the end thereof *are* the ways of death. 12:15 • Rom. 6:21

13 Even in laughter the heart is sorrowful; and the end of that mirth *is* heaviness.

14 The backslider in heart shall be [R]filled with his own ways: and a good man *shall be satisfied* from himself. 1:31; 12:14

15 The simple believeth every word: but the prudent *man* looketh well to his going.

16 [R]A wise *man* feareth, and departeth from evil: but the fool rageth, and is confident. 22:3; Job 28:28; Ps. 34:14

17 *He that is* soon angry dealeth foolishly: and a man of wicked devices is hated.

18 The simple inherit folly: but the prudent are crowned with knowledge.

19 The evil bow before the good; and the wicked at the gates of the righteous.

20 The poor is hated even of his own neighbour: but the rich *hath* many friends.

21 He that despiseth his neighbour sinneth: [R]but he that hath mercy on the poor, happy *is* he. Ps. 41:1; 112:9

22 [R]Do they not err that devise evil? but mercy and truth *shall be* to them that devise good. Ps. 36:4; Mic. 2:1

23 In all labour there is profit: but the talk of the lips *tendeth* only to penury.

(24) [R]The crown of the wise *is* their riches: *but* the foolishness of fools *is* folly. 10:22

25 A true witness delivereth souls: but a deceitful *witness* [R]speaketh lies. *v.* 5

26 In the [R]fear of the LORD *is* strong confidence: and his children shall have a place of refuge. 18:10; Is. 33:6

27 The fear of the LORD *is* a fountain of life, to depart from the snares of death.

28 In the [R]multitude of people *is* the king's honour: but in the want of people *is* the destruction of the prince. 1 Kin. 4:20

29 [R]*He that is* slow to wrath *is* of great understanding: but *he that is* hasty of spirit exalteth folly. Eccl. 7:9; James 1:19

30 A sound heart *is* the life of the flesh: but envy the rottenness of the bones.

31 [R]He that oppresseth the poor reproacheth his Maker: but he that honoureth him hath mercy on the poor. 17:5

32 [R]The wicked is driven away ·in his wickedness: but [R]the righteous hath hope in his death. 6:15 • 2 Cor. 1:9; 5:8

33 Wisdom resteth in the heart of him that hath understanding: but *that which is* in the midst of fools is made known.

34 Righteousness exalteth a [R]nation: but sin *is* a reproach to any people. 11:11

35 [R]The king's favour *is* toward a wise servant: but his wrath is *against* him that causeth shame. Matt. 24:45

CHAPTER 15

A SOFT answer turneth away wrath: but grievous words stir up anger.

2 The tongue of [R]the wise useth knowledge aright: but the mouth of fools poureth out foolishness. 12:23

3 The eyes of the LORD *are* in every place, beholding the evil and the good.

4 A wholesome tongue *is* a tree of life: but perverseness therein *is* a breach in the spirit.

5 A fool [T]despiseth his father's instruction: but he that regardeth reproof is prudent. *rejects*

6 In the house of the [R]righteous *is* much treasure: but in the revenues of the wicked is trouble. 8:21

7 The lips of the wise disperse knowledge: but the heart of the foolish *doeth* not so.

8 [R]The sacrifice of the wicked *is* an abomination to the LORD: but the prayer of the upright *is* his delight. Eccl. 5:1

9 The way of the wicked *is* an abomination unto the LORD: but he loveth him that [R]followeth after righteousness. 21:21

10 [T]Correction *is* grievous unto him that forsaketh the way: *and* he that hateth reproof shall die. *stern discipline*

11 [R]Hell and destruction *are* before the LORD: how much more then the hearts of the children of men? Job 26:6; Ps. 139:8

12 A scorner loveth not one that reproveth him: neither will he go unto the wise.

13 [R]A merry heart maketh a cheerful countenance: but by sorrow of the heart the spirit is broken. 12:25; 17:22

14 The heart of him that hath understanding seeketh knowledge: but the mouth of fools feedeth on foolishness.

15 [R]All the days of the afflicted *are* evil: but he that is of a merry heart *hath* a continual feast. 17:22

16 [R]Better *is* little with the fear of the LORD than great treasure and trouble therewith. 16:8; Ps. 37:16; 1 Tim. 6:6

17 Better *is* a dinner of herbs where love is, than a stalled ox and hatred therewith.

18 A wrathful man stirreth up strife: but *he that is* slow to anger appeaseth strife.

19 [R]The way of the slothful *man is* as an hedge of thorns: but the way of the righteous *is* made plain. 19:24

20 A wise son maketh a glad father: but a foolish man despiseth his mother.

21 [R]Folly *is* joy to *him that is* destitute of wisdom: but a man of understanding walketh uprightly. 14:8; Eph. 5:15

22 [R]Without counsel purposes are disappointed: but in the multitude of counsellors they are established. 11:14

23 A man hath joy by the answer of his mouth: and [R]a word *spoken* in due season, how good *is* it! 25:11; Is. 50:4

24 The way of life *is* above to the wise, that he may depart from hell beneath.

25 [R]The LORD will destroy the house of the proud: but [R]he will establish the border of the widow. 12:7 • Deut. 19:14

26 The thoughts of the wicked *are* an abomination to the LORD: ^Rbut *the words* of the pure *are* pleasant words.   Ps. 37:30

27 ^RHe that is greedy of gain troubleth his own house; but he that hateth ^Tgifts shall live.   [Is. 5:8] · *bribes*

28 The heart of the righteous ^Rstudieth to answer: but the mouth of the wicked poureth out evil things.   1 Pet. 3:15

29 The LORD *is* far from the wicked: but he heareth the prayer of the righteous.

30 The light of the eyes rejoiceth the heart: *and* a good report maketh the bones fat.

31 The ear that heareth the reproof of life abideth among the wise.

32 He that refuseth instruction despiseth his own soul: but he that ^Theareth reproof getteth understanding.   *heeds*

33 The fear of the LORD *is* the instruction of wisdom; and before honour *is* humility.

CHAPTER 16

Proverbs Encouraging Godly Lives

THE ^Rpreparations^T of the heart in man, ^Rand the answer of the tongue, *is* from the LORD.   Jer. 10:23 · *inclinations* · Matt. 10:19

2 All the ways of a man *are* clean in his own eyes; but the LORD weigheth the spirits.

3 Commit thy works unto the LORD, and thy thoughts shall be established.

4 ^RThe LORD hath made all *things* for himself: yea, even the wicked for the day of evil.   Gen. 1:31; [Eccl. 3:11]

5 Every one *that is* proud in heart *is* an abomination to the LORD: *though* hand *join* in hand, he shall not be unpunished.

6 ^RBy mercy and truth iniquity is ^Tpurged: and by the fear of the LORD *men* depart from evil.   Dan. 4:27 · *taken away*

7 When a man's ways please the LORD, he ^Rmaketh even his enemies to be at peace with him.   Gen. 33:4; 2 Chr. 17:10

8 Better *is* a little with righteousness than great revenues without right.

9 A man's heart ^Tdeviseth his way: but the LORD directeth his steps.   *schemes*

10 ^TA divine sentence *is* in the lips of the king: his mouth transgresseth not ^Rin judgment.   *a decision* · 1 Kin. 3:28

11 ^RA just weight and balance *are* the LORD's: all the weights of the bag *are* his ^Twork.   [11:1] · *concern*

12 *It is* an abomination to kings to commit wickedness: for ^Rthe throne is established by righteousness.   25:5

13 ^RRighteous lips *are* the delight of kings; and they love him that speaketh right.   [14:35]

14 The wrath of a king *is as* messengers of death: but a wise man will pacify it.

15 In the light of the king's countenance *is* life; and his favour *is* as a ^Rcloud of the latter rain.   Job 29:23

16 How much ^Rbetter *is it* to get wisdom than gold! and to get understanding rather to be chosen than silver!   8:10

17 The ^Rhighway of the upright *is* to depart from evil: he that keepeth his way preserveth his soul.   Is. 35:8

18 ^RPride *goeth* before destruction, and an haughty spirit before a fall.   Jer. 49:16

19 Better *it is to be* of an ^Rhumble spirit with the lowly, than to divide the spoil with the proud.   29:23; Is. 57:15

20 He that handleth a matter wisely shall ^Rfind good: and whoso ^Rtrusteth in the LORD, happy *is* he.   19:8 · Ps. 2:12

21 The ^Rwise in heart shall be called prudent: ^Rand the sweetness of the lips increaseth learning.   Hos. 14:9 · 16:23

22 Understanding *is* a wellspring of life unto him that hath it: but the instruction of fools *is* folly.

23 The heart of the wise teacheth his mouth, and addeth learning to his lips.

24 Pleasant words *are as* an honeycomb, sweet to the soul, and health to the bones.

25 There is a way that seemeth right unto a man; but the end thereof *are* the ways of ^Rdeath.   14:12

26 He that laboureth laboureth for himself; for his mouth craveth it of him.

27 An ungodly man diggeth up evil: and in his lips *there is* as a burning fire.

28 A froward man soweth strife: and ^Ra whisperer separateth chief friends.   [17:9]

29 A violent man ^Renticeth his neighbour,

16:3 Commitment—Dedication is the foundation of commitment. Without it the believer is unable to offer God anything else. Paul explains this dedication process in Romans 12:1 and 2. He emphasizes three things. First, it is our body which is to be dedicated as a living sacrifice to God. Second, we are to avoid being conformed to this world, but strive to be transformed by the Word. Finally, by doing this we can discover God's perfect will for our lives.

After the dedication of our bodies, what are we to commit? We are to commit our salvation to God (Page 1200—2 Tim. 1:12). Second, we are to commit our works (Prov. 16:3). Then, our goals in life are to be given to Him (Page 521—Job 5:8; Page 562—Ps. 37:5). It is difficult but vital to commit our suffering experiences to God (Page 1239—1 Pet. 4:19). Our Lord Jesus did this very thing when He was on earth (Page 1237—1 Pet. 2:23). Finally, in the hour of death we can with confidence commit our very souls to God (Page 559—Ps. 31:5). Paul the apostle assures us that any and all such commitments to the Lord will be accepted and honored. See First Corinthians 15:58.

Now turn to Page 1134—1 Cor. 12:1–10: Using Spiritual Gifts.

and leadeth him into the way *that is* not good.   12:26

30 He shutteth his eyes to devise ᵀfroward things: moving his lips he bringeth evil to pass.   *perverse*

31 The hoary head *is* a crown of glory, *if* it be found in the way of righteousness.

32 ᴿ*He that is* slow to anger *is* better than the mighty; and he that ruleth his spirit than he that taketh a city.   19:11; 25:28

33 The lot is cast into the lap; but the whole disposing thereof *is* of the LORD.

CHAPTER 17

B ETTER *is* ᴿa dry morsel, and quietness therewith, than an house full of sacrifices *with* strife.   15:17

2 A wise servant shall have rule over ᴿa son that causeth shame, and shall have part of the inheritance among the brethren.   10:5

3 The ᵀfining pot *is* for silver, and the furnace for gold: ᴿbut the LORD ᵀtrieth the hearts.   *smelter* • [Jer. 17:10] • *tests*

4 A wicked doer giveth heed to false lips; *and* a liar giveth ear to a naughty tongue.

5 ᴿWhoso mocketh the poor reproacheth his Maker: *and* he that is glad at calamities shall not be unpunished.   [14:31]

6 ᴿChildren's children *are* the crown of old men; and the ᴿglory of children *are* their fathers.   Gen. 48:11 • [Ex. 20:12]

7 ᴿExcellent speech becometh not a fool: much less do lying lips a prince.   24:7

8 ᴿA gift *is as* a precious stone in the eyes of him that hath it: whithersoever it turneth, it prospereth.   21:14; Amos 5:12

9 ᴿHe that covereth a transgression seeketh love; but he that repeateth a matter separateth *very* friends.   [James 5:20]

10 A reproof entereth more into a wise man than an hundred stripes into a fool.

11 An evil *man* seeketh only rebellion: therefore a cruel messenger shall be sent against him.

12 Let a bear robbed of her whelps meet a man, rather than a fool in his folly.

13 Whoso ᴿrewardeth evil for good, evil shall not depart from his house.   Jer. 18:20

14 The beginning of strife *is as* when one letteth out water: therefore leave off contention, before it be meddled with.

15 ᴿHe that justifieth the wicked, and he that condemneth the just, even they both *are* abomination to the LORD.   18:5

16 ᵀWherefore *is there* a price in the hand of a fool to ᴿget wisdom, seeing *he hath* no heart *to it*?   *why* • 23:3

17 ᴿA friend loveth at all times, and a brother is born for adversity.   Ruth 1:16

18 ᴿA man ᵀvoid of understanding striketh hands, *and* becometh surety in the presence of his friend.   6:1 • *lacking*

19 ᴿHe loveth transgression that loveth strife: *and* ᴿhe that exalteth his gate seeketh destruction.   29:22 • [11:2]

20 He that hath a froward heart findeth no good: and he that hath ᴿa perverse tongue falleth into mischief.   James 3:8

21 He that begetteth a fool *doeth it* to his sorrow: and the father of a fool hath no joy.

22 A merry heart doeth good *like* a medicine: but a broken spirit drieth the bones.

23 A wicked *man* taketh a gift out of the bosom to pervert the ways of judgment.

24 ᴿWisdom *is* before him that hath understanding; but the eyes of a fool *are* in the ends of the earth.   Eccl. 2:14

25 A ᴿfoolish son *is* a grief to his father, and bitterness to her that bare him.   [10:1]

26 Also to punish the just *is* not good, *nor* to strike princes for equity.

27 ᴿHe that hath knowledge spareth his words: *and* a man of understanding is of an excellent spirit.   [10:19]

28 Even a fool, when he holdeth his peace, is counted wise: *and* he that shutteth his lips *is esteemed* a man of understanding.

CHAPTER 18

T HROUGH desire a man, having separated himself, seeketh *and* ᵀintermeddleth with all wisdom.   *quarrels*

2 A fool hath no delight in understanding, but that his heart may discover itself.

3 When the wicked cometh, *then* cometh also contempt, and with ignominy reproach.

4 ᴿThe words of a man's mouth *are as* deep waters, *and* the wellspring of wisdom *as* a flowing brook.   20:5

5 ᴿ*It* is not good to accept the person of the wicked, to overthrow the righteous in judgment.   24:23; Lev. 19:15

6 A fool's lips enter into contention, and his mouth calleth for strokes.

7 A fool's mouth *is* his destruction, and his lips *are* the snare of his soul.

8 ᴿThe words of a talebearer *are* as wounds, and they go down into the innermost parts of the belly.   26:22

9 He also that is slothful in his work is brother to him that is a great waster.

10 ᴿThe name of the LORD *is* a ᴿstrong tower: the righteous runneth into it, and is safe.   Ex. 3:15 • 2 Sam. 22:3

11 The rich man's wealth *is* his strong city, and as an high wall in his own conceit.

12 Before destruction the heart of man is haughty; and before honour *is* humility.

13 He that answereth a matter before he heareth *it*, it *is* folly and shame unto him.

14 The spirit of a man will sustain his infirmity; but a wounded spirit who can bear?

15 The heart of the prudent getteth knowledge; and the ear of the wise seeketh knowledge.

16 A man's ᴿgift maketh room for him, and bringeth him before great men.   17:8

17 *He that is* first in his own cause *seemeth* just; but his neighbour cometh and ᵀsearcheth him.   *examines*

18 The ᴿlot causeth contentions to cease, and parteth between the mighty.   [16:33]

19 A brother offended *is harder to be won* than a strong city: and *their* contentions *are* like the bars of a castle.

20 ᴿA man's belly shall be satisfied with the fruit of his mouth; *and* with the increase of his lips shall he be filled.   14:14

21 ᴿDeath and life *are* in the power of the tongue: and they that love it shall eat the fruit thereof.   12:13; Matt. 12:37

22 *Whoso* findeth a wife findeth a good *thing*, and obtaineth favour of the Lᴏʀᴅ.

23 The poor useth intreaties; but the rich answereth ᴿroughly.   1 Kin. 12:13

24 A man *that hath* friends must shew himself friendly: ᴿand there is a friend *that* sticketh closer than a brother.   17:17

CHAPTER 19

B ETTER ᴿ*is* the poor that walketh in his integrity, than *he that is* ᵀperverse in his lips, and is a fool.   28:6 · *crooked*

2 Also, *that* the ᴿsoul *be* without knowledge, *it is* not good; and he that hasteth with *his* feet sinneth.   [Hos. 4:6]

3 The foolishness of man perverteth his way: and his heart fretteth against the Lᴏʀᴅ.

4 ᴿWealth maketh many friends; but the poor is separated from his neighbour.   14:20

5 A false witness shall not be unpunished, and *he that* speaketh lies shall not escape.

6 ᴿMany will intreat the favour of the prince: and every man *is* a friend to him that giveth gifts.   [29:26]

7 All the brethren of the poor do hate him: how much more do his friends go far from him? he pursueth *them with* words, *yet* they *are* wanting *to him.*

8 He that getteth wisdom loveth his own soul: he that keepeth understanding ᴿshall find good.   16:20

9 A ᴿfalse witness shall not be unpunished, and *he that* speaketh lies shall perish.   *v.* 5

10 Delight is not seemly for a fool; much less for a servant to have rule over princes.

11 ᴿThe ᵀdiscretion of a man deferreth his anger; and *it is* his glory to pass over a transgression.   James 1:19 · *good sense*

12 The king's wrath *is* as the roaring of a lion; but his favour *is* as dew upon the grass.

13 A foolish son *is* the calamity of his father: ᴿand the contentions of a wife *are* a continual dropping.   21:9, 19

14 ᴿHouse and riches *are* the inheritance of fathers: and a prudent wife *is* from the Lᴏʀᴅ.   2 Cor. 12:14

15 ᴿSlothfulness casteth into a deep sleep; and an idle soul shall suffer hunger. 6:9, 10; 24:33

16 ᴿHe that keepeth the commandment keepeth his own soul; *but* he that despiseth his ways shall die.   16:17; Luke 10:28

17 ᴿHe that hath pity upon the poor lendeth unto the Lᴏʀᴅ; and that which he hath given will he pay him again.   [2 Cor. 9:6]

18 Chasten thy son while there is hope, and let not thy soul spare for his crying.

19 A man of great wrath shall suffer punishment: for if thou deliver *him*, yet thou must do it again.

20 Hear counsel, and receive instruction, that thou mayest be wise in thy latter end.

21 *There are* many devices in a man's heart; ᴿnevertheless the counsel of the Lᴏʀᴅ, that shall stand.   [Ps. 33:10]

22 The desire of a man *is* his kindness: and a poor man *is* better than a liar.

23 ᴿThe fear of the Lᴏʀᴅ *tendeth* to life: and *he that hath it* shall abide satisfied; he shall not be visited with evil.   [1 Tim. 4:8]

24 ᴿA slothful *man* hideth his hand in *his* bosom, and will not so much as bring it to his mouth again.   Matt. 26:23; Mark 14:20

25 Smite a scorner, and the simple will beware: and reprove one that hath understanding, *and* he will understand knowledge.

26 He that wasteth *his* father, *and* chaseth away *his* mother, *is* a son that causeth shame, and bringeth reproach.

27 Cease, my son, ᴿto hear the instruction *that causeth* to err from the words of knowledge.   Eph. 4:14

28 An ungodly witness scorneth judgment: and ᴿthe mouth of the wicked devoureth iniquity.   Job 15:16

29 Judgments are prepared for scorners, ᴿand stripes for the back of fools.   [10:13]

CHAPTER 20

W INE ᴿ*is* a mocker, strong drink *is* raging: and whosoever is deceived thereby is not wise.   Gen. 9:21

2 The fear of a king *is* as the roaring of a lion: *whoso* ᴿprovoketh him to anger sinneth *against* his own soul.   Num. 16:38

3 *It is* an honour for a man to cease from strife: but every fool will be meddling.

4 ᴿThe sluggard will not plow by reason of the cold; ᴿ*therefore* shall he beg in harvest, and *have* nothing.   [10:4] · 19:15

5 Counsel in the heart of man *is like* deep water; but a man of understanding will draw it out.

6 Most men will ᴿproclaim every one his own goodness: but a faithful man who can find?   Matt. 6:2; Luke 18:11

7 The just *man* walketh in his integrity: his children *are* blessed after him.

8 A king that sitteth in the throne of judgment ᵀscattereth away all evil with his eyes.   *disperses*

9 ᴿWho can say, I have made my heart clean, I am pure from my sin?   [1 Kin. 8:46]

10 ᴿDiversᵀ weights, *and* ᵀdivers measures, both of them *are* alike abomination to the LORD.   Deut. 25:13 · *unequal · diverse*

11 Even a child is ᴿknown by his doings, whether his work *be* pure, and whether *it be* right.   Matt. 7:16

12 The hearing ear, and the seeing eye, the LORD hath made even both of them.

13 ᴿLove not sleep, lest thou come to poverty; open thine eyes, *and* thou shalt be satisfied with bread.   Rom. 12:11

14 *It is* ᵀnaught, *it is* naught, saith the buyer: but when he is gone his way, then he boasteth.   *nothing*

15 There is gold, and a multitude of rubies: but ᴿthe ᵀlips of knowledge *are* a precious jewel.   3:15 · *thoughts*

16 ᴿTake his garment that is surety *for* a stranger: and take a pledge of him for a strange woman.   22:26

17 ᴿBread of deceit *is* sweet to a man; but afterwards his mouth shall be filled with gravel.   9:17

18 *Every* purpose is established by counsel: and with good advice make war.

19 He that goeth about *as* a talebearer revealeth secrets: therefore meddle not with him that flattereth with his lips.

20 ᴿWhoso curseth his father or his mother, ᴿhis lamp shall be put out in obscure darkness.   Matt. 15:4 · Job 18:5, 6

21 ᴿAn inheritance *may be* gotten hastily at the beginning; but the end thereof shall not be blessed.   [28:20]

22 ᴿSay not thou, I will ᵀrecompense evil; *but* ᴿwait on the LORD, and he shall save thee.   Rom. 12:17 · *repay* · 2 Sam. 16:12

23 ᴿDivers weights *are* an abomination unto the LORD; and a false balance *is* not good.   Deut. 25:13

24 Man's goings *are* of the LORD; how can a man then understand his own way?

25 *It is* a snare to the man *who* devoureth *that* which *is* holy, and ᴿafter vows to make enquiry.   [Eccl. 5:4, 5]

26 ᴿA wise king scattereth the wicked, and bringeth the wheel over them.   Ps. 101:8

27 ᴿThe spirit of man *is* the candle of the LORD, searching all the inward parts of the belly.   1 Cor. 2:11

28 Mercy and truth preserve the king: and his throne is upholden by mercy.

29 The glory of young men *is* their strength: and ᴿthe beauty of old men *is* the grey head.   16:31

30 The blueness of a wound cleanseth away evil: so *do* stripes the inward parts of the belly.

CHAPTER 21

THE king's heart *is* in the hand of the LORD, *as* the rivers of water: he ᴿturneth it whithersoever he will.   Ezra 6:22

2 Every way of a man *is* right in his own eyes: but the LORD pondereth the hearts.

3 To do justice and judgment *is* more acceptable to the LORD than sacrifice.

4 An high look, and a proud heart, *and* the plowing of the wicked, *is* sin.

5 The thoughts of the diligent *tend* only to plenteousness; but of every one *that is* hasty only to want.

6 ᴿThe getting of treasures by a lying tongue *is* a vanity tossed to and fro of them that seek death.   2 Pet. 2:3

7 The robbery of the wicked shall destroy them; because they refuse to do judgment.

8 The way of man is ᴿfroward and strange: but *as for* the pure, his work *is* right. Ps. 27:14

9 *It is* better to dwell in a corner of the housetop, than with a ᴿbrawling woman in a wide house.   19:13

10 The soul of the wicked desireth evil: his neighbour findeth no favour in his eyes.

11 When the scorner is punished, the simple is made wise: and when the wise is instructed, he receiveth knowledge.

12 The righteous *man* wisely considereth the house of the wicked: *but God* overthroweth the ᴿwicked for *their* wickedness.   21:7

13 ᴿWhoso stoppeth his ears at the cry of the poor, he also shall cry himself, but shall not be heard.   [Matt. 7:2]

14 A gift in secret pacifieth anger: and a reward in the bosom strong wrath.

15 *It is* joy to the just to do judgment: but ᴿdestruction *shall be* to the workers of iniquity.   10:29

16 The man that wandereth out of the way of understanding shall ᴿremain in the congregation of the dead.   Ps. 49:14

17 He that ᴿloveth pleasure *shall be* a poor man: he that loveth wine and oil shall not be rich.   23:21

18 The wicked *shall be* a ᴿransom for the righteous, and the transgressor for the upright.   Is. 43:3

19 ᴿ*It is* better to dwell in the wilderness, than with a contentious and an angry woman.   *v. 9*

20 ᴿ*There is* treasure to be desired and oil in the dwelling of the wise; but a foolish man ᴿspendeth it up.   Ps. 112:3 · Job 20:15

21 ᴿHe that followeth after righteousness and mercy findeth life, righteousness, and honour.   Matt. 5:6

22 A ᴿwise *man* scaleth the city of the

mighty, and casteth down the strength of the confidence thereof.   24:5; 2 Sam. 5:6

23 Whoso keepeth his mouth and his tongue keepeth his soul from troubles.

24 Proud *and* haughty scorner *is* his name, who dealeth in proud ^Rwrath.   Is. 16:6

25 The ^Rdesire of the slothful killeth him; for his hands refuse to labour.   [13:4]

26 He coveteth greedily all the day long: but the righteous giveth and spareth not.

27 ^RThe sacrifice of the wicked *is* abomination: how much more, *when* he bringeth it with a wicked mind?   Jer. 6:20

28 A false witness shall perish: but the man that heareth speaketh constantly.

29 A wicked man hardeneth his face: but *as for* the upright, he directeth his way.

30 ^R*There is* no wisdom nor understanding nor counsel against the LORD.   Is. 8:9, 10

31 The horse *is* prepared against the day of battle: but safety *is* of the LORD.

CHAPTER 22

A^RGOOD name *is* rather to be chosen than great riches, *and* loving favour rather than silver and gold.   Eccl. 7:1

2 The rich and poor meet together: the LORD *is* the ^Rmaker of them all.   Job 31:15

3 A prudent *man* foreseeth the evil, and hideth himself: but the simple pass on, and are ^Rpunished.   27:12

4 ^TBy humility *and* the fear of the LORD *are* riches, and honour, and life.   reward of

5 Thorns *and* snares *are* in the way of the ^Tfroward: he that doth keep his soul shall be far from them.   perverse

6 ^RTrain up a child in the way he should go: and when he is old, he will not depart from it.   [Eph. 6:4]

7 The rich ruleth over the poor, and the borrower *is* servant to the lender.

8 He that soweth iniquity shall reap vanity: and the rod of his anger shall fail.

9 ^RHe that hath a bountiful eye shall be blessed; ^Rfor he giveth of his bread to the poor.   [2 Cor. 9:6] • Luke 14:13

10 ^RCast out the scorner, and contention shall go out; yea, strife and reproach shall cease.   Gen. 21:9; Ps. 101:5

11 ^RHe that loveth pureness of heart, ^T*for* the grace of his lips the king *shall be* his friend.   Ps. 101:6 • *good will of his thoughts*

12 The eyes of the LORD preserve knowledge, and he overthroweth the words of the transgressor.

13 The slothful *man* saith, *There is* a lion without, I shall be slain in the streets.

14 ^RThe mouth of strange women *is* a deep pit: ^Rhe that is abhorred of the LORD shall fall therein.   2:16; 5:3 • [Eccl. 7:26]

15 Foolishness *is* bound in the heart of a child; *but* ^Rthe rod of correction shall drive it far from him.   [13:24]

16 He that oppresseth the poor to increase his *riches, and* he that giveth to the rich, *shall* surely *come* to want.

Proverbs Concerning Various Situations

17 Bow down thine ear, and hear the words of the wise, and apply thine heart unto my knowledge.

22:6 A Prescription for Rearing Children—This verse reveals two ingredients in the prescription for rearing children: first, the command, "Train up a child in the way he should go"; and second, the promise, "when he is old, he will not depart from it."
The command involves three parts:
a. The concept of training—"Train up." This does not denote corporal punishment but rather includes three ideas: *Dedication*—this is the consistent meaning of the word in its other Old Testament occurrences (Page 197—Deut. 20:5; Page 349—1 Kin. 8:63; Page 444—2 Chr. 7:5). Child training must begin with dedication of the child to God; the parent must realize that the child belongs exclusively to God and is given to the parent only as a stewardship. *Instruction*—this is the meaning of this word as it is used in the Jewish writings; the parents are to instruct or cause their children to learn everything essential in pleasing God. *Motivation*—this is the meaning of the word in Arabic, as it is used to describe the action of a midwife who stimulates the palate of the newborn babe so it will take nourishment. Parents are to create a taste or desire within the child so that he is internally motivated (rather than externally compelled) to do what God wants him to do.
b. The recipient of training—"a child." This is one of seven Hebrew words translated by the English word *child* and would better be translated by our word *dependent.* As long as the child is dependent on his parents he is to be the recipient of training, regardless of his age.
c. The content of the training—"in the way that he should go." The thought is that at each stage of his development the parents or guardians are to dedicate, instruct, and motivate the child to do what God evidently has best equipped the child to do for Him. This is graphically illustrated by Joshua when he said, "but as for me and my house, we will serve the LORD" (Page 240—Josh. 24:15).
If the command has been kept, the promise can be claimed. The promise includes the time of realization—"when he is old"—this is best understood as being parallel with "a child," hence, "when he is independent," i.e., no longer economically dependent upon his parents, referring to the time when he leaves their home to establish his own. The promise includes the certainty of realization—"he will not depart from it." If the command has been kept, the promise will be realized. If the command has not been kept, the promise will not be realized. Rearing children is not an overnight occurrence; it takes careful forethought and conscious obedience on the part of the parents.
Now turn to Page 12—Gen. 9:5: The Origin of Human Government.

18 For *it is* a ᵀpleasant thing if thou keep them within thee; they shall withal be fitted in thy lips.   *good*

19 That thy trust may be in the LORD, I have made known to thee this day, ᵀeven to thee.   *especially to you*

20 Have not I written to thee excellent things in counsels and knowledge,

21 ᴿThat I might make thee know the certainty of the words of truth; that thou mightest answer the words of truth to them that send unto thee?   Luke 1:3, 4

22 Rob not the poor, because he *is* poor: neither oppress the afflicted in the gate:

23 For the LORD will plead their cause, and spoil the soul of those that spoiled them.

24 Make no friendship with an angry man; and with a furious man thou shalt not go;

25 Lest thou ᴿlearn his ways, and get a snare to thy soul.   [1 Cor. 15:33]

26 Be not thou *one* of them that strike hands, *or* of them that are sureties for debts.

27 If thou hast nothing to pay, why should he take away thy bed from under thee?

28 ᴿRemove not the ancient landmark, which thy fathers have set.   Deut. 19:14

29 Seest thou a man diligent in his business? he shall stand before kings; he shall not stand before mean *men*.

CHAPTER 23

WHEN thou sittest to eat with a ruler, consider diligently what *is* before thee:

2 And put a knife to thy throat, if thou *be* a man given to appetite.

3 Be not desirous of his ᴿdainties: for they *are* deceitful meat.   Ps. 141:4; Dan. 1:5

4 ᴿLabour not to be rich: ᴿcease from thine own wisdom.   [1 Tim. 6:9] • Rom. 12:16

5 Wilt thou set thine eyes upon that which is not? for ᴿ*riches* certainly make themselves wings; they fly away as an eagle toward heaven.   [1 Tim. 6:17]

6 ᴿEat thou not the bread of *him that hath* ᴿan evil eye, neither desire thou his dainty ᵀmeats: Ps. 141:4 • 28:22 • *foods*

7 For as he thinketh in his heart, so *is* he: Eat and drink, ᴿsaith he to thee; but his heart *is* not with thee.   Ps. 12:2

8 The morsel *which* thou hast eaten shalt thou vomit up, and lose thy sweet words.

9 Speak not in the ears of a fool: for he will despise the wisdom of thy words.

10 Remove not the old landmark; and enter not into the fields of the fatherless:

11 ᴿFor their redeemer *is* mighty; he shall plead their cause with thee.   22:23

12 Apply thine heart unto instruction, and thine ears to the words of knowledge.

13 ᴿWithhold not correction from the child: for *if* thou beatest him with the rod, he shall not die.   [13:24; 22:6]

14 Thou shalt beat him with the rod, and shalt deliver his soul from ᵀhell.   *Sheol*

15 My son, if thine heart be wise, my heart shall rejoice, even mine.

16 Yea, my ᵀreins shall rejoice, when thy lips speak right things.   *heart*

17 ᴿLet not thine heart envy sinners: but *be thou* in the fear of the LORD all the day long.   24:1, 19; Ps. 37:1

18 For surely there is an end; and thine expectation shall not be cut off.

19 Hear thou, my son, and be wise, and guide thine heart in the way.

20 ᴿBe not among winebibbers; among riotous eaters of flesh: 20:1; Is. 5:22

21 For the drunkard and the glutton shall come to poverty: and drowsiness shall clothe *a man* with rags.

22 ᵀHearken unto thy father that begat thee, and despise not thy mother when she is old.   *listen*

23 Buy the truth, and sell *it* not; *also* wisdom, and instruction, and understanding.

24 ᴿThe father of the righteous shall greatly rejoice: and he that begetteth a wise *child* shall have joy of him.   [10:1]

25 Thy father and thy mother shall be glad, and she that bare thee shall rejoice.

22:21 God's Word Equips—In a general sense it can be said that the Bible was written to convict sinners of sin and to equip believers for service.
a. It equips for evangelism. Philip the evangelist uses the fifty-third chapter of Isaiah to point the Ethiopian eunuch to Christ in Acts 8:26–35.
b. It equips for counseling others. In his two letters to Timothy, Paul constantly urges this young man to preach the Word of God (Page 1194—1 Tim. 1:3, 18; 4:13–15; Page 1201—2 Tim. 2:1, 2, 15). "If thou put the brethren in remembrance of these things, thou shalt be a good minister of Jesus Christ, nourished up in the words of faith and of good doctrine, whereunto thou hast attained" (Page 1196—1 Tim. 4:6).
c. It equips for using one's spiritual gifts from God. A spiritual gift is an ability given by the Holy Spirit to the believer for the purpose of edifying the church and glorifying God. In Ephesians 1:17–19 and 4:7, 11–14 Paul says a knowledge of God's Word will provide us with the maturity we need to use our gifts in the most effective way.
d. It equips us for doing battle with Satan. In Ephesians 6:10–17 Paul likens the believers' armor to that used by Roman foot soldiers. In this comparison the Word of God is likened to the soldier's sword (Page 1167—Eph. 6:17).
    Now turn to Page 836—Dan. 11:32: We Know God Through His Word.

26 My son, give me thine heart, and let thine eyes ^Robserve my ways.   Ps. 119:24

27 ^RFor a whore is a deep ditch; and a strange woman is a narrow pit.   22:14

28 She also lieth in wait as for a prey, and increaseth the transgressors among men.

29 ^RWho hath woe? who hath sorrow? who hath contentions? who hath babbling? who hath wounds without cause? who hath redness of eyes?   Is. 5:11, 22

30 ^RThey that tarry long at the wine; they that go to seek mixed wine.   Ps. 75:8

31 Look not thou upon the ^Rwine when it is red, when it giveth his colour in the cup, when it moveth itself aright.   Song 7:9

32 At the last it ^Rbiteth like a serpent, and stingeth like an adder.   Job 20:16

33 Thine eyes shall behold strange ^Twomen, and thine ^Theart shall utter perverse things.   things • mind

34 Yea, thou shalt be as he that lieth down in the midst of the sea, or as he that lieth upon the top of a mast.

35 ^RThey have stricken me, shalt thou say, and I was not sick; they have beaten me, and I felt it not: when shall I awake? I will seek it yet again.   Jer. 5:3

CHAPTER 24

BE not thou ^Renvious against evil men, neither desire to be with them.   Ps. 37:1

2 For their heart studieth destruction, and their ^Tlips talk of mischief.   thoughts

3 Through wisdom is an house builded; and by understanding it is established:

4 And by knowledge shall the chambers be filled with all precious and pleasant riches.

5 ^RA wise man is strong; yea, a man of knowledge increaseth strength.   Eccl. 9:16

6 ^RFor by wise counsel thou shalt make thy war: and in multitude of counsellors there is safety.   Luke 14:31

7 ^RWisdom is too high for a fool: he openeth not his mouth in the gate.   Ps. 10:5

8 He that ^Rdeviseth to do evil shall be called a mischievous person.   Rom. 1:30

9 The thought of foolishness is sin: and the scorner is an abomination to men.

10 If thou ^Rfaint in the day of adversity, thy strength is small.   Deut. 20:8; Job 4:5

11 ^RIf thou forbear to deliver them that are drawn unto death, and those that are ready to be slain;   Ps. 82:4; Is. 58:6, 7

12 If thou sayest, Behold, we knew it not; doth not he that pondereth the heart consider it? and he that keepeth thy soul, doth not he know it? and shall not he render to every man ^Raccording to his works?   Ps. 62:12

13 My son, ^Reat thou honey, because it is good; ^Rand the honeycomb, which is sweet to thy taste: Song 5:1 • 16:24

14 So shall the knowledge of wisdom be unto thy soul: when thou hast found it, ^Rthen there shall be a reward, and thy expectation shall not be cut off.   Ps. 58:11

15 ^RLay not wait, O wicked man, against the dwelling of the righteous; ^Tspoil not his resting place: Ps. 10:9, 10 • destroy

16 ^RFor a just man falleth seven times, and riseth up again: ^Rbut the wicked shall fall into mischief.   Job 5:19 • Jer. 18:17

17 ^RRejoice not when thine enemy falleth, and let not thine heart be glad when he stumbleth: Job 31:29; Obad. 12

18 Lest the LORD see it, and it displease him, and he turn away his wrath from him.

19 Fret not thyself because of evil men, neither be thou envious at the wicked;

20 For ^Rthere shall be no reward to the evil man; ^Rthe candle of the wicked shall be put out.   Job 15:31 • Job 18:5, 6

21 My son, ^Rfear thou the LORD and the king: and meddle not with them that are given to change: [Rom. 13:1–7]

22 For their calamity shall rise suddenly; and who knoweth the ruin of them both?

24:6 Knowing the Will of God Through Circumstances and Counsel—While the Christian is to live above his circumstances, he is not to be unaware of them. God often works through circumstances in revealing His perfect will for us. Certainly Paul's wonderful statement that "all things work together for good to them that love God" (Page 1115—Rom. 8:28) takes into account our circumstances. A number of biblical examples can be given to illustrate this.
a. God directed Abraham to substitute a ram, whose horns had somehow become entangled in a thicket, for the life of Isaac (Page 23—Gen. 22:13).
b. God arranged for Pharaoh's daughter to be bathing in the river Nile at the exact time the baby Moses floated by in a little ark of bulrushes (Page 57—Ex. 2:1–10).
c. Paul's young nephew happened to overhear a plot to kill his famous uncle. He then reported it to the authorities, thus saving the apostle's life (Page 1098—Acts 23:12–22).
Surely the above circumstances were providentially arranged. So the Christian should ask, when attempting to discover God's will, "Is the Lord showing me something through my circumstances?"
Counselors also play an important role in finding God's will. "In multitude of counselors there is safety" (Prov. 24:6). However, three things must be kept in mind at this point:
a. Counsel must come from a godly source. "Confidence in an unfaithful man in time of trouble is like a broken tooth, and a foot out of joint" (Page 632—Prov. 25:19).
b. Sometimes even the godliest person can unknowingly give us wrong advice. Nathan the prophet did this when he encouraged David to build the temple (Page 314—2 Sam. 7:1–13).
c. In the final analysis, each person is responsible for knowing God's revealed purpose for his own life. Now turn to Page 766—Lam. 5:20: Occasions of Doubt.

23 These *things* also *belong* to the wise. ^{R}*It is* not good to have respect of persons in judgment.   Lev. 19:15; Deut. 16:19

24 ^{R}He that saith unto the wicked, Thou *art* righteous; him shall the people curse, nations shall abhor him: Is. 5:23

25 But to them that rebuke *him* shall be delight, and a good blessing shall come upon them.

26 *Every man* shall ^{T}kiss *his* lips that giveth a right answer.   approve

27 ^{R}Prepare thy work without, and make it fit for thyself in the field; and afterwards build thine house.   1 Kin. 5:17

28 Be not a witness against thy neighbour without cause; and deceive *not* with thy lips.

29 ^{R}Say not, I will do so to him as he hath done to me: I will render to the man according to his work.   [Matt. 5:39]

30 I went by the field of the slothful, and by the vineyard of the man ^{R}void^T of understanding;   6:32 · lacking

31 And, lo, ^{R}it was all grown over with thorns, *and* nettles had covered the face thereof, and the stone ^{R}wall thereof was broken down.   Job 30:7 · Is. 5:5

32 Then I saw, *and* considered *it* well: I looked upon *it, and* received instruction.

33 ^{R}Yet a little sleep, a little slumber, a little folding of the hands to sleep: 6:9, 10

34 So shall thy poverty come *as* one that travelleth; and thy want as an armed man.

CHAPTER 25

Relationships with Kings

THESE *are* also ^{R}proverbs of Solomon, which the men of Hez-e-ki′-ah king of Judah copied out.   1:1

2 *It is* the glory of God to ^{R}conceal a thing: but the honour of kings *is* to search out a matter.   Deut. 29:29; Rom. 11:33

3 The heaven for height, and the earth for depth, and the heart of kings *is* unsearchable.

4 ^{R}Take away the dross from the silver, and there shall come forth a vessel for the ^{T}finer.   2 Tim. 2:21 · refiner

5 Take away the ^{R}wicked *from* before the king, and his throne shall be established in righteousness.   20:8

6 ^{T}Put not forth thyself in the presence of the king, and stand not in the place of great men: do not claim honour

7 For better *it is* that it be said unto thee, Come up hither; than that thou shouldest be put lower in the presence of the prince whom thine eyes have seen.

Relationships with Neighbours

8 Go not forth hastily to strive, lest *thou know not* what to do in the end thereof, when thy neighbour hath put thee to shame.

9 ^{R}Debate thy cause with thy neighbour

himself; and ^{R}discover^T not a secret to another: [Matt. 18:15 · 11:13] · reveal

10 Lest he that heareth *it* put thee to shame, and thine infamy turn not away.

11 A ^{R}word fitly spoken *is like* apples of gold in pictures of silver.   15:23

12 *As* an ^{R}earring of gold, and an ornament of fine gold, *so is* a wise reprover upon an obedient ear.   Ex. 32:2; 35:22

13 As the cold of snow in the time of harvest, *so is* a faithful messenger to them that send him: for he refresheth the soul of his masters.

14 Whoso boasteth himself of a false gift *is like* clouds and wind without rain.

15 By long forbearing is a prince persuaded, and a soft tongue breaketh the bone.

16 ^{R}Hast thou found honey? eat so much as is sufficient for thee, lest thou be filled therewith, and vomit it.   Judg. 14:8

17 Withdraw thy foot from thy neighbour's house; lest he be weary of thee, and *so* hate thee.

18 ^{R}A man that beareth false witness against his neighbour *is* a maul, and a sword, and a sharp arrow.   24:28; Ex. 20:16

19 Confidence in an ^{R}unfaithful man in time of trouble *is like* a broken tooth, and a foot out of joint.   Job 6:15

20 *As* he that taketh away a garment in cold weather, *and as* vinegar upon nitre, so *is* he that singeth songs to an heavy heart.

Relationships with Enemies

21 ^{R}If thine enemy be hungry, give him bread to eat; and if he be thirsty, give him water to drink: Ex. 23:4; 2 Kin. 6:22

22 For thou shalt heap coals of fire upon his head, and the LORD shall reward thee.

23 The north wind driveth away rain: so *doth* an angry countenance ^{R}a backbiting tongue.   Ps. 101:5

24 ^{R}*It is* better to dwell in the corner of the housetop, than with a brawling woman and in a wide house.   19:13

Relationships with Yourself

25 *As* cold waters to a thirsty soul, so *is* good news from a far country.

26 A righteous man falling down before the wicked *is as* a ^{R}troubled fountain, and a corrupt spring.   Ezek. 32:2; 34:18

27 *It is* not good to eat much honey: so *for* men to search their own glory *is not* glory.

28 ^{R}He that *hath* no rule over his own spirit *is like* a city *that is* broken down, *and* without walls.   16:32

CHAPTER 26

Relationships with Fools

AS snow in summer, and as rain in harvest, so honour is not ^{T}seemly for a fool.   proper

2 As the ᴿbird by wandering, as the swallow by flying, so ᴿthe curse causeless shall not come.   Is. 16:2 • Num. 23:8

3 ᴿA whip for the horse, a bridle for the ass, and a rod for the fool's back.   Ps. 32:9

4 Answer not a fool according to his folly, lest thou also be like unto him.

5 ᴿAnswer a fool according to his folly, lest he be wise in his own conceit.   Matt. 16:1

6 He that sendeth a message by the hand of a fool cutteth off the feet, and drinketh damage.

7 The legs of the lame are not equal: so is a parable in the mouth of fools.

8 As he that bindeth a stone in a sling, so is he that giveth honour to a fool.

9 As a thorn goeth up into the hand of a drunkard, so is a parable in the mouth of fools.

10 The great God that formed all things both rewardeth the fool, and rewardeth transgressors.

11 ᴿAs a dog returneth to his vomit, so a fool returneth to his folly.   2 Pet. 2:22

12 ᴿSeest thou a man wise in his own conceit? there is more hope of a fool than of him.   3:7

Relationships with Sluggards

13 The slothful man saith, There is a lion in the way; a lion is in the streets.

14 As the door turneth upon his hinges, so doth the slothful upon his bed.

15 The ᴿslothful hideth his hand in his bosom; it grieveth him to bring it again to his mouth.   19:24

16 ᴿThe sluggard is wiser in his own conceit than seven men that can render a reason.   27:11; 1 Pet. 3:15

Relationships with Gossips

17 He that passeth by, and meddleth with strife belonging not to him, is like one that taketh a dog by the ears.

18 As a mad man who casteth ᴿfirebrands, arrows, and death,   Is. 50:11

19 So is the man that deceiveth his neighbour, and saith, Am not I in sport?

20 Where no wood is, there the fire goeth out: so where there is no ᴿtalebearer, the strife ceaseth.   16:28

21 ᴿAs coals are to burning coals, and wood to fire; so is a contentious man to kindle strife.   15:18; 29:22

22 The words of a ᴿtalebearer are as wounds, and they go down into the innermost parts of the belly.   18:8

23 Burning lips and a wicked heart are like a potsherd covered with silver dross.

24 He that hateth dissembleth with his lips, and layeth up deceit within him;

25 ᴿWhen he speaketh fair, believe him

not: for there are seven abominations in his heart.   Ps. 28:3; Jer. 9:8

26 Whose hatred is ᴿcovered by deceit, his wickedness shall be shewed before the whole congregation.   Matt. 23:28

27 ᴿWhoso diggeth a pit shall fall therein: and he that rolleth a stone, it will return upon him.   Ps. 7:15, 16; 9:15

28 A lying tongue hateth those that are afflicted by it; and a flattering mouth worketh ᴿruin.   29:5

CHAPTER 27

Proverbs Regulating Various Activities

BOASTᴿ not thyself of to morrow; for thou ᴿknowest not what a day may bring forth.   Luke 12:19 • James 4:14

2 Let another man ᴿpraise thee, and not thine own mouth; a stranger, and not thine own lips.   2 Cor. 10:12, 18; 12:11

3 A stone is heavy, and the sand weighty; but a fool's wrath is heavier than them both.

4 Wrath is cruel, and anger is outrageous; but who is able to stand before envy?

5 Open rebuke is better than secret love.

6 Faithful are the wounds of a friend; but the kisses of an enemy are deceitful.

7 The full soul loatheth an honeycomb; but to the hungry soul every bitter thing is sweet.

8 As a bird that wandereth from her nest, so is a man that wandereth from his place.

9 ᴿOintment and perfume rejoice the heart: so doth the sweetness of a man's friend by hearty counsel.   Ps. 23:5

10 Thine own friend, and thy father's friend, ᴿforsake not; neither go into thy brother's house in the day of thy calamity: for ᴿbetter is a neighbour that is near than a brother far off.   1 Kin. 12:6-8 • 18:24

11 My son, ᴿbe wise, and make my heart glad, ᴿthat I may answer him that reproacheth me.   [10:1] • Ps. 119:42

12 A prudent man foreseeth the evil, and hideth himself; but the simpleᵀ pass on, and are punished.   naive

13 Take his garment that is ᵀsurety for a stranger, and take a pledge of him for a strange woman.   guarantee

14 He that blesseth his friend with a loud voice, rising early in the morning, it shall be counted a curse to him.

15 A continual dropping in a very rainy day and a contentious woman are alike.

16 Whosoever ᵀhideth her hideth the wind, and the ointment of his right hand, which ᵀbewrayeth itself.   restrain • betrays

17 Iron sharpeneth iron; so a man sharpeneth the countenance of his friend.

18 ᴿWhoso ᵀkeepeth the fig tree shall eat the fruit thereof: so he that waiteth on his master shall be honoured.   1 Cor. 9:7 • takes care

19 As in water face *answereth* to face, so the heart of man to man.

20 Hell and destruction are never full; so the eyes of man are never satisfied.

21 *As* the fining pot for silver, and the furnace for gold; so *is* a man to his praise.

22 RThough thou shouldest Tbray a fool in a mortar among wheat with a pestle, *yet* will not his foolishness depart from him. 23:35 • *crush*

23 Be thou diligent to know the state of thy flocks, *and* look well to thy herds.

24 For riches *are* not for ever: and doth the crown *endure* to every generation?

25 RThe hay appeareth, and the tender grass sheweth itself, and herbs of the mountains are gathered.   Is. 17:5

26 The lambs *are* for thy clothing, and the goats *are* the price of the field.

27 And *thou shalt have* goats' milk enough for thy food, for the food of thy household, and *for* the maintenance for thy maidens.

CHAPTER 28

THE wicked flee when no man pursueth: but the righteous are bold as a lion.

2 For the transgression of a land Rmany *are* the princes thereof: but by a man of understanding *and* knowledge the state *thereof* shall be prolonged.   1 Kin. 16:8–28

3 A poor man that oppresseth the poor *is like* a sweeping rain which leaveth no food.

4 RThey that forsake the law praise the wicked: Rbut such as keep the law contend with them.   Ps. 49:18; Rom. 1:32 • Eph. 5:11

5 REvil men understand not judgment: but Rthey that seek the LORD understand all things.   Is. 6:9; 44:18 • 1 Cor. 2:15

6 Better *is* the poor that walketh in his uprightness, than *he that is* perverse *in his* ways, though he *be* rich.

7 Whoso keepeth the law *is* a wise son: but he that is a companion of Triotous *men* shameth his father.   *gluttonous*

8 He that by Rusury and unjust gain increaseth his substance, he shall gather it for him that will pity the poor.   Ex. 22:25

9 He that turneth away his ear from hearing the law, Reven his prayer *shall be* abomination.   [15:8]

10 Whoso causeth the righteous to go astray in an evil way, Rhe shall fall himself into his own pit: but the upright shall have good *things* in possession.   Ps. 7:15

11 The rich man *is* wise in his own conceit; but the poor that hath understanding searcheth him out.

12 When righteous *men* do rejoice, *there is* great glory: but Rwhen the wicked rise, a man is hidden.   Eccl. 10:5, 6

13 RHe that covereth his sins shall not prosper: but whoso confesseth and forsaketh *them* shall have mercy.   Job 31:33

14 Happy *is* the man that Rfeareth alway: but he that Rhardeneth his heart shall fall into mischief.   23:17 • Rom. 2:5

15 *As* a roaring lion, and a ranging bear; *so is* a wicked ruler over the poor people.

16 The prince that wanteth understanding *is* also a great oppressor: *but* he that hateth covetousness shall prolong *his* days.

17 RA man that doeth violence to the blood of *any* person shall flee to the pit; let no man stay him.   Gen. 9:6; Ex. 21:14

18 Whoso walketh uprightly shall be saved: but *he that is* perverse *in his* ways shall fall at once.

19 RHe that tilleth his land shall have plenty of bread: but he that followeth after vain *persons* shall have poverty enough. 20:13

20 A faithful man shall abound with blessings: Rbut he that maketh haste to be rich shall not be innocent.   1 Tim. 6:9

21 RTo have respect of persons *is* not good: Rfor for a piece of bread *that* man will transgress.   24:23 • Ezek. 13:19

22 He that Rhasteth to be rich *hath* an evil eye, and considereth not that poverty shall come upon him.   23:6

23 RHe that rebuketh a man afterwards shall find more favour than he that flattereth with the tongue.   27:5, 6

24 Whoso robbeth his father or his mother, and saith, *It is* no transgression; the same *is* the companion of a destroyer.

25 He that is of a proud heart stirreth up strife: but he that putteth his trust in the LORD shall be made fat.

26 He that trusteth Rin his own heart is a fool: but whoso walketh wisely, he shall be delivered.   3:5

27 RHe that giveth unto the poor shall not lack: but he that hideth his eyes shall have many a curse.   11:24; 19:17

28 When the wicked rise, men hide themselves: but when they perish, the righteous increase.

CHAPTER 29

HE, Rthat being often reproved hardeneth *his* neck, shall suddenly be destroyed, and that without remedy.   1:24

2 RWhen the righteous are in authority, the people rejoice: but when the wicked beareth rule, the people mourn.   11:10; 28:12

3 Whoso Rloveth wisdom rejoiceth his father: but he that keepeth company with harlots spendeth *his* substance.   10:1; 15:20

4 The Rking by judgment establisheth the land: but he that receiveth gifts overthroweth it.   28:14; 8:15; 2 Chr. 9:8

5 A man that Rflattereth his neighbour spreadeth a net for his feet.   1 Thess. 2:5

6 In the transgression of an evil man *there* Ris a snare: but the righteous doth Rsing and rejoice.   22:5; Eccl. 9:12 • Ex. 15:1

7 The ᴿrighteous considereth the cause of the poor: *but* the wicked regardeth not to know *it*.   [Ps. 41:1]

8 Scornful men bring a city into ᴿa snare: but wise *men* turn away wrath.   1 Tim. 6:9

9 *If* a wise man contendeth with a foolish man, whether he rage or laugh, *there is* no rest.

10 ᴿThe bloodthirsty hate the upright: but the just seek his soul.   Gen. 4:5–8

11 ᴿA fool uttereth all his mind: but a wise *man* keepeth it in till afterwards.   19:11

12 If a ᴿruler hearken to lies, all his servants *are* wicked.   1 Kin. 12:14

13 The poor and the deceitful man meet together: the LORD ᴿlighteneth both their eyes.   Ezra 9:8; Ps. 13:3; Is. 29:18

14 The ᴿking that faithfully judgeth the ᴿpoor, his throne shall be established for ever.   Ps. 72:4; Is. 11:4; 16:5 · Jer. 22:16

15 The ᴿrod and ᴿreproof give wisdom: but a child left *to himself* bringeth his mother to shame.   [13:24] · Eccl. 7:5

16 When the wicked are multiplied, transgression increaseth: but the ᴿrighteous shall see their fall.   21:12; Ps. 37:34, 36

17 Correct thy son, and he shall give thee rest; yea, he shall give delight unto thy soul.

18 ᴿWhere *there is* no vision, the people perish: but he that keepeth the law, happy *is* he.   1 Sam. 3:1; Ps. 74:9; Amos 8:11, 12

19 A servant will not be corrected by words: for though he understand he will not answer.

20 Seest thou a man *that is* ᴿhasty in his words? *there is* more hope of a fool than of him.   [Eccl. 5:2; James 1:19]

21 He that delicately bringeth up his servant from a child shall have him become his son at the length.

22 An angry man stirreth up strife, and a furious man aboundeth in transgression.

23 A man's pride shall bring him low: but honour shall uphold the humble in spirit.

24 Whoso is partner with a thief hateth his own soul: ᴿhe heareth cursing, and bewrayeth *it* not.   Lev. 5:1

25 ᴿThe fear of man bringeth a snare: but whoso putteth his ᴿtrust in the LORD shall be safe.   Gen. 12:12; Luke 12:4 · 18:10; 28:25

26 Many seek the ruler's favour; but *every* man's judgment *cometh* from the LORD.

27 An ᴿunjust man *is* an abomination to the just: and *he that is* upright in the way *is* abomination to the wicked.   12:8

CHAPTER 30

The Words of Agur

THE words of A'-gur the son of Ja'-keh, *even* the prophecy: the man spake unto Ith'-i-el, even unto Ith'-i-el and U'-cal,

2 ᴿSurely I *am* more ᵀbrutish than *any* man, and have not the understanding of a man.   [12:1] · *stupid*

3 I neither learned wisdom, nor have the knowledge of the holy.

4 ᴿWho hath ascended up into heaven, or descended? who hath gathered the wind in his fists? who hath bound the waters in a garment? who hath established all the ends of the earth? what *is* his name, and what *is* his son's name, if thou canst tell?   Ps. 68:18

5 Every word of God *is* pure: he *is* a shield unto them that put their trust in him.

6 Add thou not unto his words, lest he reprove thee, and thou be found a liar.

7 Two *things* have I required of thee; deny me *them* not before I die:

8 Remove far from me vanity and lies: give me neither poverty nor riches; feed me with food convenient for me:

9 Lest I be full, and deny *thee*, and say, Who *is* the LORD? or lest I be poor, and steal, and take the name of my God *in vain*.

10 Accuse not a servant unto his master, lest he curse thee, and thou be found guilty.

11 *There is* a generation *that* curseth their father, and doth not bless their mother.

12 *There is* a generation ᴿ*that are* pure in their own eyes, and *yet* is not washed from their filthiness.   [16:2]

13 *There is* a generation, O how ᴿlofty are their eyes! and their eyelids are lifted up. 6:17

14 *There is* a generation, whose teeth *are* as swords, and their jaw teeth *as* knives, to devour the poor from off the earth, and the needy from *among* men.

15 The ᴿhorseleach hath two daughters, *crying*, Give, give. There are three *things that* are never satisfied, *yea*, four *things* say not, *It is* enough: Hab. 2:5

16 ᴿThe grave; and the barren womb; the earth *that* is not filled with water; and the fire *that* saith not, *It is* enough.   27:20

17 ᴿThe eye *that* mocketh at *his* father, and despiseth to obey *his* mother, the ravens of the valley shall pick it out, and the young eagles shall eat it.   Gen. 9:22

18 There be three *things which* are too wonderful for me, yea, four which I know not:

19 The way of an ᴿeagle in the air; the way of a serpent upon a rock; the way of a ship in the midst of the sea; and the way of a man with a maid.   Deut. 28:49; Jer. 48:40

20 Such *is* the way of an adulterous woman; she eateth, and wipeth her mouth, and saith, I have done no wickedness.

21 For three *things* the earth is disquieted, and for four *which* it cannot bear:

22 For a servant when he reigneth; and a fool when he is filled with meat;

23 ᴿFor an odious *woman* when she is married; ᴿand an handmaid that is heir to her mistress.   [12:4] · 29:21

24 There be four *things which are* little upon the earth, but they *are* exceeding wise:

25 The ants *are* a people not strong, yet they prepare their meat in the summer;

26 The conies *are but* a feeble folk, yet make they their houses in the rocks;

27 The ᴿlocusts have no king, yet go they forth all of them ᴿby bands;   Is. 33:4 • Joel 2:7

28 The spider taketh hold with her hands, and is in kings' palaces.

29 There be three *things* which go well, yea, four are ᵀcomely in going: *stately*

30 A lion *which is* strongest among beasts, and turneth not away for any;

31 A greyhound; an he goat also; and a king, against whom *there is* no rising up.

32 If thou hast done foolishly in lifting up thyself, or if thou hast thought evil, *lay* thine hand upon thy mouth.

33 Surely the churning of milk bringeth forth ᴿbutter, and the wringing of the nose bringeth forth blood: so the forcing of wrath bringeth forth strife.   Is. 7:22; Is. 7:15

CHAPTER 31

Wisdom for Leaders

THE words of king Lem'-u-el, the prophecy that his mother taught him.

2 What, my son? and what, the son of my womb? and what, the son of my vows?

3 Give not thy strength unto women, nor thy ways to that which destroyeth kings.

4 ᴿ*It is* not for kings, O Lem'-u-el, *it is* not for kings ᴿto drink wine; nor for princes strong drink: Eccl. 10:17 • [20:1]

5 Lest they drink, and forget the law, and pervert the judgment of any of the afflicted.

6 ᴿGive strong drink unto him that is ready to perish, and wine unto those that be ᵀof heavy hearts.   Ps. 104:15 • *in despair*

7 Let him drink, and forget his poverty, and remember his misery no more.

8 ᴿOpen thy mouth for the dumb in the cause of all such as are appointed to destruction.   24:11; Job 29:15, 16

9 Open thy mouth, judge righteously, and plead the cause of the poor and needy.

Wise Woman

10 Who can find ᴿa virtuous woman? for her price *is* far above rubies.   [12:4]

11 ᴿThe heart of her husband doth safely trust in her, so that he shall have no need of spoil.   18:22; 19:14

12 ᴿShe will do him good and not evil all the days of her life.   Esth. 1:20

13 She seeketh wool, and flax, and worketh willingly with her hands.

14 She is like the ᴿmerchants' ships; she bringeth her food from afar.   Ezek. 27:25

15 She riseth also while it is yet night, and giveth ᵀmeat to her household, and a portion to her maidens.   *food*

16 ᴿShe considereth a field, and ᵀbuyeth it: with the fruit of her hands she planteth a vineyard.   Rom. 12:11 • *procures*

17 She girdeth her loins with strength, and strengtheneth her arms.

18 She perceiveth that her merchandise *is* good: her candle goeth not out by night.

19 She layeth her hands to the spindle, and her hands hold the distaff.

20 ᴿShe ᵀstretcheth out her hand to the poor; yea, she reacheth forth her hands to the needy.   Eph. 4:28 • *is ready to help*

21 She is not afraid of the snow for her household: for all her household *are* clothed with ᵀscarlet.   *the best*

22 She maketh herself coverings of tapestry; her clothing *is* silk and purple.

23 Her husband is known in the gates, when he sitteth among the elders of the land.

24 She maketh fine linen, and selleth *it;* and delivereth girdles unto the merchant.

25 Strength and honour *are* her clothing; and she shall rejoice in time to come.

26 She openeth her mouth with wisdom; and in her tongue *is* the law of kindness.

27 ᴿShe looketh well to the ways of her household, and eateth not the bread of idleness.   1 Tim. 5:14

28 Her children arise up, and call her blessed; her husband *also,* and he praiseth her.

29 Many daughters have done ᵀvirtuously, but thou excellest them all.   *well*

30 Favour *is* deceitful, and ᴿbeauty *is* vain: *but* a woman *that* feareth the LORD, she shall be praised.   Is. 28:1

31 Give her of the fruit of her hands; and let her own works praise her in the gates.

ECCLESIASTES;

OR, THE PREACHER

📖 THE BOOK OF ECCLESIASTES

The key word in Ecclesiastes is *vanity*, the futile emptiness of trying to be happy apart from God. The Preacher (traditionally taken to be Solomon—1:1, 12—the wisest, richest, most influential king in Israel's history) looks at life "under the sun" (1:9) and, from the human perspective, declares it all to be empty. Power, popularity, prestige, pleasure—nothing can fill the God-shaped void in man's life but God Himself! But once seen from God's perspective, life takes on meaning and purpose, causing Solomon to exclaim, "Eat . . . drink . . . rejoice . . . do good . . . live joyfully . . . fear God . . . keep His commandments!" Skepticism and despair melt away when life is viewed as a daily gift from God.

The Hebrew title *Qoheleth* is a rare term, found only in Ecclesiastes (1:1, 2, 12; 7:27; 12:8-10). It comes from the word *qahal*, "to convoke an assembly, to assemble." Thus, it means "one who addresses an assembly, a preacher." The Septuagint used the Greek word *Ekklesiastes* as its title for this book. Derived from the word *ekklesia*, "assembly, congregation, church," it simply means "preacher." The Latin *Ecclesiastes* means "speaker before an assembly."

THE AUTHOR OF ECCLESIASTES

There are powerful arguments that the author of Ecclesiastes was Solomon.

External Evidence: Jewish talmudic tradition attributes the book to Solomon but suggests that Hezekiah's scribes may have edited the text (see Prov. 25:1). Solomonic authorship of Ecclesiastes is the standard Christian position, although some scholars, along with the Talmud, believe the work was later edited during the time of Hezekiah or possibly Ezra.

Internal Evidence: The author calls himself "the son of David, king in Jerusalem" in 1:1, 12. Solomon was the best qualified Davidic descendant for the quest in this book. He was the wisest man who ever taught in Jerusalem (see 1:16; 1 Kin. 4:29, 30). The descriptions of Qoheleth's exploration of pleasure (2:1-3), impressive accomplishments (2:4-6), and unparalleled wealth (2:7-10) were fulfilled only by King Solomon. The proverbs in this book are similar to those in the Book of Proverbs (e.g., Eccl. 7; 10). According to 12:9, Qoheleth collected and arranged many proverbs, perhaps referring to the two Solomonic collections in Proverbs. The unity of authorship of Ecclesiastes is supported by the seven references to Qoheleth.

⬛ THE TIME OF ECCLESIASTES

Some scholars argue that the literary forms in Ecclesiastes are postexilic, but they are, in fact, unique, and cannot be used in dating this book. The phrase "all *they* that have been before me in Jerusalem" in 1:16 has been used to suggest a date after Solomon's time, but there were many kings and wise men in Jerusalem before the time of Solomon. However, Solomon was the only son of David who reigned over Israel from Jerusalem (1:12).

Ecclesiastes was probably written late in Solomon's life, about 935 B.C. If this is so, the great glory that Solomon ushered in early in his reign was already beginning to fade; and the disruption of Israel into two kingdoms would soon take place. Jewish tradition asserts that Solomon wrote Song of Solomon in his youthful years, Proverbs in his middle years, and Ecclesiastes in his latter years. This book may be expressing his regret for his folly and wasted time due to carnality and idolatry (cf. 1 Kin. 11).

There are no references to historical events other than to personal aspects of Qoheleth's life. The location was Jerusalem (1:1, 12, 16), the seat of Israel's rule and authority.

✝ THE CHRIST OF ECCLESIASTES

Ecclesiastes convincingly portrays the emptiness and perplexity of life without a relationship with the Lord. Each person has eternity in his heart (3:11), and only Christ can provide ultimate satisfaction, joy, and wisdom. Man's highest good is found in the "one shepherd" (12:11) who offers abundant life (John 10:9, 10).

🗝 KEYS TO ECCLESIASTES

Key Word: Vanity—Ecclesiastes reports the results of a diligent quest for purpose, meaning, and satisfaction in human life. The Preacher poignantly sees the emptiness and futility of power, popularity, prestige, and pleasure apart from God. The word *vanity* appears thirty-seven times to express the many things that cannot be understood about life. All earthly goals and ambitions when pursued as ends in themselves lead to dissatisfaction and frustration. Life "under the sun" (used twenty-nine times) seems to be filled with inequities, uncertainties, changes in fortune, and violations of justice. But Ecclesiastes does not give an answer of atheism or skepticism; God is referred to throughout. In fact, it claims that the search for man's *summum bonum* must end in God. Satisfaction in life can be found only by looking beyond this world. Ecclesiastes gives an analysis

of negative themes but it also develops the positive theme of overcoming the vanities of life by fearing a God who is good, just, and sovereign (12:13, 14). Wisdom involves seeing life from a divine perspective and trusting God in the face of apparent futility and lack of purpose. Life is a daily gift from God and it should be enjoyed as much as possible (see 2:24–26; 3:12, 13, 22; 5:18–20; 8:15; 9:7–10; 11:8, 9). Our comprehension is indeed limited, but there are many things we can understand. Qoheleth recognized that ultimately God will judge all people. Therefore he exhorted: "Fear God, and keep his commandments" (12:13).

Key Verses: Ecclesiastes 2:24 and 12:13, 14— "There is nothing better for a man, than that he should eat and drink, and that he should make his soul enjoy good in his labour. This also I saw, that it was from the hand of God" (2:24).

"Let us hear the conclusion of the whole matter: Fear God, and keep his commandments: for this is the whole duty of man. For God shall bring every work into judgment, with every secret thing, whether it be good, or whether it be evil" (12:13, 14).

Key Chapter: Ecclesiastes 12—At the end of the Book of Ecclesiastes, the Preacher looks at life through "binoculars." On the other hand, from the perspective of the natural man who only sees life "under the sun," the conclusion is, "All is vanity." Life's every activity, even though pleasant for the moment, becomes purposeless and futile when viewed as an end in itself.

The Preacher carefully documents the latter view with a long list of his own personal pursuits in life. No amount of activities or possessions has satisfied the craving of his heart. Every earthly prescription for happiness has left the same bitter aftertaste. Only when the Preacher views his life from God's perspective "above the sun" does it take on meaning as a precious gift "from the hand of God" (2:24).

Chapter 12 resolves the book's extensive inquiry into the meaning of life with the single conclusion, "Fear God, and keep his commandments: for this is the whole duty of man" (12:13).

SURVEY OF ECCLESIASTES

Ecclesiastes is a profound and problematic book. It is the record of an intense search for meaning and satisfaction in life on this earth, especially in view of all the iniquities and apparent absurdities that surround us. It takes the perspective of the greatest answers that wisdom under the sun can produce. If the Preacher is identified as Solomon, Ecclesiastes was written from a unique vantage point. Possessing the greatest mental, material, and political resources ever combined in one man, he was qualified beyond all others to write this book. Ecclesiastes is extremely difficult to synthesize, and several alternate approaches have been used. The one used here is: the thesis that "all is vanity" (1:1–11), the proof that "all is vanity" (1:12–6:12), the counsel for living with vanity (7:1–12:14).

The Thesis That "All Is Vanity" (1:1–11): After a one-verse introduction, the Preacher states his theme: "Vanity of vanities; all is vanity" (1:2). Life under the sun appears to be futile and perplexing. Verses 3–11 illustrate this theme in the endless and apparently meaningless cycles found in nature and history.

The Proof That "All Is Vanity" (1:12–6:12): The Preacher describes his multiple quest for meaning and satisfaction as he explores his vast personal resources. He begins with wisdom (1:12–18) but finds that "he that increaseth knowledge increaseth sorrow." Due to his intense perception of reality he experiences just the reverse of "ignorance is bliss." The Preacher moves from wisdom to laughter, hedonism, and wine (2:1–3) and then turns to works, women, and wealth (2:4–11); but all lead to emptiness. He

FOCUS	THESIS: "ALL IS VANITY"		PROOF: "LIFE IS VAIN"		COUNSEL: "FEAR GOD"		
REFERENCE	1:1————1:4————		1:12————3:1————		7:1————10:1————		12:9————12:14
DIVISION	INTRODUCTION OF VANITY	ILLUSTRATIONS OF VANITY	PROOF FROM SCRIPTURE	PROOF FROM OBSERVATIONS	COPING IN A WICKED WORLD	COUNSEL FOR UNCERTAINTY	CONCLUSION: FEAR AND OBEY GOD
TOPIC	DECLARATION OF VANITY		DEMONSTRATION OF VANITY		FROM VANITY		
	SUBJECT		SERMONS		SUMMARY		
LOCATION	UNIVERSE: "UNDER THE SUN"						
TIME	c. 935 B.C.						

realizes that wisdom is far greater than foolishness, but both seem to lead to futility in view of the brevity of life and universality of death (2:12–17). He concludes by acknowledging that contentment and joy are found only in God.

At this point, Ecclesiastes turns from his situation in life to a philosophical quest; but the conclusion remains the same. The Preacher considers the unchanging order of events and the fixed laws of God. Time is short, and there is no eternity on earth (3:1–15). The futility of death seems to cancel the difference between righteousness and wickedness (3:16–22). Chapters 4 and 5 explore the futility in social relationships (oppression, rivalry, covetousness, power) and in religious relationships (formalism, empty prayer, vows). In addition, the world's offerings produce disappointment, not satisfaction. Ultimate meaning can be found only in God.

The Counsel for Living with Vanity (7:1— 12:14): A series of lessons on practical wisdom are given in 7:1—9:12. Levity and pleasure-seeking are seen as superficial and foolish; it is better to have sober depth of thought. Wisdom and self-control provide perspective and strength in coping with life. One should enjoy prosperity and consider in adversity that God made both. Avoid the twin extremes of self-righteousness and immorality. Sin invades all men, and wisdom is cut short by evil and death. The human mind cannot grasp ultimate meaning. Submission to authority helps one avoid unnecessary hardship, but real justice is often lacking on earth. The uncertainties of life and certainty of the grave show that God's purposes and ways often cannot be grasped. One should, therefore, magnify opportunities while they last, because fortune can change suddenly.

Observations on wisdom and folly are found in 9:13—11:6. Wisdom, the most powerful human resource, is contrasted with the meaningless talk and effort of fools. In view of the unpredictability of circumstances, wisdom is the best course to follow in order to minimize grief and misfortune. Wisdom involves discipline and diligence. In 11:7—12:7 the Preacher offers exhortations on using life well. Youth is too brief and precious to be squandered in foolishness or evil. A person should live well in the fullness of each day before God and acknowledge Him early in life. This section closes with an exquisite allegory of old age (12:1–7).

The Preacher concludes that the "good life" is only attained by revering God. Those who fail to take God and His will seriously into account are doomed to lives of foolishness and futility. Life will not wait upon the solution of all its problems; nevertheless, real meaning can be found by looking not "under the sun" but beyond the sun to the "one shepherd" (12:11).

OUTLINE OF ECCLESIASTES

Part One: The Thesis That "All Is Vanity" (1:1–11)

Part Two: The Proof That "All Is Vanity" (1:12—6:12)

CHAPTER 1

Introduction of Vanity

THE words of the ᴿPreacher, the son of David, king in Jerusalem.   7:27; 12:8-10

2 ᴿVanity of vanities, saith the Preacher, vanity of vanities; all is vanity.   12:8

3 What profit hath a man of all his labour which he ᵀtaketh under the sun?   performs

Illustrations of Vanity

4 One generation passeth away, and another generation cometh: ᴿbut the earth abideth for ever.   Ps. 104:5; 119:90

5 ᴿThe sun also ariseth, and the sun goeth down, and hasteth to his place where he arose.   Ps. 19:4-6; John 3:8

6 ᴿThe wind goeth toward the south, and turneth about unto the north; it whirleth about continually, and the wind returneth again according to his circuits.   11:5; John 3:8

7 All the rivers run into the sea; yet the sea is not full; unto the place from whence the rivers come, thither they return again.

8 All things are full of ᵀlabour; man cannot utter it: the eye is not satisfied with seeing, nor the ear filled with hearing.   weariness

9 ᴿThe thing that hath been, it is that which shall be; and that which is done is that which shall be done: and there is no new thing under the sun.   2:12; 3:15; 6:10

10 Is there any thing whereof it may be said, See, this is new? it hath been already of old time, which was before us.

11 There is ᴿno remembrance of former things; neither shall there be any remembrance of things that are to come with those that shall come after.   2:16; 9:5

Vanity of Striving After Wisdom

12 I the ᴿPreacher was king over Israel in Jerusalem.   v. 12; 7:27; 12:8-10

13 And I ᴿgave my heart to seek and ᴿsearch out by wisdom concerning all things that are done under heaven: this sore travail hath God given to the sons of man to be ᵀexercised therewith.   v. 17 · 3:10 · busy with

14 I have seen all the works that are done under the sun; and, behold, all is ᴿvanity and vexation of spirit.   2:11, 17

15 ᴿThat which is crooked cannot be made straight: and that which is ᵀwanting cannot be numbered.   7:13 · lacking

16 I communed with mine own heart, saying, Lo, I am come to great estate, and have gotten ᴿmore wisdom than all they that have been before me in Jerusalem: yea, my heart had ᵀgreat experience of wisdom and knowledge.   2:9; 1 Kin. 3:12, 13 · learned much

17 And I gave my heart to know wisdom, and to know madness and folly: I perceived that this also is vexation of spirit.

18 For ᴿin much wisdom is much grief: and he that increaseth knowledge increaseth sorrow.   2:23; 12:12; 2 Tim. 3:7

CHAPTER 2

Vanity of Striving After Pleasure

I SAID in mine heart, Go to now, I will prove thee with mirth, therefore enjoy pleasure: and, behold, this also is vanity.

2 I said of laughter, It is mad: and of ᴿmirth, What doeth it?   [7:3, 6]

3 I sought in mine heart ᴿto give myself unto wine, yet acquainting mine heart with wisdom; and to lay hold on folly, till I might see what was that good for the sons of men, which they should do under the heaven all the days of their life.   Ps. 104:15

Vanity of Great Accomplishments

4 I made me great works; ᴿI builded me houses; I planted me vineyards: 1 Kin. 7:1-12

5 I made me gardens and orchards, and I planted trees in them of all kind of fruits:

6 I made me pools of water, to water therewith the wood that bringeth forth trees:

7 I got me servants and maidens, and had ᵀservants born in my house; also I had great possessions of great and small cattle above all that were in Jerusalem before me: slaves

8 I gathered me also silver and gold, and the peculiar treasure of kings and of the provinces: I gat me men singers and women singers, and the delights of the sons of men, *as* musical instruments, and that of all sorts.

9 So I was great, and increased more than all that were ^Rbefore me in Jerusalem: also my wisdom remained with me.   1:16

10 And ^Rwhatsoever mine eyes desired I kept not from them, I withheld not my heart from any joy; for my heart rejoiced in all my labour: and ^Rthis was my portion of all my labour.   6:2 • 3:22; 5:18; 9:9

11 Then I looked on all the works that my hands had wrought, and on the labour that I had laboured to do: and, behold, all *was* ^Rvanity and vexation of spirit, and *there was* no profit under the sun.   1:3, 14

12 And I turned myself to behold wisdom, and madness, and folly: for what *can* the man *do* that cometh after the king? *even* that which hath been already done.

13 Then I saw that wisdom excelleth folly, as far as light excelleth darkness.

14 ^RThe wise man's eyes *are* in his head; but the fool walketh in darkness: and I myself perceived also that ^Rone event happeneth to them all.   8:1 • 9:2, 3, 11; Ps. 49:10

15 Then said I in my heart, As it happeneth to the fool, so it happeneth even to me; and why was I then more wise? Then I said in my heart, that this also *is* vanity.

16 For *there is* ^Rno remembrance of the wise more than of the fool for ever; seeing that which now *is* in the days to come shall all be forgotten. ^RAnd how dieth the wise *man?* as the fool.   4:16; 9:5 • v. 14; 2 Sam. 3:33

17 Therefore I ^Rhated life; because the work that is wrought under the sun *is* grievous unto me: for all *is* vanity and vexation of spirit.   4:2

Vanity of Hard Labour

18 Yea, I hated all my labour which I had taken under the sun: because I should leave it unto the man that shall be after me.

19 And who knoweth whether he shall be a wise *man* or a fool? yet shall he have rule over all my labour wherein I have laboured, and wherein I have shewed myself wise under the sun. This *is* also vanity.

20 ^RTherefore I went about to cause my heart to despair of all the labour which I took under the sun.   Deut. 28:39

21 For there is a man whose labour *is* in wisdom, and in knowledge, and in ^Tequity; yet to a man that hath not laboured therein shall he leave it *for* his ^Tportion. This also *is* vanity and a great evil.   skill • inheritance

22 ^RFor what hath man of all his labour, and of the vexation of his heart, wherein he hath laboured under the sun?   v. 11; 1:3; 3:9

23 For all his days *are* sorrows, and his travail grief; yea, his heart ^Ttaketh not rest in the night. This is also vanity.   finds no relief

Conclusion: Be Content

24 ^R*There is* nothing better for a man, *than* that he should eat and drink, and *that* he should ^Tmake his soul enjoy good in his labour. This also I saw, that it *was* from the hand of God.   3:12, 13, 22 • delight his senses

25 For who can eat, or who else can hasten *hereunto,* more than I?

26 For *God* giveth to a man ^Tthat *is* good in his sight wisdom, and knowledge, and joy: but to the sinner he giveth travail, to gather and to heap up, that ^Rhe may give to *him that is* good before God. This also *is* vanity and vexation of spirit.   what • Prov. 28:8

CHAPTER 3

God Predetermines the Events of Life

TO every *thing there is* a season, and a time to every purpose under the heaven:

2 A time to be born, and ^Ra time to die; a time to plant, and a time to pluck up *that which is* planted;   2 Sam. 14:14; Job 14:5; Heb. 9:27

3 A time to kill, and a time to heal; a time to break down, and a time to build up;

4 A time to weep, and a time to laugh; a time to mourn, and a time to dance;

5 A time to cast away stones, and a time to gather stones together; a time to embrace, and a time to refrain from embracing;

6 A time to ^Tget, and a time to lose; a time to keep, and a time to cast away;   gain

7 A time to rend, and a time to sew; a time to keep silence, and a time to speak;

8 A time to love, and a time to ^Rhate; a time of war, and a time of peace.   Luke 14:26

9 ^RWhat profit hath he that worketh in that wherein he laboureth?   1:3; 2:11; 5:16

God Predetermines the Conditions of Life

10 ^RI have seen the ^Ttravail, which God hath given to the sons of men to be ^Texercised in it.   1:13; 2:26 • work • occupied

11 He hath ^Rmade every *thing* beautiful in his time: also he hath set the world in their heart, so that ^Rno man can find out the work that God maketh from the beginning to the end.   Gen. 1:31 • 8:17; Rom. 11:33

12 I know that *there* ^R*is* ^Tno good in them, but for *a man* to rejoice, and to do good in his life.   2:24 • nothing better for them than

13 And also ^Rthat every man should eat and drink, and enjoy the good of all his labour, it *is* the gift of God.   2:24; 5:19

14 I know that, whatsoever God doeth, it shall be for ever: ^Rnothing can be put to it, nor any thing taken from it: and God doeth *it,* that *men* should fear before him.   James 1:17

15 That which hath been is now; and that which is to be hath already been; and God ᵀrequireth that which is past.   *seeks*

God Judges All

16 And moreover ᴿI saw under the sun the place of judgment, *that* wickedness *was* there; and the place of righteousness, *that* iniquity *was* there.   4:1; 5:8; 8:9

17 I said in mine heart, ᴿGod shall judge the righteous and the wicked: for *there is* a time there for every purpose and for every work.   Rom. 2:6–8; 2 Cor. 5:10; 2 Thess. 1:5, 6

18 I said in mine heart concerning the estate of the sons of men, that God ᵀmight manifest them, and that they might see that they themselves are beasts.   *may prove*

19 ᴿFor that which befalleth the sons of men befalleth beasts; even one thing befalleth them: as the one dieth, so dieth the other; yea, they have all one breath; so that a man hath no preeminence above a beast: for all *is* vanity.   9:12; Ps. 49:12, 20; 73:22

20 All go unto one place; ᴿall are of the dust, and all turn to dust again.   12:7; Gen. 3:19

21 ᴿWho knoweth the spirit of man that goeth upward, and the spirit of the beast that goeth downward to the earth?   12:7

22 ᴿWherefore I perceive that *there is* nothing better, than that a man should rejoice in his own works; for ᴿthat *is* his ᵀportion: for who shall bring him to see what shall be after him?   2:24; 5:18 • 2:10 • *share*

CHAPTER 4

Evil Oppression

SO I returned, and considered all the oppressions that are done under the sun: and behold the tears of *such as were* oppressed, and they had no comforter; and on the ᵀside of their oppressors *there was* power; but they had no comforter.   *hand*

2 ᴿWherefore I praised the dead which are already dead more than the living which are yet alive.   2:17; Job 3:11–26

3 ᴿYea, better *is* he than both they, which hath not yet been, who hath not seen the evil work that is done under the sun.   6:3

Folly of Hard Work

4 ᴿAgain, I considered all travail, and every ᵀright work, that for this a man is envied of his neighbour. This *is* also vanity and vexation of spirit.   *v. 16 • skilful*

5 ᴿThe fool foldeth his hands together, and eateth his own flesh.   Prov. 6:10; 24:33

6 ᴿBetter *is* an handful *with* quietness, than both the hands full *with* ᵀtravail and ᵀvexation of spirit.   Prov. 15:16 • *hard labour • anxiety*

7 Then I returned, and I saw vanity under the sun.

8 There is one *alone,* and *there is* not a second; yea, he hath neither child nor brother: yet *is there* no end of all his labour; neither is his eye satisfied with riches; neither *saith he,* For whom do I labour, and bereave my soul of good? This *is* also vanity, yea, it *is* a ᵀsore travail.   *grievous burden*

9 ᴿTwo *are* better than one; because they have a good reward for their labour.   Ex. 17:12

10 ᴿFor if they fall, the one will lift up his fellow: ᴿbut woe to him *that is* alone when he falleth; ᴿfor *he hath* not another to help him up.   John 15:13 • 2 Chr. 28:15 • Ps. 31:11

11 Again, if two lie together, then they have heat: but how can one be warm *alone?*

12 ᴿAnd if one prevail against him, two shall withstand him; and a threefold cord is not quickly broken.   1 Cor. 1:10

Transience of Popularity

13 Better *is* a ᴿpoor and a wise child than an old and foolish king, who ᵀwill no more be admonished.   7:19 • *will not accept advice*

14 For ᴿout of prison he cometh to reign; whereas also *he that is* born in his kingdom becometh poor.   Gen. 41:14, 41–43

15 I considered all the living which walk under the sun, with the second child that shall stand up in his stead.

16 *There is* no end of all the people, *even* of all that have been before them: they also that come after shall not rejoice in him. ᴿSurely this also *is* vanity and vexation of spirit.   *v. 4*

CHAPTER 5

Insufficiencies of Human Religion

KEEP thy foot when thou goest to the house of God, and be more ready to hear, than to give the sacrifice of fools: for they consider not that they do evil.

2 Be not rash with thy mouth, and let not thine heart be hasty to utter *any* thing before God: for God *is* in heaven, and thou upon earth: therefore let thy words be few.

3 For a dream cometh through the multitude of business; and ᴿa fool's voice *is known* by multitude of words.   [Prov. 10:19]

4 When thou vowest a vow unto God, defer not to pay it; for *he hath* no pleasure in fools: pay that which thou hast vowed.

5 Better *is it* that thou shouldest not vow, than that thou shouldest vow and not pay.

6 Suffer not thy mouth to cause thy flesh to sin; neither say thou before the angel, that it *was* an ᴿerror: wherefore should God be angry at thy voice, and destroy the work of thine hands?   Lev. 4:2, 22

7 For in the multitude of dreams and many words *there are* also ᵀdivers vanities: but ᴿfear thou God.   *various foolishnesses* • [12:13]

Wealth Does Not Satisfy

8 If thou ᴿseest the oppression of the poor, and violent perverting of judgment and justice in a province, marvel not at the matter: for *he that is* higher than the highest regardeth; and *there be* higher than they. 3:16

9 Moreover the profit of the earth is for all: the king *himself* is served by the field.

10 He that loveth silver shall not be satisfied with silver; nor he that loveth abundance with increase: this *is* also vanity.

11 ᴿWhen goods increase, they are increased that eat them: and what good *is there* to the owners thereof, saving the beholding *of them* with their eyes? 2:9

12 The sleep of a labouring man *is* sweet, whether he eat little or much: but the abundance of the rich will not suffer him to sleep.

Wealth Brings Difficulties

13 ᴿThere is a sore evil *which* I have seen under the sun, *namely,* riches kept for the owners thereof to their hurt. 6:1, 2

14 But those riches perish by evil ᵀtravail: and he begetteth a son, and *there is* nothing in his hand. *adventure*

15 As he came forth of his mother's womb, naked shall he return to go as he came, and shall take nothing of his labour, which he may carry away in his hand.

16 And this also *is* a sore evil, *that* in all points as he came, so shall he go: and ᴿwhat profit hath he ᴿthat hath laboured for the wind? 1:3; 2:11; 3:9 • [Luke 12:16–21]

17 All his days also ᴿhe eateth in darkness, and he ᴿhath much sorrow and wrath with his ᴿsickness. Ps. 127:2 • 2:23 • Mic. 6:13

Wealth Comes Ultimately from God

18 Behold *that* which I have seen: *it is* good and comely *for one* to eat and to drink, and to enjoy the good of all his labour that he taketh under the sun all the days of his life, which God giveth him: for it *is* his portion.

19 ᴿEvery man also to whom ᴿGod hath given riches and wealth, and hath given him power to eat thereof, and to take his portion, and to rejoice in his labour; this *is* the gift of God. 2:24; 3:13 • [6:2]

20 For he shall not much remember the days of his life; because God answereth *him* in the joy of his heart.

CHAPTER 6

No Satisfaction in Wealth

THERE is an evil which I have seen under the sun, and it *is* common among men:

2 A man to whom God hath given riches, wealth, and honour, so that he wanteth nothing for his soul of all that he desireth, yet

God giveth him not power to eat thereof, but a stranger eateth it: this *is* ᵀvanity, and it *is* an evil disease. *emptiness*

No Satisfaction in Children

3 If a man beget an hundred *children,* and live many years, so that the days of his years be many, and his soul be not filled with good, and also *that* he have no burial; I say, *that* an untimely birth *is* better than he.

4 ᴿFor he cometh in with vanity, and departeth in darkness, and his name shall be covered with darkness. 8:10

5 Moreover he hath not seen the sun, nor known *any thing:* this hath more ᵀrest than the other. *comfort*

6 Yea, though he live a thousand years twice *told,* yet hath he seen no good: ᴿdo not all go to one place? 2:14, 15

No Satisfaction in Labour

7 ᴿAll the labour of man *is* for his mouth, and yet the appetite is not filled. Prov. 16:26

8 For ᴿwhat hath the wise more than the fool? what hath the poor, that knoweth to walk before the living? 2:15

No Satisfaction in the Future

9 Better *is* the ᴿsight of the eyes ᴿthan the wandering of the desire: ᴿthis *is* also vanity and vexation of spirit. 11:9 • 4:4 • 1:14

10 That which hath been is named already, and it is known that it *is* man: ᴿneither may he contend with him that is mightier than he. Job 9:32; Is. 45:9; Jer. 49:19

11 Seeing there be many things that increase vanity, what *is* man the better?

12 For who knoweth what *is* good for man in *this* life, all the days of his vain life which he spendeth as a shadow? for who can tell a man what shall be after him under the sun?

CHAPTER 7

Wisdom and Folly Contrasted

A ᴿGOOD name *is* better than precious ointment; and the ᴿday of death than the day of one's birth. Prov. 22:1 • *v.* 8; 4:2

2 *It is* better to go to the house of mourning, than to go to the house of feasting: for that is the ᴿend of all men; and the living will lay *it* to his heart. 2:16; 3:19, 20; 6:6; 9:2, 3

3 ᴿSorrow *is* better than laughter: ᴿfor by the sadness of the countenance the heart is made ᵀbetter. 2:2 • [2 Cor. 7:10] • *glad*

4 The heart of the wise *is* in the house of mourning; but the heart of fools *is* in the house of mirth.

5 *It is* better to hear the rebuke of the wise, than for a man to hear the song of fools.

6 ᴿFor as the ᵀcrackling of ᴿthorns under a

pot, so is the [R]laughter of the fool: this also is vanity.   2:2 • *sound* • Ps. 58:9; 118:12 • Luke 6:25

7 Surely oppression maketh a wise man mad; and a gift destroyeth the heart.

8 Better is the end of a thing than the beginning thereof: *and* the patient in spirit is better than the proud in spirit.

9 Be not hasty in thy spirit to be angry: for anger resteth in the bosom of fools.

10 Say not thou, What is *the cause* that the former days were better than these? for thou dost not enquire [T]wisely concerning this.   *out of wisdom*

11 Wisdom is [T]good with an inheritance: and [R]by it there is profit [R]to them that see the sun.   *as good as* • Prov. 8:10, 11 • 11:7

12 For wisdom is [T]a defence, *and* money is a defence: but the [T]excellency of knowledge is, *that* [R]wisdom giveth life to them that have it.   *an asset* • *best part* • Prov. 3:18; 8:35

13 [R]Consider the work of God: for [R]who can make *that* straight, which he hath made crooked?   3:11; 8:17 • 1:15; Job 12:14

14 [R]In the day of prosperity be joyful, but in the day of adversity consider: God also hath set the one [T]over against the other, to the end that man should find nothing after him.   3:22; Deut. 28:47 • *to balance*

Wisdom of Moderation

15 [R]All *things* have I seen in the days of my vanity: [R]there is a just *man* that perisheth in his righteousness, and there is a [R]wicked *man* that prolongeth *his life* in his wickedness.   6:12; 9:9 • 8:14 • [8:12, 13]

16 Be not righteous over much; [R]neither make thyself over wise: why shouldest thou [T]destroy thyself?   Matt. 6:1 • *be desolate*

17 Be not over much wicked, neither be thou foolish: [R]why shouldest thou die before thy time?   Job 22:16; 15:23, 32; Ps. 55:23

18 *It is* good that thou shouldest [R]take hold of this; yea, also from this withdraw not thine hand: for he that feareth God shall come forth of them all.   *v.* 16

Strength of Wisdom

19 Wisdom strengtheneth the wise more than ten mighty *men* which are in the city.

20 For *there is* not a just man upon earth, that doeth good, and sinneth not.

21 Also [T]take no heed unto all words that are spoken; lest thou hear thy servant curse thee: *do not pay attention*

22 For oftentimes also thine own heart knoweth that thou thyself likewise hast [R]cursed others.   Rom. 3:14

23 All this have I proved by wisdom: I said, I will be wise; but it *was* far from me.

24 [R]That which is far off, and exceeding deep, who can find it out?   Rom. 11:33

25 I applied mine heart to know, and to search, and to seek out wisdom, and the reason *of things,* and to know the wickedness of folly, even of foolishness *and* madness:

26 And I find more [R]bitter than death the woman, whose heart is snares and nets, *and* her hands *as* bands: whoso pleaseth God shall escape from her; but the sinner shall be taken by her.   Prov. 5:4

27 Behold, this have I found, saith [R]the preacher, [T]counting one by one, to find out the account: 1:1, 2 • *checking each one*

28 Which yet my soul seeketh, but I find not: [R]one man among a thousand have I found; but a [R]woman among all those have I not found.   Job 33:23 • 1 Kin. 11:1–8

29 Lo, this only have I found, that God hath made man upright; but [R]they have sought out many inventions.   Gen. 3:6, 7

CHAPTER 8

Submit to Authority

WHO is as the wise *man?* and who knoweth the interpretation of a thing? a man's wisdom maketh his face to shine, and the boldness of his face shall be changed.

2 I *counsel thee* to keep the king's commandment, [R]and *that* in regard of the [R]oath of God.   1 Chr. 29:24 • Ex. 22:11; 2 Sam. 21:7

3 Be not hasty to go out of [R]his sight: [T]stand not in an evil thing; for he doeth whatsoever pleaseth him.   10:4 • *persist*

4 Where the word of a king *is, there is* power: and [R]who may say unto him, What doest thou?   Job 9:12; Dan. 4:35

5 Whoso keepeth the commandment shall feel no evil thing: and a wise man's heart discerneth both time and judgment.

6 Because [R]to every purpose there is time and judgment, therefore the misery of man is great upon him.   3:1, 17

7:20 Individual Sin—Each individual man, woman, and child who composes mankind is a sinner. Paul points out in Romans 3:13–16 that "Their throat is an open sepulcher . . . the poison of asps [a small deadly poisonous snake] is under their lips: Whose mouth is full of cursing and bitterness: Their feet are swift to shed blood [consider the high incidence of violent crime, murder, and abortion that infects our society]: Destruction and misery are in their ways [whatever man touches he corrupts]." All of this shows that there is no person who seeks after God and no person does what is right (Page 1110—Rom. 3:10, 11). Each individual man, woman, and child needs the righteousness of God. Without God's righteousness no one can ever enter or stand in God's presence. Plainly, every man, woman, and child needs to have a new life because each is a sinner.

Now turn to Page 1113—Rom. 6:23: New Life: A Free Gift.

7 For he knoweth not that which shall be: for who can tell him when it shall be?

8 *There is* no man that hath power over the spirit to retain the spirit; neither *hath he* power in the day of death: and *there is* no discharge in *that* war; neither shall wickedness deliver those that are given to it.

9 All this have I seen, and applied my heart unto every work that is done under the sun: ^R*there is* a time wherein one man ruleth over another to his own hurt.   5:8

Inability to Understand All God's Doing

10 And so I saw the wicked buried, who had come and gone from the place of the holy, and they were forgotten in the city where they had so done: this *is* also vanity.

11 ^RBecause sentence against an evil work is not executed speedily, ^Rtherefore the heart of the sons of men is fully set in them to do evil.   Ps. 50:21 • Ps. 10:6; Is. 26:10; Rom. 2:4, 5

12 Though ^Ra sinner do evil an hundred times, and his *days* be prolonged, yet surely I know that it shall be well with them that fear God, which fear before him: Is. 65:20

13 But it shall not be well with the wicked, neither shall he prolong *his* days, *which are* as a ^Rshadow; because he feareth not before God.   Job 14:2

14 There is a vanity which is done upon the earth; that there be just *men*, unto whom it ^Rhappeneth according to the work of the wicked; again, there be ^Rwicked *men*, to whom it happeneth according to the work of the righteous: I said that this also *is* vanity.   2:14; 7:15; 9:1–3; Ps. 73:14 • Mal. 3:15

15 ^RThen I commended mirth, because a man hath no better thing under the sun, than to eat, and to drink, and to be merry: for that shall abide with him of his labour the days of his life, which God giveth him under the sun.   2:24; 3:12, 22; 5:18; 9:7

16 When I applied mine heart to know wisdom, and to see the business that is done upon the earth: (for also *there is that* ^Rneither day nor night seeth sleep with his eyes:) 2:23

17 Then I beheld all the work of God, that a man cannot find out the work that is done under the sun: because though a man labour to seek *it* out, yet he shall not find *it*; yea further; though a wise *man* think to know *it*, yet shall he not be able to find *it*.

CHAPTER 9

Judgment Comes to All Men

FOR all this I considered in my heart even to declare all this, that the righteous, and the wise, and their works, *are* in the hand of God: no man knoweth either love or hatred *by* all *that is* before them.

2 ^RAll *things come* alike to all: *there is* one event to the righteous, and to the wicked; to the good and to the clean, and to the unclean; to him that sacrificeth, and to him that sacrificeth not: as *is* the good, so *is* the sinner; *and* he that sweareth, as *he* that feareth an oath.   Ps. 73:3, 12, 13; Mal. 3:15

3 This *is* an ^Revil among all *things* that are done under the sun, that *there is* one event unto all: yea, also the heart of the sons of men is full of evil, and ^Tmadness *is* in their heart while they live, and after that *they* go to the dead.   7:20 • *wickedness*

4 For to him that is ^Tjoined to all the living there is hope: for a living dog is better than a dead lion.   *involved with*

5 For the living know that they shall die: but ^Rthe dead know not any thing, neither have they any more a reward; for the memory of them is forgotten.   Job 14:21

6 Also their love, and their hatred, and their envy, is now perished; neither have they any more a ^Rportion for ever in any *thing* that is done under the sun.   3:22

Enjoy Life While You Have It

7 Go thy way, ^Reat thy bread with joy, and drink thy wine with a merry heart; for God now accepteth thy works.   8:15

8 Let thy ^Rgarments be always white; and let thy head lack no ointment.   Rev. 3:4

9 ^TLive joyfully with the wife whom thou lovest all the days of the life of thy vanity, which he hath given thee under the sun, all the days of thy vanity: for that *is* thy portion in *this* life, and in thy labour which thou takest under the sun.   *see; or, enjoy life*

10 Whatsoever thy hand findeth to do, do *it* with thy might; for *there is* no work, nor device, nor knowledge, nor wisdom, in the ^Tgrave, whither thou goest.   *world of the dead*

11 I returned, and saw under the sun, that the race *is* not to the swift, nor the battle to the strong, neither yet bread to the wise, nor yet riches to men of understanding, nor yet favour to men of skill; but time and chance happeneth to them all.

12 For ^Rman also knoweth not his time: as the fishes that are taken in an evil net, and as the birds that are caught in the snare; so *are* the sons of men snared in an evil time, when it falleth suddenly upon them.   8:7

Value of Wisdom

13 This wisdom have I seen also under the sun, and it *seemed* great unto me:

14 ^R*There was* a little city, and few men within it; and there came a great king against it, and besieged it, and built great bulwarks against it: 2 Sam. 20:16–22

15 Now there was found in it a poor wise man, and he by ^Rhis wisdom delivered the city; yet no man ^Tremembered that same poor man.   2 Sam. 20:22 • *appreciated*

16 Then said I, Wisdom *is* better than

strength: nevertheless the poor man's wisdom *is* despised, and his words are not heard.

17 The ᴿwords of wise *men are* heard in quiet more than the ᵀcry of him that ruleth among fools.　　　　7:5; 10:12 • *shouting*

18 Wisdom *is* better than weapons of war: but one sinner destroyeth much good.

CHAPTER 10

Wisdom's Characteristics

DEAD flies cause the ointment of the apothecary to send forth a stinking ᵀsavour: *so doth* a little folly him that is in reputation for wisdom *and* honour.　　*odour*

2 A wise man's heart *is* at his right hand; but a fool's heart at his left.

3 Yea also, when he that is a fool walketh by the way, his wisdom faileth *him,* and he saith to every one *that* he *is* a fool.

4 If the spirit of the ruler rise up against thee, ᴿleave not thy place; for ᴿyielding pacifieth great offences.　　8:3 • Prov. 25:15

5 There is an evil *which* I have seen under the sun, as an ᴿerror ᵀwhich proceedeth from the ruler:　　5:6 • *which comes to the notice of*

6 ᴿFolly is set ᵀin great dignity, and the rich sit in low place.　　Esth. 3:1 • *in great heights*

7 I have seen servants upon horses, and princes walking as servants upon the earth.

8 ᴿHe that diggeth a pit shall fall into it; and whoso breaketh an hedge, ᵀa serpent shall bite him.　　Prov. 26:27 • *will reap an evil result*

9 Whoso ᵀremoveth stones shall be hurt therewith; *and* he that ᵀcleaveth wood shall be endangered thereby.　　*cuts out • splits*

10 If the iron be blunt, and he do not whet the edge, then must he put to more strength: but ᴿwisdom *is* profitable to direct.　　Prov. 8:11

11 Surely the serpent will bite without enchantment; and a babbler is no better.

12 ᴿThe words of a wise man's mouth *are* gracious; but ᴿthe lips of a fool will swallow up himself.　　Prov. 10:32; Luke 4:22 • Prov. 10:14

13 The beginning of the words of his mouth *is* foolishness: and the end of his talk *is* mischievous madness.

14 ᴿA fool also is full of words: a man cannot tell what shall be; and what shall be after him, who can tell him?　　[Prov. 15:2]

15 The labour of the foolish wearieth every one of them, because he knoweth not how to go to the city.

Wisdom Related to the King

16 Woe to thee, O land, when thy king *is* a child, and thy princes eat in the morning!

17 Blessed *art* thou, O land, when thy king *is* the son of nobles, and ᴿthy princes eat in due season, for strength, ᴿand not for drunkenness!　　Prov. 31:4 • Is. 5:11

18 By much ᴿslothfulness the building decayeth; and through idleness of the hands the house droppeth through.　　Prov. 24:30–34

19 A feast is made for laughter, and ᴿwine ᵀmaketh merry: but money answereth all things.　　Judg. 9:13; Ps. 104:15 • *makes glad the life*

20 ᴿCurse not the king, no not in thy thought; and curse not the rich ᴿin thy bedchamber: for a bird of the air shall carry the voice, and that which hath wings shall tell the matter.　　Ex. 22:28; Acts 23:5 • 2 Kin. 6:12

CHAPTER 11

Wisdom Related to Business

CAST thy bread upon the waters: for thou shalt find it after many days.

2 ᴿGive a portion to seven, and also to eight; ᴿfor thou knowest not what evil shall ᵀbe upon the earth.　　Ps. 112:9 • Eph. 5:16 • *come*

3 If the clouds be full of rain, they empty *themselves* upon the earth: and if the tree fall toward the south, or toward the north, in the place where the tree falleth, there it shall be.

4 He that observeth the wind shall not sow; and he that ᵀregardeth the clouds shall not ᵀreap.　　*is waiting for good weather • harvest*

5 As ᴿthou knowest not what *is* the way of the ᵀspirit, ᴿnor how the bones *do* grow in the womb of her that is with child: even so thou knowest not the works of God who maketh all.　　John 3:8 • *wind* • Ps. 139:14–16

6 In the morning sow thy seed, and in the evening withhold not thine hand: for thou knowest not ᵀwhether shall prosper, either this or that, or whether they both *shall be* alike good.　　*which will work out successfully*

Rejoice in Your Youth

7 Truly the light *is* sweet, and a pleasant *thing it is* for the eyes to behold the sun:

8 But if a man live many years, *and* rejoice in them all; yet let him remember the days of ᴿdarkness; for they shall be many. All that cometh *is* vanity.　　12:1

9 Rejoice, O young man, in thy youth; and let thy heart cheer thee in the days of thy youth, and walk ᵀin the ways of thine heart, and in the sight of thine eyes: but know thou, that for all these *things* God will bring thee into judgment.　　*as you want to*

10 ᴿTherefore remove sorrow from thy heart, and put away evil from thy flesh: for childhood and youth *are* vanity.　　2 Cor. 7:1

CHAPTER 12

Remember God in Your Youth

REMEMBER now thy Creator in the days of thy youth, while the evil days come not, nor the years draw nigh, when thou shalt say, I have no pleasure in them;

2 While the sun, ᴿor the light, or the moon, or the stars, be not darkened, nor the clouds return after the rain: Is. 5:30; 13:10

3 In the day when the keepers of the house shall tremble, and the strong men shall bow themselves, and the ᵀgrinders cease because they are few, and those that look out of the windows be darkened,   *teeth*

4 And the doors shall be shut in the streets, when the ᴿsound of the grinding is low, and he shall rise up at the voice of the bird, and all ᴿthe daughters of musick shall be brought low;   Jer. 25:10 • 2 Sam. 19:35

5 Also *when* they shall be afraid of *that which is* high, and fears *shall be* in the way, and the almond tree shall ᵀflourish, and the grasshopper shall be a burden, and desire shall fail: because man goeth to ᴿhis long home, and ᴿthe mourners go about the streets: *blossom* • Job 17:13 • Jer. 9:17

6 Or ever the silver cord be loosed, ᴿor the golden bowl be broken, or the pitcher be broken at the fountain, or the wheel broken at the cistern.   Zech. 4:2, 3

7 ᴿThen shall the dust return to the earth as it was: ᴿand the spirit shall return unto God ᴿwho gave it.   Gen. 3:19 • 3:21 • Num. 16:22

8 ᴿVanity of vanities, saith the preacher, all *is* vanity.   Ps. 62:9

Conclusion: "Fear God, and Keep His Commandments"

9 And moreover, because the preacher was wise, he still taught the people knowledge; yea, he gave good heed, and sought out, *and* set in order many proverbs.

10 The preacher sought to find out ᵀacceptable words: and *that which was* written *was* upright, *even* words of truth.   *suitable*

11 The ᴿwords of the wise *are* as goads, and as ᴿnails fastened *by* the masters of assemblies, *which* are given from one shepherd.   Prov. 1:6; 22:17 • Acts 2:37; Ezra 9:8

12 And further, by these, my son, be admonished: of ᴿmaking many books *there is* no end; and ᴿmuch ᵀstudy *is* a weariness of the flesh.   1 Kin. 4:32, 33 • 1:18 • *reading*

13 Let us hear the ᵀconclusion of the whole matter: ᴿFear God, and keep his commandments: for this *is* the whole *duty* of man.   *the end of the matter* • Deut. 10:12

14 For ᴿGod shall bring every work into judgment, with every secret thing, whether *it be* good, or whether *it be* evil.   Matt. 12:36

SONG OF SOLOMON

📖 **THE BOOK OF SONG OF SOLOMON**
The Song of Solomon is a love song written by Solomon and abounding in metaphors and oriental imagery. Historically, it depicts the wooing and wedding of a shepherdess by King Solomon, and the joys and heartaches of wedded love.

Allegorically, it pictures Israel as God's espoused bride (Hos. 2:19, 20), and the church as the bride of Christ. As human life finds its highest fulfillment in the love of man and woman, so spiritual life finds its highest fulfillment in the love of God for His people and Christ for His church.

The book is arranged like scenes in a drama with three main speakers: the bride (Shulamite), the king (Solomon), and a chorus (daughters of Jerusalem).

The Hebrew title *Shir Hashirim* comes from 1:1, "The song of songs." This is in the superlative and speaks of Solomon's most exquisite song. The Greek title *Asma Asmaton* and the Latin *Canticum Canticorum* also mean "Song of Songs" or "The Best Song." The name *Canticles* ("Songs") is derived from the Latin title. Because Solomon is mentioned in 1:1, the book is also known as the Song of Solomon.

✍ **THE AUTHOR OF SONG OF SOLOMON**
Solomonic authorship is rejected by critics who claim it is a later collection of songs. Many take 1:1 to mean "which is about or concerning Solomon." But the internal evidence of the book strongly favors the traditional position that Solomon is its author. Solomon is specifically mentioned seven times (1:1, 5; 3:7, 9, 11; 8:11, 12), and he is identified as the groom. There is evidence of royal luxury and rich imported goods (e.g., 3:6–11). The king by this time also had sixty queens and eighty concubines (6:8). Solomon's harem at its fullest extent reached seven hundred queens and three hundred concubines (1 Kin. 11:3).

First Kings 4:32, 33 says that Solomon composed 1,005 songs and had intimate knowledge of the plant and animal world. This greatest of his songs alludes to twenty-one species of plants and fifteen species of animals. It cites geographical locations in the north and in the south, indicating that they were still one kingdom. For example, 6:4 mentions both Tirzah and Jerusalem, the northern and southern capitals (after Solomon's time, Samaria became the northern capital). Because of the poetic imagery, the Song of Solomon uses forty-nine words that occur nowhere else in Scripture.

⏳ **THE TIME OF SONG OF SOLOMON**
This song was written primarily from the point of view of the Shulamite, but Solomon was its author, probably early in his reign, about 965 B.C. There is a problem regarding how a man with a harem of 140 women (6:8) could extol the love of the Shulamite as though she was his only bride. It may be that Solomon's relationship with the Shulamite was the only pure romance he ever experienced. The bulk of his marriages were political arrangements. It is significant that the Shulamite was a vineyard keeper of no great means. This book was also written before Solomon plunged into gross immorality and idolatry. "For it came to pass, when Solomon was old, *that* his wives turned away his heart after other gods: and his heart was not perfect with the LORD his God" (1 Kin. 11:4).

The Shulamite addresses the king as "my beloved" and the king addresses his bride as "my love." The daughters of Jerusalem were probably attendants to the Shulamite. The term *Shulamite* appears only in 6:13, and it may be derived from the town of Shunem which was southwest of the Sea of Galilee in the tribal area of Issachar. The song refers to fifteen geographic locations from Lebanon in the north to Egypt in the south: Kedar (1:5), Egypt (1:9), En-gedi (1:14), Sharon (2:1), Jerusalem (2:7), Lebanon (3:9), Mount Gilead (4:1), Amana (4:8), Shenir (4:8), Hermon (4:8), Tirzah (6:4), Heshbon (7:4), Damascus (7:4), Carmel (7:5), and Baal-hamon (8:11).

✝ **THE CHRIST OF SONG OF SOLOMON**
In the Old Testament, Israel is regarded as the bride of Yahweh (see Is. 54:5, 6; Jer. 2:2; Ezek. 16:8–14; Hos. 2:16–20). In the New Testament, the church is seen as the bride of Christ (see 2 Cor. 11:2; Eph. 5:23–25; Rev. 19:7-9; 21:9). The Song of Solomon illustrates the former and anticipates the latter.

🔑 **KEYS TO SONG OF SOLOMON**
Key Word: Love in Marriage—The purpose of this book depends on the viewpoint taken as to its primary thrust. Is it fictional, allegorical, or historical?

(1) *Fictional:* Some hold that this song is a fictional drama that portrays Solomon's attraction and marriage to a poor but beautiful girl from the country. However, the book gives every indication that the story really happened.

(2) *Allegorical:* In this view, the primary purpose of the Song is to illustrate the truth of God's love for His people whether the events were fictional or not. Some commentators insist

that the book is indeed historical, but its primary purpose is typical, that is, to present God's love for His bride Israel or Christ's love for His church. However, this interpretation is subjective and lacking in evidence. In other Scriptures the husband and wife relationship is used symbolically (cf. Ezek. 16; 23; Hos. 1—3), but these are always indicated as symbols. This may be an application of the book, but it should not be the primary interpretation.

(3) *Historical:* The Song of Songs is a poetic record of Solomon's actual romance with a Shulamite woman. The various scenes in the book exalt the joys of love in courtship and marriage and teach that physical beauty and sexuality in marriage should not be despised as base or unspiritual. It offers a proper perspective of human love and avoids the extremes of lust and asceticism. Only when sexuality is viewed in the wrong way, as something akin to evil, is an attempt made to allegorize the book. But this is part of God's creation with its related desires and pleasures, and it is reasonable that He would provide us with a guide to a pure sexual relationship between a husband and wife. In fact, the union of the two sexes was originally intended to illustrate the oneness of the Godhead (see Gen. 1:27; 2:24; 1 Cor. 6:16-20). Thus, the Song is a bold and positive endorsement by God of marital love in all its physical and emotional beauty. This interpretation does not mean that the book has no spiritual illustrations and applications. It certainly illustrates God's love for His covenant people Israel, and anticipates Christ's love for His bride, the church.

Key Verses: Song of Solomon 7:10 and 8:7—"I am my beloved's, and his desire *is* toward me" (7:10).

"Many waters cannot quench love, neither can the floods drown it: if a man would give all the substance of his house for love, it would utterly be contemned" (8:7).

Key Chapter: Song of Solomon—Since the whole book is a unity, there is no Key Chapter; rather, all eight chapters beautifully depict the love of a married couple.

SURVEY OF SONG OF SOLOMON
Solomon wrote 1,005 songs (1 Kin. 4:32), but this beautiful eulogy of love stood out among them as the "song of songs" (1:1). The great literary value of this song can be seen in its rich use of metaphor and oriental imagery as it extols the purity, beauty, and satisfaction of love. It is never crass, but often intimate, as it explores the dimensions of the relationship between two lovers: attraction, desire, companionship, pleasure, union, separation, faithfulness, and praise. Like Ecclesiastes, this little book is not easily outlined, and various schemes can be used. It abounds with sudden changes of speakers, and they are not identified. The beginning of love is seen in 1:1—5:1, and the broadening of love is found in 5:2—8:14.

The Beginning of Love (1:1–5:1): King Solomon has a vineyard in the country of the Shulamite (6:13; 8:11). The Shulamite must work in the vineyard with her brothers (1:6; 8:11, 12); and when Solomon visits the area, he wins her heart and eventually takes her to the palace in Jerusalem as his bride. She is tanned from hours of work outside in the vineyard, but she is "fairest among women" (1:6, 8).

This song is arranged like scenes in a one-act drama with three main speakers—the bride (the Shulamite), the king (Solomon), and a chorus (the daughters of Jerusalem). It is not always clear who is speaking, but this is a likely arrangement:

The bride: 1:2-4, 5-7, 12-14, 16, 17; 2:1, 3-6, 8-17; 3:1-4; 4:16; 5:2-8, 10-16; 6:2, 3, 11, 12; 7:9-13; 8:1-3, 6, 7, 10-12, 14.

The groom: 1:8-10, 15; 2:2, 7; 3:5; 4:1-15; 5:1; 6:4-10, 13; 7:1-9; 8:4, 5, 13.

FOCUS	BEGINNING OF LOVE		BROADENING OF LOVE	
REFERENCE	1:1————————3:6		5:2————————7:11————————8:14	
DIVISION	FALLING IN LOVE	UNITED IN LOVE	STRUGGLING IN LOVE	GROWING IN LOVE
TOPIC	COURTSHIP	WEDDING	PROBLEM	PROGRESS
	FOSTERING OF LOVE	FULFILLMENT OF LOVE	FRUSTRATION OF LOVE	FAITHFULNESS OF LOVE
LOCATION	ISRAEL			
TIME	c. 1 YEAR			

The chorus: 1:4, 11; 3:6-11; 5:9; 6:1, 13; 8:5, 8, 9.

Chapters 1—3 give a series of recollections of the courtship: (1) the bride's longing for affection at the palace before the wedding (1:2-8), (2) expressions of mutual love in the banquet hall (1:9—2:7), (3) a springtime visit of the king to the bride's home in the country (2:8-17), (4) the Shulamite's dream of separation from her beloved (3:1-5), and (5) the ornate wedding procession from the bride's home to Jerusalem (3:6-11).

In 4:1—5:1, Solomon praises his bride from head to foot with a superb chain of similes and metaphors. Her virginity is compared to "a garden inclosed" (4:12), and the garden is entered when the marriage is consummated (4:16—5:1). The union is commended, possibly by God, in 5:1.

The Broadening of Love (5:2—8:14): Some time after the wedding, the Shulamite has a troubled dream (5:2) in the palace while Solomon is away. In her dream Solomon comes to her door, but she answers too late—he is gone. She panics and searches for him late at night in Jerusalem. Upon his return, Solomon assures her of his love and praises her beauty (6:4—7:10). The Shulamite begins to think of her country home and tries to persuade her beloved to return there with her (7:11—8:4). The journey takes place in 8:5-7 and their relationship continues to deepen. Their love will not be overthrown by jealousy or circumstances. At her homecoming (8:8-14) the Shulamite reflects on her brothers' care for her when she was young (8:8, 9). She remains virtuous ("I *am* a wall," 8:10) and is now in a position to look out for her brothers' welfare (8:11, 12). The song concludes with a dual invitation of lover and beloved (8:13, 14).

OUTLINE OF SONG OF SOLOMON

CHAPTER 1

Bride's Longing for Affection

THE song of songs, which *is* Solomon's.
2 Let him kiss me with the kisses of his mouth: for thy love *is* better than wine.
3 Because of the savour of thy good ointments thy name *is as* ointment poured forth, therefore do the virgins love thee.
4 Draw me, we will run after thee: ᴿthe king hath brought me into his chambers: we will be glad and rejoice in thee, we will remember thy ᴿlove more than wine: the upright love thee.   Ps. 45:14, 15 • *v.* 1; 4:10
5 I *am* black, but comely, O ye daughters of Jerusalem, as the ᴿtents of ᴿKe'-dar, as the curtains of Solomon.   Ps. 120:5 • Is. 60:7
6 Look not upon me, because I *am* black, because the sun hath looked upon me: my ᴿmother's children were angry with me; they

made me the keeper of the vineyards; *but* mine own vineyard have I not kept.   Ps. 69:8
7 Tell me, O thou whom my soul loveth, where thou feedest, where thou ᴿmakest *thy* flock to rest at noon: for why should I be ᵀas one that turneth aside by the flocks of thy companions?   2:16; 3:1-4 • *bashful*
8 If thou know not, ᴿO thou fairest among women, go thy way forth by the footsteps of the flock, and feed thy kids beside the shepherds' tents.   5:9; 6:1

Expressions of Mutual Love

9 I have compared thee, O my love, to a company of horses in Pharaoh's chariots.
10 Thy cheeks are comely with rows *of jewels,* thy neck with chains *of gold.*
11 We will make thee ᵀborders of gold with ᵀstuds of silver.   *ornaments • beads*

12 While the king *sitteth* at his table, my spikenard sendeth forth the smell thereof.

13 A bundle of ᴿmyrrh *is* my wellbeloved unto me; he shall lie all night betwixt my breasts.   Ps. 45:8; John 19:39

14 My beloved *is* unto me *as* a cluster of camphire in the vineyards of En-ge'-di.

15 Behold, thou *art* fair, my love; behold, thou *art* fair; thou *hast* doves' eyes.

16 Behold, thou *art* fair, my beloved, yea, pleasant: also our ᵀbed *is* green.   *couch*

17 The beams of our house *are* ᴿcedar, *and* our rafters of fir.   1 Kin. 6:9, 10; Jer. 22:14

CHAPTER 2

I AM the ᴿrose of ᴿShar'-on, *and* the ᴿlily of the valleys.   Is. 35:1 · Is. 33:9; 35:2 · 5:13; 7:2

2 As the lily among thorns, so *is* ᴿmy love among the daughters.   1:9

3 As the apple tree among the trees of the wood, so *is* my beloved among the sons. I sat down under his shadow with great delight, and his fruit *was* sweet to my taste.

4 He brought me to the banqueting house, and his banner over me *was* love.

5 Stay me with flagons, comfort me with apples: for I *am* ᵀsick of love.   *faint*

6 ᴿHis left hand *is* under my head, and his right hand doth embrace me.   8:3

7 ᴿIᵀ charge you, O ye daughters of Jerusalem, by the roes, and by the hinds of the field, that ye stir not up, nor awake *my* love, till he please.   3:5; 8:4 · *I put you on oath*

Visit of the King to the Bride's Home

8 The voice of my beloved! behold, he cometh leaping ᴿupon the mountains, skipping upon the hills.   *v.* 17; Is. 52:7

9 My beloved is like a roe or a young hart: behold, he standeth behind our wall, he looketh forth at the windows, shewing himself through the lattice.

10 My beloved spake, and said unto me, ᴿRise up, my love, my fair one, and come away.   *v.* 13

11 For, lo, the winter is past, the rain is over *and* gone;

12 The flowers appear on the earth; the time of the singing *of birds* is come, and the voice of the turtle is heard in our land;

13 The ᴿfig tree putteth forth her green figs, and the ᴿvines *with* the tender grape give a *good* smell. Arise, my love, my fair one, and come away.   Matt. 24:32 · 7:12

14 O my dove, *that art* in the clefts of the rock, in the secret *places* of the stairs, let me see thy ᵀcountenance, let me hear thy voice; for sweet *is* thy voice, and thy ᵀcountenance *is* comely.   *face · face is lovely*

15 Take us ᴿthe foxes, the little foxes, that spoil the vines: for our ᴿvines *have* tender grapes.   Luke 13:32 · *v.* 13

16 ᴿMy beloved *is* mine, and I *am* his: he ᴿfeedeth among the lilies.   6:3; 7:10 · 4:5

17 ᴿUntil the day break, and the shadows flee away, turn, my beloved, and be thou like a ᴿroe or a young hart ᴿupon the mountains ᵀof Be'-ther.   4:6 · *v.* 9 · *v.* 8 · *of division*

CHAPTER 3

Bride's Dream of Separation

BY ᴿnight on my bed I sought him ᴿwhom my soul loveth: I ᴿsought him, but I found him not.   Is. 26:9 · 1:7 · 5:6

2 I will rise now, and go about the city in the ᴿstreets, and in the broad ways I will seek him whom my soul loveth: I sought him, but I found him not.   Jer. 5:1

3 ᴿThe watchmen that go about the city found me: *to whom I said,* Saw ye him whom my soul loveth?   5:7

4 *It was* but a little that I passed from them, but I found him whom my soul loveth: I held him, and would not let him go, until I had ᴿbrought him into my mother's house, and into the ᵀchamber of her that conceived me.   8:2 · *room*

5 ᴿI charge you, O ye daughters of Jerusalem, by the ᴿroes, and by the hinds of the field, that ye stir not up, nor awake *my* love, till he please.   8:4 · 2:7

Wedding Procession

6 ᴿWho *is* this that cometh out of the wilderness like ᴿpillars of smoke, perfumed with ᴿmyrrh and frankincense, with all powders of the merchant?   8:5 · Ex. 13:21 · 1:13

7 Behold his ᵀbed,ᴿ which *is* Solomon's; threescore valiant men *are* about it, of the valiant of Israel.   *litter* · Amos 6:4

8 They all hold swords, *being* ᵀexpert in war: every man *hath* his sword upon his thigh because of fear in the night.   *skilled*

9 King Solomon made himself ᵀa chariot of the wood of Leb'-a-non.   *a bed*

10 He made the pillars thereof *of* silver, the bottom thereof *of* gold, the covering of it *of* purple, the midst thereof being paved *with* love, for the daughters of Jerusalem.

11 Go forth, O ye ᴿdaughters of Zion, and behold king Solomon with the crown wherewith his mother crowned him in the day of his espousals, and ᴿin the day of the gladness of his heart.   Is. 3:16, 17; 4:4 · Is. 62:5

CHAPTER 4

Bride's Beauty Is Praised

BEHOLD, thou *art* fair, my love; behold, thou *art* fair; thou *hast* doves' eyes within thy locks: ᴿthy hair *is* as a flock of goats, that appear from mount Gil'-e-ad.   6:7

2 Thy teeth *are* like a flock *of sheep that are even* shorn, which came up from the washing; whereof every one bear twins, and none *is* barren among them.

3 Thy lips *are* like a thread of scarlet, and thy speech *is* comely: thy temples *are* like a piece of a pomegranate within thy locks.

4 ᴿThy neck *is* like the tower of David builded ᴿfor an armoury, whereon there ᴿhang a thousand bucklers, all shields of mighty men.   7:4 • Neh. 3:19 • Ezek. 27:10, 11

5 Thy two breasts *are* like two young roes that are twins, which feed among the lilies.

6 Until the day break, and the shadows flee away, I will get me to the mountain of myrrh, and to the hill of frankincense.

7 ᴿThou *art* all fair, my love; *there is* no ᴿspot in thee.   1:15 • Eph. 5:27

8 Come with me from Leb′-a-non, *my* spouse, with me from Leb′-a-non: look from the top of Am′-a-na, from the top of She′-nir and Hermon, from the lions' dens, from the mountains of the leopards.

9 Thou hast ravished my heart, ᴿmy sister, *my* spouse; thou hast ravished my heart with one of thine eyes, with ᴿone chain of thy neck.   *vv.* 10, 12; 5:1 • Gen. 41:42

10 How fair is thy love, my sister, *my* spouse! ᴿhow much better is thy love than wine! and the ᵀsmell of thine ᵀointments than all spices!   1:2 • *fragrance • perfume*

11 Thy lips, O *my* spouse, drop *as* the honeycomb: ᴿhoney and milk *are* under thy tongue; and the smell of thy garments *is* like the smell of Leb′-a-non.   Prov. 24:13

12 A garden inclosed *is* my sister, *my* spouse; a spring shut up, a fountain sealed.

13 Thy plants *are* an ᴿorchard of pomegranates, with pleasant fruits; ᵀcamphire, with spikenard,   Eccl. 2:5 • *henna*

14 Spikenard and saffron; calamus and cinnamon, with all trees of frankincense; myrrh and aloes, with all the chief spices:

15 A fountain of gardens, a well of living waters, and streams from Leb′-a-non.

The Marriage Is Consummated

16 Awake, O north wind; and come, thou south; blow upon my garden, *that* the spices thereof may flow out. Let my beloved come into his garden, and eat his pleasant fruits.

CHAPTER 5

I AM come into my garden, my sister, *my* spouse: I have gathered my myrrh with my spice; I have eaten my honeycomb with my honey; I have drunk my wine with my milk: eat, O friends; drink, yea, drink abundantly, O beloved.

Bride's Second Dream of Separation

2 I sleep, but my heart waketh: *it is* the voice of my beloved that knocketh, *saying,*

Open to me, my sister, my love, my dove, my undefiled: for my head is filled with dew, *and* my locks with the drops of the night.

3 I have ᴿput off my coat; how shall I put it on? I have ᴿwashed my feet; how shall I ᵀdefile them?   Luke 11:7 • Gen. 19:2 • *soil*

4 My beloved put in his hand by the hole of the door, and my ᴿbowelsᵀ were moved for him.   Jer. 31:20 • *feelings*

5 I rose up to open to my beloved; and my hands ᴿdropped *with* myrrh, and my fingers *with* sweet smelling myrrh, upon the handles of the lock.   *v.* 13

6 I opened to my beloved; but my beloved had withdrawn himself, *and* was gone: my soul failed when he spake: I sought him, but I could not find him; I called him, but he gave me no answer.

7 ᴿThe watchmen that went about the city found me, they smote me, they wounded me; the keepers of the walls took away my veil from me.   3:3

Bridegroom's Handsomeness Is Praised

8 I charge you, O daughters of Jerusalem, if ye find my beloved, that ye tell him, that I *am* ᵀsick of love.   *faint with desire*

9 What *is* thy beloved more than *another* beloved, ᴿO thou fairest among women? what *is* thy beloved more than *another* beloved, that thou dost so charge us?   1:8

10 My beloved *is* white and ruddy, the ᵀchiefest among ten thousand.   *leader*

11 His head *is as* the most fine gold, his locks *are* bushy, *and* black as a raven.

12 ᴿHis eyes *are* as *the eyes* of doves by the rivers of waters, washed with milk, *and* ᵀfitly set.   1:15; 4:1 • *beautiful*

13 His cheeks *are* as a ᴿbed of spices, *as* ᵀsweet flowers: his lips *like* ᴿlilies, ᴿdropping sweet smelling myrrh.   6:2 • *fragrant* • 2:1 • v. 5

14 His hands *are as* gold rings set with the ᴿberyl: his belly *is as* bright ivory overlaid *with* sapphires.   Ex. 28:20; 39:13

15 His legs *are as* pillars of marble, set upon sockets of fine gold: his countenance *is* as Leb′-a-non, excellent as the cedars.

16 His mouth *is* most sweet: yea, he *is* altogether lovely. This *is* my beloved, and this *is* my friend, O daughters of Jerusalem.

CHAPTER 6

WHITHER is thy beloved gone, ᴿO thou fairest among women? whither is thy beloved turned aside? that we may seek him with thee.   1:8; 5:6

2 My beloved is gone down into his ᴿgarden, to the beds of spices, to feed in the gardens, and to gather lilies.   4:16; 5:1

3 ᴿI *am* my beloved's, and my beloved *is* mine: he feedeth among the lilies.   2:16; 7:10

Bride's Beauty Is Praised

4 [R]Thou *art* beautiful, O my love, as [R]Tir'-zah, comely as Jerusalem, [T]terrible as *an army* with banners.   1:15 • 1 Kin. 14:17 • *glorious*

5 Turn away thine eyes from me, for they have overcome me: thy hair *is* as a flock of goats that appear from Gil'-e-ad.

6 [R]Thy teeth *are* as a flock of sheep which go up from the washing, whereof every one beareth twins, and *there is* not one [T]barren among them.   4:2 • *missing*

7 [R]As a piece of a pomegranate *are* thy temples within thy [T]locks.   4:3 • *veil*

8 There are threescore [R]queens, and fourscore concubines, and [R]virgins without number.   1 Kin. 11:3 • 1:3

9 My dove, my [T]undefiled is *but* one; she *is* the *only* one of her mother, she *is* the choice one of her that bare her. The daughters saw her, and blessed her; *yea*, the queens and the concubines, and they praised her.   *pure one*

10 Who *is* she *that* looketh forth as the morning, fair as the moon, clear as the sun, *and* terrible as *an army* with banners?

11 I went down into the garden of nuts to see the fruits of the valley, *and* [R]to see whether the vine flourished, *and* the [R]pomegranates budded.   7:12 • 4:13

12 Or ever I was aware, my soul made me *like* the chariots of Am-mi'-na-dib.

13 Return, return, O Shu'-lam-ite; return, return, that we may look upon thee. What will ye see in the Shu'-lam-ite? As it were the company of two armies.

CHAPTER 7

H OW beautiful are thy feet with shoes, [R]O prince's daughter! the joints of thy thighs *are* like jewels, the work of the hands of a cunning workman.   Ps. 45:13

2 Thy navel *is like* a round goblet, *which* wanteth not liquor: thy belly *is like* an heap of wheat set about with lilies.

3 [R]Thy two breasts *are* like two young roes *that are* twins.   4:5

4 [R]Thy neck *is* as a tower of ivory; thine eyes *like* the fishpools in [R]Hesh'-bon, by the gate of Bath-rab'-bim: thy nose *is* as the tower of Leb'-a-non which looketh toward Damascus.   4:4 • Num. 21:26

5 Thine head upon thee *is* like Carmel, and the hair of thine head like purple; the king *is* [T]held in the galleries.   *enslaved*

6 How [R]fair and how pleasant art thou, O love, for delights!   1:15, 16; 4:10

7 This thy stature is like to a palm tree, and thy breasts to clusters *of grapes*.

8 I said, I will go up to the palm tree, I will take hold of the boughs thereof: now also thy breasts shall be as clusters of the vine, and the smell of thy nose like apples;

9 And the roof of thy mouth like the best wine for my beloved, that goeth *down* sweetly, causing the lips of those that are asleep to speak.

10 [R]I *am* my beloved's, and [R]his desire *is* toward me.   2:16; 6:3 • Ps. 45:11

Bride's Desire to Visit Her Home

11 Come, my beloved, let us go forth into the field; let us lodge in the villages.

12 Let us get up early to the vineyards; let us [R]see if the vine flourish, *whether* the tender grape appear, *and* the pomegranates bud forth: there will I give thee my loves.   6:11

13 The [R]mandrakes give a smell, and at our gates [R]*are* all manner of pleasant *fruits*, new and old, *which* I have laid up for thee, O my beloved.   Gen. 30:14 • 2:3; 4:13

CHAPTER 8

O THAT thou *wert* as my brother, that sucked the breasts of my mother! *when* I should find thee without, I would kiss thee; yea, I should not be despised.

2 I would lead thee, *and* bring thee into my mother's house, *who* would instruct me: I would cause thee to drink of spiced wine of the juice of my pomegranate.

3 [R]His left hand *should be* under my head, and his right hand should embrace me.   2:6

4 [R]I charge you, O daughters of Jerusalem, that ye stir not up, nor awake *my* love, until he please.   2:7; 3:5

Journey and Homecoming

5 [R]Who *is* this that cometh up from the wilderness, leaning upon her beloved? I raised thee up under the [R]apple tree: there thy mother brought thee forth: there she brought thee forth *that* bare thee.   3:6 • 2:3

6 Set me as a seal upon thine heart, as a [R]seal upon thine arm: for love *is* strong as death; jealousy *is* cruel as the grave: the coals thereof *are* coals of fire, *which hath* a most vehement flame.   Is. 49:16

7 Many waters cannot quench love, neither can the floods drown it: if a man would give all the substance of his house for love, it would utterly be contemned.

8 We [R]have a little sister, and she hath no breasts: what shall we do for our sister in the day when she shall be spoken for?   Ezek. 16:7

9 If she *be* a wall, we will build upon her a palace of silver: and if she *be* a door, we will inclose her with boards of cedar.

10 I *am* a wall, and my breasts like towers: then was I in his eyes as one that found [T]favour.   *peace*

11 Solomon had a vineyard at Ba'-al-ha'-mon; he let out the vineyard unto keepers; every one for the fruit thereof was to bring a [T]thousand *pieces* of silver. $128,000

12 My vineyard, which *is* mine, *is* before me: thou, O Solomon, *must have* a thousand, and those that keep the fruit thereof two hundred.

13 Thou that dwellest in the gardens, the

[R]companions hearken to thy voice: [R]cause me to hear *it*.   1:7 · 2:14

14 [T]Make haste, my beloved, and [R]be thou like to a roe or to a young hart upon the mountains of spices.   *hurry* · 2:17

The Jewish Calendar

The Jews used two kinds of calendars:
   Civil Calendar—official calendar of kings, childbirth, and contracts.
   Sacred Calendar—from which festivals were computed.

NAMES OF MONTHS	CORRESPONDS WITH	NO. OF DAYS	MONTH OF CIVIL YEAR	MONTH OF SACRED YEAR	
TISHRI	Sept.–Oct.	30 days	1st	7th	The Jewish day was from sunset to sunset, in 8 equal parts:
HESHVAN	Oct.–Nov.	29 or 30	2nd	8th	
CHISLEV	Nov.–Dec.	29 or 30	3rd	9th	
TEBETH	Dec.–Jan.	29	4th	10th	FIRST WATCH ..... SUNSET TO 9 P.M.
SHEBAT	Jan.–Feb.	30	5th	11th	SECOND WATCH ... 9 P.M. TO MIDNIGHT
ADAR	Feb.–Mar.	29 or 30	6th	12th	THIRD WATCH ..... MIDNIGHT TO 3 A.M.
NISAN	Mar.–Apr.	30	7th	1st	FOURTH WATCH ... 3 A.M. TO SUNRISE
IYAR	Apr.–May	29	8th	2nd	
SIVAN	May–June	30	9th	3rd	FIRST WATCH ..... SUNRISE TO 9 A.M.
TAMMUZ	June–July	29	10th	4th	SECOND WATCH ... 9 A.M. TO NOON
AB	July–Aug.	30	11th	5th	THIRD WATCH ..... NOON TO 3 P.M.
*ELUL	Aug.–Sept.	29	12th	6th	FOURTH WATCH ... 3 P.M. TO SUNSET

*Hebrew months were alternately 30 and 29 days long. Their year, shorter than ours, had 354 days. Therefore, about every 3 years (7 times in 19 years) an extra 29-day-month, VEADAR, was added between ADAR and NISAN.

ISAIAH

THE BOOK OF ISAIAH

Isaiah is like a miniature Bible. The first thirty-nine chapters (like the thirty-nine books of the Old Testament) are filled with judgment upon immoral and idolatrous men. Judah has sinned; the surrounding nations have sinned; the whole earth has sinned. Judgment must come, for God cannot allow such blatant sin to go unpunished forever. But the final twenty-seven chapters (like the twenty-seven books of the New Testament) declare a message of hope. The Messiah is coming as a Saviour and a Sovereign to bear a cross and to wear a crown.

Isaiah's prophetic ministry, spanning the reigns of four kings of Judah, covers at least forty years. *Yesha'yahu* and its shortened form *yeshaiah* mean "Yahweh Is Salvation." This name is an excellent summary of the contents of the book. The Greek form in the Septuagint is *Hesaias*, and the Latin form is *Esaias* or *Isaias*.

THE AUTHOR OF ISAIAH

Isaiah, the "St. Paul of the Old Testament," was evidently from a distinguished Jewish family. His education is evident in his impressive vocabulary and style. His work is comprehensive in scope and beautifully communicated. Isaiah maintained close contact with the royal court, but his exhortations against alliances with foreign powers were not always well received. This great poet and prophet was uncompromising, sincere, and compassionate. His wife was a prophetess and he fathered at least two sons (7:3; 8:3). He spent most of his time in Jerusalem, and talmudic tradition says his persecutors sawed him in two during the reign of Manasseh (cf. Heb. 11:37).

The unity of this book has been challenged by critics who hold that a "Deutero-Isaiah" wrote chapters 40—66 after the Babylonian captivity. They argue that 1—39 has an Assyrian background, while 40—66 is set against a Babylonian background. But Babylon is mentioned more than twice as often in 1—39 as in 40—66. The only shift is one of perspective from present time to future time. Critics also argue that there are radical differences in the language, style, and theology of the two sections. Actually, the resemblances between 1—39 and 40—66 are greater than the differences. These include similarities in thoughts, images, rhetorical ornaments, characteristic expressions, and local coloring. It is true that the first section is more terse and rational, while the second section is more flowing and emotional, but much of this is caused by the different subject matter, condemnation versus consolation. Critics often forget that content, time, and circumstances typically affect any author's style. In addition, there is no theological contradiction between the emphasis on the Messiah as King in 1—39 and as suffering Servant in 40—66. While the thrust is different, the Messiah is seen in both sections as Servant and King. Another critical argument is that Isaiah could not have predicted the Babylonian captivity and the return under Cyrus (mentioned by name in 44 and 45) 150 years in advance. This view is based on the mere assumption that divine prophecy is impossible, rejecting the predictive claims of the book (see 42:9). The theory cannot explain the amazing messianic prophecies of Isaiah that were literally fulfilled in the life of Christ (see "The Christ of Isaiah").

The unity of Isaiah is supported by the book of Ecclesiasticus, the Septuagint, and the Talmud. The New Testament also claims that Isaiah wrote both sections. John 12:37—41 quotes from Isaiah 6:9, 10 and 53:1 and attributes it all to Isaiah. In Romans 9:27 and 10:16-21, Paul quotes from Isaiah 10, 53, and 65 and gives the credit to Isaiah. The same is true of Matthew 3:3 and 12:17-21, Luke 3:4-6, and Acts 8:28.

If 40—66 was written by another prophet after the events took place, it is a misleading and deceptive work. Furthermore, it would lead to the strange conclusion that Israel's greatest prophet is the only writing prophet of the Old Testament to go unnamed.

THE TIME OF ISAIAH

Isaiah's long ministry ranged from about 740 to 680 B.C. (1:1). He began his ministry near the end of Uzziah's reign (790-739 B.C.) and continued through the reigns of Jotham (739-731 B.C.), Ahaz (731-715 B.C.), and Hezekiah (715-686 B.C.). Assyria was growing in power under Tiglath-pileser who turned toward the west after his conquests in the east. He plucked up the small nations that dotted the Mediterranean coast including Israel and much of Judah. Isaiah lived during this time of military threat to Judah, and warned its kings against trusting in alliances with other countries rather than the power of Yahweh. As a contemporary of Hosea and Micah, he prophesied during the last years of the northern kingdom but ministered to the southern kingdom of Judah who was following the sins of her sister Israel. After Israel's demise in 722 B.C., he warned Judah of judgment not by Assyria but by Babylonia, even though Babylonia had not yet risen to power.

Isaiah ministered from the time of Tiglath-pileser (745-727 B.C.) to the time of Sennacherib (705-681 B.C.) of Assyria. He outdated Hezekiah

by a few years because 37:38 records the death of Sennacherib in 681 B.C. Hezekiah was succeeded by his wicked son Manasseh who overthrew the worship of Yahweh and no doubt opposed the work of Isaiah.

✝ THE CHRIST OF ISAIAH

When he speaks about Christ, Isaiah sounds more like a New Testament writer than an Old Testament prophet. His messianic prophecies are clearer and more explicit than those in any other Old Testament book. They describe many aspects of the person and work of Christ in His first and second advents, and often blend the two together. Here are a few of the Christological prophecies with their New Testament fulfillments: 7:14 (Matt. 1:22, 23); 9:1, 2 (Matt. 4:12–16); 9:6 (Luke 2:11; Eph. 2:14–18); 11:1 (Luke 3:23, 32; Acts 13:22, 23); 11:2 (Luke 3:22); 28:16 (1 Pet. 2:4–6); 40:3–5 (Matt. 3:1–3); 42:1–4 (Matt. 12:15–21); 42:6 (Luke 2:29–32); 50:6 (Matt. 26:67; 27:26, 30); 52:14 (Phil. 2:7–11); 53:3 (Luke 23:18; John 1:11; 7:5); 53:4, 5 (Rom. 5:6, 8); 53:7 (Matt. 27:12–14; John 1:29; 1 Pet. 1:18, 19); 53:9 (Matt. 27:57–60); 53:12 (Mark 15:28); 61:1, 2 (Luke 4:17–19, 21). The Old Testament has over three hundred prophecies about the first advent of Christ, and Isaiah contributes a number of them. The odds that even ten of them could be fulfilled by one person is a statistical marvel. Isaiah's messianic prophecies that await fulfillment in the Lord's second advent include: 4:2; 11:2–6, 10; 32:1–8; 49:7; 52:13, 15; 59:20, 21; 60:1–3; 61:2, 3.

Isaiah 52:13—53:12 is the central passage of the consolation section (40—66). Its five stanzas present five different aspects of the saving work of Christ: (1) 52:13–15—His wholehearted sacrifice (burnt offering); (2) 53:1–3—His perfect character (meal offering); (3) 53:4–6—He brought atonement that issues in peace with God (peace offering); (4) 53:7–9—He paid for the transgression of the people (sin offering); (5) 53:10–12—He died for the effects of sin (trespass offering).

🗝 KEYS TO ISAIAH

Key Word: Salvation Is of The Lord—
The basic theme of this book is found in Isaiah's name: "Salvation Is of the Lord." The word *salvation* appears twenty-six times in Isaiah but only seven times in all the other prophets combined. Chapters 1—39 portray man's great need for salvation, and chapters 40—66 reveal God's great provision of salvation. Salvation is of God, not man; and He is seen as the supreme Ruler, the sovereign Lord of history, and the only Saviour. Isaiah solemnly warns Judah of approaching judgment because of moral depravity, political corruption, social injustice, and especially spiritual idolatry. Because the nation does not turn away from its sinful practice, Isaiah announces the ultimate overthrow of Judah. Nevertheless, God will remain faithful to His covenant by preserving a godly remnant and promises salvation and deliverance through the coming Messiah. The Saviour will come out of Judah and accomplish the dual work of redemption and restoration. The Gentiles will come to His light and universal blessing will finally take place.

Key Verses: Isaiah 9:6, 7 and 53:6—"For unto us a child is born, unto us a son is given: and the government shall be upon his shoulder: and his name shall be called Wonderful, Counsellor, The mighty God, The everlasting Father, The Prince of Peace. Of the increase of *his* government and peace *there shall be* no end, upon the throne of David, and upon his kingdom, to order it, and to establish it with judgment and with justice from henceforth even for ever. The zeal of the LORD of hosts will perform this" (9:6, 7).

"All we like sheep have gone astray; we have turned every one to his own way; and the LORD hath laid on him the iniquity of us all" (53:6).

FOCUS	PROPHECIES OF CONDEMNATION				HISTORICAL PARENTHESIS	PROPHECIES OF COMFORT		
REFERENCE	1:1———13:1———		24:1———28:1———		36:1———	40:1———49:1———		58:1–66:24
DIVISION	PROPHECIES AGAINST		PROPHECIES OF		HEZEKIAH'S SALVATION, SICKNESS, AND SIN	ISRAEL'S DELIVERANCE	ISRAEL'S DELIVERER	ISRAEL'S GLORIOUS FUTURE
	JUDAH	THE NATIONS	DAY OF LORD	JUDGMENT & BLESSING				
TOPIC	PROPHETIC				HISTORIC	MESSIANIC		
	JUDGMENT				TRANSITION	HOPE		
LOCATION	ISRAEL AND JUDAH							
TIME	c. 740–680 B.C.							

Key Chapter: Isaiah 53—Along with Psalm 22, Isaiah 53 lists the most remarkable and specific prophecies of the atonement of the Messiah. Fulfilling each clear prophecy, the Jewish nation later proved the messiahship of Jesus.

SURVEY OF ISAIAH

Isaiah, the "Shakespeare of the prophets," has often been called the "evangelical prophet" because of his incredibly clear and detailed messianic prophecies. The "gospel according to Isaiah" has three major sections: prophecies of condemnation (1—35), historical parenthesis (36—39), and prophecies of comfort (40—66).

Prophecies of Condemnation (1—35): Isaiah's first message of condemnation is aimed at his own countrymen in Judah (1—12). Chapter 1 is a capsulized message of the entire book. Judah is riddled with moral and spiritual disease; the people are neglecting God as they bow to ritualism and selfishness. But Yahweh graciously invites them to repent and return to Him because this is their only hope of avoiding judgment. Isaiah's call to proclaim God's message is found in chapter 6, and this is followed by the book of Immanuel (7—12). These chapters repeatedly refer to the Messiah (see 7:14; 8:14; 9:2, 6, 7; 11:1, 2) and anticipate the blessing of His future reign.

The prophet moves from local to regional judgment as he proclaims a series of oracles against the surrounding nations (13—23). The eleven nations are Babylon, Assyria, Philistia, Moab, Damascus (Syria), Ethiopia, Egypt, Babylon (again), Edom, Arabia, Jerusalem (Judah), and Tyre. Isaiah's little apocalypse (24—27) depicts universal tribulation followed by the blessings of the kingdom. Chapters 28—33 pronounce six woes on Israel and Judah for specific sins. Isaiah's prophetic condemnation closes with a general picture of international devastation that will precede universal blessing (34 and 35).

Historical Parenthesis (36—39): This historical parenthesis looks back to the Assyrian invasion of Judah in 701 B.C. and anticipates the coming Babylonian invasion of Judah. Judah escapes captivity by Assyria (36 and 37; 2 Kin. 18 and 19), but they will not escape from the hands of Babylon (38 and 39; 2 Kin. 20). God answers King Hezekiah's prayers and delivers Judah from Assyrian destruction by Sennacherib. Hezekiah also turns to the Lord in his illness and is granted a fifteen-year extension of his life. But he foolishly shows all his treasures to the Babylonian messengers, and Isaiah tells him that the Babylonians will one day carry his treasure and descendants to their land.

Prophecies of Comfort (40—66): Having pronounced Judah's divine condemnation, Isaiah comforts them with God's promises of hope and restoration. The basis for this hope is the sovereignty and majesty of God (40—48). Of the 216 verses in these nine chapters, 115 speak of God's greatness and power. The Creator is contrasted with idols, the creations of men. His sovereign character is Judah's assurance of future restoration. Babylon will indeed carry them off; but Babylon will finally be judged and destroyed, and God's people will be released from captivity.

Chapters 49—57 concentrate on the coming Messiah who will be their Saviour and suffering Servant. This rejected but exalted One will pay for their iniquities and usher in a kingdom of peace and righteousness throughout the earth. All who acknowledge their sins and trust in Him will be delivered (58—66). In that day Jerusalem will be rebuilt, Israel's borders will be enlarged, and the Messiah will reign in Zion. God's people will confess their sins and His enemies will be judged. Peace, prosperity, and justice will prevail, and God will make all things new.

OUTLINE OF ISAIAH

Part One: Prophecies of Condemnation (1:1—35:10)

Part Two: The Historical Parenthesis (36:1—39:8)

Part Three: The Prophecies of Comfort (40:1—66:24)

CHAPTER 1

The Judgment of Judah

THE vision of Isaiah the son of Amoz, which he saw concerning Judah and Jerusalem in the days of Uz-zi'-ah, Jo'-tham, Ahaz, and Hez-e-ki'-ah, kings of Judah.

2 ᴿHear, O heavens, and give ear, O ᴿearth: for the LORD hath spoken, I have nourished and brought up children, and they have rebelled against me.   Jer. 2:12 • Mic. 1:2

3 The ox knoweth his owner, and the ass his master's crib: but Israel doth not know, my people doth not consider.

4 Ah sinful nation, a people laden with iniquity, a seed of evildoers, children that are corrupters: they have forsaken the LORD, they have provoked the Holy One of Israel unto anger, they are gone away backward.

5 Why should ye be stricken any more? ye will revolt more and more: the whole head is sick, and the whole heart faint.

6 From the sole of the foot even unto the head there is no soundness in it; but wounds,

and bruises, and putrifying sores: they have not been ^{T}closed, neither bound up, neither mollified with ointment.   *healed*

7 Your country is desolate, ^{R}your cities are burned with fire: your land, strangers ^{T}devour it in your presence, and it is desolate, as overthrown by strangers.   2 Chr. 36:19 · *destroy*

8 And the daughter of Zion is left as a ^{T}cottage in a vineyard, as a lodge in a garden of cucumbers, as a besieged city.   *booth*

9 ^{R}Except the LORD of hosts had left unto us a very small remnant, we should have been as ^{R}Sodom, *and* we should have been like unto Go-mor'-rah.   Lam. 3:22 · Gen. 19:24

10 Hear the word of the LORD, ye rulers ^{R}of Sodom; give ear unto the law of our God, ye people of Go-mor'-rah.   Deut. 32:32

11 To what purpose *is* the multitude of your sacrifices unto me? saith the LORD: I am full of the burnt offerings of rams, and the fat of fed beasts; and I delight not in the blood of bullocks, or of lambs, or of he goats.

12 When ye come ^{R}to appear before me, who hath required this at your hand, to ^{T}tread my courts?   Ex. 23:17 · *trample*

13 Bring no more vain ^{T}oblations; incense is an abomination unto me; the new moons and sabbaths, the calling of assemblies, I cannot away with; *it is* iniquity, even the solemn meeting.   *offerings*

14 Your new moons and your ^{R}appointed feasts my soul hateth: they are a trouble unto me; I am weary to bear *them*.   Lam. 2:6

15 And when ye spread forth your hands, I will hide mine eyes from you: yea, when ye make many prayers, I will not hear: your hands are full of ^{T}blood.   *evil deeds*

16 ^{R}Wash you, make you clean; put away the evil of your doings from before mine eyes; ^{R}cease to do evil;   Jer. 4:14 · Rom. 12:9

17 Learn to do well; seek judgment, ^{T}relieve the oppressed, judge the fatherless, plead for the widow.   *deal righteously with*

18 Come now, and ^{R}let us reason together, saith the LORD: though your sins be as scarlet, ^{R}they shall be as white as snow; though they be red like crimson, they shall be as wool.   41:1, 21; 43:26 · Ps. 51:7

19 ^{R}If ye be willing and obedient, ye shall eat the good of the land: Deut. 30:15, 16

20 But if ye refuse and rebel, ye shall be ^{T}devoured with the sword: ^{R}for the mouth of the LORD hath spoken it.   *destroyed* · [Titus 1:2]

21 How is the faithful city become an harlot! it was full of judgment; righteousness lodged in it; but now murderers.

22 ^{R}Thy silver is become ^{R}dross, thy wine mixed with water: Jer. 6:28 · Prov. 25:4

23 ^{R}Thy princes are rebellious, and companions of thieves: every one loveth ^{T}gifts, and followeth after rewards: they judge not the fatherless, neither doth the cause of the widow come unto them.   Hos. 9:15 · *bribes*

24 Therefore saith the Lord, the LORD of hosts, the mighty One of Israel, Ah, ^{R}I will ^{T}ease me of mine adversaries, and avenge me of mine enemies: Deut. 28:63 · *get rid of*

25 And I will turn my hand upon thee, and ^{R}purely^T purge away thy dross, and take away all thy tin: Mal. 3:3 · *thoroughly*

26 And I will restore thy judges as at the first, and thy counsellors as at the beginning: afterward thou shalt be called, The city of righteousness, the faithful city.

27 Zion shall be redeemed with judgment, and her converts with righteousness.

28 And the ^{R}destruction of the transgressors and of the sinners ^{R}shall be together, and they that forsake the LORD shall be ^{T}consumed.   Job 31:3 · [66:24] · *destroyed*

29 For they shall be ashamed of the ^{T}oaks which ye have ^{T}desired, and ye shall be ^{T}confounded for the gardens that ye have chosen.   *pagan shrines · chosen · brought to confusion*

30 For ye shall be as an oak whose leaf fadeth, and as a garden that hath no water.

31 ^{R}And the strong shall be as tow, and ^{T}the maker of it as a spark, and they shall both ^{R}burn together, and none shall quench them.   Ezek. 32:21 · *his work* · 5:24; 9:19

CHAPTER 2

The Day of the Lord

THE word that Isaiah the son of Amoz saw concerning Judah and Jerusalem.

2 And it shall come to pass in the last days, *that* the mountain of the LORD's house shall be established in the top of the mountains, and shall be exalted above the hills; and all nations shall flow unto it.

3 And many people shall go and say, ^{R}Come ye, and let us go up to the mountain of the LORD, to the house of the God of Jacob; and he will teach us of his ways, and we will walk in his paths: for out of Zion shall go forth the law, and the word of the LORD from Jerusalem.   Jer. 50:5 ☆

4 And he shall judge among the nations, and shall rebuke many people: and ^{R}they shall beat their swords into plowshares, and their spears into pruninghooks: nation shall not lift up sword against nation, neither shall they learn war any more.   Is. 32:17, 18 ☆

5 O house of Jacob, come ye, and let us ^{R}walk in the light of the LORD.   Eph. 5:8

6 Therefore thou hast forsaken thy people the house of Jacob, because they be replenished from the east, and *are* soothsayers like the Phi-lis'-tines, and they please themselves in the children of strangers.

7 ^{R}Their land also is full of silver and gold, neither *is there any* end of their treasures; their land is also full of horses, neither *is there any* end of their chariots: Deut. 17:16

8 ^{R}Their land also is full of idols; they

worship the work of their own hands, that which their own fingers have made: Jer. 2:28

9 And the ᵀmean ᴿman ᵀboweth down, and the great man humbleth himself: therefore forgive them not.   common • 5:15 • is humbled

10 ᴿEnter into the rock, and hide thee in the dust, for fear of the LORD, and for the glory of his majesty.   vv. 19, 20; Rev. 6:15

11 The ᵀlofty looks of man shall be humbled, and the haughtiness of men shall be bowed down, and the LORD alone shall be exalted ᴿin that day.   proud • Hos. 2:16

12 For the day of the LORD of hosts shall be upon every one that is proud and lofty, and upon ᴿevery one that is lifted up; and he shall be brought low: 24:4, 21; Job 40:11

13 And upon all ᴿthe cedars of Leb'-a-non, that are high and lifted up, and upon all the oaks of Ba'-shan,   14:8; 1 Kin. 4:33; Zech. 11:1, 2

14 And ᴿupon all the high mountains, and upon all the hills that are lifted up,   30:25

15 And upon every ᴿhigh tower, and upon every ᵀfenced wall,   25:12 • fortified

16 And upon all the ships of Tar'-shish, and upon all pleasant ᵀpictures.   imagery

17 And the ᵀloftiness of man shall be bowed down, and the ᴿhaughtiness of men shall be made low: and the LORD alone shall be exalted in that day.   pride; v. 11 • Ps. 10:2

18 And the idols he shall utterly abolish.

19 And they shall go into the ᴿholes of the rocks, and into the caves of the earth, ᴿfor fear of the LORD, and for the glory of his majesty, when he ariseth ᴿto shake terribly the earth.   [Rev. 9:6] • [2 Thess. 1:9] • Hag. 2:6, 21

20 In that day a man shall ᵀcast his idols of silver, and his idols of gold, which they made each one for himself to worship, to the moles and to the bats;   discard; 30:22

21 To go into the clefts of the rocks, and into the tops of the ragged rocks, for fear of the LORD, and for the glory of his majesty, when he ariseth to shake terribly the earth.

22 ᴿCease ye from man, whose ᴿbreath is in his nostrils: for wherein is he to be ᴿaccounted of?   Ps. 146:3 • Job 27:3 • 40:15, 17

CHAPTER 3

FOR, behold, the Lord, the LORD of hosts, doth take away from Jerusalem and from Judah the stay and the staff, the whole stay of bread, and the whole stay of water,

2 The ᴿmighty man, and the man of war, the judge, and the prophet, and the ᵀprudent, and the ᵀancient,   9:14, 15; 2 Kin. 24:14 • diviner • elder

3 The captain of fifty, and the honourable man, and the counsellor, and the cunning ᵀartificer, and the eloquent orator.   enchanter

4 And I will give children to be their princes, and babes shall rule over them.

5 And the people shall be oppressed, every one by another, and every one by his neighbour: the child shall behave himself proudly against the ᵀancient, and the ᵀbase against the honourable.   old man • frivolous

6 When a man shall ᴿtake hold of his brother of the house of his father, saying, Thou hast clothing, be thou our ruler, and let this ruin be under thy hand: 4:1

7 In that day shall he ᵀswear, saying, I will not be an ᵀhealer; for in my house is neither bread nor clothing: make me not a ruler of the people.   declare • helper; Ezek. 34:4

8 For ᴿJerusalem is ruined, and Judah is fallen: ᴿbecause their tongue and their doings are against the LORD, to provoke ᵀthe eyes of his glory.   Mic. 3:12 • 2 Chr. 36:16, 17 • his anger

9 The shew of their countenance doth witness against them; and they ᵀdeclare their sin as ᴿSodom, they hide it not. Woe unto their soul! for they have rewarded evil unto themselves.   reveal • Gen. 13:13

10 Say ye to the righteous, ᴿthat it shall be well with him: ᴿfor they shall eat the fruit of their doings.   [Eccl. 8:12] • Ps. 128:2

11 Woe unto the wicked! ᴿit shall be ill with him: ᴿfor the reward of his hands shall be ᵀgiven him.   [Ps. 11:6] • 65:6, 7 • his share

12 As for my people, ᴿchildren are their oppressors, and women rule over them. O my people, ᴿthey which lead thee cause thee to err, and destroy the way of thy paths.   v. 4 • 9:16

13 The LORD standeth up ᴿto plead, and standeth to judge the people.   Mic. 6:2

14 The LORD will ᴿenter into judgment with the ᵀancients of his people, and the princes thereof: for ye have ᵀeaten up ᴿthe vineyard; the spoil of the poor is in your houses.   Ezek. 20:35, 36 • elders • burnt • Matt. 21:33

15 What mean ye that ye ᴿbeat my people to pieces, and grind the faces of the poor? saith the Lord GOD of hosts.   Ps. 94:5

16 Moreover the LORD saith, Because the daughters of Zion are haughty, and walk with stretched forth necks and wanton eyes, walking and ᵀmincing as they go, and making a tinkling with their feet: tripping

17 Therefore the Lord will smite with ᴿa scab the crown of the head of the daughters of Zion, and the LORD will ᴿdiscoverᵀ their secret parts.   Deut. 28:27 • Jer. 13:22 • uncover

18 In that day the Lord will take away the ᵀbravery of their ᵀtinkling ornaments about their feet, and their ᵀcauls, and their round tires like the moon,   beauty • anklets • lace

19 The ᴿchains,ᵀ and the ᴿbracelets, and the ᵀmufflers,   Gen. 41:42 • earrings • Gen. 24:22 • vails

20 The ᴿbonnets, and the ornaments of the legs, and the ᵀheadbands, and the ᵀtablets, and the earrings,   Ex. 39:28 • sashes • perfume boxes

21 The rings, and ᴿnose jewels,   Gen. 24:47

22 The changeable suits of apparel, and the mantles, and the ᵀwimples, and the ᵀcrisping pins,   shawls • handbags

23 The ᵀglasses, and the fine linen, and the ᵀhoods, and the vails.   mirrors • turbans

24 And it shall come to pass, *that* instead of ᴿsweet smell there shall be stink; and instead of a girdle a ᵀrent; and instead of well set hair ᴿbaldness; and instead of a ᵀstomacher a girding of sackcloth; *and* burning instead of beauty.   Esth. 2:12 • *rope* • 22:12 • *robe*

25 Thy men shall ᴿfall by the sword, and thy mighty in the war.   1:20; 65:12

26 ᴿAnd her gates shall lament and mourn; and she *being* ᵀdesolate ᴿshall sit upon the ground.   Jer. 14:2 • *deserted* • Lam. 2:10

CHAPTER 4

AND ᴿin that day seven women shall take hold of one man, saying, We will eat our own bread, and wear our own apparel: only let us be called by thy name, to take away ᴿour reproach.   2:11, 17 • Luke 1:25

2 In that day shall the branch of the Lord be beautiful and glorious, and the fruit of the earth *shall be* excellent and comely for them that are escaped of Israel.

3 And it shall come to pass, *that he that is* ᴿleft in Zion, and *he that* remaineth in Jerusalem, ᴿshall be called holy, *even* every one that is ᴿwritten among the living in Jerusalem: Rom. 11:4, 5 • 60:21 • Phil. 4:3

4 When the Lord shall have washed away the filth of the daughters of Zion, and shall have purged the blood of Jerusalem from the midst thereof by the spirit of judgment, and by the spirit of burning.

5 And the Lord will create upon every dwelling place of mount Zion, and upon her assemblies, a cloud and smoke by day, and the shining of a flaming fire by night: for ᵀupon all the glory *shall be* a defence.   over

6 And there shall be a tabernacle for a shadow in the daytime from the heat, and ᴿfor a place of refuge, and for a ᵀcovert from storm and from rain.   25:4 • *covering*

CHAPTER 5

The Parable of the Vineyard

NOW will I sing to my wellbeloved a song of my beloved touching his vineyard. My wellbeloved hath a ᴿvineyard in a very ᵀfruitful hill: Mark 12:1 • *fertile spot*

2 And he fenced it, and gathered out the stones thereof, and planted it with the choicest vine, and built a tower in the midst of it, and also made a winepress therein: and he looked that it should bring forth grapes, and it brought forth wild grapes.

3 And now, O inhabitants of Jerusalem, and men of Judah, ᴿjudge, I pray you, betwixt me and my vineyard.   Matt. 21:40

4 What could have been done more to my vineyard, that I have not done in it? wherefore, when I looked that it should bring forth grapes, brought it forth wild grapes?

5 And now ᵀgo to; I will tell you what I will do to my vineyard: I will take away the hedge thereof, and it shall be eaten up; *and* break ᴿdown the wall thereof, and it shall be trodden down: *listen to me* • 2 Chr. 36:19

6 And I will lay it waste: it shall not be pruned, nor digged; but there shall come up briers and thorns: I will also command the clouds that they rain no rain upon it.

7 For the vineyard of the Lord of hosts *is* the house of Israel, and the men of Judah his pleasant plant: and he looked for judgment, but behold oppression; for righteousness, but behold a cry.

8 Woe unto them that join ᴿhouse to house, *that* lay field to field, till *there be* no place, that they may be placed alone in the midst of the earth!   Jer. 22:13–17

9 In mine ears *said* the Lord of hosts, Of a truth many houses shall be desolate, *even* great and fair, without inhabitant.

10 Yea, ten acres of vineyard shall yield one ᵀbath, and the seed of an ᵀho′-mer shall yield an ᵀe′-phah.   6 gal. • 6.5 bu. • .65 bu.

11 Woe unto them that rise up early in the morning, *that* they may ᵀfollow ᴿstrong drink; that continue until night, *till* wine inflame them!   *devote themselves to* • Prov. 23:29, 30

12 And the harp, and the viol, the tabret, and pipe, and wine, are in their feasts: but they regard not the work of the Lord, neither consider the operation of his hands.

13 Therefore my people are gone into captivity, because *they have* no knowledge: and their honourable men *are* famished, and their multitude dried up with thirst.

14 Therefore hell hath enlarged herself, and opened her mouth without measure: and ᴿtheir glory, and their multitude, and their pomp, and he that rejoiceth, shall descend into it.   14:9

15 And ᴿthe mean man shall be brought down, and the mighty man shall be humbled, and ᴿthe eyes of the lofty shall be humbled: 2:9, 11 • 2:11; 10:33

16 But the ᴿLord of hosts shall be exalted in judgment, and God that is holy shall be sanctified in righteousness.   8:13; 1 Pet. 1:16

17 ᴿThen shall the lambs feed after their manner, and the waste places of the fat ones shall strangers eat.   7:25; Mic. 2:12

18 Woe unto them that ᴿdrawᵀ iniquity with cords of vanity, and sin as it were with a cart rope: 59:7, 8; Jer. 23:10–14 • *promote*

19 That say, Let him make speed, *and* hasten his work, that we may see *it:* and let the counsel of the Holy One of Israel draw nigh and come, that we may know *it!*

20 Woe unto them that ᴿcall evil good, and good evil; that put darkness for light, ᴿand

light for darkness; that put bitter for sweet, and sweet for bitter! Prov. 17:15 • 8:20

21 Woe unto *them that are* wise in their own eyes, and prudent in their own sight!

22 ᴿWoe unto *them that are* mighty to drink wine, and men of strength to mingle strong drink: v. 11; 56:12; Prov. 23:20; Hab. 2:15

23 Which justifyᵀ the wicked for ᵀreward, and take away the righteousness of the righteous from him! declare innocent • bribes

24 Therefore ᴿas ᵀthe fire devoureth the stubble, and the flame consumeth the chaff, so their root shall be as rottenness, and their blossom shall go up as dust: because they have cast away the law of the LORD of hosts, and despised the word of the Holy One of Israel. 9:18, 19; Ex. 15:7 • the tongue of fire

25 Therefore is the anger of the LORD kindled against his people, and he hath stretched forth his hand against them, and hath smitten them: and the hills did tremble, and their carcases *were* torn in the midst of the streets. For all this his anger is not turned away, but his hand *is* stretched out still.

26 And he will lift up an ensign to the nations from far, and will hissᵀ unto them from the end of the earth: and, behold, they shall come with speed swiftly: call

27 ᴿNone shall be weary nor stumble among them; none shall slumber nor sleep; neither ᴿshall the girdle of their loins be loosed, nor the latchet of their shoes be broken: Joel 2:7, 8 • Job 12:18; Dan. 5:6

28 ᴿWhose arrows *are* sharp, and all their bows bent, their horses' hoofs shall be counted like flint, and their wheels like a whirlwind: 13:18; Ps. 7:12, 13; 45:5

29 Their roaring *shall be* like a lion, they shall roar like young lions: yea, they shall roar, and lay hold of the prey, and shall carry *it* away safe, and none shall deliver *it*.

30 And in that day they shall ᴿroar against them like the roaring of the sea: and if *one* ᴿlook unto the land, behold darkness *and* sorrow, and the light is darkened in the heavens thereof. 17:12; Jer. 6:23 • 8:22

CHAPTER 6

The Commission of Isaiah

IN the year that king Uz-zi'-ah died I ᴿsaw also the Lord sitting upon a throne, high and lifted up, and ᵀhis train filled the temple. John 12:41; Rev. 4:2, 3; 20:11 • skirts

2 Above it stood the ser'-a-phims: each one ᴿhad six wings; with ᵀtwain he covered his face, and with twain he covered his feet, and with twain he did fly. Rev. 4:8 • two

3 And one cried unto another, and said, Holy, holy, holy, *is* the LORD of hosts: ᴿthe whole earth *is* full of his glory. Num. 14:21

4 And the posts of the door moved at the voice of him that cried, ᴿand the house was filled with smoke. Ex. 40:34; 1 Kin. 8:10

5 Then said I, ᴿWoe *is* me! for I am undone; because I *am* a man of unclean lips, and I dwell in the midst of a people of unclean lips: for mine eyes have seen the King, the LORD of hosts. [Ex. 33:20]; Luke 5:8

6 Then flew one of the ser'-a-phims unto me, having a live coal in his hand, *which* he had taken with the tongs from off the altar:

7 And he laid *it* upon my mouth, and said, Lo, this hath touched thy lips; and thine iniquity is taken away, and thy sin purged.

8 Also I heard the voice of the Lord, saying, Whom shall I send, and who will go for us? Then said I, Here *am* I; send me.

6:3 Holiness of God—Our greatest failing is in not realizing who God is and what His character is like. God is NOT human. He is God, and as such there is an infinite gap between the highest in us and the lowest in God. The gap between God and us is unbridgeable from our side. If the gap is to be bridged, it must be from God's side—for God is holy. To be holy means "to be set apart." God is set apart *from* the power, practice, and presence of sin, and is set apart *to* absolute righteousness and goodness. There is no sin in God and God can have nothing to do with sin. If we are to approach God, we must do so on God's terms. Somehow, we must be made holy—just as holy as God is. Any holiness which falls short of God's holiness will not be able to stand in the presence of God. Therefore, because of the holiness of God, we must have a new life in which our sins have been forgiven and done away with so that we actually can be separated from sin as God is. This is the good news of the gospel— that Christ died for our sins, having taken them upon Himself, and has set us apart from them. This is our position before God which will never change. Because of what God has done, we can enter boldly into the presence of God.

Now turn to Page 6—Gen. 3:6, 7: Adam's Sin.

6:8 Knowing the Will of God Through Submission to the Spirit—The moment a repenting sinner receives Christ by faith into his heart the Holy Spirit immediately does five things for him:

a. He regenerates the believer, that is, He gives him a new nature (Page 1044—John 3:5, 6; Page 1207—Titus 3:5).

b. He baptizes the believer into the body of Christ (Page 1134—1 Cor. 12:13).

c. He indwells the believer (Page 1114—Rom. 8:9; Page 1129—1 Cor. 6:19).

d. He seals the believer (Page 1172—Eph. 1:13; 4:30).

e. He fills the believer (Page 1073—Acts 2:4; 4:8; 7:55; 13:52).

All five of these ministries often occur at the moment of conversion. The fifth ministry, however, should be asked for as many times as needed: See Ephesians 5:18; Galatians 5:16. Actually the word

9 And he said, Go, and tell this people, ᴿHear ye indeed, but understand not; and see ye indeed, but perceive not.   Matt. 13:14, 15 ☆

10 ᴿMake the heart of this people fat, and make their ears heavy, and shut their eyes; lest they see with their eyes, and hear with their ears, and understand with their heart, and convert, and be healed.   Mark 6:1–6 ☆

11 Then said I, Lord, how long? And he answered, Until the cities be wasted without inhabitant, and the houses without man, and the land be utterly desolate,

12 ᴿAnd the Lᴏʀᴅ have removed men far away, and there be a great ᴿforsaking in the midst of the land.   2 Kin. 25:21 • Jer. 4:29

13 But yet in it shall be a tenth, and it shall return, and shall be eaten: as a teil tree, and as an oak, whose substance is in them, when they cast their leaves: so the holy seed shall be the substance thereof.

CHAPTER 7

Sign of Immanuel—2 Kin. 16:5; 2 Chr. 28:5–15

AND it came to pass in the days of ᴿAhaz the son of Jo'-tham, the son of Uz-zi'-ah, king of Judah, that Re'-zin the king of Syria, and Pe'-kah the son of Rem-a-li'-ah, king of Israel, went up toward Jerusalem to war against it, but could not ᵀprevail against it.   2 Kin. 16:5; 2 Chr. 28:5, 6 • conquer

2 And it was told the ᴿhouse of David, saying, Syria is ᵀconfederate with E'-phra-im. And his heart was moved, and the heart of his people, as the trees of the wood are moved with the wind.   v. 13; 22:22 • allied

3 Then said the Lᴏʀᴅ unto Isaiah, Go forth now to meet Ahaz, thou, and She'-ar-jash'-ub thy son, at the end of the ᴿconduit of the upper pool in the highway of the fuller's field;   36:2; 2 Kin. 18:17

4 And say unto him, ᵀTake heed, and be quiet; fear not, neither be fainthearted for the two tails of these smoking firebrands, for the fierce anger of Re'-zin with Syria, and of the son of Rem-a-li'-ah.   be very careful

5 Because ᴿSyria, E'-phra-im, and the son of Rem-a-li'-ah, have ᵀtaken evil counsel against thee, saying,   v. 2 • made plans to harm

6 Let us go up against Judah, and ᵀvex it, and let us ᵀmake a breach therein for us, and set a king in the midst of it, even the son of Ta'-be-al: attack • force an entrance

7 Thus saith the Lord Gᴏᴅ, ᴿIt shall not stand, neither shall it come to pass.   8:10

8 For the head of Syria is Damascus, and the head of Damascus is Re'-zin; and ᴿwithin ᵀthreescore and five years shall E'-phra-im be broken, that it be not a people.   2 Kin. 17:6 • 65

9 And the head of E'-phra-im is Sa-ma'-ri-a, and the head of Sa-ma'-ri-a is Rem-a-li'-ah's son. If ye will not believe, surely ye shall not be ᵀestablished.   made secure

10 Moreover the Lᴏʀᴅ spake again unto Ahaz, saying,

11 ᴿAsk thee a sign of the Lᴏʀᴅ thy God; ask it either in the ᵀdepth, or in the ᵀheight above.   38:7; Matt. 12:38 • of hell • of heaven

12 But ᴿAhaz said, I will not ask, neither will I ᵀtempt the Lᴏʀᴅ.   Matt. 4:7 • test

13 And he said, Hear ye now, O ᴿhouse of David; Is it a small thing for you to weary men, but will ye weary my God also?   v. 2

14 ᴿTherefore the Lord himself shall give you a sign; Behold, a virgin shall conceive, and bear a son, and shall call his name ᴿIm-man'-u-el.   Matt. 1:23; Luke 1:31, 34, 35 ☆ • 8:8–10

15 ᴿButter and honey shall he eat, ᵀthat he may know to refuse the evil, and choose the good.   v. 22; 11:3 • when he knows enough to refuse evil

16 ᴿFor before the child shall know to refuse the evil, and choose the good, the land that thou ᵀabhorrest shall be forsaken of ᴿboth her kings.   8:4 • do dislike • 2 Kin. 15:30

17 ᴿThe Lᴏʀᴅ shall bring upon thee, and upon thy people, and upon thy father's house, days that have not come, from the day that ᴿE'-phra-im departed from Judah; even the king of Assyria.   2 Chr. 28:19 • 1 Kin. 12:16

18 And it shall come to pass in that day, that the Lᴏʀᴅ shall hiss for the fly that is in the uttermost part of the rivers of Egypt, and for the bee that is in the land of Assyria.

19 And they shall come, and shall rest all of them in the desolate valleys, and in ᴿthe holes of the rocks, and upon all thorns, and upon all bushes.   2:19; Jer. 16:16

20 In the same day shall the Lord shave with a razor that is hired, namely, by them beyond the river, by the king of Assyria, the

---

control is a better term than fill in describing this fifth ministry. It does not mean that we get more of the Spirit, but rather that He gets more of us. The fifth ministry is lost when the believer either quenches (Page 1185—1 Thess. 5:19) or grieves (Page 1165—Eph. 4:30) the Holy Spirit. The fifth ministry can be regained by following the command of 1 John 1:9, "If we confess our sins, he is faithful and just to forgive us our sins, and to cleanse us from all unrighteousness."

How can a Christian be certain that he is indeed controlled by the Holy Spirit on a daily basis? First, he must consecrate his body as a living sacrifice to the Holy Spirit (Page 1118—Rom. 12:1, 2). Second, he must depend upon the Holy Spirit to convict him of sin (Page 608—Ps. 139:23, 24; 19:12–14). Finally, he must look to the Holy Spirit for divine power in serving Christ (Page 1072—Acts 1:8; Page 1158—Gal. 5:16, 17; Page 1163—Eph. 3:16).

Now turn to Page 631—Prov. 24:6: Knowing the Will of God Through Circumstances and Counsel.

head, and the hair of the feet: and it shall also ^Tconsume the beard.   *take away*

21 And it shall come to pass in that day, *that* a man shall ^Tnourish a young ^Rcow, and two sheep;   *feed* · 27:10

22 And it shall come to pass, for the abundance of milk *that* they shall give he shall eat butter: for ^Rbutter and honey shall every one eat that is left in the land.   *v.* 15

23 And it shall come to pass in that day, *that* every place shall be, where there were a thousand vines at a ^Tthousand silverlings, it shall *even* be for briers and thorns. $128,000

24 ^RWith arrows and with bows shall *men* come thither; because all the land shall become briers and thorns.   Lev. 26:25

25 And *on* all hills that shall be digged with the mattock, there shall not come thither the fear of briers and thorns: but it shall be for the ^Rsending forth of oxen, and for the treading of ^Tlesser cattle.   5:17 · *sheep*

CHAPTER 8

Sign of Maher-shalal-hash-baz

M OREOVER the LORD said unto me, Take thee a great roll, and ^Rwrite in it with a man's pen concerning ^TMa′-her–shal′-al–hash′-baz.   Hab. 2:2 · longest Bible word

2 And I took unto me faithful witnesses to record, ^RU-ri′-ah the priest, and Zech-a-ri′-ah the son of Je-ber-e-chi′-ah.   2 Kin. 16:10

3 And I ^Twent unto the prophetess; and she conceived, and bare a son. Then said the LORD to me, Call his name ^TMa′-her–shal′-al–hash′-baz.   *married · prey speeds*

4 For before the child shall ^Thave knowledge to cry, My father, and my mother, the riches of Damascus and the spoil of Sa-ma′-ri-a ^Rshall be taken away ^Tbefore the king of Assyria.   *be old enough to understand* · 2 Kin. 17:6 · *by*

5 The LORD spake also unto me again, saying,

6 Forasmuch as this people refuseth the waters of Shi-lo′-ah that go softly, and rejoice in Re′-zin and Rem-a-li′-ah's son;

7 Now therefore, behold, the Lord bringeth up upon them the waters of the river, strong and many, *even* the king of Assyria, and all his glory: and he shall come^T up over all his channels, and go over all his banks: *overflow*

8 And he shall pass through Judah; he shall overflow and go over, he shall reach *even* to the neck; and ^Tthe stretching out of his wings shall fill the breadth of thy land, O Im-man′-u-el.   *he shall extend his power over*

9 Associate yourselves, O ye people, and ye shall be broken in pieces; and give ear, all ye of far countries: gird yourselves, and ye shall be broken in pieces; gird yourselves, and ye shall be broken in pieces.

10 Take counsel together, and it shall

come to nought; speak the word, ^Rand it shall not stand: for God *is* with us.   7:14

11 For the LORD spake thus to me ^Twith^R a strong hand, and instructed me that I should ^Rnot walk in the way of this people, saying,   *with emphasis* · Ezek. 3:14 · Ezek. 2:8

12 Say ye not, A confederacy, to all *them to* whom this people shall say, A confederacy; neither fear ye their fear, nor be afraid.

13 ^TSanctify^R the LORD of hosts himself; and *let* him *be* your fear, and *let* him *be* your dread.   *give the highest honour to* · 5:16; 29:23

14 And he shall be for a sanctuary; but for a ^Rstone of stumbling and for a rock ^Tof offence to both the houses of Israel, for a gin and for a snare to the inhabitants of Jerusalem.   1 Pet. 2:8 ☆ · *that will cause confusion*

15 ^RAnd many among them shall stumble, and fall, and be broken, and be snared, and be taken.   Luke 20:18; [Rom. 9:32]

16 ^TBind up the ^Ttestimony, ^Rseal the law among my disciples.   *protect · records* · Dan. 12:4

17 And I will ^Twait upon the LORD, that ^Rhideth his face from the house of Jacob, and I ^Rwill look for him.   *call* · 54:8 · Hab. 2:3

18 ^RBehold, I and the children whom the LORD hath given me *are* for signs and for wonders in Israel from the LORD of hosts, which dwelleth in mount Zion.   Heb. 2:13

19 And when they shall say unto you, Seek unto them that have familiar spirits, and unto wizards that ^Tpeep, and that mutter: should not a people seek unto their God? for the living to the dead?   *whisper*

20 To the law and to the testimony: if they speak not according to this word, *it is* because ^R*there is* no light in them.   Mic. 3:6

21 And they shall pass through it, ^Thardly bestead and hungry: and it shall come to pass, that when they shall be hungry, they shall fret themselves, and curse their king and their God, and look upward.   *in trouble*

22 And they shall look unto the earth; and behold trouble and darkness, dimness of anguish; and *they shall be* driven to darkness.

CHAPTER 9

Prophecy of the Messiah's Birth

N EVERTHELESS the dimness *shall* not *be* such as *was* in her ^Tvexation, when at the first he lightly afflicted the land of Zeb′-u-lun and ^Rthe land of Naph′-ta-li, and afterward did more grievously afflict her by the way of the sea, beyond Jordan, in Galilee of the nations.   *trouble* · Matt. 4:14–16 ☆

2 The ^Rpeople that walked in darkness have seen a great light: they that dwell in the land of the ^Tshadow of death, upon them hath the light shined.   Luke 1:79 ☆ · *deep darkness*

3 Thou hast multiplied the nation, *and* not increased the joy: they joy before thee

according to the joy in harvest, *and* as *men* rejoice when they divide the spoil.

4 For thou ᵀhast broken the yoke of his burden, and the staff of his shoulder, the rod of his ᴿoppressor, as in the day of ᴿMid'-i-an. *has delivered from* · 14:4; 49:26 · Judg. 7:22

5 ᵀFor every battle of the warrior *is* with confused noise, and garments rolled in blood; ᴿbut *this* shall be with burning *and* ᵀfuel of fire. *usually* · 66:15 · *material for*

6 ᴿFor unto us a child is born, unto us a son is given: and the government shall be upon his shoulder: and his name shall be called Wonderful, Counsellor, ᴿThe mighty God, The everlasting Father, ᴿThe Prince of Peace. [7:14; Luke 2:11] ☆ · Titus 2:13 · Eph. 2:14

7 Of the increase of *his* government and peace *there* shall be no end, upon the throne of David, and upon his kingdom, to order it, and to establish it with judgment and with justice from henceforth even for ever. The zeal of the LORD of hosts will perform this.

Judgment on Ephraim

8 The Lord sent a word into Jacob, and it hath ᵀlighted upon Israel. *come to be known*

9 And all the people shall know, *even* E'-phra-im and the inhabitant of Sa-mar'-i-a, that say in the pride and stoutness of heart,

10 The bricks are fallen down, but we will ᴿbuild with ᵀhewn stones: the sycomores are cut down, but we will ᵀchange *them into* cedars. Mal. 1:4 · *smooth* · *replace them with*

11 Therefore the LORD shall ᵀset up the adversaries of Re'-zin against him, and ᵀjoin his enemies together; *raise* · *unite*

12 The Syrians before, and the Phi-lis'-tines behind; and they shall devour Israel with open mouth. For all this his anger ᵀis not turned away, but his hand ᵀis stretched out still. *does not cease* · *continues to chasten*

13 For the people turneth not unto him that ᵀsmiteth them, ᴿneither do they seek the LORD of hosts. *chastens* · Jer. 5:3; Hos. 7:10

14 Therefore the LORD will cut off from Israel ᴿhead and tail, branch and ᵀrush, ᴿin one day. 19:15 · *bulrush* · Rev. 18:8

15 The ᵀancient ᴿand honourable, he *is* the head; and the prophet that teacheth lies, he *is* the tail. *elder* · 3:2, 3

16 For the ᴿleaders of this people cause *them* to err; and *they that are* led of them *are* destroyed. Mic. 3:1, 5, 9; Matt. 15:14

17 Therefore the Lord ᴿshall have no joy in their young men, neither shall have mercy on their fatherless and widows: for every one *is* an hypocrite and an evildoer, and every mouth speaketh folly. ᴿFor all this his anger is not turned away, but his hand *is* stretched out still. Ps. 147:10 · 5:25

18 For wickedness burneth as the fire: it shall devour the briers and thorns, and shall kindle in the thickets of the forest, and they shall mount up *like* the lifting up of smoke.

9:6 The Person of the Son of God—It is crucial to remember that the existence of the Son of God did not commence with His birth in Beth-lehem. He is spoken of as the Son before He became a man (Is. 9:6; Page 1156—Gal. 4:4). Micah prophesies of His birth, but yet states that His "goings forth *have been* from of old, from everlasting" (Page 873—Mic. 5:2). John says that He existed "in the beginning" before anything was created (Page 1042—John 1:1–3).

Even before He was born of Mary, He appeared to men in the Old Testament as the "Angel of the LORD." It is clear that this Angel was no ordinary angel because He is identified as God (Page 58—Ex. 3:1, 4); He pardons sin (Page 78—Ex. 23:20, 21); and He is worshiped (Page 221—Josh. 5:13–15). While these passages do not say that this member of the Godhead was the preincarnate Christ, we may conclude that they are the same person since their work is the same.

While Christ was preexistent and appeared occasionally to men in the Old Testament, He took on a body permanently when He was conceived in Mary's womb. This incomparable event of God's becoming man in Jesus Christ is called the Incarnation. This miracle was prophesied hundreds of years previously (Page 663—Is. 7:14) and was fulfilled historically in Mary, in whose womb the Holy Spirit's power conceived a child (Page 942—Matt. 1:23; Page 1005—Luke 1:35). Thus Christ, the sinless God-man, was qualified to become our Redeemer (Page 1146—2 Cor. 5:21).

Having been born of a woman, Jesus Christ was fully man apart from sin (Page 1042—John 1:14). As a man He experienced the normal physical, mental, social, and spiritual growth as others did (Page 1007—Luke 2:52). He suffered pain, hunger, thirst, fatigue, temptation, pleasure, and rest. Because of His complete humanity He can be sympathetic and compassionate toward us (Page 1217—Heb. 4:15).

While Christ was fully man He was also fully God, as these facts indicate: He is called God (Page 1042—John 1:1; Page 1215—Heb. 1:8); He did works that only God could do, such as forgive sins (Page 980—Mark 2:7) and create (Page 1177—Col. 1:16); He had attributes that only God could have, such as truth (Page 1059—John 14:6) and omniscience, all-knowing (Page 1044—John 2:24, 25); and He claimed equality with God (Page 1055—John 10:30).

The question may then be raised as to whether Christ lost anything of deity when He became a man (Page 1171—Phil. 2:6–8). While there is an inscrutable mystery involved in this unparalleled act of condescension, one can be certain that He lost none of God's attributes, because He was still God (Page 1066—John 20:28). He was fully God and fully man united in one person forever. Even now, at the right hand of God, He is the God-man (Page 1194—1 Tim. 2:5). The great condescension of the Son of God's becoming a man serves eternally as a perfect model of humility and self-giving love (Page 1171—Phil. 2:5).

Now turn to Page 1054—John 10:10: The Earthly Life of the Son of God.

19 Through the wrath of the LORD of hosts is the land darkened, and the people shall be as the fuel of the fire: ^Rno man shall spare his brother. Mic. 7:2, 6

20 And he shall snatch on the right hand, and be hungry; and he shall eat on the left hand, and they shall not be satisfied: they shall eat every man the flesh of his own arm:

21 Ma-nas'-seh, E'-phra-im; and E'-phra-im, Ma-nas'-seh: and they together shall be ^Ragainst Judah. ^RFor all this his anger is not turned away, but his hand is stretched out still. 2 Chr. 28:6, 8 • vv. 12, 17

CHAPTER 10

WOE unto them that ^Rdecree unrighteous decrees, and that write grievousness which they have prescribed; Ps. 58:2

2 To turn aside the needy from judgment, and to take away the right from the poor of my people, that widows may be their prey, and that they may rob the fatherless!

3 And what will ye do in the day of visitation, and in the desolation which shall come from far? to whom will ye flee for help? and where will ye leave your glory?

4 Without me they shall bow down under the prisoners, and they shall fall under the slain. For all this his anger is not turned away, but his hand is stretched out still.

Destruction of Assyria

5 O Assyrian, the rod of mine anger, and the staff in their hand is mine indignation.

6 I ^Rwill send him against an ^Thypocritical nation, and against the people of my wrath will I give him a charge, to take the spoil, and to take the prey, and to tread them down like the mire of the streets. 2 Kin. 17:6 • profane

7 Howbeit he meaneth not so, neither doth his heart think so; but it is in his heart to destroy and cut off nations not a few.

8 ^RFor he saith, Are not my princes ^Taltogether kings? 2 Kin. 18:24; 19:10 • as great as

9 Is not ^RCal'-no as^T Car'-che-mish? is not Ha'-math as Ar'-pad? is not Sa-ma'-ri-a ^Ras Damascus? Amos 6:2 • as good as • 2 Kin. 16:9

10 As my hand hath found the kingdoms of the idols, and whose graven images did excel them of Jerusalem and of Sa-ma'-ri-a;

11 Shall I not, as I have done unto Sa-ma'-ri-a and her ^Tidols, so do to Jerusalem and ^Rher idols? images • 2:8

12 Wherefore it shall come to pass, that when the Lord hath performed his whole work upon mount Zion and on Jerusalem, ^RI will punish the fruit of the stout heart of the king of Assyria, and the glory of his ^Thigh looks. 2 Kin. 19:35; 2 Chr. 32:21; Jer. 50:18 • proud attitude

13 ^RFor he saith, By the strength of my hand I have done it, and by my wisdom; for I am prudent: and I have removed the bounds of the people, and have robbed their treasures, and I have put down the inhabitants like a ^Tvaliant man: 37:24 • mighty

14 And my hand hath found as a nest the riches of the people: and as one gathereth eggs that are left, have I gathered all the earth; and there was none that moved the wing, or opened the mouth, or peeped.

15 Shall ^Rthe ax boast itself against him that heweth therewith? or shall the saw magnify itself against him that shaketh it? as if the rod should shake itself against them that lift it up, or as if the staff should lift up itself, as if it were no wood. Jer. 51:20

16 Therefore shall the Lord, the Lord of hosts, send among his fat ones ^Rleanness; and under his glory he shall kindle a burning like the burning of a fire. Ps. 106:15

17 And the ^Rlight of Israel shall be for a fire, and his ^RHoly One for a flame: ^Rand it shall burn and devour his thorns and his briers in one day; 30:33; 31:9 • 37:23 • 9:18

18 And shall consume the glory of his forest, and of ^Rhis fruitful field, ^Tboth soul and body: and they shall be as when a standard-bearer fainteth. 2 Kin. 19:23 • utterly

19 And the rest of the trees of his forest shall be few, that a child may write them.

Remnant of Israel

20 And it shall come to pass in that day, that the remnant of Israel, and such as are escaped of the house of Jacob, shall no more again ^Tstay upon him that smote them; but shall ^Rstay upon the LORD, the Holy One of Israel, in truth. depend • 17:7

21 The remnant shall return, even the remnant of Jacob, unto the mighty God.

22 For though thy people Israel be as the sand of the sea, yet a remnant of them shall return: the ^Tconsumption decreed shall overflow with righteousness. destruction

23 ^RFor the Lord GOD of hosts shall make a consumption, even determined, in the midst of all the land. 28:22; Dan. 9:27; Rom. 9:28

24 Therefore thus saith the Lord GOD of hosts, O my people that dwellest in Zion, be not afraid of the Assyrian: he shall smite thee with a rod, and shall lift up his staff against thee, after the manner of Egypt.

25 For yet a very little while, ^Rand the indignation shall ^Tcease, and mine anger in their destruction. Dan. 11:36 • be accomplished

26 And the LORD of hosts shall stir up ^Ta scourge for him according to the slaughter of Mid'-i-an at the rock of O'-reb: and as his rod was upon the sea, so shall he lift it up after the manner of Egypt. an enemy

27 And it shall come to pass in that day, that his burden shall be taken away from off thy shoulder, and his ^Tyoke from off thy neck, and the yoke shall be destroyed because of ^Rthe anointing. control • Ps. 105:15

28 He is come to A'-iath, he is passed to Mig'-ron; at Mich'-mash he hath laid up his ᵀcarriages: *baggage;* Judg. 18:21; 1 Sam. 17:22

29 They are gone over the passage: they have taken up their lodging at Ge'-ba; Ra'-mah is afraid; Gib'-e-ah of Saul is fled.

30 Lift up thy voice, O daughter ᴿof Gal'-lim: cause it to be heard unto ᴿLa'-ish, O poor An'-a-thoth. 1 Sam. 25:44 • Judg. 18:7

31 Mad-me'-nah is removed; the inhabitants of Ge'-bim gather themselves to flee.

32 As yet shall he remain ᴿat Nob that day: he shall ᴿshake his hand *against* the mount of ᴿthe daughter of Zion, the hill of Jerusalem. Neh. 11:32 • 13:2 • 37:22

33 Behold, the Lord, the LORD of hosts, shall ᵀlop the bough with terror: and the high ones of stature *shall be* hewn down, and the haughty shall be humbled. *cut off*

34 And he shall cut down the thickets of the forest with ᵀiron, and Leb'-a-non shall fall by a mighty one. *an iron axe*

CHAPTER 11

Restoration of the Messiah's Kingdom

AND there shall come forth a rod out of the stem of Jesse, ᴿand a Branch shall ᵀgrow out of his roots: [Acts 13:23] ☆ • *bear fruit*

2 ᴿAnd the spirit of the LORD shall rest upon him, the spirit of wisdom and understanding, the spirit of ᵀcounsel and might, the spirit of knowledge and of the fear of the LORD; [42:1; 61:1]; John 1:32 ☆ • *advice*

3 ᴿAnd shall make him of quick understanding in the fear of the LORD: and he shall not judge after the sight of his eyes, neither reprove after the hearing of his ears: John 2:25 ☆

4 But ᴿwith righteousness shall he judge the poor, and ᵀreprove with equity for the meek of the earth: and he shall smite the earth with the rod of his mouth, and with the breath of his lips shall he ᵀslay the wicked. Rev. 19:11 ☆ • *take up the cause fairly • destroy*

5 And righteousness shall be the girdle ᴿof his ᵀloins, and ᴿfaithfulness the girdle of his ᵀreins. Eph. 6:14 • *strength* • 25:1 • *emotions*

6 The ᴿwolf also shall dwell with the lamb, and the leopard shall lie down with the kid; and the calf and the young lion and the fatling together; and a little child shall lead them. 65:25; Hos. 2:18

7 And the cow and the bear shall feed; their young ones shall lie down together: and the lion shall eat straw like the ox.

8 And the sucking child shall play on the hole of the asp, and the weaned child shall put his hand on the ᵀcockatrice' den. *adder's*

9 ᴿThey shall not hurt nor destroy in all my holy ᵀmountain: for the earth shall be full of the knowledge of the LORD, as the waters cover the sea. Job 5:23 • *kingdom*

10 And in that day there shall be a ᴿroot of Jesse, which shall stand for ᵀan ensign of the people; to it shall the Gentiles seek: and his rest shall be glorious. 11:1 ☆ • *a signal*

11 And it shall come to pass in that day, *that* the Lord shall set his hand again the second time to ᵀrecover the remnant of his people, which shall be left, ᴿfrom Assyria, and from Egypt, and from Path'-ros, and from Cush, and from E'-lam, and from Shi'-nar, and from Ha'-math, and from the ᴿislands of the sea. *restore* • Zech. 10:10 • 24:15

12 And he shall set up an ensign for the nations, and shall assemble the outcasts of Israel, and gather together the dispersed of Judah from the four corners of the earth.

13 ᴿThe envy also of E'-phra-im shall depart, and the adversaries of Judah shall be cut off: E'-phra-im shall not envy Judah, and Judah shall not vex E'-phra-im. Jer. 3:18

14 But they shall fly upon the shoulders of the Phi-lis'-tines toward the west; they shall spoil them of the east together: they shall lay their hand upon E'-dom and Moab; and the children of Ammon shall obey them.

15 And the LORD shall utterly destroy the tongue of the Egyptian sea; and with his mighty wind shall he shake his hand over the river, and shall smite it in the seven streams, and make *men* go over ᵀdryshod. *dry land*

16 And ᴿthere shall be an highway for the remnant of his people, which shall be left, from Assyria; ᴿlike as it was to Israel in the day that he came up out of the land of Egypt. 19:23; Ex. 14:16 • Ex. 14:29

CHAPTER 12

Thanksgiving in the Messiah's Kingdom

AND ᴿin that day thou shalt say, O LORD, I will praise thee: though thou wast angry with me, thine anger is turned away, and thou comfortedst me. Zech. 14:20, 21

2 Behold, God *is* my salvation; I will trust, and not be afraid: for the LORD JE-HO'-VAH *is* my ᴿstrength and *my* song; he also is become my salvation. Ex. 15:2

3 Therefore with joy shall ye draw ᴿwater out of the wells of salvation. Jer. 2:13

4 And in that day shall ye say, ᴿPraise the LORD, call upon his name, declare his doings among the people, make mention that his name is exalted. Ps. 105:1

5 ᴿSing unto the LORD; for he hath done excellent things: ᵀthis *is* known in all the earth. 24:14; 42:10; Ex. 15:1; Ps. 98:1 • *let this be*

6 ᴿCry out and shout, thou inhabitant of Zion: for great *is* ᴿthe Holy One of Israel in the midst of thee. Zeph. 3:14 • Ps. 89:18

CHAPTER 13

Prophecies Against Babylon

THE [R]burden of Babylon, which Isaiah the son of Amoz did see.   Jer. 50; 51

2 [R]Lift ye up a banner upon the high mountain, [T]exalt the voice unto them, [R]shake the hand, that they may go into the gates of the nobles.   18:3 · *call loudly* · 10:32

3 I have commanded my [T]sanctified ones, I have also called [R]my mighty ones for mine anger, *even* them that [R]rejoice in my [T]highness.   *dedicated* · Joel 3:11 · Ps. 149:2 · *prestige*

4 The noise of a multitude in the mountains, like as of a great people; a tumultuous noise of the kingdoms of nations gathered together: the LORD of hosts [T]mustereth the host of the battle.   *calls together*

5 They come from a far country, from the end of heaven, *even* the [R]LORD, and the [T]weapons of his [R]indignation, to destroy the whole land.   42:13 · *instruments* · 26:20

6 [T]Howl ye; [R]for the day of the LORD *is* at hand; [R]it shall come as a destruction from the Almighty.   *wail* · Rev. 6:17 · Job 31:23; Joel 1:15

7 Therefore shall all hands be [T]faint, and every man's heart shall melt: *weak*

8 And they shall be [R]afraid: [R]pangs and sorrows shall take hold of them; they shall be in pain as a woman that travaileth: they shall be amazed one at another; their faces *shall be as* flames.   Ps. 48:6 · 1 Thess. 5:3

9 Behold, the [R]day of the LORD cometh, cruel both with wrath and fierce anger, to lay the land desolate: and he shall destroy the sinners thereof out of it.   Mal. 4:1

10 For the stars of heaven and the constellations thereof shall not give their light: the sun shall be [R]darkened in his going forth, and the moon shall not cause her light to shine.   Joel 2:31; Matt. 24:29; Mark 13:24

11 And I will [R]punish the world for *their* evil, and the wicked for their iniquity; [R]and I will cause the arrogancy of the proud to cease, and will lay low the haughtiness of the [T]terrible.   26:21 · [2:17] · *ruthless*

12 I will make a man [T]more precious than fine gold; even a man than the [T]golden wedge of O'-phir.   *rarer* · *pure gold*

13 [R]Therefore I will shake the heavens, and the earth shall remove out of her place, in the wrath of the LORD of hosts, and in [R]the day of his fierce anger.   Hag. 2:6 · Ps. 110:5

14 And it shall be as the chased roe, and as a sheep that no man taketh up: they shall every man turn to his own people, and flee every one into his own land.

15 Every one that is found shall be thrust through; and every one that is joined *unto them* shall fall by the sword.

16 [R]Their children also shall be dashed to pieces before their eyes; their houses shall be spoiled, and their wives ravished.   14:21

17 Behold, I will stir up the Medes against them, which shall not regard silver; and *as for* gold, they shall not delight in it.

18 [R]Their bows also shall dash the young men to pieces; and they shall have no pity on the fruit of the womb; their eye shall not spare children.   2 Kin. 8:12

19 [R]And Babylon, the glory of kingdoms, the beauty of the Chal'-dees' excellency, shall be as when God overthrew [R]Sodom and Go-mor'-rah.   14:4 · Deut. 29:23; Jer. 50:40

20 [R]It shall never be inhabited, neither shall it be dwelt in from generation to generation: neither shall the A-ra'-bi-an pitch tent there; neither shall the shepherds make their fold there.   Jer. 50:3

21 But wild beasts of the desert shall lie there; and their houses shall be full of [T]doleful creatures; and owls shall dwell there, and satyrs shall dance there.   *weird*

22 And the wild beasts of the islands shall cry in their desolate houses, and dragons in *their* pleasant palaces: and her time *is* near to come, and her days shall not be prolonged.

CHAPTER 14

FOR the LORD will have mercy on Jacob, and will yet [R]choose Israel, and set them in their own land: and the strangers shall be joined with them, and they shall [T]cleave to the house of Jacob.   54:7, 8 · *unite*

2 And the people shall take them, [R]and bring them to their place: and the house of Israel shall possess them in the land of the LORD for servants and handmaids: and they shall take them captives, whose captives they [T]were; [R]and they shall rule over their oppressors.   49:22 · *had been* · 60:14

3 And it shall come to pass in the day that the LORD shall give thee rest from thy sorrow, and from thy fear, and from the hard bondage wherein thou wast made to serve,

4 That thou [R]shalt take up this [T]proverb against the [R]king of Babylon, and say, How hath the oppressor ceased! the [R]golden[T] city ceased!   Hab. 2:6 · *saying* · *v.* 12 · Rev. 18:16 · *greedy*

5 The LORD hath broken [R]the staff of the wicked, *and* the sceptre of the rulers.   Ps. 125:3

6 He who smote the people in wrath with a continual stroke, he that ruled the nations in anger, is persecuted, *and* none hindereth.

7 The whole earth is at rest, *and* is quiet: they [R]break forth into singing.   Ps. 47:1–3

8 Yea, the fir trees rejoice at thee, *and* the cedars of Leb'-a-non, *saying,* Since thou art laid down, no feller is come up against us.

9 [T]Hell[R] from beneath is moved for thee to meet *thee* at thy coming: it stirreth up the dead for thee, *even* all the [T]chief ones of the earth; it hath raised up from their thrones all the kings of the nations.   Sheol · 5:14 · *leaders*

10 All they shall [R]speak and say unto thee,

Art thou also become weak as we? art thou become like unto us?   Ezek. 32:21

11 Thy [R]pomp is brought down to the [T]grave, *and* the noise of thy [T]viols: the worm is spread under thee, and the worms cover thee.   Ezek. 28:13 • *Sheol • lutes*

12 [R]How art thou fallen from heaven, [T]O Lu'-ci-fer, son of the morning! *how* art thou cut down to the ground, which didst weaken the nations!   *v. 4; 34:4 • O day star*

13 For thou hast said in thine heart, I will ascend into heaven, I will exalt my throne above the stars of God: I will sit also [T]upon the mount of the congregation, in the sides of the north: *in the place of control*

14 I will ascend above the heights of the clouds; I will be like the most High.

15 Yet thou [R]shalt be brought down to [T]hell, to the sides of the pit.   Matt. 11:23 • *Sheol*

16 They that see thee shall [T]narrowly look upon thee, *and* consider thee, *saying, Is* this the man that made the earth to tremble, that did shake kingdoms;   *study*

17 *That* made the world as a wilderness, and destroyed the cities thereof; *that* opened not the house of his prisoners?

18 All the kings of the nations, *even* all of them, lie in [R]glory, every one in his own [T]house.   2 Chr. 32:33; [Ps. 49:17] • *tomb*

19 But thou art cast out of thy grave like an abominable branch, *and as* the raiment of those that are slain, thrust through with a sword, that go down to the stones of the pit; as a carcase trodden under feet.

20 Thou shalt not be joined with them in burial, because thou hast destroyed thy land, *and* slain thy people: the seed of evildoers shall never be [T]renowned.   *honoured*

21 Prepare slaughter for his children [T]for the iniquity of their fathers; that they do not rise, nor possess the land, nor fill the face of the world with cities.   *because of the sin*

22 For I will rise up against them, saith the LORD of hosts, and cut off from Babylon the name, and [R]remnant, [R]and son, and nephew, saith the LORD.   1 Kin. 14:10 • Job 18:19

23 I will also make it a possession for the bittern, and pools of water: and I will sweep it with the [T]besom of destruction, saith the LORD of hosts.   *broom*

Prophecies Against Assyria

24 The LORD of hosts hath sworn, saying, Surely [R]as I have thought, so shall it come to pass; and as I have purposed, *so* shall it stand: 46:11; [55:8, 9]; Job 23:13; Acts 4:28

25 That I will break the Assyrian in my land, and upon my mountains tread him under foot: then shall [R]his yoke [T]depart from off them, and his burden depart from off their shoulders.   10:27 • *be removed*

26 This *is* the purpose that is purposed upon the whole earth: and this *is* the hand that is stretched out upon all the nations.

27 For the LORD of hosts hath purposed, and who shall disannul *it?* and his hand *is* stretched out, and who shall turn it back?

Prophecies Against Philistia

28 In the year that [R]king Ahaz died [T]was this burden.   2 Kin. 16:20 • *came this message*

29 Rejoice not thou, whole Pal-es-ti'-na, because the rod of [R]him that smote thee is broken: for out of the serpent's root shall come forth [T]a cockatrice, and his fruit *shall be* a fiery flying serpent.   2 Kin. 18:8 • *an adder*

30 And the firstborn of the [R]poor shall feed, and the needy shall lie down in safety: and I will kill thy root with famine, and he shall slay thy remnant.   3:14, 15

31 Howl, O [R]gate; cry, O city; thou, whole Pal-es-ti'-na, *art* dissolved: for there shall come from the north a smoke, and none *shall be* alone in his appointed times.   3:26

32 What shall *one* then answer the messengers of the nation? That the LORD hath founded Zion, and [R]the poor of his people shall [T]trust in it.   Zech. 11:11 • *take refuge*

CHAPTER 15

Prophecies Against Moab

THE burden of Moab. Because in the night Ar of Moab is laid waste, *and* brought to silence; because in the night Kir of Moab is laid waste, *and* brought to silence;

2 He is gone up to Ba'-jith, and to Di'-bon, the high places, to weep: Moab shall howl over Ne'-bo, and over Med'-e-ba: [R]on all their heads *shall be* [R]baldness, *and* every beard cut off.   Lev. 21:5 • Jer. 48:37

3 [R]In their streets they shall gird themselves with sackcloth: on the tops of their houses, and in their streets, every one shall howl, weeping abundantly.   Jer. 48:38

4 And Hesh'-bon shall cry, and E-le-a'-leh: their voice shall be heard *even* unto Ja'-haz: therefore the armed soldiers of Moab shall cry out; his life shall be grievous unto him.

5 My heart shall cry out for Moab; [T]his fugitives *shall flee* unto Zo'-ar, an heifer of three years old: for by the mounting up of Lu'-hith with weeping shall they go it up; for in the way of Hor-o-na'-im they shall raise up a cry of destruction.   *her nobles*

6 For the waters of Nim'-rim shall be desolate: for the hay is withered away, the grass faileth, there is no green thing.

7 Therefore the [R]abundance they have gotten, and that which they have laid up, shall they carry away to [T]the brook of the willows.   30:6; Jer. 48:36 • *the place of destruction*

8 For the [T]cry is gone round about the borders of Moab; the [T]howling thereof unto Eg'-la-im, and the howling thereof unto Be'-er-e'-lim.   *of distress • wailing*

9 For the waters of Di'-mon shall be full of blood: for I will bring more upon Di'-mon, lions upon him that escapeth of Moab, and upon the remnant of the land.

CHAPTER 16

SEND ye the lamb to the ruler of the land from Se'-la to the wilderness, unto the mount of the daughter of Zion.

2 For it shall be, *that*, as a wandering bird cast out of the nest, so the daughters of Moab shall be at the fords of Arnon.

3 Take counsel, execute judgment; make thy Rshadow as the night in the midst of the noonday; hide the outcasts; Tbewray not him that wandereth.   25:4 · betray

4 Let mine outcasts dwell with thee, Moab; be thou a covert to them from the face of the spoiler: for the Textortioner is at an end, the spoiler ceaseth, the oppressors are consumed out of the land.   ruthless creditor

5 And in mercy shall the throne be established: and he shall sit upon it in truth in the tabernacle of David, judging, and seeking judgment, and Thasting righteousness. prompt

6 We have heard of the Rpride of Moab; *he is* very proud: *even* of his haughtiness, and his pride, and his wrath: Rbut his lies shall not be so.   Jer. 48:29, 30; Amos 2:1 · 28:15

7 Therefore shall Moab howl for Moab, every one shall howl: for the foundations of RKir-har'-e-seth shall ye mourn; surely *they are* stricken.   2 Kin. 3:25

8 For Rthe fields of Hesh'-bon languish, *and* Rthe vine of Sib'-mah: the lords of the heathen have broken down the principal plants thereof, they are come *even* unto Ja'-zer, they wandered *through* the wilderness: her branches are Tstretched out, they are gone over the sea.   24:7 · v. 9 · plucked up

9 Therefore I will bewail with the weeping of Ja'-zer the vine of Sib'-mah: I will water thee with my tears, O Hesh'-bon, and E-le-a'-leh: for the shouting for thy summer fruits and for thy harvest is fallen.

10 And Rgladness is taken away, and joy out of the plentiful field; and in the vineyards there shall be no singing, neither shall there be shouting: the treaders shall tread out no wine in *their* presses; I have made *their* vintage shouting to cease.   24:8

11 Wherefore Rmy bowels shall sound like an harp for Moab, and mine inward parts for Kir-ha'-resh.   15:5; Jer. 48:36

12 And it shall come to pass, when it is seen that Moab is weary on Rthe high place, that he shall come to his sanctuary to pray; but he shall not Tprevail.   15:2 · have power

13 This *is* the word that the LORD hath spoken concerning Moab since that time.

14 RBut now the LORD hath spoken, saying, Within three years, Ras the years of an hireling, and the glory of RMoab shall be Tcontemned, with all that great multitude; and the remnant *shall be* very small *and* feeble.   v. 6 · Job 7:1; 21:16 · 25:10 · despised

CHAPTER 17

Prophecies Against Damascus and Samaria

THE Rburden of Damascus. Behold, Damascus is taken away from *being* a city, and it shall be a ruinous heap.   Zech. 9:1

2 The cities of Ar'-o-er *are* forsaken: they shall be for flocks, which shall lie down, and Rnone shall make *them* afraid.   Jer. 7:33

3 RThe fortress also shall cease from E'-phra-im, and the kingdom from Damascus, and the remnant of Syria: they shall be as the Rglory of the children of Israel, saith the LORD of hosts.   7:16; 8:4 · Hos. 9:11

4 And in that day it shall come to pass, *that* the glory of Jacob shall be made thin, and the fatness of his flesh shall wax lean.

5 And it shall be as when the harvestman gathereth the corn, and reapeth the ears with his arm; and it shall be as he that gathereth ears in the valley of Reph'-a-im.

6 Yet Rgleaning grapes shall be left in it, as the shaking of an olive tree, two or three berries in the top of the uppermost bough, four or five in the outmost fruitful branches thereof, saith the LORD God of Israel. 24:13

7 At that day Rshall a man look to his Maker, and his eyes Tshall have respect to the Holy One of Israel.   10:20 · give honour to

8 And he shall not look to the Raltars, the work of his hands, neither shall respect *that* which his fingers have made, Reither the groves, or the Timages.   27:9 · Deut. 16:21 · idols

9 RIn that day shall his strong cities be as a forsaken bough, and an uppermost branch, which they left because of the children of Israel: and there shall be Tdesolation. 7:25 · ruin

10 Because thou hast forgotten Rthe God of thy salvation, and hast not been mindful of the rock of thy strength, therefore shalt thou plant pleasant plants, and shalt set it with strange slips: 12:2; Ps. 68:19

11 RIn the day shalt thou make thy plant to grow, and in the morning shalt thou make thy seed to flourish: *but* the harvest *shall be* Ta heap in the day of grief and of desperate sorrow.   Ps. 90:6 · a failure

12 Woe to the multitude of many people, *which* make a noise like the noise of the seas; and to the rushing of nations, *that* make a rushing like the rushing of mighty waters!

13 The Rnations shall rush like the rushing of many waters: but God shall Rrebuke them, and they shall flee far off, and Rshall be chased as the chaff of the mountains before the wind, and like a rolling thing before the whirlwind.   33:3 · 41:11 · Hos. 13:3

14 And behold at eveningtide trouble; *and* before the morning ᵀhe *is* not. This *is* the portion of them that spoil us, and the lot of them that rob us.   *he is destroyed*

CHAPTER 18

Prophecies Against Ethiopia

WOE ᴿto the land ᵀshadowing with wings, which *is* beyond the rivers of E-thi-o′-pi-a: 20:4, 5 • *with outstretched wings*
2 That sendeth ambassadors by the sea, even in vessels of bulrushes upon the waters, *saying,* Go, ye swift messengers, to a nation scattered and peeled, to a people terrible from their beginning hitherto; a nation meted out and trodden down, whose land the rivers have spoiled!
3 All ye inhabitants of the world, and dwellers on the earth, see ye, when he lifteth up an ensign on the mountains; and when he bloweth a trumpet, hear ye.
4 For so the LORD said unto me, I will ᵀtake my rest, and ᴿI will ᵀconsider in my dwelling place like a clear heat ᵀupon herbs, *and* like a cloud of dew in the heat of harvest.   *be silent* • 26:21 • *look* • *in sunshine*
5 For ᴿafore the harvest, when the bud is perfect, and the sour grape is ripening in the flower, he shall both cut off the sprigs with pruninghooks, and take away *and* cut down the branches.   17:10, 11; Ezek. 17:6–10
6 They shall be left together unto the ᴿfowls of the mountains, and to the beasts of the earth: and the fowls shall summer upon them, and all the beasts of the earth shall winter upon them.   46:11; 56:9; Jer. 7:33
7 In that time ᴿshall the present be brought unto the LORD of hosts of a people ᵀscattered and peeled, and from a people terrible from their beginning hitherto; a nation meted out and trodden under foot, whose land the rivers have spoiled, to the place of the name of the LORD of hosts, the mount Zion.   16:1; Mal. 1:11 • *stripped*

CHAPTER 19

Prophecies Against Egypt

THE burden of Egypt. Behold, the LORD rideth upon a swift cloud, and shall come into Egypt: and the idols of Egypt shall be moved at his presence, and the heart of Egypt shall melt in the midst of it.
2 And I will ᴿset the Egyptians against the Egyptians: and they shall fight every one against his brother, and every one against his neighbour; city against city, *and* kingdom against kingdom.   2 Chr. 20:23
3 And the spirit of Egypt shall fail in the midst thereof; and I will destroy the counsel thereof: and they shall ᴿseek to the idols, and

to the charmers, and to them that have familiar spirits, and to the wizards.   8:19; 47:12
4 And the Egyptians will I give over ᴿinto the hand of a cruel lord; and a fierce king shall rule over them, saith the Lord, the LORD of hosts.   20:4; Jer. 46:26; Ezek. 29:19
5 And the waters shall fail from the sea, and the river shall be wasted and dried up.
6 And they shall turn the rivers far away; *and* the brooks of defence shall be emptied and dried up: the reeds and flags shall wither.
7 The ᵀpaper reeds by the ᵀbrooks, ᴿby the ᵀmouth of the brooks, and every thing sown by the brooks, shall wither, be driven away, and be no *more.*   *meadows* • *Nile* • 23:3, 10 • *brink*
8 The ᴿfishers also shall mourn, and all they that cast ᵀangle into the brooks shall lament, and they that spread nets upon the waters shall languish.   Ezek. 47:10 • *hooks*
9 Moreover they that work in fine flax, and they that weave ᵀnetworks, shall be ᵀconfounded.   *white works* • *troubled*
10 And they shall be ᵀbroken in the purposes thereof, all that make ᵀsluices *and* ponds for fish.   *defeated in their plans* • *dams*
11 Surely the princes of Zo′-an *are* fools, the counsel of the wise counsellors of Pharaoh is become ᵀbrutish: how say ye unto Pharaoh, I *am* the son of the ᴿwise, the son of ancient kings?   *like animals* • Gen. 41:38, 39
12 ᴿWhere *are* they? where *are* thy wise *men?* and let them tell thee now, and let them know what the LORD of hosts hath ᵀpurposed upon Egypt.   1 Cor. 1:20 • *planned for*
13 The princes of Zo′-an are become fools, ᴿthe princes of Noph are deceived; they have also seduced Egypt, *even they that are* the stay of the tribes thereof.   Jer. 2:16
14 The LORD hath mingled a perverse spirit in the midst thereof: and they have caused Egypt to err in every work thereof, as a drunken *man* staggereth in his vomit.
15 Neither shall there be *any* work for Egypt, which ᴿthe head or tail, branch or rush, may do.   9:14, 15
16 In that day shall Egypt be like unto women: and it shall be afraid and fear because of the shaking of the hand of the LORD of hosts, which he shaketh over it.
17 And the land of Judah shall be a terror unto Egypt, every one that maketh mention thereof shall be afraid in himself, because of the counsel of the LORD of hosts, which he hath determined against it.
18 In that day shall five cities in the land of Egypt speak ᵀthe language of Canaan, and swear to the LORD of hosts; one shall be called, The city of destruction.   *the lip*
19 In that day ᴿshall there be an altar to the LORD in the midst of the land of Egypt, and a pillar at the border thereof to the LORD.   56:7; Gen. 28:18; Ex. 24:4; Josh. 22:10, 26, 27
20 And ᴿit shall be for a sign and for a

witness unto the LORD of hosts in the land of Egypt: for they shall cry unto the LORD because of the oppressors, and he shall send them a ᴿsaviour, and a great one, and he shall deliver them.   Josh. 4:20; 22:27 • 43:3, 11

21 And the LORD shall be ᵀknown to Egypt, and the Egyptians shall know the LORD in that day, and shall do sacrifice and oblation; yea, they shall vow a vow unto the LORD, and perform it.   *recognized in*

22 And the LORD shall smite Egypt: he shall smite and ᴿheal it: and they shall return *even* to the LORD, and he shall be intreated of them, and shall heal them.   30:26

23 In that day ᴿshall there be a highway out of Egypt to Assyria, and the Assyrian shall come into Egypt, and the Egyptian into Assyria, and the Egyptians shall serve with the Assyrians.   11:16; 35:8; 49:11; 62:10

24 In that day shall Israel be the ᵀthird with Egypt and with Assyria, *even* a blessing in the midst of the land: *third party*

25 Whom the LORD of hosts shall bless, saying, Blessed *be* Egypt my people, and Assyria ᴿthe work of my hands, and Israel mine inheritance.   29:23; Hos. 2:23; [Eph. 2:10]

CHAPTER 20

IN the year that ᴿTar′-tan came unto Ash′-dod, (when Sar′-gon the king of Assyria sent him,) and fought against Ash′-dod, and took it;   2 Kin. 18:17

2 At the same time spake the LORD by Isaiah the son of Amoz, saying, Go and loose ᴿthe sackcloth from off thy loins, and put off thy shoe from thy foot. And he did so, walking naked and barefoot.   Zech. 13:4

3 And the LORD said, Like as my servant Isaiah hath walked naked and barefoot three years ᴿ*for* a sign and wonder upon Egypt and upon E-thi-o′-pi-a;   8:18

4 So shall the king of Assyria lead away the Egyptians prisoners, and the E-thi-o′-pi-ans captives, young and old, naked and barefoot, ᴿeven with *their* buttocks uncovered, to the ᵀshame of Egypt.   3:17 • *disgrace*

5 ᴿAnd they shall be ᴿafraid and ashamed of E-thi-o′-pi-a their expectation, and of Egypt their glory.   30:3–5; 31:1 • 2 Kin. 18:21

6 And the inhabitant of this isle shall say in that day, Behold, such *is* our expectation, whither we flee for help to be delivered from the king of Assyria: and how shall we escape?

CHAPTER 21

Prophecies Against Babylon

THE ᵀburden of the desert of the sea. As ᴿwhirlwinds in the south pass through; *so* it cometh from the desert, from a terrible land.   *message to* • Zech. 9:14

2 A grievous vision is declared unto me; the treacherous dealer dealeth treacherously, and the ᵀspoiler spoileth. Go up, O E′-lam: besiege, ᴿO Me′-di-a; all the sighing thereof have I made to cease.   *robber robs* • Dan. 5:28, 31

3 Therefore ᴿare my loins filled with pain: pangs have taken hold upon me, as the pangs of a woman that travaileth: I was bowed down at the hearing *of it;* I was dismayed at the seeing *of it.*   13:8; 16:11

4 My heart panted, fearfulness affrighted me: the night of my pleasure hath he ᵀturned into fear unto me.   *changed into fright*

5 ᴿPrepare the table, watch in the watchtower, eat, drink: arise, ye princes, *and* anoint the shield.   Jer. 51:39, 57; Dan. 5:1

6 For thus hath the Lord said unto me, Go, set a watchman, let him ᵀdeclareᴿ what he seeth.   *tell* • 2 Kin. 9:17–20

7 And he saw a chariot *with* a couple of horsemen, a chariot of asses, *and* a ᵀchariot of camels; and he hearkened diligently with much heed: *wagon*

8 And ᵀhe cried, A lion: My lord, I stand continually upon the ᴿwatchtower in the daytime, and I am set in my ᵀward whole nights: *cried as a lion* • Hab. 2:1 • *place*

9 And, behold, here cometh a chariot of men, *with* a couple of horsemen. And he answered and said, Babylon is fallen, is fallen; and all the ᵀgraven images of her gods he hath broken unto the ground.   *idols*

10 ᴿO my threshing, and the corn of my floor: that which I have heard of the LORD of hosts, the God of Israel, have I declared unto you.   Jer. 51:33; Mic. 4:13

Prophecies Against Dumah (Edom)

11 ᴿThe burden of Du′-mah. He calleth to me out of Se′-ir, Watchman, what of the night? Watchman, what of the night? Obad. 1

12 The watchman said, The ᴿmorning cometh, and also the night: if ye will enquire, enquire ye: return, come.   [Mal. 4:2]

Prophecies Against Arabia

13 ᴿThe burden upon Arabia. In the forest in Arabia shall ye lodge, O ye travelling companies ᴿof Ded′-a-nim.   Jer. 49:28 • 1 Chr. 1:9

14 The inhabitants of the land of Te′-ma brought water to him that was thirsty, they prevented with their bread him that fled.

15 For they fled ᵀfrom the swords, from the drawn sword, and from the bent bow, and from the grievousness of war.   *in fear*

16 For thus hath the Lord said unto me, Within a year, ᴿaccording to the years of an hireling, and all the glory of ᴿKe′-dar shall fail: 16:14 • 60:7; Ps. 120:5

17 And the ᵀresidue of the number of archers, the mighty men of the children of Ke′-dar, shall be diminished: for the LORD God of Israel hath spoken it.   *rest;* 10:19

CHAPTER 22

Prophecies Against Jerusalem

THE burden of the ᴿvalley of vision. What aileth thee now, that thou art wholly gone up to the housetops?   Ps. 125:2; Jer. 21:13

2 Thou that art full of stirs, a tumultuous city, a joyous city: thy slain *men are* not slain with the sword, nor dead in battle.

3 All thy rulers are ᴿfled together, they are bound ᵀby the archers: all that are found in thee are bound together, *which* have fled from far.   21:15 • *together*

4 Therefore said I, ᵀLook away from me; ᴿI will weep bitterly, labour not to comfort me, because of the ᵀspoiling of the daughter of my people.   *do not look at* • Jer. 4:19 • *robbing*

5 For *it is* a day of trouble, and of treading down, and of perplexity by the Lord Goᴅ of hosts in the valley of vision, breaking down the walls, and of crying to the mountains.

6 ᴿAnd E'-lam bare the quiver with chariots of men *and* horsemen, and ᴿKir uncovered the shield.   Jer. 49:35 • 15:1

7 And it shall come to pass, *that* thy choicest valleys shall be full of chariots, and the horsemen shall set themselves in array ᵀat the gate.   *in front of the entrance*

8 And he discovered the covering of Judah, and thou didst look in that day to the armour ᴿof the house of the forest.   1 Kin. 7:2

9 ᴿYe have seen also the breaches of the city of David, that they are many: and ye ᴿgathered together the waters of the lower pool.   2 Kin. 20:20; 2 Chr. 32:4 • Neh. 3:16

10 And ye have numbered the houses of Jerusalem, and the houses have ye broken down to fortify the wall.

11 ᴿYe made also a ᵀditchᴿ between the two walls for the water of the old pool: but ye have not looked unto the maker thereof, neither had respect unto him that fashioned it long ago.   Neh. 3:16 • *reservoir* • 2 Kin. 25:4

12 And in that day did the Lord Goᴅ of hosts call to weeping, and to mourning, and to baldness, and to girding with sackcloth:

13 And behold joy and gladness, slaying oxen, and killing sheep, eating flesh, and drinking wine: ᴿlet us eat and drink; for to morrow we shall die.   56:12; 1 Cor. 15:32

14 ᴿAnd it was revealed in mine ears by the Loʀᴅ of hosts, Surely this iniquity ᴿshall not be purged from you till ye die, saith the Lord Goᴅ of hosts.   5:9 • 1 Sam. 3:14

15 Thus saith the Lord Goᴅ of hosts, Go, get thee unto this treasurer, *even* unto Sheb'-na, which *is* over the house, *and say,*

16 What hast thou here? and whom hast thou here, that thou hast hewed thee out a sepulchre here, *as* he ᴿthat heweth him out a sepulchre on high, *and* that graveth an habitation for himself in a rock?   Matt. 27:60

17 Behold, the Loʀᴅ will carry thee away with a mighty captivity, ᴿand will ᵀsurely cover thee.   Esth. 7:8 • *wrap thee up*

18 He will surely violently turn and toss thee *like* a ball into a large country: there shalt thou die, and there the chariots of thy glory *shall be* the shame of thy lord's house.

19 And I will drive thee from thy station, and from thy state shall he pull thee down.

20 And it shall come to pass in that day, that I will call my servant ᴿE-li'-a-kim the son of Hil-ki'-ah: 36:3, 22; 37:2; 2 Kin. 18:18

21 And I will clothe him with thy robe, and strengthen him with thy girdle, and I will commit thy government into his hand: and he shall be a father to the inhabitants of Jerusalem, and to the house of Judah.

22 And ᴿthe key of the ᴿhouse of David will I lay upon his shoulder; so he shall open, and none shall shut; and he shall shut, and none shall open.   Rev. 3:7 ☆ • Job 12:14

23 And I will fasten him *as* ᴿa nail in a sure place; and he shall be for a glorious throne to his father's house.   Ezra 9:8

24 And they shall hang upon him all the glory of his father's house, the offspring and the issue, all vessels of small quantity, from the vessels of ᵀcups, even to all the vessels of ᵀflagons.   *bowls • bottles* or *jars*

25 In that day, saith the Loʀᴅ of hosts, shall the nail that is fastened in the sure place be removed, and be cut down, and fall; and the burden that *was* upon it shall be cut off: for the Loʀᴅ hath spoken *it.*

CHAPTER 23

Prophecies Against Tyre

THE burden of Tyre. Howl, ye ships of Tar'-shish; for it is laid waste, so that there is no house, no entering in: from the land of Chit'-tim it is revealed to them.

2 Be still, ye inhabitants of the isle; thou whom the merchants of Zi'-don, that pass over the sea, have ᵀreplenished.   *satisfied*

3 And by great waters the seed of Si'-hor, the harvest of the river, *is* her revenue; and she is a ᵀmart of nations.   *trading center*

4 Be thou ashamed, ᴿO Zi'-don: for the sea hath spoken, *even* the strength of the sea, saying, I travail not, nor bring forth children, neither do I nourish up young men, *nor* bring up virgins.   Josh. 11:8; Joel 3:4

5 ᴿAs at the report concerning Egypt, *so* shall they be ᴿsorely pained at the report of Tyre.   19:16 • Ex. 15:14–16; Josh. 2:9–11

6 Pass ye over to Tar'-shish; howl, ye inhabitants of the ᵀisle.   *coast*

7 *Is* this your joyous *city,* whose antiquity *is* of ancient days? her own feet shall carry her ᵀafar off to sojourn.   *into captivity*

8 Who hath taken this counsel against Tyre, ᴿthe crowning *city,* whose merchants

are princes, whose ᵀtraffickers *are* the honourable of the earth? Ezek. 28:2, 12 · *traders*

9 The LORD of hosts hath purposed it, to stain the pride of all glory, *and* to bring into contempt all the honourable of the earth.

10 ᵀPass through thy land as a river, O daughter of Tar′-shish: *there* is no more ᵀstrength. *overflow · restraint*

11 He stretched out his hand over the sea, he shook the kingdoms: the LORD hath given a commandment against the merchant *city*, to destroy the strong holds thereof.

12 And he said, ᴿThou shalt no more rejoice, O thou oppressed virgin, daughter of Zi′-don: arise, pass over to Chit′-tim; there also shalt thou have no rest. Rev. 18:22

13 Behold the land of the Chal-de′-ans; this people was not, *till* the Assyrian founded it for ᴿthem that dwell in the wilderness: they set up the towers thereof, they ᵀraised up the palaces thereof; *and* ᴿhe brought it to ruin. Ps. 72:9 · *overthrew* · 10:7

14 ᴿHowl, ye ships of Tar′-shish: for your strength is ᵀlaid waste. 2:16 · *destroyed*

15 And it shall come to pass in that day, that Tyre shall be forgotten ᴿseventy years, according to the days of one king: after the end of seventy years shall Tyre sing as an harlot. Jer. 25:11, 12

16 Take an harp, go about the city, thou harlot that hast been forgotten; make sweet melody, sing many songs, that thou mayest be remembered.

17 And it shall come to pass after the end of seventy years, that the LORD will visit Tyre, and she shall turn to her hire, and shall commit fornication with all the kingdoms of the world upon the face of the earth.

18 And her merchandise and her hire shall be holiness to the LORD: it shall not be treasured nor laid up; for her merchandise shall be for them that dwell before the LORD, to eat sufficiently, and for durable clothing.

CHAPTER 24

Judgments of the Tribulation

BEHOLD, the LORD ᴿmaketh the earth empty, and maketh it waste, and turneth it upside down, and scattereth abroad the inhabitants thereof. *vv.* 19, 20; 2:19

2 And it shall be, as with the people, so with the priest; as with the servant, so with his master; as with the maid, so with her mistress; as with the buyer, so with the seller; as with the lender, so with the borrower: as with the taker of ᴿusury, so with the giver of usury to him. Lev. 25:36, 37

3 ᴿThe land shall be utterly emptied, and utterly ᵀspoiled: for the LORD hath spoken this word. 6:11 · *robbed*

4 The earth mourneth *and* fadeth away,

the world languisheth *and* fadeth away, the haughty people of the earth do languish.

5 The earth also is defiled under the inhabitants thereof; because they have transgressed the laws, changed the ordinance, broken the everlasting covenant.

6 Therefore hath the curse devoured the earth, and they that dwell therein are ᵀdesolate: therefore the inhabitants of the earth are burned, and few men left. *guilty*

7 The new wine mourneth, the vine languisheth, all the merryhearted do sigh.

8 The mirth ᴿof ᵀtabrets ceaseth, the noise of them that rejoice endeth, the joy of the harp ceaseth. Hos. 2:11; Rev. 18:22 · *tambourines*

9 They shall not drink wine with a song; ᴿstrong drink shall be ᴿbitter to them that drink it. 5:11, 22 · 5:20

10 The ᴿcity of confusion is broken down: ᴿevery house is shut up, that no man may come in. 34:11 · 23:1

11 *There is* a crying ᵀfor wine in the streets; ᴿall joy is darkened, the mirth of the land is gone. *because of the* · Jer. 14:2; 46:12

12 In the city is left desolation, and the ᴿgate is smitten with destruction. 14:31; 45:2

13 When thus it shall be in the midst of the land among the people, *there shall be* as the shaking of an olive tree, *and* as the gleaning grapes when the vintage is done.

14 ᴿThey shall lift up their voice, they shall sing for the majesty of the LORD, they shall cry aloud from the sea. 48:20; 52:8

15 Wherefore ᴿglorify ye the LORD ᵀin the fires, *even* the name of the LORD God of Israel in the isles of the sea. 25:3 · *in the east*

16 From the uttermost part of the earth have we heard songs, *even* glory to the righteous. But I said, My leanness, my leanness, woe unto me! the treacherous dealers have dealt treacherously; yea, the treacherous dealers have dealt very treacherously.

17 Fear, and the pit, and the snare, *are* upon thee, O inhabitant of the earth.

18 And it shall come to pass, *that* he who fleeth from the noise of the fear shall fall into the pit; and he that cometh up out of the midst of the pit shall be taken in the snare: for the windows from on high are open, and the foundations of the earth do shake.

19 The earth is utterly broken down, the ᴿearth is ᵀclean dissolved, the earth is moved exceedingly. Num. 16:31 · *completely*

20 The earth shall ᴿreelᵀ to and fro like a drunkard, and shall be removed like a cottage; and the ᴿtransgression thereof shall be heavy upon it; and it shall fall, and not rise again. *v.* 1 · *stagger* · 1:28; 19:14; 28:7; 43:27

21 And it shall come to pass in that day, *that* the LORD shall ᵀpunish the host of the high ones *that are* on high, and the kings of the earth upon the earth. *judge*

22 And they shall be gathered together, *as* prisoners are gathered in the pit, and shall be shut up in the prison, and after many days shall they be visited.

23 Then the moon shall be confounded, and the sun ashamed, when the LORD of hosts shall reign in mount Zion, and in Jerusalem, and before his ancients gloriously.

CHAPTER 25

Israel's Praise for Kingdom Blessings

O LORD, thou *art* my God; ^RI will exalt thee, I will praise thy name; for thou hast done wonderful *things; thy* counsels of old *are* faithfulness *and* truth.   Ex. 15:2

2 For thou hast made of a city an heap; *of* a defenced city a ruin: a palace of strangers to be no city; it shall never be built.

3 Therefore shall the strong people ^Rglorify thee, the city of the ^Tterrible nations shall fear thee.   24:15; Rev. 11:13 · *impressive*

4 For thou hast been a strength to the poor, a strength to the needy in his distress, ^Ra refuge from the storm, a shadow from the heat, when the blast of the terrible ones *is* as a storm *against* the wall.   4:6

5 Thou shalt bring down the noise of strangers, as the heat in a dry place; *even* the heat with the shadow of a cloud: the branch of the terrible ones shall be brought low.

6 And in ^Rthis mountain shall ^Rthe LORD of hosts make unto all people a feast of fat things, a feast of wines on the lees, of fat things full of marrow, of wines on the lees well refined.   [2:2, 3] · Matt. 22:4

7 And he will destroy in this mountain the face of the covering cast over all people, and the vail that is spread over all nations.

8 He will swallow up death in victory; and the Lord GOD will wipe away tears from off all faces; and the rebuke of his people shall he take away from off all the earth: for the LORD hath spoken *it*.

9 And it shall be said in that day, Lo, ^Rthis *is* our God; ^Rwe have waited for him, and he will save us: this *is* the LORD; we have waited for him, ^Rwe will be glad and rejoice in his salvation.   Gen. 28:21 · Gen. 49:18 · Ps. 20:5

10 ^RFor ^Tin this mountain shall the hand of the LORD rest, and Moab shall be ^Ttrodden down under him, even as straw is trodden down for the dunghill.   Job 9:13 · *on* · *crushed*

11 And he shall spread forth his hands in the midst of them, as he that swimmeth spreadeth forth *his* hands to swim: and he shall ^Rbring down their pride together with the ^Tspoils of their hands.   16:6, 14 · *craft of his*

12 And the ^Rfortress of the high fort of thy walls shall he bring down, lay low, *and* bring to the ground, *even* to the dust.   26:5

CHAPTER 26

Israel's Kingdom Song

I N ^Rthat day shall this song be sung in the land of Judah; We have a strong city; ^Rsalvation will God appoint *for* walls and bulwarks.   4:2; 12:1, 2 · 60:18

2 Open ye the gates, that the righteous nation which keepeth the truth may enter in.

3 Thou wilt keep *him* in perfect ^Rpeace, *whose* mind *is* stayed *on thee:* because he trusteth in thee.   27:5

4 Trust ye in the LORD for ever: for in the LORD JE-HO'-VAH *is* everlasting strength:

5 For he bringeth down them that dwell on high; ^Rthe lofty city, he layeth it low; he layeth it low, *even* to the ground; he bringeth it *even* to the dust.   25:12

6 The foot shall tread it down, *even* the feet of the poor, *and* the steps of the needy.

7 The way of the just *is* uprightness: thou, most upright, dost weigh the path of the just.

8 Yea, ^Rin the way of thy judgments, O LORD, have we waited for thee; the desire of *our* soul *is* to ^Rthy name, and to the remembrance of thee.   64:5 · v. 13

9 ^RWith my soul have I desired thee in the night; yea, with my spirit within me will I seek thee early: for when thy judgments *are* in the earth, the inhabitants of the world will learn righteousness.   Song 3:1; Luke 6:12

10 Let favour be shewed to the wicked, *yet* will ^Rhe not learn righteousness: in the land of uprightness will he deal unjustly, and will not behold the majesty of the LORD. [Rom. 2:4]

11 LORD, *when* thy hand is lifted up, they will not see: *but* they shall see, and be ashamed for *their* envy at the people; yea, the fire of thine enemies shall devour them.

12 LORD, thou wilt ordain peace for us: for thou also hast wrought all our works in us.

13 O LORD our God, *other* lords beside thee have had dominion over us: *but* by thee only will we make mention of thy name.

14 *They are* dead, they shall not live; *they are* deceased, they shall not rise: therefore hast thou ^Tvisited and destroyed them, and made all their memory to perish.   *judged*

15 ^RThou hast increased the nation, O LORD, thou hast increased the nation: thou art glorified: thou hadst removed *it* far *unto* all the ends of the earth.   9:3; 33:17; 54:2, 3

16 LORD, ^Rin trouble have they visited thee, they poured out a prayer *when* thy chastening *was* upon them.   37:3

17 Like as ^Ra woman with child, *that* draweth near the time of her delivery, is in pain, *and* crieth out in her pangs; so have we been in thy sight, O LORD.   13:8; 21:3

18 We have been with child, we have been in pain, we have as it were brought forth wind; we have ^Tnot wrought any deliverance

in the earth; neither have ^Rthe inhabitants of the world fallen.   *accomplished nothing* • Ps. 17:14

19 Thy ^Rdead *men* shall live, *together with* my dead body shall they arise. Awake and sing, ye that dwell in dust: for thy dew *is as* the dew of herbs, and the earth shall cast out the dead.   25:8; [Ezek. 37:1–14] ✫

20 Come, my people, enter thou into thy chambers, and shut thy doors about thee: hide thyself as it were for a little moment, until the indignation be overpast.

21 For, behold, the LORD ^Rcometh out of his place to punish the inhabitants of the earth for their iniquity: the earth also shall disclose her blood, and shall no more cover her slain.   Mic. 1:3; [Jude 14]

CHAPTER 27

Israel Blossoms in the Kingdom

IN that day the LORD with his sore and great and strong sword shall punish le-vi′-a-than the piercing serpent, even le-vi′-a-than that crooked serpent; and he shall slay the dragon that *is* in the sea.

2 In that day ^Rsing ye unto her, ^RA vineyard of red wine.   5:1 • Ps. 80:8; Jer. 2:21

3 ^RI the LORD do ^Tkeep it; I will water it every moment: lest *any* hurt it, ^RI will keep it night and day.   31:5 • *protect* • Ps. 121:4, 5

4 Fury *is* not in me: who would set ^Rthe briers *and* thorns against me in battle? I would ^Tgo through them, I would burn them together.   9:18; 2 Sam. 23:6 • *march against*

5 Or let him ^Ttake hold of my strength, *that* he may ^Rmake peace with me; *and* he shall make peace with me.   *call upon* • Job 22:21

6 He shall cause them that come of Jacob to take root: Israel shall blossom and bud, and fill the face of the world with fruit.

7 Hath he smitten him, as he smote those that smote him? or is he slain according to the slaughter of them that are slain by him?

8 In measure, when it shooteth forth, thou wilt debate with it: he stayeth his rough wind in the day of the east wind.

9 By this therefore shall the iniquity of Jacob be ^Rpurged; and this *is* all the fruit to take away his sin; when he maketh all the stones of the altar as chalkstones that are beaten in sunder, the groves and ^Timages shall not stand up.   1:25; 48:10 • *idols*

10 Yet the defenced city *shall be* desolate, *and* the habitation forsaken, and left like a wilderness: ^Rthere shall the calf feed, and there shall he lie down, and ^Tconsume the branches thereof.   17:2; 32:14 • *destroy*

11 When the boughs thereof are withered, they shall be broken off: the women come, *and* set them on fire: for it *is* a people of no understanding: therefore he that made them will not have mercy on them, and he that formed them will shew them no favour.

12 And it shall come to pass in that day, *that* the ^RLORD shall ^Tbeat off from the channel of the river unto the stream of Egypt, and ye shall be gathered one by one, O ye children of Israel.   11:11; 17:6; 24:13 • *thresh*

13 And it shall come to pass in that day, *that* the great trumpet shall be blown, and they shall come which were ready to perish in the land of Assyria, and the outcasts in the land of Egypt, and shall worship the LORD in the holy mount at Jerusalem.

CHAPTER 28

Woe to Ephraim

WOE to the crown of pride, to the ^Rdrunkards of E′-phra-im, whose glorious beauty *is* a fading flower, which *are* on the head of the ^Tfat valleys of them that are overcome with wine!   Nah. 1:10 • *rich*

2 Behold, the Lord hath a ^Rmighty and strong one, ^R*which* as a tempest of hail *and* a destroying storm, as a flood of mighty waters overflowing, shall cast down to the earth with the hand.   8:7 • 30:30; Ezek. 13:11

3 The crown of pride, the drunkards of E′-phra-im, shall be trodden under feet:

4 And the glorious beauty, which *is* on the head of the fat valley, shall be a fading flower, *and* as the hasty fruit before the summer; which *when* he that looketh upon it seeth, while it is yet in his hand he eateth it up.

5 In that day shall the LORD of hosts be for a crown of glory, and for a diadem of beauty, unto the residue of his people,

6 And for a spirit of judgment to him that sitteth in judgment, and for strength to them that turn the battle to the gate.

7 But they also ^Rhave ^Terred through wine, and through strong drink are out of the way: the priest and the prophet have erred through strong drink, they are swallowed up of wine, they are out of the way through strong drink; they err in vision, they stumble *in* judgment.   Hos. 4:11 • *sinned*

8 For all tables are full of vomit *and* filthiness, *so that there is* no place clean.

9 ^RWhom shall he teach knowledge? and whom shall he make to understand ^Tdoctrine? *them that are* weaned from the milk, *and* drawn from the breasts.   v. 26 • *the message*

10 For precept *must be* upon precept, precept upon precept; line upon line, line upon line; here a little, *and* there a little:

11 For with ^Tstammering lips and another tongue will he speak to this people.   *strange*

12 To whom he said, This *is* the ^Rrest *wherewith* ye may cause the weary to rest; and this *is* the refreshing: yet they would not hear.   [11:10]; 30:15; Jer. 6:16; [Matt. 11:28, 29]

13 But the word of the LORD was unto them ^Tprecept upon precept, precept upon

precept; line upon line, line upon line; here a little, *and* there a little; that they might go, and ᴿfall backward, and be broken, and snared, and taken.   *order* • 8:15; Matt. 21:44

14 Wherefore hear the word of the LORD, ye ᴿscornful men, that ᴿrule this people which is in Jerusalem.   29:20 • Ezek. 22:27

15 Because ye have said, We have made a covenant with death, and with hell are we at agreement; when the overflowing scourge shall pass through, it shall not come unto us: for we have made lies our refuge, and under falsehood have we hid ourselves:

16 Therefore thus saith the Lord GOD, Behold, I lay in Zion for a foundation ᴿa stone, a tried stone, a precious corner *stone*, a sure foundation: he that believeth shall not ᵀmake haste.   1 Pet. 2:6–8 ☆ • *be forced to flee*

17 ᵀJudgment also will I lay to the line, and righteousness to the plummet: and the hail shall sweep away the refuge of lies, and the waters shall overflow the hiding place.   *justice*

18 And your covenant with death shall be disannulled, and your agreement with hell shall not stand; when the overflowing scourge shall pass through, then ye shall be ᵀtrodden down by it.   *brought into defeat*

19 From the time that it goeth forth it shall take you: for morning by morning shall it pass over, by day and by night: and it shall be a vexation only to understand the report.

20 ᴿFor the bed is shorter than that a *man* can stretch himself *on it:* and the ᵀcovering ᵀnarrower than that he can wrap himself *in it.*   [Num. 32:23] • *blanket* • *too small*

21 For the LORD shall rise up as *in* mount ᴿPer′-a-zim, he shall be wroth as *in* the valley of Gib′-e-on, that he may do his work, his ᵀstrange work; and bring to pass his act, his strange act.   2 Sam. 5:20 • *remarkable*

22 Now therefore be ye not mockers, lest your bands be made strong: for I have heard from the Lord GOD of hosts a consumption, even determined upon the whole earth.

23 Give ye ear, and hear my voice; ᴿhearken, and hear my speech.   Prov. 7:24

24 Doth the ᵀplowman plow all day to sow? doth he ᵀopen and break the clods of his ground?   *farmer* • *turn and harrow the ground*

25 When he hath made plain the face thereof, doth he not ᵀcast abroad the ᵀfitches, and scatter the cummin, and cast in the principal wheat and the appointed barley and the ᴿrie in their place?   *sow* • *dill* • Ex. 9:32

26 For his God doth ᴿinstruct him to discretion, *and* doth teach him.   Jer. 32:33

27 For the ᵀfitchesᴿ are not threshed with a threshing instrument, neither is a cart wheel turned about upon the ᴿcummin; but the fitches are beaten out with a staff, and the cummin with a rod. *dill* • [Amos 1:3] • Matt. 23:23

28 Bread ᵀcorn is ᵀbruised; because he will not ever be threshing it, nor break *it with* the

wheel of his cart, nor ᵀbruise it *with* his horsemen.   *grain* • *ground* • *grind*

29 This also cometh forth from the LORD of hosts, ᴿwhich is wonderful in counsel, *and* excellent in working.   Ps. 92:5; Jer. 32:19

CHAPTER 29

Woe to Ariel (Jerusalem)

WOE to ᵀA′-ri-el, to A′-ri-el, the city *where* David dwelt! add ye year to year; let them kill sacrifices.   *Jerusalem*

2 Yet I will distress A′-ri-el, and there shall be heaviness and sorrow: and it shall be unto me as ᵀA′-ri-el.   *the lion of God*

3 And I will camp against thee round about, and will lay siege against thee with a mount, and I will raise forts against thee.

4 And thou shalt be brought down, *and* shalt speak out of the ground, and thy speech shall be low out of the dust, and thy voice shall be, as of one that hath a familiar spirit, out of the ground, and thy speech shall whisper out of the dust.

5 Moreover the multitude of thy ᴿstrangersᵀ shall be like small dust, and the multitude of the ᵀterrible ones *shall be* as chaff that passeth away: yea, it shall be at an instant suddenly.   25:5 • *foes* • *impressive persons*

6 ᴿThou shalt be visited of the LORD of hosts with thunder, and with earthquake, and great noise, with storm and tempest, and the flame of devouring fire.   28:2; 30:30

7 ᴿAnd the multitude of all the nations that fight against A′-ri-el, even all that fight against her and her ᵀmunition, and that distress her, shall be ᴿas a dream of a night vision.   37:36 • *military equipment* • Job 20:8

8 ᴿIt shall even be as when an hungry *man* dreameth, and, behold, he eateth; but he awaketh, and his soul is empty: or as when a thirsty man dreameth, and, behold, he drinketh; but he awaketh, and, behold, *he is* faint, and his soul hath appetite: so shall the multitude of all the nations be, that fight against mount Zion.   Ps. 73:20

9 Stay yourselves, and wonder; cry ye out, and cry: they are drunken, but not with wine; they stagger, but not with strong drink.

10 For ᴿthe LORD hath poured out upon you the spirit of deep sleep, and hath closed your eyes: the prophets and your ᵀrulers, the seers hath he covered.   Rom. 11:8 • *leaders*

11 And the vision of all is become unto you as the words of a book that is sealed, which *men* deliver to one that is learned, saying, Read this, I pray thee: ᴿand he saith, I cannot; for it *is* sealed: Dan. 12:4

12 And the book is delivered to him that is not learned, saying, Read this, I pray thee: and he saith, I am not learned.

13 Wherefore the Lord said, ᴿForasmuch

as this people draw near *me* with their mouth, and with their lips do honour me, but have removed their heart far from me, and their fear toward me is taught by ᴿthe precept of men: Ezek. 33:31; Mark 7:6, 7 • Col. 2:22

14 ᴿTherefore, behold, I will proceed to do a marvellous work among this people, *even* a marvellous work and a wonder: ᴿfor the wisdom of their wise *men* shall perish, and the understanding of their prudent *men* shall be hid.   Hab. 1:5 • Obad. 8; 1 Cor. 1:19

15 Woe unto them that seek deep to hide their ᵀcounsel from the LORD, and their works are in the dark, and they say, Who seeth us? and who knoweth us?   *intentions*

16 Surely your turning of things upside down shall be esteemed as the potter's clay: for shall the ᴿwork say of him that made it, He made me not? or shall the thing framed say of him that framed it, He had no understanding?   45:9; Rom. 9:20

17 *Is* it not yet a very ᴿlittle while, and ᴿLeb'-a-non shall be turned into a fruitful field, and the fruitful field shall be esteemed as a forest?   35:1, 2 • 32:15

18 And ᴿin that day shall the deaf hear the words of the book, and the ᴿeyes of the blind shall see out of obscurity, and out of darkness.   35:5 • 32:3; Ps. 119:18; Prov. 20:12

19 The meek also shall increase *their* joy in the LORD, and ᴿthe poor among men shall rejoice in the Holy One of Israel.   [James 2:5]

20 For the terrible one is brought to nought, and the scorner is consumed, and all that watch for iniquity are cut off:

21 That make a man an offender for a word, and lay a snare for him that reproveth in the gate, and turn aside the just ᴿforᵀ a thing of nought.   Prov. 28:21 • *nothing*

22 Therefore thus saith the LORD, ᴿwho redeemed Abraham, concerning the house of Jacob, Jacob shall not now be ashamed, neither shall his face now wax pale.   Josh. 24:3

23 But when he seeth his children, the work of mine hands, in the midst of him, they shall sanctify my name, and sanctify the Holy One of Jacob, and shall fear the God of Israel.

24 They also that erred in spirit shall come to understanding, and they that ᵀmurmured shall learn doctrine.   *rebelled*

CHAPTER 30

Woe to Egyptian Alliance

WOE to the rebellious children, saith the LORD, that take counsel, but not of me; and that cover with a covering, but not of my spirit, that they may add sin to sin:

2 ᴿThat walk to go down into Egypt, and ᴿhave not asked at my mouth; to strengthen themselves in the strength of Pharaoh, and to trust in the shadow of Egypt!   31:1 • Num. 27:21

3 ᴿTherefore shall the strength of Pharaoh be your shame, and the trust in the shadow of Egypt *your* confusion.   Jer. 37:5, 7

4 For his ᴿprinces were at Zo'-an, and his ambassadors came to Ha'-nes.   19:11

5 They were all ashamed of a people *that* could not profit them, nor be an help nor profit, but a shame, and also a reproach.

6 The burden of the beasts of the ᵀsouth: into the land of trouble and anguish, from whence *come* the young and old lion, ᴿthe viper and fiery flying serpent, they will carry their riches upon the shoulders of young asses, and their treasures upon the ᵀbunches of camels, to a people *that* shall not profit them.   Negev • Deut. 8:15 • *humps*

7 For the Egyptians shall help in vain, and to no purpose: therefore have I cried concerning this, Their strength *is* to sit still.

8 Now go, write it before them in a ᵀtable, and note it in a book, that it may be for the time to come for ever and ever: *tablet*

9 That ᴿthis *is* a rebellious people, lying children, children *that* will not ᵀhear the law of the LORD: 1:4; 65:2; Deut. 32:20 • *obey*

10 ᴿWhich say to the seers, See not; and to the prophets, Prophesy not unto us right things, ᴿspeak unto us smooth things, prophesy deceits: Amos 2:12; Mic. 2:6, 11 • 2 Tim. 4:3

11 Get you out of the way, ᴿturn aside out of the path, cause the Holy One of Israel to cease from before us.   Deut. 13:5

12 Wherefore thus saith the Holy One of Israel, Because ye ᴿdespise this word, and trust in ᵀoppression and perverseness, and ᵀstay thereon: 5:24; 7:9; 8:6 • *fraud* • *trust*

13 Therefore this iniquity shall be to you ᴿas a breach ready to fall, swelling out in a high wall, whose breaking ᴿcometh suddenly at an instant.   Ps. 62:3 • 29:5

14 And ᴿhe shall break it as the breaking of the potters' vessel that is broken in pieces; he shall not spare: so that there shall not be found in the bursting of it a sherd to take fire from the hearth, or to take water *withal* out of the pit.   Jer. 19:11

15 For thus saith the Lord GOD, the Holy One of Israel; In returning and rest shall ye be saved; in quietness and in confidence shall be your strength: and ye would not.

16 But ye said, No; for we will flee upon ᴿhorses; therefore shall ye flee: and, We will ride upon the swift; therefore shall they that pursue you be swift.   2:7; 31:1, [3]

17 One thousand *shall flee* at the rebuke of one; at the rebuke of five shall ye flee: till ye be left as a beacon upon the top of a mountain, and as an ensign on an hill.

18 And therefore will the LORD wait, that he may be gracious unto you, and therefore will he be exalted, that he may have mercy upon you: for the LORD *is* a God of judgment: blessed *are* all they that wait for him.

19 For the people [R]shall dwell in Zion at Jerusalem: thou shalt weep no more: he will be very gracious unto thee at the voice of thy cry; when he shall hear it, he will answer thee.   25:8; [60:20; 61:1-3]; 65:9; [Ezek. 37:25]

20 And *though* the Lord give you [R]the bread of adversity, and the water of [T]affliction, yet shall not [R]thy teachers be removed into a corner any more, but thine eyes shall see thy teachers: Ps. 127:2 • *trouble* • Ps. 74:9

21 And thine ears shall hear a word behind thee, saying, This *is* the [R]way, walk ye in it, when ye [R]turn to the right hand, and when ye turn to the left.   [35:8, 9] • Josh. 1:7

22 Ye shall defile also the covering of thy graven images of silver, and the ornament of thy molten images of gold: thou shalt cast them away as a menstruous cloth; [R]thou shalt say unto it, Get thee hence.   Hos 14:8

23 [R]Then shall he give the rain of thy seed, that thou shalt sow the ground withal; and bread of the increase of the earth, and it shall be fat and plenteous: in that day shall thy cattle feed in large pastures. [Matt. 6:33; 1 Tim. 4:8]

24 The oxen likewise and the young asses that [T]ear the ground shall eat [T]clean provender, which hath been winnowed with the shovel and with the fan.   *till* • *good fodder*

25 And there shall be upon every high mountain, and upon every high hill, rivers *and* streams of waters in the day of the great slaughter, when the towers fall.

26 Moreover [R]the light of the moon shall be as the light of the sun, and the light of the sun shall be sevenfold, as the light of seven days, in the day that the LORD bindeth up the breach of his people, and healeth the stroke of their wound.   [24:23; 60:19, 20]

27 [R]Behold, the name of the LORD cometh from far, burning *with* his anger, and the burden [T]thereof *is* heavy: [R]his lips are full of indignation, and his tongue as a devouring fire: 59:19 • *of flame* • [10:5; 13:5]

28 And his breath, as an overflowing stream, shall reach to the midst of the neck, to sift the nations with the sieve of vanity: and *there shall be* a bridle in the jaws of the people, causing *them* to err.

29 Ye shall have a song, as in the night *when* a holy solemnity is kept; and gladness of heart, as when one goeth with a pipe to come into [R]the mountain of the LORD, to the mighty One of Israel.   [2:3]

30 And the LORD shall cause his glorious voice to be heard, and shall shew the lighting down of his arm, with the indignation of *his* anger, and *with* the flame of a devouring fire, *with* scattering, and tempest, and hailstones.

31 For [R]through the voice of the LORD shall the Assyrian be [T]beaten down, [R]*which* smote with a rod.   37:36 • *crushed* • 10:5, 24

32 [R]And *in* every place where the grounded staff shall pass, which the LORD

shall lay upon him, *it* shall be with tabrets and harps: and in battles of [R]shaking will he fight [T]with it.   10:24 • 11:15 • *against them*

33 For To'-phet *is* ordained of old; yea, for the king it is prepared; he hath made *it* deep *and* large: the pile thereof *is* fire and much wood; the breath of the LORD, like a stream of brimstone, doth kindle it.

CHAPTER 31

WOE to them that go down to Egypt for help; and stay[T] on horses, and trust in chariots, because *they are* many; and in horsemen, because they are very strong; but they look not unto the Holy One of Israel, neither seek the LORD!   *depend*

2 Yet he also *is* wise, and will bring evil, and will not call back his words: but will arise against the house of the evildoers, and against the help of them that work iniquity.

3 Now the Egyptians *are* [R]men, and not God; and their [R]horses flesh, and not spirit. When the LORD shall stretch out his hand, both he that helpeth shall fall, and he that is [T]holpen shall fall down, and they all shall fail together.   Ezek. 28:9; 2 Thess. 2:4 • 36:9 • *helped*

4 For thus hath the LORD spoken unto me, [R]Like as the lion and the young lion roaring on his prey, when a multitude of shepherds is called forth against him, *he* will not be afraid of their voice, nor abase himself for the noise of them: so shall the LORD of hosts come down to fight for mount Zion, and for the hill thereof.   Num. 24:9

5 [R]As birds flying, so will the LORD of hosts defend Jerusalem; defending also he will deliver *it; and* passing over he will preserve *it.*   Deut. 32:11

6 [R]Turn ye unto *him from* whom the children of Israel have deeply revolted. [44:22]

7 For in that day every man shall [R]cast away his idols of silver, and his idols of gold, which your own hands have made unto you *for* [R]a sin.   2:20; 30:22 • 1 Kin. 12:30

8 Then shall the [R]Assyrian fall with the sword, not of a mighty man; and the sword, not of a mean man, shall devour him: but he shall flee from the sword, and his young men shall be [T]discomfited.   10:12 • *slaves*

9 And he shall pass over to his strong hold for fear, and his princes shall be afraid of the ensign, saith the LORD, whose fire *is* in Zion, and his furnace in Jerusalem.

CHAPTER 32

Behold the Coming King

BEHOLD, [R]a king shall reign in righteousness, and princes shall rule in judgment.   [9:6, 7; 11:4, 5; Ps. 72; Jer. 23:5]

2 And a man shall be as an hiding place from the wind, and a covert from the tempest; as rivers of water in a dry place, as the shadow of a great rock in a weary land.

3 And ᴿthe eyes of them that see shall not be ᵀdim, and the ears of them that hear shall hearken.   29:18 • *blind*

4 The heart also of the rash shall understand knowledge, and the tongue of the stammerers shall be ready to speak plainly.

5 The vile person shall be no more called liberal, nor the churl said *to be* bountiful.

6 For the vile person will speak villany, and his ᴿheart will work iniquity, to practise hypocrisy, and to utter error against the LORD, to make empty the soul of the hungry, and he will cause the drink of the thirsty to fail.   59:7, 13; Prov. 19:3

7 The instruments also of the ᵀchurl *are* evil: he ᴿdeviseth wicked devices to destroy the poor with lying words, even when the needy speaketh right.   *greedy one* • Jer. 5:26–28

8 But the ᵀliberal deviseth liberal things; and by liberal things shall he stand.   *noble*

9 Rise up, ye ᴿwomen ᴿthat are at ease; hear my voice, ye careless daughters; give ear unto my speech.   47:8; Zeph. 2:15 • Amos 6:1

10 Many days and years shall ye be troubled, ye careless women: for the vintage shall fail, the gathering shall not come.

11 Tremble, ye women that are at ease; ᴿbe troubled, ye careless ones: strip you, and make you bare, and gird *sackcloth* upon *your* loins.   22:12

12 They shall lament for the teats, for the pleasant fields, for the fruitful vine.

13 Upon the land of my people shall come up thorns *and* briers; yea, upon all the houses of joy *in* the joyous city:

14 Because the palaces shall be forsaken; the multitude of the city shall be left; the forts and towers shall be for dens for ever, a joy of wild asses, a pasture of flocks;

15 Until ᴿthe spirit be poured upon us from on high, and ᴿthe wilderness be a fruitful field, and the fruitful field be counted for a forest.   [11:2; Joel 2:28] • 29:17

16 Then ᴿjudgment shall dwell in the wilderness, and righteousness remain in the fruitful field.   1:26; 33:5

17 ᴿAnd the work of righteousness shall be peace; and the effect of righteousness quietness and assurance for ever.   James 3:18

18 And my people shall dwell in a ᴿpeaceable habitation, and in ᵀsure dwellings, and in quiet resting places;   [26:3, 12] • *safe*

19 ᴿWhen it shall hail, coming down ᴿon the forest; and the city shall be ᵀlow in a low place.   30:30 • Zech. 11:2 • *brought down*

20 Blessed *are* ye that ᴿsow beside all waters, that send forth *thither* the feet of ᴿthe ox and the ass.   [1 Cor. 9:22] • [Eccl. 11:1]

CHAPTER 33

Woe to the Spoiler of Jerusalem (Assyria)

WOE to thee that spoilest, and thou *wast* not spoiled; and dealest treacherously, and they dealt not treacherously with thee! when thou shalt cease to spoil, thou shalt be ᵀspoiled; *and* when thou shalt make an end to deal treacherously, they shall deal treacherously with thee.   *robbed*

2 O LORD, ᴿbe gracious unto us; ᴿwe have waited for thee: ᴿbe thou their arm every morning, our salvation also in the time of trouble.   30:18, 19 • 25:9 • 40:10; 51:5; 59:16

3 ᴿAt the noise of the tumult the people fled; at the lifting up of thyself the nations were scattered.   10:33; 17:13; 59:16–18

4 And your spoil shall be gathered *like* the gathering of the caterpiller: as the running to and fro of locusts shall he run upon them.

5 ᴿThe LORD is exalted; for he dwelleth on high: ᴿhe hath filled Zion with judgment and righteousness.   Ps. 97:9 • 1:26; 28:6; 32:16

6 And wisdom and knowledge shall be the ᵀstabilityᴿ of thy times, ᴿand strength of salvation: ᴿthe fear of the LORD *is* his treasure.   *security* • 33:20 • 45:17 • Matt. 6:19–21

7 Behold, their ᵀvaliant ones shall cry without: ᴿthe ambassadors of peace shall weep bitterly.   *champions* • 2 Kin. 18:18, 37

8 ᴿThe highways lie waste, the wayfaring man ceaseth: ᴿhe hath broken the covenant, he hath despised the cities, he regardeth no man.   Judg. 5:6 • 2 Kin. 18:14–17

9 The earth mourneth *and* languisheth: Leb′-a-non is ashamed *and* ᵀhewn down: Shar′-on is like a wilderness; and Ba′-shan and Carmel shake off *their fruits*.   *destroyed*

10 Now will I rise, saith the LORD; now will I be exalted; now will I lift up myself.

11 ᴿYe shall conceive chaff, ye shall bring forth stubble: your breath, *as* fire, shall devour you.   [59:4; James 1:15; Ps. 7:14]

12 And the people shall be *as* the burnings of lime: ᴿas thorns cut up shall they be burned in the fire.   27:4; 2 Sam. 23:6, 7

13 Hear, ᴿye *that are* far off, what I have done; and, ye *that are* near, acknowledge my might.   49:1; Ps. 48:10

14 The ᴿsinners in Zion are afraid; fearfulness hath ᵀsurprised the ᵀhypocrites. Who among us shall dwell with the devouring fire? who among us shall dwell with everlasting burnings?   [1:28] • *seized* • *godless ones*

15 He that walketh righteously, and speaketh uprightly; he that despiseth the gain of ᵀoppressions, that shaketh his hands from holding of bribes, that stoppeth his ears from hearing of ᵀblood, and shutteth his eyes from seeing evil;   *deceits* • *violence*

16 He shall dwell on ᵀhigh: his place of defence *shall be* the munitions of rocks: ᴿbread shall be given him; his waters *shall be* sure.   *heights; high places* • 49:10

17 Thine eyes shall see Rthe king in his beauty: they shall behold the land Tthat is very far off. [vv. 21, 22]; 6:5 • of far distances

18 Thine heart shall meditate terror. RWhere is the scribe? where is the receiver? where is he that counted the towers? 1 Cor. 1:20

19 RThou shalt not see a fierce people, a people of a deeper speech than thou canst perceive; of a Tstammering tongue, that thou canst not understand. 2 Kin. 19:32 • strange

20 RLook upon Zion, the city of our solemnities: thine eyes shall see Jerusalem a quiet habitation, a tabernacle that shall not be taken down; not one of the stakes thereof shall ever be removed, neither shall any of the cords thereof be broken. Ps. 48:12

21 But there the glorious LORD will be unto us a place of broad rivers and streams; wherein shall go no Tgalley with oars, neither shall gallant ship pass thereby. ship

22 For the LORD is our Rjudge, the LORD is our Rlawgiver, Rthe LORD is our king; he will save us. 2:4; [11:4; 16:5] • James 4:12 • Ps. 89:18

23 Thy tacklings are loosed; they could not well strengthen their mast, they could not spread the sail: then is the prey of a great spoil divided; the Rlame take the prey. [35:6]

24 And the inhabitant shall not say, I am sick: Rthe people that dwell therein shall be forgiven their iniquity. 40:2; Jer. 50:20

CHAPTER 34

Woe to the Nations

COME near, Rye nations, to hear; and hearken, ye people: Rlet the earth hear, and all that is therein; the world, and all things that come forth of it. 41:1 • Deut. 32:1

2 For the indignation of the LORD is upon all nations, and his fury upon all their armies: he hath utterly destroyed them, he hath delivered them to the slaughter.

3 Their slain also shall be cast out, and Rtheir stink shall come up out of their carcases, and the mountains shall be melted with their Rblood. Joel 2:20 • Ezek. 14:19; 35:6

4 And all the host of heaven shall be dissolved, and the heavens shall be rolled together as a scroll: and all their host shall fall down, as the leaf falleth off from the vine, and as a falling fig from the fig tree.

5 For my sword shall be bathed in heaven: behold, it shall come down upon Id-u-me'-a, and Rupon the people of my curse, to judgment. 24:6; 43:28

6 The sword of the LORD is filled with blood, it is made fat with fatness, and with the blood of lambs and goats, with the fat of the kidneys of rams: for Rthe LORD hath a sacrifice in RBoz'-rah, and a great slaughter in the land of Id-u-me'-a. Zeph. 1:7 • Jer. 48:24

7 And the unicorns shall come down with them, and the bullocks with the bulls; and their land shall be soaked with blood, and their dust made fat with fatness.

8 For it is the day of the LORD's Rvengeance, and the year of recompences for the controversy of Zion. 13:6; 35:4; 47:3; 61:2

9 RAnd the streams thereof shall be turned into pitch, and the dust thereof into brimstone, and the land thereof shall become burning pitch. Deut. 29:23

10 It shall not be quenched night nor day; Rthe smoke thereof shall go up for ever: Rfrom generation to generation it shall lie waste; none shall Tpass through it for ever and ever. Rev. 14:11; 18:18; 19:3 • Mal. 1:4 • live

11 But the Tcormorant and the bittern shall possess it; the owl also and the raven shall dwell in it: and Rhe shall stretch upon it the line of confusion, and the stones of emptiness. pelican • 2 Kin. 21:13

12 RThey shall call the nobles thereof to the kingdom, but none shall be there, and all her princes shall be nothing. Jer. 27:20

13 And thorns shall come up in her palaces, nettles and brambles in the fortresses thereof: and it shall be an habitation of dragons, and a court for owls.

14 The Twild beasts of the desert shall also meet with the wild beasts of the island, and the satyr shall cry to his fellow; the screech owl also shall rest there, and find for herself a place of rest. hyenas

15 There shall the great owl make her nest, and lay, and hatch, and gather under her shadow: there shall the vultures also be gathered, every one with her mate.

16 Seek ye out of Rthe book of the LORD, and read: no one of these shall fail, none shall want her mate: Rfor my mouth it hath commanded, and his spirit it hath gathered them. 30:8; [Mal. 3:16] • 1:20; 40:5; 58:14

17 And he hath cast the lot for them, and his hand hath divided it unto them by line: they shall possess it for ever, from generation to generation shall they dwell therein.

CHAPTER 35

Behold the Coming Kingdom

THE wilderness and the solitary place shall be glad for them; and the desert shall rejoice, and blossom as the rose.

2 RIt shall blossom abundantly, and Rrejoice even with joy and singing: the glory of Leb'-a-non shall be given unto it, the excellency of Carmel and Shar'-on, they shall see the glory of the LORD, and the excellency of our God. [27:6]; 32:15 • v. 10

3 RStrengthen ye the weak hands, and confirm the feeble knees. Job 4:3, 4; Heb. 12:12

4 Say to them that are of a fearful heart, Be strong, fear not: behold, your God will

come *with* vengeance, *even* God *with* a recompence; he will come and save you.

5 Then the ᴿeyes of the blind shall be opened, and ᴿthe ears of the deaf shall be ᵀunstopped.   John 9:6, 7 ✩ • [Matt. 11:5] • *opened*

6 Then shall the ᴿlame *man* leap as ᵀan hart, and the tongue of the dumb sing: for in the wilderness shall waters break out, and streams in the desert.   Matt. 15:30 ✩ • *a deer*

7 And the parched ground shall become a pool, and the thirsty land springs of water: in the habitation of dragons, where each lay, *shall be* grass with reeds and rushes.

8 And an highway shall be there, and a way, and it shall be called The way of holiness; the unclean shall not pass over it; but it *shall be* for those: the wayfaring men, though fools, shall not err *therein.*

9 ᴿNo lion shall be there, nor *any* ravenous beast shall go up thereon, it shall not be found there; but the ᴿredeemed shall walk *there:*   Lev. 26:6; Ezek. 34:25 • 51:10; 62:12

10 And the ᴿransomed of the LORD shall return, and come to Zion with songs and everlasting joy upon their heads: they shall obtain joy and gladness, and ᴿsorrow and sighing shall flee away.   51:11 • 25:8

CHAPTER 36

Assyria Challenges God
2 Kin. 18:13–37; 2 Chr. 32:1–19

N OW ᴿit came to pass in the fourteenth year of king Hez-e-ki′-ah, *that* Sen-nach′-e-rib king of Assyria came up against all the defenced cities of Judah, and took them.   2 Kin. 18:13, 17; 2 Chr. 32:1

2 And the king of Assyria sent Rab′-sha-keh from La′-chish to Jerusalem unto king Hez-e-ki′-ah with a great army. And he stood by the conduit of the upper pool in the highway of the fuller's field.

3 Then came forth unto him E-li′-a-kim, Hil-ki′-ah's son, which was over the house, and Sheb′-na the ᵀscribe, and Jo′-ah, A′-saph's son, the recorder.   *secretary*

4 And Rab′-sha-keh said unto them, Say ye now to Hez-e-ki′-ah, Thus saith the great king, the king of Assyria, What confidence *is* this wherein thou trustest?

5 I say, *sayest thou,* (but *they are but* ᵀvain words) *I have* counsel and strength for war: now on whom dost thou trust, that thou rebellest against me?   *shallow*

6 Lo, thou trustest in the ᴿstaff of this broken reed, on Egypt; whereon if a man lean, it will go into his hand, and pierce it: ᴿso *is* Pharaoh king of Egypt to all that trust in him.   Ezek. 29:6, 7 • 30:3, 5, 7; Ps. 146:3

7 But if thou say to me, We trust in the LORD our God: *is it* not he, whose high places and whose altars Hez-e-ki′-ah hath taken

away, and said to Judah and to Jerusalem, Ye shall worship before this altar?

8 Now therefore give pledges, I pray thee, ᵀto my master the king of Assyria, and I will give thee two thousand horses, if thou be able on thy part to set riders upon them.   *with*

9 How then wilt thou turn away the face of one captain of the least of my master's servants, and put thy ᴿtrust on Egypt for chariots and for horsemen?   20:5; 30:2–5, 7

10 And am I now come up without the LORD against this land to destroy it? ᴿthe LORD said unto me, Go up against this land, and destroy it.   1 Kin. 13:18; 22:6, 12

11 Then said E-li′-a-kim and Sheb′-na and Jo′-ah unto Rab′-sha-keh, Speak, I pray thee, unto thy servants in the Syrian language; for we understand *it:* and speak not to us in the Jews' language, in the ᵀears of the people that *are* on the wall.   *hearing*

12 But Rab′-sha-keh said, Hath my master sent me to thy master and to thee to speak these words? *hath he* not *sent me* to the men that sit upon the wall, that they may eat their own ᵀdung, and drink their own ᵀpiss with you?   *refuse • urine*

13 Then Rab′-sha-keh stood, and ᴿcried with a loud voice in the Jews' language, and said, Hear ye the words of the great king, the king of Assyria.   2 Chr. 32:18

14 Thus saith the king, Let not Hez-e-ki′-ah ᴿdeceive you: for he shall not be able to deliver you.   37:10

15 Neither let Hez-e-ki′-ah make you trust in the LORD, saying, The LORD will surely deliver us: this city shall not be delivered into the hand of the king of Assyria.

16 Hearken not to Hez-e-ki′-ah: for thus saith the king of Assyria, Make *an agreement* with me *by* a present, and come out to me: and eat ye every one of his vine, and every one of his fig tree, and drink ye every one the waters of his own cistern;

17 Until I come and take you away to a land like your own land, a land of ᵀcorn and wine, a land of bread and vineyards.   *grain*

18 *Beware* lest Hez-e-ki′-ah persuade you, saying, The LORD will deliver us. Hath any of the gods of the nations delivered his land out of the hand of the king of Assyria?

19 Where *are* the gods of ᴿHa′-math and Ar′-phad? where *are* the gods of Seph-ar-va′-im? and have they delivered ᴿSa-mar′-i-a out of my hand?   10:9–11; 37:11–13 • 2 Kin. 17:6

20 Who *are they* among all the gods of these lands, that have delivered their land out of my hand, that ᴿthe LORD should deliver Jerusalem out of my hand?   2 Chr. 32:15

21 But they held their peace, and answered him not a word: for the king's commandment was, saying, Answer him not.

22 Then came E-li′-a-kim, the son of Hil-ki′-ah, that *was* over the household, and

Sheb'-na the scribe, and Jo'-ah, the son of A'-saph, the recorder, to Hez-e-ki'-ah with ᴿtheir clothes rent, and told him the words of Rab'-sha-keh.   33:7; 2 Kin. 18:18, 37

CHAPTER 37

God Destroys Assyria—2 Kin. 19:1-37

AND it came to pass, when king Hez-e-ki'-ah heard it, that he rent his clothes, and covered himself with sackcloth, and went into the house of the LORD.

2 ᴿAnd he sent ᴿE-li'-a-kim, who was over the household, and ᴿSheb'-na the scribe, and the elders of the priests covered with sackcloth, unto ᴿIsaiah the prophet the son of Amoz.   2 Kin. 19:2 · 22:20 · 22:15 · 1:1

3 ᴿAnd they said unto him, Thus saith Hez-e-ki'-ah, This day is a day of trouble, and of rebuke, and of blasphemy: for the children are come to the birth, and there is not strength to bring forth.   2 Kin. 19:3

4 It may be the LORD thy God will hear the words of Rab'-sha-keh, whom the king of Assyria his master hath sent to reproach the living God, and will reprove the words which the LORD thy God hath heard: wherefore lift up thy prayer for the remnant that is left.

5 ᴿSo the servants of king Hez-e-ki'-ah came to Isaiah.   2 Kin. 19:5

6 And Isaiah said unto them, Thus shall ye say unto your master, Thus saith the LORD, Be not afraid of the words that thou hast heard, wherewith the servants of the king of Assyria have blasphemed me.

7 Behold, ᴿI will send a blast upon him, and he shall hear a rumour, and return to his own land; and I will cause him ᵀto fall by the sword in his own land.   2 Chr. 32:21 · to be killed

8 ᴿSo Rab'-sha-keh returned, and found the king of Assyria warring against ᴿLib'-nah: for he had heard that he was departed from La'-chish.   2 Kin. 19:8 · Num. 33:20

9 And he heard say concerning Tir'-ha-kah king of E-thi-o'-pi-a, He is come forth to make war with thee. And when he heard it, he sent messengers to Hez-e-ki'-ah, saying,

10 ᴿThus shall ye speak to Hez-e-ki'-ah king of Judah, saying, ᴿLet not thy God, in whom thou trustest, deceive thee, saying, Jerusalem shall not be given into the hand of the king of Assyria.   2 Kin. 19:10 · 36:15

11 ᴿBehold, thou hast heard what the kings of Assyria have done to all lands by destroying them utterly; and shalt thou be delivered?   10:9-11; 36:18-20; 2 Kin. 19:11

12 Have the gods of the nations delivered them which my fathers have destroyed, as Go'-zan, and Ha'-ran, and Re'-zeph, and the children of Eden which were in Te-las'-sar?

13 Where is the king of Ha'-math, and the

king of Ar'-phad, and the king of the city of Seph-ar-va'-im, He'-na, and I'-vah?

14 And Hez-e-ki'-ah received the letter from the hand of the messengers, and read it: and Hez-e-ki'-ah went up unto the house of the LORD, and spread it before the LORD.

15 ᴿAnd Hez-e-ki'-ah prayed unto the LORD, saying,   2 Kin. 19:15

16 O LORD of hosts, God of Israel, ᴿthat dwellest between the cher'-u-bims, thou art the God, even thou alone, of all the kingdoms of the earth: thou hast made heaven and earth.   Ex. 25:22; 1 Sam. 4:4; Ps. 80:1

17 ᴿIncline thine ear, O LORD, and hear; open thine eyes, O LORD, and see: and hear all the words of Sen-nach'-e-rib, which hath sent to reproach the living God.   Dan. 9:18

18 Of a truth, LORD, the kings of Assyria have laid waste all the nations, and their ᵀcountries,ᴿ   lands · 2 Kin. 15:29; 16:9; 17:24

19 And have ᴿcast their gods into the fire: for they were no gods, but the work of men's hands, wood and stone: therefore they have destroyed them.   Ex. 32:20

20 Now therefore, O LORD our God, save us from his hand, that ᴿall the kingdoms of the earth may know that thou art the LORD, even thou only.   v. 16; 25:9

21 Then Isaiah the son of Amoz sent unto Hez-e-ki'-ah, saying, Thus saith the LORD God of Israel, Whereas thou hast prayed to me against Sen-nach'-e-rib king of Assyria:

22 This is the word which the LORD hath spoken concerning him; The virgin, the daughter of Zion, hath despised thee, and laughed thee to scorn; the daughter of Jerusalem hath shaken her head at thee.

23 Whom hast thou reproached and blasphemed? and against whom hast thou exalted thy voice, and lifted up thine eyes on high? even against the Holy One of Israel.

24 By thy servants hast thou reproached the Lord, and hast said, By the multitude of my chariots am I come up to the height of the mountains, to the sides of ᴿLeb'-a-non; and I will cut down the tall cedars thereof, and the choice fir trees thereof: and I will enter into the height of his border, and the forest of his Carmel.   10:33, 34

25 I have digged, and drunk water; and with the sole of my feet have I dried up all the rivers of the besieged places.

26 Hast thou not heard long ago, how I have done it; and of ancient times, that I have formed it? now have I brought it to pass, that thou shouldest be to ᵀlay waste defenced cities into ruinous heaps.   destroy

27 ᵀTherefore their inhabitants were ᵀof small power, they were dismayed and confounded: they were as the grass of the field, and as the green herb, as the grass on the housetops, and as corn ᵀblasted before it be grown up.   for this reason · weak · withered

28 But I know thy ^Tabode,^R and thy going out, and thy coming in, and thy rage against me.   *dwelling place* • Ps. 139:1

29 Because thy rage against me, and thy tumult, is come up into mine ears, therefore will I put my hook in thy nose, and my bridle in thy lips, and I will turn thee back by the way by which thou camest.

30 And this *shall be* a sign unto thee, Ye shall eat *this* year such as ^Rgroweth of itself; and the second year that which springeth of the same: and in the third year sow ye, and reap, and plant vineyards, and eat the fruit thereof.   Lev. 25:5, 11

31 And the remnant that is escaped of the house of Judah shall again take root downward, and bear fruit upward:

32 For out of Jerusalem shall go forth a ^Rremnant, and they that escape out of mount Zion: the ^Rzeal of the LORD of hosts shall do this.   v. 4; 2 Kin. 19:31 • 9:7; 59:17

33 Therefore thus saith the LORD concerning the king of Assyria, He shall not come into this city, nor shoot an arrow there, nor come before it with shields, nor ^Tcast a bank against it.   set up attacking devices

34 ^RBy the way that he came, by the same shall he return, and shall not come into this city, saith the LORD.   v. 29, 37

35 For I will ^Rdefend this city to save it ^Rfor mine own sake, and for my servant David's sake.   38:6; 2 Kin. 20:6 • 43:25

36 Then the angel of the LORD went forth, and smote in the camp of the Assyrians a ^Thundred and fourscore and five thousand: and when they arose early in the morning, behold, they *were* all dead corpses.   185,000

37 So Sen-nach′-e-rib king of Assyria departed, and went and returned, and dwelt at ^RNin′-e-veh.   Gen. 10:11; Zeph. 2:13

38 And it came to pass, as he was worshipping in the house of Nis′-roch his god, that A-dram′-me-lech and Sha-re′-zer his sons smote him with the sword; and they escaped into the land of ^TAr-me′-ni-a: and E′-sar-had′-don his son reigned in his stead.   Ararat

CHAPTER 38

Hezekiah's Salvation from Sickness

IN those days was Hez-e-ki′-ah sick unto death. And Isaiah the prophet the son of Amoz came unto him, and said unto him, Thus saith the LORD, Set thine house in order: for thou shalt die, and not live.

2 Then Hez-e-ki′-ah turned his face toward the wall, and prayed unto the LORD,

3 And said, Remember now, O LORD, I beseech thee, how I have walked before thee in truth and with a perfect heart, and have done *that which is* good in thy sight. And Hez-e-ki′-ah wept ^Tsore.   very much

4 Then came the word of the LORD to Isaiah, saying,

5 Go, and say to Hez-e-ki′-ah, Thus saith the LORD, the God of David thy father, I have heard thy prayer, I have seen thy tears: behold, I will add unto thy days ^Rfifteen years.   2 Kin. 18:2, 13

6 And I will deliver thee and this city out of the hand of the king of Assyria: and ^RI will defend this city.   37:35; 2 Chr. 32:21

7 And this *shall be* ^Ra sign unto thee from the LORD, that the LORD will do this thing that he hath spoken;   7:11; 2 Kin. 20:8

8 Behold, I will bring again the shadow of the degrees, which is gone down in the ^Rsun dial of Ahaz, ten ^Tdegrees backward. So the sun returned ten degrees, by which degrees it was gone down.   Josh. 10:12-14 • steps

9 The writing of Hez-e-ki′-ah king of Judah, when he had been sick, and was recovered of his sickness:

10 I said in the cutting off of my days, I shall go to the gates of the grave: I am deprived of the residue of my years.

11 I said, I shall not see the LORD, *even* the LORD, ^Rin the land of the living: I shall behold man no more with the inhabitants of the world.   Ps. 27:13

12 Mine age is departed, and is removed from me as a shepherd's tent: I have cut off like a weaver my life: he will ^Tcut me off with pining sickness: from day *even* to night wilt thou make an end of me.   cut me off from the loom

13 I reckoned till morning, *that,* as a lion, so will he break all my bones: from day *even* to night wilt thou make an end of me.

14 Like a crane *or* a swallow, so did I chatter: ^RI did mourn as a dove: mine eyes fail *with looking* upward: O LORD, I am oppressed; undertake for me.   59:11

15 ^RWhat shall I say? He hath both spoken unto me, and himself hath done *it:* I shall go softly all my years ^Rin the bitterness of my soul.   Ps. 39:9 • 38:17; Job 7:11; 10:1

16 O Lord, by these *things men* live, and in all these *things is* the life of my spirit: so wilt thou ^Trecover me, and make me to live. restore

17 Behold, for peace I had great bitterness: but thou hast in love to my soul *delivered it* from the pit of corruption: for thou hast cast all my sins behind thy back.

18 For the grave cannot praise thee, death can *not* celebrate thee: they that go down into the pit cannot hope for thy truth.

19 The living, the living, he shall praise thee, as I *do* this day: the father to the children shall make known thy truth.

20 The LORD *was ready* to save me: therefore we will sing my songs to the stringed instruments all the days of our life in the house of the LORD.

21 For ^RIsaiah had said, Let them take a

lump of figs, and lay *it* for a plaister upon the boil, and he shall recover.   2 Kin. 20:7

22 ᴿHez-e-ki'-ah also had said, What *is* the sign that I shall go up to the house of the LORD?   2 Kin. 20:8

CHAPTER 39

Hezekiah's Sin

AT ᴿthat time Me-ro'-dach–bal'-a-dan, the son of Bal'-a-dan, king of Babylon, sent letters and a present to Hez-e-ki'-ah: for he had heard that he had been sick, and was recovered.   2 Kin. 20:12; 2 Chr. 32:31

2 And Hez-e-ki'-ah was glad of them, and shewed them the house of his ᵀprecious things, the silver, and the gold, and the spices, and the precious ointment, and all the house of his armour, and all that was found in his treasures: there was nothing in his house, nor in all his dominion, that Hez-e-ki'-ah shewed them not.   *special treasures*

3 Then came Isaiah the ᴿprophet unto king Hez-e-ki'-ah, and said unto him, What said these men? and from whence came they unto thee? And Hez-e-ki'-ah said, They are come from a ᴿfar country unto me, *even* from Babylon.   2 Sam. 12:1 • Deut. 28:49

4 Then said he, What have they seen in thine house? And Hez-e-ki'-ah answered, All that *is* in mine house have they seen: there is nothing among my treasures that I have not shewed them.

5 Then said Isaiah to Hez-e-ki'-ah, Hear the ᴿword of the LORD of hosts: 1 Sam. 13:13, 14

6 Behold, the days come, ᴿthat all that *is* in thine house, and *that* which thy fathers have laid up in store until this day, shall be ᴿcarried to Babylon: nothing shall be left, saith the LORD.   Jer. 20:5 • 2 Kin. 24:13; 25:13–15

7 And ᴿof thy sons that shall issue from thee, which thou shalt beget, shall they take away; and they shall be eunuchs in the palace of the king of Babylon.   Dan. 1:3–5

8 Then said Hez-e-ki'-ah to Isaiah, ᴿGood *is* the word of the LORD which thou hast spoken. He said moreover, For there shall be peace and truth in my days.   1 Sam. 3:18

CHAPTER 40

Comfort Because of Israel's Deliverance

COMFORTᴿ ye, comfort ye my people, saith your God.   12:1; 49:13; 51:3, 12; 52:9

2 Speak ye ᵀcomfortably to Jerusalem, and cry unto her, that her ᵀwarfare is accomplished, that her iniquity is pardoned: for she hath received of the LORD's hand double for all her sins.   *kindly • conflict is over*

3 ᴿThe voice of him that crieth in the wilderness, Prepare ye the way of the LORD,

make straight in the desert a highway for our God.   Matt. 3:3; Mark 1:3; Luke 3:4–6; John 1:23 ☆

4 Every valley shall be exalted, and every mountain and hill shall be made low: ᴿand the crooked shall be made ᵀstraight, and the rough places plain: 45:2 • *a straight place*

5 And the glory of the LORD shall be revealed, and all flesh shall see *it* together: for the mouth of the LORD hath spoken *it*.

6 The voice said, Cry. And he said, What shall I cry? ᴿAll flesh *is* grass, and all the goodliness thereof *is* as the flower of the field: Job 14:2; Ps. 102:11; 103:15; 1 Pet. 1:24, 25

7 The ᴿgrass withereth, the flower fadeth: because the ᵀspirit of the LORD bloweth upon it: surely the people *is* grass.   Ps. 90:5, 6 • *breath*

8 The grass withereth, the flower fadeth: but ᴿthe word of our God shall stand for ever.   59:21; Matt. 5:18; [John 12:34]; 1 Pet. 1:25

9 O Zion, that bringest good tidings, get thee up into the high mountain; O Jerusalem, that bringest good tidings, lift up thy voice with strength; lift *it* up, be not afraid; say unto the cities of Judah, Behold your God!

10 Behold, the Lord GOD will come ᵀwith strong *hand*, and his ᴿarm shall rule for him: behold, his reward *is* with him, and his work before him.   *in strength* • 59:16, 18 ☆

11 He shall ᴿfeed his flock like a shepherd: he shall gather the lambs with his arm, and carry *them* in his bosom, *and* shall gently lead those that are with young.   Mic. 5:4 ☆

Comfort Because of God's Character

12 ᴿWho hath measured the waters in the hollow of his hand, and ᵀmeted out heaven with the span, and comprehended the dust of the earth in a measure, and weighed the mountains in scales, and the hills in a balance?   Prov. 30:4 • *measured to 1½ pecks*

13 ᴿWho hath directed the ᵀSpirit of the LORD, or *being* his counsellor hath taught him?   Job 21:22; Rom. 11:34; [1 Cor. 2:16] • *Holy Spirit*

14 With whom took he counsel, and *who* instructed him, and taught him in the path of judgment, and taught him knowledge, and shewed to him the way of understanding?

15 Behold, the nations *are* as a drop of a bucket, and are counted as the small dust of the balance: behold, he ᵀtaketh up the ᵀisles as a very little thing.   *considers • coasts*

16 And ᴿLeb'-a-non *is* not sufficient to burn, nor the beasts thereof sufficient for a burnt offering.   Deut. 3:25

17 All nations before him *are* as ᴿnothing; and ᴿthey are counted to him less than nothing, and vanity.   Dan. 4:35 • Ps. 62:9

18 To whom then will ye liken God? or what likeness will ye compare unto him?

19 The workman melteth a graven image, and the goldsmith spreadeth it over with gold, and casteth silver chains.

20 He that *is* so impoverished that he hath

no ᵀoblation chooseth a tree *that* will not rot; he seeketh unto him a ᵀcunning workman to prepare a graven image, *that* shall not be moved.   *offering • skilful*

21 ᴿHave ye not known? have ye not heard? hath it not been told you from the beginning? have ye not understood from the foundations of the earth?   Rom. 1:19

22 *It is* he that sitteth upon the circle of the earth, and the inhabitants thereof *are* as grasshoppers; that ᴿstretcheth out the heavens as a curtain, and spreadeth them out as a tent to dwell in: Job 9:8; Jer. 10:12

23 That bringeth the princes to nothing: he maketh the judges of the earth as vanity.

24 Yea, they shall not be planted; yea, they shall not be sown: yea, their stock shall not take root in the earth: and he shall also blow upon them, and they shall wither, and the ᴿwhirlwind shall take them away as stubble.   17:13; 41:16

25 ᴿTo whom then will ye liken me, or shall I be equal? saith the Holy One.   *v.* 18

26 Lift up your eyes on high, and behold who hath created these *things*, that bringeth out their host by number: he calleth them all by names by the greatness of his might, for that *he is* strong in power; not one faileth.

27 ᴿWhy sayest thou, O Jacob, and speakest, O Israel, My way is hid from the LORD, and my ᵀjudgment is passed over from my God?   [54:7, 8] • *the justice due to me is passed away*

28 Hast thou not known? hast thou not heard, *that* the everlasting God, the LORD, the Creator of the ends of the earth, fainteth not, neither is weary? ᴿ*there is* no searching of his understanding.   Ps. 147:5

29 He giveth power to the ᴿfaint; and to *them that have* no might he ᴿincreaseth strength.   50:4; Jer. 31:25 • 41:10

30 Even the youths shall faint and be weary, and the young men shall utterly fall:

31 But they that ᵀwait upon the LORD ᴿshall ᵀrenew *their* strength; they shall mount up with wings as eagles; they shall run, and not be weary; *and* they shall walk, and not faint.   *hope in* • Ps. 103:5 • *be refreshed in*

CHAPTER 41

Comfort Because of God's Greatness

KEEP silence before me, O islands; and let the people renew *their* strength: let them come near; then let them speak: let us come near together to judgment.

2 Who raised up the righteous *man* from the east, called him to his foot, gave the nations before him, and made *him* rule over kings? he gave *them* as the dust to his sword, *and* as driven stubble to his bow.

3 He pursued them, *and* passed ᵀsafely;

even by the way *that* he had not gone with his feet.   *in peace*

4 Who hath wrought and done *it*, calling the generations from the beginning? I the LORD, the first, and with the last; I *am* he.

5 The isles saw *it*, and feared; the ends of the earth were afraid, drew near, and came.

6 ᴿThey helped every one his neighbour; and *every one* said to his brother, ᵀBe of good courage.   40:19; Joel 3:9–11 • *be strong*

7 ᴿSo the carpenter encouraged the goldsmith, *and* he that smootheth *with* the hammer him that smote the anvil, saying, It *is* ready for the sodering: and he fastened it with nails, *that* it should not be moved.   40:19

8 But thou, Israel, *art* my servant, Jacob whom I have ᴿchosen, the seed of Abraham my ᴿfriend.   [43:1]; Ps. 135:4 • 2 Chr. 20:7; James 2:23

9 ᴿ*Thou* whom I have taken from the ends of the earth, and called thee from the ᵀchief men thereof, and said unto thee, Thou *art* my servant; I have chosen thee, and not cast thee away.   43:5–7 • *corners*

10 ᴿFear thou not; ᴿfor I *am* with thee: be not dismayed; for I *am* thy God: I will strengthen thee; yea, I will help thee; yea, I will uphold thee with the right hand of my righteousness.   *vv.* 13, 14; 43:5 • [Deut. 31:6]

11 Behold, all they that were incensed against thee shall be ashamed and confounded: they shall be as nothing; and they that strive with thee shall perish.

12 ᴿThou shalt seek them, and shalt not find them, *even* them that contended with thee: they that war against thee shall be as nothing, and as a thing of nought.   17:14

13 ᴿFor I the LORD thy God will hold thy right hand, saying unto thee, Fear not; I will help thee.   42:6; 45:1

14 ᴿFear not, thou ᴿworm Jacob, *and* ye ᵀmen of Israel; I will help thee, saith the LORD, and thy ᴿredeemer, the Holy One of Israel.   [44:6, 22–24] • Job 25:6 • *few men* • [35:10]; 43:14

15 Behold, I will make thee a new sharp threshing instrument having teeth: thou shalt thresh the mountains, and beat *them* small, and shalt make the hills as chaff.

16 Thou shalt ᴿfan them, and the wind shall carry them away, and the whirlwind shall scatter them: and thou shalt ᴿrejoice in the LORD, *and* ᴿshalt glory in the Holy One of Israel.   Jer. 51:2 • 25:9; 35:10 ☆ • 45:25

17 *When* the poor and needy seek water, and *there is* none, *and* their tongue faileth for thirst, I the LORD will hear them, *I* the God of Israel will not forsake them.

18 I will open rivers in high places, and fountains in the midst of the valleys: I will make the ᴿwilderness a pool of water, and the dry land springs of water.   Ps. 107:35

19 I will plant in the wilderness the cedar, the shit'-tah tree, and the myrtle, and the oil

tree; I will set in the desert the fir tree, *and* the pine, and the box tree together:

20 RThat they may see, and know, and consider, and understand together, that the hand of the LORD hath done this, and the Holy One of Israel hath created it.   Job 12:9

21 TProduce your cause, saith the LORD; bring forth your strong *reasons,* saith the RKing of Jacob.   *Set forth your plans* • 43:15

22 Let them bring *them* forth, and shew us what shall happen: let them shew the former things, what they *be,* that we may consider them, and know the latter end of them; or declare us things for to come.

23 RShew the things that are to come hereafter, that we may know that ye *are* gods: yea, do good, or do evil, that we may be dismayed, and behold *it* together.   42:9

24 Behold, ye *are* Tof nothing, and your work Tof nought: an abomination *is he that* chooseth you.   *of no account • amounts to nothing*

25 I have raised up *one* from the north, and he shall come: from the Trising of the sun shall he call upon my name: Rand he shall come upon princes as *upon* morter, and as the potter treadeth clay.   *east • v. 2*

26 RWho hath declared from the beginning, that we may know? and beforetime, that we may say, *He is* righteous? yea, *there is* Rnone that sheweth, yea, *there is* none that declareth, yea, *there is* none that heareth your words.   43:9 • Hab. 2:18, 19

27 RThe first Rshall say to Zion, Behold, behold them: and I will give to Jerusalem one that bringeth good tidings.   *v.* 4 • 40:9

28 RFor I beheld, and *there was* no man; even among them, and *there was* no Rcounsellor, that, when I asked of them, could Tanswer a word.   63:5 • 40:13, 14 • *make a reply*

29 RBehold, they *are* all vanity; their works *are* Tnothing: their Tmolten images *are* wind and confusion.   *v.* 24 • *worthless • melted*

CHAPTER 42

Comfort Because of God's Servant

BEHOLDR my servant, whom I uphold; mine elect, *in whom* my soul delighteth; I have put my spirit upon him: he shall bring forth judgment to the Gentiles.   Luke 3:22 ☆

2 RHe shall not cry, nor lift up, nor cause his voice to be heard in the street. Matt. 12:19 ☆

3 A bruised reed shall he not break, and the smoking flax shall he not quench: he shall bring forth judgment unto truth.

4 He shall not fail nor be discouraged, till he have set judgment in the earth: Rand the isles shall wait for his law.   [Gen. 49:10] ☆

5 Thus saith God the LORD, Rhe that created the heavens, and stretched them out; he that spread forth the earth, and that which cometh out of it; Rhe that giveth

breath unto the people upon it, and spirit to them that walk therein: 44:24 • Acts 17:25

6 I the LORD have called thee in Rrighteousness, and will hold thine hand, and will keep thee, and give thee for a covenant of the people, for a light of the Gentiles;   Jer. 23:5, 6 ☆

7 RTo open the blind eyes, to bring out the prisoners from the prison, *and* them that sit in darkness out of the prison house.   35:5 ☆

8 I *am* the LORD: that *is* my name: and my Rglory will I not give to another, neither my praise to Tgraven images.   48:11 • *idols*

9 Behold, the former things are come to pass, and Rnew things do I declare: before they spring forth I tell you of them.   43:19

10 Sing unto the LORD a new song, *and* his praise from the end of the earth, ye that go down to the sea, and all that is therein; the Tisles, and the inhabitants thereof.   *coasts*

11 Let the Rwilderness and the cities thereof lift up *their voice,* the villages *that* RKe'-dar doth inhabit: let the inhabitants of the Rrock sing, let them shout from the top of the mountains.   32:16; 35:1 • 21:16 • 52:7

12 Let them give glory unto the LORD, and declare his praise in the islands.

13 The LORD shall go forth as a mighty man, he shall Tstir up jealousy like a man of war: he shall cry, yea, roar; he shall prevail against his enemies.   *arouse fury*

14 I have long time Tholden my peace; I have been still, *and* refrained myself: *now* will I cry like a travailing woman; I will destroy and Tdevour at once.   *held • consume*

15 I will make waste mountains and hills, and dry up all their herbs; and I will make the rivers islands, and I will dry up the pools.

16 And I will bring the blind by a way *that* they knew not; I will lead them in paths *that* they have not known: I will make darkness light before them, and crooked things straight. These things will I do unto them, and not forsake them.

17 They shall be Rturned back, they shall be greatly ashamed, that trust in Tgraven images, that say to the molten images, Ye *are* our gods.   1:29; 44:11; 45:16; Ps. 97:7 • *idols*

18 RHear, ye deaf; and look, ye blind, that ye may see.   29:18; 35:5

19 RWho *is* blind, but my servant? or deaf, as my messenger *that* I sent? who *is* blind as *he that is* perfect, and blind as the LORD's servant?   43:8; Ezek. 12:2; [John 9:39, 41]

20 Seeing many things, but thou observest not; opening the ears, but he heareth not.

21 The LORD is well pleased Rfor his righteousness' sake; he will Rmagnify the law, and make *it* honourable.   43:25 • Ps. 138:2

22 But this *is* a people robbed and Tspoiled; *they are* all of them snared in holes, and they are hid in prison houses: they are for a prey, and none delivereth; for a spoil, and none saith, Restore.   *stripped*

23 Who among you will give ear to this? who will ᵀhearken and hear for the time to come? *listen*

24 ᴿWho gave Jacob for ᵀa spoil, and Israel to the robbers? did not the Lᴏʀᴅ, he against whom we have sinned? ᴿfor they would not walk in his ways, neither were they obedient unto his law. 10:5 • *loot* • 65:2

25 Therefore he hath poured upon him the fury of his anger, and the strength of battle: and it hath set him on fire round about, ᴿyet he knew not; and it burned him, yet he laid *it* not to heart. Hos. 7:9

CHAPTER 43

Comfort Because of Israel's Restoration

BUT now thus saith the Lᴏʀᴅ that created thee, O Jacob, and he that formed thee, O Israel, Fear not: ᴿfor I have redeemed thee, ᴿI have called *thee* by thy name; thou *art* mine. 44:6 • 42:6; 45:4

2 ᴿWhen thou passest through the waters, ᴿI *will be* with thee; and through the rivers, they shall not overflow thee: when thou ᴿwalkest through the fire, thou shalt not be burned; neither shall the flame kindle upon thee. [Ps. 66:12; 91:3] • [Deut. 31:6] • Dan. 3:25

3 For I *am* the Lᴏʀᴅ thy God, the Holy One of Israel, thy ᴿSaviour: ᴿI gave Egypt *for* thy ransom, E-thi-o'-pi-a and Se'-ba for thee. 19:20; 43:11; 45:15, 21 • [Prov. 11:8; 21:18]

4 Since thou wast ᴿprecious in my sight, thou hast been honourable, and I have ᴿloved thee: therefore will I give men for thee, and people for thy life. [Ex. 19:5, 6] • 63:9

5 ᴿFear not: for I *am* with thee: I will bring thy seed from the east, and gather thee from the west; 41:10; Jer. 30:10; 46:27, 28

6 I will say to the ᴿnorth, Give up; and to the south, Keep not back: bring my ᴿsons from far, and my daughters from the ends of the earth; 49:12 • 2 Cor. 6:18

7 *Even* every one that is called by my name: for I have created him for my glory, I have formed him; yea, I have made him.

8 ᴿBring forth the blind people that have eyes, and the deaf that have ears. Ezek. 12:2

9 Let all the nations be gathered together, and let the people be assembled: who among them can declare this, and shew us ᴿformer things? let them bring forth their witnesses, that they may be justified: or let them hear, and say, It is truth. 41:22

10 Ye *are* my witnesses, saith the Lᴏʀᴅ, and my servant whom I have chosen: that ye may know and believe me, and understand that I *am* he: before me there was no God formed, neither shall there be after me.

11 I, *even* I, ᴿ*am* the Lᴏʀᴅ; and beside me *there is* no saviour. 45:21; Hos. 13:4

12 I have declared, and have saved, and I have shewed, when *there was* no strange *god* among you: therefore ye *are* my witnesses, saith the Lᴏʀᴅ, that I *am* God.

13 Yea, before the day *was* I *am* he; and *there is* none that can deliver out of my hand: I will work, and who shall let it?

14 Thus saith the Lᴏʀᴅ, your redeemer, the Holy One of Israel; For your sake I have sent to Babylon, and have brought down all their nobles, and the Chal-de'-ans, whose cry *is* in the ᴿships. Jer. 51:13

15 I *am* the Lᴏʀᴅ, your Holy One, the creator of Israel, your ᴿKing. Hos. 13:10

16 Thus saith the Lᴏʀᴅ, which ᴿmaketh a way in the sea, and a ᴿpath in the mighty waters; Ex. 14:16 • Josh. 3:13

17 Which bringeth forth the chariot and horse, the army and the power; they shall lie down together, they shall not rise: they are extinct, they are quenched as tow.

18 ᴿRemember ye not the former things, neither consider the things of old. Jer. 16:14

19 Behold, I will do a ᴿnew thing; now it shall spring forth; shall ye not know it? ᴿI will even make a way in the wilderness, *and* rivers in the desert. [Rev. 21:5] • Ex. 17:6

20 The beast of the field shall honour me, the ᵀdragons and the ᵀowls: because ᴿI give waters in the wilderness, *and* rivers in the desert, to give drink to my people, my ᴿchosen. *jackals* • *ostriches* • 48:21 • Ezek. 20:5

21 ᴿThis people have I formed for myself; they shall shew forth my praise. Ps. 102:18

22 But thou hast not called upon me, O Jacob; but thou ᴿhast been weary of me, O Israel. Mic. 6:3; Mal. 1:13; 3:14

23 Thou hast not brought me the ᵀsmall cattle of thy burnt offerings; neither hast thou honoured me with thy sacrifices. I have not caused thee to serve with an offering, nor ᵀwearied thee with incense. *sheep* • *troubled*

24 Thou hast bought me no sweet cane with money, neither hast thou filled me with the fat of thy sacrifices: but thou hast made me to ᵀserve with thy sins, thou hast wearied me with thine iniquities. *be satisfied*

25 I, *even* I, *am* he that blotteth out thy transgressions ᴿfor mine own sake, and will not remember thy sins. Ezek. 36:22

26 ᵀPut me in remembrance: let us plead together: ᵀdeclare thou, that thou mayest be justified. *report to me* • *speak out*

27 Thy first father hath sinned, and thy teachers have transgressed against me.

28 Therefore ᴿI have profaned the princes of the sanctuary, and have given Jacob to the curse, and Israel to reproaches. Jer. 24:9

CHAPTER 44

YET now hear, ᴿO Jacob my servant; and Israel, whom I have chosen: 41:8

2 Thus saith the Lᴏʀᴅ that made thee, and

formed thee from the womb, which will help thee; Fear not, O Jacob, my servant; and thou, Jes'-u-run, Rwhom I have chosen. [43:1, 7]

3 For I will pour water upon him that is thirsty, and floods upon the dry ground: I will Rpour my spirit upon thy seed, and my blessing upon thine offspring;   [Acts 2:18]

4 And they shall spring up as among the grass, as willows by the water courses.

5 One shall say, I am the LORD's; and another shall call himself by the name of Jacob; and another shall Tsubscribe with his hand unto the LORD, and surname himself by the name of Israel.   write on

6 Thus saith the LORD the King of Israel, and his redeemer the LORD of hosts; RI am the first, and I am the last; and beside me there is no God.   41:4; [Rev. 1:8, 17; 22:13]

7 And Rwho, as I, shall call, and shall Tdeclare it, and set it in order for me, since I appointed the ancient people? and the things that are coming, and shall come, let them shew unto them.   41:4, 22 • speak it out

8 Fear ye not, neither be afraid: have not I told thee from that time, and have declared it? ye are even my witnesses. Is there a God beside me? yea, Rthere is no TGod; I know not any.   Deut. 4:35; 32:39 • Rock

9 RThey that make a graven image are all of them vanity; and their Tdelectable things shall not profit; and they are their own witnesses; they see not, nor know; that they may be ashamed.   41:24 • desirable

10 Who hath formed a god, or molten a graven image that is profitable for nothing?

11 Behold, all his fellows shall be Rashamed: and the workmen, they are of men: let them all be gathered together, let them stand up; yet they shall fear, and they shall be ashamed together.   Ps. 97:7

12 The smith with the tongs both worketh in the coals, and fashioneth it with hammers, and worketh it with the strength of his arms: yea, he is hungry, and his strength faileth: he drinketh no water, and is faint.

13 The carpenter stretcheth out his Trule; he marketh it out with a Tline; he fitteth it with planes, and he marketh it out with the compass, and maketh it after the figure of a man, according to the beauty of a man; that it may remain in the house.   line • pencil

14 He heweth him down cedars, and taketh the cypress and the oak, which he Tstrengtheneth for himself among the trees of the forest; he planteth an ash, and the rain doth nourish it.   lets grow strong

15 Then shall it be for a man to burn: for he will take thereof, and warm himself; yea, he kindleth it, and baketh bread; yea, he maketh a god, and worshippeth it; he maketh it a graven image, and falleth down thereto.

16 He burneth part thereof in the fire; with part thereof he eateth flesh; he roasteth roast,

and is satisfied: yea, he warmeth himself, and saith, Aha, I am warm, I have seen the fire:

17 And the residue thereof he maketh a god, even his Tgraven image: he falleth down unto it, and worshippeth it, and Rprayeth unto it, and saith, Deliver me; for thou art my god.   idol • 45:20; 1 Kin. 18:26, 28

18 RThey have not known nor understood: for Rhe hath shut their eyes, that they cannot see; and their hearts, that they cannot understand.   45:20 • 2 Thess. 2:11

19 And none considerethT in his heart, neither is there knowledge nor understanding to say, I have burned part of it in the fire; yea, also I have baked bread upon the coals thereof; I have roasted flesh, and eaten it: and shall I make the residue thereof an abomination? shall I fall down to the stock of a tree?   is deeply concerned

20 He feedeth on ashes: Ra deceived heart hath turned him aside, that he cannot Tdeliver his soul, nor say, Is there not a lie in my right hand?   Rom. 1:21; 2 Thess. 2:11 • free

21 Remember these, O Jacob and Israel; for thou art my servant: I have formed thee; thou art my servant: O Israel, Rthou shalt not be forgotten of me.   46:4

22 I have blotted out, as a thick cloud, thy transgressions, and, as a cloud, thy sins: return unto me; for I have redeemed thee.

23 RSing, O ye heavens; for the LORD hath done it: shout, ye lower parts of the earth: break forth into singing, ye mountains, O forest, and every tree therein: for the LORD hath redeemed Jacob, and glorified himself in Israel.   42:10; 49:13; Jer. 51:48; Rev. 18:20

24 Thus saith the LORD, thy redeemer, and he that formed thee from the womb, I am the LORD that maketh all things; that stretcheth forth the heavens alone; that spreadeth abroad the earth by myself;

25 That Rfrustrateth the tokens Rof the liars, and maketh diviners mad; that turneth wise men backward, Rand maketh their knowledge foolish;   47:13 • Jer. 50:36 • 1 Cor. 1:20

26 RThat confirmeth the word of his servant, and performeth the counsel of his messengers; that saith to Jerusalem, Thou shalt be inhabited; and to the cities of Judah, Ye shall be built, and I will raise up the Tdecayed places thereof: Zech. 1:6 • waste

27 RThat saith to the deep, Be dry, and I will dry up thy rivers: Jer. 50:38; 51:32, 36

28 That saith of Cyrus, He is my shepherd, and shall perform all my pleasure: even saying to Jerusalem, RThou shalt be built; and to the temple, Thy foundation shall be laid.   2 Chr. 36:22; Ezra 1:1

CHAPTER 45

Comfort Because of God's Use of Cyrus

THUS saith the LORD to his anointed, to Cyrus, whose right hand I have holden, to

subdue nations before him; and I will loose the loins of kings, to open before him the two leaved gates; and the gates shall not be shut;

2 I will go before thee, ᴿand make the crooked places straight: ᴿI will break in pieces the gates of ᵀbrass, and cut in sunder the bars of iron: 40:4 · Ps. 107:16 · *bronze*

3 And I will give thee the treasures of darkness, and hidden riches of secret places, ᴿthat thou mayest know that I, the LORD, which ᴿcall *thee* by thy name, *am* the God of Israel.   41:23 · Ex. 33:12

4 For ᴿJacob my servant's sake, and Israel mine elect, I have even called thee by thy name: I have surnamed thee, though thou hast not known me.   41:8, 9; 44:1

5 I *am* the LORD, and *there is* none else, *there* is no God beside me: ᴿI girded thee, though thou hast not known me: Ps. 18:32

6 ᴿThat they may know from the rising of the sun, and from the west, that *there is* none beside me. I *am* the LORD, and *there is* none else.   Ps. 102:15; Mal. 1:11

7 ᴿI form the light, and create darkness: I make peace, and ᴿcreate evil: I the LORD do all these *things*.   42:16 · Amos 3:6

8 Drop down, ye heavens, from above, and let the skies pour down righteousness: let the earth open, and let them bring forth salvation, and let righteousness spring up together; I the LORD have created it.

9 Woe unto him that striveth with his Maker! *Let* the potsherd *strive* with the potsherds of the earth. Shall the clay say to him that fashioneth it, What makest thou? or thy work, He hath no hands?

10 Woe unto him that saith unto *his* father, What begettest thou? or to the woman, What hast thou brought forth?

11 Thus saith the LORD, the Holy One of Israel, and his Maker, Ask me of things to come concerning my sons, and concerning the work of my hands command ye me.

12 I have made the earth, and ᴿcreated man upon it: I, *even* my hands, have stretched out the heavens, and ᴿall their host have I commanded.   Gen. 1:26 · Gen. 2:1

13 ᴿI have raised him up in righteousness, and I will ᵀdirect all his ways: he shall build my city, and he shall let go my captives, ᵀnot for price nor reward, saith the LORD of hosts.   41:2 · *guide* · *without payment*

14 Thus saith the LORD, The labour of Egypt, and merchandise of E-thi-o'-pi-a and of the Sa-be'-ans, men of stature, shall come over unto thee, and they shall be thine: they shall come after thee; ᴿin chains they shall come over, and they shall fall down unto thee, they shall make supplication unto thee, saying, ᴿSurely God *is* in thee; and *there is* none else, *there* is no God.   Ps. 149:8 · 1 Cor. 14:25

15 Verily thou *art* a God ᴿthat hidest thyself, O God of Israel, the Saviour.   57:17

16 They shall be ashamed, and also confounded, all of them: they shall go to confusion together *that are* makers of idols.

17 ᴿBut Israel shall be saved in the LORD with an everlasting salvation: ye shall not be ashamed nor confounded world without end.   26:4; 56:1; [Rom. 11:26]

18 For thus saith the LORD ᴿthat created the heavens; God himself that formed the earth and made it; he hath established it, he created it not ᵀin vain, he formed it to be inhabited: ᴿI *am* the LORD; and *there is* none else.   42:5 · *without purpose* · v. 5

19 I have not spoken in ᴿsecret, in a dark place of the earth: I said not unto the seed of Jacob, Seek ye me ᵀin vain: ᴿI the LORD speak righteousness, I ᵀdeclare things that are right.   Deut. 30:11 · *with no success* · Ps. 19:8 · *say*

20 Assemble yourselves and come; draw near together, ye *that are* escaped of the nations: ᴿthey have no knowledge that set up the wood of their graven image, and pray unto a god *that* cannot save.   46:7

21 Tell ye, and bring *them* near; yea, let them take counsel together: who hath declared this from ancient time? *who* hath told it from that time? *have* not I the LORD? and *there is* no God else beside me; a just God and a Saviour; *there is* none beside me.

22 ᴿLook unto me, and be ye saved, all the ends of the earth: for I *am* God, and *there is* none else.   Num. 21:8; Ps. 22:27; 65:5

23 I have sworn by myself, the word is gone out of my mouth *in* righteousness, and shall not return, That unto me every knee shall bow, every tongue shall swear.

24 Surely, shall *one* say, in the LORD have I righteousness and strength: *even* to him shall *men* come; and all that are incensed against him shall be ashamed.

25 In the LORD shall all the seed of Israel be justified, and ᴿshall glory.   1 Cor. 1:31

CHAPTER 46

Destruction of Babylon's Idols

BEL boweth down, Ne'-bo stoopeth, their idols were upon the beasts, and upon the cattle: your carriages *were* heavy loaden; *they are* a burden to the weary *beast.*

2 They stoop, they bow down together; they could not deliver the burden, ᴿbut themselves are gone into captivity.   Jer. 48:7

3 Hearken unto me, O house of Jacob, and all the remnant of the house of Israel, ᴿwhich are borne *by me* from the belly, which are carried from the womb: Ps. 71:6

4 And *even* to *your* old age ᴿI *am* he; and *even* to ᵀhoar hairs will I carry *you:* I have made, and I will bear; even ᴿI will carry, and will deliver *you.*   Mal. 3:6 · *gray hairs* · Ezra 8:31

5 ᴿTo whom will ye liken me, and make *me* equal, and compare me, that we may be like?   40:18

6 ^RThey lavish gold out of the bag, and weigh silver in the balance, *and* hire a goldsmith; and he maketh it a god: they ^Tfall down, yea, they worship. 40:19; 41:6 · *bow*

7 They bear him upon the shoulder, they carry him, and set him in his place, and he standeth; from his place shall he not remove: yea, *one* shall cry unto him, yet can he not answer, nor save him out of his trouble.

8 Remember this, and ^Tshew yourselves men: ^Rbring it again to mind, O ye transgressors. *be responsible* · 44:19

9 ^RRemember the former things of old: for I *am* God, and *there is* none else; I *am* God, and *there is* none like me, Deut. 32:7

10 ^RDeclaring the end from the beginning, and from ancient times *the things* that are not *yet* done, saying, My counsel shall stand, and I will do all my pleasure: 45:21

11 Calling a ravenous bird from the ^Reast, the man ^Rthat^T executeth my counsel from a far country: yea, I have spoken *it,* I will also bring it to pass; I have purposed *it,* I will also do it. 41:2 · 44:28 · *carries out my advice*

12 Hearken unto me, ye ^Rstouthearted, that *are* far from righteousness: Ps. 76:5

13 I bring near my righteousness; it shall not be far off, and my salvation shall not ^Ttarry: and I will place ^Rsalvation in Zion for Israel my glory. *be delayed* · [Heb. 12:22, 23]

CHAPTER 47

Destruction of Babylon

COME down, and ^Rsit in the dust, O virgin daughter of Babylon, sit on the ground: *there is* no throne, O daughter of the Chal-de'-ans: for thou shalt no more be called tender and ^Tdelicate. 3:26 · *genteel*

2 ^RTake the millstones, and grind meal: uncover thy locks, make bare the leg, uncover the thigh, pass over the rivers. Ex. 11:5

3 Thy nakedness shall be uncovered, yea, thy shame shall be seen: I will take vengeance, and I will not meet *thee as* a man.

4 *As for* our redeemer, the LORD of hosts *is* his name, the Holy One of Israel.

5 Sit thou ^Rsilent, and get thee into darkness, O daughter of the Chal-de'-ans: ^Rfor thou shalt no more be called, The lady of ^Rkingdoms. 1 Sam. 2:9 · [Dan. 2:37] · Rev. 17:18

6 I was ^Twroth with my people, ^RI have polluted mine inheritance, and given them into thine hand: thou didst shew them no mercy; upon the ^Tancient hast thou very heavily laid thy yoke. *angry* · 43:28 · *old men*

7 And thou saidst, I shall be ^Ra lady for ever: *so* that thou didst not ^Rlay these *things* to thy heart, neither didst remember the latter end of it. Rev. 18:7 · 46:8

8 Therefore hear now this, *thou that art* given to pleasures, that dwellest carelessly,

that sayest in thine heart, I *am,* and none else beside me; I shall not sit *as* a widow, neither shall I know the loss of children:

9 But these two *things* shall come to thee in a moment in one day, the loss of children, and widowhood: they shall come upon thee in their perfection for the multitude of thy sorceries, *and* for the great abundance of thine enchantments.

10 For thou hast trusted in thy wickedness: thou hast said, None seeth me. Thy wisdom and thy knowledge, it hath perverted thee; and thou hast said in thine heart, I *am,* and none else beside me.

11 Therefore shall evil come upon thee; thou shalt not know from ^Twhence it riseth: and mischief shall fall upon thee; thou shalt not be able to put it off: and ^Rdesolation shall come upon thee suddenly, *which* thou shalt not know. *where* · *v.* 9; 1 Thess. 5:3

12 Stand now with thine ^Renchantments, and with the multitude of thy sorceries, wherein thou hast laboured from thy youth; if so be thou shalt be able to profit, if so be thou mayest prevail. Deut. 18:10; 2 Kin. 17:17

13 Thou art wearied in the multitude of thy ^Tcounsels. Let now the astrologers, the stargazers, the monthly prognosticators, stand up, and save thee from *these things* that shall come upon thee. *advisors*

14 Behold, they shall be ^Ras stubble; the fire shall burn them; they shall not deliver themselves from ^Tthe power of the flame: *there shall* not *be* a coal to warm at, *nor* fire to sit before it. Nah. 1:10 · *the judgment of God*

15 Thus shall they be unto thee with whom thou hast laboured, *even* ^Rthy merchants, from thy youth: they shall wander every one to his ^Tquarter; none shall save thee. Rev. 18:11 · *own place*

CHAPTER 48

Declaration of Judah's Chastening

HEAR ye this, O house of Jacob, which are called by the name of Israel, and are come forth out of the waters of Judah, ^Rwhich swear by the name of the LORD, and make mention of the God of Israel, *but* not in truth, nor in righteousness. Deut. 6:13

2 For they call themselves of the holy city, and ^Tstay themselves upon the God of Israel; The LORD of hosts *is* his name. *trust*

3 I have declared the former things from the beginning; and they went forth out of my mouth, and I shewed them; I did *them* suddenly, ^Rand they came to pass. Josh. 21:45

4 Because I knew that thou *art* ^Tobstinate, and ^Rthy neck *is* an iron ^Tsinew, and thy brow ^Tbrass; *hard* · Deut. 31:27 · *muscle* · *bronze*

5 I have even from the beginning declared *it* to thee; before it came to pass I shewed *it* thee: lest thou shouldest say, Mine idol hath

done them, and my graven image, and my molten image, hath commanded them.

6 Thou hast heard, see all this; and will not ye declare it? I have shewed thee ᴿnew things from this time, even hidden things, and thou didst not know them.   42:9

7 They are created now, and not from the beginning; even before the day when thou heardest them not; lest thou shouldest say, Behold, I knew them.

8 Yea, thou heardest not; yea, thou knewest not; yea, from that time that thine ear was not opened: for I knew that thou wouldest deal very treacherously, and wast called a transgressor from the womb.

9 ᴿFor my name's sake will I ᵀdefer mine anger, and for my praise will I refrain for thee, that I cut thee not off.   Ps. 79:9 • hold back

10 Behold, ᴿI have refined thee, but not ᵀwith silver; I have chosen thee in the furnace of affliction.   Ps. 66:10; Jer. 9:7 • as

11 For mine own sake, even for mine own sake, will I do it: for ᴿhow should my name be ᵀpolluted? and ᴿI will not give my glory unto another.   Ezek. 20:9 • smeared • 42:8

12 Hearken unto me, O Jacob and Israel, my called; ᴿI am he; I am the ᴿfirst, I also am the last.   Deut. 32:29 • 44:6; [Rev. 22:13]

13 Mine hand also hath ᴿlaid the foundation of the earth, and my right hand hath ᵀspanned the heavens: when I call unto them, they stand up together.   42:5 • spread

14 All ye, assemble yourselves, and ᵀhear; which among them hath declared these things? ᴿThe Lᴏʀᴅ hath loved him: he will do his pleasure on Babylon, and his arm shall be on the Chal-de′-ans.   listen • 45:1

15 I, even I, have spoken; yea, I have ᴿcalled him: I have brought him, and he shall make his way prosperous.   41:2; 45:1, 2

16 ᴿCome ye near unto me, hear ye this; ᴿI have not spoken in secret from the beginning; from the time that it was, there am I: and now ᴿthe Lord Gᴏᴅ, and his Spirit, hath sent me.   34:1 • 45:19 • Zech. 2:8

17 Thus saith ᴿthe Lᴏʀᴅ, thy Redeemer, the Holy One of Israel; I am the Lᴏʀᴅ thy God which teacheth thee to profit, ᴿwhich leadeth thee by the way that thou shouldest go.   41:14; 43:14; 49:7 • Ps. 32:8

18 ᴿO that thou hadst ᵀhearkened to my commandments! ᴿthen had thy peace been as a river, and thy righteousness as the waves of the sea.   Ps. 81:13 • listened • Ps. 119:165

19 Thy seed also had been as the sand, and the offspring of thy bowels like the gravel thereof; his name should not have been cut off nor destroyed from before me.

20 Go ye forth of Babylon, flee ye from the Chal-de′-ans, with a voice of singing declare ye, tell this, utter it even to the end of the earth; say ye, The Lᴏʀᴅ hath ᴿredeemed his servant Jacob.   [Ex. 19:4–6]

21 And they ᴿthirsted not when he led them through the deserts: he ᴿcaused the waters to flow out of the rock for them: he clave the rock also, and the waters gushed out.   [41:17, 18] • Ex. 17:6; Ps. 105:41

22 ᴿThere is no peace, saith the Lᴏʀᴅ, unto the wicked.   [57:21]

CHAPTER 49

The Messiah's Mission

LISTEN, ᴿO isles, unto me; and hearken, ye people, from far; ᴿThe Lᴏʀᴅ hath called me from the womb; from the bowels of my mother hath he made mention of my name.   41:1 • Jer. 1:5; Matt. 1:18–25; John 10:36

2 And he hath made ᴿmy mouth like a sharp sword; in the shadow of his hand hath he hid me, and made me a polished shaft; in his quiver hath he hid me;   11:4; Rev. 1:16; 2:12 ☆

3 And said unto me, Thou art my servant, O Israel, in whom I will be glorified.

4 Then I said, I have laboured in vain, I have spent my strength for nought, and in vain: yet surely my judgment is with the Lᴏʀᴅ, and my work with my God.

5 And now, saith the Lᴏʀᴅ that formed me from the womb to be his servant, to bring Jacob again to him, Though Israel ᴿbe not gathered, yet shall I be ᴿglorious in the eyes of the Lᴏʀᴅ, and my God shall be my ᴿstrength.   Matt. 23:37 ☆ • 43:4 • 12:2

6 And he said, It is a light thing that thou shouldest be my servant to raise up the tribes of Jacob, and to restore the preserved of Israel: I will also give thee for ᴿa light to the Gentiles, that thou mayest be my salvation unto the end of the earth.   Luke 2:32 ☆

7 Thus saith the Lᴏʀᴅ, the Redeemer of Israel, and his Holy One, to him ᴿwhom man despiseth, to him whom the nation abhorreth, to a servant of rulers, Kings shall see and arise, princes also shall worship, because of the Lᴏʀᴅ that is faithful, and the Holy One of Israel, and he shall choose thee.   Ps. 22:6–8 ☆

8 Thus saith the Lᴏʀᴅ, ᴿIn an acceptable time have I heard thee, and in a day of salvation have I helped thee: and I will preserve thee, and give thee for a covenant of the people, to establish the earth, to cause to inherit the desolate heritages;   2 Cor. 6:2 ☆

9 That thou mayest say to the prisoners, Go forth; to them that are in darkness, Shew yourselves. They shall feed in the ways, and their pastures shall be in all high places.

10 They shall not ᴿhunger nor thirst; ᴿneither shall the heat nor sun smite them: for he that hath mercy on them ᴿshall lead them, even by the springs of water shall he guide them.   Rev. 7:16 ☆ • Ps. 121:6 • Ps. 23:2

11 And I will make all my mountains a way, and my highways shall be exalted.

12 Behold, these shall come from far: and, lo, these from the north and from the west; and these from the land of Si'-nim.

13 RSing, O heavens; and be joyful, O earth; and break forth into singing, O mountains: for the RLORD hath comforted his people, and will have mercy upon his Tafflicted.   44:23 · 40:1; 51:3, 12 · *troubled ones*

14 But Zion said, The LORD hath forsaken me, and my Lord hath forgotten me.

15 Can a woman forget her sucking child, that she should not have compassion on the son of her womb? yea, they may forget, Ryet will I not forget thee.   Rom. 11:29

16 Behold, RI have graven thee upon the palms of my hands; thy walls are Tcontinually before me.   Ex. 13:9 · *always in my memory*

17 Thy children shall make haste; Rthy destroyers and they that made thee waste shall go Tforth of thee.   10:6; 37:18 · *away from*

18 RLift up thine eyes round about, and behold: all these gather themselves together, and come to thee. As I live, saith the LORD, thou shalt surely clothe thee with them all, as with an ornament, and bind them on thee, as a bride doeth.   60:4

19 For thy Twaste and thy Tdesolate places, and the land of thy destruction, shall even now be too narrow by reason of the inhabitants, and they that swallowed thee up shall be far away.   *empty · uninhabited*

20 The children which thou shalt have, after thou hast lost the other, shall say again in thine ears, The place is too strait for me: give place to me that I may dwell.

21 Then shalt thou say in thine heart, Who hath begotten me these, seeing I have lost my children, and am desolate, a captive, and Tremoving to and fro? and who hath brought up these? Behold, I was left alone; these, where had they been?   *wandering*

22 Thus saith the Lord GOD, Behold, I will lift up mine hand to the Gentiles, and set up my standard to the people: and they shall bring thy sons in their arms, and thy daughters shall be carried upon their shoulders.

23 And kings shall be thy nursing fathers, and their queens thy nursing mothers: they shall Tbow down to thee with their face toward the earth, and lick up the dust of thy feet; and thou shalt know that I am the LORD: for they shall not be ashamed that wait for me.   *respect*

24 Shall the prey be taken from the mighty, or the lawful captive delivered?

25 But thus saith the LORD, REven the captives of the mighty shall be taken away, and the prey of the terrible shall be delivered: for I will contend with him that contendeth with thee, and I will save thy children. [14:1, 2]

26 And I will feed them that oppress thee with their own flesh; and they shall be drunken with their own blood, as with Tsweet wine: and all flesh shall know that I the LORD am thy Saviour and thy Redeemer, the mighty One of Jacob.   *new wine*

CHAPTER 50

The Messiah's Obedience

THUS saith the LORD, Where is the bill of your mother's divorcement, whom I have put away? or which of my Rcreditors is it to whom I have sold you? Behold, for your Tiniquities Rhave ye sold yourselves, and for your Ttransgressions is your mother put away.   2 Kin. 4:1 · *sins* · 52:3 · *wrongdoings*

2 Wherefore, when I came, was there no man? Rwhen I called, was there none to answer? RIs my hand shortened at all, that it cannot redeem? or have I no power to deliver? behold, at my rebuke I dry up the sea, I make the rivers a wilderness: their fish stinketh, because there is no water, and dieth for thirst.   65:12; Jer. 7:13 · 59:1

3 I Rclothe the heavens with blackness, and I make sackcloth their covering.   13:10

4 The Lord GOD hath given me the tongue of the learned, that I should know how to speak a word in season to him that is weary: he wakeneth morning by morning, he wakeneth mine ear to hear as the learned.

5 The Lord GOD Rhath opened mine ear, and I was not Rrebellious, neither turned away back.   Ps. 40:6–8 · Matt. 26:39; John 14:31 ☆

6 I gave my back to the smiters, and my cheeks to them that plucked off the hair: RI hid not my face from shame and spitting.   Matt. 26:67 ☆

7 For the Lord GOD will help me; therefore shall I not be confounded: therefore have RI set my face like a flint, and I know that I shall not be Tashamed.   Luke 9:51 ☆ · *disappointed*

8 He is near that justifieth me; who will contend with me? let us stand together: who is mine adversary? let him come near to me.

9 Behold, the Lord GOD Rwill help me; who is he that shall condemn me? Rlo, they all shall wax old as a garment; Rthe moth shall eat them up.   Acts 2:24 ☆ · Job 13:28 · 51:8

10 Who is among you that feareth the LORD, that obeyeth the voice of his servant, that Rwalketh in darkness, and hath no light? let him trust in the name of the LORD, and Tstay upon his God.   Ps. 23:4 · *rest*

11 Behold, all ye that kindle a fire, that compass yourselves about with sparks: walk in the light of your fire, and in the sparks that ye have kindled. This shall ye have of mine hand; ye shall lie down in sorrow.

CHAPTER 51

The Messiah's Encouragement to Israel

HEARKEN to me, ye that follow after righteousness, ye that seek the LORD: look unto the rock *whence* ye are hewn, and to the hole of the pit *whence* ye are digged.

2 Look unto Abraham your father, and unto Sarah *that* bare you: for I called him alone, and blessed him, and increased him.

3 For the LORD shall comfort Zion: he will comfort all her waste places; and he will make her wilderness like Eden, and her desert like the garden of the LORD; joy and gladness shall be found therein, thanksgiving, and the voice of melody.

4 Hearken unto me, my people; and give ear unto me, O my nation: for a law shall proceed from me, and I will make my judgment to rest for a light of the people.

5 RMy righteousness *is* near; my salvation is gone forth, and mine arms shall judge the people; the isles shall wait upon me, and on mine arm shall they trust.   46:13

6 Lift up your eyes to the heavens, and look upon the earth beneath: for the heavens shall vanish away like smoke, and the earth shall wax old like a garment, and they that dwell therein shall die in like manner: but my salvation shall be for ever, and my righteousness shall not be Tabolished.   *put away*

7 Hearken unto me, ye that know righteousness, the people in whose heart *is* my law; fear ye not the reproach of men, neither be ye afraid of their revilings.

8 For Rthe moth shall eat them up like a garment, and the Rworm shall eat them like wool: but my righteousness shall be for ever, and my salvation from generation to generation.   50:9 • 14:11; 66:24

9 Awake, awake, put on strength, O arm of the LORD; awake, as in the ancient days, in the generations of old. *Art* thou not it that hath cut Ra′-hab, *and* wounded the dragon?

10 TArt thou not it which hath Rdried the sea, the waters of the great deep; that hath made the depths of the sea a way for the ransomed to pass over?   *was it not thou* • Ex. 14:21

11 Therefore Rthe redeemed of the LORD shall return, and come with singing unto Zion; and everlasting joy *shall be* upon their head: they shall obtain gladness and joy; *and* sorrow and mourning shall flee away. [Rev. 7:17]

12 I, *even* I, *am* he that comforteth you: who *art* thou, that thou shouldest be afraid Rof a man *that* shall die, and of the son of man *which* shall be made *as* grass;   Ps. 118:6

13 And forgettest the LORD thy maker, Rthat hath stretched forth the heavens, and laid the foundations of the earth; and hast feared continually every day because of the fury of the oppressor, as if he Twere ready to destroy? Rand where *is* the fury of the oppressor?   Ps. 104:2 • *made himself ready* • Job 20:7

14 The captive exile hasteneth that he may be loosed, and that he should not die in the pit, nor that his bread should fail.

15 But I *am* the LORD thy God, that Rdivided the sea, whose waves roared: The LORD of hosts *is* his name.   Ex. 14:21; Job 26:12

16 And I have put my words in thy mouth, and I have covered thee in the shadow of mine hand, that I may plant the heavens, and lay the foundations of the earth, and say unto Zion, Thou *art* my people.

17 RAwake, awake, stand up, O Jerusalem, which Rhast drunk at the hand of the LORD the cup of his fury; thou hast drunken the dregs of the cup of trembling, *and* wrung *them* out.   52:1 • 29:9; Job 21:20

18 *There is* none to guide her among all the sons *whom* she hath brought forth; neither *is there any* that taketh her by the hand of all the sons *that* she hath brought up.

19 These two *things* are come unto thee; who shall be sorry for thee? desolation, and destruction, and the famine, and the sword: by whom shall I comfort thee?

20 RThy sons have fainted, they lie at the head of all the streets, as a wild bull in a net: they are full of the Tfury of the LORD, the rebuke of thy God.   Lam. 2:11 • *judgment*

21 Therefore hear now this, thou afflicted, and drunken, Rbut not with wine: *v.* 17

22 Thus saith thy Lord the LORD, and thy God *that* pleadeth the cause of his people, Behold, I have taken out of thine hand the cup of trembling, *even* the dregs of the cup of my fury; thou shalt no more drink it again:

23 But I will put it into the hand of them that afflict thee; which have said to thy soul, Bow down, that we may go over: and thou hast laid thy body as the ground, and as the street, to them that went over.

CHAPTER 52

AWAKE, awake; put on thy strength, O Zion; put on thy beautiful garments, O Jerusalem, the holy city: for henceforth there shall no more come into thee the Tuncircumcised and the unclean.   *unbelieving*

2 RShake thyself from the dust; Rarise, *and* sit down, O Jerusalem: Rloose thyself from the bands of thy neck, O captive daughter of Zion.   3:26 • 60:1 • Zech. 2:7

3 For thus saith the LORD, RYe have sold yourselves for Tnought; and ye shall be redeemed without money.   Ps. 44:12 • *nothing*

4 For thus saith the Lord GOD, My people went down aforetime into REgypt to Tsojourn there; and the Assyrian oppressed them without cause.   Gen. 46:6 • *live*

5 Now therefore, what have I here, saith the LORD, that my people is taken away for nought? they that rule over them make them

to howl, saith the LORD; and my name continually every day is blasphemed.

6 Therefore my people shall know my name: therefore they shall know in that day that I am he that doth speak: behold, it is I.

7 How beautiful upon the mountains are the feet of him that bringeth good tidings, that publisheth peace; that bringeth good tidings of good, that publisheth salvation; that saith unto Zion, Thy God reigneth!

8 Thy watchmen shall lift up the Rvoice; with the voice together shall they sing: for they shall Tsee eye to eye, when the LORD shall bring again Zion.   62:6 • be of one mind

9 RBreak forth into joy, sing together, ye waste places of Jerusalem: for the LORD hath comforted his people, he hath redeemed Jerusalem.   44:23; Ps. 98:4

10 The LORD hath Tmade bare his holy arm in the eyes of all the nations; and Rall the ends of the earth shall see the salvation of our God.   revealed his power • Luke 3:6

11 RDepart ye, depart ye, go ye out from thence, touch no unclean thing; go ye out of the midst of her; Rbe ye clean, that bear the vessels of the LORD.   48:20 • Lev. 22:2

12 For ye shall not go out with haste, nor go by flight: for the LORD will go before you; and the God of Israel will be your rereward.

The Messiah's Atonement

13 Behold, Rmy servant shall deal prudently, Rhe shall be exalted and extolled, and be very high.   42:1 • Phil. 2:9 ☆

14 As many were astonied at thee; his visage was so marred more than any man, and his form more than the sons of men:

15 So Rshall he Tsprinkle many nations; the kings shall shut their mouths at him: for Rthat which had not been told them shall they see; and that which they had not heard shall they consider. 1 Pet. 1:2 ☆ • startle • Rom. 15:21 ☆

CHAPTER 53

WHO Rhath believed our Treport? and to whom is the arm of the LORD revealed?   John 12:38; Rom. 10:16 ☆ • doctrine?

2 For he shall grow up before him as a tender plant, and as a root out of a dry ground: he hath no form nor comeliness; and Rwhen we shall see him, there is no beauty that we should desire him.   Mark 15:32 ☆

3 He is despised and rejected of men; a man of sorrows, and acquainted with grief: and we hid as it were our faces from him; he was despised, and we esteemed him not.

4 Surely he hath borne our griefs, and carried our sorrows: yet we did esteem him stricken, smitten of God, and afflicted.

5 But Rhe was wounded for our transgressions, he was bruised for our iniquities: the chastisement of our peace was upon him; and with his stripes we are healed.   [1 Pet. 2:24] ☆

6 RAll we like sheep have gone astray; Rwe have turned every one to his own way; and the LORD hath Rlaid on him the iniquity of us all.   Gen. 6:5 • Ps. 119:176; Jer. 50:6 • Heb. 9:28 ☆

7 He was oppressed, and he was afflicted, yet Rhe opened not his mouth: Rhe is brought as a lamb to the slaughter, and as a sheep before her shearers is dumb, so he openeth not his mouth. Matt. 26:63; Mark 15:4, 5 ☆ • Acts 8:32 ☆

8 He was taken from prison and from judgment: and who shall declare his generation? for Rhe was cut off out of the land of the living: Rfor the transgression of my people was he Tstricken. [Dan. 9:26] • 1 Cor. 15:3 ☆ • punished

9 And he made his grave Rwith the wicked, and with the rich in his death; because he had done no violence, neither was any Rdeceit in his mouth.   Matt. 27:38, 57–60 ☆ • 1 John 3:5 ☆

10 Yet it pleased the LORD to bruise him; he hath put him to grief: when thou shalt make his soul.Ran offering for sin, he shall see Rhis seed, Rhe shall prolong his days, and the pleasure of the LORD shall prosper in his hand.   [John 1:29; 2 Cor. 5:21] ☆ • Ps. 22:30 • Acts 2:24 ☆

11 He shall see of the Ttravail of his soul, and shall be satisfied: Rby his knowledge shall my righteous servant justify many; for he shall bear their iniquities. suffering • Rom. 5:18, 19 ☆

12 Therefore will I divide him a portion with the great, and he shall divide the spoil with the strong; because he hath Rpoured out his soul unto death: and he was Rnumbered with the transgressors; and he bare the sin of many, and Rmade intercession for the transgressors.   50:6 • Luke 22:37 ☆ • Luke 23:34 ☆

CHAPTER 54

The Messiah's Promise of Israel's Restoration

SING, O barren, thou that didst not bear; break forth into singing, and cry aloud, thou that didst not Ttravail with child: Rfor more are the children of the desolate than the children of the married wife, saith the LORD.   suffer • Gal. 4:27

2 REnlarge the place of thy tent, and let them stretch forth the curtains of thine habitations: spare not, lengthen thy Rcords, and strengthen thy stakes;   49:19, 20 • Ex. 35:18

3 For thou shalt break forth on the right hand and on the left; and thy seed shall Tinherit the TGentiles, and make the desolate cities to be inhabited.   possess • nations

4 Fear not; for thou shalt not be ashamed: neither be thou confounded; for thou shalt not be put to shame: for thou shalt forget the shame of thy youth, and shalt not remember the reproach of thy widowhood any more.

5 RFor thy Maker is thine husband; the LORD of hosts is his name; and thy Redeemer

the Holy One of Israel; The God of the whole earth shall he be called.   Jer. 3:14

6 For the LORD Rhath called thee as a woman forsaken and grieved in spirit, and a wife of youth, when thou wast Trefused, saith thy God.   49:14–21; 50:1; 62:4 · *cast off*

7 RFor a small moment have I forsaken thee; but with great mercies will I Rgather thee.   26:20; 60:10; 2 Cor. 4:17 · [43:5; 56:8]

8 In a little wrath I hid my face from thee for a moment; Rbut with everlasting kindness will I have mercy on thee, saith the LORD thy Redeemer.   55:3; Jer. 31:3

9 For this *is as* the waters of Noah unto me: for *as* RI have sworn that the waters of Noah should no more go over the earth; so have I sworn that I would not be Twroth with thee, nor rebuke thee.   Gen. 8:21; 9:15 · *angry*

10 For Rthe mountains shall depart, and the hills be removed; but my kindness shall not depart from thee, neither shall the covenant of my peace be removed, saith the LORD that hath mercy on thee.   Ps. 46:2

11 O thou afflicted, tossed with tempest, *and* not comforted, behold, I will lay thy stones with Rfair colours, and lay thy foundations with sapphires. 1 Chr. 29:2; Rev. 21:18

12 And I will make thy Twindows of agates, and thy gates of carbuncles, and all thy borders of pleasant stones.   *pinnacles*

13 And all thy children *shall be* Rtaught of the LORD; and Rgreat *shall be* the peace of thy children.   11:9; [1 John 2:20] · Ps. 119:165

14 In righteousness shalt thou be Testablished: thou shalt be far from oppression; for thou shalt not fear: and from terror; for it shall not come near thee.   *made secure*

15 Behold, they shall surely gather together, *but* not by me: Rwhosoever shall gather together against thee shall fall for thy sake.   41:11-16

16 Behold, I have created the smith that bloweth the coals in the fire, and that bringeth forth an instrument for his work; and I have created the waster to destroy.

17 RNo weapon that is formed against thee shall prosper; and every tongue *that* shall rise against thee in judgment thou shalt condemn. This *is* the heritage of the servants of the LORD, and their righteousness *is* of me, saith the LORD.   29:8; 50:8, 9

CHAPTER 55

The Messiah's Invitation to the World

HO, every one that thirsteth, come ye to the waters, and he that hath no money; come ye, buy, and eat; yea, come, buy wine and milk without money and without price.

2 Wherefore do ye spend money for *that which is* not bread? and your labour for *that which* satisfieth not? hearken diligently unto

me, and eat ye *that which is* good, and let your soul delight itself in fatness.

3 Incline your ear, and come unto me: hear, and your soul shall live; and I will make an everlasting covenant with you, *even* the sureT mercies of David.   *confirmed*

4 Behold, I have given him *for* Ra witness to the people, Ra leader and commander to the people.   [John 18:37; Rev. 1:5] · [Dan. 9:25]

5 RBehold, thou shalt call a nation *that* thou knowest not, and nations *that* knew not thee shall run unto thee because of the LORD thy God, and for the Holy One of Israel; for he hath glorified thee.   52:15 ✻

6 Seek ye the LORD while he may be found, call ye upon him while he is near:

7 RLet the wicked forsake his way, and the unrighteous man his thoughts: and let him return unto the LORD, and he will have mercy upon him; and to our God, for he will Tabundantly pardon.   1:16 · *fully*

8 RFor my thoughts *are* not your thoughts, neither *are* Ryour ways my ways, saith the LORD.   2 Sam. 7:19 · [53:6]

9 For *as* the heavens are higher than the earth, so are my ways higher than your ways, and my thoughts than your thoughts.

10 For as the rain cometh down, and the snow from heaven, and returneth not thither, but watereth the earth, and maketh it bring forth and bud, that it may give seed to the sower, and bread to the eater:

11 RSo shall my word be that goeth forth out of my mouth: it shall not return unto me Tvoid, but it shall accomplish that which I please, and it shall prosper *in the thing* whereto I sent it.   45:23; 54:9 · *without fruit*

12 RFor ye shall go out with joy, and be led forth with peace: the mountains and the hills shall Rbreak forth before you into singing, and Rall the trees of the field shall clap *their* hands.   35:10 · Ps. 98:8 · 1 Chr. 16:33

13 RInstead of Rthe thorn shall come up the fir tree, and instead of the brier shall come up the myrtle tree: and it shall be to the LORD for a name, for an everlasting sign *that* shall not be cut off.   41:19 · Mic. 7:4

CHAPTER 56

THUS saith the LORD, TKeep ye judgment, and do justice: Rfor my salvation *is* near to come, and my righteousness to be revealed.   *be fair* · Matt. 4:17; Rom. 13:11, 12

2 Blessed *is* the man that doeth this, and the son of man that layeth hold on it; that keepeth the sabbath from polluting it, and keepeth his hand from doing any evil.

3 Neither let the son of the stranger, that hath joined himself to the LORD, speak, saying, The LORD hath utterly separated me from his people: neither let the eunuch say, Behold, I *am* a dry tree.

4 For thus saith the LORD unto the eunuchs that keep my sabbaths, and choose *the things* that please me, and ᵀtake hold of my covenant;   *hold fast by*

5 Even unto them will I give in mine house and within my walls a place ᴿand a name better than of sons and of daughters: ᴿI will give them an everlasting name, that shall not be cut off.   [John 1:12] • [Acts 11:26]

6 Also the sons of the stranger, that join themselves to the LORD, to serve him, and to love the name of the LORD, to be his servants, every one that keepeth the sabbath from ᵀpolluting it, and ᵀtaketh hold of my covenant;   *desecrating • accepts for himself*

7 Even them will I bring to my holy mountain, and make them joyful in my house of prayer: their burnt offerings and *sacrifices shall be* accepted upon mine altar; for mine house shall be called an house of prayer ᴿfor all people.   [Mal. 1:11]

8 The Lord GOD which ᴿgathereth the outcasts of Israel saith, ᴿYet will I gather *others* to him, beside those that are gathered unto him.   Ps. 147:2 • [John 10:16]

The Messiah's Rebuke of the Wicked

9 All ye beasts of the field, come to ᵀdevour, *yea*, all ye beasts in the forest. *destroy*

10 His watchmen *are* ᴿblind: they are all ignorant, ᴿthey *are* all dumb dogs, they cannot bark; sleeping, lying down, loving to slumber.   [Jer. 14:13, 14]; Matt. 15:14 • Phil. 3:2

11 Yea, *they are* ᴿgreedy dogs *which* ᴿcan never have enough, and they *are* shepherds *that* cannot understand: they all look to their own way, every one for his gain, from ᵀhis quarter.   [Mic. 3:11] • Ezek. 34:2 • *every*

12 Come ye, *say they*, I will fetch wine, and we will fill ourselves with strong drink; ᴿand to morrow shall be as this day, *and* much more abundant.   Prov. 23:35; Luke 12:19

CHAPTER 57

THE righteous perisheth, and no man layeth *it* to heart: and merciful men *are* taken away, none considering that the righteous is taken away from the evil *to come.*

2 He shall ᵀenter into peace: they shall rest in ᴿtheir beds, *each one* walking ᵀin his uprightness.   *go in peace* • 2 Chr. 16:14 • *honestly*

3 But draw near ᵀhither, ᴿye sons of the sorceress, the seed of the adulterer and the ᵀwhore.   *here* • Matt. 16:4; Mal. 3:5 • *harlot*

4 Against whom do ye sport yourselves? against whom make ye a wide mouth, *and* ᵀdraw out the tongue? *are* ye not children of transgression, a seed of falsehood,   *stick*

5 Enflaming yourselves with idols under every green tree, slaying the children in the valleys under the clifts of the rocks?

6 Among the smooth *stones* of the stream *is* thy portion; they, they *are* thy lot: even to them hast thou poured a drink offering, thou hast offered a ᵀmeat offering. Should I ᵀreceive comfort in these?   *meal • be appeased for*

7 Upon a lofty and high mountain hast thou set ᴿthy bed: even thither wentest thou up to offer sacrifice.   Ezek. 23:41

8 Behind the doors also and the posts hast thou set up thy remembrance: for thou hast discovered *thyself to another* than me, and art gone up; thou hast enlarged thy bed, and made thee *a covenant* with them; thou lovedst their bed where thou sawest *it.*

9 And ᴿthou wentest to the king with ointment, and didst increase thy perfumes, and didst send thy messengers far off, and didst debase *thyself even* unto hell.   Hos. 7:11

10 Thou art wearied in the greatness of thy way; *yet* saidst thou not, There is no hope: thou hast found the life of thine hand; therefore thou wast not grieved.

11 And of whom hast thou been afraid or feared, that thou hast lied, and hast not remembered me, nor laid *it* to thy heart? ᴿhave not I ᵀheld my peace even of old, and thou fearest me not?   Ps. 50:21 • *remained silent*

12 I will declare thy righteousness, and thy works; for they shall not profit thee.

13 When thou criest, let thy companies deliver thee; but the wind shall carry them all away; vanity shall take *them:* but he that putteth his trust in me shall possess the land, and shall inherit my holy mountain;

14 And shall say, ᴿCast ye up, cast ye up, prepare the way, take up the stumblingblock out of the way of my people.   40:3

15 For thus saith the high and lofty One that inhabiteth eternity, whose name *is* Holy; I dwell in the high and holy *place*, with him also *that is* of a contrite and humble spirit, to revive the spirit of the humble, and to revive the heart of the contrite ones.

16 ᴿFor I will not contend for ever, neither will I be always ᵀwroth: for the spirit should fail before me, and the souls ᴿwhich I have made.   [Mic. 7:18] • *angry* • Num. 16:22

17 For the iniquity of his covetousness was I wroth, and ᵀsmote him: I hid me, and was wroth, and he went on ᵀfrowardly in the way of his heart.   *punished • rebelliously*

18 I have seen his ways, and will heal him: I will lead him also, and restore comforts unto him and to ᴿhis mourners.   61:2

19 I create the fruit of the lips; Peace, peace to *him that is* far off, and to *him that is* near, saith the LORD; and I will heal him.

20 ᴿBut the wicked *are* like the troubled sea, when it cannot rest, whose waters cast up mire and dirt.   Job 15:20; Prov. 4:16; Jude 13

21 ᴿThere is no peace, saith my God, to the wicked.   48:22; 59:8

CHAPTER 58

Blessings of True Worship

CRY aloud, [T]spare not, lift up thy voice like a trumpet, and [R]shew my people their transgression, and the house of Jacob their sins. *have no pity* • 40:6, 8; Mic. 3:8

2 Yet they [R]seek me daily, and delight to know my ways, as a nation that did [R]righteousness, and forsook not the ordinance of their God: they ask of me the ordinances of justice; they take delight in [R]approaching to God. 1:11; Titus 1:16 • Jer. 7:9, 10 • 29:13

3 Wherefore have we fasted, *say they,* and thou seest not? *wherefore* have we afflicted our soul, and thou takest no knowledge? Behold, in the day of your fast ye find pleasure, and exact all your labours.

4 [R]Behold, ye fast for strife and debate, and to smite with the fist of wickedness: ye shall not fast as *ye do this* day, to make your voice to be heard on high. 1 Kin. 21:9

5 Is it such a fast that I have chosen? a day for a man to [T]afflict his soul? *is it* to bow down his head as a bulrush, and to spread sackcloth and ashes *under him?* wilt thou call this a fast, and an acceptable day to the LORD? *discipline his inner emotions?*

6 *Is* not this the fast that I have chosen? to loose the bands of wickedness, to undo the heavy burdens, and [R]to let the oppressed go free, and that ye break every yoke? Jer. 34:9

7 *Is it* not to [T]deal thy bread to the hungry, and that thou bring the poor that are cast out to thy house? when thou seest the naked, that thou cover him; and that thou hide not thyself from thine own flesh? *share*

8 Then shall thy light break forth as the morning, and thine health shall spring forth speedily: and thy righteousness shall go before thee; [R]the glory of the LORD shall be thy [T]rereward. 52:12; Ex. 14:19 • *protection*

9 Then shalt thou call, and the LORD shall answer; thou shalt cry, and he shall say, Here I *am.* If thou take away from the midst of thee the yoke, the putting forth of the finger, and [R]speaking vanity; Ps. 12:2

10 And *if* thou draw out thy soul to the hungry, and satisfy the [T]afflicted soul; then

shall thy light rise in obscurity, and thy darkness *be* as the noon day: *suffering*

11 And the LORD shall guide thee continually, and [R]satisfy thy soul in drought, and make [T]fat thy bones: and thou shalt be like a watered garden, and like a spring of water, whose waters fail not. 41:17 • *strong*

12 And *they that shall be* of thee shall build the old waste places: thou shalt raise up the foundations of many generations; and thou shalt be called, The repairer of the breach, The restorer of paths to dwell in.

13 If [R]thou turn away thy foot from the sabbath, *from* doing thy pleasure on my holy day; and call the sabbath a delight, the holy of the LORD, honourable; and shalt honour him, not doing thine [R]own ways, nor finding thine own pleasure, nor speaking *thine own* words: 56:2 • 55:8

14 Then shalt thou delight thyself in the LORD; and I will cause thee to ride upon the high places of the earth, and feed thee with the heritage of Jacob thy father: for the mouth of the LORD hath spoken *it.*

CHAPTER 59

Sins of Israel

BEHOLD, the LORD's hand is not [R]shortened, that it cannot save; neither his ear heavy, that it cannot hear: 50:2

2 But your [T]iniquities[R] have separated between you and your God, and your sins [T]have hid *his* face from you, that he will not hear. *sins* • 1:15; 50:1 • *come between*

3 For [R]your hands are defiled with [T]blood, and your fingers with iniquity; your lips have spoken lies, your tongue hath muttered [T]perverseness. 1:15 • *wrongdoing* • *error*

4 [R]None calleth for [T]justice, nor *any* pleadeth [T]for truth: they trust in vanity, and speak lies; they conceive mischief, and bring forth iniquity. 5:7 • *righteousness* • *in*

5 They hatch [T]cockatrice' eggs, and weave the spider's web: he that eateth of their eggs dieth, and that which is crushed breaketh out into a viper. *adders'*

59:2 What Sin Does—Sin, regardless of its degree, always has an effect—separation. Sin separates one from God. This separation from God is death. Adam was told that if he ate of the tree of the knowledge of good and evil that he would die (Page 6—Gen. 3:3). Adam ate of the tree and immediately died spiritually—his soul was separated from God—and he began to die physically. The entrance of sin into the human race brought with it death (Page 1112—Rom. 5:12; 6:23). That man is a sinner is proven by the fact that he dies—where there is death, there is sin. Sin's penalty, death, can be remedied by life—union with God. This is achieved by belief in Jesus, who died to pay the penalty of man's sin (Page 1112—Rom. 5:21). For the one who believes in Jesus, the penalty of sin is broken. Yes, he will die physically (unless he is alive when Jesus returns to take all believers to heaven with Himself, Page 1185—1 Thess. 4:14-18), but physical death for him is only the doorway into the presence of God. Sin, however, does have an effect upon the believer, for it mars his fellowship with God. Sin in the believer's life is a terrible thing and is not to be tolerated. While it is probable that the believer will sin, it is never necessary for him to do so (Page 1249—1 John 2:1).
Now turn to Page 560—Ps. 32:5: What Should Be Done About Sin.

6 Their webs shall not become garments, neither shall they cover themselves with their works: their works *are* works of iniquity, and the act of violence *is* in their hands.

7 Their feet run to evil, and they make haste to shed innocent blood: their thoughts *are* thoughts of iniquity; wasting and ^Tdestruction *are* in their paths.   *violence*

8 The way of peace they know not; and *there is* no ^Tjudgment in their goings: they have made them crooked paths: whosoever goeth therein shall not know peace. *justice*

9 Therefore is judgment far from us, neither doth justice overtake us: ^Rwe wait for light, but behold obscurity; for brightness, *but* we walk in darkness.   Jer. 8:15

10 ^RWe grope for the wall like the blind, and we grope as if *we had* no eyes: we stumble at noon day as in the night; *we are* in desolate places as dead *men.*   Amos 8:9

11 We roar all like bears, and mourn sore like doves: we look for judgment, but *there is* none; for salvation, *but* it is far off from us.

12 For our transgressions are multiplied before thee, and our sins testify against us: for our transgressions *are* with us; and *as for* our iniquities, we ^Tknow them; *recognize*

13 In transgressing and ^Tlying against the LORD, and departing away from our God, ^cpeaking oppression and revolt, conceiving and uttering ^Rfrom the heart words of falsehood. *denying;* Josh. 24:27; Prov. 30:9 · Matt. 12:34

14 And ^Rjudgment is turned away backward, and ^Rjustice standeth afar off: for truth is fallen in the street, and equity cannot enter.   1:21; 5:7 · 46:12; Hab. 1:4

15 Yea, truth faileth; and he *that* departeth from evil maketh himself ^Ta prey: and the LORD saw *it,* and it displeased him that *there* was no judgment. *an easy victim*

16 And he saw that *there was* no man, and wondered that *there was* no intercessor: therefore his arm brought salvation unto him; and his righteousness, it sustained him.

17 ^RFor he put on righteousness as a breastplate, and an helmet of salvation upon his head; and he put on the garments of vengeance *for* clothing, and was clad with zeal as a cloke.   Eph. 6:14, 17; 1 Thess. 5:8

18 ^RAccording to *their* deeds, accordingly he will repay, fury to his adversaries, recompence to his enemies; to the islands he will repay recompence.   63:6; 65:6, 7

19 So shall they fear the name of the LORD from the west, and his glory from the rising of the sun. When the enemy shall come in like a flood, the Spirit of the LORD shall lift up a standard against him.

20 And ^Rthe Redeemer shall come to Zion, and unto them that turn from transgression in Jacob, saith the LORD.   Rom. 11:26 ☆

21 As for me, this *is* my covenant with them, saith the LORD; My spirit that *is* upon thee, and my words which I have put in thy mouth, shall not depart out of thy mouth, nor out of the mouth of thy seed, nor out of the mouth of thy seed's seed, saith the LORD, from henceforth and for ever.

CHAPTER 60

Glory of Israel in the Kingdom

ARISE, shine; for thy light is come, and the glory of the LORD is risen upon thee.

2 For, behold, the ^Rdarkness shall cover the earth, and gross darkness the people: but the LORD shall arise upon thee, and his glory shall be seen upon thee.   58:10

3 And the ^RGentiles ^Tshall come to thy light, and kings to the brightness of thy rising. 2:3; 49:6, 23; Rev. 21:24 ☆ · *nations*

4 ^RLift up thine eyes round about, and see: all they gather themselves together, ^Rthey come to thee: thy sons shall come from far, and thy daughters shall be nursed at *thy* side.   49:18 · 49:20–22

59:21 Inspiration of God's Word—The word *inspiration* is found but once in the New Testament. This occurs in Second Timothy 3:16, where Paul says "All scripture *is* given by inspiration of God," literally "God-breathed." Divine inspiration logically follows divine revelation. In revelation God speaks to man's ear while by inspiration He guides the pen to ensure that the imparted message is correctly written down.

There are several ideas about the process of inspiration. One is called the natural theory. This says that the Bible authors were inspired in the same sense that William Shakespeare was inspired. Another theory, called the content theory, suggests that God merely gave the writer the main content or idea, allowing him to choose his own words to express that concept. In contrast Jesus Himself said that the very letters of the words were also chosen by God (Page 945—see Matt. 5:18). This position is referred to as the plenary-verbal view, which says that all (plenary) the very words (verbal) of the Bible are inspired by God. Jesus once told the devil that the Christian is to live by each of these inspired words (Page 944—Matt. 4:4). The Bible authors understood that their writings were being guided by the Spirit of God, even as they wrote them. Peter said this was true of the Old Testament authors (Page 1243—2 Pet. 1:20, 21). He then stated that his own letters (Page 1235—1 and 2 Pet.) were inspired by God (Page 1244—2 Pet. 3:1, 2). Finally, he pointed out that this was also true concerning Paul's writings (Page 1244—2 Pet. 3:15, 16).

One final thing should be said about inspiration. Plenary-verbal inspiration does not guarantee the inspiration of any translation, but only of the original Hebrew and Greek manuscripts.

Now turn to Page 618—Prov. 6:23: Illumination of God's Word.

5 Then thou shalt see, and flow together, and thine heart shall fear, and be enlarged; because Rthe abundance of the sea shall be converted unto thee, the forces of the Gentiles shall come unto thee.   [Rom. 11:25]

6 The multitude of camels shall cover thee, the dromedaries of Mid'-i-an and E'-phah; all they from She'-ba shall come: they shall bring Rgold and incense; and they shall shew forth the praises of the LORD.   Matt. 2:11

7 All the flocks of Ke'-dar shall be gathered together unto thee, the rams of Ne-bai'-oth shall minister unto thee: they shall come up with acceptance on mine Raltar, and I will glorify the house of my glory.   19:19; 56:7

8 RWho are these that fly as a cloud, and as the doves to their windows?   49:21

9 RSurely the isles shall wait for me, and the ships of Tar'-shish first, to bring thy sons from far, their silver and their gold with them, unto the name of the LORD thy God, and to the Holy One of Israel, Rbecause he hath glorified thee.   Ps. 72:10 • 55:5

10 And the sons of strangers shall build up thy walls, and their kings shall minister unto thee: for in my wrath I smote thee, but in my favour have I had mercy on thee.

11 Therefore thy gates Rshall be open continually; they shall not be shut day nor night; that men may bring unto thee the Tforces of the Gentiles, and that their kings may be brought.   Rev. 21:25 • strength

12 For the nation and kingdom that will not serve thee shall perish; yea, those nations shall be utterly Twasted.   destroyed

13 RThe glory of Leb'-a-non shall come unto thee, the fir tree, the pine tree, and the box together, to beautify the place of my sanctuary; and I will make Rthe place of my feet glorious.   35:2 • 1 Chr. 28:2; Ps. 132:7

14 The sons also of them that afflicted thee shall come bending unto thee; and all they that despised thee shall bow themselves down at the soles of thy feet; and they shall call thee, The city of the LORD, The Zion of the Holy One of Israel.

15 Whereas thou hast been Rforsaken and hated, so that no man went through thee, I will make thee an eternal excellency, a joy of many generations.   1:7-9; 6:11-13

16 Thou shalt also suck the milk of the Gentiles, Rand shalt suck the breast of kings: and thou shalt know that RI the LORD am thy Saviour and thy Redeemer, the mighty One of Jacob.   49:23 • 43:3

17 For brass I will bring gold, and for iron I will bring silver, and for wood brass, and for stones iron: I will also make thy officers peace, and thine exactors righteousness.

18 RViolence shall no more be heard in thy land, wasting nor destruction within thy borders; but thou shalt call Rthy walls Salvation, and thy gates Praise.   54:14 • 26:1

19 The Rsun shall be no more thy light by day; neither for brightness shall the moon give light unto thee: but the RLORD shall be unto thee an everlasting light, and Rthy God thy glory.   Rev. 21:23 • 2:5; 9:2 • Zech. 2:5

20 Thy sun shall no more go down; neither shall thy moon withdraw itself: for the LORD shall be thine everlasting light, and the days of thy mourning shall be ended.

21 Thy people also shall be all righteous: Rthey shall inherit the land for ever, the branch of my planting, the work of my hands, that I may be glorified.   Rev. 21:27

22 RA little one shall become a thousand, and a small one a strong nation: I the LORD will hasten it in his time.   Hos. 1:10

CHAPTER 61

Advents of the Messiah

THE Spirit of the Lord GOD is upon me; because the LORD hath anointed me to preach good tidings unto the meek; he hath sent me to bind up the brokenhearted, to proclaim liberty to the captives, and the opening of the prison to them that are bound;

2 RTo proclaim the acceptable year of the LORD, and the day of vengeance of our God; to comfort all that mourn;   Lev. 25:9

3 To Tappoint unto them that mourn in Zion, Rto give unto them beauty for ashes, the oil of joy for mourning, the garment of praise for the spirit of heaviness; that they might be called trees of righteousness, Rthe planting of the LORD, Rthat he might be glorified.   assign • Ps. 30:11 • 60:21 • [John 15:8]

4 And they shall Rbuild the old wastes, they shall raise up the former desolations, and they shall repair the waste cities, the desolations of many generations.   Ezek. 36:33

5 And strangers shall stand and feed your flocks, and the sons of the alien shall be your plowmen and your vinedressers.

6 But ye shall be named the Priests of the LORD: men shall call you the Ministers of our God: ye shall eat the riches of the Gentiles, and in their glory shall ye boast yourselves.

7 RFor your shame ye shall have double; and for confusion they shall rejoice in their portion: therefore in their land they shall possess the double: everlasting joy shall be unto them.   40:2; Zech. 9:12

8 For RI the LORD love judgment, I hate robbery for burnt offering; and I will direct their work in truth, and I will make an everlasting covenant with them.   Ps. 11:7

9 And their seed shall be known among the TGentiles, and their offspring among the people: all that see them shall acknowledge them, Rthat they are the seed which the LORD hath blessed.   nations • 65:23

10 ᴿI will greatly rejoice in the Lᴏʀᴅ, my soul shall be joyful in my God; for he hath clothed me with the garments of salvation, he hath covered me with the robe of righteousness, ᴿas a bridegroom decketh *himself* with ornaments, and as a bride adorneth *herself* with her jewels. Hab. 3:18 • 49:18

11 For as the earth bringeth forth her bud, and as the garden causeth the things that are sown in it to spring forth; so the Lord Gᴏᴅ will cause ᴿrighteousness and praise to spring forth before all the nations. Ps. 72:3; 85:11

CHAPTER 62

Future of Jerusalem

FOR Zion's sake will I not ᵀhold my peace, and for Jerusalem's sake I will not rest, until the righteousness thereof go forth as brightness, and the ᴿsalvation thereof as a lamp *that* burneth. keep quiet • 46:13

2 And the Gentiles shall see thy righteousness, and all kings thy glory: ᴿand thou shalt be called by a new name, which the mouth of the Lᴏʀᴅ shall name. Acts 11:26

3 Thou shalt also be ᴿa crown of ᵀglory in the hand of the Lᴏʀᴅ, and a royal diadem in the hand of thy God. Zech. 9:16 • beauty

4 ᴿThou shalt no more be termed Forsaken; neither shall thy land any more be termed ᴿDesolate: but thou shalt be called Heph′-zi–bah, and thy land ᵀBeu′-lah: for the Lᴏʀᴅ delighteth in thee, and thy land shall be married. Hos. 1:10 • 54:1 • married

5 For *as* a young man marrieth a virgin, *so* shall thy sons marry thee: and *as* the bridegroom rejoiceth over the bride, *so* ᴿshall thy God rejoice over thee. 65:19

6 I have set watchmen upon thy walls, O Jerusalem, *which* shall never ᵀhold their peace day nor night: ye that make mention of the Lᴏʀᴅ, keep not silence, stay quiet

7 And give him no ᵀrest, till he establish, and till he make Jerusalem ᴿa praise in the earth. silence • 61:11; Zeph. 3:20

8 The Lᴏʀᴅ hath sworn by his right hand,

and by the arm of his strength, Surely I will no more ᴿgive thy corn *to be* meat for thine enemies; and the sons of the stranger shall not drink thy wine, for the which thou hast laboured: Deut. 28:31

9 But they that have gathered it shall eat it, and praise the Lᴏʀᴅ; and they that have brought it together shall drink it ᴿin the courts of my ᵀholiness. Deut. 12:11 • presence

10 Go through, go through the gates; prepare ye the way of the people; cast up, cast up the highways; gather out the stones; ᴿlift up a standard for the people. 11:12

11 Behold, the Lᴏʀᴅ hath proclaimed unto the end of the ᵀworld, ᴿSay ye to the daughter of Zion, Behold, thy salvation cometh; behold, his reward *is* with him, and his ᵀwork before him. earth • Zech 9:9 ☆ • deeds

12 And they shall call them, ᴿThe holy people, The redeemed of the Lᴏʀᴅ: and thou shalt be called, Sought out, A city ᴿnot forsaken. 4:3; Deut. 7:6; 1 Pet. 2:9 • 41:17; 62:4

CHAPTER 63

Vengeance of God

WHO *is* this that cometh from E′-dom, with dyed garments from Boz′-rah? this *that is* glorious in his apparel, travelling in the greatness of his strength? I that speak in righteousness, mighty to save.

2 ᵀWherefore ᴿart *thou* red in thine apparel, and thy garments like him that treadeth in the winefat? why • [Rev. 19:13] ☆

3 I have ᴿtrodden the winepress alone; and of the people *there was* none with me: for I will tread them in mine anger, and trample them in my fury; and their blood shall be sprinkled upon my garments, and I will stain all my raiment. Mark 14:50; Rev. 14:20; 19:15 ☆

4 For the day of vengeance *is* in mine heart, and the year of my redeemed is come.

5 ᴿAnd I looked, and ᴿ*there was* none to help; and I wondered that *there was* none to uphold: therefore mine own ᴿarm brought salvation unto me; and my fury, it upheld me. 41:28 • [John 16:32] • 59:16; Ps. 98:1

6 And I will ᴿtread down the people in

mine anger, and make them drunk in my ᵀfury, and I will bring down their strength to the earth. 22:5; 34:2 • *aroused feelings*

Prayer of the Remnant

7 I will mention the lovingkindnesses of the Lᴏʀᴅ, *and* the praises of the Lᴏʀᴅ, according to all that the Lᴏʀᴅ hath bestowed on us, and the great goodness toward the house of Israel, which he hath bestowed on them according to his mercies, and according to the multitude of his lovingkindnesses.

8 For he said, Surely they *are* ᴿmy people, children *that* will not ᵀlie: so he was their ᴿSaviour. 3:15; 51:4; Ex. 6:7 • *deal falsely* • 60:16 ☆

9 ᴿIn all their affliction he was afflicted, and the angel of his presence saved them: in his love and in his pity he redeemed them; and ᴿhe bare them, and carried them all the days of old. Judg. 10:16 • Ex. 19:4

10 But they rebelled, and ᴿvexed his holy Spirit: therefore he was turned to be their enemy, *and* he fought against them. Ps. 78:40

11 Then he remembered the days of old, Moses, *and* his people, *saying,* Where *is* he that ᴿbrought them up out of the sea with the shepherd of his flock? where *is* he that put his holy Spirit within him? Ex. 14:30

12 That led *them* by the right hand of Moses ᴿwith his ᵀglorious arm, ᴿdividing the water before them, to make himself an everlasting name? Ex. 15:16 • *mighty* • Josh. 3:16

13 ᴿThat led them through the deep, as an horse in the wilderness, *that* they should not ᴿstumble? Ps. 106:9 • Jer. 31:9

14 As ᵀa beast goeth down into the valley, the Spirit of the Lᴏʀᴅ caused him to rest: so didst thou lead thy people, ᴿto make thyself a glorious name. *the cattle* • 2 Sam. 7:23

15 Look down from heaven, and behold from the habitation of thy holiness and of thy glory: where *is* thy zeal and thy strength, the sounding of thy bowels and of thy mercies toward me? are they restrained?

16 Doubtless thou *art* our father, though Abraham be ignorant of us, and Israel acknowledge us not: thou, O Lᴏʀᴅ, *art* our father, our redeemer; ᵀthy name *is* from everlasting. *from everlasting is thy name*

17 O Lᴏʀᴅ, why hast thou made us to err from thy ways, *and* hardened our heart from thy fear? Return for thy servants' sake, the tribes of thine inheritance.

18 The people of thy holiness have possessed *it* but a little while: our adversaries have trodden down thy sanctuary.

19 We are *thine:* thou never barest rule over them; ᵀthey were not called by thy name. *they never belonged to you*

CHAPTER 64

OH that thou wouldest ᵀrend the heavens, ᴿthat thou wouldest come down, that the mountains might flow down at thy ᴿpresence, *open* • Ex. 19:18; Judg. 5:5 • Mic. 1:3, 4

2 As *when* the melting fire burneth, the fire causeth the waters to boil, to make thy name known to thine adversaries, *that* the nations may tremble at thy presence!

3 When thou didst terrible things *which* we looked not for, thou camest down, the mountains flowed down at thy presence.

4 For since the beginning of the world ᴿmen have not heard, nor perceived by the ear, neither hath the eye seen, O God, beside thee, ᴿwhat he hath prepared for him that waiteth for him. Ps. 31:19 • 1 Cor. 2:9

5 Thou meetest him that rejoiceth and worketh righteousness, *those that* remember thee in thy ways: behold, thou art ᵀwroth; for we have sinned: in those is continuance, and we shall be saved. *angry*

6 But we are all as an unclean *thing,* and all our righteousnesses *are* as filthy rags; and we all do fade as a leaf; and our iniquities, like the wind, have taken us away.

7 And *there is* none that calleth upon thy name, that stirreth up himself to take hold of thee: for thou hast hid thy face from us, and hast consumed us, because of our iniquities.

8 But now, O Lᴏʀᴅ, thou *art* our father; we *are* the clay, and ᴿthou our potter; and we all *are* the work of thy hand. Jer. 18:6

9 Be not wroth very sore, O Lᴏʀᴅ, neither remember iniquity for ever: behold, see, we beseech thee, we *are* all thy people.

10 Thy holy cities are a wilderness, Zion is a wilderness, Jerusalem a desolation.

11 Our holy and our beautiful house, where our fathers praised thee, is burned up with fire: and all ᴿour pleasant things are ᵀlaid waste. Ezek. 24:21 • *turned into ruins*

12 Wilt thou refrain thyself for these *things,* O Lᴏʀᴅ? wilt thou hold thy peace, and ᵀafflict us very ᵀsore? *trouble* • *badly*

CHAPTER 65

The Lord's Answer to the Remnant

I AM sought of *them that* asked not *for me;* I am found of *them that* sought me not: I said, Behold me, behold me, unto a nation *that* was not called by my name.

2 ᴿI have spread out my hands all the day unto a ᴿrebellious people, which ᴿwalketh in a way *that was* not good, after their own thoughts; Rom. 10:21 ☆ • 1:2, 23 • Deut. 32:5

3 A people that provoketh me to anger continually to my face; ᴿthat sacrificeth in ᵀgardens, and burneth incense upon ᵀaltars of brick; 1:29 • *pagan shrines* • *pagan altars*

4 ᴿWhich remain among the graves, and lodge in the monuments, ᴿwhich eat swine's flesh, and ᴿbroth of abominable *things is in* their vessels; Deut. 18:11 • 66:17 • Lev. 11:7

5 ^RWhich say, Stand by thyself, come not near to me; for I am ^Rholier than thou. These *are* a smoke in my nose, a fire that burneth all the day.   Jude 19 · Luke 18:9–12

6 Behold, ^R*it is* written before me: I will not keep silence, but will recompense, even recompense into their bosom,   Mal. 3:16

7 Your iniquities, and the iniquities of your fathers together, saith the LORD, which have burned incense upon the mountains, and blasphemed me upon the hills: therefore will I measure their former work into their bosom.

8 Thus saith the LORD, As the new wine is found in the cluster, and *one* saith, Destroy it not; for ^Ra blessing *is* in it: so will I do for my servants' sakes, that I may not destroy them all.   Joel 2:14

9 And I will bring forth a seed out of Jacob, and out of Judah an inheritor of my mountains: and mine elect shall inherit it, and my servants shall dwell there.

10 And ^RShar'-on shall be a fold of flocks, and ^Rthe valley of A'-chor a place for the herds to lie down in, for my people that have sought me.   33:9 · Josh. 7:24; Hos. 2:15

11 But ye *are* they that forsake the LORD, that forget my holy mountain, that prepare a table for that troop, and that furnish the drink offering unto that number.

12 Therefore will I number you to the sword, and ye shall all bow down to the slaughter: ^Rbecause when I called, ye did not answer; when I spake, ye did not hear; but did evil before mine eyes, and did choose that wherein I delighted not.   Jer. 7:13

13 Therefore thus saith the Lord GOD, Behold, my servants shall eat, but ye shall be hungry: behold, my servants shall drink, but ye shall be thirsty: behold, my servants shall rejoice, but ye shall be ashamed:

14 Behold, my servants shall sing for joy of heart, but ye shall cry for sorrow of heart, and shall ^Thowl for vexation of spirit.   wail

15 And ye shall leave your name ^Rfor a curse unto ^Rmy chosen: for the Lord GOD shall slay thee, and ^Rcall his servants by another name: Zech. 8:13 · *vv.* 9, 22 · [Acts 11:26]

16 ^RThat he who blesseth himself in the earth shall bless himself in the God of truth; and he that sweareth in the earth shall swear by the God of truth; because the former troubles are forgotten, and because they are hid from mine eyes.   Jer. 4:2

Glorious Consummation of History

17 For, behold, I create ^Rnew heavens and a new earth: and the former shall not be remembered, nor come into mind.   Rev. 21:1

18 But be ye glad and rejoice for ever in that which I create: for, behold, I create Jerusalem a rejoicing, and her people a joy.

19 And ^RI will rejoice in Jerusalem, and joy in my people: and the ^Rvoice of weeping shall be no more heard in her, nor the voice of crying.   62:5 · 35:10; Rev. 7:17

20 There shall be no more thence an infant of days, nor an old man that hath not filled his days: for the child shall die an hundred years old; but the sinner *being* an hundred years old shall be accursed.

21 And they shall build houses, and inhabit *them;* ^Rand they shall plant vineyards, and eat the fruit of them.   Amos 9:14

22 They shall not build, and another inhabit; they shall not plant, and another eat: for as the days of a tree *are* the days of my people, and ^Rmine elect shall long enjoy the work of their hands.   *vv.* 9, 15

23 They shall not labour in vain, ^Rnor bring forth for trouble; for ^Rthey *are* the seed of blessed of the LORD, and their offspring with them.   Hos. 9:12 · 61:9

24 And it shall come to pass, that ^Rbefore they call, I will answer; and while they are yet speaking, I will hear.   [Ps. 32:5]; Dan. 9:21

25 The wolf and the lamb shall feed together, and the lion shall eat straw like the bullock: and dust *shall be* the serpent's meat. They shall not hurt nor destroy in all my holy mountain, saith the LORD.

CHAPTER 66

THUS saith the LORD, ^RThe heaven *is* my throne, and the earth *is* my footstool: where *is* the house that ye build unto me? and where *is* the place of my rest?   Matt. 5:34

2 For all those *things* hath mine hand made, and all those *things* have been, saith the LORD: but to this *man* will I look, *even to* him *that is* poor and of a contrite spirit, and ^Rtrembleth at my word.   1 Cor. 2:3

3 He that killeth an ox *is as if* he slew a man; he that sacrificeth a lamb, *as if* he cut off a dog's neck; he that offereth an oblation, *as if he offered* swine's blood; he that burneth incense, *as if* he blessed an idol. Yea, they have chosen their own ways, and their soul delighteth in their abominations.

4 I also will ^Tchoose their delusions, and will bring their fears upon them; ^Rbecause when I called, none did answer; when I spake, they did not hear: but they did evil before mine eyes, and chose *that* in which I delighted not.   *select their own ideas* · 65:12

5 Hear the word of the LORD, ye that tremble at his word; ^RYour brethren that hated you, that cast you out for my name's sake, said, Let the LORD be glorified: but ^Rhe shall appear to your joy, and they shall be ashamed.   5:19 · [2 Thess. 1:10; Titus 2:13]

6 A voice of noise from the city, a voice from the temple, a voice of the LORD that rendereth recompence to his enemies.

7 Before she ^Ttravailed,^R she brought forth;

before her pain came, she was delivered of a man child.   *suffered • v. 8*

8 Who hath heard such a thing? who hath seen such things? Shall the earth be made to bring forth in one day? *or* shall a nation be born at once? for as soon as Zion travailed, she brought forth her children.

9 Shall I bring to the birth, and ᴿnot ᵀcause to bring forth? saith the LORD: shall I cause to bring forth, and shut *the womb?* saith thy God.   37:3 • *enable*

10 Rejoice ye with Jerusalem, and be glad with her, all ye that love her: rejoice for joy with her, all ye that mourn for her:

11 That ye may suck, and be satisfied with the breasts of her ᵀconsolations; that ye may milk out, and be delighted with the abundance of her glory.   *comforts*

12 For thus saith the LORD, Behold, I will extend peace to her like a river, and the glory of the Gentiles like a flowing stream: then shall ye suck, ye shall be borne upon *her* sides, and be dandled upon *her* knees.

13 As one whom his mother comforteth, so will I ᴿcomfort you; and ye shall be comforted in Jerusalem.   51:3

14 And when ye ᴿsee *this,* your heart shall rejoice, and ᴿyour bones shall flourish like an herb: and the hand of the LORD shall be known toward his servants, and *his* indignation toward his enemies.   33:20 • Ezek. 37:1

15 ᴿFor, behold, the LORD will come with fire, and with his chariots like a whirlwind, to render his anger with fury, and his rebuke with flames of fire.   9:5; [2 Thess. 1:8]

16 For by fire and by ᴿhis sword will the LORD plead with all flesh: and the slain of the LORD shall be ᴿmany.   27:1 • 34:6

17 They that sanctify themselves, and purify themselves in the gardens behind one *tree* in the midst, eating swine's flesh, and the abomination, and the mouse, shall be consumed together, saith the LORD.

18 ᴿFor I *know* their works and their thoughts: it shall come, that I will ᴿgather all nations and tongues; and they shall come, and see my glory.   Heb. 4:13 • Jer. 3:17

19 And I will set a sign among them, and I will send those that escape of them unto the nations, *to* Tar'-shish, Pul, and Lud, that draw the bow, *to* Tu'-bal, and Ja'-van, *to* the ᵀisles afar off, that have not heard my fame, neither have seen my glory; and they shall declare my glory among the Gentiles.   *coasts*

20 And they shall bring all your brethren ᴿ*for* an offering unto the LORD out of all nations upon horses, and in chariots, and in litters, ᵀand upon mules, and upon swift beasts, to my holy mountain Jerusalem, saith the LORD, as the children of Israel bring an offering in a clean vessel into the house of the LORD.   [Rom. 15:16] • *drawn by*

21 And I will also take of them for priests *and* for Levites, saith the LORD.

22 For as ᴿthe new heavens and the new earth, which I will make, shall remain before me, saith the LORD, so shall your seed and your name remain.   2 Pet. 3:13; Rev. 21:1

23 And it shall come to pass, *that* from one new moon to another, and from one sabbath to another, ᴿshall all flesh come to worship before me, saith the LORD.   Ps. 65:2

24 And they shall go forth, and look upon the carcases of the men that have transgressed against me: for their worm shall not die, neither shall their fire be quenched; and they shall be an abhorring unto all flesh.

Weights

Unit	Weight	Equivalents	Translations
Jewish Weights Talent	c. 75 pounds for common talent, c. 150 pounds for royal talent	60 minas; 3,000 shekels	talent
Mina	1.25 pounds	50 shekels	maneh, pound
Shekel	c. .4 ounce (11.4 grams) for common shekel c. .8 ounce for royal shekel	2 bekas; 20 gerahs	shekel
Beka	c. .2 ounce (5.7 grams)	½ shekel; 10 gerahs	half a shekel
Gerah	c. .02 ounce (.57 grams)	¹⁄₂₀ shekel	gerah
Roman Weight Litra	12 ounces		pound

THE BOOK OF THE PROPHET

JEREMIAH

THE BOOK OF JEREMIAH

The Book of Jeremiah is the prophecy of a man divinely called in his youth from the priest-city of Anathoth. A heartbroken prophet with a heartbreaking message, Jeremiah labors for more than forty years proclaiming a message of doom to the stiff-necked people of Judah. Despised and persecuted by his countrymen, Jeremiah bathes his harsh prophecies in tears of compassion. His broken heart causes him to write a broken book, which is difficult to arrange chronologically or topically. But through his sermons and signs he faithfully declares that surrender to God's will is the only way to escape calamity.

Yirmeyahu or *Yirmeyah* literally means "Yahweh Throws," perhaps in the sense of laying a foundation. It may effectively mean "Yahweh establishes, appoints, or sends." The Greek form of the Hebrew name in the Septuagint is *Hieremias*, and the Latin form is *Jeremias*.

THE AUTHOR OF JEREMIAH

Jeremiah was the son of Hilkiah the priest and lived just over two miles north of Jerusalem in Anathoth. As an object lesson to Judah he was not allowed to marry (16:2). Because of his radical message of God's judgment through the coming Babylonian invasion, he led a life of conflict. He was threatened in his hometown of Anathoth, tried for his life by the priests and prophets of Jerusalem, put in stocks, forced to flee from king Jehoiakim, publicly humiliated by the false prophet Hananiah, and thrown into a cistern.

The book clearly states that Jeremiah is its author (1:1). Jeremiah dictated all his prophecies to his secretary Baruch from the beginning of his ministry until the fourth year of Jehoiakim. After this scroll was destroyed by the king, Jeremiah dictated a more complete edition to Baruch (see 36—38), and later sections were also composed. Only chapter 52 was evidently not written by Jeremiah. This supplement is almost identical to Second Kings 24:18—25:30, and it may have been added by Baruch.

Daniel alludes to Jeremiah's prophecy of the seventy-year captivity (25:11–14; 29:10; Dan. 9:2), and Jeremiah's authorship is also confirmed by Ecclesiasticus, Josephus, and the Talmud. The New Testament makes explicit and implicit references to Jeremiah's prophecy: Matthew 2:17, 18 (31:15); Matthew 21:13; Mark 11:17; Luke 19:4 (7:11); Romans 11:27 (31:33); and Hebrews 8:8–13 (31:31–34).

THE TIME OF JEREMIAH

Jeremiah was a contemporary of Zephaniah, Habakkuk, Daniel, and Ezekiel. His ministry stretched from 627 to about 580 B.C. Josiah, Judah's last good king (640–609 B.C.), instituted spiritual reforms when the Book of the Law was discovered in 622 B.C. Jeremiah was on good terms with Josiah and lamented when he was killed in 609 B.C. by Pharaoh–necho of Egypt. By this time, Babylon had already overthrown Nineveh, the capital city of Assyria (612 B.C.). Jehoahaz replaced Josiah as king of Judah, but reigned only three months before he was deposed and taken to Egypt by Necho. Jehoiakim (609–597 B.C.) was Judah's next king, but he reigned as an Egyptian vassal until 605 B.C., when Egypt was defeated by Babylon at Carchemish. Nebuchadnezzar took Palestine and deported key persons such as Daniel to Babylon. Judah's king Jehoiakim was now a Babylonian vassal, but he rejected Jeremiah's warnings in 601 B.C. and rebelled against Babylon. Jehoiachin became Judah's next king in 597 B.C., but was replaced by Zedekiah three months later when Nebuchadnezzar captured Jerusalem and deported Jehoiachin to Babylon. Zedekiah was the last king of Judah; his attempted alliance with Egypt led to Nebuchadnezzar's occupation and overthrow of Jerusalem in 586 B.C.

Thus, there were three stages in Jeremiah's ministry: (1) From 627 to 605 B.C. he prophesied while Judah was threatened by Assyria and Egypt. (2) From 605 to 586 B.C. he proclaimed God's judgment while Judah was threatened and besieged by Babylon. (3) From 586 to about 580 B.C. he ministered in Jerusalem and Egypt after Judah's downfall.

THE CHRIST OF JEREMIAH

The Messiah is clearly seen in 23:1–8 as the coming Shepherd and righteous Branch who "shall reign and prosper, and shall execute judgment and justice in the earth. In his days Judah shall be saved, and Israel shall dwell safely: and this *is* his name whereby he shall be called, THE LORD OUR RIGHTEOUSNESS" (23:5, 6). He will bring in the new covenant (31:31–34), which will fulfill God's covenants with Abraham (Gen. 12:1–3; 17:1–8), Moses and the people (Deut. 28—30), and David (2 Sam. 7:1–17).

The curse on Jehoiachin (Jeconiah, Coniah) in 22:28–30 meant that no physical descendant would succeed him to the throne. Matthew 1:1–17 traces the genealogy of Christ through Solomon and Jeconiah to His legal (but not His physical) father, Joseph. However, no son of Joseph could sit upon the throne of David, for he

would be under the curse of Jehoiachin. Luke 3:23–38 traces Christ's lineage backward from Mary (His physical parent) through David's other son, Nathan (3:31), thereby avoiding the curse. The righteous Branch will indeed reign on the throne of David.

KEYS TO JEREMIAH

Key Word: Judah's Last Hour—In Jeremiah, God is seen as patient and holy: He delays judgment and appeals to His people to repent before it is too late. As the object lesson at the potter's house demonstrates, a ruined vessel can be repaired while still wet (18:1–4); but once dried, a marred vessel is fit only for the garbage heap (19:10, 11). God's warning is clear: Judah's time for repentance will soon pass. Because they defy God's words and refuse to repent, the Babylonian captivity is inevitable. Jeremiah lists the moral and spiritual causes for their coming catastrophe, but he also proclaims God's gracious promise of hope and restoration. There will always be a remnant, and God will establish a new covenant.

Key Verses: Jeremiah 7:23, 24 and 8:11, 12— "But this thing commanded I them, saying, Obey my voice, and I will be your God, and ye shall be my people: and walk ye in all the ways that I have commanded you, that it may be well unto you. But they hearkened not, nor inclined their ear, but walked in the counsels *and* in the imagination of their evil heart, and went backward, and not forward" (7:23, 24).

"For they have healed the hurt of the daughter of my people slightly, saying, Peace, peace; when *there is* no peace. Were they ashamed when they had committed abomination? nay, they were not at all ashamed, neither could they blush: therefore shall they fall among them that fall: in the time of their visitation they shall be cast down, saith the LORD" (8:11, 12).

Key Chapter: Jeremiah 31—Amid all the judgment and condemnation by Jeremiah are the wonderful promises of Jeremiah 31. Even though Judah has broken the covenants of her great King, God will make a new covenant when He will "put my law in their inward parts, and write it in their hearts; and will be their God, and they shall be my people" (31:33). The Messiah instituted that new covenant with His death and resurrection (cf. Matt. 26:26–29).

SURVEY OF JEREMIAH

Jeremiah is a record of the ministry of one of Judah's greatest prophets during its darkest days. He is called as a prophet during the reign of Josiah, the last of Judah's good kings. But even Josiah's well-intentioned reforms cannot stem the tide of apostasy. The downhill slide of the nation continues virtually unabated through a succession of four godless kings during Jeremiah's ministry. The people wallow in apostasy and idolatry and grow even more treacherous than Israel was before its captivity (3:11). They pervert the worship of the true God and give themselves over to spiritual and moral decay. Because they refuse to repent or even listen to God's prophet, the divine cure requires radical surgery. Jeremiah proclaims an approaching avalanche of judgment. Babylon will be God's instrument of judgment, and this book refers to that nation 164 times, more references than the rest of the Bible.

Jeremiah faithfully proclaims the divine condemnation of rebellious Judah for forty years and is rewarded with opposition, beatings, isolations, and imprisonment. His sympathy and sensitivity cause him to grieve over the rebelliousness and imminent doom of his nation. He often desires to resign from his prophetic office because of the harshness of his message and his reception, but he perseveres to Judah's bitter end. He is the weeping prophet (9:1; 13:17)—lonely, rejected, and persecuted.

FOCUS	CALL OF JEREMIAH	PROPHECIES TO JUDAH				PROPHECIES TO THE GENTILES	FALL OF JERUSALEM
REFERENCE	1:1——2:1——	26:1——	30:1——	34:1——	46:1——	52:1—52:34	
DIVISION	PROPHETIC COMMISSION	CONDEMNATION OF JUDAH	CONFLICTS OF JEREMIAH	FUTURE RESTORATION OF JERUSALEM	PRESENT FALL OF JERUSALEM	CONDEMNATION OF NINE NATIONS	HISTORIC CONCLUSION
TOPIC		BEFORE THE FALL			THE FALL	AFTER THE FALL	
	CALL	MINISTRY					RETROSPECT
LOCATION		JUDAH				SURROUNDING NATIONS	BABYLON
TIME	c. 627–580 B.C.						

Although Jeremiah is not easily arranged chronologically or thematically, its basic message is clear: surrender to God's will is the only way to escape calamity. Judgment cannot be halted, but promises of restoration are sprinkled through the book. Its divisions are: the call of Jeremiah (1); the prophecies to Judah (2—45); the prophecies to the Gentiles (46—51); and the fall of Jerusalem (52).

The Call of Jeremiah (1): Jeremiah is called and sanctified before birth to be God's prophet. This introductory chapter surveys the identification, inauguration, and instructions of the prophet.

The Prophecies to Judah (2—45): Jeremiah's message is communicated through a variety of parables, sermons, and object lessons. The prophet's life becomes a daily illustration to Judah, and most of the book's object lessons are found in this section (13:1-14; 14:1-9; 16:1-9; 18:1-8; 19:1-13; 24:1-10; 27:1-11; 32:6-15; 43:8-13). In a series of twelve graphic messages, Jeremiah lists the causes of Judah's coming judgment. The gentile nations are more faithful to their false gods than Judah is to God. They become a false vine by following idols and are without excuse. The people are condemned for their empty profession, disobedience to God's covenant, and spiritual harlotry. God has bound Judah to Himself; but like a rotten girdle (waistband), they have become corrupt and useless. Jeremiah offers a confession for the people, but their sin is too great; the prophet can only lament for them. As a sign of imminent judgment Jeremiah is forbidden to marry and participate in the feasts. Because the nation does not trust God or keep the Sabbath, the land will receive a sabbath rest when they are in captivity. Jerusalem will be invaded and the rulers and

people will be deported to Babylon. Restoration will only come under the new Shepherd, the Messiah, the nation's future King. Jeremiah announces the duration of the captivity as seventy years, in contrast to the messages of the false prophets who insist it will not happen.

Because of his message (2:25), Jeremiah suffers misery and opposition (26—45). He is rejected by the prophets and priests who call for his death, but he is spared by the elders and officials. In his sign of the yoke he proclaims the unpopular message that Judah must submit to divine discipline. But he assures the nation of restoration and hope under a new covenant (30—33). A remnant will be delivered and there will be a coming time of blessing. Jeremiah's personal experiences and sufferings are the focal point of 34—45 as opposition against the prophet mounts. Since he is no longer allowed in the temple, he sends his assistant Baruch to read his prophetic warnings. His scroll is burned by Jehoiakim, and Jeremiah is imprisoned. After the destruction of the city, Jeremiah is taken to Egypt by fleeing Jews, but he prophesies that Nebuchadnezzar will invade Egypt as well.

The Prophecies to the Gentiles (46—51): These chapters are a series of prophetic oracles against nine nations: Egypt, Philistia, Moab, Ammon, Edom, Damascus (Syria), Arabia, Elam, and Babylon. Only Egypt, Moab, Ammon, and Elam are given a promise of restoration.

The Fall of Jerusalem (52): Jeremiah's forty-year declaration of doom was finally vindicated in an event so significant that it is recorded in detail four times in the Scriptures (2 Kin. 25; 2 Chr. 36; Jer. 39; 52). In this historical supplement, Jerusalem is captured, destroyed, and plundered. The leaders are killed and the captives taken to Babylon.

OUTLINE OF JEREMIAH

Part One: The Call of Jeremiah (1:1-19)

Part Two: The Prophecies to Judah (2:1—45:5)

JEREMIAH

708

CHAPTER 1

Jeremiah's Call

THE words of Jer-e-mi'-ah the son of Hil-ki'-ah, of the priests that *were* Rin An'-a-thoth in the land of Benjamin: 1 Chr. 6:60

2 To whom the word of the LORD came in the days of Jo-si'-ah the son of Amon king of Judah, in the thirteenth year of his reign.

3 It came also in the days of Je-hoi'-a-kim the son of Jo-si'-ah king of Judah, unto the end of the eleventh year of Zed-e-ki'-ah the son of Jo-si'-ah king of Judah, Runto the carrying away of Jerusalem captive Rin the fifth month.   52:12 • 2 Kin. 25:8

4 Then the word of the LORD came unto me, saying,

5 Before I formed thee in the belly I knew thee; and before thou camest forth out of the womb I sanctified thee, *and* I ordained thee a prophet unto the nations.

6 Then said I, RAh, Lord GOD! behold, I cannot speak: for I *am* a child. Ex. 3:11; 4:10; 6:12

7 But the LORD said unto me, Say not, I *am* a child: Rfor thou shalt go to all that I shall send thee, and Rwhatsoever I command thee thou shalt speak.   Ex. 7:1, 2 • Matt. 28:20

8 Be not afraid of their faces: for I *am* with thee to deliver thee, saith the LORD.

9 Then the LORD put forth his Rhand, and Rtouched my mouth. And the LORD said unto me, Behold, I have Rput my words in thy mouth.   Mark 7:33–35 • Is. 6:7 • Is. 51:16

10 See, I have this day set thee over the nations and over the kingdoms, to root out, and to pull down, and to destroy, and to throw down, to build, and to plant.

Jeremiah's Signs

11 Moreover the word of the LORD came unto me, saying, Jer-e-mi'-ah, Rwhat seest thou? And I said, I see a Rrod of an almond tree.   Amos 7:8 • Num. 17:8

12 Then said the LORD unto me, Thou hast well seen: for I will Thasten Rmy word to perform it.   watch over • Deut. 32:35

13 And the word of the LORD came unto me the second time, saying, RWhat seest thou? And I said, I see a seething pot; and the face thereof *is* toward the north.   Zech. 4:2

14 Then the LORD said unto me, Out of the Rnorth an evil shall break forth upon all the inhabitants of the land.   4:6; 6:1; 10:22

15 For, lo, I will Rcall all the families of the kingdoms of the north, saith the LORD; and they shall come, and they shall Rset every one his throne at the Tentering of the gates of Jerusalem, and against all the walls thereof round about, and against all the cities of Judah.   6:22 • 39:3 • entrance

16 And I will utter my judgments against them Ttouching all their wickedness, Rwho have forsaken me, and have burned incense unto other gods, and worshipped the works of their own hands.   about • Deut. 28:20

Jeremiah's Assurance

17 Thou therefore gird up thy loins, and arise, and speak unto them all that I command thee: be not dismayed at their faces, lest I confound thee before them.

18 For, behold, I have made thee this day Ra defenced city, and an iron pillar, and brasen walls against the whole land, against the kings of Judah, against the princes thereof, against the priests thereof, and against the people of the land.   Is. 50:7

19 And they shall fight against thee; but they shall not prevail against thee; for I *am* with thee, saith the LORD, to deliver thee.

CHAPTER 2

Jeremiah's First Sermon:
Judah Sinned Wilfully

MOREOVER the word of the LORD came to me, saying,

2 Go and cry in the ears of Jerusalem, saying, Thus saith the LORD; I remember Tthee, the kindness of thy youth, the love of thine Tespousals, when thou Twentest after me in the wilderness, in a land *that was* not sown.   for thy sake • betrothals • followed

3 Israel *was* holiness unto the LORD, *and* the firstfruits of his increase: Rall that devour him shall Toffend; evil shall come upon them, saith the LORD.   12:14 • be held guilty

4 Hear ye the word of the LORD, O house of Jacob, and all the families of the house of Israel:

5 Thus saith the LORD, What iniquity have your fathers found in me, that they are gone far from me, and have Twalked after vanity, and are become vain?   followed

6 Neither said they, Where *is* the LORD that Rbrought us up out of the land of Egypt, that led us through Rthe wilderness, through a land of deserts and of pits, through a land of drought, and of the shadow of death, through a land that no man passed through, and where no man dwelt? Is. 63:9; Hos. 13:4 • Deut. 8:15

7 And I brought you into a plentiful country, to eat the fruit thereof and the goodness thereof; but when ye entered, ye defiled my land, and made mine heritage Tan abomination.   something to be despised

8 The priests said not, Where *is* the LORD? and they that handle the law knew me not: the pastors also transgressed against me, and the prophets prophesied by Ba'-al, and walked after *things that* do not profit.

9 Wherefore RI will yet plead with you, saith the LORD, and with your children's children will I plead.   Ezek. 20:35, 36; Mic. 6:2

10 For pass over the isles of Chit'-tim, and see; and send unto Ke'-dar, and consider diligently, and see if there be such a thing.

11 ᴿHath a nation changed *their* gods, which *are* ᴿyet no gods? ᴿbut my people have changed their glory for *that which* doth not profit.   Mic. 4:5 · Is. 37:19 · Ps. 106:20

12 Be ᵀastonished, O ye heavens, ᴿat this, and be horribly afraid, be ye very ᵀdesolate, saith the LORD.   *appalled* · Is. 1:2 · *downhearted*

13 For my people have committed two evils; they have forsaken me the fountain of living waters, *and* hewed them out cisterns, broken cisterns, that can hold no water.

14 *Is* Israel ᴿa servant? *is* he a homeborn *slave?* why is he ᵀspoiled?   [Ex. 4:22] · *robbed*

15 ᴿThe young lions roared upon him, *and* yelled, and they made his land waste: his cities are burned without inhabitant.   50:17

16 Also ᴿthe children of Noph and ᴿTa-hap'-a-nes have ᴿbroken the crown of thy head.   2 Kin. 23:29–37 · 43:7–9 · Deut. 33:20; Is. 8:8

17 Hast thou not procured this unto thyself, in that thou hast forsaken the LORD thy God, when he led thee by the way?

18 And now what hast thou to do in the way of Egypt, to drink the waters of Si'-hor? or what hast thou to do in the way of Assyria, to drink the waters of the river?

19 Thine own wickedness shall correct thee, and thy backslidings shall reprove thee: know therefore and see that *it is* an evil *thing* and bitter, that thou hast forsaken the LORD thy God, and that my fear *is* not in thee, saith the Lord GOD of hosts.

20 For of old time I have broken thy yoke, *and* burst thy bands; and thou saidst, I will not transgress; when upon every high hill and under every green tree thou wanderest, ᴿplaying the harlot.   Ex. 34:15

21 Yet I had ᴿplanted thee a noble vine, wholly a right seed: how then art thou turned into ᴿthe degenerate plant of a strange vine unto me?   Ex. 15:17; Ps. 80:8 · Is. 5:4

22 For though thou wash thee with nitre, and take thee much sope, *yet* thine iniquity is marked before me, saith the Lord GOD.

23 ᴿHow canst thou say, I am not ᵀpolluted, I have not gone after Ba'-a-lim? see thy way in the valley, know what thou hast done: *thou art* a swift ᵀdromedary traversing her ways;   Prov. 30:12 · *unclean* · *young camel*

24 A wild ass used to the wilderness, *that* snuffeth up the wind at her pleasure; in her occasion who can turn her away? all they that seek her will not weary themselves; in her month they shall find her.

25 Withhold thy foot from being unshod, and thy throat from thirst: but thou saidst, There is no hope: no; for I have loved ᴿstrangers, and after them will I go.   3:13

26 As the ᴿthief is ashamed when he is found, so is the house of Israel ashamed; they, their kings, their princes, and their priests, and their prophets,   48:27

27 Saying to a stock, Thou *art* my father; and to a stone, Thou hast brought me forth: for they have turned *their* back unto me, and not *their* face: but in the time of their trouble they will say, Arise, and save us.

28 But where *are* thy gods that thou hast made thee? let them arise, if they ᴿcan save thee in the time of thy ᵀtrouble: for ᴿ*according to* the number of thy cities are thy gods, O Judah.   Is. 45:20 · *evil* · 11:13

29 Wherefore will ye plead with me? ye ᴿall have transgressed against me, saith the LORD.   5:1; 6:13; Dan. 9:11

30 In vain have I ᴿsmitten your children; they received no correction: your own sword hath ᴿdevoured your prophets, like a destroying lion.   5:3; Is. 9:13 · Acts 7:52

31 O generation, see ye the word of the LORD. Have I been a wilderness unto Israel? a land of ᴿdarkness? wherefore say my people, We are ᵀlords; ᴿwe will come no more unto thee?   Is. 45:19 · *independent* · Deut. 32:15

32 Can a maid forget her ornaments, *or* a bride her attire? yet my people ᴿhave forgotten me days without number.   Ps. 106:21

33 Why ᵀtrimmest thou thy way to seek love? therefore hast thou also taught the wicked ᵀones thy ways.   *adjust* · *women*

34 Also in thy skirts is found the blood of the souls of the poor innocents: I have not found it by secret search, but upon all these.

35 ᴿYet thou sayest, Because I am innocent, surely his anger shall turn from me. Behold, I will plead with thee, because thou sayest, I have not sinned.   vv. 23, 29

36 Why gaddest thou about so much to change thy way? thou also shalt be ashamed of Egypt, as thou wast ashamed of Assyria.

37 Yea, thou shalt go forth from him, and ᴿthine hands upon thine head: for the LORD hath rejected thy confidences, and thou shalt not prosper in them.   2 Sam. 13:19

CHAPTER 3

THEY say, If a man put away his wife, and she go from him, and become another man's, ᴿshall he return unto her again? shall not that land be greatly polluted? but thou hast played the harlot with many lovers; yet return again to me, saith the LORD.   Deut. 24:4

2 Lift up thine eyes unto the high places, and see where thou hast not been lien with. In the ways hast thou sat for them, as the A-ra'-bi-an in the wilderness; and thou ᵀhast polluted the land with thy whoredoms and with thy wickedness.   *made unclean*

3 Therefore the ᴿshowers have been withholden, and there hath been no latter rain; and thou hadst a whore's ᵀforehead, thou refusedst to be ashamed.   Zeph. 3:5 · *brow*

4 Wilt thou not from this time cry unto me, RMy father, thou *art* Rthe guide of Rmy youth?   *v.* 19; 31:9 • Prov. 2:17 • Hos. 2:15

5 Will he reserve *his anger* for ever? will he keep *it* to the end? Behold, thou hast spoken and done evil things as thou couldest.

Judah Ignores Israel's Example

6 The LORD said also unto me in the days of Jo-si'-ah the king, Hast thou seen *that* which Rbacksliding Israel hath done? she is Rgone up upon every high mountain and under every green tree, and there hath played the harlot.   7:24 • 2:20; 17:2

7 RAnd I said after she had done all these *things,* Turn thou unto me. But she returned not. And her treacherous Rsister Judah saw *it.*   2 Kin. 17:13 • *v.* 11; Ezek. 16:46–48

8 And I saw, when for all the causes whereby backsliding Israel committed adultery I had Rput her away, and given her a bill of divorce; Ryet her treacherous sister Judah feared not, but went and played the harlot also.   2 Kin. 17:6 • Ezek. 23:11

9 And it came to pass through the Tlightness of her whoredom, that she Rdefiled the land, and committed adultery with Rstones and with stocks.   *easy acceptance* • 2:7 • 2:27

10 And yet for all this her treacherous sister Judah hath not turned unto me Rwith her whole heart, but Tfeignedly, saith the LORD.   Hosea 7:14 • *only in false manner;* 12:2

Judah Is Called from Backsliding

11 And the LORD said unto me, RThe backsliding Israel hath justified herself more than treacherous Judah.   Ezek. 16:51

12 Go and proclaim these words toward Rthe north, and say, Return, thou backsliding Israel, saith the LORD; *and* I will not cause mine anger to fall upon you: for I *am* merciful, saith the LORD, *and* I will not keep *anger* for ever.   2 Kin. 17:6

13 Only acknowledge thine iniquity, that thou hast transgressed against the LORD thy God, and hast scattered thy ways to the strangers under every green tree, and ye have not obeyed my voice, saith the LORD.

14 Turn, O backsliding children, saith the LORD; Rfor I am married unto you: and I will take you one of a city, and two of a family, and I will bring you to Zion: Hos. 2:19

15 And I will give you pastors according to mine heart, which shall Rfeed you with knowledge and understanding.   Acts 20:28

16 And it shall come to pass, when ye be multiplied and increased in the land, in those days, saith the LORD, they shall say no more, The ark of the covenant of the LORD: Rneither shall it come to mind: neither shall they remember it; neither shall they visit *it;* neither shall *that* be done any more.   Is. 65:17

17 At that time they shall call Jerusalem the throne of the LORD; and all the nations shall be gathered unto it, Rto the name of the LORD, to Jerusalem: neither shall they Rwalk any more after the Timagination of their evil heart.   Is. 60:9 • 11:8 • *willfulness*

18 In those days Rthe house of Judah shall walk Twith the house of Israel, and they shall come together out of the land of the north to the land that I have given for an inheritance unto your fathers.   Is. 11:13 • *beside*

19 But I said, How shall I put thee among the children, and give thee a pleasant land, a goodly heritage of the hosts of nations? and I said, Thou shalt call me, RMy father; and shalt not turn away from me.   Is. 63:16

20 Surely *as* a wife treacherously departeth from her Thusband, so Rhave ye dealt treacherously with me, O house of Israel, saith the LORD.   *companion* • Is. 48:8

21 A voice was heard upon Rthe high places, weeping *and* supplications of the children of Israel: for they have perverted their way, *and* they have forgotten the LORD their God.   Judg. 3:7; 1 Kin. 3:2; Is. 15:2

22 Return, ye backsliding children, *and* I will heal your backslidings. Behold, we come unto thee; for thou *art* the LORD our God.

23 RTruly in vain *is salvation hoped for* from the hills, *and from* the multitude of mountains: Rtruly in the LORD our God *is* the salvation of Israel.   Ps. 121:1, 2 • Ps. 3:8

24 For shame hath devoured the labour of our fathers from our youth; their flocks and their herds, their sons and their daughters.

25 We lie down in our shame, and our confusion covereth us: Rfor we have sinned against the LORD our God, we and our fathers, from our youth even unto this day, and Rhave not obeyed the voice of the LORD our God.   Ezra 9:7 • 22:21

CHAPTER 4

I F thou wilt return, O Israel, saith the LORD, Rreturn unto me: and if thou wilt put away thine abominations out of my sight, then shalt thou not remove.   Joel 2:12

2 RAnd thou shalt swear, The LORD liveth, in truth, in judgment, and in righteousness; and the nations shall bless themselves in him, and in him shall they glory.   Is. 45:23

3 For thus saith the LORD to the men of Judah and Jerusalem, Break up your fallow ground, and sow not among thorns.

4 RCircumcise yourselves to the LORD, and take away the foreskins of your heart, ye men of Judah and inhabitants of Jerusalem: lest my fury come forth like fire, and burn that none can quench *it,* because of the evil of your doings.   Deut. 10:16

Judah's Destruction from the North

5 Declare ye in Judah, and publish in Jerusalem; and say, Blow ye the trumpet in

the land: cry, ᵀgather together, and say, ᴿAssemble yourselves, and let us go into the ᵀdefenced cities. *aloud • 8:14 • fortified*

6 Set up the standard toward Zion: retire, ᵀstay not: for I will bring evil from the north, and a great destruction. *delay*

7 The lion is come up from his thicket, and the destroyer of the Gentiles is on his way; he is gone forth from his place to make thy land desolate; *and* thy cities shall be laid waste, without an inhabitant.

8 For this ᴿgird you with sackcloth, lament and howl: for the fierce anger of the LORD is not turned back from us. *Is. 22:12*

9 And it shall come to pass at that day, saith the LORD, *that* the ᴿheart of the king shall perish, and the heart of the princes; and the priests shall be ᵀastonished, and the prophets shall wonder. *48:41 • astounded*

10 Then said I, Ah, Lord GOD! surely thou hast greatly deceived this people and Jerusalem, saying, Ye shall have peace; whereas the sword reacheth unto the soul.

11 At that time shall it be said to this people and to Jerusalem, ᴿA dry wind of the high places in the wilderness toward the daughter of my people, not to fan, nor to cleanse, *51:1; Ezek. 17:10; Hos. 13:15*

12 *Even* a full wind from those *places* shall come unto me: now also ᴿwill I ᵀgive sentence against them. *1:16 • utter judgment*

13 Behold, he shall come up as clouds, and his chariots *shall be* as a whirlwind: ᴿhis horses are swifter than eagles. Woe unto us! for we are ᵀspoiled. *Hab. 1:8 • robbed*

14 O Jerusalem, ᴿwash thine heart from wickedness, that thou mayest be saved. How long shall thy ᵀvain thoughts lodge within thee? *Is. 1:16; James 4:8 • wicked*

15 For a voice declareth ᴿfrom Dan, and ᵀpublisheth affliction from ᵀmount E'-phra-im. *8:16 • announces trouble • the hills of*

16 Make ye mention to the nations; behold, publish against Jerusalem, *that* watchers come from a far country, and give out their voice against the cities of Judah.

17 ᴿAs keepers of a field, are they against her round about; because she hath been rebellious against me, saith the LORD. *2 Kin. 25:1*

18 ᴿThy way and thy doings have procured these *things* unto thee; this *is* thy wickedness, because it is bitter, because it reacheth unto thine heart. *2:17, 19; Is. 50:1*

19 My bowels, my bowels! I am pained at my very heart; my heart maketh a noise in me; I cannot hold my peace, because thou hast heard, O my soul, the sound of the trumpet, the alarm of war.

20 ᴿDestruction upon destruction is cried; for the whole land is ᵀspoiled: suddenly are ᴿmy tents spoiled, *and* my curtains in a moment. *Ps. 42:7; Ezek. 7:26 • robbed • 10:20*

21 How long shall I see the standard, *and* hear the sound of the trumpet?

22 For my people *is* foolish, they have not known me; they *are* ᵀsottish children, and they have ᵀnone understanding: ᴿthey *are* wise to do evil, but to do good they have no knowledge. *stupid • no • Rom. 16:19*

23 ᴿI beheld the earth, and, lo, *it was* ᴿwithout form, and void; and the heavens, and they *had* no light. *Is. 24:19 • Gen. 1:2*

24 I beheld the mountains, and, lo, they trembled, and all the hills moved lightly.

25 I beheld, and, lo, *there was* no man, and all the birds of the heavens were fled.

26 I beheld, and, lo, the fruitful place *was* a ᴿwilderness, and all the cities thereof were broken down at the presence of the LORD, *and* by his fierce anger. *9:10*

27 For thus hath the LORD said, The whole land shall be ᵀdesolate; ᴿyet will I not make a full end. *forsaken • 5:10, 18; 30:11*

28 For this shall the earth mourn, and the heavens above be black: because I have spoken *it,* I have purposed *it,* and will not repent, neither will I turn back from it.

29 ᴿThe whole city shall flee for the noise of the horsemen and bowmen; they shall go into thickets, and climb up upon the rocks: every city *shall be* forsaken, and not a man dwell therein. *2 Kin. 25:4*

30 And *when* thou *art* ᵀspoiled, what wilt thou do? Though thou clothest thyself with crimson, though thou deckest thee with ornaments of gold, ᴿthough thou rentest thy face with painting, in vain shalt thou make thyself fair; *thy* lovers will despise thee, they will seek thy life. *robbed • 2 Kin. 9:30*

31 For I have heard a voice as of a woman in travail, *and* the anguish as of her that bringeth forth her first child, the voice of the daughter of Zion, *that* bewaileth herself, *that* spreadeth her hands, *saying,* Woe *is* me now! for my soul is wearied because of murderers.

CHAPTER 5

Judah's Sins

RUN ye to and fro through the streets of Jerusalem, and see now, and know, and seek in the broad places thereof, if ye can find a man, if there be *any* that ᵀexecuteth judgment, that seeketh the truth; ᴿand I will pardon ᵀit. *doeth justly • Gen. 18:26 • her*

2 And though they say, ᴿThe LORD liveth; surely they ᴿswear falsely. *4:2 • 7:9*

3 O LORD, *are* not thine eyes upon the truth? thou hast ᴿstricken them, but they have not grieved; thou hast consumed them, *but* ᴿthey have refused to receive correction: they have made their faces harder than a rock; they have refused to return. *2:30 • 7:28*

4 Therefore I said, Surely these *are* poor;

they are foolish: for they know not the way of the Lord, *nor* the judgment of their God.

5 I will get me unto the great men, and will speak unto them; for they have known the way of the Lord, *and* the ᵀjudgment of their God: but these have altogether broken the yoke, *and* burst the bonds.   *law*

6 ᴿWherefore a lion out of the forest shall slay them, *and* a wolf of the evenings shall ᵀspoil them, a leopard shall watch over their cities: every one that goeth out thence shall be torn in pieces: because their transgressions are many, *and* their backslidings are increased.   50:17 • *take away their goods*

7 How shall I pardon thee for this? thy children have forsaken me, and sworn by *them that are* no gods: when I had fed them to the full, they then committed adultery, and assembled themselves ᵀby troops in the harlots' houses.   *in companies*

8 They were *as* fed horses in the morning: every one neighed ᴿafter his neighbour's wife.   Ezek. 22:11

9 Shall I not ᵀvisit for these *things?* saith the Lord: ᴿand shall not my soul be avenged on such a nation as this?   *punish* • 44:2; Is. 1:24

10 Go ye up upon her walls, and destroy; but make not a full end: take away her battlements; for they *are* not the Lord's.

11 For ᴿthe house of Israel and the house of Judah have dealt very treacherously against me, saith the Lord.   3:20

12 They have belied the Lord, and said, *It is* not he; neither shall evil come upon us; neither shall we see sword nor famine:

13 And the prophets shall become ᵀwind,ᴿ and the word *is* not in them: thus shall it be done unto them.   *of no consequence* • 14:13, 15

14 Wherefore thus saith the Lord God of hosts, Because ye speak this word, behold, I will make my words in thy mouth fire, and this people wood, and it shall devour them.

15 Lo, I will bring a ᴿnation upon you from far, O house of Israel, saith the Lord: it *is* a mighty nation, it *is* an ancient nation, a nation whose language thou knowest not, neither understandest what they say. 1:15; 50:17

16 ᴿTheir quiver *is* as an open ᴿsepulchre, they *are* all mighty men.   Is. 13:18 • Ps. 5:9

17 And they shall eat up thine ᴿharvest, and thy bread, *which* thy sons and thy daughters should eat: they shall eat up thy flocks and thine herds: they shall eat up thy vines and thy fig trees: they shall impoverish thy ᵀfenced cities, wherein thou trustedst, with the sword. Deut. 28:31, 33 • *fortified*

18 Nevertheless in those days, saith the Lord, I will not make a full end with you.

19 And it shall come to pass, when ye shall say, Wherefore doeth the Lord our God all these *things* unto us? then shalt thou answer them, Like as ye have forsaken me, and served strange gods in your land, so shall ye serve strangers in a land *that is* not your's.

20 Declare this in the house of Jacob, and publish it in Judah, saying,

21 Hear now this, O foolish people, and without understanding; which have eyes, and see not; which have ears, and hear not:

22 Fear ye not me? saith the Lord: will ye not tremble at my presence, which have placed the sand *for* the bound of the sea by a perpetual decree, that it cannot pass it: and though the waves thereof toss themselves, yet can they not prevail; though they roar, yet can they not pass over it?

23 But this people hath a revolting and a rebellious ᴿheart; they are revolted and gone.   6:28; Deut. 21:18; Ps. 78:8

24 Neither say they in their heart, Let us now fear the Lord our God, that giveth rain, both the former and the latter, in his season: ᴿhe reserveth unto us the appointed weeks of the harvest.   [Gen. 8:22]

25 ᴿYour iniquities have turned away these *things*, and your sins have ᵀwithholden good *things* from you.   3:3 • *withheld*

26 For among my people are found wicked *men:* they lay wait, as he that setteth snares; they set a trap, they catch men.

27 As a ᵀcage is full of birds, so *are* their houses full of deceit: therefore they are become great, and ᵀwaxen rich.   *coop* • *grown*

28 They are ᵀwaxen fat, they shine: yea, they ᵀoverpass the deeds of the wicked: they judge not the cause, the cause of the fatherless, yet they prosper; and the right of the needy do they not judge.   *grown* • *overlook*

29 ᴿShall I not visit for these *things?* saith the Lord: shall not my soul be avenged on such a nation as this?   Mal. 3:5

30 ᵀA wonderful and horrible thing is committed in the land;   *An appalling*

31 The prophets prophesy falsely, and the priests bear rule by their means; and my people ᴿlove to have it so: and what will ye do in the end thereof?   Mic. 2:11; 2 Tim. 4:3

CHAPTER 6

Jerusalem to Be Destroyed

O YE children of Benjamin, gather yourselves to flee out of the midst of Jerusalem, and blow the trumpet in Te-ko′-a, and set up a sign of fire in ᴿBeth–hac′-ce-rem: ᴿfor evil appeareth out of the north, and great destruction.   Neh. 3:14 • 4:6

2 I have likened the daughter of Zion to a comely and ᴿdelicate *woman.*   Deut. 28:56

3 The shepherds with their flocks shall come unto her; ᴿthey shall pitch *their* tents against her round about; they shall feed every one in his place.   2 Kin. 25:1; 2 Chr. 36:3, 6

4 ᴿPrepare ye war against her; arise, and let us go up ᴿat noon. Woe unto us! for the day goeth away, for the shadows of the evening are stretched out.   Joel 3:9 • 15:8

5 Arise, and let us go by night, and let us [R]destroy her palaces.   52:13; Is. 32:14

6 For thus hath the LORD of hosts said, Hew ye down trees, and [T]cast a mount against Jerusalem: this is the city to be visited; she is wholly [R]oppression in the midst of her.   build a tower for attacking • 2 Kin. 21:16

7 As a fountain casteth out her waters, so she casteth out her wickedness: violence and spoil is heard in her; before me continually is [T]grief and wounds.   sickness

8 Be thou instructed, O Jerusalem, lest [R]my soul depart from thee; lest I make thee desolate, a land not inhabited.   Hos. 9:12

9 Thus saith the LORD of hosts, They shall [R]throughly glean the [R]remnant of Israel as a vine: turn back thine hand as a grapegatherer into the baskets.   16:16; 49:9 • 8:3

10 To whom shall I speak, and give warning, that they may hear? behold, their ear is uncircumcised, and they cannot hearken: behold, the word of the LORD is unto them a reproach; they have no delight in it.

11 Therefore I am full of the fury of the LORD; [R]I am weary with holding in: I will pour it out [R]upon the children [T]abroad, and upon the assembly of young men together: for even the husband with the wife shall be taken, the aged with him that is full of days.   20:9 • 9:21 • in the street

12 And [R]their houses shall be turned unto others, with their fields and wives together: for I will stretch out my hand upon the inhabitants of the land, saith the LORD.   8:10

13 For from the least of them even unto the greatest of them every one is given to covetousness; and from the prophet even unto the priest every one dealeth falsely.

14 They have [R]healed also the hurt of the daughter of my people slightly, saying, Peace, peace; when there is no peace.   8:11

15 Were they [R]ashamed when they had committed abomination? nay, they were not at all ashamed, neither could they blush: therefore they shall fall among them that fall: at the time that I visit them they shall be cast down, saith the LORD.   3:3

16 Thus saith the LORD, Stand ye in the ways, and see, and ask for the [R]old paths, where is the good way, and walk therein, and ye shall find rest for your souls. But they said, We will not walk therein.   Is. 8:20

17 Also I set [R]watchmen over you, saying, Hearken to the sound of the trumpet. But they said, We will not hearken.   25:4; Hab. 2:1

18 Therefore hear, ye nations, and [T]know, O congregation, what is among them.   realize

19 [R]Hear, O earth: behold, I will bring evil upon this people, even the fruit of their thoughts, because they have not hearkened unto my words, nor to my law, but rejected it.   Is. 1:2

20 [R]To what purpose cometh there to me incense [R]from She'-ba, and the sweet cane

from a far country? [R]your burnt offerings are not acceptable, nor your sacrifices sweet unto me.   Mic. 6:6, 7 • Is. 60:6 • 7:21

21 Therefore thus saith the LORD, Behold, [R]I will lay stumblingblocks before this people, and the fathers and the sons together shall fall upon them; the neighbour and his friend shall perish.   [Job 5:12]; Is. 8:14

22 Thus saith the LORD, Behold, a people cometh from the [R]north country, and a great nation shall be raised from the [T]sides of the earth.   1:15 • uttermost parts

23 They shall lay hold on bow and spear; they are cruel, and have no mercy; their voice [R]roareth like the sea; and they ride upon horses, set in array as men for war against thee, O daughter of Zion.   Is. 5:30

24 We have heard the fame thereof: our hands wax feeble: anguish hath taken hold of us, and pain, as of a woman in travail.

25 [R]Go not forth into the field, nor walk by the way; for the sword of the enemy and fear is on every side.   14:18

26 O daughter of my people, gird thee with sackcloth, and wallow thyself in ashes: make thee mourning, as for an only son, most bitter lamentation: for the [T]spoiler shall suddenly come upon us.   raider

27 I have set thee for a tower and [R]a fortress among my people, that thou mayest know and [T]try their way.   1:18 • test

28 They are all grievous revolters, [R]walking with slanders: they are [R]brass and iron; they are all corrupters.   9:4 • Ezek. 22:18

29 The bellows are burned, the lead is consumed of the fire; the founder melteth in vain: for the wicked are not plucked away.

30 [T]Reprobate silver shall men call them, because the LORD hath rejected them.   inferior

CHAPTER 7

Judah's Sin of External Religion

THE word that came to Jer-e-mi'-ah from the LORD, saying,

2 Stand in the gate of the LORD's house, and proclaim there this word, and say, Hear the word of the LORD, all ye of Judah, that enter in at these gates to worship the LORD.

3 Thus saith the LORD of hosts, the God of Israel, Amend your ways and your doings, and I will cause you to dwell in this place.

4 Trust ye not in lying words, saying, The temple of the LORD, The temple of the LORD, The temple of the LORD, are these.

5 For if ye throughly amend your ways and your doings; if ye throughly execute judgment between a man and his neighbour;

6 If ye oppress not the stranger, the fatherless, and the widow, and shed not innocent blood in this place, [R]neither walk after other gods to your hurt: Deut. 6:14, 15

7 ᴿThen will I cause you to dwell in this place, in ᴿthe land that I gave to your fathers, for ever and ever.   Deut. 4:40 · 3:18

8 Behold, ye trust in ᴿlying words, that cannot profit.   5:31; 14:13, 14

9 ᴿWill ye steal, murder, and commit adultery, and swear falsely, and ᵀburn incense unto Ba'-al, and walk after other gods whom ye know not;   Zeph. 1:5 · worship

10 And come and stand before me in this house, which ᵀis called by my name, and say, We are delivered to do all these abominations?   whereupon my name is called

11 Is this house, which is called by my name, become a den of robbers in your eyes? Behold, even I have seen it, saith the LORD.

12 But go ye now unto my place which was in Shi'-loh, where I set my name at the first, and see ᴿwhat I did to it for the wickedness of my people Israel.   1 Sam. 4:10

13 And now, because ye have done all these works, saith the LORD, and I spake unto you, ᴿrising up early and speaking, but ye ᵀheard not; and I ᴿcalled you, but ye answered not;   11:7 · did not listen · Prov. 1:24

14 Therefore will I do unto this house, which is called by my name, ᴿwherein ye trust, and unto the place which I gave to you and to your fathers, as I have done to ᴿShi'-loh.   [4:1, 2; Is. 1:19] · 1 Sam. 4:10; Ps. 78:60

15 And I will ᴿcast you out of my sight, ᴿas I have cast out all your brethren, even the whole seed of E'-phra-im.   15:1 · 2 Kin. 17:23

16 Therefore ᴿpray not thou for this people, neither lift up cry nor prayer for them, neither make intercession to me: ᴿfor I will not hear thee.   11:14; 14:11; Ex. 32:10 · 15:1

17 Seest thou not what they do in the cities of Judah and in the streets of Jerusalem?

18 ᴿThe children gather wood, and the fathers kindle the fire, and the women knead their dough, to make cakes to the queen of heaven, and to ᴿpour out drink offerings unto other gods, that they may ᴿprovoke me to anger.   44:17 · 19:13 · 11:17

19 ᴿDo they provoke me to anger? saith the LORD: do they not provoke themselves to the confusion of their own faces?   Job 35:6

20 Therefore thus saith the Lord GOD; Behold, mine anger and my fury shall be poured out upon this place, upon man, and upon beast, and upon the ᴿtrees of the field, and upon the fruit of the ground; and it shall burn, and shall not be quenched.   8:13

21 Thus saith the LORD of hosts, the God of Israel; ᴿPut your burnt offerings unto your sacrifices, and eat flesh.   Is. 1:11; Hos. 8:13

22 ᴿFor I spake not unto your fathers, nor commanded them in the day that I brought them out of the land of Egypt, concerning burnt offerings or sacrifices: 1 Sam. 15:22

23 But this thing commanded I them, saying, ᴿObey my voice, and I will be your God, and ye shall be my people: and walk ye in all the ways that I have commanded you, that it may be well unto you.   Ex. 15:26

24 But they hearkened not, nor inclined their ear, but walked in the counsels and in the imagination of their evil heart, and ᵀwent backward, and not forward.   were

25 Since the day that your fathers came forth out of the land of Egypt unto this day I have even ᴿsent unto you all my servants the prophets, daily rising up early and sending them: 2 Chr. 36:15; [Neh. 9:30]

26 Yet they hearkened not unto me, nor inclined their ear, but hardened their neck: they did worse than their fathers.

27 Therefore ᴿthou shalt speak all these words unto them; but they will not hearken to thee: thou shalt also call unto them; but they will not answer thee.   1:7; Ezek. 2:7

28 But thou shalt say unto them, This is a nation that obeyeth not the voice of the LORD their God, nor receiveth correction: truth is perished, and is cut off from their mouth.

29 ᴿCut off thine hair, O Jerusalem, and cast it away, and take up a lamentation on high places; for the LORD hath rejected and forsaken the generation of his wrath.   Is. 15:2

30 For the children of Judah have done evil in my sight, saith the LORD: ᴿthey have set their abominations in the house which is called by my name, to pollute it.   2 Kin. 21:4

31 And they have built the high places of To'-phet, which is in the valley of the son of Hin'-nom, to burn their sons and their daughters in the fire; which I commanded them not, neither came it into my heart.

32 Therefore, behold, ᴿthe days come, saith the LORD, that it shall no more be called To'-phet, nor the valley of the son of Hin'-nom, but the valley of slaughter: for they shall bury in To'-phet, till there be no place.   19:6

33 And the ᴿcarcasesᵀ of this people shall be meat for the fowls of the heaven, and for the beasts of the earth; and none shall ᵀfray them away.   Deut. 28:26 · corpses · frighten

34 Then will I cause to ᴿcease from the cities of Judah, and from the streets of Jerusalem, the voice of mirth, and the voice of gladness, the voice of the bridegroom, and the voice of the bride: for ᴿthe land shall be desolate.   Is. 24:7, 8; Hos. 2:11 · Lev. 26:33

CHAPTER 8

AT that time, saith the LORD, they shall bring out the bones of the kings of Judah, and the bones of his princes, and the bones of the priests, and the bones of the prophets, and the bones of the inhabitants of Jerusalem, out of their graves:

2 And they shall spread them before the sun, and the moon, and all the host of

heaven, whom they have loved, and whom they have served, and after whom they have walked, and whom they have sought, and whom they have worshipped: they shall not be gathered, nor be buried; they shall be for dung upon the face of the earth.

3 And ᴿdeath shall be chosen rather than life by all the ᵀresidue of them that remain of this evil family, which remain in all the places whither I have driven them, saith the LORD of hosts.   Job 3:21; Rev. 9:6 · *remainder*

Judah's Judgment Imminent

4 Moreover thou shalt say unto them, Thus saith the LORD; Shall they fall, and not arise? shall he turn away, and not return?

5 Why *then* is this people of Jerusalem slidden back by a perpetual backsliding? they hold fast deceit, they refuse to return.

6 ᴿI hearkened and heard, *but* they spake not aright: no man repented him of his wickedness, saying, What have I done? every one turned to his course, as the horse rusheth into the battle.   Ps. 14:2; [Is. 30:18; 2 Pet 3:9]

7 Yea, the stork in the heaven knoweth her appointed times; and ᴿthe turtle and the crane and the swallow observe the time of their coming; but ᴿmy people know not the judgment of the LORD.   Song 2:12 · 5:4, 5

8 How do ye say, We *are* wise, ᴿand the law of the LORD *is* with us? Lo, certainly in vain made he *it*; the pen of the scribes ᵀis in vain.   Rom. 1:22; 2:17 · *hath wrought falsely*

9 ᴿThe wise *men* are ashamed, they are dismayed and taken: lo, they have rejected the word of the LORD; and ᴿwhat wisdom *is* in them?   Is. 19:11; [1 Cor. 1:27] · 4:22; Is. 44:25

10 Therefore will I give their wives unto others, *and* their fields to them that shall inherit *them:* for every one from the least even unto the greatest is given to ᴿcovetousness, from the prophet even unto the priest every one dealeth falsely.   Is. 56:11

11 For they have healed the hurt of the daughter of my people slightly, saying, ᴿPeace, peace; when *there is* no peace.   6:14

12 Were they ᴿashamed when they had committed abomination? nay, they were not at all ashamed, neither could they blush: therefore shall they fall among them that fall: in the time of their visitation they shall be cast down, saith the LORD.   6:15

13 I will surely consume them, saith the LORD: *there shall be* no grapes on the vine, nor figs on the ᴿfig tree, and the leaf shall fade; and *the things that* I have given them shall pass away from them.   Matt. 21:19

14 Why do we sit still? assemble yourselves, and let us enter into the defenced cities, and let us be silent there: for the LORD our God hath put us to silence, and given us ᵀwater of gall to drink, because we have sinned against the LORD.   *bitter water*

15 We ᴿlooked for peace, but no good *came; and* for a time of health, and behold trouble!   8:11; 14:19

16 The snorting of his horses was heard from ᴿDan: the whole land trembled at the sound of the neighing of his ᴿstrong ones; for they are come, and have devoured the land, and all that is in it; the city, and those that dwell therein.   4:15 · 47:3; Judg. 18:29

17 For, behold, I will send serpents, ᵀcockatrices, among you, which *will* not *be* ᴿcharmed,ᵀ and they shall bite you, saith the LORD.   *adders* · Ps. 58:4, 5 · *stopped by any charm*

Jeremiah's Lament for Judah

18 ᴿWhen I would comfort myself against sorrow, my heart *is* faint in me.   Lam. 1:16, 17

19 Behold the voice of the cry of the daughter of my people because of them that dwell in a far country: *Is* not the LORD in Zion? *is* not her king in her? Why have they provoked me to anger with their graven images, *and* with strange vanities?

20 ᴿThe harvest is past, the summer is ended, and we are not saved.   Matt. 25:10, 11

21 ᴿFor the hurt of the daughter of my people am I hurt; I am ᴿblack; astonishment hath taken hold on me.   9:1 · Joel 2:6

22 *Is there* no ᴿbalm in Gil'-e-ad; *is there* no physician there? why then is not the health of the daughter of my people ᵀrecovered?   46:11; Gen. 37:25; 43:11 · *restored?*

CHAPTER 9

OH ᴿthat my head were waters, and mine eyes a fountain of tears, that I might ᴿweep day and night for the slain of the daughter of my people!   Is. 22:4 · 10:19

2 Oh that I had in the wilderness a lodging place of wayfaring men; that I might leave my people, and go from them! for ᴿthey *be* all adulterers, an assembly of ᵀtreacherous men.   5:7, 8; 23:10 · *deceitful*

3 And ᴿthey bend their tongues *like* their bow *for* lies: but they are not valiant for the truth upon the earth; for they proceed from evil to evil, and they ᴿknowᵀ not me, saith the LORD.   Ps. 64:3 · 1 Sam. 2:12 · *respect*

4 Take ye heed every one of his neighbour, and trust ye not in any brother: for every brother will utterly supplant, and every neighbour will walk with slanders.

5 And they will deceive every one his neighbour, and will not speak the truth: they have taught their tongue to speak lies, *and* weary themselves to commit iniquity.

6 Thine ᴿhabitation *is* in the midst of deceit; through deceit they refuse to know me, saith the LORD.   5:27; 8:5; Ps. 120:5

7 Therefore thus saith the LORD of hosts, Behold, ᴿI will ᵀmelt them, and ᵀtry them;

Rfor how shall I do for the daughter of my people? Is. 1:25 • *put them in the fire* • *test* • Hos. 11:8

8 Their tongue *is as* an arrow shot out; it speaketh Rdeceit: *one* speaketh Rpeaceably to his neighbour with his mouth, but in heart he layeth his wait. Ps. 12:2 • Ps. 55:21

Judah's Judgment Is Described

9 RShall I not visit them for these *things?* saith the LORD: shall not my soul be avenged on such a nation as this? 5:9, 29

10 For the mountains will I take up a weeping and wailing, and for the habitations of the wilderness a lamentation, because they are burned up, so that none can pass through *them;* neither can *men* hear the voice of the cattle; both the fowl of the heavens and the beast are fled; they are gone.

11 And I will make Jerusalem heaps, *and* a den of dragons; and I will make the cities of Judah desolate, without an inhabitant.

12 RWho *is* the wise man, that may understand this? and *who is* he to whom the mouth of the LORD hath spoken, that he may declare it, for what the land perisheth *and* is burned up like a wilderness, that none passeth through? Ps. 107:43; Hos. 14:9

13 And the LORD saith, Because they have Rforsaken my law which I set before them, and have not obeyed my voice, neither walked therein; 5:19; 22:9; 2 Chr. 7:19

14 But have walked after the Timagination of their own heart, and after Ba'-a-lim, which their fathers taught them: *wilfulness*

15 Therefore thus saith the LORD of hosts, the God of Israel; Behold, I will feed them, *even* this people, with wormwood, and give them Twater of gall to drink. *bitter water*

16 I will scatter them also among the heathen, whom neither they nor their fathers have known: and I will send a sword after them, till I have consumed them.

17 Thus saith the LORD of hosts, Consider ye, and call for Rthe mourning women, that they may come; and send for cunning *women,* that they may come: Job 3:8; Matt. 9:23

18 And let them make haste, and take up a wailing for us, that Rour eyes may run down with tears, and our eyelids gush out with waters. *v.* 1; 14:17; Is. 22:4

19 For a voice of wailing is heard out of Zion, How are we spoiled! we are greatly confounded, because we have forsaken the land, because our dwellings have cast us out.

20 Yet hear the word of the LORD, O ye women, and let your ear receive the word of his mouth, and teach your daughters wailing, and every one her neighbour lamentation.

21 For Rdeath is come up into our windows, *and* is entered into our palaces, to cut off Rthe children from without, *and* the young men from the streets. 2 Chr. 36:17 • 6:11

22 Speak, Thus saith the LORD, Even the

carcases of men shall fall as dung upon the open field, and as the handful after the harvestman, and none shall gather *them.*

23 Thus saith the LORD, RLet not the wise *man* glory in his wisdom, neither let the mighty *man* glory in his might, let not the rich *man* glory in his riches: [Eccl. 9:11]

24 But Rlet him that glorieth glory in this, that he understandeth and knoweth me, that I *am* the LORD which exercise lovingkindness, judgment, and righteousness, in the earth: Rfor in these *things* I delight, saith the LORD. 1 Cor. 1:31; 2 Cor. 10:17 • Mic. 7:18

25 Behold, the days come, saith the LORD, that I will punish all *them which are* circumcised with the uncircumcised;

26 Egypt, and Judah, and E'-dom, and the children of Ammon, and Moab, and all *that are* in the utmost corners, that dwell in the wilderness: for all *these* nations *are* uncircumcised, and all the house of Israel *are* Runcircumcised in the heart. Lev. 26:41

CHAPTER 10

Judah's Futile Idolatry

HEAR ye the word which the LORD speaketh unto you, O house of Israel:

2 Thus saith the LORD, RLearn not the way of the heathen, and be not dismayed at the signs of heaven; Tfor the heathen are dismayed at them. [Lev. 18:3] • *just because*

3 For the customs of the people *are* Tvain: for Rone cutteth a tree out of the forest, the work of the hands of the workman, with the ax. *of no value* • Is. 40:19; 45:20

4 They Rdeck it with silver and with gold; they Rfasten it with nails and with hammers, that it move not. *v.* 14 • Is. 41:7

5 They *are* upright as the palm tree, but speak not: they must needs be Rborne, because they cannot go. Be not afraid of them; for Rthey cannot do evil, neither also *is* it in them to do good. Is. 46:1, 7 • Is. 41:23

6 RForasmuch as *there is* none Rlike unto thee, O LORD; thou *art* great, and thy name *is* great in might. Deut. 33:26 • Ex. 15:11

7 RWho would not fear thee, O King of nations? for to thee doth it appertain: forasmuch as Ramong all the wise *men* of the nations, and in all their kingdoms, *there is* none like unto thee. Rev. 15:4 • [Ps. 22:28; 89:6]

8 But they are altogether brutish and foolish: the stock *is* a doctrine of vanities.

9 RSilver spread into plates is brought from Tar'-shish, and gold from U'-phaz, the work of the workman, and of the hands of the founder: blue and purple *is* their clothing: they *are* all the work of cunning men. Ps. 72:10

10 But the LORD *is* the Ttrue God, he *is* the living God, and an everlastingT king: at his wrath the earth shall tremble, and the

nations shall not be able to ^Rabide his indignation.   *God of truth • king of eternity • Ps. 76:7*

11 Thus shall ye say unto them, ^RThe gods that have not made the heavens and the earth, *even* they shall perish from the earth, and from under these heavens.   Ps. 96:5

12 He ^Rhath made the earth by his power, he hath ^Restablished the world by his wisdom, and ^Rhath stretched out the heavens by his discretion.   Ps. 136:5 • Ps. 93:1 • Job 9:8

13 ^RWhen he uttereth his voice, *there is* a multitude of waters in the heavens, and ^Rhe causeth the vapours to ascend from the ends of the earth; he maketh lightnings with rain, and bringeth forth the wind out of his treasures.   Job 38:34; [Ps. 29:3–9] • Ps. 135:7

14 Every man is brutish in *his* knowledge: every founder is confounded by the graven image: for his molten image is falsehood, and *there is* no breath in them.

15 ^RThey *are* vanity, *and* the work of ^Terrors: in the time of their visitation they shall perish.   8:12, 19; 14:22; Is. 41:24 • *delusions*

16 The portion of Jacob *is* not like them: for he *is* the former of all *things;* and ^RIsrael *is* the ^Trod of his inheritance: ^RThe LORD of hosts *is* his name.   Deut. 32:9 • *tribe* • Is. 47:4

17 Gather up thy wares out of the land, O ^Tinhabitant of the fortress.   *inhabitress*

18 For thus saith the LORD, Behold, I will ^Rsling out the inhabitants of the land at this once, and will distress them, ^Rthat they may find *it so.*   1 Sam. 25:29 • Ezek. 6:10

Jeremiah's Prayer for Correction

19 ^RWoe is me for my hurt! my wound is grievous: but I said, ^RTruly this *is* a grief, and ^RI must bear it.   8:21 • Ps. 77:10 • Mic. 7:9

20 ^RMy tabernacle is spoiled, and all my cords are broken: my children are gone forth of me, and they *are* not: ^R*there is* none to stretch forth my tent any more, and to set up my curtains.   4:20; 2 Kin. 25:9–11 • Is. 51:18

21 For the ^Tpastors are become ^Tbrutish, and have not sought the LORD: therefore they shall not prosper, and ^Rall their flocks shall be scattered.   *shepherds • stupid* • 23:2

22 Behold, the ^Tnoise of the ^Tbruit is come, and a great commotion out of the north country, to make the cities of Judah desolate, *and* a den of dragons.   *voice • tidings*

23 O LORD, I know that the ^Rway of man *is* not in himself: *it is* not in man that walketh to direct his steps.   Prov. 20:24; [Is. 26:7]

24 O LORD, ^Tcorrect^R me, but with judgment; not in thine anger, lest thou ^Tbring me to nothing.   *diminish me* • 30:11 • *reduce*

25 ^RPour out thy fury upon the heathen ^Rthat know thee not, and upon the families that call not on thy name: for they have eaten up Jacob, and ^Rdevoured him, and consumed him, and have made his habitation desolate.   Ps. 79:6 • Job 18:21 • 8:16

CHAPTER 11

Judah's Curse
Because of the Broken Covenant

THE word that came to Jer-e-mi'-ah from the LORD, saying,

2 Hear ye the words of this ^Tcovenant, and speak unto the men of Judah, and to the inhabitants of Jerusalem;   *agreement*

3 And say thou unto them, Thus saith the LORD God of Israel; Cursed *be* the man that obeyeth not the words of this covenant,

4 Which I commanded your fathers in the day *that* I brought them forth out of the land of Egypt, from the iron furnace, saying, Obey my voice, and do them, according to all which I command you: so shall ye be my people, and I will be your God:

5 That I may ^Tperform the ^Roath which I have sworn unto your fathers, to give them a land flowing with milk and honey, as *it is* this day. Then answered I, and said, ^TSo be it, O LORD.   *fulfil* • Deut. 7:12 • *Amen*

6 Then the LORD said unto me, ^TProclaim all these words in the cities of Judah, and in the streets of Jerusalem, saying, Hear ye the words of this covenant, and do them.   *preach*

7 For I ^Rearnestly protested unto your fathers in the ^Rday *that* I brought them up out of the land of Egypt, *even* unto this day, ^Rrising early and protesting, saying, Obey my voice.   1 Sam. 8:9 • Ex. 15:26 • 35:15

8 ^RYet they obeyed not, nor inclined their ear, but ^Rwalked every one in the ^Timagination of their evil heart: therefore I will bring upon them all the words of this covenant, which I commanded *them* to do; but they did *them* not.   7:26 • 9:14 • *stubbornness*

9 And the LORD said unto me, A conspiracy is found among the men of Judah, and among the inhabitants of Jerusalem.

10 They are turned back to ^Rthe iniquities of their forefathers, which refused to hear my words; and they went after other gods to serve them: the house of Israel and the house of Judah have broken my covenant which I made with their fathers.   Ezek. 20:18

11 Therefore thus saith the LORD, Behold, I will bring evil upon them, which they shall not be able to escape; and though they shall cry unto me, I will not hearken unto them.

12 Then shall the cities of Judah and inhabitants of Jerusalem go, and ^Rcry unto the gods unto whom they offer incense: but they shall not save them at all in the time of their ^Ttrouble.   Deut. 32:37; Is. 45:20 • *evil*

13 For *according to* the number of thy cities were thy gods, O Judah; and *according to* the number of the streets of Jerusalem have ye set up altars to *that* shameful thing, *even* altars to burn incense unto Ba'-al.

14 Therefore ^Rpray not thou for this people, neither lift up a cry or prayer for

them: for I will not hear *them* in the time that they cry unto me for their ᵀtrouble.   7:16 • *evil*

15 ᴿWhat hath my beloved to do in mine house, *seeing* she hath wroughtᵀ lewdness with many, and the holy flesh is passed from thee? when thou doest evil, then thou ᵀrejoicest.   Ps. 50:16 • *done evil things • are happy*

16 The Lᴏʀᴅ called thy name, A green olive tree, fair, *and* of goodly fruit: with the noise of a great tumult he hath kindled fire upon it, and the branches of it are broken.

17 For the Lᴏʀᴅ of hosts, ᴿthat planted thee, hath pronounced evil against thee, for the evil of the house of Israel and of the house of Judah, which they have done against themselves to provoke me to anger in offering incense unto Ba'-al.   Is. 5:2

Anathoth's Conspiracy Against Jeremiah

18 And the Lᴏʀᴅ ᴿhath given me knowledge *of it,* and I know *it:* then thou shewedst me their doings.   2 Kin. 6:9, 10

19 But I *was* like a lamb *or* an ox *that* is brought to the slaughter; and I knew not that they had devised devices against me, *saying,* Let us destroy the tree with the fruit thereof, ᴿand let us cut him off from ᴿthe land of the living, that his name may be no more remembered.   Ps. 83:4 • Ps. 27:13

20 But, O Lᴏʀᴅ of hosts, that judgest righteously, that triest the reins and the heart, let me see thy vengeance on them: for unto thee have I revealed my cause.

21 Therefore thus saith the Lᴏʀᴅ of the men of An'-a-thoth, that seek thy life, saying, ᴿProphesy not in the name of the Lᴏʀᴅ, that thou die not by our hand: Mic. 2:6

22 Therefore thus saith the Lᴏʀᴅ of hosts, Behold, I will punish them: the young men shall die by the sword; their sons and their daughters shall ᴿdie by famine: 9:21

23 And there shall be no remnant of them: for I will bring evil upon the men of An'-a-thoth, *even* the year of their visitation.

CHAPTER 12

Jeremiah's Complaint to God

RIGHTEOUS *art* thou, O Lᴏʀᴅ, when I plead with thee: yet let me talk with thee of *thy* judgments: Wherefore doth the way of the wicked prosper? *wherefore* are all they happy that deal very treacherously?

2 Thou hast planted them, yea, they have taken root: they grow, yea, they bring forth fruit: ᴿthou *art* near in their mouth, and far from their reins.   Matt. 15:8

3 But thou, O Lᴏʀᴅ, knowest me: thou hast seen me, and ᵀtried mine heart toward thee: pull them out like sheep for the slaughter, and prepare them for the day of slaughter.   *tested my personal attitudes toward you*

4 How long shall ᴿthe land mourn, and the herbs of every field wither, for the wickedness of them that dwell therein? the beasts are consumed, and the birds; because they said, He shall not see our last end.   Hosea 4:3

God's Reply to Jeremiah

5 If thou hast run with the footmen, and they have wearied thee, then how canst thou contend with horses? and *if* in the land of peace, *wherein* thou trustedst, *they wearied thee,* then how wilt thou do in ᴿthe ᵀswelling of Jordan?   Josh. 3:15; 1 Chr. 12:15 • *pride*

6 For even thy brethren, and the house of thy father, even they have dealt treacherously with thee; yea, they have called a multitude after thee: believe them not, though they speak fair words unto thee.

7 I have ᴿforsaken mine house, ᴿI have left mine heritage; I have given ᵀthe ᴿdearly beloved of my soul into the hand of her enemies.   [7:29; 23:39] • Is. 2:6 • *the love* • 11:15

8 ᴿMine heritage is unto me as a lion in the forest; it crieth out against me: therefore ᴿhave I hated it.   Amos 6:8 • [2 Chr. 36:16]

9 Mine heritage *is* unto me *as* a ᵀspeckled bird, the ᴿbirds round about *are* against her; come ye, assemble all the beasts of the field, ᴿcome to devour.   *spotted* • 2 Kin. 24:2 • Is. 56:9

10 Many ᴿpastors have destroyed my vineyard, they have trodden my portion under foot, they have made my pleasant ᵀportion a desolate wilderness.   6:3 • *place*

11 They have made it desolate, *and* ᴿbeing desolate it mourneth unto me; the whole land is made desolate, because ᴿno man layeth *it* to heart.   14:2; 25:11 • Is. 42:25; Mal. 2:2

12 The ᵀspoilers are come upon all high places through the wilderness: for the sword of the Lᴏʀᴅ shall devour from the *one* end of the land even to the *other* end of the land: no flesh shall have peace.   *robbers*

13 ᴿThey have sown wheat, but shall reap thorns: they have put themselves to pain, *but* shall not profit: and ᵀthey shall be ashamed of your ᵀrevenues because of the fierce anger of the Lᴏʀᴅ.   Mic. 6:15 • *ye* • *fruits*

14 Thus saith the Lᴏʀᴅ against all mine evil neighbours, that ᴿtouch the inheritance which I have caused my people Israel to inherit; Behold, I will ᴿpluck them out of their land, and pluck out the house of Judah from among them.   Zech. 2:8 • 32:37

15 ᴿAnd it shall come to pass, after that I have plucked them out I will return, and have compassion on them, ᴿand will bring them again, every man to his heritage, and every man to his land.   Ezek. 28:25 • Amos 9:14

16 And it shall come to pass, if they will diligently learn the ways of my people, ᴿto swear by my name, The Lᴏʀᴅ liveth; as they taught my people to ᴿswear by Ba'-al; then shall they be ᴿbuilt in the midst of my people.   [4:2] • Josh. 23:7 • [Eph. 2:20, 21; 1 Pet. 2:5]

17 But if they will not ᴿobey, ᵀI will utterly pluck up and destroy that nation, saith the LORD.   Ps. 2:8, 9; Is. 60:12 · hear

CHAPTER 13

Sign of the Marred Girdle

THUS saith the LORD unto me, Go and ᵀget thee a linen ᵀgirdle, and put it upon thy loins, and put it not in water.   buy · belt

2 So I got a girdle according to the word of the LORD, and put it on my loins.

3 And the word of the LORD came unto me the second time, saying,

4 Take the ᵀgirdle that thou hast ᵀgot, which is upon thy loins, and arise, go to Eu-phra'-tes, and hide it there in a ᵀhole of the rock.   belt · bought · cleft

5 So I went, and hid it by Eu-phra'-tes, ᴿas the LORD commanded me.   Ex. 39:42

6 And it came to pass after many days, that the LORD said unto me, Arise, go to Eu-phra'-tes, and take the ᵀgirdle from thence, which I commanded thee to hide there.   belt

7 Then I went to Eu-phra'-tes, and digged, and took the girdle from the place where I had hid it: and, behold, the girdle was marred, it was profitable for nothing.

8 Then the word of the LORD came unto me, saying,

9 Thus saith the LORD, After this manner ᴿwill I ᵀmar the pride of Judah, and the great pride of Jerusalem.   Lev. 26:19 · ruin

10 This evil people, which refuse to hear my words, which walk in the imagination of their heart, and walk after other gods, to serve them, and to worship them, shall even be as this girdle, which is good for nothing.

11 For as the ᵀgirdle cleaveth to the loins of a man, so have I caused to cleave unto me the whole house of Israel and the whole house of Judah, saith the LORD; that they might be unto me for a people, and ᴿfor a name, and for a praise, and for a glory: but they would not hear.   belt · 33:9

Sign of the Wine Bottles

12 Therefore thou shalt speak unto them this word; Thus saith the LORD God of Israel, Every bottle shall be filled with wine: and they shall say unto thee, Do we not certainly know that every bottle shall be filled with wine?

13 Then shalt thou say unto them, Thus saith the LORD, Behold, I will fill all the inhabitants of this land, even the kings that sit upon David's throne, and the priests, and the prophets, and all the inhabitants of Jerusalem, with drunkenness.

14 And I will dash them one against another, even the fathers and the sons

together, saith the LORD: I will not pity, nor spare, nor have mercy, but destroy them.

15 Hear ᴿye, and give ear; be not ᴿproud: for the LORD hath spoken.   Is. 42:23 · [Prov. 16:5]

16 Give glory to the LORD your God, before he cause darkness, and before your feet stumble upon the dark mountains, and, while ye ᴿlook for light, he turn it into the shadow of death, and make it gross darkness.   Is. 59:9

17 But if ye will not hear it, my soul shall weep in secret places for your pride; and ᴿmine eye shall weep sore, and run down with tears, because the LORD's flock is carried away captive.   9:1; Lam. 1:2, 16; 2:18

18 Say unto ᴿthe king and to the queen, Humble yourselves, sit down: for your ᵀprincipalities shall come down, even the crown of your glory.   22:26; 2 Kin. 24:12 · prestige

19 The cities of the south shall be shut up, and none shall open them: Judah shall be carried away ᴿcaptive all of it, it shall be wholly carried away captive.   Lev. 26:21

20 Lift up your eyes, and behold them ᴿthat come from the north: where is the ᴿflock that was given thee, thy beautiful flock?   6:22, 10:22; 46:20; Hab. 1:6 · v. 17; 23:2

21 What wilt thou say when he shall punish thee? for thou hast taught them to be captains, and as chief over thee: shall not sorrows take thee, as a woman in travail?

22 And if thou say in thine heart, ᴿWherefore come these things upon me? For the greatness of thine iniquity are thy skirts discovered, and thy heels made bare.   16:10

23 Can the E-thi-o'-pi-an change his skin, or the leopard his spots? then may ye also do good, that are accustomed to do evil.

24 Therefore will I ᴿscatter them ᴿas the stubble that passeth away by the wind of the wilderness.   9:16; Lev. 26:33 · Ps. 1:4; Hos. 13;3

25 ᴿThis is thy lot, the portion of thy measures from me, saith the LORD; because thou hast forgotten me, and trusted in ᴿfalsehood.   Job 20:29; Ps. 11:6 · 10:14

26 Therefore will I discover thy skirts upon thy face, that thy shame may appear.

27 I have seen thine adulteries, and thy ᴿneighings, the lewdness of thy whoredom, and thine abominations on the ᴿhills in the fields. Woe unto thee, O Jerusalem! ᵀwilt thou not be made clean? when shall it once be?   5:8 · 2:20 · how long before you will be made clean?

CHAPTER 14

Judah's Dearth Is Described

THE word of the LORD that came to Jer-e-mi'-ah concerning the ᵀdearth.   drought

2 Judah mourneth, and ᴿthe gates thereof languish; they are black unto the ground; and the cry of Jerusalem is gone up.   Is. 3:26

3 And their nobles have sent their little ones to the waters: they came to the pits, *and* found no water; they returned with their vessels empty; they were ashamed and confounded, and covered their heads.

4 Because the ground is ᵀchapt, for there was no rain in the earth, the plowmen were ashamed, they covered their heads.   parched

5 Yea, the hind also calved in the field, and forsook *it*, because there was no grass.

6 And the wild asses did stand in the high places, they ᵀsnuffed up the wind like ᵀdragons; their eyes ᵀdid fail, because *there was* no grass.   pant for air • jackals • were weakened

Jeremiah's First Intercession

7 O Lord, though our ᴿiniquities testify against us, do thou *it* ᴿfor thy name's sake: for our backslidings are many; we have sinned against thee.   Is. 59:12; Hos. 5:5 • Ps. 25:11

8 ᴿO the hope of Israel, the ᴿsaviour thereof in time of trouble, why shouldest thou be as a ᵀstranger in the land, and as a wayfaring man *that* turneth aside to tarry for a night?   17:13; Acts 28:20 • Ps. 46:1 • sojourner

9 Why shouldest thou be as a man astonied, as a mighty man *that* cannot save? yet thou, O Lord, *art* in the midst of us, and we are called by thy name; leave us not.

10 Thus saith the Lord unto this people, ᴿThus have they loved to wander, they have not refrained their feet, therefore the Lord doth not accept them; he will now remember their iniquity, and visit their sins.   2:23-25

11 Then said the Lord unto me, ᴿPray not for this people for *their* good.   Ex. 32:10

12 When they fast, I will not hear their cry; and when they offer burnt offering and an oblation, I will not accept them: but I will consume them by the sword, and by the famine, and by the pestilence.

Jeremiah's Second Intercession

13 Then said I, Ah, Lord God! behold, the prophets say unto them, Ye shall not see the sword, neither shall ye have famine; but I will give you assured peace in this place.

14 Then the Lord said unto me, The prophets prophesy lies in my name: I sent them not, neither have I commanded them, neither spake unto them: they prophesy unto you a false vision and ᵀdivination, and a thing of nought, and the deceit of their heart.   insight

15 Therefore thus saith the Lord concerning the prophets that prophesy in my name, and I sent them not, yet they say, Sword and famine shall not be in this land; By sword and famine shall those prophets be consumed.

16 And the people to whom they prophesy shall be cast out in the streets of Jerusalem because of the famine and the sword; ᴿand they shall have none to bury them, them, their wives, nor their sons, nor their daughters: for I will ᵀpour their wickedness upon them.   7:32; 16:4; Ps. 79:3 • bring

17 Therefore thou shalt say this word unto them; ᴿLet mine eyes run down with tears night and day, and let them not cease: ᴿfor the virgin daughter of my people is broken with ᵀa great breach, with a very grievous blow.   9:1 • 8:21 • much damage

18 If I go forth into the field, then behold the slain with the sword! and if I enter into the city, then behold them that are sick with famine! yea, both the prophet and the priest go about into a land that they know not.

Jeremiah's Third Intercession

19 Hast thou utterly rejected Judah? hath thy soul lothed Zion? why hast thou smitten us, and *there is* no healing for us? we looked for peace, and *there is* no good; and for the time of healing, and behold trouble!

20 We acknowledge, O Lord, our wickedness, *and* the iniquity of our fathers: for ᴿwe have sinned against thee.   Ps. 106:6; Dan. 9:8

21 Do not abhor *us*, ᴿfor thy name's sake, do not disgrace the ᴿthrone of thy glory: ᴿremember, break not thy covenant with us.   14:7; Ps. 25:11 • 3:17; 17:12 • Ps. 106:45

22 Are there any among the vanities of the Gentiles that can cause rain? or can the heavens give showers? *art* not thou he, O Lord our God? therefore we will wait upon thee: for thou hast made all these *things*.

CHAPTER 15

THEN said the Lord unto me, Though ᴿMoses and ᴿSamuel stood before me, *yet* my mind *could* not *be* ᵀtoward this people: cast *them* out of my sight, and let them go forth.   Ps. 99:6 • 1 Sam. 7:9 • favourable to

2 And it shall come to pass, if they say unto thee, Whither shall we go forth? then thou shalt tell them, Thus saith the Lord; Such as *are* for death, to death; and such as *are* for the sword, to the sword; and such *are* for the famine, to the famine; and such as *are* for the captivity, to the captivity.

3 And I will appoint over them four ᵀkinds, saith the Lord: the sword to slay, and the dogs to tear, and ᴿthe fowls of the heaven, and the beasts of the earth, to devour and destroy.   possibilities • Deut. 28:26

4 And I will cause them to be removed into all kingdoms of the earth, because of Manas'-seh the son of Hez-e-ki'-ah king of Judah, for *that* which he did in Jerusalem.

5 For who shall have pity upon thee, O Jerusalem? or who shall bemoan thee? or who shall go aside to ask how thou doest?

6 Thou hast forsaken me, saith the Lord, thou art gone backward: therefore will I stretch out my hand against thee, and destroy thee; I am weary with repenting.

7 And I will fan them with a fan in the gates of the land; I will bereave *them* of ^Tchildren, I will destroy my people, *since* they return not from their ways.   *their loved ones*

8 Their widows are increased to me above the sand of the seas: I have brought upon them against the mother of the young men a spoiler at noonday: I have caused *him* to fall upon it suddenly, and terrors upon the city.

9 She that hath borne seven languisheth: she hath given up the ghost; her sun is gone down while *it was* yet day: she hath been ashamed and confounded: and the residue of them will I deliver to the sword before their enemies, saith the LORD.

God Encourages Jeremiah

10 ^RWoe is me, my mother, that thou hast borne me a man of strife and a man of contention to the whole ^Tearth! I have neither lent on ^Tusury, nor men have lent to me on usury; *yet* every one of them doth curse me.   20:14; Job 3:1 · *land · interest*

11 The LORD said, Verily it shall be well with thy remnant; verily I will cause ^Rthe enemy to entreat thee *well* in the time of evil and in the time of affliction.   40:4, 5

12 Shall iron break the northern iron and the ^Tsteel?   *bronze*

13 Thy substance and thy treasures will I give to the spoil without price, and *that* for all thy sins, even in all thy borders.

14 And I will make *thee* to ^Tpass with thine enemies into a land *which* thou knowest not: for a ^Rfire is kindled in mine anger, *which* shall burn upon you.   *go* · Deut. 32:22

15 O LORD, ^Rthou knowest: remember me, and ^Tvisit me, and ^Rrevenge me of my persecutors; take me not away in thy longsuffering: know that ^Rfor thy sake I have suffered rebuke.   Ps. 17:3 · *come to* · 20:12 · Ps. 69:7

16 Thy words were found, and I did eat them; and thy word was unto me the joy and rejoicing of mine heart: for I am called by thy name, O LORD God of hosts.

17 ^RI sat not in the assembly of ^Tthe mockers, nor rejoiced; I sat alone because of thy hand: for thou hast filled me with indignation.   Ps. 1:1; Ps. 26:4 · *them that make merry*

18 Why is my ^Rpain perpetual, and my wound incurable, *which* refuseth to be healed? wilt thou be altogether unto me as a liar, *and as* waters *that* fail?   [30:15]

19 Therefore thus saith the LORD, ^RIf thou return, then will I bring thee again, *and* thou shalt ^Rstand before me: and if thou take forth the precious from the vile, thou shalt be as my mouth: let them return unto thee; but return not thou unto them.   Zech. 3:7 · *v.* 1

20 And I will make thee unto this people a fenced brasen wall: and they shall fight against thee, but they shall not prevail against thee: for I *am* with thee to save thee and to deliver thee, saith the LORD.

21 And I will ^Rdeliver thee out of the hand of the wicked, and I will redeem thee out of the hand of the terrible.   20:13; 39:11, 12

CHAPTER 16

Jeremiah Is Not to Marry

THE word of the LORD came also unto me, saying,

2 Thou shalt ^Rnot take thee a wife, neither shalt thou have sons or daughters in this place.   1 Cor. 7:26, 27

3 For thus saith the LORD concerning the sons and concerning the daughters that are born in this place, and concerning their mothers that bare them, and concerning their fathers that begat them in this land;

4 They shall die of grievous deaths; they shall not be lamented; neither shall they be buried; *but* they shall be as dung upon the face of the earth: and they shall be consumed by the sword, and by famine; and their carcases shall be meat for the fowls of heaven, and for the beasts of the earth.

5 For thus saith the LORD, Enter not into the house of mourning, neither go to lament nor bemoan them: for I have taken away my peace from this people, saith the LORD, *even* lovingkindness and mercies.

6 Both the great and the small shall die in this land: they shall not be buried, neither shall *men* lament for them, nor cut themselves, nor make themselves bald for them:

7 Neither shall *men* ^Ttear *themselves* for them in mourning, to comfort them for the dead; neither shall *men* give them the cup of consolation to ^Rdrink for their father or for their mother.   *break bread* · Prov. 31:6

8 Thou shalt not also go into the house of feasting, ^Rto sit with them to eat and to drink.   15:17; Eccl. 7:2–4; Is. 22:12–14; Amos 6:4–6

9 For thus saith the LORD of hosts, the God of Israel; Behold, I will cause to cease out of this place in your eyes, and in your days, the voice of ^Tmirth, and the voice of gladness, the voice of the bridegroom, and the voice of the bride.   *happiness*

Judah's Idolatry

10 And it shall come to pass, when thou shalt shew this people all these words, and they shall say unto thee, ^RWherefore hath the LORD pronounced all this great evil against us? or what *is* our iniquity? or what *is* our sin that we have committed against the LORD our God?   5:19; Deut. 29:24

11 Then shalt thou say unto them, ^RBecause your fathers have forsaken me, saith the LORD, and have walked after other gods, and have served them, and have worshipped

them, and have forsaken me, and have not kept my law;   22:9; Deut. 29:25

12 And ye have done ᴿworse than your fathers; for, behold, ye walk every one after the imagination of his evil heart, that they may not hearken unto me: 7:26

13 Therefore will I cast you out of this land ᴿinto a land that ᵀye know not, *neither* ye nor your fathers; and there shall ye serve other gods day and night; where I will not shew you favour.   15:14 · *is foreign*

God's Promise of Judah's Restoration

14 Therefore, behold, the days come, saith the LORD, that it shall no more be said, The LORD liveth, that brought up the children of Israel out of the land of Egypt;

15 But, The LORD liveth, that brought up the children of Israel from the land of the north, and from all the lands whither he had driven them: and I will bring them again into their land that I gave unto their fathers.

16 Behold, I will send for many ᴿfishers,ᵀ saith the LORD, and they shall fish them; and after will I send for many hunters, and they shall hunt them from every mountain, and from every hill, and out of the ᵀholes of the rocks.   Amos 4:2; Hab. 1:15 · *fishermen · clefts*

17 For mine eyes *are* upon all their ways: they are not hid from my face, neither is their iniquity hid from mine eyes.

18 And first I will recompense their iniquity and their sin ᴿdouble; because they have defiled my land, they have filled mine inheritance with the carcases of their detestable and abominable things.   Is. 40:2

19 O LORD, ᴿmy strength, and my fortress, and my refuge in the day of affliction, the Gentiles shall come unto thee from the ends of the earth, and shall say, Surely our fathers have inherited lies, vanity, and *things* wherein *there* is no profit.   Ps. 18:2

20 Shall a man make gods unto himself, and ᴿthey *are* no gods?   2:11; Is. 37:19; Gal. 4:8

21 Therefore, behold, I will this once cause them to know, I will cause them to know mine hand and my might; and they shall know that my name *is* The LORD.

CHAPTER 17

Judah's Sins Are Listed

THE sin of Judah *is* written with a pen of iron, *and* with the point of a diamond: *it is* graven upon the table of their heart, and upon the horns of your altars;

2 Whilst their children remember ᵀtheir altars and their ᴿgroves by the green trees upon the high hills.   *their pagan shrines* · Judg. 3:7

3 O my ᵀmountain in the field, I will give thy substance *and* all thy treasures ᵀto the spoil, *and* thy high places for sin, throughout all thy borders.   *own people · to be taken as loot*

4 And thou, even thyself, shalt ᵀdiscontinue from thine heritage that I gave thee; and I ᴿwill cause thee to serve thine enemies in the land which thou knowest not: for ye have kindled a fire in mine anger, *which* shall burn for ever.   *not live any longer in* · 2 Chr. 36:20

5 Thus saith the LORD; ᴿCursed *be* the man that trusteth in man, and maketh ᴿflesh his arm, and whose heart departeth from the LORD.   Is. 30:1, 2; 31:1 · Is. 31:3; Ps. 146:3

6 For he shall be like the heath in the desert, and shall not see when good cometh; but shall inhabit the parched places in the wilderness, *in* a salt land and not inhabited.

7 ᴿBlessed *is* the man that trusteth in the LORD, and whose hope the LORD is.   Is. 30:18

8 For he shall be as a tree planted by the waters, and *that* spreadeth out her roots by the river, and shall not ᵀsee when heat cometh, but her leaf shall be green; and shall not be careful in the year of drought, neither shall cease from yielding fruit.   *fear*

9 The heart *is* deceitful above all *things,* and desperately wicked: who can know it?

10 I the LORD ᴿsearch the heart, *I* ᵀtry the reins, ᴿeven to ᵀgive every man according to his ways, *and* according to the fruit of his doings.   Ps. 7:9 · *test the emotions* · Ps. 62:12 · *repay*

11 *As* the partridge sitteth on eggs, ᵀand hatcheth *them* not; *so* he that getteth riches, and not by right, ᴿshall leave them in the midst of his days, and at his end shall be ᴿa fool.   *she laid not* · Ps. 55:23 · Luke 12:20

12 ᴿA glorious high throne from the beginning *is* the place of our sanctuary.   [3:17]

13 O LORD, ᴿthe hope of Israel, all that forsake thee shall be ashamed, *and* they that depart from me shall be written in the earth, because they have forsaken the LORD, the fountain of living waters.   14:8

14 ᴿHeal me, O LORD, and I shall be healed; save me, and I shall be saved: for ᴿthou *art* my praise.   [30:17; 33:6] · Deut. 10:21

15 Behold, they say unto me, Where *is* the word of the LORD? let it come now.

16 As for me, ᴿI have not ᵀhastened from *being* a ᵀpastor to follow thee: neither have I desired the woeful day; thou knowest: that which came out of my lips was *right* before thee.   1:4–12 · *forsaken · shepherd*

17 Be not a ᴿterror unto me: ᴿthou *art* my ᵀhope in the day of evil.   Ps. 88:15 · 16:19 · *refuge*

18 Let them be confounded that persecute me, but ᴿlet not me be confounded: let them be dismayed, but let not me be dismayed: bring upon them the day of evil, and destroy them with double destruction.   Ps. 25:2

Jeremiah's Call for Sabbath Observance

19 Thus said the LORD unto me; Go and stand in the gate of the children of the people, whereby the kings of Judah come in, and by the which they go out, and in all the gates of Jerusalem;

20 And say unto them, ᴿHear ye the word of the LORD, ye kings of Judah, and all Judah, and all the inhabitants of Jerusalem, that enter in by these gates: 19:3

21 Thus saith the LORD; ᴿTake heed to yourselves, and bear no burden on the sabbath day, nor bring it in by the gates of Jerusalem;   Num. 15:32; Neh. 13:19; [John 5:10]

22 Neither carry forth a burden out of your houses on the sabbath day, neither do ye any work, but hallow ye the sabbath day, as I commanded your fathers.

23 But they obeyed not, neither inclined their ear, but made their neck stiff, that they might not hear, nor receive instruction.

24 And it shall come to pass, if ye diligently hearken unto me, saith the LORD, to bring in no burden through the gates of this city on the sabbath day, but hallow the sabbath day, to do no work therein;

25 Then shall there enter into the gates of this city kings and princes sitting upon the throne of David, riding in chariots and on horses, they, and their princes, the men of Judah, and the inhabitants of Jerusalem: and this city shall remain for ever.

26 And they shall come from the cities of Judah, and from the places about Jerusalem, and from the land of Benjamin, and from the plain, and from the mountains, and from the south, bringing burnt offerings, and sacrifices, and meat offerings, and incense, and bringing ᴿsacrifices of praise, unto the house of the LORD.   Ps. 107:22; 116:17

27 But if ye will not hearken unto me to hallow the sabbath day, and not to bear a burden, even entering in at the gates of Jerusalem on the sabbath day; then ᴿwill I kindle a fire in the gates thereof, and ᴿit shall devour the palaces of Jerusalem, and it shall not be quenched.   Lam. 4:11 • 2 Kin. 25:9

CHAPTER 18

Sign of the Potter

THE word which came to Jer-e-mi'-ah from the LORD, saying,

2 Arise, and go down to the potter's ᴿhouse, and there I will cause thee to hear my words.   19:1, 2; 23:22

3 Then I went down to the potter's house, and, behold, he ᵀwrought a work on the ᵀwheels.   made • stones

4 And the vessel that he made of clay was marred in the hand of the potter: so he ᵀmade it again another vessel, as seemed good to the potter to make it.   reworked it as

5 Then the word of the LORD came to me, saying,

6 O house of Israel, ᴿcannot I do with you as this potter? saith the LORD. Behold, as the clay is in the potter's hand, so are ye in mine hand, O house of Israel.   Is. 45:9

7 At what instant I shall speak concerning a nation, and concerning a kingdom, to ᴿpluck up, and to pull down, and to destroy it;   1:10

8 ᴿIf that nation, against whom I have pronounced, turn from their evil, ᴿI will repent of the evil that I thought to do unto them.   [Ezek. 18:21; 33:11] • 26:3; Jon. 3:10

9 And at what instant I shall speak concerning a nation, and concerning a kingdom, to build ᴿand to plant it;   Amos 9:11-15

10 If it do evil in my sight, that it obey not my voice, then I will repent of the good, wherewith I said I would benefit them.

11 Now therefore go to, speak to the men of Judah, and to the inhabitants of Jerusalem, saying, Thus saith the LORD; Behold, I ᴿframe evil against you, and devise a device against you: ᴿreturn ye now every one from his evil way, and make your ways and your doings good.   4:6 • 7:3; 2 Kin. 17:13

12 And they said, ᴿThere is no hope: but we will walk after our own ᵀdevices, and we will every one do the ᵀimagination of his evil heart.   2:25 • plans • stubbornness

13 Therefore thus saith the LORD; ᴿAsk ye now among the ᵀheathen, who hath heard such things: the virgin of Israel hath done a very horrible thing.   2:10; 5:30 • nations

14 Will a man ᵀleave the snow of Leb'-a-non which cometh from the rock of the field? or shall the cold flowing waters that come from another place be forsaken?   forsake

15 Because my people hath ᴿforgotten me, they have ᵀburned incense to vanity, and they have caused them to stumble in their ways from the ancient paths, to walk in paths, in a way not cast up;   2:13 • worshipped

16 To make their land ᴿdesolate, and a perpetual ᴿhissing; every one that passeth thereby shall be astonished, and wag his head.   19:8; 49:13 • 1 Kin. 9:8; Lam. 2:15; Mic. 6:16

17 ᴿI will scatter them ᴿas with an east wind before the enemy; ᴿI will shew them ᵀthe back, and not the face, in the day of their calamity.   13:24; 2 Chr. 36:17 • Ps. 48:7 • 2:27 • my

18 Then said they, ᴿCome, and let us devise devices against Jer-e-mi'-ah; ᴿfor the law shall not perish from the priest, nor counsel from the wise, nor the word from the prophet. Come, and let us smite him ᵀwith the tongue, and let us not give heed to any of his words.   11:19 • [John 7:48] • for the tongue

19 Give heed to me, O LORD, and hearken to the voice of them that contend with me.

20 ᴿShall evil be recompensed for good? for ᴿthey have digged a pit for my soul. Remember that I stood before thee to ᵀspeak good for them, and to turn away thy wrath from them.   Ps. 109:4 • Ps. 35:7 • pray

21 Therefore deliver up their children to the famine, and pour out their blood by the force of the sword; and let their wives be

bereaved of their children, and *be* widows; and let their men be put to death; *let* their young men *be* slain by the sword in battle.

22 Let a ᴿcry be heard from their houses, when thou shalt bring a troop suddenly upon them: for they have digged a pit to take me, and hid snares for my feet.   6:26

23 Yet, Lᴏʀᴅ, thou knowest all their counsel against me to slay *me:* ᴿforgive not their iniquity, neither blot out their sin from thy sight, but let them be overthrown before thee; deal *thus* with them in the time of thine anger.   11:20; Ps. 35:4; 109:14

CHAPTER 19

Sign of the Broken Bottle

THUS saith the Lᴏʀᴅ, Go and ᵀget a potter's earthen ᵀbottle, and *take* of the ᵀancients of the people, and of ᴿthe ancients of the priests;   *buy • flask • elders •* Ezek. 8:11

2 And go forth unto the valley of the son of Hin'-nom, which *is* by the entry of ᵀthe east gate, and proclaim there the words that I shall tell thee,   *the sun gate*

3 ᴿAnd say, Hear ye the word of the Lᴏʀᴅ, O kings of Judah, and inhabitants of Jerusalem; Thus saith the Lᴏʀᴅ of hosts, the God of Israel; Behold, I ᴿwill bring evil upon this place, the which whosoever heareth, his ears shall ᴿtingle.   17:20 • 2 Chr. 36 • 2 Kin. 21:12

4 Because they ᴿhave forsaken me, and have estranged this place, and have burned incense in it unto other gods, whom neither they nor their fathers have known, nor the kings of Judah, and have filled this place with the blood of innocents;   Deut. 28:20

5 ᴿThey have built also the high places of Ba'-al, to burn their sons with fire *for* burnt offerings unto Ba'-al, ᴿwhich I commanded not, nor spake *it,* neither came *it* into my mind: 7:31; 32:35; Num. 22:41 • Lev. 18:21

6 Therefore, behold, the days come, saith the Lᴏʀᴅ, that this place shall no more be called To'-phet, nor The valley of the son of Hin'-nom, but The valley of slaughter.

7 And I will make void the counsel of Judah and Jerusalem in this place; and I will cause them to fall by the sword before their enemies, and by the hands of them that seek their lives: and their carcases will I give to be meat for the fowls of the heaven, and for the beasts of the earth.

8 And I will make this city desolate, and ᵀan hissing; every one that passeth thereby shall be astonished and hiss because of all the plagues thereof.   *a shame*

9 And I will cause them to eat the flesh of their sons and the flesh of their daughters, and they shall eat every one the flesh of his friend in the siege and ᵀstraitness, wherewith their enemies, and they that seek their lives, shall straiten them.   *famine*

10 Then shalt thou break the bottle in the sight of the men that go with thee,

11 And shalt say unto them, Thus saith the Lᴏʀᴅ of hosts; Even so will I break this people and this city, as *one* breaketh a potter's vessel, that cannot be made whole again: and they shall bury *them* in To'-phet, till *there be* no place to bury.

12 Thus will I do unto this place, saith the Lᴏʀᴅ, and to the inhabitants thereof, and *even* make this city as To'-phet:

13 And the houses of Jerusalem, and the houses of the kings of Judah, shall be defiled as the place of To'-phet, because of all the houses upon whose ᴿroofs they have ᵀburned incense unto all the host of heaven, and ᴿhave poured out drink offerings unto other gods.   32:29 • *worshipped •* 7:18

14 Then came Jer-e-mi'-ah from To'-phet, whither the Lᴏʀᴅ had sent him to prophesy; and he stood in the court of the Lᴏʀᴅ's house; and said to all the people,

15 Thus saith the Lᴏʀᴅ of hosts, the God of Israel; Behold, I will bring upon this city and upon all her towns all the evil that I have pronounced against it, because ᴿthey have hardened their necks, that they might not hear my words.   7:26; 17:23

CHAPTER 20

Jeremiah Is Persecuted by Pashur

NOW Pash'-ur the son of ᴿIm'-mer the priest, who *was* also chief governor in the house of the Lᴏʀᴅ, heard that Jer-e-mi'-ah prophesied these things.   1 Chr. 24:14

2 Then Pash'-ur ᵀsmote Jer-e-mi'ah the prophet, and put him in ᵀthe stocks that *were* in the high gate of Benjamin, which *was* by the house of the Lᴏʀᴅ.   *beat • prison*

3 And it came to pass on the morrow, that Pash'-ur brought forth Jer-e-mi'-ah out of the stocks. Then said Jer-e-mi'-ah unto him, The Lᴏʀᴅ hath not called thy name Pash'-ur, but ᵀMa'-gor–mis'-sa-bib.   *terror*

4 ᴿFor thus saith the Lᴏʀᴅ, Behold, I will make thee a ᴿterror to thyself, and to all thy friends: and they shall fall by the sword of their enemies, and thine eyes shall behold *it:* and I will give all Judah into the hand of the king of Babylon, and he ᴿshall carry them captive into Babylon, and shall slay them with the sword.   Ezek. 26:21 • Job 18:11 • 2 Chr. 36:20

5 Moreover I ᴿwill deliver all the strength of this city, and all the labours thereof, and all the precious things thereof, and all the treasures of the kings of Judah will I give into the hand of their enemies, which shall ᵀspoil them, and take them, and carry them to Babylon.   2 Kin. 20:17; 24:12–16; 25:13–21 • *rob*

6 And thou, Pash'-ur, and all that dwell in thine house shall go into captivity: and thou

shalt come to Babylon, and there thou shalt die, and shalt be buried there, thou, and all thy friends, to whom thou hast ᴿprophesied lies.   14:13, 14; 28:15; 29:21

Jeremiah Complains to God

7 O LORD, thou hast deceived me, and I was ᵀdeceived: ᴿthou art stronger than I, and hast prevailed: ᴿI am in derision daily, every one mocketh me.   fooled • 1:6, 7 • Lam. 3:14

8 For since I spake, I cried out, ᴿI cried violence and spoil; because the word of the LORD was made a reproach unto me, and a ᴿderision, ᵀdaily.   6:7 • 2 Chr. 36:16 • all the day

9 Then I said, I will not make mention of him, nor speak any more in his name. But his word was in mine heart as a burning fire shut up in my bones, and I was weary with forbearing, and ᴿI could not stay.   Job 32:18

10 For I heard the defaming of many, fear on every side. Report, say they, and we will report it. All my familiars watched for my halting, saying, ᵀPeradventure he will be enticed, and we shall prevail against him, and we shall take our revenge on him.   perhaps

11 But the LORD is with me as a mighty terrible one: therefore my persecutors shall stumble, and they shall not prevail: they shall be greatly ashamed; for they shall not prosper: their ᴿeverlasting confusion shall never be forgotten.   23:40

12 But, O LORD of hosts, that triest the righteous, and seest the reins and the heart, ᴿlet me see thy vengeance on them: for unto thee have I opened my cause.   Ps. 54:7

13 Sing unto the LORD, praise ye the LORD: for he hath delivered the ᵀsoul of the poor from the hand of evildoers.   life

14 ᴿCursed be the day wherein I was born: let not the day wherein my mother bare me be blessed.   15:10; Job 3:3

15 Cursed be the man who brought tidings to my father, saying, A man child is born unto thee; making him very glad.

16 And let that man be as the cities which the LORD overthrew, and repented not: and let him hear the cry in the morning, and the shouting at noontide;

17 ᴿBecause he slew me not from the womb; or that my mother might have been my grave, and her womb to be always great with me.   Job 3:10, 11; 10:18, 19

18 ᴿWherefore came I forth out of the womb to see labour and sorrow, that my days should be consumed with shame?   Job 3:20

CHAPTER 21

Message Against Zedekiah

THE word which came unto Jer-e-mi'-ah from the LORD, when king Zed-e-ki'-ah sent unto him ᴿPash'-ur the son of Mel-chi'-

ah, and ᴿZeph-a-ni'-ah the son of Ma-a-se'-iah the priest, saying,   38:1 • 2 Kin. 25:18

2 Enquire, I pray thee, of the LORD for us; for Neb-u-chad-rez'-zar king of Babylon maketh war against us; if so be that the LORD will deal with us according to all his wondrous works, that he may go up from us.

3 Then said ᴿJer-e-mi'-ah unto them, Thus shall ye say to Zed-e-ki'-ah: 24:3

4 Thus saith the LORD God of Israel; Behold, I will ᵀturn back the weapons of war that are in your hands, wherewith ye fight against the king of Babylon, and against the Chal-de'-ans, which besiege you without the walls, and ᴿI will assemble them into the midst of this city.   work against • Is. 13:4

5 And ᴿI myself will fight against you with an ᴿoutstretched hand and with a strong arm, even in anger, and in ᵀfury, and in great wrath.   32:24; 33:5; Is. 63:10 • Ex. 6:6 • violence

6 And I will smite the inhabitants of this city, both man and beast: they shall die of a great ᴿpestilence.   14:12; 32:24

7 And afterward, saith the LORD, ᴿI will deliver Zed-e-ki'-ah king of Judah, and his servants, and the people, and such as are left in this city from the pestilence, from the sword, and from the famine, into the hand of Neb-u-chad-rez'-zar king of Babylon, and into the hand of their enemies, and into the hand of those that seek their life: and he shall smite them with the edge of the sword; he shall not spare them, neither have pity, nor have mercy.   37:17; 2 Kin. 25:7; 2 Chr. 36:17

8 And unto this people thou shalt say, Thus saith the LORD; Behold, I set before you the way of life, and the way of death.

9 He that abideth in this city shall die by the sword, and by the famine, and by the pestilence: but he that goeth out, and ᵀfalleth to the Chal-de'-ans that besiege you, he shall live, and ᴿhis life shall be unto him for a ᵀprey.   surrenders • 39:18; 45:5 • gift

10 For I have set my face against this city for evil, and not for good, saith the LORD: it shall be given into the hand of the king of Babylon, and he shall burn it with fire.

11 And touching the house of the king of Judah, say, Hear ye the word of the LORD;

12 O house of David, thus saith the LORD; Execute judgment in the morning, and deliver him that is ᵀspoiled out of the hand of the oppressor, lest my fury go out like fire, and burn that none can quench it, because of the evil of your doings.   robbed

13 Behold, ᴿI am against thee, O inhabitant of the valley, and rock of the plain, saith the LORD; which say, Who shall come down against us? or who shall enter into our habitations?   49:4; [Ezek. 13:8]; Obad. 3

14 But I will punish you according to the fruit of your doings, saith the LORD: and I will

kindle a fire in the forest thereof, and it shall devour all things round about it.

CHAPTER 22

THUS saith the LORD; Go down to the house of the king of Judah, ᴿand speak there this word,   21:11; 34:2; 2 Chr. 25:15, 16

2 And say, Hear the word of the LORD, O king of Judah, that ᴿsittest upon the throne of David, thou, and thy servants, and thy people that enter in by these gates: 22:4, 30

3 Thus saith the LORD; ᴿExecute ye judgment and righteousness, and deliver the ᵀspoiled out of the hand of the oppressor: and do no wrong, do no violence to the stranger, the fatherless, nor the widow, neither shed innocent blood in this place.   7:23; 21:12 · robbed

4 For if ye do this thing ᵀindeed, then shall there enter in by the gates of this house kings sitting upon the throne of David, riding in chariots and on horses, he, and his servants, and his people.   really

5 But if ye will not hear these words, I swear by myself, saith the LORD, that ᴿthis house shall become a desolation.   Matt. 23:38 ☆

6 For thus saith the LORD unto the king's house of Judah; Thou art Gil′-e-ad unto me, and the head of Leb′-a-non: yet surely I will ᴿmake thee a ᴿwilderness, and cities which are not inhabited.   Ps. 107:34 · Mic. 3:12

7 And I will prepare destroyers against thee, every one with his weapons: and they shall cut down ᴿthy choice cedars, ᴿand cast them into the fire.   Is. 37:24 · 21:14

8 And many nations shall pass by this city, and they shall say every man to his neighbour, ᴿWherefore hath the LORD done thus unto this great city?   Deut. 29:24, 25

9 Then they shall answer, ᴿBecause they have forsaken the covenant of the LORD their God, and worshipped other gods, and served them.   11:3; 2 Kin. 22:17; 2 Chr. 34:25

Message Against Shallum

10 Weep ye not for ᴿthe dead, neither bemoan him: but weep sore for him ᴿthat goeth away: for he shall return no more, nor see his native country.   2 Kin. 22:20 · v. 11

11 For thus saith the LORD touching Shal′-lum the son of Jo-si′-ah king of Judah, which reigned instead of Jo-si′-ah his father, which went forth out of this place; He shall not return thither any more:

12 But he shall ᴿdie in the place whither they have led him captive, and shall see this land no more.   22:18; 2 Kin. 23:34

Message Against Jehoiakim

13 ᴿWoe unto him that buildeth his house by unrighteousness, and his ᵀchambers by wrong; that useth his neighbour's service

without ᵀwages, and giveth him not for his work;   2 Kin. 23:35 · dwellingplace · paying him

14 That saith, I will build me a wide house and large ᵀchambers, and cutteth him out windows; and it is cieled with cedar, and painted with vermilion.   rooms

15 Shalt thou reign, because thou ᵀclosest thyself in cedar? did not thy father eat and drink, and do judgment and justice, and then it was well with him?   tries to excell

16 He judged the cause of the poor and needy; then it was well with him: ᴿwas not this to know me? saith the LORD.   [Ps. 9:10]

17 ᴿBut thine eyes and thine heart are not but for thy covetousness, and for to shed innocent blood, and for oppression, and for ᵀviolence, to do it.   Ezek. 19:6 · injustice

18 Therefore thus saith the LORD concerning ᴿJe-hoi′-a-kim the son of Jo-si′-ah king of Judah; They shall not lament for him, saying, ᴿAh my brother! or, Ah sister! they shall not lament for him, saying, Ah lord! or, Ah his glory!   25:1 · 1 Kin. 13:30

19 ᴿHe shall be buried with the ᴿburial of an ass, drawn and cast forth beyond the gates of Jerusalem.   2 Chr. 36:6 · 8:2; 36:30

20 Go up to Leb′-a-non, and cry; and lift up thy voice in Ba′-shan, and cry from the passages: for all thy lovers are destroyed.

21 I spake unto thee in thy ᵀprosperity; but thou saidst, I will not hear. This hath been thy manner from thy youth, that thou obeyedst not my voice.   prosperous days

22 The wind shall eat up all thy pastors, and thy ᵀlovers shall go into captivity: surely then shalt thou be ashamed and confounded for all thy wickedness.   friends

23 O inhabitant of Leb′-a-non, that makest thy nest in the cedars, how gracious shalt thou be when pangs come upon thee, the pain as of a woman in travail!

Message Against Coniah (Jehoiachin)

24 As I live, saith the LORD, though Co-ni′-ah the son of Je-hoi′-a-kim king of Judah were the ᵀsignet upon my right hand, yet would I pluck thee thence;   ring

25 And I will give thee into the hand of them that seek thy life, and into the hand of them whose face thou fearest, even into the hand of Neb-u-chad-rez′-zar king of Babylon, and into the hand of the Chal-de′-ans.

26 ᴿAnd I will cast thee out, and thy mother that bare thee, into another country, ᵀwhere ye were not born; and there shall ye die.   2 Kin. 24:15; 2 Chr. 36:10 · where you will be an alien

27 But to the land whereunto they desire to return, thither shall they not return.

28 Is this man Co-ni′-ah a despised broken idol? is he ᴿa vessel wherein is no pleasure? wherefore are they cast out, he and his seed, and are cast into a land which they know not?   Ps. 31:12; 48:38; Hos. 8:8

29 ^RO earth, earth, earth, hear the word of the LORD.   6:19; Deut. 32:1; Is. 1:2; 34:1; Mic. 1:2

30 Thus saith the LORD, Write ye this man childless, a man *that* shall not prosper in his days: for no man of his seed shall prosper, sitting upon the throne of David, and ruling any more in Judah.

CHAPTER 23

Message of the Righteous King

WOE ^Rbe unto the ^Tpastors that destroy and scatter the sheep of my pasture! saith the LORD.   10:21; Ezek. 34:2 · *shepherds*

2 Therefore thus saith the LORD God of Israel against the pastors that feed my people; Ye have scattered my flock, and driven them away, and have not visited them: behold, I will ^Tvisit upon you the evil of your doings, saith the LORD.   *bring*

3 And ^RI will gather the remnant of my flock out of all countries whither I have driven them, and will bring them again to their folds; and they shall be fruitful and increase.   vv. 3–8; 31:7; 32:37; Is. 1:9

4 And I will set up ^Rshepherds over them which shall feed them: and they shall fear no more, nor be dismayed, neither shall they be lacking, saith the LORD.   3:15

5 Behold, ^Rthe days come, saith the LORD, that I ^Rwill raise unto David a righteous Branch, and a King shall reign and prosper, ^Rand shall execute judgment and justice in the earth.   33:14; [John 1:45] · Matt. 1:1, 6 ☆ · Ps. 72:2

6 In his days Judah shall be saved, and Israel ^Rshall dwell safely: and ^Rthis *is* his name whereby he shall be called, THE LORD OUR RIGHTEOUSNESS.   32:37 · 33:16 ☆

7 Therefore, behold, the days come, saith the LORD, that they shall no more say, The LORD liveth, which brought up the children of Israel out of the land of Egypt;

8 But, The LORD liveth, which brought up and which led the seed of the house of Israel out of the north country, ^Rand from all countries whither I had driven them; and they shall dwell in their own land.   Is. 43:5

Jeremiah's Tenth Sermon:
Against Judah's False Prophets

9 Mine heart within me is broken because of the prophets; all my bones shake; I am like a drunken man, and like a man whom wine hath overcome, because of the LORD, and because of the words of his holiness.

10 For ^Rthe land is full of adulterers; for because of ^Tswearing the land mourneth; ^Rthe pleasant places of the wilderness are dried up, and their course is evil, and their force *is* not right.   9:2 · *ungodliness* · 9:10

11 For ^Rboth prophet and priest are profane; yea, ^Rin my house have I found their wickedness, saith the LORD.   7:30 · Zeph. 3:4

12 Wherefore their way shall be unto them as slippery *ways* in the darkness: they shall be driven on, and fall therein: for I will bring evil upon them, *even* the year of their visitation, saith the LORD.

13 And I have seen folly in the prophets of Sa-ma'-ri-a; ^Rthey prophesied ^Tin Ba'-al, and caused my people Israel to err.   2:8 · *by*

14 I have seen also in the prophets of Jerusalem an horrible thing: ^Rthey commit adultery, and walk in lies: they ^Rstrengthen also the hands of evildoers, that none doth return from his wickedness: they are all of them unto me as Sodom, and the inhabitants thereof as Go-mor'-rah.   29:23 · Is. 1:9

15 Therefore thus saith the LORD of hosts concerning the prophets; Behold, I will feed them with ^Rwormwood, and make them drink the water of gall: for from the prophets of Jerusalem is ^Tprofaneness gone forth into all the land.   9:15 · *sacrilege*

16 Thus saith the LORD of hosts, Hearken not unto the words of the prophets that prophesy unto you: they make you vain: they speak a vision of their own heart, *and* not out of the mouth of the LORD.

17 They say still unto them that despise me, The LORD hath said, ^RYe shall have peace; and they say unto every one that walketh after the imagination of his own heart, No evil shall come upon you.   8:11

18 For ^Rwho ^Thath stood in the counsel of the LORD, and hath perceived and heard his word? who hath ^Tmarked his word, and heard *it?*   Job 15:8 · *has the private thoughts* · *noted*

19 Behold, a ^Rwhirlwind of the LORD is gone forth in fury, even a grievous whirlwind: it shall fall grievously upon the head of the wicked.   25:32; 30:23; Amos 1:14

20 The anger of the LORD shall not return, until he have executed, and till he have performed the thoughts of his heart: in the latter days ye shall consider it perfectly.

21 ^RI have not sent these prophets, yet they ran: I have not spoken to them, yet they prophesied.   14:14; 27:15; 29:9

22 But if they had ^Tstood in my counsel, and had caused my people to hear my words, then they should have ^Rturned them from their evil way, and from the evil of their doings.   *understood my mind* · 25:5

23 ^RAm I a God at hand, saith the LORD, and not a God afar off?   [Ps. 139:1–10]

24 Can any ^Rhide himself in secret places that I shall not see him? saith the LORD. ^RDo not I fill heaven and earth? saith the LORD.   [Ps. 139:7]; Amos 9:2, 3 · [1 Kin. 8:27]

25 I have ^Rheard what the prophets said, that prophesy lies in my name, saying, I have dreamed, I have dreamed.   8:6

26 How long shall *this* be in the heart of the prophets that prophesy lies? yea, *they are* prophets of the deceit of their own heart;

27 Which think to cause my people to

forget my name by their dreams which they tell every man to his neighbour, as their fathers have forgotten my name for Ba'-al.

28 The prophet that hath a dream, let him tell a dream; and he that hath my word, let him speak my word faithfully. What is the chaff to the wheat? saith the LORD.

29 Is not my word like as a ᴿfire? saith the LORD; and like a ᴿhammer that breaketh the rock in pieces?   5:14 • [2 Cor. 10:4, 5; Heb. 4:12]

30 Therefore, behold, I am against the prophets, saith the LORD, that ᵀsteal my words every one from his neighbour. take away

31 ᴿBehold, I am against the prophets, saith the LORD, ᵀthat use their tongues, and say, He saith.   Ezek. 13:9 • that use oratory

32 Behold, I am against them that prophesy false dreams, saith the LORD, and do tell them, and cause my people to err by their lies, and by ᴿtheir lightness;ᵀ yet I sent them not, nor commanded them: therefore they shall not profit this people at all, saith the LORD.   Zeph. 3:4 • vain boasting

33 ᴿAnd when this people, or the prophet, or a priest, shall ask thee, saying, What is the ᵀburden of the LORD? thou shalt then say unto them, What burden? I will even forsake you, saith the LORD.   v. 39 • message

34 And as for the prophet, and the priest, and the people, that shall say, The ᴿburdenᵀ of the LORD, I will even ᵀpunish that man and his house.   Zech. 13:3 • message • visit upon

35 Thus shall ye say every one to his neighbour, and every one to his brother, What hath the LORD answered? and, ᴿWhat hath the LORD spoken?   33:3; 42:4

36 And the ᵀburden of the LORD shall ye mention no more: for every ᴿman's word shall be his burden; for ye have ᴿperverted the words of the living God, of the LORD of hosts our God.   message • [Matt. 12:36] • Deut. 4:2

37 Thus shalt thou say to the prophet, What hath the LORD answered thee? and, What hath the LORD spoken?

38 But since ye say, The burden of the LORD; therefore thus saith the LORD; Because ye say this word, The burden of the LORD, and I have sent unto you, saying, Ye shall not say, The burden of the LORD;

39 Therefore, behold, I, even I, will utterly forget you, and I will forsake you, and the city that I gave you and your fathers, and cast you out of my presence:

40 And I will bring ᴿan everlasting reproach upon you, and a perpetual ᴿshame, which shall not be forgotten.   20:11 • Mic. 3:5-7

CHAPTER 24

Jeremiah's Eleventh Sermon:
The Two Baskets of Figs

THE LORD shewed me, and, behold, two baskets of figs were set before the temple of the LORD, after that Neb-u-chad-rez'-zar king of Babylon had carried away captive Jec-o-ni'-ah the son of Je-hoi'-a-kim king of Judah, and the princes of Judah, with the carpenters and smiths, from Jerusalem, and had brought them to Babylon.

2 One basket had very good figs, even like the figs that are first ripe: and the other basket had very naughty figs, which could not be eaten, they were so bad.

3 Then said the LORD unto me, What seest thou, Jer-e'mi'-ah? And I said, Figs; the good figs, very good; and the evil, very evil, that cannot be eaten, they are so evil.

4 Again the word of the LORD came unto me, saying,

5 Thus saith the LORD, the God of Israel; Like these good figs, so will I acknowledge them that are carried away captive of Judah, whom I have sent out of this place into the land of the Chal-de'-ans for their good.

6 For I will set mine eyes upon them for good, and ᴿI will bring them again to this land: and ᴿI will build them, and not pull them down; and I will plant them, and not pluck them up.   12:15; 29:10 • 32:41; 33:7

7 And I will give them ᴿan heart to know me, that I am the LORD: and they shall be ᴿmy people, and I will be their God: for they shall return unto me ᴿwith their whole heart.   [Deut. 30:6; Ezek. 11:19] • [30:22] • [29:13]

8 And as the evil figs, which cannot be eaten, they are so evil; surely thus saith the LORD, So will I give Zed-e-ki'-ah the king of Judah, and his princes, and the residue of Jerusalem, that remain in this land, and them that dwell in the land of Egypt:

9 And I will deliver them to ᴿbe removed into all the kingdoms of the earth for their hurt, ᴿto be a reproach and a proverb, a taunt and a curse, in all places whither I shall drive them.   Deut. 28:25, 37 • Ps. 44:13, 14

10 And I ᴿwill send the sword, the famine, and the pestilence, among them, till they be ᵀconsumed from off the land that I gave unto them and to their fathers.   32:24 • destroyed

CHAPTER 25

Jeremiah's Twelfth Sermon:
The Seventy-year Captivity

THE word that came to Jer-e-mi'-ah concerning all the people of Judah ᴿin the fourth year of Je-hoi'-a-kim the son of Jo-si'-ah king of Judah, that was the first year of Neb-u-chad-rez'-zar king of Babylon;   36:1

2 The which Jer-e-mi'-ah the prophet spake unto all the ᴿpeople of Judah, and to all the inhabitants of Jerusalem, saying,   18:11

3 From the thirteenth year of Jo-si'-ah the son of Amon king of Judah, even unto this day, that is the three and twentieth year, the word of the LORD hath come unto me, and I

have spoken unto you, rising early and speaking; but ye have not ᵀhearkened. *listened*

4 And the LORD hath sent unto you all his servants the prophets, ᴿrising early and sending *them;* but ye have not hearkened, nor inclined your ear to hear.   7:13, 25

5 They said, ᴿTurn ye again now every one from his evil way, and from the evil of your doings, and dwell in the land that the LORD hath given unto you and to your fathers for ever and ever: 18:11; [Jon. 3:8]

6 And go not after other gods to serve them, and to worship them, and provoke me not to anger with the works of your hands; and I will do you no ᵀhurt.   *harm*

7 Yet ye have not ᵀhearkened unto me, saith the LORD; that ye might ᴿprovoke me to anger with the works of your hands to your own hurt.   *listened* • 7:19; 32:30; Deut. 32:21

8 Therefore thus saith the LORD of hosts; Because ye have not heard my words,

9 Behold, I will send and take ᴿall the families of the north, saith the LORD, and Neb-u-chad-rez'-zar the king of Babylon, my servant, and will bring them against this land, and against the inhabitants thereof, and against all these nations round about, and will utterly destroy them, and make them an astonishment, and ᵀan hissing, and perpetual desolations.   1:15; 2 Chr. 36 • *a shame*

10 Moreover I will take from them the ᴿvoice of mirth, and the voice of gladness, the voice of the bridegroom, and the voice of the bride, ᴿthe sound of the millstones, and the light of the candle.   Is. 24:7 • Eccl. 12:4

11 And this whole land shall be a desolation, *and* an ᵀastonishment; and these nations shall serve the king of Babylon seventy ᴿyears.   *horror* • Ezra 1:1; Dan. 9:2; Zech. 7:5

12 And it shall come to pass, when seventy years are accomplished, *that* I ᴿwill punish the king of Babylon, and that nation, saith the LORD, for their iniquity, and the land of the Chal-de'-ans, ᴿand will make it perpetual desolations.   Dan. 5:28, 31 • Is. 13:20

13 And I will bring upon that land all my words which I have pronounced against it, *even* all that is written in ᴿthis book, which Jer-e-mi'-ah hath prophesied against all the nations.   36:4, 29, 32

14 ᴿFor many nations ᴿand great kings shall ᴿserve themselves of them also: ᴿand I will recompense them according to their deeds, and according to the works of their own hands.   50:9 • 51:27 • 27:7 • 50:29

15 For thus saith the LORD God of Israel unto me; Take the wine cup of this ᵀfury at my hand, and cause all the nations, to whom I send thee, to drink it.   *violent anger*

16 And ᴿthey shall drink, and ᵀbe moved, and be mad, because of the sword that I will send among them.   Nah. 3:11 • *reel to and fro*

17 Then took I the cup at the LORD's hand,

and ᴿmade all the nations to drink, unto whom the LORD had sent me: *v.* 28

18 *To wit,* ᴿJerusalem, and the cities of Judah, and the kings thereof, and the princes thereof, to make them a desolation, an astonishment, ᵀan hissing, and ᴿa curse; as *it is* this day;   Ezek. 9:8 • *a shame* • 24:9

19 Pharaoh king of Egypt, and his servants, and his princes, and all his people;

20 And all the mingled people, and all the kings of ᴿthe land of Uz, and all the kings of the land of the Phi-lis'-tines, and Ash'-ke-lon, and Az'-zah, and Ek'-ron, and ᴿthe remnant of Ash'-dod,   Job 1:1 • Is. 20:1

21 ᴿE'-dom, and ᴿMoab, and the children of ᴿAmmon,   49:7–22 • Amos 2:1–3 • Amos 1:13–15

22 And all the kings of Ty'-rus, and all the kings of Zi'-don, and the kings of the isles which *are* beyond the ᴿsea,   49:23

23 ᴿDe'-dan, and Te'-ma, and Buz, and all *that are* in the utmost corners,   49:8

24 And all the kings of ᴿArabia, and all the kings of the ᴿmingled people that dwell in the desert,   2 Chr. 9:14 • 50:37; Ezek. 30:5

25 And all the kings of Zim'-ri, and all the kings of ᴿE'-lam, and all the kings of the Medes,   49:34; Gen. 10:22; Is. 11:11

26 ᴿAnd all the kings of the north, far and near, one with another, and all the kingdoms of the world, which *are* upon the face of the earth: ᴿand the king of She'-shach shall drink after them.   50:9 • 51:41

27 Therefore thou shalt say unto them, Thus saith the LORD of hosts, the God of Israel; Drink ye, and be drunken, and spue, and fall, and rise no more, because of the sword which I will send among you.

28 And it shall be, if they ᴿrefuse to take the cup at thine hand to drink, then shalt thou say unto them, Thus saith the LORD of hosts; Ye shall certainly drink.   Job 34:33

29 For, lo, I begin to bring ᵀevil on the city ᴿwhich is called by my name, and should ye be utterly unpunished? Ye shall not be unpunished: for I will call for a sword upon all the inhabitants of the earth, saith the LORD of hosts.   *disaster* • Dan. 9:18

30 Therefore prophesy thou against them all these words, and say unto them, The LORD shall roar from on high, and utter his voice from his holy habitation; he shall mightily roar upon his habitation; he shall give a shout, as they that tread *the grapes,* against all the inhabitants of the earth.

31 A noise shall come *even* to the ends of the earth; for the LORD hath a controversy with the nations, ᴿhe will plead with all flesh; he will give them *that are* wicked to the sword, saith the LORD.   Joel 3:2

32 Thus saith the LORD of hosts, Behold, evil shall go forth from nation to nation, and ᴿa great whirlwind shall be raised up from the coasts of the earth.   23:19; 30:23

33 And the slain of the LORD shall be at that day from *one* end of the earth even unto the *other* end of the earth: they shall not be lamented, neither gathered, nor buried; they shall be dung upon the ground.

34 ᵀHowl, ye shepherds, and cry; and wallow yourselves *in the ashes*, ye principal of the flock: for the days of your slaughter and of your dispersions are accomplished; and ye shall fall like a pleasant vessel.   *wail*

35 And the shepherds shall have ᴿno way to flee, nor the ᵀprincipal of the flock to escape.   11:11; [Job 11:20]; Amos 2:14 • *chief*

36 A voice of the cry of the shepherds, and an ᵀhowling of the ᵀprincipal of the flock, *shall be heard*: for the LORD hath ᵀspoiled their pasture.   *wailing • chief • ruined*

37 And the peaceable ᵀhabitations ᴿare ᵀcut down because of the fierce ᴿanger of the LORD.   *folds • 5:17 • brought to silence • Is. 66:15*

38 He hath forsaken his ᵀcovert, as the lion: for their land is desolate because of the fierceness of the ᵀoppressor, and because of his fierce anger.   *hiding • oppressing sword*

CHAPTER 26

Conflict with the Nation

IN the beginning of the reign of Je-hoi'-a-kim the son of Jo-si'-ah king of Judah came this word from the LORD, saying,

2 Thus saith the LORD; Stand in the court of the LORD'S house, and speak unto all the cities of Judah, which come to worship in the LORD'S house, ᴿall the words that I command thee to speak unto them; ᴿdiminish not a word: Ezek. 3:10 • Acts 20:27

3 If so be they will hearken, and turn every man from his evil way, that I may repent me of the evil, which I purpose to do unto them because of the evil of their doings.

4 And thou shalt say unto them, Thus saith the LORD; ᴿIf ye will not ᵀhearken to me, to walk in my law, which I have set before you,   17:27; Lev. 26:14, 15; Deut. 28:15 • *listen*

5 To hearken to the words of my servants the prophets, ᴿwhom I sent unto you, both rising up early, and sending *them*, but ye have not hearkened;   7:13, 25; 11:7; 25:3, 4

6 Then will I make this house like Shi'-loh, and will make this city a curse to all the nations of the earth.

7 So the ᴿpriests and the prophets and all the people heard Jer-e-mi'-ah speaking these words in the house of the LORD.   5:31; Mic. 3:11

8 Now it came to pass, when Jer-e-mi'-ah had made an end of speaking all that the LORD had commanded *him* to speak unto all the people, that the ᴿpriests and the prophets

and all the people took him, saying, Thou shalt surely die.   Amos 5:10

9 Why hast thou prophesied in the name of the LORD, saying, This house shall be like Shi'-loh, and this city shall be ᴿdesolate without an inhabitant? And ᴿall the people were gathered against Jer-e-mi'-ah in the house of the LORD.   9:11 • Acts 3:11; 5:12

10 When the princes of Judah heard these things, then they came up from the king's house unto the house of the LORD, and sat down ᵀin the entry of the ᴿnew gate of the LORD'S *house*.   *in the doorway* • 2 Kin. 15:35

11 Then spake the priests and the prophets unto the princes and to all the people, saying, This man *is* worthy to die; ᴿfor he hath prophesied against this city, as ye have heard with your ears.   38:4; Matt. 26:66

12 Then spake Jer-e-mi'-ah unto all the princes and to all the people, saying, The LORD ᴿsent me to prophesy against this house and against this city all the words that ye have heard.   Num. 16:28

13 Therefore now amend your ways and your doings, and obey the voice of the LORD your God; and the LORD will repent him of the evil that he hath pronounced against you.

14 As for me, behold, ᴿI *am* in your hand: do with me ᵀas seemeth good and meet unto you.   38:5 • *as it is good and right in your eyes*

15 But know ye for certain, that if ye put me to death, ye shall surely bring ᴿinnocent blood upon yourselves, and upon this city, and upon the inhabitants thereof: for of a truth the LORD hath sent me unto you to speak all these words in your ears.   7:6

16 Then said the princes and all the people unto the priests and to the prophets; This man *is* not worthy to die: for he hath spoken to us in the name of the LORD our God.

17 ᴿThen rose up certain of the elders of the land, and spake to all the assembly of the people, saying,   Acts 5:34

18 Mi'-cah the Mo'-ras-thite prophesied in the days of Hez-e-ki'-ah king of Judah, and spake to all the people of Judah, saying, Thus saith the LORD of hosts; Zion shall be plowed *like* a field, and Jerusalem shall become heaps, and the mountain of the house as the high places of a forest.

19 Did Hez-e-ki'-ah king of Judah and all Judah put him at all to death? did he not fear the LORD, and besought the LORD, and the LORD repented him of the evil which he had pronounced against them? Thus might we procure great evil against our souls.

20 And there was also a man that prophesied in the name of the LORD, U-ri'-jah the son of She-ma'-iah of Kir'-jath-je'-a-rim, who prophesied against this city and against this land according to all the words of Jer-e-mi'-ah:

21 And when Je-hoi'-a-kim the king, with

all his mighty men, and all the princes, heard his words, the king sought to put him to death: but when U-ri'-jah heard it, he was afraid, and fled, and went into Egypt;

22 And Je-hoi'-a-kim the king sent men into Egypt, namely, ^REl-na'-than the son of Ach'-bor, and certain men with him into Egypt.   36:12

23 And they fetched forth U-ri'-jah out of Egypt, and brought him unto Je-hoi'-a-kim the king; who ^Rslew him with the sword, and cast his dead body into the graves of the common people.   2:30

24 Nevertheless the hand of A-hi'-kam the son of Sha'-phan was with Jer-e-mi'-ah, that they should not give him into the hand of the people to put him to death.

CHAPTER 27

Conflict with the False Prophets

IN the beginning of the reign of ^RJe-hoi'-a-kim the son of Jo-si'-ah ^Rking of Judah came this word unto Jer-e-mi'-ah from the LORD, saying,   2 Kin. 23:34 • vv. 3, 12, 20

2 Thus ^Tsaith the LORD to me; Make thee bonds and yokes, ^Rand put them upon thy neck,   hath the LORD said • Ezek. 4:1; 12:3; 24:3

3 And send them to the king of E'-dom, and to the king of Moab, and to the king of the Am'-mon-ites, and to the king of Ty'-rus, and to the king of Zi'-don, by the hand of the messengers which come to Jerusalem unto Zed-e-ki'-ah king of Judah;

4 And command them ^Tto say unto their masters, Thus saith the LORD of hosts, the God of Israel; Thus shall ye say unto your masters;   concerning their masters, saying

5 ^RI have made the earth, the man and the beast that are upon the ground, by my great power and by my outstretched arm, and ^Rhave given it unto whom it seemed ^Tmeet unto me.   Is. 45:12 • Dan. 4:17, 25, 32 • right

6 And now have I given all these lands into the hand of Neb-u-chad-nez'-zar the king of Babylon, my servant; and the beasts of the field have I given him also to serve him.

7 And all nations shall serve him, and his son, and his son's son, until the very time of his land come: and then many nations and great kings shall serve themselves of him.

8 ^RAnd it shall come to pass, that the nation and kingdom which will not serve the same Neb-u-chad-nez'-zar the king of Babylon, and that will not put their neck under the yoke of the king of Babylon, that nation will I punish, saith the LORD, with the sword, and with the famine, and with the pestilence, until I have consumed them by his hand.   25:12

9 Therefore hearken not ye to your prophets, nor to your diviners, nor to your dreamers, nor to your enchanters, nor to your sorcerers, which speak unto you, saying, Ye shall not serve the king of Babylon:

10 For they prophesy a lie unto you, to remove you far from your land; and that I should drive you out, and ye should perish.

11 But the nations that ^Tbring their neck under the yoke of the king of Babylon, and serve him, those will I let remain still in their own land, saith the LORD; and they shall till it, and dwell therein.   yield to

12 I spake also to ^RZed-e-ki'-ah king of Judah according to all these words, saying, ^TBring your necks under the yoke of the king of Babylon, and serve him and his people, and live.   28:1; 38:17 • yield to

13 ^RWhy will ye die, thou and thy people, by the sword, by the famine, and by the pestilence, as the LORD hath spoken against the nation that will not serve the king of Babylon?   v. 8; 38:23; [Ezek. 18:31]

14 Therefore hearken not unto the words of the prophets that speak unto you, saying, Ye shall not serve the king of Babylon: for they prophesy ^Ra lie unto you.   14:14

15 ^RFor I have not sent them, saith the LORD, yet they prophesy ^Ta lie in my name; that I might drive you out, and that ye might perish, ye, and the prophets that prophesy unto you.   23:21 • what is untrue

16 Also I spake to the priests and to all this people, saying, Thus saith the LORD; Hearken not to the words of your prophets that prophesy unto you, saying, Behold, the vessels of the LORD'S house shall now shortly be brought again from Babylon: for they prophesy a lie unto you.

17 Hearken not unto them; serve the king of Babylon, and live: wherefore should this city be laid waste?

18 But if they be prophets, and if the word of the LORD be with them, let them now make intercession to the LORD of hosts, that the vessels which are left in the house of the LORD, and in the house of the king of Judah, and at Jerusalem, go not to Babylon.

19 For thus saith the LORD of hosts ^Rconcerning the ^Rpillars, and concerning the sea, and concerning the bases, and concerning the residue of the vessels that remain in this city,   2 Kin. 25:13–17 • 52:17, 20, 21

20 Which Neb-u-chad-nez'-zar king of Babylon took not, when he carried away captive Jec-o-ni'-ah the son of Je-hoi'-a-kim king of Judah from Jerusalem to Babylon, and all the nobles of Judah and Jerusalem;

21 Yea, thus saith the LORD of hosts, the God of Israel, concerning the vessels that remain in the house of the LORD, and in the house of the king of Judah and of Jerusalem;

22 They shall be carried to Babylon, and there shall they be until the day that I visit them, saith the LORD; then will I bring them up, and restore them to this place.

CHAPTER 28

Conflict with Hananiah

AND ^Rit came to pass the same year, in the beginning of the reign of Zed-e-ki'-ah king of Judah, in the fourth year, *and* in the fifth month, *that* ^RHan-a-ni'-ah the son of A'-zur the prophet, which *was* of Gib'-e-on, spake unto me in the house of the LORD, in the presence of the priests and of all the people, saying,   27:1; 49:34 • 36:12

2 Thus speaketh the LORD of hosts, the God of Israel, saying, I have ^Tbroken the yoke of the king of Babylon.   *destroyed the power*

3 ^RWithin two full years will I bring again into this place ^Rall the vessels of the LORD'S house, that Neb-u-chad-nez'-zar king of Babylon took away from this place, and carried them to Babylon: 27:16 • 2 Kin. 24:13

4 And I will bring again to this place Jec-o-ni'-ah the son of Je-hoi'-a-kim king of Judah, with all the captives of Judah, that went into Babylon, saith the LORD: for I will break the yoke of the king of Babylon.

5 Then the prophet Jer-e-mi'-ah said unto the prophet Han-a-ni'-ah in the presence of the priests, and in the presence of all the people that stood in the house of the LORD,

6 Even the prophet Jer-e-mi'-ah said, ^RA'-men: the LORD do so: the LORD perform thy words which thou hast prophesied, to bring again the vessels of the LORD'S house, and all that is carried away captive, from Babylon into this place.   Ps. 41:13

7 Nevertheless ^Rhear thou now this word that I speak in thine ears, and in the ears of all the people;   1 Kin. 22:28

8 ^RThe prophets that have been before me and before thee of old prophesied both against many countries, and against great kingdoms, of war, and of evil, and of pestilence.   1 Kin. 14:15; Is. 5:5-7; Joel 1:20; Amos 1:2

9 The prophet which prophesieth of peace, when the word of the prophet shall come to pass, *then* shall the prophet be known, that the LORD hath truly sent him.

10 Then Han-a-ni'-ah the prophet took the ^Ryoke from off the prophet Jer-e-mi'-ah's neck, and brake it.   27:2; 1 Kin. 22:24

11 And Han-a-ni'-ah spake in the presence of all the people, saying, Thus saith the LORD; Even so will I break the yoke of Neb-u-chad-nez'-zar king of Babylon from the neck of all nations within the space of two full years. And the prophet Jer-e-mi'-ah went his way.

12 Then the word of the LORD came unto Jer-e-mi'-ah *the prophet*, after that Han-a-ni'-ah the prophet had broken the yoke from off the neck of the prophet Jer-e-mi'-ah, saying,

13 Go and tell Han-a-ni'-ah, saying, Thus saith the LORD; Thou hast broken the yokes of wood; but thou shalt make for them ^Ryokes of iron.   Ps. 107:16; Is. 45:2

14 For thus saith the LORD of hosts, the God of Israel; ^RI have put a yoke of iron upon the neck of all these nations, that they may serve Neb-u-chad-nez'-zar king of Babylon; and they shall serve him: and I have given him the beasts of the field also.   Deut. 28:48

15 Then said the prophet Jer-e-mi'-ah unto Han-a-ni'-ah the prophet, Hear now, Han-a-ni'-ah; The LORD hath not sent thee; but thou makest this people to trust in a lie.

16 Therefore thus saith the LORD; Behold, I will cast thee from off the face of the earth: this ^Ryear thou shalt die, because thou hast taught rebellion against the LORD.   28:17

17 So Han-a-ni'-ah the prophet died the same year in the seventh month.

CHAPTER 29

First Letter to the Exiles

NOW these *are* the words of the ^Rletter that Jer-e-mi'-ah the prophet sent from Jerusalem unto the ^Tresidue of the elders which were carried away captives, and to the priests, and to the prophets, ^Rand to all the people whom Neb-u-chad-nez'-zar had ^Rcarried away captive from Jerusalem to Babylon;   22:24-28 • *rest* • 2 Kin. 24:12-16 • 27:20

2 (After that Jec-o-ni'-ah the king, and the queen, and the eunuchs, the princes of Judah and Jerusalem, and the carpenters, and the smiths, were departed from Jerusalem;)

3 By the hand of El'-a-sah the son of ^RSha'-phan, and Gem-a-ri'-ah the son of ^RHil-ki'-ah, (whom Zed-e-ki'-ah king of Judah sent unto Babylon to Neb-u-chad-nez'-zar king of Babylon) saying,   2 Chr. 34:8 • 1 Chr. 6:13

4 Thus saith the LORD of hosts, the God of Israel, unto all that are carried away captives, whom I have ^Rcaused to be carried away from Jerusalem unto Babylon;   24:5

5 Build ye houses, and dwell *in them;* and plant gardens, and eat the fruit of them;

6 Take ye ^Rwives, and beget sons and daughters; and take wives for your sons, and give your daughters to husbands, that they may bear sons and daughters; that ye may be increased there, and not diminished.   16:2-4

7 And seek the peace of the city whither I have caused you to be carried away captives, and pray unto the LORD for it: for in the peace thereof shall ye have peace.

8 For thus saith the LORD of hosts, the God of Israel; Let not your prophets and your diviners, that *be* in the midst of you, ^Rdeceive you, neither hearken to your dreams which ye cause to be dreamed.   23:21

9 For they prophesy ^Tfalsely^R unto you in my name: ^RI have not sent them, saith the LORD.   *deceitfully* • 27:15 • v. 31

10 For thus saith the LORD, That after ^Rseventy years be accomplished at Babylon I will visit you, and perform my good word

toward you, in causing you to return to this place.   25:12; 27:22; 2 Chr. 36:21, 22; Ezra 1:1

11 For I know the Rthoughts that I think toward you, saith the LORD, thoughts of peace, and not of evil, to give you Tan expected end.   30:18-22 • hope in your latter end

12 Then shall ye Rcall upon me, and ye shall go and pray unto me, and I will Rhearken unto you.   Dan. 9:3 • Ps. 145:19

13 And Rye shall seek me, and find me, when ye shall search for me Rwith all your heart.   Lev. 26:39, 40; Deut. 4:29; 30:1 • 24:7

14 And RI will be found of you, saith the LORD: and I will turn away your captivity, and I will gather you from all the nations, and from all the places whither I have driven you, saith the LORD; and I will bring you again into the place whence I caused you to be carried away captive.   [Deut. 4:7]

15 Because ye have said, The LORD hath raised us up prophets in RBabylon;   vv. 21, 24

16 RKnow that thus saith the LORD of the king that sitteth upon the throne of David, and of all the people that dwelleth in this city, and of your brethren that are not gone forth with you into captivity;   38:2, 3

17 Thus saith the LORD of hosts; Behold, I will send upon them the Rsword, the famine, and the pestilence, and will make them like Rvile T figs, that cannot be eaten, they are so Tevil.   v. 18; 24:10; 32:24 • 24:8 • rotten • bad

18 And I will persecute them with the sword, with the famine, and with the pestilence, and will deliver them to be removed to all the kingdoms of the earth, to be a curse, and an astonishment, and an hissing, and a reproach, among all the nations whither I have driven them:

19 Because they have not hearkened to my words, saith the LORD, which RI sent unto them by my servants the prophets, rising up early and sending them; but ye would not hear, saith the LORD.   25:4; 32:33

20 Hear ye therefore the word of the LORD, all ye of the captivity, whom RI have sent from Jerusalem to Babylon: Mic. 4:10

21 Thus saith the LORD of hosts, the God of Israel, of Ahab the son of Ko-la′-iah, and of Zed-e-ki′-ah the son of Ma-a-se′-iah, which prophesy a lie unto you in my name; Behold, I will deliver them into the hand of Neb-u-chad-rez′-zar king of Babylon; and he shall slay them before your eyes;

22 And of them shall be taken up a curse by all the captivity of Judah which are in Babylon, saying, The LORD make thee like Zed-e-ki′-ah and like Ahab, whom the king of Babylon roasted in the fire;

23 Because Rthey have committed villany in Israel, and have committed adultery with their neighbours' wives, and have spoken lying words in my name, which I have not

commanded them; even I know, and am a witness, saith the LORD.   23:14

Letter from Shemaiah

24 Thus shalt thou also speak to She-ma′-iah the TNe-hel′-a-mite, saying,   dreamer

25 Thus speaketh the LORD of hosts, the God of Israel, saying, Because thou hast sent letters in thy name unto all the people that are at Jerusalem, Rand to Zeph-a-ni′-ah the son of Ma-a-se′-iah the priest, and to all the priests, saying,   21:1; 2 Kin. 25:18

26 The LORD hath made thee priest in the stead of Je-hoi′-a-da the priest, that ye should be officers in the house of the LORD, for every man that is mad, Tand maketh himself a prophet, that thou shouldest put him in prison, and in the stocks.   unbalanced

27 Now therefore why hast thou not Rreproved Jer-e-mi′-ah of An′-a-thoth, which maketh himself a prophet to you?   Num. 16:3

28 For therefore he sent unto us in Babylon, saying, This captivity is long: build ye houses, and dwell in them; and plant gardens, and eat the fruit of them.

29 And Zeph-a-ni′-ah the priest read this letter in the ears of Jer-e-mi′-ah the prophet.

Second Letter to the Exiles

30 Then came the word of the LORD unto Jer-e-mi′-ah, saying,

31 Send to all them of the captivity, saying, Thus saith the LORD concerning She-ma′-iah the Ne-hel′-a-mite; Because that She-ma′-iah hath prophesied unto you, and I sent him not, and he caused you to trust in a lie:

32 Therefore thus saith the LORD; Behold, I will punish She-ma′-iah the Ne-hel′-a-mite, and his seed: he shall not have a man to dwell among this people; neither shall he behold the good that I will do for my people, saith the LORD; because he hath taught rebellion against the LORD.

CHAPTER 30

Restoration to the Land

THE word that came to Jer-e-mi′-ah from the LORD, saying,

2 Thus speaketh the LORD God of Israel, saying, RWrite thee all the words that I have spoken unto thee in a book.   25:13; 36:4

3 For, lo, the days come, saith the LORD, that RI will bring again the captivity of my people Israel and Judah, saith the LORD: Rand I will cause them to return to the land that I gave to their fathers, and they shall possess it.   v. 18; Amos 9:14, 15 • 16:15

4 And these are the words that the LORD spake concerning Israel and concerning Judah.

5 For thus saith the LORD; We have heard a voice of ᴿtrembling, ᵀof fear, and not of peace.　6:25; 8:16; Is. 5:30; Amos 5:16–18 • *of fright*

6 Ask ye now, and see whether a man doth ᵀtravail with child? wherefore do I see every man with his hands on his loins, ᴿas a woman in travail, and all faces are turned into paleness?　*have labour pains* • 4:31; 6:24

7 Alas! for that day *is* great, so that none *is* like it: it *is* even the time of Jacob's trouble; but he shall be saved out of it.

8 For it shall come to pass in that day, saith the LORD of hosts, *that* I will break ᵀhis yoke from off thy neck, and will burst thy bonds, and strangers shall no more serve themselves of him:　*his power over you*

9 But they shall serve the LORD their God, and ᴿDavid their king, whom I will ᴿraise up unto them.　Hos. 3:5 • [Luke 1:69] ✩

10 Therefore fear thou not, O my servant Jacob, saith the LORD; neither be dismayed, O Israel: for, lo, I will save thee from afar, and thy seed ᴿfrom the land of their captivity; and Jacob shall return, and shall be in rest, and be quiet, and none shall make *him* afraid.　3:18

11 For I *am* with thee, saith the LORD, to save thee: ᴿthough I make a full end of all nations whither I have scattered thee, yet will I not make a full end of thee: but I will correct thee in measure, and will not leave thee altogether unpunished.　Amos 9:8

12 For thus saith the LORD, Thy bruise *is* incurable, *and* thy wound *is* grievous.

13 *There is* none to plead thy cause, that thou mayest be bound up: ᴿthou hast no healing medicines.　8:22; 14:19; 46:11

14 ᴿAll thy lovers have forgotten thee; they seek thee not; for I have wounded thee with the wound of an enemy, with the chastisement ᴿof a cruel one, for the multitude of thine iniquity; ᴿ*because* thy sins were increased.　Lam. 1:2 • Job 30:21 • 5:6

15 Why criest thou for thine affliction? thy sorrow *is* incurable for the multitude of thine iniquity: *because* thy sins were increased, I have done these things unto thee.

16 Therefore all they that devour thee shall be devoured; and all thine adversaries, every one of them, shall go into captivity; and they that spoil thee shall be a spoil, and all that prey upon thee will I give for a prey.

17 ᴿFor I will restore health unto thee, and I will heal thee of thy wounds, saith the LORD; because they called thee an Outcast, *saying*, This *is* Zion, whom no man seeketh after.　8:22; 33:6; Ps. 107:20

18 Thus saith the LORD; Behold, I will bring again the captivity of Jacob's tents, and have mercy on his dwellingplaces; and the city shall be builded ᵀupon her own heap, and the palace shall remain after the manner thereof.　*upon her own site*

19 And out of them shall proceed thanks-giving and the voice of them that make merry: and I will multiply them, and they shall not be few; I will also glorify them, and they shall not be small.

20 Their children also shall be ᴿas ᵀaforetime, and their congregation shall be ᴿestablished before me, and I will punish all that oppress them.　Is. 1:26 • *beforetime* • [Is. 54:14]

21 And their nobles shall be of themselves, and their governor shall proceed from the midst of them; and I will ᴿcause him to draw near, and he shall approach unto me: for who *is* this that engaged his heart to approach unto me? saith the LORD.　50:44; Num. 16:5; Ps. 65:4

22 And ye shall be ᴿmy people, and I will be your God.　32:38; Ex. 6:7; Hos. 2:23

23 Behold, the whirlwind of the LORD goeth forth with ᵀfury, a ᵀcontinuing whirlwind: it shall ᵀfall with pain upon the head of the wicked.　*violent anger* • *cutting* • *remain*

24 The fierce anger of the LORD shall not return, until he have done *it*, and until he have performed the intents of his heart: in the latter days ye shall consider it.

CHAPTER 31

Israel Is Restored

AT ᴿthe same time, saith the LORD, will I be the God of all the families of Israel, and they shall be my people.　30:24

2 Thus saith the LORD, The people *which were* left of the sword found grace in the wilderness; *even* Israel, when ᴿI went to cause him to rest.　Deut. 1:33; Ps. 95:11; Is. 63:14

3 The LORD hath appeared of old unto me, *saying*, Yea, ᴿI have loved thee with an everlasting love: therefore with lovingkindness have I drawn thee.　Mal. 1:2

4 Again I will build thee, and thou shalt be built, O virgin of Israel: thou shalt again be adorned with thy tabrets, and shalt go forth in the dances of them that ᴿmake merry.　30:19

5 Thou shalt yet plant vines upon the mountains of Sa-ma′-ri-a: the planters shall plant, and shall eat *them* as common things.

6 For there shall be a day, *that* the watchmen upon the mount E′-phra-im shall cry, ᴿArise ye, and let us go up to Zion unto the LORD our God.　[Is. 2:3; Mic. 4:2]

7 For thus saith the LORD: ᴿSing with gladness for Jacob, and shout among the ᴿchief of the nations: publish ye, praise ye, and say, O LORD, save thy people, the remnant of Israel.　Ps. 14:7; Is. 12:5, 6 • [Deut. 28:13]

8 Behold, I will bring them from the north country, and ᴿgather them from the coasts of the earth, *and* with them the blind and the lame, the woman with child and her that travaileth with child together: a great company shall return thither.　Ezek. 20:34, 41; 34:13

9 They shall come with weeping, and with Tsupplications will I lead them: I will cause them to walk by the rivers of waters in a straight way, wherein they shall not stumble: for I am a father to Israel, and E'-phra-im is my Rfirstborn.   blessings • Ex. 4:22

10 Hear the word of the LORD, O ye nations, and declare it in the Risles afar off, and say, He that scattered Israel Rwill gather him, and keep him, as a shepherd doth his flock.   25:22; Is. 66:19 • Is. 40:11

11 For the LORD hath redeemed Jacob, and ransomed him Rfrom the hand of him that was Rstronger than he.   Is. 49:24 • Ps. 142:6

12 Therefore they shall come and sing in the height of Zion, and shall flow together to the goodness of the LORD, for wheat, and for wine, and for oil, and for the young of the flock and of the herd: and their soul shall be as a watered garden; and they shall not sorrow any more at all.

13 RThen shall the virgin rejoice in the dance, both young men and old together: for I will turn their mourning into joy, and will comfort them, and make them rejoice from their sorrow.   Judg. 21:21; Is. 51:11

14 And I will Tsatiate the soul of the priests with fatness, and my people shall be satisfied with my goodness, saith the LORD.   satisfy

15 Thus saith the LORD; A voice was heard in Ra'-mah, lamentation, and bitter weeping; Ra'-hel weeping for her children refused to be comforted for her children, because Rthey were not.   Gen. 42:13; Matt. 2:17 ☆

16 Thus saith the LORD; Refrain thy voice from weeping, Rand thine eyes from tears: for thy work shall be rewarded, saith the LORD; and they shall come again from the land of the enemy.   Ruth 2:12; [Is. 30:19]

17 And there is hope in thine end, saith the LORD, that thy children shall come again to their own border.

18 I have surely heard E'-phra-im bemoaning himself thus; Thou hast chastised me, and I was chastised, as a bullock unaccustomed to the yoke: turn thou me, and I shall be turned; for thou art the LORD my God.

19 Surely after that I was turned, I repented; and after that I was instructed, I Tsmote upon my thigh: I was ashamed, yea, even confounded, because I did bear the reproach of my youth.   acknowledged my sin

20 Is E'-phra-im my dear son? is he a pleasant child? for since I spake against him, I do earnestly remember him still: Rthere-

fore Tmy bowels are troubled for him; RI will surely have mercy upon him, saith the LORD.   Is. 63:15 • my emotions are stirred • Is. 57:18

21 Set thee up waymarks, make thee Thigh heaps: Rset thine heart toward the highway, even the way which thou wentest: turn again, O virgin of Israel, turn again to these thy cities.   guideposts • 50:5

Judah Is Restored

22 How long wilt thou Rgo about, O thou Rbacksliding daughter? for the LORD hath created a new thing in the earth, A woman shall compass a man.   2:18, 23, 36 • 3:6, 8

23 Thus saith the LORD of hosts, the God of Israel; As yet they shall use this speech in the land of Judah and in the cities thereof, when I shall bring again their captivity; RThe LORD bless thee, O habitation of justice, and mountain of holiness.   Is. 1:26

24 And there shall dwell in Judah itself, and in all the cities thereof together, husbandmen, and they that go forth with flocks.

25 RFor I have Tsatiated the weary soul, and I have Rreplenished every sorrowful soul.   Ps. 107:9; [Matt. 5:6] • satisfied • [John 4:14]

26 Upon this I Rawaked, and beheld; and my sleep was sweet unto me.   Zech. 4:1

27 Behold, the days come, saith the LORD, that RI will sow the house of Israel and the house of Judah with the seed of man, and with the seed of beast.   Ezek. 36:9–11; Hos. 2:23

28 And it shall come to pass, that like as I have Rwatched over them, Rto pluck up, and to break down, and to throw down, and to destroy, and to afflict; so will I watch over them, Rto build, and to plant, saith the LORD.   44:27 • 1:10; 18:7 • 24:6

29 In those days they shall say no more, The fathers have eaten a sour grape, and the children's teeth are set on edge.

30 But every one shall die for his own iniquity: every man that eateth the sour grape, his teeth shall be set on edge.

31 Behold, the days come, saith the LORD, that I will make a new covenant with the house of Israel, and with the house of Judah:

32 RNot according to the covenant that I made with their fathers in the day that RI took them by the hand to bring them out of the land of Egypt; which my covenant they brake, although I was an husband unto them, saith the LORD: [Luke 22:20] ☆ • Deut. 1:31

33 But this shall be the covenant that I will

31:31–34 The New Covenant—The New Covenant is the fifth and last of the theocratic covenants (pertaining to the rule of God). Four provisions are made in this covenant: (1) regeneration—God will put His law in their inward parts and write it in their hearts, 31:33; (2) a national restoration—Yahweh will be their God and the nation will be His people, 31:33; (3) personal ministry of the Holy Spirit—they will all be taught individually by God, 31:34; and (4) full justification—their sins will be forgiven and completely removed, 31:34. The New Covenant is made sure by the blood that Jesus shed on Calvary's cross. That blood which guarantees to Israel its New Covenant also provides for the forgiveness of sins

make with the house of Israel; After those days, saith the LORD, ^RI will put my law in their inward parts, and write it in their hearts; ^Rand will be their God, and they shall be my people.   Ps. 40:8 • Heb. 10:15–17 ☆

34 And they shall teach no more every man his neighbour, and every man his brother, saying, Know the LORD: for ^Rthey shall all ^Tknow me, from the least of them unto the greatest of them, saith the LORD: for I will forgive their iniquity, and I will remember their sin no more.   Is. 11:9 ☆ • honor

35 Thus saith the LORD, ^Rwhich giveth the sun for a light by day, and the ordinances of the moon and of the stars for a light by night, which divideth ^Rthe sea when the waves thereof roar; ^RThe LORD of hosts is his name: Ps. 72:5, 17; 89:2, 36 • Is. 51:15 • 10:16

36 ^RIf those ordinances depart from before me, saith the LORD, then the seed of Israel also shall cease from being a nation before me for ever.   33:20; Ps. 148:6; Is. 54:9, 10

37 Thus saith the LORD; ^RIf heaven above can be measured, and the foundations of the earth searched out beneath, I will also cast off all the seed of Israel for all that they have done, saith the LORD.   33:22

38 Behold, the days come, saith the LORD, that the city shall be built to the LORD ^Rfrom the tower of Ha-nan'-e-el unto ^Rthe gate of the corner.   Zech. 14:10 • 2 Kin. 14:13

39 And ^Rthe measuring line shall yet go forth over against it upon the hill Ga'-reb, and shall compass about to Go'-ath.   Zech. 2:1

40 And the whole valley of the dead bodies, and of the ashes, and all the fields unto the brook of Kid'-ron, unto the corner of the horse gate toward the east, shall be holy unto the LORD; it shall not be plucked up, nor thrown down any more for ever.

CHAPTER 32

Rebuilding of Jerusalem

THE word that came to Jer-e-mi'-ah from the LORD in the tenth year of Zed-e-ki'-ah king of Judah, which was the eighteenth year of Neb-u-chad-rez'-zar.

2 For then the king of Babylon's army besieged Jerusalem: and Jer-e-mi'-ah the prophet was shut up in the court of the prison, which was in the king of Judah's house.

3 For Zed-e-ki'-ah king of Judah had shut him up, saying, Wherefore dost thou prophesy, and say, Thus saith the LORD, Behold, I

will give this city into the hand of the king of Babylon, and he shall take it;

4 And Zed-e-ki'-ah king of Judah ^Rshall not escape out of the hand of the Chal-de'-ans, but shall surely be delivered into the hand of the king of Babylon, and shall speak with him mouth to mouth, and his eyes shall behold his eyes;   34:3; 38:18, 23; 39:4–7

5 And he shall lead Zed-e-ki'-ah to Babylon, and there shall he be ^Runtil I visit him, saith the LORD: though ye fight with the Chal-de'-ans, ye shall not prosper.   27:22

6 And Jer-e-mi'-ah said, The word of the LORD came unto me, saying,

7 Behold, Ha-nam'-e-el the son of Shal'-lum thine uncle shall come unto thee, saying, Buy thee my field that is in An'-a-thoth: for the right of redemption is thine to buy it.

8 So Ha-nam'-e-el mine uncle's son came to me in the court of the prison according to the word of the LORD, and said unto me, Buy my field, I pray thee, that is in An'-a-thoth, which is in the country of Benjamin: for the right of inheritance is thine, and the redemption is thine; buy it for thyself. Then I knew that this was the word of the LORD.

9 And I bought the field of Ha-nam'-e-el my uncle's son, that was in An'-a-thoth, and weighed him the money, even ^Tseventeen shek'-els of silver. $2,176

10 And I ^Rsubscribed the ^Tevidence, and sealed it, and took witnesses, and weighed him the money in the balances.   v. 44 • deed

11 So I took the evidence of the purchase, both that which was sealed according to the law and custom, and that which was open:

12 And I gave the evidence of the purchase unto Ba'-ruch the son of Ne-ri'-ah, the son of Ma-a-se'-iah, in the sight of Ha-nam'-e-el mine uncle's son, and in the presence of the witnesses that subscribed the book of the purchase, before all the Jews that sat in the court of the prison.

13 And I charged Ba'-ruch before them, saying,

14 Thus saith the LORD of hosts, the God of Israel; Take these evidences, this ^Tevidence of the purchase, both which is sealed, and this evidence which is open; and put them in an earthen vessel, that they may continue many days.   deed

15 For thus saith the LORD of hosts, the God of Israel; Houses and fields and vineyards shall be possessed again in this land.

16 Now when I had delivered the ^Tevidence of the purchase unto Ba'-ruch the son

---

for the believers who comprise the church. Jesus' payment for sins is more than adequate to pay for the sins of all who will believe in Him. The New Covenant is called "new" in contrast to the covenant with Moses which is called "old" (Jer. 31:32; Page 1219—Heb. 8:6–13) because it actually accomplishes what the Mosaic Covenant could only point to, that is, the child of God living in a manner that is consistent with the character of God.
Now turn to Page 20—THE CHRISTIAN'S GUIDE: Understanding God's Being.

of Ne-ri'-ah, I ᴿprayed unto the LORD, saying,   *deed* • 12:1; Gen. 32:9–12; [Phil. 4:6, 7]

17 Ah Lord GOD! behold, thou hast made the heaven and the earth by thy great power and stretched out arm, *and* there is nothing ᵀtoo hard for thee: *hid from thee*

18 Thou shewest lovingkindness unto thousands, and recompensest the iniquity of the fathers into the bosom of their children after them: the Great, ᴿthe Mighty God, the LORD of hosts, *is* his name,   [Is. 9:6]

19 ᴿGreat in counsel, and mighty in ᵀwork: for thine eyes *are* open upon all the ways of the sons of men: to give every one according to his ways, and according to the fruit of his doings: [Is. 9:6; 28:29] • *doing*

20 Which hast set signs and wonders in the land of Egypt, *even* unto this day, and in Israel, and among *other* men; and hast made thee ᴿa name, as at this day;   Ex. 9:16

21 And ᴿhast brought forth thy people Israel out of the land of Egypt with signs, and with wonders, and with a strong hand, and with a stretched out arm, and with great terror;   2 Sam. 7:23; 1 Chr. 17:21; Ps. 136:11, 12

22 And hast given them this land, which thou didst swear to their fathers to give them, a land flowing with milk and honey;

23 And they came in, and possessed it; but ᴿthey obeyed not thy voice, neither walked in thy law; they have done nothing of all that thou commandedst them to do: therefore thou hast caused all this evil to come upon them: 11:8; [Neh. 9:26; Dan. 9:10–14]

24 Behold the mounts, they are come unto the city to take it; and the city is given into the hand of the Chal-de'-ans, that fight against it, because of the ᴿsword, and of the famine, and of the pestilence: and what thou hast spoken is come to pass; and, behold, thou seest *it*.   *v.* 36; 29:17

25 And thou hast said unto me, O Lord GOD, Buy thee the field for money, and take witnesses; ᵀfor the city is given into the hand of the Chal-de'-ans.   *though*

26 Then came the word of the LORD unto Jer-e-mi'-ah, saying,

27 Behold, I *am* the LORD, the God of all flesh: is there any thing too hard for me?

28 Therefore thus saith the LORD; Behold, I will give this city into the hand of the Chal-de'-ans, and into the hand of ᴿNeb-u-chad-rez'-zar king of Babylon, and he shall take it: *vv.* 3, 24, 36; 19:7–12; 34:2, 3

29 And the Chal-de'-ans, that fight against this city, shall ᴿcome and set fire on this city, and burn it with the houses, upon whose roofs they have offered incense unto Ba'-al, and poured out drink offerings unto other gods, to provoke me to anger.   2 Kin. 25:9

30 For the children of Israel and the children of Judah have only done evil before me from their youth: for the children of Israel

have only provoked me to anger with the work of their hands, saith the LORD.

31 For this city hath been to me *as* ᵀa ᴿprovocation of mine anger and of my fury from the day that they built it even unto this day; ᴿthat I should remove it from before my face,   *an irritation* • 5:9–11 • 2 Kin. 24:3

32 Because of all the evil of the children of Israel and of the children of Judah, which they have done to provoke me to anger, they, their kings, their princes, their priests, and their prophets, and the men of Judah, and the inhabitants of Jerusalem.

33 And they have turned unto me the ᴿback, and not the face: though I taught them, ᴿrising up early and ᴿteaching *them*, yet they have not hearkened to receive instruction.   2:27; 7:24 • 25:3; 26:5 • 7:13

34 But they ᴿset their ᵀabominations in ᵀthe house, which is called by my name, to defile it.   23:11; Ezek. 8:5, 6 • *idols* • *the temple*

35 And they built the high places of Ba'-al, which *are* in the valley of the son of Hin'-nom, to cause their sons and their daughters to pass through *the fire* unto Mo'-lech; which I commanded them not, neither came it into my mind, that they should do this abomination, to cause Judah to sin.

36 And now therefore thus saith the LORD, the God of Israel, concerning this city, whereof ye say, It shall be delivered into the hand of the king of Babylon by the sword, and by the famine, and by the pestilence;

37 Behold, I will gather them out of all countries, whither I have driven them in mine anger, and in my fury, and in great wrath; and I will bring them again unto this place, and I will cause them to dwell safely:

38 And they shall be ᴿmy people, and I will be their God: [24:7; 30:22; 31:33]

39 And I will ᴿgive them one heart, and one way, that they may fear me for ever, for the good of them, and of their children after them: [24:7; 31:33; Ezek. 11:19; Eph. 4:4–6]

40 And ᴿI will make an everlasting covenant with them, that I will not turn away from them, to do them good; but ᴿI will put my fear in their hearts, that they shall not depart from me.   31:31; Is. 55:3 • [31:33]

41 Yea, I will ᴿrejoice over them to do them good, and I will plant them in this land ᵀassuredly with my whole heart and with my whole soul.   Deut. 30:9 • *in truth*

42 For thus saith the LORD; ᴿLike as I have brought all this great evil upon this people, so will I bring upon them all the good that I have promised them.   31:28

43 And ᴿfields shall be bought in this land, ᴿwhereof ye say, *It is* desolate without man or beast; it is given into the hand of the Chal-de'-ans.   [Ezek. 37:11–14] • 33:10

44 Men shall buy fields for money, and subscribe ᵀevidences, and seal *them*, and take

witnesses in Rthe land of Benjamin, and in the places about Jerusalem, and in the cities of Judah, and in the cities of the mountains, and in the cities of the valley, and in the cities of the south: for RI will cause their captivity to return, saith the LORD. *the deeds* • 17:26 • 33:7, 11

CHAPTER 33

Reconfirming the Covenant

MOREOVER the word of the LORD came unto Jer-e-mi'-ah the second time, while he was yet Rshut up in the court of the prison, saying,   32:2, 3

2 Thus saith the LORD the Rmaker thereof, the LORD that formed it, to establish it; Tthe LORD *is* his name;   Is. 37:26 • *Yahweh*

3 Call unto me, and I will answer thee, and shew thee great and Tmighty Rthings, which thou knowest not.   *hidden* • Is. 48:6

4 For thus saith the LORD, the God of Israel, concerning the houses of this city, and concerning the Rhouses of the kings of Judah, which are thrown down by the Tmounts, and by the sword;   2 Kin. 25:9 • *siege mounds*

5 They come to fight with the Chal-de'-ans, but *it is* to fill them with the dead bodies of men, whom I have slain in mine anger and in my fury, and for all whose wickedness I have hid my face from this city.

6 Behold, I will bring it health and cure, and I will cure them, and will reveal unto them the abundance of peace and truth.

7 And I will cause the captivity of Judah and the captivity of Israel to return, and will build them, Ras at the first.   Is. 1:26

8 And I will cleanse them from all their iniquity, whereby they have sinned against me; and I will Rpardon all their iniquities, whereby they have sinned, and whereby they have transgressed against me.   [31:34]

9 And it shall be to me a name of joy, a praise and an honour before all the nations of the earth, which shall hear all the good that I do unto them: and they shall fear and tremble for all the goodness and for all the prosperity that I procure unto it.

10 Thus saith the LORD; Again there shall be heard in this place, Rwhich ye say *shall be* desolate without man and without beast, *even* in the cities of Judah, and in the streets of Jerusalem, that are Tdesolate, without man, and without inhabitant, and without beast,   32:43 • *a waste*

11 The Rvoice of joy, and the voice of gladness, the voice of the bridegroom, and the voice of the bride, the voice of them that shall say, Praise the LORD of hosts: for the LORD *is* good; for his mercy *endureth* for ever: *and* of them that shall bring the sacrifice of praise into the house of the LORD.

For I will cause to return the captivity of the land, as at the first, saith the LORD. Rev. 18:23

12 Thus saith the LORD of hosts; Again in this place, which is desolate without man and without beast, and in all the cities thereof, shall be an habitation of shepherds causing *their* flocks to lie down.

13 RIn the cities of the mountains, in the cities of the vale, and in the cities of the south, and in the land of Benjamin, and in the places about Jerusalem, and in the cities of Judah, shall the flocks Rpass again under the hands of him that Ttelleth *them*, saith the LORD.   17:26 • 32:44 • *counts*

14 Behold, the days come, saith the LORD, that RI will perform that good thing which I have promised unto the house of Israel and to the house of Judah.   29:10

15 In those days, and at that time, will I cause the RBranch of righteousness to grow up unto David; and he shall execute judgment and righteousness in the land.   Zech. 6:12, 13 ☆

16 In those days shall RJudah be saved, and Jerusalem shall dwell safely: and this *is* the name wherewith she shall be called, RThe LORD our righteousness. Is. 45:17, 22 ☆ • [1 Cor. 1:30]

17 For thus saith the LORD; David shall never Rwant T a man to sit upon the throne of the house of Israel;   [Luke 1:32] • *be without*

18 Neither shall the priests the Levites want a man before me to Roffer burnt offerings, and to Tkindle meat offerings, and to do sacrifice continually.   [Rev. 1:6] • *burn*

19 And the word of the LORD came unto Jer-e-mi'-ah, saying,

20 Thus saith the LORD; If ye can Rbreak my covenant of the day, and my covenant of the night, and that there should not be day and night in their season;   *v.* 25; 31:35–37

21 *Then* may also my covenant be broken with David my servant, that he should not have a son to reign upon his throne; and with the Levites the priests, my ministers.

22 As Rthe host of heaven cannot be numbered, neither the Rsand of the sea measured: so will I multiply the seed of David my servant, and the Levites that minister unto me.   Gen. 15:5; Ezek. 36:10, 11 • Gen. 22:17

23 Moreover the word of the LORD came to Jer-e-mi'-ah, saying,

24 Considerest thou not what this people have spoken, saying, The two families which the LORD hath chosen, he hath even cast them off? thus they have Rdespised my people, that they should be no more a nation before them.   Neh. 4:2–4; Esth. 3:6, 8

25 Thus saith the LORD; If Rmy covenant T*be* not with day and night, *and if* I have not appointed the ordinances of heaven and earth;   31:35–37 • *of day and night stand out*

26 Then will I cast away the seed of Jacob, and David my servant, *so* that I will not take

any of his seed *to be* ᴿrulers over the seed of Abraham, Isaac, and Jacob: for I will cause their captivity to return, and have ᴿmercy on them. 　　　　　　　　Gen. 49:10 • 31:20

CHAPTER 34

Message to Zedekiah

THE word which came unto Jer-e-mi′-ah from the LORD, when Neb-u-chad-nez′-zar king of Babylon, and all his army, and all the kingdoms of the earth of his dominion, and all the people, fought against Jerusalem, and against all the cities thereof, saying,

2 Thus saith the LORD, the God of Israel; Go and speak to Zed-e-ki′-ah king of Judah, and tell him, Thus saith the LORD; Behold, I will give this city into the hand of the king of Babylon, and he shall burn it with fire:

3 And ᴿthou shalt not escape out of his hand, but shalt surely be taken, and delivered into his hand; and thine eyes shall behold the eyes of the king of Babylon, and he shall speak with thee mouth to mouth, and thou shalt go to Babylon. 　　　　　2 Kin. 25:4–7

4 Yet hear the word of the LORD, O Zed-e-ki′-ah king of Judah; Thus saith the LORD of thee, Thou shalt not die by the sword:

5 *But* thou shalt die in peace: and with the burnings of thy fathers, the former kings which were before thee, so shall they burn *odours* for thee; and they will lament thee, *saying*, Ah lord! for I have pronounced the word, saith the LORD.

6 Then Jer-e-mi′-ah the prophet spake ᴿall these words unto Zed-e-ki′-ah king of Judah in Jerusalem, 　　　1 Sam. 3:18; 15:16–24

7 When the king of Babylon's army fought against Jerusalem, and against all the cities of Judah that were left, against ᴿLa′-chish, and against A-ze′-kah: for these defenced cities remained of the cities of Judah. 　　Josh. 10:3, 5

Message to the People

8 *This is* the word that came unto Jer-e-mi′-ah from the LORD, after that the king Zed-e-ki′-ah had ᴿmade a covenant with all the people which *were* at Jerusalem, to proclaim liberty unto them; 　　2 Kin. 11:17

9 That every man should let his manservant, and every man his maidservant, *being* an Hebrew or an Hebrewess, go free; ᴿthat none should serve himself of them, *to wit*, of a Jew his brother. 　　　　　Lev. 25:39–46

10 Now when all the princes, and all the people, which had entered into the covenant, heard that every one should let his manservant, and every one his maidservant, go free, that none should serve themselves of them any more, then they obeyed, and let *them* go.

11 But ᴿafterward they turned, and caused the servants and the handmaids, whom they had let go free, to return, and brought them into subjection for servants and for handmaids. 　　　v. 21; 37:5; Ps. 78:34–36; Hos. 6:1

12 Therefore the word of the LORD came to Jer-e-mi′-ah from the LORD, saying,

13 Thus saith the LORD, the God of Israel; I ᴿmade a covenant with your fathers in the day that I brought them forth out of the land of Egypt, out of the house of bondmen, saying, 　　　　31:32; Ex. 24:3, 7, 8

14 At the end of seven years let ye go every man his brother an Hebrew, which hath been sold unto thee; and when he hath served thee six years, thou shalt let him go free from thee: but your fathers hearkened not unto me, neither inclined their ear.

15 And ye were now turned, and had done right in my sight, in proclaiming liberty every man to his neighbour; and ye had ᴿmade a covenant before me in the house which is called by my name: 　　　　2 Kin. 23:3

16 But ye turned and ᴿpolluted my name, and caused every man his servant, and every man his handmaid, whom he had set at liberty at their pleasure, to return, and brought them into subjection, to be unto you for servants and for handmaids. 　　Ex. 20:7

17 Therefore thus saith the LORD; Ye have not hearkened unto me, in proclaiming liberty, every one to his brother, and every man to his neighbour: behold, I ᴿproclaim a liberty for you, saith the LORD, to the sword, to the pestilence, and to the famine; and I will make you to be removed into all the kingdoms of the earth. 　　2 Kin. 25; 2 Chr. 36

18 And ᴿI will give the men that have transgressed my covenant, which have not performed the words of the covenant which they had made before me, when ᴿthey cut the calf in ᵀtwain, and passed between the parts thereof, 　　　　Hos. 6:7 • Gen. 15:10, 17 • *two*

19 The ᴿprinces of Judah, and the princes of Jerusalem, the eunuchs, and the priests, and all the people of the land, which passed between the parts of the calf; 　　Ezek. 22:27

20 I will even give them into the hand of their enemies, and into the hand of them that seek their life: and their dead bodies shall be for meat unto the fowls of the heaven, and to the beasts of the earth.

21 And ᴿZed-e-ki′-ah king of Judah and his princes will I give into the hand of their enemies, and into the hand of them that seek their life, and into the hand of the king of Babylon's army, ᴿwhich are gone up from you. 　　32:3, 4; 39:6; 52:10, 24–27 • 37:5, 11

22 ᴿBehold, I will command, saith the LORD, and cause them to return to this city; and they shall fight against it, ᴿand take it, and burn it with fire: and I will make the cities of Judah a ᵀdesolation without an inhabitant. 　　　　37:8 • 38:23 • *ruin*

CHAPTER 35

Message to the Rechabites

THE word which came unto Jer-e-mi'-ah from the LORD in the days of Je-hoi'-a-kim the son of Jo-si'-ah king of Judah, saying,

2 Go unto the house of the Re'-chab-ites, and speak unto them, and bring them into the house of the LORD, into one of the chambers, and give them wine to drink.

3 Then I took Ja-az-a-ni'-ah the son of Jer-e-mi'-ah, the son of Hab-a-zi-ni'-ah, and his brethren, and all his sons, and the whole house of the Re'-chab-ites;

4 And I brought them into the house of the LORD, into the chamber of the sons of Ha'-nan, the son of Ig-da-li'-ah, a ᴿman of God, which was by the chamber of the princes, which was above the chamber of Ma-a-se'-iah the son of Shal'-lum, the keeper of the ᵀdoor: Josh. 14:6 · threshold

5 And I set before the sons of the house of the Re'-chab-ites pots full of wine, and cups, and I said unto them, Drink ye wine.

6 But they said, We will drink no wine: for Jon'-a-dab the son of Re'-chab our father commanded us, saying, Ye shall drink no wine, neither ye, nor your sons for ever:

7 Neither shall ye build house, nor sow seed, nor plant vineyard, nor have any: but all your days ye shall dwell in tents; ᴿthat ye may live many days in the land where ye be strangers.   Ex. 20:12; Eph. 6:2, 3

8 Thus have we ᴿobeyed the voice of Jon'-a-dab the son of Re'-chab our father in all that he hath charged us, ᴿto drink no wine all our days, we, our wives, our sons, nor our daughters;   [Prov. 1:8, 9; 4:1, 2, 10] · [Col. 3:20]

9 Nor to build houses for us to dwell in: neither ᴿhave we vineyard, nor field, nor seed: v. 7; [Ps. 37:16; 1 Tim. 6:6]

10 But we have dwelt in tents, and have obeyed, and done according to all that Jon'-a-dab our father commanded us.

11 But it came to pass, when Neb-u-chad-rez'-zar king of Babylon came up into the land, that we said, Come, and let us go to Jerusalem for fear of the army of the Chal-de'-ans, and for fear of the army of the Syrians: so we dwell at Jerusalem.

12 Then came the word of the LORD unto Jer-e-mi'-ah, saying,

13 Thus saith the LORD of hosts, the God of Israel; Go and tell the men of Judah and the inhabitants of Jerusalem, Will ye not ᴿreceive instruction to ᵀhearken to my words? saith the LORD.   32:33 · listen

14 The words of Jon'-a-dab the son of Re'-chab, that he commanded his sons not to drink wine, are performed; for unto this day they drink none, but obey their father's commandment: notwithstanding I have spoken unto you, rising early and speaking; but ye hearkened not unto me.

15 I have sent also unto you all my servants the prophets, rising up early and sending them, saying, ᴿReturn ye now every man from his evil way, and amend your doings, and go not after other gods to serve them, and ye shall dwell in the land which I have given to you and to your fathers: but ye have not inclined your ear, nor hearkened unto me.   18:11; 25:5, 6

16 Because the sons of Jon'-a-dab the son of Re'-chab have ᴿperformed the command-ment of their father, which he commanded them; but this people hath not hearkened unto me: Mal. 1:6

17 Therefore thus saith the LORD God of hosts, the God of Israel; Behold, I ᴿwill bring upon Judah and upon all the inhabitants of Jerusalem all the evil that I have pronounced against them: ᴿbecause I have spoken unto them, but they have not heard; and I have called unto them, but they have not an-swered.   2 Kin. 25; 2 Chr. 36 · 7:13; Prov. 1:24

18 And Jer-e-mi'-ah said unto the house of the Re'-chab-ites, Thus saith the LORD of hosts, the God of Israel; Because ye have obeyed the commandment of Jon'-a-dab your father, and kept all his precepts, and done according unto all that he hath commanded you:

19 Therefore thus saith the LORD of hosts, the God of Israel; Jon'-a-dab the son of Re'-chab shall ᵀnot want a man to ᴿstand before me for ever.   never lack · 15:19

CHAPTER 36

Message of the Scroll

AND it came to pass in the ᴿfourth year of Je-hoi'-a-kim the son of Jo-si'-ah king of Judah, that this word came unto Jer-e-mi'-ah from the LORD, saying,   2 Kin. 24:1

2 Take thee a ᴿroll of a book, and write therein all the words that I have spoken unto thee against Israel, and against Judah, and against all the nations, from the day I spake unto thee, from the days of Jo-si'-ah, even into this day.   Is. 8:1

3 It may be that the house of Judah will hear all the evil which I purpose to do unto them; that they may return every man from his evil way; that I may forgive their iniquity and their sin.

4 Then Jer-e-mi'-ah ᴿcalled Ba'-ruch the son of Ne-ri'-ah: and ᴿBa'-ruch wrote from the mouth of Jer-e-mi'-ah all the words of the LORD, which he had spoken unto him, upon a roll of a ᴿbook.   32:12 · 45:1 · Ezek. 2:9

5 And Jer-e-mi'-ah commanded Ba'-ruch, saying, I am ᵀshut up; I cannot go into the house of the LORD: restricted

6 Therefore go thou, and read in the roll, which thou hast written from my mouth, the words of the LORD in the ears of the people in the LORD's house upon the fasting day: and also thou shalt read them in the ears of all Judah that come out of their cities.

7 It may be they will present their supplication before the LORD, and will return every one from his evil way: for great is the anger and the fury that the LORD hath pronounced against this people.

8 And Ba'-ruch the son of Ne-ri'-ah did according to all that Jer-e-mi'-ah the prophet commanded him, reading in the book the words of the LORD in the LORD's house.

9 And it came to pass in the fifth year of Je-hoi'-a-kim the son of Jo-si'-ah king of Judah, in the ninth month, that they proclaimed a ᴿfast before the LORD to all the people in Jerusalem, and to all the people that came from the cities of Judah unto Jerusalem.   Esth. 4:16; Joel 1:14

10 Then read Ba'-ruch in the book the words of Jer-e-mi'-ah in the house of the LORD, in the chamber of Gem-a-ri'-ah the son of Sha'-phan the scribe, in the higher court, at the entry of the new gate of the LORD's house, in the ears of all the people.

11 When Mi-cha'-iah the son of Gem-a-ri'-ah, the son of Sha'-phan, had heard out of the book all the words of the LORD,

12 Then he went down into the king's house, into the scribe's chamber: and, ᵀlo, all the princes sat there, even ᴿE-lish'-a-ma the scribe, and De-la'-iah the son of She-ma'-iah, and El-na'-than the son of Ach'-bor, and Gem-a-ri'-ah the son of Sha'-phan, and Zed-e-ki'-ah the son of Han-a-ni'-ah, and all the princes.   look • 41:1

13 Then Mi-cha'-iah declared unto them all the words that he had heard, when Ba'-ruch read the book in the ears of the people.

14 Therefore all the princes sent Je-hu'-di the son of Neth-a-ni'-ah, the son of Shel-e-mi'-ah, the son of Cu'-shi, unto Ba'-ruch, saying, Take in thine hand the roll wherein thou hast read in the ears of the people, and come. So Ba'-ruch the son of Ne-ri'-ah took the roll in his hand, and came unto them.

15 And they said unto him, Sit down now, and read it in our ears. So Ba'-ruch ᴿread it in their ears.   v. 21

16 Now it came to pass, when they had heard all the words, they were afraid both one and other, and said unto Ba'-ruch, We will surely tell the king of all these words.

17 And they asked Ba'-ruch, saying, Tell us now, ᴿHow didst thou write all these words at his mouth?   John 9:10, 15, 26

18 Then Ba'-ruch answered them, He ᴿpronounced all these words unto me with his mouth, and I wrote them with ᴿink in the book.   v. 4; 43:2, 3 • [2 Cor. 3:3]

19 ᴿThen said the princes unto Ba'-ruch, Go, hide thee, thou and Jer-e-mi'-ah; and let no man know where ye be.   1 Kin. 17:3; 18:4

20 And they went in to the king into the court, but they laid up the roll in the chamber of E-lish'-a-ma the scribe, and told all the words in the ears of the king.

21 So the king sent Je-hu'-di to fetch the roll: and he took it out of E-lish'-a-ma the scribe's chamber. And Je-hu'-di read it in the ears of the king, and in the ears of all the princes which stood beside the king.

22 Now the king sat in ᴿthe winterhouse in the ninth month: and there was a fire on the hearth burning before him.   Amos 3:15

23 And it came to pass, that when Je-hu'-di had read three or four leaves, he cut it with the penknife, and cast it into the fire that was on the hearth, until all the roll was consumed in the fire that was on the hearth.

24 Yet they were not afraid, nor rent their garments, neither the king, nor any of his servants that heard all these words.

25 Nevertheless El-na'-than and De-la'-iah and Gem-a-ri'-ah had made ᴿintercession to the king that he would not burn the roll: but he would not hear them.   Gen. 37:22, 26, 27

26 But the king commanded Je-rah'-me-el the son ᵀof Ham'-me-lech, ᴿand Se-ra'-iah the son of Az'-ri-el, and Shel-e-mi'-ah the son of Ab'-de-el, to ᴿtake Ba'-ruch the scribe and Jer-e-mi'-ah the prophet: but the LORD hid them.   1 Kin. 19:1–3, 10, 14 • of the king • 38:6

27 Then the word of the LORD came to Jer-e-mi'-ah, after that the king had burned the roll, and the words which Ba'-ruch wrote at the mouth of Jer-e-mi'-ah, saying,

28 ᴿTake thee again another roll, and write in it all the former words that were in the first roll, which Je-hoi'-a-kim the king of Judah hath burned.   36:4

29 And thou shalt say to Je-hoi'-a-kim king of Judah, Thus saith the LORD; Thou hast ᴿburned this roll, saying, Why hast thou written therein, saying, The king of Babylon shall certainly come and destroy this land, and shall cause to cease from thence man and beast?   [Deut. 29:19; Job 15:24, 25]

30 Therefore thus saith the LORD of Je-hoi'-a-kim king of Judah; He shall have none to sit upon the throne of David: and his dead body shall be cast out in the day to the heat, and in the night to the frost.

31 And I ᴿwill punish him and his seed and his servants for their iniquity; and I will bring upon them, and upon the inhabitants of Jerusalem, and upon the men of Judah, all the evil that I have pronounced against them; but they hearkened not.   2 Kin. 25; 2 Chr. 36

32 Then took Jer-e-mi'-ah another roll, and gave it to Ba'-ruch the scribe, the son of Ne-ri'-ah; who wrote therein from the mouth of Jer-e-mi'-ah all the words of the book which

Je-hoi'-a-kim king of Judah had burned in the fire: and there were added besides unto them many like words.

CHAPTER 37

First Interview with Zedekiah
2 Kin. 24:17; 2 Chr. 36:10

AND king ᴿZed-e-ki'-ah the son of Jo-si'-ah reigned instead of Co-ni'-ah the son of Je-hoi'-a-kim, whom Neb-u-chad-rez'-zar king of Babylon made king in the land of Judah.   22:24; 2 Kin. 24:17; 2 Chr. 36:10

2 ᴿBut neither he, nor his servants, nor the people of the land, did ᵀhearken unto the words of the LORD, which he spake by the prophet Jer-e-mi'-ah.   2 Chr. 36:12, 14 · *obey*

3 And Zed-e-ki'-ah the king sent Je-hu'-cal the son of Shel-e-mi'-ah and ᴿZeph-a-ni'-ah the son of Ma-a-se'-iah the priest to the prophet Jer-e-mi'-ah, saying, Pray now unto the LORD our God for us.   21:1, 2

4 Now Jer-e-mi'-ah came in and went out among the people: for they had not put him into prison.

5 Then Pharaoh's army was come forth out of Egypt: and when the Chal-de'-ans that besieged Jerusalem heard tidings of them, they departed from Jerusalem.

6 Then came the word of the LORD unto the prophet Jer-e-mi'-ah, saying,

7 Thus saith the LORD, the God of Israel; Thus shall ye say to the king of Judah, ᴿthat sent you unto me to enquire of me; Behold, ᴿPharaoh's army, which is come forth to help you, shall return to Egypt into their own land.   21:2 · 21:1, 2; 2 Kin. 22:18

8 ᴿAnd the Chal-de'-ans shall come again, and fight against this city, and take it, and burn it with fire.   34:22; 38:23; 39:2–8

9 Thus saith the LORD; Deceive not yourselves, saying, The Chal-de'-ans shall surely depart from us: for they shall not depart.

10 ᴿFor though ye had smitten the whole army of the Chal-de'-ans that fight against you, and there remained *but* ᵀwounded men among them, *yet* should they rise up every man in his tent, and burn this city with fire.   Lev. 26:36–38; Is. 30:17 · *thrust through*

Jeremiah Is Imprisoned in a Dungeon

11 And it came to pass, that when the army of the Chal-de'-ans was broken up from Jerusalem for fear of Pharaoh's army,

12 Then Jer-e-mi'-ah went forth out of Jerusalem to go into the ᴿland of Benjamin, to ᵀseparate himself thence in the midst of the people.   1 Kin. 19:3, 9 · *receive his portion there*

13 And when he was in the gate of Benjamin, a captain of the ward *was* there, whose name *was* I-ri'-jah, the son of Shel-e-mi'-ah, the son of Han-a-ni'-ah; and he took Jer-e-mi'-ah the prophet, saying, Thou ᵀfallest away to the Chal-de'-ans.   *deserted*

14 Then said Jer-e-mi'-ah, It *is* false; I fall not away to the Chal-de'-ans. But he hearkened not to him: so I-ri'-jah took Jer-e-mi'-ah, and brought him to the princes.

15 Wherefore the princes were wroth with Jer-e-mi'-ah, and smote him, and put him in prison in the house of Jonathan the scribe: for they had made that the prison.

16 When Jer-e-mi'-ah was entered into the dungeon, and into the ᵀcabins, and Jer-e-mi'-ah had remained there many days;   *cells*

Second Interview of Zedekiah

17 Then Zed-e-ki'-ah the king sent, and took him out: and the king asked him secretly in his house, and said, Is there *any* word from the LORD? And Jer-e-mi'-ah said, There is: for, said he, thou shalt be delivered into the hand of the king of Babylon.

18 Moreover Jer-e-mi'-ah said unto king Zed-e-ki'-ah, What have I offended against

---

37:15 Examples of Suffering—In the Word of God there are four great examples of believers' suffering for the sake of righteousness. These are: Joseph, Job, Jeremiah, and Paul.

The *sufferings of Joseph:* he was hated by his brothers (Page 39—Gen. 37:4, 5, 8); he was sold into slavery (Page 39—Gen. 37:28); he was severely tempted (Page 41—Gen. 39:7); and he was imprisoned (Page 41—Gen. 39:20).

The *sufferings of Job:* his oxen and donkeys were stolen and his farmhands killed (Page 518—Job 1:14, 15); his sheep and herdsmen were burned by a fire (Page 519—Job 1:16); his camels were stolen and his servants killed (Page 519—Job 1:17); his sons and daughters died in a windstorm (Page 519—Job 1:18, 19); and he was struck with boils (Page 519—Job 2:7).

The *sufferings of Jeremiah:* he was persecuted by his own family (Page 719—Jer. 12:6); he was plotted against by his own hometown (Page 719—Jer. 11:18–23); he was rejected and ridiculed by his religious peers (Page 725—Jer. 20:1–3, 7–9); and he was arrested, beaten, and accused of treason (Page 743—Jer. 37:11–16).

The *sufferings of Paul:* he plotted against (Page 1082—Acts 9:23, 29; 20:3; 21:30; 23:10, 12; 25:3); he was stoned and left for dead (Page 1088—Acts 14:19); he was subjected to satanic pressure (Page 1184—1 Thess. 2:18); he was beaten and jailed at Philippi (Page 1090—Acts 16:19–24); he was ridiculed (Page 1091—Acts 17:16–18; 26:24); he was falsely accused (Page 1096—Acts 21:21, 28; 24:5–9); he endured a number of violent storms at sea (Page 1150—2 Cor. 11:25; Page 1102—Acts 27:14–20); he was bitten by a serpent (Page 1103—Acts 28:3, 4); and he was forsaken by all (Page 1202—2 Tim. 4:10, 16).

Now turn to Page 396—2 Kin. 23:3: Knowing the Will of God Through the Scriptures.

thee, or against thy servants, or against this people, that ye have put me in prison?

19 ᴿWhere *are* now your prophets which prophesied unto you, saying, The king of Babylon shall not come against you, nor against this land?   2:28; 6:14; Deut. 32:37, 38

20 Therefore hear now, I pray thee, O my lord the king: let my supplication, I pray thee, be accepted before thee; that thou cause me not to return to the house of Jonathan the scribe, lest I die there.

21 Then Zed-e-ki′-ah the king commanded that they should commit Jer-e-mi′-ah ᴿinto the court of the prison, and that they should give him daily a piece of bread out of the bakers' street, until all the bread in the city were spent. Thus Jer-e-mi′-ah remained in the court of the prison.   32:2

CHAPTER 38

Jeremiah Is Imprisoned in a Cistern

THEN Sheph-a-ti′-ah the son of Mat′-tan, and Ged-a-li′-ah the son of Pash′-ur, and ᴿJu′-cal the son of Shel-e-mi′-ah, and Pash′-ur the son of Mal-chi′-ah, heard the words that Jer-e-mi′-ah had spoken unto all the people, saying,   37:3

2 Thus saith the LORD, ᴿHe that remaineth in this city shall die by the sword, by the famine, and by the pestilence: but he that ᵀgoeth forth to the Chal-de′-ans shall live; for he shall have his life for a prey, and shall live.   21:9; 39:18; 45:5; 2 Chr. 36:17 • *surrenders to*

3 Thus saith the LORD, This ᴿcity shall surely be given into the hand of the king of Babylon's army, which shall take it.   2 Kin. 25

4 Therefore the princes said unto the king, We beseech thee, ᴿlet this man be put to death: for thus he weakeneth the hands of the men of war that remain in this city, and the hands of all the people, in speaking such words unto them: for this man seeketh not the welfare of this people, but the hurt. 26:11

5 Then Zed-e-ki′-ah the king said, Behold, he *is* in your hand: for the king *is* not *he that* can do *any* thing against you.

6 Then took they Jer-e-mi′-ah, and cast him into the dungeon of Mal-chi′-ah the son of Ham′-me-lech, that *was* in the court of the prison: and they let down Jer-e-mi′-ah with cords. And in the dungeon *there was* no water, but mire: so Jer-e-mi′-ah sunk in the mire.

7 ᴿNow when E′-bed–me′-lech the E-thi-o′-pi-an, one of the eunuchs which was in the king's house, heard that they had put Jer-e-mi′-ah in the dungeon; the king then sitting in the gate of Benjamin;   39:16

8 E′-bed–me′-lech went forth out of the king's house, and spake to the king, saying,

9 My lord the king, these men have done evil in all that they have done to Jer-e-mi′-ah the prophet, whom they have cast into the dungeon; and he is ᵀlike to die for hunger in the place where he is: for *there is* ᴿno more bread in the city.   *likely to die* • 37:21; 52:6

10 ᴿThen the king commanded E′-bed–me′-lech the E-thi-o′-pi-an, saying, Take from hence thirty men with thee, and take up Jer-e-mi′-ah the prophet out of the dungeon, before he die.   [Prov. 16:15]

11 So E′-bed–me′-lech took the men with him, and went into the house of the king under the treasury, and took thence old cast clouts and old rotten rags, and let them down by cords into the dungeon to Jer-e-mi′-ah.

12 And E′-bed–me′-lech the E-thi-o′-pi-an said unto Jer-e-mi′-ah, Put now *these* old cast clouts and rotten rags under thine armholes under the cords. And Jer-e-mi′-ah did so.

13 So they drew up Jer-e-mi′-ah with cords, and took him up out of the dungeon: and Jer-e-mi′-ah remained in the court of the prison.

Third Interview of Zedekiah

14 Then Zed-e-ki′-ah the king sent, and took Jer-e-mi′-ah the prophet unto him into the third entry that *is* in the house of the LORD: and the king said unto Jer-e-mi′-ah, I will ask thee a thing; hide nothing from me.

15 Then Jer-e-mi′-ah said unto Zed-e-ki′-ah, If I declare *it* unto thee, wilt thou not surely put me to death? and if I give thee counsel, wilt thou not hearken unto me?

16 So Zed-e-ki′-ah the king sware secretly unto Jer-e-mi′-ah, saying, *As* the LORD liveth, that made us this soul, I will not put thee to death, neither will I give thee into the hand of these men that seek thy life.

17 Then said Jer-e-mi′-ah unto Zed-e-ki′-ah, Thus saith the LORD, the God of hosts, the God of Israel; If thou wilt assuredly goᵀ forth ᴿunto the king of Babylon's princes, then thy soul shall live, and this city shall not be burned with fire; and thou shalt live, and thine house: *surrender* • 39:3

18 But if thou wilt not go forth to the ᴿking of Babylon's princes, then shall this city be given into the hand of the Chal-de′-ans, and they shall burn it with fire, and thou shalt not escape out of their hand.   27:8

19 And Zed-e-ki′-ah the king said unto Jer-e-mi′-ah, I am afraid of the Jews that are fallen to the Chal-de′-ans, lest they deliver me into their hand, and they mock me.

20 But Jer-e-mi′-ah said, They shall not deliver *thee*. Obey, I beseech thee, the voice of the LORD, which I speak unto thee: so it shall be well unto thee, and thy soul shall live.

21 But if thou refuse to go forth, this *is* the word that the LORD hath shewed me:

22 And, behold, all the women that are left

in the king of Judah's house *shall be* brought forth to the king of Babylon's princes, and those *women* shall say, Thy friends have set thee on, and have prevailed against thee: thy feet are sunk in the mire, *and* they are turned away back.

23 So they shall bring out all thy wives and ᴿthy children to the Chal-de'-ans: and thou shalt not escape out of their hand, but shalt be taken by the hand of the king of Babylon: and thou shalt cause this city to be burned with fire. 39:6; 41:10; 2 Kin. 25:7

24 Then said Zed-e-ki'-ah unto Jer-e-mi'-ah, Let no man know of these words, and thou shalt not die.

25 But if the princes hear that I have talked with thee, and they come unto thee, and say unto thee, Declare unto us now what thou hast said unto the king, hide it not from us, and we will not put thee to death; also what the king said unto thee:

26 Then thou shalt say unto them, I presented my supplication before the king, that he would not cause me to return ᴿto Jonathan's house, to die there. 37:15

27 Then came all the princes unto Jer-e-mi'-ah, and asked him: and he told them according to all these words that the king had commanded. So they left off speaking with him; for the matter was not perceived.

28 So ᴿJer-e-mi'-ah abode in the court of the prison until the day that Jerusalem was taken: and he was *there* when Jerusalem was taken. *v.* 13; 15:20, 21; 37:21; 39:14

CHAPTER 39

Jerusalem Falls—2 Kin. 25:1-12; Jer. 52:4-14

IN the ᴿninth year of Zed-e-ki'-ah king of Judah, in the tenth month, came Neb-u-chad-rez'-zar king of Babylon and all his army against Jerusalem, and they besieged it. 52:4; 2 Kin. 25:1-4; Ezek. 24:1, 2

2 *And* in the eleventh year of Zed-e-ki'-ah, in the fourth month, the ninth *day* of the month, the city was broken up.

3 And all the princes of the king of Babylon came in, and sat in the middle gate, *even* Ner'-gal-sha-re'-zer, Sam'-gar-ne'-bo, Sar-se'-chim, Rab'-sa-ris, Ner'-gal-sha-re'-zer, Rab'-mag, with all the ᵀresidue of the princes of the king of Babylon. *rest*

4 And it came to pass, *that* when Zed-e-ki'-ah the king of Judah saw them, and all the men of war, then they fled, and went forth out of the city by night, by the way of the king's garden, by the gate betwixt the two walls: and he went out the way of the plain.

5 But the Chal-de'-ans' army pursued after them, and ᴿovertook Zed-e-ki'-ah in the plains of Jericho: and when they had taken

him, they brought him up to Neb-u-chad-nez'-zar king of Babylon to ᴿRib'-lah in the land of Ha'-math, where he ᵀgave judgment upon him. 32:4 · 2 Kin. 23:33 · *passed*

6 Then the king of Babylon slew the sons of Zed-e-ki'-ah ᴿin Rib'-lah before his eyes: also the king of Babylon slew all the nobles of Judah. 34:19-21; 52:10; Deut. 28:34; 2 Kin. 25:7

7 Moreover ᴿhe put out Zed-e-ki'-ah's eyes, and bound him ᵀwith chains, to carry him to Babylon. 52:11 · *with two brasen chains*

8 And the Chal-de'-ans burned the king's house, and the houses of the people, with fire, and brake down the walls of Jerusalem.

9 Then Neb'-u-zar-a'-dan the ᵀcaptain of the guard carried away captive into Babylon the remnant of the people that remained in the city, and those that ᵀfell away, that fell to him, with the rest of the people that remained. *chief marshal · surrendered*

10 But Neb'-u-zar-a'-dan the captain of the guard left of the poor of the people, which had nothing, in the land of Judah, and gave them vineyards and fields at the same time.

Jeremiah Is Released

11 Now Neb-u-chad-rez'-zar king of Babylon gave charge ᴿconcerning Jer-e-mi'-ah to Neb'-u-zar-a'-dan the captain of the guard, saying, 15:20, 21; [Job 5:15, 16]; Acts 24:23

12 Take him, and ᵀlook well to him, and ᴿdo him no harm; but do unto him even as he shall say unto thee. *take care of · Ps.* 105:14

13 So Neb'-u-zar-a'-dan the captain of the guard sent, and Neb-u-shas'-ban, Rab'-sa-ris, and Ner'-gal-sha-re'-zer, Rab'-mag, and all the king of Babylon's princes;

14 Even they sent, and took Jer-e-mi'-ah out of the court of the prison, and committed him unto Ged-a-li'-ah the son of A-hi'-kam the son of Sha'-phan, that he should carry him home: so he dwelt among the people.

Ebed-melech Is Rewarded

15 ᴿNow the word of the LORD came unto Jer-e-mi'-ah, while he was shut up in the court of the prison, saying, 38:28

16 Go and speak to E'-bed-me'-lech the E-thi-o'-pi-an, saying, Thus saith the LORD of hosts, the God of Israel; Behold, ᴿI will bring my words upon this city for evil, and not for good; and they shall be *accomplished* in that day before thee. [Dan. 9:12]

17 But I will deliver thee in that day, saith the LORD: and thou shalt not be given into the hand of the men of whom thou *art* afraid.

18 For I will surely deliver thee, and thou shalt not fall by the sword, but thy life shall be for a prey unto thee: because thou hast put thy trust in me, saith the LORD.

CHAPTER 40

Ministry to Remnant in Judah

THE word that came to Jer-e-mi'-ah from the LORD, Rafter that Neb'-u-zar-a'-dan the captain of the guard had let him go from RRa'-mah, when he had taken him being bound in Rchains^T among all that were carried away captive of Jerusalem and Judah, which were carried away captive unto Babylon. 39:14 · 31:15 · Acts 12:6, 7; 21:13 · *manacles*

2 And the captain of the guard took Jer-e-mi'-ah, and Rsaid unto him, The LORD thy God hath pronounced this evil upon this place. 22:8, 9; 50:7; Deut. 29:24–28

3 Now the LORD hath brought *it*, and done according as he hath said: Rbecause ye have sinned against the LORD, and have not obeyed his voice, therefore this thing is come upon you. Deut. 29:24, 25; Dan. 9:11

4 And now, behold, I loose thee this day from the chains which *were* upon thine hand. If it seem good unto thee to come with me into Babylon, come; and I will look well unto thee: but if it seem ill unto thee to come with me into Babylon, forbear: behold, all the land *is* before thee: whither it seemeth good and convenient for thee to go, thither go.

5 Now while he was not yet gone back, *he* said, Go back also to Ged-a-li'-ah the son of A-hi'-kam the son of Sha'-phan, Rwhom the king of Babylon hath made governor over the cities of Judah, and dwell with him among the people: or go wheresoever it seemeth convenient unto thee to go. So the captain of the guard gave him Rvictuals and a Treward, and let him go. 41:10; 2 Ki. 25:23 · 52:34 · *bonus*

6 RThen went Jer-e-mi'-ah unto Ged-a-li'-ah the son of A-hi'-kam to RMiz'-pah; and dwelt with him among the people that were left in the land. 39:14 · Judg. 20:1; 21:1; 1 Sam. 7:5

7 RNow when all the captains of the forces which *were* in the fields, *even* they and their men, heard that the king of Babylon had made Ged-a-li'-ah the son of A-hi'-kam governor in the land, and had committed unto him men, and women, and children, and of the poor of the land, of them that were not carried away captive to Babylon; 2 Kin. 25:23–26

8 Then they came to Ged-a-li'-ah to Miz'-pah, even Ish'-ma-el the son of Neth-a-ni'-ah, and Jo-ha'-nan and Jonathan the sons of Ka-re'-ah, and Se-ra'-iah the son of Tan'-hu-meth, and the sons of E'-phai the Ne-toph'-a-thite, and Jez-a-ni'-ah the son of a Ma-ach'-a-thite, they and their men.

9 And Ged-a-li'-ah the son of A-hi'-kam the son of Sha'-phan Rsware unto them and to their men, saying, Fear not Tto serve the Chal-de'-ans: dwell in the land, and serve the king of Babylon, and it shall be well with you. 1 Sam. 20:16 · *to stand before*

10 As for me, behold, I will dwell at Miz'-pah, to Rserve the Chal-de'-ans, which will come unto us: but ye, gather ye wine, and summer Rfruits, and oil, and put *them* in your vessels, and dwell in your cities that ye have taken. Deut. 1:38; 1 Kin. 10:8 · Is. 16:9

11 Likewise when all the Jews that *were* in RMoab, and among the Am'-mon-ites, and in E'-dom, and that *were* in all the countries, heard that the king of Babylon had left a remnant of Judah, and that he had set over them Ged-a-li'-ah the son of A-hi'-kam the son of Sha'-phan; Num. 22:1

12 Even all the Jews Rreturned out of all places whither they were driven, and came to the land of Judah, to Ged-a-li'-ah, unto Miz'-pah, and gathered wine and summer fruits very much. 43:5

13 Moreover Jo-ha'-nan the son of Ka-re'-ah, and all the captains of the forces that *were* in the fields, came to Ged-a-li'-ah to Miz'-pah,

14 And said unto him, Dost thou Tcertainly know that Ba'-al-is the king of the Am'-mon-ites hath sent Ish'-ma-el the son of Neth-a-ni'-ah to slay thee? But Ged-a-li'-ah the son of A-hi'-kam believed them not. *realize*

15 Then Jo-ha'-nan the son of Ka-re'-ah spake to Ged-a-li'-ah in Miz'-pah secretly, saying, RLet me go, I pray thee, and I will slay Ish'-ma-el the son of Neth-a-ni'-ah, and no man shall know *it:* Rwherefore should he slay thee, that all the Jews which are gathered unto thee should be scattered, and the remnant in Judah perish? 1 Sam. 26:8 · 2 Sam. 21:17

16 But Ged-a-li'-ah the son of A-hi'-kam said unto Jo-ha'-nan the son of Ka-re'-ah, Thou shalt not do this thing: for thou speakest falsely of Ish'-ma-el.

CHAPTER 41

NOW it came to pass in the seventh month, *that* Ish'-ma-el the son of Neth-a-ni'-ah the son of E-lish'-a-ma, of the seed royal, and the princes of the king, even ten men with him, came unto Ged-a-li'-ah the son of A-hi'-kam to Miz'-pah; and there they did eat bread together in Miz'-pah.

2 Then arose Ish'-ma-el the son of Neth-a-ni'-ah, and the ten men that were with him, and smote Ged-a-li'-ah the son of A-hi'-kam the son of Sha'-phan with the sword, and slew him, whom the king of Babylon had made governor over the land.

3 Ish'-ma-el also slew all the Jews that were with him, *even* with Ged-a-li'-ah, at Miz'-pah, and the Chal-de'-ans that were found there, *and* the Tmen of war. *soldiers*

4 And it came to pass the Tsecond day after he had slain Ged-a-li'-ah, and no man knew *it,* *next*

5 That there came certain from She'-chem, from Shi'-loh, and from Sa-ma'-ri-a, *even* fourscore men, having their beards shaven,

and their clothes rent, and having cut themselves, with offerings and incense in their hand, to bring *them* to the house of the LORD.

6 And Ish'-ma-el the son of Neth-a-ni'-ah went forth from Miz'-pah to meet them, weeping all along as he went: and it came to pass, as he met them, he said unto them, Come to Ged-a-li'-ah the son of A-hi'-kam.

7 And it was *so,* when they came into the midst of the city, that Ish'-ma-el the son of Neth-a-ni'-ah slew them, ᴿ*and cast them* into the midst of the pit, he, and the men that *were* with him.   Ps. 55:23; Is. 59:7; Ezek. 22:27

8 But ten men were found among them that said unto Ish'-ma-el, Slay us not: for we have ᴿtreasures in the field, of wheat, and of barley, and of oil, and of honey. So he forbare, and slew them not among their brethren.   [Is. 45:3]

9 Now the pit wherein Ish'-ma-el had cast all the dead bodies of the men, whom he had slain because of Ged-a-li'-ah, *was* it which A'-sa the king had made for fear of Ba-ash'-a king of Israel: *and* Ish'-ma-el the son of Neth-a-ni'-ah filled it with *them that were* slain.

10 Then Ish'-ma-el carried away captive all the residue of the people that *were* in Miz'-pah, *even* the king's daughters, and all the people that remained in Miz'-pah, whom Neb'-u-zar-a'-dan the captain of the guard had committed to Ged-a-li'-ah the son of A-hi'-kam: and Ish'-ma-el the son of Neth-a-ni'-ah carried them away captive, and departed to go over to the Am'-mon-ites.

11 But when Jo-ha'-nan the son of Ka-re'-ah, and all the captains of the forces that *were* with him, heard of all the evil that Ish'-ma-el the son of Neth-a-ni'-ah had done,

12 ᴿThen they took all the men, and went to fight with Ish'-ma-el the son of Neth-a-ni'-ah, and found him by ᴿthe great waters that *are* in Gib'-e-on.   Gen. 14:14-16 • 2 Sam. 2:13

13 Now it came to pass, *that* when all the people which *were* with Ish'-ma-el saw Jo-ha'-nan the son of Ka-re'-ah, and all the captains of the forces that *were* with him, then they were glad.

14 So all the people that Ish'-ma-el had carried away captive from Miz'-pah ᵀcast about and returned, and went unto Jo-ha'-nan the son of Ka-re'-ah.   *deserted*

15 But Ish'-ma-el the son of Neth-a-ni'-ah escaped from Jo-ha'-nan with eight men, and went to the Am'-mon-ites.

16 Then took Jo-ha'-nan the son of Ka-re'-ah, and all the captains of the forces that *were* with him, all the remnant of the people whom he had recovered from Ish'-ma-el the son of Neth-a-ni'-ah, from Miz'-pah, after *that* he had slain Ged-a-li'-ah the son of A-hi'-kam, *even* mighty men of war, and the

women, and the children, and the eunuchs, whom he had brought again from Gib'-e-on:

17 And they departed, and dwelt in the habitation of Chim'-ham, which is by Beth'-le-hem, to go to enter into Egypt,

18 Because of the Chal-de'-ans: for they were afraid of them, because Ish'-ma-el the son of Neth-a-ni'-ah had slain Ged-a-li'-ah the son of A-hi'-kam, ᴿwhom the king of Babylon made governor in the land.   40:5

CHAPTER 42

THEN all the captains of the forces, ᴿand Jo-ha'-nan the son of Ka-re'-ah, and Jez-a-ni'-ah the son of Ho-sha'-iah, and ᴿall the people from the least even unto the greatest, came near,   40:8, 13; 41:11 • v. 8; 6:13

2 And said unto Jer-e-mi'-ah the prophet, ᵀLet, we beseech thee, our supplication be accepted before thee, and pray for us unto the LORD thy God, *even* for all this remnant; (for we are left *but* a few of many, as thine eyes do behold us:)   *grant our request*

3 That the LORD thy God may shew us ᴿthe way wherein we may walk, and the thing that we may do.   Ezra 8:21; Ps. 86:11

4 Then Jer-e-mi'-ah the prophet said unto them, I have heard *you;* behold, I will pray unto the LORD your God according to your words; and it shall come to pass, *that* ᴿwhatsoever thing the LORD shall answer you, I will declare *it* unto you; I will ᴿkeep nothing back from you.   1 Kin. 22:14 • Acts 20:20

5 Then they said to Jer-e-mi'-ah, ᴿThe LORD be a true and faithful witness between us, if we do not even according to all things for the which the LORD thy God shall send thee to us.   43:2; Gen. 31:50; Judg. 11:10; Mic. 1:2

6 Whether *it be* good, or whether *it be* evil, we will obey the voice of the LORD our God, to whom we send thee; ᴿthat it may be well with us, when we obey the voice of the LORD our God.   7:23; Deut. 6:3

7 And it came to pass after ten days, that the word of the LORD came unto Jer-e-mi'-ah.

8 Then called he Jo-ha'-nan the son of Ka-re'-ah, and all the captains of the forces which *were* with him, and all the people from the least even to the greatest,

9 And said unto them, Thus saith the LORD, the God of Israel, unto whom ye sent me to present your supplication before him;

10 If ye will still abide in this land, then ᴿwill I build you, and not pull *you* down, and I will plant you, and not pluck *you* up: for I repent me of the evil that I have done unto you.   24:6; 31:28; Ezek. 36:36

11 Be not afraid of the king of Babylon, of whom ye are afraid; be not afraid of him, saith the LORD: for I *am* with you to save you, and to deliver you from his hand.

12 And I will shew mercies unto you, that he may have mercy upon you, and cause you to return to your own land.

13 But if ^Rye say, We will not dwell in this land, neither obey the voice of the LORD your God,   44:16; Ex. 5:2

14 Saying, No; but we will go into the land of Egypt, where we shall see no war, nor hear the sound of the trumpet, nor have hunger of bread; and there will we dwell:

15 And now therefore hear the word of the LORD, ye remnant of Judah; Thus saith the LORD of hosts, the God of Israel; If ye wholly set ^Ryour faces to enter into Egypt, and go to sojourn there;   Luke 9:51

16 Then it shall come to pass, *that* the ^Rsword, which ye feared, shall overtake you there in the land of Egypt, and the famine, whereof ye were afraid, shall follow ^Tclose after you there in Egypt; and there ye shall die.   44:13, 27; Ezek. 11:8; Amos 9:1–4 • *soon*

17 So shall it be with all the men that ^Tset their faces to go into Egypt to sojourn there; they shall die by the sword, by the famine, and by the pestilence: and none of them shall remain or escape from the evil that I will bring upon them.   *decide*

18 For thus saith the LORD of hosts, the God of Israel; As mine anger and my fury hath been poured forth upon the inhabitants of Jerusalem; so shall my fury be poured forth upon you, when ye shall enter into Egypt: and ye shall be an execration, and an astonishment, and a curse, and a reproach; and ye shall see this place no more.

19 The LORD hath said concerning you, O ye remnant of Judah; ^RGo ye not into Egypt: know certainly that I have ^Tadmonished you this day.   Deut. 17:16 • *warned*

20 ^RFor ye ^Tdissembled in your hearts, when ye sent me unto the LORD your God, saying, Pray for us unto the LORD our God; and according unto all that the LORD our God shall say, so declare unto us, and we will do *it*.   41:17; 43:2; Ezek. 14:3 • *were deceitful*

21 And *now* I have this day declared *it* to you; but ye have not obeyed the voice of the LORD your God, nor any *thing* for the which he hath sent me unto you.

22 Now therefore know certainly that ye shall die by the sword, by the famine, and by the pestilence, in the place whither ye ^Tdesire to go *and* to sojourn.   *are planning*

CHAPTER 43

Ministry to Remnant in Egypt

AND it came to pass, *that* when Jer-e-mi'-ah had made an end of speaking unto all the people all the words of the LORD their God, for which the LORD their God had sent him to them, *even* all these words,

2 ^RThen spake Az-a-ri'-ah the son of Ho-sha'-iah, and Jo-ha'-nan the son of Ka-re'-ah, and all the proud men, saying unto Jer-e-mi'-ah, Thou speakest falsely: the LORD our God hath not sent thee to say, Go not into Egypt to sojourn there: 42:1

3 But Ba'-ruch the son of Ne-ri'-ah ^Tsetteth thee on against us, for to deliver us into the hand of the Chal-de'-ans, that they might put us to death, and carry us away captives into Babylon.   *has influenced you*

4 So ^RJo-ha'-nan the son of Ka-re'-ah, and all the captains of the forces, and all the people, ^Robeyed not the voice of the LORD, to dwell in the land of Judah.   42:8 • 42:5, 6

5 But Jo-ha'-nan the son of Ka-re'-ah, and all the captains of the forces, took all the remnant of Judah, that were returned from all nations, whither they had been driven, to dwell in the land of Judah;

6 *Even* men, and women, and children, and the ^Rking's daughters, and every person that Neb'-u-zar-a'-dan the captain of the guard had left with Ged-a-li'-ah the son of A-hi'-kam the son of Sha'-phan, and Jer-e-mi'-ah the prophet, and Ba'-ruch the son of Ne-ri'-ah.   41:10

7 So they came into the land of Egypt: for they obeyed not the voice of the LORD: thus came they *even* to Tah'-pan-hes.

8 Then came the word of the LORD unto Jer-e-mi'-ah in Tah'-pan-hes, saying,

9 Take great stones in thine hand, and ^Thide them in the clay in the brickkiln, which *is* at the entry of Pharaoh's house in Tah'-pan-hes, in the sight of the men of Judah;   *bury*

10 And say unto them, Thus saith the LORD of hosts, the God of Israel; Behold, I will send and take Neb-u-chad-rez'-zar the king of Babylon, my servant, and will set his throne upon these stones that I have hid; and he shall spread his royal pavilion over them.

11 ^RAnd when he cometh, he shall smite the land of Egypt, *and deliver* ^Rsuch *as are* for death to death; and such *as are* for captivity to captivity; and such *as are* for the sword to the sword.   44:13 • Zech. 11:9

12 And I will kindle a fire in the houses of the gods of Egypt; and he shall burn them, and carry them away captives: and he shall ^Rarray himself with the land of Egypt, as a shepherd putteth on his garment; and he shall go forth from thence in peace.   Ps. 104:2

13 He shall break also the ^Timages of Beth–she'-mesh, that *is* in the land of Egypt; and the houses of the gods of the Egyptians shall he burn with fire.   *pillars*

CHAPTER 44

THE word that came to Jer-e-mi'-ah concerning all the Jews which dwell in the land of Egypt, which dwell at ^RMig'-dol,

and at Tah'-pan-hes, and at Noph, and in the country of Path'-ros, saying,   Ex. 14:2

2 Thus saith the LORD of hosts, the God of Israel; Ye have seen all the evil that I have brought upon Jerusalem, and upon all the cities of Judah; and, behold, this day they *are* a desolation, and no man dwelleth therein,

3 Because of their wickedness which they have committed to provoke me to anger, in that they went to ᴿburn incense, *and* to serve other gods, whom they knew not, *neither* they, ye, nor your fathers.   *worship*

4 Howbeit ᴿI sent unto you all my servants the prophets, rising early and sending *them*, saying, Oh, do not this abominable thing that I hate.   7:25; 25:4; 26:5; 29:19

5 But they hearkened not, nor inclined their ear to turn from their wickedness, to burn no incense unto other gods.

6 Wherefore my fury and mine anger was poured forth, and was kindled in the cities of Judah and in the streets of Jerusalem; and they are wasted *and* desolate, as at this day.

7 Therefore now thus saith the LORD, the God of hosts, the God of Israel; ᴿWherefore commit ye *this* great evil ᴿagainst your souls, to cut off from you man and woman, child and suckling, out of Judah, to leave you none to remain;   26:19; Num. 16:38 • 7:19

8 In that ye provoke me unto wrath with the works of your hands, burning incense unto other gods in the land of Egypt, whither ye be gone to dwell, that ye might cut yourselves off, and that ye might be a curse and a reproach among all the nations of the earth?

9 Have ye forgotten the wickedness of your fathers, and the wickedness of the kings of Judah, and the wickedness of their wives, and your own wickedness, and the wickedness of your wives, which they have committed in the land of Judah, and in the streets of Jerusalem?

10 They are not ᴿhumbled *even* unto this day, neither have they feared, nor walked in my law, nor in my statutes, that I set before you and before your fathers.   6:15

11 Therefore thus saith the LORD of hosts, the God of Israel; Behold, I will set my face against you for evil, and to cut off all Judah.

12 And I will take the remnant of Judah, that have set their faces to go into the land of Egypt to sojourn there, and they shall all be consumed, *and* fall in the land of Egypt; they shall *even* be consumed by the sword *and* by the famine: they shall die, from the least even unto the greatest, by the sword and by the famine: and they shall be an execration, *and* an astonishment, and a curse, and a reproach.

13 ᴿFor I will punish them that dwell in the land of Egypt, as I have punished Jerusalem, by the sword, by the famine, and by the pestilence: *v.* 27; 11:22; 43:11

14 So that ᴿnone of the remnant of Judah, which are gone into the land of Egypt to sojourn there, shall escape or remain, that they should return into the land of Judah, to the which they ᵀhave a desire to return to dwell there: for none shall return but such as shall escape.   22:10 • *lift up their soul*

15 Then ᴿ all the men which knew that their wives had ᵀburned incense unto other gods, and all the women that stood by, a great multitude, even all the people that dwelt in the land of Egypt, in Path'-ros, answered Jer-e-mi'-ah, saying,   5:1-5 • *worshipped*

16 *As for* the word that thou hast spoken unto us in the name of the LORD, ᴿwe will not hearken unto thee.   6:16

17 But we will certainly do whatsoever thing ᵀgoeth forth out of our own mouth, to burn incense unto the queen of heaven, and to pour out drink offerings unto her, as we have done, we, and our fathers, our kings, and our princes, in the cities of Judah, and in the streets of Jerusalem: for *then* had we plenty of victuals, and were well, and saw no evil.   *is our own idea*

18 But since we left off to ᵀburn incense to the queen of heaven, and to pour out drink offerings unto her, we have ᵀwanted all *things*, and have been consumed by the sword and by the famine.   *worship • lacked*

19 And when we burned incense to the queen of heaven, and poured out drink offerings unto her, did we make her cakes to worship her, and pour out drink offerings unto her, without our ᵀmen?   *husbands*

20 Then Jer-e-mi'-ah said unto all the people, to the men, and to the women, and to all the people which had given him *that* answer, saying,

21 The incense that ye ᴿburned in the cities of Judah, and in the streets of Jerusalem, ye, and your fathers, your kings, and your princes, and the people of the land, did not the LORD remember them, and came it *not* into his mind?   Ezek. 8:10, 11

22 So that the LORD could no longer bear, because of the evil of your doings, *and* because of the abominations which ye have committed; therefore is your land a desolation, and an astonishment, and a curse, without an inhabitant, as at this day.

23 Because ye have burned incense, and because ye have sinned against the LORD, and have not obeyed the voice of the LORD, nor walked in his law, nor in his statutes, nor in his testimonies; therefore this evil is happened unto you, as at this day.

24 Moreover Jer-e-mi'-ah said unto all the people, and to all the women, ᴿHear the word of the LORD, all Judah that ᴿare in the land of Egypt: *v.* 16; 42:15 • *vv.* 15, 26

25 Thus saith the LORD of hosts, the God of

Israel, saying; Ye and your wives have both spoken with your mouths, and fulfilled with your hand, saying, We will surely perform our vows that we have vowed, to burn incense to the queen of heaven, and to pour out drink offerings unto her: ye will surely accomplish your vows, and surely perform your vows.

26 Therefore hear ye the word of the LORD, all Judah that dwell in the land of Egypt; Behold, ^RI have sworn by my great name, saith the LORD, that ^Rmy name shall no more be named in the mouth of any man of Judah in all the land of Egypt, saying, The Lord GOD liveth.   Gen. 22:16 • Ezek. 20:39

27 Behold, I will watch over them for evil, and not for good: and all the men of Judah that are in the land of Egypt shall be consumed by the sword and by the famine, until there be an end of them.

28 Yet ^Ra small number that escape the sword shall return out of the land of Egypt into the land of Judah, and all the remnant of Judah, that are gone into the land of Egypt to sojourn there, shall know whose words shall stand, mine, or their's.   Is. 27:13

29 And this shall be a sign unto you, saith the LORD, that I will punish you in this place, that ye may know that ^Rmy words shall surely stand against you for evil: Prov. 19:21

30 Thus saith the LORD; Behold, ^RI will give Pha'-raoh-hoph'-ra king of Egypt into the hand of his enemies, and into the hand of them that seek his life; as I gave ^RZed-e-ki'-ah king of Judah into the hand of Neb-u-chad-rez'-zar king of Babylon, his enemy, and that sought his life.   Ezek. 29:3; 30:21 • 39:5

CHAPTER 45

Message to Baruch

THE ^Rword that Jer-e-mi'-ah the prophet spake unto Ba'-ruch the son of Ne-ri'-ah, when he had written these words in a book at the mouth of Jer-e-mi'-ah, in the fourth year of Je-hoi'-a-kim the son of Jo-si'-ah king of Judah, saying,   36:1, 4, 32

2 Thus saith the LORD, the God of Israel, unto thee, O Ba'-ruch;

3 Thou didst say, Woe is me now! for the LORD hath added grief to my sorrow; I fainted in my sighing, and I find no rest.

4 Thus shalt thou say unto him, The LORD saith thus; Behold, that which I have built will I break down, and that which I have planted I will pluck up, even this whole land.

5 And seekest thou great things for thyself? seek them not: for, behold, I will bring evil upon all flesh, saith the LORD: but thy life will I give unto thee for a prey in all places whither thou goest.

CHAPTER 46

Prophecies Against Egypt

THE word of the LORD which came to Jer-e-mi'-ah the prophet ^Tagainst ^Rthe ^TGentiles;   concerning • 1:10; 25:15 • nations

2 Against Egypt, against the army of Pha'-raoh-ne'-cho king of Egypt, which was by the river Eu-phra'-tes in Car'-che-mish, which Neb-u-chad-rez'-zar king of Babylon smote in the fourth year of Je-hoi'-a-kim the son of Jo-si'-ah king of Judah.

3 ^ROrder^T ye the buckler and shield, and draw near to battle.   Nah. 2:1 • put on your armour

4 Harness the horses; and get up, ye horsemen, and stand forth with your helmets; ^Rfurbish the spears, and put on the ^Tbrigandines.   Ezek. 21:9–11 • coats of mail

5 Wherefore have I seen them dismayed and ^Rturned away back? and their mighty ones are ^Tbeaten down, and are fled apace, and look not back: for fear was round about, saith the LORD.   v. 21 • broken in pieces

6 Let not the ^Rswift flee away, nor the mighty man escape; they shall ^Rstumble, and fall toward the north by the river Eu-phra'-tes.   Is. 30:16 • vv. 12, 16; Dan. 11:19

7 Who is this that cometh up as a flood, whose waters are moved as the rivers?

8 Egypt riseth up like a ^Tflood, and his waters are moved like the rivers; and he saith, ^RI will go up, and will cover the earth; I will ^Rdestroy the city and the inhabitants thereof.   the Nile • Is. 37:24 • Is. 10:13

9 Come up, ye horses; and rage, ye chariots; and let the mighty men come forth; the E-thi-o'-pi-ans and the Lib'-y-ans, that handle the shield; and the Lyd'-i-ans, that handle and bend the bow.

10 For this is the day of the Lord GOD of hosts, a day of vengeance, that he may avenge him of his adversaries: and the sword shall devour, and it shall be satiate and made drunk with their blood: for the Lord GOD of hosts hath a sacrifice in the north country by the river Eu-phra'-tes.

11 ^RGo up into Gil'-e-ad, and take balm, ^RO virgin, the daughter of Egypt: in vain shalt thou use many medicines; for thou ^Tshalt not be cured.   8:22 • Is. 47:1 • are incurable

12 The nations have heard of thy shame, and thy cry hath filled the land: for the mighty man hath stumbled against the mighty, and they are fallen both together.

13 The word that the LORD spake to Jer-e-mi'-ah the prophet, how Neb-u-chad-rez'-zar king of Babylon should come and ^Rsmite the land of Egypt.   Is. 19:1; Ezek. 29, 30, 32

14 Declare ye in Egypt, and publish in Mig'-dol, and publish in Noph and in Tah'-pan-hes: say ye, Stand fast, and prepare thee; for the sword shall devour round about thee.

15 Why are thy ᴿvaliant *men* swept away? they stood not, because the Lᴏʀᴅ did ᴿdrive them. Is. 66:15, 16 • Ps. 18:14, 39; 68:1, 2

16 He made many to fall, yea, one fell upon another: and they said, Arise, and let us go again to our own people, and to the land of our nativity, from the oppressing sword.

17 They did cry there, Pharaoh king of Egypt *is* ᴿ*but* a noise; he hath passed the time appointed. Ex. 15:8, 10; 1 Kin. 20:10, 11

18 *As* I live, saith the King, ᴿwhose name *is* the Lᴏʀᴅ of hosts, Surely as Ta′-bor *is* among the mountains, and as Carmel by the sea, *so* shall he come. 48:15; Is. 47:4

19 O ᴿthou daughter dwelling in Egypt, ᵀfurnish thyself ᴿto go into captivity: for Noph shall be waste and desolate without an inhabitant. 48:18 • *prepare* • Is. 20:4

20 Egypt *is like* a very fair ᴿheifer, *but* destruction cometh; it cometh ᴿout of the north. Hos. 10:11 • 1:14

21 Also her hired men *are* in the midst of her like fatted bullocks; for they also ᵀare turned back, *and* are fled away together: they did not stand, because the day of their calamity was come upon them, *and* the time of their visitation. *have deserted*

22 ᴿThe voice thereof shall go like a serpent; for they shall march ᵀwith an army, and come against her with axes, as hewers of wood. [Is. 29:4] • *in force*

23 They shall ᴿcut down her forest, saith the Lᴏʀᴅ, though it cannot be searched; because they are more than ᴿthe grasshoppers, and *are* innumerable. Is. 10:34 • Judg. 6:5

24 The daughter of Egypt shall be confounded; she shall be delivered into the hand of ᴿthe people of the north. 1:15

25 The Lᴏʀᴅ of hosts, the God of Israel, saith; Behold, I will punish the multitude of ᴿNo, and Pharaoh, and Egypt, with their gods, and their kings; even Pharaoh, and *all* them that trust in him: Ezek. 30:14

26 And I will deliver them into the hand of those that seek their lives, and into the hand of Neb-u-chad-rez′-zar king of Babylon, and into the hand of his servants: and ᴿafterward it shall be inhabited, as in the days of old, saith the Lᴏʀᴅ. Ezek. 29:11, 13, 14

27 But fear not thou, O my servant Jacob, and be not dismayed, O Israel: for, behold, I will save thee from afar off, and thy seed from the land of their captivity; and Jacob shall return, and be in rest and at ease, and none shall make *him* afraid.

28 Fear thou not, O Jacob my servant, saith the Lᴏʀᴅ: for I *am* with thee; for I will make a full end of all the nations whither I have driven thee: but I will not make a full end of thee, but correct thee in measure; yet will I not leave thee wholly unpunished.

CHAPTER 47

Prophecies Against Philistia

THE word of the Lᴏʀᴅ that came to Jer-e-mi′-ah the prophet against the Phi-lis′-tines, before that Pharaoh smote Ga′-za.

2 Thus saith the Lᴏʀᴅ; Behold, waters rise up ᴿout of the north, and shall be an overflowing flood, and shall overflow the land, and all that is therein; the city, and them that dwell therein: then the men shall cry, and all the inhabitants of the land shall howl. Is. 8:7

3 At the noise of the stamping of the hoofs of his strong ᵀhorses, at the rushing of his chariots, *and at* the rumbling of his wheels, the fathers shall not look back to *their* children for feebleness of hands; *ones*

4 Because of the day that cometh to spoil all the Phi-lis′-tines, *and* to cut off from ᴿTy′-rus and Zi′-don every helper that remaineth: for the Lᴏʀᴅ will spoil the Phi-lis′-tines, the remnant of the country of Caph′-tor. 25:22

5 Baldness is come upon Ga′-za; Ash′-ke-lon is cut off *with* the remnant of their valley: how long wilt thou cut thyself?

6 O thou sword of the Lᴏʀᴅ, how long *will it be* ere thou be quiet? put up thyself into thy scabbard, rest, and be still.

7 ᵀHow can it be quiet, seeing the Lᴏʀᴅ hath ᴿgiven it a charge against Ash′-ke-lon, and against the sea shore? there hath he appointed it. *how can you* • Ezek. 14:17; Mic. 6:9

CHAPTER 48

Prophecies Against Moab

AGAINST Moab thus saith the Lᴏʀᴅ of hosts, the God of Israel; Woe unto ᴿNe′-bo! for it is ᵀspoiled: Kir-i-a-tha′-im is confounded *and* taken: Mis′-gab is confounded and dismayed. Num. 32:3 • *the high fort*

2 *There shall be* no more praise of Moab: in Hesh′-bon they have devised evil against it; come, and let us cut it off from *being* a nation. Also thou shalt be cut down, O Mad′-men; the sword shall pursue thee.

3 A voice of crying *shall be* from Hor-o-na′-im, spoiling and great destruction.

4 Moab is destroyed; her little ones have caused a cry to be heard.

5 For in the going up of Lu′-hith ᵀcontinual weeping shall go up; for in the going down of Hor-o-na′-im the enemies have heard a cry of destruction. *constant lament*

6 Flee, save your lives, and be like the heathᵀ in the wilderness. *naked object*

7 For because thou hast trusted in thy works and in thy treasures, thou shalt also be taken: and ᴿChe′-mosh shall go forth into captivity *with* his ᴿpriests and his princes together. Judg. 11:24; Is. 46:1, 2 • 49:3

8 And the ᵀspoiler shall come upon every city, and no city shall escape: the valley also shall perish, and the plain shall be destroyed, as the LORD hath spoken.   *robber*

9 Give wings unto Moab, that it may flee and get away: for the cities thereof shall be desolate, without any to dwell therein.

10 Cursed *be* he that doeth the work of the LORD deceitfully, and cursed *be* he that keepeth back his sword from blood.

11 Moab hath been at ease from his youth, and he hath settled on his lees, and hath not been emptied from vessel to vessel, neither hath he gone into captivity: therefore ᵀthis taste remained in him, and his scent is not changed.   *he is the same as before*

12 Therefore, behold, the days come, saith the LORD, that I will send unto him wanderers, that shall cause him to wander, and shall empty his vessels, and break their bottles.

13 And Moab shall be ashamed of Che'-mosh, as the house of Israel was ashamed of Beth'-el their confidence.

14 How say ye, ᴿWe *are* mighty and strong men for the war?   Ps. 33:16

15 Moab is spoiled, and gone up *out of* her cities, and his chosen young men are gone down to the slaughter, saith the King, whose name *is* the LORD of hosts.

16 The calamity of Moab *is* near to ᴿcome, and his affliction hasteth fast.   Is. 13:22

17 All ye that are about him, bemoan him; and all ye that know his name, say, ᴿHow is the strong staff broken, *and* the beautiful rod!   Is. 9:4; 14:4, 5

18 ᴿThou daughter that dost inhabit ᴿDi'-bon, come down from *thy* glory, and sit in thirst; for the ᵀspoiler of Moab shall come upon thee, *and* he shall destroy thy strong holds.   Is. 47:1 · Num. 21:30; Is. 15:2 · *destroyer*

19 O inhabitant of Ar'-o-er, stand by the way, and espy; ask him that fleeth, and her that escapeth, *and* say, What is done?

20 Moab is confounded; for it is broken down: ᴿhowl and cry; tell ye it in ᴿArnon, that Moab is spoiled,   Is. 16:7 · Num. 21:13

21 And judgment is come upon the plain country; upon Ho'-lon, and upon Ja'-ha-zah, and upon Meph'-a-ath,

22 And upon Di'-bon, and upon Ne'-bo, and upon Beth–dib-la-tha'-im,

23 And upon Kir-i-a-tha'-im, and upon Beth–ga'-mul, and upon Beth–me'-on,

24 And upon ᴿKe'-ri-oth, and upon ᴿBoz'-rah, and upon all the cities of the land of Moab, far or near.   Amos 2:2 · Is. 34:6

25 The ᵀhorn of Moab is cut off, and his arm is broken, saith the LORD.   *strength*

26 ᴿMake ye him drunken: for he magnified *himself* against the LORD: Moab also shall wallow in his vomit, and he also shall be in derision.   25:15

27 For ᴿwas not Israel a derision unto thee? ᴿwas he found among thieves? for ᵀsince thou spakest of him, thou ᵀskippedst for joy.   Zeph. 2:8 · 2:26 · *as often as* · *jump*

28 O ye that dwell in Moab, leave the cities, and ᴿdwell in the rock, and be like ᴿthe dove *that* maketh her nest in the sides of the hole's mouth.   Ps. 55:6, 7 · Song 2:14

29 We have heard the ᴿpride of Moab, (he is exceeding proud) his loftiness, and his arrogancy, and his pride, and the haughtiness of his heart.   Is. 16:6; Zeph. 2:8

30 I know his wrath, saith the LORD; but *it* shall not *be* so; ᴿhisᵀ lies shall not so effect *it*.   50:36 · *his boastings have done nothing*

31 Therefore will I howl for Moab, and I will cry out for all Moab; *mine heart* shall mourn for the men of Kir-he'-res.

32 ᴿO vine of Sib'-mah, I will weep for thee with the weeping of Ja'-zer: thy plants are gone over the sea, they reach *even* to the sea of Ja'-zer: the spoiler is fallen upon thy summer fruits and upon thy vintage.   Is. 16:8, 9

33 And joy and gladness is taken from the plentiful field, and from the land of Moab; and I have caused wine to fail from the winepresses: none shall tread with shouting; *their* shouting *shall be* no shouting.

34 ᴿFrom the cry of Hesh'-bon *even* unto E-le-a'-leh, *and even* unto Ja'-haz, have they uttered their voice, ᴿfrom Zo'-ar *even* unto Hor-o-na'-im, *as* an heifer of three years old: for the waters also of Nim'-rim shall be ᵀdesolate.   Is. 15:4-6 · Is. 15:5, 6 · *ruined*

35 Moreover I will cause to cease in Moab, saith the LORD, him that offereth in the ᵀhigh places, and him that ᵀburneth incense to his gods.   *pagan shrines* · *worships*

36 Therefore mine heart shall sound for Moab like pipes, and mine heart shall sound like pipes for the men of Kir-he'-res: because the riches *that* he hath gotten are perished.

37 For every head *shall be* bald, and every beard clipped: upon all the hands *shall be* cuttings, and upon the loins sackcloth.

38 *There shall be* ᵀlamentation generally upon all the ᴿhousetops of Moab, and in the streets thereof: for I have broken Moab like ᴿa vessel wherein *is* no pleasure, saith the LORD.   *weeping* · Is. 22:1 · 22:28

39 They shall howl, *saying,* How is it broken down! how hath Moab turned the back with shame! so shall Moab be a derision and a dismaying to all them about him.

40 For thus saith the LORD; Behold, ᴿhe shall fly as an eagle, and shall ᴿspread his wings over Moab.   Deut. 28:49; Hab. 1:8 · Is. 8:8

41 ᵀKe'-ri-oth is taken, and the strong holds are surprised, and the mighty men's hearts in Moab at that day shall be as the heart of a woman in her pangs.   *the cities are*

42 And Moab shall be ᴿdestroyed from *being* a people, because he hath ᴿmagnified *himself* against the LORD.   Ps. 83:4 · Is. 37:23

43 ℝFear, and the pit, and the snare, *shall be* upon thee, O inhabitant of Moab, saith the LORD.   Is. 24:17, 18; Lam. 3:47

44 He that fleeth from the fear shall fall into the pit; and he that getteth up out of the pit shall be taken in the snare: for I will bring upon it, *even* upon Moab, the year of their visitation, saith the LORD.

45 They that fled stood under the shadow of Hesh'-bon because of the force: but a fire shall come forth out of Hesh'-bon, and a flame from the midst of Si'-hon, and shall devour the corner of Moab, and the crown of the head of the tumultuous ones.

46 ℝWoe be unto thee, O Moab! the people of ℝChe'-mosh perisheth: for thy sons are taken captives, and thy daughters captives.   Num. 21:29 · v. 7; Judg. 11:24; 1 Kin. 11:7

47 Yet will I bring again the captivity of Moab ℝin the latter days, saith the LORD. Thus far *is* the judgment of Moab.   49:6

CHAPTER 49

Prophecies Against Ammon

CONCERNINGᵀ the ℝAm'-mon-ites, thus saith the LORD; Hath Israel no sons? hath he no heir? why *then* doth ℝtheir ᵀking inherit Gad, and his people dwell in his cities?   *against* · Amos 1:13 · 1 Kin. 11:5, 33 · *Malcam*

2 Therefore, behold, the days come, saith the LORD, that I will cause an alarm of war to be heard in ℝRab'-bah of the Am'-mon-ites; and it shall be a desolate ᵀheap, and her daughters shall be burned with fire: then shall Israel be heir unto them that were his heirs, saith the LORD.   Ezek. 25:5 · *ruin*

3 Howl, O Hesh'-bon, for A'-i is spoiled: cry, ye daughters of Rab'-bah, gird you with sackcloth; lament, and run to and fro by the hedges; for their king shall go into captivity, *and* his priests and his princes together.

4 Wherefore gloriest thou in the valleys, thy flowing valley, O backsliding daughter? that trusted in her treasures, *saying*, Who shall come unto me?

5 Behold, I will bring a fear upon thee, saith the Lord GOD of hosts, from all those that be about thee; and ye shall be driven out every man right forth; and none shall ᵀgather up him that wandereth.   *rescue*

6 And afterward I will bring again the captivity of the children of Ammon, saith the LORD.

Prophecies Against Edom

7 ℝConcerning E'-dom, thus saith the LORD of hosts; Is wisdom no more in Te'-man? is counsel perished from the prudent? is their wisdom vanished?   Ezek. 25:12

8 Flee ye, ᵀturn back, dwell deep, O inhabitants of ℝDe'-dan; for I will bring the calamity of Esau upon him, the time *that* I will visit him.   *they are turned back* · 25:23

9 If ℝgrapegatherers come to thee, would they not leave *some* gleaning grapes? if thieves by night, they will destroy ᵀtill they have enough.   Obad. 5 · *as much as they wish*

10 ℝBut I have made Esau bare, I have uncovered his secret places, and he shall not be able to hide himself: his seed is ᵀspoiled, and his brethren, and his neighbours, and ℝhe *is* not.   Mal. 1:3 · *ruined* · Is. 17:14

11 Leave thy fatherless children, I will preserve *them* alive; and let thy ℝwidows trust in me.   Ps. 68:5; Zech. 7:10

12 For thus saith the LORD; Behold, ℝthey whose judgment *was* not to drink of the cup have assuredly drunken; and *art* thou he *that* shall altogether go ℝunpunished? thou shalt not go unpunished, but thou shalt surely drink *of it.*   Obad. 16 · [1 Pet. 4:17]

13 For I have sworn by myself, saith the LORD, that Boz'-rah shall become a desolation, a reproach, a waste, and a curse; and all the cities thereof shall be perpetual wastes.

14 I have heard a rumour from the LORD, and an ambassador is sent unto the heathen, *saying*, Gather ye together, and come against her, and rise up to the battle.

15 For, lo, I will make thee small among the heathen, *and* despised among men.

16 Thy ᵀterribleness hath deceived thee, *and* the pride of thine heart, O thou that dwellest in the clefts of the rock, that holdest the height of the hill: though thou shouldest make thy ℝnest as high as the eagle, ℝI will bring thee down from thence, saith the LORD.   *prestige* · Job 39:27 · Amos 9:2

17 Also E'-dom shall be a ℝdesolation: ℝevery one that goeth by it shall be astonished, and shall ᵀhiss at all the plagues thereof.   *v.* 13; Ezek. 35:7 · 18:16; 50:13 · *scorn*

18 As in the overthrow of Sodom and Gomor'-rah and the neighbour *cities* thereof, saith the LORD, no man shall abide there, neither shall a son of man dwell in it.

19 Behold, he shall come up like a lion from the swelling of Jordan against the habitation of the strong: but I will suddenly make him run away from her: and who *is* a chosen *man, that* I may appoint over her? for who *is* like me? and who will ᵀappoint me the time? and who *is* that shepherd that will stand before me?   *decide*

20 ℝTherefore hear the counsel of the LORD, that he hath taken against E'-dom; and his purposes, that he hath purposed against the inhabitants of Te'-man: Surely the least of the flock shall draw them out: surely he shall make their habitations ℝdesolate with them.   Is. 14:24, 27 · Mal. 1:3, 4

21 ℝThe earth is moved at the noise of their fall, at the cry the noise thereof was heard in the ᵀRed sea.   50:46 · *Weedy Sea*

22 Behold, ^Rhe shall come up and fly as the eagle, and spread his wings over Boz'-rah: and at that day shall the heart of the mighty men of E'-dom be as the heart of a woman in her pangs.   4:13; 48:40, 41; Hos. 8:1

Prophecies Against Damascus

23 Concerning Damascus. Ha'-math is confounded, and Ar'-pad: for they have heard evil tidings: they are ^Tfainthearted; *there is* sorrow on the sea; it cannot be quiet.   *weak*

24 Damascus is waxed feeble, *and* turneth herself to flee, and fear hath seized on *her:* ^Ranguish and sorrows have taken her, as a woman in ^Ttravail.   4:31; Is. 13:8 · *suffering*

25 How is ^Rthe city of praise not left, the city of my joy!   33:9; 51:41

26 Therefore her young men shall fall in her streets, and all the men of war shall be cut off in that day, saith the LORD of hosts.

27 And I will kindle a ^Rfire in the wall of Damascus, and it shall consume the palaces of Ben-ha'-dad.   1 Kin. 15:18-20; Amos 1:4

Prophecies Against Kedar and Hazor

28 Concerning Ke'-dar, and concerning the kingdoms of Ha'-zor, which Neb-u-chad-rez'-zar king of Babylon shall smite, thus saith the LORD; Arise ye, go up to Ke'-dar, and ^Tspoil the men of the east.   *rob*

29 Their ^Rtents and their flocks shall they take away: they shall take to themselves their curtains, and all their vessels, and their camels; and they shall cry unto them, ^RFear *is* on every side.   Ps. 120:5 · 46:5

30 Flee, get you far off, dwell deep, O ye inhabitants of Ha'-zor, saith the LORD; for Neb-u-chad-rez'-zar king of Babylon hath ^Ttaken counsel against you, and hath conceived a purpose against you.   *made plans*

31 Arise, get you up unto ^Tthe wealthy nation, that dwelleth without care, saith the LORD, which have neither gates nor bars, *which* ^Rdwell alone.   *strong* · Num. 23:9

32 And their camels shall be a booty, and the multitude of their cattle a ^Tspoil: and I will scatter into all winds them *that are* ^Tin the utmost corners; and I will bring their calamity from all sides thereof, saith the LORD.   *prize of war · cut off into corners*

33 And Ha'-zor ^Rshall be a dwelling for ^Tdragons, *and* a desolation for ever: there shall no man abide there, nor *any* son of man dwell in it.   9:11; 10:22; Mal. 1:3 · *jackals*

Prophecies Against Elam

34 The word of the LORD that came to Jer-e-mi'-ah the prophet against ^RE'-lam in the beginning of the reign of Zed-e-ki'-ah king of Judah, saying,   25:25; Gen. 10:22; 14:1, 9

35 Thus saith the LORD of hosts; Behold, I will break ^Rthe ^Tbow of E'-lam, the chief of their might.   Is. 22:6 · *power*

36 And upon E'-lam will I bring the four winds from the four quarters of heaven, and will scatter them toward all those winds; and there shall be no nation whither the outcasts of E'-lam shall not come.

37 For I will cause E'-lam to be ^Tdismayed before their enemies, and before them that seek their life: and I will bring evil upon them, *even* my fierce anger, saith the LORD; and I will send the sword after them, till I have consumed them: *frightened*

38 And I will ^Rset my throne in E'-lam, and will destroy from thence the king and the princes, saith the LORD.   43:10

39 But it shall come to pass ^Rin the latter days, *that* I will bring again the captivity of E'-lam, saith the LORD.   48:47

CHAPTER 50

Babylon's Defeat

T HE word that the LORD spake against Babylon *and* against the land of the Chal-de'-ans by Jer-e-mi'-ah the prophet.

2 Declare ye among the nations, and publish, and ^Tset up a standard; publish, *and* conceal not: say, Babylon is taken, Bel is confounded, Me-ro'-dach is broken in pieces; her idols are confounded, her images are broken in pieces.   *lift up*

3 For out of the north there cometh up ^Ra nation against her, which shall make her land ^Tdesolate, and none shall dwell therein: they shall remove, they shall depart, both man and beast.   Is. 13:17, 18, 20 · *empty*

4 In those days, and in that time, saith the LORD, the children of Israel shall come, they and the children of Judah together, ^Rgoing and weeping: they shall go, ^Rand seek the LORD their God.   Ezra 3:12 · Hos. 3:5

5 They shall ask the way to Zion with their faces thitherward, *saying,* Come, and let us join ourselves to the LORD in a perpetual covenant *that* shall not be forgotten.

6 My people hath been lost sheep: their shepherds have caused them to go astray, they have turned them away *on* the mountains: they have gone from mountain to hill, they have forgotten their ^Trestingplace.   *refuge*

7 All that found them have ^Rdevoured them: and their adversaries said, We offend not, because they have sinned against the LORD, the habitation of justice, even the LORD, the hope of their fathers.   Ps. 79:7

8 Remove out of the midst of Babylon, and go forth out of the land of the Chal-de'-ans, and be as the he goats before the flocks.

9 ^RFor, lo, I will raise and cause to come up against Babylon an assembly of great nations from the north country: and they shall set themselves in array against her; from thence she shall be taken: their arrows *shall be* as of a mighty expert man; ^Rnone shall return in vain.   15:14 · 2 Sam. 1:22

10 And ᴿChal-de'-a shall be ᵀa spoil: ᴿall that ᵀspoil her shall be satisfied, saith the LORD.   Ezek. 11:24 • *for loot* • [Rev. 17:16] • *rob*

11 Because ye were glad, because ye rejoiced, O ye destroyers of mine heritage, because ye are grown fat as the heifer at grass, and ᵀbellow as bulls;   *neigh as steeds*

12 Your mother shall be sore confounded; she that bare you shall be ashamed: behold, the hindermost of the nations *shall be* a wilderness, a dry land, and a desert.

13 Because of the wrath of the LORD it shall not be inhabited, ᴿbut it shall be wholly desolate: ᴿevery one that goeth by Babylon shall be astonished, and ᵀhiss at all her plagues.   25:12 • 49:17 • *sneer*

14 Put yourselves in array against Babylon round about: all ye that bend the bow, shoot at her, spare no arrows: for she hath sinned against the LORD.

15 Shout against her round about: she hath given her hand: her foundations are fallen, her walls are thrown down: for it *is* the vengeance of the LORD: take vengeance upon her; as she hath done, do unto her.

16 Cut off the sower from Babylon, and him that handleth the sickle in the time of harvest: for fear of the oppressing sword they shall turn every one to his people, and they shall flee every one to his own land.

17 Israel *is* a scattered sheep; ᴿthe lions have driven *him* away: first ᴿthe king of Assyria hath devoured him; and last this ᴿNeb-u-chad-rez'-zar king of Babylon hath broken his bones.   2:15 • 2 Kin. 17:6 • 2 Kin. 24:10, 14

18 Therefore thus saith the LORD of hosts, the God of Israel; Behold, I will punish the king of Babylon and his land, as I have punished the king of Assyria.

19 And I will ᴿbring Israel again to his habitation, and he shall feed on Carmel and Ba'-shan, and his soul shall be satisfied upon mount E'-phra-im and Gil'-e-ad.   31:10

20 In those days, and in that time, saith the LORD, the iniquity of Israel shall be sought for, and *there shall be* none; and the sins of Judah, and they shall not be found: for I will pardon them whom I ᵀreserve.   *save*

Babylon's Desolation

21 Go up against the land of Mer-a-tha'-im, *even* against it, and against the inhabitants of ᴿPe'-kod: waste and utterly destroy after them, saith the LORD, and do according to all that I have commanded thee.   Ezek. 23:23

22 ᴿA sound of battle *is* in the land, and of great destruction.   4:19-21; 51:54-56

23 How is the hammer of the whole earth cut asunder and broken! how is Babylon become a desolation among the nations!

24 I have laid a snare for thee, and thou art also taken, O Babylon, and thou wast not aware: thou art found, and also caught, because thou hast striven against the LORD.

25 The LORD hath opened his armoury, and hath brought forth the weapons of his indignation: for this *is* the work of the Lord GOD of hosts in the land of the Chal-de'-ans.

26 Come against her from ᵀthe utmost border, open her storehouses: cast her up as heaps, and ᴿdestroy her utterly: let nothing of her be left.   *the whole land* • Is. 14:23

27 Slay all her bullocks; let them go down to the slaughter: woe unto them! for their day is come, the time of ᴿtheir visitation.   48:44

28 The voice of them that flee and escape out of the land of Babylon, ᴿto declare in Zion the ᴿvengeance of the LORD our God, the vengeance of his temple.   51:10 • Lam. 1:10

29 Call together the archers against Babylon: all ye that bend the bow, camp against it round about; let none thereof escape: recompense her according to her work; according to all that she hath done, do unto her: for she hath been proud against the LORD, against the Holy One of Israel.

30 Therefore shall her young men fall in the streets, and all her men of war shall be cut off in that day, saith the LORD.

31 Behold, I *am* against thee, *O thou* most proud, saith the Lord GOD of hosts: for thy day is come, the time *that* I will visit thee.

32 And the most proud shall stumble and fall, and none shall raise him up: and ᴿI will kindle a fire in his cities, and it shall ᵀdevour all round about him.   21:14 • *destroy*

33 Thus saith the LORD of hosts; The children of Israel and the children of Judah *were* oppressed together: and ᴿall that took them captives held them fast; they refused to let them go.   [Is. 14:17; 58:6]

34 Their Redeemer *is* strong; ᴿthe LORD of hosts *is* his name: he shall throughly plead their cause, that he may give rest to the land, and disquiet the inhabitants of Babylon. Is. 47:4

35 A ᴿsword *is* upon the Chal-de'-ans, saith the LORD, and upon the inhabitants of Babylon, and ᴿupon her princes, and upon ᴿher wise *men*.   47:6 • Dan. 5:30 • Is. 47:13

36 A sword *is* upon the liars; and they shall ᵀdote: a sword *is* upon her mighty men; and they shall be dismayed.   *despair*

37 A sword *is* upon their horses, and upon their chariots, and upon all the mingled people that *are* in the midst of her; and they shall become as women: a sword *is* upon her treasures; and they shall be robbed.

38 A drought *is* upon her waters; and they shall be dried up: for it *is* the land of graven images, and they are mad upon *their* idols.

39 ᴿTherefore the wild beasts of the desert with the wild beasts of the islands shall dwell *there*, and the owls shall dwell therein: ᴿand it shall be no more inhabited for ever; neither shall it be dwelt in from generation to generation.   Rev. 18:2 • Is. 13:20

40 As God overthrew Sodom and Go-mor'-rah and the neighbour *cities* thereof, saith the

LORD; so shall no man abide there, neither shall any son of man dwell therein.

41 ᴿBehold, a people shall come from the north, and a great nation, and ᴿmany kings shall be raised up from the coasts of the earth. *v. 3; 6:22; 25:14; 51:27 • Rev. 17:16*

42 They shall hold the bow and the lance: they *are* cruel, and will not shew mercy: ᴿtheir voice shall roar like the sea, and they shall ride upon horses, *every one* put in array, like a man to the battle, against thee, O daughter of Babylon. *Is. 5:30*

43 The king of Babylon hath heard the report of them, and his hands ᵀwaxed feeble: anguish took hold of him, *and* pangs as of a woman in travail. *grew weak*

44 Behold, he shall come up like a lion from the ᵀswelling of Jordan unto the habitation of the strong: but I will make them suddenly run away from her: and who *is* a chosen *man, that* I may appoint over her? for who *is* like me? and who will ᵀappoint me the time? and who *is* that shepherd that will stand before me? *flood • decide*

45 Therefore hear ye ᴿthe ᵀcounsel of the LORD, that he hath taken against Babylon; and his purposes, that he hath purposed against the land of the Chal-de′-ans: Surely the least of the flock shall draw them out: surely he shall make *their* habitation desolate with them. *51:11 • word*

46 ᴿAt the noise of the taking of Babylon the earth is moved, and the cry is heard among the nations. *4:11, 12; Rev. 18:9*

CHAPTER 51

Babylon's Destiny

THUS saith the LORD; Behold, I will raise up against Babylon, and against them that dwell in the midst of them that rise up against me, a destroying wind;

2 And will send unto Babylon ᴿfanners, that shall fan her, and shall empty her land: ᴿfor in the day of trouble they shall be against her round about. *15:7 • 50:14*

3 Against *him that* bendeth ᴿlet the archer bend his bow, and against *him that* lifteth himself up in his ᵀbrigandine: and spare ye not her young men; ᴿdestroy ye utterly all her host. *50:14 • armour • 50:21*

4 Thus the slain shall fall in the land of the Chal-de′-ans, ᴿand *they that are* thrust through in her streets. *49:26; 50:30, 37*

5 For ᴵIsrael *hath* not *been* forsaken, nor Judah of his God, of the LORD of hosts; though their land was filled with sin against the Holy One of Israel. *[33:24-26]*

6 ᴿFlee out of the midst of Babylon, and deliver every man his ᵀsoul: be not cut off in her iniquity; for ᴿthis *is* the time of the LORD's vengeance; ᴿhe will render unto her a recompence. *Rev. 18:4 • life • 50:15 • 25:14*

7 Babylon *hath been* a golden cup in the LORD's hand, that made all the earth drunken: the nations have drunken of her wine; therefore the nations are ᵀmad. *crazed*

8 Babylon is suddenly fallen and destroyed: ᵀhowl for her; take balm for her pain, if so be she may be healed. *lament*

9 We would have healed Babylon, but she is not healed: forsake her, and ᴿlet us go every one into his own country: ᴿfor her judgment reacheth unto heaven, and is lifted up *even* to the skies. *Is. 13:14 • Rev. 18:5*

10 The LORD hath ᴿbrought forth our righteousness: come, and let us declare in Zion the work of the LORD our God. *Ps. 37:6*

11 ᴿMake ᵀbright the arrows; gather the shields: the LORD hath raised up the spirit of the kings of the Medes: for his ᵀdevice *is* against Babylon, to destroy it; because it *is* the vengeance of the LORD, the vengeance of his temple. *46:4 • polish • plan*

12 Set up the standard upon the walls of Babylon, make the watch strong, set up the watchmen, prepare the ambushes: for the LORD hath both devised and done that which he spake against the inhabitants of Babylon.

13 O thou that dwellest upon many waters, abundant in treasures, thine end is come, *and* the measure of thy covetousness.

14 The LORD of hosts hath sworn by himself, *saying,* Surely I will fill thee with men, as with caterpillers; and they shall ᵀlift up a shout against thee. *raise a battle cry*

15 ᴿHe hath made the earth by his power, he hath established the world by his wisdom, and ᴿhath stretched out the heaven by his understanding. *Gen. 1:1, 6 • Job 9:8*

16 When he uttereth *his* ᴿvoice, *there is a* ᵀmultitude of waters in the heavens; and ᴿhe causeth the vapors to ascend from the ends of the earth: he maketh lightnings with rain, and bringeth forth the wind out of his treasures. *Job 37:2-6 • tumult • Ps. 135:7*

17 Every man is brutish by *his* knowledge; every founder is confounded by the graven image: for his molten image *is* falsehood, and *there is* no breath in them.

18 They *are* vanity, the work of errors: in the time of their visitation they shall perish.

19 The ᴿportion of Jacob *is* not like them; for he *is* the former of all things: and *Israel is* the ᵀrod of his inheritance: the LORD of hosts *is* his name. *Ps. 73:26 • tribe*

20 ᴿThou *art* my battle ax *and* weapons of war: for with thee will I ᴿbreak in pieces the nations, and with thee will I destroy kingdoms; *Is. 10:5, 15 • Mic. 4:12, 13*

21 And with thee will I break in pieces the horse and his rider; and with thee will I break in pieces the chariot and his rider;

22 With thee also will I break in pieces man and woman; and with thee will I break in pieces ᴿold and young; and with thee will I

break in pieces the ᴿyoung man and the maid;   2 Chr. 36:17 · Is. 13:15, 16, 18

23 I will also break in pieces with thee the shepherd and his flock; and with thee will I break in pieces the husbandman and his yoke of oxen; and with thee will I break in pieces captains and rulers.

24 ᴿAnd I will render unto Babylon and to all the inhabitants of Chal-de′-a all their evil that they have done in Zion in your sight, saith the LORD.   50:15

25 Behold, I am against thee, ᴿO destroying ᵀmountain, saith the LORD, which destroyest all the earth: and I will stretch out mine hand upon thee, and roll thee down from the rocks, and will make thee ᵀa burnt mountain.   Is. 13:2 · power · a ruined power

26 And they shall not take of thee a stone for a corner, nor a stone for foundations; ᴿbut thou shalt be ᵀdesolate for ever, saith the LORD.   50:13, 40 · ruined

27 ᴿSet ye up a standard in the land, blow the trumpet among the nations, prepare the nations against her, call together against her ᴿthe kingdoms of A′-ra-rat, Min′-ni, and Ash′-che-naz; appoint a captain against her; cause the horses to come up as the rough caterpillers.   Is. 13:2 · 50:41

28 Prepare against her the nations with the kings of the Medes, the captains thereof, and all the rulers thereof, and all the land of his dominion.

29 And the land shall tremble and sorrow: for every purpose of the LORD shall be performed against Babylon, to make the land of Babylon a desolation without an inhabitant.

30 The mighty men of Babylon have forborn to fight, they have remained in their ᵀholds: their might hath failed; they became as women: they have burned her dwellingplaces; her bars are broken.   forts

31 ᴿOne post shall run to meet another, and one messenger to meet another, to shew the king of Babylon that his city is taken ᵀat one end,   50:24 · on every quarter

32 And that the passages are ᵀstopped, and the reeds they have burned with fire, and the men of war are affrighted.   seized

33 For thus saith the LORD of hosts, the God of Israel; The daughter of Babylon is like a threshingfloor, itᵀ is time to thresh her: yet a little while, and the time of her harvest shall come.   at the time when it is trampled

34 Neb-u-chad-rez′-zar the king of Babylon hath ᴿdevoured me, he hath crushed me, he hath made me an empty vessel, he hath swallowed me up like a dragon, he hath filled his belly with my ᵀdelicates, he hath cast me out.   50:17 · delicious foods

35 The violence done to me and to my ᵀflesh be upon Babylon, shall the inhabitant

of Zion say; and my blood upon the inhabitants of Chal-de′-a, shall Jerusalem say. kinfolk

36 Therefore thus saith the LORD; Behold, ᴿI will plead thy cause, and take vengeance for thee; ᴿand I will dry up her sea, and make her springs dry.   50:34 · 50:38

37 And Babylon shall become heaps, a dwellingplace for dragons, an astonishment, and ᵀan hissing, without an inhabitant. a shame

38 They shall roar together like ᴿlions: they shall yell as lions' whelps.   2:15

39 In their heat I will make their feasts, and ᴿI will make them drunken, that they may rejoice, and sleep a perpetual sleep, and not wake, saith the LORD.   v. 57; Ps. 76:5

40 I will bring them down like lambs to the slaughter, like rams with he goats.

41 ᴿHow is She′-shach taken! and how is the praise of the whole earth surprised! how is Babylon become an ᵀastonishment among the nations!   25:26 · desolation

42 ᴿThe sea is come up upon Babylon: she is covered with the multitude of the waves thereof.   Is. 8:7; Dan. 9:26

43 ᴿHer cities are a desolation, a dry land, and a wilderness, a land wherein no man dwelleth, neither doth any son of man pass thereby.   50:39; Is. 13:20

44 And I will punish Bel in Babylon, and I will bring forth out of his mouth that which he hath swallowed up: and the nations shall not flow together any more unto him: yea, the wall of Babylon shall fall.

45 ᴿMy people, go ye out of the midst of her, and deliver ye every man his soul from the fierce anger of the LORD.   [50:8; Rev. 18:4]

46 And ᵀlest your heart faint, and ye fear ᴿfor the rumour that shall be heard in the land; a rumour shall both come one year, and after that in another year shall come a rumour, and violence in the land, ᴿruler against ruler.   let not · 2 Kin. 19:7 · Is. 19:2

47 Therefore, behold, the days come, that I will ᵀdo judgment upon the ᴿgraven images of Babylon: and her whole land shall be confounded, and all her slain shall fall in the midst of her.   bring · Is. 21:9; 46:1, 2

48 Then ᴿthe heaven and the earth, and all that is therein, shall sing for Babylon: ᴿfor the spoilers shall come unto her from the north, saith the LORD.   Is. 44:23 · 50:3, 41

49 ᴿAs Babylon hath caused the slain of Israel to fall, so at Babylon shall fall the slain of all the ᵀearth.   50:29; Ps. 137:8 · land

50 ᴿYe that have escaped the sword, go away, stand not still: ᴿremember the LORD afar off, and let Jerusalem come into your mind.   44:28 · [Deut. 4:29–31]; Ps. 137:6

51 We are confounded, because we have heard reproach: shame hath covered our faces: for strangers are come into the ᵀsanctuaries of the LORD'S house.   holy places

52 Wherefore, behold, the days come, saith

the LORD, that I will ᵀdo judgment upon her graven images: and through all her land the wounded shall groan. _bring_

53 Though Babylon should mount up to heaven, and though she should fortify the height of her strength, _yet_ from me shall spoilers come unto her, saith the LORD.

54 ᴿA sound of a cry _cometh_ from Babylon, and great destruction from the land of the Chal-de′-ans: 50:22

55 Because the LORD hath spoiled Babylon, and destroyed out of her the great voice; when her waves do roar like great waters, a noise of their voice is uttered:

56 Because the ᵀspoiler is come upon her, _even_ upon Babylon, and her mighty men are taken, every one of their bows is broken: ᴿfor the LORD God of recompences shall surely ᵀrequite. _robber • 50:29 • pay back_

57 And I will make drunk her princes, and her wise _men,_ her captains, and her rulers, and her mighty men: and they shall sleep a perpetual sleep, and not wake, saith the King, whose name _is_ the LORD of hosts.

58 Thus saith the LORD of hosts; The broad walls of Babylon shall be utterly broken, and her high gates shall be burned with fire; and the people shall labour in vain, and the ᵀfolk in the fire, and they shall be weary. _nations for_

59 The word which Jer-e-mi′-ah the prophet commanded Se-ra′-iah the son of Ne-ri′-ah, the son of Ma-a-se′-iah, when he went with Zed-e-ki′-ah the king of Judah into Babylon in the fourth year of his reign. And _this_ Se-ra′-iah _was_ a quiet prince.

60 So Jer-e-mi′-ah wrote in a book all the evil that should come upon Babylon, _even_ all these words that are written against Babylon.

61 And Jer-e-mi′-ah said to Se-ra′-iah, When thou comest to Babylon, and shalt see, and shalt read all these words;

62 Then shalt thou say, O LORD, thou hast spoken against this place, to cut it off, that none shall remain in it, neither man nor beast, but that it shall be desolate for ever.

63 And it shall be, when thou hast made an end of reading this book, ᴿthat thou shalt bind a stone to it, and ᴿcast it into the midst of Eu-phra′-tes: _Rev. 18:21 • 19:10, 11_

64 And thou shalt say, Thus shall Babylon sink, and shall not rise from the evil that I will bring upon her: and they shall be ᴿweary. Thus far _are_ the words of Jer-e-mi′-ah. _v. 58_

CHAPTER 52

The Capture of Jerusalem
2 Kin. 24:18—25:30; 2 Chr. 36:11-20; Jer. 39:1-8

ZED-E-KI′-AH _was_ one and twenty years old when he ᵀbegan to reign, and he reigned eleven years in Jerusalem. And his mother's name _was_ Ha-mu′-tal the daughter of Jer-e-mi′-ah of Lib′-nah. _became king_

2 And he did _that which was_ ᴿevil in the eyes of the LORD, ᴿaccording to all that Je-hoi′-a-kim had done. _1 Kin. 14:22 • 36:30, 31_

3 For through the ᴿanger of the LORD it came to pass in Jerusalem and Judah, till he had cast them out from his presence, that Zed-e-ki′-ah ᴿrebelled against the king of Babylon. _Is. 3:1, 4, 5 • 2 Chr. 36:13_

4 And it came to pass in the ninth year of his reign, in the tenth month, in the tenth _day_ of the month, _that_ Neb-u-chad-rez′-zar king of Babylon came, he and all his army, against Jerusalem, and ᵀpitched against it, and built forts against it round about. _besieged_

5 So the city was besieged unto the eleventh year of king Zed-e-ki′-ah.

6 And in the ᴿfourth month, in the ninth _day_ of the month, the ᴿfamine was sore in the city, so that there was no bread for the people of the land. _39:2 • 38:9; 2 Kin. 25:3_

7 Then the city ᵀwas broken up, and all the men of war fled, and went forth out of the city by night by the way of the gate between the two walls, which _was_ by the king's garden; (now the Chal-de′-ans _were_ by the city round about:) and they went by the way of the plain. _fell to the attackers_

8 But the army of the Chal-de′-ans pursued after the king, and ᴿovertook Zed-e-ki′-ah in the plains of Jericho; and all his army was scattered from him. _21:7; 32:4_

9 ᴿThen they took the king, and ᴿcarried him up unto the king of Babylon to ᴿRib′-lah in the land of Ha′-math; where he gave judgment upon him. _32:4 • 39:5; 2 Kin. 25:6 • 39:5_

10 And the king of Babylon slew the sons of Zed-e-ki′-ah before his eyes: he slew also all the princes of Judah in Rib′-lah.

11 Then he put out the eyes of Zed-e-ki′-ah; and the king of Babylon bound him in chains, and carried him to Babylon, and put him in prison till the day of his death.

The Destruction of Jerusalem

12 ᴿNow in the fifth month, in the tenth _day_ of the month, which _was_ the nineteenth year of Neb-u-chad-rez′-zar king of Babylon, came Neb′-u-zar-a′-dan, captain of the guard, _which_ served the king of Babylon, into Jerusalem, _2 Kin. 25:8-21_

13 And ᴿburned the house of the LORD, and the king's house; and all the houses of Jerusalem, and all the houses of the great _men,_ burned he with fire: _2 Chr. 36:19_

14 And all the army of the Chal-de′-ans, that _were_ with the captain of the guard, ᴿbrake down all the walls of Jerusalem round about. _2 Kin. 25:10; Neh. 1:3_

15 Then Neb′-u-zar-a′-dan the captain of the guard carried away captive _certain_ of the poor of the people, and the residue of the people that remained in the city, and those that ᵀfell away, that fell to the king of Babylon, and the rest of the multitude. _deserted_

16 But Neb'-u-zar-a'-dan the captain of the guard left *certain* of the poor of the land for vinedressers and for husbandmen.

17 Also the pillars of brass that *were* in the house of the LORD, and the bases, and the brasen sea that *was* in the house of the LORD, the Chal-de'-ans ᵀbrake, and carried all the brass of them to Babylon.　　　*smashed*

18 The caldrons also, and the shovels, and the snuffers, and the ᵀbowls, and the spoons, and all the vessels of brass wherewith they ministered, took they away.　　　*basons*

19 And the ᴿbasons, and the ᵀfirepans, and the bowls, and the caldrons, and the candlesticks, and the spoons, and the cups; *that* which *was* of gold *in* gold, and *that* which *was* of silver *in* silver, took the captain of the guard away.　　　1 Kin. 7:49, 50 • *censers*

20 The two pillars, one sea, and twelve brasen bulls that *were* under the bases, which king Solomon had made ᵀin the house of the LORD: ᴿthe brass of all these vessels was ᵀwithout weight.　　　*for* • 1 Kin. 7:47 • *not weighed*

21 And *concerning* the pillars, the height of one pillar *was* ᵀeighteen cubits; and a fillet of ᵀtwelve cubits did ᵀcompass it; and the thickness thereof *was* ᵀfour fingers: *it was* hollow.　　　*27 ft.* • *18 ft.* • *circumference* • *3 in.*

22 And a chapiter of brass *was* upon it; and the height of one ᵀchapiter *was* ᵀfive cubits, with network and pomegranates upon the chapiters round about, all of brass. The second pillar also and the pomegranates *were* like unto these.　　　*capital* • *7.5 ft.*

23 And there were ninety and six pomegranates on a side; *and* ᴿall the pomegranates upon the network *were* an hundred round about.　　　1 Kin. 7:20

The Exile to Babylon

24 And the captain of the guard took Se-ra'-iah the chief priest, ᴿand Zeph-a-ni'-ah the second priest, and the three keepers of the ᵀdoor:　　　21:1; 29:25 • *entrance*

25 He took also out of the city a eunuch, which had the charge of the men of war; and seven men of them that were near the king's person, which were found in the city; and the principal scribe of the host, who mustered the people of the land; and threescore men of the people of the land, that were found in the midst of the city.

26 So Neb'-u-zar-a'-dan the captain of the guard took them, and brought them to the king of Babylon to Rib'-lah.

27 And the king of Babylon ᵀsmote them, and put them to death in Rib'-lah in the land of Ha'-math. Thus Judah was carried away captive out of his own land.　　　*struck*

28 ᴿThis *is* the people whom Neb-u-chad-rez'-zar carried away captive: in the ᴿseventh year ᴿthree thousand Jews and three and twenty:　　　2 Kin. 24:2 • 2 Kin. 24:12 • 2 Kin. 24:14

29 ᴿIn the eighteenth year of Neb-u-chad-rez'-zar he carried away captive from Jerusalem eight hundred thirty and two persons:　　　39:9

30 ᴿIn the three and twentieth year of Neb-u-chad-rez'-zar Neb'-u-zar-a'-dan the captain of the guard carried away captive of the Jews seven hundred forty and five persons: all the persons *were* four thousand and six hundred.　　　2 Kin. 25:11

The Liberation of Jehoiachin

31 And it came to pass in the seven and thirtieth year of the captivity of Je-hoi'-a-chin king of Judah, in the twelfth month, in the five and twentieth *day* of the month, *that* E'-vil-me-ro'-dach king of Babylon in the *first* year of his reign ᵀlifted up the head of Je-hoi'-a-chin king of Judah, and brought him forth out of prison,　　　*favoured*

32 And spake kindly unto him, and set his throne above the throne of the kings that *were* with him in Babylon,

33 And changed his prison garments: ᴿand he did continually eat bread before him all the days of his life.　　　2 Sam. 9:13

34 And *for* his ᵀdiet, there was a continual diet given him of the king of Babylon, every day a portion until the day of his death, all the days of his life.　　　*allowance*

THE
LAMENTATIONS
OF JEREMIAH

📖 THE BOOK OF LAMENTATIONS

Lamentations describes the funeral of a city. It is a tearstained portrait of the once proud Jerusalem, now reduced to rubble by the invading Babylonian hordes. In a five-poem dirge, Jeremiah exposes his emotions. A death has occurred; Jerusalem lies barren.

Jeremiah writes his lament in acrostic or alphabetical fashion. Beginning each chapter with the first letter A (aleph) he progresses verse by verse through the Hebrew alphabet, literally weeping from A to Z. And then, in the midst of this terrible holocaust, Jeremiah triumphantly cries out, "Great is thy faithfulness" (3:23). In the face of death and destruction, with life seemingly coming apart, Jeremiah turns tragedy into a triumph of faith. God has never failed him in the past. God has promised to remain faithful in the future. In the light of the God he knows and loves, Jeremiah finds hope and comfort.

The Hebrew title of this book comes from the first word of chapters 1, 2, and 4: *Ekah*, "How!" Another Hebrew word *Ginoth* ("Elegies" or "Lamentations") has also been used as the title because it better represents the contents of the book. The Greek title *Threnoi* means "Dirges" or "Laments," and the Latin title *Threni* ("Tears" or "Lamentations") was derived from this word. The subtitle in Jerome's Vulgate reads: *"Id est lamentationes Jeremiae prophetae,"* and this became the basis for the English title "The Lamentations of Jeremiah."

✒ THE AUTHOR OF LAMENTATIONS

The author of Lamentations is unnamed in the book, but internal and external evidence is consistently in favor of Jeremiah.

External Evidence: The universal consensus of early Jewish and Christian tradition attributes this book to Jeremiah. The superscription to Lamentations in the Septuagint says: "And it came to pass, after Israel had been carried away captive, and Jerusalem had become desolate, that Jeremiah sat weeping, and lamented with this lamentation over Jerusalem, saying. . . ." This is also the position of the Talmud, the Aramaic Targum of Jonathan, and early Christian writers, such as Origen and Jerome. In addition, Second Chronicles 35:25 says that "Jeremiah lamented for Josiah." This was an earlier occasion, but Jeremiah was obviously familiar with the lament form.

Internal Evidence: The scenes in this graphic book were clearly portrayed by an eyewitness to Jerusalem's siege and fall soon after the destruction took place (cf. 1:13–15; 2:6, 9; 4:1–12). Jeremiah witnessed the fall of Jerusalem and remained behind after the captives were deported (see Jer. 39). Although some critics claim that the style of Lamentations is different from the Book of Jeremiah, the similarities are in fact striking and numerous, especially in the poetic sections of Jeremiah. Compare these passages from Lamentations and Jeremiah: 1:2 (Jer. 30:14); 1:15 (Jer. 8:21); 1:16 and 2:11 (Jer. 9:1, 18); 2:22 (Jer. 6:25); 4:21 (Jer. 49:12). The same compassion, sympathy, and grief over Judah's downfall are evident in both books.

⧗ THE TIME OF LAMENTATIONS

The historical background of Lamentations can be found in "The Time of Jeremiah." The book was written soon after Jerusalem's destruction (Jer. 39; 52) at the beginning of the Exile. Nebuchadnezzar laid siege to Jerusalem from January 588 B.C. to July 586 B.C. It fell on July 19, and the city and temple were burned on August 15. Jeremiah probably wrote these five elegies before he was taken captive to Egypt by his disobedient countrymen not long after the destruction (Jer. 43:1–7).

✝ THE CHRIST OF LAMENTATIONS

The weeping prophet Jeremiah is a figure of Christ, the Prophet who wept over the same city six centuries later. "O Jerusalem, Jerusalem, *thou* that killest the prophets, and stonest them which are sent unto thee, how often would I have gathered thy children together, even as a hen gathereth her chickens under *her* wings, and ye would not! Behold, your house is left unto you desolate" (Matt. 23:37, 38). Like Christ, Jeremiah identified himself personally with the plight of Jerusalem and with human suffering caused by sin.

Lamentations also includes elements that picture Christ's life and ministry as the Man of Sorrows who was acquainted with grief. He was afflicted (1:12; 3:19), despised, and derided by His enemies (2:15, 16; 3:14, 30).

🔑 KEYS TO LAMENTATIONS

Key Word: Lamentations—Three themes run through the five laments of Jeremiah. The most prominent is the theme of mourning over Jerusalem's holocaust. The Holy City has been laid waste and desolate: God's promised judgment for sin has come. In his sorrow, Jeremiah speaks for himself, for the captives, and sometimes for the personified city. The second theme is a confession of sin and acknowledgment

of God's righteous and holy judgment upon Judah. The third theme is least prominent but very important: it is a note of hope in God's future restoration of His people. Yahweh has poured out His wrath, but in His mercy He will be faithful to His covenant promises.

Key Verses: Lamentations 2:5, 6 and 3:22, 23—"The Lord was as an enemy: he hath swallowed up Israel, he hath swallowed up all her palaces: he hath destroyed his strong holds, and hath increased in the daughter of Judah mourning and lamentation. And he hath violently taken away his tabernacle, as *if it were of* a garden: he hath destroyed his places of the assembly: the LORD hath caused the solemn feasts and sabbaths to be forgotten in Zion, and hath despised in the indignation of his anger the king and the priest" (2:5, 6).

"*It is of* the LORD's mercies that we are not consumed, because his compassions fail not. *They are* new every morning: great *is* thy faithfulness" (3:22, 23).

Key Chapter: Lamentations 3—In the midst of five chapters of ruin, destruction, and utter hopelessness, Jeremiah rises and grasps with strong faith the promises and character of God. Lamentations 3:22-25 expresses a magnificent faith in the mercy of God—especially when placed against the dark backdrop of chapters 1, 2, 4, and 5.

SURVEY OF LAMENTATIONS

For forty years Jeremiah suffers rejection and abuse for his warnings of coming judgment. When Nebuchadnezzar finally comes and destroys Jerusalem in 586 B.C., a lesser man might say, "I told you so!" But Jeremiah compassionately identifies with the tragic overthrow of Jerusalem and composes five beautiful and emotional lament poems as a requiem for the once proud city. These dirges reflect the tender heart of the man who was divinely commissioned to communicate a harsh message to a sinful and stiff-necked people. The city, the temple, the palace, and the walls have been reduced to rubble and its inhabitants have been deported to distant Babylon. Jeremiah's five mournful poems can be entitled: the destruction of Jerusalem (1), the anger of Yahweh (2), the prayer for mercy (3), the siege of Jerusalem (4), and the prayer for restoration (5).

The Destruction of Jerusalem (1): This poem consists of a lamentation by Jeremiah (1:1-11) and a lamentation by the personified Jerusalem (1:12-22). The city has been left desolate because of its grievous sins, and her enemies "did mock at her sabbaths" (1:7). Jerusalem pleads with God to regard her misery and repay her adversaries.

The Anger of Yahweh (2): In his second elegy, Jeremiah moves from Jerusalem's desolation to a description of her destruction. Babylon has destroyed the city, but only as the Lord's instrument of judgment. Jeremiah presents an eyewitness account of the thoroughness and severity of Jerusalem's devastation. Through the Babylonians, God has terminated all religious observances, removed the priests, prophets, and kings, and razed the temple and palaces. Jeremiah grieves over the suffering the people brought on themselves through rebellion against God, and Jerusalem's supplications complete the lament.

The Prayer for Mercy (3): In the first eighteen verses, Jeremiah enters into the miseries and despair of his people and makes them his own. However, there is an abrupt turn in verses 19-39 as the prophet reflects on the faithfulness and loyal love of the compassionate God of Israel. These truths enable him to find comfort and hope in spite of his dismal circumstances. Jeremiah expresses his deep sorrow and petitions God for deliverance and for God to avenge Jerusalem's misery.

The Siege of Jerusalem (4): The prophet rehearses the siege of Jerusalem and remembers the suffering and starvation of rich and poor. He

FOCUS	DESTRUCTION OF JERUSALEM	ANGER OF JEHOVAH	PRAYER FOR MERCY	SIEGE OF JERUSALEM	PRAYER FOR RESTORATION
REFERENCE	1:1—————2:1	————3:1	————4:1	————5:1	————5:22
DIVISION	MOURNING CITY	BROKEN PEOPLE	SUFFERING PROPHET	RUINED KINGDOM	PENITENT NATION
TOPIC	GRIEF	CAUSE	HOPE	REPENTANCE	PRAYER
LOCATION	JERUSALEM				
TIME	C. 586 B.C.				

also reviews the causes of the siege, especially the sins of the prophets and priests and their foolish trust in human aid. This poem closes with a warning to Edom of future punishment and a glimmer of hope for Jerusalem.

The Prayer for Restoration (5): Jeremiah's last elegy is a melancholy description of his people's lamentable state. Their punishment is complete, and Jeremiah prayerfully desires the restoration of his nation.

OUTLINE OF LAMENTATIONS

CHAPTER 1

The Desolation of Jerusalem

HOW doth the city sit solitary, *that was* full of people! *how* is she become as a widow! she *that was* great among the nations, *and* princess ᴿamong the provinces, *how* is she become tributary!   Ezra 4:20

2 She ᴿweepeth sore in the night, and her tears *are* on her cheeks: among all her lovers she hath none to comfort *her:* all her friends have dealt treacherously with her, they are become her enemies.   Jer. 13:17

3 Judah is gone into captivity because of affliction, and ᵀbecause of great servitude: ᴿshe dwelleth among the heathen, she findeth no rest: all her persecutors overtook her between the straits.   *under* · Lam. 2:9

4 The ways of Zion do mourn, because none come to the solemn feasts: all her gates are ᴿdesolate: her priests sigh, her virgins are afflicted, and she *is* in bitterness.   Jer. 9:11

5 Her adversaries ᴿare the chief, her enemies prosper; for the LORD hath afflicted her for the multitude of her transgressions: her children are gone into captivity before the enemy.   Deut. 28:43

6 And from the daughter of Zion all her beauty is departed: her princes are become like harts *that* find no pasture, and they are gone without strength before the pursuer.

7 Jerusalem remembered in the days of her affliction and of her miseries all her pleasant things that she had in the days of old, when her people fell into the hand of the enemy, and ᴿnone did help her: the adversaries saw her, *and* did mock at her sabbaths. 4:17; Jer. 37:7

The Cause of Jerusalem's Desolation

8 Jerusalem hath ᴿgrievously sinned; therefore she is removed: all that honoured her despise her, because they have seen her nakedness: yea, she sigheth, and turneth backward.   1:5, 20; [Is. 59:2–13]

9 Her filthiness *is* in her skirts; she remembereth not her last end; therefore she came down wonderfully: she had no comforter. O LORD, behold my affliction: for the enemy hath magnified *himself.*

10 The adversary hath spread out his hand upon all her pleasant things: for she hath seen *that* the heathen entered into her sanctuary, whom thou didst command *that* they should not enter into thy congregation.

11 All her people sigh, they seek bread; they have given their pleasant things for meat to relieve the soul: see, O LORD, and consider; for I am become vile.

The Contrition of Jerusalem

12 *Is it* nothing to you, all ye that pass by? behold, and see ᴿif there be any sorrow like unto my sorrow, which is done unto me, wherewith the LORD hath afflicted *me* in the day of his fierce anger.   Dan. 9:12

13 From above hath he sent fire into my bones, and it prevaileth against them: he hath spread a net for my feet, he hath turned me back: he hath made me ^Tdesolate *and* faint all the day. *downhearted*

14 ^RThe yoke of my transgressions is bound by his hand: they are wreathed, *and* come up upon my neck: he hath made my strength to fall, the Lord hath delivered me into *their* hands, *from whom* I am not able to rise up. Deut. 28:48; [Prov. 5:22]

15 The Lord hath ^Ttrodden under foot all my mighty *men* in the midst of me: he hath called an assembly against me to crush my young men: ^Rthe Lord hath trodden the virgin, the daughter of Judah, *as* in a winepress. *trampled* • Jer. 6:11; 18:21

16 For these *things* I weep; mine eye, mine eye runneth down with water, because the comforter that should relieve my soul is far from me: my children are desolate, because the enemy prevailed.

17 Zion spreadeth forth her hands, *and* there is none to comfort her: the LORD hath commanded concerning Jacob, *that* his adversaries *should be* round about him: Jerusalem is as a menstruous woman among them.

18 The LORD is righteous; for I have ^Rrebelled against his commandment: hear, I pray you, all people, and behold my sorrow: my virgins and my young men are gone into captivity. 1 Sam. 12:14

19 I called for my lovers, *but* they deceived me: my priests and mine elders gave up their ghost in the city, while they sought their meat to relieve their souls.

The Confession of Jerusalem

20 Behold, O LORD; for I *am* in distress: my ^Tbowels are troubled; mine heart is turned within me; for I have grievously rebelled: abroad the sword bereaveth, at home *there is* as death. *emotions are disturbed*

21 They have heard that I sigh: *there is* none to comfort me: all mine enemies have heard of my trouble; they are glad that thou hast done *it:* thou wilt bring ^Rthe day *that* thou hast ^Tcalled, and they shall be ^Rlike unto me. [Jer. 46] • *predicted* • Is. 14:5, 6; 47:6, 11

22 Let all their wickedness come before thee; and do unto them, as thou hast done unto me for all my transgressions: for my sighs *are* many, and my heart *is* faint.

CHAPTER 2

The Anger of God

HOW hath the Lord covered the daughter of Zion with a cloud in his anger, *and* cast down from heaven unto the earth the beauty of Israel, and remembered not his footstool in the day of his anger!

2 The Lord hath swallowed up all the habitations of Jacob, and hath not pitied: he hath thrown down in his wrath the strong holds of the daughter of Judah; he hath brought *them* down to the ground: he hath polluted the kingdom and the princes thereof.

3 He hath cut off in *his* fierce anger all the horn of Israel: he hath drawn back his right hand from before the enemy, and he burned against Jacob like a flaming fire, *which* devoureth round about.

4 He hath bent his bow like an enemy: he stood with his right hand as an adversary, and slew all *that were* pleasant to the eye in the tabernacle of the daughter of Zion: he poured out his fury like fire.

5 ^RThe Lord was as an enemy: he hath swallowed up Israel, he hath swallowed up all her palaces: he hath destroyed his strong holds, and hath increased in the daughter of Judah mourning and lamentation. Jer. 30:14

6 And he hath violently taken away his ^Ttabernacle, as *if it were of* a garden: he hath destroyed his places of the assembly: the LORD hath caused the solemn feasts and sabbaths to be forgotten in Zion, and hath despised in the indignation of his anger the king and the priest. *hedge*

7 The Lord hath cast off his altar, he hath abhorred his sanctuary, he hath given up into the hand of the enemy the walls of her palaces; they have made a noise in the house of the LORD, as in the day of a solemn feast.

8 The LORD ^Thath purposed to destroy the wall of the daughter of Zion: he hath stretched out a line, he hath not withdrawn his hand from destroying: therefore he made the rampart and the wall to lament; they languished together. *planned*

9 Her gates are sunk into the ground; he hath destroyed and broken her bars: her king and her princes *are* among the Gentiles: the law *is* no *more;* her prophets also find no vision from the LORD.

The Agony of Jerusalem

10 The elders of the daughter of Zion sit upon the ground, *and* keep silence: they have ^Rcast up dust upon their heads; they have ^Rgirded themselves with sackcloth: the virgins of Jerusalem hang down their heads to the ground. Job 2:12 • Is. 15:3

11 Mine eyes do fail with tears, my bowels are troubled, my liver is poured upon the earth, for the destruction of the daughter of my people; because the children and the sucklings swoon in the streets of the city.

12 They say to their mothers, Where *is* corn and wine? when they ^Tswooned as the wounded in the streets of the city, when their ^Tsoul was poured out into their mothers' bosom. *fainted* • *sorrow was confessed*

13 What thing shall I take to witness for

thee? what thing ᴿshall I liken to thee, O daughter of Jerusalem? what shall I equal to thee, that I may comfort thee, O virgin daughter of Zion? for thy ᵀbreach *is* great like the sea: who can heal thee?   1:12 • *wound*

14 Thy ᴿprophets have seen vain and foolish things for thee: and they have not discovered thine iniquity, to turn away thy captivity; but have seen for thee false burdens and causes of banishment.   Jer. 2:8

15 All that pass by clap *their* hands at thee; they hiss and wag their head at the daughter of Jerusalem, *saying, Is* this the city that *men* call The perfection of beauty, The joy of the whole earth?

16 ᴿAll thine enemies have opened their mouth against thee: they hiss and gnash the teeth: they say, We have swallowed *her* up: certainly this *is* the day that we looked for; we have found, we have seen *it*.   Job 16:10

17 The LORD hath done *that* which he had devised; he hath fulfilled his word that he had commanded in the days of old: he hath thrown down, and hath not pitied: and he hath caused *thine* enemy to ᴿrejoice over thee, he hath set up the horn of thine adversaries.   1:5; Deut. 28:43, 44

The Appeal of Jerusalem

18 Their heart cried unto the Lord, O wall of the daughter of Zion, let tears run down like a river day and night: give thyself no rest; let not the apple of thine eye cease.

19 Arise, ᴿcry out in the night: in the beginning of the watches pour out thine heart like water before the face of the Lord: lift up thy hands toward him for the life of thy young children, that faint for hunger in the top of every street.   Ps. 119:55

20 Behold, O LORD, and consider to whom thou hast done this. Shall the women eat their ᵀfruit, *and* children of a span long? shall the priest and the prophet be slain in the sanctuary of the Lord?   *children*

21 ᴿThe young and the old lie on the ground in the streets: my virgins and my young men are fallen by the sword; thou hast slain *them* in the day of thine anger; thou hast killed, *and* not pitied.   2 Chr. 36:17

22 Thou hast called as in a solemn day ᴿmy terrors round about, so that in the day of the LORD'S anger none escaped nor remained: ᴿthose that I have swaddled and brought up hath mine enemy consumed.   Is. 24:17 • Jer. 16:2–4

CHAPTER 3

Jeremiah's Cry of Despair

I AM the man *that* hath seen affliction by the rod of his wrath.

2 He hath led me, and brought *me into* ᴿdarkness, but not *into* light.   Job 30:26

3 Surely against me is he turned; he turneth his hand *against me* all the day.

4 ᴿMy flesh and my skin hath he made old; he hath broken my bones.   Job 16:8

5 He hath builded against me, and compassed *me* with gall and travel.

6 ᴿHe hath set me in dark places, as *they that be* dead of old.   [Ps. 88:5, 6; 143:3]

7 He hath hedged me about, that I cannot get out: he hath made my chain heavy.

8 Also ᴿwhen I cry and shout, he shutteth out my prayer.   Job 30:20; Ps. 22:2

9 He hath inclosed my ways with hewn stone, he hath made my paths crooked.

10 ᴿHe *was* unto me *as* a bear lying in wait, *and as* a lion in secret places.   Is. 38:13

11 He hath turned aside my ways, and ᴿpulled me in pieces: he hath made me ᵀdesolate.   Job 16:12, 13 • *ruined*

12 He hath bent his bow, and ᴿset me as a ᵀmark for the arrow.   Job 7:20 • *target*

13 He hath caused the arrows of his quiver to enter into my ᵀreins.   *heart*

14 I was a ᴿderision to all my people; *and* their song all the day.   Jer. 20:7

15 He hath filled me with bitterness, he hath made me drunken with wormwood.

16 He hath also ᴿbroken my teeth ᴿwith gravel stones, he hath ᴿcovered me with ashes.   Ps. 3:7; 58:6 • [Prov. 20:17] • Jer. 6:26

17 And thou hast removed my soul far off ᴿfrom peace: I forgat prosperity.   Is. 59:11

18 ᴿAnd I said, My strength and my hope is perished from the LORD: Ps. 31:22

Jeremiah's Confession of Faith

19 Remembering mine affliction and my misery, the wormwood and the gall.

20 My soul hath *them* still in remembrance, and is ᴿhumbled in me.   Ps. 42:5, 6, 11

21 This I ᵀrecall to my mind, therefore have I ᴿhope.   *remember* • Ps. 130:7

22 ᴿ*It is of* the LORD'S mercies that we are not consumed, because his compassions fail not.   Ps. 78:38; Jer. 3:12; [Mal. 3:6]

23 *They are* new ᴿevery morning: great *is* thy faithfulness.   Is. 33:2; Zeph. 3:5

24 The LORD *is* my ᴿportion, saith my soul; therefore will I hope in him.   Ps. 16:5

25 The LORD *is* good unto them that wait for him, to the soul *that* seeketh him.

26 *It is* good that *a* man should both hope ᴿand quietly wait for the salvation of the LORD.   [Rom. 4:16–18]

27 ᴿ*It is* good for a man that he bear the yoke in his youth.   Ps. 94:12; Eccl. 12:1

28 He sitteth alone and keepeth silence, because he hath borne *it* upon him.

29 He ᵀputteth his mouth in the dust; if so be there may be hope.   *speaks humbly*

30 He giveth *his* cheek to him that smiteth him: he is filled full with reproach.

31 For the Lord will not cast off for ever:

32 But though he cause grief, yet will he have [R]compassion according to the multitude of his mercies.   Ps. 78:38

33 For he doth not afflict willingly nor grieve the children of men.

34 [R]To crush under his feet all the prisoners of the earth,   Is. 14:17

35 [R]To turn aside the right of a man before the face of the most High,   [Ps. 140:12]

36 To subvert a man in his cause, [R]the Lord approveth not.   [Jer. 22:3; Hab. 1:13]

37 Who is he that saith, and it cometh to pass, when the Lord commandeth it not?

38 Out of the mouth of the most High proceedeth not [R]evil and good?   Job 2:10

39 Wherefore doth a living man complain, a man for the punishment of his sins?

Jeremiah's Condition of Need

40 Let us [R]search [T]and try our ways, and turn again to the Lord.   Ps. 119:59 · test

41 [R]Let us lift up our heart with our hands unto God in the heavens.   Ps. 86:4

42 [R]We have transgressed and have rebelled: thou hast not pardoned.   Dan. 9:5

43 [R]Thou hast covered with anger, and persecuted us: thou hast slain, thou hast not pitied.   Ps. 83:15

44 Thou hast covered thyself with a cloud, that our prayer should not pass through.

45 Thou hast made us as the offscouring and refuse in the midst of the people.

46 [R]All our enemies have opened their mouths against us.   2:16; Job 30:9, 10

47 Fear and a snare is come upon us, [R]desolation and destruction.   Is. 51:19

48 [R]Mine eye runneth down with rivers of water for the destruction of the daughter of my people.   Jer. 4:19

49 [R]Mine eye trickleth down, and ceaseth not, without any intermission,   Ps. 77:2

50 Till the Lord [R]look down, and behold from heaven.   5:1; Ps. 80:14; Is. 63:15

51 Mine eye affecteth mine heart because of all the daughters of my city.

52 Mine enemies chased me sore, [R]like a bird, [R]without cause.   Ps. 11:1 · Ps. 35:7, 19

53 They have cut off my life in the dungeon, and cast a stone upon me.

54 [R]Waters flowed over mine head; then [R]I said, I am cut off.   Jon. 2:3–5 · Is. 38:10

Jeremiah's Confidence in God

55 [R]I called upon thy name, O Lord, out of the low dungeon.   Ps. 130:1

56 Thou hast heard my voice: hide not thine ear at my breathing, at my cry.

57 Thou drewest near in the day that I called upon thee: thou saidst, Fear not.

58 O Lord, thou hast pleaded the causes of my soul; thou hast redeemed my life.

59 O Lord, thou hast seen my wrong: [R]judge thou my cause.   Ps. 9:4; 26:1; 43:1

60 Thou hast seen all their vengeance and all their imaginations against me.

61 Thou hast heard their reproach, O Lord, and all their imaginations against me;

62 The lips of those that rose up against me, and their device against me all the day.

63 Behold their [R]sitting down, and their rising up; I am their musick.   Ps. 139:2

64 Render unto them a recompence, O Lord, according to the work of their hands.

65 Give them [R]sorrow of heart, thy curse unto them.   Ex. 14:8; Deut. 2:30

66 Persecute and destroy them in anger from under the heavens of the Lord.

CHAPTER 4

The Conditions During the Siege

HOW[R] is the gold become dim! how is the most fine gold changed! the stones of the sanctuary are poured out in the top of every street.   2 Kin. 25:9, 10

2 The precious sons of Zion, comparable to fine gold, how are they esteemed as earthen pitchers, the work of the hands of the potter!

3 Even the [T]sea monsters draw out the breast, they give suck to their young ones: the daughter of my people is become cruel, like the ostriches in the wilderness.   jackals

4 The tongue of the sucking child [R]cleaveth to the roof of his mouth for thirst: the young children ask bread, and no man breaketh it unto them.   Ps. 22:15

5 They that did feed delicately are desolate in the streets: they that were brought up in scarlet embrace dunghills.

6 For the punishment of the iniquity of the daughter of my people is greater than the punishment of the sin of Sodom, that was [R]overthrown as in a moment, and no hands [T]stayed on her.   Gen. 19:25 · laid

7 Her [T]Nazarites were [R]purer than snow, they were whiter than milk, they were more ruddy in body than rubies, their polishing was of sapphire: nobles · Ps. 51:7

8 Their visage is [R]blacker than a coal; they are not known in the streets: their skin cleaveth to their bones; it is withered, it is become like a stick.   5:10; Job 30:30

9 They that be slain with the sword are better than they that be slain with hunger: for these pine away, stricken through for want of the fruits of the field.

10 The hands of the [R]pitiful women have [T]sodden their own children: they were their [T]meat in the destruction of the daughter of my people.   2:20 · boiled · food

The Cause of the Siege

11 The Lord hath accomplished his fury; [R]he hath poured out his fierce anger, and

hath kindled a fire in Zion, and it hath devoured the foundations thereof.   Jer. 7:20

12 The kings of the earth, and all the inhabitants of the world, would not have believed that the adversary and the enemy should have Rentered into the gates of Jerusalem.   Jer. 21:13

13 For the sins of her prophets, *and* the iniquities of her priests, that have shed the blood of the just in the midst of her,

14 They have wandered *as* blind *men* in the streets, Rthey have polluted themselves with blood, Rso that men could not touch their garments.   Jer. 2:34 • Num. 19:16

15 They cried unto them, Depart ye; Tit *is* Runclean; depart, depart, touch not: when they fled away and wandered, they said among the heathen, They shall no more sojourn *there*.   *yet polluted* • Lev. 13:45, 46

16 The anger of the LORD hath divided them; he will no more regard them: Rthey respected not the persons of the priests, they favoured not the elders.   5:12; Is. 9:14–16

17 As for us, our eyes as yet failed for our vain help: in our watching we have watched for a nation *that* could not save *us*.

18 They hunt our steps, that we cannot go in our streets: our end is near, our days are fulfilled; for our end is come.

19 Our persecutors are Rswifter than the eagles of the heaven: they pursued us upon the mountains, they laid wait for us in the wilderness.   Deut. 28:49; Is. 5:26–28; Hab. 1:8

20 The Rbreath of our nostrils, the anointed of the LORD, was taken in their pits, of whom we said, Under his shadow we shall live among the heathen.   Gen. 2:7

The Consequences of the Siege

21 Rejoice and be glad, O daughter of E'-dom, that dwellest in the land of Uz; the cup also shall pass through unto thee: thou shalt be drunken, and shalt make thyself naked.

22 The punishment of thine iniquity is accomplished, O daughter of Zion; he will no more carry thee away into captivity: he will visit thine iniquity, O daughter of E'-dom; he will Tdiscover thy sins.   *reveal*

CHAPTER 5
The Review of the Need for Restoration

REMEMBER, O LORD, what is come upon us: consider, and behold our reproach.

2 ROur inheritance is turned to Rstrangers, our houses to aliens.   Ps. 79:1 • Is. 1:7

3 We are orphans and Rfatherless, our mothers *are* as widows.   Ex. 22:24; Jer. 15:8

4 We have drunken our Rwater for money; our wood is sold unto us.   Is. 3:1

5 TOur necks *are* under persecution: we labour, *and* have no rest.   *we suffer*

6 RWe have given the hand Rto the Egyptians, *and* to the Assyrians, to be satisfied with bread.   Gen. 24:2 • Hos. 12:1

7 Our fathers have sinned, *and are* not; and we have borne their iniquities.

8 Servants have ruled over us: *there is* none that doth deliver *us* out of their hand.

9 We gat our bread with *the peril of* our lives because of the sword of the wilderness.

10 Our skin was black like an oven because of the Tterrible famine.   *terrors*

11 They ravished the women in Zion, *and* the maids in the cities of Judah.

12 Princes are hanged up by their hand: the faces of Relders were not honoured.   4:16

13 They took the young men to grind, and the children fell under the wood.

14 The elders have ceased from the gate, the young men from their Rmusick.   Is. 24:8

15 The joy of our heart is Rceased; our dance is turned into mourning.   Jer. 25:10

The Repentance of Sin

16 RThe crown is fallen *from* our head: woe unto us, that we have sinned!   Ps. 89:39

17 For this our Rheart is faint; Rfor these *things* our eyes are dim.   Is. 1:5 • Ps. 6:7

18 Because of the mountain of Zion, which is desolate, the foxes walk upon it.

The Request for Restoration

19 Thou, O LORD, remainest for ever; thy throne from generation to generation.

20 RWherefore dost thou forget us for ever, *and* forsake us so long time?   Ps. 13:1

5:20 Occasions of Doubt—Doubt may be defined as an uncertainty of belief or lack of confidence in something. Applied to the Christian life, doubt refers to the unbelief in God and His Word that Christians occasionally exhibit. It is possible that in a moment of infirmity a Christian may doubt the existence of God in spite of the fact that it is not reasonable for a person to disbelieve this obvious truth (Page 552—Ps. 14:1). A Christian is more likely to doubt his salvation after sinning or after a spiritual defeat. A misunderstanding of such verses as First John 3:9 contributes to this doubt: "Whosoever is born of God doth not commit sin." It is crucial to note that this verse speaks of a life-style of sin, not instances of sin.

A Christian may also doubt God's sovereignty or His goodness. In such circumstances as sickness, suffering, injustice, opposition, economic problems, family problems, national calamity, or apparently unanswered prayer, a Christian may be tempted to doubt the goodness of God. One must remember that it is not always possible to discern God's good hand in the affairs of life. The person of faith believes God even when circumstances appear to the contrary.

All doubt may be traced ultimately to unbelief in the Word of God, which affirms beyond question the existence and character of God. To regard doubt as the sin of unbelief and then confess it to God as sin is therefore the first step toward conquering it.

Now turn to Page 882—Hab. 1:2: Sources of Doubt.

21 RTurn thou us unto thee, O LORD, and we shall be turned; Rrenew our days as of old.   Ps. 80:3; Jer. 31:18 • [Is. 60:20–22]

22 But thou hast utterly rejected us; thou art very Twroth against us.   angry

Measures of Length

Unit	Length	Equivalents	Translations
Day's journey	c. 20 miles		day's journey
Roman mile	4,854 feet	8 stadia	mile
Sabbath day's journey	3,637 feet	6 stadia	sabbath day's journey
Stadion	606 feet	⅛ Roman mile	furlong
Rod	9 feet (10.5 feet in Ezekiel)	3 paces; 6 cubits	measuring reed, reed
Fathom	6 feet	4 cubits	fathom
Pace	3 feet	⅓ rod; 2 cubits	pace
Cubit	18 inches	½ pace; 2 spans	cubit
Span	9 inches	½ cubit; 3 hand-breadths	span
Handbreadth	3 inches	⅓ span; 4 fingers	handbreadth
Finger	.75 inches	¼ handbreadth	finger

Liquid Measures

Unit	Measure	Equivalents	Translations
Kor	60 gallons	10 baths	cor
Metretes	10.2 gallons		firkin
Bath	6 gallons	6 hins	measure, bath
Hin	1 gallon	2 kabs	hin
Kab	2 quarts	4 logs	cab
Log	1 pint	¼ kab	log

EZEKIEL

THE BOOK OF EZEKIEL

Ezekiel, a priest and a prophet, ministers during the darkest days of Judah's history: the seventy-year period of Babylonian captivity. Carried to Babylon before the final assault on Jerusalem, Ezekiel uses prophecies, parables, signs, and symbols to dramatize God's message to His exiled people. Though they are like dry bones in the sun, God will reassemble them and breathe life into the nation once again. Present judgment will be followed by future glory so that "ye shall know that I *am* the LORD" (6:7).

The Hebrew name *Yehezke'l* means "God Strengthens" or "Strengthened by God." Ezekiel is indeed strengthened by God for the prophetic ministry to which he is called (3:8, 9). The name occurs twice in this book and nowhere else in the Old Testament. The Greek form in the Septuagint is *Iezekiel* and the Latin form in the Vulgate is *Ezechiel*.

THE AUTHOR OF EZEKIEL

Ezekiel, the son of Buzi (1:3), had a wife who died as a sign to Judah when Nebuchadnezzar began his final siege on Jerusalem (24:16–24). Like Jeremiah, he was a priest who was called to be a prophet of the Lord. His prophetic ministry shows a priestly emphasis in his concern with the temple, priesthood, sacrifices, and Shekinah (the glory of God). Ezekiel was privileged to receive a number of visions of the power and plan of God, and he was careful and artistic in his written presentation.

Some objections have been raised, but there is not a good reason to overthrow the strong evidence in favor of Ezekiel's authorship. The first person singular is used throughout the book, indicating that it is the work of a single personality. This person is identified as Ezekiel in 1:3 and 24:24, and internal evidence supports the unity and integrity of Ezekiel's prophetic record. The style, language, and thematic development are consistent throughout the book; and several distinctive phrases are repeated throughout, such as, "They shall know that I *am* the LORD," "Son of man," "the word of the LORD came unto me," and the "glory of the LORD."

THE TIME OF EZEKIEL

Nebuchadnezzar destroyed Jerusalem in three stages. First, in 605 B.C., he overcame Jehoiakim and carried off key hostages including Daniel and his friends. Second, in 597 B.C., the rebellion of Jehoiakim and Jehoiachin brought further punishment; and Nebuchadnezzar made Jerusalem submit a second time. He carried off ten thousand hostages including

Jehoiachin and Ezekiel. Third, in 586 B.C., Nebuchadnezzar destroyed the city after a long siege and disrupted all of Judah. If "thirtieth year" in 1:1 refers to Ezekiel's age, he was twenty-five years old when he was taken to Babylon and thirty years old when he received his prophetic commission (1:2, 3). This means he was about seventeen when Daniel was deported in 605 B.C., so that Ezekiel and Daniel were about the same age. Both men were about twenty years younger than Jeremiah who was ministering in Jerusalem. According to this chronology, Ezekiel was born in 622 B.C., deported to Babylon in 597 B.C., prophesied from 592 B.C. to at least 570 B.C., and died about 560 B.C. Thus, he overlapped the end of Jeremiah's ministry and the beginning of Daniel's ministry. By the time Ezekiel arrived in Babylon, Daniel was already well known; and he is mentioned three times in Ezekiel's prophecy (14:14, 20; 28:3). Ezekiel's Babylonian home was at Tel-abib, the principal colony of Jewish exiles along the river Chebar, Nebuchadnezzar's "Grand Canal" (1:1; 3:15, 23).

From 592 to 586 B.C., Ezekiel found it necessary to convince the disbelieving Jewish exiles that there was no hope of immediate deliverance. But it was not until they heard that Jerusalem was destroyed that their false hopes of returning were abandoned.

Ezekiel no doubt wrote this book shortly after the incidents recorded in it occurred. His active ministry lasted for at least twenty-two years (1:2; 29:17), and his book was probably completed by 565 B.C.

THE CHRIST OF EZEKIEL

Ezekiel 17:22–24 depicts the Messiah as a tender twig that becomes a stately cedar on a lofty mountain, as He is similarly called the Branch in Isaiah (11:1), Jeremiah (23:5; 33:15), and Zechariah (3:8; 6:12). The Messiah is the King who has the right to rule (21:26, 27), and He is the true Shepherd who will deliver and feed His flock (34:11–31).

KEYS TO EZEKIEL

Key Word: The Future Restoration of Israel—The broad purpose of Ezekiel is to remind the generation born during the Babylonian exile of the cause of Israel's current destruction, of the coming judgment on the gentile nations, and of the coming national restoration of Israel. Central to that hope is the departure of the glory of God from Israel and the prediction of its ultimate return (43:2).

Key Verses: Ezekiel 36:24-26 and 36:33-35— "For I will take you from among the heathen, and

gather you out of all countries, and will bring you into your own land. Then will I sprinkle clean water upon you, and ye shall be clean: from all your filthiness, and from all your idols, will I cleanse you. A new heart also will I give you, and a new spirit will I put within you: and I will take away the stony heart out of your flesh, and I will give you an heart of flesh" (36:24-26).

"Thus saith the Lord GOD; In the day that I shall have cleansed you from all your iniquities I will also cause *you* to dwell in the cities, and the wastes shall be builded. And the desolate land shall be tilled, whereas it lay desolate in the sight of all that passed by. And they shall say, This land that was desolate is become like the garden of Eden; and the waste and desolate and ruined cities *are become* fenced, *and* are inhabited" (36:33-35).

Key Chapter: Ezekiel 37—Central to the hope of the restoration of Israel is the vision of the valley of dry bones. Ezekiel 37 outlines with clear steps Israel's future.

SURVEY OF EZEKIEL

Ezekiel prophesies among the Jewish exiles in Babylon during the last days of Judah's decline and downfall. His message of judgment is similar to that of his older contemporary Jeremiah, who has remained in Jerusalem. Judah will be judged because of her unfaithfulness, but God promises her future restoration and blessing. Like Isaiah and Jeremiah, Ezekiel proclaims a message of horror and hope, of condemnation and consolation. But Ezekiel places special emphasis on the glory of Israel's sovereign God who says, "They shall know that I *am* the LORD." The book breaks into four sections: the commission of Ezekiel (1—3), the judgment on Judah (4—24), the judgment on the Gentiles (25—32), and the restoration of Israel (33—48).

The Commission of Ezekiel (1—3): God gives Ezekiel an overwhelming vision of His divine glory and commissions him to be His prophet (cf. the experiences of Moses in Ex. 3:1-10, Isaiah in 6:1-10, Daniel in 10:5-14, and John in Rev. 1:12-19). Ezekiel is given instruction, enablement, and responsibility.

The Judgment on Judah (4—24): Ezekiel directs his prophecies against the nation God chose for Himself. The prophet's signs and sermons (4—7) point to the certainty of Judah's judgment. In 8—11, Judah's past sins and coming doom are seen in a series of visions of the abominations in the temple, the slaying of the wicked, and the departing glory of God. The priests and princes are condemned as the glory leaves the temple, moves to the Mount of Olives, and disappears in the east. Chapters 12—24 speak of the causes and extent of Judah's coming judgment through dramatic signs, powerful sermons, and parables. Judah's prophets are counterfeits and her elders are idolatrous. They have become a fruitless vine and an adulterous wife. Babylon will swoop down like an eagle and pluck them up, and they will not be aided by Egypt. The people are responsible for their own sins, and they are not being unjustly judged for the sins of their ancestors. Judah has been unfaithful, but God promises that her judgment ultimately will be followed by restoration.

The Judgment on the Gentiles (25—32): Judah's nearest neighbors may gloat over her destruction, but they will be next in line. They too will suffer the fate of siege and destruction by Babylon. Ezekiel shows the full circle of judgment on the nations that surround Judah by following them in a clockwise circuit: Ammon, Moab, Edom, Philistia, Tyrus, and Sidon (25—28). He spends a disproportionate amount of time on Tyrus, and many scholars believe that the "king of Tyrus" in 28:11-19 may be Satan, the real

FOCUS	COMMISSION OF EZEKIEL		JUDGMENT ON JUDAH	JUDGMENT ON GENTILES	RESTORATION OF ISRAEL		
REFERENCE	1:1———————2:1————————		4:1————————	25:1————————	33:1—————	40:1—————	48:35
DIVISION	EZEKIEL SEES THE GLORY	EZEKIEL IS COMMISSIONED TO THE WORK	SIGNS, MESSAGES, VISIONS, AND PARABLES OF JUDGMENT	JUDGMENT ON SURROUNDING NATIONS	RETURN OF ISRAEL TO THE LORD	RESTORATION OF ISRAEL IN THE KINGDOM	
TOPIC	BEFORE THE SIEGE (c. 592-587 B.C.)			DURING THE SIEGE (c. 586 B.C.)	AFTER THE SIEGE (c. 585-570 B.C.)		
	JUDAH'S FALL			JUDAH'S FOES	JUDAH'S FUTURE		
LOCATION	BABYLON						
TIME	c. 592-570 B.C.						

power behind the nation. Chapters 29—32 contain a series of oracles against Egypt. Unlike the nations in chapters 25—28 that were destroyed by Nebuchadnezzar, Egypt will continue to exist, but as "the basest of the kingdoms" (29:15). Since that time it has never recovered its former glory or influence.

The Restoration of Israel (33—48): The prophecies in these chapters were given after the overthrow of Jerusalem. Now that the promised judgment has come, Ezekiel's message no longer centers on coming judgment but on the positive theme of comfort and consolation. Just as surely as judgment has come, blessing will also come; God's people will be regathered and restored. The mouth of Ezekiel, God's watchman, is opened when he is told that Jerusalem has been taken. Judah has had false shepherds (rulers), but the true Shepherd will lead them in the future. The vision of the valley of dry bones pictures the reanimation of the nation by the Spirit of God. Israel and Judah will be purified and reunited. There will be an invasion by the northern armies of God, but Israel will be saved because the Lord will destroy the invading forces.

In 572 B.C., fourteen years after the destruction of Jerusalem, Ezekiel returns in a vision to the fallen city and is given detailed specifications of the reconstruction of the temple, the city, and the land (40—48). After an intricate description of the new outer court, inner court, and temple (40—42), Ezekiel views the return of the glory of the Lord to the temple from the east. Regulations concerning worship in the coming temple (43—46) are followed by revelations concerning the new land and city (47; 48).

OUTLINE OF EZEKIEL

Part Three: Judgment on Gentiles (25:1—32:32)

Part Four: Restoration of Israel (33:1—48:35)

CHAPTER 1

Time of the Vision

NOW it came to pass in the thirtieth year, in the fourth *month*, in the fifth *day* of the month, as I *was* among the captives by the river of Che'-bar, *that* ᴿthe heavens were opened, and I saw visions of God.   Acts 7:56

2 In the ᴿfifth *day* of the month, which *was* the fifth year of king Je-hoi'-a-chin's captivity,   8:1; 20:1; 2 Kin. 24:12–15

3 ᴿThe word of the LORD came expressly unto E-ze'-ki-el the priest, the son of Bu'-zi, in the land of the Chal-de'-ans by the river Che'-bar; and ᴿthe hand of the LORD was there upon him.   [Zech. 7:12] • 3:14

The Four Living Creatures

4 And I looked, and, behold, a whirlwind came out of the north, a great cloud, and a fire infolding itself, and a brightness was about it, and out of the midst thereof as the colour of amber, out of the midst of the fire.

5 ᴿAlso out of the midst thereof came the likeness of four living creatures. And ᴿthis was their appearance; they had ᴿthe likeness of a man.   10:4–22; Rev. 4:6–9 • 10:8 • 10:14

6 And every one had ᴿfour faces, and every one had ᴿfour wings.   v. 10; 10:14, 21 • v. 23

7 And their feet were straight feet; and the sole of their feet was like the sole of a calf's foot: and they sparkled like the colour of ᴿburnished brass.   Rev. 1:15; 2:13

8 And they had the hands of a man under their wings on their four sides; and they four had their faces and their wings.

9 Their wings were joined one to another; they turned not when they went; they went every one straight forward.

10 As for the likeness of their faces, they four had the face of a man, and the face of a lion, on the right side: and they four had the face of an ox on the left side; they four also had the face of an eagle.

11 Thus were their faces: and their wings were ᵀstretched upward; two wings of every one were joined one to another, and ᴿtwo covered their bodies.   divided above • Is. 6:2

12 And they went every one straight forward: whither the spirit was to go, they went; and they turned not when they went.

13 As for the likeness of the living creatures, their appearance was like burning coals of fire, and like the appearance of lamps: it went up and down among the living creatures; and the fire was bright, and out of the fire went forth lightning.

14 And ᴿthe living creatures ran and returned ᴿas the appearance of a flash of lightning.   [Ps. 104:4] • [Matt. 24:27; Luke 17:24]

The Four Wheels

15 Now as I beheld the living creatures, behold ᴿone wheel upon the earth by the living creatures, with his four faces.   10:9

16 The appearance of the wheels and their work was like unto the colour of a beryl: and they four had one likeness: and their appearance and their work was as it were a wheel in the middle of a wheel.

17 When they went, they went upon their four sides: and they ᴿturned not when they went.   vv. 9, 12; 10:11

18 As for their rings, they were so high that they were dreadful; and their rings were full of eyes round about them four.

19 And ᴿwhen the living creatures went, the wheels went by them: and when the

living creatures were lifted up from the earth, the wheels were lifted up.   10:16, 17

20 ᴿWhithersoever the spirit was to go, they went, thither was their spirit to go; and the wheels were lifted ᵀup over against them: for the spirit of the living creature was in the wheels.   v. 12 • at the same time

21 ᴿWhen those went, these went; and when those stood, these stood; and when those were lifted up from the earth, the wheels were lifted up over against them: for the spirit of the living creature was in the wheels.   10:17

The Firmament

22 And the likeness of the firmament upon the heads of the living creature was as the colour of the terrible crystal, stretched forth over their heads above.

23 And under the firmament were their wings straight, the one toward the other: ᴿevery one had two, which covered on this side, and every one had two, which covered on that side, their bodies.   vv. 6, 11

24 And when they went, I heard the noise of their wings, like the noise of great waters, as the voice of the Almighty, the voice of speech, as the noise of an host: when they stood, they ᵀlet down their wings.   rested

25 And there was a voice from the firmament that was over their heads, when they stood, and had let down their wings.

The Appearance of a Man

26 And above the ᴿfirmament that was over their heads was the likeness of a throne, as the appearance of a ᴿsapphire stone: and upon the likeness of the throne was the likeness as the appearance of a man above upon it.   v. 22; 10:1 • Ex. 24:10

27 And I saw as the colour of ᴿamber, as the appearance of fire round about within it, from the appearance of his loins even upward, and from the appearance of his loins even downward, I saw as it were the appearance of fire, and it had brightness round about.   v. 4; 8:2

28 As the appearance of the ᴿbow that is in the cloud in the day of rain, so was the appearance of the brightness round about. This was the appearance of the likeness of the ᴿglory of the LORD. And when I saw it, ᴿI fell upon my face, and I heard a voice of one that spake.   Rev. 4:3 • 3:23 • Acts 9:4

CHAPTER 2

Ezekiel Is Sent to Israel

AND he said unto me, Son of man, ᴿstand upon thy feet, and I will speak unto thee.   Dan. 10:11; Acts 9:6

2 And the spirit entered into me when he spake unto me, and set me upon my feet, that I heard him that spake unto me.

3 And he said unto me, Son of man, I send thee to the children of Israel, to a rebellious nation that hath ᴿrebelled against me: they and their fathers have transgressed against me, *even* unto this very day.　1 Sam. 8:7, 8

4 For *they are* ᴿimpudentᵀ children and stiffhearted. I do send thee unto them; and thou shalt say unto them, Thus saith the Lord GOD.　3:7; Ps. 95:8 • *hard headed*

5 And they, whether they will hear, or whether they will forbear, (for they *are* a rebellious house,) yet shall know that there hath been a prophet among them.

6 And thou, son of man, be not afraid of them, neither be afraid of their words, though briers and thorns *be* with thee, and thou dost dwell among scorpions: ᴿbe not afraid of their words, nor be dismayed at their looks, though they *be* a rebellious house.　[1 Pet. 3:14]

7 ᴿAnd thou shalt speak my words unto them, whether they will ᵀhear, or whether they will forbear: for they *are* ᵀmost rebellious.　[3:10]; Jer. 1:7, 17 • *listen or not • very*

8 But thou, son of man, hear what I say unto thee; Be not thou rebellious like that rebellious house: open thy mouth, and ᴿeat that I give thee.　3:3; [Jer. 15:16]; Rev. 10:9

9 And when I looked, behold, an hand *was* ᵀsent unto me; and, lo, ᴿa roll of a book *was* therein;　*put forth • 3:1*

10 And he spread it before me; and it *was* written ᵀwithin and without: and *there was* written therein lamentations, and mourning, and ᴿwoe.　*front and back • Rev. 8:13*

CHAPTER 3

MOREOVER he said unto me, Son of man, eat that thou findest; eat this roll, and go speak unto the house of Israel.

2 So I ᴿopened my mouth, and he caused me to eat that ᵀroll.　Jer. 25:17 • *scroll*

3 And he said unto me, Son of man, cause thy belly to eat, and fill thy bowels with this roll that I give thee. Then did I eat *it;* and it was in my mouth as honey for sweetness.

Ezekiel Is Instructed About His Ministry

4 And he said unto me, Son of man, go, get thee unto the house of Israel, and speak with ᴿmy words unto them.　Jer. 1:7

5 For thou *art* not sent to a people of a ᵀstrange speech and of an hard language, *but* to the house of Israel;　*foreign language*

6 Not to many people of a strange speech and of an hard language, whose words thou canst not understand. Surely, ᴿhad I sent thee to them, they ᴿwould have hearkened unto thee.　Matt. 11:21 • [Acts 28:27, 28]

7 But the house of Israel will not hearken unto thee; for they will not hearken unto me: for all the house of Israel *are* impudent and hardhearted.

8 Behold, I have made thy face ᵀstrong against their faces, and thy forehead strong against their foreheads.　*hard*

9 ᴿAs ᵀan adamant harder than flint have I made thy forehead: ᴿfear them not, neither be dismayed at their looks, though they *be* a rebellious house.　Is. 50:7 • *stone • 2:6*

10 Moreover he said unto me, Son of man, all my ᴿwords that I shall speak unto thee receive in thine heart, and hear with thine ears.　2:8; 3:1-3; Job 22:22

11 And go, get thee to them of the captivity, unto the children of thy people, and speak unto them, and tell them, Thus saith the Lord GOD; ᴿwhether they will hear, or whether they will forbear.　2:5, 7

12 Then ᴿthe spirit took me up, and I heard behind me a voice of a great rushing, *saying,* Blessed *be* the glory of the LORD from his place.　8:3; 1 Kin. 18:12

13 *I heard* also the noise of the wings of the living creatures that touched one another, and the noise of the wheels over against them, and a noise of a great rushing.

14 So the spirit lifted me up, and took me away, and I went in bitterness, in the ᵀheat of my spirit; but ᴿthe hand of the LORD was strong upon me.　*anger • 2 Kin. 3:15*

15 Then I came to them of the captivity at Tel-a'-bib, that dwelt by the river of Che'-bar, and I sat where they sat, and remained there astonished among them seven days.

16 ᴿAnd it came to pass at the end of seven days, that the word of the LORD came unto me, saying,　Jer. 42:7

17 ᴿSon of man, I have made thee ᴿa watchman unto the house of Israel: therefore hear the word at my mouth, and give them warning from me.　33:7 • Jer. 6:17

18 When I say unto the wicked, Thou shalt surely die; and thou givest him not warning, nor speakest to warn the wicked from his wicked way, to save his life; the same wicked *man* shall die in his iniquity; but his blood will I require at thine hand.

19 ᴿYet if thou warn the wicked, and he turn not from his wickedness, nor from his wicked way, he shall die in his iniquity; but thou hast delivered thy soul.　33:8, 9

20 Again, When a ᴿrighteous *man* doth turn from his righteousness, and commit iniquity, and I lay a stumblingblock before him, he shall die: because thou hast not given him warning, he shall die in his sin, and his righteousness which he hath done shall not be remembered; but his blood will I require at thine hand.　18:24

21 Nevertheless if thou warn the righteous *man,* that the righteous sin not, and he doth

not sin, he shall surely live, because he is warned; also thou hast delivered thy soul.

22 ᴿAnd the hand of the LORD was there upon me; and he said unto me, Arise, go forth ᴿinto the plain, and I will there ᴿtalk with thee.   1:3; 2 Chr. 30:12 • 8:4 • Acts 9:6

23 Then I arose, and went forth into the plain: and, behold, the glory of the LORD stood there, as the glory which I saw by the river of Che'-bar: and I fell on my face.

24 Then ᴿthe ᵀspirit entered into me, and set me upon my feet, and spake with me, and said unto me, Go, shut thyself within thine house.   2:2 • Spirit

25 But thou, O son of man, behold, ᴿthey shall put ᵀbands upon thee, and shall ᵀbind thee with them, and thou shalt not go out among them: 4:8 • you under arrest • hold

26 And I will make thy tongue cleave to the roof of thy mouth, that thou shalt be dumb, and shalt not be to them a reprover: for they are a rebellious house.

27 But when I speak with thee, I will open thy mouth, and thou shalt say unto them, Thus saith the Lord GOD; ᴿHe that heareth, let him hear; and he that forbeareth, let him forbear: for they are a rebellious house.   v. 11

CHAPTER 4

Sign of the Tile

THOU also, son of man, take thee a ᵀtile, and lay it before thee, and pourtray upon it the city, even Jerusalem: brick

2 And ᴿlay siege against it, and build a fort against it, and cast a mount against it; set the camp also against it, and set battering rams against it round about.   2 Kin. 25:1

3 Moreover take thou unto thee ᵀan iron pan, and set it for a wall of iron between thee and the city: and set thy face against it, and it shall be besieged, and thou shalt lay siege against it. ᴿThis shall be a sign to the house of Israel.   a flat plate • 12:6, 11; 24:24, 27

Sign of Ezekiel's Lying on His Side

4 Lie thou also upon thy left side, and lay the iniquity of the house of Israel upon it: according to the number of the days that thou shalt lie upon it thou shalt ᴿbear their iniquity.   [Lev. 10:17; 16:22]; Num. 18:1

5 For I have laid upon thee the years of their ᴿiniquity, according to the number of the days, three hundred and ninety days: ᴿso shalt thou bear the iniquity of the house of Israel.   [Job 15:16] • Num. 14:34

6 And when thou hast accomplished them, lie again on thy right side, and thou shalt bear the iniquity of the house of Judah forty days: I have appointed thee ᴿeach day for a year.   Num. 14:34; [Dan. 9:24–26]

7 Therefore thou shalt ᵀset thy face toward the siege of Jerusalem, and thine arm shall be

uncovered, and thou shalt ᴿprophesy against it.   take as an objective • 21:2

8 And, behold, ᴿI will ᵀlay bands upon thee, and thou shalt not turn thee from one side to another, till thou hast ended the days of thy siege.   3:25 • put you under restrictions

Sign of the Defiled Bread

9 Take thou also unto thee wheat, and barley, and beans, and lentiles, and millet, and ᵀfitches,ᴿ and put them in one vessel, and make thee bread thereof, according to the number of the days that thou shalt lie upon thy side, three hundred and ninety days shalt thou eat thereof.   rie • Is. 28:25

10 And thy meat which thou shalt eat shall be by weight, ᵀtwenty shek'-els a day: from time to time shalt thou eat it.   8 oz.

11 Thou shalt drink also water by measure, the ᵀsixth part of an hin: from time to time shalt thou drink.   21.3 oz.

12 And thou shalt eat it as barley cakes, and thou shalt bake it with ᵀdung that cometh out of man, in their sight.   manure

13 And the LORD said, Even thus shall the children of Israel ᴿeat their ᴿdefiled bread among the Gentiles, whither I will drive them.   Hos. 9:3 • Dan. 1:8

14 Then said I, Ah Lord GOD! behold, my soul hath not been polluted: for from my youth up even till now have I not eaten of that which dieth of itself, or is torn in pieces; neither came there ᴿabominableᵀ flesh into my mouth.   Is. 65:4 • unclean food

15 Then he said unto me, Lo, I have given thee cow's dung for man's dung, and thou shalt prepare thy bread therewith.

16 Moreover he said unto me, Son of man, behold, I will break the staff of bread in Jerusalem: and they shall eat bread by weight, and with care; and they shall drink water by measure, and with astonishment:

17 That they may want bread and water, and be astonied one with another, and consumeᵀ awayᵀ for their iniquity.   waste • in

CHAPTER 5

Sign of the Razor and the Hair

AND thou, son of man, take thee a sharp knife, take thee a barber's razor, ᴿand cause it to pass upon thine head and upon thy beard: then take thee balances to weigh, and divide the hair.   44:20; Is. 7:20

2 ᴿThou shalt burn with fire a third part in the midst of the city, when the days of the siege are fulfilled: and thou shalt take a third part, and smite about it with a knife: and a third part thou shalt scatter in the wind; and I will draw out a sword after them.   2 Kin. 25

3 Thou shalt also take thereof a few in number, and bind them in thy skirts.

4 Then take of them again, and cast them into the midst of the fire, and burn them in the fire; *for* thereof shall a fire come forth into all the house of Israel.

Explanation of the Signs

5 Thus saith the Lord GOD; This *is* ^RJerusalem: I have set it in the midst of the nations and countries *that are* round about her.   4:1
6 And she hath changed my judgments ^Tinto wickedness more than the nations, and my statutes more than the countries that *are* round about her: for they have refused my judgments and my statutes, they have not walked in them.   *in doing*
7 Therefore thus saith the Lord GOD; Because ye ^Tmultiplied more than the nations that *are* round about you, *and* have not walked in my statutes, neither have kept my judgments, ^Rneither have done according to the judgments of the nations that *are* round about you;   *are turbulent* · 16:47
8 ^RTherefore thus saith the Lord GOD; Behold, I, even I, *am* against thee, and will execute judgments in the midst of thee in the sight of the nations.   15:7; 21:3; Zech. 14:2
9 ^RAnd I will do in thee that which I have not done, and whereunto I will not do any more the like, because of all thine abominations.   Lam. 4:6; Dan. 9:12; [Amos 3:2]
10 Therefore the fathers shall eat the sons in the midst of thee, and the sons shall eat their fathers; and I will execute judgments in thee, and the whole remnant of thee will I scatter into all the winds.
11 Wherefore, *as* I live, saith the Lord GOD; Surely, because thou hast defiled my sanctuary with all thy detestable things, and with all thine abominations, therefore will I also diminish *thee;* neither shall mine eye spare, neither will I have any pity.
12 A third part of thee ^Rshall die with the pestilence, and with famine shall they be consumed in the midst of thee: and a third part shall fall by the sword round about thee; and I will scatter a third part into all the winds, and I will ^Rdraw out a sword after them.   6:12; Jer. 15:2; 21:9 · Jer. 9:16
13 Thus shall mine anger be accomplished, and I will cause my fury to rest upon them, and I will be comforted: and they shall know that I the LORD have spoken *it* in my zeal, when I have accomplished my fury in them.
14 Moreover ^RI will make thee waste, and a reproach among the nations that *are* round about thee, in the sight of all that pass by.   22:4; Lev. 26:31; Neh. 2:17; Ps. 74:3–10
15 So it shall be a ^Rreproach and a taunt, an instruction and an astonishment unto the nations that *are* round about thee, when I shall execute judgments in thee in anger and in fury and in ^Rfurious rebukes. I the LORD have spoken *it*.   Ps. 79:4 · 25:17

16 When I shall send upon them the evil arrows of famine, which shall be for *their* destruction, *and* which I will send to destroy you: and I will increase the famine upon you, and will break your staff of bread:
17 So will I send upon you famine and evil beasts, and they shall bereave thee; and pestilence and blood shall pass through thee; and I will bring the sword upon thee. I the LORD have spoken *it*.

CHAPTER 6

Destruction of High Places

AND the word of the LORD came unto me, saying,
2 Son of man, ^Rset^T thy face toward the ^Rmountains of Israel, and prophesy against them,   20:46; 21:2 · *take as an objective* · 36:1
3 And say, Ye mountains of Israel, hear the word of the Lord GOD; Thus saith the Lord GOD to the mountains, and to the hills, to the rivers, and to the valleys; Behold, I, even I, ^Rwill bring a sword upon you, and I will destroy your high places.   2 Kin. 25; 2 Chr. 36
4 And your altars shall be desolate, and your images shall be broken: and I will cast down your slain *men* before your idols.
5 And I will lay the dead ^Tcarcases of the children of Israel before their idols; ^Rand I will scatter your bones round about your altars.   *corpses* · 2 Kin. 23:14, 16, 20; Jer. 8:1, 2
6 In all your dwellingplaces the ^Rcities shall be laid waste, and the high places shall be desolate; that your altars may be laid waste and made desolate, and your idols may be broken and cease, and ^Ryour ^Timages may be cut down, and your works may be abolished.   5:14; Lev. 26:31 · Mic. 1:7 · *idols*
7 And the slain shall fall in the midst of you, and ye shall know that I *am* the LORD.

Salvation of the Remnant

8 ^RYet will I leave a remnant, that ye may have *some* that shall escape the sword among the nations, when ye shall be scattered through the countries.   5:2, 12
9 And they that escape of you shall remember me among the nations whither they shall be carried captives, because I am broken with their whorish heart, which hath departed from me, and with their eyes, which go a whoring after their idols: and they shall lothe themselves for the evils which they have committed in all their abominations.
10 And they shall know that I *am* the LORD, *and that* I have not said in vain that I would do this evil unto them.

Desolation of the Land

11 Thus saith the Lord GOD; ^TSmite with thine hand, and stamp with thy foot, and say,

Alas for all the evil abominations of the house of Israel! for they shall fall by the sword, by the famine, and by the pestilence. *clap your hands*

12 He that is far off shall die of the pestilence; and he that is near shall fall by the sword; and he that remaineth and is besieged shall die by the famine: Rthus will I accomplish my fury upon them.   5:13

13 Then shall ye know that I *am* the LORD, when their slain *men* shall be among their idols round about their altars, upon every high hill, in all the tops of the mountains, and under every green tree, and under every thick oak, the place where they did offer sweet savour to all their idols.

14 So will I Rstretch out my hand upon them, and make the land desolate, yea, more desolate than the wilderness toward Dib'-lath, in all their habitations: and they shall know that I *am* the LORD.   Is. 5:25

CHAPTER 7

Description of the Babylonian Conquest

MOREOVER the word of the LORD came unto me, saying,

2 Also, thou son of man, thus saith the Lord GOD unto the land of Israel; RAn end, the end is come upon the Rfour corners of the land.   Amos 8:2; [Matt. 24:6, 13, 14] • Rev. 7:1

3 Now *is* the end *come* upon thee, and I will send mine anger upon thee, and will Rjudge thee according to thy ways, and will Trecompense upon thee all thine abominations.   [Ps. 62:12] • *repay you for*

4 And Rmine eye shall not spare thee, neither will I have pity: but I will recompense thy ways upon thee, and thine abominations shall be in the midst of thee: and ye shall know that I *am* the LORD.   5:11

5 Thus saith the Lord GOD; An Revil, an only evil, behold, is come.   2 Kin. 21:12, 13

6 An end is come, the end is come: it watcheth for thee; behold, it is come.

7 The morning is come unto thee, O thou that dwellest in the land: the time is come, the day of trouble *is* near, and not the Tsounding again of the mountains.   *echo*

8 Now will I shortly Rpour out my fury upon thee, and accomplish mine anger upon thee: and I will judge thee according to thy ways, and will recompense thee for all thine abominations.   9:8; 14:19; 20:8, 21

9 And mine eye shall not spare, neither will I have pity: I will recompense thee according to thy ways and thine abominations *that* are in the midst of thee; and ye shall know that I *am* the LORD that smiteth.

10 Behold the day, behold, it is come: the morning is gone forth; the Rrod hath blossomed, pride hath budded.   Is. 10:5

11 Violence is risen up into a rod of wickedness: none of them *shall remain,* nor of their multitude, nor of any of their's: neither *shall there be* wailing for them.

12 The Rtime is come, the day draweth near: let not the buyer rejoice, nor the seller mourn: for wrath *is* upon all the multitude thereof.   *vv.* 5-7, 10; 1 Cor. 7:29-31

13 For the seller shall not return to that which is sold, although they were yet alive: for the vision *is* touching the whole multitude thereof, *which* shall not return; neither shall any strengthen himself Tin the iniquity of his life.   *in the evil manner*

14 They have Rblown the trumpet, even to make all ready; but none goeth to the battle: for my wrath *is* upon all the multitude thereof.   Num. 10:9; Jer. 4:5

15 RThe sword *is* without, and the pestilence and the famine within: he that *is* in the field shall die with the sword; and he that *is* in the city, famine and pestilence shall devour him.   Deut. 32:25; Lam. 1:20

16 But they that Rescape of them shall escape, and shall be on the mountains like doves of the valleys, all of them mourning, every one for his iniquity.   6:8; 14:22

17 All Rhands shall be feeble, and all knees shall be weak *as* water.   Is. 13:7; Jer. 6:24

18 They shall also Rgird *themselves* with sackcloth, and horror shall cover them; and shame *shall be* upon all faces, and baldness upon all their heads.   Jer. 6:26; Amos 8:10

19 They shall cast their silver in the streets, and their gold shall be removed: their Rsilver and their gold shall not be able to deliver them in the day of the wrath of the LORD: they shall not satisfy their souls, neither fill their bowels: because it is the stumblingblock of their iniquity.   [Prov. 11:4]

20 As for the beauty of his ornament, he set it in majesty: Rbut they made the images of their abominations *and* of their detestable things therein: therefore have I Tset it far from them.   Jer. 7:30 • *taken it away*

21 RAnd I will give it into the hands of the Tstrangers for a prey, and to the wicked of the earth for a spoil; and they shall pollute it.   2 Kin. 24:12, 13; Ps. 74:2-8 • *foreigners*

22 My face will I turn also from them, and they shall pollute my secret *place:* for the robbers shall enter into it, and defile it.

23 Make a chain: for the land is full of bloody crimes, and the city is full of violence.

24 Wherefore I will bring the worst of the heathen, and they shall possess their houses: I will also make the pomp of the strong to cease; and their holy places shall be defiled.

25 TDestruction cometh; and they shall seek peace, and *there shall be* none.   *disaster*

26 RMischief shall come upon mischief, and rumour shall be upon rumour; Rthen shall they seek a vision of the prophet; but the law

shall perish from the priest, and counsel from the ancients.   Jer. 4:20 • 20:1, 3; Ps. 74:9

27 The king shall mourn, and the prince shall be ᴿclothed with desolation, and the hands of the people of the land shall be troubled: I will do unto them after their way, and according to their deserts will I judge them; and they shall know that I *am* the LORD.   26:16; Job 8:22; Ps. 35:26

CHAPTER 8

Vision of the Glory of God

AND it came to pass in the sixth year, in the sixth *month,* in the fifth *day* of the month, *as* I sat in mine house, and the elders of Judah sat before me, that the hand of the Lord GOD fell there upon me.

2 Then I beheld, and lo a likeness as the appearance of fire: from the appearance of his loins even downward, fire; and from his loins even upward, as the appearance of brightness, ᴿas the colour of amber.   1:4

3 And he put forth the form of an hand, and took me by a lock of mine head; and the spirit lifted me up between the earth and the heaven, and brought me in the visions of God to Jerusalem, to the door of the inner gate, that looketh toward the north; where *was* the seat of the image of jealousy, which provoketh to jealousy.

4 And, behold, the glory of the God of Israel *was* there, according to the vision that I ᴿsaw in the plain.   1:28; 3:22, 23

Image of Jealousy

5 Then said he unto me, Son of man, lift up thine eyes now the way toward the north. So I lifted up mine eyes the way toward the north, and behold northward at the gate of the altar this image of jealousy in the entry.

6 He said furthermore unto me, Son of man, seest thou what they do? *even* the great ᴿabominations that the house of Israel committeth here, that I should go far off from my sanctuary? but turn thee yet again, *and* thou shalt see greater abominations.
                                   2 Kin. 23:4, 5

Paintings on the Wall

7 And he brought me to the door of the court; and when I looked, behold a hole in the wall.

8 Then said he unto me, Son of man, ᴿdig now in the wall: and when I had digged in the wall, behold a door.   Job 34:22; Is. 29:15

9 And he said unto me, Go in, and behold the wicked abominations that they do here.

10 So I went in and saw; and behold every ᴿform of creeping things, and abominable beasts, and all the ᴿidols of the house of Israel, pourtrayedᵀ upon the wall round about.   Ex. 20:4 • Jer. 2:26, 27 • *pictured*

11 ᴿAnd there stood before them seventy men of the ᵀancients of the house of Israel, and in the midst of them stood Ja-az-a-ni'-ah the son of Sha'-phan, with every man his censer in his hand; and a thick cloud of incense went up.   Ex. 24:1, 9 • *elders*

12 Then said he unto me, Son of man, hast thou seen what the ancients of the house of Israel do in the dark, every man in the chambers of his ᵀimagery? for they say, ᴿThe LORD seeth us not; the LORD hath forsaken the earth.   *imagination* • 9:9

Weeping for Tammuz

13 ᴿHe said also unto me, Turn thee yet again, *and* thou shalt see greater ᵀabominations that they do.   Jer. 9:3 • *evils*

14 Then he brought me to the door of the gate of the LORD's house which *was* toward the north; and, behold, there sat women weeping for ᵀTam'-muz.   *god of flocks*

Sun Worship

15 Then said he unto me, Hast thou seen *this,* O son of man? turn thee yet again, *and* thou shalt see greater ᴿabominations than these.   Deut. 7:25

16 And he brought me into the inner court of the LORD's house, and, behold, at the door of the temple of the LORD, ᴿbetween the porch and the altar, *were* about five and twenty men, with their backs toward the temple of the LORD, and their faces toward the east; and theyᴿ worshipped the sun toward the east.   Joel 2:17 • Jer. 44:17

17 Then he said unto me, Hast thou seen *this,* O son of man? Is it a light thing to the house of Judah that they commit the abominations which they commit here? for they have filled the land with violence, and have returned to provoke me to anger: and, lo, they put the branch to their nose.

18 Therefore will I also deal in fury: mine eye shall not spare, neither will I have pity: and though they cry in mine ears with a loud voice, *yet* will I not hear them.

CHAPTER 9

Call to the Six Men

HE cried also in mine ears with a loud voice, saying, Cause them that have charge over the city to draw near, even every man *with* his destroying weapon in his hand.

2 And, behold, six men came from the way of the higher gate, which lieth toward the north, and every man a slaughter weapon in his hand; and one man among them *was* clothed with linen, with a writer's inkhorn by his side: and they went in, and stood beside the brasen altar.

3 And the glory of the God of Israel was gone up from the cherub, whereupon he was, to the threshold of the house. And he called to the man clothed with linen, which *had* the writer's inkhorn by his side;

Command to Slay the Wicked

4 And the LORD said unto him, Go through the midst of the city, through the midst of Jerusalem, and ᵀset ᴿa mark upon the foreheads of the men that sigh and that cry for all the ᵀabominations that be done in the midst thereof.   *put · Ex. 12:7 · evils*

5 And to the others he said in ᵀmine hearing, Go ye after him through the city, and smite: ᴿlet not your eye spare, neither have ye pity: *mine ears · 5:11*

6 Slayᵀ utterly old *and* young, both maids, and little children, and women: but come not near any man upon whom *is* the mark; and begin at my ᵀsanctuary. Then they began at the ᵀancient men which *were* before the house.   *destroy completely · temple · elders*

7 And he said unto them, ᴿDefile the house, and fill the courts with the slain: go ye forth. And they went forth, and slew in the city.   *7:20–22; 2 Chr. 36:17*

Weeping of Ezekiel

8 And it came to pass, while they were slaying them, and I was left, that I fell upon my face, and cried, and said, Ah Lord GOD! wilt thou destroy all the residue of Israel in thy pouring out of thy fury upon Jerusalem?

9 Then said he unto me, The iniquity of the house of Israel and Judah *is* exceeding great, and the land is full of blood, and the city full of perverseness: for they say, The LORD hath forsaken the earth, and the LORD seeth not.

10 And as for me also, mine eye shall not spare, neither will I have pity, *but* I will recompense their way upon their head.

11 And, behold, the man clothed with linen, which *had* the inkhorn by his side, reported the matter, saying, ᴿI have done as thou hast commanded me.   *Gen. 6:22*

CHAPTER 10

Departure of the Glory of God to the Threshold

THEN I looked, and, behold, in the ᴿfirmament that was above the head of the cher'-u-bims there appeared over them as it were a sapphire stone, as the appearance of the likeness of a throne.   *1:22, 26*

2 And he spake unto the man clothed with linen, and said, Go in between the wheels, *even* under the cherub, and fill thine hand with coals of fire from between the cher'-u-bims, and scatter *them* over the city. And he went in in my sight.

3 Now the cher'-u-bims stood on the right side of the house, when the man went in; and the cloud filled ᴿthe inner court.   *8:3, 16*

4 ᴿThen the glory of the LORD went up from the cherub, *and stood* over the threshold of the house; and the house was filled with the cloud, and the court was full of the brightness of the LORD's glory.   *v. 18*

5 And the ᴿsound of the cher'-u-bims' wings was heard *even* to the outer court, as ᴿthe voice of the Almighty God when he speaketh.   *1:24 · [Job 40:9; Ps. 29:3; Rev. 1:10–16]*

6 And it came to pass, *that* when he had commanded the man clothed with linen, saying, Take fire from between the wheels, from between the cher'-u-bims; then he went in, and stood beside the wheels.

7 And one cherub stretched forth his hand from between the cher'-u-bims unto the fire that *was* between the cher'-u-bims, and took *thereof*, and put *it* into the hands of *him that was* clothed with linen: who took *it*, and went out.

8 And there appeared in the cher'-u-bims the form of a man's hand under their wings.

Vision of the Wheels and Cherubims

9 ᴿAnd when I looked, behold the four wheels by the cher'-u-bims, one wheel by one cherub, and another wheel by another cherub: and the appearance of the wheels *was* as the colour of a beryl stone.   *1:15*

10 And *as for* their appearances, they four had ᵀone likeness, as if a wheel had been in the midst of a wheel.   *the same image*

11 When they went, they went upon their four sides; they turned not as they went, but to the place whither the head looked they followed it; they turned not as they went.

12 And their whole body, and their backs, and their hands, and their wings, and the wheels, *were* ᴿfull of eyes round about, *even* the wheels that they four had.   *1:18*

13 As for the wheels, ᵀit was cried unto them in my hearing, O wheel.   *they were called*

14 ᴿAnd every one had four faces: the first face *was* the face of a ᴿcherub, and the second face *was* the face of a man, and the third the face of a lion, and the fourth the face of an eagle.   *v. 21; 1:6, 10 · 1 Kin. 7:29, 36*

15 And the cher'-u-bims were ᵀlifted up. This *is* ᴿthe living creature that I saw by the river of Che'-bar.   *mounted · 1:5*

16 ᴿAnd when the cher'-u-bims went, the wheels went by them: and when the cher'-u-bims lifted up their wings to mount up from the earth, the same wheels also turned not from beside them.   *1:19*

17 ᴿWhen they stood, *these* stood; and when they were lifted up, *these* lifted up themselves *also*: for the spirit ᵀof the living creature *was* in them.   *1:12, 20, 21 · of life*

18 Then ᴿthe glory of the LORD ᴿdeparted

from off the threshold of the house, and stood over the cher'-u-bims.   *v.* 4 • Hos. 9:12

19 And the cher'-u-bims lifted up their wings, and mounted up from the earth in my sight: when they went out, the wheels also *were* beside them, and *every* one stood at the door of the ᴿeast gate of the Loʀᴅ's house; and the glory of the God of Israel *was* over them above.   11:1, 22

20 ᴿThis *is* the living creature that I saw under the God of Israel ᴿby the river of Che'-bar; and I knew that they *were* the cher'-u-bims.   *v.* 15; 1:22 • 1:1

21 Every one had four faces apiece, and every one four wings; and the likeness of the hands of a man *was* under their wings.

22 And the likeness of their faces *was* the same faces which I saw by the river of Che'-bar, their appearances and themselves: they went every one straight forward.

CHAPTER 11

Vision of the Twenty-five Wicked Rulers

MOREOVER the spirit lifted me up, and brought me unto the east gate of the Loʀᴅ's house, which looketh eastward: and behold at the door of the gate five and twenty men; among whom I saw Ja-az-a-ni'-ah the son of A'-zur, and Pel-a-ti'-ah the son of Be-na'-iah, princes of the people.

2 Then said he unto me, Son of man, these *are* the men that devise mischief, and give wicked counsel in this city:

3 Which say, *It is* not ᵀnear; let us build houses: this *city is* the ᵀcaldron, and we *be* the flesh.   *for us to build houses now* • *kettle*

4 Therefore ᴿprophesy against them, prophesy, O son of man.   3:4, 17

5 And ᴿthe Spirit of the Loʀᴅ fell upon me, and said unto me, Speak; Thus saith the Loʀᴅ; Thus have ye said, O house of Israel: for I know the things that come into your mind, *every one of* them.   2:2

6 ᴿYe have multiplied your slain in this city, and ye have filled the streets thereof with the slain.   7:23; Is. 1:15; Jer. 7:9

7 Therefore thus saith the Lord Goᴅ; ᴿYour slain whom ye have laid in the midst of it, they *are* the flesh, and this *city is* the caldron: ᴿbut I will bring you forth out of the midst of it.   24:3, 6; Mic. 3:3 • *v.* 9

8 Ye haveᴿ feared the sword; and I will bring a sword upon you, saith the Lord Goᴅ.   2 Kin. 25; 2 Chr. 36; Job 3:25; Is. 24:17, 18

9 And I will bring you out of the midst thereof, and deliver you into the hands of ᴿstrangers, and ᴿwill execute judgments among you.   Deut. 28:36, 49, 50 • 5:8

10 Ye shall fall by the sword; I will judge you in ᴿthe border of Israel; and ye shall know that I *am* the Loʀᴅ.   1 Kin. 8:65

11 ᴿThis *city* shall not be your ᵀcaldron, neither shall ye be the ᵀflesh in the midst thereof; *but* I will judge you in the border of Israel: *v.* 3; 24:3, 6 • *kettle* • *meat*

12 And ye shall know that I *am* the Loʀᴅ: for ye have not walked in my statutes, neither executed my judgments, but ᴿhave done after the manners of the heathen that *are* round about you.   Lev. 18:3

Promise of the Restoration of the Remnant

13 ᴿAnd it came to pass, when I prophesied, that ᴿPel-a-ti'-ah the son of Be-na'-iah died. Then ᴿfell I down upon my face, and cried with a loud voice, and said, Ah Lord Goᴅ! wilt thou make a full end of the remnant of Israel?   Acts 5:5 • *v.* 1 • 9:8

14 Again the word of the Loʀᴅ came unto me, saying,

15 Son of man, thy brethren, *even* thy brethren, the men of thy kindred, and all the house of Israel wholly, *are* they unto whom the inhabitants of Jerusalem have said, Get you far from the Loʀᴅ: ᴿunto us is this land given in possession.   33:24

16 Therefore say, Thus saith the Lord Goᴅ; Although I have cast them far off among the heathen, and although I have scattered them among the countries, yet will I be to them as a little ᵀsanctuary in the countries where they shall come.   *refuge*

17 Therefore say, Thus saith the Lord Goᴅ; ᴿI will even gather you from the people, and assemble you out of the countries where ye have been scattered, and I will give you the land of Israel.   Jer. 24:5

18 And they shall come thither, and ᴿthey shall take away all the ᵀdetestable things thereof and all the ᵀabominations thereof from thence.   37:23 • *wrong* • *evils*

19 And ᴿI will give them one heart, and I will put a new spirit within you; and I will take the stony heart out of their flesh, and will give them an heart of flesh: 36:26

20 ᴿThat they may walk in my statutes, and keep mine ordinances, and do them: ᴿand they shall be my people, and I will be their God.   36:27; Ps. 105:45 • Jer. 24:7

21 But *as for them* whose heart walketh after the heart of their ᵀdetestable things and their ᵀabominations, ᴿI will recompense their way upon their own heads, saith the Lord Goᴅ.   *wrong* • *evils* • 9:10

Departure of the Glory of God from the Mount of Olives

22 Then did the cher'-u-bims ᴿlift up their wings, and the wheels beside them; and the glory of the God of Israel *was* over them above.   1:19; 10:19

23 And ᴿthe glory of the Loʀᴅ went up from the midst of the city, and stood ᴿupon the mountain ᴿwhich *is* on the east side of the city.   8:4; 9:3 • Zech. 14:4 • 43:2

24 Afterwards ᴿthe ᵀspiritᴿ took me up, and brought me in a vision by the Spirit of God into Chal-de'-a, to them of the captivity. So the vision that I had seen went up from me.   8:3 • Spirit • Acts 10:16

25 Then I ᴿspake unto them of the captivity all the things that the LORD had shewed me.   2:7; 3:4, 17, 27

CHAPTER 12

Sign of Stuff (Baggage) for Removing

THE word of the LORD also came unto me, saying,

2 Son of man, thou dwellest in the midst of a rebellious house, which have eyes to see, and see not; they have ears to hear, and hear not: for they *are* a rebellious house.

3 Therefore, thou son of man, prepare thee ᵀstuff for removing, and remove by day in their sight; and thou shalt remove from thy place to another place in their sight: it may be they will consider, though they *be* a rebellious house.   exile's baggage

4 Then shalt thou bring forth thy stuff by day in their sight, as stuff for removing: and thou shalt go forth at even in their sight, as they that go forth into captivity.

5 Dig thou through the wall in their sight, and carry out thereby.

6 In their sight shalt thou bear *it* upon *thy* shoulders, *and* carry *it* forth in the twilight: thou shalt cover thy face, that thou see not the ground: ᴿfor I have set thee *for* a sign unto the house of Israel.   Is. 8:18

7 And I ᴿdid so as I was commanded: I brought forth my stuff by day, as stuff for ᵀcaptivity, and in the even I digged through the wall with mine hand; I brought *it* forth in the twilight, *and* I bare *it* upon *my* shoulder in their sight.   24:18 • exile

8 And in the morning came the word of the LORD unto me, saying,

9 Son of man, hath not the house of Israel, the rebellious house, said unto thee, ᴿWhat doest thou?   17:12; 24:19

10 Say thou unto them, Thus saith the Lord GOD; This ᴿburdenᵀ *concerneth* the prince in Jerusalem, and all the house of Israel that *are* among them.   Mal. 1:1 • message

11 Say, ᴿI *am* your sign: like as I have done, so shall it be done unto them: they shall remove *and* go into captivity.   v. 6

12 And ᴿthe prince that *is* among them shall bear upon *his* shoulder in the twilight, and shall go forth: they shall dig through the wall to carry out thereby: he shall cover his face, that he see not the ground with *his* eyes.   12:6; 2 Kin. 25:4; Jer. 39:4

13 My ᴿnet also will I spread upon him, and he shall be taken in my snare: and ᴿI will bring him to Babylon *to* the land of the Chal-de'-ans; yet shall he not see it, though he shall die there.   Job 19:6 • 2 Kin. 25:7

14 And ᴿI will scatter toward every wind all that *are* about him to help him, and all his ᵀbands; and ᴿI will draw out the sword after them.   5:10; 2 Kin. 25:4, 5 • troops • 5:2, 12

15 And they shall know that I *am* the LORD, when I shall scatter them among the nations, and disperse them in the countries.

16 ᴿBut I will leave a few men of them from the sword, from the famine, and from the pestilence; that they may ᵀdeclare all their ᵀabominations among the ᵀheathen whither they come; and they shall know that I *am* the LORD.   6:8–10 • shew • evils • nations

Sign of Trembling

17 Moreover the word of the LORD came to me, saying,

18 Son of man, ᴿeat thy bread with ᵀquaking, and drink thy water with trembling and with carefulness;   4:16 • trembling

19 And say unto the people of the land, Thus saith the Lord GOD of the inhabitants of Jerusalem, *and* of the land of Israel; They shall eat their bread with ᵀcarefulness, and drink their water with astonishment, that her land may be desolate from all that is therein, because of the violence of all them that dwell therein.   anxiety

20 And the cities that are inhabited shall be laid waste, and the land shall be desolate; and ye shall know that I *am* the LORD.

21 And the word of the LORD came unto me, saying,

22 Son of man, what *is* that ᴿproverb *that* ye have in the land of Israel, saying, The days are prolonged, and every vision faileth?   16:44

23 Tell them therefore, Thus saith the Lord GOD; I will make this proverb to cease, and they shall no more use it as a proverb in Israel; but say unto them, The days are at hand, and the ᵀeffect of every vision.   result

24 For there shall be no more any ᴿvainᵀ vision nor flattering ᵀdivination within the house of Israel.   Lam. 2:14 • empty • prediction

25 For I *am* the LORD: I will speak, and ᴿthe word that I shall speak shall come to pass; it shall be no more prolonged: for in your days, O rebellious house, will I say the word, and will perform it, saith the Lord GOD.   v. 28; [Is. 55:11]; Dan. 9:12; [Luke 21:33]

26 Again the word of the LORD came to me, saying,

27 ᴿSon of man, behold, *they of* the house of Israel say, The vision that he seeth *is* for many days *to come,* and he prophesieth of the times *that are* far off.   v. 22; Dan. 10:14

28 ᴿTherefore say unto them, Thus saith the Lord GOD; There shall none of my words be ᵀprolonged any more, but the word which I have spoken shall be done, saith the Lord GOD.   vv. 23, 25 • delayed

CHAPTER 13

Judgment upon False Prophets

AND the word of the LORD came unto me, saying,

2 Son of man, prophesy against the prophets of Israel that prophesy, and say thou unto them that prophesy out of their own hearts, Hear ye the word of the LORD;

3 Thus saith the Lord GOD; Woe unto the foolish prophets, that follow their own ᵀspirit, and have seen nothing!   mind

4 O Israel, thy prophets are ᴿlike the foxes in the ᵀdeserts.   Song 2:15 · waste places

5 Ye ᴿhave not gone up into the ᵀgaps, neither ᵀmade up the hedge for the house of Israel to stand in the battle in the day of the LORD.   22:30 · broken places · repaired

6 They have seen ᵀvanity and lying divination, saying, The LORD saith: and the LORD hath not sent them: and they have made others to hope that they would confirm the word.   empty ideas and misleading insights

7 ᴿHave ye not seen a vain vision, and have ye not spoken a lying divination, whereas ye say, The LORD saith it; ᵀalbeit I have not spoken?   22:28 · although

8 Therefore thus saith the Lord GOD; Because ye have spoken vanity, and seen lies, therefore, behold, I am ᴿagainst you, saith the Lord GOD.   5:8; 21:3; Nah. 2:13

9 And mine hand shall be upon the prophets that see vanity, and that divine lies: they shall not be in the assembly of my people, neither shall they be written in the writing of the house of Israel, neither shall they enter into the land of Israel; and ye shall know that I am the Lord GOD.

10 Because, even because they have seduced my people, saying, Peace; and there was no peace; and one built up a wall, and, lo, others daubed it with untempered morter:

11 Say unto them which daub it with untempered morter, that it shall fall: ᴿthere shall be an overflowing shower; and ye, O great hailstones, shall fall; and a stormy wind shall rend it.   38:22

12 Lo, when the wall is fallen, shall it not be said unto you, Where is the daubing wherewith ye have daubed it?

13 Therefore thus saith the Lord GOD; I will even ᵀrend it with a stormy wind in my fury; and there shall be an overflowing shower in mine anger, and great ᴿhailstones in my fury to consume it.   tear · Ps. 18:12

14 So will I break down the wall that ye have daubed with untempered morter, and bring it down to the ground, so that the ᴿfoundation thereof shall be discovered, and it shall fall, and ye shall be consumed in the midst thereof: ᴿand ye shall know that I am the LORD.   Mic. 1:6; Hab. 3:13 · [vv. 9, 21, 23]

15 Thus will I accomplish my wrath upon the wall, and upon them that have daubed it with untempered morter, and will say unto you, The wall is no more, neither they that daubed it;

16 To wit, the prophets of Israel which prophesy concerning Jerusalem, and which ᴿsee visions of peace for her, and there is no peace, saith the Lord GOD.   Jer. 6:14; 28:9

Judgment upon False Prophetesses

17 Likewise, thou son of man, set thy face against the daughters of thy people, ᴿwhich prophesy out of their own heart; and prophesy thou against them,   v. 2

18 And say, Thus saith the Lord GOD; Woe to the women that sew pillows to all armholes, and make kerchiefs upon the head of every stature to hunt souls! Will ye hunt the souls of my people, and will ye save the souls alive that come unto you?

19 And will ye pollute me among my people for handfuls of barley and for pieces of bread, to slay the souls that should not die, and to ᴿsave the souls alive that should not live, by your lying to my people that hear your lies?   Jer. 23:14, 17

20 Wherefore thus saith the Lord GOD; Behold, I am against your pillows, wherewith ye there hunt the souls to make them fly, and I will tear them from your arms, and will let the souls go, even the souls that ye hunt to make them fly.

21 Your kerchiefs also will I tear, and ᴿdeliver my people out of your hand, and they shall be no more in your hand to be hunted; ᴿand ye shall know that I am the LORD.   Ps. 91:3; 124:7 · v. 9

22 Because with ᵀlies ye have made the heart of the righteous sad, whom I have not made sad; and strengthened the hands of the wicked, that he should not return from his wicked way, by promising him life: error

23 Therefore ᴿye shall see no more vanity, nor divine divinations: for I will deliver my people out of your hand: and ye shall know that I am the LORD.   12:24; Mic. 3:6; Zech. 13:3

CHAPTER 14

Idolatry of the Elders

THEN ᴿcame certain of the elders of Israel unto me, and sat before me.   8:1

2 And the word of the LORD came unto me, saying,

3 Son of man, these men have set up their idols in their heart, and put the stumblingblock of their iniquity before their face: should I be enquired of at all by them?

4 Therefore speak unto them, and say unto them, Thus saith the Lord GOD; Every man of the house of Israel that setteth up his idols in his heart, and putteth the stumblingblock of

his iniquity before his face, and cometh to the prophet; ᴿI the LORD will answer him that cometh according to the multitude of his idols;   1 Kin. 21:20

5 That I may take the house of Israel in their own heart, because they are all estranged from me through their idols.

6 Therefore say unto the house of Israel, Thus saith the Lord GOD; Repent, and turn *yourselves* from your idols; and turn away your faces from all your abominations.

7 For every one of the house of Israel, or of the stranger that sojourneth in Israel, which separateth himself from me, and setteth up his idols in his heart, and putteth the stumblingblock of his iniquity before his face, and cometh to a prophet to enquire ᵀof him ᵀconcerning me; I the LORD will answer him by myself: *for himself · of*

8 And ᴿI will set my face against that man, and will make him a ᴿsign and a proverb, and I will cut him off from the midst of my people; ᴿand ye shall know that I *am* the LORD.   Jer. 44:11 · 5:15 · 6:7

9 And if the prophet be deceived when he hath spoken a thing, I the LORD have deceived that prophet, and I will stretch out my hand upon him, and will destroy him from the midst of my people Israel.

10 And they shall bear the punishment of their iniquity: the punishment of the prophet shall be even as the ᵀpunishment of him that seeketh *unto him;*   *iniquity*

11 That the house of Israel may go no more astray from me, neither be ᵀpolluted any more with all their transgressions; but that they may be my people, and I may be their God, saith the Lord GOD.   *made unclean*

Jerusalem to Be Destroyed

12 The word of the LORD came again to me, saying,

13 Son of man, when the land sinneth against me by trespassing ᵀgrievously, then will I stretch out mine hand upon it, and will break the ᴿstaff of the bread thereof, and will send famine upon it, and will cut off man and beast from it: *greatly · Lev. 26:26*

14 Though these three men, Noah, Daniel, and Job, were in it, they should deliver *but* their own souls ᴿby their righteousness, saith the Lord GOD.   [Prov. 11:4]

15 If I cause ᵀnoisome beasts to pass through the land, and they ᵀspoil it, so that it be desolate, that no man may pass through because of the beasts: *violent · ravage*

16 *Though* these three men *were* in it, *as* I live, saith the Lord GOD, they shall deliver neither sons nor daughters; they only shall be delivered, but the land shall be desolate.

17 Or *if* I bring a sword upon that land,

and say, Sword, go through the land; so that I cut off man and beast from it:

18 Though these three men *were* in it, *as* I live, saith the Lord GOD, they shall deliver neither sons nor daughters, but they only shall be delivered themselves.

19 Or *if* I send a pestilence into that land, and pour out my fury upon it in blood, to cut off from it man and beast:

20 ᴿThough Noah, Daniel, and ᴿJob, *were* in it, *as* I live, saith the Lord GOD, they shall deliver neither son nor daughter; they shall *but* deliver their own souls by their righteousness.   *v. 14; Job 1:1 · James 5:11*

21 For thus saith the Lord GOD; How much more when ᴿI send my four ᵀsore judgments upon Jerusalem, the sword, and the famine, and the noisome beast, and the pestilence, to cut off from it man and beast? 5:17; 33:27 · *severe*

22 Yet, behold, therein shall be left a ᴿremnant that shall be brought forth, *both* sons and daughters: behold, they shall come forth unto you, and ye shall see their way and their doings: and ye shall be comforted concerning the evil that I have brought upon Jerusalem, *even* concerning all that I have brought upon it.   Ezra 2:1

23 And they shall ᴿcomfort you, when ye see their ways and their doings: and ye shall know that I have not done ᴿwithout cause all that I have done in it, saith the Lord GOD.   Gen. 50:21 · Jer. 22:8, 9

CHAPTER 15

Parable of the Vine Tree

AND the word of the LORD came unto me, saying,

2 Son of man, What is the ᴿvine tree more than any tree, *or than* a branch which is among the trees of the forest?   Hos. 10:1

3 Shall wood be taken thereof to do any work? or will *men* take a pin of it to hang any vessel thereon?

4 Behold, ᴿit is cast into the fire for fuel; the fire devoureth both the ends of it, and the midst of it is burned. Is it ᵀmeet for *any* work?   *v. 6; 19:4; [John 15:6] · good enough*

5 Behold, when it was whole, it was ᵀmeet for no work: how much less shall it be meet yet for *any* work, when the fire hath devoured it, and it is burned?   *good enough*

6 Therefore thus saith the Lord GOD; As the vine tree among the trees of the forest, which I have given to the fire for fuel, so will I give the inhabitants of Jerusalem.

7 And ᴿI will set my face against them; ᴿthey shall go out from *one* fire, and *another* fire shall devour them; ᴿand ye shall know that I *am* the LORD, when I set my face against them.   Lev. 17:10; 2 Kin. 25 · Is. 24:18 · 7:4

8 And I will make the land ᵀdesolate,

because they have ^Tcommitted a trespass, saith the Lord GOD. *uninhabited · sinned*

CHAPTER 16

God Has Mercy on Israel

AGAIN the word of the LORD came unto me, saying,

2 Son of man, ^Rcause Jerusalem to ^Tknow her abominations,   *20:4 · realize her evil deeds*

3 And say, Thus saith the Lord GOD unto Jerusalem; Thy birth and thy ^Tnativity *is* of the land of Canaan; thy father *was* an Am'-or-ite, and thy mother an Hit'-tite.   *origin*

4 And *as for* thy nativity, in the day thou wast born thy navel was not cut, neither wast thou washed in water to supple *thee;* thou wast not salted at all, nor swaddled at all.

5 ^RNone eye pitied thee, to do any of these unto thee, to have compassion upon thee; but thou wast cast out in the ^Ropen field, to the ^Tlothing of thy person, in the day that thou wast born.   *v. 22 · Deut. 32:10 · disgust*

6 And when I passed by thee, and saw thee ^Tpolluted in thine own blood, I said unto thee *when thou wast* in thy blood, ^RLive; yea, I said unto thee *when thou wast* in thy blood, Live.   *wallowing · Ex. 19:4*

7 I have caused thee to multiply as the bud of the field, and thou hast increased and waxen great, and thou ^Tart come to excellent ornaments: *thy* breasts are fashioned, and thine hair is grown, whereas thou *wast* naked and bare.   *become attractive*

8 Now when I passed by thee, and looked upon thee, behold, thy time *was* the time of love; and I spread my skirt over thee, and covered thy nakedness: yea, I sware unto thee, and entered into a covenant with thee, saith the Lord GOD, and thou becamest mine.

9 Then washed I thee with water; yea, I throughly washed away thy blood from thee, and I anointed thee with oil.

10 I clothed thee also with ^Rbroidered work, and shod thee with ^Tbadgers' skin, and I girded thee about with fine linen, and I covered thee with silk.   *vv. 13, 18 · seal skin*

11 I decked thee also with ornaments, and I ^Rput bracelets upon thy hands, ^Rand a chain on thy neck.   *Gen. 24:22 · Prov. 1:9*

12 And I put a ^Tjewel on thy forehead, and earrings in thine ears, and a beautiful crown upon thine head.   *ring upon thy nose*

13 Thus wast thou decked with gold and silver; and thy raiment *was of* fine linen, and silk, and broidered work; ^Rthou didst eat fine flour, and honey, and oil: and thou wast exceeding ^Rbeautiful, and thou didst prosper into a kingdom.   *Deut. 32:13, 14 · Ps. 48:2*

14 And thy renown went forth among the heathen for thy beauty: for it *was* perfect through my comeliness, which I had put upon thee, saith the Lord GOD.

Israel Rejects God

15 ^RBut thou didst trust in thine own beauty, ^Rand playedst the harlot because of thy ^Trenown, and pouredst out thy fornications on every one that passed by; his it was.   *Jer. 7:4; Mic. 3:11 · Is. 1:21; 57:8 · good name*

16 ^RAnd of thy garments thou didst take, and deckedst thy ^Thigh places with divers colours, and playedst the harlot thereupon: *the like things* shall not come, neither shall it be *so.*   *7:20; 2 Kin. 23:7; Hos. 2:8 · pagan shrines*

17 Thou hast also taken thy fair jewels of my gold and of my silver, which I had given thee, and madest to thyself images of men, and didst commit whoredom with them,

18 And tookest thy broidered garments, and coveredst them: and thou hast set mine oil and mine incense before them.

19 ^RMy meat also which I gave thee, fine flour, and oil, and honey, wherewith I fed thee, thou hast even set it before them ^Tfor a sweet savour: and *thus* it was, saith the Lord GOD.   *Hos. 2:8 · as an offering*

20 ^RMoreover thou hast taken thy sons and thy daughters, whom thou hast borne unto me, and these hast thou sacrificed unto them ^Tto be devoured. *Is this* of thy whoredoms a small matter,   *Is. 57:5 · to be killed*

21 That thou hast slain my children, and delivered them to ^Rcause them to pass through *the fire* for them?   *2 Kin. 17:17; Jer. 19:5*

22 And in all thine abominations and thy whoredoms thou hast not remembered the days of thy youth, when thou wast naked and bare, *and* wast polluted in thy blood.

23 And it came to pass after all thy wickedness, ^R(woe, woe unto thee! saith the Lord GOD;)   *24:6*

24 *That* ^Rthou hast also built unto thee an eminent place, and hast made thee ^Tan high place in every street.   *v. 31 · a pagan shrine*

25 Thou hast built thy ^Rhigh place at every head of the way, and hast made thy beauty to be ^Tabhorred, and hast opened thy feet to every one that passed by, and multiplied thy whoredoms.   *Prov. 9:14 · despised*

26 Thou hast also committed fornication with ^Rthe Egyptians thy neighbours, great of flesh; and hast increased thy whoredoms, to provoke me to anger.   *8:10*

27 Behold, therefore I have stretched out my hand over thee, and have diminished thine ordinary *food,* and delivered thee unto the will of them that hate thee, the daughters of the ^RPhi-lis'-tines, which are ashamed^T of thy lewd way.   *v. 57 · shocked*

28 Thou hast played the whore also with the Assyrians, because thou wast unsatiable; yea, thou hast played the harlot with them, and yet couldest not be satisfied.

29 Thou hast moreover multiplied thy fornication in the land of Canaan ^Runto Chal-

de'-a; and yet thou wast not satisfied herewith. 23:14-17

30 How weak is thine heart, saith the Lord GOD, seeing thou doest all these *things*, the work of an imperious whorish woman;

31 In that thou buildest thine eminent place in the head of every way, and makest thine high place in every street; and hast not been as an harlot, in that thou scornest hire;

32 But *as* a wife that committeth Radultery, *which* taketh strangers instead of her husband! Ex. 20:14

33 They give gifts to all whores: but Rthou givest thy gifts to all thy lovers, and hirest them, that they may come unto thee on every side for thy whoredom. Is. 30:6

34 And the contrary is in thee from *other* women in thy whoredoms, whereas none followeth thee to commit whoredoms: and Rin that thou givest a reward, and no reward is given unto thee, therefore thou art contrary. Ex. 32:25

God Punishes Israel

35 Wherefore, O harlot, hear the word of the LORD:

36 Thus saith the Lord GOD; Because thy filthiness was poured out, and thy nakedness discovered through thy whoredoms with thy lovers, and with all the idols of thy abominations, and by Rthe blood of thy children, which thou didst give unto them; *v.* 20; Jer. 2:34

37 Behold, therefore I will gather all thy lovers, with whom thou hast taken pleasure, and all *them* that thou hast loved, with all *them* that thou hast hated; I will even gather them round about against thee, and will discover thy nakedness unto them, that they may see all thy nakedness.

38 RAnd I will judge thee, Tas women that break wedlock and Rshed blood are judged; and I will give thee blood in fury and jealousy. Lev. 20:10 • *with judgments of* • Ex. 21:12

39 And RI will also give thee into their hand, and they shall throw down thine eminent place, and shall break down thy high places: Rthey shall strip thee also of thy clothes, and shall take thy fair jewels, and leave thee naked and bare. 2 Kin. 25 • Hos. 2:3

40 RThey shall also bring up a company against thee, Rand they shall stone thee with stones, and thrust thee through with their swords. 23:46 • John 8:5, 7

41 And they shall Rburn thine houses with fire, and execute judgments upon thee in the sight of many women: and I will cause thee to cease from playing the harlot, and thou also shalt give no hire any more. 2 Kin. 25:9

42 So will I make my fury toward thee to rest, and my jealousy shall depart from thee, and I will be quiet, and will be no more angry.

43 Because thou hast not remembered the days of thy youth, but hast fretted me in all

these *things;* behold, therefore I also will recompense thy way upon *thine* head, saith the Lord GOD: and thou shalt not commit this lewdness above all thine abominations.

44 Behold, every one that useth proverbs shall use *this* proverb against thee, saying, As *is* the mother, *so is* her daughter.

45 Thou *art* thy mother's daughter, that Tlotheth her husband and her children; and thou *art* the Rsister of thy sisters, which lothed their husbands and their children: Ryour mother *was* an Hit'-tite, and your father an Am'-or-ite. *despised* • 23:2, 37 • *v.* 3

46 And thine Relder sister *is* Sa-ma'-ri-a, she and her daughters that dwell at thy left hand: and Rthy younger sister, that dwelleth at thy right hand, *is* Sodom and her daughters. 23:4 • Deut. 32:32; Is. 1:10

47 Yet hast thou not walked after their ways, nor done after their abominations: but, as *if that were* a very little *thing*, thou wast corrupted more than they in all thy ways.

48 As I live, saith the Lord GOD, RSodom thy sister hath not done, she nor her daughters, as thou hast done, thou and thy daughters. Matt. 10:15; 11:24

49 Behold, this was the iniquity of thy sister Sodom, pride, Rfulness of bread, and abundance of idleness was in her and in her daughters, neither did she strengthen the hand of the poor and needy. Gen. 13:10

50 And they were haughty, and committed abomination before me: therefore RI took them away as I saw good. Gen. 19:24

51 Neither hath Sa-ma'-ri-a committed half of thy sins; but thou hast multiplied thine abominations more than they, and Rhast justified thy sisters in all thine abominations which thou hast done. Jer. 3:11

52 Thou also, which hast judged thy sisters, bear thine own shame for thy sins that thou hast committed more abominable than they: they are more righteous than thou: yea, be thou confounded also, and bear thy shame, in that thou hast justified thy sisters.

53 When I shall bring again their captivity, the captivity of Sodom and her daughters, and the captivity of Sa-ma'-ri-a and her daughters, then *will I bring again* the captivity of thy captives in the midst of them:

54 That thou mayest bear thine own shame, and mayest be confounded in all that thou hast done, in that thou art Ra comfort unto them. 14:22

55 When thy sisters, Sodom and her daughters, shall return to their former estate, and Sa-ma'-ri-a and her daughters shall return to their former estate, then thou and thy daughters shall return to your former estate.

56 For thy sister Sodom was not mentioned by thy mouth in the day of thy pride,

57 Before thy wickedness was discovered, as at the time of *thy* reproach of the daughters of Syria, and all *that are* round about her, the daughters of the Phil-is'-tines, which despise thee round about.

58 ^RThou hast borne thy lewdness and thine abominations, saith the LORD.   23:49

59 For thus saith the Lord GOD; I will even deal with thee as thou hast done, which hast despised the ^Roath in ^Rbreaking the ^Rcovenant.   17:13 • Is. 24:5 • Deut. 29:12

God Remembers His Covenant

60 Nevertheless I will ^Rremember my covenant with thee in the days of thy youth, and I will establish unto thee ^Ran everlasting covenant.   Ps. 106:45 • Jer. 32:40

61 Then thou shalt remember thy ways, and be ashamed, when thou shalt receive thy sisters, thine elder and thy younger: and I will give them unto thee for daughters, but not by thy ^Tcovenant.   *agreement*

62 ^RAnd I will establish my covenant with thee; and thou shalt know that I *am* the LORD: 20:37; 34:25; 37:26; Hos. 2:19

63 That thou mayest remember, and be confounded, and never open thy mouth any more because of thy shame, when I am ^Tpacified toward thee for all that thou hast done, saith the Lord GOD.   *have forgiven*

CHAPTER 17

Parable of the Two Eagles

AND the word of the LORD came unto me, saying,

2 Son of man, put forth a riddle, and speak a parable unto the house of Israel;

3 And say, Thus saith the Lord GOD; A great eagle with great wings, longwinged, full of feathers, which had ^Tdivers colours, came unto Leb'-a-non, and ^Rtook the highest branch of the cedar: *various* • 2 Kin. 24:12

4 He cropped off the top of his young twigs, and carried it into a land of traffick; he set it in a city of merchants.

5 He took also of the seed of the land, and planted it in a fruitful field; he placed *it* by great waters, *and* set it *as* a willow tree.

6 And it grew, and became a spreading vine ^Rof low stature, whose branches turned toward him, and the roots thereof were under him: so it became a vine, and brought forth branches, and shot forth sprigs.   *v.* 14

7 There was also another great eagle with great wings and many feathers: and, behold, this vine did bend her roots toward him, ^Rand shot forth her branches toward him, that he might ^Rwater it by the furrows of her plantation.   *v.* 15 • 31:4

8 It was planted in a good ^Tsoil by great waters, that it might bring forth branches, and that it might bear fruit, that it might be a goodly vine.   *field*

9 Say thou, Thus saith the Lord GOD; ^RShall it prosper? ^Rshall he not pull up the roots thereof, and cut off the fruit thereof, that it wither? it shall wither in all the leaves of her spring, even without great power or many people to pluck it up by the roots thereof.   *vv.* 10, 15–21 • 2 Kin. 25:7

10 Yea, behold, *being* planted, shall it prosper? ^Rshall it not utterly wither, when the east wind toucheth it? it shall wither in the furrows where it grew.   Hos. 13:15

11 Moreover the word of the LORD came unto me, saying,

12 Say now to the rebellious house, Know ye not what these *things mean?* tell *them,* Behold, ^Rthe king of Babylon is come to Jerusalem, and hath taken the king thereof, and the princes thereof, and led them with him to Babylon;   2 Kin. 24:11–16

13 And hath taken of the king's seed, and made a covenant with him, and hath ^Ttaken an oath of him: he hath also taken the mighty of the land: *put him under oath*

14 That the kingdom might be base, that it might not lift itself up, *but* that by keeping of his covenant it might stand.

15 But ^Rhe rebelled against him in sending his ambassadors into Egypt, that they might give him horses and much people. Shall he prosper? shall he escape that doeth such *things?* or shall he break the covenant, and be delivered?   2 Kin. 24:20

16 *As* I live, saith the Lord GOD, surely in the place *where* the king *dwelleth* that made him king, whose oath he despised, and whose covenant he brake, *even* with him in the midst of Babylon he shall die.

17 Neither shall Pharaoh with *his* mighty army and great company make for him in the war, by casting up mounts, and building forts, to cut off many persons:

18 Seeing he despised the oath by breaking the ^Tcovenant, when, lo, he ^Thad ^Rgiven his hand, and hath done all these *things,* he shall not escape.   *agreement* • *had promised* • Lam. 5:6

19 Therefore thus saith the Lord GOD; *As* I live, surely mine oath that he hath despised, and my covenant that he hath broken, even it will I recompense upon his own head.

20 And I will ^Rspread my net upon him, and he shall be taken in my snare, and I will bring him to Babylon, and ^Rwill plead with him there for his trespass that he hath trespassed against me.   12:13 • 20:36

21 And all his fugitives with all his bands shall fall by the sword, and they that remain shall be scattered toward all winds: and ye shall know that I the LORD have spoken *it.*

22 Thus saith the Lord GOD; I will also

take of the highest ᴿbranch of the high cedar, and will set *it;* I will crop off from the top of his young twigs ᴿa tender one, and will ᴿplant *it* upon an high mountain and eminent: [Jer. 23:5; Zech. 3:8] • [Is. 53:2, 3] • [Ps. 2:6, 7]

23 ᴿIn the mountain of the height of Israel will I plant it: and it shall bring forth boughs, and bear fruit, and be a goodly cedar: and under it shall dwell all fowl of every wing; in the shadow of the branches thereof shall they dwell.   [Is. 2:2, 3]

24 And all the trees of the field shall know that I the LORD have brought down the high tree, have exalted the low tree, have dried up the green tree, and have made the dry tree to flourish: ᴿI the LORD have spoken and have done *it.*   22:14

CHAPTER 18

Message of Personal Judgment
for Personal Sin

THE word of the LORD came unto me again, saying,

2 What mean ye, that ye use this proverb concerning the land of Israel, saying, The ᴿfathers have eaten sour grapes, and the children's teeth are set on edge?   Jer. 31:29

3 *As* I live, saith the Lord GOD, ye shall not have *occasion* any more to use this proverb in Israel.

4 Behold, all souls are mine; as the soul of the father, so also the soul of the son is mine: the soul that sinneth, it shall die.

5 But if a man be ᴿjust, and do that which is lawful and right,   Gen. 6:9; [Hab. 2:4]

6 ᴿAnd hath not eaten upon the mountains, neither hath lifted up his eyes to the idols of the house of Israel, neither hath defiled his neighbour's wife, neither hath come near to a menstruous woman,   22:9

7 And hath not oppressed any, *but* hath restored to the debtor his ᴿpledge, hath ᵀspoiled none by violence, hath given his bread to the hungry, and hath covered the naked with a garment;   Deut. 24:12 • *robbed*

8 He *that* hath not given forth upon ᵀusury,ᴿ neither hath taken any increase, *that* hath withdrawn his hand from iniquity, hath executed true judgment between man and man,   *interest* • Lev. 25:36

9 Hath walked in my statutes, and hath kept my judgments, to deal truly; he *is* just, he shall surely live, saith the Lord GOD.

10 If he beget a son *that is* a robber, ᴿa shedder of blood, and *that* doeth the like to *any* one of these *things,*   Gen. 9:6; Ex. 21:12

11 And that doeth not any of those *duties,* but even hath eaten upon the mountains, and defiled his neighbour's wife,

12 Hath oppressed the poor and needy, hath spoiled by violence, hath not restored the pledge, and hath lifted up his eyes to the idols, hath committed abomination,

13 Hath given forth upon usury, and hath taken increase: shall he then live? he shall not live: he hath done all these abominations; he shall surely die; his blood shall be upon him.

14 Now, lo, *if* he beget a son, that seeth all his father's sins which he hath done, and considereth, and doeth not such like,

15 ᴿ*That* hath not eaten ᵀupon the mountains, neither hath lifted up his eyes to the idols of the house of Israel, hath not defiled his neighbour's wife,   v. 6 • in company with heathen

16 Neither hath oppressed any, hath not withholden the pledge, neither hath ᵀspoiled by violence, ᴿ*but* hath given his bread to the hungry, and hath covered the naked with a garment,   *robbed* • Is. 58:7, 10

17 *That* hath taken off his hand from the poor, *that* hath not received usury nor increase, hath executed my judgments, hath walked in my statutes; he shall not die for the iniquity of his father, he shall surely live.

18 *As for* his father, because he cruelly oppressed, spoiled his brother by violence, and did *that* which *is* not good among his people, lo, even he shall die in his iniquity.

19 Yet say ye, Why? doth not the son bear the iniquity of the father? When the son hath done that which is lawful and right, *and* hath kept all my statutes, and hath done them, he shall surely live.

20 The soul that sinneth, it shall die. The son shall not bear the iniquity of the father, neither shall the father bear the iniquity of the son: the righteousness of the righteous shall be upon him, and ᴿthe wickedness of the wicked shall be upon him.   [Rom. 2:5–9]

21 But if the wicked will turn from all his sins that he hath committed, and keep all my statutes, and do that which is lawful and right, he shall surely live, he shall not die.

22 ᴿAll his transgressions that he hath committed, they shall not be mentioned unto him: in his righteousness that he hath done he shall ᴿlive.   33:16 • [Ps. 18:20–24]

23 ᴿHave I any pleasure at all that the wicked should die? saith the Lord GOD: *and* not that he should return from his ways, and live?   [33:11; 1 Tim. 2:4; 2 Pet. 3:9]

24 But when the righteous turneth away from his righteousness, and committeth iniquity, *and* doeth according to all the abominations that the wicked *man* doeth, shall he live? All his righteousness that he hath done shall not be mentioned: in his trespass that he hath trespassed, and in his sin that he hath sinned, in them shall he die.

25 Yet ye say, The way of the Lord is not equal. Hear now, O house of Israel; Is not my way equal? are not your ways unequal?

26 ᴿWhen a righteous *man* turneth away from his righteousness, and committeth iniquity, and dieth in them; for his iniquity that he hath done shall he die.   Prov. 14:14

27 Again, ᴿwhen the wicked *man* turneth away from his wickedness that he hath committed, and doeth that which is lawful and right, he shall save his soul alive.   *v.* 21

28 Because ᴿhe considereth, and turneth away from all his transgressions that he hath committed, he shall surely live, he shall not die.   Ps. 119:59; Hag. 1:7

29 Yet saith the house of Israel, The way of the Lord is not ᵀequal.ᴿ O house of Israel, are not my ways equal? are not your ways ᵀunequal?   *fair* • [Ps. 98:9] • *unfair*

30 Thereforeᴿ I will judge you, O house of Israel, every one according to his ways, saith the Lord GOD. Repent, and turn *yourselves* from all your transgressions; so iniquity shall not be your ruin.   7:3; 33:20

31 Cast away from you all your transgressions, whereby ye have transgressed; and make you a new heart and a new spirit: for why will ye die, O house of Israel?

32 For ᴿI have no pleasure in the death of him that dieth, saith the Lord GOD: wherefore turn *yourselves*, and live ye.   [2 Pet. 3:9]

CHAPTER 19

Lament for the Princes of Israel

MOREOVER ᴿtake thou up a lamentation for the princes of Israel,   26:17

2 And say, What *is* thy mother? A lioness: she lay down among lions, she nourished her ᴿwhelpsᵀ among young lions.   Gen. 49:9 • *kittens*

3 And she brought up one of her whelps: it became a young lion, and it learned to catch the prey; it devoured men.

4 The nations also heard of him; ᴿhe was taken in their pit, and they brought him with chains unto the land of Egypt.   2 Kin. 23:33

5 Now when she saw that she had waited, *and* her hope was lost, then she took ᴿanother of her whelps, *and* made him a young lion.   2 Kin. 23:34

6 And he went up and down among the lions, he became a young lion, and learned to catch the prey, *and* devoured men.

7 And he knew their desolate palaces, and he laid waste their cities; and the land was desolate, and the fulness thereof, by the noise of his roaring.

8 Then the nations set against him on every side from the provinces, and spread their net over him: he was taken in their pit.

9 And they put him in ward ᵀin chains, and brought him to the king of Babylon: they brought him into holds, that his voice should no more be heard upon ᴿthe mountains of Israel.   *with hooks* • 6:2

Parable of the Withered Vine

10 Thy mother *is* like a vine in thy blood, planted by the waters: she was fruitful and full of branches by reason of many waters.

11 And she had strong rods for the sceptres of them that bare rule, and her ᴿstature was exalted among the thick branches, and she appeared in her height with the multitude of her branches.   Dan. 4:11

12 But she was plucked up in fury, she was cast down to the ground, and the ᴿeast wind dried up her fruit: her strong rods were broken and withered; the fire consumed them.   17:10; Hos. 13:15

13 And now she *is* planted in the wilderness, in a dry and thirsty ground.

14 ᴿAnd fire is gone out of a rod of her branches, *which* hath devoured her fruit, so that she hath no strong rod *to be* a sceptre to rule. ᴿThis *is* a lamentation, and shall be for a lamentation.   2 Kin. 24:20 • Lam. 1:2

CHAPTER 20

In Egypt

AND it came to pass in the seventh year, in the fifth *month*, the tenth *day* of the month, *that* ᴿcertain of the elders of Israel came to ᵀenquire of the LORD, and sat before me.   8:1 • *ask for guidance*

2 Then came the word of the LORD unto me, saying,

3 Son of man, speak unto the elders of Israel, and say unto them, Thus saith the Lord GOD; Are ye come to enquire of me? *As* I live, saith the Lord GOD, ᴿI will not be enquired of by you.   14:3

4 Wilt thou judge them, son of man, wilt thou judge *them*? ᴿcause them to know the abominations of their fathers: 16:2

5 And say unto them, Thus saith the Lord GOD; In the day when I chose Israel, and ᵀlifted up mine hand unto the seed of the house of Jacob, and made myself known unto them in the land of Egypt, when I lifted up mine hand unto them, saying, I *am* the LORD your God;   *promised*

6 In the day *that* I lifted up mine hand unto them, to bring them forth of the land of Egypt into a land that I had ᵀespied for them, flowing with milk and honey, which *is* the glory of all lands: *searched out;* 13:5

7 Then said I unto them, Cast ye away every man the abominations of his eyes, and defile not yourselves with the idols of Egypt: I *am* the LORD your God.

8 But they rebelled against me, and would not hearken unto me: they did not every man cast away the abominations of their eyes, neither did they forsake the idols of Egypt: then I said, I will ᴿpour out my fury upon

them, to accomplish my anger against them in the midst of the land of Egypt. 7:8

9 But I wrought for my name's sake, that it should not be polluted before the heathen, among whom they *were*, in whose sight I made myself known unto them, in bringing them forth out of the land of Egypt.

In the Wilderness

10 Wherefore I ^Rcaused them to go forth out of the land of Egypt, and brought them into the wilderness. Ex. 13:18

11 And I gave them my statutes, and ^Tshewed them my judgments, which *if* a man do, he shall even live in them. *revealed*

12 Moreover also I gave them my ^Rsabbaths, to be a sign between me and them, that they might know that I *am* the LORD that sanctify them. Ex. 20:8; Deut. 5:12; Neh. 9:14

13 But the house of Israel rebelled against me in the wilderness: they walked not in my statutes, and they ^Rdespised my judgments, which *if* a man do, he shall even live in them; and my sabbaths they greatly polluted: then I said, I would pour out my fury upon them in the wilderness, to consume them. Prov. 1:25

14 But I wrought for my name's sake, that it should not be polluted before the heathen, in whose sight I brought them out.

15 Yet also I ^Tlifted up my hand unto them in the wilderness, that I would not bring them into the land which I had given *them*, flowing with milk and honey, which *is* the glory of all lands; *promised*

16 ^RBecause they despised my judgments, and walked not in my statutes, but ^Tpolluted my sabbaths: for ^Rtheir heart went after their idols. *vv. 13, 24 • made unclean • Acts 7:42*

17 ^RNevertheless mine eye spared them from destroying them, neither did I make an end of them in the wilderness. [Ps. 78:38]

18 But I said unto their children in the wilderness, Walk ye not in the statutes of your fathers, neither observe their judgments, nor defile yourselves with their idols:

19 I *am* the LORD your God; ^Rwalk in my statutes, and keep my judgments, and do them; Deut. 5:32; 6:6, 7

20 And hallow my sabbaths; and they shall be a sign between me and you, that ye may know that I *am* the LORD your God.

21 Notwithstanding ^Rthe children rebelled against me: they walked not in my statutes, neither kept my judgments to do them, which *if* a man do, he shall even live in them; they ^Tpolluted my sabbaths: then I said, I would pour out my fury upon them, to accomplish my anger against them in the wilderness. Num. 25:1 • made unclean

22 ^RNevertheless I ^Twithdrew mine hand, and wrought for my name's sake, that it should not be polluted in the sight of the heathen, in whose sight I brought them forth. vv. 9, 14, 17; [Ps. 78:38] • refrained from judgment

23 I ^Tlifted up mine hand unto them also in the wilderness, that ^RI would scatter them among the heathen, and disperse them through the countries; *promised • Jer. 15:4*

24 Because they had not executed my judgments, but had despised my statutes, and had polluted my sabbaths, and ^Rtheir eyes were after their fathers' idols. 6:9

25 Wherefore ^RI gave them also statutes *that were* not good, and judgments whereby they should not live; Rom. 1:24; 2 Thess. 2:11

26 And I polluted them in their own gifts, in that they caused to pass through *the fire* all that openeth the womb, that I might make them desolate, to the end that they might know that I *am* the LORD.

In Canaan

27 Therefore, son of man, speak unto the house of Israel, and say unto them, Thus saith the Lord GOD; Yet in this your fathers have blasphemed me, in that they have committed a trespass against me.

28 *For* when I had brought them into the land, *for* the which I ^Tlifted up mine hand to give it to them, then they saw every high hill, and all the thick trees, and they offered there their sacrifices, and there they presented the provocation of their offering: there also they made their sweet savour, and poured out there their drink offerings. *promised*

In Ezekiel's Time

29 Then I said unto them, What *is* the high place whereunto ye go? And the name thereof is called Ba'-mah unto this day.

30 Wherefore say unto the house of Israel, Thus saith the Lord GOD; Are ye polluted after the manner of your fathers? and commit ye whoredom after their abominations?

31 For when ye offer your gifts, when ye make your sons to pass through the fire, ye pollute yourselves with all your idols, even unto this day: and shall I be enquired of by you, O house of Israel? *As* I live, saith the Lord GOD, I will not be enquired of by you.

32 And that which cometh into your mind shall not be at all, that ye say, We will be as the heathen, as the families of the countries, to serve wood and stone.

Message of God's Future Restoration of Israel

33 *As* I live, saith the Lord GOD, surely with a mighty hand, and ^Rwith a stretched out arm, and with fury poured out, will I rule over you: Jer. 21:5; 51:57

34 And I will ^Rbring you out from the people, and will gather you out of the countries wherein ye are scattered, with a mighty hand, and with a stretched out arm, and with fury poured out. Is. 27:12

35 And I will bring you into the wilderness of the people, and there ^Rwill I plead with you face to face. 17:20; Jer. 2:9, 35

36 Like as I pleaded with your fathers in the wilderness of the land of Egypt, so will I plead with you, saith the Lord God.

37 And I will cause you to pass under the rod, and I will bring you into ^Tthe bond of the covenant: *obligation of the agreement*

38 And I will purge out from among you the rebels, and them that transgress against me: I will bring them forth out of the country where they sojourn, and ^Rthey shall not enter into the land of Israel: and ye shall know that I *am* the Lord. *Jer. 44:14*

39 As for you, O house of Israel, thus saith the Lord God; ^RGo ye, serve ye every one his idols, and hereafter *also*, if ye will not hearken unto me: ^Rbut ^Tpollute ye my holy name no more with your gifts, and with your idols. *Ps. 81:12 · 23:38 · made unclean*

40 For in mine holy mountain, in the mountain of the height of Israel, saith the Lord God, there shall all the house of Israel, all of them in the land, serve me: there will I accept them, and there will I require your offerings, and the ^Tfirstfruits of your ^Toblations, with all your holy things. *chief · gifts*

41 I will accept you with your sweet savour, when I bring you out from the people, and gather you out of the countries wherein ye have been scattered; and I will be sanctified in you before the heathen.

42 And ye shall know that I *am* the Lord, when I shall bring you into the land of Israel, into the country *for* the which I lifted up mine hand to give it to your fathers.

43 And there shall ye remember your ways, and all your doings, wherein ye have been defiled; and ^Rye shall ^Tlothe yourselves in your own sight for all your evils that ye have committed. *Hos. 5:15 · despise*

44 And ye shall know that I *am* the Lord, when I have wrought with you for my name's sake, not according to your wicked ways, nor according to your corrupt doings, O ye house of Israel, saith the Lord God.

Sign of the Forest Fire

45 Moreover the word of the Lord came unto me, saying,

46 ^RSon of man, set thy face toward the south, and drop *thy word* toward the ^Rsouth, and prophesy against the ^Rforest of the south field; *21:2 · Jer. 13:19 · Is. 30:6-11*

47 And say to the forest of the south, Hear the word of the Lord; Thus saith the Lord God; Behold, I will kindle a fire in thee, and it shall devour every green tree in thee, and every dry tree: the flaming flame shall not be ^Tquenched, and all faces ^Rfrom the south to the north shall be burned therein. *put out · 21:4*

48 And all flesh shall see that I the Lord have kindled it: it shall not be quenched.

49 Then said I, Ah Lord God! they say of me, ^RDoth he not speak parables? *Matt. 13:13, 14*

CHAPTER 21

Sign of the Drawn Sword

AND the word of the Lord came unto me, saying,

2 Son of man, ^Tset thy face toward Jerusalem, and ^Rdrop^T thy *word* toward the holy places, and ^Tprophesy against the land of Israel, *think about · Amos 7:16 · talk about · preach*

3 And say to the land of Israel, Thus saith the Lord; Behold, ^RI *am* against thee, and will draw forth my sword out of his sheath, and will cut off from thee ^Rthe righteous and the wicked. *5:8; 2 Kin. 25; 2 Chr. 36 · Job 9:22*

4 Seeing then that I will cut off from thee the righteous and the wicked, therefore shall my sword go forth out of his sheath against all flesh from the south to the north:

5 That all flesh may know that I the Lord have drawn forth my sword out of his sheath: it shall not return any more.

6 ^RSigh therefore, thou son of man, with the ^Tbreaking of *thy* loins; and with bitterness sigh before their eyes. *Is. 22:4 · pain*

7 And it shall be, when they say unto thee, Wherefore sighest thou? that thou shalt answer, For the tidings; because it cometh: and every heart shall melt, and ^Rall hands shall be feeble, and every spirit shall faint, and all knees shall be weak *as* water: behold, it cometh, and shall be brought to pass, saith the Lord God. *7:17*

8 Again the word of the Lord came unto me, saying,

9 Son of man, prophesy, and say, Thus saith the Lord; Say, A sword, a sword is sharpened, and also ^Tfurbished: *polished*

10 It is sharpened to make a sore slaughter; it is furbished that it may glitter: should we then make mirth? it contemneth the rod of my son, *as* every tree.

11 And he hath given it to be ^Tfurbished, that it may be handled: this sword is sharpened, and it is furbished, to give it into the hand of ^Rthe slayer. *polished · v. 19*

12 Cry and howl, son of man: for ^Tit shall be upon my people, it *shall be* upon all the princes of Israel: terrors by reason of the sword shall be upon my people: smite therefore upon *thy* thigh. *it is coming to*

13 Because *it is* ^Ra trial, and what if *the sword* contemn even the rod? ^Rit shall be no more, saith the Lord God. *Job 9:23 · v. 27*

14 Thou therefore, son of man, prophesy, and smite *thine* hands together, and let the sword be doubled the third time, the sword of the slain: it *is* the sword of the great *men that are* slain, which entereth into their ^Tprivy chambers. *private quarters*

15 I have set the point of the sword against all their gates, that *their* heart may faint, and *their* ruins be multiplied: ah! *it is* made bright, *it is* wrapped up for the slaughter.

16 Go thee one way or other, *either* on the right hand, *or* on the left, ^Twhithersoever thy face *is* set. *which way is your face set*

17 I will also ^Rsmite mine hands together, and ^RI will cause my fury to rest: I the LORD have said *it*. 22:13 • 5:13

Sign of the Double Stroke of the Sword

18 The word of the LORD came unto me again, saying,

19 Also, thou son of man, ^Rappoint thee two ways, that the sword of the king of Babylon may come: ^Tboth twain shall come forth out of one land: and choose thou a place, choose *it* at the head of the way to the city. 4:1–3 • *they*

20 Appoint a way, that the sword may come to Rab′-bath of the Am′-mon-ites, and to Judah in Jerusalem the defenced.

21 For the king of Babylon stood at the parting of the way, at the head of the two ways, to use divination: he made *his* arrows bright, he consulted with images, he ^Tlooked in the liver. *tried to foretell the future*

22 At his right hand was the divination for Jerusalem, ^Rto appoint captains, to open the mouth in the slaughter, to lift up the voice with shouting, ^Rto appoint *battering* rams against the gates, to cast ^Ta mount, *and* to build a fort. Jer. 51:14 • 4:2 • *up mounds*

23 And it shall be unto them as a false divination in their sight, to them that have sworn oaths: but he will call to remembrance the iniquity, that they may be taken.

24 Therefore thus saith the Lord GOD; Because ye have made your iniquity to be remembered, in that your ^Rtransgressions are ^Tdiscovered, so that in all your doings your sins do appear; because, *I say*, that ye are come to remembrance, ye shall be taken with the hand. [Num. 32:23] • *revealed*

25 And thou, ^Rprofane wicked prince of Israel, ^Rwhose day is come, when iniquity *shall have* an end, 2 Chr. 36:13; Jer. 52:2 • *v.* 29

26 Thus saith the Lord GOD; Remove the ^Tdiadem, and take off the crown: this *shall* not *be* the same: ^Rexalt *him that is* low, and abase *him that is* high. *turban* • Luke 1:52

27 I will overturn, overturn, overturn, it: and it shall be no *more*, until he come whose right it is; and I will give it *him*.

28 And thou, son of man, prophesy and say, Thus saith the Lord GOD concerning the Am′-mon-ites, and concerning their reproach; even say thou, The sword, the sword *is* drawn: for the slaughter *it is* ^Tfurbished, to consume because of the glittering: *polished*

29 Whiles they ^Rsee vanity unto thee, whiles they divine a lie unto thee, to bring thee upon the necks of *them that are* slain, of the wicked, whose day is come, when their iniquity *shall have* an end. 12:24

30 ^RShall I cause *it* to return into his

sheath? I will judge thee in the place where thou wast created, in the land ^Tof thy nativity. Jer. 47:6, 7 • *where you were born*

31 And I will pour out mine indignation upon thee, I will blow against thee in the fire of my wrath, and deliver thee into the hand of ^Tbrutish men, *and* skilful to destroy. *cruel*

32 Thou shalt be for ^Rfuel to the fire; thy blood shall be in the midst of the land; ^Rthou shalt be no *more* remembered: for I the LORD have spoken *it*. 20:47, 48 • 25:10

CHAPTER 22

Message of Judgment on Jerusalem

MOREOVER the word of the LORD came unto me, saying,

2 Now, thou son of man, ^Rwilt thou judge, wilt thou judge the bloody city? yea, thou shalt shew her all her abominations. 20:4

3 Then say thou, Thus saith the Lord GOD, The city sheddeth blood in the midst of it, that her time may come, and maketh idols against herself to defile herself.

4 Thou art become ^Rguilty in thy blood that thou hast shed; and hast defiled thyself in thine idols which thou hast made; and thou hast caused thy days to draw near, and art come *even* unto thy years: therefore have I made thee a reproach unto the heathen, and a mocking to all countries. 24:7

5 *Those that be* near, and *those that be* far from thee, shall mock thee, *which art* ^Tinfamous *and* much ^Tvexed. *notorious* • *troubled*

6 Behold, the princes of Israel, every one were in thee to their power to shed blood.

7 In thee have they ^Rset light by father and mother: in the midst of thee have they ^Rdealt by ^Toppression with the stranger: in thee have they vexed the fatherless and the widow. Lev. 20:9; Deut. 27:16 • Ex. 22:21 • *extortion*

8 Thou hast despised mine holy things, and hast ^Rprofaned my sabbaths. Lev. 19:30

9 In thee are ^Rmen that carry tales to shed blood: ^Rand in thee they eat upon the mountains: in the midst of thee they ^Rcommit lewdness. Lev. 19:16 • 18:6, 11 • Hos. 4:2, 10, 14

10 In thee have they discovered their fathers' nakedness: in thee have they humbled her that was set apart for pollution.

11 And one hath committed ^Tabomination with his neighbour's wife; and another hath ^Tlewdly defiled his daughter in law; and another in thee hath humbled his sister, his father's daughter. *evil* • *immorally*

12 In thee ^Rhave they taken gifts to shed blood; thou hast taken usury and increase, and thou hast greedily ^Tgained of thy neighbours by extortion, and hast forgotten me, saith the Lord GOD. Ex. 23:8 • *taken advantage*

13 Behold, therefore I have ^Rsmitten mine hand at thy dishonest gain which thou hast

made, and at thy blood which hath been in the midst of thee.   21:17; Is. 33:15

14 RCan thine heart endure, or can thine hands be strong, in the days that I shall deal with thee? RI the LORD have spoken *it*, and will do *it*.   21:7 · 17:24

15 And I will scatter thee among the heathen, and disperse thee in the countries, and will consume thy filthiness out of thee.

16 And thou shalt take thine inheritance in thyself in the sight of the heathen, and Rthou shalt know that I *am* the LORD.   Ps. 9:16

17 And the word of the LORD came unto me, saying,

18 Son of man, the house of Israel is to me become dross: all they *are* brass, and tin, and iron, and lead, in the midst of the furnace; they are *even* the dross of silver.

19 Therefore thus saith the Lord GOD; Because ye are all become dross, behold, therefore I will gather you into the midst of Jerusalem.

20 *As* they gather silver, and brass, and iron, and lead, and tin, into the midst of the furnace, to blow the fire upon it, to Rmelt *it*; so will I gather *you* in mine anger and in my fury, and I will leave *you there*, and melt you.   Is. 1:25; Jer. 9:7

21 Yea, I will gather you, and blow upon you in the Rfire of my wrath, and ye shall be melted in the midst thereof.   2 Kin. 22:13

22 As silver is melted in the midst of the furnace, so shall ye be melted in the midst thereof; and ye shall know that I the LORD have Rpoured out my fury upon you.   20:8

23 And the word of the LORD came unto me, saying,

24 Son of man, say unto her, Thou *art* the land that is Rnot cleansed, nor rained upon in the day of indignation.   24:13; Jer. 2:30

25 *There is* a conspiracy of her prophets in the midst thereof, like a roaring lion ravening the prey; they have devoured souls; Rthey have taken the treasure and precious things; they have made her many widows in the midst thereof.   Mic. 3:11

26 Her priests have violated my law, and have profaned mine holy things: they have put no difference between the holy and profane, neither have they shewed *difference* between the unclean and the clean, and have hid their eyes from my sabbaths, and I am profaned among them.

27 Her princes in the midst thereof *are* like wolves ravening the prey, to shed blood, *and* to destroy souls, to get dishonest gain.

28 And Rher prophets have Tdaubed them with untempered *morter*, Rseeing vanity, and divining lies unto them, saying, Thus saith the Lord GOD, when the LORD hath not spoken.   13:10 · *clouted up* · 13:6, 7

29 The people of the land have used Toppression, and exercised robbery, and have

vexed the poor and needy: yea, they have oppressed the stranger wrongfully.   *deceit*

30 And I sought for a man among them, that should make up the hedge, and stand in the gap before me for the land, that I should not destroy it: but I found none.

31 Therefore have I Rpoured out mine indignation upon them; I have consumed them with the fire of my wrath: Rtheir own way have I recompensed upon their heads, saith the Lord GOD.   *v.* 22 · 9:10

CHAPTER 23

Parable of Two Sisters

THE word of the LORD came again unto me, saying,

2 Son of man, there were Rtwo women, the daughters of one mother: Jer. 3:7, 8

3 And they committed whoredoms in Egypt; they committed whoredoms in their youth: there were their breasts pressed, and there they bruised the teats of their virginity.

4 And the names of them *were* A-ho'-lah the elder, and A-hol'-i-bah her sister: and they were mine, and they bare sons and daughters. Thus *were* their names; Sa-mar'-i-a *is* A-ho'-lah, and Jerusalem A-hol'-i-bah.

5 And A-ho'-lah played the harlot when she was mine; and she doted on her lovers, on Rthe Assyrians *her* neighbours,   Hos. 8:9

6 *Which were* clothed with blue, captains and rulers, all of them Tdesirable young men, horsemen riding upon horses.   *handsome*

7 RThus she committed her whoredoms with them, with all them *that were* the chosen men of Assyria, and with all Ton whom she doted: with all their idols she defiled herself.   Hos. 5:3 · *she loved*

8 RNeither left she her whoredoms Tbrought from Egypt: for in her youth they lay with her, and they bruised the breasts of her virginity, and poured their whoredom upon her.   *vv.* 3, 19 · *since the days of*

9 Wherefore I have delivered her into the hand of her lovers, into the hand of the RAssyrians, upon whom she doted.   2 Kin. 17:3

10 RThese discovered her nakedness: they took her sons and her daughters, and slew her with the sword: and she became Tfamous among women; for they had executed judgment upon her.   Hos. 2:10 · *a byword*

11 And when her sister A-hol'-i-bah saw *this*, she was more corrupt in her inordinate love than she, and in her whoredoms more than her sister in *her* whoredoms.

12 She doted upon the Assyrians *her* neighbours, captains and rulers clothed most gorgeously, horsemen riding upon horses, all of them desirable young men.

13 Then I saw that she was defiled, *that* they took both one way,

14 And *that* she increased her whoredoms: for when she saw men pourtrayed upon the wall, the images of the Chal-de'-ans pourtrayed with vermilion,

15 Girded with ᵀgirdles upon their loins, exceeding in dyed attire upon their heads, all of them princes to look to, after the manner of the Babylonians of Chal-de'-a, the land of their nativity: *belts*

16 And as soon as she saw them with her eyes, she ᵀdoted upon them, and sent messengers unto them into Chal-de'-a.   *loved*

17 And the ᵀBabyloniansᴿ came to her into the bed of love, and they defiled her with their whoredom, and she was polluted with them, and her mind was ᵀalienated from them.   *children of Babel • 2 Kin. 24:17 • led astray*

18 So she discovered her whoredoms, and discovered her nakedness: then ᴿmy mind was alienated from her, like as my mind was alienated from her sister.   Ps. 78:59; Jer. 6:8

19 Yet she multiplied her whoredoms, in calling to remembrance the days of her youth, ᴿwherein she had played the harlot in the land of Egypt.   v. 3; Lev. 18:3

20 For she ᵀdoted upon their paramours, whose flesh *is as* the flesh of asses, and whose issue *is like* the issue of horses.   *loved*

21 ᴿThus thou calledst to remembrance the ᵀlewdness of thy youth, in bruising thy teats by the ᴿEgyptians for the paps of thy youth.   v. 3; Jer. 3:9 • *immoral conduct* • 16:26

22 Therefore, O A-hol'-i-bah, thus saith the Lord GOD; ᴿBehold, I will raise up thy lovers against thee, from whom thy mind is alienated, and I will bring them against thee on every side;   v. 28; 16:37; Is. 10:5, 6

23 The Babylonians, and all the ᴿChal-de'-ans, Pe'-kod, and Sho'-a, and Ko'-a, *and* all the Assyrians with them: ᴿall of them desirable young men, captains and rulers, great lords and renowned, all of them riding upon horses.   2 Kin. 24:2 • v. 12

24 And they shall come against thee with ᴿchariots, wagons, and wheels, and with an assembly of people, *which* shall set against thee buckler and shield and helmet round about: and I will set ᴿjudgment before them, and they shall judge thee according to their judgments.   Nah. 2:3, 4 • v. 45; Jer. 39:5

25 And I will set my jealousy against thee, and they shall deal furiously with thee: they shall take away thy nose and thine ears; and thy remnant shall fall by the sword: they shall take thy sons and thy daughters; and thy residue shall be devoured by the fire.

26 They shall also strip thee out of thy clothes, and take away thy fair jewels.

27 Thus ᴿwill I make thy lewdness to cease from thee, and thy whoredom *brought* from the land of Egypt: so that thou shalt not lift up thine eyes unto them, nor remember Egypt any more.   16:41

28 For thus saith the Lord GOD; Behold, I will deliver thee into the hand *of them* whom thou hatest, into the hand *of them* ᴿfrom whom thy mind is alienated: v. 17

29 And they shall deal with thee hatefully, and shall take away all thy labour, and shall leave thee naked and bare: and the nakedness of thy whoredoms shall be discovered, both thy lewdness and thy whoredoms.

30 I will do these *things* unto thee, because thou hast ᴿgone a whoring after the heathen, *and* because thou art polluted with their idols.   6:9

31 Thou hast walked in the way of thy sister; therefore will I give her ᴿcup into thine hand.   2 Kin. 21:13; Jer. 7:14; 25:15

32 Thus saith the Lord GOD; Thou shalt ᴿdrink of thy sister's cup deep and large: ᴿthou shalt be laughed to scorn and had in derision; it containeth much.   Ps. 60:3 • 22:4, 5

33 Thou shalt be filled with ᴿdrunkenness and sorrow, with the cup of astonishment and desolation, with the cup of thy sister Sa-ma'-ri-a.   Jer. 25:15, 16, 27; Hab. 2:16

34 Thou shalt even drink it and suck *it* out, and thou shalt break the sherds thereof, and pluck off thine own breasts: for I have spoken *it*, saith the Lord GOD.

35 Therefore thus saith the Lord GOD; Because thou hast forgotten me, and cast me behind thy back, therefore bear thou also thy lewdness and thy whoredoms.

36 The LORD said moreover unto me; Son of man, wilt thou ᴿjudge A-ho'-lah and A-hol'-i-bah? yea, ᴿdeclare unto them their abominations;   20:4; 22:2 • Is. 58:1; Mic. 3:8

37 That they have committed adultery, and ᴿblood *is* in their hands, and with their idols have they committed adultery, and have also caused their sons, ᴿwhom they bare unto me, to pass for them through *the* fire, to devour *them*.   16:38 • 16:20

38 Moreover this they have done unto me: they have defiled my sanctuary in the same day, and have profaned my sabbaths.

39 For when they had slain their children to their idols, then they came the same day into my sanctuary to profane it; and, lo, thus have they done in the midst of mine house.

40 And furthermore, that ye have sent for men to come from far, unto whom a messenger *was* sent; and, lo, they came: for whom thou didst wash thyself, paintedst thy eyes, and ᴿdeckedst thyself with ornaments, Is. 3:18

41 And satest upon a stately ᴿbed, and a table prepared before it, whereupon thou hast set mine incense and mine oil.   Is. 57:7

42 And a voice of a multitude being at ease *was* with her: and with the ᵀmen of the common sort *were* brought ᵀSa-be'-ans from the wilderness, which put bracelets upon their hands, and beautiful crowns upon their heads.   *multitude of mankind • drunkards*

43 Then said I unto *her that was* ^Rold in adulteries, Will they now commit whoredoms with her, and she *with them?*   Ps. 106:6

44 Yet they went in unto her, as they go in unto a woman that playeth the harlot: so went they in unto A-ho'-lah and unto A-hol'-i-bah, the ^Tlewd women.   *immoral*

45 And the righteous men, they shall ^Rjudge them after the manner of adulteresses, and after the manner of women that shed blood; because they *are* adulteresses, and blood *is* in their hands.   16:38

46 For thus saith the Lord GOD; I will bring up a company upon them, and will give them to be removed and ^Tspoiled.   *robbed*

47 ^RAnd the company shall stone them with stones, and dispatch them with their swords; ^Rthey shall slay their sons and their daughters, and burn up their houses with fire.   16:40 · 24:21; 2 Chr. 36:17, 19

48 Thus will I cause lewdness to cease out of the land, that all women may be taught not to do after your lewdness.

49 And they shall recompense your lewdness upon you, and ye shall ^Rbear the sins of your idols: ^Rand ye shall know that I *am* the Lord GOD.   *v.* 35 · 20:38, 42, 44; 25:5

CHAPTER 24

Parable of the Boiling Pot

AGAIN in the ninth year, in the tenth month, in the tenth *day* of the month, the word of the LORD came unto me, saying,

2 Son of man, write thee the name of the day, *even* of this same day: ^Rthe king of Babylon set himself against Jerusalem this same day.   2 Kin. 25:1; Jer. 39:1; 52:4

3 ^RAnd utter a parable unto the rebellious house, and say unto them, ^RThus saith the Lord GOD; ^RSet on a pot, set *it* on, and also pour water into it: 17:12 · Jer. 11:3 · Jer. 1:13

4 ^RGather the pieces thereof into it, *even* every good piece, the thigh, and the shoulder; fill *it* with the choice bones.   Mic. 3:2, 3

5 Take the ^Rchoice of the flock, and ^Tburn also the bones under ^Tit, *and* make it boil well, and let them seethe the bones of it therein.   Jer. 39:6; 52:10, 24–27 · *pile* · *the caldron*

6 Wherefore thus saith the Lord GOD; Woe to ^Rthe bloody city, to the pot whose scum *is* therein, and whose scum is not gone out of it! bring it out piece by piece; let no ^Rlot fall upon it.   22:3 · Joel 3:3; Nah. 3:10

7 For her blood is in the midst of her; she set it upon the top of a rock; she poured it not upon the ground, to cover it with dust;

8 That it might ^Rcause fury to come up to take vengeance; I have set her blood upon the top of a rock, that it should ^Rnot be covered.   Is. 26:21 · Jer. 22:8, 9

9 Therefore thus saith the Lord GOD; ^RWoe to the bloody city! I will even make the pile for fire great.   *v.* 6; Nah. 3:1; Hab. 2:12

10 Heap on wood, kindle the fire, ^Tconsume the flesh, and spice it well, and let the bones be burned.   *completely cook*

11 Then set it empty upon the coals thereof, that the brass of it may be hot, and ^Rmay burn, and *that* ^Rthe filthiness of it may be molten in it, *that* the scum of it may be ^Tconsumed.   Jer. 21:10 · 22:15 · *burned*

12 She hath ^Rwearied *herself* with ^Tlies, and her great scum went not forth out of her: her scum *shall be* in the fire.   Jer. 9:5 · *toil*

13 In thy filthiness *is* ^Tlewdness: because I have purged thee, and thou wast not purged, thou shalt not be purged from thy filthiness any more, till I have caused my fury to rest upon thee.   *immorality*

14 ^RI the LORD have spoken *it:* it shall come to pass, and I will do *it;* I will not go back, ^Rneither will I spare, neither will I repent; ^Raccording to thy ways, and according to thy doings, shall they judge thee, saith the Lord GOD.   [1 Sam. 15:29] · 5:11 · Is. 3:11

Sign Through the Death of Ezekiel's Wife

15 Also the word of the LORD came unto me, saying,

16 Son of man, behold, I take away from thee the ^Tdesire of thine eyes with a stroke: yet neither shalt thou mourn nor weep, neither shall thy tears run down.   *pleasure*

17 ^TForbear to cry, make no mourning for the dead, bind the ^Ttire of thine head upon thee, and put on thy shoes upon thy feet, and cover not *thy* lips, and eat not the bread of men.   *sigh, but not aloud* · *turban*

18 So I spake unto the people in the morning: and at even my wife died; and I did in the morning as I was commanded.

19 And the people said unto me, ^RWilt thou not tell us what these *things are* to us, that thou ^Rdoest so?   12:9; 37:18 · *vv.* 16, 17

20 Then I answered them, The word of the LORD came unto me, saying,

21 Speak unto the house of Israel, Thus saith the Lord GOD; Behold, I will profane my sanctuary, the excellency of your strength, the desire of your eyes, and that which your soul pitieth; and your sons and your daughters whom ye have left shall fall by the sword.

22 And ye shall do as I have done: ye shall not cover *your* lips, nor eat the bread of men.

23 And your ^Ttires *shall be* upon your heads, and your shoes upon your feet: ^Rye shall not mourn nor weep; but ^Rye shall pine away for your iniquities, and mourn one toward another.   *turbans* · Ps. 78:64 · Lev. 26:39

24 Thus ^RE-ze'-ki-el is unto you a sign: according to all that he hath done shall ye do: ^Rand when this cometh, ye shall know that I *am* the Lord GOD.   Is. 20:3 · John 13:19

25 Also, thou son of man, *shall it* not *be* in

the day when I take from them their strength, the joy of their glory, the desire of their eyes, and that whereupon they set their minds, their sons and their daughters,

26 *That* Rhe that escapeth in that day shall come unto thee, to cause *thee* to hear *it* with *thine* ears?   33:21; 1 Sam. 4:12; Job 1:15

27 RIn that day shall thy mouth be opened to him which is escaped, and thou shalt speak, and be no more dumb: and thou shalt be a sign unto them; and they shall know that I *am* the LORD.   3:26; 33:22

CHAPTER 25

Judgment on Ammon

THE word of the LORD came again unto me, saying,

2 Son of man, set thy face against the Am'-mon-ites, and prophesy against them;

3 And say unto the Am'-mon-ites, Hear the word of the Lord GOD; Thus saith the Lord GOD; Because thou saidst, Aha, against my sanctuary, when it was profaned; and against the land of Israel, when it was desolate; and against the house of Judah, when they went into captivity;

4 Behold, therefore I will deliver thee to the men of the east for a possession, and they shall set their palaces in thee, and make their dwellings in thee: they shall eat thy fruit, and they shall drink thy milk.

5 And I will make RRab'-bah Ra stable for camels, and the Am'-mon-ites a Tcouching-place for flocks: Rand ye shall know that I *am* the LORD.   21:20 · Is. 17:2 · *resting* · 24:24

6 For thus saith the Lord GOD; Because thou hast clapped *thine* hands, and stamped with the feet, and rejoiced in heart with all thy Tdespite against the land of Israel;   *spite*

7 Behold, therefore I will Rstretch out mine hand upon thee, and will deliver thee for a Tspoil to the Theathen; and I will cut thee off from the people, and I will cause thee to perish out of the countries: I will destroy thee; and thou shalt know that I *am* the LORD.   Zeph. 1:4 · *loot* · *nations*

Judgment on Moab

8 Thus saith the Lord GOD; Because that Moab and Se'-ir do say, Behold, the house of Judah *is* like unto all the heathen;

9 Therefore, behold, I will open the side of Moab from the cities, from his cities *which are* on his frontiers, the glory of the country, RBeth-jesh'-i-moth, Ba'-al-me'-on, and Kir-i-a-tha'-im,   Num. 33:49

10 RUnto the men of the east with the Am'-mon-ites, and will give them in possession, that the Am'-mon-ites Rmay not be remembered among the nations.   *v.* 4 · 21:32

11 And I will execute judgments upon

Moab; and they shall know that I *am* the LORD.

Judgment on Edom

12 Thus saith the Lord GOD; Because that E'-dom hath dealt against the house of Judah by taking vengeance, and hath greatly offended, and revenged himself upon them;

13 Therefore thus saith the Lord GOD; I will also stretch out mine hand upon E'-dom, and will cut off man and beast from it; and I will make it desolate from Te'-man; and they of De'-dan shall fall by the sword.

14 And RI will lay my vengeance upon E'-dom by the hand of my people Israel: and they shall do in E'-dom according to mine Ranger and according to my fury; and they shall know my vengeance, saith the Lord GOD.   Is. 11:14 · 35:11

Judgment on Philistia

15 Thus saith the Lord GOD; Because the Phi-lis'-tines have dealt by revenge, and have taken vengeance with a despiteful heart, to destroy *it* for the old hatred;

16 Therefore thus saith the Lord GOD; Behold, RI will stretch out mine hand upon the Phi-lis'-tines, and I will cut off the RCher'-e-thims, Rand destroy the remnant of the sea coast.   Zeph. 2:4 · 1 Sam. 30:14 · Jer. 47:4

17 And I will Rexecute great vengeance upon them with furious rebukes; and they shall know that I *am* the LORD, when I shall lay my vengeance upon them.   5:15

CHAPTER 26

Destruction of Tyrus

AND it came to pass in the eleventh year, in the first *day* of the month, *that* the word of the LORD came unto me, saying,

2 Son of man, Rbecause that Ty'-rus hath said against Jerusalem, Aha, she is broken *that was* the gates of the people: she is turned unto me: I shall be Treplenished, *now* she is laid waste: Is. 23 · *filled with her goods*

3 Therefore thus saith the Lord GOD; Behold, I *am* against thee, O Ty'-rus, and will cause many nations to come up against thee, as the sea causeth his waves to come up.

4 And they shall Rdestroy the walls of Ty'-rus, and break down her towers: I will also scrape her dust from her, and make her like the top of a rock.   Is. 23:11; Amos 1:10

5 It shall be *a place for* the spreading of nets Rin the midst of the sea: for I have spoken *it*, saith the Lord GOD: and it shall become a Tspoil to the nations.   27:32 · *loot*

6 And her daughters which *are* in the field shall be slain by the sword; Rand they shall know that I *am* the LORD.   25:5

7 For thus saith the Lord GOD; Behold, I

will bring upon Ty'-rus Neb-u-chad-rez'-zar king of Babylon, ^Ra king of kings, from the north, with horses, and with ^Rchariots, and with horsemen, and companies, and much people.   Ezra 7:12; Dan. 2:37 • Nah. 2:3, 4

8 He shall slay with the sword thy daughters in the field: and he shall make a fort against thee, and cast a mount against thee, and lift up the buckler against thee.

9 And he shall set engines of war against thy walls, and with his axes he shall break down thy towers.

10 By reason of the abundance of his horses their dust shall cover thee: thy walls shall shake at the noise of the horsemen, and of the wheels, and of the chariots, when he shall enter into thy gates, as men enter into a city wherein is made a breach.

11 With the hoofs of his horses shall he tread down all thy streets: he shall slay thy people by the sword, and thy strong garrisons shall go down to the ground.

12 And they shall make a spoil of thy riches, and make a prey of thy merchandise: and they shall break down thy walls, and destroy thy pleasant houses: and they shall lay thy stones and thy timber and thy dust in the midst of the water.

13 And I will cause the ^Rnoise of thy songs to cease; and the sound of thy harps shall be no more heard.   Is. 14:11; 24:8; Rev. 18:22

14 And I will make thee like the top of a rock: thou shalt be *a place* to spread nets upon; thou shalt be built no more: for I the LORD have spoken *it,* saith the Lord GOD.

15 Thus saith the Lord GOD to Ty'-rus; Shall not the isles shake at the sound of thy fall, when the wounded cry, when the slaughter is made in the midst of thee?

16 Then all the ^Rprinces of the sea shall come down from their thrones, and lay away their robes, and put off their broidered garments: they shall clothe themselves with trembling; they shall sit upon the ground, and shall tremble at *every* moment, and be astonished at thee.   Is. 23:8

17 And they shall take up a lamentation for thee, and say to thee, How art thou destroyed, *that wast* inhabited of seafaring men, the renowned city, which wast strong in the sea, she and her inhabitants, which cause their terror *to be* on all that haunt it!

18 Now shall ^Rthe isles tremble in the day of thy fall; yea, the isles that *are* in the sea shall be troubled at thy departure.   *v.* 15

19 For thus saith the Lord GOD; When I shall make thee a desolate city, like the cities that are not inhabited; when I shall ^Rbring up the deep upon thee, and great waters shall cover thee;   *v.* 3; Is. 8:7, 8

20 When I shall bring thee down with them that descend into the pit, with the people of old time, and shall set thee in the low parts of the earth, in places desolate of old, with them that go down to the pit, that thou be not inhabited; and I shall set glory ^Rin the land of the living;   32:23

21 ^RI will make thee a terror, and thou *shalt be no more:* ^Rthough thou be sought for, yet shalt thou never be found again, saith the Lord GOD.   *vv.* 15, 16; 28:19 • Ps. 37:36

CHAPTER 27

Lament over Tyrus

THE word of the LORD came again unto me, saying,

2 Now, thou son of man, ^Rtake up a ^Rlamentation for Ty'-rus;   26:17 • Jer. 4:8

3 And say unto Ty'-rus, O thou that art ^Tsituate at the entry of the sea, *which art* a merchant of the people for many isles, Thus saith the Lord GOD; O Ty'-rus, thou hast said, I *am* of perfect beauty.   *placed*

4 Thy borders *are* in the midst of the seas, thy builders have perfected thy beauty.

5 They have made all thy *ship* boards of fir trees of Se'-nir: they have taken cedars from Leb'-a-non to make masts for thee.

6 *Of* the ^Roaks of Ba'-shan have they made thine oars; the company of the Ash'-ur-ites have made thy benches *of* ivory, *brought* out of ^Rthe isles of Chit'-tim.   Is. 2:13 • Jer. 2:10

7 Fine linen with broidered work from Egypt was that which thou spreadest forth to be thy sail; blue and purple from the isles of E-li'-shah was that which covered thee.

8 The inhabitants of Zi'-don and Ar'-vad were thy mariners: thy wise *men,* O Ty'-rus, *that* were in thee, were thy pilots.

9 The ancients of Ge'-bal and the wise *men* thereof were in thee thy calkers: all the ships of the sea with their mariners were in thee to occupy thy merchandise.

10 They of ^RPersia and of Lud and of Phut were in thine army, thy men of war: they hanged the shield and helmet in thee; they set forth thy comeliness.   38:5

11 The men of Ar'-vad with thine army *were* upon thy walls round about, and the Gam'-ma-dims were in thy towers: they hanged their shields upon thy walls round about; they have made thy beauty perfect.

12 ^RTar'-shish *was* thy merchant by reason of the multitude of all *kind of* riches; with silver, iron, tin, and lead, they traded in thy fairs.   38:13; Gen. 10:4; 2 Chr. 20:36

13 ^RJa'-van, Tu'-bal, and Me'-shech, they *were* thy merchants: they traded ^Rthe persons of men and vessels of brass in thy market.   *v.* 19; Gen. 10:2; Is. 66:19 • Joel 3:3; Rev. 18:13

14 They of the house of ^RTo-gar'-mah traded in thy fairs with horses and ^Thorsemen and mules.   38: 6; Gen. 10:3 • *war-horses*

15 The men of ^RDe'-dan *were* thy mer-

chants; many isles *were* the merchandise of thine hand: they brought thee *for* a present horns of ivory and ebony.   Gen. 10:7

16 Syria *was* thy merchant by reason of the multitude of ᵀthe wares of thy making: they occupied in thy fairs with emeralds, purple, and broidered work, and fine linen, and coral, and ᵀagate.   *thy works · rubies*

17 Judah, and the land of Israel, they *were* thy merchants: they traded in thy market wheat of Min′-nith, and Pan′-nag, and honey, and oil, and ᴿbalm.ᵀ   Jer. 8:22 · *rosin*

18 ᴿDamascus *was* thy merchant in the multitude of the wares of thy making, for the multitude of all riches; in the wine of Hel′-bon, and white wool.   47:16-18; Is. 7:8

19 Dan also and Ja′-van going to and fro occupied in thy fairs: bright iron, cassia, and calamus, were in thy market.

20 De′-dan *was* thy merchant in ᵀprecious clothes for chariots.   *cloths for riding*

21 Arabia, and all the princes of Ke′-dar, they occupied with thee in lambs, and rams, and goats: in these *were they* thy merchants.

22 The merchants of She′-ba and Ra′-a-mah, they *were* thy merchants: they occupied in thy fairs with chief of all spices, and with all precious stones, and gold.

23 ᴿHa′-ran, and Can′-neh, and Eden, the merchants of ᴿShe′-ba, Assh′-ur, *and* Chil′-mad, *were* thy merchants.   Gen. 11:31 · Gen. 25:3

24 These *were* thy merchants in ᵀall sorts *of things,* ᴿin blue clothes, and broidered work, and in chests of rich apparel, bound with cords, and made of cedar, among thy merchandise.   *excellent things · Esth. 6:8*

25 ᴿThe ships of ᴿTar′-shish did sing of thee in thy market: and thou wast replenished, and made very glorious ᴿin the midst of the seas.   Ps. 48:7; Is. 2:16 · 1 Kin. 10:22 · *v. 4*

26 Thy ᵀrowers have brought thee into great waters: ᴿthe east wind hath broken thee in the midst of the seas.   *sailors · Ps. 48:7*

27 Thy riches, and thy fairs, thy merchandise, thy mariners, and thy pilots, thy calkers, and the occupiers of thy merchandise, and all thy men of war, that *are* in thee, and in all thy company which *is* in the midst of thee, shall fall into the midst of the seas in the day of thy ruin.

28 The suburbs ᵀshall ᴿshake at the sound of the cry of thy pilots.   *waves · 26:15*

29 And ᴿall that handle the oar, the mariners, *and* all the pilots of the sea, shall come down from their ships, they shall stand upon the land;   Rev. 18:17-19

30 And shall cause their voice to be heard against thee, and shall cry bitterly, and shall cast up dust upon their heads, they shall wallow themselves in the ashes:

31 And they shall make themselves utterly bald for thee, and gird them with sackcloth, and they shall weep for thee with bitterness of heart *and* bitter wailing.

32 And in their wailing they shall take up a lamentation for thee, and lament over thee, *saying,* What *city is* like Ty′-rus, like the destroyed in the midst of the sea?

33 When thy wares went forth out of the seas, thou filledst many people; thou didst enrich the kings of the earth with the multitude of thy riches and of thy merchandise.

34 In the time *when* thou shalt be broken by the seas in the depths of the waters thy merchandise and all thy company in the midst of thee shall fall.

35 ᴿAll the inhabitants of the isles shall be astonished at thee, and their kings shall be sore afraid, they shall be troubled in *their* countenance.   26:15; Is. 23:6

36 The merchants among the ᵀpeople shall hiss at thee; ᴿthou shalt be a terror, and never *shalt be* any more.   *peoples · 26:21*

CHAPTER 28

Fall of the Prince of Tyrus

THE word of the Lᴏʀᴅ came again unto me, saying,

2 Son of man, say unto the prince of Ty′-rus, Thus saith the Lord Gᴏᴅ; Because thine heart *is* ᵀlifted up, and thou hast said, I *am* a ᴿGod, I sit *in* the seat of God, in the midst of the seas; yet thou *art* a man, and not God, though thou set thine heart as the heart of God: *proud · 28;9; Is. 14:14*

3 Behold, thou *art* ᴿwiser than Daniel; there is no secret that they can hide from thee: Dan. 1:20; [2:20-23, 28]; 5:11, 12

4 With thy wisdom and with thine understanding thou hast gotten thee ᴿriches, and hast gotten gold and silver into thy treasures: 27:33; Zech. 9:2, 3

5 By thy great wisdom *and* by thy ᵀtraffick hast thou increased thy riches, and thine heart is lifted up because of thy riches: *trade*

6 Therefore thus saith the Lord Gᴏᴅ; Because thou hast ᴿset thine heart as the heart of God;   *v. 2;* Ex. 9:17

7 Behold, therefore I will bring strangers upon thee, ᴿthe terrible of the nations: and they shall draw their swords against the beauty of thy wisdom, and they shall defile thy brightness.   30:11; 31:12; 32:12

8 They shall ᴿbring thee down to the pit, and thou shalt die the deaths of *them that are* slain in the midst of the seas.   Job 33:18

9 Wilt thou yet ᴿsay before him that slayeth thee, I *am* God? but thou *shalt be* a man, and ᵀno God, in the hand of him that ᵀslayeth thee.   *v. 2;* Dan. 4:31 · *not · woundeth*

10 Thou shalt die the deaths of the ᵀuncircumcised by the hand of strangers: for I have spoken *it,* saith the Lord Gᴏᴅ.   *ungodly*

11 Moreover the word of the LORD came unto me, saying,

12 Son of man, ᴿtake up a lamentation upon the king of Ty'-rus, and say unto him, Thus saith the Lord GOD; ᴿThou sealest up the sum, full of wisdom, and ᴿperfect in beauty.   19:1; 26:17; 27:2 • v. 3 • 27:3

13 Thou hast been in ᴿEden the garden of God; every precious stone was thy covering, the ᵀsardius, topaz, and the diamond, the beryl, the onyx, and the jasper, the sapphire, the emerald, and the carbuncle, and gold: the workmanship of thy tabrets and of thy pipes was prepared in thee in the day that thou wast created.   31:8, 9 • ruby

14 Thou art the anointed ᴿcherub that covereth; and I have set thee so: thou wast upon ᴿthe holy mountain of God; thou hast walked up and down in the midst of the ᵀstones of fire.   Ex. 25:20 • 20:40 • brilliant stones

15 Thou wast ᴿperfect in thy ways from the day that thou wast created, till iniquity was found in thee.   vv. 3–6

16 By the multitude of thy ᵀmerchandiseᴿ they have filled the midst of thee with violence, and thou hast sinned: therefore I will cast thee as profane out of the mountain of God: and I will destroy thee, ᴿO covering cherub, from the midst of the stones of fire.   possessions • 26:17 • v. 14

17 Thine heart was lifted up because of thy beauty, thou hast corrupted thy wisdom by reason of thy brightness: I will cast thee to the ground, I will lay thee before kings, that they may behold thee.

18 Thou hast defiled thy sanctuaries by the multitude of thine iniquities, by the iniquity of thy ᵀtraffick; therefore will I bring forth a ᴿfire from the midst of thee, it shall devour thee, and I will bring thee to ashes upon the earth in the sight of all them that behold thee.   trade • Amos 1:9, 10

19 All they that know thee among the people shall be astonished at thee: ᴿthou shalt be a terror, and never shalt thou be ᴿany more.   26:21; 27:36 • Jer. 51:64

Judgment on Zidon

20 Again the word of the LORD came unto me, saying,

21 Son of man, set thy face against ᴿZi'-don, and prophesy against it,   Is. 23:4

22 And say, Thus saith the Lord GOD; ᴿBehold, I am against thee, O Zi'-don; and I will be glorified in the midst of thee: and they shall know that I am the LORD, when I shall have executed judgments in her, and shall be sanctified in her.   Ex. 14:4, 17

23 For I will send into her ᵀpestilence, and blood into her street; and the wounded shall be judged in the midst of her by ᵀthe sword upon her on every side; and they shall know that I am the LORD.   epidemics • war

24 And there shall be no more aᵀ pricking brier unto the house of Israel, nor any grieving thorn of all that are round about them, that despised them; and they shall know that I am the Lord GOD.   an irritation

25 Thus saith the Lord GOD; When I shall have gathered the house of Israel from the people among whom they are scattered, and shall be sanctified in them in the sight of the heathen, then shall they dwell in their land that I have given to my servant Jacob.

26 And they shall dwell safely therein, and shall build houses, and plant vineyards; yea, they shall dwell with confidence, when I have executed judgments upon all those that despise them round about them; and they shall know that I am the LORD their God.

CHAPTER 29

Egypt to Be Desolate

IN the ᴿtenth year, in the tenth month, in the twelfth day of the month, the word of the LORD came unto me, saying,   v. 17

2 Son of man, set thy face against Pharaoh king of Egypt, and ᵀprophesy against him, and against all Egypt: preach

3 Speak, and say, Thus saith the Lord GOD; ᴿBehold, I am against thee, Pharaoh king of Egypt, the great ᴿdragon that lieth in the midst of his rivers, ᴿwhich hath said, My river is mine own, and I have made it for myself.   v. 10 • 32:2; Ps. 74:13, 14 • 28:2

4 But I will put hooks in thy jaws, and I will cause the fish of thy rivers to stick unto thy scales, and I will bring thee up out of the midst of thy rivers, and all the fish of thy rivers shall stick unto thy scales.

5 And I will leave thee thrown into the wilderness, thee and all the fish of thy rivers: thou shalt fall upon the open fields; thou shalt not be brought together, nor gathered: I have given thee for ᵀmeat to the beasts of the field and to the fowls of the heaven.   food

6 And all the inhabitants of Egypt shall know that I am the LORD, because they have been a staff of reed to the house of Israel.

7 ᴿWhen they took hold of thee by thy hand, thou didst break, and ᵀrend all their shoulder: and when they leaned upon thee, thou brakest, and madest all their loins to be at a stand.   17:17; Jer. 37:5, 7, 11 • tear

8 Therefore thus saith the Lord GOD; Behold, I will bring a sword upon thee, and cut off man and beast out of thee.

9 And the land of Egypt shall be desolate and waste; and they shall know that I am the LORD: because he hath ᴿsaid, The river is mine, and I have made it.   v. 3

10 Behold, therefore I am against thee, and against thy rivers, ᴿand I will make the land of Egypt utterly waste and desolate, from the

tower of ᵀSy-e′-ne even unto the border of E-thi-o′-pi-a.   30:12 · *seventh*

11 No foot of man shall pass through it, nor foot of beast shall pass through it, neither shall it be inhabited forty years.

12 ᴿAnd I will make the land of Egypt ᵀdesolate in the midst of the countries *that are* desolate, and her cities among the cities *that are* laid waste shall be desolate forty years: and I will scatter the Egyptians among the nations, and will disperse them through the countries.   30:7, 26 · *empty*

13 Yet thus saith the Lord GOD; At the ᴿend of forty years will I gather the Egyptians from the people whither they were scattered: Jer. 46:26

14 And I will ᵀbring again the captivity of Egypt, and will cause them to return *into* the land of Path′-ros, into the land of their ᵀhabitation; and they shall be there a ᴿbaseᵀ kingdom.   *release · birth · 17:6, 14 · low*

15 It shall be the basest of the kingdoms; neither shall it exalt itself any more above the nations: for I will diminish them, that they shall no more rule over the nations.

16 And it shall be no more ᴿthe confidence of the house of Israel, which bringeth *their* iniquity to remembrance, when they shall look after them: but they shall know that I *am* the Lord GOD.   Is. 30:2, 3

Egypt to Be Taken by Babylon

17 And it came to pass in the ᴿseven and twentieth year, in the first *month*, in the first *day* of the month, the word of the LORD came unto me, saying,   *v.* 1; 24:1

18 Son of man, Neb-u-chad-rez′-zar king of Babylon caused his army to serve a great service against Ty′-rus: every head *was* made bald, and every shoulder *was* peeled: yet had he no wages, nor his army, for Ty′-rus, for the service that he had served against it:

19 Therefore thus saith the Lord GOD; Behold,ᴿ I will give the land of Egypt unto Neb-u-chad-rez′-zar king of Babylon; and he shall take her multitude, and take her spoil, and take her prey; and it shall be the wages for his army.   30:10, 24, 25; 32:11

20 ᴿI have given him the land of Egypt ᵀ*for* his labour wherewith he served against it, because they wrought for me, saith the Lord GOD.   Is. 10:6, 7; Jer. 25:9 · *for his hire*

21 In that day ᴿwill I cause the ᵀhorn of the house of Israel to bud forth, and I will give thee ᴿthe opening of the mouth in the midst of them; and they shall know that I *am* the LORD.   Ps. 132:17 · *strength* · 24:27

CHAPTER 30

Egypt to Be Destroyed

THE word of the LORD came again unto me, saying,

2 Son of man, prophesy and say, Thus saith the Lord GOD; ᴿHowlᵀ ye, ᵀWoe worth the day!   21:12; Is. 13:6 · *wail · alas for*

3 For ᴿthe day *is* near, even the day of the LORD *is* near, a cloudy day; it shall be the time of the heathen.   Joel 2:1; Zeph. 1:7

4 And the sword shall come upon Egypt, and great ᵀpain shall be in E-thi-o′-pi-a, when the slain shall fall in Egypt, and they shall take away her multitude, and her foundations shall be broken down.   *anguish*

5 E-thi-o′-pi-a, and ᵀLib′-y-a, and Lyd′-i-a, and all the mingled people, and Chub, and the men of the land that is in league, shall fall with them by the sword.   *Put*

6 Thus saith the LORD; They also that uphold Egypt shall fall; and the pride of her power shall come down: ᵀfrom the tower of Sy-e′-ne shall they fall in it by the sword, saith the Lord GOD.   *from Migdol to Syene*

7 ᴿAnd they shall be ᵀdesolate in the midst of the countries *that are* desolate, and her cities shall be in the midst of the cities *that are* wasted.   29:12 · *empty*

8 And they shall know that I *am* the LORD, when I have set a fire in Egypt, and *when* all her helpers shall be destroyed.

9 In that day ᴿshall messengers go forth from me in ships to make the ᵀcareless E-thi-o′-pi-ans afraid, and great pain shall come upon them, as in the day of Egypt: for, ᵀlo, it cometh.   Is. 18:1, 2 · *carefree · look*

10 Thus saith the Lord GOD; I will also make the multitude of Egypt to cease by the hand of Neb-u-chad-rez′-zar king of Babylon.

11 He and his people with him, the terrible of the nations, shall be brought to destroy the land: and they shall draw their swords against Egypt, and fill the land with the slain.

12 And ᴿI will make the rivers dry, and ᴿsell the land into the hand of the wicked: and I will make the land waste, and all that is therein, by the hand of strangers: I the LORD have spoken *it*.   Is. 19:5, 6 · Is. 19:4

13 Thus saith the Lord GOD; I will also destroy the idols, and I will cause *their* images to cease out of Noph; and there shall be no more a prince of the land of Egypt: and I will put a fear in the land of Egypt.

14 And I will make Path′-ros ᵀdesolate, and will set fire in ᵀZo′-an, and will execute judgments in No.   *a ruin · Tanis*

15 And I will pour my fury upon ᵀSin, the strength of Egypt; and ᴿI will ᵀcut off the multitude of No.   *pelusium* · Jer. 46:25 · *destroy*

16 And I will set fire in Egypt: Sin shall have great pain, and No shall be rent asunder, and Noph *shall have* distresses daily.

17 The young men of A′-ven and of ᵀPi-be′-seth shall fall by the sword: and these *cities* shall go into captivity.   *Bubastum*

18 ᴿAt Te-haph′-ne-hes also the day shall be darkened, ᴿwhen I shall break there the

yokes of Egypt: and the pomp of her strength shall cease in her: as for her, a cloud shall cover her, and her daughters shall go into captivity.   Jer. 2:16 • Jer. 43:8–13

19 Thus will I ^Rexecute judgments in Egypt: and they shall know that I *am* the LORD.   *v.* 14; 5:8, 15; 25:11; [Ps. 9:16]

20 And it came to pass in the ^Releventh year, in the first *month,* in the seventh *day* of the month, *that* the word of the LORD came unto me, saying,   26:1; 29:1; 31:1

21 Son of man, I have broken the arm of Pharaoh king of Egypt; and, lo, it shall not be bound up to be healed, to put a roller to bind it, to make it strong to hold the sword.

22 Therefore thus saith the Lord GOD; Behold, I *am* against Pharaoh king of Egypt, and will break his arms, the strong, and that which was broken; and I will cause the sword to fall out of his hand.

23 ^RAnd I will scatter the Egyptians among the nations, and will disperse them through the countries.   *vv.* 17, 18, 26; 29:12

24 And I will ^Rstrengthen the arms of the king of Babylon, and put my sword in his hand: but I will break Pharaoh's arms, and he shall groan before him with the groanings of a deadly wounded *man.*   *vv.* 10, 25

25 But I will strengthen the arms of the king of Babylon, and the arms of Pharaoh shall fall down; and they shall know that I *am* the LORD, when I shall put my sword into the hand of the king of Babylon, and he shall stretch it out upon the land of Egypt.

26 ^RAnd I will scatter the Egyptians among the nations, and ^Rdisperse them among the countries; and they shall know that I *am* the LORD.   *v.* 23; 29:12 • Gen. 11:8

CHAPTER 31

Egypt Is Cut Down Like Assyria

AND it came to pass in the ^Releventh year, in the third *month,* in the first *day* of the month, *that* the word of the LORD came unto me, saying,   30:20

2 Son of man, speak unto Pharaoh king of Egypt, and to his multitude; ^RWhom art thou like in thy greatness?   *v.* 18

3 Behold, the Assyrian *was* a cedar in Leb'-a-non with fair branches, and with a shadowing shroud, and of an high stature; and his top was among the thick boughs.

4 The waters made him great, the deep set him up on high with her rivers running round about his plants, and sent out her little rivers unto all the trees of the field.

5 Therefore ^Rhis height was exalted above all the trees of the field, and his boughs were multiplied, and his branches became long because of the ^Rmultitude of waters, when he ^Tshot forth.   Dan. 4:11 • 17:5 • *grew up*

6 All the fowls of heaven made their nests in his boughs, and under his branches did all the beasts of the field bring forth their young, and under his shadow dwelt all great nations.

7 Thus was he fair in his greatness, in the length of his branches: for his ^Rroot was by great waters.   Ps. 1:3

8 The cedars in the garden of God could not hide him: the fir trees were not like his boughs, and the chesnut trees were not like his branches; nor any tree in the garden of God was like unto him in his beauty.

9 I have made him fair by the multitude of his branches: so that all the trees of Eden, that *were* in the garden of God, envied him.

10 Therefore thus saith the Lord GOD; Because thou hast ^Tlifted up thyself in height, and he hath shot up his top among the thick boughs, and ^Rhis heart is ^Tlifted up in his height;   *prided* • Dan. 5:20 • *proud*

11 I have therefore delivered him into the hand of the ^Rmighty one of the heathen; he shall surely deal with him: I have driven him out for his wickedness.   30:10, 11

12 And strangers, ^Rthe terrible of the nations, have cut him off, and have left him: upon the mountains and in all the valleys his branches are fallen, and his boughs are broken by all the rivers of the land; and all the people of the earth are gone down from his shadow, and have left him.   28:7

13 ^RUpon his ruin shall all the fowls of heaven remain, and all the beasts of the field shall be upon his branches: Is. 18:6

14 To the end that none of all the trees by the waters exalt themselves for their height, neither shoot up their top among the thick boughs, neither their trees stand up in their height, all that drink water: for they are all delivered unto death, to the ^Tnether parts of the earth, in the midst of the children of men, with them that go down to the pit.   *lower*

15 Thus saith the Lord GOD; In the day when he went down to the grave I caused a mourning: I covered the ^Tdeep for him, and I restrained the floods thereof, and the great waters were stayed: and I caused Leb'-a-non to mourn for him, and all the trees of the field fainted for him.   *sea*

16 I made the nations to shake at the sound of his fall, when I cast him down to hell with them that descend into the pit: and all the trees of Eden, the choice and best of Leb'-a-non, all that drink water, shall be comforted in the nether parts of the earth.

17 They also went down into hell with him unto *them that be* slain with the sword; and *they that were* his arm, *that* dwelt under his shadow in the midst of the heathen.

18 ^RTo whom art thou thus like in glory and in greatness among the trees of Eden? yet shalt thou be brought down with the trees of Eden unto the nether parts of the earth: ^Rthou shalt lie in the midst of

the uncircumcised with *them that be* slain by the sword. This *is* Pharaoh and all his multitude, saith the Lord GOD.   32:18, 19 • 28:10

CHAPTER 32

Egypt Is Lamented

AND it came to pass in the ᴿtwelfth year, in the twelfth month, in the first *day* of the month, *that* the word of the LORD came unto me, saying,   *v. 17*

2 Son of man, ᴿtake up a lamentation for Pharaoh king of Egypt, and say unto him, Thou art like a young lion of the nations, and thou *art* as a ᵀwhale in the seas: and thou camest forth with thy rivers, and troubledst the waters with thy feet, and ᴿfouledst their rivers.   *v. 16 • monster • 34:18*

3 Thus saith the Lord GOD; I will therefore ᴿspread out my net over thee with a company of many people; and they shall bring thee up in my net.   12:13; Hos. 7:12

4 Then ᴿwill I leave thee upon the land, I will cast thee forth upon the open field, and will cause all the fowls of the heaven to remain upon thee, and I will fill the beasts of the whole earth with thee.   29:5

5 And I will lay thy flesh upon the mountains, and fill the valleys with thy height.

6 I will also water with thy blood the land wherein thou swimmest, *even* to the mountains; and the rivers shall be full of thee.

7 And when I shall ᵀput thee out, I will cover the heaven, and make the stars thereof dark; I will cover the sun with a cloud, and the moon shall not give her light.   *destroy you*

8 All the bright ᴿlights of heaven will I make dark over thee, and set darkness upon thy land, saith the Lord GOD.   Gen. 1:14

9 I will also ᵀvex ᴿthe hearts of many people, when I shall bring thy destruction among the nations, into the countries which thou hast not known.   *trouble • 27:29-31*

10 Yea, I will make many people ᴿamazed at thee, and their kings shall be horribly afraid for thee, when I shall brandish my sword before them; and ᴿthey shall tremble at *every* moment, every man for his own life, in the day of thy fall.   27:35 • 26:16

11 For thus saith the Lord GOD; The ᴿsword of the king of Babylon shall come upon thee.   30:4; Lev. 26:25

12 By the swords of the mighty will I cause thy multitude to fall, the terrible of the nations, all of them: and they shall ᵀspoil the pomp of Egypt, and all the multitude thereof shall be destroyed.   *ravage*

13 I will destroy also all the beasts thereof from beside the great waters; neither shall the foot of man trouble them any more, nor the hoofs of beasts trouble them.

14 Then will I make their waters ᵀdeep, and cause their rivers to run like oil, saith the Lord GOD.   *clear*

15 When I shall make the land of Egypt desolate, and the country shall be destitute of that whereof it was full, when I shall smite all them that dwell therein, then shall they know that I *am* the LORD.

16 This *is* the ᴿlamentation wherewith they shall lament her: the daughters of the nations shall lament her: they shall lament for her, *even* for Egypt, and for all her multitude, saith the Lord GOD.   26:17

Egypt in Sheol

17 It came to pass also in the twelfth year, in the fifteenth *day* of the month, *that* the word of the LORD came unto me, saying,

18 Son of man, wail for the multitude of Egypt, and ᴿcast them down, *even* her, and the daughters of the famous nations, unto the ᵀnether parts of the earth, with them that go down into the pit.   Jer. 1:10 • *lower*

19 ᴿWhom dost thou pass in beauty? ᴿgo down, and be thou laid with the ᵀuncircumcised.   31:2, 18 • vv. 21, 24; 28:10 • *ungodly*

20 They shall fall in the midst of *them that are* slain by the sword: she is delivered to the sword: draw her and all her multitudes.

21 The strong among the mighty shall speak to him out of the midst of hell with them that help him: they are gone down, they lie uncircumcised, slain by the sword.

22 ᴿAssh'-ur *is* there and all her company: his graves *are* about him: all of them slain, fallen by the sword: 27:23; 31:3, 16

23 Whose graves are set in the sides of the pit, and her company is round about her grave: all of them slain, fallen by the sword, which caused terror in the land of the living.

24 There *is* E'-lam and all her multitude round about her grave, all of them slain, fallen by the sword, which are gone down uncircumcised into the ᵀnether parts of the earth, which caused their terror in the land of the living; yet have they borne their shame with them that go down to the pit.   *lower*

25 They have set her a bed in the midst of the slain with all her multitude: her graves *are* round about ᵀhim: all of them uncircumcised, slain by the sword: though their terror was caused in the land of the living, yet have they borne their shame with them that go down to the pit: he is put in the midst of *them that be* slain.   *her*

26 There *is* ᴿMe'-shech, Tu'-bal, and all her multitude: her graves *are* round about him: all of them ᴿuncircumcised, slain by the sword, though they caused their terror in the land of the living.   27:13 • vv. 19, 20

27 And they shall not lie with the mighty *that are* fallen of the ᵀuncircumcised, which are gone down to hell with their weapons of

war: and they have laid their swords under their heads, but their iniquities shall be upon their bones, though *they were* the terror of the mighty in the land of the living.   *ungodly*

28 Yea, thou shalt be broken in the midst of the uncircumcised, and shalt lie with *them that are* slain with the sword.

29 There *is* E'-dom, her kings, and all her princes, which with their might ᴿare laid by *them that were* slain by the sword: they shall lie with the uncircumcised, and with them that go down to the pit.   Is. 34:5-15

30 There *be* the princes of the north, all of them, and all the Zi-do'-ni-ans, which are gone down with the slain; with their terror they are ashamed of their might; and they lie ᵀuncircumcised with *them that be* slain by the sword, and bear their shame with them that go down to the pit.   *ungodly*

31 Pharaoh shall see them, and shall be ᴿcomforted over all his multitude, *even* Pharaoh and all his army slain by the sword, saith the Lord Gᴏᴅ.   14:22; 31:16

32 For I have caused my terror in the land of the living: and he shall be laid in the midst of the ᵀuncircumcised with *them that are* slain with the sword, *even* Pharaoh and all his multitude, saith the Lord Gᴏᴅ.   *ungodly*

CHAPTER 33

The Appointment of Ezekiel as Watchman

AGAIN the word of the Lᴏʀᴅ came unto me, saying,

2 Son of man, speak to ᴿthe children of thy people, and say unto them, ᴿWhen I bring the sword upon a land, if the people of the land take a man of their coasts, and set him for their watchman: 3:11 • 14:17

3 If when he seeth the sword come upon the land, he ᴿblow the trumpet, ᴿand warn the people;   Hos. 8:1; Neh. 4:18–20 • Is. 58:1

4 Then whosoever heareth the sound of the trumpet, and taketh not warning; if the sword come, and take him away, ᴿhis blood shall be upon his own head.   18:13

5 He heard the sound of the trumpet, and took not warning; his blood shall be upon him. ᴿBut he that taketh warning shall ᵀdeliver his soul.   Ex. 9:19–21; Heb. 11:7 • *save*

6 But if the watchman see the sword come, and blow not the trumpet, and the people be not warned; if the sword come, and take *any* person from among them, ᴿhe is taken away in his iniquity; but his blood will I require at the watchman's hand.   *v.* 8

7 ᴿSo thou, O son of man, I have set thee a watchman unto the house of Israel; therefore thou shalt hear the word at my mouth, and warn them from me.   3:17

8 When I say unto the wicked, O wicked *man,* thou shalt surely die; if thou dost not speak to warn the wicked from his way, that wicked *man* shall die in his iniquity; but his blood will I require at thine hand.

9 Nevertheless, if thou warn the wicked of his way to turn from it; if he do not turn from his way, he shall die in his iniquity; but thou hast ᴿdelivered thy soul.   Acts 20:26

10 Therefore, O thou son of man, speak unto the house of Israel; Thus ye speak, saying, If our transgressions and our sins *be* upon us, and we ᴿpineᵀ away in them, how should we then live?   24:23 • *waste*

11 Say unto them, *As* I live, saith the Lord Gᴏᴅ, ᴿI have no pleasure in the death of the wicked; but that the wicked turn from his way and live: turn ye, turn ye from your evil ways; for ᴿwhy will ye die, O house of Israel?   [2 Sam. 14:14; 2 Pet. 3:9] • 18:31

12 Therefore, thou son of man, say unto the children of thy people, The ᴿrighteousness of the righteous shall not deliver him in the day of his transgression: as for the wickedness of the wicked, ᴿhe shall not fall thereby in the day that he turneth from his wickedness; neither shall the righteous be able to live for his *righteousness* in the day that he sinneth.   3:20 • 18:21; [2 Chr. 7:14]

13 When I shall say to the righteous, *that* he shall surely live; ᴿif he trust to his own righteousness, and ᴿcommit iniquity, all his righteousnesses shall not be remembered; but for his iniquity that he hath committed, he shall die for it.   3:20; 18:24 • [Heb. 10:38]

14 Again, when I say unto the wicked, Thou shalt surely die; if he turn from his sin, and do that which is lawful and right;

15 *If* the wicked restore the pledge, give again that he had robbed, walk in the statutes of life, without committing iniquity; he shall surely live, he shall not die.

16 ᴿNone of his sins that he hath committed shall be mentioned unto him: he hath done that which is lawful and right; he shall surely live.   18:22; [Is. 1:18; 43:25]

17 ᴿYet the children of thy people say, The way of the Lord is not ᵀequal: but as for them, their way is not equal.   *v.* 20 • *just*

18 ᴿWhen the righteous turneth from his righteousness, and committeth iniquity, he shall even die thereby.   *vv.* 12, 13; 3: 20; 18:24, 26

19 ᴿBut if the wicked turn from his wickedness, and do that which is lawful and right, he shall live thereby.   Jer. 18:1–10

20 Yet ye say, The way of the Lord is not ᵀequal. O ye house of Israel, I will judge you every one after his ways.   *just*

21 And it came to pass in the twelfth year ᴿof our captivity, in the tenth *month,* in the fifth *day* of the month, *that* one that had escaped out of Jerusalem came unto me, saying, The city is smitten.   1:2

22 Now the hand of the Lᴏʀᴅ was upon me in the evening, afore he that was escaped

came; and had opened my mouth, until he came to me in the morning; and my mouth was opened, and I was no more dumb.

23 Then the word of the LORD came unto me, saying,

24 Son of man, they that inhabit those wastes of the land of Israel speak, saying, RAbraham was one, and he inherited the land: Rbut we *are* many; the land is given us for inheritance.   Is. 51:2; [Rom. 4:12, 13] • Mic. 3:11

25 Wherefore say unto them, Thus saith the Lord GOD; Ye eat with the blood, and lift up your eyes toward your idols, and shed blood: and shall ye possess the land?

26 Ye Rstand upon your sword, ye work abomination, and ye Rdefile every one his neighbour's wife: and shall ye possess the land?   Mic. 2:1, 2; Zeph. 3:3 • 18:6; 22:11

27 Say thou thus unto them, Thus saith the Lord GOD; *As* I live, surely Rthey that *are* in the Rwastes shall fall by the sword, and him that *is* in the open field will I give to the beasts to be devoured, and they that *be* in the forts and Rin the caves shall die of the pestilence.   v. 24 • 2 Kin. 25; 2 Chr. 36 • 1 Sam. 13:6

28 For I will lay the land most desolate, and the Rpomp of her strength shall cease; and the mountains of Israel shall be desolate, that none shall pass through.   7:24

29 Then shall they know that I *am* the LORD, when I have laid the land most desolate because of all their Tabominations which they have committed.   evil deeds

30 RAlso, thou son of man, the children of thy people Tstill are talking against thee by the walls and in the doors of the houses, and speak one to another, every one to his brother, saying, Come, I pray you, and hear what is the word that cometh forth from the LORD.   14:3; 20:3; Is. 29:13; 58:2 • talk of

31 And they come unto thee as the people cometh, and they Rsit before thee *as* my people, and they hear thy words, but they will not do them: for with their mouth they shew much love, *but* their heart goeth after their covetousness.   8:1

32 And, Tlo, thou *art* unto them as Ta very lovely song of one that hath a Rpleasant voice, and can play well on an instrument: for they hear thy words, but they do them not.   look • a popular singer • Mark 6:20; John 5:35

33 And when this cometh to pass, (lo, it will come,) then Rshall they know that a prophet hath been among them.   1 Sam. 3:20

CHAPTER 34

The False Shepherds

AND the word of the LORD came unto me, saying,

2 Son of man, Tprophesy against the shepherds of Israel, prophesy, and say unto them, Thus saith the Lord GOD unto the shepherds; Woe *be* to the shepherds of Israel that do feed themselves! should not the shepherds feed the flocks?   preach

3 RYe eat the fat, and ye clothe you with the wool, Rye kill them that are fed: *but* ye feed not the flock.   Is. 56:11; Zech. 11:5, 16 • 22:25

4 RThe diseased have ye not strengthened, neither have ye healed that which was sick, neither have ye bound up *that which was* broken, neither have ye brought again that which was driven away, neither have ye sought that which was lost; but with force and with cruelty have ye ruled them. Zech. 11:16

5 And they were scattered, because Tthere is no shepherd: and they became Tmeat to all the beasts of the field, when they were scattered.   they were without • the prey of

6 My sheep Rwandered through all the mountains, and upon every high hill: yea, my Rflock was scattered upon all the face of the earth, and Rnone did search or seek *after* them.   Jer. 40:11, 12 • [John 10:16] • Ps. 142:4

7 Therefore, ye shepherds, hear the word of the LORD;

8 *As* I live saith the Lord GOD, surely because my flock became a prey, and my flock Rbecame Tmeat to every beast of the field, because *there was* no shepherd, neither did my shepherds search for my flock, Rbut the shepherds fed themselves, and fed not my flock;   vv. 5, 6 • food • vv. 2, 10

9 Therefore, O ye shepherds, hear the word of the LORD;

10 Thus saith the Lord GOD; Behold, I Ram against the shepherds; and I will require my flock at their hand, and cause them to cease from feeding the flock; neither shall the shepherds feed themselves any more; for I will deliver my flock from their mouth, that they may not be meat for them.   Jer. 52:24-27

The True Shepherd

11 For thus saith the Lord GOD; Behold, RI, *even* I, will both search my sheep, and seek them out.   11:17; 20:41; Is. 51:12

12 RAs a shepherd seeketh out his flock in the day that he is among his sheep *that are* scattered; so will I Rseek out my sheep, and will deliver them out of all places where they have been scattered in Rthe cloudy and dark day.   Jer. 31:10 • Is. 40:10, 11; 56:8 • 30:3

13 And I will bring them out from the people, and gather them from the countries, and will bring them to their own land, and feed them upon the mountains of Israel by the rivers, and in all the inhabited places of the country.

14 I will feed them in a good pasture, and upon the high mountains of Israel shall their fold be: there shall they lie in a good fold, and in a Tfat pasture shall they feed upon the mountains of Israel.   rich

15 ᴿI will feed my flock, and I will cause them to lie down, saith the Lord GOD.   Ps. 23:1

16 I will seek that which was lost, and bring again that which was driven away, and will bind up *that which was* broken, and will strengthen that which was sick: but I will destroy the ᵀfat and the strong; I will feed them with judgment.   *prosperous*

17 And *as for* you, O my flock, thus saith the Lord GOD; ᴿBehold, I judge between ᵀcattle and cattle, between the rams and the he goats.   Mal. 4:1; [Matt. 25:31, 32] · *sheep and sheep*

18 *Seemeth* it a ᴿsmall thing unto you to have eaten up the good pasture, but ye must tread down with your feet the ᵀresidue of your pastures? and to have drunk of the deep waters, but ye must foul the residue with your feet?   Num. 16:9 · *remainder*

19 And *as for* my flock, they eat that which ye have trodden with your feet; and they drink that which ye have fouled with your feet.

20 Therefore thus saith the Lord GOD unto them; Behold, I, *even* I, will judge between the fat cattle and between the lean cattle.

21 Because ye have ᴿthrust with side and with shoulder, and pushed all the diseased with your horns, till ye have scattered them ᵀabroad;   Deut. 33:17; Luke 13:14 · *to the outside*

22 Therefore will I ᴿsave my flock, and they shall no more be a prey; and I will judge between cattle and cattle.   Ps. 72:12

23 And I will set up one ᴿshepherd over them, and he shall feed them, ᴿ*even* my servant David; he shall feed them, and he shall be their shepherd.   Is. 40:10, 11 · Jer. 30:9

24 And I the LORD will be their God, and my servant ᴿDavid a prince among them; I the LORD have spoken *it.*   37:22, 24; Is. 55:3

25 And I will make with them ᵀa covenant of peace, and ᴿwill cause the evil beasts to cease out of the land: and they shall dwell safely in the wilderness, and sleep in the woods.   *an agreement* · Lev. 26:6

26 And I will make them and the places round about my hill a blessing; and I will cause the shower to come down in his season; there shall be showers of blessing.

27 And ᴿthe tree of the field shall yield her fruit, and the earth shall yield her increase, and they shall be safe in their land, and shall know that I *am* the LORD, when I have broken the bands of their yoke, and delivered them out of the hand of those that served themselves of them.   Lev. 26:4

28 And they shall no more be a prey to the heathen, neither shall the beast of the land devour them; but they shall dwell safely, and none shall make *them* afraid.

29 And I will raise up for them a plant of renown, and they shall be no more consumed with hunger in the land, neither bear the shame of the heathen any more.

30 Thus shall they know that ᴿI the LORD their God *am* with them, and *that* they, *even* the house of Israel, *are* my people, saith the Lord GOD.   14:11; 36:28; Ps. 46:7, 11

31 And ye my ᴿflock, the flock of my pasture, *are* men, *and* I *am* your God, saith the Lord GOD.   Ps. 78:52; 80:1; 100:3; [John 10:7, 11]

CHAPTER 35

The Judgment of Edom

MOREOVER the word of the LORD came unto me, saying,

2 Son of man, ᴿset thy face against mount Se'-ir, and prophesy against it,   Obad. 1, 10

3 And say unto it, Thus saith the Lord GOD; Behold, O mount Se'-ir, I *am* against thee, and ᴿI will stretch out mine hand against thee, and I will ᵀmake thee most desolate.   6:14; Jer. 6:12; 15:6 · *strip you bare*

4 I will ᴿlay thy cities waste, and thou shalt be ᵀdesolate, and thou shalt know that I *am* the LORD.   v. 9; 6:6; Mal. 1: 3, 4 · *empty*

5 Because thou hast had ᵀa perpetual hatred, and hast shed *the blood of* the children of Israel by the force of the sword in the time of their calamity, in the time *that* their iniquity *had* an end: *an old feud*

6 Therefore, *as* I live, saith the Lord GOD, I will prepare thee unto blood, and blood shall pursue thee: sith thou hast not hated blood, even blood shall pursue thee.

7 Thus will I make mount Se'-ir most desolate, and cut off from it ᴿhim that passeth out and him that returneth.   Judg. 5:6

8 And I will fill his mountains with his ᴿslain *men:* in the hills, and in thy valleys, and in all thy rivers, shall they ᵀfall that are slain with the sword.   Is. 34:5, 6 · *fall in them*

9 ᴿI will make thee perpetual desolations, and thy cities shall not return: and ye shall know that I *am* the LORD.   Jer. 49:17

10 Because thou hast said, ᴿThese two nations and these two countries shall be mine, and we will possess it; ᵀwhereas ᴿthe LORD was there: Ps. 83:4–12 · *though* · [Ps. 48:1–3]

11 Therefore, *as* I live, saith the Lord GOD, I will even do according to thine anger, and according to thine envy which thou hast used out of thy hatred against them; and I will make myself known among them, when I have judged thee.

12 And thou shalt know that I *am* the LORD, *and that* I have heard all thy blasphemies which thou hast spoken against the mountains of Israel, saying, They are laid desolate, they are given us to consume.

13 Thus with your mouth ye have boasted against me, and have multiplied your words against me: I have heard *them.*

14 Thus saith the Lord GOD; ᴿWhen the whole earth rejoiceth, I will make thee ᵀdesolate.   Is. 44:23; 49:13; 65:13, 14; Jer. 51:48 · *a ruin*

15 ᴿAs thou didst rejoice at the inheritance of the house of Israel, because it was desolate, so will I do unto thee: thou shalt be desolate, O mount Se'-ir, and all ᵀId-u-me'-a, *even* all of it: and they shall know that I *am* the LORD.   Obad. 12, 15 · *Edom*

CHAPTER 36

Judgment on the Nations

ALSO, thou son of man, prophesy unto the mountains of Israel, and say, Ye mountains of Israel, hear the word of the LORD:
2 Thus saith the Lord GOD; Because the enemy hath said against you, Aha, ᴿeven the ᵀancient high places ᴿare our's in possession: Deut. 32:13 · *old shrines* · 35:10
3 Therefore prophesy and say, Thus saith the Lord GOD; Because they have made *you* desolate, and swallowed you up on every side, that ye might be a possession unto the residue of the heathen, and ye are ᵀtaken up in the lips of talkers, and *are* an infamy of the people: *made a subject of gossip*
4 Therefore, ye mountains of Israel, hear the word of the Lord GOD; Thus saith the Lord GOD to the mountains, and to the ᴿhills, to the rivers, and to the valleys, to the desolate wastes, and to the cities that are forsaken, which became a prey and ᴿderision to the residue of the heathen that *are* round about;   Deut. 11:11 · Ps. 79:4
5 Therefore thus saith the Lord GOD; Surely in the fire of my jealousy have I spoken against the residue of the heathen, and against all Id-u-me'-a, which have appointed my land into their possession with the joy of all *their* heart, with despiteful minds, to cast it out for a prey.
6 ᵀProphesy therefore concerning the land of Israel, and say unto the mountains, and to the hills, to the rivers, and to the valleys, Thus saith the Lord GOD; Behold, I have spoken in my jealousy and in my fury, because ye have ᴿborne the shame of the heathen: *preach* · *v.* 15; 34:29; Ps. 123:3, 4
7 Therefore thus saith the Lord GOD; I have lifted up mine hand, Surely the heathen that *are* about you, they shall bear their shame.

Israel Returns to the Lord

8 But ye, O mountains of Israel, ye shall ᴿshoot forth your branches, and yield your fruit to my people of Israel; for they are at hand to come.   17:23; 34:26–29; Is. 4:2; 27:6
9 For, behold, I *am* for you, and I will turn unto you, and ye shall be tilled and sown:
10 And I will multiply men upon you, all the house of Israel, *even* all of it: and the cities shall be inhabited, and ᴿthe wastes shall be builded: *v.* 33; Is. 58:12; 61:4; Amos 9:14

11 And ᴿI will multiply upon you man and beast; and they shall increase and bring fruit: and I will settle you after your old estates, and will do better *unto you* than at your beginnings: ᴿand ye shall know that I *am* the LORD.   Jer. 31:27, 28 · 35:9
12 Yea, I will cause ᴿmen to walk upon you, *even* my people Israel; and they shall possess thee, and thou shalt be their inheritance, and thou shalt no more henceforth bereave them *of men.*   34:13, 14
13 Thus saith the Lord GOD; Because they say unto you, Thou *land* devourest up men, and hast bereaved thy nations;
14 Therefore thou shalt ᵀdevour men no more, neither ᵀbereave thy nations any more, saith the Lord GOD.   *use up* · *strip*
15 Neither will I cause *men* to hear in thee the shame of the heathen any more, neither shalt thou bear the reproach of the people any more, neither shalt thou cause thy nations to fall any more, saith the Lord GOD.
16 Moreover the word of the LORD came unto me, saying,
17 Son of man, when the house of Israel dwelt in their own land, they defiled it by their own way and by their doings: ᴿtheir way was before me as the uncleanness of a ᵀremoved woman.   Lev. 15:19 · *an impure woman*
18 Wherefore I ᴿpoured my fury upon them for the blood that they had shed upon the land, and for their idols *wherewith* they had polluted it: 22:20
19 And I scattered them among the heathen, and they were dispersed through the countries: according to their way and according to their doings I judged them.
20 And when they entered unto the heathen, whither they went, they ᵀprofaned my holy name, when they said to them, These *are* the people of the LORD, and are gone forth out of his land.   *smeared*
21 But I had pity for mine holy name, which the house of Israel had profaned among the heathen, whither they went.
22 Therefore say unto the house of Israel, Thus saith the Lord GOD; I do not *this* for your sakes, O house of Israel, but for mine holy name's sake, which ye have profaned among the heathen, whither ye went.
23 And I will sanctify my great name, which was profaned among the heathen, which ye have profaned in the midst of them; and the heathen shall know that I *am* the LORD, saith the Lord GOD, when I shall be ᵀsanctified in you before their eyes.   *honoured*
24 For I will take you from among the ᵀheathen, and gather you out of all countries, and will bring you into your own land.   *nations*
25 ᴿThen will I sprinkle clean water upon you, and ye shall be clean: ᴿfrom all your filthiness, and from all your idols, will I cleanse you.   Ps. 51:7; Is. 52:15; Heb. 10:22 · Jer. 33:8

26 A new heart also will I give you, and a new spirit will I put within you: and I will take away the stony heart out of your flesh, and I will give you an heart of flesh.

27 And I will put my spirit within you, and cause you to walk in my statutes, and ye shall keep my judgments, and do *them*.

28 And ye shall dwell in the land that I gave to your fathers; Rand ye shall be my people, and I will be your God.   Jer. 30:22

29 I will also Rsave you from all your uncleannesses: and RI will call for the corn, and will increase it, and Rlay no famine upon you.   [Rom. 11:26] • Hos. 2:22 • Ps. 105:16

30 RAnd I will multiply the fruit of the tree, and the increase of the field, that ye shall receive no more reproach of famine among the heathen.   34:27; Lev. 26:4; Amos 9:13

31 Then Rshall ye remember your own evil ways, and your doings that *were* not good, and Rshall Tlothe yourselves in your own sight for your iniquities and for your abominations.   16:61, 63 • Lev. 26:39 • *despise*

32 RNot for your sakes do I *this*, saith the Lord GOD, be it known unto you: be ashamed and confounded for your own ways, O house of Israel.   *v. 22;* Deut. 9:5

33 Thus saith the Lord GOD; In the day that I shall have cleansed you from all your iniquities I will also cause *you* to dwell in the cities, and the wastes shall be builded.

34 And the Tdesolate land shall be tilled, whereas it lay desolate in the sight of all that passed by.   *forsaken*

35 And they shall say, This land that was desolate is become like the garden of Eden; and the waste and desolate and ruined cities *are become* Tfenced, *and* are inhabited. *rebuilt*

36 Then the heathen that are left round about you shall know that I the LORD build the ruined *places, and* plant that Tthat was Tdesolate: RI the LORD have spoken *it*, and I will do *it*.   *which • barren •* 17:24; 22:14; 37:14

37 Thus saith the Lord GOD; RI will yet *for* this be enquired of by the house of Israel, to do *it* for them; I will Rincrease them with men like a flock.   14:3 • *v. 10*

38 As the holy flock, as the flock of Jerusalem in her solemn feasts; so shall the waste cities be filled with flocks of men: and they shall know that I *am* the LORD.

CHAPTER 37

Vision of Dry Bones

THE Rhand of the LORD was upon me, and carried me out Rin the spirit of the LORD, and set me down in the midst of the valley which *was* full of bones,   1:3 • 3:14

2 And caused me to pass by them round about: and, behold, *there were* very many in the open valley; and, lo, *they were* very dry.

3 RAnd he said unto me, Son of man, can these bones live? And I answered, O Lord GOD, thouT knowest. [John 5:21; 2 Cor. 1:9] • *only you*

4 Again he said unto me, TProphesy upon these bones, and say unto them, O ye dry bones, hear the word of the LORD.   *preach*

5 Thus saith the Lord GOD unto these bones; Behold, I will Rcause breath to enter into you, and ye shall live: *v. 9;* [Ps. 104:1, 30]

6 And I will lay sinews upon you, and will bring up flesh upon you, and cover you with skin, and put breath in you, and ye shall live; and ye shall know that I *am* the LORD.

7 So I Tprophesied Ras I was commanded: and as I prophesied, there was a noise, and behold a shaking, and the bones came together, bone to his bone.   *preached •* Jer. 13:5-7

8 And when I beheld, Tlo, the sinews and the flesh came up upon them, and the skin covered them above: but *there was* no breath in them.   *look*

9 Then said he unto me, Prophesy unto the Twind, prophesy, son of man, and say to the wind, Thus saith the Lord GOD; Come from the four winds, O breath, and breathe upon these slain, that they may live.   *breath*

10 So I prophesied as he commanded me, Rand the breath came into them, and they lived, and stood up upon their feet, Ran exceeding great army.   Rev. 11:11 • Jer. 30:19; 33:22

11 Then he said unto me, Son of man, these bones are the Rwhole house of Israel: behold, they say, ROur bones are dried, and our hope is lost: we are cut off for our parts.   Jer. 33:24 • Ps. 141:7; Is. 49:14

12 Therefore prophesy and say unto them, Thus saith the Lord GOD; Behold, O my people, I will open your graves, and cause you to come up out of your graves, and bring you into the land of Israel.

13 And ye shall know that I *am* the LORD, when I have opened your graves, O my people, and brought you up out of your graves,

14 And Rshall put my Tspirit in you, and ye shall live, and I shall place you in your own land: then shall ye know that I the LORD have spoken *it*, and performed *it*, saith the LORD.   *v. 9;* 11:19; 39:29; 36:27 • *Spirit*

Sign of the Two Sticks

15 The word of the LORD came again unto me, saying,

16 Moreover, thou son of man, take thee one stick, and write upon it, For Judah, and for the children of Israel his companions: then take another stick, and write upon it, For Joseph, the stick of E'-phra-im, and *for* all the house of Israel his companions:

17 And Rjoin them one to another into one stick; and they shall become one in thine hand.   *vv.* 22, 24; Is. 11:13; Jer. 50:4; Hos. 1:11

18 And when the children of thy people

shall speak unto thee, saying, Wilt thou not shew us what thou *meanest* by these?

19 Say unto them, Thus saith the Lord God; Behold, I will take ᴿthe stick of Joseph, which *is* in the hand of E'-phra-im, and the tribes of Israel his fellows, and will put them with him, *even* with the stick of Judah, and make them one stick, and they shall be one in mine hand.   *vv.* 16, 17

20 And the sticks whereon thou writest shall be in thine hand before their eyes.

21 And say unto them, Thus saith the Lord God; Behold, I will take the children of Israel from among the heathen, whither they be gone, and will gather them on every side, and bring them into their own land:

22 And ᴿI will make them one nation in the land upon the mountains of Israel; and ᴿone king shall be king to them all: and they shall be no more two nations, neither shall they be divided into two kingdoms any more at all: Is. 11:13; Hos. 1:11 • John 10:14–16

23 ᴿNeither shall they defile themselves any more with their idols, nor with their ᵀdetestable things, nor with any of their transgressions: but I will save them out of all their dwellingplaces, wherein they have sinned, and will cleanse them: so shall they be my people, and I will be their God.   36:25 • *evil*

24 And ᴿDavid my servant *shall be* king over them; and ᴿthey all shall have one shepherd: ᴿthey shall also walk in my judgments, and observe my statutes, and do them.   [Jer. 23:5; Luke 1:32] ☆ • [John 10:14–16] • 36:27

25 ᴿAnd they shall dwell in the land that I have given unto Jacob my servant, wherein your fathers have dwelt; and they shall dwell therein, *even* they, and their children, and their children's children ᴿfor ever: and ᴿmy servant David *shall be* their prince for ever.   36:28 • Is. 60:21 • John 12:34 ☆

26 Moreover I will make a covenant of peace with them; it shall be an everlasting covenant with them: and I will place them, and multiply them, and will set my sanctuary in the midst of them for evermore.

27 My ᵀtabernacle also shall be with them: yea, I will be ᴿtheir God, and they shall be my people.   *dwellingplace* • 11:20

28 ᴿAnd the heathen shall know that I the Lord do ᴿsanctify Israel, when my sanctuary shall be in the midst of them for evermore.   36:23 • 20:12; Ex. 31:13

CHAPTER 38

Attack by Gog

AND the word of the Lord came unto me, saying,

2 ᴿSon of man, set thy face against Gog, the land of Ma'-gog, ᵀthe chief prince of Me'-shechᴿ and Tu'-bal, and prophesy against him,   39:1 • *prince of the chief* • 32:26

3 And say, Thus saith the Lord God; Behold, I *am* against thee, ᴿO Gog, the chief prince of Me'-shech and Tu'-bal: 39:1

4 And I will turn thee back, and put hooks into thy jaws, and I will bring thee forth, and all thine army, horses and horsemen, all of them clothed with all sorts *of armour, even* a great company *with* bucklers and shields, all of them handling swords:

5 Persia, E-thi-o'-pi-a, and Lib'-y-a with them; all of them with shield and helmet:

6 Go'-mer, and all his bands; the house of To-gar'-mah of the north quarters, and all his bands: *and* many people with thee.

7 ᴿBe thou prepared, and prepare for thyself, thou, and all thy company that are assembled unto thee, and be thou a guard unto them.   Is. 8:9, 10; Jer. 46:3, 4

8 After many days thou shalt be visited: in the latter years thou shalt come into the land *that is* brought back from the sword, *and is* gathered out of many people, against ᴿthe mountains of Israel, which have been always waste: but it is brought forth out of the nations, and they shall ᴿdwell safely all of them.   36:1, 4 • Jer. 23:6

9 Thou shalt ascend and come ᴿlike a storm, thou shalt be ᴿlike a cloud to cover the land, thou, and all thy bands, and many people with thee.   Is. 28:2 • Jer. 4:13

10 Thus saith the Lord God; It shall also come to pass, *that* at the same time shall things come into thy mind, and thou shalt ᵀthink ᴿan evil thought: *devise* • Ps. 36:4

11 And thou shalt say, I will go up to the land of unwalled villages; I will ᴿgo to them that are at rest, that dwell ᵀsafely, all of them dwelling without walls, and having neither bars nor gates,   Jer. 49:31 • *confidently*

12 To take a spoil, and to ᵀtake a prey; to turn thine hand upon the desolate places *that are now* inhabited, and upon the people *that are* gathered out of the nations, which have gotten cattle and goods, that dwell in the midst of the land.   *enslave them*

13 She'-ba, and De'-dan, and the merchants of Tar'-shish, with all the young lions thereof, shall say unto thee, Art thou come to take a spoil? hast thou gathered thy company to ᵀtake a prey? to carry away silver and gold, to take away cattle and goods, to take a great ᵀspoil?   *enslave* • *loot*

14 Therefore, son of man, prophesy and say unto Gog, Thus saith the Lord God; In that day when my people of Israel dwelleth safely, shalt thou not know *it*?

15 And thou shalt come from thy place out of the north parts, thou, and many people with thee, all of them riding upon horses, a great company, and a mighty army:

16 And thou shalt come up against my people of Israel, as a cloud to cover the land; it shall be in the latter days, and I will bring

thee against my land, that the Theathen may Rknow me, when I shall be sanctified in thee, O Gog, before their eyes. *nations • v. 23; 36:23*

Judgment of God

17 Thus saith the Lord GOD; *Art* thou he of whom I have spoken in old time by my servants the prophets of Israel, which Rprophesied in those days *many* years that I would bring thee against them? *Is. 5:26–29*

18 And it shall come to pass at the same time when Gog shall come against the land of Israel, saith the Lord GOD, *that* my Rfury shall come up in my face. *Ps. 18:8, 15*

19 For in my jealousy Rand in the fire of my wrath have I spoken, RSurely in that day there shall be a great shaking in the land of Israel; *Ps. 89:46 • Hag. 2:6, 7; Rev. 16:18*

20 So that the fishes of the sea, and the fowls of the heaven, and the beasts of the field, and all creeping things that creep upon the earth, and all the men that *are* upon the face of the earth, shall shake at my presence, and the mountains shall be thrown down, and the steep places shall fall, and every wall shall fall to the ground.

21 And I will Rcall for a sword against him throughout all my mountains, saith the Lord GOD: Revery man's sword shall be against his brother. *Ps. 105:16 • Judg. 7:22*

22 And I will plead against him with pestilence and with blood; and RI will rain upon him, and upon his bands, and upon the many people that *are* with him, and overflowing rain, and Rgreat hailstones, fire, and brimstone. *Ps. 11:6 • Is. 28:17; Rev. 16:21*

23 Thus will I magnify myself, and Rsanctify^T myself; Rand I will be known in the eyes of many nations, and they shall know that I *am* the LORD. *36:23 • honour • 37:28*

CHAPTER 39

THEREFORE, Rthou son of man, prophesy against Gog, and say, Thus saith the Lord GOD; Behold, I *am* against thee, O Gog, the chief prince of Me'-shech and Tu'-bal: *38:2, 3*

2 And I will Rturn thee back, and leave but the sixth part of thee, Rand will cause thee to come up from the north parts, and will bring thee upon the mountains of Israel: *38:8 • 38:15*

3 RAnd I will smite thy bow out of thy left hand, and will cause thine arrows to fall out of thy right hand. *Hos. 1:5*

4 Thou shalt fall upon the mountains of Israel, thou, and all thy bands, and the people that *is* with thee: I will give thee unto the ravenous birds of every sort, and *to* the beasts of the field to be devoured.

5 Thou shalt fall upon the open field: for I have spoken *it*, saith the Lord GOD.

6 RAnd I will send a fire on Ma'-gog, and among them that dwell Tcarelessly in Rthe

isles: and they shall know that I *am* the LORD. *Amos 1:4; Nah. 1:6 • securely • Ps. 72:10; Is. 66:19*

7 So will I make my holy name known in the midst of my people Israel; and I will not *let them* pollute my holy name any more: and the heathen shall know that I *am* the LORD, the Holy One in Israel.

8 Behold, Rit is come, and it is done, saith the Lord GOD; this *is* the day Rwhereof I have spoken. *7:3–8; Rev. 16:17; 21:6 • 38:17*

9 And they that dwell in the cities of Israel shall Rgo forth, and shall Rset on fire and burn the weapons, both the shields and the bucklers, the bows and the arrows, and the handstaves, and the spears, and they shall burn them with fire seven years: *Is. 66:24 • Ps. 46:9*

10 So that they shall take no wood out of the field, neither cut down *any* out of the forests; for they shall burn the weapons with fire: Rand they shall Tspoil those that spoiled them, and rob those that robbed them, saith the Lord GOD. *Is. 14:2; Mic. 5:8 • loot*

11 And it shall come to pass in that day, *that* I will give unto Gog a place there of graves in Israel, the valley of the passengers on the east of the sea: and it shall stop the *noses* of the passengers: and there shall they bury Gog and all his multitude: and they shall call *it* The valley of Ha'-mon-gog.

12 And seven months shall the house of Israel be burying of them, Rthat they may cleanse the land. *v. 14; Deut. 21:23*

13 Yea, all the people of the land shall bury *them;* and it shall be to them a Trenown the day that RI shall be glorified, saith the Lord GOD. *famous day when • 28:22*

14 And they shall Tsever out men of Tcontinual employment, passing through the land to bury with the Tpassengers those that remain upon the face of the earth, to cleanse it: after the end of seven months shall they search. *choose • constant labour • travellers*

15 And the passengers *that* pass through the land, when *any* seeth a man's bone, then shall he set up a sign by it, till the buriers have buried it in the valley of Ha'-mon-gog.

16 And also the name of the city *shall be* THa-mo'-nah. Thus shall they Rcleanse the land. *multitude • v. 12*

17 And, thou son of man, thus saith the Lord GOD; Speak unto every feathered fowl, and to every Rbeast of the field, Assemble yourselves, and come; gather yourselves on every side to my Tsacrifice that I do sacrifice for you, *even* a great sacrifice upon the mountains of Israel, that ye may eat flesh, and drink blood. *Is. 56:9 • slaughter*

18 Ye shall eat the flesh of the mighty, and drink the blood of the princes of the earth, of rams, of lambs, and of goats, of bullocks, all of them fatlings of Ba'-shan.

19 And ye shall eat fat till ye be full, and

drink blood till ye be drunken, of my sacrifice which I have sacrificed for you.

20 Thus ye shall be filled at my table with horses and chariots, with mighty men, and with all men of war, saith the Lord GOD.

21 And I will set my glory among the heathen, and all the heathen shall see my judgment that I have executed, and Rmy hand that I have laid upon them.   Ex. 7:4

22 So the Rhouse of Israel shall Rknow that I am the LORD their God from that day and forward.   vv. 7 • Jer. 24:7

23 And the heathen shall know that the house of Israel went into captivity for their iniquity: because they trespassed against me, therefore hid I my face from them, and gave them into the hand of their enemies: so fell they all by the sword.

24 According to their uncleanness and according to their transgressions have I done unto them, and hid my face from them.

25 Therefore thus saith the Lord GOD; RNow will I Tbring again the captivity of Jacob, and have mercy upon the Rwhole house of Israel, and will be Tjealous for my holy name;   Jer. 30:3, 18 • restore • Hos. 1:1 • zealous

26 RAfter that they have borne their shame, and all their trespasses whereby they have trespassed against me, when they Rdwelt safely in their land, and none made them afraid.   Dan. 9:16 • Lev. 26:5, 6

27 When I have brought them again from the people, and gathered them out of their enemies' lands, and am Tsanctified in them in the sight of many nations;   honoured

28 Then shall they know that I am the LORD their God, which caused them to be led into captivity among the heathen: but I have gathered them unto their own land, and have left none of them any more there.

29 RNeither will I hide my face any more from them: for I have Rpoured out my spirit upon the house of Israel, saith the Lord GOD.   Is. 54:8 • [Joel 2:28; Zech. 12:10]; Acts 2:17

CHAPTER 40

Vision of the Man with the Measuring Rod

IN the Rfive and twentieth year of our captivity, in the beginning of the year, in the tenth day of the month, in the fourteenth year after that Rthe city was smitten, in the selfsame day Rthe hand of the LORD was upon me, and brought me thither.   32:1, 17 • 33:21 • 1:3

2 In the visions of God brought he me into the land of Israel, and set me upon a very high mountain, by which was Tas the frame of a city on the south.   a structure like a city

3 And he brought me thither, and, behold, there was a man, whose appearance was Rlike the appearance of brass, Rwith a line of flax in his hand, and a measuring reed; and he stood in the gate.   1:7 • 47:3

4 And the man said unto me, Son of man, behold with thine eyes, and hear with thine ears, and Tset thine heart upon all that I shall shew thee; for to the intent that I might shew them unto thee art thou brought hither: declare all that thou seest to the house of Israel.   consider earnestly

The Outer Court

5 And behold Ra wall on the outside of the house round about, and in the man's hand a measuring reed of Tsix cubits long by the cubit and an hand breadth: so he measured the breadth of the building, Tone reed; and the height, one reed.   42:20 • 10.5 ft. • 10.5 ft.

6 Then came he unto the gate Twhich looketh toward the east, and went up the stairs thereof, and measured the threshold of the gate, which was Tone reed broad; and the other threshold of the gate, which was one reed broad.   on the east side • 10.5 ft.

7 And every little chamber was one reed long, and Tone reed broad; and between the little Tchambers were Tfive cubits; and the threshold of the gate by the porch of the gate within was one reed.   10.5 ft. • lodges • 8 ft. 9 in.

8 He measured also the porch of the gate within, Tone reed.   10.5 ft.

9 Then measured he the porch of the gate, Teight cubits; and the posts thereof, Ttwo cubits; and the porch of the gate was Tinward.   14 ft. • 42 in. • from the house

10 And the little chambers of the gate eastward were three on this side, and three on that side; they three were of one measure: and the posts had one measure on this side and on that side.

11 And he measured the breadth of the entry of the gate, Tten cubits; and the length of the gate, Tthirteen cubits.   17.5ft. • 22.75ft.

12 The space also before the little chambers was Tone cubit on this side, and the space was one cubit on that side: and the little chambers were Tsix cubits on this side, and six cubits on that side.   21 in. • 10.5 ft.

13 He measured then the gate from the roof of one little chamber to the roof of another: the breadth was Tfive and twenty cubits, door against door.   43.75 ft.

14 He made also posts of Tthreescore cubits, even unto the post of the Rcourt round about the gate.   105 ft. • 1 Chr. 28:6

15 And from the face of the gate of the entrance unto the face of the porch of the inner gate were Tfifty cubits.   87.5 ft.

16 And there were narrow windows to the little chambers, and to their posts within the gate round about, and likewise to the arches: and windows were round about Tinward: and upon each post were palm trees. facing the court

17 Then brought he me into the outward

court, and, lo, *there were* chambers, and a pavement made for the court round about: thirty chambers *were* upon the pavement.

18 And the pavement by the side of the ᴿgates over against the length of the gates was the lower pavement.   *vv.* 23, 27; 46:1, 2

19 Then he measured the breadth from the forefront of the lower gate unto the forefront of the inner court without, an ᵀhundred cubits eastward and northward.   *175 ft.*

20 And the ᴿgate of the outward court that looked toward the north, he measured the length thereof, and the breadth thereof.   *v.* 6

21 And the little chambers thereof *were* three on this side and three on that side; and the posts thereof and the arches thereof were after the measure of the first gate: the length thereof *was* ᵀfifty cubits, and the breadth ᵀfive and twenty cubits.   *87.5 ft.* · *43.75 ft.*

22 And their windows, and their arches, and their palm trees, *were* after the measure of the gate that looketh toward the east; and they went up unto it by seven steps; and the arches thereof *were* before them.

23 And the gate of the inner court *was* ᵀover against the gate toward the north, and toward the east; and he measured from gate to gate an ᵀhundred cubits.   *opposite* · *175 ft.*

24 After that he brought me toward the south, and behold a gate toward the south: and he measured the posts thereof and the arches thereof according to these measures.

25 And *there were* windows in it and in the arches thereof round about, like those windows: the length *was* fifty cubits, and the breadth five and twenty cubits.

26 And *there were* seven steps to go up to it, and the arches thereof *were* before them: and it had palm trees, one on this side, and another on that side, upon the posts thereof.

27 And *there was* a gate in the ᴿinner court toward the south: and he measured from gate to gate toward the south an ᵀhundred cubits.   *vv.* 23, 32 · *175 ft.*

The Inner Court

28 And he brought me to the inner court by the south gate: and he measured the south gate according to these measures;

29 And ᴿthe little chambers thereof, and the posts thereof, and the arches thereof, according to these measures: and *there were* windows in it and in the arches thereof round about: it *was* ᵀfifty cubits long, and five and twenty cubits broad.   *vv.* 7, 10, 21 · *87.5 ft.*

30 And the ᴿarches round about *were* ᵀfive and twenty cubits long, and ᵀfive cubits broad.   *vv.* 16, 21 · *43.75 ft.* · *8.75 ft.*

31 And the arches thereof *were* toward the utter court; and ᴿpalm trees *were* upon the posts thereof: and the going up to it *had* eight steps.   *vv.* 16, 22, 26, 34, 37

32 And he brought me into the ᴿinner court toward the east: and he measured the gate according to these measures.   *v.* 28

33 And ᴿthe little chambers thereof, and the posts thereof, and the arches thereof, *were* according to these measures: and *there were* ᴿwindows therein and in the arches thereof round about: *it was* fifty cubits long, and five and twenty cubits broad.   *v.* 29 · *v.* 16

34 And the arches thereof *were* toward the outward court; and palm trees *were* upon the posts thereof, on this side, and on that side: and the going up to it *had* eight steps.

35 And he brought me to the north gate, and measured *it* according to these measures;

36 The ᴿlittle chambers thereof, the posts thereof, and the ᴿarches thereof, and the windows to it round about: the length *was* ᵀfifty cubits, and the breadth ᵀfive and twenty cubits.   *vv.* 7, 29 · *v.* 16 · *87.5 ft.* · *43.75 ft.*

37 And the posts thereof *were* toward the utter court; and ᴿpalm trees *were* upon the posts thereof, on this side, and on that side: and the going up to it *had* eight steps.   *v.* 16

38 And the ᴿchambers and the entries thereof *were* by the posts of the gates, where they washed the burnt offering.   *v.* 17

39 And in the porch of the gate *were* two tables on this side, and two tables on that side, to slay thereon the burnt offering and the sin offering and the trespass offering.

40 And at the side without, as one goeth up to the entry of the north gate, *were* two tables; and on the other side, which *was* at the porch of the gate, *were* two tables.

41 Four ᴿtables *were* on this side, and four tables on that side, by the side of the gate; eight tables, whereupon they slew *their* sacrifices.   *vv.* 39, 40

42 And the four tables *were* of hewn stone for the burnt offering, of a ᵀcubit and an half long, and a cubit and an half broad, and ᵀone cubit high: whereupon also they laid the instruments wherewith they slew the burnt offering and the sacrifice. *31.5 in.* · *21 in.*

43 And within *were* hooks, an ᵀhand broad, fastened round about: and upon the tables *was* the flesh of the offering.   *3 in.*

44 And without the inner gate *were* the chambers of ᴿthe singers in the inner court, which *was* at the side of the north gate; and their prospect *was* toward the south: one at the side of the east gate *having* the prospect toward the north.   1 Chr. 6:31, 32

45 And he said unto me, This chamber, whose prospect *is* toward the south, *is* for the priests, ᴿthe keepers of the ᵀcharge of the house.   1 Chr. 9:23; 2 Chr. 13:11; Ps. 134:1 · *rule*

46 And the chamber ᵀwhose prospect *is* toward the north *is* for the priests, ᴿthe keepers of the charge of the altar: these *are* the sons of ᴿZa′-dok among the sons of Levi,

which come near to the LORD to minister unto him. *which is facing* · Num. 18:5 · 1 Kin. 2:35

47 So he measured the court, an ᵀhundred cubits long, and an hundred cubits broad, foursquare; and the altar *that was* before the house. *175 ft.*

The Temple Porch

48 And he brought me to the porch of the house, and measured *each* post of the porch, ᵀfive cubits on this side, and five cubits on that side: and the breadth of the gate *was* ᵀthree cubits on this side, and three cubits on that side. *8.75 ft.* · *5.25 ft.*

49 The length of the porch *was* twenty cubits, and the breadth eleven cubits; and *he brought me* by the steps whereby they went up to it: and *there were* pillars by the posts, one on this side, and another on that side.

CHAPTER 41

The Temple Itself

AFTERWARD ᴿhe brought me to the temple, and measured the posts, ᵀsix cubits broad on the one side, and six cubits broad on the other side, *which was* the breadth of the tabernacle. 40:2, 3 · *10.5 ft.*

2 And the breadth of the door *was* ᵀten cubits; and the sides of the door *were* ᵀfive cubits on the one side, and five cubits on the other side: and he measured the length thereof, ᵀforty cubits: and the breadth, ᵀtwenty cubits. *17.5 ft.* · *8.75 ft.* · *70 ft.* · *35 ft.*

3 Then went he ᵀinward, and measured the post of the door, ᵀtwo cubits; and the door, ᵀsix cubits; and the breadth of the door, ᵀseven cubits. *inside* · *3.5 ft.* · *10.5 ft.* · *12.25 ft.*

4 So he measured the length thereof, twenty cubits; and the breadth, ᵀtwenty cubits, before the temple: and he said unto me, This *is* the most holy *place*. *35 ft.*

5 After he measured the wall of the house, ᵀsix cubits; and the breadth of *every* side chamber, ᵀfour cubits, ᴿround about the house on every side. *10.5 ft.* · *7 ft.* · 1 Kin. 6:5

6 And the side chambers *were* three, one over another, and thirty in order; and they entered into the wall which *was* of the house for the side chambers round about, that they might have hold, but they had not hold in the wall of the house.

7 And *there was* an enlarging, and a winding about still upward to the side chambers: for the winding about of the house went still upward round about the house: therefore the breadth of the house *was still* upward, and so increased *from* the lowest *chamber* to the highest by the midst.

8 I saw also the height of the house round about: the foundations of the side chambers *were* ᵀa full reed of six great cubits. *10.5 ft.*

9 The thickness of the wall, which *was* for the side chamber without, *was* ᵀfive cubits: and *that* which *was* left *was* the place of the side chambers that *were* within. *8.75 ft.*

10 And between the ᴿchambers *was* the wideness of ᵀtwenty cubits round about the house on every side. 40:17 · *35 ft.*

11 And the doors of the side chambers *were* toward *the place that was* left, one door toward the north, and another door toward the south: and the breadth of the place that was left *was* ᵀfive cubits round about. *8.75 ft.*

12 Now the building that *was* before the separate place at the end toward the west *was* seventy cubits broad; and the wall of the building *was* five cubits thick round about, and the length thereof ninety cubits.

13 So he measured the house, ᴿan hundred cubits long;ᵀ and the separate place, and the building, with the walls thereof, an hundred cubits long; 40:47 · *175 ft.*

14 Also the breadth of the face of the house, and of the separate place toward the east, an hundred cubits.

15 And he measured the length of the building over against the separate place which *was* behind it, and the galleries thereof on the one side and on the other side, an hundred cubits, with the inner temple, and the porches of the court;

16 The door posts, and ᴿthe narrow windows, and the galleries round about on their three stories, over against the door, ᵀcieled with wood round about, and from the ground up to the windows, and the windows *were* covered; 40:16 · *covered*

17 To that above the door, even unto the inner house, and without, and by all the wall round about within and without, ᵀby measure. *exactly*

18 And *it was* made ᴿwith cher'-u-bims and palm trees, so that a palm tree *was* between a cherub and a cherub; and *every* cherub had two faces; 1 Kin. 6:29

19 ᴿSo that the face of a man *was* toward the palm tree on the one side, and the face of a young lion toward the palm tree on the other side: *it was* made through all the house round about. 1:10; 10:14

20 From the ground unto above the door *were* ᴿcher'-u-bims and palm trees made, and *on* the wall of the temple. 41:18

21 The ᵀpostsᴿ of the ᴿtemple *were* squared, *and* the face of the sanctuary; the appearance *of the one* as the appearance *of the other*. *door posts* · 1 Kin. 6:33 · *v.* 1

22 The altar of wood *was* ᵀthree cubits high, and the length thereof ᵀtwo cubits; and the corners thereof, and the length thereof, and the walls thereof, *were* of wood: and he said unto me, This *is* the table that *is* before the LORD. *5.25 ft.* · *3.5 ft.*

23 ᴿAnd the temple and ᴿthe sanctuary had ᴿtwo doors. *v.* 1 · *v.* 4 · 1 Kin. 6:31–35

24 And the doors had two leaves *apiece*, two turning leaves; two *leaves* for the one door, and two leaves for the other *door*.

25 And *there were* made on them, on the doors of the temple, cher'-u-bims and palm trees, like as *were* made upon the walls; and *there were* ᵀthick planks upon the face of the porch without.   *canopy of wood over*

26 And *there were* ᴿnarrow windows and palm trees on the one side and on the other side, on the sides of the porch, and *upon* the side chambers of the house, and ᵀthick planks.   *v. 16; 40:16; 1 Kin. 6:4 • the thresholds*

CHAPTER 42

The Chamber in the Outer Court

THEN he brought me forth into the utter court, the way toward the north: and he brought me into ᴿthe chamber that *was* over against the separate place, and which *was* before the building toward the north. *v. 4; 40:17*

2 Before the length of an ᵀhundred cubits *was* the north door, and the breadth *was* ᵀfifty cubits.   *175 ft. • 87.5 ft.*

3 Over against the twenty *cubits* which *were* for the inner court, and over against the pavement which *was* for the utter court, *was* gallery against gallery in three *stories*.

4 And before the chambers *was* a walk of ten cubits breadth inward, a way of ᵀone cubit; and their doors toward the north. *21 in.*

5 Now the upper chambers *were* shorter: for the ᴿgalleries were higher than these, than the lower, and than the middlemost of the building.   *v. 3*

6 For they *were* in ᴿthree *stories*, but had not pillars as the pillars of the courts: therefore *the* ᵀ*building* was ᵀstraitened more than the lowest and the middlemost from the ground.   *41:6 • uppermost • set back*

7 And the wall that *was* without over against the chambers, toward the utter court on the forepart of the chambers, the length thereof *was* ᵀfifty cubits.   *87.5 ft.*

8 For the length of the chambers that *were* in the utter court *was* fifty cubits: and, lo, before the temple *were* an hundred cubits.

9 And from under these chambers *was* the entry on the east side, as one goeth into them from the ᵀutter court.   *outside*

10 The chambers *were* in the thickness of the wall of the court toward the east, over against ᴿthe ᵀseparate place, and over against the building.   *41:14 • temple yard*

11 And ᴿthe way before them *was* like the appearance of the chambers which *were* toward the north, as long as they, *and* as broad as they: and all their goings out *were* both according to their fashions, and according to their doors.   *v. 4*

12 And according to the doors of the chambers that *were* toward the south *was* a door in the head of the way, *even* the way directly before the ᴿwall toward the east, as one entereth into them.   *v. 7*

13 Then said he unto me, The north chambers *and* the south chambers, which *are* before the separate place, they *be* holy chambers, where the priests that approach unto the LORD shall eat the most holy things: there shall they lay the most holy things, and the meat offering, and the sin offering, and the trespass offering; for the place *is* holy.

14 ᴿWhen the priests enter therein, then shall they not go out of the holy *place* into the utter court, but there they shall lay their ᴿgarments wherein they minister; for they *are* holy; and shall put on other garments, and shall approach to *those things* which *are* for the people.   *44:19 • Ex. 29:4-9*

The Place of Separation

15 Now when he had made an end of measuring the inner house, he brought me forth toward the ᴿgate whose prospect *is* toward the east, and measured it round about.   *40:6; 43:1*

16 He measured the east side with the measuring reed, ᵀfive hundred reeds, with the measuring reed round about.   *about 1 mi.*

17 He measured the north side, five hundred reeds, with the measuring reed round about.

18 He measured the south side, five hundred reeds, with the measuring reed.

19 He turned about to the west side, *and* measured five hundred reeds with the measuring reed.

20 He measured it by the four sides: it had a wall round about, five hundred *reeds* long, and five hundred broad, to make a separation between the sanctuary and the ᵀprofane place.   *for the common people*

CHAPTER 43

The Return of the Glory of God to the Temple

AFTERWARD he brought me to the gate, *even* the gate ᴿthat looketh toward the east: *10:19; 40:6; 42:15; 46:1*

2 And, behold, the glory of the God of Israel came from the way of the east: and ᴿhis voice *was* like a noise of many waters: and the earth shined with his glory.   *1:24*

3 And *it was* according to the appearance of the vision which I saw, *even* according to the vision that I saw when I came to destroy the city: and the visions *were* like the vision that I saw by the river Che'-bar; and I fell upon my face.

4 ᴿAnd the glory of the LORD came into the house by the way of the gate whose prospect *is* toward the east.   *10:19; 11:23*

5 RSo the spirit took me up, and brought me into the inner court; and, behold, the glory of the LORD filled the house.   3:12

6 And I heard Thim speaking unto me out of the house; and the man stood by me.   one

7 And he said unto me, Son of man, the place of my throne, and the place of the soles of my feet, where I will dwell in the midst of the children of Israel for ever, and my holy name, shall the house of Israel no more defile, neither they, nor their kings, by their whoredom, nor by Rthe carcases of their kings in their high places.   Lev. 26:30

8 In their setting of their threshold by my thresholds, and their post by my posts, and the wall between me and them, they have even defiled my holy name by their abominations that they have committed: wherefore I have consumed them in mine anger.

9 Now let them Rput away their whoredom, and the Tcarcases of their kings, far from me, and I will dwell in the midst of them for ever.   16:61, 63 • corpses

10 Thou son of man, shew the house to the house of Israel, that they may be ashamed of their iniquities: and let them Tmeasure the pattern.   take note of the requirements

11 And if they be ashamed of all that they have done, shew them the form of the house, and the fashion thereof, and the goings out thereof, and the comings in thereof, and all the forms thereof, and all the ordinances thereof, and all the forms thereof, and all the laws thereof: and write it in their sight, that they may keep the whole form thereof, and all the ordinances thereof, and do them.

12 This is the law of the house; Upon Rthe top of the mountain the whole limit thereof round about shall be most holy. Behold, this is the law of the house.   40:2

The Altar of Burnt Offerings

13 And these are the measures of the altar after the cubits: TThe cubit is a cubit and an hand breadth; even the bottom shall be a cubit, and the breadth a cubit, and the border thereof by the Tedge thereof round about shall be a Tspan: and this shall be the Thigher place of the altar.   21 in. • rim • 9 in. • base

14 And from the bottom upon the ground even to the lower settle shall be two cubits, and the breadth one cubit; and from the lesser settle even to the greater settle shall be four cubits, and the breadth one cubit.

15 So Tthe altar shall be Tfour cubits; and from Tthe altar and upward shall be four Rhorns.   upper altar • 7 ft. • lower altar • Ex. 27:2

16 And the Raltar shall be Ttwelve cubits long, twelve broad, square in the four squares thereof.   Ex. 27:1 • 21 ft.

17 And the Tsettle shall be Tfourteen cubits long and fourteen broad in the four squares thereof; and the border about it shall be Thalf a cubit; and the bottom thereof shall be a

Tcubit about; and his stairs shall look toward the east.   ledge • 24.5 ft. • 10.5 in. • 21 in.

18 And he said unto me, Son of man, thus saith the Lord GOD; These are the ordinances of the altar in the day when they shall make it, to offer burnt offerings thereon, and to sprinkle blood thereon.

19 And thou shalt give to the priests the Levites that be of the seed of Za'-dok, which approach unto me, Rto minister unto me, saith the Lord GOD, Ra young bullock for a sin offering.   44:16 • 45:18; Lev. 8:14

20 And Rthou shalt take of the blood thereof, and put it on the four horns of it, and on the four corners of the Tsettle, and upon the border round about: thus shalt thou cleanse and purge it.   Lev. 8:15 • ledge

21 Thou shalt take the Tbullock also of the sin offering, and he Rshall burn it in the appointed place of the house, RwithoutT the sanctuary.   bull • Ex. 29:14 • Heb. 13:11 • outside

22 And on the second day thou shalt offer a kid of the goats without blemish for a sin offering; and they shall Rcleanse the altar, as they did cleanse it with the bullock.   vv. 20, 26

23 When thou hast made an end of cleansing it, thou shalt offer a young Rbullock without blemish, and a ram out of the flock without blemish.   45:18; Ex. 29:1, 10

24 And thou shalt offer them before the LORD, Rand the priests shall cast salt upon them, and they shall offer them up for a burnt offering unto the LORD.   Lev. 2:13

25 RSeven days shalt thou prepare every day a goat for a sin offering: they shall also prepare a young bullock, and a ram out of the flock, without blemish.   Ex. 29:35

26 Seven days shall they Tpurge the altar and purify it; and they shall Tconsecrate themselves.   make atonement for • fill its hands

27 And when these days are expired, it shall be, that Rupon the eighth day, and so forward, the priests shall make your burnt offerings upon the altar, and your Tpeace offerings; and I will Raccept you, saith the Lord GOD.   Lev. 9:1 • thank offerings • 20:40, 41

CHAPTER 44

Duties of Temple Priests

THEN he brought me back the way of the gate of the outward sanctuary which looketh toward the east; and it was shut.

2 Then said the LORD unto me; This gate shall be shut, it shall not be opened, and no man shall enter in by it; Rbecause the LORD, the God of Israel, hath entered in by it, therefore it shall be shut.   43:2-4

3 It is for the prince; the prince, he shall sit in it to eat bread before the LORD; he shall enter by the way of the porch of that gate, and shall go out by the way of the same.

4 Then brought he me the way of the north gate before the house: and I looked, and, behold, the glory of the LORD filled the house of the LORD: and I fell upon my face.

5 And the LORD said unto me, Son of man, mark well, and behold with thine eyes, and hear with thine ears all that I say unto thee concerning all the Rordinances of the house of the LORD, and all the laws thereof; and mark well the entering in of the house, with every going forth of the sanctuary. Deut. 12:32

6 And thou shalt say to the Rrebellious, *even* to the house of Israel, Thus saith the Lord GOD; O ye house of Israel, let it suffice you of all your abominations, 2:5

7 In that ye have brought *into my sanctuary* strangers, uncircumcised in heart, and uncircumcised in flesh, to be in my sanctuary, to pollute it, *even* my house, when ye offer my bread, the fat and the blood, and they have broken my Tcovenant because of all your abominations. *agreement*

8 And ye have not kept the charge of mine holy things: but ye have set keepers of my charge in my sanctuary for yourselves.

9 Thus saith the Lord GOD; No stranger, uncircumcised in heart, nor uncircumcised in flesh, shall enter into my sanctuary, of any stranger that *is* among the children of Israel.

10 And the Levites that are gone away far from me, when Israel went astray, which went astray away from me after their idols; they shall even bear their iniquity.

11 Yet they shall be ministers in my sanctuary, *having* charge at the gates of the house, and ministering to the house: they shall slay the burnt offering and the sacrifice for the people, and they shall stand before them to minister unto them.

12 Because they ministered unto them before their idols, and caused the house of Israel to fall into iniquity; therefore have I lifted up mine hand against them, saith the Lord GOD, and they shall bear their iniquity.

13 And they shall Rnot come near unto me, to do the office of a priest unto me, nor to come near to any of my holy things, in the most holy *place*: but they shall bear their shame, and their abominations which they have committed. Num. 18:3

14 But I will make them keepers of the charge of the house, for all the service thereof, and for all that shall be done therein.

15 RBut the priests the Levites, the sons of Za'-dok, that kept the charge of my sanctuary when the children of Israel went astray from me, they shall come near to me to minister unto me, and they shall stand before me to offer unto me the fat and the blood, saith the Lord GOD: 40:46

16 They shall Renter into my Tsanctuary, and they shall come near to Rmy table, to minister unto me, and they shall Rkeep my charge. Num. 18:5, 7, 8 · *holy place* · 41:22 · Mal. 2:7

17 And it shall come to pass, *that* when they enter in at the gates of the inner court, Rthey shall be clothed with linen garments; and no wool shall come upon them, whiles they minister in the gates of the inner court, and within. Ex. 28:39; Rev. 19:8

18 They shall have linen bonnets upon their heads, and shall have linen breeches upon their loins; they shall not gird *themselves* with any thing that causeth sweat.

19 And when they go forth into the utter court, *even* into the utter court to the people, they shall Rput off their garments wherein they ministered, and lay them in the holy chambers, and they shall put on other garments; and they shall not sanctify the people with their garments. 42:14

20 RNeither shall they shave their heads, nor Rsuffer their locks to grow long; they shall only poll their heads. Lev. 21:5 · Num. 6:5

21 Neither shall any priest drink wine, when they enter into the inner court.

22 Neither shall they take for their wives a widow, nor her that is put away: but they shall take maidens of the seed of the house of Israel, or a widow that had a priest before.

23 RAnd they shall teach my people the Rdifference between the holy and Tprofane, and cause them to discern between the unclean and the clean. Mal. 2:7 · Lev. 10:10 · *common*

24 And in controversy they shall stand in judgment; *and* they shall judge it according to my judgments: and they shall keep my laws and my statutes in all mine assemblies; and they shall hallow my sabbaths.

25 And they shall Tcome at no dead person to defile themselves: but for father, or for mother, or for son, or for daughter, for brother, or for sister that hath had no husband, they may defile themselves. *touch*

26 And Rafter he is cleansed, they shall reckon unto him seven days. Num. 6:9, 10

27 And in the day that he goeth into the sanctuary, unto the inner court, to minister in the sanctuary, Rhe shall offer his sin offering, saith the Lord GOD. Lev. 4:3; 5:3, 6

28 And it shall be unto them for an inheritance: I Ram their inheritance: and ye shall give them no possession in Israel: I *am* their possession. Num. 18:20; Josh. 13:14, 33

29 RThey shall eat the meat offering, and the sin offering, and the trespass offering; and Revery T dedicated thing in Israel shall be their's. Lev. 7:6 · Lev. 27:21, 28 · *all offerings*

30 And the firstT of all the firstfruits of all *things*, and every oblation of all, of every *sort* of your oblations, shall be the priest's: ye shall also give unto the priest the first of your dough, that he may cause the blessing to rest in thine house. *best*

31 The priests shall not eat of any thing that is Rdead of itself, or torn, whether it be fowl or beast. Ex. 22:31; Lev. 22:8; Deut. 14:21

CHAPTER 45

Land of the Temple Priests

MOREOVER, when ye shall divide by lot the land for inheritance, ye shall offer an oblation unto the LORD, an holy portion of the land: the length *shall be* the length of five and twenty *reeds*, and the breadth *shall be* ten thousand. This *shall be* holy in all the borders thereof round about.

2 Of this there shall be for the sanctuary Tfive hundred *in length*, with five hundred *in breadth*, square round about; and fifty cubits round about for the suburbs thereof.   *875 ft.*

3 And of this measure shalt thou measure the length of five and twenty thousand, and the breadth of ten thousand: and in it shall be the sanctuary *and* the most holy place.

4 The holy *portion* of the land shall be for the priests the ministers of the sanctuary, which shall come near to minister unto the LORD: and it shall be a place for their houses, and Tan holy place for the sanctuary. *a separated*

5 RAnd the Tfive and twenty thousand of length, and the Tten thousand of breadth, shall also the Levites, the ministers of the house, have for themselves, for a possession for Rtwenty chambers. *48:13 • 8.75 mi. • 3.3 mi. • 40:17*

6 RAnd ye shall appoint the possession of the city Tfive thousand broad, and Tfive and twenty thousand long, over against the oblation of the holy *portion:* it shall be for the whole house of Israel.   *48:15 • 1.6 mi. • 8.75 mi.*

7 And *a portion shall be* for the prince on the one side and on the other side of the oblation of the holy *portion*, and of the possession of the city, before the oblation of the holy *portion*, and before the possession of the city, from the west side westward, and from the east side eastward: and the length *shall be* over against one of the portions, from the west border unto the east border.

8 In the land shall be his possession in Israel: and Rmy princes shall no more oppress my people; and *the rest of* the land shall they give to the house of Israel according to their tribes.   *19:7; 22:27; Jer. 22:15-17*

Offerings of the Temple Priests

9 Thus saith the Lord GOD; Let it suffice you, O princes of Israel: remove violence and Tspoil, and execute judgment and justice, take away your Texactions from my people, saith the Lord GOD.   *robbery • evictions*

10 Ye shall have just balances, and a just Te'-phah, and a just Tbath.   *.65 bu. • 6 gal.*

11 The e'-phah and the bath shall be of one measure, that the bath may contain the tenth part of an Tho'-mer, and the e'-phah the tenth part of an ho'-mer: the measure thereof shall be after the ho'-mer.   *6.5 bu. or 60 gal.*

12 And the Tshek'-elR *shall be* twenty ge'-rahs: twenty shek'-els, five and twenty shek'-els, fifteen shek'-els, shall be your Tma'-neh.   *.4 oz. • Num. 3:47 • 24 oz.*

13 This *is* the oblation that ye shall offer; the Tsixth part of an e'-phah of an ho'-mer of wheat, and ye shall give the sixth part of an e'-phah of an ho'-mer of barley: *1.1 bu.*

14 Concerning the ordinance of oil, the bath of oil, *ye shall offer* the tenth part of a bath out of the Tcor, *which is* an ho'-mer of ten baths; for ten baths *are* an ho'-mer: *60 gal.*

15 And one lamb out of the flock, out of two hundred, out of the fat pastures of Israel; for a meat offering, and for a burnt offering, and for peace offerings, to make reconciliation for them, saith the Lord GOD.

16 All the people of the land shall give this oblation for the prince in Israel.

17 And it shall be the prince's part *to give* burnt offerings, and meat offerings, and drink offerings, in the feasts, and in the new moons, and in the sabbaths, in all solemnities of the house of Israel: he shall prepare the sin offering, and the meat offering, and the burnt offering, and the peace offerings, to make reconciliation for the house of Israel.

18 Thus saith the Lord GOD; In the first *month*, in the first *day* of the month, thou shalt take a young bullock without blemish, and Rcleanse the sanctuary: *Lev. 16:16*

19 And the priest shall take of the blood of the sin offering, and put *it* upon the posts of the house, and upon the four corners of the settle of the altar, and upon the posts of the gate of the inner court.

20 And so thou shalt do the seventh *day* of the month Rfor every one that Terreth, and for *him that is* Tsimple: so shall ye reconcile the house.   *Lev. 4:27 • sins • ignorant*

21 RIn the first *month*, in the fourteenth day of the month, ye shall have the passover, a feast of seven days; unleavened bread shall be eaten.   *Num. 9:2, 3; 28:16, 17*

22 And upon that day shall the prince prepare for himself and for all the people of the land a bullock *for* a sin offering.

23 And Rseven days of the feast he shall prepare a burnt offering to the LORD, seven bullocks and seven rams without blemish daily the seven days; and a kid of the goats daily *for* a sin offering.   *Num. 28:16-25*

24 And he shall prepare a meat offering of an e'-phah for a bullock, and an e'-phah for a ram, and an Thin of oil for an e'-phah. *1 gal.*

25 In the seventh *month*, in the fifteenth day of the month, shall he do the like in the Rfeast of the seven days, according to the sin offering, according to the burnt offering, and according to the meat offering, and according to the oil.   *Deut. 16:13*

CHAPTER 46

THUS saith the Lord GOD; The gate of the Rinner court that looketh toward the east

shall be shut the six working days; but on the sabbath it shall be opened, and in the day of the new moon it shall be opened.   8:16; 10:3

2 And the prince shall enter by the way of the porch of *that* gate without, and shall stand by the ᴿpost of the gate, and the priests shall prepare his burnt offering and his peace offerings, and he shall worship at the threshold of the gate: then he shall go forth; but the gate shall not be shut until the evening.   45:19

3 Likewise the people of the land shall worship at the door of this gate before the Lᴏʀᴅ in the sabbaths and in the new moons.

4 And the burnt offering that ᴿthe prince shall offer unto the Lᴏʀᴅ in the sabbath day *shall be* ᴿsix lambs without blemish, and a ram without blemish.   45:17 • Num. 28:9, 10

5 ᴿAnd the meat offering *shall be* an ᵀe′-phah for a ram, and the meat offering for the lambs as he shall be able to give, and an ᵀhin of oil to an e′-phah.   *vv.* 7, 11; 45:24 • .65 bu. • 1 gal.

6 And in the day of the new moon *it shall be* a young bullock without blemish, and six lambs, and a ram: they shall be without blemish.

7 And he shall prepare a meat offering, an ᵀe′-phah for a bullock, and an e′-phah for a ram, and for the lambs according as ᵀhis hand shall attain unto, and an ᵀhin of oil to an e′-phah.   .65 bu. • he is able • 1 gal.

8 ᴿAnd when the prince shall enter, he shall go in by the way of the porch of *that* gate, and he shall go forth by the way thereof.   v. 2; 44:3

9 But when the people of the land shall come before the Lᴏʀᴅ in the solemn feasts, he that entereth in by the way of the north gate to worship shall go out by the way of the south gate; and he that entereth by the way of the south gate shall go forth by the way of the north gate: he shall not return by the way of the gate whereby he came in, but shall go ᵀforth over against it.   out

10 And the prince in the ᴿmidst of them, when they go in, shall go in; and when they go forth, shall go forth.   2 Sam. 6:14, 15

11 And in the feasts and in the solemnities ᴿthe meat offering shall be an ᵀe′-phah to a bullock, and an e′-phah to a ram, and to the lambs as he is able to give, and an ᵀhin of oil to an e′-phah.   v. 5 • .65 bu. • 1 gal.

12 Now when the prince shall prepare a voluntary burnt offering or peace offerings voluntarily unto the Lᴏʀᴅ, *one* shall then open him the gate that ᵀlooketh toward the east, and he shall prepare his burnt offering and his peace offerings, as he did on the sabbath day: then he shall go forth; and after his going forth *one* shall shut the gate.   faces

13 ᴿThou shalt daily prepare a burnt offering unto the Lᴏʀᴅ *of* a lamb of the first year without blemish: thou shalt prepare it ᵀevery morning.   Num. 28:3–5 • morning by morning

14 And thou shalt prepare a meat offering for it every morning, the ᵀsixth part of an e′-phah, and the ᵀthird part of an hin of oil, to temper with the fine flour; a meat offering continually by a ᵀperpetual ordinance unto the Lᴏʀᴅ.   3.5 qt. • 42.7 oz. • continual

15 Thus shall they prepare the lamb, and the meat offering, and the oil, every morning *for* a ᴿcontinual burnt offering.   Ex. 29:42

16 Thus saith the Lord Gᴏᴅ; If the prince give a ᴿgift unto any of his sons, the inheritance thereof shall be his sons′; it *shall be* their possession by inheritance.   2 Chr. 21:3

17 But if he give a gift of his inheritance to one of his servants, then it shall be his to ᴿthe year of liberty; after it shall return to the prince: but his inheritance shall be his sons′ for them.   Lev. 25:10

18 Moreover the prince shall not take of the people′s inheritance by oppression, to thrust them out of their possession; *but* he shall give his sons inheritance out of his own possession: that my people be not scattered every man from his possession.

19 After he brought me through the entry, which *was* at the side of the gate, into the holy chambers of the priests, which looked toward the north: and, behold, there *was* a place on the two sides westward.

20 Then said he unto me, This *is* the place where the priests shall ᴿboil the trespass offering and the sin offering, where they shall bake the meat offering; that they bear *them* not out into the utter court, to sanctify the people.   2 Chr. 35:13

21 Then he brought me forth into the utter court, and caused me to pass by the four corners of the court; and, behold, in every corner of the court *there was* a court.

22 In the four corners of the court *there were* courts joined of ᵀforty *cubits* long and ᵀthirty broad: these four corners *were* of ᵀone measure.   70 ft. • 52.5 ft. • the same size

23 And *there was* a row *of building* round about in them, round about them four, and *it was* made with ᵀboiling places under the rows round about.   cooking

24 Then said he unto me, These *are* the places of them that ᵀboil, where ᴿthe ministers of the house shall ᴿboil the sacrifice of the people.   boiling-houses • 44:11 • v. 20

CHAPTER 47

River from the Temple

AFTERWARD he brought me again unto the ᴿdoor of the house; and, behold, ᴿwaters issued out from under the ᵀthreshold of the house eastward: for the forefront of the house *stood toward* the east, and the waters came down from under from the right side of the house, at the south *side* of the altar.   41:2 • [Rev. 22:1] • doorway

2 Then brought he me out of the way of the gate northward, and led me about the way without unto the utter gate by the way that looketh eastward; and, behold, there ran out waters on the right side.

3 And when the man that had the line in his hand went forth eastward, he measured a thousand cubits, and he brought me through the waters; the waters *were* to the ancles.

4 Again he measured a ᵀthousand, and brought me through the waters; the waters *were* to the knees. Again he measured a thousand, and brought me through; the waters *were* to the loins.   *.33 mi.*

5 Afterward he measured a thousand; *and it was* a river that I could not pass over: for the waters were risen, waters to swim in, a river that could not be ᵀpassed over.   *forded*

6 And he said unto me, Son of man, hast thou seen *this?* Then he brought me, and caused me to return to the brink of the river.

7 Now when I had returned, behold, at the bank of the river *were* very many ᴿtrees on the one side and on the other.   [Rev. 22:2]

8 Then said he unto me, These waters issue out toward the east country, and go down into the ᵀdesert, and go into ᴿthe sea: *which being* brought forth into the sea, the waters shall be healed.   *plain* • Deut. 3:17; 4:49

9 And it shall come to pass, *that* every thing that liveth, which moveth, whithersoever the rivers shall come, shall live: and there shall be a very great multitude of fish, because these waters shall come thither: for they shall be healed; and every thing shall live whither the river cometh.

10 And it shall come to pass, *that* the fishers shall stand upon it from En-ge'-di even unto En-eg'-la-im; they shall be a *place* to spread forth nets; their fish shall be according to their kinds, as the fish ᴿof the great sea, exceeding many.   Num. 34:3

11 But the ᵀmiry places thereof and the marishes thereof shall not be healed; they shall be given to ᴿsalt.   *swampy* • Deut. 29:23

12 And by the river upon the bank thereof, on this side and on that side, shall grow all trees for meat, whose leaf shall not fade, neither shall the fruit thereof be consumed: it shall bring forth new fruit according to his months, because their waters they issued out of the sanctuary: and the fruit thereof shall be for meat, and the leaf thereof for medicine.

Boundaries of the Land

13 Thus saith the Lord GOD; This *shall be* the border, whereby ye shall inherit the land according to the twelve tribes of Israel: Joseph *shall have two* portions.

14 And ye shall inherit it, one as well as another: *concerning* the which I lifted up

mine hand to give it unto your fathers: and this land shall fall unto you for inheritance.

15 And this *shall be* the border of the land toward the north side, from the great sea, the way of Heth'-lon, as men go to Ze'-dad;

16 Ha'-math, Be-ro'-thah, Sib-ra'-im, which *is* between the border of Damascus and the border of Ha'-math; Ha'-zar-hat'-ti-con, which *is* by the coast of Hau'-ran.

17 And the border from the sea shall be Ha'-zar-e'-nan, the border of Damascus, and the north northward, and the border of Ha'-math. And *this is* the north side.

18 And the east side ye shall measure ᵀfrom Hau'-ran, and from Damascus, and from Gil'-e-ad, and from the land of Israel *by* Jordan, from the border unto the east sea. And *this is* the east side.   *from between*

19 And the ᴿsouth side southward, from Ta'-mar *even* to the waters of strife *in* Ka'-desh, the river to the great sea. And *this is* the south side southward.   Num. 34:3-5

20 The west side also *shall be* the great sea from the border, till a man come over against Ha'-math. This *is* the west side.

21 So shall ye divide this land unto you according to the tribes of Israel.

22 And it shall come to pass, *that* ye shall divide it by lot for an inheritance unto you, and to the strangers that sojourn among you, which shall beget children among you: ᴿand they shall be unto you as born in the country among the children of Israel; they shall have inheritance with you among the tribes of Israel.   [Eph. 3:6]

23 And it shall come to pass, *that* in what tribe the stranger sojourneth, there shall ye give *him* his inheritance, saith the Lord GOD.

CHAPTER 48

Divisions of the Land

NOW ᴿthese *are* the names of the tribes. ᴿFrom the north end to the coast of the way of Heth'-lon, as one goeth to Ha'-math, Ha'-zar-e'-nan, the border of Damascus northward, to the coast of Ha'-math; for these are his sides east *and* west; a *portion for* ᴿDan.   Ex. 1:1 • 47:15 • Josh. 19:40-48

2 And by the border of Dan, from the east side unto the west side, a *portion for* Asher.

3 And by the border of Asher, from the east side even unto the west side, a *portion for* ᴿNaph'-ta-li.   Josh. 19:32-39

4 And by the border of Naph'-ta-li, from the east side unto the west side, a *portion for* ᴿMa-nas'-seh.   Josh. 13:29-31; 17:1-12

5 And by the border of Ma-nas'-seh, from the east side unto the west side, a *portion for* ᴿE'-phra-im.   Josh. 16:5-9; 17:8-10, 14-18

6 And by the border of E'-phra-im, from the east side even unto the west side, a *portion for* RReuben.   Josh. 13:15-21

7 And by the border of Reuben, from the east side unto the west side, a *portion for* RJudah.   Josh. 15:1-63; 19:9

8 And by the border of Judah, from the east side unto the west side, shall be the offering which ye shall offer of Tfive and twenty thousand *reeds in* breadth, and *in* length as one of the *other* parts, from the east side unto the west side: and the sanctuary shall be in the midst of it.   8.3 mi.

9 The oblation that ye shall offer unto the LORD *shall be* of five and twenty thousand in length, and of ten thousand in breadth.

10 And for them, *even* for the Rpriests, shall be *this* holy oblation; toward the north Tfive and twenty thousand *in length*, and toward the west Tten thousand in breadth, and toward the east ten thousand in breadth, and toward the south five and twenty thousand in length: and the sanctuary of the LORD shall be in the midst thereof.   45:4 · 8.3 mi. · 3.3 mi.

11 *It shall be* for the priests that are sanctified of the sons of Za'-dok; which have kept my Tcharge, which went not astray when the children of Israel went astray, as the Levites went astray.   ordinance

12 And *this* Toblation of the land that is offered shall be unto them a thing most holy by the border of the Levites.   offering

13 And over against the border of the priests the RLevites *shall have* Tfive and twenty thousand in length, and Tten thousand in breadth: all the length *shall be* five and twenty thousand, and the breadth ten thousand.   45:5 · 8.3 mi. · 3.3 mi.

14 And they shall not sell of it, neither exchange, nor alienate the firstfruits of the land: for *it is* holy unto the LORD.

15 And the Tfive thousand, that are left in the breadth over against the Tfive and twenty thousand, shall be a profane *place* for the city, for dwelling, and for suburbs: and the city shall be in the midst thereof. 1.6 mi. · 8.3 mi.

16 And these *shall be* the measures thereof; the north side Tfour thousand and five hundred, and the south side four thousand and five hundred, and on the east side four thousand and five hundred, and the west side four thousand and five hundred.   1.5 mi.

17 And the suburbs of the city shall be toward the north two hundred and fifty, and toward the south two hundred and fifty, and toward the east two hundred and fifty, and toward the west two hundred and fifty.

18 And the residue in length over against the Toblation of the holy *portion shall be* Tten thousand eastward, and ten thousand westward: and it shall be over against the oblation of the holy *portion;* and the increase thereof shall be for food unto them that serve the city.   offering · 3.3 mi.

19 And they that serve the city shall Tserve it out of all the tribes of Israel.   till

20 All the oblation *shall be* Tfive and twenty thousand by five and twenty thousand: ye shall offer the holy oblation foursquare, with the possession of the city. 8.3 mi.

21 And the residue *shall be* for the prince, on the one side and on the other of the holy oblation, and of the possession of the city, over against the five and twenty thousand of the oblation toward the east border, and westward over against the five and twenty thousand toward the west border, over against the portions for the prince: and it shall be the holy oblation; and the sanctuary of the house *shall be* in the midst thereof.

22 Moreover from the possession of the Levites, and from the possession of the city, *being* in the midst *of that* which is the prince's, between the border of Judah and the border of Benjamin, shall be for the prince.

23 As for the rest of the tribes, from the east side unto the west side, Benjamin *shall have* Ta portion.   one portion

24 And by the border of Benjamin, from the east side unto the west side, RSimeon *shall have* a portion.   Josh. 19:1-9

25 And by the border of Simeon, from the east side unto the west side, RIs'-sa-char a portion.   Josh. 19:17-23

26 And by the border of Is'-sa-char, from the east side unto the west side, RZeb'-u-lun a portion.   Josh. 19:10-16

27 And by the border of Zeb'-u-lun, from the east side unto the west side, RGad a portion.   Josh. 13:24-28

28 And by the border of Gad, at the south side southward, the border shall be even from Ta'-mar *unto* the waters of strife *in* Ka'-desh, *and* to the river toward the great sea.

29 RThis *is* the land which ye shall divide by lot unto the tribes of Israel for inheritance, and these *are* their portions, saith the Lord GOD.   47:14, 21, 22

Gates of the City

30 And these *are* the goings out of the city on the Rnorth side, Tfour thousand and five hundred measures.   vv. 32-34 · 1.5 mi.

31 And the gates of the city *shall be* after the names of the tribes of Israel: three gates northward; one gate of Reuben, one gate of Judah, one gate of Levi.

32 And at the east side Tfour thousand and five hundred: and three gates; and one gate of Joseph, one gate of Benjamin, one gate of Dan.   1.5 mi.

33 And at the south side four thousand and five hundred measures: and three gates; one gate of Simeon, one gate of Is'-sa-char, one gate of Zeb'-u-lun.

34 At the west side four thousand and five hundred, with their three gates; one gate of Gad, one gate of Asher, one gate of ᴿNaph'-ta-li.   Gen. 30:8

Name of the City

35 It was round about ᵀeighteen thousand measures: and the name of the city from that day shall be, The LORD is there.   6 mi.

The Jewish Calendar

The Jews used two kinds of calendars:

Civil Calendar—official calendar of kings, childbirth, and contracts.

Sacred Calendar—from which festivals were computed.

NAMES OF MONTHS	CORRESPONDS WITH	NO. OF DAYS	MONTH OF CIVIL YEAR	MONTH OF SACRED YEAR			
TISHRI	Sept.–Oct.	30 days	1st	7th	The Jewish day was from sunset to sunset, in 8 equal parts:		
HESHVAN	Oct.–Nov.	29 or 30	2nd	8th			
CHISLEV	Nov.–Dec.	29 or 30	3rd	9th			
TEBETH	Dec.–Jan.	29	4th	10th	FIRST WATCH	.....	SUNSET TO 9 P.M.
SHEBAT	Jan.–Feb.	30	5th	11th	SECOND WATCH	...	9 P.M. TO MIDNIGHT
ADAR	Feb.–Mar.	29 or 30	6th	12th	THIRD WATCH	.....	MIDNIGHT TO 3 A.M.
NISAN	Mar.–Apr.	30	7th	1st	FOURTH WATCH	...	3 A.M. TO SUNRISE
IYAR	Apr.–May	29	8th	2nd			
SIVAN	May–June	30	9th	3rd	FIRST WATCH	.....	SUNRISE TO 9 A.M.
TAMMUZ	June–July	29	10th	4th	SECOND WATCH	...	9 A.M. TO NOON
AB	July–Aug.	30	11th	5th	THIRD WATCH	.....	NOON TO 3 P.M.
*ELUL	Aug.–Sept.	29	12th	6th	FOURTH WATCH	...	3 P.M. TO SUNSET

*Hebrew months were alternately 30 and 29 days long. Their year, shorter than ours, had 354 days. Therefore, about every 3 years (7 times in 19 years) an extra 29-day-month, VEADAR, was added between ADAR and NISAN.

THE BOOK OF

DANIEL

📖 **THE BOOK OF DANIEL**
Daniel's life and ministry bridge the entire seventy-year period of Babylonian captivity. Deported to Babylon at the age of sixteen, and handpicked for government service, Daniel becomes God's prophetic mouthpiece to the gentile and Jewish world declaring God's present and eternal purpose. Nine of the twelve chapters in his book revolve around dreams, including God-given visions involving trees, animals, beasts, and images. In both his personal adventures and prophetic visions, Daniel shows God's guidance, intervention, and power in the affairs of men.

The name *Daniye'l* or *Dani'el* means "God Is My Judge," and the book is, of course, named after the author and principal character. The Greek form *Daniel* in the Septuagint is the basis for the Latin and English titles.

✍️ **THE AUTHOR OF DANIEL**
Daniel and his three friends were evidently born into noble Judean families and were "Children in whom *was* no blemish, but well favoured, and skilful in all wisdom, and cunning in knowledge, and understanding science" (1:4). He was given three years of training in the best of Babylon's schools (1:5). As part of the reidentification process, he was given a new name that honored one of the Babylonian deities: *Belteshazzar* meant "Bel Protect His Life" (see 1:7; 4:8; Jer. 51:44). Daniel's wisdom and divinely given interpretive abilities brought him into a position of prominence, especially in the courts of Nebuchadnezzar and Darius. He is one of the few well-known Bible characters about whom nothing negative is ever written. His life was characterized by faith, prayer, courage, consistency, and lack of compromise. This "greatly beloved" man (9:23; 10:11, 19) mentioned three times by his sixth-century B.C. contemporary Ezekiel as an example of righteousness.

Daniel claimed to write this book (12:4), and he used the autobiographical first person from 7:2 onward. The Jewish Talmud agrees with this testimony, and Christ attributed a quote from 9:27 to "Daniel the prophet" (Matt. 24:15).

⏳ **THE TIME OF DANIEL**
Babylon rebelled against the Assyrian Empire in 626 B.C. and overthrew the Assyrian capital of Nineveh in 612 B.C. Babylon became the master of the Middle East when it defeated the Egyptian armies in 605 B.C. Daniel was among those taken captive to Babylon that year when Nebuchadnezzar subdued Jerusalem. He ministered for the full duration of the

Babylonian captivity as a prophet and a government official and continued on after Babylon was overcome by the Medes and Persians in 539 B.C. His prophetic ministry was directed to the gentile courts of Babylon (Nebuchadnezzar and Belshazzar) and Persia (Darius and Cyrus), as well as to his Jewish countrymen. Zerubbabel led a return of the Jews to Jerusalem in the first year of Cyrus, and Daniel lived and ministered at least until the third year of Cyrus (536 B.C.; 10:1). Daniel's book was no doubt written by Cyrus's ninth year (c. 530 B.C.). As he predicted, the Persian Empire continued until Alexander the Great (11:2, 3) who extended the boundaries of the Greek Empire as far east as India. The Romans later displaced the Greeks as rulers of the Middle East.

For various reasons, many critics have argued that Daniel is a fraudulent book that was written in the time of the Maccabees in the second century B.C., not the sixth century B.C. as it claims. But their arguments are not compelling:

(1) *The prophetic argument* holds that Daniel could not have made such accurate predictions; it must be a "prophecy after the events." Daniel 11 alone contains over one hundred specific prophecies of historical events that literally came true. The author, the critics say, must have lived at the time of Antiochus Epiphanes (175–163 B.C.) and probably wrote this to strengthen the faith of the Jews. But this argument was developed out of a theological bias that assumes true prophecy cannot take place. It also implies that the work was intentionally deceptive.

(2) *The linguistic argument* claims that the book uses a late Aramaic in 2—7 and that the Persian and Greek words also point to a late date. But recent discoveries show that Daniel's Aramaic is actually a form of the early Imperial Aramaic. Daniel's use of some Persian words is no argument for a late date since he continued living in the Persian period under Cyrus. The only Greek words are names of musical instruments in chapter 3, and this comes as no surprise since there were Greek mercenaries in the Assyrian and Babylonian armies. Far more Greek words would be expected if the book were written in the second century B.C.

(3) *The historical argument* asserts that Daniel's historical blunders argue for a late date. But recent evidence has demonstrated the historical accuracy of Daniel. Inscriptions found at Haran show that Belshazzar reigned in Babylon while his father Nabonidus was fighting the invading Persians. And Darius the Mede (5:31; 6:1) has been identified as Gubaru, a governor appointed by Cyrus.

✝ THE CHRIST OF DANIEL

Christ is the Great Stone who will crush the kingdoms of this world (2:34, 35, 44), the Son of Man who is given dominion by the Ancient of Days (7:13, 14), and the coming Messiah who will be cut off (9:25, 26). It is likely that Daniel's vision in 10:5–9 was an appearance of Christ (cf. Rev. 1:12–16).

The vision of the sixty-nine weeks in 9:25, 26 pinpoints the coming of the Messiah. The decree of 9:25 took place on March 4, 444 B.C. (Neh. 2:1–8). The sixty-nine weeks of seven years equals 483 years, or 173,880 days (using 360-day prophetic years). This leads to March 29, A.D. 33, the date of the Triumphal Entry. This is checked by noting that 444 B.C. to A.D. 33 is 476 years, and 476 times 365.24219 days per year equals 173,855 days. Adding twenty-five for the difference between March 4 and March 29 gives 173,880 days.

🗝 KEYS TO DANIEL

Key Word: God's Program for Israel— Daniel was written to encourage the exiled Jews by revealing God's sovereign program for Israel during and after the period of gentile domination. The "Times of the Gentiles" began with the Babylonian captivity, and Israel would suffer under gentile powers for many years. But this period is not permanent, and a time will come when God will establish the messianic kingdom which will last forever. Daniel repeatedly emphasizes the sovereignty and power of God over human affairs. "The most High ruleth in the kingdom of men, and giveth it to whomsoever he will" (4:25). The God who directs the forces of history has not deserted His people. They must continue to trust in Him, because His promises of preservation and ultimate restoration are as sure as the coming of the Messiah.

Key Verses: Daniel 2:20–22 and Daniel 2:44— "Daniel answered and said, Blessed be the name of God for ever and ever: for wisdom and might are his: And he changeth the times and the seasons: he removeth kings, and setteth up kings: he giveth wisdom unto the wise, and knowledge to them that know understanding: He revealeth the deep and secret things: he knoweth what *is* in the darkness, and the light dwelleth with him" (2:20–22).

"And in the days of these kings shall the God of heaven set up a kingdom, which shall never be destroyed: and the kingdom shall not be left to other people, *but* it shall break in pieces and consume all these kingdoms, and it shall stand for ever" (2:44).

Key Chapter: Daniel 9—Daniel's prophecy of the seventy weeks (9:24–27) provides the chronological frame for messianic prediction from the time of Daniel to the establishment of the kingdom on earth. It is clear that the first sixty-nine weeks were fulfilled at Christ's first coming. Some scholars affirm that the last week has not yet been fulfilled because Christ relates its main events to His second coming (Matt. 24:6, 15). Others perceive these words of Christ as applying to the Roman desecration of the temple in A.D. 70.

⍾ SURVEY OF DANIEL

Daniel, the "Apocalypse of the Old Testament," presents a surprisingly detailed and comprehensive sweep of prophetic history. After an introductory chapter in Hebrew, Daniel switches to Aramaic in chapters 2—7 to describe the future course of the gentile world powers. Then in 8—12, Daniel reverts to his native language to survey the future of the Jewish nation under gentile dominion. The theme of God's sovereign control in the affairs of world history clearly emerges and provides comfort to the future church, as well as to the Jews whose nation was destroyed by the Babylonians. The Babylonians, Persians, Greeks, and Romans will

FOCUS	HISTORY OF DANIEL	PROPHETIC PLAN FOR THE GENTILES				PROPHETIC PLAN OF ISRAEL		
REFERENCE	1:1————2:1——————————5:1————————6:1————7:1————8:1————9:1————10:1-12:13							
DIVISION	PERSONAL LIFE OF DANIEL	VISIONS OF NEBUCHADNEZZAR	VISION OF BELSHAZZAR	DECREE OF DARIUS	FOUR BEASTS	VISION OF RAM AND HE-GOAT	VISION OF SEVENTY WEEKS	VISION OF ISRAEL'S FUTURE
TOPIC	DANIEL'S BACKGROUND	DANIEL INTERPRETS OTHERS' DREAMS				ANGEL INTERPRETS DANIEL'S DREAMS		
	HEBREW	ARAMAIC				HEBREW		
LOCATION	BABYLON OR PERSIA							
TIME	c. 605-536 B.C.							

come and go, but God will establish His kingdom through His redeemed people forever. Daniel's three divisions are: the personal history of Daniel (1), the prophetic plan for the Gentiles (2—7), and the prophetic plan for Israel (8—12).

The Personal History of Daniel (1): This chapter introduces the book by giving the background and preparation of the prophet. Daniel is deported along with other promising youths and placed in an intensive training program in Nebuchadnezzar's court. Their names and diets are changed so that they will lose their Jewish identification, but Daniel's resolve to remain faithful to the Lord is rewarded. He and his friends are granted wisdom and knowledge.

The Prophetic Plan for the Gentiles (2—7): Only Daniel can relate and interpret Nebuchadnezzar's disturbing dream of the great statue (2). God empowers Daniel to foretell the way in which He will sovereignly raise and depose four gentile empires. The Messiah's kingdom will end the times of the Gentiles. Because of his position revealed in the dream, Nebuchadnezzar erects a golden image and demands that all bow to it (3). The persecution and preservation of Daniel's friends in the fiery furnace again illustrate the power of God. After Nebuchadnezzar refuses to respond to the warning of his vision of the tree (4), he is humbled until he acknowledges the supremacy of God and the foolishness of his

pride. The feast of Belshazzar marks the end of the Babylonian kingdom (5). Belshazzar is judged because of his arrogant defiance of God. In the reign of Darius, a plot against Daniel backfires when he is divinely delivered in the den of lions (6). Daniel's courageous faith is rewarded, and Darius learns a lesson about the might of the God of Israel. The vision of the four beasts (7) supplements the four-part statue vision of chapter 2 in its portrayal of the Babylonian, Persian, Greek, and Roman empires. But once again, "the saints of the most High shall take the kingdom, and possess the kingdom for ever" (7:18).

The Prophetic Plan for Israel (8—12): The focus in chapter 8 narrows to a vision of the ram and goat that shows Israel under the Medo-Persian and Grecian empires. Alexander the Great is the great horn of 8:21 and Antiochus Epiphanes is the little horn of 8:9. After Daniel's prayer of confession for his people, he is privileged to receive the revelation of the seventy weeks, including the Messiah's atoning death (9). This gives the chronology of God's perfect plan for the redemption and deliverance of His people. Following is a great vision that gives amazing details of Israel's future history (10 and 11). Chapter 11 chronicles the coming kings of Persia and Greece, the wars between the Ptolemies of Egypt and the Seleucids of Syria, and the persecution led by Antiochus. God's people will be saved out of tribulation and resurrected (12).

OUTLINE OF DANIEL

Part One: The Personal History of Daniel (1:1-21)

Part Two: The Prophetic Plan for the Gentiles (2:1—7:28)

Part Three: The Prophetic Plan for Israel (8:1—12:13)

CHAPTER 1

The Deportation of Daniel to Babylon

IN the third year of the reign of Je-hoi'-a-kim king of Judah ᴿcame Neb-u-chad-nez'-zar king of Babylon unto Jerusalem, and besieged it.   2 Kin. 24:1; 2 Chr. 36:6

2 And the Lord gave Je-hoi'-a-kim king of Judah into his hand, with ᴿpart of the vessels of the house of God: which he carried into the land of Shi'-nar to the house of his god; and he brought the vessels into the treasure house of his god.   Jer. 27:18-20

3 And the king spake unto Ash'-pe-naz the master of his eunuchs, that he should bring certain of the children of Israel,ᴿ and of the king's seed, and of the princes;   Is. 39:5-7

4 Children in whom was no blemish, but ᵀwell favoured, and skilful in all wisdom, and cunning in knowledge, and understanding science, and such as had ability in them to ᵀstand in the king's palace, and whom they might teach the learning and the tongue of the Chal-de'-ans.   gifted · serve

5 And the king appointed them a daily provision of the king's meat, and of the wine which he drank: so nourishing them three years, that at the end thereof they might ᴿstandᵀ before the king.   v. 19 · serve

6 Now among these were of the children of Judah, ᵀDaniel, Han-a-ni'-ah, Mish'-a-el, and Az-a-ri'-ah: God is my Judge

7 Unto whom the prince of the eunuchs gave names: for he gave unto Daniel the name of Bel-te-shaz'-zar; and to Han-a-ni'-ah, of Sha'-drach; and to Mish'-a-el, of Me'-shach; and to Az-a-ri'-ah, of A-bed'-ne-go.

The Faithfulness of Daniel in Babylon

8 But Daniel purposed in his heart that he would not defile himself with the portion of the king's meat, nor with the wine which he drank: therefore he requested of the prince of the eunuchs that he might not defile himself.

9 Now ᴿGod had brought Daniel into favour and tender love with the prince of the eunuchs.   Gen. 39:21; Ps. 106:46; [Prov. 16:7]

10 And the prince of the eunuchs said unto Daniel, I fear my lord the king, who hath appointed your ᵀmeat and your drink: for why should he see your faces ᵀworse liking than the children which are of your ᵀsort? then shall ye make me endanger my head to the king.   food · less attractive · age

11 Then said Daniel to Mel'-zar, whom the prince of the eunuchs had set over Daniel, Han-a-ni'-ah, Mish'-a-el, and Az-a-ri'-ah,

12 ᵀProve thy servants, I beseech thee, ten days; and let them give us ᵀpulse to eat, and water to drink.   test · beans

13 Then let our countenances be looked upon before thee, and the countenance of the children that eat of the portion of the king's

Tmeat: and as thou seest, deal with thy servants.   *food*

14 So he consented to them in this matter, and Tproved them ten days.   *tested*

15 And at the end of ten days their countenances appeared fairer and Tfatter in flesh than all the children which did eat the portion of the king's meat.   *better looking*

16 Thus Mel'-zar took away the portion of their meat, and the wine that they should drink; and gave them Tpulse.   *beans*

The Reputation of Daniel in Babylon

17 As for these four children, God gave them Rknowledge and skill in all learning and wisdom: and Daniel had understanding in all visions and dreams.   Acts 7:22

18 Now at the end of the days that the king had said he should bring them in, then the prince of the eunuchs brought them in before Neb-u-chad-nez'-zar.

19 And the king communed with them; and among them all was found none like Daniel, Han-a-ni'-ah, Mish'-a-el, and Az-a-ri'-ah: therefore stood they before the king.

20 And in all matters of wisdom *and* understanding, that the king enquired of them, he found them ten times better than all the magicians *and* Tastrologers that *were* in all his realm.   *enchanters*

21 RAnd Daniel continued *even* unto the first year of king Cyrus.   6:28; 10:1

CHAPTER 2

Nebuchadnezzar Conceals His Dream

AND in the second year of the reign of Neb-u-chad-nez'-zar Neb-u-chad-nez'-zar dreamed dreams, wherewith his spirit was troubled, and his sleep brake from him.

2 RThen the king commanded to call the magicians, and the astrologers, and the sorcerers, and the Chal-de'-ans, for to shew the king his dreams. So they came and stood before the king.   5:7; Ex. 7:11; Is. 47:12, 13

3 And the king said unto them, I have dreamed a dream, and my spirit was troubled to Tknow the dream.   *understand*

4 Then spake the Chal-de'-ans to the king in Syr'-i-ack, RO king, live for ever: tell thy servants the dream, and we will shew the interpretation.   3:9; 5:10; 6:6, 21

5 The king answered and said to the Chal-de'-ans, TThe thing is gone from me: if ye will not make known unto me the dream, with the interpretation thereof, ye shall be cut in pieces, and your houses shall be made a dunghill.   *I have forgotten it*

6 RBut if ye Tshew the dream, and the interpretation thereof, ye shall receive of me Rgifts and rewards and great honour: therefore shew me the dream, and the interpretation thereof.   5:16 • *tell* • 5:7

7 They answered again and said, Let the king tell his servants the dream, and we will shew the interpretation of it.

8 The king answered and said, I know of certainty that ye would gain the time, because ye see the thing is gone from me.

9 But if ye will not make known unto me the dream, *there is but* Rone decree for you: for ye have prepared lying and corrupt words to speak before me, till the time be changed: therefore tell me the dream, and I shall know that ye can shew me the interpretation thereof.   Esth. 4:11

10 The Chal-de'-ans answered before the king, and said, There is not a man upon the earth that can Tshew the king's matter: therefore *there is* no king, lord, nor ruler, *that* asked such things at any magician, or astrologer, or Chal-de'-an.   *reveal*

11 And *it is* a rare thing that the king requireth, and there is none other that can shew it before the king, except the gods, whose dwelling is not with flesh.

12 For this cause the king was Rangry and very furious, and commanded to destroy all the wise *men* of Babylon.   3:13; Ps. 76:10

13 And the decree went forth that the wise *men* should be slain; Rand they sought Daniel and his fellows to be slain.   1:19, 20

God Reveals the Dream

14 Then Daniel answered with counsel and wisdom to A'-ri-och the Tcaptain of the king's guard, which was gone forth to slay the wise *men* of Babylon: *chief marshall*

15 He answered and said to A'-ri-och the king's captain, Why *is* the decree *so* Thasty from the king? Then A'-ri-och Tmade the thing known to Daniel.   *urgent • explained*

16 Then Daniel went in, and desired of the king that he would give him time, and that he would shew the king the interpretation.

17 Then Daniel went to his house, and made the thing known to Han-a-ni'-ah, Mish'-a-el, and Az-a-ri'-ah, his companions:

18 That they would desire mercies of the God of heaven concerning this secret; that Daniel and his fellows should not perish with the rest of the wise *men* of Babylon.

19 Then was the secret revealed unto Daniel Rin a night vision. Then Daniel blessed the God of heaven.   Num. 12:6; Job 33:15

20 Daniel answered and said, Blessed be the name of God for ever and ever: Rfor wisdom and might are his: [Jer. 32:19]

21 And he changeth Rthe times and the seasons: Rhe removeth kings, and setteth up kings: Rhe giveth Rwisdom unto the wise, and knowledge to them that know understanding: Esth. 1:13 • [Ps. 75:6, 7] • [Jer. 27:5] • [James 1:5]

22 RHe revealeth the deep and secret things: he knoweth what *is* in the darkness, and the light dwelleth with him.   Job 12:22

23 I thank thee, and praise thee, RO thou God of my fathers, who hast given me wisdom and might, and hast made known unto me now what we desired of thee: Rfor thou hast now made known unto us the king's matter.   Gen. 31:42 • Ps. 21:2, 4

Daniel Interprets the Dream

24 Therefore Daniel went in unto A'-ri-och, whom the king had ordained to destroy the wise men of Babylon: he went and said thus unto him; Destroy not the wise men of Babylon: bring me in before the king, and I will shew unto the king the interpretation.

25 Then A'-ri-och Rbrought in Daniel before the king in haste, and said thus unto him, I have found a man of the captives of Judah, that will Tmake known unto the king the interpretation.   Gen. 41:14 • reveal

26 The king answered and said to Daniel, whose name was RBel-te-shaz'-zar, Art thou able to make known unto me the dream which I have seen, and the interpretation thereof?   4:8; 5:12

27 Daniel answered in the presence of the king, and said, The secret which the king hath demanded cannot the Rwise men, the astrologers, the magicians, the soothsayers, Tshew unto the king;   5:7, 8 • explain

28 But there is a God in heaven that revealeth secrets, and maketh known to the king Neb-u-chad-nez'-zar what shall be in the Rlatter days. Thy dream, and the visions of thy head upon thy bed, are these;   Mic. 4:1

29 As for thee, O king, thy thoughts came into thy mind upon thy bed, what should come to pass hereafter: Rand he that reveal-eth secrets maketh known to thee what shall come to pass.   [vv. 22, 28]

30 RBut as for me, this secret is not revealed to me for any wisdom that I have more than any living, but for their sakes that shall make known the interpretation to the king, and that thou mightest Tknow the thoughts of thy heart.   Acts 3:12 • understand

31 Thou, O king, sawest, and behold a great image. This great image, whose brightness was excellent, stood before thee; and the form thereof was Tterrible.   magnificent

32 RThis image's head was of fine gold, his breast and his arms of silver, his belly and his Tthighs of brass,   vv. 38, 45 • loins

33 His legs of iron, his feet part of iron and part of clay.

34 Thou Tsawest till that a stone was cut out without hands, which smote the image upon his feet that were of iron and clay, and brake them to pieces.   was seeing

35 Then was the iron, the clay, the brass, the silver, and the gold, broken to pieces together, and became like the chaff of the summer threshingfloors; and the wind carried them away, that no place was found for

them: and the stone that smote the image Rbecame a great mountain, Rand filled the whole earth.   [Is. 2:2, 3] • Ps. 80:9

36 This is the dream; and we will tell the interpretation thereof before the king.

37 RThou, O king, art a king of kings: for the God of heaven hath given thee a king-dom, power, and strength, and glory.   Is. 47:5

38 RAnd wheresoever the children of men dwell, the beasts of the field and the fowls of the heaven hath he given into thine hand, and hath made thee ruler over them all. Thou art this head of gold.   4:21, 22

39 And after thee shall arise Ranother kingdom Rinferior to thee, and another third kingdom of brass, which shall bear rule over all the earth.   5:28, 31 • v. 32

40 And Rthe fourth kingdom shall be strong as iron: forasmuch as iron breaketh in pieces and subdueth all things: and as iron that breaketh all these, shall it break in pieces and bruise.   7:7, 23

41 And whereas thou sawest the feet and toes, part of potters' clay, and part of iron, the kingdom shall be divided; but there shall be in it of the strength of the iron, forasmuch as thou sawest the iron mixed with Tmiry clay.   common

42 And as the toes of the feet were part of iron, and part of clay, so the kingdom shall be partly strong, and partly broken.

43 And whereas thou sawest iron mixed with miry clay, they shall mingle themselves with the seed of men: but they shall not Tcleave one to another, even as iron is not mixed with clay.   be united

44 And in the days of these kings shall the God of heaven set up a Rkingdom, which shall never be destroyed: and the kingdom shall not be left to other people, but it shall break in pieces and consume all these kingdoms, and it shall stand for ever.   Is. 9:7 ✶

45 Forasmuch as thou sawest that the stone was cut out of the mountain without hands, and that it brake in pieces the iron, the brass, the clay, the silver, and the gold; the great God hath made known to the king what shall come to pass Thereafter: and the dream is Tcertain, and the interpretation thereof sure.   in the future • genuine

Nebuchadnezzar Promotes Daniel

46 Then the king Neb-u-chad-nez'-zar fell upon his face, and worshipped Daniel, and commanded that they should offer an oblation and sweet odours unto him.

47 The king answered unto Daniel, and said, Of a truth it is, Rthat your God is a RGod of gods, and a Lord of kings, and a revealer of secrets, seeing thou couldst reveal this secret.   [4:25] • [Deut. 10:17; Ps. 136:2]

48 Then the king made Daniel a great man, and gave him many great gifts, and made him

ruler over the whole province of Babylon, and [R]chief of the governors over all the wise *men* of Babylon.   4:9; 5:11

49 Then Daniel requested of the king, and he set Sha'-drach, Me'-shach, and A-bed'-ne-go, over the affairs of the province of Babylon: but Daniel *sat* in the gate of the king.

CHAPTER 3

Nebuchadnezzar's Image Is Erected

NEB-U-CHAD-NEZ'-ZAR the king made an image of gold, whose height *was* [T]threescore cubits, *and* the breadth thereof [T]six cubits: he set it up in the plain of Du'-ra, in the province of Babylon.   90 ft. • 9 ft.

2 Then Neb-u-chad-nez'-zar the king sent to gather together the princes, the [T]gover-nors, and the captains, the judges, the treasurers, the counsellors, the sheriffs, and all the rulers of the provinces, to come to the dedication of the image which Neb-u-chad-nez'-zar the king had set up.   *deputies*

3 Then the princes, the governors, and captains, the judges, the treasurers, and all the rulers of the provinces, were gathered together unto the dedication of the image that Neb-u-chad-nez'-zar the king had set up; and they stood before the image that Neb-u-chad-nez'-zar had set up.

4 Then [R]an herald cried [T]aloud, To you it is commanded, [R]O people, nations, and lan-guages,   Is. 58:1 • *with might* • 4:1; 6:25

5 *That* at what time ye hear the sound of the cornet, flute, harp, sackbut, psaltery, dulcimer, and all kinds of musick, ye fall down and worship the golden image that Neb-u-chad-nez'-zar the king hath set up:

6 And whoso falleth not down and wor-shippeth shall the same hour be cast into the midst of a [R]burning fiery furnace.   Rev. 9:2

7 Therefore at that time, when all the people heard the sound of the cornet, flute, harp, sackbut, psaltery, and all kinds of musick, all the people, the nations, and the languages, fell down *and* worshipped the golden image that Neb-u-chad-nez'-zar the king had set up.

Daniel's Friends Refuse to Worship

8 Wherefore at that time certain Chal-de'-ans came near, and accused the Jews.

9 They spake and said to the king Neb-u-chad-nez'-zar, [R]O king, live for ever.   2:4

10 Thou, O king, hast made a decree, that every man that shall hear the sound of the cornet, flute, harp, sackbut, psaltery, and dulcimer, and all kinds of musick, shall fall down and worship the golden image:

11 And whoso falleth not down and worshippeth, *that* he should be cast into the midst of a burning fiery furnace.

12 [R]There are certain Jews whom thou hast set over the affairs of the province of Babylon, Sha'-drach, Me'-shach, and A-bed'-ne-go; these men, O king, have not regarded thee: they serve not thy gods, nor worship the golden image which thou hast set up.   2:49

Daniel's Friends Trust God

13 Then Neb-u-chad-nez'-zar in *his* rage and fury commanded to bring Sha'-drach, Me'-shach, and A-bed'-ne-go. Then they brought these men before the king.

14 Neb-u-chad-nez'-zar spake and said unto them, *Is it* true, O Sha'-drach, Me'-shach, and A-bed'-ne-go, [R]do not ye serve my gods, nor worship the golden image which I have set up?   Is. 46:1; Jer. 50:2

15 Now if ye be ready that at what time ye hear the sound of the cornet, flute, harp, sackbut, psaltery, and dulcimer, and all kinds of musick, ye fall down and worship the image which I have made; *well:* but if ye worship not, ye shall be cast the same hour into the midst of a burning fiery furnace; [R]and who *is* that God that shall deliver you out of my hands?   Ex. 5:2; 2 Kin. 18:35

16 Sha'-drach, Me'-shach, and A-bed'-ne-go, answered and said to the king, O Neb-u-chad-nez'-zar, [T]we *are* not careful to answer thee in this matter.   *we have no need*

17 If it [T]be *so,* our [R]God whom we serve is able to deliver us from the burning fiery furnace, and he will deliver *us* out of thine hand, O king.   *be his will* • Job 5:19; [Ps. 27:1, 2]

18 [R]But if not, be it known unto thee, O king, that we will not serve thy gods, nor worship the golden image which thou hast set up.   Job 13:15; Acts 4:19

Daniel's Friends Are Protected in the Furnace

19 Then was Neb-u-chad-nez'-zar full of [R]fury, and [T]the form of his visage was changed against Sha'-drach, Me'-shach, and A-bed'-ne-go: *therefore* he spake, and commanded that they should heat the furnace one seven times more than it was [T]wont to be heated.   *v. 13 • his attitude • usually*

20 And he commanded the most mighty men that *were* in his army to bind Sha'-drach, Me'-shach, and A-bed'-ne-go, *and* to cast *them* into the burning fiery furnace.

21 Then these men were bound in their coats, their [T]hosen, and their hats, and their *other* garments, and were cast into the midst of the burning fiery furnace.   *socks*

22 Therefore because the king's command-ment was [R]urgent, and the furnace exceeding hot, the flame of the fire slew those men that took up Sha'-drach, Me'-shach, and A-bed'-ne-go.   2:15; Ex. 12:33

23 And these three men, Sha'-drach, Me'-shach, and A-bed'-ne-go, fell down bound into the midst of the burning fiery furnace.

24 Then Neb-u-chad-nez'-zar the king was ^Rastonied, and rose up in haste, *and* spake, and said unto his ^Tcounsellors, Did not we cast three men bound into the midst of the fire? They answered and said unto the king, True, O king.   Matt. 13:54 • *nobles*

25 He answered and said, Lo, I see four men loose, walking in the midst of the fire, and they have no hurt; and the form of the fourth is like ^Rthe Son of God.   [Ps. 34:7]

Daniel's Friends Are Promoted

26 Then Neb-u-chad-nez'-zar came near to the mouth of the burning fiery furnace, *and* spake, and said, Sha'-drach, Me'-shach, and A-bed'-ne-go, ye servants of the most high God, come forth, and come *hither.* Then Sha'-drach, Me'-shach, and A-bed'-ne-go, came forth of the midst of the fire.

27 And the princes, governors, and captains, and the king's counsellors, being gathered together, saw these men, upon whose bodies the ^Rfire had no power, nor was an hair of their head singed, neither were their ^Rcoats changed, nor the smell of fire had passed on them.   [Is. 43:2]; Heb. 11:34 • *v.* 21

28 *Then* Neb-u-chad-nez'-zar spake, and said, Blessed *be* the God of Sha'-drach, Me'-shach, and A-bed'-ne-go, who hath sent his angel, and delivered his servants that ^Rtrusted in him, and have ^Tchanged the king's word, and yielded their bodies, that they might not serve nor worship any god, except their own God.   [Jer. 17:7] • *disobeyed*

29 Therefore I make a decree, That every people, nation, and language, which speak any thing ^Tamiss against the God of Sha'-drach, Me'-shach, and A-bed'-ne-go, shall be cut in pieces, and their houses shall be made a ^Tdunghill: because there is no other God that can deliver after this sort.   *contrary • ruin*

30 Then the king ^Rpromoted^T Sha'-drach, Me'-shach, and A-bed'-ne-go, in the province of Babylon.   *v.* 12; 2:49 • *made to prosper*

CHAPTER 4

Nebuchadnezzar's Proclamation

NEB-U-CHAD-NEZ'-ZAR the king, ^Runto all people, nations, and languages, that dwell in all the earth; ^RPeace be multiplied unto you.   3:4; 6:25 • Ezra 4:17

2 I thought it good to shew the signs and wonders ^Rthat the high God hath wrought toward me.   [*vv.* 17, 24, 25, 32, 34]; 3:26

3 ^RHow great *are* his signs! and how mighty *are* his wonders! his kingdom *is* ^Ran everlasting kingdom, and his dominion *is* from generation to generation.   6:27 • [*v.* 34]

Nebuchadnezzar's Vision

4 I Neb-u-chad-nez'-zar was at rest in mine house, and flourishing in my palace:

5 I saw a dream which made me afraid, and the thoughts upon my bed and the visions of my head ^Rtroubled me.   2:1

6 Therefore made I a decree to ^Rbring in all the wise *men* of Babylon before me, that they might ^Tmake known unto me the interpretation of the dream.   2:2 • *reveal*

7 ^RThen came in the magicians, the ^Tastrologers, the Chal-de'-ans, and the soothsayers: and I told the dream before them; but they did not make known unto me the interpretation thereof.   2:2, 10, 27 • *enchanters*

8 But at the last Daniel came in before me, ^Rwhose name *was* Bel-te-shaz'-zar, according to the name of my god, and in whom *is* the spirit of the holy gods: and before him I told the dream, *saying,*   1:7

9 O Bel-te-shaz'-zar, master of the magicians, because I know that the spirit of the holy gods *is* in thee, and no secret troubleth thee, tell me the visions of my dream that I have seen, and the interpretation thereof.

10 Thus *were* the visions of mine head in my bed; ^TI saw, and behold ^Ra tree in the midst of the earth, and the height thereof *was* great.   *I was having a vision* • Ezek. 31:14

11 The tree grew, and was strong, and the height thereof reached unto heaven, and the sight thereof to the end of all the earth:

12 The leaves thereof *were* fair, and the fruit thereof much, and in it *was* meat for all: the beasts of the field had shadow under it, and the fowls of the heaven dwelt in the boughs thereof, and all flesh was fed of it.

13 I saw in the visions of my head upon my bed, and, behold, ^Ra watcher and an holy one came down from heaven;   [*vv.* 17], 23

14 He cried aloud, and said thus, ^RHew down the tree, and cut off his branches, shake off his leaves, and scatter his fruit: let the beasts get away from under it, and the fowls from his branches: Ezek. 31:10-14

15 Nevertheless ^Rleave the stump of his roots in the earth, even with a band of iron and brass, in the tender grass of the field; and let it be wet with the dew of heaven, and *let* his portion *be* with the beasts in the grass of the earth: Job 14:7-9

16 Let his heart be changed from man's, and let a beast's heart be given unto him; and let seven ^Ttimes pass over him.   *years*

17 This matter *is* by the decree of the watchers, and the demand by the word of the holy ones: to the intent ^Rthat the living may know ^Rthat the most High ruleth in the kingdom of men, and giveth it to whomsoever he will, and setteth up over it the basest of men.   Ps. 9:16 • [*vv.* 25, 32]

18 This dream I king Neb-u-chad-nez'-zar have seen. Now thou, O Bel-te-shaz'-zar,

declare the interpretation thereof, forasmuch as all the wise *men* of my kingdom are not able to ᵀmake known unto me the interpretation: but thou *art* able; ᴿfor the spirit of the holy gods *is* in thee. *reveal • v. 8*

Daniel's Interpretation of the Vision

19 Then Daniel, whose name *was* Bel-te-shaz'-zar, was astonied for one hour, and his thoughts troubled him. The king spake, and said, Bel-te-shaz'-zar, let not the dream, or the interpretation thereof, trouble thee. Bel-te-shaz'-zar answered and said, My lord, the dream *be* to them that hate thee, and the interpretation thereof to thine enemies.

20 ᴿThe tree that thou sawest, which grew, and was strong, whose height reached unto the heaven, and the sight thereof to all the earth; *vv. 10–12*

21 Whose leaves *were* fair, and the fruit thereof much, and in it *was* meat for all; under which the beasts of the field dwelt, and upon whose branches the fowls of the heaven had their habitation:

22 It *is* thou, O king, that art grown and become strong: for thy greatness is grown, and reacheth unto heaven, ᴿand thy dominion to the end of the earth. *Jer. 27:6–8*

23 ᴿAnd whereas the king saw a watcher and an holy one coming down from heaven, and saying, Hew the tree down, and destroy it; yet leave the stump of the roots thereof in the earth, even with a band of iron and brass, in the tender grass of the field; and let it be wet with the dew of heaven, ᴿand *let* his portion *be* with the beasts of the field, till seven ᵀtimes pass over him; *v. 13 • 5:21 • years*

24 This *is* the interpretation, O king, and this *is* the decree of the most High, which is ᴿcome upon my lord the king: *Job 40:11, 12*

25 That ᴿthey shall drive thee from men, and thy dwelling shall be with the beasts of the field, and they shall make thee to eat grass as oxen, and they shall wet thee with the dew of heaven, and seven times shall pass over thee, till thou know that the most High ruleth in the kingdom of men, and giveth it to whomsoever he will. *vv. 28, 33*

26 And whereas they commanded to leave the stump of the tree roots; thy kingdom shall be ᵀsure unto thee, after that thou shalt have known that the heavens do rule. *secured*

27 Wherefore, O king, let my counsel be acceptable unto thee, and break off thy sins by righteousness, and thine iniquities by ᴿshewing mercy to the poor; if it may be a lengthening of thy tranquillity. *[Ps. 41:1]*

Nebuchadnezzar's Humiliation

28 All this ᴿcame upon the king Neb-u-chad-nez'-zar. *Zech. 1:6*

29 At the end of ᴿtwelve months he walked in the palace of the kingdom of Babylon. *[2 Pet. 3:9]*

30 The king spake, and said, Is not this great Babylon, that I have built for the house of the kingdom by the might of my power, and for the honour of my majesty?

31 While the word *was* in the king's mouth, there fell a voice from heaven, *saying*, O king Neb-u-chad-nez'-zar, to thee it is spoken; The kingdom is departed from thee.

32 And they shall drive thee from men, and thy dwelling *shall be* with the beasts of the field: they shall make thee to eat grass as oxen, and seven ᵀtimes shall pass over thee, until thou know that ᴿthe most High ruleth in the kingdom of men, and giveth it to whomsoever he will. *years • [vv. 25, 33]*

33 The same hour was the thing fulfilled upon Neb-u-chad-nez'-zar: ᴿand he was driven from men, and did eat grass as oxen, and his body was wet with the dew of heaven, till his hairs were grown like eagles' *feathers*, and his nails like birds' *claws*. *[5:21]*

Nebuchadnezzar's Restoration

34 And at the end of the days I Neb-u-chad-nez'-zar lifted up mine eyes unto heaven, and mine ᵀunderstanding returned unto me, and I blessed the most High, and I praised and honoured him ᴿthat liveth for ever, whose dominion *is* ᴿan everlasting dominion, and his kingdom *is* from generation to generation: *reason • [Rev. 4:10] • [Ps. 10:16]*

35 And all the inhabitants of the earth *are* ᵀreputed as nothing: and he doeth according to his will in the army of heaven, and *among* the inhabitants of the earth: and none can ᵀstay his hand, or say unto him, What doest thou? *to be considered • stop*

36 At the same time my reason returned unto me; and for the glory of my ᴿkingdom, mine honour and brightness returned unto me; and my counsellors and my lords sought unto me; and I was established in my kingdom, and excellent majesty was ᴿadded unto me. *v. 26 • [Prov. 22:4; Matt. 6:33]*

37 Now I Neb-u-chad-nez'-zar praise and extol and honour the King of heaven, ᴿall whose works *are* truth, and his ways judgment: ᴿand those that walk in pride he is able to ᵀabase. *[Ps. 33:4; Rev. 15:3] • Ex. 18:11 • humble*

CHAPTER 5

Belshazzar Defiles the Temple Vessels

BEL-SHAZ'-ZAR the king ᴿmade a great feast to a thousand of his lords, and drank wine before the thousand. *Esth. 1:3*

2 Bel-shaz'-zar, whiles he tasted the wine, commanded to bring the golden and silver vessels which his ᵀfather Neb-u-chad-nez'-zar had ᵀtaken out of the temple which *was* in Jerusalem; that the king, and his princes, his

wives, and his concubines, might drink therein. *grandfather · robbed from*

3 Then they brought the golden ^Rvessels that were taken out of the temple of the house of God which *was* at Jerusalem; and the king, and his princes, his wives, and his concubines, drank in them. 2 Chr. 36:10

4 They drank wine, ^Rand praised the gods of gold, and of silver, of brass, of iron, of wood, and of stone. Ps. 115:4; 135:15; Rev. 9:20

Belshazzar Sees the Handwriting

5 ^RIn the same hour came forth fingers of a man's hand, and wrote over against the candlestick upon the plaister of the wall of the king's palace: and the king saw the part of the hand that wrote. 4:31

6 Then the king's countenance was changed, and his thoughts troubled him, so that the joints of his loins were loosed, and his knees smote one against another.

7 The king cried aloud to bring in the astrologers, the Chal-de'-ans, and the soothsayers. *And* the king spake, and said to the wise *men* of Babylon, Whosoever shall read this writing, and shew me the interpretation thereof, shall be ^Tclothed with scarlet, and *have* a chain of gold about his neck, and shall be the third ruler in the kingdom. *honoured*

8 Then came in all the king's wise *men:* ^Rbut they could not read the writing, nor ^Tmake known to the king the interpretation thereof. 2:27 · *reveal*

9 Then was king Bel-shaz'-zar greatly troubled, and his ^Tcountenance was changed in him, and his lords were astonied. *colour*

Daniel Interprets the Handwriting

10 *Now* the queen by reason of the words of the king and his lords came into the banquet house: *and* the queen spake and said, O king, ^Rlive for ever: let not thy thoughts trouble thee, nor let thy ^Tcountenance be changed: 2:4; 3:9 · *colour*

11 There is a man in thy kingdom, in whom *is* the spirit of the holy gods; and in the days of thy ^Tfather light and understanding and wisdom, like the wisdom of the gods, was found in him; whom the king Neb-u-chad-nez'-zar thy father, the king, I *say*, thy father, made master of the magicians, astrologers, Chal-de'-ans, *and* soothsayers; *grandfather*

12 Forasmuch as an excellent spirit, and knowledge, and understanding, interpreting of dreams, and shewing of hard sentences, and dissolving of doubts, were found in the same Daniel, whom the king named Bel-te-shaz'-zar: now let Daniel be called, and he will shew the interpretation.

13 Then was Daniel brought in before the king. *And* the king spake and said unto Daniel, *Art* thou that Daniel, which *art* of the children of the captivity of Judah, whom the king my father brought out of Jewry?

14 I have even heard of thee, that ^Rthe spirit of the ^Rgods *is* in thee, and *that* light and understanding and excellent wisdom is found in thee. *vv.* 11, 12 · [1 Cor. 8:5, 6]

15 And now ^Rthe wise *men*, the ^Tastrologers, have been brought in before me, that they should read this writing, and ^Tmake known unto me the interpretation thereof: but they ^Rcould not shew the interpretation of the thing: *vv.* 7, 8 · *enchanters · reveal ·* Is. 47:12

16 And I have heard of thee, that thou canst make interpretations, and dissolve doubts: now if thou canst read the writing, and ^Tmake known to me the interpretation thereof, thou shalt be clothed with scarlet, and *have* a chain of gold about thy neck, and shalt be the third ruler in the kingdom. *reveal*

17 Then Daniel answered and said before the king, Let thy gifts be to thyself, and give thy rewards to another; yet I will read the writing unto the king, and make known to him the interpretation.

18 O thou king, ^Rthe most high God gave Neb-u-chad-nez'-zar thy father a kingdom, and majesty, and glory, and honour: 2:37

19 And for the majesty that he gave him, ^Rall people, nations, and languages, trembled and feared before him: whom he would he slew; and whom he would he kept alive; and whom he would he set up; and whom he would he put down. Jer. 27:7

20 ^RBut when his heart was ^Tlifted up, and his mind hardened in pride, he was deposed from his kingly throne, and they took his glory from him: 4:30, 37 · *made vain*

21 And he was ^Rdriven from the sons of men; and his ^Theart was made like the beasts, and his dwelling *was* with the wild asses: they fed him with grass like oxen, and his body was wet with the dew of heaven; ^Rtill he knew that the most high God ruled in the kingdom of men, and *that* he appointeth over it whomsoever he will. 4:32, 33 · *mind ·* [4:17, 25]

22 And thou his son, O Bel-shaz'-zar, ^Rhast not humbled thine heart, though thou knewest all this; 2 Chr. 33:23; 36:12

23 ^RBut hast lifted up thyself against the Lord of heaven; and they have brought the vessels of his house before thee, and thou, and thy lords, thy wives, and thy concubines, have drunk wine in them; and thou hast praised the gods of silver, and gold, of brass, iron, wood, and stone, which see not, nor hear, nor know: and the God in whose hand thy breath *is*, and whose *are* all thy ways, hast thou not glorified: *vv.* 3, 4

24 Then was the part of the hand sent from him; and this writing was written.

25 And this *is* the writing that was written, ME'-NE, ME'-NE, TE'-KEL, U-PHAR'-SIN.

26 This *is* the interpretation of the ^Tthing:

ME'-NE; God hath numbered thy kingdom, and Rfinished it. *word* • Is. 13:6, 17; Jer. 50:41, 42

27 TE'-KEL; RThou art weighed in the balances, and art found wanting. Ps. 62:9; Jer. 6:30

28 PE'-RES; Thy kingdom is divided, and given to the Medes and RPersians.   6:28

29 Then commanded Bel-shaz'-zar, and they clothed Daniel with scarlet, and *put* a chain of gold about his neck, and made a proclamation concerning him, that he should be the third ruler in the kingdom.

Belshazzar Is Killed

30 RIn that night was Bel-shaz'-zar the king of the Chal-de'-ans slain.   Jer. 51:31, 39, 57

31 RAnd Da-ri'-us the Me'-di-an took the kingdom, *being* about threescore and two years old.   6:1; 9:1

CHAPTER 6

Daniel Is Promoted

IT pleased Da-ri'-us to set over the kingdom an hundred and twenty princes, which should be over the whole kingdom;

2 And over these three presidents; of whom Daniel *was* first: that the princes might Tgive accounts unto them, and the king should have no Tdamage.   *report* • *loss*

3 Then this Daniel was preferred above the presidents and princes, because an excellent spirit *was* in him; and the king thought to set him over the whole realm.

Darius Signs the Foolish Decree

4 Then the presidents and princes Rsought to find occasion against Daniel concerning the kingdom; but they could find Rnone occasion nor fault; forasmuch as he *was* faithful, neither was there any error or fault found in him.   Eccl. 4:4; Gen. 43:18 • Luke 20:26

5 Then said these men, We shall not find any occasion against this Daniel, except we find *it* against him concerning the Rlaw of his God.   Acts 24:13–16, 20, 21

6 Then these presidents and princes assembled together to the king, and said thus unto him, King Da-ri'-us, live for ever.

7 All the presidents of the kingdom, the governors, and the princes, the counsellors, and the captains, have consulted together to establish a royal statute, and to make a firm Rdecree,T that whosoever shall ask a petition of any God or man for thirty days, save of thee, O king, he shall be cast into the Tden of lions.   Is. 10:1 • *interdict* • *pit*

8 Now, O king, establish the decree, and sign the writing, that it be not changed, according to the Rlaw of the Medes and Persians, which altereth not.   *vv.* 12, 15

9 Wherefore king Da-ri'-us Rsigned the writing and the decree.   [Ps. 118:9; 146:3]

Daniel Prays Faithfully

10 Now when Daniel knew that the writing was signed, he went into his house; and his windows being open in his chamber Rtoward Jerusalem, he kneeled upon his knees three times a day, and prayed, and gave thanks before his God, as he did aforetime.   Jon. 2:4

11 Then these men Rassembled, and found Daniel praying and making supplication before his God.   *v.* 6; [Ps. 37:32, 33]

12 RThen they came near, and spake before the king concerning the king's decree; Hast thou not signed a decree, that every man that shall ask *a petition* of any God or man within thirty days, save of thee, O king, shall be cast into the den of lions? The king answered and said, The thing *is* true, according to the law of the Medes and Persians, which altereth not.   3:8

13 Then answered they and said before the king, That Daniel, which *is* of the children of the captivity of Judah, regardeth not thee, O king, nor the decree that thou hast signed, but maketh his petition three times a day.

14 Then the king, when he heard *these* words, was sore displeased with himself, and Tset *his* heart on Daniel to deliver him: and he Tlaboured till the going down of the sun to deliver him.   *made up his mind about* • *tried*

15 Then these men assembled unto the king, and said unto the king, Know, O king, that Rthe law of the Medes and Persians *is,* That no decree nor statute which the king establisheth may be changed.   *v.* 8; Esth. 8:8

Daniel Is Saved in the Lions' Den

16 Then the king commanded, and they brought Daniel, and cast *him* into the den of lions. Now the king spake and said unto Daniel, RThy God whom thou servest continually, he will deliver thee.   [Ps. 37:39, 40]

17 And a stone was brought, and laid upon the mouth of the den; and the king sealed it with his own signet, and with the signet of his lords; that the purpose might not be changed concerning Daniel.

18 Then the king went to his palace, and passed the night fasting: neither were instruments of musick brought before him: Rand his sleep went from him.   2:1

19 Then the Rking arose very early in the morning, and went in haste unto the den of lions.   3:24

20 And when he came to the den, he cried with a Tlamentable voice unto Daniel: *and* the king spake and said to Daniel, O Daniel, servant of the living God, Ris thy God, whom thou servest continually, able to deliver thee from the lions?   *pitiful* • 3:15

21 Then said Daniel unto the king, RO king, live for ever.   2:4

22 My God hath sent his angel, and hath

Rshut the lions' mouths, that they have not hurt me: forasmuch as before him innocency was found in me; and also before thee, O king, have I done no hurt.   Heb. 11:33

23 Then was the king exceeding glad for him, and commanded that they should take Daniel up out of the den. So Daniel was taken up out of the den, and no manner of hurt was found upon him, because he Rbelieved in his God.   1 Chr. 5:20; [Is. 26:3]

24 And the king commanded, and they brought those men which had accused Daniel, and they cast them into the den of lions, them, their children, and their wives; and the lions had the mastery of them, and brake all their bones in pieces or ever they came at the bottom of the den.

Darius' Wise Decree

25 Then king Da-ri'-us wrote unto all people, nations, and languages, that dwell in all the earth; Peace be multiplied unto you.

26 I make a decree, That in every dominion of my kingdom men tremble and fear before the God of Daniel: Rfor he is the living God, and stedfast for ever, and his kingdom that which shall not be destroyed, and his dominion shall be even unto the end.   4:34

27 He delivereth and rescueth, Rand he worketh signs and wonders in heaven and in earth, who hath delivered Daniel from the Tpower of the lions.   4:3 · paw

28 So this Daniel prospered in the reign of Da-ri'-us, Rand in the reign of RCyrus the Persian.   1:21 · Ezra 1:1, 2

CHAPTER 7

Four Beasts

IN the first year of Bel-shaz'-zar king of Babylon Daniel had a dream and visions of his head upon his bed: then he wrote the dream, and told the sum of the matters.

2 Daniel spake and said, I saw in my vision by night, and, behold, the four winds of the heaven strove upon the great sea.

3 And four great beasts Rcame up from the sea, diverse one from another.   Rev. 13:1

4 The first was like a lion, and had eagle's wings: I beheld till the wings thereof were plucked, and it was lifted up from the earth, and made stand upon the feet as a man, and a man's Theart was given to it.   mind

5 And behold another beast, a second, like to a bear, and it raised up itself on one side, and it had three ribs in the mouth of it between the teeth of it: and they said thus unto it, Arise, devour much flesh.

6 After this I beheld, and lo another, like a leopard, which had upon the back of it four wings of a fowl; the beast had also four heads; and dominion was given to it.

7 After this I saw in the night visions, and behold a fourth beast, dreadful and terrible, and strong exceedingly; and it had great Riron teeth: it devoured and brake in pieces, and stamped the residue with the feet of it: and it was diverse from all the beasts that were before it; and it had ten horns.   2:41

8 I considered the horns, and, behold, there came up among them another little horn, before whom there were three of the first horns plucked up by the roots: and, behold, in this horn were eyes like the eyes of man, and a mouth speaking great things.

"Ancient of Days"

9 RI beheld till the thrones were cast down, and the Ancient of days did sit, whose garment was white as snow, and the hair of his head like the pure wool: his throne was like the fiery flame, Rand his wheels as burning fire.   [Rev. 20:4] · Ezek. 1:15

10 A fiery stream issued and came forth from before him: thousand thousands ministered unto him, and ten thousand times ten thousand stood before him: Rthe judgment was set, and the books were opened. [Rev. 20:4]

11 I beheld then because of the voice of the great words which the horn spake: RI beheld even till the beast was slain, and his body destroyed, and given to the burning flame.   [Rev. 19:20; 20:10]

12 As concerning the rest of the beasts, they had their dominion taken away: yet their lives were prolonged for a Tseason and time.   while

13 I saw in the night visions, and, behold, Rone like the Son of man came with the Rclouds of heaven, and came to the Ancient of days, and they brought him near before him.   Ezek. 1:26; [Matt. 24:30; Rev. 1:7] ✶ · Acts 1:9

14 And there was given him dominion, and glory, and a kingdom, that all people, nations, and languages, should serve him: Rhis dominion is an everlasting dominion, which shall not pass away, and his kingdom that which shall not be destroyed.
                    Mic. 4:7; [Luke 1:33] ✶

Interpretation of the Four Beasts

15 I Daniel was grieved in my spirit Tin the midst of my body, and the visions of my head Rtroubled me.   within me · 4:19

16 I came near unto one of them that stood by, and asked him the truth of all this. So he told me, and made me Tknow the interpretation of the things.   understand

17 These great beasts, which are four, are four kings, which shall arise out of the earth.

18 But Rthe saints of the most High shall take the kingdom, and possess the kingdom for ever, even for ever and ever.   Is. 60:12

19 Then I would know the truth of the fourth beast, which was Tdiverse from all the others, exceeding dreadful, whose teeth were

of iron, and his nails of brass; which devoured, brake in pieces, and stamped the residue with his feet; *different*

20 And of the ten horns that *were* in his head, and of the other which came up, and before whom three fell; even of that horn that had eyes, and a mouth that spake very great things, whose look *was* more stout than his fellows.

21 I beheld, and the same horn made war with the saints, and prevailed against them;

22 Until the Ancient of days came, and judgment was given to the saints of the most High; and the time came that the ᴿsaints possessed the kingdom.   [Rev. 1:6]

Interpretation of the Fourth Beast

23 Thus he said, The fourth beast shall be the fourth kingdom upon earth, which shall be diverse from all kingdoms, and shall devour the whole earth, and shall tread it down, and break it in pieces.

24 ᴿAnd the ten horns out of this kingdom *are* ten kings *that* shall arise: and another shall rise after them; and he shall be ᵀdiverse from the first, and he shall subdue three kings.   Rev. 17:12 · *different*

25 And he shall speak *great* words against the most High, and shall ᵀwear out the saints of the most High, and think to change times and laws: and they shall be given into his hand until a time and times and the dividing of time.   *persecute*

26 ᴿBut the judgment shall sit, and they shall take away his dominion, to consume and to destroy *it* unto the end.   [vv. 10, 22]

27 And the kingdom and dominion, and the greatness of the kingdom under the whole heaven, shall be given to the people of the saints of the most High, whose kingdom is an everlasting kingdom, and all ᵀdominions shall serve and obey him.   *powers*

28 Hitherto *is* the end of the matter. As for me Daniel, ᴿmy cogitations much troubled me, and my countenance changed in me: but I ᴿkept the matter in my heart.   8:27 · Luke 2:19

CHAPTER 8

The Ram

IN the third year of the reign of king Bel-shaz'-zar a vision appeared unto me, *even* unto me Daniel, after that which appeared unto me ᴿat the first.   7:1

2 And I saw in a vision; and it came to pass, when I saw, that I *was* at ᴿShu'-shan *in* the palace, which *is* in the ᴿprovince of E'-lam; and I saw in a vision, and I was by the river of U'-lai.   Esth. 1:2 · Gen. 10:22; 14:1

3 Then I lifted up mine eyes, and saw, and, behold, there stood before the river a ram

which had *two* horns: and the *two* horns *were* high; but one *was* higher than the other, and the higher came up last.

4 I saw the ram pushing westward, and northward, and southward; so that no beasts might stand before him, neither *was there* *any* that could deliver out of his hand; ᴿbut he did according to his will, and ᵀbecame great.   5:19 · *magnified himself*

The He Goat

5 And as I was considering, behold, an he goat came from the west on the face of the whole earth, and ᵀtouched not the ground: and the goat had a ᵀnotable horn between his eyes.   *without touching · conspicuous*

6 And he came to the ram that had *two* horns, which I had seen standing before the river, and ran unto him in the fury of his power.

7 And I saw him come close unto the ram, and he was moved with ᵀcholer against him, and smote the ram, and brake his two horns: and there was no power in the ram to stand before him, but he cast him down to the ground, and stamped upon him: and there was none that could deliver the ram out of his hand.   *anger*

8 Therefore the he goat waxed very great: and when he was strong, the great horn was broken; and for it came up ᴿfour notable ones toward the four winds of heaven.   v. 22

The Little Horn

9 And out of one of them came forth a little horn, which waxed exceeding great, toward the south, and toward the east, and toward the ᴿpleasantᵀ *land.*   Ps. 48:2 · *glorious*

10 And it waxed great, *even* ᵀto the host of heaven; and it ᵀcast down *some* of the host and of the stars to the ground, and stamped upon them.   *in opposition to · defeated*

11 Yea, he magnified *himself* even to the prince of the host, and by him the daily *sacrifice* was taken away, and the place of his sanctuary was cast down.

12 And an host was given *him* against the daily *sacrifice* by reason of transgression, and it cast down the truth to the ground; and it practised, and prospered.

The Length of the Vision

13 Then I heard ᴿone saint speaking, and another saint said unto that certain *saint* which spake, How long *shall be* the vision *concerning* the daily *sacrifice*, and the transgression of desolation, to ᵀgive both the sanctuary and the host to be ᴿtrodden under foot?   4:13 · *yield* · Jer. 12:10; Rev. 11:2

14 And he said unto me, Unto ᴿtwo thousand and three hundred days; then shall the sanctuary be ᵀcleansed.   7:25 · *delivered*

Interpretation of the Vision

15 And it came to pass, when I, *even* I Daniel, had seen the vision, and sought for the meaning, then, behold, there stood before me as the appearance of a man.

16 And I heard a man's voice ᴿbetween *the banks of* U'-lai, which called, and said, ᴿGabriel, make this *man* to understand the vision.   12:5-7 • Luke 1:19

17 So he came near where I stood: and when he came, I was afraid, and ᴿfell upon my face: but he said unto me, Understand, O son of man: for at the time of the end *shall be* the vision.   Ezek. 1:28; Rev. 1:17

18 Now as he was speaking with me, I was in a deep ᴿsleep on my face toward the ground: ᴿbut he touched me, and ᵀset me upright.   Luke 9:32 • Ezek. 2:2 • *made me stand up*

19 And he said, Behold, I will make thee know what shall be in the last end of the indignation: ᴿfor at the time appointed the end *shall be*.   Hab. 2:3

Interpretation of the Ram

20 The ram which thou sawest having *two* horns *are* the kings of Me'-di-a and Persia.

Interpretation of the He Goat

21 And the rough goat *is* the king of Gre'-ci-a: and the great horn that *is* between his eyes ᴿis the first king.   11:3

22 Now that being broken, whereas four stood up for it, four kingdoms shall stand up out of the nation, but not in his power.

Interpretation of the Little Horn

23 And in the latter time of their kingdom, when the transgressors are come to the full, a king of fierce countenance, and understanding dark sentences, shall stand up.

24 And his power shall be mighty, ᴿbut not by his own power: and he shall destroy wonderfully, ᴿand shall prosper, and practise, ᴿand shall destroy the mighty and the holy people.   Rev. 17:13 • 11:36 • 7:25

25 And through his policy also he shall cause craft to prosper in his hand; and he shall magnify *himself* in his heart, and by ᵀpeace shall destroy many: he shall also stand up against the Prince of princes; but he shall be broken without hand.   *prosperity*

26 And the vision of the evening and the morning which was told *is* true: wherefore ᵀshutᴿ thou up the vision; for it *shall be* for many days.   *keep it to yourself* • Rev. 22:10

Response of Daniel

27 And I Daniel fainted, and was sick *certain* days; afterward I rose up, and did the king's business; and I was astonished at the vision, but none understood *it*.

CHAPTER 9

The Understanding of Daniel

IN the ᴿfirst year of Da-ri'-us the son of A-has-u-e'-rus, of the seed of the Medes, which was made king over the realm of the Chal-de'-ans;   1:21

2 In the first year of his reign I Daniel understood by books the number of the years, whereof the word of the LORD came to ᴿJer-e-mi'-ah the prophet, that he would accomplish ᴿseventy years in the ᵀdesolations of Jerusalem.   2 Chr. 36:21 • Zech. 7:5 • *ruin*

The Intercession of Daniel

3 ᴿAnd I set my face unto the Lord God, to seek by prayer and supplications, with fasting, and sackcloth, and ashes: Neh. 1:4

4 And I prayed unto the LORD my God, and made my confession, and said, O Lord, the great and dreadful God, keeping the covenant and mercy to them that love him, and to them that keep his commandments;

5 ᴿWe have sinned, and have committed iniquity, and have done wickedly, and have rebelled, even by departing from thy precepts and from thy judgments: 1 Kin. 8:47

6 Neither have we hearkened unto thy servants the prophets, which spake in thy

---

9:3, 4 Knowing the Will of God Through Prayer and Fasting—Soon after Israel had invaded Palestine in the days of Joshua, the Israelites were tricked into signing an unscriptural peace treaty with a group of deceitful pagans. The cause for this tragic error is clearly stated in God's Word, "And the men . . . asked not *counsel* at the mouth of the LORD" (Page 2251—Josh. 9:14). These pagans, the Gibeonites, brought only trouble to Israel. See Joshua 10:4–15; Second Samuel 21:1–14.

It therefore becomes immediately obvious that one of the most important factors in knowing God's will for our lives is to pray. "If any of you lack wisdom, let him ask of God, that giveth to all *men* liberally, and upbraideth not; and it shall be given him" (Page 1228—James 1:5). See also Psalm 143:8, 10; James 4:2.

In the light of these passages it is evident a Christian must pray to know God's will. In other Bible verses fasting is linked with prayer.

a. Meaning of fasting: to fast is to abstain for a period of time from some important and necessary activity in our lives.

b. Purpose of fasting: this is done that we might spend that time in prayer before God.

c. Kinds of fasting: one may, for a time, refrain from sleep (Page 1146—2 Cor. 6:5; 11:27), marital sex (Page 1130—1 Cor. 7:1–5), or food (Page 943—Matt. 4:1, 2).

d. Examples of biblical fasting: Moses (Page 187—Deut. 9:9, 18, 25–29); Elijah (Page 362—1 Kin. 19:8); Daniel (Page 832—Dan. 9:3; 10:3); Ezra (Page 484—Ezra 10:6); Nehemiah (Page 489—Neh. 1:4); and Paul (Page 1146—2 Cor. 6:5, 11:27).

Now turn to Page 662—Is. 6:8: Knowing the Will of God Through Submission to the Spirit.

name to our kings, our princes, and our fathers, and to all the people of the land.

7 O Lord, righteousness *belongeth* unto thee, but unto us confusion of faces, as at this day; to the men of Judah, and to the inhabitants of Jerusalem, and unto all Israel, *that are* near, and *that are* far off, through all the countries whither thou hast driven them, because of their trespass that they have trespassed against thee.

8 ᴿO Lord, to us *belongeth* ᵀconfusion of face, to our kings, to our princes, and to our fathers, because we have sinned against thee.   Ps. 25:3 • *shame*

9 ᴿTo the Lord our God *belong* mercies and forgivenesses, though we have ᴿrebelled against him; [Neh. 9:17; Ps. 130:4, 7] • *vv*. 5, 6; Ps. 106:43

10 Neither have we obeyed the voice of the Lᴏʀᴅ our God, to walk in his laws, which he set before us by his servants the prophets.

11 Yea, all Israel have transgressed thy law, even by departing, that they might not obey thy voice; therefore the curse is poured upon us, and the oath that *is* written in the law of Moses the servant of God, because we have sinned against him.

12 And he hath ᴿconfirmed his words, which he spake against us, and against our judges that judged us, by bringing upon us a great evil: ᴿfor under the whole heaven hath not been done as hath been done upon Jerusalem.   Zech. 1:6 • Lam. 1:12

13 As *it is* written in the law of Moses, all this evil is come upon us: yet ᵀmade we not our prayer before the Lᴏʀᴅ our God, that we might turn from our iniquities, and understand thy truth.   *we did not pray to*

14 Therefore hath the Lᴏʀᴅ watched upon the evil, and brought it upon us: for the Lᴏʀᴅ our God is righteous in all his works which he doeth: for we obeyed not his voice.

15 And now, O Lord our God, that hast brought thy people forth out of the land of Egypt with a mighty hand, and hast ᵀgotten thee renown, as at this day; we have sinned, we have done wickedly.   *became famous*

16 O Lord, according to all thy righteousness, I beseech thee, let thine anger and thy fury be turned away from thy city Jerusalem, thy holy mountain: because for our sins, and for the iniquities of our fathers, Jerusalem and thy people *are become* a reproach to all *that are* about us.

17 Now therefore, O our God, hear the prayer of thy servant, and his supplications, and cause thy face to shine upon thy sanctuary that is desolate, for the Lord's sake.

18 O my God, ᴿincline thine ear, and hear; open thine eyes, and behold our ᵀdesolations, and the city which is called by thy name: for we do not present our supplications before thee for our righteousnesses, but for thy great mercies.   Ex. 3:7 • *ruins*

19 ᴿO Lord, hear; O Lord, forgive; O Lord, hearken and do; defer not, for thine own sake, O my God: for thy city and thy people are called by thy name.   Ps. 44:23; 79:9, 10

The Intervention of Gabriel

20 And whiles I *was* speaking, and ᴿpraying, and ᴿconfessing my sin and the sin of my people Israel, and presenting my supplication before the Lᴏʀᴅ my God for the holy mountain of my God;   *v.* 3 • 10:12

21 Yea, whiles I *was* speaking in prayer, even the man Gabriel, whom I had seen in the vision at the beginning, being caused ᵀto fly swiftly, touched me about the time of the evening ᵀoblation.   *to come quickly • offering*

22 And he informed *me*, and talked with me, and said, O Daniel, I am now come forth to give thee skill and understanding.

23 At the beginning of thy supplications the commandment came forth, and I am come to shew *thee;* for thou *art* greatly beloved: therefore understand the matter, and ᴿconsider the vision.   Matt. 24:15

The Revelation of the Seventy Weeks

24 Seventy weeks are determined upon thy people and upon thy holy city, to finish the transgression, and to make an end of sins, and to make reconciliation for iniquity, and to bring in everlasting righteousness, and to seal up the vision and prophecy, and to anoint the most Holy.

25 Know therefore and understand, *that* from the going forth of the commandment to restore and to build Jerusalem unto ᴿthe Messi′-ah ᴿthe Prince *shall be* seven weeks, and threescore and two weeks: the street shall be built again, and the wall, even in troublous times.   John 1:41 ☆ • Is. 55:4

26 And after threescore and two weeks ᴿshall Mes-si′-ah be ᵀcut off, but not for himself: and the people of the prince that shall come shall destroy the city and the sanctuary; and the end thereof *shall be* with a flood, and unto the end of the war desolations are determined.   Matt. 27:50 ☆ • *killed*

27 And he shall confirm the covenant with many for one week: and in the midst of the week he shall cause the sacrifice and the oblation to cease, and for the overspreading of abominations he shall make *it* desolate, even until the consummation, and that determined shall be poured upon the desolate.

CHAPTER 10

Time of the Vision

Iᴺ the third year of Cyrus king of Persia a thing was revealed unto Daniel, whose

name was called Bel-te-shaz'-zar; and the thing *was* true, but the time appointed *was* ᵀlong: and he understood the thing, and had understanding of the vision.   *great*

2 In those days I Daniel was ᴿmourning three full weeks.   Ezra 9:4, 5; Neh. 1:4

3 I ate no ᵀpleasant bread, neither came flesh nor wine in my mouth, neither did I anoint myself at all, till three whole weeks were fulfilled.   *desirable food*

4 And in the four and twentieth day of the first month, as I was by the side of the great ᴿriver, which *is* Hid'-de-kel;   Ezek. 1:3

Vision of the Heavenly Messenger

5 Then I lifted up mine eyes, and looked, and behold a certain man ᴿclothed in linen, whose loins *were* ᴿgirded with ᵀfine gold of U'-phaz: Ezek. 9:2 • Rev. 1:13; 15:6 • *pure*

6 His body also *was* like the beryl, and his face as the appearance of lightning, and his eyes as lamps of fire, and his arms and his feet like in colour to polished brass, ᴿand the voice of his words like the voice of a multitude.   [Rev. 1:15, 16]

7 And I Daniel ᴿalone saw the vision: for the men that were with me saw not the vision; but a great quaking fell upon them, so that they fled to hide themselves.   Acts 9:7

8 Therefore I was left alone, and saw this great vision, and there remained no strength in me: for my comeliness was turned in me into corruption, and I retained no strength.

9 Yet heard I the voice of his words: and when I heard the voice of his words, then was I in a ᴿdeep sleep on my face, and my face toward the ground.   Gen. 15:12; Job 4:13

Touch of the Heavenly Messenger

10 And, behold, ᴿan hand touched me, which ᵀset me upon my knees and *upon* the palms of my hands.   9:21 • *brought me*

11 And he said unto me, O Daniel, ᴿa man greatly beloved, understand the words that I speak unto thee, and stand upright: for unto thee am I now sent. And when he had spoken this word unto me, I stood trembling.   9:23

12 Then said he unto me, Fear not, Daniel: for from the first day that thou didst set thine heart to understand, and to chasten thyself before thy God, thy words were heard, and I am come for thy words.

13 But the prince of the kingdom of Persia withstood me one and twenty days: but, lo, ᴿMi'-cha-el, ᵀone of the chief princes, came to help me; and I remained there with the kings of Persia.   [Rev. 12:7] • *the first*

14 Now I am come to make thee understand what shall befall thy people ᴿin the latter days: ᴿfor yet the vision *is* for *many* days.   2:28; Gen. 49:1 • *v.* 1; 8:26; Hab. 2:3

15 And when he had spoken such words unto me, I ᵀset my face toward the ground, and I became ᵀdumb.   *turned • silent*

16 And, behold, *one* like the similitude of the sons of men touched my lips: then I opened my mouth, and spake, and said unto him that stood before me, O my lord, by the vision ᴿmy sorrows are turned upon me, and I have retained no strength.   *v.* 8

17 For how can the servant of this my lord talk with this my lord? for as for me, straightway there remained no strength in me, neither is there breath left in me.

Strengthening by the Heavenly Messenger

18 Then there came again and touched me *one* like the appearance of a man, and he ᴿstrengthened me,   Is. 35:3

19 And said, O man greatly beloved, ᴿfear not: peace *be* unto thee, be strong, yea, be strong. And when he had spoken unto me, I was strengthened, and said, Let my lord speak; for thou hast strengthened me. Judg. 6:23

20 Then said he, Knowest thou ᵀwherefore I come unto thee? and now will I return to fight with the ᴿprince of Persia: and when I am gone forth, lo, the prince of Gre'-ci-a shall come.   *why • v.* 13

21 But I will shew thee that which is noted in the scripture of truth: and *there is* none that holdeth with me in these things, but ᴿMi'-cha-el your prince.   *v.* 13

CHAPTER 11

The Rule of Persia

ALSO I ᴿin the first year of ᴿDa-ri'-us the Mede, *even* I, stood to confirm and to strengthen him.   9:1 • 5:31

2 And now will I shew thee the truth. Behold, there shall stand up yet three kings in Persia; and the fourth shall be far richer than *they* all: and ᴿby his strength through his riches he shall stir up all against the realm of Gre'-ci-a.   10:20, 21

The Rule of Greece

3 And ᴿa mighty king shall stand up, that shall rule with great dominion, and ᴿdo according to his will.   7:6; 8:5 • 8:4

4 And when he shall stand up, ᴿhis kingdom shall be broken, and shall be divided toward the four winds of heaven; and not to his posterity, nor according to his dominion which he ruled: for his kingdom shall be plucked up, even for others beside those.   8:8

5 And the king of the south shall be strong, and *one* of his princes; and he shall be strong above him, and have dominion; his dominion *shall be* a great dominion.

6 And in the end of years they shall ᵀjoin

themselves together; for the king's daughter of the south shall come to the king of the north to make an agreement: but she shall not retain the power of the arm; neither shall he stand, nor his arm: but she shall be given up, and they that brought her, and he that begat her, and he that strengthened her in *these* times.   unite

7 But out of a branch of her roots shall *one* stand up in his estate, which shall come with an army, and shall enter into the fortress of the king of the north, and shall deal against them, and shall prevail:

8 ᴿAnd shall also carry captives into Egypt their gods, with their princes, *and* with their ᵀprecious vessels of silver and of gold; and he shall continue *more* years than the king of the north.   Is. 37:18 · *valuable*

9 So the king of the south shall come into *his* kingdom, and shall return into his own land.

10 But his sons shall be stirred up, and shall assemble a multitude of great forces: and *one* shall certainly come, ᴿand overflow, and pass through: then shall he return, and be stirred up, *even* to his fortress.   9:26; Is. 8:8

11 ᴿAnd the king of the south shall be moved with ᵀcholer, and shall come forth and fight with him, *even* with the king of the north: and he shall set forth a great multitude; but the multitude shall be given into his hand.   8:7 · *anger*

12 *And* when he hath taken away the multitude, his heart shall be lifted up; and he shall cast down *many* ten thousands: but he shall not be strengthened *by it*.

13 ᴿFor the king of the north shall return, and shall set forth a multitude greater than the former, and shall certainly come ᵀafter certain years with a great army and with much riches.   v. 11 · *in due time*

14 And in those times there shall many stand up against the king of the south: also the robbers of thy people shall exalt themselves to ᵀestablish the vision; but they shall fall.   *achieve the plan*

15 So the king of the north shall come, and cast up a mount, and take the most fenced cities: and the arms of the south shall not withstand, neither his chosen people, neither *shall there be any* strength to withstand.

16 But he that cometh against him shall do according to his own will, and ᴿnone shall stand before him: and he shall stand in the glorious land, which by his hand shall be ᵀconsumed.   Josh. 1:5 · *conquered*

17 He shall also set his face to enter with the strength of his whole kingdom, and upright ones with him; thus shall he do: and he shall give him the daughter of women, corrupting her: but she shall not stand *on his* side, neither be for him.

18 After this shall he turn his face unto the ᴿisles, and shall take many: but a prince for his own behalf shall cause the reproach offered by him to cease; without his own reproach ᴿhe shall cause *it* to turn upon him.   Is. 66:19; Jer. 2:10; Zeph. 2:11 · Hos. 12:14

19 Then he shall turn his face toward the fort of his own land: but he shall stumble and fall, ᴿand ᵀnot be found.   Ps. 37:36 · *be lost*

20 Then shall stand up in his ᴿestateᵀ a raiser of taxes *in* the glory of the kingdom: but within few days he shall be destroyed, neither in anger, nor in battle.   Is. 60:17 · *place*

21 And in his estate shall stand up a vile person, to whom they shall not give the honour of the kingdom: ᴿbut he shall come in ᵀpeaceably, and obtain the kingdom by ᴿflatteries.   v. 24 · *time of security* · vv. 32, 34

22 And with the arms of a flood shall they be ᴿoverflown from before him, and shall be ᴿbroken; yea, also the prince of the covenant.   7:8 · 8:10, 11

23 And after the league *made* with him ᴿhe shall work deceitfully: for he shall come up, and shall become strong with a small people.   8:25; Gen. 3:1

24 He shall enter peaceably even upon the ᵀfattest places of the province; and he shall do *that* which his fathers have not done, nor his fathers' fathers; he shall scatter among them the prey, and spoil, and riches: *yea*, and he shall ᵀforecast his devices against the strong holds, even for a time.   richest · *aim his plans*

25 And he shall ᵀstir up his power and his courage against the king of the south with a great army; and the king of the south shall be stirred up to battle with a very great and mighty army; but he shall not stand: for they shall forecast devices against him.   *muster*

26 Yea, they that feed of the portion of his ᵀmeat shall destroy him, and his army shall overflow: and many shall fall down slain. *food*

27 And both these kings' hearts *shall be* to do mischief, and they shall speak lies at one table; but it shall not prosper: for yet the end *shall be* at the time appointed.

28 Then shall he return into his land with great riches; and his heart *shall be* against the holy covenant; and he shall do *exploits*, and return to his own land.

29 At the time appointed he shall return, and come toward the south; but it shall not be as the former, or as the latter.

30 For the ships of Chit'-tim shall come against him: therefore he shall be grieved, and return, and have indignation against the holy covenant: so shall he do; he shall even return, and have intelligence with them that forsake the holy covenant.

31 And arms shall stand on his part, and ᴿthey shall pollute the sanctuary of strength, and shall take away the daily *sacrifice*, and

they shall place the abomination that
^Tmaketh desolate.   8:11 · *causes ruin*

32 And such as do wickedly against the
covenant shall he ^Tcorrupt by flatteries: but
the people that do know their God shall be
strong, and do *exploits.*   *deceive*

33 And they that understand among the
people shall instruct many: yet they ^Rshall fall
by the sword, and by flame, by captivity, and
by spoil, *many* days.   Heb. 11:36–38

34 Now when they shall fall, they shall be
^Tholpen with a little help: but many shall
cleave to them with flatteries.   *helped*

35 And *some* of them of understanding
shall fall, to try them, and to purge, and to
make *them* white, *even* to the time of the
end: because *it is* yet for a time appointed.

Prophecy of the Willful King

36 And the king shall do according to his
will; and he shall exalt himself, and magnify
himself above every god, and shall speak
marvellous things against the God of gods,
and shall prosper till the ^Tindignation be
accomplished: for that that is determined
shall be done.   *time of judgment*

37 Neither shall he regard the ^TGod of his
fathers, nor the desire of women, ^Rnor regard
any god: for he shall ^Rmagnify himself above
all.   *gods* · [1 Cor. 8:5, 6] · Is. 14:13

38 But in his estate shall he honour the
God of forces: and a god whom his fathers
knew not shall he honour with gold, and
silver, and with precious stones, and ^Tpleas-
ant things.   *things desired*

39 Thus shall he do in the most strong
holds with a strange god, whom he shall
acknowledge *and* increase with glory: and he

shall cause them to rule over many, and shall
divide the land for ^Tgain.   *profit*

40 And at the time of the end shall the
king of the south push at him: and the king of
the north shall come against him ^Rlike a
whirlwind, with chariots, ^Rand with horsemen, and with many ships; and he shall enter
into the countries, and shall overflow and
pass over.   Is. 21:1 · Ezek. 38:4

41 He shall enter also into the ^Tglorious
land, and   many *countries* shall be overthrown: but these shall escape out of his
hand, *even* E′-dom, and Moab, and the chief
of the children of Ammon.   *goodly land*

42 He shall ^Tstretch forth his hand also
upon the countries: ^Rand the land of Egypt
shall not escape.   *extend his control* · Joel 3:19

43 But he shall have power over the
treasures of gold and of silver, and over all
the precious things of Egypt: and the Lib′-y-
ans and the E-thi-o′-pi-ans *shall be* at his
steps.

44 But tidings out of the east and out of
the north shall trouble him: therefore he shall
go forth with great fury to destroy, and
utterly to ^Tmake away many.   *sweep*

45 And he shall plant the tabernacles of his
palace between the seas in the ^Tglorious holy
mountain; yet he shall come to his end, and
none shall help him.   *goodly*

CHAPTER 12

Prophecy of the Great Time of Trouble

AND at that time shall Mi′-cha-el stand up,
the great prince which standeth for the
children of thy people: ^Rand there shall be a
time of trouble, such as never was since there
was a nation *even* to that same time: and at

11:32 We Know God Through His Word—One of the most vital teachings of Scripture is that God
can be known. The highest knowledge to which men and women can attain is a personal knowledge of
God (Page 717—Jer. 9:24). People do not naturally possess this knowledge (Page 1110—Rom. 3:10,
11), even though they know that He exists (Page 552—Ps. 14:1; Page 1109—Rom. 1:19, 20). Knowing
that God exists is not the same as knowing God personally, just as knowing about the President does
not mean that you necessarily know him personally. This knowledge of God is crucial, however, since
to know God personally is to be saved and have eternal life (Page 1062—John 17:3). People should
rejoice in the fact that God earnestly wants them to attain this knowledge. That is why He has spoken
to us in His Word, revealing Himself and disclosing the means by which we may know Him.
    While God surely can be known, there is always more to be learned about Him. There are many
Scriptures which teach that our knowledge of God is partial. It is said to be "too wonderful" (Page
607—Ps. 139:6), "unsearchable" (Page 609—Ps. 145:3; Page 1118—Rom. 11:33), and "infinite" (Page
610—Ps. 147:5). Since our knowledge of God is incomplete, we must increase it through spiritual
growth. Paul, for example, prays to know God better (Page 1172—Phil. 3:10). We are even commanded
to grow in the knowledge of Christ (Page 1245—2 Pet. 3:18). The development of one's intimate
knowledge of God constitutes one of the greatest delights of the Christian life.
    The Bible also reveals that God cannot be known personally apart from His Word. It contains the
gospel which must be believed (Page 1162—Eph. 1:13), and the gospel brings forth saving faith in itself
(Page 1116—Rom. 10:17). The gospel can therefore be called "the power of God unto salvation" (Page
1109—Rom. 1:16). The part that the Scriptures and the gospel contained within them play in bringing
men to know God is described in three important illustrations: the gospel is the agent of the new birth
(Page 1228—James 1:18), that is, it is like the implanted seed without which the conception of new life
cannot occur; it is also a cleansing agent through which God gives the believing sinner a spiritual bath
that results in salvation (Page 1166—Eph. 5:26); the Scriptures are like an educator bringing the
wisdom that leads to salvation (Page 1202—2 Tim. 3:15).
    Now turn to Page 564—Ps. 40:8: We Know God's Will Through His Word.

that time thy people shall be delivered, every one that shall be found written in the ^Rbook.   Is. 26:20 • v. 4

Prophecy of the Resurrections

2 And many of them that sleep in the dust of the earth shall awake, ^Rsome to everlasting life, and some to shame ^Rand everlasting contempt.   [Matt. 25:46] • [Rom. 9:21]

3 And they that be ^Twise shall shine as the brightness of the firmament; and they that turn many to righteousness as the ^Rstars for ever and ever.   teachers • 1 Cor. 15:41

Sealing of the Book

4 But thou, O Daniel, ^Rshut up the words, and seal the book, even to the time of the end: many shall run to and fro, and ^Rknowledge shall be increased.   Rev. 22:10 • 2 Tim. 3:7

Questions Regarding the Great Time of Trouble

5 Then I Daniel looked, and, behold, there stood other two, the one on this side of the bank of the river, and the other on that ^Rside of the bank of the river.   10:4

6 And one said to the man clothed in linen, which was upon the waters of the river, ^RHow long shall it be to the end of these wonders?   8:13; Mark 13:4

7 And I heard the man clothed in linen, which was upon the waters of the river, when he held up his right hand and his left hand unto heaven, and sware by him that liveth for ever ^Rthat it shall be for a time, times, and an half; and when he shall have accomplished to scatter the power of the holy people, all these things shall be finished.   7:25

8 And I heard, but I understood not: then said I, O my Lord, what shall be the end of these things?

9 And he said, Go thy way, Daniel: for the words are closed up and ^Tsealed till the time of the end.   kept secret

10 Many shall be purified, and made white, and tried; but the wicked shall do wickedly: and none of the wicked shall understand; but the wise shall understand.

11 And from the time that the daily sacrifice shall be taken away, and the abomination that maketh desolate set up, there shall be a thousand two hundred and ninety days.

12 ^RBlessed is he that waiteth, and cometh to the ^Rthousand three hundred and five and thirty days.   [Is. 30:18] • Rev. 12:6

13 But go thou thy way till the end be: ^Rfor thou shalt rest, and stand in thy ^Rlot at the end of the days.   Rev. 14:13 • Ps. 16:5

THE BOOK OF

HOSEA

THE BOOK OF HOSEA

Hosea, whose name means "Salvation," ministers to the northern kingdom of Israel (also called Ephraim, after its largest tribe). Outwardly, the nation is enjoying a time of prosperity and growth; but inwardly, moral corruption and spiritual adultery permeate the people. Hosea, instructed by God to marry a woman named Gomer, finds his domestic life to be an accurate and tragic dramatization of the unfaithfulness of God's people. During his half century of prophetic ministry, Hosea repeatedly echoes his threefold message: God abhors the sins of His people; judgment is certain; but God's loyal love stands firm.

The names Hosea, Joshua, and Jesus are all derived from the same Hebrew root word. The word *hoshea* means "salvation," but "Joshua" and "Jesus" include an additional idea: "Yahweh Is Salvation" (see "The Book of Joshua"). As God's messenger, Hosea offers the possibility of salvation if only the nation will turn from idolatry back to God.

Israel's last king, Hoshea, has the same name as the prophet even though the English Bible spells them differently. Hosea in the Greek and Latin is *Osee*.

THE AUTHOR OF HOSEA

Few critics refute the claim in 1:1 that Hosea is the author of this book. His place of birth is not given, but his familiarity and obvious concern with the northern kingdom indicate that he lived in Israel, not Judah. This is also seen when he calls the king of Samaria "our king" (7:5). Hosea was the son of Beeri (1:1), husband of Gomer (1:3), and father of two sons and a daughter (1:4, 6, 9). Nothing more is known of him since he is not mentioned elsewhere in the Bible.

Hosea has a real compassion for his people, and his personal suffering because of Gomer gives him some understanding of God's grief over their sin. Thus, his words of coming judgment are passionately delivered but tempered with a heart of tenderness. He upbraids his people for their lying, murder, insincerity, ingratitude, idolatry, and covetousness with cutting metaphors and images; but his messages are punctuated with consolation and future hope.

THE TIME OF HOSEA

Hosea addressed the northern kingdom of Israel (5:1), often called Ephraim after the largest tribe (5:3, 5, 11, 13). According to 1:1, he ministered during the reigns of Uzziah (767–739 B.C.), Jotham (739–731 B.C.), Ahaz (731–715 B.C.),

and Hezekiah (715–686 B.C.), kings of Judah. When Hosea began his ministry, Jeroboam II (782–753 B.C.) was still reigning in Israel. This makes Hosea a younger contemporary of Amos, another prophet to the northern kingdom. Hosea was also a contemporary of Isaiah and Micah who ministered to the southern kingdom. Hosea's long career continued after the time of Jeroboam II and spanned the reigns of the last six kings of Israel from Zechariah (753–752 B.C.) to Hoshea (732–722 B.C.). Hosea evidently compiled this book during the early years of Hezekiah, and his ministry stretched from about 755 B.C. to about 710 B.C. The Book of Hosea represents approximately forty years of prophetic ministry.

When Hosea began his ministry, Israel was enjoying a temporary period of political and economic prosperity under Jeroboam II. However, the nation began to crumble after Tiglath-pileser III (745–727 B.C.) strengthened Assyria. The reigns of Israel's last six kings were relatively brief since four were murdered and a fifth was carried captive to Assyria. Confusion and decline characterized the last years of the northern kingdom, and her people refused to heed Hosea's warning of imminent judgment. The people were in a spiritual stupor, riddled with sin and idolatry.

THE CHRIST OF HOSEA

Matthew 2:15 applies Hosea 11:1 to Christ in Egypt: "When Israel *was* a child, then I loved him, and called my son out of Egypt." Matthew quotes the second half of this verse to show that the Exodus of Israel from Egypt as a new nation was a prophetic figure of Israel's Messiah who was also called out of Egypt in His childhood. Both Israel and Christ left Palestine to take refuge in Egypt.

Christ's identification with our plight and His loving work of redemption can be seen in Hosea's redemption of Gomer from the slave market.

KEYS TO HOSEA

Key Word: The Loyal Love of God for Israel—The themes of chapters 1—3 echo throughout the rest of the book. The adultery of Gomer (1) illustrates the sin of Israel (4—7); the degradation of Gomer (2) represents the judgment of Israel (8—10); and Hosea's redemption of Gomer (3) pictures the restoration of Israel (11—14). More than any other Old Testament prophet, Hosea's personal experiences illustrate his prophetic message. In his relationship to Gomer, Hosea portrays God's faithfulness, justice, love, and forgiveness toward His people. The

theme of God's holiness is developed in contrast to Israel's corruption and apostasy. Hosea utters about 150 statements concerning the sins of Israel, and more than half deal specifically with idolatry. The theme of God's justice is contrasted with Israel's lack of justice. There has never been a good king in Israel, and judgment is long overdue. The theme of God's love is seen in contrast to Israel's hardness and empty ritual. God's loyal love is unconditional and ceaseless; in spite of Israel's manifold sins, God tries every means to bring His people back to Himself. He pleads with the people to return to Him, but they will not. "O Israel, return unto the LORD thy God; for thou hast fallen by thine iniquity" (14:1).

Key Verses: Hosea 4:1; 11:7-9—"Hear the word of the LORD, ye children of Israel: for the LORD hath a controversy with the inhabitants of the land, because *there is* no truth, nor mercy, nor knowledge of God in the land" (4:1).

"And my people are bent to backsliding from me: though they called them to the most High, none at all would exalt *him*. How shall I give thee up, Ephraim? *how* shall I deliver thee, Israel? how shall I make thee as Admah? *how* shall I set thee as Zeboim? mine heart is turned within me, my repentings are kindled together. I will not execute the fierceness of mine anger, I will not return to destroy Ephraim: for I *am* God, and not man; the Holy One in the midst of thee: and I will not enter into the city" (11:7-9).

Key Chapter: Hosea 4—The nation of Israel has left the knowledge of the truth and followed the idolatrous ways of their pagan neighbors. Central to the book is Hosea 4:6—"My people are destroyed for lack of knowledge: because thou hast rejected knowledge, I will also reject thee, that thou shalt be no priest to me: seeing thou hast forgotten the law of thy God, I will also forget thy children."

SURVEY OF HOSEA

Hosea is called by God to prophesy during Israel's last hours, just as Jeremiah will prophesy years later to the crumbling kingdom of Judah. As one commentator has noted, "What we see in the prophecy of Hosea are the last few swirls as the kingdom of Israel goes down the drain." This book represents God's last gracious effort to plug the drain. Hosea's personal tragedy is an intense illustration of Israel's national tragedy. It is a story of one-sided love and faithfulness that represents the relationship between Israel and God. As Gomer is married to Hosea, so Israel is betrothed to God. Both relationships gradually disintegrate—Gomer runs after other men, and Israel runs after other gods. Israel's spiritual adultery is illustrated in Gomer's physical adultery. The development of the book can be traced in two parts: the adulterous wife and faithful husband (1—3) and the adulterous Israel and faithful Lord (4—14).

The Adulterous Wife and Faithful Husband (1—3): Hosea marries a woman named Gomer who bears him three children appropriately named by God as signs to Israel. Jezreel, Lo-ruhamah, and Lo-ammi mean "God Scatters," "Not Pitied," and "Not My People." Similarly, God will judge and scatter Israel because of her sin.

Gomer seeks other lovers and deserts Hosea. In spite of the depth to which her sin carries her, Hosea redeems her from the slave market and restores her.

The Adulterous Israel and Faithful Lord (4—14): Because of his own painful experience, Hosea can feel some of the sorrow of God over the sinfulness of His people. His loyal love for Gomer is a reflection of God's concern for Israel. However, Israel has fallen into the dregs of sin

FOCUS	ADULTEROUS WIFE AND FAITHFUL HUSBAND			ADULTEROUS ISRAEL AND FAITHFUL LORD			
REFERENCE	1:1———2:2———3:1———4:1———6:4———9:1———11:1———14:9						
DIVISION	PROPHETIC MARRIAGE	APPLICATION OF GOMER TO ISRAEL	RESTORATION OF GOMER	SPIRITUAL ADULTERY OF ISRAEL	REFUSAL OF ISRAEL TO REPENT	JUDGMENT OF ISRAEL BY GOD	RESTORATION OF ISRAEL TO GOD
TOPIC	MARRIAGE OF HOSEA			MESSAGE OF HOSEA			
	PERSONAL			NATIONAL			
LOCATION	NORTHERN KINGDOM OF ISRAEL						
TIME	c. 755—710 B.C.						

and is hardened against God's gracious last appeal to return. The people have flagrantly violated all of God's commandments, and they are indicted by the holy God for their crimes. Even now God wants to heal and redeem them (7:1, 13), but in their arrogance and idolatry they rebel.

Chapters 9 and 10 give the verdict of the case God has just presented. Israel's disobedience will lead to her dispersion. "For they [sow] the wind" (4—7), "and they . . . reap the whirlwind" (8—

10). Israel spurns repentance, and the judgment of God can no longer be delayed.

God is holy (4—7) and just (8—10), but He is also loving and gracious (11—14). God must discipline, but because of His endless love, He will ultimately save and restore His wayward people. "How shall I give thee up, Ephraim? . . . I will heal their backsliding, I will love them freely: for mine anger is turned away from him" (11:8; 14:4).

OUTLINE OF HOSEA

CHAPTER 1

The Introduction to the Book of Hosea

THE word of the LORD that came unto Ho-se'-a, the son of Be-e'-ri, in the days of Uz-zi'-ah, Jo'-tham, Ahaz, *and* Hez-e-ki'-ah, kings of Judah, and in the days of Jer-o-bo'-am the son of Jo'-ash, king of Israel.

Hosea's Marriage to Gomer

2 The beginning of the word of the LORD by Ho-se'-a. And the LORD said to Ho-se'-a, RGo, take unto thee a wife of whoredoms and children of Twhoredoms: for the land hath committed great whoredom, *departing* from the LORD.   3:1 • *harlotry*

The Children of Hosea and Gomer

3 So he went and took Go'-mer the daughter of Dib'-la-im; which conceived, and bare him a son.

4 And the LORD said unto him, Call his name Jez'-re-el; for yet a little *while,* and I will avenge the blood of Jez'-re-el upon the

house of Je'-hu, and will Rcause to cease the kingdom of the house of Israel. 2 Kin. 17:6; 18:11

5 And it shall come to pass at that day, that I will break the bow of Israel in the valley of Jez'-re-el.

6 And she conceived again, and bare a daughter. And God said unto him, Call her name Lo-ru'-ha-mah: Rfor I will no more have mercy upon the house of Israel; but I will utterly take them away.   2 Kin. 17:6

7 RBut I will have mercy upon the house of Judah, and will save them by the LORD their God, and Rwill not save them by bow, nor by sword, nor by battle, by horses, nor by horsemen.   2 Kin. 19:35 • [Zech. 4:6]

8 Now when she had weaned Lo-ru'-ha-mah, she conceived, and bare a son.

9 Then said *God,* Call his name TLo-am'-mi: for ye *are* not my people, and I will not be your *God.*   *not my people*

The Application of Future Restoration

10 Yet the number of the children of Israel shall be as the sand of the sea, which cannot

be measured nor numbered; and it shall come to pass, *that* in the place where it was said unto them, ᴿYe *are* not my people, *there* it shall be said unto them, Ye *are* the sons of the living God. Rom. 9:25-28

11 ᴿThen shall the children of Judah and the children of Israel be gathered together, and appoint themselves one head, and they shall come up out of the land: for great *shall be* the day of Jez'-re-el. Is. 11:12

CHAPTER 2

SAY ye unto your brethren, Am'-mi; and to your sisters, Ru'-ha-mah.

Israel's Sin of Spiritual Adultery

2 Plead with your mother, plead: for ᴿshe *is* not my wife, neither *am* I her husband: let her therefore put away her whoredomsᵀ out of her sight, and her adulteries from between her breasts; Is. 50:1 · *harlotry*

3 Lest I strip her naked, and set her as in the day that she was born, and make her as a wilderness, and set her like a dry land, and slay her with ᴿthirst. Amos 8:11

4 And I will not have mercy upon her children; for they *be* the ᴿchildren of ᵀwhoredoms. John 8:41 · *harlotry*

5 For their mother hath played the harlot: she that conceived them hath done shamefully: for she said, I will go after my lovers, that give *me* my bread and my water, my wool and my flax, mine oil and my drink.

Judgment of God

6 Therefore, behold, I will hedge up thy way with thorns, and ᵀmake a wall, that she shall not find her paths. *put up a hindrance*

7 And she shall follow after her lovers, but she shall not overtake them; and she shall seek them, but shall not find *them:* then shall she say, ᴿI will go and return to my ᴿfirst husband; for then *was it* better with me than now. Luke 15:18 · Ezek. 16:8

8 For she ᴿdid not know that I gave her corn, and ᵀwine, and oil, and multiplied her silver and gold, *which* they ᵀprepared for Ba'-al. Is. 1:3 · *new wine* · *considered as belonging to*

9 Therefore will I return, and take away my corn in the time thereof, and my wine in the season thereof, and will recover my wool and my flax *given* to cover her nakedness.

10 And now will I ᵀdiscover her lewdness in the sight of her lovers, and none shall deliver her out of mine hand. *reveal her sin*

11 I will also cause all her mirth to cease, her feast days, her new moons, and her sabbaths, and all her solemn feasts.

12 And I will destroy her vines and her fig trees, whereof she hath said, These *are* my rewards that my lovers have given me: and I

will make them a forest, and the beasts of the field ᴿshall eat them. Is. 5:5

13 And I will visit upon her the days of Ba'-al-im, wherein she burned incense to them, and she decked herself with her earrings and her jewels, and she went after her lovers, and forgat me, saith the Lᴏʀᴅ.

Restoration of Israel

14 Therefore, behold, I will allure her, and ᴿbring her into the wilderness, and speak comfortably unto her. [Ezek. 20:33-38]

15 And I will give her her vineyards from thence, and the valley of A'-chor for a door of hope: and she shall sing there, as in the days of her youth, and as in the day when she came up out of the land of Egypt.

16 And it shall be at that day, saith the Lᴏʀᴅ, *that* thou shalt call me Ish'-i; and shalt call me no more ᵀBa'-al-i. *my lord*

17 For I will take away the names of Ba'-al-im out of her mouth, and they shall no more be remembered by their name.

18 And in that day will I make a covenant for them with the beasts of the field, and with the fowls of heaven, and *with* the creeping things of the ground: and I will break the bow and the sword and the battle out of the earth, and will make them to lie down safely.

19 And ᴿI will betroth thee unto me for ever; yea, I will betroth thee unto me in righteousness, and in judgment, and in lovingkindness, and in mercies. Is. 62:4, 5

20 I will even betroth thee unto me in faithfulness: and ᴿthou shalt know the Lᴏʀᴅ. [Jer. 31:33; John 17:3]

21 And it shall come to pass in that day, I will hear, saith the Lᴏʀᴅ, I will hear the heavens, and they shall hear the earth;

22 And the ᴿearth ᵀshall hear the corn, and the wine, and the oil; and they ᵀshall hear Jez'-re-el. Jer. 31:12; Joel 2:19 · *will respond* · *answer*

23 And I will ᵀsow her unto me in the earth; ᴿand I will have mercy upon her that had not obtained mercy; and I will say to *them* which *were* not my people, Thou *art* my people; and they shall say, Thou *art* my God. *start her like a new crop* · 1:6

CHAPTER 3

The Restoration of Gomer to Hosea

THEN said the Lᴏʀᴅ unto me, Go yet, love a woman beloved of *her* friend, yet ᴿan adulteress, according to the love of the Lᴏʀᴅ toward the children of Israel, who look to other gods, and love flagons of wine. Jer. 3:20

2 So ᴿI bought her to me for fifteen *pieces* of silver, and *for* an ᵀho'-mer of barley, and an half ho'-mer of barley: Ruth 4:10 · *9.8 bushels*

3 And I said unto her, Thou shalt abide for me many days; ᴿthou shalt not play the

harlot, and thou shalt not be for *another* man: so *will* I also *be* for thee.   Deut. 21:13

4 For the children of Israel shall abide many days ᴿwithout a king, and without a prince, and ᴿwithout a sacrifice, and without ᵀan image, and without an e'-phod, and *without* ter'-a-phim: 10:3 • [Dan. 9:25–27] • *pillar*

5 Afterward shall the children of Israel return, and seek the LORD their God, and David their king; and shall fear the LORD and his goodness in the ᴿlatter days.   [Is. 2:2]

CHAPTER 4

Rejection of the Knowledge of God

HEAR ᴿthe word of the LORD, ye children of Israel: for the LORD hath a controversy with the inhabitants of the land, because *there is* no truth, nor mercy, nor knowledge of God in the land.   Is. 50:4

2 By swearing, and lying, and killing, and stealing, and committing adultery, they break out, and blood toucheth blood.

3 Therefore shall the land mourn, and ᴿevery one that dwelleth therein shall languish, with the beasts of the field, and with the fowls of heaven; yea, the fishes of the sea also shall be taken away.   Zeph. 1:3

4 Yet let no man ᴿstrive, nor reprove another: for thy people *are* as they ᴿthat strive with the priest.   Ezek. 3:26 • Deut. 17:12

5 Therefore shalt thou fall in the day, and the prophet also shall fall with thee in the night, and I will destroy thy mother.

6 ᴿMy people are destroyed for lack of knowledge: because thou hast rejected knowledge, I will also reject thee, that thou shalt be no priest to me: seeing thou hast forgotten the law of thy God, I will also forget thy children.   Is. 5:13; 2 Pet. 1:5

7 As they were ᴿincreased, so they sinned against me: ᴿtherefore will I change their glory into shame.   Is. 56:11; Mic. 3:11 • 1 Sam. 2:30

8 They eat up the sin of my people, and they set their heart on their iniquity.

9 And there shall be, like people, like priest: and I will punish them for their ways, and ᵀreward them their doings.   *punish*

10 For they shall eat, and not have enough: they shall commit ᵀwhoredom, and shall not increase: because they have left off to take heed to the LORD.   *harlotry*

11 ᴿWhoredom and wine and new wine take away the heart.   Is. 5:12; 28:7

Idolatry of Israel

12 My people ask counsel at their stocks, and their ᵀstaff declareth unto them: for the spirit of whoredoms hath caused *them* to err, and they have gone a whoring from under their God.   *pagan charm*

13 They sacrifice upon the tops of the mountains, and burn incense upon the hills, under oaks and poplars and elms, because the shadow thereof *is* good: therefore your daughters shall commit ᵀwhoredom, and your spouses shall commit adultery.   *harlotry*

14 I will not punish your daughters when they commit whoredom, nor your spouses when they commit adultery: for themselves are separated with whores, and they sacrifice with harlots: therefore the people *that* doth not understand shall fall.

15 Though thou, Israel, play the harlot, *yet* let not Judah offend; ᴿand come not ye unto Gil'-gal, neither go ye up to Beth-a'-ven, nor swear, The LORD liveth.   9:15

16 For Israel ᴿslideth back as a ᵀbacksliding heifer: now the LORD will feed them as a lamb in a large place.   Jer. 3:6 • *stubborn*

17 E'-phra-im *is* ᵀjoined to ᴿidols: ᴿlet him alone.   *united* • 13:2 • v. 4; Ps. 81:12

18 Their drink is sour: they have committed whoredom continually: her ᵀrulers *with* shame do love, Give ye.   *leaders in sin*

19 ᴿThe wind hath bound her up in her wings, and ᴿthey shall be ashamed because of their sacrifices.   12:1; 13:15; Jer. 51:1 • Is. 1:29

CHAPTER 5

Judgment on Israel

HEAR ye this, O priests; and hearken, ye house of Israel; and give ye ear, O house of the king; for judgment *is* toward you, because ᴿye have been a snare on Miz'-pah, and a net spread upon Ta'-bor.   6:9

2 And the revolters are ᴿprofoundᵀ to make slaughter, though I *have been* a rebuker of them all.   4:6, 14; Is. 29:15 • *determined*

3 I know E'-phra-im, and Israel is not hid from me: for now, O E'-phra-im, thou committest whoredom, *and* Israel is defiled.

4 They will not frame their doings to turn unto their God: for the spirit of whoredoms *is* in the midst of them, and they have not ᵀknown the LORD.   *respected*

5 And the ᴿpride of Israel doth testify to his face: therefore shall Israel and E'-phra-im fall in their iniquity; ᴿJudah also shall fall with them.   *v.* 10 • Ezek. 23:31–35

6 ᴿThey shall go with their flocks and with their herds to seek the LORD; ᴿbut they shall not find *him;* he hath withdrawn himself from them.   Prov. 1:28; Mic. 6:6 • Is. 1:15

7 They have ᴿdealt treacherously against the LORD: for they have begotten strange children: now shall a month ᵀdevour them with their ᵀportions.   Jer. 3:20 • *destroy* • *fields*

8 Blow ye the cornet in Gib'-e-ah, *and* the trumpet in Ra'-mah: cry aloud *at* Beth-a'-ven, after thee, O Benjamin.

9 E'-phra-im shall be desolate in the day of rebuke: among the tribes of Israel have I made known that which shall surely be.

10 The princes of Judah were like them that remove the bound: *therefore* I will pour out my wrath upon them like water.

11 E'-phra-im *is* oppressed *and* broken in judgment, because he willingly walked ᵀafter ᴿthe commandment.   *away from* • Mic. 6:16

12 Therefore *will* I *be* unto E'-phra-im as ᴿa moth, and to the house of Judah ᴿas ᵀrottenness.   [Ps. 39:11; Is. 51:8] • Prov. 12:4 • *a worm*

13 When E'-phra-im saw his sickness, and Judah *saw* his ᴿwound, then ᴿwent E'-phra-im to the Assyrian, and sent to king Ja'-reb: yet could he not heal you, nor cure you of your wound.   Jer. 30:12 • 7:11

14 For I *will be* unto E'-phra-im as a lion, and as a young lion to the house of Judah: I, *even* I, will tear and go away; I will take away, and ᴿnone shall rescue *him.*   Mic. 5:8

Eventual Restoration of Israel

15 I will go *and* return to my place, till they ᵀacknowledge their offence, and seek my face: in their affliction they ᴿwill seek me ᵀearly.   *admit their guilt* • Ps. 50:15 • *earnestly*

CHAPTER 6

COME, and let us return unto the LORD: for he hath torn, and he will heal us; he hath smitten, and he will bind us up.

2 ᴿAfter two days will he revive us: in the third day he will raise us up, and we shall live in his sight.   [Luke 24:46; 1 Cor. 15:4] ✿

3 ᴿThen shall we know, *if* we follow on to ᵀknow the LORD: his going forth is prepared as the morning; and he shall come unto us as the rain, as the latter *and* former rain unto the earth.   Is. 54:13 • *recognize*

Willful Transgression of the Covenant

4 O E'-phra-im, what shall I do unto thee? O Judah, what shall I do unto thee? for your ᵀgoodness *is* as a morning cloud, and as the early dew it goeth away.   *virtue*

5 Therefore have I ᵀhewed *them* by the prophets; I have slain them by ᴿthe words of my mouth: and thy judgments *are as* the light *that* goeth forth.   *cut down* • [Jer. 23:29]

6 For I desired mercy, and ᴿnot sacrifice; and the ᴿknowledgeᵀ of God more than burnt offerings.   Is. 1:11 • [John 17:3] • *reverence*

7 But they ᵀlikeᴿ men have transgressed the covenant: there have they dealt treacherously against me.   *like Adam* • Job 31:33

8 Gil'-e-ad *is* a city of them that work iniquity, *and is* ᵀpolluted with blood.   *guilty*

9 And as troops of robbers wait for a man, *so* the company of priests murder in the way by consent: for they commit lewdness.

10 I have seen an horrible thing in the house of Israel: there *is* the whoredom of E'-phra-im, Israel is defiled.

11 Also, O Judah, he hath set an ᴿharvest

for thee, when I ᵀreturned the captivity of my people.   Jer. 51:33; Joel 3:13 • *bring back*

CHAPTER 7

Willful Refusal to Return to the Lord

WHEN ᴿI would have healed Israel, then the iniquity of E'-phra-im was discovered, and the wickedness of Sa-ma'-ri-a: for ᴿthey commit falsehood; and the thief cometh in, *and* the troop of robbers ᵀspoileth without.   *v.* 13 • 5:1 • *carries away the goods*

2 And they ᵀconsider not in their hearts *that* I ᴿremember all their wickedness: now their own doings have beset them about; they are before my face.   *say not to* • Jer. 17:1

3 They make the king glad with their wickedness, and the princes with their lies.

4 ᴿThey *are* all adulterers, as an oven heated by the baker, *who* ceaseth ᵀfrom raising after he hath kneaded the dough, until it be leavened.   Jer. 9:2 • *to stir the fire*

5 In the day of our king the princes have made *him* sick with bottles of wine; he stretched out his hand with scorners.

6 For they have made ready their heart like an oven, whiles they lie in wait: their baker sleepeth all the night; in the morning it burneth as a flaming fire.

7 They are all hot as an oven, and have devoured their judges; all their kings are fallen: ᴿ*there is* none among them that calleth unto me.   Is. 9:13; 64:7

8 E'-phra-im, he ᴿhath mixed himself among the ᵀpeople; E'-phra-im is a cake not turned.   Ps. 106:35 • *nations*

9 ᴿStrangers have devoured his strength, and he knoweth *it* ᴿnot: yea, gray hairs are ᵀhere and there upon him, yet he knoweth not.   8:7 • Is. 42:25 • *sprinkled*

10 And the pride of Israel testifieth to his face: and they do not return to the LORD their God, nor seek him for all this.

11 ᴿE'-phra-im also is like a silly dove without heart: ᴿthey call to Egypt, they go to Assyria.   5:13 • 11:11; Is. 30:3

12 When they shall go, I ᴿwill spread my net upon them; I will bring them down as the fowls of the heaven; I will chastise them, as their congregation hath heard.   2 Kin. 17; 18

13 Woe unto them! for they have ᴿfled from me: destruction unto them! because they have transgressed against me: though ᴿI have redeemed them, yet they have spoken lies against me.   Jer. 14:10 • Mic. 6:4

14 And they have not cried unto me with their heart, when they howled upon their beds: they assemble themselves for corn and wine, *and* they rebel against me.

15 Though I have ᵀbound *and* strengthened their arms, yet do they ᴿimagine mischief against me.   *trained* • Nah. 1:9

16 They return, *but* not to the most High: ^Rthey are like a deceitful bow: their princes shall fall by the sword for the ^Rrage of their tongue: this *shall be* their derision ^Rin the land of Egypt.   Ps. 78:57 • Ps. 73:9 • 9:3, 6

CHAPTER 8

Willful Idolatry

SET the trumpet to thy mouth. *He shall come* as an eagle against the house of the LORD, because they have transgressed my covenant, and trespassed against my law.

2 ^RIsrael shall cry unto me, My God, ^Rwe ^Tknow thee.   5:15; Ps. 78:34 • Titus 1:16 • *reverence*

3 Israel hath cast off *the thing that is* good: the enemy shall pursue him.

4 They have set up kings, but ^Tnot by me: they have made princes, and I ^Tknew *it* not: of their silver and their gold have they made them idols, that they may be cut off.   *consented*

5 Thy calf, O Sa-ma'-ri-a, hath cast *thee* off; mine anger is kindled against them: how long *will it be* ere they attain to innocency?

6 For from Israel *was* it also: the workman made it; therefore it *is* not God: but the calf of Sa-ma'-ri-a shall be broken in pieces.

7 For they have sown the wind, and they shall reap the whirlwind: it hath no stalk: the bud shall yield no meal: if so be it yield, the strangers shall swallow it up.

8 ^RIsrael is swallowed up: now shall they be among the ^TGentiles ^Ras a vessel wherein *is* no pleasure.   2 Kin. 17:6 • *nations* • Jer. 22:28

9 For they are gone up to Assyria, ^Ra wild ass alone by himself: E'-phra-im ^Rhath hired ^Tlovers.   Jer. 2:24 • Ezek. 16:33, 34 • *loves*

10 Yea, though they have hired among the nations, now will I gather them, and they shall ^Tsorrow a little for the burden of the king of princes.   *be in some distress*

11 Because E'-phra-im hath made many altars to sin, altars shall be unto him to sin.

12 I have written to him ^Rthe great things of my law, *but* they were counted as ^Ta strange thing.   [Deut. 4:6, 8]; Ps. 119:18 • *an unknown*

13 ^RThey sacrifice flesh *for* the sacrifices of mine offerings, and eat *it;* ^Rbut the LORD accepteth them not; now will he remember their iniquity, and visit their sins: they shall return to Egypt.   Zech. 7:6 • Jer. 14:10

14 ^RFor Israel hath forgotten ^Rhis Maker, and buildeth temples; and Judah hath multiplied fenced cities: but ^RI will send a fire upon his cities, and it shall devour the palaces thereof.   Deut. 32:18 • Is. 29:23 • Jer. 17:27

CHAPTER 9

Judgment of Dispersion

REJOICE not, O Israel, for joy, as *other* people: for thou hast gone ^Ta whoring from thy God, thou hast loved a reward upon every cornfloor.   *in an unfaithful way*

2 The floor and the winepress shall not feed them, and the new wine shall fail in her.

3 They shall not dwell in the LORD's land; but E'-phra-im shall return to Egypt, and they shall eat unclean *things* in Assyria.

4 They shall not offer wine *offerings* to the LORD, neither shall they be pleasing unto him: their sacrifices *shall be* unto them as the bread of mourners; all that eat thereof shall be polluted: for their bread for their soul shall not come into the house of the LORD.

5 ^RWhat will ye do in the solemn day, and in the day of the feast of the LORD?   Is. 10:3

6 For, lo, they are gone because of destruction: Egypt shall gather them up, Mem'-phis shall bury them: the pleasant *places* for their silver, nettles shall possess them: thorns *shall be* in their tabernacles.

7 The ^Rdays of visitation are come, the days of recompence are come; Israel shall know *it:* the prophet *is* a fool, the spiritual man *is* mad, for the multitude of thine iniquity, and the great hatred.   2 Kin. 17; 18

8 The ^Rwatchman of E'-phra-im *was* with my God: *but* the prophet *is* a snare of a fowler in all his ways, *and* ^Thatred in the house of his God.   Jer. 6:17; 31:6 • *opposed to*

9 ^RThey have deeply corrupted *themselves,* as in the days of ^RGib'-e-ah: *therefore* he will remember their iniquity, he will visit their sins.   10:9; Is. 31:6 • Judg. 19:22

Judgment of Barrenness

10 I found Israel like grapes in the wilderness; I saw your fathers as the firstripe in the fig tree at her first time: *but* they went to ^RBa'-al-pe'-or, and separated themselves unto *that* shame; and *their* abominations were according as they loved.   Ps. 106:28

11 *As for* E'-phra-im, their glory shall fly away like a bird, from the birth, and from the womb, and from the conception.

12 Though they bring up their children, yet will I bereave them, *that there shall* not *be* a man *left:* yea, ^Rwoe also to them when I depart from them!   Deut. 31:17

13 E'-phra-im, as I saw Ty'-rus, *is* planted in a pleasant place: but E'-phra-im shall bring forth his children to the murderer.

14 Give them, O LORD: what wilt thou give? ^Tgive them ^Ra miscarrying womb and dry breasts.   *let their women be barren* • Luke 23:29

15 All their wickedness *is* in Gil'-gal: for there I hated them: for the wickedness of their doings I will drive them out of mine house, I will love them no more: ^Rall their princes *are* ^Trevolters.   Is. 1:23 • *rebels*

16 E'-phra-im is smitten, their root is dried up, they shall bear no fruit: yea, though they bring forth, yet will I slay *even* the beloved *fruit* of their womb.

17 My God will cast them away, because they did not hearken unto him: and they shall be wanderers among the nations.

CHAPTER 10

Judgment of Destruction

ISRAEL is ᴿan empty vine, he bringeth forth fruit unto himself: according to the multitude of his fruit ᴿhe hath increased the altars; according to the goodness of his land they have made goodly images.   Nah. 2:2 • 8:11

2 Their heart is divided; now shall they be found faulty: he shall break down their altars, he shall ᵀspoil their images.   destroy

3 For now they shall say, We have ᴿno king, because we feared not the LORD; what then should a king do to us?   Ps. 12:4

4 They have spoken words, swearing falsely in making ᵀa covenant: thus ᴿjudgment springeth up as hemlock in the furrows of the field.   an agreement • Amos 5:7

5 The inhabitants of Sa-ma′-ri-a shall fear because of the ᴿcalvesᵀ of Beth-a′-ven: for the people thereof shall mourn over it, and the priests thereof that rejoiced on it, for the glory thereof, because it is departed from it.   1 Kin. 12:28, 29 • calf idols

6 It shall be also ᴿcarried unto Assyria for a present to king Ja′-reb: ᴿE′-phra-im shall receive shame, and Israel shall be ashamed of his ᴿown ᵀcounsel.   2 Kin. 17:6 • 5:13 • Jer. 7:24 • advice

7 As for Sa-ma′-ri-a, her ᴿking is cut off as the foam upon the water.   13:11

8 The high places also of A′-ven, the sin of Israel, shall be destroyed: the thorn and the thistle shall come up on their altars; and they shall say to the mountains, Cover us; and to the hills, Fall on us.

9 O Israel, thou hast sinned from the days of Gib′-e-ah: there they stood: the battle in Gib′-e-ah against the children of iniquity did not ᵀovertake them.   overcome

10 It is in my desire that I should chastise them; and ᴿthe people shall be gathered against them, when they shall bind themselves in their two furrows.   Jer. 16:16

11 And E′-phra-im is as an heifer that is taught, and loveth to tread out the corn; but I passed over upon her fair neck: I will make E′-phra-im to ride; Judah shall plow, and Jacob shall break his clods.

12 Sow to yourselves in righteousness, reap in mercy; break up your fallow ground: for it is time to seek the LORD, till he come and rain righteousness upon you.

13 Ye have plowed wickedness, ye have reaped iniquity; ye have eaten the fruit of lies: because thou didst trust in thy way, in the multitude of thy mighty men.

14 Therefore shall a ᵀtumult arise among thy people, and all thy fortresses shall be spoiled, as Shal′-man spoiled Beth-ar′-bel in the day of battle: the mother was dashed in pieces upon her children.   mutiny

15 So shall Beth′-el do unto you because of your great wickedness: in a morning shall the king of Israel utterly be cut off.

CHAPTER 11

God's Love for Israel

WHEN Israel was a child, then I loved him, and called my son out of Egypt.

2 As they called them, so they went from them: they sacrificed unto Ba′-al-im, and burned incense to ᵀgraven images.   carved

3 ᴿI taught E′-phra-im also to go, taking them by ᵀtheir arms; but they knew not that ᴿI healed them.   Deut. 1:31 • my • Ex. 15:26

4 I drew them with cords of a man, with bands of love: and I was to them as they that ᵀtake off the yoke on their jaws, and I ᵀlaid meat unto them.   set them free • gave food

5 He shall not return into the land of Egypt, but ᴿthe Assyrian shall be his king, because they refused to return.   2 Kin. 17:6

6 And the sword shall abide on his cities, and shall consume his branches, and devour them, because of their own counsels.

7 And my people are bent to backsliding from me: though they called them to the most High, none at all would exalt him.

8 How shall I give thee up, E′-phra-im? how shall I deliver thee, Israel? how shall I make thee as Ad′-mah? how shall I set thee as Ze-bo′-im? mine heart is turned within me, my repentings are kindled together.

9 ᴿI will not execute the fierceness of mine anger, I will not return to destroy E′-phra-im: ᴿfor I am God, and not man; the Holy One in the midst of thee: and I will not enter into the city.   Deut. 13:17 • Num. 23:19

10 They shall walk after the LORD: he shall roar like a lion: when he shall roar, then the children shall tremble from the west.

11 They shall tremble as a bird out of Egypt, and as a dove out of the land of Assyria: ᴿand I will ᵀplace them in their houses, saith the LORD.   Ezek. 28:25, 26 • restore

12 E′-phra-im compasseth me about with lies, and the house of Israel with deceit: but Judah yet ruleth with God, and is faithful with the saints.

CHAPTER 12

Israel's Continuing Sin

E′-PHRA-IM feedeth on wind, and followeth after the east wind: he daily increaseth lies and ᵀdesolation; and they do make a covenant with the Assyrians, and oil is carried into Egypt.   violence

2 ᴿThe LORD hath also a ᵀcontroversy with Judah, and ᴿwill punish Jacob according to

his ways; according to his doings will he recompense him.   Mic. 6:2 • *complaint* • 2 Kin. 17, 18

3 He took his brother ᴿby the heel in the womb, and by his strength he ᴿhadᵀ power with God: Gen. 25:26 • Gen. 32:28 • *prevailed*

4 Yea, he had power over the angel, and prevailed: he wept, and made supplication unto him: he found him *in* ᴿBeth'-el, and there he spake with us;   [Gen. 28:12-15]

5 Even the Lᴏʀᴅ God of hosts; the Lᴏʀᴅ *is* his ᴿmemorial.   Ex. 3:15

6 ᴿTherefore turn thou to thy God: keep mercy and judgment, and ᵀwait on thy God continually.   Mic. 6:8 • *serve*

7 *He is* a merchant, the balances of deceit *are* in his hand: he loveth to oppress.

8 And E'-phra-im said, ᴿYet I am become rich, I have found me out substance: *in* all my labours they shall find none iniquity in me that *were* sin.   Ps. 62:10; Rev. 3:17

9 And I *that am* the Lᴏʀᴅ thy God from the land of Egypt ᴿwill yet make thee to dwell in tabernacles, as in the days of the solemn feast.   Lev. 23:42

10 I have also spoken by the prophets, and I have multiplied visions, and used similitudes, by the ministry of the prophets.

11 *Is there* iniquity *in* Gil'-e-ad? surely they are vanity: they sacrifice bullocks in Gil'-gal; yea, their altars *are* as heaps in the furrows of the fields.

12 And Jacob ᴿfled into the ᵀcountry of Syria, and Israel served for a wife, and for a wife he kept *sheep.*   Gen. 28:5 • *field of Aram*

13 ᴿAnd by a prophet the Lᴏʀᴅ brought Israel out of Egypt, and by a prophet was he preserved.   Ex. 12:50, 51; Ps. 77:20; Mic. 6:4

14 E'-phra-im provoked *him* to anger ᵀmost bitterly: therefore shall he leave his blood upon him, and his reproach shall his Lord return unto him.   *with bitternesses*

6 According to their pasture, so were they filled; they were filled, and their heart was exalted; therefore have they forgotten me.

7 Therefore ᴿI will be unto them as a lion: as ᴿa leopard by the way will I ᵀobserve *them:*   Lam. 3:10 • Jer. 5:6 • *look at them*

8 I will meet them as a bear *that is* bereaved *of her whelps,* and will rend the caul of their heart, and there will I devour them like a lion: the wild beast shall tear them.

9 O Israel, ᴿthou hast destroyed thyself; but in me *is* thine help.   Jer. 2:17, 19; Mal. 1:12

10 I will be thy king: ᴿwhere is *any other* that may save thee in all thy cities? and thy judges of whom ᴿthou saidst, Give me a king and princes?   Deut. 32:38 • 1 Sam. 8:5

11 ᴿI gave thee a king in mine anger, and took *him* away in my wrath.   1 Sam. 8:7

12 ᴿThe iniquity of E'-phra-im *is* bound up; his sin *is* ᵀhid.   Deut. 32:34 • *laid up in store*

13 The sorrows of a ᴿtravailing woman shall come upon him: he *is* an unwise son; for he should not stay long in *the place of* the breaking forth of children.   Mic. 4:9, 10

14 I will ransom them from ᵀthe power of the grave; I will redeem them from death: O death, I will be thy plagues; O grave, I will be thy destruction: ᴿrepentance shall be hid from mine eyes.   *the hand* • Jer. 15:6

15 Though he be fruitful among his brethren, ᴿan east wind shall come, the wind of the Lᴏʀᴅ shall come up from the wilderness, and his spring shall become dry, and his fountain shall be dried up: he shall ᵀspoil the treasure of all pleasant vessels.   Jer. 4:11 • *destroy*

16 ᴿSa-ma'-ri-a shall ᵀbecome desolate; for she hath rebelled against her God: ᴿthey shall fall by the sword: their infants shall be dashed in pieces, and their women with child shall be ripped up.   2 Kin. 17 • *be held guilty* • 2 Kin. 8:12

CHAPTER 13

W HEN ᴿE'-phra-im spake trembling, he exalted himself in Israel; but when he offended in Ba'-al, he died.   Judg. 12:1

2 And now they sin more and more, and have made them molten images of their silver, *and* idols according to their own understanding, all of it the work of the craftsmen: they say of them, Let the men that sacrifice ᵀkiss the calves.   *worship*

3 Therefore they shall be as the morning cloud, and as the early dew that passeth away, ᴿas the chaff *that* is driven with the whirlwind out of the floor, and as the smoke out of the chimney.   Is. 17:13; Dan. 2:35

4 Yet I *am* the Lᴏʀᴅ thy God from the land of Egypt, and thou shalt know no god but me: for *there is* no saviour beside me.

5 I did ᴿknow thee in the wilderness, in the land of great drought.   Deut. 32:10

CHAPTER 14

God's Promise to Restore Israel

O ISRAEL, ᴿreturn unto the Lᴏʀᴅ thy God; for thou hast fallen by thine ᵀiniquity.   [Joel 2:13] • *sin*

2 Take with you words, and turn to the Lᴏʀᴅ: say unto him, Take away all iniquity, and receive *us* graciously: so will we render the ᵀcalves of our lips.   *offerings*

3 Assh'-ur shall not save us; ᴿwe will not ride upon horses: neither will we say any more to the work of our hands, Ye are our gods: ᴿfor in thee the fatherless findeth mercy.   [Ps. 33:17]; Is. 31:1 • Ps. 10:14; 68:5

4 ᴿI will heal their backsliding, ᴿI will love them freely: for ᴿmine anger is turned away from him.   Is. 57:18 • Zeph. 3:17 • Is. 12:1

5 I will be as the dew unto Israel: he shall ᵀgrow as the lily, and ᵀcast forth his roots as Leb'-a-non.   *blossom* • *strike*

6 His branches ᵀshall spread, and his beauty shall be as the olive tree, and ᴿhis ᵀsmell as Leb′-a-non.   *sprout • Gen. 27:27 • fragrance*

7 They that dwell under his shadow shall return; they shall revive *as* the corn, and grow as the vine: the ᵀscent thereof *shall be* as the wine of Leb′-a-non.   *fragrance*

8 E′-phra-im *shall say,* What have I to do

any more with idols? I have ᵀheard *him,* and observed him: I *am* like a green fir tree. From me is thy fruit found.   *answered*

9 Who *is* wise, and he shall understand these *things?* prudent, and he shall know them? for ᴿthe ways of the LORD *are* right, and the just shall walk in them: but the transgressors shall fall therein.   [Prov. 10:29]

THE BOOK OF

JOEL

THE BOOK OF JOEL

Disaster strikes the southern kingdom of Judah without warning. An ominous black cloud descends upon the land—the dreaded locusts. In a matter of hours, every living green thing has been stripped bare. Joel, God's spokesman during the reign of Joash (835-796 B.C.), seizes this occasion to proclaim God's message. Although the locust plague has been a terrible judgment for sin, God's future judgments during the day of the Lord will make that plague pale by comparison. In that day, God will destroy His enemies, but bring unparalleled blessing to those who faithfully obey Him.

The Hebrew name *Yo'el* means "Yahweh Is God." This name is appropriate to the theme of the book, which emphasizes God's sovereign work in history. The courses of nature and nations are in His hand. The Greek equivalent is *Ioel*, and the Latin is *Joel*.

THE AUTHOR OF JOEL

Although there are several other Joels in the Bible, the prophet Joel is known only from this book. In the introductory verse, Joel identifies himself as the son of Pethuel (1:1), meaning "persuaded of God." His frequent references to Zion and the house of the Lord (1:9, 13, 14; 2:15-17, 23, 32; 3:1, 5, 6, 16, 17, 20, 21) suggest that he probably lived not far from Jerusalem. Because of his statements about the priesthood in 1:13, 14 and 2:17, some think Joel was a priest as well as a prophet. In any case, Joel was a clear, concise, and uncompromising preacher of repentance.

THE TIME OF JOEL

Since this book includes no explicit time references, it cannot be dated with certainty. Some commentators assign a late date (usually postexilic) to Joel for these reasons: (1) It does not mention the northern kingdom and indicates it was written after the 722 B.C. demise of Israel. (2) The references to priests but not kings fit the postexilic period. (3) Joel does not refer to Assyria, Syria, or Babylon, perhaps because these countries had already been overthrown. (4) If Joel 3:2 refers to the Babylonian captivity, this also supports the postexilic date. (5) The mention of the Greeks in 3:6 argues for a late date.

Commentators who believe Joel was written in the ninth century B.C. answer the above arguments in this way: (1) Joel's failure to mention the northern kingdom is an argument from silence. His prophecy was directed to Judah, not Israel. (2) Other early prophets omit

references to a king (Obadiah, Jonah, Nahum, and Habakkuk). This also fits the political situation during 841-835 B.C. when Athaliah usurped the throne upon the death of her husband Ahaziah. Joash, the legitimate heir to the throne, was a minor and protected by the high priest Jehoiada. When Athaliah was removed from power in 835, Joash came to the throne but ruled under the regency of Jehoiada. Thus, the prominence of the priests and lack of reference to a king in Joel fit this historical context. (3) It is true that Joel does not refer to Assyria or Babylon, but the countries Joel mentions are more crucial. They include Phoenicia, Philistia, Egypt, and Edom—countries prominent in the ninth century but not later. Assyria and Babylon are not mentioned because they had not yet reached a position of power. Also, if Joel had been postexilic, a reference to Persia would be expected. (4) Joel 3:2 does not refer to the Babylonian captivity but to an event that has not yet occurred. (5) Greeks are mentioned in Assyrian records from the eighth century B.C. It is just an assumption to state that the Hebrews had no knowledge of the Greeks at an early time.

Evidence also points to a sharing of material between Joel and Amos (cf. Joel 3:16 and Amos 1:2; Joel 3:18 and Amos 9:13). The context of the books suggests that Amos, an eighth-century prophet, borrowed from Joel. Also, Joel's style is more like that of Hosea and Amos than of the postexilic writers. The evidence seems to favor a date of about 835 B.C. for Joel. Since Joel does not mention idolatry, it may have been written after the purge of Baal worship and most other forms of idolatry in the early reign of Joash under Jehoiada the priest. As an early prophet of Judah, Joel would have been a contemporary of Elisha in Israel.

THE CHRIST OF JOEL

Christ promised to send the Holy Spirit after His ascension to the Father (John 16:7-15; Acts 1:8). When this was fulfilled on the Day of Pentecost, Peter said, "This is that which was spoken by the prophet Joel" (Joel 2:28-32; Acts 2:16-21). Joel also portrays Christ as the One who will judge the nations in the valley of Jehoshaphat in 3:2, 12.

KEYS TO JOEL

Key Word: The Great and Terrible Day of the Lord—The key theme of Joel is the day of the Lord in retrospect and prospect. Joel uses the terrible locust plague that has recently occurred in Judah to illustrate the coming day of

judgment when God will directly intervene in human history to vindicate His righteousness. This will be a time of unparalleled retribution upon Israel (2:1–11) and the whole nation (3:1–17), but this time will culminate in great blessing and salvation for all who trust in the Lord (2:18–32; 3:18–21). "And it shall come to pass, *that* whosoever shall call on the name of the Lord shall be delivered" (2:32).

Joel is written as a warning to the people of Judah of their need to turn humbly to the Lord with penitent hearts (2:12–17) so that God can bless rather than buffet them. If they continue to spurn God's gracious call to repentance, judgment will be inevitable. Joel stresses the sovereign power of God over nature and nations, and points out how God uses nature to get the attention of people.

Key Verses: Joel 2:11, 28, 29—"And the Lord shall utter his voice before his army: for his camp *is* very great: for *he is* strong that executeth his word: for the day of the Lord *is* great and very terrible; and who can abide it?" (2:11).

"And it shall come to pass afterward, *that* I will pour out my spirit upon all flesh; and your sons and your daughters shall prophesy, your old men shall dream dreams, your young men shall see visions: And also upon the servants and upon the handmaids in those days will I pour out my spirit" (2:28, 29).

Key Chapter: Joel 2—The prophet calls for Judah's repentance and promises God's repentance (2:13, 14) from His planned judgment upon Judah if they do indeed turn to Him. Though the offer is clearly given, Judah continues to rebel against the Lord, and judgment is to follow. In that judgment, however, is God's promise of His later outpouring, fulfilled initially on the Day of Pentecost (Acts 2:16ff.) and ultimately when Christ returns for the culmination of the day of the Lord.

SURVEY OF JOEL

The brief Book of Joel develops the crucial theme of the coming day of the Lord (1:15; 2:1, 2, 11, 31; 3:14, 18). It is a time of awesome judgment upon people and nations that have rebelled against God. But it is also a time of future blessing upon those who have trusted in Him. The theme of disaster runs throughout the book (locust plagues, famine, raging fires, invading armies, celestial phenomena), but promises of hope are interspersed with the pronouncements of coming judgment. The basic outline of Joel is: the day of the Lord in retrospect (1:1–20) and the day of the Lord in prospect (2:1—3:21).

The Day of the Lord in Retrospect (1:1-20): Joel begins with an account of a recent locust plague that has devastated the land. The black cloud of insects has stripped the grapevines and fruit trees and ruined the grain harvest. The economy has been brought to a further standstill by a drought and the people are in a desperate situation.

The Day of the Lord in Prospect (2:1—3:21): Joel makes effective use of this natural catastrophe as an illustration of a far greater judgment to come. Compared to the terrible day of the Lord, the destruction by the locusts will seem insignificant. The land will be invaded by a swarming army; like locusts they will be speedy and voracious. The desolation caused by this army will be dreadful: "The day of the Lord *is* great and very terrible; and who can abide it?" (2:11).

Even so, it is not too late for the people to avert disaster. The prophetic warning is designed to bring them to the point of repentance (2:12–17). "Therefore also now, saith the Lord, turn ye *even* to me with all your heart, and with fasting, and with weeping, and with mourning" (2:12). But God's gracious offer falls on deaf ears.

Ultimately, the swarming, creeping, stripping,

FOCUS	DAY OF THE LORD IN RETROSPECT		DAY OF THE LORD IN PROSPECT	
REFERENCE	1:1——————————1:13———————		2:1——————————2:28—————————3:21	
DIVISION	PAST DAY OF THE LOCUST	PAST DAY OF THE DROUGHT	IMMINENT DAY OF THE LORD	ULTIMATE DAY OF THE LORD
TOPIC	HISTORICAL INVASION		PROPHETIC INVASION	
	PAST JUDGMENT ON JUDAH		FUTURE JUDGMENT AND RESTORATION OF JUDAH	
LOCATION	SOUTHERN KINGDOM OF JUDAH			
TIME	c. 835 B.C.			

and gnawing locusts (1:4; 2:25) will come again in a fiercer form. But God promises that judgment will be followed by great blessing in a material (2:18–27) and spiritual (2:28–32) sense.

These rich promises are followed by a solemn description of the judgment of all nations in the valley of decision (3:14) in the end times. The nations will give an account of themselves to the God of Israel who will judge those who have rebelled against Him. God alone controls the course of history. "So shall ye know that I *am* the LORD your God dwelling in Zion, my holy mountain" (3:17). Joel ends with the kingdom blessings upon the remnant of faithful Judah: "But Judah shall dwell for ever, and Jerusalem from generation to generation" (3:20).

OUTLINE OF JOEL

CHAPTER 1

The Past Day of the Locust

THE ᴿword of the LORD that came to Jo'-el the son of Pe-thu'-el.   Luke 3:2

2 Hear this, ye old men, and give ear, all ye inhabitants of the land. ᴿHath this been in your days, or even in the days of your fathers?   2:2; Jer. 30:7

3 ᴿTell ye your children of it, and *let* your children *tell* their children, and their children another generation.   Ex. 10:2; Ps. 78:4

4 That which the ᴿpalmerworm hath left hath the locust eaten; and that which the locust hath left hath the cankerworm eaten; and that which the cankerworm hath left hath the caterpiller eaten.   Amos 4:9

5 Awake, ye drunkards, and ᴿweep; and ᵀhowl, all ye drinkers of wine, because of the new wine; ᴿfor it is ᵀcut off from your mouth.   James 4:9 • groan • Is. 32:10 • stopped

6 For a nation is come up upon my land, ᴿstrong, and without number, ᴿwhose teeth *are* the teeth of a lion, and he hath the cheek teeth of a great lion.   Prov. 30:25 • Rev. 9:8

7 He hath ᴿlaid my vine waste, and ᵀbarked my fig tree: he hath made it clean bare, and cast it away; the branches thereof are made white.   Is. 5:6 • chewed off the bark

8 Lament like a virgin girded with sackcloth for the husband of her youth.

9 The meat offering and the drink offering is cut off from the house of the LORD; the priests, the LORD's ministers, mourn.

10 The field is wasted, the land mourneth; for the corn is wasted: the new wine ᵀis dried up, the oil languisheth.   is all gone

11 ᴿBe ye ashamed, O ye husbandmen; ᵀhowl, O ye vinedressers, for the wheat and for the barley; because the ᴿharvest of the field is perished.   Jer. 8:20 • groan • Jer. 14:3, 4

12 The vine is dried up, and the fig tree languisheth; the pomegranate tree, the palm tree also, and the apple tree, *even* all the trees of the field, are withered: because joy is ᵀwithered away from the sons of men. dried up

The Past Day of the Drought

13 ᴿGird yourselves, and lament, ye priests: howl, ye ministers of the altar: come, lie all night in ᴿsackcloth, ye ministers of my God: for the meat offering and the drink offering is ᵀwithholden from the house of your God.   Jer. 4:8 • 1 Kin. 21:27 • absent

14 Sanctify ye a fast, call a solemn assembly, gather the elders *and* all the inhabitants of the land *into* the house of the LORD your God, and cry unto the LORD.

15 ᴿAlas for the day! for ᴿthe day of the LORD *is* at hand, and as a destruction from the Almighty shall it come.   [Jer. 30:7] • [Is. 13:6, 9]

16 ᴿIs not the ᵀmeat cut off before our eyes, *yea*, ᴿjoy and gladness from the house of our God?   Amos 4:6 • food • Deut. 12:6, 7

17 The seed is rotten under their clods, the garners are laid desolate, the barns are broken down; for the corn is withered.

18 How do ᴿthe beasts groan! the herds of cattle are ᵀperplexed, because they have no pasture; yea, the flocks of sheep are ᵀmade desolate.   Hos. 4:3 • troubled • ruined

19 O LORD, ᴿto thee will I cry: for ᴿthe fire

hath devoured the pastures of the wilderness, and the flame hath burned all the ᴿtrees of the field.   Rev. 8:7 • [Ps. 50:15] • Jer. 9:10

20 The beasts of the field ᴿcry also unto thee: for ᴿthe rivers of waters are dried up, and the fire hath devoured the pastures of the wilderness.   Job 38:41; Ps. 104:21 • 1 Kin. 17:7

CHAPTER 2

Prophecy of the Imminent Invasion of Judah

BLOW ye the trumpet in Zion, and sound an alarm in my holy mountain: let all the inhabitants of the land tremble: for the day of the LORD cometh, for *it is* nigh at hand;

2 A day of darkness and of gloominess, a day of clouds and of thick darkness, as the morning spread upon the mountains: ᴿa great people and a strong; there hath not been ever the like, neither shall be any more after it, *even* to the years of many generations.   1:6

3 A fire devoureth before them; and behind them a flame burneth: the land *is* as ᴿthe garden of Eden before them, ᴿand behind them a desolate wilderness; yea, and nothing shall escape them.   Is. 51:3 • Zech. 7:14

4 ᴿThe appearance of them *is* as the appearance of horses; and as horsemen, so shall they run.   Rev. 9:7

5 Like the noise of chariots on the tops of mountains shall they leap, like the noise of a flame of fire that devoureth the stubble, as a strong people set in battle array.

6 Before their face the people shall be much pained: ᴿall faces shall gather ᵀblackness.   Jer. 8:21; Lam. 4:8; Nah. 2:10 • *sorrow*

7 They shall run like mighty men; they shall climb the wall like men of war; and they shall march every one on his ways, and they shall not break their ranks:

8 Neither shall one thrust another; they shall walk every one in his path: and *when* they ᵀfall upon the sword, they shall not be wounded.   *burst through the weapons*

9 They shall run to and fro in the city; they shall run upon the wall, they shall climb up upon the houses; they shall enter in at the windows ᴿlike a thief.   John 10:1

10 ᴿThe earth shall quake before them; the heavens shall tremble: ᴿthe sun and the moon shall be dark, and the stars shall withdraw their shining: Ps. 18:7 • Is. 13:10

11 ᴿAnd the LORD shall utter his voice before his army: for his camp *is* very great: for *he is* strong that executeth his word: for the day of the LORD is great and very terrible; and who can abide it?   Jer. 25:30

Conditional Promise of the Salvation of Judah

12 Therefore also now, saith the LORD, ᴿturn ye *even* to me with all your heart, and with fasting, and with weeping, and with mourning: [Deut. 4:29]; Jer. 4:1; Hos. 12:6

13 And ᴿrendᵀ your heart, and not your garments, and turn unto the LORD your God: for he *is* ᴿgracious and merciful, slow to anger, and of great kindness, and repenteth him of the evil.   [Ps. 34:18] • *tear* • [Ex. 34:6]

14 ᴿWho knoweth *if* he will return and repent, and leave ᴿa blessing behind him; *even* a meat offering and a drink offering unto the LORD your God?   2 Kin. 19:4 • Hag. 2:19

15 ᴿBlow the trumpet in Zion, sanctify a fast, call a solemn assembly: Num. 10:3

16 Gather the people, sanctify the congregation, assemble the elders, gather the children, and ᵀthose that suck the breasts: let the bridegroom go forth of his chamber, and the bride out of her closet.   *infants*

17 Let the priests, the ministers of the LORD, weep between the porch and the altar, and let them say, Spare thy people, O LORD, and give not thine heritage to reproach, that the ᵀheathen should ᵀrule over them: wherefore should they say among the people, Where *is* their God?   *nations • win*

18 Then will the LORD ᴿbe jealous for his land, and pity his people.   Is. 60:10; Zech. 1:14

19 Yea, the LORD will answer and say unto his people, Behold, I will send you corn, and wine, and oil, and ye shall be satisfied therewith: and I will no more make you a reproach among the heathen:

20 But I will remove far off from you the northern *army*, and will drive him into a land barren and desolate, with his face toward the east sea, and his hinder part toward the utmost sea, and his stink shall come up, and his ᵀill savour shall come up, because he hath done great things.   *foul smell*

21 ᴿFear not, O land; be glad and rejoice: for the LORD will do great things.   Is. 54:4

22 Be not afraid, ye beasts of the field: for the pastures of the wilderness do spring, for the tree beareth her fruit, the fig tree and the vine do yield their strength.

23 Be glad then, ye children of Zion, and ᴿrejoice in the LORD your God: for he hath given you the former rain moderately, and he ᴿwill cause to come down for you the rain, the former rain, and the latter rain in the first *month*.   Zech. 10:7 • Lev. 26:4; Deut. 11:14

24 And the ᴿfloors shall be full of wheat, and the fats shall overflow with wine and oil.   Lev. 26:10; Amos 9:13; [Mal. 3:10]

25 And I will restore to you the years ᴿthat the locust hath eaten, the cankerworm, and the caterpiller, and the palmerworm, my great army which I sent among you.   1:4

26 And ye shall eat in plenty, and be satisfied, and praise the name of the LORD your God, that hath dealt wondrously with you: and my people shall never be ashamed.

27 And ye shall ᵀknow that I *am* in the midst of Israel, and *that* ᴿI *am* the LORD your

God, and none else: and my people shall never be ashamed.   *realize* • [Is. 45:5]

Last Events Before the Terrible Day of the Lord

28 And it shall come to pass afterward, *that* I will pour out my spirit upon all flesh; and your sons and your daughters shall prophesy, your old men shall dream dreams, your young men shall see visions:

29 And also upon ᴿthe servants and upon the handmaids in those days will I ᴿpour out my spirit.   [1 Cor. 12:13; Gal. 3:28] • Acts 2:16-21

30 And ᴿI will shew wonders in the heavens and in the earth, blood, and fire, and pillars of smoke.   Matt. 24:29

31 The sun shall be turned into darkness, and the moon into blood, before the great and the terrible day of the LORD come.

32 And it shall come to pass, *that* whosoever shall call on the name of the LORD shall be ᵀdelivered: for in mount Zion and in Jerusalem shall be ᵀdeliverance, as the LORD hath said, and in ᴿthe remnant whom the LORD shall call.   *saved* • *salvation* • Is. 11:11

CHAPTER 3

Judgment on the Gentiles

FOR, behold, ᴿin those days, and in that time, when I shall bring again the captivity of Judah and Jerusalem,   Ezek. 38:14

2 I will also gather all nations, and will bring them down into the valley of Je-hosh'-a-phat, and ᴿwill plead with them there for my people and *for* my heritage Israel, whom they have scattered among the nations, and parted my land.   Is. 66:16

3 And they have cast lots for my people; and have given a boy for an harlot, and sold a girl for wine, that they might drink.

4 Yea, and what have ye to do with me, ᴿO Tyre, and Zi'-don, and all the coasts of ᵀPalestine? will ye render me a recompence? and if ye recompense me, swiftly *and* speedily will I return your recompence upon your own head;   Josh. 19:29 • *Philistia*

5 Because ye have taken my silver and my gold, and have carried into your temples my goodly ᵀpleasant things: *precious*

6 The children also of Judah and the children of Jerusalem have ye sold unto the Gre'-cians, that ye might ᵀremove them far from their border.   *send them far away*

7 Behold, I will raise them out of the place whither ye have sold them, and will return your recompence upon your own head:

8 And I will sell your sons and your daughters into the hand of the children of Judah, and they shall sell them to the ᴿSa-be'-ans, to a people ᴿfar off: for the LORD hath spoken *it*.   Ezek. 23:42 • Jer. 6:20

9 ᴿProclaim ye this among the ᵀGentiles; ᴿPrepare war, wake up the mighty men, let all the men of war draw near; let them come up: Jer. 51:27, 28 • *nations* • Ezek. 38:7

10 ᴿBeat your plowshares into swords, and your ᵀpruninghooks into spears: let the weak say, I *am* strong.   [Mic. 4:3] • *scythes*

11 Assemble yourselves, and come, all ye heathen, and gather yourselves together round about: thither cause ᴿthy mighty ones to come down, O LORD.   Is. 13:3

12 Let the heathen be wakened, and come up to the ᴿvalley of Je-hosh'-a-phat: for there will I sit to ᴿjudge all the heathen round about.   *v. 2, 14* • Ps. 7:6; [98:9]

13 ᴿPut ye in the sickle, for ᴿthe harvest is ripe: come, get you down; for the ᴿpress is full, the fats overflow; for their wickedness *is* great.   Rev. 14:15 • Jer. 51:33 • [Is. 63:3, 4]

14 Multitudes, multitudes in the valley of ᵀdecision: for ᴿthe day of the LORD *is* near in the valley of decision.   *judgment* • 2:1

15 The sun and the moon shall be darkened,ᴿ and the stars shall ᴿwithdraw their shining.   2:10, 31 • Is. 13:10

Restoration of Judah

16 The LORD also shall roar out of Zion, and utter his voice from Jerusalem; and the heavens and the earth shall shake: but the LORD *will be* the hope of his people, and the strength of the children of Israel.

17 So shall ye ᵀknow that I *am* the LORD your God dwelling in Zion, ᴿmy holy mountain: then shall Jerusalem be ᵀholy, and there shall no strangers pass through her any more.   *realize* • [Is. 11:9] • *set apart for the LORD*

18 And it shall come to pass in that day, *that* the ᴿmountains shall drop down new wine, and the hills shall flow with milk, and all the ᵀrivers of Judah shall flow with waters, and a fountain shall come forth of the house of the LORD, and shall water the valley of ᵀShit'-tim.   Amos 9:13 • *brooks* • *acacias*

19 Egypt shall be a ᴿdesolation, and E'-dom shall be a desolate wilderness, ᴿfor the violence *against* the children of Judah, because they have shed innocent blood in their land.   Jer. 49:17 • Obad. 10

20 But Judah shall dwell for ever, and Jerusalem from generation to generation.

21 For I will ᴿcleanse their blood *that* I have not cleansed: for the LORD dwelleth in Zion.   Is. 4:4

THE BOOK OF

AMOS

THE BOOK OF AMOS

Amos prophesies during a period of national optimism in Israel. Business is booming and boundaries are bulging. But below the surface, greed and injustice are festering. Hypocritical religious motions have replaced true worship, creating a false sense of security and a growing callousness to God's disciplining hand. Famine, drought, plagues, death, destruction—nothing can force the people to their knees.

Amos, the farmer-turned-prophet, lashes out at sin unflinchingly, trying to visualize the nearness of God's judgment and mobilize the nation to repentance. The nation, like a basket of rotting fruit, stands ripe for judgment because of its hypocrisy and spiritual indifference.

The name *Amos* is derived from the Hebrew root *amas,* "to lift a burden, to carry." Thus, his name means "Burden" or "Burden-Bearer." Amos lives up to the meaning of his name by bearing up under his divinely given burden of declaring judgment to rebellious Israel. The Greek and Latin titles are both transliterated in English as *Amos.*

THE AUTHOR OF AMOS

The only Old Testament appearance of the name *Amos* is in this book. (He should not be confused with Amoz, the father of Isaiah.) Concerning his background, Amos said, "I *was* no prophet, neither *was* I a prophet's son; but I *was* an herdman, and a gatherer of sycomore fruit" (7:14). But he was gripped by God and divinely commissioned to bring his prophetic burden to Israel (3:8; 7:15). He came from the rural area of Tekoa in Judah, twelve miles south of Jerusalem, where he tended a special breed of small sheep that produced wool of the best quality. As a grower of sycamore figs, he had to puncture the fruit before it ripened to allow the insects inside to escape. Amos lived a disciplined life, and his knowledge of the wilderness often surfaces in his messages (cf. 3:4, 5, 12; 5:8, 19; 9:9). Amos was from the country, but he was well-educated in the Scriptures. His keen sense of morality and justice is obvious, and his objective appraisal of Israel's spiritual condition was not well received, especially since he was from Judah. He delivered his message in Beth-el because it was the residence of the king of Israel and a center of idolatry. His frontal attack on the greed, injustice, and self-righteousness of the people of the northern kingdom made his words unpopular.

THE TIME OF AMOS

Amos prophesied "in the days of Uzziah king of Judah, and in the days of Jeroboam the son of Joash king of Israel, two years before the earthquake" (1:1). Uzziah reigned from 767 to 739 B.C. and Jeroboam II reigned from 782 to 753 B.C., leaving an overlap from 767 to 753 B.C. Over two hundred years later, Zechariah referred to this earthquake in Uzziah's reign (Zech. 14:5). Amos 7:11 anticipates the 722 B.C. Assyrian captivity of Israel and indicates that at the time of writing, Jeroboam II was not yet dead. Thus, Amos prophesied in Beth-el about 755 B.C. Astronomical calculations indicate that a solar eclipse took place in Israel on June 15, 763 B.C. This event was probably fresh in the minds of Amos's hearers (see 8:9).

Amos ministered after the time of Obadiah, Joel, and Jonah and just before Hosea, Micah, and Isaiah. At this time Uzziah reigned over a prosperous and militarily successful Judah. He fortified Jerusalem and subdued the Philistines, the Ammonites, and the Edomites. In the north, Israel was ruled by the capable king Jeroboam II. Economic and military circumstances were almost ideal, but prosperity only increased the materialism, immorality, and injustice of the people (2:6–8; 3:10; 4:1; 5:10–12; 8:4–6). During these years, Assyria, Babylon, Syria, and Egypt were relatively weak. Thus, the people of Israel found it hard to imagine the coming disaster predicted by Amos. However, it was only three decades until the downfall of Israel.

THE CHRIST OF AMOS

The clearest anticipation of Christ in Amos is found at the end of the book. He has all authority to judge (1:1—9:10), but He will also restore His people (9:11–15).

KEYS TO AMOS

Key Word: The Judgment of Israel—The basic theme of Amos is the coming judgment of Israel because of the holiness of Yahweh and the sinfulness of His covenant people. Amos unflinchingly and relentlessly visualizes the causes and course of Israel's quickly approaching doom. God is gracious and patient, but His justice and righteousness will not allow sin to go unpunished indefinitely. The sins of Israel are heaped as high as heaven: empty ritualism, oppression of the poor, idolatry, deceit, self-righteousness, arrogance, greed, materialism, and callousness. The people have repeatedly broken every aspect of their covenant relationship with God. Nevertheless, God's mercy and love are evident in His offer of deliverance if the people will only turn back to Him. God graciously sends

Amos as a reformer to warn the people of Israel of their fate if they refuse to repent. But they reject his plea, and the course of judgment cannot be altered.

Key Verses: Amos 3:1, 2; 8:11, 12—"Hear this word that the LORD hath spoken against you, O children of Israel, against the whole family which I brought up from the land of Egypt, saying, You only have I known of all the families of the earth: therefore I will punish you for all your iniquities" (3:1, 2).

"Behold, the days come, saith the Lord GOD, that I will send a famine in the land, not a famine of bread, nor a thirst for water, but of hearing the words of the LORD: And they shall wander from sea to sea, and from the north even to the east, they shall run to and fro to seek the word of the LORD, and shall not find *it*" (8:11, 12).

Key Chapter: Amos 9—Set in the midst of the harsh judgments of Amos are some of the greatest prophecies of restoration of Israel anywhere in Scripture. Within the scope of just five verses the future of Israel becomes clear, as the Abrahamic, Davidic, and Palestinian covenants are focused on their climactic fulfillment in the return of the Messiah.

SURVEY OF AMOS

Amos's message of the coming doom of the northern kingdom of Israel seems preposterous to the people. Unsurprisingly, Amos's earnest and forceful message against Israel's sins and abuses is poorly received. The prophet of Israel's Indian summer presents a painfully clear message: "prepare to meet thy God, O Israel" (4:12). The four divisions of Amos are: the eight prophecies (1:1—2:16), the three sermons (3:1—6:14), the five visions (7:1—9:10), and the five promises (9:11-15).

The Eight Prophecies (1:1—2:16): Amos is called by God to the unenviable task of leaving his homeland in Judah to preach a harsh message of judgment to Israel. Each of his eight oracles in chapters 1 and 2 begins with the statement "For three transgressions of . . . and for four." The fourth transgression is equivalent to the last straw; the iniquity of each of the eight countries is full. Amos begins with the nations that surround Israel as his catalog of catastrophes gradually spirals in on Israel herself. Seven times God declares, "I will send a fire" (1:4, 7, 10, 12, 14; 2:2, 5), a symbol of judgment.

The Three Sermons (3:1—6:14): In these chapters, Amos delivers three sermons, each beginning with the phrase "Hear this word" (3:1; 4:1; 5:1). The first sermon (3) is a general pronouncement of judgment because of Israel's iniquities. The second sermon (4) exposes the crimes of the people and describes the ways God has chastened them in order to draw them back to Himself. Five times He says, "Yet have ye not returned unto me" (4:6, 8, 9, 10, 11). The third sermon (5 and 6) lists the sins of the house of Israel and calls the people to repent. But they hate integrity, justice, and compassion, and their refusal to turn to Yahweh will lead to their exile. Although they arrogantly wallow in luxury, their time of prosperity will suddenly come to an end.

The Five Visions (7:1—9:10): Amos's three sermons are followed by five visions of coming judgment upon the northern kingdom. The first two judgments of locusts and fire do not come to pass because of Amos's intercession. The third vision of the plumbline is followed by the only narrative section in the book (7:10-17). Amaziah, the priest of Beth-el, wants Amos to go back to Judah. The fourth vision pictures Israel as a basket of rotten fruit, overripe for judgment. The fifth vision is a relentless portrayal of Israel's unavoidable judgment.

The Five Promises (9:11-15): Amos has

FOCUS	EIGHT PROPHECIES		THREE SERMONS		FIVE VISIONS		FIVE PROMISES
REFERENCE	1:1		3:1		7:1		9:11 ——— 9:15
DIVISION	JUDGMENT OF ISRAEL AND SURROUNDING NATIONS		SIN OF ISRAEL: PRESENT, PAST, AND FUTURE		PICTURES OF THE JUDGMENT OF ISRAEL		RESTORATION OF ISRAEL
TOPIC	PRONOUNCEMENTS OF JUDGMENT		PROVOCATIONS FOR JUDGMENT		FUTURE OF JUDGMENT		PROMISES AFTER JUDGMENT
			JUDGMENT				HOPE
LOCATION	SURROUNDING NATIONS			NORTHERN KINGDOM OF ISRAEL			
TIME			c. 760 – 753 B.C.				

hammered upon the theme of divine retribution with oracles, sermons, and visions. Nevertheless, he ends his book on a note of consolation, not

condemnation. God promises to reinstate the Davidic line, to renew the land, and to restore the people.

OUTLINE OF AMOS

CHAPTER 1

Introduction to Amos

THE words of Amos, who was among the herdmen of Te-ko'-a, which he saw concerning Israel in the days of Uz-zi'-ah king of Judah, and in the days of Jer-o-bo'-am the son of Jo'-ash king of Israel, two years before the ᴿearthquake.   Zech. 14:5

2 And he said, The LORD will roar from Zion, and utter his voice from Jerusalem; and the habitations of the shepherds shall mourn, and the top of Carmel shall wither.

Judgment on Damascus

3 Thus saith the LORD; For three transgressions of Damascus, ᵀand for four, I will not turn away the punishment thereof; because they have threshed Gil'-e-ad with threshing instruments of iron: yea, for four

4 ᴿBut I will send a fire into the house of Haz'-a-el, which ᵀdevour the ᴿpalaces of Ben–ha'-dad.   Jer. 49:27 • destroy • Jer. 17:27

5 I will break also the ᴿbar of Damascus, and cut off the inhabitant from the plain of A'-ven, and him that ᵀholdeth the sceptre from ᵀthe house of Eden: and the people of Syria shall go into captivity unto Kir, saith the LORD.   Jer. 51:30 • rules • Beth-Eden

Judgment on Gaza

6 Thus saith the LORD; For three transgressions of Ga'-za, and for four, I will not turn

away the punishment thereof; because they carried away captive the whole captivity, to deliver them up to E'-dom:

7 But I will send a fire on the wall of Ga'-za, which shall devour the palaces thereof:

8 And I will cut off the inhabitant from Ash'-dod, and him that holdeth the sceptre from Ash'-ke-lon, and I will turn mine hand against Ek'-ron: and the remnant of the Phi-lis'-tines shall perish, saith the Lord GOD.

Judgment on Tyrus

9 Thus saith the LORD; For three transgressions of Ty'-rus, and for four, I will not turn away the punishment thereof; because they delivered up the whole captivity to E'-dom, and remembered not ᵀthe brotherly covenant: agreement between relatives

10 But I will send a ᴿfire on the wall of ᴿTy'-rus, ᴿwhich shall devour the palaces thereof.   Jer. 47:4 • 1 Kin. 18:38 • Zech. 9:4

Judgment on Edom

11 Thus saith the LORD; For three transgressions of E'-dom, and for four, I will not turn away the punishment thereof; because he did pursue his brother with the sword, and did cast off all pity, and his anger did tear perpetually, and he kept his wrath for ever:

12 But I will send a fire upon Te'-man, which shall devour the palaces of Boz'-rah.

Judgment on Ammon

13 Thus saith the LORD; For three transgressions of the children of Ammon, and for four, I will not turn away *the punishment* thereof; because they have ᵀripped up the women with child of Gil'-e-ad, that they might enlarge their border: *mutilated*

14 But I will kindle a fire in the wall of Rab'-bah, and it shall devour the palaces thereof, with shouting in the day of battle, with a tempest in the day of the whirlwind:

15 And their king shall go into captivity, he and his princes together, saith the LORD.

CHAPTER 2

Judgment on Moab

THUS saith the LORD; ᴿFor three transgressions of Moab, and for four, I will not turn away *the punishment* thereof; because he burned the bones of the king of E'-dom into lime: 2 Kin. 3:26, 27

2 But I will send a fire upon Moab, and it shall devour the palaces of Kir'-i-oth: and Moab shall die with ᴿtumult, with shouting, *and* with the sound of the trumpet: Jer. 48:45

3 And I will cut off the judge from the midst thereof, and will slay all the ᴿprinces thereof with him, saith the LORD.   Jer. 48:7

Judgment on Judah

4 Thus saith the LORD; For three transgressions of Judah, and for four, I will not turn away *the punishment* thereof; because they have despised the law of the LORD, and have not kept his commandments, and their lies caused them to err, after the which their fathers have walked:

5 But I will send a fire upon Judah, and it shall devour the palaces of Jerusalem.

Judgment on Israel

6 Thus saith the LORD; For three transgressions of Israel, and for four, I ᴿwill not turn away *the punishment* thereof; because ᴿthey sold the righteous for silver, and the poor for a pair of shoes;   2 Kin. 17; 18 · Is. 29:21

7 That pant after the dust of the earth on the head of the poor, and turn aside the way of the meek: and a man and his father will go in unto the *same* ᵀmaid, to ᵀprofane my holy name: *young woman · desecrate*

8 And they lay *themselves* down upon clothes ᴿlaid to pledge by every altar, and they drink the wine of the ᵀcondemned *in* the house of their ᵀgod.   Ex. 22:26 · *fined · God*

9 Yet destroyed I the ᴿAm'-or-ite before them, whose height *was* like the height of the cedars, and he *was* strong as the oaks; yet I ᴿdestroyed his fruit from above, and his roots from beneath.   Deut. 2:31 · [Mal. 4:1]

10 Also ᴿI brought you up from the land of Egypt, and ᴿled you forty years through the wilderness, to possess the land of the Am'-or-ite.   Ex. 12:51 · Deut. 2:7

11 And I raised up of your sons for prophets, and of your young men for ᴿNazarites. *Is it* not even thus, O ye children of Israel? saith the LORD.   Num. 6:2

12 But ye gave the ᵀNazarites wine to drink; and commanded the prophets, ᴿsaying, Prophesy not.   *Nazirites · Jer. 11:21; Mic. 2:6*

13 Behold, I am pressed under you, as a cart is pressed *that is* full of sheaves.

14 Therefore the ᴿflight shall perish from the swift, and the strong shall not strengthen his force, ᴿneither shall the mighty ᵀdeliver himself: Is. 30:16 · Ps. 33:16 · *save*

15 Neither shall he stand that handleth the bow; and *he that is* swift of foot shall not ᵀdeliver *himself:* neither shall he that rideth the horse deliver ᵀhimself.   *save · soul*

16 And *he that is* ᵀcourageous among the mighty shall ᴿflee away naked in that day, saith the LORD.   *strong of his heart · Judg. 4:17*

CHAPTER 3

Israel's Judgment Is Deserved (Present)

HEAR this word that the LORD hath spoken against you, O children of Israel, against the whole family which I brought up from the land of Egypt, saying,

2 ᴿYou only have I known of all the families of the earth: therefore I will punish you for all your iniquities.   [Deut. 7:6]

3 Can two walk together, ᴿexcept they be agreed?   [Lev. 26:23, 24]

3:2 Selection of Israel—The selection of Israel as a special nation to God was part of God's plan (Page 1117—Rom. 11:2). Historically, the selection of Israel began with the Lord's promise to Abraham, "I will make of thee a great nation" (Page 14—Gen. 12:2). The name *Israel* actually is from the new name which God gave to Abraham's grandson, Jacob. It was occasioned by Jacob's spiritual victory at the ford of Jabbok (Page 35—Gen. 32:28). This fact explains why his descendants are often called the children of Israel.

The motivation for the Lord's choice of Israel as His select nation did not lie in any special attraction it possessed. Its people were, in fact, the least in number among all the nations (Page 185—Deut. 7:6-8). Rather, the Lord chose them because of His love for them and because of His covenant with Abraham. This fact does not mean that God did not love other nations, because it was through Israel that He intended to bring forth the Saviour and to bless the entire world (Page 15—Gen. 12:3).

Now turn to Page 580—Ps. 78:4: History of Israel.

4 Will a lion roar in the forest, when he hath no prey? will a young lion cry out of his den, if he have taken nothing?

5 Can a bird fall in a snare upon the earth, where no ^{T}gin is for him? shall one take up a snare from the earth, and have taken nothing at all?   *trap*

6 Shall a trumpet be blown in the city, and the people not be afraid? shall there be evil in a city, and the LORD hath not done it?

7 Surely the Lord GOD will do nothing, ^{T}but ^{R}he revealeth his secret unto his servants the prophets. *unless* • Gen. 6:13; [John 15:15]

8 The lion hath roared, who will not fear? the ^{R}Lord GOD hath spoken, ^{R}who can but prophesy?   1:2; Jon. 1:1-3 • Acts 4:20; 1 Cor. 9:16

9 Publish in the palaces at Ash'-dod, and in the palaces in the land of Egypt, and say, Assemble yourselves upon the ^{R}mountains of Sa-ma'-ri-a, and behold the great tumults in the midst thereof, and the ^{R}oppressed in the midst thereof.   Is. 28:1 • 8:6

10 For they ^{R}know not to do right, saith the LORD, who ^{R}store up violence and ^{T}robbery in their palaces. Jer. 4:22 • Hab. 2:8-11 • *loot*

Israel's Judgment Is Described (Present)

11 Therefore thus saith the Lord GOD; An adversary *there shall be* even round about the land; ^{R}and he shall bring down thy strength from thee, and thy palaces shall be ^{T}spoiled.   2 Kin. 17:3, 6 • *looted*

12 Thus saith the LORD; ^{R}As the shepherd ^{T}taketh out of the mouth of the lion two legs, or a piece of an ear; so shall the children of Israel be taken out that dwell in Sa-ma'-ri-a in the corner of a bed, and in Damascus in a couch.   1 Sam. 17:34 • *delivers*

13 Hear ye, and testify in the house of Jacob, saith the Lord GOD, the God of hosts,

14 That in the day that I shall ^{T}visit the transgressions of Israel upon him I will also visit the altars of ^{R}Beth'-el: and the horns of the altar shall be cut off, and fall to the ground.   *bring judgment for* • Hos. 10:5

15 And I will smite ^{R}the winter house with the summer house; and the houses of ivory shall perish, and the great houses shall have an end, saith the LORD.   Jer. 36:22

CHAPTER 4

Israel's Judgment Is Deserved (Past)

HEAR this word, ye ^{R}kine^T of Ba'-shan, that are in the mountain of Sa-ma'-ri-a, which oppress the poor, which crush the needy, which say to their masters, Bring, and let us drink.   Ezek. 39:18 • *idols*

2 The Lord GOD hath sworn by his holiness, that, lo, the days shall come upon you, that he will take you away with hooks, and your posterity with fishhooks.

3 And ye shall ^{R}go out at the ^{T}breaches, ^{T}every cow at that which is before her; and ye shall ^{T}cast them into the palace, saith the LORD.   Jer. 52:7 • *ruins* • *one* • *put them in prison*

4 Come to Beth'-el, and transgress; at Gil'-gal multiply transgression; and ^{R}bring your sacrifices every morning, ^{R}and your tithes after three years: Num. 28:3 • Deut. 14:28

5 And offer a sacrifice of thanksgiving with leaven, and proclaim and publish the free offerings: for this liketh you, O ye children of Israel, saith the Lord GOD.

Israel's Judgment Is Demonstrated (Past)

6 And I also have given you ^{T}cleanness of teeth in all your cities, and want of bread in all your places: yet have ye not returned unto me, saith the LORD.   *dullness*

7 And also I have withholden the rain from you, when there were yet three months to the harvest: and I caused it to rain upon one city, and caused it not to rain upon another city: one piece was rained upon, and the piece whereupon it rained not withered.

8 So two or three cities wandered unto one city, to drink ^{R}water; but they were ^{R}not satisfied: yet have ^{R}ye not returned unto me, saith the LORD.   1 Kin. 18:5 • Hag. 1:6 • Jer. 3:7

9 I have smitten you with ^{T}blasting and mildew: when your gardens and your vineyards and your fig trees and your olive trees increased, the ^{T}palmerworm devoured them: yet have ye not returned unto me, saith the LORD.   *plant disease* • *locust*

10 I have sent among you the pestilence after ^{T}the manner of Egypt: your young men have I slain with the sword, and have taken away your horses; and I have made the stink of your camps to come up unto your nostrils: yet have ye not returned unto me, saith the LORD.   *as it was in*

11 I have overthrown some of you, as God overthrew ^{R}Sodom and Go-mor'-rah, and ye were as a firebrand plucked out of the burning: ^{R}yet have ye not returned unto me, saith the LORD.   Gen. 19:24; Is. 13:19 • Jer. 23:14

Israel's Judgment Is Described (Past)

12 Therefore thus will I do unto thee, O Israel: and because I will do this unto thee, prepare to meet thy God, O Israel.

13 For, lo, he that formeth the mountains, and createth the ^{T}wind, and declareth unto man what is his thought, that maketh the morning darkness, and treadeth upon the high places of the earth, The LORD, The God of hosts, is his name.   *spirit*

CHAPTER 5

Israel's Judgment Is Deserved (Future)

HEAR ye this word which I ^{R}take up against you, even a lamentation, O house of Israel.   Jer. 7:29; 9:10; Ezek. 19:1

2 The virgin of Israel is fallen; she shall no more rise: she is forsaken upon her land; *there is* ^Rnone to raise her up.   Is. 51:18

3 For thus saith the Lord GOD; The city that went out *by* a thousand shall leave ^Ran hundred, and that which went forth *by* an hundred shall leave ten, to the house of Israel.   Is. 6:13

4 For thus saith the LORD unto the house of Israel, Seek ye me, and ye shall live:

5 But seek not Beth'-el, nor enter into Gil'-gal, and pass not to Be'-er-she'-ba: for Gil'-gal shall surely go into captivity, and Beth'-el shall come to ^Tnought.   *nothing*

6 ^RSeek the LORD, and ye shall live; lest he break out like ^Rfire in the house of Joseph, and devour *it,* and *there be* none to quench *it* in Beth'-el.   [Is. 55:3 • Deut. 4:24]

7 Ye who turn judgment to wormwood, and leave off righteousness in the earth,

8 *Seek him* that maketh the seven stars and O-ri'-on, and turneth the shadow of death into the morning, and maketh the day dark with night: that calleth for the waters of the sea, and poureth them out upon the face of the earth: ^RThe LORD *is* his name: [4:13]

9 That strengtheneth the ^Tspoiled against the strong, so that the spoiled shall come against the fortress.   *robbed ones*

10 ^RThey hate him that rebuketh in the gate, and they ^Rabhor him that speaketh uprightly.   Is. 29:21; 66:5 • 1 Kin. 22:8

11 Forasmuch therefore as your treading *is* upon the poor, and ye take from him burdens of wheat: ye have built houses of hewn stone, but ye shall not dwell in them; ye have planted pleasant vineyards, but ye shall not drink wine of them.

12 For I know your manifold transgressions and your mighty sins: they afflict the just, they take a bribe, and they turn aside the poor in the gate *from their right.*

13 Therefore the prudent shall keep silence in that time; for it *is* an evil time.

14 Seek good, and not evil, that ye may live: and so the LORD, the God of hosts, shall be with you, as ye have spoken.

15 ^RHate the evil, and love the good, and establish judgment in the gate: it may be that the LORD God of hosts will be gracious unto the remnant of Joseph.   Rom. 12:9

The First Woe of Judgment

16 Therefore the LORD, the God of hosts, the Lord, saith thus; Wailing *shall be* in all streets; and they shall say in all the highways, Alas! alas! and they shall call the husbandman to mourning, and such as are skilful of lamentation to wailing.

17 And in all vineyards *shall be* wailing: for I will pass through thee, saith the LORD.

18 Woe unto you that desire the day of the LORD! to what end *is* it for you? the day of the LORD *is* darkness, and not light.

19 ^RAs if a man did flee from a lion, and a bear met him; or went into the house, and leaned his hand on the wall, and a serpent bit him.   Job 20:24; Is. 24:17; Jer. 48:44

20 *Shall* not the day of the LORD *be* darkness, ^Rand not light? even very dark, and no brightness in it?   Is. 13:10; [Zeph. 1:15]

21 I hate, I despise your feast days, and I will not smell in your solemn assemblies.

22 Though ye ^Roffer me burnt offerings and your ^Tmeat offerings, I will not accept *them:* neither will I regard the ^Tpeace offerings of your fat beasts.   Mic. 6:6 • *meal* • *thank*

23 Take thou away from me the noise of thy songs; for I will not hear the melody of thy ^Tviols.   *harps*

24 But let judgment ^Trun down as waters, and righteousness as a mighty stream.   *abound*

25 ^RHave ye offered unto me sacrifices and offerings in the wilderness forty years, O house of Israel?   Deut. 32:17; Josh. 24:14

26 But ye have borne the tabernacle ^Rof your ^TMo'-loch and ^TChi'-un your images, the star of your god, which ye made to yourselves.   1 Kin. 11:33 • *king* • *the shrine of*

27 Therefore ^Rwill I cause you to go into captivity beyond Damascus, saith the LORD, whose name *is* The God of hosts.   2 Kin. 17; 18

CHAPTER 6

The Second Woe of Judgment

WOE to them *that are* at ease in Zion, and trust in the mountain of Sa-ma'-ri-a, *which are* named chief of the nations, to whom the house of Israel came!

2 Pass ye unto Cal'-neh, and see; and from thence go ye to Ha'-math the great: then go down to Gath of the Phi-lis'-tines: *be they* better than these kingdoms? or their border greater than your border?

3 Ye that put far away the evil day, and cause the seat of violence to come near;

4 That lie upon beds of ivory, and ^Tstretch themselves upon their couches, and eat the lambs out of the flock, and the calves out of the midst of the stall;   *enjoy*

5 That ^Tchant to the sound of the viol, *and* invent to themselves instruments of musick, ^Rlike David;   *sing idle songs* • 1 Chr. 23:5

6 That drink wine in ^Tbowls, and anoint themselves with the chief ointments: ^Rbut they are not ^Rgrieved for the ^Taffliction of Joseph.   *sacred bowls* • Gen. 37:25 • Ezek. 9:4 • *breach*

7 Therefore now shall they go captive with the first that go captive, and the banquet of them ^Rthat ^Tstretched themselves shall be removed.   1 Kin. 20:16–20 • *enjoyed*

8 ^RThe Lord GOD hath sworn by himself, saith the LORD the God of hosts, I abhor the excellency of Jacob, and hate his palaces: ^Rtherefore will I deliver up the city with all that is therein.   Jer. 51:14 • Ezek. 24:21

9 And it shall come to pass, if there ᵀremain ᴿten men in one house, that they shall die. *survive after the siege* • 5:5

10 And a man's uncle shall take him up, and he that burneth him, to bring out the bones out of the house, and shall say unto him that is by the sides of the house, Is there yet any with thee? and he shall say, No. Then shall he say, Hold thy tongue: for we may not make mention of the name of the LORD.

11 For, behold, the LORD commandeth, and he will smite the great house with breaches, and the little house with clefts.

12 Shall horses run upon the rock? will one plow there with oxen? for ᴿye have turned judgment into gall, and the fruit of righteousness into hemlock: *Hos. 10:4*

13 ᴿYe which rejoice in a thing of nought, which say, Have we not taken to us ᵀhorns by our own strength? *Job 8:14, 15 • power*

14 But, behold, I will raise up against you a nation, O house of Israel, saith the LORD the God of hosts; and they shall afflict you from the entering in of He'-math unto the ᵀriver of the wilderness. *brook*

CHAPTER 7

Vision of the Grasshoppers

THUS hath the Lord GOD shewed unto me; and, behold, he formed grasshoppers in the beginning of the shooting up of the latter growth; and, lo, it was the latter growth after the king's mowings.

2 And it came to pass, that when they had made an end of eating the grass of the land, then I said, O Lord GOD, forgive, I beseech thee: by whom shall Jacob arise? for he is small.

3 ᴿThe LORD repented for this: It shall not be, saith the LORD. *Jon. 3:10; [James 5:16]*

Vision of the Fire

4 Thus hath the Lord GOD shewed unto me: and, behold, the Lord GOD ᵀcalled to contend by fire, and it devoured the great deep, and did eat up a part. *decided to chastise*

5 Then said I, ᴿO Lord GOD, cease, I beseech thee: ᴿby whom shall Jacob arise? for he is small. *Ps. 85:4; Joel 2:17 • vv. 2, 3*

6 The LORD ᴿrepented for this: This also shall not be, saith the Lord GOD. *Ps. 106:45*

Vision of the Plumbline

7 Thus he shewed me: and, behold, the Lord stood upon a wall made by a plumbline, with a plumbline in his hand.

8 And the LORD said unto me, Amos, what seest thou? And I said, A plumbline. Then said the Lord, Behold, I will set a plumbline in the midst of my people Israel: I will not again pass by them any more:

9 And the high places of Isaac shall be desolate, and the sanctuaries of Israel shall be laid waste; and I will rise against the house of Jer-o-bo'-am with the sword.

Opposition of Amaziah (Historical Parenthesis)

10 Then Am-a-zi'-ah the priest of Beth'-el sent to Jer-o-bo'-am king of Israel, saying, Amos hath conspired against thee in the midst of the house of Israel: the land is not able to ᵀbear all his words. *endure*

11 For thus Amos saith, Jer-o-bo'-am shall die by the sword, and Israel shall surely be led away captive out of their own land.

12 Also Am-a-zi'-ah said unto Amos, O thou seer, ᴿgo, flee thee away into the land of Judah, and there ᵀeat bread, and prophesy there: *Matt. 8:34 • make your home*

13 But prophesy not again any more at Beth'-el: for it is the king's ᵀchapel, and it is the ᵀking's court. *sanctuary • royal residence*

14 Then answered Amos, and said to Am-a-zi'-ah, I was no prophet, neither was I a prophet's son; but I was an herdman, and a gatherer of ᵀsycomore fruit: *wild figs*

15 And the LORD took me as I followed the flock, and the LORD said unto me, ᴿGo, prophesy unto my people Israel. *Jer. 1:7*

16 Now therefore hear thou the word of the LORD: Thou sayest, Prophesy not against Israel, and ᴿdrop not thy word against the house of Isaac. *Ezek. 21:2; Mic. 2:6*

17 Therefore thus saith the LORD; Thy wife shall be an harlot in the city, and thy sons and thy daughters shall fall by the sword, and thy land shall be divided by line; and thou shalt die in a polluted land: and Israel shall surely go into captivity forth of his land.

CHAPTER 8

Vision of the Summer Fruit

THUS hath the Lord GOD shewed unto me: and behold a basket of summer fruit.

2 And he said, Amos, what seest thou? And I said, A basket of summer fruit. Then said the LORD unto me, ᴿThe end is come upon my people of Israel; ᴿI will not again pass by them any more. *Ezek. 7:2 • 7:8*

3 And ᴿthe songs of the temple shall be ᵀhowlings in that day, saith the Lord GOD: ᴿthere shall be many dead bodies in every place; they shall ᵀcast them forth with silence. *5:23 • wailings • 6:9, 10 • burn them*

4 Hear this, O ye that ᴿswallow up the needy, even to make the poor of the land to fail, *2:7; 5:11; Ps. 14:4; Prov. 30:14*

5 Saying, When will the ᵀnew moon be gone, that we may sell corn? and the sabbath, that we may set forth wheat, making the e'-phah small, and the shek'-el great, and falsifying the balances by deceit? *month*

6 That we may buy the poor for Rsilver, and the needy for a pair of shoes; *yea,* and sell the refuse of the wheat? 2:6

7 The LORD hath sworn by Rthe excellency of Jacob, Surely RI will never forget any of their works. 6:8 • Hos. 8:13

8 RShall not the land tremble for this, and every one mourn that dwelleth therein? and it shall rise up wholly as a flood; and it shall be cast out and drowned, Ras *by* the Tflood of Egypt. Hos. 4:3 • 9:5 • *river*

9 And it shall come to pass in that day, saith the Lord GOD, Rthat I will cause the sun to go down at noon, and I will darken the earth in the clear day: Job 5:14; Is. 13:10

10 And I will turn your feasts into mourning, and all your songs into lamentation; Rand I will bring up sackcloth upon all loins, and baldness upon every head; and I will make it as the mourning of an only *son,* and the end thereof as a bitter day. Ezek. 27:31

11 Behold, the days come, saith the Lord GOD, that I will send a famine in the land, not a famine of bread, nor a thirst for water, but of hearing the words of the LORD:

12 And they shall wander from sea to sea, and from the north even to the east, they shall run to and fro to Rseek the word of the LORD, and shall not find *it.* Ezek. 20:3

13 In that day shall the fair virgins and young men faint for thirst.

14 They that swear by the sin of Samaria, and say, Thy god, O Dan, liveth; and, The Tmanner of Be′-er-she′-ba liveth; even they shall fall, and never rise up again. *way*

CHAPTER 9

Vision of the Smitten Lintels of the Door

I SAW the Lord standing upon the altar: and he said, Smite the lintel of the door, that the posts may shake: and cut them in the head, all of them; and I will slay the last of them with the sword: he that fleeth of them shall not flee away, and he that escapeth of them shall not be delivered.

2 Though they dig into hell, thence shall mine hand take them; though they climb up to heaven, thence will I bring them down:

3 And though they hide themselves in the top of Carmel, RI will search and take them out thence; and Rthough they be hid from my sight in the bottom of the sea, thence will I command the serpent, and he shall bite them: Jer. 16:16 • [Job 34:22; Ps. 139:9–12]

4 And though they go into captivity before their enemies, thence will I command the Rsword, and it shall slay them: and RI will set mine eyes upon them for evil, and not for good. Lev. 26:33 • Lev. 17:10; Jer. 21:10

5 And the Lord GOD of hosts *is* he that toucheth the land, and it shall melt, Rand all that dwell therein shall mourn: and it shall rise up wholly like a flood; and shall be drowned, as *by* the flood of Egypt. 8:8

6 *It is* he that buildeth his stories in the heaven, and hath founded his troop in the earth; he that calleth for the waters of the sea, and poureth them out upon the face of the earth: The LORD *is* his name.

7 *Are* ye not as children of the E-thi-o′-pi-ans unto me, O children of Israel? saith the LORD. Have not I brought up Israel out of the land of Egypt? and the Phi-lis′-tines from Caph′-tor, and the Syrians from Kir?

8 Behold, the eyes of the Lord GOD *are* upon the sinful kingdom, and I Rwill destroy it from off the face of the earth; saving that I will not utterly destroy the house of Jacob, saith the LORD. [Obad. 16, 17]

9 For, lo, I will command, and I will Tsift the house of Israel among all nations, like as *corn* is sifted in a sieve, yet shall not the least grain fall upon the earth. *scatter around*

10 All the sinners of my people shall die by the sword, Rwhich say, The evil shall not overtake nor Tprevent us. 6:3 • *meet*

The Five Promises of the Restoration of Israel

† 11 In that day will I raise up the tabernacle of David that is fallen, and Tclose up the breaches thereof; and I will raise up his ruins, and I will build it as in the days of old: *repair*

12 That they may possess the remnant of E′-dom, and of all the heathen, Twhich are called by my name, saith the LORD that doeth this. *upon whom my name is called*

13 Behold, the days come, saith the LORD, that the plowman shall overtake the reaper, and the treader of grapes him that soweth seed; Rand the mountains shall drop sweet wine, and all the hills shall melt. Joel 3:18

14 RAnd I will bring again the captivity of my people of Israel, and they shall build the waste cities, and inhabit *them;* and they shall plant vineyards, and drink the wine thereof; they shall also make gardens, and eat the fruit of them. Jer. 30:3

15 And I will plant them upon their land, and Rthey shall no more be pulled up out of their land which I have given them, saith the LORD thy God. Ezek. 34:28

THE BOOK OF

OBADIAH

THE BOOK OF OBADIAH

A struggle that began in the womb between twin brothers, Esau and Jacob, eventuates in a struggle between their respective descendants, the Edomites and the Israelites. For the Edomites' stubborn refusal to aid Israel, first during the time of wilderness wandering (Num. 20:14–21) and later during a time of invasion, they are roundly condemned by Obadiah. This little-known prophet describes their crimes, tries their case, and pronounces their judgment: total destruction.

The Hebrew name *Obadyah* means "Worshiper of Yahweh" or "Servant of Yahweh." The Greek title in the Septuagint is *Obdiou*, and the Latin title in the Vulgate is *Abdias*.

THE AUTHOR OF OBADIAH

Obadiah was an obscure prophet who probably lived in the southern kingdom of Judah. Nothing is known of his hometown or family, but it is not likely that he came out of the kingly or priestly line, because his father is not mentioned (1:1). There are thirteen Obadiahs in the Old Testament, and some scholars have attempted to identify the author of this book with one of the other twelve. Four of the better prospects are: (1) the officer in Ahab's palace who hid God's prophets in a cave (1 Kin. 18:3); (2) one of the officials sent out by Jehoshaphat to teach the law in the cities of Judah (2 Chr. 17:7); (3) one of the overseers who took part in repairing the temple under Josiah (2 Chr. 34:12); or (4) a priest in the time of Nehemiah (Neh. 10:5).

THE TIME OF OBADIAH

Obadiah mentions no kings, so verses 10–14 provide the only historical reference point to aid in determining the book's time and setting. However, scholars disagree about which invasion of Jerusalem Obadiah had in mind. There are four possibilities: (1) In 926 B.C., Shishak of Egypt plundered the temple and palace of Jerusalem in the reign of Rehoboam (1 Kin. 14:25, 26). At this time, Edom was still subject to Judah. This does not fit Obadiah 10–14, which indicates that Edom was independent of Judah. (2) During the reign of Jehoram (848–841 B.C.), the Philistines and Arabians invaded Judah and looted the palace (2 Chr. 21:16, 17). Edom revolted during the reign of Jehoram and became a bitter antagonist (2 Kin. 8:20–22; 2 Chr. 21:8–20). This fits the description of Obadiah. (3) In 790 B.C., King Jehoash of Israel invaded Judah (2 Kin. 14; 2 Chr. 25). However, Obadiah in verse 11 calls the invaders "strangers." This would be

an inappropriate term for describing the army of the northern kingdom. (4) In 586 B.C., Nebuchadnezzar of Babylon defeated and destroyed Jerusalem (2 Kin. 24; 25).

The two best candidates are (2) and (4). Obadiah 10–14 seems to fit (2) better than (4) because it does not indicate the total destruction of the city, which took place when Nebuchadnezzar burned the palace and temple and razed the walls. And Nebuchadnezzar certainly would not have "cast lots upon Jerusalem" (11) with anyone. Also, all of the other prophets who speak of the destruction of 586 B.C. identify Nebuchadnezzar and the Babylonians as the agents; but Obadiah leaves the enemy unidentified. For these and other reasons, it appears likely that the plundering of Jerusalem written of in Obadiah was by the Philistines between 848 and 841 B.C. This would make the prophet a contemporary of Elisha, and Obadiah would be the earliest of the writing prophets, predating Joel by a few years.

The history of Edom began with Esau who was given the name Edom ("Red") because of the red stew for which he traded his birthright. Esau moved to the mountainous area of Seir and absorbed the Horites, the original inhabitants. Edom refused to allow Israel to pass through their land on the way to Canaan. The Edomites opposed Saul and were subdued under David and Solomon. They fought against Jehoshaphat and successfully rebelled against Jehoram. They were again conquered by Judah under Amaziah, but they regained their freedom during the reign of Ahaz. Edom was later controlled by Assyria and Babylon; and in the fifth century B.C. the Edomites were forced by the Nabateans to leave their territory. They moved to the area of southern Palestine and became known as Idumeans. Herod the Great, an Idumean, became king of Judea under Rome in 37 B.C. In a sense, the enmity between Esau and Jacob was continued in Herod's attempt to murder Jesus. The Idumeans participated in the rebellion of Jerusalem against Rome and were defeated along with the Jews by Titus in A.D. 70. Ironically, the Edomites applauded the destruction of Jerusalem in 586 B.C. (see Ps. 127:7) but died trying to defend it in A.D. 70. After that time they were never heard of again. As Obadiah predicted, they would be "cut off for ever" (10); "there shall not be *any* remaining of the house of Esau" (18).

THE CHRIST OF OBADIAH

Christ is seen in Obadiah as the Judge of the nations (15–16), the Saviour of Israel (17–20), and the Possessor of the kingdom (21).

KEYS TO OBADIAH

Key Word: The Judgment of Edom—The major theme of Obadiah is a declaration of Edom's coming doom because of its arrogance and cruelty to Judah: "I have made thee small among the heathen" (2); "The pride of thine heart hath deceived thee" (3); "How art thou cut off!" (5); "How are *the things* of Esau searched out!" (6); "Thy mighty *men*, O Teman, shall be dismayed" (9); "Shame shall cover thee" (10); "Thou shalt be cut off for ever" (10); "As thou hast done, it shall be done unto thee" (15). Even the last few verses, which primarily deal with Israel, speak of Edom's downfall (17–21). The secondary theme of Obadiah is the future restoration of Israel and faithfulness of Yahweh to His covenant promises. God's justice will ultimately prevail.

Key Verses: Obadiah 10 and 21—"For *thy* violence against thy brother Jacob shame shall cover thee, and thou shalt be cut off for ever" (10).

"And saviours shall come up on mount Zion to judge the mount of Esau; and the kingdom shall be the LORD's" (21).

SURVEY OF OBADIAH

Obadiah is the shortest book in the Old Testament (twenty-one verses), but it carries one of the strongest messages of judgment in the Old Testament. For Edom there are no pleas to return, no words of consolation or hope. Edom's fate is sealed, and there are no conditions for possible deliverance. God will bring total destruction upon Edom, and there will be no remnant. Obadiah is Edom's day in court, complete with Edom's arraignment, indictment, and sentence. This prophet of poetic justice describes how the Judge of the earth will overthrow the pride of Edom and restore the house of Jacob. The two sections of Obadiah are: the judgment of Edom (1–18) and the restoration of Israel (19–21).

The Judgment of Edom (1–18): The first section of Obadiah makes it clear that the coming overthrow of Edom is a certainty, not a condition. Edom is arrogant (3) because of its secure position in Mount Seir, a mountainous region south of the Dead Sea. Its capital city of Sela (Petra) is protected by a narrow canyon that prevents invasion by an army. But God says this will make no difference. Even a thief does not take everything, but when God destroys Edom it will be totally ransacked. Nothing will avert God's complete judgment. Verses 10–14 describe Edom's major crime of gloating over the invasion of Jerusalem. Edom rejoiced when foreigners plundered Jerusalem, and became as one of them. On the day when she should have been allies with Judah, she instead became an aggressor against Judah. Edom will eventually be judged during the coming day of the Lord when Israel "shall be a fire, . . . and the house of Esau for stubble" (18).

The Restoration of Israel (19–21): The closing verses give hope to God's people that they will possess not only their own land, but also that of Edom and Philistia.

FOCUS	JUDGMENT OF EDOM			RESTORATION OF ISRAEL
REFERENCE	1 10	15	19	21
DIVISION	PREDICTIONS OF JUDGMENT	REASONS FOR JUDGMENT	RESULTS OF JUDGMENT	POSSESSION OF EDOM BY ISRAEL
TOPIC	DEFEAT OF ISRAEL			VICTORY OF ISRAEL
	PREDICTION OF JUDGMENT			PREDICTION OF POSSESSION
LOCATION	EDOM AND ISRAEL			
TIME	c. 840 B.C.			

OUTLINE OF OBADIAH

The Predictions of Judgment on Edom

THE vision of O-ba-di'-ah. Thus saith the Lord GOD ᴿconcerning E'-dom; We have ᴿheard a ᵀrumour from the LORD, and an ambassador is sent among the heathen, Arise ye, and let us rise up against her in battle. Joel 3:19; Mal. 1:3 • Jer. 49:14 • *message*
2 Behold, I have made thee small among the heathen: thou art greatly despised.
3 The pride of thine heart hath deceived thee, thou that dwellest in the clefts of the rock, whose habitation *is* high; ᴿthat saith in his heart, Who shall bring me down to the ground? Is. 14:13–15; Rev. 18:7
4 ᴿThough thou exalt *thyself* as the eagle, and though thou ᴿset thy nest among the stars, thence will I bring thee down, saith the LORD. Job 20:6 • Hab. 2:9
5 If thieves came to thee, if robbers by night, (how art thou cut off!) would they not have stolen till they had enough? if the grapegatherers came to thee, would they not leave ᵀ*some* grapes? *gleanings*
6 How are the things of Esau searched out! how are his hidden things sought up!
7 All the men of thy confederacy have brought thee *even* to the border: the men that were at peace with thee have deceived thee, *and* prevailed against thee; *they that eat* thy bread have laid a wound under thee: *there is* none understanding in him.
8 Shall I not in that day, saith the LORD, even destroy the wise *men* out of E'-dom, and understanding out of the mount of Esau?
9 And thy mighty *men*, O Te'-man, shall be dismayed, to the end that every one of the mount of Esau may be cut off by slaughter.

The Reasons for the Judgment on Edom

10 For thy ᴿviolence against thy brother Jacob shame shall cover thee, and ᴿthou shalt be cut off for ever. Gen. 27:41 • Ezek. 35:9
11 In the day that thou stoodest on the other side, in the day that the strangers carried away captive his forces, and foreigners entered into his gates, and cast lots upon Jerusalem, even thou *wast* as one of them.
12 But thou shouldest not have ᵀlooked on the day of thy brother in the day that he became a stranger; neither shouldest thou have rejoiced over the children of Judah in

the day of their destruction; neither shouldest thou have spoken proudly in the day of distress. *gloated over*
13 Thou shouldest not have entered into the gate of my people in the day of their calamity; yea, thou shouldest not have looked on their affliction in the day of their calamity, nor have laid *hands* on their substance in the day of their calamity;
14 Neither shouldest thou have ᴿstood in the crossway, to cut off those of his that did escape; neither shouldest thou have ᵀdelivered up those of his that did remain in the day of distress. Is. 16:3, 4 • *made captive*

The Results of the Judgment on Edom

15 ᴿFor the day of the LORD *is* near upon all the heathen: ᴿas thou hast done, it shall be done unto thee: thy reward shall return upon thine own head. Ezek. 30:3 • Hab. 2:8
16 ᴿFor as ye have drunk upon my holy mountain, *so* shall all the heathen drink continually, yea, they shall drink, and they shall ᵀswallow down, and they shall be as though they had not been. Joel 3:17 • *eat*
17 But upon mount Zion ᴿshall be ᵀdeliverance, and ᵀthere shall be holiness; and the house of Jacob shall possess their possessions. Amos 9:8 • *salvation • it shall be holy*
18 And the house of Jacob shall be a fire, and the house of Joseph a flame, and the house of Esau for stubble, and they shall kindle in them, and devour them; and there shall not be *any* remaining of the house of Esau; for the LORD hath spoken *it*.

The Possession of Edom by Israel

19 And *they of* the south shall possess the mount of Esau; ᴿand *they of* the plain the Phi-lis'-tines: ᴿand they shall possess the fields of E'-phra-im, and the fields of Sa-ma'-ri-a: and Benjamin *shall possess* Gil'-e-ad. Zeph. 2:7; Is. 11:14 • Jer. 31:5; 32:44
20 And the captivity of this host of the children of Israel *shall possess* that of the Ca'-naan-ites, *even* unto Zar'-e-phath;* and the captivity of Jerusalem, which *is* in Seph'-a-rad, shall possess the cities of the south.
21 And ᴿsaviours ᵀ shall come up on mount Zion to judge the mount of Esau; and the kingdom shall be the LORD'S. [James 5:20] • *judges*

THE BOOK OF

JONAH

THE BOOK OF JONAH
Nineveh is northeast; Tarshish is west. When God calls Jonah to preach repentance to the wicked Ninevites, the prophet knows that God's mercy may follow. He turns down the assignment and heads for Tarshish instead. But once God has dampened his spirits (by tossing him out of the boat and into the water) and has demonstrated His protection (by moving him out of the water and into the fish), Jonah realizes God is serious about His command. Nineveh must hear the word of the Lord; therefore Jonah goes. Although the preaching is a success, the preacher comes away angry and discouraged and must learn firsthand of God's compassion for sinful men.

Yonah is the Hebrew word for "dove." The Septuagint Hellenized this word into *Ionas*, and the Latin Vulgate used the title *Jonas*.

THE AUTHOR OF JONAH
The first verse introduces Jonah as "the son of Amittai." Nothing more would be known about him were it not for another reference to him in Second Kings 14:25 as a prophet in the reign of Jeroboam II of Israel. Under Jeroboam, the borders of Israel were expanded "according to the word of the LORD God of Israel, which he spake by the hand of his servant Jonah, the son of Amittai, the prophet, which *was* of Gath-hepher." Gath-hepher was three miles north of Nazareth in lower Galilee, making Jonah a prophet of the northern kingdom. The Pharisees were wrong when they said, "Search, and look: for out of Galilee ariseth no prophet" (John 7:52), because Jonah was a Galilean. One Jewish tradition says that Jonah was the son of the widow of Zarephath whom Elijah raised from the dead (1 Kin. 17:8-24).

Some critics claim that Jonah was written during the fifth to third centuries B.C. as a historical fiction to oppose the "narrow nationalism" of Ezra and Nehemiah by introducing universalistic ideas. They say an anonymous writer created this work to counteract the Jewish practice of excluding the Samaritans from worship and of divorcing foreign wives. To support this view, it is noted that the book is written in the third person with no claim that Jonah wrote it. The use of Aramaic words and the statement that "Nineveh was an exceeding great city" (3:3) indicate a late date after Nineveh's fall in 612 B.C.

Conservative scholars refute this claim with these arguments: (1) The idea of God's inclusion of the Gentiles in His program is found elsewhere in the Scripture (cf. Gen. 9:27; 12:3; Lev. 19:33, 34; 1 Sam. 2:10; Is. 2:2; Joel 2:28-32). (2) Aramaic words occur in early as well as late Old Testament books. Aramaic is found in Near Eastern texts as early as 1500 B.C. (3) The fact that the book does not explicitly say that it was written by Jonah is an argument from silence. (4) Use of the third-person style was common among biblical writers. (5) The text in 3:3 literally means "had become." At the time of the story, Nineveh had already become a very large city. (6) Jonah was a historical prophet (2 Kin. 14:25), and there are no hints that the book is fictional or allegorical. (7) Christ supported the historical accuracy of the book (Matt. 12:39-41).

THE TIME OF JONAH
Jonah was a contemporary of Jeroboam II of Israel (782-753 B.C.) who ministered after the time of Elisha and just before the time of Amos and Hosea. Israel under Jeroboam II was enjoying a period of resurgence and prosperity (see "The Time of Amos"). Conditions looked promising after many bleak years, and nationalistic fervor was probably high. During these years, Assyria was in a period of mild decline. Weak rulers had ascended the throne, but Assyria remained a threat. By the time of Jonah, Assyrian cruelty had become legendary. Graphic accounts of their cruel treatment of captives have been found in ancient Assyrian records, especially from the ninth and seventh centuries B.C. The repentance of Nineveh probably occurred in the reign of Ashurdan III (773-755 B.C.). Two plagues (765 and 759 B.C.) and a solar eclipse (763 B.C.) may have prepared the people for Jonah's message of judgment.

THE CHRIST OF JONAH
Jonah is the only prophet whom Jesus likened to Himself. "But he answered and said unto them, An evil and adulterous generation seeketh after a sign; and there shall no sign be given to it, but the sign of the prophet Jonas: For as Jonas was three days and three nights in the whale's belly; so shall the Son of man be three days and three nights in the heart of the earth. The men of Nineveh shall rise in judgment with this generation, and shall condemn it: because they repented at the preaching of Jonas; and, behold, a greater than Jonas *is* here" (Matt. 12:39-41). Jonah's experience is a figure of the death, burial, and resurrection of Christ. (The Hebrew idiom, "three days and three nights," only requires a portion of the first and third days.)

KEYS TO JONAH

Key Word: The Revival in Nineveh— God's loving concern for the Gentiles is not a truth disclosed only in the New Testament. More than seven centuries before Christ, God commissioned the Hebrew prophet Jonah to proclaim a message of repentance to the Assyrians. Jewish nationalism, however, blinded both God's prophets and covenant people to God's worldwide purposes of salvation. The story of Jonah is one of the clearest demonstrations of God's love and mercy for all mankind in the entire Scriptures.

Key Verses: Jonah 2:8, 9; 4:2—"They that observe lying vanities forsake their own mercy. But I will sacrifice unto thee with the voice of thanksgiving; I will pay *that* that I have vowed. Salvation *is* of the LORD" (2:8, 9).

"And he prayed unto the LORD, and said, I pray thee, O LORD, *was* not this my saying, when I was yet in my country? Therefore I fled before unto Tarshish: for I knew that thou *art* a gracious God, and merciful, slow to anger, and of great kindness, and repentest thee of the evil" (4:2).

Key Chapter: Jonah 3—The third chapter of Jonah records perhaps the greatest revival of all time as the entire city of Nineveh "[believes] God, and [proclaims] a fast," and cries out to God.

SURVEY OF JONAH

Jonah is an unusual book because of its message and messenger. Unlike other Old Testament books, it revolves exclusively around a gentile nation. God is concerned for the Gentiles as well as for His covenant people Israel. But God's messenger is a reluctant prophet who does not want to proclaim his message for fear that the Assyrians will respond and be spared by the compassionate God of Israel. Of all the people and things mentioned in the book—the storm, the lots, the sailors, the fish, the Ninevites, the plant,

the worm, and the east wind—only the prophet himself fails to obey God. All these were used to teach Jonah a lesson in compassion and obedience. The four chapters divide: the first commission of Jonah (1 and 2) and the second commission of Jonah (3 and 4).

The First Commission of Jonah (1 and 2): This chapter records the commission of Jonah (1:1, 2), the disobedience of Jonah (1:3), and the judgment on Jonah (1:4-17). Jonah does not want to see God spare the notoriously cruel Assyrians. To preach a message of repentance to them would be like helping Israel's enemy. In his patriotic zeal, Jonah put his country before his God and refused to represent Him in Nineveh. Instead of going five hundred miles northeast to Nineveh, Jonah attempts to go two thousand miles west to Tarshish (Spain). But the Lord uses a creative series of counter-measures to accomplish His desired result. Jonah's efforts to thwart God's plan are futile.

God prepares a "great fish" to preserve Jonah and deliver him on dry land. The fish and its divinely appointed rendezvous with the sinking prophet became a powerful reminder to Jonah of the sovereignty of God in every circumstance. While inside the fish (2), Jonah utters a declarative praise psalm which alludes to several psalms that were racing through his mind (Ps. 3:8; 31:22; 42:7; 69:1). In his unique "prayer closet," Jonah offers thanksgiving for his deliverance from drowning. When he acknowledges that "Salvation *is* of the LORD" (2:9), he is finally willing to obey and be used by God. After he is cast up on the shore, Jonah has a long time to reflect on his experiences during his eastward trek of five hundred miles to Nineveh.

The Second Commission of Jonah (3 and 4): Jonah obeys his second commission to go to Nineveh (3:1-4) where he becomes "a sign unto the Ninevites" (Luke 11:30). The prophet is a walking object lesson from God, his skin no doubt

FOCUS	FIRST COMMISSION OF JONAH				SECOND COMMISSION OF JONAH			
REFERENCE	1:1———1:4	———2:1—	——2:10—		——3:1———3:5	————	4:1——4:4	——4:11
DIVISION	DISOBEDIENCE TO THE FIRST CALL	JUDGMENT ON JONAH EXACTED	PRAYER OF JONAH IN THE FISH	DELIVERANCE OF JONAH FROM THE FISH	OBEDIENCE TO THE SECOND CALL	JUDGMENT ON NINEVEH AVERTED	PRAYER OF JONAH	REBUKE OF JONAH
TOPIC	GOD'S MERCY UPON JONAH				GOD'S MERCY UPON NINEVEH			
	"I WON'T GO."		"I WILL GO."		"I'M HERE."		"I SHOULDN'T HAVE COME."	
LOCATION	THE GREAT SEA				THE GREAT CITY			
TIME	c. 760 B.C.							

bleached from his stay in the fish. As he proceeds through the city, his one-sentence sermon brings incredible results: it is the most responsive evangelistic effort in history. Jonah's words of coming judgment are followed by a proclamation by the king of the city to fast and repent. Because of His great mercy, God "repented of the evil, that he had said he would do unto them" (3:10).

In the final chapter, God's love and grace are contrasted with Jonah's anger and lack of compassion. He is unhappy with the good results of his message because he knows God will now spare Nineveh. God uses a plant, a worm, and a wind to teach Jonah a lesson in compassion. Jonah's emotions shift from fierce anger (4:1), to despondency (4:3), then to great joy (4:6), and finally to despair (4:8). In a humorous but meaningful account, Jonah is forced to see that he has more concern for a plant than for hundreds of thousands of people (if 120,000 children are in mind in 4:11, the population of the area may have been 600,000). Jonah's lack of a divine perspective makes his repentance a greater problem than the repentance of Nineveh.

OUTLINE OF JONAH

CHAPTER 1

The Disobedience to the First Call

NOW the word of the LORD came unto Jonah the son of A-mit'-tai, saying,

2 Arise, go to RNin'-e-veh, that great city, and Tcry against it; for Rtheir wickedness is come up before me.   Gen. 10:11 • preach • Gen. 18:20

3 But Jonah rose up to flee unto Tar'-shish from the presence of the LORD, and went down to Jop'-pa; and he found a ship going to Tar'-shish: so he paid the fare thereof, and went down into it, to go with them unto Tar'-shish Rfrom the presence of the LORD. Gen. 4:16

The Great Storm

4 But the LORD sent out a great wind into the sea, and there was a mighty tempest in the sea, so that the ship was Tlike to be broken.   in danger of being wrecked

5 Then the mariners were afraid, and cried every man unto his god, and cast forth the wares that were in the ship into the sea, to lighten it of them. But Jonah was gone down Rinto the sides of the ship; and he lay, and was fast asleep.   1 Sam. 24:3

6 So the shipmaster came to him, and said unto him, What meanest thou, O sleeper? arise, call upon thy God, if so be that God will think upon us, that we perish not.

7 And they said every one to his fellow, Come, and let us Rcast lots, that we may know for whose cause this evil is upon us.

So they cast lots, and Rthe lot fell upon Jonah.   1 Sam. 14:41, 42; Prov. 16:33 • [Num. 32:23]

8 Then said they unto him, RTell us, we Tpray thee, for whose cause this evil is upon us; What is thine occupation? and whence comest thou? what is thy country? and of what people art thou?   Josh. 7:19 • ask

9 And he said unto them, I am an Hebrew; and I fear the LORD, the God of heaven, which hath made the sea and the dry land.

10 Then were the men Texceedingly afraid, and said unto him, Why hast thou done this? For the men knew that he Rfled from the presence of the LORD, because he had told them.   with great fear • Job 27:22

11 Then said they unto him, What shall we do unto thee, that the sea may be calm Tunto us? for the sea Twrought, and was tempestuous.   for • raged

12 And he said unto them, Take me up, and cast me forth into the sea; so shall the sea be calm unto you: for I know that for my sake this great tempest is upon you.

13 Nevertheless the men rowed hard to bring it to the land; Rbut they could not: for the sea Twrought, and was tempestuous against them.   [Prov. 21:30] • raged

14 Wherefore they cried unto the LORD, and said, We beseech thee, O LORD, we beseech thee, let us not perish for this man's life, and Rlay not upon us innocent blood: for thou, O LORD, Rhast done as it pleased thee.   Deut. 21:8 • [Ps. 115:3]

15 So they took up Jonah, and cast him forth into the sea: ᴿand the sea ᵀceased from her raging.   [Ps. 89:9]; Luke 8:24 · *stopped*

16 Then the men ᴿfeared the Lᴏʀᴅ exceedingly, and offered a sacrifice unto the Lᴏʀᴅ, and made vows.   Mark 4:41; Acts 5:11

The Great Salvation of Jonah by the Fish

17 Now the Lᴏʀᴅ had prepared a great fish to swallow up Jonah. And Jonah was in the belly of the fish three days and three nights.

CHAPTER 2

The Prayer of Jonah

THEN Jonah prayed unto the Lᴏʀᴅ his God out of the fish's ᴿbelly,   Ps. 130:1, 2
2 And said, I ᴿcried by reason of mine affliction unto the Lᴏʀᴅ, and he heard me; out of the belly of ᵀhell cried I, *and* thou heardest my voice.   [Ps. 18:4–6; 22:24] · *the grave*
3 ᴿFor thou hadst cast me into the deep, in the midst of the seas; and the floods compassed me about: ᴿall thy billows and thy waves passed over me.   Ps. 69:1 · Ps. 42:7
4 Then I said, I am cast out of thy sight; yet I will look again toward thy holy temple.
5 The waters compassed me about, *even* to the soul: the depth closed me round about, the weeds were wrapped about my head.
6 I went down to the bottoms of the mountains; the earth with her bars *was* about me for ever: yet hast thou brought up my life from corruption, O Lᴏʀᴅ my God.
7 When my soul fainted within me I remembered the Lᴏʀᴅ: and my prayer came in unto thee, into thine holy temple.
8 They that observe ᴿlying vanities forsake their own mercy.   2 Kin. 17:15; Jer. 10:8
9 But I will sacrifice unto thee with the voice of thanksgiving; I will pay *that* that I have vowed. Salvation *is* of the Lᴏʀᴅ.

The Deliverance of Jonah

10 And the Lᴏʀᴅ spake unto the fish, and it vomited out Jonah upon the dry *land*.

CHAPTER 3

The Obedience to the Second Call

AND the word of the Lᴏʀᴅ came unto Jonah the second time, saying,
2 Arise, go unto Nin'-e-veh, that great city, and ᴿpreach unto it the preaching that I bid thee.   Jer. 1:17; Ezek. 2:7
3 So Jonah arose, and went unto Nin'-e-veh, according to the word of the Lᴏʀᴅ. Now Nin'-e-veh was an ᴿexceeding great city of ᵀthree days' journey.   1:2; 4:11 · *60 mi.*
4 And Jonah began to enter into the city a ᵀday's journey, and ᴿhe cried, and said, Yet

forty days, and Nin'-e-veh shall be overthrown.   20 mi. · [Deut. 18:22]

The Great Fast

5 So the people of Nin'-e-veh ᴿbelieved God, and proclaimed a fast, and put on sackcloth, from the greatest of them even to the least of them.   [Matt. 12:41; Luke 11:32]
6 For word came unto the king of Nin'-e-veh, and he arose from his throne, and he laid his robe from him, and covered *him* with sackcloth, ᴿand sat in ashes.   Job 2:8
7 And he caused *it* to be proclaimed and published through Nin'-e-veh by the decree of the king and his nobles, saying, Let neither man nor beast, herd nor flock, taste any thing: let them not feed, nor drink water:
8 But let man and beast be covered with sackcloth, and cry mightily unto God: yea, let them turn every one from his evil way, and from the violence that *is* in their hands.
9 ᴿWho can tell *if* God will turn and repent, and turn away from his fierce anger, that we perish not?   2 Sam. 12:22; Joel 2:14

The Great Salvation of Nineveh by God

10 And God saw their works, that they turned from their evil way; and God repented of the evil, that he had said that he would do unto them; and he did *it* not.

CHAPTER 4

The Prayer of Jonah

BUT it displeased Jonah exceedingly, and he was very angry.
2 And he prayed unto the Lᴏʀᴅ, and said, I pray thee, O Lᴏʀᴅ, *was* not this my saying, when I was yet in my country? Therefore I ᴿfled before unto Tar'-shish: for I knew that thou *art* a gracious God, and merciful, slow to anger, and of great kindness, and repentest thee of the evil.   1:3
3 ᴿTherefore now, O Lᴏʀᴅ, take, I beseech thee, my life from me; for ᴿit *is* better for me to die than to live.   1 Kin. 19:4 · *v.* 8

The Rebuke of Jonah by God

4 Then said the Lᴏʀᴅ, ᴿDoestᵀ thou well to be angry?   *v.* 9 · *art thou greatly angry?*
5 So Jonah went out of the city, and sat on the east side of the city, and there made him a booth, and sat under it in the shadow, till he might see what would become of the city.
6 And the Lᴏʀᴅ God prepared a gourd, and made *it* to come up over Jonah, that it might be a shadow over his head, to ᵀdeliver him from his ᵀgrief. So Jonah was exceeding glad of the gourd.   *save* · *discomfort*
7 But God prepared a worm when the morning rose the next day, and it ᵀsmote the ᵀgourd that it withered.   *struck* · *plant*

8 And it came to pass, when the sun did arise, that God prepared a ᵀvehement ᴿeast wind; and the sun beat upon the head of Jonah, that he fainted, and wished in himself to die, and said, ᴿIt is better for me to die than to live.   sultry · Ezek. 19:13 · v. 3

9 And God said to Jonah, Doest thou well to be angry for the gourd? And he said, I do well to be angry, even unto death.

10 Then said the LORD, Thou hast had pity on the gourd, for the which thou hast not laboured, neither madest it grow; which came up in a night, and perished in a night:

11 And should not I spare Nin'-e-veh, that great city, wherein are more than sixscore thousand persons ᴿthat cannot discern between their right hand and their left hand; and also much cattle?   Deut. 1:39

THE BOOK OF

MICAH

THE BOOK OF MICAH

Micah, called from his rustic home to be a prophet, leaves his familiar surroundings to deliver a stern message of judgment to the princes and people of Jerusalem. Burdened by the abusive treatment of the poor by the rich and influential, the prophet turns his verbal rebukes upon any who would use their social or political power for personal gain. One-third of Micah's book exposes the sins of his countrymen; another third pictures the punishment God is about to send; and the final third holds out the hope of restoration once that discipline has ended. Through it all, God's righteous demands upon His people are clear: "to do justly, and to love mercy, and to walk humbly with thy God" (6:8).

The name *Michayahu* ("Who Is Like Yahweh?") is shortened to *Michaia*. In 7:18, Micah hints at his own name with the phrase "Who *is* a God like unto thee?" The Greek and Latin titles of this book are *Michaias* and *Micha*.

THE AUTHOR OF MICAH

Micah's home town of Moresheth-gath (1:1, 14) was located about twenty-five miles southwest of Jerusalem on the border of Judah and Philistia, near Gath. Like Amos, Micah was from the country. His family and occupation are unknown, but Moresheth was in a productive agricultural belt. Micah was not as aware of the political situation as Isaiah or Daniel, but he showed a profound concern for the sufferings of the people. His clear sense of prophetic calling is seen in 3:8: "But truly I am full of power by the spirit of the LORD, and of judgment, and of might, to declare unto Jacob his transgression, and to Israel his sin."

THE TIME OF MICAH

The first verse indicates that Micah prophesied in the days of Jotham (739–731 B.C.), Ahaz (731–715 B.C.), and Hezekiah (715–686 B.C.), kings of Judah. Although Micah deals primarily with Judah, he also addresses the northern kingdom of Israel and predicts the fall of Samaria (1:6). Much of his ministry, therefore, took place before the Assyrian captivity of Israel in 722 B.C. His strong denunciations of idolatry and immorality also suggest that his ministry largely preceded the sweeping religious reforms of Hezekiah. Thus, Micah's prophecies ranged from about 735 to 710 B.C. He was a contemporary of Hosea in the northern kingdom, and of Isaiah in the court of Jerusalem.

After the prosperous reign of Uzziah in Judah (767–739 B.C.), his son, Jotham, came to power

and followed the same policies (739–731 B.C.). He was a good king, although he failed to remove the idolatrous high places. Under the wicked King Ahaz (731–715 B.C.), Judah was threatened by the forces of Assyria and Syria. Hezekiah (715–686 B.C.) opposed the Assyrians and successfully withstood an Assyrian siege with the help of God. He was an unusually good king who guided the people of Judah back to a proper course in their walk with God.

During the ministry of Micah, the kingdom of Israel continued to crumble inwardly and outwardly until its collapse in 722 B.C. The Assyrian Empire under Tiglath-pileser III (745–727 B.C.), Shalmeneser V (727–722 B.C.), Sargon II (722–705 B.C.), and Sennacherib (705–681 B.C.) reached the zenith of its power and became a constant threat to Judah. Babylon was still under Assyrian domination, and Micah's prediction of future Babylonian captivity for Judah (4:10) must have seemed unlikely.

THE CHRIST OF MICAH

Micah 5:2 is one of the clearest and most important of all Old Testament prophecies: "But thou, Beth-lehem Ephratah, *though* thou be little among the thousands of Judah, *yet* out of thee shall he come forth unto me *that is* to be ruler in Israel; whose goings forth *have been* from of old, from everlasting." This prophecy about the birthplace and eternity of the Messiah was made seven hundred years before His birth. The chief priests and scribes paraphrased this verse in Matthew 2:5, 6 when questioned about the birthplace of the Messiah. Micah 2:12, 13; 4:1–8; and 5:4, 5 offer some of the best Old Testament descriptions of the righteous reign of Christ over the whole world.

KEYS TO MICAH

Key Word: The Judgment and Restoration of Judah—Micah exposes the injustice of Judah and the righteousness and justice of Yahweh. About one-third of the book indicts Israel and Judah for specific sins, including oppression; bribery among judges, prophets, and priests; exploitation of the powerless; covetousness; cheating; violence; and pride. Another third of Micah predicts the judgment that will come as a result of those sins. The remaining third of the book is a message of hope and consolation. God's justice will triumph and the divine Deliverer will come. True peace and justice will prevail only when the Messiah reigns. The "goodness and severity of God" (Rom. 11:22) are illustrated in Micah's presentation of divine judgment and pardon. This book emphasizes the integral

relationship between true spirituality and social ethics. Micah 6:8 summarizes what God wants to see in His people: justice and equity tempered with mercy and compassion, as the result of a humble and obedient relationship with Him.

Key Verses: Micah 6:8; 7:18—"He hath shewed thee, O man, what *is* good; and what doth the LORD require of thee, but to do justly, and to love mercy, and to walk humbly with thy God?" (6:8).

"Who *is* a God like unto thee, that pardoneth iniquity, and passeth by the transgression of the remnant of his heritage? he retaineth not his anger for ever, because he delighteth *in* mercy" (7:18).

Key Chapters: Micah 6; 7—The closing section of Micah describes a courtroom scene. God has a controversy against His people, and He calls the mountains and hills together to form the jury as He sets forth His case. The people have replaced heartfelt worship with empty ritual, thinking that this is all God demands. They have divorced God's standards of justice from their daily dealings in order to cover their unscrupulous practices. They have failed to realize what the Lord requires of man. There can only be one verdict: guilty.

Nevertheless, the book closes on a note of hope. The same God who executes judgment also delights to extend mercy (7:18). No wonder the prophet exclaims, "Therefore I will look unto the LORD; I will wait for the God of my salvation: my God will hear me" (7:7).

SURVEY OF MICAH

Micah is the prophet of the downtrodden and exploited people of Judean society. He prophesies during a time of great social injustice and boldly opposes those who imposed their power upon the poor and weak for selfish ends. Corrupt rulers, false prophets, and ungodly priests all become targets for Micah's prophetic

barbs. Micah exposes judges who are bought by bribes and merchants who use deceptive weights. The pollution of sin has permeated every level of society in Judah and Israel. The whole earth is called to witness God's indictment against His people (1:2; 6:1, 2), and the guilty verdict leads to a sentence of destruction and captivity. However, while the three major sections begin with condemnation (1:2—2:11; 3:6), they all end on a clear note of consolation (2:12, 13; 4; 5; 7). After sin is punished and justice is established, "he will have compassion upon us; he will subdue our iniquities; and thou wilt cast all their sins into the depths of the sea" (7:19). The three sections of Micah are: the prediction of judgment (1—3), the prediction of restoration (4 and 5), and the plea for repentance (6 and 7).

The Prediction of Judgment (1—3): Micah begins by launching into a general declaration of the condemnation of Israel (Samaria) and Judah (Jerusalem). Both kingdoms will be overthrown because of their rampant treachery. Micah uses a series of wordplays on the names of several cities of Judah in his lamentation over Judah's coming destruction (1:10–16). This is followed by some of the specific causes for judgment: premeditated schemes, covetousness, and cruelty. Nevertheless, God will regather a remnant of His people (2:12, 13). The prophet then systematically condemns the princes (3:1–4) and the prophets (3:5–8) and concludes with a warning of coming judgment (3:9–12).

The Prediction of Restoration (4 and 5): Micah then moves into a two-chapter message of hope, which describes the reinstitution of the kingdom (4:1–5) and the intervening captivity of the kingdom (4:6—5:1), concluding with the coming Ruler of the Kingdom (5:2–15). The prophetic focus gradually narrows from the nations to the remnant to the King.

The Plea for Repentance (6 and 7): In His two

FOCUS	PREDICTION OF JUDGMENT		PREDICTION OF RESTORATION			PLEA FOR REPENTANCE		
REFERENCE	1:1————3:1	————4:1	————4:6	————5:2	———6:1	———6:10	———7:7	——7:20
DIVISION	JUDGMENT OF PEOPLE	JUDGMENT OF LEADERSHIP	PROMISE OF COMING KINGDOM	PROMISE OF COMING CAPTIVITIES	PROMISE OF COMING KING	FIRST PLEA OF GOD	SECOND PLEA OF GOD	PROMISE OF FINAL SALVATION
TOPIC	PUNISHMENT		PROMISE			PARDON		
	RETRIBUTION		RESTORATION			REPENTANCE		
LOCATION	JUDAH—ISRAEL							
TIME	c. 735 – 710 B.C.							

controversies with His people, God calls them into court and presents an unanswerable case against them. The people have spurned God's grace, choosing instead to revel in wickedness.

Micah concludes with a sublime series of promises that the Lord will pardon their iniquity and renew their nation in accordance with His covenant.

OUTLINE OF MICAH

CHAPTER 1

Introduction to the Book of Micah

THE word of the LORD that came to ᴿMi'-cah the Mo'-ras-thite in the days of ᴿJo'-tham, Ahaz, and Hez-e-ki'-ah, kings of Judah, which he saw concerning Sa-mar'-i-a and Jerusalem.   Jer. 26:18 • 2 Kin. 15:5

Judgment on Samaria

2 Hear, all ye people; ᴿhearken, O earth, and all that therein is: and let the Lord GOD be witness against you, the Lord from ᴿhis holy temple.   Jer. 6:19; 22:29 • [Ps. 11:4]

3 ᴿFor, behold, the LORD cometh forth out of his place, and will come down, and tread upon the high places of the earth.   Is. 26:21

4 And the mountains shall be molten under him, and the valleys shall be cleft, as wax before the fire, and as the waters that are poured down a steep place.

5 For the transgression of Jacob is all this, and for the sins of the house of Israel. What is the transgression of Jacob? is it not Sa-ma'-ri-a? and what are the high places of Judah? are they not Jerusalem?

6 Therefore ᴿI will make Sa-ma'-ri-a as an heap of the field, and as plantings of a vineyard: and I will pour down the stones thereof into the valley, and I will ᵀdiscover the foundations thereof.   2 Kin. 17; 18 • uncover

7 And all the graven images thereof shall be beaten to pieces, and all the hires thereof shall be burned with the fire, and all the

ᴿidols thereof will I lay desolate: for she gathered it of the hire of an harlot, and they shall return to the hire of an harlot.   Hos. 2:5

8 Therefore I will wail and howl, I will go stripped and naked: I will make a wailing like the dragons, and mourning as the owls.

Judgment on Judah

9 For her wound is incurable; for it is come unto Judah; he is come unto the ᴿgate of my people, even to Jerusalem.   v. 12

10 Declare ye it not at Gath, weep ye not at all: in the house of ᵀAph'-rah roll thyself in the dust.   dust

11 Pass ye away, thou inhabitant of Sa'-phir, having thy shame naked: the inhabitant of ᵀZa'-a-nan came not forth in the mourning of Beth-e'-zel; he shall receive of you his standing.   the country of flocks

12 For the inhabitant of Ma'-roth waited carefully for good: but evil came down from the LORD unto the gate of Jerusalem.

13 O thou inhabitant of ᴿLa'-chish, bind the chariot to the swift beast: she is the beginning of the sin to the daughter of Zion: for the ᴿtransgressions of Israel were found in thee.   Is. 36:2 • Ezek. 23:11

14 Therefore shalt thou give presents to Mor'-esh-eth-gath: the houses of Ach'-zib shall be a ᵀlie to the kings of Israel.   snare

15 Yet will I bring an heir unto thee, O inhabitant of Ma-re'-shah: he shall come unto A-dul'-lam the glory of Israel.

16 ᵀMake thee bald, and poll thee for thy delicate children; enlarge thy baldness as the

eagle; for they are gone into captivity from thee.   *shave your head in mourning*

CHAPTER 2

Cause of the Judgment

WOE to them that devise iniquity, and ᵀwork evil upon their beds! when the morning is light, they practise it, because it is in the power of their hand.   *plan*

2 And they covet fields, and take *them* by violence; and houses, and take *them* away: so they ᵀoppress a man and his house, even a man and his heritage.   *defraud*

3 Therefore thus saith the LORD; Behold, against this family do I ᵀdevise an evil, from which ye shall not remove your necks; neither shall ye go ᴿhaughtily: for this time *is* evil.   *purpose to make trouble* • [Is. 2:11, 12]

4 In that day shall *one* take up a parable against you, and ᴿlament with a doleful lamentation, *and* say, We be utterly spoiled: he hath changed the portion of my people: how hath he removed *it* from me! turning away he hath divided our fields.   2 Sam. 1:17

5 ᴿTherefore thou shalt have none that shall cast a cord by lot in the congregation of the LORD.   [Deut. 32:8, 9]

6 ᴿProphesy ye not, *say they to them that* prophesy: they shall not prophesy to them, *that* they shall not take shame.   Amos 2:12

7 O *thou that art* named the house of Jacob, is the spirit of the LORD straitened? *are* these his doings? do not my words do good to him that walketh uprightly?

8 Even of late my people is risen up as an enemy: ye pull off the robe with the garment from them that pass by ᵀsecurely as men averse from war.   *peaceably*

9 The women of my people have ye cast out from their pleasant houses; from their children have ye taken away my glory for ever.

10 Arise ye, and depart; for this *is* not *your* rest: because it is polluted, it shall destroy *you*, even with a sore destruction.

11 If a man walking in the spirit ᵀand falsehood do lie, *saying*, I will prophesy unto thee of wine and of strong drink; he shall even be the prophet of this people.   *of*

Promise of Future Restoration

12 ᴿI will surely assemble, O Jacob, all of thee; I will surely gather the remnant of Israel; I will put them together as the sheep of Boz'-rah, as the flock in the midst of their fold: they shall make great noise by reason of the multitude of men.   [4:6, 7]

13 The ᵀbreaker is come up before them: they have broken up, and have passed through the gate, and are gone out by it: and their king shall pass before them, and the LORD on the head of them.   *destroyer*

CHAPTER 3

Judgment on Princes

AND I said, Hear, I pray you, O heads of Jacob, and ye princes of the house of Israel; ᴿIs it not for you to know judgment?   Jer. 5:4, 5

2 ᴿWho hate the good, and love the evil; who pluck off their skin from off them, and their flesh from off their bones;   Ps. 53:4

3 Who also ᴿeat the flesh of my people, and flay their skin from off them; and they break their bones, and chop them in pieces, as for the pot, and as flesh within the caldron. Ps. 14:4

4 Then shall they cry unto the LORD, but he will not hear them: he will even hide his face from them at that time, as they have behaved themselves ill in their doings.

Judgment on Prophets

5 Thus saith the LORD concerning the prophets that make my people err, that ᵀbite with their teeth, and cry, Peace; and he that putteth not into their mouths, they even prepare war against him.   *do harm*

6 Therefore night *shall be* unto you, that ye shall not have a vision; and it shall be dark unto you, that ye shall not divine; and the sun shall go down over the prophets, and the day shall be dark over them.

7 Then shall the seers ᴿbe ashamed, and the ᴿdiviners confounded: yea, they shall all cover their ᵀlips; ᴿfor *there is* no answer of God.   Zech. 13:4 • [Is. 44:24, 25] • *upper lip* • Amos 8:11

8 But truly I am full of power by the ᵀspirit of the LORD, and of judgment, and of might, ᴿto declare unto Jacob his transgression, and to Israel his sin.   *Spirit* • Is. 58:1

Promise of Future Judgment

9 Hear this, I pray you, ye heads of the house of Jacob, and princes of the house of Israel, that ᵀabhor judgment, and ᵀpervert all equity.   *hate* • *miscarry justice all the time*

10 ᴿThey build up Zion with ᵀblood, and Jerusalem with iniquity.   Jer. 22:13 • *violence*

11 ᴿThe heads thereof judge for reward, and the priests thereof teach for hire, and the prophets thereof ᵀdivine for money: yet will they lean upon the LORD, ᵀand say, *Is* not the LORD among us? none evil can come upon us.   Jer. 6:13; Is. 1:23 • *preach* • *saying*

12 Therefore ᴿshall Zion for your sake be plowed *as* a field, and Jerusalem shall become ᵀheaps, and the mountain of the house as the high places of the forest.   2 Kin. 25 • *ruins*

CHAPTER 4

The Promise of the Coming Kingdom

BUT in the last days it shall come to pass, that the mountain of the house of the

LORD shall be established in the top of the mountains, and it shall be exalted above the hills; and ᵀpeople shall flow unto it. *peoples*

2 ᴿAnd many nations shall come, and say, Come, and let us go up to the mountain of the LORD, and to the house of the God of Jacob; and he will teach us of his ways, and we will walk in his paths: for the law shall go forth ᴿof Zion, and the word of the LORD from Jerusalem.   Is. 2:3; [Luke 24:47] • Is. 42:1

3 And he shall judge among many people, and rebuke strong nations afar off; and they shall beat their swords into ᴿplowshares, and their spears into pruninghooks: nation shall not lift up a sword against nation, neither shall they learn war any more.   Is. 2:4; Joel 3:10

4 ᴿBut they shall sit every man under his vine and under his fig tree; and none shall make *them* afraid: for the mouth of the LORD of hosts hath spoken it.   Zech. 3:10

5 For all people will ᴿwalk every one in the name of his god, and we will walk in ᴿthe name of the LORD our God for ever and ever.   2 Kin. 17:29 • Zech. 10:12

The Promise of the Coming Captivities

6 In that day, saith the LORD, will I ᵀassemble her that ᵀhalteth, ᴿand I will gather her that is driven out, and her that I have afflicted;   *call together • is lame •* Ps. 147:2

7 And I will make her that halted ᴿa remnant, and her that was cast far off a strong nation: and the LORD ᴿshall reign over them in mount Zion from henceforth, even for ever.   [2:12] • [Is. 9:6, 7; Luke 1:31–33; Rev. 11:15]

8 And thou, O ᴿtower of the flock, the strong hold of the daughter of Zion, unto thee shall it come, even the ᴿfirst dominion; the kingdom shall come to the daughter of Jerusalem.   [Ps. 48:3] • Is. 1:26; [Zech. 9:9, 10]

9 Now why dost thou cry out aloud? ᴿ*is there* no king in thee? is thy counsellor perished? for ᴿpangs have taken thee as a woman in travail.   Jer. 8:19 • Is. 13:8; Jer. 30:6

10 Be in pain, and labour to bring forth, O daughter of Zion, like a woman in travail: ᴿfor now shalt thou go forth out of the city, and thou shalt dwell in the field, and thou shalt go *even* to Babylon; there shalt thou be delivered; there the LORD shall redeem thee from the hand of thine enemies.   Hos. 2:14

11 ᴿNow also many nations are gathered against thee, that say, Let her be defiled, and let our eye look upon Zion.   Lam. 2:16

12 But they know not ᴿthe thoughts of the LORD, neither understand they his ᵀcounsel: for he shall gather them ᴿas the sheaves into the floor.   [Is. 55:8] • *guidance •* Is. 21:10

13 Arise and thresh, O daughter of Zion: for I will make thine horn iron, and I will make thy hoofs brass: and thou shalt beat in pieces many people: and I will consecrate their gain unto the LORD, and their substance unto ᴿthe Lord of the whole earth.   Zech. 4:14

CHAPTER 5

NOW gather thyself in troops, O daughter of troops: he hath laid siege against us: they shall ᴿsmite the judge of Israel with a rod upon the cheek.   Matt. 27:30; Mark 15:19 ☆

Birth of the Messiah

2 But thou, ᴿBeth′-le-hem Eph′-ra-tah, *though* thou be little among the thousands of Judah, *yet* out of thee shall he come forth unto me *that is* to be ruler in Israel; whose goings forth *have been* from of old, from ᵀeverlasting.   Matt. 2:6; Luke 2:4–7 ☆ • *eternity*

Rejection of the Messiah

3 Therefore will he give them up, until the time *that* ᴿshe which ᵀtravaileth hath brought forth: then ᴿthe remnant of his brethren shall return unto the children of Israel.   4:10; Hos. 11:8 • *is in labour •* 4:7; Is. 10:20

Work of the Messiah

4 And he shall stand and ᴿfeedᵀ in the strength of the LORD, in the majesty of the name of the LORD his God; and they shall abide: for now ᴿshall he be great unto the ends of the earth. [Is. 40:10, 11] • *be nourished •* Ps. 72:8

5 And this *man* ᴿshall be the peace, when the Assyrian shall come into our land: and when he shall tread in our palaces, then shall we raise against him seven shepherds, and eight ᵀprincipal men.   Ps. 72:7; [Is. 9:6] • *princes*

6 ᴿAnd they shall ᵀwaste the land of Assyria with the sword, and the land of Nimrod in the entrances thereof: thus shall he deliver *us* from the Assyrian, when he cometh into our land, and when he treadeth within our borders.   Nah. 2:11, 13 • *eat up*

7 And ᴿthe remnant of Jacob shall be in the midst of many people ᴿas a dew from the LORD, as the showers upon the grass, that tarrieth not for man, nor waiteth for the sons of men.   *v.* 3 • Deut. 32:2; Ps. 72:6

8 ᴿAnd the remnant of Jacob shall be among the Gentiles in the midst of many people as a ᴿlion among the beasts of the forest, as a young lion among the flocks of sheep: who, if he go through, both treadeth down, and teareth in pieces, and none can deliver.   Is. 41:15, 16 • Gen. 49:9

9 Thine hand shall be lifted up upon thine adversaries, and all thine ᴿenemies shall be cut off.   Is. 26:11

10 ᴿAnd it shall come to pass in that day, saith the LORD, that I will ᵀcut off thy horses out of the midst of thee, and I will destroy thy chariots: Zech. 9:10 • *destroy*

11 And I will cut off the cities of thy land, and throw down all thy strong holds:

12 ᴿAnd I will cut off witchcrafts out of thine hand; and thou shalt have no *more* ᴿsoothsayers: Deut. 18:10–12 • Is. 2:6

13 Thy graven images also will I cut off,

and thy Tstanding images out of the midst of thee; and thou shalt Rno more worship the work of thine hands. statues • Is. 2:8

14 And I will pluck up thy Rgroves out of the midst of thee: so will I destroy thy Tcities. Ex. 34:13; Is. 27:9 • enemies

15 And I will execute vengeance in anger and fury upon the heathen, Tsuch as they have not heard. which hearkened not

CHAPTER 6

God Pleads

HEAR ye now what the LORD saith; Arise, contend thou before the mountains, and let the hills hear thy voice.

2 Hear ye, O mountains, the LORD's controversy, and ye strong foundations of the earth: for the LORD hath a controversy with his people, and he will plead with Israel.

3 RO my people, Rwhat have I done unto thee? and wherein have I wearied thee? testify against me. Ps. 50:7 • Jer. 2:5, 31

4 RFor I brought thee up out of the land of Egypt, and redeemed thee out of the house of servants; and I sent before thee Moses, Aaron, and Miriam. Ex. 20:2; [Deut. 4:20]

5 O my people, remember now what Ba'-lak king of Moab consulted, and what Ba'-laam the son of Be'-or answered him from Shit'-tim unto Gil'-gal; that ye may know the righteousness of the LORD.

Micah Replies

6 RWherewith shall I come before the LORD, and bow myself before the high God? shall I come before him with burnt offerings, with calves of a year old? Ps. 40:6–8

7 Will the LORD be pleased with thousands of rams, or with ten thousands of rivers of oil? Rshall I give my firstborn for my transgression, Tthe fruit of my body for the sin of my soul? Ezek. 23:37 • my child

8 He hath shewed thee, O man, what is good; and what doth the LORD require of thee, but Rto do justly, and to love mercy, and to walk humbly with thy God? Is. 1:17

9 The LORD's voice crieth unto the city, and the man of wisdom shall see thy name: hear ye the rod, and who hath appointed it.

God Pleads

10 Are there yet the treasures of wickedness in the house of the wicked, and the Tscant measure that is abominable? lawless

11 TShall I count them pure with Rthe wicked balances, and with the bag of deceitful weights? Shall I be pure with • Hos. 12:7

12 For the rich men thereof are full of violence, and the inhabitants thereof have spoken lies, and Rtheir tongue is deceitful in their mouth. Is. 3:8; Jer. 9:3, 5

13 Therefore also will I Rmake thee sick in smiting thee, in making thee desolate because of thy sins. Lev. 26:16; Ps. 107:17

14 RThou shalt eat, but not be satisfied; and thy casting down shall be in the midst of thee; and thou shalt take hold, but shalt not deliver; and that which thou deliverest will I give up to the sword. Lev. 26:26; Is. 9:20

15 RThou shalt sow, but thou shalt not reap; thou shalt tread the olives, but thou shalt not anoint thee with oil; and sweet wine, but shalt not drink wine. Amos 5:11

16 For the statutes of Om'-ri are kept, and all the works of the house of Ahab, and ye walk in their counsels; that I should make thee a desolation, and the inhabitants thereof an hissing: therefore ye shall bear the reproach of my people.

CHAPTER 7

Micah Replies

WOE is me! for I am as when they have gathered the summer fruits, as Rthe grapegleanings of the vintage: there is no cluster to eat: Rmy soul desired the firstripe fruit. Is. 17:6; 24:13 • Is. 28:4; Hos. 9:10

2 The good man is perished out of the earth: and there is none upright among men: they all lie in wait for blood; they hunt every man his brother with a net.

3 That they may do evil with both hands earnestly, the prince asketh, and the judge asketh for a Rreward; and the great man, he uttereth his Rmischievous desire: so they Twrap it up. 3:11 • Amos 5:12 • weave it together

4 The best of them is as a brier: the most upright is sharper than a thorn hedge: the day of thy watchmen and thy visitation cometh; now shall be Rtheir perplexity. Is. 22:5

5 Trust ye not in a friend, put ye not confidence in a guide: keep the doors of thy mouth from her that lieth in thy bosom.

6 For Rthe son dishonoureth the father, the daughter riseth up against her mother, the daughter in law against her mother in law; a man's enemies are the men of his own house. Matt. 10:21, 36; Luke 12:53; [2 Tim. 3:1–3]

The Promise of Final Salvation

7 Therefore I will Rlook unto the LORD; I will wait for the RGod of my salvation: Rmy God will hear me. Hab. 2:1 • Ps. 18:46 • [Ps. 4:3]

8 Rejoice not against me, O mine enemy: when I fall, I shall arise; when I sit in darkness, the LORD shall be a light unto me.

9 I will bear the indignation of the LORD, because I have sinned against him, until he plead my cause, and execute judgment for me: he will bring me forth to the light, and I shall behold his righteousness.

10 Then she that is mine enemy shall see it, and shame shall cover her which said unto

me, Where is the Lord thy God? mine eyes shall behold her: now shall she be trodden down as the mire of the streets.

11 In the day that thy walls are Rto be built, in that day shall the Rdecree be far removed.　　Is. 54:11; [Amos 9:11] • Zeph. 2:2

12 In that day also Rhe shall come even to thee from Assyria, Tand from the fortified cities, and from the fortress even to the river, and from sea to sea, and from mountain to mountain.　[Is. 11:16; 19:23–25] • even to

13 RNotwithstanding the land shall be Tdesolate because of them that dwell therein, for the fruit of their doings.　[Is. 3:10] • empty

14 TFeed thy people with thy rod, the flock of thine heritage, which dwell Tsolitarily in the wood, in the midst of RCarmel: let them feed in Ba'-shan and Gil'-e-ad, as in the days of old.　rule • by themselves • Is. 37:24

15 According to the days of thy coming out of the land of Egypt will I shew unto him Rmarvellous things.　Ex. 3:20; 34:10

16 The nations Rshall see and be confounded at all their might: Rthey shall lay their hand upon their mouth, their ears shall be deaf.　Is. 26:11 • Job 21:5; 3:7

17 They shall lick the Rdust like a serpent, they shall move out of their holes like Tworms of the earth: they shall Rbe afraid of the Lord our God, and shall fear because of thee.　Ps. 72:9 • creeping things • Ps. 18:45

18 Who is a God like unto thee, that pardoneth iniquity, and passeth by the transgression of Rthe remnant of his heritage? he Tretaineth not his anger for ever, because he delighteth in mercy.　[4:7] • keeps

19 RHe will turn again, he will have compassion upon us; he will subdue our iniquities; and thou wilt cast all their sins into the depths of the sea.　[Is. 38:17; Jer. 31:34]

20 RThou wilt perform the truth to Jacob, and the mercy to Abraham, Rwhich thou hast sworn unto our fathers from the days of old.　Luke 1:72 ☆ • Ps. 105:9; [Deut. 7:8, 12]

THE BOOK OF
NAHUM

📖 **THE BOOK OF NAHUM**
"For unto whomsoever much is given, of him shall be much required" (Luke 12:48). Nineveh had been given the privilege of knowing the one true God. Under Jonah's preaching this great gentile city had repented, and God had graciously stayed His judgment. However, a hundred years later, Nahum proclaims the downfall of this same city. The Assyrians have forgotten their revival and have returned to their habits of violence, idolatry, and arrogance. As a result, Babylon will so destroy the city that no trace of it will remain—a prophecy fulfilled in painful detail.

The Hebrew word *nahum* ("comfort, consolation") is a shortened form of Nehemiah ("Comfort of Yahweh"). The destruction of the capital city of Assyria is a message of comfort and consolation to Judah and all who live in fear of the cruelty of the Assyrians. The title of this book in the Greek and Latin Bibles is *Naoum* and *Nahum*.

✍️ **THE AUTHOR OF NAHUM**
The only mention of Nahum in the Old Testament is found in 1:1 where he is called an Elkoshite. At least four locations have been proposed for Elkosh: (1) A sixteenth-century tradition identifies Elkosh with Al-Qush in Iraq, north of the site of Nineveh on the Tigris River. (2) Jerome believed that Elkesi, a city near Ramah in Galilee, was Elkosh because of the similarity of the consonants. (3) Capernaum means "City of Nahum" *(Kephar-Nahum)*, and many believe that the name Elkosh was changed to Capernaum in Nahum's honor. (4) Most conservative scholars believe that Elkosh was a city of southern Judah (later called Elcesei) between Jerusalem and Gaza. This would make Nahum a prophet of the southern kingdom and may explain his interest in the triumph of Judah (1:15; 2:2).

⏳ **THE TIME OF NAHUM**
The fall of Nineveh to the Babylonians in 612 B.C. is seen by Nahum as a future event. Critics who deny predictive prophecy naturally date Nahum after 612 B.C., but this is not based upon exegetical or historical considerations. Nahum 3:8–10 refers to the fall of Thebes as a recent event, so this book must be dated after 664 B.C., the year when this took place. Thus, Nahum can safely be placed between 663 and 612 B.C. Thebes was restored a decade after its defeat, and Nahum's failure to mention this restoration has led several scholars to the conclusion that Nahum was written before 654 B.C. The fact that Nahum mentions no king in the

introduction to his book (1:1) may point to the reign of the wicked King Manasseh (686–642 B.C.).

The conversion of the Ninevites in response to Jonah's message of judgment took place about 760 B.C. The revival was evidently short-lived, because the Assyrians soon returned to their ruthless practices. In 722 B.C., Sargon II of Assyria destroyed Samaria, the capital of the northern kingdom of Israel, and scattered the ten tribes. Led by Sennacherib, the Assyrians also came close to capturing Jerusalem in the reign of King Hezekiah in 701 B.C. By the time of Nahum (c. 660 B.C.), Assyria reached the peak of its prosperity and power under Ashurbanipal (669–633 B.C.). This king extended Assyria's influence farther than had any of his predecessors. Nineveh became the mightiest city on earth with walls 100 feet high and wide enough to accommodate three chariots riding abreast. Dotted around the walls were huge towers that stretched an additional 100 feet above the top of the walls. In addition, the walls were surrounded by a moat 150 feet wide and 60 feet deep. Nineveh appeared impregnable and could withstand a 20-year siege. Thus, Nahum's prophecy of Nineveh's overthrow seemed unlikely indeed.

Assyrian power faded under Ashurbanipal's sons, Ashuretililani (633–629 B.C.) and Sinshar-ishkun (629–612 B.C.). Nahum predicted that Nineveh would end "with an overrunning flood" (1:8), and this is precisely what occurred. The Tigris River overflowed its banks and the flood destroyed part of Nineveh's wall. The Babylonians invaded through this breach in the wall, plundered the city, and set it on fire. Nahum also predicted that Nineveh would "be hid" (3:11). After its destruction in 612 B.C. the site was not discovered until A.D. 1842.

✝️ **THE CHRIST OF NAHUM**
While there are no direct messianic prophecies in Nahum, the divine attributes in 1:2–8 are consistent with Christ's work as the Judge of the nations in His Second Advent.

🔑 **KEYS TO NAHUM**
Key Word: The Judgment of Nineveh—If ever a city deserved the title "Here to Stay," Nineveh was that city. The great city appeared invincible. But into the scene steps Nahum—a prophet of God's judgment—to declare that Nineveh will fall. Less than half a century later the prediction of God's spokesman comes true as the great city topples before the Babylonian onslaught, never again to be rebuilt.

Key Verses: Nahum 1:7, 8; 3:5-7—"The LORD *is* good, a strong hold in the day of trouble; and he knoweth them that trust in him. But with an overrunning flood he will make an utter end of the place thereof, and darkness shall pursue his enemies" (1:7, 8).

"Behold, I *am* against thee, saith the LORD of hosts; and I will discover thy skirts upon thy face, and I will shew the nations thy nakedness, and the kingdoms thy shame. And I will cast abominable filth upon thee, and make thee vile, and will set thee as a gazingstock. And it shall come to pass, *that* all they that look upon thee shall flee from thee, and say, Nineveh is laid waste: who will bemoan her? whence shall I seek comforters for thee?" (3:5-7).

Key Chapter: Nahum 1—The first chapter of Nahum records the principles of divine judgment resulting in the decree of the destruction of Nineveh and the deliverance and celebration of Judah. Beginning with 1:9, the single thrust of Nahum's prophecy is the retribution of God upon the wickedness of Nineveh. Nineveh's judgment is irreversibly decreed by the righteous God who will no longer delay His wrath. Assyria's arrogance and cruelty to other nations will come to a sudden end: her power will be useless against the mighty hand of Yahweh.

Nahum 1:2-8 portrays the patience, power, holiness, and justice of the living God. He is slow to wrath, but God settles His accounts in full. This book concerns the downfall of Assyria, but it is written for the benefit of the surviving kingdom of Judah. (Israel had already been swallowed up by Assyria.) The people in Judah who trust in the Lord will be comforted to hear of God's judgment upon the proud and brutal Assyrians (1:15; 2:2).

SURVEY OF NAHUM
When God finally convinces His prophet Jonah to preach to the people of Nineveh, the whole city responds with repentance and

Nineveh escapes destruction. The people humble themselves before the one true God, but their humility soon changes to arrogance as Assyria reaches its zenith as the most powerful empire in the world. About a century after the preaching of Jonah, God calls Nahum to proclaim the coming destruction of Nineveh. This time there will be no escape, because their measure of wickedness is full. Unlike Jonah, Nahum does not go to the city but declares his oracle from afar. There is no hope of repentance. Nineveh's destruction is decreed (1), described (2), and deserved (3).

The Destruction of Nineveh Is Decreed (1): Nahum begins with a very clear description of the character of Yahweh. Because of His righteousness, He is a God of vengeance (1:2). God is also characterized by patience (1:3) and power (1:3-6). He is gracious to all who respond to Him, but those who rebel against Him will be overthrown (1:7, 8). God is holy, and Nineveh stands condemned because of her sins (1:9-14). Nothing can stand in the way of judgment, and this is a message of comfort to the people of Judah (1:15). The threat of Assyrian invasion will soon be over.

The Destruction of Nineveh Is Described (2): Assyria will be conquered, but Judah will be restored (2:1, 2). Nahum's description of the siege of Nineveh (2:3-7) and the sack of Nineveh (2:8-13) is one of the most vivid portraits of battle in Scripture. The storming warriors and chariots can almost be seen as they enter the city through a breach in the wall. As the Ninevites flee in terror, the invading army plunders the treasures of the city. Nineveh is burned and cut off forever.

The Destruction of Nineveh Is Deserved (3): Nahum closes his brief book of judgment with God's reasons for Nineveh's coming overthrow. The city is characterized by cruelty and corruption (3:1-7). Just as Assyria crushed the Egyptian capital city of Thebes (No), Assyria's capital city will also be destroyed (3:8-10).

FOCUS	DESTRUCTION OF NINEVEH DECREED		DESTRUCTION OF NINEVEH DESCRIBED		DESTRUCTION OF NINEVEH DESERVED	
REFERENCE	1:1 ——————— 1:9 ——————— 2:1 ———————		2:3 ——————— 3:1 ———————		3:12 ——————— 3:19	
DIVISION	GENERAL PRINCIPLES OF DIVINE JUDGMENT	DESTRUCTION OF NINEVEH AND DELIVERANCE OF JUDAH	THE CALL TO BATTLE	DESCRIPTION OF THE DESTRUCTION OF NINEVEH	REASONS FOR THE DESTRUCTION OF NINEVEH	INEVITABLE DESTRUCTION OF NINEVEH
TOPIC	VERDICT OF VENGEANCE		VISION OF VENGEANCE		VINDICATION OF VENGEANCE	
	WHAT GOD WILL DO		HOW GOD WILL DO IT		WHY GOD WILL DO IT	
LOCATION	IN JUDAH AGAINST NINEVEH, CAPITAL OF ASSYRIA					
TIME	c. 660 B.C.					

Nineveh is fortified so well that defeat seems impossible, but God proclaims that its destruction is inevitable (3:11–19). None of its resources can deter divine judgment.

OUTLINE OF NAHUM

CHAPTER 1

God's Vengeance in Judgment

THE burden of Nin'-e-veh. The book of the vision of Na'-hum the El'-kosh-ite.

2 God is jealous, and the LORD revengeth; the LORD revengeth, and is furious; the LORD will take vengeance on his adversaries, and he reserveth wrath for his enemies.

God's Power in Judgment

3 The LORD is slow to anger, and Rgreat in power, and will not at all acquit the wicked: Rthe LORD hath his way in the whirlwind and in the storm, and the clouds are the dust of his feet.   [Job 9:4] · Ps. 18:7

4 RHe rebuketh the sea, and maketh it dry, and drieth up all the rivers: RBa'-shan languisheth, and Carmel, and the flower of Leb'-a-non languisheth.   Matt. 8:26 · Is. 33:9

5 The Rmountains quake at him, and the hills melt, and the earth is Tburned at his presence, yea, the world, and all that dwell therein.   Mic. 1:4 · upheaved

6 Who can stand before his indignation? and who can abide in the fierceness of his anger? his fury is poured out like fire, and the rocks are thrown down by him.

7 RThe LORD is good, a Tstrong hold in the day of trouble; and he Tknoweth them that trust in him.   [Jer. 33:11] · refuge · cherishes

8 But with an overrunning flood he will make an utter end of the place thereof, and darkness shall pursue his enemies.

The Destruction of Nineveh and Deliverance of Judah

9 RWhat do ye imagine against the LORD? Rhe will make an utter end: affliction shall not rise up the second time.   Ps. 2:1 · 1 Sam. 3:12

10 For while they be Tfolden together as thorns, and while they are Rdrunken as drunkards, Rthey shall be devoured as stubble fully dry.   closely knit · 3:11 · Mal. 4:1

11 There is one come out of thee, that Timagineth evil against the LORD, Ta wicked counsellor.   plans · a counsellor of Belial

12 Thus saith the LORD; Though they be quiet, and likewise many, yet thus shall they be cut down, when he shall pass through. Though I have afflicted thee, I will afflict thee no more.

13 For now will I break his yoke from off thee, and will burst thy bonds in sunder.

14 And the LORD hath given a commandment concerning thee, that no more of thy name Tbe sown: out of the house of thy gods will I cut off the Rgraven image and the molten image: I will make thy grave; for thou art Tvile.   bear children · Mic. 5:13, 14 · evil

15 Behold upon the mountains the feet of him that bringeth good tidings, that publisheth peace! O Judah, keep thy solemn feasts, perform thy vows: for the wicked shall no more pass through thee; he is utterly cut off.

CHAPTER 2

The Call to Battle

HET that dasheth in pieces is come up before thy face: keep the munition, watch the way, make thy loins strong, fortify thy power mightily.   the destroyer

2 For the LORD hath turned away the excellency of Jacob, as the excellency of Israel: for the emptiers have emptied them out, and marred their vine branches.

The Destruction of Nineveh

3 The shield of his mighty men is made Tred, the valiant men are Tin scarlet: the

chariots *shall be* with ᵀflaming torches in the day of his preparation, and the fir trees shall be terribly shaken.   *bloody · like flames · fiery*
4 The chariots shall rage in the streets, they shall justle one against another in the broad ways: they shall seem like torches, they shall run like the lightnings.
5 He shall recount his worthies: they shall stumble in their walk; they shall make haste to the wall thereof, and the defence shall be prepared.
6 The gates of the rivers shall be opened, and the palace shall be dissolved.
7 And Huz'-zab shall be led away captive, she shall be brought up, and her maids shall ᵀlead *her* as with the voice of doves, tabering upon their ᵀbreasts.   *mourn · hearts*
8 But Nin'-e-veh *is* of old like a pool of water: yet they shall flee away. Stand, stand, *shall they cry;* but none shall look back.
9 Take ye the spoil of silver, take the spoil of gold: for *there is* none end of the store *and* glory out of all the pleasant furniture.
10 She is ᴿempty, and void, and waste: and the heart melteth, and the knees smite together, and much pain *is* in all loins, and the faces of them all gather blackness. Is. 24:1
11 Where *is* the dwelling of the lions, and the feedingplace of the young lions, where the lion, *even* the old lion, walked, *and* the lion's whelp, and none made *them* afraid?
12 The lion did tear in pieces enough for his whelps, ᴿand strangled for his lionesses, and ᴿfilled his holes with prey, and his dens with ᵀravin.   Is. 10:14 · Jer. 51:34 · *torn flesh*
13 Behold, ᴿI *am* against thee, saith the LORD of hosts, and I will burn her chariots in the smoke, and the sword shall devour thy young lions: and I will cut off thy prey from the earth, and the voice of thy messengers shall no more be heard.   Jer. 21:13

CHAPTER 3

Nineveh's Great Ungodliness

WOEᴿ to the bloody city! ᴿit *is* all full of lies *and* robbery; the prey departeth not;   Ezek. 22:2, 3; 24:6, 9 · Hab. 2:12
2 The noise of a whip, and the noise of the rattling of the wheels, and of the pransing horses, and of the jumping chariots.
3 The horseman lifteth up both the bright sword and the glittering spear: and *there is* a multitude of slain, and a great number of carcases; and *there is* none end of *their* corpses; they stumble upon their corpses:
4 Because of the multitude of the whoredoms of the wellfavoured harlot, ᴿthe mistress of witchcrafts, that selleth nations through her whoredoms, and families through her witchcrafts.   Is. 47:9, 12
5 Behold, I *am* against thee, saith the LORD of hosts; and I will discover thy skirts upon

thy face, and I will shew the nations thy nakedness, and the kingdoms thy shame.
6 And I will ᴿcast abominable filth upon thee, and make thee ᵀvile, and will set thee as a ᵀgazingstock.   Job 9:31 · *evil · horrible example*
7 And it shall come to pass, *that* all they that look upon thee ᴿshall flee from thee, and say, Nin'-e-veh is laid waste: ᴿwho will bemoan her? whence shall I seek comforters for thee?   Rev. 18:19 · Is. 51:19; Jer. 15:5

Comparison of Nineveh to No

8 Art thou better than populous No, that was ᵀsituate among the rivers, *that had* the waters round about it, whose rampart *was* the sea, *and* her wall *was* from the sea? *located*
9 ᴿE-thi-o'-pi-a and Egypt *were* her strength, and *it was* infinite; ᴿPut and Lu'-bim were thy helpers.   Is. 20:5 · Ezek. 27:10
10 Yet *was* she carried away, she went into captivity: her young children also were dashed in pieces at the top of all the streets: and they cast lots for her honourable men, and all her great men were bound in chains.
11 Thou also shalt be ᴿdrunken: thou shalt be hid, thou also shalt seek strength because of the enemy.   1:10; Jer. 25:17

Nineveh's Strong Holds Are Weak

12 All thy ᵀstrong holds *shall be* like ᴿfig trees with the firstripe figs: if they be shaken, they shall even fall into the mouth of the eater.   *fortresses* · Is. 28:4; Hab. 1:10; Rev. 6:13
13 Behold, ᴿthy people in the midst of thee *are* women: the gates of thy land shall be set wide open unto thine enemies: the fire shall devour thy bars.   Jer. 50:37
14 Draw thee waters for the siege, ᴿfortify thy strong holds: go into clay, and tread the morter, make strong the brickkiln.   2:1
15 There ᴿshall the fire devour thee; the sword shall cut thee off, it shall eat thee up like ᴿthe cankerworm: make thyself many as the cankerworm, make thyself many as the locusts.   Is. 66:15 · Joel 1:4

Nineveh's Leaders Are Weak

16 Thou hast multiplied thy merchants above the stars of heaven: the cankerworm ᵀspoileth, and fleeth away.   *destroys*
17 Thy crowned *are* as the locusts, and thy captains as the great grasshoppers, which camp in the hedges in the cold day, *but* when the sun ariseth they flee away, and their place is not known where they *are*.
18 Thy shepherds slumber, O king of Assyria: thy nobles shall dwell *in the dust:* thy people is scattered upon the mountains, and no man gathereth *them*.
19 *There is* no healing of thy bruise; ᴿthy wound is grievous: ᴿall that hear the ᵀbruit of thee shall clap the hands over thee: for upon whom hath not thy wickedness passed continually?   Mic. 1:9 · Zeph. 2:15 · *news*

THE BOOK OF
HABAKKUK

📖 THE BOOK OF HABAKKUK

Habakkuk ministers during the "death throes" of the nation of Judah. Although repeatedly called to repentance, the nation stubbornly refuses to change her sinful ways. Habakkuk, knowing the hardheartedness of his countrymen, asks God how long this intolerable condition can continue. God replies that the Babylonians will be His chastening rod upon the nation—an announcement that sends the prophet to his knees. He acknowledges that the just in any generation shall live by faith, not by sight (2:4). Habakkuk concludes by praising God's wisdom even though he doesn't fully understand God's ways.

Habaqquq is an unusual Hebrew name derived from the verb *habaq*, "embrace." Thus his name probably means "One Who Embraces" or "Clings." At the end of his book this name becomes appropriate because Habakkuk chooses to cling firmly to God regardless of what happens to his nation (3:16-19). The Greek title in the Septuagint is *Ambakouk*, and the Latin title in Jerome's Vulgate is *Habacuc*.

🖋️ THE AUTHOR OF HABAKKUK

In the introduction to the book (1:1) and in the closing psalm (3:1), the author identifies himself as "Habakkuk the prophet." This special designation seems to indicate that Habakkuk was a professional prophet. The closing statement at the end of the psalm ("To the chief singer on my stringed instruments") suggests that Habakkuk may have been a priest connected with the temple worship in Jerusalem. He mentions nothing of his genealogy or location, but speculative attempts have been made to identify him with certain unnamed Old Testament characters. In the apocryphal Book of Bel and the Dragon, Daniel is rescued a second time by the prophet Habakkuk.

⧗ THE TIME OF HABAKKUK

The only explicit time reference in Habakkuk is to the Babylonian invasion as an imminent event (1:6; 2:1; 3:16). Some scholars suggest Habakkuk was written during the reign of Manasseh (686-642 B.C.) or Amon (642-640 B.C.) because of the list of Judah's sins in 1:2-4. However, the descriptions of the Chaldeans indicate that Babylon had become a world power; and this was not true in the time of Manasseh when Babylon was under the thumb of Assyria. It is also unlikely that this prophecy took place in the time of King Josiah (640-609 B.C.), because the moral and spiritual reforms of Josiah do not fit the situation in 1:2-4. The most likely date for the

book is in the early part of Jehoiakim's reign (609-597 B.C.). Jehoiakim was a godless king who led the nation down the path of destruction (cf. 2 Kin. 23:34—24:5; Jer. 22:17).

The Babylonians began to rise in power during the reign of Nabopolassar (626-605 B.C.), and in 612 B.C. they destroyed the Assyrian capital of Nineveh. By the time of Jehoiakim, Babylon was the uncontested world power. Nabopolassar's successor, Nebuchadnezzar, came to power in 605 B.C. and carried out successful military expeditions in the west, advancing into Palestine and Egypt. Nebuchadnezzar's first invasion of Judah occurred in his first year, when he deported ten thousand of Jerusalem's leaders to Babylon. The nobles who oppressed and extorted from the poor were the first to be carried away. Since Habakkuk prophesied prior to the Babylonian invasion, the probable date for this book is about 607 B.C.

✝️ THE CHRIST OF HABAKKUK

The word *salvation* appears three times in 3:13, 18 and is the root word from which the name *Jesus* is derived (cf. Matt. 1:21). When He comes again, "the earth shall be filled with the knowledge of the glory of the LORD, as the waters cover the sea" (2:14).

🗝️ KEYS TO HABAKKUK

Key Word: "The Just Shall Live by His Faith"—The circumstances of life sometimes appear to contradict God's revelation concerning His power and purposes. Habakkuk struggles in his faith when he sees men flagrantly violate God's law and distort justice on every level, without fear of divine intervention. He wants to know why God allows this growing iniquity to go unpunished. When God reveals His intention to use Babylon as His rod of judgment, Habakkuk is even more troubled, because that nation is more corrupt than Judah. God's answer satisfies Habakkuk that he can trust Him even in the worst of circumstances because of His matchless wisdom, goodness, and power. God's plan is perfect, and nothing is big enough to stand in the way of its ultimate fulfillment. In spite of appearances to the contrary, God is still on the throne as the Lord of history and the Ruler of the nations. God may be slow to wrath, but all iniquity will be punished eventually. He is the worthiest object of faith, and the righteous man will trust in Him at all times.

Key Verses: Habakkuk 2:4; 3:17-19—"Behold, his soul *which* is lifted up is not upright in him: but the just shall live by his faith" (2:4).

"Although the fig tree shall not blossom, neither *shall* fruit *be* in the vines; the labour of the olive shall fail, and the fields shall yield no meat; the flock shall be cut off from the fold, and *here shall be* no herd in the stalls: Yet I will rejoice in the LORD, I will joy in the God of my salvation. The LORD God *is* my strength, and he will make my feet like hinds' *feet,* and he will make me to walk upon mine high places" 3:17-19).

Key Chapter: Habakkuk 3—The Book of Habakkuk builds to a triumphant climax reached n the last three verses (3:17-19). The beginning f the book and the ending stand in stark ontrast: mystery to certainty, questioning to ffirming, and complaint to confidence. Chapter 3 s one of the most majestic of all Scripture and ecords the glory of God in past history and in uture history (prophecy).

SURVEY OF HABAKKUK

Habakkuk is a freethinking prophet who is not afraid to wrestle with issues that test his faith. He openly and honestly directs his problems to God and waits to see how He will respond to his probing questions. After two ounds of dialogue with the Lord, Habakkuk's ncreased understanding of the person, power, nd plan of God cause him to conclude with a psalm of unqualified praise. The more he knows bout the Planner, the more he can trust His plans. No matter what God brings to pass, "the ust shall live by his faith" (2:4). The two divisions f this book are: the problems of Habakkuk (1 and) and the praise of Habakkuk (3).

The Problems of Habakkuk (1 and 2): Habakkuk's first dialogue with God takes place in :1-11. In 1:1-4, the prophet asks God how long Ie will allow the wickedness of Judah to go

unpunished. The people of Judah sin with impunity, and justice is perverted. God's startling answer is given in 1:5-11: He is raising up the fierce Babylonians as His rod of judgment upon sinful Judah. The Chaldeans will come against Judah swiftly, violently, and completely. The coming storm from the east will be God's answer to Judah's crimes.

This answer leads to Habakkuk's second dialogue with God (1:12—2:20). The prophet is more perplexed than ever and asks how the righteous God can punish Judah with a nation that is even more wicked (1:12—2:1). Will the God whose eyes are too pure to approve evil reward the Babylonians for their cruelty and idolatry? Habakkuk stands upon a watchtower to wait for God's reply. The Lord answers with a series of five woes—of greed and aggression (2:5-8), exploitation and extortion (2:9-11), violence (2:12-14), immorality (2:15-17), and idolatry (2:18-20). God is aware of the sins of the Babylonians, and they will not escape His terrible judgment. But Judah is guilty of the same offenses and stands under the same condemnation. Yahweh concludes His answer with a statement of His sovereign majesty: "But the LORD *is* in his holy temple: let all the earth keep silence before him" (2:20).

The Praise of Habakkuk (3): Habakkuk begins by questioning God, but he concludes his book with a psalm of praise for the person (3:1-3), power (3:4-12), and plan (3:13-19) of God. He now acknowledges God's wisdom in the coming invasion of Judah, and although it terrifies him, he will trust the Lord. God's creative and redemptive work in the past gives the prophet confidence in the divine purposes, and hope at a time when he would otherwise despair. "Yet I will rejoice in the LORD, I will joy in the God of my salvation" (3:18).

FOCUS	PROBLEMS OF HABAKKUK				PRAISE OF HABAKKUK
REFERENCE	1:1————1:5	————1:12	————2:2	————3:1	————3:19
DIVISION	FIRST PROBLEM OF HABAKKUK	FIRST REPLY OF GOD	SECOND PROBLEM OF HABAKKUK	SECOND REPLY OF GOD	PRAYER OF PRAISE OF HABAKKUK
TOPIC	FAITH TROUBLED				FAITH TRIUMPHANT
	WHAT GOD IS DOING				WHO GOD IS
LOCATION	THE NATION OF JUDAH				
TIME	c. 607 B.C.				

OUTLINE OF HABAKKUK

CHAPTER 1

The First Problem of Habakkuk

THE ᴿburden which Ha-bak'-kuk the prophet did see.   Is. 13:1; Nah. 1:1

2 O Lᴏʀᴅ, how long shall I cry, ᴿand thou wilt not hear! *even* cry out unto thee *of* violence, and thou wilt not save!   Lam. 3:8

3 ᴿWhy dost thou shew me iniquity, and cause *me* to behold grievance? for spoiling and violence *are* before me: and there are *that* raise up strife and contention.   Jer. 15:10

4 Therefore the law is slacked, and judgment doth never go forth: for the wicked doth compass about the righteous; therefore ᵀwrong judgment proceedeth.   *twisted*

God's First Reply

5 ᴿBehold ye among the heathen, and regard, and wonder marvellously: for *I* will work a work in your days, *which* ye will not believe, though it be told *you.*   Is. 29:14

6 For, lo, I raise up the Chal-de'-ans, *that* bitter and hasty nation, which shall march through the breadth of the land, to possess the dwellingplaces *that are* not their's.

7 They *are* ᴿterrible and dreadful: their judgment and their dignity shall proceed of themselves.   Is. 18:2, 7; Jer. 39:5–9

8 Their horses also are swifter than the leopards, and are more fierce than the evening wolves: and their horsemen shall spread themselves, and their horsemen shall come from far; they shall fly as the ᴿeagle *that* hasteth to eat.   Ezek. 17:3; Hos. 8:1

9 They shall come all for violence: their faces shall sup up *as* the east wind, and they shall gather the captivity as the sand.

10 And they shall ᴿscoff at the kings, and the princes shall be a scorn unto them: they shall deride every strong hold; for they shall heap dust, and take it.   2 Chr. 36:6

11 Then shall *his* mind change, and he shall pass over, and offend, ᴿ*imputing* this his power unto his god.   *v.* 16; Dan. 4:30

The Second Problem of Habakkuk

12 *Art* thou not from everlasting, O Lᴏʀᴅ my God, mine Holy One? we shall not die. O Lᴏʀᴅ, thou hast ordained ᵀthem for judgment; and, O mighty God, thou hast ᵀestablished them for correction.   *him • chosen*

13 *Thou art* of purer eyes than to behold evil, and canst not look on ᵀiniquity: wherefore lookest thou upon them that deal treacherously, *and* holdest thy ᵀtongue when the wicked devoureth *the man that is* more righteous than he?   *evil doings • peace*

14 And makest men as the fishes of the sea, as the ᵀcreeping things, *that have* no ruler over them?   *moving*

15 ᴿThey take up all of them with the ᵀangle, they catch them in their net, and

---

1:2 Sources of Doubt—One of the most potent sources of doubt is introduced in the early chapters of Genesis. It is Satan himself who causes Eve to doubt God by questioning His Word: "Yea, hath God said, Ye shall not eat of every tree of the garden?" (Page 6—Gen. 3:1). Satan even tries to get the long-suffering Job to curse God (Page 518—Job 1:11). Satan is said to be seeking to devour Christians (Page 1239—1 Pet. 5:8). This statement must not be taken literally, but means that Satan wants to devour the Christian's commitment to God and testimony before others. One way he does this is by introducing doubt into the mind.

    The world system is another source of doubt. Since it has its own set of values and objectives that are opposed to God, it also has its own worldly wisdom (Page 1127—1 Cor. 2:6). This wisdom stands in direct opposition to the wisdom of God taught by the Holy Spirit (Page 1127—1 Cor. 2:13). It is clearly revealed, for example, in the opposition of the evolutionary theory to the truth of the creation of man (Page 1197—1 Tim. 6:20).

    Probably the greatest source of doubt Christians face is simply their own spiritual immaturity. James traces doubting in prayer to double-mindedness and instability (Page 1228—James 1:8). Paul explains that when Christians doubt sound doctrine, it is because they are children in the faith and thus are easily deceived (Page 1164—Eph. 4:14). Conquering this kind of doubt demands a growing, obedient relationship with God.

    Now turn to Page 360—1 Kin. 18:21: Cure for Doubt.

gather them in their ^Tdrag: therefore they rejoice and are glad.   Jer. 16:16 • hook • seine

16 Therefore ^Rthey sacrifice unto their net, and burn incense unto their drag; because by them their portion *is* fat, and their meat plenteous.   Deut. 8:17; Is. 10:13

17 Shall they therefore empty their ^Rnet, and not spare continually to ^Rslay the nations?   Is. 19:8 • Is. 14:5, 6

CHAPTER 2

I WILL ^Rstand upon my watch, and set me upon the tower, and will watch to see what he will say unto me, and what I shall answer when I am reproved.   Is. 21:8, 11

God's Second Reply

2 And the LORD answered me, and said, Write the vision, and make *it* plain upon tables, that he may run that readeth it.

3 For the vision *is* yet for an appointed time, but at the end it shall speak, and not lie: though it tarry, wait for it; because it will surely come, it will not tarry.

4 Behold, his soul *which* is lifted up is not upright in him: but the ^Rjust shall live by his faith.   [John 3:36]; Rom. 1:17; Gal. 3:11

5 ^TYea also, because he transgresseth by wine, *he is* a proud man, neither keepeth at home, who enlargeth his desire as hell, and *is* as death, and cannot be satisfied, but gathereth unto him all nations, and heapeth unto him all people: *and moreover*

6 Shall not all these ^Rtake up a parable against him, and a taunting proverb against him, and say, Woe to him that increaseth *that which is* not his! how long? and to him that ladeth himself with thick clay!   Is. 14:4

7 Shall they not rise up suddenly that shall bite thee, and awake that shall vex thee, and thou shalt be for ^Tbooties unto them?   *spoils*

8 Because^R thou hast spoiled many nations, all the remnant of the people shall spoil thee; because of men's blood, and *for* the violence of the land, of the city, and of all that dwell therein.   *v.* 17; Is. 33:1; Jer. 27:7

9 Woe to him that coveteth an evil covetousness to his house, that he may ^Rset his nest on high, that he may be delivered from the power of ^Tevil!   Obad. 4 • *harm*

10 Thou hast consulted ^Rshame to thy house by cutting off many people, and hast sinned *against* thy soul.   2 Kin. 9:26; Nah. 1:14

11 For the ^Rstone shall cry out of the wall, and the beam out of the timber shall ^Tanswer it.   Josh. 24:27; Luke 19:40 • *respond*

12 Woe to him that buildeth a town with blood, and stablisheth a city by iniquity!

13 Behold, *is it* not of the LORD of hosts that the people shall labour in the very ^Rfire, and ^Rthe people shall weary themselves ^Tfor very vanity?   Is. 50:11 • Is. 55:2 • *in vain?*

14 ^RFor the earth shall be filled with the knowledge of the glory of the LORD, as the waters cover the sea.   [Ps. 22:27; Zech. 14:8, 9]

15 Woe unto him that giveth his neighbour drink, that puttest thy ^Rbottle to *him,* and makest *him* drunken also, that thou mayest look on their nakedness!   Hos. 7:5

16 Thou art filled with shame for glory: drink thou also, and let thy foreskin be uncovered: the cup of the LORD's right hand shall be turned unto thee, and ^Tshameful spewing *shall be* on thy glory.   *a foul shame*

17 For the ^Tviolence of Leb'-a-non shall cover thee, and the spoil of beasts, *which* made them afraid, because of men's blood, and for the violence of the land, of the city, and ^Tof all that dwell therein.   *done to • to*

18 What profiteth the graven image that the maker thereof hath graven it; the molten image, and a teacher of lies, that the maker of his work trusteth therein, to make ^Rdumb idols?   Is. 44:9; Jer. 10:3–5; 1 Cor. 12:2

19 Woe unto him that saith to the wood, ^RAwake; to the dumb stone, Arise, it shall teach! Behold, it *is* laid over with ^Rgold and silver, and *there is* ^Rno breath at all in the midst of it.   1 Kin. 18:26 • Jer. 10:9 • Ps. 135:17

20 But the LORD *is* in his holy temple: let all the earth keep silence before him.

CHAPTER 3

Habakkuk Prays for God's Mercy

A PRAYER of Ha-bak'-kuk the prophet upon Shig-i-o'-noth.

2 O LORD, I have heard thy speech, *and* was afraid: O LORD, revive thy work in the midst of the years, in the midst of the years make known; in wrath remember mercy.

The Glory of the Person of God

3 God came from Te'-man, and the Holy One from mount Pa'-ran.   Selah. His ^Rglory covered the heavens, and the earth was full of his praise.   [Ps. 113:4]

4 And *his* ^Rbrightness was as the light; he had horns *coming* out of his hand: and there *was* the hiding of his power.   Ps. 18:12

The Power of the Saving Acts of God

5 Before him went the ^Rpestilence, and burning coals went forth at his feet.   Ex. 5:3

6 He stood, and ^Rmeasured the earth: he beheld, and drove asunder the nations; ^Rand the everlasting mountains were scattered, the perpetual hills did bow: his ways *are* everlasting.   [Deut. 32:8] • Nah. 1:5

7 I saw the tents of Cu'-shan ^Tin affliction: *and* the curtains of the land of Mid'-i-an did tremble.   *being troubled*

8 Was the LORD displeased against the rivers? *was* thine anger against the ^Rrivers?

was thy wrath against the ᴿsea, that thou didst ride upon thine horses *and* thy chariots of salvation?   Ex. 7:19 • Ex. 14:16

9 Thy bow was made quite naked, *according* to the oaths of the tribes, *even thy* word. Selah. Thou didst cleave the earth with rivers.

10 The mountains saw thee, *and* they trembled: the overflowing of the water passed by: the deep ᴿuttered his voice, *and* lifted up his hands on high.   Ps. 93:3

11 ᴿThe sun *and* moon stood still in their habitation: at the light of thine arrows they went, *and* at the shining of thy glittering spear.   Josh. 10:13; Ps. 18:9

12 Thou didst ᴿmarch through the land in indignation, thou didst thresh the heathen in anger.   Ps. 68:7

13 Thou wentest forth for the salvation of thy people, *even* for salvation with thine anointed; thou woundedst the head out of the house of the wicked, by discovering the foundation unto the neck.   Selah.

14 Thou didst strike through with his staves the head of his villages: they came out as a whirlwind to scatter me: their rejoicing *was* as to ᴿdevour the poor secretly.   Ps. 10:8

15 Thou didst walk through the sea with thine horses, *through* the ᵀheap of great waters.   *surging*

Habakkuk Trusts in God's Salvation

16 When I heard, my belly ᴿtrembled; my lips quivered at the voice: rottenness entered into my ᴿbones, and I trembled in myself, that I might rest in the day of trouble: when he cometh up unto the people, he will invade them with his troops.   [*v.* 6] • Jer. 23:9

17 Although the fig tree shall not blossom, neither *shall* fruit *be* in the vines; the labour of the olive shall fail, and the fields shall yield no meat; the flock shall be cut off from the fold, and *there shall be* no herd in the stalls:

18 ᴿYet I will rejoice in the Lᴏʀᴅ, I will joy in the God of my salvation.   [Ps. 42:5]

19 The Lᴏʀᴅ God *is* my strength, and he will make my feet like hinds' *feet*, and he will make me to walk upon mine high places. To the chief singer on my stringed instruments.

THE BOOK OF

ZEPHANIAH

THE BOOK OF ZEPHANIAH

During Judah's hectic political and religious history, reform comes from time to time. Zephaniah's forceful prophecy may be a factor in the reform that occurs during Josiah's reign—a "revival" that produces outward change, but does not fully remove the inward heart of corruption which characterizes the nation. Zephaniah hammers home his message repeatedly that the day of the Lord, Judgment Day, is coming when the malignancy of sin will be dealt with. Israel and her gentile neighbors will soon experience the crushing hand of God's wrath. But after the chastening process is complete, blessing will come in the person of the Messiah, who will be the cause for praise and singing.

Tsephan-yah means "Yahweh Hides" or "Yahweh Has Hidden." Zephaniah was evidently born during the latter part of the reign of King Manasseh. His name may mean that he was "hidden" from Manasseh's atrocities. The Greek and Latin title is *Sophonias*.

THE AUTHOR OF ZEPHANIAH

The first verse is very unusual in that Zephaniah traces his lineage back four generations to Hezekiah. This is probably Hezekiah the king of Judah, since this would best explain the genealogy. If Zephaniah was the great-great-grandson of the godly King Hezekiah, he was the only prophet of royal descent. This may have given the prophet freer access to the court of King Josiah in whose reign he ministered. Because Zephaniah used the phrase "this place" (1:4) to refer to Jerusalem and was quite familiar with its features (cf. 1:9, 10; 3:1-7), he was probably an inhabitant of Judah's royal city.

THE TIME OF ZEPHANIAH

Zephaniah solves the dating problem by fixing his prophecy "in the days of Josiah the son of Amon, king of Judah" (1:1). Josiah reigned from 640 to 609 B.C., and 2:13 indicates that the destruction of Nineveh (612 B.C.) was still a future event. Thus, Zephaniah's prophecy can be dated between 640 and 612 B.C.

However, the sins catalogued in 1:3-13 and 3:1-7 indicate a date prior to Josiah's reforms when the sins from the reign of Manasseh and Amon still predominated. It is therefore likely that Zephaniah's ministry played a significant role in preparing Judah for the revivals that took place in the reign of the nation's last righteous king. Josiah became king of Judah at the age of eight, and by the age of sixteen his heart had already begun to turn toward God. His first reform took place in the twelfth year of his reign (628 B.C.; 2

Chr. 34:3-7) when he tore down all the altars of Baal, destroyed the foreign incense altars, burned the bones of the false prophets on their altars, and broke the Asherim (carved images) and molten images in pieces. Six years later (622 B.C.), Josiah's second reform was kindled when Hilkiah the priest found the Book of the Law in the temple (2 Chr. 34:8—35:19). Thus, Zephaniah's prophecy can be dated more precisely as occurring between 630 and 625 B.C.

The evil reigns of Manasseh and Amon (a total of fifty-five years) had such a profound effect upon Judah that it never recovered. Josiah's reforms were too little and too late, and the people reverted to their crass idolatry and teaching soon after Josiah was gone. As a contemporary of Jeremiah and Habakkuk, Zephaniah was one of the eleventh-hour prophets to Judah.

THE CHRIST OF ZEPHANIAH

Jesus alluded to Zephaniah on two occasions (cf. Zeph. 1:3; Matt. 13:41 and cf. Zeph. 1:15; Matt. 24:29). Both of these passages about the day of the Lord are associated with Christ's Second Advent. Although the Messiah is not specifically mentioned in Zephaniah, it is clear that He is the One who will fulfill the great promises of 3:9-20. He will gather His people and reign in victory: "The LORD hath taken away thy judgments, he hath cast out thine enemy: the king of Israel, *even* the LORD, *is* in the midst of thee: thou shalt not see evil any more" (3:15).

KEYS TO ZEPHANIAH

Key Word: The Day of the Lord—Zephaniah discusses the coming day of judgment upon Judah and the nations. God is holy and must vindicate His righteousness by calling all the nations of the world into account before Him. The sovereign God will judge not only His own people but also the whole world: no one escapes from His authority and dominion. The day of the Lord will have universal impact. To some degree, that day has already come for Judah and all the nations mentioned in 2:4-15, but there is also a future aspect, when all the earth will be judged. Zephaniah 3:9-20 speaks of another side of the day of the Lord: it will be a day of blessing after the judgment is complete. A righteous remnant will survive and all who call upon Him, Jew or Gentile, will be blessed. God will regather and restore His people, and there will be worldwide rejoicing.

Zephaniah is also written as a warning to Judah

and as a call to repentance (2:1–3). God wants to spare the people, but they ultimately reject Him. His judgment will be great; but God promises His people a future day of hope and joy. Wrath and mercy, severity and kindness, cannot be separated in the character of God.

Key Verses: Zephaniah 1:14, 15; 2:3—"The great day of the LORD is near, it is near, and hasteth greatly, even the voice of the day of the LORD: the mighty man shall cry there bitterly. That day is a day of wrath, a day of trouble and distress, a day of wasteness and desolation, a day of darkness and gloominess, a day of clouds and thick darkness" (1:14, 15).

"Seek ye the LORD, all ye meek of the earth, which have wrought his judgment; seek righteousness, seek meekness: it may be ye shall be hid in the day of the LORD's anger" (2:3).

Key Chapter: Zephaniah 3—The last chapter of Zephaniah records the two distinct parts of the day of the Lord: judgment and restoration. Following the conversion of the nation, Israel finally is fully restored. Under the righteous rule of God, Israel fully inherits the blessings contained in the biblical covenants.

SURVEY OF ZEPHANIAH

On the whole, Zephaniah is a fierce and grim book of warning about the coming day of the Lord. Desolation, darkness, and ruin will strike Judah and the nations because of the wrath of God upon sin. Zephaniah looks beyond judgment, however, to a time of joy when God will cleanse the nations and restore the fortunes of His people Israel. The book begins with God's declaration, "I will utterly consume all things from off the land" (1:2); but it ends with this promise, "At that time will I bring you again" and "turn back your captivity before your eyes" (3:20). Zephaniah moves three times from the general to the specific: (1) from universal judgment (1:1–3) to judgment upon Judah (1:4—2:3); (2) from judgment upon surrounding nations

(2:4–15) to judgment upon Jerusalem (3:1–7); (3) from judgment and cleansing of all nations (3:8–10) to restoration of Israel (3:11–20). The two broad divisions of the book are: the judgment in the day of the Lord (1:1—3:8), and the salvation in the day of the Lord (3:9–20).

The Judgment in the Day of the Lord (1:1—3:8): The prophetic oracle begins with an awesome statement of God's coming judgment upon the entire earth because of the sins of men (1:2, 3). Zephaniah then concentrates on the judgment of Judah (1:4–18), listing some of the offenses that will cause it to come. Judah is polluted with idolatrous priests who promote the worship of Baal and nature, and her officials and princes are completely corrupt. Therefore, the day of the Lord is imminent; and it will be characterized by terror, desolation, and distress. However, by His grace, Yahweh appeals to His people to repent and humble themselves to avert the coming disaster before it is too late (2:1-3).

Zephaniah pronounces God's coming judgment upon the nations that surround Judah (2:4–15). He looks in all four directions: Philistia (west), Moab and Ammon (east), Ethiopia (south), and Assyria (north). Then he focuses on Jerusalem, the center of God's dealings (3:1–7). Jerusalem is characterized by spiritual rebellion and moral treachery. "She obeyed not the voice; she received not correction; she trusted not in the LORD; she drew not near to her God" (3:2).

The Salvation in the Day of the Lord (3:9-20): After a broad statement of the judgment of all nations (3:8), Zephaniah changes the tone of the remainder of his book to blessing; for this, too, is an aspect of the day of the Lord. The nation will be cleansed and will call on the name of the Lord (3:9, 10). The remnant of Israel will be regathered, redeemed, and restored (3:11-20). They will rejoice in their Redeemer, and He will be in their midst. Zephaniah opens with idolatry, wrath, and judgment, but closes with true worship, rejoicing, and blessing.

FOCUS	JUDGMENT IN THE DAY OF THE LORD					SALVATION IN THE DAY OF THE LORD	
REFERENCE	1:1———1:4———2:4———3:1———3:8					3:9———3:14———3:20	
DIVISION	JUDGMENT ON THE WHOLE EARTH	JUDGMENT ON THE NATION OF JUDAH	JUDGMENT ON THE NATIONS SURROUNDING JUDAH	JUDGMENT ON THE CITY OF JERUSALEM	JUDGMENT ON THE WHOLE EARTH	PROMISE OF CONVERSION	PROMISE OF RESTORATION
TOPIC	DAY OF WRATH					DAY OF JOY	
	JUDGMENT ON JUDAH					RESTORATION FOR JUDAH	
LOCATION	JUDAH AND THE NATIONS						
TIME	c. 630 B.C.						

OUTLINE OF ZEPHANIAH

CHAPTER 1

The Judgment on the Whole Earth

THE word of the LORD which came unto Zeph-a-ni'-ah the son of Cu'-shi, the son of Ged-a-li'-ah, the son of Am-a-ri'-ah, the son of Hiz-ki'-ah, in the days of Jo-si'-ah the son of Amon, king of Judah.

2 I will ᵀutterly consume all *things* from off the land, saith the LORD.   *completely destroy*

3 I will consume man and beast; I will consume the fowls of the heaven, and the fishes of the sea, and the ᵀstumblingblocks with the wicked; and I will cut off man from off the land, saith the LORD.   *shrines*

Causes of the Judgment

4 ᴿI will also stretch out mine hand upon Judah, and upon all the inhabitants of Jerusalem; and I will cut off the remnant of Ba'-al from this place, *and* the name of the Chem'-a-rims with the priests;   Jer. 6:12

5 And them that worship the host of heaven upon the housetops; and them that worship *and* that swear by the LORD, and that swear ᴿby Mal'-cham;   Josh. 23:7

6 And them that are ᵀturned back from the LORD; and *those* that have not sought the LORD, nor enquired for him.   *fallen away*

7 Hold thy peace at the presence of the Lord GOD: for the day of the LORD *is* at hand: for the LORD hath prepared a sacrifice, he hath ᵀbid his guests.   *consecrated*

8 And it shall come to pass in the day of the LORD's sacrifice, that I will ᵀpunish the princes, and the king's children, and all such as are clothed with strange apparel.   *visit upon*

9 In the same day also will I punish all those that ᵀleap on the ᴿthreshold, which fill their masters' houses with ᴿviolence and deceit.   *worship the pagans* • 1 Sam. 5:5 • Amos 3:10

10 And it shall come to pass in that day, saith the LORD, *that there shall be* the noise of a cry from the ᴿfish gate, and an howling from the second, and a great crashing from the hills.   2 Chr. 33:14

11 ᴿHowl, ye inhabitants of Mak'-tesh, for all the merchant people are cut down; all they that bear silver are cut off.   James 5:1

12 And it shall come to pass at that time, *that* I will search Jerusalem with candles, and punish the men that are ᴿsettled on their lees: that say in their heart, The LORD will not do good, neither will he do evil.   Jer. 48:11

13 Therefore their goods shall become a booty, and their houses a desolation: they shall also build houses, but not inhabit *them*; and they shall plant vineyards, ᴿbut not drink the wine thereof.   Amos 5:11; Mic. 6:15

Description of the Judgment

14 The great day of the LORD *is* near, *it is* near, and ᵀhasteth greatly, *even* the voice of the day of the LORD: the mighty man shall cry there bitterly.   *comes quickly*

15 That day *is* a day of wrath, a day of trouble and distress, a day of wasteness and desolation, a day of darkness and gloominess, a day of clouds and thick darkness,

16 A day of ᴿthe trumpet and alarm against the ᵀfenced cities, and against the ᵀhigh towers.   Jer. 4:19 • *fortified* • *fortifications*

17 And I will bring distress upon men, that they shall ᴿwalk like blind men, because they have sinned against the LORD: and their blood shall be poured out as dust, and their flesh as the dung.   Deut. 28:29

18 ᴿNeither their silver nor their gold shall be able to deliver them in the day of the LORD's wrath; but the whole land shall be devoured by the fire of his jealousy: for he shall make even a speedy riddance of all them that dwell in the land.   Ezek. 7:19

CHAPTER 2

Call to Repentance

GATHER yourselves together, yea, gather together, O nation not desired;

2 Before the decree ᵀbring forth, *before* the day pass as the chaff, before the fierce anger of the LORD come upon you, before the day of the LORD's anger come upon you.   *is born*

3 ᴿSeek ye the Lᴏʀᴅ, ᴿall ye meek of the earth, which have ᵀwrought his judgment; seek righteousness, seek meekness: ᴿit may be ye shall be hid in the day of the Lᴏʀᴅ's anger.   Ps. 105:4; Amos 5:6 • Ps. 76:9 • *worked* • Amos 5:15

Judgment Against Philistia (West)

4 For ᴿGa'-za shall be forsaken, and Ash'-ke-lon a desolation: they shall drive out Ash'-dod ᴿat the noon day, and Ek'-ron shall be rooted up.   Amos 1:7; Zech. 9:5, 6 • Jer. 6:4

5 Woe unto the inhabitants of the sea coast, the nation of the ᴿCher'-e-thites! the word of the Lᴏʀᴅ *is* ᴿagainst you; O ᴿCanaan, the land of the Phi-lis'-tines, I will even destroy thee, that there shall be no inhabitant.   Ezek. 25:16 • Amos 3:1 • Josh. 13:3

6 And the sea coast shall be dwellings *and* cottages for shepherds, and folds for flocks.

7 And the coast shall be for ᴿthe remnant of the house of Judah; they shall feed thereupon: in the houses of Ash'-ke-lon shall they lie down in the evening: ᵀfor the Lᴏʀᴅ their God shall visit them, and turn away their captivity.   [Mic. 5:7, 8] • *when*

Judgment Against Moab and Ammon (East)

8 ᴿI have heard the reproach of Moab, and ᴿthe revilings of the children of Ammon, whereby they have reproached my people, and ᴿmagnified *themselves* against their border.   Jer. 48:27 • Ezek. 25:3 • Jer. 49:1

9 Therefore *as* I live, saith the Lᴏʀᴅ of hosts, the God of Israel, Surely Moab shall be as Sodom, and the children of Ammon as Go-mor'-rah, *even* the breeding of nettles, and saltpits, and a perpetual desolation: the residue of my people shall spoil them, and the remnant of my people shall possess them.

10 This shall they have for their ᴿpride, because they have reproached and magnified *themselves* against the people of the Lᴏʀᴅ of hosts.   Is. 16:6; Jer. 48:29

11 The Lᴏʀᴅ *will be* terrible unto them: for he will famish all the gods of the earth; and *men* shall worship him, every one from his place, *even* all the isles of the heathen.

Judgment Against Ethiopia (South)

12 ᴿYe E-thi-o'-pi-ans also, ye *shall be* slain by my ᴿsword.   Is. 18:1; 20:4 • Ps. 17:13

Judgment Against Assyria (North)

13 And he will stretch out his hand against the north, and ᴿdestroy Assyria; and will make Nin'-e-veh a desolation, *and* dry like a wilderness.   Is. 10:12; Ezek. 31:3

14 And flocks shall lie down in the midst of her, all the beasts of the nations: both the cormorant and the ᵀbittern shall lodge in the upper ᵀlintels of it; *their* voice shall sing in the windows; desolation *shall be* in the thresholds: for he shall ᵀuncover the cedar work.   *porcupine* • *columns* • *destroy*

15 This *is* the rejoicing city ᴿthat dwelt carelessly, that said in her heart, I *am*, and *there is* none beside me: how is she become a desolation, a place for beasts to lie down in! every one that passeth by her shall ᵀhiss, *and* wag his hand.   Is. 47:8 • *sneer*

CHAPTER 3

Jerusalem's Injustice

WOE to her that is ᵀfilthy and polluted, to the oppressing city!   *rebellious*

2 She obeyed not the voice; she received not correction; she trusted not in the Lᴏʀᴅ; she drew not near to her God.

3 Her princes within her *are* roaring lions; her judges *are* evening wolves; they gnaw not the bones till the morrow.

4 Her prophets *are* light *and* treacherous persons: her priests have polluted the sanctuary, they have done violence to the law.

The Lord's Justice

5 The just Lᴏʀᴅ *is* in the midst thereof; he will not do iniquity: every morning doth he bring his judgment to light, he faileth not; but ᴿthe unjust knoweth no shame.   Jer. 3:3

6 ᴿI have cut off the nations: their ᵀtowers are desolate; I made their streets waste, that none passeth by: their cities are destroyed, so that there is no man, that there is none inhabitant.   Job 22:16 • *battlements*

7 I said, Surely thou wilt fear me, thou wilt receive instruction; so their dwelling should not be cut off, howsoever I punished them: but they rose early, *and* ᴿcorrupted all their doings.   Jer. 8:6; Gen. 6:12

The Judgment on the Whole Earth

8 Therefore wait ye upon me, saith the Lᴏʀᴅ, until the day that I rise up to the prey: for my determination *is* to ᴿgather the nations, that I may assemble the kingdoms, to pour upon them mine indignation, *even* all my fierce anger: for all the earth shall be devoured with the fire of my jealousy.   Joel 3:2

The Promise of Conversion

9 For then will I turn to the ᵀpeople a pure language, that they may all call upon the name of the Lᴏʀᴅ, to serve him with one consent.   *peoples*

10 From beyond the rivers of E-thi-o'-pi-a my suppliants, *even* the daughter of my dispersed, shall bring mine offering.

11 In that day shalt thou ᴿnot be ashamed for all thy doings, wherein thou hast transgressed against me: for then I will take away out of the midst of thee them that rejoice in thy pride, and thou shalt no more be haughty because of my holy mountain.   [Is. 45:17; 54:4]

12 I will also leave in the midst of thee an afflicted and ᴿpoor people, and they shall trust in the name of the LORD.   Is. 14:32

13 ᴿThe remnant of Israel shall not do iniquity, nor speak lies; neither shall a deceitful tongue be found in their mouth: for they shall feed and lie down, and ᵀnone shall make them afraid.   [Mic. 4:7] • be secure

The Promise of Restoration

14 Sing, O daughter of Zion;ᴿ shout, O Israel; be glad and rejoice with all the heart, O daughter of Jerusalem.   Is. 12:6

15 The LORD hath taken away thy judgments, he hath cast out thine enemy: ᴿthe king of Israel, even the LORD, ᴿis in the midst of thee: thou shalt not see evil any more.   [John 1:49] • [3:5]; Ezek. 48:35; [Rev. 7:13–17]

16 In that day it shall be said to Jerusalem, ᴿFear thou not: and to Zion, ᴿLet not thine hands ᵀbe slack.   Is. 35:4 • Heb. 12:12 • falter

17 The LORD thy God in the midst of thee is mighty; he will save, he will rejoice over thee with joy; he will rest in his love, he will joy over thee with singing.

18 I will gather them that are sorrowful for the solemn assembly, who are of thee, to whom the reproach of it was a burden.

19 Behold, at that time I will undo all that afflict thee: and I will save her that halteth, and gather her that was driven out; and I will ᵀget them praise and fame in every land where they have been put to shame.   bring

20 At that time will I bring you again, even in the time that I gather you: for I will make you a name and a praise among all people of the earth, when I ᵀturn back your captivity before your eyes, saith the LORD.   deliver you

The Jewish Calendar

The Jews used two kinds of calendars:
 Civil Calendar—official calendar of kings, childbirth, and contracts.
 Sacred Calendar—from which festivals were computed.

NAMES OF MONTHS	CORRESPONDS WITH	NO. OF DAYS	MONTH OF CIVIL YEAR	MONTH OF SACRED YEAR	
TISHRI	Sept.–Oct.	30 days	1st	7th	The Jewish day was from sunset to sunset, in 8 equal parts:
HESHVAN	Oct.–Nov.	29 or 30	2nd	8th	
CHISLEV	Nov.–Dec.	29 or 30	3rd	9th	
TEBETH	Dec.–Jan.	29	4th	10th	FIRST WATCH ..... SUNSET TO 9 P.M.
SHEBAT	Jan.–Feb.	30	5th	11th	SECOND WATCH ... 9 P.M. TO MIDNIGHT
ADAR	Feb.–Mar.	29 or 30	6th	12th	THIRD WATCH ...... MIDNIGHT TO 3 A.M.
NISAN	Mar.–Apr.	30	7th	1st	FOURTH WATCH ... 3 A.M. TO SUNRISE
IYAR	Apr.–May	29	8th	2nd	
SIVAN	May–June	30	9th	3rd	FIRST WATCH ..... SUNRISE TO 9 A.M.
TAMMUZ	June–July	29	10th	4th	SECOND WATCH ... 9 A.M. TO NOON
AB	July–Aug.	30	11th	5th	THIRD WATCH ...... NOON TO 3 P.M.
***ELUL**	Aug.–Sept.	29	12th	6th	FOURTH WATCH ... 3 P.M. TO SUNSET

*Hebrew months were alternately 30 and 29 days long. Their year, shorter than ours, had 354 days. Therefore, about every 3 years (7 times in 19 years) an extra 29-day-month, VEADAR, was added between ADAR and NISAN.

HAGGAI

THE BOOK OF HAGGAI

With the Babylonian exile in the past, and a newly returned group of Jews back in the land, the work of rebuilding the temple can begin. However, sixteen years after the process is begun, the people have yet to finish the project, for their personal affairs have interfered with God's business. Haggai preaches a fiery series of sermonettes designed to stir up the nation to finish the temple. He calls the builders to renewed courage in the Lord, renewed holiness of life, and renewed faith in God who controls the future.

The etymology and meaning of *haggay* is uncertain, but it is probably derived from the Hebrew word *hag*, "festival." It may also be an abbreviated form of *haggiah*, "festival of Yahweh." Thus, Haggai's name means "Festal" or "Festive," possibly because he was born on the day of a major feast, such as Tabernacles (Haggai's second message takes place during that feast, 2:1). The title in the Septuagint is *Aggaios*, and in the Vulgate it is *Aggaeus*.

THE AUTHOR OF HAGGAI

Haggai's name is mentioned nine times (1:1, 3, 12, 13; 2:1, 10, 13, 14, 20); the authorship and date of the book are virtually uncontested. The unity of theme, style, and dating is obvious. Haggai is known only from this book and from two references to him in Ezra 5:1 and 6:14. There he is seen working alongside the younger prophet Zechariah in the ministry of encouraging the rebuilding of the temple. Haggai returned from Babylon with the remnant under Zerubbabel and evidently lived in Jerusalem. Some think 2:3 may mean that he was born in Judah before the 586 B.C. Captivity and was one of the small company who could remember the former temple before its destruction. This would mean Haggai was about seventy-five when he prophesied in 520 B.C. It is equally likely, however, that he was born in Babylon during the Captivity.

THE TIME OF HAGGAI

In 538 B.C. Cyrus of Persia issued a decree allowing the Jews to return to their land and rebuild their temple. The first return was led by Zerubbabel, and in 536 B.C. work on the temple began. Ezra 4—6 gives the background to the Book of Haggai and describes how the Samaritans hindered the building of the temple

and wrote a letter to the Persian king. This opposition only added to the growing discouragement of the Jewish remnant. Their initial optimism upon returning to their homeland was dampened by the desolation of the land, crop failure, hard work, hostility, and other hardships. They gave up the relative comfort of Babylonian culture to pioneer in a land that seemed unproductive and full of enemies. Finding it easier to stop building than to fight their neighbors, the work on the temple ceased in 534 B.C. The pessimism of the people led to spiritual lethargy, and they became preoccupied with their own building projects. They used political opposition and a theory that the temple was not to be rebuilt until some later time (perhaps after Jerusalem was rebuilt) as excuses for neglecting the house of the Lord.

It was in this context that God called His prophets Haggai and Zechariah to the same task of urging the people to complete the temple. Both books are precisely dated: Haggai 1:1, September 1, 520 B.C.; Haggai 1:15, September 24, 520 B.C.; Haggai 2:1, October 21, 520 B.C.; Zechariah 1:1, November, 520 B.C.; Haggai 2:10, 20, December 24, 520 B.C.; Zechariah 1:7, February 24, 519 B.C.; Zechariah 7:1, December 4, 518 B.C. Zechariah's prophecy commenced between Haggai's second and third messages. Thus, after fourteen years of neglect, work on the temple was resumed in 520 B.C. and was completed in 516 B.C. (Ezra 6:15). The Talmud indicates that the ark of the covenant, the Shekinah glory, and the Urim and Thummim were not in the rebuilt temple.

Darius I (521–486 B.C.) was king of Persia during the ministries of Haggai and Zechariah. He was a strong ruler who consolidated his kingdom by defeating a number of revolting nations.

THE CHRIST OF HAGGAI

The promise of Haggai 2:9 points ahead to the crucial role the second temple is to have in God's redemptive plan. Herod the Great later spent a fortune on the project of enlarging and enriching this temple, and it was filled with the glory of God incarnate every time Christ came to Jerusalem.

The Messiah is also portrayed in the person of Zerubbabel: "In that day . . . will I take thee, O Zerubbabel . . . and will make thee as a signet: for I have chosen thee" (2:23). Zerubbabel becomes the center of the Messianic line and is like a signet ring, sealing both branches together.

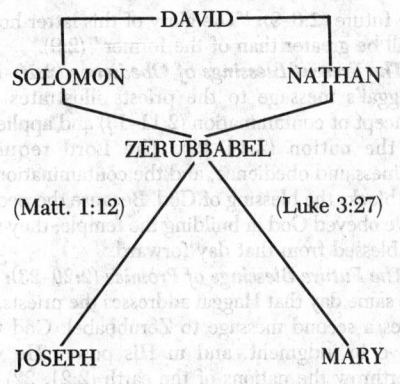

DAVID

SOLOMON   NATHAN

ZERUBBABEL

(Matt. 1:12)   (Luke 3:27)

JOSEPH   MARY

hosts. The glory of this latter house shall be greater than of the former, saith the LORD of hosts: and in this place will I give peace, saith the LORD of hosts" (2:7-9).

Key Chapter: Haggai 2—Verses 6-9 record some of the most startling prophecies in Scripture: "I will shake the heavens, and the earth, and the sea, and the dry *land*" (the Tribulation) and "the desire of all nations shall come" and "In this place will I give peace" (the Second Coming of the Messiah).

KEYS TO HAGGAI

Key Word: The Reconstruction of the Temple—Haggai's basic theme is clear: the remnant must reorder its priorities and complete the temple before it can expect the blessing of God upon its efforts. Because of spiritual indifference the people fail to respond to God's attempts to get their attention. In their despondency they do not realize that their hardships are divinely given symptoms of their spiritual disease. Haggai brings them to an understanding that circumstances become difficult when people place their own selfish interests before God's. When they put God first and seek to do His will, He will bring His people joy and prosperity.

Key Verses: Haggai 1:7, 8; 2:7-9—"Thus saith the LORD of hosts; Consider your ways. Go up to the mountain, and bring wood, and build the house; and I will take pleasure in it, and I will be glorified, saith the LORD" (1:7, 8).

"And I will shake all nations, and the desire of all nations shall come: and I will fill this house with glory, saith the LORD of hosts. The silver *is* mine, and the gold *is* mine, saith the LORD of

SURVEY OF HAGGAI

Haggai is second only to Obadiah in brevity among Old Testament books, but this strong and frank series of four terse sermons accomplishes its intended effect. The work on the temple has ceased, and the people have become more concerned with the beautification of their own houses than with the building of the central sanctuary of God. Because of their misplaced priorities, their labor is no longer blessed by God. Only when the people put the Lord first by completing the task He has set before them will His hand of blessing once again be upon them. Haggai acts as God's man in God's hour, and his four messages are: the completion of the latter temple (1:1-15), the glory of the latter temple (2:1-9), the present blessings of obedience (2:10-19), and the future blessings of promise (2:20-23).

The Completion of the Latter Temple (1:1-15): When the remnant returns from Babylon under Zerubbabel, they begin to rebuild the temple of the Lord. However, the work soon stops and the people find excuses to ignore it as the years pass. They have no problem in building rich dwellings for themselves ("cieled houses," 1:4) while they claim that the time for building the temple has not yet come (1:2). God withdraws

FOCUS	COMPLETION OF THE LATTER TEMPLE	GLORY OF THE LATTER TEMPLE	PRESENT BLESSING OF OBEDIENCE	FUTURE BLESSING THROUGH PROMISE
REFERENCE	1:1	2:1	2:10	2:20 2:23
DIVISION	"CONSIDER YOUR WAYS . . . MY HOUSE WHICH LIES DESOLATE.	"THE LATTER GLORY OF THIS HOUSE WILL BE GREATER."	"FROM THIS DAY ON I WILL BLESS YOU."	"I AM GOING TO SHAKE THE HEAVENS AND THE EARTH."
TOPIC	THE TEMPLE OF GOD		THE BLESSINGS OF GOD	
	FIRST REBUKE (PRESENT)	FIRST ENCOURAGEMENT (FUTURE)	SECOND REBUKE (PRESENT)	SECOND ENCOURAGEMENT (FUTURE)
LOCATION	JERUSALEM			
TIME	SEPTEMBER 1 520 B.C.	OCTOBER 21 520 B.C.	DECEMBER 24 520 B.C.	DECEMBER 24 520 B.C.

his blessing and they sink into an economic depression. However, they do not recognize what is happening because of their indifference to God and indulgence of self; so God communicates directly to the remnant through His prophet Haggai. Zerubbabel the governor, Joshua the high priest, and all the people respond; and twenty-three days later they again begin to work on the temple.

The Glory of the Latter Temple (2:1-9): In a few short weeks, the enthusiasm of the people sours into discouragement; the elders remember the glory of Solomon's temple and bemoan the puniness of the present temple (see Ezra 3:8-13). Haggai's prophetic word of encouragement reminds the people of God's covenant promises in the past (2:4, 5), and of His confident plans for

the future (2:6-9): "The glory of this latter house shall be greater than of the former" (2:9).

The Present Blessings of Obedience (2:10-19): Haggai's message to the priests illustrates the concept of contamination (2:11-13) and applies it to the nation (2:14-19). The Lord requires holiness and obedience, and the contamination of sin blocks the blessing of God. Because the people have obeyed God in building the temple, they will be blessed from that day forward.

The Future Blessings of Promise (2:20-23): On the same day that Haggai addresses the priests, he gives a second message to Zerubbabel. God will move in judgment, and in His power He will overthrow the nations of the earth (2:21, 22). At that time, Zerubbabel, a symbol of the Messiah to come, will be honored.

OUTLINE OF HAGGAI

CHAPTER 1

The Temple Is Not Complete—Ezra 5:1

IN the second year of Da-ri'-us the king, in the sixth month, in the first day of the month, came the word of the LORD by Hag'-gai the prophet unto ᴿZe-rub'-ba-bel the son of She-al'-ti-el, ᵀgovernor of Judah, and to ᴿJoshua the son of Jos'-e-dech, the high priest, saying,   1 Chr. 3:17 · *captain* · Ezra 5:2

2 Thus speaketh the LORD of hosts, saying, This people say, The time is not come, the time that the LORD'S house should be built.

3 Then came the word of the LORD ᴿby Hag'-gai the prophet, saying,   Ezra 5:1

4 *Is it* time for you, O ye, to dwell in your cieled houses, and this house *lie* waste?

5 Now therefore thus saith the LORD of hosts; ᵀConsider your ways.   *give attention to*

6 Ye have ᴿsown much, and bring in little; ye eat, but ye have not enough; ye drink, but ye are not filled with drink; ye clothe you, but there is none warm; and he that earneth wages earneth wages *to put it* into a bag with holes.   Deut. 28:38

The Temple Must Be Completed

7 Thus saith the LORD of hosts; ᵀConsider your ways.   *give attention to*

8 ᴿGo up to the ᵀmountain, and bring wood, and build the house; and I will take pleasure in it, and I will be glorified, saith the LORD.   2:7, 9; Ezra 3:7; [Ps. 132:13, 14] · *hill country*

9 ᴿYe looked for much, and, lo, *it came* to little; and when ye brought *it* home, ᴿI did blow upon it. Why? saith the LORD of hosts. Because of mine house that *is* waste, and ye run every man unto his own house. 2:16 · 2:17

10 Therefore ᴿthe heaven over you is stayed from dew, and the earth is ᵀstayed *from* her fruit.   Lev. 26:19; Deut. 28:23 · *withholds*

11 And I called for a drought upon the land, and upon the mountains, and upon the corn, and upon the new wine, and upon the oil, and upon *that* which the ground bringeth forth, and upon men, and upon cattle, and upon all the labour of the hands.

12 Then Ze-rub'-ba-bel the son of She-al'-ti-el, and Joshua the son of Jos'-e-dech, the high priest, with all the remnant of the people, obeyed the voice of the LORD their

God, and the words of Hag'-gai the prophet, as the LORD their God had sent him, and the people ᴿdid fear before the LORD.   Is. 50:10

13 Then spake Hag'-gai the LORD's messenger in the LORD's message unto the people, saying, I *am* with you, saith the LORD.

14 And the LORD stirred up the spirit of Ze-rub'-ba-bel the son of She-al'-ti-el, governor of Judah, and the spirit of Joshua the son of Jos'-e-dech, the high priest, and the spirit of all the remnant of the people; ᴿand they came and did work in the house of the LORD of hosts, their God,   Ezra 5:2, 8

15 In the four and twentieth day of the sixth month, in the second year of Da-ri'-us the king.

CHAPTER 2

The Latter Temple Is Not as Glorious as the First

IN the seventh *month*, in the ᵀone and twentieth *day* of the month, came the word of the LORD ᵀby the prophet ᴿHag'-gai, saying,   *twenty-first* • *by the hand of* • 1:1

2 Speak now to Ze-rub'-ba-bel the son of She-al'-ti-el, governor of Judah, and to Joshua the son of Jos'-e-dech, the high priest, and to the residue of the people, saying,

3 ᴿWho *is* left among you that saw this house in her first glory? and how do ye see it now? ᴿ*is it* not in your eyes in comparison of it as nothing?   Ezra 3:12 • Zech. 4:10

The Latter Temple Will Be More Glorious than the First

4 ᴿYet now be strong, O Ze-rub'-ba-bel, saith the LORD; and be strong, O Joshua, son of Jos'-e-dech, the high priest; and be strong, all ye people of the land, saith the LORD, and work: for I *am* with you, saith the LORD of hosts: Deut. 31:23; Zech. 8:9

5 *According to* the word that I ᵀcove-nanted with you when ye came out of Egypt, so ᴿmy ᵀspirit remaineth among you: fear ye not.   *promised* • Is. 63:11 • *Spirit*

6 For thus saith the LORD of hosts; ᴿYet once, ᵀit *is* a little while, and ᴿI will shake the heavens, and the earth, and the sea, and the dry *land*;   Heb. 12:26 • *in* • [Joel 3:16]

7 ᴿAnd I will shake all nations, and the ᵀdesire of all nations shall come: and ᴿI will fill this house with glory, saith the LORD of hosts.   [Is. 60:4–9; Dan. 2:44] • *precious things* • 1 Kin. 8:11

8 ᴿThe silver *is* mine, and the gold *is* mine, saith the LORD of hosts.   [Ps. 24:1; 50:10]

9 ᴿThe glory of this latter house shall be greater than the former, saith the LORD of hosts: and in this place will I ᵀgive peace, saith the LORD of hosts.   [Zech. 2:5] • *bless*

The Disobedience of the Remnant

10 ᴿIn the ᵀfour and twentieth *day* of the ninth *month*, in the second year of Da-ri'-us,

came the word of the LORD by Hag'-gai the prophet, saying,   1:1, 15 • *twenty-fourth*

11 Thus saith the LORD of hosts; Ask now the priests *concerning* the law, saying,

12 ᴿIf one bear holy flesh in the ᵀskirt of his garment, and with his skirt do touch bread, or pottage, or wine, or oil, or any meat, shall it be holy? And the priests answered and said, No.   Lev. 6:27, 29; Ezek. 44:19 • *wing*

13 Then said Hag'-gai, ᴿIf *one that is* unclean by a dead body touch any of these, shall it be unclean? And the priests answered and said, It shall be unclean.   Lev. 22:4

14 Then answered Hag'-gai, and said, ᴿSo *is* this people, and so *is* this nation before me, saith the LORD; and so *is* every work of their hands; and that which they offer there *is* unclean.   [Prov. 15:8; Is. 1:11–15; Titus 1:15]

The Solution: The Obedience of the Remnant

15 And now, I pray you, ᴿconsiderᵀ from this day and ᵀupward, ᴿfrom before a stone was laid upon a stone in the temple of the LORD: 1:5 • *review* • *backward* • Ezra 3:10; 4:24

16 ᴿSince those *days* were, when *one* came to an heap of twenty *measures*, there were *but* ten: when *one* came to the pressfat for to draw out fifty *vessels* out of the press, there were *but* twenty.   Zech. 8:10

17 ᴿI smote you with ᵀblasting and with mildew and with hail ᴿin all the labours of your hands; ᴿyet ye *turned* not to me, saith the LORD.   Amos 4:9 • *blight* • 1:11 • Amos 4:6–11

18 ᵀConsider now from this day and ᵀupward, from the four and twentieth day of the ninth *month, even* from the day that the foundation of the LORD's temple ᴿwas laid, consider *it*.   *think* • *backward* • Zech. 8:9

19 Is the seed yet in the barn? yea, as yet the vine, and the fig tree, and the pomegranate, and the olive tree, hath not brought forth: from this day will I bless *you.*

The Future Destruction of the Nations

20 And again the word of the LORD came unto Hag'-gai in the four and twentieth *day* of the month, saying,

21 Speak to Ze-rub'-ba-bel, ᴿgovernor of Judah, saying, ᴿI will shake the heavens and the earth;   1:14; Zech. 4:6–10 • *vv.* 6, 7

22 And ᴿI will overthrow the throne of kingdoms, and I will destroy the strength of the kingdoms of the heathen; and ᴿI will overthrow the chariots, and those that ride in them; and the horses and their riders shall come down, every one by the sword of his brother.   [Dan. 2:44] • Zech. 9:10

The Future Recognition of Zerubbabel

23 In that day, saith the LORD of hosts, will I take thee, O Ze-rub'-ba-bel, my servant, the son of She-al'-ti-el, saith the LORD, and will make thee as a signet: for I have chosen thee, saith the LORD of hosts.

THE BOOK OF

ZECHARIAH

📖 **THE BOOK OF ZECHARIAH**
For a dozen years or more, the task of rebuilding the temple has been half completed. Zechariah is commissioned by God to encourage the people in their unfinished responsibility. Rather than exhorting them to action with strong words of rebuke, Zechariah seeks to encourage them to action by reminding them of the future importance of the temple. The temple must be built, for one day the Messiah's glory will inhabit it. But future blessing is contingent upon present obedience. The people are not merely building a building; they are building the future. With that as their motivation, they can enter into the building project with wholehearted zeal, for their Messiah is coming.

Zekar-yah means "Yahweh Remembers" or "Yahweh Has Remembered." This theme dominates the whole book: Israel will be blessed because Yahweh remembers the covenant He made with the fathers. The Greek and Latin version of his name is *Zacharias*.

✍ **THE AUTHOR OF ZECHARIAH**
Zechariah ("Yahweh Remembers") was a popular name shared by no fewer than twenty-nine Old Testament characters. It may have been given out of gratitude for God's gift of a baby boy. Like his predecessors, Jeremiah and Ezekiel, Zechariah was of priestly lineage as the son of Berechiah and grandson of Iddo (1:1, 7; Ezra 5:1; 6:14; Neh. 12:4, 16). He was born in Babylon and was brought by his grandfather to Palestine when the Jewish exiles returned under Zerubbabel and Joshua the high priest. If he was the "young man" of 2:4, he was called to prophesy at an early age in 520 B.C. According to Jewish tradition, Zechariah was a member of the Great Synagogue that collected and preserved the canon of revealed Scripture. Matthew 23:35 indicates he was slain "between the temple and the altar" in the same way that an earlier Zechariah was martyred (see 2 Chr. 24:20, 21). The universal testimony of Jewish and Christian tradition affirms Zechariah as the author of the entire book.

⏳ **THE TIME OF ZECHARIAH**
Zechariah was a younger contemporary of Haggai the prophet, Zerubbabel the governor, and Joshua the high priest. The historical setting for chapters 1—8 (520–518 B.C.) is identical to that of Haggai (see "The Time of Haggai"). Work was resumed on the temple in 520 B.C., and the project was completed in 516 B.C. Chapters 9—14 are undated, but stylistic differences and references to Greece indicate a date of between 480 and 470 B.C. This would mean that Darius I (521–486 B.C.) had passed from the scene and had been succeeded by Xerxes (486–464 B.C.), the king who deposed Queen Vashti and made Esther queen of Persia.

✝ **THE CHRIST OF ZECHARIAH**
Very clear messianic passages abound in this book. Christ is portrayed in His two Advents as both Servant and King, Man and God. The following are a few of Zechariah's explicit anticipations of Christ: the Angel of the Lord (3:1, 2); the righteous Branch (3:8; 6:12, 13), the stone with seven eyes (3:9); the King-Priest (6:13); the lowly King (9:9, 10); the cornerstone, nail, and battle bow (10:4); the Good Shepherd who is rejected and sold for thirty shekels of silver, the price of a slave (11:4–13); the pierced One (12:10); the cleansing fountain (13:1); the smitten Shepherd who is abandoned (13:7); the coming Judge and righteous King (14).

🔑 **KEYS TO ZECHARIAH**
Key Word: Prepare for the Messiah—The first eight chapters frequently allude to the temple and encourage the people to complete their great work on the new sanctuary. As they build the temple, they are building their future, because that very structure will be used by the Messiah when He comes to bring salvation. Zechariah eloquently attests to Yahweh's covenant faithfulness toward Israel through the work of the Messiah, especially in chapters 9—14. This book outlines God's program for His people during the times of the Gentiles until the Messiah comes to deliver them and reign upon the earth. This hope of glory provides a source of reassurance to the Jewish remnant at a time when circumstances are trying. Zechariah also seeks to promote spiritual revival so that the people will call upon the Lord with humble hearts and commit their ways to Him.

Key Verses: Zechariah 8:3; 9:9—"Thus saith the LORD; I am returned unto Zion, and will dwell in the midst of Jerusalem: and Jerusalem shall be called a city of truth; and the mountain of the LORD of hosts the holy mountain" (8:3).

"Rejoice greatly, O daughter of Zion; shout, O daughter of Jerusalem: behold, thy King cometh unto thee: he *is* just, and having salvation; lowly, and riding upon an ass, and upon a colt the foal of an ass" (9:9).

Key Chapter: Zechariah 14—Zechariah builds to a tremendous climax in the fourteenth chapter where he discloses the last siege of Jerusalem, the initial victory of the enemies of Israel, the cleaving of the Mount of Olives, the Lord's

defense of Jerusalem with His visible appearance on Olivet, judgment on the confederated nations, the topographical changes in the land of Israel, the Feast of Tabernacles, and the ultimate holiness of Jerusalem and her people.

SURVEY OF ZECHARIAH

Zechariah uses a series of eight visions, four messages, and two burdens to portray God's future plans for His covenant people. The first eight chapters were written to encourage the remnant while they were rebuilding the temple; the last six chapters were written after the completion of the temple to anticipate Israel's coming Messiah. Zechariah moves from gentile domination to messianic rule, from persecution to peace, and from uncleanness to holiness. The book divides into: the eight visions (1—6), the four messages (7 and 8), and the two burdens (9—14).

The Eight Visions (1—6): The book opens with an introductory appeal to the people to repent and return to God, unlike their fathers who rejected the warnings of the prophets (1:1-6). A few months later, Zechariah has a series of eight night visions, evidently in one troubled night (February 15, 519 B.C.; 1:7). The angel who speaks with him interprets the visions, but some of the symbols are not explained. The visions mix the work of the Messiah in both Advents, and like the other prophets, Zechariah sees only the peaks of God's program without the intervening valleys. The first five are visions of comfort, and the last three are visions of judgment: (1) The horsemen among the myrtle trees—God will rebuild Zion and His people (1:7-17). (2) The four horns and craftsmen—Israel's oppressors will be judged (1:18-21). (3) The man with a measuring line— God will protect and glorify Jerusalem (2:1-13).

(4) The cleansing of Joshua the high priest—Israel will be cleansed and restored by the coming Branch (3:1-10). (5) The golden lampstand— God's Spirit is empowering Zerubbabel and Joshua (4:1-14). (6) The flying scroll—individual sin will be judged (5:1-4). (7) The woman in the ephah—national sin will be removed (5:5-11). (8) The four chariots—God's judgment will descend on the nations (6:1-8). The crowning of Joshua (6:9-15) anticipates the coming of the Branch who will be King and Priest (the composite crown).

The Four Messages (7 and 8): In response to a question about the continuation of the fasts (7:1-3), God gives Zechariah a series of four messages: (1) a rebuke of empty ritualism (7:4-7); (2) a reminder of past disobedience (7:8-14); (3) the restoration and consolation of Israel (8:1-17); and (4) the recovery of joy in the kingdom (8:18-23).

The Two Burdens (9—14): The first burden (9—11) concerns the First Advent and rejection of Israel's coming King. Alexander the Great will conquer Israel's neighbors, but will spare Jerusalem (9:1-8) which will be preserved for her King (the Messiah; 9:9, 10). Israel will succeed against Greece (the Maccabean revolt; 9:11-17), and although they will later be scattered, the Messiah will bless them and bring them back (10:1—11:3). Israel will reject her Shepherd-King and be led astray by false shepherds (11:4-17). The second burden (12—14) concerns the Second Advent of Christ and the acceptance of Israel's King. The nations will attack Jerusalem, but the Messiah will come and deliver His people (12). They will be cleansed of impurity and falsehood (13), and the Messiah will come in power to judge the nations and reign in Jerusalem over the whole earth (14).

FOCUS	EIGHT VISIONS			FOUR MESSAGES	TWO BURDENS	
REFERENCE	1:1————1:7————6:9————			7:1————9:1————	12:1————14:21	
DIVISION	CALL TO REPENTANCE	EIGHT VISIONS	CROWNING OF JOSHUA	QUESTION OF THE FASTS	FIRST BURDEN: REJECTION OF THE MESSIAH	SECOND BURDEN: REIGN OF THE MESSIAH
TOPIC	PICTURES			PROBLEM	PREDICTION	
	ISRAEL'S FORTUNE			ISRAEL'S FASTINGS	ISRAEL'S FUTURE	
LOCATION	JERUSALEM					
TIME	WHILE BUILDING THE TEMPLE (520 – 518 B.C.)				AFTER BUILDING THE TEMPLE (c. 480 – 470 B.C.)	

OUTLINE OF ZECHARIAH

CHAPTER 1

The Call to Repentance—Ezra 5:1

IN the eighth month, in the second year of Da-ri'-us, came the word of the LORD unto Zech-a-ri'-ah, the son of Ber-e-chi'-ah, the son of Id'-do the prophet, saying,

2 The LORD hath been ᵀsore displeased with your fathers.   *very unhappy; v.15; 2 Chr. 36:16*

3 Therefore say thou unto them, Thus saith the LORD of hosts; ᴿTurn ye unto me, saith the LORD of hosts, and I will turn unto you, saith the LORD of hosts.   [James 4:8]

4 Be ye not as your fathers, unto whom the former prophets have cried, saying, Thus saith the LORD of hosts; ᴿTurn ye now from your evil ways, and *from* your evil doings: but they did not hear, nor hearken unto me, saith the LORD.   [Hos. 14:1]

5 Your ᴿfathers, where *are* they? and the prophets, do they live for ever?   John 8:52

6 But my words and my statutes, which I commanded my servants the prophets, did they not take hold of your fathers? and they returned and said, Like as the LORD of hosts thought to do unto us, according to our ways, and according to our doings, so hath he dealt with us.

The Horses Among the Myrtle Trees

7 Upon the four and twentieth day of the eleventh month, which *is* the month Se'-bat, in the second year of Da-ri'-us, came the word of the LORD unto Zech-a-ri'-ah, the son of Ber-e-chi'-ah, the son of Id'-do the prophet, saying,

8 I saw by night, and behold a man riding upon a red horse, and he stood among the myrtle trees that *were* in the bottom; and behind him *were there* ᴿred horses, ᵀspeckled, and white.   [6:2–7] • *sorrel*

9 Then said I, O my lord, what *are* these? And the angel that talked with me said unto me, I will shew thee what these *be.*

10 And the man that stood among the myrtle trees answered and said, ᴿThese *are they* whom the LORD hath sent to walk to and fro through the earth.   [Job 1:7; Heb. 1:14]

11 ᴿAnd they answered the angel of the LORD that stood among the myrtle trees, and said, We have walked to and fro through the earth, and, behold, all the earth sitteth still, and is at rest.   [Ps. 103:20]

12 Then the angel of the LORD answered and said, O LORD of hosts, how long wilt thou ᵀnot have mercy on Jerusalem and on the cities of Judah, against which thou hast had indignation ᴿthese threescore and ten years?   *have no* • Jer. 25:11, 12; Dan. 9:2

13 And the LORD answered the ᴿangel that talked with me *with* ᴿgood words *and* ᵀcomfortable words.   4:1 • Jer. 29:10 • *comforting*

14 So the angel that communed with me said unto me, Cry thou, saying, Thus saith the LORD of hosts; I am jealous for Jerusalem and for Zion with a great jealousy.

15 And I am very ᵀsore displeased with the heathen *that are* at ease: for I was but a little displeased, and they ᵀhelped forward the affliction.   *angry* • *made matters worse*

16 Therefore thus saith the LORD; ᴿI am returned to Jerusalem with mercies: my house shall be built in it, saith the LORD of hosts, and ᴿa line shall be stretched forth upon Jerusalem.   [2:10]; Is. 12:1; [54:8] • 2:1, 2

17 Cry yet, saying, Thus saith the LORD of hosts; My cities through Tprosperity shall yet be Tspread abroad; Rand the LORD shall yet comfort Zion, and shall yet choose Jerusalem.   *good • increased • [Is. 51:3]*

The Four Horns and Four Carpenters

18 Then lifted I up mine eyes, and saw, and behold four Thorns.   *units of power*
19 And I said unto the angel that talked with me, What be these? And he answered me, RThese are the horns which have scattered Judah, Israel, and Jerusalem. Ezra 4:1
20 And the LORD shewed me four Tcarpenters.R   *smiths • 2 Sam. 5:11*
21 Then said I, What come these to do? And he spake, saying, These are the horns which have scattered Judah, so that no man did lift up his head: but these are come to Tfray them, to cast out the horns of the Gentiles, which lifted up their horn over the land of Judah to scatter it.   *terrify*

CHAPTER 2

The Man with the Measuring Line

I LIFTED up mine eyes again, and looked, and behold a man with a Rmeasuring line in his hand.   Jer. 31:39; Ezek. 40:3
2 Then said I, Whither goest thou? And he said unto me, RTo measure Jerusalem, to see what is the breadth thereof, and what is the length thereof.   Ezek. 40:3; Rev. 11:1
3 And, behold, the Rangel that talked with me went forth, and another angel went out to meet him,   Gen. 32:1; Matt. 1:20
4 And said unto him, Run, speak to this young man, saying, Jerusalem shall be inhabited as towns without walls for the multitude of men and cattle therein:
5 For I, saith the LORD, will be unto her Ra wall of fire round about, Rand will be the glory in the midst of her.   [Is. 26:1 • Is. 60:19]
6 Ho, ho, come forth, and flee from the land of the north, saith the LORD: for I have Rspread you abroad as the four winds of the heaven, saith the LORD.   [Deut. 28:64]
7 RDeliver thyself, O Zion, that dwellest with the daughter of Babylon.   [Rev. 18:4]
8 For thus saith the LORD of hosts; After the glory hath he sent me unto the nations which Tspoiled you: for he that toucheth you toucheth the apple of his eye.   *robbed*
9 For, behold, I will shake mine hand upon them, and they shall be a Tspoil to their servants: and ye shall know that the LORD of hosts hath sent me.   *booty*
10 Sing and rejoice, O daughter of Zion: for, lo, I come, and I Rwill dwell in the midst of thee, saith the LORD.   [Lev. 26:12]
11 RAnd many nations shall be joined to the LORD in that day, and shall be my people:

and I will dwell in the midst of thee, and thou shalt know that the LORD of hosts hath sent me unto thee.   [Is. 56:3-7]
12 And the LORD shall Rinherit Judah his portion in the holy land, and Rshall choose Jerusalem again.   [Deut. 32:9 • 1:17; 2 Chr. 6:6]
13 RBe silent, O all flesh, before the LORD: for he is raised up out of Rhis holy Thabitation.   Hab. 2:20; Zeph. 1:7 • [Ps. 68:5] • *dwelling*

CHAPTER 3

The Cleansing of Joshua, the High Priest

AND he shewed me RJoshua the high priest standing before the angel of the LORD, and Satan standing at his right hand to Tresist him.   Hag. 1:1 • *oppose*
2 And the LORD said unto Satan, The LORD rebuke thee, O Satan; even the LORD that hath chosen Jerusalem rebuke thee: is not this a brand plucked out of the fire?
3 Now Joshua was clothed with filthy garments, and stood before the angel.
4 And he answered and spake unto those that stood before him, saying, Take away the filthy garments from him. And unto him he said, Behold, I have caused thine iniquity to pass from thee, and I will clothe thee with Tchange of raiment.   *rich*
5 And I said, Let them set a fair mitre upon his head. So they set a fair mitre upon his head, and clothed him with garments. And the angel of the LORD stood by.
6 And the angel of the LORD Tprotested unto Joshua, saying,   *ordered*
7 Thus saith the LORD of hosts; If thou wilt walk in my ways, and if thou wilt Tkeep my Tcharge, then thou shalt also judge my house, and shalt also keep my courts, and I will give thee places to walk among these that stand by.   *obey • instruction*
8 Hear now, O Joshua the high priest, thou, and thy fellows that sit before thee: for they are Rmen T wondered at: for, behold, I will bring forth Rmy servant the BRANCH.   Ps. 71:7 • *men of wonder* • Is. 42:1 ☆
9 For behold the stone that I have laid before Joshua; Rupon one stone shall be Rseven eyes: behold, I will engrave the graving thereof, saith the LORD of hosts, and RI will remove the iniquity of that land in one day.   Ps. 118:22 • Rev. 5:6 • Jer. 31:34
10 RIn that day, saith the LORD of hosts, shall ye call every man his neighbour under the vine and under the fig tree.   [2:11]

CHAPTER 4

The Golden Candlestick and Olive Trees

AND the angel that talked with me came again, and waked me, Ras a man that is wakened out of his sleep,   Dan. 8:18

2 And said unto me, What seest thou? And I said, I have looked, and behold ᴿa candlestick all of gold, with a bowl upon the top of it, ᴿand his seven lamps thereon, and seven ᵀpipes to the seven lamps, which are upon the top thereof: Rev. 1:12 • [Rev. 4:5] • lips

3 ᴿAnd two olive trees by it, one upon the right side of the bowl, and the other upon the left side thereof.   4:11; Rev. 11:4

4 So I answered and spake to the angel that talked with me, saying, What are these, my lord?

5 Then the angel that talked with me answered and said unto me, Knowest thou not what these be? And I said, No, my lord.

6 Then he answered and spake unto me, saying, This is the word of the LORD unto Ze-rub'-ba-bel, saying, ᴿNot by might, nor by power, ᴿbut by my ᵀspirit, saith the LORD of hosts.   [Is. 11:2–4; 30:1]; Hos. 1:7 • [Eph. 6:17] • Spirit

7 Who art thou, ᴿO great ᵀmountain? before Ze-rub'-ba-bel thou shalt become a plain: and he shall bring forth the headstone thereof with shoutings, crying, Grace, grace unto it.   Is. 40:3, 4 • military power

8 Moreover the word of the LORD came unto me, saying,

9 The hands of Ze-rub'-ba-bel have laid the foundation of this house; his hands shall also finish it; and ᴿthou shalt know that the LORD of hosts hath sent me unto you.   2:9, 11; 6:15

10 For who hath despised the day of small things? for they shall rejoice, and shall see the ᵀplummet in the hand of Ze-rub'-ba-bel with those seven; they are ᴿthe eyes of the LORD, which run to and fro through the whole earth.   authority • 2 Chr. 16:9

11 Then answered I, and said unto him, What are these ᴿtwo olive trees upon the right side of the candlestick and upon the left side thereof?   v. 3

12 And I answered again, and said unto him, What be these two olive branches which through the two golden pipes empty the golden oil out of themselves?

13 And he answered me and said, Knowest thou not what these be? And I said, No, my lord.

14 Then said he, ᴿThese are the two ᵀanointed ones, ᴿthat stand by ᴿthe Lord of the whole earth.   Rev. 11:4 • chosen • 3:7 • 6:5

CHAPTER 5

The Flying Roll

THEN I turned, and lifted up mine eyes, and looked, and behold a flying roll.

2 And he said unto me, What seest thou? And I answered, I see a flying roll; the length thereof is ᵀtwenty cubits, and the breadth thereof ᵀten cubits.   30 ft. • 15 ft.

3 Then he said unto me, This is the ᴿcurse that goeth forth over the face of the whole earth: for every one that stealeth shall be cut off as on this side according to it; and every one that sweareth shall be cut off as on that side according to it.   Mal. 4:6

4 I will bring it forth, saith the LORD of hosts, and it shall enter into the house of the thief, and into the house of ᴿhim that ᵀsweareth falsely by my name: and it shall remain in the midst of his house, and shall ᵀconsume it with the timber thereof and the stones thereof.   Mal. 3:5 • is deceitful • destroy

The Woman in the Ephah

5 Then the ᴿangel that talked with me went forth, and said unto me, Lift up now thine eyes, and see what is this that goeth forth.   v. 10; 12:8

6 And I said, What is it? And he said, This is an ᵀe'-phah that goeth forth. He said moreover, This is their ᵀresemblance through all the earth.   bushel container • appearance

7 And, behold, there was lifted up a ᵀtalent of lead: and this is a woman that sitteth in the midst of the e'-phah.   75 lb.

8 And he said, This is ᴿwickedness. And he cast it into the midst of the e'-phah; and he cast the weight of lead upon the mouth thereof.   Hos. 12:7; Amos 8:5; Mic. 6:11

9 Then lifted I up mine eyes, and looked, and, behold, there came out two women, and the wind was in their wings; for they had wings like the wings of a ᴿstork: and they lifted up the e'-phah between the earth and the heaven.   Lev. 11:13, 19; Ps. 104:17

10 Then said I to the angel that talked with me, Whither do these bear the e'-phah?

11 And he said unto me, To ᴿbuildᵀ it an house in the land of ᴿShi'-nar: and it shall be established, and set there upon her own base.   Jer. 29:5, 28 • her • Gen. 10:10

CHAPTER 6

The Four Chariots

AND I turned, and lifted up mine eyes, and looked, and, behold, there came four chariots out from between two mountains; and the mountains were mountains of brass.

2 In the first chariot were red horses; and in the second chariot black horses;

3 And in the third chariot white ᴿhorses; and in the fourth chariot ᵀgrisled and ᵀbay horses.   1:8; Rev. 6:2 • dappled • strong

4 Then I answered ᴿand said unto the angel that talked with me, What are these, my lord?   5:10

5 And the angel answered and said unto me, These are the four ᵀspirits of the heavens, which go forth from standing before the Lord of all the earth.   winds

6 The black horses which *are* therein go forth into the north country; and the white go forth after them; and the ᵀgrisled go forth toward the south country.   *dappled*

7 And the bay went forth, and sought to go that they might ᴿwalk to and fro through the earth: and he said, Get you hence, walk to and fro through the earth. So they walked to and fro through the earth.   1:10; Gen. 13:17

8 Then cried he upon me, and spake unto me, saying, Behold, these that go toward the north country have ᴿquieted my spirit in the north country.   Eccl. 10:4

The Crowning of Joshua

9 And the word of the LORD came unto me, saying,

10 Take of *them* of the captivity, *even* of Hel'-dai, of To-bi'-jah, and of Je-da'-iah, which are come from Babylon, and come thou the same day, and go into the house of Jo-si'-ah the son of Zeph-a-ni'-ah;

11 Then take silver and gold, and make ᴿcrowns, and set *them* upon the head of ᴿJoshua the son of Jos'-e-dech, the high priest;   Ex. 29:6; 2 Sam. 12:30; Ps. 21:3 • Hag. 1:1

12 And speak unto him, saying, Thus speaketh the LORD of hosts, saying, Behold the man whose name is The ᴿBRANCH; and he shall grow up out of his place, and he shall build the temple of the LORD: Is. 4:2; 11:1 ☆

13 Even he shall build the temple of the LORD; and he shall bear the glory, and shall sit and rule upon his throne; and ᴿhe shall be a priest upon his throne: and the counsel of peace shall be between them both. [Ps. 110:4–7] ☆

14 And the crowns shall be to He'-lem, and to To-bi'-jah, and to ᵀJe-da'-iah, and to Hen the son of Zeph-a-ni'-ah, for a memorial in the temple of the LORD.   *Josiah*

15 And ᴿthey *that are* far off shall come and build in the temple of the LORD, and ye shall know that the LORD of hosts hath sent me unto you. And *this* shall come to pass, if ye will diligently ᴿobey the voice of the LORD your God.   Is. 57:19 • [Is. 58:10–14]

CHAPTER 7

The Question of Fasting

AND it came to pass in the fourth year of king Da-ri'-us, *that* the word of the LORD came unto Zech-a-ri'-ah in the fourth *day* of the ninth month, *even* in Chis'-leu;

2 When they had sent unto the house of God She-re'-zer and Re'-gem-me'-lech, and their men, to pray before the LORD,

3 *And* to speak unto the priests which *were* in the house of the LORD of hosts, and to the prophets, saying, Should I weep in the fifth month, ᵀseparating myself, as I have done these so many years?   *fasting*

Rebuke of Hypocrisy

4 Then came the word of the LORD of hosts unto me, saying,

5 Speak unto all the people of the land, and to the priests, saying, When ye fasted and mourned in the fifth and seventh *month,* even those seventy years, did ye at all fast ᵀunto me, *even* to me?   *for my sake?*

6 And when ye did eat, and when ye did drink, ᵀdid not ye eat *for yourselves,* and drink *for yourselves?*   *be not ye they that*

7 *Should* ye not *hear* the words which the LORD hath cried by the former prophets, when Jerusalem was inhabited and in prosperity, and the cities thereof round about her, when *men* inhabited the south and the plain?

Repent of Disobedience

8 And the word of the LORD came unto Zech-a-ri'-ah, saying,

9 Thus speaketh the LORD of hosts, saying, ᴿExecuteᵀ true judgment, and ᴿshew mercy and compassions every man to his brother: Is. 58:6, 7; Jer. 7:23 • *bring to pass* • Job 6:14

10 And ᴿoppress not the widow, nor the fatherless, the stranger, nor the poor; ᴿand let none of you imagine evil against his brother in your heart.   Jer. 5:28 • Ps. 36:4

11 But they refused to hearken, and pulled away the shoulder, and ᵀstopped their ears, that they should not hear.   *closed*

12 Yea, they made their ᴿhearts *as* an adamant stone, ᴿlest they should hear the law, and the words which the LORD of hosts hath sent in his ᵀspirit by the former prophets: therefore came a great wrath from the LORD of hosts.   Jer. 17:1 • Neh. 9:29 • *Spirit*

13 Therefore it is come to pass, *that* as he cried, and they would not hear; so ᴿthey cried, and I would not hear, saith the LORD of hosts: Prov. 1:24; Is. 1:15; Mic. 3:4

14 But ᴿI scattered them with a whirlwind among all the nations whom they knew not. Thus the land was desolate after them, that no man passed through nor returned: for they laid the pleasant land desolate. Deut. 28:64

CHAPTER 8

Restoration of Israel

AGAIN the word of the LORD of hosts came to *me,* saying,

2 Thus saith the LORD of hosts; I was jealous for Zion with great jealousy, and I was jealous for her with great fury.

3 Thus saith the LORD; I am returned unto Zion, and will dwell in the midst of Jerusalem: and Jerusalem shall be called a city of truth; and ᴿthe mountain of the LORD of hosts the holy mountain.   [Is. 2:3]

4 Thus saith the LORD of hosts; There shall yet old men and old women dwell in the streets of Jerusalem, and every man with his staff in his hand for very age.

5 ᴿAnd the streets of the city shall be full of boys and girls playing in the streets thereof.   Jer. 30:19, 20; 31:12, 13

6 Thus saith the LORD of hosts; If it be ᵀmarvellous in the eyes of the remnant of this people in these days, ᴿshould it also be marvellous in mine eyes? saith the LORD of hosts.   wonderful • [Gen. 18:14; Luke 1:37]

7 Thus saith the LORD of hosts; Behold, ᴿI will save my people from the east country, and from the west country;   Is. 11:11

8 And I will bring them, and they shall dwell in the midst of Jerusalem: ᴿand they shall be my people, and I will be their God, in truth and in righteousness.   [Jer. 31:1, 33]

9 Thus saith the LORD of hosts; Let your hands be strong, ye that hear in these days these words by the mouth of the prophets, which were in the day that the foundation of the house of the LORD of hosts was laid, that the temple might be built.

10 For before these days there was no hire for man, nor any hire for beast; neither was there any peace to him that went out or came in because of the affliction: for I set all men every one against his neighbour.

11 But now ᴿI will not be unto the ᵀresidue of this people as in the former days, saith the LORD of hosts.   [Ps. 103:9]; Is. 12:1 • remnant

12 ᴿFor the seed shall be prosperous; the vine shall give her fruit, and ᴿthe ground shall give her increase, and ᴿthe heavens shall give their dew; and I will cause the remnant of this people to possess all these things.   Joel 2:22 • Ps. 67:6 • Hag. 1:10

13 And it shall come to pass, that as ye were a curse among the heathen, O house of Judah, and house of Israel; so will I save you, and ᴿye shall be a blessing: fear not, but let your hands be strong.   Ruth 4:11

14 For thus saith the LORD of hosts; ᴿAs I thought to punish you, when your fathers provoked me to wrath, saith the LORD of hosts, and I repented not: [2 Chr. 36:16]

15 So again have I thought in these days to ᴿdo well unto Jerusalem and to the house of Judah: fear ye not.   Jer. 29:11; [Mic. 7:18]

16 These are the things that ye shall do; ᴿSpeak ye every man the truth to his neighbour; ᵀexecute the judgment of truth and peace in your gates: Eph. 4:25 • carry out

17 ᴿAnd let none of you imagine evil in your hearts against his neighbour; and love no false oath: for all these are things that I hate, saith the LORD.   7:10; Prov. 3:29

Rejoice in Israel's Future

18 And the word of the LORD of hosts came unto me, saying,

19 Thus saith the LORD of hosts; The fast of the fourth month, and the fast of the fifth, and the fast of the seventh, and the fast of the tenth, shall be to the house of Judah joy and gladness, and cheerful feasts; therefore love the truth and peace.

20 Thus saith the LORD of hosts; It shall yet come to pass, that there shall come people, and the inhabitants of many cities:

21 And the inhabitants of one city shall go to another, saying, ᴿLet us go ᵀspeedily to pray before the LORD, and to seek the LORD of hosts: I will go also.   [Is. 2:3] • at once

22 Yea, many people and strong nations shall come to seek the LORD of hosts in Jerusalem, and to pray before the LORD.

23 Thus saith the LORD of hosts; In those days it shall come to pass, that ten men shall ᴿtake hold out of all languages of the nations, even shall take hold of the skirt of him that is a Jew, saying, We will go with you: for we have heard that God is with you.   [Is. 45:14, 24]

CHAPTER 9

Judgment on Surrounding Nations

THE ᴿburden of the word of the LORD in the land of Ha'-drach, and ᴿDamascus shall be the rest thereof: when ᴿthe eyes of man, as of all the tribes of Israel, shall be toward the LORD.   Jer. 23:33 • Amos 1:3 • Ps. 145:15

2 And ᴿHa'-math also shall border thereby; ᴿTy'-rus, and ᴿZi'-don, though it be very ᴿwise.   Jer. 49:23 • Is. 23 • 1 Kin. 17:9 • Ezek. 28:3

3 And Ty'-rus did build herself a strong hold, and heaped up silver as the dust, and fine gold as the mire of the streets.

4 Behold, the Lord will cast her out, and he will smite ᴿher power in the sea; and she shall be devoured with fire.   Ezek. 26:17

5 Ash'-ke-lon shall see it, and fear; Ga'-za also shall see it, and be very sorrowful, and ᴿEk'-ron; for her expectation shall be ashamed; and the king shall perish from ᴿGa'-za, and Ash'-ke-lon shall not be inhabited.   Zeph. 2:4, 5 • Amos 1:6–8

6 And a ᵀbastard shall dwell ᴿin Ash'-dod, and I will cut off the pride of the ᴿPhi-lis'-tines.   a bastard race • Amos 1:8 • Ezek. 25:15, 16

7 ᴿAnd I will take away his blood out of his mouth, and his abominations from between his teeth: but he that remaineth, even he, shall be for our God, and he shall be as a ᵀgovernor in Judah, and Ek'-ron as a Jeb'-u-site.   [Ezek. 25:15–17] • chieftain

8 And ᴿI will encamp about mine house because of the army, because of him that passeth by, and because of him that returneth: and no ᴿoppressor shall pass through them any more: for now have I seen with mine eyes.   2:5; Is. 52:1 • Is. 54:14

First Coming of the Messiah

9 Rejoice ᴿgreatly, O daughter of Zion; shout, O daughter of Jerusalem: behold, thy King cometh unto thee: he is just, and having salvation; lowly, and riding upon an ass, and upon a colt the foal of an ass.   Matt. 21:4, 5 ☆

Second Coming of the Messiah

10 And I will cut off the chariot from E′-phra-im, and the horse from Jerusalem, and the battle bow shall be cut off: and he shall ᴿspeak peace unto the heathen: and his dominion shall be from sea even to sea, and from the river even to the ends of the earth.   Mic. 4:2-4 ☆

11 As for thee also, by the blood of thy covenant I have sent forth thy ᴿprisoners out of the pit wherein is no water.   Is. 42:7

12 Turn you to the strong hold, ᴿye prisoners of hope: even to day do I declare that I will render double unto thee;   Is. 49:9

13 ᵀWhen I have bent Judah for me, ᴿfilled the bow with E′-phra-im, and raised up thy sons, O Zion, against thy sons, ᴿO Greece, and made thee as the sword of a mighty man.   for • Ps. 45:5; Jer. 51:20 • Joel 3:6

14 And the LORD shall be seen over them, and his arrow shall go forth as the lightning: and the Lord GOD shall blow the trumpet, and shall go ᴿwith whirlwinds of the south. [66:15]

15 The LORD of hosts shall defend them; and they shall devour, and ᵀsubdue with sling stones; and they shall drink, and make a noise as through wine; and they shall be ᵀfilled like bowls, and as the corners of the altar.   conquer • completely victorious

16 And the LORD their God shall save them in that day as the flock of his people: for ᴿthey shall be as the stones of a crown, lifted up as an ensign upon his land.   Is. 62:3

17 For ᴿhow great is his goodness, and how great is his ᴿbeauty! ᴿcorn shall make the young men ᵀcheerful, and new wine the maids.   [Ps. 31:19] • Ps. 27:4; Is. 33:17 • Joel 3:18 • flourish

CHAPTER 10

ASK ye of the LORD rain in the time of the latter rain; so the LORD shall make bright clouds, and give them showers of rain, to every one grass in the field.

2 For the idols have spoken vanity, and the diviners have seen a lie, and have told false dreams; they comfort in vain: therefore they went their way as a flock, they were troubled, because there was no shepherd.

3 Mine anger was kindled against the shepherds, and I punished the goats: for the LORD of hosts hath visited his flock the house of Judah, and ᴿhath made them as his goodly horse in the battle.   Song 1:9

4 Out of him came forth the corner, out of

him the nail, out of him the battle bow, out of him every oppressor together.

5 And they shall be as mighty men, which tread down their enemies in the mire of the streets in the battle: and they shall fight, because the LORD is with them, and the riders on horses shall be confounded.

6 And I will strengthen the house of Judah, and I will save the house of Joseph, and I will bring them again to place them; for I have mercy upon them: and they shall be as though ᴿI had not cast them off: for I am the LORD their God, and will hear them.   Is. 54:4

7 And they of E′-phra-im shall be like a mighty man, and their ᴿheart shall rejoice as through wine: yea, ᴿtheir children shall see it, and be glad; their heart shall rejoice in the LORD.   9:15; Ps. 104:15 • [Is. 54:13]; Ezek. 37:25

8 I will ᴿhissᵀ for them, and gather them; for I have redeemed them: and they shall increase as they have increased.   Is. 5:26 • call

9 And I will ᵀsow them among the people: and they shall remember me in far countries; and they shall live with their children, and turn again.   make them to grow

10 ᴿI will bring them again also out of the land of Egypt, and gather them out of Assyria; and I will bring them into the land of Gil′-e-ad and Leb′-a-non; and ᴿplace shall not be found for them.   Is. 11:11 • Is. 49:20

11 ᴿAnd he shall pass through the sea with affliction, and shall smite the waves in the sea, and all the deeps of the river shall dry up: and ᴿthe pride of Assyria shall be brought down, and ᴿthe sceptre of Egypt shall depart away.   Is. 11:15 • Is. 14:25 • Ezek. 30:13

12 And I will strengthen them in the LORD; and ᴿthey shall walk up and down in his name, saith the LORD.   Mic. 4:5

CHAPTER 11

Rejection of the Messiah

OPEN thy doors, O Leb′-a-non, that the fire may ᵀdevour thy cedars.   burn

2 Howl, fir tree; for the cedar is fallen; because the ᵀmighty are spoiled: howl, O ye oaks of Ba′-shan; ᴿfor the forest of the vintage is come down.   gallants • Is. 32:19

3 There is a voice of the howling of shepherds; for their glory is ᵀspoiled: a voice of the ᴿroaring of young lions; for the pride of Jordan is spoiled.   ruined • Jer. 2:15

4 Thus saith the LORD my God; Feed the flock of the slaughter;

5 Whose possessors slay them, and ᴿhold themselves not guilty: and they that sell them say, Blessed be the LORD; for I am rich: and their own shepherds pity them not.   [Jer. 2:3]

6 For I will no more pity the inhabitants of the land, saith the LORD: but, lo, I will deliver the men every one into his ᴿneighbour's hand, and into the hand of his king: and they

shall smite the land, and out of their hand I will not deliver *them*. 14:13

7 And I will feed the flock of slaughter, ᵀeven you, ᴿO poor of the flock. And I took unto me two staves; the one I called Beauty, and the other I called ᵀBands; and I fed the flock. *verily the poor* • Matt. 11:5 • *binders*

8 Three shepherds also I ᵀcut off in one month; and my soul ᵀlothed them, and their soul also abhorred me. *destroyed* • *despised*

9 Then said I, I will not feed you: ᴿthat that dieth, let it die; and that that is to be cut off, let it be cut off; and let the rest eat every one the flesh of another. Jer. 15:2

10 And I took my staff, *even* Beauty, and cut it asunder, that I might break my covenant which I had made with all the people.

11 And it was broken in that day: and so the poor of the flock that waited upon me knew that it *was* the word of the LORD.

12 And I said unto them, If ye think good, give *me* my price; and if not, forbear. So they ᴿweighed for my price ᵀthirty *pieces* of silver. Matt. 27:9 ☆ • *$3840*

13 And the LORD said unto me, Cast it unto the ᴿpotter: a goodly price that I was ᵀprised at of them. And I took the thirty *pieces* of silver, and cast them to the potter in the house of the LORD. Matt. 27:7, 10 ☆ • *valued by*

14 Then I cut asunder mine other staff, *even* ᵀBands, that I might break the brotherhood between Judah and Israel. *Binders*

15 And the LORD said unto me, ᴿTake unto thee yet the instruments of a ᴿfoolishᵀ shepherd. Ezek. 34:2 • *v. 17* • *naïve*

16 For, lo, I will raise up a shepherd in the land, which shall not visit those that be cut off, neither shall seek the young one, nor heal that that is broken, nor feed that that standeth still: but he shall eat the flesh of the fat, and tear their claws in pieces.

17 ᴿWoe to the ᵀidol shepherd that leaveth the flock! the sword *shall be* upon his arm, and upon his right eye: his arm shall be clean dried up, and his right eye shall be utterly darkened. John 10:12 • *worthless*

CHAPTER 12

Physical Salvation of Judah

THE burden of the word of the LORD for Israel, saith the LORD, ᴿwhich stretcheth forth the heavens, and ᴿlayeth the foundation of the earth, and ᴿformeth the spirit of man within him. Is. 42:5 • Job 26:7 • [Is. 57:16]

2 Behold, I will make Jerusalem a cup of trembling unto all the people round about, when they shall be in the siege both against Judah *and* against Jerusalem.

3 And in that day will I make Jerusalem a burdensome stone for all people: all that burden themselves with it shall be cut in pieces, though all the people of the earth be gathered together against it.

4 In that day, saith the LORD, ᴿI will smite every horse with astonishment, and his rider with madness: and I will open mine eyes upon the house of Judah, and will smite every horse of the people with blindness. Ps. 76:6

5 And the ᵀgovernors of Judah shall say in their heart, The inhabitants of Jerusalem ᵀ*shall be* my strength in the LORD of hosts their God. *chieftains* • *are*

6 In that day will I make the governors of Judah ᴿlike an hearth of fire among the wood, and like a torch of fire in a sheaf; and they shall devour all the people round about, on the right hand and on the left: and Jerusalem shall be inhabited again in her own place, *even* in Jerusalem. Obad. 18

7 The LORD also shall ᴿsave the tents ᴿof Judah first, that the glory of the house of David and the glory of the inhabitants of Jerusalem do not magnify *themselves* against Judah. Jer. 30:18 • [Amos 9:11]

8 In that day shall the LORD ᴿdefend the inhabitants of Jerusalem; and he that is ᴿfeebleᵀ among them at that day shall be as David; and the house of David *shall be* as God, as the ᴿangel of the LORD before them. Lev. 26:8 • Josh. 23:10 • *weak* • [Ps. 8:5]

9 And it shall come to pass in that day, *that* I will seek to ᴿdestroy all the nations that come against Jerusalem. Hag. 2:22

Spiritual Salvation of Judah

10 And I will pour upon the house of David, and upon the inhabitants of Jerusalem, the spirit of grace and of supplications: and ᴿthey shall look upon me whom they have pierced, and they shall mourn for him, as one mourneth for *his* only *son*, and shall be in bitterness for him, as one that is in bitterness for *his* firstborn. John 19:34; 20:27 ☆

11 In that day shall there be a great ᴿmourning in Jerusalem, as the mourning of Ha-dad-rim'-mon in the valley of ᴿMe-gid'-don. [Matt. 24:30] • 2 Kin. 23:29

12 And the land shall mourn, every family apart; the family of the house of David apart, and their wives apart; the family of the house of Nathan apart, and their wives apart;

13 The family of the house of Levi apart, and their wives apart; the family of Shim'-e-i apart, and their wives apart;

14 All the families that remain, every family apart, and their wives apart.

CHAPTER 13

IN that day there shall be a ᴿfountain opened to the house of David and to the inhabitants of Jerusalem for ᴿsin and for uncleanness. Jer. 2:13 • [John 1:29; Eph. 1:7]

2 And it shall come to pass in that day, saith the LORD of hosts, *that* I will cut off the names of the idols out of the land, and they shall no more be remembered: and also I will cause the prophets and the unclean spirit to pass out of the land.

3 And it shall come to pass, *that* when any shall yet prophesy, then his father and his mother that begat him shall say unto him, Thou shalt not live; for thou speakest lies in the name of the LORD: and his father and his mother that begat him shall thrust him through when he prophesieth.

4 And it shall come to pass in that day, *that* the prophets shall be Rashamed every one of his vision, when he hath prophesied; neither shall they wear Ra Trough garment to deceive: Jer. 6:15 • 2 Kin. 1:8 • *hairy mantle*

5 But he shall say, RI *am* no prophet, I *am* an husbandman; for man taught me to keep cattle from my youth.   Amos 7:14

6 And *one* shall say unto him, RWhat *are* these wounds in thine hands? Then he shall answer, *Those* with which I was wounded *in* the house of my friends.   John 20:25, 27 ☆

7 Awake, O sword, against my shepherd, and against the man *that is* my fellow, saith the LORD of hosts: Rsmite the shepherd, and the sheep shall be scattered: and I will turn mine hand upon the little ones.   Matt. 26:56 ☆

8 And it shall come to pass, *that* in all the land, saith the LORD, two parts therein shall be cut off *and* die; Rbut the third shall be left therein.   [Rom. 11:5]

9 And I will bring the third part through the fire, and will Rrefine them as silver is refined, and will try them as gold is tried: they shall call on my name, and I will hear them: I will say, It *is* my people: and they shall say, The LORD *is* my God. Is. 48:10; Mal. 3:3

CHAPTER 14

Final Siege of Jerusalem

BEHOLD, Rthe day of the LORD cometh, and thy Tspoil shall be divided in the midst of thee.   [Is. 13:9; Joel 2:1; Mal. 4:1] • *property*

2 For I will gather all nations against Jerusalem to battle; and the city shall be taken, and the Rhouses rifled, and the women ravished; and half of the city shall go forth into captivity, and the residue of the people shall not be cut off from the city.   Is. 13:16

Second Coming of the Messiah

3 Then shall the LORD go forth, and Rfight against those nations, as when he fought in the day of battle.   [Rev. 19:17]

4 And his feet shall stand in that day upon the mount of Olives, which is before Jerusalem on the east, and the mount of Olives shall

Rcleave in the midst thereof toward the east and toward the west, *and there shall be* a very great valley; and half of the mountain shall remove toward the north, and half of it toward the south.   Is. 64:1

5 And ye shall flee *to* the valley of the mountains; for the valley of the mountains shall reach unto A'-zal: yea, ye shall flee, like as ye fled from before the Rearthquake in the days of Uz-zi'-ah king of Judah: Rand the LORD my God shall come, *and* all the saints with thee.   Is. 29:6 • Joel 3:11

6 And it shall come to pass in that day, *that* the light shall not be clear, nor dark:

7 But Rit shall be one day which shall be known to the LORD, not day, nor night: but it shall come to pass, *that* Rat evening time it shall be light.   Jer. 30:7 • [Rev. 22:5]

8 And it shall be in that day, *that* living waters shall go out from Jerusalem; half of them toward the Tformer sea, and half of them toward the Thinder sea: in summer and in winter shall it be.   *eastern • western*

Kingdom of the Messiah

9 And the LORD shall be Rking over all the earth: in that day shall there be Rone LORD, and his name one.   [Rev. 11:15 • Deut. 6:4]

10 All the land shall be turned as a plain from Ge'-ba to Rim'-mon south of Jerusalem: and it shall be lifted up, and inhabited in her place, from Benjamin's gate unto the place of the first gate, unto the corner gate, and *from* the tower of Ha-nan'-e-el unto the king's winepresses.

11 And *men* shall dwell in it, and there shall be no more utter destruction; but Jerusalem shall be safely inhabited.

12 And this shall be the plague wherewith the LORD will smite all the people that have fought against Jerusalem; Their flesh shall Rconsume away while they stand upon their feet, and their eyes shall consume away in their holes, and their tongue shall consume away in their mouth.   Lev. 26:16

13 And it shall come to pass in that day, *that* Ra great Ttumult from the LORD shall be among them; and they shall lay hold every one on the hand of his neighbour, and his hand shall rise up against the hand of his neighbour.   1 Sam. 14:15, 20 • *disturbance*

14 And Judah also shall fight Tat Jerusalem; and the wealth of all the heathen round about shall be gathered together, gold, and silver, and apparel, in great abundance. *against*

15 And Rso shall be the plague of the horse, of the mule, of the camel, and of the ass, and of all the beasts that shall be in Tthese tents, as this plague.   *v. 12 • those camps*

16 And it shall come to pass, *that* every one that is left of all the nations which came against Jerusalem shall even Rgo up from

year to year to worship the King, the LORD of hosts, and to keep Rthe feast of tabernacles.   [Is. 60:6; 66:23] • Hos. 12:9; John 7:2

17 And it shall be, *that* whoso will not come up of *all* the families of the earth unto Jerusalem to worship the King, the LORD of hosts, even upon them shall be no rain.

18 And if the family of REgypt go not up, and come not, that *have no rain;* there shall be the plague, wherewith the LORD will smite the heathen that come not up to keep the feast of tabernacles.   Deut. 11:10

19 This shall be the Tpunishment of Egypt, and the punishment of all nations that come not up to keep the feast of tabernacles.   sin

20 In that day shall there be upon the bells of the horses, HOLINESS UNTO THE LORD; and the pots in the LORD's house shall be like the bowls before the altar.

21 Yea, every pot in Jerusalem and in Judah shall be Rholiness unto the LORD of hosts: and all they that sacrifice shall come and take of them, and Tseethe therein: and in that day there shall be no more the RCa'-naan-ite in the house of the LORD of hosts.   [Rom. 14:6] • boil • Joel 3:17

THE BOOK OF
MALACHI

THE BOOK OF MALACHI

Malachi, a prophet in the days of Nehemiah, directs his message of judgment to a people plagued with corrupt priests, wicked practices, and a false sense of security in their privileged relationship with God. Using the question-and-answer method, Malachi probes deeply into their problems of hypocrisy, infidelity, mixed marriages, divorce, false worship, and arrogance. So sinful has the nation become that God's words to the people no longer have any impact. For four hundred years after Malachi's ringing condemnations, God remains silent. Only with the coming of John the Baptist (3:1) does God again communicate to His people through a prophet's voice.

The meaning of the name *Mal'aki* ("My Messenger") is probably a shortened form of *Mal'ak-ya*, "Messenger of Yahweh," and it is appropriate to the book which speaks of the coming of the "messenger of the covenant" ("messenger" is mentioned three times in 2:7; 3:1). The Septuagint used the title *Malachias* even though it also translated it "by the hand of his messenger." The Latin title is *Maleachi*.

THE AUTHOR OF MALACHI

The only Old Testament mention of Malachi is in 1:1. The authorship, date, and unity of Malachi have never been seriously challenged. The unity of the book can be seen in the dialectic style that binds it together. Nothing is known of Malachi (not even his father's name), but a Jewish tradition says that he was a member of the Great Synagogue (see "The Author of Zechariah").

THE TIME OF MALACHI

Although an exact date cannot be established for Malachi, internal evidence can be used to deduce an approximate date. The Persian term for governor, *pechah* (1:8; cf. Neh. 5:14; Hag. 1:1, 14; 2:21), indicates that this book was written during the Persian domination of Israel (539–333 B.C.). Sacrifices were being offered in the temple (1:7–10; 3:8), which was rebuilt in 516 B.C. Evidently many years had passed since the offerings were instituted, because the priests had grown tired of them and corruptions had crept into the system. In addition, Malachi's oracle was inspired by the same problems that Nehemiah faced: corrupt priests (1:6—2:9; Neh. 13:1-9), neglect of tithes and offerings (3:7–12; Neh. 13:10–13), and intermarriage with pagan wives (2:10–16; Neh. 13:23–28). Nehemiah came to Jerusalem in 444 B.C. to rebuild the city walls, thirteen years after

Ezra's return and reforms (457 B.C.). Nehemiah returned to Persia in 432 B.C., but came back to Palestine about 425 B.C. and dealt with the sins described in Malachi. It is therefore likely that Malachi proclaimed his message while Nehemiah was absent between 432 B.C. and 425 B.C., almost a century after Haggai and Zechariah began to prophesy (520 B.C.).

THE CHRIST OF MALACHI

The book of Malachi is the prelude to four hundred years of prophetic silence, broken finally by the words of the next prophet, John the Baptist: "Behold the Lamb of God, which taketh away the sin of the world" (John 1:29). Malachi predicts the coming of the messenger who will clear the way before the Lord (3:1; cf. Is. 40:3). John the Baptist later fulfills this prophecy, but the next few verses (3:2-5) jump ahead to Christ in His Second Advent. This is also true of the prophecy of the appearance of "Elijah the prophet" (4:5). John the Baptist was this Elijah (Matt. 3:3; 11:10–14; 17:9–13; Mark 1:3; 9:10, 11; Luke 1:17; 3:4; John 1:23), but Elijah will also appear before the second coming of Christ.

KEYS TO MALACHI

Key Word: An Appeal to Backsliders— The divine dialogue in Malachi's prophecy is designed as an appeal to break through the barrier of Israel's disbelief, disappointment, and discouragement. The promised time of prosperity has not yet come, and the prevailing attitude that it is not worth serving God becomes evident in their moral and religious corruption. However, God reveals His continuing love in spite of Israel's lethargy. His appeal in this oracle is for the people and priests to stop and realize that their lack of blessing is not caused by God's lack of concern, but by their disobedience of the covenant law. When they repent and return to God with sincere hearts, the obstacles to the flow of divine blessing will be removed. Malachi also reminds the people that a day of reckoning will surely come when God will judge the righteous and the wicked.

Key Verses: Malachi 2:17—3:1; 4:5, 6—"Ye have wearied the LORD with your words. Yet ye say, Wherein have we wearied *him?* When ye say, Every one that doeth evil *is* good in the sight of the LORD, and he delighteth in them; or, Where *is* the God of judgment? Behold, I will send my messenger, and he shall prepare the way before me: and the Lord, whom ye seek, shall suddenly come to his temple, even the messenger of the covenant, whom ye delight in: behold, he shall come, saith the LORD of hosts" (Mal. 2:17—3:1).

"Behold, I will send you Elijah the prophet before the coming of the great and dreadful day of the LORD: And he shall turn the heart of the fathers to the children, and the heart of the children to their fathers, lest I come and smite the earth with a curse" (Mal. 4:5, 6).

Key Chapter: Malachi 3—The last book of the Old Testament concludes with a dramatic prophecy of the coming of the Lord and John the Baptist: "I will send my messenger, and he shall prepare the way before me" (3:1). Israel flocked to the Jordan four hundred years later when "The voice of one crying in the wilderness, Prepare ye the way of the Lord" (Matt. 3:3) appeared, breaking the long silence of prophetic revelation. Malachi 3 and 4 record the coming of the Messiah and His forerunner.

SURVEY OF MALACHI

The great prophecies of Haggai and Zechariah are not yet fulfilled, and the people of Israel become disillusioned and doubtful. They begin to question God's providence as their faith imperceptibly degenerates into cynicism. Internally, they wonder whether it is worth serving God after all. Externally, these attitudes surface in mechanical observances, empty ritual, cheating in tithes and offerings, and crass indifference to God's moral and ceremonial law. Their priests are corrupt and their practices wicked, but they are so spiritually insensitive that they wonder why they are not being blessed by God.

Using a probing series of questions and answers, God seeks to pierce their hearts of stone. In each case the divine accusations are denied: How has God loved us? (1:2-5); How have we (priests) despised God's name? (1:6—2:9); How have we (people) profaned the covenant? (2:10-16); How have we wearied God? (2:17—3:6); How have we robbed God? (3:7-12); How

have we spoken against God? (3:13-15). In effect, the people sneer, "Oh, come on now: it's not that bad!" However, their rebellion is quiet, not open. As their perception of God grows dim, the resulting materialism and externalism become settled characteristics that later grip the religious parties of the Pharisees and Sadducees. In spite of all this, God still loves His people and once again extends His grace to any who will humbly turn to Him. Malachi explores: the privilege of the nation (1:1-5), the pollution of the nation (1:6—3:15), and the promise to the nation (3:16—4:16).

The Privilege of the Nation (1:1-5): The Israelites blind themselves to God's love for them. Wallowing in the problems of the present, they are forgetful of God's works for them in the past. God gives them a reminder of His special love by contrasting the fates of Esau (Edom) and Jacob (Israel).

The Pollution of the Nation (1:6—3:15): The priests have lost all respect for God's name and in their greed offer only diseased and imperfect animals on the altar. They have more respect for the Persian governor than they do for the living God. Moreover, God is withholding His blessings from them because of their disobedience to God's covenant and because of their insincere teaching.

The people are indicted for their treachery in divorcing the wives of their youth in order to marry foreign women (2:10-16). In response to their questioning the justice of God, they receive a promise of the Messiah's coming but also a warning of the judgment that He will bring (2:17—3:6). The people have robbed God of the tithes and offerings due Him, but God is ready to bless them with abundance if they will put Him first (3:7-12). The final problem is the arrogant challenge to the character of God (3:13-15), and this challenge is answered in the remainder of the book.

The Promise to the Nation (3:16—4:6): The Lord assures His people that a time is coming

FOCUS	PRIVILEGE OF THE NATION	POLLUTION OF THE NATION		PROMISE TO THE NATION		
REFERENCE	1:1 ——————— 1:6	———— 2:10 ————	3:16 ————	4:1 ————	4:4 ———— 4:6	
DIVISION	LOVE OF GOD FOR THE NATION	SIN OF THE PRIESTS	SIN OF THE PEOPLE	BOOK OF REMEMBRANCE	COMING OF CHRIST	COMING OF ELIJAH
TOPIC	PAST	PRESENT		FUTURE		
	CARE OF GOD	COMPLAINT OF GOD		COMING OF GOD		
LOCATION	JERUSALEM					
TIME	c. 432 – 425 B.C.					

when the wicked will be judged and those who fear Him will be blessed. The day of the Lord will reveal that it is not "vain to serve God" (3:14). Malachi ends on the bitter word *curse*.

Although the people are finally cured of idolatry, there is little spiritual progress in Israel's history. Sin abounds, and the need for the coming Messiah is greater than ever.

OUTLINE OF MALACHI

CHAPTER 1

The Privilege of the Nation

THE ᵀburden of the word of the LORD to Israel by Mal′-a-chi.   *message*

2 ᴿI have loved you, saith the LORD. Yet ye say, Wherein hast thou loved us? *Was* not Esau Jacob's brother? saith the LORD: yet ᴿI loved Jacob,   Deut. 7:8 · Rom. 9:13

3 And I hated Esau, and ᴿlaid his mountains and his ᵀheritage waste for the ᵀdragons of the wilderness.   Jer. 49:18 · *estate* · *jackals*

4 Whereas E′-dom saith, We are impoverished, but we will return and build the desolate places; thus saith the LORD of hosts, They shall build, but I will throw down; and they shall call them, The border of wickedness, and, The people against whom the LORD hath indignation for ever.

5 And your eyes shall see, and ye shall say, ᴿThe LORD will be ᵀmagnified from the border of Israel.   Ps. 35:27 · *honoured*

The Priests Despise the Name of the Lord

6 A son honoureth *his* father, and a servant his master: if then I *be* a father, where *is* mine honour? and if I *be* a master, where *is* my fear? saith the LORD of hosts unto you, O priests, that ᵀdespise my name. And ye say, Wherein have we despised thy name?   *abhor*

7 Ye offer polluted bread upon mine altar; and ye say, Wherein have we ᵀpolluted thee? In that ye say, The table of the LORD *is* contemptible.   *made unclean*

8 And ᴿif ye offer the blind for sacrifice, *is it* not evil? and if ye offer the lame and sick, *is it* not evil? offer it now unto thy governor;

will he be pleased with thee, or accept thy person? saith the LORD of hosts.   Lev. 22:22

9 And now, I pray you, beseech God that he will be gracious unto us: this hath been by ᵀyour means: will he regard your persons? saith the LORD of hosts.   *your work*

10 Who *is there* even among you that would shut the doors *for nought?* ᴿneither do ye kindle *fire* on mine altar ᵀfor nought. I have no pleasure in you, saith the LORD of hosts, ᴿneither will I accept an offering at your hand.   1 Cor. 9:13 · *in vain* · Is. 1:11

11 For from the rising of the sun even unto the going down of the same my name *shall be* great among the Gentiles; and in every place incense *shall be* offered unto my name, and a pure offering: for my name *shall be* great among the heathen, saith the LORD of hosts.

12 But ye have profaned it, in that ye say, The table of the LORD *is* polluted; and the fruit thereof, *even* his meat, *is* contemptible.

13 Ye said also, Behold, what a weariness *is it!* and ye have snuffed at it, saith the LORD of hosts; and ye brought *that which was* torn, and the lame, and the sick; thus ye brought an offering: should I accept this of your hand? saith the LORD.

14 But cursed *be* ᴿthe deceiver, ᵀwhich hath in his flock a male, and voweth, and sacrificeth unto the Lord a ᵀcorrupt thing: for ᴿI *am* a great King, saith the LORD of hosts, and my name *is* dreadful among the heathen.   *v. 8 · in whose flock is · blemished · Ps. 47:2*

CHAPTER 2

The Lord Curses the Priests

AND now, O ye priests, this commandment is for you.

2 ℞If ye will not hear, and if ye will not lay it to heart, to give glory unto my name, saith the LORD of hosts, I will even send a curse upon you, and I will curse your blessings: yea, I have cursed them already, because ye do not lay it to heart.   [Deut. 28:15]

3 Behold, I will ᵀcorrupt your seed, and ᵀspread dung upon your faces, even the dung of your solemn feasts; and one shall take you away with it.   bring to ruin • humiliate you

4 And ye shall know that I have sent this commandment unto you, that my covenant might be with Levi, saith the LORD of hosts.

5 ℞My ᵀcovenant was with him of life and peace; and I gave them to him for the fear wherewith he feared me, and was afraid before my name.   Deut. 33:9 • agreement

6 The law of truth was in his mouth, and iniquity was not found in his lips: he walked with me in peace and equity, and did ℞turn many away from iniquity.   [James 5:19, 20]

7 ℞For the priest's lips should keep knowledge, and they should seek the law at his mouth: ℞for he is the messenger of the LORD of hosts.   Num. 27:21; Deut. 17:9 • Gal. 4:14

8 But ye are departed out of the way; ye have caused many to ℞stumble at the law; ℞ye have corrupted the covenant of Levi, saith the LORD of hosts.   Jer. 18:15 • Neh. 13:29

9 Therefore ℞have I also made you contemptible and base before all the people, according as ye have not kept my ways, but have been partial in the law.   1 Sam. 2:30

The People Commit Idolatry

10 Have we not all one father? hath not one God created us? why do we deal treacherously every man against his brother, by profaning the covenant of our fathers?

11 Judah hath dealt treacherously, and an abomination is committed in Israel and in Jerusalem; for Judah hath profaned the holiness of the LORD which he loved, and hath married the daughter of a strange god.

12 The LORD will cut off the man that doeth this, the master and the scholar, out of the tabernacles of Jacob, and him that offereth an offering unto the LORD of hosts.

13 And this have ye done again, covering the altar of the LORD with tears, with weeping, and with crying out, insomuch that he regardeth not the offering any more, or receiveth it with good will at your hand.

The People Divorce

14 Yet ye say, Wherefore? Because the LORD hath been witness between thee and the wife of thy youth, against whom thou hast dealt treacherously: yet is she thy companion, and the wife of thy covenant.

15 And did not he make one? Yet had he the residue of the spirit. And wherefore one? That he might seek a godly seed. Therefore take heed to your spirit, and let none deal treacherously against the wife of his youth.

16 For the LORD, the God of Israel, saith that he hateth putting away: for one covereth violence with his garment, saith the LORD of hosts: therefore take heed to your spirit, that ye deal not treacherously.

The Lord Will Judge at His Coming

17 ℞Ye have wearied the LORD with your words. Yet ye say, Wherein have we wearied him? When ye say, ℞Every one that doeth evil is good in the sight of the LORD, and he delighteth in them; or, ℞Where is the God of judgment?   Is. 43:24 • Is. 5:20, 21 • Jer. 17:15

CHAPTER 3

BEHOLD, ℞I will send my messenger, and he shall prepare the way before me: and the Lord, whom ye seek, shall suddenly come to his temple, even the messenger of the covenant, whom ye delight in: behold, he shall come, saith the LORD of hosts. Luke 1:76 ☆

2 But who may abide ℞the day of his coming? and ℞who shall stand when he appeareth? for ℞he is like a refiner's fire, and like fullers' sope: [4:1] • Rev. 6:17 • Matt. 3:10

3 And he shall sit as a refiner and purifier of silver: and he shall purify the sons of Levi, and ᵀpurge them as gold and silver, that they may ℞offer unto the LORD an offering in righteousness.   cleanse • [1 Pet. 2:5]

4 Then shall the offering of Judah and Jerusalem be pleasant unto the LORD, as in the days of old, and as in former years.

5 And I will come near to you to judgment;

2:10 God the Father of All—The Fatherhood of God applies in a general sense to everyone since all men and women are created by God in His image. Thus their creaturehood is derived from His Fatherhood. This fact is demonstrated by Hebrews 12:9, which speaks of God as "the Father of spirits" (cf. Page 153—Num. 16:22; Page 647—Eccl. 12:7). Paul even agrees with a heathen poet that all men are God's offspring (Page 1092—Acts 17:28). He does not mean, of course, that everyone will have eternal life but that all men and women are the offspring of God in their created natures. James says that men still bear this image (Page 1229—James 3:9).

God is also the Father of all as sustainer of life. Every person is an object of His fatherly care (Page 960—Matt. 18:10) and a candidate for His kingdom (Page 1028—Luke 18:16). Furthermore, God is not willing that any should perish (Page 960—Matt. 18:14; Page 1194—1 Tim. 2:4). Even when men and women reject God, He still provides for them as He does for believers with rain, fruitful seasons, food, and gladness (Page 946—Matt. 5:45; Page 1088—Acts 14:17).

Now turn to Page 943—Matt. 3:17: God the Father of Christ.

and I will be a swift witness against the sorcerers, and against the adulterers, and against false swearers, and against those that oppress the hireling in *his* wages, the widow, and the fatherless, and that turn aside the stranger *from his right,* and fear not me, saith the LORD of hosts.

The People Rob God

6 For I *am* the LORD, I change not; therefore ye sons of Jacob are not consumed.

7 Even from the days of ᴿyour fathers ye are gone away from mine ordinances, and have not kept *them.* Return unto me, and I will return unto you, saith the LORD of hosts. But ye said, Wherein shall we return? Acts 7:51

8 Will a man rob God? Yet ye have robbed me. But ye say, Wherein have we robbed thee? In tithes and offerings.

9 Ye *are* cursed with a curse: for ye have robbed me, *even* this whole nation.

10 ᴿBring ye all the tithes into the storehouse, that there may be meat in mine house, and ᵀprove me now herewith, saith the LORD of hosts, if I will not open you the windows of heaven, and ᵀpour you out a blessing, that *there shall* not *be room* enough *to receive it.*   Prov. 3:9 • *test* • *empty out*

11 And I will rebuke the devourer for your sakes, and he shall not ᵀdestroy the fruits of your ground; neither shall your vine cast her fruit before the time in the field, saith the LORD of hosts.   *corrupt*

12 And ᴿall nations shall call you blessed: for ye shall be ᴿa ᵀdelightsome land, saith the LORD of hosts.   Is. 61:9 • Dan. 8:9 • *delightful*

The People Doubt the Character of God

13 Your words have been ᵀstout against me, saith the LORD. Yet ye say, What have we spoken *so much* against thee?   *strong*

14 Ye have said, It is vain to serve God: and what profit *is it* that we have kept his ᵀordinance, and that we have walked mournfully before the LORD of hosts?   *laws*

15 And now we call the proud happy; yea, they that work wickedness are set up; yea, *they that* tempt God are even delivered.

The Rewards of the Book of Remembrance

16 Then they that feared the LORD ᴿspake often one to another: and the LORD hearkened, and heard *it,* and ᴿa book of remembrance was written before him for them that feared the LORD, and that thought upon his name.   Heb. 3:13 • Ps. 56:8

17 And they shall be mine, saith the LORD of hosts, in that day when I make up my jewels; and I will spare them, as a man spareth his own son that serveth him.

18 ᴿThen shall ye return, and discern between the righteous and the wicked, between him that serveth God and him that serveth him not.   [Gen. 18:25; Ps. 58:11]; Amos 5:15

CHAPTER 4

The Rewards of the Coming of Christ

FOR, behold, ᴿthe day cometh, that shall burn as an oven; and all the proud, yea, and all that do wickedly, shall be stubble: and the day that cometh shall burn them up, saith the LORD of hosts, that it shall leave them neither root nor branch.   [2 Pet. 3:7]

2 But unto you that fear my name shall the Sun of righteousness arise with healing in his wings; and ye shall go forth, and grow up as calves of the stall.

3 ᴿAnd ye shall tread down the wicked; for they shall be ᴿashes under the soles of your feet in the day that I shall do *this,* saith the LORD of hosts.   Mic. 7:10 • Ezek. 28:18

The Prophecy of the Coming of Elijah

4 Remember ye the ᴿlaw of Moses my servant, which I commanded unto him ᴿin Ho'-reb for all Israel, *with* ᴿthe statutes and judgments.   Ex. 20:3 • Deut. 4:10 • Ps. 147:19

5 Behold, I will send you ᴿE-li'-jah the prophet before the coming of the great and dreadful day of the LORD: [Matt. 11:14] ☆

6 And he shall turn the heart of the fathers to the children, and the heart of the children to their fathers, lest I come and ᴿsmite the earth with a curse.   Is. 11:4 ☆

Introduction to the Visual Survey of the Bible

The book introductions in **The Open Bible** provide background information and a survey of each book. But this Visual Survey of the Bible takes a further step by giving a perspective on the whole of Scripture.

Take a moment to familiarize yourself with the first chart, which compares the Old and New Testaments. Note particularly the time-line at the bottom of the page. This time-line divides the Old Testament into five periods and the New Testament into two. It is the key to the rest of the charts.

As you look through the following pages, notice that each chart has its own time-line containing both biblical and extrabiblical events. The maps portray the major movement of each period; the boxes present the key topics. The charts also summarize the themes of the Old Testament poetic and prophetic books, and the themes of the New Testament Epistles.

The ten Life Applications are an important part of this Survey. Based on the flow of each period, they crystallize the central spiritual truths of Scripture. Each principle leads into the next, and all of them relate to your own life.

VISUAL SURVEY...

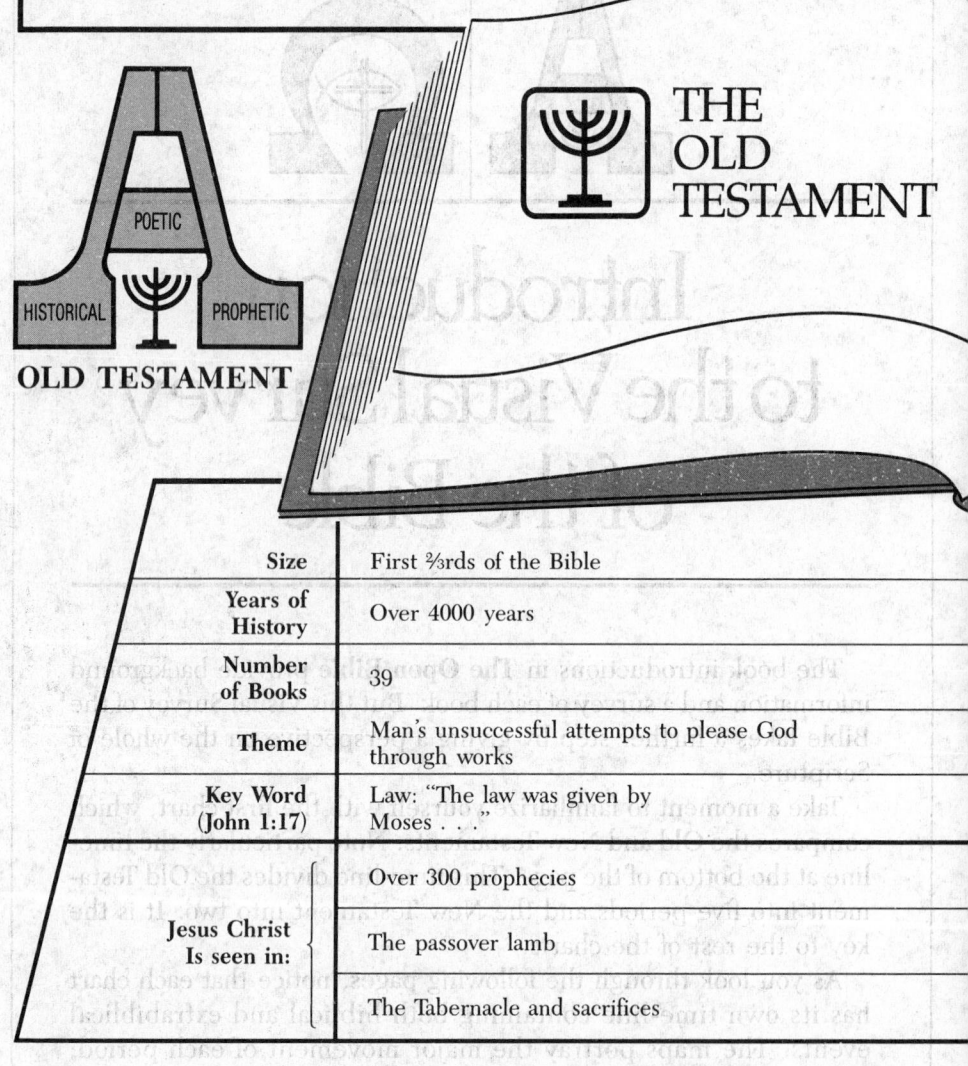

OLD TESTAMENT

THE OLD TESTAMENT

Size	First ⅔rds of the Bible
Years of History	Over 4000 years
Number of Books	39
Theme	Man's unsuccessful attempts to please God through works
Key Word (John 1:17)	Law: "The law was given by Moses . . ."
Jesus Christ Is seen in:	Over 300 prophecies
	The passover lamb
	The Tabernacle and sacrifices

Adam	Noah	Abraham	Moses	David	Ezra
Before 4000 B.C.	?	2000 B.C.	1500 B.C.	1000 B.C.	500 B.C.

History of the Early World		History of Israel			
Pre-Flood	After the Flood	The People	The Land	The Kingdom	The Remnant
11 Chapters (Gen. 1—11)		Over 38 Books (Gen. 12—Mal.)			

...OF THE BIBLE

THE NEW TESTAMENT

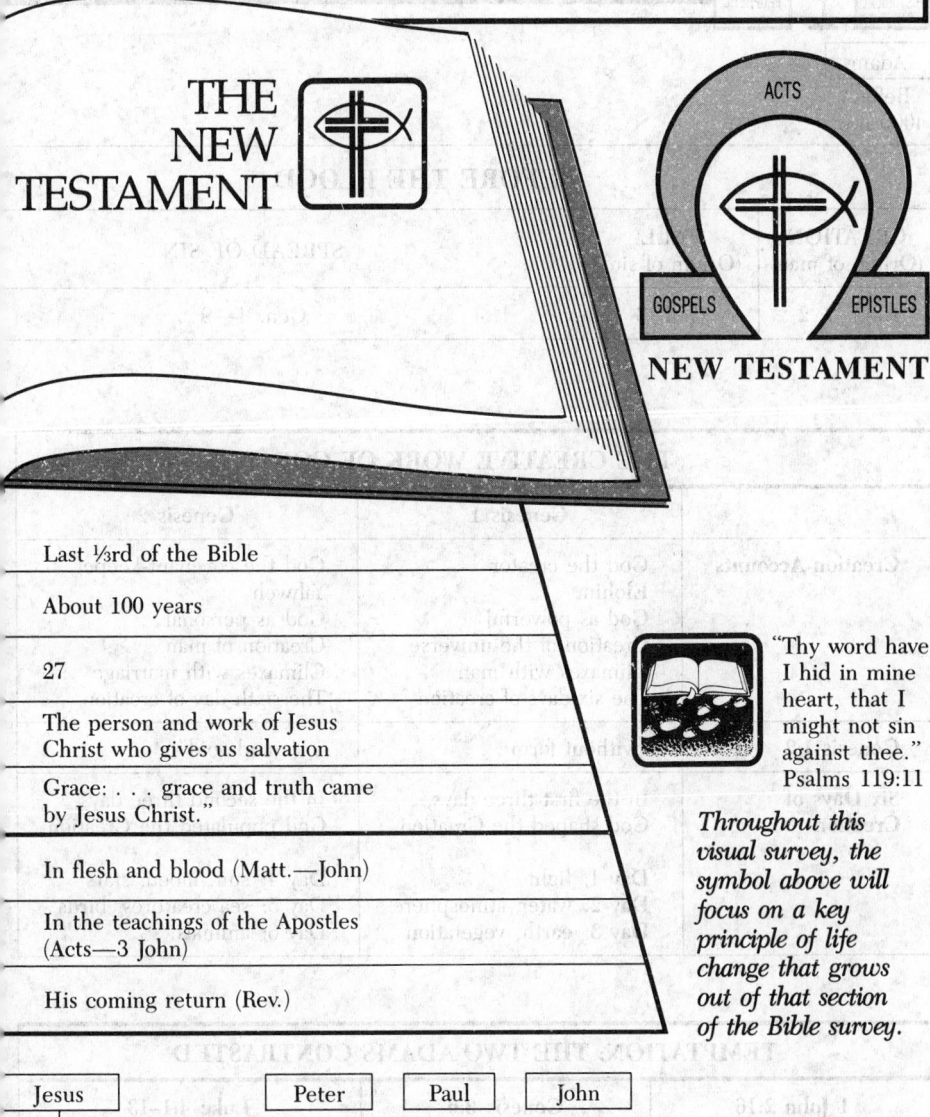

ACTS

GOSPELS   EPISTLES

NEW TESTAMENT

Last ⅓rd of the Bible

About 100 years

27

The person and work of Jesus Christ who gives us salvation

Grace: . . . grace and truth came by Jesus Christ."

In flesh and blood (Matt.—John)

In the teachings of the Apostles (Acts—3 John)

His coming return (Rev.)

"Thy word have I hid in mine heart, that I might not sin against thee."
Psalms 119:11

Throughout this visual survey, the symbol above will focus on a key principle of life change that grows out of that section of the Bible survey.

Jesus		Peter	Paul	John
4 B.C.	A.D. 33			A.D. 100

History of the Messiah	History of the Early Church		
The Life of Christ	In all Jerusalem	In all Judea & Samaria	To all the Earth
(Matt.—John)	(Acts—Rev.)		

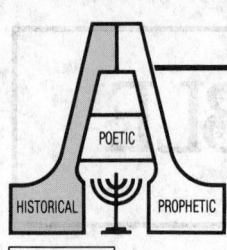

POETIC

HISTORICAL   PROPHETIC

HISTORY OF THE EARLY WORLD

Adam

Before
4000 B.C.

BEFORE THE FLOOD		
CREATION (Origin of man)	FALL (Origin of sin)	SPREAD OF SIN
Gen. 1; 2	Gen. 3	Gen. 4—9

THE CREATIVE WORK OF GOD		
	Genesis 1	**Genesis 2**
Creation Accounts	God the creator Elohim God as powerful Creation of the universe Climaxes with man The six days of creation	God the covenant-keeper Yahweh God as personal Creation of man Climaxes with marriage The sixth day of creation
Genesis 1:2	"without form . . ."	". . . and void"
Six Days of Creation	In the first three days, God shaped the Creation Day 1: light Day 2: water, atmosphere Day 3: earth, vegetation	In the second three days, God populated the Creation Day 4: sun, moon, stars Day 5: sea creatures, birds Day 6: animals

TEMPTATION: THE TWO ADAMS CONTRASTED		
1 John 2:16	**Genesis 3:6** (First Adam)	**Luke 4:1–13** (Second Adam—Christ)
"the lust of the flesh"	"the tree was good for food"	"command this stone that it be made bread"
"the lust of the eyes"	"it was pleasant to the eyes"	"the devil . . . shewed unto him all the kingdoms"
"the pride of life"	"a tree to be desired to make one wise"	"cast thyself down from hence"

4000+ B.C.	2000	Christ

Noah		Abraham
2500 B.C. ?		2000 B.C.

AFTER THE FLOOD

FLOOD (Judgment of sin)	SPREAD OF NATIONS
Gen. 6—9	Gen. 10—11

AGES OF THE PATRIARCHS
(Before and after the Flood)

The patriarchs who lived before the Flood had an average life span of about 900 years (Gen. 5). The ages of post-Flood patriarchs dropped rapidly and gradually leveled off (Gen. 11). Some suggest that this is due to major environmental changes brought about by the Flood.

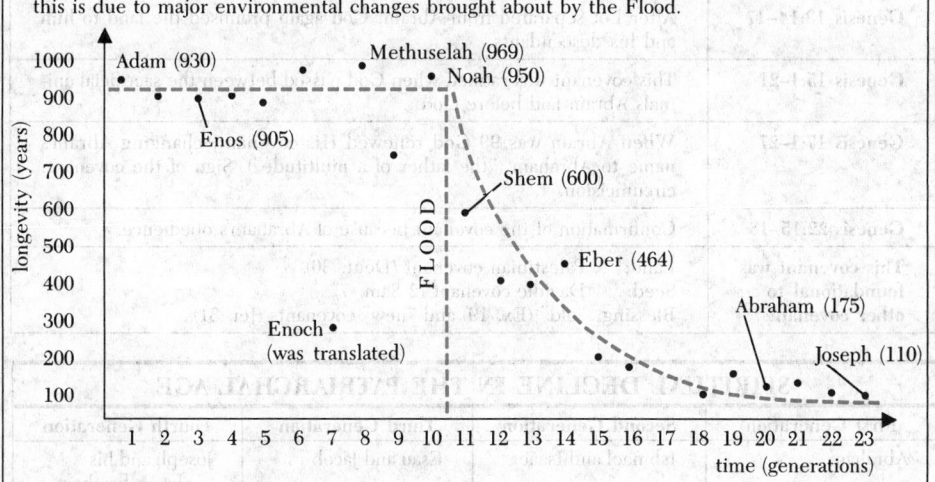

Principle: Righteousness is creative; sin is destructive (Gen. 2:17; Rom. 6:23).

Practice: Genesis 1—11, the prologue not only to Genesis, but to the entire Bible, begins with the ordered and life-giving activity of the holy Creator. The fall of man and the consequent spread of sin stand in stark contrast to the work of God and illustrate the disorder and death that always accompanies rebellion against the purposes of the Lord. God is not mocked; in a moral and spiritual universe, sin must be judged. What must you do, according to Romans 3:21–26, to escape the condemnation of your Creator?

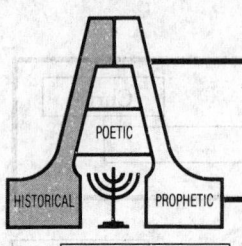

POETIC

HISTORICAL

PROPHETIC

HISTORY OF ISRAEL:

Abraham	Joseph
2000 B.C.	1975 B.C.

THE PEOPLE

THE PATRIARCHS	BONDAGE IN EGYPT

2135 Birth of Abraham	1991 Beginning of Egyptian Middle Kingdom	Jacob Enters Egypt with His Family	1790 Code of Hammurabi

THE ABRAHAMIC COVENANT

Genesis 12:1–3	God initiated His covenant with Abram when he was living in Ur of the Chaldeans, promising a land, descendants, and blessing.
Genesis 12:4, 5	Abram went with his family to Haran, lived there for a time, and left at the age of 75.
Genesis 13:14–17	After Lot separated from Abram, God again promised the land to him and his descendants.
Genesis 15:1–21	This covenant was ratified when God passed between the sacrificial animals Abram laid before God.
Genesis 17:1–27	When Abram was 99 God renewed His covenant, changing Abram's name to Abraham ("the father of a multitude"). Sign of the covenant: circumcision.
Genesis 22:15–18	Confirmation of the covenant because of Abraham's obedience.
This covenant was foundational to other covenants.	Land: Palestinian covenant (Deut. 30). Seed: Davidic covenant (2 Sam. 7). Blessing: "old" (Ex. 19) and "new" covenants (Jer. 31).

SPIRITUAL DECLINE IN THE PATRIARCHAL AGE

First Generation	Second Generation	Third Generation	Fourth Generation
Abraham	Ishmael and Isaac	Esau and Jacob	Joseph and his eleven brothers

Abraham:
  man of faith
  believed God
	Ishmael:
	  not son of
	  promise
	Isaac:
	  called on God
	  believed God
		Esau:
		  unspiritual
		  little faith
		Jacob:
		  at first compro-
		  mised, later
		  turned to the
		  Lord
			Joseph:
			  man of God
			  showed faith
			Brothers:
			  treachery, immo-
			  rality, lack of sep-
			  aration from
			  Canaanites

Abraham:
  built altars to
  God (Gen. 12:7,
  8; 13:4, 18; 22:9)
	Isaac:
	  built an altar to
	  God (Gen. 26:25)
		Jacob:
		  built altars to
		  God (Gen. 33:20;
		  35:1, 3, 7)
			No altars were built
			to God in the fourth
			generation

	Moses
	1500 B.C.

430 years until Exodus, Ex. 12:40; Gal. 3:17)

c. 1750	1570	1525	1445
Beginning of Hittite Empire	Beginning of Egyptian New Kingdom	Birth of Moses	The Exodus

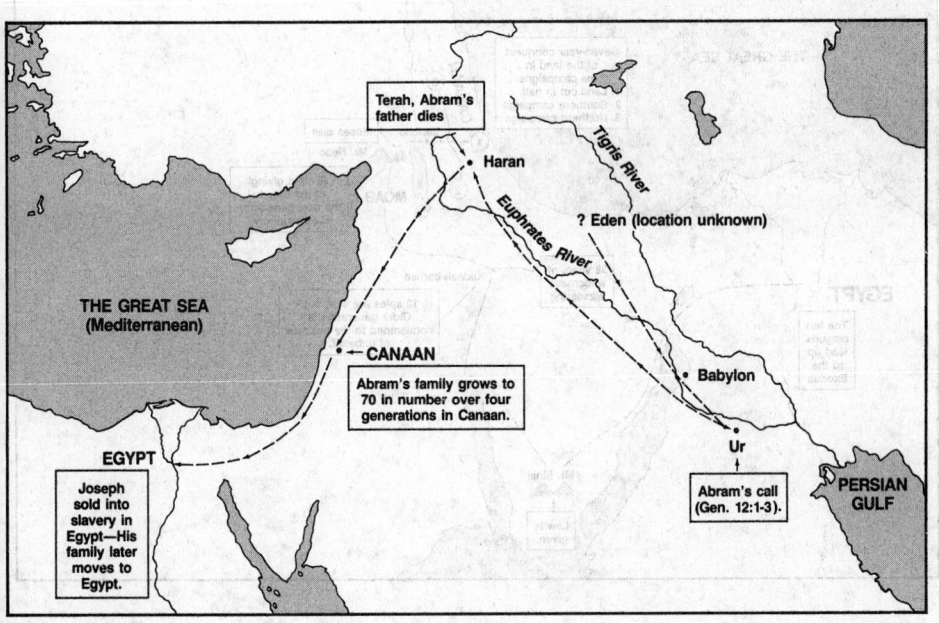

Principle: The destructiveness of sin is overcome by a faith that takes God at His word in spite of appearances and circumstances to the contrary (Gen. 15:6; John 3:16; Heb. 11:8–22).

Practice: Beginning in Genesis 12, God drew forth a man who would be the father of the people from whom and to whom the Messiah would come. Abraham became a friend of God through faith. In spite of appearances to the contrary, he went to a land he had not seen, believed God's promise of a son, and offered up that son at the same area where God's own Son would be crucified. Because he believed God, his faith was accounted to him for righteousness. In the same way, you can enter into a relationship with God by placing your trust in the person and work of His Son. Have you made that decision?

917

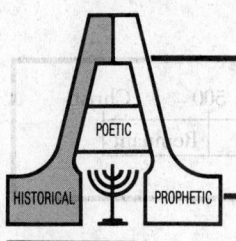

POETIC

HISTORICAL

PROPHETIC

HISTORY OF ISRAEL:

Moses
1500 B.C.

⟶ Shang Dynasty c. 1000 ⟶
⟶ Mycenaean Civilization c. 1100 ⟶

THE LAND

EXODUS	CONQUEST	PERIOD OF THE JUDGES

1445   1405   1398
1450 ——————— 1423   Reign of Amenhotep II of Egypt

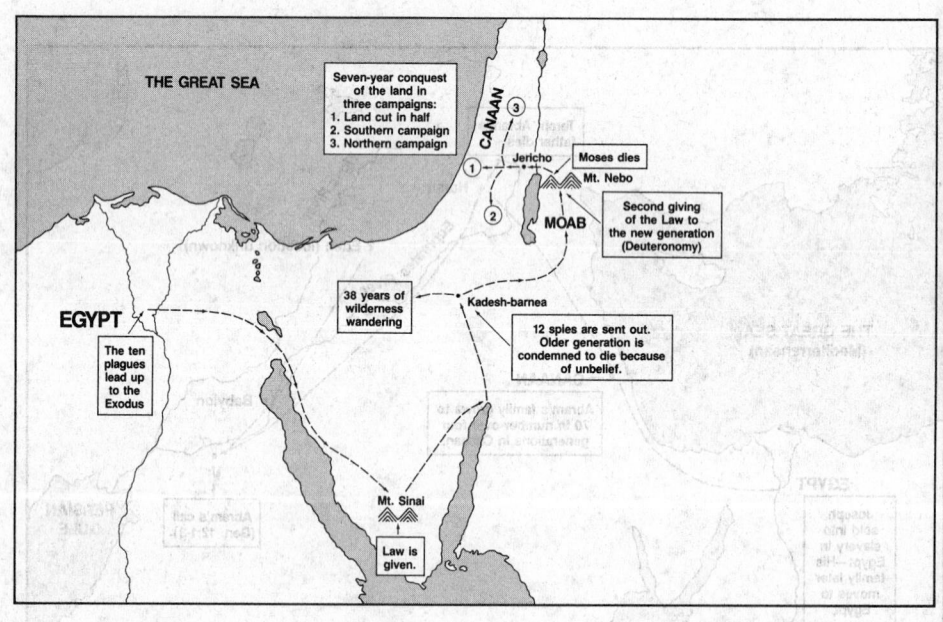

THE GREAT SEA

Seven-year conquest
of the land in
three campaigns:
1. Land cut in half
2. Southern campaign
3. Northern campaign

CANAAN

③

①   Jericho   Moses dies
            Mt. Nebo

②   MOAB   Second giving
                of the Law to
                the new generation
                (Deuteronomy)

EGYPT

The ten
plagues
lead up
to the
Exodus

38 years of
wilderness
wandering   Kadesh-barnea

12 spies are sent out.
Older generation is
condemned to die because
of unbelief.

Mt. Sinai

Law is
given.

Principle: Revelation demands obedience, and obedience brings blessing (Deut. 6:1–15; Josh. 1:8; John 15:12–17).

Practice: After redeeming His people from bondage, the Lord spoke to them in power and glory at Mt. Sinai. The revelation of the Mosaic law required a response of obedience. Their success as individuals and as a nation would depend on the degree of their conformity to God's moral, civil, and ceremonial law. Likewise, disobedience would lead to disaster (e.g., the wilderness wandering and servitude in the time of the Judges). As believers in Christ, our success is measured by the degree of our conformity to His character. To what extent is Christ the Lord of your life?

918

THE LAND		2000	1500	1000	500	Christ
			People	Land	Kingdom	Remnant

	Samuel	David
	1105–1020	1000 B.C.

c. 1100 Greek Dark Ages ⟶

1191
Gideon beats Midianites

1043
Saul anointed King

THE LAW After their deliverance from Egyptian bondage, the children of Israel needed to learn to walk with their God. The Law was given to instruct the people about the person and the ways of their Redeemer so that they could be set apart to a life of holiness and obedience, not to save anyone but to reveal the people's need to trust in the Lord. As Paul told the Galatians, "Wherefore the law was our schoolmaster to bring us unto Christ, that we might be justified by faith (Gal. 3:24).

The Law combines poetry, salvation history, legislation, and exhortation. The three major divisions of the Law (Deut. 4:44) are the testimonies (moral duties), the statutes (ceremonial duties), and the judgments or ordinances (civil and social duties). The moral portion of the Law is summarized in the Ten Commandments (Ex. 20:1–17; Deut. 5:6–21):

THE TEN COMMANDMENTS (Moral Law)

1–4	Duties to God	"Thou shalt love the Lord thy God" (Matt. 22:37).
5–10	Duties to man	"Thou shalt love thy neighbour" (Matt. 22:39).

THE JUDGES: A CASE STUDY IN DISOBEDIENCE

Each of the seven cycles found in Judges 3:5—16:31 has five steps: sin, servitude, supplication, salvation, and silence. The cycles connect as a descending spiral of sin (2:19), with Israel vacillating between obedience and apostasy.

Cycle	Oppressor	Years of Oppression	Judge/Deliverer	Years of Peace
1. (3:7–11)	Mesopotamians	8	Othniel	40
2. (3:12–30)	Moabites	18	Ehud	80
(3:31)	Philistines		Shamgar	
3. (4:1—5:31)	Canaanites	20	Deborah/Barak	40
4. (6:1—8:32)	Midianites	7	Gideon	40
5. (8:33—10:5)	Abimelech	3	Tola/Jair	45
6. (10:6—12:15)	Ammonites	18	Jephthah/Ibzan/Elon/Abdon	6/7/10/8
7. (13:1—16:31)	Philistines	40	Samson	20

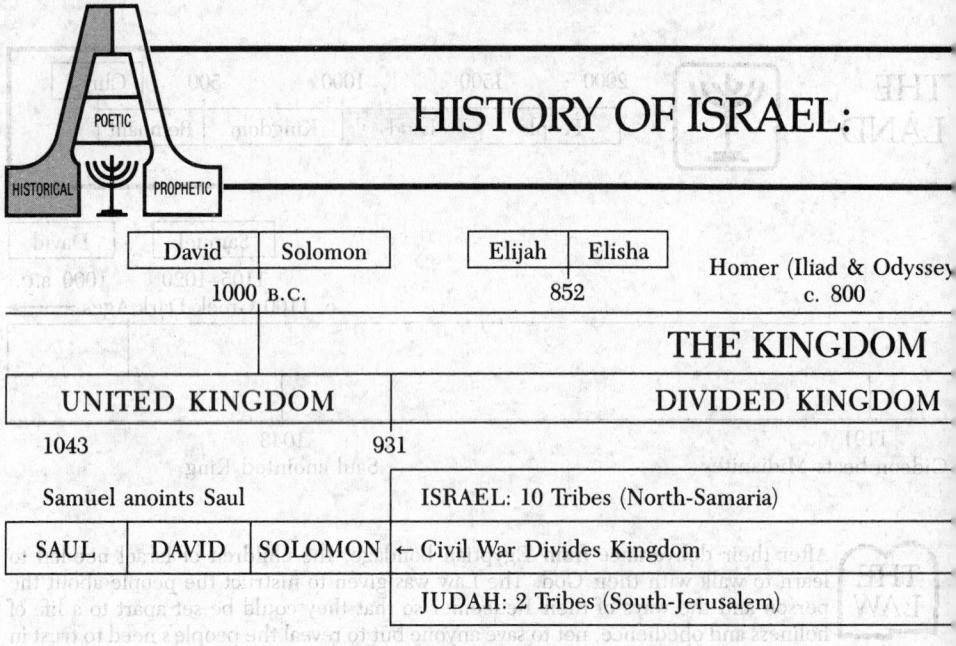

HISTORY OF ISRAEL:

David	Solomon		Elijah	Elisha	Homer (Iliad & Odyssey)
1000 B.C.			852		c. 800

THE KINGDOM

UNITED KINGDOM	DIVIDED KINGDOM
1043 931	
Samuel anoints Saul	ISRAEL: 10 Tribes (North-Samaria)
SAUL DAVID SOLOMON	← Civil War Divides Kingdom
	JUDAH: 2 Tribes (South-Jerusalem)

THE LIFE OF DAVID: A Man after God's own heart

1041 B.C.				1011			971 B.C.
DAVID'S 70 YEARS							
David as Subject (30 Years)				David as King (40 Years)			
As a son to his father	As a servant to King Saul			King over the South		King over all 12 tribes	
	His rise over Saul	Rejected by Saul	Refuge with Philistines	Growing		Growing	
	17–18	19–26	27–31	⟍Success			Crisis⟍
Psalms	1 Samuel			2 Samuel			1 Kings
23	17	19:1–10	31	7	11 14–18 24		2:10

David the Shepherd	Kills Goliath		Saul and Jonathan killed at Gilboa	Promise of Christ		Absalom's Rebellion	David Dies
		Protected by Jonathan			Sins with Bathsheba	David's Census	

Principle: Obedience grows out of a heart for God (Deut. 6:5; 1 Sam. 13:14; 1 Chr. 28:9; Acts 13:22).

Practice: Saul and David are a study in contrasts. The key to Saul's failure was his lack of a heart for God; the key to David's greatness was his obvious love for the Lord. David's relationship with God became the standard by which all the kings of Judah would be measured. To know God is to love Him, and to love Him is to desire to obey Him. Read Psalms 23 as a model of a man who was intimate with God. What are the things that may be hindering your growth in the knowledge of God?

THE
KINGDOM

2000	1500	1000	500	Christ
People	Land	Kingdom	Remnant	

Rome Founded
753

Births of Buddha, Confucius
563   551

Ezra

500 B.C.

	EXILE	RETURN
722	586	516

← Assyria Conquers Israel

Babylon Conquers Judah →

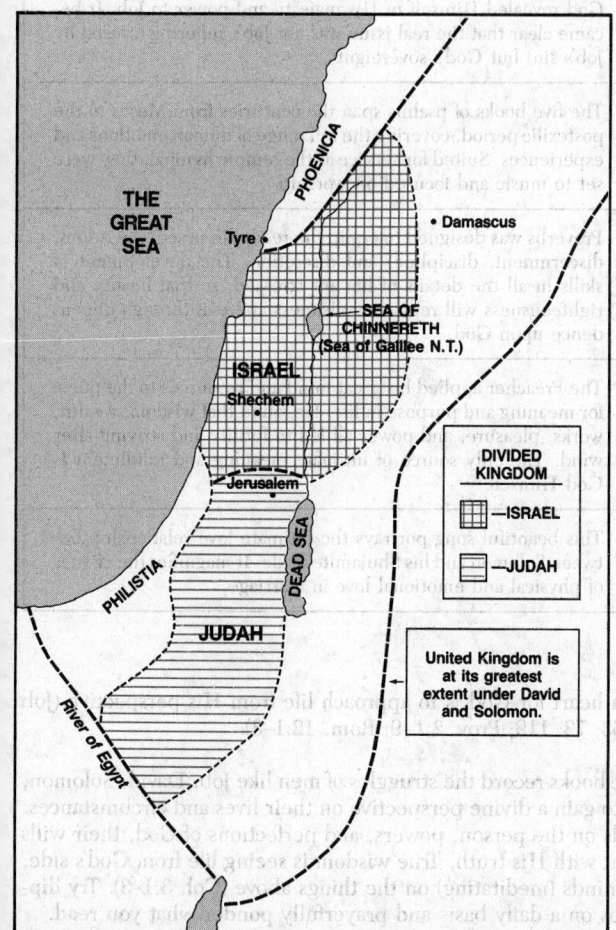

THE
GREAT
SEA

Tyre

PHOENICIA

• Damascus

SEA OF
CHINNERETH
(Sea of Galilee N.T.)

ISRAEL
Shechem

Jerusalem

DEAD SEA

PHILISTIA

JUDAH

River of Egypt

DIVIDED
KINGDOM

—ISRAEL

—JUDAH

United Kingdom is
at its greatest
extent under David
and Solomon.

KINGS OF ISRAEL
1. Jeroboam I
2. Nadab
3. Baasha
4. Elah
5. Zimri
6. Omri
7. Ahab
8. Ahaziah
9. Jehoram
10. Jehu
11. Jehoahaz
12. Jehoash
13. Jeroboam II
14. Zachariah
15. Shallum
16. Menahem
17. Pekahiah
18. Pekah
19. Hoshea

KINGS OF JUDAH
1. Rehoboam
2. Abijam
3. Asa
4. Jehoshaphat
5. Jehoram
6. Ahaziah
7. Athaliah
8. Joash
9. Amaziah
10. Azariah
11. Jotham
12. Ahaz
13. Hezekiah
14. Manasseh
15. Amon
16. Josiah
17. Jehoahaz
18. Jehoiakim
19. Jehoiachin
20. Zedekiah

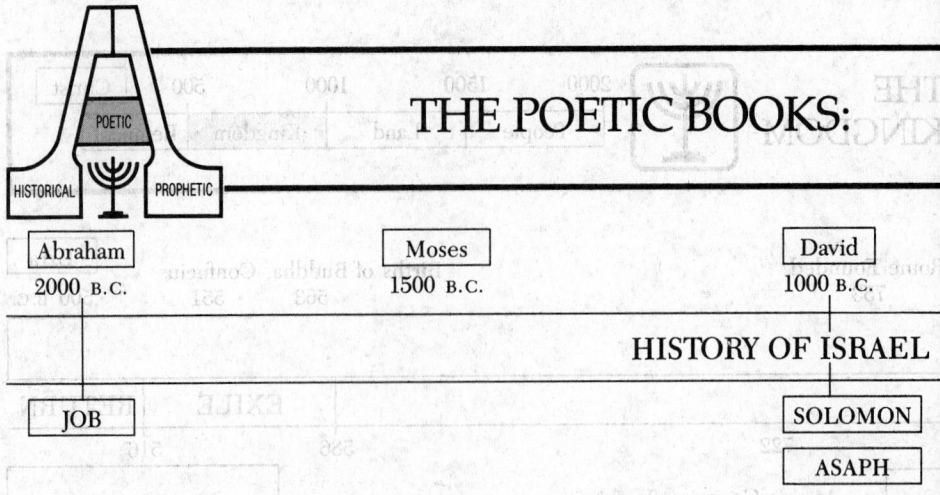

THE POETIC BOOKS:

Abraham	Moses	David
2000 B.C.	1500 B.C.	1000 B.C.

HISTORY OF ISRAEL

JOB		SOLOMON
		ASAPH

THEMES OF THE POETIC BOOKS

BOOK	KEY WORD	THEME
Job	Sovereignty	God revealed Himself in His majesty and power to Job. It became clear that the real issue was not Job's suffering (caused by Job's sin) but God's sovereignty.
Psalms	Worship	The five books of psalms span the centuries from Moses to the postexilic period, covering the full range of human emotions and experiences. Suited for service as the temple hymnal, they were set to music and focused on worship.
Proverbs	Wisdom	Proverbs was designed to equip the reader in practical wisdom, discernment, discipline, and discretion. The development of skills in all the details of life are stressed, so that beauty and righteousness will replace foolishness and evil through dependence upon God.
Ecclesiastes	Vanity	The Preacher applied his great mind and resources to the quest for meaning and purpose in life. He found that wisdom, wealth, works, pleasure, and power all led to futility and striving after wind. The only source of ultimate meaning and fulfillment is God Himself.
Song of Solomon	Love in Marriage	This beautiful song portrays the intimate love relationship between Solomon and his Shulamite bride. It magnifies the virtues of physical and emotional love in marriage.

Principle: To have a heart for God is to approach life from His perspective (Job 42:1-6; Ps. 1; 19; 63; 73; 119; Prov. 2:1-9; Rom. 12:1-3).

Practice: The poetic books record the struggles of men like Job, David, Solomon, Asaph, and others to gain a divine perspective on their lives and circumstances. As they learned to set their minds on the person, powers, and perfections of God, their wills and emotions came into alignment with His truth. True wisdom is seeing life from God's side, and this is rooted in setting our minds (meditating) on the things above (Col. 3:1-3). Try dipping into the Psalms and Proverbs on a daily basis and prayerfully ponder what you read.

THE HEART OF THE JEWS

Ezra		Christ
500 B.C.		4 B.C.

THE PATH TO TRUE SUCCESS

Question	Principle
1. What is wisdom?	Wisdom is the key to a life of beauty, fulfillment, and purpose (Prov. 3:15–18). Wisdom is the skill in the art of living life with every area under the dominion of God. It is the ability to use the best means at the best time to accomplish the best ends.
2. How do we pursue wisdom?	The treasure of wisdom rests in the hands of God. Since it comes from above (Prov. 2:6; cf. James 3:17), we cannot attain it apart from Him.
3. What are the conditions for attaining wisdom?	True wisdom can only be gained by cultivating the fear of the Lord (Job 28:28; Ps. 86:11; 111:10; Prov. 1:7; 9:10).
4. What is the fear of the Lord?	To fear God is to have an attitude of awe and humility before Him (Prov. 15:33). It is to recognize Him as our Creator and our complete dependence upon Him in every activity of our lives.
5. Why have so few people developed this fear of God?	The temporal value system of this world is based on what is seen, while the eternal value system of Scripture is based on what is unseen (2 Cor. 4:16–18; 5:7). The former exerts a powerful influence upon us, and we struggle with giving up the seen for the unseen.
6. What can enable us to choose the eternal value system?	This choice is based on faith (believing God in spite of appearances and circumstances), and faith is based on trust.
7. How do we grow in faith?	Our ability to trust God is directly proportional to our knowledge of God. The better we know Him, the more we can trust Him.
8. How can we increase in our knowledge of God?	We become intimate with God as we talk with Him in prayer and listen to His voice in Scripture. The better we know God, the more we love Him and want to respond to His desires for our lives. Faith in God is simply trusting Him as a person, and trust is manifested in action.

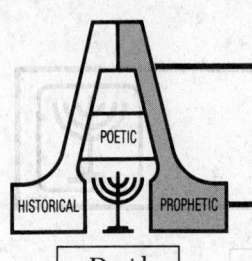

POETIC

HISTORICAL   PROPHETIC

THE PROPHETIC BOOKS:

David		Elijah	Elisha		Zerubbabel	Ezra	Nehemiah
1000 B.C.			852			500	

THE KINGDOM

UNITED KINGDOM	DIVIDED KINGDOM	EXILE	RETURN

	ISRAEL	← 722	70	3 stage return
UNITED KINGDOM	← 931		Years in	1st Zerubbabel
		586 →	Babylon	2nd Ezra
	JUDAH			3rd Nehemiah

PROPHETS BEFORE THE EXILE		EXILE PROPHETS	PROPHETS AFTER THE EXILE
To Israel:	To Judah:	To Jews in Babylon:	To the Remnant after returning:
Amos (760)	Joel (835)	Daniel (605)	
Hosea (755)	Isaiah (740)	Ezekiel (592)	Haggai (520)
	Micah (735)		Zechariah (520)
To Nineveh:	Zephaniah (630)		Malachi (432)
	Jeremiah (627)		
Jonah (760)	Habakkuk (607)		
Nahum (660)	Lamentations (586)		
To Edom:			
Obadiah (840)			

Principle: God's disciplines are designed to restore a heart for Himself (Jer. 17:5, 7; Joel 2:12, 13; Heb. 12:5–11).

Practice: God had to discipline His people because of their moral and spiritual rebellion and their refusal to heed the warnings of His prophets. Reproof is designed to bring repentance and repentance brings restoration. The same prophets who pronounced the condemnation of God also announced the consolation of God. Similarly, because God loves us, He must sometimes chasten us as His children to train us in the ways of righteousness. How do you respond during these times? Are you teachable or intractable?

924

THE HOPE OF THE JEWS

Christ
4 B.C.

THE REMNANT
400 YEARS UNTIL CHRIST

415

THEMES OF THE PROPHETIC BOOKS

The Major Prophets

BOOK	KEY WORD	THEME
Isaiah	Salvation Is of the Lord	Twofold message of condemnation (1–39) and consolation (40–66). God's judgment on the sins of Judah, the surrounding nations, and the world, followed by future salvation and restoration.
Jeremiah	Judah's Last Hour	Declaration of certain judgment of God against Judah. God promises to establish a new covenant with His people.
Lamenta-tions	Lamentations	This beautifully structured series of five lament poems is a funeral dirge for the fallen city of Jerusalem.
Ezekiel	Future Resto-ration	Ministry to the Jewish captives in Babylon before and after the fall of Jerusalem. The fate of Judah's foes and an apocalyptic vision of Judah's future.
Daniel	God's Program for Israel	Outlines God's plan for the gentile nations (2–7) and portrays Israel during the time of gentile domination (8–12).

The Minor Prophets

BOOK	KEY WORD	THEME
Hosea	God's Love for Israel	The story of Hosea and his faithless wife illustrates the loyal love of God and the spiritual adultery of Israel.
Joel	Day of the Lord	A recent locust plague illustrates the far more terrifying day of the Lord. God appeals to the people to repent in order to avert the coming disaster.
Amos	Judgment of Israel	In eight pronouncements of judgment, Amos spirals around the surrounding countries before landing on Israel. He lists the sins of Israel and calls for repentance.
Obadiah	Judgment of Edom	Condemns the nation of Edom (descended from Esau) for refusing to act as a brother toward Judah (descended from Jacob).
Jonah	Revival in Nineveh	The repentant response of the people of Nineveh to Jonah's one-line prophetic message caused the God of mercy to spare the city.
Micah	Judgment and Restoration of Judah	In spite of divine retribution against the corruption of Israel and Judah, God's covenant with them will be fulfilled in Messiah's future kingdom.
Nahum	Judgment of Nineveh	About 125 years after Nineveh repented under the preaching of Jonah, Micah predicted the destruction of the city because of its idolatry and brutality.
Habak-kuk	Live by Faith	Troubled with God's plan to use the Babylonians as His rod of judgment on Judah, Habakkuk praises the Lord after gaining a better perspective on His power and purposes.
Zepha-niah	Day of the Lord	The coming day of the Lord is a time of awesome judgment followed by great blessing. Judah stands con-demned, but God will restore the fortunes of the remnant.
Haggai	Reconstruction of the Temple	After the Babylonian exile, Haggai urges the Jews to put God first and finish the Temple they had begun so that they can enjoy God's blessing.
Zecha-riah	Prepare for the Messiah	Like Haggai, Zechariah exhorts the Jews to complete the construction of the Temple. He relates it to the coming of Messiah in a series of visions and messianic prophecies.
Malachi	Appeal to Backsliders	The spiritual climate of the people had grown cold, and Malachi rebukes them for their religious and social compromise. If they return to God with sincere hearts, they will be blessed.

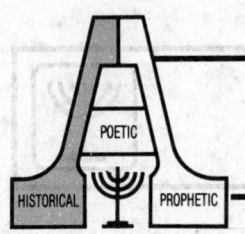

POETIC

HISTORICAL · PROPHETIC

HISTORY OF ISRAEL: THE REMNANT

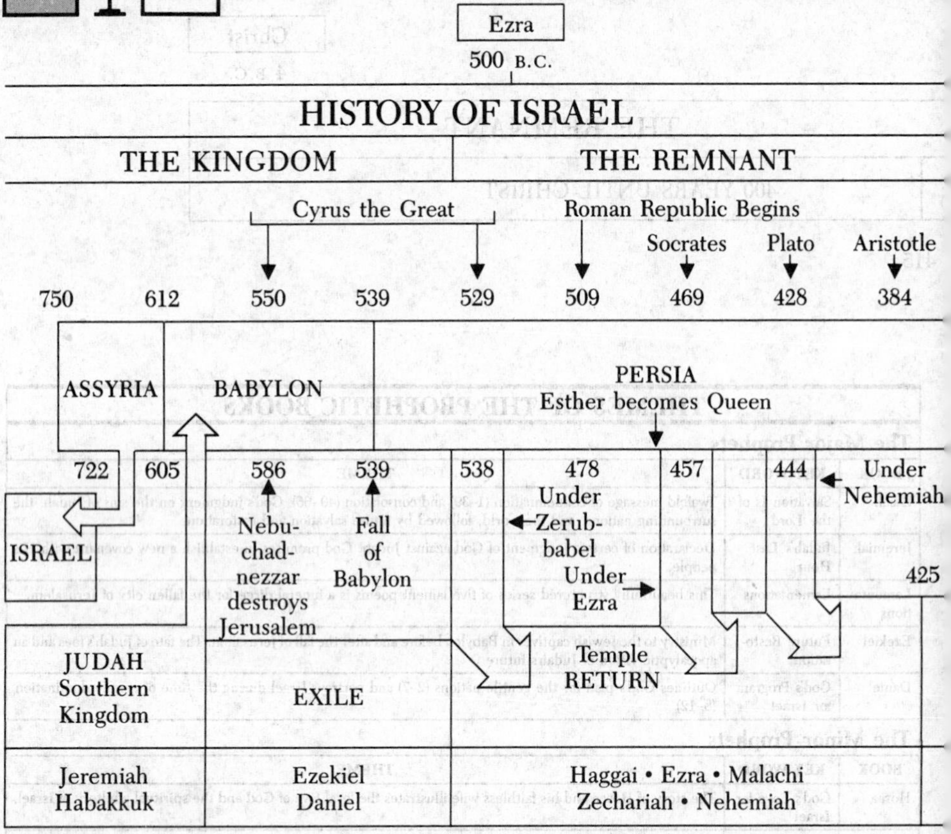

Ezra
500 B.C.

HISTORY OF ISRAEL

THE KINGDOM	THE REMNANT

Cyrus the Great

Roman Republic Begins

Socrates · Plato · Aristotle

750	612	550	539	529	509	469	428	384

ASSYRIA	BABYLON	PERSIA

Esther becomes Queen

722	605	586	539	538	478	457	444	Under Nehemiah

ISRAEL

Nebu-chad-nezzar destroys Jerusalem

Fall of Babylon

Under Zerub-babel

Under Ezra

425

JUDAH Southern Kingdom	EXILE	Temple RETURN

Jeremiah Habakkuk	Ezekiel Daniel	Haggai · Ezra · Malachi Zechariah · Nehemiah

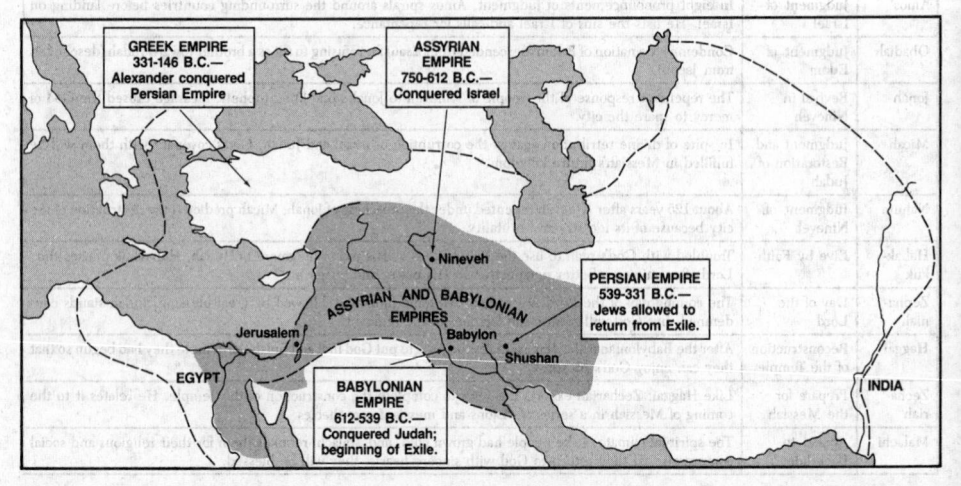

GREEK EMPIRE
331-146 B.C.—
Alexander conquered
Persian Empire

ASSYRIAN
EMPIRE
750-612 B.C.—
Conquered Israel

• Nineveh

ASSYRIAN AND BABYLONIAN EMPIRES

Jerusalem

Babylon

• Shushan

PERSIAN EMPIRE
539-331 B.C.—
Jews allowed to
return from Exile.

EGYPT

BABYLONIAN
EMPIRE
612-539 B.C.—
Conquered Judah;
beginning of Exile.

INDIA

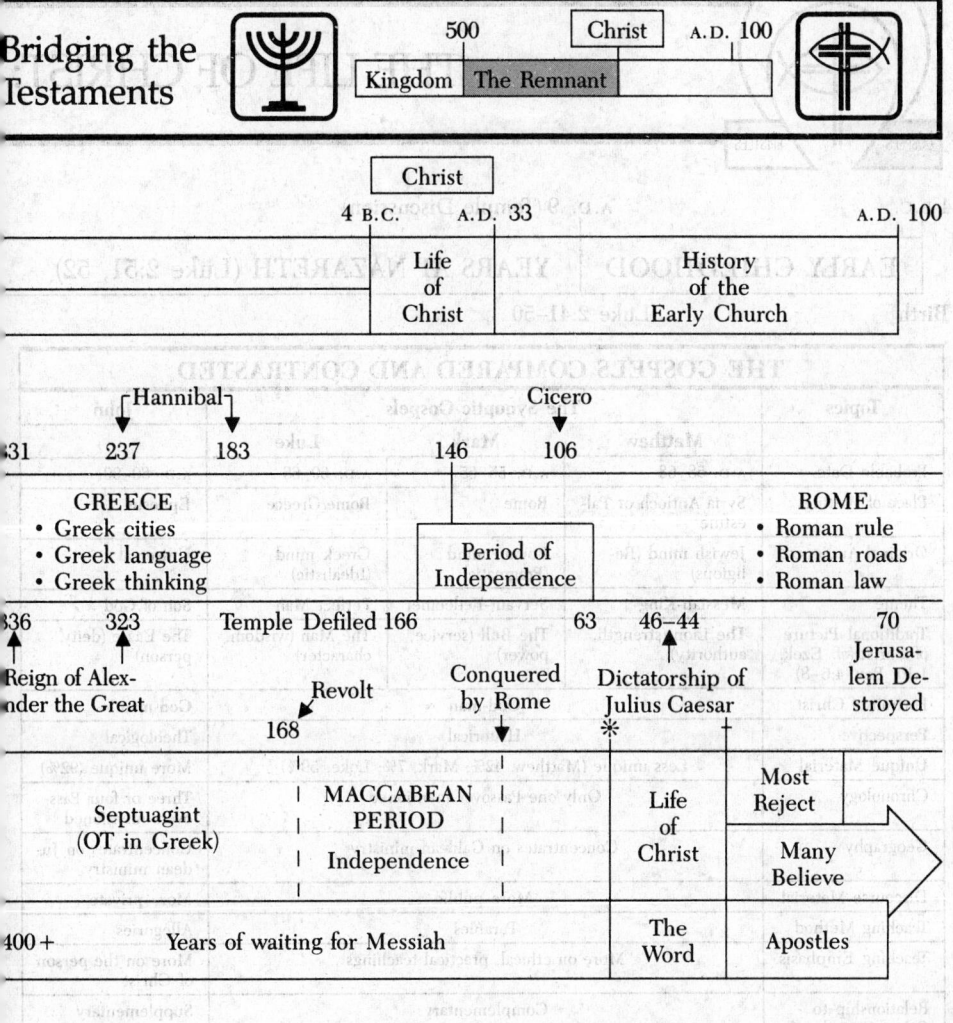

Bridging the Testaments

		500		Christ	A.D. 100
		Kingdom	The Remnant		

Christom

	Christ					
	4 B.C.	A.D. 33				A.D. 100
	Life of Christ		History of the Early Church			

Hannibal			Cicero		
31	237	183	146	106	

GREECE		Period of Independence		ROME	
• Greek cities				• Roman rule	
• Greek language				• Roman roads	
• Greek thinking				• Roman law	

36	323	Temple Defiled 166		63	46–44	70
Reign of Alexander the Great		Revolt 168	Conquered by Rome	Dictatorship of Julius Caesar *		Jerusalem Destroyed

Septuagint (OT in Greek)	MACCABEAN PERIOD Independence	Life of Christ	Most Reject / Many Believe
400 + Years of waiting for Messiah		The Word	Apostles

Principle: True restoration results from being molded by the Word within rather than the world without (Ezra 7:10; 9:10–15; Is. 46:3, 4; Acts 7:51–53).

Practice: Even after the chastening of the Exile, most of the returning Jews became enmeshed once again in the affairs of the world and neglected their relationship with God. For some, the problem was external religiosity without internal reality; for others, the problem was being more influenced by culture than Scripture. God has always had to work with a faithful minority who love Him enough to stand against the tide of the world system. Is your quality of life different from that of those who love the world more than the Lord?

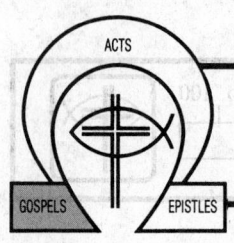

THE LIFE OF CHRIST:

4 B.C.   A.D. 9 (Temple Discussion)

EARLY CHILDHOOD	YEARS AT NAZARETH (Luke 2:51, 52)
Birth	Luke 2:41–50

THE GOSPELS COMPARED AND CONTRASTED

Topics	The Synoptic Gospels			John
	Matthew	Mark	Luke	
Probable Date	A.D. 58–68	A.D. 55–65	A.D. 60–68	A.D. 80–90
Place of Writing	Syria Antioch or Palestine	Rome	Rome/Greece	Ephesus
Original Audience	Jewish mind (Religious)	Roman mind (Pragmatic)	Greek mind (Idealistic)	Universal
Theme	Messiah-King	Servant-Redeemer	Perfect Man	Son of God
Traditional Picture of Christ (cf. Ezek. 1:10; Rev. 4:6–8)	The Lion (strength, authority)	The Bull (service, power)	The Man (wisdom, character)	The Eagle (deity, person)
Portrait of Christ	God-man			God-man
Perspective	Historical			Theological
Unique Material	Less unique (Matthew, 42%; Mark, 7%; Luke, 59%)			More unique (92%)
Chronology	Only one Passover mentioned			Three or four Passovers mentioned
Geography	Concentrates on Galilean ministry			Concentrates on Judean ministry
Discourse Material	More public			More private
Teaching Method	Parables			Allegories
Teaching Emphasis	More on ethical, practical teachings			More on the person of Christ
Relationship to Other Gospels	Complementary			Supplementary

CHRIST'S PUBLIC MINISTRY

Masses drawn to His miracles and teachings →

Popularity peaks

Leaders attribute His miracles

A.D. 29	30	31
Opening events	Early Judaean ministry	Great Galilean ministry
Year of curious acceptance		Year of growing hostility

↑ Baptized by John Matt. 3

↑ First miracle John 2

↑ Nicodemus learns of new birth John 3

↑ Woman at well John 4

↑ Rejected at Nazareth Luke 4

↑ Apostles selected Mark 3

Sermon on Mount Matt. 5—7

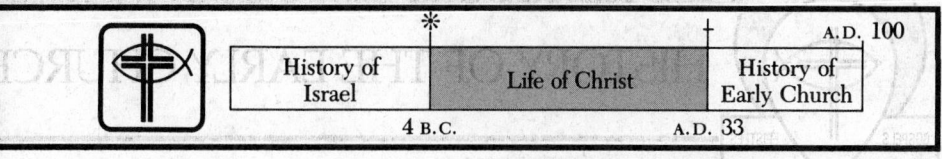

A.D. 29   A.D. 33

PUBLIC MINISTRY

Principle: Jesus, the living Word, lives His life in and through us as we walk in dependence upon Him (John 1:11, 12; 10:10; 15:4, 5; Gal. 2:20).

Practice: In Christ, God personally revealed Himself in human flesh: to see Him is to see God (John 12:45; 14:9), to know Him is to know God (John 8:19), to receive Him is to receive God (Mark 9:37), to honor Him is to honor God (John 5:23), and to reject Him is to reject God (Luke 10:16). He is the vine, the source of life; we are the branches, the channels of life. It is only as we draw our life from Him that we bear lasting fruit. To what extent are you looking to Jesus as the true source of your security, significance, and fulfillment?

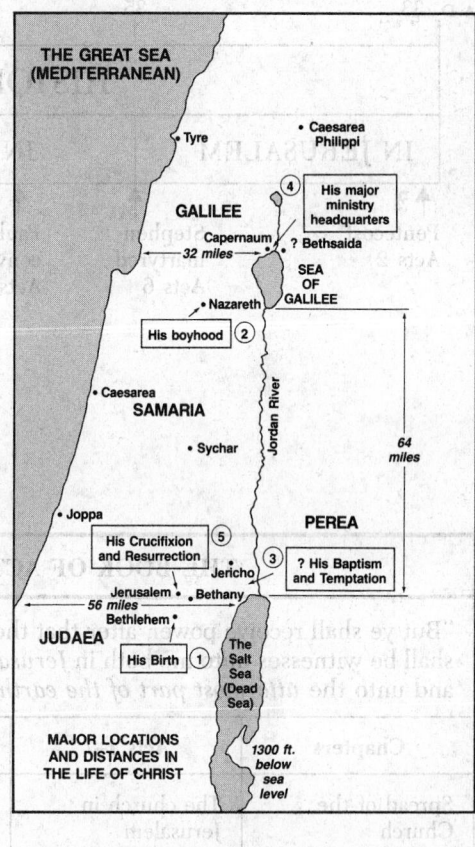

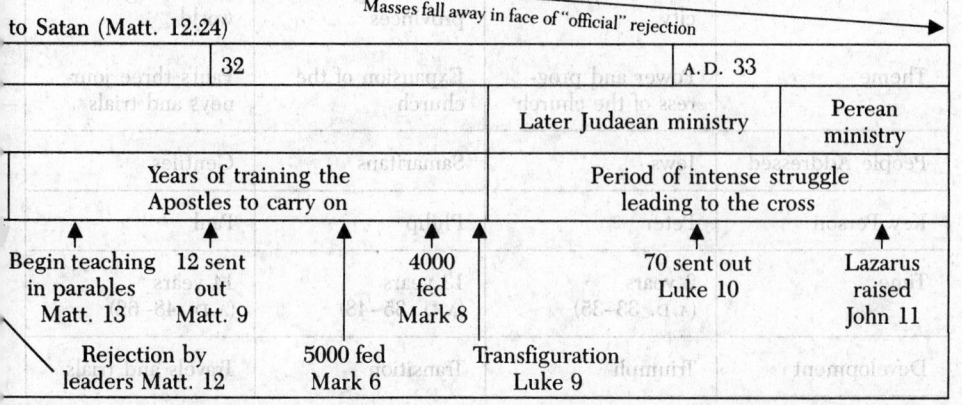

to Satan (Matt. 12:24)   Masses fall away in face of "official" rejection

32		A.D. 33	
		Later Judaean ministry	Perean ministry
Years of training the Apostles to carry on		Period of intense struggle leading to the cross	

| Begin teaching in parables Matt. 13 | 12 sent out Matt. 9 | 4000 fed Mark 8 | 70 sent out Luke 10 | Lazarus raised John 11 |
| Rejection by leaders Matt. 12 | 5000 fed Mark 6 | Transfiguration Luke 9 | | |

929

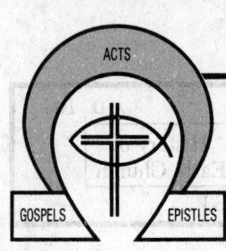

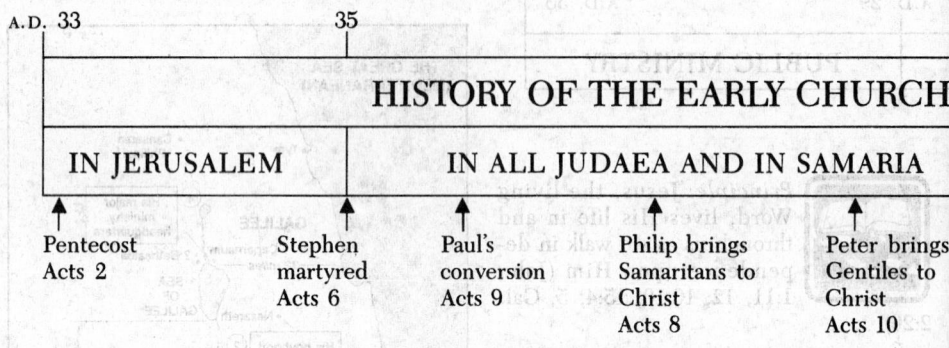

A.D. 33 ———————————— 35

HISTORY OF THE EARLY CHURCH

IN JERUSALEM	IN ALL JUDAEA AND IN SAMARIA

↑ Pentecost
Acts 2

↑ Stephen
martyred
Acts 6

↑ Paul's
conversion
Acts 9

↑ Philip brings
Samaritans to
Christ
Acts 8

↑ Peter brings
Gentiles to
Christ
Acts 10

THE BOOK OF ACTS IN OVERVIEW

"But ye shall receive power, after that the Holy Ghost is come upon you: and ye shall be witnesses unto me both in *Jerusalem*, and in all *Judaea*, and in *Samaria*, and unto the *uttermost part of the earth*" (Acts 1:8).

Chapters	Acts 1–7	Acts 8–12	Acts 13–28
Spread of the Church	The church in Jerusalem	The church in all Judaea and Samaria	The church to all the earth
The Gospel	Witnessing in the city	Witnessing in the provinces	Witnessing in the world
Theme	Power and progress of the church	Expansion of the church	Paul's three journeys and trials
People Addressed	Jews	Samaritans	Gentiles
Key Person	Peter	Philip	Paul
Time	2 years (A.D. 33–35)	13 years (A.D. 35–48)	14 years (A.D. 48–62)
Development	Triumph	Transition	Travels and trials

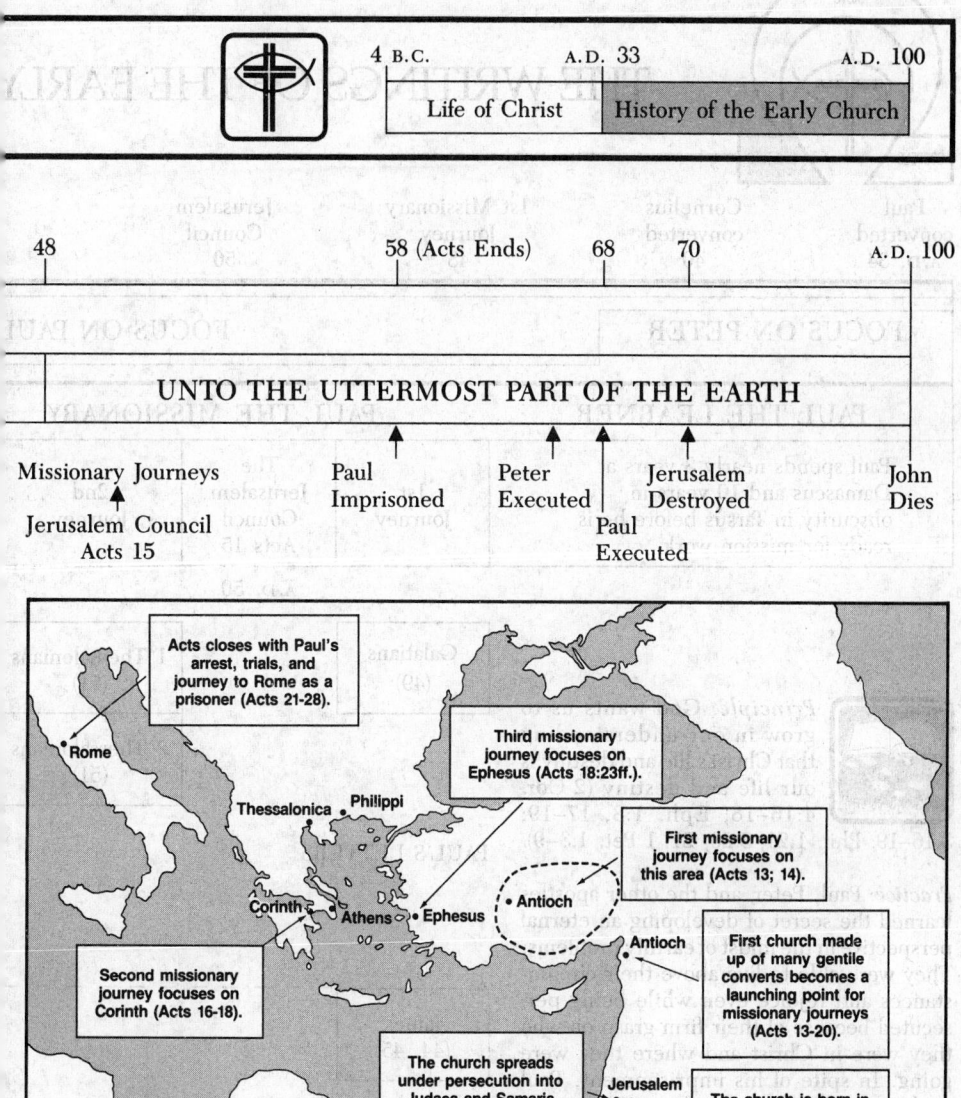

4 B.C.	A.D. 33	A.D. 100
Life of Christ	History of the Early Church	

48	58 (Acts Ends)	68	70	A.D. 100

UNTO THE UTTERMOST PART OF THE EARTH

Missionary Journeys
▲
Jerusalem Council
Acts 15

Paul
Imprisoned

Peter
Executed

Jerusalem
Destroyed
Paul
Executed

John
Dies

Acts closes with Paul's arrest, trials, and journey to Rome as a prisoner (Acts 21-28).

• Rome

Third missionary journey focuses on Ephesus (Acts 18:23ff.).

Thessalonica • Philippi

First missionary journey focuses on this area (Acts 13; 14).

Corinth • Athens • Ephesus • Antioch

• Antioch

First church made up of many gentile converts becomes a launching point for missionary journeys (Acts 13-20).

Second missionary journey focuses on Corinth (Acts 16-18).

The church spreads under persecution into Judaea and Samaria (Acts 8-12).

Jerusalem

The church is born in Jerusalem (Acts 2).

Principle: Christ's life is reproduced in others when we take the initiative to witness in the power of the Holy Spirit (Matt. 28:18–20; Acts 1:8; Col. 4:2–6).

Practice: The Book of Acts records the spread of the gospel from the city of Jerusalem to the whole province of Judea and Samaria, and ultimately through the Roman Empire and beyond. These first-century Christians were sold out for the cause of Christ and transformed their world as their lives became living epistles of the Good News. God has called us to a life-style of evangelism in which we build relationships with non-Christians. These friendships in turn become natural bridges for communicating the gospel. Take a close look at Colossians 4:2–6 to learn how to become more effective as an instrument of the Holy Spirit to reproduce the life of Christ in others.

931

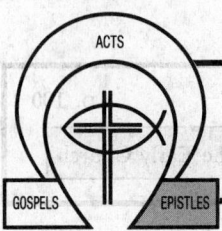

THE WRITINGS OF THE EARLY

Paul converted A.D. 34	Cornelius converted 40	1st Missionary Journey 48	Jerusalem Council 50

FOCUS ON PETER		FOCUS ON PAUL

PAUL THE LEARNER		PAUL THE MISSIONARY	
Paul spends nearly 3 years at Damascus and 10 years in obscurity in Tarsus before he is ready for mission work.	1st Journey	The Jerusalem Council Acts 15	2nd Journey

A.D. 50

Galatians (49)	1 Thessalonians (51)
	2 Thessalonians (51)

Principle: God wants us to grow in our understanding that Christ's life and destiny is our life and destiny (2 Cor. 4:16–18; Eph. 1:3, 17–19; 3:16–19; Phil. 1:21; 3:20, 21; 1 Pet. 1:3–9).

PAUL'S LETTERS

Practice: Paul, Peter, and the other apostles learned the secret of developing an eternal perspective in the midst of earthly problems. They were able to live above their circumstances and rejoice even while being persecuted because of their firm grasp on who they were in Christ and where they were going. In spite of his imprisonment, Paul could write, "For to me, to live is Christ, and to die is gain" (Phil. 1:21). Are you looking more at "the things which are seen" or at "the things which are not seen"? The former are temporary, but the latter are eternal (2 Cor. 4:18).

James
(44, 45)

**LETTERS
BY
OTHERS**

GOSPELS & ACTS

Matthew
(c. 40's)

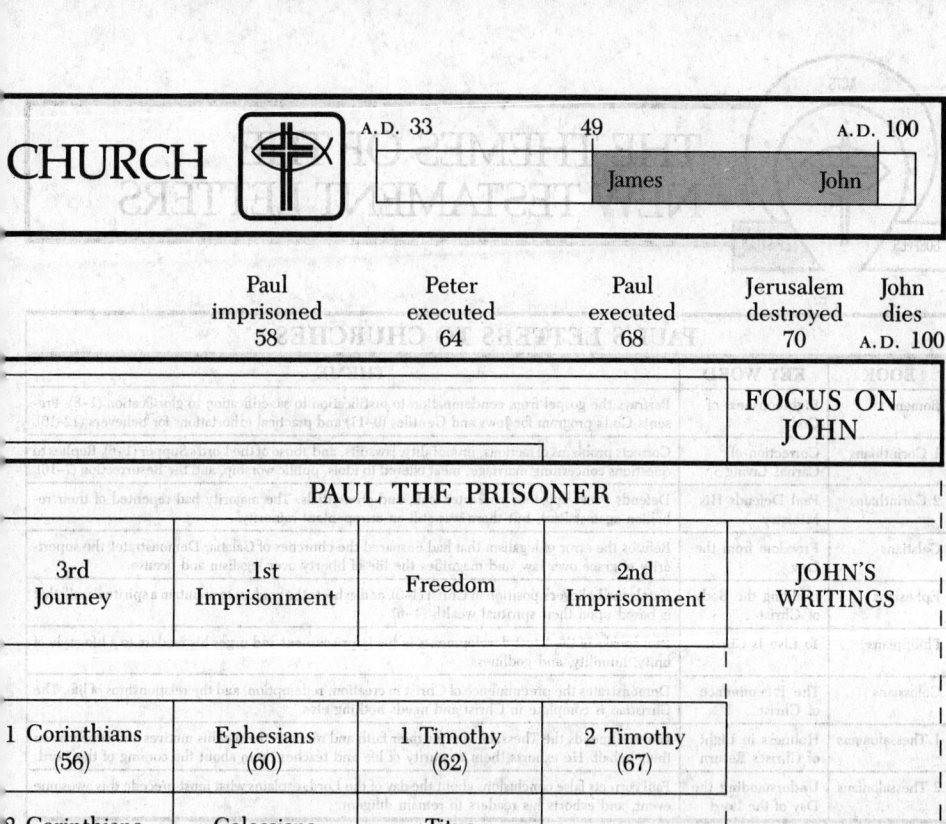

A.D. 33 — 49 — A.D. 100

James — John

| Paul imprisoned 58 | Peter executed 64 | Paul executed 68 | Jerusalem destroyed 70 | John dies A.D. 100 |

FOCUS ON JOHN

PAUL THE PRISONER

3rd Journey	1st Imprisonment	Freedom	2nd Imprisonment	JOHN'S WRITINGS
1 Corinthians (56)	Ephesians (60)	1 Timothy (62)	2 Timothy (67)	
2 Corinthians (56)	Colossians (61)	Titus (66)		
Romans (56, 57)	Philemon (61)			
	Philippians (62)			
		1 Peter (64)	Hebrews (66–69)	1 John (85–90)
		2 Peter (64)	Jude (75)	2 John (85–90)
				3 John (85–90)
				Revelation (95–96)
	Acts (62)			
	Luke (58–60)	Mark (60)		John (65–70)

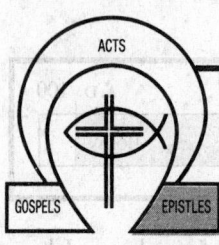

THE THEMES OF THE NEW TESTAMENT LETTERS

PAUL'S LETTERS TO CHURCHES

BOOK	KEY WORD	THEME
Romans	Righteousness of God	Portrays the gospel from condemnation to justification to sanctification to glorification (1–8). Presents God's program for Jews and Gentiles (9–11) and practical exhortations for believers (12–16).
1 Corinthians	Correction of Carnal Living	Corrects problems of factions, immorality, lawsuits, and abuse of the Lord's Supper (1–6). Replies to questions concerning marriage, meat offered to idols, public worship, and the Resurrection (7–16).
2 Corinthians	Paul Defends His Ministry	Defends Paul's apostolic character, call, and credentials. The majority had repented of their rebellion against Paul, but there was still an unrepentant minority.
Galatians	Freedom from the Law	Refutes the error of legalism that had ensnared the churches of Galatia. Demonstrates the superiority of grace over law, and magnifies the life of liberty over legalism and license.
Ephesians	Building the Body of Christ	Extols the believer's position in Christ (1–3), and exhorts the readers to maintain a spiritual walk that is based upon their spiritual wealth (4–6).
Philippians	To Live Is Christ	Paul speaks of the latest developments in his imprisonment and urges his readers to a life-style of unity, humility, and godliness.
Colossians	The Preeminence of Christ	Demonstrates the preeminence of Christ in creation, redemption, and the relationships of life. The Christian is complete in Christ and needs nothing else.
1 Thessalonians	Holiness in Light of Christ's Return	Paul commends the Thessalonians for their faith and reminds them of his motives and concerns on their behalf. He exhorts them to purity of life and teaches them about the coming of the Lord.
2 Thessalonians	Understanding the Day of the Lord	Paul corrects false conclusions about the day of the Lord, explains what must precede this awesome event, and exhorts his readers to remain diligent.

PAUL'S LETTERS TO PEOPLE

BOOK	KEY WORD	THEME
1 Timothy	Leadership Manual for Churches	Paul counsels Timothy on the problems of false teachers, public prayer, the role of women, and the requirements for elders and deacons.
2 Timothy	Endurance in Ministry	A combat manual designed to build up and encourage Timothy to boldness and steadfastness in view of the hardships of the spiritual warfare.
Titus	Conduct Manual for Churches	Lists the requirements for elders and instructs Titus in his duties relative to the various groups in the churches.
Philemon	Forgiveness from Slavery	Paul appeals to Philemon to forgive Onesimus and to regard him no longer as a slave but as a brother in Christ.

LETTERS FROM OTHERS

BOOK	KEY WORD	THEME
Hebrews	Superiority of Christ	Demonstrates the superiority of Christ's person, priesthood, and power over all that preceded Him to encourage the readers to mature and to become stable in their faith.
James	Faith that Works	A practical catalog of the characteristics of true faith written to exhort James' Hebrew-Christian readers to examine the reality of their own faith.
1 Peter	Suffering for Christ	Comfort and counsel to those who were being maligned for their faith in Christ. They are encouraged to develop an attitude of submission in view of their suffering.
2 Peter	Guard Against False Prophets	Copes with internal opposition in the form of false teachers who were enticing believers into their errors of belief and conduct. Appeals for growth in the true knowledge of Christ.
1 John	Fellowship with God	Explores the dimensions of fellowship between redeemed people and God. Believers must walk in His light, manifest His love, and abide in His life.
2 John	Avoid Fellowship with False Teachers	John commends his readers for remaining steadfast in apostolic truth and reminds them to walk in love and avoid false teachers.
3 John	Enjoy Fellowship with the Brethren	John thanks Gaius for his support of traveling teachers of the truth, in contrast to Diotrephes, who rejected them and told others to do the same.
Jude	Contend for the Faith	This expose of false teachers reveals their conduct and character and predicts their judgment. Jude encourages his readers to build themselves up in the truth and contend earnestly for the faith.
Revelation	Revelation of the Coming Christ	The glorified Christ gives seven messages to the church (1–3). Visions of unparalleled judgment upon rebellious mankind are followed by the Second Advent (4–19). The Apocalypse concludes with a description of the new heaven and new earth and the marvels of the new Jerusalem (20–22).

The

New Testament

of

The Open Bible®

EXPANDED EDITION

King James Version

MATTHEW

THE BOOK OF MATTHEW

Matthew is the gospel written by a Jew to Jews about a Jew. Matthew is the writer, his countrymen are the readers, and Jesus Christ is the subject. Matthew's design is to present Jesus as the King of the Jews, the long-awaited Messiah. Through a carefully selected series of Old Testament quotations, Matthew documents Jesus Christ's claim to be Messiah. His genealogy, baptism, messages, and miracles all point to the same inescapable conclusion: Christ is King. Even in His death, seeming defeat is turned to victory by the Resurrection, and the message again echoes forth: the King of the Jews lives.

At an early date this gospel was given the title *Kata Matthaiōn*, "According to Matthew." As this title suggests, other gospel accounts were known at that time (the word *Gospel* was added later). Matthew ("Gift of the Lord") was also surnamed Levi (Mark 2:14; Luke 5:27).

THE AUTHOR OF MATTHEW

The early church uniformly attributed this gospel to Matthew, and no tradition to the contrary ever emerged. This book was known early and accepted quickly. In his Ecclesiastical History (A.D. 323), Eusebius quoted a statement by Papias (c. A.D. 140) that Matthew wrote *logia* ("sayings") in Aramaic. No Aramaic Gospel of Matthew has been found, and it is evident that Matthew is not a Greek translation of an Aramaic original. Some believe that Matthew wrote an abbreviated version of Jesus' sayings in Aramaic before writing his gospel in Greek for a larger circle of readers.

Matthew, the son of Alphaeus (Mark 2:14), occupied the unpopular post of tax collector in Capernaum for the Roman government. As a publican he was no doubt disliked by his Jewish countrymen. When Jesus called him to discipleship (9:9–13; Mark 2:14; Luke 5:27, 28), his quick response probably meant that he had already been stirred by Jesus' public preaching. He gave a large reception for Jesus in his house so that his associates could meet Jesus. He was chosen as one of the twelve apostles, and the last appearance of his name in the Bible is in Acts 1:13. Matthew's life from that point on is veiled in tradition.

THE TIME OF MATTHEW

Like all the Gospels, Matthew is not easy to date: suggestions have ranged from A.D. 40 to 140. The two expressions "unto this day" (27:8) and "until this day" (28:15) indicate that a substantial period of time has passed since the events described in the book, but they also point to a date prior to the destruction of Jerusalem in A.D. 70. The Olivet Discourse (24 and 25) also anticipates this event. The strong Jewish flavor of this gospel is another argument for a date prior to A.D. 70. If Matthew depended on Mark's gospel as a source, the date of Mark would determine the earliest date for Matthew. The likely time frame for this book is A.D. 58–68. It may have been written in Palestine or Syrian Antioch.

THE CHRIST OF MATTHEW

Matthew presents Jesus as Israel's promised messianic King (1:23; 2:2, 6; 3:17; 4:15–17; 21:5, 9; 22:44, 45; 26:64; 27:11, 27–37). The phrase "the kingdom of heaven" appears thirty-two times in Matthew but nowhere else in the New Testament. To show that Jesus fulfills the qualifications for the Messiah, Matthew uses more Old Testament quotations and allusions than any other book (almost 130). Often used in this gospel is the revealing phrase "that what was spoken through the prophet might be fulfilled," which appears nine times in Matthew and not once in the other Gospels. Jesus is the climax of the prophets (12:39, 40; 13:13–15, 35; 17:5–13), "the Son of man" (24:30ff.), the "servant" of the Lord (12:17–21), and the "son of David" (the Davidic reference occurs nine times in Matthew, but only six times in all of the other Gospels).

KEYS TO MATTHEW

Key Word: Jesus the King—A Jewish tax collector named Matthew writes to a Jewish audience to convince them that the King of Jews has come. By quoting repeatedly from the Old Testament, Matthew validates Christ's claims that He is, in fact, the prophesied Messiah (the Anointed One) of Israel. Everything about this King is unique: His miraculous birth and obscure yet carefully prophesied birthplace, His flight into Egypt, His announcement by John, His battle with Satan in the wilderness, all support the only possible conclusion—Jesus is the culmination of promises delivered by the prophets over a period of a thousand years. Thus God's redemptive plan is alive and well, even after four hundred years of prophetic silence.

Key Verses: Matthew 16:16-19 and 28:18-20—"And Simon Peter answered and said, Thou art the Christ, the Son of the living God. And Jesus answered and said unto him, Blessed art thou, Simon Bar-jona: for flesh and blood hath not revealed *it* unto thee, but my Father which is in heaven. And I say also unto thee, That thou art Peter, and upon this rock I will build my church; and the gates of hell shall not prevail against it. And I will give unto thee the keys of the kingdom of heaven: and whatsoever thou shalt bind on

earth shall be bound in heaven: and whatsoever thou shalt loose on earth shall be loosed in heaven" (16:16–19).

"And Jesus came and spake unto them, saying, All power is given unto me in heaven and in earth. Go ye therefore, and teach all nations, baptizing them in the name of the Father, and of the Son, and of the Holy Ghost: Teaching them to observe all things whatsoever I have commanded you: and, lo, I am with you alway, *even* unto the end of the world. Amen" (28:18–20).

Key Chapter: Matthew 12—The turning point of Matthew comes in the twelfth chapter when the Pharisees, acting as the leadership of the nation of Israel, formally reject Jesus Christ as the Messiah, saying that His power comes not from God but from Satan. Christ's ministry changes immediately with His new teaching of parables, increased attention given to His disciples, and His repeated statement that His death is now near.

SURVEY OF MATTHEW

The Old Testament prophets predicted and longed for the coming of the Anointed One who would enter history to bring redemption and deliverance. The first verse of Matthew succinctly announces the fulfillment of Israel's hope in the coming of Christ: "The book of the generation of Jesus Christ, the son of David, the son of Abraham." Matthew was placed first in the canon of New Testament books by the early church because it is a natural bridge between the Testaments. This gospel describes the person and work of Israel's messianic King. An important part of Matthew's structure is revealed in the phrase "when Jesus had finished" (7:28; 11:1; 13:53; 19:1; 26:1), which is used to conclude the five key discourses of the book: the Sermon on the Mount (5:3—7:27), Instruction to the Disciples (10:5–42), Parables of the Kingdom (13:3-52), Terms of Discipleship (18:3-35), and the Olivet Discourse (24:4—25:46). Matthew can

be outlined as follows: the presentation of the King (1:1—4:11); the proclamation of the King (4:12—7:29); the power of the King (8:1—11:1); the progressive rejection of the King (11:2—16:12); the preparation of the King's disciples (16:13—20:28); the presentation and rejection of the King (20:29—27:66); the proof of the King (28:1-20).

The Presentation of the King (1:1—4:11): The promise to Abraham was that "in thee shall all families of the earth be blessed" (Gen. 12:3). Jesus Christ, the Saviour of the world, is "the son of Abraham" (1:1). However, He is also "the son of David"; and as David's direct descendant, He is qualified to be Israel's King. The magi know that the "King of the Jews" (2:2) has been born and come to worship Him. John the Baptist, the messianic forerunner who breaks the four hundred years of prophetic silence, also bears witness of Him (cf. Mal. 3:1). The sinlessness of the King is proved when He overcomes the satanic temptations to disobey the will of the Father.

The Proclamation of the King (4:12—7:29): In this section, Matthew uses a topical rather than a chronological arrangement of his material in order to develop a crucial pattern in Christ's ministry. The words of the Lord are found in the Sermon on the Mount (5—7). This discourse requires less than fifteen minutes to read, but its brevity has not diminished its profound influence on the world. The Sermon on the Mount presents new laws and standards for God's people.

The Power of the King (8:1—11:1): The works of the Lord are presented in a series of ten miracles (8 and 9) that reveal His authority over every realm (disease, demons, death, and nature). Thus, the words of the Lord are supported by His works; His claims are verified by His credentials.

The Progressive Rejection of the King (11:2—16:12): Here we note a series of reactions

FOCUS	OFFER OF THE KING			REJECTION OF THE KING			
REFERENCE	1:1———————4:12———————8:1———			—11:2———————16:13———————20:29———————28:1———28:20			
DIVISION	PRESENTATION OF THE KING	PROCLAMATION OF THE KING	POWER OF THE KING	PROGRESSIVE REJECTION OF THE KING	PREPARATION OF THE KING'S DISCIPLES	PRESENTATION AND REJECTION OF THE KING	PROOF OF THE KING
TOPIC	TEACHING THE THRONGS			TEACHING THE TWELVE			
	CHRONOLOGICAL	THEMATIC		CHRONOLOGICAL			
LOCATION	BETHLEHEM AND NAZARETH	GALILEE				JUDEA	
TIME	c. 4 B.C. — A.D. 33						

to Christ's words and works. Because of increasing opposition, Jesus begins to spend proportionately more time with His disciples as He prepares them for His coming death and departure.

The Preparation of the King's Disciples (16:13—20:28): In a series of discourses, Jesus communicates the significance of accepting or rejecting His offer of righteousness. His teaching in 16:13—21:11 is primarily directed to those who accept Him.

The Presentation and Rejection of the King (20:29—27:66): The majority of Christ's words in this section are aimed at those who reject their King. The Lord predicts the terrible judgment that will fall on Jerusalem, resulting in the dispersion of the Jewish people. Looking beyond these events (fulfilled in A.D. 70), He also describes His second coming as the Judge and Lord of the earth.

The Proof of the King (28): Authenticating His words and works are the empty tomb, resurrection, and appearances, all proving that Jesus Christ is indeed the prophesied Messiah, the very Son of God.

Christ's final ministry in Judea (beginning in 19:1) reaches a climax at the cross as the King willingly gives up His life to redeem sinful persons. Jesus endures awesome human hatred in this great demonstration of divine love (cf. Rom. 5:7, 8). His perfect sacrifice is acceptable, and this gospel concludes with His glorious resurrection.

OUTLINE OF MATTHEW

Part Four: The Progressive Rejection of the King (11:2—16:12)

Part Five: The Preparation of the King's Disciples (16:13—20:28)

Part Six: The Presentation and Rejection of the King (20:29—27:66)

Part Seven: The Proof of the King (28:1–20)

CHAPTER 1

Genealogy of Christ
Ruth 4:18–22; I Chr. 1:34; 2:1–15; Luke 3:31–34

THE book of the generation of Jesus Christ, Rthe son of David, Rthe son of Abraham.   Ps. 132:11; Jer. 23:5; Acts 2:30 * • Gen. 12:3

2 AbrahamR begat Isaac; and RIsaac begat Jacob; and RJacob begat Judas and his brethren;   Gen. 17:19 * • Gen. 25:26 • Luke 3:33, 34

3 And RJudas begat Pha'-res and Za'-ra of Tha'-mar; and Pha'-res begat Es'-rom; and Es'-rom begat A'-ram;   Gen. 38:27

4 And A'-ram begat A-min'-a-dab; and A-min'-a-dab begat Na-as'-son; and Na-as'-son begat Sal'-mon;

5 And Sal'-mon begat Bo'-oz of Ra'-chab; and Bo'-oz begat O'-bed of Ruth; and O'-bed begat RJesse;   Is. 11:1, 10 *

6 And RJesse begat David the king; and

David the king begat Solomon of her that had been the wife of U-ri'-as;   1 Sam. 16:1

7 And Solomon begat Ro-bo'-am; and Ro-bo'-am begat A-bi'-a; and A-bi'-a begat A'-sa;

8 And A'-sa begat Jos'-a-phat; and Jos'-a-phat begat Jo'-ram; and Jo'-ram begat RO-zi'-as;   2 Kin. 15:13

9 And O-zi'-as begat Jo'-a-tham; and Jo'-a-tham begat A'-chaz; and RA'-chaz begat Ez-e-ki'-as;   2 Kin. 15:38

10 And REz-e-ki'-as begat Ma-nas'-ses; and Ma-nas'-ses begat Amon; and Amon begat Jo-si'-as;   2 Kin. 20:21

11 And Jo-si'-as begat Jech-o-ni'-as and his brethren, about the time they were Rcarried away to Babylon: 2 Kin. 24:14–16

12 And after they were brought to Babylon, RJech-o-ni'-as begat Sa-la'-thi-el; and Sa-la'-thi-el begat Zo-rob'-a-bel;   1 Chr. 3:17

13 And Zo-rob'-a-bel begat A-bi'-ud; and

A-bi'-ud ^Rbegat E-li'-a-kim; and E-li'-a-kim begat A'-zor;   Luke 3:30

14 And A'-zor begat Sa'-doc; and Sa'-doc begat A'-chim; and A'-chim begat E-li'-ud;

15 And E-li'-ud begat E-le-a'-zar; and E-le-a'-zar begat Mat'-than; and Mat'-than begat Jacob;

16 And Jacob begat Joseph the husband of Mary, of whom was born Jesus, who is called Christ.

17 So all the generations from Abraham to David *are* fourteen generations; and from David until the carrying away into Babylon *are* fourteen generations; and from the ^Rcarrying away into Babylon unto Christ *are* fourteen generations.   2 Kin. 24:14

Birth of Christ

18 Now the birth of Jesus Christ was on this wise: When as his mother Mary was ^Tespoused to Joseph, ^Rbefore they came together, she was found with child of the Holy Ghost.   betrothed • Is. 7:14; 49:1, 5 *

19 Then Joseph her husband, being a ^Tjust *man,* and not willing ^Rto make her a publick example, was minded to put her away ^Tprivily.   fair • Deut. 24:1 • secretly

20 But while he thought on these things, behold, the angel of the Lord appeared unto him in a dream, saying, Joseph, thou son of David, fear not to take unto thee Mary thy wife: for that which is ^Tconceived in her is of the Holy Ghost.   begotten

21 And she shall bring forth a son, and thou shalt call his name JESUS: for he ^Rshall save his people from their sins.   Rom. 5:18, 19 ☆

22 Now all this was done, that it might be fulfilled which was spoken of the Lord by the prophet, ^Rsaying,   Is. 7:14 *

23 BEHOLD, A VIRGIN SHALL BE WITH CHILD, AND SHALL BRING FORTH A SON, AND THEY SHALL CALL HIS NAME EM-MAN'-U-EL, which being interpreted is, God with us.

24 Then Joseph being raised from sleep did as the angel of the Lord had bidden him, and took unto him his wife:

25 And knew her not till she had brought forth her firstborn son: and he ^Rcalled his name JESUS.   1:21 *

CHAPTER 2

Visit of Wise Men

NOW when Jesus was ^Rborn in Beth'-le-hem of Ju-dae'-a in the days of Herod the king, behold, there came wise men ^Rfrom the east to Jerusalem,   Mic. 5:2 * • 1 Kin. 4:30

2 Saying, Where is he that is born ^RKing of the Jews? for we have seen his star in the east, and are come to worship him.   Jer. 23:5 *

3 When Herod the king had heard *these things,* he was troubled, and all Jerusalem with him.

4 And when he had gathered all ^Rthe chief priests and ^Rscribes of the people together, ^Rhe demanded of them where Christ should be born.   2 Chr. 36:14 • 2 Chr. 34:13 • Mal. 2:7

5 And they said unto him, In Beth'-le-hem of Ju-dae'-a: ^Rfor thus it is written by the prophet,   Mic. 5:2; John 7:42 *

6 AND THOU BETH'-LE-HEM, *IN* THE LAND OF JUDA, ART NOT THE LEAST AMONG THE PRINCES OF JUDA: FOR ^ROUT OF THEE SHALL COME A GOVERNOR, THAT SHALL RULE MY PEOPLE ISRAEL.   Gen. 49:10 *

7 Then Herod, when he had ^Tprivily called the wise men, enquired of them diligently what time the star appeared.   secretly

8 And he sent them to Beth'-le-hem, and said, Go and search diligently for the young child; and when ye have found *him,* bring me word again, that I may come and worship him also.

9 When they had heard the king, they departed; and, lo, the star, which they saw in the east, went before them, till it came and stood over where the young child was.

10 When they saw the star, they rejoiced with exceeding great joy.

11 And when they were come into the house, they saw the young child with Mary his mother, and fell down, and worshipped him: and when they had opened their treasures, they ^Tpresented unto him gifts; gold, and frankincense, and myrrh.   offered

12 And being warned of God in a dream that they should not return to Herod, they departed into their own country another way.

Flight into Egypt

13 And when they were departed, behold, the angel of the Lord appeareth to Joseph in a dream, saying, Arise, and take the young child and his mother, and flee into Egypt, and be thou there until I bring thee word: for ^RHerod will seek the young child to destroy him.   2:16 ☆

14 When he arose, he took the young child and his mother by night, and departed into Egypt:

15 And was there until the death of Herod: that it might be fulfilled which was spoken of the Lord by the prophet, ^Rsaying, OUT OF EGYPT HAVE I CALLED MY SON.   Hos. 11:1 *

Herod Kills the Children

16 Then Herod, when he saw that he was mocked of the wise men, was exceeding wroth, and sent forth, and slew all the ^Tchildren that were in Beth'-le-hem, and in all the coasts thereof, from two years old and under, according to the time which he had diligently enquired of the wise men.   male children

17 Then was fulfilled that which was spoken by Jeremy the prophet, saying,

18 ^RIN RA'-MA WAS THERE A VOICE HEARD, LAMENTATION, AND WEEPING, AND GREAT

MOURNING, RA'-CHEL WEEPING FOR HER
CHILDREN, AND WOULD NOT BE COMFORTED,
BECAUSE THEY ARE NOT.   Jer. 31:15 ✴

Jesus Returns to Nazareth—Luke 2:39

19 But when Herod was dead, behold, an
angel of the Lord ᴿappeareth in a dream to
Joseph in Egypt,   *vv.* 12, 13, 22
20 Saying, Arise, and take the young child
and his mother, and go into the land of Israel:
for they are dead which ᵀsought the young
child's life.   *tried to kill*
21 And he arose, and took the young child
and his mother, and ᵀcame into the land of
Israel.   *went back*
22 But when he heard that Ar-che-la'-us
did reign in Ju-dae'-a in the room of his father
Herod, he was afraid to go ᵀthither: notwithstanding, being warned of God in a dream, he
turned aside into the parts of Galilee: *there*
23 And he came and dwelt in a city called
Nazareth: that it might be fulfilled ᴿwhich
was spoken by the prophets, He shall be
called a Nazarene.   John 1:45; Judg. 13:5 ✴

CHAPTER 3

*The Person of John the Baptist
Mark 1:2–6; Luke 3:3–6*

IN those days came John the Baptist,
preaching in the wilderness of Ju-dae'-a,
2 And saying, Repent ye: for ᴿthe kingdom
of heaven is at hand.   Mal. 4:5, 6 ✴
3 For this is he that was spoken of by the
prophet E-sa'-ias, saying, THE VOICE OF ONE
CRYING IN THE WILDERNESS, PREPARE YE THE
WAY OF THE LORD, MAKE HIS PATHS STRAIGHT.
4 And the same John had his raiment of
camel's hair, and a leathern girdle about his
loins; and his ᵀmeat was ᴿlocusts and ᴿwild
honey.   *food* · Lev. 11:22 · 1 Sam. 14:25, 26
5 ᴿThen ᵀwent out to him Jerusalem, and
all Ju-dae'-a, and all the region round about
Jordan,   Mark 1:5 · *came to*
6 ᴿAnd were baptized of him in Jordan,
confessing their sins.   Acts 19:4, 18

*The Preaching of John the Baptist
Mark 1:7–9; Luke 3:7–9, 16, 17*

7 But when he saw many of the Pharisees
and Sad'-du-cees come to his baptism, he said

unto them, O generation of vipers, who hath
warned you to flee from the wrath to come?
8 ᵀBring forth therefore ᵀfruits ᵀmeet for
repentance: *do · things · suitable*
9 And think not to say within yourselves,
ᴿWe have Abraham to *our* father: for I say
unto you, that God is able of these stones to
raise up children unto Abraham.   John 8:33
10 And now also the ax is laid unto the
root of the trees: ᴿtherefore every tree which
bringeth not forth good fruit is hewn down,
and cast into the fire.   7:19; John 15:6
11 ᴿI indeed baptize you with water unto
repentance: but he that cometh after me is
mightier than I, whose shoes I am not worthy
to bear: he shall baptize you with the Holy
Ghost, and *with* fire: Acts 2:4, 33 ✴
12 Whose fan *is* in his hand, and he will
throughly purge his floor, and gather his
wheat into the ᵀgarner; but he will burn up
the chaff with unquenchable fire.   *barn*

Baptism of Jesus—Mark 1:9–11; Luke 3:21–23

13 Then cometh Jesus from Galilee to
Jordan unto John, to be baptized of him.
14 But John ᵀforbad him, saying, I have
need to be baptized of thee, and ᵀcomest thou
to me?   *would have hindered · you come*
15 And Jesus answering said unto him,
Suffer *it to be so* now: for thus it becometh us
to fulfil all ᴿrighteousness. Then he ᵀsuffered
him.   [Ps. 119:172; Acts 10:34, 35] · *permitted*
16 And Jesus, when he was baptized, went
up straightway out of the water: and, lo, the
heavens were opened unto him, and he saw
the ᴿSpirit of God descending like a dove, and
lighting upon him: Is. 11:2; 42:1; 61:1 ✴

17 ᴿAnd lo a voice from heaven, saying,
ᴿThis is my beloved Son, in whom I am well
pleased.   John 12:28 · Ps. 2:7; Luke 9:35; Col. 1:13

CHAPTER 4

First Temptation—Mark 1:12, 13; Luke 4:1–4

THEN was Jesus led up of the spirit into
the wilderness to be tempted of the devil.
2 And when he had fasted forty days and
forty nights, he was afterward an hungred.
3 And when the ᵀtempter came to him, he

3:17 God the Father of Christ—Every new Christian eventually wonders as to what sense God may
be called the Father of Christ and Christ the Son of God. The answer to this question is not a simple
one. First, one must recognize that the title Son of God does not speak of physical nature, for God is
spirit (Page 1045—John 4:24), and Christ was the Son of God before He assumed a human body in
Beth-lehem (Page 1044—John 3:16; Page 1156—Gal. 4:4). Passages which use terms implying
physical origin must be taken in a figurative sense (Page 1215—Heb. 1:5).
   Second, the title expresses a unique relationship. Christ distinguished His sonship from that of His
disciples (Page 1065—John 20:17). He is begotten of God in a sense that no one else is (Page 1042—
John 1:14; 3:16). Some call this "eternal generation," signifying the timelessness of this "God from God"
relationship.

(continued on next page)

said, If thou be the Son of God, command that these stones be made bread. *devil*

4 But he answered and said, It is written, RMAN SHALL NOT LIVE BY BREAD ALONE, BUT BY EVERY WORD THAT PROCEEDETH OUT OF THE MOUTH OF GOD. Deut. 8:3

Second Temptation—Luke 4:9–12

5 Then the devil taketh him up Rinto the holy city, and setteth him on a Tpinnacle of the temple, 27:53; Neh. 11:1 · *highest point*
6 And saith unto him, If thou be the Son of God, cast thyself down: for it is written, RHE SHALL GIVE HIS ANGELS CHARGE CONCERNING THEE: and IN THEIR HANDS THEY SHALL BEAR THEE UP, LEST AT ANY TIME THOU DASH THY FOOT AGAINST A STONE. Ps. 91:11, 12 ★
7 Jesus said unto him, It is written again, THOU SHALT NOT TEMPT THE LORD THY GOD.

Third Temptation—Mark 1:13; Luke 4:5–8, 13

8 Again, the devil taketh him up into an exceeding high mountain, and sheweth him all the kingdoms of the world, and the Tglory of them; *greatness*
9 And saith unto him, All these things will I give thee, if thou wilt Tfall down and worship me. *kneel*
10 Then saith Jesus unto him, Get thee hence, Satan: for it is written, RTHOU SHALT WORSHIP THE LORD THY GOD, AND HIM ONLY SHALT THOU SERVE. Deut. 6:13
11 Then the devil leaveth him, and, behold, angels came and Tministered unto him. *helped*

Jesus Begins His Ministry
Mark 1:14, 15; Luke 4:14, 31

12 RNow when Jesus had heard that John was Tcast into prison, he departed into Galilee; Luke 3:20; John 4:43 · *delivered up*
13 And leaving Nazareth, he came and dwelt in Ca-per'-na-um, which is upon the sea coast, in the borders of Zab'-u-lon and Neph'-tha-lim:
14 That it might be fulfilled which was spoken by E-sa'-ias the prophet, saying,
15 RTHE LAND OF ZAB'-U-LON, AND THE LAND OF NEPH'-THA-LIM, BY THE WAY OF THE SEA, BEYOND JORDAN, GALILEE OF THE GEN-TILES; Is. 9:1 ★

16 RTHE PEOPLE WHICH SAT IN DARKNESS SAW GREAT LIGHT; AND TO THEM WHICH SAT IN THE REGION AND SHADOW OF DEATH LIGHT TIS SPRUNG UP. Is. 9:2 ★ · *has dawned*
17 From that time Jesus began to preach, and to say, Repent: for the kingdom of heaven is Tat hand. *near*

Jesus Calls His First Disciples—Mark 1:16–20

18 And Jesus, walking by the sea of Galilee, saw two brethren, Simon called Peter, and Andrew his brother, casting a net into the sea: for they were fishers.
19 And he saith unto them, Follow me, and I will make you fishers of men.
20 RAnd they Tstraightway left *their* nets, and followed him. Mark 10:28 · *at once*
21 And going on from Tthence, he saw other two brethren, James *the son* of Zeb'-e-dee, and John his brother, in a ship with Zeb'-e-dee their father, mending their nets; and he called them. *there*
22 And they Timmediately left the ship and their father, and followed him. *at once*

Jesus Ministers in Galilee
Mark 1:39; Luke 4:44

23 And Jesus went about all Galilee, Rteaching in their synagogues, and preaching the gospel of the kingdom, and Rhealing all manner of sickness and all manner of disease among the people. Ps. 22:22 ★ · Mark 1:34
24 And his fame went throughout all Syria: and they brought unto him all sick people that were taken with Tdivers diseases and torments, and those which were possessed with Tdevils, and those which were lunatick, and those that had the palsy; and he healed them. *various · demons*
25 And there followed him great multitudes of people from Galilee, and *from* De-cap'-o-lis, and *from* Jerusalem, and *from* Ju-dae'-a, and *from* beyond Jordan.

CHAPTER 5

The Beatitudes—Luke 6:20–26

AND seeing the multitudes, Rhe went up into a mountain: and when he was set, his disciples came unto him: Mark 3:13

(continued from previous page)
    Third, the title describes a relationship of equality. The Son of God is no less than God. When Jesus claimed to be "one" with the Father, He was speaking of a unity of "substance" with the Father and thus equality in all the attributes of deity (Page 1055—John 10:30). The Jews certainly understood this claim, for they took up stones to stone Him, protesting that "thou . . . makest thyself God" (Page 1055—John 10:33).
    Fourth, the title especially emphasizes Christ's role as the revealer of God. He alone possesses the knowledge of the Father (Page 1059—John 14:6–9; Page 1249—1 John 1:2) and He is the sole mediator of that knowledge (Page 1194—1 Tim. 2:5). Therefore no one can know the Father except through the Son (Page 1059—John 14:6). The narrowness of this way to God should be a sober incentive to take to all the world the message that the Son of God has come to impart to every person the life of the Father.
    Now turn to Page 1114—Rom. 8:15: God the Father of Believers.

2 And he opened his mouth, and taught them, saying,

3 Blessed[R] *are* the poor in spirit: for their's is the kingdom of heaven.   James 2:5

4 [R]Blessed *are* they that mourn: for they shall be comforted.   Is. 61:2; [2 Cor. 1:7]

5 [R]Blessed *are* the meek: for [R]they shall inherit the [T]earth.   Ps. 37:11 • [Rom. 4:13] • *land*

6 [T]Blessed *are* they which do hunger and thirst after righteousness: [R]for they shall be filled.   *happy* • [Is. 55:1; 65:13]

7 Blessed *are* the merciful: [R]for they shall obtain mercy.   6:14; Ps. 41:1; Mark 11:25

8 [R]Blessed *are* the [T]pure in heart: for they shall see God.   1 John 3:2, 3; Heb. 12:14 • *sincere*

9 Blessed *are* the peacemakers: for they shall be called the children of God.

10 [R]Blessed *are* they which are persecuted for righteousness' sake: for their's is the kingdom of heaven.   2 Tim. 3:12

11 [R]Blessed are ye, when *men* shall revile you, and persecute *you*, and shall say all manner of [R]evil against you [T]falsely, for my sake.   Luke 6:22 • 1 Pet. 4:14 • *in deceitful fashion*

12 [R]Rejoice, and be exceeding glad: for great *is* your reward in heaven: for [R]so persecuted they the prophets which were before you.   Acts 5:41; 1 Pet. 4:13 • Neh. 9:26; Acts 7:52

The Similitudes

13 Ye are the salt of the earth: [R]but if the salt have lost his [T]savour, wherewith shall it be salted? it is thenceforth good for nothing, but to be cast out, and to be trodden under foot of men.   Mark 9:50 • *strength*

14 [R]Ye are the light of the world. A city that is set on an hill cannot be hid.   Phil. 2:15

15 Neither do men light a candle, and put it under a bushel, but on a candlestick; and it giveth light unto all that are in the house.

16 Let your light so shine before men, that they may see your good works, and glorify your Father which is in heaven.

Jesus Fulfills the Law

17 [R]Think not that I am come to destroy the law, or the prophets: I am not come to destroy, but to fulfil.   Rom. 3:31; 10:4

18 For verily I say unto you, Till heaven and earth pass, one jot or one tittle shall in no wise pass from the law, till all be fulfilled.

19 Whosoever therefore shall break one of these least commandments, and shall teach men so, he shall be called the least in the kingdom of heaven: but whosoever shall do and teach *them,* the same shall be called great in the kingdom of heaven.

Murder

20 For I say unto you, That except your righteousness shall exceed *the righteousness* of the scribes and Pharisees, ye shall in no case enter into the kingdom of heaven.

21 Ye have heard that it was said [T]by them of old time, [R]Thou shalt not kill; and whosoever shall kill shall be in danger of the judgment: *in former times* • Ex. 20:13

22 But I say unto you, That whosoever [R]is angry with his brother without a cause shall be in danger of the judgment: and whosoever shall say to his brother, [T]Ra'-ca, shall be in danger of the council: but whosoever shall say, Thou fool, shall be in danger of hell fire.   [1 John 3:15] • *vain fellow*

23 Therefore if thou bring thy gift to the altar, and there rememberest that thy brother hath [T]ought against thee;   *anything*

24 Leave there thy gift before the altar, and go thy way; first be reconciled to thy brother, and then come and offer thy gift.

25 Agree with thine adversary quickly, whiles thou art in the way with him; lest at any time the adversary deliver thee to the judge, and the judge deliver thee to the officer, and thou be cast into prison.

26 Verily I say unto thee, Thou shalt by no means come out thence, till thou hast paid the uttermost [T]farthing.   *1/64 of a day's wage*

Adultery

27 Ye have heard that it was said by them of old time, THOU SHALT NOT COMMIT ADULTERY:

28 But I say unto you, That whosoever [R]looketh on a woman to lust after her hath committed adultery with her already in his heart.   Job 31:1; Prov. 6:25; 2 Pet. 2:14

29 [R]And if thy right eye offend thee, pluck it out, and cast *it* from thee: for it is profitable for thee that one of thy members should perish, and not *that* thy whole body should be cast into hell.   [Col. 3:5]

30 And if thy right hand offend thee, cut it off, and cast *it* from thee: for it is profitable for thee that one of thy members should perish, and not *that* thy whole body should be cast into hell.

Divorce

31 It hath been said, [R]WHOSOEVER SHALL [T]PUT AWAY HIS WIFE, LET HIM GIVE HER A WRITING OF DIVORCEMENT: Deut. 24:1 • *divorce*

32 But I say unto you, That whosoever shall put away his wife, saving for the cause of fornication, causeth her to commit adultery: and whosoever shall marry her that is divorced committeth adultery.

Oaths

33 Again, ye have heard that it hath been said of them of old time, Thou shalt not forswear thyself, [R]but shalt perform unto the Lord thine oaths: Lev. 19:12

34 But I say unto you, Swear not at all; neither by heaven; for it is God's throne:

35 Nor by the earth; for it is his footstool: neither by Jerusalem; for it is ᴿthe city of the great ᴿKing.   Ps. 48:2 • 87:3

36 Neither shalt thou swear by thy head, because thou canst not make one hair white or black.

37 But let your communication be, Yea, yea; Nay, nay: for whatsoever is more than these cometh ᵀof evil.   *out of an evil heart*

Retaliation

38 Ye have heard that it hath been said, AN EYE FOR AN EYE, AND A TOOTH FOR A TOOTH:

39 But I say unto you, That ye resist not evil: but whosoever shall ᵀsmite thee on thy right cheek, turn to him the other also. *hit you*

40 And if any man will sue thee at the law, and take away thy coat, let him have *thy* cloke also.

41 And whosoever shall compel thee to go a mile, go with him ᵀtwain.   *two*

42 Give to him that asketh thee, and ᴿfrom him that would borrow of thee turn not thou away.   Deut. 15:8

Love—Luke 6:27, 32

43 Ye have heard that it hath been said, ᴿTHOU SHALT LOVE THY NEIGHBOUR, AND HATE THINE ENEMY.   Lev. 19:18

44 But I say unto you, Love your enemies, bless them that curse you, do good to them that hate you, and pray for them which despitefully use you, and persecute you;

45 That ye may be the children of your Father which is in heaven: for he maketh his sun to rise on the evil and on the good, and sendeth rain on the just and on the unjust.

46 For if ye love them which love you, what reward have ye? do not even the ᵀpublicans the same?   *tax collectors*

47 And if ye ᵀsalute your brethren only, what do ye more than *others*? do not even the publicans so?   *act graciously toward*

48 ᴿBe ye therefore perfect, even as your Father which is in heaven is perfect. James 1:4

CHAPTER 6

Almsgiving

TAKE heed that ye do not your ᵀalms before men, to be seen of them: otherwise ye have no reward of your Father which is in heaven.   *gifts to the poor and needy*

2 Therefore ᴿwhen thou doest *thine* ᵀalms, do not sound a trumpet before thee, as the hypocrites do in the synagogues and in the streets, that they may have glory of men. Verily I say unto you, They have their reward.   Rom. 12:8 • *acts of charity*

3 But when thou doest alms, let not thy left hand know what thy right hand doeth:

4 That thine alms may be in secret: and thy Father which seeth in secret himself ᴿshall reward thee openly.   Luke 14:14

Prayer—Luke 11:2-4

5 And when thou prayest, thou shalt not be as the ᵀhypocrites *are*: for they love to pray standing in the synagogues and in the corners of the streets, that they may be seen of men. Verily I say unto you, They have their reward.   *insincere*

6 But thou, when thou prayest, ᴿenter into thy closet, and when thou hast shut thy door, pray to thy Father which is in secret; and thy Father which seeth in secret shall reward thee openly.   2 Kin. 4:33

7 But when ye pray, ᴿuse not ᵀvain repetitions, as the heathen *do*: ᴿfor they think that they shall be heard for their much speaking.   Eccl. 5:2 • *meaningless words* • 1 Kin. 18:26

8 Be not ye therefore like unto them: for ᴿyour Father knoweth what things ye have need of, before ye ask him.   6:32; Ps. 139:2

9 After this manner therefore pray ye: ᴿOur Father which art in heaven, Hallowed be thy name.   Luke 11:2

10 Thy kingdom come. Thy will be done in earth, as *it is* in heaven.

11 Give us this day our daily bread.

12 And forgive us our debts, as we forgive our debtors.

13 And lead us not into temptation, but deliver us from ᵀevil: For thine is the kingdom, and the power, and the glory, for ever. A-men'.   *the evil one*

14 For if ye forgive men their trespasses, your heavenly Father will also forgive you:

15 But ᴿif ye forgive not men their trespasses, neither will your Father forgive your trespasses.   18:35; James 2:13

Fasting

16 Moreover ᴿwhen ye fast, be not, as the hypocrites, of a sad countenance: for they disfigure their faces, that they may appear unto men to fast. Verily I say unto you, They have their reward.   Is. 58:5

17 But thou, when thou fastest, ᴿanoint thine head, and wash thy face;   Ruth 3:3

18 That thou appear not unto men to fast, but unto thy Father which is in ᵀsecret: and thy Father, which seeth in secret, shall reward thee openly.   *private*

Wealth—Luke 11:34-36; 12:22-34

19 Lay not up for yourselves treasures upon earth, where moth and rust doth ᵀcorrupt, and where thieves break through and steal: *ruin*

20 ᴿBut lay up for yourselves treasures in heaven, where neither moth nor rust doth corrupt, and where thieves do not break through nor steal: 19:21; 1 Tim. 6:19; 1 Pet. 1:4

21 For ᴿwhere your treasure is, there will your heart be also.   Luke 12:34

22 ᴿThe light of the body is the eye: if therefore thine eye be ᵀsingle, thy whole body shall be full of light.   Luke 11:34 • clear

23 But if thine eye be ᵀevil, thy whole body shall be full of darkness. If therefore the light that is in thee be darkness, how ᵀgreat is that darkness!   foggy • terrible

24 ᴿNo man can serve two masters: for either he will hate the one, and love the other; or else he will hold to the one, and despise the other. ᴿYe cannot serve God and mammon.   Luke 16:13 • [James 4:4; 1 John 2:15]

25 Therefore I say unto you, Take no thought for your life, what ye shall eat, or what ye shall drink; nor yet for your body, what ye shall put on. Is not the life more than meat, and the body than ᵀraiment?   clothing

26 Behold the fowls of the air: for they sow not, neither do they reap, nor gather into barns; yet your heavenly Father feedeth them. Are ye not much better than they?

27 Which of you by ᵀtaking thought can add one cubit unto his stature?   being anxious

28 And why take ye thought for raiment? Consider the lilies of the field, how they grow; they toil not, neither do they spin:

29 And yet I say unto you, That even Solomon in all his glory was ᵀnot arrayed like one of these.   not dressed

30 Wherefore, if God so clothe the grass of the field, which to day is, and to morrow is cast into the oven, shall he not much more clothe you, O ye of little faith?

31 Therefore take no thought, saying, What shall we eat? or, What shall we drink? or, Wherewithal shall we be clothed?

32 (For after all these things do the Gentiles seek:) for your heavenly Father knoweth that ye have need of all these things.

33 But ᴿseek ye first the kingdom of God, and his righteousness; and all these things shall be added unto you.   Phil. 4:19

34 ᵀTake therefore no thought for the morrow: for the morrow shall take thought for the things of itself. Sufficient unto the day is the evil thereof.   do not worry about

CHAPTER 7

Judging—Luke 6:37–42

JUDGE not, that ye be not judged.
2 For with what judgment ye judge, ye shall be judged: and with what measure ye mete, it shall be measured to you again.

3 And why beholdest thou the mote that is in thy brother's eye, but considerest not the beam that is in thine own eye?

4 Or how wilt thou say to thy brother, Let me pull out the mote out of thine eye; and, behold, a beam is in thine own eye?

5 Thou hypocrite, first cast out the ᵀbeam out of thine own eye; and then shalt thou see clearly to cast out the ᵀmote out of thy brother's eye.   log • sliver

6 Give not that which is holy unto the dogs, neither cast ye your pearls before swine, lest they trample them under their feet, and turn again and ᵀrend you.   tear

"Ask and It Shall Be Given"—Luke 11:9–13

7 ᴿAsk, and it shall be given you; seek, and ye shall find; knock, and it shall be opened unto you: Luke 11:9, 10; [John 14:13]

8 For every one that asketh receiveth; and ᴿhe that seeketh findeth; and to him that knocketh it shall be opened.   Prov. 8:17

9 Or what man is there of you, whom if his son ask bread, will he give him a stone?

10 Or if he ask a fish, will he give him a serpent?

11 If ye then, being evil, know how to give good gifts unto your children, how much more shall your Father which is in heaven give good things to them that ask him?

Golden Rule—Luke 6:31

12 Therefore all things whatsoever ye would that men should do to you, do ye even so to them: for ᴿthis is the law and the prophets.   Gal. 5:14; [1 Tim. 1:5]

Two Ways of Life

13 Enter ye in at the strait gate: ᴿfor wide is the gate, and broad is the way, that leadeth to destruction, and many there be which go in thereat: Luke 13:24

14 ᵀBecause strait is the gate, and narrow is the way, which leadeth unto life, and few there be that find it.   for narrow

False and True Teaching—Luke 6:43–45

15 Beware of false prophets, which come to you in sheep's clothing, but inwardly they are ᵀravening wolves.   hungry

16 ᴿYe shall know them by their ᵀfruits. Do men gather grapes of thorns, or figs of thistles?   v. 20 • actions

17 Even so ᴿevery good tree bringeth forth good fruit; but a ᵀcorrupt tree bringeth forth evil fruit.   Jer. 11:19; 12:33 • bad

18 A ᵀgood tree cannot bring forth ᵀevil fruit, neither can a ᵀcorrupt tree bring forth good fruit.   healthy • bad • poor

19 ᴿEvery tree that bringeth not forth good fruit is hewn down, and cast into the fire.   3:10; Luke 3:9; [John 15:2]

20 Wherefore by ᴿtheir fruits ye shall know them.   7:16; 12:33; James 3:12

True Way into the Kingdom—Luke 6:46

21 Not every one that saith unto me, ᴿLord, Lord, shall enter into the kingdom of heaven; but he that doeth the will of my Father which is in heaven.   25:11

22 Many will say to me in that day, Lord, Lord, have we not prophesied in thy name? and in thy name have cast out devils? and in thy name done many wonderful works?

23 And ᴿthen will I profess unto them, I never knew you: ᴿdepart from me, ye that work iniquity.   Luke 13:25, 27 • Ps. 6:8 ☆

Parable of the Two Builders—Luke 6:47–49

24 Therefore whosoever heareth these sayings of mine, and doeth them, I will liken him unto a wise man, which built his house upon a rock:

25 And the ᴿrain descended, and the floods came, and the winds blew, and beat upon that house; and ᴿit fell not: for it was founded upon a rock.   [Acts 14:22] • [2 Tim. 2:19]

26 And every one that heareth these ᵀsayings of mine, and doeth them not, shall be ᵀlikened unto a foolish man, which built his house upon the sand: words • the same as

27 And the rain descended, and the floods came, and the winds blew, and beat upon that house; and it fell: and ᵀgreat ᴿwas the fall of it.   terrible • [Heb. 10:31]

Response to the Sermon

28 And it came to pass, when Jesus had ended these sayings, ᴿthe people were astonished at his ᵀdoctrine: 13:54 • teaching

29 ᴿFor he taught them as one having authority, and not as the scribes.   [John 7:46]

CHAPTER 8

The Leper Is Cleansed
Mark 1:40–44; Luke 5:12–14

WHEN he was come down from the mountain, ᵀgreat multitudes followed him.   large crowds

2 And, behold, there came a leper and ᵀworshipped him, saying, Lord, if thou wilt, thou canst make me clean.   bowed down to

3 And Jesus put forth his hand, and touched him, saying, I will; be thou clean. And immediately his leprosy was cleansed.

4 And Jesus saith unto him, See thou tell no man; but go thy way, shew thyself to the priest, and offer the gift that Moses commanded, for a testimony unto them.

The Centurion's Servant Is Healed
Luke 7:1–10

5 And when Jesus was entered into Ca-per'-na-um, there came unto him a centurion, beseeching him,

6 And saying, Lord, my servant lieth at home ᵀsick of the palsy, ᵀgrievously tormented.   paralyzed • suffering pain

7 And Jesus saith unto him, I will come and ᵀheal him.   make him well

8 The centurion answered and said, Lord, I am not worthy that thou shouldest come under my roof: but ᴿspeak the word only, and my servant shall be healed.   Ps. 107:20

9 For I am a man under ᴿauthority, having soldiers under me: and I say to this man, Go, and he goeth; and to another, Come, and he cometh; and to my servant, Do this, and he doeth it.   [Mark 1:27; Luke 9:1]

10 When Jesus heard it, he ᴿmarvelled, and said to them that followed, Verily I say unto you, I have not found so great faith, no, not in Israel.   [15:21–28]

11 And I say unto you, That many shall come from the east and west, ᴿand shall sit down with Abraham, and Isaac, and Jacob, in the kingdom of heaven. Is. 49:12; 59:19; [Eph. 3:6]

12 But the children of the ᴿkingdom shall be cast out into outer darkness: there shall be weeping and gnashing of teeth.   [21:43]

13 And Jesus said unto the centurion, Go thy way; and as thou hast believed, so be it done unto thee. And his servant was healed in the selfsame ᴿhour.   [9:22, 29]

Peter's Mother-in-Law Is Healed
Mark 1:29–34; Luke 4:38–41

14 And when Jesus was come into Peter's house, he saw ᴿhis wife's mother laid, and sick of a fever.   1 Cor. 9:5

15 And he touched her hand, and the fever left her: and she arose, and ᵀministered unto them.   waited on • him

16 When the even was come, they brought unto him many that were possessed with ᵀdevils: and he cast out the spirits with his word, and healed all that were sick: demons

17 That it ᵀmight be fulfilled which was spoken by E-sa'-ias the prophet, saying, ᴿHIMSELF TOOK OUR INFIRMITIES, AND BARE OUR SICKNESSES. make come true • Is. 53:4; 1 Pet. 2:24 ★

Demands of Discipleship—Luke 9:57–62

18 Now when Jesus saw great multitudes about him, he gave ᵀcommandment to depart unto the other side.   ordered his disciples

19 And a certain scribe came, and said unto him, Master, I will follow thee whithersoever thou goest.

20 And Jesus saith unto him, The foxes have holes, and the birds of the air have nests; but the Son of man hath ᵀnot where to lay his head.   no place

21 And another of his disciples said unto him, Lord, ᴿsuffer me first to go and bury my father.   1 Kin. 19:20

22 But Jesus said unto him, ᴿFollow me; and let the dead bury their dead.   Mark 2:14

The Sea Is Stilled—Mark 4:35–41; Luke 8:22–25

23 And when he was entered into a ship, his disciples ᵀfollowed him.   went with

24 And, behold, there arose a great tempest in the sea, insomuch that the ship

was covered with the waves: but he was asleep.

25 And his disciples came to *him*, and awoke him, saying, Lord, save us: we perish.

26 And he saith unto them, Why are ye fearful, O ye of little faith? Then ᴿhe arose, and rebuked the winds and the sea; and there was a great calm.   Ps. 65:7; 89:9; 107:29

27 But the men ᵀmarvelled, saying, What manner of man is this, that even the winds and the sea obey him!   *were surprised*

Devils Are Cast into Swine
Mark 5:1–17; Luke 8:26–37

28 And when he was come to the other side into the country of the Ger-ge-senes', there met him two possessed with devils, coming out of the tombs, exceeding fierce, so that no man might pass by that way.

29 And, behold, they cried out, saying, What have we to do with thee, Jesus, thou Son of God? art thou come hither to torment us before the time?

30 And there was a good way off from them an herd of many ᵀswine feeding.   *hogs*

31 So the ᵀdevils besought him, saying, If thou cast us out, ᵀsuffer us to go away into the herd of swine.   *demons begged • permit*

32 And he said unto them, Go. And when they were come out, they went into the herd of swine: and, behold, the whole herd of swine ran violently down a steep place into the sea, and perished in the waters.

33 And they that kept them fled, and went their ways into the city, and told every thing, and what was befallen to ᵀthe possessed of the devils.   *them that were*

34 And, behold, the whole city came out to meet Jesus: and when they saw him, ᴿthey besought *him* that he would depart out of their coasts.   Luke 5:8

CHAPTER 9

The Paralytic Is Forgiven
Mark 2:1–12; Luke 5:17–26

AND he entered into a ship, and passed over, and came into his own city.

2 And, behold, they brought to him a man ᵀsick of the palsy, lying on a bed: ᴿand Jesus seeing their faith said unto the sick of the palsy; Son, be of good cheer; thy sins be forgiven thee.   *paralyzed • 8:10*

3 And, behold, certain of the scribes said within themselves, This *man* blasphemeth.

4 And Jesus knowing their thoughts said, Wherefore think ye evil in your hearts?

5 For whether is easier, to say, Thy sins be forgiven thee; or to say, Arise, and walk?

6 But that ye may know that the Son of man hath power on earth to forgive sins,

(then saith he to the sick of the palsy,) Arise, take up thy bed, and go unto thine house.

7 And he arose, and departed to his house.

8 But when the multitudes saw *it*, they ᵀmarvelled, and glorified God, which had given such power unto men.   *were afraid*

Matthew Is Called—Mark 2:14; Luke 5:27, 28

9 And as Jesus passed forth from thence, he saw a man, named Matthew, sitting at the receipt of custom: and he saith unto him, Follow me. And he arose, and followed him.

The Disciples Eat with Sinners
Mark 2:15–17; Luke 5:29–32

10 And it came to pass, as Jesus sat ᵀat meat in the house, behold, many ᵀpublicans and sinners came and sat down with him and his disciples.   *eating • tax collectors*

11 And when the Pharisees saw *it*, they said unto his disciples, Why eateth your Master with publicans and sinners?

12 But when Jesus heard *that*, he said unto them, They that be ᵀwhole need not a physician, but they that are sick.   *well*

13 But go ye and learn what *that* meaneth, ᴿI WILL HAVE MERCY, AND NOT SACRIFICE: for I am not come to call the righteous, ᴿbut sinners to repentance.   Hos. 6:6; 12:7 • 1 Tim. 1:15

The Disciples Do Not Fast
Mark 2:18–22; Luke 5:33–39

14 Then came to him the disciples of John, saying, Why do we and the Pharisees fast oft, but thy disciples fast not?

15 And Jesus said unto them, Can the children of the bridechamber mourn, as long as the bridegroom is with them? but the days will come, when the bridegroom shall be taken from them, and then shall they fast.

16 No man putteth a piece of ᵀnew cloth unto an old garment, for that which is put in to fill it up taketh from the garment, and the ᵀrent is made worse.   *unshrunk cloth • tear*

17 Neither do men put new wine into old ᵀbottles: else the bottles break, and the wine runneth out, and the bottles ᵀperish: but they put new wine into new bottles, and both are preserved.   *wine-skins • are ruined*

Life Is Restored—Mark 5:21–43; Luke 8:40–56

18 While he spake these things unto them, behold, there came a certain ruler, and worshipped him, saying, My daughter is even now dead: but come and lay thy hand upon her, and she shall live.

19 And Jesus arose, and followed him, and so did his ᴿdisciples.   10:2–4

20 And, behold, a woman, which was diseased with an issue of blood twelve years, came behind *him*, and touched the hem of his garment:

21 For she said within herself, If I may but touch his garment, I shall be whole.

22 But Jesus turned him about, and when he saw her, he said, Daughter, be of good comfort; Rthy faith hath made thee whole. And the woman was made whole from that hour.   Luke 7:50; 17:19; 18:42

23 And when Jesus came into the ruler's house, and saw the Tminstrels and the people making a noise,   *flute players*

24 He said unto them, Give place: Rfor the maid is not dead, but sleepeth. And they laughed him to scorn.   Acts 20:10

25 But when the people were put Tforth, he went in, and took her by the hand, and the maid arose.   *out*

26 And the fame Thereof went abroad into all that land.   *of this thing*

Sight Is Restored

27 And when Jesus departed thence, two blind men followed him, crying, and saying, Thou son of David, have mercy on us.

28 And when he was come into the house, the blind men came to him: and Jesus saith unto them, Believe ye that I am able to do this? They said unto him, Yea, Lord.

29 Then touched he their eyes, saying, According to your faith be it unto you.

30 And their eyes were opened; and Jesus Tstraitly charged them, saying, RSee that no man know it.   *strictly instructed* • 8:4

31 But they, when they were departed, spread abroad his fame in all that country.

Speech Is Restored

32 RAs they went out, behold, they brought to him a dumb man possessed with a Tdevil.   12:22; Luke 11:14 • *demon*

33 And when the Tdevil was cast out, the dumb spake: and the multitudes marvelled, saying, It was never so seen in Israel.   *demon*

34 But the Pharisees said, He casteth out devils through the prince of the devils.

The Need for Delegation of Power

35 And Jesus went about all the cities and villages, Rteaching in their synagogues, and preaching the gospel of the kingdom, and healing Tevery sickness and every disease among the people.   4:23 • *all manner of*

36 But when he saw the multitudes, he was moved with compassion on them, because they fainted, and were scattered abroad, as sheep having no shepherd.

37 Then saith he unto his disciples, RThe harvest truly is Tplenteous, but the labourers are few;   Luke 10:2; John 4:35 • *large*

38 RPray ye therefore the Lord of the harvest, that he will Tsend forth labourers into his harvest.   2 Thess. 3:1 • *send out*

CHAPTER 10

The Twelve Apostles Are Sent
Mark 6:7; Luke 9:1

AND Rwhen he had called unto *him* his twelve disciples, he gave them power *against* unclean spirits, to cast them out, and to heal all manner of sickness and all manner of disease.   Mark 3:13; Luke 6:13

2 Now the names of the twelve apostles are these; The first, Simon, who is called Peter, and Andrew his brother; James *the son* of Zeb'-e-dee, and John his brother;

3 RPhilip, and Bartholomew; Thomas, and Matthew the publican; James *the son* of Al-phae'-us, and Leb-bae'-us, whose surname was Thad-dae'-us;   Mark 3:14–19

4 Simon the Ca'-naan-ite, and Judas RIscar'-i-ot, who also betrayed him.   John 13:26

The Twelve Apostles Are Instructed
Mark 6:8–13; Luke 9:2–6; 12:2–10

5 These twelve Jesus sent forth, and commanded them, saying, Go not into the Tway of the Gentiles, and into *any* city of the Sa-mar'-i-tans enter ye not: *region*

6 RBut go rather to the Rlost sheep of the house of Israel.   Acts 13:46 • Is. 53:6; Jer. 50:6

7 And as ye go, preach, saying, RThe kingdom of heaven is Tat hand.   3:2 • *near*

8 Heal the sick, cleanse the lepers, raise the dead, cast out devils: Rfreely ye have received, Tfreely give.   [Acts 8:18] • *without charge*

9 TProvide neither gold, nor silver, nor brass in your purses,   *take along*

10 Nor scrip for *your* journey, neither two coats, neither shoes, nor yet staves: for the workman is worthy of his meat.

11 RAnd into whatsoever city or town ye shall enter, enquire who in it is worthy; and there abide till ye go thence.   Luke 10:8

12 And when ye come into an house, Tsalute Rit.   *greet* • 1 Sam. 25:6; Ps. 122:7, 8

13 And if the house be worthy, let your peace come upon it: but if it be not worthy, let your peace return to you.

14 And whosoever shall not receive you, nor hear your words, when ye depart out of that house or city, Rshake off the dust of your feet.   Neh. 5:13; Acts 13:51

15 Verily I say unto you, It shall be more tolerable for the land of Sodom and Go-mor'-rha in the day of judgment, than for that city.

16 Behold, I send you forth as sheep in the midst of wolves: be ye therefore wise as serpents, and Tharmless as doves.   *innocent*

17 RBut beware of men: for they will deliver you up to the councils, and they will scourge you in their synagogues;   Acts 5:40

18 And Rye shall be brought before governors and kings for my sake, for a testimony against them and the Gentiles.   Acts 12:1

19 ^RBut when they deliver you up, take no thought how or what ye shall speak: for ^Rit shall be given you in that same hour what ye shall speak.   Luke 21:14 · Ex. 4:12

20 ^RFor it is not ye that speak, but the Spirit of your Father which speaketh in you.   2 Sam. 23:2; [John 12:44; 1 Cor. 1:17; 2 Tim. 4:17]

21 And the brother shall deliver up the brother to death, and the father the child: and the children shall rise up against *their* parents, and cause them to be put to death.

22 And ye shall be hated of all *men* for my name's sake: ^Rbut he that ^Tendureth to the end shall be saved.   [Dan. 12:12] · *persists*

23 But ^Rwhen they persecute you in this city, flee ye into another: for verily I say unto you, Ye shall not have gone over the cities of Israel, till the Son of man be come.   2:13; Acts 8:1

24 ^RThe disciple is not above *his* master, nor the servant above his lord.   Luke 6:40

25 It is enough for the disciple that he be as his master, and the servant as his lord. If they have called the master of the house ^TBe-el'-ze-bub, how much more *shall they call* them of his household?   *beelzebul*

26 Fear them not therefore: for there is nothing covered, that shall not be revealed; and hid, that shall not be known.

27 What I tell you in darkness, *that* speak ye in light: and what ye hear in the ear, *that* preach ye upon the housetops.

28 And fear not them which kill the body, but are not able to kill the soul: but rather fear ^Thim which is able to destroy both soul and body in hell.   *God who*

29 Are not two sparrows sold for a ^Tfarthing? and one of them shall not fall on the ground without your Father.   *1/16 of a day's wage*

30 ^RBut the very ^Rhairs of your head are all numbered.   1 Sam. 14:45; Luke 21:18 · Acts 27:34

31 Fear ye not therefore, ye are of more ^Tvalue than many sparrows.   *worth*

32 ^RWhosoever therefore shall confess me before men, him will I confess also before my Father which is in heaven.   Luke 12:8

33 ^RBut whosoever shall deny me before men, him will I also deny before my Father which is in heaven.   [Luke 9:26]; 2 Tim. 2:12

34 ^RThink not that I am come to send peace on earth: I came not to ^Tsend peace, but a sword.   [Luke 12:49] · *bring*

35 For I am come to ^RSET A MAN AT VARIANCE AGAINST HIS FATHER, AND THE DAUGHTER AGAINST HER MOTHER, AND THE DAUGHTER IN LAW AGAINST HER MOTHER IN LAW.   Mic. 7:6 ☆

36 And ^RA MAN'S FOES *SHALL BE* THEY OF HIS OWN ^THOUSEHOLD.   Ps. 41:9; John 13:18 ☆ · *family*

37 ^RHe that loveth father or mother more than me is not worthy of me: and he that loveth son or daughter more than me is not worthy of me.   Luke 14:26

38 And he that taketh not his cross, and followeth after me, is not worthy of me.

39 ^RHe that findeth his life shall lose it: and he that loseth his life for my sake shall find it.   16:25; Mark 8:35; Luke 9:24; 17:33; John 12:25

40 ^RHe that receiveth you receiveth me, and he that receiveth me receiveth him that sent me.   Luke 9:48; John 12:44; Gal. 4:14

41 ^RHe that receiveth a prophet in the name of a prophet shall receive a prophet's reward; and he that receiveth a righteous man in the name of a righteous man shall receive a righteous man's reward.   1 Kin. 17:10

42 ^RAnd whosoever shall give to drink unto one of these little ones a cup of cold *water* only in the name of a disciple, verily I say unto you, he shall in no wise lose his reward.   [25:40]; Mark 9:41; Heb. 6:10

CHAPTER 11

AND it came to pass, when Jesus had made an end of commanding his twelve disciples, he departed thence to teach and to preach in their cities.

Rejection of John the Baptist—Luke 7:19-30

2 Now when John had heard ^Rin the prison the works ^Tof Christ, he sent two of his disciples,   14:3 · *by*

3 And said unto him, Art thou he that should come, or do we look for another?

4 Jesus answered and said unto them, Go and shew John again those ^Rthings which ye do hear and see: Is. 29:18, 19; 35:4-6 ☆

5 The blind receive their sight, and the lame walk, the lepers are cleansed, and the deaf hear, the dead are raised up, and the poor have the gospel preached to them.

6 And blessed is *he,* whosoever shall not be ^Toffended in me.   *moved to oppose*

7 And as they departed, Jesus began to say unto the multitudes concerning John, What went ye out into the wilderness to see? A reed shaken with the wind?

8 But what went ye out for to see? A man clothed in soft raiment? behold, they that wear soft *clothing* are in kings' houses.

9 But what went ye out for to see? A ^Tprophet? yea, I say unto you, ^Rand more than a prophet.   *preacher* · Luke 1:76

10 For this is *he,* of whom it is written, ^RBEHOLD, I SEND MY MESSENGER BEFORE THY FACE, WHICH SHALL PREPARE THY WAY BEFORE THEE.   Mal. 3:1 ☆

11 Verily I say unto you, Among them that are born of women there hath not risen a greater than John the Baptist: notwithstanding he that is least in the kingdom of heaven is greater than he.

12 And from the days of John the Baptist until now the kingdom of heaven suffereth violence, and the violent take it by force.

13 For all the prophets and the law prophesied until John.

14 And if ye will receive *it*, this is [R]E-li'-as, which was for to come.   Mal. 4:5

15 He that hath ears to hear, let him hear.

Rejection by Jesus' Generation—Luke 7:31-35

16 But whereunto shall I liken this generation? It is like unto children sitting in the markets, and calling unto their fellows,

17 And saying, We have piped unto you, and ye [T]have not danced; we have mourned unto you, and ye have not lamented.   *would not*

18 For John came neither eating nor drinking, and they say, He hath a devil.

19 The Son of man came eating and drinking, and they say, Behold a man gluttonous, and a [T]winebibber, a friend of publicans and sinners. But wisdom is justified of her children.   *wine drinker*

Rejection of Chorazin, Bethsaida, and Capernaum—Luke 10:12-15

20 Then began he to [T]upbraid the cities wherein most of his mighty works were done, because they repented not: *accuse*

21 Woe unto thee, Cho-ra'-zin! woe unto thee, Beth-sa'-i-da! for if the mighty works, which were done in you, had been done in Tyre and Si'-don, they would have repented long ago in sackcloth and ashes.

22 But I say unto you, [R]It shall be more tolerable for Tyre and Si'-don at the day of judgment, than for you.   10:15

23 And thou, Ca-per'-na-um, which art exalted unto heaven, shalt be brought down to hell: for if the [T]mighty works, which have been done in thee, had been done in Sodom, it would have remained until this day.   *miracles*

24 But I say unto you, [R]That it shall be more tolerable for the land of Sodom in the day of judgment, than for thee.   10:15

Invitation to Come unto Jesus

25 At that time Jesus answered and said, I thank thee, O Father, Lord of heaven and earth, because thou hast hid these things from the wise and prudent, and hast revealed them unto babes.

26 [T]Even so, [R]Father: for so it seemed good in thy sight.   *this was done* • John 11:41; 12:27, 28

27 All things are delivered unto me of my Father: and no man knoweth the Son, but the Father; neither knoweth any man the Father, [T]save the Son, and *he* to whomsoever the Son will reveal *him*.   *except*

28 Come unto me, all ye that labour and are heavy laden, and I will give you rest.

29 Take my yoke upon you, and learn of me; for I am meek and lowly in heart: and ye shall find rest unto your souls.

30 [R]For my yoke *is* easy, and my [T]burden is light.   [1 John 5:3] • *load*

CHAPTER 12

Controversy over Sabbath-Labour
Mark 2:23-28, Luke 6:1-5

AT that time [R]Jesus went on the sabbath day through the corn; and his disciples were an hungred, and began to pluck the ears of corn, and to eat.   Deut. 23:25

2 But when the Pharisees saw *it*, they said unto him, Behold, thy disciples do that which is not lawful to do upon the sabbath day.

3 But he said unto them, Have ye not read what David did, when he was an hungred, and they that were with him;

4 How he entered into the house of God, and did eat the shewbread, which was not lawful for him to eat, neither for them which were with him, but only for the priests?

5 Or have ye not read in the law, how that on the sabbath days the priests in the temple profane the sabbath, and are blameless?

6 But I say unto you, That in this place is [R]one greater than the temple.   [Mal. 3:1]

7 But if ye had known what *this* meaneth, I WILL HAVE MERCY, AND NOT SACRIFICE, ye would not have condemned the guiltless.

8 For the [R]Son of man is Lord even of the sabbath day.   Dan. 7:13

Controversy over Sabbath-Healing
Mark 3:1-5; Luke 6:6-10

9 And when he was departed thence, he went into their synagogue:

10 And, behold, there was a man which had *his* hand withered. And they asked him, saying, Is it lawful to heal on the sabbath days? that they might accuse him.

11 And he said unto them, What man shall there be among you, that shall have one sheep, and [R]if it fall into a pit on the sabbath day, will he not [T]lay hold on it, and lift *it* out?   Deut. 22:4; Luke 14:5 • *take*

12 How much then is a man [T]better than a sheep? Wherefore it is lawful to do [T]well on the sabbath days.   *worth more* • *good*

13 Then saith he to the man, Stretch forth thine hand. And he stretched *it* forth; and it was restored whole, like as the other.

Pharisees Plan to Destroy Christ
Mark 3:6-12; Luke 6:11

14 Then [R]the Pharisees went out, and [T]held a council against him, how they might destroy him.   27:1 • *took counsel*

15 But when Jesus knew *it*, he withdrew himself from thence: and great multitudes followed him, and he healed them all;

16 And [R]charged[T] them that they should not make him known: 9:30 • *requested*

17 That it might be fulfilled which was spoken by E-sa'-ias the prophet, saying,

18 [R]BEHOLD MY SERVANT, WHOM I HAVE CHOSEN; MY BELOVED, IN WHOM MY SOUL IS

WELL PLEASED: I WILL PUT MY SPIRIT UPON HIM, AND HE SHALL SHEW JUDGMENT TO THE GENTILES. Is. 42:1,2 *

19 ᴿHE SHALL NOT STRIVE, NOR CRY; NEITHER SHALL ANY MAN HEAR HIS VOICE IN THE STREETS. Is. 42:2 *

20 A BRUISED REED SHALL HE NOT BREAK, AND SMOKING FLAX SHALL HE NOT QUENCH, TILL HE SEND FORTH JUDGMENT UNTO VICTORY.

21 ᴿAND IN HIS NAME SHALL THE GENTILES TRUST. Is. 42:3, 4 *

Pharisees Blaspheme the Holy Spirit
Mark 3:22-27; Luke 11:17-23

22 ᴿThen was brought unto him one possessed with a ᵀdevil, blind, and dumb: and he healed him, insomuch that the blind and dumb both spake and saw. Luke 11:14 · demon

23 And all the people were amazed, and said, Is not this the son of David?

24 But when the Pharisees heard it, they said, This fellow doth not cast out devils, but by Be-el'-ze-bub the prince of the devils.

25 And Jesus ᴿknew their thoughts, and said unto them, Every kingdom divided against itself is brought to ᵀdesolation; and every city or house divided against itself shall not stand: 9:4; John 2:25; Rev. 2:23 · ruin

26 And if Satan ᵀcast out Satan, he is divided against himself; how shall then his kingdom stand? fights

27 And if I by Be-el'-ze-bub cast out devils, by whom do your children cast them out? therefore they shall be your judges.

28 But if I cast out devils by the Spirit of God, then ᴿthe kingdom of God is come unto you. [Dan. 2:44; Luke 1:33]; 11:20; [17:20, 21]

29 Or else how can one enter into a strong man's house, and ᵀspoil his goods, except he first bind the strong man? and then he will ᵀspoil his house. take away · rob

30 He that is not ᵀwith me is against me; and he that ᵀgathereth not with me scattereth abroad. for · does not help

Pharisees Commit the Unpardonable Sin
Mark 3:28, 29

31 Wherefore I say unto you, All manner of sin and blasphemy shall be forgiven unto men: but the blasphemy against the Holy Ghost shall not be forgiven unto men.

32 And whosoever ᴿspeaketh a word against the Son of man, ᴿit shall be forgiven him: but whosoever speaketh against the Holy Ghost, it shall not be forgiven him, neither in this world, neither in the world to come. 11:19; 13:55; John 7:12, 52 · 1 Tim. 1:13

33 Either make the tree good, and ᴿhis fruit good; or else make the tree ᵀcorrupt, and his fruit corrupt: for the tree is known by his fruit. 7:17; Luke 6:43 · bad

34 O generation of vipers, how can ye, being evil, speak good things? for out of the abundance of the heart the mouth speaketh.

35 A good man out of the ᵀgood treasure of the heart bringeth forth good things: and an evil man out of the evil treasure bringeth forth evil things. his

36 But I say unto you, That every idle word that men shall speak, they shall give account thereof in the day of judgment.

37 For by thy words thou shalt be justified, and by thy words thou shalt be condemned.

Pharisees Demand a Sign
Luke 11:24-26, 29-32

38 ᴿThen certain of the scribes and of the Pharisees answered, saying, Master, we would see a sign from thee. 16:1; Mark 8:11

39 But he answered and said unto them, An evil and adulterous generation seeketh after a sign; and there shall no sign be given to it, but the sign of the prophet Jo'-nas:

40 ᴿFor as Jo'-nas was three days and three nights in the whale's belly; so shall the Son of man be three days and three nights in the heart of the earth. Jon. 1:17 ☆

41 The men of Nin'-e-veh shall rise in judgment with this generation, and shall condemn it: ᴿbecause they repented at the preaching of Jo'-nas; and, behold, a greater than Jo'-nas is here. · Jon. 3:5

42 ᴿThe queen of the south shall rise up in the judgment with this generation, and shall condemn it: for she came from the uttermost parts of the earth to hear the wisdom of Solomon; and, behold, a greater than Solomon is here. 2 Chr. 9:1; Luke 11:31

43 WhenR the unclean spirit is gone out of a man, he walketh through dry places, seeking rest, and findeth none. Luke 11:24

44 Then he saith, I will return into my house from whence I came out; and when he is come, he findeth it empty, swept, and ᵀgarnished. put in order

45 Then goeth he, and taketh with himself seven other spirits more wicked than himself, and they enter in and dwell there: ᴿand the last state of that man is worse than the first. Even so shall it be also unto this wicked generation. [Heb. 6:4; 2 Pet. 2:20-22]

Jesus and the True Brethren—Mark 3:31-35

46 While he yet talked to the people, behold, his mother and ᴿhis brethren stood without, desiring to speak with him. 13:55

47 Then one said unto him, Behold, thy mother and thy brethren stand ᵀwithout, desiring to speak with thee. outside

48 But he answered and said unto him that told him, Who is my mother? and who are my brethren?

49 And he stretched forth his hand toward his disciples, and said, ᵀBehold my mother and my brethren! *here are*

50 For ᴿwhosoever shall do the will of my Father which is in heaven, the same is my brother, and sister, and mother. [Heb. 2:11]

CHAPTER 13

Parable of the Soils—Mark 4:1-20; Luke 8:4-15

THE same day went Jesus out of the house, and sat by the sea side.

2 And great multitudes were gathered together unto him, so that ᴿhe went into a ship, and sat; and the whole multitude stood on the shore. Luke 5:3

3 And he spake many things unto them in ᵀparables, saying, Behold, a sower went forth to sow; *illustrations*

4 And when he sowed, some *seeds* fell by the way side, and the fowls came and devoured them up:

5 Some fell upon ᵀstony places, where they had not much earth: and ᵀforthwith they sprung up, because they had no deepness of earth: *little soil • soon*

6 And when the sun was up, they were ᵀscorched; and because they had no root, they ᵀwithered away. *burned • dried up*

7 And some fell among thorns; and the thorns sprung up, and choked them:

8 But other fell into good ground, and brought forth fruit, some ᴿan hundredfold, some sixtyfold, some thirtyfold. Gen. 26:12

9 Who hath ears to hear, let him hear.

10 And the disciples came, and said unto him, Why ᵀspeakest thou unto them in parables? *talk to*

11 He answered and said unto them, Because ᴿit is given unto you to know the ᵀmysteries of the kingdom of heaven, but to them it is not given. [1 John 2:27] • *hidden truths*

12 ᴿFor whosoever hath, to him shall be given, and he shall have more abundance: but whosoever hath not, from him shall be taken away even that he hath. 25:29

13 Therefore speak I to them in parables: because they seeing see not; and hearing they hear not, neither do they understand.

14 And in them is fulfilled the prophecy of E-sa'-ias, which saith, BY HEARING YE SHALL HEAR, AND SHALL NOT UNDERSTAND; AND SEEING YE SHALL SEE, AND SHALL NOT PERCEIVE:

15 FOR THIS PEOPLE'S HEART IS WAXED ᵀGROSS, AND *THEIR* EARS ᴿARE DULL OF HEARING, AND THEIR EYES THEY HAVE CLOSED; LEST AT ANY TIME THEY SHOULD SEE WITH *THEIR* EYES AND HEAR WITH *THEIR* EARS, AND SHOULD UNDERSTAND WITH *THEIR* HEART, AND SHOULD BE CONVERTED, AND I SHOULD HEAL THEM. *callous* • Is. 6:9, 10; Heb. 5:11 *

16 But ᴿblessed *are* your eyes, for they see: and your ears, for they hear. [vv. 11, 17]

17 For verily I say unto you, That many prophets and righteous *men* have desired to see *those things* which ye see, and have not seen *them;* and to hear *those things* which ye hear, and have not heard *them.*

18 ᵀHear ye therefore the parable of the sower. *learn what it means*

19 When any one heareth the word of the kingdom, and understandeth *it* not, then cometh the wicked *one,* and catcheth away that which was sown in his heart. This is he which received seed by the way side.

20 But he that received the seed into stony places, the same is he that heareth the word, and anon with joy receiveth it;

21 Yet hath he not root in himself, but dureth for a while: for when tribulation or persecution ariseth because of the word, by and by he is offended.

22 ᴿHe also that received seed ᴿamong the thorns is he that heareth the word; and the care of this world, and the deceitfulness of riches, choke the word, and he becometh unfruitful. 2 Tim. 4:10 • Jer. 4:3

23 But he that received seed into the good ground is he that heareth the word, and understandeth *it;* which also beareth ᴿfruit, and bringeth forth, some an hundredfold, some sixty, some thirty. Phil. 1:11

Parable of the Wheat and Tares

24 Another parable put he forth unto them, saying, The kingdom of heaven is likened unto a man which sowed ᴿgood seed in his field: [1 Pet. 1:23]

25 But while men slept, his enemy came and sowed ᵀtares among the wheat, and went his way. *weeds*

26 But when the ᵀblade was sprung up, and brought forth fruit, then appeared the ᵀtares also. *grass • weeds*

27 So the servants of the householder came and said unto him, Sir, didst not thou sow good seed in thy field? from ᵀwhence then hath it tares? *where*

28 He said unto them, An enemy hath done this. The servants said unto him, Wilt thou then that we go and gather them up?

29 But he said, Nay; lest while ye gather up the ᵀtares, ye root up also the wheat with them. *injurious weeds*

30 Let both grow together until the harvest: and in the time of harvest I will say to the reapers, Gather ye together first the tares, and bind them in bundles to burn them: but gather the wheat into my barn.

Parable of the Mustard Seed
Mark 4:30–32; Luke 13:18, 19

31 Another parable put he forth unto them, saying, The kingdom of heaven is like

to a grain of mustard seed, which a man took, and sowed in his field:

32 Which indeed is the ᵀleast of all seeds: but when it is grown, it is the ᵀgreatest among herbs, and becometh a tree, so that the birds of the air come and lodge in the branches thereof.   *smallest · biggest*

Parable of the Leaven—Luke 13:20, 21

33 Another parable spake he unto them; The kingdom of heaven is like unto leaven, which a woman took, and hid in ᵀthree measures of meal, till the whole was leavened.   *6.52 bushels*

34 All these things spake Jesus unto the multitude in parables; and without a parable spake he not unto them:

35 That it might be fulfilled which was spoken by the prophet, saying, ᴿI WILL OPEN MY MOUTH IN PARABLES; I WILL UTTER THINGS WHICH HAVE BEEN KEPT SECRET FROM THE FOUNDATION OF THE WORLD.   Ps. 78:2 ⋆

Parable of the Tares Explained

36 Then Jesus sent the multitude away, and went into the house: and his disciples came unto him, saying, Declare unto us the parable of the tares of the field.

37 He answered and said unto them, He that soweth the good seed is the Son of man;

38 The field is the world; the good seed are the children of the kingdom; but the tares are the children of the wicked *one;*

39 The enemy that sowed them is the devil; ᴿthe harvest is the end of the world; and the reapers are the angels.   Rev. 14:15

40 As therefore the tares are gathered and burned in the fire; so shall it be in the ᴿend of this world.   1 Cor. 10:11; Heb. 9:26

41 The Son of man shall send forth his angels, ᴿand they shall gather out of his kingdom all ᵀthings that offend, and them which do ᵀiniquity;   18:7 · *scandals · wrong*

42 ᴿAnd shall cast them into a furnace of fire: ᴿthere shall be wailing and gnashing of teeth.   3:12; Rev. 19:20; 20:10 · v. 50; 8:12

43 Then shall the righteous shine forth as the sun in the kingdom of their Father. ᴿWho hath ears to hear, let him hear.   v. 9

Parable of the Hidden Treasure

44 Again, the kingdom of heaven is like unto treasure hid in a field; the which when a man hath found, he hideth, and for joy thereof goeth and ᴿselleth all that he hath, and buyeth that field.   Phil. 3:7, 8

Parable of the Pearl of Great Price

45 Again, the kingdom of heaven is like unto a ᵀmerchant man, seeking ᵀgoodly pearls: *buyer · fine*

46 Who, when he had found ᴿone pearl of great price, went and sold all that he had, and bought it.   Prov. 2:4; 3:14, 15; 8:10, 19

Parable of the Net

47 Again, the kingdom of heaven is like unto a net, that was cast into the sea, and ᴿgathered of every kind: 22:10

48 Which, when it was full, they drew to shore, and sat down, and gathered the good into vessels, but cast the bad away.

49 So shall it be at the end of the world: the angels shall come forth, and ᴿseverᵀ the wicked from among the just,   25:32 · *separate*

50 And shall cast them into the furnace of fire: there shall be wailing and gnashing of teeth.

Parable of the Householder

51 Jesus saith unto them, Have ye understood all these things? They say unto him, ᵀYea, Lord.   *yes*

52 Then said he unto them, Therefore every ᵀscribe *which is* instructed unto the kingdom of heaven is like unto a man *that is* an householder, which bringeth forth out of his treasure *things* new and old.   *scholar*

53 And it came to pass, *that* when Jesus had finished these parables, he ᵀdeparted thence.   *went to his home town*

Rejection at Nazareth—Mark 6:1-6

54 ᴿAnd when he was come into his own country, he ᴿtaught them in their synagogue, insomuch that they were astonished, and said, Whence hath this *man* this wisdom, and *these* mighty works?   2:23 · Ps. 22:22 ⋆

55 Is not this the carpenter's son? is not his mother called Mary? and his brethren, James, and Jo′-ses, and Simon, and Judas?

56 And his sisters, are they not all ᵀwith us? Whence then hath this *man* all these ᴿthings?   *living here* · 1:25

57 And they were ᴿoffended in him. But Jesus said unto them, ᴿA prophet is not without honour, save in his own country, and in his own house.   11:6 · John 4:44

58 And he did not many mighty works there because of their unbelief.

CHAPTER 14

Present Response to Jesus
Mark 6:14-16; Luke 9:7-9

AT that time Herod the te′-trarch heard of the fame of Jesus,

2 And said unto his servants, This is John the Baptist; he is risen from the dead; and therefore mighty works ᵀdo shew forth themselves in him.   *are done by him*

Recount of the Murder of John the Baptist
Mark 6:17–29

3 For Herod had laid hold on John, and bound him, and put *him* in prison for He-ro'-di-as' sake, his brother Philip's wife.

4 For John said unto him, ᴿIt is not ᵀlawful for thee to have her. Lev. 18:16; 20:21 • *right*

5 And when he would have put him to death, he feared the multitude, ᴿbecause they counted him as a prophet. Luke 20:6

6 But when Herod's birthday was kept, the daughter of He-ro'-di-as danced ᵀbefore them, and pleased Herod. *in the midst*

7 Whereupon he promised with an oath to give her whatsoever she would ask.

8 And she, being before instructed of her mother, said, Give me here John Baptist's head in a ᵀcharger. *platter*

9 And the king was sorry: ᴿnevertheless for the oath's sake, and them which ᵀsat with him at meat, he commanded *it* to be given her. [Eccl. 5:2] • *dined with him*

10 And he sent, and beheaded John in the prison.

11 And his head was brought in a ᵀcharger, and given to the ᵀdamsel: and she ᵀbrought *it* to her mother. *large plate • girl • took*

12 And his disciples came, and took up the body, and buried it, and went and told Jesus.

Jesus Feeds 5,000
Mark 6:31–44; Luke 9:11–17; John 6:1–13

13 When Jesus heard *of it*, he departed thence by ship into a desert place apart: and when the people had heard *thereof*, they followed him on foot out of the cities.

14 And Jesus went forth, and saw a great multitude, and was moved with compassion toward them, and he healed their sick.

15 And when it was evening, his disciples came to him, saying, This is a desert place, and the time is now past; send the multitude away, that they may go into the villages, and buy themselves ᵀvictuals. *food*

16 But Jesus said unto them, They need not depart; give ye them to eat.

17 And they say unto him, We have here but five loaves, and two fishes.

18 He said, Bring them hither to me.

19 And he commanded ᴿthe multitude to sit down on the grass, and took the five loaves, and the two fishes, and looking up to heaven, he ᵀblessed, and brake, and gave the loaves to *his* disciples, and the disciples to the multitude. *v. 13 • thanked God*

20 And they did all eat, and were filled: and they took up of the ᵀfragments that remained twelve baskets full. *leftovers*

21 And they that had eaten were about five thousand men, ᵀbeside women and children. *not counting*

Jesus Walks on Water
Mark 6:45–52; John 6:14–21

22 And ᵀstraightway Jesus ᵀconstrained his disciples to get into a ship, and to go before him unto the other side, while he sent the multitudes away. *immediately • urged*

23 And when he had sent the multitudes away, he went up into a mountain apart to pray: ᴿand when the evening was come, he was there alone. John 6:16

24 But the ship was now in the midst of the sea, tossed with waves: for the wind was ᵀcontrary. *blowing against it*

25 And in the fourth watch of the night Jesus went unto them, walking on the sea.

26 And when the disciples saw him ᴿwalking on the sea, they were troubled, saying, It is a spirit; and they cried out for fear. Job 9:8

27 But ᵀstraightway Jesus spake unto them, saying, ᵀBe of good cheer; it is I; be not afraid. *at once • courage*

28 And Peter answered him and said, Lord, if it be thou, ᵀbid me come unto thee on the water. *command*

29 And he said, Come. And when Peter was come down out of the ship, he walked on the water, to go to Jesus.

30 But when he saw the wind ᵀboisterous, he was afraid; and beginning to sink, he cried, saying, Lord, save me. *strong*

31 And immediately Jesus stretched forth *his* hand, and caught him, and said unto him, ᴿO thou of little faith, wherefore didst thou doubt? 6:30; 8:26; James 1:6, 7

32 And when they ᵀwere come into the ship, the wind ᵀceased. *got into • stopped*

33 Then they that were in the ship came and ᵀworshipped him, saying, Of a truth ᴿthou art the Son of God. *honoured • Rom. 1:4*

Jesus Heals Many—Mark 6:53–56

34 And when they were gone over, they came into the land of Gen-nes'-a-ret.

35 And when the men of that place had ᵀknowledge of him, they sent out into all that country round about, and brought unto him all that were diseased; *heard about*

36 And besought him that they might only touch the hem of his garment: and ᴿas many as touched were made perfectly whole. 9:20

CHAPTER 15

Debate over Tradition—Mark 7:1–23

THEN came to Jesus scribes and Pharisees, which were of Jerusalem, saying,

2 Why do thy disciples transgress the tradition of the elders? for they wash not their hands when they eat bread.

3 But he answered and said unto them, Why do ye also ᵀtransgress the commandment of God by your tradition? *disobey*

4 For God commanded, saying, ᴿHONOUR

THY FATHER AND MOTHER: and, ᴿHE THAT CURSETH FATHER OR MOTHER, LET HIM DIE THE DEATH.   Ex. 20:12 • Ex. 21:17

5 But ye say, Whosoever shall say to his father or his mother, It is a gift, by whatsoever thou mightest be profited by me;

6 And honour not his father or his mother, he shall be free. Thus have ye made the commandment of God of none effect by your tradition.

7 Ye hypocrites, ᵀwell did E-sa′-ias prophesy of you, saying,   rightly

8 THIS PEOPLE DRAWETH NIGH UNTO ME WITH THEIR MOUTH, AND HONOURETH ME WITH THEIR LIPS; BUT THEIR HEART IS FAR FROM ME.

9 ᴿBUT IN VAIN THEY DO WORSHIP ME, ᴿTEACHING FOR DOCTRINES THE COMMANDMENTS OF MEN.   Is. 29:13 • [Col. 2:18–22]; Titus 1:14

10 And he called the multitude, and said unto them, Hear, and understand:

11 ᴿNot that which goeth into the mouth defileth a man; but that which cometh out of the mouth, this defileth a man.   [Titus 1:15]

12 Then came his disciples, and said unto him, Knowest thou that the Pharisees were offended, after they heard this saying?

13 But he answered and said, Every plant, which my heavenly Father hath not planted, shall be rooted up.

14 Let them alone: ᴿthey be blind leaders of the blind. And if the blind lead the blind, both shall fall into the ditch.   Luke 6:39

15 Then answered Peter and said unto him, ᵀDeclare unto us this parable.   explain

16 And Jesus said, Are ye also yet without understanding?

17 Do not ye yet understand, that whatsoever entereth in at the mouth goeth into the belly, and is cast out into the draught?

18 But ᴿthose things which proceed out of the mouth come forth from the heart; and they defile the man.   [James 3:6]

19 ᴿFor out of the heart proceed evil thoughts, murders, adulteries, fornications, thefts, false witness, blasphemies: Jer. 17:9

20 These are the things which ᵀdefile a man: but to eat with unwashen hands defileth not a man.   make a man unclean

Jesus Heals the Gentile Woman's Daughter
Mark 7:24–30

21 Then Jesus went thence, and departed into the coasts of Tyre and Si′-don.

22 And, behold, a woman of Canaan came out of the same coasts, and cried unto him, saying, Have mercy on me, O Lord, thou son of David; my daughter is ᵀgrievously vexed with a devil.   sadly troubled by a demon

23 But he answered her not a word. And his disciples came and besought him, saying, Send her away; for she crieth after us.

24 But he answered and said, ᴿI am ᵀnot sent but unto the lost sheep of the house of Israel.   10:5, 6 • sent only to

25 Then came she and ᵀworshipped him, saying, Lord, help me.   fell at his feet

26 But he answered and said, It is not meet to take the children's bread, and to cast it to ᴿdogsᵀ.   Phil. 3:2 • puppies

27 And she said, Truth, Lord: yet the ᵀdogs eat of the crumbs which fall from their masters' table.   puppies

28 Then Jesus answered and said unto her, O woman, great is thy faith: be it unto thee even as thou wilt. And her daughter was made ᵀwhole from that very hour.   well

Jesus Heals Many—Mark 7:31–37

29 And Jesus departed from thence, and came nigh unto the sea of Galilee; and went up into a mountain, and sat down there.

30 ᴿAnd great multitudes came unto him, having with them those that were lame, blind, dumb, ᵀmaimed, and many others, and cast them down at Jesus' feet; and he healed them: Is. 35:5, 6; Luke 7:22 • crippled

31 Insomuch that the multitude wondered, when they saw the dumb to speak, the maimed to be ᵀwhole, the lame to walk, and the blind to see: and they ᵀglorified the God of Israel.   well or healthy • praised

Jesus Feeds 4,000—Mark 8:1–10

32 Then Jesus called his disciples unto him, and said, I have compassion on the multitude, because they continue with me now three days, and have nothing to eat: and I will not send them away fasting, lest they faint in the way.

33 And his disciples say unto him, Whence should we have so much bread in the wilderness, as to fill so great a multitude?

34 And Jesus saith unto them, How many loaves have ye? And they said, Seven, and a few little fishes.

35 And he ᵀcommanded the multitude to sit down on the ground.   ordered

36 And ᴿhe took the seven loaves and the fishes, and ᴿgave thanks, and brake them, and gave to his disciples, and the disciples to the multitude.   14:19 • Luke 22:19

37 And they did all eat, and were filled: and they took up of the broken meat that was left seven baskets full.

38 And they that did eat were four thousand men, beside women and children.

39 And he sent away the multitude, and took ship, and came into the coasts of ᵀMag′-da-la.   Magadan

CHAPTER 16

Debate over a Sign from Heaven
Mark 8:11, 12

THE Pharisees also with the Sad′-du-cees came, and tempting ᵀdesired him that he would shew them a sign from heaven.   asked

2 He answered and said unto them, [R]When it is [T]evening, ye say, It will be fair weather: for the sky is red.   Luke 12:54 · sunset

3 And in the morning, It will be foul weather to day: for the sky is red and lowring. O ye hypocrites, ye can discern the face of the sky; but can ye not discern the signs of the times?

4 [R]A wicked and adulterous generation seeketh after a sign; and there shall no sign be given unto it, but the sign of the prophet Jo′-nas. And he left them, and departed. 12:39

Withdrawal of Jesus—Mark 8:13-21

5 And when his disciples [T]were come to the other side, they had forgotten to take bread.   crossed over

6 Then Jesus said unto them, Take heed and beware of the [T]leaven of the Pharisees and of the Sad′-du-cees.   teaching

7 And they reasoned among themselves, saying, It is because we have taken no bread.

8 Which when Jesus perceived, he said unto them, O ye of little faith, why reason ye among yourselves, because ye have brought no bread?

9 Do ye not yet understand, neither remember the five loaves of the five thousand, and how many baskets ye took up?

10 [R]Neither the seven loaves of the four thousand, and how many baskets ye [T]took up?   15:34 · filled

11 How is it that ye do not understand that I spake it not to you concerning bread, that ye should beware of the [T]leaven of the Pharisees and of the Sad′-du-cees?   yeast

12 Then understood they how that he bade them not beware of the leaven of bread, but of the [T]doctrine of the Pharisees and of the Sad′-du-cees.   teaching

Revelation of the Person of the King
Mark 8:27-30; Luke 9:18-21

13 When Jesus came into the coasts of Caes-a-re′-a Phi-lip′-pi, he asked his disciples, saying, Whom[T] do men say that I the Son of man am?   who

14 And they said, Some say that thou art John the Baptist: some, E-li′-as; and others, Jer-e-mi′-as, or one of the prophets.

15 He saith unto them, But whom say ye that I am?

16 And Simon Peter answered and said, [R]Thou art the Christ, the Son of the living God.   Acts 8:37; Heb. 1:2, 5; 1 John 4:15

17 And Jesus answered and said unto him, Blessed art thou, [T]Simon Bar-jo′-na: for flesh and blood hath not revealed it unto thee, but my Father which is in heaven.   son of John

Revelation of the Church

18 And I say also unto thee, That thou art Peter, and upon this [R]rock I will [R]build my church; and the gates of hell shall not prevail against it.   [1 Cor. 3:11; Eph. 2:20] · Acts 2:41, 47 ☆

19 [R]And I will give unto thee the keys of the kingdom of heaven: and whatsoever thou shalt bind on earth shall be bound in heaven: and whatsoever thou shalt loose on earth shall be loosed in heaven.   18:18

20 [R]Then [T]charged he his disciples that they should tell no man that he was [T]Jesus the Christ.   17:9 · warned · the Messiah

Revelation of Jesus' Death
Mark 8:31-33; Luke 9:22

21 From that time forth began Jesus [R]to shew unto his disciples, how that he must go unto Jerusalem, and suffer many things of the elders and chief priests and scribes, and be killed, and be [R]raised again the third day.   20:17-19 · Acts 10:40; 1 Cor. 15:4 ☆

22 Then Peter took him, and began to rebuke him, saying, [T]Be it far from thee, Lord: this shall not be unto thee.   God forbid!

23 But he turned, and said unto Peter, Get thee behind me, Satan: thou art an offence unto me: for thou savourest not the things that be of God, but those that be of men.

Revelation of Jesus' Reward
Mark 8:34-37; Luke 9:23-25

24 [R]Then said Jesus unto his disciples, If any man will come after me, let him deny himself, and take up his cross, and follow me.   Luke 9:23; [Acts 14:22; 1 Thess. 3:3; 2 Tim. 3:12]

25 For [R]whosoever will save his life shall lose it: and [R]whosoever will lose his life for my sake shall find it.   Luke 17:33 · John 12:25

26 For what is a man profited, if he shall gain the whole world, and lose his own [T]soul? or [R]what shall a man give in exchange for his soul?   life · Ps. 49:7, 8

16:18 The Origin of the Church—The church was a mystery (i.e., hidden, not revealed) in the Old Testament. It was first prophesied in these words spoken to Peter, "upon this rock I will build my church." In this prophecy there is a play on the word rock which also happens to be Peter's name. Jesus said, "thou art Peter" (masculine, petros) and "upon this rock (feminine, petra) I will build my church." But when did the church actually begin? Again, many suggestions are offered for varying reasons. The simplest view is to understand the New Testament church as beginning on the Day of Pentecost in response to Peter's pentecostal sermon when "the same day there were added unto them [i.e., the apostles] about three thousand souls" (Page 1074—Acts 2:41). This group for the first time is called "the church" in Acts 2:47, and God added to their number daily those who were saved.
Now turn to Page 1163—Eph. 3:21: The Purpose of the Church.

The Prophecy of the Second Coming
Mark 8:38—9:1; Luke 9:26, 27

27 For ᴿthe Son of man shall come in the glory of his Father ᴿwith his angels; and then he shall reward every man according to his works. 26:64 · Zech. 14:5

28 Verily I say unto you, ᴿThere be some standing here, which shall not taste of death, till they see the Son of man coming in his kingdom. 26:64; Job 34:11; Dan. 7:13

CHAPTER 17

The Transfiguration
Mark 9:2-13; Luke 9:28-36; 2 Pet. 1:17, 18

AND after six days Jesus taketh Peter, James, and John his brother, and bringeth them up into an high mountain apart,

2 And was ᵀtransfigured before them: and his face did shine as the sun, and his raiment was white as the light. *changed*

3 And, behold, there appeared unto them Moses and E-li′-as talking with him.

4 Then answered Peter, and said unto Jesus, Lord, it is good for us to be here: if thou wilt, let us make here three ᵀtabernacles; one for thee, and one for Moses, and one for E-li′-as. *sacred tents*

5 While he yet spake, behold, a bright cloud overshadowed them: and behold ᴿa voice out of the cloud, which said, This is my beloved Son, in whom I am well pleased; hear ye him. Is. 42:1; 2 Pet. 1:17 ☆

6 And when the disciples heard *it*, they fell on their face, and were sore afraid.

7 And Jesus came and ᴿtouched them, and said, Arise, and be not afraid. Dan. 8:18

8 And when they had lifted up their eyes, they saw no man, ᵀsave Jesus only. *except*

9 And as they came down from the mountain, Jesus ᵀcharged them, saying, Tell the vision to no man, until the Son of man be risen again from the dead. *commanded*

10 And his disciples asked him, saying, ᴿWhy then say the scribes that E-li′-as must first come? Mal. 4:5

11 And Jesus answered and said unto them, E-li′-as truly shall first come, and ᴿrestore all things. [Mal. 4:6]

12 But I say unto you, That ᴿE-li′-as is come already, and they knew him not, but have done unto him whatsoever they ᵀlisted. Likewise ᴿshall also the Son of man suffer of them. 11:14 · *desired* · 16:21

13 Then the disciples understood that he spake unto them of John the Baptist.

Instruction About Faith
Mark 9:14-29; Luke 9:37-42

14 And when they were come to the multitude, there came to him a *certain* man, kneeling down to him, and saying,

15 Lord, have mercy on my son: for he is lunatick, and sore vexed: for ofttimes he falleth into the fire, and oft into the water.

16 And I brought him to thy disciples, and they could not cure him.

17 Then Jesus answered and said, O faithless and perverse generation, how long shall I be with you? how long shall I suffer you? bring him hither to me.

18 And Jesus rebuked the ᵀdevil; and he departed out of him: and the child was cured from that very hour. *demon*

19 Then came the disciples to Jesus apart, and said, Why could not we cast him out?

20 And Jesus said unto them, Because of your unbelief: for verily I say unto you, If ye have faith as a grain of mustard seed, ye shall say unto this mountain, Remove hence to yonder place; and it shall remove; and nothing shall be impossible unto you.

21 ᵀHowbeit this kind goeth not out but by prayer and fasting. *however*

Instruction About Jesus' Death
Mark 9:30-32; Luke 9:43-45

22 And while they abode in Galilee, Jesus said unto them, The Son of man ᴿshall be betrayed into the hands of men: 26:57 ☆

23 And they shall ᴿkill him, and the third day he shall be raised again. And they were exceeding ᵀsorry. Mark 15:37; Acts 10:40 ☆ · *sad*

Instruction About Taxes

24 And when they were come to Ca-per′-na-um, they that received ᵀtribute *money* came to Peter, and said, Doth not your master pay tribute? *2 days' wages*

25 He saith, Yes. And when he was come into the house, Jesus prevented him, saying, What thinkest thou, Simon? of whom do the kings of the earth ᵀtake custom or tribute? of their own children, or of strangers? *levy taxes*

26 Peter saith unto him, Of strangers. Jesus saith unto him, Then are the ᵀchildren free. *citizens*

27 Notwithstanding, lest we should offend them, go thou to the sea, and cast an hook, and take up the fish that first cometh up; and when thou hast opened his mouth, thou shalt find a ᵀpiece of money: that take, and give unto them for me and thee. *4 days' wages*

CHAPTER 18

Instruction About Humility
Mark 9:33-37; Luke 9:46-48

AT the same time came the disciples unto Jesus, saying, Who is the greatest in the kingdom of heaven?

2 And Jesus called a little child unto him, and set him in the midst of them,

3 And said, Verily I say unto you, RExcept ye be converted, and become as little children, ye shall not enter into the kingdom of heaven. Ps. 131:2; [1 Cor. 14:20; 1 Pet. 2:2]

4 RWhosoever therefore shall humble himself as this little child, the same is greatest in the kingdom of heaven. [20:27]

5 And Rwhoso shall receive one such little child in my name receiveth me. [10:42]

Punishment of Offenders—Mark 9:42–48

6 RBut whoso shall Toffend one of these little ones which believe in me, it were better for him that a millstone were hanged about his neck, and that he were drowned in the depth of the sea. Luke 17:1, 2 • hurt

7 RWoe unto the world because of Toffences! for it Tmust needs be that offences come; but woe to that man by whom the offence cometh! 27:4, 5 • harmful events • is unavoidable

8 RWherefore if thy hand or thy foot offend thee, cut them off, and cast them from thee: it is better for thee to enter into life halt or maimed, rather than having two hands or two feet to be cast into everlasting fire. 5:29, 30

9 And if thine eye offend thee, pluck it out, and cast it from thee: it is better for thee to enter into life with one eye, rather than having two eyes to be cast into hell fire.

10 Take heed that ye despise not one of these little ones; for I say unto you, That in heaven their angels do always behold the face of my Father which is in heaven.

Parable of the Lost Sheep—Luke 15:4–7

11 RFor the Son of man is come to save that which was lost. Luke 9:56; John 3:17

12 RHow think ye? if a man have an hundred sheep, and one of them be gone astray, doth he not leave the ninety and nine, and goeth into the mountains, and seeketh that which is gone astray? Luke 15:4

13 TAnd if so be that he find it, verily I say unto you, he rejoiceth more of that sheep, than of the ninety and nine which went not astray. when he finds it

14 Even so it is not the will of your Father which is in heaven, that one of these little ones should perish.

The Offended Brother

15 Moreover if thy brother shall trespass against thee, go and tell him his fault between thee and him alone: if he shall hear thee, thou hast gained thy brother.

16 But if he will not hear thee, then take with thee one or two more, that in RTHE MOUTH OF TWO OR THREE WITNESSES EVERY WORD MAY BE ESTABLISHED. Deut. 19:15; John 8:17

17 And if he shall neglect to hear them, tell it unto the church: but if he neglect to hear the church, let him be unto thee as an Rheathen man and a publican. 1 Cor. 5:9

18 Verily I say unto you, RWhatsoever ye shall bind on earth shall be bound in heaven: and whatsoever ye shall loose on earth shall be loosed in heaven. 16:19

19 Again I say unto you, That if two of you shall agree on earth as touching any thing that they shall ask, it shall be done for them of my Father which is in heaven.

20 For where two or three are gathered Rtogether in my name, there am I in the midst of them. Acts 20:7; 1 Cor. 14:26

Instruction About Forgiveness

21 Then came Peter to him, and said, Lord, how oft shall my brother sin against me, and I forgive him? till seven times?

22 Jesus saith unto him, I say not unto thee, Until seven times: Rbut, Until seventy times seven. [6:14; Mark 11:25]; Col. 3:13

23 Therefore is the kingdom of heaven likened unto a certain king, which Twould take account of his servants. wanted to check

24 And when he had begun to reckon, one was brought unto him, which owed him Tten thousand talents. $3,840,000,000, if silver

25 But forasmuch as he had not to pay, his lord commanded him Rto be sold, and his wife, and children, and all that he had, and payment to be made. 2 Kin. 4:1; Neh. 5:8

26 The servant therefore fell down, and worshipped him, saying, Lord, have patience with me, and I will pay thee all.

27 Then the lord of that servant was moved with compassion, and Tloosed him, and forgave him the debt. released him

28 But the same servant went out, and found one of his fellowservants, which owed him an Thundred pence: and he laid hands on him, and took him by the throat, saying, Pay me Tthat thou owest. $3200 • what

29 And his fellowservant fell down at his feet, and besought him, saying, Have patience with me, and I will pay thee all.

30 And he would not: but went and cast him into prison, till he should pay the debt.

31 So when his fellowservants saw what was done, they were very sorry, and came and told unto their lord all that was done.

32 Then his lord, after that he had called him, said unto him, O thou wicked servant, I forgave thee all that debt, because thou Tdesiredst me: did ask

33 Shouldest not thou also have had Tcompassion on thy fellowservant, even as I had pity on thee? mercy

34 And his lord was wroth, and Tdelivered him to the tormentors, till he should pay all that was due unto him. put him in jail

35 RSo likewise shall my heavenly Father do also unto you, if ye from your hearts

'orgive not every one his brother their respasses. 6:12; Mark 11:26; James 2:13

CHAPTER 19

Instruction About Divorce
Mark 10:1–16; Luke 18:15–17

AND it came to pass, Rthat when Jesus had finished these sayings, he departed from Galilee, and came into the coasts of Ju-dae'-a beyond Jordan; John 10:40

2 RAnd great multitudes followed him; and he healed them there. 12:15

3 The Pharisees also came unto him, Ttempting him, and saying unto him, Is it lawful for a man to Tput away his wife for Tevery cause? testing · divorce · any

4 And he answered and said unto them, Have ye not read, that he which made them at the beginning MADE THEM MALE AND FEMALE,

5 And said, FOR THIS CAUSE SHALL A MAN LEAVE FATHER AND MOTHER, AND SHALL CLEAVE TO HIS WIFE: AND THEY TWAIN SHALL BE ONE FLESH?

6 Wherefore they are no more twain, but one flesh. What therefore God hath joined together, let not man put asunder.

7 They say unto him, RWhy did Moses then command to give a writing of divorcement, and to put her away? 5:31 · Deut. 24:1

8 He saith unto them, Moses because of the hardness of your hearts Tsuffered you to put away your wives: but from the beginning it was not so. allowed

9 RAnd I say unto you, Whosoever shall put away his wife, except it be for fornication, and shall marry another, committeth adultery: and whoso marrieth her which is put away doth commit adultery. 1 Cor. 7:10

10 His disciples say unto him, RIf the case of the man be so with his wife, it is not good to marry. [Prov. 21:19]

11 But he said unto them, RAll men Tcannot receive this saying, save they to whom it is given. [1 Cor. 7:2, 7, 9, 17] · are not in position to

12 For there are some eunuchs, which were so born from their mother's womb: and there are some eunuchs, which were made eunuchs of men: and Rthere be eunuchs, which have made themselves eunuchs for the kingdom of heaven's sake. He that is able to receive it, let him receive it. [1 Cor. 7:32]

13 Then were there brought unto him little children, that he should put his hands on them, and pray: and the disciples Trebuked them. turned them away

14 But Jesus said, Suffer little children, and forbid them not, to come unto me: for Rof such is the kingdom of heaven. 18:3

15 And he Tlaid his hands on them, and departed Tthence. placed (in prayer) · from there

Rich Young Ruler
Mark 10:17–27; Luke 18:18–27

16 And, behold, one came and said unto him, Good Master, what good thing shall I do, that I may have eternal life?

17 And he said unto him, Why callest thou me Tgood? there is none good but one, that is, God: but if thou wilt enter into life, keep the commandments. perfect

18 He saith unto him, Which? Jesus said, RTHOU SHALT DO NO MURDER, THOU SHALT NOT COMMIT ADULTERY, THOU SHALT NOT STEAL, THOU SHALT NOT BEAR FALSE WITNESS, Ex. 20:13

19 RHONOUR THY FATHER AND THY MOTHER: and, RTHOU SHALT LOVE THY NEIGHBOUR AS THYSELF. Ex. 20:12 · Lev. 19:18

20 The young man saith unto him, All these things have I kept from my youth up: Twhat lack I yet? what else do I need?

21 Jesus said unto him, If thou wilt be perfect, go and sell that thou hast, and give to the poor, and thou shalt have treasure in heaven: and come and follow me.

22 But when the young man heard that saying, he went away sorrowful: for he Thad great possessions. was very rich

23 Then said Jesus unto his disciples, Verily I say unto you, That a rich man shall hardly enter into the kingdom of heaven.

24 And again I say unto you, It is easier for a camel to go through the eye of a needle, than for a rich man Rto enter into the kingdom of God. [1 Tim. 6:9]

25 When his disciples heard it, they were exceedingly amazed, saying, RWho then can be saved? [Rom. 1:16]

26 But Jesus beheld them, and said unto them, With men this is impossible; but with God all things are possible.

The Apostles' Reward
Mark 10:28–30; Luke 18:28–30

27 Then answered Peter and said unto him, Behold, we have forsaken all, and followed thee; what shall we have therefore?

28 And Jesus said unto them, Verily I say unto you, That ye which have followed me, in the regeneration when the Son of man shall sit in the throne of his glory, Rye also shall sit upon twelve thrones, judging the twelve tribes of Israel. 20:21

29 And every one that hath forsaken houses, or brethren, or sisters, or father, or mother, or wife, or children, or lands, for my name's sake, shall receive an hundredfold, and shall inherit everlasting life.

30 RBut many that are first shall be last; and the last shall be first. 20:16; [21:31, 32]

CHAPTER 20

Parable of the Labourers—Mark 10:31

FOR the kingdom of heaven is like unto a man *that is* an householder, which went out early in the morning to hire labourers into his vineyard.

2 And when he had agreed with the labourers for a ᵀpenny a day, he sent them into his vineyard.   *$32*

3 And he went out about the third hour, and saw others standing idle in the market-place,

4 And said unto them; Go ye also into the vineyard, and whatsoever is right I will give you. And they went their way.

5 Again he went out about the ᵀsixth and ᵀninth hour, and did likewise.   *noon · 3 p.m.*

6 And about the ᵀeleventh hour he went out, and found others standing idle, and saith unto them, Why stand ye here all the day idle?   *5 p.m.*

7 They say unto him, Because no man hath hired us. He saith unto them, Go ye also into the vineyard; and whatsoever is right, *that* shall ye receive.

8 So when ᵀeven was come, the lord of the vineyard saith unto his steward, Call the labourers, and give them *their* hire, beginning from the last unto the first.   *evening*

9 And when they came that *were hired* about the eleventh hour, they ᴿreceived every man a ᵀpenny.   [2 Tim. 4:7, 8] · *$32*

10 But when the first came, they supposed that they should have received more; and they likewise received every man a penny.

11 And when they had received *it*, they ᵀmurmured against the ᵀgoodman of the house,   *complained · landowner*

12 Saying, These last ᵀhave wrought *but* one hour, and thou hast made them equal unto us, which have borne the burden and heat of the day.   *have continued one hour only*

13 But he answered one of them, and said, Friend, I do thee no wrong: didst not thou agree with me for a ᵀpenny?   *$32*

14 Take *that* thine *is*, and go thy way: I will give unto this last, even as unto thee.

15 ᴿIs it not lawful for me to do what I will with mine own? ᴿIs thine eye ᵀevil, because I am good?   [Rom. 9:21] · Deut. 15:9 · *bad*

16 So the last shall be first, and the first last: for many be called, but few chosen.

Instruction About Jesus' Death
Mark 10:32-34; Luke 18:31-34

17 ᴿAnd Jesus going up to Jerusalem took the twelve disciples apart in the way, and said unto them,   John 12:12

18 ᴿBehold, we go up to Jerusalem; and the Son of man shall be ᴿbetrayed unto the chief priests and unto the scribes, and they shall condemn him to death,   16:21 · 26:46, 66 ✻

19 ᴿAnd shall deliver him to the Gentiles to mock, and to scourge, and to crucify *him:* and the third day he shall rise again.
          Acts 2:23, 24 ✻

Instruction About Ambition—Mark 10:35-45

20 Then came to him the mother of ᴿZeb'-e-dee's children with her sons, worshipping *him,* and desiring a certain thing of him.   4:21

21 And he said unto her, What wilt thou? She saith unto him, Grant that these my two sons ᴿmay sit, the one on thy right hand, and the other on the left, in thy kingdom.   [19:28]

22 But Jesus answered and said, Ye know not what ye ask. Are ye able to drink of the cup that I shall drink of, and to be baptized with ᴿthe baptism that I am baptized with? They say unto him, We are able.   Luke 12:50

23 And he saith unto them, Ye shall drink indeed of my cup, and be baptized with the baptism that I am baptized with: but to sit on my right hand, and on my left, is not mine to ᴿgive, but *it shall be given to them* for whom it is prepared of my Father.   25:34

24 ᴿAnd when the ten heard *it,* they were moved with indignation against the two brethren.   Luke 22:24, 25

25 But Jesus called them *unto him,* and said, Ye know that the princes of the Gentiles exercise dominion over them, and they that are great exercise authority upon them.

26 But it shall not be so among you: but ᴿwhosoever will be great among you, let him be your ᵀminister;   23:11 · *servant*

27 ᴿAnd whosoever will be chief among you, let him be your servant: [18:4]

28 Even as the Son of man came not to be ministered unto, but to minister, and ᴿto give his life a ransom for many.   Is. 53:12 ✻

The Blind Men Recognize the King
Mark 10:46-52; Luke 18:35-43

29 And as they departed from Jericho, a great multitude followed him.

30 And, behold, ᴿtwo blind men sitting by the way side, when they heard that Jesus passed by, cried out, saying, Have mercy on us, O Lord, *thou* son of David.   9:27

31 And the multitude rebuked them, because they should ᵀhold their peace: but they cried the more, saying, Have mercy on us, O Lord, *thou* son of David.   *keep quiet*

32 And Jesus stood still, and called them, and said, What ᵀwill ye that I shall do ᵀunto you?   *do you want · for*

33 They say unto him, Lord, that our eyes may be opened.

34 So Jesus had compassion *on them,* and touched their eyes: and immediately their eyes received sight, and they followed him.

CHAPTER 21

The Triumphal Entry
Mark 11:1-10; Luke 19:29-38; John 12:12-15

AND when they drew nigh unto Jerusalem, and were come to Beth'-pha-ge, unto ^Rthe mount of Olives, then sent Jesus two disciples,   Zech. 14:4

2 Saying unto them, Go into the village over against you, and ^Tstraightway ye shall find an ass tied, and a colt with her: loose *them,* and bring *them* unto me.   *at once*

3 And if any *man* say ^Tought unto you, ye shall say, The Lord hath need of them; and straightway he will send them.   *anything*

4 All this was done, that it ^Tmight be fulfilled which was spoken by the prophet, saying,   *make come true*

5 ^RTELL YE THE DAUGHTER OF SI'-ON, BEHOLD, THY KING COMETH UNTO THEE, MEEK, AND SITTING UPON AN ASS, AND A COLT THE FOAL OF AN ASS.   Is. 62:11; Zech. 9:9 *

6 And the disciples went, and did as Jesus commanded them,

7 And brought the ^Tass, and the colt, and ^Rput on them their clothes, and they set *him* thereon.   *donkey* · 2 Kin. 9:13

8 And a very great multitude spread their garments in the way; others cut down branches from the trees, and ^Tstrawed *them* in the ^Tway.   *threw · road*

9 And the multitudes that went before, and that followed, cried, saying, ^RHO-SAN'-NA TO THE SON OF DAVID: ^RBLESSED *IS* HE THAT COMETH IN THE NAME OF THE LORD; HO-SAN'-NA IN THE HIGHEST.   Ps. 118:26 * · 23:39

10 ^RAnd when he was come into Jerusalem, all the city was moved, saying, Who is this?   Mark 11:15-19; Luke 19:45-48; John 2:13, 15

11 And the multitude said, This is Jesus ^Rthe prophet of Nazareth of Galilee.   2:23

The Cleansing of the Temple
Mark 11:15-17; Luke 19:45, 46

12 And^R Jesus went into the temple of God, and cast out all them that sold and bought in the temple, and overthrew the tables of the moneychangers, and the seats of them that sold doves,   Mal. 3:1 *

13 And said unto them, It is written, ^RMY HOUSE SHALL BE CALLED THE HOUSE OF PRAYER; but ye have made it a DEN OF THIEVES.   Is. 56:7

14 And the blind and the lame came to him in the temple; and he healed them.

15 And when the chief priests and scribes saw the wonderful things that he did, and the children crying in the temple, and saying, Ho-san'-na to the son of David; they were ^Tsore displeased,   *very unhappy*

16 And said unto him, Hearest thou what these say? And Jesus saith unto them, Yea;

have ye never read, ^ROUT OF THE MOUTH OF BABES AND SUCKLINGS THOU HAST PERFECTED PRAISE?   Ps. 8:2 *

17 And he left them, and went out of the city into Beth'-a-ny; and he lodged there.

Cursing of the Fig Tree—Mark 11:11-14, 20-24

18 Now in the morning as he returned into the city, he ^Thungered.   *was hungry*

19 And when he saw a fig tree in the way, he came to it, and found nothing thereon, but leaves only, and said unto it, Let no fruit grow on thee henceforward for ever. And presently the fig tree withered away.

20 And when the disciples saw *it,* they marvelled, saying, How soon is the fig tree ^Twithered away!   *dried up*

21 Jesus answered and said unto them, Verily I say unto you, ^RIf ye have faith, and doubt not, ye shall not only do this *which is done* to the fig tree, but also if ye shall say unto this mountain, Be thou removed, and be thou cast into the sea; it shall be done.   17:20

22 And all things, whatsoever ye shall ask in prayer, believing, ye shall receive.

Question of Jesus' Authority
Mark 11:27-33; Luke 20:1-18

23 And when he was come into the temple, the chief priests and the elders of the people came unto him as he was teaching, and ^Rsaid, By what ^Tauthority doest thou these things? and who gave thee this authority?   Acts 4:7 · *right*

24 And Jesus ^Ranswered and said unto them, I also will ask you one thing, which if ye tell me, I in like wise will tell you by what authority I do these things.   Job 5:13

25 The baptism of John, ^Twhence was it? from heaven, or of men? And they reasoned with themselves, saying, If we shall say, From heaven; he will say unto us, Why did ye not then believe him?   *from whom*

26 But if we shall say, Of men; we fear the people; ^Rfor all hold John as a prophet.   14:5

27 And they answered Jesus, and said, We ^Tcannot tell. And he said unto them, Neither tell I you by what ^Tauthority I do these things.   *don't know · right*

Parable of the Two Sons

28 But what think ye? A *certain* man had two sons; and he came to the first, and said, Son, go work to day in my vineyard.

29 He answered and said, I will not: but afterward he ^Rrepented, and went.   [Acts 17:30]

30 And he came to the second, and said likewise. And he answered and said, I go, sir: and went not.

31 Whether of them twain did the will of *his* father? They say unto him, The first. Jesus saith unto them, Verily I say unto you, That the publicans and the harlots go into the kingdom of God before you.

32 For John came unto you in the way of righteousness, and ye believed him not: but the publicans and the harlots believed him: and ye, when ye had seen *it*, ^Trepented not afterward, that ye might believe him.   *regretted*

Parable of the Householder
Mark 12:1-12; Luke 20:9-19

33 Hear another parable: There was a certain householder, which planted a vineyard, and hedged it round about, and digged a winepress in it, and built a tower, and ^Tlet it out to ^Thusbandmen, and ^Rwent into a far country: *rented • farmers • 25:14*

34 And when the time of the fruit drew near, he sent his servants to the husbandmen, that they might receive the fruits of it.

35 ^RAnd the husbandmen took his servants, and beat one, and killed another, and stoned another.   [23:34, 37; Acts 7:52; 1 Thess. 2:15]

36 Again, he sent other servants more than the first: and they did unto them likewise.

37 But last of all he sent unto them his son, saying, They will reverence my son.

38 But when the ^Thusbandmen saw the son, they said among themselves, ^RThis is the heir; ^Rcome, let us kill him, and let us seize on his inheritance.   *farmers • [Ps. 2:8] • [Ps. 2:2]*

39 ^RAnd they caught him, and cast *him* out of the vineyard, and slew *him*.   [26:50]

40 When the lord therefore of the vineyard cometh, what will he do unto those ^Thusbandmen?   *farmers*

41 They say unto him, He will miserably destroy those wicked men, and will let out *his* vineyard unto other husbandmen, which shall render him the fruits in their seasons.

42 Jesus saith unto them, Did ye never read in the scriptures, THE STONE WHICH THE BUILDERS REJECTED, THE SAME IS BECOME THE HEAD OF THE CORNER: THIS IS THE LORD'S DOING, AND IT IS MARVELLOUS IN OUR EYES?

43 Therefore say I unto you, ^RThe kingdom of God shall be taken from you, and given to a ^Tnation bringing forth the fruits thereof.   [8:12] • *people*

44 ^RAnd whosoever shall fall on this stone shall be broken: but on whomsoever it shall fall, it will grind him to powder.   Is. 8:14, 15 *

45 And when the chief priests and Pharisees had heard his parables, they ^Tperceived that he spake of them.   *understood*

46 But when they sought to lay hands on him, they feared the multitude, because ^Rthey took him for a prophet.   John 7:40

CHAPTER 22

Parable of the Marriage Feast

AND Jesus answered and spake unto them again by parables, and said,

2 The kingdom of heaven is like unto a certain king, which made a marriage for his son,

3 And sent forth his servants to call them that were ^Tbidden to the wedding: and they would not come.   *invited*

4 Again, he sent forth other servants, saying, Tell them which are bidden, Behold, I have prepared my dinner: my oxen and *my* fatlings *are* killed, and all things *are* ready: come unto the marriage.

5 But they ^Tmade light of *it*, and went their ways, one to his farm, another to his merchandise: *paid no attention*

6 And the remnant took his servants, and entreated *them* spitefully, and slew *them*.

7 But when the king heard *thereof*, he was wroth: and he sent forth ^Rhis armies, and destroyed those murderers, and burned up their city.   [Dan. 9:26]; Luke 19:27

8 Then saith he to his servants, The wedding is ready, but they which were bidden were not ^Rworthy.   [Acts 13:46]; 10:11

9 Go ye therefore into the highways, and as many as ye shall find, bid to the marriage.

10 So those servants went out into the highways, and gathered together all as many as they found, both bad and good: and the wedding was furnished with guests.

11 And when the king came in to see the guests, he saw there a man which had not on a wedding garment:

12 And he saith unto him, Friend, how camest thou in hither not having a wedding garment? And he was speechless.

13 Then said the king to the servants, ^TBind him hand and foot, and take him away, and cast *him* into outer darkness; there shall be weeping and gnashing of teeth.   *tie*

14 ^RFor many are called, but few *are* chosen.   20:16; 2 Pet. 1:10

Conflict with Pharisees and Herodians
Mark 12:13-17; Luke 20:20-26

15 Then went the Pharisees, and took counsel how they might entangle him in *his* talk.

16 And they sent out unto him their disciples with the He-ro'-di-ans, saying, Master, we know that thou art true, and teachest the way of God in truth, neither carest thou for any *man*: for thou ^Tregardest not the person of men.   *do not pay attention to*

17 Tell us therefore, What thinkest thou? Is it ^Tlawful to give ^Rtribute unto Caesar, or not?   *right* • 17:25; Luke 2:1

18 But Jesus perceived their wickedness, and said, Why tempt ye me, *ye* hypocrites?

19 Shew me the tribute money. And they brought unto him a ^Tpenny.   *1 day's wage*

20 And he saith unto them, Whose *is* this image and ^Tsuperscription?   *inscription*

21 They say unto him, Caesar's. Then saith

he unto them, ᵀRender therefore unto Caesar the things which are Caesar's; and unto God the things that are God's.   pay

22 When they had heard *these words,* they marvelled, and left him, and went their way.

Conflict with Sadducees
Mark 12:18–27; Luke 20:27–40

23 The same day came to him the Sad'-du-cees, ᴿwhich say that there is no resurrection, and asked him,   Acts 23:8

24 Saying, Master, ᴿMoses said, If a man die, having no children, his brother shall marry his wife, and raise up ᵀseed unto his brother.   Deut. 25:5 · *children*

25 Now there were with us seven brethren: and the first, when he had married a wife, ᵀdeceased, and, having no ᵀissue, left his wife unto his brother: *died · child*

26 Likewise the second also, and the third, unto the seventh.

27 And last of all the woman died also.

28 Therefore in the resurrection ᴿwhose wife shall she be of the seven? for they all had her.   [1 Tim. 1:4; 4:7; 6:4; 2 Tim. 2:23–26]

29 Jesus answered and said unto them, Ye ᵀdo err, not ᵀknowing the scriptures, nor the power of God.   *make a mistake · recognizing*

30 For in the resurrection they neither marry, nor are given in marriage, but ᴿare as the angels of God in heaven.   [1 John 3:2]

31 But as ᵀtouching the resurrection of the dead, have ye not read that which was spoken unto you by God, saying,   *concerning*

32 I ᴀᴍ ᴛʜᴇ Gᴏᴅ ᴏғ Aʙʀᴀʜᴀᴍ, ᴀɴᴅ ᴛʜᴇ Gᴏᴅ ᴏғ Iꜱᴀᴀᴄ, ᴀɴᴅ ᴛʜᴇ Gᴏᴅ ᴏғ Jᴀᴄᴏʙ? God is not the God of the dead, but of the living.

33 And when the multitude heard *this,* they were astonished at his doctrine.

The Greatest Commandment—Mark 12:28–34

34 But when the Pharisees had heard that he had put the Sad'-du-cees to silence, they were gathered together.

35 Then one of them, *which was* a lawyer, asked *him a question,* ᵀtempting him, and saying,   *testing*

36 Master, which *is* the great commandment in the law?

37 Jesus said unto him, Tʜᴏᴜ ꜱʜᴀʟᴛ ʟᴏᴠᴇ ᴛʜᴇ Lᴏʀᴅ ᴛʜʏ Gᴏᴅ ᴡɪᴛʜ ᴀʟʟ ᴛʜʏ ʜᴇᴀʀᴛ, ᴀɴᴅ ᴡɪᴛʜ ᴀʟʟ ᴛʜʏ ꜱᴏᴜʟ, ᴀɴᴅ ᴡɪᴛʜ ᴀʟʟ ᴛʜʏ ᴍɪɴᴅ.

38 This is the first and great commandment.

39 And the second is like unto it, Tʜᴏᴜ ꜱʜᴀʟᴛ ʟᴏᴠᴇ ᴛʜʏ ɴᴇɪɢʜʙᴏᴜʀ ᴀꜱ ᴛʜʏꜱᴇʟғ.

40 ᴿOn these two commandments hang all the law and the prophets.   [7:12] · [1 Tim. 1:5]

The Son of David
Mark 12:35–37; Luke 20:41–44

41 While the Pharisees were gathered together, Jesus asked them,

42 Saying, What think ye of Christ? whose son is he? They say unto him, *The son* of David.

43 He saith unto them, How then doth David in spirit call him Lord, saying,

44 ᴿTʜᴇ Lᴏʀᴅ ꜱᴀɪᴅ ᴜɴᴛᴏ ᴍʏ Lᴏʀᴅ, Sɪᴛ ᴛʜᴏᴜ ᴏɴ ᴍʏ ʀɪɢʜᴛ ʜᴀɴᴅ, ᴛɪʟʟ I ᴍᴀᴋᴇ ᴛʜɪɴᴇ ᴇɴᴇᴍɪᴇꜱ ᴛʜʏ ғᴏᴏᴛꜱᴛᴏᴏʟ?   Ps. 110:1

45 If David then call him Lord; how is he his son?

46 And no man was able to answer him a word, neither durst any *man* from that day forth ask him any more *questions.*

CHAPTER 23

Jesus Characterizes the Pharisees
Mark 12:38–40; Luke 20:45–47

THEN spake Jesus to the multitude, and to his disciples,

2 Saying, The scribes and the Pharisees sit in Moses' seat:

3 All therefore whatsoever they bid you observe, *that* observe and do; but do not ye ᵀafter their works: for ᴿthey say, and do not.   *in the same manner as* · [Rom. 2:19]

4 For they bind heavy burdens and grievous to be borne, and lay *them* on men's shoulders; but they *themselves* will not move them with one of their fingers.

5 But all their works they do for to be seen of men: they make broad their phylacteries, and enlarge the borders of their garments,

6 And love the uppermost rooms at feasts, and the chief seats in the synagogues,

7 And greetings in the markets, and to be called of men, Rabbi, ᵀRabbi.   *teacher*

8 ᴿBut be not ye called Rabbi: for one is your Master, *even* Christ; and all ye are brethren.   [James 3:1; 2 Cor. 1:24; 1 Pet. 5:3]

9 And call no *man* your father upon the earth: ᴿfor one is your Father, which is in heaven.   [Mal. 1:6]

10 Neither be ye called ᵀmasters: for one is your Master, *even* Christ.   *leader*

11 But ᴿhe that is greatest among you shall be your servant.   20:26, 27

12 ᴿAnd whosoever shall exalt himself shall be ᵀabased; and he that shall humble himself shall be exalted.   Luke 14:11 · *humbled*

Jesus Condemns the Pharisees

13 But ᴿwoe unto you, scribes and Pharisees, hypocrites! for ye ᵀshut up the kingdom of heaven against men: for ye neither go in *yourselves,* neither suffer ye them that are entering to go in.   Luke 11:52 · *close*

14 Woe unto you, scribes and Pharisees, hypocrites! for ye devour widows' houses, and for a pretence make long prayer: therefore ye shall receive the greater damnation.

15 Woe unto you, scribes and Pharisees, hypocrites! for ye ᵀcompass sea and land to make one ᵀproselyte, and when he is made, ye make him twofold more the child of hell than yourselves.   *go over • convert to Judaism*

16 Woe unto you, ᴿye blind guides, which say, Whosoever shall swear by the temple, it is nothing; but whosoever shall swear by the gold of the temple, he is a debtor!   *v. 24*

17 Ye fools and blind: for whether is greater, the gold, ᴿor the temple that ᵀsanctifieth the gold?   Ex. 30:29 • *sets it apart as holy*

18 And, Whosoever shall swear by the altar, it is nothing; but whosoever sweareth by the gift that is upon it, he is guilty.

19 Ye fools and blind: for whether is greater, the gift, or ᴿthe altar that sanctifieth the gift?   Ex. 29:37

20 Whoso therefore shall ᵀswear by the altar, sweareth by it, and by all ᵀthings thereon.   *give his word • gifts*

21 And whoso shall swear by the temple, sweareth by it, and by ᴿhim that dwelleth therein.   Ps. 26:8; 132:14

22 And he that shall ᴿswear by heaven, sweareth by ᴿthe throne of God, and by him that sitteth thereon.   5:34 • Acts 7:49

23 Woe unto you, scribes and Pharisees, hypocrites! for ye pay tithe of mint and anise and cummin, and have omitted the weightier *matters* of the law, judgment, mercy, and faith: these ought ye to have done, and not to leave the other undone.

24 Ye blind guides, which strain at a gnat, and swallow a camel.

25 Woe unto you, scribes and Pharisees, hypocrites! for ye make clean the outside of the cup and of the platter, but within they are full of extortion and excess.

26 Thou blind Pharisee, cleanse first that *which is* within the cup and platter, that the outside of them may be clean also.

27 Woe unto you, scribes and Pharisees, hypocrites! for ye are ᵀlike unto whited sepulchres, which indeed appear beautiful outward, but are within full of dead *men's* bones, and of all uncleanness.   *just like*

28 Even so ye also outwardly appear ᵀrighteous unto men, but within ye are full of hypocrisy and ᵀiniquity.   *good • sin*

29 ᴿWoe unto you, scribes and Pharisees, hypocrites! because ye build the tombs of the prophets, and ᵀgarnish the sepulchres of the righteous,   Luke 11:47 • *decorate*

30 And say, If we had been in the days of our fathers, we would not have been partakers with them in the blood of the prophets.

31 Wherefore ye be witnesses unto yourselves, that ᴿye are the children of them which killed the prophets.   1 Thess. 2:15

32 Fill ye up then the measure of your fathers.

33 Ye serpents, ye generation of vipers, how can ye escape the damnation of hell?

34 ᴿWherefore, behold, I send unto you prophets, and wise men, and scribes: and ᴿsome of them ye shall kill and crucify; and ᴿsome of them shall ye scourge in your synagogues, and persecute *them* from city to city: Luke 11:49 • Acts 5:40; 7:58, 59 • 10:17

35 That upon you may come all the righteous blood shed upon the earth, from the blood of righteous Abel unto the blood of Zach-a-ri'-as son of Bar-a-chi'-as, whom ye slew between the temple and the altar.

36 Verily I say unto you, All these ᵀthings shall come upon this generation.   *punishment*

Jesus Laments over Jerusalem

37 Oᴿ Jerusalem, Jerusalem, *thou* that killest the prophets, and stonest them which are sent unto thee, how often would I have gathered thy children together, even as a hen gathereth her chickens under *her* wings, and ye ᴿwould not!   Luke 13:34 • Is. 49:5 ★

38 Behold, ᴿyour house is left unto you ᵀdesolate.   Jer. 22:5 ★ ★ *empty*

39 For I say unto you, Ye shall not see me henceforth, till ye shall say, BLESSED IS HE THAT COMETH IN THE NAME OF THE LORD.

CHAPTER 24

The Temple to Be Destroyed
Mark 13:1, 2; Luke 21:5, 6

AND Jesus went out, and departed from the temple: and his disciples came to *him* for to shew him the buildings of the temple.

2 And Jesus said unto them, See ye not all these things? verily I say unto you, There shall not be left here one stone upon another, that shall not be thrown down.

The Disciples' Two Questions
Mark 13:3, 4; Luke 21:7

3 And as he sat upon the mount of Olives, the disciples came unto him privately, saying, Tell us, when shall these things be? and what *shall be* the sign of thy coming, and of the end of the world?

The Tribulation—Mark 13:5-23; Luke 21:5-24

4 And Jesus answered and said unto them, Take heed that no man deceive you.

5 For many shall come in my name, saying, I am Christ; and shall deceive many.

6 And ye shall hear of ᴿwars and rumours of wars: see that ye be not troubled: for all *these things* must come to pass, but the end ᵀis not yet.   [Rev. 6:2-4] • *has not come*

7 For nation shall rise against nation, and kingdom against kingdom: and there shall be famines, and pestilences, and earthquakes, in ᵀdivers places.   *various*

8 All these *are* the beginning of sorrows.

9 Then shall they deliver you up to be afflicted, and shall kill you: and ye shall be hated of all nations for my name's sake.

10 And ᴿthen shall many be ᵀoffended, and shall betray one another, and shall hate one another.   2 Tim. 1:15 • *stumble*

11 And ᴿmany false prophets shall rise, and ᴿshall deceive many.   Acts 20:29 • [1 Tim. 4:1]

12 And because ᵀiniquity shall abound, the love of many shall wax cold.   *sin*

13 ᴿBut he that shall endure unto the end, the same shall be saved.   10:22; [Rev. 2:10]

14 And this gospel of the kingdom shall be preached in all the world for a witness unto all nations; and then shall the end come.

15 When ye therefore shall see the ABOMI-NATION OF DESOLATION, spoken of by Daniel the prophet, stand in the holy place, (whoso readeth, let him understand:)

16 Then let them which be in Ju-dae'-a flee into the mountains:

17 Let him which is on the housetop not come down to take any thing out of his house:

18 Neither let him which is in the field return back to take his ᵀclothes.   *cloke*

19 And ᴿwoe unto them that are with child, and to them that ᵀgive suck in those days!   Luke 23:29 • *have babies*

20 But pray ye that your flight be not in the winter, neither on the sabbath day:

21 For then shall be great tribulation, such as was not since the beginning of the world to this time, no, nor ever shall be.

22 And except those days should be shortened, there should no flesh be saved: ᴿbut for the ᵀelect's sake those days shall be shortened.   [Zech. 14:2, 3] • *chosen of God*

23 Then if any man shall say unto you, Lo, here is Christ, or there; believe *it* not.

24 For there shall arise false Christs, and false prophets, and shall shew great signs and wonders; insomuch that, if *it* were possible, they shall deceive the very elect.

25 Behold, I have told you before.

26 Wherefore if they shall say unto you, Behold, ᵀhe is in the desert; go not forth: behold, *he is* in the ᵀsecret chambers; believe *it* not.   *the Messiah* • *inner rooms*

The Second Coming
Mark 13:24–27; Luke 21:25–28

27 For as the lightning cometh out of the east, and shineth even unto the west; so shall also the coming of the Son of man be.

28 For wheresoever the carcase is, there will the eagles be gathered together.

29 Immediately after the ᵀtribulation of those days shall the sun be darkened, and the moon shall not give her light, and the stars shall fall from heaven, and the powers of the heavens shall be shaken: *trouble*

30 And then shall appear the sign of the Son of man in heaven: and then shall all the tribes of the earth mourn, and ᴿthey shall see the Son of man coming in the clouds of heaven with power and great glory. Rev. 1:7 ☆

31 And he shall send his angels with a great sound of a trumpet, and they shall gather together his elect from the four winds, from one end of heaven to the other.

Parable of the Fig Tree
Mark 13:28–31; Luke 21:29–33

32 Now learn a parable of the fig tree; When his branch is yet tender, and putteth forth leaves, ye know that summer *is* nigh:

33 So likewise ye, when ye shall see all these things, know ᴿthat ᵀit is near, *even* at the doors.   [James 5:8, 9] • *he*

34 Verily I say unto you, This generation shall not pass, till all these things be fulfilled.

35 ᴿHeaven and earth shall pass away, but my words shall not pass away.   Ps. 102:25, 26

Illustration of the Days of Noah
Mark 13:32–37; Luke 21:34–36

36 ᴿBut of that day and hour knoweth no *man*, no, not the angels of heaven, ᴿbut my Father only.   1 Thess. 5:2; 2 Pet. 3:10 • Zech. 14:7

37 But as the days of No'-e *were*, so shall also the coming of the Son of man be.

38 For as in the days that were before the flood they were eating and drinking, marrying and giving in marriage, until the day that No'-e entered into the ark,

39 And ᵀknew not until the flood came, and took them all away; so shall also the coming of the Son of man be.   *did not realize*

40 ᴿThen shall two be in the field; the one shall be taken, and the other left.   Luke 17:34

41 Two *women shall be* grinding at the ᴿmill; the one shall be taken, and the other left.   Deut. 24:6; Ex. 11:5; Is. 47:2

42 ᴿWatch therefore: for ye know not what hour your Lord doth come.   25:13

43 ᴿBut know this, that if the goodman of the house had known in what watch the thief would come, he would have watched, and would not have ᵀsuffered his house to be broken ᵀup.   Luke 12:39; Rev. 3:3 • *allowed* • *into*

44 ᴿTherefore be ye also ready: for in such an hour as ye think not the Son of man cometh.   [1 Thess. 5:6]

Illustration of the Two Servants
Luke 12:41–48

45 Who then is a faithful and wise servant, whom his lord hath made ruler over his household, to give them meat in due season?

46 Blessed *is* that servant, whom his lord when he cometh shall find so doing.

47 Verily I say unto you, That ᴿhe shall make him ruler over all his goods.   25:21

48 But and if that evil servant shall say in his heart, My lord delayeth his coming;

49 And shall begin to ᵀsmite *his* fellow-servants, and to eat and drink with the drunken;   *beat*

50 The lord of that servant shall come in a day when he looketh not for *him*, and in an hour that he is not aware of,

51 And shall cut him asunder, and appoint *him* his portion with the hypocrites: there shall be weeping and gnashing of teeth.

CHAPTER 25

Parable of the Ten Virgins

THEN shall the kingdom of heaven be likened unto ten virgins, which took their lamps, and went forth to meet ᴿthe bridegroom.   [Rev. 19:7; 21:2, 9]

2 And five of them were wise, and five *were* foolish.

3 They that *were* foolish took their lamps, and took no oil with them:

4 ᴿBut the wise took oil in their ᵀvessels with their lamps.   1 Thess. 5:6 • *containers*

5 While the bridegroom ᵀtarried, they all slumbered and slept.   *was late*

6 And at midnight ᴿthere was a cry made, Behold, the bridegroom cometh; go ye out to meet him.   [24:31; 1 Thess. 4:16]

7 Then all those virgins arose, and ᴿtrimmed their lamps.   Luke 12:35

8 And the foolish said unto the wise, Give us of your oil; for our lamps are gone out.

9 But the wise answered, saying, *Not so;* lest there be not enough for us and you: but go ye rather to ᵀthem that sell, and buy for yourselves.   *the store*

10 And while they went to buy, the bridegroom came; and they that were ready went in with him to the ᵀmarriage: and ᴿthe door was shut.   *marriage feast* • Luke 13:25

11 Afterward came also the other virgins, saying, ᴿLord, Lord, open to us.   [7:21-23]

12 But he answered and said, Verily I say unto you, I ᵀknow you not.   *do not recognize*

13 ᴿWatch therefore, for ye know neither the day nor the hour wherein the Son of man cometh.   24:42, 44; Mark 13:33, 35; [Luke 21:36]

Parable of the Talents

14 ᴿFor *the kingdom of heaven is* ᴿas a man travelling into a far country, *who* called his own servants, and delivered unto them his goods.   Luke 19:12 • 21:33

15 And unto one he gave five talents, to another two, and to another one; to every man according to his ᵀseveral ability; and straightway took his journey.   *individual*

16 Then he that had received the ᵀfive talents went and traded with the same, and ᵀmade *them* other five talents. *$1,920,000 • earned*

17 And likewise he that *had received* ᵀtwo, he also ᵀgained other two.   *$768,000 • earned*

18 But he that had received one went and digged in the earth, and hid his lord's money.

19 After a long time the lord of those servants cometh, and reckoneth with them.

20 And so he that had received ᵀfive talents came and brought other five talents, saying, Lord, thou deliveredst unto me five talents: behold, I have gained beside them five talents more.   *$1,920,000*

21 His lord said unto him, Well done, *thou* good and faithful servant: thou hast been faithful over a few things, ᴿI will make thee ruler over many things: enter thou into the joy of thy lord.   Luke 12:44

22 He also that had received ᵀtwo talents came and said, Lord, thou deliveredst unto me two talents: behold, I have gained two other talents beside them.   *$768,000*

23 His lord said unto him, ᴿWell done, good and faithful servant; thou hast been faithful over a ᵀfew things, I will make thee ruler over many things: enter thou into the joy of thy lord.   *v. 21 • small*

24 Then he which had received the ᵀone talent came and said, Lord, I knew thee that thou art an hard man, reaping where thou hast not sown, and gathering where thou ᵀhast not strawed: *$384,000 • did not scatter*

25 And I was afraid, and went and hid thy talent in the earth: lo, *there* thou hast *that is* thine.

26 His lord answered and said unto him, *Thou* wicked and ᵀslothful servant, thou knewest that I reap where I sowed not, and gather where I have not strawed: *lazy*

27 Thou oughtest therefore to have put my money to the ᵀexchangers, and *then* at my coming I should have received mine own with ᵀusury.   *bankers • interest*

28 Take therefore the talent from him, and give *it* unto him which hath ten talents.

29 ForᴿR unto every one that hath shall be given, and he shall have abundance: but from him that hath not shall be taken away even that which he hath.   13:12

30 And cast ye the unprofitable servant ᴿinto outer darkness: there shall be weeping and gnashing of teeth.   8:12; 24:51

Judgment of the Gentiles

31 When the Son of man shall come in his glory, and all the holy angels with him, then shall he sit upon the throne of his glory:

32 And ᴿbefore him shall be gathered all nations: and ᴿhe shall separate them one from another, as a shepherd divideth *his* sheep from the goats: [Rom. 14:10] • Ezek. 20:38

33 And he shall ᵀset the sheep on his right hand, but the goats on the left.   *put*

34 Then shall the King say unto them on his right hand, Come, ye blessed of my

Father, inherit the kingdom prepared for you from the foundation of the world:

35 ^RFor I was ^Tan hungred, and ye gave me ^Tmeat: I was thirsty, and ye gave me drink: ^RI was a stranger, and ye took me in: Is. 58:7; [James 1:27] • *hungry* • *food* • [Heb. 13:2]

36 ^RNaked, and ye clothed me: I was sick, and ye visited me: ^RI was in prison, and ye came unto me.   [James 2:15, 16] • 2 Tim. 1:16

37 Then shall the righteous answer him, saying, Lord, when saw we thee ^Tan hungred, and fed *thee?* or thirsty, and gave *thee* drink?   *hungry*

38 When saw we thee a stranger, and took *thee* in? or naked, and clothed *thee?*

39 Or when saw we thee sick, or in prison, and came unto thee?

40 And the King shall answer and say unto them, Verily I say unto you, Inasmuch as ye have done *it* unto one of the least of these my brethren, ye have done *it* unto me.

41 Then shall he say also unto them on the left hand, Depart from me, ye cursed, ^Rinto everlasting fire, prepared for ^Rthe devil and his angels: 13:40, 42 • [2 Pet. 2:4]

42 For I was ^Tan hungred, and ye gave me no ^Tmeat: I was thirsty, and ye gave me no drink: *hungry • food*

43 I was a stranger, and ye took me not in: naked, and ye clothed me not: sick, and in prison, and ye visited me not.

44 Then shall they also answer him, saying, Lord, when saw we thee an hungred, or athirst, or a stranger, or naked, or sick, or in prison, and did not ^Tminister unto thee? *help*

45 Then shall he answer them, saying, Verily I say unto you, ^RInasmuch as ye did *it* not to one of the least of these, ye did *it* not to me.   Prov. 14:31; Zech. 2:8; Acts 9:5

46 And ^Rthese shall go away into everlasting punishment: but the righteous into life eternal.   [Dan. 12:2; John 5:29; Rom. 2:7]

CHAPTER 26

The Religious Leaders Plot to Kill Jesus
Mark 14:1, 2; Luke 22:1, 2

AND it came to pass, ^Rwhen Jesus had finished all these sayings, he said unto his disciples,   7:28

2 Ye know that after two days is *the feast of* the passover, and the Son of man is ^Rbetrayed to be ^Rcrucified.   26:15 • 27:35

3 ^RThen assembled together the chief priests, and the scribes, and the elders of the people, unto the palace of the high priest, who was called Ca'-ia-phas,   Ps. 2:2

4 And consulted that they might take Jesus by ^Tsubtilty, and kill *him.*   *trickery*

5 But they said, Not on the feast *day,* lest there be an uproar among the people.

Mary Anoints Jesus for Burial
Mark 14:3–9; Luke 12:2–8

6 Now when Jesus was in Beth'-a-ny, in the house of Simon the leper,

7 There came unto him a woman having an alabaster box of very precious ointment, and poured it on his head, as he sat *at meat.*

8 ^RBut when his disciples saw *it,* they ^Thad indignation, saying, To what purpose *is* this waste?   John 12:4 • *became angry*

9 For this ointment might have been sold for much, and given to the poor.

10 When Jesus understood *it,* he said unto them, Why trouble ye the woman? for she hath wrought a good work upon me.

11 ^RFor ye have the poor always with you; but me ye have not always.   John 12:8

12 For in that she hath poured this ointment on my body, she did *it* for my burial.

13 Verily I say unto you, Wheresoever this gospel shall be preached in the whole world, *there* shall also this, that this woman hath done, be told for a memorial of her.

Judas Agrees to Betray Jesus
Mark 14:10, 11; Luke 22:3–6

14 Then one of the twelve, called ^RJudas Is-car'-i-ot, went unto the chief priests,   10:4

15 And said *unto them,* ^RWhat will ye give me, and I will deliver him unto you? And they ^Tcovenanted with him for ^Tthirty pieces of silver.   Zech. 11:12 ⋆ • *weighed unto* • $3,840

16 And from that time he sought opportunity to betray him.

The Passover Is Prepared
Mark 14:12–16; Luke 22:7–13

17 ^RNow the first *day* of the *feast of* unleavened bread the disciples came to Jesus, saying unto him, Where wilt thou that we prepare for thee to eat the passover?   Ex. 12:6

18 And he said, Go into the city to such a man, and say unto him, The Master saith, My time is at hand; I will keep the passover at thy house with my disciples.

19 And the disciples did as Jesus had appointed them; and they ^Tmade ready the passover.   *prepared*

The Passover Is Celebrated
Mark 14:17–21; Luke 22:14, 21–23; John 13:21, 22

20 Now when the even was come, he sat down with the twelve.

21 And as they did eat, he said, Verily I say unto you, that one of you shall betray me.

22 And they were ^Texceeding sorrowful, and began every one of them to say unto him, Lord, is it I?   *very upset*

23 And he answered and said, ^RHe that dippeth *his* hand with me in the dish, the same shall betray me.   Ps. 41:9 ⋆

24 The Son of man goeth as it is written of him: but ᴿwoe unto that man by whom the Son of man is betrayed! it had been good for that man if he had not been born.   27:4, 5

25 Then Judas, which betrayed him, answered and said, Master, is it I? He said unto him, ᵀThou hast said.   *you said it*

The Lord's Supper Is Instituted
Mark 14:22–25; Luke 22:19, 20; 1 Cor. 11:23–26

26 And as they were eating, Jesus took bread, and ᵀblessed *it*, and brake *it*, and gave *it* to the disciples, and said, Take, eat; ᴿthis is my body.   *gave thanks* • 1 Cor. 10:16

27 And he took the cup, and gave thanks, and gave *it* to them, saying, Drink ye ᵀall of it;   *all of you*

28 For this is my blood of the new testament, which is shed ᴿfor many for the ᵀremission of sins.   [Acts 2:38] • *forgiveness*

29 But I say unto you, I will not drink henceforth of this fruit of the vine, ᴿuntil that day when I drink it new with you in my Father's kingdom.   Acts 10:41

Peter's Denial Is Predicted
Mark 14:26–31; Luke 22:34, 39; John 13:37, 38

30 And when they had sung an hymn, they went out into the mount of Olives.

31 Then saith Jesus unto them, All ye shall be offended because of me this night: for it is written, ᴿI WILL SMITE THE SHEPHERD, AND THE SHEEP OF THE FLOCK SHALL BE SCATTERED ABROAD.   26:56; Zech. 13:7 ☆

32 But after I am risen again, ᴿI will go before you into Galilee.   28:7, 10, 16 ☆

33 Peter answered and said unto him, Though all men shall be ᵀoffended because of thee, *yet* will I never be offended.   *confused*

34 Jesus said unto him, ᴿVerily I say unto thee, That this night, before the cock crow, thou shalt deny me thrice.   26:74, 75 ☆

35 Peter said unto him, Though I should die with thee, yet will I not deny thee. Likewise also said all the disciples.

Jesus' Three Prayers
Mark 14:32–42; Luke 22:40–46

36 Then cometh Jesus with them unto a place called Geth-sem′-a-ne, and saith unto the disciples, Sit ye here, while I go and pray yonder.

37 And he took with him Peter and ᴿthe two sons of Zeb′-e-dee, and began to be sorrowful and very ᵀheavy.   4:21 • *downhearted*

38 Then saith he unto them, ᴿMy soul is exceeding sorrowful, even unto death: tarry ye here, and watch with me.   John 12:27

39 And he went a little farther, and fell on his face, and prayed, saying, O my Father, if it be possible, let this cup pass from me: nevertheless ᴿnot as I will, but as thou wilt.   Ps. 50:5 ★

40 And he cometh unto the disciples, and findeth them asleep, and saith unto Peter, ᵀWhat, could ye not watch with me one hour?   *how is it*

41 ᴿWatch and pray, that ye enter not into temptation: the spirit indeed *is* willing, but the flesh *is* weak.   Mark 13:33; 14:38

42 He went away again the second time, and prayed, saying, O my Father, if this cup may not ᵀpass away from me, except I drink it, ᴿthy will be done.   *be taken away* • Is. 50:5 ★

43 And he came and found them asleep again: for their eyes were ᵀheavy.   *sleepy*

44 And he left them, and went away again, and prayed the third time, saying the same words.

45 Then cometh he to his disciples, and saith unto them, Sleep on now, and take *your* rest: behold, the hour is at hand, and the Son of man is betrayed into the hands of sinners.

46 Rise, let us be going: behold, ᵀhe is at hand that doth ᴿbetray me.   *the man* • 20:18; 26:21 ★

Jesus' Betrayal and Arrest
Mark 14:43–52; Luke 22:47–53; John 18:1–11

47 And while he yet spake, lo, Judas, one of the twelve, came, and with him a great multitude with swords and staves, from the chief priests and elders of the people.

48 Now he that betrayed him gave them a sign, saying, Whomsoever I shall kiss, that same is he: hold him ᵀfast.   *firmly*

49 And forthwith he came to Jesus, and said, Hail, ᵀmaster; and kissed him.   *Rabbi*

50 And Jesus said unto him, Friend, wherefore art thou come? Then came they, and laid hands on Jesus, and took him.

51 And, behold, one of them which were with Jesus stretched out *his* hand, and drew his sword, and struck a servant of the high priest's, and smote off his ear.

52 Then said Jesus unto him, Put up again thy sword into his place: for all they that take the sword shall perish with the sword.

53 Thinkest thou that I cannot now pray to my Father, and he shall presently give me more than ᵀtwelve legions of angels?   *72,000*

54 But how then shall the scriptures be fulfilled, ᴿthat thus it must be?   Is. 53:7

55 In that same hour said Jesus to the multitudes, Are ye come out as against a thief with swords and ᵀstaves for to take me? I sat daily with you teaching in the temple, and ye laid no hold on me.   *clubs*

56 But all this was done, that the scriptures of the prophets might be fulfilled. ᴿThen all the disciples forsook him, and fled.   26:31 ★

Two False Witnesses
Mark 14:53–65; Luke 22:54, 55, 63–65; John 18:12, 18, 24

57 And they that had laid hold on Jesus led *him* away to Ca′-ia-phas the high priest,

where the scribes and the elders were assembled.

58 But Peter followed him afar off unto the high priest's palace, and went in, and sat with the servants, to see the end.

59 Now the chief priests, and elders, and all the council, sought false ᵀwitness against Jesus, to put him to death;   evidence

60 But found none: yea, though ᴿmany false witnesses came, yet found they none. At the last came two false witnesses,   Ps. 27:12 ★

61 And said, This fellow said, ᴿI am able to destroy the temple of God, and to build it in three days.   27:40; John 2:19

62 And the high priest arose, and said unto him, Answerest thou nothing? what is it which these witness against thee?

63 But ᴿJesus held his peace. And the high priest answered and said unto him, ᴿI adjure thee by the living God, that thou tell us whether thou be the Christ, the Son of God.   Ps. 38:13, 14; Is. 53:7 ★ · Lev. 5:1; 1 Sam. 14:24, 26

64 Jesus saith unto him, ᵀThou hast said: nevertheless I say unto you, Hereafter shall ye see ᴿTHE SON OF MAN SITTING ON THE RIGHT HAND OF POWER, and ᴿCOMING IN THE CLOUDS OF HEAVEN.   you said it · Ps. 110:1 · Dan. 7:13

65 ᴿThen the high priest rent his clothes, saying, He hath spoken blasphemy; what further need have we of witnesses? behold, now ye have heard his blasphemy.   2 Kin. 18:37

66 What think ye? They answered and said, ᴿHe is guilty of death.   Lev. 24:16; John 19:7

67 ᴿThen did they spit in his face, and buffeted him; and others smote him with the palms of their hands,   27:30; Job 16:10; Is. 50:6 ★

68 Saying, Prophesy unto us, thou Christ, Who is he that smote thee?

Three Denials of Peter
Mark 14:66–72; Luke 22:55–62; John 18:15–18, 25–27

69 Now Peter sat without in the palace: and a damsel came unto him, saying, Thou also wast with Jesus of Galilee.

70 But he denied before them all, saying, I know not what thou sayest.

71 And when he was gone out into the porch, another maid saw him, and said unto them that were there, This ᵀfellow was also with Jesus of Nazareth.   man

72 And again he denied with an oath, I do not know the man.

73 And after a while came unto him they that stood by, and said to Peter, Surely thou also art one of them; for thy ᴿspeech ᵀbewrayeth thee.   Luke 22:59 · makes you known

74 Then began he to curse and to swear, saying, ᴿI know not the man. And immediately the cock crew.   26:34 ★

75 And Peter remembered the word of Jesus, which said unto him, ᴿBefore the cock crow, thou shalt deny me thrice. And he went out, and wept bitterly.   v. 34

CHAPTER 27

Jesus Is Delivered to Pilate
Mark 15:1; Luke 22:66; 23:1; John 18:28

WHEN the morning was come, ᴿall the chief priests and elders of the people ᵀtook counsel against Jesus to put him to death: Ps. 2:2 ★ · consulted

2 And when they had bound him, they led him away, and ᴿdelivered him to Pon'-tius Pilate the governor.   20:19; Luke 18:32; Acts 3:13 ★

Judas Repents—Acts 1:18, 19

3 ᴿThen Judas, which had betrayed him, when he saw that he was condemned, ᵀrepented himself, and brought again the ᵀthirty pieces of silver to the chief priests and elders,   26:14 · having regretted it · $3,840

4 Saying, I have sinned in that I have betrayed the innocent blood. And they said, What is that to us? see thou to that.

5 And he ᵀcast down the pieces of silver in the temple, ᴿand departed, and went and hanged himself.   threw down · 18:7; 26:24 ★

6 And the chief priests took the silver pieces, and said, It is not ᵀlawful for to put them into the treasury, because it is ᵀthe price of blood.   legal · blood money

7 And they took counsel, and bought with them the potter's field, to bury strangers in.

8 Wherefore that field was called, ᵀThe field of blood, unto this day.   Aceldama

9 Then was fulfilled that which was spoken by Jeremy the prophet, saying, ᴿAND THEY TOOK THE THIRTY PIECES OF SILVER, THE PRICE OF HIM THAT WAS VALUED, whom they of the children of Israel did value;   Zech. 11:12 ★

10 ᴿAND GAVE THEM FOR THE POTTER'S FIELD, AS THE LORD APPOINTED ME.   Zech. 11:13 ★

Jesus Is Examined
Mark 15:2–5; Luke 23:2–5; John 18:29–38

11 And Jesus stood before the governor: and the governor asked him, saying, Art thou the King of the Jews? And Jesus said unto him, ᵀThou sayest.   you say so

12 And when he was accused of the chief priests and elders, he answered nothing.

13 Then said Pilate unto him, ᴿHearest thou not how many things they witness against thee?   26:62; John 19:10

14 And ᴿhe answered him to never a word; insomuch that the governor ᵀmarvelled greatly.   Ps. 38:13, 14 ★ · was greatly surprised

Barabbas Is Freed
Mark 15:6–14; Luke 23:17–23; John 18:39, 40

15 Now at that feast the governor was ᵀwont to ᵀrelease unto the people a prisoner, whom they would.   accustomed · free

16 And they had then a ᵀnotable prisoner, called Bar-ab'-bas.   *well-known*

17 Therefore when they were gathered together, Pilate said unto them, Whom will ye that I ᵀrelease unto you? Bar-ab'-bas, or Jesus which is called Christ?   *free*

18 For he knew that for ᴿenvy they had ᵀdelivered him.   James 3:14 · *given him over*

19 When he was set down on the judgment seat, his wife sent unto him, saying, Have thou nothing to do with that just man: for I have suffered many things this day in a dream because of him.

20 ᴿBut the chief priests and elders persuaded the multitude that they should ask Bar-ab'-bas, and destroy Jesus.   Acts 3:14

21 The governor answered and said unto them, Whether of the twain will ye that I release unto you? They said, Bar-ab'-bas.

22 Pilate saith unto them, What shall I do then with Jesus which is called Christ? *They* all say unto him, Let him be crucified.

23 And the governor said, Why, what evil hath he done? But they cried out the more, saying, Let him be crucified.

24 When Pilate saw that he could prevail nothing, but *that* rather a tumult was made, he ᴿtook water, and washed *his* hands before the multitude, saying, I am innocent of the blood of this just person: see ye *to it.*   Deut. 21:6

25 Then answered all the people, and said, His blood *be* on us, and on our children.

Jesus Is Scourged
Mark 15:15–17; Luke 23:24, 25; John 19:16

26 Then released he Bar-ab'-bas unto them: and when he had ᴿscourgedᵀ Jesus, he delivered *him* to be crucified. Is. 50:6 ★ · *whipped*

27 ᴿThen the soldiers of the governor took Jesus into the common hall, and gathered unto him the whole band *of soldiers.*   John 19:2

28 And they stripped him, and ᴿput on him a scarlet robe.   Luke 23:11

Jesus Is Led to Golgotha
Mark 15:18–22; Luke 23:26–33; John 19:17

29 ᴿAnd when they had platted a crown of thorns, they put *it* upon his head, and a reed in his right hand: and they bowed the knee before him, and mocked him, saying, Hail, King of the Jews!   Ps. 69:19; Is. 53:3 ★

30 And ᴿthey spit upon him, and took the reed, and ᵀsmote him on the head. Is. 50:6 ★ · *hit*

31 And after that they had ᵀmocked him, they took the robe off from him, and put his own raiment on him, ᴿand led him away to crucify *him.*   made fun · Is. 53:7 ★

32 And as they came out, they found a man of Cy-re'-ne, Simon by name: him they compelled to bear his cross.

33 And when they were come unto a place called Gol'-go-tha, that is to say, a place of a skull,

Jesus Is Crucified
Mark 15:23–32; Luke 23:33–43; John 19:18–24

34 ᴿThey gave him ᵀvinegar to drink mingled with gall: and when he had tasted *thereof,* he would not drink.   Ps. 69:21 ★ · *wine*

35 And they crucified him, and parted his garments, casting lots: that it might be fulfilled which was spoken by the prophet, THEY PARTED MY GARMENTS AMONG THEM, AND UPON MY VESTURE DID THEY CAST LOTS.

36 ᴿAnd sitting down they watched him there;   v. 54; Ps. 22:17 ★

37 And set up over his head his accusation written, THIS IS JESUS THE KING OF THE JEWS.

38 ᴿThen were there two ᵀthieves crucified with him, one on the right hand, and another on the left.   Is. 53:9 ★ · *robbers*

39 And ᴿthey that passed by ᵀreviled him, wagging their heads,   Ps. 22:7 ★ · *taunted*

40 And saying, ᴿThou that destroyest the temple, and buildest *it* in three days, save thyself. ᴿIf thou be the Son of God, come down from the cross.   26:61; John 2:19 · 26:63

41 Likewise also the chief priests ᴿmocking *him,* with the scribes and elders, said,   20:19 ★

42 He saved others; himself he cannot save. ᴿIfᵀ he be the King of Israel, let him now come down from the cross, and we will ᵀbelieve him.   Ps. 22:6; 69:9 ★ · *He is* · *believe in*

43 ᴿHe trusted in God; let him deliver him now, if he ᵀwill have him: for he said, I am the Son of God.   Ps. 22:8 ☆ · *wants*

44 The thieves also, which were crucified with him, cast the sameᵀ in his teeth.   *insult*

Jesus Dies
Mark 15:33–37; Luke 23:44–46; John 19:28–30

45 ᴿNow from the sixth hour there was darkness over all the land unto the ninth hour.   Amos 8:9

46 And about the ninth hour Jesus cried with a loud voice, saying, *E'-li, E'-li, la'-ma sa-bach'-tha-ni?* that is to say, ᴿMY GOD, MY GOD, WHY HAST THOU FORSAKEN ME? Ps. 22:1 ★

47 Some of them that stood there, when they heard *that,* said, This *man* calleth for E-li'-as.

48 And straightway one of them ran, and took a spunge, and filled *it* with vinegar, and put *it* on a reed, and gave him to drink.

49 The rest said, Let be, let us see whether E-li'-as will come to save him.

50 Jesus, when he had cried again with a loud voice, yielded up the ghost.

Signs Accompanying Jesus' Death
Mark 15:38–41; Luke 23:45, 47–49

51 And, behold, the veil of the temple was rent in twain from the top to the bottom; and the earth did quake, and the rocks rent;

52 And the graves were opened; and many bodies of the saints which slept arose,

53 And came out of the graves after his ᵀresurrection, and went into the holy city, and appeared unto many.   *He arose*

54 Now when the centurion, and they that were with him, watching Jesus, saw the earthquake, and those things that were done, they feared greatly, saying, Truly this was the Son of God.

55 And many women were there beholding afar off, ᴿwhich followed Jesus from Galilee, ministering unto him: Luke 8:2, 3

56 Among which was Mary Mag-da-le'-ne, and ᴿMary the mother of James and Jo'-ses, and the mother of Zeb'-e-dee's children. *v.* 61

Jesus Is Buried
Mark 15:42–47; Luke 23:50–55; John 19:38–42

57 When the even was come, there came a rich man of Ar-i-ma-thae'-a, named Joseph, who also himself was Jesus' disciple:

58 He went to Pilate, and ᵀbegged the body of Jesus. Then Pilate commanded the body to be delivered.   *requested*

59 And when Joseph had taken the body, he wrapped it in a clean linen cloth,

60 And ᴿlaid it in his own new tomb, which he had hewn out in the rock: and he rolled a great stone to the door of the sepulchre, and departed.   Is. 53:9 ★

61 And there was Mary Mag-da-le'-ne, and ᴿthe other Mary, sitting ᵀover against the sepulchre.   *v.* 56 · *in front of*

62 Now the next day, that followed the day of the preparation, the chief priests and Pharisees came together unto Pilate,

63 Saying, Sir, we remember that that ᵀdeceiver said, while he was yet alive, After three days I will rise again.   *impostor*

64 Command therefore that the sepulchre be ᵀmade sure until the third day, lest his disciples come by night, and steal him away, and say unto the people, He is risen from the dead: so the last error shall be worse than the first.   *guarded*

65 Pilate said unto them, Ye have a ᵀwatch: go your way, make *it* as sure as ye can.   *guard*

66 So they went, and made the sepulchre sure, ᴿsealingᵀ the stone, and setting a ᵀwatch.   Dan. 6:17 · *put a seal upon* · *guard*

CHAPTER 28

The Empty Tomb—Mark 16:1–8; Luke 24:1–11

IN the end of the sabbath, as it began to dawn toward the first *day* of the week,

came Mary Mag-da-le'-ne ᴿand the other Mary to see the sepulchre.   27:56

2 And, behold, there was a great earthquake: for the angel of the Lord descended from heaven, and came and rolled back the stone from the door, and sat upon it.

3 His countenance was like lightning, and his ᵀraiment white as snow: *clothing*

4 And for fear of him the keepers did shake, and became as dead *men*.

5 And the angel answered and said unto the women, Fear not ye: for I know that ye seek Jesus, which was crucified.

6 He is not here: for he is risen, as he said. Come, see the place where the Lord lay.

7 And go quickly, and tell his disciples that he is ᴿrisen from the dead; and, behold, ᴿhe goeth before you into Galilee; there shall ye see him: lo, I have told you.   16:21 ★ · 26:32

8 And they departed quickly from the ᵀsepulchre with fear and great joy; and did run to bring his disciples word.   *tomb*

The Appearance of Jesus to the Women

9 And as they went to tell his disciples, behold, ᴿJesus met them, saying, All hail. And they came and held him by the feet, and worshipped him.   Mark 16:9; John 20:14

10 Then said Jesus unto them, Be not afraid: go tell my brethren that they go into Galilee, and there shall they see me.

The Bribery of the Soldiers

11 Now when they were going, behold, some of the watch came into the city, and shewed unto the chief priests all the things that were done.

12 And when they were assembled with the elders, and had taken counsel, they gave large money unto the soldiers,

13 Saying, Say ye, His disciples came by night, and stole him *away* while we slept.

14 And if this come to the governor's ears, we will persuade him, and ᵀsecure you. *protect*

15 So they took the money, and did as they were taught: and ᴿthis saying is commonly reported among the Jews until this day.   Luke 2:34 ★

The Appearance of Jesus to the Disciples

16 Then the eleven disciples went away into Galilee, into a mountain ᴿwhere Jesus had appointed them.   *v.* 7; 26:32; Mark 14:28

17 And when they saw him, they worshipped him: but some ᴿdoubted. John 20:24–29

The Great Commission

18 And Jesus came and spake unto them, saying, ᴿAll power is given unto me in heaven and in earth.   11:27; [Dan. 7:13, 14]

19 Go ye therefore, and teach all nations, baptizing them in the name of the Father, and of the Son, and of the Holy Ghost:

20 ᴿTeaching them to observe all things whatsoever I have commanded you: and, lo, I am with you alway, *even* unto the end of the world. A-men'.   [18:20; Acts 2:42]

28:19 Sharing Our Faith: Why?—There are at least six compelling reasons for sharing our faith in Christ with those who have not experienced new life in Christ.
a. Because God has commanded us to do so. The final words of Jesus while on earth (Page 1072—Acts 1:8) and also the Bible (Page 1283—Rev. 22:17) speak concerning this.
b. Because it demonstrates our love for God. Christ said that if we truly loved Him we would keep His commandments (Page 1059—John 14:15).
c. Because all are lost (Page 1110—Rom. 3:10, 23).
d. Because our sharing is God's chosen method to tell all people. He could have used angels, but He didn't. Only redeemed sinners can tell lost sinners about Christ. See Romans 10:14–17; Acts 8:3.
e. Because God desires to save all people (Page 1075—Acts 4:12; Page 1244—2 Pet. 3:9; Page 1194—1 Tim. 2:4).
f. Because someone once shared his faith with us. It may have been a faithful Bible teacher, or a godly pastor, or a praying parent. In other words, they have the right to expect that we will do for others what they have done for us.
    Now turn to Page 1137—1 Cor. 15:3, 4: Sharing Our Faith: What?

Monies

Unit	Monetary Value	Equivalents	Translations
Jewish Weights			
Talent	gold—$5,760,000[1]	3,000 shekels; 6,000 bekas	talent
	silver—$384,000		
Shekel	gold—$1,920	4 days' wages; 2 bekas;	shekel
	silver—$128	20 gerahs	
Beka	gold—$960	½ shekel; 10 gerahs	bekah
	silver—$64		
Gerah	gold—$96	1⁄20 shekel	gerah
	silver—$6.40		
Persian Coins			
Daric	gold—$1,280[2]	2 days' wages; ½ Jewish	dram
	silver—$64	silver shekel	
Greek Coins			
Tetradrachma (Stater)	$128	4 drachmas	piece of money
Didrachma	$64	2 drachmas	tribute
Drachma	$32	1 day's wage	piece of silver
Lepton	$.25	½ of a Roman kodrantes	mite
Roman Coins			
Aureus	$800	25 denarii	
Denarius	$32	1 day's wage	pence, penny
Assarius	$2	1⁄16 of a denarius	farthing
Kodrantes	$.50	¼ of an assarius	farthing

[1]Value of gold is fifteen times the value of silver.
[2]Value of gold is twenty times the value of silver.

THE GOSPEL ACCORDING TO

MARK

📖 THE BOOK OF MARK

The message of Mark's gospel is captured in a single verse: "For even the Son of man came not to be ministered unto, but to minister, and to give his life a ransom for many" (10:45). Chapter by chapter, the book unfolds the dual focus of Christ's life: service and sacrifice.

Mark portrays Jesus as a Servant on the move, instantly responsive to the will of the Father. By preaching, teaching, and healing, He ministers to the needs of others even to the point of death. After the Resurrection, He commissions His followers to continue His work in His power—servants following in the steps of the perfect Servant.

The ancient title for this gospel was *Kata Markōn*, "According to Mark." The author is best known by his Latin name *Marcus*, but in Jewish circles he was called by his Hebrew name *John*. Acts 12:12, 25 and 15:37 refer to him as "John, whose surname was Mark."

✍️ THE AUTHOR OF MARK

According to Acts 12:12, Mark's mother Mary had a large house that was used as a meeting place for believers in Jerusalem. Peter apparently went to this house often because the servant girl recognized his voice at the gate (Acts 12:13–16). Barnabas was Mark's cousin (Col. 4:10), but Peter may have been the person who led him to Christ (Peter called him "Marcus my son," 1 Pet. 5:13). It was this close association with Peter that lent apostolic authority to Mark's gospel, since Peter was evidently Mark's primary source of information. It has been suggested that Mark was referring to himself in his account of "a certain young man" in Gethsemane (14:51, 52). Since all the disciples had abandoned Jesus (14:50), this little incident may have been a firsthand account.

Barnabas and Saul took Mark along with them when they returned from Jerusalem to Antioch (Acts 12:25) and again when they left on the first missionary journey (Acts 13:5). However, Mark left early and returned to Jerusalem (Acts 13:13). When Barnabas wanted to bring Mark on the second missionary journey, Paul's refusal led to a disagreement. The result was that Barnabas took Mark to Cyprus and Paul took Silas through Syria and Cilicia (Acts 15:36–41). Nevertheless, Paul wrote that Mark was with him during his first Roman imprisonment (Col. 4:10; Philem. 24) about twelve years later, so there must have been a reconciliation. In fact, at the end of his life Paul sent for Mark, saying, "He is profitable to me for the ministry" (2 Tim. 4:11).

The early church uniformly attested that Mark wrote this gospel. Papias, Irenaeus, Clement of Alexandria, and Origen are among the church fathers who affirmed Marcan authorship.

⌛ THE TIME OF MARK

Many scholars believe that Mark was the first of the four Gospels, but there is uncertainty over its date. Because of the prophecy about the destruction of the temple (13:2), it should be dated before A.D. 70, but early traditions disagree as to whether it was written before or after the martyrdom of Peter (c. A.D. 64). The probable range for this book is A.D. 55–65.

Mark was evidently directed to a Roman readership and early tradition indicates that it originated in Rome. This may be why Mark omitted a number of items that would not have been meaningful to Gentiles, such as the genealogy of Christ, fulfilled prophecy, references to the Law, and certain Jewish customs that are found in other gospels. Mark interpreted Aramaic words (3:17; 5:41; 7:34; 15:22) and used a number of Latin terms in place of their Greek equivalents (4:21; 6:27; 12:14, 42; 15:15, 16, 39).

✝️ THE CHRIST OF MARK

The Lord is presented as an active, compassionate, and obedient Servant who constantly ministers to the physical and spiritual needs of others. Because this is the story of a Servant, Mark omits Jesus' ancestry and birth and moves right into His busy public ministry. The distinctive word of this book is *euthus*, translated "immediately" or "straightway," and it appears more often in this compact gospel (forty-two times) than in the rest of the New Testament. Christ is constantly moving toward a goal that is hidden to almost all. Mark clearly shows the power and authority of this unique Servant, identifying Him as no less than the Son of God (1:1, 11; 3:11; 5:7; 9:7; 13:32; 14:61; 15:39).

🔑 KEYS TO MARK

Key Word: Jesus the Servant—Even in the first verse it is obvious that this Gospel centers on the person and mission of the Son of God. Mark's theme is captured well in 10:45 because Jesus is portrayed in this book as a Servant and as the Redeemer of men (cf. Phil. 2:5–11). Like the other Gospels, Mark is not a biography but a topical narrative. Mark juxtaposes Christ's teachings and works to show how they authenticate each other. Miracles are

predominant in this book (there are eighteen), and they are used to demonstrate not only the power of Christ but also His compassion. Mark shows his gentile readers how the Son of God—rejected by His own people—achieved ultimate victory through apparent defeat. There was no doubt an evangelistic purpose behind this gospel as Mark directed his words to a gentile audience that knew little about Old Testament theology.

Key Verses: Mark 10:43-45 and 8:34-37—"But so shall it not be among you: but whosoever will be great among you, shall be your minister: And whosoever of you will be the chiefest, shall be servant of all. For even the Son of man came not to be ministered unto, but to minister, and to give his life a ransom for many" (10:43-45).

"And when he had called the people unto him with his disciples also, he said unto them, Whosoever will come after me, let him deny himself, and take up his cross, and follow me. For whosoever will save his life shall lose it; but whosoever shall lose his life for my sake and the gospel's, the same shall save it. For what shall it profit a man, if he shall gain the whole world, and lose his own soul? Or what shall a man give in exchange for his soul?" (8:34-37).

Key Chapter: Mark 8—As in Matthew, Mark's gospel contains a pivotal chapter showing the change of emphasis in Jesus' ministry. In Matthew it is chapter 12; in Mark it is chapter 8. The pivotal event lies in Peter's confession, "Thou art the Christ." That faith-inspired response triggers a new phase in both the content and the course of Jesus' ministry. Until this point He has sought to validate His claims as Messiah. But now He begins to fortify His men for His forthcoming suffering and death at the hands of the religious leaders. Jesus' steps begin to take Him daily closer to Jerusalem—the place where the Perfect Servant will demonstrate the full extent of His servanthood.

SURVEY OF MARK

Mark, the shortest and simplest of the four gospels, gives a crisp and fast-moving look at the life of Christ. With few comments, Mark lets the narrative speak for itself as it tells the story of the Servant who constantly ministers to others through preaching, healing, teaching, and, ultimately, His own death. Mark traces the steady building of hostility and opposition to Jesus as He resolutely moves toward the fulfillment of His earthly mission. Almost forty percent of this gospel is devoted to a detailed account of the last eight days of Jesus' life, climaxing in His resurrection. The Lord is vividly portrayed in this book in two parts: to serve (1—10); to sacrifice (11—16).

To Serve (1—10): Mark passes over the birth and early years of Jesus' life and begins with the events that immediately precede the inauguration of His public ministry—His baptism by John and His temptation by Satan (1:1–13). The first four chapters emphasize the words of the Servant while chapters 5—7 accent His works. However, in both sections there is a frequent alternation between Christ's messages and miracles in order to reveal His person and power. Though He has come to serve others, Jesus' authority prevails over many realms.

Although Jesus has already been teaching and testing His disciples (see ch. 4), His ministry with them becomes more intense from this point on as He begins to prepare them for His departure. The religious leaders are growing more antagonistic, and Christ's "hour" is only about six months away. Mark 8:31 is the pivotal point in the gospel as the Son of Man speaks clearly to His disciples about His coming death and resurrection. The disciples struggle with this difficult revelation, but Jesus' steps head inexorably to Jerusalem.

To Sacrifice (11—16): Mark allots a disproportionate space to the last weeks of the Servant's

FOCUS	TO SERVE			TO SACRIFICE	
REFERENCE	1:1————2:13————		8:27————11:1————		16:1————16:20
DIVISION	PRESENTATION OF THE SERVANT	OPPOSITION TO THE SERVANT	INSTRUCTION BY THE SERVANT	REJECTION OF THE SERVANT	RESURRECTION OF THE SERVANT
TOPIC	SAYINGS AND SIGNS			SUFFERINGS	
	c. 3 YEARS		c. 6 MONTHS	8 DAYS	
LOCATION	GALILEE AND PERAEA			JUDEA AND JERUSALEM	
TIME	c. A.D. 29 – 33				

redemptive ministry. During the last seven days in Jerusalem, hostility from the chief priests, scribes, elders, Pharisees, Herodians, and Sadducees reaches crisis proportions as Jesus publicly refutes their arguments in the temple.

After His last supper with the disciples, Jesus offers no resistance to His arrest, abuse, and agonizing crucifixion. His willingness to bear countless human sins is the epitome of servanthood.

OUTLINE OF MARK

CHAPTER 1

The Forerunner of the Servant
Matt. 3:1-11; Luke 3:3-16; John 1:19-34

THE beginning of the gospel of Jesus Christ, ^Rthe Son of God;   Matt. 14:33

2 As it is written in the prophets, ^RBEHOLD, I SEND MY MESSENGER BEFORE THY FACE, WHICH SHALL PREPARE THY WAY BEFORE THEE.   Mal. 3:1 ★

3 ^RTHE VOICE OF ONE CRYING IN THE WILDERNESS, PREPARE YE THE WAY OF THE LORD, MAKE HIS PATHS STRAIGHT.   Is. 40:3 ★

4 John did baptize in the wilderness, and preach the ^Rbaptism of repentance ^Tfor the remission of sins.   Mal. 4:6 ★ • *unto*

5 And there went out unto him all the land of Ju-dae'-a, and they of Jerusalem, and were all baptized of him in the river of Jordan, confessing their sins.

6 And John was clothed with camel's hair, and with a girdle of a skin about his loins; and he did eat locusts and wild honey;

7 And preached, saying, ^RThere cometh one mightier than I after me, the latchet of whose shoes I am not worthy to stoop down and unloose.   John 1:27

8 ^RI indeed have baptized you ^Twith water: but he shall baptize you ^Rwith the Holy Ghost.   vv. 4, 9, 10 • *in* • [Acts 2:4; 10:45, 46; 1 Cor. 12:13] ★

The Baptism of the Servant
Matt. 3:13-17; Luke 3:21-23

9 ^RAnd it came to pass in those days, that Jesus came from Nazareth of Galilee, and was baptized of John in Jordan.   Matt. 3:13

10 And straightway coming up out of the water, he saw the heavens opened, and the Spirit like a dove descending upon him:

11 And there came a voice from heaven, saying, ^RThou art my beloved Son, in whom I am well pleased.   [Ps. 2:7]; Is. 42:1 ★

The Temptation of the Servant
Matt. 4:1-11; Luke 4:1-13

12 ^RAnd immediately the spirit ^Tdriveth him into the wilderness.   Matt. 4:1 • *impelled*

13 And he was there in the wilderness forty days, ^Ttempted of Satan; and was with the wild beasts; ^Rand the angels ^Tministered unto him.   *tested* • Matt. 4:11 • *helped*

The Work of the Servant
Matt. 4:12-17; Luke 4:14, 15

14 Now after that John was put in prison, Jesus came into Galilee, preaching the gospel of the kingdom of God,

15 And saying, ^RThe time is fulfilled, and the kingdom of God is ^Tat hand: repent ye, and believe the gospel.   Dan. 9:25 • *near*

The First Disciples Are Called—Matt. 4:18–22

16 ᴿNow as he walked by the sea of Galilee, he saw Simon and Andrew his brother casting a net into the sea: for they were ᵀfishers.   Matt. 4:18; Luke 5:4 · *fishermen*

17 And Jesus said unto them, Come ye after me, and I will make you to become fishers of men.

18 And ᵀstraightway they ᵀforsook their nets, and followed him.   *immediately · left*

19 And when he had gone a little farther thence, he saw James the *son* of Zeb'-e-dee, and John his brother, who also were in the ship mending their nets.

20 And straightway he called them: and they left their father Zeb'-e-dee in the ship with the hired servants, and went after him.

Demons Are Cast Out—Luke 4:31–37

21 And they went into Ca-per'-na-um; and straightway on the sabbath day he entered into the synagogue, and taught.

22 And they were astonished at his ᵀdoctrine: for he taught them as one that had authority, and not as the scribes.   *teaching*

23 And there was in their synagogue a man with an ᵀunclean spirit; and ᵀhe ᵀcried out,   *evil · the spirit · screamed*

24 Saying, Let *us* alone; what have we to do with thee, thou Jesus of Nazareth? art thou come to destroy us? I know thee who thou art, the Holy One of God.

25 And Jesus ᴿrebuked him, saying, Hold thy peace, and come out of him.   *v. 34*

26 And when the unclean spirit ᴿhad ᵀtorn him, and cried with a loud voice, he came out of him.   *9:20 · shook*

27 And they were all amazed, insomuch that they questioned among themselves, saying, What thing is this? what new ᵀdoctrine is this? for with authority commandeth he even the unclean spirits, and they do obey him.   *teaching*

28 And immediately his ᵀfame spread abroad throughout all the region round about Galilee.   *news*

Peter's Mother-in-Law Is Healed
Matt. 8:14, 15; Luke 4:38, 39

29 And forthwith, when they ᵀwere come out of the synagogue, they entered into the house of Simon and Andrew, with James and John.   *left*

30 But Simon's wife's mother lay sick of a fever, and anon they tell him of her.

31 And he came and took her by the hand, and lifted her up; and immediately the fever left her, and she ᵀministered unto them. *served*

Many Healings
Matt. 8:16, 17; 4:23; Luke 4:40–44

32 And at even, when the sun did set, they brought unto him all that were diseased, and them that were possessed with ᵀdevils. *demons*

33 And all the city was gathered together at the ᵀdoor.   *front of the house*

34 And he healed many that were sick of divers diseases, and cast out many devils; and suffered not the devils to speak, because they knew him.

35 And in the morning, rising up a great while before day, he went out, and departed into a ᵀsolitary place, and there prayed. *lonely*

36 And Simon and they that were with him ᵀfollowed after him.   *searched for*

37 And when they had found him, they said unto him, All *men* seek for thee.

38 And he said unto them, Let us go into the next towns, that I may preach there also: for therefore came I forth.

39 And he preached in their synagogues throughout all Galilee, and cast out devils.

A Leper Is Cleansed
Matt. 8:1–4; Luke 5:12–16

40 ᴿAnd there came a leper to him, ᵀbeseeching him, and kneeling down to him, and saying unto him, If thou wilt, thou canst make me clean.   *Matt. 8:2 · urgently asking*

41 And Jesus, moved with compassion, put forth *his* hand, and touched him, and saith unto him, I will; be thou clean.

42 And as soon as he had spoken, immediately the leprosy departed from him, and he was cleansed.

43 And he ᵀstraitly charged him, and forthwith sent him away;   *strictly directed*

44 And saith unto him, See thou say nothing to any man: but go thy way, shew thyself to the priest, and offer for thy cleansing those things which Moses commanded, for a testimony unto them.

45 But he went out, and began to publish *it* much, and to blaze abroad the matter, insomuch that Jesus could no more openly enter into the city, but was ᵀwithout in desert places: ᴿand they came to him from every quarter.   *outside the city · 2:13*

CHAPTER 2

A Paralytic Is Healed
Matt. 9:1–8; Luke 5:17–26

AND again ᴿhe entered into Ca-per'-na-um after *some* days; and it was ᵀnoised that he was in the house.   *Matt. 9:1 · reported*

2 And ᵀstraightway many were gathered together, insomuch that there was no room to receive *them*, no, not so much as ᵀabout the door: and he preached the word unto them.   *immediately · in front of*

3 And they come unto him, bringing one sick of the palsy, which was borne of four.

4 And when they could not come ᵀnigh unto him for the ᵀpress, they uncovered the roof where he was: and when they had

broken it up, they let down the bed wherein the sick of the palsy lay. near • crowd

5 When Jesus saw their faith, he said unto the ᵀsick of the palsy, Son, thy sins be forgiven thee. paralyzed

6 But there were certain of the scribes sitting there, and reasoning in their hearts,

7 Why doth this man thus speak blasphemies? who can forgive sins but God only?

8 And immediately when Jesus perceived in his spirit that they so reasoned within themselves, he said unto them, Why reason ye these things in your hearts?

9 Whether is it easier to say to the sick of the palsy, Thy sins be forgiven thee; or to say, Arise, and take up thy bed, and walk?

10 But that ye may know that the Son of man hath power on earth to forgive sins, (he saith to the sick of the palsy,)

11 I say unto thee, Arise, and take up thy bed, and go thy way into thine house.

12 And immediately he arose, took up the bed, and went forth before them all; insomuch that they were all amazed, and glorified God, saying, We never saw it on this fashion.

Call of Matthew—Matt. 9:9–13; Luke 5:27–32

13 And he went forth again by the sea side; and all the multitude resorted unto him, and he taught them.

14 And as he passed by, he saw Levi the son of Al-phae'-us sitting at the ᵀreceipt of custom, and said unto him, Follow me. And he arose and followed him. place of toll

15 And it came to pass, that, as Jesus sat at meat in his house, many ᵀpublicans and sinners sat also together with Jesus and his disciples: for there were many, and they followed him. tax collectors

16 And when the scribes ᵀand Pharisees saw him eat with publicans and ᵀsinners, they said unto his disciples, How is it that he eateth and drinketh with publicans and sinners? of the • outcasts

17 When Jesus heard it, he saith unto them, ᴿThey that are whole have no need of the physician, but they that are sick: I came not to call the righteous, but sinners to repentance. Matt. 18:11; 1 Tim. 1:15

Parable of Cloth and Wine Bottles
Matt. 9:14–17; Luke 5:33–39

18 And the disciples of John and of the Pharisees ᵀused to fast: and they come and say unto him, Why do the disciples of John and of the Pharisees fast, but thy disciples fast not? were fasting

19 And Jesus said unto them, Can the ᵀchildren of the bridechamber ᵀfast, while the bridegroom is with them? as long as they have the bridegroom with them, they cannot fast. guests • go without food

20 But the days will come, when the bridegroom shall be taken away from them, and then shall they fast in those days.

21 No man also seweth a piece of ᵀnew cloth on an old garment: else the new piece that filled it up taketh away from the old, and the rent is made worse. unshrunk

22 And no man putteth new wine into old ᵀbottles: else the new wine doth burst the bottles, and the wine is spilled, and the bottles will ᵀbe marred: but new wine must be put into new bottles. wineskins • burst

Controversy over Sabbath-Work
Matt. 12:1–8; Luke 6:1–5

23 And it came to pass, that he went through the ᵀcorn fields on the sabbath day; and his disciples began, as they went, ᴿto pluck the ears of corn. grain • Deut. 23:25

24 And the Pharisees said unto him, Behold, why do they on the sabbath day that which is not lawful?

25 And he said unto them, Have ye never read ᴿwhat David did, when he had need, and was ᵀan hungred, he, and they that were with him? 1 Sam. 21:6 • hungry

26 How he went into the house of God in the days of A-bi'-a-thar the high priest, and did eat the ᵀshewbread, which is not lawful to eat but for the priests, and gave also to them which were with him? sacred bread

27 And he said unto them, The sabbath was made ᵀfor man, and not man for the sabbath: for the good of

28 Therefore ᴿthe Son of man is Lord ᵀalso of the sabbath. Matt. 12:8 • even

CHAPTER 3

Controversy over Sabbath-Healing
Matt. 12:9–13; Luke 6:6–10

AND he entered again into the synagogue; and there was a man there which had a withered hand.

2 And they watched him, whether he would heal him on the sabbath day; that they might ᵀaccuse him. criticize

3 And he saith unto the man which had the withered hand, Stand forth.

4 And he saith unto them, Is it lawful to do good on the sabbath days, or to do evil? to save life, or to kill? But they held their peace.

5 And when he had looked round about on them with anger, being ᵀgrieved for the hardness of their hearts, he saith unto the man, Stretch forth thine hand. And he stretched it out: and his hand ᵀwas restored whole as the other. saddened • became well

Pharisees Counsel to Destroy Jesus
Matt. 12:14–16; Luke 6:11

6 ᴿAnd the Pharisees went forth, and ᵀstraightway took counsel with ᴿthe He-ro'-

di-ans against him, how they might destroy him. Ps. 2:2 * • immediately consulted • Matt. 22:16

7 But Jesus ᵀwithdrew himself with his disciples to the sea: and a great multitude from Galilee followed him, ᴿand from Ju-dae′-a,   went away • Matt. 4:25; Luke 6:17

8 And from Jerusalem, and from Id-u-mae′-a, and from beyond Jordan; ᴿand they about Tyre and Si′-don, a great multitude, when they had heard what great things he did, came unto him.   Matt. 11:21

9 And he spake to his disciples, that a small ship should wait on him because of the multitude, lest they should throng him.

10 For he had healed many; insomuch that they ᵀpressed upon him for to touch him, as many as had plagues.   crowded

11 ᴿAnd unclean spirits, when they saw him, fell down before him, and cried, saying, Thou art the Son of God.   1:23, 24

12 And he straitly charged them that they should not make him known.

Selection of the Twelve—Luke 6:12–16

13 ᴿAnd he goeth up into a mountain, and calleth unto him ᵀwhom he would: and they came unto him.   Matt. 10:1 • such as he wanted

14 And he ᵀordained twelve, that they should be with him, and that he might send them forth to preach,   appointed

15 And to have ᵀpower to heal sicknesses, and to cast out ᵀdevils: authority • demons

16 And Simon he surnamed Peter;

17 ᴿAnd James the son of Zeb′-e-dee, and John the brother of James; and he surnamed them Bo-a-ner′-ges, which is, The sons of thunder: Matt. 10:2-4

18 ᴿAnd Andrew, and Philip, and Bartholo-mew, and Matthew, and Thomas, and James the son of Al-phae′-us, and Thad-dae′-us, and Simon the Ca′-naan-ite,   Acts 1:13

19 And Judas Is-car′-i-ot, which also betrayed him: and they went into an house.

Opposition of His Friends

20 And the multitude cometh together again, ᴿso that they ᵀcould not so much as eat bread.   6:31 • did not have time to

21 And when his friends heard of it, they went out to ᵀlay hold on him: for they said, He is ᵀbeside himself.   restrain • unbalanced

Scribes Commit the Unpardonable Sin Matt. 12:24–32; Luke 11:17–23

22 And the scribes which came down from Jerusalem said, ᴿHe hath Be-el′-ze-bub, and by the prince of the ᵀdevils casteth he out devils.   Matt. 9:34; 10:25 • demons

23 ᴿAnd he called them unto him, and said unto them in parables, How can Satan cast out Satan?   Matt. 4:10; 12:25

24 And if a kingdom be divided against itself, that kingdom cannot stand.

25 And if a house be ᵀdivided against itself, that house cannot stand.   fights

26 And if Satan rise up against himself, and be divided, ᵀhe cannot stand, but hath an end.   he will fall apart

27 No man can enter into a strong man's house, and ᵀspoil his goods, except he will first bind the strong man; and then he will ᵀspoil his house.   take away • rob

28 ᴿVerily I say unto you, All sins shall be forgiven unto the sons of men, and blas-phemies wherewith soever they shall blas-pheme: Luke 12:10; [1 John 5:16]

29 But he that shall blaspheme against the Holy Ghost hath never forgiveness, but is in danger of eternal damnation:

30 Because they said, He hath an ᵀunclean spirit.   evil spirit in him

New Relationships Are Defined Matt. 12:46–50; Luke 8:19–21

31 There came then his brethren and his mother, and, ᵀstanding without, sent unto him, calling him.   waiting outside

32 And the multitude sat about him, and they said unto him, Behold, thy mother and thy brethren without seek for thee.

33 And he answered them, saying, Who is my mother, or my brethren?

34 And he looked round about on them which sat about him, and said, Behold my mother and my ᵀbrethren!   brothers

35 For whosoever shall do the will of God, the same is my brother, and my sister, and mother.

CHAPTER 4

Parable of the Soils Matt. 13:1–23; Luke 8:4–15

AND he began again to teach by the sea side: and there was gathered unto him a great multitude, so that he entered into a ship, and sat in the sea; and the whole multitude was by the sea on the land.

2 And he taught them many things by parables, ᴿand said unto them in his ᵀdoc-trine,   12:38 • teaching

3 ᵀHearken; Behold, there went out a sower to sow: listen

4 And it came to pass, as he sowed, some fell by the way side, and the fowls of the air came and devoured it up.

5 And some fell on stony ground, where it had not much earth; and immediately it sprang up, because it had no depth of earth:

6 But when the sun was up, it was scorched; and because it had no root, it ᵀwithered away.   dried up

7 And some fell among thorns, and the thorns grew up, and choked it, and it yielded no ᵀfruit.   grain

8 And other fell on good ground, and did yield fruit that sprang up and increased; and brought forth, some thirty, and some sixty, and some an hundred.

9 And he said unto them, He that hath ears to hear, let him hear.

10 And when he was alone, they that were about him with the twelve asked of him the parable.

11 And he said unto them, Unto you it is given to know the mystery of the kingdom of God: but unto ᴿthem that are without, all *these* things are done in parables: [1 Tim. 3:7]

12 That ᴿSEEING THEY MAY SEE, AND NOT PERCEIVE; AND HEARING THEY MAY HEAR, AND NOT UNDERSTAND; LEST AT ANY TIME THEY SHOULD BE CONVERTED, AND *THEIR* SINS SHOULD BE FORGIVEN THEM.   Is. 6:9

13 And he said unto them, ᵀKnow ye not this parable? and how then will ye know all parables?   *understand*

14 ᴿThe sower soweth the word.   Matt. 13:9

15 And these are they by the way side, where the word is sown; but when they have heard, Satan cometh immediately, and taketh away the word that was sown in their hearts.

16 And these are they likewise which are sown on stony ground; who, when they have heard the word, immediately receive it with gladness;

17 And have no root in themselves, and so endure but for a time: afterward, when affliction or persecution ariseth for the word's sake, immediately they ᵀare offended.   *stumble*

18 And these are they which are sown among thorns; such as hear the word,

19 And the ᵀcares of this world, ᴿand the deceitfulness of riches, and the lusts of other things entering in, choke the word, and it becometh unfruitful.   *burdens* • 1 Tim. 6:9

20 And these are they which are sown on good ground; such as hear the word, and receive *it*, and bring forth fruit, some thirtyfold, some sixty, and some an hundred.

Parable of the Lamp—Luke 8:16–18

21 And he said unto them, Is a candle brought to be put under a bushel, or under a bed? and not to be set on a candlestick?

22 For there is nothing hid, which shall not be manifested; neither was any thing kept secret, but that it should come abroad.

23 ᴿIf any man have ears to hear, let him hear.   *v.* 9; Matt. 11:15

24 And he said unto them, Take heed what ye hear: with what measure ye mete, it shall be measured to you: and unto you that hear shall more be given.

25 For he that hath, to him shall be given: and he that hath not, from him shall be taken even that which he hath.

Parable of the Growing Seed

26 And he said, So is the kingdom of God, as if a man should cast seed into the ground;

27 And should ᵀsleep, and rise night and day, and the seed should spring and grow up, he knoweth not how.   *sleep at night*

28 For the earth bringeth forth fruit of herself; first the blade, then the ear, after that the full corn in the ear.

29 But when the fruit is ᵀbrought forth, immediately ᴿhe putteth in the sickle, because the harvest is come.   *ripe* • Rev. 14:15

Parable of the Mustard Seed—Matt. 13:31–35

30 And he said, Whereunto shall we liken the kingdom of God? or with what comparison shall we compare it?

31 *It is* like a grain of mustard seed, which, when it is sown in the earth, is less than all the seeds that be in the earth:

32 But when it is sown, it groweth up, and becometh ᵀgreater than all herbs, and shooteth out great branches; so that the fowls of the air may lodge under the shadow of it.   *larger*

33 ᴿAnd with many such parables spake he the word unto them, as they were able to hear *it*.   [John 16:12]

34 But without a parable spake he not unto them: and when they were alone, he expounded all things to his disciples.

The Sea Is Stilled—Matt. 8:23–27; Luke 8:22–25

35 And the same day, when the even was come, he saith unto them, Let us pass over unto the other side.

36 And when they had sent away the multitude, they took him even as he was in the ship. And there were also with him other little ᵀships.   *boats*

37 And there arose a great storm of wind, and the waves beat into the ship, so that it was now full.

38 And he was in the hinder part of the ship, asleep on a pillow: and they awake him, and say unto him, ᵀMaster, carest thou not that we perish?   *Teacher*

39 And he arose, and rebuked the wind, and said unto the sea, Peace, be still. And the wind ceased, and there was a great calm.

40 And he said unto them, Why are ye so fearful? how is it that ye have no faith?

41 And they feared exceedingly, and said one to another, What manner of man is this, that even the wind and the sea obey him?

CHAPTER 5

Devils Are Cast into Swine
Matt. 8:28–34; Luke 8:26–39

AND they came over unto the other side of the sea, into the country of the ᵀGad-a-renes'.   *Gerasenes*

2 And when he was come out of the ship, immediately there met him out of the tombs a man with an unclean spirit,

3 Who had *his* dwelling ᵀamong the tombs; and no man could bind him, no, not with chains: *in the graveyard*

4 Because that he had been often bound with fetters and chains, and the chains had been ᵀplucked asunder by him, and the fetters broken in pieces: neither could any *man* ᵀtame him.   *broken • stop*

5 And always, night and day, he was in the mountains, and in the tombs, crying, and cutting himself with stones.

6 But when he saw Jesus afar off, he ran and ᵀworshipped him,   *bowed down to*

7 And cried with a loud voice, and said, What have I to do with thee, Jesus, *thou* Son of the most high God? I ᵀadjure thee by God, that thou torment me not.   *command*

8 For he said unto him, Come out of the man, *thou* unclean spirit.

9 And he asked him, What *is* thy name? And he answered, saying, My name *is* Legion: for we are many.

10 And he ᵀbesought him much that he would not send them away out of the country.   *begged*

11 Now there was there nigh unto the mountains a great herd of swine feeding.

12 And all the ᵀdevils besought him, saying, Send us into the ᵀswine, that we may enter into them.   *demons • hogs*

13 And forth with Jesus gave them leave. And the unclean spirits went out, and entered into the swine: and the herd ran violently down a steep place into the sea, (they were about two thousand;) and were ᵀchoked in the sea.   *drowned*

14 And they that fed the swine fled, and told *it* in the city, and in the country. And they went out to see what it was that was ᵀdone.   *happening*

15 And they come to Jesus, and see him that was possessed with the devil, and had the legion, sitting, and clothed, and in his right mind: and they were afraid.

16 And they that saw *it* told them how it befell to him that was possessed with the devil, and *also* concerning the swine.

17 And ᴿthey began to ᵀpray him to depart out of their coasts.   *Acts 16:39 • ask*

18 And when he was come into the ship, he that had been possessed with the devil prayed him that he might be with him.

19 Howbeit Jesus ᵀsuffered him not, but saith unto him, Go home to thy friends, and tell them how great things the Lord hath done for thee, and hath had compassion on thee.   *would not let him*

20 And he departed, and began to publish in De-cap'-o-lis how great things Jesus had done for him: and all *men* did marvel.

Jairus Pleads for His Daughter
Matt. 9:18, 19; Luke 8:41, 42

21 ᴿAnd when Jesus was passed over again by ship unto the other side, much people gathered unto him: and he was nigh unto the sea.   *Matt. 9:1*

22 And, behold, there cometh one of the rulers of the synagogue, Ja-i'-rus by name; and when he saw him, he fell at his feet,

23 And besought him greatly, saying, My little daughter lieth at the point of death: *I pray thee*, come and lay thy hands on her, that she may be healed; and she shall live.

24 And *Jesus* went with him; and much people followed him, and thronged him.

A Woman with Issue Is Healed
Matt. 9:20-22; Luke 8:43-48

25 And a certain woman, ᴿwhich had an issue of blood twelve years,   *Lev. 15:25*

26 And had suffered many ᵀthings of many physicians, and had spent all that she had, and was ᵀnothing bettered, but rather grew worse,   *treatments • not improved*

27 When she had heard of Jesus, came in the press behind, and touched his garment.

28 For she said, If I may touch but his clothes, I shall be ᵀwhole.   *well*

29 And straightway the fountain of her blood was dried up; and she felt in *her* body that she was healed of that plague.

30 And Jesus, immediately knowing in himself that ᴿvirtue had gone out of him, turned him about in the ᵀpress, and said, Who touched my clothes?   *Luke 6:19 • crowd*

31 And his disciples said unto him, Thou seest the multitude thronging thee, and sayest thou, Who touched me?

32 And he looked round about to see ᵀher that had done this thing.   *who*

33 But the woman fearing and trembling, ᵀknowing what was done ᵀin her, came and fell down before him, and told him all the truth.   *realizing • to*

34 And he said unto her, Daughter, ᴿthy faith hath made thee whole; go in peace, and be whole of thy plague.   *Mark 10:52*

Jairus's Daughter Is Healed
Matt. 9:23-26; Luke 8:49-56

35 While he yet spake, there came from the ruler of the synagogue's *house certain* which said, Thy daughter is dead: why troublest thou the Master any further?

36 As soon as Jesus heard the word that was spoken, he saith unto the ruler of the synagogue, Be not afraid, only believe.

37 And he ᵀsuffered no man to follow him, ᴿsave Peter, and James, and John the brother of James.   *allowed • Matt. 17:1*

38 And he cometh to the house of the ruler of the synagogue, and seeth the ᵀtumult, and them that wept and wailed greatly.   *confusion*

39 And when he was come in, he saith unto them, Why make ye this ado, and weep? the damsel is not dead, but sleepeth.

40 And they laughed him to scorn. RBut when he had put them all out, he taketh the father and the mother of the damsel, and them that were with him, and entereth in where the damsel was lying.   Acts 9:40

41 And he took Tthe damsel by the hand, and said unto her, Tal'-i-tha cu'-mi; which is, being interpreted, TDamsel, I say unto thee, arise.   her · maid

42 And Tstraightway the damsel arose, and walked; for she was of the age of twelve years. And they were astonished with a great astonishment.   immediately

43 And he charged them straitly that no man should know it; and commanded that something should be given her to eat.

CHAPTER 6

Jesus Is Rejected at Nazareth—Matt. 13:54-58

AND Rhe went out from thence, and came into his own country; and his disciples follow him.   Luke 4:16

2 And when the sabbath day was come, he began to teach in the synagogue: and many hearing him were astonished, saying, From Twhence hath this man these things? and what wisdom is this which is given unto him, that even such mighty works are wrought by his hands?   where did this man get

3 Is not this the carpenter, the son of Mary, Rthe brother of James, and Jo'-ses, and of Juda, and Simon? and are not his sisters here with us? And they Rwere Toffended at him.   Matt. 12:46 · [Matt. 11:6] · repelled by

4 But Jesus said unto them, RA prophet is not without honour, but in his own country, and among his own Tkin, and in his own Thouse.   John 4:44 · relatives · home

5 And he could there do no mighty work, save that he laid his hands upon a few sick folk, and healed them.

6 And Rhe marvelled because of their unbelief. RAnd he went round about the villages, teaching.   Is. 59:16 · Luke 13:22

Twelve Are Sent to Serve
Matt. 10:1-42; Luke 9:1-6

7 And he called unto him the twelve, and began to send them forth by two and two; and gave them power over unclean spirits;

8 And commanded them that they should take nothing for their journey, save a staff only; no Tscrip, no bread, no money in their purse: bag

9 But Rbe shod with sandals; and not put on two coats.   Acts 12:8

10 And he said unto them, In what place soever ye enter into an house, there abide till ye depart from that place.

11 And whosoever shall not receive you, nor hear you, when ye depart thence, shake off the dust under your feet for a testimony against them. Verily I say unto you, It shall be more tolerable for Sodom and Go-mor'-rha in the day of judgment, than for that city.

12 And they went out, and preached that men should Trepent.   turn away from their sins

13 And they cast out many Tdevils, Rand anointed with oil many that were sick, and healed them.   demons · [James 5:14]

John the Baptist Is Murdered
Matt. 14:1-12; Luke 9:7-9

14 And king Herod heard of him; (for his name was spread abroad:) and he said, That John the Baptist was risen from the dead, and therefore mighty works do shew forth themselves in him.

15 ROthers said, That it is E-li'-as. And others said, That it is a Tprophet, or as one of the prophets.   Matt. 16:14 · preacher from God

16 RBut when Herod heard thereof, he said, It is John, whom I beheaded: he is risen from the dead.   Luke 3:19

17 For Herod himself had sent forth and laid hold upon John, and bound him in prison for He-ro'-di-as' sake, his brother Philip's wife: for he had married her.

18 For John had said unto Herod, RIt is not Tlawful for thee to have thy brother's wife.   Lev. 18:16; 20:21 · right

19 Therefore He-ro'-di-as Thad a quarrel against him, and would have killed him; but she could not: resented

20 For Herod feared John, knowing that he was a just man and an holy, and observed him; and when he heard him, he did many things, and heard him gladly.

21 And when a convenient day was come, that Herod Ron his birthday made a supper to his lords, high captains, and chief estates of Galilee;   Gen. 40:20

22 And when the daughter of the said He-ro'-di-as came in, and danced, and pleased Herod and them that sat with him, the king said unto the damsel, Ask of me whatsoever thou wilt, and I will give it thee.

23 And he sware unto her, RWhatsoever thou shalt ask of me, I will give it thee, unto the half of my kingdom.   Esth. 5:3, 6; 7:2

24 And she went forth, and said unto her mother, What shall I ask? And she said, The head of John the Baptist.

25 And she came in straightway with haste unto the king, and asked, saying, I will that thou give me by and by in a charger the head of John the Baptist.

26 And the king was exceeding sorry; yet for his oath's sake, and for their sakes which sat with him, he would not Treject her.   deny

27 And immediately the king sent Tan executioner, and commanded his head to be

brought: and he went and beheaded him in the prison, *one of his guard*

28 And brought his head ^Tin a charger, and gave it to the damsel: and the damsel gave it to her mother. *on a platter*

29 And when his disciples heard of it, they came and took up his corpse, and laid it in a tomb.

Twelve Return—Luke 9:10

30 And the apostles ^Tgathered themselves together unto Jesus, and told him all things, both what they had done, and what they had taught. *returned*

31 And he said unto them, Come ye yourselves apart into a desert place, and rest a while: for ^Rthere were many coming and going, and they had no ^Tleisure so much as to eat. 3:20 • *time*

Five Thousand Are Fed
Matt. 14:13–21; Luke 9:11–17; John 6:1–14

32 And they departed into a desert place by ^Tship privately. *boat*

33 And the people saw them departing, and many knew him, and ran afoot thither out of all cities, and ^Toutwent them, and came together unto him. *ran ahead*

34 And Jesus, when he came out, saw much people, and was moved with compassion toward them, because they were as sheep not having a shepherd: and he began to teach them many things.

35 And when the day was now far spent, his disciples came unto him, and said, This is a ^Tdesert place, and now the time is ^Tfar passed: *lonely • late*

36 Send them away, that they may go into the country round about, and into the villages, and buy themselves bread: for they have nothing to eat.

37 He answered and said unto them, Give ye them to eat. And they say unto him, Shall we go and buy two hundred pennyworth of bread, and give them to eat?

38 He saith unto them, How many loaves have ye? go and see. And when they knew, they say, Five, and two fishes.

39 And he commanded them to make all sit down by companies upon the green grass.

40 And they sat down in ^Tranks, by hundreds, and by fifties. *companies*

41 And when he had taken the five loaves and the two fishes, he looked up to heaven, and blessed, and brake the loaves, and gave them to his disciples to set before them; and the two fishes divided he among them all.

42 And they did all eat, and were filled.

43 And they took up twelve baskets full of the fragments, and of the fishes.

44 And they that did eat of the loaves were about five thousand men.

Jesus Walks on Water
Matt. 14:22–33; John 6:15–21

45 And ^Tstraightway he constrained his disciples to get into the ship, and to go to the other side before unto Beth-sa′-i-da, while he sent away the people. *immediately*

46 And when he had sent them away, he departed into a mountain to pray.

47 And when even was come, the ^Tship was in the midst of the sea, and he alone on the land. *boat*

48 And he saw them toiling in rowing; for the wind was contrary unto them: and about the fourth watch of the night he cometh unto them, walking upon the sea, and ^Rwould have passed by them. Luke 24:28

49 But when they saw him walking upon the sea, they supposed it ^Thad been a spirit, and cried out: *was an apparition*

50 For they all saw him, and were ^Ttroubled. And immediately he talked with them, and saith unto them, Be of good cheer: it is I; be not afraid. *disturbed*

51 And he went up unto them into the ship; and the wind ceased: and they were ^Tsore amazed in themselves beyond measure, and wondered. *very much astonished*

52 For ^Rthey considered not the miracle of the loaves: for their heart was hardened. 8:17, 18

Jesus Heals at Gennesaret—Matt. 14:34–36

53 And when they had ^Tpassed over, they came into the land of Gen-nes′-a-ret, and drew to the shore. *crossed*

54 And when they were come out of the ship, straightway they knew him,

55 And ran through that whole region round about, and began to ^Tcarry about in beds those that were sick, ^Twhere they heard he was. *bring • wherever*

56 And whithersoever he entered, into villages, or cities, or country, they laid the sick in the streets, and ^Tbesought him that ^Rthey might touch if it were but the border of his garment: and as many as touched ^Thim were made whole. *begged* • [Acts 19:12] • *it*

CHAPTER 7

Pharisees and Defilement—Matt. 15:1–20

THEN came together unto him the Pharisees, and certain of the scribes, which came from Jerusalem.

2 And when they saw some of his disciples eat bread with defiled, that is to say, with unwashen, hands, they found fault.

3 For the Pharisees, and all the Jews, except they wash their hands ^Toft, eat not, holding the tradition of the elders. *much*

4 ^RAnd when they come from the market, except they wash, they eat not. And many

other things there be, which they have received to hold, *as* the washing of cups, and pots, brasen vessels, and of tables.   Lev. 6:28

5 Then the Pharisees and scribes asked him, Why walk not thy disciples according to the tradition of the elders, but eat bread with ^Tunwashen hands?   *defiled*

6 He answered and said unto them, Well hath E-sa'-ias prophesied of you hypocrites, as it is written, <small>RTHIS PEOPLE HONOURETH ME WITH *THEIR* LIPS, BUT THEIR HEART IS FAR FROM ME.</small>   Is. 29:13 ★

7 <small>HOWBEIT IN VAIN DO THEY WORSHIP ME, TEACHING FOR DOCTRINES THE COMMANDMENTS OF MEN.</small>

8 For laying aside the commandment of God, ^Rye hold the tradition of men, *as* the washing of pots and cups: and many other such like things ye do.   vv. 5, 9, 13; Gal. 1:14

9 And he said unto them, Full well ye ^Treject the commandment of God, that ye may keep your own tradition.   *disobey*

10 For Moses said, <small>RHONOUR THY FATHER AND THY MOTHER;</small> and, <small>RWHOSO CURSETH FATHER OR MOTHER, LET HIM DIE THE DEATH:</small>   Ex. 20:12 • Ex. 21:17

11 But ye say, If a man shall say to his father or mother, *It is* Cor'-ban, that is to say, a gift, by whatsoever thou mightest be profited by me; *he shall be free.*

12 And ye ^Tsuffer him no more to do ought for his father or his mother;   *allow*

13 Making the word of God ^Tof none effect through your tradition, which ye have delivered: and many such like things do ye.   *useless*

14 And when he had called all the people unto *him,* he said unto them, Hearken unto me every one of you, and understand:

15 There is nothing from ^Twithout a man, that entering into him can ^Tdefile him: but the things which come out of him, those are they that defile the man.   *outside • make unclean*

16 ^RIf any man have ears to hear, let him hear.   Matt. 11:15

17 And when he was entered into the house from the people, his disciples asked him concerning the parable.

18 And he saith unto them, Are ye so without understanding also? Do ye not perceive, that whatsoever thing from without entereth into the man, *it* cannot defile him;

19 Because it entereth not into his heart, but into the belly, and goeth out into the draught, ^Tpurging all ^Tmeats?   *cleansing • food*

20 And he said, ^RThat which cometh out of the man, that defileth the man.   v. 23

21 ^RFor from within, out of the heart of men, proceed evil thoughts, adulteries, fornications, murders,   Gen. 6:5; 8:21

22 Thefts, covetousness, wickedness, deceit, lasciviousness, an evil eye, ^Tblasphemy, pride, foolishness: *railing*

23 All these evil things come from within, and ^Tdefile the man.   *make unclean*

Syrophenician Woman Is Healed
Matt. 15:21–28

24 And from thence he arose, and went into the borders of Tyre and Si'-don, and entered into an house, and ^Twould have no man know *it:* but he could not be hid.   *wanted*

25 For a *certain* woman, whose young daughter had an unclean spirit, heard of him, and came and fell at his feet:

26 The woman was a Greek, a Sy-ro-phe-ni'-cian by nation; and she besought him that he would cast forth the ^Tdevil out of her daughter.   *demon*

27 But Jesus said unto her, Let the children first be filled: for it is not meet to take the children's bread, and to cast *it* unto the dogs.

28 And she answered and said unto him, Yes, Lord: yet the dogs under the table eat of the children's ^Tcrumbs.   *leftovers*

29 And he said unto her, For this ^Tsaying go thy way; the devil is gone out of thy daughter.   *understanding answer*

30 And when she was come to her house, she found the ^Tdevil gone out, and her daughter laid upon the bed.   *demon*

Deaf and Dumb Man Is Healed

31 ^RAnd again, departing from the coasts of Tyre and Si'-don, he came unto the sea of Galilee, through the midst of the coasts of De-cap'-o-lis.   Matt. 15:29

32 And ^Rthey bring unto him one that was deaf, and had an impediment in his speech; and they ^Tbeseech him to put his hand upon him.   Matt. 9:32; Luke 11:14 • *asked*

33 And he took him aside from the multitude, and put his fingers into his ears, and he spit, and touched his tongue;

34 And ^Rlooking up to heaven, ^Rhe sighed, and saith unto him, Eph'-pha-tha, that is, Be opened.   6:41; John 11:41; 17:1 • John 11:33, 38

35 ^RAnd straightway his ears were opened, and the ^Tstring of his tongue was loosed, and he spake plain.   Is. 35:5, 6 • *bond*

36 And ^Rhe ^Tcharged them that they should tell no man: but the more he charged them, so much the more a great deal they published *it;*   5:43 • *instructed*

37 And were beyond measure astonished, saying, He hath done all things well: he maketh both the deaf to hear, and the dumb to speak.

CHAPTER 8

Four Thousand Are Fed—Matt. 15:32–38

IN those days the multitude being very great, and having nothing to eat, Jesus

called his disciples *unto him,* and saith unto them,

2 I have compassion on the multitude, because they have now been with me three days, and Thave nothing to eat: *now have*

3 And if I send them away fasting to their own houses, they will faint by the way: for divers of them came from far.

4 And his disciples Tanswered him, From whence can a man satisfy these *men* with bread here in the wilderness?   *asked*

5 And he asked them, How many loaves have ye? And they said, Seven.

6 And he commanded the people to sit down on the ground: and he took the seven loaves, and gave thanks, and brake, and gave to his disciples to set before *them;* and they did set *them* before the people.

7 And they had a few small fishes: and Rhe Tblessed, and commanded to set them also before *them.*   6:41; Matt. 14:19 • *gave thanks*

8 So they did eat, and Twere filled: and they took up of the broken *meat* that was left seven baskets.   *had enough*

9 And they that had eaten were about four thousand: and he sent them away.

Pharisees Seek a Sign
Matt. 15:39—16:4

10 And straightwayT he entered into a ship with his disciples, and came into the parts of Dal-ma-nu'-tha.   *immediately*

11 RAnd the Pharisees came forth, and began to question with him, seeking of him a sign from heaven, tempting him.   John 6:30

12 And he sighed deeply in his spirit, and saith, Why doth this generation seek after a sign? verily I say unto you, There shall no sign be given unto this generation.

13 And he left them, and entering into the ship again departed to the other side.

Disciples Do Not Understand—Matt. 16:5–12

14 Now the disciples had forgotten to take bread, neither had they in the ship with them more than one loaf.

15 And he charged them, saying, Take heed, beware of the Tleaven of the Pharisees, and of the leaven of Herod.   *yeast*

16 And they reasoned among themselves, saying, It is because we have no bread.

17 And when Jesus knew it, he saith unto them, Why reason ye, because ye have no bread? Rperceive ye not yet, neither understand? have ye your heart yet hardened? 6:52

18 Having eyes, see ye not? and having ears, hear ye not? and do ye not remember?

19 RWhen I brake the five loaves among five thousand, how many baskets full of fragments took ye up? They say unto him, Twelve.   6:43; Matt. 14:20; Luke 9:17; John 6:13

20 And when the seven among four thousand, how many baskets full of fragments took ye up? And they said, Seven.

21 And he said unto them, How is it that Rye do not understand?   *v.* 17; [6:52]

A Blind Man Is Healed

22 And he cometh to Beth-sa'-i-da; and they bring a blind man unto him, and Tbesought him to touch him.   *begged*

23 And he took the blind man by the hand, and led him out of the town; and when Rhe had spit on his eyes, and put his hands upon him, he asked him if he saw ought.   7:33

24 And he looked up, and said, I see men Tas trees, walking.   *who look like*

25 After that he put *his* hands again upon his eyes, and made him look up: and he was restored, and saw every man clearly.

26 And he sent him away to his house, saying, Neither go into the town, Rnor tell *it* to any in the town.   5:43; Matt. 8:4

Peter's Confession of Christ
Matt. 16:13–23; Luke 9:18–22

27 And Jesus went Tout, and his disciples, into the towns of Caes-a-re'-a Phi-lip'-pi: and by the way he asked his disciples, saying unto them, Whom do men say that I am?   *away*

28 And they answered, RJohn the Baptist: but some say, E-li'-as; and others, One of the prophets.   Matt. 14:2

29 And he saith unto them, But whom say ye that I am? And Peter answereth and saith unto him, Thou art the Christ.

30 And he Tcharged them that they should tell no man of him.   *instructed*

31 And he began to teach them, that the Son of man must suffer many things, and be rejected of the elders, and of the chief priests, and scribes, and be Rkilled, and after three days Rrise again.   Matt. 27:50 • Luke 24:46 ✰

32 And he spake that saying openly. And Peter took him, and began to rebuke him.

33 But when he had turned about and looked on his disciples, he rebuked Peter, saying, Get thee behind me, Satan: for thou savourest not the things that be of God, but the things that be of men.

Cost of Discipleship
Matt. 16:24–27; Luke 9:22–26

34 And when he had called the people *unto him* with his disciples also, he said unto them, RWhosoever will come after me, let him deny himself, and take up his cross, and follow me.   [Matt. 10:38]; 14:27

35 For Rwhosoever will save his Tlife shall lose it; but whosoever shall lose his life for Tmy sake and the gospel's, the same shall save it.   John 12:25 • *own life* • *me*

36 For what shall Tit profit a man, if he shall Tgain the whole world, and lose his own soul?   *a man gain* • *win*

37 Or what shall a man give in Texchange for his soul?   *to regain his life*

38 ᴿWhosoever therefore ᴿshall be ashamed of me and of my words in this adulterous and sinful generation; of him also shall the Son of man be ashamed, when he cometh in the glory of his Father with the holy angels. Matt. 10:33 • Rom. 1:16

CHAPTER 9

The Transfiguration
Matt. 16:28—17:3; Luke 9:27-36

AND he said unto them, ᴿVerily I say unto you, That there be some of them that stand here, which shall not taste of death, till they have seen ᴿthe kingdom of God come with power. Acts 7:55, 56 ☆ • [Matt. 24:30]

2 And after six days Jesus taketh with him Peter, and James, and John, and leadeth them up into an high mountain apart by themselves: and he was ᵀtransfigured before them. changed

3 And his raiment became shining, exceeding white as snow; so as no ᵀfuller on earth can ᵀwhite them. laundryman • bleach

4 And there appeared unto them E-li'-as with Moses: and they were talking with Jesus.

5 And Peter answered and said to Jesus, Master, it is good for us to be here: and let us make three tabernacles; one for thee, and one for Moses, and one for E-li'-as.

6 For he ᵀwist not what to say; for they were ᵀsore afraid. knew • very much

7 And there was a cloud that ᵀovershadowed them: and a voice came out of the cloud, saying, ᴿThis is my beloved Son: hear him. covered them in a shadow • Ps. 2:7; Is. 42:1; Luke 1:35 ☆

8 And suddenly, when they had looked round about, they saw no man any more, ᵀsave Jesus only with themselves. except

9 And as they came down from the mountain, he charged them that they should tell no man what things they had seen, till the Son of man were risen from the dead.

10 And they kept that saying with themselves, questioning one with another what the rising from the dead should mean.

11 And they asked him, saying, Why say the scribes that E-li'-as must first come?

12 And he answered and told them, E-li'-as verily cometh first, and restoreth all things; and ᴿhow it is written of the Son of man, that he must suffer many things, and ᴿbe ᵀset at nought. Ps. 22:6; Is. 53:3 ☆ • Phil. 2:7 • destroyed

13 But I say unto you, That ᴿE-li'-as is indeed come, and they have done unto him whatsoever they ᵀlisted, as it is written of him. Mal. 4:5; Matt. 11:14; 17:12; Luke 1:17 • desired

Demon-Possessed Son Is Delivered
Matt. 17:14-21; Luke 9:37-42

14 And when he came to his disciples, he saw a great multitude about them, and the scribes questioning with them.

15 And straightway all the people, when they beheld him, were greatly amazed, and running to him ᵀsaluted him. greeted

16 And he asked the scribes, What question ye ᵀwith them? among yourselves

17 And one of the multitude answered and said, Master, I have brought unto thee my son, which hath a dumb spirit;

18 And wheresoever he taketh ᵀhim, he teareth him: and he foameth, and gnasheth with his teeth, and ᵀpineth away: and I spake to thy disciples that they should cast him out; and they could not. it • convulses

19 He answereth him, and saith, O ᵀfaithless generation, how long shall I be with you? how long shall I ᵀsuffer you? bring him unto me. unbelieving • put up with

20 And they brought him unto him: and ᴿwhen he saw him, straightway the spirit ᵀtare him; and he fell on the ground, and wallowed foaming. 1:26 • convulsed

21 And he asked his father, How long ᵀis it ago since this came unto him? And he said, Of a child. has he been like this

22 And ᵀofttimes it hath cast him into the fire, and into the waters, to destroy him: but if thou canst do any thing, have compassion on us, and help us. many times

23 Jesus said unto him, ᴿIf thou canst believe, all things are possible to him that believeth. 11:23; Luke 17:6; John 11:40

24 And straightway the father of the child cried out, and said with tears, Lord, I believe; help thou mine unbelief.

25 When Jesus saw that the people came running together, he rebuked the foul spirit, saying unto him, Thou dumb and deaf spirit, I ᵀcharge thee, come out of him, and enter no more into him. command

26 And the spirit cried, and ᵀrent him ᵀsore, and came out of him: and he was as one dead; insomuch that many said, He is dead. convulsed • severely

27 But Jesus took him by the hand, and lifted him up; and he arose.

28 And when he was come into the house, his disciples asked him privately, Why could not we cast him out?

29 And he said unto them, This kind can ᵀcome forth by nothing, but by prayer and fasting. be driven out

Jesus Foretells His Death
Matt. 17:22, 23; Luke 9:43-45

30 And they departed thence, and passed through Galilee; and he ᵀwould not that any man should know it. wanted no

31 For he taught his disciples, and said unto them, The Son of man is delivered into the hands of men, and they shall ᴿkill him; and after that he is killed, he shall ᴿrise the third day. 15:37 • Luke 24:46 ☆

32 But they understood not that saying, and were afraid to ask him.

Attitude of Servanthood
Matt. 18:1–5; Luke 9:46–50

33 ᴿAnd he came to Ca-per'-na-um: and being in the house he asked them, What was it that ye ᵀdisputed among yourselves by the way?   [22:24] • *argued*
34 But they ᵀheld their peace: for by the way they had disputed among themselves, who *should be* the greatest.   *could not answer*
35 And he sat down, and called the twelve, and saith unto them, ᴿIf any man desire to be first, *the same* shall be last of all, and servant of all.   Matt. 20:26, 27
36 And ᴿhe took a child, and set him in the midst of them: and when he had taken him in his arms, he said unto them,   10:16
37 Whosoever shall receive one of such children in my name, receiveth me: and ᴿwhosoever shall receive me, receiveth not me, but him that sent me.   Matt. 10:40
38 And John answered him, saying, Master, we saw one casting out devils in thy name, and he followeth not us: and we forbad him, because he followeth not us.
39 But Jesus said, Forbid him not: for there is no man which shall do a miracle in my name, that can lightly speak evil of me.
40 For ᴿhe that is not against us is on our ᵀpart.   [Matt. 12:30] • *side*
41 ᴿFor whosoever shall give you a cup of water to drink in my name, because ye belong to Christ, verily I say unto you, he shall not lose his reward.   Matt. 10:42

Warning About Hell—Matt. 18:6–9

42 And whosoever shall offend one of *these* little ones that believe in me, it is better for him that a millstone were hanged about his neck, and he were cast into the sea.
43 And if thy hand offend thee, cut it off: it is better for thee to enter into life ᵀmaimed, than having two hands to go into hell, into the fire that never shall be quenched: *crippled*
44 Where ᴿTHEIR WORM DIETH NOT, AND THE FIRE IS NOT ᵀQUENCHED.   Is. 66:24 • *put out*
45 And if thy foot offend thee, cut it off: it is better for thee to enter halt into life, than having two feet to be cast into hell, into the fire that never shall be quenched:
46 Where ᴿTHEIR WORM DIETH NOT, AND THE FIRE IS NOT QUENCHED.   Is. 66:24
47 And if thine eye ᵀoffend thee, pluck it out: it is better for thee to enter into the kingdom of God with one eye, than having two eyes to be cast into hell fire: *does not see*
48 Where ᴿTHEIR WORM DIETH NOT, AND THE FIRE IS NOT QUENCHED.   Is. 66:24
49 For every one shall be salted with fire, and every sacrifice shall be salted with salt.
50 ᴿSalt *is* good: but if the salt have lost his saltness, wherewith will ye season it? ᴿHave salt in yourselves, and have peace one with another.   Luke 14:34 • [Eph. 4:29]

CHAPTER 10

Marriage and Divorce—Matt. 19:1–9

AND ᴿhe arose from thence, and cometh into the coasts of Ju-dae'-a by the farther side of Jordan: and the people resort unto him again; and, as he was wont, he taught them again.   John 10:40; 11:7
2 And the Pharisees came to him, and asked him, Is it lawful for a man to put away *his* wife? tempting him.
3 And he answered and said unto them, What did Moses command you?
4 And they said, Moses suffered to write a bill of divorcement, and to put *her* away.
5 And Jesus answered and said unto them, For the ᵀhardness of your heart he wrote you this ᵀprecept.   *callous nature • ruling*
6 But from the beginning of the creation God ᴿMADE THEM MALE AND FEMALE.   Gen. 1:27
7 FOR THIS CAUSE SHALL A MAN LEAVE HIS FATHER AND MOTHER, AND CLEAVE TO HIS WIFE;
8 AND THEY TWAIN SHALL BE ONE FLESH: SO then they are no more twain, but one flesh.
9 What therefore God hath ᵀjoined together, let not man put asunder.   *united*
10 And in the house his disciples asked him again of the same *matter*.
11 And he saith unto them, ᴿWhosoever shall put away his wife, and marry another, committeth adultery against her.   [Matt. 5:32]
12 And if a woman shall put away her husband, and be married to another, she committeth adultery.

Children and the Kingdom
Matt. 19:13–15; Luke 18:15–17

13 And they brought young children to him, that he should touch them: and *his* disciples rebuked those that brought them.
14 But when Jesus saw *it,* he was ᵀmuch displeased, and said unto them, Suffer the little children to come unto me, and forbid them not: for ᴿof such is the kingdom of God.   *moved with indignation • [1 Cor. 14:20; 1 Pet. 2:2]*
15 Verily I say unto you, Whosoever shall not receive the kingdom of God as a little child, he shall not enter therein.
16 And he took them up in his arms, put *his* hands upon them, and blessed them.

Rich Young Ruler
Matt. 19:16–22; Luke 18:18–23

17 And when he was gone forth into the way, there came one running, and kneeled to him, and asked him, Good Master, what shall I do that I may inherit eternal life?
18 And Jesus said unto him, Why callest thou me good? ᴿthere is none good but one, *that is,* God.   1 Sam. 2:2
19 Thou knowest the commandments, Do NOT COMMIT ADULTERY, DO NOT KILL, DO NOT

STEAL, DO NOT BEAR FALSE WITNESS, Defraud not, HONOUR THY FATHER AND MOTHER.

20 And he answered and said unto him, Master, all these have I ᵀobserved from my youth.   *kept*

21 Then Jesus beholding him loved him, and said unto him, One thing thou lackest: go thy way, sell whatsoever thou hast, and give to the poor, and thou shalt have ᴿtreasure in heaven: and come, take up the cross, and follow me.   Matt. 6:19, 20; 19:21

22 And he was sad at that saying, and went away grieved: for he ᵀhad great possessions.   *was rich*

Difficulty of Riches
Matt. 19:23-26; Luke 18:24-27

23 And Jesus looked round about, and saith unto his disciples, ᵀHow hardly shall they that have riches enter into the kingdom of God!   *with what difficulty*

24 And the disciples were astonished at his words. But Jesus answereth again, and saith unto them, Children, how ᵀhard is it for them ᴿthat trust in riches to enter into the kingdom of God!   *difficult* · Job 31:24; Ps. 52:7

25 It is easier for a camel to go through the eye of a needle, than for a rich man to enter into the kingdom of God.

26 And they were astonished ᵀout of measure, saying among themselves, Who then can be saved?   *beyond*

27 And Jesus looking upon them saith, With men it is impossible, but not with God: for with God all things are possible.

Eternal Reward
Matt. 19:27-30; Luke 18:28-30

28 Then Peter began to say unto him, ᵀLo, we have left all, and have followed thee. *look*

29 And Jesus answered and said, Verily I say unto you, There is no man that hath left house, or brethren, or sisters, or father, or mother, or wife, or children, or lands, for my sake, and the gospel's,

30 ᴿBut he shall receive an hundredfold now in this time, houses, and brethren, and sisters, and mothers, and children, and lands, with persecutions; and in the world to come eternal life.   2 Chr. 25:9

31 ᴿBut many that are first shall be last; and the last first.   Matt. 20:16; Luke 13:30

Coming Crucifixion
Matt. 20:17-19; Luke 18:31-34

32 And they were in the way going up to Jerusalem; and Jesus went before them: and

they were amazed; and as they followed, they were afraid. And he took again the twelve, and began to tell them what things should happen unto him,

33 *Saying,* Behold, we go up to Jerusalem; and the Son of man shall be ᴿdelivered unto the chief priests, and unto the scribes; and they shall condemn him to death, and shall deliver him to the Gentiles: 14:53, 64 ✶

34 ᴿAnd they shall mock him, and shall scourge him, and shall spit upon him, and shall kill him: and the third day he shall rise again.   14:65; 15:15, 20, 31, 37; Luke 24:46 ✶

"Whosoever Will Be Great"—Matt. 20:20-28

35 And James and John, the sons of Zeb'-e-dee, come unto him, saying, Master, we would that thou shouldest do for us whatsoever we shall desire.

36 And he said unto them, What ᵀwould ye that I should do for you?   *do you want*

37 They said unto him, Grant unto us that we may sit, one on thy right hand, and the other on thy left hand, in thy glory.

38 But Jesus said unto them, Ye know not what ye ask: can ye drink of the cup that I drink of? and be baptized with the baptism that I am baptized with?

39 And they said unto him, We can. And Jesus said unto them, Ye shall indeed drink of the cup that I drink of; and with the baptism that I am baptized withal shall ye be baptized:

40 But to sit on my right hand and on my left hand is not ᵀmine to give; but it shall be given to them for whom it is prepared. *my right*

41 ᴿAnd when the ten heard it, they ᵀbegan to be much displeased with James and John.   Matt. 20:24 · *became angry*

42 But Jesus called them to him, and saith unto them, Ye know that they which are accounted to rule over the Gentiles exercise lordship over them; and their great ones exercise authority upon them.

43 ᴿBut so shall it not be among you: but whosoever will be great among you, shall be your ᵀminister: 9:35; Luke 9:48 · *servant*

44 And whosoever of you will be the chiefest, shall be servant of all.

45 For even the Son of man came not to be ᵀministered unto, but to minister, and to give ᴿhis life a ransom for many.   *served* · Is. 53:12 ✶

Blind Bartimaeus Is Healed
Matt. 20:29-34; Luke 18:35-43

46 And they came to Jericho: and as he went out of Jericho with his disciples and a

---

10:45 The Ministry of the Son of God—The ministry of Christ is threefold:
a. He is Saviour. The title *Saviour* implies many important and interrelated truths: the need of sinful men to be saved (Page 1194—1 Tim. 1:15); the qualifications of Christ as God-man to be our Saviour (Page 1055—John 10:18); the humiliating death He experienced to become our Saviour (Page 1064—John 19:18); the victorious, bodily resurrection He experienced as a sure guarantee of our

great number of people, blind Bar-ti-mae'-us, the son of Ti-mae'-us, sat by the highway side begging.

47 And when he heard that it was Jesus of Nazareth, he began to cry out, and say, Jesus, *thou* son of David, have mercy on me.

48 And many Tcharged him that he should Thold his peace: but he cried the more Ta great deal, Thou son of David, have mercy on me. *scolded • keep quiet • loudly*

49 And Jesus stood still, and commanded him to be called. And they call the blind man, saying unto him, TBe of good comfort, rise; he calleth thee. *cheer up*

50 And he, casting away his garment, Trose, and came to Jesus. *jumped up*

51 And Jesus answered and said unto him, What wilt thou that I should do unto thee? The blind man said unto him, TLord, that I might receive my sight. *Rabboni*

52 And Jesus said unto him, Go thy way; Rthy faith hath Tmade thee whole. And immediately he received his sight, and followed Jesus in the way. Matt. 9:22 • *saved you*

CHAPTER 11

The Triumphal Entry
Matt. 21:1-11; Luke 19:29-40

AND Rwhen they came nigh to Jerusalem, unto Beth'-pha-ge and Beth'-a-ny, at the mount of Olives, he sendeth forth two of his disciples, John 12:14

2 And saith unto them, Go your way into the village Tover against you: and as soon as ye be entered into it, ye shall find a colt tied, whereon never man sat; loose him, and bring him. *ahead of*

3 And if any man say unto you, Why do ye this? say ye that the Lord hath need of him; and straightway he will send him hither.

4 And they went their way, and found the colt tied by the door without in a place where two ways met; and they loose him.

5 And certain of them that stood there said unto them, What do ye, loosing the colt?

6 And they said unto them even as Jesus had commanded: and they let them go.

7 And they brought the colt to Jesus, and Tcast their garments on him; and Rhe sat upon him. *put • Zech. 9:9 ★*

8 And many spread their garments in the way: and others cut down branches off the trees, and strawed *them* in the Tway. *road*

9 And they that went before, and they that followed, cried, saying, RHOSANNA; BLESSED IS HE THAT COMETH IN THE NAME OF THE LORD: Ps. 118:26 ★

10 Blessed *be* the kingdom of our father David, that cometh in the name of the Lord: RHosanna in the highest. Ps. 148:1

11 RAnd Jesus entered into Jerusalem, and into the temple: and when he had looked round about upon all things, and now the eventide was come, he went out unto Beth'-a-ny with the twelve. Matt. 21:12

A Fig Tree Is Cursed—Matt. 21:18, 19

12 And on the morrow, when they were come from Beth'-a-ny, he was hungry:

13 And seeing a fig tree afar off having leaves, he came, if Thaply he might find any thing thereon: and when he came to it, he found nothing but leaves; for the time of figs was not *yet.* *maybe*

14 And Jesus answered and said unto it, No man eat fruit of thee hereafter for ever. And his disciples heard *it.*

The Temple Is Cleansed
Matt. 21:12, 13; Luke 19:45, 46

15 RAnd they come to Jerusalem: and Jesus Rwent into the temple, and began to cast out them that sold and bought in the temple, and Toverthrew the tables of the moneychangers, and the seats of them that sold doves; John 2:14 • Mal. 3:1 ★ • *overturned*

16 And would not suffer that any man should carry *any* vessel through the temple.

---

salvation (Page 1137—1 Cor. 15:13-22); and the glorious results of salvation (Page 1047—John 5:24). It is no wonder that in light of these precious realities Paul speaks of Christ as "the great God and our Saviour" (Page 1207—Titus 2:13).

b. He is High Priest. The high priest was of supreme importance in the Old Testament. It was on the basis of his mediation for the people before God on the Day of Atonement that they were brought near to God and protected from judgment (Page 116—Lev. 16:16). Therefore his qualifications were exacting: appointed by God, physically perfect, ceremonially pure, etc. (Page 120—Lev. 21). Jesus is eminently qualified to be our High Priest: He was appointed by God (Page 1217—Heb. 5:5); He is eternal (Page 1218—Heb. 7:24, 25); He is sinless (Page 1218—Heb. 7:26); His offering was final (Page 1220—Heb. 9:28); and His mediation is effective (Page 1115—Rom. 8:34; Page 1218—Heb. 7:25; Page 1249—1 John 2:1). As the only qualified High Priest for men and women, Jesus Christ thus constitutes the only way to God (Page 1194—1 Tim. 2:5).

c. He is King. The position of king implies sovereign authority and rule over all. The Scriptures clearly teach that this right belongs only to Jesus Christ, who is called "KING OF KINGS, AND LORD OF LORDS" (Page 1281—Rev. 19:16). This title means that He is destined to rule as king and that every knee must ultimately bow and acknowledge His authority (Page 1171—Phil. 2:10). Those who acknowledge Christ as King and Lord in this life will reign with Him; those who do not will be judged by Him (Page 1281—Rev. 20:11-15). The weight of eternity hangs on this solemn decision.
Now turn to Page 1164—Eph. 4:3: The Person of the Holy Spirit.

17 And he taught, saying unto them, Is it not written, ᴿMY HOUSE SHALL BE CALLED OF ALL NATIONS THE HOUSE OF PRAYER? but ye have made it a DEN OF THIEVES.   Is. 56:7

18 And the scribes and chief priests heard *it*, and sought how they might destroy him: for they feared him, because all the people was astonished at his ᵀdoctrine.   *teaching*

19 And when ᵀeven was come, he went out of the city.   *evening*

Power of Faith—Matt. 21:20–22

20 And in the morning, as they passed by, they saw the fig tree dried up from the roots.

21 And Peter calling to remembrance saith unto him, Master, behold, the fig tree which thou cursedst is withered away.

22 And Jesus answering saith unto them, Have faith in God.

23 For verily I say unto you, That whosoever shall say unto this mountain, Be thou removed, and be thou cast into the sea; and shall not doubt in his heart, but shall believe that those things which he saith shall come to pass; he shall have whatsoever he saith.

24 Therefore I say unto you, What things soever ye desire, when ye pray, believe that ye receive *them*, and ye shall have *them*.

Necessity of Forgiveness

25 And when ye stand praying, ᴿforgive, if ye have ought against any: that your Father also which is in heaven may forgive you your trespasses.   Matt. 6:14; [Col. 3:13]

26 But ᴿif ye do not forgive, neither will your Father which is in heaven forgive your trespasses.   Matt. 18:35

Question of Authority
Matt. 21:23–27; Luke 20:1–8

27 And they come again to Jerusalem: and as he was walking in the temple, there come to him the chief priests, and the scribes, and the elders,

28 And say unto him, By what authority doest thou these things? and who gave thee this authority to do these things?

29 And Jesus answered and said unto them, I will also ask of you one ᵀquestion, and answer me, and I will tell you by what authority I do these things.   *thing*

30 The baptism of John, was *it* from heaven, or of men? answer me.

31 And they reasoned with themselves, saying, If we shall say, From heaven; he will say, Why then did ye not believe him?

32 But if we shall say, Of men; they feared the people: for ᴿall *men* counted John, that he was a prophet indeed.   6:20

33 And they answered and said unto Jesus, We cannot tell. And Jesus answering saith unto them, Neither do I tell you by what authority I do these things.

CHAPTER 12

Parable of the Vineyard Owner
Matt. 21:33–46, Luke 20:9–19

AND he began to speak unto them by parables. A *certain* man planted a vineyard, and set an hedge about *it*, and digged *a place for* the winefat, and built a tower, and ᵀlet it out to ᵀhusbandmen, and went into a far country.   *rented • tenant farmers*

2 And at the ᵀseason he sent to the ᵀhusbandmen a servant, that he might receive from the husbandmen of the fruit of the vineyard.   *harvest time • tenants*

3 And they caught *him*, and beat him, and sent *him* away ᵀempty.   *with no pay*

4 And again he sent unto them another servant; and at him they cast stones, and wounded *him* in the head, and sent *him* away shamefully ᵀhandled.   *treated*

5 And again he sent another; and him they killed, and many others; beating some, and killing some.

6 Having yet therefore one son, his wellbeloved, he sent him also last unto them, saying, They will ᵀreverence my son.   *respect*

7 But those husbandmen said among themselves, This is the heir; come, let us kill him, and the inheritance shall be our's.

8 And they took him, and killed *him*, and cast *him* out of the vineyard.

9 What shall therefore the ᵀlord of the vineyard do? he will come and destroy the husbandmen, and will ᵀgive the vineyard unto others.   *owner • lease*

10 And have ye not read this scripture; ᴿTHE STONE WHICH THE BUILDERS REJECTED IS BECOME THE HEAD OF THE CORNER: Ps. 118:22 *

11 ᴿTHIS WAS THE LORD'S DOING, AND IT IS MARVELLOUS IN OUR EYES?   Ps. 118:23 *

12 And they sought to lay hold on him, but feared the people: for they knew that he had spoken the parable against them: and they left him, and went their way.

Question of Taxes
Matt. 22:15–22; Luke 20:20–26

13 And they send unto him certain of the Pharisees and of the He-ro'-di-ans, to ᵀcatch him in *his* words.   *find some fault*

14 And when they were come, they say unto him, Master, we know that thou art true, and ᵀcarest for no man: for thou regardest not the person of men, but teachest the way of God in truth: Is it ᵀlawful to give tribute to Caesar, or not?   *fearest • right*

15 Shall we give, or shall we not give? But he, knowing their hypocrisy, said unto them, Why ᵀtempt ye me? bring me a ᵀpenny, that I may see *it*.   *test • 1 day's wage ($32)*

16 And they brought *it*. And he saith unto them, Whose *is* this ᵀimage and superscription? And they said unto him, Caesar's.   *face*

17 And Jesus answering said unto them, ᵀRender to Caesar the things that are Caesar's, and to God the things that are God's. And they marvelled at him.   *pay*

Question of the Resurrection
Matt. 22:23–33; Luke 20:27–40

18 Then come unto him the Sad'-du-cees, ᴿwhich say there is no resurrection; and they asked him, saying,   Acts 23:8

19 Master, Moses wrote unto us, ᴿIF A MAN'S BROTHER DIE, and leave *his* wife *behind him*, AND LEAVE NO CHILDREN, THAT HIS BROTHER SHOULD TAKE HIS WIFE, AND RAISE UP SEED UNTO HIS BROTHER.   Deut. 25:5

20 Now there were seven brethren: and the first took a wife, and dying left no seed.

21 And the second took her, and died, neither left he any seed: and the third likewise.

22 And the seven had her, and left no seed: last of all the woman died also.

23 In the resurrection therefore, when they shall rise, whose wife shall she be of them? for the seven had her to wife.

24 And Jesus answering said unto them, Do ye not therefore err, because ye know not the scriptures, neither the power of God?

25 For when they shall rise from the dead, they neither marry, nor are given in marriage; but ᴿare as the angels which are in heaven.   [1 Cor. 15:42, 49, 52]

26 And as touching the dead, that they rise: have ye not read in the book of Moses, how in the bush God spake unto him, saying, ᴿI AM THE GOD OF ABRAHAM, AND THE GOD OF ISAAC, AND THE GOD OF JACOB?   Ex. 3:6

27 He is not the God of the dead, but the God of the living: ye therefore do greatly err.

Question of the Greatest Commandment
Matt. 22:34–40

28 And one of the scribes came, and having heard them ᵀreasoning together, and ᵀperceiving that he had answered them well, asked him, Which is the ᵀfirst commandment of all?   *arguing • seeing • most important*

29 And Jesus answered him, The first of all the commandments *is*, ᴿHEAR, O ISRAEL; THE LORD OUR GOD IS ONE LORD: Deut. 6:4

30 ᴿAND THOU ᵀSHALT LOVE THE LORD THY GOD WITH ALL THY HEART, AND WITH ALL THY SOUL, AND WITH ALL THY MIND, AND WITH ALL THY STRENGTH: this *is* the first commandment.   Deut. 6:5 • *must*

31 And the second *is* like, *namely* this, ᴿTHOU SHALT LOVE THY NEIGHBOUR AS THYSELF. There is none other commandment greater than these.   Lev. 19:18; [Rom. 13:9]; Gal. 5:14

32 And the scribe said unto him, Well, Master, thou hast said the truth: for there is one God; and there is none other but he:

33 And to love him with all the heart, and with all the understanding, and with all the soul, and with all the strength, and to love *his* neighbour as himself, is more than all whole burnt offerings and sacrifices.

34 And when Jesus saw that he answered discreetly, he said unto him, Thou art not far from the kingdom of God. And no man after that ᵀdurst ask him *any question*.   *dared*

Jesus Questions the Leaders
Matt. 22:41–45; Luke 20:41–44

35 And Jesus answered and said, while he taught in the temple, How say the scribes that Christ is the son of David?

36 For David himself said by the Holy Ghost, ᴿTHE LORD SAID TO MY LORD, SIT THOU ON MY RIGHT HAND, TILL I MAKE THINE ENEMIES THY FOOTSTOOL.   Ps. 110:1

37 David therefore himself calleth him Lord; and whence is he *then* his son? And the common people heard him gladly.

Jesus Condemns the Leaders
Matt. 23:1–14; Luke 20:45—21:4

38 And ᴿhe said unto them in his doctrine, Beware of the scribes, which love to go in long clothing, and ᴿlove ᵀsalutations in the marketplaces,   4:2 • Luke 11:43 • *greetings*

39 And the chief seats in the synagogues, and the ᵀuppermost rooms at feasts: *chief*

40 Which ᵀdevour widows' houses, and for ᵀa pretence make long prayers: these shall receive greater damnation.   *eat up • a show*

41 And Jesus sat ᵀover against the treasury, and ᵀbeheld how the people cast money into the treasury: and many that were rich cast in much.   *opposite • noticed*

42 And there came a certain poor widow, and she threw in ᵀtwo mites, which make a farthing.   *about 50 cents*

43 And he called *unto him* his disciples, and saith unto them, Verily I say unto you, That ᴿthis poor widow hath ᵀcast more in, than ᵀall they which have cast into the treasury: [2 Cor. 8:12] • *put • all others*

44 For all *they* did cast in of their abundance; but she of her want did cast in all that she had, *even* all her living.

CHAPTER 13

Questions from the Disciples
Matt. 24:1–3; Luke 21:5-7

AND as he went out of the temple, one of his disciples saith unto him, Master, see what manner of stones and what buildings *are here!*

2 And Jesus answering said unto him, Seest thou these great buildings? ᴿthere shall not be left one stone upon another, that shall not be thrown down.   Luke 19:44

3 And as he sat upon the mount of Olives over against the temple, Peter and James and John and Andrew asked him privately,

4 Tell us, when shall these things be? and what *shall be* the sign when all these things shall be fulfilled?

The Tribulation—Matt. 24:4–26; Luke 21:8–24

5 And Jesus answering them began to say, Take heed lest any *man* deceive you:
6 For many shall come in my name, saying, I am *Christ;* and shall deceive many.
7 And when ye shall hear of wars and rumours of wars, be ye not troubled: for *such things* must needs be; but the end *shall* not *be* yet.
8 For nation shall rise against nation, and kingdom against kingdom: and there shall be earthquakes in ^Tdivers places, and there shall be famines and troubles: these *are* the beginnings of sorrows.   *various*
9 But take heed to yourselves: for they shall deliver you up to councils; and in the synagogues ye shall be beaten: and ye shall be brought before rulers and kings for my sake, for a testimony against them.
10 And the gospel must first be published among all nations.
11 But when they shall lead *you,* and deliver you up, take no thought beforehand what ye shall speak, neither do ye premeditate: but whatsoever shall be given you in that hour, that speak ye: for it is not ye that speak, but the Holy Ghost.
12 Now the brother shall betray the brother to death, and the father the son; and children shall rise up against *their* parents, and shall cause them to be put to death.
13 And ye shall be hated of all *men* for my name's sake: but he that shall endure unto the end, the same shall be saved.
14 But when ye shall see the ABOMINATION OF DESOLATION, spoken of by Daniel the prophet, standing where it ought not, (let him that readeth understand,) then let them that be in Ju-dae'-a flee to the mountains:
15 And let him that is on the housetop not go down into the house, neither enter *therein,* to take any thing out of his house:
16 And let him that is in the field not turn back again for to take up his garment.
17 But woe to them that are with child, and to them that give suck in those days!
18 And pray ye that your flight be not in the winter.
19 For^R *in* those days shall be ^Taffliction, such as was not from the beginning of the creation which God created unto this time, neither shall be.   Joel 2:2 • *trouble*
20 And except that the Lord had shortened those days, no flesh should be saved: but for the elect's sake, whom he hath chosen, he hath shortened the days.
21 ^RAnd then if any man shall say to you, Lo, here *is* Christ; or, lo, *he is* there; believe *him* not: Luke 17:23; 21:8

22 For false Christs and false prophets shall rise, and shall shew signs and wonders, to seduce, if *it were* possible, even the elect.
23 But ^Rtake ye heed: behold, I have foretold you all things.   [2 Pet. 3:17]

The Second Coming
Matt. 24:29–31; Luke 21:25–28

24 But in those days, after that tribulation, the sun shall be darkened, and the moon shall not give her light,
25 And the stars of heaven shall fall, and the powers that are in heaven shall be ^Tshaken.   *driven from their courses*
26 And^R then shall they see the Son of man coming in the clouds with great power and glory.   [Matt. 16:27; 2 Thess. 1:7, 10] ✫
27 And then shall he send his angels, and shall gather together his elect from the four winds, from the uttermost part of the earth to the uttermost part of heaven.

Parable of the Fig Tree—Matt. 24:32–35

28 Now learn a parable of the fig tree; When her branch is yet tender, and putteth forth leaves, ye know that summer is near:
29 So ye in like manner, when ye shall see these things come to pass, know that it is ^Tnigh, *even* at the doors.   *near*
30 ^TVerily I say unto you, that this generation shall not pass, till all these things be done.   *remember*
31 Heaven and earth shall pass away: but ^Rmy words shall not pass away.   Is. 40:8

Exhortation to Watch
Matt. 24:36–51; Luke 21:34–36

32 But of that day and *that* hour knoweth no man, no, not the angels which are in heaven, neither the Son, but the Father.
33 Take ye heed, watch and pray: for ye know not when the time is.
34 ^R*For the Son of man is* as a man taking a ^Tfar journey, who left his house, and gave authority to his servants, and to every man his work, and commanded the porter to watch.   Matt. 24:45; 25:14 • *long trip*
35 Watch ye therefore: for ye know not when the master of the house cometh, at even, or at midnight, or at the cockcrowing, or in the morning:
36 Lest coming suddenly he find you sleeping.
37 And what I say unto you I say unto all, Watch.

CHAPTER 14

Leaders Plot to Kill Jesus
Matt. 26:1–5; Luke 22:1, 2

AFTER ^Rtwo days was *the feast of* the passover, and of unleavened bread: and the chief priests and the scribes sought how

they might take him by ᵀcraft, and put *him* to death.　　　　　　　　John 11:55; 13:1 • *some trick*

2 But they said, Not on the feast *day*, lest there be an uproar of the people.

Mary Anoints Jesus
Matt. 26:6–13; John 12:2–8

3 And being in Beth'-a-ny in the house of Simon the leper, as he sat at meat, there came a woman having an alabaster box of ointment of spikenard very precious; and she brake the box, and poured *it* on his head.

4 And there were some that had indignation within themselves, and said, Why was this waste of the ointment made?

5 For it might have been sold for more than ᵀthree hundred ᴿpence, and have been given to the poor. And they murmured against her.　　　*300 days' wages* • 12:15; Matt. 18:28

6 And Jesus said, Let her alone; why trouble ye her? she hath wrought a ᵀgood work on me.　　　　　　　　　*beautiful thing*

7 ᴿFor ye have the poor with you always, and whensoever ye will ye may do them good: but me ye have not always.　　Deut. 15:11

8 She hath done what she could: she is come aforehand to ᵀanoint my body to ᵀthe ᴿburying.　　*perfume • its burial* • 15:46; John 19:40–42 ✶

9 Verily I say unto you, Wheresoever this gospel shall be preached throughout the whole world, *this* also that she hath done shall be spoken of for a memorial of her.

Judas Plans to Betray Jesus
Matt. 26:14–16; Luke 22:3–6

10 And Judas Is-car'-i-ot, one of the twelve, went unto the chief priests, to betray him unto them.

11 And when they heard *it*, they were glad, and promised to give him money. And he sought how he might conveniently betray him.

The Passover Is Prepared
Matt. 26:17–19; Luke 22:7–13

12 And the first day of unleavened bread, when they ᵀkilled the passover, his disciples said unto him, Where ᵀwilt thou that we go and prepare that thou mayest eat the passover?　　　*sacrificed • do you want*

13 And he sendeth forth two of his disciples, and saith unto them, Go ye into the city, and there shall meet you a man bearing a pitcher of water: follow him.

14 And wheresoever he shall go in, say ye to the goodman of the house, The Master saith, Where is the guestchamber, where I shall eat the passover with my disciples?

15 And he will shew you a large upper room furnished *and* prepared: there make ready for us.

16 And his disciples went forth, and came into the city, and found as he had said unto them: and they made ready the passover.

The Passover Is Celebrated
Matt. 26:20–25; Luke 22:14–16; John 13:21–30

17 And in the evening he cometh with the twelve.

18 And as they sat and did eat, Jesus said, Verily I say unto you, ᴿOne of you which eateth with me shall betray me.　14:42; Ps. 41:9 ✶

19 And they began to be sorrowful, and to say unto him one by one, *Is* it I? and another said, ᵀ*Is* it I?　　　　　　　*you don't mean me?*

20 And he answered and said unto them, *It* *is* one of ᵀthe twelve, that dippeth with me in the dish.　　　　　　　　　　　　*you*

21 The Son of man indeed goeth, as it is written of him: but ᴿwoe to that man by whom the Son of man is betrayed! good were it for that man if he had never been born.　　　　　　　Matt. 27:4, 5; Acts 1:16–20

The Lord's Supper Is Instituted
Matt. 26:26–29; Luke 22:17–23

22 And as they did eat, Jesus took bread, and blessed, and brake *it*, and gave to them, and said, Take, eat: this is my body.

23 And he took the cup, and when he had given thanks, he gave *it* to them: and they all drank of it.

24 And he said unto them, This is my blood of the new testament, which is ᵀshed for many.　　　　　　　　　　　　　　*poured out*

25 Verily I say unto you, I will drink no more of the fruit of the vine, until that day that I drink it new in the kingdom of God.

Jesus Predicts Peter's Denial
Matt. 26:30–35; Luke 22:31–39; John 13:36–38

26 And when they had sung an hymn, they went out into the mount of Olives.

27 And Jesus saith unto them, All ye shall be offended because of me this night: for it is written, ᴿI WILL SMITE THE SHEPHERD, AND THE SHEEP SHALL BE SCATTERED.　　　Zech. 13:7

28 But ᴿafter that I am risen, I will go before you into Galilee.　16:7; Matt. 28:16; John 21:1

29 But Peter said unto him, Although all shall be offended, yet *will* not I.

30 And Jesus saith unto him, Verily I say unto thee, ᴿThat this day, *even* in this night, before the cock crow twice, thou shalt ᵀdeny me thrice.　　14:72; Luke 22:61 ✶ • *say you don't know me*

31 But he spake the more vehemently, If I should die with thee, I will not deny thee in any ᵀwise. Likewise also said they all.　　*way*

Jesus Prays in Gethsemane
Matt. 26:36–46; Luke 22:39–46

32 And they came to a place which was named Geth-sem'-a-ne: and he saith to his disciples, Sit ye here, while I shall pray.

33 And he taketh with him Peter and James and John, and began to be sore amazed, and to be very heavy;

34 And saith unto them, ᴿMy soul! is exceeding sorrowful unto death: tarry ye here, and watch.　　　　　　　　　John 12:27

35 And he went forward a little, and fell on the ground, and prayed that, if it were possible, the hour might pass from him.

36 And he said, RAb'-ba, Father, all things *are* possible unto thee; take away this cup from me: nevertheless Rnot what I will, but what thou wilt.   Rom. 8:15 • Is. 50:5 *

37 And he cometh, and findeth them sleeping, and saith unto Peter, Simon, sleepest thou? couldest not thou watch one hour?

38 Watch ye and pray, lest ye enter into temptation. RThe spirit truly *is* ready, but the flesh *is* weak.   [Rom. 7:23; Gal. 5:17]

39 And again he went away, and prayed, and spake the same words.

40 And when he returned, he found them asleep again, (for their eyes were heavy,) neither Twist they what to answer him.   *knew*

41 And he cometh the third time, and saith unto them, Sleep on now, and take *your* rest: it is enough, RtheT hour is come; behold, the Son of man is betrayed into the hands of sinners.   John 13:1 • *the time is here*

42 Rise up, let us go; lo, he that Rbetrayeth me is at hand.   14:18; Matt. 20:18; 26:21 *

Judas Betrays Jesus
Matt. 26:47-56; Luke 22:47-53; John 18:1-11

43 And immediately, while he yet spake, cometh Judas, one of the twelve, and with him a great multitude with swords and Tstaves, from the chief priest and the scribes and the elders.   *spears*

44 And he that betrayed him had given them a Ttoken, saying, Whomsoever I shall kiss, that same is he; take him, and lead *him* away Tsafely.   *sign • without trouble*

45 And as soon as he Twas come, he goeth straightway to him, and saith, Master, master; and kissed him.   *arrived*

46 And they Tlaid their hands on him, and took him.   *arrested him*

47 And one of them that stood by drew a sword, and smote a servant of the high priest, and cut off his ear.

48 And Jesus answered and said unto them, Are ye come out, as against a thief, with swords and *with* staves to take me?

49 I was daily with you in the temple teaching, and ye took me not: but Rthe scriptures must be fulfilled.   Ps. 22:6; Is. 53:7

50 And they all forsook him, and fled.

51 And there followed him a certain young man, having a linen cloth cast about *his* naked *body;* and the young men Tlaid hold on him: *tried to arrest*

52 And he left the linen cloth, and fled from them naked.

The Sanhedrin Tries Jesus
Matt. 26:57-68; Luke 22:54, 55, 63-65; John 18:12, 18, 24

53 And they led Jesus away to the high priest: and with him were assembled all the chief priests and the elders and the scribes.

54 And Peter followed him Tafar off, even into the palace of the high priest: and he sat with the servants, and warmed himself at the fire.   *at a great distance*

55 And the chief priests and all the council Tsought for witness against Jesus to put him to death; and found none.   *hunted*

56 For many bare false witness against him, but their witness agreed not together.

57 And Rthere arose certain, and bare false witness against him, saying,   Ps. 27:12; 35:11 *

58 We heard him say, RI will destroy this temple that is made with hands, and within three days I will build another made without hands.   15:29; John 2:19

59 But neither so did their Twitness agree together.   *stories*

60 And the high priest stood up in the midst, and asked Jesus, saying, Answerest thou nothing? what *is it which* these Twitness against thee?   *testify*

61 But Rhe held his peace, and answered nothing. Again the high priest asked him, and said unto him, Art thou the Christ, the Son of the Blessed?   Is. 53:7

62 And Jesus said, I am: and ye shall see RTHE SON OF MAN SITTING ON THE RIGHT HAND OF POWER, and COMING IN THE CLOUDS OF HEAVEN.   Dan. 7:13

63 Then the high priest Trent his clothes, and saith, What need we any further witnesses?   *tore*

14:38 Temptation by the Flesh—*Flesh* in the Bible often means something other than the substance of the human body. It is used constantly to refer to the carnal, sinful principle within man that is opposed to God (Page 1114—Rom. 8:7). The actions produced by the flesh are given in detail in Galatians 5:19–21. Among these are all types of sexual immorality, impurity, hatred, anger, false religions, envy, and drunkenness. A person whose life is characterized by these sins cannot be a true Christian and is under the wrath of God (Page 1158—Gal. 5:21; Page 1162—Eph. 2:3).

Though the flesh is not eradicated for the Christian, he does not have to obey it (Page 1113—Rom. 7:15–25). He possesses a new nature empowered by the Holy Spirit. Since the flesh and the Spirit are totally opposed to each other, the one whom the believer allows to dominate him will take charge in his life and produce its own fruit. The solution to the urges of the flesh lies in acknowledging that the power of sin was nullified by Jesus' death (Page 1112—Rom. 6:11) and in living under the control of the Spirit's power (Page 1158—Gal. 5:16). The latter is a moment-by-moment dependence in faith on the Spirit's power. The believer must choose by an act of his will to benefit from the Spirit's enablement.

Now turn to Page 424—1 Chr. 21:1: Temptation by Satan.

64 Ye have heard the ᵀblasphemy: what think ye? And they all ᴿcondemned him to be guilty of death.   *wicked words* • 10:33; Matt. 20:18 ★

65 And some began to spit on him, and to cover his face, and to ᵀbuffet him, and to say unto him, Prophesy: and the servants did strike him with the palms of their hands. *beat*

Peter Denies Jesus
Matt. 26:69–75; Luke 22:55–62; John 18:15–18, 25–27

66 And as Peter was beneath in the palace, there cometh one of the maids of the high priest:

67 And when she saw Peter warming himself, she looked upon him, and said, And thou also wast with Jesus of Nazareth.

68 But he denied, saying, ᵀI know not, neither understand I what thou sayest. And he went out into the porch; and the cock crew.   *I do not know what you are talking about*

69 And a maid saw him again, and began to say to them that stood by, This is *one* of them.

70 And he denied it again. And a little after, they that stood by said again to Peter, Surely thou art *one* of them: ᴿfor thou art a Gal-i-lae'-an, and thy ᵀspeech agreeth *thereto*.   Acts 2:7 • *accent shows that*

71 But he began to curse and ᵀto swear, *saying*, I know not this man of whom ye speak.   *made a vow*

72 And the second time the cock crew. And Peter called to mind ᴿthe word that Jesus said unto him, Before the cock crow twice, thou shalt deny me thrice. And when he thought thereon, he wept.   14:30; John 13:38 ★

CHAPTER 15

Pilate Tries Jesus
Matt. 27:1, 2, 11–23; Luke 23:1–5, 13–23; John 18:28—19:15

AND straightway in the morning the chief priests held a ᵀconsultation with the elders and scribes and the whole council, and bound Jesus, and carried *him* away, and ᴿdelivered *him* to Pilate.   *conference* • Is. 53:7 ★

2 ᴿAnd Pilate asked him, Art thou the King of the Jews? And he answering said unto him, Thou sayest *it*.   Matt. 27:11

3 And the chief priests accused him of many things: but he answered nothing.

4 And Pilate asked him again, saying, Answerest thou nothing? behold how many things they ᵀwitness against thee.   *testify*

5 ᴿBut Jesus yet answered nothing; so that Pilate marvelled.   Ps. 38:13, 14; Is. 53:7; John 19:9 ★

6 Now ᴿat *that* feast he ᵀreleased unto them one prisoner, whomsoever they ᵀdesired.   Luke 23:17; John 18:39 • *set free* • *wanted*

7 And there was *one* named Bar-ab'-bas, ᵀwhich *lay* bound with them that had made insurrection with him, who had committed murder in the insurrection.   *who was in jail*

8 And the multitude crying aloud began to ᵀdesire *him to do* as he had ever done unto them.   *ask*

9 But Pilate answered them, saying, Will ye that I ᵀrelease unto you the King of the Jews?   *set free*

10 For he knew that the chief priests had delivered him ᵀfor envy.   *because of*

11 But ᴿthe chief priests ᵀmoved the people, that he should rather release Bar-ab'-bas unto them.   Acts 3:14 • *influenced*

12 And Pilate answered and said again unto them, What will ye then that I shall do *unto him* whom ye call the King of the Jews?

13 And they cried out again, Crucify him.

14 Then Pilate said unto them, Why, what evil hath he done? And they cried out the more exceedingly, Crucify him.

Jesus Is Beaten
Matt. 27:26–34; Luke 23:24–32; John 19:16–22

15 And *so* Pilate, willing to content the people, released Bar-ab'-bas unto them, and delivered Jesus, when he had ᴿscourgedᵀ *him*, to be crucified.   10:34; Is. 50:6; Matt. 20:19 • *whipped*

16 And the soldiers led him away into the hall, called Prae-to'-ri-um; and they call together the whole band.

17 And they clothed him with ᵀpurple, and platted a crown of thorns, and put it ᵀabout his *head*,   *a purple robe* • *on*

18 And began to salute him, ᵀHail, King of the Jews!   *long live*

19 And they ᴿsmote him on the head with a reed, and did spit upon him, and bowing *their* knees worshipped him.   Is. 52:14; Mic. 5:1 ★

20 And when they had ᴿmockedᵀ him, they took off the purple from him, and put his own clothes on him, and led him out to crucify him.   Ps. 69:19; Is. 53:3; Luke 18:32 ★ • *made fun of*

21 And they compel one Simon a Cy-re'-ni-an, who passed by, coming out of the country, the father of Alexander and Rufus, to bear his cross.

22 ᴿAnd they bring him unto the place Gol'-go-tha, which is, being interpreted, The place of a skull.   John 19:17

23 And they gave him to drink wine mingled with myrrh: but he received *it* not.

Jesus Is Crucified
Matt. 27:35–56; Luke 23:33–49; John 19:18, 23–30

24 ᴿAnd when they had crucified him, they parted his garments, casting lots upon them, what every man should take.   Ps. 22:16–18 ★

25 And it was the third hour, and they crucified him.

26 And the superscription of his accusation was written over, THE KING OF THE JEWS.

27 And ^Rwith him they crucify two ^Tthieves; the one on his right hand, and the other on his left. Is. 53:9, 12 ★ · *robbers*

28 And the scripture was fulfilled, which saith, ^RAND HE WAS NUMBERED WITH THE TRANSGRESSORS. Is. 53:12; Luke 22:37 ★

29 And ^Rthey that passed by railed on him, wagging their heads, and saying, Ah, ^Rthou that destroyest the temple, and buildest *it* in three days, Ps. 22:7 ★ · John 2:19

30 ^RSave thyself, and come down from the cross. Ps. 22:8 ★

31 Likewise also the chief priests ^Rmocking said among themselves with the scribes, He saved others; himself he cannot save. Ps. 69:19 ★

32 ^RLet Christ the King of Israel descend now from the cross, that we may see and believe. And they that were crucified with him ^Treviled him. Ps. 22:8 ★ · *scorned*

33 And ^Rwhen the sixth hour was come, there was darkness over the whole land until the ninth hour. Amos 8:9 ★

34 And at the ninth hour Jesus cried with a loud voice, saying, ^RE-lo'-i, E-lo'-i, la'-ma sa-bach'-tha-ni? which is, being interpreted, MY GOD, MY GOD, WHY HAST THOU FORSAKEN ME? Ps. 22:1 ★

35 And some of them that stood by, when they heard *it*, said, Behold, he calleth E-li'-as.

36 And one ran and filled a spunge full of vinegar, and put *it* on a reed, and ^Rgave him to drink, saying, Let alone; let us see whether E-li'-as will come to take him down. Ps. 69:21 ★

37 ^RAnd Jesus cried with a loud voice, and gave up the ghost. Matt. 17:23 ★

38 And the veil of the temple was rent in twain from the top to the bottom.

39 And when the centurion, which stood ^Tover against him, saw that he so cried out, and gave up the ghost, he said, Truly this man was the Son of God. *opposite*

40 There were also women looking on afar off: among whom was Mary Mag-da-le'-ne, and Mary the mother of James the less and of Jo'-ses, and Sa-lo'-me;

41 (Who also, when he was in Galilee, ^Rfollowed him, and ministered unto him;) and many other women which came up with him unto Jerusalem. Luke 8:2, 3

Jesus Is Buried
Matt. 27:57–61; Luke 23:50–55; John 19:38–42

42 And now when the even was come, because it was the preparation, that is, the day before the sabbath,

43 Joseph of Ar-i-ma-thae'-a, an honourable counsellor, which also waited for the kingdom of God, came, and went in boldly unto Pilate, and craved the body of Jesus.

44 And Pilate marvelled if he were already dead: and calling *unto him* the centurion, he asked him whether he had been ^Tany while dead. *dead a long time*

45 And when he ^Tknew *it* of the centurion, he gave the body to Joseph. *heard from*

46 And he bought fine linen, and took him down, and wrapped him in the linen, and ^Rlaid him in a sepulchre which was hewn out of a rock, and rolled a stone unto the door of the sepulchre. 14:8; Matt. 26:12 ★

47 And Mary Mag-da-le'-ne and Mary the mother of Jo'-ses beheld where he was laid.

CHAPTER 16

The Resurrection of Jesus
Matt. 28:1–8; Luke 24:1–9

AND when the sabbath was past, Mary Mag-da-le'-ne, and Mary the mother of James, and Sa-lo'-me, had bought sweet spices, that they might come and anoint him.

2 And very early in the morning the first *day* of the week, they came unto the sepulchre at the rising of the sun.

3 And they said among themselves, Who shall roll us away the stone from the ^Tdoor of the sepulchre? *entrance*

4 And when they looked, they saw that the stone was rolled ^Taway: for it was very ^Tgreat. *back · large*

5 ^RAnd entering into the sepulchre, they saw a young man sitting on the right side, clothed in a long white garment; and they were ^Taffrighted. John 20:11 · *amazed*

6 And he saith unto them, Be not affrighted: Ye seek Jesus of Nazareth, which was crucified: he is ^Rrisen; he is not here: behold the place where they laid him. Hos. 6:2 ★

7 But go your way, tell his disciples and Peter that he goeth before you into Galilee: there shall ye see him, as he said unto you.

8 And they went out quickly, and fled from the sepulchre; for they trembled and were amazed: neither said they any thing to any *man*; for they were afraid.

The Appearances of Jesus
Luke 24:13–48; John 20:1–10

9 Now when *Jesus* was risen early ^Tthe first *day* of the week, he appeared first to Mary Mag-da-le'-ne, ^Rout of whom he had cast seven devils. *on Sunday* · Luke 8:2

10 *And* she went and told them that had been with him, as they mourned and wept.

11 And they, when they had heard that he was alive, and had been seen of her, ^Tbelieved not. *believed her not*

12 After that he appeared in another form unto two of them, as they walked, and went into the country.

13 And they went and told *it* unto the ^Tresidue: neither believed they them. *remainder*

14 Afterward he appeared unto the eleven as they sat at meat, and upbraided them with

their unbelief and hardness of heart, because they believed not them which had seen him after he was risen.

15 ᴿAnd he said unto them, Go ye into all the world, ᴿand preach the gospel to every creature.   Matt. 28:19; [John 15:16] • [Col. 1:23]

16 ᴿHe that believeth and is baptized shall be saved; ᴿbut he that believeth not shall be ᵀdamned.   [John 3:15] • [Acts 2:38] • *condemned*

17 And these signs shall follow them that believe; In my name shall they cast out devils; they shall speak with new tongues;

18 ᴿThey shall take up serpents; and if they drink any deadly thing, it shall not hurt them; they shall lay hands on the sick, and they shall recover.   [Luke 10:19]

The Ascension of Jesus
Luke 24:49–53; Acts 1:9

19 So then after the Lord had spoken unto them, he was ᴿreceived up into heaven, and sat on the right hand of God.   Is. 9:7 ★

20 And they went forth, and preached every where, the Lord working with *them*, ᴿand confirming the word with signs following. A-men'.   Acts 5:12; [1 Cor. 2:4, 5; Heb. 2:4]

Measures of Length

Unit	Length	Equivalents	Translations
Day's journey	c. 20 miles		day's journey
Roman mile	4,854 feet	8 stadia	mile
Sabbath day's journey	3,637 feet	6 stadia	sabbath day's journey
Stadion	606 feet	⅛ Roman mile	furlong
Rod	9 feet (10.5 feet in Ezekiel)	3 paces; 6 cubits	measuring reed, reed
Fathom	6 feet	4 cubits	fathom
Pace	3 feet	⅓ rod; 2 cubits	pace
Cubit	18 inches	½ pace; 2 spans	cubit
Span	9 inches	½ cubit; 3 handbreadths	span
Handbreadth	3 inches	⅓ span; 4 fingers	handbreadth
Finger	.75 inches	¼ handbreadth	finger

LUKE

THE BOOK OF LUKE

Luke, a physician, writes with the compassion and warmth of a family doctor as he carefully documents the perfect humanity of the Son of Man, Jesus Christ. Luke emphasizes Jesus' ancestry, birth, and early life before moving carefully and chronologically through His earthly ministry. Growing belief and growing opposition develop side by side. Those who believe are challenged to count the cost of discipleship. Those who oppose will not be satisfied until the Son of Man hangs lifeless on a cross. But the resurrection insures that His purpose will be fulfilled: "to seek and to save that which was lost" (19:10).

Kata Loukōn, "According to Luke," is the ancient title that was added to this gospel at a very early date. The Greek name *Luke* appears only three times in the New Testament (Col. 4:14; 2 Tim. 4:11; Philem. 24).

THE AUTHOR OF LUKE

It is evident from the prologues to Luke and Acts (Luke 1:1–4; Acts 1:1–5) that both books were addressed to Theophilus as a two-volume work (Luke is called "the former treatise"). Acts begins with a summary of Luke and continues the story from where the Gospel of Luke concludes. The style and language of both books are quite similar. The "we" portions of Acts (Acts 16:1–17; 20:5—21:18; 27:1—28:16) reveal that the author was a close associate and traveling companion of Paul. Because all but two of Paul's associates are named in the third person, the list can be narrowed to Titus and Luke. Titus has never been seriously regarded as a possible author of Acts, and Luke best fits the requirements. He was with Paul during his first Roman imprisonment, and Paul referred to him as "Luke, the beloved physician" (Col. 4:14; cf. Philem. 24). During his second Roman imprisonment, Paul wrote "Only Luke is with me" (2 Tim. 4:11), an evidence of Luke's loyalty to the apostle in the face of profound danger.

Luke may have been a Hellenistic Jew, but it is more likely that he was a Gentile (this would make him the only gentile contributor to the New Testament). In Colossians 4:10–14, Paul lists three fellow workers who are "of the circumcision" (vv. 10, 11) and then includes Luke's name with two Gentiles (vv. 12–14). Luke's obvious skill with the Greek language and his phrase "their proper tongue" in Acts 1:19 also imply that he was not Jewish. It has been suggested that Luke may have been a Greek physician to a Roman family who at some point was set free and given Roman citizenship. Another guess is that he was

the "brother" referred to in Second Corinthians 8:18, 19. Ancient traditions (including the Muratorian Fragment, Irenaeus, Tertullian, Clement of Alexandria, Origen, Eusebius, and Jerome) strongly support Luke as the author of Luke and Acts. Tradition also says that Luke was from Syrian Antioch, remained unmarried, and died at the age of eighty-four.

THE TIME OF LUKE

Luke was not an eyewitness of the events in his gospel, but he relied on the testimony of eyewitnesses and written sources (1:1–4). He carefully investigated and arranged his material and presented it to Theophilus ("Friend of God"). The title "most excellent," or "most noble" (see Acts 23:26; 24:3; 26:25), indicates that Theophilus was a man of high social standing. He probably assumed responsibility for publishing Luke and Acts so that they would be available to gentile readers. Luke translates Aramaic terms with Greek words and explains Jewish customs and geography to make his gospel more intelligible to his original Greek readership. During Paul's two-year Caesarean imprisonment, Luke may have traveled in Palestine to gather information from eyewitnesses of Jesus' ministry. The date of this gospel depends on that of Acts since this was the first volume (see "The Time of Acts"). If Luke was written during Paul's first imprisonment in Rome it would be dated in the early 60s. However, it may have been given final form in Greece. In all probability, its publication preceded the destruction of Jerusalem (A.D. 70).

THE CHRIST OF LUKE

The humanity and compassion of Jesus are repeatedly stressed in Luke's gospel. Luke gives the most complete account of Christ's ancestry, birth, and development. He is the ideal Son of Man who identified with the sorrow and plight of sinful men in order to carry our sorrows and offer us the priceless gift of salvation. Jesus alone fulfills the Greek ideal of human perfection.

KEYS TO LUKE

Key Word: Jesus the Son of Man—Luke clearly states his purpose in the prologue of his gospel: "to write unto thee in order, . . . That thou mightest know the certainty of those things, wherein thou hast been instructed" (1:3, 4). Luke wanted to create an accurate, chronological, and comprehensive account of the unique life of Jesus the Christ to strengthen the faith of gentile believers and stimulate saving faith among nonbelievers. Luke also had another purpose, and that was to show that Christ was not only divine

but also human. Luke portrays Christ in His fullest humanity by devoting more of his writing to Christ's feelings and humanity than any other gospel.

Key Verses: Luke 1:3, 4 and 19:10—"It seemed good to me also, having had perfect understanding of all things from the very first, to write unto thee in order, most excellent Theophilus, That thou mightest know the certainty of those things, wherein thou hast been instructed" (1:3, 4).

"For the Son of man is come to seek and to save that which was lost" (19:10).

Key Chapter: Luke 15—Captured in the three parables of the Lost Sheep, Lost Coin, and Lost Son is the crux of this gospel: that God through Christ has come to seek and to save that which was lost.

SURVEY OF LUKE

Luke builds the gospel narrative on the platform of historical reliability. His emphasis on chronological and historical accuracy makes this the most comprehensive of the four gospels. This is also the longest and most literary gospel, and it presents Jesus Christ as the Perfect Man who came to seek and to save sinful men. This book can be divided into four sections: the introduction of the Son of Man (1:1—4:13); the ministry of the Son of Man (4:14—9:50); the rejection of the Son of Man (9:51—19:27); the crucifixion and resurrection of the Son of Man (19:28—24:53).

The Introduction of the Son of Man (1:1—4:13): Luke places a strong emphasis on the ancestry, birth, and early years of the Perfect Man and of His forerunner John the Baptist. Their infancy stories are intertwined as Luke records their birth announcements, advents, and temple presentations. Jesus prepares over thirty years (summarized in one verse, 2:52) for a public ministry of only three years. The ancestry of the Son of Man is traced back to the first man Adam, and His ministry commences after His baptism and temptation.

The Ministry of the Son of Man (4:14—9:50): The authority of the Son of Man over every realm is demonstrated in 4:14—6:49. In this section His authority over demons ("devils"), disease, nature, the effects of sin, tradition, and all people is presented as a prelude to His diverse ministry of preaching, healing, and discipling (7:1—9:50).

The Rejection of the Son of Man (9:51—19:27): The dual response of growing belief and growing rejection has already been introduced in the gospel (cf. 4:14 and 6:11), but from this time forward the intensity of opposition to the ministry of the Son of Man increases. When the religious leaders accuse Him of being demonized, Jesus pronounces a series of divine woes upon them (11). Knowing that He is on His last journey to Jerusalem, Jesus instructs His disciples on a number of practical matters including prayer, covetousness, faithfulness, repentance, humility, discipleship, evangelism, money, forgiveness, service, thankfulness, the second advent, and salvation (12:1—19:27).

The Crucifixion and Resurrection of the Son of Man (19:28—24:53): After His triumphal entry into Jerusalem, Jesus encounters the opposition of the priests, Sadducees, and scribes, and predicts the overthrow of Jerusalem (19:28—21:38). The Son of Man instructs His disciples for the last time before His betrayal in Gethsemane. The three religious and three civil trials culminate in His crucifixion. The glory and foundation of the Christian message is the historical resurrection of Jesus Christ. The Lord conquers the grave as He has promised, and appears on a number of occasions to His disciples before His ascension to the Father.

FOCUS	INTRODUCTION OF THE SON OF MAN	MINISTRY OF THE SON OF MAN	REJECTION OF THE SON OF MAN	CRUCIFIXION AND RESUR-RECTION OF THE SON OF MAN
REFERENCE	1:1 —————— 4:14 ——————		9:51 —————— 19:28 ——————	24:53
DIVISION	ADVENT	ACTIVITIES	ANTAGONISM AND ADMONITION	APPLICATION AND AUTHENTICATION
TOPIC	SEEKING THE LOST		SAVING THE LOST	
	MIRACLES PROMINENT		TEACHING PROMINENT	
LOCATION	ISRAEL	GALILEE	ISRAEL	JERUSALEM
TIME	c. 4 B.C.–A.D. 33			

CHAPTER 1

The Purpose and Method of Luke's Gospel

FORASMUCH as many have ᵀtaken in hand to set forth in order a declaration of those things which are most surely believed among us,   *undertaken*

2 Even as they delivered them unto us, which ᴿfrom the beginning were eyewitnesses, and ministers of the word;   Heb. 2:3

3 It seemed good to me also, having had perfect understanding of all things from the very first, to write unto thee in order, ᴿmost excellent The-oph′-i-lus,   Acts 1:1

4 ᴿThat thou mightest know the certainty of those things, wherein thou hast been instructed.   [John 20:31]

Zacharias Ministers in the Temple

5 THERE was in the days of Herod, the king of Ju-dae′-a, a certain priest named Zach-a-ri′-as, ᴿof the course of A-bi′-a: and his wife *was* of the daughters of Aaron, and her name *was* Elisabeth.   1 Chr. 24:10

6 And they were both righteous before God, walking in all the commandments and ordinances of the Lord blameless.

7 And they had no child, because that Elisabeth was barren, and they both were now well ᵀstricken in years.   *along*

8 And it came to pass, that while he ᵀexecuted the priest's office before God in the order of his course,   *performed*

9 According to the custom of the priest's office, his ᵀlot was to burn incense when he went into the temple of the Lord.   *duty*

10 And the whole multitude of the people were praying without at the time of incense.

An Angel Announces
the Birth of John the Baptist

11 And there appeared unto him an ᴿangel of the Lord standing on the right side of ᴿthe altar of incense.   Acts 5:19 • Ex. 30:1

12 And when Zach-a-ri′-as saw *him,* he was troubled, and fear fell upon him.

13 But the angel said unto him, Fear not, Zach-a-ri′-as: for thy prayer is heard; and thy wife Elisabeth shall bear thee a son, and ᴿthou shalt call his name John.   vv. 60, 63

14 And thou shalt have joy and gladness; and ᴿmany shall rejoice at his birth.   v. 58

15 For he shall be great in the sight of the Lord, and ᴿshall drink neither wine nor strong drink; and he shall be filled with the Holy Ghost, ᴿeven from his mother's womb.   Num. 6:3; Judg. 13:4 • Jer. 1:5; Gal. 1:15

16 And many of the children of Israel shall he turn to the Lord their God.

17 ᴿAnd he shall go before him in the spirit and power of E-li′-as, TO TURN THE HEARTS OF THE FATHERS TO THE CHILDREN, and the disobedient to the wisdom of the just; to make ready a people prepared for the Lord.   Mal. 4:5, 6 ✫

Zacharias Is Unable to Speak

18 And Zach-a-ri′-as said unto the angel, Whereby shall I know this? for I am an old man, and my wife well stricken in years.

19 And the angel answering said unto him, I am Gabriel, that stand in the presence of God; and am sent to speak unto thee, and to shew thee these glad tidings.

20 And, behold, ᴿthou shalt be dumb, and not able to speak, until the day that these things shall be performed, because thou believest not my words, which shall be fulfilled in their season.   Ezek. 3:26; 24:27

21 And the people waited for Zach-a-ri′-as, and marvelled that he tarried so long in the temple.

22 And when he came out, he could not speak unto them: and they perceived that he had seen a vision in the temple: for he beckoned unto them, and remained speechless.

23 And it came to pass, that, as soon as the days of his ministration were accomplished, he departed to his own house.

24 And after those days his wife Elisabeth ᴿconceived, and hid herself five months, saying,   Gen. 21:2

25 Thus hath the Lord dealt with me in the days wherein he looked on *me,* to ᴿtake away my reproach among men.   Gen. 30:23

Gabriel Announces Christ's Birth

26 And in the sixth month the angel Gabriel was sent from God unto a city of Galilee, named Nazareth,

27 To a ᴿvirgin ᵀespoused to a man whose name was Joseph, of the house of David; and the virgin's name *was* Mary.   Is. 7:14 ✱ • *betrothed*

28 And the angel came in unto her, and said, ᴿHail, *thou that art* ᵀhighly favoured, ᴿthe Lord *is* with thee: blessed *art* thou among women.   Dan. 9:23 • *very fortunate* • Judg. 6:12

29 And when she saw *him*, ^Rshe was troubled at his saying, and cast in her mind what manner of salutation this should be. *v.* 12

30 And the angel said unto her, Fear not, Mary: for thou hast found favour with God.

31 ^RAnd, behold, thou shalt conceive in thy womb, and bring forth a son, and shalt call his name JESUS. 2:21; Matt. 1:21, 25 ☆

32 He shall be great, ^Rand shall be called the Son of the Highest: and ^Rthe Lord God shall give unto him the throne of his father David: Mark 5:7 ☆ • Ps. 132:11; [Is. 9:6, 7; 16:5]

33 ^RAnd he shall reign over the house of Jacob ^Rfor ever; and of his kingdom there shall be no end. [Obad. 21; Mic. 4:7] • Ps. 89:36, 37 ☆

Mary Miraculously Conceives

34 Then said Mary unto the angel, How shall this be, seeing I know not a man?

35 And the angel answered and said unto her, ^RThe Holy Ghost shall come upon thee, and the power of the Highest shall overshadow thee: therefore also that holy thing which shall be born of thee shall be called ^Rthe Son of God. Matt. 1:20 • Matt. 14:33 ☆

36 And, behold, thy cousin Elisabeth, she hath also conceived a son in her old age: and this is the sixth month with her, who was called ^Tbarren. *childless*

37 For ^Rwith God nothing shall be impossible. Gen. 18:14; Mark 10:27; Rom. 4:21

38 And Mary said, Behold the ^Thandmaid of the Lord; be it unto me according to thy word. And the angel departed from her. *servant*

Mary Visits Elisabeth

39 And Mary arose in those days, and went into the hill country with haste, ^Rinto a city of Juda; Josh. 21:9

40 And entered into the house of Zach-a-ri'-as, and ^Tsaluted Elisabeth. *greeted*

41 And it came to pass, that when Elisabeth heard the ^Tsalutation of Mary, the babe leaped in her womb; and Elisabeth was filled with the Holy Ghost: *greeting*

42 And she spake out with a loud voice, and said, Blessed *art* thou among women, and blessed *is* the fruit of thy womb.

43 And whence *is* this to me, that the mother of my Lord should come to me?

44 For, lo, as soon as the voice of thy salutation sounded in mine ears, the babe leaped in my womb for joy.

45 And blessed *is* she that believed: for there shall be a performance of those things which were told her from the Lord.

46 And Mary said, My soul doth ^Tmagnify the Lord, *praise*

47 And my spirit hath rejoiced in God my Saviour.

48 For he hath regarded the low estate of his handmaiden: for, behold, from henceforth ^Rall generations shall call me blessed. 11:27

49 For he that is mighty hath done to me great things; and ^Rholy *is* his name. Ps. 111:9

50 And ^Rhis mercy *is* on them that fear him from generation to generation. Ex. 20:6

51 ^RHe hath shewed strength with his arm; ^Rhe hath scattered the proud in the imagination of their hearts. Is. 40:10 • [1 Pet. 5:5]

52 He hath put down the mighty from *their* seats, and exalted them of low degree.

53 He hath filled the hungry with good things; and the rich he hath sent empty away.

54 He hath holpen his servant Israel, in remembrance of *his* mercy;

55 ^RAs he spake to our fathers, to Abraham, and to his seed for ever. [Gal. 3:16]

56 And Mary abode with her about three months, and returned to her own house.

Elisabeth Gives Birth to John

57 Now Elisabeth's full time came that she should be delivered; and she ^Rbrought^T forth a son. *v.* 13 • *gave birth to*

58 And her neighbours and her cousins heard how the Lord had shewed great mercy upon her; and they rejoiced with her.

59 And it came to pass, that ^Ron the eighth day they came to circumcise the child; and they called him Zach-a-ri'-as, after the name of his father. Gen. 17:12

60 And his mother answered and said, ^RNot *so;* but he shall be called John. *v.* 13

61 And they said unto her, There is none of thy kindred that is called by this name.

62 And they made signs to his father, how he would have him ^Tcalled. *named*

63 And he asked for a writing table, and wrote, saying, His name is John. And they ^Tmarvelled all. *were astonished*

64 And his mouth was opened immediately, and his tongue *loosed,* and he spake, and praised God.

65 And fear came on all that dwelt round about them: and all these ^Tsayings were ^Tnoised abroad throughout all the hill country of Ju-dae'-a. *things • reported*

66 And all they that heard *them* ^Rlaid *them* up in their hearts, saying, What manner of child shall ^Rthis be! And ^Rthe hand of the Lord was with him. 2:19 • Acts 11:21

Zacharias Prophesies of John's Ministry

67 And his father Zach-a-ri'-as ^Rwas filled with the Holy Ghost, and ^Tprophesied, saying, Joel 2:28 • *preached*

68 Blessed *be* the Lord God of Israel; for he hath visited and redeemed his people,

69 And hath raised up an horn of salvation for us in the house of his servant David;

70 As he spake by the mouth of his holy prophets, which have been since the world began:

71 That we should be saved from our enemies, and from the hand of all that hate us;

72 To perform the mercy *promised* to our fathers, and to remember his holy covenant;

73 RThe oath which he sware to our father Abraham,   Gen. 12:3; [Heb. 6:13]

74 That he would grant unto us, that we being delivered out of the hand of our enemies might serve him without fear,

75 RIn holiness and righteousness before him, all the days of our life.   [Eph. 4:24]

76 And thou, child, shalt be called the prophet of the Highest: for Rthou shalt go before the face of the Lord to prepare his ways;   Matt. 11:9, 10 ☆

77 To give knowledge of salvation unto his people Rby the remission of their sins, Mark 1:4

78 Through the tender mercy of our God; Twhereby the dayspring from on high hath visited us,   *in which the dawn*

79 To give light to them that sit in darkness and *in* the shadow of death, to guide our feet into the way of Rpeace.   John 14:27 ☆

80 And the child grew, and waxed strong in spirit, and Rwas in the deserts till the day of his shewing unto Israel.   Matt. 3:1

CHAPTER 2

Christ Is Born

AND it came to pass in those days, that there went out a decree from Caesar Augustus, that all the world should be taxed.

2 (RAnd this taxing was first made when Cy-re'-ni-us was governor of Syria.)   Acts 5:37

3 And all went to be Ttaxed, every one into his own city.   *registered*

4 And Joseph also went up from Galilee, out of the city of Nazareth, into Ju-dae'-a, unto the city of David, which is called RBeth'-le-hem; (because he was of the Thouse and Tlineage of David:)   Mic. 5:2 ☆ • *family • descent*

5 To be taxed with Mary his Tespoused wife, being great with child.   *betrothed*

6 And so it was, that, while they were there, the days were accomplished that she should be delivered.

7 And Rshe brought forth her firstborn son, and wrapped him in swaddling clothes, and laid him in a manger; because there was no room for them in the inn.   1:31; Matt. 1:25

The Angels Announce Jesus to the Shepherds

8 And there were in the same country shepherds Tabiding in the field, keeping watch over their flock by night.   *staying*

9 And, lo, the angel of the Lord came upon them, and the glory of the Lord shone round about them: Rand they were sore afraid. 1:12

10 And the angel said unto them, Fear not:

for, behold, I bring you good tidings of great joy, which shall be to all people.

11 RFor unto you is born this day in the city of David Ra Saviour, Rwhich is Christ the Lord.   Is. 9:6 ☆ • Matt. 1:21 • Acts 2:36; Phil. 2:11

12 And Rthis *shall be* a sign unto you; Ye shall find the babe wrapped in swaddling clothes, lying in a manger.   1 Sam. 2:34

13 RAnd suddenly there was with the angel a multitude of the heavenly host praising God, and saying,   [Heb. 1:14]; Rev. 5:11

14 Glory to God in the highest, and on earth peace, Rgood will toward men. John 3:16

The Shepherds Visit Jesus

15 And it came to pass, as the angels were gone away from them into heaven, the shepherds said one to another, Let us now go even unto Beth'-le-hem, and see this thing which is come to pass, which the Lord hath made known unto us.

16 And they came with haste, and found Mary, and Joseph, and the babe lying in a manger.

17 And when they had seen *it*, they made known abroad the saying which was told them concerning this child.

18 And all they that heard *it* wondered at those things which were told them by the shepherds.

19 RBut Mary kept all these things, and pondered *them* in her heart.   1:66

20 And the shepherds returned, glorifying and praising God for all the things that they had heard and seen, as it was told unto them.

Christ Is Circumcised

21 RAnd when eight days were accomplished for the circumcising of the child, his name was called RJESUS, which was so named of the angel before he was conceived in the womb.   Lev. 12:3 • Matt. 1:21; 1:31 ☆

22 And when Rthe days of her purification according to the law of Moses were Taccomplished, they brought him to Jerusalem, to present *him* to the Lord;   Lev. 12:2 • *ended*

23 (As it is written in the law of the Lord, REVERY MALE THAT OPENETH THE WOMB SHALL BE CALLED HOLY TO THE LORD;)   Ex. 13:2; Num. 3:13

24 And to offer a sacrifice according to that which is said in the law of the Lord, A PAIR OF TURTLEDOVES, OR TWO YOUNG PIGEONS.

Simeon's Prophecy

25 And, behold, there was a man in Jerusalem, whose name *was* Simeon; and the same man *was* just and devout, Rwaiting for the consolation of Israel: and the Holy Ghost was upon him.   Mark 15:43

26 RAnd it was revealed unto him by the Holy Ghost, that he should not see death, before he had seen the Lord's Christ.   *v.* 30 ☆

27 And he came ᴿbyᵀ the Spirit into the temple: and when the parents brought in the child Jesus, to do for him after the custom of the law,   Matt. 4:1 · *in*

28 Then took he him up in his arms, and blessed God, and said,

29 Lord, now lettest thou thy servant depart in peace, according to thy word:

30 For mine eyes have seen thy salvation,

31 Which thou hast prepared before the face of all people;

32 ᴿA light to lighten the Gentiles, and the glory of thy people Israel.   Is 9:2; 42:6 ✰

33 And Joseph and his mother marvelled at those things which were spoken of him.

34 And Simeon blessed them, and said unto Mary his mother, Behold, this *child* is set for the ᴿfall and rising again of many in Israel; and for ᴿa sign which shall be spoken against;   Is. 8:14; [1 Pet. 2:7, 8] ✰ · Acts 28:22

35 (Yea, ᴿa sword shall pierce through thy own soul also,) that the thoughts of many hearts may be revealed.   Ps. 42:10

Anna's Testimony

36 And there was one Anna, a prophetess, the daughter of Phan'-u-el, of the tribe of A'-ser: she was of a great age, and had lived with an husband seven years from her virginity;

37 And she *was* a widow of about fourscore and four years, which departed not from the temple, but served God with fastings and prayers ᴿnight and day.   1 Tim. 5:5

38 And she coming in that instant gave thanks likewise unto the Lord, and spake of him to all them that ᴿlooked for redemption in ᵀJerusalem.   24:21 · *Israel*

Jesus Returns to Nazareth—Matt. 2:19-23

39 And when they had ᵀperformed all things according to the law of the Lord, they returned into Galilee, to their own city Nazareth.   *done*

40 ᴿAnd the child grew, and ᵀwaxed strong in spirit, filled with wisdom: and the grace of God was upon him.   1:80; *v.* 52 · *became*

Jesus Celebrates the Passover

41 Now his parents went to Jerusalem every year at the feast of the passover.

42 And when he was twelve years old, they went up to Jerusalem after the ᴿcustom of the feast.   Ex. 23:14, 15

43 And when they had fulfilled the days, as they returned, the child Jesus tarried behind in Jerusalem; and ᵀJoseph and his mother knew not *of it.*   *his parents*

44 But they, supposing him to have been in the ᵀcompany, went a ᵀday's journey; and they sought him among *their* ᵀkinsfolk and acquaintance.   *group* · 20 mi. · *relatives*

45 And when they found him not, they turned back again to Jerusalem, seeking him.

46 And it came to pass, that after three days they found him in the temple, sitting in the midst of the ᵀdoctors, both hearing them, and asking them questions.   *teachers*

47 And all that heard him were astonished at his understanding and answers.

48 And when they saw him, they were amazed: and his mother said unto him, Son, why hast thou thus dealt with us? behold, thy father and I have sought thee sorrowing.

49 And he said unto them, How is it that ye sought me? ᵀwist ye not that I must be about my Father's business?   *knew*

50 And ᴿthey understood not the saying which he spake unto them.   John 7:15, 46

Jesus Grows in Wisdom

51 And he went down with them, and came to Nazareth, and was ᵀsubject unto them: but his mother ᴿkept all these sayings in her heart.   *obedient* · *v.* 19; Dan. 7:28

52 And Jesus increased in wisdom and stature, and in favour with God and man.

CHAPTER 3

The Ministry of John the Baptist
Matt. 3:1-12; Mark 1:2-8; John 1:19-31

NOW in the fifteenth year of the reign of Ti-be'-ri-us Caesar, Pon'-tius Pilate being governor of Ju-dae'-a, and Herod being te'-trarch of Galilee, and his brother Philip te'-trarch of It-u-rae'-a and of the region of Trach-o-ni'-tis, and Ly-sa'-ni-as the ᵀte'-trarch of Ab-i-le'-ne,   *governor*

2 An'-nas and Ca'-ia-phas being the high priests, the word of God came unto John the son of Zach-a-ri'-as in the wilderness.

3 And he came into all the country about Jordan, ᴿpreaching the baptism of repentance for the remission of sins;   1:17, 77 ✰

4 As it is written in the book of the words of E-sa'-ias the prophet, saying, ᴿTHE VOICE OF ONE CRYING IN THE WILDERNESS, PREPARE YE THE WAY OF THE LORD, MAKE HIS PATHS STRAIGHT.   Is. 40:3 ✰

5 ᴿEVERY VALLEY SHALL BE FILLED, AND EVERY MOUNTAIN AND HILL SHALL BE BROUGHT LOW; AND THE CROOKED SHALL BE MADE STRAIGHT, AND THE ROUGH WAYS *SHALL BE* MADE SMOOTH;   Is. 40:4 ✰

6 ᴿAND ALL FLESH SHALL SEE THE SALVA-TION OF GOD.   Is. 40:5 ✰

7 Then said he to the multitude that came forth to be baptized of him, O generation of vipers, who hath warned you to flee from the wrath to come?

8 Bring forth therefore fruits worthy of repentance, and begin not to say within yourselves, We have Abraham to *our* father: for I say unto you, That God is able of these stones to raise up children unto Abraham.

9 And now also the axe is laid unto the root of the trees: Revery tree therefore which bringeth not forth good fruit is hewn down, and cast into the fire.   Matt. 7:19

10 And the people asked him, saying, RWhat shall we do then?   [Acts 2:37, 38]

11 He answereth and saith unto them, RHe that hath two coats, let him Timpart to him that hath none; and he that hath Tmeat, let him do likewise.   11:41 · give · food

12 Then Rcame also Tpublicans to be baptized, and said unto him, Master, what shall we do?   7:29; Matt. 21:32 · tax collectors

13 And he said unto them, Exact no more than that which is appointed you.

14 And the soldiers likewise demanded of him, saying, And what shall we do? And he said unto them, TDo violence to no man, Rneither accuse any falsely; and be content with your Twages.   act roughly · Ex. 23:1 · allowance

15 And as the people were in expectation, and all men mused in their hearts of John, whether he were the Christ, or not;

16 John answered, saying unto them all, I indeed baptize you Twith water; but one mightier than I cometh, the Tlatchet of whose shoes I am not worthy to unloose: Rhe shall baptize you with the Holy Ghost and with fire: in · straps · John 20:22; Acts 2:4 ☆

17 Whose fan is in his hand, and he will throughly purge his floor, and will gather the wheat into his garner; but the chaff he will burn with fire unquenchable.

18 And many other things in his exhortation preached he unto the people.

19 ButR Herod the te'-trarch, being Treproved by him for He-ro'-di-as his brother Philip's wife, and for all the evils which Herod had done,   Matt. 14:3; Mark 6:17 · criticized

20 Added yet this above all, that he shut up John in prison.

The Baptism of Christ
Matt. 3:13–17; Mark 1:9–11; John 1:32–34

21 Now when all the people were baptized, it came to pass, that Jesus also being baptized, and praying, the heaven was opened,

22 And the Holy Ghost descended in a bodily shape like a dove upon him, and a voice came from heaven, which said, Thou art my beloved Son; in thee I am well pleased.

The Genealogy of Christ Through Mary
Gen. 5:1–32; 11:10–26; Ruth 4:18–22;
1 Chr. 1:1–4, 24–27, 34; 2:1–15; Matt. 1:2–6

23 And Jesus himself began to be Rabout thirty years of age, being (as was supposed) Rthe son of Joseph, which was the son of He'-li,   [Num. 4:3, 35] · Matt. 13:55; John 6:42

24 Which was the son of Mat'-that, which was the son of Levi, which was the son of Mel'-chi, which was the son of Jan'-na, which was the son of Joseph,

25 Which was the son of Mat-ta-thi'-as, which was the son of Amos, which was the son of Na'-um, which was the son of Es'-li, which was the son of Nag'-ge,

26 Which was the son of Ma'-ath, which was the son of Mat-ta-thi'-as, which was the son of Sem'-e-i, which was the son of Joseph, which was the son of Juda,

27 Which was the son of Jo-an'-na, which was the son of Rhe'-sa, which was the son of Zo-rob'-a-bel, which was the son of Sa-la'-thi-el, which was the son of Ne'-ri,

28 Which was the son of Mel'-chi, which was the son of Ad'-di, which was the son of Co'-sam, which was the son of El-mo'-dam, which was the son of Er,

29 Which was the son of Jo'-se, which was the son of E-li-e'-zer, which was the son of Jo'-rim, which was the son of Mat'-that, which was the son of Levi,

30 Which was the son of Simeon, which was the son of Juda, which was the son of Joseph, which was the son of Jo'-nan, which was the son of E-li'-a-kim,

31 Which was the son of Me'-le-a, which was the son of Me'-nan, which was the son of Mat'-ta-tha, which was the son of Nathan, which was the son Rof David,   Is. 9:7 ☆

32 Which was the son Rof Jesse, which was the son of O'-bed, which was the son of Bo'-oz, which was the son of Sal'-mon, which was the son of Na-as'-son,   Is. 11:1, 10 ☆

33 Which was the son of A-min'-a-dab, which was the son of A'-ram, which was the son of Es'-rom, which was the son of Pha'-res, which was the son Rof Juda,   Gen. 49:10 ☆

34 Which was the son of Jacob, which was the son of Isaac, which was the son of Abraham, Rwhich was the son of Tha'-ra, which was the son of Na'-chor,   Gen. 11:24, 26

35 Which was the son of Sa'-ruch, which was the son of Ra'-gau, which was the son of Pha'-lec, which was the son of He'-ber, which was the son of Sa'-la,

36 RWhich was the son of Ca-i'-nan, which was the son of Ar-phax'-ad, which was the son of Sem, which was the son of No'-e, which was the son of La'-mech,   Gen. 11:12

37 Which was the son of Ma-thu'-sa-la, which was the son of E'-noch, which was the son of Ja'-red, which was the son of Ma-le'-le-el, which was the son of Ca-i'-nan,

38 Which was the son of E'-nos, which was the son of Seth, which was the son of Adam, Rwhich was the son of God.   Gen. 5:1, 2

CHAPTER 4

The Temptation of Christ
Matt. 4:1–11; Mark 1:12, 13

AND Jesus being full of the Holy Ghost returned from Jordan, and was led by the Spirit into the wilderness,

2 Being forty days ᵀtempted of ᵀthe devil. And ᴿin those days he did eat nothing: and when they were ended, he afterward hungered.   *tested • Satan* • Ex. 34:28; 1 Kin. 19:8

3 ᴿAnd the devil said unto him, If thou be the Son of God, command this stone that it be made bread.   [Heb. 4:15; James 1:14]

4 And Jesus answered him, saying, It is written, ᴿTHAT MAN SHALL NOT LIVE BY BREAD ALONE, BUT BY EVERY WORD OF GOD. Deut. 8:3

5 And the devil, taking him up into an high mountain, shewed unto him all the kingdoms of the world in a moment of time.

6 And the devil said unto him, All this power will I give thee, and the glory of them: for that is delivered unto me; and to whomsoever I will I give it.

7 If thou therefore wilt ᵀworship me, all shall be thine.   *bow down to me*

8 And Jesus answered and said unto him, Get thee behind me, Satan: for it is written, ᴿTHOU SHALT WORSHIP THE LORD THY GOD, AND HIM ONLY SHALT THOU SERVE.   Deut. 6:13

9 And he brought him to Jerusalem, and set him on a pinnacle of the temple, and said unto him, If thou be the Son of God, cast thyself down from hence:

10 For it is written, HE SHALL GIVE HIS ANGELS CHARGE OVER THEE, TO KEEP THEE:

11 ᴿAND IN *THEIR* HANDS THEY SHALL BEAR THEE UP, LEST AT ANY TIME THOU DASH THY FOOT AGAINST A STONE.   Ps. 91:11, 12 ★

12 And Jesus answering said unto him, It is said, ᴿTHOU SHALT NOT ᵀTEMPT THE LORD THY GOD.   Deut. 6:16 • *test*

13 And when ᵀthe devil had ended all the temptation, he departed from him ᴿfor ᵀa season.   *Satan* • [John 14:30; Heb. 4:15] • *a while*

Acceptance Throughout Galilee
Matt. 4:12; Mark 1:14

14 And Jesus returned ᴿin the power of the Spirit into ᴿGalilee: and there went out a ᵀfame of him through all the region round about.   John 4:43 • Acts 10:37 • *report*

15 And he ᴿtaught in their synagogues, being ᴿglorified of all.   Ps. 22:22 • Is. 52:13 ★

Rejection at Nazareth

16 And he came to Nazareth, where he had been brought up: and, as his custom was, ᴿhe went into the synagogue on the sabbath day, and stood up for to read.   Ps. 22:22 ★

17 And there was delivered unto him the ᵀbook of the prophet E-sa'-ias. And when he had opened the book, he found the place where it was written,   *scroll*

18 ᴿTHE SPIRIT OF THE LORD *IS* UPON ME, BECAUSE HE HATH ANOINTED ME TO PREACH THE GOSPEL TO THE POOR; HE HATH SENT ME TO HEAL THE BROKENHEARTED, TO PREACH DELIVERANCE TO THE CAPTIVES, AND RECOVERING OF

SIGHT TO THE BLIND, TO SET AT LIBERTY THEM THAT ARE BRUISED,   Is. 61:1 ★

19 ᴿTO PREACH THE ACCEPTABLE YEAR OF THE LORD.   Is. 61:1, 2 ★

20 And he closed the book, and he gave *it* again to the ᵀminister, and sat down. And the eyes of all them that were in the synagogue were fastened on him.   *attendant*

21 And he began to say unto them, This day is this scripture fulfilled in your ears.

22 And all bare him witness, and ᴿwondered at the gracious words which proceeded out of his mouth. And they said, ᴿIs not this Joseph's son?   2:47; [Ps. 45:2] • John 6:42

23 And he said unto them, Ye will surely say unto me this proverb, Physician, heal thyself: whatsoever we have heard done in ᴿCa-per'-na-um, do also here in ᴿthy country.   Matt. 4:13; 11:23 • Matt. 13:54; Mark 6:1

24 And he said, Verily I say unto you, No prophet is accepted in his own country.

25 But I tell you of a truth, ᴿmany widows were in Israel in the days of E-li'-as, when the heaven was shut up three years and six months, when great famine was throughout all the land;   1 Kin. 17:9

26 But unto none of them was E-li'-as sent, save unto Sa-rep'-ta, *a city* of Si'-don, unto a woman *that was* a widow.

27 ᴿAnd many lepers were in Israel in the time of El-i-se'-us the prophet; and none of them was ᵀcleansed, saving Na'-a-man the Syrian.   2 Kin. 5:14 • *made clean*

28 And all they in the synagogue, when they heard these things, were ᵀfilled with wrath,   *very indignant*

29 And rose up, and thrust him out of the city, and led him unto the ᵀbrow of the hill whereon their city was built, that they might cast him down headlong.   *edge*

30 But he ᴿpassing through the midst of them went his way,   John 8:59; 10:39

Demons Are Cast Out—Mark 1:21-28

31 And ᴿcame down to Ca-per'-na-um, a city ᴿof Galilee, and taught them on the sabbath days.   Matt. 4:13 • Is. 9:1, 2

32 And they were astonished at his ᵀdoctrine: for his word was with power.   *teaching*

33 And in the synagogue there was a man, which had a spirit of an unclean devil, and cried out with a loud voice,

34 Saying, Let *us* alone; what have we to do with thee, *thou* Jesus of Nazareth? art thou come to destroy us? I know thee who thou art; the Holy One of God.

35 And Jesus rebuked him, saying, Hold thy peace, and come out of him. And when the ᵀdevil had thrown him in the midst, he came out of him, and hurt him not.   *demon*

36 And they were all amazed, and spake among themselves, saying, What a word *is*

this! for with authority and power he commandeth the ᵀunclean spirits, and they come out.   *evil*

37 And the fame of him went out into every place of the country round about.

Peter's Mother in Law Is Healed
Matt. 8:14, 15; Mark 1:29–31

38 And he arose out of the synagogue, and entered into Simon's house. And Simon's wife's mother was taken with a great fever; and they ᵀbesought him for her.   *petitioned*

39 And he stood over her, and rebuked the fever; and it left her: and immediately she arose and ministered unto them.

Jesus Ministers Throughout Galilee
Matt. 4:23–25; 8:16, 17; Mark 1:32–39

40 Now when the sun was setting, all they that had any sick with ᵀdivers diseases brought them unto him; and he laid his hands on every one of them, and healed them. *various*

41 And ᵀdevils also came out of many, crying out, and saying, Thou art Christ the Son of God. And he rebuking *them* ᵀsuffered them not to speak: for they knew that he was Christ.   *demons · allowed*

42 And when it was day, he departed and went into a desert place: and the people sought him, and came unto him, and stayed him, that he should not depart from them.

43 And he said unto them, I must preach the kingdom of God to other cities also: for ᵀtherefore am I sent.   *this reason have I come*

44 And he preached in the synagogues ᵀof Galilee.   *all over the country*

CHAPTER 5

The First Disciples Are Called

AND it came to pass, that, as the people pressed upon him to hear the word of God, he stood by the lake of Gen-nes'-a-ret,

2 And saw two ships standing by the lake: but the fishermen were gone out of them, and were washing *their* nets.

3 And he entered into one of the ᵀships, which was Simon's, and ᵀprayed him that he would ᵀthrust out a little from the land. And he sat down, and taught the people out of the ship.   *boats · asked · push*

4 Now when he had left speaking, he said unto Simon, ᴿLaunch out into the deep, and let down your nets for a draught.   John 21:6

5 And Simon answering said unto him, Master, we have ᵀtoiled all the night, and have taken nothing: nevertheless at thy word I will let down the net.   *worked*

6 And when they had this done, they ᵀinclosed a great multitude of fishes: and their net brake.   *caught*

7 And they ᵀbeckoned unto *their* partners, which were in the other ship, that they should come and help them. And they came, and filled both the ships, so that they began to sink.   *motioned*

8 When Simon Peter saw *it*, he fell down at Jesus' knees, saying, Depart from me; for I am a sinful man, O Lord.

9 For he was astonished, and all that were with him, at the ᵀdraught of the fishes which they had taken: *catch*

10 And so *was* also James, and John, the sons of Zeb'-e-dee, which were partners with Simon. And Jesus said unto Simon, Fear not; from henceforth thou shalt catch men.

11 And when they had brought their ships to land, they forsook all, and followed him.

A Leper Is Cleansed
Matt. 8:2–4; Mark 1:40–45

12 And it came to pass, when he was in a certain city, behold a man full of leprosy: who seeing Jesus fell on *his* face, and ᵀbesought him, saying, Lord, if thou wilt, thou canst make me clean.   *petitioned*

13 And he put forth *his* hand, and touched him, saying, I will: be thou clean. And immediately the leprosy departed from him.

14 And he charged him to tell no man: but go, and shew thyself to the priest, and offer for thy cleansing, according as Moses commanded, for a testimony unto them.

15 But so much the more went there ᵀa fame abroad of him: ᴿand great multitudes came together to hear, and to be healed by him of their infirmities.   *a report · Matt. 4:25*

A Paralytic Is Healed
Matt. 9:1–8; Mark 2:1–12

16 ᴿAnd he withdrew himself into the wilderness, and prayed.   Matt. 14:23; Mark 6:46

17 And it came to pass on a certain day, as he was teaching, that there were Pharisees and ᵀdoctors of the law sitting by, which were come out of every town of Galilee, and Ju-dae'-a, and Jerusalem: and the power of the Lord was *present* to heal them.   *teachers*

18 And, behold, men brought in a bed a man which was ᵀtaken with a palsy: and they sought *means* to bring him in, and to lay *him* before him.   *paralyzed*

19 And when they could not find by what *way* they might bring him in because of the multitude, they went upon the housetop, and let him down through the tiling with *his* couch into the midst before Jesus.

20 And when he saw their faith, he said unto him, Man, thy sins are forgiven thee.

21 And the scribes and the Pharisees began to ᵀreason, saying, Who is this which speaketh blasphemies? ᴿWho can forgive sins, but God alone?   *question · Ps. 32:5*

22 But when Jesus perceived their

thoughts, he answering said unto them, What ᵀreason ye in your hearts?   *think*

23 Whether is easier, to say, Thy sins be forgiven thee; or to say, Rise up and walk?

24 But that ye may know that the ᴿSon of man hath power upon earth to forgive sins, (he said unto the sick of the palsy,) I say unto thee, Arise, and take up thy couch, and go into thine house.   [Acts 5:31]

25 And immediately he rose up before them, and took up that whereon he lay, and departed to his own house, glorifying God.

26 And they were all amazed, and they glorified God, and were filled with fear, saying, We have seen strange things to day.

Matthew Is Called—Matt. 9:9; Mark 2:13, 14

27 And after these things he went forth, and saw a ᵀpublican, named Levi, sitting at the receipt of custom: and he said unto him, Follow me.   *tax collector*

28 And he left ᵀall, rose up, and followed him.   *everything*

Jesus Eats with Sinners
Matt. 9:10–13; Mark 2:15–17

29 And Levi made him a great feast in his own house: and ᴿthere was a great company of publicans and of others that sat down with them.   15:1

30 But their scribes and Pharisees murmured against his disciples, saying, Why do ye eat and drink with publicans and sinners?

31 And Jesus answering said unto them, They that are ᵀwhole need not a physician; but they that are sick.   *healthy*

32 ᴿI came not to call the righteous, but sinners to repentance.   1 Tim. 1:15

Jesus Teaches About Fasting
Matt. 9:14, 15; Mark 2:18–20

33 And they said unto him, Why do the disciples of John fast often, and make prayers, and likewise the disciples of the Pharisees; but thine eat and drink?

34 And he said unto them, Can ye make the children of the bridechamber fast, while the bridegroom is with them?

35 But the days will come, when the bridegroom shall be taken away from them, and then shall they fast in those days.

Parable of the Cloth and Wine Bottles
Matt. 9:16, 17; Mark 2:21, 22

36 And he spake also a parable unto them; No man putteth a piece of a new garment upon an old; if otherwise, then both the new maketh a rent, and the piece that was *taken* out of the new agreeth not with the old.

37 And no man putteth new wine into old ᵀbottles; else the new wine will burst the bottles, and be spilled, and the bottles shall ᵀperish.   *wineskins • be ruined*

38 But new wine must be put into new ᵀbottles; and both are preserved.   *wineskins*

39 No man also having drunk old *wine* ᵀstraightway desireth new: for he saith, The old is better.   *then*

CHAPTER 6

Jesus Works on the Sabbath
Matt. 12:1–8; Mark 2:23–28

AND it came to pass on the second sabbath after the first, that he went through the ᵀcorn fields; and his disciples plucked the ears of corn, and did eat, rubbing *them* in *their* hands.   *grain*

2 And certain of the Pharisees said unto them, Why do ye that ᴿwhich is not ᵀlawful to do on the sabbath days?   Ex. 20:10 • *right*

3 And Jesus answering them said, Have ye not read so much as this, what David did, when himself was ᵀan hungred, and they which were with him;   *hungry*

4 How he went into the house of God, and did take and eat the shewbread, and gave also to them that were with him; which it is not lawful to eat but for the priests alone?

5 And he said unto them, That the Son of man is Lord also of the sabbath.

Jesus Heals on the Sabbath
Matt. 12:9–14; Mark 3:1–6

6 And it came to pass also on another sabbath, that he entered into the synagogue and taught: and there was a man whose right hand was ᵀwithered.   *drawn up*

7 And the scribes and Pharisees watched him, whether he would heal on the sabbath day; that they might find an ᴿaccusation against him.   20:20

8 But he knew their thoughts, and said to the man which had the withered hand, Rise up, and ᵀstand forth in the midst. And he arose and stood forth.   *come forward*

9 Then said Jesus unto them, I will ask you one thing; Is it ᵀlawful on the sabbath days to do good, or to do evil? to save life, or to destroy *it*?   *right*

10 And looking round about upon them all, he said unto the man, Stretch forth thy hand. And he did so: and his hand ᵀwas restored whole as the other.   *made well*

11 And they were filled with madness; and ᵀcommuned one with another what they might do to Jesus.   *conferred*

Selection of the Twelve Apostles
Mark 3:13–19

12 And it came to pass in those days, that he went out into a mountain to pray, and continued all night in prayer to God.

13 And when it was day, he called *unto him* his disciples: and of them he chose twelve, whom also he named apostles;

14 Simon, (^Rwhom he also named Peter,) and Andrew his brother, James and John, Philip and Bartholomew,   John 1:42

15 Matthew and Thomas, James the *son* of Al-phae'-us, and Simon called Ze-lo'-tes,

16 And Judas *the brother* of James, and Judas Is-car'-i-ot, which also was the traitor.

17 And he came down with them, and stood in the plain, and the company of his disciples, and a great multitude of people out of all Ju-dae'-a and Jerusalem, and from the sea coast of Tyre and Si'-don, which came to hear him, and to be healed of their diseases;

18 And they that were ^Tvexed with unclean spirits: and they were healed.   *troubled*

19 And the whole multitude ^Rsought to touch him: for ^Rthere went virtue out of him, and healed *them* all.   Matt. 14:36 • Mark 5:30

The Beatitudes—Matt. 5:1-12

20 And he lifted up his eyes on his disciples, and said, ^RBlessed *be* ye poor: for your's is the kingdom of God.   Matt. 5:3; [11:5]

21 Blessed *are* ye that hunger now: for ye shall be ^Tfilled. ^RBlessed *are* ye that weep now: for ye shall laugh.   *satisfied* • [Is. 61:3]

22 ^RBlessed are ye, when men shall hate you, and when they ^Rshall separate you *from their company*, and shall reproach *you*, and cast out your name as evil, for the Son of man's sake.   1 Pet. 2:19 • [John 16:2]

23 ^RRejoice ye in that day, and leap for joy: for, behold, your reward *is* great in heaven: for ^Rin the like manner did their fathers unto the prophets.   James 1:2 • Acts 7:51

24 ^RBut woe unto you that are rich! for ye have received your consolation.   James 5:1

25 ^RWoe unto you that are full! for ye shall hunger. Woe unto you that laugh now! for ye shall mourn and weep.   [Is. 65:13]

26 ^RWoe unto you, when all men shall speak well of you! for so did their fathers to the false prophets.   [John 15:19; 1 John 4:5]

Rules of Kingdom Life
Matt. 5:39–48; 7:1, 2, 12

27 ^RBut I say unto you which hear, Love your enemies, do good to them which hate you,   Ex. 23:4; Prov. 25:21; Rom. 12:20

28 Bless them that curse you, and pray for them which despitefully use you.

29 And unto him that smiteth thee on the *one* cheek offer also the other; ^Rand him that taketh away thy cloke forbid not *to take thy* coat also.   [1 Cor. 6:7]

30 Give to every man that asketh of thee; and of him that taketh away thy goods ask *them* not again.

31 And as ye would that men should do to you, do ye also to them likewise.

32 For if ye love them which love you, what thank have ye? for sinners also love those that love them.

33 And if ye do good to them which do good to you, what ^Tthank have ye? for sinners also do even the same.   *blessing*

34 ^RAnd if ye lend ^Tto *them* of whom ye hope to receive, what thank have ye? for sinners also lend to sinners, to receive as much again.   Matt. 5:42 • *only to them*

35 But love ye your enemies, and do good, and ^Rlend, hoping for nothing again; and your reward shall be great, and ye shall be the children of the Highest: for he is kind unto the unthankful and *to* the evil.   [Ps. 37:26]

36 Be ye therefore merciful, as your Father also is merciful.

37 Judge not, and ye shall not be judged: condemn not, and ye shall not be condemned: ^Tforgive, and ye shall be forgiven: *forgive others*

38 Give, and it shall be given unto you; good measure, pressed down, and shaken together, and running over, shall men give into your bosom. For with the same measure that ye ^Tmete withal it shall be measured to you again.   *use in measuring anything*

Parable of the Blind Leading the Blind
Matt. 7:3-5, 16-18

39 And he spake a parable unto them, ^RCan the blind lead the blind? shall they not both fall into the ditch?   Matt. 15:14

40 ^RThe disciple is not above his master: but every one that is ^Tperfect shall be as his master.   Matt. 10:24; [John 13:16; 15:20] • *mature*

41 And why beholdest thou the mote that is in thy brother's eye, but perceivest not the ^Tbeam that is in thine own eye?   *log*

42 Either how canst thou say to thy brother, Brother, let me pull out the mote that is in thine eye, when thou thyself beholdest not the beam that is in thine own eye? Thou hypocrite, cast out first the ^Tbeam out of thine own eye, and then shalt thou see clearly to pull out the ^Tmote that is in thy brother's eye.   *log • tiny splinter*

43 For a good tree bringeth not forth ^Tcorrupt fruit; neither doth a corrupt tree bring forth good fruit.   *bad*

44 For every tree is known by his own fruit. For of thorns men do not gather figs, nor of a bramble bush gather they grapes.

45 ^RA good man out of the good treasure of his heart bringeth forth that which is good; and an evil man out of the evil treasure of his heart bringeth forth that which is evil: for ^Rof the abundance of the heart his mouth speaketh.   Matt. 12:35 • Matt. 12:34

Parable of the Two Foundations—Luke 7:21-27

46 ^RAnd why call ye me, Lord, Lord, and do not the things which I say?   Mal. 1:6

47 Whosoever cometh to me, and heareth my sayings, and doeth them, I will shew you to whom he is like:

48 He is like a man which built an house,

and digged deep, and laid the foundation on a rock: and when the flood arose, the stream beat vehemently upon that house, and could not shake it: for it was founded upon a rock.

—49 But he that heareth, and doeth not, is like a man that without a foundation built an house upon the earth; against which the stream did beat vehemently, and immediately it fell; and the Rruin of that house was great.   [Job 8:13; Heb. 10:28–31]

CHAPTER 7

A Centurion's Servant Is Healed—Matt. 8:5–13

NOW when he had ended all his sayings in the audience of the people, he entered into Ca-per'-na-um.

2 And a certain Tcenturion's servant, who was dear unto him, was sick, and Tready to die.   Roman officer's · about

3 And when he heard of Jesus, he sent unto him the elders of the Jews, beseeching him that he would come and heal his servant.

4 And when they came to Jesus, they besought him instantly, saying, That he was worthy for whom he should do this:

5 For he loveth our Tnation, and he hath built us a synagogue.   people

6 Then Jesus went with them. And when he was now not far from the house, the centurion sent friends to him, saying unto him, Lord, trouble not thyself: for I am not worthy that thou shouldest Tenter under my roof: enter my house

7 Wherefore neither thought I myself worthy to come unto thee: but say in a word, and my servant shall be healed.

8 For I also am a man Tset under authority, having under me soldiers, and I say unto one, Go, and he goeth; and to another, Come, and he cometh; and to my servant, Do this, and he doeth it.   placed

9 When Jesus heard these things, he marvelled at him, and turned him about, and said unto the people that followed him, I say unto you, I have not found so great faith, no, not in Israel.

10 And they that were sent, returning to the house, found the servant Twhole that had been sick.   cured

A Widow's Son Is Raised

11 And it came to pass the day after, that he went into a city called Na'-in; and many of his disciples went with him, and Tmuch people.   many

12 Now when he Tcame nigh to the gate of the city, behold, there was a dead man carried out, the only son of his mother, and she was a widow: and much people of the city was with her.   arrived at

13 And when the Lord saw her, he had Tcompassion on her, and said unto her, TWeep not.   pity for her · don't cry

14 And he came and touched the bier: and they that bare him stood still. And he said, Young man, I say unto thee, Arise.

15 And he that was dead sat up, and began to speak. And he Tdelivered him to his mother.   gave him back

16 RAnd there came a fear on all: and they glorified God, saying, That a great prophet is risen up among us; and, RThat God hath visited his people.   1:65 · 1:68

John's Questions Are Answered—Matt. 11:2–6

17 And this Trumour of him went forth throughout all Ju-dae'-a, and throughout all the region round about.   report

18 And the disciples of John Tshewed him of all these things.   told

19 And John calling unto him two of his disciples sent them to Jesus, saying, Art thou he that should come? or Tlook we for another?   should we expect someone else

20 When the men were come unto him, they said, John Baptist hath sent us unto thee, saying, Art thou he that should come? or look we for another?

21 And in that same hour he cured many of their Tinfirmities and Tplagues, and of evil spirits; and unto many that were blind he gave sight.   sicknesses · diseases

22 Then Jesus answering said unto them, Go your way, and tell John what things ye have seen and heard; how that THE BLIND SEE, THE LAME WALK, THE LEPERS ARE CLEANSED, THE DEAF HEAR, THE DEAD ARE RAISED, TO THE POOR THE GOSPEL IS PREACHED.

23 And Rblessed is he, whosoever shall not be Toffended in me.   Ps. 2:12 ★ · doubtful of

Jesus Praises John—Matt. 11:7–15

24 And when the messengers of John were departed, he began to speak unto the people concerning John, What went ye out into the wilderness for to see? A reed Tshaken with the wind?   bending

25 But what went ye out for to see? A man clothed in soft raiment? Behold, they which are gorgeously Tapparelled, and live delicately, are in kings' courts.   dressed

26 But what went ye out for to see? A Tprophet? Yea, I say unto you, and much more than a prophet.   preacher

27 This is he, of whom it is written, BEHOLD, I SEND MY MESSENGER BEFORE THY FACE, WHICH SHALL PREPARE THY WAY BEFORE THEE.

28 For I say unto you, Among those that are born of women there is not a greater Tprophet than John the Baptist: but he that is Tleast in the kingdom of God is greater than he.   preacher · little

29 And all the people that heard *him*, and the publicans, justified God, ^Rbeing baptized with the baptism of John.   Matt. 3:5

30 But the Pharisees and lawyers ^Trejected the counsel of God against themselves, being not baptized of him.   *opposed*

Jesus Criticizes His Generation
Matt. 11:16–19

31 And the Lord said, Whereunto then shall I liken the men of this generation? and to what are they like?

32 They are like unto children sitting in the marketplace, and calling one to another, and saying, We have ^Tpiped unto you, and ye have not danced; we have mourned to you, and ye have not wept.   *played funeral music*

33 For ^RJohn the Baptist came neither eating bread nor drinking wine; and ye say, He hath a devil.   1:15; [Matt. 3:4; Mark 1:6]

34 The Son of man is come eating and drinking; and ye say, Behold a gluttonous man, and a ^Twinebibber, a friend of publicans and ^Tsinners!   *drunkard • outcasts*

35 But wisdom is ^Tjustified of all her children.   *shown true*

A Woman Anoints Jesus' Feet

36 And one of the Pharisees desired him that he would eat with him. And he went into the Pharisee's house, and sat down to meat.

37 And, behold, a woman in the city, which was a sinner, when she knew that *Jesus* sat at meat in the Pharisee's house, brought an alabaster box of ointment,

38 And stood at his feet behind *him* weeping, and began to wash his feet with tears, and did wipe *them* with the hairs of her head, and kissed his feet, and ^Tanointed *them* with the ^Tointment.   *wet • perfume*

39 Now when the Pharisee which had ^Tbidden him saw *it*, he spake within himself, saying, This man, if he were a ^Tprophet, would have known who and what manner of woman *this is* that toucheth him: for she is a sinner.   *invited • true preacher*

The Parable of the Two Debtors

40 And Jesus answering said unto him, Simon, I have somewhat to say unto thee. And he saith, Master, say ^Ton.   *it*

41 There was a certain creditor which had two debtors: the one owed five hundred pence, and the other ^Tfifty.   *50 days' wages*

42 And when they had nothing to pay, he ^Tfrankly forgave them both. Tell me therefore, which of them will love him most? *freely*

43 Simon answered and said, I suppose that *he*, to whom he forgave most. And he said unto him, Thou hast rightly judged.

44 And he turned to the woman, and said unto Simon, Seest thou this woman? I entered into thine house, thou gavest me no

^Rwater for my feet: but she hath washed my feet with tears, and wiped *them* with the hairs of her head.   Gen. 18:4; 1 Tim. 5:10

45 Thou gavest me no kiss: but this woman since the time I came in hath not ^Tceased to kiss my feet.   *stopped kissing*

46 ^RMy head with oil thou didst not anoint: but this woman hath anointed my feet with ^Tointment.   Ps. 23:5 • *perfume*

47 ^RWherefore I say unto thee, Her sins, which are many, are forgiven; for she ^Tloved much: but to whom little is forgiven, *the same* loveth little.   [1 Tim. 1:14] • *showed her love*

48 And he said unto her, ^RThy sins are forgiven.   Matt. 9:2; Mark 2:5

49 And they that sat at meat with him began to say within themselves, ^RWho is this that forgiveth sins also?   [Mark 2:7]

50 And he said to the woman, ^RThy faith hath saved thee; go in peace.   Matt. 9:22

CHAPTER 8

Certain Women Minister to Christ

AND it came to pass afterward, that he went throughout every city and village, preaching and ^Rshewing the glad tidings of the kingdom of God: and the twelve *were* with him,   Matt. 4:23

2 And certain women, which had been healed of evil spirits and ^Tinfirmities, Mary called Mag-da-le′-ne, ^Rout of whom went seven ^Tdevils,   *sicknesses • Mark 16:9 • demons*

3 And Jo-an′-na the wife of Chu′-za Herod's steward, and Susanna, and many others, which ^Tministered unto him of their ^Tsubstance.   *served him with • goods*

Parable of the Sower and Soils
Matt. 13:1–23; Mark 4:1–20

4 And when much people were gathered together, and were come to him out of every city, he spake by a parable:

5 A sower went out to sow his seed: and as he sowed, some fell by the way side; and it was ^Ttrodden down, and the fowls of the air devoured it.   *stepped on*

6 And some fell upon a rock; and as soon as it was sprung up, it ^Twithered away, because it lacked moisture.   *dried up*

7 And some fell among thorns; and the thorns sprang up with it, and choked it.

8 And other fell on good ground, and sprang up, and bare fruit an hundredfold. And when he had said these things, he cried, He that hath ears to hear, let him ^Thear. *listen*

9 And his disciples asked him, saying, What might this parable be?

10 And he said, Unto you it is given to know the mysteries of the kingdom of God: but to others in parables; ^RTHAT SEEING THEY MIGHT NOT SEE, AND HEARING THEY MIGHT NOT UNDERSTAND.   Is. 6:9 •

11 Now the parable is this: The seed is the word of God.

12 Those by the way side are they that hear; then cometh the devil, and ᴿtaketh away the word out of their hearts, lest they should believe and be saved.   2 Cor. 2:11

13 They on the rock *are they*, which, when they hear, receive the word with joy; and these have no root, which for a while believe, and in time of ᵀtemptation fall away.   *testing*

14 And that which fell among thorns are they, which, when they have heard, go forth, and are choked with cares and riches and pleasures of *this* life, and bring no fruit to ᵀperfection.   *harvest*

15 But that on the good ground are they, which in an honest and good heart, having heard the word, keep *it*, and bring forth fruit ᵀwith patience.   *in due time*

Parable of the Lamp—Mark 4:21-25

16 No man, when he hath lighted a candle, covereth it with a vessel, or putteth *it* under a bed; but setteth *it* on a candlestick, that they which enter in may see the light.

17 For nothing is secret, that shall not be made manifest; neither *any thing* hid, that shall not be known and come abroad.

18 Take heed therefore how ye hear: for whosoever hath, to him shall be given; and whosoever hath not, from him shall be taken even that which he seemeth to have.

Christ's True Brethren
Matt. 12:46-50; Mark 3:31-35

19 Then came to him *his* mother and his brethren, and ᴿcould not come at him for the ᵀpress.   Ps. 69:8 • *crowd*

20 And it was told him by *certain* which said, Thy mother and thy brethren stand ᵀwithout, desiring to see thee.   *outside*

21 And he answered and said unto them, My mother and my brethren are these which hear the word of God, and do it.

The Storm Is Stilled
Matt. 8:23-27; Mark 4:35-41

22 Now it came to pass on a certain day, that he went into a ship with his disciples: and he said unto them, Let us go over unto the other side of the lake. And they launched forth.

23 But as they sailed he fell asleep: and there came down a storm of wind on the lake; and ᵀthey were filled *with water*, and were in ᵀjeopardy.   *the boat was • danger*

24 And they came to him, and awoke him, saying, Master, master, we perish. Then he arose, and ᵀrebuked the wind and the raging of the water: and they ceased, and there was a calm.   *commanded*

25 And he said unto them, Where is your faith? And they being afraid wondered,

saying one to another, What manner of man is this! for he commandeth even the winds and water, and they obey him.

Devils Are Cast into Swine
Matt. 8:28-34; Mark 5:1-20

26 And they arrived at the country of the Gad-a-renes', which is over against Galilee.

27 And when he went forth to land, there met him out of the city a certain man, which had ᵀdevils long time, and ᴿware no clothes, neither ᵀabode in *any* house, but in the tombs.   *demons • v. 35 • lived*

28 When he saw Jesus, he ᴿcried out, and fell down before him, and with a loud voice said, What have I to do with thee, Jesus, *thou* Son of God most high? I beseech thee, torment me not.   Acts 16:16, 17

29 (For he had commanded the unclean spirit to come out of the man. For oftentimes it had caught him: and he was kept bound with chains and in ᵀfetters; and he brake the bands, and was driven of the devil into the wilderness.)   *shackles*

30 And Jesus asked him, saying, What is thy name? And he said, Legion: because many devils were entered into him.

31 And they besought him that he would not command them to go out into the deep.

32 And there was there an herd of many swine feeding on the mountain: and they besought him that he would suffer them to enter into them. And he suffered them.

33 Then went the devils out of the man, and entered into the ᵀswine: and the herd ran violently down a steep place into the lake, and were ᵀchoked.   *hogs • drowned*

34 When they that fed *them* saw what was done, they fled, and went and told *it* in the city and in the country.

35 Then they went out to see what was done; and came to Jesus, and found the man, out of whom the devils were departed, sitting ᴿat the feet of Jesus, clothed, and in his right mind: and they were afraid.   Luke 10:39

36 They also which saw *it* told them by what means he that was possessed of the devils was ᵀhealed.   *delivered*

37 Then the whole multitude of the country of the Gad-a-renes' round about besought him to depart from them; for they were taken with great fear: and he went up into the ship, and returned back again.

38 Now the man out of whom the devils were departed besought him that he might be with him: but Jesus sent him away, saying,

39 Return to thine own house, and shew how great things God hath done unto thee. And he went his way, and ᵀpublished throughout the whole city how great things Jesus had done unto him.   *told*

40 And it came to pass, that, when Jesus was returned, the people *gladly* received him: for they were all waiting for him.

A Woman Is Healed
Matt. 9:18–22; Mark 5:21–34

41 And, behold, there came a man named Ja-i′-rus, and he was a ruler of the synagogue: and he fell down at Jesus' feet, and ᵀbesought him that he would come into his house: *asked*

42 For he had one only daughter, about twelve years of age, and she lay a dying. But as he went the people thronged him.

43 And a woman having an issue of blood twelve years, which had spent all her living upon physicians, neither could be ᵀhealed of any,   *cured by*

44 Came behind *him*, and touched the border of his garment: and immediately her issue of blood ᵀstanched.   *dried up*

45 And Jesus said, Who touched me? When all denied, Peter and they that were with him said, Master, the multitude throng thee and ᵀpress *thee*, and sayest thou, Who touched me?   *crowd*

46 And Jesus said, Somebody hath touched me: for I perceive that ᴿvirtueᵀ is gone out of me.   *6:19 • power*

47 And when the woman saw that she was not ᵀhid, she came trembling, and falling down before him, she declared unto him before all the people for what cause she had touched him, and how she was healed immediately.   *unnoticed*

48 And he said unto her, Daughter, be of good comfort: thy faith hath made thee ᵀwhole; go in peace.   *well*

Jairus's Daughter Is Raised
Matt. 9:23–26; Mark 5:35–43

49 While he yet spake, there cometh one from the ruler of the synagogue's *house*, saying to him, Thy daughter is dead; trouble not the Master.

50 But when Jesus heard *it*, he answered him, saying, Fear not: believe only, and she shall be made whole.

51 And when he came into the house, he ᵀsuffered no man to go in, ᵀsave Peter, and James, and John, and the father and the mother of the maiden.   *allowed • except*

52 And all wept, and bewailed her: but he said, Weep not; she is not dead, but sleepeth.

53 And they laughed him to scorn, knowing that she was dead.

54 And he put them all out, and took her by the hand, and called, saying, Maid, arise.

55 And her spirit came again, and she arose ᵀstraightway: and he commanded to give her ᵀmeat.   *immediately • food*

56 And her parents were astonished: but ᴿhe ᵀcharged them that they should tell no man what was done.   *Mark 5:43; 9:30 • instructed*

CHAPTER 9

Twelve Are Sent to Preach
Matt. 10:1–14; 14:1–14; Mark 6:7–16, 30–34

THEN he called his twelve disciples together, and gave them power and authority over all devils, and to cure diseases.

2 And ᴿhe sent them to preach the kingdom of God, and to heal the sick. *Mark 6:12*

3 And he said unto them, Take nothing for *your* journey, neither ᵀstaves, nor ᵀscrip, neither bread, neither money; neither have two coats apiece.   *staff • bag*

4 And whatsoever house ye enter into, there abide, and thence depart.

5 And whosoever will not receive you, when ye go out of that city, ᴿshake off the very dust from your feet for a testimony against them.   *Acts 13:51*

6 And they departed, and went through the towns, preaching the ᵀgospel, and healing every where.   *good news*

7 Now Herod the te′-trarch heard of all that was done by him: and he was ᵀperplexed, because that it was said of some, that John was risen from the dead;   *puzzled*

8 And of some, that E-li′-as had appeared; and ᵀof others, that one of the old prophets was risen again.   *by*

9 And Herod said, John have I beheaded: but who is this, of whom I hear such things? And he ᵀdesired to see him.   *wanted*

10 And the apostles, when they were returned, told him all that they had done. ᴿAnd he took them, and went aside privately into a desert place belonging to the city called Beth-sa′-i-da.   *Matt. 14:13*

11 And the people, when they knew *it*, followed him: and he received them, and spake unto them of the kingdom of God, and healed them that had need of healing.

Five Thousand Are Fed
Matt. 14:15–21; Mark 6:35–44; John 6:1–14

12 And when the day began to ᵀwear away, then came the twelve, and said unto him, Send the multitude away, that they may go into the towns and country round about, and lodge, and get ᵀvictuals: for we are here in a desert place.   *come to an end • food*

13 But he said unto them, Give ye them to eat. And they said, We have no more but five loaves and two fishes; except we should go and buy meat for all this people.

14 For they were about five thousand men. And he said to his disciples, Make them sit down by fifties in a company.

15 And they did so, and made them all sit down.

16 Then he took the five loaves and the two fishes, and looking up to heaven, he blessed them, and brake, and gave to the disciples to set before the multitude.

17 And they did eat, and were all ᵀfilled: and there was taken up of fragments that remained to them twelve baskets.   *satisfied*

Peter's Confession of Faith
Matt. 16:13–21; Mark 8:27–31

18 And it came to pass, as he was alone praying, his disciples were with him: and he asked them, saying, ᵀWhom say the people that I am?   *who*

19 They answering said, John the Baptist; but some *say*, E-li'-as; and others *say*, that one of the old prophets is risen again.

20 He said unto them, But whom say ye that I am? Peter answering said, ᴿThe Christ of God.   John 6:69

21 And he straitly charged them, and commanded *them* to tell no man that thing;

22 Saying, ᴿThe Son of man must suffer many things, and be rejected of the elders and chief priests and scribes, and be slain, and be raised the third day.   24:46; John 19:7 ✶

True Cost of Discipleship
Matt. 16:24–27; Mark 9:34–38

23 And he said to *them* all, If any *man* will come after me, let him deny himself, and take up his cross daily, and follow me.

24 For whosoever will save his life shall lose it: but whosoever will lose his life for my sake, the same shall save it.

25 For what is a man ᵀadvantaged, if he gain the whole world, and lose himself, or be cast away?   *better off*

26 ᴿFor whosoever shall be ashamed of me and of my words, of him shall the Son of man be ashamed, when he shall come in his own glory, and in *his* Father's, and of the holy angels.   2 Tim. 2:12

The Transfiguration
Matt. 16:28—17:9; Mark 9:1-9; 2 Pet. 1:17, 18

27 But I tell you of a truth, ᴿthere be some standing here, which shall not taste of death, till they see the kingdom of God. Acts 7:55, 56 ✶

28 And it came to pass about an eight days after these ᵀsayings, he took Peter and John and James, and went up into a mountain to pray.   *things*

29 And as he prayed, the fashion of his countenance was altered, and his ᵀraiment *was* white *and* ᵀglistering.   *clothing • shining*

30 And, behold, there talked with him two men, which were Moses and E-li'-as:

31 Who appeared in glory, and spake of his ᵀdecease which he should accomplish at Jerusalem.   *death*

32 But Peter and they that were with him were heavy with sleep: and when they ᵀwere awake, they saw his glory, and the two men that stood with him.   *woke up*

33 And it came to pass, as they departed from him, Peter said unto Jesus, Master, it is good for us to be here: and let us make three ᵀtabernacles; one for thee, and one for Moses, and one for E-li'-as: not ᵀknowing what he said.   *tents • realizing*

34 While he thus spake, there came a cloud, and overshadowed them: and they feared as they entered into the cloud.

35 And there came a voice out of the cloud, saying, ᴿThis is my beloved Son: hear him.   Ps. 2:7; Is. 42:1; Matt. 3:17 ✶

36 And when the voice was past, Jesus was found alone. And they kept *it* ᵀclose, and told no man in those days any of those things which they had seen.   *to themselves*

Demoniac Son Is Healed
Matt. 17:14–18; Mark 9:14–27

37 And it came to pass, that on the next day, when they were come down from the hill, much people met him.

38 And, behold, a man of the company cried out, saying, Master, I beseech thee, look upon my son: for he is mine only child.

39 And, lo, a spirit taketh him, and he suddenly crieth out; and it teareth him that he foameth again, and bruising him ᵀhardly departeth from him.   *scarcely*

40 And I ᵀbesought thy disciples to cast him out; and they could not.   *begged*

41 And Jesus answering said, O ᵀfaithless and ᵀperverse generation, how long shall I be with you, and ᵀsuffer you? Bring thy son hither.   *unbelieving • crooked • endure*

42 And as he was yet a coming, the devil threw him down, and tare *him*. And Jesus rebuked the unclean spirit, and healed the child, and delivered him again to his father.

Christ Prophesies His Coming Death
Matt. 17:22, 23; Mark 9:30-32

43 And they were all amazed at the ᵀmighty power of God. But while they wondered every one at all things which Jesus did, he said unto his disciples,   *majesty*

44 Let these sayings sink down into your ears: for the Son of man shall be ᴿdelivered into the ᵀhands of men.   22:54 ✶ • *power*

45 But they understood not this saying, and it was ᵀhid from them, that they perceived it not: and they ᵀfeared to ask him of that saying.   *unknown to • hesitated*

True Greatness—Matt. 18:1-5; Mark 9:33-40

46 Then there arose a reasoning among them, which of them should be greatest.

47 And Jesus, perceiving the thought of their heart, took a child, and set him by him,

48 And said unto them, Whosoever shall receive this child in my name receiveth me: and whosoever shall receive me receiveth him that sent me: for he that is least among you all, the same shall be great.

49 And John answered and said, Master, we saw one casting out ᵀdevils in thy name; and we forbad him, because he followeth not with us.   *demons*

50 And Jesus said unto him, Forbid *him* not: for he that is not against us is for us.

Samaria Rejects Christ

51 And it came to pass, when the time was come that he should be received up, he stedfastly set his face to go to Jerusalem,

52 And sent messengers before his face: and they went, and entered into a village of the Sa-mar'-i-tans, to make ready for him.

53 And ᴿthey did not receive him, because his ᵀface was as though he would go to Jerusalem.   John 4:4, 9 · *plan*

54 And when his disciples James and John saw *this*, they said, Lord, wilt thou that we command fire to come down from heaven, and consume them, even as E-li'-as did?

55 But he turned, and ᵀrebuked them, and said, Ye know not what manner of ᵀspirit ye are of.   *reprimanded · nature*

56 For ᴿthe Son of man is not come to destroy men's lives, but to save *them*. And they went to another village.   John 3:17

True Cost of Discipleship—Matt. 8:18–22

57 And it came to pass, that, as they went in the way, a certain *man* said unto him, Lord, I will follow thee ᵀwhithersoever thou goest.   *wherever*

58 And Jesus said unto him, Foxes have holes, and birds of the air *have* nests; but the Son of man hath not where to lay *his* head.

59 And he said to another, Follow me. But he said, Lord, ᵀsuffer me first to go and bury my father.   *allow*

60 Jesus said unto him, Let the dead bury their ᵀdead: but go thou and preach the kingdom of God.   *own dead*

61 And another also said, Lord, I will follow thee; but let me first go bid them farewell, which are at home at my house.

62 And Jesus said unto him, No man, having put his hand to the plough, and looking back, is fit for the kingdom of God.

CHAPTER 10

Mission of the Seventy

AFTER these things the Lord appointed other seventy also, and sent them two and two before his face into every city and place, whither he himself would come.

2 Therefore said he unto them, ᴿThe harvest truly *is* great, but the labourers *are* few: ᴿpray ye therefore the Lord of the harvest, that he would send forth labourers into his harvest.   Matt. 9:37; John 4:35 · 2 Thess. 3:1

3 Go your ways: ᴿbehold, I send you forth as lambs among wolves.   Matt. 10:16

4 Carry neither purse, nor scrip, nor shoes: and salute no man by the way.

5 ᴿAnd into whatsoever house ye enter, first say, Peace *be* to this house.   Matt. 10:12

6 And if ᵀthe son of peace be there, your peace shall rest upon it: if not, it shall turn to you again.   *they are ready to receive you graciously*

7 ᴿAnd in the same house remain, eating and drinking such things as they give: for ᴿthe labourer is worthy of his hire. Go not from house to house.   Matt. 10:11 · [Matt. 10:10]

8 And into whatsoever city ye enter, and they ᵀreceive you, eat such things as are set before you: *welcome*

9 ᴿAnd heal the sick that are therein, and say unto them, ᴿThe kingdom of God is come nigh unto you.   9:2, 11 · Matt. 3:2

10 But into whatsoever city ye enter, and they receive you not, go your ways out into the streets of the same, and say,

11 Even the very dust of your city, which cleaveth on us, we do wipe off against you: notwithstanding be ye sure of this, that the kingdom of God is come ᵀnigh unto you. *near*

12 But I say unto you, that ᴿit shall be more ᵀtolerable in that day for Sodom, than for that city.   Matt. 10:15; Mark 6:11 · *merciful*

13 ᴿWoe unto thee, Cho-ra'-zin! woe unto thee, Beth-sa'-i-da! ᴿfor if the mighty works had been done in Tyre and Si'-don, which have been done in you, they had a great while ago repented, sitting in sackcloth and ashes.   Matt. 11:21 · Ezek. 3:6

14 But it shall be more tolerable for Tyre and Si'-don at the judgment, than for you.

15 ᴿAnd thou, Ca-per'-na-um, which art ᴿexalted to heaven, ᴿshalt be thrust down to hell.   Matt. 11:23 · Is. 14:13–15; Jer. 51:53 · Ezek. 26:20

16 ᴿHe that heareth you heareth me; and ᴿhe that despiseth you despiseth me; ᴿand he that despiseth me despiseth him that sent me.   John 13:20 · 1 Thess. 4:8 · John 5:23

Return of the Seventy

17 And ᴿthe seventy returned again with joy, saying, Lord, even the devils are subject unto us through thy name.   *v. 1*

18 And he said unto them, I beheld Satan as lightning fall from heaven.

19 Behold, ᴿI give unto you power to tread on serpents and scorpions, and over all the power of the enemy: and nothing shall by any means hurt you.   Mark 16:18

20 Notwithstanding in this rejoice not, that the spirits are subject unto you; but rather rejoice, because ᴿyour names are written in heaven.   [Ex. 32:32, 33]; Ps. 69:28; Rev. 13:8

21 In that hour Jesus rejoiced in spirit, and said, I thank thee, O Father, Lord of heaven and earth, that thou hast hid these things from the wise and prudent, and hast revealed

them unto babes: Reven so, Father; for so it seemed good in thy sight.   Matt. 11:25

22 RAll things are delivered to me of my Father: and Rno man knoweth who the Son is, but the Father; and who the Father is, but the Son, and *he* to whom the Son will reveal *him.*   Matt. 28:18 • John 1:18; [6:44, 46]

23 And he turned him unto *his* disciples, and said privately, RBlessed *are* the eyes which see the things that ye see: Matt. 13:16

24 For I tell you, Rthat many prophets and kings have desired to see those things which ye see, and have not seen *them;* and to hear those things which ye hear, and have not heard *them.*   1 Pet. 1:10

How to Inherit Eternal Life

25 And, behold, a certain lawyer stood up, and Ttempted him, saying, Master, what shall I do to inherit eternal life?   *tested*

26 He said unto him, What is written in the law? how readest thou?

27 And he answering said, THOU SHALT LOVE THE LORD THY GOD WITH ALL THY HEART, AND WITH ALL THY SOUL, AND WITH ALL THY STRENGTH, AND WITH ALL THY MIND; AND RTHY NEIGHBOUR AS THYSELF.   Lev. 19:18

28 And he said unto him, Thou hast answered right: this do, and thou shalt live.

Parable of the Good Samaritan

29 But he, willing to justify himself, said unto Jesus, And who is my neighbour?

30 And Jesus answering said, A certain *man* went down from Jerusalem to Jericho, and fell among thieves, which stripped him of his raiment, and wounded *him,* and departed, leaving *him* half dead.

31 And by chance there came down a certain priest that way: and when he saw him, he passed by on the other side.

32 And likewise a Levite, when he was at the place, came and looked Ton *him,* and Tpassed by on the other side.   *at • walked*

33 But a certain Sa-mar'-i-tan, as he journeyed, came where he was: and when he saw him, he had compassion on him,

34 And went to *him,* and bound up his wounds, pouring in oil and wine, and set him on his own Tbeast, and brought him to an inn, and took care of him.   *animal*

35 And on the morrow when he departed, he took out Ttwo pence, and gave *them* to the host, and said unto him, Take care of him; and whatsoever thou spendest more, when I come again, I will repay thee.   *$64*

36 Which now of these three, Tthinkest thou, was neighbour unto him that fell among the thieves?   *in your opinion*

37 And he said, He that shewed Tmercy on him. Then said Jesus unto him, Go, and do thou likewise.   *kindness to*

Mary and Martha Are Contrasted

38 Now it came to pass, as they went, that he entered into a certain village: and a certain woman named RMartha received him into her house.   John 11:1; 12:2, 3

39 And she had a sister called Mary, Rwhich also Rsat at Jesus' feet, and Theard his word.   [1 Cor. 7:32] • 8:35; Acts 22:3 • *listened to*

40 But Martha was Tcumbered about much serving, and came to him, and said, Lord, dost thou not care that my sister hath left me to serve alone? bid her therefore that she help me.   *burdened*

41 And Jesus answered and said unto her, Martha, Martha, thou art Tcareful and troubled about many things: *anxious*

42 But Rone thing is needful: and Mary hath chosen that good part, which shall not be taken away from her.   [Ps. 27:4]

CHAPTER 11

The Lord's Prayer—Matt. 6:9–13

AND it came to pass, that, as he was praying in a certain place, when he ceased, one of his disciples said unto him, Lord, teach us to pray, as John also taught his disciples.

2 And he said unto them, When ye pray, say, Our Father which art in heaven, Hallowed be thy name. Thy kingdom come. Thy will be done, as in heaven, so in earth.

3 Give us day by day our daily Tbread. *food*

4 And forgive us our sins; for we also forgive every one that is indebted to us. And Tlead us not into temptation; but deliver us from evil.   *bring*

Parable of the Persistent Friend

5 And he said unto them, Which of you shall have a friend, and shall go unto him at midnight, and say unto him, Friend, lend me three loaves;

6 For a friend of mine in his journey is come to me, and I have nothing to Tset before him?   *feed him*

7 And he from within shall answer and say, TTrouble me not: the door is now shut, and my children are with me in bed; I cannot rise and give thee.   *don't bother me*

8 I say unto you, RThough he will not rise and give him, because he is his friend, yet because of his importunity he will rise and give him as many as he needeth.   [18:1]

9 And I say unto you, Ask, and it shall be given you; seek, and ye shall find; knock, and it shall be opened unto you.

10 For every one that asketh receiveth; and he that seeketh findeth; and to him that knocketh it shall be opened.

Parable of the Good Father—Matt. 7:7–11

11 ᴿIf a son shall ask bread of any of you that is a father, will he give him a stone? or if *he ask* a fish, will he for a fish give him a serpent? Matt. 7:9

12 Or if he shall ask an egg, will he ᵀoffer him a scorpion? *give*

13 If ye then, being evil, know how to give good gifts unto your children: how much more shall *your* heavenly Father give the Holy Spirit to them that ask him?

Christ Heals the Demoniac

14 ᴿAnd he was casting out a ᵀdevil, and it was dumb. And it came to pass, when the devil was gone out, the dumb spake; and the people wondered. Matt. 9:32 • *demon*

Christ's Power Not from Satan
Matt. 12:25–30, 43–45; Mark 3:22–27

15 But some of them said, ᴿHe casteth out devils ᴿthrough ᵀBe-el'-ze-bub the chief of the devils. Matt. 9:34 • *vv.* 18, 19 • Beelzebul

16 And others, ᵀtempting *him,* ᵀsought of him a sign from heaven. *testing • asked*

17 But ᴿhe, knowing their thoughts, said unto them, Every kingdom divided against itself is brought to ᵀdesolation; and a house *divided* against a house falleth. John 2:25 • *ruin*

18 If Satan also be ᵀdivided against himself, how shall his kingdom stand? because ye say that I cast out devils ᵀthrough Be-el'-ze-bub. *fighting • with power from*

19 And if I by Be-el'-ze-bub cast out devils, by whom do your sons cast *them* out? therefore shall they be your judges.

20 But if I ᴿwith the ᵀfinger of God cast out devils, ᵀno doubt the kingdom of God is come upon you. Ex. 8:19 • *power • that proves*

21 When a strong man armed keepeth his palace, his goods are in peace:

22 But when a stronger than he shall come upon him, and overcome him, he taketh from him all his armour wherein he trusted, and divideth his ᵀspoils. *goods*

23 He that is not with me is against me: and he that gathereth not with me scattereth.

24 When the ᵀunclean spirit is gone out of a man, ᵀhe walketh through dry places, seeking rest; and finding none, ᵀhe saith, I will return unto my house whence I came out. *evil • it • it*

25 And when he cometh, he findeth *it* swept and ᵀgarnished. *decorated*

26 Then goeth he, and taketh *to him* seven other spirits more wicked than himself; and they enter in, and dwell there: and the last *state* of that man is worse than the first.

27 And it came to pass, as he spake these things, a certain woman of the company lifted up her voice, and said unto him,

ᴿBlessed *is* the womb that bare thee, and the paps which thou hast sucked. 1:28, 48

28 But he said, Yea ᴿrather, blessed *are* they that hear the word of God, and keep it. [8:21; Matt. 7:21]; James 1:25

Christ's Only Sign Is Jonah—Matt. 12:39–42

29 And when the people were gathered thick together, he began to say, This is an evil generation: they seek a sign; and there shall no sign be given it, but ᴿthe sign of Jo'-nas the prophet. 24:46; Acts 10:40 ✿

30 For as ᴿJo'-nas was a sign unto the Nin'-e-vites, ᴿso shall also the Son of man be to this generation. Jon. 1:17; 2:10 • 1 Cor. 15:4 ✿

31 ᴿThe queen of the south shall rise up in the judgment with the men of this generation, and condemn them: for she came from the utmost parts of the earth to hear the wisdom of Solomon; and, behold, a greater than Solomon *is* here. 1 Kin. 10:1

32 The men of Nin'-e-ve shall rise up in the judgment with this generation, and shall condemn it: for ᴿthey repented at the preaching of Jo'-nas; and, behold, a greater than Jo'-nas *is* here. Jon. 3:5

Parable of the Lighted Candle

33 No man, when he hath lighted a candle, putteth *it* in a secret place, neither under a bushel, but on a candlestick, that they which come in may see the light.

34 The light of the body is the eye: therefore when thine eye is ᵀsingle, thy whole body also is full of light; but when *thine eye* is evil, thy body also *is* full of darkness. *clear*

35 Take heed therefore that the light which is in thee be not darkness.

36 If thy whole body therefore *be* full of ᴿlight, having no part dark, the whole shall be full of light, as when the bright shining of a candle doth give thee light. [Ps. 119:18]

"Woes" on the Pharisees

37 And as he spake, a certain Pharisee ᵀbesought him to dine with him: and he went in, and sat down to ᵀmeat. *invited • food*

38 And ᴿwhen the Pharisee saw *it,* he ᵀmarvelled that he had not first washed before dinner. Mark 7:3 • *was surprised*

39 And the Lord said unto him, Now do ye Pharisees make clean the outside of the cup and the platter; but your inward part is full of ravening and wickedness.

40 ᴿYe fools, did not ᵀhe that made that which is without make that which is within also? 1 Cor. 15:36 • *God*

41 ᴿBut rather give alms ᵀof such things as ye have; and, behold, all things are clean unto you. [12:33]; Is. 58:7 • *as you are able*

42 ᴿBut woe unto you, Pharisees! for ye tithe mint and rue and all manner of herbs, and pass over judgment and the love of God:

these ought ye to have done, and not to leave the other undone.   Matt. 23:23

43 ᴿWoe unto you, Pharisees! for ye love the ᵀuppermost seats in the synagogues, and greetings in the markets.   Matt. 23:6 • chief

44 Woe unto you, scribes and Pharisees, hypocrites! for ye are as graves which ᵀappear not, and the men that walk over them are not aware of them.   are invisible

"Woes" on the Lawyers

45 Then answered one of the ᵀlawyers, and said unto him, Master, thus saying thou ᵀreproachest us also.   Mosaic expert • insult

46 And he said, Woe unto you also, ye lawyers! for ye lade men with burdens grievous to be borne, and ye yourselves touch not the burdens with one of your fingers.

47 ᴿWoe unto you! for ye build the ᵀsepulchres of the prophets, and your fathers killed them.   Matt. 23:29 • tombs

48 Truly ye bear witness that ye allow the deeds of your fathers: for they indeed killed them, and ye build their sepulchres.

49 Therefore also said the ᴿwisdom of God, ᴿI will send them prophets and apostles, and some of them they shall slay and persecute: [1 Cor. 1:24, 30; Col. 2:3] • Matt. 23:34

50 That the blood of all the prophets, which was shed from the foundation of the world, may be required of this generation;

51 ᴿFrom the blood of Abel unto ᴿthe blood of Zach-a-ri'-as, which perished between the altar and the temple: verily I say unto you, It shall be required of this generation.   Gen. 4:8 • 2 Chr. 24:20, 21

52 Woe unto you, lawyers! for ye have taken away the key of knowledge: ye entered not in yourselves, and them that were entering in ye ᵀhindered.   kept out

53 And as he said these things unto them, the scribes and the Pharisees began to ᵀurge him vehemently, and to provoke him to speak of many things: criticize

54 Laying wait for him, and ᴿseeking to catch something out of his mouth, that they might accuse him.   Mark 12:13

CHAPTER 12

Christ Warns About Hypocrisy—Matt. 10:26-33

IN the mean time, when there were gathered together an innumerable multitude of people, insomuch that they trode one upon another, he began to say unto his disciples first of all, Beware ye of the leaven of the Pharisees, which is hypocrisy.

2 ᴿFor there is nothing covered, that shall not be revealed; neither hid, that shall not be known.   8:17; Matt. 10:26; Mark 4:22

3 Therefore whatsoever ye have spoken in darkness shall be heard in the light; and that which ye have spoken in the ear in closets shall be proclaimed upon the housetops.

4 And I say unto you my friends, Be not afraid of them that kill the body, and after that have no more that they can do.

5 But I will forewarn you whom ye shall fear: Fear ᵀhim, which after he hath killed hath power to cast into ᵀhell; yea, I say unto you, Fear him.   God, who • destruction

6 Are not five sparrows sold for ᵀtwo farthings, and not one of them is forgotten before God?   1/8 day's wage

7 But even the very hairs of your head are all numbered. Fear not therefore: ye are of more value than many sparrows.

8 ᴿAlso I say unto you, Whosoever shall confess me before men, him shall the Son of man also confess before the angels of God: Matt. 10:32; [Mark 8:38; 2 Tim. 2:12; 1 John 2:23]

9 But he that denieth me before men shall be denied before the angels of God.

10 And whosoever shall speak a word against the Son of man, it shall be forgiven him: but unto him that blasphemeth against the Holy Ghost it shall not be forgiven.

11 And when they bring you unto the synagogues, and unto magistrates, and powers, take ye no thought how or what thing ye shall answer, or what ye shall say:

12 For the Holy Ghost shall teach you in the same hour what ye ought to say.

Parable of the Rich Fool

13 And one of the company said unto him, Master, ᵀspeak to my brother, that he divide the inheritance with me.   tell

14 And he said unto him, Man, who made me a judge or a divider over you?

15 And he said unto them, Take heed, and beware of ᵀcovetousness: for a man's life consisteth not in the abundance of the things which he possesseth.   greed

16 And he spake a parable unto them, saying, The ground of a certain rich man brought forth ᵀplentifully: good crops

17 And he thought within himself, saying, What shall I do, because I have no room where to bestow my fruits?

18 And he said, This will I do: I will pull down my barns, and build greater; and there will I bestow all my fruits and my goods.

19 And I will say to my soul, Soul, thou hast much goods laid up for many years; take thine ease, eat, drink, and be merry.

20 But God said unto him, Thou fool, this night ᴿthy soul shall be required of thee: ᴿthen whose shall those things be, which thou hast provided?   Ps. 52:7 • Jer. 17:11

21 So is he that ᵀlayeth up treasure for himself, and is not rich toward God.   saves

Seek the Kingdom of God—Matt. 6:25-33

22 And he said unto his disciples, Therefore I say unto you, ᵀTake no thought for your life, what ye shall eat; neither for the body, what ye shall put on.   *do not worry*

23 The life is more than ᵀmeat, and the body *is more* than ᵀraiment.   *food · clothes*

24 Consider the ravens: for they neither sow nor reap; which neither have storehouse nor barn; and God feedeth them: how much more are ye ᵀbetter than the fowls?   *worth*

25 And which of you with taking thought can add to his stature one cubit?

26 If ye then be not able to do that thing which is least, why ᵀtake ye thought for the rest?   *do you worry*

27 Consider the lilies how they grow: they toil not, they spin not; and yet I say unto you, that Solomon in all his glory was not ᵀarrayed like one of these.   *dressed*

28 If then God so clothe the grass, which is to day in the field, and to morrow is cast into the oven; how much more *will he clothe* you, ᴿO ye of little faith?   Matt. 6:30

29 And seek not ye what ye shall eat, or what ye shall drink, neither ᵀbe ye of doubtful mind.   *be filled with anxiety*

30 For all these things do the ᵀnations of the world seek after: and your Father knoweth that ye have need of these things.   *heathen*

31 ᴿBut rather ᵀseek ye the kingdom of God; and all these things shall be added unto you.   Matt. 6:33 · *be concerned with*

32 Fear not, little ᴿflock; for ᴿit is your Father's good pleasure to give you the kingdom.   Is. 40:11; Zech. 13:7 ✶ · [Matt. 11:25, 26]

33 ᴿSell that ye have, and give alms; ᴿprovide yourselves bags which wax not old, a treasure in the heavens that faileth not, where no thief approacheth, neither moth ᵀcorrupteth.   Matt. 19:21 · [1 Tim. 6:19] · *ruins*

34 For ᴿwhere your treasure is, there will your heart be also.   Matt. 6:21

Parable of the Expectant Steward

35 ᴿLet your loins be girded about, and ᴿyour lights burning;   [1 Pet. 1:13] · [Matt. 25:1-13]

36 And ye yourselves like unto men that wait for their lord, when he will return from the ᵀwedding; that when he cometh and knocketh, they may open unto him immediately.   *marriage feast*

37 Blessed *are* those servants, whom the lord when he cometh shall find watching: verily I say unto you, that he shall gird himself, and make them to sit down to meat, and will come forth and serve them.

38 And if he shall come in the second watch, or come in the third watch, and find *them* so, blessed are those servants.

39 ᴿAnd this know, that if the ᵀgoodman of the house had known what hour the thief

would come, he would have watched, and not have ᵀsuffered his house to be broken ᵀthrough.   Matt. 24:43 · *owner · allowed · into*

40 ᴿBe ye therefore ready also: for the Son of man cometh at an hour when ye think not.   [21:34, 36]; 1 Thess. 5:6; [2 Pet. 3:12]

Parable of the Faithful Steward
Matt. 24:45-51

41 Then Peter said unto him, Lord, speakest thou this parable unto us, or even to all?

42 And the Lord said, Who then is that faithful and wise steward, whom *his* lord shall make ruler over his household, to give *them their* portion of meat in due season?

43 Blessed *is* that servant, whom his lord when he cometh shall find so doing.

44 Of a truth I say unto you, that he will make him ruler over all that he hath.

45 ᴿBut and if that servant say in his heart, My lord delayeth his coming; and shall begin to beat the menservants and maidens, and to eat and drink, and to be drunken;   Matt. 24:48

46 The lord of that servant will come in a day when he looketh not for *him*, and at an hour when he is not aware, and will ᵀcut him in sunder, and will appoint him his portion with the unbelievers.   *separate him*

47 And ᴿthat servant, which knew his lord's will, and prepared not *himself*, neither did according to his will, shall be beaten with many *stripes*.   Num. 15:30; [John 9:41]

48 But he that knew not, and did commit things worthy of stripes, shall be beaten with few *stripes*. For unto whomsoever much is given, of him shall be much required: and to whom men have committed much, of him they will ask the more.

Christ Warns of the Costs of Discipleship

49 I am come to send fire on the earth; and what will I, if it be already kindled?

50 But ᴿI have a baptism to be baptized with; and how am I ᵀstraitened till it be accomplished!   Matt. 20:22; Mark 10:38 · *burdened*

51 ᴿSuppose ye that I am come to give peace on earth? I tell you, Nay; ᴿbut rather division: *v. 49*; Matt. 10:34 · Mic. 7:6

52 ᴿFor from henceforth there shall be five in one house divided, three against two, and two against three.   Matt. 10:35

53 The father shall be divided against the son, and the son against the father; the mother against the daughter, and the daughter against the mother; the mother in law against her daughter in law, and the daughter in law against her mother in law.

Christ Warns of Not Discerning the Times

54 And he said also to the people, ᴿWhen ye see a cloud rise out of the west, ᵀstraightway ye say, There cometh a shower; and so it is.   Matt. 16:2 · *immediately*

55 And when ye ᵀsee the south wind blow, ye say, There will be heat; and it cometh to pass.   *feel*

56 Ye hypocrites, ye can discern the face of the sky and of the earth; but how is it that ye do not discern this time?

57 Yea, and why even of yourselves ᵀjudge ye not what is right?   *decide*

58 When thou goest with thine adversary to the magistrate, *as thou art* in the way, give diligence that thou mayest be delivered from him; lest he ᵀhale thee to the judge, and the judge deliver thee to the officer, and the officer cast thee into prison.   *bring*

59 I tell thee, thou shalt not depart thence, till thou hast paid the very last mite.

CHAPTER 13

Christ Teaches on Repentance

THERE were present at that season some that told him of the Gal-i-lae'-ans, ᵀwhose blood Pilate had ᵀmingled with their sacrifices.   *whom Pilate killed · mixed*

2 And Jesus answering said unto them, ᵀSuppose ye that these Gal-i-lae'-ans were sinners above all the Gal-i-lae'-ans, because they suffered such things?   *do you think*

3 ᴿI tell you, Nay: but, except ye repent, ye shall all likewise perish.   *v. 5*

4 Or those eighteen, upon whom the tower in Si-lo'-am fell, and slew them, think ye that they were ᵀsinnersᴿ above all men that dwelt in Jerusalem?   *debtors · [Matt. 18:24]*

5 I tell you, Nay: but, ᵀexcept ye repent, ye shall all likewise perish.   *unless*

6 He spake also this parable; ᴿA certain *man* had a fig tree planted in his vineyard; and he came and sought fruit thereon, and found none.   Is. 5:2; Matt. 21:19

7 Then said he unto the dresser of his vineyard, Behold, these three years I come seeking fruit on this fig tree, and find none: cut it down; why cumbereth it the ground?

8 And he answering said unto him, Lord, let it alone this year also, till I shall dig about it, and ᵀdung *it:*   *fertilize*

9 And if it bear fruit, *well:* and if not, *then* after that thou shalt cut it down.

Christ Heals the Crippled Woman

10 And he was teaching in one of the synagogues on the sabbath.

11 And, behold, there was a woman which had ᵀa spirit of infirmity eighteen years, and was bowed together, and could in no wise ᵀlift up *herself.*   *been crippled · straighten up*

12 And when Jesus saw her, he called *her* to *him,* and said unto her, Woman, thou art ᵀloosed from thine infirmity.   *free*

13 ᴿAnd he laid *his* hands on her: and

immediately she was made straight, and ᵀglorified God.   Mark 16:18; Acts 9:17 · *praised*

14 And the ruler of the synagogue answered with indignation, because that Jesus had healed on the sabbath day, and said unto the people, ᴿThere are six days in which men ought to work: in them therefore come and be healed, and not on the sabbath day. Ex. 20:9

15 The Lord then answered him, and said, *Thou* hypocrite, doth not each one of you on the sabbath loose his ox or *his* ass from the stall, and lead *him* away to watering?

16 And ought not this woman, ᴿbeing a daughter of Abraham, whom Satan hath bound, lo, these eighteen years, be loosed from this bond on the sabbath day?   19:9

17 And when he had said these things, all his adversaries were ashamed: and all the people rejoiced for all the ᵀglorious things that were done by him.   *wonderful*

Parable of the Mustard Seed
Matt. 13:31, 32; Mark 4:30–32

18 ᴿThen said he, Unto what is the kingdom of God like? and whereunto shall I resemble it?   Matt. 13:31; Mark 4:30

19 It is like a grain of mustard seed, which a man took, and cast into his garden; and it grew, and waxed a great tree; and the fowls of the air lodged in the branches of it.

Parable of the Leaven—Matt. 13:33–35

20 And again he said, Whereunto shall I liken the kingdom of God?

21 It is like leaven, which a woman took and hid in ᵀthree ᴿmeasures of meal, till the whole was leavened.   6.52 bushels · Matt. 13:33

The Way into the Kingdom

22 ᴿAnd he went through the cities and villages, teaching, and journeying toward Jerusalem.   Matt. 9:35; Mark 6:6

23 Then said one unto him, Lord, are there few that be saved? And he said unto them,

24 Strive to enter in at the ᵀstrait gate: for many, I say unto you, will seek to enter in, and shall not be able.   *narrow*

25 ᴿWhen once the master of the house is risen up, and hath shut to the door, and ye begin to stand without, and to knock at the door, saying, Lord, Lord, open unto us; and he shall answer and say unto you, I know you not whence ye are: [Ps. 32:6]

26 Then shall ye begin to say, We have eaten and drunk ᵀin thy presence, and thou hast taught in our streets.   *with you*

27 ᴿBut he shall say, I tell you, I know you not whence ye are; ᴿdepart from me, all *ye* workers of iniquity.   *v. 25 · Ps. 6:8*

28 ᴿThere shall be weeping and gnashing of teeth, ᴿwhen ye shall see Abraham, and Isaac, and Jacob, and all the prophets, in the

kingdom of God, and you *yourselves* thrust out.   Matt. 8:12; 13:42; 24:51 • Matt. 8:11

29 And they shall come from the east, and *from* the west, and from the north, and *from* the south, and shall sit ᵀdown in the kingdom of God.   *at the table*

30 ᴿAnd, behold, there are last which shall be first, and there are first which shall be last.   Matt. 19:30; [20:16]; Mark 10:31

Christ Mourns over Jerusalem

31 The same day there came certain of the Pharisees, saying unto him, Get thee out, and depart hence: for Herod ᵀwill kill thee.   *wants to*

32 And he said unto them, Go ye, and tell that fox, Behold, I cast out devils, and I do cures to day and to morrow, and ᴿthe third *day* I shall be perfected.   24:46; Acts 10:40 ☆

33 Nevertheless I must walk to day, and to morrow, and the *day* following: for it cannot be that a prophet perish out of Jerusalem.

34 ᴿO Jerusalem, Jerusalem, which killest the prophets, and stonest them that are sent unto thee; how often would I have gathered ᵀthy children together, as a hen *doth gather* her brood under *her* wings, and ye would not!   Matt. 23:37 • *all your people*

35 ᴿBehold, your house is left unto you ᵀdesolate: and verily I say unto you, Ye shall not see me, until *the time* come when ye shall say, ᴿBLESSED *IS* HE THAT COMETH IN THE NAME OF THE LORD.   Jer. 22:5 ☆ • *empty* • Ps. 118:26

CHAPTER 14

Instruction on the Sabbath

AND it came to pass, as he went into the house of one of the chief Pharisees to eat bread on the sabbath day, that they ᵀwatched him.   *watched him closely*

2 And, behold, there was a certain man before him which had the dropsy.

3 And Jesus answering spake unto the lawyers and Pharisees, saying, ᴿIs it ᵀlawful to heal on the sabbath day?   Matt. 12:10 • *right*

4 And they held their peace. And he took *him*, and healed him, and let him go;

5 And answered them, saying, ᴿWhich of you shall have an ass or an ox fallen into a pit, and will not straightway pull him out on the sabbath day?   13:15; [Ex. 23:5; Deut. 22:4]

6 And they ᵀcould not answer him ᵀagain to these things.   *were not able* • *back*

Parable of the Ambitious Guest

7 And he put forth a parable to those which were bidden, when he marked how they chose out the ᵀchief ᵀrooms; saying unto them,   *best* • *seats*

8 When thou art bidden of any *man* to a ᵀwedding, sit not down in the ᵀhighest room; lest a more honourable man than thou be bidden of him;   *marriage feast* • *chief seat*

9 And ᵀhe that bade thee and him come and say to thee, Give this man place; and thou begin with ᵀshame to take the lowest ᵀroom.   *the host* • *embarrassment* • *place*

10 ᴿBut when thou art bidden, go and sit down in the lowest room; that when he that bade thee cometh, he may say unto thee, Friend, go up higher: then shalt thou have ᵀworship in the presence of them that sit at meat with thee.   Prov. 25:6, 7 • *honour*

11 ᴿFor whosoever exalteth himself shall be ᵀabased; and he that humbleth himself shall be exalted.   Ps. 18:27; [1 Pet. 5:5] • *humbled*

12 Then said he also to him that bade him, When thou makest a dinner or a supper, call not thy friends, nor thy brethren, neither thy kinsmen, nor *thy* rich neighbours; lest they also bid thee again, and a recompence be made thee.

13 But when thou makest a feast, call the poor, the maimed, the lame, the blind:

14 And thou shalt be blessed; for they cannot recompense thee: for thou shalt be recompensed at the resurrection of the just.

Parable of the Great Supper

15 And when one of them that ᵀsat at meat with him heard these things, he said unto him, ᴿBlessed *is* he that shall eat bread in the kingdom of God.   *ate* • Rev. 19:9

16 Then said he unto him, A certain man made a great supper, and bade many:

17 And ᴿsent his servant at supper time to say to them that were bidden, Come; for all things are now ready.   Prov. 9:2, 5

18 And they all with one *consent* began to make excuse. The first said unto him, I have bought a piece of ground, and I must needs go and see it: I pray thee have me excused.

19 And another said, I have bought five yoke of oxen, and I go to ᵀprove them: I pray thee have me excused.   *try*

20 And another said, ᴿI have married a wife, and therefore I cannot come.   Deut. 24:5

21 So that servant came, and shewed his lord these things. Then the master of the house being angry said to his servant, Go out quickly into the streets and lanes of the city, and bring in hither the poor, and the maimed, and the halt, and the blind.

22 And the servant said, Lord, it is done as thou hast commanded, and yet there is ᵀroom.   *more room*

23 And the lord said unto the servant, Go out into the highways and hedges, and ᵀcompel *them* to come in, that my house may be filled.   *urge*

24 For I say unto you, ᴿThat none of those men which were bidden shall taste of my supper.   [Matt. 21:43; 22:8; Acts 13:46]

Christ Teaches on Discipleship

25 And there went great multitudes with him: and he turned, and said unto them,

26 If any *man* come to me, and hate not his father, and mother, and wife, and children, and brethren, and sisters, yea, and his own life also, he cannot be my disciple.

27 And ᴿwhosoever doth not bear his cross, and come after me, cannot be my disciple.   9:23; Matt. 16:24; Mark 8:34; [2 Tim. 3:12]

28 For ᴿwhich of you, intending to build a tower, sitteth not down first, and ᵀcounteth the cost, whether he have ᵀ*sufficient* to finish *it?*   Prov. 24:27 • *figures • enough money*

29 Lest haply, after he hath laid the foundation, and is not able to finish *it*, all that behold *it* begin to ᵀmock him,   *ridicule*

30 Saying, This man began to build, and was not able to finish.

31 Or what king, going to make war against another king, sitteth not down first, and ᵀconsulteth whether he be able with ten thousand to meet him that cometh against him with twenty thousand?   *considers*

32 Or else, while the other is yet a great way off, he sendeth ᵀan ambassage, and desireth conditions of peace.   *a delegation*

33 So likewise, whosoever he be of you that ᵀforsaketh not all that he hath, he cannot be my disciple.   *does not give up all*

34 Salt *is* good: but if the salt have lost his savour, wherewith shall it be seasoned?

35 It is neither fit for the land, nor yet for the dunghill; *but* men cast it out. He that hath ears to hear, let him hear.

CHAPTER 15

Parable of the Lost Sheep—Matt. 18:12-14

THEN drew near unto him all the publicans and sinners for to hear him.

2 And the Pharisees and scribes murmured, saying, This man ᵀreceiveth sinners, and eateth with them.   *is friendly with*

3 And he spake this ᵀparable unto them, saying,   *illustration*

4 What man of you, having an hundred sheep, if he lose one of them, doth not leave the ninety and nine in the wilderness, and go after that which is lost, until he find it?

5 And when he hath found *it*, he layeth *it* on his shoulders, rejoicing.

6 And when he cometh home, he calleth together *his* friends and neighbours, saying unto them, Rejoice with me; for I have found my sheep ᴿwhich was lost.   [1 Pet. 2:10]

7 I say unto you, that likewise joy shall be in heaven over one sinner that repenteth, more than over ninety and nine ᵀjust persons, which need no repentance.   *good*

Parable of the Lost Coin

8 Either what woman having ten pieces of silver, if she lose ᵀone piece, doth not light a candle, and sweep the house, and seek diligently till she find *it?*   *1 day's wages*

9 And when she hath found *it*, she calleth *her* friends and *her* neighbours together, saying, Rejoice with me; for I have found the ᵀpiece which I had lost.   *coin*

10 Likewise, I say unto you, there is ᴿjoy in the presence of the angels of God over one sinner that repenteth.   Acts 11:18

Parable of the Lost Son

11 And he said, A certain man had two sons:

12 And the younger of them said to *his* father, Father, give me the ᵀportion of goods that falleth *to me.* And he divided unto them ᴿhis ᵀliving.   *share • Mark 12:44 • estate*

13 And not many days after the younger son gathered all together, and took his journey into a far country, and there wasted his substance with riotous living.

14 And when he had spent all, there arose a ᵀmighty famine in that land; and he ᵀbegan to be in want.   *severe • had nothing*

15 And he went and ᵀjoined himself to a citizen of that country; and he sent him into his fields to feed swine.   *united*

16 And he ᵀwould fain have filled his belly with the husks that the swine did eat: and no man gave unto him.   *longed to*

17 And when he came to himself, he said, How many hired servants of my father's have bread enough and to spare, and I ᵀperish with hunger!   *die*

18 I will arise and go to my father, and will say unto him, Father, I have sinned against heaven, and ᵀbefore thee,   *against*

19 And am no more ᵀworthy to be called thy son: make me as one of thy hired ᵀservants.   *fit • workers*

20 And he arose, and came to his father. But when he was yet a great way off, his father saw him, and had compassion, and ran, and fell on his neck, and kissed him.

21 And the son said unto him, Father, I have sinned against heaven, ᴿand in thy sight, and am no more worthy to be called thy son.   Ps. 51:4

22 But the father said to his servants, Bring forth the best robe, and put *it* on him; and put a ring on his ᵀhand, and shoes on *his* feet: *finger*

23 ᴿAnd bring hither the fatted calf, and kill *it;* and let us eat, and be merry: *v.* 32

24 ᴿFor this my son was dead, and is alive again; he was lost, and is found. And they began to be merry.   [Eph. 2:15; 5:14]

25 Now his elder son was in the field: and as he came and drew ᵀnigh to the house, he heard musick and dancing.   *near*

26 And he called one of the servants, and asked what these things meant.

27 And he said unto him, Thy brother is ᵀcome; and thy father hath killed the ᵀfatted calf, because he hath ᵀreceived him safe and sound.   *home • prize • returned*

28 And he was angry, and would not go in: therefore came his father out, and ᵀintreated him.   *called for*

29 And he answering said to *his* father, Lo, these many years do I serve thee, neither transgressed I at any time thy commandment: and yet thou never gavest me a kid, that I might make merry with my friends:

30 But as soon as this thy son was come, which hath devoured thy living with harlots, thou hast killed for him the fatted calf.

31 And he said unto him, Son, thou art ever with me, and all that I have is thine.

32 It was ᵀmeet that we should make merry, and be glad: ᴿfor this thy brother was dead, and is alive again; and was lost, and is found.   *fitting • v. 24*

CHAPTER 16

Parable of the Unjust Servant

AND he said also unto his disciples, There was a certain rich man, which had a steward; and the same was accused unto him that he had wasted his goods.

2 And he called him, and said unto him, How is it that I hear this of thee? give an account of thy ᵀstewardship; for thou mayest be no longer steward.   *management*

3 Then the steward said within himself, What shall I do? for my lord ᵀtaketh away from me the stewardship: I cannot dig; to beg I am ashamed.   *dismissed me from*

4 I am resolved what to do, that, when I am put out of the stewardship, they may receive me into their houses.

5 So he called every one of his lord's debtors *unto him*, and said unto the first, How much owest thou unto my lord?

6 And he said, An ᵀhundred measures of oil. And he said unto him, Take thy bill, and sit down quickly, and write fifty.   *600 gal.*

7 Then said he to another, And how much owest thou? And he said, An ᵀhundred measures of wheat. And he said unto him, Take thy bill, and write fourscore.   *65.2 bushels*

8 And the lord commended the unjust steward, because he had done wisely: for the children of this world are in their generation wiser than the children of light.

9 And I say unto you, Make to yourselves friends of the mammon of unrighteousness; that, when ye fail, they may receive you into everlasting habitations.

10 He that is faithful in that which is least is faithful also in much: and he that is unjust in the least is unjust also in much.

11 If therefore ye have not been faithful in the unrighteous ᵀmammon, who will commit to your trust the true *riches*?   *riches*

12 And if ye have not been faithful in that which is another man's, who shall give you that which is your ᴿown?   [1 Pet. 1: 3, 4]

13 ᴿNo servant can serve two masters: for either he will hate the one, and love the other; or else he will hold to the one, and despise the other. Ye cannot serve God and ᵀmammon.   Matt. 6:24 • *money*

Christ Warns the Pharisees

14 And the Pharisees also, who were ᵀcovetous, heard all these things: and they ᵀderided him.   *money lovers • turned up their noses at*

15 And he said unto them, Ye are they which justify yourselves before men; but God ᵀknoweth your hearts: for that which is highly esteemed among men is abomination in the sight of God.   *understands*

16 The law and the prophets *were* until John: since that time the kingdom of God is preached, and every man presseth into it.

17 And it is easier for heaven and earth to pass, than one tittle of the law to fail.

Christ Teaches on Divorce

18 Whosoever putteth away his wife, and marrieth another, committeth adultery: and whosoever marrieth her that is put away from *her* husband committeth adultery.

Parable of the Rich Man and Lazarus

19 There was a certain rich man, which was clothed in purple and fine linen, and fared ᵀsumptuously every day: *lavishly*

20 And there was a certain beggar named Laz'-a-rus, which was ᵀlaid at his gate, full of sores,   *brought to*

21 And desiring to be fed with the crumbs which fell from the rich man's table: moreover the dogs came and licked his sores.

22 And it came to pass, that the beggar died, and ᴿwas carried by the angels into Abraham's bosom: the rich man also died, and was buried;   Matt. 8:11; Heb. 1:14

23 And in hell he lift up his eyes, being in ᵀtorments, and seeth Abraham afar off, and Laz'-a-rus in his bosom.   *pain*

24 And he cried and said, Father Abraham, have mercy on me, and send Laz'-a-rus, that he may dip the tip of his finger in water, and cool my tongue; for I ᴿam ᵀtormented in this flame.   [Is. 66:24] • *suffering*

25 But Abraham said, Son, ᴿremember that thou in thy lifetime receivedst thy good things, and likewise Laz'-a-rus evil things: but now he is comforted, and thou art ᵀtormented.   6:24; Job 21:13 • *in pain*

26 And beside all this, between us and you there is a great gulf fixed: so that they which would pass from ᵀhence to you cannot; neither can they pass to us, that *would come* from ᵀthence.   *here • there*

27 Then he said, I pray thee therefore, father, that thou wouldest send ᵀhim to my father's house: *Lazarus*

28 For I have five brethren; that he may ᵀtestify unto them, lest they also come into this place of ᵀtorment.   *witness • suffering*

29 Abraham saith unto him, They have Moses and the prophets; let them hear them.

30 And he said, ᵀNay, father Abraham: but if one went unto them from the dead, they will repent.   *that is not enough*

31 And he said unto him, If they hear not Moses and the prophets, neither will they be persuaded, though one rose from the dead.

CHAPTER 17

Christ Teaches on Offences

THEN said he unto the disciples, It is impossible but that offences will come: but woe *unto him*, through whom they come!

2 It were better for him that a millstone were hanged about his neck, and he cast into the sea, than that he should ᵀoffend one of these little ones.   *bring injury to*

3 Take heed to yourselves: If thy brother trespass against thee, ᵀrebuke him; and if he repent, forgive him.   *confront*

4 And if he ᵀtrespass against thee seven times in a day, and seven times in a day turn again to thee, saying, I repent; thou shalt forgive him.   *sin*

5 And the apostles said unto the Lord, ᵀIncrease our faith.   *make our faith greater*

6 ᴿAnd the Lord said, If ye had faith as a grain of mustard seed, ye might say unto this sycamine tree, Be thou plucked up by the root, and be thou planted in the sea; and it should obey you.   [Mark 9:23]; 11:23

7 But which of you, having a servant plowing or feeding cattle, will say unto him by and by, when he is come from the field, Go and sit down to ᵀmeat?   *eat*

8 And will not rather say unto him, Make ready wherewith I may ᵀsup, and ᵀgird thyself, ᴿand serve me, till I have eaten and drunken; and afterward thou shalt eat and drink?   *eat • put on your apron • [12:37]*

9 Doth he thank that servant because he did the things that were commanded him? I ᵀtrow not.   *think*

10 So likewise ye, when ye shall have done all those things which are commanded you, say, We are unprofitable servants: we have done that which was our duty to do.

Christ Cleanses Ten Lepers

11 And it came to pass, ᴿas he went to Jerusalem, that he passed through the midst of Sa-ma'-ri-a and Galilee.   John 4:4

12 And as he entered into a certain village, there met him ten men that were lepers, ᴿwhich stood afar off: Lev. 13:46

13 And they lifted up *their* voices, and said, Jesus, Master, have mercy on us.

14 And when he saw *them*, he said unto them, ᴿGo shew yourselves unto the priests. And it came to pass, that, as they went, they were cleansed.   5:14; Matt. 8:4

15 And one of them, when he saw that he was healed, turned back, and with a loud voice ᵀglorified God,   *thanked*

16 And ᵀfell down on *his* face at his feet, giving him thanks: and he was a Sa-mar'-i-tan.   *threw himself to the ground*

17 And Jesus answering said, Were there not ten cleansed? but where *are* the nine?

18 There are not found that returned to give glory to God, save this stranger.

19 And he said unto him, Arise, go thy way: thy faith hath made thee whole.

Christ Teaches on the Second Coming

20 And when he was demanded of the Pharisees, when the kingdom of God should come, he answered them and said, The kingdom of God cometh not with observation:

21 Neither shall they say, Lo here! or, lo there! for, behold, ᴿthe kingdom of God is ᵀwithin you.   [Rom. 14:17] • *among you*

22 And he said unto the disciples, ᴿThe days will come, when ye shall desire to see one of the days of the Son of man, and ye shall not see *it*.   Matt. 9:15; [John 17:12]

23 ᴿAnd they shall say to you, See here; or, see there: go not after *them*, nor follow *them*.   [21:8]; Matt. 24:23; Mark 13:21

24 ᴿFor as the lightning, that lighteneth out of the one *part* under heaven, shineth unto the other *part* under heaven; so shall also the Son of man be in his day.   Matt. 24:27

25 But first must he ᵀsuffer many things, and be rejected of this generation.   *endure*

26 ᴿAnd as it was in the days of No'-e, so shall it be also in the days of the Son of man.   [Gen. 6]; Matt. 24:37

27 They did eat, they drank, they married wives, they were given in marriage, until the ᴿday that No'-e entered into the ark, and the flood came, and destroyed them all.   Gen. 7:1-16

28 Likewise also as it was in the days of Lot; they did eat, they drank, they bought, they sold, they planted, they builded;

29 But ᴿthe same day that Lot went out of Sodom it rained fire and brimstone from heaven, and destroyed *them* all.   Gen. 19:16, 24

30 Even thus shall it be in the day when the Son of man ᴿis revealed.   [2 Thess. 1:7]

31 In that day, he ᴿwhich shall be upon the housetop, and his ᵀstuff in the house, let him not come down to take it away: and he that is in the field, let him likewise not return back.   Matt. 24:17; Mark 13:15 • *property*

32 ᴿRemember Lot's wife.   Gen. 19:26

33 ᴿWhosoever shall seek to save his life shall lose it; and whosoever shall lose his life shall ᵀpreserve it.   9:24; John 12:25 • *save*

34 [R]I tell you, in that night there shall be two *men* in one bed; the one shall be taken, and the other shall be left.   Matt. 24:40

35 Two *women* shall be grinding together; the one shall be taken, and the other left.

36 Two *men* shall be in the field; the one shall be taken, and the other left.

37 And they answered and said unto him, [R]Where, Lord? And he said unto them, Wheresoever the body *is*, thither will the [T]eagles be gathered together. Matt. 24:28 • *vultures*

CHAPTER 18

Parable of the Woman and the Judge

AND he spake a parable unto them *to this end*, that men ought [R]always to pray, and not to [T]faint;   Col. 4:2 • *lose heart*

2 Saying, There was [T]in a city a judge, which feared not God, neither [T]regarded man: *in a certain city • respected*

3 And there was a widow in that city; and she came unto him, saying, [T]Avenge me of mine adversary.   *help me against*

4 And he would not for a while: but afterward he said within himself, Though I fear not God, nor [R]regard man;   Heb. 12:9

5 [R]Yet because this widow troubleth me, I will [T]avenge her, lest by her continual coming she weary me.   11:8 • *give her justice*

6 And the Lord said, Hear what the [T]unjust judge saith.   *corrupt*

7 And shall not God [T]avenge his own elect, which cry day and night unto him, though he bear long with them?   *protect*

8 I tell you that he will avenge them speedily. Nevertheless when the Son of man cometh, shall he find faith on the earth?

Parable of the Pharisee and the Publican

9 And he spake this parable unto certain [R]which trusted in themselves that they were righteous, and despised others: 10:29

10 Two men went up into the temple to pray; the one a Pharisee, and the other a [T]publican.   *tax collector*

11 The Pharisee stood and prayed thus with himself, God, I thank thee, that I am not as other men *are*, extortioners, unjust, adulterers, or even as this publican.

12 I fast twice in the week, I give [T]tithes of all that I possess.   *one tenth*

13 And the publican, standing afar off, would not lift up so much as *his* eyes unto heaven, but smote upon his breast, saying, God be merciful to me a sinner.

14 I tell you, this man went down to his house justified *rather* than the other: [R]for every one that exalteth himself shall be abased; and he that humbleth himself shall be exalted.   14:11; Matt. 23:12; [James 4:6; 1 Pet. 5:5]

Christ Blesses the Children
Matt. 19:13–15; Mark 10:13–16

15 And they brought unto him also infants, that he would touch them: but when *his* disciples saw *it*, they rebuked them.

16 But Jesus called them *unto him*, and said, Suffer little children to come unto me, and forbid them not: for [R]of such is the kingdom of God.   [1 Pet. 2:2]

17 Verily I say unto you, Whosoever shall not receive the kingdom of God as a little child shall in no wise enter therein.

Rich Young Ruler
Matt. 19:16–26; Mark 10:17–27

18 And a certain ruler asked him, saying, Good Master, what shall I do to [T]inherit eternal life?   *acquire*

19 And Jesus said unto him, Why callest thou me good? none *is* good, save [T]one, *that is*, God.   *one alone*

20 Thou knowest the commandments, [R]Do NOT COMMIT ADULTERY, DO NOT KILL, DO NOT STEAL, DO NOT BEAR FALSE WITNESS, [R]HONOUR THY FATHER AND THY MOTHER.   Eph. 6:2

21 And he said, All these have I [T]kept from my youth up.   *honoured*

22 Now when Jesus heard these things, he said unto him, Yet lackest thou one thing: sell all that thou hast, and distribute unto the poor, and thou shalt have treasure in heaven: and come, follow me.

23 And when he heard this, he was very [T]sorrowful: for he was very rich.   *sad*

24 And when Jesus saw that he was very sorrowful, he said, [T]How hardly shall they that have riches enter into the kingdom of God!   *with what difficulty*

25 For it is easier for a camel to go through a needle's eye, than for a rich man to enter into the kingdom of God.

26 And they that heard *it* said, Who then can be saved?

27 And he said, The things which are impossible with men are possible with God.

Christ Will Reward Sacrifice
Matt. 19:27–29; Mark 10:28–30

28 Then Peter said, Lo, we have left [T]all, and followed thee.   *our homes*

29 And he said unto them, Verily I say unto you, There is no man that hath left house, or parents, or brethren, or wife, or children, for the kingdom of God's sake,

30 [R]Who shall not receive [T]manifold more in this present time, and in the world to come life everlasting.   Job 42:10 • *many times*

Christ Foretells His Death and Resurrection
Matt. 20:17–19; Mark 10:32–34

31 [R]Then he took *unto him* the twelve, and said unto them, Behold, we go up to Jerusa-

lem, and all things ^Rthat are written by the prophets concerning the Son of man shall be ^Taccomplished. Matt. 16:21 • Ps. 22 • *done*

32 ^RFor he shall be delivered unto the Gentiles, and shall be mocked, and spitefully entreated, and spitted on: 23:1, 11, 36; Mark 15:19 ☆

33 ^RAnd they shall ^Tscourge *him*, and put him to death: and the third day he shall rise ^Tagain. 23:46; 24:46; John 19:1 ☆ • *whip • to life*

34 ^RAnd they understood none of these things: and this saying was ^Thid from them, neither knew they the things which were spoken. Mark 9:32; John 10:6; [12:16] • *unknown to*

Christ Heals Bartimaeus
Matt. 20:29–34; Mark 10:46–52

35 And it came to pass, that as he was come nigh unto Jericho, a certain blind man sat by the way side begging:

36 And hearing the multitude pass by, he asked ^Twhat it meant. *what is this?*

37 And they told him, that Jesus of Nazareth passeth by.

38 And he cried, saying, Jesus, *thou* son of David, ^Thave mercy on me. *heal*

39 And they which went before ^Trebuked him, that he should hold his peace: but he cried so much the more, *Thou* son of David, have mercy on me. *tried to silence*

40 And Jesus ^Tstood, and commanded him to be brought unto him: and when he was come near, he asked him, *stopped*

41 Saying, What wilt thou that I shall do unto thee? And he said, Lord, that ^TI may receive my sight. *I want to see*

42 And Jesus said unto him, Receive thy sight: ^Rthy faith hath saved thee. 17:19

43 And immediately he received his sight, and followed him, ^Rglorifying^T God: and all the people, when they saw *it*, gave praise unto God. 5:26; Acts 4:21; 11:18 • *praising*

CHAPTER 19

Christ Abides with Zacchaeus

A ND Jesus entered and ^Tpassed through Jericho. *was passing*

2 And, behold, *there was* a man named Zac-chae'-us, which was the chief among the ^Tpublicans, and he was rich. *tax collectors*

3 And he sought to see Jesus who he was; and could not for the ^Tpress, because he was ^Tlittle of stature. *crowd • a short man*

4 And he ran before, and climbed up into a ^Tsycomore tree to see him: for he was to pass that *way*. *inferior fig tree*

5 And when Jesus came to the place, he looked up, and saw him, and said unto him, Zac-chae'-us, ^Tmake haste, and come down; for to day I must abide at thy house. *hurry*

6 And he ^Tmade haste, and came down, and received him joyfully. *hurried*

7 And when they saw *it*, they all ^Tmurmured, saying, That he was gone to be guest with a man that is a sinner. *complained*

8 And Zac-chae'-us stood, and said unto the Lord; Behold, Lord, the half of my goods I give to the poor; and if I have taken any thing from any man by false accusation, ^RI restore *him* fourfold. Ex. 22:1

9 And Jesus said unto him, This day is salvation come to this house, forsomuch as he also is ^Ra son of Abraham. [13:16]

10 ^RFor the Son of man is come to seek and to save that which was lost. Matt. 18:11

Christ Gives the Parable of the Ten Pounds

11 And as they heard these things, he added and spake a parable, because he was ^Tnigh to Jerusalem, and because ^Rthey thought that the kingdom of God should immediately appear. *almost • Acts 1:6*

12 He said therefore, A certain nobleman went into a far country to receive for himself a kingdom, and to return.

13 And he called his ten servants, and delivered them ^Tten pounds, and said unto them, ^TOccupy till I come. *$64,000 • trade with this*

14 ^RBut his citizens hated him, and sent a message after him, saying, We will not have this *man* to reign over us. [John 1:11]

15 And it came to pass, that when he was returned, having received the kingdom, then he commanded these servants to be called unto him, to whom he had given the ^Tmoney, that he might know how much every man had gained by trading. *silver*

16 Then came the first, saying, Lord, thy ^Tpound hath gained ten pounds. *$6,400*

17 And he said unto him, ^TWell, thou good servant: because thou hast been ^Rfaithful in a very little, have thou authority over ten cities. *well done • 16:10; Matt. 25:21*

18 And the second came, saying, Lord, thy pound hath gained ^Tfive pounds. *$32,000*

19 And he said likewise to him, Be thou also ^Tover five cities. *in charge of*

20 And another came, saying, Lord, behold, *here is* thy ^Tpound, which I have kept ^Tlaid up in a napkin: *$6,400 • hidden*

21 ^RFor I feared thee, because thou art ^Tan austere man: thou takest up that thou layedst not down, and reapest that thou didst not sow. *Matt. 25:24 • a harsh*

22 And he saith unto him, ^ROut of thine own mouth will I judge thee, *thou* wicked servant. Thou knewest that I was an austere man, taking up that I laid not down, and reaping that I did not sow: 2 Sam. 1:16

23 Wherefore then gavest not thou my money into the bank, that at my coming I might have required mine own with usury?

24 And he said unto them that stood by, Take from him the ^Tpound, and give *it* to him that hath ten pounds. *$6,400*

25 (And they said unto him, Lord, he hath ᵀten pounds.)   *$64,000*

26 For I say unto you, ᴿThat unto every one which hath shall be given; and from him that hath not, even that he hath shall be taken away from him.   Matt. 13:12; 25:29

27 But those mine enemies, which would not that I should ᵀreign over them, bring hither, and slay *them* before me.   *be king*

The Triumphal Entry
Matt. 21:1-9; Mark 11:1-10; John 12:12-19

28 And when he had thus spoken, he went before, ascending up to Jerusalem.

29 And it came to pass, when he was come nigh to Beth'-pha-ge and Beth'-a-ny, at the mount called *the mount* of Olives, he sent two of his disciples,

30 Saying, Go ye into the village over against *you*; in the which at your entering ye shall find a colt tied, whereon yet never man sat: loose him, and bring *him hither*.

31 And if any man ask you, Why do ye loose *him*? thus shall ye say unto him, Because the Lord hath need of him.

32 And they that were sent went their way, and found ᵀeven as he had said unto them.   *everything*

33 And as they were ᵀloosing the colt, the owners thereof said unto them, ᵀWhy loose ye the colt?   *untying • why do you untie the colt*

34 And they said, The ᵀLord hath need of him.   *Master*

35 And they brought him to Jesus: ᴿand they cast their garments upon the colt, and they set Jesus thereon.   2 Kin. 9:13

36 And as he went, they spread their ᵀclothes in the ᵀway.   *cloaks • road*

37 And when he was come nigh, even now at the descent of the mount of Olives, the whole multitude of the disciples began to rejoice and praise God with a loud voice for all the mighty works that they had seen;

38 Saying, ᴿBLESSED BE THE KING THAT COMETH IN THE NAME OF THE LORD: peace in heaven, and glory in the highest.   Ps. 118:26 *

39 And some of the Pharisees from among the multitude said unto him, ᵀMaster, ᵀrebuke thy disciples.   *teacher • stop*

40 And he answered and said unto them, I tell you that, if these should ᵀhold their peace, ᴿthe stones would immediately cry out.   *keep quiet • Hab. 2:11*

41 And when he was come near, he beheld the city, and ᴿwept over it,   John 11:35; Heb. 5:7

42 Saying, If thou hadst known, even thou, at least in this thy day, the things ᵀwhich belong unto thy peace! but now they are hid from thine eyes.   *needed for peace*

43 For the days shall come upon thee, that thine enemies shall cast a trench about thee, and ᵀcompass thee round, and ᵀkeep thee in on every side,   *encircle • besiege you*

44 And shall ᵀlay thee even with the ground, and thy children within thee; and ᴿthey shall not leave in thee one stone upon another; because thou knewest not the time of thy visitation.   *demolish you • 21:6*

Cleansing the Temple
Matt. 21:12, 13; Mark 11:15-17

45 ᴿAnd he went into the temple, and began to cast out them that sold therein, and them that bought;   Mal. 3:1 *

46 Saying unto them, It is written, ᴿMY HOUSE IS THE HOUSE OF PRAYER: but ye have made it a ᴿDEN OF THIEVES.   Is. 56:7 • Jer. 7:11

47 And he taught daily in the temple. But the chief priests and the scribes and the chief of the people sought to destroy him,

48 And could not find what they might do: for all the people were very ᵀattentive to hear him.   *responsive*

CHAPTER 20

Religious Leaders Question Christ's
Authority—Matt. 21:23-27; Mark 11:27-33

AND it came to pass, *that* on one of those days, as he taught the people in the temple, and preached the gospel, the chief priests and the scribes came upon *him* with the elders,

2 And spake unto him, saying, Tell us, by what ᵀauthority doest thou these things? or who is he that gave thee this authority? *right*

3 And he answered and said unto them, I will also ask you one thing; and answer me:

4 The baptism of John, was ᵀit from heaven, or of men?   *the authority*

5 And they reasoned with themselves, saying, If we shall say, From heaven; he will say, Why then believed ye him not?

6 But and if we say, Of men; all the people will stone us: ᴿfor they be persuaded that John was a prophet.   7:29; Matt. 14:5

7 And they answered, that they could not tell ᵀwhence *it was*.   *where it came from*

8 And Jesus said unto them, Neither tell I you by what authority I do these things.

Parable of the Vineyard Owner
Matt. 21:33-44; Mark 12:1-11

9 Then began he to speak to the people this parable; A certain man planted a vineyard, and let it forth to husbandmen, and went into a far country for a long time.

10 And at the season he sent a servant to the husbandmen, that they should give him of the fruit of the vineyard: but the husbandmen beat him, and sent *him* away empty.

11 And again he sent another servant: and they beat him also, and ᵀentreated *him* shamefully, and sent *him* away empty. *handled*

12 And again he sent a third: and they wounded him also, and cast *him* out.

13 Then said the lord of the vineyard, What shall I do? I will send my beloved son: it may be they will ^Treverence *him* when they see him.   *respect*

14 But when the ^Thusbandmen saw him, they reasoned among themselves, saying, This is the heir: come, let us kill him, that the inheritance may be our's.   *tenants*

15 So they cast him out of the vineyard, and killed *him*. What therefore shall the lord of the vineyard do unto them?

16 He shall come and destroy these ^Thusbandmen, and shall give the vineyard to others. And when they heard *it*, they said, God forbid.   *tenant farmers*

17 And he beheld them, and said, What is this then that is written, ^RTHE STONE WHICH THE BUILDERS REJECTED, THE SAME IS BECOME THE HEAD OF THE CORNER?   Is. 8:14, 15 ✶

18 Whosoever shall fall upon that stone shall be broken; but on whomsoever it shall fall, it will grind him to ^Tpowder.   *dust*

Herodians Question Tribute Money
Matt. 21:45, 46; 22:15–22; Mark 12:12–17

19 And the chief priests and the scribes the same hour sought to lay hands on him; and they feared the people: for they perceived that he had spoken this parable against them.

20 And they watched *him*, and sent forth spies, which should ^Tfeign themselves just men, that they might take hold of his words, that so they might deliver him unto the power and authority of the governor.   *pretend*

21 And they asked him, saying, Master, we know that thou sayest and teachest rightly, neither acceptest thou the person *of any*, but teachest the way of God truly:

22 Is it ^Tlawful for us to give ^Ttribute unto Caesar, or no?   *right • taxes*

23 But he perceived their craftiness, and said unto them, Why tempt ye me?

24 Shew me a ^Tpenny. Whose image and ^Tsuperscription hath it? They answered and said, Caesar's.   *$32 • inscription*

25 And he said unto them, ^TRender therefore unto Caesar the things which be Caesar's, and ^Tunto God the things which be God's.   *give • pay to*

26 And they could not take hold of his words before the people: and they marvelled at his answer, and held their peace.

Sadducees Question Resurrection
Matt. 22:23–32; Mark 12:18–27

27 Then came to *him* certain of the Sad'-du-cees, which deny that there is any resurrection; and they asked him,

28 Saying, Master, Moses wrote ^Tunto us, ^RIf any man's brother die, having a wife, and he die without children, that his brother should take his wife, and raise up seed unto his brother.   *this law for • Deut. 25:5*

29 There were therefore seven ^Tbrethren: and the first took a wife, and died without children.   *brothers*

30 And the second ^Ttook her to wife, and he died childless.   *married her*

31 And the third took her; and in like manner the seven also: and they left no children, and died.

32 Last of all the woman died also.

33 Therefore in the resurrection whose wife of them is she? for seven had her to wife.

34 And Jesus answering said unto them, The children of this ^Tworld marry, and are given in marriage: *age*

35 But they which shall be accounted worthy to obtain that world, and ^Tthe resurrection from the dead, neither marry, nor are given in marriage: *rise*

36 Neither can they die any more: for ^Rthey are equal unto the angels; and are the children of God, ^Rbeing the children of the resurrection.   [1 Cor. 15:42, 49, 52] • Rom. 8:23

37 Now that the dead are raised, even Moses shewed at the bush, when he calleth the Lord THE GOD OF ABRAHAM, AND THE GOD OF ISAAC, AND THE GOD OF JACOB. Ex. 3:6

38 For he is not ^Ta God of the dead, but of the living: for all live unto him.   *the*

Christ Questions the Scribes
Matt. 22:41—23:14; Mark 12:35–40

39 Then certain of the scribes answering said, Master, thou hast well said.

40 And after that they ^Tdurst not ask him any *question at all*.   *dared*

41 And he said unto them, How say they that Christ is David's son?

42 And David himself saith in the book of Psalms, ^RTHE LORD SAID UNTO MY LORD, SIT THOU ON MY RIGHT HAND,   Ps. 110:1 ✶

43 ^RTILL I MAKE THINE ENEMIES THY FOOTSTOOL.   Ps. 110:1 ✶

44 David therefore calleth him Lord, how is he then his son?

45 Then in the audience of all the people he said unto his disciples,

46 Beware of the scribes, which desire to walk in long robes, and love greetings in the markets, and the highest seats in the synagogues, and the chief rooms at feasts;

47 Which devour widows' houses, and for a ^Tshew make long prayers: the same shall receive greater damnation.   *pretence*

CHAPTER 21

Christ Teaches on the Widow's Mites
Mark 12:41–44

AND he looked up, and saw the rich men casting their gifts into the treasury.

2 And he saw also a certain poor widow casting in thither ᵀtwo mites.   *about 50 cents*
3 And he said, Of a truth I say unto you, ᴿthat this poor widow hath ᵀcast in more than they all: [2 Cor. 8:12] • *put*
4 For all these have of their abundance ᵀcast in unto the offerings of God: but she of her ᵀpenury hath cast in all the living that she had.   *put into • poverty*

The Disciples' Two Questions
Matt. 24:1–3; Mark 13:1–4

5 And as some spake of the temple, how it was ᵀadorned with goodly stones and gifts, he said,   *decorated*
6 As for these things which ye behold, the days will come, in the which ᴿthere shall not be left one stone upon another, that shall not be thrown down.   19:44
7 And they asked him, saying, Master, but when shall these things be? and what ᵀsign will there be when these things shall come to pass?   *will happen to show*

Signs of Christ's Coming
Matt. 24:4–13; Mark 13:5–13

8 And he said, Take heed that ye be not deceived: for many shall come in my name, saying, I am Christ; and the time draweth near: ᵀgo ye not therefore after them.   *follow*
9 But when ye shall hear of wars and commotions, be not terrified: for these things must first ᵀcome to pass; but the end is not ᵀby and by.   *take place • just yet*
10 Then said he unto them, Nation shall rise against nation, and kingdom against kingdom:
11 And great earthquakes shall be in ᵀdivers places, and famines, and pestilences; and fearful sights and great signs shall there be from heaven.   *various*
12 ᴿBut before all these, they shall ᵀlay their hands on you, and persecute you, delivering you up to the synagogues, and into prisons, being brought before kings and rulers for my name's sake.   [Rev. 2:10] • *arrest*
13 And ᴿit shall turn to you for a ᵀtestimony.   [Phil. 1:28; 2 Thess. 1:5] • *to hear the Gospel*
14 Settle it therefore in your hearts, not to meditate before what ye shall answer:
15 For I will give you a mouth and wisdom, ᴿwhich all your adversaries shall not be able to gainsay nor resist.   Acts 6:10
16 And ye shall be betrayed both by parents, and brethren, and kinsfolks, and friends; and ᴿsome of you shall they cause to be put to death.   Acts 7:59; 12:2
17 And ᴿye shall be hated of all men ᵀfor my name's sake.   Matt. 10:22 • *because of me*
18 ᴿBut there shall not an hair of your head ᵀperish.   Matt. 10:30 • *be lost*
19 In your patience possess ye your souls.

Destruction of Jerusalem
Matt. 24:15–21; Mark 13:14–19

20 And when ye shall see Jerusalem compassed with armies, then ᵀknow that the desolation thereof is ᵀnigh.   *recognize • near*
21 Then let them which are in Ju-dae'-a flee to the mountains; and let them which are in the midst of ᵀit depart out; and let not them that are in the ᵀcountries enter thereinto.   *the city • country*
22 For these be the days of ᵀvengeance, that ᴿall things which are written may be fulfilled.   *justice* • [Dan. 9:26, 27; Zech. 11:1]
23 But woe unto them that are with child, and to them that give suck, in those days! for there shall be great distress in the land, and wrath upon this people.
24 And they shall fall by the edge of the sword, and shall be led away captive into all nations: and Jerusalem shall be trodden down of the Gentiles, ᴿuntil the times of the Gentiles be fulfilled.   [Dan. 9:27; Rom. 11:25]

The Second Coming
Matt. 24:29–31; Mark 13:24–27

25 And there shall be signs in the sun, and in the moon, and in the stars; and upon the earth distress of nations, with perplexity; the sea and the waves roaring;
26 Men's hearts failing them for fear, and for looking after those things which are coming on the earth: for the powers of heaven shall be shaken.
27 And then shall they see ᴿTHE SON OF MAN COMING IN A CLOUD with power and great glory.   Dan. 7:13; Rev. 1:7; 14:14
28 And when these things begin to ᵀcome to pass, then look up, and lift up your heads; for your redemption draweth nigh.   *happen*

Parable of the Fig Tree
Matt. 24:32–35; Mark 13:28–31

29 And he spake to them a parable; Behold the fig tree, and all the trees;
30 When they now shoot forth, ye see and know of your own selves that summer is ᵀnow nigh at hand.   *near*
31 So likewise ye, when ye see these things ᵀcome to pass, know ye that the kingdom of God is nigh at hand.   *happen*
32 Verily I say unto you, This generation shall not pass away, till all be fulfilled.
33 Heaven and earth shall pass away: but my words shall not pass away.

Warning to Watch for His Coming
Matt. 24:36–44; Mark 13:32–37

34 And ᴿtake heed to yourselves, lest at any time your hearts be overcharged with ᵀsurfeiting, and drunkenness, and cares of this life, and so that day come upon you ᵀunawares.   1 Pet. 4:7 • *overeating • unexpectedly*

35 For as a snare shall it come on all them that dwell on the face of the whole earth.

36 Watch ye therefore, and pray always, that ye may be accounted worthy to escape all these things that shall come to pass, and to stand before the Son of man.

37 ^RAnd in the day time he was teaching in the temple; and ^Rat night he went out, and ^Tabode in the mount that is called the mount of Olives.   John 8:1, 2 • 22:39 • stayed

38 And all the people came early in the morning to him in the temple, for to hear him.

CHAPTER 22

Judas Agrees to Betray Christ
Matt. 26:1-5, 14-16; Mark 14:1, 2, 10, 11

NOW the feast of unleavened bread drew nigh, which is called the Passover.

2 And ^Rthe chief priests and scribes ^Tsought how they might kill him; for they feared the people.   Ps. 2:2; Acts 4:27 • planned

3 ^RThen entered Satan into Judas surnamed Is-car'-i-ot, being of the number of the twelve.   John 13:2, 27

4 And he went his way, and ^Tcommuned with the chief priests and captains, how he might betray him unto them.   conferred

5 And they were glad, and ^Rcovenanted^T to give him money.   Zech. 11:12 • promised

6 And he promised, and sought opportunity to betray him unto them ^Tin the absence of the multitude.   without people knowing

The Upper Room Is Prepared
Matt. 26:17-19; Mark 14:12-16

7 Then came the day of unleavened bread, when the passover must be killed.

8 And he sent ^RPeter and John, saying, Go and prepare us the ^Tpassover, that we may eat.   Acts 3:1, 11; 4:13, 19; 8:14 • passover meal

9 And they said unto him, Where wilt thou that we prepare?

10 And he said unto them, Behold, when ye are entered into the city, there shall a man meet you, bearing a pitcher of water; follow him into the house where he entereth in.

11 And ye shall say unto the ^Tgoodman of the house, The Master saith unto thee, Where is the guestchamber, where I shall eat the passover with my disciples?   owner

12 And he shall shew you a large upper room furnished: there make ready.

13 And they went, and found ^Tas he had said unto them: and they made ready the passover.   everything

The Passover Is Celebrated
Matt. 26:20, 29; Mark 14:17, 25

14 And when the hour was come, he sat down, and the twelve apostles with him.

15 And he said unto them, ^TWith desire I have desired to eat this passover with you before I suffer: I have wanted very much

16 For I say unto you, I will not any more eat thereof, ^Runtil it be fulfilled in the kingdom of God.   14:15; [Acts 10:41; Rev. 19:9]

17 And he took the cup, and gave ^Tthanks, and said, Take this, and ^Tdivide it among yourselves: thanks to God • share

18 For I say unto you, I will not drink of the fruit of the vine, until the kingdom of God shall come.

The Lord's Supper Is Instituted
Matt. 26:26-28; Mark 14:22-24

19 And he took bread, and gave thanks, and brake it, and gave unto them, saying, This is my body which is given for you: this do in remembrance of me.

20 Likewise also the cup after supper, saying, ^RThis cup is the new testament in my blood, which is shed for you.   1 Cor. 10:16

Christ Predicts His Betrayer
Matt. 26:21-25; Mark 14:18-21; John 13:21-26

21 ^RBut, behold, the hand of him that betrayeth me is with me on the table. Ps. 41:9 ☆

22 And truly the Son of man goeth, as it was determined: but ^Rwoe unto that man by whom he is betrayed!   Matt. 27:4, 5; Acts 1:16-20

23 And they began to enquire among themselves, which of them it was that should do this thing.

The Disciples Argue over Who Is the Greatest

24 ^RAnd there was also a strife among them, which of them should be ^Taccounted the greatest.   Mark 9:34 • considered

25 ^RAnd he said unto them, The kings of the Gentiles exercise lordship over them; and they that exercise authority upon them are called benefactors.   Mark 10:42

26 ^RBut ye shall not be so: ^Rbut he that is greatest among you, let him be as the younger; and he that is chief, as he that doth serve.   Matt. 20:26; [1 Pet. 5:3] • 9:48

27 For ^Twhether is greater, he that sitteth ^Tat meat, or he that serveth? is not he that sitteth at meat? but ^RI am among you as he that serveth.   who • to eat • Matt. 20:28

28 Ye are they which have ^Tcontinued with me in my ^Ttemptations.   stayed • trials

29 And I appoint unto you a kingdom, as my Father hath appointed unto me;

30 That ^Rye may eat and drink at my table in my kingdom, and sit on thrones judging the twelve tribes of Israel.   [Matt. 8:11]

Christ Predicts Peter's Denial
Matt. 26:31-35; Mark 14:27-31; John 13:36-38

31 And the Lord said, Simon, Simon, behold, ^RSatan hath desired to have you, that he may ^Rsift you as wheat: 1 Pet. 5:8 • Amos 9:9

32 But I have prayed for thee, that thy faith fail not: and ^{R}when thou art converted, strengthen thy brethren.   Acts 1:15; 2:14

33 And he said unto him, Lord, I am ready to go with thee, both into prison, and to death.

34 And ^{R}he said, I tell thee, Peter, the cock shall not crow this day, before that thou shalt thrice deny that thou knowest me.   *v.* 61 ☆

Christ Predicts Coming Conflict

35 And he said unto them, When I sent you without purse, and scrip, and shoes, lacked ye any thing? And they said, Nothing.

36 Then said he unto them, But now, he that hath a purse, let him take *it*, and likewise *his* scrip: and he that hath no sword, let him sell his garment, and buy one.

37 For I say unto you, that this that is written must yet be accomplished in me, ^{R}AND HE WAS RECKONED AMONG THE TRANS-GRESSORS: for the things concerning me have an end.   23:32; Is. 53:12; John 19:18 ☆

38 And they said, Lord, behold, here *are* two ^{R}swords. And he said unto them, It is enough.   22:36, 49

Christ Prays in Gethsemane
Matt. 26:36–46; Mark 14:32–42; John 18:1

39 And he came out, and went, as he was ^{T}wont, to the mount of Olives; and his disciples also followed him.   *accustomed*

40 ^{R}And when he was at the place, he said unto them, Pray that ye ^{T}enter not into temptation.   *v.* 46 • *will not fall*

41 And he ^{T}was withdrawn from them about a stone's ^{T}cast, and kneeled down, and prayed,   *went away* • *throw*

42 Saying, Father, if thou be willing, remove this cup from me: nevertheless ^{R}not my will, but thine, be done.   Is. 50:5 ✱

43 And there appeared an angel unto him from heaven, strengthening him.

44 And being in an agony he prayed more earnestly: and his sweat was as it were great drops of blood falling down to the ground.

45 And when he rose up from prayer, and was come to his disciples, he found them sleeping for sorrow,

46 And said unto them, Why sleep ye? rise and pray, lest ye enter into temptation.

Judas Betrays Christ
Matt. 26:47–56; Mark 14:43–50; John 18:2–11

47 And while he yet spake, behold a multitude, and he that was called Judas, one of the twelve, went before them, and drew near unto Jesus to kiss him.

48 But Jesus said unto him, Judas, ^{R}betrayest thou the Son of man with a kiss? Ps. 41:9 ✱

49 And when they which were about him saw what would follow, they said unto him, Lord, shall we ^{T}smite with the sword?   *fight*

50 And one of them smote the servant of the high priest, and cut off his right ear.

51 And Jesus answered and said, ^{T}Suffer ye thus far. And he touched his ear, and healed him.   *allow this to happen*

52 Then Jesus said unto the chief priests, and captains of the temple, and the elders, which were come to him, Be ye come out, as against a thief, with swords and ^{T}staves? *clubs*

53 When I was daily with you in the temple, ye ^{T}stretched forth no hands against me: but this is your hour, and the power of darkness.   *did not try to arrest*

Peter Denies Christ
Matt. 26:57, 58, 69–75; Mark 14:53, 54, 66–72; John 18:15–18, 25–27

54 Then took they him, and led *him*, and brought him into the high priest's house. And Peter followed afar off.

55 And when they had kindled a fire in the midst of the hall, and were set down together, Peter sat down among them.

56 But a certain maid beheld him as he sat by the fire, and earnestly looked upon him, and said, This man was also with him.

57 And he denied him, saying, Woman, I know him not.

58 And after a little while another saw him, and said, Thou art also of them. And Peter said, Man, I am not.

59 And about the space of one hour after another confidently ^{T}affirmed, saying, Of a truth this *fellow* also was with him: for he is a Gal-i-lae'-an.   *insisted*

60 And Peter said, Man, I know not what thou sayest. And ^{R}immediately, while he yet spake, the cock crew.   *v.* 34; John 13:38 ✱

61 And the Lord turned, and looked upon Peter. And Peter remembered the word of the Lord, how he had said unto him, Before the cock crow, thou shalt deny me thrice.

62 And Peter went out, and wept bitterly.

Christ Is Beaten—Matt. 26:67, 68; Mark 14:65

63 ^{R}And the men that held Jesus mocked him, and smote *him*.   Ps. 69:19; Is. 50:6; 52:14 ✱

64 And when they had blindfolded him, they struck him on the face, and asked him, saying, Prophesy, who is it that smote thee?

65 ^{R}And many other things blasphemously spake they against him.   Is. 53:3 ✱

The Sanhedrin Tries Christ
Matt. 27:1; Mark 15:1

66 ^{R}And as soon as it was day, ^{R}the elders of the people and the chief priests and the scribes came together, and led him into their council, saying,   Matt. 27:1 • Acts 4:26

67 ^{R}Art thou the ^{T}Christ? tell us. And he said unto them, If I tell you, ye will not believe: Matt. 26:63; Mark 14:61 • *Messiah*

68 And if I ᵀalso ask you, ye will not ᵀanswer me, nor let me go.   tell you · believe
69 Hereafter shall the Son of man SIT ON THE RIGHT HAND OF THE POWER OF GOD.
70 Then said they all, Art thou then the Son of God? And he said unto them, ᴿYe ᵀsay that I am.   1:35 ⋆ · you said it
71 And they said, What need we any further witness? for we ourselves have heard of his own mouth.

CHAPTER 23

Pilate Tries Christ
Matt. 27:2, 11–14; Mark 15:1–5; John 18:28–38

A ND ᴿthe whole multitude of them arose, and led him unto Pilate.   18:32 ⋆
2 And they began to accuse him, saying, We found this *fellow* perverting the nation, and forbidding to give tribute to Caesar, saying that he himself is Christ a King.
3 And Pilate asked him, saying, Art thou the King of the Jews? And he answered him and said, ᵀThou sayest it.   you said it
4 Then said Pilate to the chief priests and to the people, I find no fault in this man.
5 And they were the more ᵀfierce, saying, He ᵀstirreth up the people, teaching throughout all Jewry, beginning from Galilee to this place.   insistent · excites
6 When Pilate heard of ᴿGalilee, he asked whether the man were a Gal-i-lae'-an. John 7:41
7 And as soon as he knew that he belonged unto ᴿHerod's ᵀjurisdiction, he sent him to Herod, who himself also was at Jerusalem at that time.   3:1 · region

Herod Tries Christ

8 And when Herod saw Jesus, he was exceeding glad: for he was desirous to see him of a long *season*, because ᴿhe had heard many things of him; and he hoped to have seen some miracle done by him.   Matt. 14:1
9 Then he questioned with him in many words; but he answered him nothing.
10 And the chief priests and scribes stood and ᵀvehemently accused him.   vigorously
11 ᴿAnd Herod with his ᵀmen of war set him at nought, and mocked him, and arrayed him in a gorgeous robe, and sent him again to Pilate.   Ps. 69:19; Is. 53:3 ⋆ · soldiers
12 And the same day Pilate and Herod were made friends together: for before they were at enmity between themselves.

Pilate Tries Christ Again
Matt. 27:15–26; Mark 15:6–15; John 18:39—19:16

13 And Pilate, when he had called together the chief priests and the rulers and the people,
14 Said unto them, ᴿYe have brought this man unto me, as one that ᵀperverteth the

people: and, behold, I, having examined *him* before you, have found no ᵀfault in this man touching those things whereof ye accuse him: vv. 1, 2 · misleads · crime
15 No, nor yet Herod: for ᵀI sent you to him; and, lo, nothing worthy of death is done unto him.   he sent him back to us
16 I will therefore ᵀchastise him, and ᵀrelease *him*.   whip · set him free
17 (For of necessity he must release one unto them at the feast.)
18 And ᴿthey cried out all at once, saying, Away with this *man*, and release unto us Barab'-bas: Is. 53:3; Acts 3:14 ⋆
19 (Who for a certain sedition made in the city, and for murder, was cast into prison.)
20 Pilate therefore, ᵀwilling to release Jesus, spake again to them.   wanted
21 But they cried, saying, ᵀCrucify *him*, crucify him.   to the cross with him
22 And he said unto them the third time, Why, what ᵀevil hath he done? I have found no cause of death in him: I will therefore chastise him, and let *him* go.   crime
23 And they were ᵀinstant with loud voices, requiring that he might be crucified. And the voices of them and of the chief priests ᵀprevailed.   urgent · won
24 And ᴿPilate ᵀgave sentence that it should be as they required.   [Ex. 23:2] · assented
25 And he released unto them him that for ᵀsedition and murder was cast into prison, whom they had desired; but he delivered Jesus to their will.   insurrection

Christ Is Crucified
Matt. 27:31–56; Mark 15:20–41; John 19:16–30

26 And as they led him away, they laid hold upon one Simon, a Cy-re'-ni-an, coming out of the country, and on him they laid the cross, that he might bear it after Jesus.
27 And there followed him a great company of people, and of women, which also ᵀbewailed and lamented him. wailing and weeping
28 But Jesus turning unto them said, Daughters of Jerusalem, ᵀweep not for me, but weep for yourselves, and for your children.   don't cry
29 For, behold, the days are coming, in the which they shall say, Blessed *are* the barren, and the wombs that never bare, and the paps which never gave suck.
30 Then shall they begin ᴿTO SAY TO THE MOUNTAINS, FALL ON US; AND TO THE HILLS, COVER US.   Is. 2:19; Hos. 10:8; Rev. 6:16; 9:6
31 ᴿFor if they do these things in a green tree, what shall be done in the dry? [Jer. 25:29]
32 And there were also two others, malefactors, led with him to be put to death.
33 And when they were come to the place, which is called Calvary, there they ᴿcrucified him, and the malefactors, one on the right hand, and the other on the left. Ps. 22:16–18 ⋆

34 Then said Jesus, Father, forgive them; for they know not what they do. ᴿAND THEY PARTED HIS RAIMENT, AND CAST LOTS. Ps. 22:18 *

35 ᴿAnd the people stood beholding. And the rulers also with them derided *him*, saying, He saved others; let him save himself, if he be Christ, the chosen of God. Ps. 22:7, 8 *

36 And the soldiers also mocked him, coming to him, and offering him vinegar,

37 And saying, If thou be the king of the Jews, save thyself.

38 And a superscription also was written over him in letters of Greek, and Latin, and Hebrew, THIS IS THE KING OF THE JEWS.

39 And one of the ᵀmalefactors which were hanged railed on him, saying, ᴿIf thou be Christ, save thyself and us.   *criminals* · Ps. 22:8 *

40 But the other answering rebuked him, saying, Dost not thou fear God, seeing thou art in the same ᵀcondemnation?   *sentence*

41 And we indeed ᵀjustly; for we receive the due reward of our deeds: but this man hath done nothing ᵀamiss.   *rightly · wrong*

42 And he said unto Jesus, Lord, remember me when thou comest into thy kingdom.

43 And Jesus said unto him, Verily I say unto thee, ᴿto day shalt thou be with me in ᴿparadise.   Eph. 4:8-10 · [2 Cor. 12:2, 4]

44 ᴿAnd it was about the sixth hour, and there was a darkness over all the ᵀearth until the ninth hour.   Amos 8:9 * · *land*

45 And the sun was darkened, and the veil of the temple was rent in the midst.

46 And when Jesus had cried with a loud voice, he said, Father, ᴿINTO THY HANDS I COMMEND MY SPIRIT: ᴿand having said thus, he gave up the ghost.   Ps. 31:5 · Matt. 17:23 *

47 Now when the centurion saw what was done, he glorified God, saying, Certainly this was a righteous man.

48 ᴿAnd all the people that came together to that ᵀsight, beholding the things which ᵀwere done, smote their breasts, and ᵀreturned.   John 16:20-22 * · *spectacle · happened · went home*

49 And all his acquaintance, and the women that followed him from Galilee, stood afar off, beholding these things.

Christ Is Buried
Matt. 27:57-61; Mark 15:42-47; John 19:38-42

50 And, behold, *there was* a man named Joseph, a counsellor; *and he was* a good man, and a just:

51 (The same had not consented to the counsel and deed of them;) *he was* of Ar-i-ma-thae'-a, a city of the Jews: who also himself waited for the kingdom of God.

52 ᴿThis *man* went unto Pilate, and ᵀbegged the body of Jesus.   Is. 53:9 * · *asked for*

53 ᴿAnd he took it down, and wrapped it in linen, and laid it in a ᵀsepulchre that was hewn in stone, wherein never man before was laid.   Matt. 26:12; Mark 14:8 * · *grave*

54 And that day was ᵀthe ᴿpreparation, and the sabbath drew on.   *Friday* · Matt. 27:62

55 And the women also, which came with him from Galilee, followed after, and beheld the sepulchre, and how his body was laid.

In the Grave

56 And they returned, and prepared spices and ointments; and rested the sabbath day according to the commandment.

CHAPTER 24

The Resurrection
Matt. 28:1-8; Mark 16:1-8; John 20:1-10

NOW upon the first *day* of the week, very early in the morning, they came unto the sepulchre, ᴿbringing the spices which they had prepared, and certain *others* with them.   23:56

2 And they found the stone rolled away from the sepulchre.

3 ᴿAnd they entered in, and found not the body of the Lord Jesus.   v. 23

4 And it came to pass, as they were much ᵀperplexed thereabout, behold, two men stood by them in shining garments: *puzzled*

5 And as they were ᵀafraid, and bowed down *their* faces to the earth, they said unto them, Why seek ye ᵀthe living among the dead?   *full of fear · him that liveth*

6 He is not here, but is risen: ᴿremember how he spake unto you when he was yet in Galilee,   9:22; Matt. 16:21; Mark 8:31 *

7 Saying, The Son of man must be delivered into the hands of sinful men, and be crucified, ᴿand the third day rise again.   v. 21

8 And they remembered his words,

9 And returned from the sepulchre, and told all these things unto the ᵀeleven, and to all the rest.   *eleven disciples*

10 It was Mary Mag-da-le'-ne, and ᴿJo-an'-na, and Mary *the mother* of James, and other *women that were* with them, which told these things unto the apostles.   8:3

11 And their words seemed to them as idle tales, and they believed them not.

12 Then arose Peter, and ran unto the sepulchre; and stooping down, he beheld the linen clothes laid by themselves, and departed, wondering in himself at that which was come to pass.

Christ Appears on the Road to Emmaus
Mark 16:12, 13

13 And, behold, two of them went that same day to a village called Em-ma'-us, which was from Jerusalem *about* ᵀthreescore furlongs.   7.5 mi.

14 And they talked ᵀtogether of all these things which had happened.   *to each other*

15 And it came to pass, that, while they

communed *together* and reasoned, Jesus himself drew near, and went with them.

16 But their eyes were holden that they ^Tshould not know him.   *were unable to see him*

17 And he said unto them, What manner of communications *are* these that ye have one to another, as ye walk, and are sad?

18 And the one of them, ^Rwhose name was Cle′-o-pas, answering said unto him, Art thou only a stranger in Jerusalem, and hast not known the things which are come to pass there in these days?   John 19:25

19 And he said unto them, What things? And they said unto him, Concerning Jesus of Nazareth, ^Rwhich was a prophet ^Rmighty in deed and word before God and all the people: 7:16; John 3:2; Acts 2:22 • Acts 7:22

20 ^RAnd how the chief priests and our rulers delivered him to be condemned to death, and have crucified him.   Acts 13:27

21 But we trusted ^Rthat it had been he which should have redeemed Israel: and beside all this, to day is the third day since these things were done.   1:68; 2:38; [Acts 1:6]

22 Yea, and ^Rcertain women also of our company made us astonished, which were early at the sepulchre;   Matt. 28:8; Mark 16:10

23 And when they found not his body, they came, saying, that they had also seen a vision of angels, which said that he was alive.

24 And ^Rcertain of them which were with us went to the sepulchre, and found *it* ^Teven so as the women had said: but him they saw not.   *v. 12 • exactly*

25 Then he said unto them, ^TO fools, and slow of heart to believe all that the prophets have spoken: *how foolish*

26 Ought not Christ to have suffered these things, and to enter into his glory?

27 And beginning at Moses and all the prophets, he expounded unto them in all the scriptures the things concerning himself.

28 And they drew nigh unto the village, ^Twhither they went: and he made as though he would have gone further.   *where*

29 But ^Rthey constrained him, saying, Abide with us: for it is toward evening, and the day is far spent. And he went in to tarry with them.   Gen. 19:3; Acts 16:15

30 And it came to pass, as he sat at meat with them, ^Rhe took bread, and blessed *it,* brake, and gave to them.   Matt. 14:19

31 And their eyes were opened, and they ^Tknew him; and he ^Tvanished out of their sight.   *recognized • ceased to be seen of them*

32 And they said one to another, Did not our heart burn within us, while he talked with us ^Tby the way, and while he ^Topened to us the scriptures?   *on the road • explained*

The Proof of His Resurrection
Mark 16:4; John 20:19-23; 1 Cor. 15:5

33 And they rose up the same hour, and returned to Jerusalem, and found the eleven gathered together, and them that were with them,

34 Saying, The Lord is risen indeed, and ^Rhath appeared to Simon.   1 Cor. 15:5

35 And they told what things *were done* in the way, and how he was ^Tknown of them in breaking of bread.   *recognized*

36 ^RAnd as they thus spake, Jesus himself stood in the midst of them, and saith unto them, Peace *be* unto you.   1 Cor. 15:5

37 But they were terrified and affrighted, and supposed that they had seen a spirit.

38 And he said unto them, Why are ye troubled? and why do ^Tthoughts arise in your ^Thearts?   *doubts • minds*

39 Behold my hands and my feet, that it is I myself: handle me, and see; for a spirit hath not flesh and bones, as ye see me have.

40 And when he had thus spoken, he shewed them *his* hands and *his* feet.

41 And while they yet believed not ^Rfor joy, and wondered, he said unto them, ^RHave ye here any meat?   Gen. 45:26 • John 21:5

42 And they gave him a piece of a broiled fish, and of an honeycomb.

43 ^RAnd he took *it,* and did eat before them.   Acts 10:41

The Great Commission—Acts 1:3-8

44 And he said unto them, ^RThese *are* the words which I spake unto you, while I was yet with you, that all things must be fulfilled, which were written in the law of Moses, and in the prophets, and in the psalms, concerning me.   *v. 6; 9:22; 18:31*

45 Then opened he their understanding, that they might understand the scriptures,

46 And said unto them, Thus it is written, and thus it behoved Christ to suffer, and ^Rto rise from the dead the third day: Hos. 6:1, 2 ✶

47 And that repentance and remission of sins should be preached in his name ^Ramong all nations, beginning at Jerusalem.   [Mic. 4:2]

48 And ye are witnesses of these things.

The Ascension—Mark 16:19; Acts 1:9

49 ^RAnd, behold, I send the promise of my Father upon you: but ^Ttarry ye in the city of Jerusalem, until ye be endued with power from on high.   Is. 44:3; Joel 2:28; Acts 2:4 ✶ • *wait*

50 And he led them ^Tout as far as to Beth′-a-ny, and he lifted up his hands, and blessed them.   *out of the city*

51 ^RAnd it came to pass, while he blessed them, he was ^Tparted from them, and carried up into heaven.   Ps. 68:18, 110:1 ✶ • *departed*

52 ^RAnd they worshipped him, and returned to Jerusalem with great joy: Matt. 28:9

53 And were continually ^Rin the temple, praising and blessing God. A-men′.   Acts 2:46

THE GOSPEL ACCORDING TO
JOHN

THE BOOK OF JOHN

Just as a coin has two sides, both valid, so Jesus Christ has two natures, both valid. Luke presents Christ in His humanity as the Son of Man; John portrays Him in His deity as the Son of God. John's purpose is crystal clear: to set forth Christ in His deity in order to spark believing faith in his readers. John's gospel is topical, not primarily chronological, and it revolves around seven miracles and seven "I am" statements of Christ.

Following an extended eyewitness description of the Upper Room meal and discourse, John records events leading up to the Resurrection, the final climactic proof that Jesus is who He claims to be—the Son of God.

The title of the Fourth Gospel follows the same format as the titles of the synoptic Gospels: *Kata Ioannen,* "According to John." As with the others, the word "Gospel" was later added. *Ioannes* is derived from the Hebrew name *Johanan,* "Yahweh Has Been Gracious."

THE AUTHOR OF JOHN

Jesus nicknamed John and his brother, James, "Sons of Thunder" (Mark 3:17). Their father was Zebedee; and their mother, Salome, served Jesus in Galilee and was present at His crucifixion (Mark 15:40, 41). John was evidently among the Galileans who followed John the Baptist until they were called to follow Jesus at the outset of His public ministry (1:19–51). These Galileans were later called to become full-time disciples of the Lord (Luke 5:1–11), and John was among the twelve men who were selected to be apostles (Luke 6:12–16). After Christ's ascension, John became one of the "pillars" of the church in Jerusalem along with James and Peter (Gal. 2:9). He is mentioned three times by name in Acts (3:1; 4:13; 8:14), each time in association with Peter. Tradition says that John later went to Ephesus (perhaps just before the destruction of Jerusalem). He was eventually exiled by the Romans for a time to the island of Patmos (Rev. 1:9).

The author of this gospel is identified only as the disciple "whom Jesus loved" (13:23; 19:26; 20:2; 21:7, 20). His knowledge of Palestinian geography and Jewish customs makes it clear that he was a Palestinian Jew, and his meticulous attention to numbers (2:6; 6:13, 19; 21:8, 11) and names (1:45; 3:1; 11:1; 18:10) indicates that he was an eyewitness. This fits his own claim to be a witness of the events he described (1:14; 19:35; 21:24, 25). The disciple "whom Jesus loved" was part of the inner circle of disciples and was closely associated with Peter. The synoptic Gospels name this inner circle as Peter, James, and John. Since Peter is separate from the beloved disciple, only James and John are left. James was martyred too early to be the author (Acts 12:1, 2), so the apostle John was the author of this gospel. This conclusion from internal evidence is consistent with the external testimony of the early church. Irenaeus (c. A.D. 185) was a disciple of Polycarp who was in turn a disciple of the apostle John. In his *Against Heresies,* Irenaeus bore witness to Johannine authorship of this gospel and noted that John lived until the time of the emperor Trajan (A.D. 98–117). Clement of Alexandria, Theophilus of Antioch, Origen, and others also ascribe this book to John.

THE TIME OF JOHN

In spite of the strong internal and external testimony supporting Johannine authorship of this gospel, theological assumptions have motivated a number of critics to deny this claim. Until recently it was popular to propose a second-century date for this book. The discovery of the John Rylands Papyrus 52 containing portions of John 18:31–33, 37, 38 has overthrown this conjecture. This fragment has been dated at about A.D. 135, and a considerable period of time must have been required for John's gospel to be copied and circulated before it reached Egypt, where this papyrus was found.

On the other hand, John was written after the last of the synoptic Gospels (c. A.D. 66–68). His familiarity with the topography of Jerusalem (e.g., 5:2; 19:13) does not necessarily require a date before A.D. 70. Since John's three epistles and Revelation were written after his gospel, the probable range for this work is A.D. 60–90. By this time, John would have been one of the last surviving eyewitnesses of the Lord. According to tradition, John wrote this gospel in Ephesus.

THE CHRIST OF JOHN

This book presents the most powerful case in all the Bible for the deity of the incarnate Son of God. "A man that is called Jesus" (9:11) is also "Christ, the Son of the living God" (6:69). The deity of Christ can be seen in His seven "I am" statements: "I am the bread of life" (6:35, 48); "I am the light of the world" (8:12; 9:5); "I am the door" (10:7, 9); "I am the good shepherd" (10:11, 14); "I am the resurrection, and the life" (11:25); "I am the way, the truth, and the life" (14:6); "I am the true vine" (15:1–5). The seven signs (1—12) and the five witnesses (5:30–40) also point to His divine character. On certain occasions, Jesus equates Himself with the Old Testament "I AM," or Yahweh (see 4:25, 26; 8:24, 28, 58; 13:19; 18:5, 6,

8). Some of the most crucial affirmations of His deity are in 1:1; 8:58; 10:30; 14:9; 20:28.

The Word was God (1:1), but the Word also became flesh (1:14). The humanity of Jesus can be seen in His weariness (4:6), thirst (4:7), dependence (5:19), grief (11:35), troubled soul (12:27), and His anguish and death (19).

KEYS TO JOHN

Key Word: Believe That Jesus Is the Son of God—The Fourth Gospel has the clearest statement of purpose in the Bible: "But these are written, that ye might believe that Jesus is the Christ, the Son of God; and that believing ye might have life through his name" (20:31). John selected the signs he used for the specific purpose of creating intellectual ("that ye might believe") and spiritual ("that believing ye might have life") conviction about the Son of God. The key verb in John is "believe," and requires both knowledge (8:32; 10:38) and volition (1:12; 3:19; 7:17).

The predominant theme of this gospel is the dual response of faith and unbelief to the person of Jesus Christ. Those who place their faith in the Son of God have eternal life, but those who reject Him are under the condemnation of God (3:36; 5:24-29; 10:27-29): this is the basic issue. John 1:11, 12 summarizes the responses of accepting or rejecting the Son of God that are traced through the rest of the book. The rejection of Jesus by His own people can be seen over and over in chapters 2 through 19 ("his own received him not"), but John also lists a number of men and women who believed in Him ("But as many as received him").

Key Verses: John 1:11-13 and John 20:30, 31—"He came unto his own, and his own received him not. But as many as received him, to them gave he power to become the sons of God, *even* to them that believe on his name: Which were born, not of blood, nor of the will of the flesh, nor of the will of man, but of God" (1:11-13).

"And many other signs truly did Jesus in the presence of his disciples, which are not written in this book: But these are written, that ye might believe that Jesus is the Christ, the Son of God; and that believing ye might have life through his name" (20:30, 31).

Key Chapter: John 3—John 3:16 is without doubt the most quoted and preached verse in all of Scripture. Captured in it is the gospel in its clearest and simplest form: that salvation is a gift of God and is obtainable only through belief. The conversation with Nicodemus and the testimony of John the Baptist provide the setting that clearly points out that being "born again" is the only way to find the "kingdom of God."

SURVEY OF JOHN

This most unusual gospel, with its distinct content and style, serves as a supplement to the three synoptics. It is easily the simplest and yet the most profound of the gospels, and for many people it is the greatest and most powerful. John writes his gospel for the specific purpose of bringing people to spiritual life through belief in the person and work of Jesus Christ. The five basic sections of this gospel are: the incarnation of the Son of God (1:1-18); the presentation of the Son of God (1:19—4:54); the opposition to the Son of God (5:1—12:50); the preparation of the disciples by the Son of God (13:1—17:26); the crucifixion and resurrection of the Son of God (18:1—21:25).

The Incarnation of the Son of God (1:1-18): This prologue introduces the rest of the book and gives the background for the historical narrative that follows. It dates the nature of Jesus, introduces His forerunner, clarifies His mission, and notes the rejection and acceptance He will find during His ministry.

The Presentation of the Son of God (1:19—4:54): In this section Christ is under careful consideration and scrutiny by Israel. He is introduced by John the Baptist who directs his

FOCUS	INCARNATION OF THE SON OF GOD	PRESENTATION OF THE SON OF GOD	OPPOSITION TO THE SON OF GOD	PREPARATION OF THE DISCIPLES	CRUCIFIXION AND RESURRECTION OF THE SON OF GOD
REFERENCE	1:1———————1:19————5:1——————13:1——————18:1———21:25				
DIVISION	INTRODUCTION TO CHRIST	REVELATION OF CHRIST	REJECTION OF CHRIST	REVELATION OF CHRIST	REJECTION OF CHRIST
TOPIC	SEVEN MIRACLES			UPPER ROOM DISCOURSE	SUPREME MIRACLE
	THAT YOU MIGHT BELIEVE			THAT YOU MIGHT HAVE LIFE	
LOCATION	ISRAEL				
TIME	A FEW YEARS			A FEW HOURS	A FEW WEEKS

own disciples to Christ. Shortly the author begins listing the seven signs, which continue through the next section. John carefully selects seven miracles out of the many that Christ accomplished (cf. John 21:25) in order to build a concise case for His deity. They are called signs because they symbolize the life-changing results of belief in Jesus—(1) water to wine: the ritual of law is replaced by the reality of grace (2:1–11); (2) healing the nobleman's son: the gospel brings spiritual restoration (4:46–54); (3) healing the paralytic: weakness is replaced by strength (5:1–16); (4) feeding the multitude: Christ satisfies spiritual hunger (6:1–13); (5) walking on water: the Lord transforms fear to faith (6:16–21); (6) sight to the man born blind: Jesus overcomes darkness and brings in light (9:1–7); (7) raising of Lazarus: the gospel brings people from death to life (11:1–44). These signs combine to show that Jesus is indeed the Son of God.

The Opposition to the Son of God (5:1—12:50): John's unusual pattern in these chapters is to record the reactions of belief and disbelief after the performance of one miracle before moving to the next. In a series of growing confrontations, John portrays the intense opposition that will culminate in the Lord's final rejection on the cross. Even though many people receive Him, the inevitable crucifixion is foreshadowed in several places (2:4, 21, 22; 7:6, 39; 11:51, 52; 12:16).

The Preparation of the Disciples by the Son of God (13:1—17:26): John surveys the incarnation

and public ministry of Jesus in twelve chapters, but radically changes the pace in the next five chapters to give a detailed account of a few crucial hours. In this clear and vivid recollection of Jesus' last discourse to His intimate disciples, John captures the Lord's words of comfort and assurance to a group of fearful and confused followers. Jesus knows that in less than twenty-four hours He will be on the cross. Therefore, His last words speak of all the resources that will be at the disciples' disposal after His departure. They will be indwelt and empowered by the Triune Godhead. The Upper Room Discourse contains the message of the Epistles in capsule form as it reveals God's pattern for Christian living. In it, the key themes of servanthood, the Holy Spirit, and abiding in Christ are developed.

The Crucifixion and Resurrection of the Son of God (18:1—21:25): After recording Christ's High Priestly Prayer on behalf of His disciples and all who believe in Him "through their word" (17:20), John immediately launches into a dramatic description of Christ's arrest and trials before Annas, Caiaphas, and Pilate. In His crucifixion, Jesus willingly fulfills John the Baptist's prophetic words: "Behold the Lamb of God, which taketh away the sin of the world" (1:29). John closes his profound gospel with a particularly detailed account of the post-resurrection appearances of the Lord. The Resurrection is the ultimate sign that points to Jesus as the Son of God.

OUTLINE OF JOHN

Part One: The Incarnation of the Son of God (1:1-18)

Part Two: The Presentation of the Son of God (1:19—4:54)

Part Three: The Opposition to the Son of God (5:1—12:50)

Part Four: The Preparation of the Disciples by the Son of God (13:1—17:26)

Part Five: The Crucifixion and Resurrection of the Son of God (18:1—21:25)

CHAPTER 1

The Deity of Christ

IN the beginning ᴿwas the Word, and the Word was with God, and the Word was God. [v. 14; 17:5, 24]; Eph. 1:4

2 ᴿThe same was in the beginning with God. Gen. 1:1

The Preincarnate Work of Christ

3 ᴿAll things were made by him; and without him was not any thing made that was made. Ps. 33:6; [Eph. 3:9; Col. 1:16, 17]; Heb. 1:10

4 ᴿIn him was life; and ᴿthe life was the light of men. [1 John 5:11] • 8:12

5 And ᴿthe light shineth in darkness; and the darkness comprehended it not. [3:19]

The Forerunner of Christ

6 There was a ᵀman sent from God, whose name was John. messenger

7 The same came for a witness, to ᵀbear witness of the Light, that all men through him might believe. tell about

8 He was not that Light, but ᵀwas sent to bear witness of that Light. came

The Rejection of Christ

9 That was the true Light, which lighteth every man that cometh into the world.

10 ᵀHe was in the world, and ᴿthe world was made by him, and the world ᵀknew him not. The Word • Heb. 1:2 • recognized

11 ᴿHe came unto his own, and his ᵀown received him not. Is. 53:3; [Luke 19:14] ✶ • own people

The Acceptance of Christ

12 But as many as received him, to them gave he power to become the sons of God, even to them that believe on his name:

13 ᴿWhich were born, not of blood, nor of the will of the flesh, nor of the will of man, but of God. [1 Pet. 1:23]; 1 John 5:1

The Incarnation of Christ

14 ᴿAnd the Word was made flesh, and dwelt among us, (and we beheld his glory, the glory as of the only begotten of the Father,) full of grace and truth. Matt. 1:16

15 John bare witness of him, and cried, saying, This was he of whom I spake, He that cometh after me is ᵀpreferred before me: for he ᵀwas before me. greater • existed

16 And of his ᴿfulness have all we received, and grace for grace. Col. 1:19

17 For the law was given by Moses, but grace and truth came by Jesus Christ.

18 No man hath seen God at any time; ᴿthe only begotten Son, which is in the bosom of the Father, he hath declared him. Ps. 2:7 ✶

John's Witness to the Priests and Levites
Matt. 3:1–12; Mark 1:2–8; Luke 3:3–16

19 And this is ᴿthe record of John, when the Jews sent priests and Levites from Jerusalem to ask him, Who art thou? 5:33

20 And he ᵀconfessed, and denied not; but confessed, I am not the Christ. admitted

21 And they asked him, What then? Art thou E-li'-as? And he saith, I am not. Art thou that prophet? And he answered, No.

22 Then said they unto him, Who art thou? that we may give an answer to them that sent us. What sayest thou of thyself?

23 He said, I AM THE VOICE OF ONE CRYING IN THE WILDERNESS, ᴿMAKE STRAIGHT THE WAY OF THE LORD, as said the prophet E-sa'-ias. Is. 40:3 ✶

24 And ᵀthey which were sent were of the Pharisees. the messengers

25 And they asked him, and said unto him, Why baptizest thou then, if thou be not that Christ, nor E-li'-as, neither that prophet?

26 John answered them, saying, ᴿI baptize with water: but there standeth one among you, whom ye know not; Matt. 3:11

27 He it is, who coming after me is preferred before me, whose ᵀshoe's latchet I am not worthy to ᵀunloose. sandals • untie

28 These things were done ᴿin ᵀBeth-ab'-a-ra ᵀbeyond Jordan, where John was baptizing. Judg. 7:24 • Bethany • on the east side

John's Witness at Christ's Baptism
Matt. 3:13–17; Mark 1:9–11; Luke 3:21, 22

29 The next day John seeth Jesus coming unto him, and saith, Behold ᴿthe Lamb of God, ᴿwhich taketh away the sin of the world. [Ex. 12:3; 1 Pet. 1:19] • [Is. 53:11; 1 John 2:2]

30 This is he of whom I said, After me cometh a man which is ᴿpreferred before me: for he was before me. [Col. 1:17, 18]

31 And I knew him not: but that he should be made manifest to Israel, therefore am I come baptizing with water.

32 And John bare record, saying, ᴿI saw the Spirit descending from heaven like a dove, and it abode upon him.   Is. 42:1; 61:1 *

33 And I knew him not: but he that sent me to baptize with water, the same said unto me, Upon whom thou shalt see the Spirit descending, and remaining on him, the same is he which baptizeth with the Holy Ghost.

34 And I saw, and ᵀbare record that ᴿthis is the Son of God.   gave my testimony • Ps. 2:7; Luke 1:35 *

Andrew and Peter Follow Christ

35 Again the next day ᵀafter John stood, and two of his disciples;   John was there

36 And looking upon Jesus as he walked, he saith, ᴿBehold the Lamb of God!   v. 29

37 And the two disciples heard him speak, and they followed Jesus.

38 Then Jesus turned, and saw them following, and saith unto them, What seek ye? They said unto him, Rabbi, (which is to say, being interpreted, Master,) ᵀwhere dwellest thou?   where do you live?

39 He saith unto them, Come and see. They came and saw where he dwelt, and abode with him that day: for it was ᵀabout the tenth hour.   two hours before evening

40 One of the two which heard John speak, and followed ᵀhim, was Andrew, Simon Peter's brother.   Jesus

41 He first findeth his own brother Simon, and saith unto him, ᴿWe have found the Mes-si′-as, which is, being interpreted, ᵀthe Christ.   Dan. 9:25 * • the Anointed

42 And he brought him to Jesus. And when Jesus beheld him, he said, Thou art Simon the son of Jona: ᴿthou shalt be called Ce′-phas, which is by interpretation, A stone. Matt. 16:18

Philip and Nathanael Follow Christ

43 The day following Jesus ᵀwould go forth into Galilee, and findeth Philip, and saith unto him, Follow me.   planned to

44 Now ᴿPhilip was of Beth-sa′-i-da, the city of Andrew and Peter.   12:21

45 Philip findeth Na-than′-a-el, and saith unto him, We have found him, of whom Moses in the law, and the prophets, did write, Jesus of Nazareth, the son of Joseph.

46 And Na-than′-a-el said unto him, Can there any good thing come out of Nazareth? Philip saith unto him, Come and see.

47 Jesus saw Na-than′-a-el coming to him, and saith of him, Behold an Israelite indeed, in whom is no ᵀguile!   dishonesty

48 Na-than′-a-el saith unto him, ᵀWhence knowest thou me? Jesus answered and said unto him, Before that Philip called thee, when thou wast under the fig tree, I saw thee.   how do you know

49 Na-than′-a-el answered and saith unto him, Rabbi, ᴿthou art the Son of God; thou art ᴿthe King of Israel.   Ps. 2:7 * • Matt. 21:5

50 Jesus answered and said unto him, Because I said unto thee, I saw thee under the fig tree, believest thou? thou shalt see greater things than these.

51 And he saith unto him, Verily, verily, I say unto you, ᴿHereafter ye shall see heaven open, and the angels of God ascending and descending upon the Son of man. [Luke 2:9, 13]

CHAPTER 2

Christ Changes Water to Wine

AND the third day there was a ᴿmarriage in ᴿCana of Galilee; and the mother of Jesus was there: [Heb. 13:4] • Josh. 19:28

2 And both Jesus was ᵀcalled, and his disciples, to the marriage.   invited

3 And when they ᵀwanted wine, the mother of Jesus saith unto him, They have no wine.   needed

4 Jesus saith unto her, ᴿWoman, what have I to do with thee? ᴿmine hour is not yet come.   19:26 • 7:6

5 His mother saith unto the servants, Whatsoever he saith unto you, do it.

6 And there were set there six waterpots of stone, ᴿafter the manner of the purifying of the Jews, containing ᵀtwo or three firkins apiece.   [Mark 7:3] • 20 or 30 gallons

7 Jesus saith unto them, Fill the waterpots with water. And they filled them up to the brim.

8 And he saith unto them, Draw out now, and bear unto the ᵀgovernor of the feast. And they bare it.   man in charge

9 When the ruler of the feast had tasted ᴿthe water that was made wine, and knew not whence it was: (but the servants which drew the water knew;) the governor of the feast called the bridegroom,   4:46

10 And saith unto him, Every man at the beginning doth set forth good wine; and when men have ᵀwell drunk, then that which is worse: but thou hast kept the good wine until now.   drunk freely

The Disciples Believe

11 This beginning of miracles did Jesus in Cana of Galilee, ᴿand manifested forth his glory; and his disciples believed on him. 1:14

12 After this he went down to Ca-per′-na-um, he, and his mother, and ᴿhis brethren, and his disciples: and they continued there not many days.   Matt. 12:46

Christ Cleanses the Temple

13 ᴿAnd the Jews' passover was at hand, and Jesus went up to Jerusalem,   Ex. 12:14

14 ᴿAnd found in the temple those that sold oxen and sheep and doves, and the changers of money sitting: Mal. 3:1 *

What are you teaching?

15 And when he had made a ᵀscourge of small cords, he ᴿdrove them all out of the temple, and the sheep, and the oxen; and poured out the changers' money, and overthrew the tables; *whip* • [Jer. 10:10]

16 And said unto them that sold doves, Take these things hence; make not my Father's house an house of merchandise.

17 And his disciples remembered that it was written, ᴿTHE ZEAL OF THINE HOUSE HATH EATEN ME UP. Ps. 69:9 ✶

18 Then answered the Jews and said unto him, What sign shewest thou unto us, seeing that thou doest these things?

19 Jesus answered and said unto them, ᴿDestroy this temple, and in three days I will raise it up. Matt. 26:61; [Mark 14:58]; Acts 10:40 ✶

20 Then said the Jews, Forty and six years was this temple in building, and wilt thou ᵀrear it up in three days? *build*

21 But he spake ᴿof the temple of his body. [1 Cor. 3:16; 6:19; 2 Cor. 6:16; Col. 2:9; Heb. 8:2]

22 When therefore he was risen from the dead, his disciples remembered that he had said this unto them; and they believed the scripture, and the word which Jesus had said.

23 ᴿNow when he was in Jerusalem at the passover, in the feast *day*, many believed in his name, when they saw the miracles which he did. Mark 16:20

24 But Jesus did not commit himself unto them, because he knew all *men*,

25 And needed not that any should testify of man: for he knew what was in man.

CHAPTER 3

Christ Witnesses to Nicodemus

THERE was a man ᵀof the Pharisees, named ᴿNic-o-de'-mus, a ruler of the Jews: *who belonged to* • 7:50; 19:39

2 ᴿThe same came to Jesus by night, and said unto him, Rabbi, we know that thou art a teacher come from God: for no man can do these miracles that thou doest, except ᴿGod be with him. 7:50 • [Acts 10:38]

3 Jesus answered and said unto him, Verily, verily, I say unto thee, ᴿExcept a man be born ᵀagain, he cannot see the kingdom of God. [Gal. 6:15; 1 John 3:9] • *from above*

4 Nic-o-de'-mus saith unto him, How can a man be born when he is old? can he enter the second time into his mother's womb, and be born?

5 Jesus answered, Verily, verily, I say unto thee, ᴿExcept a man be born of ᴿwater and *of* the Spirit, he cannot enter into the kingdom of God. [Eph. 5:26] • [Titus 3:5]

6 That which is born of the flesh is flesh; and that which is born of the Spirit is spirit.

7 Marvel not that I said unto thee, Ye must be born ᵀagain. *from above*

8 The wind bloweth where it listeth, and thou hearest the sound thereof, but canst not tell whence it cometh, and whither it goeth: so is every one that is born of the Spirit.

9 Nic-o-de'-mus answered and said unto him, ᴿHow can these things be? 6:52, 60

10 Jesus answered and said unto him, Art thou a ᵀmaster of Israel, and knowest not these things? *great teacher*

11 Verily, verily, I say unto thee, We speak that we do know, and testify that we have seen; and ye receive not our witness.

12 If I have told you ᵀearthly things, and ye believe not, how shall ye believe, if I tell you *of* heavenly things? *things of this world*

13 And no man hath ᵀascended up to heaven, but he that came down from heaven, *even* the Son of man which is in heaven.

14 ᴿAnd as Moses lifted up the serpent in the wilderness, even so ᴿmust the Son of man be lifted up: Num. 21:9 • 8:28; 19:18 ✶

15 That whosoever believeth in him should not perish, but have eternal life.

16 ᴿFor God so loved the world, that he gave his only begotten Son, that whosoever believeth in him should not perish, but have everlasting life. Rom. 5:8; 1 John 4:9

17 For God sent not his Son into the world to condemn the world; but ᴿthat the world through him might be saved. Matt. 1:21 ✶

18 ᴿHe that believeth on him is not condemned: but he that believeth not is condemned already, because he hath not believed in the name of the only begotten Son of God. 5:24; [6:40], 47; 20:31

19 And this is the ᵀcondemnation, ᴿthat light is come into the world, and men loved darkness rather than light, because their deeds were evil. *judgment* • [1:4, 9–11]

20 For every one that doeth evil hateth the light, neither cometh to the light, lest his deeds should be ᵀreproved. *examined*

21 But he that doeth truth cometh to the light, that his deeds may be made manifest, that they are wrought in God.

John the Baptist Witnesses Concerning Christ

22 After these things came Jesus and his disciples into the land of Ju-dae'-a; and there he ᵀtarried with them, and baptized. *stayed*

23 And John also was baptizing in Ae'-non near to ᴿSa'-lim, because there was much water there: ᴿand they came, and were baptized. 1 Sam. 9:4 • Matt. 3:5, 6

24 For John was not yet cast into prison.

25 Then there arose a question between *some* of John's disciples and the Jews about ᵀpurifying. *religious washing*

26 And they came unto John, and said unto him, Rabbi, he that was with thee beyond Jordan, ᴿto whom thou barest witness, behold, the same baptizeth, and all *men* come to him. 1:7, 15, 27, 34

27 John answered and said, ᴿA man can ᵀreceive nothing, except it be given him from heaven. [James 1:17] • *take unto himself nothing*

28 Ye yourselves bear me witness, that I said, ᴿI am not the Christ, but ᴿthat I am sent before him. 1:20, 27; Mark 1:2 • [Luke 1:17]

29 ᴿHe that hath the bride is the bridegroom: but the friend of the bridegroom, which standeth and heareth him, rejoiceth greatly because of the bridegroom's voice: this my joy therefore is fulfilled. Rev. 21:9

30 He must increase, but I *must* decrease.

31 ᴿHe that cometh from above ᴿis above all: he that is of the earth is earthly, and speaketh of the earth: he that cometh from heaven is above all. *v.* 13 • Rom. 9:5

32 And what he hath seen and heard, that he testifieth; ᴿand no man ᵀreceiveth his testimony. Is. 53:1, 3 ★ • *will believe what he says*

33 He that hath received his testimony hath set to his seal that God is true.

34 For ᴿhe whom God hath sent speaketh the words of God: for God giveth not the Spirit by measure *unto him.* Deut. 18:18 ★

35 ᴿThe Father loveth the Son, and hath given all things into his hand. Luke 10:22

36 ᴿHe that believeth on the Son hath everlasting life: and he that believeth not the Son shall not see life; but the wrath of God ᵀabideth on him. 1 John 5:10 • *will stay*

CHAPTER 4

Christ Witnesses to the Woman at the Well

WHEN therefore the Lord knew how the Pharisees had heard that Jesus made and baptized more disciples than John,

2 (Though Jesus himself baptized not, but his disciples,)

3 He left Ju-dae'-a, and ᵀdeparted again into Galilee. *went back*

4 And he must ᵀneeds ᵀgo through Sa-ma'-ri-a. *of necessity • pass*

5 Then cometh he to a city of Sa-ma'-ri-a, which is called Sy'-char, near to the parcel of ground that Jacob gave to his son Joseph.

6 Now ᴿJacob's well was there. Jesus therefore, being wearied with *his* journey, sat thus on the well: *and* it was about the ᵀsixth hour. Gen. 33:19 • *noon*

7 There cometh a woman of Sa-ma'-ri-a to draw water: Jesus saith unto her, Give me to drink.

8 (For his disciples were gone away unto the city to buy ᵀmeat.) *food*

9 Then saith the woman of Sa-ma'-ri-a unto him, How is it that thou, being a Jew, askest drink of me, which am a woman of Sa-ma'-ri-a? for ᴿthe Jews have no dealings with the Sa-mar'-i-tans. Luke 9:52, 53

10 Jesus answered and said unto her, If thou knewest the gift of God, and who it is

that saith to thee, Give me to drink; thou wouldest have asked of him, and he would have given thee living water.

11 The woman saith unto him, Sir, thou hast nothing to draw with, and the well is deep: from whence then hast thou that ᴿliving water? Rev. 21:6; 22:17

12 Art thou greater than our father Jacob, which ᴿgave us the well, and drank thereof himself, and his children, and his cattle? *v.* 6

13 Jesus answered and said unto her, Whosoever drinketh of this water shall thirst again:

14 But ᴿwhosoever drinketh of the water that I shall give him shall never thirst; but the water that I shall give him ᴿshall be in him a well of water springing up into ᴿeverlasting life. [6:35, 58] • 7:38 • [1 John 5:20]

15 ᴿThe woman saith unto him, Sir, give me this water, that I thirst not, neither come hither to draw. [Rom. 6:23]

16 Jesus saith unto her, Go, call thy husband, and come ᵀhither. *here*

17 The woman answered and said, I have no husband. Jesus said unto her, Thou hast well said, I have no husband:

18 For thou hast had five husbands; and he whom thou now hast is not thy husband: in that saidst thou truly.

19 The woman saith unto him, Sir, I ᵀperceive that thou art a prophet. *recognize*

20 Our fathers worshipped in ᴿthis mountain; and ye say, that in Jerusalem is the place where men ought to worship. Judg. 9:7

21 Jesus saith unto her, Woman, believe me, the hour cometh, ᴿwhen ye shall neither in this mountain, nor yet at Jerusalem, worship the Father. [Mal. 1:11]

22 Ye worship ᴿye know not what: we know what we worship: for ᴿsalvation is of the Jews. [2 Kin. 17:29] • [Luke 24:47; Rom. 9:4, 5]

23 But the hour cometh, and now is, when the true worshippers shall worship the Father in spirit ᴿand in truth: for the Father seeketh such to worship him. [1:17]

24 God *is* a Spirit: and they that worship him must worship *him* in spirit and in truth.

25 The woman saith unto him, I know that Mes-si'-as cometh, which is called Christ: when he is come, he will tell us all things.

26 Jesus saith unto her, ᴿI that speak unto thee am *he.* Dan. 9:25; Matt. 26:63, 64; Mark 14:61, 62 ★

Christ Witnesses to the Disciples

27 And upon this came his disciples, and ᵀmarvelled that he talked with the woman: yet no man said, What seekest thou? or, Why talkest thou with her? *were amazed*

28 The woman then left her waterpot, and went her way into the city, and saith to the men,

29 Come, see a man, which told me all things that ever I did: is not this the Christ?

30 Then they went out of the city, and came unto him.

31 In the mean while his disciples ^Tprayed him, saying, Master, eat.   *urged*

32 But he said unto them, I have ^Tmeat to eat that ye know not of.   *food*

33 Therefore said the disciples one to another, Hath any man brought him ^Tought to eat?   *something*

34 Jesus saith unto them, ^RMy meat is to do the will of him that sent me, and to finish his work.   6:38; [17:4; 19:30]; Job 23:12

35 Say not ye, There are yet four months, and *then* cometh harvest? behold, I say unto you, Lift up your eyes, and look on the fields; for they are ^Twhite already to harvest.   *ripe*

36 ^RAnd he that reapeth receiveth wages, and gathereth fruit unto life eternal: that both he that soweth and he that reapeth may rejoice together.   Dan. 12:3

37 And herein is that saying true, One soweth, and another reapeth.

38 I sent you to reap that whereon ye ^Tbestowed no labour: other men laboured, and ye are entered into their labours.   *put*

Christ Witnesses to the Samaritans

39 And many of the Sa-mar'-i-tans of that city believed on him ^Rfor the saying of the woman, which testified, He told me all that ever I did.   *v. 29*

40 So when the Sa-mar'-i-tans were come unto him, they ^Tbesought him that he would ^Ttarry with them: and he abode there two days.   *asked • stay*

41 And many more believed because of his own word;

42 And said unto the woman, Now we believe, not because of thy saying: for ^Rwe have heard *him* ourselves, and ^Tknow that this is indeed the Christ, the Saviour of the world.   17:8; 1 John 4:14 • *recognize*

Christ Is Received by the Galilaeans

43 Now after two days he departed thence, and went into Galilee.

44 For Jesus himself testified, that a prophet hath no honour in his own country.

45 Then when he was come into Galilee, the Gal-i-lae'-ans received him, having seen all the things that he did at Jerusalem at the feast: for they also went unto the feast.

Christ Heals the Nobleman's Son

46 So Jesus came again into Cana of Galilee, where he made the water wine. And there was a certain ^Tnobleman, whose son was sick at Ca-per'-na-um.   *ruler*

47 When he heard that Jesus was come out of Ju-dae'-a into Galilee, he went unto him, and ^Tbesought him that he would come down, and heal his son: for he was at the point of death.   *begged*

48 Then said Jesus unto him, Except ye see signs and wonders, ye will not believe.

49 The nobleman saith unto him, Sir, come down ^Tere my child die.   *before*

50 Jesus saith unto him, Go thy way; thy son liveth. And the man believed the word that Jesus had spoken unto him, and he went his way.

51 And as he was now going down, his servants met him, and told *him*, saying, ^RThy son liveth.   [Ps. 111:7; Ezek. 12:25]

52 Then enquired he of them the hour when he began to ^Tamend. And they said unto him, Yesterday at the seventh hour the fever left him.   *improve*

53 So the father knew that *it was* at the same hour, in the which Jesus said unto him, Thy son liveth: and himself believed, and ^Rhis whole house.   *v. 50;* Acts 11:14

54 This *is* again the second miracle *that* Jesus did, when he was come out of Ju-dae'-a into Galilee.

CHAPTER 5

Christ Heals the Impotent Man

AFTER this there was a feast of the Jews; and Jesus went up to Jerusalem.

2 Now there is at Jerusalem by the sheep ^T*market* a pool, which is called in the Hebrew tongue Be-thes'-da, having five porches.   *gate*

3 In these lay a great multitude of ^Timpotent folk, of blind, halt, withered, waiting for the moving of the water.   *crippled*

4 For an angel went down at a certain season into the pool, and troubled the water: whosoever then first after the troubling of the water stepped in was made whole of whatsoever disease he had.

5 And a certain man was there, which had an infirmity thirty and eight years.

6 When Jesus saw him lie, and knew that he had been now a long time *in that case,* he saith unto him, Wilt thou be made whole?

7 The impotent man answered him, Sir, I have no man, when the water is troubled, to put me into the pool: but while I am coming, another steppeth down before me.

8 Jesus saith unto him, ^RRise, take up thy bed, and walk.   Matt. 9:6; Mark 2:11; Luke 5:24

9 And immediately the man was made whole, and took up his bed, and walked: and on the same day was the sabbath.

Christ Breaks the Sabbath

10 The Jews therefore said unto him that was cured, It is the sabbath day: it is not ^Tlawful for thee to carry *thy* bed.   *right*

11 He answered them, He that made me ^Twhole, the same said unto me, Take up thy ^Tbed, and walk.   *well • pallet*

12 Then asked they him, What man is that

which said unto thee, Take up thy bed, and walk?

13 And he that was healed Twist not who it was: for Jesus had conveyed himself away, a multitude being in *that* place.   *knew*

14 Afterward Jesus findeth him in the temple, and said unto him, Behold, Tthou art made whole: sin no more, lest a worse thing come unto thee.   *you have been healed*

15 The man departed, and told the Jews that it was Jesus, which had made him Twhole.   *well*

16 And therefore did the Jews persecute Jesus, and sought to slay him, because he had done these things on the sabbath day.

Equality with God in Nature

17 But Jesus answered them, RMy Father worketh hitherto, and I work.   [9:4; 14:10]

18 Therefore the Jews Rsought the more to kill him, because he not only had broken the sabbath, but said also that God was his Father, making himself equal with God.   7:19

Equality with God in Power

19 Then answered Jesus and said unto them, Verily, verily, I say unto you, The Son can do nothing of himself, but what he seeth the Father do: for what things soever he doeth, these also doeth the Son likewise.

20 For the Father loveth the Son, and sheweth him all things that himself doeth: and he will shew him greater works than these, that ye may Tmarvel.   *be surprised*

21 For as the Father raiseth up the dead, and Tquickeneth *them;* even so the Son quickeneth whom he will.   *gives back life*

Equality with God in Authority

22 For the Father judgeth no man, but Rhath committed all judgment unto the Son: 3:35; 17:2; Matt. 11:27; [Acts 17:31; 1 Pet. 4:5]

23 That all *men* should honour the Son, even as they honour the Father. He that honoureth not the Son honoureth not the Father which hath sent him.

24 Verily, verily, I say unto you, RHe that heareth my word, and believeth on him that

sent me, hath everlasting life, and shall not come into condemnation; but is passed from death unto life.   3:16

25 Verily, verily, I say unto you, The hour is coming, and now is, when Rthe dead shall hear the voice of the Son of God: and they that hear shall live.   [Eph. 2:1, 5; Col. 2:13]

26 For as the Father hath life in himself; so hath he given to the Son to Thave life in himself;   *be the source of life*

27 And Rhath given him authority to Texecute judgment also, Rbecause he is the Son of man.   [Acts 10:42] • *carry out* • Dan. 7:13

28 Marvel not at this: for the hour is coming, in the which all Tthat are in the graves shall hear his voice,   *the dead*

29 And shall come forth; they that have done good, unto the resurrection of life; and they that have done evil, unto the resurrection of Tdamnation.   *judgment*

30 I can of mine own self do nothing: as I hear, I judge: and my judgment is just; because I seek not mine own will, but the will of the Father which hath sent me.

Witness of John the Baptist

31 RIf I bear witness of myself, my witness is not true.   [8:14, 28; 12:49]; Rev. 3:14

32 RThere is another that beareth witness of me; and I know that the witness which he witnesseth of me is true.   [8:18]

33 Ye sent unto John, Rand he bare witness unto the truth.   [1:15, 19, 27, 32]

34 But I receive not Ttestimony from man: but these things I say, that ye might be saved.   *witness*

35 He was a burning and Ra shining light: and Rye were willing for Ta season to rejoice in his light.   2 Pet. 1:19 • Mark 6:20 • *a while*

Witness of the Works of Christ

36 But RI have greater witness than *that* of John: for Rthe works which the Father hath given me to finish, the same works that I do, bear witness of me, that the Father hath sent me.   1 John 5:9 • 3:2; 10:25

5:24 Everlasting Life—One benefit of finding new life in Christ is called in the Bible "everlasting [eternal!] life." The character of this great reality may be summarized by carefully looking at each word. The word *life* stresses the quality of this new relationship to God (Page 1054—John 10:10). It does not mean, of course, that we are not physically alive before salvation; it simply stresses the fact that we enter a new, personal relationship with God that gives us a fullness of spiritual vitality that we lacked before (Page 1062—John 17:3).

The word *everlasting* emphasizes life without end. Though it will not be completely fulfilled until our future bodily redemption (see Page 1115—Rom. 8:23), it is still a present possession that can never perish (Page 1055—John 10:28).

Everlasting life must not be conceived of as an exclusively future possession. Rather, its possession is clearly seen in our actions. Thus, "no murderer hath eternal life abiding in him" (Page 1251—1 John 3:15). Indeed, love is the confirming evidence that we do, in fact, have eternal life (Page 1251—1 John 3:14).

The greatness of this spiritual reality constitutes a wonderful incentive to vigorously proclaim the gospel to those who are still "dead in trespasses and sins" (Page 1162—Eph. 2:1).

Now turn to Page 1145—2 Cor. 5:17: New Nature.

Witness of the Father

37 And the Father himself, which hath sent me, [R]hath borne witness of me. Ye have neither heard his voice at any time, [R]nor seen his shape.   6:27; 8:18 • Deut. 4:12

38 And [T]ye have not his word abiding in you: for whom he hath sent, him ye believe not.   *you do not honour his word*

Witness of the Scriptures

39 [T]Search the scriptures; [T]for in them ye think ye have eternal life: and they are they which testify of me.   *ye search • because*

40 [R]And ye will not come to me, that ye might have life.   1:11; [3:19]

41 [R]I receive not honour from men.   *v. 34*

42 But I [T]know you, that ye have not the love of God in you.   *understand*

43 I am come in my Father's name, and ye receive me not: if another shall come in his own name, him ye will receive.

44 [R]How can ye believe, which receive honour one of another, and seek not the honour that *cometh* from God only?   12:43

45 Do not think that I will accuse you to the Father: there is *one* that accuseth you, *even* Moses, in whom ye [T]trust.   *hope*

46 For had ye believed Moses, ye would have believed me: for he wrote of me.

47 But if ye [T]believe not his writings, how shall ye believe my words?   *do not believe*

CHAPTER 6

Christ Feeds 5,000
Matt. 14:13–21; Mark 6:31–44; Luke 9:11–17

AFTER these things Jesus went over the sea of Galilee, which is *the sea* of Ti-be′-ri-as.

2 And a great multitude followed him, because they [T]saw his miracles which he did on them that were diseased.   *beheld the signs*

3 And Jesus went up into a mountain, and there he sat with his disciples.

4 [R]And the passover, a feast of the Jews, was [T]nigh.   Lev. 23:5, 7; Deut. 16:1 • *near at hand*

5 When Jesus then lifted up *his* eyes, and saw a great company come unto him, he saith unto Philip, Whence shall we buy bread, that these may eat?

6 And this he said to [T]prove him: for he himself knew what he would do.   *test*

7 Philip answered him, [R]Two[T] hundred pennyworth of bread is not sufficient for them, that every one of them may take a little.   Num. 11:21, 22 • *200 days' wages*

8 One of his disciples, Andrew, Simon Peter's brother, saith unto him,

9 There is a lad here, which hath five barley loaves, and two small fishes: [R]but what are they among so many?   2 Kin. 4:43

10 And Jesus said, Make the men sit down. Now there was much grass in the place. So the men sat down, in number about [R]five thousand.   Matt. 14:21

11 And Jesus took the loaves; and when he had given thanks, he distributed to the disciples, and the disciples to them that were set down; and likewise of the fishes as much as they [T]would.   *wanted*

12 When they were filled, he said unto his disciples, Gather up the [T]fragments that remain, that nothing be lost.   *pieces*

13 Therefore they gathered *them* together, and filled twelve baskets with the fragments of the five barley loaves, which remained over and above unto them that had eaten.

14 Then those men, when they had seen the miracle that Jesus did, said, This is of a truth [R]that prophet that [T]should come into the world.   Deut. 18:15, 18 ★ • *was expected to*

Christ Walks on the Water
Matt. 14:22–33; Mark 6:45–52

15 When Jesus therefore [T]perceived that they would come and take him by force, to make him a king, he departed again into a mountain himself alone.   *understood*

16 And when even was now come, his disciples went down unto the sea,

17 And entered into a ship, and went over the sea toward Ca-per′-na-um. And it was now dark, and Jesus was not come to them.

18 And the sea [T]arose by reason of a great wind that blew.   *stirred*

19 So when they had rowed about [T]five and twenty or thirty furlongs, they see Jesus walking on the sea, and drawing nigh unto the ship: and they were afraid.   3 to 3.5 miles

20 But he saith unto them, It is I; be not afraid.

21 Then they willingly [T]received him into the ship: and immediately the ship was at the land whither they went.   *took*

"I Am the Bread of Life"

22 The day following, when the people which stood on the other side of the sea saw that there was none other [T]boat there, save that one whereinto his disciples were entered, and that Jesus went not with his disciples into the boat, but *that* his disciples were gone away alone;   *little boat*

23 (Howbeit there came other [T]boats from Ti-be′-ri-as nigh unto the place where they did eat bread, after that the Lord had given thanks:)   *little boats*

24 When the people therefore saw that Jesus was not there, neither his disciples, they also took [T]shipping, and came to Ca-per′-na-um, seeking for Jesus.   *to the boats*

25 And when they had found him on the other side of the sea, they said unto him, Rabbi, when camest thou hither?

26 Jesus answered them and said, Verily, verily, I say unto you, Ye seek me, not because ye saw the miracles, but because ye did eat of the loaves, and were filled.

27 ᵀLabour not for the meat which perisheth, but ᴿfor that meat which endureth unto everlasting life, which the Son of man shall give unto you: ᴿfor him hath God the Father sealed.　　　　　　　work not • 4:14 • 2 Pet. 1:17

28 Then said they unto him, What shall we do, that we might work the works of God?

29 Jesus answered and said unto them, ᴿThis is the work of God, that ye believe on him whom he hath sent.　　　　　Acts 10:35

30 They said therefore unto him, What sign shewest thou then, that we may see, and believe thee? what dost thou work?

31 ᴿOur fathers did eat man'-na in the desert; as it is written, ᴿHE GAVE THEM BREAD FROM HEAVEN TO EAT.　　　Ex. 16:15 • Ps. 78:24

32 Then Jesus said unto them, ᵀVerily, verily, I say unto you, Moses gave you not that bread from heaven; but my Father giveth you the true bread from heaven.　　　　　　　　　truly, truly

33 For the ᵀbread of God is he which cometh down from heaven, and giveth life unto the world.　　　　bread which God gives

34 ᴿThen said they unto him, Lord, evermore give us this bread.　　　　4:15

35 And Jesus said unto them, ᴿI am the bread of life: ᴿhe that cometh to me shall never hunger; and he that believeth on me shall never thirst.　　vv. 48, 58 • 4:14; 7:37

36 ᴿBut I said unto you, That ye also have seen me, and believe not.　　　vv. 26, 64

37 ᴿAll that the Father giveth me shall come to me; and him that cometh to me I will in no wise cast out.　　　　　　　v. 45

38 For I came down from heaven, ᴿnot to do mine own will, ᴿbut the will of him that sent me.　　　　　Matt. 26:39 • 4:34; 5:30

39 And this is the Father's will which hath sent me, that of all which he hath given me I should lose nothing, but should raise it up again ᴿat the last day.　　　vv. 40, 44, 54

40 And this is the will of him that sent me, that every one which seeth the Son, and believeth on him, may have everlasting life: and I will raise him up at the last day.

41 The Jews then ᵀmurmured at him, because he said, I am the bread which came down from heaven.　　　　　complained

42 And they said, ᴿIs not this Jesus, the son of Joseph, whose father and mother we know? how is it then that he saith, I came down from heaven?　　Matt. 13:55; Mark 6:3

43 Jesus therefore answered and said unto them, Murmur not among yourselves.

44 ᴿNo man can come to me, except the Father which hath sent me draw him: and I will raise him up at the last day.　　　v. 65

45 It is written in the prophets, ᴿAND THEY

SHALL BE ALL TAUGHT OF GOD. Every man therefore that hath heard, and hath learned of the Father, cometh unto me.　　Is. 54:13 ★

46 ᴿNot that any man hath seen the Father, ᴿsave he which is of God, he hath seen the Father.　　1:18 • 7:29; [Luke 10:22]

47 Verily, verily, I say unto you, He that believeth on me hath everlasting life.

48 ᴿI am that bread of life.　　vv. 33, 35

49 ᴿYour fathers did eat man'-na in the wilderness, and are dead.　　　　v. 31

50 ᵀThis is the ᴿbread which cometh down from heaven, that a man may eat thereof, and not die.　　　　this new bread • vv. 33, 35

51 I am the living bread ᴿwhich came down from heaven: if any man eat of this bread, he shall live for ever: and ᴿthe bread that I will give is my flesh, which I will give for the life of the world.　　　3:13 • Heb. 10:5

52 The Jews therefore ᴿstroveᵀ among themselves, saying, How can this man give us his flesh to eat?　　7:43; 9:16; 10:19 • argued

53 Then Jesus said unto them, Verily, verily, I say unto you, Except ᴿye eat the flesh of the Son of man, and drink his blood, ye have no life in you.　　　Matt. 26:26

54 Whoso eateth my flesh, and drinketh my blood, hath eternal life; and I will raise him up ᴿat the last day.　　vv. 39, 40, 44; 11:24

55 For my flesh is ᵀmeat indeed, and my blood is ᵀdrink indeed.　the real food • the real drink

56 He that eateth my flesh, and drinketh my blood, dwelleth in me, and I in him.

57 As the living Father hath sent me, and I live by the Father: so he that eateth me, even he shall live ᵀby me.　　　　because of

58 ᴿThis is that bread which came down from heaven: not as your fathers did eat man'-na, and are dead: he that eateth of this bread shall live for ever.　　　vv. 49–51

59 These things said he in the synagogue, as he taught in Ca-per'-na-um.

Rejection by Many Followers

60 Many therefore of his disciples, when they had heard this, said, This is ᵀan hard saying; who can ᵀhear it?　a difficult • understand

61 When Jesus knew in himself that his disciples ᵀmurmured at it, he said unto them, Doth this offend you?　　　complained

62 What and if ᴿye shall see the Son of man ascend up where he was before? Acts 1:9 ★

63 ᴿIt is the spirit that ᵀquickeneth; the flesh ᵀprofiteth nothing: the words that I speak unto you, they are spirit, and they are life.　2 Cor. 3:6 • makes alive • helps nothing

64 But ᴿthere are some of you that believe not. For ᴿJesus knew from the beginning who they were that believed not, and who should betray him.　　　v. 36 • 2:24, 25

65 And he said, Therefore ᴿsaid I unto you, that no man can come unto me, except it were given unto him of my Father.　　v. 44

66 From that *time* many of his disciples went back, and walked no more with him.

Confession by Peter

67 Then said Jesus unto the twelve, ᵀWill ye also go away?   *would you like*

68 Then Simon Peter answered him, Lord, to whom shall we go? thou hast ᴿthe words of eternal life.   Acts 5:20

69 And we believe and are sure that thou art that Christ, the Son of the living God.

70 Jesus answered them, Have not I chosen you twelve, and one of you is a devil?

71 He spake of Judas Is-car'-i-ot *the son* of Simon: for he it was that should betray him, ᵀbeing one of the twelve.   *though*

CHAPTER 7

Christ's Brothers Do Not Believe

AFTER these things Jesus walked in Galilee: for he would not walk in Jewry, ᴿbecause the Jews sought to kill him.   5:16, 18

2 ᴿNow the Jews' feast of tabernacles was at hand.   Lev. 23:34

3 ᴿHis brethren therefore said unto him, Depart hence, and go into Ju-dae'-a, that thy disciples also may see the works that thou doest.   Matt. 12:46; Mark 3:31; Acts 1:14

4 For *there is* no man *that* doeth any thing in ᵀsecret, and he himself seeketh to be known openly. If thou do these things, shew thyself to the world.   *hiding*

5 For ᵀneither ᴿdid his brethren believe in him.   *not even* · Ps. 69:8; Mic. 7:6; Mark 3:21 *

6 Then Jesus said unto them, My time is not yet come: but your time is alway ready.

7 ᴿThe world cannot hate you; but me it hateth, ᴿbecause I testify of it, that the works thereof are evil.   [15:18–19] · 3:19

8 Go ye up unto this feast: I go not up yet unto this feast; ᴿfor ᵀmy time is not yet full come.   8:20 · *the right time*

9 When he had said these words unto them, he ᵀabode *still* in Galilee.   *stayed*

Christ Secretly Goes to the Feast

10 But when his brethren ᵀwere gone up, then went he also up unto the feast, not openly, but as it were in secret.   *went*

11 Then ᴿthe Jews sought him at the feast, and said, Where is he?   11:56

12 And there was much ᵀmurmuring among the people concerning him: for some said, He is a good man: others said, Nay; but he deceiveth the people.   *discussion*

13 Howbeit no man spake openly of him ᴿfor fear of the Jews.   [9:22; 12:42]; 19:38

Christ's Authority from the Father

14 Now about the midst of the feast ᴿJesus went up into the temple, and taught. Ps. 22:22 *

15 ᴿAnd the Jews marvelled, saying, How knoweth this man letters, having never learned?   Matt. 13:54; Mark 6:2; [Luke 4:22]; Acts 2:7

16 Jesus answered them, and said, My doctrine is not mine, but his that sent me.

17 ᴿIf any man will do his will, he shall know of the doctrine, whether it be of God, or *whether* I speak of myself.   8:43

18 He that speaketh of himself seeketh his own glory: but he that seeketh his glory that sent him, the same is ᵀtrue, and no ᵀunrighteousness is in him.   *genuine* · *deceit*

19 ᴿDid not Moses give you the law, and *yet* none of you keepeth the law? ᴿWhy go ye about to kill me?   Acts 7:38 · Matt. 12:14

20 The people answered and said, Thou hast a devil: who goeth about to kill thee?

21 Jesus answered and said unto them, I have done one work, and ye all marvel.

22 ᴿMoses therefore gave unto you circumcision; (not because it is of Moses, ᴿbut of the fathers;) and ye on the sabbath day circumcise a man.   Lev. 12:3 · Gen. 17:10

23 If a man on the sabbath day receive circumcision, that the law of Moses should not be broken; are ye angry at me, because ᴿI have made a man every ᵀwhit whole on the sabbath day?   5:8, 9, 16 · *bit healthy*

24 ᴿJudge not according to the appearance, but judge righteous judgment.   James 2:1

Christ's Origin from the Father

25 Then said some of them of Jerusalem, Is not this he, whom they seek to kill?

26 But, lo, he speaketh boldly, and they say nothing unto him. ᴿDo the rulers know indeed that this is the very Christ?   *v. 48*

27 ᴿHowbeit we know this man whence he is: but when Christ cometh, no man knoweth whence he is.   Mark 6:3; Luke 4:22

28 Then cried Jesus in the temple as he taught, saying, ᴿYe both know me, and ye know whence I am: and I am not come of myself, but he that sent me ᴿis ᵀtrue, whom ye know not.   8:14 · Rom. 3:4 · *genuine*

29 But ᴿI ᵀknow him: for I am from him, and he hath sent me.   Matt. 11:27 · *honour*

30 Then they sought to take him: but ᴿno man laid hands on him, because his hour was not yet come.   *v. 44*

31 And ᴿmany of the people believed on him, and said, When Christ cometh, will he do more ᵀmiracles than these which this *man* hath done?   Matt. 12:23 · *signs*

Christ's Departure to the Father

32 The Pharisees heard that the people ᵀmurmured such things concerning him; and the Pharisees and the chief priests sent officers to take him.   *rumored*

33 Then said Jesus unto them, ᴿYet a little while am I with you, and *then* I go unto him that sent me.   13:33; Mark 16:19; Acts 1:9 ☆

34 Ye shall seek me, and shall not find *me:* and where I am, *thither* ye cannot come.

35 Then said the Jews among themselves, Whither will he go, that we shall not find

him? will he go unto the dispersed among the ᵀGentiles, and teach the Gentiles?   *Greeks*

36 What *manner of* saying is this that he said, Ye shall seek me, and shall not find *me:* and where I am, *thither* ye cannot come?

Christ Reveals the "Living Water"

37 In the last day, that great *day* of the feast, Jesus stood and cried, saying, If any man thirst, let him come unto me, and drink.

38 ᴿHe that believeth on me, as the scripture hath said, out of his belly shall flow rivers of ᵀliving water.   *Deut. 18:15 · running*

39 (ᴿBut this spake he of the Spirit, which they that believe on him should receive: for the Holy Ghost was not yet *given;* because that Jesus was not yet glorified.)   *Acts 5:32*

Israel Is Divided over Christ

40 Many of the people therefore, when they heard this saying, said, Of a truth this is ᴿthe Prophet.   *Deut. 18:15*

41 Others said, This is the Christ. But some said, Shall Christ come out of Galilee?

42 ᴿHath not the scripture said, That Christ cometh of the seed of David, and out of the town of Beth'-le-hem, ᴿwhere David was?   *Mic. 5:2; [Luke 2:4] · 1 Sam. 16:1, 4*

43 So ᴿthere was a division ᵀamong the people because of him.   *v. 12 · in the crowd*

44 And ᴿsome of them would have taken him; but no man laid hands on him.   *v. 30*

The Sanhedrin Is Confused over Christ

45 Then came the officers to the chief priests and Pharisees; and they said unto them, Why have ye not brought him?

46 The officers answered, Never man ᵀspake like this man.   *talked*

47 Then answered them the Pharisees, Are ye also ᵀdeceived?   *fooled*

48 ᴿHave any of the rulers or of the Pharisees believed on him?   *vv. 50–53*

49 But this people who ᵀknoweth not the ᵀlaw are cursed.   *understands · law of Moses*

50 Nic-o-de'-mus saith unto them, (ᴿHe that came to Jesus by night, being one of them,)   *3:2; 19:39*

51 Doth our law judge *any* man, before it hear him, and know what he doeth?

52 They answered and said unto him, Art thou also of Galilee? Search, and look: for ᴿout of Galilee ariseth no prophet.   *[Is. 9:1, 2]*

53 And every man went ᵀunto his own house.   *home*

CHAPTER 8

A Woman Is Caught in Adultery

JESUS went unto the mount of Olives.
2 And early in the morning he came ᵀagain into the temple, and all the people came unto him; and he sat down, and taught them.   *back*

3 And the scribes and Pharisees brought unto him a woman taken in adultery; and when they had set her in the midst,

4 They say unto him, Master, this woman was taken in adultery, in the very act.

5 ᴿNow Moses in the law commanded us, that such should be ᵀstoned: but what sayest thou?   *Lev. 20:10; Deut. 22:22 · stoned to death*

6 This they said, tempting him, that they might have to accuse him. But Jesus stooped down, and with *his* finger wrote on the ground, *as though he heard them not.*

7 So when they continued asking him, he lifted up himself, and said unto them, ᴿHe that is without sin among you, let him first cast a stone at her.   *Deut. 17:7; [Rom. 2:1]*

8 And again he stooped down, and wrote on the ground.

9 And they which heard *it,* being convicted by *their own* conscience, went out one by one, beginning at the eldest, *even* unto the last: and Jesus was left alone, and the woman standing in the midst.

10 When Jesus had lifted up himself, and saw none but the woman, he said unto her, Woman, where are those thine accusers? ᵀhath no man ᵀcondemned thee?   *did · condemn*

11 She said, No man, Lord. And Jesus said unto her, ᴿNeither do I condemn thee: go, and ᴿsin no more.   *[3:17; Luke 9:56] · [5:14]*

"I Am the Light of the World"

12 Then spake Jesus again unto them, saying, I am the light of the world: he that followeth me shall not walk in darkness, but shall have the light of life.

13 The Pharisees therefore said unto him, Thou ᵀbearest record of thyself; thy record is not ᵀtrue.   *gives testimony · testimony*

14 Jesus answered and said unto them, Though I bear record of myself, *yet* my record is true: for I know whence I came, and whither I go; but ᴿye cannot tell whence I come, and whither I go.   *7:28*

15 ᴿYe judge ᵀafter the flesh; ᴿI judge no man.   *7:24 · according to human ideas · [3:17; Acts 10:42]*

16 And yet if I judge, my judgment is true: for ᴿI am not alone, but I and the Father that sent me.   *16:32*

17 ᴿIt is also written in your law, that the testimony of two men is true.   *Heb. 10:28*

18 I am one that bear witness of myself, and ᴿthe Father that sent me ᵀbeareth witness of me.   *5:37 · testifies*

19 Then said they unto him, Where is thy Father? Jesus answered, ᴿYe neither know me, nor my Father: if ye had known me, ye should have known my Father also.   *16:3*

20 These words spake Jesus in ᴿthe treasury, as he taught in the temple: and ᴿno man laid hands on him; for ᴿhis hour was not yet come.   *Mark 12:41 · 7:30 · 7:8*

21 Then said Jesus again unto them, I go my way, and ᴿye shall seek me, and ᴿshall

die in your sins: ^Rwhither I go, ye cannot come.   7:34; 13:33 • Mark 16:19; Acts 1:9 ✩ • v. 24

22 Then said the ^TJews, Will he kill himself? because he saith, Whither I go, ye cannot come.   *Jewish authorities*

23 And he said unto them, Ye are from beneath; I am from above: ^Rye are of this world; I am not of this world.   1 John 4:5

24 ^RI said therefore unto you, that ye shall die in your sins: for if ye believe not that I am *he,* ye shall die in your sins.   v. 21

25 Then said they unto him, Who art thou? And Jesus saith unto them, Even *the same* that I said unto you from the beginning.

26 I have many things to say and to judge of you: but ^Rhe that sent me is ^Ttrue; and I speak to the world those things which I have heard of him.   7:28 • *reliable*

27 They understood not that he spake to them of the Father.

28 Then said Jesus unto them, When ye have ^Rlifted^T up the Son of man, then shall ye know that I am *he,* and *that* I do nothing of myself; but as my Father hath taught me, I speak these things.   19:18; Matt. 27:35 • *crucified*

29 And he that sent me is with me: the Father hath not left me alone; for I do always those things that please him.

30 As he spake these words, ^Rmany believed ^Ton him.   7:31; 10:42; 11:45 • *in*

31 Then said Jesus to those Jews which believed on him, If ye continue in my word, then are ye my disciples indeed;

32 And ye shall know the truth, and ^Rthe truth shall make you free.   [James 1:25]

33 They answered him, We be Abraham's seed, and were never in bondage to any man: how sayest thou, Ye shall be made free?

34 Jesus answered them, Verily, verily, I say unto you, ^RWhosoever committeth sin is the servant of sin.   Rom. 6:16; 2 Pet. 2:19

35 And the servant abideth not in the house for ever: *but* the Son abideth ever.

36 ^RIf the Son therefore shall make you free, ye shall be free indeed.   [Rom. 8:2]; Gal. 5:1

37 I ^Tknow that ye are Abraham's seed; but ye seek to kill me, because my word ^Thath no place in you.   *realize • you do not accept*

38 ^RI speak that which I have seen with my Father: and ye do that which ye have seen with your father.   3:32; [5:19, 30; 14:10]

39 They answered and said unto him, ^RAbraham is our father. Jesus saith unto them, If ye were Abraham's children, ye would do the works of Abraham.   [Rom. 2:28]

40 ^RBut now ye seek to kill me, a man that hath told you the truth, which I have heard of God: this did not Abraham.   v. 37

41 Ye do the deeds of your father. Then said they to him, We be not born of fornication; we have one Father, *even* God.

42 Jesus said unto them, ^RIf God were your Father, ye would love me: for I proceeded forth and came from God; neither came I of myself, but he sent me.   1 John 5:1

43 ^RWhy do ye not understand my speech? *even* because ye cannot hear my word.   [7:17]

44 ^RYe are of *your* father the devil, and the ^Tlusts of your father ye will do. He was a murderer from the beginning, and ^Rabode^T not in the truth, because there is no truth in him. When he speaketh a lie, he speaketh of his own: for he is a liar, and the father of it.   1 John 3:8 • *desires* • [Jude 6] • *lived*

45 And because I tell *you* the truth, ye ^Tbelieve me not.   *choose not to believe me*

46 Which of you ^Tconvinceth me of sin? And if I say the truth, why do ye not believe me?   *can prove I sin*

47 ^RHe that is of God heareth God's words: ye therefore hear *them* not, because ye are not of God.   10:27; 1 John 4:6

48 Then answered the Jews, and said unto him, Say we not well that thou art a Sa-mar'-i-tan, and ^Thast a devil?   *are crazy?*

49 Jesus answered, I have not a devil; but I honour my Father, and ye do dishonour me.

50 And ^RI seek not mine own glory: there is one that seeketh and judgeth.   5:41

51 Verily, verily, I say unto you, If a man keep my saying, he shall never see death.

52 Then said the Jews unto him, Now we

8:31 God's Word Confirms—To confirm means to fully establish a truth or fact. The Bible should be used to confirm the truth in our own hearts.

a. It confirms our salvation. Often Christians are troubled with doubts about their conversion experience. Did God really save them when they asked Him to do so? Are they still saved today? A number of verses may be used to confirm our salvation. One of the strongest is Jesus' own words in the gospel of John: "Verily, verily, I say unto you, He that heareth my word, and believeth on him that sent me, hath everlasting life, and shall not come into condemnation; but is passed from death unto life" (Page 1047—John 5:24). Compare John 3:16; 6:27, 35, 37, 40; 10:27–29; Romans 8:1.

b. It confirms the hand of God in all of life's bitter disappointments. Undoubtedly a most important verse of reassurance and comfort in the hour of great need is Romans 8:28: "And we know that all things work together for good to them that love God, to them who are the called according to *his* purpose."

c. It confirms our forgiveness when we sin. Sometimes believers carry with them an unnecessary burden of guilt over past sins and failures. Even though these have been confessed, they have difficulty believing God has truly forgiven and cleansed them. But time and again the Bible assures us that all confessed sin is instantly and eternally forgiven (Page 560—Ps. 32:5; 103:12; Page 684—Is. 38:17).

Now turn to Page 630—Prov. 22:21: God's Word Equips.

know that thou ᵀhast a devil. Abraham is dead, and the prophets; and thou sayest, If a man keep my saying, he shall never ᵀtaste of death.   *are possessed of a demon • die*

53 Art thou greater than our father Abraham, which is dead? and the prophets are dead: whom makest thou thyself?

54 Jesus answered, If I honour myself, my honour is nothing: ᴿit is my Father that honoureth me; of whom ye say, that he is your God: 5:41

55 Yet ye have not ᵀknown him; but I know him: and if I should say, I know him not, I shall be a liar like unto you: but I know him, and keep his saying.   *appreciated*

56 Your father Abraham rejoiced to see my day: and he saw *it*, and was glad.

57 Then said the ᴿJews unto him, Thou art not yet fifty years old, and hast thou seen Abraham?   1:19

58 Jesus said unto them, Verily, verily, I say unto you, Before Abraham was, I am.

59 Then ᴿtook they up stones to cast at him: but Jesus hid himself, and went out of the temple, ᴿgoing through the midst of them, and so passed by.   10:31, 39 • Luke 4:30

CHAPTER 9

Christ Heals the Blind Man

AND as *Jesus* passed by, he saw a man which was blind from *his* birth.

2 And his disciples asked him, saying, Master, ᴿwho did sin, this man, or his parents, that he was born blind?   *v. 34*

3 Jesus answered, Neither hath this man sinned, nor his parents: ᴿbut that the works of God should be made manifest in him. 11:4

4 ᴿI must ᵀwork the works of him that sent me, while it is day: the night cometh, when no man can work.   4:34; [5:19] • *do*

5 As long as I am in the world, ᴿI am the light ᵀof the world.   [1:5, 9] • *for*

6 When he had thus spoken, ᴿhe spat on the ground, and made clay of the spittle, and he ᵀanointed the eyes of the blind man with the clay,   Mark 7:33 • *rubbed*

7 And said unto him, Go, wash in the pool of Si-lo′-am, (which is by interpretation, Sent.) ᴿHe went his way therefore, and washed, and came seeing.   2 Kin. 5:14

8 The neighbours therefore, and they which before had seen him ᵀthat he was blind, said, Is not this he that ᴿsat and begged?   *when* • Acts 3:2, 10

9 Some said, This is he: others *said,* He ᵀis like him: *but* he said, I am *he.*   *looks*

10 Therefore said they unto him, How were thine eyes opened?

11 He answered and said, A man that is called Jesus made clay, and ᵀanointed mine eyes, and said unto me, Go to the pool of Si-

lo′-am, and wash: and I went and washed, and I received sight.   *put clay on*

12 Then said they unto him, Where is he? He said, I know not.

13 They brought to the Pharisees him that ᵀaforetime was blind.   *had been*

14 And it was the sabbath day when Jesus made the clay, and opened his eyes.

15 Then ᴿagain the Pharisees also asked him how he had received his sight. He said unto them, He put clay upon mine eyes, and I washed, and do see.   9:10

16 Therefore said some of the Pharisees, This man is not of God, because he keepeth not the sabbath day. Others said, ᴿHow can a man that is a sinner do such miracles? And there was a division among them.   *v. 33*

17 They say unto the blind man again, What sayest thou of him, that he hath opened thine eyes? He said, ᴿHe is a prophet.   4:19; [6:14]

18 But the Jews did not believe concerning him, that he had been blind, and received his sight, until they called the parents of him that had received his sight.

19 And they asked them, saying, Is this your son, who ye say was born blind? how then doth he now ᵀsee?   *have vision*

20 His parents answered them and said, We know that this is our son, and that he was born ᵀblind: *without sight*

21 But by what means he now seeth, we know not; or who ᵀhath opened his eyes, we know not: he is of age; ask him: he shall speak for himself.   *gave him sight*

22 These *words* spake his parents, because they feared the Jews: for the Jews had agreed already, that if any man did confess that he was Christ, he should be ᵀput out of the synagogue.   *excluded from*

23 ᵀTherefore said his parents, He is of age; ask him.   *that is why his parents said*

24 Then again called they the man that was blind, and said unto him, Give God the praise: we know that this man is a sinner.

25 He answered and said, Whether he be a sinner *or no,* I know not: one thing I know, that, whereas I was blind, now I see.

26 Then said they to him again, What did he to thee? how opened he thine eyes?

27 He answered them, I have told you already, and ye did not ᵀhear: wherefore would ye hear *it* again? will ye ᵀalso be his disciples?   *accept what I say • like to*

28 Then they reviled him, and said, Thou art his disciple; but we are Moses' disciples.

29 We know that God spake unto Moses: *as for* this ᵀfellow, ᴿwe ᵀknow not from whence he is.   *man* • 8:14 • *understand*

30 The man answered and said unto them, ᴿWhy herein is a marvellous thing, that ye know not from whence he is, and *yet* he hath opened mine eyes.   3:10

31 Now we know that God heareth not

sinners: but if any man be a worshipper of God, and doeth his will, him he heareth.

32 Since the world began ᵀwas it not heard that any man opened the eyes of one that was born blind.   *it has never been heard*

33 ᴿIf this man ᵀwere not of God, he could do nothing.   *v. 16 • came not from*

34 They answered and said unto him, ᴿThou wast altogether born in sins, and dost thou teach us? And they cast him out.   *v. 2*

35 Jesus heard that they had cast him out; and when he had found him, he said unto him, Dost thou believe on the Son of God?

36 He answered and said, Who is he, Lord, that I might believe on him?

37 And Jesus said unto him, Thou hast both seen him, and ᴿit is he that ᵀtalketh with thee.   *4:26 • is speaking to you now*

38 And he said, ᴿLord, I believe. And he ᵀworshipped him.   *Mark 9:24 • knelt before*

39 And Jesus said, ᴿFor judgment I am come into this world, ᴿthat they which see not might see; and that they which see might be made blind.   *[5:22, 27] • Matt. 13:13*

40 And *some* of the Pharisees which were with him heard these words, ᴿand said unto him, Are we blind also?   *[Rom. 2:19]*

41 Jesus said unto them, If ye were blind, ye should have no sin: but now ye say, We see; therefore your sin remaineth.

CHAPTER 10

"I Am the Good Shepherd"

VERILY, verily, I say unto you, He that entereth not by the door into the sheepfold, but climbeth up some other way, the same is a thief and a robber.

2 But he that ᵀentereth in by the door is the shepherd of the sheep.   *goes*

3 To him the porter openeth; and the sheep hear his voice: and he calleth his own sheep by name, and leadeth them out.

4 And when he putteth forth his own sheep, he goeth before them, and the sheep follow him: for they know his voice.

5 And a ᴿstranger will they not follow, but will flee from him: for they know not the voice of strangers.   *[2 Cor. 11:13-15]*

6 This ᵀparable spake Jesus unto them: but they understood not what things they were which he spake unto them.   *allegory*

7 Then said Jesus unto them again, ᵀVerily, verily, I say unto you, I am the door ᵀof the sheep.   *Truly, truly • for*

8 All that ever came before me are thieves and robbers: but the sheep did not ᵀhear them.   *listen*

9 ᴿI am the door: by me if any man enter in, he shall be saved, and shall go in and out, and ᵀfind pasture.   *[Eph. 2:18] • be nourished*

10 The thief cometh not, but for to steal, and to kill, and to destroy: I am come that they might have life, and that they might have *it* ᵀmore abundantly.   *in fullest measure*

11 I am the good shepherd: the good shepherd giveth his life for the sheep.

12 But he that is ᵀan hireling, and not ᵀthe shepherd, whose own the sheep are not, seeth the wolf coming, and leaveth the sheep, and fleeth: and the wolf catcheth them, and scattereth the sheep.   *an • a*

13 The hireling fleeth, because he is an hireling, and careth not for the sheep.

14 I am the good ᴿshepherd, and know my *sheep,* and am known of mine.   *Is. 40:11 ★*

15 ᴿAs the Father knoweth me, even so

10:10 The Earthly Life of the Son of God—Since the gospel narratives are mainly concerned with Jesus' earthly ministry, it is important that the main aspects of His teaching be recognized. The most important of these are: the kingdom of God (Page 944—Matt. 5—7; 24—25); His divine authority over men (Page 948—Matt. 7:28, 29; Page 980—Mark 2:10); His own role as God and Messiah demonstrated by miracles and signs (Page 958—Matt. 16:15–20); the significance of His death and resurrection (Page 958—Matt. 16:21; Page 1037—Luke 24:26); the relationship which His disciples and subsequent believers are to share with Him (Page 1058—John 13—16); and the urgency of His commission to believers to make disciples (Page 974—Matt. 28:19, 20).

Of the many events of His earthly life the most significant, without a doubt, are His death and resurrection. On these two pivotal, historical incidents rests the validity of the entire Christian faith (Page 1137—1 Cor. 15:14). It is vital then to understand the nature of these two events. The death of Christ was first of all a humiliating physical death (Page 1064—John 19:18, 33). More than that, for a brief time it constituted a spiritual separation from God (Page 972—Matt. 27:46). Within this moment there occurred the inexplicable mystery of the Father punishing the Son for the sins of the world (Page 1238—1 Pet. 3:18; Page 1146—2 Cor. 5:21). This event, though it was the greatest crime of human history, was in the plan of God (Page 1073—Acts 2:23), and thus became the basis of salvation for sinners (Page 695—Is. 53:5).

The power of the death of Christ would be nullified without His bodily resurrection. Though it does not justify us, the resurrection demonstrated that His death, by which believing sinners are justified, was valid (Page 1137—1 Cor. 15:12–20). While skeptics have denied the bodily resurrection of Christ, the historical evidence for it is overwhelming: the many separate accounts of post-resurrection appearances, the empty tomb, and the transformed disciples. Every life that has been dramatically and wonderfully changed by believing in Christ since the first century is a testimony to its historical reality. Furthermore, it is the power of the resurrection that marvelously empowers Christians today to live the Christian life (Page 1162—Eph. 1:19, 20; Page 1172—Phil. 3:10).

Now turn to Page 990—Mark 10:45: The Ministry of the Son of God.

know I the Father: ^Rand I lay down my life for the sheep.   Matt. 11:27 • [15:13]; Matt. 27:50 ☆

16 And ^Rother sheep I have, which are not of this fold: them also I must bring, and they shall hear my voice; and there shall be one fold, *and* one shepherd.   Is. 42:6; 56:8; Acts 10:45 ★

17 Therefore doth my Father love me, ^Rbecause I ^Tlay down my life, that I might take it again.   [Is. 53:7, 8, 12; Heb. 2:9] • *give up*

18 No man taketh it from me, but I lay it down of myself. I have power to lay it down, and I have power to take it again. This commandment have I received of my Father.

19 There was a division therefore again among the Jews for these ^Tsayings.   *remarks*

20 And many of them said, He hath a devil, and is ^Tmad; why hear ye him?   *crazy*

21 Others said, These are not the words of him that hath a devil. ^RCan a ^Tdevil open the eyes of the blind?   [Ex. 4:11] • *demon*

The Opposition at the Feast of Dedication in Jerusalem

22 And it was at Jerusalem the feast of the dedication, and it was winter.

23 And Jesus ^Twalked in the temple ^Rin Solomon's porch.   *was walking* • Acts 3:11

24 Then came the Jews round about him, and said unto him, How long dost thou ^Tmake us to doubt? If thou be the Christ, tell us plainly.   *hold us in suspense?*

25 Jesus answered them, I told you, and ye believed not: ^Rthe works that I do in my Father's name, they bear witness of me.   *v. 38*

26 But ^Rye believe not, because ye are not of my sheep, as I said unto you.   [8:47]

27 ^RMy sheep hear my voice, and I ^Tknow them, and they follow me: vv. 4, 14 • *recognize*

28 And I give unto them eternal life; and they shall never perish, neither shall any *man* pluck them out of my hand.

29 My Father, which gave *them* me, is greater than all; and no *man* is able to pluck *them* out of my Father's hand.

30 ^RI and *my* Father are one.   17:11, 22

31 Then ^Rthe Jews took up stones again to ^Tstone him.   8:59 • *throw at*

32 Jesus answered them, Many good works have I shewed you from my Father; for which of those works do ye stone me?

33 The Jews answered him, saying, For a good work we stone thee not; but for blasphemy; and because that thou, being a man, ^Rmakest thyself God.   5:18

34 Jesus answered them, ^RIs it not written in your law, I SAID, YE ARE GODS?   Ps. 82:6

35 If he called them gods, unto whom the word of God came, and the scripture ^Tcannot be broken;   *is true forever*

36 Say ye of him, whom the Father hath sanctified, and ^Rsent into the world, Thou blasphemest; because I said, I am ^Rthe Son of God?   3:17 • 5:17, 18 • Luke 1:35

37 ^RIf I do not ^Tthe works of my Father, believe me not.   15:24 • *the will*

38 But if I do, though ye believe not me, ^Rbelieve^T the works: that ye may know, and believe, ^Rthat the Father is in me, and I in him.   5:36 • *accept the evidence of* • 14:10, 11

39 Therefore they sought again to take him: but he escaped out of their hand,

40 And went away again beyond Jordan into the place ^Rwhere John at first baptized; and there he ^Tabode.   1:28 • *stayed*

41 And many resorted unto him, and said, John did no miracle: but all things that John spake of this man were true.

42 And many believed on him there.

CHAPTER 11

Christ Raises Lazarus

NOW a certain *man* was sick, *named* Laz'-a-rus, of Beth'-a-ny, the town of ^RMary and her sister Martha.   Luke 10:38, 39

2 (It was *that* Mary which anointed the Lord with ointment, and wiped his feet with her hair, whose brother Laz'-a-rus was sick.)

3 Therefore his sisters sent unto him, saying, Lord, behold, ^The whom thou lovest is sick.   *your dear friend*

4 When Jesus heard *that,* he said, This sickness is not unto death, but for the glory of God, that the Son of God might be ^Tglorified thereby.   *honoured*

5 Now Jesus loved Martha, and her sister, and Laz'-a-rus.

6 When he had heard therefore that he was sick, ^Rhe ^Tabode two days still in the same place where he was.   10:40 • *stayed*

7 Then after that saith he to *his* disciples, Let us go into Ju-dae'-a again.

8 *His* disciples say unto him, Master, ^Rthe Jews of late ^Tsought to stone thee; and goest thou thither again?   10:31 • *wanted*

9 Jesus answered, Are there not twelve hours in the day? ^RIf any man walk in the day, he stumbleth not, because he seeth the ^Tlight of this world.   9:4 • *sunlight*

10 But if a man walk in the night, he stumbleth, because there is no light in him.

11 These things said he: and after that he saith unto them, Our friend Laz'-a-rus ^Rsleepeth; but I go, that I may awake him out of sleep.   Matt. 9:24; Acts 7:60; [1 Cor. 15:18, 51]

12 Then said his disciples, Lord, if he sleep, he ^Tshall do well.   *will recover*

13 Howbeit Jesus spake of his ^Tdeath: but they thought that he had spoken of taking of rest in ^Tsleep.   *actual death* • *natural sleep*

14 Then said Jesus unto them ^Rplainly, Laz'-a-rus is dead.   10:24

15 And I am glad for your sakes that I was not there, to the intent ye may believe; nevertheless let us go unto him.

16 Then said Thomas, which is called ᵀDid'-y-mus, unto his fellowdisciples, Let us also go, that we may die with him.   *twin*

17 Then when Jesus came, he found that he had *lain* in the grave four days already.

18 Now Beth'-a-ny was nigh unto Jerusalem, about ᵀfifteen furlongs off: *1.75 mi.*

19 And many of the Jews came to Martha and Mary, to comfort them ᵀconcerning their brother.   *about their brother's death*

20 Then Martha, as soon as she heard that Jesus was coming, went and met him: but Mary ᵀsat *still* in the house.   *stayed home*

21 Then said Martha unto Jesus, Lord, if thou hadst been here, my brother ᵀhad not died.   *would not have died*

22 But I know, that even now, ᴿwhatsoever thou wilt ask of God, God will give it thee.   [9:31]

23 Jesus saith unto her, Thy brother shall ᵀrise again.   *rise to life*

24 Martha saith unto him, ᴿI ᵀknow that he shall rise again in the resurrection at the last day.   [5:29; 12:48] • *understand*

25 Jesus said unto her, I am the resurrection, and the life: he that believeth in me, though he were dead, yet shall he live:

26 And whosoever liveth and believeth in me shall never die. Believest thou this?

27 She saith unto him, Yea, Lord: I believe that thou art the Christ, the Son of God, which should come into the world.

28 And when she had so said, she went her way, and called Mary her sister ᵀsecretly, saying, The Master is come, and calleth for thee.   *privately*

29 As soon as she heard *that,* she arose quickly, and ᵀcame unto him.   *hurried out*

30 Now Jesus was not yet come into the town, but was in that place where Martha ᵀmet him.   *had met*

31 ᴿThe Jews then which were with her in the house, and comforted her, when they saw Mary, that she rose up ᵀhastily and went out, followed her, saying, She goeth unto the grave to weep there.   *v. 19 • in a hurry*

32 Then when Mary was come where Jesus was, and saw him, she fell down at his feet, saying unto him, Lord, if thou hadst been here, my brother had not died.

33 When Jesus therefore saw her weeping, and the Jews also weeping which came with her, he groaned in the spirit, and ᵀwas troubled,   *was deeply moved*

34 And said, Where have ye laid him? They said unto him, Lord, come and see.

35 ᴿJesus wept.   Luke 19:41; Heb. 5:7

36 Then said the Jews, ᵀBehold how he loved him!   *see*

37 And some of them said, Could not this man, ᴿwhich opened the eyes of the blind, have ᵀcaused that even this man should not have died?   *9:6 • kept this man from dying*

38 Jesus therefore again ᵀgroaning in himself cometh to the grave. It was a cave, and a stone lay upon it.   *deeply moved*

39 Jesus said, Take ye away the stone. Martha, the sister of him that was dead, saith unto him, Lord, by this time he stinketh: for he hath been *dead* four days.

40 Jesus saith unto her, Said I not unto thee, that, if thou wouldest believe, thou shouldest ᴿsee the glory of God?   vv. 4, [23]

41 Then they took away the stone *from the place* where the dead was laid. And Jesus lifted up *his* eyes, and said, Father, I thank thee that thou hast heard me.

42 And I knew that thou hearest me always: but ᴿbecause of the people which stand by I said *it,* that they may believe that thou hast sent me.   12:30

43 And when he thus had spoken, he cried with a loud voice, Laz'-a-rus, come ᵀforth.   *out*

44 And he that was dead came forth, bound hand and foot with graveclothes: and ᴿhis face was bound about with a napkin. Jesus saith unto them, ᵀLoose him, and let him go.   20:7 • *untie*

The Pharisees Plan to Kill Christ

45 Then many of the Jews which came to Mary, ᴿand had seen the things which Jesus did, believed on him.   2:23; 10:42

46 But some of them ᵀwent their ways to the Pharisees, and told them what things Jesus had done.   *returned*

47 Then gathered the chief priests and the Pharisees a council, and said, What do we? for this man doeth many miracles.

48 If we let him thus alone, all *men* will believe on him: and the Romans shall come and take away both our place and nation.

49 And one of them, *named* Ca'-ia-phas, being the high priest that same year, said unto them, Ye know nothing at all,

50 Nor consider that it is expedient for us, that one man should die for the people, and that the whole nation perish not.

51 And this spake he not of himself: but being high priest that year, he prophesied that Jesus should die for that nation;

52 And not for that nation only, but that also he should gather together in one the children of God that were scattered abroad.

53 Then from that day forth they took counsel together for to put him to death.

54 Jesus therefore walked no more openly among the Jews; but went thence unto a country near to the wilderness, into a city called E'-phra-im, and there ᵀcontinued with his disciples.   *spent some time*

55 And the Jews' passover was ᵀnigh at hand: and many went out of the country up to Jerusalem before the passover, to purify themselves.   *near*

56 ᴿThen ᵀsought they for Jesus, and spake

among themselves, as they stood in the temple, What think ye, that he will not come to the feast? 7:11 · looked

57 Now both the chief priests and the Pharisees had given a commandment, that, if any man knew where he were, he should shew it, that they might take him.

CHAPTER 12

Mary Anoints Christ
Matt. 26:6–12; Mark 14:3–8

THEN Jesus six days before the passover came to Beth'-a-ny, Rwhere Laz'-a-rus was which had been dead, whom he raised from the dead. 11:1, 43

2 There they made him a supper; and Martha served: but Laz'-a-rus was one of them that sat at the table with him.

3 Then took RMary a Tpound of ointment of spikenard, very costly, and anointed the feet of Jesus, and wiped his feet with her hair: and the house was filled with the odour of the ointment. Matt. 26:7 · 12 oz.

4 Then saith one of his disciples, Judas Is-car'-i-ot, Simon's son, Twhich should betray him, who was going to

5 Why was not this ointment sold for three hundred pence, and given to the poor?

6 This he said, not that he cared for the poor; but because he was a thief, and had the bag, and bare what was put therein.

7 Then said Jesus, Let her alone: against the day of my burying hath she kept this.

8 For the poor always ye have with you; but me ye have not always.

9 Much people of the Jews therefore knew that he was there: and they came not for Jesus' sake only, but that they might see Laz'-a-rus also, Rwhom he had raised from the dead. 11:43, 44

10 But the chief priests consulted that they might put Laz'-a-rus also to death;

11 Because that by reason of him many of the Jews went away, and believed on Jesus.

The Triumphal Entry
Matt. 21:1–9; Mark 11:1–10; Luke 19:29–38

12 On the next day Tmuch people that were come to the feast, when they heard that Jesus was coming to Jerusalem, many

13 Took branches of palm trees, and went forth to meet him, and cried, RHosanna: BLESSED IS THE KING OF ISRAEL THAT COMETH IN THE NAME OF THE LORD. Ps. 118:26 ★

14 And Jesus, when he had found a young ass, sat thereon; as it is Rwritten, Zech. 9:9 ★

15 FEAR NOT, DAUGHTER OF SI'-ON: BEHOLD, THY KING COMETH, SITTING ON AN ASS'S COLT.

16 These things understood not his disciples at the first: but when Jesus was glorified, then remembered they that these things were

written of him, and that they had done these things unto him.

17 The people therefore that was with him when he called Laz'-a-rus out of his grave, and raised him from the dead, bare record.

18 RFor this cause the people also met him, for that they heard that he had done this miracle. v. 11

19 The Pharisees therefore said among themselves, RPerceive Tye how ye Tprevail nothing? behold, Tthe world is gone after him. 11:47 · see · accomplish · everybody is following

20 And there were certain Greeks among them that came up to worship at the feast:

21 The same came therefore to Philip, Rwhich was of Beth-sa'-i-da of Galilee, and Tdesired him, saying, Sir, we Twould see Jesus. 1:44 · asked · want to

22 Philip cometh and telleth Andrew: and again Andrew and Philip tell Jesus.

The Messiah Teaches

23 And Jesus answered them, saying, RThe hour is come, Rthat the Son of man should be Tglorified. 13:32 · Acts 3:13 ☆ · honoured

24 Verily, verily, I say unto you, RExcept a corn of wheat fall into the ground and die, it abideth alone: but if it die, it bringeth forth much fruit. 1 Cor. 15:36

25 RHe that loveth his life shall lose it; and he that hateth his life in this world shall keep it unto life eternal. [Matt. 10:39]

26 If any man serve me, let him follow me; and Rwhere I am, there shall also my servant be: if any man serve me, him will my Father honour. 14:3; [1 Thess. 4:17]

27 Now is my soul troubled; and what shall I say? Father, save me from this hour: but for this cause came I unto this hour.

28 Father, glorify thy name. Then came there a voice from heaven, saying, I have both glorified it, and will glorify it again.

29 The people therefore, that stood by, and heard it, said that it thundered: others said, RAn angel spake to him. Acts 23:9

30 Jesus answered and said, This voice came not because of me, but for your sakes.

31 Now is the judgment of this world: now shall Rthe prince of this world be cast out. Luke 10:18; [Acts 26:18]; 2 Cor. 4:4

32 And I, if I be Tlifted up from the earth, will draw all men unto me. crucified

33 RThis he said, signifying what Tdeath he should die. 18:32 · type

34 The people answered him, We have heard out of the law that Christ abideth for ever: and how sayest thou, The Son of man must be lifted up? who is this Son of man?

35 Then Jesus said unto them, Yet a little while Ris the light with you. Walk while ye have the light, lest darkness come upon you: for he that walketh in darkness knoweth not whither he goeth. [1:9; 8:12]

36 While ye have light, believe in the light, that ye may be [R]the children of light. These things spake Jesus, and departed, and did hide himself from them.   Luke 16:8

37 But though he had done so many [T]miracles before them, yet they [T]believed not on him: *signs • did not commit themselves to*

38 That the saying of E-sa′-ias the prophet might be fulfilled, which he spake, [R]LORD, WHO HATH BELIEVED OUR REPORT? AND TO WHOM HATH THE ARM OF THE LORD BEEN REVEALED?   Is. 53:1 ⋆

39 [T]Therefore they could not believe, because that E-sa′-ias said again, *for this reason*

40 HE HATH BLINDED THEIR EYES, AND HARDENED THEIR HEART; THAT THEY SHOULD NOT SEE WITH *THEIR* EYES, NOR UNDERSTAND WITH *THEIR* HEART, AND BE CONVERTED, AND I SHOULD HEAL THEM.

41 [R]These things said E-sa′-ias, when he saw his glory, and spake of him.   Is. 6:10 ⋆

42 Nevertheless among the chief rulers also many believed on him; but because of the Pharisees they did not confess *him*, lest they should be put out of the synagogue:

43 [R]For they loved the praise of men more than the praise of God.   5:44

44 Jesus cried and said, [R]He that believeth on me, believeth [T]not on me, but on him that sent me.   Mark 9:37 • *not only*

45 And [R]he that seeth me [T]seeth him that sent me.   [14:9] • *also sees*

46 [R]I am come a light into the world, that [T]whosoever believeth on me should not [T]abide in darkness.   *vv. 35, 36 • everyone who • live*

47 And if any man hear my words, and believe not, I judge him not: for I came not to judge the world, but to save the world.

48 [R]He that rejecteth me, and receiveth not my words, hath one that judgeth him: the word that I have spoken, the same shall judge him in the last day.   [Luke 10:16]

49 For [R]I have not spoken of myself; but the Father which sent me, he gave me a commandment, [R]what I should say, and what I should speak.   8:38 • Deut. 18:18

50 And I know that his commandment is life [T]everlasting: whatsoever I speak therefore, even as the Father [T]said unto me, so I speak.   *eternal • told*

CHAPTER 13

Christ Washes the Disciples' Feet

NOW [R]before the feast of the passover, when Jesus knew that [R]his hour was come that he should depart out of this world unto the Father, having loved his own which were in the world, he loved them unto the end.   Matt. 26:2 • 12:23

2 And supper being ended, the devil having now put into the heart of Judas Is-car′-i-ot, Simon's *son*, to betray him;

3 Jesus knowing that the Father had given all things into his hands, and that he was come from God, and went to God;

4 [R]He riseth from supper, and laid aside his [T]garments; and took a towel, and girded himself.   [Luke 22:27; Phil. 2:7, 8] • *outer garment*

5 After that he poureth water into a bason, and began to wash the disciples' feet, and to [T]wipe *them* with the towel wherewith he was girded.   *dry*

6 Then cometh he to Simon Peter: and Peter saith unto him, Lord, [R]dost[T] thou wash my feet?   Matt. 3:14 • *do you intend to*

7 Jesus answered and said unto him, What I do thou [T]knowest not now; [R]but thou shalt know hereafter.   *does not realize • v. 19*

8 Peter saith unto him, Thou shalt never wash my feet. Jesus answered him, If I wash thee not, thou hast no part with me.

9 Simon Peter saith unto him, Lord, not my feet only, but also *my* hands and *my* [T]head.   *head too!*

10 Jesus saith to him, He that is washed needeth not [T]save to wash *his* feet, but is clean every [T]whit: and [R]ye are clean, [T]but not all.   *wash except • bit • [15:3] • except one*

11 For he knew who should betray him; therefore said he, Ye are not all clean.

12 So after he had washed their feet, and had taken his garments, and was set down again, he said unto them, [T]Know ye what I have done to you?   *do you realize*

13 [R]Ye call me Master and Lord: and ye say [T]well; for *so* I am.   Matt. 23:8 • *the right thing*

14 If[R] I then, *your* Lord and Master, have washed your feet; [R]ye also ought to wash one another's feet.   Luke 22:27 • [1 Pet. 5:5]

15 For I have given you an example, that ye should do as I have done to you.

16 [R]Verily, verily, I say unto you, The servant is not greater than his lord; neither [T]he that is sent greater than he that sent him.   Matt. 10:24; [Luke 6:40] • *the messenger*

17 [R]If ye [T]know these things, happy are ye if ye [T]do them.   [James 1:25] • *realize • practise*

18 I speak not of you all: I know whom I have chosen: but that the scripture may be fulfilled, [R]HE THAT EATETH BREAD WITH ME HATH LIFTED UP HIS HEEL AGAINST ME.   Ps. 41:9 ⋆

19 [R]Now[T] I tell you before it come, that, when it is come to pass, ye may believe that I am *he*.   14:29 • *from henceforth*

20 [R]Verily, verily, I say unto you, He that receiveth whomsoever I send receiveth me; and he that receiveth me receiveth him that sent me.   Matt. 10:40; Luke 10:16

Christ Announces Judas, the Betrayer
Matt. 26:21, 22; Mark 14:18, 19; Luke 22:21–23

21 When Jesus had thus said, [R]he was troubled in spirit, and testified, and said, Verily, verily, I say unto you, that [R]one of you shall betray me.   12:27 • John 18:2 ⋆

22 Then the disciples looked one on another, ᵀdoubting of whom he spake. *uncertain*

23 Now ᴿthere was ᵀleaning on Jesus' ᵀbosom one of his disciples, whom Jesus loved.   19:26 • *sitting next to • breast*

24 Simon Peter therefore ᵀbeckoned to him, that he should ask who it ᵀshould be of whom he spake.   *motioned • is*

25 He then ᵀlying on Jesus' breast saith unto him, Lord, who is it?   *moved closer*

26 Jesus answered, He it is, to whom I shall give a sop, when I have dipped *it*. And when he had dipped the sop, he gave *it* to Judas Is-car'-i-ot, *the son* of Simon.

27 ᴿAnd after the sop Satan entered into him. Then said Jesus unto him, ᵀThat thou doest, do quickly.   Luke 22:3 • *what you do*

28 Now no man at the table knew for what intent he spake this unto him.

29 For some *of them* thought, because ᴿJudas had the bag, that Jesus had said unto him, Buy *those things* that we have need of against the feast; or, that he should give something to the poor.   12:6

30 He then having received the ᵀsop went immediately out: and it was night.   *bread*

Christ Announces His Departure

31 Therefore, when he was gone out, Jesus said, Now is the Son of man ᵀglorified, and God is glorified in him.   *honoured*

32 If God be ᵀglorified in him, God shall also glorify him in himself, and ᴿshall straightway glorify him.   *revealed • 12:23*

33 Little children, yet a little while I am with you. Ye shall seek me: and as I said unto the Jews, ᴿWhither I go, ye cannot come; so now I say to you.   Mark 16:19; Acts 1:9 ☆

34 A new commandment I give unto you, That ye love one another; as I have loved you, that ye also love one another.

35 By this shall all *men* know that ye are my disciples, if ye have love one to another.

Christ Foretells Peter's Denial
Matt. 26:34, 35; Mark 14:30, 31; Luke 22:33, 34

36 Simon Peter said unto him, Lord, whither goest thou? Jesus answered him, Whither I go, thou canst not follow me now; but thou shalt follow me afterwards.

37 Peter said unto him, Lord, why cannot I follow thee now? I will ᴿlay down my life for thy sake.   Matt. 26:33; Mark 14:29

38 Jesus answered him, Wilt thou lay down thy life for my sake? ᴿVerily, verily, I say unto thee, The cock shall not crow, till thou hast denied me thrice.   18:27; Luke 22:61 ☆

CHAPTER 14

Christ Comforts His Disciples

LET ᴿnot your heart be troubled: ye believe in God, believe also in me.   [v. 27]

2 In my Father's house are many mansions: if *it were* not so, I would have told you. I go to prepare a place for you.

3 And if I go and prepare a place for you, ᴿI will come again, and receive you unto myself; that ᴿwhere I am, *there* ye may be also.   [Acts 1:11] • [12:26; 1 Thess. 4:17]

4 And whither I go ye ᵀknow, and the way ye know.   *understand*

Christ Answers Thomas

5 ᴿThomas saith unto him, Lord, we know not whither thou goest; and how can we know the way?   11:16

6 Jesus saith unto him, I am the way, ᴿthe truth, and the life: ᴿno man cometh unto the Father, but by me.   [8:32] • [10:9]

7 If ye had known me, ye should have known my Father also: and from henceforth ye know him, and have seen him.

Christ Answers Philip

8 Philip saith unto him, Lord, shew us the Father, and it ᵀsufficeth us.   *will satisfy*

9 Jesus saith unto him, Have I been so long time with you, and yet hast thou not known me, Philip? ᴿhe that hath seen me hath seen the Father; and how sayest thou *then*, Shew us the Father?   Col. 1:15; Heb. 1:3

10 Believest thou not that ᴿI am in the Father, and the Father in me? the words that I speak unto you ᴿI speak not of myself: but the Father that dwelleth in me, he doeth the works.   10:38 • 5:19; Deut. 18:18 ☆

11 Believe me that I *am* in the Father, and the Father in me: or else believe me for the very ᴿworks' sake.   5:36

12 Verily, verily, I say unto you, He that believeth on me, the works that I do shall he do also; and greater *works* than these shall he do; because I go unto my Father.

13 ᴿAnd whatsoever ye shall ask in my name, that will I do, that the Father may be ᵀglorified in the Son.   [1 John 3:22] • *honoured*

14 If ye shall ask any thing in my ᴿname, I will do *it*.   15:16; 16:23

15 ᴿIf ye love me, keep my commandments.   1 John 5:3

16 And I will pray the Father, and ᴿhe shall give you another Comforter, that he may ᵀabide with you for ever;   [15:26]; Acts 2:4, 33 ☆ • *stay*

17 *Even* the Spirit of truth; ᴿwhom the world cannot receive, because it seeth him not, neither ᵀknoweth him: but ye know him; for he dwelleth with you, ᴿand shall be in you.   [1 Cor. 2:14] • *appreciates* • [1 John 2:27]

18 ᴿI will not leave you ᵀcomfortless: ᴿI will come to you.   [Matt. 28:20] • *orphans* • v. 3, 28

19 Yet a little while, and the world seeth me no more; but ᴿye see me: ᴿbecause I live, ye shall live also.   16:16 • [1 Cor. 15:20]

20 At that day ye shall know that I *am* in my Father, and ye in me, and I in you.

21 ᴿHe that hath my commandments, and ᵀkeepeth them, he it is that loveth me: and he that loveth me shall be loved of my Father, and I will love him, and will ᵀmanifest myself to him.   1 John 2:5 • obeys • show

Christ Answers Judas

22 Judas saith unto him, not Is-car′-i-ot, Lord, how is it that thou wilt manifest thyself unto us, and not unto the world?

23 Jesus answered and said unto him, If a man love me, he will keep my words: and my Father will love him, ᴿand we will come unto him, and make our abode with him. [1 John 2:24]

24 He that loveth me not keepeth not my sayings: and the word which ye hear is not mine, but the Father's which sent me.

25 These things have I spoken unto you, being yet present with you.

26 But the Comforter, which is the Holy Ghost, whom the Father will send in my name, ᴿhe shall teach you all things, and bring all things to your remembrance, whatsoever I have said unto you.   2:22

27 ᴿPeace I leave with you, my peace I give unto you: not as the world giveth, give I unto you. Let not your heart be troubled, neither let it be afraid.   Luke 1:79; [Phil. 4:7] ★

28 Ye have heard how ᴿI said unto you, I go away, and come again unto you. If ye loved me, ye would rejoice, because I said, ᴿI go unto the Father: for ᴿmy Father is greater than I.   vv. 3, 18 • 16:16 • [Phil. 2:6]

29 And ᴿnow I have told you before it come to pass, that, when it is come to pass, ye might believe.   13:19

30 Hereafter I will not talk much with you: for the prince of this world cometh, and ᵀhath nothing in me.   has no interest in me

31 But that the world may ᵀknow that I love the Father; and ᴿas the Father gave me commandment, even so I do. Arise, let us go hence.   understand • 10:18; Is. 50:5 ★

CHAPTER 15

The Relationship of Believers to Christ

I AM the ᵀtrue vine, and my Father is the ᵀhusbandman.   genuine • gardener

2 Every ᴿ branch in me that beareth not fruit he taketh away: and every branch that beareth fruit, he ᵀpurgeth it, that it may bring forth more fruit.   Matt. 15:13 • prunes

3 Now ye are ᵀclean through the word which I have spoken unto you.   pruned

4 ᴿAbide in me, and I in you. As the branch cannot bear fruit of itself, except it ᵀabide in the vine; no more can ye, except ye abide in me.   [Col. 1:23] • remains attached to

5 I am the vine, ye are the branches: He that abideth in me, and I in him, the same bringeth forth much ᴿfruit: for ᵀwithout me ye can do nothing.   Hos. 14:8 • apart from

6 If a man abide not in me, ᴿhe is cast forth as a branch, and is withered; and men gather them, and cast them into the fire, and they are burned.   Matt. 3:10

7 If ye ᵀabide in me, and my words ᵀabide in you, ye shall ask what ye will, and it shall be done unto you.   remain attached to • affect

8 ᴿHerein is my Father ᵀglorified, that ye bear much fruit; ᴿso shall ye be my disciples.   [Matt. 5:16; Phil. 1:11] • honoured • 8:31

9 As the Father hath loved me, so have I loved you: continue ye in my love.

10 ᴿIf ye ᵀkeep my commandments, ye shall ᵀabide in my love; even as I have kept my Father's commandments, and ᵀabide in his love.   14:15 • obey • live • remain

11 These things have I spoken unto you, that my joy might remain in you, and ᴿthat your joy might be full.   [16:24]; 1 John 1:4

The Relationship of Believers to Each Other

12 This is my commandment, That ye love one another, as I have loved you.

13 Greater love hath no man than this, that a man lay down his life for his friends.

14 ᴿYe are my friends, if ye do ᵀwhatsoever I command you.   [Matt. 12:50] • what

15 Henceforth I call you not servants; for the servant knoweth not what his lord doeth: but I have called you friends; for all things that I have heard of my Father I have ᵀmade known unto you.   explained

16 Ye have not chosen me, but I have chosen you, and ᵀordained you, that ye should go and bring forth fruit, and that your fruit should ᵀremain: that whatsoever ye shall ask of the Father in my name, he may give it you.   appointed • abide

17 ᵀThese things I command you, that ye love one another.   this; then

The Relationship of Believers to the World

18 ᴿIf the world hate you, ye know that it hated me before it hated you.   1 John 3:13

19 If ye were of the world, the world would love his own: but ᴿbecause ye are not of the world, but I have chosen you out of the world, therefore the world hateth you.   17:14

20 Remember the word that I said unto you, ᴿThe servant is not greater than his lord. If they have persecuted me, they will also persecute you; if they have kept my saying, they will keep your's also.   Matt. 10:24

21 But ᴿall these things will they do unto you for my name's sake, because they know not him that sent me.   Matt. 10:22

22 ᴿIf I had not come and spoken unto them, they had not had sin: but now they have no ᵀcloke for their sin.   9:41 • covering

23 ᴿHe that ᵀhateth me hateth my Father also.   1 John 2:23 • despise

24 If I had not done among them the works which none other man did, they had not had sin: but now have they both seen and hated both me and my Father.

25 But *this cometh to pass*, that the word might be fulfilled that is written in their law, RTHEY HATED ME WITHOUT A CAUSE. Ps. 69:4 ✱

The Promise of the Holy Spirit

26 But when the Comforter is come, whom I will send unto you from the Father, *even* the Spirit of truth, which proceedeth from the Father, he shall testify of me:

27 And Rye also shall bear witness, because Rye have been with me from the beginning. 1 Pet. 5:1; 2 Pet. 1:16 • Luke 1:2

CHAPTER 16

THESE things have I spoken unto you, that ye should not be Toffended. *upset*

2 RThey shall put you out of the synagogues: yea, the time cometh, Rthat whosoever killeth you will think that he doeth God service. Acts 8:1; 26:11 • 1 Tim. 1:13

3 And Rthese things will they do unto you, because they have not known the Father, nor me. 15:21; Rom. 10:2

4 But these things have I told you, that when the time shall come, ye may remember that I told you of them. And these things I Tsaid not unto you at the beginning, because I was with you. *did not tell*

5 But now I go my way to him that sent me; and none of you asketh me, TWhither goest thou? *where are you going?*

6 But because I have said these things unto you, sorrow hath filled your heart.

7 Nevertheless I tell you the truth; It is Texpedient for you that I go away: for if I go not away, the TComforter will not come unto you; but Rif I depart, I will send him unto you. *advantageous • helper • Acts 2:33 ✱*

8 And when he is come, Rhe will Treprove the world of sin, and of Trighteousness, and of judgment: Acts 2:37 ✱ • *convict • about what is right*

9 Of sin, because they believe not on me;

10 ROf righteousness, because I go to my Father, and ye see me no more; Acts 2:32

11 ROf judgment, because Rthe prince of this world is judged.

12 I have yet many things to say unto you, but ye cannot Tbear them now. *grasp*

13 Howbeit when he, the Spirit of truth, is come, he will guide you into all truth: for he shall not speak of himself; but whatsoever he shall hear, *that* shall he speak: and Rhe will shew you things to come. Acts 11:28; Rev. 1:19 ✱

14 He shall glorify me: for he shall receive of mine, and shall shew *it* unto you.

15 RAll things that the Father hath are mine: therefore said I, that he shall take of mine, and shall shew *it* unto you. 3:35

The Predictions of Christ's Death and Resurrection

16 RA little while, and ye shall not see me: and again, a little while, and ye shall see me, Rbecause I go to the Father. 19:42; 20:19 ✱ • 13:3

17 Then said *some* of his disciples among themselves, What is this that he saith unto us, A little while, and ye shall not see me: and again, a little while, and ye shall see me: and, Because I go to the Father?

18 They said therefore, What is this that he saith, A little while? we cannot Ttell what he Tsaith. *understand • is saying*

19 Now Jesus knew that they were desirous to ask him, and said unto them, Do ye enquire among yourselves of that I said, A little while, and ye shall not see me: and again, a little while, and ye shall see me?

20 RVerily, verily, I say unto you, That ye shall weep and lament, but the world shall rejoice: and ye shall be sorrowful, but your sorrow shall be turned into joy. 20:20 ✱

21 A woman when she is in Ttravail hath sorrow, because her hour is come: but as soon as she is delivered of the child, she remembereth no more the anguish, for joy that a man is born into the world. *labour*

22 And ye now therefore have sorrow: but I will see you again, and Ryour heart shall rejoice, and your joy no man Ttaketh from you. 20:20; Acts 2:46; 13:52; 1 Pet. 1:8 ✱ • *can rob*

23 And in that day ye shall ask me nothing. RVerily, verily, I say unto you, Whatsoever ye shall ask the Father in my name, he will give *it* you. 14:13; [15:16]; Matt. 7:7

24 THitherto have ye asked nothing in my name: ask, and ye shall receive, Rthat your Tjoy may be full. *until now • 15:11 • happiness*

25 These things have I spoken unto you in proverbs: but the time cometh, when I shall no more speak unto you in proverbs, but I shall shew you plainly of the Father.

26 At that day ye shall ask in my name: and I say not unto you, that I will pray the Father Tfor you: *on your behalf*

27 RFor the Father himself loveth you, because ye have loved me, and have believed that I came out from God. [14:21]

28 RI came forth from the Father, and am come into the world: again, I leave the world, and go to the Father. 13:3

29 His disciples said unto him, TLo, now speakest thou Tplainly, and speakest no Tproverb. *look • openly • illustration*

30 Now are we sure that thou knowest all things, and needest not that any man should ask thee: by this Rwe believe that thou camest forth from God. 17:8

31 Jesus answered them, TDo ye now believe? *do you believe now?*

32 RBehold, the hour cometh, yea, is now come, that ye shall be scattered, every man to This own, and shall leave me alone: and Ryet

I am not alone, because the Father is with me.   Matt. 26:56; Mark 14:50 ☆ • *his own home* • 8:29

33 These things I have spoken unto you, that in me ye might have peace. In the world ye shall have tribulation: but be of good cheer; I have overcome the world.

CHAPTER 17

Christ Prays for Himself

THESE words spake Jesus, and lifted up his eyes to heaven, and said, Father, Rthe hour is come; Tglorify thy Son, that thy Son also may glorify thee: 12:23 • *honour*

2 RAs thou hast given him power over all flesh, that he should give eternal life to as many as thou hast given him.   Dan. 7:14

3 And Rthis is life eternal, that they might know thee the only true God, and Jesus Christ, whom thou hast sent.   [Is. 53:11]

4 RI have glorified thee on the earth: RI have finished the work Rwhich thou gavest me to do.   13:31; Is. 49:3; 50:5 ★ • 4:34 • 14:31

5 And now, O Father, glorify thou me with thine own self with the glory which I had with thee before the world was.

Christ Prays for His Disciples

6 I have manifested thy name unto the men which thou gavest me out of the world: thine they were, and thou gavest them me; and they have kept thy word.

7 Now they have known that all things whatsoever thou hast given me are of thee.

8 For RI have given unto them the words which thou gavest me; and they have received *them*, and have Tknown surely that I came out from thee, and they have believed that thou didst send me.   Deut. 18:18 ★ • *realized*

9 I pray for them: RI pray not for the world, but for them which thou hast given me; for they are thine.   [1 John 5:19]

10 And all mine are thine, and thine are mine; and I am Tglorified in them.   *honoured*

11 And now I am no more in the world, but these are in the world, and I come to thee. Holy Father, keep through thine own name those whom thou hast given me, that they may be one, Ras we *are*.   Eph. 4:25

12 While I was with them in the world, I kept them in thy name: those that thou gavest me I have kept, and none of them is lost, Rbut the son of perdition; Rthat the scripture might be fulfilled.   Matt. 27:4, 5 • Acts 1:20

13 And now come I to thee; and these things I speak in the world, that they might have my joy fulfilled in themselves.

14 I have given them thy word; and the world hath hated them, because they are not of the world, even as I am not of the world.

15 I pray not that thou shouldest take them out of the world, but that thou shouldest Tkeep them from the evil.   *protect*

16 They are not of the world, even as I Tam not of the world.   *do not belong to*

17 RSanctifyT them through thy truth: thy word is truth.   [1 Pet. 1:22] • *make them holy*

18 As thou hast sent me into the world, even so have I also sent them into the world.

19 And Rfor their sakes I sanctify myself, that they also might be sanctified through the truth.   1 Cor. 1:2; 1 Thess. 4:7; [Heb. 10:10]

Christ Prays for All Believers

20 Neither pray I for these Talone, but for them also which shall believe on me through their Tword;   *only* • *message*

21 RThat they all may be one; as thou, Father, *art* in me, and I in thee, that they also may be one in us: that the world may believe that thou hast sent me.   [10:16]

22 And the Tglory which thou gavest me I have given them; Rthat they may be one, even as we are one: *blessing* • 14:20; 1 John 1:3

23 I in them, and thou in me, that they may be made perfect in one; and that the world may know that thou hast sent me, and hast loved them, as thou hast loved me.

24 Father, I will that they also, whom thou hast given me, be with me where I am; Rthat they may behold my glory, which thou hast given me: for thou lovedst me before the foundation of the world.   *v.* 5

25 O righteous Father, Rthe world Thath not known thee: but RI have known thee, and Rthese have known that thou hast sent me.   15:21 • *does* • 7:29; 8:55 • *v.* 8

26 RAnd I have Tdeclared unto them thy name, and will declare *it:* that the love Rwherewith thou hast loved me may be in them, and I in them.   *v.* 6 • *made known* • 15:9

CHAPTER 18

The Arrest of Christ
Matt. 26:47–56; Mark 14:43–52; Luke 22:47–53

WHEN Jesus had spoken these words, he went forth with his disciples over the brook Ce′-dron, where was a garden, into the which he entered, and his disciples.

2 And Judas also, which betrayed him, knew the place: for Jesus ofttimes Tresorted thither with his disciples.   *went there*

3 RJudas then, having received a band *of men* and officers from the chief priests and Pharisees, Tcometh thither with lanterns and torches and weapons.   Acts 1:16 • *came there*

4 Jesus therefore, knowing all things that should Tcome upon him, went forth, and said unto them, Whom seek ye?   *happen*

5 They answered him, Jesus of Nazareth. Jesus saith unto them, I am *he.* And Judas also, which betrayed him, stood with them.

6 As soon then as he had said unto them, I am he, ᴿthey ᵀwent backward, and fell to the ground.   Ps. 27:2 ⋆ • moved

7 Then asked he them again, Whom seek ye? And they said, Jesus of Nazareth.

8 Jesus answered, I have told you that I am he: if therefore ye seek me, let ᵀthese go ᵀtheir way: these others • free

9 That the saying might be fulfilled, which he spake, ᴿOf them which thou gavest me have I lost none.   [17:12]

10 Then Simon Peter having a sword drew it, and smote the high priest's servant, and cut off his right ear. The servant's name was Mal'-chus.

11 Then said Jesus unto Peter, Put up thy sword into the ᵀsheath: ᴿthe ᵀcup which my Father hath given me, shall I not drink it?   scabbard • Matt. 20:22 • cup of suffering

First Jewish Trial Before Annas
Matt. 26:69, 70; Mark 14:66–68; Luke 22:55–57

12 Then the ᵀband and the captain and officers of the Jews took Jesus, and ᵀbound him,   group of soldiers • tied

13 And led him away to An'-nas first; for he was father in law to Ca'-ia-phas, which was the high priest that same year.

14 Now Ca'-ia-phas was he, which gave counsel to the Jews, that it was expedient that one man should die for the people.

15 And Simon Peter followed Jesus, and so did another disciple: that disciple was known unto the high priest, and went in with Jesus into the ᵀpalace of the high priest.   court

16 But Peter stood at the door without. Then went out that other disciple, which was known unto the high priest, and spake unto her that kept the door, and brought in Peter.

17 Then saith the damsel that kept the door unto Peter, Art not thou also one of this man's disciples? He saith, I am not.

18 And the servants and ᵀofficers stood there, who had made a fire of coals; for it was cold: and they warmed themselves: and Peter stood with them, and warmed himself.   guards

19 The high priest then asked Jesus of his disciples, and of his ᵀdoctrine.   teaching

20 Jesus answered him, I spake openly to the world; I ever taught in the synagogue, and in the temple, whither the Jews always resort; and in secret have I said nothing.

21 Why askest thou me? ask them which heard me, what I have said unto them: behold, they know what I said.

22 And when he had thus spoken, one of the officers which stood by ᴿstruck Jesus with the palm of his hand, saying, Answerest thou the high priest so?   Job 16:10; Lam. 3:30 ⋆

23 Jesus answered him, If I have spoken ᵀevil, ᵀbear witness of the evil: but if well, why smitest thou me?   wrong • point out

Second Jewish Trial Before Caiaphas
Matt. 26:57–68, 73–75; Mark 14:53–65, 70–72; Luke 22:59–65

24 Now An'-nas had sent him bound unto Ca'-ia-phas the high priest.

25 And Simon Peter stood and warmed himself. They said therefore unto him, Art not thou also one of his disciples? He denied it, and said, I am not.

26 ᴿOne of the servants of the high priest, being his kinsman whose ear Peter cut off, saith, Did not I see thee in the garden with him?   Matt. 26:51; Mark 14:47; Luke 22:49, 50

27 ᴿPeter then denied again: and ᴿimmediately the cock crew. Matt. 26:34; Mark 14:30 ⋆ • 13:38

First Roman Trial Before Pilate
Matt. 27:2, 11–14; Mark 15:1–5; Luke 23:1–5

28 ᴿThen led they Jesus from Ca'-ia-phas unto the hall of judgment: and it was early; and they themselves went not into the judgment hall, lest they should be defiled; but that they might eat the passover.   18:32 ⋆

29 Pilate then went ᵀout unto them, and said, What accusation bring ye against this man?   outside

30 They answered and said unto him, If he were not a ᵀmalefactor, we would not have delivered him up unto thee.   criminal

31 Then said Pilate unto them, Take ye him, and judge him according to your law. The Jews therefore said unto him, It is not lawful for us to put any man to death:

32 ᴿThat the saying of Jesus might be fulfilled, which he spake, signifying what death he should die.   12:32, 33; Matt. 20:19

33 Then Pilate entered into the judgment hall again, and called Jesus, and said unto him, Art thou the King of the Jews?

34 Jesus answered him, Sayest thou this ᵀthing of thyself, or did others tell ᵀit thee of me?   question • you about me?

35 Pilate answered, Am I a Jew? Thine own nation and the chief priests have delivered thee unto me: what hast thou done?

36 Jesus answered, ᴿMy kingdom is not of this world: if my kingdom were of this world, then would my servants fight, that I should not be delivered to the Jews: but now is my kingdom not from hence.   6:15

37 Pilate therefore said unto him, Art thou a king then? Jesus answered, Thou sayest that I am a king. To this end was I born, and for this cause came I into the world, that I should bear witness unto the truth. Every one that is of the truth heareth my voice.

38 Pilate saith unto him, What is truth? And when he had said this, he went out again unto the Jews, and saith unto them, ᴿI find in him no fault at all.   19:4, 6

Second Roman Trial Before Pilate
Matt. 27:15–31; Mark 15:6–20; Luke 23:13–25

39 But ye have a custom, that I should release unto you one at the passover: will ye therefore that I ᵀrelease unto you the King of the Jews? *free*

40 ᴿThen cried they all again, saying, Not this man, but Bar-ab′-bas. Now Bar-ab′-bas was a robber. Is. 53:3; Acts 3:14 ✱

CHAPTER 19

THEN ᴿPilate therefore took Jesus, and scourged *him*. Is. 50:6 ✱

2 And the soldiers ᵀplatted a crown of thorns, and put *it* on his head, and they put on him a purple robe, *made*

3 And said, Hail, King of the Jews! and they ᵀsmote him with their hands. *struck*

4 Pilate therefore went forth again, and saith unto them, Behold, I bring him forth to you, ᴿthat ye may ᵀknow that I find no ᵀfault in him. v. 6; 18:38 • *realize • crime*

5 Then came Jesus forth, wearing the crown of thorns, and the purple robe. And *Pilate* saith unto them, Behold the man!

6 ᴿWhen the chief priests therefore and officers saw him, they cried out, saying, Crucify *him*, crucify *him*. Pilate saith unto them, Take ye him, and crucify *him*: for I find no ᵀfault in him. Acts 3:13 • *misdeed*

7 The Jews answered him, We have a law, and by our law ᴿhe ought to die, because he made himself the Son of God. Matt. 20:18 ✱

8 When Pilate therefore heard ᵀthat saying, he was the more afraid; *this accusation*

9 And went again into the judgment hall, and saith unto Jesus, Whence art thou? ᴿBut Jesus gave him no answer. Ps. 38:13, 14; Is. 53:7 ✱

10 Then saith Pilate unto him, Speakest thou not unto me? knowest thou not that I have ᵀpower to crucify thee, and have power to ᵀrelease thee? *authority • free*

11 Jesus answered, ᴿThou couldest have no power *at all* against me, except it were given thee from above: therefore he that ᵀdelivered me unto thee hath the greater sin. 7:30; [Luke 22:53] • *handed me over*

12 And from thenceforth Pilate sought to release him: but the Jews cried out, saying, If thou let this man go, thou art not Caesar's friend: whosoever maketh himself a king speaketh against Caesar.

13 When Pilate therefore heard that saying, he brought Jesus ᵀforth, and sat down in the ᵀjudgment seat in a place that is called the Pavement, but in the Hebrew, Gab′-ba-tha. *out • judge's*

14 And it was the preparation of the passover, and about the sixth hour: and he saith unto the Jews, Behold your King!

15 ᴿBut they cried out, ᵀAway with *him*, away with *him*, crucify him. Pilate saith unto them, Shall I crucify your King? The chief priests answered, ᴿWe have no king but Caesar. Is. 53:3 ✱ • *kill him! kill him!* • [Gen. 49:10]

16 ᴿThen delivered he him therefore unto them to be crucified. And they took Jesus, and led *him* away. Mark 15:15; Luke 23:24, 25

The Crucifixion of Christ
Matt. 27:32–38, 48, 50; Mark 15:21–26, 36, 37; Luke 23:26–33, 38, 46

17 And he bearing his cross went forth into a place called *the place* of a skull, which is called in the Hebrew Gol′-go-tha:

18 Where they ᴿcrucified him, and two other with him, on either side one, and Jesus in the midst. Ps. 22:16–18; Matt. 20:19; 26:2 ✱

19 And Pilate wrote a title, and put *it* on the cross. And the writing was, JESUS OF NAZARETH THE KING OF THE JEWS.

20 This title then read many of the Jews: for the place where Jesus was crucified was ᵀnigh to the city: and it was written in Hebrew, *and* Greek, *and* Latin. *close*

21 Then said the chief priests of the Jews to Pilate, Write not, The King of the Jews; but that he said, I am King of the Jews.

22 Pilate answered, What I have written ᵀI have written. *stays written*

23 Then the soldiers, when they had crucified Jesus, took his garments, and made four parts, to every soldier a part; and also *his* coat: now the coat was without seam, woven from the top throughout.

24 They said therefore among themselves, Let us not rend it, but cast lots for it, whose it shall be: that the scripture might be fulfilled, which saith, ᴿTHEY PARTED MY RAIMENT AMONG THEM, AND FOR MY VESTURE THEY DID CAST LOTS. These things therefore the soldiers did. Ps. 22:18 ✱

25 ᴿNow there stood by the cross of Jesus his mother, and his mother's sister, Mary the *wife* of ᴿCle′-o-phas,ᵀ and Mary Mag-da-le′-ne. Luke 2:35 ✱ • Luke 24:18 • *Clopas*

26 When Jesus therefore saw his mother, and ᴿthe disciple standing by, whom he loved, he saith unto his mother, Woman, ᵀbehold thy son! 13:23; 20:2 • *here is your son!*

27 Then saith he to the disciple, Behold thy mother! And from that hour that disciple took her ᴿunto his own *home*. 1:11

28 After this, Jesus knowing that all things were now accomplished, ᴿthat the scripture might be fulfilled, saith, I thirst. Ps. 22:15 ✱

29 Now there was set a vessel full of ᵀvinegar: and ᴿthey filled a spunge with vinegar, and put *it* upon ᵀhyssop, and put *it* to his mouth. *sour wine* • Ps. 69:21 ✱ • *a branch*

30 When Jesus therefore had received the vinegar, he said, It is finished: and ᴿhe bowed his head, and gave up the ghost. Zech. 11:10, 11 ✱

31 The Jews therefore, because it was the preparation, that the bodies should not remain upon the cross on the sabbath day, (for that sabbath day was an high day,) besought Pilate that their legs might be broken, and *that* they might be taken away.

32 Then came the soldiers, and brake the legs of the first, and of the other which was ᵀcrucified with him.   *put to death*

33 But when they came to Jesus, and ᵀsaw that he was dead already, ᴿthey brake not his legs: *realized* • Ps. 34:20 ⋆

34 But one of the soldiers with a spear pierced his side, and ᵀforthwith ᴿcame there out blood and water.   *at once* • [1 John 5:6, 8]

35 And he that saw *it* bare record, and his record is true: and he knoweth that he ᵀsaith true, that ye might believe.   *speaks truth*

36 For these things were done, ᴿthat the scripture should be fulfilled, A BONE OF HIM SHALL NOT BE BROKEN.   Ps. 34:20 ⋆

37 And again another scripture saith, ᴿTHEY SHALL LOOK ON HIM WHOM THEY PIERCED.   Zech. 12:10 ⋆

The Burial of Christ
Matt. 27:57–60; Mark 15:42–46; Luke 23:50–54

38 ᴿAnd after this Joseph of Ar-i-ma-thae′-a, being a disciple of Jesus, but secretly ᴿfor fear of the Jews, ᵀbesought Pilate that he might take away the body of Jesus: and Pilate gave *him* leave. He came therefore, and took the body of Jesus.   Is. 53:9 ⋆ • 9:22; [12:42] • *requested*

39 And there came also ᴿNic-o-de′-mus, which at the first came to Jesus by night, and brought a mixture of myrrh and aloes, about an ᵀhundred pound *weight*.   3:1, 2; 7:50 • 75 lb.

40 Then took they the body of Jesus, and ᴿwoundᵀ it in linen clothes with the spices, as the manner of the Jews is to bury.   Acts 5:6

41 Now in the place where he was crucified there was a garden; and in the garden ᴿa new ᵀsepulchre, wherein was never man ᵀyet laid.   Is. 53:9 ⋆ • *tomb* • *buried*

42 ᴿThere laid they Jesus therefore because of the Jews' preparation *day;* for the sepulchre was nigh at hand.   Mark 14:8 ⋆

CHAPTER 20

The Resurrection of Christ
Matt. 28:1–8; Mark 16:1–8; Luke 24:1–12

THE first *day* of the week cometh Mary Mag-da-le′-ne early, when it was yet dark, unto the ᵀsepulchre, and seeth the stone taken away from the sepulchre.   *tomb*

2 Then she runneth, and cometh to Simon Peter, and to the ᴿother disciple, whom Jesus loved, and saith unto them, They have taken away the Lord out of the sepulchre, and we know not where they have laid him.   [21:24]

3 Peter therefore went forth, and that other disciple, and came to the sepulchre.

4 So they ran both together: and the other disciple did outrun Peter, and came first to the ᵀsepulchre.   *tomb*

5 And he stooping down, *and looking in,* saw ᴿthe linen clothes lying; yet went he not in.   19:40

6 Then cometh Simon Peter following him, and ᵀwent into the sepulchre, and seeth the linen clothes lie,   *went straight*

7 And the napkin, that was about his head, not lying with the linen clothes, but wrapped together in a place by itself.

8 Then went in also that other disciple, which ᵀcame first to the ᵀsepulchre, and saw, and believed.   *reached* • *tomb*

9 For as yet they knew not the scripture, that he must rise again from the dead.

10 Then the disciples went ᵀaway again unto their own home.   *back*

Christ Appears to Mary Magdalene

11 But Mary stood without at the sepulchre weeping: and as she wept, she stooped down, *and looked* into the ᵀsepulchre,   *tomb*

12 And seeth two angels in white sitting, the one at the head, and the other at the feet, where the body of Jesus had lain.

13 And they say unto her, Woman, why weepest thou? She saith unto them, Because they have taken away my Lord, and I know not where they have laid him.

14 And when she had thus said, she turned herself back, and saw Jesus standing, and knew not that it was Jesus.

15 Jesus saith unto her, Woman, why weepest thou? whom seekest thou? She, supposing him to be the gardener, saith unto him, Sir, if thou have borne him hence, tell me where thou hast laid him, and I will ᵀtake him away.   *go get him*

16 Jesus saith unto her, Mary. She turned herself, and saith unto him, Rab-bo′-ni; which is to say, ᵀMaster.   *Teacher*

17 Jesus saith unto her, Touch me not; for I am not yet ascended to my Father: but go to my brethren, and say unto them, ᴿI ascend unto my Father, and your Father; and *to* my God, and your God.   Mark 16:19; Acts 1:9 ⋆

18 Mary Mag-da-le′-ne came and told the disciples that she had seen the Lord, and *that* he had spoken these things unto her.

Christ Appears to the Disciples
(Thomas Absent)—Mark 16:14; Luke 24:36–43

19 ᴿThen the same day at evening, being the first *day* of the week, when the doors were shut where the disciples were assembled for fear of the Jews, ᴿcame Jesus and stood in the midst, and saith unto them, Peace *be* unto you.   1 Cor. 15:5 • 16:16 ⋆

20 And when he had so said, he shewed unto them *his* hands and his side. ᴿThen

were the disciples ᵀglad, when they saw the Lord.   12:21; 16:22 ★ • *filled with joy*

21 Then said Jesus to them again, Peace *be* unto you: ᴿas *my* Father hath sent me, even so send I you.   [Matt. 28:19; 2 Tim. 2:2]

22 ᴿAnd when he had said this, he breathed on *them*, and saith unto them, Receive ye the Holy Ghost: 16:20-22 ★

23 ᴿWhose soever sins ye remit, they are remitted unto them; *and* whose soever *sins* ye retain, they are retained.   Matt. 16:19; 18:18

24 But Thomas, one of the twelve, ᴿcalled ᵀDid'-y-mus, was not with them when Jesus ᵀcame.   11:16 • *twin* • *returned*

25 The other disciples therefore said unto him, We have seen the Lord. But he said unto them, Except I shall see in his hands the print of the nails, and put my finger into the print of the nails, and thrust my hand into his side, I will not believe.

Christ Appears to the Disciples (Thomas Present)—1 Cor. 15:5

26 And after eight days again his disciples were within, and Thomas with them: *then* came Jesus, the doors being shut, and stood in the midst, and said, Peace *be* unto you.

27 Then saith he to Thomas, Reach hither thy finger, and behold my hands; and ᴿreach hither thy hand, and thrust *it* into my side: and be not faithless, but believing.   1 John 1:1

28 And Thomas answered and said unto him, ᴿMy Lord and my God.   [Ps. 73:25, 26]

29 Jesus saith unto him, Thomas, because thou hast seen me, thou hast believed: ᴿblessed *are* they that have not seen, and *yet* have believed.   1 Pet. 1:8

The Purpose of John's Gospel

30 And many other ᵀsigns truly did Jesus in the presence of his disciples, which are not written in this book: *miracles*

31 ᴿBut these are written, that ye might believe that Jesus is the Christ, the Son of God; ᴿand that believing ye might have life through his name.   Luke 1:4 • [1 Pet. 1:8, 9]

CHAPTER 21

Christ Appears to the Seven Disciples

AFTER these things Jesus shewed himself ᵀagain to the disciples at the sea of Ti-be'-ri-as; and ᵀon this wise shewed he *himself*.   *once more* • *in this fashion*

2 There were together Simon Peter, and Thomas called Did'-y-mus, and Na-than'-a-el of Cana in Galilee, and the *sons* of Zeb'-e-dee, and two other of his disciples.

3 Simon Peter saith unto them, I go a fishing. They say unto him, We also go with thee. They went forth, and entered into a ᵀship immediately; and that night they caught nothing.   *boat*

4 But when the morning was now come, Jesus stood on the shore: but the disciples ᵀknew not that it was Jesus.   *recognized*

5 Then Jesus saith unto them, Children, have ye any meat? They answered him, No.

6 And he said unto them, Cast the net on the right side of the ship, and ye shall find. They cast therefore, and now they were not able to draw it for the multitude of fishes.

7 Therefore that disciple whom Jesus loved saith unto Peter, It is the Lord. Now when Simon Peter heard that it was the Lord, he girt *his* fisher's coat *unto him,* (for he was naked,) and did cast himself into the sea.

8 And the other disciples came in a little ship; (for they were not far from land, but as it were ᵀtwo hundred cubits,) dragging the net ᵀwith fishes.   *300 ft.* • *full of fish*

9 As soon then as they were come to land, they saw a fire of ᵀcoals there, and fish laid thereon, and bread.   *charcoal*

10 Jesus saith unto them, Bring ᵀof the fish which ye have now caught.   *some of*

11 Simon Peter went up, and drew the net to land full of great fishes, an hundred and fifty and three: and for all there were so many, yet was not the net ᵀbroken.   *torn*

12 Jesus saith unto them, Come *and* dine. And none of the disciples durst ask him, Who art thou? knowing that it was the Lord.

13 Jesus then cometh, and taketh bread, and giveth them, and fish likewise.

14 This is now ᴿthe third time that Jesus shewed himself to his disciples, after that he was risen from the dead.   20:19, 26

Christ Speaks to Peter

15 So when they had dined, Jesus saith to Simon Peter, Simon, *son* of Jo'-nas, lovest thou me more than these? He saith unto him, Yea, Lord; thou knowest that I love thee. He saith unto him, Feed my lambs.

16 He saith to him again the second time, Simon, *son* of Jo'-nas, lovest thou me? He saith unto him, Yea, Lord; thou knowest that I ᵀlove thee. ᴿHe saith unto him, Feed my sheep.   *have affection for you* • Heb. 13:20

17 He saith unto him the third time, Simon, *son* of Jo'-nas, lovest thou me? Peter was grieved because he said unto him the third time, Lovest thou me? And he said unto him, Lord, thou knowest all things; thou knowest that I love thee. Jesus saith unto him, Feed my sheep.

18 Verily, verily, I say unto thee, When thou wast young, thou ᵀgirdedst thyself, and walkedst whither thou wouldest: but when thou shalt be old, thou shalt stretch forth thy hands, and another shall gird thee, and carry *thee* whither thou wouldest not.   *did dress*

19 This spake he, signifying ᴿby what death ᵀhe should ᵀglorify God. And when he

had spoken this, he saith unto him, Follow me. *2 Pet. 1:14 · Peter · bring glory to*

20 Then Peter, turning about, seeth the disciple ᴿwhom Jesus loved following; which also leaned on his breast at supper, and said, Lord, which is he that betrayeth thee? *13:23, 25*

21 Peter seeing him saith to Jesus, Lord, and what ᵀshall this man do? *about this man*

22 Jesus saith unto him, If I will that he ᵀtarry ᴿtill I come, what *is that* to thee? follow thou me. *wait · Rev. 2:25; [3:11; 22:7, 20]*

23 Then went this saying abroad among the brethren, that that disciple should not die: yet Jesus said not unto him, He shall not die; but, If I ᵀwill that he ᵀtarry till I come, what *is that* to thee? *decide · wait*

The Conclusion of John's Gospel

24 This is the disciple which testifieth of these things, and wrote these things: and we know that his testimony is true.

25 And there are also many other things which Jesus did, the which, if they should be written every one, I suppose that even the world itself could not contain the books that should be written. A-men'.

Jewish Feasts

Feast of	Month on Jewish Calendar	Day	Corresponding Month	References
*Passover (Unleavened Bread)	Nisan	14–21	Mar.–Apr.	Ex. 12:43—13:10; Matt. 26:17–20
*Pentecost (Firstfruits or Weeks)	Sivan	6 (50 days after Passover)	May–June	Deut. 16:9–12; Acts 2:1
Trumpets, *Rosh Hashanah*	Tishri	1, 2	Sept.–Oct.	Num. 29:1–6
Day of Atonement, *Yom Kippur*	Tishri	10	Sept.–Oct.	Lev. 23:26–32; Heb. 9:7
*Tabernacles (Booths or Ingathering)	Tishri	15–22	Sept.–Oct.	Neh. 8:13–18; John 7:2
Dedication (Lights), *Hanukkah*	Chislev	25 (8 days)	Nov.–Dec.	John 10:22
Purim (Lots)	Adar	14, 15	Feb.–Mar.	Esth. 9:18–32

*The three major feasts for which all males of Israel were required to travel to the Temple in Jerusalem (Ex. 23:14–19).

THE ACTS

OF THE APOSTLES

THE BOOK OF ACTS

Jesus' last recorded words have come to be known as the Great Commission: "Ye shall be witnesses unto me both in Jerusalem, and in all Judaea, and in Samaria, and unto the uttermost part of the earth" (1:8). The Book of Acts, written by Luke, is the story of the men and women who took that commission seriously and began to spread the news of a risen Saviour to the most remote corners of the known world.

Each section of the book (1—7; 8—12; 13—28) focuses on a particular audience, a key personality, and a significant phase in the expansion of the gospel message.

As the second volume in a two-part work by Luke, this book probably had no separate title. But all available Greek manuscripts designate it by the title *Praxeis*, "Acts," or by an expanded title like "The Acts of the Apostles." *Praxeis* was commonly used in Greek literature to summarize the accomplishments of outstanding men. While the apostles are mentioned collectively at several points, this book really records the acts of Peter (1—12) and of Paul (13—28).

THE AUTHOR OF ACTS

Acts 1:1 refers Theophilus to "The former treatise," that is, the Gospel of Luke. (See "The Author of Luke" for the internal and external support for Lucan authorship of Luke.) Luke's source for the "we" sections in this book (16:10-17; 20:5—21:18; 27:1—28:16) was his own memory if not some kind of diary. For the remainder of this book, Luke no doubt followed the same careful investigative procedures that he used in writing his gospel (Luke 1:1-4). As a close traveling companion of Paul, Luke had access to the principal eyewitness for chapters 13—28. It is also likely that he had opportunities to interview such key witnesses in Jerusalem as Peter and John for the information in chapters 1—12. Acts 15:23-29 and 23:26-30 indicate that Luke may have used written documents as well.

THE TIME OF ACTS

Suggested dates for the writing of Acts range from A.D. 62 to the middle of the second century. Twentieth-century archaeological discoveries have strikingly confirmed the trustworthiness and precision of Luke as a historian and show that his work should be dated in the first century. Luke's perplexingly abrupt ending with Paul awaiting trial in Rome has led many to believe that Acts was completed prior to Paul's trial (A.D. 62). If it was written after this crucial event, why didn't Luke mention the outcome? Luke may have had a reason, but the simplest explanation of his silence is that Paul had not yet stood before Caesar. Acts gives no hint of the persecution under Nero (A.D. 64), Paul's death (A.D. 68), or the destruction of Jerusalem (A.D. 70).

THE CHRIST OF ACTS

The resurrected Saviour is the central theme of the sermons and defenses in Acts. The Old Testament Scriptures, the historical Resurrection, the apostolic testimony, and the convicting power of the Holy Ghost, or Spirit, all bear witness that Jesus is both Lord and Christ (see Peter's sermons in 2:22–36 and 10:34-43). "To him give all the prophets witness, that through his name whosoever believeth in him shall receive remission of sins" (10:43). "Neither is there salvation in any other: for there is none other name under heaven given among men, whereby we must be saved" (4:12).

KEYS TO ACTS

Key Word: The Growth of the Church— While there are four accounts of the life of Jesus, this is the only book that carries on the story from His ascension to the period of the New Testament Epistles. Thus, Acts is the historical link between the Gospels and the Epistles. Because of Luke's strong emphasis on the ministry of the Holy Spirit, this book could be regarded as "the Acts of the Spirit of Christ Working in and Through the Apostles." As a missionary himself, Luke's interest in the progressive spread of the gospel is obviously reflected in this apostolic history. Luke was personally involved as a participant in this story, so it was not written from a detached point of view.

From a theological standpoint, Acts was written to trace the development of the body of Christ over the one-generation transition from a primarily Jewish to a predominantly gentile membership. This apologetic work presents Christianity as distinct from Judaism but also as its fulfillment.

Key Verses: Acts 1:8 and 2:42-47—"But ye shall receive power, after that the Holy Ghost is come upon you: and ye shall be witnesses unto me both in Jerusalem, and in all Judaea, and in Samaria, and unto the uttermost part of the earth" (1:8).

"And they continued stedfastly in the apostles' doctrine and fellowship, and in breaking of bread, and in prayers. And fear came upon every soul: and many wonders and signs were done by the apostles. And all that believed were together, and had all things common; And sold their possessions and goods, and parted them to all *men*, as every

man had need. And they, continuing daily with one accord in the temple, and breaking bread from house to house, did eat their meat with gladness and singleness of heart, Praising God, and having favour with all the people. And the Lord added to the church daily such as should be saved" (2:42–47).

Key Chapter: Acts 2—Chapter 2 records the earth-changing events of the Day of Pentecost when the Holy Spirit comes, fulfilling Christ's promise to wait until the Holy Spirit arrives to empower and direct the witness. The Spirit transforms a small group of fearful men into a thriving, worldwide church that is ever moving forward and fulfilling the Great Commission.

SURVEY OF ACTS

Luke begins the Book of Acts where he left off in his gospel. Acts records the initial fulfillment of the Great Commission of Matthew 28:19, 20 as it traces the beginning and growth of the New Testament church (this growth pattern can be seen in 1:15; 2:41, 47; 4:4; 5:14; 6:7; 9:31; 12:24; 13:49; 16:5; 19:20). Acts traces important events in the early history of Christianity from the ascension of Christ to the outpouring of the Holy Spirit to the rapid progress of the gospel, beginning in Jerusalem and spreading throughout the Roman Empire.

Acts is a pivotal book of transitions: from the Gospels to the Epistles (history), from Judaism to Christianity (religion), from law to grace (divine dealing), from Jews alone to Jews and Gentiles (people of God), and from kingdom to church (program of God).

The three movements in Acts follow its key verse (1:8): witness in Jerusalem (1:1—8:4); witness in Judaea and Samaria (8:5—12:25); witness to the uttermost part of the earth (13—28).

Witness in Jerusalem (1:1—8:4): After appearing to His disciples for "forty days" (1:3), the Lord tells them to wait in Jerusalem for the

fulfillment of His promise concerning the Holy Spirit. Ten days after His ascension, this promise is significantly fulfilled as the disciples are suddenly empowered and filled with the Holy Spirit. The disciples are transformed and filled with courage to proclaim the brand new message of the resurrected Saviour. Peter's powerful sermon, like all the sermons in Acts, is built upon the Resurrection, and 3,000 persons respond with saving faith. After dramatically healing a man who was lame from birth, Peter delivers a second crucial message to the people of Israel resulting in thousands of additional responses. The religious leaders arrest the apostles, and this gives Peter an opportunity to preach a special sermon to them.

The enthusiasm and joy of the infant church are marred by internal and external problems. Ananias and Sapphira receive the ultimate form of discipline because of their treachery, and the apostles are imprisoned and persecuted because of their witness. Seven men, including Stephen and Philip, are selected to assist the apostles. Stephen is brought before the Sanhedrin; in his defense, Stephen surveys the Scriptures to prove that the Man they condemned and killed was the Messiah Himself. The members of the Sanhedrin react to Stephen's words by dragging him out of the city and making him the first Christian martyr.

Witness in Judaea and Samaria (8:5—12:25): Philip goes to the province of Samaria and successfully proclaims the new message to a people hated by the Jews. Peter and John confirm his work and exercise their apostolic authority by imparting the Holy Spirit to these new members of the body of Christ. God sovereignly transforms Saul the persecutor into Paul the Apostle to the Gentiles, but He uses Peter to introduce the gospel to the Gentiles. In a special vision Peter realizes that Christ has broken down the barrier between Jew and Gentile. After Cornelius and other Gentiles come to Christ through his preaching, Peter convinces the Jewish believers in

FOCUS	WITNESS IN JERUSALEM		WITNESS IN JUDEA AND SAMARIA	WITNESS TO THE REMOTEST PART OF THE EARTH	
REFERENCE	1:1 —————— 3:1 ————————		8:5 —————————————	13:1 ————— 21:17 —— 28:31	
DIVISION	POWER OF THE CHURCH	PROGRESS OF THE CHURCH	EXPANSION OF THE CHURCH	PAUL'S THREE JOURNEYS	PAUL'S TRIALS
TOPIC	JEWS		SAMARITANS	GENTILES	
	PETER		PHILIP	PAUL	
LOCATION	JERUSALEM		JUDEA AND SAMARIA	UTTERMOST PART	
TIME	2 YEARS (A.D.33–35)		13 YEARS (A.D. 35–48)	14 YEARS (A.D. 48–62)	

Jerusalem that "the Gentiles had also received the word of God" (11:1). Even while experiencing more and more persecution, the church continues to increase, spreading throughout the Roman Empire.

Witness to the Uttermost Part of the Earth (13—28): Beginning with chapter 13, Luke switches the focus of Acts from Peter to Paul. Antioch in Syria gradually replaces Jerusalem as the headquarters of the church, and all three of Paul's missionary journeys originate from that city. The first journey (A.D. 48–49) concentrates on the Galatian cities of Pisidian Antioch, Iconium, Lystra, and Derbe. After this journey, a council is held among the apostles and elders of the church in Jerusalem to determine that the gentile converts need not submit to the law of Moses. The second missionary journey (A.D. 50–52) brings Paul once again to the Galatian churches, and then for the first time on to Macedonia and Greece. Paul spends much of his time in the cities of Philippi, Thessalonica, and Corinth, and later returns to Jerusalem and Antioch. In his third missionary journey (A.D. 53–57), Paul spends almost three years in the Asian city of Ephesus before visiting Macedonia and Greece for the second time. Although he is warned not to go to Jerusalem, Paul cannot be dissuaded.

It is not long before Paul is falsely accused of bringing Gentiles into the temple. Only the Roman commander's intervention prevents his being killed by the mob. Paul's defense before the people and before the Sanhedrin evokes violent reactions. When the commander learns of a conspiracy to assassinate Paul, he sends his prisoner to Felix, the governor in Caesarea. During his two-year imprisonment there (A.D. 57–59), Paul defends the Christian faith before Felix, Festus, and Agrippa. His appeal to Caesar requires a long voyage to Rome, where he is placed under house arrest until his trial.

OUTLINE OF ACTS

Part One: The Witness in Jerusalem (1:1—8:4)

Part Two: The Witness in Judaea and Samaria (8:5—12:25)

theo = God
ophi - love [handwritten annotations]

CHAPTER 1

Prologue to Acts

THE ᴿformer ᵀtreatise have I ᵀmade, O The-oph'-i-lus, of all that Jesus began both to do and teach,   Luke 1:3 · *book* · *written*

2 Until the day in which he ᵀwas taken up, after that he through the Holy Ghost had given commandments unto the apostles whom he had chosen: *ascended into heaven*

Appearances of the Resurrected Christ
Luke 24:44–49

3 ᴿTo whom also he shewed himself alive after his passion by many ᵀinfallible proofs, being seen of them forty days, and speaking of the things ᵀpertaining to the kingdom of God: Mark 16:14 · *unmistakable* · *concerning*

4 And, ᵀbeing assembled together with *them*, commanded them that they should not depart from Jerusalem, ᴿbut wait for the promise of the Father, which, *saith he*, ye have heard of me.   *when they came* · Luke 24:49

5 For John truly baptized with water; ᴿbut ye shall be baptized with the Holy Ghost not many days hence.   2:4, 33; Matt. 3:11

6 ᴿWhen they therefore were come together, they asked of him, saying, Lord, wilt thou at this time ᵀrestore again the kingdom to Israel?   Amos 9:11 · *give back*

7 And he said unto them, It is not for you to know the times or the seasons, which the Father hath put in his own power.

8 ᴿBut ye shall receive power, after that the Holy Ghost is come upon you: and ye shall be witnesses unto me both in Jerusalem, and in all Ju-dae'-a, and in Sa-ma'-ri-a, and unto the uttermost part of the earth.   2:4, 33

Ascension of Christ
Mark 16:19; Luke 24:50, 51

9 And when he had spoken these things, while they beheld, he was taken up; and a cloud received him out of their sight.

10 And while they looked stedfastly toward heaven as he went up, behold, two men stood by them in white apparel;

11 Which also said, Ye men of Galilee, why stand ye gazing up into heaven? this same Jesus, which is taken up from you into heaven, ᴿshall so come in like manner as ye have seen him go into heaven.   Rev. 1:7 ☆

Anticipation of the Spirit—Luke 24:52

12 Then returned they unto Jerusalem from the mount called Olivet, which is from Jerusalem a sabbath day's journey.

13 ᴿAnd when they were come in, they went up into an upper room, where abode both Peter, and James, and John, and Andrew, Philip, and Thomas, Bartholomew, and Matthew, James *the son* of Al-phae'-us, and Simon Ze-lo'-tes, and Judas *the brother* of James.   Matt. 10:2–4; Luke 6:13–16

14 These all continued ᵀwith one accord in prayer and supplication, with the women, and Mary the mother of Jesus, and with ᴿhis brethren.   *united* · Matt. 13:55

Appointment of Matthias—Matt. 27:7, 8

15 And in those days Peter ᴿstood up in the midst of the disciples, and said, (the number of names together were about an hundred and twenty,)   2:14; Luke 22:32

16 Men *and* brethren, this scripture must needs have been fulfilled, ᴿwhich the Holy Ghost by the mouth of David spake before concerning Judas, ᴿwhich was guide to them that took Jesus.   Ps. 41:9 ☆ · Luke 22:47

17 For he was numbered with us, and had obtained part of ᴿthis ministry.   *v. 25*

18 ᴿNow this man purchased a field with ᴿthe reward of iniquity; and falling headlong, he burst asunder in the midst, and all his bowels gushed out.   Matt. 27:5 · Matt. 26:15

19 And it was known unto all the ᵀdwellers at Jerusalem; insomuch as that field is called in their proper tongue, A-cel'-da-ma, that is to say, The field of blood.   *people*

1:8 Empowered by God—One of the most common excuses for not becoming a Christian is the fear of failure to live the Christian life. Besides overlooking the fact that men cannot be saved on the basis of good works (Page 1207—Titus 3:5), this objection neglects the truth that God provides the power to live the Christian life. Before Christ was crucified He promised the coming of the Holy Spirit to help believers (Page 1061—John 16:13, 14). The subsequent events of the Book of Acts supply ample evidence of the fulfillment of this prophecy (Page 1075—Acts 4:7, 33; 6:8).

The power of the Holy Spirit was not designed solely for the first-century church. Rather, all Christians are indwelt by the Spirit and thus have His power available (Page 1129—1 Cor. 6:19). However, living the Christian life under the Spirit's power must not be thought of as simply allowing the Spirit to take control while the believer does nothing. The believer still must live the Christian life, though he does it through the Spirit's power. Romans 8:13 says, "If ye through the Spirit do mortify the deeds of the body, ye shall live." It is "ye" who are to put to death the sinful deeds of the body, but you are to do it through the Spirit's power.

The Christian who struggles in his own strength to live the Christian life will fail. He must by faith appropriate daily the power of the Holy Spirit (Page 1114—Rom. 8:4, 5). Described practically, this means that the believer trusts the Spirit to empower him in specific instances such as sharing his faith with others, resisting temptation, being faithful, etc. There is no *secret formula* that makes the Spirit's power available. It is simply a reliance on the Spirit to help.

Now turn to Page 1206—Titus 1:2: Promise of God.

20 For it is written in the book of Psalms, [R]LET HIS HABITATION BE DESOLATE, AND [R]LET NO MAN DWELL THEREIN: AND HIS BISHOPRICK LET ANOTHER TAKE.   Ps. 69:25 · Ps. 109:8 *

21 Wherefore of these men which have companied with us all the time that the Lord Jesus went in and out among us,

22 Beginning from the baptism of John, unto that same day that he was taken up from us, must one be [T]ordained to be a witness with us of his resurrection.   *chosen*

23 And they [T]appointed two, Joseph called [R]Bar'-sa-bas, who was surnamed Justus, and Mat-thi'-as.   *nominated* · 15:22

24 And they prayed, and said, Thou, Lord, which knowest the hearts of all *men*, shew whether of these two thou hast chosen,

25 [R]That he may take [T]part of this ministry and apostleship, from which Judas by transgression fell, that he might go to his own [T]place.   *v. 17 · the place in · reward*

26 And they gave forth their lots; and the lot fell upon Mat-thi'-as; and he was [T]numbered with the eleven apostles.   *added to*

CHAPTER 2

Filling with the Holy Ghost

AND when [R]the day of Pentecost [T]was fully come, [R]they were all with one accord in one place.   20:16 · had come · 1:14

2 And suddenly there came a sound from heaven as of a rushing mighty wind, and it filled all the house where they were sitting.

3 And there appeared unto them [T]cloven tongues [T]like as of fire, and it [T]sat upon each of them.   *divided · which looked like · rested*

4 And they were all filled with the Holy Ghost, and began to speak with other tongues, as the Spirit gave them utterance.

Speaking with Other Tongues

5 And there were dwelling at Jerusalem Jews, devout men, [R]out of every [T]nation under heaven.   [Zech. 2:11, 12] · *country*

6 Now when this was noised abroad, the multitude came together, and were [T]confounded, because that every man heard them speak in his own language.   *disturbed*

7 And they were all amazed and marvelled, saying one to another, Behold, are not all these which [T]speak Gal-i-lae'-ans?   *talk*

8 [R]And how hear we every man in our own [T]tongue, wherein we were born?   *v. 4 · Lit. dialect*

9 Par'-thi-ans, and Medes, and E'-lam-ites, and the [T]dwellers in Mes-o-po-ta'-mi-a, and in Ju-dae'-a, and Cap-pa-do'-ci-a, in Pon'-tus, and Asia,   *citizens of*

10 Phryg'-i-a, and Pam-phyl'-i-a, in Egypt, and in the parts of Lib'-y-a about Cy-re'-ne, and strangers of Rome, Jews and proselytes,

11 Cretes and A-ra'-bi-ans, we do hear them speak in our [T]tongues the wonderful [T]works of God.   *dialects · things God has done*

12 And they were all amazed, and were in [T]doubt, saying one to another, What meaneth this?   *confused*

13 Others [T]mocking said, These men are full of new wine.   *made fun of the believers*

Peter Explains Pentecost

14 But Peter, standing up with the eleven, lifted up his voice, and said unto them, Ye men of Ju-dae'-a, and all ye that dwell at Jerusalem, be this known unto you, and [T]hearken to my words: *listen*

15 For these are not drunken, as ye suppose, [R]seeing it is *but* [T]the third hour of the day.   1 Thess. 5:7 · *9 a.m.*

16 [R]But this is [T]that which was spoken by the prophet Jo'-el;   Joel 2:28–32 · *the Spirit*

17 AND IT SHALL COME TO PASS IN THE LAST DAYS, SAITH GOD, I WILL POUR OUT OF MY SPIRIT UPON ALL FLESH: AND YOUR SONS AND YOUR DAUGHTERS SHALL PROPHESY, AND YOUR YOUNG MEN SHALL SEE VISIONS, AND YOUR OLD MEN SHALL DREAM DREAMS:

18 AND ON MY SERVANTS AND ON MY HANDMAIDENS I WILL POUR OUT IN THOSE DAYS OF MY SPIRIT; AND THEY SHALL PROPHESY:

19 AND I WILL SHEW WONDERS IN HEAVEN ABOVE, AND SIGNS IN THE EARTH BENEATH; BLOOD, AND FIRE, AND VAPOUR OF SMOKE:

20 THE SUN SHALL BE TURNED INTO DARKNESS, AND THE MOON INTO BLOOD, BEFORE THAT GREAT AND NOTABLE DAY OF THE LORD COME:

21 AND IT SHALL COME TO PASS, *THAT* WHOSOEVER SHALL CALL ON THE NAME OF THE LORD SHALL BE SAVED.

22 Ye men of Israel, hear these words; Jesus of Nazareth, [R]a man approved of God among you by miracles and wonders and signs, which God did by him in the midst of you, as ye yourselves also know: Is. 50:5 *

23 Him, [R]being delivered by the determinate counsel and foreknowledge of God, [R]ye have taken, and by wicked hands have crucified and slain: Matt. 26:24; Luke 22:22 · 5:30

24 Whom God hath raised up, having loosed the pains of death: because it was not possible that he should be holden of it.

25 For David speaketh concerning him, [R]I FORESAW THE LORD ALWAYS BEFORE MY FACE, FOR HE IS ON MY RIGHT HAND, THAT I SHOULD NOT BE [T]MOVED;   Ps. 16:8–11 * · *troubled*

26 THEREFORE DID MY HEART REJOICE, AND MY TONGUE WAS GLAD; MOREOVER ALSO MY FLESH SHALL REST IN HOPE:

27 BECAUSE THOU WILT NOT LEAVE MY SOUL IN HELL, NEITHER WILT THOU SUFFER THINE HOLY ONE TO SEE CORRUPTION.

28 THOU HAST MADE KNOWN TO ME THE WAYS OF LIFE; THOU SHALT MAKE ME FULL OF JOY WITH THY COUNTENANCE.

29 Men *and* brethren, let me freely speak unto you of the patriarch David, that he is both dead and buried, and his ᵀsepulchre is with us unto this day. *tomb*

30 Therefore being a prophet, and knowing that God had sworn with an ᴿoath to him, that of the fruit of his loins, according to the flesh, he would raise up Christ to sit on his throne; Ps. 132:11 *

31 ᵀHe seeing this before spake of the resurrection of Christ, ᴿthat his soul was not left in hell, neither his flesh did see corruption. *David* • 13:35; Ps. 16:10 *

32 ᴿThis Jesus hath God raised up, ᴿwhereof we all are witnesses. Ps. 68:18 * • 1:8

33 Therefore ᴿbeing by the right hand of God exalted, and ᴿhaving received of the Father the promise of the Holy Ghost, he ᴿhath shed forth this, which ye now see and hear. Ps. 16:11; [Phil. 2:9] * • [John 14:26] • 10:45

34 For David is not ascended into the heavens: but he saith himself, ᴿTHE LORD SAID UNTO MY LORD, SIT THOU ON MY RIGHT HAND, Ps. 110:1 *

35 UNTIL I MAKE THY FOES THY FOOTSTOOL.

36 Therefore let all the house of Israel ᵀknow assuredly, that God hath made that same Jesus, whom ye have crucified, both Lord and ᵀChrist. *understand completely • Messiah*

37 Now when they heard *this*, they were ᴿpricked in their heart, and said unto Peter and to the rest of the apostles, Men *and* brethren, what shall we do? 9:6; 16:30; John 16:8 *

38 Then Peter said unto them, ᴿRepent, and be baptized every one of you in the name of Jesus Christ ᵀfor the remission of sins, ᴿand ye shall receive the gift of the Holy Ghost. [3:19] • *unto* • [Matt. 26:28]; Mark 1:4

39 For the promise is unto you, and to your children, and to all that are afar off, *even* as many as the Lord our God shall call.

40 And with many other words did he testify and exhort, saying, Save yourselves from this ᵀuntoward generation. *crooked*

41 ᴿThen they that gladly received his word were baptized: and the same day there were added ᵀunto *them* about three thousand souls. *v.* 47; Matt. 16:18 * • *to the group*

Practices of the Early Church

42 ᴿAnd they continued stedfastly in the apostles' doctrine and fellowship, and in breaking of bread, and in prayers. 1:14

43 And fear came upon every soul: and ᴿmany wonders and ᵀsigns were done by the apostles. 4:33; 5:12; Mark 16:17 • *miracles*

44 And all that believed were together, and ᴿhad all things common; 4:32, 34

45 And sold their possessions and goods, and ᴿpartedᵀ them to all *men*, as every man ᵀhad need. Is. 58:7 • *shared • was in need*

46 And they, continuing daily with one accord in the temple, and breaking bread from house to house, did eat their meat with gladness and singleness of heart,

47 ᴿPraising God, and having favour with all the people. And the Lord added to the church daily such as should be saved. *v.* 41

CHAPTER 3

Peter Heals the Lame Man

NOW Peter and John went up together ᴿinto the temple at the hour of prayer, ᴿ*being* the ninth *hour*. 2:46 • Ps. 55:17

2 And ᴿa certain man lame from his mother's womb was carried, whom they laid daily at the gate of the temple which is called Beautiful, to ᵀask alms of them that entered into the temple; 14:8 • *beg*

3 Who seeing Peter and John about to go into the temple asked an alms.

4 And Peter, fastening his eyes upon him with John, said, Look ᵀon us. *at*

5 And he gave heed unto them, expecting to receive something of them.

6 Then Peter said, Silver and gold have I none; but such as I have give I thee: ᴿIn the name of Jesus Christ of Nazareth rise up and walk. 4:10

7 And he took him by the right hand, and lifted *him* up: and immediately his feet and ancle bones received strength.

8 And he leaping up stood, and walked, and entered with them into the temple, walking, and leaping, and praising God.

9 ᴿAnd ᵀall the people saw him walking and praising God: 4:16, 21 • *the whole crowd*

2:42–47 Benefits of Participation in the Local Church—The benefits of participation in a local church are immediately apparent. This passage records the first meeting of the first local church. From this passage seven benefits of participation in the local church are immediately apparent: instruction—"continued stedfastly in the apostles' doctrine"; fellowship—"and fellowship"; observance of the ordinances—"breaking of bread"; corporate prayer—"prayers"; effective outreach—"fear came upon every soul"; common cause—"had all things common"; and mutual assistance—"parted them to all *men*, as every man had need." In addition to these, four other benefits of participation in the local church are clear: worship (Page 1095—Acts 20:7); discipline (Page 960—Matt. 18:15–17; Page 1151—2 Cor. 13:1–10); pastoral oversight (Page 1239—1 Pet. 5:1–3); and obedience to God's command (Page 1221—Heb. 10:25). Participation in the local church is not optional for the child of God. It is imperative and yields eternal benefits.

Now turn to Page 974—Matt. 28:19: Sharing Our Faith: Why?

10 And they ^Tknew that it was he which ^Rsat for alms at the Beautiful gate of the temple: and they were filled with wonder and ^Tamazement at that which had happened unto him. *recognized · John 9:8 · surprise*

11 And as the lame man which was healed held Peter and John, all the people ran together unto them in the porch that is called Solomon's, greatly wondering.

Peter's Second Sermon

12 And when Peter saw *it*, he answered unto the people, Ye men of Israel, why marvel ye at this? or why look ye so earnestly on us, ^Ras though by our own power or holiness we had made this man to walk? [10:26]

13 ^RThe God of Abraham, and of Isaac, and of Jacob, the God of our fathers, hath glorified his Son Jesus; whom ye delivered up, and denied him in the presence of Pilate, when he was determined to let *him* go. 5:30

14 But ye denied ^Rthe Holy One ^Rand the Just, and desired a murderer to be granted unto you; *Mark 1:24; Luke 1:35 · 7:52*

15 And killed the ^TPrince of life, ^Rwhom God hath raised from the dead; ^Rwhereof we are witnesses. *author · 2:24 · 2:32*

16 ^RAnd his name through faith in his name hath made this man strong, whom ye see and know: yea, the faith which is by him hath given him this perfect soundness in the presence of you all. *Matt. 9:22*

17 And now, brethren, I ^Twot that ^Rthrough ignorance ye did *it*, as *did* also your rulers. *know · Luke 23:34; 1 Cor. 2:8*

18 But ^Rthose things, which God before had shewed ^Rby the mouth of all his prophets, that Christ should suffer, he hath so fulfilled. *26:22; Luke 24:44 · Ps. 22: 1; Is. 53:3 ★*

19 ^RRepent ye therefore, and be converted, that your sins may be blotted out, when the times of refreshing shall come from the presence of the Lord; [2:38]

20 And he shall send Jesus Christ, ^Rwhich before was preached unto you: *Mal. 3:1 ★*

21 Whom the heaven must receive until the times of restitution of all things, which God hath spoken by the mouth of all his holy prophets since the world began.

22 For Moses truly said unto the fathers, A PROPHET SHALL THE LORD YOUR GOD RAISE UP UNTO YOU OF YOUR BRETHREN, LIKE UNTO ME; HIM SHALL YE HEAR IN ALL THINGS WHATSOEVER HE SHALL SAY UNTO YOU.

23 ^RAND IT SHALL COME TO PASS, *THAT* EVERY SOUL, WHICH WILL NOT HEAR THAT PROPHET, SHALL BE DESTROYED FROM AMONG THE PEOPLE. *Deut. 18:19 ★*

24 Yea, and all the prophets from Samuel and those that follow after, as many as have spoken, have likewise foretold of these days.

25 Ye are the children of the prophets, and of the covenant which God made with our fathers, saying unto Abraham, ^RAND IN THY SEED SHALL ALL THE ^TKINDREDS OF THE EARTH BE BLESSED. *Gen. 12:3; 18:18 ★ · nations*

26 ^RUnto you first God, having raised up his Son Jesus, sent him to bless you, in turning away every one of you from his iniquities. *13:32, 33; Ps. 16:10, 11; Is. 42:1; Matt. 1:21 ★*

CHAPTER 4

Peter and John Are Put into Custody

AND as they spake unto the people, the priests, and the captain of the temple, and the Sad'-du-cees, came upon them,

2 ^RBeing ^Tgrieved that they taught the people, and preached through Jesus the resurrection from the dead. *[23:8] · unhappy*

3 And they ^Tlaid hands on them, and put *them* in ^Thold unto the next day: for it was now ^Teventide. *arrested · jail · late*

4 ^RHowbeit many of them which heard the word believed; and the number of the men was about five thousand. 6:7

Peter Preaches to the Sanhedrin

5 And it came to pass on the morrow, that their rulers, and elders, and scribes,

6 And An'-nas the high priest, and Ca'-ia-phas, and John, and Alexander, and as many as were of the kindred of the high priest, were gathered together at Jerusalem.

7 And when they had set them in the midst, they asked, By what power, or by what name, have ye done this?

8 ^RThen Peter, filled with the Holy Ghost, said unto them, Ye rulers of the people, and elders of Israel, *Matt. 5:6; Luke 12:11, 12*

9 If we this day be ^Texamined of the good deed done to the ^Timpotent man, by what means he is made whole; *questioned · helpless*

10 Be it known unto you all, and to all the people of Israel, ^Rthat by the name of Jesus Christ of Nazareth, whom ye crucified, ^Rwhom God raised from the dead, *even* by him doth this man stand here before you ^Twhole. *3:6, [16] · 2:24 · well*

11 ^RTHIS IS THE STONE WHICH WAS SET AT NOUGHT OF YOU BUILDERS, WHICH IS BECOME THE HEAD OF THE CORNER. *Is. 28:16; Matt. 21:42 ★*

12 ^RNeither is there salvation in any other: for there is none other name under heaven given among men, ^Twhereby we must be saved. *[10:43]; 19:5; 1 Tim. 2:5, 6] · by which*

Sanhedrin Commands Peter Not to Preach

13 Now when they saw the boldness of Peter and John, and perceived that they were unlearned and ignorant men, they marvelled; and they took knowledge of them, that they had been with Jesus.

14 And beholding the man which was ^Thealed standing with them, ^Rthey could say nothing against it. *made whole · v. 16*

15 But when they had commanded them to ᵀgo aside out of the council, they ᵀconferred among themselves,   *leave · talked it over*

16 Saying, What shall we do to these men? for that indeed a notable miracle hath been done by them *is* manifest to all them that dwell in Jerusalem; and we cannot deny *it*.

17 But that it spread no further among the people, let us ᵀstraitly threaten them, that they speak henceforth to no man in ᵀthis name.   *sternly · Jesus' name*

18 ᴿAnd they called them, and commanded them not to speak at all nor teach in the name of Jesus.   5:40

19 But Peter and John answered and said unto them, ᴿWhether it be right in the sight of God to hearken unto you more than unto God, judge ye.   [Gal. 1:10]

20 For we cannot but speak the things which ᴿwe have seen and heard.   [1 John 1:1, 3]

21 So when they had further threatened them, they let them go, finding nothing how they might punish them, ᴿbecause of the people: for all *men* ᵀglorified God for ᴿthat which was done.   5:26 · *praised* · 3:7, 8

22 For the man was ᵀabove forty years old, on whom this miracle of healing ᵀwas shewed.   *over · was seen*

Apostles' Prayer for Boldness

23 And being let go, they went to their own company, and reported all that the chief priests and elders had said unto them.

24 And when they heard that, they ᵀlifted up their voice to God with one accord, and said, Lord, ᴿthou *art* God, which hast made heaven, and earth, and the sea, and all that in them is: *prayed* · 2 Kin. 19:15

25 Who by the mouth of thy servant David hast said, ᴿWʜʏ ᴅɪᴅ ᴛʜᴇ ʜᴇᴀᴛʜᴇɴ ʀᴀɢᴇ, ᴀɴᴅ ᴛʜᴇ ᴘᴇᴏᴘʟᴇ ɪᴍᴀɢɪɴᴇ ᴠᴀɪɴ ᴛʜɪɴɢs?   Ps. 2:1,2 *

26 Tʜᴇ ᴋɪɴɢs ᴏꜰ ᴛʜᴇ ᴇᴀʀᴛʜ sᴛᴏᴏᴅ ᴜᴘ, ᴀɴᴅ ᴛʜᴇ ʀᴜʟᴇʀs ᴡᴇʀᴇ ɢᴀᴛʜᴇʀᴇᴅ ᴛᴏɢᴇᴛʜᴇʀ ᴀɢᴀɪɴsᴛ ᴛʜᴇ Lᴏʀᴅ, ᴀɴᴅ ᴀɢᴀɪɴsᴛ ʜɪs Cʜʀɪsᴛ.

27 For of a truth against thy holy child Jesus, whom thou hast anointed, both Herod, and Pon′-tius Pilate, with the Gentiles, and the people of Israel, were gathered together,

28 For to do whatsoever thy hand and thy counsel determined before to be done.

29 And now, Lord, behold their threatenings: and grant unto thy servants, that with all boldness they may speak thy word,

30 By stretching forth thine hand to heal; and that signs and wonders may be done by the name of thy holy child Jesus.

31 And when they had prayed, ᴿthe place was shaken where they were assembled together; and they were all ᴿfilled with the Holy Ghost, ᴿand they spake the word of God with boldness.   2:2, 4; 16:26 · Matt. 5:6 · *v.* 29

Early Church Voluntarily Shares

32 And the multitude of them that believed were of one heart and of one soul: neither said any *of them* that ᵀought of the things which he possessed was his own; but they had all things common.   *anything*

33 And with great power gave the apostles witness of the resurrection of the Lord Jesus: and great grace was upon them all.

34 Neither was there any among them ᵀthat lacked: ᴿfor as many as were ᵀpossessors of lands or houses sold them, and brought the ᵀprices of the things that were sold,   *in need* · 2:45 · *owned* · *money*

35 ᴿAnd laid *them* down at the apostles' feet: and distribution was made unto every man according as he had need.   *v.* 37

36 And Jo′-ses, who by the apostles was surnamed Barnabas, (which is, being interpreted, The son of ᵀconsolation,) a Levite, *and* of the country of Cyprus,   *comfort*

37 ᴿHaving land, sold *it*, and brought the money, and laid *it* at the apostles' feet.   *v.* 34

CHAPTER 5

Ananias and Sapphira Lie

Bᴜᴛ a certain man named An-a-ni′-as, with Sap-phi′-ra his wife, sold ᵀa possession,   *some property*

2 ᴿAnd kept back *part* of the price, his wife also being privy *to it*, and brought a certain part, and laid *it* at the apostles' feet.   4:37

3 ᴿBut Peter said, An-a-ni′-as, why hath ᴿSatan ᵀfilled thine heart to lie to the Holy Ghost, and to keep back *part* of the price of the land?   Eccl. 5:4 · Luke 22:3 · *controlled*

4 Whiles it remained, was it not thine own? and after it was sold, was it not in thine own power? why hast thou ᵀconceived this thing in thine heart? thou hast not lied unto men, but unto God.   *decided*

5 And An-a-ni′-as hearing these words fell down, and gave up the ghost: and great fear came on all them that heard these things.

6 And the young men arose, wound him up, and carried *him* out, and buried *him*.

7 And it was about the space of three hours after, when his wife, not knowing what ᵀwas done, came in.   *had happened*

8 And Peter answered unto her, Tell me whether ye sold the land for so much? And she said, Yea, for ᵀso much.   *this amount*

9 Then Peter said unto her, How is it that ye have agreed together to ᵀtempt the Spirit of the Lord? behold, the feet of them which have buried thy husband *are* at the door, and shall carry thee out.   *try*

10 ᴿThen fell she down ᵀstraightway at his feet, and ᵀyielded up the ghost: and the young men came in, and found her dead, and, carrying *her* forth, buried *her* by her husband.   *v.* 5 · *immediately* · *died*

11 ᴿAnd great fear came upon all the church, and upon as many as heard these things.   v. 5; 2:43; 19:17

Apostles' Mighty Miracles

12 And by the hands of the apostles were many signs and wonders ᵀwrought among the people; (and they were all with one accord in Solomon's porch.   worked
13 And ᴿof the rest ᵀdurst no man ᴿjoin himself to them: ᴿbut the people magnified them.   John 9:22 · dared · 2:47 · 4:21
14 And believers were the more ᴿadded to the Lord, multitudes both of men and women.)   [John 14:12]; 2:41, 47; 11:24; [1 Cor. 3:6]
15 Insomuch that they brought forth the sick into the streets, and laid them on beds and couches, ᴿthat at the least the shadow of Peter passing by might overshadow some of them.   19:12; Matt. 9:21
16 There came also a multitude out of the cities round about unto Jerusalem, bringing ᴿsick folks, and them which were ᵀvexed with unclean spirits: and they were healed every one.   Mark 16:17; [John 14:12] · troubled

Apostles Are Miraculously Freed from Prison

17 ᴿThen the high priest rose up, and all they that were with him, (which is the sect of the Sad'-du-cees,) and were filled with ᵀindignation,   4:1, 2, 6 · jealousy
18 And ᵀlaid their hands on the apostles, and put them in the common prison.   arrested
19 But ᴿthe angel of the Lord by night opened the prison doors, and brought them forth, and said,   12:7; 16:26
20 Go, stand and speak in the temple to the people ᴿall the words of this life.   John 6:68
21 And when they heard that, they entered into the temple early in the morning, and taught. ᴿBut the high priest came, and they that were with him, and called the council together, and all the senate of the children of Israel, and sent to the prison to have them brought.   4:5, 6
22 But when the officers ᵀcame, and found them not in the prison, they returned, and ᵀtold,   arrived · reported
23 Saying, The prison truly found we shut with all safety, and the keepers standing without before the doors: but when we had opened, we found no man within.
24 Now when the high priest and the captain of the temple and the chief priests heard these things, they ᵀdoubted of them whereunto this would grow.   were uncertain
25 Then came one and told them, saying, Behold, the men whom ye put in prison are standing in the temple, and teaching the people.
26 Then went the captain with the officers, and brought them ᵀwithout violence: ᴿfor

they feared the people, lest they should have been stoned.   quietly · Matt. 21:26
27 And when they had brought them, they ᵀset them before the council: and the high priest asked them,   made them stand
28 Saying, Did not we ᵀstraitly command you that ye should not teach in this name? and, behold, ye have filled Jerusalem with your doctrine, and intend to bring this man's blood upon us.   sternly

Apostles Preach to the Council

29 Then Peter and the other apostles answered and said, ᴿWe ought to obey God ᵀrather than men.   4:19 · not
30 The God of our fathers raised up Jesus, whom ye slew and hanged on a tree.
31 ᴿHim hath God exalted with his right hand to be ᴿa Prince and ᴿa Saviour, ᴿfor to give repentance to Israel, and forgiveness of sins.   [2:33, 36] · 3:15 · Matt. 1:21 · [Col. 1:14]
32 And ᴿwe are his witnesses of these things; and so is also the Holy Ghost, whom God hath given to them that obey him.   2:38

Gamaliel's Advice

33 When they heard that, they were cut to the heart, and took counsel to slay them.
34 Then stood there up one in the council, a Pharisee, named ᴿGa-ma'-li-el, a doctor of the law, had in reputation among all the people, and commanded to put the apostles forth a little space;   22:3
35 And said unto them, Ye men of Israel, ᵀtake heed to yourselves what ye intend to do as touching these men.   be careful
36 For before these days rose up Theu'-das, boasting himself to be somebody; to whom a number of men, about four hundred, joined themselves: who was slain; and all, as many as ᴿobeyed him, were scattered, and brought to nought.   v. 14
37 After this man rose up Judas of Galilee in the days of the ᵀtaxing, and drew away much people after him: he also perished; and all, even as many as obeyed him, were ᵀdispersed.   census · scattered
38 And now I say unto you, ᵀRefrain from these men, and let them alone: for if this ᵀcounsel or this work be of men, it will come to ᵀnought: hold back · message · nothing
39 ᴿBut if it be of God, ye cannot overthrow it; lest haply ye be found even ᴿto fight against God.   Luke 21:15 · 7:51; 9:5

Apostles Are Beaten

40 And to him they agreed: and when they had ᴿcalled the apostles, and beaten them, they commanded that they should not speak in the name of Jesus, and let them go.   4:18
41 And they departed from the presence of the council, rejoicing that they were counted worthy to suffer shame for his name.

42 And daily ᴿin the temple, and in every house, ᴿthey ceased not to teach and preach Jesus Christ.   2:46 · 4:20, 29

CHAPTER 6

Deacons Are Appointed

AND in those days, when the number of the disciples was multiplied, there arose a murmuring of the Gre'-cians against the Hebrews, because their widows were neglected in the daily ministration.

2 Then the twelve called the multitude of the disciples *unto them*, and said, ᵀIt is not reason that we should leave the word of God, and serve tables.   *it does not make sense*

3 Wherefore, brethren, ᴿlook ye out among you seven men of honest report, full of the Holy Ghost and wisdom, whom we may appoint over this business.   Deut. 1:13

4 But we will give ourselves continually to prayer, and to the ministry of the word.

5 And the saying pleased the whole multitude: and they chose Stephen, a man full of faith and of the Holy Ghost, and ᴿPhilip, and Proch'-o-rus, and Ni-ca'-nor, and Ti'-mon, and Par'-me-nas, and Nic'-o-las a proselyte of An'-ti-och: 8:26; 21:8

6 Whom they set before the apostles: and when they had prayed, they laid ᵀ*their* hands on them.   *this responsibility on them*

7 And the word of God increased; and the number of the disciples multiplied in Jerusalem greatly; and a great company of the priests were obedient to the faith.

8 And Stephen, full of faith and power, ᵀdid great wonders and miracles among the people.   *performed*

Stephen Is Brought Before the Council

9 Then there arose certain of the synagogue, which is called *the synagogue* of the Lib'-er-tines, and Cy-re'-ni-ans, and Al-ex-an'-dri-ans, ᴿand of them of Ci-li'-ci-a and of Asia, disputing with Stephen.   22:3

10 And they were not able to resist the wisdom and the spirit by which he spake.

11 Then they suborned men, which said, We have heard him speak blasphemous words against Moses, and *against* God.

12 And they ᵀstirred up the people, and the elders, and the scribes, and came upon *him*, and ᵀcaught him, and brought *him* ᵀto the council,   *excited · seized · before*

13 And set up false witnesses, which said, This man ceaseth not to speak blasphemous words against this holy place, and the law:

14 ᴿFor we have heard him say, that this Jesus of Nazareth shall ᴿdestroy this place, and shall change the ᵀcustoms which Moses delivered us.   25:8 · [Dan. 9:26] · *rites*

15 And all that sat in the council, looking stedfastly on him, ᴿsaw his face as it had been the face of an angel.   Ex. 34:29, 30, 35

CHAPTER 7

Stephen Preaches to the Council

THEN ᵀsaid the high priest, ᴿAre these things so?   *asked* · Prov. 18:13; John 7:51

2 And he said, ᴿMen, brethren, and fathers, hearken; The God of glory appeared unto our father Abraham, when he was in Mes-o-po-ta'-mi-a, before he dwelt in Char'-ran,   22:1

3 And said unto him, GET THEE OUT OF THY COUNTRY, AND FROM THY KINDRED, AND COME INTO THE LAND WHICH I SHALL SHEW THEE.

4 Then ᴿcame he out of the land of the Chal-dae'-ans, and dwelt in Char'-ran: and from thence, when his father was dead, ᵀhe removed him into this land, wherein ye now dwell.   Gen. 11:31; 12:4, 5 · *God made him move*

5 And he gave him none inheritance in it, no, not *so much as* to set his foot on: ᴿyet he promised that he would give it to him for a possession, and to his seed after him, when *as yet* he had no child.   Gen. 12:7; 13:15

6 And God spake on this wise, ᴿTHAT HIS SEED SHOULD SOJOURN IN A STRANGE LAND; AND THAT THEY SHOULD BRING THEM INTO BONDAGE, AND ENTREAT *THEM* EVIL FOUR HUNDRED YEARS.   Gen. 15:13

7 AND THE NATION TO WHOM THEY SHALL BE IN BONDAGE WILL I ᵀJUDGE, said God: AND AFTER THAT SHALL THEY COME FORTH, AND ᴿSERVE ME IN THIS PLACE.   *pass judgment* · Ex. 3:12

8 And he gave him the covenant of circumcision: and so *Abraham* begat Isaac, and circumcised him the eighth day; ᴿand Isaac *begat* Jacob; and ᴿJacob *begat* the twelve patriarchs.   Gen. 25:26 · Gen. 35:22–26

9 ᴿAnd the patriarchs, moved with envy, sold Joseph into Egypt: ᴿbut God was with him,   Gen. 37:4, 11, 28; Ps. 105:17 · Gen. 39:2, 21, 23

10 And delivered him out of all his ᵀafflictions, ᴿand gave him favour and wisdom in the sight of Pharaoh king of Egypt; and he made him governor over Egypt and all his house.   *troubles* · Gen. 41:37; 42:6

11 ᴿNow there came a ᵀdearth over all the land of Egypt and Cha'-naan, and great ᵀaffliction: and our fathers found no ᵀsustenance.   Gen. 41:54 · *famine · suffering · food*

12 But when Jacob heard that there was corn in Egypt, he sent out our fathers first.

13 And at the second *time* Joseph was made known to his brethren; and Joseph's kindred was made known unto Pharaoh.

14 Then sent Joseph, and called his father Jacob to *him*, and ᴿall his kindred, ᵀthreescore and fifteen souls.   Deut. 10:22 · 75

15 ᴿSo Jacob went down into Egypt, ᴿand died, he, and our fathers,   Gen. 46:5 • Ex. 1:6

16 And were carried over into Sy'-chem, and laid in the sepulchre that Abraham bought for a sum of money of the sons of Em'-mor *the father* of Sy'-chem.

17 But when ᴿthe time of the promise drew nigh, which God had sworn to Abraham, the people grew and multiplied in Egypt,   v. 6

18 Till another king arose, which knew not Joseph.

19 The same dealt ᵀsubtilly with our ᵀkindred, and evil entreated our fathers, so that they cast out their young children, to the end they might not live.   *craftily • family*

20 In which time Moses was born, and was exceeding fair, and ᵀnourished up in his father's house three months: *brought*

21 And ᴿwhen he was ᵀcast out, Pharaoh's daughter took him up, and nourished him for her own son.   Ex. 2:3–10 • *put out of his home*

22 And Moses was ᵀlearned in all the wisdom of the Egyptians, and was mighty in words and in deeds.   *educated*

23 ᴿAnd when he was ᵀfull forty years old, it came into his heart to visit his brethren the children of Israel.   Ex. 2:11, 12 • *well-nigh*

24 And seeing one *of them* suffer wrong, he defended *him*, and avenged him that was oppressed, and smote the Egyptian:

25 For he supposed his brethren would have understood how that God by his hand would deliver them: but they understood not.

26 And the next day he shewed himself unto them as they strove, and would have set them at one again, saying, Sirs, ye are brethren; why do ye wrong one to another?

27 But he that did his neighbour wrong thrust him away, saying, ᴿWHO MADE THEE A RULER AND A JUDGE OVER US?   Luke 12:14

28 ᵀWILT THOU KILL ME, AS THOU DIDST THE EGYPTIAN YESTERDAY?   *do you want to*

29 ᴿThen fled Moses at this saying, and was a stranger in the land of Ma'-di-an, where he begat two sons.   Ex. 2:15, 22; 4:20

30 ᴿAnd when forty years were ᵀexpired, there appeared to him in the wilderness of mount Si'-na an angel of the Lord in a flame of fire in a bush.   Ex. 3:2 • *passed*

31 When Moses saw *it*, he wondered at the sight: and as he drew near to behold *it*, the voice of the Lord came unto him,

32 *Saying*, I AM THE GOD OF THY FATHERS, THE GOD OF ABRAHAM, AND THE GOD OF ISAAC, AND THE GOD OF JACOB. Then Moses trembled, and ᵀdurst not behold.   *dared not look*

33 Then said the Lord to him, PUT OFF THY SHOES FROM THY FEET: FOR THE PLACE WHERE THOU STANDEST IS HOLY GROUND.

34 ᴿI ᵀHAVE SEEN, I HAVE SEEN THE AFFLIC-TION OF MY PEOPLE WHICH IS IN EGYPT, AND I HAVE HEARD THEIR GROANING, AND AM COME DOWN TO DELIVER THEM. AND NOW COME, I WILL SEND THEE INTO EGYPT. Ex. 3:5, 7 • *have looked*

35 This Moses whom they refused, saying, WHO MADE THEE A RULER AND A JUDGE? the same did God send *to be* a ruler and a deliverer ᴿby the hand of the angel which appeared to him in the bush.   Num. 20:16

36 He brought them out, after that he had shewed wonders and signs in the land of Egypt, ᴿand in the Red sea, ᴿand in the wilderness forty years.   Ex. 14:21 • Ex. 16:1

37 This is that Moses, which said unto the children of Israel, A PROPHET SHALL THE LORD YOUR GOD RAISE UP UNTO YOU OF YOUR BRETHREN, LIKE UNTO ME; HIM SHALL YE HEAR.

38 ᴿThis is he, that was in the church in the wilderness with the angel which spake to him in the mount Si'-na, and *with* our fathers: who received the ᵀlively ᴿoracles to give unto us: Ex. 19:3 • *living words* • Rom. 3:2

39 To whom our fathers would not obey, but thrust *him* from them, and in their hearts turned back again into Egypt,

40 Saying unto Aaron, ᴿMAKE US GODS TO GO BEFORE US: FOR *AS FOR* THIS MOSES, WHICH BROUGHT US OUT OF THE LAND OF EGYPT, WE ᵀWOT NOT WHAT IS BECOME OF HIM.   Ex. 32:1 • *know*

41 And they made a calf in those days, and offered sacrifice unto the idol, and rejoiced in the works of their own hands.

7:38 The Meaning of the Word *Church*—In modern English the word *church* is used in five ways: (1) a building designated as a place of worship, i.e., a church building; (2) all who profess faith in Christ regardless of particular theological beliefs; (3) a denomination; (4) a single organized Christian group, i.e., a local church; and (5) the Body of Christ, i.e., the universal church. While all of these are legitimate uses for modern English, the word *church* is used in the New Testament in only the last two senses— a local church, or the Body of Christ, the universal church. At its root, the word *church* means a "called-out group." It is used of the nation Israel (Acts 7:38) which was a group of people who were called out of the rest of the people of the world to have a special national relationship to God. It is used of a local church (Page 1183—1 Thess. 1:1, church of the Thessalonians; Page 1269—Rev. 2:1, church of Ephesus, etc.), and of the universal church, the Body of Christ (Page 1177—Col. 1:18). The universal church comprises all believers from the Day of Pentecost until the time God takes the church out of the world, and at which time His program for the church will be complete. The local church is a local, visible, temporal manifestation of the universal church. At one point in history the local and universal churches were identical (Page 1074—Acts 2:41). The universal church will not meet until "we all get to heaven" and once in session will never cease.

Now turn to Page 958—Matt. 16:18: The Origin of the Church.

42 Then God turned, and gave them up to worship the host of heaven; as it is written in the book of the prophets, ᴿO YE HOUSE OF ISRAEL, HAVE YE OFFERED TO ME SLAIN BEASTS AND SACRIFICES *BY THE SPACE OF FORTY YEARS IN THE WILDERNESS?*   Amos 5:25

43 YEA, YE TOOK UP THE TABERNACLE OF MO'-LOCH, AND THE STAR OF YOUR GOD REM'-PHAN, FIGURES WHICH YE MADE TO WORSHIP THEM: AND I WILL CARRY YOU AWAY BEYOND BABYLON.

44 Our fathers had the tabernacle of witness in the wilderness, as he had appointed, speaking unto Moses, that he should make it according to the fashion that he had seen.

45 Which also our fathers that came after brought in with Jesus into the possession of the Gentiles, whom God drave out before the face of our fathers, unto the days of David;

46 ᴿWho found favour before God, and desired to find a tabernacle for the God of Jacob.   2 Sam. 7:1; 1 Kin. 8:17

47 But Solomon built him an house.

48 Howbeit ᴿthe ᵀmost High dwelleth not in temples made with hands; as saith the prophet,   17:24, 25; 1 Kin. 8:27 · *Most*

49 ᴿHEAVEN *IS* MY THRONE, AND EARTH *IS* MY FOOTSTOOL: WHAT HOUSE WILL YE BUILD ME? SAITH THE LORD: OR WHAT *IS* THE PLACE OF MY REST?   Is. 66:1

50 ᴿHATH NOT MY HAND MADE ALL THESE THINGS?   Is. 66:2

51 ᴿYe stiffnecked and uncircumcised in heart and ears, ye do always resist the Holy Ghost: as your fathers *did,* so *do* ye.   Is. 6:10

52 Which of the prophets have not your fathers persecuted? and they have slain them which shewed before of the coming of ᴿthe Just One; of whom ye have been now the betrayers and murderers: 3:14

53 Who have received the law by the disposition of angels, and have not kept *it.*

54 ᴿWhen they heard these things, they were ᵀcut to the heart, and they gnashed on him with *their* teeth.   5:33 · *deeply affected*

55 But he, ᴿbeing full of the Holy Ghost, looked up stedfastly into heaven, and ᴿsaw the glory of God, and Jesus standing on the right hand of God,   6:5; Matt. 5:6 · Matt. 5:8; 16:28

56 And said, Behold, ᴿI see the heavens opened, and the ᴿSon of man standing on the right hand of God.   Matt. 3:16 · Dan. 7:13

57 ᴿThen they cried out with a loud voice, and stopped their ears, and ran upon him ᵀwith one accord,   Is. 6:10 · *together*

58 And cast *him* out of the city, and stoned *him:* and ᴿthe witnesses laid down their clothes at a young man's feet, whose name was Saul.   22:20; Luke 4:29; Heb. 13:12

59 And they stoned Stephen, ᵀcalling upon God, and saying, Lord Jesus, ᴿreceive my spirit.   *who was calling* · Ps. 31:5; [2 Tim. 4:6-8]

60 ᴿAnd he kneeled down, and cried with a loud voice, Lord, lay not this sin to their charge. And when he had said this, he fell asleep.   Matt. 5:44; Luke 23:34

CHAPTER 8

Saul Persecutes the Church

AND ᴿSaul was consenting unto his death. And at that time there was a great persecution against the church which was at Jerusalem; and they were all scattered abroad throughout the regions of Ju-dae'-a and Sa-ma'-ri-a, except the apostles.   John 16:2

2 And ᵀdevout men carried Stephen *to his* burial, and made great ᵀlamentation over him.   *godly · weeping*

3 ᴿAs for Saul, he ᵀmade havock of the church, entering into every house, and ᵀhaling men and women committed *them* to prison.   1 Tim. 1:13 · *laid waste · arresting*

4 Therefore ᴿthey ᵀthat were scattered abroad went every where preaching the ᵀword.   Matt. 10:23 · *the believers · message*

Philip Witnesses to the Samaritans

5 Then Philip went down to the city of Sa-ma'-ri-a, and preached Christ unto them.

6 And the people with one accord ᵀgave heed unto those things which Philip spake, hearing and seeing the miracles which he ᵀdid.   *paid attention · performed*

7 For unclean spirits, crying with loud voice, came out of many that were possessed *with them:* and many taken with palsies, and that were lame, were healed.

8 And there was great joy in that city.

9 But there was a certain man, called Simon, which beforetime in the same city used ᵀsorcery, and ᵀbewitched the people of Sa-ma'-ri-a, ᴿgiving out that himself was some great one: *witchcraft · amazed · 5:36*

10 To whom they all gave heed, from ᵀthe least to the greatest, saying, This man is the great power of God.   *all classes of society*

11 And to him they ᵀhad regard, because that of long time he had ᵀbewitched them with ᵀsorceries.   *gave respect · astounded · witchcraft*

12 But when they believed Philip preaching the things ᴿconcerning the kingdom of God, and the name of Jesus Christ, they were baptized, both men and women.   1:3

13 Then Simon himself believed also: and when he was baptized, he continued with Philip, and wondered, beholding the miracles and signs which were done.

14 Now when the apostles which were at Jerusalem heard that ᵀSa-ma'-ri-a had received the word of God, they sent unto them Peter and John: *the people of Samaria*

15 Who, when they ᵀwere come down, prayed for them, that they might receive the Holy ᵀGhost: *arrived · Spirit*

16 (For ᴿas yet he was fallen upon none of them: only they were baptized ᵀin the name of the Lord Jesus.)   19:2 · *into*

17 Then ᴿlaid they *their* hands on them, and they received the Holy Ghost.   Heb. 6:2

18 And when Simon saw that through laying on of the apostles' hands the Holy Ghost was given, he offered them money,

19 Saying, Give me also this power, that on whomsoever I lay hands, he may receive the Holy ᵀGhost.   *Spirit*

20 But Peter said unto him, Thy money perish with thee, because thou hast thought that ᴿthe gift of God may be purchased with money.   2 Kin. 5:16; [Matt. 10:8]

21 Thou hast neither part nor ᵀlot in this matter: for thy ᴿheart is not right in the sight of God.   *share* · Jer. 17:9

22 ᴿRepent therefore of this thy wickedness, and pray God, if perhaps the thought of thine heart may be forgiven thee.   James 5:19

23 For I perceive that thou art in the gall of bitterness, and *in* the bond of iniquity.

24 Then answered Simon, and said, ᴿPray ye to the Lord for me, that none of these things which ye have spoken come upon me.   Gen. 20:7, 17; Ex. 8:8; 1 Kin. 13:6; Job 42:8

25 And they, when they had testified and preached the word of the Lord, returned to Jerusalem, and preached the gospel in many villages of the Sa-mar′-i-tans.

Philip Witnesses to the Ethiopian Treasurer

26 And the angel of the Lord spake unto Philip, saying, Arise, and go toward the south unto the way that goeth down from Jerusalem unto Ga′-za, which is desert.

27 And he arose and went: and, behold, ᴿa man of E-thi-o′-pi-a, an eunuch of great authority under Can-da′-ce queen of the E-thi-o′-pi-ans, ᴿwho had the charge of all her treasure, and ᴿhad come to Jerusalem for to worship,   Zeph. 3:10 · Ps. 68:31 · John 12:20

28 Was returning, and sitting in his chariot read E-sa′-ias the prophet.

29 Then the Spirit said unto Philip, Go near, and join thyself to this chariot.

30 And Philip ran thither to *him*, and heard him read the prophet E-sa′-ias, and said, Understandest thou what thou readest?

31 ᴿAnd he said, How can I, except some man should ᵀguide me? And he ᵀdesired Philip that he would come up and sit with him.   [Is. 56:3–7] · *explain to* · *asked*

32 The place of the scripture which he read was this, Hᴇ ᴡᴀs ʟᴇᴅ ᴀs ᴀ sʜᴇᴇᴘ ᴛᴏ ᴛʜᴇ sʟᴀᴜɢʜᴛᴇʀ; ᴀɴᴅ ʟɪᴋᴇ ᴀ ʟᴀᴍʙ ᴅᴜᴍʙ ʙᴇғᴏʀᴇ ʜɪs sʜᴇᴀʀᴇʀ, sᴏ ᴏᴘᴇɴᴇᴅ ʜᴇ ɴᴏᴛ ʜɪs ᴍᴏᴜᴛʜ:

33 Iɴ ʜɪs ʜᴜᴍɪʟɪᴀᴛɪᴏɴ ʜɪs ᴊᴜᴅɢᴍᴇɴᴛ ᴡᴀs ᴛᴀᴋᴇɴ ᴀᴡᴀʏ: ᴀɴᴅ ᴡʜᴏ sʜᴀʟʟ ᴅᴇᴄʟᴀʀᴇ ʜɪs ɢᴇɴᴇʀᴀᴛɪᴏɴ? ᴿғᴏʀ ʜɪs ʟɪғᴇ ɪs ᴛᴀᴋᴇɴ ғʀᴏᴍ ᴛʜᴇ ᴇᴀʀᴛʜ.   Is. 53:8

34 And the eunuch ᵀanswered Philip, and said, ᵀI pray thee, of whom speaketh the prophet this? of himself, or of some other man?   *asked · tell me*

35 Then Philip opened his mouth, ᴿand began at the same scripture, and preached unto him Jesus.   18:28; Luke 24:27

36 And as they went on *their* way, they came unto a certain water: and the eunuch said, ᵀSee, *here is* water; ᴿwhat doth hinder me to be baptized?   *behold* · 10:47

37 And Philip said, ᴿIf thou believest with all thine heart, thou mayest. And he answered and said, ᴿI believe that Jesus Christ is the Son of God.   [Rom. 10:9] · Matt. 16:16

38 And he commanded the chariot to stand still: and they went down both into the water, ᴿboth Philip and the eunuch; and he baptized him.   Matt. 3:16; Mark 1:10; [10:47]

39 And when they were come up out of the water, the Spirit of the Lord caught away Philip, that the eunuch saw him no more: and he went on his way rejoicing.

40 But Philip was found at A-zo′-tus: and passing through he preached in all the cities, till he came to Caes-a-re′-a.

CHAPTER 9

Saul Is Converted and Blinded
Acts 22:4–11; 26:13–18

AND Saul, yet breathing out threatenings and slaughter against the disciples of the Lord, went unto the high priest,

2 And desired of him letters to Damascus to the synagogues, that if he found any of this way, whether they were men or women, he might bring them bound unto Jerusalem.

3 And as he journeyed, he came near Damascus: and suddenly there shined round about him a light from heaven:

4 And he fell to the earth, and heard a voice saying unto him, Saul, Saul, ᴿwhy persecutest thou me?   22:7; [Matt. 25:40]

5 And he said, ᴿWho art thou, Lord? And the Lord said, I am Jesus whom thou persecutest: *it is* hard for thee to kick against the ᵀpricks.   *join*   22:8 · *oxgoads*

6 And he trembling and astonished said, Lord, ᴿwhat wilt thou have me to do? And the Lord *said* unto him, Arise, and go into the city, and it shall be told thee what thou must do.   2:37; 16:30; 22:10, 16

7 And ᴿthe men which journeyed with him stood speechless, hearing a voice, but seeing no man.   [22:9; 26:13]; Dan. 10:7

8 ᴿAnd Saul arose from the earth; and when his eyes were opened, he saw ᵀno man: but they led him by the hand, and brought *him* into Damascus.   22:11 · *nothing*

9 And he was three days without sight, and neither did eat nor drink.

Saul Is Filled with the Spirit

10 And there was a certain disciple at Damascus, ^Rnamed An-a-ni'-as; and to him said the Lord in a vision, An-a-ni'-as. And he said, Behold, I *am here*, Lord.   22:12

11 And the Lord *said* unto him, Arise, and go into the street which is called Straight, and ^Tenquire in the house of Judas for *one* called Saul, ^Rof Tar'-sus: for, behold, he prayeth,   *ask* • 21:39; 22:3

12 And hath seen in a vision a man named An-a-ni'-as coming in, and putting *his* hand on him, that he might receive his sight.

13 Then An-a-ni'-as answered, Lord, I have heard by many of this man, how much evil he hath done to thy saints at Jerusalem:

14 And here he hath authority from the chief priests to bind all that call on thy name.

15 But the Lord said unto him, Go thy way: for he is a chosen vessel ^Runto me, to bear my name before the Gentiles, and kings, and the children of Israel: [2 Cor. 4:7]

16 For I will shew him how ^Tgreat things he must suffer for my name's sake.   *many*

17 ^RAnd An-a-ni'-as went his way, and entered into the house; and ^Rputting his hands on him said, Brother Saul, the Lord, *even* Jesus, that appeared unto thee in the way as thou camest, hath sent me, that thou mightest receive thy sight, and be filled with the Holy Ghost.   22:12, 13 • 8:17

18 And immediately there fell from his eyes as it had been scales: and he received sight forthwith, and arose, and was baptized.

19 And when he had ^Treceived meat, he was strengthened. ^RThen was Saul ^Tcertain days with the disciples which were at Damascus.   *eaten food* • 26:20 • *several*

Saul Preaches at Damascus

20 And straightway he preached Christ in the synagogues, that he is the Son of God.

21 But all that heard *him* were amazed, and said; Is not this he that destroyed them which called on this name in Jerusalem, and came hither for that intent, that he might bring them bound unto the chief priests?

22 But Saul ^Tincreased the more in strength, ^Rand ^Tconfounded the Jews which dwelt at Damascus, proving that this is very Christ.   *preached* • 18:28 • *confused*

Saul Witnesses in Jerusalem

23 And after that many days were fulfilled, the Jews took counsel to kill him:

24 ^RBut their ^Tlaying await was known ^Tof Saul. And they watched the ^Tgates day and night to kill him.   2 Cor. 11:32 • *plot • to • city gates*

25 Then the disciples took him by night, and let *him* down by the wall in a basket.

26 And when Saul was come to Jerusalem, he assayed to join himself to the disciples: but they were all afraid of him, and believed not that he was a disciple.

27 ^RBut Barnabas took him, and brought *him* to the apostles, and declared unto them how he had seen the Lord in the way, and that he had spoken to him, ^Rand how he had preached boldly at Damascus in the name of Jesus.   4:36; 13:2 • *vv.* 20, 22

28 And ^Rhe was with them coming in and going out at Jerusalem.   Gal. 1:18

29 And he spake boldly in the name of the Lord Jesus, and disputed against the Gre'-cians: but they went about to slay him.

30 *Which* when the brethren ^Tknew, they brought him down to Caes-a-re'-a, and sent him forth to Tar'-sus.   *found out*

31 Then had the ^Tchurches rest throughout all Ju-dae'-a and Galilee and Sa-ma'-ri-a, and were ^Tedified; and walking in the fear of the Lord, and in the comfort of the Holy Ghost, were multiplied.   *church • built up*

Peter Heals Aeneas at Lydda

32 And it came to pass, as Peter passed throughout all *quarters*, he came down also to the saints which dwelt at Lyd'-da.

33 And there he found a certain man named Ae'-ne-as, which had kept his bed eight years, and was sick of the palsy.

34 And Peter said unto him, Ae'-ne-as, Jesus Christ maketh thee whole: arise, and make thy bed. And he arose immediately.

35 And all that dwelt at Lyd'-da and Sa'-ron saw him, and turned to the Lord.

Peter Raises Dorcas at Joppa

36 Now there was at Jop'-pa a certain disciple named Tab'-i-tha, which by interpretation is called Dor'-cas: this woman was full ^Rof good works and ^Talmsdeeds which she did.   1 Tim. 2:10; Titus 3:8 • *works of mercy*

37 And it came to pass in those days, that she was sick, and died: whom when they had ^Twashed, they laid *her* in ^Ran upper ^Tchamber.   *washed her body* • 1:13 • *room*

38 And forasmuch as Lyd'-da was ^Tnigh to Jop'-pa, and the disciples had heard that Peter was there, they sent unto him two men, ^Tdesiring *him* that he would not delay to come to them.   *close • with a message*

39 Then Peter arose and went with them. When he was come, they brought him into the upper chamber: and all the widows stood ^Tby him weeping, and shewing the coats and garments which Dor'-cas made, while she was with them.   *around*

40 But Peter put them all forth, and kneeled down, and prayed; and turning *him* to the body ^Rsaid, Tab'-i-tha, arise. And she opened her eyes: and when she saw Peter, she sat up.   John 11:43

41 And he gave her *his* hand, and lifted her up, and when he had called the ^Tsaints and widows, presented her alive.   *believers*

42 And it was known throughout all Jop'-pa; and many believed in the Lord.

43 And it came to pass, that he tarried many days in Jop'-pa with one ᴿSimon a ᵀtanner.   10:6 · *leather-worker*

CHAPTER 10

Cornelius Sends for Peter

THERE was a certain man in Caes-a-re'-a called Cornelius, ᴿa ᵀcenturion of the band called the Italian *band*,   *v. 22 · captain*

2 *A* devout *man*, and one that feared God with all his house, which gave much alms to the people, and prayed to God alway.

3 ᴿHe saw in a vision ᵀevidently about the ᵀninth hour of the day an angel of God coming in to him, and saying unto him, Cornelius.   *v. 30 · openly, as it were · 3 p.m.*

4 And when he looked on him, he was afraid, and said, What is it, Lord? And he said unto him, Thy prayers and thine alms are come up for a memorial before God.

5 And now send men to Jop'-pa, and call for *one* Simon, whose surname is Peter:

6 He lodgeth with one Simon a tanner, whose house is by the sea side: ᴿhe shall tell thee what thou oughtest to do.   11:14

7 And when the angel which spake unto Cornelius was departed, he called two of his household servants, and a ᵀdevout soldier of them that waited on him continually;   *godly*

8 And when he had declared all *these* things unto them, he sent them to Jop'-pa.

Peter Sees the Great Sheet

9 On the morrow, as they went on their journey, and drew nigh unto the city, ᴿPeter went up upon the housetop to pray about the ᵀsixth hour: 11:5 · *noon*

10 And he became very hungry, and would have eaten: but while they made ready, he ᵀfell into a trance,   *had a vision*

11 And ᴿsaw heaven opened, and a certain vessel descending unto him, as it had been a great sheet knit at the four corners, and let down to the earth: 7:56; Rev. 19:11

12 Wherein were all manner of fourfooted beasts of the earth, and wild beasts, and creeping things, and fowls of the air.

13 ᴿAnd there came a voice to him, Rise, Peter; kill, and eat.   11:7

14 But Peter said, Not so, Lord; for I have never eaten any thing that is ᵀcommon or unclean.   *outside the regulations of the law*

15 And the voice *spake* unto him again the second time, What God hath cleansed, *that* call not thou common.

16 This was done thrice: and the vessel was received ᵀup again into heaven.   *back*

17 Now while Peter doubted in himself what this vision which he had seen should

mean, behold, the men which were sent from Cornelius had made enquiry for Simon's house, and stood before the gate,

18 ᴿAnd called, and asked whether Simon, which was surnamed Peter, ᵀwere lodged there.   *vv. 5, 6 · was a guest*

19 While Peter thought on the vision, ᴿthe Spirit said unto him, Behold, three men ᵀseek thee.   11:12 · *look for you*

20 ᴿArise therefore, and get thee down, and go with them, ᵀdoubting nothing: for I have sent them.   15:7 · *questioning*

21 Then Peter went down to the men which were sent unto him from Cornelius; and said, Behold, I am he whom ye seek: what *is* the cause wherefore ye are come?

22 And they said, Cornelius the centurion, a just man, and one that feareth God, and ᴿof good report among all the nation of the Jews, was warned from God by an holy angel to send for thee into his house, and to hear words of thee.   22:12

Peter Preaches to the Gentiles

23 Then called he them in, and lodged *them*. And on the morrow Peter went away with them, ᴿand certain brethren from Jop'-pa accompanied him.   11:12

24 And the morrow after they entered into Caes-a-re'-a. And Cornelius waited for them, and had ᵀcalled together his ᵀkinsmen and ᵀnear friends.   *invited · relatives · neighbours*

25 ᴿAnd as Peter was coming in, Cornelius met him, and fell down at his feet, and ᵀworshipped *him*.   Rev. 19:10; 22:7 · *honoured*

26 But Peter took him up, saying, ᴿStand up; I myself also am a man.   3:12; 14:15

27 And as he talked with him, he went in, and found many that were come together.

28 And he said unto them, Ye know how ᴿthat it is an unlawful thing for a man that is a Jew to keep company, or come unto one of another nation; but God hath shewed me that I should not call any man ᵀcommon or unclean.   John 4:9 · *unfit*

29 Therefore came I *unto you* without ᵀgainsaying, as soon as I was sent for: ᴿI ask therefore ᵀfor what intent ye have sent for me?   *argument · v. 33 · why did you send*

30 And Cornelius said, Four days ago I was fasting until this hour; and at the ninth hour I prayed in my house, and, behold, a man stood before me in bright clothing,

31 And said, Cornelius, ᴿthy prayer is heard, and thine ᵀalms are had in remembrance in the sight of God.   *v. 4 · charity*

32 Send therefore to Jop'-pa, and call ᵀhither Simon, whose surname is Peter; he is lodged in the house of *one* Simon a tanner by the sea side: who, when he cometh, shall speak unto thee.   *for*

33 Immediately therefore I sent to thee; and thou hast well done that thou art come. Now therefore are we all here present before

God, ^Rto hear all things that are commanded thee of ^TGod.   *v. 29 • the Lord*

34 Then Peter opened *his* mouth, and said, ^ROf a truth I perceive that God is no respecter of persons: Rom. 2:11; Gal. 2:6; Eph. 6:9

35 But ^Rin every nation he that feareth him, and ^Tworketh righteousness, is accepted with him.   [1 Cor. 12:13; Eph. 2:13] • *practises*

36 The word which *God* sent unto the children of Israel, ^Rpreaching peace by Jesus Christ: (he is Lord of all:)   Is. 57:19

37 That ^Tword, *I say,* ye know, which was published throughout all Ju-dae'-a, and ^Rbegan from Galilee, after the baptism which John preached;   *great event* • Luke 4:14

38 How ^RGod anointed Jesus of Nazareth with the Holy Ghost and with power: who went about doing good, and healing all that were ^Toppressed of the devil; for God was with him.   Luke 4:18 • *under the power*

39 ^RAnd we are witnesses of all things which he did both in the land of the Jews, and in Jerusalem; whom they slew and hanged on a tree: 2:32; 5:30

40 Him ^RGod raised up the third day, and shewed him openly;   [2:24]; Hos. 6:2; Matt. 12:39, 40 ★

41 ^RNot to all the people, but unto witnesses chosen before of God, *even* to us, ^Rwho did eat and drink with him after he rose from the dead.   [John 14:17, 22, 23] • Luke 24:30

42 And he commanded us to preach unto the people, and to testify ^Rthat it is he which was ordained of God *to be* the Judge of ^Tquick and dead.   John 5:22 • *living*

43 To him give all the prophets witness, that through his name whosoever believeth in him shall receive remission of sins.

Gentiles Are Converted and Speak in Tongues

44 While Peter yet spake these words, ^Rthe Holy ^TGhost fell on all them which heard the word.   4:31; 15:8 • *Spirit*

45 ^RAnd ^Tthey of the circumcision which believed were astonished, as many as came with Peter, ^Rbecause that on the Gentiles also was poured out the gift of the Holy Ghost.   v. 23 • *the Jews* • [11:18]; Is. 42:1, 6; 49:6

46 For they heard them speak with ^Ttongues, and ^Tmagnify God. Then answered Peter,   *strange tongues* • *praise*

47 Can any man forbid water, that these should not be baptized, which have received the Holy Ghost as well as we?

48 And he commanded them to be baptized in the name of the Lord. Then prayed they him to tarry certain days.

CHAPTER 11

Peter Defends His Ministry to the Gentiles

AND the apostles and brethren that were in Ju-dae'-a heard that the Gentiles had also received the word of God.

2 And when Peter was come up to Jerusalem, ^Rthey that were of the circumcision ^Tcontended with him,   10:45 • *argued*

3 Saying, Thou wentest in to men uncircumcised, and didst eat with them.

4 But Peter rehearsed *the matter* from the beginning, and ^Texpounded *it* ^Rby order unto them, saying,   *explained it* • Luke 1:3

5 ^RI was in the city of Jop'-pa praying: and in a trance I saw a vision, A certain vessel descend, as it had been a great sheet, let down from heaven by four corners; and it ^Tcame even to me: 10:9 • *stopped next*

6 Upon the which when I had fastened mine eyes, I considered, and saw fourfooted beasts of the earth, and wild beasts, and creeping things, and fowls of the air.

7 ^RAnd I heard a voice saying unto me, Arise, Peter; slay and eat.   10:13

8 But I said, Not so, Lord: for nothing ^Tcommon or unclean hath at any time entered into my mouth.   *defiled*

9 But the voice answered me again from heaven, What God hath cleansed, *that* call not thou ^Tcommon.   *unclean*

10 And this was done three times: and all were drawn up again into heaven.

11 And, behold, immediately there were three men already come unto the house where I ^Twas, sent from Caes-a-re'-a unto me.   *was staying*

12 And ^Rthe Spirit bade me go with them, nothing doubting. Moreover ^Rthese six brethren accompanied me, and we entered into the man's house: [John 16:13] • 10:23

13 ^RAnd he shewed us how he had seen an angel in his house, which stood and said unto him, Send men to Jop'-pa, and call for Simon, whose surname is Peter;   10:30

14 Who shall tell thee words, whereby thou and all thy house shall be saved.

15 And as I began to speak, the Holy ^TGhost fell on them, ^Ras on us at the beginning.   *Spirit came down* • 2:4

16 Then remembered I the word of the Lord, how that he said, ^RJohn indeed baptized with water; but ^Rye shall be baptized with the Holy Ghost.   Matt. 3:11 • Is. 44:3

17 ^RForasmuch then as God gave them the like gift as *he did* unto us, who believed on the Lord Jesus Christ; what was I, that I could withstand God?   15:8, [9]

18 ^RWhen they heard these things, they held their peace, and ^Tglorified God, saying, Then ^Rhath God also to the Gentiles granted repentance unto life.   15:3 • *praised* • Is. 42:1; 49:6

The Witness of the Antioch Church

19 Now they which were scattered abroad upon the persecution that arose about Stephen travelled as far as Phe-ni'-ce, and Cyprus, and An'-ti-och, preaching the word to none but unto the Jews only.

20 And some of them were men of Cyprus and Cy-re'-ne, which, when they were come to An'-ti-och, spake unto Rthe Gre'-cians, preaching the Lord Jesus. 　6:1; 9:29

21 And Rthe hand of the Lord was with them: and a great number believed, and Rturned unto the Lord. 　Luke 1:66 • 9:35

22 Then Ttidings of these things came unto the ears of the church which was in Jerusalem: and they sent forth Barnabas, that he should go as far as An'-ti-och. 　reports

23 Who, when he came, and had seen the grace of God, was glad, and Rexhorted[T] them all, that with purpose of heart they would cleave unto the Lord. 　13:43 • urged

24 For he was a good man, and full of the Holy Ghost and of faith: Rand much people was added unto the Lord. 　2:41, 47

25 Then Tdeparted Barnabas to RTar'-sus, for to Tseek Saul: 　went • 9:30 • look for

26 And when he had found him, he brought him unto An'-ti-och. And it came to pass, that a whole year they assembled themselves with the church, and taught much people. RAnd the disciples were called Christians first in An'-ti-och. 　[Is. 62:2; 65:15]

27 And in these days came Tprophets from Jerusalem unto An'-ti-och. 　preachers

28 And there stood up one of them named RAg'-a-bus, and Tsignified by the Spirit that there should be great dearth throughout all the world: which came to pass in the days of Claudius Caesar. 　21:10; John 16:13 • predicted

29 Then the disciples, every man according to his ability, determined to send relief unto the brethren which dwelt in Ju-dae'-a:

30 Which also they did, and sent it to the elders by the hands of Barnabas and Saul.

CHAPTER 12

Herod Kills James

NOW about that time Herod the king Tstretched forth his hands to Tvex certain of the church. 　began • trouble

2 And he killed James Rthe brother of John with the sword. 　Matt. 4:21; 20:23

Peter Is Miraculously Released from Prison

3 And because he saw it pleased the Jews, he proceeded further to take Peter also. (Then were the days of unleavened bread.)

4 And when he had Tapprehended him, he put him in prison, and delivered him to four Tquaternions of soldiers to keep him; intending after TEaster to bring him forth to the people. 　arrested • sixteen • the Passover

5 Peter therefore was kept in prison: but prayer was made without ceasing Tof the church unto God for him. 　by the people

6 And when Herod Twould have brought him forth, the same night Peter was sleeping

between two soldiers, bound with two chains: and the keepers before the door Tkept the prison. 　planned to bring • guarded

7 And, behold, Rthe angel of the Lord came upon him, and a light shined in the Tprison: and he Tsmote Peter on the side, and raised him up, saying, Arise up quickly. And his chains fell off from his hands. 　5:19 • cell • shook

8 And the angel said unto him, Gird thyself, and bind on thy sandals. And so he did. And he saith unto him, Cast thy garment about thee, and follow me.

9 And he went out, and followed him; and wist not that it was true which was done by the angel; but thought he saw a vision.

10 When they were past the first and the second ward, they came unto the iron gate that leadeth unto the city; which opened to them of his own accord: and they went out, and passed on through one street; and forthwith the angel departed from him.

11 And when Peter was come to himself, he said, Now I know of a surety, that Rthe Lord hath sent his angel, and hath delivered me out of the hand of Herod, and from all the expectation of the people of the Jews. 　[Ps. 34:7]

12 And when he had considered the thing, he came to the house of Mary the mother of John, whose surname was Mark; where many were gathered together praying.

13 And as Peter knocked at the door of the gate, a Tdamsel[R] came to Thearken, named Rhoda. 　maid • John 18:16 • answer

14 And when she knew Peter's voice, she opened not the gate for gladness, but ran in, and told how Peter stood before the gate.

15 And they said unto her, Thou art mad. But she constantly affirmed that it was even so. Then said they, RIt is his angel. 　[Matt. 18:10]

16 But Peter continued knocking: and when they had opened the door, and saw him, they were Tastonished. 　amazed

17 But he, beckoning unto them with the hand to hold their peace, declared unto them how the Lord had brought him out of the prison. And he said, Go shew these things unto James, and to the brethren. And he departed, and went into another place.

18 Now as soon as it was day, there was Tno small stir among the soldiers, what was become of Peter. 　excitement

19 And when Herod had sought for him, and found him not, he examined the keepers, Rand commanded that they should be put to death. And he went down from Ju-dae'-a to Caes-a-re'-a, and there abode. 　16:27

Herod Blasphemes and Dies

20 And Herod was highly displeased with them of Tyre and Si'-don: but they came Twith one accord to him, and, having made Blas'-tus the king's chamberlain their friend,

desired peace; because their country was nourished by the king's *country*.   *unitedly*

21 And upon a set day Herod, ᵀarrayed in royal apparel, sat upon his throne, and made an ᵀoration unto them.   *dressed · speech*

22 And the people gave a shout, *saying, It is* the voice of a god, and not of a man.

23 And immediately the angel of the Lord smote him, because ᴿhe gave not God the glory: and he was eaten of worms, and ᵀgave up the ghost.   Ps. 115:1 · *he died*

24 But ᴿthe word of God ᵀgrew and multiplied.   6:7; 19:20; Col. 1:6 · *brought results*

25 And Barnabas and Saul returned from Jerusalem, when they had fulfilled *their* ᵀministry, and took with them ᴿJohn, whose surname was Mark.   *mission · v. 12*

CHAPTER 13

Barnabas and Saul Are Sent from Antioch

NOW there were in the church that was at An'-ti-och certain prophets and teachers; as Barnabas, and Simeon that was called Ni'-ger, and Lu'-cius of Cy-re'-ne, and Man'-a-en, which had been brought up with Herod the te'-trarch, and Saul.

2 As they ministered to the Lord, and fasted, the Holy Ghost said, ᴿSeparate me Barnabas and Saul for the work ᴿwhereunto I have called them.   Rom. 1:1 · Matt. 9:38

3 And ᴿwhen they had fasted and prayed, and ᵀlaid *their* hands on them, they sent *them* ᵀaway.   6:6 · *commissioned · off*

Preaching in the Synagogues

4 So they, being sent forth by the Holy Ghost, departed unto Se-leu'-ci-a; and from thence they sailed to ᴿCyprus.   4:36

5 And when they were at Sal'-a-mis, ᴿthey preached the word of God in the synagogues of the Jews: and they had also John ᵀto *their* minister.   [v. 46] · *as their assistant*

Controversy with Bar-jesus

6 And when they had gone through the isle unto Pa'-phos, they found ᴿa certain sorcerer, a false prophet, a Jew, whose name *was* ᵀBar-je'-sus: 8:9 · *son of Jesus*

7 Which was with the ᵀdeputy of the country, Ser'-gi-us Pau'-lus, a ᵀprudent man; who called for Barnabas and Saul, and desired to hear the word of God. *proconsul · wise*

8 But ᴿEl'-y-mas the sorcerer (for so is his name by interpretation) ᵀwithstood them, seeking to turn away the deputy from the faith.   Ex. 7:11; 2 Tim. 3:8 · *opposed*

9 Then Saul, (who also *is called* Paul,) ᴿfilled with the Holy Ghost, set his eyes on ᵀhim,   4:8 · *the sorcerer*

10 And said, O full of all subtilty and all mischief, ᴿthou child of the devil, *thou* enemy of all righteousness, wilt thou not cease to pervert the right ways of the Lord? [1 John 3:8]

11 And now, behold, ᴿthe hand of the Lord *is* upon thee, and thou shalt be blind, not seeing the sun for a ᵀseason. And immediately there fell on him a mist and a darkness; and he went about seeking some to lead him by the hand.   1 Sam. 5:6 · *while*

12 Then the deputy, when he saw what was done, believed, being astonished at the ᵀdoctrine of the Lord.   *teaching about Jesus*

13 Now when Paul and his company ᵀloosed from Pa'-phos, they came to Per'-ga in Pam-phyl'-i-a: and John departing from them returned to Jerusalem.   *departed*

Paul Preaches on First Sabbath

14 But when they departed from Per'-ga, they came to An'-ti-och in Pi-sid'-i-a, and ᴿwent into the synagogue on the sabbath day, and sat down.   16:13; 17:2; 18:4

15 And ᴿafter the reading of the law and the prophets the rulers of the synagogue sent unto them, saying, Ye men *and* brethren, if ye have any word of exhortation for the people, say on.   Luke 4:16

16 Then Paul stood up, and beckoning with *his* hand said, Men of Israel, and ᴿye that fear God, give audience.   10:35

17 The God of this people of Israel ᴿchose our fathers, and exalted the people ᴿwhen they dwelt as strangers in the land of Egypt, and with ᵀan high arm brought he them out of it.   Deut. 7:6, 7 · 7:17 · *power*

18 And about the time of forty years suffered he their manners in the wilderness.

19 And when he had destroyed seven nations in the land of Cha'-naan, ᴿhe divided their land to them by lot.   Josh. 14:1

20 And after that he gave *unto them* judges about the space of four hundred and fifty years, until Samuel the prophet.

21 ᴿAnd afterward they desired a king: and God gave unto them Saul the son of Cis, a man of the tribe of Benjamin, ᵀby the space of forty years.   1 Sam. 8:5 · *for about*

22 And when he had removed him, he raised up unto them David to be their king; to whom also he gave testimony, and said, ᴿI HAVE FOUND DAVID THE *SON* OF JESSE, ᴿA MAN AFTER MINE OWN HEART, which shall fulfil all my will.   [Ps. 89:20] · 1 Sam. 13:14

23 ᴿOf this man's seed hath God according ᴿto *his* promise raised unto Israel ᴿa Saviour, Jesus: Is. 11:1 ✶ · Ps. 132:11 · Matt. 1:21

24 ᴿWhen John had first preached before his coming the baptism of repentance to all the people of Israel.   Matt. 3:1; [Luke 3:3]

25 And as John fulfilled his course, ᴿhe said, ᴿWhom think ye that I am? I am not *he*. But, behold, there cometh one after me, whose shoes of *his* feet I am not worthy to ᵀloose.   [John 3:30] · Mark 1:7 · *remove*

26 Men *and* brethren, children of the stock of Abraham, and whosoever among you feareth God, ᴿto you is the ᵀword of this salvation sent.   Matt. 10:6 • *message*

27 For they that dwell at Jerusalem, and their rulers, ᴿbecause they knew him not, nor yet the voices of the prophets which are read every sabbath day, they have fulfilled *them* in condemning *him*.   Luke 23:34

28 ᴿAnd though they found no ᵀcause of death *in him*, yet desired they Pilate that he should be slain.   Matt. 27:22 • *reason*

29 And when they had fulfilled all that was written of him, they took *him* down from the tree, and laid *him* in a sepulchre.

30 But God raised him from the dead:

31 And ᴿhe was seen many days of them which came up with him from Galilee to Jerusalem, who are his witnesses unto the people.   Matt. 28:16

32 And we declare unto you glad tidings, how that ᴿthe promise which was made unto the fathers,   Gen. 12:3; [Rom. 4:13; Gal. 3:16]

33 God hath fulfilled the same unto us their children, in that he hath raised up Jesus again; as it is also written in the second psalm, ᴿTʜᴏᴜ ᴀʀᴛ ᴍʏ Sᴏɴ, ᴛʜɪs ᴅᴀʏ ʜᴀᴠᴇ I ʙᴇɢᴏᴛᴛᴇɴ ᴛʜᴇᴇ.   Ps. 2:7; Heb. 1:5 ★

34 And as concerning that he raised him up from the dead, *now* no more to return to corruption, he said on this wise, ᴿI ᴡɪʟʟ ɢɪᴠᴇ ʏᴏᴜ ᴛʜᴇ sᴜʀᴇ ᴍᴇʀᴄɪᴇs ᴏғ Dᴀᴠɪᴅ.   Is. 55:3 ★

35 Wherefore he saith also in another *psalm*, ᴿTʜᴏᴜ sʜᴀʟᴛ ɴᴏᴛ sᴜғғᴇʀ ᴛʜɪɴᴇ Hᴏʟʏ Oɴᴇ ᴛᴏ sᴇᴇ ᴄᴏʀʀᴜᴘᴛɪᴏɴ.   2:31; Ps. 16:10 ★

36 For David, after he had served his own generation by the will of God, ᴿfell on sleep, and was laid unto his fathers, and ᵀsaw corruption: 2:29 • *his body decayed*

37 But he, whom God raised again, saw no ᵀcorruption.   *decay*

38 Be it known unto you therefore, men *and* brethren, that through this man is preached unto you the forgiveness of sins:

39 And ᴿby him all that believe are justified from all things, from which ye could not be justified by the law of Moses. [Is. 53:11]

40 Beware therefore, lest that come upon you, which is spoken of in the prophets;

41 Bᴇʜᴏʟᴅ, ʏᴇ ᴅᴇsᴘɪsᴇʀs, ᴀɴᴅ ᴡᴏɴᴅᴇʀ, ᴀɴᴅ ᴘᴇʀɪsʜ: ғᴏʀ I ᴡᴏʀᴋ ᴀ ᴡᴏʀᴋ ɪɴ ʏᴏᴜʀ ᴅᴀʏs, ᴀ ᴡᴏʀᴋ ᴡʜɪᴄʜ ʏᴇ sʜᴀʟʟ ɪɴ ɴᴏ ᴡɪsᴇ ʙᴇʟɪᴇᴠᴇ, ᴛʜᴏᴜɢʜ ᴀ ᴍᴀɴ ᴅᴇᴄʟᴀʀᴇ ɪᴛ ᴜɴᴛᴏ ʏᴏᴜ.

42 ᴿAnd when the Jews were gone out of the synagogue, the Gentiles ᵀbesought that these words might be preached to them the next sabbath.   v. 44 • *invited*

43 Now when the congregation was broken up, many of the Jews and religious ᵀproselytes followed Paul and Barnabas: who, speaking to them, persuaded them to continue in the grace of God.   *converts*

Paul Preaches on Second Sabbath

44 ᴿAnd the next sabbath day came almost the whole city together to hear the word of ᵀGod.   v. 42 • *the Lord*

45 But when the Jews saw the multitudes, they were filled with envy, and spake against those things which were spoken by Paul, contradicting and blaspheming.

46 Then Paul and Barnabas waxed bold, and said, ᴿIt was necessary that the word of God should first have been spoken to you: but seeing ye put it from you, and judge yourselves unworthy of everlasting life, lo, we turn to the Gentiles.   Matt. 10:5, 6

47 For so hath the Lord commanded us, *saying*, I ʜᴀᴠᴇ sᴇᴛ ᴛʜᴇᴇ ᴛᴏ ʙᴇ ᴀ ʟɪɢʜᴛ ᴏғ ᴛʜᴇ Gᴇɴᴛɪʟᴇs, ᴛʜᴀᴛ ᴛʜᴏᴜ sʜᴏᴜʟᴅᴇsᴛ ʙᴇ ғᴏʀ sᴀʟᴠᴀᴛɪᴏɴ ᴜɴᴛᴏ ᴛʜᴇ ᴇɴᴅs ᴏғ ᴛʜᴇ ᴇᴀʀᴛʜ.

48 And when the Gentiles heard this, they were glad, and ᵀglorified the word of the Lord: ᴿand as many as were ordained to eternal life believed.   *praised* • [2:47]

49 And the word of the Lord was published throughout all the region.

50 But the Jews stirred up the devout and honourable women, and the chief men of the city, and ᴿraised persecution against Paul and Barnabas, and expelled them out of their ᵀcoasts.   2 Tim. 3:11 • *borders*

Ministry at Iconium

51 ᴿBut they shook off the dust of their feet against them, and came unto I-co'-ni-um.   Matt. 10:14; Mark 6:11; [Luke 9:5]

52 And the disciples ᴿwere filled with joy, and with the Holy Ghost.   Matt. 5:12; John 16:22

CHAPTER 14

Aɴᴅ it came to pass in I-co'-ni-um, that they went both together into the synagogue of the Jews, and so spake, that a great multitude both of the Jews and also of the Greeks believed.

2 But the unbelieving Jews stirred up the Gentiles, and made their minds ᵀevil affected against the brethren.   *opposed to*

3 Long time therefore abode they speaking boldly in the Lord, which gave testimony unto the word of his grace, and granted signs and wonders to be done by their hands.

4 But the ᵀmultitude of the city was divided: and part held with the Jews, and part with the ᴿapostles.   *crowd* • 13:2, 3

5 And when there was an assault made both of the Gentiles, and also of the Jews with their rulers, to use *them* ᵀdespitefully, and to stone them,   *in hostility*

A Lame Man Is Healed

6 They were ware of *it*, and fled unto Lys'-tra and Der'-be, cities of Lyc-a-o'-ni-a, and unto the region that lieth round about:

7 And there they preached the gospel.

8 [R]And there sat a certain man at Lys'-tra, impotent in his feet, being a cripple from his mother's womb, who never had walked: 3:2

9 The same heard Paul speak: who stedfastly beholding him, and [T]perceiving that he had faith to be healed,   noting

10 Said with a loud voice, [R]Stand upright on thy feet. And he leaped and walked. [Is. 35:6]

Paul and Barnabas Are Deified

11 And when the people saw what Paul had done, they lifted up their voices, saying in the speech of Lyc-a-o'-ni-a, The gods are come down to us in the likeness of men.

12 And they called Barnabas, Jupiter; and Paul, Mer-cu'-ri-us, because he was the chief speaker.

13 Then the priest of Jupiter, which was before their city, brought oxen and garlands unto the gates, and would have [T]done sacrifice with the people.   worshipped

14 Which when the apostles, Barnabas and Paul, heard of, they rent their clothes, and ran in among the people, crying out,

15 And saying, Sirs, why do ye these things? We also are men of like passions with you, and preach unto you that ye should turn from these vanities unto the living God, which made heaven, and earth, and the sea, and all things that are therein:

16 Who in times past [T]suffered all nations to walk in their own ways.   allowed

17 Nevertheless he left not himself without witness, in that he did good, and gave us rain from heaven, and fruitful seasons, filling our hearts with food and gladness.

18 And with these sayings scarce restrained they the people, that they had not [T]done sacrifice unto them.   offered

Paul Is Stoned

19 [R]And there came thither certain Jews from An'-ti-och and I-co'-ni-um, who persuaded the people, and, having stoned Paul, drew him out of the city, [T]supposing he had been dead.   13:45 · thinking he was

20 Howbeit, as the disciples stood round about him, he [T]rose up, and came [T]into the city: and the next day he departed with Barnabas to Der'-be.   revived · back into

Ministry on the Return Trip

21 And when they had preached the gospel to that city, [R]and had taught many, they returned again to Lys'-tra, and to I-co'-ni-um, and An'-ti-och,   Matt. 28:19

22 Confirming the souls of the disciples, and exhorting them to continue in the faith, and that we must through much tribulation enter into the kingdom of God.

23 And when they had [R]ordained them elders in every church, and had prayed [R]with

fasting, they commended them to the Lord, on whom they believed.   Titus 1:5 · Matt. 9:15

24 And after they had passed throughout Pi-sid'-i-a, they came to Pam-phyl'-i-a.

25 And when they had preached the word in Per'-ga, they went down into At-ta-li'-a:

Report on the First Missionary Journey

26 And thence sailed to An'-ti-och, from whence they had been [T]recommended [R]to the grace of God for the work which they [T]fulfilled.   committed · 13:2; 18:22 · completed

27 And when they were come, and had gathered the church together, [R]they [T]rehearsed all that God had done with them, and how he had [R]opened the door of faith unto the Gentiles.   15:4, 12 · reviewed · Col. 4:3

28 And there they abode long time with the [T]disciples.   believers

CHAPTER 15

Debate over Gentiles Keeping the Law

AND certain men which came down from Ju-dae'-a taught the brethren, and said, [R]Except ye be circumcised after the manner of Moses, ye cannot be saved.   v. 5

2 When therefore Paul and Barnabas had no small [T]dissension and [T]disputation with them, they determined that Paul and Barnabas, and certain other of them, should [R]go up to Jerusalem unto the apostles and elders about this question.   argument · debate · Gal. 2:1

3 And being [T]brought on their way by the church, they passed through Phe-ni'-ce and Sa-ma'-ri-a, declaring the conversion of the Gentiles: and they caused great joy unto all the brethren.   sent

4 And when they were come to Jerusalem, they were received of the church, and of the apostles and elders, and they declared all things that God had done with them.

5 But there rose up certain of the sect of the Pharisees which believed, saying, That it was needful to circumcise them, and to command them to keep the law of Moses.

Peter Preaches Salvation Through Grace

6 And the apostles and elders came together for to consider of this matter.

7 And when there had been much disputing, Peter rose up, and said unto them, Men and brethren, ye know how that a good while ago God made choice among us, that the Gentiles by my mouth should hear the word of the gospel, and believe.

8 And God, [R]which knoweth the hearts, bare them witness, giving them the Holy Ghost, even as he did unto us;   1 Chr. 28:9

9 And put no difference between us and them, purifying their hearts by faith.

10 Now therefore why [T]tempt ye God, [R]to put a [T]yoke upon the neck of the disciples,

which neither our fathers nor we were able to bear?   *test · Matt. 23:4; Gal. 5:1 · burden*

11 But ᴿwe believe that through the grace of the Lord Jesus Christ we shall be saved, even as they.   Rom. 3:24; [Eph. 2:8; Titus 2:11]

Paul and Barnabas Testify

12 Then all the multitude kept silence, and gave audience to Barnabas and Paul, declaring what miracles and wonders God had ᴿwrought among the Gentiles by them.   14:27

James Proves Gentiles Are Free from the Law

13 And after they had ᵀheld their peace, James answered, saying, Men *and* brethren, hearken unto me: *finished their report*

14 ᴿSimeon hath declared how God at the first did visit the Gentiles, to take out of them a people for his name.   *v. 7*

15 And to this ᵀagree the words of the prophets; as it is written,   *agree completely*

16 ᴿAFTER THIS I WILL RETURN, AND WILL BUILD AGAIN THE TABERNACLE OF DAVID, WHICH IS FALLEN DOWN; AND I WILL BUILD AGAIN THE RUINS THEREOF, AND I WILL SET IT UP: Amos 9:11, 12

17 THAT THE RESIDUE OF MEN MIGHT SEEK AFTER THE LORD, AND ALL THE GENTILES, UPON WHOM MY NAME IS CALLED, SAITH THE LORD, WHO DOETH ALL THESE THINGS.

18 Known unto God are all his works from the beginning of the world.

19 Wherefore my ᵀsentence is, that we trouble not them, which from among the Gentiles ᴿare turned to God: *judgment · v. 28*

20 ᴿBut that we write unto them, that they abstain from pollutions of idols, and *from* fornication, and *from* things strangled, and *from* blood.   [1 Cor. 6:9, 18; 8:1]

21 For Moses of old time hath in every city them that preach him, ᴿbeing read in the synagogues every sabbath day.   13:15

The Council Sends an Official Letter

22 Then pleased it the apostles and elders, with the whole church, to send chosen men of their own company to An'-ti-och with Paul and Barnabas; *namely,* Judas surnamed ᴿBar'-sa-bas, and Silas, ᵀchief men among the brethren: 1:23 · *respected*

23 And they wrote *letters* by them after this manner; The apostles and elders and brethren *send* greeting unto the brethren which are of ᵀthe Gentiles in An'-ti-och and Syria and Ci-li'-ci-a: *Gentile birth*

24 Forasmuch as we have heard, that ᴿcertain which went out from us have troubled you with words, ᵀsubverting your souls, saying, Ye must be circumcised, and keep the law: to whom we gave no *such* commandment: *v. 1 · misleading your hearts*

25 It seemed good unto us, being assembled ᵀwith one accord, to send chosen men

unto you ᵀwith our beloved Barnabas and Paul,   *in a united spirit · to go with*

26 Men that have hazarded their lives for the name of our Lord Jesus Christ.

27 We have sent therefore Judas and Silas, who shall also ᵀtell *you* the same things by ᵀmouth.   *tell in person · word of mouth*

28 For it seemed good to the Holy Ghost, and to us, to lay upon you no ᵀgreater burden than these necessary things;   *more*

29 ᴿThat ye abstain from meats offered to idols, and ᴿfrom blood, and from things strangled, and from fornication: from which if ye keep yourselves, ye shall do well. Fare ye well.   *v. 20; Rev. 2:14, 20 · Lev. 17:14*

Report to Antioch

30 So when they were dismissed, they came to An'-ti-och: and when they had gathered the ᵀmultitude together, they delivered the ᵀepistle: *whole group · letter*

31 Which when they had read, they rejoiced for the ᵀconsolation.   *comfort*

32 And Judas and Silas, being prophets also themselves, exhorted the brethren with many words, and confirmed *them.*

33 And after they had tarried *there* a space, they were let ᴿgo in peace from the brethren unto the apostles.   Heb. 11:31

34 Notwithstanding it pleased Silas to abide there ᵀstill.   *awhile*

35 Paul also and Barnabas continued in An'-ti-och, teaching and preaching the word of the Lord, with many others also.

Contention over John Mark

36 And some days after Paul said unto Barnabas, Let us go again and visit our brethren in every city where we have preached the word of the Lord, *and see* how they ᵀdo.   *are getting along*

37 And Barnabas determined to take with them John, whose surname was Mark.

38 But Paul thought not good to take him with them, who ᵀdeparted from them from Pam-phyl'-i-a, and went not with them ᵀto the work.   *deserted · in their program*

39 And the contention was so sharp between them, that they ᵀdeparted asunder one from the other: and so Barnabas took Mark, and sailed unto Cyprus;   *separated*

40 And Paul chose Silas, and departed, ᴿbeing ᵀrecommended by the brethren unto the grace of God.   Gal. 2:9 · *given*

41 And he went through Syria and Ci-li'-ci-a, ᵀconfirming the churches.   *strengthening*

CHAPTER 16

Derbe and Lystra: Timotheus Is Circumcised

THEN came he to Der'-be and Lys'-tra: and, behold, a certain disciple was there, named Ti-mo'-the-us, the son of a certai⸢

woman, which was a Jewess, Tand believed; but his father *was* a Greek: who

2 Which Rwas well reported of by the brethren that were at Lys'-tra and I-co'-ni-um.   [2 Tim. 3:15]

3 Him would Paul have to go forth with him; and took and circumcised him because of the Jews which were in those quarters: for they knew all that his father was a Greek.

4 And as they went through the cities, they delivered them the decrees for to keep, that were ordained of the apostles and elders which were at Jerusalem.

5 And so were the churches established in the faith, and increased in number daily.

Troas: Macedonian Call

6 Now when they had gone throughout Phryg'-i-a and the region of Ga-la'-ti-a, and were forbidden of the Holy Ghost to preach the word in Asia,

7 After they were come to My'-si-a, they Tassayed to go into Bi-thyn'-i-a: but the Spirit suffered them not.   tried

8 And they passing by My'-si-a Rcame down to Tro'-as.   2 Cor. 2:12; 2 Tim. 4:13

9 And a vision appeared to Paul in the night; There stood a man of Mac-e-do'-ni-a, and prayed him, saying, Come over into Mac-e-do'-ni-a, and help us.

10 And after he had seen the vision, immediately we endeavoured to go Rinto Mac-e-do'-ni-a, Tassuredly gathering that Tthe Lord had called us for to preach the gospel unto them.   2 Cor. 2:13 • being satisfied • God

Lydia Is Converted

11 Therefore loosing from Tro'-as, we came with a straight course to Sam-o-thra'-ci-a, and the next *day* to Ne-ap'-o-lis;

12 And from thence to Phi-lip'-pi, which is the Tchief city of that part of Mac-e-do'-ni-a, *and* a colony: and we were in that city abiding certain days.   most important

13 And on the sabbath we went out of the city by a river side, where prayer was Twont to be made; and we sat down, and spake unto the women which resorted *thither.*   accustomed

14 And a certain woman named Lyd'-i-a, a seller of purple, of the city of Thy-a-ti'-ra, which worshipped God, heard *us:* whose heart the Lord opened, that she attended unto the things which were spoken of Paul.

15 And when she was baptized, and her household, she besought *us,* saying, If ye have judged me to be faithful to the Lord, come into my house, and abide *there.* RAnd she Tconstrained us.   v. 40 • prevailed upon

A Spirit of Divination Is Cast Out

16 And it came to pass, as we went to prayer, a certain damsel possessed with a spirit of divination met us, which brought her masters much gain by soothsaying:

17 The same followed Paul and us, and cried, saying, These men are the servants of the most high God, which shew unto us Tthe way of salvation.   how to be saved

18 And this did she many days. But Paul, being grieved, turned and said to the spirit, I command thee in the name of Jesus Christ to come out of her. RAnd he came out the same hour.   Mark 16:17

19 And when her masters saw that the hope of their gains was gone, they caught Paul and Silas, and drew *them* into the Tmarketplace unto the rulers,   court

20 And brought them to the magistrates, saying, These men, being Jews, Rdo exceedingly trouble our city,   17:8; 1 Kin. 18:17

21 And teach customs, which are Tnot lawful for us to receive, neither to observe, being Romans.   against our law

22 And the multitude rose up together against them: and the magistrates rent off their clothes, and commanded to beat *them.*

23 And when they had laid many stripes upon them, they cast *them* into prison, charging the jailor to keep them safely:

24 Who, having received such a charge, thrust them into the inner prison, and made their feet Tfast in the stocks.   firm

Philippian Jailor Is Converted

25 RAnd at midnight Paul and Silas prayed, and sang praises unto God: and the prisoners heard them.   Rom. 15:9

26 And suddenly there was a great earthquake, so that the foundations of the prison were shaken: and immediately Rall the doors were opened, and every one's bands were loosed.   5:19; 12:7, 10

27 And the keeper Rof the prison awaking out of his sleep, and seeing the prison doors open, he drew out his sword, and would have killed himself, supposing that the prisoners had Tbeen fled.   v. 36 • escaped

28 But Paul cried with a loud voice, saying, Do thyself no harm: for we are all here.

29 Then he called for a light, and sprang in, and came trembling, and fell down before Paul and Silas,

30 And brought them out, and said, RSirs, what must I do to be saved?   2:37; 9:6

31 And they said, RBelieve on the Lord Jesus Christ, and thou shalt be saved, and thy house.   v. 34; [John 3:16, 36; 6:47; 1 John 5:10]

16:31 New Life: Received by Faith—The words spoken to the Philippian jailer are the best news human ears have ever heard, for they clearly tell how we receive God's gift of eternal life. When we receive God's gift of eternal life we are said to be "saved." The basic concept underlying "salvation" or "being saved" is deliverance. We are delivered from the penalty of sin (death, separation from God)

32 And they spake unto him the word of the Lord, and to all that were in his house.

33 And he took them the same hour of the night, and washed *their* stripes; and was baptized, he and all his, straightway.

34 And when he had brought them into his house, he set meat before them, and rejoiced, believing in God with all his house.

Paul Is Released from Prison

35 And when it was day, the magistrates sent the serjeants, saying, Let those men go.

36 ᴿAnd the keeper of the prison told this saying to Paul, The magistrates have ᵀsent to let you go: now therefore depart, and go in peace.   *v. 27 • sent an order*

37 But Paul said unto them, They have beaten us openly uncondemned, ᴿbeing Romans, and have cast *us* into prison; and now do they ᵀthrust us out ᵀprivily? nay verily; but let them come themselves and ᵀfetch us out.   *22:25 • put • in secret • bring*

38 And the serjeants told these words unto the magistrates: and they feared, when they heard that they were Romans.

39 And they came and besought them, and brought *them* out, and ᴿdesired *them* to depart out of the city.   *Matt. 8:34*

40 And they went out of the prison, ᴿand entered into *the house of* Lyd′-i-a: and when they had seen the brethren, they comforted them, and departed.   *vv. 14, 15*

CHAPTER 17

Thessalonica: "Turned the World Upside Down"

NOW when they had passed through Am-phip′-o-lis and Ap-ol-lo′-ni-a, they came to ᴿThes-sa-lo-ni′-ca, where was a synagogue of the Jews: *1 Thess. 1:1; 2 Thess. 1:1*

2 And Paul, as his manner was, ᴿwent in unto them, and three sabbath days reasoned with them out of the scriptures,   *9:20*

3 Opening and ᵀalleging, ᴿthat Christ must needs have suffered, and risen again from the dead; and that this Jesus, whom I preach unto you, is Christ.   *proving • Gal. 3:1*

4 And some of them believed, and ᵀcon-sorted with Paul and Silas; and of the ᵀdevout Greeks a great multitude, and of the chief women not a few.   *joined • religious*

5 But the Jews which believed not, moved with envy, took unto them certain lewd fellows of the baser sort, and gathered a company, and set all the city on an uproar, and assaulted the house of Ja′-son, and sought to bring them out to the people.

6 And when they found them not, they drew Ja′-son and certain brethren unto the rulers of the city, crying, ᴿThese that have ᵀturned the world upside down are come hither also;   *[16:20] • caused trouble everywhere*

7 Whom Ja′-son hath received: and these all do contrary to the decrees of Caesar, saying that there is another king, one Jesus.

8 And they ᵀtroubled the people and the rulers of the city, when they heard these ᵀthings.   *disturbed • words*

9 And when they had taken security of Ja′-son, and of the other, they let them go.

Berea: Many Receive the Word

10 And ᴿthe brethren immediately sent away Paul and Silas by night unto Be-re′-a: who coming *thither* went into the synagogue of the Jews.   *v. 14; 9:25*

11 These were more noble than those in Thes-sa-lo-ni′-ca, in that they received the word with all readiness of mind, and ᴿsearched the scriptures daily, whether those things were so.   *Luke 16:29; John 5:39*

12 Therefore many of them believed; also of honourable women which were Greeks, and of men, not a few.

13 But when the Jews of Thes-sa-lo-ni′-ca had knowledge that the word of God was preached of Paul at Be-re′-a, they came thither also, and stirred up the ᵀpeople.   *mobs*

14 And then immediately the brethren sent away Paul to go as it were to the sea: but Silas and Ti-mo′-the-us abode there still.

15 And they that conducted Paul brought him unto Athens: and receiving a command-ment unto Silas and Ti-mo′-the-us for to come to him with all speed, they departed.

Athens: Paul's Sermon on Mars' Hill

16 Now while Paul waited for them at Athens, his spirit was stirred in him, when he saw the city wholly given to idolatry.

---

and from the power of sin. Ultimately we will be delivered from the very presence of sin and will be delivered into the very presence of God. We receive new life by faith—believing that Jesus died for our sins, that His death was in our place, and that His payment for sin is fully acceptable in God's sight. Faith can be summarized in the acrostic:

     F orsaking
     A ll
     I
     T ake
     H im

We are to forsake all (repent of our sins) and to take Him (by faith turn to God for our salvation) (Page 1095—Acts 20:21).

Now turn to Page 1047—John 5:24: Everlasting Life.

17 Therefore ᵀdisputed he in the synagogue with the Jews, and with the ᵀdevout
persons, and in the market daily with them
that met with him.   *argued • religious*

18 Then certain philosophers of the Ep-i-
cu-re'-ans, and of the Sto'-icks, ᵀencountered
him. And some said, What will this babbler
say? other some, He seemeth to be a setter
forth of strange gods: because he preached
unto them Jesus, and the resurrection.   *met*

19 And they took him, and brought him
unto ᵀAr-e-op'-a-gus, saying, May we know
what this new doctrine, whereof thou
speakest, *is?*   *Mars' hill*

20 For thou bringest certain strange things
to our ears: we would ᵀknow therefore what
these things mean.   *like to know*

21 (For all the A-the'-ni-ans and strangers
which were there spent their time in nothing
else, but either to tell, or to hear ᵀsome new
thing.)   *the latest*

22 Then Paul stood in the midst of Mars'
hill, and said, *Ye* men of Athens, I perceive
that in all things ye are too superstitious.

23 For as I passed by, and beheld ᵀyour
devotions, I found an altar with this inscription, TO THE UNKNOWN GOD. Whom
therefore ye ignorantly worship, him declare
I unto you.   *the objects of your worship*

24 ᴿGod that made the world and all things
therein, seeing that he is Lord of heaven and
earth, ᴿdwelleth not in temples made with
hands;   14:15 • 7:48

25 ᴿNeither is worshipped with men's
hands, as though he needed any thing, seeing he giveth to all life, and breath, and all
things;   Ps. 50:12; Is. 42:5; [Zech. 12:1]

26 And hath made of one blood all nations
of men for to dwell on all the face of the
earth, and hath determined the ᵀtimes before
appointed, and ᴿthe bounds of their habitation;   *seasons • Deut. 32:8*

27 ᴿThat they should seek the Lord, if
ᵀhaply they might feel after him, and find
him, ᴿthough he be not far from every one of
us: [Rom. 1:20] • *perhaps* • [14:17]

28 For in him we live, and move, and have
our being; as certain also of your own poets
have said, For we are also his offspring.

29 Forasmuch then as we are the offspring
of God, we ought not to think that the
Godhead is like unto gold, or silver, or stone,
graven by art and man's device.

30 And the times of this ignorance God
ᵀwinked at; but ᴿnow commandeth all men
every where to repent: *overlooked • Luke 24:47*

31 Because he hath appointed a day, in the
which he will judge the world in righteousness by *that* man whom he hath ᵀordained;
whereof he hath given assurance unto all
men, in that he hath raised him from the
dead.   *commissioned*

32 And when they heard of the resurrection of the dead, some mocked: and others
said, We will hear thee again of this *matter.*

33 So Paul departed from among them.

34 Howbeit certain men clave unto him,
and believed: among the which *was* Di-o-
nys'-i-us the Ar-e-op'-a-gite, and a woman
named Dam'-a-ris, and others with them.

CHAPTER 18

Paul Works with Aquila and Priscilla

AFTER these things Paul departed from
Athens, and came to Corinth;

2 And found a certain Jew named ᴿAq'-ui-
la, born in Pon'-tus, lately come from Italy,
with his wife Priscilla; (because that Claudius
had commanded all Jews to depart from
Rome:) and came unto them.   2 Tim. 4:19

3 And because he was of the same craft, he
abode with them, and wrought: for by their
occupation they were tentmakers.

Jews Reject Paul

4 ᴿAnd he ᵀreasoned in the synagogue
every sabbath, and ᵀpersuaded the Jews and
the Greeks.   17:2 • *argued* • *convinced*

5 And when Silas and Ti-mo'-the-us were
come from Mac-e-do'-ni-a, Paul was pressed
in the spirit, and testified to the Jews *that*
Jesus ᵀwas Christ.   *is the Christ*

6 And ᴿwhen they opposed themselves,
and blasphemed, he shook *his* raiment, and
said unto them, Your blood *be* upon your
own heads; I *am* clean: from henceforth I will
go unto the Gentiles.   13:45

Crispus, the Gentile, Is Converted

7 And he departed thence, and entered
into a certain *man's* house, named Justus,
one that worshipped God, whose house
joined ᵀhard to the synagogue.   *close by*

8 And Cris'-pus, the chief ruler of the
synagogue, believed on the Lord with all his
house; and many of the Corinthians hearing
believed, and were baptized.

9 Then spake the Lord to Paul in the night
by a vision, Be not afraid, but speak, and
ᵀhold not thy peace: *do not keep quiet*

10 ᴿFor I am with thee, and no man shall
ᵀset on thee to hurt thee: for I have much
people in this city.   *v. 8*; Jer. 1:18, 19 • *be able*

11 And he ᵀcontinued *there* a year and six
months, teaching the word of God among
them.   *sat there*

Gallio Will Not Try Paul

12 And when Gal'-li-o was the deputy of A-
cha'-ia, the Jews ᵀmade insurrection with one
accord against Paul, and brought him to the
judgment seat,   *created an uproar*

13 Saying, This ᵀ*fellow* persuadeth men to worship God contrary to the law.   *man*

14 And when Paul was now about to open *his* mouth, Gal'-li-o said unto the Jews, If it were a matter of wrong or wicked lewdness, O *ye* Jews, reason would that I should bear with you:

15 But if it be a ᵀquestion of words and names, and *of* your law, look ye *to it;* for I will be no judge of such *matters.*   *argument*

16 And he drave them ᵀfrom the judgment seat.   *out of the court*

17 Then all the Greeks took Sos'-the-nes, the chief ruler of the synagogue, and beat *him* before the judgment seat. And Gal'-li-o cared for none of those things.

Return Trip to Antioch

18 And Paul *after this* ᵀtarried *there* yet a ᵀgood while, and then took his leave of the brethren, and sailed thence into Syria, and with him Priscilla and Aq'-ui-la; having ᴿshorn *his* head in ᴿCen'-chre-a: for he had a vow.   *stayed · long time · 21:24 · Rom. 16:1*

19 And he came to Eph'-e-sus, and left them there: but he himself entered into the synagogue, and reasoned with the Jews.

20 When they desired *him* to tarry longer time with them, he consented not;

21 But bade them farewell, saying, I must by all means keep this feast that cometh in Jerusalem: but I will return again unto you, if God will. And he sailed from Eph'-e-sus.

22 ᴿAnd when he had landed at Caes-a-re'-a, and gone up, and saluted the church, he went down to An'-ti-och.   *14:26*

Galatia and Phrygia: Strengthening the Disciples

23 And after he had spent some time *there*, he departed, and went over *all* the country of Ga-la'-ti-a and Phryg'-i-a in order, ᴿstrengthening all the disciples.   *14:22*

Apollos Teaches Effectively

24 ᴿAnd a certain Jew named A-pol'-los, born at Alexandria, ᵀan eloquent man, *and* mighty in the scriptures, came to Eph'-e-sus.   *1 Cor. 1:12; 3:5, 6; 4:6; Titus 3:13 · a learned*

25 This man was instructed in the way of the Lord; and being ᴿferventᵀ in the spirit, he spake and taught diligently the things of the Lord, ᴿknowingᵀ only the baptism of John.   *Rom. 12:11 · zealous · 19:3 · understanding*

26 And he began to speak boldly in the synagogue: whom when Aq'-ui-la and Priscilla had heard, they took him unto *them*, and ᵀexpounded unto him the way of God more ᵀperfectly.   *explained · accurately*

27 And when he was disposed to pass into A-cha'-ia, the brethren wrote, exhorting the disciples to receive him: who, when he was come, ᴿhelped them much which had believed through grace: *1 Cor. 3:6*

28 For he mightily convinced the Jews, *and that* publickly, shewing by the ᵀscriptures that Jesus was Christ.   *the Old Testament*

CHAPTER 19

Disciples of John Receive the Holy Ghost

AND it came to pass, that, while A-pol'-los was at Corinth, Paul having passed through the upper coasts came to Eph'-e-sus: and finding certain disciples,

2 He said unto them, Have ye received the Holy Ghost since ye believed? And they said unto him, We have not so much as heard whether there be any Holy Ghost.

3 And he said unto them, ᵀUnto what then were ye baptized? And they said, ᴿUnto John's baptism.   *into · 18:25*

4 Then said Paul, ᴿJohn verily baptized with the baptism of repentance, saying unto the people, that they should believe on him which should come after him, that is, on Christ Jesus.   *Matt. 3:11; [John 1:15, 27, 30]*

5 When they heard *this*, they were baptized ᵀin the name of the Lord Jesus.   *into*

6 And when Paul had laid *his* hands upon them, the Holy Ghost came on them; and they spake with tongues, and prophesied.

7 And all the men were about twelve.

Paul Teaches in Tyrannus's School

8 ᴿAnd he went into the synagogue, and spake boldly for the space of three months, disputing and persuading the things concerning the kingdom of God.   *17:2; 18:4*

9 But ᴿwhen divers were hardened, and believed not, but spake evil of that way before the multitude, he departed from them, and separated the disciples, disputing daily in the school of one Ty-ran'-nus.   *2 Tim. 1:15*

10 And ᴿthis continued by the space of two years; so that all they which dwelt in Asia heard the word of the Lord Jesus, both Jews and Greeks.   *20:31*

Miracles Are Performed at Ephesus

11 And ᴿGod wrought special miracles by the hands of Paul: *14:3; Mark 16:20*

12 ᴿSo that from his body were brought unto the sick handkerchiefs or aprons, and the diseases departed from them, and the evil spirits went out of them.   *2 Kin. 4:29*

13 Then certain of the vagabond Jews, ᵀexorcists, took upon them to call over them which had evil spirits the name of the Lord Jesus, saying, We adjure you by Jesus whom Paul preacheth.   *witch doctors*

14 And there were seven sons of *one* Sce'-va, a Jew, *and* chief of the priests, which ᵀdid so.   *were doing th*

15 And the evil spirit answered and said, [R]Jesus I know, and Paul I know; but who are ye? Matt. 8:29; [James 2:19]

16 And the man in whom the evil spirit was leaped on them, and overcame them, and prevailed against them, so that they fled out of that house naked and wounded.

17 And this was known to all the Jews and Greeks also dwelling at Eph'-e-sus; and [R]fear fell on them all, and the name of the Lord Jesus was magnified. Luke 1:65

18 And many that believed came, and [R]confessed, and shewed their deeds. Matt. 3:6

19 Many of them also which used [T]curious arts brought their books together, and burned them before all *men*: and they counted the price of them, and found *it* [T]fifty thousand *pieces* of silver. *magic* • *$6,400,000*

20 [R]So mightily [T]grew the word of God and [T]prevailed. 6:7; 12:24 • *spread* • *had power*

Timotheus and Erastus Are Sent to Macedonia

21 After these things were ended, Paul purposed in the spirit, when he had passed through Mac-e-do'-ni-a and A-cha'-ia, to go to Jerusalem, saying, After I have been there, I must also see Rome.

22 So he sent into Mac-e-do'-ni-a two of them that ministered unto him, Ti-mo'-the-us and [R]E-ras'-tus; but he himself stayed in Asia for a [T]season. Rom. 16:23; 2 Tim. 4:20 • *while*

Demetrius Causes Uproar at Ephesus

23 And [R]the same time there arose no small stir about [R]that way. 2 Cor. 1:8 • 9:2

24 For a certain *man* named De-me'-tri-us, a silversmith, which made silver shrines for Diana, brought no [T]small gain unto the [T]craftsmen; *little business* • *tradesmen*

25 Whom he called together with the workmen of like occupation, and said, Sirs, ye know that by this craft we have our wealth.

26 Moreover ye see and hear, that not alone at Eph'-e-sus, but almost throughout all Asia, this Paul hath persuaded and turned away much people, saying that they be no gods, which are made with hands:

27 So that not only this our craft is in danger to be [T]set at nought; but also that the temple of the great goddess Diana should be despised, and her magnificence should be destroyed, whom all Asia and the world worshippeth. *reduced to nothing*

28 And when they heard *these sayings*, they were full of wrath, and cried out, saying, Great *is* Diana of the E-phe'-sians.

29 And the whole city was filled with confusion: and having caught [R]Ga'-ius and Ar-is-tar'-chus, men of Mac-e-do'-ni-a, Paul's companions in travel, they rushed with one accord into the theatre. Rom. 16:23

30 And when Paul would have entered in unto the people, [R]the disciples [T]suffered him not. v. 9 • *allowe*

31 And certain of the chief of Asia, which were his friends, sent unto him, desiring *him* that he would not [T]adventure himself into the theatre. *risk goin*

32 [R]Some therefore cried one thing, and some another: for the assembly was con fused; and the more part knew not wherefore they were come together. vv. 39, 41

33 And they drew Alexander out of the multitude, the Jews putting him forward. And [R]Alexander [R]beckoned with the hand, and would have made his defence unto the people. 1 Tim. 1:20; 2 Tim. 4:14 • 12:17

34 But when they knew that he was a Jew, all with one voice about the space of two hours cried out, Great *is* Diana of the E-phe'-sians.

35 And when the townclerk had appeased the people, he said, Ye men of Eph'-e-sus, what man is there that knoweth not how that the city of the E-phe'-sians is [T]a worshipper of the great goddess Diana, and of the *image* which fell down from Jupiter? *the temple keeper*

36 Seeing then that these things cannot be spoken against, ye ought to be quiet, and to do nothing [T]rashly. *reckless*

37 For ye have brought hither these men, which are neither robbers of [T]churches, nor yet blasphemers of your goddess. *temples*

38 Wherefore if De-me'-tri-us, and the craftsmen which are with him, have a [T]matter against any man, [T]the law is open, and there are deputies: let them [T]implead one another. *complaint* • *courts are available* • *accuse*

39 But if ye enquire any thing concerning other matters, it shall be [T]determined in a lawful [R]assembly. *settled orderly* • vv. 32, 41

40 For we are in danger to be [T]called in question for this day's [T]uproar, there being no cause whereby we may give an account of this [T]concourse. *accused* • *riot* • *tumult*

41 And when he had thus spoken, [R]he dismissed the [T]assembly. vv. 32, 39 • *meeting*

CHAPTER 20

Macedonia: Three Months of Ministry

AND after the uproar was [T]ceased, Paul called unto *him* the disciples, and [T]embraced *them*, and [R]departed for to go into Mac-e-do'-ni-a. *quieted down* • *exhorted* • 1 Cor. 16:5

2 And when he had gone over those parts, and had given them much [T]exhortation, he came into Greece, *encouragement*

3 And *there* [T]abode three months. And [R]when the Jews laid wait for him, as he was about to sail into Syria, he purposed to return through Mac-e-do'-ni-a. *stayed* • 9:23

4 And there accompanied him into Asia Sop'-a-ter of Be-re'-a; and of the Thes-sa-lo'-

ni-ans, Ar-is-tar'-chus and Se-cun'-dus; and Ga'-ius of Der'-be, and Ti-mo'-the-us; and of Asia, Tych'-i-cus and Troph'-i-mus.

5 These going before ᵀtarried for us at Tro'-as.　　　　　　　　　　　　*waited*

Troas: Eutychus Falls from Loft

6 And we sailed away from Phi-lip'-pi after the days of unleavened bread, and came unto them to Tro'-as in five days; where we ᴿabode seven days.　　　　　　　　21:4; 28:14

7 And upon ᴿthe first *day* of the week, when the disciples came together ᴿto break bread, Paul preached unto them, ready to depart on the morrow; and continued his speech until midnight.　　Rev. 1:10 · 1 Cor. 10:16

8 And there were many lights ᴿin the upper chamber, where they were ᵀgathered together.　　　　　　1:13; 2:1, 2 · *meeting*

9 And there sat in a window a certain young man named Eu'-ty-chus, being fallen into a deep sleep: and as Paul was long preaching, he sunk down with sleep, and fell down from the third ᵀloft, and was taken up dead.　　　　　　　　　　　　*story*

10 And Paul went down, and fell on him, and embracing *him* said, ᴿTrouble not yourselves; for his life is in him.　Matt. 9:24

11 When he therefore was come up again, and had broken bread, ᴿand eaten, and talked a long while, even till break of day, so he departed.　　　　　　　　　　　　*v. 7*

12 And they brought the young man alive, and were ᵀnot a little comforted.　　*much*

Miletus: Paul Bids Farewell to Ephesian Elders

13 And we went before to ship, and sailed unto As'-sos, there intending to take in Paul: for so had he ᵀappointed, minding himself to go ᵀafoot.　　　　　　*arranged · by land*

14 And when he met with us at As'-sos, we took him in, and came to Mit-y-le'-ne.

15 And we sailed thence, and came the next *day* ᵀover against Chi'-os; and the next *day* we arrived at Sa'-mos, and tarried at Tro-gyl'-li-um; and the next *day* we came to ᴿMi-le'-tus.　　　　　*opposite* · 2 Tim. 4:20

16 For Paul had determined to sail by Eph'-e-sus, because he would not spend the time in Asia: for he ᵀhasted, if it were possible for him, to be at Jerusalem ᴿthe day of Pente-cost.　　　　　　*hurried* · 2:1; 1 Cor. 16:8

17 And from Mi-le'-tus he sent to Eph'-e-sus, and called the elders of the church.

18 And when they were come to him, he said unto them, Ye know, ᴿfrom the first day that I came into Asia, after what manner I have been with you at all seasons,　18:19; 19:1, 10

19 Serving the Lord with all humility of mind, and with many tears, and temptations, which befell me ᴿby the ᵀlying in wait of the Jews:　　　　　　　　　　　*v. 3 · plots*

20 *And* how ᴿI kept back nothing that was profitable *unto you*, but have shewed you, and have taught you publickly, and from house to house,　　　　　　　　　*v. 27*

21 Testifying both to the Jews, and also to the Greeks, repentance toward God, and faith toward our Lord Jesus Christ.

22 And now, behold, ᴿI go bound in the spirit unto Jerusalem, not knowing the things that shall befall me there:　　　19:21

23 Save that ᴿthe Holy Ghost witnesseth in every city, saying that bonds and afflictions ᵀabide me.　　21:4, 11; 1 Thess. 3:3 · *await*

24 But none of these things ᵀmove me, neither count I my life dear unto myself, so that I might finish my course with joy, ᴿand the ministry, which I have received of the Lord Jesus, to ᵀtestify the gospel of the grace of God.　　　　　　*affect · 1:17 · preach*

25 And now, behold, I know that ye all, among whom I have gone preaching the kingdom of God, shall see my face no more.

26 Wherefore I take you to record this day, that I *am* ᴿpure from the blood of all *men*.　　　　　　　　18:6; 2 Cor. 7:2

27 For I have not ᵀshunned to declare unto you all the counsel of God.　　*hesitated*

28 Take heed therefore unto yourselves, and to all the flock, over the which the Holy Ghost hath made you ᵀoverseers, to feed the church of God, which he hath purchased with his own blood.　　　　　*bishops*

29 For I know this, that after my departing shall grievous wolves enter in among you, ᵀnot sparing the flock.　　*with no mercy for*

30 Also of your own selves ᴿshall men arise, speaking ᵀperverse things, to draw away disciples after them.　Rev. 2:2 · *contrary*

31 Therefore watch, and remember, that by the space of three years I ceased not to warn every one night and day with tears.

32 And now, brethren, I commend you to God, and ᴿto the word of his grace, which is able ᴿto build you up, and to give you ᴿan inheritance among all them which are sanctified.　Heb. 13:9 · 9:31 · 26:18; Eph. 1:18

33 ᴿI have coveted no man's silver, or gold, or apparel.　　　1 Cor. 9:12; [2 Cor. 7:2]

34 Yea, ye yourselves know, ᴿthat these hands have ministered unto my necessities, and to them that were with me.　　18:3

35 I have shewed you all things, ᴿhow that so labouring ye ought to support the weak, and to remember the words of the Lord Jesus, how he said, It is more blessed to give than to receive.　　　1 Thess. 4:11; 2 Thess. 3:8

36 And when he had thus spoken, he kneeled down, and prayed with them all.

37 And they all wept sore, and fell on Paul's neck, and kissed him,

38 Sorrowing most of all for the words which he spake, that they ᵀshould see his face no more. ᴿAnd they accompanied him unto the ship.　*would see him no more · v. 25*

CHAPTER 21

Tyre: Paul Is Warned About Jerusalem

AND it came to pass, that after we were gotten from them, and had launched, we came with a straight course unto Co'-os, and the *day* following unto Rhodes, and from thence unto Pat'-a-ra:

2 And finding a ship sailing over unto Phe-ni'-ci-a, we went aboard, and set ᵀforth.   *sail*

3 Now when we had ᵀdiscovered Cyprus, we left it on the left hand, and sailed into Syria, and landed at Tyre: for there the ship was to unlade her burden.   *seen*

4 And finding disciples, we tarried there seven days: who said to Paul through the Spirit, that he should not go up to Jerusalem.

5 And when we had accomplished those days, we departed and went our way; and they all brought us on our way, with wives and children, till *we were* out of the city: and we kneeled down on the shore, and prayed.

6 And when we had taken our leave one of another, we took ship; and they returned home again.

Caesarea: Agabus's Prediction

7 And when we had finished ᵀour course from Tyre, we came to Ptol-e-ma'-is, and saluted the brethren, and ᵀabode with them one day.   *the voyage · stayed*

8 And the next *day* we that were of Paul's company ᴿdeparted, and came unto Caes-a-re'-a: and we entered into the house of Philip the evangelist, which was *one* of the seven; and abode with him.   6:5

9 And the same man had four daughters, virgins, ᴿwhich ᵀdid prophesy.   2:17 · *preached*

10 And as we tarried *there* many days, there came down from Ju-dae'-a a certain prophet, named ᴿAg'-a-bus.   11:28

11 And when he was come unto us, he took Paul's ᵀgirdle, and bound his own hands and feet, and said, Thus saith the Holy Ghost, So shall the Jews at Jerusalem bind the man that owneth this girdle, and shall deliver *him* into the hands of the Gentiles.   *belt*

12 And when we heard these things, both we, and they of that place, ᵀbesought him not to go up to Jerusalem.   *begged*

13 Then Paul answered, What mean ye to weep and to break mine heart? for I am ready not to be bound only, but also to die at Jerusalem for the name of the Lord Jesus.

14 And when he would not be persuaded, we ᵀceased, saying, ᴿThe will of the Lord be done.   *stopped* · Matt. 6:10; 26:42; Luke 11:2; 22:42

15 And after those days we took up our carriages, and went up to Jerusalem.

16 There went with us also *certain* of the disciples of Caes-a-re'-a, and brought with them one Mna'-son of Cyprus, an ᵀold disciple, with whom we should lodge.   *early*

Paul Conforms to Jewish Customs

17 And when we were come to Jerusalem, the brethren received us gladly.

18 And the *day* following Paul went in with us unto ᴿJames; and all the elders were present.   15:13; Gal. 1:19; 2:9

19 And when he had saluted them, ᴿhe ᵀdeclared particularly what things God had wrought among the Gentiles ᴿby his ministry.   Rom. 15:18, 19 · *told in detail* · 1:17; 20:24

20 And when they heard *it*, they glorified the Lord, and said unto him, Thou seest, brother, how many thousands of Jews there are which believe; and they are all ᵀzealous of the law: *eager to keep the law*

21 And they are informed of thee, that thou teachest all the Jews which are among the Gentiles to forsake Moses, saying that they ought not to circumcise *their* children, neither to walk after the customs.

22 What is it therefore? the multitude ᵀmust needs come together: for they will hear that thou art come.   *will certainly*

23 Do therefore this that we say to thee: We have four men which have ᵀa ᴿvow on them;   *taken a vow* · Num. 6:1–7

24 Them take, and purify thyself with them, and be at charges with them, that they may ᴿshave *their* heads: and all may know that those things, whereof they were informed concerning thee, are nothing; but *that* thou thyself also walkest orderly, and keepest the law.   Num. 6:2, 13, 18

25 ᴿAs touching the Gentiles which believe, we have written *and* concluded that they observe no such thing, save only that they keep themselves from *things* offered to idols, and from blood, and from strangled, and from fornication.   15:29

26 Then Paul took the men, and the next day purifying himself with them ᴿentered into the temple, ᴿto signify the ᵀaccomplishment of the days of purification, until that an offering should be offered for every one of them.   24:18 · Num. 6:13 · *completion*

Paul's Arrest

27 And when the seven days were almost ended, the Jews which were of Asia, when they saw him in the temple, stirred up all the people, and laid hands on him,

28 Crying out, Men of Israel, help: This is the man, ᴿthat teacheth all *men* every where against the people, and the law, and this place: and further brought Greeks also into the temple, and hath ᵀpolluted this holy place.   24:5, 6 · *made unclean*

29 (For they had seen before with him in the city ᴿTroph'-i-mus an E-phe'-sian, whom they supposed that Paul had brought into the temple.)   20:4

30 And ᴿall the city was ᵀmoved, and the people ran together: and they took Paul, and

drew him out of the temple: and forthwith the doors were shut.   26:21 · *disturbed*

31 And as they went about to kill him, tidings came unto the chief captain of the band, that all Jerusalem was in an uproar.

32 Who immediately took soldiers and centurions, and ran down unto them: and when they saw the chief captain and the soldiers, they Tleft beating of Paul.   *stopped*

33 Then the chief captain came near, and took him, and commanded *him* to be bound with two chains; and Tdemanded who he was, and what he had done.   *asked*

34 And some cried one thing, some another, among the multitude: and when he could not Tknow the certainty for the tumult, he commanded him to be carried into the castle.   *find out for sure what caused the riot*

35 And when he came upon the stairs, so it was, that he was borne of the soldiers Tfor the violence of the people.   *because of*

36 For the multitude of the people followed after, crying, RAway with him.   22:22

37 And as Paul was to be led into the castle, he said unto the chief captain, May I speak unto thee? Who said, TCanst thou speak Greek?   *dost thou know*

38 Art not thou that Egyptian, which before these days Tmadest an uproar, and leddest out into the wilderness four thousand men that were murderers?   *caused a riot*

39 But Paul said, I am a man *which am* a Jew of Tar′-sus, *a city* in Ci-li′-ci-a, a citizen of no mean city: and, I beseech thee, Tsuffer me to speak unto the people.   *allow*

Paul's Defence Before the Crowd
Acts 9:1–8, 17, 18; 26:13–18

40 And when he had given him licence, Paul stood on the stairs, and beckoned with the hand unto the people. And when there was made a great silence, he spake unto *them* in the Hebrew tongue, saying,

CHAPTER 22

MEN, brethren, and fathers, hear ye my defence *which I make* now unto you.

2 (RAnd when they heard that he spake in the Hebrew tongue to them, they kept the more silence: and he saith,)   21:40

3 I am verily a man *which am* a Jew, born in Tar′-sus, *a city* in Ci-li′-ci-a, yet brought up in this city at the feet of Ga-ma′-li-el, *and* taught according to the perfect manner of the law of the fathers, and was zealous toward God, as ye all are this day.

4 RAnd I persecuted this way unto the death, binding and delivering into prisons both men and women.   Phil. 3:6; 1 Tim. 1:13

5 As also the high priest doth bear me witness, and all the Testate of the elders:

Rfrom whom also I received letters unto the brethren, and went to Damascus, to bring them which were there bound unto Jerusalem, for to be punished.   *council* · 9:2

6 And it came to pass, that, as I made my journey, and was come nigh unto Damascus about noon, suddenly there shone from heaven a great light round about me.

7 RAnd I fell unto the ground, and heard a voice saying unto me, Saul, Saul, why persecutest thou me?   9:4

8 RAnd I answered, Who art thou, Lord? And he said unto me, I am Jesus of Nazareth, whom thou persecutest.   9:5

9 And Rthey that were with me saw indeed the light, and were afraid; but they heard not the voice of him that spake to me.   9:7; Dan. 10:7

10 And I said, What shall I do, Lord? And the Lord said unto me, Arise, and go into Damascus; and there it shall be told thee of all things which are Tappointed Rfor thee to do.   *determined* · 9:6

11 And when I could not see for the glory of that light, being led by the hand Rof them that were with me, I came into Damascus. 9:8

12 RAnd one An-a-ni′-as, a devout man according to the law, having a good report of all the Jews which dwelt *there*,   9:17, 18

13 Came unto me, and stood, and said unto me, Brother Saul, receive thy sight. And the same hour I looked up upon him.

14 And he said, The God of our fathers hath chosen thee, that thou shouldest know his will, and see that Just One, and shouldest hear the voice of his mouth.

15 For thou shalt be his witness unto all men of what thou hast seen and heard.

16 And now why Ttarriest thou? arise, and be baptized, and wash away thy sins, calling on the name of the Lord.   *do you delay?*

17 And it came to pass, that, when I was come again to Jerusalem, even while I prayed in the temple, I was in a trance;

18 And Rsaw him saying unto me, RMake Thaste, and get thee quickly out of Jerusalem: for they will not receive thy testimony concerning me.   *v.* 14 · Matt. 10:14 · *hurry*

19 And I said, Lord, Rthey know that I imprisoned and Rbeat in every synagogue them that believed on thee: *v.* 4 · Matt. 10:17

20 RAnd when the blood of thy martyr Stephen was shed, I also was standing by, and consenting unto his death, and kept the raiment of them that slew him.   7:58; 8:1

21 And he said unto me, Depart: for I will send thee far hence unto the Gentiles.

22 And they gave him audience unto this word, and *then* lifted up their voices, and said, Away with such a *fellow* from the earth: for it is not fit that he should live.

23 And as they cried out, and cast off *their* clothes, and threw dust into the air,

Paul's Defence Before the Centurion

24 The chief captain commanded him to be brought into the castle, and bade that he should be examined by ᵀscourging; that he might ᵀknow wherefore they cried so against him.   *whipping • find out why*

25 And as they bound him with thongs, Paul said unto the centurion that stood by, Is it lawful for you to ᵀscourge a man that is a Roman, and uncondemned?   *whip*

26 When the centurion heard *that*, he went and told the chief captain, saying, ᵀTake heed what thou doest: for this man is a Roman.   *what are you about to do?*

27 Then the chief captain came, and said unto him, Tell me, art thou a Roman? He said, Yea.

28 And the chief captain answered, With a great sum obtained I this freedom. And Paul said, But I was ᵀfree born.   *a Roman*

29 Then straightway they departed from him which should have ᵀexamined him: and the chief captain also was afraid, after he knew that he was a Roman, and because he had bound him.   *investigated him*

Paul's Defence Before the Sanhedrin

30 On the morrow, because he would have known the certainty ᵀwherefore he was accused of the Jews, he loosed him from *his* bands, and commanded the chief priests and all their council to appear, and brought Paul down, and set him before them.   *why*

CHAPTER 23

AND Paul, earnestly beholding the council, said, Men *and* brethren, ᴿI have lived in all good conscience before God until this day.   2 Tim. 1:3; Heb. 13:18

2 And the high priest An-a-ni'-as commanded them that stood by him ᴿto ᵀsmite him on the mouth.   Jer. 20:2; John 18:22 • *hit*

3 Then said Paul unto him, God shall smite thee, *thou* whited wall: for sittest thou to judge me after the law, and commandest me to be smitten contrary to the law?

4 And they that stood by said, ᵀRevilest thou God's high priest?   *insult*

5 Then said Paul, I ᵀwist not, brethren, that he was the high priest: for it is written, ᴿTHOU SHALT NOT SPEAK EVIL OF THE RULER OF THY PEOPLE.   *knew* • Ex. 22:28; [Jude 8]

6 But when Paul perceived that the one part were Sad'-du-cees, and the other Pharisees, he cried out in the council, Men *and* brethren, I am a Pharisee, the son of a Pharisee: of the hope and resurrection of the dead I am called in question.

7 And when he had so said, there arose a dissension between the Pharisees and the Sad'-du-cees: and the multitude was divided.

8 ᴿFor the Sad'-du-cees say that there is no resurrection, neither angel, nor spirit: but the Pharisees confess both.   Matt. 22:23

9 And there arose a great cry: and the scribes *that were* of the Pharisees' part arose, and strove, saying, We find no evil in this man: but if a spirit or an angel hath spoken to him, let us not fight against God.

10 And when there arose a great ᵀdissension, the chief captain, fearing lest Paul should have been pulled in pieces of them, commanded the soldiers to go down, and to take him by force from among them, and to bring *him* into the castle.   *quarrel*

11 And ᴿthe night following the Lord stood by him, and said, Be of good cheer, Paul: for as thou hast testified of me in Jerusalem, so must thou bear witness also at Rome. 27:23, 24

Jews' Plan to Kill Paul

12 And when it was day, certain of the Jews banded together, and bound themselves under a curse, saying that they would neither eat nor drink till they had killed Paul.

13 And they were more than forty which had ᵀmade this conspiracy.   *planned*

14 And they came to the chief priests and elders, and said, We have bound ourselves under a great ᵀcurse, that we will eat nothing until we have slain Paul.   *vow*

15 Now therefore ye with the council signify to the chief captain that he bring him down unto you to morrow, as though ye would enquire something more ᵀperfectly concerning him: and we, ᵀor ever he come near, are ready to kill him.   *fully • if*

16 And when Paul's ᵀsister's son heard of their ᵀlying in wait, he went and entered into the castle, and told Paul.   *nephew • plan*

17 Then Paul called one of the centurions unto *him*, and said, Bring this young man unto the ᵀchief captain: for he hath a certain thing to tell him.   *commander*

18 So he took him, and brought *him* to the chief captain, and said, Paul the prisoner called me unto *him*, and prayed me to bring this young man unto thee, who hath something to say unto thee.

19 Then the chief captain took him by the hand, and went *with him* aside privately, and asked *him*, What is that thou hast to tell me?

20 And he said, The Jews have agreed to desire thee that thou wouldest bring down Paul to morrow into the council, as though they would enquire somewhat ᵀof him more perfectly.   *more exactly concerning him*

21 But do not thou yield unto them: for there lie in wait for him of them more than forty men, which have bound themselves with an oath, that they will neither eat nor drink till they have killed him: and now are they ready, looking for a promise from thee.

22 So the chief captain *then* let the young man depart, and charged *him, See thou* tell no man that thou hast ᵀshewed these things to me. *told*

Paul's Rescue

23 And he called unto *him* two centurions, saying, Make ready two hundred soldiers to go to Caes-a-re'-a, and horsemen threescore and ten, and spearmen two hundred, at the ᵀthird hour of the night; *9 p.m.*

24 And provide *them* ᵀbeasts, that they may set Paul on, and bring *him* safe unto Felix the governor. *horses*

25 And he wrote a letter after this manner:

26 Claudius Lys'-i-as unto the most excellent governor Felix *sendeth* greeting.

27 This man was taken of the Jews, and should have been killed of them: then came I with an army, and rescued him, having understood that he was a Roman.

28 ᴿAnd when I would have known the cause wherefore they accused him, I brought him forth into their council: *22:30*

29 Whom I perceived to be accused ᴿof questions of their law, ᴿbut to have nothing laid to his charge worthy of death or of bonds. *18:15; 25:19 • 26:31*

30 And ᴿwhen it was told me how that the Jews laid wait for the man, I sent straightway to thee, and gave commandment to his accusers also to say before thee what *they* had against him. Farewell. *v. 20*

31 Then the soldiers, as it was commanded them, took Paul, and brought *him* by night to An-tip'-a-tris.

32 On the morrow they left the horsemen to go with him, and returned to the castle:

33 Who, when they came to Caes-a-re'-a, and delivered the ᵀepistle to the governor, presented Paul also before him. *letter*

Paul Is Tried Before Felix

34 And when the governor had read *the letter*, he asked of what province he was. And when he understood that *he was* of ᴿCi-li'-ci-a; *21:39*

35 I will hear thee, said he, when thine accusers are also come. And he commanded him to be kept in Her'-od's judgment hall.

CHAPTER 24

AND after five days An-a-ni'-as the high priest descended with the elders, and *with* a certain orator *named* Ter-tul'-lus, who informed the governor against Paul.

2 And when he was called forth, Ter-tul'-lus began to accuse *him*, saying, Seeing that by thee we enjoy great quietness, and that very worthy deeds are done unto this nation by thy ᵀprovidence, *provision*

3 We accept *it* always, and in all places, most noble Felix, with all thankfulness.

4 Notwithstanding, that I be not further ᵀtedious unto thee, I pray thee that thou wouldest hear us of thy ᵀclemency a few words. *tiring • kindness*

5 ᴿFor we have found this man *a* pestilent *fellow*, and a mover of sedition among all the Jews throughout the world, and a ringleader of the sect of the Nazarenes: *Luke 23:2*

6 Who also hath gone about to ᵀprofane the temple: whom we took, and would have judged according to our law. *desecrate*

7 ᴿBut the chief captain Lys'-i-as came *upon us*, and with great violence took *him* away out of our hands, *21:33*

8 ᴿCommanding his accusers to come unto thee: by examining of whom thyself mayest take knowledge of all these things, whereof we accuse him. *23:30*

9 And the Jews also ᵀassented, saying that these things were so. *agreed*

10 Then Paul, after that the governor had ᵀbeckoned unto him to speak, answered, Forasmuch as I know that thou hast been of many years a judge unto this nation, I do the more cheerfully answer for myself: *nodded*

11 Because that thou mayest understand, that there are yet but twelve days since I went up to Jerusalem for to worship.

12 ᴿAnd they neither found me in the temple disputing with any man, neither raising up the people, neither in the synagogues, nor in the city: *25:8; 28:17*

13 ᴿNeither can they prove the things whereof they now accuse me. *vv. 4–6*

14 But this I confess unto thee, that after the way which they call ᵀheresy, so worship I the God of my fathers, believing all things which are written in ᴿthe law and in the prophets: *a sect • 26:22*

15 And have hope toward God, which they themselves also ᵀallow, ᴿthat there shall be a resurrection of the dead, both of the just and unjust. *look for • [Dan. 12:2]*

16 And ᴿherein do I exercise myself, to have always a conscience ᵀvoid of offence toward God, and *toward* men. *23:1 • free*

17 Now after many years ᴿI came to bring alms to my nation, and offerings. *Gal. 2:10*

18 Whereupon certain Jews from Asia found me purified in the temple, neither with multitude, nor with ᵀtumult. *disorder*

19 ᴿWho ought to have been here before thee, and object, if they had ᵀought against me. *23:30; [25:16] • anything*

20 Or else let these same *here* say, if they have found any ᵀevil doing in me, while I stood before the council, *wrong*

21 Except it be for this one voice, that I cried standing among them, ᴿTouching the resurrection of the dead I am called in question by you this day. *23:6; [28:20]*

22 And when Felix heard these things, having more ᵀperfect knowledge of *that* way, he deferred them, and said, When Lys'-i-as the chief captain shall come down, I will know the uttermost of your matter.   *exact*

23 And he commanded a centurion to keep Paul, and to let *him* have liberty, and that he should forbid none of his acquaintance to minister or come unto him.

24 And after certain days, when Felix came with his ᴿwife Dru-sil'-la, which was a Jewess, he sent for Paul, and heard him concerning the faith in Christ.   20:21

25 And as he reasoned of righteousness, ᵀtemperance, and judgment to come, Felix trembled, and answered, Go thy way for this time; when I have a convenient season, I will call for thee.   *self-control*

26 He hoped also that ᴿmoney should have been given him of Paul, that he might loose him: wherefore he sent for him the oftener, and communed with him.   Ex. 23:8

27 But after two years Por'-cius Festus came into Felix' room: and Felix, willing to shew the Jews a pleasure, left Paul bound.

CHAPTER 25

Paul Is Tried Before Festus

NOW when Festus was come into the province, after three days he ascended from Caes-a-re'-a to Jerusalem.

2 ᴿThen the high priest and the chief of the Jews informed him against Paul, and ᵀbesought him,   *v. 15; 24:1 • begged*

3 And desired favour against him, that he would send for him to Jerusalem, ᴿlaying wait in the way to kill him.   23:12, 15

4 But Festus answered, that Paul should be kept at Caes-a-re'-a, and that he himself would depart shortly *thither.*

5 Let them therefore, said he, which ᵀamong you are able, go down with *me*, and accuse this man, ᴿif there be any wickedness in him.   *of power among you • v. 18; 18:14*

6 And when he had tarried among them more than ten days, he went down unto Caes-a-re'-a; and the next day sitting on the ᴿjudgment seat commanded Paul to be brought.   John 19:13

7 And when he was come, the Jews which came down from Jerusalem stood round about, ᴿand laid many and ᵀgrievous complaints against Paul, which they could not prove.   24:5, 13; Mark 15:3; Luke 23:2, 10 • serious

8 While he answered for himself, ᴿNeither against the law of the Jews, neither against the temple, nor yet against Caesar, have I offended any thing at all.   6:13; 24:12; 28:17

9 But Festus, ᴿwilling to do the Jews a pleasure, answered Paul, and said, Wilt thou go up to Jerusalem, and there be judged of these things before me?   24:27

10 Then said Paul, I stand at Caesar's judgment seat, where I ought to be ᵀjudged: to the Jews have I done no wrong, as thou very well knowest.   *tried*

11 For if I be an offender, or have committed any thing worthy of death, I refuse not to die: but if there be none of these things whereof these accuse me, no man may deliver me unto them. I appeal unto Caesar.

12 Then Festus, when he had conferred with the council, answered, Hast thou appealed unto Caesar? unto Caesar shalt thou go.

13 And after certain days king A-grip'-pa and Ber-ni'-ce came unto Caes-a-re'-a to ᵀsalute Festus.   *visit*

14 And when they had been there many days, Festus declared Paul's cause unto the king, saying, ᴿThere is a certain man left in bonds by Felix: 24:27

15 ᴿAbout whom, when I was at Jerusalem, the chief priests and the elders of the Jews informed *me*, desiring *to have* judgment against him.   *vv. 2, 3*

16 ᴿTo whom I answered, It is not the manner of the Romans to deliver any man to die, before that he which is accused have the accusers face to face, and have ᵀlicence to answer for himself concerning the crime laid against him.   *vv. 4, 5 • opportunity*

17 Therefore, when they were come hither, ᴿwithout any delay on the morrow I sat on the judgment seat, and commanded the man to be brought forth.   *v. 6*

18 Against whom when the accusers stood up, they brought none accusation of such things as I ᵀsupposed: *expected*

19 ᴿBut had certain questions against him of their own ᵀsuperstition, and of one Jesus, which was dead, whom Paul affirmed to be alive.   18:15; 23:29 • religion

20 And because I ᵀdoubted of such manner of questions, I asked *him* whether he would go to Jerusalem, and there be judged of these matters.   *was uncertain*

21 But when Paul had appealed to be reserved unto the ᵀhearing of ᵀAugustus, I commanded him to be kept till I might send him to Caesar.   *judgment • the emperor*

22 Then ᴿA-grip'-pa said unto Festus, I would also hear the man myself. To morrow, said he, thou shalt hear him.   9:15

Paul Is Tried Before Agrippa

23 And on the morrow, when A-grip'-pa was come, and Ber-ni'-ce, with great ᵀpomp, and was entered into the place of hearing, with the chief captains, and principal men of the city, at Festus' commandment Paul was brought forth.   *ceremony*

24 And Festus said, King A-grip'-pa, and all men which are here present with us, ye see this man, about whom ᴿall the multitude of the Jews have dealt with me, both at Jerusalem, and *also* here, crying that he ought not to live any longer. *vv. 2, 3, 7*

25 But when I found that he had committed nothing worthy of death, ᴿand that he himself hath appealed to Augustus, I have determined to send him. *vv. 11, 12*

26 Of whom I have no ᵀcertain thing to write unto my lord. Wherefore I have brought him forth before you, and specially before thee, O king A-grip'-pa, that, after ᵀexamination had, I might have somewhat to write. *specific · investigation had occurred*

27 For it seemeth to me unreasonable to send a prisoner, and not ᵀwithal to signify the crimes *laid* against him. *to show charges*

CHAPTER 26

THEN A-grip'-pa said unto Paul, Thou art permitted to speak for thyself. Then Paul stretched forth the hand, and ᵀanswered for himself: *defended himself*

2 I think myself happy, king A-grip'-pa, because I shall ᵀanswer for myself this day before thee touching all the things whereof I am accused of the Jews: *make my defence*

3 Especially *because I know* thee to be ᴿexpert in all customs and questions which are among the Jews: wherefore I beseech thee to hear me patiently. *Deut. 17:14-20*

4 My manner of life from my youth, which was at the first among mine own nation at Jerusalem, know all the Jews;

5 Which knew me from the beginning, if they would testify, that after ᴿthe ᵀmost straitest sect of our religion I lived a Pharisee. *22:3; 23:6; [24:15, 21]; Phil. 3:5 · strictest*

6 ᴿAnd now I stand and am judged for the hope of ᴿthe promise made of God unto our fathers: *23:6 · 13:32; Rom. 15:8; [Titus 2:13]*

7 Unto which *promise* ᴿour twelve tribes, instantly serving *God* day and night, hope to come. For which hope's sake, king A-grip'-pa, I am accused of the Jews. *James 1:1*

8 Why should it be thought a thing ᵀincredible with you, that ᴿGod should raise the dead? *impossible · Dan. 12:2*

9 ᴿI verily thought with myself, that I ought to do many things ᵀcontrary to the name of Jesus of Nazareth. *John 16:2 · opposed*

10 Which thing I also did in Jerusalem: and many of the saints did I shut up in prison, having received authority from the chief priests; and when they were put to death, I gave my voice against *them*.

11 ᴿAnd I punished them oft in every synagogue, and ᵀcompelled *them* to blaspheme; and being exceedingly mad against

them, I persecuted *them* even unto ᵀstrange cities. *22:19 · strove to make · foreign*

12 ᴿWhereupon as I went to Damascus with authority and commission from the chief priests, *22:6*

13 At midday, O king, I saw in the way a light from heaven, above the brightness of the sun, ᴿshining round about me and them which journeyed with me. *9:3; 22:6*

14 And when we were all fallen to the earth, I heard a voice speaking unto me, and saying in the Hebrew tongue, Saul, Saul, why persecutest thou me? *it is* hard for thee to kick against the ᵀpricks. *goads*

15 And I said, Who art thou, Lord? And he said, I am Jesus whom thou persecutest.

16 But rise, and stand upon thy feet: for I have appeared unto thee for this purpose, ᴿto make thee a minister and a witness both of these things which thou hast seen, and of those things in the which I will appear unto thee; *22:15; 1 Cor. 9:1; 15:5-8*

17 ᵀDelivering thee from the people, and *from* the Gentiles, ᴿunto whom now I send thee, *saving · 22:21*

18 ᴿTo open their eyes, *and* ᴿto turn *them* from darkness to light, and *from* the power of Satan unto God, that they may receive forgiveness of sins, and inheritance among them which are ᵀsanctified by faith that is in me. *Is. 35:5; 42:7 · 2 Cor. 6:14 · set apart*

19 Whereupon, O king A-grip'-pa, I was not disobedient unto the heavenly vision:

20 But shewed first unto them of Damascus, and at Jerusalem, and throughout all the coasts of Ju-dae'-a, and *then* to the Gentiles, that they should repent and turn to God, and do works meet for repentance.

21 For these causes the Jews caught me in the temple, and went about to kill *me*.

22 Having therefore obtained help of God, I continue unto this day, ᵀwitnessing both to small and great, saying none other things than those which the prophets and Moses did say should come: *giving testimony*

23 ᴿThat Christ should suffer, *and* that he should be the first that should rise from the dead, and should shew light unto the people, and to the Gentiles. *Luke 24:26*

24 And as he thus spake for himself, Festus said with a loud voice, Paul, ᴿthou art beside thyself; much learning doth make thee ᵀmad. *2 Kin. 9:11; John 10:20; 1 Cor. 1:23 · crazy*

25 But he said, I am not mad, most ᵀnoble Festus; but speak forth the words of truth and soberness. *excellent*

26 For the king ᵀknoweth of these things, before whom also I speak freely: for I am persuaded that none of these things are hidden from him; for this thing was not done in a corner. *understands*

27 King A-grip'-pa, believest thou the prophets? I know that thou believest.

28 Then A-grip'-pa said unto Paul, Almost thou persuadest me to be a RChristian.   11:26

29 And Paul said, RI would to God, that not only thou, but also all that hear me this day, were both almost, and altogether such as I am, except these bonds.   I Cor. 7:7

30 And when he had thus spoken, the king rose up, and the governor, and Ber-ni'-ce, and they that sat with them:

31 And when they were Tgone aside, they talked between themselves, saying, RThis man doeth nothing worthy of death or of bonds.   leaving • 23:9, 29; 25:25

32 Then said A-grip'-pa unto Festus, This man might have been set at liberty, Rif he had not appealed unto Caesar.   25:11

CHAPTER 27

Paul's Witness During the Shipwreck

AND when Rit was determined that we should sail into Italy, they delivered Paul and certain other prisoners unto *one* named Julius, a Tcenturion of Augustus' band.   25:12, 25 • *commander of 100 soldiers*

2 And entering into a ship of Ad-ra-myt'-ti-um, we launched, meaning to sail by the coasts of Asia; *one* Ar-is-tar'-chus, a Mac-e-do'-ni-an of Thes-sa-lo-ni'-ca, being with us.

3 And the next *day* we touched at Si'-don. And Julius Rcourteously Tentreated Paul, and gave *him* liberty to go unto his friends to refresh himself.   24:23 • *treated*

4 And when we had Tlaunched from thence, we sailed under Cyprus, because the winds were contrary.   *set sail*

5 And when we had sailed over the sea of Ci-li'-ci-a and Pam-phyl'-i-a, we came to My'-ra, *a city* of Ly'-ci-a.

6 And there the centurion found a ship of Alexandria sailing into Italy; and he put us therein.

7 And when we had sailed slowly many days, and scarce were come over against Cni'-dus, the wind not suffering us, we sailed Tunder Crete, over against Sal-mo'-ne;   *near*

8 And, hardly passing it, came unto a place which is called The fair havens; nigh whereunto was the city *of* La-se'-a.

9 Now when much time was spent, and when sailing was now dangerous, because the fast was now already past, Paul Tadmonished *them*,   *advised*

10 RAnd said unto them, Sirs, I perceive that this voyage will be with Thurt and much damage, not only of the Tlading and ship, but also of our lives.   27:14-20 • *danger* • *cargo*

11 Nevertheless the Tcenturion believed the master and the owner of the ship, more than those things which were spoken by Paul.   *commander of 100 soldiers*

12 And because the haven was not commodious to winter in, the more part advised to depart thence also, if by any means they might attain to Phe-ni'-ce, *and there* to winter; *which is* an Thaven of Crete, and lieth toward the south west and north west.   *harbour*

13 And when the south wind blew softly, supposing that they had obtained *their* purpose, Tloosing *thence*, they sailed close by Crete.   *pulling anchor*

14 But not long after there arose against it a tempestuous wind, called Eu-roc'-ly-don.

15 And when the ship was caught, and could not bear up into the wind, we let *her* Tdrive.   *run before the wind*

16 And running Tunder a certain island which is called Clauda, we had much work to Tcome by the boat: *near • secure*

17 Which when they had taken up, they used helps, undergirding the ship; and, fearing lest they should fall into the quicksands, strake sail, and so were driven.

18 And we being exceedingly tossed with a tempest, the next *day* they Tlightened the ship;   *threw freight overboard*

19 And the third *day* we cast out with our own hands the tackling of the ship.

20 And when neither sun nor stars in many days appeared, and no small tempest lay on *us*, all hope that we should be saved was then Ttaken away.   *given up*

21 But after long Tabstinence Paul stood forth in the midst of them, and said, Sirs, ye should have hearkened unto me, and not have loosed from Crete, and to have gained this harm and loss.   *being without food*

22 And now I Texhort you to be of good cheer: for Rthere shall be no loss of *any man's* life among you, but of the ship.   *urge • v. 44*

23 RFor there stood by me this night the angel of God, whose I am, and Rwhom I serve,   23:11 • Dan. 6:16; Rom. 1:9; 2 Tim. 1:3

24 Saying, Fear not, Paul; thou must be brought before Caesar: and, lo, God hath given thee all them that sail with thee.

25 Wherefore, sirs, be of good cheer: Rfor I believe God, that it shall be even as it was told me.   Luke 1:45; Rom. 4:20, 21; 2 Tim. 1:12

26 Howbeit Rwe must be cast upon a certain island.   28:1

27 But when the fourteenth night was come, as we were driven up and down in A'-dri-a, about midnight the shipmen deemed that they drew near to some Tcountry;   *land*

28 And sounded, and found *it* Ttwenty fathoms: and when they had gone a little further, they sounded again, and found *it* Tfifteen fathoms.   *120 ft. • 90 ft.*

29 Then fearing lest we should have fallen upon rocks, they cast four anchors out of the stern, and wished for the day.

30 And as the shipmen were about to flee out of the ship, when they had let down the

boat into the sea, Tunder colour as though they would have cast anchors out of the foreship,   *under the pretence*

31 Paul said to the centurion and to the soldiers, Except Tthese abide in the ship, ye cannot be saved.   *these sailors*

32 Then the soldiers cut off the ropes of the boat, and let her fall off.

33 And while the day was coming on, Paul Tbesought *them* all to take Tmeat, saying, This day is the fourteenth day that ye have Ttarried and continued fasting, having taken nothing.   *begged • food • waited*

34 Wherefore I pray you to take *some* Tmeat: for this is for your Thealth: for Rthere shall not an hair fall from the head of any of you.   *food • safety •* [Luke 12:7; 21:18]

35 And when he had thus spoken, he took bread, and Rgave thanks to God in presence of them all: and when he had broken *it*, he began to eat.   Mark 8:6; John 6:11; [1 Tim. 4:3, 4]

36 Then were they all of good cheer, and they also took *some* Tmeat.   *food*

37 And we were in all in the ship Ttwo hundred threescore and sixteen souls.   *276*

38 And when they had eaten enough, they lightened the ship, and Rcast out the wheat into the sea.   Jon. 1:5

39 And when it was day, they Tknew not the land: but they discovered a certain Tcreek with a shore, into the which they were minded, if it were possible, to thrust in the ship.   *did not recognize • bay*

40 And when they had Ttaken up the anchors, they Tcommitted *themselves* unto the sea, and loosed the rudder bands, and hoised up the mainsail to the wind, and made toward shore.   *cut loose • left them in*

41 And falling into a place where two seas met, they ran the ship aground; and the Tforepart stuck fast, and remained unmoveable, but the Thinder part was broken with the violence of the waves.   *prow • stern*

42 And the soldiers' Tcounsel was to kill the prisoners, lest any of them should swim out, and escape.   *advice*

43 But the centurion, Rwilling to save Paul, kept them from *their* purpose; and commanded that they which could swim should cast *themselves* first *into the sea*, and get to land: [2 Pet. 2:9]

44 And the rest, some on boards, and some on *broken pieces* of the ship. And so it came to pass, that they escaped all safe to land.

CHAPTER 28

Paul's Witness on Melita

AND when they were escaped, then Tthey knew that Rthe island was called TMel'-i-ta.   *we •* 27:26 • *Malta*

2 And the Rbarbarous people shewed us no little kindness: for they kindled a fire, and received us every one, because of the present rain, and because of the cold.   Col. 3:11

3 And when Paul had gathered a bundle of sticks, and laid *them* on the fire, there came a Tviper out of the heat, and fastened on his hand.   *snake*

4 And when the barbarians saw the *venomous* beast hang on his hand, they said among themselves, No doubt this man is a murderer, whom, though he hath escaped the sea, yet vengeance suffereth not to live.

5 And he shook off the beast into the fire, and Rfelt no harm.   Mark 16:18; Luke 10:19

6 Howbeit they looked when he should have swollen, or fallen down dead suddenly: but after they had looked a great while, and saw no harm come to him, they changed their minds, and said that he was a god.

7 In the same quarters were possessions of the chief man of the island, whose name was Pub'-li-us; who received us, and Tlodged us three days courteously.   *entertained*

8 And it came to pass, that the father of Pub'-li-us lay sick of a fever and of a bloody flux: to whom Paul entered in, and prayed, and laid his hands on him, and healed him.

9 So when this was done, others also, which had diseases in the island, came, and were healed:

10 Who also honoured us with many honours; and when we departed, they laded *us* with such things as were necessary.

11 And after three months we departed in a ship of Alexandria, which had wintered in the isle, whose sign was Castor and Pol'-lux.

12 And landing at Syr'-a-cuse, we Ttarried *there* three days.   *stayed*

13 And from thence we Tfetched a compass, and came to Rhe'-gi-um: and after one day the south wind blew, and we came the next day to Pu-te'-o-li: *made a circuit*

14 RWhere we found brethren, and were desired to tarry with them seven days: and so we went toward Rome.   20:6; 21:4

15 And from thence, when the brethren heard of us, they came to meet us as far as Ap'-pi-i for'-um, and The three taverns: whom when Paul saw, he thanked God, and took Rcourage.   [Josh. 1:6–9; Ps. 27:14]

Paul's Witness in Rome

16 And when we came to Rome, the centurion delivered the prisoners to the captain of the guard: but Paul was suffered to dwell by himself with a soldier that kept him.

17 And it came to pass, that after three days Paul called the chief of the Jews together: and when they were come together, he said unto them, Men *and* brethren, though I have committed nothing against the people, or customs of our fathers, yet was I delivered

prisoner from Jerusalem into the hands of the Romans.

18 Who, ᴿwhen they had examined me, would have let *me* go, because there was no cause of death in me.　　　　22:24; 24:10; 25:8

19 But when the Jews spake against *it*, I was constrained to appeal unto Caesar; not that I had ought to accuse my nation of.

20 For this cause therefore have I called for you, to see *you*, and to speak with *you*: because that ᴿfor the hope of Israel I am bound with ᴿthis chain.　　26:6, 7 · Philem. 10, 13

21 And they said unto him, We neither received letters out of Ju-dae'-a concerning thee, neither any of the brethren, that came shewed or spake any harm of thee.

22 But we desire to hear of thee what thou thinkest: for as concerning this sect, we know that every where it is spoken against.

23 And when they had appointed him a day, there came many to him into *his* lodging; ᴿto whom he expounded and testified the kingdom of God, persuading them concerning Jesus, ᴿboth out of the law of Moses, and *out of* the prophets, from morning till evening.　　[17:3]; 19:8 · 26:6, 22

24 And ᴿsome believed the things which were spoken, and some believed not.　　14:4

25 And when they agreed not among themselves, they departed, ᵀafter that Paul had spoken one word, Well spake the Holy Ghost by E-sa'-ias the prophet unto our fathers,　　　　　　*after Paul said this thing*

26 Saying, ᴿGO UNTO THIS PEOPLE, AND SAY, HEARING YE SHALL HEAR, AND SHALL NOT UNDERSTAND; AND SEEING YE SHALL SEE, AND NOT PERCEIVE:　　　　　Is. 6:9, 10 ✶

27 FOR THE HEART OF THIS PEOPLE IS WAXED GROSS, AND THEIR EARS ARE DULL OF HEARING, AND THEIR EYES HAVE THEY CLOSED; LEST THEY SHOULD SEE WITH *THEIR* EYES, AND HEAR WITH *THEIR* EARS, AND UNDERSTAND WITH *THEIR* HEART, AND SHOULD BE CONVERTED, AND I SHOULD HEAL THEM.

28 Be it known therefore unto you, that the salvation of God is sent ᴿunto the Gentiles, and *that* they will hear it.　　Is. 42:1 ✶

29 And when he had said these words, the Jews departed, and had great ᵀreasoning among themselves.　　　　　　　*arguing*

30 And Paul dwelt two whole years ᵀin his own hired house, and ᵀreceived all that came in unto him,　　*at his own expense · welcomed*

31 ᴿPreaching the kingdom of God, and teaching those things which concern the Lord Jesus Christ, with all confidence, no man forbidding him.　　4:31; Eph. 6:19

ROMANS

THE BOOK OF ROMANS

Romans, Paul's greatest work, is placed first among his thirteen epistles in the New Testament. While the four Gospels present the words and works of Jesus Christ, Romans explores the significance of His sacrificial death. Using a question-and-answer format, Paul records the most systematic presentation of doctrine in the Bible. Romans is more than a book of theology; it is also a book of practical exhortation. The Good News of Jesus Christ is more than facts to be believed; it is also a life to be lived—a life of righteousness befitting the person "justified freely by [God's] grace through the redemption that is in Christ Jesus" (3:24).

Although some manuscripts omit "in Rome" in 1:7, 15, the title *Pros Rōmaious*, "To the Romans," has been associated with the epistle almost from the beginning.

THE AUTHOR OF ROMANS

All critical schools agree on the Pauline authorship (1:1) of this foundational book. The vocabulary, style, logic, and theological development are consistent with Paul's other epistles. Paul dictated this letter to a secretary named Tertius (16:22), who was allowed to add his own greeting.

The problem arises not with the authorship but with the disunity of the epistle. Some Latin (but no Greek) manuscripts omit 15:1—16:24, and the closing doxology (16:25-27) is placed at the end of chapter 14 in some manuscripts. These variations have led some scholars to conclude that the last two chapters were not originally part of the epistle, or that Paul issued it in two editions. However, most scholars believe that chapter 15 fits in logically with the rest of the epistle. There is more debate over chapter 16, because Paul greets by name twenty-six persons in a church he has never visited. Some scholars contend that it was a separate letter, perhaps written to Ephesus, that was appended to this epistle. Such a letter would be surprising, to say the least (nothing but greetings), especially in the ancient world. It is simpler to understand the list of greetings as Paul's effort as a stranger to the Roman church to list his mutual friends. Paul met these people in the cities of his missionary journeys. Significantly, the only other Pauline epistle that lists individual greetings was addressed to the believers at Colosse, another church Paul had never visited. It may be that this portion was omitted from some copies of Romans because it did not seem relevant.

THE TIME OF ROMANS

Paul did not found the church at Rome, and the tradition that Peter was its founder is contrary to the evidence. It is possible that it began when some of the Jews and proselytes to Judaism who became followers of Christ on the Day of Pentecost (cf. Acts 2:10) returned to Rome, but it is more likely that Christians from churches established by Paul in Asia, Macedonia, and Greece settled in Rome and led others to Christ. According to this epistle, Gentiles were predominant in the church at Rome (1:13; 11:13, 28-31; 15:15, 16), but there were also Jewish believers (2:17—3:8; 3:21—4:1; 7:1-14; 14:1—15:12).

Rome was founded in 753 B.C., and by the time of Paul it was the greatest city in the world with over one million inhabitants (one inscription says over four million). It was full of magnificent buildings, but the majority of people were slaves: opulence and squalor coexisted in the Imperial City. The church in Rome was well known (1:8), and it had been established for several years by the time of this letter (see 14:14; 15:23). The believers there were probably numerous, and evidently they met in several places (16:1-16). The historian Tacitus referred to the Christians who were persecuted under Nero in A.D. 64 as "an immense multitude." The gospel filled the gap left by the practically defunct polytheism of Roman religion.

Paul wrote Romans in A.D. 57, near the end of his third missionary journey (Acts 18:23—21:14; cf. Rom. 15:19). It was evidently written during his three-month stay in Greece (Acts 20:3-6), more specifically, in Corinth. Paul was staying with Gaius of Corinth (16:23; cf. 1 Cor. 1:14), and he also mentioned "Erastus the chamberlain of the city" (16:23). A first-century inscription in Corinth mentions him: "Erastus, the commissioner of public works, laid this pavement at his own expense." Paul's collection from the churches of Macedonia and Achaia for the needy Christians in Jerusalem was complete (15:26), and he was ready to deliver it (15:25). Instead of sailing directly to Jerusalem, Paul avoided a plot by the Jews by first going north to Philippi. He evidently gave this letter to Phoebe from the church at Cenchrea, near Corinth, and she carried it to Rome (16:1, 2).

THE CHRIST OF ROMANS

Paul presents Jesus Christ as the Second Adam whose righteousness and substitutionary death have provided justification for all who place their faith in Him. He offers His righteousness as a gracious gift to sinful men,

having borne God's condemnation and wrath for their sinfulness. His death and resurrection are the basis for the believer's redemption, justification, reconciliation, salvation, and glorification.

KEYS TO ROMANS

Key Word: The Righteousness of God— The theme of Romans is found in 1:16, 17: God offers the gift of His righteousness to everyone who comes to Christ by faith. Paul writes Romans to reveal God's sovereign plan of salvation (1—8), to show how Jews and Gentiles fit into that plan (9—11), and to exhort them to live righteous and harmonious lives (12—16). In his sweeping presentation of God's plan of salvation, Paul moves from condemnation to glorification and from positional truth to practical truth. Key words, such as *righteousness, faith, law, all,* and *sin* each appear at least sixty times in this epistle.

Key Verses: Romans 1:16, 17 and 3:21-25— "For I am not ashamed of the gospel of Christ: for it is the power of God unto salvation to every one that believeth; to the Jew first, and also to the Greek. For therein is the righteousness of God revealed from faith to faith: as it is written, The just shall live by faith" (1:16, 17).

"But now the righteousness of God without the law is manifested, being witnessed by the law and the prophets; Even the righteousness of God *which is* by faith of Jesus Christ unto all and upon all them that believe: for there is no difference: For all have sinned, and come short of the glory of God; Being justified freely by his grace through the redemption that is in Christ Jesus: Whom God hath set forth *to be* a propitiation through faith in his blood, to declare his righteousness for the remission of sins that are past, through the forbearance of God" (3:21-25).

Key Chapters: Romans 6—8—Foundational to all teaching on the spiritual life is the central passage of Romans 6—8. The answers to the questions of how to be delivered from sin, how to live a balanced life under grace, and how to live the victorious Christian life through the power of the Holy Spirit are all contained here. Many consider this to be the principal passage on conforming to the image of Jesus Christ.

SURVEY OF ROMANS

The poet Samuel Taylor Coleridge regarded Romans as "the most profound book in existence," and the commentator Godet called it "the cathedral of the Christian faith." Because of its majestic declaration of the divine plan of salvation, Martin Luther wrote: "This epistle is the chief part of the New Testament and the very purest gospel. . . . It can never be read or pondered too much, and the more it is dealt with the more precious it becomes, and the better it tastes." The four Gospels present the words and works of the Lord Jesus, but Romans, "The Gospel According to Paul," delves more into the significance of His death and resurrection. The theology of Romans is balanced by practical exhortation, because Paul sees the believer's position as the basis for his practice. The theme of righteousness that runs through the book is reflected in the following outline: the revelation of the righteousness of God (1—8); the vindication of the righteousness of God (9—11); the application of the righteousness of God (12—16).

The Revelation of the Righteousness of God (1—8): The prologue (1:1-17) consists of a salutation (1:1-7), a statement of Paul's desire to minister in Rome (1:8-15), and the theme of the book (1:16, 17). This two-verse theme is the basic text of Romans because it combines the three crucial concepts of salvation, righteousness, and faith.

In 1:18—3:20, Paul builds a solid case for the condemnation of all people under the holy God. The Gentiles are without excuse because they have suppressed the knowledge of God they

FOCUS	REVELATION OF GOD'S RIGHTEOUSNESS			VINDICATION OF GOD'S RIGHTEOUSNESS			APPLICATION OF GOD'S RIGHTEOUSNESS	
REFERENCE	1:1————3:21————		6:1————9:1——	9:30————11:1——			12:1————14:1——16:27	
DIVISION	NEED FOR GOD'S RIGHTEOUSNESS	IMPUTATION OF GOD'S RIGHTEOUSNESS	DEMONSTRATION OF GOD'S RIGHTEOUSNESS	ISRAEL'S PAST: ELECTION	ISRAEL'S PRESENT: REJECTION	ISRAEL'S FUTURE: RESTORATION	CHRISTIAN DUTIES	CHRISTIAN LIBERTIES
TOPIC	SIN	SALVATION	SANCTIFICATION	SOVEREIGNTY			SERVICE	
	DOCTRINAL						BEHAVIORAL	
LOCATION	PROBABLY WRITTEN IN CORINTH							
TIME	C. A.D. 57							

received from nature and their conscience (1:18–32; their seven-step regression is traced in 1:21–31). The Jews are also under the condemnation of God, and Paul overcomes every objection they could raise to this conclusion (2:1—3:8). God judges according to truth (2:2–5), works (2:6–10), and impartiality (2:11–16), and both the moral and religious Jews fail to meet His standard. Paul concludes his discussion of the reasons for the guilt of the Jews by reminding them they do not obey the Law (2:17–29) nor believe the Oracles of God (3:1–8). The divine verdict (3:9–20) is universal: "all have sinned, and come short of the glory of God" (3:23).

The section on justification (3:21–5:21) centers on and develops the theme of God's provision for man's need. The first eleven verses are the core of the book (3:21–31), revealing that in Christ, God is both Judge and Saviour. Justification is by grace (the source of salvation; 3:21–24), by blood (the basis of salvation; 3:25, 26), and by faith (the condition of salvation; 3:27–31).

Chapter 4 illustrates the principle of justification by faith apart from works in the life of Abraham. Justification issues in reconciliation between God and man (5:1–11). It is brought about by the love of God which is causeless (5:6), measureless (5:7, 8), and ceaseless (5:9–11). In 5:12–21 Paul contrasts the two Adams and the opposite results of their two acts. The righteousness of the Second Adam is imputed to all who trust in Him, leading to reconciliation.

Chapter 6 describes the believer's relationship to sin: in his position he is dead to the principle of sin (6:1–14) and the practice of sin (6:15–23). The reality of identification with Christ is the basis for the sanctified Christian life. After describing the Christian's emancipation from the Law (7), Paul looks at the work of the Holy Spirit who indwells and empowers every believer (8:1–17). The next major topic after condemnation, justification, and sanctification is glorification (8:18–39). All Christians can anticipate a time when they will be perfectly conformed to Jesus Christ not only in their position (present) but also in their practice (the future resurrection).

The Vindication of the Righteousness of God (9—11): It appears that God has rejected His people, Israel, but it is really Israel who has rejected her Messiah. God's rejection of Israel is only partial (there is a spiritual remnant that has trusted in Christ) and temporary (they will be grafted back, 11:23–27). Paul appropriately quotes frequently from the Old Testament in this section, and he emphasizes that God will be faithful to His covenant promises and restore Israel.

The Application of the Righteousness of God (12—16): Paul recognizes that behavior must be built upon belief, and this is why the practical exhortations of this epistle appear after his teaching on the believer's position in Christ. The salvation described in the first eleven chapters should transform a Christian's life in relation to God (12:1, 2), society (12:3–21), higher powers (13:1–7), and one's neighbors (13:8–14). In chapters 14 and 15 the apostle discusses the whole concept of Christian liberty, noting its principles (14) and its practice (15:1–13). A changed life is not a condition for salvation, but it should be the natural outcome of saving faith. The epistle closes with Paul's statement of his plans (15:14–33), a long series of personal greetings (16:1–16), and an admonition followed by a doxology (16:17–27).

OUTLINE OF ROMANS

Part One: The Revelation of the Righteousness of God (1:1—8:39)

CHAPTER 1

Introduction

PAUL, a servant of Jesus Christ, called *to be* an apostle, separated unto the gospel of God,

2 (RWhich he had promised afore by his prophets in the holy scriptures,)   Acts 26:6

3 Concerning his Son Jesus Christ our Lord, which was Rmade of the seed of David according to the flesh;   Is. 9:7; Gal. 4:4 ★

4 RAnd declared *to be* the Son of God with power, according to the spirit of holiness, by the resurrection from the dead: Ps. 2:7; 16:10, 11 ★

5 By whom we have received grace and apostleship, for obedience to the faith among all nations, Rfor his name: Acts 9:15

6 Among whom are ye also Tthe called of Jesus Christ: called to belong to

7 To all that be in Rome, beloved of God, Rcalled *to be* saints: RGrace to you and peace from God our Father, and the Lord Jesus Christ.   1 Cor. 1:2 • 1 Cor. 1:3

8 First, I thank my God through Jesus

Christ for you all, that your faith is spoken of throughout the whole world.

9 For RGod is my witness, whom I serve Twith my spirit in the gospel of his Son, that without ceasing I make mention of you always in my prayers;   9:1 • in my spirit

10 Making request, if by any means now at length I might have a prosperous journey by the will of God to come unto you.

11 For I long to see you, that I may Timpart unto you some spiritual gift, to the end ye may be established;   share with

12 That is, that I may be comforted together Twith you by Rthe mutual faith both of you and me.   in you • Titus 1:4; 2 Pet. 1:1

13 Now I would not have you ignorant, brethren, that oftentimes I purposed to come unto you, (but was Tlet hitherto,) that I might have some fruit among you also, even as among other Gentiles.   hindered

14 TI am debtor both to the Greeks, and to the Barbarians; both to the wise, and to the unwise.   I have an obligation

15 So, as much as in me is, I am ready to

preach the [R]gospel to you that are at Rome also.   Gen. 12:3; Rev. 14:6

16 For I am not ashamed of the gospel of Christ: for it is the power of God unto salvation to every one that believeth; [R]to the Jew first, and also to the Greek.   Acts 3:26

17 For therein is the righteousness of God revealed from faith to faith: as it is written, [R]THE JUST SHALL LIVE BY FAITH.   Hab. 2:4

Reason for Gentile Guilt

18 [R]For the wrath of God is revealed from heaven against all ungodliness and unrighteousness of men, who [T]hold the truth in unrighteousness;   [Acts 17:30] · hold back

19 Because [R]that which may be known of God is [T]manifest [T]in them; for God hath shewed it unto them.   [Acts 14:17] · shown · to them

20 For the invisible things of him from the creation of the world are clearly seen, being understood by the things that are made, even his eternal power and Godhead; so that they are without excuse:

21 Because that, when they knew God, they glorified him not as God, neither were thankful; but became vain in their imaginations, and their foolish heart was darkened.

22 [R]Professing themselves to be wise, they [T]became fools,   Jer. 10:14 · are

23 And changed the glory of the uncorruptible [R]God into an image made like to corruptible man, and to birds, and fourfooted beasts, and creeping things.   Ps. 106:20

Results of Gentile Guilt

24 Wherefore God also gave them up to uncleanness through the lusts of their own hearts, [R]to dishonour their own bodies [R]between themselves: 1 Cor. 6:18 · Lev. 18:22

25 Who changed [R]the truth of God [R]into a lie, and worshipped and served the creature [T]more than the Creator, who is blessed for ever. A-men'.   1 Thess. 1:9 · Is. 44:20 · rather

26 For this cause God gave them up unto [R]vile [T]affections: for even their women did change the natural use into that which is against nature: Lev. 18:22; Eph. 5:12 · passions

27 And likewise also the men, leaving the natural use of the woman, burned in their lust one toward another; men with men working that which is unseemly, and receiving in themselves that [T]recompence of their error which was [T]meet.   reward · due

28 And even as they did not like to retain God in their knowledge, God gave them over to a reprobate mind, to do those things which are not convenient;

29 Being filled with all unrighteousness, fornication, wickedness, covetousness, maliciousness; full of envy, murder, [T]debate, deceit, malignity; whisperers,   strife

30 Backbiters, haters of God, [T]despiteful,

[T]proud, boasters, inventors of evil things, disobedient to parents,   insolent · haughty

31 Without understanding, covenant-breakers, [T]without natural affection, implacable, unmerciful: heartless

32 Who knowing the judgment of God, that they which commit such things are worthy of death, not only do the same, but have pleasure in them that do them.

CHAPTER 2

Jews Are Judged According to Truth

THEREFORE thou art [R]inexcusable, O man, whosoever thou art that [T]judgest: for wherein thou judgest another, thou condemnest thyself; for thou that judgest doest the same things.   [1:20] · criticizes anyone

2 But we are sure that the judgment of God is [T]according to truth against them which commit such things.   right

3 And [R]thinkest thou this, O man, that judgest them which do such things, and doest the same, that thou shalt escape the judgment of God?   [Prov. 11:21]

4 Or despisest thou the riches of his goodness and [R]forbearance and longsuffering; not knowing that the goodness of God leadeth thee to repentance?   [3:25]

5 But after thy hardness and impenitent heart [R]treasurest up unto thyself wrath against the day of wrath and revelation of the righteous judgment of God;   [Deut. 32:34]

Jews Are Judged by Their Works

6 [R]WHO WILL RENDER TO EVERY MAN ACCORDING TO HIS DEEDS: [Job 34:11; 2 Cor. 5:10]

7 To them who by patient continuance in well doing seek for glory and honour and [T]immortality, eternal life: incorruption

8 But unto them that are contentious, and do not obey the truth, but obey unrighteousness, indignation and wrath,

9 Tribulation and anguish, upon every soul of man that doeth evil, of the Jew first, and also of the Gentile;

10 [R]But glory, honour, and peace, to every man that worketh good, to the Jew first, and also to the Gentile: [1 Pet. 1:7]

Jews Are Judged with Impartiality

11 For [R]there is no respect of persons with God.   [Job 34:19]; Acts 10:34; [Eph. 6:9]

12 For as many as have sinned [T]without law shall also perish without law: and as many as have sinned in the law shall be judged by the law;   apart from the law

13 (For [R]not the hearers of the law are just before God, but the doers of the law shall be justified.   [James 1:22-25; 1 John 3:7]

14 For when the Gentiles, which have not the law, do by nature the things contained in

the law, these, having not the law, Rare a law unto themselves: [Deut. 12:8]

15 TWhich shew the work of the law written in their hearts, their conscience also bearing witness, and *their* thoughts Tthe mean while accusing or else excusing one another;) *their conduct · between themselves*

16 RIn the day when God shall judge the secrets of men Rby Jesus Christ Raccording to my gospel. Rev. 20:12 · John 5:22 · [2 Cor. 4:3]

Jews Do Not Obey the Law

17 Behold, Rthou art called a Jew, and RrestestT in the law, Rand makest thy boast of God, [Matt. 3:9] · Mic. 3:11 · *hast confidence* · Is. 48:1, 2

18 And Rknowest *his* will, and Tapprovest the things that are more excellent, being instructed out of the law; Deut. 4:8 · *judges*

19 And Rart confident that thou thyself art a guide of the blind, a light of them which are in darkness, Matt. 15:14; John 9:34

20 An instructor of the foolish, a teacher of babes, Rwhich hast the form of knowledge and of the truth in the law. [2 Tim. 3:5]

21 RThou therefore which teachest another, teachest thou not thyself? thou that preachest a man should not steal, dost thou steal? Ex. 20:15; Ps. 50:16; Matt. 23:3

22 Thou that sayest a man should not commit adultery, dost thou commit adultery? thou that abhorrest idols, Rdost thou Tcommit sacrilege? Mal. 3:8 · *rob temples*

23 Thou that Rmakest thy boast of the law, through breaking the law Tdishonourest thou God? v. 17 · *bring shame*

24 FOR THE NAME OF GOD IS BLASPHEMED AMONG THE GENTILES THROUGH YOU, as it is Rwritten. 2 Sam. 12:14; Is. 52:5; Ezek. 36:23

25 RFor circumcision verily profiteth, if thou keep the law: but if thou be a breaker of the law, thy circumcision is made uncircumcision. [1 Cor. 7:19; Gal. 5:3]

26 Therefore if the uncircumcision keep the righteousness of the law, shall not his uncircumcision be counted for circumcision?

27 And shall not uncircumcision which is by nature, if it fulfil the law, Rjudge thee, who Tby the Tletter and circumcision dost transgress the law? Matt. 12:41 · *with · scripture*

28 For Rhe is not a Jew, which is one outwardly; neither *is that* circumcision, which is outward in the flesh: John 8:39

29 But he *is* a Jew, which is one inwardly; and circumcision *is that* of the heart, in the spirit, *and* not in the letter; whose praise *is* not of men, but of God.

CHAPTER 3

Jews Do Not Believe the Oracles

WHAT advantage then hath the Jew? or what profit *is there* of circumcision?
2 Much Tevery way: chiefly, because that

Runto them were Tcommitted the Toracles of God. *indeed · Deut. 4:7 · trusted · words*

3 For what if Rsome did not believe? shall their unbelief make the Tfaith of God without effect? Heb. 4:2 · *faithfulness*

4 God forbid: yea, let God be true, but every man a liar; as it is written, THAT THOU MIGHTEST BE JUSTIFIED IN THY SAYINGS, AND MIGHTEST OVERCOME WHEN THOU ART JUDGED.

5 But if our unrighteousness commend the righteousness of God, what shall we say? *Is* God unrighteous who taketh vengeance? (RI speak as a man) Gal. 3:15

6 TGod forbid: for then Rhow shall God judge the world? *by no means* · [Gen. 18:25]

7 For if the truth of God hath more abounded through my lie unto his glory; why yet am I also judged as a sinner?

8 And not *rather,* (as we be slanderously reported, and as some affirm that we say,) Let us do evil, that good may come? whose Tdamnation is just. *condemnation is deserved*

Conclusion: All Are Guilty Before God

9 What then? are we better *than they?* No, in no wise: for we have before proved both Jews and Gentiles, that Rthey are all under sin; Gal. 3:22

10 As it is written, RTHERE IS NONE RIGHTEOUS, NO, NOT ONE: Ps. 14:1–3; 53:1–4

11 THERE IS NONE THAT UNDERSTANDETH, THERE IS NONE THAT SEEKETH AFTER GOD.

12 THEY ARE ALL GONE OUT OF THE WAY, THEY ARE TOGETHER BECOME UNPROFITABLE; THERE IS NONE THAT DOETH GOOD, NO, NOT ONE.

13 THEIR THROAT *IS* AN OPEN SEPULCHRE; WITH THEIR TONGUES THEY HAVE USED DECEIT; THE POISON OF ASPS *IS* UNDER THEIR LIPS:

14 RWHOSE MOUTH *IS* FULL OF CURSING AND BITTERNESS: Ps. 10:7

15 THEIR FEET *ARE* SWIFT TO SHED BLOOD:

16 RDESTRUCTION AND MISERY *ARE* IN THEIR WAYS: Is. 59:7

17 RAND THE WAY OF PEACE HAVE THEY NOT KNOWN: Is. 59:8

18 RTHERE IS NO FEAR OF GOD BEFORE THEIR EYES. Ps. 36:1

19 Now we know that what things soever the law saith, it saith to them who are under the law: that every mouth may be stopped, and all the world may become Tguilty before God. *subject to the judgment of God*

20 Therefore by the deeds of the law Rthere shall no Tflesh be justified in his sight: for by the law *is* the knowledge of sin. Ps. 143:2 · *man*

Description of Righteousness

21 But now the righteousness of God without the law is manifested, being witnessed by the law and the prophets;

22 Even the righteousness of God *which is* by faith of Jesus Christ unto all and upon

all them that believe: for ᴿthere is no ᵀdifference: [Gal. 3:28; Col. 3:11] • *distinction*

23 For ᴿall have sinned, and ᵀcome short of the glory of God;   Gal. 3:22 • *fall*

24 Being justified ᵀfreely ᴿby his grace ᴿthrough the redemption that is in Christ Jesus: *without any cost* • [Eph. 2:8] • [1 Pet. 1:18, 19]

25 ᴿWhom God hath set forth *to be* ᵀa propitiation through faith in his blood, to declare his righteousness for the ᵀremission of sins that are past, through the forbearance of God;   [Heb. 9:22] • *a mercy seat* • *passing over*

26 To declare, *I say*, ᵀat this time his righteousness: that he might be just, and the justifier of him which believeth in Jesus.   *now*

27 ᴿWhere *is* boasting then? It is excluded. By what law? of works? Nay: but by the law of faith.   2:17, 23; [1 Cor. 1:29]; Eph. 2:9

28 Therefore we conclude ᴿthat a man is ᵀjustified by faith ᵀwithout the deeds of the law.   Gal. 2:16 • *cleared of all guilt* • *apart from*

29 *Is he* the God of the Jews only? *is he* not also of the Gentiles? ᵀYes, of the Gentiles also: *of course*

30 Seeing ᴿ*it is* one God, which shall justify the circumcision by faith, and uncircumcision through faith.   [Gal. 3:8, 20]

31 Do we then make void the law through faith? God forbid: yea, we establish the law.

CHAPTER 4

Abraham's Righteousness Apart from Works

WHAT shall we say then that ᴿAbraham our father, as pertaining to the flesh, hath found?   John 8:33; 2 Cor. 11:22

2 For if Abraham were ᴿjustifiedᵀ by works, he hath *whereof* to glory; but not before God.   3:20, 27 • *cleared of guilt*

3 For what saith the scripture? ᴿABRAHAM BELIEVED GOD, AND IT WAS COUNTED UNTO HIM FOR RIGHTEOUSNESS.   Gal. 3:6; James 2:23

4 Now to him that worketh is the reward not reckoned of grace, but of debt.

5 But to him that worketh not, but believeth on him that justifieth the ungodly, his faith is counted for righteousness.

6 Even as David also describeth the blessedness of the man, unto whom God imputeth righteousness without works,

7 *Saying*, ᴿBLESSED *ARE* THEY WHOSE INIQUITIES ARE FORGIVEN, AND WHOSE SINS ARE COVERED.   Ps. 32:1

8 ᴿBLESSED *IS* THE MAN TO WHOM THE LORD WILL NOT IMPUTE SIN.   Ps. 32:2

Abraham's Righteousness Apart from Circumcision

9 *Cometh* this ᵀblessedness then upon the circumcision *only*, or upon the uncircumcision also? for we say that faith was reckoned to Abraham for righteousness.   *happiness*

10 How was it then reckoned? when he was in circumcision, or in uncircumcision? Not in circumcision, but in uncircumcision.

11 And ᴿhe received the sign of circumcision, a seal of the righteousness of the faith which *he had yet* being uncircumcised: that ᴿhe might be the father of all them that believe, though they be not circumcised; that righteousness might be imputed unto them also: Gen. 17:10 • Luke 19:9

12 And the father of circumcision to them who are not of the circumcision only, but who also walk in the steps of that faith of our father Abraham, which *he had* being *yet* uncircumcised.

Abraham's Righteousness Apart from the Law

13 For the promise, that he should be the ᴿheir of the world, *was* not to Abraham, or to his seed, through the law, but through the righteousness of faith.   Gen. 17:4

14 For ᴿif they which are of the law *be* heirs, faith is made ᵀvoid, and the promise made of ᵀnone effect: Gal. 3:18 • *empty* • *no use*

15 Because the law worketh wrath: for where no law is, *there is* no transgression.

Abraham's Righteousness Was by Faith

16 Therefore *it is* of faith, that *it might be* by grace; to the end the promise might be ᵀsure to all the seed; not to that only which is of the law, but to that also which is of the faith of Abraham; ᴿwho is the father of us all,   *certain to come* • Is. 51:2

17 (As it is written, ᴿI HAVE MADE THEE A FATHER OF MANY NATIONS,) before him whom he believed, *even* God, who quickeneth the dead, and calleth those things which be not as though they were.   Gen. 17:5

18 Who against hope believed in hope, that he might become the father of many nations, according to that which was spoken, ᴿSO SHALL THY SEED BE.   Gen. 15:5

19 And being not weak in faith, he considered not his own body now dead, when he was about an hundred years old, neither yet the deadness of Sarah's womb:

20 He ᵀstaggered not at the promise of God through unbelief; but was strong in faith, giving glory to God;   *did not doubt*

21 And being fully persuaded that, what he had promised, ᴿhe was able also to perform.   [Ps. 115:3; Luke 1:37; Heb. 11:19]

22 And therefore ᴿIT WAS ᵀIMPUTED TO HIM FOR RIGHTEOUSNESS.   Gen. 15:6 • *reckoned*

23 Now it was not written for his sake alone, that it was imputed to him;

24 But for us also, to whom it shall be imputed, if we believe on him that raised up Jesus our Lord from the dead;

25 Who was delivered for our offences, and was raised again for our justification.

CHAPTER 5

Peace with God

THEREFORE being justified by faith, we have Rpeace with God through our Lord Jesus Christ: John 16:33; [Eph. 2:14]

2 Rby whom also we have access by faith into this grace wherein we stand, and rejoice in hope of the glory of God. [John 10:9]

Joy in Tribulation

3 And not only so, but Rwe glory in tribulations also: Rknowing that tribulation worketh patience; James 1:2 · James 1:3

4 Rand Tpatience, experience; and experience, hope: [James 1:12] · steadfastness

5 Rand hope maketh not ashamed; Rbecause the love of God is shed abroad in our hearts by the Holy Ghost which is given unto us. Phil. 1:20 · 2 Cor. 1:22; Eph. 1:13

6 For when we were yet without strength, in due time Christ died for the ungodly.

7 For scarcely for a righteous man will one die: yet Tperadventure for a good man some would even dare to die. perhaps

8 But Rgod commendeth his love toward us, in that, while we were yet sinners, Christ died for us. Is. 53:5; [John 15:13]; 1 John 3:16 ★

Salvation from God's Wrath

9 Much more then, being now justified Rby his blood, we shall be saved Rfrom wrath through him. [1 John 1:7] · 1 Thess. 1:10

10 For if, when we were enemies, Rwe were reconciled to God by the death of his Son, much more, being reconciled, we shall be saved Rby his life. 2 Cor. 5:18 · John 14:19

11 And not only so, but we also Rjoy in God through our Lord Jesus Christ, by whom we have now received the atonement. [3:29, 30]

Contrast of Righteousness and Condemnation

12 Wherefore, as Rby one man sin entered into the world, and Rdeath by sin; and so death passed upon all men, Tfor that all have sinned: Gen. 3:6; [1 Cor. 15:21] · Gen. 2:17 · in

13 (For until the law sin was in the world: but Rsin is Tnot imputed when there is no law. 4:15; 1 John 3:4 · no account is kept

14 Nevertheless death reigned from Adam to Moses, even over them that had not sinned after the Tsimilitude of Adam's transgression, Rwho is the figure of him that was to come. likeness · [1 Cor. 15:21, 22]

15 But not as the offence, so also is the free gift. For if through the offence of one many be dead, much more the grace of God, and the gift by grace, which is by one man, Jesus Christ, hath abounded unto many.

16 And not as it was by one that sinned, so is the gift: for the Rjudgment was by one to condemnation, but the free gift is of many offences unto justification. 1 Cor. 11:32

17 For if Tby Rone man's offence death reigned by one; much more they which receive abundance of grace and of the gift of righteousness shall reign in life by one, Jesus Christ.) by one offence · Gen. 2:17; 3:6, 19

18 Therefore as by the offence of one judgment came upon all men to condemnation; even so Rby the righteousness of one the free gift came upon all men unto justification of life. Is. 53:11, 12; Matt. 1:21 ★

19 For as by one man's disobedience many were made sinners, so by the obedience of one shall many be made righteous.

20 Moreover the law entered, that the offence might abound. But where sin abounded, grace did much more abound:

21 That as sin hath reigned unto death, even so might Rgrace reign through righteousness unto eternal life by Jesus Christ our Lord. John 1:17

CHAPTER 6

Believer's Death to Sin in Principle

WHAT shall we say then? Shall we continue in sin, that grace may abound?

2 God forbid. How shall we, that are dead to sin, live any longer therein?

3 Know ye not, that so many of us as Twere baptized into Jesus Christ Rwere baptized into his death? are · [1 Cor. 15:29]

4 Therefore we are buried with him by baptism into death: that Rlike T as Christ was raised up from the dead by the glory of the Father, Reven so we also should walk in newness of life. Col. 2:12 · just · [Gal. 6:15]

5 For if we have been planted together in the likeness of his death, we shall be also in the likeness of his resurrection:

6 Knowing this, that Rour old man is crucified with him, that Rthe body of sin might be destroyed, that henceforth we should not serve sin. Gal. 2:20 · Col. 2:11

7 For he that is dead is freed from sin.

8 Now if we be dead with Christ, we believe that we shall also live with him:

9 Knowing that Rchrist being raised from the dead dieth no more; death hath no more dominion over him. Rev. 1:18

10 For in that he died, Rhe died Tunto sin once: but in that he liveth, Rhe liveth unto God. Heb. 9:27 · to · Luke 20:38

11 Likewise reckon ye also yourselves to be Rdead indeed unto sin, but alive unto God through Jesus Christ our Lord. v. 2

12 Rlet not sin therefore Treign in your mortal body, that ye should obey it in the Tlusts thereof. Ps. 19:13 · rule · desires

13 Neither yield ye your members as instruments of unrighteousness unto sin: but yield yourselves unto God, as those that are alive from the dead, and your members as instruments of righteousness unto God.

14 For Rsin shall not Thave dominion over

you: for ye are not under the law, but under grace. [7:4, 6; 8:2; Gal. 5:18] • *rule*

Believer's Death to Sin in Practice

15 What then? shall we sin, because we are not ᴿunder the law, but under grace? ᵀGod forbid. 1 Cor. 9:21 • *by no means*

16 Know ye not, that to whom ye yield yourselves servants to obey, his servants ye are to whom ye obey; whether of sin unto death, or of obedience unto righteousness?

17 But God be thanked, that ye were the servants of sin, but ye have obeyed from the heart that form of doctrine ᵀwhich was delivered you. *whereunto ye were delivered*

18 Being then made free from sin, ye became the servants of righteousness.

19 I speak after the manner of men because of the infirmity of your flesh: for as ye have yielded your members servants to uncleanness and to iniquity unto iniquity; even so now yield your members servants to righteousness unto ᵀholiness. *sanctification*

20 For when ye were ᴿthe servants of sin, ye were free from righteousness. John 8:34

21 ᴿWhat fruit had ye then in those things whereof ye are now ashamed? for the end of those things *is* death. 7:5

22 But now ᴿbeing ᵀmade free from sin, and become servants to God, ye have your fruit unto holiness, and the end everlasting life. [John 8:32] • *having nothing to do with sin*

23 For ᴿthe wages of sin *is* death; but ᴿthe gift of God *is* eternal life through Jesus Christ our Lord. Gen. 2:17 • 2:7; 1 Pet. 1:4

CHAPTER 7

Dead to the Law but Alive to God

KNOW ye not, brethren, (for I speak to them that know the law,) how that the law ᵀhath dominion over a man as long as he liveth? *is in force over*

2 For the woman which hath an husband is bound by the law to *her* husband so long as he liveth; but if the husband be dead, she is loosed from the law of *her* husband.

3 So then ᴿif, while *her* husband liveth, she be ᵀmarried to another man, she shall be called an adulteress: but if her husband be dead, she is free from that law; so that she is no adulteress, though she be married to another man. [Matt. 5:32] • *joined*

4 Wherefore, my brethren, ye also are become dead to the law by the body of Christ; that ye should be married to another, *even* to him who is raised from the dead, that we should bring forth fruit unto God.

5 For when we were in the flesh, the ᵀmotions of sins, which were by the law, ᴿdid work in our members ᴿto bring forth fruit unto death. *desires* • 6:13 • James 1:15

6 But now we are delivered from the law, that being dead wherein we were held; that we should serve ᴿin newness of spirit, and not *in* the oldness of the letter. 2:29

Law Cannot Deliver from Sin

7 What shall we say then? *Is* the law sin? God forbid. Nay, I had not known sin, but by the law: for I had not known lust, except the law had said, THOU SHALT NOT COVET.

8 But ᴿsin, taking occasion by the commandment, ᵀwrought in me all manner of ᵀconcupiscence. For ᵀwithout the law sin *was* dead. 4:15 • *worked* • *desire* • *apart from*

9 For I was alive without the law once: but when the commandment came, sin revived, and I ᴿdied. [James 1:14, 15]

10 And the commandment, which *was* ordained to life, I found *to be* unto death.

11 For sin, taking occasion by the commandment, deceived me, and by it slew *me.*

12 Wherefore the law *is* holy, and the commandment holy, and just, and good.

13 Was then that which is good made death unto me? God forbid. But sin, that it might appear sin, working death in me by that which is good; that sin by the commandment might become exceeding sinful.

14 For we know that the law is spiritual: but I am carnal, ᴿsold under sin. 2 Kin. 17:17

15 For that which I do I ᵀallow not: for ᴿwhat I ᵀwould, that do I not; but what I hate, that do I. *do not approve* • [Gal. 5:17] • *want*

16 If then I do that which I would not, I consent unto the law that *it is* good.

17 Now then it is ᵀno more I that do it, but sin that dwelleth in me. *not really*

18 For I know that ᴿin me (that is, in my flesh,) dwelleth no good thing: for to will is present with me; but *how* to perform that which is good I find not. [Gen. 6:5; 8:21]

19 For the good that I would I do not: but the evil which I would not, that I do.

6:23 New Life: A Free Gift—You can work for sin but it is a cruel master. When it pays you off, its wage is death—separation from God forever. In stark contrast, God does not pay wages. He has a free gift to offer—eternal life. There is nothing that one can do to earn this gift. If one could earn it, it would not be a gift; it would be wages. Eternal life is just that—eternal—it never ceases. The basic concept underlying life is *union*. There are three kinds of life mentioned in the Bible: (1) physical life—union of the soul with the body; (2) spiritual life—union of the soul with God; and (3) eternal life—eternal union of the soul with God. Jesus said, "My sheep hear my voice . . . And I give unto them eternal life; and they shall never perish" (Page 1055—John 10:27, 28). The gift of God is eternal life. One receives this gift when he believes in Jesus as his own personal Saviour. Having eternal life, he will never perish.
    Now turn to Page 1177—Col. 1:22: New Life: Based on Christ's Death.

20 Now if I do that I would not, it is no more I that do it, but sin that dwelleth in me.

21 I find then a law, that, when I would do good, evil is present with me.

22 For I ᴿdelight in the law of God after ᴿthe inward man: Ps. 1:2 • [Eph. 3:16; Col. 3:9, 10]

23 But ᴿI see another law in my members, warring against the law of my mind, and bringing me into captivity to the law of sin which is in my members.   [Gal. 5:17]

24 O wretched man that I am! who shall deliver me from the body of this death?

25 ᴿI thank God through Jesus Christ our Lord. So then with the mind I myself serve the law of God; but with the flesh the law of sin.   1 Cor. 15:57

CHAPTER 8

The Spirit Delivers from the Power of the Flesh

*T*HERE is therefore now no condemnation to them which are in Christ Jesus, who walk not after the flesh, but after the Spirit.

2 For the law of the ᴿthe Spirit of life in Christ Jesus hath made me free from ᴿthe law of sin and death.   [1 Cor. 15:45] • 7:24, 25

3 For what the law could not do, in that it was weak through the flesh, God sending his own Son in the likeness of sinful flesh, and for sin, condemned sin in the flesh:

4 That the ᵀrighteousness of the law might be fulfilled in us, ᴿwho walk not after the flesh, but after the Spirit.   ordinance • v. 1

5 For they that are after the flesh do mind the things of the flesh; but they that are after the Spirit the things of the Spirit.

6 For to be carnally minded *is* death; but to be spiritually minded *is* life and peace.

7 Because ᴿthe carnal mind *is* enmity against God: for it is not subject to the law of God, neither indeed can be.   James 4:4

8 So then they that are ᵀin the flesh cannot please God.   obey their human nature

9 But ye are not in the flesh, but in the Spirit, if so be that the Spirit of God dwell in you. Now if any man have not ᴿthe Spirit of Christ, he is none of his.   John 3:34

10 And ᴿif Christ *be* in you, the body *is* dead because of sin; but the ᵀSpirit *is* life because of righteousness.   Gal. 2:20 • spirit

11 But if the Spirit of him that raised up Jesus from the dead dwell in you, he that raised up Christ from the dead shall also quicken your mortal bodies ᵀby his Spirit that dwelleth in you.   because of his Spirit

The Spirit Gives Sonship

12 Therefore, brethren, we are debtors, not to the flesh, to live after the flesh.

13 For if ye live after the flesh, ye shall die: but if ye through the Spirit do mortify the deeds of the body, ye shall live.

14 For ᴿas many as are led by the Spirit of God, they are the sons of God.   [Gal. 5:18]

15 For ᴿye have not received the spirit of bondage again to fear; but ye have received the Spirit of adoption, whereby we cry, ᴿAb'-ba, Father.   [1 Cor. 2:12] • Mark 14:36

16 The Spirit itself beareth witness with our spirit, that we are the children of God:

17 And if children, then heirs; ᴿheirs of God, and joint-heirs with Christ; ᴿif so be that we suffer with *him*, that we may be also glorified together.   Acts 26:18 • Phil. 1:29

The Spirit Assures of Future Glory

18 For I reckon that ᴿthe sufferings of this present time *are* not worthy *to be compared* with the glory which shall be revealed in us.   2 Cor. 4:17; [1 Pet. 1:6]

19 For ᴿthe ᵀearnest expectation of the creature waiteth for the manifestation of the sons of God.   [2 Pet. 3:13] • eager hope

20 For the creature was made subject to vanity, not willingly, but by reason of him who hath subjected *the same* in hope,

---

8:15 God the Father of Believers—God is the Father of all who believe in Christ in a special sense not shared by unbelievers. God is called their Father, first of all, because they have a new standing before Him. While unbelievers are the offspring of God because He created them (Page 1092—Acts 17:28, 29), they do not have the standing of sons. Their standing is rather as condemned sinners before God the Judge (Page 1044—John 3:18; Page 1281—Rev. 20:11). When a person believes in Christ as Saviour, his estate is wonderfully changed from grim condemnation to privileged sonship. This new standing grants to all believers the legal right and spiritual privileges of divine sonship: "heirs of God, and joint-heirs with Christ" (Page 1114—Rom. 8:17).

God is the Father of believers also in the sense that He gives them new life (Page 1044—John 3:3). This relationship then is a family one involving many of the same realities that exist between an earthly father and child: birth of the child (Page 1044—John 3:3); partaking of the father's nature (Page 1243—2 Pet. 1:4); the father's care for the child (Page 947—Matt. 6:32, 33; 7:9–11); and the father's discipline of the child (Page 1223—Heb. 12:6–8). Furthermore, this new Father-child relationship carries with it new brothers and sisters (Page 1223—Heb. 13:1).

To obtain God as Father is not a result of one's own merit but a result of Christ's. The one who believes in Christ as Saviour enters into the blessed Father-child relationship with God solely on the grounds of Christ's sonship (Page 1114—Rom. 8:17; Page 1216—Heb. 2:17). It is the grand privilege and calling of those who know God as Father to graciously invite unbelievers to meet God as Father and not as Judge.

Now turn to Page 665—Is. 9:6: The Person of the Son of God.

21 Because the ᵀcreature itself also shall be delivered from the bondage of ᵀcorruption into the glorious liberty of the children of God.   *creation · decay in death*

22 For we know that ᵀthe whole creation ᴿgroaneth and ᵀtravaileth in pain together until now.   *every creature · Jer. 12:11 · suffers*

23 And not only *they*, but ourselves also, which have the firstfruits of the Spirit, even we ourselves groan within ourselves, ᴿwaiting for the adoption, *to wit*, the ᴿredemption of our body.   [Luke 20:36] · Eph. 4:30

24 For we are saved by hope: but ᴿhope that is seen is not hope: for what a man seeth, why doth he yet hope for?   2 Cor. 5:7

25 ᴿBut if we hope for that we see not, *then* do we with patience wait for *it*.   *v. 24*

26 Likewise the Spirit also helpeth our infirmities: for we know not what we should pray for as we ought: but the Spirit itself maketh intercession for us with groanings which cannot be uttered.

27 And he that searcheth the hearts knoweth what *is* the mind of the Spirit, ᵀbecause he maketh intercession for the saints according to *the will of* God.   *that*

28 And we know that all things work together for good to them that love God, to them ᴿwho are the called according to *his* purpose.   [9:11, 23, 24]; 2 Tim. 1:9

29 For whom ᴿhe did foreknow, he also did predestinate *to be* conformed to the image of his Son, that he might be the firstborn among many brethren.   2 Tim. 2:19

30 Moreover whom he did predestinate, them he also called: and whom he called, them he also justified: and whom he justified, them he also ᴿglorified.   John 17:22

The Spirit Assures of Final Victory

31 What shall we then say to these things? If God *be* for us, who *can be* against us?

32 He that spared not his own Son, but delivered him up for us all, how shall he not with him also freely give us all things?

33 Who shall lay any thing to the charge of God's elect? *It is* God that justifieth.

34 Who *is* he that condemneth? *It is* Christ that died, yea rather, that is risen again, who is even at the right hand of God, who also maketh intercession for us.

35 Who shall separate us from the love of Christ? *shall* ᵀtribulation, or distress, or persecution, or famine, or nakedness, or peril, or ᵀsword?   *trouble · war*

36 As it is written, FOR THY SAKE WE ARE KILLED ALL THE DAY LONG; WE ARE ACCOUNTED AS SHEEP FOR THE SLAUGHTER.

37 Nay, in all these things we are more than conquerors through him that loved us.

38 For I am persuaded, that neither death, nor life, nor angels, nor ᴿprincipalities, nor powers, nor things present, nor things to come,   [Eph. 1:21]

39 Nor height, nor depth, nor any other creature, shall be able to separate us from the love of God, which is in Christ Jesus our Lord.

CHAPTER 9

Paul's Sorrow

I SAY the truth in Christ, I lie not, my conscience also bearing me witness in the Holy Ghost,

2 ᴿThat I have great ᵀheaviness and continual sorrow in my heart.   10:1 · *burden*

3 For I could wish that myself were ᵀaccursed from Christ for my brethren, my kinsmen according to the flesh: *separated*

4 Who are Israelites; to whom *pertaineth* the adoption, and the glory, and the covenants, and the giving of the law, and the service *of God*, and the promises;

5 Whose *are* the fathers, and of whom as concerning the flesh Christ *came*, who is over all, God blessed for ever. A-men'.

God's Sovereignty

6 ᴿNot as though the word of God hath taken none effect. For ᴿthey *are* not all Israel, which are of Israel: [2:28, 29] · [Gal. 6:16]

7 ᴿNeither, because they are the seed of Abraham, *are they* all children: but, IN ISAAC SHALL THY SEED BE CALLED.   [Gal. 4:23]

8 That is, They which are the children of the flesh, these *are* not the children of God: but ᴿthe children of the promise are ᵀcounted for the seed.   Gal. 4:28 · *reckoned for a*

9 For this *is* the word of promise, ᴿAT THIS ᵀTIME WILL I COME, AND SARAH SHALL HAVE A SON.   Gen. 18:10 · *the right time*

10 And not only *this*; but when ᴿRebecca also had conceived by one, *even* by our father Isaac;   Gen. 25:21

11 (For *the children* being not yet born, neither having done any good or evil, that the purpose of God according to election might stand, not of works, but of him that calleth;)

12 It was said unto her, ᴿTHE ELDER SHALL SERVE THE YOUNGER.   Gen. 25:23

13 As it is written, ᴿJACOB HAVE I LOVED, BUT ESAU HAVE I ᵀHATED.   Mal. 1:2, 3 · *loved less*

14 What shall we say then? *Is there* unrighteousness with God? God forbid.

15 For he saith to Moses, ᴿI WILL HAVE MERCY ON WHOM I WILL HAVE MERCY, AND I WILL HAVE COMPASSION ON WHOM I WILL HAVE COMPASSION.   Ex. 33:19

16 So then *it is* not ᵀof him that willeth, nor of him that runneth, but of God that sheweth mercy.   *what man wants or does*

17 For the scripture saith unto Pharaoh, EVEN FOR THIS SAME PURPOSE HAVE I RAISED

THEE UP, THAT I MIGHT SHEW MY POWER IN THEE, AND THAT MY NAME MIGHT BE DECLARED THROUGHOUT ALL THE EARTH.

18 Therefore hath he mercy on whom he will *have mercy,* and whom he will he Thardeneth.   *make stubborn*

19 Thou wilt say then unto me, Why doth he yet find fault? For Rwho hath resisted his will?   2 Chr. 20:6

20 Nay but, O man, who art thou that Trepliest against God? RShall the thing formed say to him that formed *it,* Why hast thou made me thus?   *talks back to* • Is. 29:16; 45:9

21 Hath not the potter power over the clay, of the same lump to make one vessel unto honour, and another unto dishonour?

22 *What* if God, willing to Tshew *his* wrath, and to make his power known, endured with much longsuffering the vessels of wrath fitted to destruction: *demonstrate*

23 And that he might make known the riches of his glory on the vessels of mercy, which he had afore prepared unto glory,

24 Even us, whom he hath called, not of the Jews only, but also of the Gentiles?

25 As he saith also in Ō′-sēe, RI WILL CALL THEM MY PEOPLE, WHICH WERE NOT MY PEOPLE; AND HER BELOVED, WHICH WAS NOT BELOVED.   Hos. 2:23

26 AND IT SHALL COME TO PASS, *THAT* IN THE PLACE WHERE IT WAS SAID UNTO THEM, YE *ARE* NOT MY PEOPLE; THERE SHALL THEY BE CALLED THE CHILDREN OF THE LIVING GOD.

27 E-sa′-ias also crieth concerning Israel, RTHOUGH THE NUMBER OF THE CHILDREN OF ISRAEL BE AS THE SAND OF THE SEA, A REMNANT SHALL BE SAVED: Is. 10:22

28 RFOR HE WILL FINISH TTHE WORK, AND CUT *IT* SHORT IN RIGHTEOUSNESS: BECAUSE A SHORT WORK WILL THE LORD MAKE UPON THE EARTH.   Is. 10:23 • *the account*

29 And as E-sa′-ias said before, REXCEPT THE LORD OF SA-BA′-OTH HAD LEFT US A SEED, WE HAD BEEN AS SOD′-O-MA, AND BEEN MADE LIKE UNTO GO-MOR′-RHA.   Is. 1:9

Israel Seeks Righteousness by Works

30 What shall we say then? That the Gentiles, which followed not after righteousness, have attained to righteousness, even the righteousness which is of faith.

31 But Israel, Rwhich followed after the law of righteousness, Rhath not attained to the law of righteousness.   [10:2–4] • [Gal. 5:4]

32 TWherefore? Because *they sought it* not by faith, but as it were by the works of the law. For Rthey stumbled at that stumblingstone;   *why?* • Is. 8:14, 15; [Luke 2:34; 1 Cor. 1:23] ★

33 As it is written, RBEHOLD, I LAY IN SI′-ON A STUMBLINGSTONE AND ROCK OF OFFENCE: AND WHOSOEVER BELIEVETH ON HIM SHALL NOT BE ASHAMED.   Ps. 118:22; Is. 28:16 ★

CHAPTER 10

Israel Rejects Christ

BRETHREN, Rmy heart's desire and prayer to God for TIsrael is, that they might be saved.   [Matt. 9:38] • *my own people*

2 For I bear them record Rthat they have a Tzeal of God, but not according to knowledge.   Acts 21:20; Gal. 1:14 • *devotion*

3 For they being ignorant of God's righteousness, and going about to establish their own righteousness, have not submitted themselves unto the righteousness of God.

4 For Christ *is* the end of the law for righteousness to every one that believeth.

5 For Moses describeth the righteousness which is of the law, THAT THE MAN WHICH DOETH THOSE THINGS SHALL LIVE BY THEM.

6 But the righteousness which is of faith speaketh on this wise, SAY NOT IN THINE HEART, WHO SHALL ASCEND INTO HEAVEN? (that is, to bring Christ down *from above:*)

7 Or, WHO SHALL DESCEND INTO THE RDEEP? (that is, to bring up Christ again from the dead.)   Luke 8:31

8 But what saith it? THE WORD IS NIGH THEE, *EVEN* IN THY MOUTH, AND IN THY HEART: that is, the word of faith, which we preach;

9 That Rif thou shalt confess with thy mouth the Lord Jesus, and shalt believe in thine heart that God hath raised him from the dead, thou shalt be saved.   Acts 8:37

10 For with the heart man believeth unto righteousness; and with the mouth confession is made unto salvation.

11 For the scripture saith, WHOSOEVER BELIEVETH ON HIM SHALL NOT BE ASHAMED.

12 For there is no difference between the Jew and the Greek: for the same Lord over all is rich unto all that call upon him.

13 RFor WHOSOEVER SHALL CALL UPON THE NAME OF THE LORD SHALL BE SAVED.   Joel 2:32

14 How then shall they call on him in whom they have not believed? and how shall they believe in him of whom they have not heard? and how shall they hear Rwithout a preacher?   Titus 1:3

15 And how shall they preach, except they be sent? as it is written, HOW BEAUTIFUL ARE THE FEET OF THEM THAT PREACH THE GOSPEL OF PEACE, AND BRING GLAD TIDINGS OF GOOD THINGS!

Israel Rejects the Prophets

16 But they have not all obeyed the gospel. For E-sa′-ias saith, RLORD, WHO HATH BELIEVED OUR TREPORT?   Is. 53:1; John 12:38 ★ ★ • *message*

17 RSo then faith *cometh* by hearing, and hearing by the word of TGod.   Acts 15:7 • *Christ*

18 But I say, Have they not heard? Yes verily, THEIR SOUND WENT INTO ALL THE EARTH, AND THEIR WORDS UNTO THE ENDS OF THE WORLD.

19 But I say, Did not Israel know? First Moses saith, I WILL PROVOKE YOU TO JEALOUSY BY *THEM THAT ARE* NO PEOPLE, *AND BY* A FOOLISH NATION I WILL ANGER YOU.

20 But E-sa'-ias is very bold, and saith, [R]I WAS FOUND OF THEM THAT SOUGHT ME NOT; I WAS MADE [T]MANIFEST UNTO THEM THAT ASKED NOT AFTER ME.   Is. 65:1 • *known*

21 But to Israel he saith, [R]ALL DAY LONG I HAVE STRETCHED FORTH MY HANDS UNTO A DISOBEDIENT AND GAINSAYING PEOPLE. Is. 65:2

CHAPTER 11

Israel's Rejection Is Not Total

I SAY then, Hath God cast away his people? [T]God forbid. For I also am an Israelite, of the seed of Abraham, *of* the tribe of Benjamin.   *by no means!*

2 God hath not cast away his people which he foreknew. Wot ye not what the scripture saith of E-li'-as? how he maketh intercession to God against Israel, saying,

3 LORD, THEY HAVE KILLED THY PROPHETS, AND DIGGED DOWN THINE ALTARS; AND I AM LEFT ALONE, AND THEY SEEK MY LIFE.

4 But what saith the answer of God unto him? [R]I HAVE RESERVED TO MYSELF SEVEN THOUSAND MEN, WHO HAVE NOT BOWED THE KNEE TO *THE IMAGE OF* BA'-AL.   1 Kin. 19:18

5 [R]Even so then at this present time also there is a [T]remnant according to the election of grace.   9:27 • *small number*

6 And if by grace, then *is it* no more of works: otherwise grace is no more grace. But if *it be* of works, then is it no more grace: otherwise work is no more work.

7 What then? Israel hath not obtained that which he seeketh for; but the election hath obtained it, and the rest were blinded

8 (According as it is written, GOD HATH GIVEN THEM THE SPIRIT OF SLUMBER, EYES THAT THEY SHOULD NOT SEE, AND EARS THAT THEY SHOULD NOT HEAR;) UNTO THIS DAY.

9 And David saith, LET THEIR TABLE BE MADE A SNARE, AND A TRAP, AND A STUMBLINGBLOCK, AND A RECOMPENCE UNTO THEM:

10 [R]LET THEIR EYES BE DARKENED, THAT THEY MAY NOT SEE, AND BOW DOWN THEIR BACK ALWAY.   Ps. 69:22, 23 *

Purpose of Israel's Rejection

11 I say then, Have they stumbled that they should fall? God forbid: but *rather* through their fall salvation *is come* unto the Gentiles, for to provoke them to jealousy.

12 Now if the fall of them *be* the riches of the world, and the diminishing of them [R]the riches of the Gentiles; how much more their fulness?   Is. 8:14, 15; Hos. 1:10; 2:23 *

13 For I speak to you Gentiles, inasmuch as I am the apostle of the Gentiles, I [T]magnify mine office: *glorify my ministry*

14 If by any means I may provoke to [T]emulation *them which are* my flesh, and [R]might save some of them.   *jealousy* • 1 Cor. 9:22

15 For if the casting away of them *be* the reconciling of the world, what *shall* the receiving *of them be*, but life from the dead?

16 For if [R]the firstfruit *be* holy, the lump *is* also *holy*: and if the root *be* holy, so *are* the branches.   Lev. 23:10; [James 1:18]

17 And if some of the branches be broken off, [R]and thou, being a wild olive tree, wert graffed in among them, and with them partakest of the root and [T]fatness of the olive tree;   [Eph. 2:12] • *strength*

18 [R]Boast not against the branches. But if thou boast, thou [T]bearest not the root, but the root thee.   [1 Cor. 10:12] • *dost not support*

19 Thou wilt say then, The branches were broken off, that I might be graffed in.

20 Well; because of unbelief they were broken off, and thou standest by faith. Be not [T]highminded, but [T]fear: *proud • be humble*

21 For if God spared not the [T]natural branches, [T]take heed lest he also spare not thee.   *Jews • neither will he spare*

22 Behold therefore the goodness and severity of God: on them which fell, severity; but toward thee, goodness, if thou continue in *his* goodness: otherwise [R]thou also shalt be [T]cut off.   [John 15:2] • *rejected*

23 And they also, [R]if they abide not still in unbelief, shall be graffed in: for God is able to graff them in again.   [2 Cor. 3:16]

24 For if thou [T]wert cut out of the olive tree which is wild by nature, and wert graffed contrary to nature into a good olive tree: how [T]much more shall these, which be the natural *branches*, be graffed into their own olive tree?   *were • easier*

Promise of Israel's Restoration

25 For I would not, brethren, that ye should be ignorant of this mystery, lest ye should be wise in your own [T]conceits; that [R]blindness[T] in part is happened to Israel, [R]until the fulness of the Gentiles be come in.   *proud ideas* • 2 Cor. 3:14 • *hardness* • Luke 21:24

26 And [T]so all Israel shall be saved: as it is written, [R]THERE SHALL COME OUT OF SI'-ON THE DELIVERER, AND SHALL TURN AWAY UNGODLINESS FROM JACOB: *in this manner* • Is. 59:20

27 FOR THIS *IS* MY COVENANT UNTO THEM, WHEN I SHALL TAKE AWAY THEIR SINS.

28 As concerning the gospel, *they are* enemies for your sakes: but [T]as touching the election, *they are* [R]beloved for the fathers' sakes.   *insofar as this concerns* • Deut. 7:8

29 For the gifts and [R]calling of God *are* without repentance.   [Eph. 1:18; 4:14]

30 For as ye [R]in times past have not [T]believed God, yet have now [T]obtained mercy through their unbelief: [Eph. 2:2] · *obeyed* · *received*

31 Even so have these also now not [T]believed, that through your mercy they also may obtain mercy.   *obeyed*

32 [R]For God hath [T]concluded them all in unbelief, that he might have mercy upon all.   3:9; [Gal. 3:22] · *shut them all up together*

Israel's Restoration:
The Occasion for Glorifying God

33 [R]O the depth of the riches both of the wisdom and knowledge of God! [T]how unsearchable *are* his judgments, and his ways past finding out!   Ps. 36:6; 92:5 · *who can explain*

34 FOR WHO HATH KNOWN THE MIND OF THE LORD? OR WHO HATH BEEN HIS COUNSELLOR?

35 OR WHO HATH FIRST GIVEN TO HIM, AND IT SHALL BE RECOMPENSED UNTO HIM AGAIN?

36 For [R]of him, and through him, and to him, *are* all things: [R]to [T]whom *be* glory for ever. A-men'.   Col. 1:16 · Heb. 13:21 · *him*

CHAPTER 12

Responsibilities Toward God

I BESEECH you therefore, brethren, by the mercies of God, that ye present your bodies a living sacrifice, holy, acceptable unto God, *which is* your reasonable service.

2 And be not conformed to this world: but be ye transformed by the renewing of your mind, that ye may prove what *is* that good, and acceptable, and perfect, will of God.

Responsibilities Toward Society

3 For I say, through the grace given unto me, to every man that is among you, [R]not to think *of himself* more highly than he ought to think; but to think soberly, according as God hath dealt [R]to every man the measure of faith.   Prov. 25:27 · [Eph. 4:7]

4 For [R]as we have many [T]members in one body, and all members have not the same office: 1 Cor. 12:12 · *parts*

5 So [R]we, *being* many, are one body in Christ, and every one members one of another.   [1 Cor. 10:17; 12:20]

6 Having then gifts differing according to the grace that is given to us, whether [R]prophecy, *let us prophesy* according to the proportion of faith;   Acts 11:27

7 Or ministry, *let us wait* on *our* ministering: or he that teacheth, on teaching;

8 Or he that exhorteth, on exhortation: he that giveth, *let him do it* with simplicity; he that ruleth, with diligence; he that sheweth mercy, with cheerfulness.

9 *Let* love be without [T]dissimulation. [R]Abhor that which is evil; [T]cleave to that which is good.   *hypocrisy* · Ps. 34:14 · *hold fast*

10 [R]Be kindly affectioned one to another with brotherly love; [R]in honour preferring one another;   Heb. 13:1 · Phil. 2:3

11 Not [T]slothful in business; fervent in spirit; serving the Lord;   *lazy*

12 Rejoicing in hope; patient in tribulation; continuing instant in prayer;

13 [T]Distributing to the [T]necessity of saints; given to hospitality.   *giving* · *needs*

14 [T]Bless[R] them which persecute you: bless, and curse not.   *ask God to bless* · [Matt. 5:44]

15 [R]Rejoice with them that do rejoice, and weep with them that weep.   [1 Cor. 12:26]

16 [R]Be of the same mind one toward another. Mind not high things, but condescend to men of low estate. Be not wise in your own [T]conceits.   [Phil. 2:2] · *proud notions*

17 [R]Recompense[T] to no man evil for evil. [R]Provide things honest in the sight of all men.   [Matt. 5:39] · *pay back* · 2 Cor. 8:21

12:1 Walking in the Spirit: Yielding—Confession of sin in itself is not enough to enable the believer to automatically walk in the Spirit. He must then become a yielded instrument for God's service. What is to be yielded is simply himself (Page 1112—Rom. 6:13; Page 1230—James 4:7). This involves both the body (Rom. 12:1; Page 1130—1 Cor. 6:20) and the mind (Rom. 12:2), since it is with the body that actions conceived in the mind are carried out and with the mind that they are formulated. Stated another way, that which is conceived in the mind is carried out in the body; thus, one's whole being must be presented by a decisive act of the will to God for His service. Yielding must not be thought of simply as a willingness to do some specific thing. Rather, it consists of dedication by a person to do whatever God commands.

Yielding leads not only to dedication but also can result in separation: "Be not conformed to this world" (Rom. 12:2). Since the world is resolutely opposed to God, one cannot revel in its lusts and at the same time do the will of God (Page 1250—1 John 2:15-17). The same word translated "conformed" here is translated "fashioning" in First Peter 1:14. So the concept of separation involves being "unfashionable" in spirit, thought, values, and actions according to the world's standards.

Finally, yielding includes transformation of the mind. This work is said to be accomplished through a lifetime of "renewing" the mind. Man's mind has been darkened by sin (Page 1114—Rom. 8:7; Page 1177—Col. 1:21) and must be brought to the place where it thinks as God thinks (Page 1165—Eph. 4:23). This renewing is said to come especially through prayer to God in everything (Page 1172—Phil. 4:6, 7) and through constant meditation on the Word of God (Page 599—Ps. 119:1). This transformation is a lifelong process that will not be completed until we are with Christ (Page 1170—Phil. 1:6; Page 1251—1 John 3:2). Along life's way, however, it brings a peace and delight that can only come from having embraced the mind of Christ.

Now turn to Page 1165—Eph. 5:18: Walking in the Spirit: Filling.

18 If it be possible, as much as lieth in you, live peaceably with all men.

19 Dearly beloved, avenge not yourselves, but *rather* ᵀgive place unto wrath: for it is written, ᴿVENGEANCE *IS* MINE; I WILL REPAY, saith the Lord.   *give in so far as anger goes* · Deut. 32:35

20 ᴿTHEREFORE IF THINE ENEMY HUNGER, FEED HIM; IF HE THIRST, GIVE HIM DRINK: FOR IN SO DOING THOU SHALT HEAP COALS OF FIRE ON HIS HEAD.   Prov. 25:21, 22; [Matt. 5:44]

21 Be not overcome of evil, but ᵀovercome evil with good.   *conquer*

CHAPTER 13

Responsibilites Toward Higher Powers

L ET every soul be subject unto the ᵀhigher powers. ᴿFor there is no power but of God: the powers that be are ᵀordained of God.   *state authorities* · [Acts 5:29] · *commissioned*

2 Whosoever therefore resisteth ᴿthe power, resisteth the ordinance of God: and they that resist shall receive to themselves ᵀdamnation.   [Titus 3:1] · *judgment*

3 For rulers are not a terror to good works, but to the evil. Wilt thou then not be afraid of the power? do that which is good, and thou shalt have praise of the same:

4 For he is the minister of God to thee for good. But if thou do that which is evil, be afraid; for he beareth not the sword in vain: for he is the minister of God, a revenger to *execute* wrath upon him that doeth evil.

5 Wherefore ᴿye must needs be subject, not only for wrath, ᴿbut also for conscience sake.   Eccl. 8:2 · [1 Pet. 2:19]

6 For for this cause pay ye ᵀtribute also: for they are God's ministers, attending continually upon this very thing.   *taxes*

7 ᴿRender therefore to all their dues: tribute to whom tribute *is due;* custom to whom custom; fear to whom fear; honour to whom honour.   Matt. 22:21; Luke 20:25

Responsibilities Toward Neighbours

8 Owe no man any thing, but to love ᵀone another: for ᴿhe that loveth another hath fulfilled the law.   *his neighbour* · [Gal. 5:14; 1 Tim. 1:5]

9 For this, THOU SHALT NOT COMMIT ADULTERY, THOU SHALT NOT KILL, THOU SHALT NOT STEAL, THOU SHALT NOT BEAR FALSE WITNESS, THOU SHALT NOT COVET; and if *there* be any other commandment, it is briefly comprehended in this saying, namely, THOU SHALT LOVE THY NEIGHBOUR AS THYSELF.

10 Love worketh no ill to his neighbour: therefore love *is* the fulfilling of the law.

11 And that, knowing the time, that now *it* is high time ᴿto awake out of sleep: for now *is* our salvation nearer than when we believed.   [1 Cor. 15:34; Eph. 5:14]

12 The night is ᵀfar spent, the day is at hand: ᴿlet us therefore cast off the works of darkness, and ᴿlet us put on the armour of light.   *nearly over* · [Eph. 5:11] · [Eph. 6:13]

13 ᴿLet us walk ᵀhonestly, as in the day; not in rioting and drunkenness, ᴿnot in chambering and wantonness, ᴿnot in strife and envying. Phil. 4:8 · *decently* · [1 Cor. 6:9] · James 3:14

14 But put ye on the Lord Jesus Christ, and ᴿmake not provision for the flesh, to *fulfil* the ᵀlusts *thereof.*   Gal. 3:27 · *desires*

CHAPTER 14

Principles of Christian Liberty

H IM that is weak in the faith receive ye, *but* not to doubtful disputations.

2 For one believeth that he may eat all things: another, who is weak, eateth herbs.

3 Let not him that eateth ᵀdespise him that eateth not; and ᴿlet not him which eateth not judge him that eateth: for God hath received him.   *belittle* · [Col. 2:16]

4 Who art thou that judgest another man's servant? to his own master he standeth or falleth. Yea, he shall be ᵀholden up: for God is able to make him stand.   *helped*

5 ᴿOne man esteemeth one day above another: another esteemeth every day *alike.* Let every man be ᵀfully persuaded in his own mind.   Gal. 4:10 · *fully assured*

6 He that regardeth the day, regardeth *it* unto the Lord; and he that regardeth not the day, to the Lord he doth not regard *it.* He that eateth, eateth to the Lord, for he giveth God

---

13:1–4 The Function of Human Government—The general function of human government, as instituted by God, may be said to be threefold: to protect, punish, and promote.
a. The Function of Protection: The moment Adam sinned it was obvious that civilizations would need some form of restraint and rule to protect citizens from themselves. An example of this function is seen in Acts 21:27–37 where Roman soldiers step in and save Paul from being murdered by his own enraged countrymen in Jerusalem.
b. The Function of Punishment: Both Paul and Peter bring this out. Paul writes that duly appointed human officials are to be regarded as God's servants to "bear the sword," that is, to impose punishment upon criminals (vv. 3, 4). Peter tells us that governors are "sent . . . for the punishment of evildoers" (Page 1236—1 Pet. 2:13, 14).
c. The Function of Promotion: Human government is to promote the general welfare of the community where its laws are in effect. Paul commands us to pray for human leaders "that we may lead a quiet and peaceable life in all godliness and honesty" (Page 1194—1 Tim. 2:1, 2).
   Now turn to Page 1236—1 Pet. 2:13: Our Responsibility to Human Government.

thanks; and he that eateth not, to the Lord he eateth not, and giveth God thanks.

7 For ᴿnone of us liveth to himself, and no man dieth to himself.   [1 Cor. 6:19; 1 Pet. 4:2]

8 ᵀFor whether we live, we ᵀlive unto the Lord; and whether we die, we die unto the Lord: whether we live therefore, or die, we are the Lord's.   *if • belong to*

9 For to this end Christ both died, and rose, and ᵀrevived, that he might be Lord both of the dead and living.   *lived again*

10 But why dost thou judge thy brother? or why dost thou ᵀset at nought thy brother? for we shall all stand before the judgment seat of Christ.   *reduce to nothing*

11 For it is written, As I LIVE, SAITH THE LORD, EVERY KNEE SHALL BOW TO ME, AND EVERY TONGUE SHALL CONFESS TO GOD.

12 So then ᴿevery one of us shall give account of himself to God.   [Gal. 6:5]; 1 Pet. 4:5

13 Let us not therefore judge one another any more: but judge this rather, that ᴿno man put a stumblingblock or an occasion to fall in *his* brother's way.   1 Cor. 8:9

14 I know, and am persuaded by the Lord Jesus, that *there is* nothing unclean of itself: but to him that esteemeth any thing to be unclean, to him *it is* unclean.

15 But if thy brother be grieved with *thy* ᵀmeat, now walkest thou ᵀnot charitably. ᴿDestroy not him with thy meat, for whom Christ died.   *menu • no longer in love • 1 Cor. 8:11*

16 ᴿLet not then your good ᵀbe evil spoken of: [12:17] • *acquire a bad name*

17 For the kingdom of God is not ᵀmeat and drink; but righteousness, and peace, and joy in the Holy Ghost.   *eating and drinking*

18 For he that in these things serveth Christ ᴿ*is*ᵀ acceptable to God, and approved of men.   2 Cor. 8:21 • *wins God's pleasure*

19 Let us therefore follow after the things which make for peace, and things wherewith one may ᵀedify another.   *build up*

20 For meat destroy not the work of God. All things indeed *are* pure; but *it is* evil for that man who eateth with offence.

21 *It is* good neither to eat ᴿflesh, nor to drink wine, nor ᵀ*any thing* whereby thy brother stumbleth, or is offended, or is made weak.   1 Cor. 8:13 • *to do anything*

22 Hast thou faith? have it to thyself before God. Happy *is* he that condemneth not himself in that thing which he alloweth.

23 And he that doubteth is ᵀdamned if he eat, because *he eateth* not of faith: for whatsoever *is* not of faith is sin.   *condemned*

CHAPTER 15

Practices of Christian Liberty

WE ᴿthen that are strong ought to bear the ᵀinfirmities of the weak, and not to please ourselves.   [Gal. 6:1] • *inabilities*

2 Let every one of us please *his* neighbour for *his* good to ᵀedification.   *his being built up*

3 For even Christ pleased not himself; but, as it is written, ᴿTHE REPROACHES OF THEM THAT REPROACHED THEE FELL ON ME. Ps. 69:9 ★

4 For ᴿwhatsoever things were written aforetime were written for our learning, that we through patience and comfort of the scriptures might have hope.   1 Cor. 10:11

5 Now the God of patience and ᵀconsolation grant you to be likeminded one toward another according to Christ Jesus: *comfort*

6 That ye may ᵀwith one mind *and* one mouth ᵀglorify God, even the Father of our Lord Jesus Christ.   *without reservation • praise*

7 Wherefore receive ye one another, as Christ also received us to the glory of God.

8 Now I say that ᴿJesus Christ was a minister ᵀof the circumcision for the truth of God, ᴿto confirm the promises *made* unto the fathers: Matt. 15:24 • *in Israel* • 2 Cor. 1:20

9 And that the Gentiles might glorify God for *his* mercy; as it is written, ᴿFOR THIS CAUSE I WILL CONFESS TO THEE AMONG THE GENTILES, AND SING UNTO THY NAME. Ps. 18:49

10 And again he saith, ᴿREJOICE, YE GENTILES, WITH HIS PEOPLE.   Deut. 32:43

11 And again, PRAISE THE LORD, ALL YE GENTILES; AND LAUD HIM, ALL YE PEOPLE.

12 And again, E-sa'-ias saith, ᴿTHERE SHALL BE A ROOT OF JESSE, AND HE THAT SHALL RISE TO REIGN OVER THE GENTILES; IN HIM SHALL THE GENTILES ᵀTRUST.   Is. 11:10 ★ • *hope*

13 Now the God of ᵀhope fill you with all ᴿjoy and peace in believing, that ye may abound in hope, through the power of the Holy Ghost.   *source of hope • 12:12*

Paul's Purpose for Writing

14 And I myself also am persuaded of you, my brethren, that ye also are full of goodness, filled with all knowledge, able also to ᵀadmonish one another.   *instruct*

15 ᴿNevertheless, brethren, I have written the more boldly unto you in some ᵀsort, as putting you in mind, because of the grace that is given to me of God,   12:3 • *measure*

16 That I should be the minister of Jesus Christ to the Gentiles, ministering the gospel of God, that the ᴿoffering up of the Gentiles might be acceptable, being sanctified by the Holy Ghost.   [Is. 66:20]

17 I have therefore whereof I may ᵀglory through Jesus Christ ᴿin those things which pertain to God.   *rejoice • Heb. 5:1*

18 For I will not dare to speak of any of those things ᴿwhich Christ hath not wrought by me, ᴿto make the Gentiles obedient, by word and deed,   Gal. 2:8 • 1:5

19 ᴿThrough mighty signs and wonders, by the power of the Spirit of God; so that from Jerusalem, and round about unto Il-lyr'-i-

cum, I have fully preached the gospel of Christ. Acts 19:11; 2 Cor. 12:12

20 Yea, so have I strived to preach the gospel, not where Christ was named, ᴿlest I should build upon another man's foundation: [2 Cor. 10:13, 15, 16]

21 But as it is written, To WHOM HE WAS NOT SPOKEN OF, THEY SHALL SEE: AND THEY THAT HAVE NOT HEARD SHALL UNDERSTAND.

Paul's Plans for Travelling

22 For which cause also ᴿI have been much hindered from coming to you. 1:13

23 But now having no more place in these parts, and ᴿhaving a great desire these many years to come unto you; Acts 19:21

24 ᴿWhensoever I take my journey into Spain, I will come to you: for I trust to see you in my journey, and to be brought on my way thitherward by you, if first I be somewhat filled with your company. v. 28

25 But now ᴿI go unto Jerusalem to ᵀminister unto the saints. Acts 19:21 · serve

26 For ᴿit hath pleased them of Mac-e-do'-ni-a and A-cha'-ia to make a certain contribution for the poor saints which are at Jerusalem. 1 Cor. 16:1, 2; 2 Cor. 8:1; 9:2, 12

27 It hath pleased them verily; and ᵀtheir debtors they are. For if the Gentiles have been made partakers of their spiritual things, their duty is also to minister unto them in carnal things. under obligation to them

28 ᴿWhen therefore I have performed this, and have sealed to them ᴿthis fruit, I will come by you into Spain. v. 24 · Phil. 4:17

29 ᴿAnd I am sure that, when I come unto you, I shall come in the fulness of the blessing of the gospel of Christ. [1:11]

30 Now I beseech you, brethren, for the Lord Jesus Christ's sake, and ᴿfor the love of the Spirit, that ye strive together with me in your prayers to God for me; Phil. 2:1

31 That I may be delivered from them that do not believe in Ju-dae'-a; and that my service which I have for Jerusalem may be ᵀaccepted of the saints; welcomed by

32 ᴿThat I may come unto you with joy ᴿby the will of God, and may with you ᴿbe refreshed. 1:10 · Acts 18:21 · 1 Cor. 16:18

33 Now ᴿthe God of peace be with you all. A-men'. [1 Thess. 5:23]; 2 Thess. 3:16; Heb. 13:20

CHAPTER 16

Paul's Praise and Greetings

I COMMEND unto you Phe'-be our sister, which is a ᵀservant of the church which is at ᴿCen'-chre-a: deaconess · Acts 18:18

2 That ye receive her in the Lord, as ᵀbecometh saints, and that ye assist her in whatsoever ᵀbusiness she hath need of you: for she hath been a ᵀsuccourer of many, and of myself also. saints should · matter · helper

3 Greet ᴿPriscilla and Aq'-ui-la my helpers in Christ Jesus: Acts 18:2, 18, 26

4 Who have for my life ᵀlaid down their own necks: unto whom not only I give thanks, but also all the churches of the Gentiles. risked their lives

5 Likewise greet ᴿthe church that is in their house. Salute my wellbeloved Ep-ae-ne'-tus, who is ᴿthe first fruits of A-cha'-ia unto Christ. 1 Cor. 16:19 · 1 Cor. 16:15

6 ᴿGreet Mary, who bestowed much labour on ᵀus. John 11:1; 19:25; Acts 12:12 · you

7 Salute An-dro-ni'-cus and Ju'-ni-a, my kinsmen, and my fellowprisoners, who are of note among the apostles, who also ᵀwere in Christ before me. had become Christians

8 Greet Am'-pli-as my ᵀbeloved in the Lord. dear friend

9 Salute Ur'-bane, our helper in Christ, and Sta'-chys my beloved.

10 Salute A-pel'-les ᵀapproved in Christ. Salute them which are of Ar-is-to-bu'-lus' ᵀhousehold. whose loyalty to Christ · family

11 Salute He-ro'-di-on my kinsman. Greet them that be of the household of Nar-cis'-sus, which are in the Lord.

12 Salute Try-phe'-na and Try-pho'-sa, who labour in the Lord. Salute the beloved Per'-sis, which laboured much in the Lord.

13 Salute Rufus chosen in the Lord, and his mother and mine.

14 Salute A-syn'-cri-tus, Phle'-gon, Her'-mas, Pat'-ro-bas, Her'-mes, and the brethren which are with them.

15 Salute Phi-lol'-o-gus, and Julia, Ne'-reus, and his sister, and O-lym'-pas, and all the saints which are with them.

16 ᵀSalute one another with an holy kiss. The churches of Christ salute you. greet

17 Now I beseech you, brethren, mark them ᴿwhich cause divisions and offences

---

16:5 Definition of the Local Church—The local church is a geographically located, temporally limited, and visibly evident manifestation of the universal church, the body of Christ. In the early New Testament days the local church met in the Jewish synagogue and had a very simple organization (Page 1229—James 2:2). A little later the church met in the homes of believers (Rom. 16:5), and it was not uncommon to have a number of churches in an area (Page 1154—Gal. 1:2). The idea of meeting in a building constructed for that exclusive purpose is a post–New Testament idea. (For a more complete discussion of the church turn to Page 1079 and read Acts 7:38 and the footnote: THE MEANING OF THE WORD CHURCH.)

Now turn to Page 1221—Heb. 10:25: The Reason for Participation in the Local Church.

contrary to the doctrine which ye have learned; and ᴿavoid them.   [Acts 15:1] • [1 Cor. 5:9]

18 For they that are such serve not our Lord Jesus Christ, but their own belly; and by good words and fair speeches deceive the hearts of the ᵀsimple.   *innocent*

19 For ᴿyour obedience is come abroad unto all *men*. I am glad therefore on your behalf: but yet I would have you ᴿwise unto that which is good, and ᵀsimple concerning evil.   1:8 • Matt. 10:16 • *harmless*

20 And the God of peace shall bruise Satan under your feet shortly. The grace of our Lord Jesus Christ *be* with you. A-men'.

21 ᴿTi-mo'-the-us my workfellow, and Lu'-cius, and Ja'-son, and ᴿSo-sip'-a-ter, my kinsmen, ᵀsalute you.   Acts 16:1 • Acts 20:4 • *greet*

22 ᴿI Ter'-tius, who wrote *this* ᵀepistle, salute you in the Lord.   1:1 • *letter*

23 ᴿGa'-ius mine host, and of the whole church, saluteth you. ᴿE-ras'tus the ᵀchamberlain of the city saluteth you, and Quar'-tus a brother.   1 Cor. 1:14 • Acts 19:22 • *treasurer*

24 ᴿThe grace of our Lord Jesus Christ *be* with you all. A-men'.   1 Thess. 5:28

25 Now to him that is of power to ᵀstablish you according to my gospel, and the preaching of Jesus Christ, according to the revelation of the mystery, which was kept secret since the world began,   *strengthen*

26 But ᴿnow is made manifest, and by the scriptures of the prophets, according to the commandment of the everlasting God, made known to all nations for ᴿthe obedience of faith: Eph. 1:9 • [Acts 6:7]

27 To ᴿGod only wise, *be* glory through Jesus Christ for ever. A-men'.   Jude 25

CORINTHIANS

THE BOOK OF FIRST CORINTHIANS

Corinth, the most important city in Greece during Paul's day, was a bustling hub of worldwide commerce, degraded culture, and idolatrous religion. There Paul founded a church (Acts 18:1–17), and two of his letters are addressed "Unto the church of God which is at Corinth."

First Corinthians reveals the problems, pressures, and struggles of a church called out of a pagan society. Paul addresses a variety of problems in the life-style of the Corinthian church: factions, lawsuits, immorality, questionable practices, abuse of the Lord's Supper, and spiritual gifts. In addition to words of discipline, Paul shares words of counsel in answer to questions raised by the Corinthian believers.

The oldest recorded title of this epistle is *Pros Korinthious A*, in effect, the "First to the Corinthians." The *A* was no doubt a later addition to distinguish this book from Second Corinthians.

THE AUTHOR OF FIRST CORINTHIANS

Pauline authorship of First Corinthians is almost universally accepted. Instances of this widely held belief can be found as early as A.D. 95, when Clement of Rome wrote to the Corinthian church and cited this epistle in regard to their continuing problem of factions among themselves.

THE TIME OF FIRST CORINTHIANS

Corinth was a key city in ancient Greece until it was destroyed by the Romans in 146 B.C. Julius Caesar rebuilt it as a Roman colony in 46 B.C. and it grew and prospered, becoming the capital of the province of Achaia. Its official language was Latin, but the common language remained Greek. In Paul's day Corinth was the metropolis of the Peloponnesus, since it was strategically located on a narrow isthmus between the Aegean Sea and the Adriatic Sea that connects the Peloponnesus with northern Greece. Because of its two seaports it became a commercial center, and many small ships were rolled or dragged across the Corinthian isthmus to avoid the dangerous 200-mile voyage around southern Greece. Nero and others attempted to build a canal at the narrowest point, but this was not achieved until 1893. The city was filled with shrines and temples, but the most prominent was the Temple of Aphrodite on top of a 1,800-foot promontory called the Acrocorinthus. Worshipers of the "goddess of love" made free use of the 1,000 Hieroduli (consecrated prostitutes). This cosmopolitan center thrived on commerce,

entertainment, vice, and corruption; pleasure-seekers came there to spend money on a holiday from morality. Corinth became so notorious for its evils that the term *Korinthiazomai* ("to act like a Corinthian") became a synonym for debauchery and prostitution.

In Paul's day the population of Corinth was approximately 700,000, about two-thirds of whom were slaves. The diverse population produced no philosophers, but Greek philosophy influenced any speculative thought that was there. In spite of these obstacles to the gospel, Paul was able to establish a church in Corinth on his second missionary journey (3:6, 10; 4:15; Acts 18:1–7). Persecution in Macedonia drove him south to Athens, and from there he proceeded to Corinth. He made tents with Aquila and Priscilla and reasoned with the Jews in the synagogue. Silas and Timothy joined him (they evidently brought a gift from Philippi; 2 Cor. 11:8, 9; Phil. 4:15), and Paul began to devote all his time to spreading the gospel. Paul wrote First and Second Thessalonians, moved his ministry from the synagogue to the house of Justus because of opposition, and converted Crispus, the leader of the synagogue. Paul taught the Word of God in Corinth for eighteen months in A.D. 51 and 52. After Paul's departure, Apollos came from Ephesus to minister in the Corinthian church (3:6; Acts 18:24–28).

When Paul was teaching and preaching in Ephesus during his third missionary journey, he was disturbed by reports from the household of Chloe concerning quarrels in the church at Corinth (1:11). The church sent a delegation of three men (16:17), who apparently brought a letter that requested Paul's judgment on certain issues (7:1). Paul wrote this epistle as his response to the problems and questions of the Corinthians (he had already written a previous letter; 5:9). It may be that the men who came from Corinth took this letter back with them. Paul was planning to leave Ephesus (16:5–8), indicating that First Corinthians was written in A.D. 56.

THE CHRIST OF FIRST CORINTHIANS

This book proclaims the relevance of Christ Jesus to every area of the believer's life. He "is made unto us wisdom, and righteousness, and sanctification, and redemption" (1:30), and these are the themes Paul addresses in this epistle.

KEYS TO FIRST CORINTHIANS

Key Word: Correction of Carnal Living—The basic theme of this epistle is the application of Christian principles to carnality in the individual as well as in the church. The cross

of Christ is a message that is designed to transform the lives of believers and make them different as people and as a corporate body from the surrounding world. However, the Corinthians are destroying their Christian testimony because of immorality and disunity. Paul writes this letter as his corrective response to the news of problems and disorders among the Corinthians. It is designed to refute improper attitudes and conduct and to promote a spirit of unity among the brethren in their relationships and worship. Paul's concern as their spiritual father (4:14, 15) is tempered with love, and he wants to avoid visiting them "with a rod" (4:21).

Key Verses: First Corinthians 6:19, 20 and 10:12, 13—"What? know ye not that your body is the temple of the Holy Ghost *which is* in you, which ye have of God, and ye are not your own? For ye are bought with a price: therefore glorify God in your body, and in your spirit, which are God's" (6:19, 20).

"Wherefore let him that thinketh he standeth take heed lest he fall. There hath no temptation taken you but such as is common to man: but God *is* faithful, who will not suffer you to be tempted above that ye are able; but will with the temptation also make a way to escape, that ye may be able to bear *it*" (10:12, 13).

Key Chapter: First Corinthians 13—Read at weddings and often the text for sermons, First Corinthians 13 has won the hearts of people across the world as the best definition of "love" ever penned. Standing in stark contrast to the idea that love is an emotion, that one can fall into or fall out of love, this chapter clearly reveals that true love is primarily an action. This is why when "God so loved the world, that he gave" (John 3:16).

SURVEY OF FIRST CORINTHIANS
Through the missionary efforts of Paul and others, the church has been established in Corinth, but Paul finds it very difficult to

keep Corinth out of the church. The pagan lifestyle of Corinth exerts a profound influence upon the Christians in that corrupt city—problems of every kind plague them. In this disciplinary letter, Paul is forced to exercise his apostolic authority as he deals firmly with problems of divisiveness, immorality, lawsuits, selfishness, abuses of the Lord's Supper and spiritual gifts, and denials of the Resurrection. This epistle is quite orderly in its approach as it sequentially addresses a group of problems that have come to Paul's attention. Paul also gives a series of perspectives on various questions and issues raised by the Corinthians in a letter. He uses the introductory words "Now concerning" or "Now" to delineate those topics (7:1, 25; 8:1; 11:2; 12:1; 15:1; 16:1). The three divisions of First Corinthians are: answer to Chloe's report of divisions (1—4); answer to report of fornication (5 and 6); and answer to letter of questions (7—16).

Answer to Chloe's Report of Divisions (1—4): Personality cults centering around Paul, Apollos, and Peter have led to divisions and false pride among the Corinthians (1). It is not their wisdom or cleverness that has brought them to Christ, because divine wisdom is contrary to human wisdom. The truth of the gospel is spiritually apprehended (2). Factions that exist among the saints at Corinth are indications of their spiritual immaturity (3). They should pride themselves in Christ, not in human leaders who are merely His servants (4).

Answer to Report of Fornication (5 and 6): The next problem Paul addresses is that of incest between a member of the church and his stepmother (5). The Corinthians have exercised no church discipline in this matter, and Paul orders them to remove the offender from their fellowship until he repents. Another source of poor testimony is the legal action of believer against believer in civil courts (6:1-8). They must learn to arbitrate their differences within the

FOCUS	ANSWER TO CHLOE'S REPORT OF DIVISIONS		ANSWER TO REPORT OF FORNICATION			ANSWER TO LETTER OF QUESTIONS					
REFERENCE	1:1———1:18	—5:1—	6:1—	6:12—	7:1—	8:1—	11:2—	15:1—	16:1—	16:24	
DIVISION	REPORT OF DIVISIONS	REASON FOR DIVISIONS	INCEST	LITIGATION	IMMORALITY	MARRIAGE	OFFERINGS TO IDOLS	PUBLIC WORSHIP	RESUR- RECTION	COLLECTION FOR JERUSALEM	
TOPIC	DIVISIONS IN THE CHURCH		DISORDER IN THE CHURCH			DIFFICULTIES IN THE CHURCH					
	CONCERN		CONDEMNATION			COUNSEL					
LOCATION	WRITTEN IN EPHESUS										
TIME	c. A.D. 56										

Christian community. Paul concludes this section with a warning against immorality in general (6:9-20).

Answer to Letter of Questions (7—16): In these chapters the apostle Paul gives authoritative answers to thorny questions raised by the Corinthians. His first counsel concerns the issues of marriage, celibacy, divorce, and remarriage (7). The next three chapters are related to the problem of meat offered to idols (8:1—11:1). Paul illustrates from his own life the twin principles of Christian liberty and the law of love, and he concludes that believers must sometimes limit their liberty for the sake of weaker brothers (cf. Rom. 14). The apostle then turns to matters concerning public worship, including improper observance of the Lord's Supper and the selfish use of spiritual gifts (11:2—14:40). Gifts are to be exercised in love for the edification of the whole body. The Corinthians also have problems with the Resurrection, which Paul seeks to correct (15). His historical and theological defense of the Resurrection includes teaching on the nature of the resurrected body. The Corinthians probably have been struggling over this issue because the idea of a resurrected body is disdainful in Greek thought. The epistle closes with Paul's instruction for the collection he will make for the saints in Jerusalem (16:1-4), followed by miscellaneous exhortations and greetings (16:5-24).

OUTLINE OF FIRST CORINTHIANS

CHAPTER 1

Greetings of Grace

PAUL, Rcalled *to be* an apostle of Jesus Christ Rthrough the will of God, and Sos'-the-nes *our* brother,   Rom. 1:1 • 2 Cor. 1:1

2 Unto the church of God which is at Corinth, to them that are sanctified in Christ Jesus, called *to be* saints, with all that in every place call upon the name of Jesus Christ our Lord, both their's and our's:

3 Grace *be* unto you, and peace, from God our Father, and *from* the Lord Jesus Christ.

Prayer of Thanksgiving

4 RI thank my God always Ton your behalf, for the grace of God which is given you by Jesus Christ;   Rom. 1:8 • *for you*

5 That in every thing ye are enriched by him, in all utterance, and *in* all knowledge;

6 Even as Rthe testimony of Christ Twas confirmed in you: Rev. 1:2 • *brought results*

7 So that ye come behind in no gift; waiting for the coming of our Lord Jesus Christ:

8 RWho shall also confirm you unto the end, Rthat ye may be blameless in the day of our Lord Jesus Christ.   1 Thess. 3:13 • Col. 1:22

9 RGod is Tfaithful, by whom ye were called unto Rthe fellowship of his Son Jesus Christ our Lord.   Is. 49:7 • *trustworthy* • [John 15:4]

Report of Divisions

10 Now I beseech you, brethren, by the name of our Lord Jesus Christ, that ye all speak the same thing, and *that* there be no divisions among you; but *that* ye be perfectly Tjoined together in the same mind and in the same judgment.   *united*

11 For it hath been Tdeclared unto me of you, my brethren, by them *which are of the house* of Chlo'-e, that there are Tcontentions among you.   *told • quarrels*

12 Now this I say, that every one of you saith, I am of Paul; and I of A-pol'-los; and I of Ce'-phas; and I of Christ.

13 RIs Christ Tdivided? was Paul crucified for you? or were ye baptized in the name of Paul?   2 Cor. 11:4; Eph. 4:5 • *divided into groups*

14 I thank God that I baptized none of you, but RCris'-pus and Ga'-ius;   Acts 18:8

15 Lest any should say that I had baptized Tin mine own name.   *as my disciples*

16 And I baptized also the household of RSteph'-a-nas: besides, I know not whether I baptized any other.   16:15, 17

17 For Christ sent me not to baptize, but to preach the gospel: Rnot with wisdom of words, lest the cross of Christ should be made Tof none effect.   [2:4] • *void*

The Gospel Is Not Earthly Wisdom

18 For the preaching of the cross is to them that perish foolishness; but unto us which are saved it is the power of God.

19 For it is written, RI WILL DESTROY THE WISDOM OF THE WISE, AND WILL BRING TO TNOTHING THE UNDERSTANDING OF THE PRUDENT.   Is. 29:14 • *nought*

20 Where *is* the wise? where *is* the scribe? where *is* the disputer of this world? Rhath not God made foolish the Twisdom of this world?   Is. 44:25; Rom. 1:22 • *philosophy*

21 RFor after that in the wisdom of God the world by wisdom knew not God, it pleased God by the foolishness of preaching to save them that believe.   Matt. 11:25

22 For the Jews require a sign, and the Greeks seek after wisdom:

23 But we preach Christ crucified, unto the Jews Ta stumblingblock, and unto the Greeks foolishness;   *an occasion of scandal*

24 But unto them which are called, both Jews and Greeks, Christ Rthe power of God, and the wisdom of God.   [Rom. 1:4]

25 Because Tthe foolishness of God is wiser than men; and the weakness of God is stronger than men.   *what seems to be*

26 For ye see your calling, brethren, how that not many wise men after the flesh, not many mighty, not many noble, *are called:*

27 But God hath chosen the foolish things of the world to confound the wise; and God hath chosen the weak things of the world to confound the things which are mighty;

28 And Tbase things of the world, and things which are despised, hath God chosen, *yea*, and things which are not, to bring to nought things that are: *lowly*

29 RThat no flesh should glory Tin his presence.   [Rom. 3:27; Eph. 2:9] • *before God*

30 RBut of him are ye in Christ Jesus, who of God is made unto us wisdom, and righteousness, and sanctification, and redemption: [Rom. 4:25; Eph. 1:7; Phil. 3:9]

31 That, according as it is written, RHe that glorieth, let him glory in the Lord.   [Jer. 9:24]

CHAPTER 2

AND I, brethren, when I came to you, came not Twith excellency of speech or of

wisdom, declaring unto you the testimony of God. *as an orator*

2 For I determined not to [T]know any thing among you, [R]save Jesus Christ, and him crucified. *esteem as important* • Gal. 6:14

3 And I was with you in weakness, and in fear, and in much trembling.

4 And my speech and my preaching *was* not with [T]enticing words of man's [T]wisdom, [R]but in demonstration of the Spirit and of power: *persuasible* • *philosophy* • Rom. 15:19

5 That your faith should not stand in the wisdom of men, but in the power of God.

The Gospel Is Heavenly Wisdom

6 Howbeit we speak wisdom among them that are [T]perfect: yet not the wisdom of this world, nor of the princes of this world, that come to nought: *mature*

7 But we speak the [T]wisdom of God in a [T]mystery, *even* the hidden *wisdom*, which God [T]ordained before the world unto our [T]glory: *truth* • *hidden form* • *designed* • *benefit*

8 Which none of the princes of this world knew: for had they known *it*, they would not have crucified the Lord of glory.

9 But as it is written, EYE HATH NOT SEEN, NOR EAR HEARD, NEITHER HAVE ENTERED INTO THE HEART OF MAN, THE THINGS WHICH GOD HATH PREPARED FOR THEM THAT LOVE HIM.

10 But God hath revealed *them* unto us by his Spirit: for the Spirit searcheth all things, yea, the deep things of God.

11 For what man knoweth the things of a man, save the [R]spirit of man which is in him? even so the things of God knoweth no man, but the Spirit of God. Prov. 20:27

12 Now we have received, not the spirit of the world, but [R]the spirit which is of God; that we might know the things that are freely given to us of God. [Rom. 8:15]

13 Which things also we speak, not in the words which man's wisdom teacheth, but which the Holy Ghost teacheth; comparing spiritual things with spiritual.

14 But the natural man receiveth not the things of the Spirit of God: for they are foolishness unto him: neither can he know *them*, because they are spiritually discerned.

15 But he that is spiritual judgeth all things, yet he himself is judged of no man.

16 [R]For who hath known the mind of the Lord, that he may instruct him? [R]But we have the mind of Christ. Is. 40:13 • [John 15:15]

CHAPTER 3

AND I, brethren, could not speak unto you as unto spiritual, but as unto carnal, *even* as unto babes in Christ.

2 I have fed you with milk, and not with [T]meat: for hitherto ye were not able *to bear it*, neither yet now are ye able. *solid food*

3 For ye are yet carnal: for whereas *there is* among you envying, and strife, and divisions, are ye not carnal, and walk as men?

4 [R]For while one saith, I am of Paul; and another, I *am* of A-pol'-los; are ye not [T]carnal? 1:12 • *worldly men*

Ministers Are Co-labourers with God

5 Who then is Paul, and who *is* A-pol'-los, but [R]ministers by whom ye believed, even as the Lord gave to every man? 2 Cor. 3:3

6 [R]I have planted, A-pol'-los watered; but God gave the increase. Acts 2:41, 47

7 So then [R]neither is he that planteth any thing, neither he that watereth; but God that giveth the increase. 2 Cor. 12:11; [Gal. 6:3]

8 Now he that planteth and he that watereth are one: and every man shall receive his own reward according to his own labour.

9 For [R]we are labourers together with God: ye are God's [T]husbandry, *ye are* [R]God's building. 2 Cor. 6:1 • *garden* • [Eph. 2:20]; Heb. 3:3, 4

10 [R]According to the grace of God which is given unto me, as a wise masterbuilder, I have laid the foundation, and another buildeth thereon. But let every man take heed how he buildeth thereupon. Rom. 1:5

11 For other foundation can no man lay than that is laid, which is Jesus Christ.

12 [R]Now if any man build upon this foundation gold, silver, precious stones, wood, hay, stubble; [Eph. 2:20]

13 Every man's work shall be made manifest: for the day shall declare it, because it shall be revealed by fire; and the fire shall try every man's work of what sort it is.

14 If any man's work abide which he hath built thereupon, he shall receive a reward.

15 [R]If any man's work shall be burned, he shall suffer loss: but he himself shall be saved; yet so [T]as by fire. Mal. 3:3 • *through*

16 [R]Know ye not that ye are the temple of God, and *that* the Spirit of God dwelleth in you? 2 Cor. 6:16

17 If any man [T]defile the temple of God, him shall God destroy; for the temple of God is holy, which *temple* ye are. *destroy*

Ministers Are Accountable to God

18 [R]Let no man [T]deceive himself. If any man among you seemeth to be wise in this world, let him become a fool, that he may [T]be wise. Prov. 3:7 • *fool* • *become*

19 For the wisdom of this world is foolishness with God. For it is written, [R]HE TAKETH THE WISE IN THEIR OWN CRAFTINESS. Job 5:13

20 And again, THE LORD KNOWETH THE THOUGHTS OF THE WISE, THAT THEY ARE VAIN.

21 Therefore let no man glory in men. For [R]all things are your's; *v. 22; [2 Cor. 4:5]*

22 Whether Paul, or A-pol'-los, or Ce'-phas, or the world, or life, or death, or things present, or things to come; [R]all are your's; *v. 21*

23 And ᴿye are Christ's; and Christ *is* God's.   [Rom. 14:8]; 2 Cor. 10:7; [Gal. 3:29]

CHAPTER 4

LET a man so account of us, as of the ᵀministers of Christ, and stewards of the ᵀmysteries of God.   *servants · hidden things*

2 Moreover it is required in stewards, that a man be found faithful.

3 But with me it is a very small thing that I should be judged of you, or of man's judgment: yea, I judge not mine own self.

4 ᴿFor I know nothing ᵀby myself; yet am I not hereby justified: but he that judgeth me is the Lord.   Rom. 4:2 · *against*

5 Therefore judge nothing before the time, until the Lord come, who both will bring to light the hidden things of darkness, and will make manifest the counsels of the hearts: and then shall every man have praise of God.

Misunderstanding of Paul's Ministry

6 And these things, brethren, I have in a figure transferred to myself and *to* A-pol'-los for your sakes; that ye might learn in us not to think *of men* above that which is written, that no one of you be puffed up for one against another.

7 For who ᵀmaketh thee to differ *from another?* and what hast thou that thou didst not receive? now if thou didst receive *it*, why dost thou glory, as if thou hadst not received *it*?   *distinguisheth thee*

8 Now ye are full, ᴿnow ye are rich, ye have reigned as kings without us: and I ᵀwould to God ye did reign, that we also might reign with you.   Rev. 3:17 · *wish*

9 For I think that God hath set forth us the apostles last, as ᵀit were appointed to death: for we are made a spectacle unto the world, and to angels, and to men.   *men*

10 We *are* fools for Christ's sake, but ye *are* wise in Christ; we *are* weak, but ye *are* strong; ye ᵀ*are* honourable, but we ᵀ*are* despised.   *have glory · have dishonour*

11 Even unto this present hour we both hunger, and thirst, and are naked, and are buffeted, and have no certain dwellingplace;

12 ᴿAnd labour, working with our own hands: being ᵀreviled, we bless; being persecuted, we suffer it: Acts 18:3 · *criticized*

13 Being defamed, we ᵀintreat: we are made as the filth of the world, *and are* the offscouring of all things unto this day.   *pray*

14 I write not these things to shame you, but as my beloved sons I warn *you*.

15 For though ye have ten thousand instructers in Christ, yet *have ye* not many fathers: for ᴿin Christ Jesus I have begotten you through the gospel.   Acts 18:11

16 Wherefore I beseech you, ᴿbe ye ᵀfollowers of me.   [11:1; 1 Thess. 1:6] · *imitators*

17 For this cause have I sent unto you Ti-mo'-the-us, who is my beloved son, and faithful in the Lord, who shall bring you ᴿinto remembrance of my ways which be in Christ, as I teach every where in every church.   11:2

18 ᴿNow some are ᵀpuffed up, as though I would not come to you.   5:2 · *proud*

19 But I will come to you shortly, if the Lord will, and will know, not the speech of them which are puffed up, but the power.

20 For ᴿthe kingdom of God *is* not in word, but in power.   2:4; 1 Thess. 1:5

21 ᵀWhat will ye? ᴿshall I come unto you with a rod, or in love, and *in* the spirit of meekness?   *which do you prefer* · 2 Cor. 10:2

CHAPTER 5

Deliver the Fornicators for Discipline

IT is reported commonly *that there is* fornication among you, and such fornication as is not so much as named among the Gentiles, that one should have his father's wife.

2 And ye are puffed up, and have not rather mourned, that he that hath done this deed might be taken away from among you.

3 For I verily, as absent in body, but present in spirit, have judged already, as though I were present, *concerning* him that hath so done this deed,

4 In the name of our Lord Jesus Christ, when ye are gathered together, and my spirit, ᴿwith the power of our Lord Jesus Christ,   [Matt. 16:19; John 20:23]

5 To deliver such an one unto Satan for the destruction of the flesh, that the spirit may be saved in the day of the Lord Jesus.

6 ᴿYour ᵀglorying *is* not good. Know ye not that ᴿa little leaven leaveneth the whole lump?   3:21 · *feeling of confidence* · Gal. 5:9

7 ᵀPurge out therefore the old leaven, that ye may be a new lump, as ye are unleavened. For even ᴿChrist our passover is ᵀsacrificed for us: *cleanse* · Is. 53:7 · *put to death*

8 Therefore let us keep the feast, not with old leaven, neither with the leaven of malice and wickedness; but with the unleavened *bread* of sincerity and truth.

Separate Yourselves from Immoral Believers

9 I wrote unto you in an epistle not to ᵀcompany with fornicators: *associate*

10 Yet not altogether with the fornicators of this world, or with the covetous, or extortioners, or with idolaters; for then must ye needs go out of the world.

11 But now I have written unto you not to keep company, if any man that is called a brother be a fornicator, or covetous, or an

idolater, or a railer, or a drunkard, or an extortioner; with such an one no not to eat.

12 For what have I to do to judge ᴿthem also that are without? do not ye judge ᴿthem that are within?   [Mark 4:11] • [6:1–4]

13 But them that are without God judgeth. Therefore ᴿput away from among yourselves that wicked person.   Deut. 13:5

CHAPTER 6

Concerning Litigation Between Believers

DARE any of you, having a matter against another, go to law before the unjust, and not before the saints?

2 Do ye not know that ᴿthe saints shall judge the world? and if the world shall be judged by you, are ye unworthy to judge the smallest matters?   Dan. 7:22; [Rev. 2:26; 20:4]

3 Know ye not that we shall ᴿjudge angels? how much more things that ᵀpertain to this life?   2 Pet. 2:4 • belong in

4 If then ye have judgments of things pertaining to this life, set them to judge who are least esteemed in the church.

5 I speak to your shame. Is it so, that there is not a wise man among you? no, not one that shall be able to ᵀjudge between his brethren?   decide

6 But brother goeth to law with brother, and that before the ᴿunbelievers.   1 Tim. 5:8

7 Now therefore there is utterly a fault among you, because ye go to law one with another. ᴿWhy do ye not rather take wrong? why do ye not rather suffer yourselves to be defrauded?   [Prov. 20:22]

8 Nay, ye do wrong, and defraud, and ᵀthat your brethren.   even your own

9 Know ye not that the unrighteous shall not inherit the kingdom of God? Be not deceived: neither fornicators, nor idolaters,

nor adulterers, nor effeminate, nor abusers of themselves with mankind,

10 Nor thieves, ᴿnor covetous, nor drunkards, nor revilers, nor extortioners, shall inherit the kingdom of God.   [Col. 3:5]

11 And such were ᴿsome of you: but ye are washed, but ye are sanctified, but ye are justified in the name of the Lord Jesus, and by the Spirit of our God.   [12:2]

Warning Against Sexual Immorality

12 ᴿAll things are lawful unto me, but all things are not ᵀexpedient: all things are lawful for me, but I will not be brought under the power of any.   10:23 • helpful

13 ᴿMeatsᵀ for the belly, and the belly for meats: but God shall destroy both it and them. Now the body is not for fornication, but ᴿfor the Lord; ᴿand the Lord for the body.   Col. 2:22 • foods • 1 Thess. 4:3 • [Eph. 5:23]

14 And ᴿGod hath both raised up the Lord, and will also raise up us ᴿby his own power.   Rom. 6:5, 8; 2 Cor. 4:14 • Eph. 1:19

15 ᵀKnow ye not that your bodies are the members of Christ? shall I then take the members of Christ, and make them the members of an harlot? God forbid.   realize

16 What? know ye not that he which is joined to an harlot is one body? for ᴿtwo, saith he, shall be one flesh.   Gen. 2:24

17 ᴿBut he that is joined unto the Lord is one spirit.   Zech. 2:11; [John 17:21]; Eph. 4:4

18 ᵀFlee fornication. Every sin that a man doeth is without the body; but he that committeth fornication sinneth ᴿagainst his own body.   avoid • Rom. 1:24

19 What? ᴿknow ye not that your body is the temple of the Holy Ghost which is in you, which ye have of God, ᴿand ye are not your own?   2 Cor. 6:16 • Rom. 14:7

6:11 Changed Life—The first stanza of a famous Christian song begins: "What a wonderful change in my life has been wrought since Jesus came into my heart."

Without doubt the greatest proof of the new birth is a changed life. The child of God now suddenly loves the following:

a. He loves Jesus. Before conversion the sinner might hold Christ in high esteem, but after conversion he loves the Saviour (Page 1253—1 John 5:1, 2).

b. He loves the Bible. We should love God's Word as the psalmist did in Psalm 119. He expresses his great love for God's Word no less than 17 times! See verses 24, 40, 47, 48, 72, 97, 103, 111, 113, 127, 129, 140, 143, 159, 162, 165, 168.

c. He loves other Christians. "We know that we have passed from death unto life, because we love the brethren" (Page 1251—1 John 3:14).

d. He loves his enemies. See Matt. 5:43–45.

e. He loves the souls of all people. Like Paul, he too can cry out for the conversion of loved ones. "Brethren, my heart's desire and prayer to God for Israel is, that they might be saved" (Page 1116—Rom. 10:1). See also Second Corinthians 5:14.

f. He loves the pure life. John says if one loves the world, the love of the Father is not in him (Page 1250—1 John 2:15–17). See also First John 5:4.

g. He loves to talk to God. "Speaking to yourselves in psalms and hymns and spiritual songs, singing and making melody in your heart to the Lord" (Page 1166—Eph. 5:19).

Now turn to Page 21—THE CHRISTIAN'S GUIDE: Growing in the New Life.

6:19 The Work of the Holy Spirit in Christian Living—As a loving and wise mother tenderly watches over her child, so the Holy Spirit cares for the children of God.

(continued on next page)

20 For ^Rye are bought with a price: therefore glorify God in your body, and in your spirit, which are God's. 1 Pet. 1:18; 2 Pet. 2:1

CHAPTER 7

Principles for Married Life

NOW concerning the things whereof ye wrote unto me: *It is* good for a man not to ^Ttouch a woman.   *live in marriage with*

2 Nevertheless, *to avoid* fornication, let every man have his own wife, and let every woman have her own husband.

3 Let the husband render unto the wife ^Tdue benevolence: and likewise also the wife unto the husband.   *her due*

4 The wife ^Thath not power of her own body, but the husband: and likewise also the husband hath not power ^Tof his own body, but the wife.   *is not master · over*

5 ^TDefraud ye not one the other, except *it be* with consent for a time, that ye may give yourselves to fasting and prayer; and come together again, that Satan tempt you not for your incontinency.   *deprive*

6 But I speak this by permission, ^R*and* not of commandment.   *vv. 12, 25; 2 Cor. 8:8; 11:17*

7 For ^RI would that all men were even as I myself. But every man hath his ^Tproper gift of God, one after this manner, and another after that.   Acts 26:29 · *own gift from*

8 I say therefore to the unmarried and widows, ^RIt is ^Tgood for them if they ^Tabide even as I.   *vv. 1, 26 · better · live alone*

9 But if they cannot contain, let them marry: for it is better to marry than to burn.

Principles for the Married Believer

10 And unto the married I command, *yet* not I, but the Lord, ^RLet not the wife depart from *her* husband: Mal. 2:14; [Matt. 5:32]

11 But and if she depart, let her remain unmarried, or be reconciled to *her* husband: and let not the husband put away *his* wife.

12 But to the rest speak I, not the Lord: If any brother hath a wife that believeth not,

and she be pleased to dwell with him, let him not ^Tput her away.   *divorce her*

13 And the woman which hath an husband that believeth not, and if he be pleased to dwell with her, let her not leave him.

14 For the unbelieving husband is sanctified by the wife, and the unbelieving wife is sanctified by the husband: else were your children unclean; but now are they holy.

15 But if the unbelieving depart, let him depart. A brother or a sister is not under bondage in such *cases:* but God hath called us ^Rto peace.   Rom. 12:18; Heb. 12:14

16 For what knowest thou, O wife, whether thou shalt ^Rsave *thy* husband? or how knowest thou, O man, whether thou shalt save *thy* wife?   1 Pet. 3:1

Principle of Abiding in God's Call

17 But as God hath distributed to every man, as the Lord hath called every one, so let him walk. And so ordain I in all churches.

18 Is any man called being circumcised? let him not become uncircumcised. Is any called in uncircumcision? ^Rlet him not be circumcised.   Acts 15:1, 5, 19, 24

19 ^RCircumcision is nothing, and uncircumcision is nothing, but the ^Tkeeping of the commandments of God.   [Gal. 5:6] · *obeying*

20 ^RLet every man abide in the same calling wherein he was called.   Eph. 4:1

21 ^TArt thou called *being* a servant? care not for it: but if thou ^Tmayest be made free, use *it* rather.   *were · can become*

22 For he that is called in the Lord, *being* a servant, is ^Rthe Lord's freeman: likewise also he that is called, *being* free, is Christ's ^Tservant.   [John 8:36] · *slave*

23 ^RYe are bought with a price; be not ye the servants of men.   1 Pet. 1:18

24 Brethren, let every man, wherein he is called, therein abide with God.

Principles for the Unmarried

25 Now concerning virgins ^RI have no commandment of the Lord: yet I give my

---

a. The Holy Spirit indwells Christians. The Bible teaches that all believers are indwelt by the Holy Spirit (Page 1129—1 Cor. 6:19). The purpose of this indwelling ministry is to control the newly created nature given at conversion (Page 1145—2 Cor. 5:17; Page 1163—Eph. 3:16).
b. The Holy Spirit fills believers. We are admonished to "be filled with the Spirit" (Page 1165—Eph. 5:18). The word "fill" means to be controlled. The filling does not mean that the Christian gets more of the Holy Spirit, but rather, He gets more of us!
c. The Holy Spirit sanctifies the believer (Page 1120—Rom. 15:16; Page 1189—2 Thess. 2:13).
d. The Holy Spirit produces fruit in the life of the believer. This fruit is described by Paul: "But the fruit of the Spirit is love, joy, peace, longsuffering, gentleness, goodness, faith, meekness, temperance" (Page 1158—Gal. 5:22, 23).
e. The Holy Spirit imparts gifts to Christians (Page 1118—Rom. 12:6–8; Page 1134—1 Cor. 12:1–11; Page 1164—Eph. 4:7–12). A spiritual gift is an ability imparted to every Christian (Page 1130—1 Cor. 7:7; Page 1238—1 Pet. 4:10). The purpose of these gifts is twofold, namely, to glorify God (Page 1271—Rev. 4:11) and to edify the body of Christ (Page 1164—Eph. 4:12, 13).
f. The Holy Spirit teaches believers. He will instruct us in all spiritual things as we read the Word of God (Page 1060—John 14:26) and abide in the Son of God (Page 1250—1 John 2:24–27).
Now turn to Page 21—THE CHRISTIAN'S GUIDE: Beginning the New Life.

judgment, as one that hath obtained mercy of the Lord to be faithful. 2 Cor. 8:8

26 I suppose therefore that this is good for the present distress, *I say*, Rthat *it is* good for a man so to be. *vv.* 1, 8

27 Art thou bound unto a wife? seek not to be loosed. Art thou loosed from a wife? seek not a wife.

28 But and if thou marry, thou hast not sinned; and if a virgin marry, she hath not sinned. Nevertheless such shall have trouble in the flesh: but I spare you.

29 But this I say, brethren, the time *is* short: it remaineth, that both they that have wives be as though they had none;

30 And they that weep, as though they wept not; and they that rejoice, as though they rejoiced not; and they that buy, as though they possessed not;

31 And they that use this world, as not Rabusing *it*: for Rthe Tfashion of this world passeth away. 9:18 • Ps. 39:6 • *structure of things*

32 But I would have you without Tcarefulness. He that is unmarried Tcareth for the things that belong to the Lord, how he may please the Lord: *anxiety • is concerned for*

33 But he that is married Tcareth for the things that are of the world, how he may please *his* wife. *is concerned*

34 There is difference *also* between a wife and a virgin. The unmarried woman Rcareth for the things of the Lord, that she may be holy both in body and in spirit: but she that is married careth for the things of the world, how she may please *her* husband. Luke 10:40

35 And this I speak for your own profit; not that I may cast a snare upon you, but for that which is comely, and that ye may attend upon the Lord without distraction.

36 But if any man think that he behaveth himself Tuncomely toward his virgin, if she pass the flower of *her* age, and need so require, let him do what he will, he sinneth not: let them marry. *improperly*

37 Nevertheless he that standeth stedfast in his heart, having no necessity, but hath power over his own will, and hath so decreed in his heart that he will keep his Tvirgin, doeth well. *own virgin daughter*

38 RSo then he that giveth *her* in marriage doeth well; but he that giveth *her* not in marriage doeth better. Heb. 13:4

Principles for Remarriage

39 RThe wife is bound by the law as long as her husband liveth; but if her husband be dead, she is at liberty to be married to whom she will; only in the Lord. Rom. 7:2

40 But she is happier if she so abide, Rafter my judgment: and RI think also that I have the Spirit of God. *v.* 25 • 1 Thess. 4:8

CHAPTER 8

Principles of Liberty and the Weaker Brother

NOW as touching things offered unto idols, we know that we all have knowledge. Knowledge Tpuffeth up, but charity Tedifieth. *makes one proud • builds one up*

2 And Rif any man think that he Tknoweth any thing, he knoweth nothing yet as he ought to know. [1 Tim. 6:4] • *understands*

3 RBut if any man love God, the same is Tknown of him. Nah. 1:7; [Matt. 7:23] • *recognized*

4 As concerning therefore the eating of those things that are offered in sacrifice unto idols, we know that Ran idol *is* nothing in the world, Rand that *there is* none other God but one. Is. 41:24 • Deut. 4:39

5 For though there be that are called gods, whether in heaven or in earth, (as there be gods many, and lords many,)

6 But to us *there is but* one God, the Father, of whom *are* all things, and we Tin him; and one Lord Jesus Christ, by whom *are* all things, and we by him. *unto*

7 Howbeit *there is* not in every man that Tknowledge: for some Rwith conscience of the idol unto this hour eat *it* as a thing offered unto an idol; and their conscience being weak is defiled. *understanding • [10:28]*

8 But meat commendeth us not to God: for neither, if we eat, are we the better; neither, if we eat not, are we the worse.

9 But take heed lest by any means this Tliberty of your's become a stumblingblock to them that are weak. *power*

10 For if any man see thee which hast knowledge sit at meat in the idol's temple, shall not Rthe conscience of him which is weak be Temboldened to eat those things which are offered to idols; 10:28 • *encouraged*

11 And through thy knowledge shall the weak brother perish, for whom Christ died?

12 But Rwhen ye sin so against the brethren, and wound their weak conscience, ye sin against Christ. Matt. 25:40

13 Wherefore, if meat make my brother to offend, I will eat no flesh while the world standeth, lest I make my brother to offend.

CHAPTER 9

Paul Lists His Rights as a Minister

AM I not an apostle? am I not free? have I not seen Jesus Christ our Lord? are not ye my work in the Lord?

2 If I be not an apostle unto others, yet doubtless I am to you: for the Tseal of mine apostleship are ye in the Lord. *proof*

3 TMine answer to them that do Texamine me is this, *my defence • criticize*

4 RHave we Tnot power to eat and to drink? [1 Thess. 2:6] • *no right*

5 Have we not power to lead about a sister, a wife, as well as other apostles, and *as* the brethren of the Lord, and Ce'-phas?

6 Or I only and Barnabas, ᴿhave not we power to ᵀforbear working?   [2 Thess. 3:8] • *cease*

7 Who ᴿgoeth a warfare any time at his own charges? who ᴿplanteth a vineyard, and eateth not of the fruit thereof? or who ᴿfeedeth a flock, and eateth not of the milk of the flock?   2 Cor. 10:4 • Deut. 20:6 • John 21:15

8 Say I these things as a man? or saith not the law the same also?

9 For it is written in the law of Moses, ᴿTHOU SHALT NOT MUZZLE THE MOUTH OF THE OX THAT TREADETH OUT THE CORN. Doth God take care for oxen?   Deut. 25:4

10 Or saith he *it* altogether for our sakes? For our sakes, no doubt, *this* is written: that ᴿhe that ploweth should plow in hope; and that he that thresheth in hope should be partaker of his hope.   2 Tim. 2:6

11 ᴿIf we have sown unto you spiritual things, *is it* a great thing if we shall reap your carnal things?   Rom. 15:27

12 If others be partakers of *this* ᵀpower over you, *are* not we rather? ᴿNevertheless we have not used this power; but ᵀsuffer all things, lest we should hinder the gospel of Christ.   *privilege* • [Acts 20:33] • *put up with*

13 Do ye not know that they which minister about holy things live *of the things* of the temple? and they which wait at the altar are partakers with the altar?

14 Even so hath the Lord ordained ᴿthat they which preach the gospel should live of the gospel.   Num. 18:21, 26, 28

Paul Limits His Rights for Ministry

15 But I have used none of these things: neither have I written these things, that it should be so done unto me: for *it were* better for me to die, than that any man should make my glorying ᵀvoid.   *empty*

16 For though I preach the gospel, I have nothing to glory of: for ᴿnecessity is laid upon me; yea, woe is unto me, if I preach not the gospel!   [Jer. 20:9; Rom. 1:14]

17 For if I do this thing willingly, I have a reward: but if against my will, a dispensation *of the gospel* is committed unto me.

18 What is my reward then? *Verily* that, when I preach the gospel, I may make the gospel of Christ without charge, that I abuse not my ᵀpower in the gospel.   *privilege*

19 For though I be free from all *men,* yet have ᴿI made myself servant unto all, ᴿthat I might gain the more.   Gal. 5:13 • Matt. 18:15

20 And unto the Jews I became as a Jew, that I might gain the Jews; to them that are under the law, as under the law, that I might gain them that are under the law;

21 To them that are without law, as without law, (being not without law to God,

but under the law to Christ,) that I might gain them that are without law.

22 To the weak became I as weak, that I might gain the weak: ᴿI am made all things to all *men,* ᴿthat I might by all means save some.   10:33 • Rom. 11:14

23 And this I do for the gospel's sake, that I might be partaker thereof with *you.*

24 Know ye not that they which run in a race run all, but one receiveth the prize? ᴿSo run, that ye may ᵀobtain.   Gal. 2:2 • *win*

25 And every man that striveth for the mastery is temperate in all things. Now they *do it* to obtain a corruptible crown; but we ᴿan incorruptible.   James 1:12

26 I therefore so run, not as uncertainly; so fight I, not as one that beateth the air:

27 But I keep under my body, and bring *it* into subjection: lest that by any means, when I have preached to others, I myself should be ᵀa castaway.   *rejected*

CHAPTER 10

Warning Against Forfeiting Liberty

MOREOVER, brethren, ᵀI would not that ye should be ignorant, how that all our fathers were under the cloud, and all passed through the sea;   *I do not want*

2 ᴿAnd were all baptized ᵀunto Moses in the cloud and in the sea;   Ex. 14:19–31 • *into*

3 And did all eat the same spiritual meat;

4 And did all drink the same ᴿspiritual drink: for they drank of that spiritual Rock that ᵀfollowed them: and that ᵀRock was Christ.   Ex. 17:6 • *went with them* • *rock*

5 But with many of them God was not well pleased: for they ᴿwere ᵀoverthrown in the wilderness.   Num. 14:29 • *destroyed*

6 Now these things were our examples, to the intent we should not ᵀlust after evil things, as ᴿthey also lusted.   *desire* • Num. 11:4

7 Neither be ye idolaters, as *were* some of them; as it is written, The people sat down to eat and drink, and rose up to play.

8 ᴿNeither let us commit fornication, as some of them committed, and fell in one day three and twenty thousand.   Rev. 2:14

9 Neither let us ᵀtempt Christ, as ᴿsome of them also tempted, and ᴿwere destroyed of serpents.   *test* • Ex. 17:2, 7 • Num. 21:6

10 Neither murmur ye, as ᴿsome of them also murmured, and ᴿwere destroyed of ᴿthe destroyer.   Ex. 16:2 • Num. 14:37 • Ex. 12:23

11 Now all these things happened unto them for ensamples: and they are written for our ᵀadmonition, upon whom the ends of the world are come.   *instruction*

12 Wherefore ᴿlet him that thinketh he standeth take heed lest he fall.   Rom. 11:20

13 There hath no temptation taken you but such as is common to man: but God *is*

faithful, who will not suffer you to be tempted above that ye are able; but will with the temptation also make a way to escape, that ye may be able to bear it.

Exhortation to Use Liberty to Glorify God

14 Wherefore, my dearly beloved, ^Rflee from idolatry.   6:18; 2 Cor. 6:17; 2 Tim. 2:22

15 I speak as to ^Rwise men; ^Tjudge ye what I say.   8:1 · think over

16 The cup of blessing which we bless, is it not the communion of the blood of Christ? The bread which we break, is it not the communion of the body of Christ?

17 For ^Rwe being many are one bread, and one body: for we are all partakers of ^Tthat one bread.   12:27 · the

18 Behold Israel after the flesh: ^Rare not they which eat of the sacrifices ^Tpartakers of the altar?   Lev. 3:3 · identified with

19 What say I then? ^Rthat the idol is any thing, or that which is offered in sacrifice to idols is any thing?   8:4

20 But I say, that the things which the Gentiles sacrifice, they sacrifice to ^Tdevils, and not to God: and I would not that ye should have fellowship with devils.   demons

21 ^RYe cannot drink the cup of the Lord, and ^Rthe cup of devils: ye cannot be partakers of the ^RLord's table, and of the table of devils.   2 Cor. 6:15 · Deut. 32:21 · Luke 22:30

22 Do we ^Tprovoke the Lord to jealousy? are we stronger than he?   want to make

23 All things are lawful for me, but all things are not expedient: all things are lawful for me, but all things edify not.

24 Let no man seek his own, but ^Tevery man another's wealth.   each his neighbour's good

25 ^RWhatsoever is sold in the ^Tshambles, that eat, asking no question for conscience sake: [1 Tim. 4:4] · meat market

26 For ^Rthe earth is the Lord's, and the fulness thereof.   Ex. 19:5; Ps. 24:1; 50:10

27 If any of them that believe not bid you to a feast, and ye be disposed to go; ^Rwhatsoever is set before you, eat, asking no question for conscience sake.   Luke 10:7

28 But if any man say unto you, This is offered in sacrifice unto idols, eat not ^Rfor his sake that shewed it, and for conscience sake: for ^Rthe earth is the Lord's, and the fulness thereof: [8:10, 12] · Deut. 10:14; Hag. 2:8

29 Conscience, I say, not thine own, but of the other: for why is my liberty ^Tjudged of another man's conscience?   to be controlled by

30 For if I by ^Tgrace ^Tbe a partaker, why am I evil spoken of for that for which I give thanks?   thanksgiving · am identified with

31 Whether therefore ye eat, or drink, or whatsoever ye do, do all to the glory of God.

32 Give ^Tnone offence, neither to the Jews, nor to the ^TGentiles, nor to the church of God: no occasion to take offence · Greeks

33 Even as I please all men in all things, not seeking mine own profit, but the profit of many, that they may be saved.

CHAPTER 11

BE ^Rye ^Tfollowers of me, even as I also am of Christ.   Eph. 5:1 · imitators

Principles of Public Prayer

2 Now I praise you, brethren, that ye remember me in all things, and keep the ordinances, as I delivered them to you.

3 But I would have you know, that ^Rthe head of every man is Christ; and ^Rthe head of the woman is the man; and ^Rthe head of Christ is God.   [Eph. 5:23] · Gen. 3:16 · John 14:28

4 Every man praying or ^Rprophesying,^T having his head covered, dishonoureth his head.   12:10, 28; 14:1 · preaching

5 But every woman that prayeth or prophesieth with her head uncovered dishonoureth her head: for that is even all one as if she were ^Rshaven.   Deut. 21:12

6 For if the woman be not covered, let her also be shorn: but if it be ^Ra shame for a woman to be shorn or shaven, let her be ^Tcovered.   Num. 5:18 · veiled

7 For a man indeed ought not to ^Tcover his head, forasmuch as ^Rhe is the image and glory of God: but the woman is the glory of the man.   have his head veiled · Gen. 1:26

8 For the man is not of the woman; ^Rbut the woman of the man.   Gen. 2:21, 22

9 Neither was the man created for the woman; but the woman for the man.

10 For this cause ought the woman to have ^Tpower on her head because of the angels.   evidence of being under the direction of another

11 Nevertheless ^Rneither is the man without the woman, neither the woman without the man, in the Lord.   [Gal. 3:28]

12 For as the woman is ^Tof the man, even so is the man also ^Tby the woman; but all things of ^TGod.   made from · born of · come from

13 Judge in yourselves: is it comely that a woman pray unto God uncovered?

14 Doth not even nature itself teach you, that, if a man have long hair, it is a ^Tshame unto him?   disgrace

15 But if a woman have long hair, it is a glory to her: for her hair is given her for a covering.

16 But if any man ^Tseem to be contentious, we have no such custom, neither the churches of God.   seems inclined to quarrel

Rebuke of Disorders at the Lord's Supper

17 Now in this that I declare unto you I praise you not, that ye come together not for the better, but for the worse.

18 For first of all, when ye come together in the church, ᴿI hear that there be divisions among you: and I partly believe it.   1:10, 11

19 For there must be also ᵀheresies among you, that they which are approved may be made manifest among you.   errors

20 When ye come together therefore into one place, ᵀthis is not to eat the Lord's supper.   it is not possible

21 For in eating every one taketh before other his own supper: and one is hungry, and ᴿanother is drunken.   2 Pet. 2:13; Jude 12

22 What? have ye not houses to eat and to drink in? or despise ye the church of God, and shame ᵀthem that have not? What shall I say to you? shall I praise you in this? I praise you not.   them that are poor?

23 For ᴿI have received of the Lord that which also I delivered unto you, ᴿThat the Lord Jesus the same night in which he was betrayed took bread: 15:3 • Luke 22:19

24 ᴿAnd when he had given thanks, he brake it, and said, Take, eat: this is my body, which is broken for you: this do in remembrance of me.   Matt. 26:26; Mark 14:22

25 After the same manner also he took the cup, when he had supped, saying, This cup is the new testament in my blood: this do ye, as oft as ye drink it, in remembrance of me.

26 For as often as ye eat this bread, and drink this cup, ye do ᵀshew the Lord's death ᴿtill he come.   proclaim • John 14:3; [Acts 1:11]

27 Wherefore whosoever shall eat this bread, and drink this cup of the Lord, ᵀunworthily, shall be guilty of the body and blood of the Lord.   in an unworthy manner

28 But ᴿlet a man ᵀexamine himself, and so let him eat of ᵀthat bread, and drink of that cup.   2 Cor. 13:5 • prove • the

29 For he that eateth and drinketh unworthily, eateth and drinketh damnation to himself, not discerning the Lord's body.

30 For this cause many are weak and sickly among you, and many sleep.

31 For ᴿif we would ᵀjudge ourselves, we should not be judged.   [1 John 1:9] • criticize

32 But when we are judged, ᴿwe are chastened of the Lord, that we should not be condemned with the world.   Ps. 94:12

33 Wherefore, my brethren, when ye come together to eat, ᵀtarry one for another.   wait

34 And if any man hunger, let him eat at home; that ye come not together unto ᵀcondemnation. ᴿAnd the rest will I set in order when I come.   judgment • Titus 1:5

CHAPTER 12

Test of the Spirit's Control

NOW concerning spiritual gifts, brethren, I would not have you ignorant.

2 Ye know ᴿthat ye were Gentiles, carried away unto these ᴿdumb idols, even as ye were led.   Eph. 2:11 • Ps. 115:5

3 Wherefore I give you to understand, that no man speaking by the Spirit of God calleth Jesus accursed: and that no man can say that Jesus is the Lord, but by the Holy Ghost.

Diversity of the Gifts

4 Now ᴿthere are diversities of gifts, but ᴿthe same Spirit.   Rom. 12:4 • Eph. 4:4

5 And there are differences of ᵀadministrations, but the same Lord.   promotion

6 And there are ᵀdiversities of operations, but it is the same God ᴿwhich worketh all in all.   various kinds • Eph. 1:23

7 But the manifestation of the Spirit is given to every man to profit withal.

8 For to one is given by the Spirit the word of wisdom; to another ᴿthe word of knowledge by the same Spirit;   2 Cor. 8:7

9 ᴿTo another faith by the same Spirit; to another ᴿthe gifts of healing by the same Spirit;   Matt. 17:19; 2 Cor. 4:13 • Mark 16:18; James 5:14

10 To another the working of miracles; to another prophecy; to another discerning of spirits; to another divers kinds of tongues; to another the interpretation of tongues:

11 But all these worketh that one and the selfsame Spirit, ᵀdividing to every man ᵀseverally as he will.   assigning • individually

Importance of All Gifts

12 For ᴿas the body is one, and hath many members, and all the members of that one body, being many, are one body: ᴿso also is Christ.   Rom. 12:4, 5; Eph. 4:4 • [Gal. 3:16]

13 For by one Spirit are we all baptized into one body, whether we be Jews or Gentiles, whether we be bond or free; and have been all made to drink into one Spirit.

14 For the body is not one ᵀmember, but many.   part

15 If the foot shall say, Because I am not

12:1–10 **Using Spiritual Gifts**—Spiritual gifts are discussed in detail in four passages of the New Testament: Romans 12:3–8; First Corinthians 12:1–10, 28–31; Ephesians 4:11, 12; and First Peter 4:10, 11. These lists are to be regarded as representative of spiritual gifts. Spiritual gifts are those gifts given by the Spirit of God for the accomplishment of God's purpose in the world and for the edification of the church, the body of Christ. Two things are important to remember concerning spiritual gifts: (1) every believer has been given spiritual gifts (Page 1118—Rom. 12:5, 6; 1 Cor. 12:7; Page 1238—1 Pet. 4:10); and (2) the gifts belong to God and are given for the believer to use for the glory of God (Page 1238—1 Pet. 4:11).

Now turn to Page 1157—Gal. 5:13: Serving.

the hand, I am not of the body; is it therefore not of the body?

16 And if the ear shall say, Because I am not the eye, I am not of the body; is it therefore not of the body?

17 If the whole body were an eye, where were the hearing? If the whole were hearing, where were the smelling?

18 But now hath ᴿGod set the members every one of them in the body, ᴿas it hath pleased him. v. 28 • Rom. 12:3

19 And if they were all one member, ᵀwhere were the body? there would be no body

20 ᴿBut now are they many members, yet but one body. Eph. 4:4; [Col. 1:18]

21 And the eye cannot say unto the hand, I have no need of thee: nor again the head to the feet, I have no need of you.

22 ᵀNay, much more those members of the body, which seem to be more ᵀfeeble, are necessary: on the contrary • weak

23 And those ᵀmembers of the body, which we think to be less honourable, upon these we ᵀbestow more abundant honour; and our uncomely parts have more abundant comeliness. parts • put

24 For our ᵀcomely parts have no need: but God hath ᵀtempered the body together, having given more abundant honour to that part which lacked: beautiful • arranged

25 That there should be no ᵀschism in the body; but that the members should have the same care one for another. division

26 And whether one member suffer, all the members suffer with it; or one member be honoured, all the members rejoice with it.

27 Now ᴿye are the body of Christ, and ᴿmembers in particular. Rom. 12:5 • Eph. 5:30

28 And God hath set some in the church, first apostles, secondarily prophets, thirdly teachers, after that miracles, then gifts of healings, helps, governments, ᵀdiversities of tongues. different kinds

29 Are all apostles? are all prophets? are all teachers? are all workers of miracles?

30 Have all the gifts of healing? do all speak with tongues? do all interpret?

31 But covet earnestly the best gifts: and yet shew I unto you a more excellent way.

CHAPTER 13

Exercise Gifts with Love

THOUGH I speak with the ᵀtongues of men and of angels, and have not ᵀcharity, I am become as sounding brass, or a tinkling cymbal. languages • love

2 ᴿAnd though I have the gift of prophecy, and understand all mysteries, and all knowledge; and though I have all faith, so that I could remove mountains, and have not charity, I am nothing. 12:8–10

3 And ᴿthough I ᵀbestow all my goods to feed the poor, and though I give my body to be burned, and have not ᵀcharity, it profiteth me nothing. Matt. 6:1, 2 • give • love

4 Charity suffereth long, and is kind; charity envieth not; charity ᵀvaunteth not itself, is not puffed up, does not push itself forward

5 Doth not behave itself unseemly, seeketh not her own, is not easily provoked, ᵀthinketh no evil; is not ready to suspect evil

6 ᴿRejoiceth not in iniquity, but rejoiceth ᵀin the truth; Ps. 10:3 • with the truth

7 Beareth all things, believeth all things, hopeth all things, endureth all things.

8 Charity never faileth: but whether there be prophecies, they shall fail; whether there be tongues, they shall cease; whether there be knowledge, it shall vanish away.

9 ᴿFor ᵀwe know in part, and we prophesy in part. 8:2 • our knowledge is limited

10 ᴿBut when that which is ᵀperfect is come, then that which is in part shall be done away. Ps. 19:7; James 1:25 • complete

11 When I was a child, I spake as a child, I ᵀunderstood as a child, I ᵀthought as a child: but when I became a man, I put away childish things. felt • reasoned

12 For ᴿnow we see through a glass, darkly; but then ᴿface to face: now I know in part; but then shall I know even as also I am known. Phil. 3:12 • [1 John 3:2]

13 And now abideth faith, hope, charity, these three; but the greatest of these is charity.

CHAPTER 14

Superiority of Prophecy

FOLLOW after charity, and ᴿdesire spiritual gifts, ᴿbut rather that ye may ᵀprophesy. 12:31 • Num. 11:25, 29 • preach infallibly

2 For he that speaketh in an unknown tongue speaketh not unto men, but unto God: for no man understandeth him; howbeit in the spirit he speaketh mysteries.

3 But he that ᵀprophesieth speaketh unto men to ᵀedification, and exhortation, and comfort. speaks God's message • building up

4 He that speaketh in an ᵀunknown tongue edifieth himself; but he that prophesieth edifieth the church. strange

5 I would that ye all spake with tongues, but rather that ye prophesied: for greater is he that prophesieth than he that speaketh with tongues, except he interpret, that the church may receive ᵀedifying. building up

6 Now, brethren, if I come unto you speaking with tongues, what shall I profit you, except I shall speak to you either by ᴿrevelation, or by knowledge, or by prophesying, or by ᵀdoctrine? v. 26 • teaching

Gift of Tongues

7 And even things without life giving sound, whether pipe or harp, except they give a distinction in the ᵀsounds, how shall it be known what is piped or harped?   *tunes*

8 For if the trumpet give an ᵀuncertain ᵀsound, who shall prepare himself ᵀto the battle?   *unclear • voice • for war*

9 So likewise ye, except ye utter by the tongue words easy to be understood, how shall it be known what is spoken? for ye shall speak ᵀinto the air.   *to no point*

10 There are, it may be, so many kinds of voices in the world, and none of them is without ᵀsignification.   *meaning*

11 Therefore if I know not the ᵀmeaning of the voice, I shall be unto him that speaketh a barbarian, and he that speaketh *shall be* a barbarian unto me.   *language*

12 Even so ye, forasmuch as ye are zealous of spiritual *gifts,* seek that ye may excel to the edifying of the church.

13 Wherefore let him that speaketh in an *unknown* tongue pray that he may interpret.

14 ᴿFor if I pray in an *unknown* tongue, my spirit prayeth, but my understanding is unfruitful.   Eph. 5:19

15 What is it then? I will pray with the spirit, and I will pray with the understanding also: I will sing with the spirit, and I will sing with the understanding also.

16 Else when thou shalt bless with the spirit, how shall he that ᵀoccupieth the room of the unlearned say A-men' at thy giving of thanks, seeing he understandeth not what thou sayest?   *lives as an uneducated man*

17 For thou verily givest thanks well, but the other is not ᵀedified.   *helped*

18 I thank my God, I speak with tongues more than ye all:

19 Yet in the church I had rather speak five words with my understanding, that *by my voice* I might teach others also, than ten thousand words in an *unknown* tongue.

20 Brethren, be not children in understanding: howbeit in malice be ye children, but in understanding be men.

21 In the law it is written, WITH MEN OF OTHER TONGUES AND OTHER LIPS WILL I SPEAK UNTO THIS PEOPLE; AND YET FOR ALL THAT WILL THEY NOT HEAR ME, saith the Lord.

22 Wherefore tongues are for a sign, not to them that believe, but to them that believe not: but prophesying *serveth* not for them that believe not, but for them which believe.

23 If therefore the whole church be come together into one place, and all speak with tongues, and there come in *those that are* ᵀunlearned, or unbelievers, will they not say that ye are ᵀmad?   *uneducated • crazy*

24 But if all prophesy, and there come in one that believeth not, or *one* unlearned, he is convinced of all, he is judged of all:

25 And thus are the secrets of his heart made manifest; and so falling down on *his* face he will worship God, and report ᴿthat God is in you of a truth.   Is. 45:14; Zech. 8:23

Exercising Gifts in Public Worship

26 How is it then, brethren? when ye come together, every one of you hath a psalm, ᴿhath a doctrine, hath a tongue, hath a revelation, hath an interpretation. Let all things be done unto edifying.   *v. 6*

27 If any man speak in ᵀan *unknown* tongue, *let it be* by two, or at the most *by* three, and *that* ᵀby course; and let one ᵀinterpret.   *a tongue • in turn • explain*

28 But if there be no interpreter, let him keep silence in the church; and let him speak to himself, and to God.

29 Let the ᵀprophets speak two or three, and ᴿlet the other judge.   *preachers • 12:10*

30 If *any thing* be revealed to another that sitteth by, let the first hold his peace.

31 For ye may all prophesy one by one, that all may learn, and all may be comforted.

32 And ᴿthe spirits of the prophets are subject to the prophets.   [1 John 4:1]

33 ᴿFor God is not *the author* of ᵀconfusion, but of peace, ᴿas in all churches of the saints.   *v. 40 • tumult; unquietness • 11:16*

34 Let your women keep silence in the churches: for it is not permitted unto them to speak; but *they are commanded* to be under obedience, as also saith the law.

35 And if they will learn any thing, let them ask their husbands at home: for it is a shame for women to speak in the church.

36 What? came the word of God ᴿout from you? or came it unto you only?   Is. 2:3

37 ᴿIf any man think himself to be a prophet, or spiritual, let him acknowledge that the things that I write unto you are the commandments of the Lord.   2 Cor. 10:7

38 ᴿBut if any man be ignorant, let him be ignorant.   [Hos. 4:6, 17; 2 Pet. 1:5, 9]; Rev. 22:11

39 Wherefore, brethren, covet to prophesy, and forbid not to speak with tongues.

40 ᴿLet all things be done ᵀdecently and in order.   *v. 33 • properly*

CHAPTER 15

Fact of Christ's Resurrection

MOREOVER, brethren, I declare unto you the gospel ᴿwhich I preached unto you, which also ye have received, and ᴿwherein ye stand;   [Gal. 1:11] • [Rom. 5:2]

2 By which also ye are saved, if ye keep in memory what I preached unto you, unless ye have believed ᵀin vain.   *without cause*

3 For I delivered unto you first of all that which I also received, how that Christ died for our sins according to the scriptures;

4 And that he was buried, and that he rose again the third day ᴿaccording to the scriptures: Ps. 16:10, 11; Is. 53:10; Luke 24:26; Acts 2:25 ⋆

5 ᴿAnd that he was seen of Ce′-phas, then ᴿof the twelve: Luke 24:34 · Matt. 28:17; John 20:26

6 After that, he was seen of above five hundred brethren at once; of whom the greater part remain unto this present, but some ᵀare fallen asleep.   *have died*

7 After that, he was seen of James; then ᴿof all the apostles.   Luke 24:50; Acts 1:3, 4

8 ᴿAnd last of all he was seen of me also, as of one born out of due time.   [Acts 9:4, 17]

9 For I am the least of the apostles, that am not meet to be called an apostle, because I persecuted the church of God.

10 But by the grace of God I am what I am: and his grace which *was bestowed* upon me was not in vain; but I laboured more abundantly than they all: yet not I, but the grace of God which was with me.

11 Therefore whether *it were* I or they, so we preach, and so ye believed.

Importance of Christ's Resurrections

12 Now if Christ be preached that he rose from the dead, how say some among you that there is no resurrection of the dead?

13 But if there be no resurrection of the dead, ᴿthen is Christ not risen: [1 Thess. 4:14]

14 And if Christ be not risen, then is our preaching vain, and your faith *is* also vain.

15 Yea, and we are found false witnesses of God; because we have testified of God that he raised up Christ: whom he raised not up, if so be that the dead rise not.

16 For if the dead rise not, then is not Christ raised:

17 And if Christ be not raised, your faith *is* vain; ᴿye are yet in your sins.   [Rom. 4:25]

18 Then they also which ᵀare fallen asleep in Christ are perished.   *have died*

19 If in this life only we have hope in Christ, we are of all men most miserable.

Order of the Resurrections

20 But now ᴿis Christ risen from the dead, *and* become ᴿthe firstfruits of them that ᵀslept.   1 Pet. 1:3 · Acts 26:23 · *died*

21 For since by man *came* death, by man *came* also the resurrection of the dead.

22 ᴿFor as in Adam all die, even so in Christ shall all be made alive.   [John 5:28, 29]

23 But ᴿevery man in his own order: Christ the firstfruits; afterward they that are Christ's at his coming.   [1 Thess. 4:15–17]

24 Then *cometh* the end, when he ᴿshall have delivered up the kingdom to God, even the Father; when he shall have put down all rule and all authority and power.   [Dan. 2:44] ⋆

25 For he must reign, ᴿtill he hath put all enemies under his feet.   Ps. 110:1; Acts 2:34, 35 ⋆

26 ᴿThe last enemy *that* shall be destroyed *is* death.   [2 Tim. 1:10; Rev. 20:14] ⋆

27 ᴿFor he hath put all things under his feet. But when he saith all things are put under *him, it is* manifest that he is excepted, which did put all things under him.   Ps. 8:6 ⋆

28 And when ᴿall things shall be subdued unto him, then shall the Son also himself be subject unto him that put all things under him, that God may be all in all.   [Phil. 3:21] ⋆

Moral Implications of Christ's Resurrection

29 Else what shall they do which are baptized for the dead, if the dead rise not at all? why are they then baptized for the dead?

30 And ᴿwhy stand we in ᵀjeopardy ᴿevery hour?   2 Cor. 11:26 · *peril* · [Gal. 5:11]

31 I protest by your rejoicing which I have in Christ Jesus our Lord, I die daily.

32 If after the manner of men I have fought with beasts at Eph′-e-sus, what advantageth it me, if the dead rise not? let us eat and drink; for to morrow we die.

33 Be not deceived: evil ᵀcommunications corrupt good manners.   *companionships*

34 Awake to righteousness, and sin not;

15:3, 4 Sharing Our Faith: What?—Before discussing just what is to be shared concerning our faith, let us mention a few things we are not to do. We are not commanded to force Christian standards upon the unbelieving world (Page 1129—1 Cor. 5:12). We are not to confuse people by allowing them to believe that church membership, tithing, or any good works are somehow connected with becoming a Christian (Page 1162—Eph. 2:8–10).

Actually we have but one thing to share with the unsaved, and that is the gospel of Christ. According to Paul it involves the death and resurrection of Christ (1 Cor. 15:1–4). A plan for sharing your faith might be as follows:

a. God's Word says all are sinners, condemned to hell (Page 695—Is. 53:6; Page 1110—Rom. 3:10, 11, 23; 5:8, 12; Page 1281—Rev. 20:15).

b. There is nothing a lost person can do on his own to save himself (Page 702— Is. 64:6; Page 1162—Eph. 2:9).

c. Christ was born, crucified, and resurrected to save lost people from their sin (Page 1044—John 3:16; Page 1194—1 Tim. 1:15).

d. To be saved a sinner must believe God's Word and invite Christ into his heart by faith (Page 1047—John 5:24; Page 1090—Acts 16:31).

    Now turn to Page 1183—1 Thess. 1:5: Sharing Our Faith: How?

Rfor some have not the knowledge of God: I speak *this* to your shame.   6:5; [1 Thess. 4:5]

Bodies of the Resurrected Dead

35 But some *man* will say, RHow are the dead raised up? and with what body do they come?   Ezek. 37:3

36 *Thou* fool, that which thou sowest is not Tquickened, except it die: *made alive*

37 And that which thou sowest, thou sowest not that body that shall be, but bare grain, it may chance of wheat, or of some other *grain:*

38 But God giveth it a body as it hath pleased him, and to every seed his own body.

39 All flesh *is* not the same flesh: but *there is* one *kind* of flesh of men, another flesh of beasts, another of fishes, *and* another of birds.

40 *There are* also Tcelestial bodies, and bodies Tterrestrial: but the glory of the celestial *is* one, and the *glory* of the terrestrial *is* another.   *heavenly • earthly*

41 *There is* one Tglory of the sun, and another glory of the moon, and another glory of the stars: for *one* star differeth from *another* star in glory.   *beauty*

42 RSo also *is* the resurrection of the dead. It is sown in corruption; it is raised in incorruption: [Dan. 12:2; Matt. 13:43]

43 RIt is sown Tin dishonour; it is raised in Tglory: it is sown in weakness; it is raised in power: [Phil. 3:21] • *ugly • beauty*

44 It is sown a natural body; it is raised a spiritual body. TThere is a natural body, and there is Ta spiritual body.   *if there • also a*

45 And so it is written, The first man Adam was made a living soul; the last Adam *was made* a quickening spirit.

46 Howbeit that *was* not first which is spiritual, but that which is natural; and afterward that which is spiritual.

47 The first man *is* of the earth, earthy: the second man *is* the Lord from heaven.

48 As *is* the earthy, such *are* they also that are earthy: and as *is* the heavenly, such *are* they also that are heavenly.

49 And Ras we have borne the image of the earthy, Rwe shall also bear the image of the heavenly.   Gen. 5:3 • [Phil. 3:21; 1 John 3:2]

50 Now this I say, brethren, that Rflesh and blood cannot inherit the kingdom of God; neither doth corruption inherit incorruption.   Matt. 16:17; [John 3:3, 5]

Bodies of the Translated Living

51 Behold, I shew you a Tmystery; RWe shall not all sleep, Rbut we shall all be changed,   *secret* • [1 Thess. 4:15] • [Phil. 3:21]

52 In a moment, in the twinkling of an eye, at the last trump: for the trumpet shall sound, and the dead shall be raised incorruptible, and we shall be changed.

53 For this Tcorruptible must put on incorruption, and Rthis mortal *must* put on immortality.   *which can die* • 2 Cor. 5:4

54 So when this corruptible shall have put on incorruption, and this mortal shall have put on immortality, then shall be brought to pass the saying that is written, RDeath is swallowed up in victory.   Is. 25:8

55 RO death, where *is* thy sting? O Tgrave, where *is* thy victory?   Hos. 13:14 • *death*

56 The sting of death *is* sin; and Rthe strength of sin *is* the law.   [Rom. 4:15; 5:13; 7:5]

57 RBut thanks *be* to God, which giveth us Rthe victory through our Lord Jesus Christ.   [Rom. 7:25] • [1 John 5:4]

58 Therefore, my beloved brethren, be ye stedfast, unmoveable, always abounding in the work of the Lord, forasmuch as ye know that your labour is not in vain in the Lord.

CHAPTER 16

Counsel Concerning the Collection for Jerusalem

NOW concerning Rthe collection for the saints, as I have given order to the churches of Ga-la'-ti-a, even so do ye. Acts 11:29

2 RUpon the first *day* of the week let every one of you lay by him in store, as *God* hath prospered him, that there be no Tgatherings when I come.   Acts 20:7 • *collections*

3 And when I come, Rwhomsoever ye shall approve by *your* letters, them will I send to bring your liberality unto Jerusalem. 2 Cor. 8:19

4 RAnd if it be Tmeet that I go also, they shall go with me.   2 Cor. 8:4, 19 • *proper*

Conclusion

5 Now I will come unto you, Rwhen I shall pass through Mac-e-do'-ni-a: for I do pass through Mac-e-do'-ni-a.   Acts 19:21

6 And it may be that I will abide, yea, and winter with you, that ye may bring me on my journey whithersoever I go.

7 For I will not see you now by the way; but I trust to Ttarry a while with you, Rif the Lord permit.   *stay* • Acts 18:21; James 4:15

8 RBut I will Ttarry at Eph'-e-sus until Pentecost.   Acts 2:1; 20:16 • *stay*

9 For Ra great door and effectual is opened unto me, and Rthere are many adversaries.   Acts 14:27; 2 Cor. 2:12; Col. 4:3 • Acts 19:9

10 Now if Ti-mo'-the-us come, see that he may be with you without fear: for he worketh the work of the Lord, as I also *do.*

11 RLet no man therefore Tdespise him: but conduct him forth Rin peace, that he may come unto me: for I look for him with the brethren.   1 Tim. 4:12 • *belittle* • Acts 15:33

12 As touching *our* brother RA-pol'-los, I greatly desired him to come unto you with the brethren: but his will was not at all to

come at this time; but he will come when he shall have convenient time.   1:12

13 RWatch ye, stand fast in the faith, quit you like men, be strong.   Matt. 24:42

14 RLet all your Tthings be done Twith charity.   14:1; [1 Pet. 4:8] · *work* · *in love*

15 I beseech you, brethren, (ye know the house of Steph′-a-nas, that it is the firstfruits of A-cha′-ia, and *that* they have addicted themselves to the ministry of the saints,)

16 RThat ye submit yourselves unto such, and to every one that helpeth with *us*, and Rlaboureth.   Heb. 13:17 · [Heb. 6:10]

17 I am glad of the coming of Steph′-a-nas and For-tu-na′-tus and A-cha′-i-cus: Rfor that which was lacking on your part they have supplied.   2 Cor. 11:9; Philem. 13

18 RFor they have refreshed my spirit and your′s: therefore Racknowledge ye them that are such.   Col. 4:8 · Phil. 2:29

19 The churches of Asia salute you. Aq′-ui-la and Priscilla salute you much in the Lord, with the church that is in their house.

20 RAll the brethren greet you. Greet ye one another with an holy kiss.   Rom. 16:16

21 RThe salutation of *me* Paul with mine own hand.   Col. 4:18; 2 Thess. 3:17

22 If any man Rlove not the Lord Jesus Christ, let him be TAn-ath′-e-ma TMar′-an-a′-tha.   Eph. 6:24 · *accursed* · *the Lord is coming*

23 RThe grace of our Lord Jesus Christ *be* with you.   Rom. 16:20

24 My love *be* with you all in Christ Jesus. A-men′.

CORINTHIANS

THE BOOK OF SECOND CORINTHIANS

Since Paul's first letter, the Corinthian church had been swayed by false teachers who stirred the people against Paul. They claimed he was fickle, proud, unimpressive in appearance and speech, dishonest, and unqualified as an apostle of Jesus Christ. Paul sent Titus to Corinth to deal with these difficulties, and upon his return, rejoiced to hear of the Corinthians' change of heart. Paul wrote this letter to express his thanksgiving for the repentant majority and to appeal to the rebellious minority to accept his authority. Throughout the book he defends his conduct, character, and calling as an apostle of Jesus Christ.

To distinguish this epistle from First Corinthians, it was given the title *Pros Korinthious B*, the "Second to the Corinthians." The *A* and *B* were probably later additions to *Pros Korinthious*.

THE AUTHOR OF SECOND CORINTHIANS

External and internal evidence amply support the Pauline authorship of this letter. As with Romans, the problem of Second Corinthians is with its lack of unity, not with its authorship. Many critics theorize that chapters 10—13 were not a part of this letter in its original form because their tone contrasts with that of chapters 1—9. It is held that the sudden change from a spirit of joy and comfort to a spirit of concern and self-defense points to a "seam" between two different letters. Many hypotheses have been advanced to explain the problem, but the most popular is that chapters 10—13 belong to a lost letter referred to in 2:4. Several problems arise with these attempts to dissect Second Corinthians. Chapters 10—13 do not fit Paul's description of the "lost" letter of 2:4 because they are firm but not sorrowful and because they do not refer to the offender about whom that letter was written (2:5-11). Also, this earlier material would have been appended at the beginning of Second Corinthians, not at the end. There is simply no external (manuscripts, church fathers, tradition) or internal basis for challenging the unity of this epistle. The difference in tone between 1—9 and 10—13 is easily explained by the change of focus from the repentant majority to the rebellious minority.

THE TIME OF SECOND CORINTHIANS

Part of the background of Second Corinthians can be found in "The Time of First Corinthians." Paul was in Ephesus when he wrote First Corinthians and expected Timothy to visit Corinth and return to him (1 Cor. 16:10-11). Timothy apparently brought Paul a report of the opposition that had developed against him in Corinth, and Paul made a brief and painful visit to the Corinthians (this visit is not mentioned in Acts, but it can be inferred from 2 Cor. 2:1; 12:14; 13:1, 2). Upon returning to Ephesus, Paul regretfully wrote his sorrowful letter to urge the church to discipline the leader of the opposition (2:1-11; 7:8). Titus carried this letter. Paul, anxious to learn the results, went to Troas and then to Macedonia to meet Titus on his return trip (2:12, 13; 7:5-16). Paul was greatly relieved by Titus's report that the majority of the Corinthians had repented of their rebelliousness against Paul's apostolic authority. However, a minority opposition still persisted, evidently led by a group of Judaizers (10—13). There in Macedonia Paul wrote Second Corinthians and sent it with Titus and another brother (8:16-24). This took place late in A.D. 56, and the Macedonian city from which it was written may have been Philippi. Paul then made his third trip to Corinth (12:14; 13:1, 2; Acts 20:1-3) where he wrote his letter to the Romans.

There is an alternate view that the anguished letter of 2:4 and 7:8 is, in fact, First Corinthians and not a lost letter. This would require that the offender of Second Corinthians 2:5-11 and 7:12 be identified with the offender of First Corinthians 5.

THE CHRIST OF SECOND CORINTHIANS

Christ is presented as the believer's comfort (1:5), triumph (2:14), Lord (4:5), light (4:6), judge (5:10), reconciliation (5:19), substitute (5:21), gift (9:15), owner (10:7), and power (12:9).

KEYS TO SECOND CORINTHIANS

Key Word: Paul's Defense of His Ministry—The major theme of Second Corinthians is Paul's defense of his apostolic credentials and authority. This is especially evident in the portion directed to the still rebellious minority (10—13), but the theme of vindication is also clear in chapters 1—9. Certain false apostles had mounted an effective campaign against Paul in the church at Corinth, and Paul was forced to take a number of steps to overcome the opposition. This epistle expresses the apostle's joy over the triumph of the true gospel in Corinth (1—7), and it acknowledges the godly sorrow and repentance of the bulk of the believers. It also urges the Corinthians to fulfill their promise of making a liberal contribution for the poor among the Christians in Judea (8 and 9). This collection

would not only assist the poor, but it would also demonstrate the concern of gentile Christians in Macedonia and Achaia for Jewish Christians in Judea, thus displaying the unity of Jews and Gentiles in the body of Christ.

The opposition addressed in chapters 10—13 apparently consists of Jews (Palestinean or Hellenistic; 11:22) who claim to be apostles (11:5, 13; 12:11) but who preach a false gospel (11:4) and are enslaving in their leadership (11:20). Chapters 10—13 are intended to expose these "false apostles" (11:13), and defend Paul's God-given authority and ministry as an apostle of Jesus Christ.

Key Verses: Second Corinthians 4:5, 6 and 5:17-19—"For we preach not ourselves, but Christ Jesus the Lord; and ourselves your servants for Jesus' sake. For God, who commanded the light to shine out of darkness, hath shined in our hearts, to *give* the light of the knowledge of the glory of God in the face of Jesus Christ" (4:5, 6).

"Therefore if any man *be* in Christ, *he is* a new creature: old things are passed away; behold, all things are become new. And all things *are* of God, who hath reconciled us to himself by Jesus Christ, and hath given to us the ministry of reconciliation; To wit, that God was in Christ, reconciling the world unto himself, not imputing their trespasses unto them; and hath committed unto us the word of reconciliation" (5:17–19).

Key Chapters: Second Corinthians 8 and 9— Chapters 8 and 9 are really one unit and comprise the most complete revelation of God's plan for giving found anywhere in the Scriptures. Contained therein are the principles for giving (8:1–6), the purposes for giving (8:7–15), the policies to be followed in giving (8:16—9:5), and the promises to be realized in giving (9:6–15).

SURVEY OF SECOND CORINTHIANS

Second Corinthians describes the anatomy of an apostle. The Corinthian church has

been swayed by false teachers who have stirred the people against Paul, especially in response to First Corinthians, Paul's disciplinary letter. Throughout this letter (Second Corinthians) Paul defends his apostolic conduct, character, and call. The three major sections are: Paul's explanation of his ministry (1—7); Paul's collection for the saints (8 and 9); and Paul's vindication of his apostleship (10—13).

Paul's Explanation of His Ministry (1—7): After his salutation and thanksgiving for God's comfort in his afflictions and perils (1:1-11), Paul explains why he has delayed his planned visit to Corinth. It is not a matter of vacillation: the apostle wants them to have enough time to repent (1:12—2:4). Paul graciously asks them to restore the repentant offender to fellowship (2:5-13). At this point, Paul embarks on an extended defense of his ministry in terms of his message, circumstances, motives, and conduct (2:14—6:10). He then admonishes the believers to separate themselves from defilement (6:11—7:1), and expresses his comfort at Titus's news of their change of heart (7:2-16).

Paul's Collection for the Saints (8 and 9): This is the longest discussion of the principles and practice of giving in the New Testament. The example of the Macedonians' liberal giving for the needy brethren in Jerusalem (8:1-6) is followed by an appeal to the Corinthians to keep their promise by doing the same (8:7—9:15). In this connection, Paul commends the messengers he has sent to Corinth to make arrangements for the large gift they have promised. Their generosity will be more than amply rewarded by God.

Paul's Vindication of His Apostleship (10—13): Paul concludes this epistle with a defense of his apostolic authority and credentials that is directed to the still rebellious minority in the Corinthian Church. His meekness in their presence in no way diminishes his authority as an apostle (10). To demonstrate his apostolic

FOCUS	EXPLANATION OF PAUL'S MINISTRY			COLLECTION FOR THE SAINTS		VINDICATION OF PAUL'S APOSTLESHIP		
REFERENCE	1:1——2:14	——6:11	——8:1	——8:7	——10:1	——11:1	——12:14–13:14	
DIVISION	HIS CHANGE OF PLANS	PHILOSOPHY OF MINISTRY	EXHORTATIONS TO THE CORINTHIANS	EXAMPLE OF THE MACEDONIANS	EXHORTATION TO THE CORINTHIANS	ANSWERS HIS ACCUSERS	DEFENDS HIS APOSTLESHIP	ANNOUNCES HIS UPCOMING VISIT
TOPIC	CHARACTER OF PAUL			COLLECTION FOR SAINTS		CREDENTIALS OF PAUL		
	EPHESUS TO MACEDONIA: CHANGE OF ITINERARY			MACEDONIA: PREPARATION FOR VISIT		TO CORINTH: IMMINENT VISIT		
LOCATION	WRITTEN IN MACEDONIA							
TIME	C. A.D. 56							

credentials, Paul is forced to boast about his knowledge, integrity, accomplishments, sufferings, visions, and miracles (11:1—12:13). He reveals his plans to visit them for the third time and urges them to repent so that he will not have to use severity when he comes (12:14—13:10). The letter ends with an exhortation, greetings, and a benediction (13:11–14).

OUTLINE OF SECOND CORINTHIANS

Part One: Paul's Explanation of His Ministry (1:1—7:16)

Part Two: Paul's Collection for the Saints (8:1—9:15)

Part Three: Paul's Vindication of His Apostleship (10:1—13:14)

CHAPTER 1

Paul's Thanksgiving to God

PAUL, Ran apostle of Jesus Christ by the will of God, and Timothy *our* brother, unto the church of God which is at Corinth, Rwith all the saints which are in all A-cha'-ia: 1 Tim. 1:1; 2 Tim. 1:1 • Phil. 1:1; Col. 1:2

2 Grace *be* to you and peace from God our Father, and *from* the Lord Jesus Christ.

3 RBlessed *be* God, even the Father of our Lord Jesus Christ, the Father of mercies, and the God of all comfort;   Eph. 1:3; 1 Pet. 1:3

4 Who Tcomforteth us in all our Ttribulation, that we may be able to comfort them which are in any trouble, by the Tcomfort wherewith we ourselves Tare comforted of God.   *helps • trouble • help • have received*

5 For as Rthe sufferings of Christ abound in us, so our Tconsolation also aboundeth by Christ.   4:10; [Acts 9:4]; Col. 1:24 • *comfort*

6 And whether we be afflicted, Rit *is* for your consolation and salvation, which is Teffectual in the enduring of the same sufferings which we also suffer: or whether we be comforted, *it is* for your consolation and salvation.   4:15; 2 Tim. 2:10; Eph. 3:1, 13 • *working*

7 And our hope of you *is* stedfast, knowing, that as ye are partakers of the sufferings, so *shall ye be* also of the consolation.

Paul's Trouble in Asia

8 For we would not, brethren, have you ignorant of Rour trouble which came to us in Asia, that we were Tpressed out of measure, above strength, insomuch that we despaired even of life: Acts 19:23 • *burdened*

9 But we had the sentence of death in ourselves, that we should not trust in ourselves, but in God which raiseth the dead:

10 RWho delivered us from so great a death, and doth deliver: in whom we trust that he will yet deliver *us;*   [2 Pet. 2:9]

11 Ye also helping together by prayer for us, that for the gift Tbestowed upon us by the means of many persons thanks may be given by many on our behalf.   *given to*

Paul's Original Plan

12 For our rejoicing is this, the testimony of our conscience, that in Tsimplicity and godly sincerity, not with fleshly wisdom, but by the grace of God, we Thave had our conversation in the world, and more abundantly to you-ward.   *holiness • behaved ourselves*

13 For we write none other things unto you, than what ye read or acknowledge; and I trust ye shall acknowledge even to the end;

14 As also ye have acknowledged us in part, that we are your rejoicing, even as ye also *are* our's in the day of the Lord Jesus.

15 And in this confidence I was minded to come unto you before, that ye might have Ra second Tbenefit;   Rom. 1:11 • *favour*

16 And to pass by you into Mac-e-do'-ni-a, and Rto come again out of Mac-e-do'-ni-a unto you, and of you to be Tbrought on my way toward Ju-dae'-a.   1 Cor. 16:5, 6 • *helped*

17 When I therefore was thus minded, did I Tuse lightness? or the things that I purpose, do I purpose Raccording to the flesh, that with me there should be yea yea, and nay nay?   *show fickleness • 10:2*

18 But *as* God *is* Ttrue, our Tword toward you was not yea and nay.   *faithful • preaching*

19 For the Son of God, Jesus Christ, who was preached among you by us, *even* by me and Sil-va'-nus and Ti-mo'-the-us, was not yea and nay, but in him was yea.

20 RFor all the promises of God in him *are* Tyea, and in him A-men', unto the glory of God by us.   [Rom. 15:8] • *positive*

21 Now he which stablisheth us with you in Christ, and hath anointed us, *is* God;

22 Who hath also sealed us, and given the earnest of the Spirit in our hearts.

Paul's Change of Plans

23 Moreover RI call God for a record upon my soul, that to spare you I Rcame not as yet unto Corinth.   Gal. 1:20 • 1 Cor. 4:21

24 Not for Rthat we have Tdominion over your faith, but are helpers of your joy: for Rby faith ye stand.   [1 Pet. 5:3] • *rule* • Rom. 11:20

CHAPTER 2

BUT I determined this with myself, Rthat I would not come again to you in Theaviness.   1:23 • *depression of spirit*

2 For if I make you sorry, who is he then that maketh me glad, but the same which is made Tsorry by me?   *sad*

3 And I wrote this same unto you, lest, when I came, RI should have sorrow from them of whom I ought to rejoice; Rhaving confidence in you all, that my joy is *the joy* of you all.   7:16; 12:21 • 8:22; Gal. 5:10

4 For out of much Taffliction and anguish of heart I wrote unto you with many tears; Rnot that ye should be grieved, but that ye might know the love which I have more abundantly unto you.   *grief* • [7:8, 9]

Paul's Appeal to Forgive

5 But Rif any have caused grief, he hath not Rgrieved me, but in part: that I may not overcharge you all.   [1 Cor. 5:1] • Gal. 4:12

6 Sufficient to such a man *is* this Tpunishment, which *was inflicted* of many.   *rebuke*

7 RSo that contrariwise ye *ought* rather to forgive *him,* and comfort *him,* lest perhaps such a one should be Tswallowed up with overmuch sorrow.   Gal. 6:1 • *utterly discouraged*

8 Wherefore I beseech you that ye would ᵀconfirm *your* love toward him.   *give evidence of*

9 For to this end also did I write, that I might know the proof of you, whether ye be ᴿobedient in all things.   7:15; 10:6

10 To whom ye forgive any thing, I *forgive* also: for if I forgave any thing, to whom I forgave *it*, for your sakes *forgave I it* in the ᵀperson of Christ;   *presence*

11 Lest Satan should get an advantage of us: for we are not ignorant of his devices.

12 Furthermore, when I came to Tro'-as to *preach* Christ's gospel, and a ᵀdoor was opened unto me of the Lord,   *an opportunity*

13 ᴿI ᵀhad no rest in my spirit, because I found not Titus my brother: but taking my leave of them, I went from thence into Mac-e-do'-ni-a.   7:5, 6 · *was worried*

Christ Causes Us to Triumph

14 Now thanks *be* unto God, which always causeth us to triumph in Christ, and maketh ᵀmanifest the ᵀsavour of his knowledge by us in every place.   *known · fragrance*

15 For we are unto God a sweet savour of Christ, ᴿin them that are saved, and ᴿin them that perish: [1 Cor. 1:18] · [4:3]

16 ᴿTo the one *we are* the savour of death unto death; and to the other the savour of life unto life. And ᴿwho *is* sufficient for these things?   Luke 2:34 · [1 Cor. 15:10; 1 Pet. 2:7, 8]

17 For we are not as many, which corrupt the word of God: but as of sincerity, but as of God, in the sight of God speak we in Christ.

CHAPTER 3

Changed Lives Prove Ministry

DO we begin again to commend our-selves? or need we, as some *others*, ᴿepistles of commendation to you, or *letters* of commendation from you?   Acts 18:27

2 ᴿYe are our epistle written in our hearts, known and read of all men: 1 Cor. 9:2

3 *Forasmuch as ye are* manifestly declared to be the epistle of Christ ministered by us, written not with ink, but with the Spirit of the living God; not in tables of stone, but in fleshy tables of the heart.

4 And such ᵀtrust have we through Christ to God-ward: *confidence*

5 ᴿNot that we are sufficient of ourselves to think any thing as of ourselves; but ᴿour sufficiency *is* of God;   [John 15:5] · 1 Cor. 15:10

New Covenant Is the Basis of Ministry

6 Who also hath made us able ᵀministers of the new testament; not of the letter, but of the spirit: for the letter killeth, but the spirit giveth life.   *communicators*

7 But if the ᵀministration of death, written *and* engraven in stones, was glorious, so that the children of Israel could not stedfastly behold the face of Moses for the glory of his countenance; which *glory* was to be done away: *dispensation*

8 How shall not ᴿthe ministration of the spirit be rather glorious?   [Gal. 3:5]

9 For if the ministration of condemnation *be* glory, much more doth the ministration ᴿof righteousness exceed in glory.   [Rom. 1:17]

10 For even that which was made glorious had no glory in ᵀthis respect, by reason of the glory that excelleth.   *comparison to this*

11 For if that which ᵀis done away *was* ᵀglorious, much more that which remaineth *is* glorious.   *passeth · with glory*

12 Seeing then that we have such hope, we use great ᵀplainness of speech: *boldness*

13 And not as Moses, ᴿwhich put a vail over his face, that the children of Israel could not stedfastly look to ᴿthe end of that which is abolished: Ex. 34:33 · [Gal. 3:23]

14 ᴿBut their minds were blinded: for until this day remaineth the same vail untaken away in the reading of the old testament; which *vail* is done away in Christ.   Is. 29:10 ★

15 But even unto this day, when Moses is read, the vail is upon their heart.

16 Nevertheless when it shall turn to the Lord, ᴿthe vail shall be taken away.   Is. 25:7

17 Now the Lord is that Spirit: and where the Spirit of the Lord *is*, there *is* liberty.

18 But we all, with open face beholding as in a glass the glory of the Lord, are changed into the same image from glory to glory, *even* as by the Spirit of the Lord.

CHAPTER 4

Christ Is the Theme of Ministry

THEREFORE seeing we have this ministry, ᴿas we have received mercy, we ᵀfaint not;   3:6; 1 Cor. 7:25; [1 Tim. 1:13] · *do not falter*

2 But have renounced the hidden things of dishonesty, not walking in craftiness, nor handling the word of God deceitfully; but by ᵀmanifestation of the truth commending ourselves to every man's conscience in the sight of God.   *open demonstration*

3 But if ᴿour gospel be ᵀhid, ᴿit is hid to them that are lost: [Rom. 16:25] · *veiled* · [1 Cor. 1:18]

4 In whom ᴿthe god of this world hath blinded the minds of them which believe not, lest ᴿthe light of the glorious gospel of Christ, ᴿwho is the image of God, should shine unto them.   [Eph. 6:12] · [3:8, 9] · [John 1:18]

5 ᴿFor we preach not ourselves, but Christ Jesus the Lord; and ᴿourselves your servants for Jesus' sake.   1 Cor. 1:13 · 1 Cor. 9:19

6 For God, who commanded the light to shine out of darkness, hath shined in our

hearts, to *give* the light of the knowledge of the glory of God in the face of Jesus Christ.

7 But we have this treasure in earthen vessels, ᴿthat the excellency of the power may be of God, and not of us.   Acts 9:15

Trials Abound in the Ministry

8 *We are* troubled on every side, yet not distressed; *we are* ᵀperplexed, but ᵀnot in despair;   *puzzled · not altogether without help; or, means*

9 Persecuted, but not forsaken; ᴿcast down, but not destroyed;   Ps. 37:24

10 Always bearing about in the body the dying of the Lord Jesus, that the life also of Jesus might be made manifest in our body.

11 For we which live ᴿare alway delivered unto death for Jesus' sake, that the life also of Jesus might be made manifest in our mortal flesh.   Rom. 8:36

12 So then death worketh in us, but life in you.

13 We having the same spirit of faith, according as it is written, ᴿI believed, and therefore have I spoken; we also believe, and therefore speak;   Ps. 116:10; Rom. 1:12; 2 Pet. 1:1

14 Knowing that ᴿhe which raised up the Lord Jesus shall raise up us also by Jesus, and shall present *us* with you.   [Rom. 8:11]

15 For all things *are* for your sakes, that ᴿthe abundant grace might through the thanksgiving of many ᵀredound to the glory of God.   1:11 · *contribute*

Motivation of External Perspective

16 For which cause we faint not; but though our outward man perish, yet the inward *man* is renewed day by day.

17 For our light affliction, which is but for a moment, worketh for us a far more exceeding *and* eternal weight of glory;

18 ᴿWhile we look not at the things which are seen, but at the things which are not seen: for the things which are seen *are* temporal; but the things which are not seen *are* eternal.   Rom. 8:24; [Heb. 11:1]

CHAPTER 5

Motivation of the Future Presence of Christ

FOR we know that if ᴿour earthly house of this tabernacle were dissolved, we have a building of God, an house not made with hands, eternal in the heavens.   Job 4:19

2 For in this ᴿwe ᵀgroan, earnestly desiring to be clothed upon with our house which is from heaven: Rom. 8:23 · *sigh*

3 If so be that ᴿbeing clothed we shall not be found ᵀnaked.   Rev. 3:18 · *without a body*

4 For we that are in *this* tabernacle do groan, being burdened: not for that we would be unclothed, but clothed upon, that mortality might be swallowed up of life.

5 Now he that hath ᵀwrought us for the selfsame thing *is* God, who also hath given unto us the earnest of the Spirit.   *prepared*

6 Therefore *we are* always confident, knowing that, whilst we are at home in the body, we are absent from the Lord:

7 (For we walk by faith, not by sight:)

8 We are ᵀconfident, *I say,* and willing rather to be absent from the body, and to be present with the Lord.   *of good courage*

Motivation of Future Reward

9 Wherefore we ᵀlabour, that, whether present or absent, we may be ᵀaccepted of him.   *also make it our aim · well-pleasing to*

10 ᴿFor we must all appear before the judgment seat of Christ; ᴿthat every one may receive the things *done* in *his* body, according to that he hath done, whether *it be* good or bad.   Rom. 14:10 · Gal. 6:7; Eph. 6:8 ☆

Motivation of the Love of Christ

11 Knowing therefore ᴿthe terror of the Lord, we persuade men; but we are made manifest unto God; and I trust also are made manifest in your consciences.   Heb. 10:31

12 For ᴿwe commend not ourselves again unto you, but give you occasion ᴿto ᵀglory on our behalf, that ye may have somewhat to *answer* them which glory in appearance, and not in heart.   3:1 · 1:14 · *take pride*

13 For ᴿwhether we be ᵀbeside ourselves, *it is* to God: or whether we be ᵀsober, *it is* for your cause.   11:6, 16 · *insane · of sound mind*

14 For the love of Christ constraineth us; because we thus judge, that ᴿif one died for all, then were all dead: [Rom. 5:15]

15 And *that* he died for all, ᴿthat they which live should not henceforth live unto themselves, but unto him which died for them, and rose again.   [Rom. 6:11; Gal. 2:20]

16 ᴿWherefore henceforth know we no man after the flesh: yea, though we have known Christ after the flesh, yet now henceforth know we *him* no more.   [John 6:63]

Motivation of the Message of Reconciliation

17 Therefore if any man *be* in Christ, *he is* a new creature: old things are passed away; behold, all things are become new.

5:17 New Nature—The term *new nature* refers to the spiritual transformation that occurs within the inner man when a person believes in Christ as Saviour. The Christian is now a *new man* as opposed to the *old man* that he was before he became a Christian (Page 1112—Rom. 6:6; Page 1163—Eph. 2:15; 4:22–24; Page 1178—Col. 3:9, 10). This concept of *newness* may be traced to an important choice between two Greek words, both meaning "new." One word means "new" in the sense of renovation (to

(continued on next page)

18 And all things *are* of God, [R]who hath reconciled us to himself by Jesus Christ, and hath given to us the ministry of reconciliation;   Rom. 5:10; [Eph. 2:16; Col. 1:20]

19 To wit, that God was in Christ, reconciling the world unto himself, not imputing their trespasses unto them; and hath committed unto us the word of reconciliation.

20 Now then we are ambassadors for Christ, as though God did beseech *you* by us: we [T]pray *you* [T]in Christ's stead, be ye reconciled to God.   beseech • on behalf of Christ

21 For [R]he hath made him *to be* sin for us, who knew no sin; that we might be made the righteousness of God in him.   Is. 53:6, 9 *

CHAPTER 6

Giving No Offence in the Ministry

WE then, *as* workers together *with him*, beseech *you* also that ye receive not the grace of God [T]in vain.   to no good use

2 (For he saith, [R]I HAVE HEARD THEE IN A TIME ACCEPTED, AND IN THE DAY OF SALVATION HAVE I [T]SUCCOURED THEE: behold, now *is* the accepted time; behold, now *is* the day of salvation.)   Is. 49:8 * • helped

3 [R]Giving no offence in any thing, that the ministry be not blamed: Rom. 14:13

4 But in all *things* approving ourselves as the ministers of God, in much patience, in afflictions, in necessities, in distresses,

5 In stripes, in imprisonments, in tumults, in labours, in watchings, in fastings;

6 By pureness, by knowledge, by [T]longsuffering, by kindness, by the Holy Ghost, by love [T]unfeigned,   patience • genuine

7 By the word of truth, by the power of God, by [R]the armour of righteousness on the right hand and on the left,   10:4

8 By honour and [T]dishonour, by [T]evil report and [T]good report: as [T]deceivers, and *yet* true;   disagreement • insult • praise • liars

9 As unknown, and [R]yet well known; [R]as dying, and, behold, we live; [R]as chastened, and not killed;   4:2 • 1 Cor. 4:9 • Ps. 118:18

10 As sorrowful, yet alway rejoicing; as poor, yet making many rich; as having nothing, and *yet* possessing all things.

Paul's Appeal for Reconciliation

11 O *ye* Corinthians, our mouth is open unto you, [R]our heart is enlarged.   7:3

12 Ye are not straitened in us, but ye are straitened in your own [T]bowels.   emotions

13 Now for a [T]recompence in the same, (I speak as unto *my* children,) [T]be ye also enlarged.   response • let your affections grow also

Paul's Appeal for Separation from Unbelievers

14 [R]Be ye not unequally yoked together with unbelievers: for [R]what fellowship hath righteousness with unrighteousness? and what communion hath light with darkness?   Deut. 7:2, 3; 1 Cor. 5:9 • 1 Kin. 18:21

15 And what concord hath Christ with Be'-li-al? or what part hath he that believeth with an [T]infidel?   unbeliever

16 And what agreement hath the temple of God with idols? for ye are the temple of the living God; as God hath said, I WILL DWELL IN THEM, AND WALK IN *THEM;* AND I WILL BE THEIR GOD, AND THEY SHALL BE MY PEOPLE.

17 [R]WHEREFORE COME OUT FROM AMONG THEM, AND BE YE SEPARATE, saith the Lord, AND TOUCH NOT THE UNCLEAN *THING;* AND I WILL RECEIVE YOU,   Is. 52:11

18 [R]AND WILL BE A FATHER UNTO YOU, AND YE SHALL BE MY SONS AND DAUGHTERS, saith the Lord Almighty.   2 Sam. 7:14; Is. 43:6

CHAPTER 7

HAVING therefore these promises, dearly beloved, let us cleanse ourselves from all filthiness of the flesh and spirit, perfecting holiness in the fear of God.

Paul's Meeting with Titus

2 Receive us; we have wronged no man, we have [T]corrupted no man, [R]we have [T]defrauded no man.   injured • Acts 20:33 • robbed

3 I speak not *this* to condemn *you:* for [R]I have said before, that ye are in our hearts to die and live with *you.*   6:11, 12

4 [R]Great *is* my boldness of speech toward you, great *is* my [T]glorying of you: [R]I am filled with comfort, I am exceeding joyful in all our tribulation.   3:12 • pride in • Col. 1:24

(continued from previous page)
repair), the other in the sense of fresh existence. It is the latter that is used to describe the Christian. He is not the old man renovated or refreshed; he is a brand-new man with a new family, a new set of values, new motivations, and new possessions.

The old man is still present in the new life and expresses himself in corrupting deeds such as lying (Page 1165—Eph. 4:22; Page 1178—Col. 3:9). The new man, to be visible, must be *put on* as one would put on a new suit of clothes (Page 1178—Col. 3:10). In other words, the new nature must be cultivated or nurtured by spiritual decisiveness to grow in Christ. We must not revert to putting on the *old suit* of the former life; rather, we must continue to grow in this new life (Page 1165—Eph. 5:8).

The message of the new nature is a message of supreme hope: the Spirit of God can accomplish a life-changing transformation for all who will only believe in Christ.

Now turn to Page 701—Is. 61:10: Christ's Righteousness.

5 For, when we were come into Mac-e-do'-ni-a, our flesh had no rest, but ᴿwe were troubled on every side; ᴿwithout *were* fightings, within *were* fears.   4:8 · Deut. 32:25

6 Nevertheless ᴿGod, that comforteth ᵀthose that are cast down, comforted us by ᴿthe coming of Titus;   1:4 · *the lowly* · 2:13

7 And not by his coming only, but by the consolation wherewith he was comforted in you, when he told us your earnest desire, your mourning, your ᵀfervent mind toward me; so that I rejoiced the more.   *warm affection*

Corinthians' Response to Paul's Letter

8 For though I made you sorry with a letter, I do not repent, ᴿthough I did repent: for I perceive that the same epistle hath made you sorry, though *it were* but for a season. 2:4

9 Now I rejoice, not that ye were made sorry, but that ye sorrowed to repentance: for ye were made sorry ᵀafter a godly manner, that ye might ᵀreceive damage by us in nothing.   *according to* · *suffer loss*

10 For godly sorrow worketh repentance to salvation not to be repented of: but the sorrow of the world worketh death.

11 For behold this selfsame thing, that ye sorrowed after a godly sort, what ᵀcarefulness it wrought in you, yea, *what* clearing of yourselves, yea, *what* indignation, yea, *what* fear, yea, *what* vehement desire, yea, *what* zeal, yea, *what* ᵀrevenge! In all *things* ye have ᵀapproved yourselves to be ᵀclear in this matter.   *heart-searching* · *avenging* · *shown* · *pure*

12 Wherefore, though I wrote unto you, *I did it* not for his cause that had done the wrong, nor for his cause that suffered wrong, ᴿbut that our care for you in the sight of God might appear unto you.   2:4

13 Therefore we were comforted in your comfort: yea, and exceedingly the more joyed we for the joy of Titus, because his spirit ᴿwas refreshed by you all.   Rom. 15:32

14 For if I have boasted any thing to him of you, I am not ᵀashamed; but as we spake all things to you in truth, even so our boasting, which *I made* before Titus, is found ᵀa truth.   *embarrassed* · *to be*

15 And his inward affection is more abundant toward you, whilst he remembereth ᴿthe obedience of you all, how with fear and trembling ye received him.   Phil. 2:12

16 I rejoice therefore that ᴿI have confidence in you in all *things*.   Philem. 8, 21

CHAPTER 8

Example of the Macedonians

MOREOVER, brethren, we ᵀdo you to wit of the grace of God bestowed on the churches of Mac-e-do'-ni-a;   *inform*

2 How that in ᵀa great trial of affliction the abundance of their joy and ᴿtheir deep poverty abounded unto the riches of their liberality.   *a time of much trouble* · Mark 12:44

3 For to *their* power, I bear record, yea, and beyond *their* power *they* ᵀwere willing of themselves;   *gave of their own accord*

4 Praying us with much intreaty that we would receive the gift, and *take upon us* the fellowship of the ministering to the saints.

5 And *this they did,* ᵀnot as we hoped, but first gave their own selves to the Lord, and unto us by the will of God.   *more than*

6 Insomuch that ᴿwe desired Titus, that as he had begun, so he would also finish in you the same grace also.   *v.* 17; 12:18

Example of Christ

7 Therefore, as ye abound in every *thing*, *in* faith, and utterance, and knowledge, and *in* all diligence, and *in* your love to us, *see* that ye abound in this grace also.

8 ᴿI speak not by commandment, but by occasion of the forwardness of others, and to prove the sincerity of your love.   *v.* 24

9 For ye know the grace of our Lord Jesus Christ, ᴿthat, though he was rich, yet for your sakes he became poor, that ye through his poverty might be rich.   Luke 9:58

Purpose of Giving

10 And herein I give *my* advice: for this is ᵀexpedient for you, who have begun before, not only to do, but also to be ᴿforwardᵀ a year ago.   *best* · 9:2 · *aggressive*

11 Now therefore perform the doing *of it;* that as *there was* a ᵀreadiness to will, so *there may be* a performance also out of that which ye have.   *eagerness*

12 For if there be first a willing mind, *it is* accepted according to that a man hath, *and* not according to that he hath not.

13 For *I mean* not that other men be eased, and ye burdened:

14 But by an equality, *that* now at this time your abundance *may be a supply* for their ᵀwant, that their abundance also may be *a supply* for your want: that there may be equality: *need*

15 As it is written, HE THAT HAD GATHERED MUCH HAD NOTHING OVER; AND HE THAT HAD GATHERED LITTLE HAD NO LACK.

Policies in Giving

16 But thanks *be* to God, which ᴿput the same earnest care into the heart of Titus for you.   Rev. 17:17

17 For indeed he accepted ᵀthe exhortation; but being more forward, of his own accord he went unto you.   *our appeal*

18 And we have sent with him ᴿthe brother, whose praise *is* in the gospel throughout all the churches;   12:18

19 And not *that* only, but who was also chosen of the churches to travel with us with this grace, which is ᵀadministered by us to the glory of the same Lord, and *declaration of* your ready mind: *handled*

20 ᴿAvoiding this, that no man should blame us in this abundance which is ᵀadministered by us: Acts 11:30 • *handled*

21 ᴿProviding for honest things, not only in the sight of the Lord, but also in the sight of men.   Rom. 12:17; Phil. 4:8; 1 Pet. 2:12

22 And we have sent with them our brother, whom we have ᵀoftentimes proved diligent in many things, but now much more ᵀdiligent, upon the great confidence which *I* have in you.   *always • earnest*

23 Whether *any do enquire* of Titus, *he is* my partner and fellowhelper concerning you: or our brethren *be enquired of, they are* ᴿthe ᵀmessengers of the churches, *and* the glory of Christ.   Phil. 2:25 • *representatives*

24 Wherefore shew ye to them, and before the churches, the ᵀproof of your love, and of our boasting on your behalf.   *evidence*

CHAPTER 9

Readiness in Giving

FOR as ᵀtouching the ministering to the saints, it is superfluous for me to write to you: *concerning the helping of other believers*

2 ᴿFor I know the ᵀforwardness of your mind, for which I boast of you to them of Mac′-e-do′-ni-a, that A-cha′-ia was ready a year ago; and your zeal hath ᵀprovoked very many.   8:10, 19, 24 • *willingness • stirred*

3 Yet have I sent the brethren, lest our boasting of you should be in vain in this behalf; that, as I said, ye may be ready:

4 Lest haply if they of Mac-e-do′-ni-a come with me, and find you unprepared, we (that we say not, ye) should be ashamed in this same confident boasting.

5 Therefore I thought it necessary to

ᵀexhort the brethren, that they would go before unto you, and make up beforehand your bounty, whereof ye had notice before, that the same might be ready, as *a matter of* bounty, and not as *of* covetousness.   *urge*

Principles in Giving

6 ᴿBut this *I say,* He which soweth sparingly shall reap also sparingly; and he which soweth ᵀbountifully shall reap also bountifully.   Prov. 11:24; 22:9; Gal. 6:7, 9 • *plentifully*

7 Every man according as he purposeth in his heart, *so let him give;* ᴿnot grudgingly, or ᵀof necessity: for God loveth a cheerful giver.   Deut. 15:7; Philem. 14 • *unwillingly*

Promises from Giving

8 ᴿAnd God *is* able to make all grace abound toward you; that ye, always having all sufficiency in all *things,* may abound to every good work: [Prov. 28:27; Phil. 4:19]

9 (As it is written, ᴿHE HATH DISPERSED ABROAD; HE HATH GIVEN TO THE POOR: HIS RIGHTEOUSNESS REMAINETH FOR EVER.   Ps. 112:9

10 Now he that ᵀministereth seed to the sower both minister bread for *your* food, and multiply your seed sown, and increase the fruits of your righteousness;)   *gives*

11 Being enriched in every thing to all ᵀbountifulness, ᴿwhich causeth through us thanksgiving to God.   *plentifulness* • 1:11

12 For the ᵀadministration of this service not only ᴿsupplieth the ᵀwant of the saints, but is abundant also by many thanksgivings unto God;   *rendering* • 8:14 • *need*

13 Whiles by the ᵀexperiment of this ᵀministration they glorify God for your professed subjection unto the gospel of Christ, and for *your* liberal distribution unto them, and unto all *men;*   *experience • service*

14 And by their prayer for you, which ᵀlong after you ᵀfor the exceeding ᴿgrace of God in you.   *yearn for • by reason of* • 8:1

15 Thanks *be* unto God ᴿfor his ᵀunspeakable gift.   [James 1:17] • *priceless*

9:6–8 Giving—There is no better indicator of growth in the new life than in the area of giving. This passage deals with the attitude one should have in his giving—it should be cheerful. When giving is cheerful, it will also be generous. The important rule of thumb is not how much is given, but how much is left after the giving. God is not primarily occupied with the amount of the gift, but with the motive that lies behind it. All the money in the world belongs to God. My gift to Him does not make Him any richer; it makes me richer spiritually because of the realization that everything I have is His and that I am giving because I love Him and want to give.

The formula for giving is found in First Corinthians 16:2 where three principles can be seen: (1) my giving is to be regular, "Upon the first *day* of the week"; (2) my giving is to be systematic, "let every one of you lay by him in store"; and (3) my giving is to be proportionate, "as *God* hath prospered him."

Failure to give of the money which God has given is a serious matter. The person who fails to honor God with his money actually robs God (Page 909—Mal. 3:8), not because it impoverishes God but because it denies the God-ordained means for the support of His work and His ministers. For the child of God who honors God with his money God promises abundant blessing (Page 909—Mal. 3:10; Page 1012—Luke 6:38) and the provision of his every need (Page 1173—Phil. 4:19). Giving, then, is a key to growth in the new life.

Now turn to Page 421—1 Chr. 16:29: The Meaning of Worship.

CHAPTER 10

The Charge of Cowardice Is Answered

NOW I Paul myself beseech you by the meekness and gentleness of Christ, who in presence *am* ᵀbase among you, but being absent am bold toward you: *lowly*

2 But I beseech *you,* ᴿthat I may not be bold when I am present with that confidence, wherewith I think to be bold against some, which think of us as if we walked according to the flesh.   1 Cor. 4:21

The Charge of Walking in the Flesh Is Answered

3 ᴿFor though we walk in the flesh, we do not war after the flesh: [Eph. 6:11-18]

4 (ᴿFor the weapons of our warfare *are* not carnal, but mighty through God to the pulling down of strong holds;)   John 18:36

5 Casting down imaginations, and every high thing that exalteth itself against the knowledge of God, and bringing into captivity every thought to the obedience of Christ;

6 ᴿAnd having in a readiness to ᵀrevenge all disobedience, when ᴿyour obedience is fulfilled.   13:2, 10 • *avenge* • 7:15

7 ᴿDo ye look on things after the outward appearance? ᴿIf any man trust to himself that he is Christ's, let him of himself think this again, that, as he *is* Christ's, even so *are* ᴿwe Christ's.   [John 7:24] • 1 Cor. 14:37 • 1 Cor. 3:23

8 For though I should boast somewhat more of our authority, which the Lord hath given us for edification, and not for your destruction, ᴿI should not be ashamed: 7:14

9 That I may not seem as if I would ᵀterrify you by letters.   *frighten*

The Charge of Personal Weakness Is Answered

10 For *his* letters, say they, *are* weighty and powerful; but *his* bodily presence *is* weak, and *his* speech ᵀcontemptible.   *common*

11 Let such an one think this, that, such as we are in word by letters when we are absent, ᵀsuch *will we be* also in deed when we are present.   *we will be the same*

12 For we dare not make ourselves of the number, or compare ourselves with some that commend themselves: but they measuring themselves by themselves, and comparing themselves among themselves, are not wise.

13 ᴿBut we will not boast of things without *our* measure, but according to the measure of the rule which God hath distributed to us, a measure to reach even unto you.   *v. 15*

14 For we stretch not ourselves beyond *our measure,* as though we reached not unto you: for we are come as far as to you also in *preaching* the gospel of Christ:

15 Not boasting of things without *our* measure, *that is,* ᴿof other men's labours; but

having hope, when your faith is increased, that we shall be enlarged by you according to our rule abundantly,   Rom. 15:20

16 To preach the gospel in the *regions* beyond you, *and* not to boast in another man's line of things made ready to our hand.

17 ᴿBut he that ᵀglorieth, let him glory in the Lord.   Is. 65:16 • *boasts*

18 For ᴿnot he that commendeth himself is approved, but ᴿwhom the Lord commendeth.   Prov. 27:2 • Rom. 2:29; [1 Cor. 4:5]

CHAPTER 11

Paul's Declaration of His Apostleship

WOULD to God ye could bear with me ᵀa little in ᴿmy folly: and indeed bear with me.   *in a little foolishness* • *v. 16*

2 For I am jealous over you with godly jealously: for I have ᵀespoused you to one husband, ᴿthat I may present *you as* a chaste virgin to Christ.   *betrothed* • Col. 1:28

3 But I fear, lest by any means, as the serpent beguiled Eve through his subtilty, so your minds should be corrupted from the simplicity that is in Christ.

4 For if he that cometh preacheth another Jesus, whom we have not preached, or *if* ye receive another spirit, which ye have not received, or another gospel, which ye have not accepted, ye might well bear with *him.*

5 For I suppose ᴿI was not a whit behind the very chiefest apostles.   [1 Cor. 15:10]

6 But though *I* be rude in speech, yet not in knowledge; but we have been throughly made manifest among you in all things.

7 Have I committed an offence in ᵀabasing myself that ye might be ᵀexalted, because I have preached to you the gospel of God ᵀfreely?   *lowering* • *helped up* • *at no cost*

8 ᴿI robbed other churches, taking wages of them, to do you service.   12:13

9 And when I was present with you, and wanted, I ᵀwas chargeable to no man: for that which was lacking to me ᴿthe brethren which came from Mac-e-do'-ni-a supplied: and in all *things* I have kept myself from being burdensome unto you, and so will I keep *myself.*   *caused no expense to* • Phil. 4:10

10 ᴿAs the truth of Christ is in me, ᴿno man shall stop me of this boasting in the regions of A-cha'-ia.   Rom. 9:1 • 1 Cor. 9:15

11 Wherefore? ᴿbecause I love you not? God knoweth.   6:11; 7:3; 12:15

12 But what I do, that I will do, ᴿthat I may cut off occasion from them which desire occasion; that wherein they glory, they may be found even as we.   1 Cor. 9:12

13 For such ᴿare false apostles, ᴿdeceitful workers, transforming themselves into the apostles of Christ.   Rev. 2:2 • Phil. 3:2; Titus 1:10

14 And no marvel; for Satan himself is transformed into ᴿan angel of light.   Gal. 1:8

15 Therefore *it is* no great thing if his ministers also be ᵀtransformed as the ministers of righteousness; ᴿwhose end shall be according to their works. *fashioned* · [Phil. 3:19]

Paul's Sufferings Support His Apostleship

16 I say again, Let no man think me a fool; if otherwise, yet as a fool ᵀreceive me, that I may boast myself a little.   *tolerate*

17 That which I speak, ᴿI speak *it* not after the Lord, but as it were foolishly, in this confidence of boasting.   9:4

18 ᴿSeeing that many ᵀglory after the flesh, I will glory also.   [Phil. 3:3, 4] · *boast*

19 For ye ᵀsuffer fools gladly, ᴿseeing ye *yourselves* are wise.   *bear with* · 1 Cor. 4:10

20 For ye suffer, ᴿif a man bring you into bondage, if a man devour *you*, if a man ᵀtake *of you*, if a man exalt himself, if a man smite you on the face.   Gal. 2:4 · *capture*

21 I speak as concerning ᵀreproach, ᴿas though we had been weak. Howbeit ᴿwhereinsoever any is bold, (I speak foolishly,) I am bold also.   *criticism* · 10:10 · Phil. 3:4

22 Are they Hebrews? ᴿso *am* I. Are they Israelites? so *am* I. Are they the seed of Abraham? so *am* I.   Acts 22:3; Rom. 11:1; Phil. 3:5

23 Are they ministers of Christ? (I speak as a fool) I *am* more; ᴿin labours more abundant, in stripes above measure, in prisons more frequent, ᴿin deaths oft.   Acts 9:16 · 1:9

24 Of the Jews five times received I ᴿforty *stripes* save one.   Deut. 25:3; Acts 16:22

25 Thrice was I beaten with rods, once was I stoned, thrice I suffered shipwreck, a night and a day I have been in the deep;

26 *In* journeyings often, *in* perils of waters, *in* perils of robbers, ᴿin perils by *mine own* countrymen, ᴿin perils by the heathen, *in* perils in the city, *in* perils in the wilderness, *in* perils in the sea, *in* perils among false brethren;   Acts 9:23 · Acts 14:5

27 In weariness and painfulness, in watchings often, ᴿin hunger and thirst, in fastings often, in cold and nakedness.   6:5

28 Beside those things that are without, that which cometh upon me daily, ᴿthe ᵀcare of all the churches.   [Rom. 1:14] · *oversight*

29 Who is weak, and I am not weak? who is offended, and I ᵀburn not?   *grieve not*

30 If I must needs glory, I will glory of the things which concern mine infirmities.

31 The God and Father of our Lord Jesus Christ, ᴿwhich is blessed for evermore, knoweth that I lie not.   Rom. 9:5; Gal. 1:20

32 ᴿIn Damascus the governor under Ar′e-tas the king kept the city of the Dam-a-scenes′ with a garrison, ᵀdesirous to apprehend me: Acts 9:24 · *in order to take*

33 And through a window in a basket was I let down by the wall, and escaped his hands.

CHAPTER 12

Vision of Paradise

IT is not expedient for me doubtless to glory. I will come to visions and ᴿrevelations of the Lord.   [Gal. 1:12; 2:2; Eph. 3:3–6]

2 I knew a man in Christ above fourteen years ago, (whether in the body, I cannot tell; or whether out of the body, I cannot tell: God knoweth;) such an one caught up to the third heaven.

3 And I knew such a man, (whether in the body, or out of the body, I cannot tell: God knoweth;)

4 How that he was caught up into paradise, and heard unspeakable words, which it is not ᵀlawful for a man to utter.   *legal*

5 Of such an one will I glory: yet of myself I will not glory, but in mine infirmities.

6 For though I would desire to glory, I shall not be a fool; for I will say the truth: but now I ᵀforbear, lest any man should think of me above that which he seeth me *to be*, or *that* he heareth of me.   *will stop*

Thorn in the Flesh

7 And lest I should be exalted above measure through the abundance of the revelations, there was given to me a thorn in the flesh, the messenger of Satan to buffet me, lest I should be exalted above measure.

8 For this thing I besought the Lord thrice, that it might depart from me.

9 And he said unto me, My grace is sufficient for thee: for my strength is made perfect in weakness. Most gladly therefore will I rather glory in my infirmities, that the power of Christ may rest upon me.

10 Therefore ᴿI take pleasure in infirmities, in reproaches, in necessities, in persecutions, in distresses for Christ's sake: for when I am weak, then am I strong.   [Rom. 5:3]

Paul's Signs Support His Apostleship

11 I am become a fool in ᵀglorying; ye have compelled me: for I ought to have been commended of you: for in nothing am I behind the very chiefest apostles, though ᴿI be nothing.   *praising myself* · 1 Cor. 3:7

12 Truly the signs of an apostle were wrought among you in all patience, in signs, and wonders, and mighty deeds.

13 For what is it wherein ye were inferior to other churches, except *it be* that I myself was not ᵀburdensome to you? ᴿforgive me this wrong.   *costly* · [11:7–9; 1 Cor. 1:7; 9:12]

Paul's Concern Not to Be a Financial Burden

14 Behold, the third time I am ready to come to you; and I will not be burdensome to you: for I seek not your's, but you: for the children ought not to lay up for the parents, but the parents for the children.

15 And I will very gladly spend and be spent for you; though the more abundantly I love you, the less I be loved.

16 But ᵀbe it so, ᴿI did not burden you: nevertheless, being crafty, I caught you with guile.   *you will agree* • 11:9

17 Did I ᵀmake a gain of you by any of them whom I sent unto you?   *take advantage*

18 I desired Titus, and with *him* I sent a brother. Did Titus ᵀmake a gain of you? walked we not in the same spirit? *walked we* not in the same steps?   *take any advantage*

Paul's Concern Not to Find Them Carnal

19 ᴿAgain, think ye that we excuse ourselves unto you? we speak before God in Christ: but *we do* all things, dearly beloved, for your ᵀedifying.   5:12 • *upbuilding*

20 For I fear, lest, when I come, I shall not find you such as I would, and *that* I shall be found unto you such as ye would not: lest *there be* debates, envyings, wraths, strifes, backbitings, whisperings, swellings, tumults:

21 *And* lest, when I come again, my God will humble me among you, and *that* I shall ᵀbewail many which have sinned already, and have not repented of the uncleanness and fornication and lasciviousness which they have committed.   *mourn over*

CHAPTER 13

Paul's Warning to Examine Yourselves

THIS *is* the third *time* I am coming to you. In the mouth of two or three witnesses shall every word be established.

2 I told you before, and foretell you, as if I were present, the second time; and being absent now I write to them which heretofore

have sinned, and to all other, that, if I come again, I will not spare:

3 Since ye seek a proof of Christ ᴿspeaking in me, which to you-ward is not weak, but is mighty ᴿin you.   1 Cor. 5:4 • [1 Cor. 9:2]

4 ᴿFor though he was crucified through weakness, yet ᴿhe liveth by the power of God. For we also are weak ᵀin him, but we shall live with him by the power of God toward you.   [1 Pet. 3:18] • [10:3, 4] • *with him*

5 Examine yourselves, whether ye be in the faith; prove your own selves. Know ye not your own selves, how that Jesus Christ is in you, except ye be reprobates?

6 But I trust that ye shall know that we are not ᵀreprobates.   *failures*

7 Now I pray to God that ye do no evil; not that we should appear approved, but that ye should do that which is ᵀhonest, though we be as reprobates.   *honourable*

8 For we can do nothing against the truth, but ᵀfor the truth.   *only for*

9 For we are glad, when we are weak, and ye are strong: and this also we wish, ᴿeven your ᵀperfection.   [1 Thess. 3:10] • *maturity*

10 ᴿTherefore I write these things being absent, lest being present I should use sharpness, according to the ᵀpower which the Lord hath given me to edification, and not to destruction.   1 Cor. 4:21; [Titus 1:13] • *authority*

Conclusion

11 Finally, brethren, farewell. Be ᵀperfect, be of good comfort, be of one mind, live in peace; and the God of love ᴿand peace shall be with you.   *mature* • Rom. 15:33

12 Greet one another with an holy kiss.

13 All the saints ᵀsalute you.   *greet*

14 The grace of the Lord Jesus Christ, and the love of God, and the communion of the Holy Ghost, *be* with you all. A-men'.

GALATIANS

THE BOOK OF GALATIANS

The Galatians, having launched their Christian experience by faith, seem content to leave their voyage of faith and chart a new course based on works—a course Paul finds disturbing. His letter to the Galatians is a vigorous attack against the gospel of works and a defense of the gospel of faith.

Paul begins by setting forth his credentials as an apostle with a message from God: blessing comes from God on the basis of faith, not law. The law declares men guilty and imprisons them; faith sets men free to enjoy liberty in Christ. But liberty is not license. Freedom in Christ means freedom to produce the fruits of righteousness through a Spirit-led life-style.

The book is called Pros Galatas, "To the Galatians," and it is the only letter of Paul that is specifically addressed to a number of churches ("to the churches of Galatia," 1:2). The name Galatians was given to this Celtic people because they originally lived in Gaul before their migration to Asia Minor.

THE AUTHOR OF GALATIANS

The Pauline authorship and the unity of this epistle are virtually unchallenged. The first verse clearly identifies the author as "Paul, an apostle." Also in 5:2, we read, "Behold, I Paul say unto you." In fact, Paul actually wrote Galatians (6:11) instead of dictating it to a secretary, as was his usual practice.

THE TIME OF GALATIANS

The term Galatia was used in an ethnographic sense (that is, cultural and geographic origin) and in a political sense. The original ethnographic sense refers to the central part of Asia Minor where these Celtic tribes eventually settled after their conflicts with the Romans and Macedonians. Later, in 189 B.C. Galatia came under Roman domination, and in 25 B.C. Augustus declared it a Roman province. The political or provincial Galatia included territory to the south that was not originally considered part of Galatia (for example, the cities of Pisidian Antioch, Iconium, Lystra, and Derbe). There are two theories regarding the date and setting of Galatians.

The North Galatian Theory holds that Paul was speaking of Galatia in its earlier, more restricted sense. According to this theory, the churches of Galatia were north of the cities Paul visited on his first missionary journey. Paul visited the ethnographic Galatia (the smaller region to the North) for the first time on his second missionary journey, probably while he was on his way to

Troas (Acts 16:6). On his third missionary journey, Paul revisited the Galatian churches he had established (Acts 18:23) and wrote this epistle either in Ephesus (A.D. 53–56) or in Macedonia (A.D. 56).

According to the South Galatian Theory, Paul was referring to Galatia in its wider political sense as a province of Rome. This means that the churches he had in mind in this epistle were in the cities he evangelized during his first missionary journey with Barnabas (Acts 13:13–14:23). This was just prior to the Jerusalem Council (Acts 15), so the Jerusalem visit in Galatians 2:1–10 must have been the Acts 11:27–30 famine-relief visit. Galatians was probably written in Syrian Antioch in A.D. 49 just before Paul went to the Council in Jerusalem.

Paul wrote this epistle in response to a report that the Galatian churches were suddenly taken over by the false teaching of certain Judaizers who professed Jesus yet sought to place gentile converts under the requirements of the Mosaic Law (1:7; 4:17, 21; 5:2–12; 6:12, 13).

THE CHRIST OF GALATIANS

Christ has freed the believer from bondage to the law (legalism) and to sin (license) and has placed him in a position of liberty. The transforming cross provides for the believer's deliverance from the curse of sin, law, and self (1:4; 2:20; 3:13; 4:5; 5:24; 6:14).

KEYS TO GALATIANS

Key Word: Freedom from the Law—This epistle shows that the believer is no longer under the law but is saved by faith alone. It has been said that Judaism was the cradle of Christianity, but also that it was very nearly its grave as well. God raised up Paul as the Moses of the Christian church to deliver them from this bondage. Galatians is the Christian's Declaration of Independence. The power of the Holy Spirit enables the Christian to enjoy freedom within the law of love.

Key Verses: Galatians 2:20, 21 and 5:1—"I am crucified with Christ: nevertheless I live; yet not I, but Christ liveth in me: and the life which I now live in the flesh I live by the faith of the Son of God, who loved me, and gave himself for me. I do not frustrate the grace of God: for if righteousness come by the law, then Christ is dead in vain" (2:20, 21).

"Stand fast therefore in the liberty wherewith Christ hath made us free, and be not entangled again with the yoke of bondage" (5:1).

Key Chapter: Galatians 5—The impact of the truth concerning freedom is staggering: freedom

must not be used "for an occasion to the flesh, but by love serve one another" (5:13). This chapter records the power, "Walk in the Spirit" (5:16), and the results, "the fruit of the Spirit" (5:22), of that freedom.

SURVEY OF GALATIANS

The Epistle to the Galatians has been called "the Magna Carta of Christian liberty." It is Paul's manifesto of justification by faith, and the resulting liberty. Paul directs this great charter of Christian freedom to a people who are willing to give up the priceless liberty they possess in Christ. The oppressive theology of certain Jewish legalizers has been causing the believers in Galatia to trade their freedom in Christ for bondage to the law. Paul writes this forceful epistle to do away with the false gospel of works and demonstrate the superiority of justification by faith. This carefully written polemic approaches the problem from three directions: the gospel of grace defended (1 and 2), the gospel of grace explained (3 and 4), and the gospel of grace applied (5 and 6).

The Gospel of Grace Defended (1 and 2): Paul affirms his divinely given apostleship and presents the gospel (1:1–5) because it has been distorted by false teachers among the Galatians (1:6–10). Paul launches into his biographical argument for the true gospel of justification by faith in showing that he received his message not from men but directly from God (1:11–24). When he submits his teaching of Christian liberty to the apostles in Jerusalem, they all acknowledge the validity and authority of his message (2:1–10). Paul also must correct Peter on the matter of freedom from the law (2:11–21).

The Gospel of Grace Explained (3 and 4): In this section Paul uses eight lines of reasoning to develop his theological defense of justification by faith: (1) The Galatians began by faith, and their growth in Christ must continue to be by faith (3:1–5). (2) Abraham was justified by faith, and the same principle applies today (3:6–9). (3) Christ has redeemed all who trust in Him from the curse of the law (3:10–14). (4) The promise made to Abraham was not nullified by the law (3:15–18). (5) The law was given to drive men to faith, not to save them (3:19–22). (6) Believers in Christ are adopted sons of God and are no longer bound by the law (3:23—4:7). (7) The Galatians must recognize their inconsistency and regain their original freedom in Christ (4:8–20). (8) Abraham's two sons allegorically reveal the superiority of the Abrahamic promise to the Mosaic Law (4:21–31).

The Gospel of Grace Applied (5 and 6): The Judaizers seek to place the Galatians under bondage to their perverted gospel of justification by law, but Paul warns them that law and grace are two contrary principles (5:1–12). So far, Paul has been contrasting the liberty of faith with the legalism of law, but at this point he warns the Galatians of the opposite extreme of license or antinomianism (5:13—6:10). The Christian is not only set free from bondage of law, but he is also free of the bondage of sin because of the power of the indwelling Spirit. Liberty is not an excuse to indulge in the deeds of the flesh; rather, it provides the privilege of bearing the fruit of the Spirit by walking in dependence upon Him. This letter closes with a contrast between the Judaizers—who are motivated by pride and a desire to avoid persecution—and Paul, who has suffered for the true gospel, but boasts only in Christ (6:11–18).

FOCUS	GOSPEL OF GRACE DEFENDED		GOSPEL OF GRACE EXPLAINED		GOSPEL OF GRACE APPLIED	
REFERENCE	1:1 ———— 2:1 ————		3:1 ———— 4:1 ————	5:1 ————	6:1 ————	6:18
DIVISION	PAUL'S APOSTLESHIP	PAUL'S AUTHORITY	BONDAGE OF LAW	FREEDOM OF GRACE	FRUIT OF THE SPIRIT	FRUITS OF THE SPIRIT
TOPIC	BIOGRAPHICAL EXPLANATION		DOCTRINAL EXPOSITION		PRACTICAL EXHORTATION	
	AUTHENTICATION OF LIBERTY		ARGUMENTATION FOR LIBERTY		APPLICATION OF LIBERTY	
LOCATION	SOUTH GALATIAN THEORY: SYRIAN ANTIOCH NORTH GALATIAN THEORY: EPHESUS OR MACEDONIA					
TIME	SOUTH GALATIAN THEORY: A.D. 49 NORTH GALATIAN THEORY: A.D. 53–56					

OUTLINE OF GALATIANS

CHAPTER 1

Salutation: The Ground of Grace

PAUL, an apostle, (not of men, neither by man, but by Jesus Christ, and God the Father, who raised him from the dead;)

2 And all the brethren which are with me, unto the churches of Ga-la'-ti-a:

3 Grace *be* to you and peace from God the Father, and *from* our Lord Jesus Christ,

4 RWho gave himself for our sins, that he might deliver us Rfrom this present evil Tworld, according to the will of God and our Father: [Matt. 20:28] • [Heb. 2:15] • *age*

5 To Twhom *be* glory for ever and ever. A-men'.   *God*

Situation: The Departure from Grace

6 I marvel that ye are so soon removed Rfrom him that called you into the grace of Christ unto Tanother gospel: 5:8 • *a different*

7 RWhich is not another; but there be some that trouble you, and would Tpervert the gospel of Christ.   2 Cor. 11:4 • *change*

8 But though Rwe, or an angel from heaven, preach any other gospel unto you than that which we have preached unto you, let him be accursed.   1 Cor. 16:22

9 As we said before, so say I now again, If any *man* preach any other gospel unto you Rthan that ye have received, let him be Taccursed.   Deut. 4:2; Prov. 30:6; Rev. 22:18 • *anathema*

Gospel of Grace Is Given by Divine Revelation

10 For do I now persuade men, or God? or do I seek to please men? for if I yet pleased men, I should not be the servant of Christ.

11 But I Tcertify you, brethren, that the gospel which was preached of me is not Tafter man.   *assure • derived from any human source*

12 For RI neither received it of man, neither was I taught *it*, but Rby the revelation of Jesus Christ.   1 Cor. 15:1 • [Eph. 3:3–5]

13 For ye have heard of my Tconversation in time past in the Jews' religion, how that beyond measure I persecuted the church of God, and Twasted it: *manner of life • ravaged*

14 RAnd profited in the Jews' religion above many my Tequals in mine own nation, being more exceedingly zealous of the traditions of my fathers.   Acts 22:3 • *own age*

15 But when it pleased God, Rwho separated me from my mother's womb, and called *me* by his grace,   Is. 49:1, 5; Jer. 1:5; Rom. 1:1

16 To reveal his Son in me, that I might preach him among the heathen; immediately I conferred not with flesh and blood:

17 TNeither went I up to Jerusalem to them which were apostles before me; but I went into Arabia, and returned again unto Damascus.   *nor did I go*

18 Then after three years RI Twent up to Jerusalem to see Peter, and Tabode with him fifteen days.   Acts 9:26 • *returned • lived*

19 But other of the apostles saw I none, save RJames the Lord's brother.   Matt. 13:55

20 Now the things which I write unto you, behold, ᴿbefore God, I lie not. Rom. 9:1

21 ᴿAfterwards I came into the regions of Syria and Ci-li'-ci-a; Acts 9:30

22 And was unknown by face unto the churches of Ju-dae'-a which were in Christ:

23 But they had heard only, That he which persecuted us in times past now preacheth the faith which once he destroyed.

24 And they glorified God ᵀin me. *for*

CHAPTER 2

Gospel of Grace Is Approved by Jerusalem Leadership

THEN fourteen years after ᴿI went up again to Jerusalem with Barnabas, and took Titus with *me* also. Acts 15:2

2 And I went up by revelation, and communicated unto them that gospel which I preach among the Gentiles, but privately to them which were of reputation, lest by any means I should run, or had run, in vain.

3 But neither Titus, who was with me, being a Greek, was ᵀcompelled to be circumcised: *forced*

4 And that because of false brethren ᵀunawares brought in, who ᵀcame in privily to spy out our ᴿliberty which we have in Christ Jesus, that they might bring us into bondage: *secretly • slipped in • Acts 15:1, 24*

5 To whom we gave place by subjection, no, not for an hour; that ᴿthe truth of the gospel might continue with you. *v. 14; [3:1]*

6 But of these who seemed to be somewhat, (whatsoever they were, it maketh no matter to me: God accepteth no man's person:) for they who seemed *to be somewhat* in conference added nothing to me:

7 But contrariwise, when they saw that the gospel of the uncircumcision ᴿwas committed unto me, as *the gospel* of the circumcision *was* unto Peter; Acts 13:46; 1 Thess. 2:4

8 (For he that ᵀwrought effectually in Peter to the apostleship of the circumcision, ᴿthe same was ᴿmighty in me toward the Gentiles:) *worked • Acts 9:15 • [3:5]*

9 And when James, Ce'-phas, and John, who seemed to be pillars, perceived the grace that was given unto me, they gave to me and Barnabas the right hands of fellowship; that we *should* go unto the ᵀheathen, and they unto the circumcision. *Gentiles*

10 Only *they would* that we should remember the poor; ᴿthe same which I also was ᵀforward to do. Acts 11:29, 30; Rom. 15:26 • *zealous*

Gospel of Grace Is Vindicated by Rebuking Peter

11 ᴿBut when Peter was come to An'-ti-och, I withstood him to the face, because he ᵀwas to be blamed. Acts 15:35 • *stood condemned*

12 For before that certain came from James, ᴿhe did eat with the Gentiles: but when they were come, he withdrew and separated himself, fearing them which were of the ᵀcircumcision. [Acts 10:28] • *Jews*

13 And the other Jews dissembled likewise with him; insomuch that Barnabas also was carried away with their dissimulation.

14 But when I saw that they walked not uprightly according to ᴿthe truth of the gospel, I said unto Peter before *them* all, ᴿIf thou, being a Jew, livest after the manner of Gentiles, and not as do the Jews, why compellest thou the Gentiles to live as do the Jews? *v. 5 • [Acts 10:28]; 1 Tim. 5:20*

15 ᴿWe *who are* Jews by nature, and not ᴿsinners of the Gentiles, [Acts 15:10] • Matt. 9:11

16 Knowing that a man is not ᵀjustified by the works of the law, but by the faith of Jesus Christ, even we have believed in Jesus Christ, that we might be justified by the faith of Christ, and not by the works of the law: for ᴿby the works of the law shall no flesh be justified. *cleared of guilt. • 5:4*

17 But if, while we seek to be ᵀjustified by Christ, we ourselves also are found ᴿsinners, is therefore Christ the minister of sin? God forbid. *put right • [1 John 3:8]*

18 For if I build again the things which I destroyed, I make myself a transgressor.

19 For I through the law am dead to the law, that I might ᴿlive unto God. [Rom. 6:11]

20 I am crucified with Christ: nevertheless I live; yet not I, but Christ liveth in me: and the life which I now live in the flesh I live by the faith of the Son of God, who loved me, and ᴿgave himself for me. Is. 53:12 ★

21 I do not frustrate the grace of God: for if righteousness *come* by the law, then Christ ᵀis dead in vain. *died for nothing*

CHAPTER 3

Holy Spirit Is Given by Faith, Not by Works

O FOOLISH Ga-la'-tians, who hath bewitched you, ᴿthat ye should not obey the truth, before whose eyes Jesus Christ hath been ᵀevidently set forth, crucified among you? 2:14; 5:7 • *openly*

2 This only would I learn of you, Received ye the Spirit by the works of the law, ᴿor by the hearing of faith? Rom. 10:17

3 Are ye so foolish? ᴿhaving begun in the Spirit, are ye now made ᵀperfect by ᴿthe flesh? [4:9]; Heb. 9:10 • *complete* • Heb. 7:16

4 Have ye suffered so many ᵀthings ᵀin vain? if *it be* yet in vain. *much • for nothing*

5 He therefore that ᵀministereth to you in the Spirit, and worketh miracles among you, *doeth he it* by the works of the law, or by the hearing of faith? *supplieth*

Abraham Was Justified by Faith, Not by Works

6 Even as Abraham believed God, and it was accounted to him for righteousness.

7 Know ye therefore that [R]they [T]which are of faith, the same are the children of Abraham.   John 8:39; [Rom. 4:11, 12, 16] • who have

8 And the scripture, foreseeing that God would justify the heathen through faith, preached before the gospel unto Abraham, saying, In thee shall all nations be blessed.

9 So then they which be of faith are blessed with [T]faithful Abraham.   believing

Christ Redeems Us from the Curse of the Law

10 For as many as are of the works of the law are under the curse: for it is written, [R]CURSED IS EVERY ONE THAT CONTINUETH NOT IN ALL THINGS WHICH ARE WRITTEN IN THE BOOK OF THE LAW TO DO THEM.   Deut. 27:26

11 But that no man is justified by the law in the sight of God, it is evident: for, [R]The just shall live by faith.   Hab. 2:4; Rom. 1:17

12 And the law is not of faith: but, The man that doeth them shall live in them.

13 Christ hath redeemed us from the curse of the law, being made a curse for us: for it is written, [R]Cursed is every one that hangeth on a tree.   Deut. 21:23; [Rom. 8:3; 2 Cor. 5:21]

14 [R]That the blessing of Abraham might come on the Gentiles through Jesus Christ; that we might receive [R]the promise of the Spirit through faith.   Is. 49:6; Rom. 4:9 * • Is. 32:15

Abrahamic Covenant Is Not Voided by the Law

15 Brethren, I speak after the manner of men; Though it be but a man's [T]covenant, yet if it be [T]confirmed, no man disannulleth, or addeth thereto.   agreement • ratified

16 Now [R]to Abraham and his seed were the promises made. He saith not, And to seeds, as of many; but as of one, And to thy seed, which is [R]Christ.   Gen. 12:3 * • [1 Cor. 12:12]

17 And this I say, that the covenant, that was confirmed before of God in Christ, the law, which was four hundred and thirty years after, cannot disannul, [R]that it should make the promise of none effect.   [Rom. 4:13]

18 For if [R]the inheritance be of the law, [R]it is no more of promise: but God gave it to Abraham by promise.   [Rom. 8:17] • Rom. 4:14

Law Given to Drive Us to Faith

19 Wherefore then serveth the law? It was added because of transgressions, till the seed should come to whom the promise was made; and it was [R]ordained[T] by angels in the hand of a mediator.   Acts 7:53 • prepared

20 Now a mediator is not a mediator of one, [R]but God is one.   [Rom. 3:29, 30]

21 Is the law then against the promises of God? God forbid: for if there had been a law

given which could have given life, verily righteousness should have been by the law.

22 But the scripture hath concluded all under sin, that the promise by faith of Jesus Christ might be given to them that believe.

Believers Are Free from the Law

23 But before faith came, we were kept under the law, shut up unto the faith which should afterwards be revealed.

24 Wherefore the law was our schoolmaster to bring us unto Christ, that we might be [T]justified by faith.   cleared of all guilt

25 But after that faith is come, we are no longer under a [T]schoolmaster.   tutor

26 For ye [R]are all the children of God by faith in Christ Jesus.   [John 1:12; 3:5, 36]

27 For as many of you as have been baptized into Christ have put on Christ.

28 [R]There is neither Jew nor Greek, there is neither bond nor free, there is neither male nor female: for ye are all one in Christ Jesus.   [John 10:16; Eph. 2:14]

29 And [R]if ye be Christ's, then are ye Abraham's seed, and [R]heirs according to the promise.   Gen. 12:3; 18:18; 21:10; Heb. 11:18 * • Rom. 8:17

CHAPTER 4

NOW I say, That the heir, as long as he is a child, differeth nothing from a [T]servant, though he be lord of all;   slave

2 But is under tutors and [T]governors until the time appointed of the father.   managers

3 Even so we, when we were children, were in bondage [T]under the elements of the world: according to the basic principles of nature

4 But when the fulness of the time was come, God sent forth his Son, [R]made[T] of a woman, made under the law,   Is. 7:14 * • born

5 [R]To redeem them that were under the law, [R]that we might [T]receive the adoption of sons.   [Matt. 20:28] • [John 1:12] • become sons of God

6 And because ye are sons, God hath sent forth [R]the Spirit of his Son into your hearts, crying, [T]Ab'-ba, Father.   [Rom. 5:5] • Father

7 Wherefore thou art no more a [T]servant, but a son; [R]and if a son, then an heir of God through Christ.   slave • [Rom. 8:16]

8 Howbeit then, [R]when ye knew not God, [R]ye[T] did service unto them which by nature are no gods.   Rom. 1:25 • Eph. 2:12 • were in bondage

9 But now, [R]after that ye have known God, or rather are known of God, [R]how turn ye again to [R]the weak and beggarly elements, whereunto ye desire again to be in bondage?   [1 Cor. 8:3] • Col. 2:20 • Heb. 7:18

10 [R]Ye observe days, and months, and times, and years.   Matt. 1:18; Luke 2:6; Rom. 14:5

11 I am afraid of you, [R]lest I have bestowed upon you labour in vain.   1 Thess. 3:5

Galatians Receive Blessings by Faith, Not by the Law

12 Brethren, I beseech you, be as I *am;* for I *am* as ye *are:* [R]ye [T]have not injured me at all.   2 Cor. 2:5 · *did me no wrong*

13 Ye know [T]how [R]through infirmity of the flesh I preached the gospel unto you at the first.   *that because of an* · 1 Cor. 2:3

14 And my [T]temptation which was in my flesh ye despised not, nor rejected; but received me [R]as an angel of God, [R]*even* as Christ Jesus.   *trial* · Mal. 2:7 · [Luke 10:16]

15 Where is then the blessedness ye spake of? for I bear you record, that, if *it had been* possible, ye would have plucked out your own eyes, and have given them to me.

16 Am I therefore become your enemy, because I tell you the [R]truth?   2:5, 14

17 They zealously affect you, *but* not [T]well; yea, they would exclude you, that ye might [T]affect them.   *for good* · *be excited after*

18 But *it is* good to be [T]zealously affected always in a good *thing,* and not only when I am present with you.   *urgently moved*

19 My little children, of whom I travail in birth again until Christ be formed in you,

20 I desire to be present with you now, and to change my [T]voice; for I [T]stand in doubt of you.   *tone* · *am not sure about*

Law and Grace Cannot Coexist

21 Tell me, ye that desire to be under the law, do ye not hear the law?

22 For it is written, that Abraham had two sons, [R]the one by a bondmaid, [R]the other by a freewoman.   Gen. 16:15 · Gen. 21:2

23 But he *who was* of the bondwoman was born after the flesh; [R]but he of the freewoman *was* by promise.   Heb. 11:11

24 Which things are an allegory: for these are the two covenants; the one from the mount [R]Si'-nai, which [T]gendereth to bondage, which is A'-gar.   Deut. 33:2 · *leads*

25 For this A'-gar is mount Si'-nai in Arabia, and answereth to Jerusalem which now is, and is in bondage with her children.

26 But [R]Jerusalem which is above is free, which is the mother of us all.   [Is. 2:2]; Heb. 12:22

27 For it is written, [R]REJOICE, THOU BARREN THAT BEAREST NOT; BREAK FORTH AND CRY, THOU THAT TRAVAILEST NOT: FOR THE DESOLATE HATH MANY MORE CHILDREN THAN SHE WHICH HATH AN HUSBAND.   Is. 54:1

28 Now we, brethren, as Isaac was, are [R]the children of promise.   Acts 3:25

29 But as then [R]he that was born after the flesh persecuted him *that was born* after the Spirit, even so *it is* now.   Gen. 21:9

30 Nevertheless what saith the scripture? CAST OUT THE BONDWOMAN AND HER SON: FOR THE SON OF THE BONDWOMAN SHALL NOT BE HEIR WITH THE SON OF THE FREEWOMAN.

31 [R]So then, brethren, we are not children of the bondwoman, but of the free.   [John 8:36]

CHAPTER 5

Position of Liberty: "Stand Fast"

STAND fast therefore in the liberty [R]wherewith Christ hath made us free, and be not entangled again with the yoke of bondage.   John 8:32; Acts 15:10; Rom. 6:18

2 Behold, I Paul say unto you, that [R]if ye be circumcised, Christ shall [T]profit you nothing.   Acts 15:1 · *benefit*

3 For I testify again to every man that is circumcised, [R]that he is [T]a debtor to do the whole law.   [2:16; 3:10, 11] · *obligated*

4 Christ is become of no effect unto you, whosoever of you are justified by the law; [T]ye are fallen from grace.   *you have given up grace*

5 For we through the Spirit [T]wait for the hope of righteousness by faith.   *look*

6 For in Jesus Christ neither circumcision availeth any thing, nor uncircumcision; but faith which worketh by love.

7 Ye [R]did run well; who did hinder you that ye should not obey the truth?   1 Cor. 9:24

8 This persuasion *cometh* not of [R]him that calleth you.   1:6; [Rom. 8:28]

9 [R]A little leaven [T]leaveneth the whole lump.   1 Cor. 5:6 · *raises*

10 I have confidence in you through the Lord, that ye will be none otherwise minded: [R]but he that troubleth you shall bear his judgment, whosoever he be.   1:7

11 And I, brethren, if I yet preach circumcision, why do I yet suffer persecution? then is the offence of the cross ceased.

12 I would they were even cut off which trouble you.

Practice of Liberty: Love One Another

13 For, brethren, ye have been called unto liberty; only *use* not liberty for an occasion to the flesh, but by love serve one another.

5:13 Serving—God intended that the Christian life should be dynamic, not static. We should sit under the teaching of the Word of God, understand and apply its meaning and implications, and serve God and our fellow believers. The Spirit of God has given us spiritual gifts, but those gifts are worthless unless they are put to use in the service of God and His church. Paul often uses the figure of the human body to show the dependence of the members of the body upon one another and the importance of each member serving the other (Page 1118—Rom. 12:4, 5; Page 1134—1 Cor. 12:12–31). While some members of the body have more prominent places of service than others, all are equally important. The worst thing that can happen to the human body is for one of its members to become nonfunctioning.   *(continued on next page)*

14 For Rall the law is fulfilled in one word, *even* in this; RThou shalt love thy neighbour as thyself.   Lev. 19:18; Matt. 7:12 • Matt. 22:39

15 But if ye Tbite and devour one another, take heed that ye be not Tconsumed one of another.   *act like animals • destroyed*

Conflict Between the Spirit and the Flesh

16 *This* I say then, Walk in the Spirit, and ye shall not fulfil the lust of the flesh.

17 For the flesh lusteth against the Spirit, and the Spirit against the flesh: and these are contrary the one to the other: so that ye cannot do the things that ye would.

18 RBut if ye be led of the Spirit, ye are not under the law.   [Rom. 6:14; 7:6; 8:2]

"Works of the Flesh"

19 Now Rthe works of the flesh are Tmanifest, which are *these;* Adultery, fornication, uncleanness, lasciviousness, Eph. 5:3 • *plain*

20 Idolatry, witchcraft, hatred, variance, Temulations, wrath, strife, Tseditions, heresies,   *jealousies • divisions*

21 Envyings, murders, drunkenness, revellings, and such like: of the which I tell you before, as I have also told *you* in time past, Rthat they which do such things shall not inherit the kingdom of God.   1 Cor. 6:9

"Fruit of the Spirit"

22 But the fruit of the Spirit is love, joy, peace, longsuffering, Rgentleness, Rgoodness, Rfaith,   Col. 3:12 • Rom. 15:14 • 1 Cor. 13:7

23 Meekness, temperance: Ragainst such there is no law.   1 Tim. 1:9

24 And they that are Christ's have crucified the flesh with the affections and lusts.

25 RIf we live in the Spirit, let us also walk in the Spirit.   *v.* 16; [Rom. 8:4, 5]

26 RLet us not be desirous of Tvain glory, Tprovoking one another, envying one another.   Phil. 2:3 • *pride • irritating*

CHAPTER 6

"Bear Ye One Another's Burdens"

BRETHREN, if a man be overtaken in a fault, ye which are spiritual, restore such an one in the spirit of meekness; considering thyself, lest thou also be tempted.

2 RBear ye one another's burdens, and so fulfil Rthe law of Christ.   Rom. 15:1 • [James 2:8]

3 For Rif a man think himself to be something, when Rhe is nothing, he deceiveth himself.   Rom. 12:3; 1 Cor. 8:2 • [2 Cor. 3:5]

4 But let every man prove his own work, and then shall he have rejoicing in himself alone, and not in another.

5 For every man shall bear his own Tburden.   *load*

Do Not Be Weary in Well Doing

6 RLet him that is taught in the word Tcommunicate unto him that teacheth in all good things.   1 Cor. 9:11 • *share with*

7 Be not deceived; God is not mocked: for Rwhatsoever a man soweth, that shall he also reap.   Job 13:9; [Luke 16:25; Rom. 2:6]

8 RFor he that soweth to his flesh shall of the flesh reap Tcorruption; but he that soweth to the Spirit shall of the Spirit reap life everlasting.   Hos. 8:7; [10:12; Rom. 8:13] • *death*

9 And Rlet us not be weary in well doing: for in due season we shall reap, Rif we Tfaint not.   1 Cor. 15:58 • [Matt. 24:13] • *do not give up*

10 RAs we have therefore opportunity, let us do good unto all *men,* especially unto them who are of the household of faith.   [John 9:4]

Motives of the Circumcised

11 Ye see how large a letter I have written unto you with mine own hand.

12 As many as desire to make a fair shew in the flesh, they Tconstrain you to be circumcised; only lest they should suffer persecution for the cross of Christ.   *urge*

13 For neither they themselves who are circumcised Tkeep the law; but desire to have you circumcised, that they may Tglory in your flesh.   *obey • making you submit*

Motives of the Apostle Paul

14 RBut God forbid that I should glory, save in the cross of our Lord Jesus Christ, by whom the world is crucified unto me, and I unto the world.   [Rom. 2:29; 6:6; Phil. 3:3, 7, 8]

15 For Rin Christ Jesus neither circumcision availeth any thing, nor uncircumcision, but a new creature.   [5:6]; 1 Cor. 7:19

16 RAnd as many as walk according to this rule, peace *be* on them, and mercy, and upon the Israel of God.   [Rom. 2:29; 9:6–8]

17 From henceforth let no man Ttrouble me: for I bear Tin my body the marks of the Lord Jesus.   *give me trouble • branded on*

18 RBrethren, the grace of our Lord Jesus Christ *be* with your spirit. A-men'.   Philem. 25

(continued from previous page)
Paralysis, sickness, deterioration, and sometimes death occur when a body member ceases to serve the other members of the body in the particular way that God intended. To maintain strength, health, and vitality, every member of the body must function and serve all the other members of the body. This is also true of the spiritual or new life. We will grow in the new life, become strong, and maintain good spiritual health as we use the talents and abilities that God has given us to meet the needs of the other members of the body.

Now turn to Page 1148—2 Cor. 9:6–8: Giving.

EPHESIANS

THE BOOK OF EPHESIANS

Ephesians is addressed to a group of believers who are rich beyond measure in Jesus Christ, yet living as beggars, and only because they are ignorant of their wealth. Since they have yet to accept their wealth, they relegate themselves to living as spiritual paupers. Paul begins by describing in chapters 1—3 the contents of the Christian's heavenly "bank account": adoption, acceptance, redemption, forgiveness, wisdom, inheritance, the seal of the Holy Spirit, life, grace, citizenship—in short, every spiritual blessing. Drawing upon that huge spiritual endowment, the Christian has all the resources needed for living "To the praise of the glory of his grace" (1:6). Chapters 4—6 resemble an orthopedic clinic, where the Christian learns a spiritual walk rooted in his spiritual wealth. "For we are his workmanship, created in Christ Jesus [1—3] unto good works . . . that we should walk in them [4—6]" (2:10).

The traditional title of this epistle is *Pros Ephesious*, "To the Ephesians." Many ancient manuscripts, however, omit *en Ephesōi*, "at Ephesus," in 1:1. This has led a number of scholars to challenge the traditional view that this message was directed specifically to the Ephesians. The encyclical theory proposes that it was a circular letter sent by Paul to the churches of Asia. It is argued that Ephesians is really a Christian treatise designed for general use: it involves no controversy and deals with no specific problems in any particular church. This is also supported by the formal tone (no terms of endearment) and distant phraseology ("after I heard of your faith," 1:15; if they "have heard" of his message, 3:2). These things seem inconsistent with the relationship Paul must have had with the Ephesians after a ministry of almost three years among them. On the other hand, the absence of personal greetings is not a support for the encyclical theory because Paul would have done this to avoid favoritism. The only letters that greet specific people are Romans and Colossians, and they were addressed to churches Paul had not visited. Some scholars accept an ancient tradition that Ephesians is Paul's letter to the Laodiceans (Col. 4:16), but there is no way to be sure. If Ephesians began as a circular letter, it eventually became associated with Ephesus, the foremost of the Asian churches. Another plausible option is that this epistle was directly addressed to the Ephesians, but written in such a way as to make it helpful for all the churches in Asia.

THE AUTHOR OF EPHESIANS

All internal (1:1) and external evidence strongly supports the Pauline authorship of Ephesians. In recent years, however, critics have turned to internal grounds to challenge this unanimous ancient tradition. It has been argued that the vocabulary and style are different from other Pauline epistles, but this overlooks Paul's flexibility under different circumstances (cf. Rom. and 2 Cor.). The theology of Ephesians in some ways reflects a later development, but this must be attributed to Paul's own growth and meditation on the church as the body of Christ. Since the epistle clearly names the author in the opening verse, it is not necessary to theorize that Ephesians was written by one of Paul's pupils or admirers, such as Timothy, Luke, Tychicus, or Onesimus.

THE TIME OF EPHESIANS

At the end of his second missionary journey, Paul visited Ephesus where he left Priscilla and Aquila (Acts 18:18-21). This strategic city was the commercial center of Asia Minor, but heavy silting required a special canal to be maintained so that ships could reach the harbor. Ephesus was a religious center as well, famous especially for its magnificent temple of Diana (Roman name) or Artemis (Greek name), a structure considered to be one of the seven wonders of the ancient world (cf. Acts 19:35). The practice of magic and the local economy were clearly related to this temple. Paul remained in Ephesus for nearly three years on his third missionary journey (Acts 18:23—19:41); the Word of God was spread throughout the province of Asia. Paul's effective ministry began to seriously hurt the traffic in magic and images, leading to an uproar in the huge Ephesian theater. Paul then left for Macedonia, but afterward he met with the Ephesian elders while on his way to Jerusalem (Acts 20:17-38).

Paul wrote the "Prison Epistles" (Ephesians, Philippians, Colossians, and Philemon) during his first Roman imprisonment in A.D. 60-62. These epistles all refer to his imprisonment (Eph. 3:1; 4:1; 6:20; Phil. 1:7, 13, 14; Col. 4:3, 10, 18; Philem. 9, 10, 13, 23), and fit well against the background in Acts 28:16-31. This is especially true of Paul's references to "the palace" (Phil. 1:13) and "Caesar's household" (Phil. 4:22). Some commentators believe that the imprisonment in one or more of these epistles refers to Paul's Caesarean imprisonment or to a hypothetical Ephesian imprisonment, but the weight of evidence favors the traditional view that they were written in Rome. Ephesians, Colossians, and

Philemon were evidently written about the same time (cf. Eph. 6:21, 22 with Col. 4:7–9) in A.D. 60–61. Philippians was written in A.D. 62, not long before Paul's release.

✝ THE CHRIST OF EPHESIANS

Paul's important phrase "in Christ" (or its equivalent) appears about thirty-five times, more than in any other New Testament book. The believer is in Christ (1:1), in the heavenly places in Christ (1:3), chosen in Him (1:4), adopted through Christ (1:5), in the Beloved (1:6), redeemed in Him (1:7), given an inheritance in Him (1:11), given hope in Him (1:12), sealed in Him (1:13), made alive together with Christ (2:5), raised and seated with Him (2:6), created in Christ (2:10), brought near by His blood (2:13), growing in Christ (2:21), a partaker of the promise in Christ (3:6), and given access through faith in Him (3:12).

🔑 KEYS TO EPHESIANS

Key Word: Building the Body of Christ—Ephesians focuses on the believer's responsibility to walk in accordance with his heavenly calling in Christ Jesus (4:1). Ephesians was not written to correct specific errors in a local church, but to prevent problems in the church as a whole by encouraging the body of Christ to maturity in Him. It was also written to make believers more aware of their position in Christ because this is the basis for their practice on every level of life.

Key Verses: Ephesians 2:8–10 and 4:1–3— "For by grace are ye saved through faith; and that not of yourselves: it is the gift of God: Not of works, lest any man should boast. For we are his workmanship, created in Christ Jesus unto good works, which God hath before ordained that we should walk in them" (2:8–10).

"I therefore, the prisoner of the Lord, beseech you that ye walk worthy of the vocation wherewith ye are called, With all lowliness and meekness, with longsuffering, forbearing one another in love; Endeavoring to keep the unity of the Spirit in the bond of peace" (4:1–3).

Key Chapter: Ephesians 6—Even though the Christian is blessed "with all spiritual blessings in heavenly *places* in Christ" (1:3), spiritual warfare is still the daily experience of the Christian while in the world. Chapter 6 is the clearest advice for how to "be strong in the Lord, and in the power of his might" (6:10).

🅰 SURVEY OF EPHESIANS

Paul wrote this epistle to make Christians more aware of their position in Christ and to motivate them to draw upon their spiritual source in daily living: "Walk worthy of the vocation wherewith ye are called" (4:1; see 2:10). The first half of Ephesians lists the believer's heavenly possessions: adoption, redemption, inheritance, power, life, grace, citizenship, and the love of Christ. There are no imperatives in chapters 1—3, which focus only on divine gifts. But chapters 4—6 include thirty-five directives in the last half of Ephesians that speak of the believer's responsibility to conduct himself according to his individual calling. So Ephesians begins in heaven, but concludes in the home and in all other relationships of daily life. The two divisions are: the position of the Christian (1:1—3:21) and the practice of the Christian (4:1—6:20).

The Position of the Christian (1:1—3:21): After a two-verse prologue, in one long Greek sentence Paul extols the triune God for the riches of redemption (1:3–14). This hymn to God's grace praises the Father for choosing us (1:3–6), the Son for redeeming us (1:7–12), and the Spirit for sealing us (1:13, 14). The saving work of each divine Person is to the praise of the glory of His grace (1:6, 12, 14). Before continuing, Paul offers the first of two very significant prayers (1:15–23;

FOCUS	THE POSITION OF THE CHRISTIAN				THE PRACTICE OF THE CHRISTIAN			
REFERENCE	1:1——————1:15——————2:4——————3:14——				——4:1——————4:17——————5:22——————6:10——————6:24			
DIVISION	PRAISE FOR REDEMPTION	PRAYER FOR REVELATION	POSITION OF THE CHRISTIAN	PRAYER FOR REALIZATION	UNITY IN THE CHURCH	HOLINESS IN LIFE	RESPONSIBIL-ITIES AT HOME AND WORK	CONDUCT IN THE CONFLICT
TOPIC	BELIEF				BEHAVIOR			
	PRIVILEGES OF THE CHRISTIAN				RESPONSIBILITIES OF THE CHRISTIAN			
LOCATION	ROME							
TIME	A.D. 60–61							

cf. 3:14–21). Here he asks that the readers receive spiritual illumination so that they may come to perceive what is in fact true. Next, Paul describes the power of God's grace by contrasting their former condition with their present spiritual life in Christ, a salvation attained not by human works but by divine grace (2:1–10). This redemption includes Jews, yet also extends to those Gentiles who previously were "strangers from the covenants of promise" (2:12). In Christ, the two for the first time have become members of one body (2:11–22). The truth that Gentiles would become "fellowheirs, and of the same body" (3:6) was formerly a mystery that has now been revealed (3:1–13). Paul's second prayer (3:14–21) expresses his desire that the readers be strengthened with the power of the Spirit and fully apprehend the love of Christ.

The Practice of the Christian (4:1—6:20): The pivotal verse of Ephesians is 4:1, because it draws a sharp line between the doctrinal and the practical divisions of this book. There is a cause and effect relationship between chapters 1—3 and 4—6 because the spiritual walk of a Christian must be rooted in his spiritual wealth. As Paul emphasized in Romans, behavior does not determine blessing; instead, blessing should determine behavior.

Because of the unity of all believers in the body of Christ, growth and maturity come from "the effectual working in the measure of every part" (4:16). This involves the exercise of spiritual gifts in love. Paul exhorts the readers to "put off concerning the former conversation the old man" (4:22) and "put on the new man" (4:24) that will be manifested by a walk of integrity in the midst of all people. They are also to maintain a walk of holiness as children of light (5:1–21). Every relationship (wives, husbands, children, parents, slaves, and masters) must be transformed by their new life in Christ (5:22—6:9). Paul's colorful description of the spiritual warfare and the armor of God (6:10–20) is followed by a word about Tychicus and then a benediction (6:21–24).

OUTLINE OF EPHESIANS

Part One: The Position of the Christian (1:1—3:21)

Part Two: The Practice of the Christian (4:1—6:24)

CHAPTER 1

Salutation from Paul

PAUL, [R]an apostle of Jesus Christ by the will of God, to the saints which are at Eph'-e-sus, and to the [T]faithful in Christ Jesus: Rom. 1:1; 1 Cor. 4:17; Col. 1:1, 2 · *believers*

2 Grace *be* to you, and peace, from God our Father, and *from* the Lord Jesus Christ.

Chosen by the Father

3 [R]Blessed *be* the God and Father of our Lord Jesus Christ, who hath blessed us with all spiritual [T]blessings in heavenly *places* in Christ: 2 Cor. 1:3 · *gifts*

4 According as [R]he hath chosen us in him [R]before the foundation of the world, that we should [R]be holy and without blame before him in love: Rom. 8:28 · 1 Pet. 1:2 · Luke 1:75

5 [R]Having predestinated us unto [R]the adoption of children by Jesus Christ to himself, [R]according to the good pleasure of his will,   [Rom. 8:29] · John 1:12 · [1 Cor. 1:21]

6 To the praise of the glory of his grace, [R]wherein he hath made us [T]accepted in [R]the beloved.   [Rom. 3:24] · *acceptable* · Matt. 3:17

Redeemed by the Son

7 [R]In whom we have redemption through his blood, the forgiveness of sins, according to the riches of his grace;   [Heb. 9:12]

8 Wherein he hath abounded toward us in all wisdom and [T]prudence;   *understanding*

9 Having made known unto us the mystery of his will, according to his good pleasure which he hath purposed in himself:

10 That in the dispensation of the fulness of times he might gather together in one [R]all things in Christ, both which are in heaven, and which are on earth; *even* in him: Col. 1:20

11 In whom also we have obtained an inheritance, being predestinated according to the purpose of him who worketh all things after the counsel of his own will:

12 [R]That we should be to the praise of his glory, who first trusted in Christ.   2 Thess. 2:13

Sealed by the Spirit

13 In whom ye also *trusted*, after that ye heard [R]the word of truth, the gospel of your salvation: in whom also after that ye believed, [R]ye were [T]sealed with that holy Spirit of promise,   John 1:17 · [2 Cor. 1:22] · *confirmed*

14 Which is the earnest of our inheritance until the redemption of the purchased possession, unto the praise of his glory.

Prayer for Revelation

15 [T]Wherefore I also, [R]after I heard of your faith in the Lord Jesus, and love unto all the saints,   *for this cause* · Col. 1:4

16 Cease not to give thanks for you, making mention of you in my prayers;

17 [R]That the God of our Lord Jesus Christ, the Father of glory, may give unto you the spirit of wisdom and revelation in the knowledge of him: John 20:17; Col. 1:9

18 The eyes of your understanding being enlightened; that ye may know what is the hope of his calling, and what the riches of the glory of his inheritance in the saints,

19 And what *is* the exceeding greatness of his power to us-ward who believe, according to the working of his mighty power,

20 Which he wrought in Christ, when he raised him from the dead, and set *him* at his own right hand in the heavenly *places*,

21 Far above all [R]principality, and power, and might, and dominion, and every name that is named, not only in this world, but also in that which is to come: [Rom. 8:38, 39]

22 And [R]hath put all *things* under his feet, and gave him [R]to *be* the head over all *things* to the church,   Dan. 7:13, 14; Matt. 28:18 ☆ · 5:23

23 Which is his body, [R]the fulness of him [R]that filleth all in all.   Col. 2:9 · [1 Cor. 12:6]

CHAPTER 2

Old Condition: Dead to God

AND you *hath he quickened*, who were dead in trespasses and sins;

2 [R]Wherein in time past ye walked according to the course of this world, according to [R]the prince of the power of the air, the spirit that now worketh in [R]the children of disobedience: Col. 1:21 · 6:12 · Col. 3:6

3 [R]Among whom also we all [T]had our conversation in times past in the lusts of our flesh, fulfilling the desires of the flesh and of the mind; and were by nature the children of wrath, even as others.   1 Pet. 4:3 · *lived*

New Condition: Alive to God

4 But God, [R]who is rich in mercy, for his great love wherewith he loved us,   Rom. 10:12

5 Even when we were dead in sins, hath [T]quickened us together with Christ, ([T]by grace ye are saved;)   *made us alive* · *by* whose *grace*

6 And hath raised *us* up together, and made *us* sit together [R]in[T] heavenly *places* in Christ Jesus: 1:20 · *in the heavenlies*

7 That in the ages to come he might shew the exceeding riches of his grace in *his* kindness toward us through Christ Jesus.

8 [R]For by grace are ye saved [R]through faith; and that not of yourselves: *it is* the gift of God: [2 Tim. 1:9] · Rom. 4:16

9 Not of [T]works, [T]lest any man should boast.   *effort* · *that no man should glory*

10 For we are [R]his workmanship, created in Christ Jesus unto good works, which God hath before [T]ordained that we should walk in them.   Is. 19:25; [Titus 2:14] · *prepared*

Reconciliation of Jews and Gentiles

11 Wherefore remember, that ye *being* in

time past Gentiles in the flesh, who are called Uncircumcision by that which is called the Circumcision in the flesh made by hands;

12 That at that time ye were without Christ, being aliens from the commonwealth of Israel, and strangers from the ᵀcovenants of promise, having no hope, and without God in the world: *agreements*

13 ᴿBut now in Christ Jesus ye ~~who~~ sometimes were far off are made nigh by the blood of Christ. *v. 17; Acts 2:39; [Gal. 3:28]*

14 ᴿFor he is our peace, who hath made both one, and hath broken down the middle wall of partition *between us;* *Is. 9:6; Mic. 5:5 ★*

15 Having abolished in his flesh the enmity, *even* the law of commandments *contained* in ordinances; for to make in himself of twain one new man, *so* making peace;

16 And that he might reconcile both unto God in one body by the cross, ᴿhaving slain the enmity ᵀthereby: *[Rom. 6:6] · by it*

17 ᴿAnd came and preached peace to you which were afar off, and to them that were nigh. *vv. 13, 14; Acts 2:39; [Rom. 5:1]*

18 For ᴿthrough him we both have access by one Spirit unto the Father. *John 10:9*

19 Now therefore ye are no more strangers and foreigners, but fellowcitizens with the saints, and of the household of God;

20 And are built upon the foundation of the apostles and prophets, ᴿJesus Christ himself being the chief corner *stone;* *Ps. 118:22 ★*

21 In whom all the building fitly framed together groweth unto ᴿan holy temple in the Lord: *[4:15, 16]; 1 Cor. 3:17; 2 Cor. 6:16*

22 In whom ye also are builded together for an habitation of God through the Spirit.

CHAPTER 3

Revelation of the Mystery of the Church

FOR this cause I Paul, ᴿthe prisoner of Jesus Christ for you Gentiles, *Acts 21:33*

2 If ye have heard of the ᵀdispensation of the grace of God ᴿwhich is given me to you-ward: *stewardship · Acts 9:15; 13:2*

3 How that by revelation he made known unto me the ᵀmystery; (as I wrote ᵀafore in few words, *hidden truth · before*

4 ᴿWhereby, when ye read, ye may understand my knowledge in the ᵀmystery of Christ) *6:19; 1 Cor. 4:1 · secret*

5 ᴿWhich in other ages was not made known unto the sons of men, as it is now

revealed unto his holy apostles and prophets by the Spirit; *2:20; Is. 29:10; Rom. 16:25*

6 That the Gentiles should be fellowheirs, and of the same body, and partakers of his promise in Christ by the gospel:

7 Whereof I was made a ᵀminister, ᴿaccording to the gift of the grace of God given unto me by ᴿthe effectual working of his power. *servant · Rom. 1:5 · Rom. 15:18*

8 Unto me, ᴿwho am less than the least of all saints, is this grace given, that I should preach among the Gentiles ᴿthe unsearchable riches of Christ; *[1 Cor. 15:9] · [Col. 1:27]*

9 And to make all *men* see what *is* the fellowship of the mystery, which from the beginning of the world hath been hid in God, who created all things by Jesus Christ:

10 ᴿTo the intent that now unto the principalities and powers in heavenly *places* might be known by the church the manifold wisdom of God, *v. 21; 1:21*

11 According to the eternal purpose which he purposed in Christ Jesus our Lord:

12 In whom we have boldness and access ᴿwith confidence by the faith of him. *Heb. 4:16*

13 Wherefore I desire that ye ᵀfaint not at my ᵀtribulations for you, which is ᵀyour glory. *be not discouraged · trials · on your behalf*

Prayer for Realization

14 For this cause I bow my knees unto the Father of our Lord Jesus Christ,

15 ᴿOf whom the whole family in heaven and earth is named, *Acts 11:26; 26:28; 1 Pet. 4:16*

16 That he would grant you, ᴿaccording to the riches of his glory, ᴿto be strengthened with might by his Spirit in ᴿthe inner man; *[Phil. 4:19] · Col. 1:11 · Rom. 7:22*

17 ᴿThat Christ may dwell in your hearts by faith; that ye, ᴿbeing rooted and grounded in love, *John 14:23 · Col. 1:23*

18 ᴿMay be able to ᵀcomprehend with all saints what *is* the breadth, and length, and depth, and height; *1:18 · grasp*

19 And to know the love of Christ, which passeth knowledge, that ye might be filled ᴿwith all the fulness of God. *1:23*

20 Now unto him that is able to do ᵀexceeding abundantly above all that we ask or think, ᴿaccording to the power that worketh in us, *very much more than · Col. 1:29*

21 ᴿUnto him *be* ᵀglory in the church by Christ Jesus throughout all ages, world without end. A-men'. *v. 10; Rom. 11:36 · praise*

3:21 The Purpose of the Church—The ultimate purpose of the church is to bring honor and glory to its head, Jesus Christ. It does this as it fulfills its two purposes related to God's program for the world.

The one purpose of the church, as it relates to the world, is evangelism. This program is spelled out in the Great Commission (Page 974—Matt. 28:19, 20), which has never been rescinded. The program is to "teach all nations." The way this is to be done is twofold: by "baptizing them in the name of the Father, and of the Son, and of the Holy Ghost," and by "teaching them to observe all things whatsoever
(continued on next page)

CHAPTER 4

Exhortation to Unity

I THEREFORE, the prisoner of the Lord, beseech you that ye walk worthy of the vocation wherewith ye are called,

2 ᴿWith all lowliness and meekness, with longsuffering, forbearing one another in love;   Acts 20:19; Gal. 5:22, 23; Col. 3:12, 13

3 Endeavouring to keep the unity of the Spirit ᴿin the bond of peace.   Col. 3:14

Explanation of Unity

4 *There is* one body, and one Spirit, even as ye are called in one hope of your calling;

5 One Lord, one faith, one baptism,

6 One God and Father of all, who *is* above all, and through all, and in you all.

Means for Unity: The Gifts

7 But unto every one of us is given grace according to the measure of the gift of Christ.

8 Wherefore he saith, ᴿWHEN HE ASCENDED UP ON HIGH, HE LED CAPTIVITY CAPTIVE, AND GAVE GIFTS UNTO MEN.   Ps. 68:18; [Col. 2:15] *

9 ᴿ(Now that he ᵀascended, what is it but that he also descended first into the lower parts of the earth?   John 3:13; 1 Pet. 3:19 · *went up*

10 He that descended is the same also ᴿthat ascended up far above all heavens, that he might fill all things.)   John 20:17; Acts 1:9, 11 *

11 ᴿAnd he gave some, apostles; and some, prophets; and some, evangelists; and some, pastors and teachers;   Acts 20:28; Phil. 1:1

Purpose of the Gifts

12 For the ᵀperfecting of the saints, for the work of the ministry, for the ᵀedifying of the body of Christ: *equipping · building up*

13 Till we all come in the unity of the faith, ᴿand of the knowledge of the Son of God, unto a perfect man, unto the measure of the stature of the fulness of Christ: Col. 2:2

14 That we *henceforth* be no more children, tossed to and fro, and carried about with every wind of doctrine, by the ᵀsleight of men, *and* cunning ᵀcraftiness, whereby they lie in wait to deceive;   *tricks · cleverness*

15 ᴿBut speaking the truth in love, may grow up into him in all things, which is the head, *even* Christ: v. 25; 1:22; Col. 1:18

16 From whom the whole body fitly joined together and compacted by that which every joint supplieth, according to the effectual working in the measure of every part, maketh increase of the body unto the ᵀedifying of itself in love.   *building up*

Put Off the Old Man

17 This I say therefore, and testify in the Lord, that ye henceforth walk not as other Gentiles walk, in the vanity of their mind,

18 Having the understanding darkened, being alienated from the life of God through

---

(continued from previous page)
I have commanded you.'' Baptism is not an optional afterthought. It is a vital part of evangelism and making disciples. By baptism, one indicates that he has been identified with Christ in His death, burial, and resurrection (i.e., he is a member of the universal church, the Body of Christ) and wishes to be identified with the local church. A responsible parent not only brings a child into the world, but also provides what is necessary for the child's growth. So in the church, teaching must accompany evangelism so that the child of God can learn all that God expects of him and has provided for him.

Another purpose of the church, as it relates to the world, is edification. According to Ephesians 4:12 the saints need to be edified (built up) for two goals: "For the perfecting of the saints'' and "for the work of the ministry.'' The believers who compose the church's membership need to be built up so that they may realize all that God has provided for Christian living and that they may come to spiritual maturity. They also need to be equipped to perform that work in the Body of Christ that God wants them to perform. In a real sense each member of the church is to be a Christian worker so that the work that God wants to perform through the local church can be accomplished.

Now turn to Page 1195—1 Tim. 3:1-13: The Offices of the Church.

4:3 The Person of the Holy Spirit—One of the most serious errors in the minds of many people concerning the Holy Spirit is that He is simply a principle or an influence. On the contrary, the Holy Spirit is as much a person (individual existence of a conscious being) as the Father and the Son.

a. The personality of the Holy Spirit. The Bible speaks of the mind (Page 1115—Rom. 8:27) and the will (Page 1134—1 Cor. 12:11) of the Holy Spirit. He is often described as speaking directly to men in the Book of Acts. During Paul's second missionary journey the apostle was forbidden by the Spirit to visit a certain mission field (Page 1090—Acts 16:6, 7) and then was instructed to proceed toward another field of service (Page 1090—Acts 16:10). It was God's Spirit who spoke directly to Christian leaders in the Antioch church, commanding them to send Paul and Barnabas on their first missionary journey (Page 1086—Acts 13:2).

b. The deity of the Holy Spirit. He is not only a real person, but He is also God. As is God the Father, He too is everywhere at once (Page 607—Ps. 139:7). As the Son is eternal, the Holy Spirit has also existed forever (Page 1219—Heb. 9:14). He is often referred to as God in the Bible. See Acts 5:3, 4. Finally, the Holy Spirit is equal with the Father and Son. This is seen during the baptism of Christ (Page 943—Matt. 3:16, 17) and is mentioned by Jesus Himself just prior to His ascension from the Mount of Olives (Page 974—Matt. 28:19, 20).

Now turn to Page 1207—Titus 3:5: The Work of the Holy Spirit in Salvation.

the ignorance that is in them, because of the blindness of their heart:

19 Who being past feeling have given themselves over unto lasciviousness, to work all uncleanness with greediness.

20 But ye have not so learned Christ;

21 If so be that ᴿye have heard him, and have been taught by him, as the truth is in Jesus: 1:13; 2:17; Rom. 10:14; Col. 1:5; 2:7

22 That ye put off concerning the former ᵀconversation the old man, which is corrupt according to the deceitful lusts;   *life*

Put On the New Man

23 And ᴿbe ᵀrenewed in the spirit of your mind;   Rom. 12:2; Col. 3:10 • *made new*

24 And that ye ᴿput on the new man, which after God is created in righteousness and ᵀtrue holiness.   [Rom. 6:4] • *holiness of truth*

25 Wherefore putting away lying, ᴿspeak every man truth with his neighbour: for we are members one of another.   Zech. 8:16

26 ᴿBE YE ANGRY, AND SIN NOT: let not the sun go down upon your wrath: Mark 3:5

27 Neither give place to the devil.

28 Let him that stole steal no more: but rather let him labour, working with *his* hands the thing which is good, that he may have to give ᴿto him that needeth.   Luke 3:11

29 Let no corrupt communication proceed out of your mouth, but that which is good to the use of ᵀedifying, that it may minister grace unto the hearers.   *building up*

Grieve Not the Holy Spirit

30 And ᴿgrieve not the holy Spirit of God, whereby ye are sealed unto the day of redemption.   1:13, 14; Rom. 8:23; 1 Thess. 5:19

31 Let all bitterness, and wrath, and anger, and clamour, and evil speaking, be put away from you, ᴿwith all malice: Titus 3:3

32 And be ye kind one to another, tenderhearted, forgiving one another, even as God for Christ's sake hath forgiven you.

CHAPTER 5

BE ᴿye therefore ᵀfollowers of God, as dear children;   Luke 6:36 • *imitators*

2 And walk in love, ᴿas Christ also hath loved us, and hath given himself for us an offering and a sacrifice to God ᴿfor a sweetsmelling savour.   Gal. 1:4 • 2 Cor. 2:15

3 ᴿBut fornication, and all uncleanness, or covetousness, let it not be once named among you, as becometh saints;   [Rom. 6:13]

4 Neither filthiness, nor foolish talking, nor jesting, ᴿwhich are not ᵀconvenient: but rather giving of thanks.   Rom. 1:28 • *suitable*

5 For this ye know, that no whoremonger, nor unclean person, nor covetous man, who is an idolater, hath any inheritance in the kingdom of Christ and of God.

6 ᴿLet no man deceive you with ᵀvain words: for because of these things cometh the wrath of God upon the children of ᵀdisobedience.   Matt. 24:4; Rom. 1:18 • *empty • unbelief*

7 ᵀBe not ye therefore partakers with them.   *have nothing to do with them*

8 ᴿFor ye were ᵀsometimes darkness, but now *are* ye light in the Lord: walk as children of light: John 12:36 • *at one time*

9 (For the fruit of the Spirit *is* in all goodness and righteousness and truth;)

10 ᴿProvingᵀ what is ᵀacceptable unto the Lord.   Rom. 12:2 • *demonstrating • pleasing*

11 ᴿAnd have no fellowship with the unfruitful works of darkness, but rather reprove *them.*   [Rom. 6:21]; 1 Cor. 5:9, 11; [Gal. 6:8]

12 ᴿFor it is ᵀa shame even to speak of those things which are done of them in secret.   Rom. 1:24 • *too shameful*

Walk as Children of Light

13 But all things that are ᵀreproved are made manifest by the light: for whatsoever doth make manifest is light.   *exposed*

14 Wherefore he saith, ᴿAWAKE THOU THAT SLEEPEST, AND ARISE FROM THE DEAD, AND CHRIST SHALL GIVE THEE LIGHT.   Is. 26:19; 60:1 ✶

15 See then that ye walk ᵀcircumspectly, not as fools, but as wise,   *cautiously*

16 Redeeming the time, because the days are evil.

17 Wherefore be ye not unwise, but understanding what the will of the Lord *is.*

Be Filled with the Spirit

18 And be not drunk with wine, wherein is excess; but be filled with the Spirit;

5:18 Walking in the Spirit: Filling—To be filled with the Spirit is to be controlled by the Spirit and is therefore crucial to successfully living the Christian life. Unlike the indwelling of the Spirit, filling is a repeated experience. This is underscored by the use of the present tense ("be filled") as well as by biblical examples of Christians who were filled more than once (Page 1073—Acts 2:4; 4:31). Just as important, we must observe that filling is a command to be obeyed, not an option.

The next most important question is, How can someone be filled with the Spirit? The prerequisites are simply confession of sin and yielding to God. The former means to agree with God about the person's sin; the latter means primarily dedication of himself to God. As the believer chooses to obey in these areas he is filled with the Spirit and enabled to manifest Christlike character. This obedience may be accompanied by prayer but is not necessarily so.

(continued on next page)

19 Speaking to yourselves in psalms and hymns and spiritual songs, singing and making melody in your heart to the Lord;

20 ᴿGiving thanks always for all things unto God and the Father ᴿin the name of our Lord Jesus Christ; Ps. 34:1 • [1 Pet. 2:5]

21 ᴿSubmitting yourselves one to another in the fear of God. [Phil. 2:3]; 1 Pet. 5:5

Wives: Submit to Your Husbands

22 ᴿWives, submit yourselves unto your own husbands, as unto the Lord. Col. 3:18

23 For the husband is the head of the wife, even as Christ is the head of the church: and he is the saviour of the body.

24 Therefore as the church is subject unto Christ, so let the wives be to their own husbands ᴿin every thing. Titus 2:4, 5

Husbands: Love Your Wives

25 ᴿHusbands, love your wives, ᴿeven as Christ also loved the church, and ᴿgave himself for it; Col. 3:19 • 1 Cor. 6:20 • Acts 20:28

26 That he might sanctify and cleanse it with the washing of water by the word,

27 That he might present it to himself a glorious church, not having spot, or wrinkle, or any such thing; but that it should be holy and without ᵀblemish. fault

28 So ought men to love their wives ᵀas their own bodies. He that loveth his wife loveth himself. as much as

29 For no man ever yet hated his own flesh; but ᵀnourisheth and ᵀcherisheth it, even as the Lord the church: feeds • cares for

30 For ᴿwe are members of his body, of his flesh, and of his bones. Rom. 12:5

31 FOR THIS CAUSE SHALL A MAN LEAVE HIS FATHER AND MOTHER, AND SHALL BE JOINED UNTO HIS WIFE, AND THEY TWO SHALL BE ONE FLESH.

32 This is a great ᵀmystery: but I speak concerning Christ and the church. hidden truth

33 Nevertheless ᴿlet every one of you ᵀin particular so love his wife even as himself; and the wife see that she ᴿreverenceᵀ her husband. Col. 3:19 • personally • 1 Pet. 3:6 • honour

CHAPTER 6

Children: Obey Your Parents

CHILDREN, ᴿobey your parents in the Lord: for this is right. Prov. 23:22; Col. 3:20

2 HONOUR THY FATHER AND MOTHER; which is the first commandment with promise;

3 THAT IT MAY BE WELL WITH THEE, AND THOU MAYEST LIVE LONG ON THE EARTH.

4 And, ye fathers, provoke not your children to wrath: but bring them up in the nurture and admonition of the Lord.

(continued from previous page)
The certainty of being filled with the Spirit may be confirmed by the believer's faith and life. The believer must, of course, believe God's Word that meeting the conditions will result in the filling. The Spirit-filled person will exhibit the Christlike character described in Galatians 5:22, 23 as the fruit of the Spirit. Included in that list are all the vibrant, attractive qualities desired by all Christians. How delightful it is that any Christian may possess them and be transformed by the filling of the Spirit.
Now turn to Page 22—THE CHRISTIAN'S GUIDE: Facing Problems in the New Life.
5:25–29 The Relationship of the Church to Christ—The wonderful relationship that exists between Christ and the church was initiated by Christ who loved the church and gave Himself for it. The intimacies of that relationship are described with seven figures:
a. "The shepherd and the sheep" emphasizes both the warm leadership and protection of Christ and the helplessness and dependency of believers (Page 1054—John 10:1–18).
b. "The vine and the branches" points out the necessity for Christians to depend on Christ's sustaining strength for growth (Page 1060—John 15:1–8).
c. "Christ as high priest" and "the church as a kingdom of priests" stresses the joyful worship, fellowship, and service which the church can render to God through Christ (Page 1217—Heb. 5:1–10; 7:1; 8:6; Page 1236—1 Pet. 2:5–9; Page 1268—Rev. 1:6).
d. "The cornerstone and building stones" accents the foundational value of Christ to everything the church is and does, as well as Christ's value to the unity of believers. Love is to be the mortar which solidly holds the living stones together (Page 1127—1 Cor. 3:9; 13:1–13; Page 1163—Eph. 2:19–22; Page 1236—1 Pet. 2:5).
e. "The head and many-membered body" is frequently used in Scripture to illustrate several tremendous truths: the church is a vibrant organism, not merely an organization; it draws its vitality and direction from Christ, the head; and each believer has a unique and necessary place in its growth (Page 1134—1 Cor. 12:12, 13, 27; Page 1164—Eph. 4:4).
f. "The last Adam and new creation" presents Christ as the initiator of a new creation of believers as Adam was of the old creation (Page 1137—1 Cor. 15:22, 45; Page 1145—2 Cor. 5:17).
g. "The bridegroom and bride" beautifully emphasizes the intimate fellowship and co-ownership existing between Christ and the church (Eph. 5:25–33; Page 1280—Rev. 19:7, 8; 21:9).
You have now completed The Christian's Guide to the New Life.
6:4 The Role of the Parents—The father is the parent responsible for setting the pattern for the child's obedience in the family. Any disciplining the mother does is an extension of the father's authority in the home. The husband and father must take leadership in this area of the family, and the

Service on the Job

5 ᴿServants, be obedient to them that are *your* masters according to the flesh, with fear and trembling, in ᵀsingleness of your heart, as unto Christ; [1 Tim. 6:1] • *sincerity*

6 ᴿNot with eyeservice, as menpleasers; but as the servants of Christ, doing the will of God from the heart; Col. 3:22

7 With ᵀgood will doing service, as to the Lord, and not to men: *cheerfulness*

8 Knowing that whatsoever good thing any man doeth, the same shall he receive of the Lord, whether *he be* bond or free.

9 And, ye masters, do the same things unto them, forbearing threatening: knowing that your Master also is in heaven; neither is there respect of persons with him.

Put On the Armour of God

10 Finally, my brethren, be strong in the Lord, and in the power of his might.

11 ᴿPut on the whole armour of God, that ye may be able to stand against the ᵀwiles of the devil. [Rom. 13:12; 2 Cor. 6:7] • *cunning devices*

12 For we wrestle not against flesh and blood, but against principalities, against powers, against ᴿthe rulers of the darkness of this world, against spiritual wickedness in ᵀhigh *places*. Luke 22:53 • *places of authority*

13 ᴿWherefore take unto you the whole armour of God, that ye may be able to withstand in the evil day, and ᵀhaving done all, to stand. [2 Cor. 10:4] • *having overcome all*

14 Stand therefore, ᴿhaving your loins ᵀgirt about with truth, and having on the breastplate of righteousness; Is. 11:5 • *girded*

15 ᴿAnd your feet shod with the preparation of the gospel of peace; Is. 52:7

16 Above all, taking ᴿthe shield of faith, wherewith ye shall be able to quench all the fiery darts of the wicked. 1 John 5:4

17 And ᴿtake the helmet of salvation, and ᴿthe sword of the Spirit, which is the word of God: 1 Thess. 5:8 • [Heb. 4:12; Rev. 19:15]

Pray for Boldness

18 Praying always with all prayer and supplication in the Spirit, and ᴿwatching thereunto with all perseverance and ᴿsupplication for all saints; [Matt. 26:41] • Phil. 1:4

19 And for me, that ᵀutterance may be given unto me, that I may open my mouth boldly, to make known the ᵀmystery of the gospel, *freedom of speech • hidden truth*

20 For which ᴿI am an ambassador ᵀin bonds: that therein I may speak boldly, as I ought to speak. 2 Cor. 5:20 • *in prison*

Conclusion

21 But that ye also may know my affairs, *and* how I do, ᴿTych'-i-cus, a beloved brother and faithful minister in the Lord, shall make known to you all things: Acts 20:4

22 Whom I have sent unto you for the same purpose, that ye might know our affairs, and *that* he might comfort your hearts.

23 ᴿPeace *be* to the brethren, and love with faith, from God the Father and the Lord Jesus Christ. Gal. 6:16; Rom. 15:33

24 Grace *be* with all them that love our Lord Jesus Christ in sincerity. A-men'.

---

wife and mother must be in submission. The father's responsibility is set forth in two ways: First, what the father is *not* to do—"provoke not your children to wrath." He is not to over-discipline them or reign in terror, with the result that the child can only react in a blind outbreak or rage. Second, what the father *is* to do—"but bring them up in the nurture and admonition of the Lord." To "bring them up" involves three ideas:

a. It is a continuous job. As long as the child is a dependent, the father is to be responsible for providing for the child so that he becomes what God wants him to be.

b. It is a loving job. To "bring up" means literally *to nourish tenderly;* children should be objects of tender, loving care.

c. It is a twofold job involving nurture (lit., *child-training*)—all that a child needs for his development physically, mentally, and spiritually—and admonition (lit., *corrective discipline*) of the Lord.

The father is God's constituted home authority who is to discipline the child when he does not obey as God intends. The father who does not discipline his children is a father who is undisciplined himself and disobedient to God's will. A child's disobedience is not to be tolerated. See Exodus 21:15–17; Deuteronomy 21:18–21; Proverbs 13:24; 19:18; 22:15; 23:13, 14; 29:15–17.

Now turn to Page 629—Prov. 22:6: A Prescription for Rearing Children.

PHILIPPIANS

THE BOOK OF PHILIPPIANS

Paul writes a thank-you note to the believers at Philippi for their help in his hour of need, and he uses the occasion to send along some instruction on Christian unity. His central thought is simple: Only in Christ are real unity and joy possible. With Christ as your model of humility and service, you can enjoy a oneness of purpose, attitude, goal, and labor—a truth which Paul illustrates from his own life, and one the Philippians desperately need to hear. Within their own ranks, fellow workers in the Philippian church are at odds, hindering the work in proclaiming new life in Christ. Because of this, Paul exhorts the church to "stand fast . . . be of the same mind . . . rejoice in the Lord alway . . . but . . . by prayer . . . let your requests be made known . . . and the peace of God . . . shall keep your hearts and minds through Christ Jesus" (4:1, 2, 4, 6, 7).

This epistle is called *Pros Philippēsious*, "To the Philippians." The church at Philippi was the first church Paul founded in Macedonia.

THE AUTHOR OF PHILIPPIANS

The external and internal evidence for the Pauline authorship of Philippians is very strong, and there is scarcely any doubt that Paul wrote it.

THE TIME OF PHILIPPIANS

In 356 B.C., King Philip of Macedonia (the father of Alexander the Great) took this town and expanded it, renaming it Philippi. The Romans captured it in 168 B.C.; and in 42 B.C., the defeat of the forces of Brutus and Cassius by those of Anthony and Octavian (later Augustus) took place outside the city. Octavian turned Philippi into a Roman colony (cf. Acts 16:12) and a military outpost. The citizens of this colony were regarded as citizens of Rome and given a number of special privileges. Because Philippi was a military city and not a commercial center, there were not enough Jews for a synagogue when Paul came (Acts 16:13).

Paul's "Macedonian Call" in Troas during his second missionary journey led to his ministry in Philippi with the conversion of Lydia and others. Paul and Silas were beaten and imprisoned, but this resulted in the conversion of the Philippian jailer. The magistrates were placed in a dangerous position by beating Roman citizens without a trial (Acts 16:37-40), and that embarrassment may have prevented future reprisals against the new Christians in Philippi. Paul visited the Philippians again on his third missionary journey (Acts 20:1, 6). When they heard of his Roman imprisonment, the Philippian church sent Epaphroditus with financial help (4:18); they had helped Paul in this way on at least two other occasions (4:16). Epaphroditus almost died of an illness, yet remained with Paul long enough for the Philippians to receive word of his malady. Upon his recovery, Paul sent this letter back with him to Philippi (2:25-30).

Silas, Timothy, Luke, and Paul first came to Philippi in A.D. 51, eleven years before Paul wrote this letter. Philippians 1:13 and 4:22 suggest that it was written from Rome, although some commentators argue for Caesarea or Ephesus. Paul's life was at stake, and he was evidently awaiting the verdict of the Imperial Court (2:20-26).

THE CHRIST OF PHILIPPIANS

The great *kenosis* passage is one of several portraits of Christ in this epistle. In chapter 1, Paul sees Christ as his life ("For to me to live *is* Christ," 1:21). In chapter 2, Christ is the model of true humility ("Let this mind be in you, which was also in Christ Jesus," 2:5). Chapter 3 presents Him as the One "Who shall change our vile body, that it may be fashioned like unto his glorious body" (3:21). In chapter 4, He is the source of Paul's power over circumstances ("I can do all things through Christ which strengtheneth me," 4:13).

KEYS TO PHILIPPIANS

Key Word: To Live Is Christ—Central to Philippians is the concept of "For to me to live *is* Christ, and to die *is* gain" (1:21). Every chapter resounds with the theme of the centrality of Jesus in the Christian's life. High points include the following: "Let this mind be in you which was also in Christ Jesus" (2:5); "I count all things *but* loss for the excellency of the knowledge of Christ Jesus" (3:8); and "I can do all things through Christ which strengtheneth me" (4:13).

Key Verses: Philippians 1:21 and 4:12—"For to me to live *is* Christ, and to die *is* gain" (1:21).

"I know both how to be abased, and I know how to abound: every where and in all things I am instructed both to be full and to be hungry, both to abound and to suffer need" (4:12).

Key Chapter: Philippians 2—The grandeur of the truth of the New Testament seldom exceeds the revelation of the humility of Jesus Christ

when He left heaven to become a servant of man. Christ is clearly the Christian's example, and Paul encourages "Let this mind be in you, which was also in Christ Jesus" (2:5).

SURVEY OF PHILIPPIANS

Philippians is the epistle of joy and encouragement in the midst of adverse circumstances. Paul freely expresses his fond affection for the Philippians, appreciates their consistent testimony and support, and lovingly urges them to center their actions and thoughts on the pursuit of the person and power of Christ. Paul also seeks to correct the problems of disunity and rivalry (2:2–4) and to prevent the problems of legalism and antinomianism (3:1–19). Philippians focuses on: Paul's account of his present circumstances (1); Paul's appeal to have the mind of Christ (2); Paul's appeal to have the knowledge of Christ (3); Paul's appeal to have the peace of Christ (4).

Paul's Account of His Present Circumstances (1): Paul's usual salutation (1:1, 2) is followed by his thanksgiving, warm regard, and prayer on behalf of the Philippians (1:3–11). For years, they have participated in the apostle's ministry, and he prays for their continued growth in the real knowledge of Christ. Paul shares the circumstances of his imprisonment and rejoices in the spread of the gospel in spite of and because of his situation (1:12–26). As he considers the outcome of his approaching trial, he expresses his willingness to "depart, and to be with Christ" (1:23) or to continue in ministry. Paul encourages the Philippians to remain steadfast in the face of opposition and coming persecution (1:27–30).

Paul's Appeal to Have the Mind of Christ (2): Paul exhorts the Philippians to have a spirit of unity and mutual concern by embracing the attitude of humility (2:1–4), the greatest example of which is the incarnation and crucifixion of Christ (2:5–11). The *kenosis,* or "emptying," of Christ, does not mean that He divested Himself of His deity, but that He withheld His preincarnate glory and voluntarily restricted His use of certain attributes (e.g., omnipresence and omniscience). Paul asks the Philippians to apply this attitude to their lives (2:12–18), and he gives two more examples of sacrifice, the ministries of Timotheus and Epaphroditus (2:19–30).

Paul's Appeal to Have the Knowledge of Christ (3): It appears that Paul is about to close his letter ("Finally, my brethren," 3:1) when he launches into a warning about the continuing problem of legalism (3:1–9). Paul refutes this teaching with revealing autobiographical details about his previous attainments in Judaism. Compared to the goal of knowing Christ, those pursuits are as nothing. True righteousness is received through faith, not by mechanical obedience to any law. Paul yearns for the promised attainment of the resurrected body.

Paul's Appeal to Have the Peace of Christ (4): In a series of exhortations, Paul urges the Philippians to have peace with the brethren by living a life-style of unity, prayerful dependence, and holiness (4:13). In 4:4–9, Paul describes the secrets of having the peace of God as well as peace with God. He then rejoices over their gift, but explains that the power of Christ enables him to live above his circumstances (4:10–20). This joyous letter from prison closes with greetings and a benediction (4:21–23).

FOCUS	ACCOUNT OF CIRCUMSTANCES	THE MIND OF CHRIST	THE KNOWLEDGE OF CHRIST	THE PEACE OF CHRIST
REFERENCE	1:1	2:1	3:1	4:1 —— 4:23
DIVISION	PARTAKE OF CHRIST	PEOPLE OF CHRIST	PURSUIT OF CHRIST	POWER OF CHRIST
TOPIC	SUFFERING	SUBMISSION	SALVATION	SANCTIFICATION
	EXPERIENCE	EXAMPLES	EXHORTATION	
LOCATION			ROME	
TIME			C. A.D. 62	

OUTLINE OF PHILIPPIANS

CHAPTER 1

Paul's Prayer of Thanksgiving

PAUL and Ti-mo'-the-us, the servants of Jesus Christ, to all the saints in Christ Jesus which are at Phi-lip'-pi, Rwith the bishops and deacons: [1 Tim. 3:1-13; Titus 1:5-9]

2 RGrace be unto you, and peace, from God our Father, and from the Lord Jesus Christ. Rom. 1:7; 2 Cor. 1:2; 1 Pet. 1:2

3 RI thank my God upon every remembrance of you, Eph. 1:15, 16; 1 Thess. 1:2

4 RAlways in every prayer of mine for you all making request with joy, Eph. 1:16

5 RFor your fellowship in the gospel from the first day until now; [Rom. 12:13; 15:26]

6 Being confident of this very thing, that he which hath begun a good work in you will perform it until the day of Jesus Christ:

7 Even as it is Tmeet for me to think this of you all, because I have you in my heart; inasmuch as both in my bonds, and in the defence and confirmation of the gospel, ye all are Tpartakers of my grace. proper · partners

8 For God is my Trecord, Rhow greatly I long after you all in the Tbowels of Jesus Christ. witness · 2:26; Rom. 9:1 · tender mercies

9 And this I pray, Rthat your love may abound yet more and more in knowledge and in all Tjudgment; 1 Thess. 3:12 · understanding

10 That ye may approve things that are excellent; that ye may be sincere and without offence till the day of Christ;

11 Being filled with the fruits of righteousness, Rwhich are by Jesus Christ, Runto the glory and praise of God. Col. 1:6 · John 15:8

Paul's Afflictions Promote the Gospel

12 But I would ye should understand, brethren, that the things which happened unto me Thave fallen out rather unto the furtherance of the gospel; turned out

13 So that my bonds in Christ are manifest in all the palace, and in all other places;

14 And many of the brethren in the Lord, waxing confident by my bonds, are much more bold to speak the word without fear.

15 Some indeed preach Christ even of envy and strife; and some also of good will:

16 The one preach Christ of Tcontention, Tnot sincerely, supposing to add affliction to my bonds: fraction · of selfish ambition

17 But the other of love, knowing that I am set for the defence of the gospel.

18 What then? notwithstanding, every way, whether in pretence, or in truth, Christ is preached; and I therein do rejoice, yea, and will Trejoice. continue to be happy

Paul's Afflictions Exalt the Lord

19 For I know that this shall turn to my salvation through your prayer, and the supply of the Spirit of Jesus Christ,

20 According to my earnest expectation and my hope, that in nothing I shall be ashamed, but that with all boldness, as always, so now also Christ shall be magnified Tin my body, whether it be by life, or by death. in what happens to me physically

21 For to me Rto live is Christ, and to die is gain. [Gal. 2:20]

22 But if I live in the flesh, this is the fruit of my labour: Ryet what I shall choose I Twot not. Acts 7:40 · know

23 RFor I am in a strait betwixt two, having a desire to depart, and to be with Christ; which is far better: 2 Tim. 4:6

24 Nevertheless to abide in the flesh is more Tneedful for Tyou. important · your sake

25 And having this confidence, I know that I shall abide and continue with you all for your furtherance and joy of faith;

26 That Ryour rejoicing may be more abundant in Jesus Christ for me by my coming to you again. 2 Cor. 1:14; 5:12

Paul's Exhortation to the Afflicted

27 Only let your conversation be as it becometh the gospel of Christ: that whether I come and see you, or else be absent, I may hear of your affairs, that ye stand fast in one spirit, with one mind striving together for the faith of the gospel;

28 And in nothing ᵀterrified by your adversaries: ᴿwhich is to them an evident ᵀtoken of perdition, but to you of salvation, and that of God.   *dismayed · 2 Thess. 1:5 · sign*

29 For unto you ᴿit is given in the behalf of Christ, ᴿnot only to believe on him, but also to suffer for his sake;   *[Rom. 5:3] · Eph. 2:8*

30 ᴿHaving the same conflict which ye saw in me, and now hear *to be* in me.   *Col. 2:1*

CHAPTER 2

Paul's Exhortation to Humility

IF *there be* therefore any ᵀconsolation in Christ, if any comfort of love, if any fellowship of the Spirit, if any ᴿbowelsᵀ and mercies,   *comfort · Col. 3:12 · affection and compassion*

2 ᴿFulfil ye my joy, ᴿthat ye be likeminded, having the same love, *being* of one accord, of one mind.   *John 3:29 · Rom. 12:16*

3 *Let* nothing *be done* through strife or vainglory; but in lowliness of mind let each esteem other better than themselves.

4 Look not every man on his own things, but every man also on the things of others.

Christ's Example of Humility

5 ᴿLet this mind be in you, which was also in Christ Jesus: *[Matt. 11:29]; John 13:15*

6 Who, being in the form of God, thought it not robbery to be equal with God:

7 But made himself of no reputation, and took upon him the form of a servant, and was made in the likeness of men:

8 And being found in fashion as a man, he humbled himself, and became obedient unto death, even the death of the cross.

9 Wherefore God also ᴿhath highly exalted him, and ᴿgiven him a name which is above every name: *Ps. 68:18; Acts 2:33 ★ · Heb. 1:4*

10 That at the name of Jesus every knee should bow, of *things* in heaven, and *things* in earth, and *things* under the earth;

11 And ᴿ*that* every tongue should confess that Jesus Christ *is* Lord, to the glory of God the Father.   *Is. 45:23; John 13:13; Rom. 14:11*

12 Wherefore, my beloved, ᴿas ye have always obeyed, not as in my presence only, but now much more in my absence, ᵀwork out your own salvation with ᴿfear and trembling.   *1:5 · complete · Eph. 6:5*

13 For it is God which worketh in you both to will and to do of *his* good pleasure.

14 Do all things ᴿwithout ᵀmurmurings and disputings: *1 Pet. 4:9 · complaining*

15 That ye may be blameless and harmless, the sons of God, without rebuke, in the midst of a crooked and perverse nation, among whom ye shine as lights in the world;

16 Holding forth the word of life; that I may rejoice in the day of Christ, that I have not run in vain, neither laboured in vain.

Paul's Example of Humility

17 Yea, and if I be offered upon the sacrifice ᴿand service of your faith, I joy, and rejoice with you all.   *Rom. 15:16*

18 For the same cause also do ye joy, and rejoice with me.

Timothy's Example of Humility

19 But I trust in the Lord Jesus to send Ti-mo'-the-us shortly unto you, that I also may be of good comfort, when I know your state.

20 For I have no man likeminded, who will naturally care for your ᵀstate.   *welfare*

21 ᴿFor all seek their own, not the things which are Jesus Christ's.   *1 Cor. 10:24, 33; 13:5*

22 But ye know the ᵀproof of him, ᴿthat, as a son with the father, he hath served with me in the gospel.   *worth · 1 Cor. 4:17*

23 Him therefore I hope to send presently, so soon as I shall see how it will go with me.

24 ᴿBut I trust in the Lord that I also myself shall come shortly.   *1:25; Philem. 22*

Epaphroditus's Example of Humility

25 Yet I supposed it necessary to send to you E-paph-ro-di'-tus, my brother, and companion in labour, and fellowsoldier, but your messenger, and ᴿhe that ᵀministered to my wants.   *2 Cor. 11:9 · provided for*

26 For he longed after you all, and was ᵀfull of heaviness, because that ye had heard that he had been sick.   *sore troubled*

27 For indeed he was sick nigh unto death: but God had mercy on him; and not on him only, but on me also, lest I should have sorrow upon sorrow.

28 I sent him therefore the more carefully, that, when ye see him again, ye may rejoice, and that I may be the less sorrowful.

29 Receive him therefore in the Lord with all gladness; and hold such in reputation:

30 Because for the work of Christ he was nigh unto death, not regarding his life, to supply your lack of service toward me.

CHAPTER 3

Warning Against Confidence in the Flesh

FINALLY, my brethren, ᴿrejoice in the Lord. To write the same things to you, to me indeed *is* not ᵀgrievous, but for you *it is* safe.   *4:4; 2 Cor. 13:11; 1 Thess. 5:16 · irksome*

2 Beware of dogs, beware of evil workers, beware of ᵀthe concision.   *the mutilators*

3 For we are ᴿthe circumcision, ᴿwhich worship God in the spirit, and rejoice in Christ Jesus, and have no confidence in ᵀthe flesh.   Deut. 30:6 · Rom. 7:6 · *ceremonies*

4 Though ᴿI might also have confidence in the flesh. If any other man thinketh that he hath whereof he might trust in the flesh, I ᵀmore: 2 Cor. 11:18, 22 · *have more reason*

5 Circumcised the eighth day, of the stock of Israel, *of* the tribe of Benjamin, ᴿan Hebrew of the Hebrews; as touching the law, ᴿa Pharisee;   2 Cor. 11:22 · Acts 23:6

6 ᴿConcerning zeal, persecuting the church; touching the righteousness which is in the law, blameless.   Acts 8:3; 9:1; 22:3

7 But ᴿwhat things were gain to me, those I counted loss for Christ.   Matt. 13:44

8 Yea doubtless, and I count all things *but* loss for the excellency of the knowledge of Christ Jesus my Lord: for whom I have suffered the loss of all things, and do count them *but* dung, that I may win Christ,

9 And be found in him, not having mine own righteousness, which is of the law, but that which is through the faith of Christ, the righteousness which is of God by faith:

Exhortation to Know Christ

10 That I may know him, and the power of his resurrection, and ᴿthe fellowship of his sufferings, being made conformable unto his death;   [Rom. 6:3-5]; 2 Tim. 2:11, 12

11 If by any means I might ᴿattain unto the resurrection ᵀof the dead.   Acts 26:6-8 · *from*

12 Not as though I had already attained, either were already perfect: but I follow after, if that I may ᵀapprehend that for which also I am apprehended of Christ Jesus.   *grasp*

13 Brethren, I ᵀcount not myself to have apprehended: but *this* one thing I *do*, ᴿforgetting those things which are behind, and ᴿreaching forth unto those things which are before,   *do not think of* · Luke 9:62 · Heb. 6:1

14 I press toward the mark for the prize of the high calling of God in Christ Jesus.

15 Let us therefore, as many as be ᴿperfect,ᵀ ᴿbe thus minded: and if in any thing ye be otherwise minded, God shall reveal even this unto you.   1 Cor. 2:6 · *mature* · Gal. 5:10

16 Nevertheless, whereto we have already ᵀattained, let us walk by the same rule, let us mind the same thing.   *achieved*

Warning Against Living for the Flesh

17 Brethren, ᴿbe followers together of me, and mark them which walk so as ᴿye have us for an ensample.   [1 Cor. 11:1] · 1 Pet. 5:3

18 (For many walk, of whom I have told you often, and now tell you even weeping, *that they are* ᴿthe enemies of the ᵀcross of Christ: 1:15, 16; [Gal. 1:7; 2:21; 6:12] · *death*

19 Whose end *is* destruction, whose God *is their* belly, and *whose* glory *is* in their shame, who mind earthly things.)

20 For ᴿour ᵀconversation is in heaven; from whence also we look for the Saviour, the Lord Jesus Christ: Eph. 2:6 · *citizenship*

21 Who shall change our ᵀvile body, that it may be fashioned like unto his ᵀglorious body, ᴿaccording to the working whereby he is able even to subdue all things unto himself.   *body of humiliation* · *body of glory* · Eph. 1:19

CHAPTER 4

Peace with the Brethren

THEREFORE, my brethren dearly beloved and longed for, my joy and crown, so stand fast in the Lord, *my* dearly beloved.

2 I beseech Eu-o′-di-as, and ᵀbeseech Syn′-ty-che, ᴿthat they ᵀbe of the same mind in the Lord.   *beg* · 3:16 · *agree*

3 And I intreat thee also, true yokefellow, help those women which laboured with me in the gospel, with Clement also, and *with* other my fellowlabourers, whose names *are* in ᴿthe book of life.   Ex. 32:32

Peace with the Lord

4 ᴿRejoice in the Lord alway: *and* again I say, Rejoice.   Luke 10:20; Rom. 12:12; [1 Pet. 4:13]

5 Let your ᵀmoderation be known unto all men. The Lord *is* at hand.   *self-control*

6 ᴿBe ᵀcareful for nothing; but in every thing by prayer and supplication with thanksgiving let your requests be made known unto God.   Ps. 55:22; [Prov. 16:3] · *worried*

4:6 Thanksgiving—The importance and spiritual benefits of thanksgiving in our prayer life cannot be overemphasized. The Bible tells us God resists the proud, but gives grace to the humble (Page 1230—James 4:6). But the question is, how do you become humble? It is done by being thankful! A good rule is to be careful (worried) for nothing (Phil. 4:6), be prayerful in all things (Page 1185—1 Thess. 5:18), and be thankful for anything. It was the sin of thanklessness that caused the ancient world to plunge into the terrible depths of sexual depravity (Page 1109—Rom. 1:21). In the Old Testament a special group of priests was appointed to do nothing else but praise and thank the Lord (Page 465—2 Chr. 31:2).

There are two main things we are to thank God for:
a. We are to thank Him for His work in Creation. David reminds us concerning this area of thanksgiving in Psalm 100. Later, John the apostle tells us we will thank God for His work in Creation throughout all eternity. Note the words of this song of praise: "Thou art worthy, O Lord, to receive glory and honour and power: for thou hast created all things, and for thy pleasure they are and were created" (Page 1271—Rev. 4:11).

7 And ᴿthe peace of God, which passeth all understanding, shall keep your hearts and minds through Christ Jesus.   [John 14:27]

8 Finally, brethren, whatsoever things are true, whatsoever things *are* ᵀhonest, whatsoever things *are* just, whatsoever things *are* pure, whatsoever things *are* lovely, whatsoever things *are* of good report; if *there be* any virtue, and if *there be* any praise, think on these things.   *honourable*

9 Those things, which ye have both learned, and received, and heard, and seen in me, do: and ᴿthe God of peace shall be with you.   Rom. 15:33; 1 Cor. 14:33; 2 Cor. 13:11

Peace in All Circumstances

10 But I rejoiced in the Lord greatly, that now at the last your care of me hath flourished again; wherein ye were also careful, but ye lacked opportunity.

11 Not that I speak in respect of want: for I have learned, in whatsoever state I am, ᴿtherewith to be content.   1 Tim. 6:6

12 ᴿI know both how to be ᵀabased, and I know how to ᵀabound: every where and in all things I am instructed both to be full and to be hungry, both to abound and to suffer need.   1 Cor. 4:11 · *made low* · *be prosperous*

13 I can do all things ᴿthrough Christ which strengtheneth me.   John 15:5; [2 Cor. 12:9]

14 Notwithstanding ye have well done, that ye did communicate with my affliction.

15 Now ye Phi-lip'-pi-ans know also, that in the beginning of the gospel, when I departed from Mac-e-do'-ni-a, ᴿno church communicated with me as concerning giving and receiving, but ye only.   2 Cor. 11:8

16 For even in Thes-sa-lo-ni'-ca ye sent once and again unto my necessity.

17 Not because I desire a gift: but I desire fruit that may abound to your account.

18 But I have ᵀall, and abound: I am full, having received of E-paph-ro-di'-tus the things which *were sent* from you, an ᵀodour of a sweet smell, a sacrifice acceptable, wellpleasing to God.   *I have received all* · *fragrance*

19 But my God ᴿshall supply all your need according to his riches in glory by Christ Jesus.   Ps. 23:1; 24:1; 50:10; 84:11

Conclusion

20 ᴿNow unto God and our Father *be* glory for ever and ever. A-men'.   Rom. 16:27

21 Salute every saint in Christ Jesus. The brethren which are with me greet you.

22 ᴿAll the saints salute you, chiefly they that are of Caesar's household.   2 Cor. 13:13

23 The grace of our Lord Jesus Christ ᴿ*be* with ᵀyou all. A-men'.   2 Tim. 4:22 · *your spirit*

---

b. We are to thank Him for His work in redemption. John also informs us that our second song in heaven will feature thanksgiving for God's work in redemption: "And they sung a new song, saying, Thou art worthy to take the book, and to open the seals thereof: for thou wast slain, and hast redeemed us to God by thy blood" (Page 1271—Rev. 5:9).
Now turn to Page 625—Prov. 16:3: Commitment.

COLOSSIANS

THE BOOK OF COLOSSIANS

If Ephesians can be labeled the epistle portraying the "Church of Christ," then Colossians must surely be the "Christ of the Church." Ephesians focuses on the Body; Colossians focuses on the Head. Like Ephesians, the little Book of Colossians divides neatly in half with the first portion doctrinal (1 and 2) and the second practical (3 and 4). Paul's purpose is to show that Christ is preeminent—first and foremost in everything—and the Christian's life should reflect that priority. Because believers are rooted in Him, alive in Him, hidden in Him, and complete in Him, it is utterly inconsistent for them to live life without Him. Clothed in His love, with His peace ruling in their hearts, they are equipped to make Christ first in every area of life.

This epistle became known as *Pros Kolossaeis*, "To the Colossians," because of 1:2. Paul also wanted it to be read in the neighboring church at Laodicea (4:16).

THE AUTHOR OF COLOSSIANS

The external testimony to the Pauline authorship of Colossians is ancient and consistent, and the internal evidence also is very good. It not only claims to be written by Paul (1:1, 23; 4:18), but the personal details and close parallels with Ephesians and Philemon make the case even stronger. Nevertheless, the authenticity of this letter has been challenged on the internal grounds of vocabulary and thought. In its four chapters, Colossians uses fifty-five Greek words that do not appear in Paul's other epistles. However, Paul commanded a wide vocabulary; and the circumstances and subject of this epistle, especially the references to the Colossian heresy, account for these additional words. The high christology of Colossians has been compared to John's later concept that Christ is the Logos (cf. 1:15–23 and John 1:1–18), with the conclusion that these concepts were too late for Paul's time. However, there is no reason to assume that Paul was unaware of Christ's work as Creator, especially in view of Philippians 2:5–11. It is also wrong to assume that the heresy refuted in Colossians 2 refers to the fully developed form of Gnosticism that did not appear until the second century. The parallels only indicate that Paul was dealing with an early form of Gnosticism.

THE TIME OF COLOSSIANS

Colosse was a minor city about one hundred miles east of Ephesus in the region of the seven Asian churches of Revelation

1—3. Located in the fertile Lycus Valley by a mountain pass on the road from Ephesus to the East, Colosse once was a populous center of commerce, famous for its glossy black wool. By the time of Paul, it had been eclipsed by its neighboring cities, Laodicea and Hierapolis (cf. 4:13), and was on the decline. Apart from this letter, Colosse exerted almost no influence on early church history. It is evident from 1:4–8 and 2:1 that Paul had never visited the church at Colosse, which was founded by Epaphras. On his third missionary journey, Paul devoted almost three years to an Asian ministry centered in Ephesus (cf. Acts 19:10; 20:31), and Epaphras probably came to Christ during this time. He carried the gospel to the cities in the Lycus Valley and years later came to visit Paul in his imprisonment (4:12, 13; Philem. 23).

Colossians, Philemon, and Ephesians were evidently written about the same time and under the same circumstances, judging by the overlapping themes and personal names (cf. Col. 4:9–17 and Philem. 2, 10, 23, 24). Although Caesarea and Ephesus have been suggested as the location of authorship, the bulk of the evidence indicates that Paul wrote all four Prison Epistles during his first Roman imprisonment (see "The Time of Ephesians" and "The Time of Philippians"). If so, Paul wrote it in A.D. 60 or 61 and sent it with Tychicus and the converted slave Onesimus to Colosse (4:7–9; see Eph. 6:21; Philem. 10–12).

Epaphroditus's visit and report about the conditions in Colosse prompted this letter. Although the Colossians had not yet succumbed (2:1–5), an encroaching heresy was threatening the predominantly gentile (1:21, 27; 2:13) Colossian church. The nature of this heresy can only be deduced from Paul's incidental references to it in his refutation in 2:8–23. It was apparently a religious system that combined elements from Greek speculation (2:4, 8–10), Jewish legalism (2:11–17), and Oriental mysticism (2:18–23). It involved a low view of the body (2:20–23) and probably nature as a whole. Circumcision, dietary regulations, and ritual observances were included in this system, which utilized asceticism, worship of angels as intermediaries, and mystical experiences as an approach to the spiritual realm. Any attempt to fit Christ into such a system would undermine His person and redemptive work.

THE CHRIST OF COLOSSIANS

This singularly christological book is centered on the cosmic Christ—"the head of all principality and power" (2:10), the Lord of creation (1:16, 17), and the Author of reconcili-

ation (1:20–22; 2:13–15). He is the basis for the believer's hope (1:5, 23, 27), the source of the believer's power for a new life (1:11, 29), the believer's Redeemer and Reconciler (1:14, 20–22; 2:11–15), the embodiment of full deity (1:15, 19; 2:9), the Creator and Sustainer of all things (1:16, 17), the Head of the church (1:18), the resurrected God-Man (1:18; 3:1), and the all-sufficient Saviour (1:28; 2:3, 10; 3:1–4).

KEYS TO COLOSSIANS
Key Word: The Preeminence of Christ— The resounding theme in Colossians is the preeminence and sufficiency of Christ in all things. The believer is complete in Him alone and lacks nothing because "in him dwelleth all the fulness of the Godhead bodily" (2:9); He has "all the treasures of wisdom and knowledge" (2:3). There is no need for speculation, mystical visions, or ritualistic regulations as though faith in Christ were insufficient. Paul's predominant purpose, then, is to refute a threatening heresy that is devaluing Christ. This false teaching is countered by a positive presentation of His true attributes and accomplishments. A proper view of Christ is the antidote for heresy. Paul also writes this epistle to encourage the Colossians to "continue in the faith grounded and settled" (1:23), so that they will grow and bear fruit in the knowledge of Christ (1:10). A firm adherence to the true gospel will give them stability and resistance to opposing influences.

Key Verses: Colossians 2:9, 10 and 3:1, 2— "For in him dwelleth all the fulness of the Godhead bodily. And ye are complete in him, which is the head of all principality and power" (2:9, 10).

"If ye then be risen with Christ, seek those things which are above, where Christ sitteth on the right hand of God. Set your affection on things above, not on things on the earth" (3:1, 2).

Key Chapter: Colossians 3—Chapter 3 links the three themes of Colossians (see "Key Word")

together showing their cause and effect relationships. Because the believer is risen with Christ (3:1-4), he is to put off the old man and put on the new (3:5-17), which will result in holiness in all relationships (3:18-25).

SURVEY OF COLOSSIANS
Colossians is perhaps the most Christ-centered book in the Bible. In it Paul stresses the preeminence of the person of Christ and the completeness of the salvation He provides, in order to combat a growing heresy that is threatening the church at Colosse. This heresy seeks to devaluate Christ by elevating speculation, ritualism, mysticism, and asceticism. But Christ, the Lord of creation and Head of the Body, is completely sufficient for every spiritual and practical need of the believer. The last half of this epistle explores the application of these principles to daily life, because doctrinal truth (1 and 2) must bear fruit in practical conduct (3 and 4). The two major topics are: supremacy of Christ (1 and 2) and submission to Christ (3 and 4).

Supremacy of Christ (1 and 2): Paul's greeting (1:1, 2) is followed by an unusually extended thanksgiving (1:3-8) and prayer (1:9-14) on behalf of the believers at Colosse. Paul expresses his concern that the Colossians come to a deeper understanding of the person and power of Christ. Even here Paul begins to develop his major theme of the preeminence of Christ, but the most potent statement of this theme is in 1:15-23. He is supreme both in creation (1:15-18) and in redemption (1:19-23), and this majestic passage builds a positive case for Christ as the most effective refutation of the heresy that will be exposed in chapter 2. Paul describes his own ministry of proclaiming the mystery of "Christ in you, the hope of glory" (1:27) to the Gentiles and assures his readers that although he has not personally met them, he strongly desires that they become deeply rooted in Christ alone, who is preeminent in the Church (1:24—2:3). This is

FOCUS	SUPREMACY OF CHRIST			SUBMISSION TO CHRIST		
REFERENCE	1:1————1:15————2:4			3:1————3:5————4:7————4:18		
DIVISION	INTRODUCTION	PREEMINENCE OF CHRIST	FREEDOM IN CHRIST	POSITION OF THE BELIEVER	PRACTICE OF THE BELIEVER	CONCLUSION
TOPIC	DOCTRINAL			PRACTICAL		
	WHAT CHRIST DID FOR US			WHAT CHRIST DOES THROUGH US		
LOCATION	ROME					
TIME	A.D. 60 – 61					

especially important in view of false teachers who would defraud them through enticing rationalisms (2:4–7), vain philosophy (2:8–10), legalistic rituals (2:11–17), improper mysticism (2:18, 19), and useless asceticism (2:20–23). In each case, Paul contrasts the error with the corresponding truth about Christ.

Submission to Christ (3 and 4): The believer's union with Christ in His death, resurrection, and exaltation is the foundation upon which his earthly life must be built (3:1–4). Because of his death with Christ, the Christian must regard

himself as dead to the old sins and put them aside (3:5–11); because of his resurrection with Christ, the believer must regard himself as alive to Him in righteousness and put on the new qualities that are prompted by Christian love (3:12–17). Turning from the inward life (3:1–17) to the outward life (3:18—4:6), Paul outlines the transformation that faith in Christ should make in relationships inside and outside the home. This epistle concludes with a statement concerning its bearers (Tychicus and Onesimus), greetings and instructions, and a farewell note (4:7–18).

OUTLINE OF COLOSSIANS

CHAPTER 1

Paul's Greeting to the Colossians

PAUL, an apostle of Jesus Christ by the will of God, and Ti-mo'-the-us *our* brother,

2 To the saints and faithful brethren in Christ which are at Co-los'-se: RGrace *be* unto you, and peace, from God our Father and the Lord Jesus Christ.   Gal. 1:3

Paul's Thanksgiving for the Colossians

3 RWe give thanks to God and the Father of our Lord Jesus Christ, praying always for you,   1 Cor. 1:4; Eph. 1:16; Phil. 1:3

4 RSince we heard of your faith in Christ Jesus, and of Rthe love *which ye have* to all the saints,   Eph. 1:15 · [Heb. 6:10]

5 For the hope Rwhich is laid up for you in heaven, whereof ye heard before in the word of the truth of the gospel;   [1 Pet. 1:4]

6 Which is come unto you, as *it is* in all the world; and bringeth forth fruit, as *it doth* also in you, since the day ye heard *of it,* and knew the grace of God in truth:

7 As ye also learned of REp'-a-phras our dear fellowservant, who is for you a faithful minister of Christ;   Philem. 23

8 TWho also declared unto us your Rlove in the Spirit.   *he told us* · Rom. 15:30

Paul's Prayer for the Colossians

9 For this cause we also, since the day we heard *it,* do not cease to pray for you, and to desire that ye might be filled with the

knowledge of his will ᴿin all wisdom and spiritual understanding;   Eph. 1:8

10 That ye might walk worthy of the Lord ᴿunto all pleasing, ᴿbeing fruitful in every good work, and increasing in the knowledge of God;   1 Thess. 4:1 • Heb. 13:21

11 Strengthened with all might, according to his glorious power, ᴿunto all patience and longsuffering with joyfulness;   Eph. 4:2

12 Giving thanks unto the Father, which hath made us ᵀmeet to be partakers of the inheritance of the saints in light: fit

13 Who hath delivered us from ᴿthe power of darkness, and hath translated us into the kingdom of his dear Son: Eph. 6:12

14 ᴿIn whom we have ᵀredemption through his blood, even the forgiveness of sins: Eph. 1:7 • been set free

Christ Is Preeminent in Creation

15 Who is the image of the invisible God, ᴿthe firstborn of every creature: Rev. 3:14

16 For by him were all things created, that are in heaven, and that are in earth, visible and invisible, whether they be thrones, or dominions, or principalities, or powers: all things were created by him, and for him:

17 ᴿAnd he is before all things, and by him all things consist.   [John 1:1, 3; 17:5]; 1 Cor. 8:6

18 And he is the head of the body, the church: who is the beginning, ᴿthe firstborn from the dead; that in all things he might have the preeminence.   Rev. 1:5

Christ Is Preeminent in Redemption

19 For it pleased the Father that ᴿin him should all fulness dwell;   2:9; John 1:16

20 And, having made peace through the blood of his cross, by him to reconcile all things unto himself; by him, I say, whether they be things in earth, or things in heaven.

21 And you, that were sometime alienated and enemies in your mind by wicked works, yet now hath he reconciled

22 In the body of his flesh through death, ᴿto present you holy and unblameable and unreproveable in his sight: [Eph. 5:27]

23 If ye continue in the faith grounded and settled, and be not moved away from the hope of the gospel, which ye have heard, and which was preached to every creature which

is under heaven; whereof I Paul am made a minister;

Christ Is Preeminent in the Church

24 Who now rejoice in my sufferings for you, and fill up that which is behind of the afflictions of Christ in my flesh for his body's sake, which is the church:

25 Whereof I am made a ᵀminister, according to the ᵀdispensation of God which is given to me for you, ᵀto fulfil the word of God;   servant • commission • fully to preach

26 Even the mystery which hath been hid from ages and from generations, but now is made ᵀmanifest to his saints: known

27 To whom God would ᵀmake known what is the riches of the glory of this mystery among the Gentiles; which is Christ in you, the hope of glory: reveal

28 Whom we preach, ᴿwarning every man, and teaching every man in all wisdom; that we may present every man ᵀperfect in Christ Jesus: Acts 20:20 • mature

29 ᴿWhereunto I also labour, striving according to his working, which worketh in me mightily.   1 Cor. 15:10; Eph. 3:7, 20

CHAPTER 2

FOR I would that ye knew what great ᴿconflict I have for you, and for them at La-od-i-ce′-a, and for as many as have not seen my face in the flesh;   Phil. 1:30

2 ᴿThat their hearts might be comforted, being knit together in love, and unto all riches of the full assurance of understanding, to the acknowledgement of the mystery of God, and of the Father, and of Christ;   3:14

3 ᴿIn whom are hid all the treasures of wisdom and knowledge.   1 Cor. 1:24

Freedom from Enticing Words

4 And this I say, lest any man should ᵀbeguile you with enticing words.   deceive

5 For though I be absent in the flesh, yet am I with you in the spirit, joying and beholding your order, and the ᴿstedfastness of your faith in Christ.   1 Pet. 5:9

6 ᴿAs ye have therefore received Christ Jesus the Lord, so walk ye in him: 1 Thess. 4:1

1:22 New Life: Based on Christ's Death—Salvation is free, but it is not cheap. Salvation is a gift and costs me nothing, but it cost God everything—it cost Jesus His life. The wages of sin is death (separation from God). God's gift is eternal life (eternal union of the soul with God). This is possible because of the death of Jesus on Calvary's cross (Page 1113—Rom. 6:23). Jesus actually took sin's penalty for every man, woman, and child who ever has lived or ever will live. As He hung upon the cross He cried, "Eli, Eli, lama sabachthani?" Being interpreted, He cried, "My God, my God, why hast thou forsaken me?" (Page 972—Matt. 27:46). Jesus was separated from God the Father so that you and I do not have to be. This is the heart of the atonement. The marvel of it all is that He did this while we were His enemies: "But God commendeth his love toward us, in that, while we were yet sinners, Christ died for us" (Page 1112—Rom. 5:8).
Now turn to Page 1090—Acts 16:31: New Life: Received by Faith.

7 Rooted and built up in him, and stablished in the faith, as ye have been taught, abounding therein with thanksgiving.

Freedom from Vain Philosophy

8 Beware lest any man Tspoil you through philosophy and vain deceit, after the tradition of men, after the Trudiments of the world, and not after Christ.   *rob • principles*

9 For Rin him dwelleth all the fulness of the Godhead Tbodily.   [John 1:14] • *in bodily form*

10 And ye are complete in him, which is the head of all principality and power:

Freedom from the Judgment of Men

11 In whom also ye are circumcised with the circumcision made without hands, in putting off the body of the sins of the flesh by the circumcision of Christ:

12 RBuried with him in baptism, wherein also ye are risen with *him* through the faith of the operation of God, Rwho hath raised him from the dead.   Rom. 6:4 • Acts 2:24

13 And you, being dead in your sins and the uncircumcision of your flesh, hath he Tquickened together with him, having forgiven you all trespasses;   *made alive*

14 RBlotting out the Thandwriting of ordinances that was against us, which was contrary to us, and took it out of the way, nailing it to his cross;   [Eph. 2:15] • *bond*

15 RAnd having spoiled principalities and powers, he made a shew of them openly, triumphing over them in it.   [John 12:31]

16 RLet no man therefore judge you in meat, or in drink, or in respect of an Tholyday, or of the new moon, or of the sabbath *days:*   [Rom. 14:2, 3, 5, 10, 17; 1 Cor. 8:8] • *feast day*

17 RWhich are a shadow of things to come; but the body *is* of Christ.   Heb. 8:5

Freedom from Improper Worship

18 Let no man beguile you of your reward in a voluntary Thumility and worshipping of angels, intruding into those things which he hath not seen, vainly Tpuffed up by his fleshly mind,   *self-abasement • made proud*

19 And not holding Rthe THead, from Twhich all the body by joints and bands having nourishment ministered, and knit together, Tincreaseth with the increase of God.   Eph. 4:15, 16 • *Christ • whom • grows*

Freedom from the Doctrine of Men

20 Wherefore if ye be dead with Christ from the Trudiments of the world, Rwhy, as though living in the world, are ye subject to Tordinances,   *principles • Gal. 4:3, 9 • rules*

21 (Touch not; taste not; handle not;

22 Which all are to perish with the using;) Rafter the Tcommandments and doctrines of men?   Is. 29:13; Matt. 15:9 • *rules*

23 Which things have indeed a shew of wisdom in will worship, and humility, and Tneglecting of the body; not in any honour to the satisfying of the flesh.   *severity to*

CHAPTER 3

The Position of the Believer

IF ye then be risen with Christ, seek those things which are above, where RChrist sitteth on the right hand of God. Ps. 68:18; 110:1 *

2 Set your Taffection on things above, not on things on the earth.   *mind*

3 RFor ye are dead, and your life is hid with Christ in God.   [Rom. 6:2]

4 RWhen Christ, *who is* Rour life, shall appear, then shall ye also appear with him Rin glory.   [1 John 3:2] • John 14:6 • 1 Cor. 15:43

Put Off the Old Man

5 Mortify therefore Ryour members which are upon the earth; fornication, uncleanness, inordinate affection, evil concupiscence, and covetousness, which is idolatry: [Rom. 6:13]

6 RFor which things' sake the wrath of God cometh on Rthe children of disobedience: Rev. 22:15 • [Eph. 2:2]

7 In the which ye also walked Tsome time, when ye lived in them.   *at one time*

8 RBut now ye also put off all these; anger, wrath, malice, Tblasphemy, filthy communication out of your mouth.   Eph. 4:22 • *railing*

9 Lie not one to another, seeing that ye have put off the old man with his deeds;

10 And have put on the new *man*, which Ris renewed in knowledge after the image of him that Rcreated him: Rom. 12:2 • [Eph. 2:10]

11 Where there is neither RGreek nor Jew, circumcision nor uncircumcision, Barbarian, Scyth'-i-an, bond *nor* free: Rbut Christ *is* all, and in all.   Gal. 3:28 • Eph. 1:23

Put On the New Man

12 Put on therefore, Ras the Telect of God, holy and beloved, Tbowels of mercies, kindness, humbleness of mind, meekness, longsuffering;   [1 Pet. 1:2] • *called • a heart*

13 RForbearing one another, and forgiving one another, if any man have a Tquarrel against any: even as Christ forgave you, so also *do* ye.   [Mark 11:25] • *complaint*

14 And above all these things *put on* charity, which is the bond of perfectness.

15 And let the peace of God rule in your hearts, to the which also ye are called Rin one body; and be ye thankful.   Eph. 4:4

16 Let the word of Christ dwell in you richly in all wisdom; teaching and Tadmonishing one another Rin psalms and hymns and spiritual songs, singing with grace in your hearts to the Lord.   *urging.* • Eph. 5:19

17 And ᴿwhatsoever ye ᵀdo in word or deed, *do* all in the name of the Lord Jesus, giving thanks to God and the Father by him. 1 Cor. 10:31 • *say or do*

Holiness in Family Life

18 Wives, submit yourselves unto your own husbands, as it is fit in the Lord.

19 ᴿHusbands, love *your* wives, and be not ᴿbitter against them. [Eph. 5:25] • Eph. 4:31

20 Children, obey *your* parents in all things: for this is well pleasing unto the Lord.

21 ᴿFathers, provoke not your children *to* anger, lest they be discouraged. Eph. 6:4

Holiness in Work Life

22 ᴿServants, obey in all things *your* masters according to the flesh; not with eyeservice, as menpleasers; but in ᵀsingleness of heart, fearing God: [1 Tim. 6:1] • *sincerity*

23 And whatsoever ye do, do *it* heartily, as to the Lord, and not unto men;

24 ᴿKnowing that of the Lord ye shall receive the reward of the inheritance: ᴿfor ye serve the Lord Christ. Eph. 6:8 • 1 Cor. 7:22

25 But he that doeth wrong shall receive for the wrong which he hath done: and ᴿthere is no respect of persons. Rom. 2:11

CHAPTER 4

MASTERS, give unto *your* servants that which is just and equal; knowing that ye also have a Master in heaven.

Holiness in Public Life

2 ᴿContinue in prayer, and watch in the same ᴿwith thanksgiving; Luke 18:1 • 2:7

3 Withal praying also for us, that God would open unto us a door ᵀof utterance, to speak ᴿthe mystery of Christ, for which I am also in bonds: *for the word* • Eph. 6:19

4 That I may make it ᵀmanifest, as I ᵀought to speak. *plain • should*

5 Walk in wisdom toward them that are without, ᴿredeeming the time. Eph. 5:16

6 ᴿLet your speech *be* alway with grace, seasoned with salt, that ye may know how ye ought to answer every man. 3:16

Commendation of Tychicus

7 All my ᵀstate shall Tych'-i-cus declare unto you, ᴿwho *is* a beloved brother, and a faithful minister and fellowservant in the Lord: *affairs* • Eph. 6:21

8 ᴿWhom I have sent unto you for the same purpose, that he might know your estate, and comfort your hearts; Eph. 6:22

9 With ᴿO-nes'-i-mus, a faithful and beloved brother, who is *one* of you. They shall ᵀmake known unto you all things which *are done* here. Philem. 10 • *tell*

Greetings from Paul's Friends

10 ᴿAr-is-tar'-chus my fellowprisoner saluteth you, and ᴿMarcus, sister's son to Barnabas, (touching whom ye received commandments: if he come unto you, receive him;) Acts 19:29 • Acts 15:37; 2 Tim. 4:11

11 And Jesus, which is called Justus, who are of the circumcision. These only *are my* fellow workers unto the kingdom of God, which have been a comfort unto me.

12 ᴿEp'-a-phras, who is *one* of you, a servant of Christ, saluteth you, always labouring fervently for you in prayers, that ye may stand ᴿperfect and ᵀcomplete in all the will of God. Philem. 23 • 1 Cor. 2:6 • *fully assured*

13 For I bear him record, that he hath a great zeal for you, and them *that are* in La-od-i-ce'-a, and them in Hi-e-rap'-o-lis.

14 ᴿLuke, the beloved physician, and ᴿDe'-mas, greet you. 2 Tim. 4:11 • 2 Tim. 4:10

Introductions Regarding This Letter

15 Salute the brethren which are in La-od-i-ce'-a, and Nym'-phas, and ᴿthe church which is in his house. Rom. 16:5; 1 Cor. 16:19

3:19 The Role of the Husband—Paul tells the husband to love his wife (Page 1166—Eph. 5:25), while Peter tells the husband to dwell together with his wife (Page 1237—1 Pet. 3:7). The husband cannot live with his wife as Peter says unless he loves her in the way Paul means. The love that the husband is commanded to have for the wife is not primarily sexual or emotional (though both of those concepts are involved); it is a love that loves in spite of the response (or lack of it) in the one loved. It is the kind of love that God has for the world (Page 1044—John 3:16) and is the fruit of the Spirit (Page 1158—Gal. 5:22). A husband can only love his wife properly if he is a Christian and under the control of the Holy Spirit.

The two responsibilities the husband has in the family are to dwell with his wife according to knowledge, and to render to his wife the honor which is due her because she is his wife. To "dwell together" with his wife means that the husband must take his wife into *every* aspect of his life. There are to be no areas of his life where there are signs that say, "Private, husband only—wife keep out."

The husband is to perform his two duties for a spiritual purpose: "that your prayers be not hindered." The man who is not taking his wife into every aspect of his life and rendering to her the honor which is due her because she is his wife cannot communicate with her in the way that God intended; hence, he cannot communicate with God either. To make sure that the channel of communication with God is open, the husband must make sure that the channel of communication with his wife is open. Only in this way can he truly love his wife as God intended and manifest his headship properly.

Now turn to Page 615—Prov. 1:8: The Role of Children.

16 And when this epistle is read among you, cause that it be read also in the church of the La-od-i-ce'-ans; and that ye likewise read the *epistle* from La-od-i-ce'-a.

17 And say to Ar-chip'-pus, ᵀTake heed to the ministry which thou hast received in the Lord, that thou fulfil it.

18 ᴿThe salutation by the hand of me Paul. ᴿRemember my bonds. Grace *be* with you. A-men'.

be careful about

1 Cor. 16:21; 2 Thess. 3:17 · Heb. 13:3

THESSALONIANS

THE BOOK OF FIRST THESSALONIANS

Paul has many pleasant memories of the days he spent with the infant Thessalonian church. Their faith, hope, love, and perseverance in the face of persecution are exemplary. Paul's labors as a spiritual parent to the fledgling church have been richly rewarded, and his affection is visible in every line of his letter.

Paul encourages them to excel in their newfound faith, to increase in their love for one another, and to rejoice, pray, and give thanks always. He closes his letter with instruction regarding the return of the Lord, whose advent signifies hope and comfort for believers both living and dead.

Because this is the first of Paul's two canonical letters to the church at Thessalonica, it received the title *Pros Thessalonikeis A*, the "First to the Thessalonians."

THE AUTHOR OF FIRST THESSALONIANS

First Thessalonians went unchallenged as a Pauline Epistle until the nineteenth century, when radical critics claimed that its dearth of doctrinal content made its authenticity suspect. But this is a weak objection on two counts: (1) the proportion of doctrinal teaching in Paul's epistles varies widely, and (2) 4:13—5:11 is a foundational passage for New Testament eschatology (future events). Paul had quickly grounded the Thessalonians in Christian doctrine, and the only problematic issue when this epistle was written concerned the matter of Christ's return. The external and internal evidence points clearly to Paul.

THE TIME OF FIRST THESSALONIANS

In Paul's time, Thessalonica was the prominent seaport and the capital of the Roman province of Macedonia. This prosperous city was located on the Via Egnatia, the main road from Rome to the East, within sight of Mount Olympus, legendary home of the Greek pantheon. Cassander expanded and strengthened this site around 315 B.C. and renamed it after his wife, the half-sister of Alexander the Great. The Romans conquered Macedonia in 168 B.C. and organized it into a single province twenty-two years later with Thessalonica as the capital city. It became a "free city" under Augustus with its own authority to appoint a governing board of magistrates who were called "politarchs." The strategic location assured Thessalonica of commercial success, and it boasted a population of perhaps 200,000 in the

first century. Thessalonica survives under the shortened name Salonika.

Thessalonica had a sizable Jewish population, and the ethical monotheism of Judaism attracted many Gentiles who had become disenchanted with Greek paganism. These God-fearers quickly responded to Paul's reasoning in the synagogue when he ministered there on his second missionary journey (Acts 17:10). The Jews became jealous of Paul's success and organized a mob to oppose the Christian missionaries. Not finding Paul and Silas, they dragged Jason, Paul and Silas's host before the politarchs and accused him of harboring traitors of Rome. The politarchs extracted a pledge guaranteeing the departure of Paul and Silas, who left that night for Berea. After a time, the Thessalonian Jews raised an uproar in Berea so that Paul departed for Athens, leaving orders for Silas and Timotheus (Timothy) to join him there (Acts 17:11–16). Because of Luke's account in Acts some scholars have reasoned that Paul was in Thessalonica for less than a month ("three sabbath days," 17:2), but other evidence suggests a longer stay: (1) Paul received two separate offerings from Philippi, 100 miles away, while he was in Thessalonica (Phil. 4:15, 16). (2) According to 1:9 and 2:14–16, most of the Thessalonian converts were Gentiles who came out of idolatry. This would imply an extensive ministry directed to the Gentiles after Paul's initial work with the Jews and gentile God-fearers. (3) Paul worked "night and day" (2:9; 2 Thess. 3:7–9) during his time there. He may have begun to work immediately, but Paul supported himself by tent-making, which took many hours away from his ministry, requiring a longer stay to accomplish the extensive ministry of evangelism and teaching that took place in that city. After Silas and Timothy met Paul in Athens (3:1, 2), he sent Timothy to Thessalonica (Silas also went back to Macedonia, probably Philippi), and his assistants later rejoined him in Corinth (Acts 18:5; cf. 1 Thess. 1:1 where Silas is called Silvanus). There he wrote this epistle in A.D. 51 as his response to Timothy's good report.

THE CHRIST OF FIRST THESSALONIANS

Christ is seen as the believer's hope of salvation both now and at His coming. When He returns, He will deliver (1:10; 5:4–11), reward (1:19), perfect (3:13), resurrect (4:13–18), and sanctify (5:23) all who trust Him.

KEYS TO FIRST THESSALONIANS

Key Word: Holiness in Light of Christ's Return—Throughout this letter is an

unmistakable emphasis upon steadfastness in the Lord (3:8) and a continuing growth in faith and love in view of the return of Christ (1:3-10; 2:12-20; 3:10-13; 4:1—5:28). The theme is not only the returning of Christ, but also the life of the believer in every practical relationship, each aspect of which can be transformed and illuminated by the glorious prospect of His eventual return.

Key Verses: First Thessalonians 3:12, 13 and 4:16-18—"And the Lord make you to increase and abound in love one toward another, and toward all *men*, even as we *do* toward you: To the end he may stablish your hearts unblameable in holiness before God, even our Father, at the coming of our Lord Jesus Christ with all his saints" (3:12, 13).

"For the Lord himself shall descend from heaven with a shout, with the voice of the archangel, and with the trump of God: and the dead in Christ shall rise first: Then we which are alive *and* remain shall be caught up together with them in the clouds, to meet the Lord in the air: and so shall we ever be with the Lord. Wherefore comfort one another with these words" (4:16-18).

Key Chapter: First Thessalonians 4—Chapter 4 includes the central passage of the epistles on the coming of the Lord when the dead in Christ shall rise first, and those who remain are caught up together with them in the clouds.

SURVEY OF FIRST THESSALONIANS

After Paul's forced separation from the Thessalonians, he grows increasingly concerned about the progress of their faith. His great relief upon hearing Timothy's positive report prompts him to write this warm epistle of commendation, exhortation, and consolation. They are commended for remaining steadfast under afflictions, exhorted to excel still more in their Christian walk, and consoled concerning their loved ones who have died in Christ. The theme of the coming of the Lord recurs throughout this epistle, and 4:13—5:11 is one of the fullest New Testament developments of this crucial truth. The two major sections of First Thessalonians are: Paul's personal reflections of the Thessalonians (1—3) and Paul's instructions for the Thessalonians (4 and 5).

Paul's Personal Reflections of the Thessalonians (1—3): Paul's typical salutation in the first verse combines the customary Greek ("grace") and Hebrew ("peace") greetings of his day and enriches them with Christian content. The opening chapter is a declaration of thanksgiving for the Thessalonians' metamorphosis from heathenism to Christian hope. Faith, love, and hope (1:3) properly characterize the new lives of these believers. In 2:1-16, Paul reviews his brief ministry in Thessalonica and defends his conduct and motives, apparently to answer enemies who are trying to impugn his character and message. He sends Timothy to minister to them and is greatly relieved when Timothy reports the stability of their faith and love (2:17—3:10). Paul therefore closes this historical section with a prayer that their faith may continue to deepen (3:11-13).

Paul's Instructions for the Thessalonians (4 and 5): The apostle deftly moves into a series of exhortations and instructions by encouraging the Thessalonians to continue progressing. He reminds them of his previous teaching on sexual and social matters (4:1-12), since these gentile believers lack the moral upbringing in the Mosaic Law provided in the Jewish community. Now rooted in the Word of God (2:13), the readers must resist the constant pressures of a pagan society.

Paul has taught them about the return of Christ, and they have become distressed over the deaths of some among them. In 4:13-18, Paul comforts them with the assurance that all who die

FOCUS	REFLECTIONS ON THE THESSALONIANS			INSTRUCTIONS TO THE THESSALONIANS			
REFERENCE	1:1 —————— 2:1 ——————		2:17 ——————	4:1 ——————	4:13 ——————	5:1 ——————	5:12 —— 5:28
DIVISION	COMMENDATION FOR GROWTH	FOUNDING OF THE CHURCH	STRENGTHENING OF THE CHURCH	DIRECTION FOR GROWTH	THE DEAD IN CHRIST	THE DAY OF THE LORD	HOLY LIVING
TOPIC	PERSONAL EXPERIENCE			PRACTICAL EXHORTATION			
	LOOKING BACK			LOOKING FORWARD			
LOCATION	WRITTEN IN CORINTH						
TIME	C. A.D. 51						

in Christ will be resurrected at His *parousia* ("presence," "coming," or "advent"). The apostle continues his discourse on eschatology by describing the coming day of the Lord (5:1–11). In anticipation of this day, believers are to "watch and be sober" as "children of light" who are destined for salvation, not wrath. Paul requests the readers to deal with integrity toward one another and to continue growing spiritually (5:12–22). The epistle closes with a wish for their sanctification, three requests, and a benediction (5:23–28).

OUTLINE OF FIRST THESSALONIANS

CHAPTER 1

Paul's Commendation for Their Growth

PAUL, and ᴿSil-va´-nus, and Ti-mo´-the-us, ᴿunto the church of the Thes-sa-lo´-ni-ans *which is* in God the Father and *in* the Lord Jesus Christ: Grace *be* unto you, and peace, from God our Father, and the Lord Jesus Christ. 1 Pet. 5:12 • 1 Cor. 14:33

2 We give thanks to God always for you all, making mention of you in our prayers;

3 Remembering without ceasing your work of faith, ᴿand labour of love, and patience of hope in our Lord Jesus Christ, in the sight of God and our Father; Rom. 16:6

4 Knowing, brethren beloved, ᴿyour ᵀelection of God. Col. 3:12 • *call*

5 For our gospel came not unto you in word only, but also in power, and ᴿin the Holy Ghost, ᴿand in much assurance; as ye know what manner of men we were among you for your sake. 2 Cor. 6:6 • Heb. 2:3

6 And ye became followers of us, and of the Lord, having received the word in much affliction, with joy of the Holy Ghost:

7 So that we were ensamples to all that believe in Mac-e-do´-ni-a and A-cha´-ia.

8 For from you ᴿsounded out the word of the Lord not only in Mac-e-do´-ni-a and A-cha´-ia, but also in every place your faith to God-ward is spread abroad; so that we need not to speak any thing. Rom. 1:8

9 For they themselves shew of us what manner of entering in we had unto you, ᴿand how ye turned to God from idols to serve the living and true God; Acts 3:19

10 And to wait for his Son from heaven, whom he raised from the dead, *even* Jesus, which delivered us from the wrath to come.

1:5 Sharing Our Faith: How?—In order to share our faith successfully, we must keep the following rules in mind.
a. First, we must be clean vessels. God reminds Isaiah the prophet of this, "be ye clean, that bear the vessels of the LORD" (Page 695—Is. 52:11). David the sinner prays for forgiveness and cleansing. Upon receiving this he states, "*Then* will I teach transgressors thy ways; and sinners shall be converted unto thee" (Page 569—Ps. 51:13). While God does not demand golden or silver vessels, He does require clean ones.
b. We must be able to clearly give out the simple facts of the gospel without getting bogged down with profound theological concepts. Philip the evangelist demonstrated how to do this when he dealt with a sinner in the desert. "Then Philip opened his mouth, and began at the same scripture, and preached unto him Jesus" (Page 1081—Acts 8:35).
c. We must avoid arguments and stick to the basic issues of man's sin and Christ's blood. Often unbelievers will attempt to sidestep the gospel by asking unrelated questions, such as "Where did Cain get his wife?"
d. We must use the Word of God. Paul's tremendous success as an evangelist can be linked directly to his constant use of God's Word. See Acts 17:2; 18:28; Second Timothy 2:15; 3:14–17.
e. We must depend upon the Spirit of God. See John 3:15; Acts 6:10; First Corinthians 2:4.
   Now turn to Page 1202—2 Tim. 4:2: Sharing Our Faith: When?

CHAPTER 2

Paul's Founding of the Church

FOR yourselves, brethren, know our Tentrance in unto you, that it was not Tin vain: *coming · useless*

2 But even after that we had suffered before, Rand were shamefully Tentreated, as ye know, at Phi-lip'-pi, we were bold in our God to speak unto you the gospel of God with much contention. *Acts 16:22; 17:2 · treated*

3 For our exhortation *was* not Tof deceit, nor of uncleanness, nor in guile: *mislead*

4 But as we were Tallowed of God to be put in trust with the gospel, even so we speak; not as pleasing men, but God, which Ttrieth our hearts. *approved · judges*

5 For neither at any time used we flattering words, as ye know, nor a cloke of Tcovetousness; RGod *is* witness: *greed · Rom. 1:9*

6 Nor of men sought we glory, neither of you, nor *yet* of others, when we might have been burdensome, as the apostles of Christ.

7 But we were gentle among you, even as a nurse cherisheth her children:

8 So being affectionately desirous of you, we were willing to have imparted unto you, not the gospel of God only, but also our own souls, because ye were dear unto us.

9 For ye remember, brethren, our labour and Ttravail: for labouring night and day, Rbecause we would not be Tchargeable unto any of you, we preached unto you the gospel of God. *suffering · 2 Cor. 12:13 · an expense*

10 Ye *are* witnesses, and God *also*, how holily and justly and unblameably we behaved ourselves among you that believe:

11 As ye know how we Texhorted and comforted and Tcharged every one of you, as a father *doth* his children, *urged · directed*

12 RThat ye would walk worthy of God, Rwho hath called you unto his kingdom and glory. *Col. 1:10 · 1 Cor. 1:9*

13 For this cause also thank we God without ceasing, because, when ye received the word of God which ye heard of us, ye received it Rnot *as* the word of men, but as it is in truth, the word of God, which effectually worketh also in you that believe. *[Gal. 4:14]*

14 For ye, brethren, became followers Rof the churches of God which in Ju-dae'-a are in Christ Jesus: for Rye also have suffered like things of your own countrymen, even as they *have* of the Jews: *Gal. 1:22 · Acts 17:5*

15 RWho both killed the Lord Jesus, and their own prophets, and have Tpersecuted us; and they please not God, and are Tcontrary to all men: *Acts 2:23 · chased us out · opposed*

16 Forbidding us to speak to the Gentiles that they might be saved, Tto fill up their sins alway: for the wrath is come upon them to the uttermost. *to complete*

Satan Hinders Paul

17 But we, brethren, being taken from you for a short time Rin presence, not in heart, endeavoured the more abundantly to see your face with great desire. *1 Cor. 5:3*

18 Wherefore we would have come unto you, even I Paul, once and again; but RSatan hindered us. *Rom. 1:13; 15:22*

19 For what *is* our hope, or joy, or crown of rejoicing? *Are* not even ye in the presence of our Lord Jesus Christ at his coming?

20 For ye are our glory and joy.

CHAPTER 3

Paul Sends Timotheus

WHEREFORE when we could no longer Tforbear, we thought it good to be left at RAthens alone; *bear it · Acts 17:15*

2 And sent Ti-mo'-the-us, our brother, and minister of God, and our fellowlabourer in the gospel of Christ, to establish you, and to comfort you concerning your faith:

3 That no man should be moved by these afflictions: for yourselves know that we are appointed thereunto.

4 For verily, when we were with you, we told you before that we should suffer tribulation; even as it came to pass, and ye know.

5 For this cause, when I could no longer forbear, I sent to Tknow your faith, lest by some means the tempter have tempted you, and our labour be in vain. *find out about*

Timotheus's Encouraging Report

6 But now when Ti-mo'-the-us came from you unto us, and brought us good tidings of your faith and charity, and that ye have good remembrance of us always, desiring greatly to see us, as we also *to see* you:

7 Therefore, brethren, we were comforted over you in all our Taffliction and Tdistress by your faith: *suffering · trouble*

8 For now we live, if ye Rstand Tfast in the Lord. *Phil. 4:1 · firm*

9 For what thanks can we render to God again for you, for all the joy wherewith we joy for your sakes before our God;

10 Night and day praying exceedingly that we might see your face, and might perfect that which is lacking in your faith?

Paul's Desire to Visit Them

11 Now God himself and our Father, and our Lord Jesus Christ, Rdirect T our way Tunto you. *Mark 1:3 · guide · to come to*

12 And the Lord make you to increase and abound in love one toward another, and toward all *men*, even as we *do* toward you:

13 To the end he may stablish your hearts unblameable in holiness before God, even our

Father, ^Rat the coming of our Lord Jesus Christ with all his saints.　　Zech. 14:5

CHAPTER 4

Directions for Growth

FURTHERMORE then we beseech you, brethren, and exhort *you* by the Lord Jesus, that as ye have received of us how ye ought to walk and to please God, *so* ye would abound more and more.

2 For ye know what ^Tcommandments we gave you by the Lord Jesus.　　*charges*

3 For this is ^Rthe will of God, *even* your ^Tsanctification, that ye should abstain from fornication:　　[Rom. 12:2] • *being made holy*

4 That ^Revery one of you should know how to ^Tpossess his vessel in sanctification and honour;　　Rom. 6:19 • *take a wife*

5 Not in the lust of concupiscence, even as the Gentiles which know not God:

6 That no *man* go beyond and defraud his brother in *any* matter: because that the Lord *is* the avenger of all such, as we also have forewarned you and ^Ttestified.　　*preached*

7 For God hath not called us unto uncleanness, ^Rbut unto holiness.　　Lev. 11:44

8 ^RHe therefore that ^Tdespiseth, despiseth not man, but God, who hath also given unto us his holy Spirit.　　Luke 10:16 • *will not listen*

9 But as touching brotherly love ye need not that I write unto you: for ye yourselves are taught of God to love one another.

10 And indeed ye do it toward all the brethren which are in all Mac-e-do′-ni-a: but we beseech you, brethren, ^Rthat ye increase more and more;　　3:12

11 And that ye study to be quiet, and to do your own business, and to work with your own hands, as we commanded you;

12 ^RThat ye may walk honestly toward them that are without, and *that* ye may have ^Tlack of nothing.　　Rom. 13:13 • *all you need*

Revelation Concerning the Dead in Christ

13 But I would not have you to be ignorant, brethren, concerning them which ^Tare asleep, that ye sorrow not, even as others which have no hope.　　*have died*

14 For if we believe that Jesus died and rose again, even so them also which ^Tsleep in Jesus will God bring with him.　　*die*

15 For this we say unto you by the word of the Lord, that we which are alive *and* remain unto the coming of the Lord shall not ^Tprevent them which are asleep.　　*precede*

16 For the Lord himself shall descend from heaven with a shout, with the voice of the archangel, and with the trump of God: and the dead in Christ shall rise first:

17 Then we which are alive *and* remain shall be caught up together with them in the clouds, to meet the Lord in the air: and so shall we ever be with the Lord.

18 ^RWherefore ^Tcomfort one another with these words.　　5:11 • *cheer*

CHAPTER 5

Description of the Day of the Lord

BUT of ^Rthe times and the ^Tseasons, brethren, ye have no need that I write unto you.　　Matt. 24:3 • *occasions*

2 ^RFor yourselves know ^Tperfectly that ^Rthe day of the Lord so cometh as a thief in the night.　　Matt. 24:43, 44 • *full well* • [2 Pet. 3:10]

3 For when they shall say, Peace and safety; then sudden destruction cometh upon them, as ^Ttravail upon a woman with child; and they shall not escape.　　*pains*

4 But ye, brethren, are not in darkness, that that day should overtake you as a thief.

5 Ye are all ^Rthe children of light, and the children of the day: we are not of the night, nor of darkness.　　Eph. 5:8

6 Therefore let us not sleep, as *do* others; but let us watch and be sober.

7 For ^Rthey that sleep sleep in the night; and they that be drunken ^Rare drunken in the night.　　[Luke 21:34] • Acts 2:15

8 But let us, who are of the day, be sober, putting on the breastplate of faith and love; and for an helmet, the hope of salvation.

9 For God hath not appointed us to ^Twrath, but to ^Tobtain salvation by our Lord Jesus Christ,　　*condemnation* • *gain*

10 ^RWho died for us, that, whether we wake or sleep, we ^Tshould live together with him.　　[Rom. 14:8, 9]; 2 Cor. 5:15 • *might*

11 Wherefore ^Tcomfort yourselves together, and ^Tedify one another, even as also ye do.　　*encourage* • *build up*

Instruction for Holy Living

12 And we beseech you, brethren, to know them which labour among you, and are over you in the Lord, and admonish you;

13 And to ^Testeem them very highly in love for their work's sake. ^RAnd be at peace among yourselves.　　*treat* • Mark 9:50

14 Now we exhort you, brethren, warn them that are unruly, comfort the ^Tfeebleminded, support the weak, ^Rbe patient toward all *men*.　　*fainthearted* • Gal. 5:22

15 See that none render evil for evil unto any *man;* but ever follow that which is good, both among yourselves, and to all *men*.

16 ^RRejoice ^Tevermore.　　[2 Cor. 6:10] • *always*

17 ^RPray without ceasing.　　Eph. 6:18

18 ^RIn every thing give thanks: for this is the will of God in Christ Jesus concerning you.　　Eph. 5:20; [Col. 3:17]

19 ^RQuench not the Spirit.　　Eph. 4:30

20 ^RDespise not prophesyings.　　1 Cor. 14:1

21 RProve all things; Rhold Tfast that which is good.   1 John 4:1 · Phil. 4:8 · keep

22 Abstain from all appearance of evil.

Conclusion

23 And the very God of peace sanctify you wholly; and I pray God your whole spirit and soul and body be preserved blameless unto the coming of our Lord Jesus Christ.

24 RFaithful is he that calleth you, who also will do it.   1 Cor. 1:9; [10:13]; 2 Thess. 3:3

25 RBrethren, pray for us.   Col. 4:3; 2 Thess. 3:1

26 RGreet all the brethren with an THoly kiss.   Rom. 16:16 · brotherly

27 I charge you by the Lord that this epistle be read unto all the holy brethren.

28 RThe grace of our Lord Jesus Christ be with you. A-men'.   Rom. 16:20, 24; 2 Thess. 3:18

THE SECOND EPISTLE OF PAUL THE APOSTLE TO THE
THESSALONIANS

THE BOOK OF SECOND THESSALONIANS

Since Paul's first letter, the seeds of false doctrine have been sown among the Thessalonians, causing them to waver in their faith. Paul removes these destructive seeds and again plants the seeds of truth. He begins by commending the believers on their faithfulness in the midst of persecution and encouraging them that present suffering will be repaid with future glory. Therefore, in the midst of persecution, expectation can be high.

Paul then deals with the central matter of his letter: a misunderstanding spawned by false teachers regarding the coming day of the Lord. Despite reports to the contrary, that day has not yet come, and Paul recounts the events that must first take place. Laboring for the gospel, rather than lazy resignation, is the proper response.

As the second letter in Paul's Thessalonian correspondence, this was entitled *Pros Thessalonikeis B*, the "Second to the Thessalonians."

THE AUTHOR OF SECOND THESSALONIANS

The external attestation to the authenticity of Second Thessalonians as a Pauline Epistle is even stronger than that for First Thessalonians. Internally, the vocabulary, style, and doctrinal content support the claims in 1:1 and 3:17 that it was written by Paul.

THE TIME OF SECOND THESSALONIANS

See "The Time of First Thessalonians" for the background to the Thessalonian correspondence. This letter was probably written a few months after First Thessalonians, while Paul was still in Corinth with Silas and Timotheus, or Timothy (1:1; cf. Acts 18:5). The bearer of the first epistle may have brought Paul an update on the new developments, prompting him to write this letter. They were still undergoing persecution, and the false teaching about the day of the Lord led some of them to overreact by giving up their jobs. The problem of idleness recorded in First Thessalonians 4:11, 12 had become more serious (3:6-15). By this time, Paul was beginning to see the opposition he would face in his ministry in Corinth (3:2; see Acts 18:5-10).

THE CHRIST OF SECOND THESSALONIANS

The return of Christ is mentioned more times (318) in the New Testament than any other doctrine, and this is certainly the major concept in chapters 1 and 2 of this epistle. The return of the Lord Jesus is a reassuring and joyful hope for believers, but His revelation from heaven holds awesome and terrifying implications for those who have not trusted in Him (1:6-10; 2:8-12).

KEYS TO SECOND THESSALONIANS

Key Word: Understanding the Day of the Lord—The theme of this epistle is an understanding of the day of the Lord and the resulting lifestyle changes. The doctrinal error of chapter 2 has been causing the practical error that Paul seeks to overcome in chapter 3. Some of the believers have abandoned their work and have begun to live off others, apparently assuming that the end is at hand. Paul commands them to follow his example by supporting themselves and instructs the rest of the church to discipline them if they fail to do so.

Key Verses: Second Thessalonians 2:2, 3 and 3:5, 6—"That ye be not soon shaken in mind, or be troubled, neither by spirit, nor by word, nor by letter as from us, as that the day of Christ is at hand. Let no man deceive you by any means: for that day shall not come, except there come a falling away first, and that man of sin be revealed, the son of perdition" (2:2, 3).

"And the Lord direct your hearts into the love of God, and into the patient waiting for Christ. Now we command you, brethren, in the name of our Lord Jesus Christ, that ye withdraw yourselves from every brother that walketh disorderly, and not after the tradition which he received of us" (3:5, 6).

Key Chapter: Second Thessalonians 2—The second chapter is written to correct the fallacious teaching that the day of the Lord has already come upon the Thessalonian church. This teaching, coupled with the afflictions they have been suffering, is causing a great disturbance among the believers who wonder when their "gathering together unto him" (2:1; 1 Thess. 4:13-18) will take place. Paul makes it clear that certain identifiable events will precede that day and that those events have not yet occurred.

SURVEY OF SECOND THESSALONIANS

This epistle is the theological sequel to First Thessalonians, which developed the theme of the coming day of the Lord (1 Thess. 5:1-11). However, not long after the Thessalonians receive that letter, they fall prey to false teaching or outright deception, thinking the day of the Lord has already begun. Paul writes this brief letter to correct the error and also to encourage those believers whose faith is being tested by the

difficulties presented by persecution. He also reproves those who have decided to cease working because they believe the coming of Christ is near. Second Thessalonians deals with Paul's encouragement in persecution (1); Paul's explanation of the day of the Lord (2); and Paul's exhortation to the church (3).

Paul's Encouragement in Persecution (1): After his two-verse salutation, Paul gives thanks for the growing faith and love of the Thessalonians and assures them of their ultimate deliverance from those who are persecuting them (1:3–10). They are encouraged to patiently endure their afflictions, knowing that the Lord Jesus will judge their persecutors when He is "revealed from heaven with his mighty angels, In flaming fire" (1:7, 8). Before Paul moves to the next topic, he concludes this section with a prayer for the spiritual welfare of his readers (1:11, 12).

Paul's Explanation of the Day of the Lord (2): Because of the severity of their afflictions, the Thessalonians have become susceptible to false teaching (and possibly a fraudulent letter in the name of Paul), claiming that they are already in the day of the Lord (2:1, 2). This was particularly disturbing because Paul's previous letter had given them the comforting hope that they were not destined for the wrath of that day (1 Thess. 5:9). Paul therefore assures them that the day of the Lord is yet in the future and will not arrive unannounced (2:3–12). Paul then concludes with a word of encouragement and a benedictory prayer of comfort before moving to his next topic.

Paul's Exhortation to the Church (3:1–18): Paul requests the Thessalonian church to pray on his behalf and to wait patiently for the Lord (3:1–5). Having thus commended, corrected, and comforted his readers, the tactful apostle closes his letter with a sharp word of command to those who have been using the truth of Christ's return as an excuse for disorderly conduct (3:6–15; cf. 1 Thess. 4:11, 12). The doctrine of the Lord's return requires a balance between waiting and working. It is a perspective that should encourage holiness, not idleness. This final section, like the first two, closes on a benedictory note (3:16–18).

FOCUS	ENCOURAGEMENT IN PERSECUTION			EXPLANATION OF THE DAY OF THE LORD		EXHORTATION TO THE CHURCH	
REFERENCE	1:1————1:5	————1:11	—2:1	————2:13	—3:1	——3:6	——3:18
DIVISION	THANKSGIVING FOR GROWTH	ENCOURAGEMENT IN PERSECUTION	PRAYER FOR BLESSING	EVENTS PRECEDING	COMFORT OF THE BELIEVER	WAIT PATIENTLY	WITHDRAW
TOPIC	DISCOURAGED BELIEVERS			DISTURBED BELIEVERS		DISOBEDIENT BELIEVERS	
	THANKSGIVING FOR THEIR LIFE			INSTRUCTION OF THEIR DOCTRINE		CORRECTION OF THEIR BEHAVIOR	
LOCATION	WRITTEN IN CORINTH						
TIME	C. A.D. 51						

OUTLINE OF SECOND THESSALONIANS

CHAPTER 1

Thanksgiving for Their Growth

PAUL, and Sil-va'-nus, and Ti-mo'-the-us, unto the church of the Thes-sa-lo'-ni-ans in God our Father and the Lord Jesus Christ:

2 Grace unto you, and peace, from God our Father and the Lord Jesus Christ.

3 We are bound to thank God always for you, brethren, as it is ᵀmeet, because that your faith groweth exceedingly, and the charity of every one of you all toward each other ᵀaboundeth;　　　*proper • increases*

4 So that we ourselves ᵀglory in you in the churches of God for your patience and faith in all your persecutions and ᵀtribulations that ye endure:　　　*take pride • troubles*

Encouragement in Their Persecution

5 *Which is* a ᵀmanifest token of the righteous judgment of God, that ye may be counted worthy of the kingdom of God, for which ye also suffer:　　　*plain evidence*

6 ᴿSeeing *it is* a righteous thing with God to ᵀrecompense tribulation to them that trouble you;　　　Rev. 6:10 • *repay trouble*

7 And to you who are troubled rest with us, when the Lord Jesus shall be revealed from heaven with his mighty angels,

8 In flaming fire taking vengeance on them that know not God, and that obey not the gospel of our Lord Jesus Christ:

9 Who shall be punished with everlasting destruction from the presence of the Lord, and from the glory of his power;

10 When he shall come to be glorified in his saints, and to be admired in all them that believe (because our testimony among you was believed) in that day.

Prayer for God's Blessing

11 Wherefore also we pray always for you, that our God would count you worthy of *this* calling, and fulfil all the good pleasure of *his* goodness, and ᴿthe work of faith with power:　　　1 Thess. 1:3

12 ᴿThat the name of our Lord Jesus Christ may be glorified in you, and ye in him, according to the grace of our God and the Lord Jesus Christ.　　　1 Pet. 1:7

CHAPTER 2

The Events Preceding the Day of the Lord

NOW we ᵀbeseech you, brethren, by the coming of our Lord Jesus Christ, and *by* our gathering together unto him,　　　*beg*

2 ᴿThat ye be not soon ᵀshaken in mind, or be troubled, neither by spirit, nor by word, nor by letter as from us, as that the day of Christ is at hand.　　　Matt. 24:4 • *upset*

3 Let no man deceive you by any means: for *that day shall not come*, except there come a falling away first, and that man of sin be revealed, the son of perdition;

4 Who opposeth and ᴿexalteth himself ᴿabove all that is called ᵀGod, or that is worshipped; so that he as God sitteth in the temple of God, shewing himself that he is God.　　　Is. 14:13 • 1 Cor. 8:5 • *divine*

5 Remember ye not, that, when I was yet with you, I told you these things?

6 And now ye know what withholdeth that he might be revealed in his time.

7 For the mystery of iniquity doth already work: only he who now letteth *will let*, until he be taken out of the way.

8 And then shall that Wicked be revealed, whom the Lord shall consume with the spirit of his mouth, and shall destroy with the brightness of his coming:

9 *Even him*, whose coming is ᴿafter the working of Satan with all power and ᴿsigns and lying wonders,　　　John 8:41, 44 • Deut. 13:1

10 And with all ᵀdeceivableness of unrighteousness in them that perish; because they received not the love of the truth, that they might be saved.　　　*deceitfulness*

11 And ᴿfor this cause God shall send them strong ᵀdelusion, ᴿthat they should believe a lie:　　　Rom. 1:28 • *error* • [1 Tim. 4:1]

12 That they all might be ᵀdamned who believed not the truth, but ᴿhad pleasure in unrighteousness.　　　*condemned* • Rom. 1:32

The Comfort of the Believer on the Day of the Lord

13 But we are bound to give thanks alway to God for you, brethren beloved of the Lord, because God hath from the beginning chosen you to salvation through sanctification of the Spirit and belief of the truth:

14 Whereunto he called you by our gospel, to ᴿthe ᵀobtaining of the glory of our Lord Jesus Christ.　　　1 Pet. 5:10 • *gaining*

15 Therefore, brethren, stand fast, and hold the traditions which ye have been taught, whether by word, or our epistle.

16 Now our Lord Jesus Christ himself, and God, even our Father, which hath loved us, and hath given *us* everlasting consolation and good hope through grace,

17 Comfort your hearts, and ᵀstablish you in every good word and work.　　　*strengthen*

CHAPTER 3

Wait Patiently for Christ

FINALLY, brethren, ᴿpray for us, that the word of the Lord may have *free* course, and be glorified, even as *it is* with you: Eph. 6:19

2 And ᴿthat we may be delivered from unreasonable and wicked men: ᴿfor all *men* have not faith.　　　Rom. 15:31 • Acts 28:24

3 But the Lord is faithful, who shall stablish you, and keep you from evil.

4 And we have confidence in the Lord touching you, that ye both do and will do the things which we command you.

5 And ᴿthe Lord direct your hearts into the love of God, and into ᵀthe patient waiting for Christ.   1 Chr. 29:18 · *the patience of Christ*

Withdraw from the Disorderly

6 Now we command you, brethren, in the name of our Lord Jesus Christ, that ye withdraw yourselves from every brother that walketh disorderly, and not after the tradition which he received of us.

7 For yourselves know how ye ought to ᵀfollow us: for we behaved not ourselves ᵀdisorderly among you;   *imitate · irresponsibly*

8 Neither did we eat any man's bread for nought; but wrought with labour and travail night and day, that we might not be ᵀchargeable to any of you: *an expense*

9 ᴿNot because we have not ᵀpower, but to make ourselves an ensample unto you to follow us.   v. 7; 1 Cor. 9:6; 1 Thess. 2:6 · *the right*

10 For even when we were with you, this we commanded you, that if any would not work, neither ᵀshould he eat.   *be allowed*

11 For we hear that there are some which ᵀwalk among you disorderly, working not at all, but are busybodies.   *live irresponsibly*

12 Now them that are such we command and ᵀexhort by our Lord Jesus Christ, ᴿthat with quietness they work, and eat their own bread.   *warn* · Eph. 4:28

13 But ye, brethren, ᴿbe not weary in well doing.   Gal. 6:9

14 And if any man obey not our word by this epistle, note that man, and have no company with him, that he may be ashamed.

15 ᴿYet count *him* not as an enemy, but ᵀadmonish *him* as a brother.   Lev. 19:17 · *warn*

Conclusion

16 Now ᴿthe Lord of peace himself give you peace always ᵀby all means. The Lord *be* with you all.   Rom. 15:33 · *in every way*

17 ᴿThe ᵀsalutation of Paul with mine own hand, which is the ᵀtoken in every epistle: so I write.   1 Cor. 16:21 · *greeting · sign*

18 ᴿThe grace of our Lord Jesus Christ *be* with you all. A-men'.   Rom. 16:24

TIMOTHY

THE BOOK OF FIRST TIMOTHY

Paul, the aged and experienced apostle, writes to the young pastor Timothy who is facing a heavy burden of responsibility in the church at Ephesus. The task is challenging: false doctrine must be erased, public worship safeguarded, and mature leadership developed. In addition to the conduct of the church, Paul talks pointedly about the conduct of the minister. Timothy must be on his guard lest his youthfulness become a liability, rather than an asset, to the gospel. He must be careful to avoid false teachers and greedy motives, pursuing instead righteousness, godliness, faith, love, perseverance, and the gentleness that befits a man of God.

The Greek title for this letter is *Pros Timotheon A*, the "First to Timothy." *Timothy* means "honoring God" or "honored by God," and probably was given to him by his mother Eunice.

THE AUTHOR OF FIRST TIMOTHY

Since the early nineteenth century, the Pastoral Epistles have been attacked more than any other Pauline Epistles on the issue of authenticity. The similarity of these epistles requires that they be treated as a unit in terms of authorship because they stand or fall together.

The external evidence solidly supports the conservative position that Paul wrote the letters to Timothy and Titus. Postapostolic church fathers, such as Polycarp and Clement of Rome, allude to them as Paul's writing. In addition, these epistles are identified as Pauline by Irenaeus, Tertullian, Clement of Alexandria, and the Muratorian Canon. Only Romans and First Corinthians have better attestation among the Pauline Epistles.

Suggestions of an author other than Paul are supported wholly on the basis of internal evidence. Even though these letters claim to be written by Paul (1:1; 2 Tim. 1:1; Titus 1:1), critics assert that they are "pious forgeries" that appeared in the second century. There are several problems with this: (1) Pseudonymous writing was unacceptable to Paul (see 2 Thess. 2:2; 3:17) and to the early church, which was very sensitive to the problem of forgeries. (2) The adjective *pious* should deceive no one: a forgery was as deliberately deceptive then as it is now. (3) The many personal facts and names that appear in the Pastoral Epistles would have been avoided by a forger who would have taken refuge in vagueness. Nor would a forger have used expressions like those in 1:13, 15 if he had been an admirer of Paul. The doctrinal teaching and autobiographical details (cf. 1:12–17; 2:7; 2 Tim. 1:8–12; 4:9–22; Titus 1:5; 3:12, 13) fit very well with "Paul the aged" (Philem. 9). (4) What purpose or advantage would these epistles serve as forgeries written years later? There are too many personal elements, and the doctrinal refutations do not refer to second-century Gnosticism. (5) The style and content of the postapostolic writings or apocryphal books differ greatly with these three letters.

THE TIME OF FIRST TIMOTHY

Pauline authorship of the Pastoral Epistles requires Paul's release from his Roman imprisonment (Acts 28), the continuation of his missionary endeavors, and his imprisonment for a second time in Rome. Unfortunately, the order of events can only be reconstructed from hints, because there is no concurrent history paralleling Acts to chronicle the last years of the apostle. The following reconstruction, therefore, is only tentative:

As he anticipated in Philippians (1:19, 25, 26; 2:24), Paul was released from his first Roman imprisonment. It is possible that his Jewish accusers decided not to appear at his trial before Caesar. In fulfillment of his promise to the Philippians (Phil. 2:19–23), he sends Timothy to Philippi to relate the good news. Paul himself went to Ephesus (in spite of his earlier expectations in Acts 20:38) and to other Asian churches like Colosse (see Philem. 22). When Timothy rejoined him in Ephesus, Paul instructed his assistant to "abide still at Ephesus" (1:3) while he journeyed to Macedonia. When he saw that he might be delayed in Macedonia, Paul wrote First Timothy, perhaps from Philippi (3:14, 15). After he saw Timothy in Ephesus, the apostle journeyed on to the island of Crete where, after a period of ministry, he left Titus to continue the work (Titus 1:5). In Corinth, Paul decided to write a letter to Titus because Zenas and Apollos were making a journey that would take them by way of Crete (Titus 3:13). He instructed Titus to join him in Nicopolis after the arrival of his replacement in Crete, Artemas, or Tychicus (Titus 3:12).

If he went to Spain as he had planned (Rom. 15:24, 28), Paul probably departed with Titus for that western province after his winter in Nicopolis. Early church tradition holds that Paul did go to Spain. Before the end of the first century, Clement of Rome said that Paul "reached the limits of the West" (1 Clement 5:7). Since he was writing from Rome, he evidently had Spain in mind. Paul may have been in Spain from A.D. 64 to 66. He returned to Greece and Asia—to Corinth, Miletus, and Troas (2 Tim. 4:13, 20)—and may have been arrested in Troas

where he left his valuable books and parchments (2 Tim. 4:13, 15).

Now that Christianity had become an illegal religion in the Empire (the burning of Rome took place in A.D. 64), Paul's enemies were able to successfully accuse him. He was imprisoned in A.D. 67 and wrote Second Timothy from his Roman cell after his first defense before the Imperial Court (2 Tim. 1:8, 17; 2:9; 4:16, 17). He was delivered from condemnation, but he held no hope of release and expected to be executed (2 Tim. 4:6–8, 18). He urged Timothy to come before that happened (2 Tim. 4:9, 21); and, according to tradition, the apostle was beheaded west of Rome on the Ostian Way.

Paul wrote First Timothy from Macedonia in A.D. 62 or 63 while Timothy was serving as his representative in Ephesus and perhaps in other churches in the province of Asia. Timothy was to appoint elders, combat false doctrine, and supervise church life as an apostolic representative.

THE CHRIST OF FIRST TIMOTHY

Christ is the "one mediator between God and men" (2:5) and "God . . . manifest in the flesh, justified in the Spirit, seen of angels, preached unto the Gentiles, believed on in the world, received up into glory" (3:16). He is the source of spiritual strength, faith, and love (1:12, 14). He "came into the world to save sinners" (1:15) and "gave himself a ransom for all" (2:6) as "the Saviour of all men, specially of those that believe" (4:10).

KEYS TO FIRST TIMOTHY

Key Word: Leadership Manual for Church Organization—The theme of this epistle is Timothy's organization and oversight of the Asian churches as a faithful minister of God. Paul writes this letter as a reference manual for leadership so that Timothy will have effective guidance for his work during Paul's absence in Macedonia (3:14, 15). Paul wants to encourage and exhort his younger assistant to become an example to others, exercise his spiritual gifts, and "Fight the good fight of faith" (6:12; cf. 1:18; 4:12–16; 6:20). Timothy's personal and public life must be above reproach; and he must be ready to deal with matters of false teaching, organization, discipline, proclamation of the Scriptures, poverty and wealth, and the roles of various groups. Negatively, he is to refute error (1:7–11; 6:3–5); positively, he is to teach the truth (4:13–16; 6:2, 17, 18).

Key Verses: First Timothy 3:15, 16 and 6:11, 12—"But if I tarry long, that thou mayest know how thou oughtest to behave thyself in the house of God, which is the church of the living God, the pillar and ground of the truth. And without controversy great is the mystery of godliness: God

was manifest in the flesh, justified in the Spirit, seen of angels, preached unto the Gentiles, believed on in the world, received up into glory" (3:15, 16).

"But thou, O man of God, flee these things; and follow after righteousness, godliness, faith, love, patience, meekness. Fight the good fight of faith, lay hold on eternal life, whereunto thou art also called, and hast professed a good profession before many witnesses" (6:11, 12).

Key Chapter: First Timothy 3—Listed in chapter 3 are the qualifications for the leaders of God's church, the elders and deacons. Notably absent are qualities of worldly success or position. Instead, Paul enumerates character qualities demonstrating that true leadership emanates from our walk with God rather than from achievements or vocational success.

SURVEY OF FIRST TIMOTHY

Paul's last three recorded letters, written near the end of his full and fruitful life, were addressed to his authorized representatives Timothy and Titus. These were the only letters Paul wrote exclusively to individuals (Philemon was addressed primarily to its namesake, but also to others), and they were designed to exhort and encourage Timothy and Titus in their ministry of solidifying the churches in Ephesus and Crete. In the eighteenth century, these epistles came to be known as the Pastoral Epistles even though they do not use any terms such as shepherd, pastor, flock, or sheep. Still, this title is appropriate for First Timothy and Titus, since they focus on the oversight of church life. It is less appropriate in the case of Second Timothy, which is a more personal than church-oriented letter. The Pastoral Epistles abound with principles for leadership and righteous living.

In his first letter to Timothy, Paul seeks to guide his younger and less experienced assistant in his weighty responsibility as the overseer of the work at Ephesus and other Asian cities. He writes, in effect, a challenge to Timothy to fulfill the task before him: combating false teaching with sound doctrine, developing qualified leadership, teaching God's Word, and encouraging Christian conduct. Because of the personal and conversational character of this letter, it is loosely structured around five clear charges that end each section (1:18–20; 3:14–16; 4:11–20; 5:21–25; 6:20, 21): Paul's charges concerning doctrine (1); Paul's charge concerning public worship (2 and 3); Paul's charge concerning false teachers (4); Paul's charge concerning church discipline (5); and Paul's charge concerning pastoral motives (6).

Paul's Charge Concerning Doctrine (1): After his greetings (1:1, 2), Paul warns Timothy about the growing problem of false doctrines, particularly as they relate to the misuse of the Mosaic

Law (1:3–11). The aging apostle then recounts his radical conversion to Christ and subsequent calling to the ministry (1:12–17). Timothy, too, has received a divine calling, and Paul charges him to fulfill it without wavering in doctrine or conduct (1:18–20).

Paul's Charge Concerning Public Worship (2 and 3): Turning his attention to the church at large, Paul addresses the issues of church worship and leadership. Efficacious public prayer should be a part of worship, and Paul associates this with the role of men in the church (2:1–8). He then turns to the role of women (2:9–15), wherein he emphasizes the importance of the inner quality of godliness. In 3:1–7, Paul lists several qualifications for bishops or overseers. The word for "bishop" (*episkopos*) is used synonymously with the word for "elder" (*presbuteros*) in the New Testament, because both originally referred to the same office (see Acts 20:17, 28; Titus 1:5, 7). The qualifications for the office of deacon (*diakonos*, "servant") are listed in 3:8–13.

Paul's Charge Concerning False Teachers (4):

Timothy obviously had difficulties with some of the older men (5:1) who had left the faith. Paul carefully advises on the issues of marriage, food, and exercise. The closing charge exhorts Timothy not to neglect the spiritual gift given to him.

Paul's Charge Concerning Church Discipline (5): One of the most difficult pastoral duties for the young minister is to lead in the exercise of church discipline. Commencing with the general advice of treating all members of the church as family (5:1, 2), Paul concentrates on the two special areas of widows and elders, focusing on Timothy's responsibility and providing practical instruction.

Paul's Charge Concerning Pastoral Duties (6): In addition, the insidious doctrine was being taught that godliness would eventually result in material blessing. Paul, in no uncertain terms, states "from such withdraw thyself" (6:5). The book closes with an extended charge (6:11–21), which is supplemented by an additional charge that Timothy is to give to the wealthy of this age (6:17–19).

FOCUS	DOCTRINE	PUBLIC WORSHIP	FALSE TEACHERS	CHURCH DISCIPLINE	PASTORAL MOTIVES
REFERENCE	1:1———————2:1		———————4:1———————	5:1———————	6:1————————6:21
DIVISION	PROBLEM OF FALSE DOCTRINE	PUBLIC WORSHIP AND LEADERSHIP	PRESERVE TRUE DOCTRINE	PRESCRIPTIONS FOR WIDOWS AND ELDERS	PASTORAL MOTIVATIONS
TOPIC	WARNING	WORSHIP	WISDOM	WIDOWS	WEALTH
	DANGERS OF FALSE DOCTRINE	DIRECTIONS FOR WORSHIP	DEFENSE AGAINST FALSE TEACHERS	DUTIES TOWARD OTHERS	DEALINGS WITH RICHES
LOCATION	WRITTEN IN MACEDONIA				
TIME	c. A.D. 62–63				

OUTLINE OF FIRST TIMOTHY

CHAPTER 1

Paul's Past Charge to Timothy

PAUL, an apostle of Jesus Christ by the commandment of God our Saviour, and Lord Jesus Christ, *which is* our hope;

2 Unto Timothy, *my* own son in the faith: Grace, mercy, *and* peace, from God our Father and Jesus Christ our Lord.

3 As I ^Tbesought thee to abide still at Eph'-e-sus, when I went into Mac-e-do'-ni-a, that thou mightest ^Tcharge some that they teach no other doctrine,   *asked · instruct*

4 ^RNeither give heed to fables and endless ^Tgenealogies, which ^Tminister questions, rather than godly edifying which is in faith: *so do.*   Titus 1:14 · *history · cause*

5 Now the ^Tend of the commandment is charity out of a pure heart, and *of* a good conscience, and *of* faith unfeigned: *goal*

6 From which some having swerved have turned aside unto ^Rvain jangling;   6:4, 20

7 Desiring to be teachers of the law; understanding neither what they say, nor whereof they ^Taffirm.   *teach*

8 ^RBut we know that the law *is* good, if a man use it lawfully;   Rom. 7:22

9 Knowing this, that the law is not made for a righteous man, but for the lawless and ^Tdisobedient, ^Rfor the ungodly and for sinners, for unholy and profane, for murderers of fathers and murderers of mothers, for manslayers,   *unruly* · [Gal. 3:19]

10 For ^Twhoremongers, for them that defile themselves with mankind, for menstealers, for liars, for perjured persons, and if there be any other thing that is ^Tcontrary to sound doctrine;   *fornicators · opposed*

11 ^RAccording to the glorious gospel of the blessed God, which was ^Tcommitted to my trust.   6:15; Gal. 2:7; Col. 1:25 · *entrusted*

Christ's Past Charge to Paul

12 And I thank Christ Jesus our Lord, who hath enabled me, for that he counted me faithful, putting me into the ministry;

13 ^RWho was before a blasphemer, and a persecutor, and ^Tinjurious: but I obtained mercy, because I did *it* ignorantly in unbelief.   Acts 8:3 · *insulting*

14 And the grace of our Lord was exceeding abundant ^Rwith faith and love which is in Christ Jesus.   2 Tim. 1:13

15 ^RThis *is* a ^Tfaithful saying, and worthy of all acceptation, that ^RChrist Jesus came into the world to save sinners; of whom I am chief.   2 Tim. 2:11 · *true* · Is. 53:5; Matt. 1:21; 9:13 *

16 Howbeit for this cause I obtained mercy, that in me first Jesus Christ might shew forth all longsuffering, ^Rfor a pattern to them which should hereafter believe on him to life everlasting.   Acts 13:39

17 Now unto the King eternal, immortal, invisible, the only wise God, *be* honour and glory for ever and ever. A-men'.

First Charge: "War a Good Warfare"

18 This charge I commit unto thee, son Timothy, according to the prophecies which went before on thee, that thou by them mightest war a good warfare;

19 Holding faith, and a good conscience; which some having put away concerning faith have made ^Tshipwreck: *ruined*

20 Of whom is Hy-me-nae'-us and Alexander; whom I have delivered unto Satan, that they may learn not to blaspheme.

CHAPTER 2

Prayer in Public Worship

I EXHORT therefore, that, first of all, supplications, prayers, intercessions, *and* giving of thanks, be made for all men;

2 For kings, and *for* all that are in authority; that we may lead a quiet and peaceable life in all godliness and honesty.

3 For this *is* good and acceptable in the sight ^Rof God our Saviour;   2 Tim. 1:9

4 ^RWho ^Twill have all men to be saved, ^Rand to come unto the knowledge of the truth.   Ezek. 18:23; Titus 2:11 · *wants to* · [John 17:3]

5 ^RFor *there is* one God, and ^Rone mediator between God and men, ^Tthe man Christ Jesus;   Gal. 3:20 · [Heb. 9:15] · *Himself*

6 ^RWho gave himself a ransom for all, to be ^Ttestified in due time.   Mark 10:45 · *preached*

7 ^RWhereunto I am ordained a preacher, and an apostle, (I speak the truth in Christ, *and* lie not;) a teacher of the Gentiles in faith and ^Tverity.   [Gal. 1:15, 16] · *truth*

8 I will therefore that men pray every where, ^Rlifting up holy hands, without wrath and doubting.   Ps. 134:2

Women in Public Worship

9 In like manner also, that women adorn themselves in modest apparel, with shame-

facedness and sobriety; not with broided hair, or gold, or pearls, or costly array;

10 ᴿBut (which becometh women professing godliness) with good works.   1 Pet. 3:4

11 Let the woman learn in ᵀsilence with all ᵀsubjection.   *quietness · submission*

12 But ᴿI ᵀsuffer not a woman to teach, nor to ᵀusurp authority over the man, but to be in silence.   1 Cor. 14:34 · *allow · take*

13 For Adam was first formed, then Eve.

14 ᴿAnd Adam was not deceived, but the woman being deceived was in the ᵀtransgression.   Gen. 3:6; 2 Cor. 11:3 · *brake God's law*

15 Notwithstanding she shall be saved in childbearing, if they continue in faith and charity and holiness with sobriety.

CHAPTER 3

Qualifications of Bishops

THIS *is* a true saying, If a man ᴿdesire the office of ᵀa bishop, he desireth a ᵀgood work.   Acts 20:28 · *an overseer · excellent*

2 A bishop then must be blameless, the husband of one wife, vigilant, sober, of good behaviour, given to hospitality, apt to teach;

3 Not ᵀgiven to wine, no ᵀstriker, not greedy of filthy lucre; but patient, not a brawler, not covetous;   *prone · scrapper*

4 One that ᵀruleth well his own house, having his children ᵀin subjection with all gravity;   *manages · under control*

5 (For if a man know not how to rule his own ᵀhouse, how shall he take care of the church of God?)   *family*

6 Not a ᵀnovice, lest being ᵀlifted up with pride he fall into the condemnation of the devil.   *new convert · puffed up*

7 Moreover he must have a good report of them which are without; lest he fall into ᵀreproach and the snare of the devil.   *shame*

Qualifications of Deacons

8 Likewise *must* the deacons *be* grave, not ᵀdoubletongued, not given to much wine, not greedy of filthy lucre;   *two-faced*

9 Holding the ᵀmystery of the faith in a pure conscience.   *hidden truth*

10 And let these also first be ᵀproved; then let them use the office of a deacon, being *found* blameless.   *tested*

11 Even so *must their* wives *be* grave, not slanderers, sober, faithful in all things.

12 Let the ᵀdeacons be the husbands of one wife, ruling their children and their own houses well.   *church helpers*

13 For they that have ᵀused the office of a deacon well purchase to themselves a good degree, and great boldness in the faith which is in Christ Jesus.   *served in*

Second Charge:
"Behave Thyself in the House of God"

14 These things write I unto thee, hoping to come unto thee shortly:

15 But if I tarry long, that thou mayest know how ᵀthou oughtest to behave ᵀthyself in the house of God, which is the church of the living God, the pillar and ground of the truth.   *men · themselves*

16 And without controversy great is the mystery of godliness: God was ᵀmanifest in the flesh, justified in the Spirit, seen of angels, preached unto the Gentiles, believed on in the world, received up into glory.   *revealed*

CHAPTER 4

Description of False Teachers

NOW the Spirit speaketh expressly, that in the latter times some shall depart from the faith, giving heed to seducing spirits, and doctrines of devils;

3:1–13 The Offices of the Church—The New Testament uses four terms to describe the leadership of the church: (1) "elder" (Gr., *presbuteros*) which places emphasis upon the authority that the leadership has to teach or rule in the church; (2) "bishop" (Gr., *episkopos*—overseer) which emphasizes the fact that the leadership is charged with overseeing the local church and as such is responsible for the spiritual well-being of those in the church; (3) "pastor" (Gr., *poimen*—shepherd) which places emphasis upon the responsibility of the leadership of the church to shepherd the flock. No shepherd has ever given birth to his sheep. It is the responsibility of those in leadership to do for the sheep what they cannot do for themselves and to make sure that they are in good spiritual condition so that they can do what comes naturally, that is, beget other sheep; (4) "deacon" (Gr., *diakonos*—minister) which places emphasis upon the attitude that the leaders are to have in their leading. They are not to "lord it over" the flock, but are to realize that they are the ministers or servants of those whom the Lord has put under their care.

The function of the office of elder is twofold: (1) teaching and (2) ruling (Page 1196—1 Tim. 5:17). An elder is to be able to teach his people what the Word of God teaches and to give direction as to how that is to be accomplished in and through the local church.

The qualifications for the office of deacon are essentially the same as those for the elder except that the deacon need not be "apt to teach." The deacons are to be spiritual and in tune with the elders and seek to assist them in implementing the goals that the elders feel the Spirit of God is leading them to pursue through the local church.

Now turn to Page 1166—Eph. 5:25–29: The Relationship of the Church to Christ.

2 Speaking lies in hypocrisy; having their conscience seared with a hot iron;

3 Forbidding to marry, *and commanding* to abstain from meats, which God hath created to be received with thanksgiving of them which believe and know the truth.

4 ᴿFor every creature of God *is* good, and nothing to be refused, if it be received with thanksgiving: Rom. 14:14, 20; 1 Cor. 10:25

5 For it is ᵀsanctified by the word of God and prayer.   *set apart for use*

Instruction for the True Teacher

6 If thou put the brethren in remembrance of these things, thou shalt be a good ᵀminister of Jesus Christ, nourished up in the words of faith and of good doctrine, whereunto thou hast attained.   *servant*

7 But refuse profane and old wives' fables, and exercise thyself *rather* unto godliness.

8 For bodily exercise profiteth little: but godliness is profitable unto all things, having promise of the life that now is, and of that which is to come.

9 This *is* a ᵀfaithful saying and worthy of ᵀall acceptation.   *true • entire acceptance*

10 For therefore we both labour and suffer reproach, because we trust in the living God, who is the Saviour of all men, ᴿspecially of those that believe.   Eph. 5:23

Third Charge: "Neglect Not The Gift"

11 These things command and teach.

12 Let no man ᵀdespise thy youth; but be thou an example of the believers, in word, in ᵀconversation, in charity, in spirit, in faith, in purity.   *look down upon • manner of life*

13 Till I come, give attendance to reading, to ᵀexhortation, to doctrine.   *preaching*

14 Neglect not the gift that is in thee, which was given thee by prophecy, with the laying on of the hands of the presbytery.

15 ᵀMeditate upon these things; give thyself wholly to them; that thy ᵀprofiting may appear to all.   *be diligent in • progress*

16 Take heed unto thyself, and unto ᵀthe doctrine; continue in ᵀthem: for in doing this thou shalt both save thyself, and them that hear thee.   *thy teaching • these things*

CHAPTER 5

How to Treat All People

REBUKEᵀ not an ᵀelder, but intreat *him* as a father; *and* the younger men as brethren;   *do not find fault with • presbyter*

2 The elder women as mothers; the younger as sisters, with all ᵀpurity.   *honour*

How to Treat Widows

3 Honour widows that are widows indeed.

4 But if any widow have children or nephews, let them learn first to shew piety at home, and to requite their parents: for that is good and acceptable before God.

5 Now she that is a widow indeed, and desolate, trusteth in God, and continueth in supplications and prayers night and day.

6 But she that ᴿliveth ᵀin pleasure is dead while she liveth.   James 5:5 • *doing as she pleases*

7 And these things give ᵀin charge, that they may be blameless.   *as a commandment*

8 But if any provide not for his own, and specially for those of his own ᵀhouse, he hath ᵀdenied the faith, and is worse than ᵀan infidel.   *family • disowned • an unbeliever*

9 Let not a widow be ᵀtaken into the number under threescore years old, having been the wife of one man,   *put on the pay roll*

10 Well reported of for good works; if she have brought up children, if she have lodged strangers, if she have washed the saints' feet, if she have relieved the afflicted, if she have diligently followed every good work.

11 But the younger widows refuse: for when they have begun to ᵀwax wanton against Christ, they will marry;   *turn away*

12 Having damnation, because they have cast off their ᵀfirst faith.   *prior commitment*

13 And withal they learn *to be* idle, wandering about from house to house; and not only idle, but tattlers also and busybodies, speaking things which they ought not.

14 I will therefore that the younger women ᴿmarry, bear children, ᵀguide the house, give none occasion to the adversary to speak reproachfully.   1 Cor. 7:9 • *rule*

15 For some are already turned ᵀaside ᵀafter Satan.   *away • as led by*

16 If any man or woman that believeth have widows, let ᵀthem relieve them, and let not the church be charged; that it may relieve them that are widows indeed.   *her*

How to Treat Elders

17 Let the elders that rule well be counted worthy of double honour, especially they who labour in the word and doctrine.

18 For the scripture saith, ᴿTHOU SHALT NOT MUZZLE THE OX THAT TREADETH OUT THE CORN. And, THE LABOURER *IS* WORTHY OF HIS REWARD.   Deut. 25:4

19 Against an elder receive not an accusation, but before two or three witnesses.

20 Them that sin ᵀrebuke before all, that others also may fear.   *openly criticize*

Fourth Charge: "Without Preferring One Before Another"

21 I charge *thee* before God, and the Lord Jesus Christ, and the elect angels, that thou observe these things without preferring one before another, doing nothing by partiality.

22 ᵀLay hands ᴿsuddenly on no man, neither be ᵀpartaker of other men's sins: keep thyself pure.   *endorse • 4:14 • a partner in*

23 Drink no longer water, but use a little wine for thy stomach's sake and thine ᵀoften infirmities.   *frequent sicknesses*

24 Some men's sins are open beforehand, going before to judgment; and some ᵀmen they follow after.   *sins show up later*

25 Likewise also the good works *of some* are ᵀmanifest beforehand; and they that are otherwise cannot be hid.   *plainly seen*

CHAPTER 6

Exhortation to Servants

LET as many servants as are ᵀunder the yoke count their own masters worthy of all honour, that the name of God and *his* doctrine be not blasphemed.   *in slavery*

2 And they that have believing masters, let them not despise *them*, because they are brethren; but rather do *them* service, because they are faithful and beloved, partakers of the benefit. These things teach and exhort.

Exhortation to Godliness with Contentment

3 If any man teach otherwise, and consent not to wholesome words, *even* the words of our Lord Jesus Christ, and to the doctrine which is according to godliness;

4 He is ᵀproud, knowing nothing, but ᵀdoting about questions and strifes of words, whereof cometh envy, strife, railings, evil surmisings,   *a fool · acting as a fool*

5 Perverse ᵀdisputings of men of corrupt minds, and destitute of the truth, supposing that gain is godliness: from such withdraw thyself.   *misleading arguments*

6 ᴿBut godliness with contentment is great gain.   [Prov. 15:16]; Heb. 13:5

7 ᴿFor we brought nothing into *this* world, *and it is* certain we can carry nothing out.   Job 1:21; Ps. 49:17; Prov. 27:24

8 And having food and ᵀraiment ᵀlet us be therewith content.   *clothes · that is enough*

9 ᴿBut they that will be rich fall into temptation and a snare, and *into* many foolish and hurtful lusts, which drown men in destruction and perdition.   *v. 17*

10 For the love of money is the root of all evil: which while some coveted after, they have erred from the faith, and pierced themselves through with many sorrows.

11 But thou, O man of God, flee these things; and follow after righteousness, godliness, faith, love, patience, meekness.

12 Fight the good fight of faith, ᵀlay hold on eternal life, whereunto thou art also called, and hast professed a good profession before many witnesses.   *deliberately seek*

13 I give thee charge in the sight of God, who quickeneth all things, and *before* Christ Jesus, ᴿwho before Pon'-tius Pilate witnessed a good confession;   Matt. 27:11

14 That thou keep *this* commandment without spot, unrebukeable, until the ᴿappearing of our Lord Jesus Christ: [2 Thess. 2:8]

15 ᴿWhich in his times he shall shew, *who is* the blessed and only Potentate, the King of kings, and Lord of lords;   1:11, 17

16 Who only hath immortality, dwelling in the light which no man can approach unto; ᴿwhom no man hath seen, nor can see: to whom *be* honour and ᵀpower everlasting. A-men'.   John 6:46 · *eternal might*

Exhortation to the Rich

17 ᵀCharge them that are rich in this ᵀworld, that they be not ᵀhighminded, nor trust in uncertain riches, but ᵀin the living God, ᴿwho giveth us richly all things to enjoy;   *command · life · proud · on · v. 9*

18 That they do good, that they be rich in good works, ready to distribute, ᵀwilling to ᵀcommunicate;   *ready · give to the needy*

19 Laying up in store for themselves a good foundation against the time to come, that they may lay hold on eternal life.

Fifth Charge: "Keep That Which Is Committed"

20 O Timothy, keep that which is committed to thy trust, avoiding ᵀprofane *and* ᵀvain babblings, and oppositions of science falsely so called: *such as do not honour God · empty*

21 ᴿWhich some professing have ᵀerred concerning the faith. Grace *be* with thee. A-men'.   1:16, 19; 2 Tim. 2:18 · *made mistakes*

TIMOTHY

THE BOOK OF SECOND TIMOTHY

Prison is the last place from which to expect a letter of encouragement, but that is where Paul's second letter to Timothy originates. He begins by assuring Timothy of his continuing love and prayers, and reminds him of his spiritual heritage and responsibilities. Only the one who perseveres, whether as a soldier, athlete, farmer, or minister of Jesus Christ, will reap the reward. Paul warns Timothy that his teaching will come under attack as men desert the truth for ear-"itching" words (4:3). But Timothy has Paul's example to guide him and God's Word to fortify him as he faces growing opposition and glowing opportunities in the last days.

Paul's last epistle received the title *Pros Timotheon B*, the "Second to Timothy." When Paul's epistles were collected together the *B* was probably added to distinguish this letter from the first letter he wrote to Timothy.

THE AUTHOR OF SECOND TIMOTHY

Since the Pastoral Epistles have to be treated as a unit on the matter of authorship, see "The Author of First Timothy" for comments on the origin of Second Timothy.

Timothy's name is found more often in the salutations of the Pauline Epistles than any other (2 Cor.; Phil.; Col.; 1 and 2 Thess.; 1 and 2 Tim.; Philem.). His father was a Greek (Acts 16:1), but his Jewish mother Eunice and grandmother Lois reared him in the knowledge of the Hebrew Scriptures (1:5; 3:15). Timothy evidently became a convert of Paul (1 Cor. 4:17; 1 Tim. 1:2; 2 Tim. 1:2) when the apostle was in Lystra on his first missionary journey (Acts 14:8-20). When he visited Lystra on his second missionary journey, Paul decided to take Timothy along with him and circumcised him because of the Jews (Acts 16:1-3). Timothy was ordained to the ministry (1 Tim. 4:14; 2 Tim. 1:6) and served as a devoted companion and assistant to Paul in Troas, Berea, Thessalonica, and Corinth (Acts 16—18; 1 Thess. 3:1, 2). During the third missionary journey, Timothy labored with Paul and ministered for him as his representative in Ephesus, Macedonia, and Corinth. He was with Paul during his first Roman imprisonment and evidently went to Philippi (2:19-23) after Paul's release. Paul left him in Ephesus to supervise the work there (1 Tim. 1:3) and years later summoned him to Rome (4:9, 21). According to Hebrews 13:23, Timothy was imprisoned and released, but the passage does not say where. Timothy was sickly (1 Tim. 5:23), timid (2 Tim. 1:7), and youthful (1

Tim. 4:12), but he was a gifted teacher who was trustworthy and diligent.

THE TIME OF SECOND TIMOTHY

For a tentative reconstruction of the events following Paul's first Roman imprisonment, see "The Time of First Timothy." The cruel and unbalanced Nero, emperor of Rome from A.D. 54 to 68, was responsible for the beginning of the Roman persecution of Christians. Half of Rome was destroyed in July A.D. 64 by a fire, and mounting suspicion that Nero was responsible for the conflagration caused him to use the unpopular Christians as his scapegoat. Christianity thus became a *religio illicito,* and persecution of those who professed Christ became severe. By the time of Paul's return from Spain to Asia in A.D. 66, his enemies were able to use the official Roman position against Christianity to their advantage. Fearing for their own lives, the Asian believers failed to support Paul after his arrest (1:15) and no one supported him at his first defense before the Imperial Court (4:16). Abandoned by almost everyone (4:10, 11), the apostle found himself in circumstances very different from those of his first Roman imprisonment (Acts 28:16-31). At that time he was merely under house arrest, people could freely visit him, and he had the hope of release. Now he was in a cold Roman cell (4:13), regarded "as an evil doer" (2:9), and without hope of acquittal in spite of the success of his initial defense (4:6-8, 17, 18). Under these conditions, Paul wrote this epistle in the fall of A.D. 67, hoping that Timothy would be able to visit him before the approaching winter (4:21). Timothy evidently was in Ephesus at the time of this letter (see 1:18; 4:19), and on his way to Rome he would go through Troas (4:13) and Macedonia. Prisca and Aquila (4:19) probably returned from Rome (Rom. 16:3) to Ephesus after the burning of Rome and the beginning of the persecution. Tychicus may have been the bearer of this letter (4:12).

THE CHRIST OF SECOND TIMOTHY

Christ Jesus appeared on earth, "abolished death, and . . . brought life and immortality to light through the gospel" (1:10). He rose from the dead (2:8) and provides salvation and "eternal glory" (2:10); for if believers "be dead with *him*" they will "also live with *him*" (2:11). All who love His appearing will receive the "crown of righteousness" (4:8) and "reign with *him*" (2:12).

KEYS TO SECOND TIMOTHY

Key Word: Endurance in the Pastoral Ministry—In this letter, Paul commissions

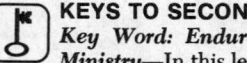

Timothy to faithfully endure and carry on the work that the condemned apostle must now relinquish. This set of instructions exhorts Timothy to use the Word of God constantly in order to overcome growing obstacles to the spread of the gospel. Timothy is in great need of encouragement because of the hardships he is facing, and Paul uses this letter to instruct him about handling persecution from the secular authorities and dissension and deception from within the church. As a spiritual father, Paul urges his young helper to overcome his natural timidity and boldly proclaim the gospel, even if it means that he will suffer for doing so.

Key Verses: Second Timothy 2:3, 4 and 3:14-17—"Thou therefore endure hardness, as a good soldier of Jesus Christ. No man that warreth entangleth himself with the affairs of *this* life; that he may please him who hath chosen him to be a soldier" (2:3, 4).

"But continue thou in the things which thou hast learned and hast been assured of, knowing of whom thou hast learned *them;* And that from a child thou hast known the holy scriptures, which are able to make thee wise unto salvation through faith which is in Christ Jesus. All scripture *is* given by inspiration of God, and *is* profitable for doctrine, for reproof, for correction, for instruction in righteousness: That the man of God may be perfect, throughly furnished unto all good works" (3:14–17).

Key Chapter: Second Timothy 2—The second chapter of Second Timothy ought to be required daily reading for every pastor and full-time Christian worker. Paul lists the keys to an enduring successful ministry: (1) a reproducing ministry (1 and 2), an enduring ministry (3—13), a studying ministry (14—18), and a holy ministry (19—26).

SURVEY OF SECOND TIMOTHY

Paul knows as he writes this final epistle that his days on earth are quickly drawing to a close. About to relinquish his heavy burdens, the godly apostle seeks to challenge and strengthen his somewhat timid but faithful associate, Timothy, in his difficult ministry in Ephesus. In spite of Paul's bleak circumstances, this is a letter of encouragement that urges Timothy on to steadfastness in the fulfillment of his divinely appointed task. Paul calls Timothy a "good solider of Jesus Christ" (2:3), and it is clear from the sharp imperatives that this letter is really a combat manual for use in the spiritual warfare: "stir up" (1:6); "Be not . . . ashamed" (1:8, 12); "be thou partaker of the afflictions" (1:8); "Hold fast . . . sound words" (1:13); "That good thing . . . unto thee keep" (1:14); "be strong" (2:1); "endure hardness" (2:3); "Study to shew thyself approved" (2:15); "Flee . . . follow" (2:22); "avoid" (2:23); "be thou ware" (4:15). Central to everything in Second Timothy is the sure foundation of the Word of God. Paul focuses on the need to persevere in present testing (1 and 2), and to endure in future testing (3 and 4).

Persevere in Present Testing (1 and 2): After his salutation to his "beloved son" (1:2), Paul expresses his thanksgiving for Timothy's "unfeigned faith" (1:5). He then encourages Timothy to stand firm in the power of the gospel and to overcome any fear in the face of opposition. At personal risk, Onesiphorus boldly sought out Paul in Rome, but most of the Asian Christians failed to stand behind Paul at the time of his arrest. Timothy must remain faithful and not fear possible persecution. Paul then exhorts his spiritual son to reproduce in the lives of others what he has received in Christ (four generations are mentioned in 2:2). He is responsible to work hard and discipline himself like a teacher, a soldier, a farmer, a workman, a vessel, and a servant, following the example of Paul's perseverance (2:1–13). In his dealings with others, Timothy must not become entangled in false speculation, foolish quarrels, or youthful lusts,

FOCUS	PERSEVERE IN PRESENT TESTINGS			ENDURE IN FUTURE TESTINGS		
REFERENCE	1:1————1:6———————2:1—			———3:1————4:1———4:6———4:22		
DIVISION	THANKSGIVING FOR TIMOTHY'S FAITH	REMINDER OF TIMOTHY'S RESPONSIBILITY	CHARACTERISTICS OF A FAITHFUL MINISTER	APPROACHING DAY OF APOSTASY	CHARGE TO PREACH THE WORD	APPROACHING DEATH OF PAUL
TOPIC	POWER OF THE GOSPEL		PERSEVERANCE OF THE GOSPEL	PROTECTOR OF THE GOSPEL	PROCLAMATION OF THE GOSPEL	
	REMINDER		REQUIREMENTS	RESISTANCE	REQUESTS	
LOCATION	ROMAN PRISON					
TIME	C. A.D. 67					

which would hamper his effectiveness. As he pursues "righteousness, faith, charity, peace" (2:22), he must know how to graciously overcome error.

Endure in Future Testing (3 and 4): Paul anticipates a time of growing apostasy and wickedness when men and women will be increasingly susceptible to empty religiosity and false teaching (3:1-9). Arrogance and godlessness will breed further deception and persecution, but Timothy must not waver in using the Scripture to combat doctrinal error and moral evil (3:10-17).

The Scriptures are inspired ("God-breathed") and with them Timothy is equipped to carry out the ministry to which he was called. Paul's final exhortation to Timothy (4:1-5) is a classic summary of the task of the man of God to proclaim the gospel in spite of opposing circumstances. This very personal letter closes with an update of Paul's situation in Rome along with certain requests (4:6-22). Paul longs to see Timothy before the end, and he also needs certain articles, especially "the parchments" (probably portions of the Old Testament Scriptures).

OUTLINE OF SECOND TIMOTHY

CHAPTER 1

Thanksgiving for Timothy's Faith

PAUL, an apostle of Jesus Christ by the will of God, according to the ᴿpromise of life which is in Christ Jesus,   Eph. 3:6

2 To Timothy, *my* dearly beloved son: Grace, mercy, *and* peace, from God the Father and Christ Jesus our Lord.

3 I thank God, whom I serve from *my* forefathers with ᵀpure conscience, that without ceasing I have remembrance of thee in my prayers night and day;   *a clear*

4 Greatly desiring to see thee, being mindful of thy tears, that I may be filled with joy;

5 When I call to remembrance ᴿthe ᵀunfeigned faith that is in thee, which dwelt first in thy grandmother Lo'-is, and ᴿthy mother Eu-ni'-ce; and I am persuaded that in thee also.   1 Tim. 1:5 • *genuine* • Acts 16:1

Reminder of Timothy's Responsibility

6 Wherefore I put thee in remembrance that thou stir up the gift of God, which is in thee by the putting on of my hands.

7 For God hath not given us the spirit of fear; ᴿbut of ᵀpower, and of love, and of ᵀa sound mind.   [Acts 1:8] • *might* • *clear thinking*

8 Be not thou therefore ashamed of the testimony of our Lord, nor of me his prisoner:

but be thou partaker of the afflictions of the gospel according to the power of God;

9 Who hath saved us, and called *us* with an holy calling, not according to our works, but according to his own purpose and grace, which was given us in Christ Jesus ᴿbefore the world began,   Rom. 16:25

10 But is now made manifest by the appearing of our Saviour Jesus Christ, who hath abolished death, and hath brought life and immortality to light through the gospel:

11 ᵀWhereunto I am appointed a ᴿpreacher, and an apostle, and a teacher of the Gentiles.   *for this reason* • Acts 9:15

12 For the which cause I also suffer these things: nevertheless I am not ashamed: for I know whom I have believed, and am persuaded that he is able to keep that which I have committed unto him against that day.

13 ᴿHold fast the form of sound words, which thou hast heard of me, in faith and love which is in Christ Jesus.   Titus 2:1, 8

14 ᴿThat good thing which was ᵀcommitted unto thee keep by the Holy Ghost which dwelleth in us.   1 Tim. 6:20 • *entrusted*

15 This thou knowest, that all they which are in Asia be turned away from me; of whom are Phy-gel'-lus and Her-mog'-e-nes.

16 ᴿThe Lord give mercy unto the house of On-e-siph'-o-rus; for he oft refreshed me, and was not ashamed of my chain: 4:19

17 But, when he was in Rome, he sought me out very diligently, and found *me*.

18 The Lord grant unto him that he may find mercy of the Lord in that day: and in how many things he ministered unto me at Eph'-e-sus, thou knowest very well.

CHAPTER 2

Discipling Teacher

THOU therefore, ᴿmy son, be strong in the grace that is in Christ Jesus.   1:2

2 And the things that thou hast heard of me among many witnesses, ᴿthe same commit thou to faithful men, who shall be able to teach others also.   Matt. 28:19, 20

Single-minded Soldier

3 Thou therefore endure hardness, ᴿas a good soldier of Jesus Christ.   1 Tim. 1:18

4 No man that warreth ᵀentangleth himself with the affairs of *this* life; that he may please him who hath chosen him to be a soldier.   *lets himself become involved*

5 ᴿAnd if a man also strive for ᵀmasteries, *yet* is he not crowned, except he ᵀstrive lawfully.   1 Cor. 9:25 • *victories • plays according to the rules*

Enduring Husbandman

6 The ᵀhusbandman that laboureth must be first partaker of the fruits.   *farmer*

7 Consider what I say; and the Lord ᴿgive thee understanding in all things.   Prov. 2:6

8 Remember that Jesus Christ of the seed of David ᴿwas raised from the dead ᴿaccording to my gospel.   1 Cor. 15:4 • Rom. 2:16

9 Wherein I suffer trouble, as an evil doer, *even* unto ᵀbonds; ᴿbut the word of God is not bound.   *being put in prison • Acts 28:31*

10 Therefore I ᵀendure all things for the ᵀelect's sakes, ᴿthat they may also ᵀobtain the salvation which is in Christ Jesus with eternal glory.   *suffer • called ones • 2 Cor. 4:17 • gain*

11 *It is* a faithful saying: For if we be dead with *him*, we shall also live with *him*:

12 If we suffer, we shall also reign with *him*: if we deny *him*, he also will deny us:

13 If we ᵀbelieve not, *yet* he abideth faithful: he cannot deny himself.   *are faithless*

Diligent Workman

14 Of these things put *them* in remembrance, charging *them* before the Lord that they strive not about words to no profit, *but* to the subverting of the hearers.

15 Study to shew thyself approved unto God, a workman that needeth not to be ashamed, rightly dividing the word of truth.

16 But shun profane *and* vain babblings: for they will increase unto more ungodliness.

17 ᴿAnd their word will eat as doth a ᵀcanker: ᵀof whom is Hy-me-nae'-us and Phi-le'-tus;   1 Tim. 1:20 • *cancer • two of these are*

18 Who concerning the truth have erred, saying that the resurrection is past already; and overthrow the faith of some.

19 Nevertheless the foundation of God standeth ᵀsure, having this seal, The Lord ᴿknoweth them that are his. And, Let every one that nameth the name of Christ depart from iniquity.   *steady • [Nah. 1:7]*

Sanctified Vessel

20 ᴿBut in a great house there are not only vessels of gold and of silver, but also of wood and of earth; and some to honour, and some to dishonour.   Rom. 9:21; 1 Tim. 3:15

21 If a man therefore purge himself from these, he shall be a vessel unto honour, sanctified, and ᵀmeet for the master's use, *and* prepared unto every good work.   *useful*

22 ᴿFlee also youthful ᵀlusts: but ᵀfollow righteousness, faith, ᵀcharity, peace, with them that call on the Lord out of a pure heart.   1 Cor. 6:18 • *passions • seek • love*

23 But foolish and unlearned questions avoid, knowing that they do gender strifes.

Gentle Servant

24 And ᴿthe servant of the Lord must not ᵀstrive; but be gentle unto all *men*, ᴿapt to teach, patient,   Titus 3:2 • *be quarrelsome • Titus 1:9*

25 ᴿIn meekness instructing those that oppose themselves; if God ᵀperadventure will give them repentance ᴿto the acknowledging of the truth;   Gal. 6:1 • *maybe • 1 Tim. 2:4*

26 And *that* they may recover themselves out of the snare of the devil, who are taken captive by him at his will.

CHAPTER 3

Coming of Apostasy

THIS know also, ᴿthat in the last days ᵀperilous times shall come.   4:3 • *dangerous*

2 ᴿFor men shall be ᵀlovers of their own selves, covetous, boasters, proud, ᵀblasphemers, disobedient to parents, unthankful, unholy,   Rom. 1:30 • *selfish • railers*

3 Without natural affection, trucebreakers, false accusers, ᵀincontinent, fierce, despisers of those that are good,   *no self-control*

4 ᴿTraitors, heady, highminded, lovers of pleasures more than lovers of God;   Jude 4, 19

5 Having a form of godliness, but denying the power thereof: from such turn away.

6 For of this sort are they which creep into houses, and lead captive silly women laden with sins, led away with divers lusts,

7 Ever learning, and never able ᴿto come to the knowledge of the truth.   1 Tim. 2:4

8 ᴿNow as Jan'-nes and Jam'-bres withstood Moses, so do these also resist the truth: men of corrupt minds, ᵀreprobate concerning the faith.   Ex. 7:11 • *counterfeit*

9 But they shall proceed no further: for their folly shall be ᵀmanifest unto all *men*, ᴿas their's also was.   *obvious* • Ex. 7:12

Confronting Apostasy

10 ᴿBut thou hast fully known my doctrine, manner of life, purpose, faith, longsuffering, ᵀcharity, patience,   1 Tim. 4:6 • *love*

11 Persecutions, afflictions, which came unto me at An'-ti-och, at I-co'-ni-um, at Lys'-tra; what persecutions I endured: but out of *them* all the Lord delivered me.

12 Yea, and all that will live godly in Christ Jesus shall suffer persecution.

13 ᴿBut evil men and ᵀseducers shall ᵀwax worse and worse, deceiving, and being deceived.   2 Thess. 2:11 • *impostors* • *go from bad to*

14 But continue thou in the things which thou hast learned and hast been assured of, knowing of whom thou hast learned *them;*

15 And that from a ᵀchild thou hast known the holy scriptures, which are able to make thee wise unto salvation through faith which is in Christ Jesus.   *babe*

16 ᴿAllᵀ scripture *is* given by inspiration of God, and *is* profitable for doctrine, for reproof, for correction, for instruction in righteousness: [2 Pet. 1:20] • *every holy*

17 That the man of God may be perfect, throughly furnished unto all good works.

CHAPTER 4

Charge to Preach the Word

I CHARGE *thee* therefore before God, and the Lord Jesus Christ, ᴿwho shall judge the ᵀquick and the dead at his appearing and his kingdom;   Acts 10:42 • *living*

2 Preach the word; be instant in season, out of season; reprove, rebuke, ᵀexhort with all longsuffering and doctrine.   *entreat*

3 For the time will come when they will not ᵀendure sound doctrine; but after their

own lusts shall they heap to themselves teachers, having itching ears;   *accept*

4 And they shall turn away *their* ears from the truth, and shall be turned unto fables.

5 But watch thou in all things, endure afflictions, do the work of ᴿan evangelist, make full proof of thy ministry.   Acts 21:8

Paul's Hope in Death

6 For I am now ready to be offered, and the time of my departure is at hand.

7 I have fought a good fight, I have finished *my* course, I have kept the faith:

8 Henceforth there is laid up for me ᴿa crown of righteousness, which the Lord, the righteous judge, shall give me ᴿat that day: and not to me only, but unto all them also that love his appearing.   James 1:12 • 1:12

Paul's Situation in Prison

9 ᴿDo ᵀthy diligence to come shortly unto me: vv. 13, 21 • *your best*

10 For De'-mas hath forsaken me, ᴿhaving loved this present world, and is departed unto Thes-sa-lo-ni'-ca; Cres'-cens to Ga-la'-ti-a, Titus unto Dal-ma'-ti-a.   1 John 2:15

11 Only ᴿLuke is with me. Take Mark, and bring him with thee: for he is ᵀprofitable to me for the ministry.   Col. 4:14 • *useful*

12 And ᴿTych'-i-cus have I sent to Eph'-e-sus.   Acts 20:4

13 The cloke that I left at Tro'-as with Carpus, when thou comest, bring *with thee,* and the books, *but* especially the parchments.

14 ᴿAlexander the coppersmith did me much evil: the Lord ᵀreward him according to his works: 1 Tim. 1:20 • *will render to*

15 Of whom ᵀbe thou ware also; for he hath greatly withstood our words.   *beware*

16 At my first answer no man stood with me, but all *men* forsook me: *I pray God* that it may not be laid to their charge.

17 Notwithstanding the Lord stood with me, and strengthened me; that by me the preaching might be fully known, and *that* all the Gentiles might hear: and I was delivered out of the mouth of the lion.

18 ᴿAnd the Lord shall deliver me from every evil work, and will preserve *me* unto

---

4:2 Sharing Our Faith: When?—A famous evangelist once ended a revival meeting in Chicago by advising the unbelievers who were present that night to go home and seriously consider the claims of the gospel, and then return on the following night prepared to make a decision for Christ. But on that same night, October 8, 1871, the tragic Chicago fire broke out. Before it was finally extinguished nearly four miles of buildings were consumed, along with 250 human fatalities. The evangelist then vowed never to end a service without giving an invitation to accept Christ immediately.

The question as to when we should share our faith is directly tied to when a sinner should accept Christ. The Bible is clear that God's accepted time is today. See Hebrews 3:15; 4:7; Second Corinthians 6:2; Isaiah 55:6. The reason for this is very simple—a sinner has no assurance whatsoever that he will live to see tomorrow. See Proverbs 27:1; Luke 12:19; James 4:13–15.

Thus, we are to witness any time, all the time, in any place and in all places. The apostle Paul shows us how this should be done. He witnesses everywhere, in a prison at midnight (Page 1090—Acts 16:25–31), and even on a sinking ship during a dark and stormy day (Page 1102—Acts 27:20–25).

Now turn to Page 578—Ps. 73:1: Walking in the Spirit: Confession.

his heavenly kingdom: ^Rto whom *be* glory for ever and ever. A-men'.   Ps. 121:7 · Rom. 11:36

Paul's Closing Greetings

19 Salute ^RPris'-ca and Aq'-ui-la, and the household of On-e-siph'-o-rus.   1:16; Rom. 16:3

20 E-ras'-tus abode at Corinth: but Troph'-i-mus have I left at Mi-le'-tum sick.

21 Do thy diligence to come before winter. Eu-bu'-lus greeteth thee, and Pu'-dens, and Li'-nus, and Claudia, and all the brethren.

22 The Lord Jesus Christ *be* with thy spirit. Grace *be* with you. A-men'.

THE EPISTLE OF PAUL TO

TITUS

THE BOOK OF TITUS

Titus, a young pastor, faces the unenviable assignment of setting in order the church at Crete. Paul writes advising him to appoint elders, men of proven spiritual character in their homes and businesses, to oversee the work of the church. But elders are not the only individuals in the church who are required to excel spiritually. Men and women, young and old, each have their vital functions to fulfill in the church if they are to be living examples of the doctrine they profess. Throughout his letter to Titus, Paul stresses the necessary, practical working out of salvation in the daily lives of both the elders and the congregation. Good works are desirable and profitable for all believers.

This third Pastoral Epistle is simply titled *Pros Titon*, "To Titus." Ironically, this was also the name of the Roman general who destroyed Jerusalem in A.D. 70 and succeeded his father Vespasian as emperor.

THE AUTHOR OF TITUS

Since the Pastoral Epistles have to be treated as a unit on the matter of authorship, see "The Author of First Timothy" for the authorship of Titus.

Titus is not mentioned in Acts, but the thirteen references to him in the Pauline Epistles make it clear that he was one of Paul's closest and most trusted companions. This convert of Paul ("*mine own son after the common faith*," 1:4) was probably from Syrian Antioch, if he was one of the disciples of Acts 11:26. Paul brought this uncircumcised Greek believer to Jerusalem (Gal. 2:3) where he became a test case on the matter of Gentiles and liberty from the law. Years later when Paul set out from Antioch on his third missionary journey (Acts 18:22), Titus must have accompanied him because he was sent by the apostle to Corinth on three occasions during that time (2 Cor. 2:12, 13; 7:5-7, 13-15; 8:6, 16-24). He is not mentioned again until Paul leaves him in Crete to carry on the work (1:5). He was with Paul during his second Roman imprisonment but left to go to Dalmatia (2 Tim. 4:10), possibly on an evangelistic mission. Paul spoke of this reliable and gifted associate as his "brother" (2 Cor. 2:13), his "partner and fellowhelper" (2 Cor. 8:23), and his "son" (1:4). He lauded Titus's character and conduct in Second Corinthians 7:13-15 and 8:16, 17.

THE TIME OF TITUS

For a tentative reconstruction of the events following Paul's first Roman imprisonment, see "The Time of First Timothy." The Mediterranean island of Crete is 156 miles long and up to 30 miles wide, and its first-century inhabitants were notorious for untruthfulness and immorality (1:12, 13). "To act the Cretan" became an idiom meaning "to play the liar." A number of Jews from Crete were present in Jerusalem at the time of Peter's sermon on the Day of Pentecost (Acts 2:11), and some of them may have believed in Christ and introduced the gospel to their countrymen. Certainly Paul would not have had opportunity to do evangelistic work during his brief sojourn in Crete while he was en route to Rome (Acts 27:7-13). The apostle spread the gospel in the cities of Crete after his release from Roman imprisonment and left Titus there to finish organizing the churches (1:5). Because of the problem of immorality among the Cretans, it was important for Titus to stress the need for righteousness in Christian living. False teachers, especially "they of the circumcision" (1:10), were also misleading and divisive. Paul wrote this letter about A.D. 63, perhaps from Corinth, taking advantage of the journey of Zenas and Apollos (3:13), whose destination would take them by way of Crete. Paul was planning to spend the winter in Nicopolis (western Greece), and he urged Titus in this letter to join him there upon his replacement by Artemas or Tychicus (3:12). Paul may have been planning to leave Nicopolis for Spain in the spring, and he wanted his useful companion Titus to accompany him.

THE CHRIST OF TITUS

The deity and redemptive work of Christ are beautifully stated in 2:13, 14: "Looking for that blessed hope, and the glorious appearing of the great God and our Saviour Jesus Christ; Who gave himself for us, that he might redeem us from all iniquity, and purify unto himself a peculiar people, zealous of good works."

KEYS TO TITUS

Key Word: Conduct Manual for Church Living—This brief letter focuses on Titus's role and responsibility in the organization and supervision of the churches in Crete. It is written to strengthen and exhort Titus to firmly exercise his authority as an apostolic representative to churches that need to be put in order, refuting false teachers and dissenters and replacing immoral behavior with good deeds. Paul uses this letter to remind Titus of some of the details related to his task, including the qualifications for elders and the behavior expected of various groups in the churches. Paul includes three doctrinal sections in this letter to stress that proper belief (orthodoxy) gives the basis for proper behavior (orthopraxy).

Key Verses: Titus 1:5 and 3:8—"For this cause left I thee in Crete, that thou shouldest set in order the things that are wanting, and ordain elders in every city, as I had appointed thee"(1:5).

"*This is* a faithful saying, and these things I will that thou affirm constantly, that they which have believed in God might be careful to maintain good works. These things are good and profitable unto men" (3:8).

Key Chapter: Titus 2—Summarized in Titus 2 are the key commands to be obeyed which insure godly relationships within the church. Paul includes all categories of people instructing them to show "all good fidelity; that they may adorn the doctrine of God our Saviour in all things" (2:10).

SURVEY OF TITUS

Titus, like First Timothy, was written by Paul after his release from Roman imprisonment and was also written to an associate who was given the task of organizing and supervising a large work as an apostolic representative. Paul left Titus on the island of Crete to "set in order the things that are wanting, and ordain elders in every city" (1:5). Not long after Paul's departure from Crete, he wrote this letter to encourage and assist Titus in his task. It stresses sound doctrine and warns against those who distort the truth, but it also is a conduct manual that emphasizes good deeds and the proper conduct of various groups within the churches. This epistle falls into two major sections: appoint elders (1); set things in order (2 and 3).

Appoint Elders (1): The salutation to Titus is actually a compact doctrinal statement, which lifts up "his word" as the source of the truth that reveals the way to eternal life (1:1–4). Paul reminds Titus of his responsibility to organize the churches of Crete by appointing elders (also called bishops; see 1:5, 7) and rehearses the qualifications these spiritual leaders must meet

(1:5–9). This is especially important in view of the disturbances that are being caused by false teachers who are upsetting a number of the believers with their Judaic myths and commandments (1:10–16). The natural tendency toward moral laxity among the Cretans coupled with that kind of deception is a dangerous force that must be overcome by godly leadership and sound doctrine.

Set Things in Order (2 and 3): Titus is given the charge to "speak thou the things which become sound doctrine" (2:1), and Paul delineates Titus's role with regard to various groups in the church, including older men, older women, young women, young men, and servants (2:2–10). The knowledge of Christ must affect a transformation in each of these groups so that their testimony will "adorn the doctrine of God" (2:10). The second doctrinal statement of Titus (2:11–14) gives the basis for the appeals Paul has just made for righteous living. God in His grace redeems believers from being slaves of sin, assuring them the "blessed hope" of the coming of Christ that will eventually be realized. Paul urges Titus to authoritatively proclaim these truths (2:15).

In chapter 3, Paul moves from conduct in groups (2:1–10) to conduct in general (3:1–11). The behavior of believers as citizens must be different from the behavior of unbelievers because of their regeneration and renewal by the Holy Spirit. The third doctrinal statement in this book (3:4–7) emphasizes the kindness, love, and mercy of God who saves us "Not by works of righteousness which we have done" (3:5). Nevertheless, the need for good deeds as a result of salvation is stressed six times in the three chapters of Titus (1:16; 2:7, 14; 3:1, 8, 14). Paul exhorts Titus to deal firmly with dissenters who would cause factions and controversies (3:9–11) and closes the letter with three instructions, a greeting, and a benediction (3:12–15).

FOCUS	APPOINT ELDERS		SET THINGS IN ORDER	
REFERENCE	1:1————————1:10		—————2:1———————	3:1————————3:15
DIVISION	ORDAIN QUALIFIED ELDERS	REBUKE FALSE TEACHERS	SPEAK SOUND DOCTRINE	MAINTAIN GOOD WORKS
TOPIC	PROTECTION OF SOUND DOCTRINE		PRACTICE OF SOUND DOCTRINE	
	ORGANIZATION	OFFENDERS	OPERATION	OBEDIENCE
LOCATION	PROBABLY WRITTEN IN CORINTH			
TIME	C. A.D. 63			

OUTLINE OF TITUS

CHAPTER 1

Introduction

PAUL, a servant of God, and an apostle of Jesus Christ, according to the faith of God's elect, and the acknowledging of the truth which is after godliness;

2 In hope of eternal life, which God, that cannot lie, promised before the world began;

3 But hath in due times ᵀmanifested his word through preaching, which is committed unto me according to the commandment of God our Saviour;   *revealed*

4 ᴿTo Titus, *mine* own son after the common faith: Grace, mercy, *and* peace, from God the Father and the Lord Jesus Christ our Saviour.   2 Cor. 2:13; Gal. 2:3

Ordain Qualified Elders

5 For this cause left I thee in Crete, that thou shouldest set in order the things that are wanting, and ordain ᵀelders in every city, as I had appointed thee: *presbyters*

6 If any be ᵀblameless, the husband of one wife, having ᵀfaithful children not accused of riot or unruly.   *above reproach • obedient*

7 For a ᵀbishop must be blameless, as the steward of God; not selfwilled, not soon angry, not given to wine, no ᵀstriker, not given to filthy lucre;   *overseer • brawler*

8 But a lover of hospitality, a lover of good men, sober, just, holy, temperate;

9 Holding fast the faithful word as he hath been taught, that he may be able by sound doctrine both to exhort and to ᵀconvince the ᵀgainsayers.   *convict • opposition*

Rebuke False Teachers

10 ᴿFor there are many ᴿunruly and vain talkers and deceivers, specially they of the ᵀcircumcision: Acts 15:1 • Rom. 16:18 • *Jews*

11 Whose mouths must be stopped, who subvert whole houses, teaching things which they ought not, for filthy lucre's sake.

12 One of themselves, *even* a prophet of their own, said, The Cre′-tians *are* alway liars, evil beasts, ᵀslow bellies.   *idle gluttons*

13 This witness is true. ᴿWherefore rebuke them sharply, that they may be sound in the faith;   2 Cor. 13:10

14 Not giving heed to Jewish ᵀfables, and ᴿcommandmentsᵀ of men, that turn from the truth.   *theories* • Is. 29:13; Matt. 15:9 • *dictates*

15 ᴿUnto the pure all things *are* pure: but unto them that are defiled and unbelieving *is* nothing pure; but even their mind and conscience is defiled.   1 Cor. 6:12

16 They profess that they know God; but in works they deny *him*, being ᵀabominable, and disobedient, and unto every good work ᵀreprobate.   *evil • worthless*

CHAPTER 2

Speak Sound Doctrine

BUT speak thou the things which ᵀbecome ᴿsound doctrine: *are suitable to • v. 9*

2 That the ᵀaged men be ᵀsober, grave, temperate, sound in faith, in ᵀcharity, in ᵀpatience.   *older • sensible • love • endurance*

3 ᴿThe aged women likewise, that *they be* in behaviour as becometh holiness, not false accusers, not given to much wine, teachers of good things;   [1 Tim. 2:9, 10; 1 Pet. 3:3, 4]

1:2 Promise of God—Often the Christian will doubt his salvation simply because he doesn't feel saved, not understanding that the basis for that salvation is the promise of God and not emotional feelings. In fact, the entire Trinity is involved in this.
a. The promise and work of the Father in our salvation. He has promised to graciously accept in Christ all repenting sinners (Page 1162—Eph. 1:6; Page 1178—Col. 3:3). This means a Christian has the right to be in heaven someday, for he is in Christ. God guarantees to us that He will work out all things for our good (Page 1115—Rom. 8:28).
b. The promise and work of the Son. He has promised us eternal life (Page 1047—John 5:24) and abundant life (Page 1054—John 10:10). This covers not only our final destiny in heaven, but also our present Christian service here on earth. He is, in fact, right now praying for us and ministering to us at His Father's right hand (Page 1218—Heb. 8:1; 9:24).
c. The promise and work of the Holy Spirit. The Holy Spirit is said to indwell the believer (Page 1059—John 14:16). In addition, He places all believing sinners into the body of Christ, thus assuring us of union with God Himself (Page 1134—1 Cor. 12:13).
   Now turn to Page 1252—1 John 3:24: Witness of the Spirit.

4 That they may ᵀteach the young women to be ᵀsober, to love their husbands, to love their children,   *train · responsible*

5 *To be* discreet, chaste, keepers at home, good, obedient to their own husbands, that the word of God be not blasphemed.

6 Young men likewise exhort to be ᵀsober minded.   *self-controlled*

7 In all things shewing thyself a pattern of good works: in doctrine *shewing* ᵀuncorruptness, gravity, sincerity,   *soundness*

8 Sound speech, that cannot be condemned; that he that is of the ᵀcontrary part may be ᵀashamed, having no evil thing to say of you.   *opposition · embarrassed in his stand*

9 *Exhort* servants to be obedient unto their own masters, *and* to please *them* well in all *things;* not answering again;

10 Not purloining, but shewing all good fidelity; that they may adorn the doctrine of God our Saviour in all things.

11 For ᴿthe grace of God that bringeth salvation hath appeared to all men,   Eph. 2:8

12 Teaching us that, denying ungodliness and worldly lusts, we should live soberly, righteously, and godly, in this present world;

13 ᴿLooking for that blessed hope, and the glorious appearing of the great God and our Saviour Jesus Christ;   1 Cor. 1:7

14 ᴿWho gave himself for us, that he might ᵀredeem us from all iniquity, and purify unto himself a peculiar people, zealous of good works.   Is. 53:12; Gal. 1:4 ★ · *rescue*

15 These things speak, and ᴿexhort,ᵀ and ᵀrebuke with all authority. Let no man despise thee.   2 Tim. 4:2 · *urge · point out error*

CHAPTER 3

Maintain Good Works

PUT them in mind to be subject to principalities and powers, to obey magistrates, to be ready to every good work,

2 To speak evil of no man, ᵀto be no brawlers, *but* gentle, shewing all ᵀmeekness unto all men.   *not to be contentious · gentleness*

3 For we ourselves also were sometimes foolish, disobedient, deceived, serving divers lusts and pleasures, living in malice and envy, hateful, *and* hating one another.

4 But after that the kindness and love of God our Saviour toward man appeared,

5 Not by works of righteousness which we have done, but according to his mercy he saved us, by the washing of regeneration, and renewing of the Holy Ghost;

6 Which he shed on us ᵀabundantly through Jesus Christ our Saviour;   *richly*

7 That being ᵀjustified by his grace, ᴿwe should be made heirs according to the hope of eternal life.   *cleared of all guilt* · [Rom. 8:23]

8 *This is* a faithful saying, and these things I will that thou affirm constantly, that they which have believed in God might be careful to maintain good works. These things are good and profitable unto men.

9 But avoid foolish questions, and genealogies, and contentions, and strivings about the law; for they are unprofitable and vain.

10 A man that is an heretick after the first and second admonition reject;

11 Knowing that ᵀhe that is such is ᵀsubverted, and sinneth, being condemned of himself.   *such a person · perverted*

Conclusion

12 When I shall send Ar'-te-mas unto thee, or ᴿTych'-i-cus, be diligent to come unto me to Ni-cop'-o-lis: for I have ᵀdetermined there to winter.   Acts 20:4 · *decided*

13 Bring Ze'-nas the lawyer and ᴿA-pol'-los on their journey diligently, that nothing be ᵀwanting unto them.   Acts 18:24 · *lacking*

14 And let ᵀour's also learn to ᵀmaintain good works for necessary uses, that they be not unfruitful.   *our people · profess honest trades*

15 All that are with me ᵀsalute thee. Greet them that love us in the faith. ᵀGrace *be* with you all. A-men'.   *greet · God's grace*

3:5 The Work of the Holy Spirit in Salvation—There are three wonderful works performed by the Holy Spirit in preparing unsaved people to become Christians.

a. The work of the Holy Spirit in restraining. Satan would enjoy nothing more than to destroy people before they make their decision to accept Christ as Saviour. But the Holy Spirit prevents this from occurring (Page 699—Is. 59:19).

b. The work of the Holy Spirit in convicting. Mankind's sin and righteousness are exposed by the Holy Spirit (Page 1061—John 16:8). There are two well-known examples of sinners being convicted by the Holy Spirit in the Book of Acts. Felix, a Roman governor, actually trembles under conviction as he hears Paul preach (Page 1100—Acts 24:25). The other case involves King Agrippa who responds to a gospel message by saying: "Almost thou persuadest me to be a Christian" (Page 1102—Acts 26:28).

c. The work of the Holy Spirit in regenerating. When a repenting sinner accepts Christ as Saviour he is given a new nature by the Holy Spirit. See Second Corinthians 5:17. Jesus carefully explained this ministry of the Holy Spirit to Nicodemus (Page 1044—John 3:3–7).

Now turn to Page 1129—1 Cor. 6:19: The Work of the Holy Spirit in Christian Living.

PHILEMON

THE BOOK OF PHILEMON

Does Christian brotherly love really work, even in situations of extraordinary tension and difficulty? Will it work, for example, between a prominent slave owner and one of his runaway slaves? Paul has no doubt! He writes a "postcard" to Philemon, his beloved brother and fellow worker, on behalf of Onesimus—a deserter, thief, and formerly worthless slave, but now Philemon's brother in Christ. With much tact and tenderness, Paul asks Philemon to receive Onesimus back with the same gentleness with which he would receive Paul himself. Any debt Onesimus owes, Paul promises to make good. Knowing Philemon, Paul is confident that brotherly love and forgiveness will carry the day.

Since this letter is addressed to Philemon in verse 1, it became known as *Pros Philēmona*, "To Philemon." Like First and Second Timothy and Titus, it is addressed to an individual, but unlike the Pastoral Epistles, Philemon is also addressed to a family and a church (v. 2).

THE AUTHOR OF PHILEMON

The authenticity of Philemon was not called into question until the fourth century, when certain theologians concluded that its lack of doctrinal content made it unworthy of the apostle Paul. But men like Jerome and Chrysostom soon vindicated this epistle, and it was not challenged again until the nineteenth century. Some radical critics who denied the authenticity of Colossians also turned against the Pauline authorship of Philemon because of the close connection between the two epistles (e.g., the same people are associated with Paul in both letters: cf. Col. 4:9, 10, 12, 14 with Philem. 10, 23, 24). The general consensus of scholarship, however, recognizes Philemon as Paul's work. There could have been no doctrinal motive for its forgery, and it is supported externally by consistent tradition and internally by no less than three references to Paul (vv. 1, 9, 19).

THE TIME OF PHILEMON

Reconstructing the background of this letter, it appears that a slave named Onesimus had robbed or in some other way wronged his master Philemon and had escaped. He had made his way from Colosse to Rome where he had found relative safety among the masses in the Imperial City. Somehow Onesimus had come into contact with Paul: it is possible that he had even sought out the apostle for help. (Onesimus no doubt had heard Philemon speak of Paul.) Paul had led him to Christ (v. 10), and although Onesimus had become a real asset to Paul, both knew that as a Christian, Onesimus had a responsibility to return to Philemon. That day came when Paul wrote his epistle to the Colossians. Tychicus was the bearer of that letter. Paul decided to send Onesimus along with Tychicus to Colosse (Col. 4:7-9; Philem. 12), knowing that it would be safer, in view of slave-catchers, to send Onesimus with a companion.

Philemon is one of the four Prison Epistles (see Ephesians, Philippians, and especially "The Time of Colossians" for background). It was written in A.D. 60 or 61 and dispatched at the same time as Colossians during Paul's first Roman imprisonment (see vv. 1, 9, 10, 13, 23). Philemon 22 reflects Paul's confident hope of release: "Prepare me also a lodging: for I trust that through your prayers I shall be given unto you."

Philemon was a resident of Colosse (Col. 4:9, 17; Philem. 1, 2) and a convert of Paul (v. 19), perhaps through an encounter with Paul in Ephesus during Paul's third missionary journey. Philemon's house was large enough to serve as the meeting place for the church there (v. 2). He was benevolent to other believers (vv. 5-7), and his son Archippus evidently held a position of leadership in the church (Col. 4:17; Philem. 2). Philemon may have had other slaves in addition to Onesimus, and he was not alone as a slave owner among the Colossian believers (Col. 4:1). Thus this letter and his response would provide guidelines for other master-slave relationships.

According to Roman law, runaway slaves such as Onesimus could be severely punished or condemned to a violent death. It is doubtful that Onesimus would have returned to Philemon even with this letter if he had not become a believer in Christ.

THE CHRIST OF PHILEMON

The forgiveness that the believer finds in Christ is beautifully portrayed by analogy in Philemon. Onesimus, guilty of a great offense (vv. 11, 18), is motivated by Paul's love to intercede on his behalf (vv. 10-17). Paul lays aside his rights (v. 8) and becomes Onesimus's substitute by assuming his debt (vv. 18, 19). By Philemon's gracious act, Onesimus is restored and placed in a new relationship (vv. 15, 16). In this analogy, we are like Onesimus. Paul's advocacy before Philemon is parallel to Christ's work of mediation before the Father. Onesimus was condemned by law but saved by grace.

KEYS TO PHILEMON

Key Word: Forgiveness from Slavery— Philemon develops the transition from bondage to brotherhood that is brought about by

Christian love and forgiveness. Just as Philemon was shown mercy through the grace of Christ, so he must graciously forgive his repentant runaway who has returned as a brother in Christ. Paul writes this letter as his personal appeal that Philemon receive Onesimus even as he would receive Paul. This letter is also addressed to other Christians in Philemon's circle, because Paul wants it to have an impact on the Colossian church as a whole.

Key Verses: Philemon 16, 17—"Not now as a servant, but above a servant, a brother beloved, specially to me, but how much more unto thee, both in the flesh, and in the Lord? If thou count me therefore a partner, receive him as myself" (vv. 16, 17).

SURVEY OF PHILEMON

This briefest of Paul's epistles (only 334 words in the Greek text) is a model of courtesy, discretion, and loving concern for the forgiveness of one who would otherwise face the sentence of death. This tactful and highly personal letter can be divided into three components: prayer of thanksgiving for Philemon (vv. 1–7); petition of Paul for Onesimus (vv. 8–16); promise of Paul to Philemon (vv. 17–25).

Prayer of Thanksgiving for Philemon (vv. 1-7): Writing this letter as a "prisoner of Jesus Christ," Paul addresses it personally to Philemon (a Christian leader in Colosse), to Apphia and Archippus (evidently Philemon's wife and son), as well as to the church that meets in Philemon's house. The main body of this compact letter begins with a prayer of thanksgiving for Philemon's faith and love.

Petition of Paul for Onesimus (vv. 8-16): Basing his appeal on Philemon's character, Paul refuses to command Philemon to pardon and receive Onesimus. Instead, Paul seeks to persuade his friend of his Christian responsibility to forgive even as he was forgiven by Christ. Paul urges Philemon not to punish Onesimus but to receive him "not now as a servant" but as "a brother beloved" (v. 16).

Promise of Paul to Philemon (vv. 17-25): Paul places Onesimus's debt on his account, but then reminds Philemon of the greater spiritual debt which Philemon himself owes as a convert to Christ (vv. 17–19).

Paul closes this effective epistle with a hopeful request (v. 22), greetings from his companions (vv. 23, 24), and a benediction (v. 25). The fact that it was preserved indicates Philemon's favorable response to Paul's pleas.

FOCUS	PRAYER OF THANKSGIVING	PETITION FOR ONESIMUS	PROMISE TO PHILEMON
REFERENCE	1 —————————————— 8	———————————————— 17	————————————————— 25
DIVISION	COMMENDATION OF PHILEMON'S LOVE	INTERCESSION FOR ONESIMUS	CONFIDENCE IN PHILEMON'S OBEDIENCE
TOPIC	PRAISE OF PHILEMON	PLEA OF PAUL	PLEDGE OF PAUL
	CHARACTER OF PHILEMON	CONVERSION OF ONESIMUS	CONFIDENCE OF PAUL
LOCATION	ROME		
TIME	c. A.D. 60 – 61		

OUTLINE OF PHILEMON

I. The Prayer of Thanksgiving for Philemon...1–7

II. The Petition of Paul for Onesimus........8–16

III. The Promise of Paul to Philemon........17–25

The Prayer of Thanksgiving for Philemon

PAUL, a prisoner of Jesus Christ, and Timothy *our* brother, unto Phi-le'-mon our dearly beloved, ᴿand fellowlabourer,   *v. 24*

2 And to *our* beloved Ap'-phi-a, and Ar-chip'-pus our fellowsoldier, ᴿand to the church in thy house: Rom. 16:5; 1 Cor. 16:19

3 Grace to you, and peace, from God our Father and the Lord Jesus Christ.

4 ᴿI thank my God, making mention of thee always in my prayers,   2 Thess. 1:3

5 ᴿHearing of thy love and faith, which thou hast toward the Lord Jesus, and toward all saints;   Eph. 1:15; Col. 1:4

6 That the ᵀcommunication of thy faith may become effectual ᴿby the acknowledging of every ᵀgood thing which is in you in Christ Jesus.   *sharing • Phil. 1:9 • blessing*

7 For we have great joy and consolation in thy love, because the bowels of the saints are refreshed by thee, brother.

The Petition of Paul for Onesimus

8 Wherefore, though I might be much bold in Christ to ᵀenjoin thee that which is ᵀconvenient,   *command • befitting*

9 Yet for love's sake I rather beseech *thee*, being such an one as Paul the aged, and now also a prisoner of Jesus Christ.

10 I beseech thee for my son O-nes'-i-mus, whom I have begotten in my bonds:

11 Which in time past was to thee unprofitable, but now profitable to thee and to me:

12 Whom I have sent again: thou therefore receive him, that is, mine own bowels:

13 Whom I would have retained with me,

that in thy stead he might have ministered unto me in the bonds of the gospel:

14 But without thy mind would I do nothing; that thy benefit should not be as it were of necessity, but willingly.

15 For perhaps ᴿhe therefore departed for a season, that thou shouldest receive him for ever;   Gen. 45:5–8

16 Not now as a servant, but ᵀabove a servant, ᴿa brother beloved, specially to me, but how much more unto thee, both in the flesh, and in the Lord?   *more than • Matt. 23:8*

The Promise of Paul to Philemon

17 ᴿIf thou count me therefore a partner, ᵀreceive him as myself.   *v. 12 • welcome*

18 If he hath wronged thee, or oweth *thee* ᵀought, put that on mine account;   *anything*

19 I Paul have written *it* with ᴿmine own hand, I will repay *it*: ᵀalbeit I do not say to thee how thou owest unto me even thine own self besides.   1 Cor. 16:21 • *that*

20 Yea, brother, let me have joy of thee in the Lord: refresh my bowels in the Lord.

21 ᴿHaving confidence in thy obedience I wrote unto thee, knowing that thou wilt also do more than I say.   2 Cor. 7:16

22 ᴿBut withal prepare me also a lodging: for I trust that through your prayers I shall be ᵀgiven unto you.   2 Kin. 4:10 • *released*

23 There salute thee ᴿEp'-a-phras, my fellowprisoner in Christ Jesus;   Col. 1:7

24 ᴿMarcus, Ar-is-tar'-chus, De'-mas, Lucas, my fellowlabourers.   Acts 12:12, 24

25 ᴿThe grace of our Lord Jesus Christ *be* with your spirit. A-men'.   2 Tim. 4:22

THE EPISTLE TO THE
HEBREWS

THE BOOK OF HEBREWS

Many Jewish believers, having stepped out of Judaism into Christianity, want to reverse their course in order to escape persecution by their countrymen. The writer of Hebrews exhorts them to "go on unto perfection" (6:1). His appeal is based on the superiority of Christ over the Judaic system. Christ is better than the angels, for they worship Him. He is better than Moses, for He created him. He is better than the Aaronic priesthood, for His sacrifice was once for all time. He is better than the Law, for He mediates a better covenant. In short, there is more to be gained in Christ than to be lost in Judaism. Pressing on in Christ produces tested faith, self-discipline, and a visible love seen in good works.

Although the King James Version uses the title "The Epistle of Paul the Apostle to the Hebrews," there is no early manuscript evidence to support it. The oldest and most reliable title is simply *Pros Ebraious*, "To Hebrews."

THE AUTHOR OF HEBREWS

Like the ancestry of Melchisedec, the origin of Hebrews is unknown. Uncertainty plagues not only its authorship, but also where it was written, its date, and its readership. The question of authorship delayed its recognition in the West as part of the New Testament canon in spite of early support by Clement of Rome. Not until the fourth century was it generally accepted as authoritative in the Western church, when the testimonies of Jerome and Augustine settled the issue. In the Eastern church, there was no problem of canonical acceptence because it was regarded as one of the "fourteen" epistles of Paul. The issue of its canonicity was again raised during the Reformation, but the spiritual depth and quality of Hebrews bore witness to its inspiration, despite its anonymity.

Hebrews 13:18–24 tells us that this book was not anonymous to the original readers; they evidently knew the author. For some reason, however, early church tradition is divided over the identity of the author. Part of the church attributed it to Paul; others preferred Barnabas, Luke, or Clement; and some chose anonymity. Thus, external evidence will not help determine the author.

Internal evidence must be the final court of appeal, but here, too, the results are ambiguous. Some aspects of the language, style, and theology of Hebrews are very similar to Paul's epistles, and the author also refers to Timothy (13:23). However, significant differences have led the majority of biblical scholars to reject Pauline authorship of this book: (1) The Greek style of Hebrews is far more polished and refined than that found in any of Paul's recognized epistles. (2) In view of Paul's consistent claims to be an apostle and an eyewitness of Christ, it is very doubtful that he would have used the phraseology found in 2:3: "which at the first began to be spoken by the Lord, and was confirmed unto us by them that heard." (3) The lack of Paul's customary salutation, which includes his name, goes against the firm pattern found in all his other epistles. (4) While Paul used both the Hebrew text and the Septuagint to quote from the Old Testament, the writer of Hebrews apparently did not know Hebrew and quoted exclusively from the Septuagint. (5) Paul's common use of compound titles to refer to the Son of God is not followed in Hebrews, which usually refers to Him as Christ, Jesus, and Lord. (6) Hebrews concentrates on Christ's present priestly ministry, but Paul's writings have very little to say about the present work of Christ. Thus, Hebrews appears not to have been written by Paul although the writer shows a Pauline influence. The authority of Hebrews in no way depends upon Pauline authorship, especially since it does not claim to have been written by Paul.

Tertullian referred to Barnabas as the author of Hebrews, but it is unlikely that this resident of Jerusalem (Acts 4:36, 37) would include himself as one of those who relied on others for eyewitness testimony about Jesus (2:3). Other suggestions include Luke, Clement of Rome, Apollos, Silvanus (Silas), Philip, and even Priscilla. Some of these are possibilities, but we must agree with the third-century theologian Origen who wrote: "Who it was that really wrote the Epistle, God only knows."

THE TIME OF HEBREWS

Because of the exclusive use of the Septuagint (Greek translation of the Hebrew Old Testament) and the elegant Greek style found in Hebrews, some recent scholars have argued that this book was written to a gentile readership. However, the bulk of the evidence favors the traditional view that the original recipients of this letter were Jewish Christians. In addition to the ancient title "To Hebrews," there is also the frequent use of the Old Testament as an unquestioned authority, the assumed knowledge of the sacrificial ritual, and the many contrasts between Christianity and Judaism, which are designed to prevent the readers from lapsing into Judaism.

Many places have been suggested for the locality of the readers, but this letter's destination cannot be determined with any certainty. In the past, Jerusalem was most frequently suggested, but this view is hindered by four problems: (1) It is unlikely that a book addressed to Palestineans would quote exclusively from the Septuagint rather than the Hebrew Old Testament. (2) Palestinean believers were poor (Rom. 15:26), but these readers were able to financially assist other Christians (6:10). (3) Residents of Jerusalem would not be characterized by the description in 2:3 because some would have been eyewitnesses of the ministry of Christ. (4) "Ye have not yet resisted unto blood" (12:4) does not fit the situation in Jerusalem. The majority view today is that the recipients of Hebrews probably lived in Rome. The statement "They of Italy salute you" in 13:24 seems to suggest that Italians away from Italy are sending their greetings home.

The recipients of this letter were believers (3:1) who had come to faith through the testimony of eyewitnesses of Christ (2:3). They were not novices (5:12), and they had successfully endured hardships because of their stand for the gospel (10:32–34). Unfortunately, they had become "dull of hearing" (5:11) and were in danger of drifting away (2:1; 3:12). This made them particularly susceptible to the renewed persecutions that were coming upon them (12:4–12), and the author found it necessary to check the downward spiral with "the word of exhortation" (13:22). While there is disagreement over the specific danger involved, the classic position that the readers were on the verge of lapsing into Judaism to avoid persecution directed at Christians seems to be supported by the whole tenor of the book. Hebrews' repeated emphasis on the superiority of Christianity over Judaism would have been pointless if the readers were about to return to Gnosticism or heathenism.

The place of writing is unknown, but a reasonable estimate of the date can be made. Hebrews was quoted in A.D. 95 by Clement of Rome, but its failure to mention the ending of the Old Testament sacrificial system with the destruction of Jerusalem in A.D. 70 indicates that it was written prior to that date. Timothy was still alive (13:23), persecution was mounting, and the old Jewish system was about to be removed (12:26, 27). All this suggests a date between A.D. 64 and 68.

✝ THE CHRIST OF HEBREWS

Christ is our eternal High Priest according to the order of Melchisedec. He identified with man in His incarnation and offered no less a sacrifice than Himself on our behalf.

Hebrews presents Christ as the divine-human Prophet, Priest, and King. His deity (1:1–3, 8) and humanity (2:9, 14, 17, 18) are asserted with equal force, and over twenty titles are used to describe His attributes and accomplishments (e.g., Heir of all things, Apostle and High Priest, Mediator, Author and Finisher of faith). He is superior to all who went before and offers the supreme sacrifice, priesthood, and covenant.

🔑 KEYS TO HEBREWS

Key Word: The Superiority of Christ— The basic theme of Hebrews is found in the word *better*, describing the superiority of Christ in His person and work (1:4; 6:9; 7:7, 19, 22; 8:6; 9:23; 10:34; 11:16, 35, 40; 12:24). The words *perfect* and *heavenly* are also prominent. He offers a better revelation, position, priesthood, covenant, sacrifice, and power. The writer develops this theme to prevent the readers from giving up the substance for the shadow by abandoning Christianity and retreating into the old Judaic system. This epistle is also written to exhort them to become mature in Christ and to put away their spiritual dullness and degeneration. Thus, it places heavy stress on doctrine, concentrating on christology and soteriology (the study of salvation).

Key Verses: Hebrews 4:14–16 and 12:1, 2— "Seeing then that we have a great high priest, that is passed into the heavens, Jesus the Son of God, let us hold fast *our* profession. For we have not an high priest which cannot be touched with the feeling of our infirmities; but was in all points tempted like as *we are, yet* without sin. Let us therefore come boldly unto the throne of grace, that we may obtain mercy, and find grace to help in time of need" (4:14–16).

"Wherefore seeing we also are compassed about with so great a cloud of witnesses, let us lay aside every weight, and the sin which doth so easily beset *us,* and let us run with patience the race that is set before us, Looking unto Jesus the author and finisher of *our* faith; who for the joy that was set before him endured the cross, despising the shame, and is set down at the right hand of the throne of God" (12:1, 2).

Key Chapter: Hebrews 11—The Hall of Fame of the Scriptures is located in Hebrews 11 and records those who willingly took God at His word even when there was nothing to cling to but His promise. Inherent to all those listed is the recognition that "without faith *it is* impossible to please *him:* for he that cometh to God must believe that he is, and *that* he is a rewarder of them that diligently seek him" (Heb. 11:6).

🅰 SURVEY OF HEBREWS

Hebrews stands alone among the New Testament Epistles in its style and approach, and it is the only New Testament book whose authorship remains a real mystery. This profound work builds a case for the superiority of Christ through a cumulative argument in which

Christ is presented as "better" in every respect. In His person He is better than the angels, Moses, and Joshua; and in His performance He provides a better priesthood, covenant, sanctuary, and sacrifice. Evidently, the readers are in danger of reverting to Judaism because of the suffering they are beginning to experience for their faith in Christ. However, by doing so, they would be retreating from the substance back into the shadow. In addition to his positive presentation of the supremacy of Christ, the writer intersperses five solemn warnings about the peril of turning away from Christ (2:1–4; 3:7—4:13; 5:11—6:20; 10:19–39; 12:25–29). These parenthetical warnings include cautions against neglect (2:1–4) and refusal (12:25–29). After using the Old Testament to demonstrate the superiority of Christ's person (1:1—4:13) and the superiority of Christ's work (4:14—10:18), the writer applies these truths in a practical way to show the superiority of the Christian's walk of faith (10:19—13:25).

The Superiority of Christ's Person (1:1—4:13): Instead of the usual salutation, this epistle immediately launches into its theme—the supremacy of Christ even over the Old Testament prophets (1:1–3). Christianity is built upon the highest form of divine disclosure: the personal revelation of God through His incarnate Son. Christ is therefore greater than the prophets, and He is also greater than the angels, the mediators of the Mosaic Law (1:4—2:18; see Acts 7:53; Heb. 2:2). This is seen in His name, His position, His worship by the angels, and His incarnation. The Son of God partook of flesh and blood and was "made like unto *his* brethren" in all things (2:17) in order to bring "many sons to glory" (2:10). Christ is also superior to Moses (3:1–6), for Moses was a servant in the house of God, but Christ is the Son over God's household. Because of these truths, the readers are exhorted to avoid

the divine judgment that is visited upon unbelief (3:7—4:13). Their disbelief had prevented the generation of the Exodus from becoming the generation of the conquest, and the rest that Christ offers is so much greater than what was provided by Joshua. The readers are therefore urged to enter the eternal rest that is possessed by faith in Christ.

The Superiority of Christ's Work (4:14—10:18): The high priesthood of Christ is superior to the Aaronic priesthood (4:14—7:28). Because of His incarnation, Christ can "be touched with the feeling of our infirmities," having been "in all points tempted as *we are, yet* without sin" (4:15). Christ was not a Levite, but He qualified for a higher priesthood according to the order of Melchisedec. The superiority of Melchisedec to Levi is seen in the fact that Levi, in effect, paid tithes through Abraham to Melchisedec (7:9, 10). Abraham was blessed by Melchisedec, and "the less is blessed of the better" (7:7). The parenthetical warning in 5:11—6:20 exhorts the readers to "go on unto perfection" by moving beyond the basics of salvation and repentance.

By divine oath (7:21), Christ has become a permanent and perfect high priest and "the mediator of a better covenant" (8:6). The new covenant has made the old covenant obsolete (8:6–13). Our great high priest similarly ministers in "a greater and more perfect tabernacle, not made with hands, that is to say, not of this building" (9:11). And unlike the former priests, He offers Himself as a sinless and voluntary sacrifice once and for all (9:1—10:18).

The Superiority of the Christian's Walk of Faith (10:19—13:25): The author applies what he has been saying about the superiority of Christ by warning his readers of the danger of discarding their faith in Christ (10:19–39). The faith that the readers must maintain is defined in 11:1–3 and illustrated in 11:4–40. The triumphs and accomplishments of faith in the lives of Old

FOCUS	CHRIST'S PERSON			CHRIST'S WORK			THE WALK OF FAITH		
REFERENCE	1:1———	1:4———	3:1———	4:14———	8:1———	9:1———	10:19———	12:1———	13:1–13:25
DIVISION	CHRIST OVER PROPHETS	CHRIST OVER ANGELS	CHRIST OVER MOSES	PRIEST-HOOD	COVENANT	SANCTUARY AND SACRIFICE	ASSURANCE OF FAITH	ENDURANCE OF FAITH	EXHORTATION TO LOVE
TOPIC	MAJESTY OF CHRIST			MINISTRY OF CHRIST			MINISTERS FOR CHRIST		
	DOCTRINE						DISCIPLINE		
LOCATION	PLACE OF WRITING UNKNOWN								
TIME	c. A.D. 64-68								

Testament believers should encourage the recipients of "some better thing" (11:40) in Christ to look "unto Jesus the author and finisher of *our* faith" (12:2). Just as Jesus endured great hostility, those who believe in Him will sometimes have to endure divine discipline for the sake of holiness (12:1–29). The readers are warned not to turn away from Christ during such times, but to place

their hope in Him. The character of their lives must be shaped by their dedication to Christ (13:1–19), and this will be manifested in their love of each other through their hospitality, concern, purity, contentment, and obedience. The author concludes this epistle with one of the finest benedictions in Scripture (13:20, 21) and some personal words (13:22–25).

OUTLINE OF HEBREWS

CHAPTER 1

The Superiority of Christ over the Prophets

GOD, who at sundry times and in ᵀdivers manners spake in time past unto the fathers by the prophets,   *various*

2 Hath in these last days spoken unto us by *his* Son, whom he hath appointed heir of all things, by whom also he made the worlds;

3 ᴿWho being the brightness of *his* glory, and the express image of his person, and upholding all things by the word of his power, ᴿwhen he had by himself ᵀpurged our sins, ᴿsat down on the right hand of the Majesty on high;   John 1:14 • [7:27] • *cleansed* • Ps. 68:18; 110:1 ★

Christ Is Superior Because of His Deity

4 Being made so much better than the angels, as ᴿhe hath by inheritance obtained a more excellent name than they.   [Phil. 2:9, 10]

5 For unto which of the angels said he at any time, ᴿTHOU ART MY SON, THIS DAY HAVE I BEGOTTEN THEE? And again, ᴿI WILL BE TO HIM A FATHER, AND HE SHALL BE TO ME A SON?   Ps. 2:7 ★ • 2 Sam. 7:14

6 And again, when he bringeth in the firstbegotten into the world, he saith, AND LET ALL THE ANGELS OF GOD WORSHIP HIM.

7 And of the angels he saith, ᴿWHO MAKETH HIS ANGELS SPIRITS, AND HIS MINISTERS A FLAME OF FIRE.   Ps. 104:4

8 But ᵀunto the Son *he saith,* ᴿTHY THRONE, O GOD, *IS* FOR EVER AND EVER: A SCEPTRE OF RIGHTEOUSNESS *IS* THE SCEPTRE OF THY KINGDOM.   *of* • Deut. 33:27; Ps. 45:6 ★

9 ᴿTHOU HAST LOVED RIGHTEOUSNESS, AND HATED INIQUITY; THEREFORE GOD, *EVEN* THY GOD, HATH ANOINTED THEE WITH THE OIL OF GLADNESS ABOVE THY FELLOWS. Ps. 45:7; Is. 61:3 ★

10 And, ᴿTHOU, LORD, IN THE BEGINNING HAST LAID THE FOUNDATION OF THE EARTH; AND THE HEAVENS ARE THE WORKS OF THINE HANDS: Ps. 102:25

11 THEYᴿ SHALL PERISH; BUT THOU REMAINEST;ᴿ AND THEY ALL SHALL WAX OLD AS DOTH A GARMENT;   Ps. 102:26 • Is. 51:6

12 ᴿAND AS A VESTURE SHALT THOU FOLD THEM UP, AND THEY SHALL BE CHANGED: BUT THOU ART THE SAME, AND THY YEARS SHALL NOT FAIL.   Ps. 102:26

13 But to which of the angels said he at any time, ᴿSIT ON MY RIGHT HAND, UNTIL I MAKE THINE ENEMIES THY FOOTSTOOL? Ps. 110:1

14 Are they not all ᵀministering spirits, sent forth to minister for them who shall be ᴿheirs of salvation?   *serving* • Rom. 8:17

CHAPTER 2

First Warning: Danger of Neglect

THEREFORE we ought to give the more earnest heed to the things which we have heard, lest at any time we ᵀshould let *them* slip.   *drift away from them*

2 For if the word spoken by angels was ᵀstedfast, and ᴿevery transgression and disobedience received a ᵀjust recompence of reward;   *certain* • Num. 15:30 • *fair repayment*

3 How shall we escape, if we neglect so great salvation; which at the first began to be spoken by the Lord, and was confirmed unto us by them that heard *him;*

4 God also bearing *them* witness, ᴿboth with signs and wonders, and with ᵀdivers miracles, and gifts of the Holy Ghost, according to his own will?   Acts 2:22 • *various*

Christ Is Superior Because of His Humanity

5 For unto the angels hath he not put ᵀin subjection ᴿthe world to come, whereof we speak.   *under control* • [2 Pet. 3:13]

6 But one in a certain place testified, saying, ᴿWHAT IS MAN, THAT THOU ART MINDFUL OF HIM? OR THE SON OF MAN, THAT THOU VISITEST HIM?   Ps. 8:4

7 ᴿTHOU MADEST HIM A LITTLE LOWER THAN THE ANGELS; THOU CROWNEDST HIM WITH GLORY AND HONOUR, AND DIDST SET HIM OVER THE WORKS OF THY HANDS: Ps. 8:5, 6

8 ᴿTHOU HAST PUT ALL THINGS IN SUBJECTION UNDER HIS FEET. For in that he put all in subjection under him, he left nothing *that is* not put under him. But now ᴿwe see not yet all things put under him.   Ps. 8:6–8 • 1 Cor. 15:25

9 But we see Jesus, who was made a little lower than the angels for the suffering of death, ᴿcrowned with glory and honour; that he by the grace of God should taste ᴿdeath for every man.   Acts 2:33 • [John 3:16]

10 For it became him, for whom *are* all things, and by whom *are* all things, in bringing many sons unto glory, to make the ᵀcaptain of their salvation ᵀperfect through sufferings.   *author* • *complete; mature*

11 For ᴿboth he that ᵀsanctifieth and they who are sanctified *are* all of one: for which cause he is not ᵀashamed to call them brethren,   10:10 • *sets apart* • *embarrassed*

12 Saying, I WILL DECLARE THY NAME UNTO MY BRETHREN, IN THE MIDST OF THE CHURCH WILL I SING PRAISE UNTO THEE.

13 And again, ᴿI WILL PUT MY TRUST IN HIM. And again, BEHOLD I AND THE CHILDREN WHICH GOD HATH GIVEN ME.   Is. 8:17, 18

14 Forasmuch then as the children are partakers of flesh and blood, he also himself likewise took part of the same; that through death he might destroy him that had the power of death, that is, the devil;

15 And ᴿdeliver them who ᴿthrough fear of death were all their lifetime ᵀsubject to bondage.   Is. 42:7; 49:9; 61:1 ★ • [Luke 1:74] • *slaves*

16 For verily he took not on *him the nature of* angels; but he ᵀtook on *him the* seed of Abraham.   *giveth help to*

17 Wherefore in all things it behoved him to be made like unto *his* brethren, that he might be a merciful and faithful high priest in things *pertaining* to God, to make reconciliation for the sins of the people.

18 ᴿFor in that he himself hath suffered being ᵀtempted, he is able to ᵀsuccour them that are tempted.   [4:15, 16] • *tested • help*

CHAPTER 3

Christ Is Superior to Moses in His Work

WHEREFORE, holy brethren, partakers of the heavenly calling, consider the Apostle and ᴿHigh Priest of our ᵀprofession, Christ Jesus;   Ps. 110:4 * • *confession*

2 Who was faithful to him that ᵀappointed him, as also ᴿMoses *was faithful* in all his house.   *chose* • Num. 12:7

3 For this *man* was counted worthy of more ᵀglory than Moses, inasmuch as ᴿhe who hath builded the house hath more honour than the house.   *praise* • Zech. 6:12

4 For every house is builded by some *man;* but he that built all things *is* God.

Christ Is Superior to Moses in His Person

5 And Moses verily *was* faithful in all his house, as a servant, for a testimony of those things which were to be spoken after;

6 But Christ as a son over his own house; whose house are we, ᴿif we hold fast ᵀthe confidence and the rejoicing of the hope firm unto the end.   [Matt. 10:22] • *our boldness*

Danger of Hardening the Heart

7 Wherefore (as the Holy Ghost saith, ᴿTO DAY IF YE WILL HEAR HIS VOICE,   Ps. 95:7

8 ᴿHARDEN NOT YOUR HEARTS, AS IN THE PROVOCATION, IN THE DAY OF TEMPTATION IN THE WILDERNESS: Ps. 95:8

9 ᴿWHEN YOUR FATHERS TEMPTED ME, PROVED ME, AND SAW MY WORKS FORTY YEARS.   Ps. 95:9, 10

10 ᴿWHEREFORE I WAS GRIEVED WITH THAT GENERATION, AND SAID, THEY DO ALWAY ERR IN *THEIR* HEART; AND THEY HAVE NOT KNOWN MY WAYS.   Ps. 95:10

11 ᴿSO I SWARE IN MY WRATH, THEY SHALL NOT ENTER INTO MY REST.)   Ps. 95:11

12 Take heed, brethren, lest there be in any of you an evil heart of unbelief, in ᵀdeparting from the living God.   *forsaking*

13 But ᵀexhort one another daily, while it is called To day; lest any of you be hardened through the deceitfulness of sin.   *urge*

14 For we are made ᵀpartakers of Christ, if we hold the beginning of our confidence ᵀstedfast unto the end;   *partners • firmly*

15 While it is said, ᴿTO DAY IF YE WILL HEAR HIS VOICE, HARDEN NOT YOUR HEARTS, AS IN THE PROVOCATION.   Ps. 95:7

16 ᴿFor some, when they had heard, did ᵀprovoke: howbeit not all that came out of Egypt by Moses.   Num. 14:2 • *rebel*

17 But with whom was he grieved forty years? *was it* not with them that had sinned, whose carcases fell in the wilderness?

18 And ᴿto whom sware he that they should not enter into his rest, but to them that ᵀbelieved not?   Num. 14:30 • *were disobedient*

19 ᴿSo we see that they could not enter in because of unbelief.   4:6

CHAPTER 4

Challenge to Enter His Rest

LET us therefore fear, lest, a promise being left *us* of entering into his rest, any of you should seem to come short of it.

2 For unto us was the gospel preached, as well as unto them: but the word preached did not profit them, not being ᵀmixed with faith in them that heard *it.*   *united by*

3 For we which have believed do enter into rest, as he said, ᴿAS I HAVE SWORN IN MY WRATH, IF THEY SHALL ENTER INTO MY REST: although the works were finished from the foundation of the world.   Ps. 95:11

4 For he spake in a certain place of the seventh *day* on this wise, AND GOD DID REST THE SEVENTH DAY FROM ALL HIS WORKS.

5 And in this *place* again, ᴿIF THEY SHALL ENTER INTO MY REST.   Ps. 95:11

6 Seeing therefore it remaineth that some must enter therein, and they to whom ᵀit was first preached entered not in because of ᵀunbelief: *the good things were • disobedience*

7 Again, he limiteth a certain day, saying in David, To day, after so long a time; as it is said, ᴿTO DAY IF YE WILL HEAR HIS VOICE, HARDEN NOT YOUR HEARTS.   Ps. 95:7

8 For if ᵀJesus ᴿhad given them rest, then would he not afterward have spoken of another day.   Joshua • Acts 7:45

9 There remaineth therefore a ᵀrest to the people of God.   *sabbath rest for*

10 For he that is entered into his rest, he also hath ᴿceased from his own works, as God *did* from his.   Rev. 14:13

11 Let us ᵀlabour therefore to enter into that rest, lest any man fall after the same example of ᵀunbelief.   *endeavour • disobedience*

12 For the word of God *is* ᵀquick, and powerful, and sharper than any twoedged sword, piercing even to the dividing asunder of soul and spirit, and of the joints and marrow, and *is* a discerner of the thoughts and intents of the heart.   *living*

13 ᴿNeither is there any creature that is ᵀnot manifest in his sight: but all things *are* naked and opened unto the eyes of him with whom we have to do.   Ps. 90:8 • *hidden*

Christ Is Superior in His Position

14 Seeing then that we have a great high priest, Rthat is passed into the heavens, Jesus the Son of God, Rlet us hold Tfast *our* profession.   7:26 • 10:23 • *firmly to*

15 For we have not an high priest which cannot be touched with the feeling of our Tinfirmities; but was in all points tempted like as *we are, yet* without sin.   *weaknesses*

16 Let us therefore come boldly unto the throne of grace, that we may obtain mercy, and find grace to help in time of need.

CHAPTER 5

Aaronic Priesthood

FOR every high priest taken from among men Ris Tordained for men in things *pertaining* to God, that he may offer both gifts and sacrifices for sins: 8:3 • *appointed*

2 Who can have compassion on the ignorant, and on them that are Tout of the way; for that he himself also is Tcompassed with infirmity.   *wayward • surrounded by weakness*

3 RAnd by reason hereof he Tought, as for the people, so also for himself, to offer for sins.   [7:27]; Lev. 9:7; 16:6, 15–17 • *is weak*

4 And no man Ttaketh this Thonour unto himself, but he that is called of God, as Rwas Aaron.   *chooses • privilege • Ex. 28:1*

Melchisedecian Priesthood

5 So also Christ Tglorified not himself to be made an high priest; but he that said unto him, RTHOU ART MY SON, TO DAY HAVE I BEGOTTEN THEE.   *exalted • Ps. 2:7 ★*

6 As he saith also in another *place*, RTHOU ART A PRIEST FOR EVER AFTER THE ORDER OF MEL-CHIS'-E-DEC.   Ps. 110:4 ★

7 Who in the days of his flesh, when he had offered up prayers and supplications with Rstrong crying and tears unto him that was able to save him from death, and was heard in that he feared;   John 11:35

8 Though he were a Son, yet learned he obedience by the things which he suffered;

9 RAnd being made perfect, he became the author of eternal salvation Runto all them that obey him;   2:10; 11:40 • Acts 5:32

10 RCalled of God an high priest after the order of Mel-chis'-e-dec.   *v. 6; 6:20; Ps. 110:4 ★*

Dullness of Hearing

11 Of whom we Rhave many things to say, and hard to be Tuttered, seeing ye are Rdull T of hearing.   [John 16:12] • *expressed* • [Matt. 13:15] • *slow*

12 For when for the time ye ought to be teachers, ye have need that one teach you again which *be* the first principles of the oracles of God; and are become such as have need of milk, and not of strong meat.

13 For every one that useth milk Tis unskilful in the word of righteousness: for he is Ra babe.   *has no experience* • Eph. 4:14

14 But strong meat belongeth to them that are of full age, *even* those who by reason of use have their senses Texercised to discern both good and evil.   *trained*

CHAPTER 6

Need for Maturity

THEREFORE Tleaving the principles of the doctrine of Christ, let us go on unto Tperfection; not laying again the foundation of repentance from dead works, and of faith toward God,   *going on from • maturity*

2 Of the doctrine of baptisms, Rand of laying on of hands, and of resurrection of the dead, and of eternal judgment.   [Acts 8:17]

3 And this will we do, if God permit.

4 For *it is* impossible for those who were once enlightened, and have tasted of Rthe heavenly gift, and Rwere made partakers of the Holy Ghost,   [John 4:10] • [Gal. 3:2, 5]

5 And have tasted the good word of God, and the powers of the Tworld to come,   *age*

6 If they shall fall away, to Trenew them again unto repentance; Rseeing they crucify to themselves the Son of God afresh, and put *him* to an open shame.   *revive* • 10:29

7 For the earth which drinketh in the rain that cometh oft upon it, and bringeth forth herbs Tmeet for them by whom it is dressed, receiveth blessing from God: *suitable*

8 RBut that which beareth thorns and briers *is* rejected, and *is* nigh unto cursing; whose end *is* to be burned.   Is. 5:6

Exhortation to Maturity

9 But, beloved, we are persuaded better things of you, and things that Taccompany salvation, though we thus speak.   *belong to*

10 For God *is* not unrighteous to forget your work and labour of love, which ye have shewed toward his name, in that ye have ministered to the saints, and do minister.

11 And we desire that every one of you do shew the same diligence Rto the full assurance of hope unto the end: Col. 2:2

12 That ye be not slothful, but Tfollowers of them who through faith and patience Rinherit the promises.   *imitators* • 10:36

13 For when God made promise to Abraham, because he could swear by no greater, Rhe sware by himself,   Gen. 22:16, 17

14 Saying, Surely blessing I will bless thee, and multiplying I will multiply thee.

15 And so, after he had patiently Tendured, he obtained the promise.   *waited*

16 For men verily swear by the greater: and Ran oath for Tconfirmation *is* to them an end of all strife.   Ex. 22:11 • *a guarantee*

17 Wherein God, willing more abundantly to shew unto the heirs of promise [T]the immutability of his counsel, confirmed it by an oath: *the permanent character of His word*

18 That by two [T]immutable things, in which it was impossible for God to lie, we might have a strong consolation, who have fled for refuge to lay hold upon the hope [R]set before us: *unchangeable • 12:1*

19 Which hope we have as an anchor of the soul, both sure and stedfast, and which entereth into that within the veil;

20 Whither the forerunner is for us entered, even Jesus, made an high priest for ever after the order of Mel-chis'-e-dec.

CHAPTER 7

Description of Melchisedec

FOR this [R]Mel-chis'-e-dec, king of Sa'-lem, priest of the most high God, who met Abraham returning from the slaughter of the kings, and blessed him;   Gen. 14:18

2 To whom also Abraham gave a tenth part of all; first being by interpretation King of righteousness, and after that also King of Sa'-lem, which is, King of peace;

3 Without father, without mother, without descent, having neither beginning of days, nor end of life; but made like unto the Son of God; abideth a priest continually.

Superiority of Melchisedec

4 Now consider how great this man was, unto whom even the [T]patriarch Abraham gave the tenth of the [T]spoils.   *father • chief spoils*

5 And verily [R]they that are of the sons of Levi, who receive the office of the priesthood, have a commandment to take tithes of the people according to the law, that is, of their brethren, though they come out of the loins of Abraham: Num. 18:21, 26

6 But he whose descent is not counted from them received tithes of Abraham, and blessed him that had the promises.

7 And without all contradiction the less is blessed [T]of the better.   *by the greater*

8 And here men that die receive tithes; but there he [T]receiveth them, [R]of whom it is [T]witnessed that he liveth.   *one • 5:6 • said*

9 And as I may so say, Levi also, who receiveth tithes, payed tithes in Abraham.

10 For he was yet in the loins of his father, when Mel-chis'-e-dec met him.

Imperfection of Aaronic Priesthood

11 If therefore perfection were by the Le-vit'-ic-al priesthood, (for under it the people received the law,) what further need was there that another priest should rise after the order of Mel-chis'-e-dec, and not be called after the order of Aaron?

12 [R]For the priesthood being changed, [T]there is made of necessity a change also of the law.   *8:4 • has to be*

13 For he of whom these things are spoken [T]pertaineth to another tribe, of which no man [T]gave attendance at the altar.   *belong • served*

14 For it is evident that [R]our Lord sprang out of Juda; of which tribe Moses spake nothing concerning priesthood.   Is. 11:1 *

15 And it is yet far more evident: for that after the [T]similitude of Mel-chis'-e-dec there ariseth another priest,   *likeness*

16 Who is made, not after the law of a [T]carnal commandment, but after the power of an endless life.   *legal requirement*

17 For he testifieth, [R]THOU ART A PRIEST FOR EVER AFTER THE ORDER OF MEL-CHIS'-E-DEC.   Ps. 110:4 *

18 For there is verily a disannulling of the commandment going before for the weakness and unprofitableness thereof.

19 For the law made nothing perfect, but the bringing in of a better hope did; by the which we draw nigh unto God.

20 And inasmuch as not without [T]an oath he was made priest: *a vow*

21 (For those priests were made without an oath; but this with an oath by him that said unto him, THE LORD SWARE AND WILL NOT REPENT, THOU ART A PRIEST FOR EVER AFTER THE ORDER OF MEL-CHIS'-E-DEC:)

22 By so much was Jesus made a [T]surety of a better [T]testament.   *guarantee • agreement*

23 And they truly were many priests, because they were not [T]suffered to continue by reason of death: *allowed*

24 But this man, because he continueth ever, hath an unchangeable priesthood.

25 Wherefore he is able also to save them to the uttermost that come unto God by him, seeing he ever liveth [R]to make intercession for them.   9:24; 1 Tim. 2:5; 1 John 2:1

26 For such an high priest became us, who is holy, harmless, undefiled, separate from sinners, and made higher than the heavens;

27 [R]Who needeth not daily, as those high priests, to offer up sacrifice, first for his own sins, and then for the people's: for this he did once, when he offered up himself.   9:12

28 For the law maketh men high priests which have infirmity; but the word of the oath, which was since the law, maketh the Son, who is consecrated for evermore.

CHAPTER 8

A Better Covenant

NOW of the things which we have spoken this is the sum: We have such an high priest, who is set on the right hand of the throne of the Majesty in the heavens;

2 A ᵀminister ᵀof the sanctuary, and of the true tabernacle, which the Lord pitched, and not man. *servant · of holy things*

3 For ᴿevery high priest is ᵀordained to offer gifts and sacrifices: wherefore ᴿit is of necessity that this man have somewhat also to offer. 5:1 · *appointed* · [9:14; Eph. 5:2]

4 ᴿFor if he were on earth, he should not be a priest, seeing that there are priests that offer gifts according to the law: [7:12]

5 Who serve unto the example and ᴿshadow of heavenly things, as Moses was admonished of God when he was about to make the tabernacle: for, See, saith he, that thou make all things according to the pattern shewed to thee in the mount. 9:23

6 But now ᴿhath he obtained a more excellent ministry, by how much also he is the mediator of a better covenant, which was established upon better promises. [2 Cor. 3:6-8]

A New Covenant

7 ᴿFor if that first covenant had been faultless, then should no place have been sought for the second. 7:11, 18

8 For finding fault with them, he saith, ᴿBEHOLD, THE DAYS COME, SAITH THE LORD, WHEN I WILL ᵀMAKE A NEW COVENANT WITH THE HOUSE OF ISRAEL AND WITH THE HOUSE OF JUDAH: Jer. 31:31 ★ · *draw up*

9 NOT ACCORDING TO THE COVENANT THAT I MADE WITH THEIR FATHERS IN THE DAY WHEN I TOOK THEM BY THE HAND TO LEAD THEM OUT OF THE LAND OF EGYPT; BECAUSE THEY CONTINUED NOT IN MY COVENANT, AND I REGARDED THEM NOT, SAITH THE LORD.

10 FOR THIS IS THE COVENANT THAT I WILL MAKE WITH THE HOUSE OF ISRAEL AFTER THOSE DAYS, SAITH THE LORD; I WILL PUT MY LAWS INTO THEIR MIND, AND WRITE THEM IN THEIR HEARTS: AND I WILL BE TO THEM A GOD, AND THEY SHALL BE TO ME A PEOPLE:

11 ᴿAND THEY SHALL NOT TEACH EVERY MAN HIS NEIGHBOUR, AND EVERY MAN HIS BROTHER, SAYING, KNOW THE LORD: FOR ALL SHALL KNOW ME, FROM THE LEAST TO THE GREATEST. Jer. 31:34

12 FOR I WILL BE MERCIFUL TO THEIR UNRIGHTEOUSNESS, AND THEIR SINS AND THEIR INIQUITIES WILL I REMEMBER NO MORE.

13 ᴿIn that he saith, A new covenant, he hath made the first old. Now that which decayeth and ᵀwaxeth old is ready to ᵀvanish away. [2 Cor. 5:17] · *grows · fade out*

CHAPTER 9
Old Covenant's Sanctuary

THEN verily the first covenant had also ᵀordinances of divine service, and ᴿa ᵀworldly sanctuary. *rites · Ex. 25:8 · material*

2 ᴿFor there was a tabernacle made; the first, wherein was the candlestick, and the table, and the shewbread; which is called the ᵀsanctuary. Ex. 25:8, 23, 30, 31 · *holy place*

3 And after the second veil, the tabernacle which is called the Holiest of all;

4 Which had the golden censer, and the ark of the covenant overlaid round about with gold, wherein was the golden pot that had man'-na, and Aaron's rod that budded, and the tables of the covenant;

5 And over it the cher'-u-bims of glory shadowing the mercyseat; of which we cannot now speak ᵀparticularly. *in detail*

Old Covenant's Sacrifice

6 Now when these things were thus ᵀordained, ᴿthe priests went always into the first tabernacle, ᵀaccomplishing the service of God. *prepared · Num. 28:3 · performing*

7 But once every year went the high priest alone ᴿonce every year, not without blood, which he offered for himself, and for the errors of the people: Ex. 30:10

8 The Holy Ghost ᵀthis signifying, that the way into the holiest of all was not yet ᵀmade manifest, while as the first tabernacle was yet standing: *showing by this · opened*

9 Which was a figure for the time then present, in which were offered both gifts and sacrifices, ᴿthat could not make him that did the service ᵀperfect, as pertaining to the conscience; [Gal. 3:21] · *complete*

10 Which stood only in meats and drinks, and ᵀdivers washings, and ᵀcarnal ordinances, imposed on them until the time of reformation. *various · fleshly regulations*

New Covenant's Sanctuary

11 But Christ being come an high priest of good things to come, by a greater and more perfect tabernacle, not made with hands, that is to say, not of this building;

New Covenant's Sacrifice

12 Neither by the blood of goats and calves, but by his own blood he entered in once into the holy place, ᴿhaving obtained eternal redemption for us. [Dan. 9:24] ★

13 For if ᴿthe blood of bulls and of goats, and ᴿthe ashes of an heifer sprinkling the unclean, ᵀsanctifieth to the ᵀpurifying of the flesh: Lev. 16:14 · Num. 19:2 · *set apart · cleansing*

14 How much more shall the blood of Christ, who through the eternal Spirit ᴿoffered himself without ᵀspot to God, ᵀpurge your ᵀconscience from dead works to serve the living God? Is. 53:12 ★ · *fault · cleanse · mind*

15 And for this cause he is the mediator of the new testament, that by means of death, for the redemption of the transgressions that were under the first testament, ᴿthey which

are called might receive the promise of eternal inheritance.   3:1

16 For where a ᵀtestament *is,* there must also ᵀof necessity be the death of ᵀthe testator.   *covenant • be proof • him that made it*

17 For ᴿa testament *is* of force after men are dead: otherwise it is of no strength at all while the ᵀtestator liveth.   Gal. 3:15 • *maker*

18 Whereupon neither the first *testament* was ᵀdedicated without blood.   *confirmed*

19 For when Moses had spoken every ᵀprecept to all the people according to the law, ᴿhe took the blood of calves and of goats, ᴿwith water, and scarlet wool, and hyssop, and sprinkled both the book, and all the people,   *rule •* Ex. 24:5, 6 • Lev. 14:4

20 Saying, This *is* the blood of the testament which God hath enjoined unto you.

21 Moreover ᴿhe sprinkled with blood both the tabernacle, and all the vessels ᵀof the ministry.   Ex. 29:12; Lev. 8:15 • *used in worship*

22 And almost all things are by the law purged with blood; and ᴿwithout shedding of blood is no remission.   Matt. 26:28; Acts 2:38

23 *It was* therefore necessary that the patterns of things in the heavens should be purified with these; but the heavenly things themselves with better sacrifices than these.

24 For ᴿChrist is not entered into the holy places made with hands, *which are* the figures of the true; but into heaven itself, now to appear in the presence of God for us: 6:20

25 Nor yet that he should offer himself often, as the high priest entereth into the holy place every year with blood of others;

26 For ᴿthen must he often have suffered since the foundation of the world: but now once in the end of ᵀthe world hath he appeared to put away sin by the sacrifice of himself.   *v.* 12; 7:27; 1 Cor. 10:11 • *ages*

27 ᴿAnd as it is appointed unto men once to die, but after this the judgment: Gen. 3:19

28 So ᴿChrist was once offered to bear the sins of many; and unto them that look for him shall he appear the second time without sin unto salvation.   Is. 53:12; Rom. 6:10 ★

CHAPTER 10

FOR the law having a shadow of good things to come, *and* not the very image of the things, can never with those sacrifices which they offered year by year continually make the comers thereunto perfect.

2 For then would they not have ceased to be offered? because that the worshippers once ᵀpurged should have had no more ᵀconscience of sins.   *cleansed • awareness*

3 But in those *sacrifices there is* a remembrance again *made* of sins every year.

4 For *it is* not possible that the blood of bulls and of goats should take away sins.

5 Wherefore when he cometh into the world, he saith, ᴿSACRIFICE AND OFFERING THOU WOULDEST NOT, BUT A BODY HAST THOU PREPARED ME: Ps. 40:6 ★

6 IN BURNT OFFERINGS AND *SACRIFICES* FOR SIN THOU HAST HAD NO PLEASURE.

7 ᴿTHEN SAID I, LO, I COME (IN THE VOLUME OF THE BOOK IT IS WRITTEN OF ME,) TO DO THY WILL, O GOD.   Ps. 40:7, 8 ★

8 Above when he said, Sacrifice and offering and burnt offerings and *offering* for sin thou wouldest not, neither hadst pleasure *therein;* which are offered by the law;

9 ᴿThen said he, Lo, I come to do thy will, O God. He taketh away the first, that he may ᵀestablish the second.   Ps. 40:8 ★ ★ • introduce

10 ᴿBy the which will we are sanctified ᴿthrough the offering of the body of Jesus Christ once *for all.*   John 17:19 • [9:12]; Is. 53:12 ★

11 And every priest standeth daily ministering and offering oftentimes the same sacrifices, which can never take away sins:

12 ᴿBut ᵀthis man, ᵀafter he had offered one sacrifice for sins for ever, sat down on the right hand of God;   Ps. 68:18; Col. 3:1 ★ • *he • when*

13 ᴿFrom henceforth ᵀexpecting till his enemies be made his footstool. Ps. 110:1 ★ • *waiting*

14 For by one offering he hath ᵀperfected for ever them that are sanctified.   *completed*

15 *Whereof* the Holy Ghost also is a witness to us: for after that he had said before,

16 ᴿTHIS IS THE COVENANT THAT I WILL MAKE WITH THEM AFTER THOSE DAYS, SAITH THE LORD, I WILL PUT MY LAWS INTO THEIR HEARTS, AND IN THEIR MINDS WILL I WRITE THEM;   Jer. 31:33 ★

17 ᴿAND THEIR SINS AND INIQUITIES WILL I REMEMBER NO MORE.   Jer. 31:34 ★

18 Now where remission of these *is, there* is no more ᵀoffering for sin.   *sacrifice*

Hold Fast the Profession of Faith

19 Having therefore, brethren, ᴿboldnessᵀ to enter ᴿinto the holiest by the blood of Jesus,   [Eph. 2:18] • *opportunity* • 9:8, 12

20 ᴿBy a new and living way, which he hath ᵀconsecrated for us, through the veil, that is to say, his flesh;   9:3, 8 • *prepared*

21 And *having* ᴿanᵀ high priest ᵀover the house of God;   Ps. 110:4 ★ • *a great • in charge*

22 Let us draw near with a true heart in full assurance of faith, having our hearts sprinkled from an evil conscience, and our bodies washed with pure water.

23 Let us ᵀhold fast the profession of *our* faith without wavering; (for ᴿhe *is* faithful that promised;)   *be persistent in* • 1 Cor. 1:9

24 And let us consider one another to provoke unto love and to good works:

25 Not forsaking the assembling of ourselves together, as the manner of some *is;* but exhorting *one another:* and so much the more, as ye see the day approaching.

Fourth Warning: Danger of Drawing Back

26 For if we sin wilfully after that we have received the knowledge of the truth, there remaineth no more sacrifice for sins,

27 But a certain fearful looking for of judgment and Rfiery indignation, which shall devour the adversaries.   Zeph. 1:18

28 He that despised Moses' law died without mercy under two or three witnesses:

29 ROf how much sorer punishment, suppose ye, shall he be thought worthy, who hath trodden under foot the Son of God, and hath counted the blood of the covenant, wherewith he was sanctified, an unholy thing, Rand hath Tdone despite unto the Spirit of grace?   [2:3] • [Matt. 12:31] • *insulted*

30 For we know him that hath said, RVENGEANCE *BELONGETH* UNTO ME, I WILL RECOMPENSE, saith the Lord. And again, THE LORD SHALL JUDGE HIS PEOPLE.   Deut. 32:35, 36

31 RIt is a Tfearful thing to fall into the hands of the living God.   [Luke 12:5] • *terrible*

32 But call to remembrance the former days, in which, after ye were illuminated, ye endured a great fight of afflictions;

33 Partly, whilst ye were made a Tgazingstock both by reproaches and afflictions; and partly, whilst ye became companions of them that were so used.   *object of ridicule*

34 For ye had compassion of me in my bonds, and took joyfully the spoiling of your Tgoods, knowing in yourselves that ye have in heaven a better and an Tenduring substance.   *property • permanent*

35 Cast not away therefore your Tconfidence, Rwhich hath great Trecompence of reward.   *boldness* • Matt. 5:12 • *promise*

36 For ye have need of Tpatience, that, after ye have done the will of God, Rye might receive the promise.   *persistence* • [Col. 3:24]

37 FOR YET A LITTLE WHILE, AND HE THAT SHALL COME WILL COME, AND WILL NOT TARRY.

38 RNOW THE JUST SHALL LIVE BY FAITH: BUT IF TANY MAN DRAW BACK, MY SOUL SHALL HAVE NO PLEASURE IN HIM.   Hab. 2:3, 4 ☆ • *he*

39 But we are not of them who draw back unto Tperdition; but of them that believe to the saving of the soul.   *destruction*

CHAPTER 11

Definition of Faith

NOW faith is the substance of things hoped for, the evidence of things not seen.

2 For by Tit the elders Tobtained a Tgood report.   *faith • won • God's approval*

3 Through faith we understand that Rthe worlds were framed by the word of God, so that things which are seen were not made of things which do appear.   Gen. 1:1

Abel

4 RBy faith Abel offered unto God a more excellent sacrifice than Cain, by which he obtained witness that he was righteous, God testifying of his gifts: and by it he being dead yet speaketh.   12:24; Gen. 4:2–10

Enoch

5 By faith RE'-noch was translated that he should not see death; and was not found, Rbecause God had translated him: for before his translation he had this testimony, that he pleased God.   Gen. 5:22 • 2 Kin. 2:11

6 But without faith *it is* impossible to please *him:* for he that cometh to God must believe that he is, and *that* he is a rewarder of them that diligently seek him.

Noah

7 By faith RNoah, being warned of God of things not seen as yet, moved with fear, Rprepared an ark to the saving of his house; by the which he condemned the world, and became heir of Rthe righteousness which is by faith.   Gen. 6:13 • 1 Pet. 3:20 • Rom. 3:22

Abraham and Sarah

8 By faith Abraham, when he was called to go out into a place which he should after receive for an inheritance, obeyed; and he went out, not knowing whither he went.

9 By faith he sojourned in the land of promise, as *in* a strange country, dwelling in Ttabernacles with Isaac and Jacob, the heirs with him of the same promise: *tents*

10 For he looked for Ra city which hath foundations, Rwhose builder and maker *is* God.   [12:22] • [Rev. 21:10]

11 Through faith also RSara herself received strength to conceive seed, and Rwas

---

10:25 The Reason for Participation in the Local Church—The ultimate reason that we should participate in a local church is because it is specifically commanded by God. Even in New Testament days there were those who yielded to the temptation of absenting themselves from the worship services of the local church. The writer of Hebrews points out that members of a local church have an obligation to one another. They are to provoke one another to good works and to exhort one another to live consistent lives worthy of God. This can best be done within the context of a local church; so believers are commanded not to forsake the assembling of themselves together.

Now turn to Page 1074—Acts 2:42–47: Benefits of Participation in the Local Church.

delivered of a child when she was past age, because she Tjudged him faithful who had promised.   Gen. 17:19 • Luke 1:36 • *considered*

12 Therefore sprang there even of one, and him as good as dead, *so many* as the stars of the sky in multitude, and as the sand which is by the sea shore innumerable.

13 These all died in faith, not having received the promises, but having seen them afar off, and were persuaded of *them*, and embraced *them*, and confessed that they were strangers and pilgrims on the earth.

14 For they that say such things Rdeclare plainly that they seek a country.   13:14

15 And truly, if they had Tbeen mindful of that *country* from whence they came out, they might have had Topportunity to have returned.   *thought back • a chance*

16 But now they desire a better *country*, that is, an heavenly: wherefore God is not ashamed Rto be called their God: for he hath prepared for them a city.   Ex. 3:6, 15

17 By faith Abraham, when he was Ttried, Roffered up Isaac: and he that had received the promises offered up his only begotten *son*,   *tested • Gen. 22:1, 7; James 2:21*

18 Of whom it was said, RThat in Isaac shall thy seed be called: Gen. 21:12 *

19 Accounting that God *was* able to raise *him* up, even from the dead; from whence also he received him in a figure.

Isaac

20 By faith RIsaac blessed Jacob and Esau concerning things to come.   Gen. 27:27, 38

Jacob

21 By faith Jacob, when he was a dying, blessed both the sons of Joseph; and worshipped, *leaning* upon the top of his staff.

Joseph

22 By faith RJoseph, when he died, Tmade mention of the departing of the children of Israel; and gave commandment concerning his bones.   Gen. 50:24 • *remembered*

Moses' Parents

23 By faith Moses, when he was born, was hid three months of his parents, because they saw *he was* a proper child; and they were not afraid of the king's commandment.

Moses

24 RBy faith Moses, when he was Tcome to years, refused to be called the son of Pharaoh's daughter;   Ex. 2:10, 11 • *grown*

25 Choosing rather to Tsuffer affliction with the people of God, than to enjoy the pleasures of sin for a season;   *endure trouble*

26 Esteeming Rthe reproach of Christ greater riches than the treasures in Egypt: for he had respect unto the recompence of the reward.   13:13

27 By faith he forsook Egypt, not fearing the wrath of the king: for he Tendured, as seeing him who is invisible.   *persevered*

28 Through faith he kept the passover, and the sprinkling of blood, lest he that destroyed the firstborn should touch them.

29 By faith they passed through the Red sea as by dry *land:* which the Egyptians Tassaying to do were drowned.   *trying*

Joshua and Rahab

30 By faith the walls of Jericho fell down, after they were compassed about seven days.

31 By faith the harlot Ra'-hab perished not with them that believed not, when she had received the spies with peace.

Many Other Heroes of Faith

32 RAnd what shall I more say? for the time would fail me to tell of Ged'-e-on, and *of* Ba'-rak, and *of* Samson, and *of* Jeph'-thae; *of* David also, and Samuel, and *of* the prophets: Judg. 4:6; 6:11; 11:1; 12:7

33 Who through faith subdued kingdoms, wrought righteousness, obtained promises, stopped the mouths of lions,

34 Quenched the violence of fire, escaped the edge of the sword, out of weakness were made strong, waxed valiant in fight, turned to flight the armies of the aliens.

35 RWomen received their dead raised to life again: and others were tortured, not accepting deliverance; that they might obtain a better resurrection: 1 Kin. 17:22

36 And others had trial of *cruel* mockings and scourgings, yea, moreover Rof bonds and imprisonment: Gen. 39:20; Jer. 20:2

37 RThey were stoned, they were sawn asunder, were tempted, were slain with the sword: Rthey wandered about Rin sheepskins and goatskins; being destitute, afflicted, tormented;   Acts 7:58 • 2 Kin. 1:8 • Zech. 13:4

38 (Of whom the world was not worthy:) they wandered in deserts, and *in* mountains, and *in* dens and caves of the earth.

39 And these all, Rhaving obtained a good Treport through faith, received not the promise: *vv.* 2, 13 • *reputation because of*

40 God having Tprovided some better thing for us, that they without us should not be Rmade Tperfect.   *foreseen • 5:9 • complete*

CHAPTER 12

Example of Christ's Endurance

WHEREFORE seeing we also are compassed about with so great a cloud of witnesses, let us lay aside every weight, and the sin which doth so easily beset *us*, and let

us run with Tpatience the race that is set before us,   *perseverance*

2 Looking unto Jesus the author and finisher of *our* faith; who for the joy that was set before him endured the cross, despising the shame, and Ris set down at the right hand of the throne of God.   Ps. 68:18 ★

3 For consider him that endured such contradiction of sinners against himself, lest ye be wearied and faint in your minds.

4 RYe have not yet resisted unto blood, striving against sin.   10:32–34; [1 Cor. 10:13]

Exhortation to Endure God's Chastening

5 And ye have forgotten the exhortation which speaketh unto you as unto children, RMY SON, DESPISE NOT THOU THE CHASTENING OF THE LORD, NOR FAINT WHEN THOU ART REBUKED OF HIM: Prov. 3:11

6 RFOR WHOM THE LORD LOVETH HE CHASTENETH, AND SCOURGETH EVERY SON WHOM HE RECEIVETH.   Prov. 3:12

7 If ye endure Tchastening, God dealeth with you as with sons; for what son is he whom the father chasteneth not?   *discipline*

8 But if ye be without chastisement, Rwhereof all are partakers, then are ye Tbastards, and not sons.   1 Pet. 5:9 • *illegitimate*

9 Furthermore we have had fathers of our flesh which corrected *us,* and we gave *them* reverence: shall we not much rather be in Tsubjection unto Rthe Father of spirits, and live?   *submission* • [Job 12:10]

10 For they verily for a few days chastened *us* Tafter their own pleasure; but he for *our* profit, that *we* might be partakers of his holiness.   *according to their own judgment*

11 Now no Tchastening for the present seemeth to be joyous, but grievous: nevertheless afterward it yieldeth the peaceable fruit of righteousness unto them which are Texercised thereby.   *infliction of pain • trained*

12 Wherefore Tlift up the hands which hang down, and the feeble knees;   *strengthen*

13 And make straight paths for your feet, lest that which is lame be turned out of the way; but let it rather be healed.

14 Follow peace with all *men,* and Tholiness, Rwithout which no man shall see the Lord: *the sanctification* • Matt. 5:8

15 TLooking diligently lest any man fail of the grace of God; lest any root of bitterness springing up trouble *you,* and thereby many be defiled;   *watching carefully*

16 Lest there *be* any fornicator, or Tprofane person, as Esau, who for one morsel of meat sold his birthright.   *God-dishonoring*

17 For ye know how that afterward, when he would have inherited the blessing, he was rejected: for he found no place Tof repentance, though he sought it carefully with tears.   *for a change of mind in his father*

18 For ye are not come unto Rthe mount that might be touched, and that burned with fire, nor unto blackness, and darkness, and tempest,   Ex. 19:12, 18, 19; Deut. 4:11

19 And the sound of a trumpet, and the voice of words; which *voice* they that heard Rintreated T that the word should not be spoken to them any more: Ex. 20:19 • *requested*

20 (For they could not endure that which was commanded, And if so much as a beast touch the mountain, it shall be stoned, or thrust through with a dart:

21 And so terrible was the sight, *that* Moses said, I exceedingly fear and quake:)

22 RBut ye are come unto mount Si'-on, and unto the city of the living God, the heavenly Jerusalem, and to an innumerable company of angels,   Ps. 68:17; [Gal. 4:26]

23 To the general assembly and church of the firstborn, which are written in heaven, and to God the Judge of all, and to the spirits of just men made perfect,

24 And to Jesus Rthe mediator of the new Tcovenant, and to Rthe blood of sprinkling, that speaketh better things Rthan *that of* Abel.   9:15 • *testament* • Ex. 24:8 • Gen. 4:10

Fifth Warning: Danger of Refusing God

25 See that ye Trefuse not him that speaketh. For Rif they escaped not who refused him that spake on earth, much more *shall not* we *escape,* if we turn away from him that *speaketh* from heaven: *disobey* • 2:2, 3

26 Whose voice then shook the earth: but now he hath promised, saying, Yet once more I shake not the earth only, but also heaven.

27 And this *word,* Yet once more, signifieth the removing of those things that are shaken, as of things that are made, that those things which cannot be shaken may remain.

28 Wherefore we receiving Ra kingdom which cannot be moved, let us have grace, whereby we may serve God acceptably with reverence and godly fear: [Dan. 2:44] ★

29 For our God *is* a consuming fire.

CHAPTER 13

Love in the Social Realm

LET Rbrotherly love continue.   Rom. 12:10
2 Be not forgetful to Tentertain strangers: for thereby some have entertained angels Tunawares.   *receive • without realizing it*

3 Remember them that are in bonds, as bound with them; *and* them which suffer adversity, as being yourselves also in the body.

4 Marriage *is* honourable in all, and the bed undefiled: Rbut whoremongers and adulterers God will judge.   1 Cor. 6:9

5 *Let your* conversation *be* without covetousness; *and be* content with such

things as ye have: for he hath said, I will never leave thee, nor forsake thee.

6 So that we may boldly say, ^RTHE LORD *IS* MY HELPER, AND I WILL NOT FEAR WHAT MAN SHALL DO UNTO ME.   Ps. 118:6

Love in the Religious Realm

7 Remember them which have the rule over you, who have spoken unto you the word of God: whose faith follow, considering the ^Tend of *their* ^Tconversation.   *goal • life*

8 Jesus Christ ^Rthe same yesterday, and to day, and for ever.   1:12; [John 8:58]

9 Be not carried about with divers and strange doctrines. For *it is* a good thing that the heart be established with grace; not with meats, which have not profited them that have been occupied therein.

10 We have an altar, whereof they have no right to eat which serve the tabernacle.

11 ^RFor the bodies of those beasts, whose blood is brought into the ^Tsanctuary by the high priest for sin, are burned ^Twithout the camp.   Lev. 6:30; Num. 19:3 • *holy place • outside*

12 Wherefore Jesus also, that he might ^Tsanctify the people with his own blood, suffered ^Twithout the gate.   *set apart • outside*

13 Let us go forth therefore unto him without the camp, bearing his reproach.

14 ^RFor here have we no continuing city, but we seek one to come.   [11:10, 16]

15 ^RBy him therefore let us offer the sacrifice of praise to God continually, that is, ^Rthe fruit of *our* lips ^Tgiving thanks to his name.   Eph. 5:20 • Hos. 14:2 • *confessing to*

16 But to do good and to ^Tcommunicate forget not: for ^Rwith such sacrifices God is well pleased.   *give to poor people* • 2 Cor. 9:12

17 Obey them that have the rule over you, and submit yourselves: for they watch for your souls, as they that must give account, that they may do it with joy, and not with grief: for that *is* unprofitable for you.

Conclusion

18 ^RPray for us: for we trust we have ^Ra good conscience, in all things ^Twilling to live honestly.   Eph. 6:19 • Acts 23:1 • *desiring*

19 But I beseech *you* the rather to do this, that I may be restored to you the sooner.

20 Now the God of peace, ^Rthat brought again from the dead our Lord Jesus, that great shepherd of the sheep, through the blood of the everlasting covenant,   Hos. 6:2 ★

21 Make you ^Tperfect in every good work to do his will, working in ^Tyou that which is wellpleasing in his sight, through Jesus Christ; to whom *be* glory for ever and ever. A-men'.   *complete • us*

22 And I beseech you, brethren, suffer the word of ^Texhortation: for I have written a letter unto you in few words.   *urging*

23 Know ye that *our* ^Rbrother Timothy is set at liberty; with whom, if he come shortly, I will see you.   Acts 16:1; Col. 1:1

24 ^TSalute all them that ^Thave the rule over you, and all the saints. They of Italy salute you.   *greet • are in authority*

25 Grace *be* with you all. A-men'.

13:15 The Expressions of Worship—Since worship encompasses thought, feeling, and deed, there are many expressions of it. Worship especially includes praise and thanksgiving which may be expressed privately or publicly, either by grateful declarations (Heb. 13:15) or by joyful singing (Page 590—Ps. 100:2; Page 1166—Eph. 5:19; Page 1178—Col. 3:16). Portions of early Christian hymns of worship actually may be preserved in the New Testament (Page 1195—1 Tim. 3:16; Page 1201—2 Tim. 2:11–13).

One very important expression of worship for the church is remembering the death of Christ through the Lord's Supper (Page 1134—1 Cor. 11:26). The Lord's Supper was instituted by Christ Himself (Page 970—Matt. 26:26–28) and judged by Paul not to be taken lightly (Page 1134—1 Cor. 11:28–32).

Since worship means giving something to God, the cheerful giving of money to God's work is certainly an act of worship (Page 1148—2 Cor. 9:7). The giving of one's time to the Lord's work may be considered worship as well. The use of one's spiritual gifts in ministry to the body of Christ constitutes an example of worship as service (Page 1134—1 Cor. 12), as does faithfully occupying a church office (Page 1164—Eph. 4:11; Page 1195—1 Tim. 3:1–13; Page 1206—Titus 1:5–9). Ministry in edifying saints and evangelizing sinners both likewise constitute services of worship.

The single most important act of worship for the Christian is the unqualified presentation of himself to God as an obedient servant. This dedication involves the body and the mind (Page 1118—Rom. 12:1, 2): the body because it contains the tools by which the will of God is carried out; the mind because it coordinates the actions to be executed by the body. When these are gladly devoted to God, they become instruments by which He effects His will on the earth. Such faithful and joyous service makes one's entire life a performance of worship.

Now turn to Page 444—2 Chr. 7:3: The Reasons for Worship.

JAMES

THE BOOK OF JAMES

Faith without works cannot be called faith. Faith without works is dead, and a dead faith is worse than no faith at all. Faith must work; it must produce; it must be visible. Verbal faith is not enough; mental faith is insufficient. Faith must be there, but it must be more. It must inspire action. Throughout his epistle to Jewish believers, James integrates true faith and everyday practical experience by stressing that true faith must manifest itself in works of faith.

Faith endures trials. Trials come and go, but a strong faith will face them head-on and develop endurance. Faith understands temptations. It will not allow us to consent to our lust and slide into sin. Faith obeys the Word. It will not merely hear and not do. Faith produces doers. Faith harbors no prejudice. For James, faith and favoritism cannot coexist. Faith displays itself in works. Faith is more than mere words; it is more than knowledge; it is demonstrated by obedience; and it overtly responds to the promises of God. Faith controls the tongue. This small but immensely powerful part of the body must be held in check. Faith can do it. Faith acts wisely. It gives us the ability to choose wisdom that is heavenly and to shun wisdom that is earthly. Faith produces separation from the world and submission to God. It provides us with the ability to resist the Devil and humbly to draw near to God. Finally, faith waits patiently for the coming of the Lord. Through trouble and trial it stifles complaining.

The name *Iakōbos* (James) in 1:1 is the basis for the early title *Iakōbou Epistole*, "Epistle of James." *Iakōbos* is the Greek form of the Hebrew name Jacob, a Jewish name common in the first century.

THE AUTHOR OF JAMES

Four men are named James in the New Testament: (1) James, the father of Judas (not Iscariot), is mentioned twice (Luke 6:16; Acts 1:13) as the father of one of the twelve disciples, but is otherwise completely unknown. (2) James, the son of Alphaeus (Matt. 10:3; Mark 3:18; Luke 6:15; Acts 1:13), elsewhere called James the less (Mark 15:40), was one of the twelve disciples. Apart from being listed with the other disciples, this James is completely obscure, and it is doubtful that he is the authoritative figure behind the epistle. Some attempts have been made to identify this James with the Lord's brother (Gal. 1:19), but this view is difficult to reconcile with the gospel accounts. (3) James, the son of Zebedee and brother of John (Matt. 4:21; 10:2; 17:1; Mark 3:17; 10:35; 13:3; Luke 9:54; Acts 1:13), was one of Jesus' intimate disciples,

but his martyrdom by A.D. 44 (Acts 12:2) makes it very unlikely that he wrote this epistle. (4) James, the Lord's brother (Matt. 13:55; Mark 6:3; Gal. 1:19), was one of the "pillars" in the church in Jerusalem (Acts 12:17; 15:13-21; 21:18; Gal. 2:9, 12). Tradition points to this prominent figure as the author of the epistle, and this best fits the evidence of Scripture. There are several clear parallels between the language of the letter drafted under his leadership in Acts 15:23-29 and the epistle of James (e.g., the unusual word *chairein*, "greeting," is found only in Acts 15:23; 23:26; and James 1:1). The Jewish character of this epistle with its stress upon the law, along with the evident influence by the Sermon on the Mount (e.g., 4:11, 12; 5:12), complement what we know about James "the Just" from Scripture and early tradition.

It has been argued that the Greek of this epistle is too sophisticated for a Galilean such as James, but this assumes that he never had the opportunity or aptitude to develop proficiency in Koine ("common") Greek. As a prominent church leader, it would have been to his advantage to become fluent in the universal language of the Roman Empire.

For various reasons, some assert that James was a stepbrother of Jesus by a previous marriage of Joseph, or that the "brothers" of Jesus mentioned in Matthew 13:55 and Mark 6:3 were really His cousins. However, the most natural understanding of the gospel accounts is that James was the half brother of Jesus, being the offspring of Joseph and Mary after the birth of Jesus (Matt. 1:24, 25). He apparently did not accept the claims of Jesus until the Lord appeared to him after His resurrection (1 Cor. 15:7). He and his brothers were among the believers who awaited the coming of the Holy Spirit on the Day of Pentecost (Acts 1:14). It was not long before he became an acknowledged leader of the Jerusalem church (Acts 12:17; Gal. 2:9, 12), and he was a central figure in the Jerusalem Council in Acts 15. Even after Paul's third missionary journey, James continued to observe the Mosaic Law as a testimony to other Jews (Acts 21:18-25). Early tradition stresses his Jewish piety and his role in bringing others to an understanding of Jesus as the Messiah. He suffered a violent martyr's death not long before the fall of Jerusalem.

The brevity and limited doctrinal emphasis of James kept it from wide circulation; and by the time it became known in the church as a whole, there was uncertainty about the identity of the James in 1:1. Growing recognition that it was written by the Lord's brother led to its acceptance as a canonical book.

THE TIME OF JAMES

James is addressed "to the twelve tribes which are scattered abroad" (1:1), and it is apparent from verses like 1:19 and 2:1, 7 that this greeting refers to Hebrew Christians outside of Palestine. Their place of meeting is called a "synagogue" in the Greek text of 2:2, and the whole epistle reflects Jewish thought and expressions (e.g., 2:19, 21; 4:11, 12; 5:4, 12). There are no references to slavery or idolatry, and this also fits an originally Jewish readership.

These Jewish believers were beset with problems that were testing their faith, and James was concerned that they were succumbing to impatience, bitterness, materialism, disunity, and spiritual apathy. As a resident of Jerusalem and a leader of the church, James no doubt had frequent contact with Jewish Christians from a number of Roman provinces. He therefore felt a responsibility to exhort and encourage them in their struggles of faith.

According to Josephus, James was martyred in A.D. 62 (Hegesippus, quoted in Eusebius, fixed the date of James's death at A.D. 66). Those who accept him as the author of this epistle have proposed a date of writing ranging from A.D. 45 to the end of his life. However, several factors indicate that this letter may have been the earliest writing of the New Testament (c. A.D. 46–49): (1) There is no mention of gentile Christians or their relationship to Jewish Christians as would be expected in a later epistle. (2) Apart from references to the person of Christ, there is practically no distinctive theology in James, suggesting an early date when Christianity was viewed in terms of Messianic Judaism. (3) The allusions to the teachings of Christ have such little verbal agreement with the synoptic Gospels that they probably preceded them. (4) James uses the word "synagogue" (assembly, 2:2) in addition to "church" and indicates a very simple organization of elders and masters, that is, teachers (3:1; 5:14), which was patterned after the early synagogue. (5) James does not mention the issues involved in the Acts 15 Council in Jerusalem (A.D. 49).

THE CHRIST OF JAMES

In 1:1 and 2:1 James refers to the "Lord Jesus Christ," and in 5:7, 8 he anticipates "the coming of the Lord." Compared to other New Testament writers, James says little about Christ, and yet his speech is virtually saturated with allusions to the teaching of Christ. The Sermon on the Mount is especially prominent in James's thinking (there are c. fifteen indirect references; e.g., James 1:2 and Matt. 5:10–12; James 1:4 and Matt. 5:48; James 2:13 and Matt. 6:14, 15; James 4:11 and Matt. 7:1, 2; James 5:2 and Matt. 6:19). This epistle portrays Christ in the context of early Messianic Judaism.

KEYS TO JAMES

Key Word: Faith That Works—Throughout his epistle, James develops the theme of the characteristics of true faith. He effectively uses these characteristics as a series of tests to help his readers evaluate the quality of their relationship to Christ. The purpose of this work is not doctrinal or apologetic but practical. James seeks to challenge these believers to examine the quality of their daily lives in terms of attitudes and actions. A genuine faith will produce real changes in a person's conduct and character, and the absence of change is a symptom of a dead faith.

Key Verses: James 1:19–22 and 2:14–17— "Wherefore, my beloved brethren, let every man be swift to hear, slow to speak, slow to wrath: For the wrath of man worketh not the righteousness of God. Wherefore lay apart all filthiness and superfluity of naughtiness, and receive with meekness the engrafted word, which is able to save your souls. But be ye doers of the word, and not hearers only, deceiving your own selves" (1:19–22).

"What *doth it* profit, my brethren, though a man say he hath faith, and have not works? can faith save him? If a brother or sister be naked, and destitute of daily food, And one of you say unto them, Depart in peace, be ye warmed and filled; notwithstanding ye give them not those things which are needful to the body; what *doth it* profit? Even so faith, if it hath not works, is dead, being alone" (2:14–17).

Key Chapter: James 1—One of the most difficult areas of the Christian life is that of testings and temptations. James reveals our correct response to both: to testings, count them all joy; to temptations, realize that God is not their source.

SURVEY OF JAMES

James is the Proverbs of the New Testament because it is written in the terse moralistic style of wisdom literature. It is evident that James was profoundly influenced by the Old Testament (especially by its wisdom literature) and by the Sermon on the Mount. But James's impassioned preaching against inequity and social injustice also earns him the title of the Amos of the New Testament. Because of the many subjects in this epistle, it is difficult to outline; suggestions have ranged from no connection between the various topics to a unified scheme. The outline used here is: the test of faith (1:1–18); the characteristics of faith (1:19–5:6); and the triumph of faith (5:7–20).

The Test of Faith (1:1–18): The first part of this epistle develops the qualities of genuine faith in regard to trials and temptations. After a one-verse salutation to geographically dispersed Hebrew Christians (1:1), James quickly intro-

duces his first subject, outward tests of faith (1:2–12). These trials are designed to produce mature endurance and a sense of dependence upon God, to whom the believer turns for wisdom and enablement. Inward temptations (1:13–18) do not come from the One who bestows "Every good gift" (1:17). These solicitations to evil must be checked at an early stage or they may result in disastrous consequences.

The Characteristics of Faith (1:19—5:6): A righteous response to testing requires that one be "swift to hear, slow to speak, slow to wrath" (1:19), and this broadly summarizes the remainder of the epistle. Quickness of hearing involves an obedient response to God's Word (1:19–27). True hearing means more than mere listening; the Word must be received and applied. After stating this principle (1:21, 22), James develops it with an illustration (1:23–25) and an application (1:26, 27). A genuine faith should produce a change in attitude from partiality to the rich to a love for the poor as well as the rich (2:1–13). True faith should also result in actions (2:14–26). In Romans 4, Paul used the example of Abraham to show that justification is by faith, not by works. But James says that Abraham was justified by works (2:21). In spite of the apparent contradiction, Romans 4 and James 2 are really two sides of the same coin. In context, Paul is writing about justification before God while James writes of the evidence of justification before men. A faith that produces no change is not saving faith.

Moving from works to words, James shows how a living faith controls the tongue ("slow to speak," 1:19). The tongue is small, but it has the power to accomplish great good or equally great evil. Only the power of God applied by an active faith can tame the tongue (3:1–12). Just as there are wicked and righteous uses of the tongue, so there are demonic and divine manifestations of wisdom (3:13–18). James contrasts seven characteristics of human wisdom with seven qualities of divine wisdom.

The strong pulls of worldliness (4:1–12) and wealth (4:13—5:6) create conflicts that are harmful to the growth of faith. The world system is at enmity with God, and the pursuit of its pleasures produces covetousness, envy, fighting, and arrogance (4:1–6). The believer's only alternative is submission to God out of a humble and repentant spirit. This will produce a transformed attitude toward others as well (4:7–12). This spirit of submission and humility should be applied to any attempts to accrue wealth (4:13–17), especially because wealth can lead to pride, injustice, and selfishness (5:1–6).

The Triumph of Faith (5:7–20): James encourages his readers to patiently endure the sufferings of the present life in view of the future prospect of the coming of the Lord (5:7–12). They may be oppressed by the rich or by other circumstances, but as the example of Job teaches, believers can be sure that God has a gracious purpose in His dealings with them. James concludes his epistle with some practical words on prayer and restoration (5:13–20). The prayers of righteous men (e.g., elders in local churches) are efficacious for the healing and restoration of believers. When sin is not dealt with, it can contribute to illness and even death.

FOCUS	TEST OF FAITH		CHARACTERISTICS OF FAITH		TRIUMPH OF FAITH		
REFERENCE	1:1————1:13		1:19——————	5:7——5:13		———————5:19———5:20		
DIVISION	PURPOSE OF TESTS	SOURCE OF TEMPTATION	OUTWARD DEMONSTRATION OF INNER FAITH	ENDURES WAITING	PRAYS FOR AFFLICTED	CONFRONTS SIN
TOPIC	DEVELOPMENT OF FAITH		WORKS OF FAITH		POWER OF FAITH		
	RESPONSE OF FAITH		REALITY OF FAITH		REASSURANCE OF FAITH		
LOCATION	PROBABLY JERUSALEM						
TIME	c. A.D. 46—49						

OUTLINE OF JAMES

CHAPTER 1

The Purpose of Tests

JAMES, a servant of God and of the Lord Jesus Christ, to the twelve tribes which are scattered abroad, greeting.

2 My brethren, count it all joy when ye fall into ᵀdivers temptations;   *various trials*

3 ᴿKnowing *this*, that the trying of your faith ᵀworketh patience.   Rom. 5:3 • *develops*

4 But let patience have *her* ᵀperfect work, that ye may be ᵀperfect and ᵀentire, ᵀwanting nothing.   *complete • mature • finished • lacking*

5 If any of you lack wisdom, let him ask of God, that giveth to all *men* liberally, and upbraideth not; and it shall be given him.

6 But let him ask in faith, nothing wavering. For he that wavereth is like a wave of the sea driven with the wind and tossed.

7 ᴿFor let not that man think that he shall receive any thing of the Lord.   [Prov. 3:5, 6]

8 ᴿA ᵀdouble minded man *is* ᵀunstable in all his ways.   4:8 • *two-faced • unreliable*

9 Let the brother of ᵀlow degree rejoice in that he is exalted: *humble circumstance*

10 But the rich, in that he is made low: because ᴿas the flower of the grass he shall pass away.   Job 14:2; Ps. 37:2; 90:5, 6; [1 Cor. 7:31]

11 For the sun is no sooner risen with a burning heat, but it withereth the grass, and the flower thereof falleth, and the grace of the fashion of it perisheth: so also shall the rich man fade away in his ways.

12 Blessed *is* the man that endureth temptation: for when he is tried, he shall receive the crown of life, which the Lord hath promised to them that love him.

The Source of Temptations

13 Let no man say when he is tempted, I am tempted of God: for God cannot be tempted ᵀwith evil, ᴿneither ᵀtempteth he any man: *by* • Gen. 22:1 • *does he tempt*

14 But every man is tempted, when he is drawn away of his own lust, and enticed.

15 Then when lust hath conceived, it bringeth forth sin: and sin, when it is finished, ᴿbringeth forth death.   Rom. 6:21

16 Do not err, my beloved brethren.

17 Every good gift and every perfect gift is from above, and cometh down from the Father of lights, with whom is no variableness, neither shadow of turning.

18 Of his own will begat he us with the word of truth, that we should be a kind of firstfruits of his creatures.

Faith Obeys the Word

19 Wherefore, my beloved brethren, let every man be swift to hear, ᴿslow to speak, ᴿslow to wrath: Prov. 10:19 • Prov. 14:17

20 For the wrath of man ᵀworketh not the righteousness of God.   *does not produce*

21 Wherefore lay apart all filthiness and ᵀsuperfluity of ᵀnaughtiness, and receive with meekness the engrafted word, which is able to save your souls.   *excess • sinfulness*

22 But be ye doers of the word, and not hearers only, deceiving your own selves.

23 For if any be a hearer of the word, and not a doer, he is like unto a man beholding his natural face in a ᵀglass: *mirror*

24 For he beholdeth himself, and goeth his way, and ᵀstraightway forgetteth what manner of man he was.   *immediately*

25 But ᴿwhoso looketh into the ᵀperfect law of liberty, and ᵀcontinueth *therein*, he being not a forgetful hearer, but a doer of the work, ᴿthis man shall be blessed in his deed.   2 Cor. 3:17 • *complete • lives in it* • John 13:17

26 If any man among you seem to be religious, and ᴿbridlethᵀ not his tongue, but deceiveth his own heart, this man's religion *is* ᵀvain.   Ps. 34:13 • *controls • useless*

27 Pure religion and undefiled before God and the Father is this, To visit the fatherless and widows in their affliction, *and* to keep himself unspotted from the world.

CHAPTER 2

Faith Removes Discrimination

MY brethren, have not the faith of our Lord Jesus Christ, ᴿ*the Lord* of glory, with ᴿrespect of persons.   1 Cor. 2:8 • Lev. 19:15

2 For if there come unto your Tassembly a man with a gold ring, in Tgoodly apparel, and there come in also a poor man in Tvile raiment;   *synagogue • nice clothes • poor garments*

3 And ye Thave respect to him that weareth the Tgay clothing, and say unto him, Sit thou here in a good place; and say to the poor, Stand thou there, or sit here under my footstool: *pay special attention • good*

4 Are ye not then partial in yourselves, and are become judges of evil thoughts?

5 Hearken, my beloved brethren, Hath not God chosen the poor of this world rich in faith, and heirs of the kingdom which he hath promised to them that love him?

6 But ye have Tdespised the poor. Do not rich men oppress you, Rand draw you before the judgment seats?   *belittled • Acts 13:50*

7 Do not they blaspheme Rthat worthy name by the which ye are called?   Acts 26:11

8 If ye fulfil the royal law according to the scripture, RTHOU SHALT LOVE THY NEIGHBOUR AS THYSELF, ye do well: Lev. 19:18

9 But if ye Thave respect to persons, ye commit sin, and are convinced of the law as transgressors.   *pay attention to special people*

10 For whosoever shall keep the whole law, and yet Toffend in one *point,* Rhe is guilty of all.   *stumble • Deut. 27:26*

11 For he that said, DO NOT COMMIT ADULTERY, said also, DO NOT KILL. Now if thou commit no adultery, yet if thou kill, thou art become a transgressor of the law.

12 So speak ye, and so do, as they that shall be judged by the law of liberty.

13 For he shall have judgment without mercy, that hath shewed no mercy; and mercy Trejoiceth against judgment.   *is a joy*

Faith Proves Itself by Works

14 What *doth it* profit, my brethren, though a man say he hath faith, and have not works? can Tfaith save him?   *that faith*

15 RIf a brother or sister be naked, and Tdestitute of daily food,   Luke 3:11 • *without*

16 And Rone of you say unto them, Depart in peace, be *ye* warmed and filled; notwithstanding ye give them not those things which are needful to the body; what *doth it* profit?   [1 John 3:18]

17 Even so Rfaith, if it hath not works, is dead, Tbeing alone.   [Gal. 5:6] • *in itself*

18 Yea, a man may say, Thou hast faith, and I have works: shew me thy faith Twithout thy works, and I will shew thee my faith by my works.   *apart from any works*

19 RThou believest that there is one God; thou doest well: the Tdevils also believe, and Ttremble.   Matt. 8:29 • *demons • shudder*

20 But wilt thou know, O vain man, that faith Twithout works is dead?   *apart from*

21 Was not Abraham our father justified by works, Rwhen he had offered Isaac his son upon the altar?   Gen. 22:9; Heb. 11:17

22 Seest thou how faith Twrought with his works, and by Tworks was faith made Tperfect?   *operated • actions • complete*

23 And the scripture was fulfilled which saith, ABRAHAM BELIEVED GOD, AND IT WAS IMPUTED UNTO HIM FOR RIGHTEOUSNESS: and he was called Rthe Friend of God.   Is. 41:8

24 Ye see then how that by works a man is Tjustified, and not by faith only.   *put right*

25 Likewise also Rwas not Ra'-hab the harlot justified by works, when she had received the messengers, and had sent *them* out another way?   Josh. 2:1; Heb. 11:31

26 For as the body without the spirit is dead, so faith without works is dead also.

CHAPTER 3

Faith Controls the Tongue

MY brethren, Rbe not many Tmasters, knowing that we shall receive the greater condemnation.   [Matt. 23:8] • *teachers*

2 For in many things we offend all. If any man Toffend not in word, the same *is* a Tperfect man, *and* able also to Tbridle the whole body.   *gives no offence • complete • control*

3 Behold, Rwe put bits in the horses' mouths, that they may obey us; and we turn about their whole body.   Ps. 32:9

4 Behold also the ships, which though *they* be so great, and *are* driven of fierce winds, yet are they turned about with a very small helm, whithersoever the governor listeth.

5 Even so the tongue is a little member, and boasteth great things. Behold, how great a matter a little fire kindleth!

6 And the tongue *is* a fire, a world of Tiniquity: so is the tongue among our members, that it defileth the whole body, and setteth on fire the course of nature; and it is set on fire of hell.   *sin*

7 For every kind of beasts, and of birds, and of serpents, and of things in the sea, is tamed, and hath been tamed of mankind:

8 But the tongue can no man tame; *it is* an unruly evil, full of deadly poison.

9 Therewith bless we God, even the Father; and therewith curse we men, which are made after the similitude of God.

10 Out of the same mouth proceedeth blessing and cursing. My brethren, these things Tought not so to be.   *should not happen*

11 Doth a fountain send forth at the same Tplace sweet *water* and bitter?   *opening*

12 Can the fig tree, my brethren, bear olive berries? either a vine, figs? so *can* no fountain both yield salt water and fresh.

Faith Produces Wisdom

13 Who *is* a wise man and [T]endued with knowledge among you? let him shew [T]out of a good conversation his works with meekness of wisdom.   *equipped · by his good life*

14 But if ye have bitter envying and [T]strife in your hearts, [T]glory not, and lie not against the truth.   *quarreling · do not be proud*

15 This wisdom descendeth not from above, but *is* earthly, sensual, devilish.

16 For where envying and strife *is,* there *is* [T]confusion and every evil work.   *disorder*

17 But the wisdom that is from above is first pure, then peaceable, gentle, *and* easy to be intreated, full of mercy and good fruits, without partiality, and without hypocrisy.

18 [R]And the fruit of righteousness is sown in peace of them that make peace.   Prov. 11:18

CHAPTER 4

Faith Produces Humility

FROM whence *come* wars and fightings among you? *come they* not hence, *even* of your lusts that war in your members?

2 Ye lust, and have not: ye [R]kill, and [T]desire to have, and cannot obtain: ye fight and war, yet ye have not, because [R]ye ask not.   [1 John 3:15] · *covet* · Ps. 10:4

3 [R]Ye ask, and receive not, [R]because ye ask amiss, that ye may consume *it* upon your [T]lusts.   Job 27:8, 9 · [Ps. 66:18] · *desires*

4 Ye adulterers and adulteresses, know ye not that the friendship of the world is enmity with God? whosoever therefore will be a friend of the world is the enemy of God.

5 Do ye think that the scripture saith in vain, The spirit that dwelleth in us [T]lusteth to envy?   *follows our desires to the point of envy*

6 But he giveth more grace. Wherefore he saith, [R]GOD RESISTETH THE PROUD, BUT GIVETH GRACE UNTO THE HUMBLE.   Prov. 3:34

7 Submit yourselves therefore to God. Resist the devil, and he will flee from you.

8 Draw nigh to God, and he will draw nigh to you. Cleanse *your* hands, *ye* sinners; and purify *your* hearts, *ye* double minded.

9 Be [T]afflicted, and mourn, and weep: let your laughter be turned to mourning, and *your* joy to [T]heaviness.   *troubled · sadness*

10 [R]Humble yourselves in the sight of the Lord, and he shall lift you up.   Job 22:29

11 [R]Speak not evil one of another, brethren. He that [T]speaketh evil of *his* brother, [R]and judgeth his brother, speaketh evil of the law, and judgeth the law: but if thou judge the law, thou art not a doer of the law, but a judge.   1 Pet. 2:1 · *criticizes* · [Matt. 7:1]

12 There is one lawgiver, [R]who is able to save and to destroy: [R]who art thou that judgest another?   [Matt. 10:28] · Rom. 14:4

Faith Produces Dependence on God

13 [R]Go to now, ye that say, To day or to morrow we will go into such a city, and continue there a year, and buy and sell, and get gain: *v. 15*; Prov. 20:18

14 Whereas ye know not what *shall be* on the morrow. For what *is* your life? It is [T]even a vapour, that appeareth for a little time, and then vanisheth away.   *like a mist*

15 For that ye *ought* to say, If the Lord will, we shall live, and do this, or that.

16 But now ye rejoice in your boastings: [R]all such rejoicing is evil.   1 Cor. 5:6

17 Therefore to him that knoweth to do good, and doeth *it* not, to him it is sin.

CHAPTER 5

GO to now, [R]ye rich men, weep and howl for your miseries that shall come upon you.   Prov. 11:28; [Luke 6:24; 1 Tim. 6:9]

2 Your riches are [T]corrupted, and [R]your garments are motheaten.   *decayed* · Job 13:28

3 Your gold and silver [T]is cankered; and the rust of them shall be a witness against you, and shall eat your flesh as it were fire. Ye have [T]heaped treasure together [T]for the last days.   *are rusted · laid up your · in*

4 Behold, the hire of the labourers who have reaped down your fields, which is of you kept back by fraud, crieth: and the cries of them which have reaped are entered into the ears of the Lord of sabaoth.

5 Ye have lived in pleasure on the earth, and been wanton; ye have nourished your hearts, as in a day of slaughter.

6 Ye have condemned *and* killed the [T]just; *and* he doth not resist you.   *good man*

Faith Endures Awaiting Christ's Return

7 Be patient therefore, brethren, unto the coming of the Lord. Behold, the husbandman waiteth for the precious fruit of the earth, and hath long patience for it, until he receive the early and latter rain.

8 Be ye also patient; stablish your hearts: for the coming of the Lord draweth nigh.

9 Grudge not one against another, brethren, lest ye be condemned: behold, the judge standeth before the door.

10 [R]Take, my brethren, the prophets, who have spoken in the name of the Lord, for an example of suffering affliction, and of [T]patience.   Matt. 5:12 · *endurance*

11 Behold, we count them happy which endure. Ye have heard of the patience of Job, and have seen the end of the Lord; that the Lord is very pitiful, and of tender mercy.

12 But above all things, my brethren, [R]swear not, neither by heaven, neither by the

earth, neither by any other oath: but let your yea be yea; and your nay, nay; lest ye fall into condemnation.　　　Matt. 5:34–37

Faith Prays for the Afflicted

13 Is any among you afflicted? let him pray. Is any merry? let him sing psalms.

14 Is any sick among you? let him call for the elders of the church; and let them pray over him, Ranointing[T] him with oil in the name of the Lord:　　　Mark 6:13 · rubbing

15 And the prayer of faith shall Tsave the sick, and the Lord shall raise him up; Rand if he have committed sins, they shall be forgiven him.　　　heal · Is. 33:24

16 Confess your faults one to another, and pray one for another, that ye may be healed.

The Teffectual fervent prayer of a righteous man availeth much.　　　unceasing

17 E-li'-as was a man Rsubject to Tlike passions as we are, and he prayed earnestly that it might not rain: and it rained not on the earth by the space of three years and six months.　　　Acts 14:15 · the same

18 RAnd he prayed again, and the Theaven gave rain, and the earth Tbrought forth her fruit.　　　1 Kin. 18:42, 45 · sky · produced

Faith Confronts the Erring Brother

19 RBrethren, if any of you do err from the truth, and one convert him;　　　Acts 8:22

20 Let him know, that he which converteth the sinner from the error of his way Rshall save a soul from death, and Rshall Thide a multitude of sins.　　　Rom. 11:14 · [1 Pet. 4:8] · cover

PETER

THE BOOK OF FIRST PETER

Persecution can cause either growth or bitterness in the Christian life. Response determines the result. In writing to Jewish believers struggling in the midst of persecution, Peter encourages them to conduct themselves courageously for the Person and program of Christ. Both their character and conduct must be above reproach. Having been born again to a living hope, they are to imitate the Holy One who has called them. The fruit of that character will be conduct rooted in submission: citizens to government, servants to masters, wives to husbands, husbands to wives, and Christians to one another. Only after submission is fully understood does Peter deal with the difficult area of suffering. The Christians are not to think it "strange concerning the fiery trial which is to try you, as though some strange thing happened unto you" (4:12), but are to rejoice as partakers of the suffering of Christ. That response to life is truly the climax of one's submission to the good hand of God.

This epistle begins with the phrase *Petros apostolos Iēsou Christou*, "Peter, an apostle of Jesus Christ." This is the basis of the early title *Petrou A*, the "First of Peter."

THE AUTHOR OF FIRST PETER

The early church universally acknowledged the authenticity and authority of First Peter. The internal evidence supports this consistent external testimony in several ways. The apostle Peter's name is given in 1:1, and there are definite similarities between certain phrases in this letter and Peter's sermons as recorded in the Book of Acts (cf. 1 Pet. 1:20 and Acts 2:23; 1 Pet. 4:5 and Acts 10:42). Twice in Acts Peter used the Greek word *xylon*, "wood, tree," to speak of the cross, and this distinctive use is also found in First Peter (see Acts 5:30; 10:39; 1 Pet. 2:24). The epistle contains a number of allusions to events in the life of Christ that held special significance for Peter (e.g., 2:23; 3:18; 4:1; 5:1; cf. 5:5 and John 13:4).

Nevertheless, critics since the nineteenth century have challenged the authenticity of First Peter on several grounds. Some claim that 1:1, 2 and 4:12—5:14 were later additions that turned an anonymous address or a baptismal sermon into a Petrine Epistle. Others argue that the sufferings experienced by readers of this letter must refer to the persecution of Christians that took place after the time of Peter in the reigns of the emperors Domitian (A.D. 81–96) and Trajan (A.D. 98–117). There is no basis for the first argument, and the second argument falsely assumes that Christians were not being reviled for their faith during the life of Peter. Another challenge asserts that the quality of the Greek of this epistle is too high for a Galilean like Peter. But Galileans were bilingual (Aramaic and Greek), and writers such as Matthew and James were skillful in their use of Greek. It is also likely that Peter used Silvanus as his scribe (5:12; Paul calls him Silvanus in 2 Cor. 1:19; 1 Thess. 1:1; 2 Thess. 1:1; Luke calls him Silas in Acts 15:40—18:5), and Silvanus may have smoothed out Peter's speech in the process.

THE TIME OF FIRST PETER

This letter is addressed "to the strangers scattered,"or more literally, "sojourners of the dispersion" (1:1). This, coupled with the injunction to keep their behavior "honest among the Gentiles" (2:12), gives the initial appearance that the bulk of the readers are Hebrew Christians. A closer look, however, forms the opposite view that most of these believers were Gentiles. They were called "out of darkness" (2:9), and they "in time past *were* not a people, but *are* now the people of God" (2:10). Their former "vain conversation *received* by tradition from [their] fathers" was characterized by ignorance and futility (1:14, 18; cf. Eph. 4:17). Because they no longer engage in debauchery and idolatry, they are maligned by their countrymen (4:3, 4). These descriptions do not fit a predominantly Hebrew Christian readership. Though Peter was an apostle "unto the circumcision" (Gal. 2:9), he also ministered to Gentiles (Acts 10:34-48; Gal. 2:12), and a letter like this would not be beyond the scope of his ministry.

This epistle was addressed to Christians throughout Asia Minor, indicating the spread of the gospel in regions not evangelized when Acts was written (Pontus, Cappadocia, Bithynia; 1:1). It is possible that Peter visited and ministered in some of these areas, but there is no evidence. He wrote this letter in response to the news of growing opposition to the believers in Asia Minor (1:6; 3:13-17; 4:12-19; 5:9, 10). Hostility and suspicion were mounting against Christians in the empire, and they were being reviled and abused for their life-styles and subversive talk about another kingdom. Christianity had not yet received the official Roman ban, but the stage was being set for the persecution and martyrdom of the near future.

Peter's life was dramatically changed after the Resurrection, and he occupied a central role in the early church and in the spread of the gospel to the Samaritans and Gentiles (Acts 2—10). After the Jerusalem Council in Acts 15, little is recorded of Peter's activities. He evidently

traveled extensively with his wife (1 Cor. 9:5) and ministered in various Roman provinces. According to tradition, Peter was crucified upside down in Rome prior to Nero's death in A.D. 68.

This epistle was written from Babylon (5:13), but scholars are divided as to whether this refers literally to Babylon in Mesopotamia or symbolically to Rome. There is no tradition that Peter went to Babylon, and in his day it had few inhabitants. On the other hand, tradition consistently indicates that Peter spent the last years of his life in Rome. As a center of idolatry, the term "Babylon" was an appropriate figurative designation for Rome (cf. the later use of Babylon in Rev. 17; 18). Peter used other figurative expressions in this epistle, and it is not surprising that he would do the same with Rome. His mention of Mark (5:13) also fits this view because Mark was in Rome during Paul's first imprisonment (Col. 4:10). This epistle was probably written shortly before the outbreak of persecution under Nero in A.D. 64.

THE CHRIST OF FIRST PETER

This epistle presents Christ as the believer's example and hope in times of suffering in a spiritually hostile world. He is the basis for the Christian's "lively hope" and "inheritance" (1:3, 4), and the love relationship available with Him by faith is a source of inexpressible joy (1:8). His suffering and death provide redemption for all who trust in Him: "His own self bare our sins in his own body on the tree, that we, being dead to sins, should live unto righteousness: by whose stripes ye were healed" (2:24; cf. 1:18, 19; 3:18). Christ is the Chief Shepherd and Guardian of believers (2:25; 5:4), and when He appears, those who know Him will be glorified.

KEYS TO FIRST PETER

Key Word: Suffering for the Cause of Christ—The basic theme of First Peter is the proper response to Christian suffering. Knowing that his readers will be facing more persecution than ever before, Peter writes this letter to give them a divine perspective on these trials so that they will be able to endure them without wavering in their faith. They should not be surprised at their ordeal because the One they follow also suffered and died (2:21; 3:18; 4:1, 12-14). Rather, they should count it a privilege to share the sufferings of Christ. Peter therefore exhorts them to be sure that their hardships are not being caused by their own wrongdoings, but for their Christian testimony. They are not the only believers who are suffering (5:9), and they must recognize that God brings these things into the lives of His children, not as a punishment but as a stimulus to "make you perfect" in Christ

(5:10). Peter wants to overcome the attitudes of bitterness and anxiety, replacing them with dependence on and confidence in God.

Another theme is stated in 5:12: "I have written briefly, exhorting, and testifying that this is the true grace of God." In this epistle, Peter frequently speaks of the believer's position in Christ and future hope, and he does so to remind his readers that they are merely sojourners on this planet: their true destiny is eternal glory "when his glory shall be revealed" (4:13). The grace of God in their salvation (1:1—2:10) shall give them an attitude of submission (2:11—3:12) in the context of suffering for the name of Christ (3:13—5:14).

Key Verses: First Peter 1:10-12 and 4:12, 13— "Of which salvation the prophets have enquired and searched diligently, who prophesied of the grace that should come unto you: Searching what, or what manner of time the Spirit of Christ which was in them did signify, when it testified beforehand the sufferings of Christ, and the glory that should follow. Unto whom it was revealed, that not unto themselves, but unto us they did minister the things, which are now reported unto you by them that have preached the gospel unto you with the Holy Ghost sent down from heaven; which things the angels desire to look into" (1:10-12).

"Beloved, think it not strange concerning the fiery trial which is to try you, as though some strange thing happened unto you: But rejoice, inasmuch as ye are partakers of Christ's sufferings; that, when his glory shall be revealed, ye may be glad also with exceeding joy" (4:12, 13).

Key Chapter: First Peter 4—Central in the New Testament revelation concerning how to handle persecution and suffering caused by one's Christian testimony is First Peter 4. Not only is Christ's suffering to be our model (4:1, 2), but also we are to rejoice in that we can share in His suffering (4:12-14).

SURVEY OF FIRST PETER

Peter addresses this epistle to "strangers" in a world that is growing increasingly hostile to Christians. These believers are beginning to suffer because of their stand for Christ, and Peter uses this letter to give them counsel and comfort by stressing the reality of their living hope in the Lord. By standing firm in the grace of God (5:12) they will be able to endure their "fiery trial" (4:12), knowing that there is a divine purpose behind their pain. This letter logically proceeds through the themes of the salvation of the believer (1:1—2:12); the submission of the believer (2:13—3:12); and the suffering of the believer (3:13—5:14).

The Salvation of the Believer (1:1—2:12): Addressing his letter to believers in several

Roman provinces, Peter briefly describes the saving work of the triune Godhead in his salutation (1:1, 2). He then extols God for the riches of this salvation by looking in three temporal directions (1:3–12). First, Peter anticipates the future realization of the Christian's manifold inheritance (1:3–5). Second, he looks at the present joy that this living hope produces in spite of various trials (1:6–9). Third, he reflects upon the prophets of the past who predicted the gospel of God's grace in Christ (1:1–12).

The proper response to this salvation is the pursuit of sanctification or holiness (1:13—2:10). This involves a purifying departure from conformity with the world to godliness in behavior and love. With this in mind, Peter exhorts his readers to "desire the sincere milk of the word, that [they] may grow" (2:2) by applying "the word of God, which liveth and abideth for ever"(1:23) and acting as a holy priesthood of believers.

The Submission of the Believer (2:13–3:12): Peter turns to the believer's relationships in the world and appeals for an attitude of submission as the Christlike way to harmony and true freedom. Submission for the Lord's sake to those in governmental (2:13–17) and social (2:18–20) authority will foster a good testimony to outsiders. Before moving on to submission in marital relationships (3:1–7), Peter again picks up the theme of Christian suffering (mentioned in 1:6, 7 and 2:12, 18–20) and uses Christ as the supreme model: He suffered sinlessly, silently, and as a substitute for the salvation of others (2:21–25; cf. Is. 52:13—53:12). Peter summarizes his appeal for Christlike submission and humility in 3:8–11.

The Suffering of the Believer (3:13–5:14): Anticipating that growing opposition to Christianity will require a number of his readers to defend their faith and conduct, Peter encourages them to be ready to do so in an intelligent and gracious way (3:13–16). Three times he tells them that if they must suffer, it should be for righteousness' sake and not as a result of sinful behavior (3:17; see 2:20; 4:15, 16). The end of this chapter (3:18–22) is an extremely difficult passage to interpret, and several options have been offered. Verses 19 and 20 may mean that Christ, during the period between His death and resurrection, addressed demonic spirits or the spirits of those who were alive before the flood. Another interpretation is that Christ preached through Noah to his pre-flood contemporaries.

As believers in Christ, the readers are no longer to pursue the lusts of the flesh as they did formerly, but rather the will of God (4:1–6). In view of the hardships that they may suffer, Peter exhorts them to be strong in their mutual love and to exercise their spiritual gifts in the power of God so that they will be built up (4:7–11). They should not be surprised when they are slandered and reviled for their faith because the sovereign God has a purpose in all things, and the time of judgment will come when His name and all who trust in Him will be vindicated (4:12–19). They must therefore "commit the keeping of their souls *to him* in well doing" (4:19).

In a special word to the elders of the churches in these Roman provinces, Peter urges them to be diligent but gentle shepherds over the flocks that have been divinely placed under their care (5:1–4). The readers as a whole are told to clothe themselves with humility toward one another and toward God who will exalt them at the proper time (5:5–7). They are to resist the adversary in the sure knowledge that their calling to God's eternal glory in Christ will be realized (5:8–11). Peter ends his epistle by stating his theme ("the true grace of God") and conveying greetings and a benediction (5:12–14).

FOCUS	SALVATION OF THE BELIEVER		SUBMISSION OF THE BELIEVER	SUFFERING OF THE BELIEVER			
REFERENCE	1:1————1:13————		2:13————	3:13————3:18————		4:7————	5:1————5:14
DIVISION	SALVATION OF THE BELIEVER	SANCTIFICA-TION OF THE BELIEVER	GOVERNMENT, BUSINESS, MARRIAGE, AND ALL OF LIFE	CONDUCT IN SUFFERING	CHRIST'S EXAMPLE OF SUFFERING	COMMANDS IN SUFFERING	MINISTER IN SUFFERING
TOPIC	BELIEF OF CHRISTIANS		BEHAVIOR OF CHRISTIANS	BUFFETING OF CHRISTIANS			
	HOLINESS		HARMONY	HUMILITY			
LOCATION	EITHER ROME OR BABYLON						
TIME	C. A.D. 63–64						

OUTLINE OF FIRST PETER

CHAPTER 1

Salutation

PETER, an apostle of Jesus Christ, to the ᵀstrangers ᴿscattered throughout Pon′-tus, Ga-la′-ti-a, Cap-pa-do′-ci-a, Asia, and Bi-thyn′-i-a,   *God's people* · John 7:35; Acts 2:9, 10

2 ᵀElect according to the foreknowledge of God the Father, through sanctification of the Spirit, unto obedience and ᴿsprinkling of the blood of Jesus Christ: Grace unto you, and peace, be multiplied.   *called* · Is. 52:15 ★

Hope for the Future

3 Blessed *be* the God and Father of our Lord Jesus Christ, which according to his ᵀabundant mercy hath begotten us again unto a ᵀlively hope by the resurrection of Jesus Christ from the dead,   *plentiful · living*

4 To an inheritance ᵀincorruptible, and undefiled, and that fadeth not away, reserved in heaven for you,   *which cannot decay*

Trials for the Present

5 ᴿWho are ᵀkept by the power of God through faith unto salvation ready to be revealed in the last time.   John 10:28 · *guarded*

6 Wherein ye greatly rejoice, though now for a season, if need be, ye are in heaviness through manifold temptations:

7 That the trial of your faith, being much more precious than of gold that perisheth, though it be tried with fire, might be found unto praise and honour and glory at the appearing of Jesus Christ:

8 ᴿWhom having not seen, ye love; ᴿin whom, though now ye see *him* not, yet believing, ye rejoice with joy unspeakable and full of glory: 1 John 4:20 · John 20:29

9 Receiving the ᴿendᵀ of your faith, *even* the salvation of *your* souls.   [Rom. 6:22] · *outcome*

Anticipation in the Past

10 ᴿOf which salvation the prophets have enquired and searched diligently, who prophesied of the grace *that should come* unto you: [Zech. 6:12]

11 Searching what, or what manner of time ᴿthe Spirit of Christ which was in them did signify, when it testified beforehand the sufferings of Christ, and the glory that should follow.   [Rom. 8:9]; 2 Pet. 1:21

12 ᴿUnto whom it was revealed, that not unto themselves, but unto ᵀus they did minister the things, which are now reported unto you by them that have ᴿpreached the gospel unto you with the Holy Ghost sent down from heaven; which things the angels desire to look into.   [Dan. 9:24] · *you* · vv. 1, 25; 4:6

"Be Ye Holy"

13 ᴿWherefore gird up the loins of your mind, be sober, and hope to the end for the grace that is to be brought unto you at the revelation of Jesus Christ;   Luke 12:35

14 As obedient children, not ᵀfashioning yourselves according to the former lusts in your ignorance: *shaping up your way of living*

15 ᴿBut as he which hath called you is holy, so be ye holy in all manner of ᵀconversation;   [2 Cor. 7:1] · living

16 Because ᵀit is written, ᵀBE YE HOLY; FOR I AM HOLY.   the Scripture says · ye shall be

17 And if ye call on the Father, who without respect of persons judgeth according to every man's work, pass the time of your ᵀsojourning here in fear: pilgrimage

18 Forasmuch as ye know that ye were not redeemed with corruptible things, as silver and gold, from your vain conversation received by tradition from your fathers;

19 But ᴿwith the precious blood of Christ, ᴿas of a ᵀlamb without blemish and without spot: Acts 20:28 · Ex. 12:5; Is. 53:7 ★ · precious sacrifice

20 Who verily was foreordained before the foundation of the world, but was ᵀmanifest in these last times for you,   revealed

21 Who by him do believe in God, that raised him up from the dead, and ᵀgave him glory; that your faith and hope might be in God.   brought him into the presence of God

"Love One Another"

22 Seeing ye have ᵀpurified your souls in obeying the truth through the Spirit unto ᵀunfeigned ᴿlove of the brethren, see that ye love one another with a pure heart ᵀfervently: cleansed · genuine · Heb. 13:1 · earnestly

23 Being born again, not of corruptible seed, but of incorruptible, by the word of God, which liveth and abideth for ever.

24 FOR ᴿALL FLESH IS AS GRASS, AND ALL THE GLORY OF MAN AS THE FLOWER OF GRASS. THE GRASS WITHERETH, AND THE FLOWER THEREOF FALLETH AWAY: Is. 40:6

25 ᴿBUT THE WORD OF THE LORD ENDURETH FOR EVER. And this is the word which by the gospel is preached unto you.   Is. 40:8

CHAPTER 2

"Desire the Sincere Milk of the Word"

WHEREFORE ᴿlaying aside all malice, and all guile, and hypocrisies, and envies, and all evil speakings,   Heb. 12:1

2 As newborn babes, desire the sincere milk of the word, that ye may grow thereby:

3 If so be ye have ᴿtasted that the Lord is ᵀgracious.   Heb. 6:5 · kind

"Offer Up Spiritual Sacrifices"

4 To whom coming, as unto ᴿa living stone, ᵀdisallowed indeed of men, but chosen of God, and precious,   Luke 20:17 · rejected

5 Ye also, as ᵀlively stones, ᵀare built up ᴿa spiritual house, an holy priesthood, to offer up spiritual sacrifices, acceptable to God by Jesus Christ.   living · be ye built · [Dan. 2:44; Matt. 16:18]

6 Wherefore also it is contained in the scripture, ᴿBEHOLD, I LAY IN SION A CHIEF CORNER STONE, ᵀELECT, PRECIOUS: AND HE THAT BELIEVETH ON HIM SHALL NOT BE ᵀCONFOUNDED.   Is. 28:16 ★ · chosen · ashamed

7 Unto you therefore which believe he is precious: but unto them which be disobedient, ᴿTHE STONE WHICH THE BUILDERS DISALLOWED, THE SAME IS MADE THE HEAD OF THE CORNER,   [Matt. 16:18]; 21:42; Ps. 118:22 ★

8 ᴿAND A STONE OF STUMBLING, AND A ROCK OF OFFENCE, even to them which stumble at the word, being disobedient: whereunto also they were appointed.   Is. 8:14 ★

9 But ye are a chosen generation, a royal priesthood, an holy nation, ᵀa peculiar people; that ye should shew forth the praises of him who hath called you out of darkness into his marvellous light: God's own

10 ᴿWhich in time past were not a people, but are now the people of God: which had not ᵀobtained mercy, but now have obtained mercy.   Hos. 1:9, 10; Rom. 9:25, 26 · received

"Abstain from Fleshly Lusts"

11 Dearly beloved, I beseech you as strangers and pilgrims, abstain from fleshly ᵀlusts, which war against the soul;   desires

12 Having your conversation honest among the Gentiles: that, whereas they speak against you as evildoers, they may by your good works, which they shall behold, glorify God in the day of visitation.

Submission to the Government

13 ᴿSubmit yourselves to every ᵀordinance of man for the Lord's sake: whether it be to the king, as supreme;   [Rom. 13:1] · regulation

14 ᴿOr unto governors, as unto them that are sent by him for the punishment of evildoers, and for the praise of them that do well.   Rom. 13:3, 4

2:13 Our Responsibility to Human Government—It is impossible for a believer to be a good Christian and a bad citizen at the same time. As children of God our responsibility to human government is threefold.

a. We are to recognize and accept that the powers that be are ordained by God. "Let every soul be subject unto the higher powers. For there is no power but of God: the powers that be are ordained of God" (Page 1119—Rom. 13:1). This truth applies even to atheistic human governments unless, of course, the law is anti-scriptural. In that situation the believer must obey God rather than man (Page 1076—Acts 4:18–20). In fact, when Paul wrote those words in Romans 13:1, the evil emperor Nero was on the throne. See also Titus 3:1.

b. We are to pay our taxes to human government (see Page 959—Matt. 17:24–27; 22:21; Page 1119—Rom. 13:7).

15 For ᴿso is the will of God, that with well doing ye may put to silence the ignorance of foolish men: [3:17]

16 ᴿAs free, and not using *your* ᵀliberty for a cloke of ᵀmaliciousness, but as the servants of God.   [Gal. 5:1] • *freedom • evil intentions*

17 Honour all *men.* Love the brotherhood. Fear God. ᵀHonour the king.   *respect*

Submission in Business

18 Servants, *be* subject to *your* masters with all fear; not only to the good and gentle, but also to the ᵀfroward.   *harsh*

19 For this *is* ᵀthankworthy, if a man for ᴿconscience toward God endure grief, suffering wrongfully.   *acceptable* • 3:14, 17

20 For what glory *is it,* if, when ye be ᵀbuffeted for your faults, ye shall take it patiently? but if, when ye do well, and suffer *for it,* ye take it patiently, this *is* ᵀacceptable with God.   *beaten • wellpleasing to*

21 For ᴿeven hereunto were ye called: because Christ also suffered ᵀfor us, ᴿleaving us an example, that ye should follow his steps: Matt. 16:24 • *on our behalf* • [1 John 2:6]

22 ᴿWʜᴏ ᵀᴅɪᴅ ɴᴏ sɪɴ, ɴᴇɪᴛʜᴇʀ ᴡᴀs ᵀɢᴜɪʟᴇ ꜰᴏᴜɴᴅ ɪɴ ʜɪs ᴍᴏᴜᴛʜ: Is. 53:9 ⋆ • *committed • deceit*

23 Who, ᴿwhen he was reviled, reviled not again; when he suffered, he threatened not; but ᴿcommitted ᵀhimself to him that judgeth righteously: Is. 53:7 ⋆ • Luke 23:46 • *committed his cause*

24 Who his own self bare our sins in his own body on the tree, that we, being dead to sins, should live unto righteousness: ᴿby whose ᵀstripes ye were healed. Is. 53:5 ⋆ • *wounds*

25 For ye were as sheep going astray; but are now returned ᴿunto the Shepherd and Bishop of your souls.   [Ezek. 34:23]; Zech. 13:7 ⋆

CHAPTER 3

Submission in Marriage

LIKEWISE, ye wives, *be* ᵀin subjection to your own husbands; that, if any ᵀobey not the word, they also may without ᵀthe word be won by the ᵀconversation of the wives;   *submissive • believe not • a • behavior*

2 ᴿWhile they behold your chaste conversation *coupled* with ᵀfear.   2:12 • *respect*

3 Whose adorning let it not be that outward *adorning* of plaiting the hair, and of wearing of gold, or of putting on of apparel;

4 But *let it be* the hidden man of the heart, in that which is not corruptible, *even the* ornament of a meek and quiet spirit, which is in the sight of God of great price.

5 For after this manner in the old time the holy women also, who trusted in God, adorned themselves, being ᵀin subjection unto their own husbands: *submissive*

6 Even as Sara obeyed Abraham, calling him lord: whose daughters ye are, as long as ye do well, and are not ᵀafraid with any ᵀamazement.   *panicked • sudden calamity*

7 Likewise, ye husbands, dwell with *them* according to knowledge, giving honour unto the wife, as unto the weaker vessel, and as being heirs together of the grace of life; that your prayers be not hindered.

8 Finally, ᴿ*be ye* all of one mind, having compassion one of another, love as brethren, *be* pitiful, *be* courteous: Rom. 12:16

Submission in All of Life

9 ᴿNot rendering evil for evil, or railing for railing: but contrariwise blessing; knowing

---

c. We are to pray for the leaders in human government. "I exhort therefore, that, first of all, supplications, prayers, intercessions, *and* giving of thanks, be made for all men; For kings, and for all that are in authority; that we may lead a quiet and peaceable life in all godliness and honesty. For this *is* good and acceptable in the sight of God our Saviour" (Page 1194—1 Tim. 2:1-3). Paul exhorts us to pray for those who are in authority that we may lead a quiet life in all godliness and honesty (Page 1194—1 Tim. 2:1-3).
Now turn to Page 856—Amos 3:2: Selection of Israel.
3:1-6 The Role of the Wife—In this passage the wife's only responsibility in the family is to "*be* in subjection" to her husband. A woman is to be in submission to her husband, not to mankind in general. To be in subjection to her husband does not imply any kind of natural inferiority on the part of the wife to the husband. In marriage two people become one. Therefore there are two intellects, two sets of emotions, and two wills that have been joined to constitute one. To keep the union from fracturing and destroying itself, one of those persons is charged with leadership in the relationship, and one is charged with submission.

The wife's submission to her husband is her "adorning," which makes her truly beautiful (3:3). This inner beauty is of great value in God's sight (3:4). The believing women of the Old Testament who hoped to be the human channel for the Messiah to come into the world made themselves beautiful by being in subjection to their own husbands. This is supremely illustrated in the relationship between Sara and Abraham. Wives are exhorted to do what Sara did, to be in subjection to their husbands, letting the consequences rest with God, and thus become Sara's daughters (3:6). For the wife who will do this God promises that, if her husband is either an unbeliever or out of fellowship with God, her subjection can be the very means God will use to bring her husband into a proper relationship with God (3:1, 2). The wife's subjection may lead to the husband's salvation.
Now turn to Page 1179—Col. 3:19: The Role of the Husband.

that ye are thereunto called, that ye should inherit a blessing. [Prov. 17:13]

10 ᴿFOR HE THAT WILL LOVE LIFE, AND SEE GOOD DAYS, LET HIM REFRAIN HIS TONGUE FROM EVIL, AND HIS LIPS THAT THEY SPEAK NO ᵀGUILE: Ps. 34:12–16 · *deceit*

11 LET HIM ESCHEW EVIL, AND DO GOOD; LET HIM SEEK PEACE, AND ENSUE IT.

12 FOR THE EYES OF THE LORD *ARE* OVER THE RIGHTEOUS, AND HIS EARS *ARE* OPEN UNTO THEIR PRAYERS: BUT THE FACE OF THE LORD *IS* AGAINST THEM THAT DO EVIL.

Conduct in Suffering

13 And who *is* he that will harm you, if ye be followers of that which is good?

14 But and if ye suffer for righteousness' sake, happy *are* ye: AND BE NOT AFRAID OF THEIR TERROR, NEITHER BE ᵀTROUBLED; *worried*

15 But ᵀsanctify the Lord God in your hearts: and ᴿ*be* ready always to *give* an answer to every man that asketh you a reason of the hope that is in you with meekness and ᵀfear: *honor* · Ps. 119:46 · *respect*

16 Having a good conscience; that, whereas they speak evil of you, as of evildoers, they may be ashamed that falsely accuse your good conversation in Christ.

17 For *it is* better, if the will of God be so, that ye suffer for well doing, than for ᵀevil doing. *wrong*

Christ's Example of Suffering

18 ᴿFor Christ also hath once suffered for sins, the just for the unjust, that he might bring us to God, being put to death in the flesh, but quickened by the Spirit: Is. 53:12

19 By which also he went and ᴿpreached unto the spirits in prison; Eph. 4:9; 4:6

20 ᴿWhich ᵀsometime were disobedient, when once the longsuffering of God waited in the days of Noah, while the ark was a preparing, wherein few, that is, eight souls were saved by water. Gen. 6:3, 14 · *aforetime*

21 The like figure whereunto *even* baptism doth also now save us (not the putting away of ᴿthe filth of the flesh, but the answer of a

good conscience toward God,) by the resurrection of Jesus Christ: [Rom. 6:1–6]

22 Who is gone into heaven, and is on the right hand of God; angels and authorities and powers being made subject unto him.

CHAPTER 4

FORASMUCH then as Christ hath suffered for us in the flesh, arm yourselves likewise with the same mind: for he that hath suffered in the flesh hath ceased from sin;

2 That he ᴿno longer should live the rest of *his* time in the flesh to the ᵀlusts of men, but to the will of God. [Rom. 6:2; Col. 3:3] · *desires*

3 For the time past of *our* life may suffice us to have wrought the will of the Gentiles, when we ᵀwalked in lasciviousness, lusts, excess of wine, revellings, banquetings, and abominable idolatries: *lived*

4 ᴿWherein they think it strange that ye run not with *them* to the same ᵀexcess of riot, speaking evil of *you*: Acts 13:45 · *extremes*

5 Who shall give account to him that is ready to judge the quick and the dead.

6 For for this cause was the gospel preached also to them that are dead, that they might be judged according to men in the flesh, but live according to God in the spirit.

Commands in Suffering

7 But the end of all things is at hand: be ye therefore sober, and watch unto prayer.

8 And above all things have fervent charity among yourselves: for CHARITY SHALL COVER THE MULTITUDE OF SINS.

9 ᴿUse hospitality one to another ᴿwithout ᵀgrudging. Heb. 13:2 · 2 Cor. 9:7 · *murmuring*

10 ᴿAs every man hath received the gift, *even* so minister the same one to another, ᴿas good stewards of ᴿthe ᵀmanifold grace of God. Rom. 12:6 · Matt. 24:45 · [1 Cor. 12:4] · *varied*

11 If any man speak, *let him speak* as the oracles of God; if any man ᵀminister, *let him do it* as of the ability which God giveth: that ᴿGod in all things may be glorified through Jesus Christ, to whom *be* praise and dominion for ever and ever. A-men'. *serve* · Eph. 5:20

3:17 Kinds of Suffering—There are three basic kinds of suffering, all of which can bring about much pain and discomfort to the believer.

a. Physical suffering. This, of course, occurs when a part of our body is injured or begins to malfunction, resulting in a disharmony between it and the rest of the body. Several factors can be involved in physical suffering. It can be caused by an accident or by carelessness (Page 312—2 Sam. 4:4). It can be due to birth deformities (Page 1053—John 9:1). It can result from internal disorders (Page 1016—Luke 8:43). Finally, physical suffering may actually be caused by Satan (Page 519—Job 2:7; Page 1023—Luke 13:16).

b. Mental suffering. In many ways this suffering is even more intense than physical suffering. Justified or unjustified concern over some matter can easily produce mental anguish. Paul himself experienced "fear, and . . . much trembling" and "anguish of heart" (Page 1127—1 Cor. 2:3; Page 1143—2 Cor. 1:8; 2:4, 13; 7:5).

c. Spiritual suffering. Spiritual suffering can come from the world (Page 1250—1 John 2:15–17), the flesh (Page 1113—Rom. 7:18–24), or the devil. Often it is the latter. See Acts 13:8–11; 16:16–18; First Thessalonians 2:18.

Now turn to Page 519—Job 2:7: Purposes of Suffering.

12 [R]Beloved, think it not strange concerning the [T]fiery trial which is to [T]try you, as though some strange thing happened unto you:　　　　[1:7; 1 Cor. 3:13] • *severe testing* • *prove*

13 [R]But rejoice, inasmuch as ye are [T]partakers of Christ's sufferings; that, when his glory shall be revealed, ye may be glad also with exceeding joy.　　　　Rom. 8:17 • *partners in*

14 If ye be [T]reproached for the name of Christ, happy *are ye;* for the spirit of [T]glory and of God resteth upon you: on their part he is [T]evil spoken of, but on your part he is [T]glorified.　　　*criticized* • *praise* • *criticized* • *praised*

15 But let none of you suffer as a murderer, or *as* a thief, or *as* an evildoer, or as a [T]busybody in other men's matters.　　　*meddler*

16 [R]Yet if *any man suffer* as a [R]Christian, let him not be ashamed; but let him glorify God on this behalf.　　　Acts 5:41 • 11:26; 26:28

17 For the time *is come* that judgment must begin at the house of God: and if *it* first *begin* at us, what shall the end *be* of them that obey not the gospel of God?

18 [R]AND IF THE RIGHTEOUS SCARCELY BE SAVED, WHERE SHALL THE UNGODLY AND THE SINNER APPEAR?　　　Prov. 11:31; Luke 23:31

19 Wherefore let them that suffer [T]according to the will of God commit the keeping of their souls *to him* in well doing, as unto a faithful Creator.　　　*as permitted by*

CHAPTER 5

Elders, Feed the Flock

THE elders which are among you I exhort, who am also an elder, and a witness of the sufferings of Christ, and also a partaker of the glory that shall be revealed:

2 Feed the flock of God which is among you, taking the oversight *thereof,* not by [T]constraint, but willingly; not for filthy lucre, but of a [T]ready mind;　　　*compulsion* • *willing*

3 Neither as being lords over *God's* heritage, but being ensamples to the flock.

4 And when the chief [T]Shepherd shall appear, ye shall receive [R]a crown of glory that fadeth not away.　　　*pastor* • 2 Tim. 4:8

Saints, Humble Yourselves

5 Likewise, ye younger, submit yourselves unto the elder. Yea, all *of you* be subject one to another, and be clothed with humility: for [R]GOD RESISTETH THE PROUD, [R]AND GIVETH GRACE TO THE HUMBLE.　　　Prov. 3:34 • Is. 57:15

6 [R]Humble yourselves therefore under the mighty hand of God, that he may [T]exalt you in due time:　　　James 4:10 • *raise you up*

7 [T]Casting all your [T]care upon him; for he careth for you.　　　*throw* • *anxiety*

8 Be sober, be vigilant; because your adversary the devil, as a roaring lion, walketh about, seeking whom he may devour:

9 Whom resist [T]stedfast in the faith, [R]knowing that the same afflictions are [T]accomplished in your brethren that are in the world.　　　*firm* • [Acts 14:22; Eph. 6:11, 13] • *suffered by*

Benediction

10 But the God of all grace, [R]who hath called us [T]unto his eternal glory by Christ Jesus, after that ye have suffered a while, make you [T]perfect, stablish, strengthen, settle *you.*　　　1 Cor. 1:9 • *to share* • *complete*

11 [R]To him *be* glory and dominion for ever and ever. A-men'.　　　Rev. 1:6

12 By [T]Sil'-va-nus, a faithful brother unto you, as I suppose, I have written briefly, exhorting, and testifying that this is the true grace of God wherein ye stand.　　　*Silas*

13 The *church that is* at [R]Babylon, elected together with *you,* saluteth you; and *so doth* Marcus my son.　　　Rev. 14:8; 16:19

14 Greet ye one another with [R]a kiss of [T]charity. [R]Peace *be* with you all that are in Christ Jesus. A-men'.　　　Rom. 16:16 • *love* • Eph. 6:23

THE SECOND EPISTLE GENERAL OF

PETER

THE BOOK OF SECOND PETER

First Peter deals with problems from the outside; Second Peter deals with problems from the inside. Peter writes to warn the believers about the false teachers who are peddling damaging doctrine. He begins by urging them to keep close watch on their personal lives. The Christian life demands diligence in pursuing virtue, knowledge, temperance, patience, godliness, brotherly kindness, and charity (selfless love). By contrast, the false teachers are sensual, arrogant, greedy, and covetous. They scoff at the thought of future judgment and live their lives as if the present would be the pattern for the future. Peter reminds them that although God may be long-suffering in sending judgment, ultimately it will come. In view of that fact, believers should live lives of godliness, blamelessness, and steadfastness.

The statement of authorship in 1:1 is very clear: "Simon Peter, a servant and an apostle of Jesus Christ." To distinguish this epistle from the first by Peter it was given the Greek title *Petrou B*, "Second of Peter."

THE AUTHOR OF SECOND PETER

No other book in the New Testament poses as many problems of authenticity as does Second Peter. Unlike First Peter, this letter has very weak external testimony, and its genuineness is hurt by internal difficulties as well. Because of these obstacles, many scholars reject the Petrine authorship of this epistle, but this does not mean that there is no case for the opposite position.

External Evidence: The external testimony for the Petrine authorship of Second Peter is weaker than that for any other New Testament book, but by the fourth century it became generally recognized as an authentic work of the apostle Peter. There are no undisputed second-century quotations from Second Peter, but in the third century it is quoted in the writings of several church fathers, notably Origen and Clement of Alexandria. Third-century writers were generally aware of Second Peter and respected its contents, but it was still cataloged as a disputed book. The fourth century saw the official acknowledgment of the authority of Second Peter in spite of some lingering doubts. For several reasons Second Peter was not quickly accepted as a canonical book: (1) Slow circulation kept it from being widely known. (2) Its brevity and contents greatly limited the number of quotations from it in the writings of early church leaders. (3) The delay in recognition meant that Second Peter had to compete with several later works which falsely claimed to be Petrine (e.g., the Apocalypse of Peter). (4) Stylistic differences between First and Second Peter also raised doubts.

Internal Evidence: On the positive side, Second Peter bears abundant testimony to its apostolic origin. It claims to be by "Simon Peter" (1:1), and 3:1 says "This second epistle, beloved, I now write unto you." The writer refers to the Lord's prediction about the apostle's death in 1:14 (cf. John 21:18, 19) and says he was an eyewitness of the Transfiguration (1:16–18). As an apostle (1:1), he places himself on an equal level with Paul (3:15). There are also distinctive words that are found in Peter's sermons in Acts, as well as unusual words and phrases shared by First and Second Peter.

On the negative side, a number of troublesome areas challenge the traditional position: (1) There are differences between the style and vocabulary of First and Second Peter. The Greek of Second Peter is rough and awkward compared to that of First Peter, and there are also differences in informality and in the use of the Old Testament. But these differences are often exaggerated, and they can be explained by Peter's use of Silvanus as his secretary for First Peter and his own hand for Second Peter. (2) It is argued that Second Peter used a passage from Jude to describe false teachers, and that Jude was written after Peter's death. However, this is a debated issue, and it is possible that Jude quoted from Peter or that both used a common source (see "The Author of Jude"). (3) The reference to a collection of Paul's letters (3:15, 16) implies a late date for this epistle. But it is not necessary to conclude that all of Paul's letters were in mind here. Peter's contact with Paul and his associates no doubt made him familiar with several Pauline Epistles. (4) Some scholars claim that the false teaching mentioned in Second Peter was a form of Gnosticism that emerged after Peter's day, but there is insufficient evidence to support this stand.

The alternative to Petrine authorship is a later forgery done in the name of Peter. Even the claim that Second Peter was written by a disciple of Peter cannot overcome the problem of misrepresentation. In addition Second Peter is clearly superior to any pseudonymous writings. In spite of the external and internal problems, the traditional position of Petrine authorship overcomes more difficulties than any other option.

THE TIME OF SECOND PETER

Most scholars regard 3:1 ("This second epistle, beloved, I now write unto you") as a reference to First Peter. If this is so, Peter had the same readers of Asia Minor in mind (see "The

Time of First Peter"), although the more general salutation in 1:1 would also allow for a wider audience. Peter wrote this epistle in response to the spread of heretical teachings which were all the more insidious because they emerged from within the churches. These false teachers perverted the doctrine of justification and promoted a rebellious and immoral way of life.

This epistle was written just before the apostle's death (1:14), probably from Rome. His martyrdom took place between A.D. 64 and 66 (if Peter were alive in 67 when Paul wrote Second Timothy during his second Roman imprisonment, it is likely that Paul would have mentioned him).

THE CHRIST OF SECOND PETER

Apart from the first verse of his epistle, Peter employs the title "Lord" every time he names the Saviour. The Lord Jesus Christ is the source of full knowledge and power for the attainment of spiritual maturity (1:2, 3, 8; 3:18). Peter recalls the glory of His transfiguration on the holy mountain and anticipates His *parousia*, "coming," when the whole world, not just three men on a mountain, will behold His glory.

KEYS TO SECOND PETER

Key Word: Guard Against False Teachers—The basic theme that runs through Second Peter is the contrast between the knowledge and practice of truth versus falsehood. This epistle is written to expose the dangerous and seductive work of false teachers, and to warn believers to be on their guard so that they will not be "led away with the error of the wicked" (3:17). It is also written to exhort the readers to "grow in grace, and *in* the knowledge of our Lord and Saviour Jesus Christ" (3:18), because this growth into Christian maturity is the best defense against spiritual counterfeits. This letter serves to remind its readers of the foundational elements in the Christian life from which they must not waver (1:12, 13; 3:1, 2). This includes the certainty of the Lord's return in power and judgment.

Key Verses: Second Peter 1:20, 21 and 3:9-11—"Knowing this first, that no prophecy of the scripture is of any private interpretation. For the prophecy came not in old time by the will of man: but holy men of God spake *as they were* moved by the Holy Ghost" (1:20, 21).

"The Lord is not slack concerning his promise, as some men count slackness; but is longsuffering to us-ward, not willing that any should perish, but that all should come to repentance. But the day of the Lord will come as a thief in the night; in the which the heavens shall pass away with a great noise, and the elements shall melt with fervent heat, the earth also and the works that are therein shall be burned up. *Seeing* then *that* all these things shall be dissolved, what manner *of persons*

ought ye to be in *all* holy conversation and godliness" (3:9-11).

Key Chapter: Second Peter 1—The Scripture clearest in defining the relationship between God and man on the issue of inspiration is contained in 1:19-21. Three distinct principles surface: (1) that the interpretation of Scriptures is not limited to a favored elect but is open for all who "rightly [divide] the word of truth" (2 Tim. 2:15); (2) that the divinely inspired prophet did not initiate the Scripture himself; and (3) that the Holy Spirit (not the emotion or circumstances of the moment) moved holy men.

SURVEY OF SECOND PETER

Peter wrote his first epistle to encourage his readers to respond properly to external opposition. His second epistle focuses on internal opposition caused by false teachers whose "damnable heresies" (2:1) can seduce believers into error and immorality. While First Peter speaks of the new birth through the living Word, Second Peter stresses the need for growth in the grace and knowledge of Christ. The best antidote for error is a mature understanding of the truth. Second Peter divides into three parts: cultivation of Christian character (1); condemnation of false teachers (2); and confidence of Christ's return (3).

Cultivation of Christian Character (1): Peter's salutation (1:1, 2) is an introduction to the major theme of chapter 1, that is, the true knowledge of Jesus Christ. The readers are reminded of the "great and precious promises" that are theirs because of their calling to faith in Christ (1:3, 4). They have been called away from the corruption of the world to conformity with Christ, and Peter urges them to progress by forging a chain of eight Christian virtues from faith to love (1:5-7). If a believer does not transform profession into practice, he becomes spiritually useless, perverting the purpose for which he was called (1:8-11).

This letter was written not long before Peter's death (1:14) to remind believers of the riches of their position in Christ and their responsibility to hold fast to the truth (1:12-21). Peter knew that his departure from this earth was imminent, and he left this letter as a written legacy. As an eyewitness of the life of Christ (he illustrates this with a portrait of the Transfiguration in 1:16-18), Peter affirms the authority and reliability of the prophetic word. The clearest biblical description of the divine-human process of inspiration is found in 1:21: "But holy men of God spake *as they were* moved by the Holy Ghost."

Condemnation of False Teachers (2): Peter's discussion of true prophecy leads him to an extended denunciation of false prophecy in the churches. These false teachers were especially dangerous because they arose within the church and undermined the confidence of believers

(2:1-3). Peter's extended description of the characteristics of these false teachers (2:10-22) exposes the futility and corruption of their strategies. Their teachings and life-styles reek of arrogance and selfishness, but their crafty words are capable of enticing immature believers.

Confidence of Christ's Return (3): Again Peter states that this letter is designed to stir up the minds of his readers "by way of remembrance" (3:1; cf. 1:13). This very timely chapter is designed to remind them of the certain truth of the imminent *parousia* (this Greek word, used in 3:4, 12, refers to the second coming or advent of Christ) and to refute those mockers who will deny this doctrine in the last days. These scoffers will claim that God does not powerfully intervene in world affairs, but Peter calls attention to two past and one future divinely induced catastrophic events: the Creation, the Flood, and the dissolution of the present heavens and earth

(3:1-7). It may appear that the promise of Christ's return will not be fulfilled, but this is untrue for two reasons: God's perspective on the passing of time is quite unlike that of men, and the apparent delay in the *parousia* is due to His patience in waiting for more individuals to come to a knowledge of Christ (3:8, 9). Nevertheless, the day of consummation will come, and all the matter of this universe will evidently be transformed from which God will fashion a new cosmos (3:10-13).

In light of this coming day of the Lord, Peter exhorts his readers to live lives of holiness, steadfastness, and growth (3:14-18). He mentions the letters of "our beloved brother Paul" and significantly places them on a level with the Old Testament Scriptures (3:15, 16). After a final warning about the danger of false teachers, the epistle closes with an appeal to growth, and a doxology.

FOCUS	CULTIVATION OF CHRISTIAN CHARACTER		CONDEMNATION OF FALSE TEACHERS			CONFIDENCE IN CHRIST'S RETURN	
REFERENCE	1:1————1:15—	—2:1—	—2:4—	—2:10—	—3:1—	—3:8—	—3:18
DIVISION	GROWTH IN CHRIST	GROUNDS OF BELIEF	DANGER	DESTRUCTION	DESCRIPTION	MOCKERY IN THE LAST DAYS	DAY OF THE LORD
TOPIC	TRUE PROPHECY		FALSE PROPHETS			PROPHECY: DAY OF THE LORD	
	HOLINESS		HERESY			HOPE	
LOCATION	PROBABLY ROME						
TIME	c. A.D. 64-66						

OUTLINE OF SECOND PETER

CHAPTER 1

Salutation

SIMON Peter, ᴿa servant and an apostle of Jesus Christ, to them that have ᵀobtained like precious faith with us through the righteousness of God and our Saviour Jesus Christ: 2 Cor. 4:13; Eph. 4:5 • received

2 ᴿGrace and peace be multiplied unto you through the knowledge of God, and of Jesus our Lord,   Dan. 4:1; Rom. 1:7

Growth in Christ

3 According as his divine power hath given unto us all things that pertain unto life and godliness, through the knowledge of him that hath called us to glory and virtue:

4 Whereby are given unto us exceeding great and precious promises: that by these ye might be partakers of the divine nature, having escaped the ᵀcorruption that is in the world through lust.   degeneration

5 And beside this, ᴿgiving all diligence, add to your faith virtue; and to virtue ᴿknowledge;   [v. 9] • 3:18; Hos. 4:6; 1 Pet. 3:7

6 ᴿAnd to knowledge ᵀtemperance; and to temperance ᵀpatience; and to patience godliness;   [v. 9] • self-control • endurance

7 And to godliness brotherly kindness; and to ᴿbrotherly kindness ᵀcharity.   [v. 9] • love

8 For if these things be in you, and abound, they make you that ye shall neither be ᵀbarren nor unfruitful in the knowledge of our Lord Jesus Christ.   idle

9 But he that lacketh these things is blind, and cannot see afar off, and hath forgotten that he was purged from his old sins.

10 ᵀWherefore the rather, brethren, give diligence to make your calling and ᵀelection sure: for if ye do these things, ye shall never ᵀfall: so then • relationship with God • stumble

11 For so an entrance shall be ᵀministered unto you abundantly into the ᴿeverlasting kingdom of our Lord and Saviour Jesus Christ.   given to • Dan. 2:44; Acts 14:22

12 Wherefore ᴿI will not be negligent to put you always in remembrance of these things, though ye know them, and be established in the present truth.   Jude 5

13 Yea, I think it ᵀmeet, as long as I am in this ᵀtabernacle, to stir you up by putting you in remembrance;   proper • body

14 ᴿKnowing that shortly I must ᵀput off this my tabernacle, even as our Lord Jesus Christ hath shewed me.   [2 Tim. 4:6] • die

Experience of the Transfiguration
Matt. 17:5; Mark 9:7; Luke 9:35

15 Moreover I will endeavour that ye may be able after my ᵀdecease to have these things always in remembrance.   death

16 For we have not followed cunningly devised fables, when we made known unto you the power and coming of our Lord Jesus Christ, but were eyewitnesses of his majesty.

17 For he received from God the Father honour and glory, when there came such a voice to him from the ᵀexcellent glory, ᴿThis is my beloved Son, in whom I am well pleased.   majestic • Matt. 3:17; Luke 9:35

18 And this voice which came from heaven we heard, when we were with him in ᴿthe holy mount.   Ex. 3:5; Josh. 5:15; Matt. 17:5, 6

Certainty of the Scriptures

19 We have also a ᵀmore sure word of prophecy; whereunto ye do well that ye take heed, as unto a light that shineth in a dark place, until the day dawn, and the day star arise in your hearts: confirmed

20 Knowing this first, that ᴿno prophecy of the scripture is of any ᵀprivate interpretation.   [Rom. 12:6] • one man's idea

21 For the prophecy came not in old time by the will of man: but holy men of God spake as they were moved by the Holy Ghost.

CHAPTER 2

Danger of False Teachers

BUT there were false prophets also among the people, even as there shall be false teachers among you, who privily shall bring in damnable heresies, even denying the Lord that bought them, and bring upon themselves swift destruction.

2 And many shall follow their ᵀpernicious ways; by ᵀreason of whom the way of truth shall be evil spoken of.   evil • because of them

3 And through ᵀcovetousness shall they with feigned words make merchandise of you: whose judgment now of a long time lingereth not, and their ᵀdamnation slumbereth not.   greed • condemnation will occur

Destruction of False Teachers

4 For if God spared not the angels that sinned, but ᴿcast them down to hell, and delivered them ᵀinto chains of darkness, to be reserved unto judgment;   Jude 6 • to pits

5 And spared not the ᵀold ᴿworld, but saved Noah the eighth person, a preacher of righteousness, bringing in the flood upon the world of the ungodly;   ancient • Ezek. 26:20

6 And turning the cities of Sodom and Go-mor'-rha into ashes condemned them with an overthrow, making them an ensample unto those that after should live ungodly;

7 And delivered just Lot, vexed with the filthy conversation of the wicked:

8 (For that righteous man dwelling among them, ᴿin seeing and hearing, vexed his

righteous soul from day to day with *their* unlawful deeds;)   Gen. 19; Ps. 119:139

9 ᴿThe Lord knoweth how to deliver the godly out of ᵀtemptations, and to reserve the unjust unto the day of judgment to be punished: Ps. 34:17 • *trials*

Description of False Teachers

10 But chiefly them that walk after the flesh in the lust of uncleanness, and ᵀdespise government. Presumptuous *are they*, self-willed, they are not afraid to speak evil of ᵀdignities.   *belittle control • prominent persons*

11 Whereas ᴿangels, which are greater in power and might, bring not railing accusation against them before the Lord.   Jude 9

12 But these, as natural brute beasts, made to be taken and destroyed, speak evil of the things that they understand not; and shall utterly perish in their own corruption;

13 And shall receive the reward of unrighteousness, *as* they that count it pleasure to riot in the day time. Spots *they are* and blemishes, sporting themselves with their own deceivings while they feast with you;

14 Having eyes full of adultery, and that cannot cease from sin; beguiling ᵀunstable souls: an heart they have exercised with covetous practices; cursed children: *weak*

15 Which have forsaken the ᴿright way, and are gone astray, following the way of Ba'-laam *the son* of Bo'-sor, who loved the wages of unrighteousness;   Acts 13:10

16 But was rebuked for his iniquity: the dumb ass speaking with man's voice forbad the madness of the prophet.

17 These are wells without water, clouds that are carried with a tempest; to whom the mist of darkness is reserved for ever.

18 For when they speak great swelling *words* of ᵀvanity, they allure through the ᵀlusts of the flesh, *through much* wantonness, those that were ᵀclean escaped from them who live in error.   *pride • desires • altogether*

19 While they promise them liberty, they themselves are the servants of corruption: for of whom a man is overcome, of the same is he brought ᵀin bondage.   *into slavery*

20 For if after they ᴿhave escaped the ᵀpollutions of the world through the knowledge of the Lord and Saviour Jesus Christ, they are again entangled therein, and overcome, the latter end is worse with them than the beginning.   *v.* 1; [1:1]; Matt. 12:45 • *sins*

21 For it had been better for them not to have known the way of righteousness, than, after they have known *it*, to turn from the holy commandment delivered unto them.

22 But it is happened unto them according to the true proverb, THE DOG IS TURNED TO HIS OWN VOMIT AGAIN; and the sow that was washed to her wallowing in the mire.

CHAPTER 3

Mockery in the Last Days

THIS second epistle, beloved, I now write unto you; in *both* which ᴿI stir up your pure minds by way of remembrance: 1:13

2 That ye may be mindful of the words which were spoken before by the holy prophets, and of the commandment of us the apostles of the Lord and Saviour:

3 Knowing this first, that there shall come in the last days scoffers, walking ᵀafter their own ᵀlusts,   *according to • desires*

4 And saying, Where is the promise of his coming? for since the fathers ᵀfell asleep, all things continue as *they were* from the beginning of the creation.   *died*

5 For this they willingly are ignorant of, that ᴿby the word of God the heavens were of old, and the earth ᵀstanding out of the water and in the water: Gen. 1:6, 9 • *emerging*

6 Whereby the world that then was, being overflowed with water, perished:

7 But the heavens and the earth, which are now, by the same word are kept in store, reserved unto fire against the day of judgment and perdition of ungodly men.

Manifestation of the Day of the Lord

8 But, beloved, ᵀbe not ignorant of this one thing, that one day *is* with the Lord as a thousand years, and ᴿa thousand years as one day.   *do not forget • Ps. 90:4*

9 ᴿThe Lord is not slack concerning his promise, as some men count slackness; but ᴿis longsuffering to us-ward, not willing that any should perish, but ᴿthat all should come to repentance.   Hab. 2:3 • Is. 30:18 • [Rom. 2:4]

10 But ᴿthe day of the Lord will come as a thief in the night; in the which the heavens shall pass away with a great noise, and the elements shall melt with fervent heat, the earth also and the works that are therein shall be burned up.   Matt. 24:43 ✧

Maturity in View of the Day of the Lord

11 *Seeing* then *that* all these things shall be ᵀdissolved, what manner *of persons* ought ye to be ᴿin *all* holy ᵀconversation and godliness,   *destroyed • 1 Pet. 1:15 • living*

12 Looking for and hasting unto the coming of the day of God, wherein the heavens being on fire shall be dissolved, and the elements shall melt with fervent heat?

13 Nevertheless we, according to his promise, look for new heavens and a new earth, wherein dwelleth righteousness.

14 Wherefore, beloved, seeing that ye ᵀlook for such things, be ᴿdiligent ᴿthat ye may be found of him in peace, without spot, and blameless.   *wait • careful • [1 Thess. 3:12, 13]*

15 And account *that* the longsuffering of our Lord *is* salvation; even as our beloved

brother Paul also according to the wisdom given unto him hath written unto you;

16 As also in all *his* epistles, ᴿspeaking in them of these things; in which are some things hard to be understood, which they that are unlearned and ᵀunstable wrest, as *they do* also the other scriptures, unto their own destruction.

Rom. 8:19 • unreliable twist

17 Ye therefore, beloved, seeing ye know *these things* before, beware lest ye also, being led away with the error of the wicked, fall from your own stedfastness.

18 ᴿBut grow in grace, and *in* the knowledge of our Lord and Saviour Jesus Christ. ᴿTo him *be* glory both now and for ever. A-men'.

Eph. 4:15 • 2 Tim. 4:18

JOHN

THE BOOK OF FIRST JOHN

God is light; God is love; and God is life. John is enjoying a delightful fellowship with that God of light, love, and life, and he desperately desires that his spiritual children enjoy the same fellowship.

God is light. Therefore, to engage in fellowship with Him we must walk in light and not in darkness. As we walk in the light, we will regularly confess our sins, allowing the blood of Christ to continually cleanse us. Christ will act as our defense attorney before the Father. Proof of our "walk in the light" will be keeping the commandments of God and replacing any hatred we have toward our brother with love. Two major roadblocks to hinder this walk will be falling in love with the world and falling for the alluring lies of false teachers.

God is love. Since we are His children we must walk in love. In fact, John says that if we do not love, we do not know God. Additionally, our love needs to be practical. Love is more than just words; it is actions. Love is giving, not getting. Biblical love is unconditional in its nature. It is an "in spite of" love. Christ's love fulfilled those qualities and when that brand of love characterizes us, we will be free of self-condemnation and experience confidence before God.

God is life. Those who fellowship with Him must possess His quality of life. Spiritual life begins with spiritual birth. Spiritual birth occurs through faith in Jesus Christ. Faith in Jesus Christ infuses us with God's life—eternal life. Therefore, one who walks in fellowship with God will walk in light, love, and life.

Although the apostle John's name is not found in this book, it was given the title *Iōannou A,* "First of John."

THE AUTHOR OF FIRST JOHN

The external evidence for the authorship of First John shows that from the beginning it was universally received without dispute as authoritative. It was used by Polycarp (who knew John in his youth) and Papias in the early second century, and later in that century Irenaeus (who knew Polycarp in his youth) specifically attributed it to the apostle John. All the Greek and Latin church fathers accepted this epistle as Johannine.

The internal evidence supports this universal tradition because the "we" (apostles), "you" (readers), and "they" (false teachers) phraseology places the writer in the sphere of the apostolic eyewitnesses (cf. 1:1–3; 4:14). John's name was well-known to the readers, and it was unnecessary for him to mention it. The style and vocabulary of First John are so similar to those of the Fourth Gospel that most scholars acknowledge these books to be by the same hand (see "The Author of John"). Both share many distinctively Johannine phrases, and the characteristics of limited vocabulary and frequent contrast of opposites are also common to them. Even so, some critics have assailed this conclusion on various grounds, but the theological and stylistic differences are not substantial enough to overcome the abundant similarities.

The traditional view is also rejected by those who hold that the Fourth Gospel and these three epistles were written by John the "elder" or "presbyter," who is to be distinguished from John the apostle. But the only basis for this distinction is Eusebius's interpretation in his *Ecclesiastical History* (A.D. 323) of a statement by Papias. Eusebius understood the passage to refer to two distinct Johns, but the wording does not require this; the elder John and the apostle John may be one and the same. Even if they were different, there is no evidence for contradicting the consistent acknowledgment by the early church that this book was written by the apostle John.

THE TIME OF FIRST JOHN

In Acts 8:14, John is associated with "the apostles which were at Jerusalem," and Paul calls him one of the "pillars" of the Jerusalem church in Galatians 2:9. Apart from Revelation 1, the New Testament is silent about his later years, but early Christian tradition uniformly tells us that he left Jerusalem (probably not long before its destruction in A.D. 70) and that he ministered in and around Ephesus. The seven churches in the Roman province of Asia, mentioned in Revelation 2 and 3, were evidently a part of this ministry. Although there is no address in First John, it is likely that the apostle directed this epistle to the Asian churches that were within the realm of his oversight.

The believers in these congregations were well established in Christian truth, and John wrote to them not as novices but as brethren grounded in apostolic doctrine (2:7, 18–27; 3:11). The apostle does not mention his own affairs, but his use of such terms of address as "beloved" and "my little children" gives this letter a personal touch that reveals his close relationship to the original recipients. First John was probably written in Ephesus after the Gospel of John, but the date cannot be fixed with certainty. No persecution is mentioned, suggesting a date prior to A.D. 95

when persecution broke out during the end of Domitian's reign (A.D. 81–96).

Advanced in years, John wrote this fatherly epistle out of loving concern for his "children," whose steadfastness in the truth was being threatened by the lure of worldliness and the guile of false teachers. The Gnostic heresy taught that matter is inherently evil, and a divine being therefore could not take on human flesh. This resulted in the distinction between the man Jesus and the spiritual Christ who came upon Jesus at His baptism but departed prior to His crucifixion. Another variation was Docetism (from *dokeō*, "to seem"), the doctrine that Christ only seemed to have a human body. The result in both cases was the same—a flat denial of the incarnation.

The Gnostics also believed that their understanding of the hidden knowledge (*gnōsis*) made them a kind of spiritual elite, who were above the normal distinctions of right and wrong. This led in most cases to deplorable conduct and complete disregard for Christian ethics.

THE CHRIST OF FIRST JOHN

The present ministry of Christ is portrayed in 1:5—2:22. His blood continually cleanses the believer from all sin, and He is our righteous Advocate before the Father. This epistle places particular stress on the incarnation of God the Son and the identity of Jesus as the Christ (2:22; 4:2, 3), in refutation of Gnostic doctrine. Jesus Christ "came by water and blood" (5:6). He was the same indivisible person from the beginning (His baptism) to the end (His crucifixion) of His public ministry.

KEYS TO FIRST JOHN

Key Word: Fellowship with God—The major theme of First John is fellowship with God. John wants his readers to have assurance of the indwelling God through their abiding relationship with Him (2:28; 5:13). Belief in Christ should be manifested in the practice of righteousness and love for the brethren, which in turn produces joy and confidence before God. John writes this epistle to encourage this kind of fellowship and to emphasize the importance of holding fast to apostolic doctrine.

First John is also written to refute the destructive teachings of the Gnostics by stressing the reality of the incarnation and the emptiness of profession without practice. These antichrists fail the three tests of righteous living, love for the brethren, and belief that Jesus is the Christ, the incarnate God-man.

Key Verses: First John 1:3, 4 and 5:11-13—"That which we have seen and heard declare we unto you, that ye also may have fellowship with us: and truly our fellowship *is* with the Father, and with his Son Jesus Christ. And these things

write we unto you, that your joy may be full" (1:3, 4).

"And this is the record, that God hath given to us eternal life, and this life is in his Son. He that hath the Son hath life; *and* he that hath not the Son of God hath not life. These things have I written unto you that believe on the name of the Son of God; that ye may know that ye have eternal life, and that ye may believe on the name of the Son of God" (5:11–13).

Key Chapter: First John 1—The two central passages for continued fellowship with God are John 15 and First John 1. John 15 relates the positive side of fellowship, that is, abiding in Christ. First John 1 unfolds the other side, pointing out that when Christians do not abide in Christ, they must seek forgiveness before fellowship can be restored.

SURVEY OF FIRST JOHN

John writes his first epistle at a time when apostolic doctrine is being challenged by a proliferation of false teachings. Like Second Peter and Jude, First John has a negative and a positive thrust: it refutes erroneous doctrine and encourages its readership to walk in the knowledge of the truth. John lists the criteria and characteristics of fellowship with God and shows that those who abide in Christ can have confidence and assurance before Him. This simply written but profound work develops the meaning of fellowship in the basis of fellowship (1:1—2:27) and the behavior of fellowship (2:28—5:21).

The Basis of Fellowship (1:1—2:27): John's prologue (1:1-4) recalls the beginning of apostolic contact with Christ. It relates his desire to transmit this apostolic witness to his readers so that they may share the same fellowship with Jesus Christ, the personification of life. This proclamation is followed by a description of the conditions of fellowship (1:5—2:14).

The readers' sins have been forgiven and they enjoy fellowship with God. As a result, they know "him *that is* from the beginning" and are strengthened to overcome the temptations of the evil one (2:12-14). The cautions to fellowship are both practical (the lusts of the corrupt world system which opposes God, 2:15-17) and doctrinal (the teachings of those who differentiate between Jesus and the Christ, 2:18-23). In contrast to these antichrists, the readers have the knowledge of the truth and an anointing from the Holy One. Therefore, it would be foolish for them to turn away from the teachings of the apostles to the innovations of the antichrists. The antidote to these heretical teachings is abiding in the apostolic truths that they "have heard from the beginning," which are authenticated by the anointing they have received (2:24-27).

The Behavior of Fellowship (2:28—5:21): The basic theme of First John is summarized in 2:28—assurance through abiding in Christ. The next verse introduces the motif of regeneration, and 2:29—3:10 argues that regeneration is manifested in the practice of righteousness. Because we are children of God through faith in Christ, we have a firm hope of being fully conformed to Him when He appears (3:1-3). Our present likeness to Christ places us in a position of incompatibility with sin, because sin is contrary to the person and work of Christ (3:4-6). The concept in 3:6 does not contradict 1:8 because it is saying that the abider, insofar as he abides, does not sin. When the believer sins, he does not reflect the regenerate new man but Satan, the original sinner (3:7-10).

Regeneration is shown in righteousness (2:29—3:10), and righteousness is manifested in love (3:10-23). The apostle uses the example of Cain to illustrate what love is not: hatred is murdering in spirit, and it arises from the worldly sphere of death. John then uses the example of Christ to illustrate what love is: love is practiced in self-sacrifice, not mere profession. This practical expression of love results in assurance before God and answered prayers because the believer is walking in obedience to God's commands to believe in Christ and love one another.

In 3:24 John introduces two important motifs, which are developed in 4:1-16: the indwelling God, and the Spirit as a mark of this indwelling. The Spirit of God confesses the incarnate Christ and confirms apostolic doctrine (4:1-6). The mutual abiding of the believer in God and God in the believer is manifested in love for others, and this love produces a divine and human fellowship that testifies to and reflects the reality of the incarnation (4:7-16). It also anticipates the perfect fellowship to come and creates a readiness to face the One from whom all love is derived (4:17-19).

John joins the concepts he has presented into a circular chain of six links that begins with love for the brethren (4:20—5:17): (1) Love for believers is the inseparable product of love for God (4:20—5:1). (2) Love for God arises out of obedience to His commandments (5:2, 3). (3) Obedience to God is the result of faith in His Son (5:4, 5). (4) This faith is in Jesus, who was the Christ not only at His baptism (the water), but also at His death (the blood; 5:6-8). (5) The divine witness to the person of Christ is worthy of complete belief (5:9-13). (6) This belief produces confident access to God in prayer (5:14-17). Since intercessory prayer is a manifestation of love for others, the chain has come full circle.

The epilogue (5:18-21) summarizes the conclusions of the epistle in a series of three certainties: (1) Sin is a threat to fellowship, and it should be regarded as foreign to the believer's position in Christ (cf. Rom. 6). (2) The believer stands with God against the satanic world system. (3) The incarnation produces true knowledge and communion with Christ. Since He is the true God and eternal life, the one who knows Him should avoid the lure of any substitute.

FOCUS	BASIS OF FELLOWSHIP		BEHAVIOR OF FELLOWSHIP	
REFERENCE	1:1————————————2:15		2:28————————————5:4	————————5:21
DIVISION	CONDITIONS FOR FELLOWSHIP	CAUTIONS TO FELLOWSHIP	CHARACTERISTICS OF FELLOWSHIP	CONSEQUENCES OF FELLOWSHIP
TOPIC	MEANING OF FELLOWSHIP		MANIFESTATIONS OF FELLOWSHIP	
	ABIDING IN GOD'S LIGHT		ABIDING IN GOD'S LOVE	
LOCATION	WRITTEN IN EPHESUS			
TIME	C. A.D. 90			

OUTLINE OF FIRST JOHN

Part One: The Basis of Fellowship (1:1—2:27)

Part Two: The Behaviour of Fellowship (2:28—5:21)

CHAPTER 1

Introduction

THAT ᴿwhich was from the beginning, which we have heard, which we have seen with our eyes, ᴿwhich we have looked upon, and ᴿour hands have handled, of the Word of life;   [John 1:1] • John 1:14 • Luke 24:39

2 (For the life was manifested, and we have seen it, and bear witness, and shew unto you that eternal life, which was with the Father, and was manifested unto us;)

3 That which we have seen and heard ᵀdeclare we unto you, that ye also may have fellowship with us: and truly our ᴿfellowship is with the Father, and with his Son Jesus Christ.   tell • [John 15:14]; 1 Cor. 1:9

4 And these things write we unto you, ᴿthat ᵀyour joy may be full.   John 16:24 • our

Walk in the Light

5 ᴿThis then is the message which we have heard of him, and ᵀdeclare unto you, that

ᴿGod is light, and in him is no darkness at all.   3:11 • announce • [John 1:9]

6 ᴿIf we say that we have fellowship with him, and walk in darkness, we lie, and ᵀdo not the truth: [John 8:12] • are not practicing

7 But if we walk in the light, as he is in the light, we have fellowship one with another, and ᴿthe blood of Jesus Christ his Son cleanseth us from all sin.   [1 Cor. 6:11]

Confession of Sin

8 If we say that we have no sin, we deceive ourselves, and the truth is not in us.

9 If we confess our sins, he is faithful and just to forgive us our sins, and to cleanse us from all unrighteousness.

10 If we say that we have not sinned, we make him a liar, and his word is not in us.

CHAPTER 2

MY little children, these things write I unto you, that ye sin not. And if any

---

1:9 Confession—One of the most remarkable chapters in the Old Testament is Psalm 51. This Psalm contains the actual words of confession uttered by King David after his great sins of adultery and murder (Page 317—2 Sam. 11).

This prayer can serve as a pattern to the Christian when he is guilty of sin in his life today.
a. David begins his prayer by freely admitting his sin (Page 569—Ps. 51:3, 4). This honesty is vital in our confession. God will graciously forgive all our sins, but not on account of our excuses.
b. He then displays real sorrow over his sin (Page 569—Ps. 51:17). Paul writes (Page 1147—2 Cor. 7:10) that the main characteristic of true confession is godly sorrow.
c. He asks God's forgiveness (Page 569—Ps. 51:1, 7-9).
d. He believes that God has heard him and will restore him (Page 569—Ps. 51:12-15).

In the New Testament the most important single verse concerning confession is First John 1:9. In essence John tells us the means of forgiveness and cleansing is the blood of Christ, while the method of this forgiveness and cleansing is the confession of the Christian.

Like David, we must admit our sin, regret the actions of our sin, plead the blood of Christ, and believe that God has indeed done what He promised, namely, to cleanse us from sin and restore us to fellowship and service.

Now turn to Page 276—1 Sam. 1:17: Petition.

man sin, we have an advocate with the Father, Jesus Christ the righteous:

2 And he is the ᵀpropitiation for our sins: and not for our's only, but ᴿalso for *the sins of* the whole world.   *expiation* • John 1:29

Obedience to His Commandments

3 And hereby we do know that we know him, if we keep his commandments.

4 ᴿHe that saith, I know him, and keepeth not his commandments, is a liar, and the truth is not in him.   [1:6, 8; 4:20]

5 But whoso keepeth his word, in him verily is the love of God perfected: hereby ᵀknow we that we are in him.   *realize*

6 He that saith he abideth in him ought himself also so to walk, even as he walked.

Love for One Another

7 Brethren, ᴿI write no new commandment unto you, but an old commandment which ye had from the beginning. The old commandment is the word which ye have heard from the beginning.   3:11; 2 John 5

8 Again, a new commandment I write unto you, which thing is true in him and in you: ᴿbecause the darkness is past, and the true light now shineth.   Rom. 13:12

9 ᴿHe that saith he is in the light, and hateth his brother, is in darkness ᵀeven until now.   [1 Cor. 13:2] • *this very hour*

10 ᴿHe that loveth his brother abideth in the light, and ᴿthere is none occasion of stumbling in him.   [3:14] • 2 Pet. 1:10

11 But he that hateth his brother is in darkness, and walketh in darkness, and ᵀknoweth not whither he goeth, because that darkness hath blinded his eyes.   *realizes*

12 I write unto you, ᵀlittle children, because ᴿyour sins are forgiven you for ᵀthis name's sake.   *my* • 1 Cor. 6:11 • *Christ's*

13 I write unto you, fathers, because ye ᵀhave known him ᵀ*that is* from the beginning. I write unto you, young men, because ye have overcome the wicked one. I write unto you, little children, because ye have known the Father.   *know* • *that existed*

14 I have written unto you, fathers, because ye have known him *that is* from the beginning. I have written unto you, young men, because ᴿye are strong, and the word of God ᵀabideth in you, and ye have overcome the wicked one.   Eph. 6:10 • *lives*

Love of the World

15 Love not the world, neither the things *that are* in the world. If any man love the world, the love of the Father is not in him.

16 For all that *is* in the world, ᴿthe ᵀlust of the flesh, ᴿand the lust of the eyes, and the pride of life, is not of the Father, but is of the world.   [Matt. 4:4–9] • *desire* • [Eccl. 5:10, 11]

17 And ᴿthe world passeth away, and the lust thereof: but he that ᵀdoeth the will of God abideth for ever.   1 Pet. 1:24 • *practices*

Spirit of the Antichrist

18 Little children, it is the last time: and as ye have heard that an'-ti-christ shall come, even now are there many an'-ti-christs; whereby we know that it is the last time.

19 They went out from us, but they were not of us; for if they had been of us, they would *no doubt* have continued with us: but *they went out,* that they might be made manifest that they were not all of us.

20 But ᴿye have an unction from the Holy One, and ye know all things.   Heb. 1:9

21 I have not written unto you because ye know not the truth, but because ye know it, and that no lie is of the truth.

22 ᴿWho is a liar but he that denieth that Jesus is the Christ? He is an'-ti-christ, that denieth the Father and the Son.   2 John 7

23 Whosoever denieth the Son, the same hath not the Father: [*but*] he that acknowledgeth the Son hath the Father also.

24 Let that therefore abide in you, ᴿwhich ye have heard from the beginning. If that which ye have heard from the beginning shall remain in you, ye also shall continue in the Son, and in the Father.   2 John 6

2:15 Temptation by the World—The term *world* does not always refer to the universe as created by God. It often is used to describe the community of sinful humanity that possesses a spirit of rebellion against God (Page 1253—1 John 5:19). Because of its opposition to God, the world values those things which are contrary to God's will: "the lust of the flesh, and the lust of the eyes, and the pride of life" (1 John 2:16). Its temptations to the believer are thus twofold: lust for the sensual and pride in mastery of his own life.

The attraction of the world is amplified by Satan who is head of its system. He is called the "prince of this world" (Page 1057—John 12:31; 14:30; 16:11), and the whole world is said to be under his power (see Page 1253—1 John 5:19, where "wickedness" can also be translated "wicked one").

Some of the tragic effects that love of the world will produce in the believer's life are:
a. A turning away from the Lord's work and other believers (Page 1202—2 Tim. 4:10);
b. Alienation from God (Page 1230—James 4:4);
c. Corrupting sins (Page 1243—2 Pet. 1:4; Page 1250—1 John 2:15–17);
d. Deception by false teachers (Page 1252—1 John 4:1; Page 1256—2 John 7).

The solution to the love of the world is to have a greater love for the Father (1 John 2:15). The Christian who seeks daily to please God in everything and who strives for spiritual growth through prayer, study of God's Word, and witnessing need not fall prey to the temptations of the world.

Now turn to Page 996—Mark 14:38: Temptation by the Flesh.

25 RAnd this is the promise that he hath promised us, *even* eternal life.   John 17:3

26 These *things* have I written unto you concerning them that Tseduce you.   *deceive*

27 But the anointing which ye have received of him abideth in you, and ye need not that any man teach you: but as the same anointing teacheth you of all things, and is truth, and is no lie, and even as it hath taught you, ye shall abide in him.

Purity of Life

28 And now, little children, abide in him; that, when he shall appear, we may have Tconfidence, and not be Tashamed before him at his coming.   *boldness • embarrassed*

29 If ye know that he is Rrighteous, ye know that every one that doeth righteousness is born of him.   [4:7; 5:1]

CHAPTER 3

BEHOLD, what manner of love the Father hath bestowed upon us, that we should be called the sons of God: therefore the world knoweth us not, because it knew him not.

2 Beloved, Rnow are we the sons of God, and it doth not yet appear what we shall be: but we know that, when he shall appear, Rwe shall be like him; for Rwe shall see him as he is.   [Is. 56:5] • Rom. 8:29 • [Ps. 16:11]

3 And every man that hath this hope in him purifieth himself, even as he is pure.

Practice of Righteousness

4 Whosoever committeth sin transgresseth also the law: for Rsin is Tthe transgression of the law.   Rom 4:15 • *lawlessness*

5 And ye know that he was manifested to take away our sins; and in him is no sin.

6 Whosoever abideth in him Tsinneth not: whosoever sinneth hath not seen him, neither known him.   *does not practice sinning*

7 Little children, let no man deceive you: he that Tdoeth righteousness is righteous, even as The is righteous.   *practises • Christ*

8 He that committeth sin is of the devil; for the devil sinneth from the beginning. For this purpose the Son of God was manifested, that he might destroy the works of the devil.

9 Whosoever is born of God doth not commit sin; for Rhis seed remaineth in him: and Rhe Tcannot sin, because he is born of God.   1 Pet. 1:23 • [Rom. 6:6, 7; Col. 3:3] • *as a usual practice*

10 In this the children of God are manifest, and the children of the devil: whosoever doeth not righteousness is not of God, neither he that loveth not his brother.

11 For this is the Tmessage that ye heard from the beginning, Rthat we should love one another.   *commandment* • [John 13:34]

12 Not as RCain, *who* was of that wicked one, and slew his brother. And wherefore slew he him? Because his own works were evil, and his brother's righteous.   Gen. 4:4, 8

Love in Deed and Truth

13 TMarvel not, my brethren, if Rthe world hate you.   *do not be surprised* • [John 17:14]

14 We know that we have passed from death unto life, because we love the Rbrethren. He that loveth not *his* brother abideth in death.   Matt. 12:50

15 Whosoever hateth his brother is a murderer: and ye know that no murderer hath eternal life Tabiding in him.   *operating*

16 RHereby Tperceive we the love of God, because he Tlaid down his life for us: and we ought to lay down *our* lives for the brethren.   [John 3:16] • *know we love • gave*

17 But whoso hath this world's good, and seeth his brother have need, and shutteth up his bowels *of compassion* from him, how dwelleth the love of God in him?

18 My little children, Rlet us not love in word, neither in Ttongue; but in Tdeed and in truth.   Ezek. 33:31 • *talk • action*

3:2 Placed into God's Family—In a general sense all men and women are the offspring of God in that He is the Creator (Page 1092—Acts 17:28, 29). This relationship, however, is not sufficient to offset the penalty of sin, because all persons are sinners separated from God (Page 1111—Rom. 3:23). Therefore, for a sinful person to become a child of God, a miraculous transformation must take place. The Bible refers to this change as being "born again" (Page 1044—John 3:3). When an individual places his faith in Christ as Saviour, he is born again into a new, spiritual, family relationship with God (Page 1156—Gal. 3:26). He gains God as Father (Page 1164—Eph. 4:6) and other Christians as brothers and sisters (Page 1216—Heb. 3:1). It is significant to note that the term "brotherly love," which Christians are commanded to have for each other (Page 1223—Heb. 13:1), is never used in the Greek language to refer to loving others as though they were your brothers. Rather, it is always used of loving those who actually are your brothers. So it is in the Christian faith: we actually are brothers and sisters with other Christians.

Not only are Christians the children of God by spiritual birth; they are adopted as well (Page 1162—Eph. 1:5). This figure implies a dramatic transformation of status from slave to son (Page 1156—Gal. 4:1-5). One is no longer in bondage to the master but becomes a free son possessing all the rights and privileges of sonship. One of these benefits is the right to call God *Abba,* an affectionate term meaning "father" (Page 1114—Rom. 8:15). This marvelous relationship carries responsibilities with it, as well as privileges. Everyone who has the hope of having his sonship perfected someday is presently purifying his own life. Since he bears the family relationship to God, he must also exhibit the family character.

Now turn to Page 1072—Acts 1:8: Empowered by God.

19 And hereby we ^Tknow ^Rthat we are of the truth, and shall ^Tassure our hearts before him.   *realize* • John 18:37 • *encourage*

20 ^RFor if our heart ^Tcondemn us, God is greater than our heart, and ^Tknoweth all things.   [1 Cor. 4:4, 5] • *makes us feel guilty* • *understands*

21 Beloved, if our heart condemn us not, *then* have we confidence toward God.

22 And ^Rwhatsoever we ask, we receive of him, because we ^Tkeep his commandments, and ^Tdo those things that are pleasing in his sight.   Ps. 34:15 • *obey* • *practice*

23 And this is his commandment, That we should believe on the name of his Son Jesus Christ, ^Rand love one another, as he gave us commandment.   Matt. 22:39; [John 13:34]

24 And he that keepeth his commandments dwelleth in him, and he in him. And hereby we know that he abideth in us, by the Spirit which he hath given us.

CHAPTER 4

Testing of the Spirits

BELOVED, ^Tbelieve not every spirit, but ^Ttry the spirits whether they are of God: because many false prophets are gone out into the world.   *trust* • *prove*

2 Hereby know ye the Spirit of God: Every spirit that confesseth that Jesus Christ is come in the flesh is of God:

3 And every spirit that confesseth not that Jesus Christ is come in the flesh is not of God: and this is that *spirit* of an'-ti-christ, whereof ye have heard that it should come; and even now already is it in the world.

4 Ye are of God, little children, and have overcome them: because greater is he that is in you, than he that is in the world.

5 ^RThey are of the world: therefore speak they of the world, and ^Rthe world ^Theareth them.   John 3:31 • John 15:19 • *listens to*

6 We are of God: he that knoweth God heareth us; he that is not of God heareth not us. Hereby ^Tknow we the spirit of truth, and the spirit of error.   *recognize*

Love as Christ Loved

7 Beloved, ^Rlet us love one another: for love is of God; and every one that loveth is born of God, and knoweth God.   [2:29]

8 ^RHe that loveth not ^Tknoweth not God; for God is love.   [v. 16; 2:4] • *does not know*

9 ^RIn this was ^Tmanifested the love of God toward us, because that God sent his only begotten Son into the world, that we might live through him.   [John 3:16] • *revealed*

10 Herein is love, not that we loved God, but that he loved us, and sent his Son *to be* the ^Tpropitiation for our sins.   *expiation*

11 Beloved, ^Rif God so loved us, we ought also to love one another.   Matt. 18:33

12 No man hath seen God at any time. If we love one another, God dwelleth in us, and his love is ^Tperfected in us.   *completed*

13 ^RHereby ^Tknow we that we ^Tdwell in him, and he in us, because he hath given us of his Spirit.   John 14:20 • *recognize* • *live*

14 And ^Rwe have seen and do ^Ttestify that ^Rthe Father sent the Son *to be* the Saviour of the world.   John 1:14 • *say* • John 3:17

15 ^RWhosoever shall ^Tconfess that Jesus is the Son of God, God dwelleth in him, and he in God.   [Rom. 10:9] • *declare*

16 And we have ^Tknown and believed the love that God hath to us. God is love; and ^Rhe that dwelleth in love dwelleth in God, and God in him.   *understood* • [3:24]

17 Herein is our love made ^Tperfect, that ^Rwe may have ^Tboldness in the day of judgment: because as he is, so are we in this world.   *complete* • [2 Cor. 5:10; James 2:13] • *assurance*

18 There is no fear in love; but ^Rperfect love casteth out fear: because fear hath ^Ttorment. He that feareth is not made perfect in love.   [Rom. 8:15; Gal. 4:30] • *punishment*

19 We love him, because he first loved us.

20 If a man say, I love God, and hateth his brother, he is a liar: for he that loveth not his brother whom he hath seen, how can he love God whom he hath not seen?

21 And ^Rthis commandment have we from him, That he who loveth God love his brother also.   Lev. 19:18; Matt. 22:37; John 13:34

3:24 Witness of the Spirit—While it is true that one need not always feel spiritual to have new life in Christ, nevertheless, feelings and emotions do play a vital role in our salvation. Both Paul (Page 1114—Rom. 8:16) and John (1 John 3:24) inform us we can experience that inner witness of the Holy Spirit to our spirit. What does this mean? It means we can enjoy the quiet confidence given by the Spirit that we have indeed passed from death unto life. It means we can now approach the mighty Creator of the vast universe and refer to Him as Abba, Father (Page 1114—Rom. 8:15). *Abba* is a very personal and intimate term for one's father. Prior to Pentecost only Christ had used the title for God (Page 996—Mark 14:36). It is almost akin to our modern title *daddy*, or *papa*. It not only means we can approach the throne of grace with a holy boldness (Page 1217—Heb. 4:16), but we can also experience the blessing of knowing that the Father will hear and answer our prayers (1 John 3:22).
    The apostle Paul experiences this witness during a crisis in his life while preaching in Corinth. See Acts 18:9, 10.
    Now turn to Page 1129—1 Cor. 6:11: Changed Life.

CHAPTER 5

WHOSOEVER believeth that Jesus is the Christ is born of God: and every one that loveth him that begat loveth him also that is begotten of him.

2 By this we ^Tknow that we love the children of God, when we love God, and ^Tkeep his commandments. *recognize • obey*

3 For this is the love of God, that we keep his commandments: and his commandments are not ^Tgrievous. *burdensome*

Victory over the World

4 For whatsoever is born of God overcometh the world: and this is the victory that overcometh the world, *even* our faith.

5 Who is he that ^Tovercometh the world, but ^Rhe that believeth that Jesus is the Son of God? *can defeat* • 1 Cor. 15:57

Assurance of Salvation

6 This is he that came by water and blood, *even* Jesus Christ; not by water only, but by water and blood. And it is the Spirit that beareth witness, because the Spirit is truth.

7 For there are three that bear record in heaven, the Father, the Word, and the Holy Ghost: ^Rand these three are one. Matt. 28:19

8 And there are three that bear witness in earth, the spirit, and the water, and the blood: and these three agree in one.

9 If we receive ^Rthe witness of men, the witness of God is greater: ^Rfor this is the witness of God which he hath ^Ttestified of his Son. John 8:17 • [Matt. 3:16] • *told about*

10 He that believeth on the Son of God ^Rhath the witness in himself: he that believeth not God ^Rhath made him a liar; because he believeth not the record that God gave of his Son. [Rom. 8:16] • John 3:33

11 And this is the record, that God hath given to us eternal life, and ^Rthis life is in his Son. John 1:4

12 ^RHe that hath the Son hath life; *and* he that hath not the Son of God hath not life. [John 3:36]

13 These things have I written unto you that believe on the name of the Son of God; that ye may ^Tknow that ye have eternal life, and that ye may believe ^Ton the name of the Son of God. *realize • in*

Guidance in Prayer

14 And this is the confidence that we have in him, that, ^Rif we ask any thing according to his will, he heareth us: 3:22

15 And if we ^Tknow that he hear us, whatsoever we ask, we know that we have the petitions that we desired of him. *understand*

16 If any man see his brother sin a sin *which is* not unto death, he shall ask, and ^The shall give him life for them that sin not unto death. There is a sin unto death: I do not say that he shall pray for it. *God*

17 ^RAll ^Tunrighteousness is sin: and there is a sin not unto death. 3:4 • *wrongdoing*

Freedom from Habitual Sin

18 We know that whosoever is born of God sinneth not; but he that is begotten of God ^Rkeepeth^T himself, and that wicked one toucheth him not. James 1:27; [Jude 21] • *guards*

19 *And* we know that we are of God, and the whole world lieth in wickedness.

20 And we ^Tknow that the Son of God is come, and hath given us an understanding, that we may ^Tknow him that is true, and we are in him that is true, *even* in his Son Jesus Christ. ^RThis is the true God, and eternal life. *realize • recognize* • Is. 9:6

21 ^RLittle children, ^Tkeep yourselves from idols. A-men'. 1 Cor. 10:4-7; 1 Thess. 1:9 • *guard*

JOHN

📖 THE BOOK OF SECOND JOHN

"Let him that thinketh he standeth take heed lest he fall" (1 Cor. 10:12). These words of the apostle Paul could well stand as a subtitle for John's little epistle. The recipients, a chosen lady and her children, were obviously standing. They were walking in truth, remaining faithful to the commandments they had received from the Father. John is deeply pleased to be able to commend them. But he takes nothing for granted. Realizing that standing is just one step removed from falling, he hesitates not at all to issue a reminder: love one another. The apostle admits that this is not new revelation, but he views it sufficiently important to repeat. Loving one another, he stresses, is equivalent to walking according to God's commandments.

John indicates, however, that this love must be discerning. It is not a naive, unthinking, open to anything and anyone kind of love. Biblical love is a matter of choice; it is dangerous and foolish to float through life with undiscerning love. False teachers abound who do not acknowledge Christ as having come in the flesh. It is false charity to open the door to false teaching. We must have fellowship with God. We must have fellowship with Christians. But we must not have fellowship with false teachers.

The "elder" of verse 1 has been traditionally identified with the apostle John, resulting in the Greek title Iōannou B, "Second of John."

✍ THE AUTHOR OF SECOND JOHN

Because of the similarity of the contents and circumstances of Second and Third John, the authorship of both will be considered here. These letters were not widely circulated at the beginning because of their brevity and their specific address to a small number of people. This limited circulation, combined with the fact that they have few distinctive ideas to add that are not found in First John, meant that they were seldom quoted in the patristic writings of the early church. Their place in the canon of New Testament books was disputed for a time, but it is significant that there was no question in the minds of those church fathers who lived closest to the time of John that these two epistles were written by the apostle. The second-century writers Irenaeus and Clement of Alexandria entertained no other view. Only as the details of their origin were forgotten did doubts arise, but the positive evidence in their favor eventually won for them the official recognition of the whole church.

It is obvious that the recipients of Second and Third John well knew the author's identity, although he did not use his name. Instead, he designated himself in the first verse of both letters as "the elder." This is not an argument against the Johannine authorship of Second and Third John, since the context of these epistles reveals that his authority was far greater than that of an elder in a local church. The apostle Peter also referred to himself as an elder (1 Pet. 5:1), and John uses the distinguishing term "the elder."

The similarity of style, vocabulary, structure, and mood between Second and Third John makes it clear that these letters were written by the same author. In addition, both (especially Second John) bear strong resemblances to First John and to the Fourth Gospel. Thus, the external and internal evidence lends clear support to the traditional view that these epistles were written by the apostle John.

⏳ THE TIME OF SECOND JOHN

The identification of the original readers of this epistle is difficult because of disagreement regarding the interpretation of "the elect lady and her children" (v. 1). Some scholars believe the address should be taken literally to refer to a specific woman and her children, while others prefer to take it as a figurative description of a local church.

The evidence is insufficient for a decisive conclusion, but in either case, the readers were well-known to John and probably lived in the province of Asia, not far from Ephesus. If the figurative view is taken, "the children of thy elect sister" (v. 13) refers to the members of a sister church.

In his first epistle, John wrote that a number of false teachers had split away from the church ("They went out from us, but they were not of us," 1 John 2:19). Some of these became traveling teachers who depended on the hospitality of individuals while they sought to infiltrate churches with their teachings.

Judging by the content and circumstances of Second John, it was evidently contemporaneous with First John or was written slightly later. It was probably written about A.D. 90. All three of John's epistles may have been written in Ephesus (see "The Time of First John").

✝ THE CHRIST OF SECOND JOHN

John refutes the same error regarding the person of Christ in this epistle as he did in his first epistle. Again he stresses that those "who confess not that Jesus Christ is come in the flesh" (v. 7) are deceivers who must be avoided. One must abide "in the doctrine of Christ" (v. 9) to have a relationship with God. The doctrine of the

person and work of Jesus Christ affects every other area of theology.

KEYS TO SECOND JOHN

Key Word: Avoid Fellowship with False Teachers—The basic theme of this brief letter is steadfastness in the practice and purity of the apostolic doctrine that the readers "have heard from the beginning" (v. 6). John writes it as a reminder to continue walking in obedience to God's commandment to love one another (practical exhortation, vv. 4–6). His primary purpose is to deliver a warning not to associate with or assist teachers who do not acknowledge the truth about Jesus Christ (doctrinal exhortation, vv. 7–11).

It has been suggested that Second and Third John were written as cover letters for First John to provide a personal word to a church (2 John) and to Gaius (3 John) that would supplement the longer epistle. However, there is no way to be sure.

Key Verses: Second John 9, 10—"Whosoever transgresseth, and abideth not in the doctrine of Christ, hath not God. He that abideth in the doctrine of Christ, he hath both the Father and the Son. If there come any unto you, and bring not this doctrine, receive him not into *your* house, neither bid him God speed" (vv. 9, 10).

SURVEY OF SECOND JOHN

This brief letter has much in common with First John, including a warning about the danger of false teachers who deny the incarnation of Jesus Christ. John encourages the readers to continue walking in love but exhorts them to be discerning in their expression of love. Second John breaks with two parts: abide in God's commandments (vv. 1–6) and abide not with false teachers (vv. 7–13).

Abide in God's Commandments (vv. 1–6): The salutation (vv. 1–3) centers on the concept of abiding in the truth (mentioned four times in these three verses). The recipients are loved for their adherence to the truth by "all they that have known the truth." The apostle commends his readers on their walk in truth in obedience to God's commandment (v. 4), and reminds them that this commandment entails the practice of love for one another (vv. 5, 6). The divine command is given in verse 5 and the human response follows in verse 6.

Abide Not with False Teachers (vv. 7–13): Moving from the basic test of Christian behavior (love for the brethren) to the basic test of Christian belief (the person of Christ), John admonishes the readers to beware of deceivers "who confess not that Jesus Christ is come in the flesh" (vv. 7–9). In no uncertain terms, the apostle enjoins the readers to deny even the slightest assistance or encouragement to itinerant teachers who promote an erroneous view of Christ (and hence of salvation; vv. 10, 11).

This letter closes with John's explanation of its brevity: he anticipates a future visit during which he will be able to "speak face to face" with his readers (v. 12). The meaning of the greeting in verse 13 relates to the interpretation of verse 1.

FOCUS	ABIDE IN GOD'S COMMANDMENTS			ABIDE NOT WITH FALSE TEACHERS		
REFERENCE	1 4	5	7	10	12	13
DIVISION	SALUTATION	WALK IN TRUTH	WALK IN LOVE	DOCTRINE OF FALSE TEACHERS	AVOID THE FALSE TEACHERS	BENEDICTION
TOPIC	WALK IN COMMANDMENTS			WATCH FOR COUNTERFEITS		
	PRACTICE THE TRUTH			PROTECT THE TRUTH		
LOCATION	WRITTEN IN EPHESUS					
TIME	C. A.D. 90					

OUTLINE OF SECOND JOHN

Salutation

THE elder unto the Telect lady and her children, whom I love in the truth; and not I only, but also all they that have Tknown Rthe truth;   *chosen · understood · Col. 1:5*

2 For the truth's sake, which Tdwelleth in us, and shall be with us for ever.   *lives*

3 RGrace be with you, mercy, *and* peace, from God the Father, and from the Lord Jesus Christ, the Son of the Father, in truth and love.   *Rom. 1:7; 1 Tim. 1:2*

Walk in Truth

4 I rejoiced greatly that I found of thy children walking in truth, as we have received a commandment from the Father.

Walk in Love

5 And now I beseech thee, lady, not as though I wrote a new commandment unto thee, but that which we had from the beginning, that we love one another.

6 And Rthis is love, that we walk after his commandments. This is the commandment, That, as ye have heard from the beginning, ye should walk in it.   *1 John 2:5*

Doctrine of the False Teachers

7 For many deceivers are entered into the world, who confess not that Jesus Christ is come in the flesh. RThis is a deceiver and an an'-ti-christ.   *1 John 2:22*

8 Look to yourselves, that we lose not those things which we have Twrought, but that we receive a full reward.   *worked for*

9 RWhosoever transgresseth, and abideth not in the doctrine of Christ, hath not God. He that abideth in the doctrine of Christ, he hath both the Father and the Son.   *1 John 2:23*

Avoid the False Teachers

10 If there come any unto you, and bring not this doctrine, receive him not into *your* house, neither bid him God speed:

11 For he that Rbiddeth him God speed is partaker of his evil deeds.   *1 Tim. 5:22; [Jude 23]*

Benediction

12 Having many things to write unto you, I would not *write* with paper and ink: but I trust to come unto you, and speak face to face, that Tour joy may be full.   *your*

13 RThe children of thy Telect sister greet thee. A-men'.   *1 Pet. 5:13 · dear*

JOHN

THE BOOK OF THIRD JOHN

In First John the apostle discusses fellowship with God; in Second John he forbids fellowship with false teachers; and in Third John he encourages fellowship with Christian brothers. Following his expression of love for Gaius, John assures him of his prayers for his health and voices his joy over Gaius's persistent walk in truth and for the manner in which he shows hospitality and support for missionaries who have come to his church. The phrase "bring forward on their journey" means to provide help for the missionaries' endeavors. Included in this help can be food, money, arrangements for companions, and means of travel. By supporting these men who are ministering for Christ, Gaius has become a fellow-helper of the truth.

But not everyone in the church feels the same way. Diotrephes' heart is one hundred and eighty degrees removed from Gaius's heart. He is no longer living in love. Pride has taken precedence in his life. He has refused a letter John has written for the church, fearing that his authority might be superseded by that of the apostle. He also has accused John of evil words and refused to accept missionaries. He forbids others to do so and even expels them from the church if they disobey him. John uses this negative example as an opportunity to encourage Gaius to continue his hospitality. Demetrius has a good testimony and may even be one of those turned away by Diotrephes. He is widely known for his good character and his loyalty to the truth. Here he is well commended by John and stands as a positive example for Gaius.

The Greek titles of First, Second, and Third John are *Iōannou A, B,* and *G.* The *G* is gamma, the third letter of the Greek alphabet; *Iōannou G* means "Third of John."

THE AUTHOR OF THIRD JOHN

The authorship of Second and Third John was considered together because the contents and circumstances of both books are similar (see "The Author of Second John"). Although the external evidence for Second and Third John is limited (there is even less for Third John than for Second John), what little there is consistently points to the apostle John as author. The internal evidence is stronger, and it, too, supports the apostolic origin of both letters.

THE TIME OF THIRD JOHN

The parallels between Second and Third John suggest that these epistles were written at about the same time (A.D. 90). Early Christian writers are unified in their testimony that the headquarters of John's later ministry was in Ephesus, the principal city of the Roman province of Asia (see "The Time of First John"). John evidently commissioned a number of traveling teachers to spread the gospel and to solidify the Asian churches, and these teachers were supported by believers who received them into their homes.

Third John, probably delivered by Demetrius, was occasioned by the report of some of these emissaries (called "brethren" in this letter), who returned to the apostle and informed him of the hospitality of Gaius and the hostility of Diotrephes. The arrogant Diotrephes seized the reins of an Asian church and vaunted himself as its preeminent authority. He maligned John's authority and rejected the teachers sent out by John, expelling those in his church who wanted to receive them.

Gaius was a common name in the Roman Empire, and three other men by that name are mentioned in the New Testament: (1) Gaius, one of Paul's traveling companions from Macedonia (Acts 19:29); (2) Gaius of Derbe (Acts 20:4); and (3) Gaius, Paul's host in Corinth, one of the few Corinthians Paul baptized (Rom. 16:23; 1 Cor. 1:14). The Gaius of Third John evidently lived in Asia, and it is best to distinguish him from these other men.

In verse 9, John alludes to a previous letter that Diotrephes had spurned. This may have been First or Second John, but it is more likely a letter that has been lost or perhaps destroyed by Diotrephes.

THE CHRIST OF THIRD JOHN

Unlike First and Second John, Third John makes no mention of the name of Jesus Christ. But verse 7 says "for his name's sake they went forth," an indirect reference to our Lord (cf. Acts 5:41, where the identical Greek construction is used to refer back to "the name of Jesus" in Acts 5:40). The concept of truth runs throughout this letter, and Christ is the source and incarnation of truth, as is obvious from John's other writings.

KEYS TO THIRD JOHN

Key Word: Enjoy Fellowship with the Brethren—The basic theme of this letter is to enjoy and continue to have fellowship (hospitality) with fellow believers, especially full-time Christian workers. This is contrasted between the truth and servanthood of Gaius and the error and selfishness of Diotrephes. Moving

through Third John, five specific purposes can be discerned from its contents: (1) to commend Gaius for his adherence to the truth and his hospitality to the emissaries sent out by John (vv. 1-6); (2) to encourage Gaius to continue his support of these brethren (vv. 6-8); (3) to rebuke Diotrephes for his pride and misconduct (vv. 9-11); (4) to provide a recommendation for Demetrius (v. 12); and (5) to inform Gaius of John's intention to visit and straighten out the difficulties (vv. 10, 13, 14).

Key Verse: Third John 11—"Beloved, follow not that which is evil, but that which is good. He that doeth good is of God: but he that doeth evil hath not seen God" (v. 11).

SURVEY OF THIRD JOHN

Third John is the shortest book in the Bible, but it is very personal and vivid. It offers a stark contrast between two men who respond in opposite ways to the itinerant teachers who have been sent out by the apostle. The faithful Gaius responds with generosity and hospitality, but the faithless Diotrephes responds with arrogance and opposition. Thus, John writes this letter to commend Gaius for walking in the truth (vv. 1-8) and to condemn Diotrephes for walking in error (vv. 9-14).

Commendation of Gaius (vv. 1-8): The "elder" writes to one of his beloved "children" whose godly behavior has given the apostles great joy (vv. 1-4). The "brethren," upon returning to John, have informed him of Gaius's faithfulness, love, and generosity in their behalf. The apostle acknowledges these actions and urges Gaius to continue supporting traveling teachers and missionaries who go out "for his [Jesus'] name's sake" (vv. 5-8).

Condemnation of Diotrephes (vv. 9-14): The epistle suddenly shifts to a negative note as John describes a man whose actions are diametrically opposed to those of Gaius (vv. 9-11). Diotrephes boldly rejects John's apostolic authority and refuses to receive the itinerant teachers sent out by the apostle. Diotrephes evidently has been orthodox in his doctrine, but his evil actions indicate a blindness to God in his practice.

By contrast, John gives his full recommendation to Demetrius, another emissary and probably the bearer of this letter to Gaius (v. 12). John expresses his hope of a personal visit in the closing remarks (vv. 13, 14), as he does in Second John.

FOCUS	COMMENDATION OF GAIUS			CONDEMNATION OF DIOTREPHES		
REFERENCE	1	2	5	9	12	13 — 14
DIVISION	SALUTATION	GODLINESS OF GAIUS	GENEROSITY OF GAIUS	PRIDE OF DIOTREPHES	PRAISE FOR DEMETRIUS	BENEDICTION
TOPIC	SERVANTHOOD			SELFISHNESS		
	DUTY OF HOSPITALITY			DANGER OF HAUGHTINESS		
LOCATION	WRITTEN IN EPHESUS					
TIME	C. A.D. 90					

OUTLINE OF THIRD JOHN

Salutation

THE elder unto the wellbeloved Ga'-ius, whom I love in the truth.

Godliness of Gaius

2 Beloved, [T]I wish above all things that thou mayest prosper and be in health, even as thy soul prospereth. *it is my earnest desire*

3 For I rejoiced greatly, when the brethren came and testified of the truth that is in thee, even as thou walkest in the truth.

4 I have no greater joy than to hear that [R]my children [T]walk in truth. [1 Cor. 4:15] • *live*

Generosity of Gaius

5 Beloved, thou doest [T]faithfully whatsoever thou doest to the [R]brethren, and to strangers; *a faithful work in* • Acts 1:15; Gal. 6:10

6 Which have borne witness of thy charity before the church: whom if thou [T]bring forward on their journey [T]after a godly sort, thou shalt do well: *help* • *for God's sake*

7 Because that for his name's sake they went forth, taking nothing of the Gentiles.

8 We therefore ought to receive such, that we might be fellowhelpers to the truth.

Pride of Diotrephes

9 I wrote unto the church: but Di-ot'-re-phes, who loveth to [T]have the preeminence among them, receiveth us not. *be leader*

10 Wherefore, if I come, I will remember his deeds which he doeth, prating against us with malicious words: and not content therewith, neither doth he himself receive the brethren, and forbiddeth them that would, and casteth *them* out of the church.

11 Beloved, [R]follow not that which is evil, but that which is good. [R]He that [T]doeth good is of God: but he that doeth evil hath not seen God. Ps. 37:27 • [1 John 2:29] • *practices*

Praise for Demetrius

12 De-me'-tri-us [R]hath good report of all *men,* and of the truth itself: yea, and we *also* [T]bear record; [R]and ye know that our record is true. 1 Tim. 3:7 • *will testify* • John 21:24

Benediction

13 I had many things to write, but I will not with ink and pen write unto thee:

14 But I trust I shall shortly see thee, and we shall speak face to face. [R]Peace *be* to thee. *Our* friends salute thee. Greet the friends by name. Eph. 6:23; 1 Pet. 5:14

JUDE

THE BOOK OF JUDE

Fight! Contend! Do battle! When apostasy arises, when false teachers emerge, when the truth of God is attacked, it is time to fight for the faith. Only believers who are spiritually "in shape" can answer the summons. At the beginning of his letter Jude focuses on the believers' common salvation, but then feels compelled to challenge them to contend for the faith. The danger is real. False teachers have crept into the church, turning God's grace into unbounded license to do as they please. Jude reminds such men of God's past dealings with unbelieving Israel, disobedient angels, and wicked Sodom and Gomorrha. In the face of such danger Christians should not be caught off guard. The challenge is great, but so is the God who is able to keep them from stumbling.

The Greek title *Iouda,* "Of Jude," comes from the name *Ioudas* which appears in verse 1. This name, which can be translated Jude or Judas, was popular in the first century because of Judas Maccabaeus (died 160 B.C.), a leader of the Jewish resistance against Syria during the Maccabean revolt.

THE AUTHOR OF JUDE

In spite of its limited subject matter and size, Jude was accepted as authentic and quoted by early church fathers. There may be some older allusions, but undisputed references to this epistle appear in the last quarter of the second century. It was included in the Muratorian Canon (c. A.D. 170) and accepted as part of Scripture by early leaders, such as Tertullian and Origen. Nevertheless, doubts arose concerning the place of Jude in the canon because of its use of the Apocrypha. It was a disputed book in some parts of the church, but it eventually won universal recognition.

The author identifies himself as "the servant of Jesus Christ, and brother of James" (v. 1). This designation, combined with the reference in verse 17 to the apostles, makes it unlikely that this is the apostle Jude, called "Judas *the brother* of James" in Luke 6:16 and in Acts 1:13. This leaves the traditional view that Jude was one of the Lord's brothers, called Judas in Matthew 13:55 and Mark 6:3 (see "The Author of James"). His older brother James (note his position on the two lists) was the famous leader of the Jerusalem church (Acts 15:13–21) and author of the epistle that bears his name. Like his brothers, Jude did not believe in Jesus before the Resurrection (John 7:1–9; Acts 1:14). The only other biblical allusion to him is in First Corinthians 9:5 where it is recorded that "the brethren of the Lord" took their wives along on their missionary journeys. (The Judas of Acts 15:22, 32 may be another reference to him.) Extrabiblical tradition adds nothing to our limited knowledge of Jude.

THE TIME OF JUDE

Jude's general address does not mark out any particular circle of readers, and there are no geographical restrictions. Nevertheless, he probably had in mind a specific region that was being troubled by false teachers. There is not enough information in the epistle to settle the question of whether his readers were predominately Jewish or gentile Christians (there is probably a mixture of both). In any case, the progress of the faith in their region was threatened by a number of apostates who rejected Christ in practice and principle. These proud libertines were especially dangerous because of their deceptive flattery (v. 16) and infiltration of Christian meetings (v. 12). They perverted the grace of God (v. 4) and caused divisions in the church (v. 19).

Jude's description of these heretics is reminiscent of that found in Second Peter and leads to the issue of the relationship between the two epistles (see "The Author of Second Peter"). The strong similarity between Second Peter 2:1—3:4 and Jude 4–18 can hardly be coincidental, but the equally obvious differences rule out the possibility that one is a mere copy of the other. It is also doubtful that both authors independently drew from an unknown third source, so the two remaining options are that Peter used Jude or Jude used Peter. Both views have their advocates, and a number of arguments have been raised in support of either side. But two arguments for the priority of Second Peter are so strong that they tip the scales in favor of this position: (1) A comparison of the two books shows that Second Peter anticipates the future rise of apostate teachers (2 Pet. 2:1, 2; 3:3) while Jude records the historical fulfillment of Peter's words (Jude 4, 11, 12, 17, 18); (2) Jude directly quotes Second Peter 3:3 and acknowledges it as a quotation from the apostles (cf. 1 Tim. 4:1; 2 Tim. 3:1).

Because of the silence of the New Testament and tradition concerning Jude's later years, we cannot know where this epistle was written. Nor is there any way to be certain of its date. Assuming the priority of Second Peter (A.D. 64–66), the probable range is A.D. 66–80. (Jude's silence concerning the destruction of Jerusalem does not prove that he wrote this letter before A.D. 70.)

THE CHRIST OF JUDE

In contrast to those who stand condemned by their licentiousness and denial of Christ (v. 4), the believer is "preserved in Jesus Christ" (v. 1). Jude tells his readers to "keep yourselves in the love of God, looking for the mercy of our Lord Jesus Christ unto eternal life" (v. 21). But at the same time, the Lord "is able to keep you from falling; and to present *you* faultless before the presence of his glory with exceeding joy" (v. 24).

KEYS TO JUDE

Key Word: Contend for the Faith—This epistle is intensely concerned with the threat of heretical teachers in the church and the believer's proper response to that threat. The contents reveal two major purposes: first, to condemn the practices of the ungodly libertines who were infesting the churches and corrupting believers; and second, to counsel the readers to stand firm, grow in their faith, and contend for the truth. Jude says little about the actual doctrines of these "raging waves of the sea," but they may have held to an antinomian version of Gnosticism (see "The Time of First John"). The readers are encouraged to reach out to those who have been misled by these men.

Key Verse: Jude 3—"Beloved, when I gave all diligence to write unto you of the common salvation, it was needful for me to write unto you, and exhort *you* that ye should earnestly contend for the faith which was once delivered unto the saints" (v. 3).

SURVEY OF JUDE

A surprisingly large number of the Pauline and non-Pauline epistles confront the problem of false teachers, and almost all of them allude to it. But Jude goes beyond all other New Testament epistles in its relentless and passionate denunciation of the apostate teachers who have "crept in unawares." With the exception of its salutation (vv. 1, 2) and doxology (vv. 24, 25), the entire epistle revolves around this alarming problem. Combining the theme of Second Peter with the style of James, Jude is potent in spite of its brevity. This urgent letter has four major sections: purpose of Jude (vv. 1-4); description of false teachers (vv. 5-16); defense against false teachers (vv. 17-23); and doxology of Jude (vv. 24, 25).

Purpose of Jude (vv. 1-4): Jude addresses his letter to believers who are "sanctified," "preserved," and "called," and wishes for them the threefold blessing of mercy, peace, and love (vv. 1, 2). Grim news about the encroachment of false teachers in the churches has impelled Jude to put aside his commentary on salvation to write this timely word of rebuke and warning (vv. 3, 4). In view of apostates who turn "the grace of our God into lasciviousness" and deny Christ, it is crucial that believers "earnestly contend for the faith."

Description of False Teachers (vv. 5-16): Jude begins his extended exposé of the apostate teachers by illustrating their ultimate doom with three examples of divine judgment from the Pentateuch (vv. 5-7).

Like unreasoning animals, these apostates are ruled by the things they revile, and they are destroyed by the things they practice (vv. 8-10). Even the archangel Michael is more careful in his dealings with superhuman powers than are these arrogant men. Jude compares these men to three spiritually rebellious men from Genesis (Cain) and Numbers (Balaam and Korah) who incurred the condemnation of God (v. 11). Verses 12 and 13 succinctly summarize their character with five highly descriptive metaphors taken from nature. After affirming the judgment of God upon such ungodly men with a quotation from the non-canonical Book of Enoch (vv. 14, 15), Jude catalogs some of their practices (v. 16).

Defense Against False Teachers (vv. 17-23): This letter has been exposing apostate teachers

FOCUS	PURPOSE	DESCRIPTION OF FALSE TEACHERS			DEFENSE AGAINST FALSE TEACHERS	DOXOLOGY
REFERENCE	1———5	———8	———14		17———24	——25
DIVISION	INTRODUCTION	PAST JUDGMENT	PRESENT CHARACTERISTICS	FUTURE JUDGMENT	DUTY OF BELIEVERS	CONCLUSION
TOPIC	REASON TO CONTEND				HOW TO CONTEND	
	ANATOMY OF APOSTASY				ANTIDOTE FOR APOSTASY	
LOCATION	UNKNOWN					
TIME	C. A.D. 66-80					

(vv. 8, 10, 12, 14, 16), but now Jude directly addresses his readers ("But, beloved, remember ye," v. 17). He reminds them of the apostolic warning that such men would come (vv. 17-19) and encourages them to protect themselves against the onslaught of apostasy (vv. 20, 21). The readers must become mature in their own faith so

that they will be able to rescue those who are enticed or already ensnared by error (vv. 22, 23).

Doxology of Jude (vv. 24, 25): Jude closes with one of the greatest doxologies in the Bible. It emphasizes the power of Christ to keep those who trust in Him from being overthrown by error.

OUTLINE OF JUDE

Purpose of Jude

JUDE, the servant of Jesus Christ, and brother of James, to them that are sanctified by God the Father, and ᵀpreserved in Jesus Christ, *and* called: *saved*

2 Mercy unto you, and ᴿpeace, and love, ᵀbe multiplied.   1 Pet. 1:2 · *in full measure*

3 ᴿBeloved, when I gave all diligence to write unto you of the ᵀcommon salvation, it was needful for me to write unto you, and ᵀexhort *you* that ye should earnestly contend for the faith which was once delivered unto the saints.   Heb. 6:9 · *mutual · urge*

4 For there are certain men crept in ᵀunawares, who were before of old ᵀordained to this condemnation, ungodly men, turning the grace of our God into ᵀlasciviousness, and denying the only Lord God, and our Lord Jesus Christ.   *secretly · prepared · evil*

Past Judgment of False Teachers

5 I will therefore put you in remembrance, though ye once knew this, how that ᴿthe Lord, having saved the people out of the land of Egypt, afterward destroyed them that believed not.   1 Cor. 10:9

6 And the angels which kept not their first estate, but left their own habitation, he hath reserved in everlasting chains under darkness unto the judgment of the great day.

7 Even as Sodom and Go-mor'-rha, and the cities about them in like manner, giving themselves over to fornication, and going after strange flesh, are set forth for an example, suffering the vengeance of eternal fire.

Present Characteristics of False Teachers

8 Likewise also these *filthy* dreamers ᴿdefile the flesh, despise dominion, and speak evil of ᵀdignities.   2 Pet. 2:10 · *authorities*

9 Yet Mi'-cha-el the archangel, when ᵀcontending with the devil he disputed about the body of Moses, ᵀdurst not bring against him a railing ᵀaccusation, but said, The Lord rebuke thee.   *arguing · dared · judgment*

10 But these speak evil of those things which they know not: but what they know naturally, as brute beasts, in those things they ᵀcorrupt themselves.   *destroy*

11 Woe unto them! for they have gone in the way of Cain, and ran greedily after the error of Ba'-laam for reward, and perished in the gainsaying of Co'-re.

12 These are spots in your feasts of charity, when they feast with you, feeding themselves without fear: clouds *they are* without water, carried about of winds; trees whose fruit withereth, without fruit, twice dead, plucked up by the roots;

13 ᴿRaging waves of the sea, ᴿfoaming out their own shame; wandering stars, ᴿto whom is reserved the blackness of darkness for ever.   Is. 57:20 · [Phil. 3:19] · 2 Pet. 2:17

Future Judgment of False Teachers

14 ᴿAnd E'-noch also, the seventh from Adam, prophesied of these, saying, Behold, the Lord cometh with ten thousands of his saints,   Gen. 5:18; Dan. 7:10; Zech. 14:5 ✻

15 ᴿTo execute judgment upon all, and to ᵀconvince all that are ungodly among them of all their ungodly deeds which they have ungodly committed, and of all their ᴿhard

speeches which ungodly sinners have spoken against him.   2 Pet. 2:6 ☆ • *convict* • 1 Sam. 2:3

16 These are murmurers, complainers, walking after their own lusts; and their mouth speaketh great swelling *words,* having men's persons in admiration ᵀbecause of advantage.   *in order to gain advantage*

Defense Against False Teachers

17 ᴿBut, beloved, remember ye the words which were spoken ᵀbefore of the apostles of our Lord Jesus Christ;   2 Pet. 3:2 • *in the past*

18 How that they told you there should be mockers in the last time, who should walk after their own ungodly ᵀlusts.   *passions*

19 These be they who separate themselves, sensual, having not the Spirit.

20 But ye, beloved, ᴿbuilding up yourselves on your most holy faith, ᴿpraying in the Holy Ghost,   [Rom. 8:26] • Eph. 6:18

21 ᵀKeep yourselves in the love of God, ᴿlooking for the mercy of our Lord Jesus Christ unto eternal life.   *guard* • 2 Pet. 3:12

22 And ᵀof some have compassion, ᵀmaking a difference: *on* • *who are doubters*

23 And others save with fear, pulling *them* out of the fire; hating even ᴿthe garment spotted by the flesh.   [Zech. 3:4, 5]

Doxology of Jude

24 ᴿNow unto him that is able to keep you from falling, and ᴿto present *you* faultless before the presence of his glory with exceeding joy,   [Eph. 3:20] • Col. 1:22

25 To the only wise God our Saviour, *be* glory and majesty, dominion and power, ᴿboth now and ever. A-men'.   Heb. 13:8

Measures of Length

Unit	Length	Equivalents	Translations
Day's journey	c. 20 miles		day's journey
Roman mile	4,854 feet	8 stadia	mile
Sabbath day's journey	3,637 feet	6 stadia	sabbath day's journey
Stadion	606 feet	⅛ Roman mile	furlong
Rod	9 feet (10.5 feet in Ezekiel)	3 paces; 6 cubits	measuring reed, reed
Fathom	6 feet	4 cubits	fathom
Pace	3 feet	⅓ rod; 2 cubits	pace
Cubit	18 inches	½ pace; 2 spans	cubit
Span	9 inches	½ cubit; 3 handbreadths	span
Handbreadth	3 inches	⅓ span; 4 fingers	handbreadth
Finger	.75 inches	¼ handbreadth	finger

THE REVELATION

OF ST. JOHN THE DIVINE

THE BOOK OF REVELATION

Just as Genesis is the book of beginnings, Revelation is the book of consummation. In it, the divine program of redemption is brought to fruition, and the holy name of God is vindicated before all creation. Although there are numerous prophecies in the Gospels and Epistles, Revelation is the only New Testament book that focuses primarily on prophetic events. Its title means "unveiling" or "disclosure." Thus, the book is an unveiling of the character and program of God. Penned by John during his exile on the island of Patmos, Revelation centers around visions and symbols of the resurrected Christ, who alone has authority to judge the earth, to remake it, and to rule it in righteousness.

The title of this book in the Greek text is *Apokalypsis Ioannou,* "Revelation of John." It is also known as the Apocalypse, a transliteration of the word *apokalypsis,* meaning "unveiling," "disclosure," or "revelation." Thus, the book is an unveiling of that which otherwise could not be known. A better title comes from the first verse: *Apokalypsis Iēsou Christou,* "Revelation of Jesus Christ." This could be taken as a revelation which came from Christ or as a revelation which is about Christ—both are appropriate. Because of the unified contents of this book, it should not be called Revelations.

THE AUTHOR OF REVELATION

The style, symmetry, and plan of Revelation show that it was written by one author, four times named "John" (1:1, 4, 9; 22:8; see "The Author of John"). Because of its contents and its address to seven churches, Revelation quickly circulated and became widely known and accepted in the early church. It was frequently mentioned and quoted by second- and third-century Christian writers and was received as part of the canon of New Testament books. From the beginning, Revelation was considered an authentic work of the apostle John, the same John who wrote the gospel and three epistles. This was held to be true by Justin Martyr, the Shepherd of Hermas, Melito, Irenaeus, the Muratorian Canon, Tertullian, Clement of Alexandria, Origen, and others.

This view was seldom questioned until the middle of the third century when Dionysius presented several arguments against the apostolic authorship of Revelation. He observed a clear difference in style and thought between Revelation and the books that he accepted as Johannine, and he concluded that the Apocalypse must have been penned by a different John. Indeed, the internal evidence does pose some problems for the traditional view: (1) The Greek grammar of Revelation is not on par with the Fourth Gospel or the Johannine Epistles. (2) There are also differences in vocabulary and expressions used. (3) The theological content of this book differs from John's other writings in emphasis and presentation. (4) John's other writings avoid the use of his name, but it is found four times in this book. While these difficulties exist, two things should be kept in mind: (1) There are a number of remarkable similarities between the Apocalypse and the other books traditionally associated with the apostle John (e.g., the distinctive use of terms, such as *word, lamb,* and *true,* and the careful development of conflicting themes, such as light and darkness, love and hatred, good and evil). (2) Many of the differences can be explained by the unusual circumstances surrounding this book. The apocalyptic subject matter demands a different treatment, and John received the contents not by reflection but by a series of startling and ecstatic visions. It is also possible that John used a secretary who smoothed out the Greek style of his other writings, and that his exile on Patmos prevented the use of such a scribe when he wrote Revelation.

Thus, the internal evidence, while problematic, need not overrule the early and strong external testimony to the apostolic origin of this important book. The author was obviously well-known to the recipients in the seven Asian churches, and this fits the unqualified use of the name John and the uniform tradition about his ministry in Asia. Alternate suggestions, such as John the Elder or a prophet named John, create more problems than they solve.

THE TIME OF REVELATION

John directed this prophetic word to seven selected churches in the Roman province of Asia (1:3, 4). The messages to these churches in chapters 2 and 3 begin with Ephesus, the most prominent, and continue in a clockwise direction until Laodicea is reached. It is likely that this book was initially carried along this circular route. While each of these messages had particular significance for these churches, they were also relevant for the church as a whole ("He that hath an ear, let him hear what the Spirit saith unto the churches").

John's effective testimony for Christ led the Roman authorities to exile him to the small, desolate island of Patmos in the Aegean Sea (1:9). This island of volcanic rock was one of several places to which the Romans banished criminals and political offenders.

Revelation was written at a time when Roman hostility to Christianity was erupting into overt persecution (1:9; 2:10, 13). Some scholars believe that it should be given an early date during the persecution of Christians under Nero after the A.D. 64 burning of Rome. The Hebrew letters for Nero Caesar *(Neron Kesar)* add up to 666, the number of the beast (13:18), and there was a legend that Nero would reappear in the East after his apparent death (cf. Rev. 13:3, 12, 14). This kind of evidence is weak, and a later date near the end of the reign of the emperor Domitian (A.D. 81–96) is preferable for several reasons: (1) This was the testimony of Irenaeus (disciple of Polycarp who was a disciple of John) and other early Christian writers. (2) John probably did not move from Jerusalem to Ephesus until about A.D. 67, shortly before the Roman destruction of Jerusalem in A.D. 70. The early dating would not give him enough time to have established an ongoing ministry in Asia by the time he wrote this book. (3) The churches of Asia appear to have been in existence for a number of years, long enough for some to reach a point of complacency and decline (cf. 2:4; 3:1, 15–18). (4) The deeds of Domitian are more relevant than those of Nero to the themes of the Apocalypse. Worship of deceased emperors had been practiced for years, but Domitian was the first emperor to demand worship while he was alive. This led to a greater clash between the state and the church, especially in Asia, where the worship of Caesar was widely practiced. The persecution under Domitian presaged the more severe persecutions to follow.

Thus, it is likely that John wrote this book in A.D. 95 or 96. The date of his release from Patmos is unknown, but he was probably allowed to return to Ephesus after the reign of Domitian. Passages such as 1:11; 22:7, 9, 10, 18, 19 suggest that the book was completed before John's release.

✝ THE CHRIST OF REVELATION

Revelation has much to say about all three persons of the Godhead, but it is especially clear in its presentation of the awesome resurrected Christ who has received all authority to judge the earth. He is called Jesus Christ (1:1), the faithful witness, the first begotten of the dead, the prince of the kings of the earth (1:5), the first and the last (1:17), he that liveth (1:18), the Son of God (2:18), holy and true (3:7), the Amen, the faithful and true witness, the beginning of the creation of God (3:14), the Lion of the tribe of Judah, the Root of David (5:5), a Lamb (5:6), Faithful and True (19:11), The Word of God (19:13), KING OF KINGS, AND LORD OF LORDS (19:16), Alpha and Omega (22:13), the bright and morning star (22:16), and the Lord Jesus Christ (22:21).

This book is indeed "The Revelation of Jesus Christ" (1:1) since it comes from Him and centers on Him. It begins with a vision of His glory, wisdom, and power (1), and portrays His authority over the entire church (2; 3). He is the Lamb who was slain and declared worthy to open the book of judgment (5). His righteous wrath is poured out upon the whole earth (6—18), and He returns in power to judge His enemies and to reign as the Lord over all (19; 20). He will rule forever over the heavenly city in the presence of all who know Him (21; 22).

The Scriptures close with His great promise: "Behold, I come quickly" (22:7, 12). "Surely I come quickly. Amen. Even so, come, Lord Jesus" (22:20).

🔑 KEYS TO REVELATION

Key Word: The Revelation of the Coming of Christ—The purposes for which Revelation was written depend to some extent on how the book as a whole is interpreted. Because of its complex imagery and symbolism, Revelation is the most difficult biblical book to interpret, and there are four major alternatives: (1) The symbolic or idealist view maintains that Revelation is not a predictive prophecy, but a symbolic portrait of the cosmic conflict of spiritual principles. (2) The preterist view (the Latin word *praeter* means "past") maintains that it is a symbolic description of the Roman persecution of the church, emperor worship, and the divine judgment of Rome. (3) The historicist view approaches Revelation as an allegorical panorama of the history of the (Western) church from the first century to the Second Advent. (4) The futurist view acknowledges the obvious influence that the first-century conflict between Roman power and the church had upon the themes of this book. It also accepts the bulk of Revelation (4—22) as an inspired look into the time immediately preceding the Second Advent (the "tribulation," usually seen as seven years; 6—18), and extending from the return of Christ to the creation of the new cosmos (19—22).

Advocates of all four interpretive approaches to Revelation agree that it was written to assure the recipients of the ultimate triumph of Christ over all who rise up against Him and His saints. The readers were facing dark times of persecution, and even worse times would follow. Therefore they needed to be encouraged to persevere by standing firm in Christ in view of God's plan for the righteous and the wicked. This plan is especially clear in the stirring words of the epilogue (22:6-21). The book was also written to challenge complacent Christians to stop compromising with the world. According to futurists, Revelation serves the additional purpose of providing a perspective on end-time events that

would have meaning and relevance to the spiritual lives of all succeeding generations of Christians.

Key Verses: Revelation 1:19 and 19:11-15— "Write the things which thou hast seen, and the things which are, and the things which shall be hereafter" (1:19).

"And I saw heaven opened, and behold a white horse; and he that sat upon him *was* called Faithful and True, and in righteousness he doth judge and make war. His eyes *were* as a flame of fire, and on his head *were* many crowns; and he had a name written, that no man knew, but he himself. And he *was* clothed with a vesture dipped in blood: and his name is called The Word of God. And the armies *which were* in heaven followed him upon white horses, clothed in fine linen, white and clean. And out of his mouth goeth a sharp sword, that with it he should smite the nations: and he shall rule them with a rod of iron: and he treadeth the winepress of the fierceness and wrath of Almighty God" (19:11-15).

Key Chapters: Revelation 19—22—When the end of history is fully understood, its impact radically affects the present. In Revelation 19—22 the plans of God for the last days and for all of eternity are recorded in explicit terms. Careful study of and obedience to them will bring the blessings that are promised (1:3). Uppermost in the mind and deep in the heart should be guarded the words of Jesus, "Behold, I come quickly."

SURVEY OF REVELATION

Revelation is written in the form of apocalyptic literature (cf. Daniel and Zechariah) by a prophet (10:11; 22:9) and refers to itself as a prophetic book (1:3; 22:7, 10, 18, 19). The three major movements in this profound unveiling are captured in 1:19: "the things which thou hast seen" (1); "the things which are" (2 and 3); and "the things which shall be hereafter" (4—22).

"The Things Which Thou Hast Seen" (1): Revelation contains a prologue (1:1-3) before the usual salutation (1:4-8). The Revelation was received by Christ from the Father and communicated by an angel to John. This is the only biblical book that specifically promises a blessing to those who read it (1:3), but it also promises a curse to those who add to or detract from it (22:18, 19). The salutation and closing benediction show that it was originally written as an epistle to seven Asian churches.

A rich theological portrait of the triune God (1:4-8) is followed by an overwhelming theophany (visible manifestation of God) in 1:9-20. The omnipotent and omniscient Christ who will subjugate all things under His authority is the central figure in this book.

"The Things Which Are" (2 and 3): The messages to the seven churches (2 and 3) refer back to an aspect of John's vision of Christ and contain a command, a commendation and/or condemnation, a correction, and a challenge.

"The Things Which Shall Be Hereafter" (4— 22): John is translated into heaven where he is given a vision of the divine majesty. In it, the Father ("*one*" sat on the throne") and the Son (The Lion/Lamb) are worshiped by the twenty-four elders, the four living creatures, and the angelic host because of who they are and what they have done (creation and redemption; 4 and 5).

Three cycles of seven judgments in chapters 6—16 consist of seven seals, seven trumpets, and seven vials. There is a prophetic insert between the sixth and seventh seal and trumpet judgments and an extended insert between the trumpet and vial judgments. Because of the similarity of the seventh judgment in each series, it is possible that the three sets of judgments take place concurrently or with some overlap so that they all terminate with the return of Christ. An alternate approach views them as three consecutive series of judgments, so that the seventh seal is the seven trumpets and the seventh trumpet is the seven vials.

The seven seals (6:1—8:5) include war, the famine and death that are associated with war, and persecution. The prophetic insert between the sixth and seventh seals (7) describes the protective sealing of 144,000 "children of Israel," 12,000 from every tribe. It also looks ahead to the multitudes from every part of the earth who come "out of the great tribulation." The catastrophic events in most of the trumpet judgments are called "woes" (8:2—11:19). The prophetic interlude between the sixth and seventh trumpets (10:1—11:14) adds more details about the nature of the tribulation period and mentions a fourth set of seven judgments (the "seven thunders"), which would have extended it if they had not been withdrawn. Two unnamed witnesses minister during three-and-a-half years of the tribulation (forty-two months or 1,260 days). At the end of their ministry they are overcome by the beast, but their resurrection and ascension confound their enemies.

Chapters 12—14 contain a number of miscellaneous prophecies that are inserted between the trumpet and vial judgments to give further background on the time of tribulation. In chapter 12 a woman gives birth to a male child, who is caught up to God. The woman flees into the wilderness and is pursued by a dragon, who is cast down to earth. Chapter 13 gives a graphic description of the beast and his false prophet, both empowered by the dragon. The first beast is

given political, economic, and religious authority; and because of his power and the lying miracles performed by the second beast, he is worshiped as the ruler of the earth. Chapter 14 contains a series of visions including the 144,000 at the end of the tribulation, the fate of those who follow the beast, and the outpouring of the wrath of God.

The seven vial judgments of chapter 16 are prefaced by a heavenly vision of the power, holiness, and glory of God in chapter 15.

Chapters 17 and 18 anticipate the final downfall of Babylon, the great harlot sitting upon a scarlet-colored beast.

The marriage banquet of the Lamb is ready and the King of Kings, Lord of Lords leads the armies of heaven into battle against the beast and his false prophet. They are cast into a lake of fire (19).

In chapter 20 the dragon—Satan—is bound for a thousand years. He is cast into a bottomless pit. During this one-thousand-year period Christ reigns over the earth with His resurrected saints,

but by the end of this millennium, many have been born who refuse to submit their hearts to Christ. At the end of the thousand years, Satan is released and a final battle ensues. This is followed by the judgment at the great white throne.

A new universe is created, this time unspoiled by sin, death, pain, or sorrow. The new Jerusalem, described in 21:9—22:5, is shaped like a gigantic cube, 1,500 miles in length, width, and height (the most holy place in the Old Testament tabernacle and the temple was also a perfect cube). Its multicolored stones will reflect the glory of God, and it will continually be filled with light. But the greatest thing of all is that believers will be in the presence of God "and they shall see his face."

Revelation concludes with an epilogue (22:6–21), which reassures the readers that Christ is coming quickly (22:7, 12, 20) and invites all who wish to "take the water of life freely" (22:17) to come to the Alpha and Omega, the Bright and Morning Star.

FOCUS	"THINGS WHICH YOU HAVE SEEN"	"THINGS WHICH ARE"	"THINGS WHICH SHALL TAKE PLACE"				
REFERENCE	1:1——————2:1	————4:1	————6:1————19:7		—20:1—	—21:1——22:21	
DIVISION	THE LORD JESUS CHRIST	SEVEN CHURCHES	THE JUDGE	TRIBULATION	SECOND COMING	MILLENNIUM	ETERNAL STATE
TOPIC	VISION OF CHRIST		VISION OF CONSUMMATION				
	THEOPHANY	TALKS	TRIBULATIONS		TRUMPETS		TOGETHER
LOCATION	WRITTEN ON THE ISLAND OF PATMOS						
TIME	C. A.D. 95 – 96						

OUTLINE OF REVELATION

Part One: "The Things Which Thou Hast Seen" (1:1–20)

Part Two: "The Things Which Are" (2:1–3:22)

Part Three: "The Things Which Shall Be Hereafter" (4:1—22:21)

CHAPTER 1

Introduction

THE Revelation of Jesus Christ, which God gave unto him, to shew unto his servants things which must ᵀshortly come to pass; and he sent and signified it by his angel unto his servant John: soon

2 ᴿWho bare record of the word of God, and of the testimony of Jesus Christ, and of all things ᴿthat he saw.   1 Cor. 1:6 · 1 John 1:1

3 ᴿBlessed is he that readeth, and they that hear the words of this prophecy, and keep those things which are written therein: ᴿfor the time is at hand.   Luke 11:28 · Rom. 13:11

4 John to the seven churches which are in Asia: Grace be unto you, and peace, from him ᴿwhich is, and which was, and which is to come; and from the seven Spirits which are before his throne;   Ex. 3:14; 8:2

5 And from Jesus Christ, who is the faithful witness, and the first begotten of the dead, and ᴿthe prince of the kings of the earth. Unto him that loved us, and washed us from our sins in his own blood,   Ps. 89:27 ★

6 And hath made us kings and priests unto God and his Father; to him be glory and dominion for ever and ever. A-men'.

7 Behold, he cometh with clouds; and every eye shall see him, and they also which pierced him: and all kindreds of the earth shall wail because of him. Even so, A-men'.

8 ᴿI am ᵀAlpha and Omega, the beginning and the ending, saith the Lord, ᴿwhich is, and which was, and which is to come, the Almighty.   Is. 41:4 · Beginning and End · 4:8

Revelation of Christ

9 I John, who also am your brother, and companion in tribulation, and in the kingdom and patience of Jesus Christ, was in the isle that is called Pat'-mos, for the word of God, and for the testimony of Jesus Christ.

10 I was in the Spirit on ᴿthe Lord's day,

and heard behind me a great voice, as of a trumpet,   [Mark 16:9; Acts 2:42; 20:7; 1 Cor. 16:1, 2]

11 Saying, I am Alpha and Omega, the first and the last: and, What thou seest, write in a book, and send *it* unto the seven churches which are in Asia; unto Eph′-e-sus, and unto Smyrna, and unto Per′-ga-mos, and unto Thy-a-ti′-ra, and unto Sar′-dis, and unto Philadelphia, and unto ^RLa-od-i-ce′-a.   Col. 2:1

12 And I turned to see the voice that spake with me. And being turned, ^RI saw seven golden candlesticks;   Ex. 25:37

13 And in the midst of the seven candlesticks *one* like unto the Son of man, clothed with a garment down to the foot, and girt about the paps with a golden girdle.

14 His head and ^Rhis hairs *were* white like wool, as white as snow; and ^Rhis eyes *were* as a flame of fire;   Dan. 7:9 · Dan. 10:6

15 ^RAnd his feet like unto fine brass, as if they burned in a furnace; and ^Rhis voice as the sound of many waters.   Ezek. 1:7 · Ezek. 43:2

16 ^RAnd he had in his right hand seven stars: and ^Rout of his mouth went a sharp twoedged sword: and his countenance *was* as the sun shineth in his strength.   2:1 · Is. 49:2 ☆

17 And ^Rwhen I saw him, I fell at his feet as dead. And ^Rhe laid his right hand upon me, saying unto me, Fear not; ^RI am the first and the last: Ezek. 1:28 · Dan. 8:18 · Is. 41:4

18 *I am* he that liveth, and was dead; and, behold, I am alive for evermore, A-men′; and have the keys of hell and of death.

19 Write the things which thou hast seen, ^Rand the things which are, ^Rand the things which shall be hereafter;   2:1 · 4:1; John 16:13

20 The ^Tmystery of the seven stars which thou sawest in my right hand, and the seven golden candlesticks. The seven stars are the ^Tangels of the seven churches: and the seven candlesticks which thou sawest are the seven churches.   *hidden truth · messengers*

CHAPTER 2

Message to Ephesus

UNTO the ^Tangel of the church of Eph′-e-sus write; These things saith ^Rhe that holdeth the seven stars in his right hand, who walketh in the midst of the seven golden candlesticks;   *messenger · 1:16*

2 I know thy works, and thy labour, and thy patience, and how thou canst not ^Tbear them which are evil: and thou hast tried them which say they are apostles, and are not, and hast found them liars: *tolerate*

3 And hast borne, and hast ^Tpatience, and for my name′s sake hast laboured, and hast ^Rnot ^Tfainted.   *persistence · Heb. 12:3, 5 · become weak*

4 Nevertheless I have *somewhat* against thee, because thou hast left thy first love.

5 Remember therefore from whence thou art fallen, and repent, and ^Tdo the first works; or else I will come unto thee quickly, and will remove thy candlestick out of his place, except thou repent.   *practise*

6 ^RBut this thou hast, that thou hatest the deeds of the ^TNic-o-la′-i-tanes, which I also hate.   *v. 15 · make believe Christians*

7 He that hath an ear, let him hear what the Spirit saith unto the churches; To him that overcometh will I give ^Rto eat of ^Rthe tree of life, which is in the midst of the ^Tparadise of God.   [22:2, 14] · Gen. 2:9 · *presence*

Message to Smyrna

8 And unto the angel of the church in Smyrna write; These things saith the first and the last, which was dead, and is alive;

9 I know thy works, and tribulation, and poverty, (but thou art ^Rrich) and *I know* the blasphemy of ^Rthem which say they are Jews, and are not, ^Rbut *are* the synagogue of Satan.   Luke 12:21 · Rom. 2:17 · 3:9

10 Fear none of those things which thou shalt suffer: behold, the devil shall cast *some* of you into prison, that ye may be ^Ttried; and ye shall have ^Ttribulation ten days: be thou faithful unto death, and I will give thee a crown of life.   *tested · trouble*

11 ^RHe that hath an ear, let him hear what the Spirit saith unto the churches; He that overcometh shall not be hurt of ^Rthe second death.   13:9 · [20:14]

Message to Pergamos

12 And to the angel of the church in Per′-ga-mos write; These things saith ^Rhe which hath the sharp sword with two edges; Is. 49:2 ☆

13 I know thy works, and where thou dwellest, *even* where Satan′s seat *is:* and thou holdest fast my name, and hast not ^Tdenied my faith, even in those days wherein An′-ti-pas *was* my faithful martyr, who was slain among you, where Satan dwelleth.   *abandoned*

14 But I have a few things against thee, because thou hast there them that hold the doctrine of ^RBa′-laam, who taught Ba′-lac to cast a stumblingblock before the children of Israel, to eat things sacrificed unto idols, and to commit fornication.   Num. 31:16

15 ^RSo hast thou also them that ^Thold the doctrine of the Nic-o-la′-i-tanes, which I hate.   *v. 6 · follow the teaching*

16 Repent; or else I will come unto thee quickly, and ^Rwill fight against them with the sword of my mouth.   Is. 11:4; 2 Thess. 2:8

17 He that hath an ear, let him hear what the Spirit saith unto the churches; To him that overcometh will I give to eat of the hidden man′-na, and will give him a white stone, and in the stone ^Ra new name written, which no man ^Tknoweth saving he that receiveth *it*.   3:12 · *recognizes*

Message to Thyatira

18 And unto the angel of the church in Thy-a-ti'-ra write; These things saith the Son of God, who hath his eyes like unto a flame of fire, and his feet *are* like fine brass;

19 I know thy works, and charity, and service, and faith, and thy patience, and thy works; and the last *to be* more than the first.

20 Notwithstanding I have a few things against thee, because thou ᵀsufferest that woman Jez'-e-bel, which calleth herself a prophetess, to teach and to ᵀseduce my servants to commit fornication, and to eat things sacrificed unto idols.   *allow • misleads*

21 And I gave her space ᴿto repent of her fornication; and she repented not.

22 Behold, I will cast her into a bed, and them that ᵀcommit adultery with her into great ᵀtribulation, except they repent of their deeds.   *promote pagan religious ideas • trouble*

23 And I will kill her children with death; and all the churches shall ᵀknow that I am he which ᵀsearcheth the ᵀreins and hearts: and I will give unto every one of you according to your works.   *realize • judges • wills*

24 But unto you I say, and unto the rest in Thy-a-ti'-ra, as many as have not this doctrine, and which have not ᵀknown the depths of Satan, as they speak; I will put upon you none other burden.   *experienced*

25 But ᴿthat which ye have *already* hold ᵀfast till I come.   *3:11; John 21:22 • firmly*

26 And he that overcometh, and ᵀkeepeth my works unto the end, to him will I give power over the nations: *maintains*

27 ᴿAnd HE SHALL RULE THEM WITH A ROD OF IRON; AS THE VESSELS OF A POTTER SHALL THEY BE BROKEN TO ᵀSHIVERS: even as I received of my Father.   *Ps. 2:8, 9 ✩ • small pieces*

28 And I will give him the morning star.

29 He that hath an ear, let him hear what the Spirit saith unto the churches.

CHAPTER 3

Message to Sardis

AND unto the angel of the church in Sar'-dis write; These things saith he that hath the seven Spirits of God, and the seven stars; I know thy works, that thou hast a name that thou livest, and art dead.

2 Be watchful, and strengthen the things ᵀwhich remain, that are ready to die: for I have not found thy works ᵀperfect before God.   *you still have • complete*

3 Remember therefore how thou hast received and heard, and hold fast, and repent. If therefore thou shalt not watch, I will come on thee as a thief, and thou shalt not know what hour I will come upon thee.

4 Thou hast a few names even in Sar'-dis which have not ᴿdefiled their garments; and

they shall walk with me ᴿin white: for they are worthy.   *[Jude 23] • 4:4*

5 He that overcometh, ᴿthe same shall be clothed in white raiment; and I will not blot out his name out of the book of life, but I will confess his name before my Father, and before his angels.   *[19:8]*

6 ᴿHe that hath an ear, let him hear what the Spirit saith unto the churches.   *2:7*

Message to Philadelphia

7 And to the angel of the church in Philadelphia write; These things saith he that is holy, he that is true, HE THAT HATH THE KEY OF DAVID, HE THAT OPENETH, AND NO MAN SHUTTETH; AND SHUTTETH, AND NO MAN OPENETH;

8 ᴿI know thy works: behold, I have set before thee ᴿan open door, and no man can shut it: for thou hast a little ᵀstrength, and hast ᵀkept my word, and hast not denied my name.   *v. 1 • 1 Cor. 16:9 • power • obeyed*

9 Behold, I will make them of the synagogue of Satan, which say they are Jews, and are not, but do lie; behold, I will make them to come and worship before thy feet, and to ᵀknow that I have loved thee.   *realize*

10 Because thou hast kept the word of my patience, I also will keep thee from the hour of temptation, which shall come upon all the world, to try them that dwell upon the earth.

11 Behold, ᴿI come quickly: ᴿhold that fast which thou hast, that no man take ᴿthy crown.   *Phil. 4:5 • 2:25 • [2:10]*

12 Him that overcometh will I make ᴿa pillar in the temple of my God, and he shall go no more out: and ᴿI will write upon him the name of my God, and the name of the city of my God, *which is* ᴿnew Jerusalem, which cometh down out of heaven from my God: ᴿand *I will write upon him* my new name.   *1 Kin. 7:21 • [14:1] • [Heb. 12:22] • [22:4]*

13 He that hath an ear, let him hear what the Spirit saith unto the churches.

Message to Laodicea

14 And unto the angel of the church of the La-od-i-ce'-ans write; These things saith the A-men', the faithful and true witness, ᴿthe beginning of the creation of God;   *[Col. 1:15]*

15 ᴿI know thy works, that thou art neither cold nor hot: I would thou wert ᵀcold or hot.   *v. 1 • one or the other*

16 So then because thou art ᵀlukewarm, and neither cold nor hot, I will ᵀspue thee out of my mouth.   *barely warm • vomit*

17 Because thou sayest, ᴿI am rich, and increased with goods, and have need of nothing; and knowest not that thou art wretched, and miserable, and poor, and blind, and naked: *Hos. 12:8; Zech. 11:5; [Matt. 5:3]*

18 I ᵀcounsel thee to buy of me gold tried in the fire, that thou mayest be rich; and

white raiment, that thou mayest be clothed, and *that* the shame of thy nakedness do not appear; and anoint thine eyes with eyesalve, that thou mayest see.   *advise*

19 ᴿAs many as I love, I rebuke and chasten: be zealous therefore, and repent. Job 5:17

20 Behold, I stand at the door, and knock: if any man hear my voice, and open the door, I will come in to him, and will sup with him, and he with me.

21 To him that ᵀovercometh ᴿwill I grant to sit with me in my throne, even as I also overcame, and am set down with my Father in his throne.   *wins the victory* · Matt. 19:28 ☆

22 He that hath an ear, let him hear what the Spirit saith unto the churches.

CHAPTER 4

The Throne of God

AFTER this I looked, and, behold, a door *was* opened in heaven: and the first voice which I heard *was* as it were of a trumpet talking with me; which said, Come up hither, and I will shew thee things which must be ᵀhereafter.   *in the future*

2 And immediately ᴿI was in the spirit: and, behold, ᴿa throne was set in heaven, and *one* sat on the throne.   1:10 · Is. 6:1

3 And he that sat was to look upon like a jasper and a sardine stone: ᴿand *there* was a rainbow round about the throne, in ᵀsight like unto an emerald.   Ezek. 1:28 · *colour*

4 ᴿAnd round about the throne *were* four and twenty seats: and upon the seats I saw four and twenty elders sitting, ᴿclothed in white ᵀraiment; and they had on their heads crowns of gold.   11:16 · 3:4, 5 · *clothing*

5 And out of the throne proceeded ᴿlightnings and thunderings and voices: ᴿand *there were* seven lamps of fire burning before the throne, which are ᴿthe seven Spirits of God.   8:5 · Ex. 37:23 · [1:4]

6 And before the throne *there was* a sea of glass like unto crystal: and in the midst of the throne, and round about the throne, *were* four beasts full of eyes before and behind.

7 ᴿAnd the first beast *was* like a lion, and the second beast like a calf, and the third beast had a face as a man, and the fourth beast *was* like a flying eagle.   Ezek. 1:10; 10:14

8 And the four beasts had each of them six wings about *him;* and *they were* full of eyes within: and they rest not day and night, saying, ᴿHOLY, HOLY, HOLY, LORD GOD ALMIGHTY, WHICH WAS, AND IS, AND IS TO COME.   Is. 6:3

9 And when those beasts give glory and honour and thanks to him that sat on the throne, ᴿwho liveth for ever and ever,   1:18

10 The four and twenty elders fall down before him that sat on the throne, and worship him that liveth for ever and ever, and cast their crowns before the throne, saying,

11 Thou art worthy, O Lord, to receive glory and honour and power: for thou hast created all things, and for thy pleasure they are and were created.

CHAPTER 5

The Sealed Book

AND I saw in the right hand of him that sat on the throne a book written within and on the backside, sealed with seven seals.

2 And I saw a strong angel proclaiming with a loud voice, Who is worthy to open the book, and to loose the seals thereof?

3 And no man in heaven, nor in earth, neither under the earth, was ᵀable to open the book, neither to look thereon.   *found*

4 And I wept ᵀmuch, because no man was found worthy to open and to read the book, neither to look thereon.   *bitterly*

5 And one of the elders saith unto me, Weep not: behold, ᴿthe Lion of the tribe of Juda, ᴿthe Root of David, hath ᵀprevailed to open the book, ᴿand to loose the seven seals thereof.   Gen. 49:9, 10 ★ · Is. 11:1, 10 · *overcome* · 6:1

6 And I beheld, and, lo, in the midst of the throne and of the four beasts, and in the midst of the elders, stood ᴿa Lamb as it had been slain, having seven horns and seven eyes, which are the seven Spirits of God sent forth into all the earth.   Is. 53:7 ☆

7 And he came and took the ᵀbook out of the right hand ᴿof him that sat upon the throne.   *scroll* · 4:2

8 And when he had taken the book, the four beasts and four *and* twenty elders fell down before the Lamb, having every one of them harps, and golden vials full of ᵀodours, which are the prayers of saints.   *incense*

9 And they sung a new song, saying, Thou art worthy to take the book, and to open the seals thereof: for thou wast slain, and hast redeemed us to God by thy blood out of every kindred, and tongue, and people, and nation;

10 And hast made us unto our God kings and priests: and we shall reign on the earth.

11 And I beheld, and I heard the voice of many angels round about the throne and the beasts and the elders: and the number of them was ten thousand times ten thousand, and thousands of thousands;

12 Saying with a loud voice, Worthy is ᴿthe Lamb that was slain to receive power, and riches, and wisdom, and strength, and honour, and glory, and blessing.   Is. 53:7 ★

13 And every creature which is in heaven, and on the earth, and under the earth, and such as are in the sea, and all that are in them, heard I saying, Blessing, and honour, and glory, and power, *be* unto him ᴿthat

sitteth upon the throne, and unto the Lamb for ever and ever.   6:16

14 And the four beasts said, A-men'. And the four *and* twenty elders fell down and worshipped him that liveth for ever and ever.

CHAPTER 6

First Seal

AND I saw when the Lamb opened one of the seals, and I heard, as it were the noise of thunder, ᴿone of the four ᵀbeasts saying, Come and see.   4:7 · *creatures*

2 And I saw, and behold ᴿa white horse: and he that sat on him had a bow; and a crown was given unto him: and he went forth conquering, and to conquer.   Zech. 6:3

Second Seal

3 And when he had opened the second seal, ᴿI heard the second ᵀbeast say, Come and see.   4:7 · *living creature*

4 And there went out another horse *that was* red: and *power* was given to him that sat thereon to take peace from the earth, and that they should kill one another: and there was given unto him a great sword.

Third Seal

5 And when he had opened the third seal, ᴿI heard the third ᵀbeast say, Come and see. And I beheld, and lo a black horse; and he that sat on him had a pair of ᵀbalances in his hand.   4:7 · *creature · scales*

6 And I heard a voice in the midst of the four beasts say, A ᵀmeasure of wheat for a ᵀpenny, and ᵀthree measures of barley for a penny; and *see* thou hurt not the oil and the wine.   *1 qt. · 1 day's wage · 3 qt.*

Fourth Seal

7 And when ᵀhe had opened the fourth seal, ᴿI heard the voice of the fourth beast say, Come and see.   *the Lamb* · 4:7

8 And I looked, and behold a pale horse: and his name that sat on him was Death, and ᵀHell followed with him. And power was given ᵀunto them over the fourth part of the earth, to kill with sword, and with hunger, and with death, and with the ᵀbeasts of the earth.   *Hades · to him · wild beasts*

Fifth Seal

9 And when he had opened the fifth seal, I saw under ᴿthe altar the souls of them that were slain for the word of God, and for the testimony which they held: 8:3

10 And they cried with a loud voice, saying, ᴿHow long, O Lord, holy and true, dost thou not judge and avenge our blood on them that dwell on the earth?   Zech. 1:12

11 And ᴿwhite robes were given unto every one of them; and it was said unto them, that they should ᵀrest yet for a little season, until their fellowservants also and their brethren, that should be killed as they *were*, should be fulfilled.   3:4 · *be quiet*

Sixth Seal

12 And I beheld when he had opened the sixth seal, ᴿand, lo, there was a ᵀgreat earthquake; and ᴿthe sun became black as sackcloth of hair, and the moon ᵀbecame as blood;   16:18 · *violent* · Joel 2:10, 28 · *turned red*

13 And the stars of heaven fell unto the earth, even as a fig tree casteth her untimely figs, when she is shaken of a mighty wind.

14 ᴿAnd the heaven departed as a scroll when it is rolled together; and ᴿevery mountain and island were moved out of their places.   Ps. 102:26 · Jer. 3:23

15 And the kings of the earth, and the great men, and the rich men, and the chief captains, and the mighty men, and every ᵀbondman, and every free man, ᴿhid themselves in the dens and ᵀin the rocks of the mountains;   *slave* · Is. 2:10, 19, 21; 24:21 · *under*

16 ᴿAnd said to the mountains and rocks, Fall on us, and hide us from the face of him that sitteth on the throne, and from the ᵀwrath of the Lamb: Luke 23:30 · *anger*

17 For the great day of his wrath is come; and who shall be able to stand?

CHAPTER 7

144,000 Jews

AND after these things I saw four angels standing on the four corners of the earth, holding the four winds of the earth, ᴿthat the wind should not blow on the earth, nor on the sea, nor on any tree.   9:4

2 And I saw another angel ascending from the ᵀeast, having the seal of the living God: and he cried with a loud voice to the four angels, to whom it was given to ᵀhurt the earth and the sea,   *sunrising · damage*

3 Saying, Hurt not the earth, neither the sea, nor the trees, till we have sealed the servants of our God in their foreheads.

4 ᴿAnd I heard the number of them which were sealed: *and there were* sealed an hundred *and* forty *and* four thousand of all the tribes of the children of Israel.   9:16; 14:1

5 Of the tribe of Juda *were* sealed twelve thousand. Of the tribe of Reuben *were* sealed twelve thousand. Of the tribe of Gad *were* sealed twelve thousand.

6 Of the tribe of A'-ser *were* sealed twelve thousand. Of the tribe of Nep'-tha-lim *were* sealed twelve thousand. Of the tribe of Ma-nas'-ses *were* sealed twelve thousand.

7 Of the tribe of Simeon *were* sealed twelve thousand. Of the tribe of Levi *were*

sealed twelve thousand. Of the tribe of Is'-sa-char *were* sealed twelve thousand.

8 Of the tribe of Zab'-u-lon *were* sealed twelve thousand. Of the tribe of Joseph *were* sealed twelve thousand. Of the tribe of Benjamin *were* sealed twelve thousand.

Great Multitude of Gentiles

9 After this I beheld, and, lo, a great multitude, which no man could number, Rof all nations, and kindreds, and people, and tongues, stood before the throne, and before the Lamb, Rclothed with white robes, and palms in their hands;   5:9 · v. 14

10 And cried with a loud voice, saying, RSALVATION TO OUR GOD WHICH SITTETH UPON THE THRONE, AND UNTO THE LAMB.   Ps. 3:8

11 And all the angels stood round about the throne, and *about* the elders and the four beasts, and fell before the throne on their faces, and Tworshipped God,   *bowed down to*

12 Saying, A-men': Blessing, and glory, and wisdom, and thanksgiving, and honour, and power, and might, *be* unto our God for ever and ever. A-men'.

13 And one of the elders answered, saying unto me, What are these which are arrayed in Rwhite robes? and whence came they?   *v. 9*

14 And I said unto him, Sir, thou knowest. And he said to me, RThese are they which came out of great tribulation, and have Rwashed their robes, and made them white in the blood of the Lamb.   6:9 · Is. 1:18

15 Therefore are they before the throne of God, and serve him day and night in his temple: and he that sitteth on the throne shall Rdwell among them.   21:3; Is. 4:5, 6

16 RThey shall hunger no more, neither thirst any more; Rneither shall the sun light on them, nor any heat.   Is. 49:10 ☆ · Ps. 121:6

17 For the Lamb which is in the midst of the throne Rshall feed them, and shall lead them unto Tliving fountains of waters: Rand God shall wipe away all tears from their eyes.   Ps. 23:1; [John 10:11, 14] ☆ · *springs* · 21:4; Is. 25:8

CHAPTER 8

Seventh Seal

AND Rwhen he had opened the seventh seal, there was silence in heaven about the space of half an hour.   6:1

2 RAnd I saw the seven angels which stood before God; Rand to them were given seven trumpets.   Luke 1:19 · 2 Chr. 29:25–28; 1:4

3 And another angel came and stood at the altar, having a golden censer; and there was given unto him much incense, that he should Toffer *it* with Rthe prayers of all saints upon Rthe golden altar which was before the throne.   *present* · 5:8 · Ex. 30:1

4 And the smoke of the incense, *which came* with the prayers of the saints, ascended up before God out of the angel's hand.

5 And the angel took the censer, and filled it with fire of the altar, and cast *it* into the earth: and there were voices, and thunderings, and lightnings, and an earthquake.

First Trumpet

6 And the seven angels which had the seven trumpets prepared themselves to Tsound.   *blow the trumpets*

7 The first angel sounded, Rand there followed hail and fire mingled with blood, and they were cast Rupon the earth: and the third part of trees was burnt up, and all green grass was burnt up.   Ezek. 38:22 · 16:2

Second Trumpet

8 And the second angel sounded, and as it were a great mountain burning with fire was cast into the sea: Rand the third part of the sea became blood;   16:3

9 And the third part of the creatures which were in the sea, and had life, died; and the third part of the ships were destroyed.

Third Trumpet

10 And the third angel sounded, and there fell a great star from heaven, burning as it were a Tlamp, Rand it fell upon the third part of the rivers, and upon the fountains of waters;   *torch* · 9:1; 16:4; Is. 14:12

11 And the name of the star is called Wormwood: and the third part of the waters became wormwood; and many men died of the waters, because they were made bitter.

Fourth Trumpet

12 And the fourth angel sounded, and the third part of the sun was smitten, and the third part of the moon, and the third part of the stars; so as the third part of them was darkened, and the day shone not for a third part of it, and the night likewise.

13 And I beheld, and heard an angel flying through the midst of heaven, saying with a loud voice, RWoe, woe, woe, to the Tinhabiters of the earth by reason of the other voices of the trumpet of the three angels, which are yet to sound!   9:12 · *people*

CHAPTER 9

Fifth Trumpet

AND the fifth angel sounded, Rand I saw a star fall from heaven unto the earth: and to him was given the key of Rthe bottomless pit.   8:10; Luke 10:18 · 17:8; Luke 8:31

2 RAnd he opened the bottomless pit; and there arose a smoke out of the pit, as the smoke of a Tgreat furnace; and the sun and

the air were darkened by reason of the smoke of the pit.   Joel 2:2, 10 · *large*

3 And there came out of the smoke ᴿlocusts upon the earth: and unto them was given power, ᴿas the scorpions of the earth have power.   Ex. 10:4; Judg. 7:12 · *v.* 10

4 And it was commanded them ᴿthat they should not hurt the grass of the earth, neither any green thing, neither any tree; but only those men which have not the seal of God in their foreheads.   6:6

5 And to them it was given that they should not kill them, ᴿbut that they should be tormented five months: and their torment *was* as the torment of a scorpion, when he striketh a man.   [*v.* 10; 11:7]

6 And in those days shall men seek death, and shall not find it; and shall desire to die, and death shall flee from them.

7 And the shapes of the locusts *were* like unto horses prepared unto battle; and on their heads *were* as it were crowns like gold, and their faces *were* as the faces of men.

8 And they had hair as the hair of women, and their teeth were as *the teeth* of lions.

9 And they had breastplates, as it were breastplates of iron; and the sound of their wings *was* ᴿas the sound of chariots of many horses running to battle.   Joel 2:5-7

10 And they had tails like unto scorpions, and there were stings in their tails: and their power *was* to hurt men five months.

11 And they had a king over them, *which* is ᴿthe angel of the bottomless pit, whose name in the Hebrew tongue *is* A-bad'-don, but in the Greek tongue hath *his* name ᵀA-pol'-ly-on.   Eph. 2:2 · that is to say, *a destroyer*

12 ᴿOne woe is past; *and*, behold, there come two woes more hereafter.   8:13

Sixth Trumpet

13 And the sixth angel sounded, and I heard a voice from the ᴿfour horns of the golden altar which is before God,   Ex. 30:2

14 Saying to the sixth angel which had the trumpet, Loose the four angels which are bound in the great river Eu-phra'-tes.

15 And the four angels were loosed, which were prepared for an hour, and a day, and a month, and a year, for to slay ᵀthe third part of men.   *one third of all mankind*

16 And the number of the army of the horsemen *were* two hundred thousand thousand: and I heard the number of them.

17 And thus I saw the horses in the vision, and them that sat on them, having breastplates of fire, and of jacinth, and brimstone: and the heads of the horses *were* as the heads of lions; and out of their mouths issued fire and smoke and brimstone.

18 By these three was the third part of men killed, by the fire, and by the smoke, and by

the brimstone, which ᵀissued out of their mouths.   *came*

19 For their power is in their mouth, and in their tails: ᴿfor their tails *were* like unto serpents, and had heads, and with them they do ᵀhurt.   Is. 9:15 · *hurt people*

20 And the rest of the men which were not killed by these plagues yet repented not of the works of their hands, that they should not worship devils, and idols of gold, and silver, and brass, and stone, and of wood: which neither can see, nor hear, nor walk:

21 Neither repented they of their murders, ᴿnor of their sorceries, nor of their fornication, nor of their thefts.   22:15

CHAPTER 10

Little Book

AND I saw another mighty angel come down from heaven, clothed with a cloud: ᴿand a rainbow *was* upon his head, and his face *was* as it were the sun, and ᴿhis feet as pillars of fire: Ezek. 1:28 · 1:15

2 And he had in his hand a little book open: ᴿand he set his right foot upon the sea, and *his* left *foot* on the earth,   Matt. 28:18

3 And cried with a loud voice, as *when* a lion roareth: and when he had cried, ᴿseven thunders uttered their voices.   8:5

4 And when the seven thunders had uttered their voices, I was about to write: and I heard a voice from heaven saying unto me, Seal up those things which the seven thunders uttered, and write them not.

5 And the angel which I saw stand upon the sea and upon the earth ᴿlifted up his hand to heaven,   Ex. 6:8; Dan. 12:7

6 And sware by him that liveth for ever and ever, who created heaven, and the things that therein are, and the earth, and the things that therein are, and the sea, and the things which are therein, that there should be time no longer:

7 But in the days of the voice of the seventh angel, when he shall begin to sound, the mystery of God should be finished, as he hath declared to his servants the prophets.

8 And the voice which I heard from heaven spake unto me again, and said, Go *and* take the ᵀlittle book which is open in the hand of the angel which standeth upon the sea and upon the earth.   *open scroll*

9 And I went unto the angel, and said unto him, Give me the little book. And he said unto me, ᴿTake *it*, and eat it up; and it shall make thy belly bitter, but it shall be in thy mouth sweet as honey.   Jer. 15:16

10 And I took the little book out of the angel's hand, and ate it up; and it was in my mouth sweet as honey: and as soon as I had eaten it, my belly was bitter.

11 And he said unto me, Thou must ᵀprophesy again before many peoples, and nations, and tongues, and kings.   *preach*

CHAPTER 11

Two Witnesses

AND there was given me a reed like unto a rod: and the angel stood, saying, Rise, and measure the temple of God, and the altar, and them that worship therein.

2 But the court which is without the temple ᵀleave out, and measure it not; for it is given unto the Gentiles: and the holy city shall they ᴿtread under foot ᴿforty *and* two months.   *cast out · Dan. 8:10 · 13:5*

3 And I will give *power* unto my two witnesses, and they shall ᵀprophesy ᴿa thousand two hundred *and* threescore days, clothed in sackcloth.   *preach · 12:6*

4 These are the ᴿtwo olive trees, and the two candlesticks standing before the God of the earth.   Ps. 52:8; Jer. 11:16; Zech. 4:3, 14

5 And if any man will hurt them, fire proceedeth out of their mouth, and devoureth their enemies: and if any man will hurt them, he must in this manner be killed.

6 These have power to shut heaven, that it rain not in the days of their ᵀprophecy: and have power over waters to turn them to blood, and to smite the earth with all plagues, as often as they will.   *prediction*

7 And when they shall have finished their ᵀtestimony, ᴿthe beast that ascendeth ᴿout of the bottomless pit ᴿshall make war against them, and shall overcome them, and kill them.   *preaching · 13:1 · 9:2 · Dan. 7:21*

8 And their dead bodies *shall lie* in the street of ᴿthe great city, which spiritually is called Sodom and Egypt, ᴿwhere also our Lord was crucified.   14:8 · Heb. 13:12

9 And they of the people and kindreds and tongues and nations shall see their dead bodies three days and an half, and shall not suffer their dead bodies to be put in graves.

10 And they that dwell upon the earth shall rejoice over them, and make merry, and shall send gifts one to another; ᴿbecause these two prophets ᵀtormented them that dwelt on the earth.   16:10 · *troubled*

11 And after ᴿthree days and an half the Spirit of life from God entered into them, and they stood upon their feet; and great fear fell upon them which saw them.   *v. 9*

12 And they heard a great voice from heaven saying unto them, Come up hither. And they ascended up to heaven in a cloud; and their enemies beheld them.

13 And the same hour ᴿwas there a great earthquake, ᴿand the tenth part of the city fell, and in the earthquake were slain of men seven thousand: and the remnant were affrighted, ᴿand gave glory to the God of heaven.   6:12 · 16:19 · Josh. 7:19

14 ᴿThe second woe is past; *and, behold,* the third woe cometh quickly.   8:13

Seventh Trumpet

15 And the seventh angel sounded; ᴿand there were great voices in heaven, saying, THE KINGDOMS OF THIS WORLD ARE BECOME THE *KINGDOMS* OF OUR LORD, AND OF HIS CHRIST; AND HE SHALL REIGN FOR EVER AND EVER.   Is. 27:13 ✶

16 And the four and twenty elders, which sat before God on their seats, fell upon their faces, and worshipped God,

17 Saying, We give thee thanks, O Lord God Almighty, which art, and wast, and art to come; because thou hast taken to thee thy great power, and hast reigned.

18 And the nations were angry, and thy wrath is come, and the time of the dead, that they should be judged, and that thou shouldest give reward unto thy servants the prophets, and to the saints, and them that fear thy name, small and great; and shouldest destroy them which destroy the earth.

19 And the temple of God was opened in heaven, and there was seen in his temple the ark of his testament: and there were lightnings, and voices, and thunderings, and an earthquake, ᴿand great hail.   16:21

CHAPTER 12

The Woman

AND there appeared a great ᵀwonder in heaven; a woman clothed with the sun, and the moon under her feet, and upon her head a crown of twelve stars: *sign*

2 And she being with child cried, travailing in birth, and pained to be delivered.

3 And there appeared another ᵀwonder in heaven; and behold ᴿa great red dragon, having seven heads and ten horns, and seven crowns upon his heads.   *sign · 17:3*

4 And his tail drew the third part of the stars of heaven, ᴿand did cast them to the earth: and the dragon stood ᴿbefore the woman which was ready to be delivered, ᴿfor to ᵀdevour her child as soon as it was born.   Dan. 8:10 · v. 2 · Ex. 1:16 · *eat up*

5 And she brought forth a man child, ᴿwho was to rule all nations with a rod of iron: and her child was caught up unto God, and *to* his throne.   19:15; Ps. 2:9 ✶

6 And ᴿthe woman fled into the wilderness, where she hath a place prepared of God, that they should feed her there ᴿa thousand two hundred *and* threescore days.   v. 4 · 11:3

The War in Heaven

7 And there was war in heaven: Mi′-cha-el and his angels fought ᴿagainst the dragon;

and the dragon fought and his angels, 20:2

8 And [T]prevailed not; neither was their place found any more in heaven.   *did not win*

9 And [R]the great dragon was cast out, that old serpent, called the Devil, and Satan, which deceiveth the whole world: he was cast out into the earth, and his angels were cast out with him.   Luke 10:18

10 And I heard a loud voice saying in heaven, Now is come salvation, and strength, and the kingdom of our God, and the power of his Christ: for the accuser of our brethren is cast down, which accused them before our God day and night.

11 And they overcame him by the blood of the Lamb, and by the word of their testimony; and they loved not their lives unto the death.

12 Therefore rejoice, *ye* heavens, and ye that dwell in them. Woe to the inhabiters of the earth and of the sea! for the devil is come down unto you, having great wrath, because he knoweth that he hath but a short time.

The War on Earth

13 And when the dragon saw that he was cast unto the earth, he persecuted the woman which brought forth the man *child.*

14 And to the woman were given two wings of a great eagle, that she might fly into the wilderness, into her place, where she is nourished for a time, and times, and half a time, from the face of the serpent.

15 And the serpent [R]cast[T] out of his mouth water as a flood after the woman, that he might cause her to be carried away of the flood.   Is. 59:19 • *poured*

16 And the earth helped the woman, and the earth opened [T]her mouth, and [T]swallowed up the flood which the dragon cast out of his mouth.   *its • drank*

17 And the dragon was [T]wroth with the woman, and went to make war with the remnant of her seed, which [T]keep the commandments of God, and have the [T]testimony of Jesus Christ.   *enraged • obey • gospel*

CHAPTER 13

The Beast Out of the Sea

AND I stood upon the sand of the sea, and saw a beast rise up out of the sea, having seven heads and ten horns, and upon his horns ten crowns, and upon his heads the [T]name of blasphemy.   *names*

2 And the beast which I saw was like unto a leopard, and his feet were as *the feet* of a bear, and his mouth as the mouth of a lion: and the dragon gave him his power, and his seat, and great authority.

3 And I saw one of his heads [R]as it were wounded to death; and his deadly wound was healed: and [R]all the world [T]wondered after the beast.   *vv. 12, 14 • 17:8 • followed*

4 And they [T]worshipped the dragon [T]which gave power unto the beast: and they worshipped the beast, saying, [R]Who *is* like unto the beast? who is able to make war with him?   *bowed down to • because he • 18:18*

5 And there was given unto him a mouth speaking great things and blasphemies; and power was given unto him to [T]continue forty *and* two months.   *exercise authority*

6 And he opened his mouth in blasphemy against God, [T]to blaspheme his name, [R]and his tabernacle, and them that dwell in heaven.   *curse • [John 1:14; Col. 2:9]*

7 And it was given unto him [R]to make war with the saints, and to overcome them: and power was given him over all kindreds, and tongues, and nations.   Dan. 7:21

8 And all that dwell upon the earth shall worship him, [R]whose names are not written in the book of life of the Lamb slain from the foundation of the world.   Ex. 32:32

9 If any man have an ear, let him hear.

10 He that leadeth into captivity shall go into captivity: he that killeth with the sword must be killed with the sword. Here is the patience and the faith of the saints.

The Beast Out of the Earth

11 And I beheld another beast coming up out of the earth; and he had two horns like a lamb, and he spake as a dragon.

12 And he exerciseth all the power of the first beast before him, and causeth the earth and them which dwell therein to worship the first beast, whose deadly wound was healed.

13 And he doeth great wonders, so that he maketh fire come down from heaven on the earth in the sight of men,

14 And deceiveth them that dwell on the earth [R]by *the means of* those miracles which he had power to do in the sight of the beast; saying to them that dwell on the earth, that they should make an image to the beast, which had the wound by a sword, [R]and did live.   2 Thess. 2:9 • 2 Kin. 20:7

15 And he had power to give [T]life unto the image of the beast, that the image of the beast should both speak, and cause that as many as would not worship the image of the beast should be killed.   *breath*

16 And he causeth all, both small and great, rich and poor, free and bond, [T]to receive a [R]mark in their right hand, or in their foreheads: *that there be given them • Gal. 6:17*

17 And that no man might buy or sell, save he that had the mark, or the name of the beast, or the number of his name.

18 Here is wisdom. Let him that hath understanding count the number of the beast: for it is the number of a man; and his number *is* Six hundred threescore *and* six.

CHAPTER 14

The 144,000

AND I looked, and, lo, a Lamb stood on the mount Si'-on, and with him an hundred forty *and* four thousand, having his Father's name written in their foreheads.

2 And I heard a voice from heaven, as the voice of many waters, and as the voice of a great thunder: and I heard the voice of ^Rharpers harping with their harps: 5:8

3 And they sung as it were a new song before the throne, and before the four beasts, and the elders: and no man could learn that song ^Rbut the hundred *and* forty *and* four thousand, which were redeemed from the earth.   5:9; 15:3

4 These are they which were not defiled with women; for they are virgins. These are they which follow the Lamb whithersoever he goeth. These ^Twere redeemed from among men, *being* the firstfruits unto God and to the Lamb.   *were bought*

5 And in their mouth was found no ^Tguile: for ^Rthey are ^Twithout fault before the throne of God.   *deceit* • Eph. 5:27 • *blameless*

The Three Angels' Announcements

6 And I saw another angel fly in the midst of heaven, having the everlasting gospel to preach unto them that dwell on the earth, ^Rand to every nation, and kindred, and tongue, and people,   13:7

7 Saying with a loud voice, ^RFear God, and give glory to him; for the hour of his judgment is come: and ^Tworship him that made heaven, and earth, and the sea, and the fountains of waters.   11:18 • *bow down to*

8 And there followed another angel, saying, Babylon is fallen, is fallen, that great city, because she made all nations drink of the wine of the wrath of her fornication.

9 And the third angel followed them, saying with a loud voice, If any man worship the beast and his image, and receive *his* mark in his forehead, or in his hand,

10 The same shall drink of the wine of the wrath of God, which is poured out without mixture into the cup of his indignation; and he shall be tormented with fire and brimstone in the presence of the holy angels, and in the presence of the Lamb:

11 And ^Rthe smoke of their torment ascendeth up for ever and ever: and they have no rest day nor night, who worship the beast and his image, and whosoever receiveth the mark of his name.   Is. 34:10

12 Here is the patience of the saints: here *are* they that ^Tkeep the commandments of God, and the faith of Jesus.   *obey*

13 And I heard a voice from heaven saying unto me, Write, Blessed *are* the dead which die in the Lord from henceforth: Yea, saith the Spirit, that they may rest from their labours; and their works do follow them.

The Harvest Judgment

14 And I looked, and behold a white cloud, and upon the cloud *one* sat like unto the Son of man, having on his head a golden crown, and in his hand a sharp sickle.

15 And another angel came out of the temple, crying with a loud voice to him that sat on the cloud, Thrust in thy sickle, and reap: for the time is come for thee to reap; for the harvest of the earth is ripe.

16 And he that sat on the cloud thrust in his sickle on the earth; and the earth was reaped.

17 And another angel came out of the temple which is in heaven, he also ^Thaving a sharp sickle.   *had*

18 And another angel came out from the altar, which had power over fire; and cried with a loud cry to him that had the sharp sickle, saying, Thrust in thy sharp sickle, and gather the clusters of the vine of the earth; for her grapes are fully ripe.

19 And the angel thrust in his sickle into the earth, and gathered the vine of the earth, and cast *it* into ^Rthe great winepress of the wrath of God.   19:15; Is. 63:2

20 And ^Rthe winepress was trodden ^Rwithout the city, and blood came out of the winepress, ^Reven unto the horse bridles, by the space of a ^Tthousand *and* six hundred furlongs.   Is. 63:3 • Heb. 13:12 • 9:16 • *184 mi.*

CHAPTER 15

Preparation for the Vial Judgments

AND I saw another sign in heaven, great and marvellous, seven angels having the seven last plagues; for in them is filled up the ^Twrath of God.   *angry judgment*

2 And I saw as it were ^Ra sea of glass mingled with fire: and them that had gotten the victory over the beast, and over his image, and over his mark, *and* over the number of his name, stand on the sea of glass, ^Rhaving the harps of God.   4:6 • 5:8

3 And they sing the song of Moses the servant of God, and the song of the Lamb, saying, GREAT AND MARVELLOUS *ARE* THY WORKS, LORD GOD ALMIGHTY; JUST AND TRUE *ARE* THY WAYS, THOU KING OF SAINTS.

4 ^RWHO SHALL NOT FEAR THEE, O LORD, AND GLORIFY THY NAME? FOR *THOU* ONLY ART HOLY: ^RFOR ALL NATIONS SHALL COME AND WORSHIP BEFORE THEE; for thy judgments are made manifest.   Jer. 10:7 • Ps. 86:9

5 And after that I looked, and, behold, ^Rthe temple of the tabernacle of the testimony in heaven was opened: Num. 1:50

6 And the seven angels came out of the temple, having the seven plagues, clothed in

pure and white linen, and having their breasts ^Tgirded with golden girdles.   *wrapped*

7 ^RAnd one of the four ^Tbeasts gave unto the seven angels seven golden ^Tvials full of the wrath of God, ^Rwho liveth for ever and ever.   4:6 • *living creatures • bowls* • 1 Thess. 1:9

8 And ^Rthe temple was filled with smoke ^Rfrom the glory of God, and from his power; and no man was able to enter into the temple, till the seven plagues of the seven angels were fulfilled.   Ex. 40:34 • 2 Thess. 1:9

CHAPTER 16

First Vial

AND I heard a great voice out of the temple saying to the seven angels, Go your ways, and pour out the ^Tvials of the wrath of God upon the earth.   *seven bowls*

2 And the first went, and poured out his vial upon the earth; and there fell a noisome and grievous sore upon the men which had the mark of the beast, and *upon* them which worshipped his image.

Second Vial

3 And the second angel poured out his ^Tvial ^Rupon the sea; and ^Rit became as the blood of a dead *man:* ^Rand every living soul died in the sea.   *bowl* • 8:8 • Ex. 7:17 • 8:9

Third Vial

4 And the third angel poured out his vial ^Rupon the rivers and fountains of waters; ^Rand they became blood.   8:10 • Ex. 7:20

5 And I heard the angel of the waters say, ^RThou art righteous, O Lord, ^Rwhich art, and wast, and shalt be, because thou hast judged thus.   15:3 • 1:4, 8

6 For they have shed the blood of saints and prophets, and thou hast given them blood to drink; for they are worthy.

7 And I heard another out of the altar say, Even so, ^RLord God Almighty, true and righteous *are* thy judgments.   15:3

Fourth Vial

8 And the fourth angel poured out his ^Tvial upon the sun; and power was given unto him to scorch men with fire.   *bowl*

9 And men were ^Tscorched with great heat, and blasphemed the name of God, which hath power over these plagues: and they repented not to give him glory.   *burned*

Fifth Vial

10 And the fifth angel poured out his vial ^Rupon the seat of the beast; ^Rand his kingdom was full of darkness; and they gnawed their tongues for pain,   13:2 • 9:2

11 And ^Tblasphemed the God of heaven because of their pains and their sores, and repented not of their ^Tdeeds.   *cursed • evil*

Sixth Vial

12 And the sixth angel poured out his vial upon the great river Eu-phra′-tes; and the water thereof was dried up, that the way of the kings of the east might be prepared.

13 And I saw three unclean spirits like frogs *come* out of the mouth of the dragon, and out of the mouth of the beast, and out of the mouth of the false prophet.

14 For they are the spirits of devils, working ^Tmiracles, *which* go forth unto the kings of the earth ^Rand of the whole world, to gather them to ^Rthe battle of that great day of God Almighty.   *signs* • Luke 2:1 • 17:14

15 ^RBehold, I come as a thief. ^TBlessed *is* he that watcheth, and keepeth his garments, ^Rlest he walk naked, and they see his shame.   Matt. 24:43 ★ • *happy* • 2 Cor. 5:3

16 ^RAnd he gathered them together into a place called in the Hebrew ^Ttongue Ar-ma-ged′-don.   19:19 • *language*

Seventh Vial

17 And the seventh angel poured out his ^Tvial into the air; and there came a great voice out of the temple of heaven, from the throne, saying, ^RIt is done.   *bowl* • 21:6

18 And ^Rthere were voices, and thunders, and lightnings; ^Rand there was a great earthquake, ^Rsuch as was not since men were upon the earth, so mighty an earthquake, *and* so great.   4:5 • 11:13 • Dan. 12:1

19 And the great city was divided into three parts, and the cities of the nations fell: and great Babylon came in remembrance before God, to give unto her the cup of the wine of the fierceness of his wrath.

20 And ^Revery island fled away, and the mountains were not found.   6:14

21 And there fell upon men a great hail out of heaven, *every stone* about the weight of a ^Ttalent: and men blasphemed God because of the plague of the hail; for the plague thereof was exceeding great.   75 *lb.*

CHAPTER 17

Great Harlot Is Described

AND there came one of the seven angels which had the seven vials, and talked with me, saying unto me, Come hither; I will shew unto thee the judgment of the great whore that sitteth upon many waters:

2 ^RWith whom the kings of the earth have committed fornication, and the inhabitants of the earth have been made drunk with the wine of her fornication.   Jer. 51:7

3 So he carried me away in the spirit ᴿinto the wilderness: and I saw a woman sit ᴿupon a scarlet coloured beast, full of ᴿnames of blasphemy, having seven heads and ten horns. 12:6, 14 · 12:3 · 13:1

4 And the woman was arrayed in purple and scarlet colour, and ᵀdecked with gold and precious stones and pearls, having a golden cup in her hand full of abominations and filthiness of her fornication: *gilded*

5 And upon her forehead *was* a name written, ᴿMYSTERY, BABYLON THE GREAT, THE MOTHER OF HARLOTS AND ABOMINATIONS OF THE EARTH. 2 Thess. 2:7

6 And I saw the woman drunken with the blood of the saints, and with the blood of the martyrs of Jesus: and when I saw her, I wondered with great admiration.

Great Harlot Is Destroyed

7 And the angel said unto me, Wherefore didst thou marvel? I will tell thee the ᵀmystery of the woman, and of the beast that carrieth her, which hath the seven heads and ten horns. *hidden truth*

8 The beast that thou sawest was, and is not; and shall ascend out of the bottomless pit, and ᴿgo into ᵀperdition: and they that dwell on the earth shall wonder, ᴿwhose names were not written in the book of life from the foundation of the world, when they behold the beast that was, and is not, and yet is. 13:10 · *doom* · 13:8

9 And here *is* the mind which hath wisdom. The seven heads are seven mountains, on which the woman sitteth.

10 And there are seven kings: five are fallen, and one is, *and* the other is not yet come; and when he cometh, he must ᵀcontinue a short space. *remain*

11 And the beast that was, and is not, even he is the eighth, and is of the seven, and goeth into ᵀperdition. *destruction*

12 And ᴿthe ten horns which thou sawest are ten kings, which have received no kingdom as yet; but receive ᵀpower as kings one hour with the beast. Dan. 7:20 · *authority*

13 These have one mind, and shall give their power and strength unto the beast.

14 These shall make war with the Lamb, and the Lamb shall overcome them: ᴿfor he is Lord of lords, and King of kings: ᴿand they that are with him *are* called, and chosen, and faithful. Deut. 10:17 · Jer. 50:44

15 And he saith unto me, ᴿThe waters which thou sawest, where the ᵀwhore sitteth, ᴿare peoples, and multitudes, and nations, and tongues. Is. 8:7 · *harlot* · 13:7

16 And the ten horns which thou sawest upon the beast, these shall hate the whore, and shall make her desolate and naked, and shall eat her flesh, and burn her with fire.

17 ᴿFor God hath put in their hearts to fulfil his will, and to agree, and give their kingdom unto the beast, ᴿuntil the words of God shall be fulfilled. 2 Thess. 2:11 · 10:7

18 And the woman which thou sawest ᴿis that great city, ᴿwhich reigneth over the kings of the earth. 16:19 · 12:4

CHAPTER 18

Babylon the Great Is Destroyed

AND ᴿafter these things I saw another angel come down from heaven, having great power; ᴿand the earth was ᵀlightened with his glory. 17:1 · Ezek. 43:2 · *bright*

2 And he cried mightily with a strong voice, saying, ᴿBabylon the great is fallen, is fallen, and ᴿis become the habitation of devils, and the hold of every foul spirit, and ᴿa cage of every unclean and hateful bird. Is. 13:19 · Is. 13:21 · Is. 14:23

3 For all nations ᴿhave drunk of the wine of the wrath of her fornication, and the kings of the earth have committed fornication with her, ᴿand the merchants of the earth are waxed rich through the ᵀabundance of her delicacies. 14:8 · Is. 47:15 · *power*

4 ᴿAnd I heard another voice from heaven, saying, Come out of her, my people, that ye be not partakers of her sins, and that ye receive not of her plagues. Is. 48:20; 2 Cor. 6:17

5 For her sins have reached unto heaven, and God hath remembered her iniquities.

6 Reward her even as she rewarded you, and double unto her double according to her works: ᴿin the cup which she hath filled ᴿfill to her double. 14:10 · 16:19

7 How much she hath glorified herself, and lived ᵀdeliciously, so much torment and sorrow give her: for she saith in her heart, I sit a ᴿqueen, and am no widow, and shall see no sorrow. *as she liked* · Is. 47:7, 8

8 Therefore shall her plagues come in one day, death, and mourning, and famine; and she shall be utterly burned with fire: for strong *is* the Lord God who judgeth her.

Earth Bewails Babylon's Destruction

9 And ᴿthe kings of the earth, who have committed fornication and lived deliciously with her, ᴿshall bewail her, and lament for her, ᴿwhen they shall see the smoke of her burning, Ezek. 26:16 · Jer. 50:46 · 19:3

10 Standing afar off for the fear of her torment, saying, ᴿAlas, alas that great city Babylon, that mighty city! ᴿfor in one hour is thy judgment come. Is. 21:9 · *vv.* 17, 19

11 And the merchants of the earth shall weep and mourn over her; for no man buyeth their merchandise any more:

12 ᴿThe ᵀmerchandise of gold, and silver, and precious stones, and of pearls, and fine

linen, and purple, and silk, and scarlet, and all ᵀthyine wood, and all manner vessels of ivory, and all manner vessels of most precious wood, and of brass, and iron, and marble,   17:4 • goods • scented

13 And cinnamon, and odours, and ointments, and frankincense, and wine, and oil, and fine flour, and wheat, and beasts, and sheep, and horses, and chariots, and slaves, and ᴿsouls of men.   Ezek. 27:13

14 And the ᵀfruits that thy soul ᵀlusted after are departed from thee, and all things which were dainty and goodly are departed from thee, and thou shalt find them no more at all.   good things • desired

15 The merchants of these things, which were made rich by her, shall stand afar off for the fear of her ᵀtorment, ᵀweeping and wailing,   suffering • mourning

16 And saying, Alas, alas that great city, ᴿthat was clothed in fine linen, and purple, and scarlet, and decked with gold, and precious stones, and pearls!   17:4

17 For in one hour so great riches is come to nought. And every shipmaster, and all the company in ships, and sailors, and as many as trade by sea, stood afar off,

18 ᴿAnd cried when they saw the smoke of her burning, saying, ᴿWhat city is like unto this great city!   Ezek. 27:30 • 13:4

19 And ᴿthey cast dust on their heads, and cried, weeping and wailing, saying, Alas, alas that great city, wherein were made rich all that had ships in the sea by reason of her costliness! ᴿfor in one hour is she made ᵀdesolate.   Ezek. 27:30 • v. 8 • a ruin

Heaven Rejoices Babylon's Destruction

20 ᴿRejoice over her, thou heaven, and ye holy apostles and ᵀprophets; for ᴿGod hath avenged you on her.   Is. 44:23 • preachers • 19:2

21 And a mighty angel took up a stone like a great millstone, and cast it into the sea, saying, ᴿThus with violence shall that great city Babylon be thrown down, and shall be found no more at all.   Jer. 51:64

22 ᴿAnd the voice of harpers, and musicians, and of pipers, and trumpeters, shall be heard no more at all in thee; and no craftsman, of whatsoever craft he be, shall be found any more in thee; and the sound of a millstone shall be heard no more at all in thee;   Jer. 7:34; 16:9; 25:10; Ezek. 26:13

23 And the light of a candle shall shine no more at all in thee; and the voice of the bridegroom and of the bride shall be heard no more at all in thee: for thy merchants were the great men of the earth; for by thy sorceries were all nations deceived.

24 And ᴿin her was found the blood of prophets, and of saints, and of all that ᴿwere slain upon the earth.   17:6 • Jer. 51:49

CHAPTER 19

AND after these things ᴿI heard a great voice of much people in heaven, saying, Al-le-lu′-ia; Salvation, and glory, and honour, and power, unto the Lord our God: 11:15

2 FOR TRUE AND RIGHTEOUS ARE HIS JUDGMENTS: for he hath judged the great whore, which did corrupt the earth with her fornication, and HATH AVENGED THE BLOOD OF HIS SERVANTS AT HER HAND.

3 And again they said, AL-LE-LU′-IA. AND HER SMOKE ROSE UP FOR EVER AND EVER.

4 And the four and twenty elders and the four beasts fell down and worshipped God that sat on the throne, saying, ᴿA-men′; ᵀAl-le-lu′-ia.   1 Chr. 16:36 • hallelujah

5 ᴿAnd a voice came out of the throne, saying, PRAISE OUR GOD, ALL YE HIS SERVANTS, AND YE THAT FEAR HIM, BOTH SMALL AND GREAT.   Ps. 115:13

6 And I heard as it were the voice of a great multitude, and as the voice of many waters, and as the voice of mighty thunderings, saying, Al-le-lu′-ia: for the Lord God omnipotent reigneth.

Marriage Supper of the Lamb

7 Let us be glad and rejoice, and give honour to him: for the marriage of the Lamb is come, and his wife hath made herself ready.

8 And to her was granted that she should be arrayed in fine linen, clean and white: for the fine linen is the righteousness of saints.

9 And he saith unto me, Write, Blessed are they which are called unto the marriage supper of the Lamb. And he saith unto me, These are the true sayings of God.

10 ᴿAnd I fell at his feet to worship him. And he said unto me, See thou do it not: I am thy fellowservant, and of thy brethren that have the testimony of Jesus: worship God: for the testimony of Jesus is the spirit of prophecy.   Acts 3:12; 10:26

Second Coming of Christ

11 And I saw heaven opened, and behold a white horse; and he that sat upon him was called Faithful and True, and in righteousness he doth judge and make war.

12 ᴿHis eyes were as a flame of fire, and on his head were many crowns; ᴿand he had a name written, that no man knew, ᵀbut he himself.   1:14 ☆ • 2:17 • except

13 ᴿAnd he was clothed with a ᵀvesture dipped in blood: and his name is called ᴿThe Word of God.   Is. 63:2, 3 ☆ • garment • [John 1:1]

14 And the armies which were in heaven followed him upon white horses, ᴿclothed in fine linen, white and clean.   Matt. 28:3

15 And out of his mouth goeth a sharp sword, that with it he should smite the

nations: and he shall rule them with a rod of iron: and he treadeth the winepress of the fierceness and wrath of Almighty God.

16 And ᴿhe hath on *his* ᵀvesture and on his thigh a name written, ᴿKING OF KINGS, AND LORD OF LORDS.   *v. 12 • robe •* Dan. 2:47

17 And I saw an angel standing in the sun; and he cried with a loud voice, saying to all the fowls that fly in the midst of heaven, Come and gather yourselves together unto the supper of the great God;

18 That ye may eat the flesh of kings, and the flesh of captains, and the flesh of mighty men, and the flesh of horses, and of them that sit on them, and the flesh of all *men, both* free and bond, both small and great.

19 ᴿAnd I saw the beast, and the kings of the earth, and their armies, gathered together to make war against him that sat on the horse, and against his army.   16:16 ☆

20 ᴿAnd the beast was taken, and with him the false prophet that wrought miracles before him, with which he deceived them that had received the mark of the beast, and them that worshipped his image. These both were cast alive into a lake of fire burning with brimstone.   16:13

21 And the remnant were slain with the sword of him that sat upon the horse, which *sword* proceeded out of his mouth: and all the fowls were filled with their flesh.

CHAPTER 20

Satan Is Bound 1,000 Years

AND I saw an angel come down from heaven, having the key of the bottomless pit and a great chain in his hand.

2 And he laid hold on ᴿthe dragon, that old serpent, which is the Devil, and Satan, and bound him a thousand years,   2 Pet. 2:4

3 And cast him into the bottomless pit, and ᵀshut him up, and ᴿset a seal upon him, that he should deceive the nations no more, till the thousand years should be fulfilled: and after that he must be ᵀloosed a little ᵀseason.   *chained him • 12:9 • released • while*

Saints Reign 1,000 Years

4 And I saw thrones, and they sat upon them, and judgment was given unto them: and *I saw* the souls of them that were beheaded for the witness of Jesus, and for the word of God, and which had not worshipped the beast, neither his image, neither had received *his* mark upon their foreheads, or in their hands; and they lived and reigned with Christ a thousand years.

5 ᴿBut the rest of the dead lived not again until the thousand years were finished. This *is* the first resurrection.   [John 6:40]

6 Blessed and holy *is* he that hath part in the first resurrection: on such ᴿthe second death hath no power, but they shall be priests of God and of Christ, and shall reign with him a thousand years.   [2:11]

Satan Is Loosed and Leads Rebellion

7 And when the thousand years are expired, Satan shall be loosed out of his prison,

8 And shall go out to deceive the nations which are in the four quarters of the earth, ᴿGog and Ma'-gog, ᴿto gather them together to battle: the number of whom *is* as the sand of the sea.   Ezek. 38:2 • 16:14

9 ᴿAnd they went up on the breadth of the earth, and ᵀcompassed the camp of the saints about, and the beloved city: and fire came down from God out of heaven, and devoured them.   Is. 8:8; Ezek. 38:9 • *surrounded*

Satan Is Tormented for Ever

10 And the devil that deceived them was cast into the lake of fire and brimstone, ᴿwhere the beast and the false prophet *are,* and ᴿshall be tormented day and night for ever and ever.   19:20 • 14:10

Great White Throne Judgment

11 And I saw a great white throne, and him that sat on it, from whose face the earth and the heaven fled away; ᴿand there was found no place for them.   Dan. 2:35

12 And I saw the dead, small and great, stand before God; and the books were opened: and another book was opened, which is *the book* of life: and the dead were judged out of those things which were written in the books, according to their works.

13 And the sea gave up the dead which were in it; and death and hell delivered up the dead which were in them: and they were judged every man according to their works.

14 And death and hell were cast into the lake of fire. This is the second death.

15 And whosoever was not found written in the ᵀbook of life ᴿwas cast into the lake of fire.   *book of the living •* 19:20

CHAPTER 21

New Heaven and Earth Are Created

AND ᴿI saw a new heaven and a new earth: ᴿfor the first heaven and the first earth were passed away; and there was no more sea.   Is. 65:17; [2 Pet. 3:13] • 20:11

New Jerusalem Descends

2 And I John saw ᴿthe holy city, new Jerusalem, coming down from God out of

heaven, prepared ᴿas a bride adorned for her husband.   Is. 52:1; [Gal. 4:26] • Is. 54:5; 2 Cor. 11:2

3 And I heard a great voice out of heaven saying, Behold, the tabernacle of God *is* with men, and he will dwell with them, and they shall be his people, and God himself shall be with them, *and be* their God.

4 ᴿAnd God shall wipe away all tears from their eyes; and there shall be no more death, ᴿneither sorrow, nor crying, neither shall there be any more pain: for the former things are passed away.   Is. 25:8 ☆ • Is. 35:10 ☆

5 And ᴿhe that sat upon the throne said, ᴿBehold, I make all things new. And he said unto me, Write: for ᴿthese words are true and faithful.   4:2, 9 • 2 Cor. 5:17 • 19:9

6 And he said unto me, It is done. I am Alpha and Omega, the beginning and the end. I will give unto him that is athirst of the fountain of the water of life freely.

7 He that overcometh shall ᵀinherit ᵀall things; and ᴿI will be his God, and he shall be my son.   *possess • these things* • Zech. 8:8 ☆

8 ᴿBut the fearful, and unbelieving, and the abominable, and murderers, and whoremongers, and sorcerers, and idolaters, and all liars, shall have their part in ᴿthe lake which burneth with fire and brimstone: which is the second death.   Gal. 5:19 • 20:14

New Jerusalem Is Described

9 And there came unto me one of the seven angels which had the seven ᵀvials full of the seven last plagues, and talked with me, saying, Come hither, I will shew thee the bride, the Lamb's wife.   *bowls*

10 And he carried me away ᴿin the spirit to a great and high mountain, and shewed me that great city, the holy Jerusalem, descending out of heaven from God,   1:10

11 Having the glory of God: and her light *was* like unto a stone most precious, even like a jasper stone, clear as crystal;

12 And had a wall great and high, *and* had ᴿtwelve gates, and at the gates twelve angels, and names written thereon, which are *the names* of the twelve tribes of the children of Israel: Ezek. 48:31–34

13 On the east three gates; on the north three gates; on the south three gates; and on the west three gates.

14 And the wall of the city had twelve foundations, and ᴿin them the names of the twelve apostles of the Lamb.   Matt. 16:18; Gal. 2:9

15 And he that talked with me ᴿhad a golden reed to measure the city, and the gates thereof, and the wall thereof.   Zech. 2:1

16 And the city lieth foursquare, and the length is as large as the breadth: and he measured the city with the reed, ᵀtwelve thousand furlongs. The length and the breadth and the height of it are equal. *1377 mi.*

17 And he measured the wall thereof, an hundred *and* forty *and* four cubits, *according to* the measure of a man, that is, of the angel.

18 And the building of the wall of it was *of* jasper: and the city *was* pure gold, like unto ᵀclear glass.   *pure*

19 ᴿAnd the foundations of the wall of the city *were* garnished with all manner of precious stones. The first foundation *was* jasper; the second, sapphire; the third, a chalcedony; the fourth, an emerald;   Is. 54:11

20 The fifth, sardonyx; the sixth, sardius; the seventh, chrysolyte; the eighth, beryl; the ninth, a topaz; the tenth, a chrysoprasus; the eleventh, a jacinth; the twelfth, an amethyst.

21 And the twelve gates *were* twelve pearls; every several gate was of one pearl: ᴿand the street of the city *was* pure gold, as it were ᵀtransparent glass.   22:2 • *clear*

22 ᴿAnd I saw no temple ᵀtherein: for the Lord God Almighty and the Lamb are the temple of it.   John 4:23 ☆ • *inside*

23 ᴿAnd the city had no need of the sun, neither of the moon, to shine in it: for the glory of God did ᵀlighten it, and the Lamb *is* the light thereof.   Is. 24:23 ☆ • *illuminate*

24 ᴿAnd the nations of them which are saved shall walk in the light of it: and the kings of the earth do bring their glory and honour into it.   Is. 60:3; 66:12 ☆

25 ᴿAnd the gates of it shall not be shut at all by day: for ᴿthere shall be no night there.   Is. 60:11 • Is. 60:20; Zech. 14:7

26 ᴿAnd they shall bring the glory and honour of the nations into it.   *v. 24*

27 And ᴿthere shall in no wise enter into it any thing that defileth, neither *whatsoever* worketh ᵀabomination, or *maketh* a lie: but they which are written in the Lamb's ᴿbook of life.   Joel 3:17 • *evil* • Phil. 4:3

CHAPTER 22

AND he shewed me a pure river of water of life, clear as crystal, proceeding out of the throne of God and of the Lamb.

2 ᴿIn the midst of the street of it, and on either side of the river, *was there* ᴿthe tree of life, which bare twelve *manner* of fruits, *and* yielded her fruit every month: and the leaves of the tree *were* ᴿfor the healing of the nations.   Ezek. 47:12 ☆ • Gen. 2:9 • 21:24

3 And ᴿthere shall be no more curse: ᴿbut the throne of God and of the Lamb shall be in it; and his servants shall ᵀserve him: Zech. 14:11 ☆ • Ezek. 48:35 ☆ • *worship*

4 And ᴿthey shall see his face; and his name *shall be* in their foreheads.   [Matt. 5:8]

5 And there shall be no night there; and they need no candle, neither light of the sun; for the Lord God giveth them light: and they shall reign for ever and ever.

Conclusion

6 And he said unto me, ᴿThese sayings *are* faithful and true: and the Lord God of the holy prophets ᴿsent his angel to shew unto his servants the things which must shortly be done.   19:9 • 1:1

7 ᴿBehold, I come quickly: ᴿblessed *is* he that keepeth the sayings of the ᵀprophecy of this book.   [3:11] • 1:3 • *message*

8 And I John saw these things, and heard *them*. And when I had heard and seen, I fell down to worship before the feet of the angel which shewed me these things.

9 Then saith he unto me, See *thou do it not*: for I am thy fellowservant, and of thy brethren the prophets, and of them which keep the sayings of this book: worship God.

10 ᴿAnd he saith unto me, Seal not the sayings of the ᵀprophecy of this book: ᴿfor the time is at hand.   Dan. 8:26 • *message* • 1:3

11 ᴿHe that is unjust, let him be unjust still: and he which is filthy, let him be filthy still: and he that is righteous, let him be righteous still: and he that is holy, let him be holy still.   [Hos. 4:6, 17; 2 Pet. 1:5, 9]

12 And, behold, I come quickly; and ᴿmy reward *is* with me, ᴿto give every man according as his work shall be. Is. 40:10 ★ • 20:12

13 ᴿI am Alpha and Omega, the beginning and the end, the first and the last.   Is. 41:4

14 ᴿBlessed *are* they that do his commandments, that they may have right to the tree of life, ᴿand may enter in through the gates into the city.   Dan. 12:12 • 21:27

15 For ᴿwithout *are* ᴿdogs, and sorcerers, and whoremongers, and murderers, and idolaters, and whosoever loveth and maketh a lie.   1 Cor. 6:9; Gal. 5:19; Col. 3:6 • Phil. 3:2

16 I Jesus have sent mine angel to testify unto you these things in the churches. I am the root and the offspring of David, *and* the bright and morning star.

17 And the Spirit and ᴿthe bride say, Come. And let ᵀhim that heareth say, Come. ᴿAnd let him that is athirst come. And whosoever will, let him take the water of life freely.   [21:2, 9] • *everyone* • Is. 55:1

18 For I ᵀtestify unto every man that heareth the words of the ᵀprophecy of this book, If any man shall add unto these things, God shall add unto him the plagues that are written in this book: *say* • *message*

19 And if any man shall take away from the words of the book of this ᵀprophecy, ᴿGod shall take away his part ᵀout of the book of life, and out of the holy city, and *from* the things which are written in this book.   *message* • Ex. 32:33 • *from the tree of life*

20 ᴿHe which ᵀtestifieth these things saith, Surely I come quickly. A-men′. Even so, come, Lord Jesus.   *v. 12; John 21:25 • says*

21 ᴿThe grace of our Lord Jesus Christ *be* with you all. A-men′.   Rom. 16:20, 24; 2 Thess. 3:18

Harmony of the Gospels

Date	Event	Location	Matthew	Mark	Luke	John	Related References
	Luke's Introduction				1:1–4		Acts 1:1
	Pre-fleshly state of Christ					1:1–18	Heb. 1:1–14
	Genealogy of Jesus Christ		1:1–17		3:23–38		Ruth 4:18–22 1 Chr. 1:1–4

BIRTH, INFANCY, AND ADOLESCENCE OF JESUS AND JOHN THE BAPTIST IN 17 EVENTS

Date	Event	Location	Matthew	Mark	Luke	John	Related References
7 B.C.	(1) Announcement of Birth of John	Jerusalem (Temple)			1:5–25		Num. 6:3
7 or 6 B.C.	(2) Announcement of Birth of Jesus to the Virgin	Nazareth			1:26–38		Is. 7:14
c. 5 B.C.	(3) Song of Elizabeth to Mary	{Hill Country {of Judah			1:39–45		
	(4) Mary's Song of Praise				1:46–56		Ps. 103:17
5 B.C.	(5) Birth, Infancy, and Purpose for Future of John the Baptist	Judea			1:57–80		Mal. 3:1
	(6) Announcement of Jesus' Birth to Joseph	Nazareth	1:18–25				Is. 9:6, 7
5–4 B.C.	(7) Birth of Jesus Christ	Bethlehem	1:24, 25		2:1–7		Is. 7:14
	(8) Proclamation by the Angels	{Near {Bethlehem			2:8–14		1 Tim. 3:16
	(9) The Visit of Homage by Shepherds	Bethlehem			2:15–20		
	(10) Jesus' Circumcision	Bethlehem			2:21		Lev. 12:3
4 B.C.	(11) First Temple Visit with Acknowledgments by Simeon and Anna	Jerusalem			2:22–38		Ex. 13:2 Lev. 12
	(12) Visit of the Wise Men	{Jerusalem & {Bethlehem	2:1–12				Num. 24:17
	(13) Flight into Egypt and Massacre of Innocents	{Bethlehem, {Jerusalem & {Egypt	2:13–18				Jer. 31:15
	(14) From Egypt to Nazareth with Jesus		2:19–23		2:39		
Afterward A.D. 7–8	(15) Childhood of Jesus	Nazareth			2:40, 51		
	(16) Jesus, 12 Years Old, Visits the Temple	Jerusalem			2:41–50		Deut. 16:1–8
Afterward	(17) 18-Year Account of Jesus' Adolescence and Adulthood	Nazareth			2:51, 52		1 Sam. 2:26

TRUTHS ABOUT JOHN THE BAPTIST

Date	Event	Location	Matthew	Mark	Luke	John	Related References
c. A.D. 25–27	John's Ministry Begins	Judean Wilderness	3:1	1:1–4	3:1, 2	1:19–28	Mal. 3:1
	Man and Message		3:2–12	1:2–8	3:3–14		Is. 40:3
	His Picture of Jesus		3:11, 12	1:7, 8	3:15–18	1:26, 27	Acts 2:38
	His Courage		14:4–12		3:19, 20		

BEGINNING OF JESUS' MINISTRY IN 12 EVENTS

Date	Event	Location	Matthew	Mark	Luke	John	Related References
c. A.D. 27	(1) Jesus Baptized	Jordan River	3:13–17	1:9–11	3:21–23	1:29–34	Ps. 2:7
	(2) Jesus Tempted	Wilderness	4:1–11	1:12, 13	4:1–13		Ps. 91:11
	(3) Calls First Disciples	Beyond Jordan				1:35–51	
	(4) The First Miracle	Cana in Galilee				2:1–11	
	(5) First Stay in Capernaum	(Capernaum is "His" city)				2:12	
A.D. 27	(6) First Cleansing of the Temple	Jerusalem				2:13–22	Ps. 69:9
	(7) Received at Jerusalem	Judea				2:23–25	
	(8) Teaches Nicodemus about Second Birth	Judea				3:1–21	Num. 21:8, 9
	(9) Co-Ministry with John	Judea				3:22–30	

Date	Event	Location	Matthew	Mark	Luke	John	Related References
A.D. 27	(10) Leaves for Galilee	Judea	4:12	1:14	4:14	4:1-4	
	(11) Samaritan Woman at Jacob's Well	Samaria				4:5-42	Josh. 24:32
	(12) Returns to Galilee			1:15	4:15	4:43-45	

A.D. 27–29	THE GALILEAN MINISTRY OF JESUS IN 55 EVENTS						

Date	Event	Location	Matthew	Mark	Luke	John	Related References
A.D. 27	(1) Healing of the Nobleman's Son	Cana				4:46-54	
	(2) Rejected at Nazareth	Nazareth			4:16-30		Is. 61:1, 2
	(3) Moved to Capernaum	Capernaum	4:13-17				Is. 9:1, 2
	(4) Four Become Fishers of Men	Sea of Galilee	4:18-22	1:16-20	5:1-11		Ps. 33:9
	(5) Demoniac Healed on the Sabbath Day	Capernaum		1:21-28	4:31-37		
	(6) Peter's Mother-in-Law Cured, Plus Others	Capernaum	8:14-17	1:29-34	4:38-41		Is. 53:4
c. A.D. 27	(7) First Preaching Tour of Galilee	Galilee	4:23-25	1:35-39	4:42-44		
	(8) Leper Healed and Response Recorded	Galilee	8:1-4	1:40-45	5:12-16		Lev. 13:49
	(9) Paralytic Healed	Capernaum	9:1-8	2:1-12	5:17-26		Rom. 3:23
	(10) Matthew's Call and Reception Held	Capernaum	9:9-13	2:13-17	5:27-32		Hos. 6:6
	(11) Disciples Defended via a Parable	Capernaum	9:14-17	2:18-22	5:33-39		
A.D. 28	(12) Goes to Jerusalem for Second Passover; Heals Lame Man	Jerusalem				5:1-47	Ex. 20:10
	(13) Plucked Grain Precipitates Sabbath Controversy	En Route to Galilee	12:1-8	2:23-28	6:1-5		Deut. 5:14
	(14) Withered Hand Healed Causes Another Sabbath Controversy	Galilee	12:9-14	3:1-6	6:6-11		
	(15) Multitudes Healed	Sea of Galilee	12:15-21	3:7-12	6:17-19		
	(16) Twelve Apostles Selected After a Night of Prayer	Near Capernaum		3:13-19	6:12-16		
	(17) Sermon on the Mt.	Near Capernaum	5:1—7:29		6:20-49		
	(18) Centurion's Servant Healed	Capernaum	8:5-13		7:1-10		Is. 49:12, 13
	(19) Raises Widow's Son from Dead	Nain			7:11-17		Job 19:25
	(20) Jesus Allays John's Doubts	Galilee	11:2-19		7:18-35		Mal. 3:1
	(21) Woes Upon the Privileged		11:20-30				Gen. 19:24
	(22) A Sinful Woman Anoints Jesus	Simon's House, Capernaum			7:36-50		
	(23) Another Tour of Galilee	Galilee			8:1-3		
	(24) Jesus Accused of Blasphemy	Capernaum	12:22-37	3:20-30	11:14-23		
	(25) Jesus' Answer to a Demand for a Sign	Capernaum	12:38-45		11:24-26, 29-36		
	(26) Mother, Brothers Seek Audience	Capernaum	12:46-50	3:31-35	8:19-21		
	(27) Famous Parables of Sower, Seed, Tares, Mustard Seed, Leaven, Treasure, Pearl, Dragnet, Lamp Told	By Sea of Galilee	13:1-52	4:1-34	8:4-18		Joel 3:13
	(28) Sea Made Serene	Sea of Galilee	8:23-27	4:35-41	8:22-25		
	(29) Gadarene Demoniac Healed	E. Shore of Galilee	8:28-34	5:1-20	8:26-39		
	(30) Jairus' Daughter Raised and Woman with Hemorrhage Healed		9:18-26	5:21-43	8:40-56		
	(31) Two Blind Men's Sight Restored		9:27-31				

Date	Event	Location	Matthew	Mark	Luke	John	Related References
A.D. 28	(32) Mute Demoniac Healed		9:32–34				
	(33) Nazareth's Second Rejection of Christ	Nazareth	13:53–58	6:1–6			
	(34) Twelve Sent Out		9:35— 11:1	6:6–13	9:1–6		1 Cor. 9:14
	(35) Fearful Herod Beheads John	Galilee	14:1–12	6:14–29	9:7–9		
Spring A.D. 29	(36) Return of 12, Jesus Withdraws, 5000 Fed	Near Bethsaida	14:13–21	6:30–44	9:10–17	6:1–14	
	(37) Walks on the Water	Sea of Galilee	14:22–33	6:45–52		6:15–21	
	(38) Sick of Gennesaret Healed	Gennesaret	14:34–36	6:53–56			
	(39) Peak of Popularity Passes in Galilee	Capernaum				6:22–71 7:1	Is. 54:13
A.D. 29	(40) Traditions Attacked		15:1–20	7:1–23			Ex. 21:17
	(41) Aborted Retirement in Phoenicia: Syro-Phoenician Healed	Phoenicia	15:21–28	7:24–30			
	(42) Afflicted Healed	Decapolis	15:29–31	7:31–37			
	(43) 4000 Fed	Decapolis	15:32–39	8:1–9			
	(44) Pharisees Increase Attack	Magdala	16:1–4	8:10–13			
	(45) Disciples' Carelessness Condemned; Blind Man Healed		16:5–12	8:14–26			Jer. 5:21
	(46) Peter Confesses Jesus is the Christ	Near Caesarea Philippi	16:13–20	8:27–30	9:18–21		
	(47) Jesus Foretells His Death	Caesarea Philippi	16:21–26	8:31–37	9:22–25		
	(48) Kingdom Promised		16:27, 28	9:1	9:26, 27		Prov. 24:12
	(49) The Transfiguration	Mountain Unnamed	17:1–13	9:2–13	9:28–36		Is. 42:1
	(50) Epileptic Healed	Mt. of Transfiguration	17:14–21	9:14–29	9:37–42		
	(51) Again Tells of Death, Resurrection	Galilee	17:22, 23	9:30–32	9:43–45		
	(52) Taxes Paid	Capernaum	17:24–27				Ex. 30:11–15
	(53) Disciples Contend About Greatness; Jesus Defines; also Patience, Loyalty, Forgiveness	Capernaum	18:1–35	9:33–50	9:46–62		
	(54) Jesus Rejects Brothers' Advice	Galilee				7:2–9	
c. Sept. A.D. 29	(55) Galilee Departure and Samaritan Rejection		19:1		9:51–56	7:10	

A.D. 29–30	LAST JUDEAN AND PEREAN MINISTRY OF JESUS IN 42 EVENTS						
Oct. A.D. 29	(1) Feast of Tabernacles	Jerusalem				7:2, 11–52	
	(2) Forgiveness of Adulteress	Jerusalem				7:53— 8:11	Lev. 20:10
A.D. 29	(3) Christ—the Light of the World	Jerusalem				8:12–20	
	(4) Pharisees Can't Meet the Prophecy Thus Try to Destroy the Prophet	Jerusalem— Temple				8:12–59	Is. 6:9
	(5) Man Born Blind Healed; Following Consequences	Jerusalem				9:1–41	
	(6) Parable of the Good Shepherd	Jerusalem				10:1–21	
	(7) The Service of the Seventy	Probably Judea			10:1–24		
	(8) Lawyer Hears the Story of the Good Samaritan	Judea (?)			10:25–37		
	(9) The Hospitality of Martha and Mary	Bethany			10:38–42		
	(10) Another Lesson on Prayer	Judea (?)			11:1–13		

Date	Event	Location	Matthew	Mark	Luke	John	Related References
A.D. 29	(11) Accused of Connection with Beelzebub				11:14–36		
	(12) Judgment Against Lawyers and Pharisees				11:37–54		Mic. 6:8
	(13) Jesus Deals with Hypocrisy, Covetousness, Worry, and Alertness				12:1–59		Mic. 7:6
	(14) Repent or Perish				13:1–5		
	(15) Barren Fig Tree				13:6–9		
	(16) Crippled Woman Healed on Sabbath				13:10–17		Deut. 5:12–15
	(17) Parables of Mustard Seed and Leaven	{Probably Perea			13:18–21		
Winter A.D. 29	(18) Feast of Dedication	Jerusalem				10:22–39	Ps. 82:6
	(19) Withdrawal Beyond Jordan					10:40–42	
	(20) Begins Teaching Return to Jerusalem with Special Words About Herod	Perea			13:22–35		Ps. 6:8
	(21) Meal with a Pharisee Ruler Occasions Healing Man with Dropsy; Parables of Ox, Best Places, and Great Supper				14:1–24		
	(22) Demands of Discipleship	Perea			14:25–35		
	(23) Parables of Lost Sheep, Coin, Son				15:1–32		1 Pet. 2:25
	(24) Parables of Unjust Steward, Rich Man and Lazarus				16:1–31		
	(25) Lessons on Service, Faith, Influence				17:1–10		
	(26) Resurrection of Lazarus	{Perea to Bethany				11:1–44	
	(27) Reaction to It: Withdrawal of Jesus					11:45–54	
A.D. 30	(28) Begins Last Journey to Jerusalem via Samaria & Galilee	{Samaria, Galilee			17:11		
	(29) Heals Ten Lepers				17:12–19		Lev. 13:45, 46
	(30) Lessons on the Coming Kingdom				17:20–37		Gen. 6—7
	(31) Parables: Persistent Widow, Pharisee and Tax Collector				18:1–14		
	(32) Doctrine on Divorce		19:1–12	10:1–12			Deut. 24:1–4 Gen. 2:23–25
	(33) Jesus Blesses Children: Objections	Perea	19:13–15	10:13–16	18:15–17		Ps. 131:2
	(34) Rich Young Ruler	Perea	19:16–30	10:17–31	18:18–30		Ex. 20:1–17
	(35) Laborers of the 11th Hour		20:1–16				
	(36) Foretells Death and Resurrection	{Near Jordan	20:17–19	10:32–34	18:31–34		Ps. 22
	(37) Ambition of James and John		20:20–28	10:35–45			
	(38) Blind Bartimaeus Healed	Jericho		10:46–52	18:35–43		
	(39) Interview with Zacchaeus	Jericho			19:1–10		
	(40) Parable: the Minas	Jericho			19:11–27		
	(41) Returns to Home of Mary and Martha	Bethany				{11:55— 12:1	
	(42) Plot to Kill Lazarus	Bethany				12:9–11	

Spring A.D. 30	JESUS' FINAL WEEK OF WORK AT JERUSALEM IN 41 EVENTS						
Sunday	(1) Triumphal Entry	Bethany, Jerusalem, Bethany	21:1–9	11:1–11	19:28–44	12:12–19	Zech. 9:9

Date	Event	Location	Matthew	Mark	Luke	John	Related References
Monday	(2) Fig Tree Cursed and Temple Cleansed	Bethany to Jerusalem	21:10–19	11:12–18	19:45–48		Jer. 7:11
	(3) The Attraction of Sacrifice	Jerusalem				12:20–50	Is. 6:10
Tuesday	(4) Withered Fig Tree Testifies	Bethany to Jerusalem	21:20–22	11:19–26			
	(5) Sanhedrin Challenges Jesus. Answered by Parables: Two Sons, Wicked Vinedressers and Marriage Feast	Jerusalem	21:23— 22:14	11:27— 12:12	20:1–19		Is. 5:1, 2
	(6) Tribute to Caesar	Jerusalem	22:15–22	12:13–17	20:20–26		
	(7) Sadducees Question the Resurrection	Jerusalem	22:23–33	12:18–27	20:27–40		Ex. 3:6
	(8) Pharisees Question Commandments	Jerusalem	22:34–40	12:28–34			
	(9) Jesus and David	Jerusalem	22:41–46	12:35–37	20:41–44		Ps. 110:1
	(10) Jesus' Last Sermon	Jerusalem	23:1–39	12:38–40	20:45–47		
	(11) Widow's Mite	Jerusalem		12:41–44	21:1–4		Lev. 27:30
	(12) Jesus Tells of the Future	Mt. Olives	24:1–51	13:1–37	21:5–36		Dan. 12:1
	(13) Parables: Ten Virgins, Talents. The Day of Judgment	Mt. Olives	25:1–46				Zech. 14:5
	(14) Jesus Tells Date of Crucifixion		26:1–5	14:1, 2	22:1, 2		
	(15) Anointing by Mary at Simon's Feast	Bethany	26:6–13	14:3–9		12:2–8	
	(16) Judas Contracts the Betrayal		26:14–16	14:10, 11	22:3–6		Zech. 11:12
Thursday	(17) Preparation for the Passover	Jerusalem	26:17–19	14:12–16	22:7–13		Ex. 12:14–28
Thursday P.M.	(18) Passover Eaten, Jealousy Rebuked	Jerusalem	26:20	14:17	22:14–16, 24–30		
	(19) Feet Washed	Upper Room				13:1–20	
	(20) Judas Revealed, Defects	Upper Room	26:21–25	14:18–21	22:21–23	13:21–30	Ps. 41:9
	(21) Jesus Warns About Further Desertion; Cries of Loyalty	Upper Room	26:31–35	14:27–31	22:31–38	13:31–38	Zech. 13:7
	(22) Institution of the Lord's Supper	Upper Room	26:26–29	14:22–25	22:17–20		1 Cor. 11:23–34
	(23) Last Speech to the Apostles and Intercessory Prayer	Jerusalem				14:1— 17:26	Ps. 35:19
Thursday-Friday	(24) The Grief of Gethsemane	Mt. Olives	26:30, 36–46	14:26, 32–42	22:39–46	18:1	Ps. 42:6
Friday	(25) Betrayal, Arrest, Desertion	Gethsemane	26:47–56	14:43–52	22:47–53	18:2–12	
	(26) First Examined by Annas	Jerusalem				18:12–14, 19–23	
	(27) Trial by Caiaphas and Council; Following Indignities	Jerusalem	26:57, 59–68	14:53, 55–65	22:54, 63–65	18:24	Lev. 24:16
	(28) Peter's Triple Denial	Jerusalem	26:58, 69–75	14:54, 66–72	22:54–62	18:15–18, 25–27	
	(29) Condemnation by the Council	Jerusalem	27:1	15:1	22:66–71		Ps. 110:1
	(30) Suicide of Judas	Jerusalem	27:3–10				Acts 1:18, 19
	(31) First Appearance Before Pilate	Jerusalem	27:2, 11–14	15:1–5	23:1–7	18:28–38	
	(32) Jesus Before Herod	Jerusalem			23:6–12		
	(33) Second Appearance Before Pilate	Jerusalem	27:15–26	15:6–15	23:13–25	18:39— 19:16	Deut. 21:6–9
	(34) Mockery by Roman Soldiers	Jerusalem	27:27–30	15:16–19			
	(35) Led to Golgotha	Jerusalem	27:31–34	15:20–23	23:26–33	19:16, 17	Ps. 69:21
	(36) 6 Events of First 3 Hours on Cross	Calvary	27:35–44	15:24–32	23:33–43	19:18–27	Ps. 22:18
	(37) Last 3 Hours on Cross	Calvary	27:45–50	15:33–37	23:44–46	19:28–30	Ps. 22:1
	(38) Events Attending Jesus' Death		27:51–56	15:38–41	23:45, 47–49		
Friday-Saturday	(39) Burial of Jesus	Jerusalem	27:57–60	15:42–46	23:50–54	19:31–37	Ex. 12:46
	(40) Tomb Sealed	Jerusalem	27:61–66		23:55, 56		Ex. 20:8–11
	(41) Women Watch	Jerusalem		15:47			

Date	Event	Location	Matthew	Mark	Luke	John	Related References
A.D. 30	**THE RESURRECTION THROUGH THE ASCENSION IN 12 EVENTS**						
Dawn of First Day (Sunday, "Lord's Day")	(1) Women Visit the Tomb	Near Jerusalem	28:1–10	16:1–8	24:1–11		
	(2) Peter and John See the Empty Tomb				24:12	20:1–10	
	(3) Jesus' Appearance to Mary Magdalene	Jerusalem		16:9–11		20:11–18	
	(4) Jesus' Appearance to the Other Women	Jerusalem	28:9, 10				
	(5) Guards' Report of the Resurrection		28:11–15				
Sunday Afternoon	(6) Jesus' Appearance to Two Disciples on Way to Emmaus			16:12, 13	24:13–35		1 Cor. 15:5
Late Sunday	(7) Jesus' Appearance to Ten Disciples Without Thomas	Jerusalem		16:14	24:36–43	20:19–25	
One Week Later	(8) Appearance to Disciples with Thomas	Jerusalem				20:26–31	
During 40 Days until Ascension	(9) Jesus' Appearance to Seven Disciples by Sea of Galilee	Galilee				21:1–25	
	(10) Appearance to 500	Mt. in Galilee					1 Cor. 15:6
	(11) Great Commission		28:16–20	16:15–18	24:44–49		
	(12) The Ascension	Mt. Olivet		16:19, 20	24:50–53		Acts 1:4–11

The Jewish Calendar

The Jews used two kinds of calendars:

Civil Calendar—official calendar of kings, childbirth, and contracts.

Sacred Calendar—from which festivals were computed.

NAMES OF MONTHS	CORRESPONDS WITH	NO. OF DAYS	MONTH OF CIVIL YEAR	MONTH OF SACRED YEAR	
TISHRI	Sept.–Oct.	30 days	1st	7th	The Jewish day was from sunset to sunset, in 8 equal parts:
HESHVAN	Oct.–Nov.	29 or 30	2nd	8th	
CHISLEV	Nov.–Dec.	29 or 30	3rd	9th	
TEBETH	Dec.–Jan.	29	4th	10th	FIRST WATCH ..... SUNSET TO 9 P.M.
SHEBAT	Jan.–Feb.	30	5th	11th	SECOND WATCH ... 9 P.M. TO MIDNIGHT
ADAR	Feb.–Mar.	29 or 30	6th	12th	THIRD WATCH ..... MIDNIGHT TO 3 A.M.
NISAN	Mar.–Apr.	30	7th	1st	FOURTH WATCH ... 3 A.M. TO SUNRISE
IYAR	Apr.–May	29	8th	2nd	
SIVAN	May–June	30	9th	3rd	FIRST WATCH ..... SUNRISE TO 9 A.M.
TAMMUZ	June–July	29	10th	4th	SECOND WATCH ... 9 A.M. TO NOON
AB	July–Aug.	30	11th	5th	THIRD WATCH ..... NOON TO 3 P.M.
*ELUL	Aug.–Sept.	29	12th	6th	FOURTH WATCH ... 3 P.M. TO SUNSET

*Hebrew months were alternately 30 and 29 days long. Their year, shorter than ours, had 354 days. Therefore, about every 3 years (7 times in 19 years) an extra 29-day-month, VEADAR, was added between ADAR and NISAN.

PROPHECIES OF THE MESSIAH FULFILLED IN JESUS CHRIST

Presented Here in Their Order of Fulfillment

PROPHETIC SCRIPTURE	SUBJECT	FULFILLED
Gen. 3:15, p. 7 And I will put enmity between thee and the woman, and between thy seed and her seed; it shall bruise thy head, and thou shalt bruise his heel.	seed of a woman	**Gal. 4:4, p. 1156** But when the fulness of the time was come, God sent forth his Son, made of a woman, made under the law.
Gen. 12:3, p. 15 And I will bless them that bless thee, and curse him that curseth thee: and in thee shall all families of the earth be blessed.	seed of Abraham	**Matt. 1:1, p. 941** The book of the generation of Jesus Christ, the Son of David, the son of Abraham.
Gen. 17:19, p. 18 And God said, Sarah thy wife shall bear thee a son indeed; and thou shalt call his name Isaac: and I will establish my covenant with him for an everlasting covenant, *and* with his seed after him.	seed of Isaac	**Luke 3:34, p. 1008** Which was *the son* of Jacob, which was *the son* of Isaac, which was *the son* of Abraham, which was *the son* of Tha'-ra, which was *the son* of Na'-chor.
Num. 24:17, p. 161 I shall see him, but not now: I shall behold him, but not nigh: there shall come a Star out of Jacob, and a Sceptre shall rise out of Israel, and shall smite the corners of Moab, and destroy all the children of Sheth.	seed of Jacob	**Matt. 1:2, p. 941** Abraham begat Isaac; and Isaac begat Jacob; and Jacob begat Judas and his brethren.
Gen. 49:10, p. 51 The sceptre shall not depart from Judah, nor a lawgiver from between his feet, until Shi'-loh come; and unto him *shall* the gathering of the people *be*.	from the tribe of Judah	**Luke 3:33, p. 1008** Which was *the son* of A-min'-a-dab, which was *the son* of A'-ram, which was *the son* of Es'-rom, which was *the son* of Pha'-res, which was *the son* of Juda.
Is. 9:7, p. 665 Of the increase of *his* government and peace *there shall be* no end, upon the throne of David, and upon his kingdom, to order it, and to establish it with judgment and with justice from henceforth even for ever. The zeal of the LORD of hosts will perform this.	heir to the throne of David	**Luke 1:32, 33, p. 1005** He shall be great, and shall be called the Son of the Highest: and the Lord God shall give unto him the throne of his father David: And he shall reign over the house of Jacob for ever; and of his kingdom there shall be no end.
Ps. 45:6, 7, p. 567; 102:25-27, p. 591 Thy throne, O God, *is* for ever and ever: the sceptre of thy kingdom *is* a right sceptre. Thou lovest righteousness, and hatest wickedness: therefore God, thy God, hath anointed thee with the oil of gladness above thy fellows. Of old hast thou laid the foundation of the earth: and the heavens *are* the work of thy hands. They shall perish, but thou shalt endure: yea, all of them shall wax old like a garment; as a vesture shalt thou change them, and they shall be changed: But thou *art* the same, and thy years shall have no end.	anointed and eternal	**Heb. 1:8-12, p. 1215** But unto the Son he saith, THY THRONE, O GOD, IS FOR EVER AND EVER: A SCEPTRE OF RIGHTEOUSNESS IS THE SCEPTRE OF THY KINGDOM. THOU HAST LOVED RIGHTEOUSNESS, AND HATED INIQUITY; THEREFORE GOD, *EVEN* THY GOD, HATH ANOINTED THEE WITH THE OIL OF GLADNESS ABOVE THY FELLOWS. AND, THOU, LORD, IN THE BEGINNING HAST LAID THE FOUNDATION OF THE EARTH; AND THE HEAVENS ARE THE WORKS OF THINE HANDS: THEY SHALL PERISH; BUT THOU REMAINEST; AND THEY ALL SHALL WAX OLD AS DOTH A GARMENT; AND AS A VESTURE SHALT THOU FOLD THEM UP, AND THEY SHALL BE CHANGED: BUT THOU ART THE SAME, AND THY YEARS SHALL NOT FAIL.

PROPHETIC SCRIPTURE	SUBJECT	FULFILLED
Mic. 5:2, p. 873 But thou, Beth'–le-hem Eph'-ra-tah, *though* thou be little among the thousands of Judah, *yet* out of thee shall he come forth unto me *that is* to be ruler in Israel; whose goings forth *have been* from of old, from everlasting.	born in Bethlehem	*Luke 2:4, 5, 7, p. 1006* And Joseph also went up from Galilee, out of the city of Nazareth, into Ju-dae'-a, unto the city of David, which is called Beth'-le-hem; (because he was of the house and lineage of David:) To be taxed with Mary his espoused wife, being great with child. And she brought forth her firstborn son, and wrapped him in swaddling clothes, and laid him in a manger; because there was no room for them in the inn.
Dan. 9:25, p. 833 Know therefore and understand, *that* from the going forth of the commandment to restore and to build Jerusalem unto the Mes-si'-ah the Prince *shall be* seven weeks, and threescore and two weeks: the street shall be built again, and the wall, even in troublous times.	time for His birth	*Luke 2:1, 2, p. 1006* And it came to pass in those days, that there went out a decree from Caesar Augustus, that all the world should be taxed. (*And* this taxing was first made when Cy-re'-ni-us was governor of Syria.)
Is. 7:14, p. 663 Therefore the Lord himself shall give you a sign; Behold, a virgin shall conceive, and bear a son, and shall call his name Im-man'-u-el.	to be born of a virgin	*Luke 1:26, 27, 30, 31, p. 1004* And in the sixth month the angel Gabriel was sent from God unto a city of Galilee, named Nazareth, To a virgin espoused to a man whose name was Joseph, of the house of David; and the virgin's name *was* Mary. And the angel said unto her, Fear not, Mary: for thou hast found favour with God. And, behold, thou shalt conceive in thy womb, and bring forth a son, and shalt call his name JESUS.
Jer. 31:15, p. 736 Thus saith the LORD: A voice was heard in Ra'-mah, lamentation, *and* bitter weeping; Ra'-hel weeping for her children refused to be comforted for her children, because they *were* not.	slaughter of the innocents	*Matt. 2:16–18, p. 942* Then Herod, when he saw that he was mocked of the wise men, was exceeding wroth, and sent forth, and slew all the children that were in Beth'-le-hem, and in all the coasts thereof, from two years old and under, according to the time which he had diligently enquired of the wise men. Then was fulfilled that which was spoken by Jeremy the prophet, saying, IN RAMA WAS THERE A VOICE HEARD, LAMENTATION, AND WEEPING, AND GREAT MOURNING. RACHEL WEEPING *FOR HER* CHILDREN, AND WOULD NOT BE COMFORTED, BECAUSE THEY ARE NOT.
Hos. 11:1, p. 845 When Israel *was* a child, then I loved him, and called my son out of Egypt.	flight to Egypt	*Matt. 2:14, 15, p. 942* When he arose, he took the young child and his mother by night, and departed into Egypt: And was there until the death of Herod: that it might be fulfilled which was spoken of the Lord by the prophet, saying, Out of Egypt have I called my son.

PROPHETIC SCRIPTURE	SUBJECT	FULFILLED
Is. 40:3–5, p. 685 The voice of him that crieth in the wilderness, Prepare ye the way of the LORD, make straight in the desert a highway for our God. Every valley shall be exalted, and every mountain and hill shall be made low: and the crooked shall be made straight, and the rough places plain: And the glory of the LORD shall be revealed, and all flesh shall see *it* together: for the mouth of the LORD hath spoken *it*.	**the way prepared**	*Luke 3:3–6, p. 1007* And he came into all the country about Jordan, preaching the baptism of repentance for the remission of sins; As it is written in the book of the words of E-sa'-ias the prophet, saying, THE VOICE OF ONE CRYING IN THE WILDERNESS, PREPARE YE THE WAY OF THE LORD, MAKE HIS PATHS STRAIGHT. EVERY VALLEY SHALL BE FILLED, AND EVERY MOUNTAIN AND HILL SHALL BE BROUGHT LOW; AND THE CROOKED SHALL BE MADE STRAIGHT, AND THE ROUGH WAYS *SHALL BE* MADE SMOOTH; AND ALL FLESH SHALL SEE THE SALVATION OF GOD.
Mal. 3:1, p. 908 Behold, I will send my messenger, and he shall prepare the way before me: and the Lord, whom ye seek, shall suddenly come to his temple, even the messenger of the covenant, whom ye delight in: behold, he shall come, saith the LORD of hosts.	**preceded by a forerunner**	*Luke 7:24, 27, p. 1013* And when the messengers of John were departed, he began to speak unto the people concerning John, What went ye out into the wilderness for to see? A reed shaken with the wind? This is *he*, of whom it is written, Behold, I send my messenger before thy face, which shall prepare thy way before thee.
Mal. 4:5, 6, p. 909 Behold, I will send you E-li'-jah the prophet before the coming of the great and dreadful day of the LORD: And he shall turn the heart of the fathers to the children, and the heart of the children to their fathers, lest I come and smite the earth with a curse.	**preceded by Elijah**	*Matt. 11:13, 14, p. 952* For all the prophets and the law prophesied until John. And if ye will receive *it*, this is E-li'-as, which was for to come.
Ps. 2:7, p. 548 I will declare the decree: the LORD hath said unto me, Thou *art* my Son; this day have I begotten thee.	**declared the Son of God**	*Matt. 3:17, p. 943* And lo a voice from heaven, saying, This is my beloved Son, in whom I am well pleased.
Is. 9:1, 2, p. 664 Nevertheless the dimness *shall* not *be* such as *was* in her vexation, when at the first he lightly afflicted the land of Zeb'-u-lun and the land of Naph'-ta-li, and afterward did more grievously afflict *her by* the way of the sea, beyond Jordan, in Galilee of the nations. The people that walked in darkness have seen a great light: they that dwell in the land of the shadow of death, upon them hath the light shined.	**Galilean ministry**	*Matt. 4:13–16, p. 944* And leaving Nazareth, he came and dwelt in Ca-per'-na-um, which is upon the sea coast, in the borders of Zab'-u-lon and Neph'-tha-lim: That it might be fulfilled which was spoken by E-sa'-ias the prophet, saying, THE LAND OF ZAB'-U-LON, AND THE LAND OF NEPH'-THA-LIM, *BY* THE WAY OF THE SEA, BEYOND JORDAN, GALILEE OF THE GENTILES; THE PEOPLE WHICH SAT IN DARKNESS SAW GREAT LIGHT; AND TO THEM WHICH SAT IN THE REGION AND SHADOW OF DEATH LIGHT IS SPRUNG UP.
Ps. 78:2–4, p. 580 I will open my mouth in a parable: I will utter dark sayings of old: Which we have heard and known, and our fathers have told us. We will not hide *them* from their children, shewing to the generation to come the praises of the LORD, and his strength, and his wonderful works that he hath done.	**speaks in parables**	*Matt. 13:34, 35, p. 955* All these things spake Jesus unto the multitude in parables; and without a parable spake he not unto them: That it might be fulfilled which was spoken by the prophet, saying, I WILL OPEN MY MOUTH IN PARABLES; I WILL UTTER THINGS WHICH HAVE BEEN KEPT SECRET FROM THE FOUNDATION OF THE WORLD.

PROPHETIC SCRIPTURE	SUBJECT	FULFILLED
Deut. 18:15, p. 196 The LORD thy God will raise up unto thee a Prophet from the midst of thee, of thy brethren, like unto me; unto him ye shall hearken.	a prophet	**Acts 3:20, 22, p. 1075** And he shall send Jesus Christ, which before was preached unto you: For Moses truly said unto the fathers, A PROPHET SHALL THE LORD YOUR GOD RAISE UP UNTO YOU OF YOUR BRETHREN, LIKE UNTO ME; HIM SHALL YE HEAR IN ALL THINGS WHATSOEVER HE SHALL SAY UNTO YOU.
Is. 61:1, 2, p. 700 The Spirit of the Lord GOD *is* upon me; because the LORD has anointed me to preach good tidings unto the meek; he hath sent me to bind up the brokenhearted, to proclaim liberty to the captives, and the opening of the prison to *them that are* bound; To proclaim the acceptable year of the LORD, and the day of vengeance of our God; to comfort all that mourn.	to heal the brokenhearted	**Luke 4:18, 19, p. 1009** THE SPIRIT OF THE LORD *IS* UPON ME, BECAUSE HE HATH ANOINTED ME TO PREACH THE GOSPEL TO THE POOR; HE HATH SENT ME TO HEAL THE BRO-KENHEARTED, TO PREACH DELIVERANCE TO THE CAPTIVES, AND RECOVERING OF SIGHT TO THE BLIND, TO SET AT LIBERTY THEM THAT ARE BRUISED, TO PREACH THE ACCEPTABLE YEAR OF THE LORD.
Is. 53:3, p. 695 He is despised and rejected of men; a man of sorrows, and acquainted with grief: and we hid as it were *our* faces from him; he was despised, and we esteemed him not.	rejected by His own people, the Jews	**John 1:11, p. 1042** He came unto his own, and his own received him not. **Luke 23:18, p. 1035** And they cried out all at once, saying, Away with this *man,* and release unto us Bar-ab'-bas.
Ps. 110:4, p. 597 The LORD hath sworn, and will not repent, Thou *art* a priest for ever after the order of Mel-chiz'-e-dek.	priest after order of Melchisedec	**Heb. 5:5, 6, p. 1217** So also Christ glorified not himself to be made an high priest; but he that said unto him, THOU ART MY SON, TO DAY HAVE I BEGOTTEN THEE. As he saith also in another *place,* THOU *ART* A PRIEST FOR EVER AFTER THE ORDER OF MEL-CHIS'-E-DEC.
Zech. 9:9, p. 901 Rejoice greatly, O daughter of Zion; shout, O daughter of Jerusalem: behold, thy King cometh unto thee: he *is* just, and having salvation; lowly, and riding upon an ass, and upon a colt the foal of an ass.	triumphal entry	**Mark 11:7, 9, 11, p. 951** And they brought the colt to Jesus, and cast their garments on him; and he sat upon him. And they that went before, and they that followed, cried, saying, HOSANNA; BLESSED *IS* HE THAT COMETH IN THE NAME OF THE LORD: And Jesus entered into Jerusalem, and into the temple: and when he had looked round about upon all things, and now the eventide was come, he went out unto Beth'-a-ny with the twelve.
Ps. 8:2, p. 550 Out of the mouth of babes and sucklings hast thou ordained strength because of thine enemies, that thou mightest still the enemy and the avenger.	adored by infants	**Matt. 21:15, 16, p. 963** And when the chief priests and scribes saw the wonderful things that he did, and the children crying in the temple, and saying, Ho-san'-na to the son of David; they were sore displeased, And said unto him, Hearest thou what these say? And Jesus saith unto them, Yea; have ye never read, OUT OF THE MOUTH OF BABES AND SUCKLINGS THOU HAST PERFECTED PRAISE?

PROPHETIC SCRIPTURE	SUBJECT	FULFILLED
Is. 53:1, p. 695 Who hath believed our report? and to whom is the arm of the LORD revealed?	**not believed**	*John 12:37, 38, p. 1058* But though he had done so many miracles before them, yet they believed not on him: That the saying of E-sa'-ias the prophet might be fulfilled, which he spake, LORD, WHO HATH BELIEVED OUR REPORT? AND TO WHOM HATH THE ARM OF THE LORD BEEN REVEALED?
Ps. 41:9, p. 565 Yea, mine own familiar friend, in whom I trusted, which did eat of my bread, hath lifted up *his* heel against me.	**betrayed by a close friend**	*Luke 22:47, 48, p. 1034* And while he yet spake, behold a multitude, and he that was called Judas, one of the twelve, went before them, and drew near unto Jesus to kiss him. But Jesus said unto him, Judas, betrayest thou the Son of man with a kiss?
Zech. 11:12, p. 902 And I said unto them, If ye think good, give *me* my price; and if not, forbear. So they weighed for my price thirty *pieces* of silver.	**betrayed for thirty pieces of silver**	*Matt. 26:14, 15, p. 969* Then one of the twelve, called Judas Iscar'-i-ot, went unto the chief priests, And said *unto them*, What will ye give me, and I will deliver him unto you? And they covenanted with him for thirty pieces of silver.
Ps. 35:11, p. 561 False witnesses did rise up; they laid to my charge *things* that I knew not.	**accused by false witnesses**	*Mark 14:57, 58, p. 996* And there arose certain, and bare false witness against him, saying, We heard him say, I will destroy this temple that is made with hands, and within three days I will build another made without hands.
Is. 53:7, p. 695 He was oppressed, and he was afflicted, yet he opened not his mouth: he is brought as a lamb to the slaughter, and as a sheep before her shearers is dumb, so he openeth not his mouth.	**silent to accusations**	*Mark 15:4, 5, p. 997* And Pilate asked him again, saying, Answerest thou nothing? behold how many things they witness against thee. But Jesus yet answered nothing; so that Pilate marvelled.
Is. 50:6, p. 693 I gave my back to the smiters, and my cheeks to them that plucked off the hair: I hid not my face from shame and spitting.	**spat upon and smitten**	*Matt. 26:67, p. 971* Then did they spit in his face, and buffeted him; and others smote *him* with the palms of their hands.
Ps. 35:19, p. 562 Let not them that are mine enemies wrongfully rejoice over me: *neither* let them wink with the eye that hate me without a cause.	**hated without reason**	*John 15:24, 25, p. 1061* If I had not done among them the works which none other man did, they had not had sin: but now have they both seen and hated both me and my Father. But *this cometh to pass*, that the word might be fulfilled that is written in their law, THEY HATED ME WITHOUT A CAUSE.
Is. 53:5, p. 695 But he *was* wounded for our transgressions, *he was* bruised for our iniquities: the chastisement of our peace *was* upon him; and with his stripes we are healed.	**vicarious sacrifice**	*Rom. 5:6, 8, p. 1112* For when we were yet without strength, in due time Christ died for the ungodly. But God commendeth his love toward us, in that, while we were yet sinners, Christ died for us.
Is. 53:12, p. 695 Therefore will I divide him a *portion* with the great, and he shall divide the spoil with the strong; because he hath poured out his soul unto death: and he was numbered with the transgressors; and he bare the sin of many, and made intercession for the transgressors.	**crucified with malefactors**	*Mark 15:27, 28, p. 998* And with him they crucify two thieves; the one on his right hand, and the other on his left. And the scripture was fulfilled, which saith, AND HE WAS NUMBERED WITH THE TRANSGRESSORS.

PROPHETIC SCRIPTURE	SUBJECT	FULFILLED
Zech. 12:10, p. 902 And I will pour upon the house of David, and upon the inhabitants of Jerusalem, the spirit of grace and of supplications: and they shall look upon me whom they have pierced, and they shall mourn for him, as one mourneth for *his* only *son*, and shall be in bitterness for him, as one that is in bitterness for *his* firstborn.	**pierced through hands and feet**	**John 20:27, p. 1066** Then saith he to Thomas, Reach hither thy finger, and behold my hands; and reach hither thy hand, and thrust *it* into my side; and be not faithless, but believing.
Ps. 22:7, 8, p. 556 All they that see me laugh me to scorn: they shoot out the lip, they shake the head, *saying,* He trusted on the LORD *that* he would deliver him: let him deliver him, seeing he delighted in him.	**scorned and mocked**	**Luke 23:35, p. 1036** And the people stood beholding. And the rulers also with them derided *him*, saying, He saved others; let him save himself, if he be Christ, the chosen of God.
Ps. 69:9, p. 576 For the zeal of thine house hath eaten me up; and the reproaches of them that reproached thee are fallen upon me.	**reproached**	**Rom. 15:3, p. 1120** For even Christ pleased not himself; but, as it is written, THE REPROACHES OF THEM THAT REPROACHED THEE FELL ON ME.
Ps. 109:4, p. 596 For my love they are my adversaries: but I *give myself unto* prayer.	**prayer for His enemies**	**Luke 23:34, p. 1036** Then said Jesus, Father, forgive them; for they know not what they do. And they parted his raiment, and cast lots.
Ps. 22:17, 18, p. 556 I may tell all my bones: they look *and* stare upon me. They part my garments among them, and cast lots upon my vesture.	**soldiers gambled for His garment**	**Matt. 27:35, 36, p. 972** And they crucified him, and parted his garments, casting lots: that it might be fulfilled which was spoken by the prophet, THEY PARTED MY GARMENTS AMONG THEM, AND UPON MY VESTURE DID THEY CAST LOTS. And sitting down they watched him there.
Ps. 22:1, p. 555 My God, my God, why hast thou forsaken me? *why art thou so* far from helping me, *and from* the words of my roaring?	**forsaken by God**	**Matt. 27:46, p. 972** And about the ninth hour Jesus cried with a loud voice, saying, E′-li, E′-li, la′-ma sa-bach′-tha-ni? that is to say, MY GOD, MY GOD, WHY HAST THOU FORSAKEN ME?
Ps. 34:20, p. 561 He keepeth all his bones: not one of them is broken.	**no bones broken**	**John 19:32, 33, 36, p. 1065** Then came the soldiers, and brake the legs of the first, and of the other which was crucified with him. But when they came to Jesus, and saw that he was dead already, they brake not his legs: For these things were done, that the scripture should be fulfilled, A BONE OF HIM SHALL NOT BE BROKEN.
Zech. 12:10, p. 902 And I will pour upon the house of David, and upon the inhabitants of Jerusalem, the spirit of grace and of supplications: and they shall look upon me whom they have pierced, and they shall mourn for him, as one mourneth for *his* only *son*, and shall be in bitterness for him, as one that is in bitterness for *his* firstborn.	**His side pierced**	**John 19:34, p. 1065** But one of the soldiers with a spear pierced his side, and forthwith came there out blood and water.

PROPHETIC SCRIPTURE	SUBJECT	FULFILLED
Is. 53:9, p. 695 And he made his grave with the wicked, and with the rich in his death; because he had done no violence, neither *was any* deceit in his mouth.	**buried with the rich**	**Matt. 27:57–60, p. 973** When the even was come, there came a rich man of Ar-i-ma-the'-a, named Joseph, who also himself was Jesus' disciple: He went to Pilate, and begged the body of Jesus. Then Pilate commanded the body to be delivered. And when Joseph had taken the body, he wrapped it in a clean linen cloth, And laid it in his own new tomb, which he had hewn out in the rock: and he rolled a great stone to the door of the sepulchre, and departed.
Ps. 16:10, p. 552 For thou wilt not leave my soul in hell; neither wilt thou suffer thine Holy One to see corruption. **Ps. 49:15, p. 568** But God will redeem my soul from the power of the grave: for he shall receive me.	**to be resurrected**	**Mark 16:6, 7, p. 998** And he saith unto them, Be not affrighted: Ye seek Jesus of Nazareth, which was crucified: he is risen; he is not here: behold the place where they laid him. But go your way, tell his disciples and Peter that he goeth before you into Galilee: there shall ye see him, as he said unto you.
Ps. 68:18, p. 575 Thou hast ascended on high, thou hast led captivity captive: thou hast received gifts for men; yea, *for* the rebellious also, that the LORD God might dwell *among* them.	**His ascension to God's right hand**	**Mark 16:19, p. 999** So then after the Lord had spoken unto them, he was received up into heaven, and sat on the right hand of God. **1 Cor. 15:4, p. 1137** And that he was buried, and that he rose again the third day according to the scriptures. **Eph. 4:8, p. 1164** Wherefore he saith, WHEN HE ASCENDED UP ON HIGH, HE LED CAPTIVITY CAPTIVE, AND GAVE GIFTS UNTO MEN.

THE PARABLES
OF JESUS CHRIST

Parable	Matthew	Mark	Luke
1. Candle Under a Bushel	5:14–16	4:21, 22	8:16, 17 11:33–36
2. A Wise Man Builds on Rock and A Foolish Man Builds on Sand	7:24–27		6:47–49
3. Unshrunk (New) Cloth on an Old Garment	9:16	2:21	5:36
4. New Wine in Old Wineskins (Bottles)	9:17	2:22	5:37, 38
5. The Sower	13:3–23	4:2–20	8:4–15
6. The Tares (Weeds)	13:24–30		
7. The Mustard Seed	13:31, 32	4:30–32	13:18, 19
8. The Leaven	13:33		13:20, 21
9. The Hidden Treasure	13:44		
10. The Pearl of Great Price	13:45, 46		
11. The Net	13:47–50		
12. The Lost Sheep	18:12–14		15:3–7
13. The Unforgiving Servant	18:23–35		
14. The Labourers in the Vineyard	20:1–16		
15. The Two Sons	21:28–32		
16. The Wicked Husbandmen	21:33–45	12:1–12	20:9–19
17. The Wedding Feast	22:2–14		
18. The Fig Tree	24:32–44	13:28–32	21:29–33
19. The Wise and Foolish Virgins	25:1–13		
20. The Talents	25:14–30		
21. The Growing Seed		4:26–29	
22. The Absent Householder		13:33–37	
23. The Creditor and Two Debtors			7:41–43
24. The Good Samaritan			10:30–37
25. A Friend in Need			11:5–13
26. The Rich Fool			12:16–21
27. The Faithful Servant and the Evil Servant			12:35–40
28. Faithful and Wise Steward			12:42–48
29. The Barren Fig Tree			13:6–9
30. The Great Supper			14:16–24
31. Building a Tower and a King Making War			14:25–35
32. The Lost Coin			15:8–10
33. The Prodigal Son			15:11–32
34. The Unjust Steward			16:1–13
35. The Rich Man and Lazarus			16:19–31
36. Unprofitable Servants			17:7–10
37. The Importunate Widow			18:1–8
38. The Pharisee and the Publican			18:9–14
39. The Minas (Pounds)			19:11–27

TEACHINGS AND ILLUSTRATIONS OF CHRIST

Subject	Reference	Subject	Reference	Subject	Reference
Abiding in Christ	John 15:4–10	Character	John 1:47	Drunkenness	Luke 21:34
Ability	Matt. 25:14, 15	Charity	Luke 12:33	Dullness	Matt. 13:13
Ablution	Matt. 6:17, 18	Cheating	Mark 10:19	Duty	Luke 17:10
Abode	John 14:23	Chosen	Matt. 22:14	Dwelling places	John 14:2, 3
Abraham	John 8:37, 56	Church	Matt. 18:17	**Earth**	Matt. 5:18
Abstinence	Luke 21:34	Circumcision	John 7:22, 23	Earthquakes	Mark 13:8
Abundant life	John 10:10	Cleansing	John 15:3	Economy	Matt. 15:37
Access to God	John 10:7, 9	Coin	Matt. 22:19–21		John 6:12
Accountability	Luke 12:47, 48	Coldness	Matt. 24:12	Elect	Matt. 24:24, 31
Accusation,		Communication	Luke 24:17	Election	Matt. 25:34
false	Matt. 5:11	Compassion	Matt. 15:32	Elijah	Matt. 17:11, 12
Adultery	Matt. 5:27, 28		Luke 10:33	Employer	Matt. 20:1–16
Adversity	Luke 24:46	Compromise	Matt. 5:25, 26	Encouragement	Matt. 9:2
Affliction	Matt. 24:7–12	Conceit	Luke 18:10–12	Endowments	Matt. 25:14, 15
Agreement	Matt. 18:19	Conduct,		Endurance	Matt. 10:22
Altar	Matt. 23:18, 19	Christian	Matt. 5:16		Luke 21:19
Ambition	Luke 22:25–30	Confessing		Enemies	Matt. 5:43, 44
Angels	Matt. 13:39, 41	Christ	Matt. 10:32, 33	Eternal life	Matt. 19:29
Anger	Matt. 5:22	Confession		Eternal sin	Mark 3:29
Anxiety	Luke 12:22–31	of sin	Luke 18:13, 14	Etiquette	Luke 10:8
Apostasy	Matt. 13:18–22	Confidence	Mark 11:24	Evil	Matt. 15:19
	Luke 8:13	Conflict	Matt. 10:34–36	Exaltation	Matt. 23:12
Apostles	Luke 11:49	Conscience	John 8:7–9	Example	John 13:15
Appearance	Matt. 6:16	Contention	Matt. 18:15–17	Excuses	Luke 14:18–20
Appearance,		Contentment	John 6:43	Extravagance	Luke 15:11–14
outward	Matt. 23:27, 28	Conversion	Matt. 13:15	**Fainting**	Mark 8:2, 3
Authority	Matt. 21:24	Convict	John 16:8	Faith	Matt. 6:25
	Luke 10:19	Corruption,			Mark 11:22
Avarice	Luke 12:16–21	moral	Luke 11:39		Luke 7:50
Backsliding	Luke 9:62	Courage	Matt. 9:22	Faithfulness	Matt. 25:21
Baptism	Matt. 28:19	Covenant	Mark 14:24	Faithlessness	Matt. 25:24–30
	Acts 1:5	Coveting	Mark 7:21, 22	False prophets	Matt. 24:11
Beatitudes	Matt. 5:3–11	Cross-bearing	Matt. 10:38	False witness	Matt. 19:18
Beelzebub	Matt. 10:25	Crucifixion	Luke 9:22	Farm	Matt. 22:2–6
Begging	Luke 16:3	Cup of water	Matt. 10:42	Fasting	Matt. 6:16–18
Beneficence	Matt. 5:42	**Dancing**	Luke 15:25–27	Faultfinding	Matt. 7:3–5
Betrayal	Matt. 26:21	Daniel	Matt. 24:15	Faults	Matt. 18:15
Bigotry	Luke 18:9–14	Darkness	Luke 11:35	Fear of God	Matt. 10:28
Birds	Matt. 8:20	David	Matt. 12:3	Feast	Luke 14:8
Blasphemy	Matt. 12:31, 32	Day	John 11:9	Feet washing	John 13:12–15
Blessings	Matt. 5:3–11	Deaf	Matt. 13:13–15	Fellowship	Matt. 8:11
Blind guides	Matt. 15:14	Death	Luke 9:22	Flattery	Luke 6:26
Borrowing	Matt. 5:42		John 8:51	Flesh	John 6:53
Bread of life	John 6:32–35	Debts	Matt. 18:24	Flock	Matt. 26:31
Brothers	Matt. 23:8	Deceivers	Matt. 24:4, 5	Following	
Builders	Matt. 7:24	Decision	Matt. 6:24	Christ	Matt. 10:37, 38
	Luke 6:47–49	Defilement	Matt. 15:11,	Food	Matt. 6:11
Burdens	Luke 11:46		18, 19		Matt. 6:25
Burial	Matt. 8:22	Devil	Matt. 13:38, 39		John 6:27
Caesar	Matt. 22:21	Diligence	John 9:4	Fool	Matt. 5:22
Call of God	Matt. 20:16	Disbelief	John 5:38	Formalism	Matt. 23:23–28
Called ones	Matt. 22:14	Discernment	Matt. 16:2, 3	Forsaking all	Luke 14:33
Capital and		Discipleship	Luke 14:33	Foxes	Luke 9:58
labor	Matt. 20:1–15	Disputes	Mark 9:33, 34	Friends	Luke 11:5–8
Capital		Distress	Luke 21:23, 25	Frugality	John 6:12
punishment	Matt. 26:52	Divorce	Matt. 5:31, 32	Fruitfulness	Matt. 13:23
Care of God	Matt. 6:30, 33	Doctrine	Mark 7:7	Fruitlessness	Luke 13:6–9
Caution	Mark 4:24	Doubt	Matt. 21:21	**Generosity**	Matt. 25:34–40
Celibacy	Matt. 19:11, 12	Drunkard	Luke 7:34	Gentiles	Matt. 10:5–7

Subject	Reference	Subject	Reference	Subject	Reference
Gentleness	Matt. 5:5	Integrity	Luke 16:10	Murder	Matt. 15:19
Giving	Luke 6:38	Intercession	John 17:9	Mysteries	
Gladness	Luke 15:32	Investment	Matt. 6:19, 20	of Heaven	Matt. 13:11
Glorifying God	Matt. 5:16	Jealousy	Luke 15:25–30	Narrow way	Matt. 7:13, 14
Gluttony	Luke 21:34	John the Baptist	Luke 7:24–28	Neglect	Luke 12:47
God	Matt. 19:17, 26	Jonah	Matt. 12:39–41	Neighbor	Matt. 19:19
Godlessness	John 5:42, 44	Joy	Matt. 25:21	Neutrality	Matt. 12:30
Golden Rule	Matt. 7:12		Luke 15:7, 10	New birth	John 3:3, 5–8
Gospel	Luke 4:18	Judge not	Matt. 7:1, 2	Noah	Luke 17:26, 27
Grace	2 Cor. 12:9	Judgment	Matt. 11:24	Oath	Matt. 5:33–37
Greatness	Matt. 5:19	Judgment day	Matt. 25:31–46	Obedience	Matt. 12:50
Grumble	John 6:43	Justice	John 5:30	Offering	Matt. 5:25
Guidance	John 16:13	Justification,		Offerings	Luke 21:3, 4
Hairs numbered	Matt. 10:30	self	Luke 16:15	Opportunity	Matt. 5:25
Hand of God	John 10:27–29	Killing	Matt. 5:21, 22	Parables	Mark 4:11, 12
Happiness	Matt. 5:12	Kindness	Luke 10:30–35	Paradise	Luke 23:43
	John 13:16, 17	Kingdom	Luke 7:28	Pardoning	Luke 6:37
Harlots	Matt. 21:31		John 18:36	Parents	Matt. 10:21
Harvest	Matt. 9:37, 38	Kiss	Luke 7:45	Patriotism	Matt. 22:21
Hatred	John 15:18, 19	Knowledge	John 8:31, 32	Peace	Mark 9:50
Healing	Matt. 10:7, 8	Labor	Matt. 20:1–14	Peacemakers	Matt. 5:9
	Mark 2:17	Laughter	Luke 6:21	Penitence	Luke 18:13
Heart	Matt. 13:19	Law	Luke 16:16	Perception	John 8:43
Heaven	Luke 16:17	Lawsuit	Matt. 5:25, 40	Perfection	Matt. 5:48
	John 3:13	Lawyers	Luke 11:46	Persecution	Matt. 24:9
Hell	Matt. 5:22	Leaven	Matt. 16:6	Perseverance	Matt. 10:22
	Matt. 10:28		Luke 13:20, 21	Pharisaism	Matt. 23:2–33
Helper	John 14:16	Lending	Luke 6:34, 35	Pharisee and	
	John 15:26	Lepers	Matt. 10:7, 8	tax collector	Luke 18:10–14
Helpless	John 6:44	Levite	Luke 10:30–32	Pharisees	Matt. 5:20
Hireling	John 10:11–13	Liars	John 8:44, 45	Philanthropy	Luke 11:41
Holy Spirit	John 14:26	Liberality	Luke 6:30, 38	Physician	Matt. 9:12
Home	Mark 5:19	Liberty	Luke 4:18	Piety	John 1:47
Honesty	Mark 10:19	Life	Matt. 6:25	Pleasing God	John 8:29
	Luke 8:15		John 5:40	Pleasures	Luke 8:14
Honor of men	Matt. 6:2	Light	Luke 11:33	Poison	Mark 16:17, 18
Honor			John 8:12	Poll tax	Matt. 22:19–21
of parents	Matt. 15:3–6	Living water	John 4:10	Polygamy	Matt. 19:8, 9
Hospitality	Luke 14:12–14	Log	Luke 6:41, 42	Poor	Mark 14:7
Humility	Matt. 11:29	Loneliness	John 16:32	Power	Matt. 6:13
	John 13:14	Lord's Supper	Matt. 26:26–29	Prayer	Matt. 6:9–13
Hunger,		Loss of soul	Matt. 16:25, 26		Matt. 7:7–11
spiritual	Matt. 5:6	Lost		Preaching	Mark 16:15, 16
	Luke 6:21	opportunity	Matt. 25:7–12	Procrastination	Matt. 25:3
Hypocrisy	Matt. 6:5	Love	Matt. 22:37–40	Profit and loss	Matt. 16:26
	Luke 6:42	Lukewarmness	Matt. 26:40, 41	Prophets	Matt. 7:15
Ignorance	Matt. 22:29	Lunatic	Matt. 17:14, 15		Matt. 10:41
Immortality	Matt. 25:46	Lust	Mark 4:18, 19	Proselyte	Luke 23:15
	John 11:25, 26	Magistrates	Luke 12:11, 58	Protection	Luke 18:3
Impartiality		Mammon	Matt. 6:24	Providence	Matt. 6:25–33
of God	Matt. 5:45	Marriage	Matt. 19:4–6	Prudence	Matt. 10:16–20
Inconsistency	Matt. 7:3–5		Mark 12:25	Punishment	Matt. 21:41
	Luke 6:41, 42	Martyrdom	John 16:1–3	Purity	Matt. 5:8
Indecision	Luke 9:62	Mary's choice	Luke 10:41, 42	Ransom	Matt. 20:28
Indifference	Matt. 24:12	Memorial	Matt. 26:13	Reaping	John 4:35–38
Industry	John 4:36	Mercy	Matt. 5:7	Receiving	
Infidelity	John 3:18		Luke 16:24	Christ	Mark 9:37
Influence	Matt. 5:13	Minister	Luke 10:2	Reconciliation	Matt. 5:23, 24
Ingratitude	Luke 17:17, 18	Miracles	Matt. 12:28	Regeneration	Matt. 19:28
Innocence	Matt. 10:16	Money lender,		Rejecting	
Insincerity	Luke 16:15	creditor	Luke 7:41, 42	Christ	John 3:18
Inspiration	Luke 12:12	Moses	Matt. 19:8	Rejoicing	Luke 10:20
Instability	Matt. 7:26, 27	Moses' Law	John 7:19	Release	Luke 4:18
Instruction	John 6:45	Mother	Matt. 10:37	Religion	Matt. 25:34–36
Insufficiency	Mark 10:21	Mourn	Matt. 5:4		Mark 7:6–8

Subject	Reference	Subject	Reference	Subject	Reference
Repentance	Matt. 11:21	Self-sacrifice	Matt. 16:25	Teaching	Matt. 28:19, 20
	Luke 13:28	Serpents	Matt. 23:33		John 13:13–15
Reproof	Matt. 11:21–23		John 3:14	Temperance	Luke 21:34
Resignation	Matt. 26:39	Service	Luke 22:27	Temptations	Matt. 4:1–11
Responsibility	Luke 12:47, 48	Sheep	Luke 15:4–7		Luke 8:13
Rest	Matt. 11:28–30	Shepherd	John 10:1–18	Thieves	Matt. 6:19
	Matt. 26:45	Sickness	Matt. 10:8		John 10:1, 8
Resurrection	John 6:40	Signs	Luke 11:16	Timidity	Mark 4:40
Retaliation	Matt. 5:39–44		John 4:48	Tithes	Luke 18:11, 12
Retribution	Matt. 23:34, 35	Silence	Matt. 17:9	Traditions	Mark 7:9, 13
Reward	Matt. 10:42	Sin	Matt. 26:28	Transgres-	
Riches	Mark 4:19		John 8:34	sions	Matt. 15:2
Righteousness	Matt. 5:6, 20	Sincerity	Matt. 5:13–16	Treasures	Matt. 6:19–21
	John 16:10	Skepticism	John 20:27, 29	Tribulation	Matt. 24:9
Robbers	Luke 10:30	Slaves	Matt. 18:23		John 16:33
	John 10:1		John 15:15	Truth	John 14:6
Robbery	Matt. 23:25	Sleep	Mark 4:26, 27	Unbelievers	Luke 12:46
Sabbath	Matt. 12:5–8		Mark 13:35, 36	Uncharitable-	
Sackcloth	Matt. 11:21	Slothfulness	Matt. 25:26–30	ness	John 7:24
Sacrifice	Matt. 12:7	Son of Man	Luke 9:22	Unchastity	Matt. 5:31, 32
Sacrilege	Matt. 21:13	Sorrow	Matt. 19:22	Uncleanness	Matt. 23:27
Sadducees	Matt. 16:6		John 16:6	Unity	John 17:20, 21
Salt	Matt. 5:13	Soul	Matt. 10:28	Unpardonable	
	Mark 9:50		Luke 12:19, 20	sin	Matt. 12:31, 32
Salvation	Luke 19:19	Soul winners	Matt. 4:19	Vengeance	Matt. 5:39, 40
	John 4:22	Sowing	Mark 4:14	Vine	John 15:1, 4, 5
Samaritan	Luke 10:30–35	Speech	John 8:43	Visions	Matt. 17:9
Sanctification	John 17:17	Spirit	Matt. 26:41	Walks of Life	John 8:12
Satan	Matt. 4:10		Mark 5:8		John 12:35
	Mark 4:15	Statement	Matt. 5:37	War	Matt. 24:26
Scripture	Matt. 21:42	Steadfastness	Matt. 10:22	Watchfulness	Matt. 24:42, 44
	Luke 4:21	Stealing	Matt. 19:18		Luke 12:37–40
Secrecy	Luke 12:2, 3	Steward	Luke 12:42, 43	Wedding	Luke 14:8–10
Security	Luke 6:47, 48		Luke 16:1–8	Widow	Mark 12:43, 44
Seduction	Mark 13:22	Stewardship	Luke 19:13–27	Wine	Luke 5:37–39
Seeking the		Stomach	Matt. 15:17	Wisdom	Luke 21:15
kingdom	Matt. 6:19, 20	Strife	Luke 22:24	Witness	John 8:14
Self-		Stubborn-		Witness, false	Matt. 19:18
condemnation	Matt. 23:29–32	ness	John 5:40	Witnessing	Acts 1:8
	Luke 19:20–24	Stumbling		Wives	Luke 14:20, 26
Self-control	Matt. 5:21	block	Matt. 23:13	Worker	Matt. 10:10
Self-deception	Luke 12:16–21	Submission	Matt. 26:39, 42	Worldliness	Luke 21:34
Self-denial	Matt. 16:24–26	Suffering	Matt. 26:38	Worm	Mark 9:43–48
Self-exaltation	Matt. 23:12	Supper,		Worries	
Self-		The Lord's	Luke 22:14–20	of the world	Matt. 13:22
examination	Matt. 7:3–5	Swearing	Matt. 23:16–22	Worship	Matt. 4:10
Selfishness	Luke 6:32–35	Talents	Matt. 18:24	Yoke	Matt. 11:28, 29
Self-		Taxes	Matt. 22:19–21	Zacchaeus	Luke 19:5
righteousness	Matt. 23:23–27	Tax collectors	Matt. 5:46, 47	Zeal	John 2:17

THE MIRACLES
OF JESUS CHRIST

Miracle	Matthew	Mark	Luke	John
1. Cleansing a Leper	8:2	1:40	5:12	
2. Healing a Centurion's Servant (of paralysis)	8:5		7:1	
3. Healing Peter's Mother-in-law	8:14	1:30	4:38	
4. Healing the Sick at Evening	8:16	1:32	4:40	
5. Stilling the Storm	8:23	4:35	8:22	
6. Devils Entering a Herd of Swine	8:28	5:1	8:26	
7. Healing a Paralytic	9:2	2:3	5:18	
8. Raising the Ruler's Daughter	9:18, 23	5:22, 35	8:40, 49	
9. Healing the Hemorrhaging Woman	9:20	5:25	8:43	
10. Healing Two Blind Men	9:27			
11. Curing a Devil-possessed, Dumb Man	9:32			
12. Healing a Man's Withered Hand	12:9	3:1	6:6	
13. Curing a Devil-possessed, Blind and Dumb Man	12:22		11:14	
14. Feeding the Five Thousand	14:13	6:30	9:10	6:1
15. Walking on the Sea	14:25	6:48		6:19
16. Healing the Gentile Woman's Daughter	15:21	7:24		
17. Feeding the Four Thousand	15:32	8:1		
18. Healing the Epileptic Boy	17:14	9:17	9:38	
19. Temple Tax in the Fish's Mouth	17:24			
20. Healing Two Blind Men	20:30	10:46	18:35	
21. Withering the Fig Tree	21:18	11:12		
22. Casting Out an Unclean Spirit		1:23	4:33	
23. Healing a Deaf and Dumb Man		7:31		
24. Healing a Blind Paralytic at Bethsaida		8:22		
25. Escape from the Hostile Multitude			4:30	
26. Draught of Fish			5:1	
27. Raising of a Widow's Son at Nain			7:11	
28. Healing the Infirm, Bowed Woman			13:11	
29. Healing the Man with Dropsy			14:1	
30. Cleansing the Ten Lepers			17:11	
31. Restoring a Servant's Ear			22:51	
32. Turning Water into Wine				2:1
33. Healing the Nobleman's Son (of fever)				4:46
34. Healing an Infirm Man at Bethesda				5:1
35. Healing the Man Born Blind				9:1
36. Raising of Lazarus				11:43
37. Second Draught of Fish				21:1

GOD'S ANSWERS TO MAN'S CONCERNS

Abiding in Christ—John 15:5;
1 John 2:28; 2 John 9

Abundance—Deut. 30:9;
John 10:10; 2 Cor. 9:8

Afflictions—Job 5:17;
2 Cor. 4:17; Heb. 12:11

Anger—Ps. 37:8; Prov. 16:32;
James 1:19

Answered Prayer—
1 Kin. 18:37; Ps. 91:15;
Luke 11:9

Backsliding—Prov. 14:14;
Matt. 24:12; Heb. 10:38

Be Still Before God—
Num. 9:8; Job 37:14;
Ps. 46:10

Believers Preserved—
John 10:28; 17:11;
Phil. 4:6, 7

Benevolence—Prov. 25:21;
Matt. 5:42; Acts 20:35

Chastisement—Deut. 8:5;
Prov. 3:11, 12; Rev. 3:19

Cheerfulness—Prov. 15:13;
John 16:33; Acts 27:25

Christ's Love—John 13:1;
Rom. 8:35; 1 John 3:16

Christ's Majesty—John 18:6;
2 Thess. 2:8; Rev. 1:17

Christian Duty—
Matt. 25:35, 36; Rom. 15:1;
1 Cor. 9:22

Confessing Christ—
Matt. 10:32; Rom. 10:9;
1 John 4:15

Contentment—Prov. 15:16;
Phil. 4:11; Heb. 13:5

Courage—Josh. 1:9;
Dan. 3:16, 17; Phil. 1:28

Death (Physical)—
Luke 16:19–26; Rom. 5:12;
Heb. 9:27

Death (Spiritual)—Gen. 2:17;
John 5:24; Rom. 5:12; 6:23;
Eph. 2:1–3

Divine Comfort—Is. 40:1;
Is. 61:1, 2; John 14:1

Divine Deliverance—
Dan. 6:22; Job 5:19;
2 Tim. 4:18

Divine Enabling—2 Cor. 9:8;
Phil. 4:13; 1 Tim. 1:12

Divine Encouragement—
Is. 41:13; Matt. 9:2;
Acts 23:11

Divine Faithfulness—Ps. 36:5;
1 Cor. 1:9; 1 Pet. 4:19

Divine Fellowship—
Matt. 18:20; Luke 24:15;
Rev. 3:20

Divine Guidance—
Ps. 25:9; 48:14; Is. 42:16

Divine Power—Rom. 4:21;
Eph. 3:20; Jude 24, 25

Divine Providence—Ps. 23:5;
Matt. 14:20; Luke 6:38

Divine Reward—Gen. 15:1;
Ps. 19:9, 11; Matt. 6:4

Divine Sympathy—
Ps. 103:13; John 11:35, 36;
Heb. 4:15

Divisions—Luke 11:17;
1 Cor. 1:10; 3:3

Doubt—Matt. 14:31;
Mark 4:40; Luke 24:25

Dying to Live—Luke 9:24;
John 12:24; Gal. 2:20

Enemies of the Soul—
Luke 22:31; Eph. 6:12;
1 Pet. 5:8

Evil Relationships—Ex. 23:2;
Ps. 1:1; 2 Cor. 6:14

Faith—Rom. 10:17; Gal. 5:16;
Eph. 2:8

Fear of God—Josh. 24:14;
Eccl. 12:13; 1 Pet. 2:17

Fear of Man—Prov. 29:25;
Is. 51:12; John 12:42

Foolishness—Ps. 53:1;
Prov. 15:14; 18:13

Forgiveness—Ps. 130:4;
Matt. 6:14; Acts 5:31

Fruitfulness—Matt. 3:8;
Luke 19:23; John 15:8

Gain Through Loss—
Matt. 19:29; John 12:24;
Phil. 3:8

Gentleness—1 Thess. 2:7;
1 Tim. 2:24; James 3:17

God Our Refuge—Ps. 57:1;
Is. 25:4; 51:16

God's Care for You—
Gen. 28:15; Ps. 121:4;
2 Tim. 1:12

God's Drawing Power—
Jer. 31:3; John 6:44; 12:32

God's Grace—
Rom. 4:16; 9:16; Titus 3:5

God's Love for You—
John 3:16; 1 Pet. 1:18, 19;
Rev. 1:5

Greed—Eccl. 5:10;
Matt. 27:5; 1 Tim. 6:9

Heaven—Matt. 6:20;
Luke 10:20; John 14:2, 3

Hell—Matt. 13:41, 42; 25:41;
Rev. 20:10, 14, 15; 21:8

Hospitality—Rom. 12:13;
Titus 1:8; Heb. 13:2

Humility—Mic. 6:8;
Luke 22:26; Rom. 12:3

Intercession—Is. 53:12;
Luke 22:32; John 17:9

Joy—Neh. 8:10; Ps. 16:11;
John 16:24

Kindness—Rom. 12:10;
1 Cor. 13:14; Eph. 4:32

Liberty—Is. 61:1; Rom. 8:2;
2 Cor. 3:17

Light in Darkness—Is. 60:1;
Mal. 4:2; 2 Pet. 1:19

Living Temples—1 Cor. 3:16;
Eph. 2:20; 1 Pet. 2:5

Living for God—
Rom. 6:11; 14:8; 2 Cor. 5:15

Looking to God—Ps. 34:5;
John 17:1; Acts 7:55

Love to Neighbors—
Mark 12:31; Rom. 13:10;
James 2:8

Man's Unfaithfulness—
Matt. 26:56; John 6:66;
1 John 2:19

Mercy—Prov. 11:17;
Matt. 5:7; Luke 6:36

Obedience—Josh. 11:15;
2 Kin. 18:6; Acts 26:19

Our Eternal Home—
John 14:2; 2 Cor. 5:1;
Rev. 7:9

Patience—Ps. 40:1; Is. 33:2;
Acts 1:4

Popularity—John 12:43;
Acts 24:7; Col. 3:22

Postponed Blessing—Ps. 40:1;
Is. 25:9; Acts 1:4

Power of Prayer—
Matt. 17:21; 21:22;
John 15:7

Praise to God—Ps. 67:3;
Heb. 13:15; 1 Pet. 2:9

Prayerfulness—
Luke 2:37; 6:12;
1 Thess. 3:10

Prayerlessness—Is. 43:22;
Dan. 9:13; Zeph. 1:6

Pride—2 Chr. 32:25;

Prov. 16:18; 1 John 2:16
Promises to the Righteous—
Job 36:7; Ps. 34:15;
Matt. 13:43
Prosperity of the Godly—
Deut. 29:9; Neh. 2:20;
Ps. 1:3
Prudence—Prov. 12:23; 14:15;
Hos. 14:9
Repentance—Luke 13:2, 3;
Acts 3:19; 17:30
Reverence—Ex. 3:5; Ps. 4:4;
Hab. 2:20
Salvation—John 3:16;
Rom. 10:9–13; Eph. 2:8–10
Satisfaction in God—
Ps. 17:15; 107:9; Is. 58:11
Seeking God—Job 23:3;
Jer. 29:13; Acts 17:27
Self-Denial—Matt. 16:24;
Luke 14:26, 27; Rom. 15:1
Simplicity—Ps. 131:2;
1 Cor. 14:20; 1 Pet. 2:2
Sin and Confession—
Prov. 28:13; Jer. 3:13;
1 John 1:9
Spiritual Blindness—
Is. 59:10; Matt. 15:14;
2 Cor. 4:4
Spiritual Carelessness—
Is. 32:9; 47:8; Amos 6:1
Spiritual Cleansing—Is. 1:16;
2 Cor. 7:1; 2 Tim. 2:21
Spiritual Fullness—
John 15:11; Eph. 3:19;
Col. 1:19

Spiritual Growth—Eph. 4:15;
1 Thess. 3:12; 1 Pet. 2:2
Spiritual Hearing—
Prov. 8:34; Luke 8:15;
James 1:19
Spiritual Hindrances—
Gen. 19:26; Matt. 13:58;
Heb. 12:1
Spiritual Hope—Rom. 4:18;
Prov. 14:32; Heb. 16:18, 19
Spiritual Imperatives—
Luke 13:2; John 3:5; 4:24
Spiritual Longing—
Ps. 42:2; 63:1; 143:6
Spiritual Nourishment—
Is. 55:2; John 6:51; Rev. 2:7
Spiritual Power—Zech. 4:6;
Acts 1:8; 6:8
Spiritual Rest—Ex. 33:14;
Ps. 116:7; Matt. 11:29
Spiritual Security—Job 11:18;
Ps. 91:5; 1 Pet. 3:13
Spiritual Stability—
2 Kin. 22:2; Job 23:11;
Acts 20:24
Spiritual Strength—
Is. 40:31; 41:10; Eph. 3:16
Spiritual Thirst—Ps. 63:1;
Is. 1:30; 41:17
Spiritual Treasure—
Matt. 6:29; 19:21; Phil. 3:8
Spiritual Understanding—
1 Kin. 3:9; 1 Cor. 2:14;
Heb. 5:14
Steadfastness—1 Cor. 15:58;
Gal. 5:1; 2 Pet. 3:17

Strength in Weakness—
1 Cor. 1:27; 2 Cor. 12:9;
Heb. 11:33, 34
Suffering for Christ—
Acts 5:41; Rom. 8:17;
1 Pet. 2:20
Teachability—Matt. 18:3;
Luke 11:1; Acts 8:31
Thankfulness—Ps. 100:4;
Col. 1:12; 1 Thess. 5:18
The Primacy of Love—
John 13:35; 1 Cor. 13:1;
1 John 3:14
True Life—Matt. 4:4;
John 6:63; Phil. 2:16
True Religion—Deut. 10:12;
Eccl. 12:13; James 1:27
True Wisdom—Job 28:28;
2 Tim. 3:15; James 3:17
Unworldliness—Rom. 12:2;
1 Cor. 7:31; 2 Tim. 2:4
Value of Godliness—
Deut. 4:40; Is. 3:10;
1 Tim. 6:6
**When You Reach
Desperation—**Ps. 116:6;
Mark 4:38, 40;
Acts 27:20, 22
Worldliness—Matt. 16:26;
Col. 3:2; Titus 2:12
Worship—1 Chr. 16:29;
Ps. 95:6; John 4:24
Zeal—Eccl. 9:10;
1 Cor. 14:12; 2 Tim. 1:6

PRAYERS OF THE BIBLE

Subject	Reference	Subject	Reference
Abijah's army—for victory	2 Chr. 13:14	Jehoahaz—for victory	2 Kin. 13:1–5
Abraham—for a son	Gen. 15:1–6	Jehoshaphat—	
Abraham—for Ishmael	Gen. 17:18–21	for protection	2 Chr. 20:5–12, 27
Abraham—for Sodom	Gen. 18:20–32	Jehoshaphat—for victory	2 Chr. 18:31
Abraham—for Abimelech	Gen. 20:17	Jeremiah—for Judah	Jer. 42:1–6
Abraham's servant—		Jeremiah—for mercy	Jer. 14:7–10
for guidance	Gen. 24:12–52	Jesus—Lord's Prayer	Matt. 6:9–13
Asa—for victory	2 Chr. 14:11	Jesus—praise for revelation	
Cain—for mercy	Gen. 4:13–15	to babes	Matt. 11:25, 26
Centurion—for his servant	Matt. 8:5–13	Jesus—at Lazarus' tomb	John 11:41, 42
Christians—for Peter	Acts 12:5–12	Jesus—for the Father's	
Christians—for kings		glory	John 12:28
in authority	1 Tim. 2:1, 2	Jesus—for the Church	John 17:1–26
Corinthians—for Paul	2 Cor. 1:9–11	Jesus—for deliverance	Matt. 26:39, 42, 44
Cornelius—			Matt. 27:46
for enlightenment	Acts 10:1–33	Jesus—for forgiveness	
Criminal—for salvation	Luke 23:42, 43	for others	Luke 23:34
Daniel—for the Jews	Dan. 9:3–19	Jesus—in submission	Luke 23:46
Daniel—for knowledge	Dan. 2:17–23	Jews—for safe journey	Ezra 8:21, 23
David—for blessing	2 Sam. 7:18–29	Jonah—for deliverance	
David—for help	1 Sam. 23:10–13	from the fish	Jon. 2:1–10
David—for guidance	2 Sam. 2:1	Joshua—for help	
David—for grace	Ps. 25:16	and mercy	Josh. 7:6–9
David—for justice	Ps. 9:17–20	Leper—for healing	Matt. 8:2, 3
Disciples—for boldness	Acts 4:24–31	Manasseh—	
Elijah—for drought		for deliverance	2 Chr. 33:12, 13
and rain	James 5:17, 18	Manoah—for guidance	Judg. 13:8–15
Elijah—for the raising to		Moses—for Pharaoh	Ex. 8:9–13
life of the widow's son	1 Kin. 17:20–23	Moses—for water	Ex. 15:24, 25
Elijah—for triumph		Moses—for Israel	Ex. 32:31–35
over Baal	1 Kin. 18:36–38	Moses—for Miriam	Num. 12:11–14
Elijah—for death	1 Kin. 19:4	Moses—that he might see	Deut. 3:23–25
Elisha—for blindness		the Promised Land	Deut. 34:1–4
and sight	2 Kin. 6:17–23	Moses—for a successor	Num. 27:15–17
Ezekiel—for undefilement	Ezek. 4:12–15	Nehemiah—for the Jews	Neh. 1:4–11
Ezra—for the sins		Paul—for the healing	
of the people	Ezra 9:6–15	of Publius' father	Acts 28:8
Gideon—for proof		Paul—for the Ephesians	Eph. 3:14–21
of his call	Judg. 6:36–40	Paul—for grace	2 Cor. 12:8, 9
Habakkuk—		People of Judah—	
for deliverance	Hab. 3:1–19	for a covenant	2 Chr. 15:12–15
Habakkuk—for justice	Hab. 1:1–4	Peter—for the raising	
Hagar—for consolation	Gen. 21:14–20	of Dorcas	Acts 9:40
Hannah—for a son	1 Sam. 1:10–17	Priests—for blessing	2 Chr. 30:27
Hezekiah—for deliverance	2 Kin. 19:15–19	Rebekah—	
Hezekiah—for health	2 Kin. 20:1–11	for understanding	Gen. 25:22, 23
Holy Spirit—		Reubenites—	
for Christians	Rom. 8:26, 27	for victory	1 Chr. 5:18–20
Isaac—for children	Gen. 25:21, 24–26	Samson—for water	Judg. 15:18, 19
Israelites—for deliverance	Ex. 2:23–25	Samson—for strength	Judg. 16:29, 30
	Ex. 3:7–10	Samuel—for Israel	1 Sam. 7:5–12
Jabez—for prosperity	1 Chr. 4:10	Solomon—for wisdom	1 Kin. 3:6–14
Jacob—all night	Gen. 32:24–30	Tax collector—	
Jacob—for deliverance		for mercy	Luke 18:13
from Esau	Gen. 32:9–12	Zechariah—for a son	Luke 1:13

THE LAWS OF THE BIBLE

BETWEEN THE TESTAMENTS

The four hundred years between the prophecy of Malachi and the advent of Christ are frequently described as "silent," but they were in fact crowded with activity. Although no inspired prophet arose in Israel during those centuries, and the Old Testament was regarded as complete, events took place which gave to later Judaism its distinctive ideology and providentially prepared the way for the coming of Christ and the proclamation of His gospel.

The Persian Period

The Jews fared well under Persian rule. Cyrus had given them permission to return to Jerusalem and rebuild their temple and, although they met opposition from the inhabitants of Palestine, it was dedicated during the reign of Darius the Great. Ezra, the scribe, and Nehemiah, the layman, sought to strengthen the Palestinian Jewish community and encourage their loyalty to the Law of God. For about a century-and-a-half after Nehemiah's time, the Persian Empire exercised control over Judaea, and the Jews were permitted to observe their religious ordinances without interference. Judaea was ruled by high priests who were responsible to the Persian government, a fact which insured the Jews a large measure of autonomy. At the same time, however, it made a political office of the priesthood and sowed the seeds of future trouble. Contests for the office of high priest were marked by jealousy, intrigue, and even murder. **Johanan, son of Joiada** (Neh. 12:22), is reported to have slain his brother, Joshua, within the temple precincts.

Johanan was succeeded as high priest by his brother, **Jaddua**, whose brother Manasseh, according to Josephus, married the daughter of **Sanballat, governor of Samaria.** It was at this time that a Samaritan temple was built on Mount Gerizim which, rather than Zion, was regarded as sacred by the Samaritan community. The sanctuary on Mount Gerizim was destroyed by the Hasmonaean ruler John Hyrcanus (134–104 B.C.), but the mount itself continues to this day to be regarded as sacred by the Samaritans. The woman of Samaria wished to dispute with Jesus concerning the merits of the rival holy places, but the Saviour chose to emphasize the spiritual attitude of the worshiper rather than the place of worship (cf. John 4:20). The Sanballat of Josephus cannot have been the same individual as the man of the same name mentioned by Nehemiah (4:1). Josephus does, however, appear to reflect a valid tradition, for a temple seems to have been built on Mount Gerizim about this time. (In 1969 the Samaritans numbered fewer than 300.)

Persia's failure to conquer Greece encouraged subject peoples to seek their independence.

Egypt was constantly atte[...] Persian yoke, and Judae[...] tween the two powers, co[...] throw off the ment. During the reign of A[...]hically be-many Jews were implicated[...]e involve-sia. When it failed, the Pers[...] Ochus), Babylonia and the southern [...]st Per-Sea.

Jews had long been in E[...]n to murder of Gedaliah, the pr[...]an forced to join a group of ref[...] asylum at Tahpanhes in the [...] 43:4–13), and other Judaean [...] their way to Egypt to avoid capt[...] **nezzar.** Migration continued d[...] Period, and by the fifth centur[...] Jewish colony of mercenary sold[...] at **Elephantine Island,** near mode[...] the First Cataract of the Nile. Cont[...] Mosaic Law, these colonists built a te[...] themselves, and they combined their devot[...] the God of their fathers with pagan elements. [...] **Elephantine Jews** had correspondence with the Samaritans as well as the Judaeans.

Alexander the Great

Persia never succeeded in subduing the Greeks, but an heir of Greek culture, **Alexander of Macedon,** eventually brought to an end the Persian Empire. Alexander was not simply a power-mad despot. A pupil of the philosopher Aristotle, he was thoroughly convinced that Greek culture was the one force that could unify the world. In 333 B.C. he passed from Macedonia into Asia Minor and defeated the Persian armies stationed there. Then he moved southward through Syria and Palestine to Egypt. Tyre and Gaza each offered stubborn resistance, but delays did not discourage Alexander, they simply strengthened his determination to win. There was no need for a campaign against the Jews, and legend makes Alexander a friend of the Jewish people. Jaddua, the high priest, is said to have come out to meet Alexander, telling him of Daniel's prophecy that the Greek army would be victorious (Dan. 8). Although historians do not take the story seriously, it does illustrate the friendly feelings between the Jews and the Macedonian conqueror. Alexander permitted the Jews to observe their laws, granted them exemption from tribute during sabbatical years, and, when he built **Alexandria** in Egypt (331 B.C.), he encouraged Jews to settle there and gave them privileges comparable to those of his Greek subjects.

Alexander was welcomed into Egypt as a deliverer from Persian oppression. His victorious armies retraced their steps through Palestine and Syria, then moved eastward. The cities of Babylonia

ander and he pressed on as
BETWEEN THE T ,on of India. Although mighty
and Persia fell ellenistic culture rather than
far as the P what was Alexander's legacy to
in battle He determined to found a new
Macel ntry of his empire, which would
th a whole along Greek lines. Mate-
ig, this meant the erection of fine
dings, a gymnasium for games, an
neater, and whatever would approxi-
life of a Greek city-state. Individuals
buraged to take Greek names, adopt
ress and language—in short, to become
ized.

material aspects of **Hellenism** must have
ed attractive for large segments of the popu-
n. Trade and commerce brought wealth to the
w merchant class. Libraries and schools were
elcomed by the scholar. Better housing and bet-
er food brought about a rise in the standard of
living. Many in Israel, as elsewhere, were glad to
accept this veneer of Greek culture. If idolatry
had been the stumbling block to Israel in the pre-
exilic period, Hellenism was the great postexilic
temptation. A third-century B.C. writer observed, "In recent times, under the foreign rule of
the Persians, and then of the Macedonians, by
whom the Persian Empire was overthrown, inter-
mingling with other races has led to many of the
traditional Jewish ordinances losing their hold."
Many Jews took Greek names, accepted a school
of Greek philosophy, and tried to combine the
wisdom of Greece with the faith of their fathers.
Others resisted Hellenism and became more and
more engrossed in the study of their Law.

At the age of thirty-three, Alexander died in
Babylon. For a number of years the future of the
Near East was uncertain, but the generals succeeded in dividing the Empire among themselves
and the tide of Hellenism increased. While the
Ptolemies of Egypt and the Seleucids of Syria
fought among themselves for land and power,
they were in complete agreement concerning
their social and cultural mission. The historian
W. W. Tarn says that Alexander "so changed the
world [that] nothing after him could be as it was
before."

The Ptolemies

Following the death of Alexander, Judaea was
first subject to Antigonus, one of his generals, but
it quickly fell to another general, **Ptolemy I, surnamed Soter, "Deliverer,"** who seized Jerusalem
on a Sabbath day in 320 B.C. Ptolemy, whose kingdom centered in Egypt, dealt kindly with the
Jews. Many of them settled in Alexandria, which
continued to be an important center of Jewish
thought for many centuries. Under **Ptolemy II**

(**Philadelphus**) the Alexandrian Jews translated
their Old Testament into Greek. This translation
was later known as the Septuagint from the legend of seventy (more correctly seventy-two, six
from each of the twelve tribes) who were sent
from Judaea to produce the Greek translation of
the Hebrew Scriptures.

The Jews in Palestine enjoyed a period of prosperity during Ptolemaic times. Tribute tax was
paid to the government in Egypt, but local affairs
were administered by high priests who had been
responsible for governing their people since Persian times. The greatest figure among the Jews of
the Ptolemaic period was **Simon the Just**, the
high priest who is the subject of highest praise in
the apocryphal book of Ecclesiasticus, which calls
him, "Great among his brethren and the glory of
his people." He is credited with rebuilding the
walls of Jerusalem, which had been demolished
by Ptolemy I, and is said to have repaired the
temple and directed the excavation of a great reservoir to provide fresh water for Jerusalem in
times of drought and siege. In addition to his reputation as high priest, Simon is also regarded as
one of the great teachers of ancient Judaism. His
favorite maxim was, "The world rests on three
things, on the Law, on Divine Service, and on
Charity" (*Pirke Aboth*, i. 2). The identity of Simon
the Just poses a historical problem. A high priest
known as Simon I lived during the middle of the
third century, and Simon II lived about 200 B.C.
One of these is doubtless the Simon the Just of
Jewish tradition and legend.

During Ptolemaic times the priestly families of
Onias and **Tobias** became bitter rivals. The house
of Tobias was pro-Egyptian and represented the
wealthy class of Jerusalem society. It may have
been related to Tobiah the Ammonite (Neh. 2:10;
4:3, 7; 6:1–19), who gave so much trouble to
Nehemiah. A papyrus from the time of Ptolemy II
speaks of a Jew named Tobias, who was a cavalry
commander in the Ptolemaic army stationed at
Ammanitis, east of the Jordan. Archaeologists
have discovered a mausoleum with the name "Tobiah" from the third century B.C. at Araq el-Emir
in central Jordan. The Tobiahs are thought to have
been tax collectors, occupying the same function
as the New Testament tax gatherers.

Josephus states that Onias II refused to pay
Ptolemy IV twenty talents of silver, which was
evidently the tribute tax demanded of the high
priests. By refusing payment, Onias seems to
have renounced allegiance to Ptolemy. Joseph, a
member of the house of Tobias, then succeeded in
having himself appointed tax collector for the
whole of Palestine. The tax collector had to go to
Alexandria each year to bid for the renewal of the
license to gather taxes. Joseph held this influential post for twenty years, under the Ptolemies
and, after the victory of Antiochus III, under the
Seleucids.

The Seleucids

The Syrian rulers are termed Seleucids because their kingdom, one of the successor states to Alexander's empire, was founded by **Seleucus I (Nicator)**. Most of the early rulers bore the names of Seleucus or Antiochus, and they ruled from Antioch on the Orontes River. The energetic ruler Antiochus III, surnamed "the Great," waged a series of battles with Egypt until, in 199 B.C., he wrested Palestine from the Ptolemies after the Battle of Panion, near the sources of the Jordan River. This marked the beginning of a new era of Jewish history for, while the Ptolemies had been tolerant of Jewish institutions, the Seleucids determined to enforce Hellenism on the Jews.

The crisis came during the reign of **Antiochus IV, surnamed Epiphanes,** who found allies in the Hellenistic party in Judaea. In the early days of the reign of Antiochus IV, Jerusalem was ruled by the high priest, Onias III, a descendant of Simon the Just and a strictly orthodox Jew. The Jews, who looked with favor on Greek culture, opposed Onias and espoused the cause of his brother, Jason. By promising large tribute to Antiochus, Jason succeeded in having himself appointed high priest. Although Antiochus looked upon the high priesthood as a political office which he had a right to fill as he pleased, pious Jews thought of the priesthood as divine in origin and considered its sale to the highest bidder a sin against God.

Jason encouraged the Hellenists who had sought his election. A gymnasium was built in Jerusalem, Greek names became commonplace, and Hebrew orthodoxy was considered obscurantist and obsolete. Yet, Jason argued with his close companion and fellow-Hellenist, **Menelaus,** of the tribe of Benjamin, who offered higher tribute to Antiochus than that paid by Jason, and had himself installed as high priest.

The orthodox Jews, who had been scandalized when Jason was named high priest, were more deeply disturbed when Menelaus, a Benjamite with no claim to priestly office, was installed. Jason raised an army to back his claim to the high priesthood, and Menelaus courted the favor of Antiochus. The Syrians, who were campaigning against Egypt, felt it essential to maintain effective control of Palestine. Antiochus staged a sneak attack on Jerusalem one Sabbath day (when the orthodox would not fight) and slaughtered a large number of the enemies of Menelaus. The city walls were destroyed, and a new fortress, the Akra, was built on the site of the citadel.

Antiochus was determined to remove all traces of orthodox Jewish faith. Israel's God was identified with Jupiter, and a bearded image of the pagan deity (perhaps in the likeness of Antiochus) was erected on the temple altar, where swine were offered in sacrifice. Jews were forbidden, under penalty of death, to practice circumcision,

Sabbath observance, or t[...] Feasts of the Jewish calend[...] tures were ordered destroy[...] forced with the utmost cru[...] named Eleazar was flogged [...] would not eat swine's flesh. [...]

By force of arms, Menelau[...] priest and the Hellenizing par[...] Yet, the Hellenizers had gone [...] zeal to annihilate the old order[...] undoing. The orthodox were [...] their faith, but not all were con[...] should die passively.

The Maccabean Revolt

The oppressed Jews were not lo[...] champion. When the emissaries of [...] rived at the village of Modin, about [...] west of Jerusalem, they expected the age[...] **Mattathias,** to set a good example to his peo[...] coming forward to offer a pagan sacrifice. Wh[...] Mattathias refused, a timid Jew came forward to perform the sacrifice. The enraged priest approached the altar and killed both the apostate Jew and the emissary of Antiochus. With his five sons, Mattathias destroyed the heathen altar and then fled to the hills to avoid reprisal. Others of orthodox persuasion joined the family of Mattathias in waging guerrilla warfare on the Syrians and the Hellenistic Jews who supported them. The orthodox would not fight on the Sabbath day, with the result that they were at a distinct military disadvantage. On one Sabbath, a group of the orthodox was surrounded and murdered, for they would not defend themselves. Following this episode, Mattathias suggested the principle that fighting in self-defense was permissible on the Sabbath day.

Soon after the beginning of the revolt, Mattathias died. He had urged his followers to choose as military leader his third son, **Judas (Hebrew Judah), known as "the Maccabee,"** a word usually interpreted to mean "the hammer." The choice was a good one, for more and more Jews rallied to the cause. The Maccabees, as the followers of Judas were called, were able to hold their own against a series of Syrian armies thrown against them. By a surprise night attack, Judas annihilated an army of Syrians and Hellenistically minded Jews at Emmaus, and then marched toward Jerusalem with the booty he had seized. The Maccabees entered the city and took everything except the Akra. They entered the temple and removed all the signs of paganism which had been installed there. The altar dedicated to Jupiter was removed and a new altar erected to Israel's God. The statue of Jupiter was ground to dust. Beginning with the twenty-fifth of Kislev (December), they celebrated an eight-day Feast of Dedication, known as Hanukkah, the Festival of Lights. In this way they marked the end of the three-year

BETWEEN TH

n the temple had been dese-
crated.

period duri rt-lived. The Syrian general,
i the Maccabees in a battle near
l besieged the city. During the
Pea r, Lysias learned of trouble at home
Ly offer of peace to the Jews. The laws
observance of Judaism would be re-
d Syria would refrain from interference
ernal affairs of Judaea. Menelaus was to
ved from office and the high priesthood
o a mild Hellenizer named **Alcimus.** Lysias
sed that Judas and his followers would not
unished. However, the walls of Jerusalem
ld be destroyed.

A council comprising Maccabean army officers,
espected scribes, and elders of the orthodox
party was convened at Jerusalem to determine
the action to be taken. Against the counsel of
Judas, the peace terms were accepted. Alcimus
became high priest; Menelaus was executed, and
Judas left the city with a few followers. The fears of
Judas proved correct, for Alcimus seized and executed many of the orthodox party. Loyal Jews
again turned to Judas and civil war was renewed.
Judas, with an ill-equipped army of eight hundred men, met a large Syrian army and died in
battle. Thus, the first phase of the Maccabean
struggle was ended.

Jonathan, a brother of Judas, fled across the
Jordan with several hundred Maccabean soldiers.
They were ill-equipped to wage battle, but the
next victories were in the field of diplomacy. Two
pretenders to the Syrian throne each sought help
from the Jews. They saw in Jonathan the man best
able to raise and lead a Jewish army. By playing a
delaying action, Jonathan was able to support the
winning candidate and at the same time make
treaties with Sparta and Rome. Before the war
was over, Jonathan was high priest, governor of
Judaea, and a member of the Syrian nobility. His
brother, Simon, became governor of the Philistine coastal area. Jonathan was able to promote
the internal prosperity of Judah, and when he
died his brother, Simon, succeeded him as ruling
high priest.

Simon was advanced in years when he came to
the throne. His major victory was in the field of
diplomacy, for by recognizing **Demetrius** as rightful king of Syria he secured for the Jews immunity
from taxation which amounted to an acknowledgment of independence. Simon was able also to
starve out the Syrian garrison at the Akra and to
occupy the cities of Joppa and Beth-zur. In recognition of his wise rule, the leaders in Israel named
Simon, "leader and high priest for ever, until
there shall arise a faithful prophet." Simon was
the last of the sons of Mattathias, and this act legit-
imized a new dynasty which is termed Hasmonaean, presumably derived from an ancestor of
the Maccabees named Asmonaeus or, in Hebrew,

Hashmon. In 134 B.C., Simon and two of his sons
were murdered by an ambitious son-in-law. A
third son, **John Hyrcanus,** managed to escape and
succeed his father as hereditary head of the Jewish state.

The Hasmonaeans

The Syrians recognized the government of John
Hyrcanus on condition that he consider himself
subject to Syria and promise help in Syrian military campaigns. Certain coastal cities annexed by
Jonathan and Simon were also to be relinquished.
The efficient rule of Hyrcanus, however, quickly
effected the re-conquest of these cities and the
addition of **Idumaea** (Old Testament Edom) to
Judaean territory. These conquests ensured the
use of ancient trade routes by the merchant class,
but they posed problems to the religiously oriented Jews. Hyrcanus compelled the Idumaeans
to become circumcised and accept the Jewish
faith, a practice which later Judaism disavows.
Hyrcanus also campaigned in Samaria, where he
destroyed the temple on Mount Gerizim. The
success of Jewish arms might be applauded by the
nationalistic element in Judaea, but the religious
fervor of the earlier Maccabees was no longer evident.

Before John Hyrcanus died in 104 B.C., the borders of the state had been extended on every side.
The Maccabean struggle was long past and new
rivalries developed. The older Hellenists were
discredited, but their ideas were perpetuated in
the party of the Sadducees. The orthodox of Maccabean times became the Pharisees of pre-Christian Judaism and the New Testament. Hyrcanus
was devout and law-abiding, but his children had
little sympathy with traditional Hebrew thought.
They numbered themselves among the aristo-
crats, and they came to look with disdain on the
rigidly orthodox Pharisees. Ironically, these heirs
of the Maccabees became thoroughly Hellenized.

The death of John Hyrcanus precipitated a dynastic struggle among his children. His eldest
son, who preferred his Greek name **Aristobulus** to
his Hebrew name, Judah, emerged as victor and
threw three of his brothers into prison—two of
whom are thought to have starved to death. Another brother was murdered in the palace. In his
short reign of but one year, Aristobulus pushed
the borders of Judaea north to Mount Lebanon
and took the title of king. His life was cut short,
however, by drink, disease, and the haunting fear
of rebellion.

At the time of Aristobulus's death he had but
one brother living, and he was in prison. Although his Hebrew name was Jonathan, history
knows him by his Greek name **Alexander Jannaeus.** Under Jannaeus the policy of territorial
expansion continued. The frontiers of Judaea
were extended along the Philistine coast toward
the Egyptian frontier and in the Trans-jordan re-

gion. The Jewish state approximated the territory controlled by Israel in the days of David and Solomon. It included the whole of Palestine and adjacent areas from the borders of Egypt to Lake Huleh, north of the Sea of Galilee. Perea in Transjordan was subject to Jannaeus, as were the cities of the Coastal Plain except for Ashkelon.

The territories incorporated into the Hasmonaean kingdom were, for the most part, quickly Judaized. The Idumaeans came to exercise an important place in Jewish life, and **Galilee** became an important center of Judaism. The Samaritans, however, continued to resist assimilation and cities such as Apollonia and Scythopolis (Old Testament Beth-shean), with only a small Jewish element in their population, kept their non-Jewish character.

Partisan strife marred the reign of Alexander Jannaeus, who showed open contempt for the Pharisees, precipitating civil war. The Pharisees accepted aid from the Syrians in their conflict with Jannaeus, and for a time Jewish independence was in the balance. When the Pharisees felt that they had gained their point, they withdrew their alliance with Syria and hoped for a Jewish state that would be both free of foreign control and tolerant of their viewpoint. Jannaeus sought out the leaders of the rebellion and crucified eight hundred Pharisees. Tradition says that Jannaeus repented on his deathbed, instructing his wife, **Salome Alexandra,** to dismiss his Sadducean advisors and reign with the help of the Pharisees. The tradition may have no historical basis, but Alexandra did turn to the Pharisees for support.

Salome Alexandra had been married successively to Aristobulus and to Alexander Jannaeus. The widow of two Hasmonaean rulers, she reigned in her own right for seven years. She was a woman of seventy when she came to the throne, dividing royal responsibilities between her two sons. **Hyrcanus,** the older son, became high priest, and his brother, **Aristobulus,** received the military command. Her brother, **Simeon ben Shetah,** was a leader among the Pharisees and this fact may have disposed her to seek peace between the opposing factions of Judaism.

Under Alexandra, the Pharisees had their opportunity to make a constructive contribution to Jewish life. In many areas, particularly education, they were eminently successful. Under the presidency of Simeon ben Shetah, the Sanhedrin (the Jewish Council of State) decreed that every young man should be educated. A comprehensive system of elementary education was inaugurated so that the larger villages, towns, and cities of Judaea would produce a literate, informed people. This education was centered in the Hebrew Scriptures.

The wounds of earlier strife were not healed during Alexandra's reign. Although the Pharisees were happy in their newfound recognition, the Sadducees were resentful... lost power. To compound... isees sought to avenge the... ers by Alexander Jannaeus... spilt and the makings of ano... the air.

The Sadducees found in Ari... ger son of Jannaeus and Alexan... could support as Alexandra's su... soldier and appealed to the party... imperial expansion and worldly powers a... the older brother and rightful heir, d of... to the Pharisees. With the death of... partisans of the two sons were read... down.

When his mother died, **Hyrcanus** (... been serving as high priest, succee... throne, but his brother, **Aristobulus,** le... of Sadducees against Jerusalem. Neith... canus nor the Pharisees were ready for war,... Hyrcanus surrendered his honors to Aristobulus (II), who became king and high priest. Hyrcanus and Aristobulus thereupon vowed eternal friendship, and Aristobulus's eldest son, Alexander, married Hyrcanus's only daughter, Alexandra. Peace between the brothers was short-lived. Hyrcanus had to flee and Antipater, governor of Idumaea, espoused his cause. With civil war threatening, Pompey appeared with his Roman legions to ensure the peace of Judaea and further the aims of Rome.

The Romans

When **Pompey** suspected Aristobulus of planning to rebel against Rome, he besieged Jerusalem. After three months, he breached the fortifications, entered the city, and reportedly murdered twelve thousand Jews. Pompey and his officers entered the Holy of Holies in the temple, but he did not touch its costly furnishings and allowed temple worship to continue. Jerusalem, however, was made tributary to the Romans, and the last vestige of Jewish independence was removed. Judaea was incorporated into the Roman province of Syria and it lost the coastal cities, the district of Samaria, and the non-Jewish cities east of the Jordan. **Hyrcanus** was named Ethnarch of Judaea, including Galilee, Idumaea, and Perea, and was confirmed again as high priest. A yearly tribute was due Rome. Aristobulus and a number of other captives were taken to Rome to grace Pompey's triumph. During the voyage, Aristobulus's son Alexander escaped and attempted to organize a revolt against Hyrcanus. With the aid of the Romans, Hyrcanus was able to meet this challenge to his authority.

During the years of strife between **Aristobulus (II)** and **Hyrcanus (II),** the Idumaean governor **Antipater** (or **Antipas**) took a lively interest in the politics of Judaea. Antipater was bitterly opposed to Aristobulus, partly through fear and partly be-

with Hyrcanus. It appears
cause of his friend much on Antipater, and that
that Hyrcanus r power behind the throne of
he was virtu esented the influence of Anti-
Judaea. Th uch as they smarted under Ro-
pater a Although the Idumaeans had
man ed into the Jewish state by John
be ey had never been assimilated and
riries were not forgotten.
risis which followed the murder of
esar, Antipater and his sons showed loy-
he new regime of **Cassius** by zealously
ing tribute taxes. **Herod,** a son of Anti-
was given the title Procurator of Judaea
the promise that he would one day be named
g. When **Anthony** defeated Brutus and Cas-
s at Philippi, Asia again fell into the hands of a
ew regime. Herod, however, quickly changed
loyalties and bribed his way into favor with Anthony.

The eastern part of the once mighty Persian
Empire was occupied by a people known as **Parthians,** who had never been subdued by Rome. In
41 B.C. they attacked Jerusalem and made **Antigonus,** son of Aristobulus II, both king and high
priest. Herod, the son of Antipater, who had inherited the throne of Judaea at the death of Hyrcanus, was forced to flee to Rome. There he won
the favor of Anthony and was officially named
"King of the Jews," although the title would have
meaning only after the Parthians were driven out.
Herod returned to Judaea with Roman arms and
triumphantly entered Jerusalem as king.

Herod's rule spanned the eventful years from
37 B.C. to 4 B.C. He is best known as the king who
feared the birth of a rival "King of the Jews" and
decreed the murder of infants in Bethlehem at the
time of the birth of Jesus. While that act of Herod
cannot be documented from secular records, his
other atrocities are well known. He had ten wives
in all, and the **Emperor Augustus** is reported to
have commented of his family life, "I'd rather be
Herod's hog than his son." The hog was an unclean animal and would not be butchered, but
Herod's wives and children were violently removed when they interfered with his plans or
were suspected of disloyalty.

Although detested by his Jewish subjects,
Herod did seek to win their favor. He built and
rebuilt cities throughout the land: Samaria became Sebaste in honor of Augustus; Straton's
Tower became Caesarea, with a harbor protected
by a moat and a wall with ten towers. Fortresses,
baths, parks, marketplaces, roads, and other luxuries of Hellenistic culture were part of his building program.

In the eighteenth year of his reign (20–19 B.C.),
Herod began the work of rebuilding, on a grand
scale, the Jewish temple in Jerusalem. The main
edifice was built by priests in a year-and-a-half,
but the work on the entire complex of courts and
buildings was not completed until the pro-
curatorship of **Albinus** (A.D. 62–64), less than a
decade before it was totally destroyed by the armies of **Titus** (A.D. 70).

The Jewish Sects

The Pharisees, Sadducees, Herodians, and
Zealots, who play so important a part in the gospel
records, all have their origin during the two centuries before the birth of Christ. They represent
different reactions to the continuing clash between Hellenism and Jewish religious life. While
the Maccabean struggle had settled the political
problem of the relationship between the Syrian
Seleucids and Judaea, it forced upon Judaism the
necessity of determining its own relationship to
the outside world.

The Pharisees

A party bearing the name of Pharisee is first
mentioned during the reign of John Hyrcanus
(134–104 B.C.), and it is evident that even then
there was an antagonism between the "orthodox"
Pharisee and the more open-minded Sadducee.
The word **Pharisee** means "separated one," and
the name probably meant, in the first instance,
one who had separated himself from the corrupting influence of Hellenism in his zeal for the biblical Law. Josephus says that the Pharisees "appear
more religious than others, and seem to interpret
the laws more accurately."

Pharisees were punctilious in observing the
laws regarding ceremonial purity. For this reason,
they could not purchase items of food or drink
from a "sinner" for fear of ceremonial defilement.
Nor could a Pharisee eat in the house of a sinner,
although he might entertain the sinner in his own
home. Under such circumstances, the Pharisee
would provide the sinner with clothes to wear, for
the sinner's clothes might be ceremonially impure.

With a sincere desire to make the Law work-
able within the changing culture of the Greco-
Roman world, the Pharisees developed systems of
tradition which sought to apply the Law to a variety of circumstances. During the first century before Christ, two influential Pharisaic teachers
gave their names to two schools of legal thought.
Hillel was the more moderate of the two, ever
considerate of the poor and willing to accept Roman rule as compatible with Jewish orthodoxy.
Shammai, on the other hand, was more strict in
his interpretation and bitterly opposed to Rome.
His viewpoint ultimately found expression in the
sect of **Zealots,** whose resistance to the Romans
brought on the destruction of Jerusalem in A.D.
70. **The Talmud** preserves the record of three
hundred sixteen controversies between the
schools of Hillel and Shammai.

Tradition, in Pharisaic thought, began as a commentary on the Law, but it was ultimately raised

to the level of Law itself. To justify this teaching, it was maintained that the "oral law" was given by God to Moses on Mount Sinai along with the "written law" or **Torah** (*Pirke Aboth*, 1.1). The ultimate in this development is reached when the **Mishna** states that oral law must be observed with greater stringency than the written law, because statutory law (that is, oral tradition) affects the life of the ordinary man more intimately than the more remote constitutional law (the written Torah) (*M. Sanhedrin*, 10.3).

In addition to the charge that Pharisaism involved little more than a concern for the minutia of the Law, the New Testament affirms that tradition had largely neglected the real intent of the Law (Matt. 15:3). As in many worthy movements, the early piety of those who had separated themselves from impurity at great cost was exchanged for an attitude of pride in the observance of legal precepts.

Men such as **Nicodemus, Joseph of Arimathea, Gamaliel,** and **Saul of Tarsus** represent some of the nobler souls from the Pharisaic tradition in the New Testament. To Saul, later Paul the apostle, the Pharisee represented the epitome of orthodoxy, "the most straitest sect of our religion" (Acts 26:5). Pharisaism began well, and its perversion is a constant reminder that self-complacency and spiritual pride are temptations to which the pious are particularly susceptible.

The Sadducees

Although Pharisees and Sadducees are frequently denounced together in the New Testament, they had little in common except their antagonism to Jesus. The Sadducees were the party of the **Jerusalem aristocracy** and the **high priesthood.** They had made their peace with the political rulers and had attained positions of wealth and influence. Temple administration and ritual were their specific responsibilities. The Sadducees held themselves aloof from the masses and were unpopular with them.

The Pharisaic attempts at applying the Law to new situations were rejected by the Sadducees, who restricted their concept of authority to the Torah, or Mosaic Law. They did not believe in resurrection, spirits, or angels (cf. Mark 12:18; Luke 20:27; Acts 23:8). Their faith was largely a series of negations with the result that they left no positive religious or political system.

While the Pharisees welcomed proselytes (Matt. 23:15), the Sadducean party was closed. None but members of the high priestly and aristocratic families of Jerusalem could become members. With the destruction of the temple in A.D. 70, the Sadducean party came to an end. Modern Judaism traces its roots to the Pharisees.

The Essenes

Essenes and Pharisees both trace their roots to the orthodox leaders of Maccabean times, who

stood their ground again[ ] maintained a strict ortho[ ] *ellenism. Pharisees* work of historical Judaism *within the frame-* separation from defileme[ ] *maintained their* ish community itself. Eve[ ] *from the Jew-* worship was conducted by [ ] *the temple* isees esteemed it a basic p[ ] *the Phar-* inheritance. While the Phari[ ] *he religious* self aloof from "sinners," he [ ] and coveted their esteem. [ ] *him-*

A more extreme reaction agai[ ] *em* which tended to corrupt Jewish sect which the ancient writers [ ] and Pliny call the Essenes. The [ ] lived for the most part in **monast**[ ] such as the one which maintained h[ ] Qumran, near the northwest corne[ ] Sea.

In seeking to explain Judaism to [ ] speaking world, Josephus spoke of three "p[ ] phies"—those of the Pharisees, Sadducees, [ ] the Essenes. The term "Essene" seems to have had quite an elastic usage, including various groups of monastically minded Jews, who varied among themselves in certain of their practices. Pliny says that the Essenes avoided women and did not marry, but Josephus speaks of an order of marrying Essenes. The excavations at Qumran indicate that women were enrolled in the Qumran community.

Ancient writers speak favorably of the Essenes, who lived a life of rigor and simplicity. Members of the community studied Scripture and other religious books. Each Essene was required to perform manual labor in order to make the community self-supporting. Community of goods was practiced, and strict discipline was enforced by an overseer. Those groups which renounced marriage adopted boys at an early age in order to inculcate and perpetuate the ideals of Essenism. Slavery and war were repudiated.

The Essenes welcomed proselytes, but the novice was required to undergo a period of strict probation before he could become a full-fledged member. Numerically, the Essenes were never large. Philo says that there were four thousand of them, and Pliny speaks of a community north of En-gedi, corresponding to the Qumran area. That there were other settlements is clear, for we are told that all members of the sect were welcome in any of the Essene colonies.

Nothing certain is known of the early history of the sect for, like all reform movements, it traces its origins back to remote times. Philo states that Moses instituted the order, and Josephus says that they existed "ever since the ancient times of the fathers." It is certain that the Essene movement was at one time an extreme protest against the corruptions which were apparent in pre-Christian Judaism, and that ultimately many members withdrew from the Palestinian community life

urification in places such as and sought spiri... elves as the only true or pure the Qumranes refused to cooperate with Regarded to be the corrupt religious ob-Israel... Jerusalem temple. The carefully substitute for the Essene center seems to have substitute for the temple in the eyes of ... es. The strictness of Essene discipline ... idity with which the Law was enforced ...sed by all who write about them. ...s says that they were stricter than all Jews ...ining from work on the Sabbath. A passage **Damascus Document** (which seems to be ...ne in origin) says that it is unlawful to lift an ...mal from a pit on the Sabbath. Such a view was ...nsidered extreme, even by legalistic Pharisees cf. Matt. 12:11).

The absence of Essenes from the main streams of Jewish life doubtless accounts for the fact that they are not mentioned in the New Testament or in the Jewish Talmud. Although the high morality of the Essenes is indeed commendable, the teaching and practice of Jesus were diametrically opposite to the legalism and asceticism of the Essene teaching. Although the Essenes considered that contact with a member of their own group of a lower order was ceremonially defiling, Jesus did not hesitate to eat and drink with "publicans and sinners" (Matt. 11:19; Luke 7:34). Although obedient to the Mosaic law, Jesus had no sympathy with those who made of the Law a burden instead of a blessing. The Sabbath, according to Jesus, was made for man, and it is lawful to do good on the Sabbath day (Matt. 12:1–12; Mark 2:23–28; Luke 6:6–11; 14:1–6).

Jesus denounced abuses in the temple and prophesied its destruction, but He did not repudiate the temple services. He came to Jerusalem for the great Jewish feasts, and after His resurrection, disciples still made their way to the temple at the hour of prayer (cf. Acts 3). While asceticism and monasticism early gained a foothold in Christian thinking, Christianity in its earliest period was in no sense an ascetic movement. The ministry of Jesus was largely to the "common people," who were rejected by both Pharisee and Essene. Jesus was not ashamed to associate with the people of His generation, so the self-righteous called Him a drunkard, a friend of publicans and sinners (Matt. 11:19).

Other Sects

The New Testament mentions **Herodians** (Mark 3:6; Matt. 22:16) and **Zealots** (Luke 6:15), groups of Jews at opposite ends of the political spectrum. The Herodians appear to have been Jews of influence and standing who were well disposed to the Herodian rule and, as a result, to the Romans who supported the Herods. The Zealots,

on the other hand, were super patriots who determined to resist Rome at all costs. Their fanaticism brought on the war during which the army of Titus destroyed Jerusalem and its temple (A.D. 70).

Chronology

Date B.C.	
612	**Nineveh** destroyed by Medes and Babylonians
587	**Jerusalem** destroyed by Nebuchadnezzar
559	**Cyrus** inherits kingdom of Anshan; beginning of Persian Empire
539	**Babylon** falls to Cyrus; end of Neo-Babylonian Empire
530–522	**Cambyses** succeeds Cyrus; conquest of Egypt
521–486	**Darius I** ruler of Persian Empire
515	**Second temple** completed by Jews in Jerusalem
486–464	**Xerxes I** attempts the conquest of Greece; time of Esther
480	**Greek naval victory** at Salamis; Xerxes flees
464–423	**Artaxerxes I** rules Persia; age of Nehemiah
334–323	**Alexander of Macedon** conquers the East
311	**Seleucus** conquers Babylon; beginning of the Seleucid dynasty
223–187	**Antiochus (III) the Great,** Seleucid ruler of Syria
198	**Antiochus III** defeats Egypt, gains control of Palestine
175–163	**Antiochus (IV) Epiphanes** rules Syria; Judaism is proscribed
167	**Mattathias** and his sons rebel against Antiochus; beginning of Maccabean revolt
166–160	**Judas** is Maccabees' Leader
160–142	**Jonathan** is high priest
142–135	**Simon** is high priest; founds Hasmonaean dynasty
134–104	**John Hyrcanus** expands holdings of independent Jewish state
103	**Aristobulus'** Rule
102–76	**Alexander Jannaeus'** Rule
75–67	**Salome Alexandra** rules; Hyrcanus II high priest
66–63	**Dynastic battle:** Aristobulus II and Hyrcanus II
63	**Pompey** invades Palestine; Roman rule begins
63–40	**Hyrcanus II** rules, subject to Rome. Antipater exercises increasing power
40–37	**Parthians** conquer Jerusalem; establish Aristobulus II as high priest and king
37–4	**Herod the Great,** son of Antipater, rules as king; subject to Rome

THE APOCRYPHA

The term Apocrypha is used to designate a collection of ancient Jewish writings which were written between about 250 B.C. and the early Christian centuries. The apocryphal books have come to be regarded as inspired Scripture in the theology of the Roman Catholic Church, but the historic Protestant and Jewish viewpoint ascribes no real inspiration to them.

Why Protestants Reject the Apocrypha

While Protestants study the Apocrypha for the light it throws on the life and thought of pre-Christian Judaism, they reject it as inspired Scripture for the following reasons:

(1) The apocryphal books were not a part of the Old Testament of Jesus and the early church. The threefold division of the Old Testament—the Law, the Prophets, and the Writings, still used in Hebrew Bibles and Jewish versions of the Old Testament—does not include the apocryphal books and never did. While the Apocrypha was known to Jesus and His disciples, they never quote from it as authoritative Scripture.

(2) Ancient Jewish writers who used the Greek Bible, notably **Philo** and **Josephus,** were acquainted with the Apocrypha but never quote it as Scripture. In fact, Josephus states that nothing had been added to Scripture "from Artaxerxes until our time." The apocryphal book of Second Esdras mentions twenty-four books, corresponding to the Hebrew Bible as it is known today, and seventy other writings which are esoteric in nature (2 Esdras 14:44—48). It is significant that this apocryphal book shows an acquaintance with the acknowledged Old Testament canon as known in the synagogue and in the Protestant churches.

(3) Church fathers, who were familiar with the Hebrew Canon, clearly distinguish between canonical and apocryphal writings. The writings of **Melito of Sardis, Cyril of Jerusalem,** and **St. Jerome** show a recognition of the difference between inspired Scripture and Apocrypha.

(4) The apocryphal books were never declared to be authoritative Scripture until the **Council of Trent** (A.D. 1546). At that time the following apocryphal books were declared canonical: Tobit, Judith, The Wisdom of Solomon, Ecclesiasticus, Baruch (including the Letter of Jeremiah), First and Second Maccabees, the additions to Esther, and the additions to Daniel (viz. Susanna, The Song of the Three Young Men, and Bel and the Dragon). Many Roman Catholic scholars distinguish between proto-canonical books (i.e., our Old Testament) and deuterocanonical books (i.e., the Apocrypha).

(5) Most readers feel that the apocryphal books represent a lower level of writing than that of the canonical Scriptures. They contain numerous his-

torical and geographical anachronisms and do not breath[e] prophe[cies and anach]-evident in canonical writi[ng]. [pro]phetic spirit so

The **Westminster Confe**[ssion] [states that] "the books commonly ca[lled] [the] being of divine inspiratio[n] ... not Canon of Scripture, and th[at] ... of the thority in the Church of Go[d] ... au-wise approved or made use o[f] ... writing." The Reformed Chu[rch]...couraged the use of the Apoc[r]...sequence it is seldom used [in] Protestantism. The Anglican Cl[urch ...] nine Articles takes a mediating [...] that "the Church doth read [these] books] for example of life and ins[truction of man]-ners; but yet doth it not apply the[m to establish any] doctrine."

In addition to the books common[ly termed] Apocrypha, there is a wide variety of ot[her an]-cient literature, both Jewish and Christian, which the name **Pseudepigrapha** is often applie[d.] Apocrypha, Pseudepigrapha, sectarian literature from the Qumran Caves, and a wide variety of other ancient writings provide helpful material for understanding the world of the New Testament and the early church. While not on a par with inspired Scripture, such writings merit close examination.

The Books Commonly Termed Apocrypha Are:

First Esdras (Vulgate, 3 Esdras). The First Book of Esdras relates a series of episodes from Old Testament history, beginning with the Passover celebrated in Jerusalem by Josiah (c. 621 B.C.) and ending with the public reading of the Law by Ezra (c. 444 B.C.). It reproduces the substance of Second Chronicles 33:1—36:23, the whole of Ezra, and Nehemiah 7:73—8:12. An addition to the biblical narrative appears in First Esdras 3:1—5:6, the **Tale of the Three Guardsmen.** Three young men who were acting as bodyguards to King Darius were keeping themselves awake by debating what was the strongest force in the world. One said wine, because of its peculiar power over men; another suggested the king, with unlimited power over his subjects; and the third (**Zerubbabel**) affirmed that woman, who gives birth to man, is strongest, but truth is victor over all things. The king, who was asked to decide the winner, favored Zerubbabel's answer and offered him any reward he might choose. Zerubbabel asked permission to return to Jerusalem to rebuild the temple. The section ends with a description of the Jews departing from Babylon en route to Jerusalem. Most scholars suggest that First Esdras was composed in Egypt some time after 150 B.C.

THE APOCRYPHA

Second Esdras gate, 4 Esdras). The core of Second Esdras (chapters 3—14) purports to describe seven apocalyptic revelations granted to Ezra in God. They are concerned with the problem of suffering and attempt "to justify God to man." The author was probably a Jew who looked forward to the advent of the Messiah and the period of blessedness it would bring. The introduction (chapters 1 and 2) and the conclusion (chapters 15 and 16) are additions written from a Christian viewpoint. The core was probably written in Aramaic toward the end of the first century A.D. About the middle of the second century, an introduction was added (in Greek), and a century later the concluding chapters were written. Oriental versions and many of the best Latin manuscripts contain only the core of the book.

Tobit. Tobit is a book of **religious fiction,** probably written in Aramaic during the second century B.C. It tells the story of a pious Jew of the tribe of Naphtali in Galilee who, with his wife Anna and their son Tobias, was taken to Nineveh by **Shalmaneser** (c. 721 B.C., 2 Kin. 18:9–12). In the land of exile they scrupulously obeyed the Jewish law. When **Tobit** lost his eyesight, he sent his son to Rages in Media to obtain payment of a debt. An angel led him on to Ecbatana, where he fell in love with a beautiful widow whose seven husbands had successively been killed on their marriage day by an evil spirit. Tobias married the virgin-widow and escaped death by burning the inner part of a fish, the smoke of which put the evil spirit to flight. As an added blessing, the gall of the fish was used to cure the blindness of the aged Tobit.

Judith. The story of Judith was probably written in Hebrew by a Palestinian Jew during the years following the Maccabean revolt. It tells how Judith, a Jewish widow, delivered her people from the Assyrian commander, **Holofernes,** who was laying siege to Bethulia. Risking great personal danger, Judith made her way to the tent of Holofernes where she beguiled the Assyrian with her charms. Getting him into a drunken stupor, Judith took the sword of Holofernes, cut off his head, and brought it back to Bethulia as evidence that God had given His people victory over the Assyrians. Judith may be compared with biblical Jael, who killed the Caananite general Sisera (Judg. 4:17–22).

The Additions to the Book of Esther. During the second or the first century B.C., an Egyptian Jew translated the canonical Book of Esther into Greek, and at the same time interpolated a total of **107 verses** into six places where he felt that a religious note should be added. These pious insertions mention the name of God and prayer, neither of which appear in the canonical Esther. The apocryphal additions add ten verses to Esther 10, and six additional chapters, numbered 11 to 16. In the Greek Septuagint, however, the supplementary verses are distributed through the text so as to make one continuous narration.

The Wisdom of Solomon. An Alexandrian Jew, sometime between 150 and 50 B.C., composed an ethical treatise which he named The Wisdom of Solomon in order to gain for it a wider reading. He sought to protect the Jews in Egypt from falling into skepticism, materialism, and idolatry, and to teach his pagan readers the truth of Judaism and the folly of heathenism. The book begins with an exhortation to the rulers of the earth to seek wisdom and follow righteousness. Its theology is based on the Old Testament with modifications derived from Greek philosophical ideas current in Alexandria. Unlike the Old and New Testaments which honor the body, The Wisdom of Solomon (The New American Bible) regards it as something that "weighs down the soul," a mere "earthly tent" which "burdens the thoughtful mind" (9:15). The preexistence (8:19, 20) and immortality (3:1–5) of the soul are maintained, although the Hebrew-Christian doctrine of bodily resurrection is absent.

Ecclesiasticus, or the Wisdom of Jesus the Son of Sirach. Ecclesiasticus, an ethical treatise extolling the virtue of wisdom, was written in Hebrew between 200 and 175 B.C. by a pious scholar from Jerusalem, Jesus the son of Sirach. The author's grandson, an Alexandrian Jew, translated the work into Greek and added a prologue (c. 132 B.C.). It is the longest of the apocryphal books, and the only one with a known author. Like the canonical Proverbs, Ecclesiasticus deals with a wide variety of practical subjects—everything from diet to domestic relationships. The longest continuous section of the book (chapters 44 to 50) is the **Praise of Famous Men,** which briefly describes a long series of Hebrew worthies from **Enoch, Noah,** and **Abraham,** down to **Zerubbabel** and **Nehemiah,** and finally the **High Priest Simon,** a contemporary and friend of the author.

Baruch. The Book of Baruch, ostensibly written by Jeremiah's friend and secretary (Jer. 32:12; 36:4; 51:59), is a composite work which was not completed until the first century B.C. or later. Although the final recension was written in Greek, some sections may be traced to Hebrew originals. The book begins with a **prayer of penitence,** recognizing that the tragedies which befell Jerusalem are the just recompense for her sins (1:1—3:8). A second poetical section explains that **Israel's misfortunes** are due to her neglect of **Wisdom** (3:9—4:4). This Wisdom, whose praises are sung by a philosophically minded writer, is equated with God's law (4:1–3). The third section of the book, also poetic, is a message of **comfort and hope for distressed Israel.** The enemy will be destroyed and the children of Jerusalem will return in triumph! Baruch is the one book of the Apocrypha which breathes something of the fire

of the Old Testament prophets, although it is lacking in originality.

The Letter of Jeremiah. Sometime about 300 B.C., or thereafter, an unknown author wrote **an impassioned sermon** based on **Jeremiah 11:10,** in which he showed the utter impotence of gods of wood, silver, and gold. This sermon, known as The Letter of Jeremiah, was originally written in Hebrew (or Aramaic), although it is extant only in Greek and translations derived from the Greek. Since many Greek and Syriac manuscripts, as well as the Latin version, attach The Letter of Jeremiah to the Book of Baruch, it appears as the sixth chapter of Baruch in most English translations of the Apocrypha. The Letter has no relation to Baruch, however, and some ancient codices place it after the biblical Book of Lamentations.

The Prayer of Azariah and the Song of the Three Young Men. (Additions to Daniel, inserted between 3:23 and 3:24.) Sometime during the second or first centuries B.C., the three "additions" to canonical Daniel, which exist as separate books of the Apocrypha, were written by unknown authors. The first of these, The Prayer of Azariah and the Song of the Three Young Men, was probably written in Hebrew by a pious Jew during the period when his people were suffering at the hand of **Antiochus Epiphanes,** or in the period of the **Maccabean revolt** which followed. During the ordeal of the fiery furnace, Azariah is represented as praising God, confessing his people's sins, and praying for national deliverance. The angel of the Lord then came into the furnace and drove out the fiery flame, so that the youths were unharmed. Then from the furnace they sang their praises to God in the Song, which is reminiscent of Psalm 148 in content and Psalm 136 in antiphonal form.

Susanna. It is uncertain whether the original of Susanna was written in Hebrew or Greek. Its unknown author lived sometime during the second or the first century B.C., but we are ignorant of other details concerning his life. Yet, the book itself is recognized as **one of the great short stories of world literature.** It tells how two immoral elders threatened to testify that they had found Susanna, the beautiful wife of an influential Babylonian Jew, in the arms of a lover, if she would not submit to them. When she repulsed them, they charged her with adultery through the testimony of two witnesses, and she was convicted and sentenced to death. A young man named Daniel, however, interrupted the proceedings and questioned the two witnesses separately. He asked each to identify the tree under which he had seen Susanna and her supposed lover. Betrayed by their own inconsistent answers, the guilty elders were put to death and Susanna was saved. In the Septuagint, the story of Susanna precedes the canonical Book of Daniel; in the Vulgate it follows it.

Bel and the Dragon. The stories of Bel and the Dragon were probably wr[itten] in Hebrew toward the middle of the first cen[tury] B.C. and added to the Book of Daniel by its [tra]nslator. In the Septuagint it directly follo[ws] while in the Vulgate it comes after Susan[na]. It is one of the world's oldest de[tective sto]ry of Bel is how Cyrus, the Persian kin[g]. It tells why he did not worship Bel, the g[od]. Cyrus told Daniel how much flour a[nd] many sheep the god Bel consume[d]. Daniel persuaded Cyrus to [seal] provisions in the temple and th[en] the temple doors. In the mean[time] scattered ashes over the temple floo[r]. [When he] came the food was gone, and the [floor covered] with footprints of the priests, thei[r chil]dren, who had used a secret ent[rance in the] table to come by night into the te[mple to con]sume the provisions. The king, co[nvinced of the] perfidy of Bel's priests, ordered th[em and] their temple destroyed. The Dragon [was a] serpent which the king worshiped unti[l Daniel] killed it by feeding it lumps of pitch, fat, an[d hair]. The Babylonians, furious at the destruction [of] their god, demanded that Daniel be put to death. The king reluctantly consented and Daniel was placed in a den of lions (cf. Dan. 6:1–28). The lions did not molest Daniel, who was miraculously fed by the prophet **Habakkuk,** who was caught up by an angel in Judea and taken to the lions' den in **Babylon.** On the seventh day the king took Daniel from the lions' den and cast his enemies into it, whereupon they were immediately devoured. The stories of Bel and the Dragon were intended to ridicule idolatry and discredit heathen priestcraft.

The Prayer of Manasseh. The apocryphal Prayer of Manasseh was probably written sometime during the last two centuries B.C. by a Palestinian Jew. Scholars are uncertain whether it was composed in Hebrew, Aramaic, or Greek. The Prayer is ascribed to Manasseh, the king of Judah who, according to Second Chronicles 33, was taken to Babylon where he repented of the idolatry that had characterized the years of his reign. Mention is made of a prayer offered by Manasseh (2 Chr. 33:19), and a pious Jew appears to have attempted to write such a prayer as Manasseh would have uttered. The Prayer is typical of ancient Jewish liturgical forms. It opens with the ascription of **praise to the Lord,** whose majesty is seen in creation (1–4) and in His mercy toward sinners (5–8). This is followed by **personal confession** (9, 10) and **supplication for pardon** (11–13). The prayer concludes with a **petition for grace** (14) and a doxology (15).

First Maccabees. First Maccabees is a valuable historical record of the forty years beginning with the accession of **Antiochus Epiphanes** to the Syrian throne (175 B.C.) and ending with the death of

THE APOCRYPHA

Simon the Macc...
written by a...
100 B.C. The...
Jewish resh
bean ...us
deno...nathan
th).

(135 B.C.). It was probably
...dian Jew, in Hebrew, about
...ves us our best account of the
...o Antiochus and the Macca-
...ultimately brought indepen-
...sh state. It relates the exploits of
...ws of Mattathias, the priest who
...us and sparked the revolt: **Judas**
...nathan (9:23—12:53), and **Simon**
... The annual Jewish festival of
...celebrated at the same season as
...commemorates the rededication of
...e as a result of the bravery of the Mac-
...he festival is mentioned in the New Tes-
...s "the feast of dedication" (John 10:22).

Second Maccabees. Second Maccabees is primarily parallel to the first seven chapters of First Maccabees, covering the period from 175 to 160 B.C. It professes to be an abridgement of a five-volume history written by **Jason of Cyrene** (2:19–23), whose identity is a matter of conjecture. The author of Second Maccabees was evidently an Alexandrian Jew who wrote in Greek. He may have written as early as 120 B.C. or as late as the early first century A.D. Second Maccabees is less historical and more rhetorical than First Maccabees. It is written from the Pharisaic viewpoint and stresses the miraculous and the marvelous in contrast to the more prosaic and objective First Maccabees.

THE ENGLISH BIBLE AND ITS DEVELOPMENT

It is from the text of the Bible printed in 1611, known as the **King James Version,** or the **Authorized Version,** that for the last three and one-half centuries the English people have derived their knowledge of the only true God, and of Jesus Christ, whom He sent; of the divine aspect of Israel's history; of the inspired ideals of the Christian life as revealed to the apostles; and any certain concept of the future; of their own souls in a life of glory; and of the earth and of the nations upon it. "So securely has it established its place in the affections of the English-speaking people, and so effectively has it imparted the great spiritual values associated with the Scriptures, that to most of its readers the **Authorized Version** *is* the Bible."

It is generally agreed that Christianity came to Britain in the second century of our era, possibly soon after the close of the apostolic age. But who brought the Christian faith first to that island, and how extensive its acceptance at that time, we may never know. "Among the many hundreds of religious monuments, civil and military, strewn about Britain from the second to the early fourth century, all are purely pagan." There were some early British martyrs, and Britain was represented at the earlier church councils, but, says the late Professor Charles Oman, "There seems every reason to believe that the main bulk of the population in this remote province of the West remained pagan until a much later date than was the case elsewhere. . . . It is very strange that a religion, which was first publicly tolerated and later encouraged by the government for nearly a hundred years before the fatal year A.D. 410, should have left so few records in stone behind it." What Bibles or parts of Bibles were in Britain in those mysteriously blacked-out decades, we do not know. The oldest book written by a Briton belongs in this period. It was a commentary on the epistles of Paul by the heretic Pelagius. But he left Britain when young, never to return, and wrote the book in Rome.

The Book of Armagh

While for the nearly two hundred years after the departure of the Roman garrison in Britain, A.D. 410, we know almost nothing of the experiences of the Christian church in England, the story is quite different for the church in Ireland, to which mountainous country the Christian faith first came in the fourth century. Within three generations, monasteries sprang up throughout the entire land. By A.D. 600 "the study of sound literature held the foremost place and was pursued

with a thoroughness and[...] elsewhere in Europe at tha[...] this period that *The Book of* unknown partly in Irish and partly in[...] during non-Vulgate text of the New [...]itten, complete copy of the New [...]ing a come down to us produced by[...]ly

The Latin Bible

It is with the coming of St. Au[...] bury in 597 that any factual histo[...] in England must begin. We do [...] Augustine actually had a Bible wit[...] we are sure that there were hundreds [...] of Scripture, especially the Psalter, stor[...] mind. Among the gifts of Pope Gregory [...] early church at Canterbury, soon thereafter, we[...] a Gregorian Bible, in two volumes, two copies o[...] the Gospels, two Psalters, an exposition of the Epistles and Gospels for several Sundays, all adorned with silver or jewels. Here is the beginning of the history of the Scriptures in Britain. What kind of Bible would Pope Gregory send to Augustine? It would have to be a *Latin* Bible, not a Hebrew Old Testament or a Greek New Testament, and this deserves brief consideration. By the third century of our era, most people in the Western provinces of the Roman Empire knew very little Greek (even in Rome). If they were to have a Bible, it must be a Latin version, the language that was spoken throughout most of the Mediterranean world. When and how Latin Bibles were replaced by English Bibles, which could be ready by the laity, is what we now want to consider.

The First English Bibles

Undoubtedly, the first translation of parts of the Bible into Anglo-Saxon were not with pen and ink, on vellum or parchment, but in song and recitation. These Christian songs began with Caedmon, whose discovery of a gift of song is so beautifully set forth by Bede. Bede says that Caedmon "sang first of the creation of the world and the beginning of mankind, and all the story of Genesis, that is the first book of Moses, and again of the Exodus of the people of Israel from the land of Egypt and of the entrance into the promised land, and of many other tales of Holy Writ . . . and of Christ's incarnation, and of His passion, and of His ascent into heaven, and of the coming of the Holy Ghost, and the teachings of the apostles; and of the day of future judgment and of the terror of punishment full of torment, and of the sweetness of the heavenly kingdom he wrote many a lay; and

y others concerning divine ...ents." Caedmon died about ...d great name in this tradition ...and died a century later in A.D. 783. ...was composed the famous Christ... as *The Christ*, showing a remark... of the life of the Saviour. The most ...of all literary compositions of this ...e exquisite *The Dream of the Rood*, ...oving interpretation of the Crucifixion ...n the first one thousand years of English ....

...reatest British scholar in the first half of ...hth century was the Venerable Bede. No ...qualed him for the next five hundred years in ...in in knowledge of the Scriptures. His own ...fession is significant. "I gave all my attention ...the study of the Scriptures. . . . From the time ...hat I received the degree of Priest's Orders unto the fifty-ninth year of my age [A.D. 731]. . . ." Bede's writings were in Latin, but he did undertake the translation of the Gospels into Anglo-Saxon and on the very day of his death was dictating his translation of John's gospel. None of these translations have come down to us. St. Aldhelm (d. 709) also translated the Psalms, but these do not exist today.

England's noble King Alfred (849–899), at the beginning of his famous code of laws for his British subjects, used as a preface his own Anglo-Saxon translation of the Ten Commandments. The earliest written translation of the Gospels into Anglo-Saxon that now exists dates from about the tenth century.

The Lindisfarne Gospels

Probably the first extant attempt to bridge this linguistic gap in literary composition is the beautiful *Lindisfarne Gospels* in Latin, originally written about A.D. 700 in an uncial Irish script, containing an interlinear translation written in Anglo-Saxon, added about A.D. 950. About A.D. 1000 appeared the celebrated Aelfric, of whom it has been rightly said, "He is among the first to stand out individually in the records of his contemporaries as one that labored to make the Scriptures available to English scholars in their native tongue." He produced sermons in the West Saxon tongue, wrote commentaries on certain books of the Bible, and composed a condensed version of the first seven books of the Old Testament.

Language changes, however, were rapid then, and by 1300 the Anglo-Saxon language of King Alfred and Aelfric had become almost obsolete. Yet, as a distinguished authority has reminded us, "From the day of Alfred to the time of Chaucer, the language of the English people had a continuous history although it underwent many vicissitudes and suffered great changes. . . . It is this persistence of an English tone and spirit grad-

ually regaining its ascendancy after having been overlaid for three centuries by the culture of the Normans that gives these Anglo-Saxon manuscripts their chief significance for us. . . . We discern in these ancient versions some permanent core of basic speech that holds over from age to age and constitutes our English idiom, the most English part of our English tongue."

For two hundred years after the Norman conquest (A.D. 1066), French remained the language of ordinary intercourse among the upper class of conquered Britain. In the thirteenth and fourteenth centuries, "its maintenance became increasingly artificial. In the fourteenth century, English won its way back into universal use, and in the fifteenth century French all but disappeared."

The Ormulum Gospels and Acts

At the beginning of the fourteenth century appeared a poetical version of the Gospels and the Acts of the Apostles, accompanied by a commentary known as the *Ormulum*, the work of an Augustinian monk, Orm. Toward the middle of that century, the stories of Genesis and Exodus were translated into rhyming English verse.

The Psalter in Early Middle English

Two prose translations of the Psalter in Early Middle English have survived. One, composed by the famous Richard Rolle, attained great popularity. As an indication of Bible study during the fourteenth century, there are 170 biblical manuscripts of this period still surviving.

The Wycliffe Version

We now come to what may be called the first great effort to place the entire Bible in the hands of the common people in their own language. This is *The Wycliffe Version*, although it is not certain that Wycliffe himself composed any part of it. John Wycliffe did (1330–1384) stir up a desire on the part of many to make available the Holy Scriptures in the language of the people. The first translation was made about 1400 and a second translation, which exercised so much influence, was a revision by John Purvey. Here the idiom is closer to the current language of the day than the earlier version. This is the only Bible in English which existed in Britain until Tyndale more than a century later. *The Wycliffe Bible* is the first complete Bible to appear in England.

The Gutenberg Bible

Between Wycliffe in 1384 and the Tyndale Version 140 years later, some stupendous events changed the whole intellectual and religious atmosphere of Europe. In 1453 Constantinople, the capital of the Eastern Roman Empire, fell. Many Greek scholars migrated to the West with their precious manuscripts. In 1456 there appeared the

first book printed with movable type, *The Guten-berg Bible,* which was to usher in a whole new era for Western man. Universal literacy and universal education were now possible, although not yet realities. Before that century ended, America had been discovered by Christopher Columbus. In 1516 Erasmus published the first Greek New Testament ever to appear in print, which exercised an enormous influence on subsequent biblical translations. In 1517 Luther nailed his ninety-five theses to the church door at Wittenberg. The Reformation may be said to have begun in Switzerland in 1519, and Calvin began his famous work in Geneva in 1541. This is the period of the reign of Henry VIII (1509–1547).

The Tyndale Bible

Tyndale, born in 1494 and educated at Oxford, became obsessed with a desire to produce a new edition of the Bible, in the English of his day, translated from original Greek and Hebrew. Tyndale was expert in seven languages. Failing to secure any encouragement from the Bishop of London, Tyndale crossed the channel to Hamburg (1524), and then to Wittenberg, where he met Luther. It was in Cologne that the first printed English New Testament was issued in 1525. Tyndale, betrayed by a friend, was deceivingly persuaded to come to England, where he was imprisoned and martyred on October 6, 1536, with those famous words upon his lips, "Lord, open the King of England's eyes."

Regarding the Old Testament, it is believed that Tyndale translated the Pentateuch and the book of Jonah. The translation of Isaiah is to be attributed to George Joye. Tyndale continued to work at revising his New Testament, with new editions appearing in 1533, 1534, and 1535. Eighty percent of the text of the *King James Version* is taken from *The Tyndale Bible.*

So harsh and constant was the denunciation of this version by ecclesiastical authorities, that of the first edition there remains only a fragment now in the British Museum. Of the second edition, only two copies are known today. Of the New Testament, printed at Worms, only two copies have survived to the present time.

The Myles Coverdale Bible

Just before Tyndale died, there appeared *the first complete Bible to be printed in the English tongue,* the work of Myles Coverdale (1485–1568), based on the Latin Vulgate, Tyndale, and the German Bible of Martin Luther. "Next to Tyndale, the man to whom lovers of the English Bible owe the greatest debt is Coverdale." He was the first to separate the Apocrypha from the Old Testament and place it as an appendix. His was the first Bible to introduce chapter summaries as distinct from brief chapter headings found in the Vulgate. So important was Coverdale's version

that his translation of the [...] self for *The Great Bible* [...] that still appears in the Boo[...]

As an illustration of th[...] Church to a Bible appearin[...] tongue, one might consider [...] the king condemning Tyndale[...] ing severe language: "And fr[...] much as it is come to the hear[...] ereign lord the king, that report[...] and many of his subjects, that as [...] not only expedient, but also nec[...] the English tongue both the New [...] the Old: and that his highness, his [...] prelates were bounden to suffer the [...] His highness hath therefore sen[...] upon consulted with the said prin[...] tuous, discrete, and well learned per[...] divinity foresaid, and by them all it is t[...] that it is not necessary, the said scripture to b[...] the English tongue, and in the hands of the com mon people; but that the distribution of the said scripture, and their permitting or denying thereof, dependeth only upon the discretion of the superiors, as they shall think it convenient. And that having respect to the malignity of this present time, with the inclination of the people to erroneous opinions, the translation of the New Testament and the Old into the vulgar tongue of English, should rather be the occasion of continuance or increase of errors among the said people, than any benefit or commodity toward the weal of their souls. And that it shall now be more convenient that the same people have the Holy Scripture expounded to them, by preachers in their sermons, according as it hath been of old time accustomed before this time."

The Cranmer Bible

In 1537 appeared a folio which in the title affirmed that the translation into English was by Thomas Matthew. The translator's name is now recognized as John Rogers, an associate of Tyndale. This translation was "set forth with the King's most gracious license." Later editions (1540 and 1541) contained a preface by Archbishop Cranmer and are known as *The Cranmer Bible.* Rogers did not know Hebrew and was dependent upon earlier translations. It is said that two-thirds of the Rogers Bible was from Tyndale and one-third from Coverdale. On the title page of the later versions appears for the first time, the words "This is the Bible appointed to the use of churches."

The Great Bible

Coverdale had a major part in a new revision of the Matthew Bible which was called *The Great Bible.* The pages measured 9x15 inches and the text was 8½x13 inches. It was commanded in 1538 that a copy of the English Bible be set up in

THE ENGLISH BIBLE

...nd this Bible was generally ... out this order. But because every parish ch... ...ate verson soon appeared *The* secured for ...ot reprinted after 1569. Rogers another ...martyrdom in 1555. "It is Rogers' ...came the foundation of all later *Great*...rized versions, and it is through h...ublication that Tyndale's 1535 version ...estament had its great influence upon ...t versions," notes L. A. Weigle.

...5 King Henry VIII issued an order that ...a or woman of what estate, condition, or [was] to receive, have, take, or keep Tyn- ...or Coverdale's New Testament." And yet *Great Bible*, for the most part made up of the ...nslations of Tyndale and Coverdale, was given ...yal approval and commanded to be placed in ...very church.

The Geneva Bible

The most accurate version until the Authorized Version of 1611 was *The Geneva Bible*. During the reign of Queen Mary (1553–1558), no Bible was printed in England, but a group of scholars in Geneva produced an English version called *The Geneva Bible* in 1560, with a second edition in 1652. The New Testament was edited by William Whittingham, who was married to Calvin's sister. Calvin wrote an introductory epistle. For the first time marginal notations called attention to variations in the Greek manuscripts. This was the first English version to use numbered verses as separate paragraphs. This was the Bible used by Shakespeare, John Bunyan, Oliver Cromwell, and so fervently used by the Puritans. Designated as "the people's book," it held a preeminent place among English versions for seventy-five years. This was the Bible brought over on the Mayflower. From 1560 to 1644, one hundred forty editions of *The Geneva Bible* appeared. The first Bible to be printed in Scotland was a Scottish edition of *The Geneva Bible* in 1579. The verse divisions of Robert Estienne, originally employed in his Greek New Testament in 1551, were used. This was the first Bible to be printed in Roman type instead of the old Black Letter.

The Bishops' Bible

The popularity of *The Geneva Bible* persuaded the Anglican authorities, after the accession of Queen Elizabeth to the throne in 1558, to produce a Bible which could bear the authority of the Church of England. This task was proposed by Archbishop Parker, who appointed a committee to begin the work. They were to use *The Great Bible* as their basis and were to compare it with the Greek and Hebrew texts. The scholarship of these Bishops was not equal to that of the group that had produced *The Geneva Bible*. The finished work was called *The Bishops' Bible*. Nineteen editions were printed from 1568–1606.

It was endorsed by Convocation in 1571. In the 1572 edition, Parker published in parallel columns the Psalter of *The Great Bible* and the Psalter of *The Bishops' Bible*. There are fewer differences between *The Bishops' Bible* and the *King James Version* than any other preceding translation.

The Rheims Bible and The Douay Bible

The last two Bibles to be considered, before the *King James Version*, are those known as *The Rheims Bible* and *The Douay Bible*, both Roman Catholic.

The New Testament was published as early as 1582 by the English College, then located at Rheims, and was thus known as *The Rheims New Testament*. The Old Testament, for the most part the work of Gregory Martin, a translation of the Latin Vulgate, was published in 1609, when the English College had returned to Douay and hence the name *The Douay Bible*. The poorest part of this version is acknowledged to be the Psalter, which has been rightly characterized as "a translation of a translation of a translation." There is, of course, a heavy emphasis in this version on ecclesiastical terms. Repentance is here translated *penance*. Here we have such unfamiliar words as *exinaninted, donances*, and *commersation*. Instead of *shewbread*, this version reads "proposition of loaves." *Deacon* is translated *minister*, and *elder* is translated *priest*. Ephesians 3:9 is made to read, "the dispensation of the sacrament." (See Eph. 3:9: "to make all *people* see what *is* the fellowship of the mystery.") The New Testament part of this Bible was extensively used by the King James revisers, but the Old Testament was published too late for any such influence.

The King James Version

It is now time to turn to a consideration of the most important English version of the Bible ever to be produced, called sometimes the *Authorized Version* and sometimes the *King James Version* (hereafter we shall refer to it with the initials KJV). In the summer of 1603, when King James was on his way to London to receive the English crown, he was presented with a petition of grievances by the clergy of Puritan convictions, which led the King to call a conference "for hearing and for the determining of things pretended to be amiss in the church." This conference was convened for three days, January 14–16, 1604, and was known as the Hampton Court Conference. During this conference Dr. John Reynolds, the leader of the Puritan party and president of Corpus Christi College, Oxford, made the motion that a new translation of the Bible be undertaken. Although the majority present were against the motion, it appealed to the king, and he ordered that such a translation be undertaken. Fifty-four

of the greatest biblical scholars in Great Britain were brought together for this great task and divided into six groups—three to work on a translation of the Old Testament and three on the New Testament. Two groups for the Old and New Testaments were to meet at Oxford, two at Cambridge, and two at Westminster. A recent writer has so well summarized the varied learning of this group that we take the liberty of quoting H. Wheeler Robinson: "The Oxford group was headed by Dr. John Hardinge, Regius Professor of Hebrew, and included Dr. John Reynolds, the originator of the project, whose 'memory and reading were near to a miracle'; Dr. Miles Smith, who 'had Hebrew at his fingers' ends'; Dr. Richard Brett, 'skilled and versed to a criticism in the Latin, Greek, Chaldee, Arabic, and Ethiopic tongues'; Sir Henry Saville, editor of the works of Chrysostom; and Dr. John Harmer, Professor of Greek, 'a most noted Latinist, Grecian, and divine.' The Cambridge committee was at first led by Edward Lively, Regius Professor of Hebrew, who died in 1605 before the work was really begun, and included Dr. Lawrence Chaderton, 'familiar with the Greek and Hebrew tongues and the numerous writings of the Rabbis'; Thomas Harrison, 'noted for his exquisite skill in Hebrew and Greek idioms'; Dr. Robert Spalding, successor to Lively as Professor of Hebrew; Andrew Downes, 'one composed of Greek and industry'; and John Bois, 'a precious Greek and Hebrew scholar.' The Westminster group was headed by Lancelot Andrewes, Dean of Westminster, afterwards Bishop of Chichester, of Ely, and finally of Winchester, 'who might have been interpreter general at Babel' . . . and included the Hebraist Hadrian Saravia; and William Bedwell, the greatest living Arabic scholar." Since there was a lapse of two or three years between the naming of these committees and the beginning of their labors, the work was begun in 1607 and completed in 1610. The Bible appeared the following year.

Fifteen rules were to bind this large number of revisers. The first reads as follows: "The ordinary Bible read in the Church, commonly called *The Bishops' Bible*, to be followed, and as little altered as the Truth of the original will permit." The fourteenth rule was more comprehensive, reading as follows: "These translations to be used when they agree better with the Text than the Bishops *Rule—Tindoll's*, Matthews, Coverdales, Whitchurch's, Geneva." In the Preface to the Reader which appeared in this version, the translators stated that they did not hesitate "to consult the Translators or Commentators, *Chaldee, Hebrewe, Syrian, Greeke,* or *Latine,* no nor the *Spanish, French, Italian,* or *Dutch.*"

The new version bore the following title: "The Holy Bible, Conteyning the Old Testament and the New; Newly Translated out of the Originall tongues, with the former Translations diligently compared and revisel, by . . . . commandement. A)poii . . . . . . Churches. Imprinted at Lc . . . . ker, Printer to the Kings mos . . . . . . Anno Dom. 1611." The New . . . . . slightly different: "The New . . . . . Lord and Saviour Jesus Christ, ... out of the Originall Greeke; an . . . . . Translations diligently compared . . . . . His Majesties speciall Comma . . . . . printed at London by Robert Ba . . . . . the Kings most Excellent Majestie . . . . . 1611. cum Privilegio." While this ve . . . . . the *Authorized Version,* no act of Pa . . . . . ever passed approving it. King Jame . . . . . promoted such an undertaking, but tl . . . . . subsequent official act. The first print . . . . . Bible was a folio 16x10½ inches. Three . . . . . quickly followed, carrying a considerable num . . . . . of misprints and variations in spelling. We must ask at this point how much of the KJV was dependent upon earlier versions? It has been said that four percent of the vocabulary goes back to the days of Wycliffe, eighteen percent came from Tyndale, thirteen percent from Coverdale, nineteen percent from the Geneva Bible, four percent from the Bishops' Bible, and three percent from all other preceding versions. Thirty-nine percent of the vocabulary of the KJV is unique. Almost nine-tenths of the New Testament portion of this version can be found word for word in the Tyndale version of 1525. All controversial notes were excluded, but there were over four thousand marginal notes, giving the literal meaning of Hebrew words, and 765 in the New Testament, indicating variant or alternative renderings. The chapter summaries and page headings were new, and some of these chapter headings are indications of current theology and then prevalent principles of biblical interpretation. The Old Testament rested upon the same Masoretic Hebrew text as all subsequent versions, but since no ancient manuscripts of the Greek New Testament arrived in England until 1628, those responsible for this greatest of all versions did not have the advantage of the best Greek text.

During subsequent decades the spelling of the KJV has been modernized, misprints have been corrected, the larger chapter summaries have been abbreviated, and the references in the margin have been examined. Chronological dates were introduced into the margin of the KJV in 1701, based on the chronology of Archbishop Ussher. As early as 1613, the text showed over 300 differences from the original of 1611. Thirty thousand new marginal references were added in versions appearing in the 1760s.

Soon the KJV crowded out all preceding translations except for students interested in specific variations and the development of the English language. For the first time, England was reading

THE ENGLISH BIBLE

...nd hearing the same Bible ...thus became bound up with one Bible at ...on. Since it stilled all contro- read in chur...st renderng, it gradually came the life of...s so far absolute that in the minds versy...ove was no distinction between this to be...he original texts, and they may al- of...to have believed in the literal inspira- very words which composed it," wrote Cook. The beauty of the KJV, as well as ...nous influence cannot easily be exagger- The translators of the *Revised Version,* ...three centuries later, declared: "We have ...to study this great Version carefully and mi- ...ely, line by line; and the longer we have been ...gaged upon it the more we have learned to ad- ...ire its simplicity, its dignity, its power, its happy turns of expression, its general accuracy, and, we must not fail to add, the music of its cadences, and the felicities of its rhythm." Even the non-Christian, Thomas Huxley, offered the following glowing tribute to this version of the Scriptures: "Consider the great historical fact that for three centuries this book has been woven into the life of all that is best and noblest in English history; that it has become the national epic of Britain, and is as familiar to noble and simple, from John-o'-Groat's House to Land's End, as Dante and Tasso once were to the Italians; that it is written in the noblest and purest English, and abounds in exquisite beauties of pure literary form; and, finally, that it forbids the veriest hind who never left his village to be ignorant of the existence of other countries and other civilizations, and of a great past stretching back to the furthest limits of the oldest civilizations of the world."

The English Revised Version

It is not necessary to discuss the translations of secondary importance offered during the next three centuries. A number of changes had occurred in the use of the English language, and a great deal of new material was available for ascertaining the Greek text of the New Testament, and much more was known about the Hebrew language. Consequently, on February 10, 1870, Bishop Wilberforce submitted the following resolution to the Upper House of Convocation of the Province of Canterbury: "That a Committee of both Houses to be appointed, with power to confer with any Committee that may be appointed by the Convocation of the Northern Province, to report upon the desirableness of a revision of the Authorized Version of the New Testament, whether by marginal notes or otherwise, in all those passages where plain and clear errors, whether in the Hebrew or Greek text originally adopted by the translators, or in the translation made from the same, shall, on due investigation, be found to exist." In May of the same year, a committee made five suggestions: "1. That it is

desirable that a revision of the Authorized Version of the Holy Scriptures be undertaken. 2. That the revision be so conducted as to comprise both marginal renderings and such emendations as it may be found necessary to insert in the text of the Authorized Version. 3. That in the above resolutions we do not contemplate any new translation of the Bible, or any alteration of the language, except when in the judgment of the most competent scholars such change is necessary. 4. That in such necessary changes, the style of the language employed in the existing version be closely followed. 5. That it is desirable that Convocation should nominate a body of its own members to undertake the work of revision, who shall be at liberty to invite the co-operation of any eminent for scholarship, to whatever nation or religious body they may belong."

Many of the finest biblical scholars in Britain were engaged to translate the Old and New Testaments—fifty-four of them. The first general principle was "to introduce as few alterations as possible into the text of the Authoized Version consistently with faithfulness." The fifth, seventh, and eighth principles were: "5. To make or retain no change in the Text on the second final revision by each Company, except *two-thirds* of those present approve of the same, but on the first revision to decide by simple majorities. 7. To revise the headings of chapters, pages, paragraphs, italics, and punctuation. 8. To refer, on the part of each Company, when considered desirable, to Divines, Scholars, and Literary Men, whether at home or abroad, for their opinions."

The New Testament was issued in May, 1881, and the Old Testament in May, 1885. Two famous Greek scholars, B. F. Westcott and F. J. A. Hort, generally influenced the adoption of what they called the "neutral text." A number of passages were taken out of the text and placed in the margin as not appearing in the earlier Greek texts, for example, John 5:3, 4; First John 5:6, 7; and John 8:1–9. Where parallel passages appeared in two or more books with identical wording in the original, the translations also were made identical. There were many criticisms of the *Revised Version,* and yet many agree with the statement of Professor F. F. Bruce that "the *Revised Version* with these marginal references is still the most useful edition of the Bible for the careful student who knows no language but English." The Old Testament is especially recognized as being a great improvement for accuracy's sake over the KJV.

The American Standard Revised Version

It was hoped that the English and American committees could be responsible for a single revised version, but so many differences arose that after some years the American Company asked to be released from further cooperation. They would

publish their own Revised Version, promising not to do so for fourteen years. In 1897, Thomas Nelson and Sons entered into an agreement with the American Company to meet the necessary expenses for the preparation of an American revision. Once again they went to work, minutely going over the entire text. Twenty-nine years later, on August 26, 1901, the *American Standard Revised Version* of the Bible was placed on sale and was at once recognized as superior in many ways to the English revision.

Other Versions

One of the more important nineteenth-century translations of the Bible was by the famous compiler of *Young's Concordance*, the British biblical scholar, Robert Young. He published at Edinburgh, as early as 1862, his *Literal Translation of the Bible*, permeated with Young's deep conviction that "every word of the original is God-breathed as the Apostle Paul says in his Second Epistle to Timothy, chapter 3:16." A third edition was issued in 1898.

The outstanding scholar among the Plymouth Brethren in their earlier days was J. N. Darby, who had immense linguistic ability and issued a translation of the Bible, first in French, then in Dutch and German, and then in English. Darby wrote in the preface to his New Testament translation, "Being profoundly convinced of the Divine inspiration of the Scriptures, we have tried in this translation to reproduce as exactly as possible what God has given us in another language. . . . ."

Coming into the twentieth century, the first new translation that need be mentioned is *The Twentieth Century New Testament*, the publication of which extended from 1898 to 1901, a careful retranslation based upon the Westcott and Hort text. Great care was taken to weigh every word in the Greek and to translate identical passages verbatim. Dr. E. H. Robertson, in his survey of the more recent versions, says, "There seems to me to be little doubt that this is one of the most careful translations ever undertaken," and reports that the result of a Bible study group which he led for some years was that here appeared "the most faithful rendering of the Greek in nearly every difficult passage we encountered."

The two most widely used translations of the New Testament, until the appearance of the RSV, were those produced by Dr. Weymouth and Dr. Moffatt. Dr. Weymouth's *New Testament in Modern Speech* first appeared in 1902, with brief introductions prefixed to each book and a considerable number of explanatory footnotes. It was frequently revised during his life and for some years after, the later revisions being increasingly liberal in theological tendency.

The New Testament: A New Translation is by Dr. James Moffatt, one of the most distinguished New Testament scholars of the earlier part of our century. This first appeared in 1913. The Old Testament followed in 1924 and the entire Bible, with a final revision, was published in 1935. His work in the Old Testament is generally recognized as being of much less value than his work in the New Testament. Even here Moffatt justly antagonized many Christians by the liberties he took with some texts. For example, the phrase occurring at the opening of John's gospel, "In the beginning was the Word and the Word was with God and the Word was God," Moffatt translates the last phrase "and the Word was divine." So also in translating the genealogy in the first chapter of Matthew in the Moffatt version, it reads: "Jacob the father of Joseph, and Joseph (to whom the virgin Mary was betrothed), the father of Jesus who is called Christ," a translation based on a late and unauthoritative Greek manuscript and contradicted by all the most ancient texts. As an illustration, however, of some of the more revealing passages in Moffatt, we might consider four verses from Second Corinthians: "I live for God as the fragrance of Christ breathed alike on those who are being saved and on those who are perishing, to the one a deadly fragrance that makes for death, to the other a vital fragrance that makes for life" (2 Cor. 2:15, 16); "Hence I never lose heart" (4:16); and "he will increase the crop of your charities—you will be enriched on all hands, so that you can be generous on all occasions, and your generosity, of which I am the agent, will make men give thanks to God" (9:11).

The last four translators we have considered were all from Great Britain. It is time now that an American version should appear, and it did, produced by scholars at the University of Chicago. In 1923 Dr. Edgar J. Goodspeed published his *The New Testament: An American Translation*, based on the Westcott and Hort text. In 1935, assisted by colleagues, a new translation of the entire Bible appeared with the simple title *The Bible: An American Translation*. It was widely used for the first twenty years after its first appearance, although it was never quoted with the same frequency as Moffatt's.

The Revised Standard Version

In 1937, the International Council of Religious Education, in which some forty of the larger denominations in North America were associated, authorized the preparation and publication of a complete new revision, which was carried through by some thirty-two different American scholars. *The New Testament Revised Version* was published in 1946 and the entire Bible in 1952. No version produced in our country has ever aroused so much antagonism, some justified and some unjustified. A number of archaisms have been removed, necessary emendations, due to a better knowledge of the meanings of the original

text, have been made. Thus, for example, Deuteronomy 32:8, which in the earlier translations stated that God had fixed the bounds of the people "according to the number of the children of Israel," now reads "according to the number of the sons of God," which is supported by the Septuagint and the Samaritan Bible and now by a fragment of the Hebrew manuscript found at Qumran.

One most commendable virtue of this version is that it returns to the familiar words of the King James translation of Second Timothy 3:16, from which the Revised Version had departed, the new version reading "All Scripture is inspired by God and *is* profitable."

A second edition of the *Revised Standard Version* was published in 1971, popularly known as RSV II. This edition includes considerable revision of the New Testament.

The Holy Scripture According to the Masoretic Text: A New Translation, and The Torah

In 1914, the Jewish Publication Society of America published a volume entitled *The Holy Scriptures According to the Masoretic Text: A New Translation* (exclusively of the Old Testament), which has not exercised extensive influence outside Jewish circles. In 1962, the same organization published a new translation of the Pentateuch with the simple title, *The Torah;* in 1978 the second section was published, *The Prophets;* and in 1982 the final portion was published, *The Writings.* This work has been very carefully done, the result of the finest Hebrew scholarship available. But there seems to be a deliberate attempt here to make the Messianic predictions of the Pentateuch void of any Messianic meaning, as for example, Genesis 3:15 which here reads: "I will put enmity between you and the woman and between your offspring and hers; they shall strike at your head and you shall strike at their heel." All other modern translations read "his heel." The modern gentile reader would certainly not get much out of the translation of Exodus 3:14, which here reads: "And God said to Moses, 'Ehyeh-Asher-Ehyeh.'" There are a number of footnotes indicating that the exact meaning of some Hebrew words is not known today, as for example, the twelve stones of Exodus 28:17–20; the creatures mentioned in Deuteronomy 14:5, 6; and the diseases of Deuteronomy 28:22.

The Amplified Bible

The Amplified Bible (1954) is a literal translation with multiple expressions using associated words to convey the original thought. The New Testament uses the Greek text of Westcott and Hort plus twenty-seven translations and revisions. The Old Testament is similarly extensive.

The version is intended to supplement other translations authentically, concisely, and in convenient form.

Good News for Modern Man

Good News for Modern Man (Today's English Version) is a translation of the New Testament by Dr. Robert G. Bratcher (and a distinguished review committee) published in 1966. This is a paraphrase which gained enormous popularity in a short period of time. It was intended to communicate the Scriptures to the masses of English-speaking people around the world and has been used as an instrument of evangelism for people outside the church.

The Jerusalem Bible

The Jerusalem Bible (1966) is a translation from the Hebrew Masoretic, Greek Septuagint, Dead Sea Scrolls, and accepted Greek and Aramaic New Testament texts—all compared with the French Version. It was produced by twenty-eight principal collaborators in translation and literary revision under Alexander Jones, general editor.

New American Bible

The *New American Bible* (1970) is a Roman Catholic translation that is a highlight of Bible publishing in the present century. All basic texts were consulted, and the work was twenty-six years in the making. Over fifty recognized biblical scholars, the majority of them college professors, labored to produce this outstanding version. Scholars were Catholic, Protestant, and Jewish. The purpose was to produce a more accurate translation from the older manuscripts, and this was made possible by the Pope in 1943. Prior to this version, Catholics had been required to use the Latin Vulgate as the basis for translation.

The Living Bible

A very popular paraphrase, *The Living Bible* (Complete Bible, 1971), is the work of a single translator, Kenneth N. Taylor. The initial source was the *American Standard Version* of 1901, but Dr. Taylor and the Greek and Hebrew specialists he consulted also used the most respected texts available.

New American Standard Bible

The New American Standard Bible was translated by an Editorial Board of fifty-four Greek and Hebrew scholars and required nearly eleven years to complete. The producers of this translation believed that interest in the *American Standard Version* of 1901 should be renewed and increased. Recognizing the values of the ASV, the Lockman Foundation, sponsor of the project, felt an urgency to update that version by incorporating recent discoveries of Hebrew and Greek textual sources and by rendering the ASV into more

current English. The editorial board has continued to function since publication of the complete Bible in 1971. Minor revisions and refinements have been inserted in more recent editions.

New International Version

The *New International Version* began with work by committees from the Christian Reformed Church and the National Association of Evangelicals. In 1967 the New York Bible Society undertook the financial sponsorship of the translation. The translation is done from the Masoretic Text in the Old Testament and an eclectic Greek text in the New Testament. This modern English version was published as a complete Bible in 1978.

New King James Version

In 1975 Thomas Nelson Publishers began the fifth revision of the *King James Version*. Over one hundred scholars worked on the translation of the *Biblia Hebraica Stuttgartensia* (Old Testament) and the Scrivener Greek Text (New Testament) into modern English using the 1611 and 1769 editions of the *King James Version* as standards. For a

more complete discussion of the *New King James Version* consult a copy of that version.

Other Major Versions Since 1950

The Holy Bible from Ancient Eastern Manuscripts (1957) was intended to convey ancient biblical customs preserved only in the Aramaic texts and to reveal the deeper biblical meanings often hidden in idioms and parables.

The Berkeley Version in Modern English (1959) translates every word using modern terms.

The *New English Bible* (Complete Bible, 1970) required twenty-four years to complete and enlisted the labors of fifty recognized biblical scholars. It is based on the original Greek and Hebrew texts.

J. B. Phillips, an English vicar, translated the New Testament into modern speech, beginning with *Letters to Young Churches* in 1947, followed by *The Gospels* in 1952, *The Young Church in Action* in 1955, the *Book of Revelation* in 1957, and in 1958 the one-volume edition of his completed translation of the New Testament, *The New Testament in Modern Speech. Four Prophets* appeared in 1963.

FIRST MENTIONED THINGS
IN THE BIBLE

Subject	Reference	Page	Subject	Reference	Page
Adultery	Ex. 20:14	75	Heir	Gen. 15:2	17
Altar	Gen. 8:20	11	Home	Gen. 27:5	28
Angel	Gen. 16:7	17	Hunter	Gen. 10:8, 9	13
Archer	Gen. 21:20	22	Husband	Gen. 3:6	6
Bird	Gen. 1:21	4	**Idols**	Gen. 31:19	33
Camp	Gen. 32:2	34	**Jail**	Gen. 39:20	41
Cave dweller	Gen. 19:30	20	Joy	Gen. 31:27	33
Chariot	Gen. 41:43	43	**Kill**	Gen. 4:8	8
Child	Gen. 11:30	14	King	Gen. 14:1	16
Child named before			Kiss	Gen. 27:26	29
birth	Gen. 16:11	17	**Man to interpret**	Gen. 41:15	42
City builder	Gen. 4:17	8	Man to wear a ring	Gen. 41:42	43
Coffin	Gen. 50:26	52	Murderer	Gen. 4:8	8
Command	Gen. 1:3	4	**Oath**	Gen. 21:23, 24	22
Congregation	Ex. 12:3	66	**Pilgrim**	Gen. 12:1–8	14
Dancing	Ex. 15:20	70	Prayer	Gen. 4:26	8
Darkness	Gen. 1:2	4	Preacher to become		
Death	Gen. 24:67	26	drunk	Gen. 9:20, 21	12
Dew	Gen. 27:28	29	Prophecy	Gen. 3:15	7
Disaster	Gen. 19:19	20	Purchase of land	Gen. 23:3–20	23
Dream	Gen. 20:3	21	**Question**	Gen. 3:1	6
Drunk	Gen. 9:21	12	**Rain**	Gen. 7:1–12	10
Dungeon	Gen. 40:15	42	Rainbow	Gen. 9:13	12
Earth	Gen. 1:1	4	**Saddle**	Gen. 22:3	22
Emancipator	Ex. 3:7–22	58	Scribe	Ex. 24:4	78
Embalming	Gen. 50:2	52	Shipbuilder	Gen. 6:14, 22	9, 10
Execution	Gen. 40:20–22	42	Sin	Gen. 3:1–24	6
Family	Gen. 8:19	11	Snake	Gen. 49:17	51
Farmer	Gen. 4:2	7	Sword	Gen. 3:24	7
Father	Gen. 2:24	6	**Temptation**	Gen. 3:1–6	6
Fear	Gen. 9:2	11	Tower	Gen. 11:4, 5	13
Food	Gen. 1:29	5	**Veil**	Gen. 24:65	26
Food control	Gen. 41:25–27	43	Violence	Gen. 6:11	9
Forgiveness	Gen. 50:17	52	**Wage contract**	Gen. 29:15–20	30
Friend	Gen. 38:12	40	War	Gen. 14:2	16
Game	Gen. 25:28	27	Wealth	Gen. 31:1	32
Gardener	Gen. 2:15	5	Well	Gen. 16:14	18
Gift	Gen. 9:3	11	Wife	Gen. 2:24	6
God	Gen. 1:1	4	Wind	Gen. 8:1	10
Gold	Gen. 2:11	5	Wine	Gen. 9:21	12
Grace of God	Ezra 9:8	483	Wish	Gen. 23:8	23
Grave	Gen. 23:6	23	Witness	Gen. 21:30	22
Guilt	Gen. 26:10	27	Woman thief	Gen. 31:19	33
Harlot	Gen. 34:31	36	Words spoken to		
Hate	Gen. 24:60	26	man	Gen. 1:28	5
Healing	Deut. 32:39	211	Worship	Gen. 4:3–5	7
Heart	Gen. 6:5	9			
Heavens	Gen. 1:1	4			

THE SCARLET THREAD OF REDEMPTION

Introduction

The Bible is a book of redemption. It is that or nothing at all. It is not merely a book of history, or of science, or of anthropology, or of cosmogony. It is a book of salvation and deliverance for lost mankind.

The idea in the word *redemption* is twofold: it refers to a deliverance; and it refers to the price paid for that deliverance, a ransom. We are redeemed from the penalty of sin, from the power of Satan and evil, by the price Jesus paid on the cross for us; and we are redeemed to a new freedom from sin, a new relationship to God, and a new life of love by the appropriation of that atonement for our sins.

The whole of the Bible, whether the Old Testament or the New Testament, looks to the mighty, redemptive atonement of Christ. His blood sacrifice is the ransom paid for our deliverance. He took our sinful nature upon Himself in order that He might satisfy the demands of the law. His sacrifice is accepted as the payment for the debt the sinner owes to God, and His death is accepted as the full payment for man's deliverance.

Our Lord's redemptive work for us is threefold: First, it is closely associated with forgiveness, since we receive forgiveness through the redemptive price of Christ's death. Second, it involves justification, since the deliverance establishes us in a restored position of favor before God. Third, it promises final deliverance from the power of sin at the coming of the Lord. This redemption is "The Scarlet Thread."

The Creation and the Fall

When God made the heavens and the earth, they must have been beautiful, perfect, and pure.

In the Garden of Eden, however, through a denial of the Word of God and through a deception of the woman, our first parents fell. Eve was deceived, but Adam chose to die by the side of the woman whom God had created and placed in his arms. When the Lord came to visit the man and his wife in the cool of the day, He could not find them. They were afraid and hid themselves from the Lord because they were naked and ashamed. To hide their guilt, they made for themselves aprons of fig leaves, but when God looked upon the covering, He said, This will not do. Covering for sin (atonement for sin) cannot be woven by human hands. Therefore, somewhere in the Garden of Eden, the Lord took an innocent animal, and before the eyes of Eve and Adam, God slew that innocent animal as the ground drank up its blood. This is the beginning of "The Scarlet Thread of Redemption." Through the slaughter of an innocent victim, God took coats of skin and covered over the shame and the nakedness of the man and his wife. This is the first sacrifice, and it was offered by the hand of Almighty God. When Adam saw the gasping, spent life of that innocent creature, and when he saw the crimson stain which soiled the ground, it was his first experience of knowing what it meant to die because of sin. So the story of atonement and sacrifice begins and unfolds throughout the Word of God until finally in glory we shall see great throngs of the saints who have washed their robes and made them white in the blood of the Lamb. This is "The Scarlet Thread of Redemption."

From the Seventh Day in Eden to the Call of Abraham

In the Garden of Eden, as the Lord covered over the nakedness of the man and the woman, He turned to Satan and said, "And I will put enmity between thee and the woman, and between thy seed and her seed; it shall bruise thy head, and thou shalt bruise his heel." (Gen. 3:15). For centuries the rabbis studied that word of Yahweh God to Satan. The Seed of the woman. *Seed* is masculine. The rabbis contemplated the promise of God that the "Seed" of the woman would bruise Satan's head. We now know that the promise is related to the long conflict and struggle betwen the hatred of Lucifer and the love of God in Christ Jesus. It speaks of Jesus at Calvary. Jesus suffered. His heel was bruised. But in that bruising, He defeated once and for all the power of that old serpent, the devil. He bruised his head.

As the man Adam and his wife, Eve, made their first home in earth cursed for their sakes, after a time there were born to them two sons. One was named Cain and the other Abel. In jealousy and insane fury, the older brother killed the younger brother. But the seed of God would be preserved. The Lord, therefore, gave to Eve another son, named Seth. Seth was a man of faith, as Cain was a man of the world. When the children of Seth, the godly remnant, intermarried with the children of Cain, the people of the world, the result was a fallen progeny that filled the earth with violence. Finally, God said it was enough. One hundred twenty years later, He would destroy the world by a flood. But a member of the line of Seth found grace in the sight of the Lord. His name was Noah. To preserve the righteous seed, God told Noah to build an ark; and into that ark of safety, salvation, and hope Noah brought his family. After the passing of the awesome judgment of the flood, the earth once again began its story of redemption through the life of this one man and his three sons.

It was not long, however, until the ravages of sin

began to waste the select family of God. Instead of carrying out the great commission of the Lord for mankind to inhabit the whole earth, the people drew together into one plain and announced their purpose to build a tower around which they were to center their civilization and their collective, communal unity. When God looked down and saw their pride, He confused their speech and caused them to "babble." From this "Tower of Babel," therefore, the different parts of the human race, being unable to understand each other, scattered in different directions and so fathered the nations of the earth that grew up from those three great family lines of Noah.

From the Call of Abraham Through the Times of the Judges

We begin the story of Abraham in a dark era. The whole world had been plunged into abysmal idolatry, but God called out this man to leave his home, his place, his country, and his family to go into another country which he would afterward receive for an inheritance. In obedience, Abraham left the Mesopotamian valley and came as a pilgrim, a stranger, and a sojourner into the land of Canaan. There he dwelt, and there God gave him two sons. But the Lord God said to Abraham that Ishmael, the son of a slave woman, would not be the promised seed. When Abraham was a hundred years old and Sarah was ninety years old, God miraculously placed in the arms of the parents the child of promise, whom they named Isaac. Isaac was the father of two sons, Esau and Jacob. The Lord, refusing Esau, chose Jacob whom He renamed, after a deep conversion experience, the "prince of God" or "Israel."

Because of a severe famine in Canaan and because Jacob's son, Joseph, was in Egypt, the entire household of Jacob went down to live in the land of the Nile. Later, there arose a Pharaoh who "knew not" Joseph. The chosen family became slaves to this new ruler of Egypt, and their heavy groaning mounted up to the ears of the Lord God in heaven. The Lord, therefore, raised up the mighty prophet, Moses, to deliver his people from the bondage and slavery of the Egyptians. God worked this deliverance by a miracle called the Passover. For the Lord had said, When I see the blood, I will pass over you and will spare you and your home. This way of salvation, through the blood, is once again "The Scarlet Thread of Redemption."

After the Lord God delivered the chosen family from Egypt, He brought them by the leadership of Moses through the parting of the Red Sea into the Sinaitic Peninsula to the base of Mount Horeb. There, for forty days and forty nights, Moses was with God, and there the Lord gave to Moses the pattern of the tabernacle, the ritual instructions of holy worship, and all of the other marvelous things in the Book of Leviticus that portray and prophesy the sacrifice of the Son of God.

After the death of Moses, Joshua went over Jordan and led the wars of conquest. In the first confrontation, at Jericho, an incident happened which gave rise to the title of this summary. The scouts sent out by Joshua to spy out Jericho were saved by the faith and kindness of Rahab. The men of Israel promised life and safety, both for her and her father's house, if she would bind a scarlet thread in her window. This she did, and, when Jericho fell into the hands of Joshua by the intervention of God, Rahab and her family were spared because of that scarlet line, "The Scarlet Thread of Redemption."

After the conquest of Canaan, under Joshua, we have the story of the Judges. The difference between a judge and a king was that a king gave to his son his throne by inheritance, but a judge was raised up in a crisis and endowed with special gifts from God for a period of time. The days of the Judges end with the birth of Samuel.

From the First of the Prophets to the Founding of the Kingdom

During the time of Samuel, the people began to cry for a king. It was the purpose of God in the beginning for the children of Israel to have a king (Deut. 17:14–20), but it hurt the heart of the Lord that the request should come in so vain and rebellious a way as they presented it to Samuel. But according to the word and instruction of God, Samuel anointed Saul to be king over Israel. In his beginning ministry, Saul was a mighty man and carried out the mandates of heaven, but he soon fell away from the instruction of Samuel and fell into gross disobedience to the will of God. The Word of the Lord, therefore, came to Samuel that he must anoint a man after God's own heart. That anointing was directed toward a lad from the shepherd field, a son of Jesse by the name of David.

David and the Kingdoms of Israel and Judah

The first part of David's life as king of Israel was magnificent. Then, in the very prime of his life, at the very height of his glory, he turned aside from the will of God and became self-indulgent and lustful like other Oriental kings. This brought to David an infinite tragedy, one by which the name of God was blasphemed. Nevertheless, God forgave the sin of David and chose him to be the father of that marvelous Son who would sit upon His throne as King forever. A type of that glorious Son of David, was the *immediate* son of David, called Solomon. Solomon also began his reign gloriously and triumphantly, but like his father, Solomon also fell into tragic decline. Upon his death, the kingdom was divided.

Thereafter, the people of God were divided into two kingdoms: that of the north was called the

kingdom of Israel and that of the south was called the kingdom of Judah. The northern kingdom of Israel was taken away into captivity by the cruel and ruthless Assyrians in 722 B.C. The southern kingdom was carried away into Babylonian captivity in 587 B.C. In the days of the Babylonian captivity, Jeremiah prophesied in Jerusalem while Daniel, the prophet-statesman, and Ezekiel, the holy seer, comforted and strengthened the people of God in Mesopotamia.

Out of the Babylonian captivity came three great establishments by which God has blessed our world. First, the Jews were never idolatrous again. Second, the synagogue was born, and from the synagogue came the church. The services of the synagogue are the same type of services we have today. Third, from the captivity came the canon of the Holy Scriptures. Out of tears and suffering came our greatest blessing, "The Scarlet Thread of Redemption."

From the Prophets to the Christ to the Preaching of Paul

Out of the agonies of the days of the kingdoms of Israel and of Judah came the predictions by the prophets of a more glorious Saviour and King, whom God would send to His people. When we read a passage like the twenty-second Psalm or the fifty-third chapter of Isaiah, we seem to be standing by the cross of the Son of God. More and more, the great spiritual leaders of Israel and of Judah began to depict the coming of a Redeemer who would save His people from their sins and bring to them the everlasting hope and righteousness of God. This messianic hope became stronger and more gloriously received as the centuries passed.

In 536 B.C. Cyrus the Persian gave the people the right to return from the Babylonian captivity to their homeland in Judah and to build their holy temple in Jerusalem. Thus, the remnant of the captivity returned under Zerubbabel, the political leader; under Joshua, the priestly leader; under Ezra, the scribe; and under Nehemiah, who had been the prime minister at the court of Shushan, the Persian capital. This holy remnant, thus seeking to restore the worship of the true God in Jerusalem and to recreate the political life of Judah, was encouraged by God's messengers, Haggai, Zechariah, and Malachi.

Of the three great restoration prophets, Zechariah is by far the greatest. Zechariah spoke much about Israel, about the end of time, and about the conversion of the people of the Lord. The last prophet is Malachi. He delivered his message from about 450 B.C. to about 425 B.C.

The four-hundred-year period between the Old Testament and the New Testament marks the rise of the Hellenistic empire. God used Alexander the Great to spread abroad throughout the civilized world one culture and one language, which made possible the later preaching of Christ to all men everywhere.

In that inter-biblical period also arose the might of the Roman Empire. When Augustus Caesar was the Roman emperor, and when Rome had the entire world in her hand, the great prophecies of Isaiah, Micah, Nathan to David, Jacob to his son Judah, and the great promise of God Almighty to Eve in the Garden of Eden, came to pass. In the seed progeny of the woman and through the seed of Abraham, all the families of the earth were to be blessed—and our Saviour was thus born into the world. "The Scarlet Thread of Redemption" has led us to the birth of Him who has come to redeem the human race from their fallen estate.

In His ministry Jesus early began to teach His disciples that He should suffer and die. When He was transfigured, there appeared Moses and Elijah talking to Him about His death, which He should accomplish in Jerusalem. When He was anointed by Mary of Bethany, He said it was for His burial. When the Greeks came to see Him from afar He said, "And I, if I be lifted up from the earth, will draw all men unto me" (John 12:32). At the Last Supper He said, This is My body; eat in remembrance of Me. And again He said, This is My blood; drink in remembrance of Me. Before He went to the cross, He gave Himself in Gethsemane in travail of soul for our redemption (Is. 53:11). And when He bowed His head and died He said, "It is finished!" (John 19:30). When we preach the cross, when we preach the blood, when we preach the sacrificial death of Christ, we are preaching the meaning of His coming into the world. The sacrifice of Christ consummated the great redemptive plan and purpose of God on the earth. This is "The Scarlet Thread of Redemption."

After the resurrection of our Lord, after the giving of the Great Commission to the apostles, and after the ascension of our Saviour into heaven, the Lord poured out His Holy Spirit upon His church in Jerusalem on the day of Pentecost. Then the disciples of Jesus began to make known throughout the earth the Good News of our hope and salvation.

The epistles of Paul are divided into four distinct groups. The first group he wrote on his second missionary journey from Athens and Corinth. They are First and Second Thessalonians. The second group of letters was born in his third missionary journey. While he was in Ephesus, he wrote First Corinthians. Somewhere between Ephesus and Corinth, he wrote Second Corinthians in Macedonia. Then, either in Antioch or on his way to Antioch, he wrote Galatians and Romans. First and Second Corinthians, Galatians, and Romans, therefore, center around the city of Ephesus. The third group of epistles Paul wrote from the prison in Rome, during his first Roman imprisonment. They are Ephesians, Phi-

lippians, Colossians, and Philemon. The fourth and last group of his epistles, written after his first Roman imprisonment were First Timothy, Titus, and Second Timothy, called the Pastoral Epistles. In all of Paul's letters, there is the constant theme of redemptive love. It is a part of "The Scarlet Thread of Redemption."

The Apocalypse and the Consummation of the Age

We come now to the conclusion of the Bible.

On the Isle of Patmos, a rocky little point in the Mediterranean Sea, several miles southwest of Ephesus, John was exiled to die of exposure and starvation. But there the Lord appears to John in a glorious vision. The vision is called the Revelation, that is, "the unveiling." "The Apocalypse," the unveiling of Jesus Christ in His glory, in His majesty, and in His kingdom, is the reward that God gave to Jesus for saving us, Adam's fallen children, from our sins.

After the vision of the exalted and glorified Christ in chapter one, and after the prophetic words in chapters two and three, John is taken up through an open door into heaven. While John, the translated saint, is with the Saviour in heaven, the judgments of Almighty God are poured out on the earth. They are depicted in the opening of the seven seals, the seven trumpets, and the seven bowls. In those dark days John sees a vision in Revelation, chapter seven, concerning the blood-washed redeemed souls in glory. Announcement is made to him through one of the elders that these are they who have come out of the great tribulation and have washed their robes and made them white in the blood of the Lamb. This is "The Scarlet Thread of Redemption" that began with the blood of covering in the Garden of Eden and finds its ultimate and final consummation in the blood-washed throng before the throne of God in glory.

After the seven seals and the judgments, the seven trumpets and the judgments, the seven bowls and the judgments, and the seven personages and the judgments, we come to the final great Judgment Day of Almighty God. The anti-Christ, who professes to be the leader of the nations of the world, is seen gathering the armies of the entire earth together. They are converging from the north, from the east, from the south, from the west, and from the islands of the sea. They are converging for that great day of the Lord. That is the Battle of Armageddon, the last great war the world is going to fight. At Megiddo, the armies of the earth by the millions will converge to face that rendezvous with God. In the midst of this holocaust, Christ will intervene in human history. He comes with His saints. He will deliver His people, shut up in the Holy City, and take Satan and bind him for a thousand years in the bottomless pit.

After the binding of Satan for a thousand years, which is called the Millennium, Satan is released, and thereafter goes forth once again to lead men in rebellion against God. This is the final conflict which ends forever man's refusal to accept the will of God for their lives. At the end time, in the final resurrection of the wicked dead and the great white throne judgment, the books are opened, and those whose names are not found written in the Lamb's Book of Life are cast out and rewarded according to their deeds. Into the abyss of hell are flung Satan and his angels, along with those who choose Satan and his way of life, plus death and the grave—all are hurled into the fiery flames where the Beast and the False Prophet have already been for a thousand years.

After the purging of the earth of Satan and his minions, and after the judgment upon those who reject Christ and His grace, and after cleansing the earth of the heartache and tears of sickness, sin, death, and the grave, will come the renovation of earth and heaven. It is a new creation with a glorious new heaven and new earth. In it is the Holy City, the heavenly Jerusalem, and in it is the dwelling place of God Himself. Tears, death, sorrow, pain, and crying are passed away. There are no graves on the hillsides of glory and no funeral wreaths on the doors of those mansions in the sky.

The book closes with the incomparable message of the hope, salvation, and redemption accomplished in the person and work of the Lord Christ.

LAST THINGS

A basic fundamental of the Christian faith is that God as Creator and Redeemer has been active in time-space events we call human history. And insofar as God has removed Himself from His transcendence to become immanent, thereby touching His creation with His divine power, so has human history been transformed and conformed to the divine purpose of God. One cannot properly understand human history without previously seeking to understand, if only minutely, the divine purposes of God. This is true whether we are speaking of God's creative act, whereby He formed man from the dust of the ground, of His mighty deliverance of Israel from Egypt, of the glorious incarnation of His Only Begotten Son, or of things to come when Jesus Christ, the Righteous Judge and King, comes to bring this present age to its final denouement.

Eschatology, the study of last things, must always keep two facets in focus: (a) the incapability of man's knowledge in foreseeing the future, and (b) the absolute certainty of God's accomplishing perfectly His divine will. We must be humble enough to say, with Paul, "For we know in part, and we prophesy in part" (1 Cor. 13:9) and "now we see through a glass, darkly" (1 Cor. 13:12). But we must also hold fast to the hope that "when that which is perfect is come, then that which is in part shall be done away" (1 Cor. 13:10), and wait with assurance that the time is coming when we shall see "face to face" (1 Cor. 13:12) the One who is to be revealed at the end of the ages.

Out of the work of scholars and students of the Scriptures have come varying interpretations of the biblical passages on the last things. The dividing line between liberal and conservative scholars is drawn along the question: Do passages of Scripture which deal with last things—for example, Daniel and Revelation—tell the events of the writer's own day, or do they foretell the events of history future to the writer's own day? Liberal scholars largely endorse the former view, while conservative scholars lean toward the latter. However, neither view by itself is sufficient to explain the kind of biblical literature Daniel and Revelation represent. It is certainly true, for example, that the apostle John, in writing the Revelation, was concerned to address the Christians of his own day. Seven churches and their present situations were addressed; they were commended, exhorted, or reproved. But in an effort to encourage them and clarify for them the purposes of God in the persecutions they were then suffering, John also says he was shown the things which "must be hereafter" (Rev. 4:1). There was still to come the vindication of those whom the Lamb "redeemed . . . to God" (Rev. 5:9). Satan and all the powers of evil were yet to be defeated in the coming judg-

ment of God, and there was still to come a "new heaven and a new earth" where the saints of God would forever reign with Him who sits upon the throne (Rev. 21:1–5).

Thus in eschatology, there is both a forth-telling and a foretelling. The point is this: While there is certainty of the coming of the last things, they should not be studied in isolation of our present situation. While holding before us the hope of things to come, the last things should also inform us about God's purpose for us now in living righteously and in readiness for the coming of the Lord (see Matt. 24 and 25; 1 Cor. 15; 1 Thess. 4:13—5:11; 2 Thess. 2; Heb. 10:23–25; 2 Pet. 3).

A central turning point for discussions of the last things among conservative scholars is the millennium, or thousand-year reign of Christ, in Revelation 20:1–10. *Postmillennialism*, popular in the early twentieth century, sees Christ's return after the millennium, which has been brought about by the spread of the church through the power of the Holy Spirit. *Premillennialism* places Christ's second coming before the millennium, which is established by the supernatural intervention of God in Christ. It is interesting that many of the early church fathers had sympathy for this view. Those who hold to *amillennialism* see the millennium as a figurative expression of the accomplishment of God's Word to Israel, fulfilled in the church. Within any of these three groups, one will find variations of thought concerning particular aspects of the viewpoint under discussion. This should lead us to be cautious about being dogmatic for any single viewpoint of the last things.

But uncertainty in these areas should not be cause for despair, as there are other things about which the Christian can be sure. First could be mentioned the resurrection of the body. The vividness of Ezekiel's vision of the valley of dry bones, while revealing the restoration of Israel, was in itself a vision of a resurrection to life from the grave (Ezek. 37). Daniel 12:2 speaks of a resurrection: "And many of them that sleep in the dust of the earth shall awake, some to everlasting life, and some to shame *and* everlasting contempt." Paul says Christ's resurrection is the assurance of our own resurrection: "But every man in his own order: Christ the firstfruits; afterward they that are Christ's at his coming" (1 Cor. 15:23). Second, we may be sure of Christ's second coming. Daniel 7 is the reference point for the New Testament doctrine of the Son of Man coming "with the clouds of heaven" (Dan. 7:13). As the disciples watched Jesus ascending into heaven, the angels told them that they would also see Him "come in like manner" (Acts 1:11). Paul told the Thessalonians that His coming would be preceded by the

man of lawlessness (2 Thess. 2:1–4). The coming of the Son of Man will be accompanied by "great power and glory" (Mark 13:26). Third, there will be judgment. Joel 3 says the Lord will enter into judgment with the nations. Peter speaks of the "judgment and perdition of ungodly men" (2 Pet. 3:7). Paul says that "we must all appear before the judgment seat of Christ; that every one may receive the things *done* in *his* body, according to that he hath done" (2 Cor. 5:10). The final judgment will take place before the very throne of God (Rev. 20:11–15). And after all is said and done, when all tribulations have been suffered, when all of Christ's foes have been defeated, when all things have been made subject to Him, then the

New Jerusalem will be "prepared as a bride adorned for her husband" (Rev. 21:2). God shall dwell among men, wiping away every tear, all death, every mourning, and pain. The saints of God will drink from the river of the water of life coming from the throne of God and of the Lamb (Rev. 22:1). The final purpose of God will then have been accomplished when the saints of God join the myriad tongues saying:

"Worthy is the Lamb that was slain to receive power, and riches, and wisdom, and strength, and honour, and glory, and blessing. . . . Blessing, and honour, and glory, and power, *be* unto him that sitteth upon the throne, and unto the Lamb for ever and ever" (Rev. 5:12, 13).

Jewish Feasts

Feast of	Month on Jewish Calendar	Day	Corresponding Month	References
*Passover (Unleavened Bread)	Nisan	14–21	Mar.–Apr.	Ex. 12:43—13:10; Matt. 26:17–20
*Pentecost (Firstfruits or Weeks)	Sivan	6 (50 days after Passover)	May–June	Deut. 16:9–12; Acts 2:1
Trumpets, *Rosh Hashanah*	Tishri	1, 2	Sept.–Oct.	Num. 29:1–6
Day of Atonement, *Yom Kippur*	Tishri	10	Sept.–Oct.	Lev. 23:26–32; Heb. 9:7
*Tabernacles (Booths or Ingathering)	Tishri	15–22	Sept.–Oct.	Neh. 8:13–18; John 7:2
Dedication (Lights), *Hanukkah*	Chislev	25 (8 days)	Nov.–Dec.	John 10:22
Purim (Lots)	Adar	14, 15	Feb.–Mar.	Esth. 9:18–32

*The three major feasts for which all males of Israel were required to travel to the Temple in Jerusalem (Ex. 23:14–19).

A GUIDE TO CHRISTIAN WORKERS

I. Commission

Give us a watchword for the hour,
A thrilling word, a word of power;
A battle cry, a flaming breath,
A call to conquest or to death;
A word to rouse the church from rest,
To heed the Master's high behest.
The call is given, ye hosts arise,
The watchword is EVANGELIZE!
To fallen men, a dying race,
Make known the gift of gospel grace.
The world that now in darkness lies,
O Church of Christ, EVANGELIZE!

"And Jesus came and spake unto them, saying, All power is given unto me in heaven and in earth. Go ye therefore, and teach all nations, baptizing them in the name of the Father, and of the Son, and of the Holy Ghost: Teaching them to observe all things whatsoever I have commanded you: and, lo, I am with you alway, *even* unto the end of the world. Amen" (Matt. 28:18–20).

"But ye shall receive power, after that the Holy Ghost is come upon you: and ye shall be witnesses unto me both in Jerusalem, and in all Judaea, and in Samaria, and unto the uttermost part of the earth" (Acts 1:8).

"So thou, O son of man, I have set thee a watchman unto the house of Israel; therefore thou shalt hear the word at my mouth, and warn them from me. When I say unto the wicked, O wicked *man*, thou shalt surely die; if thou dost not speak to warn the wicked from his way, that wicked *man* shall die in his iniquity; but his blood will I require at thine hand" (Ezek. 33:7, 8).

"Ye are the salt of the earth: but if the salt have lost his savour, wherewith shall it be salted? it is thenceforth good for nothing, but to be cast out, and to be trodden under foot of men. Ye are the light of the world. A city that is set on an hill cannot be hid. Neither do men light a candle, and put it under a bushel, but on a candlestick; and it giveth light unto all that are in the house. Let your light so shine before men, that they may see your good works, and glorify your Father which is in heaven" (Matt. 5:13–16).

II. Compassion

The story is told that Martinelli received $25,000 for singing only twice. Paul and Silas sang one night in a prison. Their song was not rendered with the skill or harmony of that of Martinelli's, but its tenderness touched the heart of the keeper of the prison and echoed through the angel-crowded streets of heaven; and the listening King of kings rewarded those who sang with crowns of glory that will gleam in beauty throughout eternal ages.

An immortal soul is beyond all price. There is no trouble too great, no humiliation too deep, no suffering too severe, no love too strong, no labor too hard, no expense too large, but that it is worth it, if it is spent in the effort to win a soul.

God loves the soul more than all creation. He fashioned it after His own image, and made it like unto Himself. Every soul has departed from God and gone astray, and God has bought the soul back again with a price.

That price was in, and through, and by Jesus Christ. God loves the soul with an everlasting love.

Satan hates the soul. In Satan's enmity toward God he is using all his energy, using every snare, his utmost cunning, employing every means *with the single purpose of ruining the soul of man*.

When a million eternities have each lived their endless ages and have rolled by into the unthinkable past and time is no more, the soul will still be living, *a conscious personality* endowed with perpetual life reunited with the body.

God has said: "He that winneth souls *is* wise" (Prov. 11:30).

The Bible says: "And they that be wise shall shine as the brightness of the firmament; and they that turn many to righteousness as the stars for ever and ever" (Dan. 12:3).

Compassion was the heartbeat of our Saviour's ministry. "But when he saw the multitudes, he was moved with compassion on them, because they fainted, and were scattered abroad, as sheep having no shepherd" (Matt. 9:36).

"But thou, O Lord, *art* a God full of compassion, and gracious, longsuffering, and plenteous in mercy and truth" (Ps. 86:15).

Heaven is geared for redemption. "I say unto you, that likewise joy shall be in heaven over one sinner that repenteth, more than over ninety and nine just persons, which need no repentance" (Luke 15:7).

No man who ever had a glimpse of hell would ever want a fellow human being to go there (see Luke 16:28).

"They that sow in tears shall reap in joy. He that goeth forth and weepeth, bearing precious seed, shall doubtless come again with rejoicing, bringing his sheaves *with him*" (Ps. 126:5, 6).

III. Concern

One of the first questions raised in recorded history was, "Am I my brother's keeper?" (Gen.

4:9). *Do I have moral obligations toward others?*

"And I sought for a man among them, that should make up the hedge, and stand in the gap before me for the land, that I should not destroy it: but I found none" (Ezek. 22:30).

"My sheep wandered through all the mountains, and upon every high hill: yea, my flock was scattered upon all the face of the earth, and none did search or seek *after them*" (Ezek. 34:6).

"And *if* thou draw out thy soul to the hungry, and satisfy the afflicted soul; then shall thy light rise in obscurity, and thy darkness *be* as the noon day" (Is. 58:10).

"I say the truth in Christ, I lie not, my conscience also bearing me witness in the Holy Ghost, That I have great heaviness and continual sorrow in my heart. For I could wish that myself were accursed from Christ for my brethren, my kinsmen according to the flesh" (Rom. 9:1–3). See also Psalm 106:23; Luke 19:41; Acts 20:31.

Intercession is the way that leads to the winning of souls. No church can prosper without it. No Christian can grow without it. The law of life demands reproduction—that kind should beget kind.

Jesus interceded for each of us. "Therefore will I divide him *a portion* with the great, and he shall divide the spoil with the strong; because he hath poured out his soul unto death: and he was numbered with the transgressors; and he bare the sin of many, and made intercession for the transgressors" (Is. 53:12).

Christ left this command to us: "Pray ye therefore the Lord of the harvest, that he will send forth labourers into his harvest" (Matt. 9:38).

IV. Contact

It began with *personal contact.*

"He first findeth his own brother Simon, and saith unto him, We have found the Messias, which is, being interpreted, the Christ" (John 1:41).

With Christ came the emphasis of *seeking the lost.* "For the Son of man is come to seek and to save that which was lost" (Luke 19:10).

The movement of Christianity in this world is scripturally based on personal contact. Anyone who really knows Jesus will want others to know Him.

The secret is in the words of Andrew, "We have *found.*" The search for satisfaction in a man's soul is completed in a living knowledge of Jesus Christ. Personal evangelism is sharing this discovery.

"And he brought him to Jesus" (John 1:42).

How is this accomplished? Christ gives the answer. "Follow me, and I will make you fishers of men" (Matt. 4:19). *A love for Christ produces a love for mankind.*

We are to be workmen "that [need] not to be ashamed" (2 Tim. 2:15). Lives today are compli-

cated by sin. They need more than slogans and formulas. They need personal help. A conscientious doctor must deal with each patient separately and so must a conscientious soul-winner.

These guidelines must be kept in mind:

1. I MUST LIVE IT. I can't say to others, "Do as I *say*, but don't do as I *do*." They must see Christ in me (1 Cor. 4:9). My strongest testimony is my daily life.

2. I MUST LOVE PEOPLE. I cannot pretend. The other person knows my motive immediately. The power of evangelism is described in Revelation 22:17, "And the Spirit and the bride say, Come." When my *concern* for others is in keeping with the concern of the Holy Spirit toward mankind, there is a community of interest in the individual that results in *compulsion.*

3. I MUST MEET THE PUBLIC. Jesus was heaven's artist at this. He never met a stranger. Paul testified, "I am made all things to all *men*, that I might by all means save some" (1 Cor. 9:22).

Kindness will open doors (Eph. 4:32). It will bring an affirmative response.

4. I MUST LOOK FOR NEED. Jesus said, "They that are whole have no need of the physician, but they that are sick: I came not to call the righteous, but sinners to repentance" (Mark 2:17).

You will be surprised how many people are ready to talk. They simply need someone in whom they can have confidence. Zacchaeus was in trouble. Uninvited, he talked about his sin. *That is my point of contact—human need.*

5. I MUST COMMUNICATE. Keep away from technicalities. Refuse to become involved in debate. The Samaritan woman quibbled: "Our fathers worshipped in this mountain; and ye say, that in Jerusalem is the place where men ought to worship" (John 4:20). It wasn't her *head* that was troubling her. It was her *heart.* She needed Christ before she needed a church; a Redeemer before she needed a ritual. "I know that Messias cometh, which is called Christ: when he is come, he will tell us all things. Jesus saith unto her, I that speak unto thee am *he*" (John 4:25, 26).

6. I MUST CONCENTRATE ON CHRIST. I can get so much "I" into my testimony that spiritual pride will offend the person to whom I am witnessing. The rule of the great Baptist still holds: "He must increase, but I *must* decrease" (John 3:30). *My business is to present Jesus* (John 12:32). Christ is the attraction.

7. I MUST USE TACT. This suggests a sensitivity to the other man's feelings. It is a spirit of discernment. "If any of you lack wisdom, let him ask of God, that giveth to all *men* liberally, and upbraideth not; and it shall be given him" (James 1:5). Be natural. Be courteous. Be a good listener. Ask wise questions.

8. I MUST BRING A PERSON TO A DECISION. This can only be accomplished through

the power and presence of the Holy Spirit (John 16:8).

The chance may never come again. *Opportunity is God-given*. Don't gamble with it. Press for a decision. "Yet ye have not, because ye ask not" (James 4:2). Don't let people say of you at Judgment Day, "He never asked me to be a Christian!"

9. I MUST TEACH THEM TO LISTEN TO GOD'S VOICE. It is my business to *introduce* them to the Saviour. So often the worker only introduces himself. "Acquaint now thyself with him, and be at peace: thereby good shall come unto thee" (Job 22:21). Let the person with whom you are dealing hear, for the first time the voice of God speaking to him or her in reassurance and comfort, and you have built strength.

This is done by teaching the person two or three primary verses of Scripture. Tie the seeker to God's Word. Let your friend know before you leave him that God has spoken these words to him. These words carry a guarantee.

Here is an *example:*

"Verily, verily, I say unto you, He that heareth my word, and believeth on him that sent me, hath everlasting life, and shall not come into condemnation; but is passed from death unto life" (John 5:24).

These are the words of the Son of God. They are spoken to *you*. They are spoken with finality and authority.

10. I MUST MAKE IT CRYSTAL CLEAR THAT THERE IS A DIFFERENCE BETWEEN KNOWING GOD AND KNOWING ABOUT GOD. Hearsay is not enough. *Birth is not something that is second-hand.* "And when he putteth forth his own sheep, he goeth before them, and the sheep follow him: for they know his voice. And a stranger will they not follow, but will flee from him: for they know not the voice of strangers" (John 10:4, 5).

I know God when I get down to business with Him. "Draw nigh to God, and he will draw nigh to you" (James 4:8). God has expressed His willingness in a covenant, contract, or testament. It bears His signature in the death and resurrection of Jesus Christ. *The moment I exercise faith toward this written word and become personally involved in agreement, that very moment the entire contract, or covenant, is in force toward me.*

If I do not associate the seeker with the Word of God, that person will miss his way. The devil will deceive the inquirer before breakfast. He will lie so cleverly that the inquirer will apologize to worldly associates before the day is over.

Remember! The authority is in the Word of God.

V. A Conversation

Dr. R. G. Lee calls this two-way conversation "convincing confutation." The following are answers to some excuses as Dr. Lee sets them forth.

1. Excuse: *"I want to get established in business first. After that I will be a Christian."*

Answer: No business should be allowed to cheat one out of heaven's blessings. Property should not kill the privilege of being a child of God. "For what shall it profit a man, if he shall gain the whole world, and lose his own soul?" (Mark 8:36). God called one man a fool to his face. "But God said unto him, *Thou* fool, this night thy soul shall be required of thee: then whose shall those things be, which thou hast provided?" (Luke 12:20). He was the man who neglected his soul's welfare by building barns, enlarging crops, and feeding his soul on corn.

Further Scriptures which may be used: Matthew 6:33; Psalm 1:1, 2; Proverbs 29:25; Mark 10:29, 30.

2. Excuse: *"I am not a sinner."*

Answer: But God says, "There is none righteous, no, not one" (Rom. 3:10). "But the scripture hath concluded all under sin" (Gal. 3:22). If you are not a sinner, are you keeping God's commands? What about Matthew 22:37? "Jesus said unto him, Thou shalt love the Lord thy God with all thy heart, and with all thy soul, and with all thy mind."

3. Excuse: *"I have no encouragement at home."*

Answer: Without families we came. Without our families we go. Guilt is personal. Then, too, if you have praying parents, a saintly wife or husband, and godly children, and you continue your selfish resistance to their accepted and your rejected Saviour, your guilt is deeper.

4. Excuse: *"I am good enough as I am."*

Answer: God says you are bad enough—by nature. Man in his natural state does wicked deeds, thinks evil thoughts, goes to bad places, rejects Jesus Christ—because he has an evil heart. No one is naturally good. If you are good, why not become acquainted with Jesus, who is supremely good?

5. Excuse: *"I am as good as others."*

Answer: Violin players do not take their tones from each other, but from the piano. Builders are constantly using the plumb line, the level, and the square. We need to live by standards—not comparisons. Nobody can claim health because he is better than another diabetic or stronger than another cancer victim. Measure yourself by Jesus if you want to know how good or bad you are. Do not be too sure you are better than many within the Church. They have confessed Jesus before men—as Jesus asked. You have not. Moreover, you are forbidden to judge to justify yourself. You are not saved or lost by the deeds of others.

6. Excuse: *"I have no feeling."*

Answer: The world isn't run by feeling. Washington did not live at Valley Forge because he felt like it. Most people do most of their worthy acts

contrary to feeling. The doctor does not deal with diseases because of feeling but because of necessity.

Scriptures which may be used: Revelation 3:20, John 3:36, Ephesians 1:13, First Peter 1:8.

7. Excuse: "I am so weak."

Answer: "Thou wilt keep *him* in perfect peace, *whose* mind *is* stayed *on thee:* because he trusteth in thee. Trust ye in the LORD for ever: for in the LORD JEHOVAH *is* everlasting strength" (Is. 26:3, 4). Who will keep? The Almighty God. How? "In perfect peace." On what condition? "Whose mind is stayed" on God—not on self, nor circumstances, failures, successes, nor on others. Trust—not try or worry, but trust. In whom? God. How long? All the time. Why? For God is everlasting strength.

Further Scriptures which may be used: Jude 24, First Corinthians 10:13, Philippians 1:6, Isaiah 41:10, 13, 14, Second Timothy 1:12.

8. Excuse: "I am doing the best I can."

Answer: How long have you been doing your best? Have you succeeded? How long will it take you to make yourself fit for heaven? Suppose you die now? The best you can do is to acknowledge you cannot do anything to save yourself—except believe.

9. Excuse: "I am too big a sinner."

Answer: Jesus came to save *all* sinners. "This *is* a faithful saying, and worthy of all acceptation, that Christ Jesus came into the world to save sinners; of whom I am chief" (1 Tim. 1:15). Are your sins scarlet? "Come now, and let us reason together, saith the LORD: though your sins be as scarlet, they shall be as white as snow; though they be red like crimson, they shall be as wool" (Is. 1:18). Are you lost? "For the Son of man is come to seek and to save that which was lost" (Luke 19:10). Are you without strength? "For when we were yet without strength, in due time Christ died for the ungodly. For scarcely for a righteous man will one die: yet peradventure for a good man some would even dare to die. But God commendeth his love toward us, in that, while we were yet sinners, Christ died for us" (Rom. 5:6–8). "All that the Father giveth me shall come to me; and him that cometh to me I will in no wise cast out" (John 6:37).

Further Scriptures which may be used: Matthew 9:13, Hebrews 7:25, Luke 23:39–43.

10. Excuse: "There are too many hypocrites."

Answer: Hypocrites are lost. If you let hypocrites keep you from being saved, you will spend eternity in hell with them. Besides, you have to be smaller than what you hide behind. If you hide behind a hypocrite, you must be smaller than a hypocrite.

Further Scriptures which may be used: Zechariah 13:6, Acts 1:6, Hebrews 12:2, Acts 17:30, 31, Romans 2:1–6; 14:12, Matthew 7:1–5, First Samuel 16:7.

11. Excuse: "A professing Christian wronged me."

Answer: Granted. But is that any reason why you should wrong God and insult Christ, who loved you and gave Himself for you? "He that believeth on the Son hath everlasting life: and he that believeth not the Son shall not see life; but the wrath of God abideth on him" (John 3:36).

12. Excuse: "There is too much to give up."

Answer: Better give up everything than lose the soul. Put Christ and your soul ahead of all else. Is it too much to give up paste pearls for glittering gems? Dirt for diamonds? Is it too much to give up rags for riches?

Further Scriptures which may be used: Psalms 16:11; 84:11, Proverbs 3:17; 13:15, Matthew 11:30, Isaiah 57:21, Romans 8:32, Mark 8:36, 37, Luke 18:29, 30.

13. Excuse: "I cannot understand."

Answer: Why let mystery cause you to refuse the Master? Do you understand the chemistry of digestion? Does your ignorance of it keep you from eating steak? Can you understand why the same sun and the same soil and the same rain get sweetness into the orange and sourness into the lemon and bitterness into the persimmon?

Lay aside your excuse of mystery and trust God as you trust the telephone to transmit your voice.

Further Scriptures which may be used: Romans 11:33, First Corinthians 1:8; 2:14.

14. Excuse: "God is unjust."

Answer: Who is God? Who are you? Injustice is sin. Do you mean to accuse God of sin? God is so just that He never demands two payments for one debt. Jesus paid your sin debt on the Cross—all of it. Therefore, when you accept Christ, you do not have that sin debt to pay.

15. Excuse: "Folks would laugh."

Answer: Better let them laugh than to have God laugh. "I also will laugh at your calamity; I will mock when your fear cometh" (Prov. 1:26). Shun evil companions. "Enter not into the path of the wicked, and go not in the way of evil *men*. The way of the wicked *is* as darkness: they know not at what they stumble" (Prov. 4:14, 19). Do not be ashamed of Christ. "Whosoever therefore shall confess me before men, him will I confess also before my Father which is in heaven. But whosoever shall deny me before men, him will I also deny before my Father which is in heaven" (Matt. 10:32, 33).

16. Excuse: "Not now."

Answer: Every time you say no, it is more difficult to say yes. The time and day is *now*. "For he saith, I have heard thee in a time accepted, and in the day of salvation have I succoured thee: behold, now *is* the accepted time; behold, now *is* the day of salvation" (2 Cor. 6:2).

Seek the Lord while He may be found. Delay is decision for the wrong way. "Today—if you will," says the Lord. Tomorrow is the day when the idle man works, the thief becomes honest, the drunk-

ard sober. Tomorrow is a period nowhere to be found except, perhaps, in the fool's calendar. God's call is not a call for tomorrow, but for *today*.

Dr. Lee says of the above, "In this manner do I deal with excuse-makers. With many excuse-makers I have had success. With some, I have not."

Further Scriptures which may be used: Proverbs 27:1; 29:1, Isaiah 55:6, Hebrews 2:3.

Some other common excuses and questions are:

17. Excuse: *"I think you are making too big a fuss about this."*

Answer: Why is Calvary such a big date in history? "But God commendeth his love toward us, in that, while we were yet sinners, Christ died for us" (Rom. 5:8).

Isn't your soul important? "For what is a man profited, if he shall gain the whole world, and lose his own soul? or what shall a man give in exchange for his soul?" (Matt. 16:26).

Isn't life uncertain? "But God said unto him, *Thou* fool, this night thy soul shall be required of thee: then whose shall those things be, which thou hast provided?" (Luke 12:20).

Death, judgment, and hell lie ahead (Gal. 6:7, Heb. 9:27).

The Son of God asks for your decision (Rev. 3:20).

18. Excuse: *"I will take my chances."*

Answer: God always has the last word. "And he saith unto him, Friend, how camest thou in hither not having a wedding garment? And he was speechless. Then said the king to the servants, Bind him hand and foot, and take him away, and cast *him* into outer darkness; there shall be weeping and gnashing of teeth" (Matt. 22:12, 13).

Nebuchadnezzar gave this testimony, "That the most High ruleth in the kingdom of men, and giveth it to whomsoever he will" (Dan. 4:17). "And all the inhabitants of the earth *are* reputed as nothing: and he doeth according to his will in the army of heaven, and *among* the inhabitants of the earth: and none can stay his hand, or say unto him, What doest thou?" (Dan. 4:35).

God's Word has eternal force (Is. 55:11).

A judgment must be rendered on each life lived (John 5:27–29).

19. Excuse: *"My friends mean so much to me."*

Answer: Are they your friends or your enemies? "Ye adulterers and adulteresses, know ye not that the friendship of the world is enmity with God? whosoever therefore will be a friend of the world is the enemy of God" (James 4:4).

Do your friends care for your soul? "And when he had spent all, there arose a mighty famine in that land; and he began to be in want. And he went and joined himself to a citizen of that country; and he sent him into his fields to feed swine. And he would fain have filled his belly with the husks that the swine did eat: and no man gave unto him" (Luke 15:14–16).

You will gain a greater Friend and friends (John 15:15, Matt. 19:29).

Your example can lead your unsaved friends to Christ (John 1:45).

20. Excuse: *"I am going to have a good time in this world and let the next world take care of itself."*

Answer: Others have followed this course before. "Son, remember that thou in thy lifetime receivedst thy good things, and likewise Lazarus evil things: but now he is comforted, and thou art tormented" (Luke 16:25).

Your life can prove to be a *charade* (Luke 12:15).

Opportunity brings responsibility (Eccl. 11:9).

21. Excuse: *"Please do not talk to me about it."*

Answer: I am simply bringing God's message to you. "Thou therefore gird up thy loins, and arise, and speak unto them all that I command thee: be not dismayed at their faces, lest I confound thee before them" (Jer. 1:17). "And go, get thee to them of the captivity, unto the children of thy people, and speak unto them, and tell them, Thus saith the Lord GOD; whether they will hear, or whether they will forbear" (Ezek. 3:11).

My business is to *witness* (2 Cor. 2:15, 16).

22. Excuse: *"I am my own boss."*

Answer: Wise men and women receive *counsel*. "There is a way which seemeth right unto a man, but the end thereof *are* the ways of death" (Prov. 14:12).

The straight way is the best way (Matt. 7:13, 14).

The easiest thing in the world to get is *a wrong answer*.

23. Excuse: *"Frankly, I am skeptical about the whole matter."*

Answer: Are you honestly looking for *answers?* Will you accept evidence as it would be accepted before a court of law? Are you an *inquirer* or a *spiritual subversive* "who changed the truth of God into a lie, and worshipped and served the creature more than the Creator" (Rom. 1:25). "And even as they did not like to retain God in *their* knowledge, God gave them over to a reprobate mind, to do those things which are not convenient" (Rom. 1:28).

Jesus Christ threw out this challenge: "He that is of God heareth God's words: ye therefore hear *them* not, because ye are not of God" (John 8:47).

You can *doubt* to your own peril (2 Thess. 2:10; 2:12).

The way to find out whether or not a thing is true and worthy of one's acceptance is to put it to *a personal test* (Ps. 34:8).

24. Excuse: *"I want to be absolutely neutral about this matter."*

Answer: There are some things you can't be neutral about—food, drink, sleep, light, for instance. That is why Christ likened Himself to the

necessities of life. "I am that bread of life" (John 6:48). "I am the light of the world: he that followeth me shall not walk in darkness, but shall have the light of life" (John 8:12).

Jesus said, "He that is not with me is against me; and he that gathereth not with me scattereth abroad" (Matt. 12:30).

25. Excuse: *"I believe God is too good to damn anyone."*

Answer: That is not what the Bible says. "Therefore the ungodly shall not stand in the judgment, nor sinners in the congregation of the righteous. For the LORD knoweth the way of the righteous: but the way of the ungodly shall perish" (Ps. 1:5, 6).

God bases your salvation or damnation on your acceptance or rejection of Jesus Christ (John 12:48).

It is not God that is hard. It is you! "But after thy hardness and impenitent heart treasurest up unto thyself wrath against the day of wrath and revelation of the righteous judgment of God" (Rom. 2:5).

Every agency of God seeks to lead you to repentance (2 Pet. 3:9).

26. Excuse: *"How can I reconcile the doctrine of hell with the Christian's God of salvation?"*

Answer: "Then shall he say also unto them on the left hand, Depart from me, ye cursed, into everlasting fire, prepared for the devil and his angels" (Matt. 25:41).

"Judas by transgression fell, that he might go to his own place" (Acts 1:25).

"The Lord is not slack concerning his promise, as some men count slackness; but is longsuffering to us-ward, not willing that any should perish, but that all should come to repentance" (2 Pet. 3:9).

"Have I any pleasure at all that the wicked should die? saith the Lord GOD: *and* not that he should return from his ways, and live?" (Ezek. 18:23).

"And these shall go away into everlasting punishment: but the righteous into life eternal" (Matt. 25:46).

"Son, remember that thou in thy lifetime receivedst thy good things, and likewise Lazarus evil things: but now he is comforted, and thou art tormented" (Luke 16:25).

"Ye serpents, *ye* generation of vipers, how can ye escape the damnation of hell?" (Matt. 23:33).

"And fear not them which kill the body, but are not able to kill the soul: but rather fear him which is able to destroy both soul and body in hell" (Matt. 10:28).

"Therefore hell hath enlarged herself, and opened her mouth without measure: and their glory, and their multitude, and their pomp, and he that rejoiceth, shall descend into it. And the mean man shall be brought down, and the mighty man shall be humbled, and the eyes of the lofty shall be humbled: but the LORD of hosts shall be exalted in judgment, and God that is holy shall be sanctified in righteousness" (Is. 5:14–16).

27. Excuse: *"I am religious."*

Answer: Religion is often something that is on the outside. "Many will say to me in that day, Lord, Lord, have we not prophesied in thy name? and in thy name have cast out devils? and in thy name done many wonderful works? And then will I profess unto them, I never knew you: depart from me, ye that work iniquity" (Matt. 7:22, 23).

No man was more religious than Paul (Gal. 1:14, Phil. 3:6, 1 Tim. 1:13, 15).

Cornelius was a religious man who needed to be saved (Acts 11:14).

28. Excuse: *"I am trying to be a Christian."*

Answer: It is not *trying*, it is *trusting* that counts. A drowning man tries with all his might and perishes, but when he trusts in the saving power of another he is rescued. "Behold, God *is* my salvation; I will trust, and not be afraid: for the LORD JEHOVAH *is* my strength and *my* song; he also is become my salvation" (Is. 12:2).

Ishmael was Abraham's fleshly attempt to fulfill the promise of God (he tried). Isaac was God's provision (he trusted) (Rom. 4:3, 5).

No work that you can do for yourself can ever substitute in merit for the work that Jesus has done for you on the Cross (Eph. 2:9).

"But we are all as an unclean *thing*, and all our righteousnesses *are* as filthy rags; and we all do fade as a leaf; and our iniquities, like the wind, have taken us away" (Is. 64:6). To try is to fail! "For whosoever shall keep the whole law, and yet offend in one *point*, he is guilty of all" (James 2:10).

29. Excuse: *"What is sin?"*

Answer: Sin is breaking God's law (1 John 3:10). All unrighteousness is sin, and there is no sin not *leading* to death (1 John 5:17).

Unbelief is sin (John 16:8, 9).

Questionable indulgences are sin (Rom. 14:23).

Missing the mark is sin (Rom. 3:23).

Undone duty is sin (James 4:17).

30. Excuse: *"My sins are small, so why worry?"*

Answer: Because any sin torments. "*There is* no peace, saith the LORD, unto the wicked" (Is. 48:22).

Because any sin separates you from God (Is. 59:2).

Because any sin enslaves you (John 8:34).

Because any sin excludes from heaven (1 Cor. 6:9).

Because any sin ends in death (Rom. 6:23).

31. Excuse: *"I may be punished but not eternally."*

Answer: If God is eternal and heaven is eternal—hell will be eternal also. "Then shall he say also unto them on the left hand, Depart from me, ye cursed, into everlasting fire, prepared for the devil and his angels" (Matt. 25:41).

There is "the resurrection of damnation" (John 5:28, 29).

Don't forget there is the "second death" (Rev. 20:13–15).

32. Excuse: "*I am too old now to become a Christian.*"

Answer: There is no age limit (2 Cor. 6:2).

God has foreseen your problem. "But if from thence thou shalt seek the LORD thy God, Thou shalt find *him*, if thou seek him with all thy heart and with all thy soul. When thou art in tribulation, and all these things are come upon thee, *even* in the latter days, if thou turn to the LORD thy God, and shalt be obedient unto his voice; (For the LORD thy God *is* a merciful God;) he will not forsake thee, neither destroy thee, nor forget the covenant of thy fathers which he sware unto them" (Deut. 4:29–31).

33. Excuse: "*I do not think I am old enough to make a decision.*"

Answer: You have reached an age of accountablity if you sense Christ's approach to your life. "Remember now thy Creator in the days of thy youth, while the evil days come not, nor the years draw nigh, when thou shalt say, I have no pleasure in them" (Eccl. 12:1).

The time to make a decision is when your conscience is tender (2 Sam. 19:35).

The best time is *now* (Heb. 3:13).

34. Excuse: "*I intend to before I die.*"

Answer: Can you determine the hour of your death? *Nothing is so uncertain as life* (Prov. 29:1, Job 34:20).

God warns against *presumption* (James 4:13–17).

There is no time like the present time. "Seek ye the LORD while he may be found, call ye upon him while he is near" (Is. 55:6).

35. Excuse: "*I am afraid I cannot hold out.*"

Answer: Jesus not only saves but He keeps. He is the Good Shepherd (John 10:11,14).

The same One who convicts you is concerned about you. "Faithful *is* he that calleth you, who also will do *it*" (1 Thess. 5:24).

Paul gives his experience. "And he said unto me, My grace is sufficient for thee: for my strength is made perfect in weakness. Most gladly therefore will I rather glory in my infirmities, that the power of Christ may rest upon me" (2 Cor. 12:9).

God has made an investment in you and He will work to protect that investment (Phil. 1:6).

To know Him is to have assurance. Commit your entire life to His care. Leave the future in your Master's hands (2 Tim. 1:12).

36. Excuse: "*I am afraid of persecution.*"

Answer: It is a cowardly thing to deny Jesus Christ. "But the fearful, and unbelieving, and the abominable, and murderers, and whoremongers, and sorcerers, and idolators, and all liars, shall have their part in the lake which burneth with fire and brimstone: which is the second death" (Rev. 21:8).

"Whosoever therefore shall be ashamed of me and of my words in this adulterous and sinful generation; of him also shall the Son of man be ashamed, when he cometh in the glory of his Father with the holy angels" (Mark 8:38).

So little is asked for so much in return. "For I reckon that the sufferings of this present time *are* not worthy *to be compared* with the glory which shall be revealed in us" (Rom. 8:18).

It is all or nothing. "If we suffer, we shall also reign with *him*: if we deny *him*, he also will deny us" (2 Tim. 2:12).

You join a select company. It is a chance of a lifetime to do something worthwhile. "Blessed are ye, when men shall hate you, and when they shall separate you *from their company*, and shall reproach *you*, and cast out your name as evil, for the Son of man's sake. Rejoice ye in that day, and leap for joy: for, behold, your reward *is* great in heaven: for in the like manner did their fathers unto the prophets" (Luke 6:22, 23).

He does not ask you to do anything for Him that He did not do for you (Heb. 12:2).

37. Excuse: "*I think that Jesus Christ is only one of the great men in history.*"

Answer: He claimed to be God ". . . Who, being in the form of God, thought it not robbery to be equal with God" (Phil. 2:6). He was put to death for this claim (Matt. 26:63–65). The resurrection substantiated this claim. ". . . Whom God hath raised up, having loosed the pains of death: because it was not possible that he should be holden of it" (Acts 2:24).

The moral grandeur of His life surpasses anything on record. "Which of you convinceth me of sin? And if I say the truth, why do ye not believe me?" (John 8:46).

No one has so influenced history (Luke 2:34).

There is the repeated testimony of personal experience. "Now we believe, not because of thy saying: for we have heard *him* ourselves, and know that this is indeed the Christ, the Saviour of the world" (John 4:42).

There is the open challenge to prove His divinity for yourself. "If any man will do his will, he shall know of the doctrine, whether it be of God, or *whether* I speak of myself" (John 7:17).

38. Question: "*Why does God allow evil in this world?*"

Answer: Freedom of choice is the Creator's great gift to the human race. "I call heaven and earth to record this day against you, *that* I have set before you life and death, blessing and cursing: therefore choose life, that both thou and thy seed may live" (Deut. 30:19).

Sin originated in man, not in God. God prevents sin's dominion (Rom. 6:14).

God has, at His own cost, provided a remedy. "I

am the way, the truth, and the life: no man cometh unto the Father, but by me" (John 14:6).

39. Excuse: "*There is so much suffering.*"

Answer: This is not the world as God planned it—the world that He said was "very good" (Gen. 1:31). It is the world in which man has spread his sin. "Even as I have seen, they that plow iniquity, and sow wickedness, reap the same" (Job 4:8).

God has provided an alternative. "For the wages of sin *is* death; but the gift of God *is* eternal life through Jesus Christ our Lord" (Rom. 6:23).

It is not the world that God intends to establish (Is. 65:20).

40. Question: "*Does this have to be done publicly?*"

Answer: God makes the rules. He has undertaken our salvation completely; therefore He has the right to say how we are to receive it. "Whosoever therefore shall confess me before men, him will I confess also before my Father which is in heaven. But whosoever shall deny me before men, him will I also deny before my Father which is in heaven" (Matt. 10:32, 33).

"For with the heart man believeth unto righteousness; and with the mouth confession is made unto salvation" (Rom. 10:10).

Like a true marriage—a miracle of trust happens in the heart first; then an open acknowledgment, through proper ordinances, is made to the public.

"Whosoever therefore shall be ashamed of me and my words in this adulterous and sinful generation; of him also shall the Son of man be ashamed, when he cometh in the glory of his Father with the holy angels" (Mark 8:38).

"Also I say unto you, Whosoever shall confess me before men, him shall the Son of man also confess before the angels of God: But he that denieth me before men shall be denied before the angels of God" (Luke 12:8, 9).

"Nevertheless among the chief rulers also many believed on him; but because of the Pharisees they did not confess *him*, lest they should be put out of the synagogue: For they loved the praise of men more than the praise of God" (John 12:42, 43).

41. Question: "*What about baptism?*"

Answer: Baptism like Communion "shows the Lord's death." It is faith you show publicly when you are baptized.

"Know ye not, that so many of us as were baptized into Jesus Christ were baptized into his death? Therefore we are buried with him by baptism into death: that like as Christ was raised up from the dead by the glory of the Father, even so we also should walk in newness of life. For if we have been planted together in the likeness of his death, we shall be also *in the likeness* of *his* resurrection" (Rom. 6:3–5).

Baptism is our open profession before the world that we are now living a miracle, supernatural life

of Christian grace by the quickening, regenerating power of God in us.

You should be baptized because like your Lord it fullfills "all righteousness." It keeps setting forth the gospel of Jesus before this world. Baptism is one of the first tests of obedience.

42. Excuse: "*I cannot break with my sins.*"

Answer: Salvation is a life-and-death choice. "I tell you, Nay: but, except ye repent, ye shall all likewise perish" (Luke 13:3).

You cannot live one way and die another way. "For he that soweth to his flesh shall of the flesh reap corruption; but he that soweth to the Spirit shall of the Spirit reap life everlasting" (Gal. 6:8, cf. Rev. 21:8).

You cannot do it in your own strength. "If the Son therefore shall make you free, ye shall be free indeed" (John 8:36).

"I can do all things through Christ which strengtheneth me" (Phil. 4:13).

Christ can reach you where you are (Heb. 7:25).

43. Excuse: "*I see no harm in worldly amusements.*"

Answer: The approach to this question should always be *positive*, and not negative. Instead of asking, "What *harm* is there in it?" I should ask, "What *good* is there in it?"

"And whatsoever ye do in word or deed, *do* all in the name of the Lord Jesus, giving thanks to God and the Father by him" (Col. 3:17).

"Whether therefore ye eat, or drink, or whatsoever ye do, do all to the glory of God" (1 Cor. 10:31).

"All things are lawful unto me, but all things are not expedient: all things are lawful for me, but I will not be brought under the power of any" (1 Cor. 6:12).

As a Christian, I am responsible to use my body and my mind in trust for God's glory (1 Cor. 6:19, 20).

Sharp warnings appear in the New Testament: "If any man defile the temple of God, him shall God destroy; for the temple of God is holy, which *temple* ye are" (1 Cor. 3:17).

"Wherefore come out from among them, and be ye separate, saith the Lord, and touch not the unclean *thing*; and I will receive you" (2 Cor. 6:17).

"They profess that they know God; but in works they deny *him*, being abominable, and disobedient, and unto every good work reprobate" (Titus 1:16).

My aim should always be to give my utmost for His highest (2 Tim. 2:4).

44. Excuse: "*I am not respectable enough to be a Christian.*"

Answer: It is your saving, active faith in Christ that counts. "And he arose, and came to his father. But when he was yet a great way off, his father saw him, and had compassion, and ran, and fell on his neck, and kissed him. And the son said unto him,

Father, I have sinned against heaven, and in thy sight, and am no more worthy to be called thy son. But the father said to his servants, Bring forth the best robe, and put *it* on him; and put a ring on his hand, and shoes on *his* feet: And bring hither the fatted calf, and kill *it;* and let us eat, and be merry: For this my son was dead, and is alive again; he was lost, and is found. And they began to be merry" (Luke 15:20–24). See also Luke 18:10–14.

We can never make ourselves good enough."But to him that worketh not, but believeth on him that justifieth the ungodly, his faith is counted for righteousness" (Rom. 4:5). See also Isaiah 41:13.

45. Excuse: "*I am afraid Jesus will not receive me.*"

Answer: You have His word on it. "All that the Father giveth me shall come to me; and him that cometh to me I will in no wise cast out" (John 6:37).

God is no respecter of persons (Rom. 10:13, Luke 15:2). See also Revelation 22:17.

46. Excuse: "*I have tried before and failed.*"

Answer: One failure need not mean final defeat. *Upon whom did you depend?* Did you make a complete surrender? Did you keep something back? Did you confess Christ publicly? Were you faithful in prayer? Did you seek guidance from the Word? "These were more noble than those in Thessalonica, in that they received the word with all readiness of mind, and searched the scriptures daily, whether those things were so" (Acts 17:11). Did you go to work for Christ? (Luke 11:24–26). See also First Peter 2:2.

Make a full surrender. "I beseech you therefore, brethren, by the mercies of God, that ye present your bodies a living sacrifice, holy, acceptable unto God, *which is* your reasonable service" (Rom. 12:1).

Keep in touch! "Watch and pray, that ye enter not into temptation: the spirit indeed *is* willing, but the flesh *is* weak" (Matt. 26:41).

Be present in church (Heb. 10:25).

47. Excuse: "*I think I have committed the unpardonable sin.*"

Answer: You will *know* if you have committed this sin. The desire to be a Christian will be forever past. No spiritual impression will ever again come to your soul. *A hardening process will have taken place.*

"Wherefore I say unto you, All manner of sin and blasphemy shall be forgiven unto men: but the blasphemy *against* the *Holy* Ghost shall not be forgiven unto men. And whosoever speaketh a word against the Son of man, it shall be forgiven him: but whosoever speaketh against the Holy Ghost, it shall not be forgiven him, neither in this world, neither in the *world* to come" (Matt. 12:31, 32).

In another passage we read: "But he that shall blaspheme against the Holy Ghost hath never forgiveness, but is in danger of eternal damnation" (Mark 3:29).

The tragedy lies in *the eternally unforgiven soul.* Since the Holy Spirit is the agent in conviction and conversion, there can be no rebirth without the Holy Spirit. To sin against the Holy Spirit is to sin against your own soul. To blaspheme against the Holy Spirit is to shut yourself off forever from access to God.

"If any man see his brother sin a sin *which is* not unto death, he shall ask, and he shall give him life for them that sin not unto death. There is a sin unto death: I do not say that he shall pray for it" (1 John 5:16).

You will *know* if you cross this line. Those who have committed this sin are completely given over to Satan and have not the slightest interest in spiritual matters. Paul describes it as being "past feeling" (Eph. 4:19).

On the other hand, Satan, *the deceiver,* will lie to you and tell you that you are unpardonable. God makes no exceptions in His offer of salvation. "And by him all that believe are justified from all things, from which ye could not be justified by the law of Moses" (Acts 13:39).

Murder is not unpardonable. David confessed his sin and was forgiven (Ps. 32:5).

Theft is not unpardonable. The penitent thief on the cross was pardoned (Luke 23:43).

Blasphemy is not unpardonable. Paul was a blasphemer and he was pardoned (1 Tim. 1:13).

Adultery is not unpardonable. The woman of Samaria was saved (John 4:18).

One of the amazing records of forgiveness is found in First Corinthians 6:9-11.

The person who sincerely asks for pardon will never be refused. "Let the wicked forsake his way, and the unrighteous man his thoughts: and let him return unto the LORD, and he will have mercy upon him; and to our God, for he will abundantly pardon" (Is. 55:7).

"Come now, and let us reason together, saith the LORD: though your sins be as scarlet, they shall be as white as snow; though they be red like crimson, they shall be as wool" (Is. 1:18). See also Acts 10:43.

Paul was a great sinner, but he obtained salvation (1 Tim. 1:15, 16).

48. Question: "*Would not suicide be the best way out of my trouble?*"

Answer: There is only one solution for guilt consciousness—forgiveness and cleansing (Job 15:20, 1 John 1:9).

Self-murder only hastens judgment. "So then every one of us shall give account of himself to God" (Rom. 14:12).

A correct relationship with Christ brings a new approach to living. "Therefore if any man *be* in Christ, *he is* a new creature: old things are passed away; behold, all things are become new" (2 Cor. 5:17).

Get the *sin-problem* settled first, and then the *trouble-problem* can be settled (Matt. 6:33).

49. Excuse: *"I am seeking but I cannot find Christ."*

Answer: Christ is not distant. His presence is noticeable, "That they should seek the Lord, if haply they might feel after him, and find him, though he be not far from every one of us: For in him we live, and move, and have our being; as certain also of your own poets have said, For we are also his offspring" (Acts 17:27, 28).

Paul says that Christ makes Himself real to a person through the exercise of faith (Rom. 10:6–11).

Be sure you are looking in the right direction! "And ye shall seek me, and find *me*, when ye shall search for me with all your heart" (Jer. 29:13).

50. Excuse: *"I am ashamed to come to Christ."*

Answer: "But when Jesus heard *that*, he said unto them, They that be whole need not a physician, but they that are sick. But go ye and learn what *that* meaneth, I will have mercy, and not sacrifice: for I am not come to call the righteous, but sinners to repentance" (Matt. 9:12, 13).

Salvation is for the *lost*. "For when we were yet without strength, in due time Christ died for the ungodly. For scarcely for a righteous man will one die: yet peradventure for a good man some would even dare to die. But God commendeth his love toward us, in that, while we were yet sinners, Christ died for us" (Rom. 5:6–8).

51. Excuse: *"I would like to be a Christian, but I cannot forgive my enemies."*

Answer: Through God's help you can do what you cannot do otherwise. "With men this is impossible; but with God all things are possible" (Matt. 19:26).

I become a recipient of God's *grace*. "And God *is* able to make all grace abound toward you; that ye, always having all sufficiency in all *things*, may abound to every good work" (2 Cor. 9:8). See also Second Corinthians 12:9.

Tell God only that *you are willing to be made willing* (Matt. 6:14, 15).

52. Excuse: *"I want to be saved, but I cannot believe."*

Answer: *Whom* does the Bible ask you to believe? "Believe on the Lord Jesus Christ, and thou shalt be saved, and thy house" (Acts 16:31).

Do you believe that God has saved *others?* Do you believe that He wants to save *you?* Do you believe that He *can* save you? Will you trust Him to save you *now?*

You are saved through the Word which is God's contract with you, and because God wants you to be saved (John 5:24). "But as many as received him, to them gave he power to become the sons of God, *even* to them that believe on his name: Which were born, not of blood, nor of the will of the flesh, nor of the will of man, but of God" (John 1:12, 13).

Use the faith that God gives you! "For by grace are ye saved through faith; and that not of yourselves: *it is* the gift of God" (Eph. 2:8). See also Romans 5:1.

53. Question: *"Does not the Bible have inconsistencies and contradictions in it?"*

Answer: Where are they? The Bible is *revelation*. "For my thoughts *are* not your thoughts, neither *are* your ways my ways, saith the LORD. For *as* the heavens are higher than the earth, so are my ways higher than your ways, and my thoughts than your thoughts" (Is. 55:8, 9).

The Bible is a *locked book* to a *locked heart*. "Many shall be purified, and made white, and tried; but the wicked shall do wickedly: and none of the wicked shall understand; but the wise shall understand" (Dan. 12:10).

"But the natural man receiveth not the things of the Spirit of God: for they are foolishness unto him: neither can he know *them*, because they are spiritually discerned" (1 Cor. 2:14).

Certainly there are mysteries presented in God's Word! "As also in all *his* epistles, speaking in them of these things; in which are some things hard to be understood, which they that are unlearned and unstable wrest, as *they do* also the other scriptures, unto their own destruction. Ye therefore, beloved, seeing ye know *these things* before, beware lest ye also, being led away with the error of the wicked, fall from your own stedfastness. But grow in grace, and *in* the knowledge of our Lord and Saviour Jesus Christ. To him *be* glory both now and for ever. Amen" (2 Pet. 3:16–18).

Know Him and you will know His book!

54. Question: *"How can I know there is a God?"*

Answer: There are *three sources* of material. First, there is the Bible. Second, there is nature. Third, there is man. These point to the Creator. None are possible by happenstance. None could have been produced by accident.

"Because that which may be known of God is manifest in them; for God hath shewed *it* unto them" (Rom. 1:19).

"When I consider thy heavens, the work of thy fingers, the moon and the stars, which thou hast ordained" (Ps. 8:3).

"By the word of the LORD were the heavens made; and all the host of them by the breath of his mouth" (Ps. 33:6).

55. Question: *"Why do I need the blood?"*

Answer: "For the life of the flesh *is* in the blood: and I have given it to you upon the altar to make an atonement for your souls: for it *is* the blood *that* maketh an atonement for the soul" (Lev. 17:11).

Jesus died for you and me (Matt. 26:28).

"And almost all things are by the law purged with blood; and without shedding of blood is no remission" (Heb. 9:22).

He tasted death for me. Thus He bore the supreme penalty of my sins (Rom. 5:9, 10).

It took the greatest price in the universe. "Forasmuch as ye know that ye were not redeemed with corruptible things, *as* silver and gold, from your vain conversation *received* by tradition from your fathers; But with the precious blood of Christ, as of a lamb without blemish and without spot" (1 Pet. 1:18, 19).

56. Question: *"Why should I accept the Bible as the final authority?"*

Answer: *The Bible has survived all unbelievers*. "For what if some did not believe? shall their unbelief make the faith of God without effect? God forbid: yea, let God be true, but every man a liar" (Rom. 3:3, 4).

"All scripture *is* given by inspiration of God, and *is* profitable for doctrine, for reproof, for correction, for instruction in righteousness" (2 Tim. 3:16).

God's character rests upon the authenticity and authority of the Bible (Mark 13:31).

57. Question: *"What must I do to be saved?"*

Answer: God, through Jesus Christ, His Son, has provided a way for you (Is. 53:5, 6). That sixth verse begins and ends with the same word, 'all." It is a universal salvation for a universal need.

Your part is to "receive." God's part is to give you "power to become." "But as many as received him, to them gave he power to become the sons of God, *even* to them that believe on his name" (John 1:12).

Conversion and regeneration go together. When you have turned to God (conversion), He will turn over your life (regeneration). God's part is as essential as your part (John 3:7).

Saving faith reaches out and believes what God's Word says about you. "Verily, verily, I say unto you, He that heareth my word, and believeth on him that sent me, hath everlasting life, and shall not come into condemnation; but is passed from death unto life" (John 5:24).

Your salvation is in your acceptance of what Christ has done for you. Did He, or did He not, die for you? (Acts 16:31).

Outward form is useless until something has happened within your life. Salvation is like marriage. All the ceremony involved can't really marry a couple unless first of all something real toward each other has happened in each of their hearts. When that occurs, they want the whole world to know (Rom. 10:9–19).

God saves sinners only. Are you a sinner? Do you need two things—(1) FORGIVENESS and (2) CLEANSING?

What God has done for others, He will do for you. "For whosoever shall call upon the name of the Lord shall be saved" (Rom. 10:13).

Jesus foretold that excuses and alibis would be given. *Excuses* are never *reasons*.

"Then said he unto him, A certain man made a great supper, and bade many: And sent his servant at supper time to say to them that were bidden, Come; for all things are now ready. And they all with one *consent* began to make excuse. The first said unto him, I have bought a piece of ground, and I must needs go and see it: I pray thee have me excused. And another said, I have bought five yoke of oxen, and I go to prove them: I pray thee have me excused. And another said, I have married a wife, and therefore I cannot come. So that servant came, and shewed his lord these things. Then the master of the house being angry said to his servant, Go out quickly into the streets and lanes of the city, and bring in hither the poor, and the maimed, and the halt, and the blind. And the servant said, Lord, it is done as thou hast commanded, and yet there is room. And the lord said unto the servant, Go out into the highways and hedges, and compel *them* to come in, that my house may be filled. For I say unto you, That none of those men which were bidden shall taste of my supper" (Luke 14:16–24).

> Let not conscience make you linger,
> Nor of fitness fondly dream;
> All the fitness he requireth
> Is to feel your need of Him.
> —Joseph Hart

VI. Conversion
Steps to the Christian Life:

1. REPENT. Turn around. Change your mind. "I tell you, Nay: but, except ye repent, ye shall all likewise perish" (Luke 13:3).

2. RECEIVE HIM. You need the Saviour. Accept Him. "But as many as received him, to them gave he power to become the sons of God, *even* to them that believe on his name" (John 1:12).

3. BE "BORN AGAIN." This is what God does for you. This is the New Birth—a miracle of spiritual life performed by the Holy Spirit. "Which were born, not of blood, nor of the will of the flesh, nor of the will of man, but of God" (John 1:13). See also John 11:25.

4. REJOICE PUBLICLY. Make your testimony for Christ, "that if thou shalt confess with thy mouth the Lord Jesus, and shalt believe in thine heart that God hath raised him from the dead, thou shalt be saved. For with the heart man believeth unto righteousness; and with the mouth confession is made unto salvation" (Rom. 10:9, 10). See also Matthew 10:32, 33.

5. REQUEST WATER BAPTISM. This is an outward testimony to an inward transaction. "He that believeth and is baptized shall be saved; but he that believeth not shall be damned" (Mark 16:16).

The Bible can never be the private and exclusive property of any one religion. God gave it to the world. It cannot be copyrighted. It is not man's product. Therefore, look for your eternal

assurance from the Bible. *It is what God says that counts.*

6. READ THE WORD. The Word is the source of your faith. "These things have I written unto you that believe on the name of the Son of God; that ye may know that ye have eternal life, and that ye may believe on the name of the Son of God" (1 John 5:13). See also Romans 10:17, Psalm 119:105.

7. REACH GOD IN PRAYER. Prayer is conversation with God. Life is sustained by union and communion (Eph. 6:18, James 4:2). "And this is the confidence that we have in him, that, if we ask any thing according to his will, he heareth us: And if we know that he hear us, whatsoever we ask, we know that we have the petitions that we desired of him" (1 John 5:14, 15).

8. RELATE YOUR EXPERIENCE TO OTHERS. You maintain strength by exercise. "Nevertheless, if thou warn the wicked of his way to turn from it; if he do not turn from his way, he shall die in his iniquity; but thou hast delivered thy soul. Therefore, O thou son of man, speak unto the house of Israel; Thus ye speak, saying, If our transgressions and our sins *be* upon us, and we pine away in them, how should we then live?" (Ezek. 33:9, 10).

9. RESIST THE DEVIL. Temptation is not sin. It is yielding to temptation that is sin. "That the trial of your faith, being much more precious than of gold that perisheth, though it be tried with fire, might be found unto praise and honour and glory at the appearing of Jesus Christ" (1 Pet. 1:7). "For we have not an high priest which cannot be touched with the feeling of our infirmities; but was in all points tempted like as *we are*, *yet* without sin" (Heb. 4:15).

10. RESTITUTION. Your guilt is gone, and you can convert your influence for good. "And Zacchaeus stood, and said unto the Lord; Behold, Lord, the half of my goods I give to the poor; and if I have taken any thing from any man by false accusation, I restore *him* fourfold" (Luke 19:8). "And herein do I exercise myself, to have always a conscience void of offence toward God, and *toward* men" (Acts 24:16).

11. "RENDER . . . UNTO GOD THE THINGS THAT ARE GOD'S." Start tithing your income immediately. "Will a man rob God? Yet ye have robbed me. But ye say, Wherein have we robbed thee? In tithes and offerings. Bring ye all the tithes into the storehouse, that there may be meat in mine house, and prove me now herewith saith the Lord of hosts, if I will not open you the windows of heaven, and pour you out a blessing, that *there shall* not *be room* enough *to receive it*" (Mal. 3:8, 10). See also First Corinthians 16:2.

12. REGULARLY ATTEND CHURCH AND SUNDAY SCHOOL. Associate yourself immediately with God's people. Become a church member (Heb. 10:25).

"And he came to Nazareth, where he had been brought up: and, as his custom was, he went into the synagogue on the sabbath day, and stood up for to read" (Luke 4:16).

"According as his divine power hath given unto us all things that *pertain* unto life and godliness, through the knowledge of him that hath called us to glory and virtue" (2 Pet. 1:3).

VII. Convincement

"In him was life; and the life was the light of men" (John 1:4).

"But that ye may know that the Son of man hath power upon earth to forgive sins" (Luke 5:24).

It is too late in another world. Forgiveness of sins must be received on this side (1 John 3:2).

What is this assurance? How can I know for certain?

There are second chances in health, money, championships, and education; but when a man passes from this life, he cannot return for a second chance. *Your religion must furnish your proof.* You have a right to demand it.

Calvary is ridiculous if your life can be changed and you do not know it. Something you may have and not know it, is something you can lose and never miss. *The proof of your salvation is not by sensation. It is by Scripture.*

Certain evidences must be manifested in our lives immediately. These evidences are recorded in the Bible.

1. THERE IS AN INFALLIBLE INSIDE WITNESS. "He that believeth on the Son of God hath the witness in himself: he that believeth not God hath made him a liar; because he believeth not the record that God gave of his Son" (1 John 5:10). The preacher and the church may tell you that you are all right. But you, *yourself*, are the final judge in that matter.

Christ asked Peter about this. He said, "Lovest thou me more than these?" (John 21:15). There was no doubt in Peter's mind about his relationship to Jesus.

2. THERE IS A FAMILY RELATIONSHIP. "We know that we have passed from death unto life, because we love the brethren" (1 John 3:14). *You sense a different and vital relationship with God's children.* You are at home with spiritual things. It is a tie stronger than any family background in this world (Gal. 6:10).

3. THERE IS A NEW IMAGE. "Therefore if any man *be* in Christ, *he is* a new creature: old things are passed away; behold, all things are become new" (2 Cor. 5:17). A New Testament Christian is not a patched-up job, a reformed sinner. There is a new will; there are new affections; there is a new purpose because there is a new nature.

The emptiest and unhappiest occupation in the world is trying to act like a Christian when you are not a Christian. You do not gradually stop stealing. You stop stealing. It is miracle, not magic.

4. THERE IS A RESPONSE OF VICTORY. "For whatsoever is born of God overcometh the world: and this is the victory that overcometh the world, *even* our faith" (1 John 5:4). See also John 17:15, 16. *The born-again man or woman is not motivated by this world-system.*

Fancy yourself on the farm. It is hot midsummer. Nearby is a big mud wallow. Here comes a pig. He grunts with contentment as he wades into the slime. You say, "Mr. Hog, why do you want to submerge in that filth? Why do you not seek a cleaner environment?" That pig has not the slightest interest in your ideas for his betterment. He loves the mud.

Now watch a sheep with long white wool. The moment a sheep notices mud it heads toward safer ground. The sheep has a different nature. So has a New Testament Christian.

These are Bible proofs. "These things have I written unto you that believe on the name of the Son of God; that ye may know that ye have eternal life, and that ye may believe on the name of the Son of God" (1 John 5:13).

Paul testified on two continents (2 Tim. 3:11).

VIII. Camouflage

Today is a day of *substitutes*. Nylon has been substituted for silk. Oleomargarine has been substituted for butter. There also are many substitutes offered for salvation. Beware.

1. SERVICE IS NOT SALVATION. "Woe unto you, scribes and Pharisees, hypocrites! for ye compass sea and land to make one proselyte, and when he is made, ye make him twofold more the child of hell than yourselves" (Matt. 23:15). How can you lead others to Christ when you do not know Christ yourself?

2. TURNING OVER A NEW LEAF IS NOT SALVATION. Man does not get saved by *reforming*, saying, "I will clean up my life, and begin life anew."

"But we are all as an unclean *thing*, and all our righteousnesses *are* as filthy rags; and we all do fade as a leaf; and our iniquities, like the wind, have taken us away" (Is. 64:6). "How ye turned to God from idols to serve the living and true God" (1 Thess. 1:9). *Notice the direction!* They did not turn from idols to God. The new birth is a divine miracle.

3. ASSERTING ONE'S MANHOOD IS NOT SALVATION. Men "dead in trespasses and sins" (Eph. 2:1) cannot throw back their shoulders and assert their manhood for righteousness. The cross of Christ does not call upon men to assert their manhood. *The cross of Christ exposes men's degradation.* That is part of the "offence of the cross" (Gal. 5:11). It does not appeal to man's pride. It unsparingly shows man that he cannot do anything for himself. He has no righteousness or decency to offer to God.

4. RIGHT THINKING IS NOT SALVATION. It is not cultivating and concentrating on a "divine spark" that is within you. "Behold, I was shapen in iniquity; and in sin did my mother conceive me" (Ps. 51:5). It is not keeping a picture of your mother, sweetheart, or your wife in your billfold, and looking at it frequently. *It is not thinking high thoughts* (Is. 55:8, 9). *How can you think high thoughts with a base nature?*

5. DENYING THE EXISTENCE OF SIN IS NOT SALVATION. God does not deny sin. *Calvary is God's recognition of sin.* "And the LORD hath laid on him the iniquity of us all" (Is. 53:6). "But the scripture hath concluded all under sin" (Gal. 3:22). One of the first steps toward salvation is to recognize your sin—not deny it.

6. TO DENY SELF IS NOT SALVATION. The heathen are masters at this. They practice all kinds of asceticism (1 Cor. 13:3). *You are not saved by crucifying yourself.* It is not proving to yourself that you can do hard things.

7. SACRIFICE IS NOT SALVATION. Dying for a great cause—the supreme sacrifice—is not salvation. *Discipline does not cleanse a man from sin.* If that were true, then everybody who entered a penitentiary would become a Christian. Paying for wrongdoing does not make a person a Christian. (1 Sam. 15:22).

There is no *side door* into heaven. Jesus said, "I am the door: by me if any man enter in, he shall be saved" (John 10:9).

"He that entereth not by the door into the sheepfold, but climbeth up some other way, the same is a thief and a robber" (John 10:1). You cannot steal your way into heaven.

IX. Christ

The Master has not asked us to do what He did not do constantly during His ministry upon earth. He says, "Follow me, and I will make you fishers of men" (Matt. 4:19).

His record is one of personal contact from when He said to Andrew, "Come and see" to His assurance to the penitent thief, "To day shalt thou be with me in paradise."

He is clear and concise about God's plan of salvation.

1. He came to meet a human need. "I came not to call the righteous, but sinners" (Luke 5:32). Salvation is for sinners only.

2. He came to be the sinner's substitute. "The good shepherd giveth his life for the sheep" (John 10:11).

3. He came to do what none other can do. "I am the way, the truth, and the life: no man cometh unto the Father, but by me" (John 14:6).

4. He came to provide assurance to the trusting sinner. "Thy sins are forgiven. . .go in peace" (Luke 7:48–50).

James remembers emphatically the passion

that his brother manifested toward the lost. He reflects this when he says, "Let him know, that he which converteth the sinner from the error of his way shall save a soul from death, and shall hide a multitude of sins" (James 5:20).

X. Condensation

The story of salvation can be told in four words:

Sin
Calvary
Faith
Life

1. Salvation is needed. "For all have sinned, and come short of the glory of God" (Rom. 3:23).

2. Salvation is provided. "Who his own self bare our sins in his own body on the tree, that we, being dead to sins, should live unto righteousness: by whose stripes ye were healed" (1 Pet. 2:24).

3. Salvation is offered. "For by grace are ye saved through faith; and that not of yourselves: *it is* the gift of God" (Eph. 2:8).

4. Salvation accepted. "He that hath the Son hath life; *and* he that hath not the Son of God hath not life" (1 John 5:12).

There is a time, we know not when,
  A place, we know not where;
Which marks the destiny of men
  To glory or despair.

There is a line, by us unseen,
  Which crosses every path,

Which marks the boundary between
  God's mercy and his wrath.

To pass that limit is to die,
  To die as if by stealth;
It does not dim the beaming eye,
  Nor pale the glow of health.

The conscience may be still at ease,
  The spirit light and gay;
And that which pleases still may please,
  And care be thrust away.

But on that forehead God hath set
  Indelibly a mark;
Unseen by man, for man as yet,
  Is blind and in the dark.

He feels perchance that all is well
  And every fear is calmed;
He lives, he dies, he walks in hell,
  Not only doomed, but damned!

O, Where is that mysterious line
  That may by men be crossed,
Beyond which God himself hath sworn,
  That he who goes is lost?

An answer from the skies repeats,
  "Ye who from God depart."
TODAY, O hear His voice,
  TODAY repent and harden not your heart.
            —Joseph Addison Alexander

THE GREATEST
ARCHAEOLOGICAL
DISCOVERIES
and Their Effects on the Bible

I
Introduction

Definition and Importance
of Biblical Archaeology

The last 150 years have witnessed the birth, growth, and phenomenal development of the science of biblical archaeology. This new science has performed many wonders in furnishing background material and in illustrating, illuminating, and in many cases authenticating the message and meaning of the Old and New Testament Scriptures.

Biblical archaeology may be defined as a study based on the excavation, decipherment, and critical evaluation of the records of the past as they affect the Bible. While the general field of archaeology is fascinating, much more so is the study of biblical archaeology, since it deals with the Holy Scriptures. This is the reason for the growing enthusiasm for biblical archaeology. The attraction lies in the supreme importance of the message and meaning of the Bible. The Scriptures, by virtue of their character as the inspired revelation of God to man and meeting man's deepest need, today as in the past, have naturally held a paramount place in the interest and affection of mankind. Biblical archaeology, illustrating the Bible in its historical background and contemporary life, attracts a measure of the interest that lies in the Bible itself. Accordingly, this science has a worthy ministry of expanding biblical horizons on the human plane.

No field of research has offered greater challenge and promise than that of biblical archaeology. Until the beginning of the 19th century very little was known of biblical times and biblical backgrounds, except what appeared on the pages of the Old Testament or what happened to be preserved in the writings of classical antiquity. This was considerable for the New Testament era but very little indeed for the Old Testament period. The reason for this is that Greek and Latin historians catalogued very little information before the 5th century B.C. As a result, the Old Testament period was very little known extrabiblically, and what was known was confined to what the Bible gave. This from the viewpoint of contemporary secular history was sparse. The result was that before the beginning of the science of modern archaeology there was practically nothing available to authenticate Old Testament history and literature. One can therefore imagine the fervor aroused among serious Bible students by illuminating discoveries in Bible lands, especially from c. 1800 to the present. In fact, modern archaeology may be said to have had its beginning in 1798, when the rich antiquities of the Nile Valley were opened up to scientific study by Napoleon's Egyptian Expedition.

II
Foundational Discoveries
of the Nineteenth Century

Although the most notable discoveries affecting the Bible and particularly the Old Testament were not made until the 20th century, foundational discoveries were made in the 19th century and prepared the way for the modern era.

1. The Rosetta Stone—Key to Egypt's
Splendid Past

This very important monument was discovered in 1798 at *Rosetta* (Rashid), near the westernmost mouth of the Nile River, by an officer in Napoleon's Expedition to Egypt. It was a slab of black basalt trilingually inscribed, which may be said to be the key that unlocked the door to knowledge of the language and literature of ancient Egypt and turned out to be the inscription that opened the modern era of scientific biblical archaeology.

The three languages in which this monument was found to be inscribed were the Greek of 200 B.C., two forms of Egyptian writing—the older, more complicated hieroglyphic script and the later simplified and more popular demotic writing, which was the common language of the people. The Greek could at once be read and provided the clue to the decipherment of the other two ancient Egyptian scripts. Sylvester de Sacy of France and J. D. Akerblad of Sweden succeeded in unraveling the demotic Egyptian by identifying the Greek personal names it contained, namely Ptolemy, Arsinoe, and Berenike. Thomas Young of England then proceeded to identify the name of Ptolemy in the hieroglyphic portion, where groups of characters enclosed in oval frames, called cartouches, had already been surmised to be royal names. From this point on, the young Frenchman Jean François Champollion, 1790–1832, was able to decipher the hiero-

glyphics of the monument, show the true nature of this script, make a dictionary, formulate a grammar, and translate numerous Egyptian texts, from the year 1818 to 1832.

Champollion's achievement formally opened up the science of Egyptology. Scholars from henceforth were able to read Egyptian monumental inscriptions and reliefs. From that time forth the literary treasures of the Nile Valley have been opened to scholarly study. Today many universities maintain chairs in the language and culture of ancient Egypt. These studies have opened up vistas of history hitherto unknown so that, from the beginning of Egypt. c. 2800 B.C. to 63 B.C. when Rome took over, the entire history of the land of the Nile can fairly well be traced.

All of this has tremendous bearing on the background of the Bible. Egypt figures largely in the patriarchal narratives and the Book of Exodus and all through the Pentateuch. As a result, the background of the story of Joseph and of the sojourn of the children of Israel in Egypt, their deliverance under Moses, and much of their sojourn in the desert and later history in Canaan can now be set in the general framework of Egyptian history. It can be said that the whole context of Old Testament history, in its broad span from Abraham to Christ, is made immeasurably clearer because of the vast strides in our knowledge of Egypt. That great nation of antiquity interacted with the mighty Assyro-Babylonian empires on the Tigris-Euphrates and with the Hittite power on the Halys across the tiny bridge that was ancient Palestine.

2. The Behistun Inscription—Gateway to Assyrian-Babylonian Antiquity

This famous monument was the key to the languages of Assyria and Babylonia. It consists of a large relief panel containing numerous columns of inscription, which was boldly carved on the face of a mountain about 500 feet above the surrounding plain of Karmanshah on the old caravan route from Babylon to Ecbatana. Unlike the Rosetta Stone written in ancient Egyptian hieroglyphics, and later in popular demotic and in the Greek of the 3rd century B.C., the *Behistun Inscription* was written in the wedge-shaped characters of ancient Assyria-Babylonia. It contained about 1200 lines of inscription. The three languages in which it was inscribed were all written in cuneiform characters, consisting of Old Persian, Elamite, and Akkadian. The third language, the Akkadian, was the wedge-shaped language of ancient Assyria and Babylonia, in which thousands upon thousands of clay tablets discovered in the Tigris-Euphrates region are inscribed.

Early excavations revealed a mass of material on which this curious wedge-shaped Babylonian-Akkadian writing appeared. But it was an unsolved riddle. Practically no progress was made

until a young English officer in the Persian army, Henry C. Rawlinson, in 1835 and the following years made the dangerous climb to the Behistun Inscription and made copies and plaster of paris impressions of it. Rawlinson knew modern Persian and set to work to decipher the old Persian, the cuneiform part of the inscription. After a decade of labor, he finally succeeded in translating the five columns, nearly 400 lines of the old Persian portion of the Behistun Inscription, and sent it to Europe in 1845. The text translation and commentary on it were published in 1847 in the *Journal of the Royal Asiatic Society*.

In conjunction with the literary part of the monument was a life-sized figure with numerous individuals bowing before it. This person turned out to be Darius the Great (522–486 B.C.), the Achemenid prince who saved the Persian Empire from a rebellion. The scene depicts the king, as Rawlinson's translation of the Persian portion of the inscription shows, receiving the submission of the rebels. The emperor is portrayed at the top of the relief accompanied by two attendants. His foot is placed upon the prostrate form of a leading rebel. The king's left hand holds a bow, while his right hand is lifted toward the winged disc symbolizing Ahura-Mazda, the spirit of good, whom Darius, an ardent follower of Zoroaster, worshiped. Behind the rebel stands a procession of rebel leaders, roped together by their necks. Beside and beneath the sculptured panel the numerous columns of the inscription appear, relating in three languages how Darius defended the throne and crushed the revolt.

Working on the supposition that the other inscriptions told the same story, scholars were soon enabled to read the second language, which was the Elamite or Susian. Then last, but most important, they could decipher the Akkadian or Assyro-Babylonian. This was a great discovery, for this wedge-shaped character of writing is recorded on numerous literary remains from the Tigris-Euphrates Valley. It opened up a vast new field of biblical background, so that today, as in the case of the Rosetta Stone opening up the science of Egyptology, the Behistun Inscription has given birth to the science of Assyriology. Moreover, both Egyptology and Assyriology offer great help in understanding biblical backgrounds and biblical history. No Bible dictionary, Bible handbook or commentary that is up to date can ignore the great findings of these sciences.

The task of deciphering cuneiform is increasing with every decade. Numerous cuneiform libraries have been discovered from antiquity. Two at Nineveh were unearthed. These contained thousands of clay tablets. *The library of Ashurbanipal* (669–625 B.C.) contained some 22,000 tablets. Among the tablets unearthed in this collection and sent to the British Museum were Assyrian copies of the Babylonian creation and flood

A gateway into Nebuchadnezzar's Palace in Babylon.
Matson Photo Service

stories. The identification and decipherment of these particular tablets by George Smith in 1872 produced great excitement in the archaeological world.

Not only in Babylonia but in many other places large bodies of cuneiform literature have been uncovered. For example, the famous *Amarna Letters* from Egypt were discovered in 1886 at Tell el-Amarna about 200 miles south of modern Cairo. These Amarna Tablets proved to be diplomatic correspondence of petty princes of Palestine in the 14th century B.C. with the Egyptian court at Amarna. The Amarna Letters give an inside glance into conditions in Palestine just before the conquest by Joshua and the Israelites. Many scholars actually think that they describe aspects of that invasion. One of the documents from the governor of Jerusalem (Urusalim) tells Amenophis IV that the "Habiru" (perhaps the Hebrews) were overrunning many Palestine cities and could not be held back.

Other important bodies of cuneiform literature bearing upon the Bible have been retrieved from Boghaz-Keui and Kanish in Asia Minor. Others come from Susa and Elam, others from the city of Mari on the middle Euphrates, others from Ras Shamra (ancient Ugarit), mentioned in the Amarna Letters and located in North Syria. Others stem from various sites within and without Babylonia. Of first-rate importance then is the Rosetta Stone from Egypt and the Behistun Inscription from Babylonia. These two monuments

may be said to have laid the foundation for the key discoveries of the 20th century.

3. The Moabite Stone—A Sensational Literary Find

This important inscription, found in 1868, offers another example of the discoveries of the 19th century that prepared the way for the great finds of the 20th century. The inscription dates from c. 850 B.C. It was erected by Mesha, king of Moab, and is often styled the *Mesha Stone*. It tells of the wars of Mesha of Moab with Omri, king of Israel, and Omri's successors. It also tells of Mesha's wars with the Edomites. The material recorded on the *Moabite Stone* parallels biblical history recorded in Second Kings, chapters 1 and 3. Numerous places mentioned in the Old Testament occur on the stele (inscribed monument). Among them are Arnon (Num. 21:13; Deut. 2:24), Ataroth (Num. 32:34), Baal-meon or Beth-baal meon (Josh. 13:17), Beth-bamoth or Bamoth-baal (Josh. 13:17), Beth-diblathaim (Jer. 48:22), Bezer (Josh. 20:8), Dibon (Num. 32:34), Jahaza (Josh. 13:18), Medeba (Josh. 13:9), and Nebo (Num. 32:38).

This inscribed monument or stele measures 3 feet 8½ inches in height, 2 feet 3½ inches in width, and 1 foot 1¾ inches in thickness. Its 34 lines constitute the longest single literary inscription yet recovered extrabiblically dealing with

A replica of the Moabite Stone.   *Matson Photo Service*

Palestine in the period 900–600 B.C. It records that Moab had been conquered by Omri and his son Ahab but was set free from the Israelite yoke by Mesha's god Chemosh. This deity is represented as commanding King Mesha to go to war against Israel, who, according to Second Kings 3:27, offered up his eldest son as a burnt offering upon the wall to propitiate the god Chemosh and to secure his favor.

The Moabite Stone is written in the language of Moab, which was very similar to the Hebrew of the time of Omri and Ahab. This inscription, therefore, has great value in tracing the development of early Hebrew through the centuries. When it was discovered, the Mesha Stone was not only the longest and oldest Phoenician-Hebrew inscription then in existence, it was the only one. Now the **Gezer Calendar** is known and it dates from c. 925 B.C. It is a school boy's exercise written in perfect classical Hebrew. This small limestone tablet, found at ancient Gezer, gives an incidental sidelight on Palestinian agriculture as well as on ancient Hebrew writing. Such discoveries as the Gezer Calendar and the Mesha Stone not only give glimpses into the background of the Bible but form important links in the culture and history of the people outside the pale of Israel.

III
Great Discoveries
of the Twentieth Century

Although such discoveries as the Rosetta Stone, the Behistun Inscription, the Mesha Stone, and the Siloam Inscription are important for their time and laid the foundations of scientific archaeology in the 19th century, it remained for the 20th century to produce the most thrilling and outstanding archaeological finds. During this period biblical archaeology came to be a refined and precise science, adding to the frontiers of biblical knowledge on the human plane and making tremendous contributions to the background, historical and cultural, of the written Word of God.

1. The Code of Hammurabi—Light on Mosaic Laws

A slab of black diorite, over 7 feet tall and some 6 feet wide, was discovered in 1901. This record of the past contains engraved upon it almost 300 paragraphs of legal provision dealing with the commercial, social, domestic, and moral life of the Babylonians of King Hammurabi's time (1728–1676 B.C.). A copy of this code was found by Jacques de Morgan at Susa in Elam, where it had been carried off by the Elamites from Babylon. At the top of the stele the king is shown receiving the laws from the sun god Shamash, patron of law and justice. At some time when Babylon was weak, an Elamite conqueror carried away the monument to

Susa. Its finding was one of the most startling legal discoveries in history.

The code is important in furnishing background material for comparison with other ancient bodies of law. It is also natural that it should offer comparative data for the study of the laws of the Pentateuch. The fact that the code is older by over three centuries than the laws of Moses has disposed of some untenable theories of the critics and given rise to others. For instance, the old critical view that detailed codes of law like those recorded in the Pentateuch are anachronistic for such an early period has been exploded by the discovery of Hammurabi's laws and much earlier codes in Mesopotamia.

A discovery of this sort illustrates how archaeology purges out radical critical views, which used to place the origin of many of the laws ascribed to Moses to much later times, such as the 9th, 8th, and 7th centuries B.C., or even later. These erroneous theories had to be drastically revised or entirely rejected. On the other hand, the discovery of the early extrabiblical legal material has led many to adopt an equally faulty view that Hebrew legislation is merely a selection and adaptation of Babylonian law. The only position that is valid as the two bodies of legal material are studied is that the Mosaic code is neither borrowed from, nor dependent upon, the Babylonian. It is divinely given, as it claims to be, and unique in those features that met Israel's peculiar need as an elect, theocratic nation.

The resemblances between the **Mosaic laws** and the **Code of Hammurabi** are clearly due to similarity of antecedents and general intellectual and cultural heritage. It is natural that in codes dealing with peoples in somewhat similar conditions, related racially and culturally, there should be some likeness in the incidents leading to litigation and likewise in the penalties imposed for infringement of common statutes. A striking difference, however, is obtained. These clearly demonstrate that there is no direct borrowing and that the Mosaic law, although later by three centuries, is in no sense dependent upon the Babylonian.

The biblical law of divorce (Deut. 24:1), for instance, permits the man to put away his wife but does not extend the same right to the wife, as does the Babylonian code. Again the so-called **Lex Talionis** is a primitive Semitic law and would be expected to be reflected in various Semitic legal codes. Mosaic injunctions (Ex. 21:23–25; Deut. 19:21) state precisely the same principle of retaliation upon which a number of Hammurabi's laws are based, namely "life for life, eye for eye, tooth for tooth, hand for hand, foot for foot, burning for burning, wound for wound, stripe for stripe."

The Mosaic and Hammurabi codes are **different in content**. The Hebrew code contains many purely religious injunctions and ritual reg-

ulations. The Code of Hammurabi, on the other hand, is civil. However, the priestly laws of Leviticus contain many points of similarity with priestly ritual and practice in western Asia, whether in Canaan or Phoenicia or Mesopotamia. But this in no sense casts doubt on the fact that Israel's religious practices as recorded in the Pentateuch are divinely given and uniquely invested with significance to fit a nation divinely called to serve the one God. In some cases similar cultic practice among surrounding peoples was divinely given to Israel. But at the same time it was invested with a special significance for the worship of the Lord.

The two codes, of course, are *different in their origin*. The Babylonian laws are alleged to have been received by Hammurabi from the sun god Shamash. Moses received his laws directly from the Lord. Hammurabi, despite his reported reception from Shamash, takes credit for them in both the prologue and epilogue of the code. He, not Shamash, established order and equity throughout the land. Moses, in contrast, is only an instrument. The legislation is "Thus saith the LORD."

The two codes govern a *different type of so-ciety*. Hammurabi's laws are fitted to the irrigation culture and highly commercialized urban society of Mesopotamia. The Mosaic injunctions, on the other hand, suit a simple, agricultural, pastoral people of a dry land like Palestine much less advanced in social and commercial development, but keenly conscious of their divine calling in all phases of their living.

The two codes *differ in their morality*. From the ethical and spiritual standpoint the Mosaic legislation, as would be expected, offers a considerable advance over the Babylonian code. Hammurabi's laws, for example, enumerate at least ten varieties of bodily mutilation prescribed for various offenses. If a doctor performs an operation that is unsuccessful, his hand is to be cut off. In the Mosaic legislation only one instance of mutilation occurs where a wife's hand is to be severed (Deut. 25:11, 12). Also in the Hebrew laws a greater value is set upon human life. A stricter regard for the honor of womanhood is seen and more humane treatment of slaves is enjoined. In addition, the Babylonian code has nothing in it corresponding to that twofold golden thread running through the Mosaic legislation, namely love to God and love to one's neighbor (Matt. 22:37–40).

Elephantine Island seen from across the Nile.   *Matson Photo Service*

The Israelite Torah and the Babylonian code may be contrasted as follows: In the Babylonian code there is no control of lust, no limitation of selfishness. The postulate of charity cannot be found. The religious motif is absent, which recognizes sin as the destruction of the people because it is in opposition to the fear of God. In the Hammurabi code every trace of religious thought is absent. Behind the Israelite laws stands the ruling will of a holy God. The laws are stamped throughout with a divine character.

2. The Elephantine Papyri—Light on the Ezra-Nehemiah Era

Discovered in 1903 on the island of Elephantine at the First Cataract of the Nile in Egypt, these important documents give an interesting glimpse of one of the outlying regions of the Persian Empire in the latter part of the 5th century B.C. *The Elephantine Papyri* come from a Jewish military colony which was settled at that place. Inscribed in Aramaic, the language of diplomacy and trade throughout western Asia in the Persian period, and which was gradually replacing Hebrew as the everyday tongue of the Jewish people, the contents are varied, ranging from the copy of the Behistun Inscription of Darius to such a document as a Jewish marriage contract. The letters tell us about the sacking of a Jewish temple at Elephantine in an anti-Jewish persecution about 411 B.C. The Jews at this far-off colony worshiped the Lord whom they referred to by the name of Yahu.

Other letters from Elephantine which have in recent years become known and have been published by the Brooklyn Museum demonstrate that the temple was rebuilt after its destruction. They contain mention of Yahu as "the god who dwells in Yeb, the fortress." Compare Psalm 31:3. These new papyri demonstrate that Egypt was still under the authority of Persia in the first years of Artaxerxes II (404–359 B.C.).

The Elephantine Papyri therefore illuminate the general background of the period of Ezra-Nehemiah and the earlier Persian period. They shed important light on the life of the Jewish dispersion in a remote frontier place such as Elephantine in Egypt. They also are invaluable in giving the scholar a knowledge of the Aramaic language of that period, and many of the customs and names that appear in the Bible are illustrated by these important literary finds.

3. The Hittite Monuments from Boghaz-Keui—Mementos of an Imperial People

In 1906 Professor Hugo Winkler of Berlin began excavations at Boghaz-Keui, a site which lies 90 miles east of Ankara in the great bend of the Halys River in Asia Minor. It was discovered that this was an ancient Hittite capital. Numerous clay tablets were dug up written in texts containing six different languages. A large number of these were inscribed in the cuneiform characters of the Hittite language. Eventually deciphered through the labors of three men and particularly of the Czech scholar Friedrich Hrozny, this language proved to be the key to a great deal of background of interest to the biblical student.

The city ruins at Ur.   *Matson Photo Service*

The Ziggurat at Ur.   *Matson Photo Service*

Before the Boghaz-Keui tablets revealed the Hittites to be an ancient people, the biblical references to them used to be regarded in critical circles as historically worthless. In the five books of Moses, references to the Hittites as inhabiting the land of Canaan and as among those whom the Israelites drove out occur in several places (Ex. 33:2; Deut. 7:1, 20:17; Josh. 3:10, 24:11). In the various lists the order varies, and there is not an inkling that one reference might be the name of a powerful imperial people and the other a small local tribe. Less than a century ago the "Hittites" meant little more to the reader of the Bible than the "Hivite" or the "Perizzite" still does.

It was commonly known from the biblical record that when Abraham settled in Hebron he had Hittites as neighbors. It was everyday knowledge that one of David's eminent soldiers was Uriah, a Hittite. But who would have expected that "Hittites" were more prominent than "Gadites" or "Beerothites"?

Now it is known that two great periods of Hittite power are to be noted. The first goes back to c. 1800 B.C., and the second is dated from c. 1400–1200 B.C. In this latter period of Hittite supremacy the powerful rulers reigned at Boghaz-Keui. One of these was named Subbiluliuma. This great conqueror extended his empire to the confines of Syria-Palestine. The great Rameses II of Egypt, in the famous battle of Kadesh, collided with Hittite power. A Hittite treaty of peace with the Pharaoh in the 21st year of the latter's reign was confirmed by a royal marriage.

About 1200 B.C. the great Hittite Empire collapsed, and the Hittite city of Boghaz-Keui fell. However, important centers of Hittite power remained at Carchemish, Sengirli, Hamath, and other places in north Syria. As a result of the excavation and decipherment of various Hittite monuments, the whole context of the ancient biblical world has been illuminated.

Because of this increased background knowledge, such allusions as those to the "kings of the Hittites" (1 Kin. 10:29; 2 Chr. 1:17) are much better understood. Also Ezekiel's reference to unfaithful Jerusalem as having an Amorite for a father and a Hittite for a mother (Ezek. 16:45) are now comprehensible. The manner in which archaeology has brought to light the ancient Hittites furnishes a good example of the way this important science is expanding biblical horizons.

4. The City of Ur—Abraham's Home

An important metropolis of the ancient world, Ur was located on the Euphrates River in lower Mesopotamia, present-day Iraq. Several centuries before Abraham lived there as a boy and grew up there as a young man, this place was a very important city under the 2nd and 3rd dynasties of Ur, an important line of kings. But the glory of the city was suddenly destroyed in the period from c. 1960–1830 B.C. Foreigners stormed down from the surrounding hills and took the reigning king, Ibi-Sin, a captive and reduced the capital *city of Ur* to ruins. So complete was the eclipse of the city that it lay buried in oblivion for centuries until, like Nineveh, it was resurrected in modern times by the work of archaeologists.

So thoroughly was the ancient city blotted out that when it was referred to in Genesis 11:28–31 and 15:7 as Abraham's ancestral home and the place from which he started on his trek to Pal-

estine, some scribe later had to append the descriptive phrase *"of the Chaldeans"* to the name of the city to give later readers some idea of where it had been located.

The long-lost and buried city was brought to the light of modern study by the work of numerous archaeologists, particularly by the work of Sir Leonard Woolley (1922–1934). Until the year 1854, the site of the ancient city was completely unknown. The Arabs used to call the location *Al-muqayyer, "Mount of bitumen."* It was a forbidding place in a climate of terrific heat and surrounded by intense desolation. In 1854, J. E. Taylor, an English archaeologist, assisted by others, made some preliminary excavations. Some cylinders turned up inscribed in cuneiform characters declaring that King Nabonidus of Babylon (556–539 B.C.) had restored the famous ziggurat of Ur-Nammu.

Later explorations were made by Campbell Thompson in 1918. H. R. Hall in 1918 continued other excavations, but it was left for the pivotal work of Sir Leonard Woolley, undertaken in 1922 as a joint expedition of the British Museum, the University of Pennsylvania, and the University Museum, to give a complete history and description of the city. The expedition completed twelve very successful archaeological campaigns, and by 1934 the long-lost and buried city of Ur, vanished from the pages of history, had become one of the best-known sites in all the ancient Near East.

Abraham's Native Town. Abraham lived in the city of Ur at the height of its splendor under the 3rd dynasty of kings. This is indicated if we follow the chronology of the Masoretic text of the Hebrew Bible. According to this system of reckoning, Abraham was born c. 2161 B.C. and entered Canaan c. 2086 B.C. Under this time arrangement, the patriarch left the city when it was near the acme of its prosperity. He entered Canaan precisely when Ur reached the pinnacle of its power, for the 3rd dynasty of kings (c. 2070–1969 B.C.) lifted the city to great prominence.

The first king was Ur-Nammu. This monarch had the title of "King of Sumer and Akkad." He built a splendid temple tower or ziggurat at this site. Today this is still preserved as the best monument of its type in all the flat alluvial territory of Lower Mesopotamia, the basin of Tigris-Euphrates rivers. It was this structure that Nabonidus, the last of the Babylonian kings, restored in the 6th century B.C.

In the famous *monument of Ur-Nammu* there is extant a contemporary record of the construction of the ziggurat at Ur. This stele is a slab of white limestone measuring 5 feet across and 10 feet in height. At the top of the monument the king is standing in an attitude of prayer. An account of the building of the monument is given, and scenes are inscribed denoting the actual construction. In the days of Ur-Nammu other buildings were built

around the ziggurat, and the entire sacred area was dedicated to Nannar, the moon god (patron deity of the city) and his consort, whose name was Nin-Gal.

A king by the name of Dungi succeeded Ur-Nammu, whom Nabonidus declared completed the ziggurat. Dungi was a great ruler who built a magnificent mortuary temple and tomb for himself. His son Bur-Sin succeeded him. He was followed on the throne at Ur by Gimil-Sin and then by Ibi-Sin.

Ur and Abraham. When Abraham lived in the city before he left for Haran and Canaan, Ur was a center of religion and industry. The city was wholly given over to the worship of the moon god cult. The Babylonians were devotees of many deities. But at Ur the moon god Sin was supreme.

Sir Leonard Woolley's lengthy excavations in twelve highly rewarding campaigns have revealed the splendor and the size of the city and also have given details of the *temonos* or the religious section of the city. In other words, Abraham was surrounded on all sides by idolatry. This we have recorded in the Bible in Joshua 24:2. "Your fathers dwelt on the other side of the flood [the Euphrates River] in old time, *even* Terah, the father of Abraham, and the father of Nachor: and they served other gods."

The moon god Sin was given such epithets as "the exalted lord" and "the beautiful lord who shines in the heavens." The immense temple tower, built like a mountain with various stages, contained the holy chamber of Nannar on its uppermost level. Here in this lofty Babylonian temple mystic ritual in honor of the deity was conducted. In front of the immense ziggurat and on the lower level was an open court, a kind of holy market where the people brought their gifts and paid their taxes to the king, who was also their landlord. Accordingly, the city was a kind of theocracy centered in the moon deity.

The sacred area was called the *temenos*. In it were located other sacred buildings and shrines, including houses for the priests and priestesses of Nannar. To the west the river Euphrates flowed near the city walls, and there were canals running around and through the city. In Abraham's day instead of being a hot, forbidding, desert-like region, Ur was a flourishing and beautiful city because of irrigation and civilization. It was surrounded by fertile farms and a busy populace engaged in agriculture and in woolen and textile industries. All of this commerce was centered in religion.

The houses of Ur have been excavated and examined. It is conceivable that Abraham grew up as a lad in one of these residences. There is presumptive evidence that Terah's father worshiped the moon god and was a devotee of Nannar and Nin-Gal. In one of the dwellings, there is a small domestic chapel with altar niche and family burial

vault. It is very likely that Terah worshiped at such an altar.

It is out of this polluted atmosphere of polytheism that God's sovereign grace called Abraham to begin a new line that was to be separated from idolatry and through which Messiah was to come, who would deliver the world from sin and idolatry.

The City Before the Time of Abraham. Ur existed as a brilliant city many hundreds of years before Abraham appeared on the scene. The lower regions of the Tigris-Euphrates basin with its flat land and very fertile soil have been the seat of many ancient empires—Sumer, Babylonia, Assyria, and Chaldea. The first of these civilizations was Sumer, one of the oldest civilized countries in the world. Wrapped in obscurity is the story of the beginnings of Sumer. At least by 3500 B.C. the Sumerians, that is the natives of the flat, alluvial lower courses of the Tigris-Euphrates plain, were advancing in civilization.

In the next thousand years the *Sumerian Empire* diffuse culture and civilization over most of western Asia. The extreme southern part of Sumer was called the land of Shinar. It was a flat, mud plain, immensely rich, formed by the sediment of the Tigris-Euphrates River. As these mighty streams flowed into the lower part of the Fertile Crescent, their current slackened, and they deposited huge amounts of a rich, sandy loam and formed a region which today is called Iraq, which is about as large as New Jersey.

With a network of canals running through this rich territory, this region blossomed like a rose. More than 150 years ago, travelers began to wonder about the strange mounds or hillocks of earth which dotted this flat region. What could they possibly be? Now and then antiquarian bits of carved marble or other remnants of bygone civilizations were exposed by the weather. Archaeologists began to dig beneath the truncated hillocks,

The Euphrates River.   *Matson Photo Service*

and it was discovered that they were long-lost and buried cities.

One of these mounds proved to be the city of Ur of biblical fame. From these regions many tablets have been resurrected with cuneiform or wedge-shaped writing on them. These tablets were made of soft mud from the riverbank and carefully inscribed with a flat pen and set out in the sun to dry, or put in the fire to bake in a more firm form. And so, under these truncated mounds were not only buried artifacts and remnants of ancient civilizations but, what is most arresting, there are vast quantities of practically indestructible materials, all inscribed on clay tablets. These have been the basis of resurrecting the history and the civilization of Bible lands in Lower Mesopotamia in the land of Sumer.

The First Dynasty of Ur. In an ancient list of kings called the Sumerian King List in *The Oxford Edition of Cuneiform Texts II*, 1923, by F. Langdon, an interesting story is told of the early rulers of Sumer. Among the line of kings who reigned at Kish, Uruk (biblical Erech, Gen. 10:10), Awan, Adap, Mari, and Akshak are listed several dynasties who ruled at Ur. The first kings at Ur witnessed the culminating phase of the early dynastic period in Mesopotamia (c. 2800–2360 B.C.).

The King List goes on to say, "Uruk was smitten with weapons. Its kingship was carried to Ur. Mes-Anne-pada became king and ruled 80 years. A-Anne-pada, a son of Mes-Anne-pada, reigned . . . years. Meskiag-Nanna, a son of Mes-Anne-pada became king and reigned 36 years. Elulu reigned 25 years. Balulu reigned 36 years. Four kings reigned 177 years. Ur was smitten with weapons."

This line of kings was very powerful and lifted the city-state, since Ur was more than a city, to a high level of culture. This is demonstrated in the discoveries of the royal tombs by Sir Leonard Woolley, dating from c. 2500 B.C. These consisted of rooms and vaults built of brick and stone. Among one of the most interesting finds was the tomb of an important lady named *Shubad of Ur.* Her name is identified by an inscribed cylinder of lapis lazuli. Near her hand was a gold cup. Her lovely artistic headdress contained 9 yards of gold band.

Another exquisite find was the so-called *"Standard of Ur."* This was a wooden panel, 22 inches long by 9 inches wide, skillfully inlaid with mosaic work on both sides depicting scenes of war and peace. In the war panel the king is seen receiving captives. In another the phalanx of the royal army advances. Scenes of fighting with chariots and javelins are depicted. The panel of peace presents a royal family feast. Musicians entertain while servants wait in the banquet hall and bring in spoils captured from the enemy.

Certainly the archaeological resurrection of

Abraham's ancient city of Ur has greatly illuminated the Bible references to the patriarch and given a much wider view of the historical horizons c. 2000 B.C. The early civilization of the Tigris-Euphrates Valley is becoming better known year after year. Bible dictionaries, encyclopedias, commentaries, and biblical works of every description are highly indebted to the restless and productive spade of the archaeologist. Certainly God has blessed, enabling scholars in our day to study these monuments and other remains of antiquity. The result is greater appreciation of the Bible on the human plane.

It must always be remembered that the Word of God is not only divine but human. It is God's Book for man. On the human side, God has so ordained that the horizons of biblical knowledge may be expanded and increased that we may on the spiritual plane better comprehend the Word of God. How unfortunate it is when the spiritual is divorced from the historical and archaeological, or vice versa, when the historical and archaeological are divorced from the spiritual. The two work hand in hand and help one another. Happy is the student of the Bible who will combine both of these disciplines in a better understanding of the Word of God.

5. The Religious Texts from Ras Shamra (Ugarit)—Canaanite Cults Exposed

One of the most important discoveries of the 20th century was the recovery of hundreds of clay tablets which have been housed in a library situated between two great temples, one dedicated to Baal and another dedicated to Dagon, in the city of *Ugarit*—modern *Ras Shamra* in north Syria. These clay tablets date from the 15th to early 14th centuries B.C. They are inscribed in the earliest-known alphabet written in wedge-shaped signs. Professor H. Bower of the University of Halle recognized this new writing as Semitic. Numbers of scholars such as E. Dhorme and Charles Virolleaud began working on the decipherment of this new Semitic language.

The tablets turned out to be religious and cultic in nature and inscribed in a dialect that was closely akin to biblical Hebrew and Phoenician. Although Semitic in form, this new writing displayed evidences of Akkadian influence, since Mesopotamians wrote on clay tablets with wedge-shaped characters from left to right. First intimations of the archaeological importance of the ancient city of Ugarit, which was unknown until 1928, came in the spring of that year when a Syrian peasant plowing in his field a little north of present-day Minet el-Beida suddenly came across some antiquities. On April 2, 1929, work began at Minet el-Beida under the direction of Claude F. Schaffer. After a month's work he changed to the nearby tell of Ras Shamra. Only a few days' work demonstrated the importance of the new location.

On May 20th the first tablets were uncovered. Schaffer continued excavations from 1929 to 1937. Between 1929 and 1933, the bulk of significant religious texts were recovered in the royal library in the area. Many of these were inscribed in an early Canaanite dialect, roughly contemporary with the Mosaic age.

The City of Ugarit. This flourishing second-millennium city, which had been known by scholars from Egyptian inscriptions from the *Tell el Amarna Letters* and *Hittite documents*, was located on the north Syrian coast opposite the island of Cyprus, about 8 miles north of Latakia and 50 miles southwest of Antioch. It was situated on a bay and had a port which could be used by seagoing trade ships. It was a harbor town known in Greek times as Leukos Limen, the white harbor. It is now called *Ras Shamra*, *"hill of fennel,"* because fennel grows there.

The hill which comprises the ruin of the ancient city has the form of a trapezium with the long side about 670 yards north and south and the longer diagonal about 1,100 yards. The hill is about 22 yards high. The site was located on the important trade route along the coast from Egypt to Asia Minor, which was connected by a road with Aleppo, Mari on the Euphrates, and Babylon. The sea route from Ugarit to Alashiya—that is, Cyprus—was a short one.

Very early, Ugarit struck up a brisk trade with the Aegean Islands. It became an important harbor. One of the main exported articles was copper, which was used in the production of bronze. Copper was imported from Asia Minor and Cyprus. Bronze was produced in Ugarit. Being a Phoenician town, Ugarit, like its sister cities, delivered timber to Egypt. Not only cedars from the interior were exported but other kinds of wood as well. There were also purple dye factories, great heaps of murex shells indicate this. These shells, abundantly found along the east Mediterranean coast, produced a famous dye of antiquity.

Literary Importance of the Texts. After preliminary work by many scholars, Cyrus Gordon worked out a **Ugaritic Grammar** and later put out an edition of the texts called **Ugaritic Literature.** The decipherment of the texts showed the important parallels between Ugaritic and Hebrew literary style and vocabulary. By 1936 H. L. Ginsberg had made some far-reaching observations with regard to common structural elements. Ginsberg's study showed that Canaanite poetry, like Hebrew, was basically accentual, that is, consisted of numbers of feet, each of which was accented. A good example of the survival of Canaanite literary elements in Hebrew religious literature is the following tricolon (unit of three lines) from the *Baal Epic of Ras Shamra:*

> "Behold, thine enemies, O Baal;
> Behold, thine enemies shalt thou crush;
> Behold, thou shalt smite thy foes."

In *Psalm 92:9* there is a striking parallel to this.

> "For, lo, thine enemies, O LORD, for, lo,
> thine enemies shall perish; all the
> workers of iniquity shall be scattered."

The following tricolon occurs frequently in the *Aqhat Epic:*

> "Do thou ask for life, O lad Aqhat;
> Do thou ask for life, I'll grant it thee,
> Eternal life, and I'll accord it thee."

A similar literary device is found in the *Song of Deborah* (Judg. 5:30).

> "To Sisera a prey of divers colours, a
> prey of divers colours of needlework,
> of divers colours of needlework on
> both sides, *meet* for the necks of *them
> that take* the spoil?"

Background material such as this is an invaluable aid in the study of Hebrew poetry and the general literary qualities of style and vocabulary in Old Testament Hebrew. Since the Ugaritic language is very closely connected with biblical Hebrew, much light has been shed upon Hebrew lexicography. Any recent lexicon of Hebrew must take into consideration the vocabulary used at Ugarit. Future Hebrew dictionaries will include many words hitherto misunderstood or only partially known.

For example, the word *beth-heber* (Prov. 21:9; 25:24) hitherto rendered "house" has been shown from Ugaritic and Assyrian to mean specifically "a storehouse." These verses must then be rendered "*It is* better to dwell in a corner of the housetop, than with a brawling woman and in a storehouse." It is of interest to note that the Egyptian proverbs of Amenemope, which have many parallels to the biblical Book of Proverbs, employs a word for "storehouse" in exactly the same sense.

Religious Significance of the Ugaritic Inscriptions. By far the most important contribution of the religious texts from Ras Shamra (Ugarit) is in giving the Bible student background material for the study of Old Testament religions. The epics set forth very clearly the *Canaanite pantheon.* We now know that this pantheon of the Canaanites was headed up by the god El, the supreme Canaanite deity. This is also a name by which God is known in the Old Testament (cf. Gen. 33:20). This name, El, often occurs in Old Testament poetry (Ps. 18:31, 32; Job 8:3). It occurs frequently also in prose in compound names, for example, El Elyon, the God Most High (Gen. 14:18); El Shaddai, Almighty God (Gen. 17:1); El Hai, the living God (Josh. 3:10). This, however, does not mean any connection, of course, with Canaanite mythology. El is simply the common Semitic word for God. In Ugaritic, El was a bloody, lustful tyrant. The description of him, as well as of other Canaanite gods, fully substantiates the testimony of the Old Testament with regard to the degeneracy and polluting influence of Canaanite religion.

Baal was the son of El. He was the active king of the gods in the Canaanite pantheon and dominated the entire list of gods. He was the deity of the storm and the rain. Thunder was thought to be the reverberation of his voice in the heavens. At Ras Shamra a stele was discovered depicting Baal holding a stylized thunderbolt. Three of the Ugaritic poems concern Baal. Baalism, the worship of this god, was one of the most debilitating and destructive influences which threatened the Hebrews in Palestine and against which they had to be continually on guard.

As the giver of rain and all fertility, Baal figures very prominently in Canaanite mythology. He struggles with Mot, the god of death and the god of drought. In the fight Baal is slain. As a consequence, the seasonal drought occurs from June to late October. Then Anath, sister and lover of Baal, goes out in search of him, discovers his body, and slays his enemy, Mot. Baal is then brought back to life, thus ensuring the revival of vegetation for a seven-year period. The great Baal Epic of Ugarit finds in this representation a central theme.

The Phoenicians at Ugarit not only had gods who were polluted and immoral but also goddesses. Three of these who are prominent are Anath, Astarte, and Asherah. They are patronesses of war and sex. Their character, like that of El and Baal, bears out the pollution and damaging effects of Canaanite religion, since they portray war in its aspect of violence and murder and sex mainly in its lustful connotation of indulgence.

The new knowledge of Canaanite religion aids the Bible student correctly to evaluate the testimony of the Old Testament to the Canaanites. Higher criticism has impugned the morality of the Old Testament writers in such episodes as the divine command to exterminate these cults. Examples are the extermination of the people of Jericho, Saul's extermination of the Amalekites, and the driving out of the Canaanites in general. All of these examples appear in a different view when adjudged in the light of the vileness of Canaanite religion. In Genesis 15:16 the Lord declares, "the iniquity of the Amorites" was not yet "full" in Abraham's day. But archaeology shows Canaanite religious immorality was complete in Joshua's day, 400 years later, and had to be destroyed.

Now, as a result of the Ras Shamra literature, the nature of Canaanite religion comes before the scholar in its real light. No longer do we have to rely on the witness of early church fathers such as Eusebius, who quotes an earlier authority, or Philo of Byblos, who in turn goes back to a much earlier authority named Sanchuniathon. No longer must we doubt the veracity of this extrabiblical witness or doubt the authenticity of the Old Testament witness. Now, as a result of archaeology, an independent witness to the effete and

degenerate nature of Canaanite cults is available. No longer can critics isolate the Old Testament and accuse it of a low morality in ordering the extermination of the Canaanites. The truth is, archeology points out that the people had become so immoral, so honeycombed with the sins of violence and sexual immorality, that had Joshua and the children of Israel not appeared to take over the land, these people would have perished under the weight of their own iniquity.

"Like priest, like people" is an old adage. Never in all the annals of history was there such a mixture of violence and lust as was combined and made an intricate part of Canaanite cults. So the Scriptures stand as a warning, corroborated by archaeology, of the judgment of God falling upon apostate and sinful religionism. Archaeology helps us to see this in an entirely different light in regard to the Canaanites.

This is especially true when we consider the low moral tone of Canaanite goddesses and gods. El was a brutal and lustful tyrant who was guilty of incest and murder. Baal also was guilty of enormous crimes. How could people worship such deities and not themselves be polluted? No wonder the warning of God was issued again and again for separation from Baalism. No wonder the history of Baal contamination of Israel is a long story of woe and suffering, as God's people were trapped into complicity with Phoenician cults.

The era of Ahab and Jezebel, and the importation of Canaanite fertility cults and intermarriage with the Canaanites, show the devastating effect of such disobedience to the plain warning of God. Exterminating the Canaanites in the time of Joshua was not a question of destroying innocent people. It was a question of destroying or being destroyed, separating or being contaminated, being quarantined from the plague or having the plague destroy everyone.

Later Excavations at Ugarit. During World War II excavations at Ras Shamra were discontinued. They were resumed in 1948 and have been going on regularly. Work under the direction of C. F. Schaffer has been centered upon uncovering the great palace. The most important discoveries in connection with this structure were the royal archives. These archives, discovered in the palace, were of a historical nature in contrast to the mythological ritual texts of the early years, 1929–1937. The archives in the west wing of the building contained administrative documents to a large degree relating to the royal estates. Those in the east wing had documents relating to the capital city. Those in the central archive were mainly legal finds. Almost all documents were inscribed in the common language of these centuries, namely Akkadian. A few were written in Hurrian and Ugaritic. The names of twelve Ugaritic kings were found in the documents which date from the 18th to the 13th centuries B.C. The seals of the royal acts are remarkable as they all are identical in design at the top, without regard to the name of the reigning king. The motif is well known from Babylonian glyptic art and shows homage being paid to the deified king.

Numbers of fine objects have been recovered from the palace, especially pieces from the king's bedroom. Especially noteworthy was the large ivory foot panel of the royal bedstead, perhaps the largest single piece of ivory carving yet recovered in the Near East. Another remarkable piece found in the campaign of 1952–1953 is the ancient Ugaritic alphabet of thirty letters. This piece is now housed in the National Museum at Damascus.

6. The Nuzi Tablets and the Biblical Horites

From this city east of ancient Asshur and a short distance west of Arrapkha, which flourished in the middle centuries of the 2nd millennium B.C., have come several thousand cuneiform texts. These texts have proved of immense value, illustrating the rise of the Hurrians and patriarchal customs. The present site of Nuzi is Yoghlan-Tepe. It is a mound 150 miles north of Baghdad near the foothills of southern Khurdistan. Nuzi was excavated in 1925–1931 by the American School of Oriental Research in Baghdad and Harvard University. The name "Nuzi" was used during its occupation by the Hurrians.

Before the time of the Hurrian settlement the site of Nuzi was occupied by a different ethnic group, called the Subarians. In this older period, the city bore the name of Gasur, and its earliest occupation goes back to prehistoric times. But the vital interest in the town stems from its occupation by the Hurrians and the cuneiform texts which have been excavated from it and from nearby Arrapkha, modern Kirkuk, some 9 miles to the east.

The Nuzi Tablets and the Hurrians. Modern archaeology has not only resurrected the ancient Hittites, who were for centuries practically unknown except for sporadic references on the pages of the Bible, but also the enigmatic Horites. In the books of the Pentateuch there are numbers of references to a perplexing people called Horites. These people were defeated by Chedorlaomer and the invading Mesopotamian army (Gen. 14:6). They were governed by chiefs (Gen. 36:20–30). They are said to have been destroyed by Esau's descendants (Deut. 2:12, 22).

This unknown people used to be thought of as a very local, restricted group of cave dwellers. The name "Horite" was thought to be derived from the Hebrew *hor,* "hole" or "cave." Other than this etymological description the Horites remained completely obscure, not appearing outside the Pentateuch or in extrabiblical literature. Within the last 35 years, however, archaeology has performed a miracle in resurrecting the ancient Hur-

rians, the biblical Horites. They are known not to be a local, restricted group but to be a prominent people who took a preeminent place on the stage of ancient history. It is now known that they not only existed but played a far-reaching role in ancient Near Eastern cultural history. As a result of the discovery of the Hurrians, the popular etymology which connects them with "cave dwellers" has had to be abandoned.

The Hurrians or Horites were non-Semitic peoples who, before the beginning of the 2nd millennium B.C., migrated into northeastern Mesopotamia. Their homeland was in the region south of the Caucasus. They appear first upon the horizon of history c. 2400 B.C. in the Zagros Mountains east of the Tigris River. In the period c. 2000–1400 B.C., the Hurrians were very common and widespread in Upper Mesopotamia.

The Nuzi Tablets and the Patriarchs. The main interest of the Nuzi Tablets lies in the illumination of patriarchal times and customs. In the patriarchal narratives, many local practices have been quite obscure to the modern reader. Numerous clay tablets from Nuzi and nearby Arrapkha have in many cases illuminated these customs, so that now we see them as they existed in the general historical background of the time. Although the Nuzi Tablets are to be dated in the 15th and 14th centuries B.C., sometime after the patriarchal period (c. 2000–1800 B.C.), nevertheless, they illustrate the times of the patriarchs. The reason is that when the patriarchs came out of Ur, they sojourned in Haran and mingled in west Hurrian society. But the same customs prevailed by extension among the west Hurrians as among the east Hurrians at Nuzi and Arrapkha. Hence, the results obtained at Nuzi are valid by extension for the west Hurrians, as well as for a period considerably later than the patriarchs.

In Genesis 15:2 Abraham laments his childless condition and the fact that his servant Eliezer was to be his heir. In the light of this situation, God assures the patriarch that he is to have a son of his own to inherit his property. The Nuzi Tablets explain this difficult matter. They tell how a trusted servant, an apparent outsider, could be heir. At ancient Nuzi, it was customary in Hurrian society for a couple who did not have a child to adopt a son to take care of his foster parents as long as they lived, take over when they died, and then in return for his filial duty to become their heir. But it is important to note that if a natural son was born, this agreement was nullified, at least in part, and the natural son became heir. Eliezer was plainly Abraham's adopted son. But the miraculous birth of Isaac, as the promised posterity, altered Eliezer's status as heir.

At Nuzi a marriage contract occasionally included the statement that a given slave girl is presented outright to a new bride, exactly as in the marriage of Leah (Gen. 29:24) and Rachel (29:29).

Other marriage provisions specify that a wife of the upper classes who was childless was to furnish her husband with a slave girl as a concubine. In such a case, however, the wife was entitled to treat the concubine's offspring as her own. This last provision illuminates the difficult statement in Genesis 16:2 with its punning: "I may obtain children by her," which means "I may be built up through her." It is interesting to note that the related law of Hammurabi, paragraph 144, offers no complete parallel. There the wife is a priestess and is not entitled to claim the children of the concubine for herself.

It is thus seen that in Nuzian law and society in which the patriarchs moved for a time, marriage was regarded primarily for bearing children and not mainly for companionship. In one way or another, it was considered necessary for the family to procreate. After Isaac's birth, Abraham's reluctance to comply with Sarah's demand that Hagar's child be driven out is illustrated by local practice at Nuzi. In the event the slave wife should have a son, that son must not be expelled. In Abraham's case, only a divine dispensation overruled human law and made the patriarch willing to comply.

Cases involving rights of the firstborn occurring in Genesis are also illustrated. In the Bible Esau sells his birthright to Jacob. In the Nuzi Tablets one brother sells a grove which he has inherited for three sheep. Evidently this in value is quite comparable to the savory food for which Esau sold his right.

In Hurrian society birthright was not so much the matter of being the firstborn as of paternal decree. Such decrees were binding above all others when handed down in the form of a deathbed declaration introduced by the following formula: "Behold now, I am old." This situation helps to illuminate Genesis 27, the chapter that tells of Jacob stealing the family blessing.

The obscure *teraphim* are also explained in Nuzian law. We now know that the teraphim were small household deities. Possession of them implied headship of family. In the case of a married daughter, they assured her husband the right to her father's property. Laban had sons of his own when Jacob left for Canaan. They alone had the right to their father's gods. The theft of these important household idols by Rachel was a notorious offense (Gen. 31:19, 30; 35). She aimed at nothing less than to preserve for her husband the cʰ title to Laban's estate.

The texts from Arrapkha and Nuzi haˌ supplied details for explaining theseˌ customs. In special circumstances tʰ could pass to a daughter's husband, ʰ father had handed over his househ son-in-law as a formal token that ꞌ had proper sanction.

Another custom illuminatˌ Genesis 12:10–20; 20:2–6; ₂

wife of a patriarch is introduced as his sister with no apparent worthy reason. The texts from Nuzi, however, show that among the Hurrians marriage bonds were most solemn, and the wife had legally, although not necessarily through ties of blood, the simultaneous status of sister, so that the term "sister" and "wife" could be interchangeable in an official use under certain circumstances. Thus, in resorting to the wife-sister relationship, both Abraham and Isaac were availing themselves of the strongest safeguards the law, as it existed then, could afford them.

Critical Value. Discoveries such as those at Nuzi and Arrapkha are forcing higher critics to abandon many radical and untenable theories. For example, not long ago it was customary for critics to view the patriarchal stories as retrojections from a much later period and not as authentic stories from the Mosaic age, namely, the 15th century B.C. But now the question rises, How could such authentic local color be retrojected from a later age? The Nuzi Letters have done a great service to students of early Bible history in not only attesting the influence of social customs in the patriarchal age and in the same portion of Mesopotamia from which the patriarchs come, but also have demonstrated these narratives are authentic to their time. Such discoveries add greatly to our historical background and enable us in our modern day to reveal them in their genuine local color and historical setting.

7. The Mari Letters—Light on the World of the Patriarchs

One of the most historically and archaeologically rewarding sites that has been discovered in Mesopotamia and Bible lands is the city of *Mari,* modern Tell el-Hariri on the Middle Euphrates, about 7 miles northwest of Abu-Kemal, a small town on the Syrian side of the Syro-Iraq frontier. The ancient city owed its importance to being a focal point on caravan routes crossing the Syrian desert and linking the city with Syria and the Mediterranean coast and with the civilizations of Assyria and Babylonia. This site was further identified by William Foxwell Albright in 1932.

Mari began to be excavated in 1933 by Andre Parrot under the auspices of the Musee du Louvre. The results were the digging up of an ancient imperial city of great importance and splendor. World War II interrupted excavations in 1939, after six highly successful campaigns had taken place. In 1951 this work was resumed. After four further campaigns it was broken off in 1956, as a result of the trouble over the Suez Canal.

Among the most important discoveries at Mari was the great *temple of Ishtar,* for the Babylonian

The excavated ruins of the capital city of Babylon.   *D. J. Wiseman*

goddess of propagation, and a temple tower or ziggurat. The temple itself had courts of the Sumerian type, columns, and a cella. The ziggurat or temple tower was similar to that at Ur and other Mesopotamian sites. Statuettes were uncovered to illustrate the popularity of the Ishtar fertility cult. One of the palace murals depicts the fact that the ruling monarch at Mari was believed to have received his staff and ring, the emblems of his authority, from Ishtar.

Another important discovery at Mari was the *royal palace.* A sprawling structure contemporary with the 1st dynasty of Babylon, it was built in the center of the mound and contained almost 300 rooms. The throne room furnished some rare specimens of well-preserved wall paintings. This huge building with its beautifully colored mural paintings, its royal apartments, administrative offices, and scribal school is considered one of the best preserved palaces of the Middle East. The structure was built by later Amorites, who worshiped the deities Adad and Dagon. In the postwar campaign the excavation centered mainly around the older strata going back to buildings of the pre-Sargonic period from the time of the dynasty of Akkad.

The Royal Archives. The most interesting finds, however, were the so-called *Mari Letters,* some 20,000 clay tablets dug up and which have revolutionized knowledge of the ancient biblical world. These documents were written in the dialect of Old Babylonian. They date from the era of Hammurabi, c. 1700 B.C., the same monarch whose code was discovered in 1901 at Susa. These records constitute memoranda of the king and governors of the city-state of Mari, and belong to the time of the kings Yasmah-Adad, under whose reign the construction of the palace was begun, and Zimri-Lim, under whom it was completed. Some of the correspondence is that of King Yasmah-Adad with his father, the powerful empire builder King Shamshi-Adad I of Assyria, as well as with the representatives of the provinces of his realm. King Zimri-Lim's correspondence also figures in exchanges of diplomatic correspondence with King Hammurabi of Babylon, as well as with the king of Aleppo and other vassals. Two letters dispatched from Aleppo to Zimri-Lim deal with prophetic utterances delivered in the name of the god Adad of Aleppo. The subject and tenor of these remind one of biblical prophecies.

Biblical Value of the Mari Texts. These records are of great value to biblical students because they stem from the region which was the home of the Hebrew patriarchs for a number of years before going on to Canaan. However, Abraham's migration from Ur, according to preserved biblical chronology, apparently took place some 400 years before the era of Zimri-Lim and the fall of Mari. At this time of the 3rd dynasty of Ur, Mari was ruled by the governors of the kings of Ur. Even-

tually, however, a prince of Mari, Ishbi-Irra, who had brought the city-state of Isin under his dominion c. 2021 B.C., was instrumental in bringing about the downfall of the city of Ur.

Nahor, which figures prominently in the patriarchal narratives (Gen. 24:10), is mentioned quite often in the Mari Letters. One letter from Nahor is sent from a woman of that town to the king and runs as follows:

To my lord say, Thus Inib-Sharrim, thy maid servant. How long must I remain in Nahor? Peace is established and the road is unobstructed. Let my lord write and let me be brought that I may see the face of my lord from whom I am separated. Further, let my lord send me an answer to my tablet.

The term "Habiru," very important since Abraham is the first individual in the Bible to be named a "Hebrew" (Gen. 14:13), is found frequently in the Mari Letters, as is also the case in the Nuzi Letters. In both instances the term apparently means "a wanderer," "one who crosses over," or "one who passes from one place to another." This explanation fits Abraham and the early patriarchs very well since they were nomadic travelers.

When Abraham left Ur in southern Mesopotamia to migrate to Canaan, he no doubt passed through the magnificent city of Mari. There can be little doubt that he and Terah with their families put up in one of the caravansaries there. Perhaps they spent days or weeks in the famous city and went sightseeing in the palace traces of whose grandeur are still visible to the eye of the modern archaeologist.

The city of Mari was idolatrous and in it there was the widespread practice of divination. A diviner was an important official in all phases of daily life at Mari. People went to him for advice in ordinary difficulties of life. Commanders saw him for help in the movement of their troops.

The patriarchs were remarkably free from occult practices and contamination from paganism and divinatory phenomena in general. This fact is true despite the teraphim (household gods) of Rachel and despite the "strange gods" which Jacob ordered put away and which he hid under a terebinth tree in Shechem (Gen. 35:2–4).

Interestingly, the Mari Letters refer to "sons of the right," that is, "sons of the south," since the directions were taken as one faced the east, and the south would be on one's right hand. These were a fierce tribe of wanderers and called Benjaminites, but they have no connection with the "Benjamites" of the Bible. The name "Benjamin," "son of the south," that is, "southerner," was a term suited to occur in various places, especially in Mari, where the parallel term "sons of the left," that is, "sons of the north," is found.

The Bible presents Benjamin as being of Pales-

tinian birth after Jacob's return from Mesopotamia. He is set forth as never having been in Mesopotamia at all. Genesis 49:27 describes Benjamin as a ravenous wolf. This fits the description of the veteran tribe at Mari remarkably well. Any connection, however, is obviously dubious and purely imaginary.

Another interesting sidelight is the fact that the word translated "chieftain," with reference to the plundering Benjaminites, is *dawidum*, meaning "leader." This sheds light on the etymology of the name of Israel's most renowned king, who evidently had a name meaning "the leader."

Historical Value of the Mari Letters. These documents establish that Shamshi-Adad I of Assyria, who ruled c. 1748–1716 B.C., and Hammurabi the Great of Babylon, were contemporaries. With these facts and other details furnished by the Mari documents, the date of Hammurabi can be fixed c. 1728–1676 B.C. This and other evidence have forced scholars to give up identifying Hammurabi of Babylon with Amraphel (Gen. 14:1). The high antiquity of Genesis 14 has been vindicated, but archaeology has not yet succeeded in furnishing the background of the four Mesopotamian kings who invaded the Trans-Jordanic country in the days of Abraham.

Hammurabi was a strong military leader and a great administrator. He was a member of the strong 1st dynasty of Babylon which reigned from 1830 to c. 1550 B.C. The power of this dynasty reached its height under Hammurabi's rule. He was the greatest of all Babylonian rulers. Hammurabi defeated Rim-Sin of Larsa and established himself over all the city-states of Lower Babylonia. His expanding military machine enabled him to destroy Mari. It was his code of laws, as we have seen, that was discovered at Susa in 1901. This famous codification has remained classic in illustrating and illuminating Israelite laws.

It was during the reign of Hammurabi that the Babylonian story of creation was composed. The poem glorified Marduk, the patron god of Babylon, whom Hammurabi established as the national god of Babylonia. In this period, the early Sumerian language became an antiquity and Semitic-Babylonian came into common usage.

The Mari Letters and the Amorites. About 2000 B.C. the Semitic-nomadic peoples, who lived along the desert fringes of the Fertile Crescent, invaded the centers of established civilization. Known as "Westerners," they are preserved in the Old Testament as "Amorites." Amorite states came into existence all over the Mesopotamian area. Nahor, Haran, Mari, Qatna, and Ugarit all appear as Amorite cities with Amorite kings. Babylon itself became the capital of an Amorite state under Hammurabi. This important historical fact is clearly reflected in the Mari Letters and in the peoples known as "Amorites" or "Westerners." In such a manner archaeology is

slowly but surely outlining the historical framework of the patriarchal age. Such discoveries as the Mari Letters prove of incalculable assistance to the historian of the ancient biblical world.

8. The Lachish Ostraca—Jeremiah's Age Lives Again

In the excavations of Lachish, a southwestern Palestinian city, the most astonishing finds were some letters embedded in a layer of burnt charcoal and ashes. They were eighteen in number and were in Hebrew writing done in the ancient Phoenician script. Three more of these letters were discovered in later campaigns in 1938.

Almost all of the letters were written by one named Hoshiah, who was stationed at some military outpost, to Jaosh, who was evidently a high ranking officer in the garrison at Lachish. It was the era of the Babylonian overrunning of Palestine several years before the fall of Jerusalem in 587 B.C. The Babylonians had attacked and partly burned Lachish some ten years before in the reign of Jehoiakim. These particular letters were in the layer of ashes which represent the final destruction of the city. Accordingly, they are to be dated from 588 B.C., when Nebuchadnezzar was making the final siege of Jerusalem and also of Lachish and Azekah.

Identification of Lachish. This large mound, one of the largest occupied in Palestine, is located 30 miles southwest of Jerusalem, 20 miles inland from the Mediterranean and 50 miles west of Hebron. It is mentioned in the Amarna Letters and in earlier Egyptian sources. Its strategic importance is attested by its being on the main route from central Palestine to Egypt. It overlooked the rich Shephelah (terrain which descended to the coastal lowland). The fortress city was an ideal barrier between the Philistine plains and the elevated Judaean country. It was one of the principal fortified cities of Judah and one of the bastions taken by the Israelites in their conquest of Palestine (Josh. 10:31–35). The site of Umm-Lakis was first thought to be Lachish. Then the location was sought at Tell el-Hesy by Sir Flinders Petrie, a pioneer archaeologist. William Foxwell Albright finally identified it correctly with the large mound of Tell el-Duweir.

Nebuchadnezzar captured Lachish in 588–586 B.C. (Jer. 34:7). Marks of a huge conflagration on the road leading up to the gate and on the adjacent wall display that the attackers relied largely upon fire, for which felled olive trees not yet harvested supplied the fuel.

Excavations at Lachish. The Wellcome-Marston Archaeological Expedition in 1933 commenced work there, under the direction of J. L. Starkey. In 1938 Starkey was killed by Arab brigands, and the work was carried on by Lankester Harding and Charles H. Inge.

The Results of the Excavation. Besides evi-

dences of earlier occupation, Lachish disclosed settlement by the Hyksos c. 1720–1550 B.C. These people overran Egypt during this period. A typical Hyksos defense ditch or *fosse*, with a ramp of clay and lime that apparently provided an enclosure for their horses, was brought to light. In the fosse three Canaanite Egyptian temples built between 1450 and 1225 B.C. were excavated. A Persian temple of a much later period was also found. Cemeteries at Lachish yielded a great quantity of pottery, jewelry, scarabs, and skeletal evidence.

A well, 200 feet deep, was located within the city, the remains of a tremendous engineering excavation for water storage, which was not completed. A shaft about 85 feet terminates in a rectangle 80 x 70 feet cut to a depth of 80 feet. The aim was a water system which would have been much larger than that provided by Hezekiah for Jerusalem in the Siloam Tunnel and comparable to similar systems at Gezer and Megiddo.

A good quantity of inscribed material has been removed from the Lachish excavations. A bronze dagger from c. 1700 B.C. contains four pictographic signs, samples of the early script. A bowl and a ewer contain specimens of the same early writing as that found at Serabit el-Khadem. The name "Gedaliah" was found on a jar handle and may be the official whom Nebuchadnezzar set over the land after the fall of Jerusalem (cf. Jer. 40—42).

Contents of the Lachish Letters. But of all the epigraphic discoveries at Lachish, the most important are the Lachish Letters. These letters may be briefly described as follows: Letter 1 lists names, the majority of which are found in the Old Testament. Letters 2 and 5 consist largely of greetings. Letter 3, the longest, contains the most information. This concerns movements of Jewish troops and also makes an interesting note to an unnamed prophet and his word of warning. Letter 4 states that Hoshiah, though observing the signals of Lachish, cannot see those of Azekah. Azekah may well have fallen earlier, for this letter states, "We are watching for the signal station at Lachish according to all the signals you are giving, because we cannot see the signals of Azekah." Letter 6 contains the biblical expression, "to weaken the hands of the people." This recalls Jeremiah, who uses a similar expression (Jer. 38:4).

Historical Importance of the Letters. The Lachish Letters give us an independent view of conditions in Judah in the last days before the fall of Jerusalem. As the Neo-Babylonian army advanced, the doom of Jerusalem was sealed, in contrast to its deliverance under the Assyrian, Sennacherib, as Isaiah had predicted (2 Kin. 19:20, 32–36). Relentlessly, Nebuchadnezzar advanced on the city after a terrible eighteen-month siege, 587 B.C. The walls of the city were broken

A clay tablet showing the colophon at the end of a typical Assyrian library tablet. Found at Ninevah.   *British Museum*

down, the houses and the temple burned, and the people carried away to exile (2 Kin. 25:1–12).

Jeremiah conducted his difficult ministry in these agonizing times. His reference to Azekah and Lachish is most interesting. "When the king of Babylon's army fought against Jerusalem, and against all the cities of Judah that were left, against Lachish, and against Azekah: for these defenced cities remained of the cities of Judah" (Jer. 34:7).

Tell Zakariya in the Shephelah region has been identified as Azekah. In 1898 it was excavated by Frederick K. Bliss of the Palestine Exploration Fund. It had a strong inner fortress buttressed with eight large towers.

The Lachish Letters concern the time just prior to the fall of the city and present the same conditions of turmoil and confusion that are revealed in the Book of Jeremiah. Numerous place names that occur in the Bible are found in the letters, as well as personal names. Hoshaiah appears in Jeremiah 42:1 and Nehemiah 12:32. God is referred to by the four-letter word YHWH, which are the consonants of the name "Jehovah" or "Yahweh." It is also interesting to note that many of the men's names have Yahweh endings. A prophet like Jeremiah is referred to in the letters. But this is most probably not Jeremiah himself.

So complete was the destruction by the Babylonians that it took many centuries for Judah to recover. The returned remnant was tiny and weak. The small Jewish state stamped its coins with the name "Yehud," that is, Judah, but not until after 300 B.C. do substantial archaeological remains appear, and then they are not abundant. Certainly the Babylonians did a thorough job of destroying Jewish power for many centuries.

The Paleographic Importance of the Letters. Being inscribed in biblical Hebrew, in which the Old Testament Scriptures were written, and with stylistic and vocabulary similarities to the Book of Jeremiah, these letters are of great paleographic importance. They help the scholar to trace the evolution of the Hebrew alphabet, noting the for-

mation of the letters and their style. They also enable him to see how the Old Testament Scriptures, which were then written, appeared.

Surely research of this type, that makes it possible for the scholar to look back, to resurrect the past, and to see how the language of the Old Testament developed, is fascinating. Great strides are being made in this field of enquiry. It is the one truly bright spot in original biblical studies. This type of study is of immense value in expanding historical backgrounds and illuminating Holy Scripture on the human plane.

9. The Dead Sea Scrolls

The middle of the 20th century saw the greatest manuscript discovery of modern times. In 1947 a young Bedouin shepherd stumbled upon a cave south of Jericho, containing many leather scrolls of Hebrew and Aramaic writing and about 600 fragmentary inscriptions. Great excitement prevailed in the archaeological world. In 1952 new caves containing fragments of later scrolls in Hebrew, Greek, and Aramaic were found. These and other startling manuscript discoveries have been followed by news of additional manuscripts found in other caves in the Dead Sea area.

A. The Date of the Scrolls. After intensive study of the manscripts from the Dead Sea area, scholars define three periods: 1. The Archaic Period c. 200–150 B.C. 2. The Hasmonaean Period c. 150–30 B.C. 3. The Herodian Period c. 30 B.C. to A.D. 70. The great majority originated in the 2nd and 3rd periods, especially the last half of the 2nd period and last half of the 3rd period.

Although attacks have been made against the antiquity and authenticity of these manuscripts, two lines of evidence substantiate their antiquity. **The evidence of radiocarbon count.** This scientific method of dating places the linen in which the scrolls were wrapped in the general era of c. 175 B.C. to A.D. 225. **Paleographic evidence.** Scholars conversant in this science date these documents by the form of the letters and the way they are written in comparison with other eras of writing. They are able to demonstrate that they come in the intermediate period between the script of the 3rd century B.C. and of the middle of the 1st century A.D. W. F. Albright observes, "All competent students of writing conversant with the available material and with paleographic method date the scrolls in the 250 years before A.D. 70."

B. The Contents of the Scrolls. The Dead Sea cave manuscripts contain material partly biblical and partly intertestamental. The biblical includes two scrolls of Isaiah, one complete, and most of the first two chapters of Habakkuk, and fragments of all Old Testament books except Esther. Large numbers of fragmentary manuscripts have been recovered from the Pentateuchal books and Isaiah. Fragments of Psalms, Jeremiah, and Daniel are numerous.

The scroll of *Isaiah,* in the initial finds from the site of Qumran, has remained the best known of

The area near the Dead Sea where the Qumran scrolls were found.   *Matson Photo Service*

the discoveries. It was the first major biblical manuscript of great antiquity to be recovered. It is earlier by a millennium than the oldest Hebrew text preserved in the Masoretic Hebrew Bible. This Masoretic Hebrew Bible is the basis of all recent translations and does not go back any earlier than A.D. 900.

This fact of the antiquity of the Hebrew text of Isaiah, dating as early as 150–125 B.C., constitutes these discoveries as the greatest of modern times. They are the oldest existing manuscripts of the Bible in any language.

In the original group of manuscripts of 1947 were a commentary on Habakkuk and so-called *Manual of Discipline* of pre-Christian Jewish sect of Essenes. Of unusual interest were manuscripts later purchased by the Hebrew University of Jerusalem, containing a later Isaiah scroll more conformed to the traditional Hebrew, and a document of great interest called *"The War Between the Children of Light and Darkness."* This composition evidently issued from the Maccabaean struggles against Greek paganism in 158–137 B.C.

In winter, 1949, the first manuscript-bearing cave was excavated by two well-known Palestinian archaeologists, Pierre de Vaux and Lankester Harding. Recovered were fragments of Genesis, Deuteronomy, and Judges with a fragment of Leviticus in Old Hebrew script. Nonbiblical finds included a fragment of the *Book of Jubilees*, a work related to the Enoch literature, and some unknown material.

C. Other Manuscript-Yielding Sites. In 1952 a cave was uncovered at Murabbaat in another part of the desert. This yielded manuscripts chiefly from the 2nd century A.D. in Hebrew, Greek, and Aramaic, including a few texts of Genesis, Exodus, Deuteronomy, and Isaiah. Several Hebrew letters were discovered from the period of Simon ben Keseba, that is, Bar Cocheba, who led the revolt in 132–135. A notable exception to the 2nd century A.D. date of this material is an archaic Hebrew papyrus piece, a palimpsest, a list of names and numbers, dated in the 6th century B.C.

In the same general area, other caves have been found, one group in Khirbet Mird, northeast of the monastery of Mar Saba. These contain Arabic papyri, Greek and Christo-Palestinian-Syrian documents, with fragments of biblical codices, all late Byzantine and early Arabic. Another group of manuscripts date from the period of the bulk of the Murabbaat material. Among them is a version of the minor prophets in Greek and a corpus of Nabataean papyri, both of great biblical and historical importance.

D. Excavations at Khirbet Qumran. Khirbet Qumran was excavated between 1951 and 1954. This Essene community, with the nearby caves, proved to be the richest manuscript-yielding center. Members of this Essenic community copied these manuscripts and preserved them by hiding them in the caves. The Essenes at Khirbet Qumran, 7 miles south of Jericho near the shores of the Dead Sea, were next to the Pharisees and Sadducees in importance in sectarian Judaism. This site has become one of the most publicized places in Palestine because of the phenomenal manuscript finds in the cave-dotted cliffs.

Excavations at Khirbet Qumran have fully authenticated this site as the center of Essenic Judaism. As the result of the recovery of coins, pottery, and architectural remains, the story of Qumran's occupation can now be told. Four periods in the later history of the site are traced.

Period 1 extends from its founding c. 110 B.C. under John Hyrcanus. Numerous coins of this ruler were dug up, as well as of other Hasmonaean rulers including Antigonus, 40–37 B.C., the last ruler of this line, to the seventh year of Herod, 31 B.C. At this time an earthquake apparently leveled the site. Indications are that during Herod's reign the place was abandoned because of his antagonism.

Period 2 at Qumran dates from rebuilding and enlargement c. A.D. 1 and Roman destruction in June A.D. 68. During this era in the lifetime of Jesus, John the Baptist, and the early Christian apostles, Qumran flourished, influencing Judaism and the early Christian church. Coins have been found dating from the reign of Archelaus, 4 B.C. to A.D. 6, and from the time of the Roman procurators down to the second year of the first Jewish revolt in A.D. 66–70.

The Roman army, which took Jericho in June, A.D. 68, evidently likewise captured Qumran. One coin, marked with an X, belonged to the Tenth Legion. Iron arrowheads were found in a layer of burned ash in the excavation.

Qumran fell to Roman occupation. Some coins describe *Judaea Capta*. These date in the reign of Titus, A.D. 79–81, and mark **Period 3** as the Roman occupation after Jerusalem's destruction in A.D. 70. Evidence that Qumran structures were converted into army barracks indicates that a Roman garrison was stationed there from A.D. 68–c. A.D. 100. At this time the site apparently was abandoned.

Period 4. Qumran is distinguished by reoccupation of the site during the 2nd Jewish revolt, A.D. 132–135. Coins dating from this era indicate that here the Jews made their last stand to drive the Romans from their country. After that Qumran sank into obscurity.

Architectural Remains at Qumran. The main edifice at Qumran is 100 feet by 120 and formed the communal center and hub of the complex. At the northwest corner was a massive defense tower with thick walls enforced by stone embankments. Some coins from the time of the 2nd Jewish revolt

(A.D. 132–135) attest its use as a fortress against Roman power.

Alongside the general meeting room is the largest hall of the main building. Here was located the scriptorium. Several inkwells of the Roman period, and even some dried ink, indicate that the manuscripts had been copied by the community's scribes.

Also in the complex were two cisterns (artificial reservoirs) carefully plastered. There were installations for ablutions and baptisms. Of the possibly 40 cisterns and reservoirs, the bulk of them must have been used for storage of water in the very hot, dry climate.

Of great interest is the cemetery, containing about 1,000 burial places. De Vaux excavated many of these tombs. They are noted for their lack of jewelry and any evidences of luxury.

E. Khirbet Qumran and the Essenes. Not only do the excavations at Khirbet Qumran demonstrate that it was the headquarters of Essenic Judaism but three authorities who were contemporary witnesses attest the same fact, namely, Josephus, Philo, and Pliny. Pliny, for example, locates the Essenes at precisely the spot where Qumran is situated, namely, "on the west side of the Dead Sea." He also designates the town of En-gedi as situated "below the Essenes."

Josephus relates their unselfish character, industry, and communal life. He extols their love for common toil, says they dressed in white, and describes their three-year probationary period before admission to the sect, and other phases of discipline. He also mentions their various lustrations and says that they numbered about 4,000. He comments on their celibacy, piety, convictions concerning immortality, and their belief in rewards for righteousness.

Philo gives a similar description of this group in Judaism. The library at Qumran attests their delight in the Bible and literature. This is reflected in information given by Philo and Josephus. The Essenes carefully copied Holy Scripture and took pains to preserve it.

There are difficulties in equating the Essenes at Qumran with the sect described by Philo, Pliny, and Josephus. Nevertheless, the likenesses far outweigh the differences. The evidence would seem to equate Qumran with the Essenes of the 1st century A.D.

F. The Essenes at Qumran and John the Baptist. Concerning John, Luke wrote: "And the child grew, and waxed strong in spirit, and was in the deserts till the day of his shewing unto Israel" (Luke 1:80). The home of John the Baptist's parents was in the hill country of Judea (Luke 1:39, 40, 65). Although nothing is known definitely, it is easy to believe that John the Baptist did in some way come in contact with the Essenes. There are many characteristics in his own life that parallel theirs.

Both John and the Qumranites feature Isaiah 40:3 with regard to preparing "the way of the LORD." But John must have early realized that there were some features of the Essenes that were not conducive to preparing the nation for the advent of the Messiah, and so if he ever had a connection with them, he must have broken with them, giving himself to an active ministry of preaching repentance and baptizing in the Jordan Valley.

John's message featured repentance (Matt. 3:2; Mark 1:4; Luke 3:3). Repentance was also a vital note in Qumran theology. They belonged to a "covenant of repentance" and they called themselves "the penitents of Israel." The baptism of repentance, which John administered, was also paralleled by the Essenes who practiced water baptism. John's baptism was an outer indication of inward spirital renovation, enabling the recipients to recognize the Messiah when He came.

Baptism among the Qumranites, however, was purely ritual, and the recipients were enjoined to separate themselves rigidly from any who did not belong to their community. The severe indictment of the Jewish nation, which was characteristic of John, was also characteristic of the Essenes. They looked upon those not belonging to their sect as "sons of darkness" connected with Belial. They regarded themselves as true Israel, living in accordance with the law. For them alone the baptismal rite could have meaning.

John featured the baptism "with the Holy Ghost, and *with* fire" (Matt. 3:11), the baptism with fire being the judgment upon the unrepentant in an eschatological sense. Such judgment of fire is described in a Qumran hymn under the figure of a fiery river overflowing in wrath "on the outcasts" and in "the time of fury for all Belial."

The baptism of the Holy Ghost, on the other hand, is prophesied by John to be the portion of those who would repent and receive the coming Messiah (John 1:33). In Qumran literature not only does God "sprinkle upon him," the Messiah, the spirit of truth as purifying water to cleanse Him from all abominations of falsehood and from the spirit of impurity, but the Messiah sprinkles His people with His Holy Spirit, constituting them His anointed ones.

John the Baptist was intensely missionary and evangelistic in his message. The Qumranites were self-centered, strictly sectarian, and did not spread their convictions. They did adopt children to train in their ways.

John the Baptist was vouchsafed the honor of preparing the way for the Messiah and being His forerunner. The Qumran community did not recognize the Messiah when He came. Their asceticism led to a deadend. It never conducted

them to Him who would take away the sin of the world (John 1:29).

G. The Essenes and Jesus the Messiah. Although the Qumran community had a messianic hope, it was strikingly different from that of the Old Testament. They could not comprehend the combination of King and Priest in *one* Person (Zech. 6:9–15). Neither could they comprehend in the union of the same Person the additional office of a Prophet, although they did feature in their writings the messianic prophecy of "a Prophet" (Deut. 18:18, 19).

Their great priest was Messiah of Aaron. Their great military leader, Messiah of Israel; their prophet comprehended in the rule of the community is set down alongside the "messiahs of Aaron and Israel," apparently as a separate messianic figure.

There are other similarities between the orgaization and teachings of the Qumran group and the teachings of Jesus and the formation of the Christian church. The passage in Matthew 18:15–17 has a striking parallel in Qumran literature.

It is easily seen that with this new material the background of the gospel stories is much more richly illustrated. The Last Supper, the Sermon on the Mount, and numerous other aspects of the earthly life and ministry of Jesus are fitted into a larger framework of historical background material, and to that extent are understood on the human side. However, it is transparently clear that the ministries of John the Baptist and Jesus remain unique. Qumran literature in no sense casts any shadow upon the unique Person and work of Jesus Christ. Christianity stands as authentically growing out of the Old Testament and not connected with later Gnosticism in a post-apostolic era that would jeopardize its historical genuineness.

H. The Dead Sea Scrolls and Literary Criticism of the New Testament. The Dead Sea material has had a stabilizing effect upon New Testament criticism. In the light of the new material, the New Testament appears as a Jewish book with a Christian theology with less Greek influence in its formation than Jewish, and there is reason to date the *synoptic gospels*, beginning with *Mark*, between A.D. 60 and 65.

Especially interesting is the dating of the *Gospel of John*. A radical criticism customarily dated this Gospel about A.D. 150 or later. Thus it was removed from apostolic tradition and treated more as an apocryphal book. Now it is well known that the Fourth Gospel reflects the genuine Jewish background of John the Baptist and Jesus and not a later 2nd-century Gnostic milieu. This is clearly attested by the parallels to the conceptual imagery of John's Gospel in the Essenic literature from Qumran.

There is every evidence to believe in the au-

Jerusalem Temple inscription warning Gentiles against intrusion.   *Matson Photo Service*

thenticity of John's Gospel, and there is not the slightest reason critically to date the Gospel after A.D. 90. Indeed, it may be quite a bit earlier. Thus the Dead Sea discoveries and the excavations at Qumran not only give additional background material to the inter-biblical and New Testament period but also help to stabilize higher criticism and purge out radical views that are now shown to be untenable.

The *Book of Hebrews* also is interesting. This is certainly to be definitely dated before the destruction of Jerusalem in A.D. 70. The treatise apparently was planned to offset the Essenic idea of "two anointed ones," one a prince and the other a priest. It was designed to present the Christian and Old Testament doctrine (cf. Zech. 6:9, 15; Ps. 110:1) that Messiah would be *both King and Priest in one Person*. Also the *Book of the Revelation* was doubtless penned toward the end of the 1st century, and, in the light of the Dead Sea Scrolls, may now possibly be dated earlier, that is before A.D. 70. This conclusion is based on its Hebraic background, being illuminated by the evidence from the Dead Sea manuscripts.

10. Jerusalem

Probably no excavation ever carried out has been as important as that carried on by Israeli institutions at the western and southern walls of the temple mountain in Jerusalem. The actual steps and entrances of Herod's temple have been uncovered as have the tiny shops and narrow streets where the merchants must have hawked their wares. The giant stone blocks from the top of the wall, which were thrown down into the streets by Titus' troops in A.D. 70, were found where they fell. In a grave in another part of the city was found the remains of a Jew who had been crucified by the Romans, the first physical evidence of this form of execution ever found. So extensive were these finds that it will be a generation before they are all deciphered and integrated into the historical framework of the Roman Age.

11. Ebla

The modern Arabic name for this 140-acre mound in the Northwest corner of Syria is Tell Mardikh. Archaeologists of the University of Rome began digging this mound in 1964 and found an inscription in 1968 that identified this site as ancient Ebla. They uncovered portions of impressive *buildings from the time of the biblical Patriarchs* (1900–1700 B.C.); and beneath these were palaces and temples of the Early Bronze Age (2400–2250 B.C.). This was the discovery of an early but advanced civilization which was previously unknown.

In 1974, 1975, and 1976, three rooms of one palace yielded almost 7000 well-preserved *clay tablets* and about 13,000 fragments of other tablets *with cuneiform writing on them.* This archive of *ancient Sumerian and Canaanite literature* is very important. The tablets contain economic, political, and legal records of Ebla. (Understanding the cultures of Israel's neighbors aids biblical interpretation.) They show that Ebla was a merchant empire. Its rulers controlled trade routes that reached into the Mesopotamian Valley, into the mountains of modern-day Turkey, and to the edge of the Nile Valley.

But more importantly, some tablets are *dictionaries*—the earliest known—providing the meanings of words used in both the Sumerian and early Canaanite (Eblaite) languages. (Languages help archaeologists understand the cultures.) Many Canaanite words at Ugarit and *Hebrew words in the Old Testament* can be understood more accurately because they also occur on these early tablets.

Many *place names* occur in the Ebla records, including those familiar to readers of the Bible: Haran, Damascus, Hazor, Beth-shan, Shechem, Joppa, Eshkelon, Jerusalem, Dor—and some scholars believe also Sodom and Gomorrah. Since the Bible itself presents these as real places, the Ebla tablets help support its historical reliability.

About 10,000 names of people are found on the tablets. Among them are *biblical names* such as Adam, Eve, Noah, Jubal, Abram, Ishmael, Hagar, Keturah, Bilhah, Israel, Micah, Michael, Saul, David, Jehorum, and Jonah. Although these names do not refer to the biblical personages, they establish that the names in Scripture are authentic.

Sometimes, however, the tablets contain mythic and legendary stories which conflict with the Scriptures (e.g., different creation accounts). Such cases illumine the biblical authors' polemics against pagan worldviews.

The excavation project continues until the present and may be expected to cast more light on the Bible's meaning and reliability.

The thrilling story of biblical archaeology is not yet completed. Other great discoveries as a result of continuous research in Bible lands promise even greater contributions to biblical studies in future years. For example, the recovery of thirteen Coptic codices from Nag Hammadi in Upper Egypt, since 1945, have almost rivaled the Dead Sea Scrolls in actual biblical importance. These even include the apocryphal "Gospel of Thomas" and are of inestimable value, especially from a critical standpoint in dating New Testament literature.

What new and exciting discovery affecting the Bible may we not expect the archaeologist's spade to turn up next? The prospect should engender a love for the Scriptures and a desire to study them employing history, linguistics, and archaeology as the means under the Holy Spirit to a more accurate understanding of the Bible's message to mankind.

Acknowledgements: The publisher gratefully acknowledges the cooperation of these sources, whose photographs appear in this article:

British Museum (80-7-19, 277)
G. Eric Matson Collection, The Episcopal House
Professor D. J. Wiseman

The Temple area in Jerusalem, showing the slope of the hill. *Matson Photo Service*

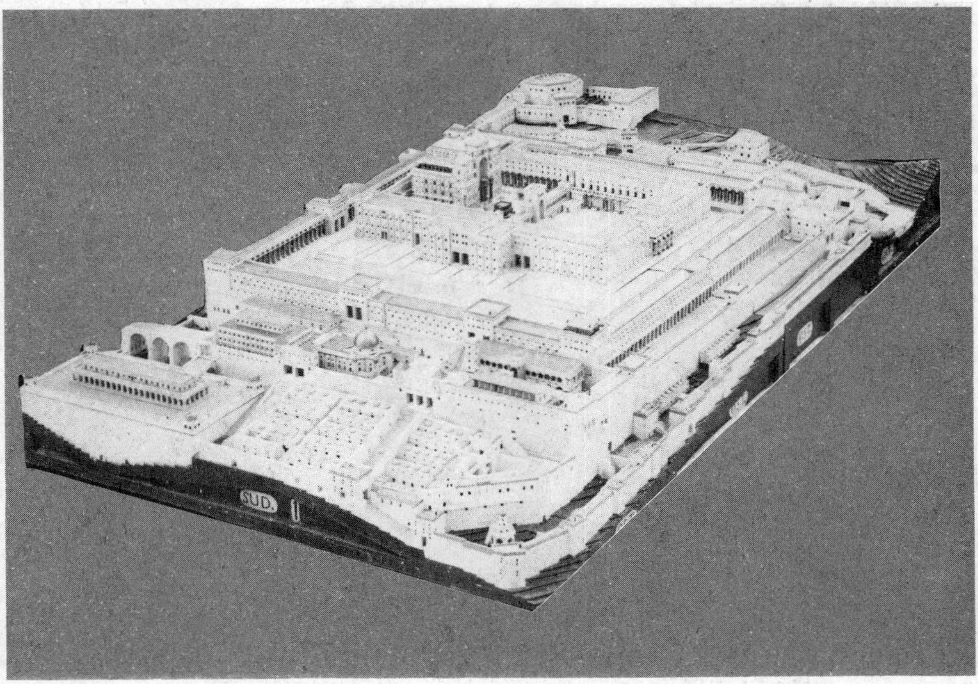

Model of the Temple of Solomon in Jerusalem. *Matson Photo Service*

Model of the Temple of Zerubbabel in Jerusalem.   *Matson Photo Service*

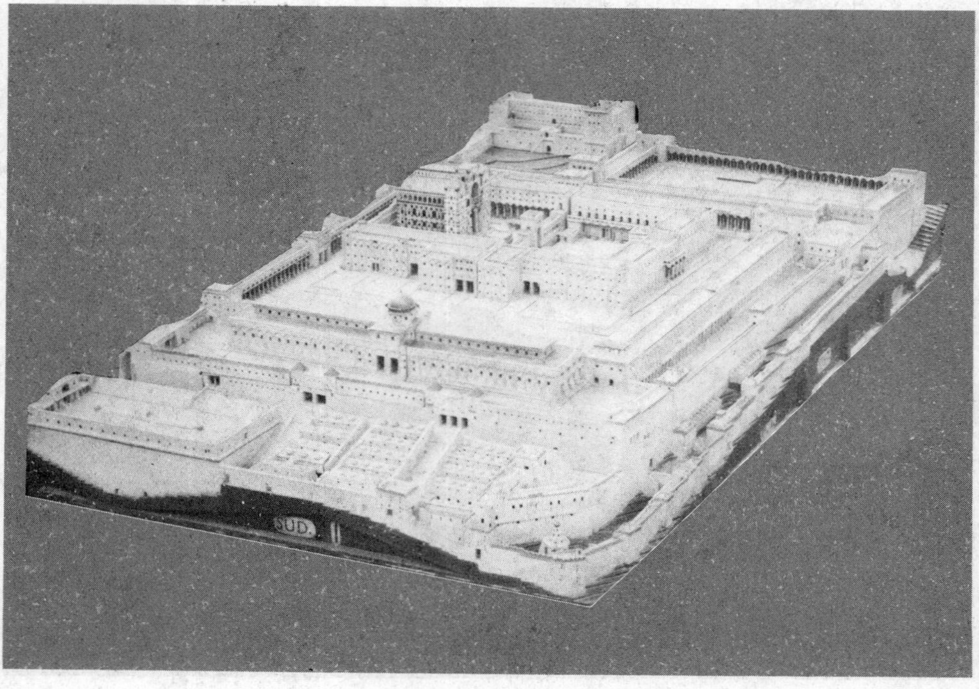

Model of the Temple of Herod in Jerusalem.   *Matson Photo Service*

Concordance

CONCORDANCE

King James Version

A

ABASE Ezek 21:26, a him that is high
Dan 4:37, he is able to a
Matt 23:12, himself shall be a
Phil 4:12, both how to be a
See Job 40:11; 2 Cor 11:7

ABIDE Ex 16:29, a ye every man
Num 31:19, a without the camp
1 Sam 5:7, shall not a with us
Ps 15:1, Lord, who shall a
91:1, shall a under the shadow
Prov 15:31, a among the wise
Eccl 1:4, the earth a for ever
Jer 42:10, a in this land
49:18, no man shall a there
Hos 3:3, thou shalt a for me
Joel 2:11, who can a it
Matt 10:11, there a till ye go
Mark 6:10, a till ye depart
Luke 9:4, there a
John 3:36, wrath of God a on him
5:38, not his word a in you
14:16, Comforter, that he may a
15:4, A in me, and I in you
15:5, He that a in me
15:10, a in my love
1 Cor 3:14, If any man's work a
13:13, now a faith, hope

ABILITY Ezra 2:69, They gave after their a
Dan 1:4, such as had a in them
Matt 25:15, his several a
1 Pet 4:11, a which God giveth
See Lev 27:8; Neh 5:8; Acts 11:29

ABLE Deut 16:17, give as he is a
Josh 23:9, hath been a to stand
1 Sam 6:20, a to stand before
1 Kin 3:9, who is a to judge
2 Chr 2:6, who is a to build
Prov 27:4, who is a to stand
Dan 3:17, a to deliver
Amos 7:10, land is not a to bear
Matt 3:9, God is a
9:28, Believe ye that I am a
20:22, Are ye a to drink
Luke 12:26, not a to do
Acts 6:10, not a to resist
Rom 4:21, had promised he was a
8:39, a to separate us
1 Cor 10:13, that ye are a
2 Cor 3:6, a ministers
Eph 3:18, a to comprehend
3:20, Now unto him that is a
Phil 3:21, a even to subdue
2 Tim 1:12, he is a to keep
Heb 2:18, a to succor them
7:25, a also to save
James 4:12, a to save
Jude 24, a to keep you
Rev 5:3, was a to open the book
6:17, who shall be a to stand
See Ex 18:21; Mark 4:33

ABOMINATION Gen 43:32, is an a unto the Egyptians
46:34, every shepherd is an a
Lev 18:26, commit any of these a
Deut 7:26, shalt thou bring an a
18:9, a of these nations
18:12, because of these a
25:16, unrighteously, are an a
Prov 3:32, the froward is a

8:7, wickedness is an a
11:20, froward is a to the Lord
15:8, an a to the Lord
15:9, way of the wicked an a
15:26, wicked are an a
21:27, of the wicked is a
28:9, his prayer shall be a
Is 44:19, residue thereof an a
Jer 4:1, put away thine a
6:15, they had committed a
Dan 11:31, place the a
Matt 24:15, the a of desolation
Mark 13:14, shall see the a
Luke 16:15, is a in the sight
Rev 21:27, worketh a, or maketh
See Lev 7:18; 11:41; Mal 2:11

ABOVE Deut 28:13, thou shalt be a only
Job 31:2, God is there from a
Prov 15:24, way of life is a
Matt 10:24, The disciple is not a
John 3:31, from a is a all
8:23, I am from a
Rom 14:5, one day a another
1 Cor 4:6, a that which
Gal 4:26, Jerusalem which is a
Phil 2:9, a name which is a
Col 3:1, things which are a
See Gen 48:22; James 1:17

ABSTAIN Acts 15:20, a from pollutions of idols
15:29, ye a from meats
1 Thess 5:22, A from all
1 Pet 2:11, a from fleshly lusts
See 1 Thess 4:3; 1 Tim 4:3

ABUNDANCE 1 Kin 18:41, sound of a of rain
Ps 52:7, a of his riches
72:7, a of peace
Jer 33:6, reveal unto them the a
Eccl 5:10, loveth a with increase
5:12, but the a of the rich
Matt 12:34, a of the heart
Luke 6:45, of the a of the heart
Matt 13:12, shall have more a
25:29, and he shall have a
Luke 12:15, in the a
2 Cor 8:2, the a of their joy
12:7, a of the revelations
See Job 36:31; Rom 5:17; Rev 18:3

ABUNDANT Job 36:28, distill upon man a
Ps 145:7, a utter the memory
Is 55:7, for he will a pardon
John 10:10, have it more a
1 Cor 15:10, I laboured more a
2 Cor 11:23, in labours more a
Eph 3:20, exceeding a above
1 Tim 1:14, was exceeding a
Titus 3:6, Which he shed on us a
2 Pet 1:11, ministered unto you a
See Ex 34:6; Is 55:7; 1 Pet 1:3

ABUSE 1 Cor 7:31, use this world, as not a it
9:18, that I a not my power
See 1 Sam 31:4; 1 Chr 10:4

ACCEPT Gen 4:7, shalt thou not be a
Ex 28:38, a before the Lord
Lev 10:19, been a in the sight
Deut 33:11, a the work
1 Sam 18:5, and he was a
2 Sam 24:23, Lord thy God a thee

Job 42:8, for him will I a
42:9, the Lord also a Job
Prov 18:5, to a the person
Jer 14:12, I will not a them
37:20, supplication . . . be a
Ezek 20:40, will I a them
43:27, I will a you
Amos 5:22, I will not a them
Mal 1:13, should I a this
Luke 4:24, No prophet is a
Acts 10:35, righteousness, is a
Rom 15:31, be a of the saints
2 Cor 5:9, we may be a
6:2, behold, now is the a time
See Ps 119:108; Eccl 12:10; Mal 1:8

ACCEPTABLE Ps 19:14, be a in thy sight, O Lord
Is 61:2, proclaim the a year
Luke 4:19, To preach the a year
Rom 12:1, holy, a unto God

ACCESS Rom 5:2, we have a by faith into this grace
Eph 2:18, a by one Spirit
3:12, a with confidence

ACCORD Acts 1:14, continued with one a in prayer
4:24, to God with one a
8:6, the people with one a
Phil 2:2, love, being of one a

ACCORDING Ex 12:25, a as he hath promised
Job 34:11, a to his ways
Jer 17:10, a to the fruit
25:14, recompense them a to
32:19, a to his ways
Matt 16:27, every man a
John 7:24, a to the appearance
Rom 2:6, a to his deeds
8:28, a to his purpose
12:6, a to the grace
2 Cor 8:12, a to that a man
2 Tim 4:14, Lord reward him a to
See Titus 3:5; 1 Pet 1:2

ACCOUNT Matt 12:36, they shall give a thereof
Luke 16:2, a of thy stewardship
20:35, a worthy to obtain
Rom 14:12, shall give a
Gal 3:6, a to him
Philem 18, put that on mine a
Heb 13:17, that must give a
See Job 33:13; 1 Pet 4:5

ACCUSATION Luke 19:8, thing from any man by false a
1 Tim 5:19, receive not an a
2 Pet 2:11, not railing a
Jude 9, a railing a
See Matt 27:37; Mark 15:26

ACCUSE Prov 30:10, A not a servant unto his master
John 5:45, I will a you
See Matt 12:10; Mark 3:2

ACKNOWLEDGE Ps 32:5, I a my sin unto thee
51:3, I a my transgressions
Prov 3:6, all thy ways a him
Is 63:16, Israel a us not
1 John 2:23, he that a the Son
See Hos 5:15; 1 Cor 14:37

ACQUIT Job 10:14, thou wilt not a
Nah 1:3, all a the wicked

ACTIONS 1 Sam 2:3, by him a are weighed

ADD Prov 10:22, he **a** no sorrow with it

Acts 2:41, there were **a**

2:47, And the Lord **a**

5:14, the more **a** to the

11:24, **a** unto the Lord

Gal 3:19, was **a** because of

ADDICTED 1 Cor 16:15, they have **a** themselves

ADMINISTER 1 Cor 12:5, are differences of **a**

2 Cor 8:19, which is **a** by us

8:20, abundance which is **a**

9:12, **a** of this service

ADMONISH Acts 27:9, Paul **a** them

Rom 15:14, able also to **a**

Col 3:16, **a** one another

1 Thess 5:12, Lord, and **a** you

2 Thess 3:15, **a** him as

Heb 8:5, Moses was **a** of God

See Eccl 4:13; 12:12; Jer 42:19

ADMONITION 1 Cor 10:11, they are written for our **a**

Eph 6:4, **a** of the Lord

Titus 3:10, second **a** reject

ADOPTION Rom 8:15, ye have received the Spirit of **a**

8:23, waiting for the **a**

9:4, whom pertaineth the **a**

Gal 4:5, receive the **a** of sons

Eph 1:5, the **a** of children

ADORN Is 61:10, bride **a** herself

1 Tim 2:9, women **a** themselves

Titus 2:10, **a** the doctrine

1 Pet 3:3, that outward **a**

3:5, **a** themselves

Rev 21:2, **a** for her husband

See Jer 31:4; Luke 21:5

ADVERSARY Ex 23:22, and an **a** unto thine **a**

Num 22:22, for an **a** against

Deut 32:43, vengeance to his **a**

1 Kin 11:14, stirred up an **a**

Job 31:35, that mine **a**

Ps 38:20, are mine **a**

69:19, **a** are all before thee

74:10, how long shall the **a**

89:42, right hand of his **a**

109:4, they are my **a**

109:20, the reward of mine **a**

109:29, mine **a** be clothed

Is 1:24, ease me of mine **a**

50:8, who is mine **a**

59:18, fury to his **a**

64:2, known to thine **a**

Jer 30:16, and all thine **a**

46:10, avenge him of his **a**

Amos 3:11, An **a** there shall be

Nah 1:2, vengeance on his **a**

Mic 5:9, upon thine **a**

Matt 5:25, Agree with thine **a**

Luke 12:58, goest with thine **a**

13:17, **a** were ashamed

18:3, Avenge me of mine **a**

1 Cor 16:9, there are many **a**

Phil 1:28, terrified by your **a**

1 Tim 5:14, occasion to the **a**

Heb 10:27, shall devour the **a**

1 Pet 5:8, your **a** the devil

See 1 Sam 2:10; Is 9:11; 11:13

ADVERSITY 1 Sam 10:19, saved you out of all your **a**

2 Sam 4:9, soul out of all **a**

2 Chr 15:6, vex them with all **a**

Ps 10:6, I shall never be in **a**

94:13, from the days of **a**

Prov 17:17, born for **a**

24:10, in the day of **a**

Is 30:20, bread of **a**

Heb 13:3, them which suffer **a**

See Ps 31:7; 35:15

ADVISE Prov 13:10, well **a** is wisdom

ADVOCATE 1 John 2:1, an **a** with the Father, Jesus Christ

AFAR Jer 23:23, the Lord, and not **a** God **a**

30:10, will save thee from **a**

Acts 2:39, all that are **a** off

Eph 2:17, you which were **a** off

Heb 11:13, seen them **a** off

AFFECTION 1 Chr 29:3, because I have set my **a** to the

Rom 1:26, up unto vile **a**

1:31, without natural **a**

12:10, Be kindly **a** one

Gal 5:24, crucified . . . with the **a**

Col 3:2, Set your **a** on things

3:5, inordinate **a**

2 Tim 3:3, Without natural **a**

See 2 Cor 7:15

AFFLICT Lev 16:29, ye shall **a** your souls

Num 11:11, hast thou **a** thy

29:7, and ye shall **a**

Ruth 1:21, Almighty hath **a** me

1 Kin 8:35, thou **a** them

11:39, **a** the seed of David

2 Chr 6:26, thou dost **a** them

Job 6:14, To him that is **a** pity

Ps 44:2, **a** the people

55:19, hear, and **a** them

82:3, do justice to the **a**

90:15, thou hast **a** us

119:67, Before I was **a**

119:71, I have been **a**

140:12, the cause of the **a**

Prov 15:15, days of the **a**

22:22, neither oppress the **a**

31:5, any of the **a**

Is 51:21, now this, thou **a**

53:4, smitten of God, and **a**

53:7, and he was **a**

54:11, thou **a**, tossed with

63:9, all their **a** he was **a**

Lam 1:5, the Lord hath **a** her

1:12, Lord hath **a** me

3:33, he doth not **a** willingly

Nah 1:12, will **a** thee no more

Zeph 3:12, **a** and poor people

2 Cor 1:6, **a**, it is for your

1 Tim 5:10, relieved the **a**

Heb 11:37, **a**, tormented

James 4:9, Be **a**, and mourn

5:13, Is any among you **a**

See Ex 1:11, 12; 22:22, 23

AFFLICTION Gen 29:32, the Lord hath looked upon my **a**

Ex 3:7, surely seen the **a**

Deut 16:3, the bread of **a**

26:7, and looked on our **a**

1 Sam 1:11, **a** of thine handmaid

2 Chr 20:9, in our **a**

33:12, in **a**, he besought

Job 5:6, **a** cometh not forth

30:16, days of **a** have taken

30:27, days of **a** prevented

36:8, cords of **a**

Ps 25:18, mine **a** and my pain

34:19, **a** of the righteous

119:50, my comfort in my **a**

132:1, David, and all his **a**

Is 30:20, water of **a**

48:10, furnace of **a**

63:9, In all their **a**

Jer 16:19, in the day of **a**

Lam 3:1, man that hath seen **a**

Hos 5:15, in their **a** they

Mark 4:17, **a** or persecution

Acts 7:10, out of all his **a**

7:11, Chanaan, and great **a**

7:34, **a** of my people

20:23, bonds and **a** abide

2 Cor 2:4, much **a** and anguish

4:17, light **a**, which is

8:2, great trial of **a**

Phil 1:16, add **a** to my bonds

4:14, communicate with my **a**

Heb 10:32, great fight of **a**

11:25, **a** with the people

James 1:27, widows in their **a**

See Col 1:24; James 5:10

AFRESH Heb 6:6, to themselves the Son of God **a**

AGES Eph 2:7, That in the **a** to come he might

3:5, Which in other **a**

3:21, throughout all **a**

Col 1:26, hid from **a**

AGREE Amos 3:3, except they be **a**

Matt 5:25, A with thine

18:19, two of you shall **a**

Mark 14:56, witness **a** not

14:59, did their witness **a**

1 John 5:8, these three **a**

See Matt 20:2; Luke 5:36

AGREEMENT Is 28:15, with hell are we at **a**

2 Cor 6:16, **a** hath the temple

AIR 1 Thess 4:17, the Lord in the **a**

ALIENATED Eph 4:18, **a** from the life

Col 1:21, that were sometime **a**

ALIVE Lev 16:10, be presented **a** before the Lord

Num 16:33, went down **a** into

Deut 4:4, are **a** every one

32:39, I kill, and I make **a**

1 Sam 2:6, The Lord . . . maketh **a**

Ezek 13:18, save the souls **a**

Mark 16:11, heard that he was **a**

Luke 15:24, dead, and is **a** again

24:23, said that he was **a**

Acts 1:3, showed himself **a**

25:19, Paul affirmed to be **a**

Rom 6:11, but **a** unto

6:13, **a** from the dead

1 Cor 15:22, all be made **a**

1 Thess 4:15, we which are **a**

Rev 1:18, I am **a** for evermore

See 2 Kin 5:7; Dan 5:19

ALMIGHTY Ex 6:3, by the name of God **A**

Ruth 1:20, A hath dealt

Job 11:7, find out the **A**

29:5, When the **A** was yet

Ezek 1:24, the voice of the **A**

10:5, **A** God when he speaketh

2 Cor 6:18, saith the Lord **A**

Rev 1:8, is to come, the **A**

4:8, holy, Lord God **A**

11:17, O Lord God **A**

See Job 21:15; Ps 91:1

ALMS Matt 6:1, do not your **a** before men

Luke 11:41, give **a** of such

12:33, have, and give **a**

Acts 10:2, **a** to the people

ALWAY Job 7:16, I would not live **a**

Prov 28:14, man that feareth **a**

Matt 28:20, I am with you **a**

Phil 4:4, in the Lord **a**

ALWAYS Gen 6:3, My spirit shall not **a** strive with

Ps 103:9, not **a** chide

Mark 14:7, the poor with you **a**

14:7, me ye have not **a**

John 12:8, the poor **a** ye have

AMBASSADOR 2 Cor 5:20, **a** for Christ

See Prov 13:17; Is 18:2

AMEN Num 5:22, the woman shall say, A, **a**

Deut 27:15-26, shall say, A

Ps 41:13, to everlasting. A

106:48, the people say, A

Matt 6:13, glory, forever. A

1 Cor 14:16, unlearned say A

2 Cor 1:20, and in him **A**
Rev 3:14, saith the **A**
See Rev 22:20
ANCHOR Heb 6:19, have as an a of the soul
ANGEL Gen 48:16, The **A** which redeemed me
Ps 34:7, a of the Lord
78:25, Man did eat a food
91:11, shall give his a
Eccl 5:6, before the a
Is 63:9, a of his presence
Dan 3:28, who hath sent his a
Hos 12:4, he had power over a
Matt 13:39, reapers are the a
Mark 12:25, are as the a which
Luke 20:36, equal unto the a
4:10, a charge over thee
22:43, there appeared an a
John 5:4, a went down
Acts 12:15, It is his a
1 Cor 6:3, we shall judge a
2 Cor 11:14, an a of light
Heb 2:2, word spoken by a
2:16, the nature of a
13:2, entertained a
1 Pet 1:12, a desire to look
See Gen 19:1; Matt 25:41; Heb 2:7
ANGER Gen 49:7, Cursed be their a, for it was fierce
Neh 9:17, slow to a
Ps 6:1, not in thine a
30:5, a endureth but a
103:8, gracious, slow to a
Prov 15:1, words stir up a
19:11, deferreth his a
Eccl 7:9, a resteth in the bosom
Mark 3:5, on them with a
Eph 4:31, and wrath, and a
Col 3:8, a, wrath, malice
3:21, your children to a
See Ps 37:8; 85:3; Prov 16:32
ANGRY Ps 7:11, God is a with the wicked
Prov 14:17, He that is soon a
22:24, with an a man
25:23, an a countenance
Jon 4:4, well to be a
Matt 5:22, a with his brother
John 7:23, are ye a at me
Eph 4:26, Be ye a, and sin not
Titus 1:7, not soon a
See Gen 18:30; Prov 21:19
ANOINT (*v.*) Deut 28:40, shalt not a thyself with the oil
1 Sam 10:1, Lord hath a thee
2 Sam 14:2, a not thyself
Is 21:5, a the shield
61:1, the Lord hath a me
Mark 14:8, a my body
Luke 4:18, hath a me to preach
7:46, thou didst not a
John 9:6, a the eyes
12:3, a the feet of Jesus
2 Cor 1:21, and hath a us
Rev 3:18, a thine eyes
See Judg 9:8; James 5:14
ANOINTED (*n.*) 1 Sam 26:9, against the Lord's a
Ps 105:15, Touch not mine a
Is 45:1, the Lord to his a
ANOTHER James 5:16, pray one for a
See 1 Sam 10:6; Job 19:27
APART Matt 14:13, desert place a
14:23, a mountain a to pray
17:1, into an high mountain a
Mark 6:31, Come ye yourselves a
See Zech 12:12; James 1:21
APPEAR 1 Sam 16:7, on the outward a
Ps 42:2, and a before God
90:16, Let thy work a

Song 2:12, flowers a on the
Matt 6:16, they may a unto men
23:28, outwardly a righteous
Rom 7:13, that it might a sin
2 Cor 5:10, all a before the
5:12, glory in a
Col 3:4, who is our life, shall a
1 Thess 5:22, all a of evil
1 Tim 4:15, profiting may a
6:14, the a of our Lord Jesus
2 Tim 1:10, the a of our Saviour
4:8, that love his a
Titus 2:13, the glorious a
Heb 9:28, for him shall he a
1 Pet 1:7, glory at the a
See Ex 23:15; Matt 24:30
APPOINT Acts 6:3, a over this business
1 Thess 5:9, not a us to wrath
See Job 14:13; Acts 17:31
ARCHANGEL 1 Thess 4:16, with the voice of the a
Jude 9, Michael the a
ARISE 1 Kin 18:44, a a little cloud out of the sea
Neh 2:20, a and build
Ps 68:1, Let God a
88:10, dead a and praise
112:4, there a light
Prov 31:28, children a up
Mal 4:2, of righteousness a
Mark 2:11, A, and take up
Luke 7:14, I say unto thee, **A**
8:54, saying, Maid, a
15:18, I will a and go
Acts 9:40, said, Tabitha, a
Eph 5:14, a from the dead
2 Pet 1:19, till the day star a
See Is 26:19; Jer 2:27
ARMOUR 1 Sam 17:54, but he put his a in his tent
1 Kin 22:38, they washed his a
Is 22:8, in that day to the a
Luke 11:22, his a wherein
Rom 13:12, the a of light
2 Cor 6:7, a of righteousness
Eph 6:11, the whole a of God
ARMS Deut 33:27, underneath are the everlasting a
See Gen 49:24; Job 22:9
ASCEND Ps 68:18, Thou hast a on high
Is 14:13, I will a into heaven
John 1:51, angels of God a
3:13, no man hath a up to
6:62, Son of man a up
20:17, I am not yet a
Rom 10:6, shall a into heaven
Eph 4:8, he a up on high
Rev 8:4, a up before God
11:12, they a up to heaven
See Ps 24:3; 139:8; Rev 17:8
ASHAMED Job 11:3, shall no man make thee a
Ps 25:3, wait on thee be a
31:2, let me never be a
34:5, their faces were not a
Is 45:17, shall not be a
65:13, ye shall be a
Jer 2:26, the thief is a
12:13, they shall be a
Rom 1:16, not a of the gospel
5:5, hope maketh not a
9:33, shall not be a
2 Cor 7:14, I am not a
2 Tim 1:8, a of the testimony
1:16, not a of my chain
2:15, needeth not to be a
Heb 2:11, not a to call them
11:16, not a to be called
1 Pet 4:16, let him not be a
1 John 2:28, not be a before him
See Gen 2:25; 2 Tim 1:12

ASHES Gen 18:27, which am but dust and a
Job 2:8, among the a
30:19, like dust and a
42:6, and repent in dust and a
See 2 Sam 3:19; Esth 4:1
ASK Ps 2:8, A of me, and I shall give thee
Is 45:11, A me of things to come
65:1, of them that a not
Matt 7:7, A, and it shall be given
7:9, if his son a bread
7:11, them that a him
21:22, ye shall a in prayer
Mark 6:22, a of me whatsoever
Luke 11:13, to them that a him
John 14:13, whatsoever ye shall a
15:7, abide in you, ye shall a
16:26, At that day ye shall a
James 1:5, let him a of God
4:2, because ye a not
1 Pet 3:15, every man that a you
1 John 3:22, whatsoever we a
5:14, if we a any thing
See Deut 32:7; John 4:9, 10
ASLEEP 1 Cor 15:6, some are fallen a
1 Thess 4:13, them which are a
2 Pet 3:4, the fathers fell a
See Song 7:9; Matt 26:48
ASSURANCE Is 32:17, quietness and a for ever
Col 2:2, a of understanding
1 Thess 1:5, and in much a
Heb 6:11, the full a of hope
10:22, in full a of faith
See Deut 28:66; Acts 17:31
ASTROLOGERS Is 47:13, Let now the a, the stargazers
Dan 2:2, magicians, and the a
5:7, to bring in the a
AUTHOR 1 Cor 14:33, God is not the a of confusion
Heb 5:9, became the a of
12:2, the a and finisher
AUTHORITY Matt 7:29, taught them as one having a
8:9, I am a man under a
21:23, what a doest thou
Mark 1:22, as one that had a
Luke 4:36, with a and power
7:8, am a man set under a
9:1, power and a over all
19:17, a over ten cities
John 5:27, a to execute
1 Cor 15:24, all a and power
1 Tim 2:2, all that are in a
2:12, nor to usurp a
Titus 2:15, rebuke with all a
1 Pet 3:22, a and powers
AVENGE Deut 32:43, he will a the blood of his servants
Josh 10:13, the people had a
1 Sam 24:12, the Lord a me
2 Sam 22:48, God that a me
Esth 8:13, to a themselves
Is 1:24, a me of mine enemies
Luke 18:3, A me of mine
18:7, not God a his own
See Gen 4:24; Lev 19:18
AVENGER Ps 8:2, still the enemy and the a
44:16, of the enemy and a
1 Thess 4:6, the Lord is the a
See Num 35:12; Deut 19:6
AVOID Prov 4:15, A it, pass not by it,
1 Tim 6:20, a profane and vain
2 Tim 2:23, questions a
Titus 3:9, But a foolish
See Rom 16:17; 2 Cor 8:20
AWAKE Ps 17:15, when I a, with thy likeness

Is 51:9, **A, a,** put on
Joel 1:5, **A,** ye drunkards
Zech 13:7, **A,** O sword
Rom 13:11, **a** out of sleep
1 Cor 15:34, **A** to righteousness
Eph 5:14, **A** thou that sleepest
See Mark 4:38; John 11:11

B

BABE Ps 8:2, of the mouth of **b** and
sucklings
Is 3:4, **b** shall rule over them
Matt 11:25, them unto **b**
21:16, the mouth of **b**
BACKSLIDER Prov 14:14, **b** in heart
shall be filled
Jer 3:6, that which **b** Israel
3:8, **b** Israel committed
3:11, The **b** Israel hath
3:12, Return, thou **b** Israel
8:5, perpetual **b**
14:7, our **b** are many
Hos 4:16, as a **b** heifer
11:7, bent to **b** from me
14:4, will heal their **b**
See Jer 2:19; 5:6; 31:22; 49:4
BALANCE Lev 19:36, Just **b,** just
weights
Prov 11:1, **b** is abomination
16:11, just weight and **b**
Is 40:12, and the hills in a **b**
Ezek 45:10, shall have just **b**
Hos 12:7, the **b** of deceit
Amos 8:5, falsifying the **b**
Rev 6:5, a pair of **b**
See Job 6:2; 31:6; Jer 32:10
BALM Jer 8:22, Is there no **b** in
Gilead
See Gen 37:25; 43:11; Jer 51:8
BANDS Ps 2:3, break their **b**
asunder
73:4, there are no **b**
107:14, and break their **b**
Hos 11:4, with **b** of love
Zech 11:7, other I called **B**
Matt 27:27, the whole **b**
See Job 38:31; Eccl 7:26
BAPTISM Matt 20:22, the **b** that I
am baptized with
21:25, The **b** of John
Mark 1:4, **b** of repentance
11:30, The **b** of John, was it
Luke 3:3, preaching the **b**
7:29, with the **b** of John
12:50, I have a **b** to be
Acts 1:22, Beginning from the **b**
18:25, knowing only the **b**
19:3, Unto John's **b**
Rom 6:4, buried with him by **b**
Eph 4:5, one faith, one **b**
Col 2:12, with him in **b**
Heb 6:2, Of the doctrine of **b**
See Matt 3:7; 1 Pet 3:21
BAPTIZE Matt 3:11, I indeed **b** you
with water
3:11, he shall **b** you
3:14, I have need to be **b**
3:16, Jesus, when he was **b**
Mark 10:39, baptism that I am **b**
16:16, believeth and is **b**
Luke 3:7, to be **b** of him
3:12, publicans to be **b**
3:16, **b** you with water
3:16, shall **b** you with
3:21, Jesus also being **b**
7:29, being **b** with the
7:30, being not **b**
John 1:26, I **b** with water
1:33, he that sent me to **b**
3:22, with them, and **b**
3:23, came and were **b**
4:1, **b** more disciples

4:2, Jesus himself **b** not
Acts 1:5, John truly **b** with
2:38, Repent, and be **b**
2:41, his word were **b**
8:12, **b,** both men
8:16, **b** in the name
8:36, hinder me to be **b**
9:18, arose, and was **b**
10:47, should not be **b**
16:15, when she was **b**
16:33, was **b,** he and all
18:8, believed, and were **b**
19:3, what then were ye **b**
19:4, John verily **b**
22:16, be **b,** and wash away
Rom 6:3, of us as were **b**
Gal 3:27, been **b** into Christ
1 Cor 1:13, were ye **b** in the
10:2, were all **b** unto Moses
12:13, all **b** into one body
15:29, **b** for the dead
See Matt 28:19; John 1:25
BATTLE 1 Sam 17:20, the fight, and
shouted for the **b**
17:47, the **b** is the Lord's
1 Chr 5:20, to God in the **b**
2 Chr 20:15, **b** is not yours
Ps 18:39, strength unto the **b**
55:18, in peace from the **b**
Eccl 9:11, **b** to the strong
Jer 50:22, sound of **b** is in
See Job 39:25; 41:8; Ps 76:3
BEAR (*v.*) Gen 4:13, greater than I
can **b**
Ex 20:16, not **b** false witness
Lev 24:15, shall **b** his sin
Num 11:14, I am not able to **b**
Deut 1:9, to **b** you myself
1 Kin 21:10, to **b** witness
Ps 91:12, shall **b** thee up
Prov 18:14, spirit who can **b**
Ezek 23:49, ye shall **b** the sins
Matt 3:11, not worthy to **b**
4:6, hands they shall **b**
27:32, to **b** his cross
Mark 15:21, Rufus, to **b** his
Luke 11:48, Truly ye **b** witness
14:27, not **b** his cross
23:26, that he might **b** it
John 1:7, to **b** witness
5:31, I **b** witness of myself
8:18, I am one that **b** witness
15:27, also shall **b** witness
16:12, cannot **b** them now
Rom 8:16, The Spirit itself **b**
13:4, **b** not the sword
15:1, **b** the infirmities
1 Cor 10:13, be able to **b** it
15:49, also **b** the image
Gal 6:2, **B** ye one another's
6:5, every man shall **b** his
6:17, for I **b** in my body
Heb 9:28, offered to **b** the sins
1 John 1:2, and **b** witness
5:8, **b** witness in earth
See Ex 28:38; Prov 12:24
BEAST Prov 12:10, the life of his **b**
Eccl 3:19, above a **b**
1 Cor 15:32, fought with **b**
James 3:7, Every kind of **b**
2 Pet 2:12, as natural brute **b**
See Lev 11:47; Ps 50:10
BEAT Is 2:4, **b** their swords into
Joel 3:10, **B** your plowshares
Luke 12:47, **b** with many stripes
1 Cor 9:26, one that **b** the air
See Prov 23:14; Mark 12:5; 13:9
BEAUTIFUL Ps 48:2, **B** for
situation, the joy of the
Eccl 3:11, **b** in his time
Song 6:4, Thou art **b,** O my love
Is 4:2, of the Lord be **b**
52:1, put on thy **b** garments

52:7, **b** upon the mountains
64:11, Our holy and our **b**
Jer 13:20, thy **b** flock
Matt 23:27, indeed appear **b**
Acts 3:2, which is called **B**
3:10, alms at the **B** gate
Rom 10:15, How **b** are the feet
BEAUTY 1 Chr 16:29, the Lord in
the **b** of holiness
2 Chr 20:21, the **b** of holiness
Ezra 7:27, to **b** the house
Ps 27:4, the **b** of the Lord
39:11, **b** to consume away
50:2, perfection of **b**
110:3, in the **b** of
Prov 31:30, **b** is vain
See 2 Sam 1:19; Zech 9:17
BEGINNING Gen 1:1, In the **b** God
created the heaven
Job 8:7, Though thy **b** was small
Ps 111:10, **b** of wisdom
119:160, is true from the **b**
Prov 1:7, the **b** of knowledge
9:10, Lord is the **b**
Eccl 7:8, than the **b** thereof
Matt 19:8, from the **b**
Luke 24:27, **b** at Moses
John 1:1, the **b** was the Word
2:11, This **b** of miracles
Heb 3:14, **b** of our confidence
Rev 1:8, the **b** and the ending
21:6, the **b** and the end
See 1 Chr 17:9; Prov 8:22, 23
BEGOTTEN John 1:14, **b** of the
Father
3:16, his only **b** Son
Heb 5:5, today have I **b** thee
1 Pet 1:3, **b** us again
1 John 4:9, his only **b** Son
See Job 38:28; Philem 10
BEHIND Is 38:17, my sins **b** thy
back
Phil 3:13, things which are **b**
Col 1:24, that which is **b**
See 1 Kin 14:9; Neh 9:26
BEHOLD Ps 37:37, **b** the upright
Matt 18:10, **b** the face
John 17:24, may **b** my glory
2 Cor 3:18, **b** as in a glass
See Num 24:17; Ps 91:8; 119:37
BELIEVE Num 14:11, how long . . .
ere they **b** me
2 Chr 20:20, **B** in the Lord
20:20, **b** his prophets
Ps 78:22, they **b** not in God
Prov 14:15, **b** every word
Matt 8:13, as thou hast **b**
9:28, **B** ye that I am able
21:25, did ye not then **b** him
27:42, and we will **b** him
Mark 5:36, not afraid, only **b**
9:23, If thou canst **b**
11:24, **b** that ye receive them
16:13, neither **b** they them
Luke 1:1, most surely **b**
8:13, which for a while **b**
8:50, **b** only, and she shall
24:25, slow of heart to **b**
24:41, while they yet **b**
John 1:7, through him might **b**
1:12, that **b** on his name
2:22, they **b** the scripture
3:12, how shall ye **b**
5:44, How can ye **b**
5:47, how shall ye **b** my words
6:36, seen me, and **b** not
7:5, did his brethren **b**
7:48, Pharisees **b** on him
10:38, **b** the works
11:15, to intent ye may **b**
11:26, **B** thou this
11:40, thou wouldest **b**
11:48, all men will **b** on him

12:36, **b** in the light
14:1, ye **b** in God, **b** also
17:21, the world may **b**
20:25, I will not **b**
20:29, and yet have **b**
Acts 4:32, them that **b**
13:39, by him all that **b**
13:48, to eternal life **b**
16:31, **B** on the Lord Jesus
16:34, **b** in God with all his
Rom 4:11, all them that **b**
4:18, against hope **b**
9:33, whosoever **b** on him
10:14, how shall they **b**
1 Cor 7:12, wife, that **b** not
2 Cor 4:13, we also **b**
Gal 3:22, given to them that **b**
2 Thess 1:10, all them that **b**
2 Tim 1:12, know whom I have **b**
Heb 10:39, but to the saving
11:6, must **b** that he is
James 2:19, devils also **b**
1 Pet 2:6, he that **b** on him
BELLY Gen 3:14, upon thy **b** shalt
thou go
Matt 15:17, goeth into the **b**
Mark 7:19, but into the **b**
John 7:38, out of his **b** shall
Rom 16:18, but their own **b**
Phil 3:19, whose God is their **b**
BELOVED Deut 33:12, The **b** of the
Lord shall dwell
Ps 127:2, giveth his **b** sleep
Dan 9:23, greatly **b**
10:11, a man greatly **b**
10:19, said, O man greatly **b**
Matt 3:17, This is my **b**
Mark 1:11, Thou art my **b** Son
Luke 3:22, Thou art my **b** Son
Rom 11:28, they are **b**
Eph 1:6, accepted in the **b**
Col 4:9, faithful and **b** brother
Philem 16, a brother **b**
2 Pet 1:17, This is my **b** Son
See Neh 13:26; Song 2:16
BENEVOLENCE 1 Cor 7:3, render
unto the wife due **b**
BESOUGHT Ex 32:11, And Moses **b**
the Lord his God
Deut 3:23, And I **b** the Lord
1 Kin 13:6, the man of God **b**
2 Chr 33:12, he **b** the Lord
Jer 26:19, and **b** the Lord
Matt 8:31, the devils **b** him
8:34, they **b** him that he
Mark 5:10, and he **b** him much
Luke 8:31, And they **b** him
8:37, **b** him to depart
2 Cor 12:8, I **b** the Lord thrice
See Gen 42:21; Esth 8:3
BEST Ps 39:5, man at his **b** state
1 Cor 12:31, the **b** gifts
See Gen 43:11; Deut 23:16
BESTOW 1 John 3:1, Father hath **b**
on us
See 1 Chr 29:25; John 4:38
BETROTH Hos 2:19, I will **b** thee
unto me for ever
BETTER 1 Sam 15:22, to obey is **b**
than sacrifice
Ps 63:3, lovingkindness is **b** than
Eccl 4:9, Two are **b** than one
7:10, former days were **b**
Phil 2:3, each esteem other **b**
Heb 1:4, much **b** than the angels
11:16, a **b** country
2 Pet 2:21, For it had been **b**
See Eccl 2:24; Song 1:2; Jon 4:3
BEWARE Matt 16:6, Take heed and
b
Mark 8:15, **b** of the leaven
12:38, **B** of the scribes
Luke 12:1, **B** ye of the leaven

12:15, **b** of covetousness
Phil 3:2, **b** of evil workers
See Deut 6:12; 8:11; 15:9
BIND Prov 6:21, **B** them continually
upon thine
Is 61:1, **b** up the brokenhearted
Matt 16:19, shalt **b** on earth
18:18, **b** on earth shall be
See Num 30:2; Job 26:8; 38:31
BIRD Jer 12:9, as a speckled **b**
See Ps 11:1; 124:7; Eccl 10:20
BIRTH Gal 4:19, whom I travail in **b**
See Eccl 7:1; Luke 1:14
BISHOP 1 Tim 3:1, If a man desire
the office of a **b**
Titus 1:7, **b** must be blameless
1 Pet 2:25, Shepherd and **B**
See Acts 1:20; Phil 1:1
BITTERNESS Job 10:1, I will speak
in the **b** of my soul
Prov 14:10, knoweth his own **b**
Eph 4:31, Let all **b**, and wrath
Heb 12:15, lest any root of **b**
See 1 Sam 15:32; Prov 17:25
BLAME 2 Cor 6:3, that the ministry
be not **b**
8:20, that no man should **b** us
Gal 2:11, he was to be **b**
Eph 1:4, be holy and without **b**
BLAMELESS 1 Cor 1:8, be **b** in the
day of
Phil 2:15, that ye may be **b**
See Matt 12:5; Phil 3:6; Titus 1:6, 7
BLASPHEME 2 Sam 12:14, the
enemies of the Lord to **b**
Is 52:5, my name . . . is **b**
Matt 9:3, themselves, This man **b**
Mark 3:29, **b** against the
Acts 26:11, compelled them to **b**
Rom 2:24, name of God is **b**
James 2:7, **b** that worthy name
See 1 Kin 21:10; 1 Tim 1:20
BLASPHEMY Matt 12:31, All
manner of sin and **b** shall be
26:65, He hath spoken **b**
Mark 14:64, Ye have heard the **b**
Luke 5:21, which speaketh **b**
See 2 Kin 19:3; Ezek 35:12
BLEMISH Eph 5:27, holy and
without **b**
1 Pet 1:19, a lamb without **b**
See Lev 21:17; Deut 15:21
BLESS Num 6:24, The Lord **b** thee,
and keep thee
Deut 28:3, **B** shalt thou be
1 Chr 4:10, thou wouldest **b** me
Ps 32:1, **B** is he whose
34:1, I will **b** the Lord
103:1, **B** the Lord, O my soul
103:1, within me, **b** his holy
Prov 10:7, the just is **b**
Is 32:20, **B** are ye that sow
65:16, **b** himself in the God
Matt 5:3, **B** are the poor in
5:44, **b** them that curse
Acts 20:35, more **b** to give than
Rom 12:14, **B** them which
1 Cor 4:12, being reviled, we **b**
2 Cor 11:31, **b** for evermore
Titus 2:13, for that **b** hope
Rev 14:13, **B** are the dead
See Hag 2:19; James 3:9
BLESSING Deut 23:5, thy God
turned the curse into a **b**
Neh 13:2, the curse into a **b**
Job 29:13, **b** of him that
Prov 10:22, **b** of the Lord
28:20, shall abound with **b**
Is 65:8, for a **b** is in it
Mal 2:2, I will curse your **b**
3:10, pour you out a **b**
Rom 15:29, the **b** of the gospel
1 Cor 10:16, cup of **b** which

James 3:10, **b** and cursing
Rev 5:12, and glory, and **b**
See Gen 27:35; Deut 11:26, 29
BLIND Ex 23:8, the gift **b** the wise
Is 35:5, eyes of the **b**
2 Cor 3:14, their minds were **b**
4:4, of this world hath **b**
1 John 2:11, darkness hath **b**
See Deut 16:19; 1 Sam 12:3
BLINDNESS Eph 4:18, because of **b**
of their heart
See Deut 28:28; Zech 12:4
BLOOD Gen 9:6, Whoso sheddeth
man's **b** . . . his **b** be shed
Ps 30:9, is there in my **b**
72:14, precious shall their **b**
Is 9:5, garments rolled in **b**
Jer 2:34, **b** of the souls
Ezek 9:9, land is full of **b**
18:13, his **b** shall be upon
Matt 16:17, flesh and **b**
27:4, the innocent **b**
27:25, His **b** be on us
Mark 14:24, **b** of the new testament
Luke 22:20, new testament in my **b**
22:44, great drops of **b**
John 1:13, not of **b**, nor of
6:54, drinketh my **b**
6:55, my **b** is drink
Acts 15:20, and from **b**
17:26, made of one **b**
20:28, with his own **b**
21:25, from **b**, and from
Rom 3:25, faith in his **b**
5:9, justified by his **b**
1 Cor 10:16, the **b** of Christ
11:25, new testament in my **b**
11:27, **b** of the Lord
15:50, flesh and **b**
Eph 1:7, through his **b**
Heb 9:22, without shedding of **b**
10:29, hath counted the **b**
13:20, **b** of the everlasting
1 Pet 1:19, precious **b** of Christ
Rev 7:14, the **b** of the Lamb
12:11, by the **b** of the Lamb
See Gen 9:4; Ex 4:9; Rev 16:6
BLOSSOM Is 35:1, desert shall
rejoice, and **b** as the rose
See Gen 40:10; Num 17:5; Is 27:6
BLOT Ex 32:32, **b** me, I pray thee,
out of thy book
Ps 51:1, mercies **b** out my
69:28, Let them be **b** out
Acts 3:19, your sins may be **b**
Col 2:14, **B** out the handwriting
Rev 3:5, I will not **b** out
See Deut 9:14; 2 Kin 14:27
BOAST (*n.*) Ps 34:2, My soul shall
make her **b**
Rom 2:17, makest thy **b** of God
2:23, that makest thy **b**
3:27, Where is **b** then
BOAST (*v.*) Ps 49:6, trust in . . . and
b
94:4, workers of iniquity **b**
Prov 27:1, **B** not thyself
2 Cor 11:16, I may **b** myself
Eph 2:9, lest any man should **b**
James 3:5, member, and **b** great
See 2 Chr 25:19; Prov 20:14
BODILY Luke 3:22, Holy Ghost
descended in a **b**
2 Cor 10:10, but his **b** presence
Col 2:9, of the Godhead **b**
1 Tim 4:8, For **b** exercise
BODY Job 19:26, worms destroy this
b
Prov 5:11, thy flesh and thy **b**
Matt 5:29, not that thy whole **b**
6:22, The light of the **b**
6:25, nor yet for your **b**
Mark 5:29, she felt in her **b**

Luke 12:22, neither for the **b**
17:37, Wheresoever the **b** is
John 2:21, the temple of his **b**
Acts 19:12, from his **b** were
Rom 6:6, **b** of sin might be
7:24, **b** of this death
12:1, present your **b** a living
12:4, many members in one **b**
1 Cor 6:19, **b** is the temple
9:27, I keep under my **b**
12:14, **b** is not one member
13:3, give my **b** to be burned
2 Cor 5:8, absent from the **b**
12:2, the **b**, I cannot tell
Gal 6:17, I bear in my **b**
Phil 3:21, unto his glorious **b**
1 Pet 2:24, own **b** on the tree
See Gen 47:18; Rom 12:5
BOLD Eccl 8:1, the **b** of his face shall
be changed
John 7:26, he speaketh **b**
Eph 3:12, we have **b** and access
Heb 4:16, therefore come **b** unto
1 John 4:17, have **b** in the day
See Prov 28:1; Acts 13:46
BOND Acts 8:23, bitterness, and in
the **b** of
Eph 4:3, **b** of peace
Col 3:14, **b** of perfectness
See Num 30:2; Ezek 20:37
BONE Ex 12:46, neither shall ye
break a **b** thereof
Num 9:12, nor break any **b** of it
Job 20:11, His **b** are full
40:18, **b** are as strong as
Ps 51:8, the **b** which thou
Prov 12:4, rottenness in his **b**
Matt 23:27, of dead men's **b**
Luke 24:39, hath not flesh and **b**
See Gen 2:23; John 19:36
BOOK Is 34:16, Seek ye out of the **b**
Mal 3:16, **b** of remembrance
Phil 4:3, the **b** of life
Rev 3:5, name out of the **b**
13:8, not written in the **b**
20:12, another **b** was opened
21:27, written in the Lamb's **b**
22:19, the words of the **b**
22:19, part out of the **b**
22:19, written in this **b**
See Ex 17:14; Ezra 4:15
BORN Job 5:7, man is **b** unto trouble
14:1, that is **b** of a woman
15:14, he which is **b** of a
Ps 87:4, this man was **b** there
Is 9:6, unto us a child is **b**
66:8, shall a nation be **b**
Matt 2:2, **b** King of the Jews
11:11, Among them that are **b**
Luke 2:11, For unto you is **b**
John 1:13, **b**, not of blood
3:3, Except a man be **b** again
3:8, is **b** of the Spirit
1 Cor 15:8, **b** out of due time
1 Pet 1:23, being **b** again, not of
1 John 4:7, loveth is **b** of God
5:1, Christ is **b** of God
5:4, whatsoever is **b** of God
5:18, **b** of God sinneth not
See Prov 17:17; Eccl 3:2
BORNE Is 53:4, he hath **b** our griefs
See Lam 5:7; Matt 20:12
BORROW Deut 15:6, nations, but
thou shalt not **b**
Ps 37:21, **b** and payeth not
Prov 22:7, the **b** is servant
Matt 5:42, him that would **b**
See Ex 3:22; 22:14; 2 Kin 4:3
BOSOM Luke 16:22, into Abraham's
b
John 1:18, **b** of the Father
13:23, leaning on Jesus' **b**
See Ex 4:6; Deut 13:6; Job 31:33

BOUGHT 1 Cor 6:20, For ye are **b**
7:23, Ye are **b** with a price
2 Pet 2:1, the Lord that **b** them
BOW Is 45:23, unto me every knee
shall **b**
Rom 14:11, every knee shall **b**
BOWELS Gen 43:30, his **b** did yearn
upon his brother
Is 63:15, the sounding of my **b**
2 Cor 6:12, in your own **b**
Col 3:12, **b** of mercies
Phil 1:8, you all in the **b**
2:1, if any **b** and mercies
1 John 3:17, **b** of compassion
See Acts 1:18; Philem 12
BRANCH Job 14:7, tender **b** thereof
will not cease
Prov 11:28, flourish as a **b**
Is 11:1, **B** shall grow out
Jer 23:5, David a righteous **B**
Matt 13:32, lodge in the **b**
21:8, **b** from the trees
John 12:13, **b** of palm trees
See Zech 3:8; John 15:2, 4–6
BREAD Deut 8:3, man doth not live
by **b** only
Ruth 1:6, in giving them **b**
1 Kin 17:6, ravens brought him **b**
Ps 132:15, her poor with **b**
Prov 9:17, **b** eaten in secret
12:11, be satisfied with **b**
28:19, have plenty of **b**
31:27, the **b** of idleness
Eccl 11:1, Cast thy **b** upon
Matt 4:3, stones be made **b**
4:4, shall not live by **b**
6:11, this day our daily **b**
Luke 4:3, that it be made **b**
11:11, ask **b** of any of you
24:35, in breaking of **b**
John 6:35, I am the **b** of life
Acts 2:42, in breaking of **b**
20:7, together to break **b**
27:35, he took **b**, and gave
1 Cor 11:23, betrayed took **b**
2 Thess 3:8, eat any man's **b**
See Josh 9:5; Judg 7:13
BREATH Gen 2:7, into his nostrils
the **b** of life
6:17, wherein is the **b**
Is 2:22, from man, whose **b**
Ezek 37:5, cause **b** to enter
37:10, **b** came into them
Acts 17:25, all life, and **b**
See Job 12:10; 33:4; Ps 146:4
BREATHE John 20:22, he **b** on them
BRETHREN Matt 23:8, all ye are **b**
Mark 10:29, or **b**, or sisters
Luke 18:29, parents, or **b**
Col 1:2, faithful **b** in Christ
Heb 2:11, to call them **b**
1 John 3:14, we love the **b**
See Gen 4:28; John 7:5
BRIDE Rev 21:2, prepared as a **b**
22:17, the Spirit and the **b**
BRIDEGROOM Matt 25:1, to meet
the **b**
John 3:29, of the **b** voice
See Ps 19:5; Is 62:5; Matt 9:15
BRIDLE Prov 26:3, a **b** for the ass
James 1:26, **b** not his tongue
3:2, to **b** the whole body
See 2 Kin 19:28; Is 37:29
BRIMSTONE Gen 19:24, Sodom and
upon Gomorrah **b**
Is 30:33, like a stream of **b**
Rev 9:17, fire and smoke and **b**
14:10, with fire and **b**
19:20, fire burning with **b**
BRING Mal 3:10, **B** ye all the tithes
into the
Matt 5:23, if thou **b** thy gift
John 15:2, that it may **b** forth

BROKEN Ps 34:18, unto them that
are of a **b** heart
51:17, are a **b** spirit
51:17, **b** and a contrite heart
69:20, Reproach hath **b**
John 10:35, cannot be **b**
19:36, bone . . . shall not be **b**
Eph 2:14, **b** down the middle
See Job 17:11; Prov 25:19
BROTHER Prov 17:17, **b** is born for
adversity
18:9, is **b** to him
18:19, **b** offended is harder
18:24, closer than a **b**
Eccl 4:8, neither child nor **b**
Matt 10:21, **b** shall deliver
1 Cor 6:6, **b** goeth to law
2 Thess 3:15, him as a **b**
See Gen 4:9; Matt 5:23
BROTHERLY Rom 12:10, one to
another with **b** love
1 Thess 4:9, as touching **b** love
Heb 13:1, Let **b** love continue
See Amos 1:9; 2 Pet 1:7
BRUISE (v.) Is 53:5, **b** for our
iniquities
See Gen 3:15; Rom 16:20
BUFFET Matt 26:67, they spit in his
face and **b** him
1 Cor 4:11, and are **b**
2 Cor 12:7, of Satan to **b** me
1 Pet 2:20, when ye be **b**
BUILD Ps 127:1, labour in vain that
b
Eccl 3:3, a time to **b** up
Is 58:12, **b** the old waste
Matt 16:18, I will **b** my church
Acts 20:32, able to **b** you up
Rom 15:20, should **b** upon another
1 Cor 3:12, if any man **b** upon
Eph 2:22, also are **b** together
See 2 Chr 6:9; Eccl 2:4
BUILDER Ps 118:22, the stone
which the **b** refused
Matt 21:42, The stone which the **b**
rejected
Acts 4:11, at nought of you **b**
1 Pet 2:7, stone which the **b**
Heb 11:10, **b** and maker is God
See 1 Kin 5:18; Ezra 3:10
BUILDING 1 Cor 3:9, husbandry, ye
are God's **b**
2 Cor 5:1, we have a **b** of God
Eph 2:21, the **b** fitly framed
Rev 21:18, the **b** of the wall
BURDEN Ps 55:22, Cast thy **b** upon
the Lord
Eccl 12:5, shall be a **b**
Matt 11:30, my **b** is light
20:12, which have borne the **b**
23:4, For they bind heavy **b**
Luke 11:46, with **b** grievous
11:46, touch not the **b**
Gal 6:2, one another's **b**
6:5, shall bear his own **b**
See Num 11:11; 2 Cor 12:16
BURN Ps 39:3, while I was musing
the fire **b**
Prov 26:23, **B** lips and a wicked
Is 9:18, wickedness **b** as a
33:14, with everlasting **b**
Mal 4:1, shall **b** as an oven
Matt 13:30, in bundles to **b**
Luke 3:17, the chaff he will **b**
12:35, and your lights **b**
24:32, Did not our heart **b**
John 5:35, He was a **b**
1 Cor 13:3, my body to be **b**
Heb 6:8, whose end is to be **b**
Rev 4:5, lamps of fire **b**
19:20, **b** with brimstone
See Gen 44:18; Ex 3:2; 21:25
BURNT-OFFERING 1 Sam 15:22,

as great delight in **b**
Ps 40:6, **b** and sin-offering
Is 61:8, I hate robbery for **b**
Jer 6:20, **b** are not acceptable
Hos 6:6, of God more than **b**
Mark 12:33, more than **b**
See Gen 22:7; Lev 1:4; 6:9
BURY Luke 9:60, dead **b** their dead
Rom 6:4, we are **b** with him
Col 2:12, **B** with him in baptism
1 Cor 15:4, he was **b**
See Gen 23:4; 47:29; Matt 14:12
BUSINESS Prov 22:29, diligent in his **b**
Luke 2:49, about my Father's **b**
Rom 12:11, Not slothful in **b**
1 Thess 4:11, to do your own **b**
See Josh 2:14; Judg 18:7; Neh 13:30

C

CALL Is 55:6, **c** ye upon him while he is near
Luke 6:46, And why **c** ye me
Rom 11:29, **c** of God
1 Cor 7:20, in the same **c**
Eph 1:18, the hope of his **c**
Phil 3:14, prize of the high **c**
2 Thess 1:11, worthy of this **c**
2 Tim 1:9, with a holy **c**
Heb 3:1, of the heavenly **c**
2 Pet 1:10, make your **c**
See Acts 7:59; 1 Cor 1:26
CANDLE Job 29:3, When his **c** shined upon my head
Ps 18:28, thou wilt light my **c**
Prov 20:27, **c** of the Lord
Luke 8:16; 11:33, lighted a **c**
Rev 18:23, **c** shall shine no more
22:5, need no **c**
See Job 18:6; 21:17; Prov 24:20
CAPTIVITY Rom 7:23, into **c** to the law of sin
2 Cor 10:5, bringing into **c**
See Job 42:10; Ps 14:7
CARE (*n.*) Jer 49:31, nation, that dwelleth without **c**
Matt 13:22, the **c** of this world
Luke 8:14, with **c** and riches
21:34, and **c** of this life
1 Cor 9:9, Doth God take **c**
12:25, **c** one for another
2 Cor 11:28, the **c** of all
1 Pet 5:7, Casting all your **c**
See 2 Kin 4:13; 2 Cor 7:12
CAREFUL Phil 4:6, Be **c** for nothing
Heb 12:17, **c** with tears
See Phil 4:10; Titus 3:8
CARNAL Rom 7:14, **c**, sold under sin
8:7, **c** mind is enmity
1 Cor 3:1, but as unto **c**
2 Cor 10:4, weapons . . . are not **c**
See 1 Cor 9:11; Heb 7:16; 9:10
CARRY 1 Kin 18:12, Spirit of the Lord shall **c** thee
Is 40:11, **c** them in
53:4, **c** our sorrows
63:9, **c** them all the days
Ezek 22:9, men that **c** tales
Heb 13:9, not **c** about
2 Pet 2:17, that are **c**
Jude 12, **c** about of winds
See Ex 33:15; Num 11:12
CAST Ps 42:5, Why art thou **c** down, O my soul
55:22, **C** thy burden upon
Prov 16:33, lot is **c** into
John 6:37, in no wise **c** out
2 Cor 10:5, **C** down imaginations
1 Pet 5:7, **C** all your care
1 John 4:18, love **c** out fear
See Ps 76:6; 3 John 10

CAUGHT 2 Cor 12:2, **c** up to the third
1 Thess 4:17, be **c** up together
See Prov 7:13; Rev 12:5
CAUSE (*v.*) Ezra 6:12, God that hath **c** his name to dwell
Ps 67:1, **c** his face to shine
80:3, and **c** thy face to shine
Rom 16:17, which **c** divisions
See Deut 1:38; 12:11; Job 6:24
CEASE Deut 15:11, poor shall never **c** out of
Job 3:17, the wicked **c**
Ps 46:9, He maketh wars to **c**
Prov 26:20, the strife **c**
Eccl 12:3, grinders **c**
Acts 20:31, I **c** not to warn
1 Cor 13:8, tongues, . . . shall **c**
1 Thess 5:17, Pray without **c**
1 Pet 4:1, hath **c** from sin
See Gen 8:22; Is 1:16; 2:22
CELESTIAL 1 Cor 15:40, There are also **c** bodies
CHAFF Matt 3:12, burn up the **c** with unquenable
Luke 3:17, the **c** he will burn
See Hos 13:3; Zeph 2:2
CHAIN Acts 12:7, his **c** fell off
2 Tim 1:16, not ashamed of my **c**
2 Pet 2:4, into **c** of darkness
Jude 6, everlasting **c** under
See Ps 73:6; Is 40:19; Lam 3:7
CHANGE (*v.*) Mal 3:6, I am the Lord, I **c** not
Rom 1:23, **c** the glory
1 Cor 15:51, we shall all be **c**
2 Cor 3:18, **c** . . . from glory
See Job 17:12; Jer 2:36; 13:23
CHARGE Job 1:22, nor **c** God foolishly
4:18, angels he **c** with folly
Acts 7:60, sin to their **c**
Rom 8:33, any thing to the **c**
1 Cor 9:18, gospel . . . without **c**
1 Tim 1:3, **c** some that they
5:21, I **c** thee before God
6:17, **C** them that are rich
2 Tim 4:1, I **c** thee therefore
4:16, be laid to their **c**
See Ex 6:13; Ps 35:11; 91:11
CHARIOT 2 Kin 2:11, a **c** of fire
Ps 20:7, Some trust in **c**
See 2 Kin 6:14, 17; Ps 68:17
CHARITY Col 3:14, put on **c**
2 Thess 1:3, the **c** of every one
1 Tim 1:5, the commandment is **c**
2 Tim 2:22, faith, **c**
Titus 2:2, sound in faith, in **c**
1 Pet 4:8, **c** shall cover the
2 Pet 1:7, brotherly kindness **c**
Jude 12, your feasts of **c**
See 1 Cor 8:1; 13:1; Rev 2:19
CHASTE 2 Cor 11:2, present you as a **c** virgin
Titus 2:5, discreet, **c**
1 Pet 3:2, your **c** conversation
CHASTEN Deut 8:5, as a man **c** his son
Ps 6:1, neither **c** me
94:12, man whom thou **c**
Prov 19:18, **C** thy son
2 Cor 6:9, as **c**, and not killed
Heb 12:6, Lord loveth he **c**
12:11, no **c** for the present
Rev 3:19, I rebuke and **c**
See Ps 69:10; 73:14; 118:18
CHASTISEMENT Deut 11:2, not seen the **c** of the Lord
Job 34:31, I have borne **c**
Is 53:5, the **c** of our peace
CHEER Prov 15:13, maketh a **c** countenance
John 16:33, be of good **c**

Rom 12:8, showeth mercy, with **c**
2 Cor 9:7, God loveth a **c** giver
See Matt 9:2; 14:27; Mark 6:50
CHERUBIM Gen 3:24, of the garden of Eden **c**
Ex 25:18, two **c** of gold
Ps 80:1, between the **c**
Ezek 10:5, sound of the **c** wings
CHIEF Matt 20:27, whosoever will be **c** among you
Eph 2:20, the **c** corner stone
1 Tim 1:15, of whom I am **c**
1 Pet 5:4, when the **c** Shepherd
CHILD Prov 20:11, a **c** is known by his
22:6, Train up a **c** in the way
22:15, in the heart of a **c**
Is 9:6, to us a **c** is born
65:20, **c** shall die an hundred
Luke 1:66, What manner of **c**
1 Cor 13:11, When I was a **c**
See Eccl 4:13; 10:16; Heb 11:23
CHILDREN Jer 31:15, weeping for her **c**
Ezek 18:2, **c** teeth are set
Matt 15:26, take the **c** bread
17:26, Then are the **c** free
19:14, Suffer little **c**
Mark 10:14, little **c** to come
Luke 16:8, **c** of this world
20:36, **c** of the resurrection
John 12:36, the **c** of light
Rom 8:16, we are the **c** of God
Gal 3:26, **c** of God by faith
Eph 4:14, no more **c**
5:6, **c** of disobedience
5:8, walk as **c** of
6:1, C, obey your parents
Col 3:6, cometh on the **c**
1 Thess 5:5, Ye are all the **c**
1 Tim 3:4, his **c** in subjection
Heb 2:13, Behold I and the **c**
1 John 3:10, In this the **c**
See Num 16:27; Esth 3:13
CHOOSE Josh 24:15, **c** you this day whom ye will serve
Heb 11:25, C rather to suffer
CHOSE Ps 33:12, people whom he hath **c** for his
Matt 20:16, called, but few **c**
22:14, but few are **c**
Luke 10:42, **c** that good part
14:7, **c** out the chief rooms
John 15:16, Ye have not **c** me
Acts 9:15, he is a **c** vessel
Rom 16:13, **c** in the Lord
1 Cor 1:27, **c** the foolish things
1:28, despised, hath God **c**
Eph 1:4, According as he hath **c**
1 Pet 2:4, **c** of God
2:9, a **c** generation
See Ex 18:25; 1 Chr 16:13
CHRIST Matt 16:16, Thou art the C
24:5, saying, I am C
John 4:25, which is called C
4:29, is not this the C
6:69, thou art that C
Rom 5:6, in due time C died
5:8, C died for us
Gal 2:20, C liveth in me
Phil 1:15, indeed preach C
1:16, C of contention
1:21, me to live is C
1 Pet 1:11, the Spirit of C
1 John 2:22, Jesus is the C
Rev 20:4, reigned with C
20:6, of God and of C
See Matt 1:16; 2:4; Luke 2:26
CHRISTIAN Acts 11:26, disciples were called C first
26:28, me to be a C
1 Pet 4:16, man suffer as a C
CHURCH Matt 18:17, tell it unto the **c**

Acts 2:47, added to the **c** daily
7:38, the **c** in the wilderness
8:3, made havock of the **c**
14:23, elders in every **c**
19:37, neither robbers of **c**
20:28, feed the **c** of God
Rom 16:5, greet the **c** that
16:16, The **c** of Christ
1 Cor 12:28, set some in the **c**
14:28, 34, silence in the **c**
16:19, with the **c** that
2 Cor 11:8, I robbed other **c**
Eph 5:24, the **c** is subject
5:25, also loved the **c**
Col 1:18, the body, the **c**
1:24, which is the **c**
1 Tim 3:5, care of the **c** of God
Heb 12:23, **c** of the firstborn
See Matt 16:18; Rev 1:4; 2:1
CIRCLE Is 40:2, sitteth upon the **c**
of the earth
CIRCUMCISE Gen 17:11, ye shall **c**
the flesh
Acts 15:1, Except ye be **c**
Rom 4:11, though they be not **c**
Gal 5:2, if ye be C, Christ
Phil 3:5, C the eighth day
See John 7:22; Gal 2:3; Col 2:11
CIRCUMCISION Acts 7:8, the
covenant of **c**
Rom 3:1, what profit is there of **c**
15:8, a minister of the **c**
Gal 5:6, neither **c**
Phil 3:3, the **c**, which worship
Col 2:11, **c** made without hands
3:11, **c** nor uncircumcision
See Ex 4:26; John 7:22; Acts 7:8
CIRCUMSPECT Ex 23:13, that I
have said unto you be **c**
Eph 5:15, that ye walk **c**
CITY Num 35:6, there shall be six **c**
for refuge
Josh 15:59, six **c** with
Ps 46:4, make glad the **c** of God
Zech 8:3, a **c** of truth
Heb. 11:10, a **c** which hath
12:22, **c** of the living God
13:14, no continuing **c**
Rev. 16:19, the **c** of the nations
20:9, the beloved **c**
See Gen 4:17; 11:4; Jon 1:2
CLAP Ps 47:1, **c** your hands, all ye
people
Is 55:12, shall **c** their hands
See 2 Kin 11:12; Job 27:23
CLAY Job 33:6, formed out of the **c**
Ps 40:2, out of the miry **c**
CLEAN Job 14:4, bring a **c** thing out
Ps 24:4, He that hath **c** hands
51:10, Create in me a **c** heart
77:8, Is his mercy **c**
Prov 16:2, **c** in his own eyes
Is 1:16, Wash you, make you **c**
52:11, be ye **c**, that bear
Ezek 36:25, I sprinkle **c** water
Matt 8:2, canst make me **c**
23:25, for ye make **c**
Luke 11:39, Pharisees make **c**
11:41, all things are **c**
John 13:11, Ye are not all **c**
15:3, **c** through the word
Acts 18:6, I am **c**
Rev 19:8, linen, **c** and white
See Josh 3:17; Prov 14:4
CLEANSE Ps 19:12, **c** thou me from
73:13, I have **c** my heart
Prov 20:30, wound **c** away evil
23:26, **c** first that
Acts 10:15, What God hath **c**
2 Cor 7:1, let us **c** ourselves
James 4:8, C your hands
1 John 1:7, his Son **c** us
1:9, to **c** us

See Ezek 36:25; Mark 1:44
CLEAVE Josh 23:8, **c** unto the Lord
your God
Acts 11:23, heart they would **c**
Rom 12:9, **c** to that which
See Gen 2:24; Matt 19:5
CLOSE Prov 18:24, sticketh **c** than a
brother
CLOSET Matt 6:6, thou prayest,
enter into thy **c**
CLOTHE Ps 109:18, **c** himself with
132:9, **c** with righteousness
Prov 23:21, shall **c** a man
31:21, household are **c**
Is 50:3, the heavens
61:10, C me with the garments
Matt 6:30, if God so **c**
6:31, shall we be **c**
25:36, Naked, and ye **c** me
25:43, naked and ye **c** me not
Luke 12:28, If then God so **c**
2 Cor 5:2, desiring to be **c**
1 Pet 5:5, be **c** with humility
Rev 3:18, that thou mayest be **c**
12:1, woman **c** with the sun
19:13, **c** with a vesture
See Ex 40:14; Esth 4:4
CLOUD Ex 13:21, them by day in a
pillar of a **c**
14:24, fire and of the **c**
1 Kin 18:44, ariseth a little **c**
18:45, was black with **c**
Neh 9:19, the pillar of the **c**
Prov 3:20, **c** drop down the dew
Dan 7:13, the **c** of heaven
Matt 17:5, a bright **c** overshadowed
24:30, in the **c** of heaven with
26:64, and coming in the **c** of
Mark 9:7, a **c** that overshadowed
13:26, man coming in the **c**
Luke 9:34, a **c**, and overshadowed
21:27, in a **c** with power
1 Cor 10:1, fathers were under the **c**
1 Thess 4:17, caught up . . . in the **c**
2 Pet 2:17, **c** that are carried with
Jude 12, **c** they are without water
Rev 1:7, he cometh with **c**
14:14, and behold a white **c**
See Gen 9:13; Ex 24:15; 40:34
COLD Matt 10:42, cup of **c** water
24:12, many shall wax **c**
2 Cor 11:27, in **c** and nakedness
Rev 3:15, neither **c** not hot
See Job 24:7; Ps 147:17
COLLECTION 2 Chr 24:6, out of
Jerusalem the **c**
1 Cor 16:1, **c** for the saints
COME Ps 40:7, Then said I, Lo, I **c**
Is 55:1, **c** ye to the waters
Matt 11:28, C unto me
18:11, the Son of man is **c**
Luke 14:23, compel them to **c**
John 14:3, I will **c** again
Rev 22:20, **c**, Lord Jesus
COMFORT (*n.*) Acts 9:31, **c** of the
Holy Ghost
Rom 15:4, patience and **c**
2 Cor 1:3, God of all **c**
7:13, comforted in your **c**
13:11, be of good **c**
Phil 2:1, if any **c** of love
See Job 10:20; Ps 94:19
COMFORT (*v.*) Ps 23:4, staff they
c me
Is 40:1, C ye, **c** ye my people
49:13; 52:9, the Lord hath **c**
61:2, **c** all that mourn
66:13, whom his mother **c**
Matt 5:4, they shall be **c**
Luke 16:25, he is **c**
John 11:19, to **c** them
2 Cor 1:4, able to **c** them
1 Thess 4:18, **c** one another

5:11, **c** yourselves together
5:14, **c** the feebleminded
See Gen 5:29; 18:5; 37:35
COMFORTER Job 16:2, miserable **c**
are ye all
Ps 69:20, looked . . . for **c**
John 14:16, give you another C
15:26, when the C is come
16:7, C will not come
See 2 Sam 10:3; 1 Chr 19:3
COMMANDMENT Ps 119:86, **c** are
faithful
119:96, **c** is exceeding broad
119:127, I love thy **c**
119:143, thy **c** are my delight
Matt 15:9, for doctrines the **c**
Luke 23:56, according to the **c**
John 13:34, A new **c** I give
Rom 7:12, **c** holy, and just
1 Cor 7:6, and not of **c**
2 Cor 8:8, I speak not by **c**
Eph 6:2, first **c** with promise
Col 2:22, after the **c**
1 Tim 1:5, end of the **c**
1 John 2:7, I write no new **c**
2 John 5, I wrote a new **c**
See Esth 3:3
COMMEND Luke 23:46, I **c** my
spirit
Rom 5:8, God **c** his love toward us
See Eccl 8:15; Acts 20:32
COMMIT Ex 20:14, Thou shalt not **c**
adultery
Ps 37:5, C thy way unto
Jer 2:13, have **c** two evils
John 2:24, Jesus did not **c**
5:22, hath **c** all judgment
Rom 3:2, **c** the oracles of God
2 Cor 5:19, **c** unto us the word
1 Tim 6:20, that which is **c**
2 Tim 1:12, which I have **c**
1 Pet 2:23, **c** himself to him
See Job 5:8; Ps 31:5; 1 Cor 9:17
COMMUNE Job 4:2, If we assay to **c**
with thee
Ps 4:4, **c** with your own heart
77:6, I **c** with mine own
Zech 1:14, angel that **c** with me
See 1 Sam 19:3; Luke 22:4
COMMUNICATION Matt 5:37, let
your **c** be, Yea
Luke 24:17, What manner of **c**
1 Cor 15:33, evil **c** corrupt
Eph 4:29, Let no corrupt **c**
See 2 Kin 9:11; Philem 6
COMMUNION 1 Cor 10:16, **c** of the
blood of Christ
10:16, **c** of the body of Christ
2 Cor 6:14, what **c** hath light
13:14, **c** of the Holy Ghost
COMPASSION Is 49:15, she should
not have **c**
Lam 3:22, his **c** fail not
3:32, will he have **c**
Mic 7:19, will have **c** upon us
Matt 9:36, he was moved with **c**
14:14, with **c** toward them
18:33, **c** on thy
20:34, had **c** on them
Mark 1:41, Jesus, moved with **c**
5:19, Lord hath . . . had **c**
9:22, have **c** on us
Luke 10:33, he had **c** on him
15:20, saw him, and had **c**
Rom 9:15, will have **c** on whom
Heb 5:2, have **c** on the ignorant
1 Pet 3:8, one mind, having **c**
Jude 22, have **c**
See Ps 78:38; 86:15; 112:4
COMPEL Matt 5:41, **c** thee to go a
mile
27:32, **c** to bear his cross

Mark 15:21, they c one Simon
Luke 14:23, c them to come in
Acts 26:11, c them to
See 2 Cor 12:11; Gal 2:3
COMPLETE Lev 23:15, seven
  sabbaths shall be c
Col 2:10, are c in him
  4:12, perfect and c in all
COMPREHEND Job 37:5, doeth he,
  which we cannot c
Is 40:12, and c the dust
John 1:5, the darkness c it not
Eph 3:18, c with all saints
CONDEMN Job 10:2, I will say unto
  God, Do not c me
Amos 2:8, drink the wine of the c
Matt 12:7, have c the guiltless
  12:37, thou shalt be c
  12:42, and shall c it
  20:18, shall c him to death
  27:3, he saw that he was c
Mark 14:64, all c him to
Luke 6:37, c not, and ye shall
John 3:17, into the world to c
  3:18, believeth not is c
  8:10, hath no man c thee
  8:11, Neither do I c thee
Rom 2:1, thou c thyself
  8:3, c sin in the flesh
  8:34, Who is he that c
  14:22, Happy is he that c
Titus 2:8, that cannot be c
James 5:6, Ye have c and killed
  5:9, lest ye be c
1 John 3:21, if our heart c us
See Job 9:20; 15:6; Matt 12:41
CONDEMNATION John 3:19, this is
  the c, that light is
  5:24, shall not come into c
2 Cor 3:9, administration of c
1 Tim 3:6, the c of the devil
James 5:12, lest ye fall into c
Jude 4, ordained to this c
See Luke 23:40; Rom 5:16; 8:1
CONFESS Prov 28:13, whoso c and
  forsaketh them
Matt 10:32, c me before men
John 9:22, c that he was Christ
  12:42, they did not c him
Acts 23:8, Pharisees c both
Rom 10:9, c with thy mouth
  14:11, every tongue shall c
Phil 2:11, c that Jesus Christ
Heb 11:13, c that they were
James 5:16, C your faults
1 John 1:9, if we c our sins
  4:2, Every spirit that c
  4:15, c that Jesus is the
Rev 3:5, will c his name
See 1 Kin 8:33; 2 Chr 6:24
CONFESSION Dan 9:4, Lord my
  God, and made my c
Rom 10:10, mouth c is made
1 Tim 6:13, witnessed a good c
CONFIDENCE Ps 65:5, the c of all
  the ends of the earth
  118:8, to put c in man
  118:9, to put c in princes
Prov 3:26, Lord shall be thy c
  14:26, Lord is strong c
Is 30:15, in c shall be your
Jer 2:37, hath rejected thy c
Eph 3:12, c by the faith
Phil 3:3, no c in the flesh
  3:4, might also have c
Heb 3:6, if we hold fast the c
  3:14, beginning of our c
  10:35, therefore your c
1 John 2:28, we may have c
  3:21, have we c toward God
  5:14, this is the c that we
See Job 4:6; Prov 25:19
CONFIDENT Ps 27:3, against me,

in this will I be c
Prov 14:16, fool rageth, and is c
2 Cor 5:6, we are always c
Phil 1:6, c of this very thing
CONFIRM Is 35:3, c the feeble
  knees
Mark 16:20, c the word
Acts 14:22, C the souls of
  15:32, words, and c them
  15:41, c the churches
Rom 15:8, c the promises made
See 2 Kin 15:19; 1 Cor 1:6
CONFORM Rom 8:29, to be c to the
  image of his Son
  12:2, not c to this world
Phil 3:10, c unto his death
CONGREGATION Neh 5:13, all the
  c said, Amen
Ps 1:5, nor sinners in the c
  26:12, in the c will I bless
Prov 21:16, the c of the dead
CONQUER Rom 8:37, we are more
  than c through him
Rev 6:2, he went forth c
CONSCIENCE Acts 24:16, c void of
  offence
Rom 2:15, their c also bearing
  9:1, my c also bearing me
  13:5, also for c sake
1 Cor 8:10, shall not the c of him
  8:12, and wounded their weak c
  10:25, question for c sake
  10:28, and for c sake
2 Cor 1:12, testimony of our c
1 Tim 1:5, a good c
  1:19, faith, and a good c
  3:9, in a pure c
  4:2, c seared with a hot iron
Heb 9:14, purge your c from
  10:22, from an evil c
  13:18, we have a good c
1 Pet 3:16, Having a good c
See John 8:9; 2 Cor 4:2
CONSIDER Ps 8:3, When I c thy
  heavens
Is 1:3, my people doth not c
Hag 1:5, 7, C your ways
Matt 6:28, C the lilies of the
  7:3, c not the beam
Luke 12:24, C the ravens
Gal 6:1, c thyself, lest thou
Heb 3:1, c the Apostle
  7:4, c how great this man was
  10:24, c one another
  12:3, c him that endured
  13:7, c the end of their
See Deut 32:29; 1 Sam 12:24
CONSOLATION Job 15:11, Are the c
  of God small
Luke 6:24, have received your c
Rom 15:5, of patience and c
Phil 2:1, any c in Christ
2 Thess 2:16, everlasting c
Heb 6:18, have a strong c
See Luke 2:25; Acts 4:36
CONSUME Ex 3:2, bush was not c
Deut 4:24, God is a c fire
  9:3, as a c fire he shall
1 Kin 18:38, and c the burnt
Job 20:26, shall c him
Ps 39:11, c away like a moth
Lam 3:22, that we are not c
Mal 3:6, are not c
Luke 9:54, c them
Gal 5:15, heed that ye be not c
Heb 12:29, For our God is a c
James 4:3, that ye may c it
See Ex 32:10; 33:3; Josh 24:20
CONSUMMATION Dan 9:27, until
  the c, and that determined
CONTAIN 1 Kin 8:27, heavens
  cannot c thee
2 Chr 2:6, heavens cannot c him

John 21:25, itself could not c
1 Cor 7:9, if they cannot c
CONTENT Mark 15:15, willing to c
  the people
Luke 3:14, be c with your wages
Phil 4:11, therewith to be c
1 Tim 6:6, godliness with c
  6:8, to be therewith c
Heb 13:5, be c with such things
See Gen 37:27; Josh 7:7
CONTINUAL Gen 6:5, of his heart
  was only evil c
Ps 34:1, praise shall c be
  40:11, and thy truth c
  71:6, be c of thee
  73:23, I am c with thee
Prov 6:21, Bind them c
  15:15, merry heart hath a c
Is 14:6, wrath with a c stroke
  52:5, c . . . is blasphemed
Luke 18:5, by her c coming
  24:53, were c in the temple
Acts 6:4, give ourselves c
Rom 9:2, I have . . . c sorrow
Heb 7:3, abideth a priest c
  10:1, offered year by year c
See Ex 29:42; Num 4:7; Job 1:5
CONTINUE Job 14:2, as a shadow,
  and c not
Ps 72:17, shall be c
Is 5:11, that c until night
Jer 32:14, may c many days
Luke 6:12, c all night
  22:28, were with me in
John 8:31, if ye c in my word
  15:9, c ye in my love
Acts 1:14, c with one accord
  2:42, they c stedfastly
  2:46, they, c daily with
  12:16, Peter c knocking
  13:43, to c in the grace
  14:22, exhorting them to c
  26:22, I c unto this day
Rom 6:1, Shall we c in sin
  12:2, c instant in prayer
Gal 3:10, c not in all things
Col 1:23, If ye c in the faith
  4:2, in prayer, and watch
1 Tim 2:15, if they c in faith
  4:16, c in them
2 Tim 3:14, c thou in
Heb 7:23, not suffered to c
  7:24, because he c ever
  13:1, Let brotherly love c
  13:14, have we no c city
James 4:13, and c there a year
2 Pet 3:4, all things c
1 John 2:19, no doubt have c
See 1 Sam 12:14; 2 Sam 7:29
CONTRITE Ps 34:18, saveth such as
  be of a c spirit
  51:17, a broken and a c heart
Is 57:15, of a c and humble
  57:15, heart of the c ones
  66:2, and of a c spirit
CONVERSATION Ps 37:14, such as
  be of upright c
  50:23, ordereth his c aright
Phil 1:27, c be as it becometh
  3:20, our c is in heaven
1 Tim 4:12, in c, in charity
Heb 13:5, c be without
  13:7, the end of their c
1 Pet 1:15, in all manner of c
  1:18, from your vain c
  2:12, your c honest
2 Pet 2:7, with the filthy c
  3:11, be in all holy c
See Eph 2:3; 4:22; James 3:13
CONVERSION Acts 15:3, declaring
  the c of the Gentiles
CONVERT Ps 19:7, perfect, c the
  soul

Is 6:10, their heart, and c
Matt 13:15, be c, and I should
18:3, Except ye be c
Mark 4:12, they should be c
Luke 22:32, when thou art c
Acts 3:19, and be c
James 5:19, and one c him
5:20, he which c
See Ps 51:13; Is 1:27; 60:5

CONVICTED John 8:9, being c by
their own conscience

CORNER Ps 118:22, become the
head stone of the c
144:12, may be as c stones
Is 28:16, precious c stone
Matt 6:5, c of the streets
Acts 26:26, not done in a c
Eph 2:20, being the chief c
1 Pet 2:6, a chief c stone
Rev 7:1, four c of the earth
See Job 1:19; Prov 7:8; 21:9

CORRECT Prov 3:12, whom the
Lord loveth he c
29:17, C thy son
29:19, not be c by words
Jer 10:24, c me, but with
30:11, I will c thee
46:28, but c thee in measure
Heb 12:9, of our flesh which c us
See Job 5:17; Ps 39:11; 94:10

CORRECTION Prov 22:15, rod of c
shall drive
Jer 2:30, they received no c
5:3, refused to receive c
7:28, nor receiveth c
Zeph 3:2, she received not c
2 Tim 3:16, for reproof, for c
See Job 37:13; Prov 3:11; 7:22

CORRUPT Deut 4:16, Lest ye c
yourselves
31:29, ye will utterly c
Matt 6:19, and rust doth c
7:17, a c tree bringeth forth
12:33, make the tree c
Luke 6:43, not forth c fruit
12:33, neither moth c
1 Cor 15:33, communications c
2 Cor 2:17, which c the word
7:2, we have c no man
11:3, your minds should be c
Eph 4:22, old man, which is c
4:29, Let no c communication
1 Tim 6:5, men of c minds
2 Tim 3:8, men of c minds
James 5:22, your riches are c
See Job 17:1; Prov 25:26

CORRUPTIBLE Rom 1:23, into an
image made like to c man
1 Cor 9:25, obtain a c crown
15:53, this c must put
1 Pet 1:18, with c things
1:23, not of c seed
3:4, in that which is not c

CORRUPTION Ps 16:10, suffer
thine Holy One to see c
49:9, and not see c
Jon 2:6, my life from c
Acts 2:31, did see c
Rom 8:21, from the bondage of c
1 Cor 15:42, It is sown in c
15:50, neither doth c
Gal 6:8, of the flesh reap c
2 Pet 1:4, the c that is in
2:12, perish in their own c
See Lev 22:25; Is 38:17

COUNSEL Ps 1:1, c of the ungodly
33:11, The c of the Lord
55:14, took sweet c together
73:24, guide me with thy c
Prov 1:25, at nought all my c
11:14, Where no c is
15:22, Without c purposes

19:21, the c of the Lord
21:30, nor c against the Lord
Eccl 8:2, I c thee
Is 28:29, wonderful in c
30:1, that take c
46:10, My c shall stand
Jer 32:19, Great in c
Hos 10:6, ashamed of his own c
Mark 3:6, took c with
John 11:53, took c together
Acts 2:23, determinate c
4:28, thy hand and thy c
20:27, all the c of God
Eph 1:11, c of his own will
Heb 6:17, of his c

COUNSELLOR Prov 11:14,
multitude of c there is safety
15:22, in the multitude of c
12:20, c of peace is joy
Is 9:6, called Wonderful, C.

COUNT Gen 15:6, he c it to him for
righteousness
Ps 44:22, c as sheep
106:31, c unto him for
Prov 17:28, is c wise
Is 32:15, be c for a forest
Matt 14:5, because they c him
Mark 11:32, men c John
Luke 14:28, and c the cost
Acts 5:41, that they were c
20:24, neither c I my life
Phil 3:7, I c loss for
3:8, I c all things
3:13, I c not myself
2 Thess 1:5, may be c worthy
1:11, God would c you worthy
1 Tim 1:12, he c me faithful
5:17, well be c worthy
Heb 10:29, c the blood
James 1:2, c it all joy
2 Pet 3:9, as some men c
See Num 23:10; Job 31:4

COUNTENANCE 1 Sam 16:7, Look
not on his c
16:12, of a beautiful c
17:42, ruddy, and of a fair c
Neh 2:2, Why is thy c sad
Job 14:20, thou changest his c
Ps 4:6, light of thy c
44:3, light of thy c
89:15, in the light of c
Prov 15:13, maketh a cheerful c
27:17, sharpeneth the c
Eccl 7:3, the sadness of the c
Is 3:9, their c doth witness
Matt 6:16, of a sad c
28:3, c was like lightning
Luke 9:29, his c was altered
Rev. 1:16, his c was as the sun
See Gen 4:5; Num 26:26; Judg 13:6

COURAGE Deut 31:6, Be strong and
of a good c
Ps 27:14, be of good c
Acts 28:15, and took c
See Num 13:20; Josh 1:7; 2:11

COURSE Acts 20:24, that I might
finish my c with joy
2 Thess 3:1, may have free c
2 Tim 4:7, I have finished my c
James 3:6, the c of nature
See Ps 82:5; Acts 13:25

COURT
Ps 65:4, dwell in thy c
84:2, the c of the Lord
92:13, flourish in the c
100:4, his c with praise
See Jer 19:14; Ezek 9:7

COVENANT Num 18:19, it is a c of
salt for ever
25:12, my c of peace
2 Chr 13:5, by a c of salt
Ps 105:8, his c for ever
106:45, for them his c

111:5, mindful of his c
Is 28:18, c with death
Matt 26:15, they c with him
Luke 22:5, and c to give him
Acts 3:25, c which God made
Rom 9:4, glory, and the c
Eph 2:12, the c of promise
Heb 8:6, mediator of a better c
12:24, mediator of the new c
13:20, of the everlasting c
See Gen 9:15; Ex 34:28; Job 31:1

COVER Ex 15:5, depths have c them
33:22, c thee with my hand
1 Sam 28:14, c with a mantle
Esth 7:8, they c Haman's face
Ps 32:1, whose sin is c
73:6, c them as a garment
91:4, He shall c thee
104:6, Thou c it with
Prov 10:6, violence c the mouth
10:12, love c all sins
12:16, a prudent man c shame
17:9, He that c a transgression
28:13, He that c sins
Is 26:21, no more c her slain
Matt 8:24, ship was c
10:26, there is nothing c
Rom 4:7, whose sins are c
1 Cor 11:4, having his head c
11:6, the woman be not c
11:7, not to c his head
1 Pet 4:8, charity shall c
See Gen 7:19; Ex 8:6; 21:33

COVET Ex 20:17, Thou shalt not c
Prov 21:26, He c greedily all the day
Hab 2:9, him that c an evil
Acts 20:33, c no man's silver
1 Cor 12:31, c earnestly
1 Tim 6:10, while some c after
See Deut 5:21; Rom 7:7

COVETOUS Prov 28:16, hateth c
shall prolong his days
Ezek 33:31, goeth after their c
Mark 7:22, Thefts, c, wickedness
Luke 12:15, beware of c
1 Cor 6:10, c, nor drunkards
Eph 5:3, all uncleanness, or c
5:5, nor c man

CREATE Gen 1:1, God c the heaven
and the earth
1:27, So God c man in his
Is 40:26, who hath c these
43:7, c him for my glory
65:17, I c new heavens
Jer 31:22, hath c a new thing
Amos 4:13, and c the wind
Mal 2:10, one God c us
1 Cor 11:9, c for the woman
Eph 2:10, c in Christ Jesus
4:24, c in righteousness
Col 1:16, were all things c
1 Tim 4:3, which God hath c
Rev 4:11, for thou hast c
See Gen 6:7; Deut 4:32; Ps 51:10

CREATION Mark 10:6, But from the
beginning of the c
13:19, beginning of the c
Rom 1:20, from the c
8:22, whole c groaneth

CREATOR Eccl 12:1, Remember
now thy C in the days
Is 40:28, the C of the ends
Rom 1:25, more than the C
1 Pet 4:19, unto a faithful C

CREATURE Ezek 1:5, came the
likeness of four living c
Mark 16:15, gospel to every c
Rom 8:19, expectation of the c
8:39, nor any other c
2 Cor 5:17, he is a new c
Gal 6:15, but a new c
Col 1:15, firstborn of every c
1:23, preached to every c

1 Tim 4:4, every c of God
See Gen 1:20; 2:19; Ezek 1:20
CROOKED Eccl 1:15, is c cannot be made straight
  7:13, which he hath made c
  Is 40:4, the c shall be
  42:16, c things straight
  45:2, make the c places
  59:8, made them c paths
  Lam 3:9, hath made my paths c
  Phil 2:15, c perverse nation
  See Deut 32:5; Job 26:13
CROSS Matt 16:24, deny himself, and take up his c
  27:32, to bear his c
  27:40, come down from the c
  Mark 10:21, take up the c
  15:21, Rufus, to bear his c
  15:30, come down from the c
  Luke 9:23, take up his c daily
  23:26, they laid the c
  John 19:25, stood by the c
  1 Cor 1:17, the c of Christ
  1:18, preaching of the c
  Gal 5:11, offence of the c
  6:12, persecution for the c
  6:14, glory, save in the c
  Eph 2:16, reconcile . . . by the c
  Phil 2:8, the death of the c
  3:18, enemies of the c
  Col 1:20, blood of his c
  2:14, nailing it to his c
  Heb 12:2, endured the c
  See Matt 10:38; John 19:17, 19
CROWN Job 19:9, taken the c from my head
  Ps 8:5, c him with glory
  65:11, c the year with
  103:4, c thee with lovingkindness
  Prov 4:9, a c of glory
  12:4, woman is a c to her
  14:18, prudent are c
  17:6, children are the c
  Is 28:1, woe to the c of pride
  Matt 27:29, platted a c of thorns
  1 Cor 9:25, corruptible c
  Phil 4:1, my joy and c
  1 Thess 2:19, or c of rejoicing
  2 Tim 2:5, not c, except he
  4:8, a c of righteousness
  Heb 2:7, thou c him with
  2:9, death, c with glory
  James 1:12, the c of life
  1 Pet 5:4, a c of glory
  Rev 2:10, I will give thee a c
  3:11, no man take thy c
  4:10, cast their c
  19:12, head were many c
  See Ex 25:25; 29:6; Job 31:36
CRUCIFY Matt 27:22, all say unto him, let him be c
  Mark 15:13, again, C him
  Luke 23:21, C him, c him
  John 19:15, away with him, c him
  Acts 2:23, wicked hands have c
  Rom 6:6, that our old man is c
  1 Cor 1:13, was Paul c for you
  1:23, we preach Christ c
  2:2 Jesus Christ, and him c
  2:8, would not have c
  2 Cor 13:4, though he was c
  Gal 2:20, I am c with Christ
  3:1, c among you
  5:24, have c the flesh
  6:14, the world is c unto me
  Heb 6:6, c to themselves
  See Matt 20:19; 23:34; 27:31
CRY (*n.*) 1 Sam 5:12, c of the city went up to heaven
  Job 34:28, he heareth the c
  Ps 9:12, c of the humble
  34:15, open to their c
  Prov 21:13, the c of the poor

CRY (*v.*) Job 29:12, poor that c
  Ps 147:9, ravens which c
  Prov 8:1, Doth not wisdom c
  Luke 18:7, c day and night
  John 7:37, Jesus stood and c
  Rom 8:15, we c, Abba, Father
CUP Ps 23:5, head with oil, my c runneth over
  Matt 10:42, c of cold water
  20:22, drink of the c
  23:25, the outside of the c
  26:27, he took the c
  26:39, let this c pass
  Mark 9:41, give you a c
  14:23, And he took the c
  14:36, this c from me
  Luke 22:20, This c is the new
  22:42, remove this c
  John 18:11, c which my Father
  1 Cor 10:16, c of blessing
  11:25, he took the c
  11:26, ye . . . drink this c
  11:27, drink this c
  See Gen 40:11; 44:2; Prov 23:31
CURE Luke 7:21, in that same hour he c many
  9:1, power to c diseases
  13:32, I do c today
  See Jer 33:6; 46:11; Hos 5:13
CURSE (*n.*) Deut 11:26, you this day a blessing and a c
  23:5, turned the c into
  Mal 3:9, ye are cursed with a c
  Matt 25:41, ye c into
  Gal 3:10, are under the c
  Rev 23:3, no more c
  See Gen 27:12; Num 5:18
CURSE (*v.*) Lev 19:14, not c the deaf
  Num 23:8, How shall I c
  Judg 5:23, c ye bitterly
  Job 2:9, c God, and die
  Ps 62:4, but they c inwardly
  Mal 2:2, c your blessings
  Matt 5:44, bless them that c
  26:74, Then began he to c
  Mark 11:21, tree which thou c
  14:71, But he began to c
  Luke 6:28, them that c you
  John 7:49, the law are c
  Rom 12:14, bless, and c not
  Gal 3:10, C is every one
  James 3:9, therewith c we men
  See Gen 8:21; 12:3; Num 22:6
CUT Dan 9:26, shall Messiah be c off
  Matt 5:30, c it off
  Luke 13:7, c it down
  Acts 5:33, c to the heart
  Gal 5:12, were even c off

D

DAILY Ps 13:2, sorrow in my heart d
  68:19, d loadeth us
  Prov 8:30, I was d his delight
  Dan 8:11, the d sacrifice
  11:31, shall take away the d
  Matt 6:11, our d bread
  Luke 9:23, take up his cross d
  11:3, us day by day our d
  Acts 2:47, added to the church d
  6:1, the d ministration
  16:5, increased in number d
  17:11, the scriptures d
  1 Cor 15:31, I die d
  James 2:15, destitute of d food
  See Num 4:16; 28:24; Neh 5:18
DAMNATION Matt 23:33, can ye escape the d of hell
  Mark 3:29, danger of eternal d
  John 5:29, resurrection of d
  Rom 13:2, to themselves d
  1 Cor 11:29, and drinketh d

2 Pet 2:3, d slumbereth not
  See Matt 23:14; Mark 12:40
DAMNED Mark 16:16, he that believeth not shall be d
  Rom 14:23, doubteth is d
  2 Thess 2:12, all might be d
DANGER Matt 5:21, shall be in d of the judgment
  Mark 3:29, is in d of eternal
DARK Job 12:25, they grope in the d
  Ps 49:4, open my d saying
  69:23, Let their eyes be d
  88:12, known in the d
  Prov 1:6, their d sayings
  Eccl 12:2, stars, be not d
  12:3, the windows be d
  Zech 14:6, be clear, nor d
  Matt 24:29, shall the sun be d
  Mark 13:24, the sun shall be d
  Luke 23:45, sun was d
  John 20:1, it was yet d
  Rom 1:21, foolish heart was d
  Eph 4:18, understanding d
  See Ex 10:15; Joel 2:10
DARKNESS Ps 18:28, enlighten my d
  91:6, that walketh in d
  107:10, Such as sit in d
  112:4, light in the d
  139:12, d and the light
  Prov 20:20, in obscure d
  Eccl. 2:13, light excelleth d
  2:14, fool walketh in d
  Is 58:10, d be as the noon day
  60:2, d shall cover the earth
  Joel 2:2, A day of d
  Matt 6:23, shall be full of d
  8:12, out into outer d
  10:27, What I tell you in d
  22:13, into outer d
  Luke 1:79, that sit in d
  11:34, is full of d
  12:3, ye have spoken in d
  22:53, the power of d
  23:44, d over all the earth
  John 1:5, d comprehended it not
  3:19, loved d rather than
  12:35, the light, lest d
  Acts 26:18, from d to light
  Rom 2:19, which are in d
  13:12, the works of d
  1 Cor 4:5, hidden things of d
  2 Cor 4:6, shine out of d
  6:14, hath light with d
  Eph 5:11, works of d
  6:12, rulers of the d
  Col 1:13, the power of d
  1 Thess 5:5, night, nor of d
  1 Pet 2:9, out of d into
  2 Pet 2:4, into chains of d
  1 John 1:5, in him is no d
  1:6, and walk in d
  2:8, the d is past
  2:9, hateth . . . is in d
  2:11, d hath blinded his eyes
  Rev 16:10, kingdom was full of d
  See Gen 1:2; 15:12; Ex 10:21
DAY 1 Chr 23:1, old and full of d
  29:15, our d on the earth
  Job 7:1, d of an hireling
  8:9, d upon earth are
  14:6, accomplish, . . . his d
  19:25, stand at the latter d
  21:30, d of destruction
  32:7, I said, D should speak
  Prov 3:2, For length of d
  3:16, Length of d is in
  4:18, unto the perfect d
  27:1, what a d may bring
  Eccl 7:1, d of death
  12:1, while the evil d
  Is 2:12, the d of the Lord
  10:3, the d of visitation

58:5, acceptable **d**
Dan 7:9, and the Ancient of **d**
Joel 1:15, for the **d**
2:11, the **d** of the Lord
Zeph 1:14, The great **d**
Zech 4:10, **d** of small things
Mal 3:2, **d** of his coming
4:5, great and dreadful **d**
Matt 6:11, Give us this **d**
24:36, **d** and hour knoweth
24:50, a **d** when he looketh
25:13, the **d** nor the hour
Mark 13:32, of that **d**
Luke 1:34, that **d** come
John 6:39, again at the last **d**
8:56, rejoiced to see my **d**
9:4, while it is **d**
Acts 2:1, the **d** of Pentecost
2:20, great and notable **d**
Rom 2:5, **d** of wrath
14:5, esteemeth every **d**
2 Cor 6:2, **d** of salvation
Phil 1:6, the **d** of Jesus Christ
1 Thess 5:2, **d** of the Lord
5:5, children of the **d**
2 Pet 3:8, **d** is with the Lord
3:10, But the **d** of
See Gen 1:5; Job 1:4; Ps 77:5
DAYSPRING Job 38:12, caused the **d**
to know his place
Luke 1:78, **d** from on high
DAY STAR 2 Pet 1:19, **d** arise in your
hearts
DEAD Lev 19:28, cuttings in your
flesh for the **d**
Ruth 1:8, dealt with the **d**
Ps 31:12, forgotten as a **d** man
115:17, **d** praise not the Lord
Prov 9:18, the **d** are there
Eccl 4:2, which are already **d**
9:5, **d** know not any thing
Is 26:19, Thy **d** men shall live
Jer 22:10, Weep ye not for the **d**
Matt 8:22, let the **d** bury
11:5, the **d** are raised up
22:32, God of the **d**
23:27, full of **d** men's bones
Mark 5:39, the damsel is not **d**
9:10, the rising from the **d**
Luke 7:22, the **d** are raised
15:24, For this my son was **d**
16:31, rose from the **d**
John 5:25, **d** shall hear
6:49, and are **d**
11:25, though he were **d**
11:44, he that was **d**
Acts 10:42, quick and **d**
26:23, rise from the **d**
Rom 6:2, that are **d** to sin
6:8, if we be **d** with Christ
6:11, **d** indeed unto sin
7:4, **d** to the law
14:9, Lord both of the **d**
1 Cor 15:15, **d** rise not
15:35, How are the **d** raised
2 Cor 1:9, raiseth the **d**
5:14, then were all **d**
Gal 2:19, through the law am **d**
Eph 2:1, were **d** in trespasses
5:14, arise from the **d**
Col 1:18, firstborn from the **d**
2:13, And you, being **d**
2:20, if ye be **d** with Christ
1 Thess 4:16, **d** in Christ
1 Tim 5:6, **d** while she liveth
2 Tim 2:11, we be **d** with him
4:1, quick and the **d**
Heb 6:1, from **d** works
9:14, your conscience from **d**
11:4, being **d** yet speaketh
13:20, again from the **d**
James 2:17, is **d**, being alone
2:20, without works is **d**

1 Pet 2:24, being **d** to sins
4:6, to them that are **d**
Jude 12, without fruit, twice **d**
Rev 1:5, begotten of the **d**
1:18, liveth, and was **d**
3:1, and art **d**
14:13, Blessed are the **d**
20:5, rest of the **d**
20:12, the **d**, small
20:13, sea gave up the **d**
See Gen 23:3; Mark 9:26
DEAF Is 29:18, shall the **d** hear
Matt 11:5, the **d** hear
Mark 7:37, both the **d** to hear
9:25, dumb and **d** spirit
DEATH Num 16:29, these men die
the common **d** of all
23:10, **d** of the righteous
Ruth 1:17, but **d** part thee
2 Sam 22:5, When the waves of **d**
Ps 6:5, in **d** there is
13:3, the sleep of **d**
18:4, The sorrows of **d**
23:4, the shadow of **d**
48:14, our guide even unto **d**
68:20, the issues from **d**
89:48, shall not see **d**
102:20, appointed to **d**
107:10, in the shadow of **d**
116:15, precious . . . is the **d**
Prov 7:27, to the chambers of **d**
8:36, that hate me love **d**
14:32, hope in his **d**
24:11, drawn unto **d**
Song 8:6, love is strong as **d**
Is 9:2, shadow of **d**
25:8, He will swallow up **d**
38:18, **d** cannot celebrate
53:9, rich in his **d**
53:12, his soul unto **d**
Jer 2:6, the shadow of **d**
8:3, **d** shall be chosen
Ezek 18:32, pleasure in the **d**
33:11, **d** of the wicked
Hos 13:14, O **d**, I will be
Matt 15:4, let him die the **d**
16:28, not taste of **d**
26:38, sorrowful, even unto **d**
Mark 5:23, at the point of **d**
14:34, sorrowful unto **d**
Luke 2:26, should not see **d**
22:33, and to **d**
John 4:47, at the point of **d**
5:24, from **d** unto life
8:51, shall never see **d**
8:52, never taste of **d**
11:4, sickness is not unto **d**
12:33, signifying what **d**
21:19, **d** he should glorify
Acts 2:24, the pains of **d**
Rom 1:32, worthy of **d**
5:10, by the **d** of his Son
5:12, **d** by sin
5:14, **d** reigned from Adam
6:5, likeness of his **d**
6:21, those things is **d**
6:23, wages of sin is **d**
8:2, law of sin and **d**
1 Cor 3:22, life, or **d**
11:26, show the Lord's **d**
15:21, by man came **d**
15:55, O **d**, where is thy
15:56, sting of **d** is sin
2 Cor 1:9, sentence of **d**
2:16, savour of **d** unto **d**
4:12, **d** worketh in us
11:23, frequent, in **d** oft
Phil 2:8, **d**, even the **d**
Col 1:22, flesh through **d**
Heb 2:9, taste **d** for every man
2:15, fear of **d**
James 1:15, bringeth forth **d**
1 John 3:14, have passed from **d**

5:16, There is a sin unto **d**
Rev 1:18, keys of hell and of **d**
2:10, be thou faithful unto **d**
2:11, of the second **d**
6:8, sat on him was D
9:6, seek **d** . . . and **d**
20:13, **d** and hell delivered up
21:4, be no more **d**
See Prov 14:12; John 18:31
DEBT Matt 18:27, forgave him the **d**
See Matt 6:12; Rom 4:4
DEBTOR Matt 6:12, as we forgive
our **d**
Rom 1:14, I am **d** both
Gal 5:3, **d** to do the whole law
DECEIT Ps 10:7, full of cursing and **d**
36:3, iniquity and **d**
55:23, **d** men shall not
Prov 12:5, the wicked are **d**
20:17, Bread of **d** is sweet
27:6, of an enemy are **d**
31:30, Favour is **d**
Jer 14:14, the **d** of their heart
17:9, heart is **d** above
23:26, **d** of their own heart
48:10, work of the Lord **d**
Hos 11:12, of Israel with **d**
Amos 8:5, balances by **d**
Zeph 1:9, with violence and **d**
Matt 13:22, the **d** of riches
Mark 7:22, wickedness, **d**
Rom 3:13, they have used **d**
2 Cor 4:2, the word of God **d**
11:13, **d** workers
Eph 4:22, the **d** lusts
Col 2:8, vain **d**, after
See Ps 50:19; Prov 12:20
DECEIVE Deut 11:16, that your
heart be not **d**
Job 12:16, **d** and the deceiver are
Prov 20:1, whosoever is **d**
Obad 3, pride . . . hath **d** thee
Matt 24:4, no man **d** you
27:63, that **d** said
John 7:12, he **d** the people
7:47, Are ye also **d**
1 Cor 6:9, Be not **d**
15:33, **d**; evil communications
2 Cor 6:8, as **d**, and yet true
Gal 6:7, Be not **d**; God is not
Eph 4:14, lie in wait to **d**
5:6, Let no man **d** you
2 Thess 2:3, **d** you by any means
1 Tim 2:14, Adam was not **d**
2 Tim 3:13, **d**, and being **d**
1 John 1:8, we **d** ourselves
3:7, let no man **d** you
2 John 7, **d** are entered into
See Gen 31:7; Ezek 14:9
DECENTLY 1 Cor 14:40, all things
be done **d**
DECISION Joel 3:14, multitudes in
the valley of **d**
DECLARE 1 Chr 16:24, D his glory
among the heathen
Job 21:31, Who shall **d** his way
31:37, I would **d** unto him
Ps 2:7, I will **d** the decree
9:11, **d** among the people
19:1, heavens **d** the glory
30:9, **d** thy truth
40:10, **d** thy faithfulness
66:16, I will **d** what he hath
75:9, I will **d** for ever
118:17, and **d** the works
145:4, **d** thy mighty acts
Is 3:9, **d** their sin as Sodom
41:26, **d** from the beginning
45:19, I **d** things
45:21, **d** this from ancient
46:10, D the end
53:8, **d** his generation

66:19, **d** my glory

John 17:26, have **d** . . . thy name

Act 13:32, we **d** unto you

17:23, him **d** I unto you

20:27, **d** unto you the counsel

Rom 1:4, **d** to be the Son

1 Cor 3:13, the day shall **d** it

See Josh 20:4; 1 John 1:3

DECREASE John 3:30, but I must **d**

DEED Ezra 9:13, for our evil **d**

Neh 13:14, out my good **d**

Ps 28:4, according to their **d**

Is 59:18, According to their **d**

Luke 11:48, **d** of your father

23:41, due reward of our **d**

24:19, mighty in **d**

John 3:19, because their **d**

8:41, Ye do the **d** of your

Acts 7:22, in words and in **d**

Rom 3:20, by the **d** of the law

3:28, faith without the **d**

8:13, the **d** of the body

Col 3:9, old man with his **d**

3:17, ye do in word or **d**

James 1:25, blessed in his **d**

1 John 3:18, in **d** and in truth

2 John 11, of his evil **d**

Jude 15, their ungodly **d**

See Gen 44:15; Acts 19:18

DEFENCE Job 22:25, the Almighty shall be thy **d**

Ps 7:10, My **d** is of God

59:9, for God is my **d**

62:2, he is my **d**

89:18, Lord is our **d**

94:22, the Lord is my **d**

Eccl 7:12, wisdom is a **d**

DEFEND Ps 5:11, shout for joy, because thou **d** them

82:3, D the poor

Zech 9:15, shall **d** them

See Ps 20:1; 59:1; Is 31:5

DEFILE Ezek 23:38, **d** my sanctuary

36:17, they **d** it by their

Dan 1:8, would not **d** himself

Matt 15:11, into the mouth **d**

15:18, they **d** the man

15:20, the things which **d**

Mark 7:15, that **d** the man

7:23, from within, and **d**

John 18:28, they should be **d**

1 Cor 3:17, **d** the temple

8:7, being weak is **d**

1 Tim 1:10, that **d** themselves

Titus 1:15, them that are **d**

1:15, conscience is **d**

Heb 12:15, thereby many be **d**

Jude 8, filthy dreamers **d**

Rev 3:4, which have not **d**

See Lev 21:4; James 3:6

DEFRAUD Mark 10:19, D not, Honour

1 Cor 6:7, yourselves to be **d**

7:5, D ye not one

See Lev 19:13; 1 Thess 4:6

DELIGHT (*n.*) Deut 10:15, Lord had a **d** in thy fathers

1 Sam 15:22, great **d** in burnt

2 Sam 15:26, no **d** in thee

Job 22:26, **d** in the Almighty

Ps 1:2, his **d** is in the law

16:3, in whom is all my **d**

119:24, Thy testimonies . . . my **d**

119:77, thy law is my **d**

119:143, commandments are my **d**

Prov 8:30, I was daily his **d**

8:31, my **d** were with

18:2, fool hath no **d**

19:10, D is not seemly

See Prov 11:1; 12:22; 15:8

DELIGHT (*v.*) Job 27:10, Will he **d** himself in the Almighty

Ps 37:4, D thyself also

37:11, **d** themselves in the

51:16, thou **d** not in burnt

Is 42:1, in whom my soul **d**

62:4, the Lord **d** in thee

Mic 7:18, he **d** in mercy

Rom 7:22, I **d** in the law

See Num 14:8; Prov 1:22; 2:14

DELIVER Ex 3:8, am come down to **d** them

Job 5:19, shall **d** thee

Ps 33:17, he **d** any

56:13, **d** my feet from

91:3, he shall **d** thee

144:10, **d** David his servant

Prov 24:11, forbear to **d** them

Eccl 9:15, by his wisdom **d**

Is 50:2, have I no power to **d**

Jer 1:8, with thee to **d** thee

39:17, **d** thee in that day

Dan 3:17, is able to **d** us

Matt 6:13, **d** us from evil

11:27, things are **d** unto me

Acts 2:23, being **d** by the

Rom 4:25, **d** for our offences

7:6, we are **d** from the law

8:21, **d** from the bondage

2 Cor 4:11, **d** unto death

2 Tim 4:18, **d** me from

See 2 Cor 1:10; Gal 1:4

DELIVERANCE 1 Chr 11:14, by a great **d**

Ps 32:7, the songs of **d**

Luke 4:18, **d** to the captives

DELUSION Is 66:4, I also will choose their **d**

2 Thess 2:11, send them strong **d**

DEN Jer 7:11, a **d** of robbers

Dan 6:16, the **d** of lions

Matt 21:13, a **d** of thieves

See Judg 6:2; Dan 6:7; Amos 3:4

DENY Josh 24:27, lest ye **d** your God

Matt 10:33, whosoever shall **d**

16:24, let him **d** himself

2 Tim 2:13, he cannot **d** himself

Titus 1:16, in works they **d** him

See 2 Tim 3:5; Titus 2:12

DEPART Gen 49:10, scepter shall not **d** from Judah

2 Sam 22:22, **d** from my God

Job 21:14, God, D from us

28:28, to **d** from evil

Ps 6:8, D from me

34:14, D from evil

Prov 15:24, he may **d** from hell

22:6, not **d** from it

Matt 7:23, **d** from me

25:41, D from me, ye cursed

John 13:1, **d** out of this world

1 Cor 7:10, not the wife **d**

Phil 1:23, desire to **d**

1 Tim 4:1, **d** from the faith

2 Tim 2:19, **d** from iniquity

See Mic 2:10; 2 Tim 4:6

DESCEND Ezek 26:20, with them that **d** into the pit

Matt 3:16, Spirit of God **d**

Mark 1:10, like a dove **d**

Luke 3:22, the Holy Ghost **d**

John 1:32, I saw the Spirit **d**

Eph 4:10, He that **d** is the

1 Thess 4:16, **d** from heaven

James 3:15, This wisdom **d** not

Rev 21:10, **d** out of heaven

See Gen 28:12; Ps 49:17; 133:3

DESERT Is 35:1, the **d** shall rejoice

35:6, streams in the **d**

40:3, make straight in the **d**

43:19, rivers in the **d**

Luke 1:80, and was in the **d**

9:10, into a **d** place

John 6:31, eat manna in the **d**

See Ex 5:3; 19:2; Is 51:3

DESIRE (*n.*) 2 Chr 15:15, sought him with their whole **d**

Ps 10:3, of his heart's **d**

37:4, **d** of thine heart

112:10, **d** of the wicked

140:8, the **d** of the

145:16, satisfiest the **d**

Prov 10:24, but the **d**

11:23, **d** of the righteous

Eccl 12:5, **d** shall fail

Ezek 24:16, **d** of thine

24:21, **d** of your eyes

Hag 2:7, the **d** of all nations

Luke 22:15, With **d** I have

Eph 2:3, **d** of the flesh

Phil 1:23, having a **d** to depart

See Gen 3:16; Job 14:15; 31:16

DESIRE (*v.*) Deut 14:26, whatsoever thy soul **d**

1 Sam 2:16, as thy soul **d**

12:13, whom ye have **d**

Job 13:3, **d** to reason with God

Ps 19:10, More to be **d**

27:4, One thing have I **d**

34:12, that **d** life

73:25, that I **d** beside

Prov 3:15, things thou canst **d**

8:11, that may be **d** are

13:4, soul of the sluggard **d**

Eccl 2:10, eyes **d** I kept

Is 53:2, that we should **d**

Hos 6:6, I **d** mercy

Mic 7:1, my soul **d** the first

Zeph 2:1, O nation not **d**

Mark 9:35, If any **d** to be first

11:24, ye **d**, when ye pray

1 Cor 14:1, **d** spiritual gifts

2 Cor 5:2, **d** to be clothed upon

Heb 11:16, **d** a better country

James 4:2, and **d** to have

1 Pet 1:12, the angels **d**

2:2, as newborn babes **d**

1 John 5:15, petitions that we **d**

See Gen 3:6; Job 7:2; Ps 51:6

DESIROUS Prov 23:3, Be not **d** of his dainties

Gal 5:26, **d** of vain glory

DESPISE Num 11:20, ye have **d** the Lord

15:31, he hath **d** the word

1 Sam 2:30, that **d** me shall be

Ps 51:17, thou wilt not **d**

53:5, God hath **d** them

102:17, not **d** their prayer

Prov 1:7, fools **d** wisdom

1:30, **d** all my reproof

5:12, heart **d** reproof

13:13, Whoso **d** the word

15:5, A fool **d** his

15:20, **d** his mother

15:32, **d** his own soul

Eccl 9:16, wisdom is **d**

Is 5:24, **d** the word of the

30:12, Because ye **d** this word

49:7, to him whom man **d**

53:3, He is **d** and rejected

Jer 49:15, **d** among men

Ezek 20:13, **d** my judgments

22:8, **d** mine holy things

Amos 2:4, they have **d** the law

Zech 4:10, who hath **d** the day

Mal 1:6, we **d** thy name

Matt 6:24, and **d** the other

18:10, **d** not one of these

Luke 10:16, that **d** you **d** me

10:16, and he that **d** me

18:9, righteous, and **d** others

Rom 2:4, **d** thou the riches

1 Cor 1:28, things which are **d**

4:10, but we are **d**

11:22, **d** ye the church of God

16:11, Let no man . . . **d** him

1 Thess 4:8, **d** not man, but God
5:20, **D** not prophesyings
1 Tim 4:12, Let no man **d**
Titus 2:15, Let no man **d** thee
Heb 12:2, **d** the shame
James 2:6, ye have **d** the poor
See Gen 16:4; 25:34; 2 Sam 6:16
DESTROY Gen 18:23, **d** the
righteous with the wicked
Ex 22:20, he shall be utterly **d**
Deut 9:14, that I may **d** them
Job 2:3, to **d** him
10:8, yet thou dost **d** me
19:10, He hath **d** me
19:26, my skin worms **d**
Ps 40:14, seek after my soul to **d** it
145:20, the wicked will he **d**
Prov 1:32, fools shall **d**
13:23, is **d** for want of judgment
31:3, that which **d** kings
Eccl 9:18, one sinner **d** much
Is 10:7, it is in his heart to **d**
11:9, shall not hurt nor **d**
19:3, I will **d** the counsel
Jer 13:14, but **d** them
23:1, pastors that **d**
Ezek 9:1, with his **d** weapon
22:27, **d** souls
Hos 13:9, thou hast **d** thyself
Matt 5:17, not come to **d**
10:28, him that is able to **d**
Mark 1:24, art thou come to **d** us
14:58, I will **d** this temple
Luke 6:9, save life, or **d** it
9:56, is not come to **d**
John 2:19, **D** this temple
2 Thess 2:8, **d** with the brightness
Heb 2:14, **d** him
James 4:12, to save and to **d**
1 John 3:8, **d** the works
See Gen 6:17; Is 65:8; Rom 6:6
DESTROYER Ex 12:23, not suffer
the **d**
Judg 16:24, delivered . . . the **d**
Job 15:21, in prosperity the **d**
Ps 17:4, the paths of the **d**
Prov 28:24, companion of a **d**
See Is 49:17; Jer 22:7
DESTRUCTION 2 Chr 22:4, to his **d**
26:16, heart was lifted up to his **d**
Job 5:21, be afraid of **d**
Prov 1:27, your **d** cometh
16:18, Pride goeth before **d**
17:19, seeketh **d**
18:7, fool's mouth is his **d**
31:8, are appointed to **d**
Is 14:23, the besom of **d**
19:18, The city of **d**
Hos 13:14, I will be thy **d**
Matt 7:13, that leadeth to **d**
Rom 3:16, **D** and misery
9:22, fitted to **d**
Phil 3:19, Whose end is **d**
1 Thess 5:3, sudden **d** cometh
2 Thess 1:9, with everlasting **d**
1 Tim 6:9, drown men in **d**
2 Pet 2:1, swift **d**
3:16, unto their own **d**
See Job 21:20; Prov 10:29; 21:15
DEVICE Ps 10:2, be taken in the **d**
DEVIL Lev 17:7, offer their
sacrifices unto **d**
Matt 4:1, tempted of the **d**
8:28, two possessed with **d**
25:41, prepared for the **d**
Luke 4:33, an unclean **d**
4:41, **d** also came out
8:2, went seven **d**
John 8:44, your father the **d**
James 2:19, the **d** also believe
4:7, Resist the **d**
1 Pet 5:8, your adversary the **d**
See Deut 32:17; Ps 106:37

DEVOTE Lev 27:21, as a field **d**
27:28, **d** unto the Lord
Num 18:14, Every thing **d**
Ps 119:38, servant, who is **d**
DEVOUT Luke 2:25, the same man
was just and **d**
Acts 2:5, Jews, **d** men
8:2, **d** men carried
See Acts 10:2; 13:50; 17:4, 17
DID Matt 13:58, he **d** not many
John 4:29, things that ever I **d**
15:24, which none other man **d**
DIE Gen 2:17, eatest thereof thou
shalt surely **d**
3:3, lest ye **d**
20:7, thou shalt surely **d**
Lev 7:24, that **d** of itself
22:8, That which **d** of itself
Num 16:29, **d** the common death
23:10, let me the death
Deut 14:21, that **d** of itself
31:14, that thou must **d**
Ruth 1:17, thou **d**, will I **d**
2 Kin 20:1, for thou shalt **d**
2 Chr 25:4, **d** for his own sin
Job 2:9, curse God, and **d**
12:2, wisdom shall **d**
14:14, If a man **d**
Prov 5:23, **d** without instruction
10:21, fools **d** for want
11:7, a wicked man **d**
Eccl 2:16, how **d** the wise man
7:17, **d** before thy time
9:5, they shall **d**
Is 66:24, worm shall not **d**
Jer 27:13, will ye **d**
28:16, this year thou shalt **d**
34:5, Thou shalt **d** in peace
Ezek 3:18, Thou shalt surely **d**
18:4, it shall **d**
18:31, why will ye **d**
33:8, thou shalt surely **d**
Matt 15:4, let him **d** the death
Mark 9:44, Where their worm **d**
John 11:26, shall never **d**
11:50, one man should **d**
Rom 5:7, will one **d**
7:9, sin revived, and I **d**
8:34, It is Christ that **d**
14:7, no man to himself
14:9, Christ both **d**, and rose
14:15, for whom Christ **d**
1 Cor 8:11, for whom Christ **d**
15:3, Christ **d** for our sins
15:22, as in Adam all **d**
15:31, I **d** daily
15:36, except it **d**
2 Cor 5:14, if one **d** for all
Phil 1:21, and to **d** is gain
1 Thess 4:14, that Jesus **d**
5:10, Who **d** for us
Heb 7:8, here men that **d**
9:27, unto men once to **d**
11:13, These all **d** in faith
Rev 3:2, ready to **d**
9:6, shall desire to **d**
14:13, the dead which **d**
See Job 14:10; Ps 118:17
DIFFERENCE Lev 10:10, And that
ye may put **d** between holy
Ezek 22:26, they have put no **d**
44:23, **d** between the holy
Rom 3:22, for there is no **d**
10:12, no **d** between the Jew
See Ex 11:7; 1 Cor 12:5; Jude 22
DINE John 21:12, Come and **d**
DIRECT Ps 5:3, will I **d** my prayer
Prov 3:6, he shall **d** thy paths
11:5, shall **d** his way
16:9, the Lord **d** his steps
21:29, he **d** his way
Eccl 10:10, profitable to **d**
Jer 10:23, to **d** his steps

2 Thess 3:5, **d** your hearts
See Gen 46:28; Is 45:13; 61:8
DISCERN 2 Sam 19:35, can I **d**
between good and evil
Eccl 8:5, a wise man's heart **d**
Jon 4:11, cannot **d** between
Matt 16:3, **d** the face of the sky
1 Cor 2:14, are spiritually **d**
11:29, not **d** the Lord's body
12:10, another **d** of spirits
Heb 4:12, a **d** of the thoughts
5:14, to **d** both good
See Gen 27:23; 2 Sam 14:17
DISCIPLE Matt 10:1, his twelve **d**
10:24, The **d** is not above
20:17, took the twelve **d**
26:56, all the **d** forsook him
28:7, tell his **d** that he is
28:13, His **d** came by night
Mark 2:18, Why do the **d** of John
4:34, all things to his **d**
7:2, his **d** eat bread
7:5, Why walk not thy **d**
10:13, his **d** rebuked those
14:14, passover with my **d**
Luke 5:30, against his **d**
5:33, of John fast
6:13, unto him his **d**
6:20, his eyes on his **d**
11:1, John also taught his **d**
14:26, he cannot be my **d**
19:37, **d** began to rejoice
John 2:11, **d** believed on him
6:66, many of his **d** went back
7:3, **d** also may see
8:31, are ye my **d** indeed
9:27, will ye also be his **d**
9:28, Thou art his **d**
13:5, to wash the **d** feet
13:35, known that ye are my **d**
15:8, so shall ye be my **d**
19:26, and the **d** standing by
19:38, being a **d** of Jesus
20:18, came and told the **d**
21:7, **d** whom Jesus loved
21:20, seeth the **d**
21:23, **d** should not die
Acts 9:1, against the **d**
9:26, to the **d**
11:26, **d** were called
20:7, the **d** came together
20:30, to draw away **d**
See Matt 11:1; John 3:25; 18:1
DISCORD Prov 6:14, continually; he
soweth **d**
6:19, that soweth **d**
DISCOURAGE Num 32:7, **d** ye the
heart of the children
Deut 1:21, neither be **d**
1:28, have **d** our heart
Col 3:21, lest they be **d**
See Num 21:4; 32:9; Is 42:4
DISEASE Ex 15:26, put none of
these **d** upon thee
Ps 103:3, who healeth all thy **d**
Eccl 6:2, it is an evil **d**
Ezek 34:4, The **d** have ye not
See Matt 4:23; 14:35; Luke 9:1
DISHONOUR Mic 7:6, son **d** the
father
John 8:49, and ye do **d** me
Rom 9:21, another unto **d**
1 Cor 15:43, It is sown in **d**
2 Cor 6:8, By honour and **d**
2 Tim 2:20, and some to **d**
See Rom 1:24; 2:23; 1 Cor 11:4, 5
DISOBEDIENCE Rom 5:19, by one
man's **d**
Eph 2:2, the children of **d**
5:6, the children of **d**
Heb 2:2, transgression and **d**
DISOBEDIENT Luke 1:17, **d** to the
wisdom

Acts 26:19, not **d** unto the . . . vision
Rom 1:30, **d** to parents
1 Tim 1:9, the lawless and **d**
2 Tim 3:2, to parents
Titus 3:3, sometimes foolish, **d**
1 Pet 2:7, unto them which be **d**
3:20, Which sometime were **d**
See 1 Kin 13:26; Rom 10:21

DISORDERLY 2 Thess 3:6, every brother that walketh **d**
3:7, behaved not ourselves **d**
3:11, walk among you **d**

DISPENSATION 1 Cor 9:17, a **d** of the gospel is committed
Eph 1:10, the **d** of the fullness
3:2, **d** of the grace of God
Col 1:25, to the **d** of God

DISSOLVE Is 34:4, host of heaven shall be **d**
Dan 5:16, and **d** doubts
2 Cor 5:1, this tabernacle were **d**
2 Pet 3:11, things shall be **d**
3:12, shall be **d**
See Job 30:22; Ps 75:3; Dan 5:12

DISTRIBUTE Luke 18:22, **d** unto the poor
Rom 12:13, **D** to the necessity
1 Cor 7:17, as God hath **d**
2 Cor 9:13, your liberal **d**
See Josh 13:32; 2 Cor 10:13

DIVERS Deut 22:11, a garment of **d** sorts
25:13, in thy bag **d** weights
Prov 20:10, **D** weights
Matt 4:24, with **d** diseases
24:7, in **d** places
Mark 1:34, sick of **d** diseases
13:8, earthquakes in **d** places
Luke 4:40, sick with **d** diseases
21:11, shall be in **d**
1 Cor 12:10, **d** kinds of tongues
1 Tim 3:6, led away with **d** lusts
Titus 3:3, serving **d** lusts
James 1:2, into **d** temptations
See Eccl 5:7; Heb 1:1; 13:9

DIVERSE 1 Cor 12:6, are **d** of operations
See Esth 1:7; 1 Cor 12:4, 28

DIVIDE Lev 11:4, 5, 6, but **d** not the hoof
1 Kin 3:25, **D** the living child
Job 27:17, the innocent shall **d**
Matt 12:25, Every kingdom **d**
12:26, Satan, he is **d**
Mark 3:24, if a kingdom be **d**
3:26, and be **d**, he cannot stand
Luke 11:17, **d** against itself
11:18, If Satan also be **d**
12:52, five in one house **d**
1 Cor 1:13, Is Christ **d**
12:11, **d** to every man
2 Tim 2:15, rightly **d** the word
Heb 4:12, the **d** asunder of soul
See Dan 7:25; Matt 25:32

DIVINATION Num 23:23, is there any **d** against Israel
Acts 16:16, a spirit of **d**
See Deut 18:10; 2 Kin 17:17

DIVINE (*v.*) Gen 44:15, I can certainly **d**
1 Sam 28:8, **d** unto me
Ezek 13:9, and that **d** lies
21:29, they **d** a lie
Mic 3:11, prophets thereof **d**
See Gen 44:5; Ezek 22:28

DIVINE (*adj.*) Prov 16:10, A **d** sentence is in the lips of the
Heb 9:1, of **d** service
2 Pet 1:3, as his **d** power hath
1:4, the **d** nature

DIVINER 1 Sam 6:2, called for the priests and the **d**

Is 44:25, and maketh **d** mad
Jer 27:9, to your **d**
29:8, your prophets and your **d**

DIVISION Ex 8:23, will put a **d** between my people
Luke 12:51, Nay; but rather **d**
Rom 16:17, them which cause **d**
See 1 Cor 1:10; 3:3; 11:18

DIVORCE Deut 24:1, then let him write her a bill of **d**
Matt 5:32, her that is **d**
Mark 10:4, write a bill of **d**

DO Eccl 3:12, to **d** good in his life
Matt 7:12, should **d** to you
Luke 10:28, this **d**
22:19, this **d** in remembrance
John 15:5, ye can **d** nothing
Rom 7:15, that **d** I not
Phil 4:13, I can **d** all things —
James 1:23, and not a **d**
See John 6:38; 10:37; Rev 19:10

DOCTRINE Prov 4:2, I give you good **d**
Is 28:9, make to understand **d**
Jer 10:8, a **d** of vanities
Matt 7:28, astonished at his **d**
16:12, the **d** of the Pharisees
Mark 1:27, what new **d** is this
John 7:17, know of the **d**
Acts 2:42, in the apostles' **d**
5:28, with your **d**
17:19, what this new **d**
Rom 6:17, form of **d**
16:17, contrary to the **d**
1 Cor 14:26, hath a **d**
Eph 4:14, every wind of **d**
1 Tim 1:10, contrary to sound **d**
4:6, and of good **d**
4:13, to exhortation, to **d**
4:16, and unto the **d**
2 Tim 3:10, fully known my **d**
3:16, profitable for **d**
4:2, all longsuffering and **d**
Titus 1:9, by sound **d**
2:1, become sound **d**
2:10, adorn the **d** of God
Heb 6:1, principles of the **d**
6:2, Of the **d** of baptisms
13:9, and strange **d**
2 John 9, abideth in the **d**
See Deut 32:2; Job 11:4

DOING Ex 15:11, **d** wonders
Ps 9:11, the people his **d**
66:5, terrible in his **d**
77:12, and talk of thy **d**
118:23, This is the Lord's **d**
Is 12:4, declare his **d**
Mic 2:7, are these his **d**
Matt 24:46, shall find so **d**
Acts 10:38, went about **d** good
Rom 2:7, continuance in well **d**
2 Cor 8:11, perform the **d** of it
Gal 6:9, not be weary in well **d**
Eph 6:6, **d** will of God
2 Thess 3:13, brethren, in well **d**
1 Pet 2:15, with well **d**
3:17, suffer for well **d**
4:19, to him in well **d**
See Lev 18:3; Prov 20:11

DOMINION Gen 1:26, let them have **d**
Num 24:19, shall have **d**
Ps 8:6, **d** over the works
19:13, let them not have **d**
72:8, He shall have **d**
119:133, have **d** over me
Dan 4:34, **d** is an everlasting
Zech 9:10, his **d** shall be from sea
Matt 20:25, Gentiles exercise **d**
Rom 6:9, death hath no more **d**
6:14, sin shall not have **d**
7:1, law hath **d** over a man
2 Cor 1:24, that we have **d**

Eph 1:21, and **d**, and every name
Col 1:16, they be thrones or **d**
See Dan 6:26; Jude 25; Rev 1:6

DOOR Gen 4:7, sin lieth at the **d**
Ex 12:7, on the upper **d** post
Ps 24:7, ye everlasting **d**
78:23, opened the **d** of heaven
141:3, the **d** of my lips
Eccl 12:4, **d** shall be shut
Hos 2:15, for a **d** of hope
Mal 1:10, shut the **d** for nought
John 10:1, by the **d**
10:2, the **d** is the shepherd
10:7, 9, I am the **d**
Acts 5:9, at the **d**
14:27, opened the **d** of faith
1 Cor 16:9, a great **d**
2 Cor 2:12, a **d** was opened
Col 4:3, open unto us a **d**
James 5:9, standeth before the **d**
Rev 3:8, thee an open **d**
3:20, I stand at the **d**
4:1, behold, a **d** was opened
See Ex 21:6; Acts 5:19; 16:26

DOUBLE Ex 22:4, he shall restore **d**
22:7, let him pay **d**
2 Kin 2:9, a **d** portion
1 Chr 12:33, not of **d** heart
Ps 12:2, and with a **d** heart
1 Tim 3:8, deacons not **d** tongued
5:17, worthy of **d** honour
James 1:8, a **d** minded man
See Gen 41:32; Is 61:7

DOUBT Ps 126:6, shall **d** come again
Dan 5:12, and dissolving of **d**
Matt 14:31, didst thou **d**
21:21, and **d** not
Mark 11:23, shall not **d**
Luke 11:20, no **d** the kingdom
John 10:24, thou make us to **d**
Rom 14:23, he that **d** is damned
Gal 4:20, I stand in **d** of you
1 Tim 2:8, without wrath and **d**
1 John 2:19, would no **d**
See Luke 12:29; Acts 2:12

DOVE Ps 55:6, wings like a **d**
Matt 3:16, descending like a **d**
Matt 10:16, and harmless as **d**

DRAGON Deut 32:33, the poison of **d**
Ps 91:13, the **d** shalt
Rev 20:2, laid hold on the **d**
See Rev 12:3; 13:2, 11; 16:13

DRAW Ps 28:3, **D** me not away
Is 5:18, **d** iniquity with cords
Luke 21:28, redemption **d** nigh
John 6:44, except the Father **d** him
12:32, will **d** all men unto me
Heb 10:22, **d** near with
10:38, but if any man **d** back
10:39, them who **d** back
James 1:14, when he is **d** away
See Acts 11:10; 20:30; Heb 7:19

DREAM Job 20:8, shall fly away as a **d**
33:15, In a **d**, in a vision
Ps 73:20, As a **d** when one
126:1, were like them that **d**
Eccl 5:3, a **d** cometh
Jer 23:28, prophet that hath a **d**
Joel 2:28, old men shall **d** dreams
Jude 8, filthy **d** defile
See Job 7:14; Is 29:8; Jer 27:9

DRESS (*v.*) Gen 2:15, of Eden to **d** it and to keep it
See Ex 30:7; Luke 13:7; Heb 6:7

DRINK (*n.*) Lev 10:9, Do not drink wine nor strong **d**
Num 6:3, wine and strong **d**
Deut 14:26, or for strong **d**
29:6, wine or strong **d**
Prov 20:1, strong **d** is raging

31:6, Give strong **d** unto him
Is 24:9, **d** shall be bitter
28:7, erred through strong **d**
Mic 2:11, of strong **d**
Matt 25:35, ye gave me **d**
John 6:55, my blood is **d** indeed
1 Cor 10:4, same spiritual **d**
Col 2:16, in meat or in **d**
See Gen 21:19; Is 5:11, 22
DRINK (*v.*) Ps 36:8, **d** of the river
60:3, **d** the wine
69:21, vinegar to **d**
80:5, givest them tears to **d**
Song 5:1, **d** yea, **d** abundantly
Amos 2:8, **d** the wine
Zech 9:15, they shall **d**
Matt 10:42, shall give to **d**
20:22, to **d** of the cup
26:27, **D** ye all of it
26:29, day when I **d** it new
26:42, except I **d** it
27:34, vinegar to **d** mingled
Mark 9:41, water to **d**
10:38, can ye **d** of the cup
14:25, I **d** it new
16:18, **d** any deadly thing
Luke 22:18, will not **d** of the
John 4:10, Give me to **d**
7:37, come unto me, and **d**
18:11, shall I not **d** it
Rom 14:21, nor to **d** wine
1 Cor 10:4, did all **d** the same
11:25, as oft as ye **d** it
12:13, to **d** into one Spirit
See Mark 2:16; Luke 7:33; 10:7
DRUNK 2 Sam 11:13, and he made
   him **d**
1 Kin 20:16, himself **d**
Job 12:25, stagger like a **d** man
Jer 23:9, I am like a **d** man
Lam 5:4, We have **d** our water
Hab 2:15, makest him **d** also
Matt 24:49, drink with the **d**
Luke 12:45, and to be **d**
Acts 2:15, these are not **d**
1 Cor 11:21, another is **d**
1 Thess 5:7, **d** in the night
See Eph 5:18; Rev 17:6
DRUNKARD Deut 21:20, he is a
   glutton, and a **d**
Prov 23:21, **d** and the glutton
26:9, hand of a **d**
1 Cor 6:10, nor **d**, nor revilers
See Ps 69:12; Is 24:20; Joel 1:5
DRUNKENNESS Deut 29:19, to
   add **d** to thirst
Eccl 10:17, and not for **d**
Ezek 23:33, filled with **d**
See Luke 21:34; Rom 13:13
DUMB Ex 4:11, who maketh the **d**
Is 35:6, the tongue of the **d**
53:7, as a sheep . . . is **d**
56:10, they are all **d** dogs
Matt 9:32, a **d** man possessed
12:22, blind, and **d**
15:30, blind, **d**, maimed
Mark 7:37, the **d** to speak
9:17, hath a **d** spirit
Acts 8:32, **d** before his shearer
See Ps 39:2; Luke 1:20; 11:14
DUST Gen 2:7, Lord God formed
   man of the **d**
3:14, **d** shalt thou eat
3:19, **d** thou art
18:27, am but **d** and ashes
Job 10:9, into **d** again
34:15, turn again unto **d**
42:6, repent in **d** and ashes
Ps 30:9, the **d** praise thee
103:14, that we are **d**
104:29, return to their **d**
Eccl 3:20, all are of the **d**
12:7, **d** return to the earth

Is 40:12, comprehended the **d**
65:25, **d** shall be bitter
Mic 7:17, lick the **d**
Matt 10:14, **d** of your feet
Mark 6:11, shake off the **d**
Luke 9:5, shake off the very **d**
10:11, **d** of your city
Acts 22:23, threw **d** into
See Ex 8:16; Num 23:10
DUTY Eccl 12:13, for this is the
   whole **d** of man
Luke 17:10, our **d** to do
Rom 15:27, their **d** is also
See Ex 21:10; 2 Chr 8:14
DWELL Deut 12:11, cause his name
   to **d** there
1 Sam 4:4, **d** between the
Ps 23:6, will **d** in the house
37:3, thou **d** in the land
84:10, than to **d** in tents
132:14, here will I **d**
133:1, brethren to **d** together
Is 33:14, shall **d** with the
33:16, He shall **d** on high
57:15, I **d** in the high
John 6:56, **d** in me
14:10, Father that **d** in me
14:17, for he **d** with you
Rom 7:17, but sin that **d** in me
Eph 3:17, **d** in your hearts
Col 1:19, all fullness **d**
3:16, word of Christ **d**
1 Tim 6:16, **d** in the light
2 Pet 3:13, **d** righteousness
1 John 3:17, how **d** the love
4:12, God **d** in us
See 2 Cor 6:16; James 4:5

E

EAGLE Ex 19:4, how I bare you on
   e wings
2 Sam 1:23, were swifter than **e**
Ps 103:5, renewed like the **e**
Is 40:31, with wings as **e**
Ezek 1:10, face of an **e**
17:3, A great **e**
Matt 24:28, the **e** be gathered
Rev 4:7, like a flying **e**
See Dan 4:33; Rev 12:14
EAR Ps 18:6, even into his **e**
34:15, his **e** are open
45:10, and incline thine **e**
58:4, stoppeth her **e**
78:1, give **e**, O my people
135:17, They have **e**
Prov 15:31, The **e** that heareth
17:4, liar giveth **e**
18:15, **e** of the wise
20:12, hearing **e**
21:13, stoppeth his **e**
22:17, bow down thine **e**
23:9, **e** of a fool
25:12, upon an obedient **e**
26:17, a dog by the **e**
Eccl 1:8, nor the **e** filled
Is 6:10, and make their **e** heavy
48:8, time that thine **e**
50:4, wakeneth my **e** to hear
55:3, incline your **e**
59:1, nor his **e** heavy
Jer 9:20, **e** receive the word
Amos 3:12, a piece of an **e**
Matt 13:15, their **e** are dull
13:16, and your **e**
Mark 7:33, fingers into his **e**
8:18, having **e**, hear ye not
Acts 7:51, in heart and **e**
17:20, things to our **e**
28:27, and their **e** are dull
1 Cor 2:9, nor **e** heard
12:16, And if the **e** shall say
2 Tim 4:3, having itching **e**

James 5:4, **e** of the Lord
1 Pet 3:12, his **e** are open
See Matt 11:15; Mark 4:9
EARLY Ps 46:5, and that right **e**
63:1, **e** will I seek thee
90:14, satisfy us **e**
Prov 1:28, they shall seek me **e**
8:17, **e** shall find me
Song 7:12, get up **e**
Hos 6:4, as the **e** dew
13:3, **e** dew that passeth away
James 5:7, **e** and latter rain
See Judg 7:3; Luke 24:22
EARNEST Rom 8:19, the **e**
   expectation
1 Cor 12:31, covet **e** the best
2 Cor 1:22, the **e** of the Spirit
5:5, given unto us the **e**
Eph 1:14, **e** of our inheritance
See Heb 2:1; James 5:17
EARTH Gen 8:22, While the **e**
   remaineth
10:25, was the **e** divided
10:25, Judge of all the **e**
Num 14:21, **e** shall be filled
16:30, the **e** open her mouth
Josh 3:11, Lord of all the **e**
23:14, way of all the **e**
Job 7:1, man upon **e**
9:24, **e** is given
38:4, foundations of the **e**
Ps 25:13, inherit the **e**
33:5, the **e** is full
34:16, them from the **e**
37:9, inherit the **e**
37:11, shall inherit the **e**
41:2, blessed upon the **e**
46:2, though **e** be removed
46:6, the **e** melted
48:2, joy of the whole **e**
60:2, made the **e** to tremble
63:9, lower parts of the **e**
68:8, The **e** shook
71:20, depths of the **e**
72:6, that water the **e**
73:25, none upon **e** that
90:2, formed the **e**
97:1, let the **e** rejoice
102:25, foundation of the **e**
104:13, the **e** is satisfied
104:24, the **e** is full
115:16, **e** hath he given
119:19, a stranger in the **e**
148:13, the **e** and heaven
Prov 3:19, founded the **e**
8:23, or ever the **e** was
8:29, foundations of the **e**
11:31, recompensed in the **e**
30:14, poor from off the **e**
Eccl 1:4, the **e** abideth for ever
3:21, downward to the **e**
12:7, return to the **e**
Is 11:9, the **e** shall be full
13:13, the **e** shall remove
14:16, the **e** to tremble
24:1, maketh the **e** empty
24:19, **e** is clean dissolved
40:22, circle of the **e**
40:28, the ends of the **e**
48:13, foundation of the **e**
49:13, be joyful, O **e**
51:6, the **e** shall wax old
66:1, the **e** is my footstool
66:8, Shall the **e** be made
Nah 1:5, and the **e** is burned
Hab 2:14, **e** shall be filled
3:3, the **e** was full
Zech 4:10, through the whole **e**
6:5, Lord of all the **e**
Mal 4:6, come and smite the **e**
Matt 5:5, meek . . . inherit the **e**
6:19, treasures upon **e**
9:6, hath power on **e**

10:34, to send peace on e
16:19, shalt bind on e
18:19, shall agree on e
23:9, father upon the e
Luke 2:14, on e peace
23:44, over all the e
John 3:12, told you e things
3:31, of the e is earthly
12:32, lifted up from the e
17:4, glorified thee on the e
Acts 8:33, taken from the e
Rom 10:18, into all the e
1 Cor 15:47, man of the e is e
15:48, As is the e
15:49, the image of the e
2 Cor 4:7, in e vessels
Col 3:2, things on the e
Phil 3:19, who mind e things
Heb 6:7, e which drinketh
8:4, if he were on e
11:13, pilgrims on the e
12:25, that spake on e
12:26, voice then shook the e
James 3:15, but is e, sensual
5:5, pleasure on the e
5:7, precious fruit of the e
5:18, e brought forth
2 Pet 3:10, the e also
Rev 5:10, shall reign on the e
7:3, Hurt not the e
18:1, the e was lightened
20:11, the e and heaven
21:1, heaven and a new e
See Gen 1:11; Ex 9:29
EARTHQUAKE 1 Kin 19:11, and
  after the wind an e
Is 29:6, e, and great noise
Amos 1:1, years before the e
Zech 14:5, the e in the days
Matt 24:7, e, in divers places
27:54, saw the e
Acts 16:26, there was a great e
Rev 8:5, lightnings, and an e
EAT Gen 2:17, the day that thou
  e thereof
9:4, shall ye not e
Lev 19:26, not e anything
Deut 12:16, not e the blood
Ps 22:26, meek shall e
69:9, hath e me up
102:9, e ashes like bread
Prov 1:31, e of the fruit
13:25, e to the satisfying
18:21, e the fruit
23:1, e with a ruler
24:13, e thou honey
25:27, not good to e
7:15, honey shall he e
11:7, the lion shall e straw
55:1, come ye, buy, and e
65:13, my servants shall e
65:25, lion shall e straw
Mark 2:16, e with publicans
7:28, dogs under the table e
Luke 10:8, e such things
12:22, what ye shall e
15:23, let us e, and be merry
John 6:52, his flesh to e
Rom 14:2, may e all things
14:6, e, e to the Lord
14:20, who e with offence
14:21, neither to e flesh
1 Cor 5:11, not to e
8:7, e it as a thing offered
8:8, neither, if we e
8:13, I will e no flesh
9:4, Have we not power to e
10:3, all e the same
10:27, set before you, e
10:31, Whether therefore ye e
11:29, that e and drinketh
2 Thess 3:10, should he e
Heb 13:10, no right to e

Rev 2:7, e of the tree of life
2:17, e of the hidden manna
19:18, e the flesh of kings
See Prov 31:27; Is 1:19; 65:4
EDIFY Rom 14:19, wherewith one
  may e another
15:2, his good to e
1 Cor 8:1, charity e
14:3, speaketh unto men to e
14:4, he that prophesieth e
10:23, all things e not
Eph 4:12, for the e of the body
See 2 Cor 10:8; 13:10; 1 Tim 1:4
EFFEMINATE 1 Cor 6:9,
  adulterers, nor e
ELDER 1 Sam 15:30, before the e of
  my people
Prov 31:23, among the e of the
Matt 15:2, the tradition of the e
Mark 7:3, the tradition of the e
1 Tim 5:17, Let the e that rule
Titus 1:5, ordain e in every
Heb 11:2, the e obtained
James 5:14, the e of the church
1 Pet 5:1, who am also an e
5:5, unto the e
See John 8:9; 1 Tim 5:2; 3 John 1
ELECT Is 42:1, mine e in whom
45:4, mine e I have
65:9, mine e shall inherit it
65:22, mine e shall long enjoy
Matt 24:22, for the e sake
24:24, deceived the very e
24:31, gather together his e
Mark 13:20, for the e sake
13:22, even the e
Luke 18:7, God avenge his own e
Rom 8:33, the charge of God's e
Col 3:12, as the e of God
1 Tim 5:21, and the e angels
1 Pet 1:2, E according to the
2:6, a chief corner stone, e
See 2 Tim 2:10; Titus 1:1; 2 John 13
ELECTION Rom 9:11, of God
  according to e
11:5, to the e of grace
1 Thess 1:4, your e of God
2 Pet 1:10, calling and e sure
ELEMENTS Gal 4:3, bondage
  under the e
4:9, the weak and beggarly e
2 Pet 3:10, the e shall melt
END Gen 6:13, The e of all flesh is
  come
Deut 8:16, at thy latter e
32:29, consider their latter e
Job 6:11, what is mine e
8:7, thy latter e should
Ps 7:9, the wicked come to an e
9:6, come to a perpetual e
37:37, the e of that man
102:27, years shall have no e
119:96, an e of all
Prov 14:12, the e thereof are
17:24, in the e of the earth
19:20, be wise in thy latter e
Eccl 3:11, beginning to the e
4:8, no e of all his labour
4:16, no e of all the people
7:2, that is the e of all
7:8, Better is the e of a
10:13, the e of his talk
Is 9:7, there shall be no e
46:10, Declaring the e from
Jer 5:31, will ye do in the e
Lam 1:9, not her last e
4:18, our e is near
Dan 8:17, time of the e shall
12:8, what shall be the e of
Matt 10:22, endureth to the e
13:39, harvest is the e of
24:3, the e of the world
24:13, shall endure unto the e

24:31, from one e of heaven to
Mark 3:26, but hath an e
13:7, but the e shall not
Luke 1:33, there shall be no e
John 13:1, them unto the e
18:37, To this e was I born
Rom 6:22, the e everlasting life
10:4, Christ is the e of the
1 Cor 10:11, upon whom the e of
15:24, Then cometh the e
Phil 3:19, Whose e is
1 Tim 1:5, the e of the
Heb 6:8, whose e is to be
9:26, e of the world hath
James 5:11, the e of the Lord
1 Pet 1:9, the e of your faith
1:13, and hope to the e
4:7, e of all things
Rev 2:26, my works unto the e
21:6, beginning and the e
See Ps 19:6; Is 45:22; Jer 4:27
ENDURE Job 8:15, but it shall not e
Ps 9:7, But the Lord shall e
19:9, e for ever
30:5, weeping may e for a
52:1, goodness of God e
72:17, His name shall e
100:5, his truth e to all
102:12, thou, O Lord, shalt e
104:31, the Lord shall e for ever
106:1, his mercy e for ever
111:3, his righteousness e
119:160, judgments e for ever
135:13, Thy name, O Lord, e
138:8, thy mercy, O Lord, e
145:13, and thy dominion e
Prov 27:24, and doth the crown e
Jer 33:11, for his mercy e
Matt 10:22, that e to the end
24:13, But he that shall e
Mark 4:17, so e but for a time
John 6:27, e unto everlasting
Rom 9:22, e with much
1 Cor 13:7, e all things
2 Tim 2:3, e hardness
4:3, they will not e sound
4:5, e afflictions
Heb 10:34, a better and e substance
12:7, If ye e chastening
James 1:12, the man that e
5:11, them happy which e
1 Pet 1:25, of the Lord e for ever
2:19, toward God e grief
See Heb 10:32; 11:27; 12:2, 3
ENEMY Ex 23:22, I will be an e
  unto thine e
Judg 5:31, all thine e perish
Ps 8:2, mightest still the e
23:5, the presence of mine e
38:19, mine e are lively
119:98, wiser than mine e
139:22, I count them mine e
Prov 16:7, maketh even his e
24:17, when thine e falleth
25:21, If thine e be hungry
27:6, kisses of an e
Is 9:11, and join his e
63:10, to be their e
Jer 15:11, will cause the e
30:14, the wound of an e
Mic 7:6, a man's e are the men
Matt 5:43, and hate thine e
5:44, Love your e, bless
13:25, his e came and sowed
13:28, An e hath done this
13:39, The e that sowed
Luke 6:27, Love your e
19:43, thine e shall cast
Acts 13:10, e of all righteousness
Rom 5:10, if when we were e
11:28, they are e for your
12:20, if thine e hunger
Gal 4:16, therefore become your e

Phil 3:18, the **e** of the cross
Col 1:21, were **e** in your mind
2 Thess 3:15, not as an **e**
James 4:4, is the **e** of God
See Ps 110:1; Is 62:8; Jer 15:14
ENJOY Eccl 2:1, therefore **e** pleasure
2:24, make his soul **e** good
5:18, and to **e** the good
1 Tim 6:17, all things to **e**
See Num 36:8; Is 65:22
ENMITY Rom 8:7, the carnal mind is **e** against God
Eph 2:15, in his flesh the **e**
2:16, having slain the **e**
James 4:4, the world is **e**
See Gen 3:15; Num 35:21
ENTER Ps 100:4, **E** into his gates with thanksgiving
Is 26:2, may **e** in
Matt 6:6, **e** into thy closet
7:13, **E** ye in
10:11, town ye shall **e**
18:8, thee to **e** into life
19:17, if thou wilt **e** into
25:21, **e** thou into the joy
Mark 5:12, that we may **e** into
9:43, for thee to **e** into
14:38, **e** into temptation
Luke 8:32, to **e** into them
9:34, **e** into the cloud
10:8, whatsoever city ye **e**
13:24, Strive to **e** in
24:26, **e** into his glory
John 3:4, can he **e** the second
4:38, ye are **e** into
10:1, **e** not by the door
10:2, But he that **e**
Rom 5:12, sin **e** into the world
1 Cor 2:9, **e** into the heart
Heb 3:11, **e** into my rest
3:18, that they should not **e**
4:10, he that is **e** into
6:20, forerunner is for us **e**
9:12, Christ is not **e**
See Ps 143:2; Matt 15:17
ENTICE Prov 1:10, if sinners **e** thee
1 Cor 2:4, with **e** words
Col 2:4, with **e** words
See Job 31:27; Prov 16:29
ENTREAT Ruth 1:16, **E** me not to leave
1 Tim 5:1, **e** him as a father
James 3:17, easy to be **e**
See Prov 18:23; Luke 15:28
ENVY Job 5:2, **e** slayeth the silly one
Prov 3:31, **E** thou not
23:17, Let not thine heart **e**
24:1, Be thou not **e**
Eccl 4:4, **e** of his neighbour
Matt 27:18, that for **e** they
Mark 15:10, delivered him for **e**
Acts 7:9, moved with **e**
13:45, were filled with **e**
Rom 1:29, full of **e**, murder
13:13, not in strife and **e**
1 Cor 3:3, **e**, and strife
13:4, charity **e** not
2 Cor 12:20, **e**, wraths, strifes
Gal 5:21, **E**, murders
5:26, **e** one another
Phil 1:15, Christ even of **e**
1 Tim 6:4, whereof cometh **e**
Titus 3:3, in malice and **e**
James 4:5, lusteth to **e**
See Ps 106:16; Ezek 31:9
EPHOD Ex 28:6, they shall make the **e** of gold
39:2, he made the **e** of gold
Judg 8:27, And Gideon made an **e**
17:5, an **e**, and teraphim
EQUAL Ps 17:2, behold the things

that are **e**
Prov 26:7, lame are not **e**
Is 40:25, or shall I be **e**
Matt 20:12, hast made them **e**
Luke 20:36, **e** unto the angels
John 5:18, **e** with God
Phil 2:6, not robbery to be **e**
Col 4:1, just and **e**
See Ex 36:22; 2 Cor 8:14
ERR Ps 95:10, people that do **e** in their heart
119:21, do **e** from thy
Is 3:12, cause thee to **e**
9:16, cause them to **e**
28:7, they **e** in vision
35:8, shall not **e**
Matt 22:29, do **e**, not knowing
Mark 12:24, ye not therefore **e**
1 Tim 6:10, have **e** from
6:21, have **e** concerning
James 1:16, Do not **e**
5:19, if any of you do **e**
See Is 29:24; Ezek 45:20
ERROR Ps 19:12, Who can understand his **e**
Eccl 5:6, it was an **e**
10:5, an **e** which proceedeth
Matt 27:64, so the last **e**
James 5:20, **e** of his way
2 Pet 3:17, **e** of the wicked
1 John 4:6, the spirit of **e**
See Job 19:4; Rom 1:27; Heb 9:7
ESCAPE Job 11:20, they shall not **e**
19:20, **e** with the skin
Prov 19:5, shall not **e**
Eccl 7:26, pleaseth God shall **e**
Is 20:6, and how shall we **e**
Matt 23:33, **e** the damnation
Luke 21:36, worthy to **e** all
John 10:39, he **e** out of their
Acts 27:44, they **e** all safe
28:4, **e** the sea
Heb 2:3, How shall we **e**
12:25, For if they **e**
2 Pet 1:4, **e** the corruption
2:20, the pollutions
See Ps 124:7; 1 Cor 10:13
ESCHEW Job 1:1; 2:3, one that feared God, and **e** evil
1 Pet 3:11, Let him **e** evil
ESTABLISH Gen 6:18, with thee will I **e** my covenant
Prov 12:19, shall be **e** for ever
16:12, **e** by righteousness
20:18, Every purpose is **e**
Jer 10:12, hath **e** the world
Rom 3:31, yea, we **e** the law
10:3, to **e** their own
1 Thess 3:2, to **e** you
See Amos 5:15; Hab 2:12
ETERNAL Deut 33:27, The **e** God is thy refuge
Is 60:15, an **e** excellency
Matt 19:16, may have **e** life
25:46, righteous into life **e**
Mark 3:29, is in danger of **e**
10:17, inherit **e** life
John 3:15, but have **e** life
4:36, unto life **e**
5:39, ye have **e** life
5:68, of **e** life
10:28, give unto them **e** life
17:2, give **e** life to as many
Acts 13:48, ordained to **e** life
Rom 2:7, immortality, **e** life
5:21, unto **e** life
6:23, gift of God is **e** life
2 Cor 4:17, **e** weight of glory
5:1, **e** in the heavens
Eph 3:11, to the **e** purpose
1 Tim 6:12, lay hold on **e** life
Titus 1:2, In hope of **e** life
3:7, the hope of **e** life

Heb 5:9, author of **e** salvation
6:2, and of **e** judgment
9:15, of **e** inheritance
1 Pet 5:10, unto his **e** glory
1 John 1:2, **e** life
2:25, even **e** life
3:15, no murderer hath **e** life
5:11, given to us **e** life
Jude 7, vengeance of **e** fire
See Rom 1:20; 1 Tim 1:17
ETERNITY Is 57:15, lofty One that inhabiteth **e**
EUNUCHS Is 56:4, thus saith the Lord unto the **e**
Matt 19:12, there are some **e**
Acts 8:27, **e** of great authority
See Is 56:3
EVANGELIST Acts 21:8, entered the house of Philip the **e**
Eph 4:11, and some, **e**
2 Tim 4:5, the work of an **e**
EVER Lev 6:13, **e** be burning upon the altar
Job 4:7, who **e** perished
Ps 37:26, He is **e** merciful
48:14, God forever and **e**
51:3, my sin is **e** before me
1 Thess 4:17, so shall we be **e**
2 Tim 3:7, **E** learning
Heb 7:25, he **e** liveth
See Matt 24:21; Luke 15:31
EVERLASTING Ex 40:15, an **e** priesthood
Deut 33:27, the **e** arms
Ps 90:2, even from **e** to **e**
139:24, lead me in the way **e**
Prov 8:23, I was set up from **e**
10:25, an **e** foundation
Is 9:6, The **e** Father
26:4, Jehovah is **e** strength
33:14, dwell with **e** burnings
35:10, and **e** joy
45:17, an **e** salvation
51:11, **e** joy shall be
54:8, with **e** kindness
55:13, an **e** sign
56:5, give them an **e** name
60:19, an **e** light
61:7, **e** joy shall
63:12, an **e** name
Jer 31:3, with an **e** love
Dan 12:2, some to **e** life
Hab 1:12, Art thou not from **e**
Matt 18:8, cast into **e** fire
19:29, shall inherit **e** life
25:41, into **e** fire
25:46, into **e** punishment
Luke 16:9, into **e** habitations
18:30, to come life **e**
John 3:16, but have **e** life
4:14, up into **e** life
6:27, endureth unto **e** life
6:40, on him, may have **e** life
12:50, commandment is life **e**
Acts 13:46, unworthy of **e** life
Rom 6:22, the end **e** life
Gal 6:8, reap life **e**
2 Thess 1:9, with **e** destruction
2:16, **e** consolation
Jude 6, in **e** chains
Rev 14:6, having the **e** gospel
See Dan 4:3; 7:27; 2 Pet 1:11
EVERMORE 1 Thess 5:16, Rejoice **e**
See 2 Kin 17:37; Ps 77:8; 106:31
EVERY Gen 6:5, **e** imagination
Ps 119:101, from **e** evil way
Prov 20:3, **e** fool will be meddling
30:5, **E** word of God is pure
Matt 4:4, but by **e** word
Luke 19:26, to **e** one which hath
Rom 14:11, **e** knee shall bow
Eph 1:21, **e** name that is named

Phil 2:9, above **e** name
2 Tim 2:19, **e** one that nameth
  2:21, unto **e** good work
Heb 12:1, lay aside **e** weight
James 1:17, **E** good gift
1 John 4:1, not **e** spirit
  4:7, **e** one that loveth
See Gen 27:29; Acts 2:38; 17:27
EVIDENCE Heb 11:1, the **e** of
  things
EVIL Gen 6:5, heart was only **e**
  continually
Deut 28:54, **e** toward his brother
Ps 34:14, Depart from **e**
  35:12, rewarded me **e**
Prov 3:7, depart from **e**
  14:19, **e** bow before the good
  15:3, beholding the **e**
  17:13, Whoso rewardeth **e**
Is 1:4, a seed of **e**
  5:20, that call **e** good
  7:15, to refuse the **e**
Matt 5:11, all manner of **e**
  6:34, day is the **e**
  7:11, If ye then, being **e**
  12:39, An **e** and adulterous
Mark 9:39, lightly speak **e**
Luke 6:22, your name as **e**
  6:35, and to the **e**
John 3:19, deeds were **e**
  18:23, If I have spoken **e**
Acts 23:5, not speak **e**
Rom 7:19, the **e** which I would
  12:9, Abhor that which is **e**
  12:21, overcome **e** with good
1 Thess 5:22, appearance of **e**
1 Tim 6:10, the root of all **e**
2 Tim 4:18, every **e** work
Titus 3:2, speak **e** of no man
James 3:16, every **e** work
1 Pet 3:9, rendering **e** for **e**
See Prov 13:21; Is 45:7
EXALT 1 Chr 29:11, **e** as head
  above all
Ps 12:8, vilest men are **e**
  34:3, let us **e** his name
  92:10, my horn shalt thou **e**
  97:9, **e** far above all gods
Prov 4:8, **E** her, and she shall
  14:34, Righteousness **e**
Is 2:2, **e** above the hills
  40:4, Every valley shall be **e**
Ezek 21:26, **e** him that is low
Mic 4:1, and it shall be **e**
Matt 11:23, which art **e**
Luke 14:11, **e** himself
2 Cor 11:20, if a man **e** himself
Phil 2:9, hath highly **e** him
2 Thess 2:4, **e** himself above
1 Pet 5:6, that he may **e** you
See Luke 1:52; James 1:9
EXAMINE Ps 26:2, **E** me, O Lord,
  and prove me
Acts 4:9, If we this day be **e**
  22:24, **e** by scourging
1 Cor 11:28, a man **e** himself
2 Cor 13:5, **E** yourselves
See Ezra 10:16; Acts 24:8; 25:26
EXAMPLE John 13:15, I have given
  you an **e**
1 Cor 10:6, things were our **e**
Phil 3:17, for an **e**
2 Thess 3:9, ourselves an **e**
1 Tim 4:12, be thou an **e**
1 Pet 2:21, leaving us an **e**
Jude 7, an **e** suffering the
See Matt 1:19; 1 Cor 10:6
EXCEEDING Ps 21:6, **e** glad with
  43:4, God my **e** joy
  119:96, commandment is **e**
Prov 30:24, they are **e** wise
Matt 2:10, with **e** great joy
  4:8, an **e** high mountain

  5:12, Rejoice, and be **e** glad
  26:38, soul is **e** sorrowful
Mark 9:3, **e** white as snow
2 Cor 4:17, a far more **e**
  7:4, am **e** joyful
Gal 1:14, **e** zealous
Eph 1:19, the **e** greatness
  2:7, **e** riches of his grace
  3:20, able to do **e** abundantly
2 Thess 1:3, faith groweth **e**
2 Pet 1:4, **e** great and precious
Jude 24, with **e** joy
See 1 Sam 26:21; Jon 3:3
EXCELLENT Job 37:23, he is **e** in
  power, and in judgment
Ps 8:1, 9, how **e** is thy name
Prov 8:6, speak of **e** things
  17:27, of an **e** spirit
  22:20, **e** things
Is 12:5, he hath done **e** things
Rom 2:18, more **e** being
1 Cor 12:31, a more **e** way
See Song 5:15; Luke 1:3; Heb 1:4
EXCEPT Matt 18:3, **E** ye be
  converted
Luke 13:3, **e** ye repent
John 3:3, **E** a man be born again
Rom 10:15, **e** they be sent
1 Cor 15:36, **e** it die
See Rom 7:7; 1 Cor 14:5; 15:27
EXCHANGE Matt 16:26, in **e** for his
  soul
EXHORT Rom 12:8, he that **e**
1 Tim 6:2, teach and **e**
Titus 1:9, **e** and to convince
  2:15, **e**, and rebuke
Heb 3:13, **e** one another daily
  10:25, but **e** one another
See 2 Cor 9:5; Titus 2:6, 9
EXPECTATION Ps 9:18, the **e** of
  the poor shall not perish
  62:5, my **e** is from him
Prov 10:28, the **e** of the wicked
  11:7, his **e** shall perish
Rom 8:19, the earnest **e**
Phil 1:20, my earnest **e**
See Jer 29:11; Acts 3:5
EXPEDIENT John 11:50, Nor
  consider that it is **e** for us
  16:7, It is **e** for you
  18:14, it was **e** that one man
1 Cor 6:12, things are not **e**
EXPRESS Heb 1:3, and the **e** image
  of his person
EXPRESSLY 1 Tim 4:1, Spirit
  speaketh **e**
EXTOL Ps 30:1, I will **e** thee
  68:4, **e** him that rideth
  145:1, **e** thee, my God
See Ps 66:17; Is 52:13; Dan 4:37
EYE Gen 3:6, pleasant to the **e**
Num 10:31, to us instead of **e**
Deut 3:27, lift up thine **e**
  12:8, right in his own **e**
  16:19, doth blind the **e**
  32:10, apple of his **e**
  34:7, his **e** was not dim
Judg 17:6, right in his own **e**
2 Chr 6:20, **e** may be open
  16:9, the **e** of the Lord
  34:28, **e** see all the evil
Job 7:8, thine **e** are upon me
  11:20, the **e** of the wicked
  15:12, what do thy **e** wink at
  19:27, mine **e** shall behold
  29:15, I was **e** to the blind
Ps 11:4, his **e** behold
  19:8, enlightening the **e**
  33:18, the **e** of the Lord
  36:1, before his **e**
  119:82, Mine **e** fail
  132:4, sleep to mine **e**
Prov 10:26, as smoke to the **e**

  20:12, the seeing **e**
  23:29, redness of **e**
  27:20, the **e** of man
  30:17, The **e** that mocketh
Eccl 1:8, **e** is not satisfied
  2:14, wise man's **e**
  6:9, sight of the **e**
  11:7, for the **e** to behold
Is 1:15, hide mine **e** from you
  29:10, hath closed your **e**
  33:17, Thine **e** shall see
  42:7, To open the blind **e**
  64:4, neither hath the **e**
Jer 5:21, which have **e**
  9:1, mine **e** a fountain
  13:17, mine **e** shall weep
Lam 2:11, Mine **e** do fail
  2:18, apple of thine **e**
Ezek 12:2, which have **e**
  24:16, desire of thine **e**
Hab 1:13, of purer **e** than
Zech 4:10, **e** of the Lord
Matt 5:29, if thy right **e**
Mark 8:18, Having **e**, see ye not
Luke 24:16, their **e** were holden
John 11:37, which opened the **e**
1 Cor 2:9, **E** hath not seen
  15:52, twinkling of an **e**
Gal 4:15, your own **e**
Eph 1:18, The **e** of your
1 Pet 3:12, **e** of the Lord
2 Pet 1:16, **e** of his majesty
1 John 2:16, the lust of the **e**
See Ezra 5:5; Matt 20:33
EYESERVICE Eph 6:6, Not with
  e, as menpleasers

F

FABLES 1 Tim 1:4, Neither give
  heed to **f**
  4:7, profane and old wives' **f**
2 Tim 4:4, turned unto **f**
Titus 1:14, to Jewish **f**
2 Pet 1:16, cunningly devised **f**
FACE Gen 4:14, from thy **f**
  32:30, seen God **f** to **f**
Ex 33:11, unto Moses **f** to **f**
  34:29, skin of his **f** shone
Ezra 9:7, to confusion of **f**
Neh 8:6, **f** to the ground
Job 1:11, curse thee to thy **f**
  4:15, passed before my **f**
  13:24, hidest thou thy **f**
Ps 13:1, thou hide thy **f**
  17:15, will behold thy **f**
  27:9, Hide not thy **f**
  34:5, **f** were not ashamed
  84:9, of thine anointed
  88:14, why hidest thou thy **f**
  102:2, Hide not thy **f** from me
Prov 27:19, **f** answereth to **f**
Eccl 8:1, his **f** to shine
Is 3:15, **f** of the poor
  50:7, set my **f** like a flint
  59:2, sins have hid his **f**
Jer 2:27, and not their **f**
  5:3, **f** harder than a rock
  30:6, all **f** are turned
Dan 9:7, us confusion of **f**
  10:6, **f** as the appearance
Hos 5:5, testify to his **f**
Matt 17:2, **f** did shine as the sun
  18:10, **f** of my Father
Luke 2:31, before the **f** of all
  9:51, set his **f** to go
  9:53, because his **f**
1 Cor 13:12, but then **f** to **f**
2 Cor 3:13, vail over his **f**
  3:18, all, with open **f**
Gal 1:22, And was unknown by **f**
  2:11, withstood him to the **f**
James 1:23, his natural **f**

Rev 20:11, from whose **f**
See 1 Kin 19:13; Dan 1:10
FADE Is 1:30, shall be as an oak
  whose leaf **f**
24:4, mourneth and **f** away
40:7, the flower **f**
64:6, **f** as a leaf
Jer 8:13, and the leaf shall **f**
James 1:11, rich man **f** away
1 Pet 1:4, that **f** not away
5:4, a crown of glory that **f**
See 2 Sam 22:46; Is 28:1
FAIL Ps 77:8, doth his promise **f**
89:33, my faithfulness to **f**
Eccl 10:3, his wisdom **f** him
12:5, desire shall **f**
Is 15:6, the grass **f**
34:16, of these shall **f**
41:17, tongue **f** for thirst
59:15, truth **f**
Jer 14:6, their eyes did **f**
15:18, as waters that **f**
Lam 3:22, his compassions **f** not
Luke 12:33, heavens that **f** not
22:32, that thy faith **f** not
1 Cor 13:8, Charity never **f**
Heb 1:12, thy years shall not **f**
See Deut 31:6; Ps 40:12; 143:7
FAINT Job 4:5, and thou **f**
107:5, their soul **f** in them
Is 1:5, the whole heart **f**
40:31, walk, and not **f**
Jer 8:18, heart is **f** in me
Lam 1:22, my heart is **f**
Amos 8:13, young men **f**
Luke 18:1, pray, and not to **f**
2 Cor 4:1, we **f** not
Gal 6:9, reap, if we **f** not
Heb 12:3, **f** in your minds
See Deut 20:8; Ps 84:2; 119:81
FAITH Deut 32:20, children in
  whom is no **f**
Matt 6:30, O ye of little **f**
8:10, found so great **f**
9:22, thy **f** hath made
14:31, O thou of little **f**
17:20, **f** as a grain
21:21, If ye have **f**
23:23, judgment, mercy, and **f**
Mark 11:22, have **f** in God
Luke 7:50, They **f** hath saved thee
8:25, Where is your **f**
17:5, Increase our **f**
18:8, **f** on the earth
22:32, that thy **f** fail not
Acts 3:16, the **f** which
6:5, a man full of **f**
11:24, Holy Ghost and of **f**
14:9, had **f** to be healed
14:27, opened the door of **f**
15:9, their hearts by **f**
16:5, established in the **f**
20:21, **f** toward our Lord
26:18, sanctified by **f**
Rom 1:5, for obedience to the **f**
1:17, revealed from **f** to **f**
3:28, justified by **f**
4:5, **f** if counted
4:20, but was strong in **f**
5:2, we have access by **f**
10:8, the word of **f**
10:17, **f** cometh by hearing
12:3, the measure of **f**
14:23, not of **f** is sin
1 Cor 13:2, though I have all **f**
13:13, And now abideth **f**
15:14, your **f** is also vain
16:13, stand fast in the **f**
2 Cor 1:24, dominion over your **f**
4:13, same spirit of **f**
5:7, we walk by **f**
13:5, be in the **f**

Gal 2:16, the **f** of Christ
2:20, **f** of the Son
3:2, by the hearing of **f**
3:12, the law is not of **f**
3:24, justified by **f**
5:6, **f** which worketh by love
6:10, of the household of **f**
Eph 3:12, by the **f** of him
3:17, in your hearts by **f**
4:5, One Lord, one **f**
4:13, in the unity of the **f**
6:16, taking the shield of **f**
Phil 1:27, for the **f**
Col 1:23, continue in the **f**
2:5, stedfastness of your **f**
1 Thess 1:3, your work of **f**
5:8, the breastplate of **f**
2 Thess 1:11, and the work of **f**
3:2, all men have not **f**
1 Tim 1:2, son in the **f**
1:5, of **f** unfeigned
2:15, if they continue in **f**
3:13, great boldness in the **f**
4:1, shall depart from the **f**
5:8, he hath denied the **f**
6:10, erred from the **f**
2 Tim 1:5, the unfeigned **f**
3:8, concerning the **f**
4:7, I have kept the **f**
Heb 4:2, not being mixed with **f**
6:1, of **f** toward God
6:12, through **f** and patience
10:22, in full assurance of **f**
11:1, **f** is the substance
11:6, without **f** it is
11:13, These all died in **f**
11:33, through **f** subdued
12:2, finisher of our **f**
13:7, whose **f** follow
James 1:3, trying of your **f**
1:6, let him ask in **f**
2:14, man say he hath **f**
2:17, **f** if it hath not works
5:15, the prayer of **f**
1 Pet 1:7, trial of your **f**
1:9, the end of your **f**
5:9, stedfast in the **f**
1 John 5:4, even our **f**
Jude 3, contend for the **f**
20, your most holy **f**
Rev 2:13, hast not denied my **f**
13:10, patience and the **f**
14:12, the **f** of Jesus
See Hab 2:4; 1 Tim 4:6
FAITHFUL Ps 89:37, a **f** witness in
  heaven
119:86, commandments are **f**
119:138, righteous and very **f**
Prov 11:13, a **f** spirit
13:17, a **f** ambassador
14:5, A **f** witness
28:20, **f** man shall abound
Jer 42:5, a true and **f** witness
Matt 24:45, **f** and wise servant
25:21, good and **f** servant
Luke 12:42, **f** and wise steward
16:10, **f** also in much
19:17, thou hast been **f**
Acts 16:15, judged me to be **f**
1 Cor 4:2, man be found **f**
4:17, **f** in the Lord
Gal 3:9, blessed with **f** Abraham
Eph 6:21, and **f** minister
Col 1:7, **f** minister in Christ
1 Thess 5:24, **F** is he that
2 Thess 3:3, Lord is **f**
1 Tim 1:15, This is a **f** saying
3:11, **f** in all things
2 Tim 2:2, thou to **f** man
2:11, It is a **f** saying
2:13, yet he abideth **f**
Titus 3:8, This is a **f** saying
Heb 2:17, and **f** high priest

3:2, **f** to him that appointed
10:23, **f** that promised
11:11, judged him **f**
1 Pet 4:19, as unto a **f** Creator
1 John 1:9, he is **f**
Rev 2:10, be thou **f** unto death
2:13, my **f** martyr
17:14, chosen, and **f**
21:5, true and **f**
22:6, **f** and true
See Deut 7:9; Dan 6:4; Rev 1:5
FAITHFULLY 3 John 5, doest **f**
  whatsoever
FAITHFULNESS Ps 5:9, no **f** in
  their mouth
40:10, declared thy **f**
Is 11:5, **f** the girdle
Lam 3:23, great is thy **f**
See 1 Sam 26:23; Ps 119:75
FAITHLESS Matt 17:17, O **f** and
  perverse generation
Mark 9:19, O **f** generation
John 20:27, and be not **f**
FALL (*n.*) Prov 16:18, haughty spirit
  before a **f**
Matt 7:27, great was the **f**
Luke 2:34, the **f** and rising
Rom 11:12, if the **f** of them
See Jer 49:21; Ezek 26:15
FALL (*v.*) Ps 5:10, let them **f**
7:15, is **f** into the ditch
37:24, Though he **f**
69:9, reproached thee are **f**
72:11, kings shall **f** down
91:7, A thousand shall **f**
Prov 10:8, fool shall **f**
11:14, the people **f**
11:28, riches shall **f**
13:17, **f** into mischief
17:20, a perverse tongue **f**
24:16, For a just man **f**
26:27, shall **f** therein
Eccl 4:10, alone when he **f**
10:8, diggeth a pit shall **f**
11:3, where the tree **f**
Is 14:12, How art thou **f**
Dan 3:5, ye **f** down and worship
11:26, many shall **f** down
Hos 10:8, and to the hills **F**
Mic 7:8, when I **f**
Matt 4:9, **f** down and worship
10:29, **f** on the ground
12:11, **f** into the pit
15:14, **f** into the ditch
21:44, **f** on the stone
24:29, **f** from heaven
Luke 6:39, they not both **f**
8:13, temptation **f** away
10:18, Satan as lightning **f**
20:18, Whosoever shall **f** upon
23:30, **F** on us
Rom 14:4, he standeth or **f**
14:13, occasion to **f**
1 Cor 10:12, heed lest he **f**
15:6, but some are **f** asleep
15:18, **f** asleep in Christ
Gal 5:4, ye are **f** from grace
1 Tim 3:6, **f** into
3:7, **f** into reproach
6:9, rich **f** into temptation
Heb 4:11, lest any man **f**
6:6, If they shall **f** away
10:31, to **f** into the hands
James 1:2, when ye **f**
1:11, flower thereof **f**
5:12, **f** into condemnation
1 Pet 1:24, flower thereof **f**
2 Pet 1:10, ye shall never **f**
3:17, **f** from your own
Rev 6:16, **F** on us
See Is 21:9; Lam 5:16; Rev 14:8
FALLING Job 4:4, have upholden
  him that was **f**

Ps 56:13, my feet from **f**
Prov 25:26, A righteous man **f**
2 Thess 2:3, a **f** away first
Jude 24, keep you from **f**
FALSE Ex 20:16, Thou shalt not
  bear **f** witness
  23:1, raise a **f** report
2 Kin 9:12, It is **f**
Ps 119:104, hate every **f** way
  120:3, thou **f** tongue
Prov 6:19, A **f** witness
  11:1, A **f** balance
  12:17, a **f** witness deceit
  14:5, but a **f** witness
  19:5, A **f** witness shall not
Matt 7:15, Beware of **f** prophets
  24:24, **f** Christs, and **f**
  26:59, sought **f** witness
Mark 13:22, **f** prophets
  14:56, many bare **f** witness
Luke 19:8, by **f** accusation
1 Cor 15:15, found **f** witnesses
2 Cor 11:13, are **f** apostles
  11:26, among **f** brethren
2 Tim 3:3, **f** accusers
Titus 2:3, not **f** accusers
See 2 Pet 2:1; 1 John 4:1
FAMILIAR Job 19:14, my **f** friends
  have forgotten me
Ps 41:9, mine own **f** friend
FAMILY Gen 12:3, shall all **f** of the
  earth be blessed
  28:14, all the **f** of the earth
Eph 3:15, **f** in heaven
See Num 27:4; Amos 3:2
FAMINE 2 Chr 20:9, pestilence, or **f**
Ps 33:19, alive in **f**
Jer 24:10, the sword, the **f**
Ezek 5:16, evil arrows of **f**
Matt 24:7, there shall be **f**
Mark 13:8, **f** and troubles
Luke 21:11, **f**, and pestilences
See Luke 15:14; Rom 8:35
FAR 2 Sam 23:17, Be it **f** from me
Ps 103:12, As **f** as the east
Prov 31:10, price is **f** above
Is 57:19, that is **f** off
Mark 12:34, **f** from the kingdom
  13:34, taking a **f** journey
2 Cor 4:17, a **f** more exceeding
Eph 1:21, **F** above all
  4:10, **f** above all heavens
Phil 1:23, which is **f** better
See Is 33:17; Mark 8:3
FASHION Job 10:8, hands have
  made me and **f** me
  31:15, **f** us in the womb
Ps 33:15, He **f** their hearts
Luke 9:29, the **f** of his
1 Cor 7:31, **f** of this world
Phil 2:8, found in **f** as a man
  3:21, be **f** like
1 Pet 1:14, not **f** yourselves
See Gen 6:15; Ezek 42:11
FAST Is 58:6, Is not this the **f**
Joel 1:14, Sanctify ye a **f**
Zech 7:5, did ye at all **f**
Matt 6:16, when ye **f**
  9:14, thy disciples **f** not
Mark 2:19, the children . . . **f**
Luke 18:12, **f** twice in the week
See Matt 4:2; Acts 13:2
FASTING Ps 35:13, I humbled my
  soul with **f**
  109:24, weak through **f**
Jer 36:6, upon the **f** day
Mark 8:3, send them away **f**
1 Cor 7:5, give yourselves to **f**
2 Cor 6:5, in watchings, in **f**
  11:27, in **f** often
See Dan 6:18; 9:3; Matt 17:21
FATHER Ex 15:2, my **f** God
  20:5, iniquity of the **f**

21:15, he that smiteth his **f**
1 Chr 28:9, the God of thy **f**
Ezra 7:27, God of our **f**
Job 29:16, a **f** to the poor
Ps 68:5, A **f** of the fatherless
Prov 4:1, instruction of a **f**
  10:1, maketh a glad **f**
  17:21, the **f** of a fool
  17:25, grief to his **f**
Is 9:6, The everlasting **F**
  63:16, thou art our **f**
  64:8, thou art our **f**
Jer 3:4, My **f**, thou art
  31:9, I am a **f** to Israel
Ezek 18:4, as the soul of the **f**
Mal 2:10, Have we not all one **f**
Matt 5:16, **f** which is in heaven
  5:45, children of your **f**
  6:9, Our **F** which art
  6:32, for your heavenly **F**
  7:21, the will of my **F**
  8:21, go and bury my **f**
  10:21, the **f** the child
  10:37, He that loveth **f**
  11:26, Even so, **F**
  12:50, shall do the will of my **F**
  18:10, the face of my **F**
  18:14, not the will of your **F**
  23:9, call no man your **f**
  25:34, Come, ye blessed of my **F**
  28:19, in the name of the **F**
Mark 14:36, he said, Abba, **F**
Luke 2:49, about my **F** business
  6:36, **F** also is merciful
  11:11, you that is a **f**
  12:30, your **F** knoweth
  12:32, your **F** good pleasure
  15:21, **F**, I have sinned
  16:27, send him to my **f** house
  22:42, **F**, if thou be willing
  23:34, **F**, forgive them
  23:46, **F**, into thy hands
John 1:14, begotten of the **F**
  5:22, the **F** judgeth no man
  5:37, And the **F** himself
  6:37, All that the **F** giveth
  6:46, hath seen the **F**
  8:16, I and the **F** that sent
  8:44, the **f** of it
  8:49, I honour my **F**
  10:15, As the **F** knoweth me
  10:30, I and my **F** are one
  12:27, **F**, save me
  12:49, the **F** which sent me
  13:1, unto the **F**
  14:6, unto the **F**, but by me
  14:9, hath seen the **F**
  14:16, And I will pray the **F**
  14:24, the **F** which sent me
  14:28, I go unto the **F**
  15:1, my **F** is the husbandman
  15:16, ye shall ask of the **F**
  16:16, because I go to the **F**
  16:26, pray the **F** for you
  16:32, the **F** is with me
  17:1, **F**, the hour is come
  20:17, I ascend unto my **F**
Acts 24:14, the God of my **f**
Rom 4:11, the **f** of all them
  8:15, we cry, Abba, **F**
1 Cor 4:15, have ye not many **f**
2 Cor 1:3, **F** of mercies
Gal 1:14, traditions of my **f**
  4:2, appointed of the **f**
Eph 4:6, One God and **F** of all
  6:4, **f**, provoke not your
Phil 2:11, glory of God the **F**
  2:22, as a son with the **f**
Col 1:19, it pleased the **F**
1 Tim 5:1, entreat him as a **f**
Heb 1:5, I will be to him a **F**
  7:3, Without **f**
  12:9, the **F** of spirits

James 1:17, **F** of lights
2 Pet 3:4, the **f** fell asleep
1 John 1:3, is with the **F**
  2:1, an advocate with the **F**
  2:15, the love of the **F**
  2:23, hath not the **F**
  3:1, of love the **F** hath
  5:7, the **F**, the Word
See 1 Chr 29:10; Luke 11:2
FATHERLESS Ps 10:14, the helper
  of the **f**
Prov 23:10, fields of the **f**
Is 1:23, they judge not the **f**
  10:2, they may rob the **f**
Jer 49:11, Leave thy **f** children
Hos 14:3, **f** findeth mercy
Mal 3:5, the widow, and the **f**
James 1:27, To visit the **f**
See Ex 22:22; Deut 10:18; 14:29
FAULTLESS Heb 8:7, if that first
  covenant had been **f**
Jude 24, and to present you **f**
FEAR (*n.*) Gen 9:2, the **f** of you and
  the dread of you
  20:11, the **f** of God is not
Deut 2:25, and the **f** of thee
Job 4:6, Is not this thy **f**
  15:4, thou castest off **f** ←
Ps 19:9, The **f** of the Lord is
  34:11, I will teach you the **f**
  36:1, no **f** of God
  111:10, The **f** of the Lord
Prov 1:26, when your **f** cometh
  3:25, not afraid of sudden **f**
  10:27, the **f** of the Lord
  14:26, In the **f** of the Lord
  15:16, with the **f** of the Lord
  19:23, **f** of the Lord
  29:25, of man bringeth
Eccl 12:5, and **f** shall be in
Is 8:12, fear ye their **f**
  14:3, and from thy **f**
  29:13, **f** toward me is taught
Jer 30:5, of, **f**, and not of peace
  32:40, I will put my **f**
Mal 1:6, where is my **f**
Matt 14:26, cried out for **f**
Luke 21:26, failing them for **f**
John 7:13, openly of him for **f**
  19:38, but secretly for **f**
  20:19, assembled for **f**
Rom 13:7, **f** to whom
1 Cor 2:3, and in **f**, and in
2 Cor 7:11, yea, what **f**
Eph 6:5, with **f** and trembling
Phil 2:12, salvation with **f**
2 Tim 1:7, the spirit of **f**
Heb 2:15, through **f** of death
  11:7, moved with **f**
  12:28, reverence and godly **f**
Jude 12, themselves without **f**
  23, others save with **f**
See Ps 2:11; 1 Pet 2:18; 3:2
FEAR (*v.*) Gen 22:12, I know that
  thou **f** God
  42:18, and live; for I **f** God
Ex 14:13, **F** ye not, stand still
  18:21, such as **f** God
Deut 4:10, they may learn to **f**
  5:29, that they would **f** me
  28:58, **f** this glorious name
1 Chr 16:30, **F** before him
Neh 7:2, and **f** God above many
Job 1:9, Doth Job **f** God for nought
Ps 23:4, I will **f** no evil
  27:1, whom shall I **f**
  34:9, **f** the Lord
  56:4, not **f** what flesh
  66:16, all ye that **f** God
  112:1, is the man that **f**
  115:11, Ye that **f** the Lord
  118:6, I will not **f**
  119:74, They that **f** thee

Prov 3:7, f the Lord
24:21, f thou the Lord
28:14, the man that f always
31:30, but a woman that f
Eccl 3:14, that men should f
5:7, but f thou God
9:2, as he that f an oath
12:13, F God, and keep his
Is 8:12, neither f ye their
35:4, Be strong, f not
41:10, F thou not
Jer 5:24, Let us now f the Lord
10:7, Who would not f thee
33:9, shall f and tremble
Dan 6:26, and f before the God
Zeph 3:7, Surely thou wilt f me
Mal 3:16, they that f the Lord
4:2, unto you that f my name
Matt 10:28, f him which is able
Luke 12:5, whom ye shall f
12:32, F not, little flock
18:2, judge, which f not God
Acts 10:22, and one that f God
Rom 8:15, again to f
11:20, not highminded, but f
2 Cor 11:3, But I f lest by
12:20, For I f, lest
1 Tim 5:20, others also may f
Heb 5:7, heard in that he f
13:6, I will not f what man
1 John 4:18, no f in love
See 1 Kin 18:12; Col 3:22
FEARFUL Heb 10:27, certain f
  looking
10:31, It is a f thing
See Deut 20:8; Luke 21:11
FEEBLE Job 4:4, strengthened the
  f
Ps 105:37, not one f person
Prov 30:26, are but a f folk
Is 35:3, confirm the f
1 Thess 5:14, comfort the f
Heb 12:12, and the f knees
See Gen 30:42; 1 Cor 12:22
FEED Prov 15:14, fools f on
  foolishness
30:8, f me with food
Is 5:17, the lambs f
11:7, the bear shall f
27:10, there shall the calf f
44:20, He f on ashes
65:25, and the lamb shall f
Zech 11:4, F the flock of the
Matt 6:26, heavenly Father f
John 21:15, F my lambs
21:16, he saith unto him, F my
21:17, Jesus saith unto him, F my
Rom 12:20, hunger, f him
1 Pet 5:2, F the flock
See Song 1:7; Acts 20:28
FEET Gen 49:10, lawgiver from
  between his f
Job 29:15, f was I to the lame
Ps 8:6, all things under his f
22:16, my hands and my f
40:2, set my f upon a rock
56:13, thou deliver my f
66:9, suffereth not our f
116:8, and my f from falling
119:105, a lamp unto my f
122:2, Our f shall stand
Prov 1:16, their f run to evil
4:26, the path of thy f
5:5, Her f go down to death
6:13, speaketh with his f
19:2, with his f sinneth
Song 5:3, washed my f
7:1, How beautiful are thy f
Is 6:2, he covered his f
26:6, even the f of the poor
52:7, the f of him that
60:13, place of my f
Lam 3:34, under his f all the

Ezek 2:1, stand upon thy f
2:2, set me upon my f
24:17, thy shoes upon thy f
25:6, stamped with the f
32:2, the waters with thy f
34:18, the residue with your f
Dan 2:33, his f part of iron
2:42, as the toes of the f
10:6, his arms and his f
Zech 14:4, And his f shall
Matt 7:6, them under their f
10:14, the dust of your f
18:8, two hands or two f
Mark 6:11, dust under your f
Luke 1:79, guide our f
7:38, kissed his f
8:35, at the f of Jesus
9:5, dust from your f
10:39, also sat at Jesus' f
24:39, my hands and my f
John 11:2, and wiped his f
12:3, anointed the f
13:5, wash the disciples' f
Acts 4:35, at the apostles' f
5:9, the f of them
13:51, the dust of their f
Rom 3:15, f are swift to shed
10:15, beautiful are the f
16:20, Satan under your f
1 Cor 12:21, the head to the f
15:25, enemies under his f
Eph 1:22, all things under his f
6:15, your f shod
Heb 12:13, paths for your f
See 2 Sam 4:4; 2 Kin 9:35
FELL Gen 4:5, his countenance f
Acts 1:25, Judas by transgression f
13:36, f on sleep
2 Pet 3:4, the fathers f asleep
Rev 16:19, of the nations f
See Matt 13:4; Acts 10:44
FELLOWSHIP Acts 2:42, and f,
  and in breaking of bread
1 Cor 1:9, unto the f of his Son
10:20, should have f with devils
2 Cor 6:14, what f hath
Eph 3:9, see what is the f of
5:11, no f with the
Phil 1:5, your f in the gospel
2:1, if any f of the Spirit
3:10, the f of his
1 John 1:3, our f is with the
1:7, we have f
See Lev 6:2; 2 Cor 8:4
FEMALE Gen 1:27, and f created
Matt 19:4, made them male and f
Mark 10:6, made them male and f
Gal 3:28, neither male nor f
See Gen 7:16; Lev 3:1; 27:4
FERVENT Acts 18:25, being f in
  the spirit
Rom 12:11, f in spirit
James 5:16, f prayer of a
1 Pet 1:22, a pure heart f
2 Pet 3:10, melt with f heat
See 2 Cor 7:7; Col 4:12
FEW Job 14:1, is of f days
Matt 7:14, and f there be
9:37, the labourers are f
20:16, but f chosen
22:14, but f are chosen
25:21, faithful over a f
Mark 6:5, upon a f sick folk
8:7, a f small fishes
Luke 12:48, with f stripes
13:23, f that be saved
Rev 2:14, a f things against thee
See Deut 7:7; Ps 109:8
FIERY Deut 33:2, a f law for them
Dan 3:6, a burning f furnace
Eph 6:16, the f darts
Heb 10:27, and f indignation
1 Pet 4:12, the f trial

See Num 21:6; Deut 8:15
FIGHT Ex 14:14, The Lord shall f
  for you, and ye
Deut 1:30, he shall f for you
3:22, he shall f for you
20:4, to f for you against
Josh 23:10, he it is that f
1 Sam 25:28, f the battles of
John 18:36, would my servants f
Acts 5:39, to f against God
23:9, not f against God
1 Cor 9:26, so f I, not as one
2 Cor 7:5, without were f
1 Tim 6:12, F the good f of
2 Tim 4:7, fought a good f
James 4:1, come wars and f
See Zech 10:5; 14:14; Rev 2:16
FILL Ex 31:3, And I have f him
  with the spirit
35:31, hath f him with
Num 14:21, shall be f
Job 23:4, f my mouth with
Ps 72:19, the whole earth be f
81:10, and I will f it
104:28, they are f with good
30:22, a fool when he is f
Matt 5:6, for they shall be f
Luke 1:15, be f with the Holy Ghost
1:41, Elisabeth was f with
1:67, Zechariah was f with
6:21, for ye shall be f
Acts 2:2, f all the house
4:8, Then Peter, f with
9:17, and be f with the
13:9, Paul,) f with the
Rom 1:29, f with all
15:14, f with all knowledge
Eph 1:23, that f all in all
3:19, might be f with all
5:18, be f with the Spirit
Phil 1:11, f with the fruits
Col 1:24, f up that which
James 2:16, be ye warmed and f
Rev 15:1, in them is f up the
See Dan 2:35; Luke 2:40; 15:16
FIND Num 32:23, your sin will f you
  out
Prov 8:35, whoso f me, f life
18:22, Whoso f a wife f a
Eccl 9:10, thy hand f to do
Jer 6:16, ye shall f rest
29:13, seek me, and f me
Matt 7:7, seek, and ye shall f
7:14, few there be that f it
10:39, shall f it
Rom 11:33, his ways past f out
Heb 4:16, and f grace to help
See John 7:34; 2 Tim 1:18
FINGER Ex 8:19, This is the f of
  God
31:18, with the f of God
Prov 7:3, Bind them upon thy f
Dan 5:5, came forth f of a
See Ps 8:3; Prov 6:13; Is 2:8
FINISH Gen 2:1, the heavens and
  the earth were f
1 Chr 28:20, thou hast f
Neh 6:15, So the wall was f
John 4:34, and to f his work
5:36, given me to f
17:4, have f the work
19:30, It is f
2 Tim 4:7, I have f my course
Heb 12:2, author and f of our
James 1:15, when it is f
See Dan 9:24; Rev 11:7; 19:7
FIRE Ex 3:2, bush burned with f
Lev 10:2, there went out f
18:21, pass through the f
Deut 18:10, pass through the f
1 Kin 19:12, not in the f
2 Kin 17:17, pass through the f
1 Chr 21:26, from heaven by f

Ps 39:3, the **f** burned
Is 24:15, Lord in the **f**
  43:2, walkest through the **f**
  44:16, I have seen the **f**
  66:15, will come with **f**
  66:24, neither shall their **f**
Jer 20:9, as a burning **f**
Zech 2:5, a wall of **f** round
Mal 3:2, like a refiner's **f**
Matt 3:11, and with **f**
  13:42, into a furnace of **f**
  18:8, into everlasting **f**
  25:41, into everlasting **f**
Mark 9:43, the **f** that never
Luke 12:49, come to send **f**
  17:29, **f** and brimstone from
John 15:6, cast them into the **f**
Acts 2:3, like as of **f**
1 Cor 3:15, yet so as by **f**
2 Thess 1:8, In flaming **f**
Heb 1:7, a flame of **f**
James 3:6, the tongue is a **f**
1 Pet 1:7, be tried with **f**
2 Pet 3:7, reserved unto **f**
Jude 7, of eternal **f**
  23, out of the **f**
Rev 3:18, gold tried in the **f**
  20:9, and **f** came down
  20:10, into the lake of **f**
  21:8, with **f** and brimstone
See Is 33:14; Jer 23:29
FIRMAMENT Gen 1:6, Let there
  be a **f** in the midst
Ps 19:1, the **f** showeth his
Ezek 1:22, likeness of the **f**
Dan 12:3, the brightness of the **f**
FIRST 1 Kin 17:13, make me thereof
  a little cake **f**
Matt 6:33, seek ye **f**
  7:5, **f** cast out the beam
  12:45, worse than the **f**
  17:10, Elijah must **f** come
  22:38, is the **f** and great
Mark 9:35, man desire to be **f**
  12:28, the **f** commandment
John 8:7, let him **f** cast a stone
Acts 11:26, Christians **f** in
Rom 2:9, the Jew **f** and also
  8:23, the **f** of the Spirit
  8:29, be the **f** among
  11:16, if the **f** be holy
1 Cor 12:28, **f** apostles
  14:30, let the **f** hold his
  15:20, and become the **f**
  15:23, Christ the **f**
  15:45, **f** man Adam was made
2 Cor 8:5, **f** gave their own
  8:12, if there be **f** a
Eph 6:2, **f** commandment with
Col 1:15, **f** of every creature
  1:18, the **f** from the dead
1 Thess 4:16, shall rise **f**
2 Thess 2:3, a falling away **f**
1 Tim 1:16, in me **f** Jesus
  2:13, Adam was **f** formed
  5:12, cast off their **f** faith
Heb 5:12, **f** principles of
  7:27, **f** for his own sins
  12:23, church of the **f**
James 3:17, is **f** pure
1 Pet 4:17, and if it **f** begin
1 John 4:19, he **f** loved us
Jude 6, not their **f** estate
Rev 2:4, left thy **f** love
  2:5, and do the **f** works
  20:5, the **f** resurrection
  21:1, **f** heaven and the **f**
See Ex 4:8; Num 18:13; John 12:16
FITLY Prov 25:11, word **f** spoken
Eph 2:21, the building **f** framed
  4:16, body **f** joined together
FIXED Ps 57:7, My heart is **f**, O
  God, my heart is **f**

108:1, my heart is **f**
112:7, his heart is **f**
Luke 16:26, a great gulf **f**
FLAME Gen 3:24, **f** sword which
  turned every way
Judg 13:20, ascended in the **f**
Is 5:24, and the **f** consumeth
  29:6, the **f** of devouring
  43:2, shall the **f** kindle
  66:15, with **f** of fire
Ezek 20:47, flaming **f** shall
Luke 16:24, tormented in this **f**
See Ps 29:7; Heb 1:7; Rev 1:14
FLEE Job 14:2, he **f** also as a
  shadow
Ps 11:1, **F** as a bird
Prov 28:1, The wicked **f**
  28:17, **f** to the pit
Song 2:17, the shadows **f** away
Is 35:10, sighing shall **f** away
  51:11, mourning shall **f**
Matt 3:7, **f** from the wrath
  24:16, **f** into the
Mark 13:14, in Judaea **f** to the
John 10:5, will **f** from him
2 Tim 2:22, **F** also youthful
James 4:7, he will **f** from you
See 1 Cor 6:18; Rev 12:6, 14
FLEECE Judg 6:37, I will put a **f** of
  wool in the floor
FLESH Gen 2:24, and they shall be
  one **f**
  6:12, all **f** had corrupted
  6:13, end of all **f** is come
  7:21, all **f** died that moved
Lev 17:14, life of all **f** is the blood
  19:28, cuttings in your **f**
Num 16:22, spirits of all **f**
Job 19:26, yet in my **f**
  33:21, **f** is consumed away
Ps 16:9, my **f** also shall rest
  65:2, shall all **f** come
Prov 5:11, thy **f** and thy body
  11:17, troubleth his own **f**
  23:20, riotous eaters of **f**
Eccl 4:5, eateth his own **f**
  12:12, weariness of the **f**
Is 40:5, and all **f** shall see
  40:6, All **f** is grass
Joel 2:28, upon all **f**
Matt 16:17, **f** and blood hath
  19:5, shall be one **f**
  24:22, no **f** be saved
  26:41, the **f** is weak
Mark 13:20, no **f** should be
Luke 24:39, not **f** and bones
John 1:14, Word was made **f**
  6:51, the bread . . . is my **f**
  6:52, his **f** to eat
  6:54, Whoso eateth my **f**
  6:63, **f** profiteth nothing
  8:15, Ye judge after the **f**
  17:2, power over all **f**
Rom 6:19, infirmity of your **f**
  8:3, condemned sin in the **f**
  8:12, live after the **f**
  9:3, according to the **f**
  13:14, provision for the **f**
1 Cor 1:29, no **f** should glory
  6:16, shall be one **f**
  15:39, All **f** is not the same
  15:50, **f** and blood
2 Cor 12:7, a thorn in the **f**
Gal 1:16, conferred not with **f**
  2:20, live in the **f**
  5:17, **f** lusteth
  6:8, soweth to his **f**
Eph 5:31, two shall be one **f**
  6:12, wrestle not against **f**
Phil 3:3, confidence in the **f**
1 Tim 3:16, manifest in the **f**
1 Pet 1:24, For all **f** is grass
  3:18, to death in the **f**

1 John 4:2, come in the **f**
Jude 8, dreamers defile the **f**
  23, spotted by the **f**
See John 1:13; 3:6; Gal 5:19
FLESHLY 2 Cor 1:12, not with **f**
  wisdom
  3:3, but in **f** tables
Col 2:18, by his **f** mind
1 Pet 2:11, from **f** lusts
FLOCK Is 40:11, He shall feed his **f**
  like a shepherd
Ezek 34:31, **f** of my pasture
Zech 11:7, O poor of the **f**
Luke 12:32, Fear not, little **f**
Acts 20:28, to all the **f**
1 Pet 5:2, the **f** of God
See Mal 1:14; Matt 26:31
FLOURISH Ps 72:7, In his days
  shall the righteous **f**
  90:6, In the morning it **f**
  92:12, righteous shall **f**
Prov 11:28, **f** as a branch
  14:11, tabernacle . . . shall **f**
See Ps 92:14; Dan 4:4
FLOWER 1 Sam 2:33, shall die in
  the **f** of their age
Job 14:2, cometh forth like a **f**
Song 2:12, The **f** appear
Is 28:1, is a fading **f**
  40:6, as the **f** of the field
See Job 15:33; 1 Cor 7:36
FLY Job 5:7, as the sparks **f** upward
Ps 55:6, then would I **f** away
  90:10, and we **f** away
Prov 23:5, **f** away as an eagle
Is 60:8, that **f** as a cloud
See Dan 9:21; Rev 14:6; 19:17
FOLLOW Num 14:24, hath **f** me
  fully, him will I bring
1 Kin 18:21, God, **f** him
Ps 23:6, mercy shall **f** me
  63:8, My soul **f** hard
  68:25, the players . . . **f** after
Prov 12:11, **f** vain persons
Is 5:11, **f** strong drink
Hos 6:3, if we **f** on to
Amos 7:15, I **f** the flock
Matt 4:19, unto them, **F** me
  8:19, I will **f** thee
Mark 10:32, and as they **f**
Luke 9:61, Lord, I will **f** thee
John 1:43, unto him, **F** me
  10:27, and they **f** me
  13:36, not **f** me now
Rom 14:19, **f** after the things
1 Cor 10:4, Rock that **f** them
  14:1, **F** after charity
Phil 3:12, I **f** after
1 Thess 5:15, ever **f** that
1 Tim 5:24, men they **f** after
  6:11, **f** after righteousness
2 Tim 2:22, **f** righteousness
Heb 12:14, **F** peace with all
  13:7, whose faith **f**
1 Pet 1:11, that should **f**
  2:21, that ye should **f**
2 Pet 2:15, **f** the way
Rev 14:4, which **f** the Lamb
  14:13, works do **f** them
See Mark 9:38; 1 Pet 3:13
FOLLOWER Eph 5:1, Be ye
  therefore **f** of God
Heb 6:12, but **f** of them
FOOD Gen 3:6, the tree was good
  for **f**
Ex 21:10, her **f**, her raiment
Deut 10:18, in giving him **f**
Ps 78:25, Man did eat angels' **f**
  136:25, **f** to all flesh
Prov 6:8, gathereth her **f**
  31:14, she bringeth her **f**
2 Cor 9:10, bread for your **f**
1 Tim 6:8, having **f** and raiment

James 2:15, destitute of daily f
See Gen 1:29; Lev 22:7
FOOL Ps 14:1, The f hath said
75:4, I said unto the f
Prov 1:7, f despise wisdom
3:35, the promotion of f
10:8, 10, but a prating f
10:21, f die for want
11:29, the f shall be servant
12:15, way of a f is right
14:9, F make a mock at sin
15:2, mouth of f poureth
20:3, f will be meddling
29:11, A f uttereth all
Eccl 2:14, the f walketh
2:16, as the f
10:14, A f also is full
Matt 5:22, say, Thou f
23:17, ye f and blind
Luke 12:20, Thou f
24:25, O f, and slow of heart
Rom 1:22, they became f
1 Cor 3:18, let him become a f
4:10, We are f for Christ's
2 Cor 11:16, man think me a f
12:11, a f in glorying
Eph 5:15, not as f
See Prov 10:18; Eccl 10:3
FOOLISH Deut 32:6, O f people
and unwise
Prov 9:6, Forsake the f
9:13, A f woman is clamorous
14:1, f plucketh it down
17:25, A f son is a grief
Eccl 7:17, neither be thou f
Jer 4:22, my people is f
Matt 7:26, unto a f man
25:2, five were f
Rom 1:21, f heart was darkened
1 Cor 1:20, made f the wisdom
Gal 3:3, Are ye so f
Eph 5:4, nor f talking
1 Tim 6:9, f and hurtful lusts
2 Tim 2:23, f and unlearned
Titus 3:9, f questions
See Job 5:3; Lam 2:14; Ezek 13:3
FOOLISHNESS Ps 69:5, thou
knowest my f
Prov 22:15, F is bound
24:9, thought of f is sin
1 Cor 1:18, them that perish f
1:21, f of preaching
1:25, f of God is wiser
2:14, they are f unto him
3:19, f with God
See 2 Sam 15:31; Prov 27:22
FOOTSTOOL Is 66:1, and the
earth is my f
Matt 5:35, for it is his f
Heb 10:13, be made his f
FORBID Num 11:28, My lord
Moses, f them
Mark 9:39, F him not
10:14, f them not
Luke 6:29, f not to take
23:2, f to give tribute
Acts 10:47, Can any man f water
1 Cor 14:39, f not to speak
1 Tim 4:3, F to marry
See Acts 16:6; 1 Thess 2:16
FOREKNOW Acts 2:23, and f of
God, ye have taken
Rom 8:29, For whom he did f
11:2, people which he f
FOREORDAINED 1 Pet 1:20, Who
verily was f before
FORESEE Prov 22:3, A prudent
man f the evil
Acts 2:25, I f the Lord always
Gal 3:8, f that God would
FORETELL Mark 13:23, behold, I
have f you all things
Acts 3:24, have likewise f

2 Cor 13:2, and f you
FORGAVE Matt 18:27, loosed him,
and f him the debt
18:32, I f thee all that debt
Luke 7:42, he frankly f them
7:43, he, to whom he f most
2 Cor 2:10, if I f any thing
Col 3:13, even as Christ f you
See Ps 32:5; 78:38; 99:8
FORGET Deut 4:9, lest thou f the
things
8:11, thou f not the Lord
Job 8:13, of all that f God
Ps 9:17, the nations that f God
10:12, f not the humble
45:10, f also thine own
50:22, ye that f God
78:7, and not f the works
88:12, the land of f
119:16, I will not f thy word
Prov 2:17, f the covenant
3:1, My son, f not my law
31:5, they drink, and f
Is 51:13, And f the Lord thy
65:11, that f my holy
Jer 23:27, cause my people to f
Phil 3:13, f those things
Heb 6:10, to f your work
13:2, Be not f to entertain
13:16, communicate f not
James 1:24, f what manner
See Gen 41:51; Lam 5:20
FORGIVE Ex 32:32, if thou wilt f
34:7, f iniquity
Num 14:18, f iniquity
1 Kin 8:30, thou hearest, f
8:39, place, and f
2 Chr 7:14, and will f
Ps 32:1, transgression is f
86:5, and ready to f
103:3, Who f all
Matt 6:12, f us our debts
6:14, For if ye f men
9:6, power on earth to f sins
18:21, and I f
18:35, from your hearts f not
Mark 2:7, who can f sins
11:25, f, if ye have ought
Luke 6:37, and ye shall be f
7:47, which are many, are f
11:4, f us our sins
17:3, if he repent, f him
23:34, Father, f them
Acts 8:22, thine heart may be f
Rom 4:7, whose iniquities are f
2 Cor 2:7, ought rather to f
2:10, To whom ye f
12:13, f me this wrong
Eph 4:32, hath f you
Col 2:13, f you all trespasses
1 John 1:9, and just to f us
2:12, your sins are f you
See Matt 9:2; 12:31; Mark 3:28
FORGIVENESS Ps 130:4, there is f
with thee
Mark 3:29, hath never f
Acts 5:31, and f of
Eph 1:7, the f of sins
Col 1:14, even the f of sins
See Dan 9:9; Acts 13:38; 26:18
FORGOTTEN Deut 32:18, f God
that formed
Ps 9:18, not always be f
10:11, God hath f
31:12, I am f
42:9, Why hast thou f me
77:9, Hath God f to be
Eccl 2:16, shall all be f
8:10, and they were f
9:5, the memory of them is f
Is 17:10, f the God
44:21, thou shalt not be f
49:14, my Lord hath f me

65:16, former troubles are f
Jer 2:32, my people have f
3:21, they have f the Lord
13:25, thou hast f me
18:15, my people have f me
44:9, f the wickedness
50:6, f their resting place
Ezek 22:12, and hast f me
23:35, thou hast f me
Matt 16:5, had f to take bread
Luke 12:6, is f before God
2 Pet 1:9, hath f that he was
See Lam 2:6; Hos 4:6; 8:14
FORM (*n.*) Gen 1:2, earth was
without f and void
Job 4:16, discern the f
Is 52:14, f more than the sons
53:2, he hath no f
Jer 4:23, it was without f
Mark 16:12, in another f
Rom 2:20, the f of knowledge
Phil 2:6, the f of God
2 Tim 1:13, f of sound words
3:5, Having a f of godliness
See 1 Sam 28:14; Ezek 43:11
FORM (*v.*) Deut 32:18, God that f
thee
2 Kin 19:25, I have f it
Job 26:5, Dead things are f
26:13, hath f the crooked
33:6, I also am f out of
Ps 90:2, or ever thou hast f
94:9, he that f the eye
Prov 26:10, great God that f
Is 43:1, he that f thee
43:7, I have f him
44:10, Who hath f a god
44:21, have f thee
54:17, No weapon that is f
Rom 9:20, the thing f say
Gal 4:19, Christ be f in you
See Gen 2:7, 19; Ps 95:5
FORMER Jer 5:24, rain, both the f
Hos 6:3, latter and f rain
Joel 2:23, given you the f
Eph 4:22, the f conversation
Rev 21:4, for the f things
See Gen 40:13; Dan 11:13
FORNICATION Matt 5:32, his
wife, saving for the cause of f
Acts 15:20, from f, and from
1 Cor 6:13, is not for f
Eph 5:3, But f
1 Thess 4:3, should abstain from f
FORSAKE Deut 4:31, he will not f
thee
12:19, that thou f not
31:6, nor f thee
32:15, he f God which made
Josh 1:5, nor f thee
1 Chr 28:9, if thou f him
2 Chr 15:2, if ye f him
Neh 10:39, not f the house
13:11, the house of God f
Job 6:14, he f the fear
20:19, hath f the poor
Ps 22:1, why hast thou f me
27:10, my mother f me
37:25, seen the righteous f
37:28, judgment, and f not
119:8, O f me not utterly
138:8, f not the works
Prov 1:8, and f not the law
2:17, f the guide of her
4:6, F her not
27:10, friend, f not
Is 6:12, a great f in the midst
54:7, have I f thee
55:7, the wicked f his way
62:4, no more be termed F
62:12, A city not f
Jer 2:13, have f me the fountain
4:29, every city shall be f

17:13, they have f theLord
Matt 19:29, every one that hath f
26:56, all the disciples f
Mark 1:18, they f their nets
14:50, And they all f him
Luke 5:11, they f all
14:33, you that f not all
2 Cor 4:9, but not f
Heb 10:25, Not f the
11:27, By faith he f Egypt
13:5, nor f thee
See Ps 71:11; Is 49:14; Jer 5:7
FORTRESS 2 Sam 22:2, rock, and
my f, and my deliverer
Jer 16:19, my strength, and my f
FORTY YEARS Ex 16:35, Israel
did eat manna f
Num 14:33, in the wilderness f
Ps 95:10, F long was I grieved
See Judg 3:11; 5:31; 8:28
FOUGHT 1 Cor 15:32, I have f
2 Tim 4:7, have f a good fight
FOUND Ps 32:6, when thou mayest
be f
Is 55:6, while he may be f
Ezek 22:30, but I f none
Dan 5:27, and art f wanting
Mal 2:6, iniquity was not f
Matt 8:10, not f so great faith
13:46, f one pearl of great
Mark 7:2, they f fault
Luke 15:6, I have f my sheep
15:9, for I have f the piece
15:24, was lost, and is f
15:32, and was lost, and is f
23:14, have f no fault
John 1:41, have f the Messiah
1 Pet 2:22, was guile f in his
See Gen 6:8; 2 Cor 5:3; Phil 3:9
FOUNDATION Job 4:19, whose f is
in the
Ps 11:3, the f be destroyed
82:5, the f of the earth
102:25, thou laid the f of
Prov 10:25, an everlasting f
Is 28:16, in Zion for a f
58:12, the f of many
Luke 6:48, the f on a rock ✓
6:49, a f built an house
Rom 15:20, upon another man's f
1 Cor 3:10, I have laid the f
3:11, other f can no man
3:12, upon this f gold
Eph 1:4, in him before the f
1 Tim 6:19, a good f against
2 Tim 2:19, the f of God
Heb 4:3, from the f of the
11:10, a city which hath f
Rev 21:14, the city had twelve f
See Matt 13:35; John 17:24
FOUNTAIN Gen 7:11, were all the f
of the great deep
8:2, f also of the deep
Deut 8:7, of f and depths
2 Chr 32:3, waters of the f
Ps 36:9, the f of life
Prov 5:16, thy f be dispersed
8:24, were no f abounding
13:14, is a f of life
Eccl 12:6, at the f
Jer 2:13, f of living waters
17:13, the f of living
Zech 13:1, shall be a f opened
James 3:11, a f send forth
3:12, no f both yield
Rev 7:17, unto living f of
14:7, the f of waters
21:6, the f of the water
See Is 12:3; Joel 3:18; Mark 5:29
FREE Gen 2:16, tree of the garden
thou mayest f eat
Ps 51:12, with thy f spirit
88:5, F among the dead

Is 58:6, let the oppressed go f
Hos 14:4, I will love them f
Matt 10:8, f ye have received
17:26, are the children f
Mark 7:11, he shall be f
John 8:32, shall make you f
Acts 22:28, But I was f born
Rom 3:24, Being justified f
5:15, so also is the f gift
6:18, Being then made f
8:2, f from the law of sin
1 Cor 9:1, am I not f
9:19, though I be f from all
12:13, we be bond or f
Gal 3:28, neither bond nor f
5:1, Christ hath made us f
Eph 6:8, he be bond or f
Rev 21:6, the water of life f
See Ex 21:2; Gal 4:22
FRIEND Ex 33:11, as a man
speaketh unto his f
2 Chr 20:7, Abraham thy f
Ps 35:14, he had been my f
41:9, familiar f in whom I
88:18, Lover and f hast thou
Prov 6:1, be surety for thy f
14:20, the rich hath many f
18:24, a f that sticketh closer
19:4, Wealth maketh many f
27:6, the wounds of a f
Song 5:16, this is my f
Is 41:8, seed of Abraham my f
Jer 20:4, and to all thy f
Mic 7:5, Trust ye not in a f
Zech 13:6, the house of my f
John 15:13, his life for his f
15:15, I have called you f
James 2:23, the F of God
4:5, f of the world is the
See Prov 22:24; Luke 14:10
FRUIT Ps 1:3, bringeth forth his f
127:3, the f of the womb
Prov 11:30, f of the righteous
Song 2:3, his f was sweet
4:16, eat his pleasant f
Amos 8:1, a basket of summer f
Matt 3:8, therefore f meet
7:16, know them by their f
7:20, by their f ye shall
12:33, and his f good
13:23, also beareth f
Mark 4:28, bringeth forth f
14:25, the f of the vine
Luke 3:8, therefore f worthy
John 4:36, f unto life eternal
12:24, bringeth forth much f
15:2, branch that beareth f
Rom 1:13, some f among you
7:4, bring forth f unto God
2 Cor 9:10, the f of your
Gal 5:22, the f of the Spirit
Eph 5:9, f of the Spirit is in
Phil 1:11, f of righteousness
1:22, the f of my labour
4:17, I desire f that may
Col 1:6, bringeth forth f
2 Tim 2:6, partaker of the f
Heb 12:11, peaceable f of
13:15, the f of our lips
James 3:17, of mercy and good f
5:7, the precious f
Jude 12, trees whose f
Rev 22:2, yielded her f
See Gen 30:2; Col 1:10
FULFILL Ps 145:19, will f the
desire
Matt 1:22, that it might be f
5:17, destroy, but to f
24:34, all these things be f
Mark 13:4, things shall be f
Luke 1:20, be f in their season
21:24, the Gentiles be f
22:16, be f in the kingdom

John 3:29, joy therefore is f
17:13, might have my joy f
Rom 8:4, the law might be f
Gal 5:14, is f in one word
6:2, so f the law of Christ
Eph 2:3, f the desires of the
Phil 2:2, F ye my joy
Col 4:17, that thou f it
2 Thess 1:11, f all the good
James 2:8, If ye f the royal
See Ex 5:13; 23:26; Gal 5:16
FULL Deut 34:9, was f of the spirit
Job 14:1, and f of trouble
Ps 10:7, is f of cursing
88:3, is f of troubles
119:64, is f of thy mercy
127:5, that hath his quiver f
Prov 27:7, f soul loatheth
27:20, are never f
Hab 3:3, f of his praise
Matt 6:22, shall be f of light
Luke 6:25, you that are f
11:36, be f of light
John 1:14, f of grace and truth
15:11, joy might be f
Acts 6:3, f of the Holy Ghost
7:55, f of the Holy Ghost
9:36, f of good works
11:24, f of the Holy Ghost
Rom 3:14, is f of cursing
15:14, f of goodness
1 Cor 4:8, Now ye are f
Phil 4:12, both to be f
4:18, I am f
2 Tim 4:5, f proof of thy ministry
Heb 5:14, that are of f
1 Pet 1:8, f of glory
1 John 1:4, joy may be f
Rev 15:7, f of the wrath of God
See Lev 2:14; Amos 2:13
FULLNESS Ps 16:11, in thy
presence is f of joy
John 1:16, of his f
Rom 11:25, much more their f
Gal 4:4, the f of the time
Eph 1:23, the f of him
3:19, filled with all the f
4:13, the f of Christ
Col 1:19, should all f dwell
2:9, f of the Godhead bodily
See Num 18:27; Ps 96:11

G

GAIN Prov 15:27, greedy of g
troubleth
Ezek 22:12, thou hast greedily g
Dan 11:39, the land for g
Mic 4:13, consecrate their g
Matt 16:26, g the whole world
18:15, g thy brother
25:22, g two other talents
Luke 19:16, hath g ten pounds
1 Cor 9:19, I might g the more
2 Cor 12:17, Did I make a g
Phil 1:21, and to die is g
3:7, But what things were g
1 Tim 6:5, g is godliness
See Job 27:8; James 4:13
GARDEN Gen 2:8, God planted a g
eastward in Eden
13:10, as the g of the Lord
Is 51:3, g of the Lord
58:11, like a watered g
61:11, and as the g
Ezek 28:13, Eden the g of God
31:8, The cedars in the g
36:35, is become like the g
See Gen 2:15; Amos 4:9; 9:14
GARMENT Ps 22:18, They part my
g

102:26, wax old like a g
Is 50:9, wax old as a g
52:1, put on thy beautiful g
61:3, g of praise
61:10, the g of salvation
Joel 2:13, and not your g
Zech 13:4, wear a rough g
Matt 9:16, unto an old g
9:20, the hem of his g
21:8, spread their g
22:11, on a wedding g
27:35, parted his g
Mark 5:27, and touched his g
11:7, cast their g on him
13:16, to take up his g
Luke 5:36, a piece of new g
8:44, border of his g
19:35, they cast their g
22:36, let him sell his g
24:4, in shining g
James 5:2, your g are motheaten
Jude 23, hating even the g
Rev 3:4, not defiled their g
16:15, keepeth his g

GATE Gen 28:17, this is the g of heaven
Deut 6:9, and on thy g
Ps 9:13, from the g of death
100:4, Enter into his g
118:19, g of righteousness
Prov 17:19, exalteth his g
31:23, known in the g
Is 26:2, Open ye the g
38:10, the g of the grave
45:1, the two leaved g
60:11, thy g shall be open
60:18, and thy g Praise
Matt 7:13, for wide is the g
16:18, the g of hell
Luke 13:24, at the strait g
Heb 13:12, without the g
Rev 21:25, And the g of it
See Ps 24:7; Is 28:6; Nah 2:6

GAVE Gen 3:12, she g me of the tree
Job 1:21, Lord g, and the Lord
Ps 21:4, thou g it him
68:11, The Lord g the word
Eccl 12:7, unto God who g it
John 3:16, g his only begotten
Acts 2:4, as the Spirit g
Rom 1:28, God g them over
1 Cor 3:6, God g the increase
Eph 4:8, g gifts unto men
4:11, he g some, apostles
5:25, g himself for it
1 Tim 2:6, Who g himself a ransom
See 2 Cor 8:5; Titus 2:14

GENERATION Deut 1:35, one of these men of this evil g
32:5, perverse and crooked g
Prov 27:24, endure to every g
Eccl 1:4, One g passeth away
Is 34:10, from g to g
Matt 3:7, O g of vipers
3:41, judgment with this g
17:17, and perverse g
23:33, ye g of vipers
23:36, come upon this g
24:34, This g shall not pass
Mark 9:19, O faithless g
Luke 16:8, in their g wiser
17:25, rejected of this g
21:32, This g shall not
1 Pet 2:9, a chosen g
See Matt 1:1; Luke 11:30

GENTILES Matt 10:5, Go not into the way of the G
John 7:35, among the G
Acts 9:15, before the G
13:42, G besought that
13:46, lo, we turn to the G
15:3, conversion of the G

18:6, go unto the G
Rom 3:29, also of the G
11:11, come unto the G
11:13, apostle of the G
1 Cor 5:1, named among the G
Eph 4:17, walk not as other G
2 Tim 1:11, teacher of the G
3 John 7, nothing of the G
See 1 Pet 2:12; Rev 11:2

GENTLE 1 Thess 2:7, we were g among you
2 Tim 2:24, but be g unto all
Titus 3:2, no brawlers, but g
James 3:17, g, and easy
1 Pet 2:18, the good and g
See 2 Sam 18:5; 22:36; Gal 5:22

GIFT Ex 23:8, for the g blindeth the wise
Deut 16:19, neither take a g
2 Sam 19:42, given us any g
2 Chr 19:7, nor taking of g
Ps 68:18, received g for men
72:10, shall offer g
Prov 6:35, givest many g
15:27, he that hateth g
17:8, A g is as
18:16, A man's g
21:14, A g in secret
Eccl 3:13, it is the g of God
7:7, g destroyeth the heart
Is 1:23, every one loveth g
Matt 5:23, bring thy g
5:24, Leave there thy g
7:11, give good g
Luke 21:1, casting their g
John 4:10, the g of God
Acts 8:20, thought that the g
Rom 1:11, some spiritual g
5:15, the g by grace
6:23, the g of God
11:29, the g and calling
12:6, g differing according
1 Cor 7:7, proper g of God
12:4, diversities of g
12:31, the best g
14:1, desire spiritual g
14:12, of spiritual g
2 Cor 9:15, his unspeakable g
Eph 2:8, it is the g of God
4:8, gave g unto men
Phil 4:17, I desire a g
1 Tim 4:14, Neglect not the g
2 Tim 1:6, stir up the g of God
James 1:17, Every good g
See Num 18:29; 1 Cor 13:2

GIVE Gen 28:22, I will surely g the tenth
Ex 30:15, rich shall not g
Deut 15:10, surely g him
16:17, Every man shall g
1 Chr 29:14, have we g thee
Ezra 9:9, to g us a reviving
Ps 2:8, I shall g thee
6:5, shall g thee thanks
29:11, Lord will g strength
37:4, g thee the desires
37:21, sheweth mercy, and g
84:11, the Lord will g grace
91:11, shall g his angels
Prov 23:26, g me thine heart
Is 9:6, a son is g
Ezek 46:5, be able to g
Matt 5:42, G to him that asketh
6:11, G us this day
7:9, will he g him a stone
10:8, freely g
16:26, a man g in exchange
19:21, g to the poor
20:23, is not mine to g
26:9, and g to the poor
Mark 4:11, you it is g to know
10:40, but it shall be g
Luke 6:38, G, and it shall

John 4:7, G me to drink
6:37, the Father g me
6:65, it were g unto him
14:27, not as the world g
Acts 3:6, such as I have g
20:35, more blessed to g
Rom 8:32, also freely g us
12:19, but rather g place
1 Cor 3:7, g the increase
11:15, for her hair is g her
2 Cor 9:7, so let him g
Phil 2:9, and g him a name
1 Tim 4:13, g attendance
4:15, g thyself wholly
6:17, g us richly
Heb 2:1, to g the more
James 1:5, that g to all men
4:6, g more grace
2 Pet 1:5, g all diligence
See Mark 12:15; Luke 12:48

GLAD Ex 4:14, he will be g in his heart
Job 3:22, g, when they can
Ps 16:9, my heart is g
31:7, be g and rejoice
34:2, hear thereof, and be g
46:4, shall make g the city
69:32, and be g
104:15, maketh g the heart
122:1, I was g
126:3, whereof we are g
Prov 10:1, maketh a g father
24:17, not thine heart be g
Lam 1:21, they are g
Luke 15:32, merry, and be g
John 8:56, saw it, and was g
11:15, And I am g for your
Acts 2:41, that g received
See Mark 6:20; 12:37; Luke 1:19

GLADNESS Num 10:10, Also in the day of your g
Deut 28:47, with g of heart
Neh 8:17, was very great g
Ps 4:7, put g in my heart
45:7, the oil of g
97:11, and g for the upright
Is 35:10, obtain joy and g
Acts 2:46, g and singleness
See Ps 100:2; Prov 10:28

GLASS 1 Cor 13:12, now we see through a g darkly
2 Cor 3:18, beholding as in a g
Rev 4:6, was a sea of g
15:2, a sea of g mingled

GLORIFY Ps 50:23, offereth praise g me
86:12, I will g thy name
Is 60:7, I will g the house
Ezek 28:22, I will be g
Matt 5:16, and g your Father
15:31, g the God of Israel
Luke 4:15, being g of all
John 7:39, Jesus was not yet g
11:4, Son of God might be g
12:16, but when Jesus was g
12:28, I have both g it
13:32, God shall also g him
15:8, Herein is my Father g
17:1, Son also may g thee
21:19, he should g God
Rom 1:21, g him not as God
8:17, that we may be also g
8:30, them he also g
1 Cor 6:20, therefore g God
Gal 1:24, And they g God in me
2 Thess 1:10, g in his saints
Heb 5:5, Christ g not himself
1 Pet 2:12, g God in the day
See Is 25:5; Luke 7:16

GLORIOUS Ps 67:3, G things are spoken
Is 11:10, his rest shall be g
63:14, make thyself a g name

Jer 17:12, A g high throne
Dan 11:16, stand in the g land
  11:45, g holy mountain
Luke 13:17, g things
Rom 8:21, g liberty
2 Cor 3:7, in stones, was g
  3:8, spirit be rather g
  4:4, light of the g gospel
Eph 5:27, to himself a g church
Phil 3:21, like unto his g body
1 Tim 1:11, the g gospel
Titus 2:13, the g appearing
See Ex 15:1; 2 Sam 6:20
GLORY Ex 33:18, I beseech thee,
    shew me thy g
Num 14:21, be filled with the g
Ps 8:1, thy g above the heavens
  24:7, and the King of g
  84:11, give grace and g
  145:11, speak of the g
Prov 3:35, shall inherit g
  17:6, the g of children
  20:29, the g of young men
  25:2, the g of God
  25:27, their own g is not g
Is 6:3, is full of his g
  24:16, g to the righteous
  42:8, my g will I not give
  43:7, created him for my g
  60:7, the house of my g
Hag 2:7, fill this house with g
Matt 6:2, that they may have g
  6:13, the power, and the g
  6:29, his g was not
  16:27, come in the g
  19:28, in the throne of his g
  24:30, with power and great g
Mark 13:26, great power and g
Luke 2:14, G to God
  9:26, come in his own g
  19:38, peace in heaven, and g
  21:27, power and great g
  24:26, to enter into his g
John 1:14, we beheld his g
  2:11, manifested forth his g
  8:50, I seek not mine own g
  11:40, see the g of God
  17:5, with the g which I had
  17:24, they may behold my g
Acts 12:23, gave not God the g
Rom 3:23, come short of the g
  8:18, the g which shall be
  11:36, to whom be g
1 Cor 1:29, no flesh should g
  10:31, to the g of God
  11:7, but the woman is the g
  11:15, it is a g to her
  15:40, g of the celestial
  15:43, it is raised in g
2 Cor 3:18, the g of the Lord
Gal 6:14, I should g
Eph 1:17, the Father of g
  3:21, Unto him be g
Phil 3:19, g is in their shame
  4:19, to his riches in g
Col 1:27, the hope of g
  3:4, appear with him in g
2 Thess 1:9, the g
1 Tim 3:16, received up into g
Heb 1:3, brightness of his g
  2:10, many sons unto g
  3:3, worthy of more g
1 Pet 1:8, full of g
  1:11, g that should follow
  1:24, the g of man
  4:14, the spirit of g
  5:10, unto his eternal g
2 Pet 1:17, from the excellent g
Rev. 4:11, received g and honour
  5:12, and honour, and g
  7:12, Blessing, and g
  18:1, lightened with his g
  21:23, the g of God

See Luke 17:18; James 2:1
GLORYING 1 Cor 5:6, Your g is not
    good
  9:15, should make my g void
2 Cor 7:4, great is my g
  12:11, become a fool in g
GNASH Matt 8:12, shall be weeping
    and g of teeth
  13:42, 50, and g of teeth
Mark 9:18, g with his teeth
See Job 16:9; Ps 35:16
GO Ruth 1:16, whither thou g
Matt 5:41, to g a mile
  28:19, G ye therefore
John 14:12, g unto my Father
See Matt 8:9; 1 Cor 9:7
GOD Gen 5:22, And Enoch walked
    with G
  6:9, and Noah walked with G
  16:13, Thou G seest me
  32:28, thou power with G
  48:21, G shall be with you
Num 23:19, G is not a man
  23:23, What hath G wrought
Deut 3:24, G is there
  33:27, The eternal G
1 Sam 17:46, that there is a G
1 Kin 18:21, If the Lord be G
  18:39, The Lord, he is the G
Job 22:13, How doth G know
Ps 14:1, There is no G
  22:1, My G, my G, why hast
  56:9, for G is for me
  86:10, thou art G alone
Eccl 5:2, before G: for G is
Is 37:16, thou art the G
  44:8, Is there a G
  45:22, for I am G
Hos 11:9, for I am G
Amos 5:27, whose name is The G
Jon 1:6, call upon thy G
Mic 6:8, walk humbly with thy G
Matt 1:23, is, G with us
  22:32, G is not the G
Mark 12:32, for there is one G
John 3:33, that G is true
  4:24, G is a Spirit
  13:3, from G, and went to G
  20:17, to my G and your G
Rom 3:4, let G be true
  8:31, If G be for us
1 Cor 1:9, G is faithful
  10:13, G is faithful
  14:25, that G is in you
  14:33, G is not the author
Gal 3:20, but G is one
  6:7, G is not mocked
Phil 4:19, my G shall supply
2 Thess 2:4, all that is called G
  2:4, he as G sitteth in the temple
1 Tim 3:16, G was manifest
Heb 8:10, I will be to them a G
  11:16, to be called their G
  12:23, G the Judge of all
1 John 1:5, that G is light
  4:8, G is love
  4:12, No man hath seen G
  5:19, know that we are of G
Rev 21:3, G himself shall be
  21:4, G shall wipe away
  21:7, I will be his G
See Job 33:12; Ps 10:4
GODHEAD Acts 17:29, G is like
    unto gold
Rom 1:20, eternal power and G
Col 2:9, fullness of the G bodily
GODLINESS 1 Tim 3:16, great is
    the mystery of g
  4:7, thyself rather unto g
  6:5, supposing that gain is g
2 Tim 3:5, Having a form of g
Titus 1:1, which is after g
2 Pet 1:3, unto life and g

  1:6, and to patience g
  3:11, conversation and g
See 1 Tim 2:2, 10; 6:6, 11
GODLY Ps 12:1, the g man ceaseth
Mal 2:15, might seek a g seed
2 Cor 1:12, simplicity and g
  7:10, g sorrow worketh
2 Tim 3:12, live g in Christ Jesus
Titus 2:12, righteously, and g
Heb 12:28, and g fear
2 Pet 2:9, deliver the g
3 John 6, after a g sort
See Ps 4:3; 2 Cor 7:9
GONE Ps 109:23, g like the shadow
  119:176, I have g astray
Is 53:6, sheep have g astray
Jer 15:9, her sun is g down
Matt 12:43, unclean spirit is g
  25:8, lamps are g out
Rom 3:12, They are all g
Jude 11, g in the way of Cain
See Ps 89:34; Song 2:11
GOOD (n.) Gen 50:20, God meant it
    unto g
Ps 14:1, none that doeth g
Prov 3:27, Withhold not g
Eccl 3:12, there is no g in them
  9:18, destroyeth much g
Acts 10:38, went about doing g
Rom 8:28, work together for g
  13:4, to thee for g
See Job 5:27; Prov 11:17
GOOD (adj.) Gen 1:4, God saw the
    light, that it was g
  1:10, God saw that it was g
Ps 34:8, the Lord is g
Prov 22:1, g name is rather
  25:25, so is g news
Eccl 6:12, what is g for men
Is 55:2, ye that which is g
Lam 3:26, It is g that a man should
  3:27, It is g for a man
Zech 1:13, g words
Matt 7:11, to give g gifts
  9:22, be of g comfort
  19:16, G Master, what g
  19:17, callest thou me g
  25:21, thou g and faithful
Mark 9:50, Salt is g
Luke 6:38, g measure, pressed
down
  10:42, chosen that g part
  12:32, Father's g pleasure
  18:19, Why callest thou me g
John 1:46, Can there any g
  10:11, I am the g shepherd
Rom 7:12, and just, and g
  7:18, dwelleth no g thing
  12:2, prove what is that g
  14:21, g neither to eat
1 Cor 7:26, g for the present
  15:33, corrupt g manners
2 Cor 9:8, to every g work
Gal 6:6, all g things
Phil 1:6, begun a g work in
Col 1:10, in every g work
1 Thess 5:15, that which is g
  5:21, which is g
1 Tim 1:8, the law is g
  3:1, he desireth a g work
  4:4, creature of God is g
  6:12, Fight the g
2 Tim 3:3, that are g
Titus 2:7, a pattern of g works
  2:14, zealous of g works
Heb 6:5, the g word
  13:9, it is a g thing
James 1:17, Every g gift
3 John 11, but that which is g
See 2 Thess. 2:17; Titus 1:16
GOODNESS Ex 33:19, make all my
    g pass before thee
  34:6, abundant in g and truth

Ps 16:2, **g** extendeth not
23:6, Surely **g** and mercy
27:13, the **g** of the Lord
33:5, earth is full of the **g**
65:11, the year with thy **g**
Prov 20:6, every one his own **g**
Hos 6:4, your **g** is as a morning
Zech 9:17, how great is his **g**
Rom 2:4, the riches of his **g**
See Neh 9:25; Is 63:7; Gal 5:22
GOSPEL Matt 11:5, have the **g**
preached to them
Mark 8:35, my sake and the **g**
Rom 1:16, ashamed of the **g**
10:15, preach the **g** of peace
2 Cor 4:3, But if our **g** be hid
Gal 1:8, preach any other **g**
2:7, **g** of the uncircumcision
Col 1:23, the hope of the **g**
1 Tim 1:11, to the glorious **g**
Rev 14:6, the everlasting **g**
See Matt 4:23; Mark 16:15
GOVERNMENT Is 9:6, the **g** shall
be upon his shoulder
1 Cor 12:28, helps, **g**, diversities
2 Pet 2:10, and despise **g**
GRACE Ps 45:2, **g** is poured into
Prov 1:9, an ornament of **g**
3:34, but he giveth **g** unto
Zech 12:10, spirit of **g** and of
John 1:14, full of **g** and truth
Rom 1:7, **G** to you and peace
3:24, freely by his **g**
4:4, not reckoned of **g**
5:20, **g** did much more abound
6:14, but under **g**
11:5, the election of **g**
1 Cor 1:3, **G** be unto you
2 Cor 1:2, **G** be to you
8:9, the **g** of our Lord Jesus
12:9, My **g** is sufficient
Gal 1:6, into the **g** of Christ
1:15, and called me by his **g**
5:4, ye are fallen from **g**
Eph 2:5, by **g** ye are saved
3:8, is this **g** given
Heb 4:16, the throne of **g**
10:29, the Spirit of **g**
James 4:6, But he giveth more **g**
1 Pet 5:5, and giveth **g** to
2 Pet 3:18, grow in **g**, and in the
See Acts 20:24; 2 Cor 6:1
GRACIOUS Ex 22:27, for I am **g**
33:19, **g** to whom I will
Neh 9:17, **g** and merciful
Ps 77:9, forgotten to be **g**
Prov 11:16, A **g** woman
Is 30:18, he may be **g** unto
Jon 4:2, thou art a **g** God
Luke 4:22, the **g** words
1 Pet 2:3, the Lord is **g**
See Ex 34:6; 2 Chr 30:9
GRAVE (*n.*) Gen 42:38, gray hairs
with sorrow to the **g**
44:31, sorrow to the **g**
Job 7:9, goeth down to the **g**
Ps 6:5, in the **g** who shall
31:27, be silent in the **g**
49:15, the power of the **g**
Eccl 9:10, in the **g**
Is 38:18, the **g** cannot praise
53:9, his **g** with the wicked
Hos 13:14, O **g**, I will be
John 5:28, that are in the **g**
11:31, to the **g** to weep
1 Cor 15:55, O **g**, where is thy
See Matt 27:52; Rev 11:9
GREAT Gen 12:2, I will make of
thee a **g** nation
18:18, **g** and mighty nation
46:3, of thee a **g** nation
2 Chr 2:5, for **g** is our God
Ps 31:19, how **g** is thy goodness
92:5, how **g** are thy works

139:17, O God! how **g** is the
Matt 5:12, for **g** is your
5:19, called **g** in the
13:46, one pearl of **g** price
15:28, **g** is thy faith
20:26, whosoever will be **g**
22:36, the **g** commandment
1 Tim 3:16, **g** is the mystery
Heb 2:3, so **g** salvation
See Deut 9:2; Eccl 2:9; Rev 7:9
GREATER Matt 12:6, **g** than the
temple
Mark 12:31, commandment **g** than
John 1:50, see **g** things than
4:12, Art thou **g** than
5:20, **g** works than these
8:53, **g** than our father
10:29, is **g** than all
14:12, **g** works than these
14:28, for my Father is **g**
13:16, The servant is not **g**
15:13, **G** love hath no man
Heb 6:13, could swear by no **g**
1 John 3:20, God is **g** than
4:4, because **g** is he that
3 John 4, I have no **g** joy
See Gen 41:40; 48:19; Heb 9:11
GREATEST Matt 18:1, the **g** in the
kingdom
Mark 9:34, who should be the **g**
Luke 9:46, should be **g**
1 Cor 13:13, but the **g** of
See Job 1:3; Jer 31:34
GRIEF Ps 31:10, life is spent with **g**
Eccl 1:18, is much **g**
Is 53:3, acquainted with **g**
See Jon 4:6; Heb 13:17
GRIEVE Mark 3:5, **g** for the
hardness
Eph 4:20, And **g** not the holy
See Neh 2:10; 13:8; Ps 119:158
GRIEVOUS Gen 21:11, the thing
was very **g** in Abraham's sight
Matt 23:4, **g** to be borne
Luke 11:46, with burdens **g** to
Phil 3:1, indeed is not **g**
Heb 12:11, be joyous, but **g**
1 John 5:3, are not **g**
See Eccl 2:17; Jer 16:4
GROAN Rom 8:22, **g** and travaileth
2 Cor 5:2, in this we **g**
See Job 23:2; Ps 6:6
GROUNDED Eph 3:17, ye, being
rooted and **g** in love
Col 1:23, in the faith **g**
GROW Is 53:2, **g** up before him
Matt 13:30, both **g** together
Eph 2:21, **g** unto an holy
4:15, may **g** up into him
2 Pet 3:18, **g** in grace
See 2 Kin 19:26; Jer 12:2
GUIDE Ps 48:14, he will be our **g**
Prov 6:7, having no **g**
Is 58:11, the Lord shall **g**
Jer 3:4, thou art the **g** of my
Luke 1:79, our feet into
John 16:13, he will **g** you
See Gen 48:14; Prov 11:3
GUILE Ps 32:2, in whose spirit
there is no **g**
John 1:47, in whom is no **g**
1 Pet 2:22, neither was **g** found
See Ex 21:14; 1 Thess 2:3
GUILTY Ex 34:7, clear the **g**
Num 14:18, clearing the **g**
Rom 3:19, become **g** before God
1 Cor 11:27, shall be **g** of
James 2:10, he is **g** of all
See Num 35:27; Prov 30:10

H

HABITATION Ps 69:25, Let their **h**
be desolate

Luke 16:9, into everlasting **h**
Acts 1:20, let his **h** be desolate
Eph 2:22, for an **h** of God
Jude 6, but left their own **h**
See Prov 8:31; Acts 1:20
HAIR Ps 40:12, the **h** of mine head
Matt 5:36, make one **h** white
10:30, the very **h** of your
1 Cor 11:14, man have long **h**
1 Tim 2:9, not with braided **h**
1 Pet 3:3, of plaiting the **h**
See 2 Sam 14:26; Hos 7:9
HALLOW Matt 6:9, **H** be thy name
HALT 1 Kin 18:21, How long **h** ye
between two
See Mic 4:6; Zeph 3:19
HAND Ex 21:24, **h** for **h**
Num 11:23, Is the Lord's **h**
Deut 33:2, from his right **h**
1 Sam 5:11, **h** of God
2 Sam 24:14, **h** of the Lord
Job 19:21, the **h** of God
19:21, the **h** of God
Ps 16:11, at thy right **h**
24:4, He that hath clean **h**
90:17, the work of our **h**
Prov 6:10, folding of the **h**
11:21, though **h** join in **h**
19:24, hideth his **h**
22:26, that strike **h**
Eccl 2:24, the **h** of God
9:10, thy **h** findeth to do
11:6, withhold not thine **h**
Is 40:12, hollow of his **h**
59:1, the Lord's **h** is not
Ezek 10:2, fill thine **h**
Zech 13:6, wounds in thine **h**
Matt 3:2, heaven is at **h**
6:3, let not thy left **h**
18:8, if thy **h** or thy foot
26:18, My time is at **h**
26:46, he is at that
Mark 9:43, thy **h** offend thee
16:19, the right **h** of God
2 Cor 5:1, not made with **h**
Phil 4:5, The Lord is at **h**
2 Thess 2:2, Christ is at **h**
1 Tim 2:8, lifting up holy **h**
Heb 10:31, **h** of the living God
James 4:8, Cleanse your **h**
1 Pet 4:7, the end . . . is at **h**
1 John 1:1, our **h** have handled
See Luke 9:62; Col 2:14
HAPPY Deut 33:29, **H** art thou
Job 5:17, **h** is the man
Ps 128:2, **h** shalt thou be
144:15, **H** is that people
Prov 3:18, **h** is every one
14:21, **h** is he
Jer 12:1, are all they **h**
Mal 3:15, call the proud **h**
John 13:17, **h** are ye
Rom 14:22, **H** is he that
James 5:11, we count them **h**
1 Pet 3:14, **h** are ye
See Prov 29:18; 1 Cor 7:40
HARDEN Ex 4:21, but I will **h** his
heart, that he
14:17, will **h** the hearts
Ps 95:8, **H** not your heart
Prov 21:29, man **h** his face
28:14, he that **h** his heart
29:1, being often reproved **h**
Is 63:17, and **h** our heart
Mark 6:52, heart was **h**
8:17, your heart yet **h**
John 12:40, and **h** their
Acts 19:9, when divers were **h**
Rom 9:18, he will he **h**
Heb 3:13, **h** through the
See Deut 15:7; Job 39:16
HARDNESS Mark 3:5, grieved for
the **h** of their hearts
16:14, and **h** of heart

2 Tim 2:3, therefore endure **h**
See Job 38:38; Mark 10:5
HARMLESS Matt 10:16, wise as
  serpents, and **h** as doves
Phil 2:15, blameless and **h**
Heb 7:26, who is holy, **h**
HARVEST Gen 8:22, seedtime and
  h
Jer 8:20, The **h** is past
  51:33, the time of her **h**
Joel 3:13, for the **h** is ripe
Matt 9:37, The **h** truly is
  9:38, Lord of the **h**
  13:30, and in the time of **h**
Mark 4:29, because the **h** is come
Luke 10:2, **h** truly is great
John 4:35, white already to **h**
Rev 14:15, the **h** of the earth
See Josh 3:15; Matt 13:39
HATE Lev 19:17, not **h** thy brother
Ps 34:21, the righteous
  97:10, love the Lord, **h** evil
Prov 1:22, and fools **h** knowledge
  13:24, **h** his son
  14:20, The poor is **h**
  15:10, he that **h** reproof
  15:27, but he that **h** gifts
Eccl 2:17, Therefore I **h** life
  3:8, and a time to **h**
Is 1:14, feasts my soul **h**
  61:8, I **h** robbery
Amos 5:15, **H** the evil
Mic 3:2, Who **h** the good
Zech 8:17, things that I **h**
Mal 1:3, I **h** Esau
Matt 5:44, to them that **h** you
  6:24, for either he will **h**
  10:22, ye shall be **h**
  24:10, shall **h** one another
Luke 6:22, men shall **h** you
  6:27, to them which **h**
  14:26, and **h** not his father
John 3:20, the light
  7:7, cannot **h** you
  12:25, he that **h** his life
  15:18, If the world **h** you
  15:24, both seen and **h**
Rom 9:13, Esau have I **h**
Eph 5:29, **h** his own flesh
1 John 2:9, **h** his brother
  3:13, if the world **h** you
  4:20, and **h** his brother
See Gen 27:41; Prov 6:16
HAUGHTY 2 Sam 22:28, thine eyes
  are upon the **h**
Ps 131:1, my heart is not **h**
Prov 16:18, and an **h** spirit
  21:24, Proud and **h** scorner
Is 10:33, **h** shall be humbled
Zeph 3:11, shalt no more be **h**
See Is 2:11; 3:11; Ezek 16:50
HEAD Gen 3:15, it shall bruise thy
  h
Josh 2:19, be upon his **h**
Ps 24:7, 9, Lift up your **h**
  110:7, he lift up the **h**
Prov 10:6, are upon the **h**
  25:22, fire upon his **h**
Eccl 2:14, eyes are in his **h**
Is 1:5, the whole **h** is sick
  35:10 joy upon their **h**
Jer 9:1, my **h** were waters
  14:3, and covered their **h**
Amos 2:7, the **h** of the poor
Zech 1:21, lift up his **h**
Luke 7:46, My **h** with oil
  21:28, lift up your **h**
1 Cor 11:3, the **h** of every man
Eph 1:22, gave him to be **h**
  4:15, which is the **h**
  5:23, the husband is the **h**
Col 1:18, the **h** of the body
  2:19, not holding the **H**
See Josh 7:6; Rev 13:1

HEAL Ex 15:26, for I am the Lord
  that **h** thee
Deut 32:39, I wound, and I **h**
2 Kin 2:22, the waters were **h**
  20:5, I will **h** thee
Ps 6:2, O Lord, **h** me
  41:4, **h** my soul
  103:3, **h** all thy diseases
  107:20, and **h** them
Is 6:10, convert, and be **h**
  53:5, stripes we are **h**
Jer 15:18, refuseth to be **h**
  17:14, **H** me, O Lord
Hos 6:1, and he will **h** us
  14:4, **h** their backsliding
Matt 10:1, and to **h** all manner
  10:8, **H** the sick
  12:10, lawful to **h**
Mark 3:2, he would **h**
Luke 4:18, **h** the brokenhearted
  4:23, Physician, **h** thyself
  5:17, present to **h** them
  10:9, **h** the sick
Acts 14:9, faith to be **h**
James 5:16, ye may be **h**
1 Pet 2:24, ye were **h**
Rev 13:3, deadly wound was **h**
See Eccl 3:3; Is 3:7; Matt 4:21
HEALING Jer 14:19, there is no **h**
  for us
Mal 4:2, **h** in his wings
Matt 4:23, **h** all manner
Luke 9:11, had need of **h**
1 Cor 12:9, gifts of **h**
  12:28, then gift of **h**
Rev 22:2, **h** of the nations
See Jer 30:13; Acts 4:22; 10:38
HEAR 2 Kin 18:28, **H** the word
Neh 8:2, **h** with understanding
Job 31:35, Oh that one would **h**
Ps 4:1, **H** me when I call
  4:3, the Lord will **h**
  10:17, thine ear to **h**
  39:12, **H** my prayer, O Lord
  54:2, **H** my prayer, O God
  66:18, Lord will not **h** me
  85:8, **h** what God
  102:1, **H** my prayer, O Lord
Prov 13:8, but the poor **h**
  18:13, before he **h** it
  22:17, **h** the words
Eccl 5:1, be more ready to **h**
  7:5, better to **h** the rebuke
Is 1:2, **H**, O heavens
  29:18, shall the deaf **h**
  33:13, **H**, ye that are far off
  34:1, ye nations, to **h**
Jer 7:16, I will not **h** thee
  14:12, not **h** their cry
Ezek 8:18, yet will I not **h**
Dan 9:17, **h** the prayer
Zech 10:6, will **h** them
Matt 7:24, whosoever **h** these
  11:5, the deaf **h**
  17:5, **h** ye him
Mark 7:37, the deaf to **h**
  9:7, beloved Son: **h** him
Luke 6:47, **h** my sayings
  7:22, the deaf **h**
  10:16, He that **h** you **h** me
  10:24, to **h** those things
John 5:25, **h** the voice of God
  6:60, who can **h** it
  9:31, we know that God **h** not
  11:42, thou **h** me always
  12:47, any man **h** my words
  14:24, the word which ye **h**
Rom 10:14, **h** without a preacher
1 John 4:5, world **h** them
  4:6, knoweth God **h** us
  5:15, that he **h** us
Rev 2:7, let him **h**
  3:20, if any man **h** my voice
See 2 Kin 19:16; 2 Chr 6:21

HEARD Gen 3:8, And they **h** the
  voice of the Lord
  21:17, And God **h** the voice
Ex 3:7, have **h** their cry
Num 11:1, and the Lord **h** it
Deut 4:12, only ye **h** a voice
Ps 6:9, **h** my supplication
  10:17, hast **h** the desire
  34:4, and he **h** me
  61:5, hast **h** my vows
  116:1, hath **h** my voice
Is 40:21, have ye not **h**
  66:8, hath **h**, such a thing
Jer 51:46, rumor that shall be **h**
Matt 6:7, be **h** for their
John 11:41, thou hast **h** me
Acts 4:4, **h** the word believed
  4:20, we have seen and **h**
Rom 10:14, they have not **h**
1 Cor 2:9, nor ear **h**
2 Cor 12:4, and **h** unspeakable
Eph 4:21, ye have **h** him
Phil 4:9, received, and **h**
Heb 2:3, by them that **h**
1 John 1:1, which we have **h**
  1:3, we have seen and **h**
See John 5:37; Rev 19:6; 22:8
HEARER Rom 2:13, For not the **h**
  of the law are just
Eph 4:29, grace unto the **h**
James 1:22, and not **h** only
HEARING Prov 20:12, The **h** ear
Eccl 1:8, ear filled with **h**
Matt 13:13, **h** they hear not
Rom 10:17, faith cometh by **h**
1 Cor 12:17, where were the **h**
Heb 5:11, ye are dull of **h**
See Gal 3:2; 2 Pet 2:8
HEART Deut 11:13, with all your **h**
1 Sam 10:9, gave him another **h**
  16:7, Lord looketh on the **h**
1 Kin 3:9, an understanding **h**
  14:8, with all his **h**
1 Chr 12:33, not of double **h**
  29:17, triest the **h**
2 Chr 32:25, **h** was lifted up
Ps 10:6, said in his **h**
  19:8, rejoicing the **h**
  27:3, **h** shall not fear
  28:7, **h** trusted in him
  64:6, the **h**, is deep
  119:11, I had in mine **h**
  139:23, and know my **h**
Prov 4:23, Keep thy **h**
  14:10, The **h** knoweth
  23:7, thinketh in his **h**
  25:20, songs to a heavy **h**
  31:11, **h** of her husband
Eccl 8:5, wise man's **h**
Is 35:4, of a fearful **h**
  65:14, sing for joy of **h**
Jer 11:20, reins and the **h**
  17:9, The **h** is deceitful
  20:9, word was in mine **h**
  24:7, will give them an **h**
  49:16, the pride of thine **h**
Ezek 11:19, take the stony **h**
  18:31, make you a new **h**
  44:7, uncircumcised in **h**
Joel 2:13, And rend your **h**
Obad 3, The pride of thine **h**
Mal 4:6, **h** of the fathers
Matt 5:8, the pure in **h**
  6:21, there will your **h** be ✓
  11:29, meek and lowly in **h**
  12:34, abundance of the **h**
  15:19, out of the **h** ✓
  18:35, from your **h**
  22:37, with all thy **h** ✓
Mark 10:5, hardness of your **h**
  12:30, with all thy **h**
  16:14, hardness of **h**
Luke 2:19, in her **h**
  6:45, abundance of the **h**

10:27, with all thy **h**
24:25, slow of **h**
24:32, our **h** burn within us
John 14:1, Let not your **h**
Acts 5:33, cut to the **h**
7:51, uncircumcised in **h**
7:54, were cut to the **h**
11:23, with purpose of **h**
Rom 10:10, For with the **h**
1 Cor 2:9, into the **h** of man
2 Cor 3:3, tables of the **h**
5:12, and not in **h**
Eph 3:17, dwell in your **h**
5:19, making melody in your **h**
6:6, from the **h**
Phil 4:7, shall keep your **h**
Col 3:22, in singleness of **h**
2 Thess 3:5, Lord direct your **h**
Heb 4:12, intents of the **h**
13:9, **h** be established
James 3:14, strife in your **h**
4:8, purify your **h**
1 Pet 3:4, hidden man of the **h**
3:15, God in your **h**
See Col 3:15; 2 Pet 1:19
HEARTILY Col 3:23, whatsoever ye do, do it **h**
HEATHEN Ps 2:1, Why do the **h** rage
Acts 4:25, Why did the **h** rage
See Lev 25:44; Neh 5:8
HEAVEN Gen 28:17, is the gate of **h**
Ex 20:22, with you from **h**
Deut 10:14, the **h** of heavens
33:13, precious things of **h**
1 Kin 8:27, **h** and **h** of heavens
2 Kin 7:2, make windows in **h**
Ps 8:3, When I consider thy **h**
14:2, looked down from **h**
119:89, word is settled in **h**
Prov 8:27, he prepared the **h**
Eccl 5:2, God is in **h**
Is 13:13, I will shake the **h**
65:17, I create new **h**
Ezek 1:1, the **h** were opened
Hag 2:6, I will shake the **h**
Mal 3:10, the windows of **h**
Matt 3:16, the **h** were opened
5:18, Till **h** and earth pass
24:35, **H** and earth shall
Mark 1:10, he saw the **h** opened
13:25, the stars of **h**
13:32, angels which are in **h**
Luke 15:18, sinned against **h**
John 1:51, shall see **h** open
6:32, true bread from **h**
Acts 4:12, name under **h** given
Rom 1:18, revealed from **h**
2 Cor 5:1, eternal in the **h**
5:2, which is from **h**
Gal 1:8, an angel from **h**
Eph 1:10, both which are in **h**
3:15, family in **h**
6:9, Master also is in **h**
Phil 3:20, conversation is in **h**
Col 4:1, a Master in **h**
Heb 12:23, are written in **h**
1 John 5:7, bear record in **h**
Rev 4:1, door was opened in **h**
21:1, I saw a new **h**
See 1 Thess 4:16; 2 Thess 1:7
HEAVENLY Luke 2:13, a multitude of the **h** host
11:13, your **h** Father
John 3:12, of **h** things
Acts 26:19, the **h** vision
1 Cor 15:48, and as is the **h**
Eph 1:3, in **h** places
2:6, together in **h** places
3:10, powers in **h** places
Heb 3:1, of the **h** calling
8:5, shadow of **h** things
9:23, but the **h** things

11:16, that is, an **h**
See 2 Tim 4:18; Heb 6:4; 12:22
HEEL Gen 3:15, head, and thou shalt bruise his **h**
HEIR Matt 21:38, This is the **h**
Rom 8:17, then **h**; **h** of God
Gal 3:29, and **h** according
4:7, then an **h** of God
Titus 3:7, should be made **h**
Heb 1:2, whom . . . appointed **h**
6:17, the **h** of promise
11:7, **h** of the righteousness
James 2:5, **h** of the kingdom
1 Pet 3:7, **h** together
See Mic 1:15; Rom 4:13
HELL Deut 32:22, shall burn unto the lowest **h**
2 Sam 22:6, The sorrows of **h**
Job 11:8, deeper than **h**
Ps 9:17, be turned into **h**
16:10, my soul in **h**
55:15, down quick into **h**
139:8, if I make my bed in **h**
Prov 5:5, take hold on **h**
7:27, is the way to **h**
9:18, the depths of **h**
15:11, **H** and destruction
15:24, he may depart from **h**
23:14, his soul from **h**
27:20, **H** and destruction
Is 14:9, **H** from beneath
28:15, and with **h** are we
Ezek 31:16, cast him down to **h**
32:21, the midst of **h**
Amos 9:2, they dig into **h**
Jon 2:2, the belly of **h**
Hab 2:5, his desire as **h**
Matt 5:22, danger of **h** fire
5:29, be cast into **h**
10:28, soul and body in **h**
11:23, brought down to **h**
16:18, and the gates of **h**
18:9, cast into **h** fire
23:15, more the child of **h**
23:33, damnation of **h**
Luke 10:15, thrust down to **h**
12:5, to cast into **h**
16:23, in **h** he lift up
Acts 2:31, nor left in **h**
James 3:6, on fire of **h**
2 Pet 2:4, them down to **h**
See Is 5:14; Rev 1:18; 20:13
HELMET Is 59:17, an **h** of salvation upon his head
Eph 6:17, the **h** of salvation
HELP Gen 2:18, will make him an **h** meet for him
Deut 33:29, shield of thy **h**
Ps 22:11, none to **h**
33:20, Lord: he is our **h**
42:5, **h** of his countenance
46:1, a very present **h**
121:1, whence cometh my **h**
124:8, Our **h** is in the name
Hos 13:9, in me is thine **h**
Matt 15:25, Lord, **h** me
Mark 9:24, **h** thou mine unbelief
Heb 4:16, find grace to **h**
See Rom 8:26; 1 Cor 1:24
HELPER Heb 13:6, Lord is my **h**, and I will not fear
HERESIES 1 Cor 11:19, there must be also **h** among you
Gal 5:20, strife, seditions, **h**
2 Pet 2:1, in damnable **h**
HERITAGE Job 20:29, the **h** appointed unto him by God
Ps 16:6, I have a goodly **h**
61:5, the **h** of those
127:3, an **h** of the Lord
Is 54:17, **h** of the servants
Jer 3:19, a goodly **h**
Mic 7:14, the flock of thine **h**

1 Pet 5:3, lords over God's **h**
See Joel 2:17; 3:2; Mal 1:3
HID 2 Kin 4:27, and the Lord hath **h** it from me
Job 3:21, for **h** treasures
Ps 32:5, have I not **h**
69:5, sins are not **h**
119:11, Thy word have I **h**
Zeph 2:3, ye shall be **h**
Matt 10:26, **h**, that shall
Mark 4:22, there is nothing **h**
Luke 19:42, **h** from thine eyes
1 Cor 2:7, the **h** wisdom
2 Cor 4:3, if our gospel be **h**
Col 3:3, your life is **h**
1 Pet 3:4, be the **h** man
Rev 2:17, of the **h** manna
See Matt 5:14; Mark 7:24
HIDE Job 14:13, thou wouldest **h** me
34:29, when he **h** his face
Ps 10:11, he **h** his face
17:8, **h** me under the shadow
139:12, the darkness **h** not
Is 1:15, I will **h** mine eyes
32:2, be as an **h** place
45:15, God that **h** thyself
James 5:20, shall **h** a multitude
Rev 6:16, **h** us from the face
See Prov 28:28; Amos 9:3
HIGH Job 11:8, It is as **h** as heaven
Ps 68:18, ascended on **h**
103:11, the heaven is **h**
131:1, too **h** for me
138:6, Though the Lord be **h**
139:6, it is **h**
Eccl 12:5, that which is **h**
Is 32:15, from on **h**
33:16, He shall dwell on **h**
Jer 49:16, make thy nest as **h**
Luke 1:78, dayspring from on **h**
24:49, power from on **h**
Rom 12:16, Mind not **h** things
13:11, it is **h** time
Phil 3:14, **h** calling of God
See Is 57:15; 2 Cor 10:5
HIGHER Is 55:9, the heavens are **h** . . . so are my ways **h**
Luke 14:10, Friend, go up **h**
Rom 13:1, unto the **h** powers
Heb 7:26, **h** than the heavens
HIGHEST Mark 11:10, of the Lord: Hosanna in the **h**
Luke 1:32, the Son of the **H**
1:35, power of the **H**
1:76, prophet of the **H**
2:14, Glory to God in the **h**
HILL Ps 2:6, holy **h** of Zion
15:1, dwell in thy holy **h**
24:3, ascend into the **h**
50:10, upon a thousand **h**
121:1, eyes unto the **h**
Prov 8:25, before the **h**
Jer 3:23, from the **h**
Hos 10:8, and to the **h**
Matt 5:14, that is set on an **h**
See Luke 4:29; 9:37; Acts 17:22
HOLD Gen 21:18, and **h** him in thine hand
Ex 20:7, not **h** him guiltless
Ps 119:117, **H** thou me up
Prov 11:12, he **h** his peace
17:28, a fool, when he **h**
Is 41:13, **h** thy right hand
Rom 1:18, **h** the truth
1 Cor 14:30, let the first **h**
Phil 2:16, **H** forth the word
Col 2:19, And not the Head
1 Thess 5:21, **h** fast that which
1 Tim 1:19, **H** faith
3:9, **H** the mystery of
2 Tim 1:13, **H** fast the form
Titus 1:9, **H** fast the faithful
Heb 3:14, **h** the beginning

4:14, **h** fast our profession
10:23, Let us **h** fast the profession
Rev 2:13, **h** fast my name
3:3, **h** fast, and repent
See Jer 2:13; 51:30; Ezek 19:9
HOLIER Is 65:5, near to me; for I
  am **h** than thou
HOLIEST Heb 9:3, which is called
  the **H** of all
10:19, into the **h**
HOLINESS Ex 15:11, who is like
  thee, glorious in **h**
28:36, **H** to the Lord
1 Chr 16:29, in the beauty of **h**
Ps 30:4, remembrance of his **h**
47:8, throne of his **h**
93:5, **h** becometh thine house
Is 35:8, The way of **h**
63:15, habitation of thy **h**
Jer 23:9, the words of his **h**
Obad 17, there shall be **h**
Zech 14:20, **H** unto the Lord
Luke 1:75, **h** and righteousness
Acts 3:12, own power or **h**
Rom 1:4, to the spirit of **h**
6:22, your fruit unto **h**
2 Cor 7:1, perfecting **h**
Eph 4:24, and true **h**
1 Thess 3:13, unblameable in **h**
4:7, but unto **h**
1 Tim 2:15, charity and **h**
Titus 2:3, as becometh **h**
Heb 12:10, partakers of his **h**
See Ps 80:35; Is 23:18; Jer 2:3
HOLY Ex 3:5, place whereon thou
  standest is **h**
19:6, an **h** nation
20:8, to keep it **h**
31:14, for it is **h**
Lev 10:10, **h** and unholy
20:7, be ye **h**
Num 16:5, and who is **h**
2 Kin 4:9, this is an **h** man
Ezra 9:2, **h** seed have
Ps 20:6, from his **h** heaven
22:3, thou art **h**
86:2, for I am **h**
99:9, worship at his **h** hill
145:17, **h** in all his works
Prov 20:25, that which is **h**
Is 6:3, said, **H, h, h**
6:13, the **h** seed
Ezek 22:26, mine **h** things
22:26, between the **h**
Matt 1:18, child of the **H** Ghost
3:11, with the **H** Ghost
7:6, not that which is **h**
12:31, against the **H** Ghost
Mark 13:11, but the **H** Ghost
Luke 1:35, The **H** Ghost shall
3:22, the **H** Ghost descended
4:1, full of the **H** Ghost
12:12, the **H** Ghost shall
John 1:33, with the **H** Ghost
7:39, the **H** Ghost was not
14:26, which is the **H** Ghost
17:11, **H** Father
20:22, Receive ye the **H** Ghost
Acts 1:8, **H** Ghost is come
2:4, were all filled with the **H**
4:27, thy **h** child Jesus
5:3, lie to the **H** Ghost
6:3, full of the **H** Ghost
7:51, resist the **H** Ghost
8:15, receive the **H** Ghost
9:31, comfort of the **H** Ghost
10:44, the **H** Ghost fell
10:47, received the **H** Ghost
15:8, giving them the **H** Ghost
15:28, good to the **H** Ghost
20:28, **H** Ghost hath made
Rom 1:2, the **h** scriptures
7:12, law is **h**

9:1, witness in the **H** Ghost
11:16, firstfruit be **h**
12:1, a living sacrifice, **h**
14:17, joy in the **H** Ghost
16:16, with an **h** kiss
1 Cor 2:13, **H** Ghost teacheth
3:17, temple of God is **h**
7:14, now are they **h**
2 Cor 13:12, with an **h** kiss
Eph 1:4, we should be **h**
2:21, unto an **h** temple
5:27, it should be **h**
Col 1:22, **h** and unblameable
3:12, **h** and beloved
1 Thess 5:27, all the **h** brethren
1 Tim 2:8, lifting up **h** hands
2 Tim 1:9, an **h** calling
Titus 1:8, sober, just, **h**
3:5, renewing of the **H** Ghost
Heb 3:1, Wherefore, **h** brethren
1 Pet 1:12, **H** Ghost sent down
1:15, called you is **h**
2:5, an **h** priesthood
2:9, an **h** nation
3:5, the **h** women
2 Pet 1:18, in the **h** mount
1:21, **h** men
3:11, in all **h** conversation
Rev 3:7, saith he that is **h**
4:8, saying, **H, h, h**
6:10, O Lord, **h** and true
20:6, Blessed and **h**
21:10, the **h** Jerusalem
22:11, he that is **h**
See 2 Tim 3:15; 1 Pet 1:16
HOME 1 Cor 11:34, let him eat at **h**
14:35, their husbands at **h**
2 Cor 5:6, at **h** in the body
1 Tim 5:4, show piety at **h**
Titus 2:5, keepers at **h**
See Jer 2:14; Luke 9:61; 15:6
HONEST Luke 8:15, in an **h** and
  good heart
Acts 6:3, men of **h** report
Rom 12:17, **h** in the sight
13:13, Let us walk **h**
2 Cor 8:21, for **h** things
Phil 4:8, things are **h**
1 Pet 2:12, your conversation **h**
See 1 Thess 4:12; 1 Tim 2:2
HONOUR (*n.*) Prov 3:16, riches and
  h
20:3, It is an **h** for a man
26:1, so **h** is not
26:8, giveth **h** to a fool
Eccl 6:2, riches, wealth, and **h**
Mal 1:6, where is mine **h**
Matt 13:57, not without **h**
John 4:44, hath no **h** in his
5:41, I receive not **h**
Rom 2:7, for glory and **h**
12:10, in **h** preferring
13:7, **h** to whom **h**
1 Tim 5:17, worthy of double **h**
2 Tim 2:20, some to **h**
1 Pet 3:7, **h** unto the wife
Rev 4:11, receive glory and **h**
See Rev 5:13; 7:12; 19:1; 21:24
HONOUR (*v.*) Ex 20:12, **H** thy
  father and thy mother
Ps 15:4, but he **h** them
Prov 3:9, **H** the Lord
12:9, he that **h** himself
Mal 1:6, A son **h** his father
Matt 15:8, **h** me with their lips
John 5:23, that **h** not the Son
1 Tim 5:3, **H** widows
1 Pet 2:17, **H** all men
See Is 29:13; 58:13; Acts 28:10
HONOURABLE Ps 45:9, were
  among thy **h** women
Is 3:3, and the **h** man
9:15, ancient and **h**

42:21, and make it **h**
See Luke 14:8; 1 Cor 4:10
HOPE (*n.*) Job 7:6, are spent
  without **h**
8:13, the hypocrite's **h**
19:10, **h** hath he removed
Ps 16:9, shall rest in **h**
39:7, my **h** is in thee
Prov 13:12, **H** deferred
14:32, righteous hath **h**
26:12, **h** of a fool
Eccl 9:4, living there is **h**
Jer 17:7, whose **h** the Lord
Rom 8:24, for we are saved by **h**
12:2, Rejoicing in **h**
1 Cor 13:13, abideth faith, **h**
Eph 1:18, **h** of his calling
2:12, having no **h**
Col 1:27, the **h** of glory
1 Thess 4:13, which have no **h**
5:8, the **h** of salvation
Titus 3:7, **h** of eternal life
Heb 6:18, lay hold upon the **h**
1 Pet 1:3, unto a lively **h**
See Col 1:5; 1 John 3:3
HOPE (*v.*) Ps 22:9, didst make me **h**
31:24, **h** in the Lord
71:14, will **h** continually
1 Pet 1:13, and **h** to the end
See Jer 3:23; Heb 11:1
HOSPITALITY Rom 12:13,
  necessity of saints; given to **h**
1 Tim 3:2, given to **h**
Titus 1:8, But a lover of **h**
1 Pet 4:9, **h** one to another
HOUR Matt 24:36, of that day and **h**
26:40, with me one **h**
Mark 13:32, day and that **h**
14:37, thou watch one **h**
Luke 12:39, known what **h**
22:53, but this is your **h**
John 5:25, The **h** is coming
12:27, save me from this **h**
16:32, the **h** cometh
Acts 3:1, the **h** of prayer
Gal 2:5, not for an **h**
Rev 3:10, **h** of temptation
See Acts 2:15; 1 Cor 4:11
HOUSE Gen 28:17, none other but
  the **h** of God
2 Kin 20:1, thine **h** in order
Neh 13:11, **h** of God forsaken
Job 30:23, to the **h** appointed
Ps 26:8, habitation of thy **h**
69:9, the zeal of thine **h**
92:13, the **h** of the Lord
Prov 12:7, **h** of the righteous
19:14, **H** and riches
Eccl 7:2, **h** of mourning
Is 5:8, join **h** to **h**
64:11, our beautiful **h**
Matt 23:38, your **h** is left
Mark 3:25, if a **h** be divided
Luke 6:48, upon that **h**
John 14:2, my Father's **h**
Acts 2:46, from **h** to **h**
2 Cor 5:1, our earthly **h**
1 Tim 5:8, those of his own **h**
See Matt 9:6; Luke 7:44; 19:5
HOUSEHOLD Gal 6:10, the **h** of
  faith
Eph 2:19, the **h** of God
See Gen 31:37; 47:12; 2 Sam 17:23
HUMBLE Ps 9:12, the cry of the **h**
34:2 the **h** shall hear
Prov 16:19, of an **h** spirit
Is 57:15, contrite and **h** spirit
Matt 18:4, therefore shall **h**
Luke 14:11, that **h** himself shall
Phil 2:8, he **h** himself
James 4:6, grace unto the **h**
1 Pet 5:6, **H** yourselves
See Is 2:11; 5:15; Lam 3:20

HUMBLY Mic 6:8, to walk **h** with
HUMILITY Prov 15:33, and before
  honour is **h**
  22:4, By **h** and the fear
  See Col 2:18, 23; 1 Pet 5:5
HUNGER Is 49:10, They shall not **h**
  Matt 5:6, they which do **h**
  Luke 6:21, ye that **h** now
  John 6:35, shall never **h**
  Rom 12:20, If thine enemy **h**
  1 Cor 4:11, both **h**, and thirst
  11:34, And if any man **h**
  Rev 7:16, shall **h** no more
  See Matt 4:2; 12:1; Luke 15:17
HUNGRY Ps 107:9, filleth the **h** soul
  146:7, food to the **h**
  Prov 25:21, if thine enemy be **h**
  27:7, to the **h** soul
  Luke 1:53, filled the **h** with good
  See Prov 6:30; Mark 11:12
HUSBAND Prov 12:4, a crown
  to her **h**
  31:23, Her **h** is known
  Is 54:5, Maker is thine **h**
  1 Cor 7:16, shalt save thy **h**
  14:35, let them ask their **h**
  Eph 5:22, unto your own **h**
  5:25, **H**, love your wives
  1 Tim 3:12, **h** of one wife
  Titus 2:4, love their **h**
  2:5, to their own **h**
  See Ruth 1:11; Esth 1:17, 20
HYMN Matt 26:30, they had sung
  an **h**
  Eph 5:19, in psalms and **h**
HYPOCRITE Job 8:13, and the **h**
  hope shall perish
  36:13, But the **h** in heart
  Is 9:17, for every one is an **h**
  Matt 6:2, as the **h** do
  6:16, be not, as the **h**
  24:51, portion with the **h**
  Mark 7:6, prophesied of you **h**
  See Job 13:16; 27:8; Prov 11:9

I

IDLE Prov 19:15, and an **i** soul
  31:27, the bread of **i**
  Matt 12:36, every **i** word
  20:3, **i** in the marketplace
  See Eccl 10:18; 1 Tim 5:13
IDOL 1 Chr 16:26, all the gods of the
  people are **i**
  Hos 4:17, joined to **i**
  Acts 15:20, pollutions of **i**
  1 Cor 8:4, an **i** is nothing
  1 Thess 1:9, to God from **i**
  1 John 5:21, yourselves from **i**
  See Gal 5:20; Col 3:5
IGNORANCE Acts 3:17, that
  through **i** ye did
  17:30, the times of this **i**
  Eph 4:18, **i** that is in them
  1 Pet 2:15, **i** of foolish men
  See Lev 4:2; Num 15:24
IGNORANT Acts 4:13, unlearned
  and **i** men
  Rom 10:3, For they being **i**
  1 Cor 14:38, if any man be **i**
  2 Cor 2:11, for we are not **i**
  Heb 5:2, compassion on the **i**
  2 Pet 3:5, they willingly are **i**
  See Num 15:28; 1 Tim 1:13
IMAGE Gen 1:26, said, Let us make
  man in our **i**
  Rom 1:23, into an **i** made
  8:29, **i** of his Son
  2 Cor 3:18, same **i** from glory
IMAGINATION Gen 6:5, every **i** of
  the thoughts of his
  8:21, the **i** of man's heart
  Deut 29:19, I walk in the **i**

1 Chr 28:9, **i** of the thoughts
Jer 23:17, **i** of his own heart
Rom 1:21, vain in their **i**
2 Cor 10:5, Casting down **i**
See Prov 6:18; Lam 3:60
IMMORTALITY Rom 2:7, glory and
  honour and **i**
  1 Cor 15:53, mortal must put on **i**
  I Tim 6:16, Who only hath **i**
  2 Tim 1:10, brought life and **i**
IMPOSSIBLE Matt 19:26, With men
  this is **i**
  Mark 10:27, it is **i**, but not with God
  Luke 1:37, nothing shall be **i**
  18:27, things which are **i**
  See Matt 17:20; Luke 17:1
IMPUTE Lev 17:4, blood shall be **i**
  unto that man
  Ps 32:2, Lord **i** not iniquity
  Hab 1:11, **i** this his power
  Rom 4:8, will not **i** sin
  5:13, sin is not **i**
  See 1 Sam 22:15; 2 Cor 5:19
INCORRUPTIBLE 1 Cor 9:25,
  corruptible crown; but we an **i**
  1 Pet 1:4, an inheritance **i**
  See Rom 1:23; 1 Cor 15:42, 50
INCREASE (*n.*) Deut 14:22, tithe
  all the **i**
  Ps 67:6, earth yield her **i**
  Is 9:7, **i** of his government
  1 Cor 3:6, God gave the **i**
  See Jer 2:3; Eph 4:16; Col 2:19
INCREASE (*v.*) Ps. 115:14, Lord
  shall **i** you
  Prov 1:5, will **i** learning
  Eccl 1:18, he that **i** knowledge
  Dan 12:4, knowledge shall be **i**
  Luke 2:52, Jesus **i** in wisdom
  17:5, **I** our faith
  Acts 6:7, word of God **i**
  16:5, **i** in number daily
  Rev 3:17, **i** with goods
  See Eccl 2:9; 5:11; Mark 4:8
INFALLIBLE Acts 1:3, by many **i**
  proofs
INFIRMITY Matt 8:17, Himself
  took our **i**
  Rom 8:26, helpeth our **i**
  See Luke 5:15; 7:21; Heb 5:2
INHERIT Ex 32:13, and they shall **i**
  it for ever
  Ps 25:13, seed shall **i**
  37:11, meek shall **i**
  Prov 14:18, simple **i** folly
  Matt 19:29, **i** everlasting life
  25:34, **i** the kingdom
  Mark 10:17, **i** eternal life
  1 Cor 6:9, shall not **i**
  15:50, cannot **i** the kingdom
  Heb 12:17, **i** the blessing
  See Heb 6:12; 1 Pet 3:9
INHERITANCE Ps 16:5, The Lord
  is the portion of mine **i**
  Eph 1:14, earnest of our **i**
  Heb 9:15, promise of eternal **i**
  See Eph 5:5; Col 1:12; Heb 1:4
INIQUITY Ex 20:5, visiting the **i**
  of the fathers
  34:7, forgiving **i**
  Job 4:8, that plow **i**
  13:26, the **i** of my youth
  34:32, if I have done **i**
  Ps 25:11, pardon mine **i**
  32:2, imputeth not **i**
  51:5, I was shapen in **i**
  103:3, forgiveth all thine **i**
  Prov 22:8, that soweth **i**
  Is 53:5, bruised for our **i**
  Hab 1:13, not look on **i**
  Matt 24:12, **i** shall abound
  Acts 1:18, the reward of **i**
  8:23, in the bond of **i**

Rom 6:19, to **i** unto **i**
2 Thess 2:7, mystery of **i**
2 Tim 2:19, depart from **i**
James 3:6, a world of **i**
See Ps 36:2; Ezek 3:18; 18:26
INNOCENT Job 27:17, **i** shall divide
  Prov 28:20, shall not be **i**
  See Ex 23:7; Matt 27:24
INSPIRATION Job 32:8, the **i**
  of the Almighty
  2 Tim 3:16, by **i** of God
INSTANT Rom 12:12, continuing **i**
  in prayer
  2 Tim 4:2, be **i** in season
INSTRUCTION Ps 50:17, Seeing
  thou hatest **i**
  Prov 1:7, despise wisdom and **i**
  4:13, Take fast hold of **i**
  8:33, Hear **i**, and be wise
  12:1, Whoso loveth **i**
  16:22, the **i** of fools
  24:32, and received **i**
  2 Tim 3:16, **i** in righteousness
  See Jer 17:23; 35:15; Zeph 3:7
INTERCESSION Is 53:12, and
  made **i** for the transgressors
  Rom 8:26, maketh **i** for us
  Heb 7:25, to make **i** for them
  See Jer 27:18; 1 Tim 2:1
INTERPRETATION 2 Pet 1:20, the
  scripture is of any private **i**
INVISIBLE Rom 1:20, For the **i**
  things of him
  Col 1:15, image of the **i** God
  1 Tim 1:17, immortal, **i**
  Heb 11:27, him who is **i**
INWARD Job 38:36, hath put
  wisdom in the **i** parts
  Ps 51:6, in the **i** parts
  64:6, **i** thought
  Jer 31:33, in their **i** parts
  Rom 7:22, after the **i** man
  2 Cor 4:16, **i** man is renewed
  See Ps 62:4; Matt 7:15; Rom 2:29

J

JEALOUS Ex 20:5, Lord thy God
  am a **j** God
  34:14, is a **j** God
  Deut 4:24, even a **j** God
  5:9, am a **j** God
  6:15, **j** God among you
  Josh 24:19, he is a **j** God
  1 Kin 19:10, have been very **j**
  Ezek 39:25, **j** for my holy name
  2 Cor 11:2, **j** over you
  See Joel 2:18; Zech 1:14; 8:2
JEALOUSY Prov 6:34, For **j** is the
  1 Cor 10:22, the Lord to **j**
  See Ps 78:58; 79:5; Is 42:13
JESUS Phil 2:21, not the things
  which are **J** Christ's
  Heb 4:14, **J** the Son of God
  1 John 4:15, confess that **J**
JOIN Is 5:8, unto them that **j**
  Hos 4:17, **j** to idols
  Matt 19:6, God hath **j** together
  Eph 4:16, fitly **j** together
  See Acts 8:29; 9:26; Eph 5:31
JOY Neh 8:10, the **j** of the Lord
  Job 41:22, turned into **j**
  Ps 16:11, fullness of **j**
  30:5, but **j** cometh
  48:2, **j** of the whole earth
  51:12, **j** of thy salvation
  126:5, shall reap in **j**
  Prov 21:15, It is **j**
  Is 51:11, everlasting **j**
  Lam 2:15, **j** of the whole earth
  Matt 25:21, 23, **j** of thy lord
  Luke 8:13, the word with **j**
  15:7, **j** shall be in heaven

24:41, believed not for j
John 3:29, this my j
  15:11, j might be full
  16:24, your j may be full
Phil 2:2, Fulfill ye my j
Heb 12:2, who for the j
James 1:2, count it all j
1 Pet 1:8, rejoice with j
  4:13, with exceeding j
2 John 12, our j may be full
See Gal 5:22; Phil 1:4
JOYFUL Ps 66:1, Make a j noise
  95:1, let us make a j noise
Eccl 7:14, prosperity be j
Is 56:7, j in my house
See 2 Cor 7:4; Heb 10:34
JUDGE (*n.*) Gen 18:25, not the J of
  all the earth
Ps 50:6, for God is j himself
  68:5, a j of the widows
  94:2, j of the earth
Acts 10:42, J of quick
2 Tim 4:8, the righteous j
Heb 12:23, God the J of all
James 5:9, the j standeth
See 2 Sam 15:4; James 4:11
JUDGE (*v.*) Deut 32:36, the Lord
  shall j
Is 1:17, j the fatherless
Matt 7:1, J not
John 7:24, j not according
Rom 14:4, Who art thou that j
See John 16:11; Rom 2:16; 3:6
JUDGMENT Deut 1:17, for the j is
  God's
Ps 1:5, not stand in the j
Prov 29:26, every man's j
Eccl 11:9, bring thee into j
  12:14, every work into j
Jer 5:1, that executeth j
Hos 12:6, keep mercy and j
Matt 5:21, danger of the j
John 5:22, committed all j
  9:39, For j I am come
  16:8, righteousness, and of j
Acts 24:25, j to come
Rom 14:10, j seat of Christ
Heb 9:27, after this the j
1 Pet 4:17, j must begin
See Heb 10:27; James 2:13
JUST Prov 3:33, habitation of the j
  10:7, The memory of the j
Is 26:7, The way of the j
Hab 2:4, the j shall live
Matt 5:45, rain on the j
Luke 14:14, of the j
  15:7, j persons
Acts 24:15, j and unjust
Rom 1:17, j shall live by faith
Gal 3:11, j shall live by faith
Phil 4:8, things are j
Heb 10:38, Now the j shall
  12:23, the spirits of j men
1 Pet 3:18, j for the unjust
See Job 34:17; Acts 3:14
JUSTICE Ps 89:14, J and judgment
Jer 23:5, judgment and j
See Job 8:3; 36:17; Is 9:7; 56:1
JUSTIFICATION Rom 4:25, and
  was raised again for our j
  5:16, offences unto j
JUSTIFY Ps 51:4, mightest be j
Is 5:23, Which j the wicked
Matt 11:19, But wisdom is j
Luke 7:35, wisdom is j
Acts 13:39, that believe are j
Rom 2:13, shall be j
  3:20, shall no flesh be j
  5:1, being j by faith
  5:9, j by his blood
Gal 2:16, not j by the works
1 Tim 3:16, j in the Spirit
James 2:21, j by works

See Is 50:8; Rom 4:5; 8:33
JUSTLY Mic 6:8, but to do j, and to
  love mercy

K

KEEP Num 6:24, and k thee
1 Sam 2:9, will k the feet
Ps 17:8, K me as the apple
Eccl 3:6, time to k
  12:13, k his commandments
Jer 3:12, not k anger for ever
Hab 2:20, the earth k silence
Mal 3:14, k his ordinance
Matt 19:17, k the commandments
Luke 11:28, of God, and k it
  19:43, and k thee
John 8:51, If a man k my saying
  14:23, will k my words
  17:11, Holy Father, k
Acts 21:25, k themselves from
1 Cor 9:27, I k under my body
Eph 4:3, to k the unity
Phil 4:7, shall k your hearts
1 Tim 5:22, k thyself pure
  6:20, k that which is
James 1:27, to k himself
1 John 5:21, k yourselves
Jude 24, k you from falling
Rev 3:10, k thee from the hour
See 1 Pet 1:5; Jude 6; Rev 3:8
KEEPER Gen 4:9, my brother's k
Ps 121:5, The Lord is thy k
Eccl 12:3, k of the house
Titus 2:5, chaste, k at home
See Matt 28:4; Acts 5:23; 16:27
KEY Matt 16:19, the k of the
  kingdom of heaven
Luke 11:52, k of knowledge
Rev 1:18, have the k of hell
See Is 22:22; Rev 3:7; 9:1
KILL Eccl 3:3, A time to k
Matt 10:28, k the body
Luke 12:4, that k the body
Rom 8:36, k all the day
2 Cor 3:6, letter k
See Matt 23:37; Mark 12:5
KIND 1 Cor 13:4, Charity . . . is k
See Eph 4:32; James 3:7
KINDNESS Prov 31:26, the law of k
Is 54:8, with everlasting k
Jer 2:2, k of thy youth
Col 3:12, k, humbleness of mind
2 Pet 1:7, brotherly k
See Josh 2:12; Joel 2:13
KING 1 Sam 10:24, God save the k
Ps 5:2, my K, and my God
  10:16, Lord is K for ever
  84:3, O Lord of hosts, my K
  102:15, the k of the earth
Prov 8:15, By me k reign
Eccl 10:20, Curse not the k
Is 32:1, a k shall reign
Jer 10:10, an everlasting k
Luke 19:38, Blessed be the K
  23:2, Christ a K
John 6:15, to make him a k
  19:14, Behold your K
1 Tim 1:17, unto the K eternal
  6:15, K of K, and Lord
Rev 1:6, k and priests
  15:3, thou K of saints
See 1 Tim 2:2; 1 Pet 2:17
KINGDOM Ex 19:6, ye shall be
  unto me a k of priests
1 Chr 29:11, thine is the k
Ps 22:28, the k is the Lord's
Dan 4:3, an everlasting k
Matt 4:23, gospel of the k
  6:13, For thine is the k
  8:12, children of the k
  12:25, k divided
  13:38, children of the k

  24:14, gospel of the k
  25:34, inherit the k
Mark 3:24, if a k be divided
Luke 11:17, Every k divided
  12:32, to give you the k
  22:29, appoint unto you a k
John 18:36, My k is not
Acts 1:6, the k to Israel
1 Cor 15:24, the k to God
Col 1:13, us into the k
2 Tim 4:18, his heavenly k
James 2:5, heirs of the k
2 Pet 1:11, the everlasting k
See Rev 1:9; 11:15; 16:10; 17:17
KISS Prov 27:6, the k of an enemy
Rom 16:16, with an holy k
KNEE Is 45:23, That unto me every
  k shall bow
Phil 2:10, every k should bow
KNOCK Matt 7:7, k, and it shall be
  opened unto you
Luke 13:25, k at the door
Rev 3:20, at the door, and k
KNOW Job 8:9, and k nothing
  19:25, k that my redeemer
Ps 46:10, k that I am God
  139:23, and k my heart
Prov 20:11, k by his doings
Eccl 9:5, living k that
Jer 17:9, who can k it
  31:34, K the Lord
Hos 2:20, shalt k the Lord
Matt 6:3, left hand k
  13:11, k the mysteries
  25:12, I k you not
Mark 1:24, I k thee
  4:11, to k the mystery
Luke 19:42, If thou hadst k
John 7:17, k of the doctrine
  10:14, k my sheep
  13:7, but thou shalt k
Acts 1:7, k the times
Rom 8:28, we k that all things
1 Cor 2:14, he k them
  13:9, we k in part
Eph 3:19, to k the love
2 Tim 1:12, for I k whom
  3:15, k the holy scriptures
1 John 2:4, saith, I k him
  3:2, we k that
Rev 2:2, I k thy works
See 2 Tim 2:19; 2 Pet 2:9
KNOWLEDGE Job 21:14, k of thy
  ways
Ps 94:10, teacheth man k
Prov 10:14, Wise men lay up k
Eccl 1:18, increaseth k
Is 53:11, by his k
Dan 1:17, God gave them k
  12:4, k shall be increased
Hos 4:6, for lack of k
Hab 2:14, of the glory
Luke 11:52, the key of k
Acts 24:22, having more perfect k
Rom 1:28, retain God in their k
1 Cor 8:1, we all have k
  8:1, K puffeth up
  13:8, k, it shall vanish
  15:34, the k of God
Eph 3:19, which passeth k
Phil 3:8, k of Christ Jesus
Col 2:3, wisdom and k
1 Tim 2:4, k of the truth
Heb 10:26, k of the truth
See 1 Sam 2:3; Hos 4:1

L

LABOUR (*n.*) Prov 14:23, all l there
  is profit
Eccl 2:22, man of all his l
  6:7, All the l of man
1 Cor 15:58, your l is not

1 Thess 1:3, and l of love
Rev 2:2, thy works, and thy l
14:13, rest from their l
See Gen 31:42; 2 Cor 6:5; 11:23
LABOUR (*v.*) Ex 20:9, Six days shalt
thou l
Ps 127:1, they l in vain
Eccl 4:8, no end of all his l
5:12, The sleep of a man
Matt 11:28, all ye that l
John 6:27, L not for . . . meat
1 Cor 3:9, we are l together
Eph 4:28, rather let him l
1 Thess 5:12, know them which l
1 Tim 5:17, who l in the word
See Matt 9:37; 20:1; Luke 10:2
LAMB Is 11:6, dwell with the l
53:7, l to the slaughter
Jer 11:19, But I was like a l
John 1:29, 36, the L of God
1 Pet 1:19, l without blemish
Rev 12:11, blood of the L
See Luke 10:3; John 21:15
LAMP Ps 119:105, Thy word is a l
unto my feet
Prov 13:9, l of the wicked
LAST Num 23:10, and let my l end
be like his
Prov 23:32, At the l it biteth
Matt 12:45, l state of that man is
19:30, first shall be l
20:16, the l shall be first
Luke 13:30, l which shall be
John 6:39, at the l day
See 2 Tim 3:1; 1 Pet 1:5
LATTER Job 19:25, stand at the l
day upon the earth
Prov 19:20, in thy l end
Hag 2:9, glory of this l house
LAUGH Prov 1:26, I also will l at
your calamity
Eccl 3:4, a time to l
Luke 6:21, for ye shall l
James 4:9, your l be turned
LAW Ps 40:8, l is within my heart
119:113, thy l do I love
119:174, thy l is my delight
Prov 13:14, l of the wise
Matt 5:17, destroy the l
Rom 3:20, by the deeds of the l
7:14, the l is spiritual
8:3, what the l could not do
Gal 3:24, the l was our
5:14, all the l is fulfilled
5:23, there is no l
6:2, fulfill the l of Christ
1 Tim 1:8, the l is good
James 1:25, l of liberty
2:8, fulfill the royal l
See Ps 1:2; 19:7; Matt 7:12
LAWFUL Matt 12:2, is not l to do
upon the sabbath day
1 Cor 6:12, All things are l
LEAD Deut 4:27, whither the Lord
shall l
Ps 23:2, he l me beside
61:2, l me to the rock
139:24, and l me in the way
Is 11:6, child shall l them
Matt 6:13, And l us not
15:14, blind l the blind
1 Tim 2:2, may l a quiet
See 1 Cor 9:5; 2 Tim 3:6
LEAN Prov 3:5, l not unto thine
own understanding
Mic 3:11, l upon the Lord
LEARN Is 1:17, L to do well
2:4, l war any more
Acts 26:24, much l doth
Rom 15:4, written for our l
Heb 5:8, yet l he obedience
See Matt 9:13; 11:29; Phil 4:11
LEAST Matt 5:19, these l

commandments . . . the l in the
11:11, is l in the kingdom
25:40, one of the l
Luke 7:28, l in the kingdom
12:26, thing which is l
16:10, that which is l
Eph 3:8, l of all saints
See Gen 32:10; 1 Cor 6:4
LEAVE Gen 2:24, man l his father
and his mother
Ps 16:10, not l my soul in hell
Matt 19:5, l father and mother
Mark 10:7, a man l his father
John 14:27, Peace I l with you
Heb 13:5, I will never l thee
See Ruth 1:16; John 16:28
LIBERTY Is 61:1, to proclaim l
Jer 34:8, l unto them
Luke 4:18, to set at l them
Rom 8:21, l of the children
1 Cor 8:9, this l of yours
2 Cor 3:17, there is l
James 1:25, perfect law of l
See Gal 5:13; 1 Pet 2:16
LIE Num 23:19, is not a man, that
he should l
Titus 1:2, that cannot l
Heb 6:18, impossible for God to l
LIFE Gen 2:7, into his nostrils the
breath of l
2:9, the tree of l
Ps 16:11, the path of l
27:1, strength of my l
36:9, fountain of l
91:16, With long l
133:3, l for evermore
Prov 3:22, l unto thy soul
8:35, findeth me findeth l
15:24, The way of l
Eccl 9:9, days of the l
Jer 21:8, the way of l
Matt 6:25, thought for your l
18:8, to enter into l
Mark 9:43, enter into l maimed
Luke 12:15, for a man's l
12:23, The l is more
John 1:4, In him was l
5:24, hath everlasting l
5:40, ye might have l
6:47, everlasting l
6:48, I am that bread of l
6:54, hath eternal l
10:10, they might have l
10:15, I lay down my l
11:25, and the l
13:37, I will lay down my l
14:6, the truth, and the l
Rom 6:4, in newness of l
11:15, l from the dead
Gal 2:20, l which I now live
Eph 4:18, alienated from the l
Col 3:3, your l is hid
James 4:14, For what is your l
1 John 1:2, l was manifested
2:16, the pride of l
3:14, from death unto l
5:11, to us eternal l
Rev 2:7, the tree of l
22:1, river of water of l
See Matt 10:39; Acts 5:20
LIGHT Ps 4:6, l of thy countenance
27:1, The Lord is my l
90:8, sins in the l
119:105, l unto my path
Is 60:1, for thy l is come
Matt 5:14, l of the world
5:16, Let your l so shine
6:22, The l of the body
Luke 12:35, your l burning
16:8, children of l
John 1:9, That was the true L
3:19, that l is come
5:35, burning and a shining l

12:35, is the l with you
Acts 26:18, from darkness to l
2 Cor 4:4, l of the glorious
4:6, commanded the l
11:14, an angel of l
1 Tim 6:16, dwelling in the l
2 Pet 1:19, l that shineth
1 John 1:5, that God is l
1:7, if we walk in the l
Rev 22:5, neither l of the sun
See 2 Tim 1:10; Rev 7:16; 18:23
LIGHTNING Ex 19:16, that there
were thunders and l
Matt 24:27, as the l cometh
Luke 10:18, I beheld Satan as l
LIKENESS Acts 14:11, in the l of
men
Rom 6:5, l of his death
8:3, his own Son in the l
Phil 2:7, in the l of men
See Gen 1:26; Deut 4:16
LION Prov 28:1, but the righteous
are bold as a l
Dan 6:16, the den of l
1 Pet 5:8, as a roaring l
LIVE Lev 18:5, he shall l
Job 7:16, not l always
14:14, shall he l again
Ps 118:17, not die, but l
Is 38:16, make me to l
55:3, soul shall l
Ezek 3:21, he shall surely l
16:6, in thy blood, L
18:9, he shall surely l
20:11, he shall even l
33:13, he shall surely l
Hos 6:2, and we shall l
Hab 2:4, l by his faith
Matt 4:4, not l by bread alone
Luke 10:28, thou shalt l
John 11:25, yet shall he l
14:19, because I l
Acts 17:28, For in him we l
Rom 1:17, The just shall l
14:8, whether we l
1 Cor 9:14, gospel should l
2 Cor 6:9, behold, we l
Gal 2:19, I might l unto God
5:25, If we l in the Spirit
Phil 1:21, me to l is Christ
1 Tim 3:12, l godly in Christ
James 4:15, we shall l
Rev 1:18, I am he that l
3:1, name that thou l
See 1 Tim 5:6; Rev 20:4
LIVING Gen 2:7, of life; and man
became a l soul
Job 28:13, land of the l
33:30, light of the l
Ps 69:28, the book of the l
Song 4:15, well of l waters
Jer 2:13, of l waters
Zech 14:8, that l waters
John 4:10, given thee l water
Rom 12:1, a l sacrifice
Heb 10:20, By a new and l way
See Matt 22:32; 1 Cor 15:43
LORD Deut 6:4, The L our God
1 Kin 18:39, L, he is the God
Ruth 2:4, The L be with you
Ps 33:12, God is the L
118:23, This is the L doing
Is 37:20, O L our God
Zech 14:9, L shall be king
Matt 7:21, saith unto me L, L
Mark 2:28, Son of man is L
Luke 6:46, why call ye me, L
Acts 2:36, both L and Christ
Eph 4:5, One L, one faith
2 Thess 3:16, L of peace
See 1 Cor 2:8; Rev 11:15
LOSE Matt 10:39, He that findeth
his life shall l it

16:26, l his own soul
Luke 9:25, l himself
See Eccl 3:6; Luke 15:4, 8
LOSS 1 Cor 3:15, shall be burned,
he shall suffer l
Phil 3:7, l for Christ
LOST Ps 119:176, I have gone astray
like a l sheep
Jer 50:6, hath been l sheep
Matt 10:6, the l sheep
18:11, that which was l
Luke 19:10, that which was l
John 17:12, none of them is l
See Deut 22:3; 2 Cor 4:3
LOVE (*n.*) 2 Sam 1:26, thy l to me
was wonderful
Prov 10:12, but l covereth
15:17, where l is
Song 2:4, banner over me was l
8:6, for l is strong
Jer 31:3, an everlasting l
Hos 11:4, with bands of l
Matt 24:12, the l of many
John 5:42, the l of God
13:35, l one to another
15:13, Greater l hath no man
Rom 13:10, L worketh no ill
2 Cor 5:14, the l of Christ
13:11, God of l and peace
Eph 3:19, And to know the l
1 Tim 6:10, l of money
Heb 13:1, brotherly l continue
1 John 4:7, l one another
4:8, for God is l
4:10, Herein is l
4:18, no fear in l
Rev 2:4, left thy first l
See Gal 5:22; 1 Thess 1:3
LOVE (*v.*) Lev 19:18, thou shalt l thy
neighbour as thyself
Deut 6:5, l the Lord thy God
19:9, to l the Lord thy God
Ps 18:1, I will l thee
69:36, they that l his name
122:6, prosper that l thee
Prov 8:17, I l them that l me
17:17, friend l at all times
Eccl 3:8, A time to l
Hos 14:4, l them freely
Amos 5:15, l the good
Mic 6:8, to l mercy
Matt 5:44, L your enemies
5:46, For if ye l
Luke 6:27, L your enemies
7:42, l him most
John 11:3, he whom thou l
15:12, That ye l one another
21:15, that I l thee
Rom 13:8, to l one another
Eph 6:24, l our Lord Jesus
1 Pet 1:8, not seen, ye l
2:17, L the brotherhood
1 John 4:19, We l him
Rev 3:19, As many as I l
See John 14:31; 1 John 4:20, 21
LOVELY Song 5:16, altogether l
Phil 4:8, things are l
LOVER Ps 88:18, l and friend
2 Tim 3:4, l of pleasures
Titus 1:8, a l of hospitality
LOVINGKINDNESS Ps 17:7,
Show thy marvelous l
36:7, How excellent is thy l
63:3, thy l is better
92:2, To shew forth thy l
Jer 31:3, with l have I drawn
LOWER Ps 8:5, him a little l than
the angels
63:9, go into the l parts
Heb 2:7, l than the angels
LUST Deut 12:15, whatsoever thy
soul l after
Ps 81:12, own hearts' l

Rom 7:7, for I had not known l
Gal 5:24, affections and l
1 Tim 6:9, and hurtful l
Titus 2:12, worldly l
James 1:14, of his own l
1 Pet 2:11, from fleshly l
1 John 2:16, l of the flesh
2:17, the l thereof
Jude 16, after their own l
18, their own ungodly l
See Matt 5:38; 1 Cor 10:6

M

MAKER Job 4:17, a man be more
pure than his m
32:22, my m would
35:10, Where is God my m
36:3, righteousness to my M
Ps 95:6, the Lord our M
Prov 14:31, reproacheth his M
22:2, the Lord is the m
Is 45:9, striveth with his M
51:13, the Lord thy m
54:5, For thy M
Heb 11:10, whose builder and m
See Is 1:31; 17:7; Hab 2:18
MAN Gen 1:26, Let us make m in
our image
8:21, imagination of m heart
Num 23:19, God is not a m
Job 5:7, Yet m is born
14:1, M that is born
Ps 10:18, m of the earth
Prov 12:2, m obtaineth favour
Eccl 6:12, what is good for m
Is 2:22, Cease ye from m
Jer 10:23, it is not in m
Hos 11:9, I am God, and not m
Matt 6:24, No m can serve two
John 1:18, No m hath seen God
2 Cor 4:16, outward m perish
Phil 2:8, in fashion as a m
1 Tim 2:5, the m Christ Jesus
See 1 Cor 15:47; Eph 4:24
MARK Gen 4:15, the Lord set a m
upon Cain
Ps 37:37, M the perfect man
Phil 3:14, press toward the m
3:17, m them which walk
See Rom 16:17; Rev 13:16; 20:4
MARRY Matt 5:32, shall m her
that is divorced
19:10, not good to m
Mark 12:25, they neither m
Luke 14:20, I have m a wife
MARVELLOUS Job 5:9, m things
without number
Ps 17:7, m lovingkindness
118:23, m in our eyes
John 9:30, is a m thing
1 Pet 2:9, his m light
See Ps 105:5; 139:14; Dan 11:36
MASTER Matt 6:24, can serve two
m
10:24, not above his m
23:8, for one is your M
Luke 16:13, can serve two m
John 13:13, Ye call me M and Lord
Col 3:22, obey . . . your m
4:1, a M in heaven
James 3:1, be not many m
1 Pet 2:18, subject to your m
See Gen 24:12; Eccl 12:11
MASTERY Ex 32:18, voice of them
that shout for m
1 Cor 9:25, striveth for the m
MEAT Matt 6:25, life more than m
John 4:32, have m to eat
4:34, My m is to do
6:27, the m which perisheth
Acts 2:46, did eat their m
15:29, abstain from m

Rom 14:15, with thy m
14:20, m destroy not
1 Cor 6:13, M for the belly
8:13, if m make my brother
10:3, same spiritual m
1 Tim 4:3, abstain from m
See Matt 3:4; Col 2:16
MEDITATE Gen 24:63, went out to
m in the field
Josh 1:8, shalt m therein
Ps 1:2, his law doth he m
63:6, m on thee
77:12, I will m also
119:148, m in thy word
143:5, I m on all thy works
Is 33:18, Thine heart shall m
Luke 21:14, not to m before
1 Tim 4:15, m upon these
See Ps 19:14; 104:34; 119:97
MEEK Num 12:3, man Moses was
very m
Ps 22:26, The m shall eat
25:9, The m will he guide
37:11, m shall inherit
149:4, will beautify the m
Is 29:19, m also shall increase
61:1, tidings unto the m
Matt 5:5, Blessed are the m
11:29, for I am m
1 Pet 3:4, ornament of a m
See Ps 76:9; 147:6; Is 11:4
MELODY Is 23:16, make sweet m,
sing many songs
Eph 5:19, making m in your
MEMBER Ps 139:16, in thy book
all my m were written
Rom 6:13, yield ye your m
12:4, many m in one body
1 Cor 6:15, the m of Christ
6:15, the m of an harlot
James 3:5, a little m
4:1, war in your m
See Matt 5:29; Eph 4:25; 5:30
MEMORY Ps 109:15, cut off the m
of them
145:7, utter the m
Prov 10:7, The m of the just
Eccl 9:5, for the m of them
MEN 1 Sam 4:9, yourselves like m
Ps 9:20, to be but m
82:7, die like m
Eccl 12:3, strong m shall bow
Is 46:8, shew yourselves m
Gal 1:10, I now persuade m
1 Thess 2:4, not as pleasing m
See 1 Tim 2:4; 1 Pet 2:17
MENTION Ps 71:16, will make m
Is 12:4, m that his name
63:7, m the lovingkindness
Rom 1:9, m of you always
1 Thess 1:2, making m of you
See Is 62:6; Ezek 18:22; 33:16
MERCIFUL Ps 37:26, He is ever
m
67:1, God be m unto us
Prov 11:17, m man doeth good
Is 57:1, m men are taken away
Jer 3:12, for I am m
Matt 5:7, Blessed are the m
Luke 6:36, m, as your Father
18:13, m to me a sinner
Heb 2:17, be a m and faithful
See Ex 34:6; Joel 2:13
MERCY Ex 33:19, shew m on
whom I will show m
1 Chr 16:34, for his m endureth
Ezra 3:11, his m endureth for ever
Ps 23:6, goodness and m shall
103:11, great is his m toward them
119:64, full of thy m
136:1, m endureth for ever
Prov 14:21, m on the poor
16:6, m and truth

Is 54:7, with great **m**
Jer 6:23, and have no **m**
Lam 3:22, of the Lord's **m**
Dan 9:4, and **m** to them
Hos 4:1, no truth, nor **m**
6:6, For I desired **m**
14:3, fatherless findeth **m**
Mic 6:8, to love **m**
7:18, he delighteth in **m**
Hab 3:2, in wrath remember **m**
Matt 5:7, they shall obtain **m**
9:13, I will have **m**
Rom 9:15, have **m** on whom
12:1, by the **m** of God
Heb 4:16, that we may obtain **m**
James 2:13, judgment without **m**
1 Pet 1:3, his abundant **m**
See Dan 4:27; 1 Tim 1:2
MIGHT Deut 6:5, all thy soul,
and with all thy **m**
Eccl 9:10, do it with thy **m**
Zech 4:6, Not by **m**
Col 1:11, with all **m**
See 2 Pet 2:11; Rev 7:12
MIGHTY Gen 10:9, was a **m** hunter
before the Lord
Ps 89:13, Thou hast a **m** arm
Is 1:24, the **m** One of Israel
63:1, **m** to save
Jer 32:19, **m** in work
Matt 11:20, **m** works were done
Acts 2:2, a rushing **m** wind
2 Cor 10:4, but **m** through God
See Eccl 6:10; Matt 3:11
MILK Ex 3:8, **m** and honey
Heb 5:12, have need of **m**
1 Pet 2:2, **m** of the word
See Judg 4:19; Job 21:24
MIND (*n.*) Is 26:3, whose **m** is
stayed
Rom 8:7, carnal **m**
12:16, same **m** one toward
2 Cor 8:12, a willing **m**
13:11, be of one **m**
Phil 1:27, with one **m**
2:2, one accord, of one **m**
2:5, Let this **m** be in you
4:7, keep your hearts and **m**
1 Tim 6:5, of corrupt **m**
2 Tim 1:7, and of sound **m**
3:8, men of corrupt **m**
See Rom 8:6; 1 Thess 5:14
MIND (*v.*) Rom 8:5, flesh do **m**
the things of the flesh
12:16, **M** not high things
Phil 3:16, **m** the same thing
3:19, who **m** earthly things
MINDFUL Ps 8:4, What is man,
that thou art **m** of him
MINISTER (*n.*) Ps 103:21, ye **m** of
his
104:4, his **m** a flaming fire
Is 61:6, **M** of our God
Joel 1:9, the Lord's **m**
Matt 20:26, let him be your **m**
Mark 10:43, shall be your **m**
Rom 13:4, is the **m** of God
2 Cor 3:6, able **m** of the new
Gal 2:17, the **m** of sin
Eph 3:7, I was made a **m**
6:21, faithful **m**
Col 1:7, faithful **m** of Christ
1:23, am made a **m**
4:7, a faithful **m**
1 Tim 4:6, shalt be a good **m**
Heb 1:7, his **m** a flame of fire
See 2 Cor 6:4; 1 Thess 3:2
MINISTRY Acts 6:4, and to the **m**
of the word
2 Cor 4:1, we have this **m**
5:18, **m** of reconciliation
6:3, that the **m**
Eph 4:12, work of the **m**

Col 4:17, Take heed to the **m**
2 Tim 4:5, proof of thy **m**
See Acts 1:17; 12:25; Rom 12:7
MIRACLE Judg 6:13, and where be
all his **m**
Mark 9:39, a **m** in my name
Luke 23:8, some **m** done
John 2:11, beginning of **m**
4:54, again the second **m**
10:41, John did no **m**
Acts 2:22, among you by **m**
1 Cor 12:10, the working of **m**
See Gal 3:5; Heb 2:4; Rev 13:14
MOCK Gal 6:7, God is not **m**
See 2 Kin 2:23; Matt 2:16
MOCKER Jude 18, there should
be **m**
MODERATION Phil 4:5, Let your
m be known unto all
MONEY Is 52:3, redeemed
without **m**
1 Tim 6:10, the love of **m**
*See Gen 23:9; Mark 6:8; Luke 9:3;
Acts 4:37*
MORTAL Job 4:17, **m** man be more
just than God
Rom 6:12, in your **m** body
1 Cor 15:53, this **m** must
See Deut 19:11; 2 Cor 4:11; 5:4
MORTIFY Rom 8:13, the Spirit do
m the deeds
Col 3:5, **M** therefore
MOTHER Job 17:14, Thou art my
m
Ps 113:9, to be a joyful **m**
Is 66:13, As one whom his **m**
Ezek 16:44, As is the **m**
Matt 12:48, Who is my **m**
John 2:1, and the **m** of Jesus
See Gal 4:26; 1 Tim 1:9; 5:2
MOURN Prov 5:11, **m** at the last
Is 61:2, all that **m**
Jer 31:13, turn their **m**
Matt 5:4, they that **m**
24:30, tribes of the earth **m**
See Zech 7:5; James 4:9
MOUTH Ps 8:2, Out of the **m** of
babes
39:1, I will keep my **m**
81:10, open thy **m** wide
Prov 10:14, **m** of the foolish
13:2, the fruit of his **m**
21:23, Whoso keepeth his **m**
Eccl 6:7, for his **m**
Mal 2:6, was in his **m**
Matt 12:34, the **m** speaketh
Luke 21:15, a **m** and wisdom
Rom 10:10, the **m** confession
Titus 1:11, **m** must be stopped
James 3:10, of the same **m**
See John 19:29; 1 Pet 2:22
MOVE Ps 10:6, said in his heart, I
shall not be **m**
16:8, I shall not be **m**
30:6, I shall never be **m**
Acts 17:28, we live, and **m**
See Prov 23:31; Is 7:2
MUCH Num 16:3, Ye take too **m**
Luke 7:47, for she loved **m**
12:48, be **m** required
16:10, faithful also in **m**
See Eccl 5:12; Jer 2:22
MULTITUDE Ex 23:2, shalt not
follow a **m** to do evil
Prov 10:19, In the **m** of words
11:14, **m** of counsellors
James 5:20, hide a **m** of sins
1 Pet 4:8, cover a **m** of sins
See Josh 11:4; Luke 2:13
MUSE Ps 39:3, while I was **m** the
fire burned
MUZZLE Deut 25:4, not **m** the ox
when he treadeth

1 Cor 9:9, not **m** the mouth
1 Tim 5:18, not **m** the ox
MYSTERY Matt 13:11, the **m**
of the kingdom of heaven
1 Cor 2:7, of God in a **m**
15:51, I show you a **m**
Eph 5:32, This is a great **m**

N

NAKED Gen 2:25, they were both
n, the man and
Ex 32:25, people were **n**
Job 1:21, N came I
Matt 25:36, N, and ye clothed
1 Cor 4:11, thirst, and are **n**
2 Cor 5:3, not be found **n**
Heb 4:13, all things are **n**
See John 21:7; Rev 3:17; 16:15
NAME Ps 20:5, in the **n** of our God
22:22, declare thy **n**
69:36, that love his **n**
138:2, praise thy **n**
Prov 10:7, **n** of the wicked
18:10, **n** of the Lord
22:1, A good **n** is rather
Eccl 7:1, A good **n** is better
Song 1:3, thy **n** is as ointment
Is 56:5, an everlasting **n**
57:15, whose **n** is Holy
62:2, by a new **n**
64:7, calleth upon thy **n**
Jer 10:6, **n** is great in might
44:26, sworn by my great **n**
Mal 4:2, fear my **n**
Matt 6:9, Hallowed be thy **n**
12:21, in his **n**
18:5, little child in my **n**
18:20, together in my **n**
19:29, for my **n** sake
24:5, come in my **n**
Mark 5:9, My **n** is Legion
9:37, children in my **n**
9:39, a miracle in my **n**
Luke 9:48, this child in my **n**
10:20, your **n** are written
21:12, for my **n** sake
John 5:43, in my Father's **n**
14:13, shall ask in my **n**
16:24, nothing in my **n**
Acts 3:16, his **n** through faith
4:12, there is none other **n**
Eph 1:21, **n** that is named
Phil 2:9, **n** which is above
2:10, at the **n** of Jesus
4:3, whose **n** are
Col 3:17, **n** of the Lord Jesus
Heb 1:4, a more excellent **n**
James 2:7, **n** by the which
Rev 2:13, holdest fast my **n**
2:17, a new **n** written
22:4, his **n** shall be
See Ex 28:9; Is 45:3; John 10:3
NATION Prov 14:34, exalteth a **n**
Is 52:15, he sprinkle many **n**
Matt 24:7, For **n** shall rise
Luke 21:10, shall rise against **n**
Phil 2:15, perverse **n**
See Deut 4:27; Jer 2:11; 4:2
NATURAL Deut 34:7, nor his **n**
force abated
Rom 1:31, without **n** affection
1 Cor 2:14, But the **n** man
2 Tim 3:3, Without **n** affection
See Phil 2:20; James 1:23
NATURE 1 Cor 11:14, Doth not
even **n** itself teach you
Eph 2:3, by **n** the children
Heb 2:16, the **n** of angels
2 Pet 1:4, of the divine **n**
See Rom 1:26; Gal 2:15; 4:8
NAY Matt 5:37, communication be,
Yea, yea; N, **n**

2 Cor 1:17, yea yea, and **n n**
1:18, was not yea and **n**
James 5:12, and your **n, n**
NEAR Prov 27:10, neighbour that is **n**
Is 50:8, come **n** to me
55:6, while he is **n**
Obad 15, day of the Lord is **n**
Zeph 1:14, great day . . . is **n**
Matt 24:33, know that it is **n**
Mark 13:28, summer is **n**
See Ezek 11:3; 22:5; Rom 13:11
NEGLECT 1 Tim 4:14, **N** not the gift
Heb 2:3, **n** so great salvation
NEIGHBOUR Lev 19:18, love thy **n**
Zech 8:16, truth to his **n**
Matt 19:19, love thy **n**
Luke 10:29, And who is my **n**
Eph 4:25, truth with his **n**
See Lev 19:13; Rom 13:10
NEVER Prov 27:20, Hell . . . are **n** full
30:15, are **n** satisfied
Is 56:11, **n** have enough
Matt 7:23, I **n** knew you
John 4:14, shall **n** thirst
6:35, shall **n** hunger
7:46, **N** man spake
8:51, **n** see death
10:28, they shall **n** perish
11:26, shall **n** die
1 Cor 13:8, **n** faileth
Heb 13:5, will **n** leave thee
See Judg 2:1; Dan 2:44
NEW Num 16:30, But if the Lord make a **n** thing
Ps 33:3, a **n** song
96:1, unto the Lord a **n**
144:9, will sing a **n** song
Eccl 1:9, Is no **n** thing
Is 65:17, create **n** heavens
66:22, the **n** earth
Lam 3:23, **n** every morning
John 13:34, A **n** commandment
2 Cor 5:17, he is a **n** creature
Eph 2:15, one **n** man
4:24, put on the **n** man
Heb 10:20, **n** and living way
1 John 2:7, no **n** commandment
Rev 2:17, a **n** name written
3:12, upon him my **n** name
5:9, they sung a **n** song
14:3, were a **n** song
21:1, I saw a **n** heaven
21:5, make all things **n**
See Is 24:7; 43:19; Acts 2:13
NEWNESS Rom 6:4, we also should walk in **n** of life
NIGH Deut 30:14, word is very **n**
Rom 10:8, The word is **n** thee
Eph 2:13, are made **n**
See Joel 2:1; Heb 6:8
NIGHT Job 35:10, songs in the **n**
Ps 77:6, song in the **n**
Luke 6:12, all **n** in prayer
John 9:4, the **n** cometh
11:10, walk in the **n**
Rom 13:12, **n** is far spent
1 Thess 5:2, a thief in the **n**
Rev 21:25, be no **n** there
See Ps 121:6; John 3:2
NOBLE Neh 3:5, but their **n** put not their necks
Job 29:10, **n** held their peace
Jer 2:21, thee a **n** vine
14:3, **n** have sent
Acts 17:11, were more **n**
1 Cor 1:26, not many **n**
See Num 21:18; Eccl 10:17
NOISE Ps 66:1, Make a joyful **n**
42:2, **n** of many waters
2 Pet 3:10, with a great **n**
See Josh 6:27; Acts 2:6

NONE Rom 3:10, there is **n** righteous, no, not one
NUMBER (*v.*) 2 Sam 24:2, **n** ye the people
1 Chr 21:2, Go, **n** Israel
Ps 90:12, to **n** our days
Eccl 1:15, wanting cannot be **n**
Is 53:12, he was **n**
Matt 10:30, very hairs . . . are all **n**
Rev 7:9, no man could **n**
See Job 14:16; Acts 1:17
NURTURE Eph 6:4, **n** and admonition of the Lord

O

OBEDIENCE Rom 5:19, so by the **o** of one
16:26, the **o** of faith
Heb 5:8, **o** by the things
See 2 Cor 10:5; 1 Pet 1:2
OBEDIENT Ex 24:7, Lord . . . said will we do, and be **o**
Prov 25:12, upon an **o** ear
Is 1:19, willing and **o**
2 Cor 2:9, **o** in all things
Eph 6:5, **o** to them that
Phil 2:8, became **o** unto death
Titus 2:9, to be **o**
1 Pet 1:14, As **o** children
See Num 27:20; Titus 2:5
OBEY Deut 11:27, if ye **o** the commandments
Josh 24:24, voice will we **o**
1 Sam 15:22, to **o** is better
Jer 7:23, **o** my voice
Acts 5:29, ought to **o** God
Rom 6:16, to whom ye **o**
Eph 6:1, **o** your parents
Col 3:22, **o** in all things
2 Thess 1:8, **o** not the gospel
Heb 13:17, **O** them that
1 Pet 1:22, in **o** the truth
4:17, **o** not the gospel
See Ex 5:2; 23:21; Dan 9:10
OBSERVATION Luke 17:20, of God cometh not with **o**
OBTAIN Prov 8:35, and shall **o** favour of the Lord
Is 35:10, they shall **o** joy
51:11, shall **o** gladness
Luke 20:35, to **o** that world
Acts 26:22, **o** help of God
1 Cor 9:24, that ye may **o**
1 Thess 5:9, to **o** salvation
1 Tim 1:13, but I **o** mercy
2 Tim 2:10, **o** the salvation
Heb 4:16, that we may **o** mercy
9:12, **o** eternal redemption
1 Pet 2:10, not **o** mercy
2 Pet 1:1, that have **o**
See Dan 11:21; Hos 2:23
OFFENCE Eccl 10:4, for yielding pacifieth great **o**
Is 8:14, a rock of **o**
Matt 16:23, an **o** unto me
18:7, by whom he **o** cometh
Luke 17:1, that **o** will come
Rom 9:33, and rock of **o**
See Rom 5:15; 16:17; Gal 5:11
OFFEND Prov 18:19, A brother **o**
Matt 5:29, if thy right eye **o**
11:6, not be **o** in me
13:41, all things that **o**
18:6, shall **o** one of these
18:9, eye **o** thee
James 2:10, yet **o** in one point
See Jer 37:18; 2 Cor 11:29
OFFER Judg 5:2, the people willingly **o** themselves
Ps 50:23, Whoso **o** praise
Matt 5:24, and **o** thy gift
Luke 6:29, **o** also the other

1 Cor 8:1, **o** unto idols
10:19, **o** in sacrifice
Phil 2:17, and if I be **o**
2 Tim 4:6, ready to be **o**
Heb 9:28, **o** to bear the sins
See Ezra 1:6; 2:68; Mal 1:8
OIL Ps 45:7, anointed thee with . . . **o** of gladness
92:10, anointed with fresh **o**
Is 61:3, the **o** of joy
See Ex 27:20; Mic 6:7
OMITTED Matt 23:23, **o** the weightier matters of the law
ONE Gen 2:24, his wife; and they shall be **o** flesh
John 10:30, I and my Father are **o**
17:11, that they may be **o**
Gal 3:28, **o** in Christ Jesus
Eph 4:5, **O** Lord, **o** faith
See Mark 12:32; 1 Tim 2:5
OPEN Num 16:30, and the earth **o** her mouth
Ps 119:18, **O** thou mine eyes
Prov 31:8, **O** thy mouth
Is 42:7, To **o** the blind eyes
Mal 3:10, I will not **o** you
Matt 25:11, Lord, **o** to us
Luke 24:32, **o** to us the scriptures
Acts 26:18, To **o** their eyes
1 Cor 16:9, is **o** unto me
Col 4:3, **o** unto us a door
See 2 Cor 2:12; Heb 4:13
OPINION 1 Kin 18:21, How long halt ye between two **o**
OPPRESS Ex 22:21, neither vex a stranger, nor **o** him
23:9, not **o** a stranger
Lev 25:14, not **o** one another
Ps 10:18, fatherless and the **o**
Prov 14:31, that **o** the poor
Jer 7:6, **o** not the stranger
Zech 7:10, **o** not the widow
See Mal 3:5; Acts 7:24; 10:38
ORDAIN Ps 8:2, thou **o** strength
Jer 1:5, I **o** thee a prophet
Mark 3:14, **o** twelve
John 15:16, and **o** you
Acts 1:22, must one be **o**
10:42, was **o** of God
13:48, **o** to eternal life
14:23, **o** them elders
16:4, **o** of the apostles
Rom 13:1, **o** of God
Gal 3:19, was **o** by angels
Eph 2:10, **o** that we should
Titus 1:5, and **o** elders
Jude 4, **o** to this
See 1 Cor 2:7; 9:14; 1 Tim 2:7
ORDER 2 Kin 20:1, set thine house in **o**
Ps 110:4, **o** of Melchizedek
1 Cor 14:40, decently and in **o**
Titus 1:5, set in **o** the things
Heb 7:11, rise after the **o**
See Ps 37:23; 1 Cor 15:23
ORDINANCE Is 58:2, forsook not the **o** of their God
Mal 3:14, have kept his **o**
Rom 13:2, the **o** of God
Eph 2:15, contained in **o**
Col 2:14, the handwriting of **o**
Heb 9:10, and carnal **o**
See Jer 31:36; 1 Pet 2:13
OUGHT Matt 23:23, **o** ye to have done
Luke 24:26, **O** not Christ
John 4:20, men **o** to worship
Acts 5:29, **o** to obey God
Rom 8:26, pray for as we **o**
Heb 5:12, **o** to be teachers
James 3:10, these things **o** not
2 Pet 3:11, **o** ye to be
See Rom 12:3; 15:1; 1 Tim 3:15

OUTWARD 1 Sam 16:7, man looketh
  on the **o** appearance
Matt 23:27, appear beautiful **o**
Rom 2:28, **o** in the flesh
2 Cor 4:16, **o** man perish
  See Matt 23:28; 1 Pet 3:3
OVERCOME John 16:33, I have **o**
  the world
Rom 12:21, Be not **o** of evil
1 John 5:4, victory that **o**
  5:5, **o** the world
Rev 2:7, To him that **o**
  2:26, he that **o**
  See Song 6:5; 2 Pet 2:19

P

PACIFY Prov 16:14, but a wise man
  will **p** it
  21:14, A gift in secret **p**
Eccl 10:4, **p** great offences
PAIN Ps 55:4, My heart is sore **p**
  within me
  116:3, the **p** of hell
Acts 2:24, the **p** of death
  See Ps 73:16; 2 Cor 11:27
PANT Ps 42:1, **p** my soul after thee
PARDON Ex 23:21, will not **p** your
  transgressions
2 Chr 30:18, Lord **p** every one
Neh 9:17, God ready to **p**
Is 55:7, he will abundantly **p**
  See Jer 33:8; Mic 7:18
PARENTS Matt 10:21, shall rise up
  against their **p**
Luke 18:29, or **p** or brethren
  21:16, betrayed both by **p**
John 9:2, this man or his **p**
Rom 1:30, disobedient to **p**
2 Cor 12:14, lay up for the **p**
Eph 6:1, Children, obey your **p**
Col 3:20, obey your **p** in all
2 Tim 3:2, disobedient to **p**
  See Luke 2:27; 8:56; 1 Tim 5:4
PARTAKER Ps 50:18, and hast been
  p with adulterers
Rom 15:27, made **p** of their
1 Cor 9:10, **p** of his hope
  9:13, **p** with the altar
  10:17, for we are all **p**
  10:21, ye cannot be **p**
1 Tim 5:22, neither be **p**
Heb 3:1, **p** of the heavenly
  6:4, **p** of the Holy Ghost
1 Pet 4:13, **p** of Christ's
  5:1, a **p** of the glory
2 Pet 1:4, might be **p**
  See Eph 3:6; Phil 1:7
PASS Ex 12:13, I see the blood, I will
  p over you
Matt 26:39, cup **p** from me
1 Cor 7:31, world **p** away
Eph 3:19, which **p** knowledge
Phil 4:7, **p** all understanding
1 John 2:17, the world **p** away
  See 2 Cor 5:17; Rev 21:2
PASSION Acts 1:3, shewed himself
  alive after his **p**
  14:15, like **p** with you
James 5:17, **p** as we are
PASTOR Jer 3:15, will give you **p**
  according to mine
  17:16, from being a **p**
  23:1, **p** that destroy
Eph 4:11, **p** and teachers
PASTURE Ps 23:2, maketh me to lie
  down in green **p**
  95:7, the people of his **p**
  100:3, sheep of his **p**
Ezek 34:14, in a good **p**
John 10:9, and find **p**
PATH Ps 16:11, the **p** of life
  77:19, **p** in the great waters

  119:105, a light unto my **p**
Prov 4:18, the **p** of the just
Is 2:3, walk in his **p**
Matt 3:3, make his **p** straight
  See Lam 3:9; Heb 12:13
PATIENCE Luke 21:19, In your **p**
  possess
Rom 5:3, worketh **p**
Heb 10:36, ye have need of **p**
  12:1, let us run with **p**
James 1:3, faith worketh **p**
  5:11, the **p** of Job
2 Pet 1:6, to **p** godliness
Rev 2:2, labour and thy **p**
  14:12, **p** of the saints
  See Eccl 7:8; 1 Thess 5:14
PATIENTLY Ps 37:7, in the Lord,
  and wait **p** for him
  40:1, waited **p** for the Lord
Heb 6:15, had **p** endured
1 Pet 2:20, shall take it **p**
PATTERN 1 Tim 1:16, **p** to them
  which should hereafter
Titus 2:7, **p** of good works
Heb 8:5, **p** shewed to thee
  9:23, **p** of things
PEACE Num 6:26, and give thee **p**
  25:12, my covenant of **p**
Deut 20:10, proclaim **p** unto it
Ps 4:8, lay me down in **p**
  37:37, end of that man is **p**
Eccl 3:8, and a time of **p**
Is 48:18, **p** been as a river
  48:22, There is no **p**
  57:21, There is no **p**
  59:8, The way of **p**
Jer 6:14, saying, **P, p**
  34:5, shalt die in **p**
Ezek 7:25, they shall seek **p**
Matt 10:34, to send **p**
Mark 9:50, **p** one with another
Luke 1:79, the way of **p**
  2:14, on earth **p**
  10:5, **p** be to this house
John 14:27, **P** I leave with you
  16:33, ye might have **p**
Rom 1:7, **p** from God
  3:17, the way of **p**
  5:1, we have **p** with God
  10:15, the gospel of **p**
2 Cor 13:11, live in **p**
Eph 2:14, For he is our **p**
  2:17, preached **p** to you
Phil 4:7, the **p** of God
Col 3:15, the **p** of God rule
1 Thess 5:13, **p** among yourselves
  3:16, the Lord of **p**
Heb 7:2, King of **p**
  12:14, Follow **p** with all men
James 2:16, Depart in **p**
1 Pet 3:11, let him seek **p**
2 Pet 1:2, **p** be multiplied
  See John 20:19; Gal 6:16
PEACEABLE Is 32:18, shall dwell
  in a **p** habitation
1 Tim 2:2, a quiet and **p** life
PEACEABLY Rom 12:18, live **p**
  with all
PEOPLE Ex 6:7, I will take you to
  me for a **p**
Deut 4:20, **p** of inheritance
  33:29, O **p** saved by the Lord
2 Sam 7:24, thy **p** Israel
  22:44, **P** which I knew not
Ps 144:15, happy is that **p**
Prov 30:25, a **p** not strong
Is 1:4, a **p** laden
  27:11, **p** of no understanding
Jer 13:11, unto me for a **p**
Luke 1:17, a **p** prepared
Titus 2:14, a peculiar **p**
  See Rom 11:2; Heb 11:25
PERCEIVE Matt 22:18, Jesus **p**

  their
Luke 8:46, I **p** that virtue
Acts 10:34, I **p** that God
1 John 3:16, **p** we the love
  See Neh 6:12; Job 33:14
PERDITION John 17:12, of them is
  lost, but the son of **p**
Phil 1:28, evident token of **p**
Heb 10:39, draw back unto **p**
PERFECT Gen 6:9, Noah was a just
  man and **p**
  17:1, and be thou **p**
Deut 18:13, **p** with the Lord
  32:4, his work is **p**
Ps 19:7, law of the Lord is **p**
  37:37, Mark the **p** man
Prov 4:18, unto the **p** day
Ezek 28:15, **p** in thy ways
Matt 5:48, Be ye therefore **p**
  19:21, If thou wilt be **p**
John 17:23, may be made **p**
Rom 12:2, acceptable, and **p**
1 Cor 2:6, them that are **p**
2 Cor 12:9, **p** in weakness
  13:11, Be **p**, be of
Eph 4:13, unto a **p** man
Phil 3:12, were already **p**
  3:15, as many as be **p**
Col 1:28, **p** in Christ Jesus
  4:12, **p** and complete
2 Tim 3:17, man of God may be **p**
Heb 2:10, their salvation **p**
  11:40, not be made **p**
  12:23, men made **p**
  13:21, Make you **p**
James 1:4, have her **p** work
  1:17, **p** gift is from above
  1:25, **p** law of liberty
  3:2, same is a **p** man
1 John 4:18, made **p** in love
  See 2 Chr 8:16; Eph 4:12
PERFECTION Job 11:7, find out the
  Almighty unto **p**
Ps 119:96, end of all **p**
2 Cor 13:9, even your **p**
Heb 6:1, go on unto **p**
PERILOUS 2 Tim 3:1, the last days
  p times shall come
PERISH Job 34:15, All flesh shall **p**
Ps 1:6, ungodly shall **p**
  37:20, the wicked shall **p**
  49:12, beasts that **p**
  102:26, They shall **p**
Prov 11:10, the wicked **p**
  31:6, ready to **p**
Jon 1:6, that we **p** not
Matt 26:52, the sword shall **p**
John 6:27, meat which **p**
Acts 8:20, Thy money **p**
Col 2:22, Which all are to **p**
2 Pet 3:9, that any should **p**
  See Ps 2:12; John 10:28
PERSECUTE Ps 7:1, them that **p**
  me
  10:2, doth **p** the poor
  143:3, hath **p** my soul
Matt 5:11, and **p** you
  5:44, and **p** you
John 15:20, will also **p** you
Acts 9:4, Saul, why **p** thou me
1 Cor 4:12, being **p**
  15:9, **p** the church
2 Cor 4:9, **P**, but not forsaken
  See Acts 7:52; Rom 12:14
PERSECUTION Matt 13:21, or **p**
  ariseth because of the word
Mark 4:17, **p** ariseth
2 Cor 12:10, **p**, distresses
2 Tim 3:12, shall suffer **p**
  See Gal 6:12; 1 Tim 1:13
PERSEVERANCE Eph 6:18, with
  all **p** and supplication
PERSON Deut 10:17, which regard-

eth not p
2 Sam 14:14, respect any p
Ps 15:4, a vile p is contemned
Prov 12:11, followeth vain p
Matt 22:16, not the p of men
2 Cor 2:10, in the p of Christ
Heb 1:3, image of his p
2 Pet 3:11, what manner of p
See Mal 1:8; Jude 16
PERSUADE Matt 28:14, we will
 p him
Acts 26:28, thou p me to be
Rom 14:5, man be fully p
2 Cor 5:11, we p men
Heb 6:9, p better things
See 2 Kin 18:32; 2 Tim 1:12
PERVERSE Deut 32:5, are a p and
 crooked generation
Prov 4:24, and p lips
12:8, is of a p heart
Phil 2:15, crooked and p nation
See Is 30:12; 1 Tim 6:5
PERVERT Deut 16:19, p the words
 of the righteous
Job 8:3, Doth God p judgment
Prov 10:9, that p his ways
19:3, foolishness of man p
Jer 3:21, have p their way
23:36, p the words
Acts 13:10, p the right ways
Gal 1:7, would p the gospel
See Eccl 5:8; Mic 3:9
PHYSICIAN Matt 9:12, They that
 be whole need not a p
Luke 4:23, P, heal thyself
See Jer 8:22; Col 4:14
PIECE Prov 6:26, a p of bread
Zech 11:12, thirty p of silver
See Luke 14:18; Acts 19:19
PIERCE Zech 12:10, whom they
 have p
Ps 22:16, p my hands
John 19:34, spear p his side
1 Tim 6:10, p themselves
See Is 27:1; Heb 4:12
PILGRIMS Heb 11:13, strangers and
 p on the earth
1 Pet 2:11, strangers and p
PILLAR Gen 19:26, and she became
 a p of salt
Prov 9:1, her seven p
Gal 2:9, seemed to be p
Rev 3:12, a p in the temple
See Joel 2:30; Rev 10:1
PIT Gen 37:20, and cast him into
 some p
Ex 21:33, open a p
21:34, owner of the p
Num 16:30, into the p
16:33, alive into the p
Job 33:24, down to the p
Ps 40:2, out of a horrible p
Prov 22:14, women is a deep p
23:27, woman is a narrow p
28:10, into his own p
Is 38:17, p of corruption
Matt 12:11, it fall into a p
Luke 14:5, ox fallen into a p
PLACE Ex 3:5, p whereon thou
 standest is holy
Ps 32:7, art my hiding p
90:1, our dwelling p
Prov 14:26, a p of refuge
15:3, are in every p
Eccl 3:20, All go unto one p
Is 66:1, p of my rest
Rom 12:19, give p unto wrath
Eph 4:27, p to the devil
Heb 12:17, no p of repentance
Rev 20:11, no p for them
See Ps 16:6; Is 40:4; Eph 1:3
PLEASE Ps 51:19, shalt thou be p
135:6, Whatsoever the Lord p

Prov 16:7, When a man's ways p
Is 2:6, p themselves
53:10, Yet it p the Lord
55:11, that which I p
Mic 6:7, Lord be p
Mal 1:8, will he be p with thee
John 8:29, things that p him
Rom 8:8, cannot p God
15:1, to p ourselves
1 Cor 1:21, it p God
10:33, Even as I p all men
Gal 1:10, I seek to p men
Heb 11:6, impossible to p him
See 1 Cor 7:32; 1 Thess 2:4
PLEASURE Job 21:21, For what p
 hath he
22:3, p to the Almighty
Ps 16:11, hand there are p
51:18, Do good in thy good p
103:21, that do his p
147:11, Lord taketh p
Prov 21:17, that loveth p
Eccl 5:4, no p in fools
12:1, no p in them
Is 44:28, perform all my p
53:10, p of the Lord
58:13, p on my holy day
Jer 22:28, wherein is no p
Ezek 18:23, Have I any p
33:11, no p in the death
Mal 1:10, I have no p in you
Luke 8:14, p of this life
12:32, your Father's good p
2 Cor 12:10, p in infirmities
Eph 1:5, p of his will
Phil 2:13, of his good p
1 Tim 5:6, in p is dead
2 Tim 3:4, lovers of p
Heb 10:38, no p in him
11:25, enjoy the p of sin
12:10, after their own p
James 5:5, Ye have lived in p
Rev 4:11, and for thy p
See Eccl 2:1; Titus 3:3
PLOW Prov 20:4, sluggard will not p
21:4, p of the wicked
Is 2:4, swords into p
Joel 3:10, Beat your p
Amos 9:13, p shall overtake
See Deut 22:10; 1 Cor 9:10
POOR Deut 15:11, p shall never cease
Job 24:4, p of the earth
29:16, a father to the p
Ps 10:14, p committeth himself
34:6, This p man cried
40:17, I am p and needy
49:2, rich and p
69:29, am p and sorrowful
70:5, I am p and needy
Prov 10:4, He becometh p
13:23, the tillage of the p
18:23, The p useth
22:2, The rich and p meet
30:9, or lest I be p
Is 41:17, p and needy seek
Amos 2:6, and the p
Zech 11:7, O p of the flock
Matt 5:3, the p in spirit
2 Cor 6:10, as p, yet making
8:9, he became p
See James 2:2; Rev 3:17
POSSESS Gen 22:17, shall p the gate
 of his enemies
24:60, let thy seed p
Prov 8:22, Lord p me
Luke 18:12, all that I p
21:19, p ye your souls
See Luke 12:15; 2 Cor 6:10
POSSESSION Gen 17:8, Canaan, for
 an everlasting p
Acts 2:45, sold their p
Eph 1:14, purchased p
See Lev 25:10; 1 Kin 21:15

POSSIBLE Matt 19:26, with God all
 things are p
24:24, if it were p
Mark 9:23, things are p
13:22, if it were p
14:36, are p unto thee
Luke 18:27, are p with God
See Acts 2:24; 20:16; Heb 10:4
POUR Job 10:10, Hast thou not p me
 out as milk
Ps 45:2, grace is p
62:8, p out your heart
Prov 1:23, p out my spirit
Is 32:15, spirit be p upon us
53:12, p out his soul
Lam 2:19, p out thine heart
Joel 2:28, p out my spirit
Nah 1:6, his fury is p out
Zech 12:10, I will p upon
Mal 3:10, p you out a blessing
Matt 26:7, p it on his head
John 2:15, p out the
Acts 2:17, p out of my Spirit
2:18, p out in those days
10:45, p out the gift
See 2 Sam 23:16; Rev 14:10; 16:1
POWER Lev 26:19, pride of your p
2 Chr 25:8, God hath p
Ps 49:15, p of the grave
Prov 3:27, p of thine hand
18:21, p of the tongue
Eccl 5:19, hath given him p
8:4, there is p
Is 40:29, p to the faint
Hos 12:3, had p with God
Mic 3:8, I am full of p
Hab 3:4, hiding of his p
Zech 4:6, nor by p
Matt 6:13, kingdom, and the p
9:6 p on earth
24:30, of heaven with p
28:18, All p is given
Luke 1:35, p of the Highest
4:6, will I give thee
4:14, p of the Spirit
12:5, hath killed hath p
21:27, a cloud with p
22:53, p of darkness
24:49, p from on high
John 1:12, p to become
10:18, p to lay it down
17:2, p over all flesh
19:10, p to crucify thee
Acts 1:8, ye shall receive p
3:12, by our own p
8:19, Give me also this p
26:18, the p of Satan
Rom 1:20, even his eternal p
1 Cor 15:43, raised in p
Eph 2:2, p of the air
3:7, working of his p
Phil 3:10, the p of his
2 Thess 1:9, glory of his p
2 Tim 1:7, of p, and of love
3:5, denying the p thereof
Heb 2:14, the p of death
6:5, the p of the world
7:16, p of an endless life
Rev 2:26, will I give p
4:11, honour and p
See Luke 22:69; Rom 1:16
POWERFUL Ps 29:4, The voice of
 the Lord is p
Heb 4:12, is quick, and p
PRAISE (*n.*) Ex 15:11, fearful in p,
 doing wonders
Deut 10:21, He is thy p
Judg 5:3, p to the Lord God
Neh 9:5, blessing and p
Ps 9:2, to thy name
22:3, the p of Israel
22:25, My p shall be
33:1, for p is comely

50:23, **p** glorifieth me
57:7, sing and give **p**
61:8, I sing **p** unto
66:2, his **p** glorious
104:33, I will sing **p**
148:14, **p** of all his saints
Prov 27:21, a man to his **p**
Is 60:18, thy gates **P**
61:3, garment of **p**
Hab 3:3, full of his **p**
Zeph 3:20, **p** among all people
John 9:24, Give God the **p**
12:43, **p** of men
Rom 2:29, **p** is not of men
13:3, **p** of the same
1 Cor 4:5, have **p** of God
2 Cor 8:18, whose **p** is
Eph 1:6, **p** of the glory
Phil 4:8, if there be any **p**
Heb 13:15, sacrifice of **p**
1 Pet 2:14, for the **p** of them
4:11, whom be **p**
See 2 Chr 29:30; 1 Pet 2:9
PRAISE (*v.*) Ps 30:9, Shall the dust **p** thee
42:5, shall yet **p** him
45:17, people **p** thee
63:3, my lips shall **p** thee
67:3, **p** thee, O God
71:14, will yet **p** thee more
72:15, daily shall he be **p**
115:17, dead **p** not the Lord
145:4, **p** thy works
Prov 27:2, another man **p** thee
31:31, her own works **p** her
Is 38:19, he shall **p** thee
See Luke 2:13; Acts 2:47; 3:8
PRAY Gen 20:7, he shall **p** for thee
1 Sam 7:5, I will **p** for you
12:23, ceasing to **p** for you
2 Chr 7:14, and **p**, and seek
Ezra 6:10, **p** for the life
Job 21:15, we **p** unto him
Ps 5:2, unto thee will I **p**
55:17, at noon will I **p**
122:6, **P** for the peace
Is 45:20, **p** unto a god
Jer 7:16, **p** not thou for
37:3, **P** now unto the Lord
42:2, **p** for us
Zech 7:2, **p** before the Lord
Matt 5:44, **p** for them
6:5, to **p** standing
6:9, therefore **p** ye
14:23, mountain apart to **p**
26:36, go and **p** yonder
Mark 11:25, when ye stand **p**
14:32, while I shall **p**
Luke 11:1, teach us to **p**
18:1, men ought always to **p**
John 14:16, will **p** the Father
16:26, **p** the Father for you
17:9, I **p** for them
17:20, Neither **p** I
Acts 9:11, Saul . . . he **p**
Rom 8:26, we should **p**
1 Cor 14:15, **p** with the spirit
Eph 6:18, **P** always
1 Thess 5:17, **P** without ceasing
1 Tim 2:8, **p** everywhere
James 5:13, let him **p**
5:16, **p** one for another
1 John 5:16, shall **p** for it
See Luke 9:29; 1 Thess 5:25
PRAYER 2 Chr 7:15, unto the **p** that is made
Job 15:4, and restrainest **p**
16:17, my **p** is pure
Ps 4:1, hear my **p**
5:3, will I direct my **p**
6:9, Lord will receive my **p**
17:1, give ear unto my **p**
35:13, **p** returned

39:12, Hear my **p**, O Lord
65:2, O thou that hearest **p**
66:19, voice of my **p**
72:15, **p** also shall
109:4, give myself unto **p**
Prov 15:8, **p** of the upright
Is 1:15, when ye make many **p**
56:7, a house of **p**
Lam 3:8, shutteth out my **p**
Matt 21:13, the house of **p**
21:22, shall ask in **p**
23:14, make long **p**
Mark 11:17, the house of **p**
Luke 6:12, night in **p** to God
19:46, the house of **p**
20:47, for a show make long **p**
Acts 3:1, the hour of **p**
6:4, continually to **p**
12:5, but **p** was made
16:13, where **p** was wont
Phil 4:6, **p** and supplication
James 5:15, the **p** of faith
5:16, **p** of a righteous man
1 Pet 4:7, watch unto **p**
Rev 5:8, the **p** of saints
8:3, offer it with the **p**
See Ps 72:20; Col 4:2
PREACH Neh 6:7, prophets to **p** of thee at Jerusalem
Is 61:1, **p** good tidings
Jon 3:2, **p** unto it
Matt 4:17, Jesus began to **p**
10:7, as ye go, **p**
11:1, to teach and to **p**
11:5, gospel **p** to them
Mark 2:2, and he **p** the word
16:20, and **p** everywhere
Luke 9:60, the **p** kingdom of God
Acts 8:5, **p** Christ unto them
10:36, Israel, **p** peace
13:38, **p** unto you
17:18, **p** unto them Jesus
Rom 2:21, that **p** a man
10:15, shall they **p**
1 Cor 1:18, **p** of the cross
1:21, of **p** to save
1:23, **p** Christ crucified
9:27, have **p** to others
15:11, so we **p**
15:14, is our **p** vain
2 Cor 4:5, For we **p** not
Phil 1:15, **p** Christ
2 Tim 4:2, **P** the word
Heb 4:2, the gospel **p**
1 Pet 3:19, **p** unto the spirits
See 2 Cor 11:4; Eph 2:17
PREACHER Rom 10:14, how shall they hear without a **p**
1 Tim 2:7, I am ordained a **p**
2 Pet 2:5, **p** of righteousness
See Eccl 1:1; 2 Tim 1:11
PRECIOUS Deut 33:13, for the **p** things of heaven
33:15, for the **p** things
2 Kin 1:13, be **p** in thy sight
Ezra 8:27, **p** as gold
Ps 49:8, their soul is **p**
72:14, **p** shall their blood be
116:15, **P** in the sight
Prov 3:15, more **p** than rubies
Eccl 7:1, than **p** ointment
Is 13:12, **p** than fine gold
28:16, a **p** corner stone
43:4, **p** in my sight
Jer 15:19, take forth the **p**
Lam 4:2, The **p** sons of Zion
1 Pet 1:7, more **p** than
1:19, **p** blood of Christ
2:6, elect, **p**
2 Pet 1:1, like **p** faith
1:4, and **p** promises
See Matt 26:7; Mark 14:3
PREDESTINATE Rom 8:29, also

did **p** to be conformed
8:30, whom he did **p**
Eph 1:5, Having **p** us
PREPARE 1 Sam 7:3, **p** your hearts unto the Lord
2 Chr 20:33, **p** their hearts
Prov 8:27, **p** the heavens
Is 40:3, **P** ye the way
62:10, **p** ye the way
Amos 4:12, **p** to meet thy God
Jon 1:17, **p** a great fish
Mal 3:1, and he shall **p**
Matt 20:23, **p** of my Father
Mark 1:2, **p** thy way
10:40, for whom it is **p**
Luke 1:76, to **p** his ways
John 14:2, I go to **p** a place
Rom 9:23, **p** unto glory
1 Cor 2:9, hath **p** for them
Heb 10:5, hast thou **p** me
See 1 Chr 22:5; Rev 21:2
PRESENCE Gen 4:16, Cain went out from the **p**
47:15, we die in thy **p**
Ex 33:15, If thy **p** go not
Job 23:15, troubled at his **p**
Ps 16:11, in thy **p**
17:2, forth from thy **p**
31:20, secret of thy **p**
51:11, not away from thy **p**
139:7, I flee from thy **p**
Prov 14:7, **p** of a foolish man
Is 63:9, his **p** saved them
Jer 23:39, you out of my **p**
52:3, out from his **p**
Jon 1:3, the **p** of the Lord
Zeph 1:7, **p** of the Lord God
See Gen 16:12; Luke 15:10
PRESENT Ps 46:1, a very **p** help
John 14:25, yet **p** with you
Acts 10:33, are we all here **p**
Rom 7:18, for to will is **p**
8:18, of this **p** time
12:1, ye **p** your bodies
1 Cor 7:26, for the **p** distress
2 Cor 5:8, be **p** with the Lord
Gal 1:4, **p** evil world
Col 1:28, may **p** every man
2 Tim 4:10, this **p** world
Jude 24, **p** you faultless
See Ps 72:10; Matt 2:11
PRESERVE Gen 32:30, God face to face, and my life is **p**
45:5, to **p** life
Job 29:2, when God **p** me
Ps 36:6, thou **p** man and beast
121:7, **p** thee from all evil
121:8, Lord shall **p**
Prov 2:8, **p** the way
2:11, Discretion shall **p**
20:28, Mercy and truth **p**
Jer 49:11, **p** them alive
Luke 17:33, life shall **p** it
See Hos 12:13; Jude 1
PRESS Luke 6:38, measure, **p** down
16:16, man **p** into it
Phil 3:14, **p** toward the mark
See Mark 2:4; 5:27; Luke 8:19
PRETENCE Matt 23:14, and for a **p** make long prayer
PREVAIL Eccl 4:12, one **p** against him
Matt 16:18, gates . . . shall not **p**
Acts 19:20, the word of God, and **p**
See Job 14:20; John 12:19
PRICE Lev 25:52, him again the **p** of his redemption
2 Sam 24:24, of thee at a **p**
1 Chr 21:22, for the full **p**
Acts 5:2, part of the **p**
1 Cor 6:20, bought with a **p**
1 Pet 3:4, of great **p**
See Deut 23:18; Zech 11:12

PRIDE Ps 31:20, thy presence from the **p** of man
Prov 8:13, **p**, and arrogancy
14:3, a rod of **p**
Is 28:1, Woe to the crown of **p**
Jer 49:16, **p** of thine heart
See Mark 7:22; 1 John 2:16
PRIEST Gen 14:18, **p** of the most high God
Ex 19:6, kingdom of **p**
1 Sam 2:35, a faithful **p**
Is 24:2, so with the **p**
28:7, the **p** and the prophet
61:6, **P** of the Lord
Jer 13:13, and the **p**
Rev 1:6, **p** unto God
5:10, kings and **p**
20:6, be **p** of God
See Heb 2:17; 3:1; 4:15; 7:26
PRIESTHOOD Ex 40:15, shall surely be an everlasting **p**
Num 16:10, seek ye the **p**
25:13, an everlasting **p**
Heb 7:24, an unchangeable **p**
1 Pet 2:5, and holy **p**
2:9, a royal **p**
See Josh 18:7; Neh 13:29
PRINCE Ps 118:9, confidence in **p**
Prov 8:15, **p** decree justice
Matt 9:34, **p** of the devils
John 12:31, **p** of this world
16:11, **p** of this world
Acts 3:15, the **P** of life
5:31, a **P** and a Saviour
1 Cor 2:6, **p** of this world
Eph 2:2, **p** of the power
See Is 3:4; Hos 7:5; Matt 20:25
PRINCIPALITY Eph 6:12, but against **p**, against powers
Titus 3:1, to **p** and powers
See Rom 8:38; Eph 1:21; 3:10
PRISON Ps 142:7, my soul out of **p**
Eccl 4:14, out of **p**
Is 53:8, He was taken from **p**
61:1, opening of the **p**
Matt 25:36, I was in **p**
1 Pet 3:19, spirits in **p**
See Jer 32:2; 39:14; Luke 3:20
PRISONER Eph 3:1, **p** of Jesus Christ
PROCLAIM Ex 33:19, I will **p** the name of the Lord
Lev 25:10, **p** liberty
Is 61:2, **p** the acceptable year
Jer 34:15, in **p** liberty
Luke 12:3, shall be **p**
See Deut 20:10; Joel 3:9
PROFANE Lev 18:21, shalt thou **p** the name of thy God
22:2, **p** not my holy name
Jer 23:11, priest are **p**
Ezek 22:26, the holy and **p**
Matt 12:5, **p** the sabbath
Acts 24:6, to **p** the temple
1 Tim 1:9, for unholy and **p**
6:20, avoiding **p** and vain
2 Tim 2:16, But shun **p**
Heb 12:16, or **p** persons
See Ps 89:39; Mal 1:12; 2:10
PROFIT (*n.*) Eccl 1:3, What **p** hath a man
2:11, no **p** under the sun
5:16, and what **p** hath he
7:11, is **p** to them
See Esth 3:8; 1 Tim 4:15
PROFIT (*v.*) Job 34:9, It **p** a man
Prov 10:2, **p** nothing
Is 30:6, shall not **p** them
Jer 2:11, which doth not **p**
23:32, they shall not **p**
Matt 16:26, what is a man **p**
Mark 8:36, shall it **p** a man
Gal 5:2, shall **p** you nothing

1 Tim 4:8, exercise **p** little
See Rom 2:25; 1 Cor 13:3
PROFITABLE Job 22:2, Can a man be **p** unto God
1 Tim 4:8, godliness is **p**
2 Tim 3:16, is **p** for doctrine
See 2 Tim 4:11; Philem 11
PROMISE (*n.*) Ps 77:8, doth his **p** fail
Luke 24:49, the **p** of my Father
Acts 1:4, wait for the **p**
2:39, the **p** is unto you
26:6, the hope of the **p**
Rom 4:14, **p** made of none effect
4:20, at the **p** of God
9:4, and the **p**
9:8, children of the **p**
2 Cor 1:20, all the **p** of God
Gal 3:21, against the **p** of God
4:28, are the children of **p**
1 Tim 4:8, **p** of the life
2 Tim 1:1, the **p** of life
Heb 6:12, inherit the **p**
9:15, the **p** of eternal
10:36, might receive the **p**
11:13, received the **p**
2 Pet 1:4, and precious **p**
3:4, **p** of his coming
3:9, concerning his **p**
See Eph 1:13; Heb 4:1; 11:9
PROMISE (*v.*) Ex 12:25, according as he hath **p**
Num 14:40, the Lord hath **p**
Deut 1:11, as he hath **p** you
15:6, as he **p** thee
Josh 23:15, your God **p** you
2 Kin 8:19, as he **p** him
Rom 4:21, what he had **p**
Heb 10:23, he is faithful that **p**
11:11, faithful who had **p**
1 John 2:25, that he hath **p** us
See 1 Kin 8:24, 25; Ezek 13:22
PROOF Acts 1:3, his passion by many infallible **p**
2 Cor 2:9, the **p** of you
8:24, **p** of your love
13:3, a **p** of Christ
Phil 2:22, know the **p** of him
2 Tim 4:5, make full **p**
PROPHECY 1 Cor 13:8, whether there be **p**
2 Pet 1:19, more sure word of **p**
1:21, the **p** came not
Rev 1:3, words of this **p**
22:7, sayings of the **p**
See Neh 6:12; 1 Tim 4:14
PROPHESY Num 11:25, spirit rested upon them, they **p**
Is 30:10, **P** not unto us
Jer 5:31, prophets **p** falsely
28:9, which **p** of peace
Ezek 37:9, **P** unto the wind
Joel 2:28, daughters shall **p**
Amos 3:8, who can but **p**
7:13, **p** not again
Mic 2:11, I will **p** unto thee
Matt 26:68, **P** unto us
Mark 14:65, unto him, **P**
Luke 22:64, **P**, who is it
Rom 12:6, let us **p** according
1 Cor 13:9, we **p** in part
14:39, covet to **p**
1 Thess 5:20, Despise not **p**
See Amos 2:12; 1 Cor 11:5
PROPHET Num 11:29, people were **p**
12:6, a **p** among you
Deut 13:1, arise among you a **p**
18:15, unto thee a **P**
34:10, arose not a **p**
1 Sam 10:12, also among the **p**
2 Kin 5:8, a **p** in Israel
2 Chr 20:20, believe his **p**

Ps 74:9, no more any **p**
Jer 29:26, maketh himself a **p**
Hos 9:7, the **p** is a fool
Amos 7:14, I was no **p**
Matt 7:15, Beware of false **p**
10:41, in the name of a **p**
13:57, A **p** is not without
23:29, the tombs of the **p**
Luke 1:76, **p** of the Highest
4:24, No **p** is accepted
7:16, great **p** is risen up
7:28, a greater **p** than John
13:33, that a **p** perish
24:19, **p** mighty in deed
John 4:19, thou art a **p**
4:44, a **p** hath no honour
7:40, this is the **P**
7:52, ariseth no **p**
1 Cor 12:29, are all **p**
14:37, himself to be a **p**
Eph 2:20, the apostles and **p**
4:11, and some, **p**
Rev 22:9, thy brethren the **p**
See 1 Kin 20:35; Neh 6:14
PROPITIATION Rom 3:25, a **p** through faith in his blood
1 John 2:2, **p** for our sins
PROSPER Num 14:41, it shall not **p**
Deut 28:29, not **p** in thy ways
2 Chr 26:5, God made him to **p**
Neh 2:20, he will **p** us
Ps 1:3, he doeth shall **p**
37:7, who **p** in his way
73:12, who **p** in the world
122:6, they shall **p**
Prov 28:13, shall not **p**
Eccl 11:6, whether shall **p**
Is 53:10, of the Lord shall **p**
54:17, thee shall **p**
Jer 2:37, shalt not **p** in them
12:1, way of the wicked **p**
22:30, man that shall not **p**
Ezek 17:9, Shall it **p**
1 Cor 16:2, as God hath **p** him
3 John 2, as thy soul **p**
See Prov 17:8; Dan 6:28; 8:12
PROUD Job 38:11, here shall thy **p** waves be stayed
40:11, one that is **p**
Ps 31:23, the **p** doer
40:4, respecteth not the **p**
94:2, a reward to the **p**
101:5, look and a **p** heart
123:4, contempt of the **p**
138:6, the **p** he knoweth
Prov 6:17, A **p** look
15:25, the house of the **p**
16:5, is **p** in heart
21:4, and a **p** heart
Eccl 7:8, the **p** in spirit
Hab 2:5, he is a **p** man
Mal 3:15, call the **p** happy
Luke 1:51, the **p** in
1 Tim 6:4, He is **p**
James 4:6, God resisteth the **p**
See Job 9:13; 26:12; 2 Tim 3:2
PROVE Ex 15:25, ordinance, and there he **p** them
Judg 6:39, let me **p**
1 Sam 17:39, he had not **p** it
1 Kin 10:1, came to **p** him
2 Chr 9:1, to **p** Solomon
Ps 17:3, hast **p** mine heart
95:9, **p** me, and saw
Mal 3:10, **p** me now herewith
2 Cor 13:5, **p** your own selves
1 Thess 5:21, **P** all things
Heb 3:9, tempted me, **p** me
See Eccl 2:1; 7:23; Dan 1:14
PRUDENT Prov 12:16, but a **p** man covereth shame
12:23, A **p** man concealeth
14:15, the **p** man looketh

16:21, shall be called **p**
19:14, and a **p** wife
22:3, A **p** man foreseeth
Is 5:21, **p** in their own sight
Jer 49:7, perished from the **p**
Hos 14:9, **p,** and he shall
Matt 11:25, the wise and **p**
See Is 52:13; Amos 5:13
PUNISH Ezra 9:13, hast **p** us less
     than our iniquities
Prov 17:26, **p** the just
Is 13:11, I will **p** the world
26:21, **p** the inhabitants
Jer 13:21, shall **p** thee
Acts 26:11, I **p** them oft
2 Thess 1:9, **p** . . . everlasting
2 Pet 2:9, judgment to be **p**
See Lev 26:18; Prov 21:11
PUNISHMENT Gen 4:13, My **p** is
     greater than I can bear
Lev 26:41, accept of the **p**
1 Sam 28:10, no **p** happen
Lam 3:39, **p** of his sins
4:6, **p** of the iniquity
4:22, **p** of thine iniquity
Ezek 14:10, shall bear the **p**
Matt 25:46, into everlasting **p**
Heb 10:29, Of how much sorer **p**
1 Pet 2:14, **p** of evildoers
See Prov 19:19; Amos 1:3; 2:1
PURCHASE Ruth 4:10, have I **p** to
     be my wife
Ps 74:2, hast **p** of old
Acts 1:18, man **p** a field
8:20, be **p** with money
20:28, **p** with his own blood
Eph 1:4, of the **p** possession
1 Tim 3:13, **p** to themselves
See Gen 49:32; Ex 15:16; Lev 25:33;
     Jer 32:11
PURE Deut 32:14, drink the **p** blood
     of the grape
2 Sam 22:27, show thyself **p**
Job 4:17, a man be more **p**
8:6, If thou wert **p**
11:4, My doctrine is **p**
16:17, my prayer is **p**
25:5, the stars are not **p**
Ps 12:6, are **p** words
19:8, of the Lord is **p**
119:140, Thy word is very **p**
Prov 15:26, words of the **p**
20:9, **p** from my sin
Mic 6:11, I count them **p**
Zeph 3:9, a **p** language
Acts 20:26, **p** from the blood
Rom 14:20, indeed are **p**
Phil 4:8, things are **p**
1 Tim 3:9, in a **p** conscience
5:22, keep thyself **p**
2 Tim 1:3, with **p** conscience
Titus 1:15, all things are **p**
James 1:27, **P** religion
3:17, is first **p**
2 Pet 3:1, your **p** minds
1 John 3:3, even as he is **p**
Rev 22:1, **p** river of water
See Ezra 6:20; Mal 1:11
PURGE 2 Chr 34:3, year he began
     to **p** Judah
Ps 51:7, **P** me with hyssop
65:3, thou shalt **p** them
Is 1:25, purely **p** away
6:7, and thy sin **p**
22:14, be **p** from you
Ezek 24:13, I have **p** thee
Mal 3:3, **p** them as gold
Matt 3:12, he will thoroughly **p**
John 15:2, he **p** it
1 Cor 5:7, **P** out therefore
2 Tim 2:21, **p** himself
Heb 9:14, **p** your conscience
9:22, **p** with blood

See Prov 16:6; Heb 1:3; 10:2
PURIFY Titus 2:14, **p** unto himself a
     peculiar people
James 4:8, **p** your hearts
1 Pet 1:22, **p** your souls
PURPOSE Job 17:11, my **p** are
     broken off
Prov 20:18, **p** is established
Is 14:27, hosts hath **p**
Matt 26:8, To what **p**
Acts 11:23, with **p** of heart
Rom 8:28, according to his **p**
9:11, the **p** of God
Eph 1:11, **p** of him
3:11, the eternal **p**
See 2 Tim 1:9; 1 John 3:8

Q

QUENCH Song 8:7, cannot **q** love
Is 34:10, It shall not be **q**
42:3, shall he not **q**
66:24, their fire be **q**
Mark 9:43, never shall be **q**
9:44, fire is not **q**
Eph 6:16, **q** all the
1 Thess 5:19, **Q** not the Spirit
Heb 11:34, **Q** the violence
See Ps 104:11; Amos 5:6
QUICK Num 16:30, and they go
     down **q** into the pit
Ps 55:15, down **q** into hell
Acts 10:42, Judge of **q**
2 Tim 4:1, shall judge the **q**
Heb 4:12, word of God is **q**
See Lev 13:10, 24; Ps 124:3
QUICKEN Ps 71:20, sore troubles,
     shalt **q** me again
80:18, **q** us
119:25, **q** thou me
119:50, word hath **q** me
Rom 8:11, **q** your mortal
1 Cor 15:36, sowest is not **q**
Eph 2:1, you hath he **q**
2:5, hath he **q** us together
Col 2:13, hath he **q**
1 Pet 3:18, **q** by the Spirit
See John 5:21; 1 Tim 6:13
QUICKLY Matt 5:25, thine
     adversary **q**
Rev 2:5, come unto thee **q**
3:11, Behold, I come **q**
22:20, Surely I come **q**
See Gen 18:6; 27:20; Luke 16:6
QUIET Prov 1:33, be **q** from fear
1 Thess 4:11, study to be **q**
1 Tim 2:2, may lead a **q**
1 Pet 3:4, and **q** spirit
See 2 Kin 11:20; Job 3:13; 21:23

R

RACE Ps 19:5, as a strong man
     to run a **r**
Eccl 9:11, the **r** is not
1 Cor 9:24, which run in a **r**
Heb 12:1, **r** that is set
RAGE Ps 2:1, do the heathen **r**
Prov 14:16, but the fool **r**
See Prov 6:34; 29:9; Dan 3:13
RAIMENT Deut 8:4, **r** waxed not
     old
Matt 6:25, the body than **r**
6:28, thought for **r**
17:2, his **r** was white
Mark 9:3, **r** became shining
Luke 9:29, his **r** was white
12:23, is more than **r**
1 Tim 6:8, food and **r**
James 2:2, in vile **r**
Rev 3:18, and white **r**
See Matt 3:4; Luke 10:30; 23:34
RAIN (*n.*) Lev 26:4, I will give you **r**

     in due season
Deut 11:11, the **r** of heaven
32:2, shall drop as the **r**
2 Sam 23:4, shining after **r**
1 Kin 18:41, abundance of **r**
Ezra 10:13, a time of much **r**
Job 5:10, Who giveth **r**
37:6, to the great **r**
38:28, Hath the **r** a father
Ps 72:6, come down like **r**
Prov 25:14, wind without **r**
25:23, wind driveth away **r**
26:1, as **r** in harvest
28:3, sweeping **r**
Eccl 11:3, clouds be full of **r**
12:2, return after the **r**
Song 2:11, the **r** is over
Is 4:6, from storm and from **r**
55:10, the **r** cometh down
Hos 6:3, unto us as the **r**
6:3, latter and former **r**
Matt 5:45, **r** on the just
7:25, the **r** descended
See Acts 14:17; 28:2; Heb 6:7
RAIN (*v.*) Ex 16:4, will **r** bread
     from heaven for you
Job 20:23, **r** it upon him
Ps 11:6, he shall **r** snares
78:24, **r** down manna
78:27, He **r** flesh
Ezek 22:24, **r** upon
Hos 10:12, **r** righteousness
See Gen 2:5; 7:4; Amos 4:7
RAISE Deut 18:15, God will **r** up
     unto thee a Prophet
Judg 2:16, Lord **r** up judges
Ps 145:14, **r** up all those
Is 45:13, I have **r** him up
Hos 6:2, he will **r** us up
Matt 10:8, **r** the dead
11:5, the dead are **r**
16:21, be **r** again
John 2:19, I will **r** it up
6:39, **r** it up again
Acts 2:24, Whom God hath **r** up
3:15, **r** from the dead
4:10, **r** from the dead
5:30, **r** up Jesus
10:40, **r** up the third day
13:30, But God **r** him
17:31, that he hath **r** him
26:8, God should **r** the dead
Rom 4:25, was **r** again
8:11, **r** up Jesus
1 Cor 15:15, whom he **r** not up
15:16, is not Christ **r**
15:35, How are the dead **r** up
15:43, is **r** in glory
2 Cor 1:9, which **r** the dead
4:14, that he which **r** up
Gal 1:1, Father, who **r** him
Eph 1:20, when he **r** him
2:6, hath **r** us up together
Heb 11:19, able to **r** him up
11:35, **r** to life again
James 5:15, shall **r** him up
See Luke 20:37; 2 Tim 2:8
RANSOM Ex 21:30, the **r** of his life
30:12, a **r** for his soul
Job 33:24, I have found a **r**
36:18, then a great **r**
Ps 49:7, nor give to God a **r**
Prov 13:8, **r** of a man's life
Is 35:10, the **r** of the Lord
43:3, Egypt for thy **r**
Hos 13:14, I will **r** them
Matt 20:28, give his life a **r**
See Prov 6:35; Is 51:10
REAP Lev 25:11, neither **r** that
     which groweth
Ps 126:5, shall **r** in joy
Eccl 11:4, clouds shall not **r**
Jer 12:13, but shall **r** thorns

Hos 8:7, r the whirlwind
10:12, r in mercy
Mic 6:15, thou shalt not r
Matt 6:26, neither do they r
25:26, r where I sowed not
Luke 12:24; neither sow nor r
19:21, and r that thou
John 4:48, to r that whereon
1 Cor 9:11, r your carnal things
2 Cor 9:6, r also sparingly
Gal 6:7, that shall he also r
James 5:4, r down your fields
See Is 17:5; John 4:36,37
REASON Job 9:14, choose out my
words to r with him
13:3, desire to r with God
15:3, Should he r with
Is 1:18, let us r together
Matt 16:7, r among themselves
Luke 5:22, What r ye
24:15, communed together and r
Acts 24:25, r of righteousness
See 1 Sam 12:7; Mark 2:6; 12:28
REBUKE (*n.*) 2 Kin 19:3, a day of
trouble, and of r
Ps 39:11, When thou with r
80:16, perish at the r
104:7, At thy r they fled
Prov 13:8, poor heareth not r
27:5, Open r is better
Eccl 7:5, r of the wise
Is 30:17, at the r of one
Jer 15:15, I have suffered r
Phil 2:15, without r
See Deut 28:20; Is 25:8; 50:2
REBUKE (*v.*) Ps 6:1, O Lord, r me
not in thine anger
38:1, O Lord, r me not
Prov 9:7, r a wicked man
9:8, r a wise man
28:23, He that r a man
Is 2:4, r many people
Mic 4:3, r strong nations
Zech 3:2, The Lord r thee
Mal 3:11, r the devourer
Matt 8:26, r the winds
16:22, began to r him
Mark 4:39, r the wind
Luke 4:39, r the fever
17:3, thee, r him
19:39, r thy disciples
1 Tim 5:1, **R** not an elder
5:20, Them that sin r
2 Tim 4:2, r, exhort with
Titus 1:13, r them sharply
2:15, exhort, and r
Heb 12:5, art r of him
See Ruth 2:16; Amos 5:10
RECEIVE 2 Kin 5:26, to r money,
and to r garments
Job 4:12, and mine ear r
22:22, **R**, I pray thee
Ps 6:9, Lord will r my prayer
49:15, he shall r me
68:18, r gifts for men
73:24, r me to glory
Prov 2:1, wilt r my words
Is 40:2, for she hath r
Jer 2:30, they r no correction
Hos 10:6, shall r shame
14:2, r us graciously
Matt 11:5, blind r their sight
11:14, if ye will r it
18:5, whoso shall r one
19:12, let him r it
21:22, believing, ye shall r
Mark 15:23, he r it not
16:19, r up into heaven
Luke 15:2, This man r sinners
18:42, **R** thy sight
John 1:11, own r him not
1:12, as many as r him
3:27, A man can r nothing

5:43, and ye r me not
5:44, which r honour
16:24, ask, and ye shall r
20:22, **R** ye the Holy Ghost
Acts 1:9, a cloud r him
7:59, r my spirit
8:17, r the Holy Ghost
10:43, shall r remission
20:24, which I have r
22:13, r thy sight
Rom 5:11, r the atonement
14:3, God hath r him
15:7, as Christ also r
1 Cor 3:8, r his own reward
11:23, I have r of the Lord
2 Cor 4:1, as we have r mercy
5:10, r the things
7:2, R us
Phil 2:29, **R** him therefore
4:15, giving and r
Col 2:6, r Christ Jesus
1 Tim 3:16, r up into glory
4:4, r with thanksgiving
1 John 3:22, we r of him
See Ezek 3:10; James 4:3
RECOMPENSE Num 5:7, he shall r
his trespass
Deut 32:35, vengeance, and r
Ruth 2:12, Lord r thy work
2 Sam 19:36, king r it me
Job 15:31, shall be his r
34:33, he will r it
Prov 20:22, I will r evil
Is 35:4, God with a r
65:6, but will r, even r
Jer 25:14, r them according
Hos 9:7, the days of r
12:2, will he r him
Joel 3:4, ye render me a r
Luke 14:12, a r be made thee
14:14, they cannot r thee
Rom 11:35, and it shall be r
12:17, **R** to no man
2 Cor 6:13, a r in the same
Heb 2:2, r of reward
10:35, great r of reward
11:26, respect unto the r
See Prov 12:14; Is 34:8
REDEEM Gen 48:16, Angel which r
me from all evil
Ex 6:6, r you with
15:13, thou hast r
Lev 27:28, shall be sold or r
2 Sam 4:9, hath r my soul
Neh 5:5, power to r them
5:8, have r our brethren
Job 5:20, r thee from death
6:23, **R** me from the hand
Ps 25:22, **R** Israel, O God
34:22, Lord r the soul
44:26, and r us
49:7, r his brother
49:15, God will r my soul
72:14, r their soul
103:4, Who r thy life
107:2, Let the r
130:8, r Israel from all
Is 1:27, be r with judgment
35:9, r shall walk there
44:22, for I have r thee
50:2, that it cannot r
51:11, the r of the Lord
52:3, r without money
63:4, the year of my r
Hos 7:13, I have r them
13:14, I will r them
Luke 1:68, r his people
24:21, have r Israel
Gal 3:13, Christ hath r us
4:5, To r them
Titus 2:14, he might r us
1 Pet 1:18, not r with
Rev 5:9, and hast r us

See Num 18:15; Col 4:5
REDEEMER Job 19:25, I know that
my r liveth
Ps 19:14, strength, and my r
78:35, high God their r
Prov 23:11, their r is mighty
Is 47:4, As for our r
49:26, Saviour and thy **R**
59:20, **R** shall come to Zion
63:16, our father, our r
See Is 41:14; 44:6; Jer 50:34
REDEMPTION Lev 25:24, ye shall
grant a r for the land
Ps 49:8, r of their soul
111:9, r unto his people
130:7, is plenteous r
Jer 32:7, the right of r
Luke 2:38, r in Jerusalem
21:28, r draweth nigh
Rom 8:23, r of our body
Eph 4:30, unto the day of r
See Num 3:49; Heb 9:12
REFRESH Ex 31:17, seventh day he
rested, and was r
Job 32:20, that I may be r
Prov 25:13, he r the soul
Acts 3:19, the times of r
1 Cor 16:18, r my spirit
See Is 28:12; 2 Cor 7:13; 13:7
REGENERATION Matt 19:28, the r
when the Son of man shall
Titus 3:5, the washing of r
REIGN Gen 37:8, Shalt thou indeed
r over us
Ex 15:18, Lord shall r for ever
Lev 26:17, shall r over you
Deut 15:6, r over many nations
Judg 9:8, **R** thou over us
1 Sam 11:12, Saul r over us
12:12, a king shall r
2 Sam 16:8, thou hast r
Job 34:30, hypocrite r not
Ps 47:8, God r over the
93:1, The Lord r
96:10, that the Lord r
97:1, The Lord r
Prov 8:15, By me kings r
30:22, a servant when he r
Eccl 4:14, he cometh to r
Is 32:1, r in righteousness
52:7, Thy God r
Jer 22:15, Shalt thou r
23:5, r and prosper
Mic 4:7, shall r over them
Luke 19:14, to r over us
19:27, not that I should r
Rom 5:14, death r from Adam
5:17, death r by one
5:21, sin hath r unto death
6:12, Let not sin . . . . r
1 Cor 4:8, to God ye did r
15:25, For he must r
2 Tim 2:12, also r with him
Rev 5:10, r on the earth
11:15, he shall r for ever
19:6, God omnipotent r
See Luke 1:33; Rev 20:4; 22:5
REJECT 1 Sam 8:7, they have not r
thee, but they have r me
10:19, r your God
15:23, thou hast r the word
16:1, r him from reigning
Is 53:3, despised and r of men
Jer 2:37, r thy confidences
7:29, the Lord hath r
8:9, have r the word
14:19, utterly r Judah
Lam 5:22, hast utterly r us
Hos 4:6, hast r knowledge
Matt 21:42, the builders r
Mark 7:9, r the commandment
Luke 7:30, lawyers r the counsel
17:25, r of this generation

Titus 3:10, admonition **r**
Heb 12:17, he was **r**
See Jer 6:19; Mark 6:26; 8:31
REJOICE Deut 12:7, shall **r** in all
that ye put your hand
26:11, **r** in every
30:9, will again **r**
1 Sam 2:1, **r** in thy salvation
1 Chr 16:10, heart of them **r**
2 Chr 6:41, saints **r** in goodness
Job 21:12, **r** at the sound
31:25, **r** because my wealth
39:21, **r** in his strength
Ps 2:11, **r** with trembling
5:11, in thee **r**
9:14, **r** in thy salvation
19:5, **r** as a strong man
33:21, shall **r** in him
35:15, adversity they **r**
51:8, bones . . . may **r**
58:10, righteous shall **r**
68:3, let them **r**
89:16, **r** all the day
96:11, Let the heavens **r**
97:1, let the earth **r**
104:31, **r** in his works
107:42, shall see it, and **r**
149:2, Israel **r** in him
Prov 2:14, Who **r** to do evil
5:18, **r** with the wife
23:15, my heart shall **r**
23:24, the righteous shall . . . **r**
24:17, **R** not when
29:2, the people **r**
31:25, and she shall **r**
Eccl 2:10, **r** in all my labour
3:12, but for a man to **r**
5:19, to **r** in his labour
11:9, **R**, O young man
Is 29:19, shall **r** in the
35:1, desert shall **r**
62:5, thy God **r** over thee
65:13, my servants shall **r**
66:14, your heart shall **r**
Jer 11:15, then thou **r**
32:41, I will **r** over them
51:39, that they may **r**
Ezek 7:12, let not the buyer **r**
Amos 6:13, Ye which **r**
Mic 7:8, **R** not against me
Hab 3:18, will **r** in the Lord
Matt 18:13, he **r** more of
Luke 1:14, **r** at his birth
6:23, **R** ye in that day
10:20, in this **r** not
10:21, Jesus **r** in spirit
15:6, **R** with me
John 5:35, to **r** in his light
8:56, **r** to see my day
14:28, ye would **r**
16:20, world shall **r**
16:22, your heart shall **r**
Rom 5:2, **r** in hope of
12:15, **R** with them
1 Cor 7:30, and they that **r**
13:6, **R** not in iniquity
Phil 1:18, I therein do **r**
2:16, that I may **r**
3:1, **r** in the Lord
4:4, **R** in the Lord always
1 Thess 5:16, **R** evermore
James 1:9, of low degree **r**
2:13, **r** against judgment
1 Pet 1:8, ye **r** with joy
See 1 Kin 1:40; 2 Kin 11:14
REJOICING Job 8:21, laughing, and
thy lips with **r**
Ps 107:22, his works with **r**
118:15, The voice of **r**
119:111, the of my heart
126:6, come again with **r**
Prov 8:31, **R** in the habitable
35:18, Jerusalem a **r**

Jer 15:16, **r** of mine heart
Zeph 2:15, is the **r** city
Acts 5:41, **r** that they
Rom 12:2, **R** in hope
2 Cor 6:10, yet always **r**
1 Thess 2:19, or crown of **r**
See Hab 3:14; James 4:16
RELIGION Acts 26:5, sect of our **r**
Gal 1:13, in the Jews' **r**
James 1:26, man's **r** is vain
1:27, Pure **r** and undefiled
REMEMBER Ex 20:8, **R** the
sabbath day
Num 15:39, **r** . . . commandments
Deut 5:15, **r** that thou wast
32:7, **R** the days of old
Neh 13:14, **R** me, O my God
Ps 9:12, he **r** them
20:7, **r** the name of
25:6, **R**, O Lord
25:7, **R** not the sins
79:8, **r** not against us
89:47, **R** how short
105:8, **r** his covenant
119:55, I have **r** thy name
136:23, **r** us in our
137:1, when we **r** Zion
Prov 31:7, **r** his misery no more
Eccl 5:20, **r** the days of his
11:8, yet let him **r**
12:1, **R** now thy Creator
Song 1:4, **r** thy love
Is 43:18, **R** ye not
46:9, **R** the former things
65:17, shall not be **r**
Jer 51:50, **r** the Lord afar off
Hab 3:2, in wrath **r** mercy
Luke 23:42, **r** me when thou comest
Gal 2:10, should **r** the poor
Col 4:18, **R** my bonds
1 Thess 1:3, **R** without ceasing
Heb 13:3, **R** them that are
Rev 2:5, **R** therefore from
See Ps 88:5; 103:14; Matt 5:23
REMEMBRANCE Num 5:15,
bringing iniquity to **r**
1 Kin 17:18, call my sin to **r**
Job 18:17, His **r** shall perish
Ps 6:5, no **r** of thee
30:4, **r** of his holiness
112:6, in everlasting **r**
Eccl 1:11, **r** of former things
2:16, no **r** of the wise
Is 43:26, Put me in **r**
57:8, set up thy **r**
Lam 3:20, them still in **r**
Ezek 23:19, calling to **r**
Mal 3:16, a book of **r**
Luke 22:19, this do in **r**
John 14:26, things to your **r**
Acts 10:31, are had in **r**
1 Cor 11:24, do in **r** of me
2 Tim 1:3, I have **r** of thee
2:14, put them in **r**
See Heb 10:3; 2 Pet 1:12; 3:1
REMISSION Matt 26:28, is shed for
many for the **r** of sins
Luke 24:47, and **r** of sins
Heb 9:22, is no **r**
REMIT John 20:23, Whose soever
sins ye **r**
REND Joel 2:13, And **r** your heart
Matt 7:6, turn again and **r** you
See Ps 7:2; Eccl 3:7; Jer 4:30
RENDER Deut 32:41, will **r**
vengeance to mine enemies
1 Sam 26:23, **r** to every man
34:11, he **r** unto him
Ps 28:4, **r** to them
38:20, **r** evil for good
79:12, **r** unto our neighbours
94:2, **r** a reward
116:12, I **r** unto the Lord

Prov 24:12, **r** to every man
26:16, can **r** a reason
Hos 14:2, so will we **r**
Joel 3:4, **r** me a recompense
Zech 9:12, I will **r** double
Matt 21:41, **r** him the fruits
Mark 12:17, **R** to Caesar
Rom 13:7, **R** therefore to all
1 Thess 3:9, we **r** to God again
5:15, **r** evil for evil
See Num 18:9; Judg 9:56
RENEW Job 10:17, Thou **r** thy
witnesses against me
29:20, and my bow was **r**
Ps 51:10, **r** a right spirit
103:5, thy youth is **r**
104:30, thou **r** the face
Is 40:31, **r** their strength
41:1, let the people **r**
Lam 5:21, **r** our days
2 Cor 4:16, **r** day by day
Eph 4:23, be **r** in the spirit
Col 3:10, is **r** in knowledge
Heb 6:6, to **r** them again
See 2 Chr 15:8; Titus 3:5
REPAY Prov 13:21, to the righteous
good shall be **r**
Deut 7:10, he will **r** him
Luke 10:35, I will **r** thee
Rom 12:19, is mine; I will **r**
See Job 21:31; 41:11; Is 59:18
REPENT Gen 6:6, **r** the Lord that
he had made man
Ex 13:17, the people **r**
32:14, Lord **r** of the evil
Num 23:19, he should **r**
Deut 32:36, and **r** himself
1 Sam 15:29, not lie nor **r**
15:29, that he should **r**
2 Sam 24:16, the Lord **r** him
Job 42:6, **r** in dust
Ps 90:13, it **r** thee
106:45, **r** according
110:4, and will not **r**
Jer 8:6, no man **r** him
18:8, **r** of the evil
26:13, and the Lord will **r**
26:19, the Lord **r** him
31:19, was turned, I **r**
Matt 3:2, **R** ye: for the
12:41, **r** at the preaching
21:29, but afterward he **r**
27:3, **r** himself
Luke 13:3, except ye **r**
15:7, one sinner that **r**
17:3, and if he **r**
Acts 8:22, **R** therefore of
Heb 7:21, and will not **r**
Rev 2:21, her space to **r**
See Acts 2:38; 17:30; Rev 2:5
REPENTANCE Hos 13:14, **r** shall be
hid from mine eyes
Matt 3:8, fruits meet for **r**
Luke 3:8, fruits worthy of **r**
Acts 26:20, works meet for **r**
Rom 2:4, leadeth thee to **r**
11:29, are without **r**
2 Cor 7:10, sorrow worketh **r**
Heb 6:1, the foundation of **r**
6:6, them again unto **r**
12:17, no place of **r**
See Luke 15:7; Acts 20:21
REPLENISH Gen 1:28, multiply,
and **r** the earth
REPROVE 1 Chr 16:21, he **r** kings
for their sakes
Job 6:25, doth your arguing **r**
13:10, He will surely **r** you
22:4, Will he **r** thee
40:2, he that **r** God
Ps 50:8, I will not **r**
141:5, and let him **r** me
Prov 9:8, **R** not a scorner

15:12, one that r him
19:25, and r one that
29:1, r hardeneth his neck
30:6, lest he r thee
Is 11:4, r with equity
Jer 2:19, shall r thee
John 3:20, deeds should be r
16:8, r the world of sin
See Luke 3:19; Eph 5:11, 13
REQUIRE Deut 10:12, r of
2 Chr 24:22, The Lord . . . r it
Ezek 3:18, I r at thine hand
33:6, blood will I r
Mic 6:8, Lord r of thee
Luke 12:48, shall be much r
See 2 Chr 8:14; Ezra 3:4
RESERVE Job 21:30, is r to the day
38:23, r against the time
Nah 1:2, and he r wrath
1 Pet 1:4, r in heaven
2 Pet 2:4, r unto judgment
3:7, r unto fire
See Num 18:9; 2 Pet 2:9
RESIST Zech 3:1, at his right hand
to r him
Matt 5:39, That ye r not evil
Luke 21:15, to gainsay nor r
Rom 9:19, r his will
13:2, r the ordinance
James 4:6, God r the proud
4:7, **R** the devil
1 Pet 5:9, Whom r steadfast
See Acts 6:10; 7:51; 2 Tim 3:8
RESPECT (*n.*) Gen 4:4, And the
Lord r unto Abel
Ex 2:25, had r unto them
1 Kin 8:28, have thou r
2 Chr 6:19, Have r therefore
19:7, nor r of persons
Ps 74:20, r unto the covenant
119:15, r unto thy ways
138:6, r unto the lowly
Prov 24:23, have r of persons
28:21, To have r of persons
Is 17:7, r to the Holy One
22:11, r unto him
Rom 2:11, no r of persons
Phil 4:11, in r of want
Col 3:25, no r of persons
See Heb 11:26; James 2:1, 3, 9
RESPECT (*v.*) Lev 19:15, not r the
person of the poor
Deut 1:17, shall not r persons
Job 37:24, r not any
See Num 16:15; Lam 4:16
REST (*n.*) Gen 49:15, he saw that r
was good
Ex 31:15, the sabbath of r
33:14, and I will give thee r
Lev 16:31, of r unto you
25:4, be a sabbath of r
Deut 12:10, he giveth you r
Job 3:17, weary be at r
11:18, thy r in safety
Ps 55:6, and be at r
95:11, enter into my r
116:7, Return unto thy r
132:8, O Lord, into thy r
132:14, This is my r for ever
Eccl 2:23, not r in the night
Is 11:10, r shall be glorious
14:7, whole earth is at r
18:4, I will take my r
28:12, This is the r
30:15, returning and r
66:1, place of my r
Jer 6:16, r for your souls
Ezek 38:11, that are at r
Mic 2:10, is not your r
Zech 1:11, and is at r
Matt 11:28, I will give you r
11:29, and ye shall find r
12:43, seeking r

26:45, and take your r
John 11:13, of r in sleep
Acts 9:31, churches r throughout
See Prov 29:17; 2 Thess 1:7
REST (*v.*) Gen 2:2, he r on the
seventh day
Num 11:25, when the spirit r
Ps 16:9, shall r in hope
37:7, **R** in the Lord
Eccl 7:9, for anger r
Is 11:2, Lord shall r
62:1, I will not r
63:14, caused him to r
Jer 47:6, r, and be still
Dan 12:13, thou shalt r
Mark 6:31, and r a while
2 Cor 12:9, may r upon me
Rev 4:8, they r not day
6:11, should r yet
14:13, that they may r
See Prov 14:33; Song 1:7
RESTORE Ex 22:4, he shall r
double
Lev 6:4, r that which
Deut 22:2, and thou shalt r
Ps 23:3, He r my soul
51:12, **R** unto me the joy
69:4, I r that which
Is 1:26, I will r thy judges
Jer 27:22, r them to
30:17, r health unto thee
Ezek 33:15, r the pledge
Matt 17:11, and r all things
Luke 19:8, I r him fourfold
Acts 1:6, r again the kingdom
Gal 6:1, r such an one
See Ruth 4:15; Mark 8:25
RETAIN Prov 4:4, heart r my words
Eccl 8:8, to r the spirit
John 20:23, sins ye r
See Mic 7:18; Philem 13
RETURN Gen 3:19, dust shalt thou r
Ps 104:29, r to their dust
Prov 26:11, dog r to his vomit
Eccl 12:7, the dust r to the earth
Is 35:10, the ransomed . . . shall r
45:23, and shall not r
55:11, r unto me void
Jer 4:1, If thou wilt r
Amos 4:6, not r unto me
Joel 2:14, if he will r
Mal 3:7, will r unto you
See Gen 31:3; Lev 25:10
REVEAL Prov 11:13, A talebearer r
Is 22:14, r in mine ears
40:5, shall be r
56:1, righteousness to be r
Dan 2:22, He r the deep
Amos 3:7, he r his secret
Matt 10:26, shall not be r
11:25, and hast r them
16:17, blood hath not r
Luke 2:35, hearts may be r
17:30, Son of man is r
John 12:38, the Lord been r
Rom 1:17, God r from faith
1:18, is r from heaven
8:18, be r in us
1 Cor 2:10, hath r them
3:13, be r by fire
14:30, If any thing be r
Gal 1:16, To r his Son
2 Thess 1:7, Jesus shall be r
2:3, that man of sin be r
2:8, shall that Wicked be r
1 Pet 1:5, ready to be r
4:13, his glory shall be r
5:1, glory that shall be r
See Eph 3:5; 2 Thess 2:6
REVELATION Rom 2:5, and r of
the righteous judgment
16:25, according to the r
1 Cor 14:26, hath a r

2 Cor 12:1, visions and r
Gal 1:12, r of Jesus Christ
See Eph 1:17; 3:3; 1 Pet 1:13
REVIVE Ps 85:6, Wilt thou not r us
again
138:7, thou wilt r me
Is 57:15, to r the spirit
Hos 6:2, will he r us
Rom 7:9, sin r
14:9, rose, and r
See Gen 45:27; 2 Kin 13:21
REWARD (*n.*) Deut 10:17, nor
taketh r
Job 7:2, the r of his work
Ps 19:11, there is great r
58:11, r for the righteous
91:8, the r of the wicked
Prov 11:18, shall be a sure r
21:14, a r in the bosom
24:20, shall be no r
Eccl 4:9, have a good r
9:5, they any more a r
Is 1:23, followeth after r
5:23, the wicked for r
40:10, his r is with him
Ezek 16:34, thou givest a r
Dan 5:17, thy r to another
Hos 9:1, loved a r upon
Mic 3:11, judge for r
7:3, judge asketh for a r
Matt 5:12, for great is your r
5:46, what r have ye
6:1, ye have no r
10:41, a prophet's r
Luke 6:23, your r is great
6:35, r shall be great
23:41, r of our deeds
Acts 1:18, r of iniquity
Rom 4:4, r not reckoned
1 Cor 3:8, receive his own r
9:18, What is my r then
Col 2:18, you of your r
3:24, receive the r
1 Tim 5:18, is worthy of his r
Heb 2:2, recompense of r
2 Pet 2:13, receive the r
See 2 John 8; Jude 11; Rev 11:18
REWARD (*v.*) Gen 44:4, Wherefore
have ye r evil for good
Deut 32:41, r them that
1 Sam 24:17, hast r me good
2 Chr 15:7, work shall be r
Job 21:19, he r him
Ps 31:23, and plentifully r
35:12, They r me evil
103:10, r us according
Prov 17:13, r evil for good
25:22, Lord shall r thee
26:10, both r the fool
Jer 31:16, work shall be r
See 2 Sam 22:21; 2 Tim 4:14
RICH 1 Sam 2:7, and maketh r
1 Kin 3:11, asked r for thyself
10:23, earth for r
1 Chr 29:12, Both r and honour
2 Chr 1:11, not asked r
Job 15:29, He shall not be r
20:15, swallowed down r
27:19, The r man
36:19, Will he esteem thy r
Ps 37:16, better than the r
49:16, one is made r
52:7, abundance of his r
62:10, if r increase
104:24, full of thy r
112:3, and r shall be
Prov 3:16, r and honour
8:18, **R** and honour
10:4, diligent maketh r
11:4, **R** profit not
13:7, yet hath great r
18:23, but the r answereth
21:17, shall not be r

RIGHT

28:11, r man is wise
30:8, poverty nor r
Eccl 5:13, r kept for
10:20, curse not the r
Is 45:3, and hidden r
53:9, and with the r
Jer 9:23, glory in his r
17:11, that getteth r
Ezek 28:5, because of thy r
Hos 12:8, I am become r
Zech 11:5, for I am r
Matt 13:22, deceitfulness of r
Mark 10:23, they that have r
12:41, r cast in much
Luke 1:53, the r he hath
6:24, that are r
8:14, with cares and r
12:21, not r toward God
14:12, thy r neighbours
18:23, he was very r
Rom 2:4, the r of his
9:23, r of his glory
10:12, is r unto all
11:12, r of the world
11:33, depth of the r
1 Cor 4:8, now ye are r
2 Cor 6:10, yet making many r
8:9, though he was r
Eph 1:7, r of his grace
2:4, who is r in mercy
2:7, shew the exceeding r
3:8, the unsearchable r
Phil 4:19, to his r in glory
Col 1:27, the r of the glory
2:2, unto all r
1 Tim 6:9, that will be r
6:17, Charge them that are r
6:18, r in good works
Heb 11:26, greater r
James 1:10, But the r
2:5, r in faith
5:2, Your r are corrupted
Rev 2:9, but thou art r
3:17, sayest, I am r
3:18, mayest be r
5:12, power, and r
See Lev 25:47; Rev 6:15
RIGHT Gen 24:48, which had led
me in the r way
Deut 32:4, just and r is he
1 Sam 12:23, good and the r way
Neh 9:13, them r judgments
Job 6:25, are r words
34:23, more than r
Ps 19:8, of the Lord are r
45:6, is a r sceptre
51:10, and renew a r spirit
107:7, by the r way
119:75, judgments are r
Prov 4:11, in r paths
8:6, be r things
12:5, thoughts . . . are r
12:15, way of a fool is r
14:12, way which seemeth r
21:2, Every way of a man is r
24:26, giveth a r answer
Is 30:10, us r things
Amos 3:10, know not to do r
Matt 20:4, whatsoever is r
Eph 6:1, for this is r
See Judg 17:6; 2 Pet 2:15
RIGHTEOUS Gen 7:1, thee have I
seen r before me
18:23, also destroy the r
20:4, also a r nation
38:26, more r than I
Ex 23:8, words of the r
Num 23:10, death of the r
Deut 25:1, justify the r
1 Sam 24:17, more r than I
1 Kin 2:32, two men more r
2 Chr 6:23, justifying the r
4:7, r cut off

9:15, though I were r
17:9, The r also
22:3, that thou art r
34:5, said, I am r
Ps 1:5, congregation of the r
7:9, for the r God trieth
11:3, what can the r do
34:17, The r cry
37:16, that a r man hath
37:29, The r shall inherit
37:39, salvation of the r
55:22, r to be moved
58:11, reward for the r
92:12, The r shall flourish
112:6, the r shall be
125:3, the lot of the r
140:13, r shall give thanks
146:8, Lord loveth the r
Prov 2:7, wisdom for the r
3:32, secret is with the r
10:11, mouth of a r man
10:16, labour of the r
10:25, r is an everlasting
10:30, The r shall
11:8, The r is delivered
12:5, The thoughts of the r
12:10, A r man regardeth
12:26, r is more excellent
13:21, but to the r good
14:32, but the r hath hope
15:19, the way of the r
15:28, heart of the r
16:13, R lips are the
18:10, r runneth into it
28:1, r are bold as a lion
29:2, r are in authority
Eccl 7:16, Be not r over much
9:1, r, and the wise
9:2, one event to the r
Is 3:10, Say ye to the r
24:16, glory to the r
26:2, r nation which
41:2, raised up the r man
53:11, shall my r servant
57:1, r perisheth
60:21, shall be all r
Jer 23:5, unto David a r Branch
Ezek 13:22, heart of the r sad
16:52, they are more r
33:12, righteousness of the r
Amos 2:6, they sold the r
Mal 3:18, between the r
Matt 9:13, to call the r
13:17, r men have desired
13:43, r shine forth
23:28, appear r unto men
23:29, sepulchres of the r
25:46, r into life eternal
Mark 2:17, not to call the r
Luke 1:6, both r before God
18:9, that they were r
23:47, this was a r man
John 7:24, judge r judgment
Rom 3:10, There is none r
5:7, scarcely for a r man
5:19, many be made r
2 Thess 1:6, it is a r thing
2 Tim 4:8, the r judge
Heb 11:4, that he was r
1 Pet 3:12, are over the r
4:18, r scarcely be saved
2 Pet 2:8, vexed his r soul
1 John 2:1, Jesus Christ the r
3:7, righteousness is r
Rev 22:11, he that is r
See Ezek 3:20; 1 Tim 1:9
RIGHTEOUSNESS Gen 30:33, shall
my r answer for me in time
Deut 33:19, sacrifices of r
1 Sam 26:23, every man his r
Job 27:6, My r I hold fast
29:14, I put on r
35:2, My r is more

36:3, ascribe r to my Maker
Ps 4:1, O God of my r
9:8, judge the world in r
15:2, and worketh r
17:15, behold thy face in r
23:3, in the paths of r
40:9, I have preached r
45:7, lovest r
50:6, declare his r
72:2, people with r
94:15, return unto r
97:2, r and judgment
111:3, his r endureth
118:19, the gates of r
132:9, be clothed with r
Prov 8:18, riches and r
10:2, but r delidereth
11:5, r of the perfect
11:19, As r tendeth to life
12:28, way of r is life
14:34, R exalteth a nation
16:12, established by r
Eccl 7:15, perisheth in his r
Is 11:5, r shall be the
26:10, will he not learn r
32:1, shall reign in r
32:17, And the work of r
59:16, and his r
62:2, shall see thy r
64:6, and all our r
Jer 23:6, The Lord our R
33:15, Branch of r
Ezek 3:20, doth turn from his r
14:14, by their r
18:24, turneth away from his r
33:13, trust to his own r
Dan 4:27, thy sins by r
9:7, r belongeth unto thee
9:24, bring in everlasting r
12:3, that turn many to r
Hos 10:12, yourselves in r
Amos 5:24, r as a mighty stream
6:12, the fruit of r
Zeph 2:3, seek r, seek meekness
Mal 4:2, Sun of r arise
Matt 3:15, fulfill all r
5:6, thirst after r
5:10, persecuted for r sake
5:20, except your r
21:32, in the way of r
Luke 1:75, In holiness and r
John 16:8, of sin, and of r
Acts 10:35, and worketh r
13:10, enemy of all r
24:25, as he reasoned of r
Rom 1:17, therein is the r
3:5, commend the r of God
4:6, God imputeth r
5:17, the gift of r
6:13, r unto God
6:20, free from r
8:10, life because of r
9:30, followed not after r
10:4, of the law for r
10:10, believeth unto r
14:17, r, and peace
1 Cor 1:30, wisdom, and r
15:34, Awake to r, and sin not
2 Cor 5:21, the r of God
6:7, the armour of r
6:14, fellowship hath r
Gal 2:21, if r come by the law
5:5, of r by faith
Eph 6:14, breastplate of r
Phil 1:11, the fruits of r
3:9, not having mine own r
1 Tim 6:11, and follow after r
2 Tim 3:16, instruction in r
4:8, a crown of r
Titus 3:5, Not by works of r
Heb 1:8, a sceptre of r
1:9, hast loved r
5:13, in the word of r

7:2, King of **r**
11:7, heir of the **r**
11:33, wrought **r**
12:11, peaceable fruit of **r**
James 1:20, not the **r** of God
3:18, And the fruit of **r**
1 Pet 2:24, should live unto **r**
2 Pet 2:5, a preacher of **r**
2:21, the way of **r**
3:13, dwelleth **r**
1 John 2:29, that doeth **r**
See Is 54:14; 63:1; Zech 8:8
RIGHTLY 2 Tim 2:15, **r** dividing the word
RISE Gen 19:2, and ye shall **r** up early
Num 24:17, a Sceptre shall **r**
Ps 127:2, to **r** up early
Prov 31:15, She **r** also
Eccl 12:4, **r** up at the voice
Is 33:10, Now will I **r**
58:10, **r** in obscurity
60:1, glory of the Lord is **r**
Jer 7:13, **r** up early
Lam 3:63, and their **r** up
Matt 5:45, **r** on the evil
17:9, be **r** again
20:19, he shall **r** again
26:32, after I am **r** again
26:46, **R**, let us be going
Mark 4:27, **r** night and day
9:9, **r** from the dead
9:10, the **r** from the dead
9:31, **r** the third day
10:49, Be of good comfort, **r**
14:28, after that I am **r**
Luke 2:34, and **r** again
11:7, I cannot **r**
22:46, **r** and pray
24:7, third day **r** again
24:34, The Lord is **r** indeed
John 11:23, shall **r** again
Acts 10:13, **R**, Peter
26:16, **r**, and stand
26:23, **r** from the dead
Rom 8:34, that is **r** again
1 Cor 15:15, the dead **r** not
15:20, **r** from the dead
Col 3:1, be with Christ
1 Thess 4:16, shall **r** first
See Is 60:3; Mark 16:2
RIVER Ex 7:19, upon their streams, upon their **r**
Job 29:6, poured me out **r**
Ps 1:3, tree planted by the **r**
46:4, There is a **r**
65:9, the **r** of God
119:136, **R** of waters
137:1, By the **r** of Babylon
Eccl 1:7, **r** run into the sea
Is 32:2, as **r** of water
43:19, **r** in the desert
48:18, peace been as a **r**
66:12, to her like a **r**
Mic 6:7, of **r** of oil
John 7:38, belly shall flow **r**
Rev 22:1, shewed me a pure **r**
See Gen 41:1; Ex 1:22; Ezek 47:9
ROARING Prov 28:15, As a **r** lion, and a ranging bear
Luke 21:25, the waves **r**
1 Pet 5:8, as a **r** lion
See Ps 22:13; Zeph 3:3
ROB Prov 22:22, **R** not the poor, because he is
Is 10:2, **r** the fatherless
10:13, **r** their treasures
42:22, this is a people **r**
Ezek 33:15, that he had **r**
Mal 3:8, man **r** God
2 Cor 11:8, I **r** other churches
See Judg 9:25; 2 Sam 17:8
ROBBER Job 12:6, The tabernacles

of **r** prosper
Is 42:24, Israel to the **r**
Jer 7:11, become a den of **r**
John 10:1, a thief and a **r**
Acts 19:37, **r** of churches
2 Cor 11:26, in perils of **r**
See Ezek 7:22; Dan 11:14
ROCK Ex 33:22, I will put thee in a clift of the **r**
Num 20:10, water out of this **r**
24:21, thy nest in a **r**
Deut 8:15, the **r** of flint
32:4, He is the **R**
32:15, **R** of his salvation
32:18, Of the **R** that
32:30, except their **R**
2 Sam 22:2, The Lord is my **r**
22:3, The God of my **r**
23:3, the **R** of Israel
Job 24:8, embrace the **r**
Ps 27:5, set me up upon a **r**
31:3, **r** and my fortress
40:2, my feet upon a **r**
61:2, lead me to the **r**
81:16, honey out of the **r**
92:15, he is my **r**
Prov 30:26, houses in the **r**
Song 2:14, clefts of the **r**
Is 8:14, a **r** of offense
17:10, **r** of thy strength
32:2, shadow of a great **r**
Matt 7:25, founded upon a **r**
16:18, upon this **r**
Luke 8:6, fell upon a **r**
Rom 9:33, **r** of offense
1 Cor 10:4, that spiritual **R**
1 Pet 2:8, a **r** of offense
Rev 6:16, the mountains and **r**
See Judg 6:20; 1 Sam 14:4
ROOT Prov 12:3, **r** of the righteous
Is 5:24, **r** shall be
11:10, a **r** of Jesse
37:31, again take **r**
53:2, **r** out of a dry ground
Ezek 31:7, for his **r** was
Mal 4:1, **r** nor branch
Matt 3:10, **r** of the trees
13:6, they had no **r**
Mark 4:6, had no **r**
11:20, dried up from the **r**
Luke 8:13, these have no **r**
Rom 11:16, the **r** be holy
1 Tim 6:10, **r** of all evil
Heb 12:15, **r** of bitterness
Jude 12, plucked up by the **r**
Rev 22:16, **r** and the offspring
See 2 Chr 7:20; Dan 4:15
ROSE (n.) Song 2:1, I am the **r** of Sharon
Is 35:1, blossom as the **r**
ROSE (v.) Gen 32:31, over Penuel the sun **r** upon him
Josh 3:16, **r** up upon a heap
Luke 16:31, **r** from the dead
Rom 14:9, both died, and **r**
1 Cor 15:4, that he **r** again
2 Cor 5:15, and **r** again
See 1 Thess 4:14; Rev 19:3
RULE (v.) Gen 1:16, light to **r** the day . . . to **r** the night
3:16, husband . . . **r** over thee
Prov 16:32, **r** his spirit
22:7, The rich **r** over
Eccl 9:17, **r** among fools
Col 3:15, peace of God **r**
See Dan 5:21; Zech 6:13
RUMOR Matt 24:6, and **r** of wars
See 2 Kin 19:7; Obad 1
RUN Ps 23:5, my cup **r** over
Dan 12:4, shall **r** to and fro
Rom 9:16, nor of him that **r**
1 Cor 9:24, **r** in a race **r** all
9:26, therefore so **r**

Gal 2:2, means I should **r**
5:7, Ye did **r** well
Heb 12:1, **r** with patience
1 Pet 4:4, ye **r** not with them
See Prov 4:12; Amos 8:12
RUST Matt 6:19, where moth and **r** doth corrupt
6:20, neither moth nor **r**

S

SABBATH Lev 25:8, thou shalt number seven s of years
2 Kin 4:23, new moon, nor s
2 Chr 36:21, she kept s
Ezek 46:1, but on the s
Amos 8:5, and the s
Mark 2:27, s was made for man
2:28, Lord also of the s
Luke 13:15, of you on the s
See Is 1:13; Matt 28:1
SACKCLOTH 2 Sam 3:31, your clothes, and gird you with s
1 Kin 20:32, So they girded s
Neh 9:1, and with s
Esth 4:1, on s with ashes
Ps 30:11, put off my s
35:13, my clothing was s
Jon 3:5, and put on s
SACRIFICE (n.) Gen 31:54, Jacob offered s upon the mount
Ex 5:17, s to the Lord
Num 25:2, s of their gods
1 Sam 15:22, better than s
Ps 4:5, s of righteousness
27:6, s of joy
40:6, S and offering
51:16, desirest not s
118:27, bind the s
Prov 15:8, s of the wicked
21:3, to the Lord than s
Eccl 5:1, the s of fools
Is 1:11, multitude of your s
Jer 6:20, nor your s sweet
Dan 8:11, by him the daily s
11:31, take away the daily s
Hos 3:4, and without a s
6:6, mercy, and not s
Amos 4:4, s every morning
Zeph 1:7, hath prepared a s
Mal 1:8, the blind for s
Mark 9:49, every s shall
12:33, offerings and s
Luke 13:1, mingled with their s
Acts 7:42, slain beasts and s
14:13, would have done s
Rom 12:1, bodies a living s
1 Cor 8:4, in s unto idols
10:19, is offered in s
Eph 5:2, and a s to God
Phil 2:17, the s and service
4:18, s acceptable
Heb 9:26, by the s of himself
10:12, one s for sins
10:26 remaineth no more s
11:4, a more excellent s
13:15, s of praise to God
13:16, with such s God is
1 Pet 2:5, offer up spiritual s
See Ezra 6:10; Jon 1:16
SACRIFICE (v.) Ex 22:20, He that s unto any god
Ezra 4:2, we do s unto him
Neh 4:2, will they s
Ps 54:6, I will freely s
106:37, s their sons
107:22, And let them s
Eccl 9:2, him that s
Is 65:3, s in gardens
Hos 8:13, They s flesh
Hab 1:16, s unto their net
1 Cor 5:7, our passover is s
10:20, they s to devils

SAFETY Prov 11:14, multitude . . .
is s
21:31, s is of the Lord
1 Thess 5:3, Peace and s
See Job 24:23; Ps 12:5; 33:17
SAINTS 1 Sam 2:9, He will keep the
feet of his s
Job 5:1, to which of the s
15:15, no trust in his s
Ps 16:3, But to the s
30:4, O ye s of his
37:28, forsaketh not his s
50:5, Gather my s
89:5, congregation of the s
97:10, souls of his s
116:15, death of his s
132:9, s shout for joy
149:9, have all his s
Dan 7:18, s of the most High
8:13, one s speaking
Matt 27:52, bodies of the s
Acts 9:13, done to thy s
Rom 1:7, called to be s
8:27, intercession for the s
12:13, the necessity of s
16:2, as becometh s
1 Cor 1:2, called to be s
6:2, the s shall judge
16:1, collection for the s
16:15, ministry of the s
Eph 1:18, inheritance in the s
2:19, citizens with the s
3:8, least of all s
4:12, perfecting of the s
5:3, as becometh s
Col 1:2, the s and faithful
1 Thess 3:13, with all his s
2 Thess 1:10, glorified in his s
1 Tim 5:10, washed the s feet
Jude 3, delivered unto the s
Rev 5:8, the prayers of s
See Phil 4:21; Rev 11:18; 13:7
SAKE Gen 3:17, cursed is the ground
for thy s
8:21, for man's s
12:13, for thy s
2 Sam 9:1, for Jonathan's s
18:5, gently for my s
Neh 9:31, great mercies' s
Ps 6:4, thy mercies' s
23:3, for his name's s
25:11, thy name's s
Matt 5:10, righteousness' s
24:22, the elect's s
Mark 13:20, for the elect's s
Luke 21:12, for my name's s
John 11:15, glad for your s
Rom 13:5, for conscience s
1 Cor 4:10, for Christ's s
10:25, 27, for conscience s
Col 1:24, for his body's s
1 Thess 5:13, for their work's s
1 Tim 5:23, thy stomach's s
Titus 1:11, filthy lucre's s
2 John 2, For the truth's s
See 2 Cor 8:9; 1 Thess 3:9
SALVATION Gen 49:18, I have
waited for thy s, O Lord
15:2, he is become my s
Deut 32:15, Rock of his s
1 Sam 11:13, s in Israel
14:45, wrought this great s
19:5, great s for all
2 Sam 22:51, the tower of s
1 Chr 16:23, show forth . . . his s
2 Chr 6:41, be clothed with s
20:17, the s of the Lord
Ps 3:8, S belongeth unto
9:14, rejoice in thy s
14:7, the s of Israel
25:5, God of my s
27:1, my light and my s
35:3, I am thy s

37:39, s of the righteous
50:23, show the s of God
51:12, joy of thy s
62:2, 6, my rock and my s
68:20, our God is the God of s
74:12, working s
85:9, his s is nigh
98:3, the s of our God
116:13, the cup of s
118:14, is become my s
119:81, fainteth for thy s
119:155, S is far from
119:174, for thy s, O Lord
144:10, he that giveth s
149:4, the meek with s
Is 12:2, Behold, God is my s
33:2, our s also
45:17, with an everlasting s
49:8, in a day of s have
51:5, my s is gone forth
52:10, see the s of our God
56:1, for my s is near
59:11, for s, but it is
59:17, helmet of s upon
60:18, call thy walls S
60:10, the garments of s
Jer 3:23, is s hoped for
Lam 3:26, the s of the Lord
Jon 2:9, S is of the Lord
Hab 3:8, thy chariots of s
3:18, the God of my s
Zech 9:9, and having s
Luke 1:69, horn of s for us
1:77, knowledge of s unto
2:30, have seen thy s
3:6, shall see the s of God
19:9, This day is s come
John 4:22, for s is of the Jews
Acts 4:12, is there s in any
16:17, the way of s
Rom 1:16, power of God unto s
13:11, s nearer than when
2 Cor 6:2, now is the day of s
7:10, repentance to s
Eph 1:13, the gospel of your s
6:17, the helmet of s
Phil 1:19, turn to my s
1:28, but to you of s
2:12, work out your own s
1 Thess 5:8, the hope of s
5:9, s by our Lord Jesus
2 Tim 3:15, make thee wise unto s
Titus 2:11, that bringeth s
Heb 1:14, be heirs of s
2:3, neglect so great s
2:10, captain of their s perfect
5:9, author of eternal s
6:9, that accompany s
9:28, without sin unto s
1 Pet 1:5, through faith unto s
1:9, the s of your souls
2 Pet 3:15, of our Lord is s
Jude 3, of the common s
Rev 7:10, S to our God
See Job 13:16; 1 Sam 2:1
SAME Rom 12:16, Be of the s mind
Phil 4:2, be of the s mind
Heb 13:8, Christ the s yesterday
See 1 Cor 10:3; 12:4; 15:39
SANCTIFY Lev 11:44, ye shall
therefore s yourselves
Num 11:18, S yourselves against
Josh 3:5, the people, S yourselves
1 Sam 16:5, s yourselves
Is 5:16, is holy shall be s
13:3, commanded my s ones
29:23, they shall s my name
66:17, that s themselves
Jer 1:5, the womb I s thee
Ezek 20:41, will be s in you
28:25, be s . . . in the sight
36:23, shall be s in you
39:27, am s in them in the

Joel 1:14, S ye a fast
John 10:36, the Father hath s
17:17, S them through
17:19, sakes I s myself
Acts 20:32, them which are s
Rom 15:16, s by the Holy Ghost
1 Cor 1:2, are s in Christ Jesus
6:11, but ye are s
7:14, husband is s by the
Eph 5:26, he might s and
1 Thess 5:23, of peace s you wholly
1 Tim 4:5, For it is s by the
2 Tim 2:21, s, and meet for
Heb 2:11, and they who are s
10:10, we are s through
10:14, them that are s
13:12, he might s the
1 Pet 3:15, But s the Lord
Jude 1, them that are s by
See Gen 2:3; Ex 13:2; Job 1:5
SATAN 1 Chr 21:1, S stood up
against Israel
Ps 109:6, and let S stand at
Matt 12:26, if S cast out S
16:23, Get thee behind me, S
Luke 10:18, S as lightning fall
Acts 5:3, hath S filled thine
26:18, power of S unto God
2 Cor 12:7, messenger of S to
2 Thess 2:9, of S with all
1 Tim 1:20, delivered unto S
5:15, turned aside after S
See Rom 16:20; 1 Cor 5:5
SAVE Gen 45:7, and to s your lives
by a great
Deut 28:29, no man shall s thee
33:29, people s by the Lord
Josh 10:6, and s us
Judg 6:15, shall I s Israel
1 Sam 14:6, the Lord to s by
Job 2:6, but s his life
22:29, and he shall s the
Ps 7:10, God, which s the
20:6, Lord s his anointed
34:18, s such as be of a
44:3, own arm s them
60:5, s with thy right
72:4, s the children
80:3, and we shall be s
86:2, s thy servant
109:31, to s him from
118:25, S now, I beseech
119:94, I am thine, s me
119:146, cried unto thee; s
138:7, hand shall s me
Prov 20:22, and he shall s thee
28:18, shall be s
Is 35:4, will come and s
43:12, and have s
45:20, that cannot s
45:22, and be ye s
47:15, none shall s thee
49:25, I will s thy children
59:1, that it cannot s
63:1, mighty to s
Jer 2:28, s thee in the time
8:20, and we are not s
11:12, shall not s them
14:9, that cannot s
15:20, for I am with thee to s thee
17:14, and I shall be s
30:10, I will s thee
30:11, to s thee
42:11, you to s you
46:27, I will s thee from
48:6, Flee, s your lives
Lam 4:17, that could not s us
Ezek 3:18, to s his life
34:22, will I s my flock
Hos 1:7, will s them by the
13:10, that may s thee in
Hab 1:2, and thou wilt not s
Zeph 3:17, he will s

Matt 1:21, shall s his
10:22, the end shall be s
16:25, whosoever will s his
18:11, is come to that
19:25, Who then can be s
24:13, the same shall be s
27:40, s thyself
27:42, himself he cannot s
Mark 3:4, to s life, or to
15:30, S thyself, and come
16:16, baptized shall be s
Luke 6:9, to s life
7:50, faith hath s thee
8:12, believe and be s
9:56, but to s them
13:23, there few that be s
19:10, seek and to s that
23:35, let him s himself
23:39, s thyself and us
John 3:17, him might be s
5:34, that ye might be s
10:9, he shall be s
12:47, but to s the world
Acts 2:21, the Lord shall be s
2:47, such as should be s
4:12, whereby we must be s
15:1, ye cannot be s
16:30, must I do to be s
16:31, thou shalt be s
27:43, willing to s Paul
Rom 5:9, shall be s from
8:24, For we are s by hope
9:27, a remnant shall be s
10:1, they might be s
10:9, thou shalt be s
11:14, might s some of them
11:26, all Israel shall be s
1 Cor 1:18, us which are s
1:21, preaching to s them
3:15, himself shall be s
5:5, the spirit may be s
7:16, shalt s thy husband
9:22, by all means s some
2 Cor 2:15, them that are s
Eph 2:5, by grace ye are s
2:8, by grace are ye s
1 Tim 1:15, the world to s sinners
2:4, all men to be s
4:16, shalt both s thyself
Heb 5:7, to s him from death
7:25, s them to the uttermost
10:39, to the s of the soul
11:7, an ark to the s
James 1:21, to s your souls
2:14, can faith s him
4:12, who is able to s
5:15, faith shall s the
5:20, s a soul from death
1 Pet 3:20, souls were s by water
4:18, scarcely be s
Jude 23, others s with fear
See Matt 14:30; John 12:27
SAVIOUR 2 Sam 22:3, tower, and
    my refuge, my s
2 Kin 13:5, gave Israel a s
Ps 106:21, forgat God their s
Is 19:20, send them a s
45:21, a just God and a S
49:26, I the Lord am thy S
63:8, so he was their S
Eph 5:23, the s of the body
1 Tim 4:10, the S of all men
Titus 2:10, God our S in all
2:13, and our S Jesus Christ
Jude 25, only wise God our S
See Neh 9:27; Obad 21
SCHOOLMASTER Gal 3:24, law
    was our s to bring us unto
SEARCH (v.) Num 13:2, that they
    may s the land of
1 Chr 28:9, Lord s all hearts
Ps 139:23, S me . . . and know
Jer 17:10, Lord s the heart

Lam 3:40, Let us s and try our ways
John 5:39, S the scriptures
Rom 8:27, he that s the hearts
1 Cor 2:10, for the Spirit s
1 Pet 1:10, and s diligently
See Job 10:6; 28:3; 1 Pet 1:11
SEASON Gen 1:14, let them be for
    signs, and for s
Eccl 3:1, there is a s
Acts 1:7, the times or the s
2 Tim 4:2, be instant in s
Heb 11:25, of sin for a s
See 1 Thess 5:1; 1 Pet 1:6
SECRET Job 11:6, the s of wisdom
Ps 25:14, The s of the Lord
27:5, s of his tabernacle
90:8, our s sins
Prov 3:32, but his s
9:17, bread eaten in s
21:14, A gift in s
27:5, than s love
Matt 6:6, Father which is in s
John 18:20, in s have I said
See Prov 11:13; Dan 2:18; 4:9
SEE Gen 11:5, Lord came down to s
    the city
Ex 12:13, when I s the blood
14:13, s the salvation
33:20, not s my face
Job 19:26, shall I s God
Ps 27:13, to s the goodness
66:5, s the works of God
Is 6:10, s with their eyes
Jer 5:21, eyes, and s not
Matt 5:8, they shall s God
John 1:50, shalt s greater
9:25, blind, now I s
Heb 2:9, we s Jesus
1 Pet 1:8, now ye s him not
1 John 3:2, s him as he is
See Matt 27:24; John 1:51
SEEK 1 Chr 28:9, if thou s him
2 Chr 19:3, heart to s God
Ezra 4:2, for we s your God
Job 5:8, I would s unto God
Ps 9:10, them that s thee
10:4, not s after God
10:15, s out his wickedness
14:2, understand, and s God
24:6, them that s him
27:4, will I s after
27:8, S ye my face
34:14, do good; s peace
63:1, early will I s thee
69:32, live that s God
83:16, they may s thy name
122:9, I will s thy good
Prov 1:28, shall s me early
11:27, s good procureth
21:6, that s death
23:30, to s mixed wine
23:35, I will s it
Eccl 1:13, my heart to s
7:25, to s out wisdom
Song 3:2, will s him
Is 1:17, s judgment
19:3, shall s to the idols
34:16, S ye out of the book
45:19, S ye me in vain
Jer 29:13, ye shall s me
30:17, no man s after
Lam 3:25, soul that s him
Ezek 34:16, they shall s peace
Dan 9:3, to s by prayer
Amos 5:4, Israel, S ye me
Zeph 2:3, S ye the Lord
Mal 2:7, Should s the law
Matt 6:33, But s ye first
7:7, s, and ye shall find
12:39, evil . . . generation s
Luke 13:7, I come s fruit
15:8, and s diligently
19:10, s and to save

24:5, s ye the living
John 4:23, the Father s such
7:25, whom they s to kill
7:34, 36, Ye shall s me
18:8, if therefore ye s me
Rom 3:11, that s after God
1 Cor 1:22, s after wisdom
10:24, no man s his own
13:5, s not her own
2 Cor 12:14, I s not yours
Phil 2:21, all s their own
Col 3:1, s those things
Heb 11:14, they s a country
13:14, s one to come
1 Pet 3:11, let him s peace
5:8, s whom he may devour
Rev 9:6, shall men s death
See Jer 45:5; 1 Cor 10:33
SEEN Gen 32:30, I have s God
    face to face
Ex 14:13, whom ye have s
Judg 6:22, I have s an angel
Job 13:1, mine eye hath s
28:7, eye hath not s
Is 6:5, have s the King
64:4, neither hath the eye s
Mark 9:1, s the kingdom
John 1:18, s God at any time
Acts 4:20, have s and heard
1 Cor 2:9, Eye hath not s
1 Tim 6:16, whom no man hath s
Heb 11:1, of things not s
1 Pet 1:8, Whom having not s
See John 5:37; 9:37; Rom 1:20
SEND Gen 24:7, he shall s his angel
    before thee
Is 6:8, Here am I; s me
Matt 9:38, s forth labourers
12:20, he s forth judgment
Mark 3:14, he might s them
John 14:26, will s in my name
17:8, thou didst s me
Rom 8:3, God s his own Son
See Luke 10:3; 2 Thess 2:11
SEPARATE Prov 16:28, s chief
    friends
19:4, the poor is s
Matt 25:32, he shall s them
Rom 8:35, shall s us
2 Cor 6:17, and be ye s
Heb 7:26, s from sinners
See Ezra 10:11; Is 56:3; 59:2
SERPENT Gen 3:1, s was more
    subtil than any beast
Job 26:13, the crooked s
Ps 58:4, the poison of a s
140:3, tongues like a s
Prov 23:32, it biteth like a s
Eccl 10:8, a s shall bite
Is 65:25, be the s meat
Jer 8:17, I will send s
Matt 7:10, give him a s
10:16, wise as s
23:33, Ye s, ye generation
Mark 16:18, shall take up s
John 3:14, lifted up the s
Rev 12:9, old s, called
See Ex 4:3; Num 21:8
SERVANT Matt 25:21, good and
    faithful s
Luke 17:10, are unprofitable s
1 Cor 7:21, called being a s
7:23, ye the s of men
Eph 6:5, S, be obedient
1 Pet 2:18, S, be subject
See 1 Tim 6:1; Rev 22:3
SERVE Deut 10:20, him shalt thou s
Josh 24:15, whom ye will s
Ps 100:2, S the Lord with gladness
Matt 6:24, s two masters
John 12:26, If any man s me
Rom 6:6, should not s sin
Gal 5:13, s one another

Col 3:24, for ye s the Lord
1 Thess 1:9, idols to s
Rev 7:15, s him day and night
See Luke 22:27; Heb 9:14; 12:28
SET Song 8:6, S me as a seal
Matt 5:14, is s on a hill
Heb 6:18, hope s before us
See Ps 75:7; 107:41; Eph 1:20
SHADOW Ps 91:1, s of the Almighty
102:11, days are like a s
144:4, s that passeth away
Eccl 6:12, spendeth as a s
8:13, which are as a s
Is 4:6, tabernacle for a s
25:4, a s from the heat
32:2, s of a great rock
Lam 4:20, Under his s
Hos 14:7, dwell under his s
See Judg 9:15, 36; Jon 4:5
SHAME Ps 4:2, long will ye turn my
glory into s
Heb 6:6, to an open s
12:2, despising the s
See 1 Thess 2:2; 1 Tim 2:9
SHED Gen 9:6, by man shall his
blood be s
Matt 26:28, S for many for
Rom 5:5, is s abroad
Titus 3:6, s on us abundantly
Heb 9:22, without s of blood
See Ezek 18:10; 22:3
SHEEP Num 27:17, as s which have
no
Ps 49:14, Like s they are
100:3, the s of his pasture
Is 53:6, like s have gone
Jer 12:3, s for the slaughter
Matt 7:15, to you in s clothing
10:6, lost s of the house
12:12, better than a s
John 10:2, shepherd of the s
10:11, life for the s
21:16, Feed my s
See Matt 10:16; 12:11
SHEPHERD Gen 46:34, every s is
an abomination
Ps 23:1, The Lord is my s
Is 13:20, the s make their fold
40:11, his flock like a s
56:11, they are s that
Jer 23:4, s over them
50:6, their s have caused
Amos 3:12, As the s taketh
Zech 11:17, Woe to the idol s
John 10:14, I am the good s
See Zech 11:3; Luke 2:8
SHIELD Ps 33:20, our help and our
s
59:11, O Lord our s
84:9, Behold, O God our s
91:4, shall be thy s
Eph 6:16, the s of faith
See Prov 30:5; Jer 51:11
SHINE Job 22:28, the light shall s
upon thy ways
29:3, When his candle s
Ps 104:15, his face to s
139:12, the night s as
Prov 4:18, s more and more
Is 9:2, hath the light s
60:1, Arise, s; for thy
Dan 12:3, wise shall s as the
Matt 5:16, your light so s
13:43, the righteous s forth
? Cor 4:6, the light to s
John 1:5; 2 Pet 1:19
R Ezek 34:26, there shall be

Job 24:8
ope deferred
t s
not s
m s of love

James 5:14, Is any s among
5:15, shall save the s
SICKNESS Matt 8:17, and bare our
s
SIGHT Ex 3:3, and see this great s
Deut 28:34, s of thine eyes
Eccl 6:9, Better is the s of
Matt 11:5, received their s
11:26, good in thy s
20:34, eyes received s
Luke 7:21, blind he gave s
18:42, Receive thy s
21:11, fearful s and great
Acts 22:13, receive thy s
Rom 12:17, the s of all men
2 Cor 5:7, not by s
See Eccl 11:9; Is 43:4
SIN (n.) Gen 4:7, doest not well, s
lieth at the door
Num 27:3, in his own s
Deut 24:16, for his own s
Job 10:6, searchest after my s
Ps 19:13, from presumptuous s
25:7, Remember not the s
32:1, whose s is covered
38:18, sorry for my s
51:3, and my s is ever
90:8, our secret s in the
103:10, with us after our s
Prov 5:22, the cords of his s
10:19, wanteth not s
14:9, make a mock at s
14:34, but s is a reproach
Is 30:1, may add s to s
43:25, not remember thy s
44:22, as a cloud, thy s
53:10, an offering for s
53:12, bare the s of many
Jer 51:5, s against the Holy
Ezek 33:16, of his s that he
Hos 4:8, They eat up the s
Mic 6:7, the s of my soul
Matt 12:31, of s and blasphemy
John 1:29, the s of the world
8:7, He that is without s
16:8, reprove the world of s
19:11, hath the greater s
Acts 7:60, lay not this s
22:16, wash away thy s
Rom 5:20, where s abounded
6:1, Shall we continue in s
6:23, wages of s is death
7:7, Is the law s
14:23, not of faith is s
2 Cor 5:21, him to be s for
2 Thess 2:3, that man of s
1 Pet 2:24, bare our s in his
See 1 John 1:8; 3:4; 4:10
SIN (v.) Gen 42:22, saying, Do not s
against the child
Ex 9:27, I have s this time
10:16, I have s against
Num 22:34, I have s; for I
Josh 7:20, I have s against
1 Sam 15:24, I have s
26:21, said Saul, I have s
2 Sam 12:13, I have s against
Job 7:20, I have s; what shall
10:14, If I s, then thou
Ps 4:4, and s not
39:1, that I s not
41:4, for I have s against
Prov 8:36, s against me
Is 43:27, first father hath s
Ezek 18:4, the soul that s
Hos 13:2, they s more and
Matt 18:21, brother s against me
27:4, I have s in that
Luke 15:18, 21, I have s against
John 5:14, s no more, lest a
8:11, go, and s no more
Rom 3:23, s, and come short of
1 Cor 15:34, and s not

Eph 4:26, Be ye angry, and s
1 John 3:9, he cannot s
See Num 15:28; Job 1:5, 22
SINGING Ps 100:2, come before his
presence with s
126:2, our tongue with s
Song 2:12, time of the s of
Eph 5:19, s and making melody
SINGLE Matt 6:22, if therefore
thine eye be s
Luke 11:34, thine eye is s
SINGLENESS Acts 2:46, with
gladness and s of heart
Eph 6:5, in s of your heart
Col 3:22, but in s of heart
SINNER Gen 13:13, men of Sodom
were wicked and s
Ps 1:1, in the way of s
25:8, he teach s in the way
26:9, my soul with s
51:13, s shall be converted
Prov 1:10, if s entice thee
13:21, Evil pursueth s
Eccl 9:18, one s destroyeth
Is 33:14, The s in Zion are
Matt 9:11, with publicans and s
9:13, but s to repentance
11:19, publicans and s
Mark 2:16, with publicans and s
Luke 7:37, which was a s
13:2, were s above all
15:2, This man receiveth s
15:7, heaven over one s
18:13, merciful to me a s
John 9:16, a s do such miracles
9:25, Whether he be a s
Rom 5:8, While we were yet s
5:19, many were made s
Heb 7:26, separate from s
See James 4:8; 1 Pet 4:18
SIT Ps 69:12, They that s in
Matt 20:23, to s on my right
See Prov 23:1; Lam 3:63
SLACK 2 Pet 3:9, The Lord is not s
SLAUGHTER Ps 44:22, We are
counted as sheep for the s
Is 53:7, a lamb to the s
See Hos 5:2; Zech 11:4
SLAY Job 13:15, Though he s me
See Gen 4:15; Ex 21:14
SLEEP (n.) 1 Sam 26:12, a deep s
from the Lord
Ps 13:3, lest I s
127:2, giveth his beloved s
Prov 3:24, and thy s shall
6:10, Yet a little s
20:13, Love not s, lest
Eccl 5:12, s of a labouring
Jer 51:39, may rejoice, and s
Luke 9:32, were heavy with s
John 11:13, of rest in s
Rom 13:11, awake out of s
See Dan 2:1; Acts 16:27
SLEEP (v.) Job 7:21, I s in the dust
Ps 4:8, in peace, and s
121:4, neither slumber nor s
Prov 4:16, For they s not
6:22, when thou s
Dan 12:2, them that s in the
1 Cor 11:30, and many s
15:51, We shall not all s
Eph 5:14, Awake thou that s
1 Thess 4:14, which s in Jesus
5:6, let us not s
See Gen 28:11; 1 Kin 18:27
SLOW Ex 4:10, s of speech
Neh 9:17, s to anger
Ps 103:8, s to anger
Prov 14:29, He that is s
Luke 24:25, and s of heart to believe
See Acts 27:7; Titus 1:12
SMITE Prov 19:25, S a scorner
Is 50:6, my back to the s

Zech 13:7, s the shepherd
Matt 5:39, shall s thee on
See Luke 6:29; Acts 23:2
SNARE 2 Sam 22:6, the s of death
Ps 91:3, thee from the s of
Prov 6:2, s with the words
  13:14, the s of death
1 Tim 3:7, reproach and the s
  6:9, temptation and a s
2 Tim 2:26, the s of the devil
See Ex 23:33; Deut 7:16
SNOW Ps 51:7, be whiter than s
Is 1:18, be as white as s
Lam 4:7, were purer than s
Dan 7:9, was white as s
Matt 28:3, raiment white as s
Mark 9:3, exceeding white as s
See Ps 68:14; 148:8; Rev 1:14
SOBER 2 Cor 5:13, we be s
1 Thess 5:6, watch and be s
1 Tim 3:2, one wife, vigilant, s
Titus 1:8, good men, s
  2:2, That the aged men be s
  2:4, women to be s
1 Pet 4:7, be ye therefore s
See Acts 26:25; Rom 12:3
SON Gen 6:2, the s of God saw the
  daughters
Job 1:6, the s of God came
  38:7, all the s of God
Ps 2:12, Kiss the S
  86:16, s of thine handmaid
Prov 10:1, A wise s maketh
  13:1, wise s heareth
  17:2, rule over a s
  17:25, foolish s is a grief
  19:13, s is the calamity
  31:2, the s of my womb
Is 9:6, unto us a s is given
  14:12, s of the morning
Jer 35:5, s of the house
Ezek 20:31, your s to pass
  23:37, also caused their s
Hos 1:10, s of the living God
Mal 3:17, spareth his own s
Matt 11:27, man knoweth the S
  13:55, the carpenter's s
  17:5, This is my beloved S
  22:42, whose s is he
Mark 6:3, the s of Mary
Luke 4:22, this Joseph's s
  10:6, the s of peace
  19:9, a s of Abraham
John 1:12, the s of God
  1:18, the only begotten S
  3:18, begotten S of God
  5:21, so the S quickeneth
  8:35, the S abideth ever
  8:36, S . . . make you free
  17:12, the s of perdition
Acts 4:36, s of consolation
Rom 1:9, gospel of his S
  8:3, sending his own S
  8:29, image of his S
  8:32, spared not his own S
1 Cor 4:14, as my beloved s
Gal 4:5, the adoption of s
  4:7, if a s, then an heir
Phil 2:15, the s of God
Col 1:13, of his dear S
2 Thess 2:3, s of perdition
Heb 2:10, in bringing many s
  5:8, Though he were a S
  11:24, the s of Pharoah's
  12:6, and scourgeth every s
1 John 2:22, the Father and the S
  3:1, the s of God
  5:12, He that hath the S
See 1 John 1:7; Rev 21:7
SONG Job 35:10, s in the night
Ps 32:7, s of deliverance
  33:3, Sing unto him a new s
  40:3, new s in my mouth

69:12, s of the drunkards
77:6, remembrance my s
119:54, have been my s
137:4, sing the Lord's s
Prov 25:20, that singeth s
Is 23:16, sing many s
  35:10, to Zion with s
  42:10, unto the Lord a new s
Ezek 33:32, a very lovely s
Amos 8:3, the s of the temple
Eph 5:19, and spiritual s
See Song 1:1; Rev 5:9; 14:3
SORROW Gen 3:16, I will greatly
  multiply thy s
Ps 127:2, eat the bread of s
Eccl 2:23, all his days are s
  7:3, S is better
Is 53:3, a man of s
Matt 24:8, the beginning of s
2 Cor 7:10, For godly s worketh
1 Thess 4:13, that ye s not
1 Tim 6:10, through with many s
See Prov 15:13; Hos 8:10
SOUL Gen 2:7, life; and man became
  a living s
Ex 30:12, a ransom for his s
Deut 11:13, with all your s
  13:6, as thine own s
  30:2, with all thy s
Judg 10:16, his s was grieved
1 Sam 18:1, as his own s
1 Kin 8:48, with all their s
1 Chr 22:19, your s to seek
Job 3:20, the bitter in s
  12:10, hand is the s
  23:13, what his s desireth
  31:30, a curse to his s
  33:22, his s draweth near
Ps 33:19, s from death
  34:22, Lord redeemeth the s
  49:8, redemption of their s
  62:1, Truly my s waiteth
  63:1, my s thirsteth
  74:19, s of thy turtledove
  103:2, the Lord, O my s
  116:8, my s from death
  119:175, Let my s live
Prov 11:25, The liberal s
  19:2, s be without knowledge
  25:25, to a thirsty s
Is 55:3, your s shall live
  58:10, the afflicted s
Jer 20:13, the s of the poor
  31:12, and their s shall
Ezek 18:4, the s that sinneth
  22:25, they have devoured s
Hab 2:10, against thy s
Matt 10:28, able to kill the s
  16:26, exchange for his s
  26:38, My s is exceeding
Luke 21:19, possess ye your s
Acts 4:32, and of one s
Rom 13:1, every s be subject
1 Thess 5:23, and s and body
Heb 6:19, an anchor of the s
  13:17, for your s
James 5:20, a s from death
1 Pet 2:11, war against the s
  4:19, keeping of their s
2 Pet 2:14, unstable s
3 John 2, as thy s prospereth
See Prov 3:22; Ezek 3:19
SOUND (*adj.*) Prov 2:7, He layeth up
  s wisdom
  3:21, keep s wisdom
  14:30, A s heart
1 Tim 1:10, to s doctrine
2 Tim 1:7, and of a s mind
  1:13, the form of s words
  4:3, not endure s doctrine
Titus 1:9, able by s doctrine
  2:1, become s doctrine
See Ps 119:80; Titus 2:2, 8

SOW Job 4:8, plow iniquity, and s
  wickedness
Ps 126:5, that s in tears
Prov 6:19, that s discord
Eccl 11:4, wind shall not s
  11:6, In the morning s
Jer 4:3, s not among thorns
Hos 10:12, S to yourselves
Matt 6:26, for they s not
  13:37, s the good seed
Gal 6:7, whatsoever a man s
See Lev 26:5; James 3:18
SPARE Joel 2:17, S thy people
Rom 8:32, s not his own Son
  11:21, if God s not
2 Pet 2:4, God s not the angels
See Prov 17:27; Is 54:2; 58:1
SPIRIT Gen 6:3, My s shall not
  always strive with
Ex 35:21, his s made willing
Num 11:17, take of the s
  14:24, another s with him
  16:22, s of all flesh
  24:2, and the s of God
  27:18, in whom is the s
Josh 5:1, was there s in them
1 Sam 10:10, and the S of God
1 Kin 22:21, there came forth a s
2 Kin 2:9, thy s be upon me
2 Chr 15:1, the S of God
Neh 9:20, good s to instruct
Job 4:15, Then a s passed
  15:13, thy s against God
  26:4, s came from thee
  32:8, there is a s in man
Ps 31:5, I commit my s
  32:2, and in whose s
  51:10, and renew a right s
  78:8, whose s was not
  104:4, maketh his angels s
  106:33, provoked his s
  139:7, I go from thy s
Prov 16:2, Lord weigheth the s
  16:18, and a haughty s
  16:19, be of a humble s
  16:32, he that ruleth his s
  29:23, the humble in s
Eccl 3:21, the s of man
  7:8, the patient in s
  8:8, to retain the s
  11:5, the way of the s
  12:7, the s shall return
Is 4:4, the s of judgment
  11:2, s of the Lord
  34:16, his s it hath
  42:1, put my s upon him
  44:3, I will pour my s
  57:15, contrite and humble s
  59:21, My s that is
  61:1, S of the Lord God
Ezek 3:14, the s lifted me up
  11:19, a new s within you
  18:31, and a new s
Joel 2:28, I will pour out my s
Mic 2:11, man walking in the s
Zech 12:10, the s of grace
Matt 3:16, S of God descending
  26:41, s indeed is willing
Mark 1:10, the S like a dove
  1:12, the s driveth him
  8:12, sighed deeply in his s
Luke 1:17, in the s and power
  2:27, came by the S
  4:14, in the power of the S
  8:55, her s came again
  9:55, not what manner of s
  10:21, Jesus rejoiced in S
  24:39, for a s hath not
John 1:32, the S descending
  3:34, the S by measure
  4:24, God is a S
  6:63, s that quickeneth
  14:17, Even the S of truth

15:26, the S of truth
Acts 2:4, the S gave them
6:10, the wisdom and the s
17:16, his s was stirred
23:8, neither angel, nor s
Rom 8:1, but after the S
8:2, the law of the S
8:11, the S of him
8:16, S itself beareth
8:26, S itself maketh
12:11, fervent in s
15:19, power of the S
1 Cor 2:4, of the S
2:10, for the S searcheth
4:21, the s of meekness
6:17, Lord is one s
6:20, and in your s
12:4, but the same S
12:10, discerning of s
14:2, in the s he speaketh
15:45, made a quickening s
2 Cor 3:6, the s giveth life
3:17, the S of the Lord is
Gal 3:3, having begun in the S
5:16, Walk in the S
5:22, fruit of the S
5:25, If we live in the S
6:8, soweth to the S
Eph 1:17, the s of wisdom
2:2, s that now worketh
2:18, access by one S
2:22, through the S
3:16, with might by his S
4:4, one body, and one S
4:23, be renewed in the s
4:30, grieve not the holy S
5:9, the S is in all
5:18, filled with the S
6:17, the sword of the S
Phil 1:27, stand fast in one s
2:1, fellowship of the S
Col 1:8, your love in the S
2:5, with you in the s
1 Thess 5:19, Quench not the S
2 Thess 2:13, of the S
1 Tim 3:16, justified in the S
4:1, S speaketh expressly
2 Tim 4:22, be with thy s
Heb 1:14, all ministering s
4:12, of soul and s
9:14, eternal s offered
12:9, unto the Father of s
12:23, the s of just men
James 2:26, body without the s
4:5, The s that dwelleth
1 Pet 3:4, a meek and quiet s
3:18, but quickened by the S
3:19, the s in prison
4:6, to God in the s
4:14, s of glory
1 John 3:24, by the S
4:1, believe not every s
4:2, know ye the S of God
4:3, s that confesseth not
4:6, the s of truth
5:6, S that beareth witness
5:8, s, and the water
Jude 19, having not the S
Rev 1:10, I was in the S
2:7, S saith unto
4:2, I was in the s
11:11, the S of life
14:13, Yea, saith the S
22:17, S and the bride say
See Matt 8:16; John 3:5
SPIRITUAL Hos 9:7, is a fool, the s
mad
you some s gift
s is s
gs
s things
s
nto s

10:3, the same s meat
12:1, concerning s gifts
14:1, and desire s gifts
15:44, raised a s body
15:46, which is s
Gal 6:1, ye which are s
Eph 5:19, hymns and s songs
6:12, against s wickedness
1 Pet 2:5, built up a s house
See 1 Cor 9:11; Col 1:9; 3:16
SPIRITUALLY Rom 8:6, but to be s
minded is life
1 Cor 2:14, are s discerned
Rev 11:8, which s is called
SPRINKLE Is 52:15, he s many
nations
Ezek 36:25, I s clean water
STAFF Ps 23:4, thy s they comfort
me
Is 3:1, the stay and the s
14:5, hath broken the s
Zech 11:10, my s, even Beauty
STAND Ex 14:13, Fear ye not, s still,
and see the
2 Kin 10:4, how then shall we s
2 Chr 20:17, ye still
Job 8:15, but it shall not s
19:25, he shall s at the
Ps 1:1, nor s in the way
1:5, shall not s
4:4, S in awe
10:1, Why s thou afar off
24:3, or who shall s in
33:11, the Lord s forever
35:2, s up for mine help
76:7, and who may s in
94:16, who will s up for
109:31, s at the right hand
122:2, Our feet shall s
130:3, who shall s
147:17, who can s before
Prov 22:29, shall s before
27:4, but who is able to s
Eccl 8:3, s not in an evil
Is 7:7, It shall not s
21:8, I s . . . upon the
28:18, hell shall not s
40:8, our God shall s
65:5, S by thyself
Jer 6:16, S ye in the ways
35:19, s before me forever
Dan 12:13, s in thy lot at the
Mic 5:4, he shall s and feed
Nah 2:8, S, s, shall they
Zech 3:1, Satan s at his
Mal 3:2, who shall s when
Matt 12:25, itself shall not s
16:28, be some s here
Mark 3:24, that kingdom cannot s
3:25, that house cannot s
Luke 11:18, shall his kingdom s
Rom 5:2, grace wherein we s
14:4, able to make him s
1 Cor 2:5, s in the wisdom of
16:13, s fast in the faith
Gal 4:20, for I s in doubt
5:1, S fast therefore
Eph 6:13, having done all, to s
Phil 1:27, that ye s fast
4:1, so s fast in the Lord
1 Thess 3:8, if ye s fast
2 Tim 2:19, God s sure
James 5:9, the judge s before
Rev 3:20, I s at the door
6:17, shall be able to s
20:12, dead . . . s before God
See 1 Cor 10:12; Rev 15:2
STATUTE Ex 18:16, do make them
know the s of God
Lev 3:17, a perpetual s for your
Ps 19:8, The s of the Lord
50:16, to declare my s
Ezek 5:6, my judgments and my s

33:15, the s of life
Zech 1:6, my words and my s
See Ps 18:22; 105:45; 119:12
STILL Ps 4:4, and be s
23:2, beside the s waters
46:10, Be s, and know
Zech 11:16, that standeth s
Mark 4:39, Peace, be s
See Num 13:30; Ps 65:7
STING 1 Cor 15:55, where is thy s
STIR Deut 32:11, eagle s up her
1 Kin 11:14, s up an adversary
1 Chr 5:26, s up the spirit
2 Chr 36:22, Lord s up the spirit
See Song 2:7; 3:5; 8:4
STONE Ps 91:12, foot against a s
118:22, s which the builders
Dan 2:34, that a s was cut
Matt 21:44, shall fall on this s
24:2, one s upon another
Luke 4:3, command this s
19:44, one s upon another
John 1:42, interpretation, A s
8:7, cast a s at her
1 Pet 2:5, as lively s, are
See 1 Sam 30:6; 1 Cor 3:12
STORE 1 Cor 16:2, lay by him in s
1 Tim 6:19, Laying up in s
See 1 Kin 10:10; 1 Chr 29:16
STOREHOUSE Mal 3:10, Bring ye
all the tithes into the s
STRAIGHT Ps 5:8, make thy way s
before my face
Prov 4:25, look s before thee
Eccl 1:15, cannot be made s
7:13, can make that s
Is 40:4, shall be made s
45:2, the crooked places s
Matt 3:3, make his paths s
Luke 13:13, she was made s
Acts 9:11, which is called S
Heb 12:13, And make s paths
See Josh 6:5; 1 Sam 6:12
STRANGER Gen 23:4, I am a s and
a sojourner with you
Ps 39:12, I am a s with thee
146:9, Lord preserveth the s
Matt 25:35, I was a s
Luke 17:18, save this s
Eph 2:12, s from the covenants
2:19, ye are no more s
Heb 11:13, they were s
13:2, to entertain s
See Matt 17:25; 1 Pet 2:11
STRENGTH Ex 15:2, The Lord is
my s and song
Judg 5:21, trodden down s
1 Sam 2:9, by s shall no man
15:29, the S of Israel
2 Sam 22:33, God is my s
Job 9:19, If I speak of s
12:13, is wisdom and s
Ps 18:2, my God, my s
18:32, girded me with s
27:1, Lord is the s
28:7, The Lord is my s
29:11, s unto his people
33:16, by much s
39:13, I may recover s
46:1, God is our refuge and s
68:34, Ascribe ye s unto God
68:35, that giveth s
73:26, s of my heart
81:1, unto God our s
84:5, whose s is in thee
96:6, s and beauty
118:14, my s and song
138:3, with s in my soul
Prov 10:29, the Lord is s
Eccl 9:16, better than s
10:17, princes eat . . . for s
Is 12:2, Jehovah is my s
25:4, a s to the poor

40:29, he increaseth s
51:9, awake, put on s
Hag 2:22, s of the kingdoms
Luke 1:51, He hath showed s
Rom 5:6, yet without s
1 Cor 15:56, and the s of sin
Rev 3:8, thou hast a little s
See Job 21:23; 2 Cor 12:9
STRENGTHEN Job 15:25, s himself
　against the Almighty
Ps 20:2, and s thee
104:15, s man's heart
Eccl 7:19, Wisdom s the wise
Is 35:3, S ye the weak hands
Luke 22:32, s thy brethren
Eph 3:16, to be s with might
Phil 4:13, which s me
Col 1:11, S with all might
See Luke 22:43; 1 Pet 5:10
STRIPES Deut 25:3, Forty s he may
　give him
1 Pet 2:24, by whose s
STRIVE Gen 6:3, My spirit shall not
　. . . s with man
Prov 3:30, S not with a man
Luke 13:24, S to enter
2 Tim 2:5, s for masteries
2:24, servant . . . must not s
See Is 45:9; Jer 50:24
STRONG 1 Sam 4:9, Be s, and quit
　yourselves like
1 Kin 2:2, be thou s therefore
Job 9:19, lo, he is s
Ps 19:5, rejoiceth as a s man
24:8, The Lord s and mighty
31:2, be thou my s rock
71:7, art my s refuge
Prov 10:15, is his s city
18:10, Lord is a s tower
Eccl 9:11, battle to the s
Is 35:4, be s, fear not
40:26, he is s in power
Dan 10:19, be s, yea, be s
Matt 12:29, a s man's house
Rom 4:20, was s in faith
1 Cor 4:10, weak, but ye are s
2 Thess 2:11, send them s delusion
Heb 5:12, not of s meat
6:18, a s consolation
See Prov 14:26; Joel 3:10
STUDY Eccl 12:12, much s is a
　weariness of the flesh
See 1 Thess 4:11; 2 Tim 2:15
STUMBLE Prov 4:19, they know not
　at what they s
Is 28:7, they s in judgment
Jer 46:6, shall s, and fall
Mal 2:8, have caused many to s
1 Pet 2:8, which s at the word
See John 11:9; Rom 9:32; 11:11
SUBDUE Mic 7:19, s our iniquities
Phil 3:21, to s all things
Heb 11:33, Who through faith s
See Zech 9:15; 1 Cor 15:28
SUBJECT Luke 10:17, devils are s
　unto us
Rom 8:7, s to the law of God
8:20, made s to vanity
13:1, every soul be s
1 Cor 14:32, s to the prophets
15:28, be s unto him
Eph 5:24, s unto Christ
Heb 2:15, s to bondage
James 5:17, s to like passions
1 Pet 2:18, s to your masters
3:22, powers being made s
5:5, all of you be s
See Luke 2:51; Titus 3:1
SUBMIT 2 Sam 22:45, Strangers
　shall s themselves
Ps 68:30, s himself
Eph 5:22, Wives, s yourselves
James 4:7, S yourselves

See Rom 10:3; Eph 5:21
SUBSTANCE Prov 3:9, with thy s
28:8, increaseth his s
Luke 15:13, wasted his s
Heb 11:1, faith is the s
See Prov 1:13; 6:31; 8:21
SUFFER Ps 55:22, s the righteous
Prov 19:15, shall s hunger
Eccl 5:12, not s him to sleep
Matt 16:21, s many things
19:14, S little children
Mark 8:31, Son of man must s
Mark 10:14, S the little children
Luke 24:46, behooved Christ to s
Acts 3:18, that Christ should s
Rom 8:17, we s with him
1 Cor 3:15, he shall s loss
12:26, one member s
Gal 6:12, should s persecution
2 Tim 2:12, If we s
3:12, shall s persecution
Heb 11:25, to s affliction
1 Pet 2:21, Christ also s
3:14, if ye s for
4:1, Christ hath s for us
See Phil 3:8; Heb 2:18; 5:8
SUFFICIENT Matt 6:34, S unto the
　day
See Deut 15:8; John 6:7
SUN Josh 10:22, S, stand thou still
　upon Gibeon
Judg 5:31, as the s when
Job 8:16, green before the s
Ps 58:8, may not see the s
84:11, a s and shield
121:6, s shall not smite
Eccl 1:9, thing under the s
11:7, to behold the s
12:2, While the s
Song 1:6, the s hath looked
6:10, clear as the s
Jer 15:9, her s is gone down
Joel 2:10, the s and the moon
Mal 4:2, S of righteousness
Matt 5:45, s to rise on
13:43, shine forth as the s
Eph 4:26, not the s go down
See 1 Cor 15:41; Rev 7:16
SUPPLICATION 1 Kin 9:3, have
　heard thy prayer and thy s
Job 9:15, s to my judge
Ps 6:9, Lord hath heard my s
Dan 9:3, seek by prayer and s
Zech 12:10, grace and of s
Eph 6:18, all prayer and s
1 Tim 2:1, s, prayers
See Ps 28:6; 31:22; Heb 5:7
SUPPLY Phil 4:19, s all your need
SWALLOW 1 Cor 15:54, Death is s
　up in victory
2 Cor 5:4, be s up of life
SWEAR Ps 15:4, He that s to his
　own hurt
Matt 5:34, S not at all
See Zeph 1:5; Matt 26:74
SWORD Ps 57:4, their tongue a
　sharp s
Is 2:4, shall not lift up s
Ezek 7:15, The s is without
Matt 10:34, but a s
Luke 2:35, a s . . . pierce
Rom 13:4, beareth not the s
Eph 6:17, s of the Spirit
Heb 4:12, any two-edged s
Rev 1:16, a sharp two-edged s
13:10, killeth with the s
19:15, goeth a sharp s
See Is 2:4; Joel 3:10; Mic 4:3

T

TABERNACLE Ps 15:1, Lord, who
　shall abide in thy t

27:5, In the secret of his t
84:1, How amiable are thy t
Is 33:20, a t that shall not
See Job 5:24; Prov 14:11
TABLE Ps 23:5, Thou preparest a t
　before me
Matt 15:27, their masters' t
Mark 7:28, dogs under the t
See Prov 3:3; Jer 17:1; Mal 1:7
TAKE Ex 6:7, I will t you to me for a
　people
Matt 6:25, T no thought
10:19, t no thought how
11:29, T my yoke upon you
26:26, and said, T, eat
Luke 6:29, t thy coat also
12:26, why t ye thought
1 Cor 6:7, rather t wrong
Rev 3:11, t thy crown
See John 1:29; Rev 22:19
TASTE Num 11:8, the t of it was as
　the t of fresh oil
Job 6:6, there any t
12:11, mouth t his meat
Ps 34:8, O t and see
119:103, sweet . . . unto my t
Jer 48:11, t remained in him
Matt 16:28, not t of death
Luke 14:24, t of my supper
John 8:52, never t of death
Col 2:21, Touch not; t not
Heb 2:9, should t death
6:4, and have t
1 Pet 2:3, ye have t
See 1 Sam 14:43; 2 Sam 19:35
TAUGHT Ps 71:17, thou hast t me
Prov 4:4, He t me also
Matt 7:29, he t them as one
Mark 1:22, for he t them
Luke 13:26, and thou hast t
John 6:45, be all t of God
8:28, as my Father hath t
Gal 1:12, neither was I t it
6:6, t in the word
Eph 4:21, been t by him
2 Thess 2:15, ye have been t
See 1 Thess 4:9; 1 John 2:27
TEACH Ex 4:15, and will t you
Deut 4:10, t their children
6:7, t them diligently
11:19, And ye shall t them
Judg 13:8, and t us
1 Sam 12:23, I will t you
2 Sam 1:18, the children of Judah
2 Chr 15:3, a t priest
Job 6:24, T me and I will
8:10, Shall not they t
12:7, they shall t thee
34:32, not t thou me
36:22, by his power: who t
Ps 25:4, t me thy paths
25:8, will he t sinners
27:11, T me thy way
34:11, will t you the fear
51:13, I t transgressors
90:12, t us to number our
94:12, and t him out
Prov 6:13, t with his fingers
Is 2:3, he will t us
28:9, shall he t knowledge
28:26, and doth t him
48:17, God which t thee
Jer 9:20, t your daughters
Ezek 44:23, t my people
Mic 3:11, thereof t for
Matt 28:19, and t all nations
Luke 11:1, Lord, t us to pray
12:12, Holy Ghost shall t
John 9:34, dost thou t us
14:26, he shall t you all
Acts 5:42, ceased not to t
Rom 12:7, or he that t
1 Cor 4:17, t every where

11:14, nature itself t
14:19, my voice I might t
Col 1:28, and t every man
3:16, t and admonishing
1 Tim 1:3, t no other doctrine
3:2, apt to t
4:11, things command and t
6:2, t and exhort
2 Tim 2:2, to t others also
Titus 1:11, t things which
2:4, t the young women
2:12, **T** us that
Heb 5:12, t you again
See Matt 22:16; Mark 6:34
TEACHER 1 Chr 25:8, as the great, the t as the scholar
Ps 119:99, than all my t
Prov 5:13, the voice of my t
Is 30:20, not thy t be removed
Hab 2:18, and a t of lies
John 3:2, t come from God
Rom 2:20, a t of babes
1 Cor 12:29, are all t
Eph 4:11, pastors and t
1 Tim 1:7, t of the law
Titus 2:3, t of good things
See 1 Tim 2:7; 2 Tim 1:11
TEARS 2 Kin 20:5, thy prayer, I have seen thy t
Ps 126:5, They that sow in t
Is 25:8, wipe away t
Mal 2:13, covering . . . with t
Luke 7:38, wash his feet with t
Acts 20:19, and with many t
20:31, and day with t
2 Tim 1:4, mindful of thy t
See 2 Cor 2:4; Heb 5:7; 12:17
TEMPLE 2 Sam 22:7, he did hear my voice out of his t
Neh 6:10, within the t
Ps 27:4, enquire in his t
29:9, in his t doth
Is 6:1, train filled the t
Amos 8:3, songs of the t
Mal 3:1, come to his t
Matt 12:6, greater than the t
John 2:19, Destroy this t
1 Cor 3:16, are the t of God
6:19, body is the t
2 Cor 6:16, t of the living God
See Hos 8:14; Rev 7:15; 11:19
TEMPORAL 2 Cor 4:18, the things which are seen are t
TEMPT Gen 22:1, that God did t Abraham
Ex 17:2, do ye t the Lord
Num 14:22, and have t me
Deut 6:16, as ye t him
Ps 78:18, they t God
Is 7:12, I t the Lord
Mal 3:15, that t God
Matt 4:7, t the Lord thy God
22:18, said, Why t ye me
Luke 10:25, and t him
Acts 5:9, to t the Spirit
15:10, why t ye God
1 Cor 10:13, you to be t
Gal 6:1, lest thou also be t
Heb 2:18, suffered being t
4:15, was in all points t
James 1:13, say when he is t
See Matt 4:1; Mark 1:13
TEMPTATION Matt 6:13, lead us not into t
'1. enter not into t
'4:38, lest ye enter into t
. . . and in time of t
. . . t taken you
. . . ⁺ which
. . . divers t
. . . dly out of t
. Pet 1:6

TEMPTER Matt 4:3, And when the t came to him
1 Thess 3:5, t have tempted you
TENTH Gen 28:22, I will surely give the t unto thee
Lev 27:32, the t shall be holy
Is 6:13, it shall be a t
TERRIBLE Deut 7:21, a mighty God and t
10:21, great and t things
Neh 1:5, the great and t God
Ps 66:3, How t art thou
68:35, O God, thou art t
Jer 15:21, the hand of the t
Joel 2:11, great and very t
Heb 12:21, so t was the sight
See Lam 5:10; Ezek 1:22; 28:7
TERROR Gen 35:5, the t of God was upon the cities
Deut 32:25, and t within
Job 6:4, t of God
18:11, **T** shall make
24:17, t of the shadow
33:7, my t shall not
Ps 55:4, the t of death
73:19, consumed with t
91:5, for the t by night
2 Cor 5:11, the t of the Lord
See Ezek 21:12; 1 Pet 3:14
TESTIMONY 2 Kin 17:15, his t which he testified
Ps 93:5, Thy t are very sure
119:22, I have kept thy t
119:24, Thy t also
119:46, will speak of thy t
119:59, feet unto thy t
119:119, I love thy t
119:129, Thy t are wonderful
Is 8:16, Bind up the t
8:20, and to the t
Matt 10:18, a t against them
Luke 21:13, to you for a t
John 3:32, receiveth his t
21:24, his t is true
Acts 14:3, t unto the word
1 Cor 2:1, the t of God
2 Cor 1:12, t of our conscience
2 Tim 1:8, ashamed of the t
Heb 11:5, had this t
See Rev 1:2; 6:9; 11:7
THANK Matt 11:25, I t thee, O Father
Luke 18:11, God I t thee
John 11:41, I t thee that
Acts 28:15, he t God
1 Cor 1:4, I t my God always
2 Thess 1:3, to t God always
1 Tim 1:12, I t Christ Jesus
See 1 Chr 23:30; Dan 2:23
THANKS Neh 12:31, companies of them that gave t
Matt 26:27, and gave t
Luke 2:38, gave t likewise
Rom 14:6, he giveth God t
1 Cor 15:57, But t be to God
Eph 5:20, Giving t always
1 Thess 3:9, For what t can we
Rev 4:9, t to him
See 2 Cor 1:11; Heb 13:15
THANKSGIVING Ps 26:7, may publish with the voice of t
95:2, his presence with t
Is 51:3, found therein, t
Amos 4:5, a sacrifice of t
Phil 4:6, supplication with t
Col 4:2, in the same with t
1 Tim 4:3, be received with t
See Neh 11:17; 12:8; 2 Cor 4:15
THIEF 1 Thess 5:2; 2 Pet 3:10, as a t in the night
See Prov 6:30; 29:24
THING Is 43:19, I will do a new t
Jer 31:22, a new t in the earth

John 5:14, a worse t come
Phil 3:16, mind the same t
See Heb 10:29; 1 Pet 4:12
THINK Gen 40:14, t on me when it shall be well
Neh 5:19, T upon me, my God
Ps 40:17, the Lord t upon me
Prov 23:7, he t in his heart
Matt 3:9, t not to say within
Rom 12:3, not to t of himself
Gal 6:3, if a man t himself
Phil 4:8, t on these things
James 1:7, that man t that he
See Job 35:2; Jer 29:11
THIRST (*v.*) Ps 42:2, My soul t for God
63:1, my soul t for thee
143:6, my soul t after thee
Is 49:10, not hunger nor t
55:1, Ho, every one that t
Matt 5:6, t after righteousness
John 4:14, him shall never t
6:35, shall never t
7:37, If any man t, let him
19:28, saith, I t
Rev 7:16, neither t any more
See Ex 17:3; Is 48:21
THORN Num 33:55, and t in your sides
Judg 2:3, as t in your sides
Song 2:2, As the lily among t
2 Cor 12:7, a t in the flesh
See Matt 13:7; 27:29
THOUGHT (*n.*) Job 42:2, no t can be withholden
Ps 10:4, in all his t
40:5, and thy t which are
92:5, thy t are very deep
94:11, the t of man
139:23, and know my t
Prov 12:5, t of the righteous
16:3, and thy t shall be
24:9, The t of foolishness
Is 55:7, unrighteous man his t
55:8, For my t are not your
Mic 4:12, the t of the Lord
Matt 6:25, Take no t for your
6:31, take no t, saying
9:4, knowing their t said
10:19, take no t how or what
12:25, Jesus knew their t
15:19, proceed evil t
Mark 7:21, proceed evil t
13:11, take no t beforehand
Luke 2:35, t of many hearts
5:22, perceived their t
6:8, he knew their t
9:47, the t of their heart
11:17, knowing their t
12:11, take ye no t how or
Acts 8:22, t of thine heart
1 Cor 3:20, the t of the wise
2 Cor 10:5, to the obedience
Heb 4:12, the t and intents of
See Gen 6:5; Jer 4:14
THOUGHT (*v.*) Mal 3:16, that t upon his name
1 Cor 13:11, I t as a child
Phil 2:6, t it not robbery
See Gen 20:11; 50:20
THRONE Ps 11:4, the Lord's t is in heaven
94:20, the t of iniquity
122:5, set t of judgment
Prov 20:28, and his t is
Is 66:1, The heaven is my t
Jer 17:12, A glorious high t
Dan 7:9, his t was like the
Matt 19:28, the t of his glory
25:31, the t of his glory
Col 1:16, be t, or dominions
Heb 4:16, the t of grace
Rev 3:21, sit with me in my t

4:2, a **t** was set in heaven
See Rev 6:16; 7:9; 14:3; 19:4
TIDINGS Ps 112:7, He shall not be
    afraid of evil **t**
Jer 20:15, man who brought **t**
Dan 11:44, But **t** out of the
Luke 1:19, thee these glad **t**
    2:10, good **t** of great joy
    8:1, glad **t** of the kingdom
Acts 13:32, unto you glad **t**
Rom 10:15, **t** of good things
See Ex 33:4; 1 Kin 14:6
TIME Gen 47:29, the **t** drew nigh
Job 22:16, down out of **t**
    38:23, the **t** of trouble
Ps 32:6, pray unto thee in a **t**
    37:19, in the evil **t**
    41:1, in **t** of trouble
    56:3, What **t** I am afraid
    69:13, an acceptable **t**
    89:47, how short my **t** is
Eccl 3:1, a **t** to every purpose
    9:11, **t** and chance happeneth
Is 49:8, an acceptable **t** have
    60:22, hasten it in his **t**
Jer 46:21, and the **t** of their
Ezek 16:8, the **t** of love
Dan 7:25, until a **t** and **t** and
Hos 10:12, **t** to seek the Lord
Mal 3:11, fruit before the the **t**
Matt 16:3, signs of the **t**
Luke 19:44, the **t** of thy visitation
Acts 3:19, the **t** of refreshing
    3:21, the **t** of restitution
Rom 13:11, high **t** to awake
1 Cor 7:29, the **t** is short
2 Cor 6:2, is the accepted **t**
Eph 5:16, Redeeming the **t**
Heb 4:16, in **t** of need
1 Pet 1:11, of **t** the Spirit
Rev 1:3, the **t** is at hand
    10:6, should be **t** no longer
See Prov 17:17; Eph 1:10
TOGETHER Ps 34:3, exalt his name
    t
Prov 22:2, the poor meet **t**
Amos 3:3, Can two walk **t**
Matt 18:20, are gathered **t**
    19:6, God hath joined **t**
Rom 8:28, work **t** for good
1 Thess 4:17, caught up **t**
See Matt 19:6; Eph 2:21
TOMORROW Prov 27:1, Boast not
    thyself of **t**
Is 22:13, drink; for **t** we shall die
    56:12, **t** shall be as this day
1 Cor 15:32, eat and drink; for **t** we
See Josh 5:12; 2 Kin 7:1
TONGUE Job 5:21, be hid from the
    scourge of the **t**
    20:12, it under his **t**
Ps 34:13, Keep thy **t** from
Prov 10:20, **t** of the just
    12:18, the **t** of the wise
    12:19, but a lying **t** is
    15:4, A wholesome **t** is a
    18:21, the power of the **t**
James 1:26, bridleth not his **t**
    3:6, the **t** is a fire
1 Pet 3:10, his **t** from evil
1 John 3:18, in word, neither in **t**
See Ps 45:1; Luke 16:24
TOOTH Ex 21:24, Eye for eye, **t** for **t**
Prov 25:19, is like a broken **t**
TRADITION Matt 15:2, transgress
    the **t** of the elders
Mark 7:3, **t** of the elders
Gal 1:14, **t** of my fathers
Col 2:8, the **t** of men
1 Pet 1:18, received by **t**
TRANSFORMED Rom 12:2, **t** by
    the renewing of your mind
2 Cor 11:13, **t** themselves

11:14, Satan himself is **t**
11:15, **t** as . . . ministers
TRANSGRESS Num 14:41, do ye **t**
    the commandment
1 Sam 2:24, Lord's people to **t**
Neh 1:8, If ye **t**
Ps 17:3, mouth shall not **t**
Prov 28:21, that man will **t**
Jer 2:8, the pastors also **t**
    3:13, hast **t** against
Hab 2:5, because he **t** by
See Matt 15:2; 1 John 3:4
TRANSGRESSION Ex 34:7,
    forgiving iniquity and **t**
1 Chr 10:13, died for his **t**
Ezra 10:6, because of the **t**
Job 7:21, not pardon my **t**
    13:23, my **t** and my sin
    14:17, My **t** is sealed
    31:33, If I covered my **t**
Ps 19:13, from the great **t**
    25:7, nor my **t**
    32:1, whose **t** is forgiven
    51:1, blot out my **t**
    65:3, as for our **t**, thou
    107:17, because of their **t**
Prov 17:9, a **t** seeketh love
Is 43:25, blotteth out thy **t**
    44:22, thy **t**
    53:5, wounded for our **t**
    53:8, the **t** of my people
    58:1, people their **t**
Ezek 18:22, All his **t** that
Mic 1:5, For the **t** of Jacob
See Rom 4:15; 5:14
TRANSGRESSOR Prov 13:15, way
    of **t** is hard
Is 48:8, a **t** from the womb
    53:12, numbered with the **t**
Luke 22:37, reckoned among the **t**
See Dan 8:23; Hos 14:9
TRANSLATE Col 1:13, hath **t** us into
Heb 11:5, Enoch was **t**
TRAVAIL Is 53:11, the **t** of his soul
Rom 8:22, and **t** in pain
Gal 4:19, I **t** in birth again
See Job 15:20; Is 13:8
TREASURE Ex 19:5, a peculiar **t**
    unto me
Deut 28:12, thee his good **t**
Ps 135:4, his peculiar **t**
Eccl 2:8, the peculiar **t**
Matt 6:21, where your **t** is
    19:21, shalt have **t** in heaven
See Deut 32:34; 33:19
TREE Ps 1:3, be like a **t** planted
    104:16, The **t** of the Lord
Ezek 31:9, the **t** of Eden
See Mark 8:24; Luke 21:29; Rev 22:2
TREMBLE Deut 2:25, and shall **t**,
    and be in anguish
Judg 5:4, earth **t**, and the
2 Sam 22:8, shook and **t**
Ezra 9:4, every one that **t**
Job 9:6, pillars thereof **t**
    26:11, pillars of heaven **t**
Ps 2:11, rejoice with **t**
    60:2, the earth to **t**
    77:18, the earth **t**
    97:4, earth saw, and **t**
    99:1, let the people **t**
    104:32, the earth, and it **t**
Eccl 12:3, house shall **t**
Is 14:16, the earth to **t**
    64:2, **t** at thy presence
    66:5, **t** at his word
Jer 5:22, **t** at my presence
    33:9, shall fear and **t**
Amos 8:8, not the land **t**
Acts 24:25, Felix **t**, and
James 2:19, believe, and **t**
See Acts 9:6; 16:29
TRESPASS Gen 31:36, what is my **t**?

what is my sin
    50:17, **t** of thy servants
Ezra 9:2, chief in this **t**
Ps 68:21, still in his **t**
Matt 6:14, forgive men their **t**
    18:15, shall **t** against thee
Luke 17:3, If thy brother **t**
2 Cor 5:19, **t** unto them
Eph 2:1, who were dead in **t**
Col 2:13, forgiven you all **t**
See Num 5:6; 1 Kin 8:31
TRIAL Job 9:23, laugh at the **t** of the
    innocent
2 Cor 8:2, great **t** of affliction
See Ezek 21:13; Heb 11:36
TRIBULATION Matt 24:21, shall be
    great **t**
John 16:33, ye shall have **t**
Acts 14:22, much **t** enter into
Rom 5:3, that **t** worketh patience
    12:12, patient in **t**
See 2 Cor 1:4; 7:4; Eph 3:13
TRIED 2 Sam 22:31, the word of the
    Lord is **t**
James 1:12, for when he is **t**
TRIUMPH Ex 15:1, 21, the Lord, for
    he hath **t** gloriously
Ps 25:2, enemies **t** over me
    92:4, I will **t** in the
2 Cor 2:14, to **t** in Christ
Col 2:15, **t** over them in
See 2 Sam 1:20; Job 20:5
TROUBLE (*n.*) Job 5:7, man is born
    unto **t**
    14:1, and full of **t**
Ps 27:5, in the time of **t**
    46:1, present help in **t**
    138:7, in the midst of **t**
I Cor 7:28, have **t** in the flesh
See Prov 15:6; 25:19
TRUE Gen 42:11, we are **t** men, thy
    servants
1 Kin 22:16, that which is **t**
2 Chr 15:3, without the **t** God
Neh 9:13, and **t** laws
Ps 119:160, Thy word is **t**
Prov 14:25, A **t** witness
Jer 10:10, is the **t** God
Matt 22:16, that thou art **t**
Luke 16:11, the **t** riches
John 1:9, the **t** Light
    4:23, the **t** worshippers
    5:31, witness is not **t**
    6:32, you the **t** bread
    10:41, this man were **t**
    15:1, I am the **t** vine
    17:3, the only **t** God
2 Cor 6:8, and yet **t**
Eph 4:24, and **t** holiness
Phil 4:8, things are **t**
Heb 10:22, with a **t** heart
1 John 5:20, him that is **t**
See Rev 3:7; 6:10; 15:3
TRUST Job 13:15, he slay me, yet
    will I **t** in him
    39:11, Wilt thou **t** him
Ps 25:2, I **t** in thee
    31:6, I **t** in the Lord
    37:3, **T** in the Lord
    40:3, shall **t** in the Lord
    55:23, I will **t** in thee
    56:3, I will **t** in thee
    62:8, **T** in him at all
    115:9, **t** thou in the Lord
    118:8, It is better to **t**
    143:8, in thee do I **t**
    144:2, he in whom I **t**
Prov 3:5, **T** in the Lord
    28:26, He that **t** in his
Is 50:10, let him **t** in the
Jer 49:11, thy widows **t** in me
Mic 7:5, **T** ye not in a
Nah 1:7, that **t** in him

Matt 27:43, He **t** in God
Luke 18:9, which **t** in themselves
See Jer 17:5; 2 Cor 1:9
TRUTH Deut 32:4, a God of **t** and
without iniquity
Ps 15:2, the **t** in his heart
51:6, thou desirest **t**
91:4, his **t . . .** be thy
117:2, the **t** of the Lord
119:30, the way of **t**
Prov 23:23, Buy the **t**
Is 59:14, for **t** is fallen
Jer 9:3, valiant for the **t**
Zech 8:16, the **t** to his
Mal 2:6, The law of **t**
John 1:14, of grace and **t**
8:32, know the **t**
14:6, the **t**, and the life
16:13, the Spirit of **t**
17:17, thy word is **t**
18:38 What is **t**
Rom 1:18, the **t** in unrighteousness
1 Cor 5:8, sincerity and **t**
2 Cor 13:8, against the **t**
Eph 4:15, the **t** in love
1 Tim 3:15, ground of the **t**
2 Tim 2:15, the word of **t**
James 5:19, err from the **t**
See 1 Cor 13:6; 2 Tim 3:7
TRY 2 Chr 32:31, God left him, to **t**
him
Job 23:10, he hath **t** me
Ps 26:2, **t** my reins and
1 John 4:1, **t** the spirits
See Prov 17:3; Is 28:16
TURN Job 23:13, in one mind, and
who can **t** him
Ps 7:12, If he **t** not
Prov 1:23, **T** you at my
Jer 31:18, **t** thou me
Lam 5:21, **t** thou us unto
Ezek 14:6, **t** yourselves from
18:30, and **t** yourselves
33:9, to **t** from it
Dan 12:3, **t** many to righteousness
Hos 12:6, **t** thou to thy God
Joel 2:12, **t** ye even to me
Zech 9:12, **T** you to the
Matt 5:39, **t** to him the other
Acts 26:18, to **t** them from
See Prov 21:1; 26:14; Hos 7:8
TWINKLING 1 Cor 15:52, in the **t** of
an eye

U

UNBELIEF Mark 9:24, Lord, I
believe; help thou mine **u**
Rom 3:3, shall their **u**
11:32, shall all in **u**
Heb 3:12, evil heart of **u**
See Matt 13:58; Mark 6:6
UNBLAMEABLE Col 1:22, to
present you holy and **u**
1 Thess 3:13, **u** in holiness
UNCLEAN Acts 10:28, not call any
man common or **u**
Rom 14:14, nothing **u** of itself
2 Cor 6:17, touch not the **u**
UNCTION 1 John 2:20, ye have an **u**
from the Holy One
UNDEFILED Ps 119:1, Blessed are
the **u** in the way
James 1:27, **u** before God
1 Pet 1:4, incorruptible, and **u**
～ Song 5:2; 6:9; Heb 7:26
～R Rom 3:9, Gentiles, that
～re all **u** sin
～keep **u** my body
～rse
～ 24:15, readeth,
～ney might **u**

John 8:43, not **u** my speech
Rom 3:11, There is none that **u**
15:21, not heard shall **u**
1 Cor 13:2, **u** all mysteries
13:11, I **u** as a child
See 1 Cor 14:2; 2 Pet 2:12; 3:16
UNDERSTANDING Ex 31:3, of
God, in wisdom, and in **u**
Deut 4:6, **u** in the sight
1 Kin 3:11, **u** to discern
4:29, wisdom and **u**
1 Chr 12:32, **u** of the times
2 Chr 26:5, who had **u**
Job 12:13, counsel and **u**
12:20, **u** of the aged
17:4, heart from **u**
28:12, the place of **u**
32:8, giveth them **u**
Ps 47:7, praises with **u**
49:3, heart shall be of **u**
119:34, Give me **u**
119:169, give me **u**
147:5, his **u** is infinite
Prov 2:11, **u** shall keep thee
3:5, unto thine own **u**
4:5, Get wisdom, get **u**
4:7, thy getting get **u**
9:6, in the way of **u**
14:29, is of great **u**
16:22, **U** is a wellspring
17:24, him that hath **u**
19:8, he that keepeth **u**
21:30, no wisdom nor **u**
30:2, not the **u** of a man
Eccl 9:11, riches to men of **u**
Is 11:2, of wisdom and **u**
40:14, the way of **u**
Jer 3:15, with knowledge and **u**
Ezek 28:4, with thine **u**
Dan 4:34, mine **u** returned
Matt 15:16, yet without **u**
Mark 7:18, so without **u**
12:33, and with all the **u**
Luke 2:47, at his **u**
24:45, opened he their **u**
1 Cor 1:9, **u** of the prudent
14:15, pray with the **u**
14:20, be not children in **u**
Eph 4:18, the **u** darkened
Phil 4:7, passeth all **u**
See Col 1:9; 2:2; 1 John 5:20
UNFAITHFUL Ps 78:57, and dealt **u**
like their fathers
Prov 25:19, in an **u** man
UNFEIGNED 2 Cor 6:6, by the
Holy Ghost, by love **u**
1 Tim 1:5, and of faith **u**
2 Tim 1:5, the **u** faith
1 Pet 1:22, Spirit unto **u** love
UNFRUITFUL Matt 13:22, the word
and he becometh **u**
Eph 5:11, **u** works of darkness
Titus 3:14, they be not **u**
2 Pet 1:8, **u** in the knowledge
UNGODLINESS Rom 1:18, from
heaven against all **u**
11:26, shall turn away **u**
2 Tim 2:16, unto more **u**
Titus 2:12, denying **u**
UNGODLY 2 Chr 19:2, Shouldest
thou help the **u**
Job 16:11, me to the **u**
Ps 1:1, counsel of the **u**
1:6, **u** shall perish
43:1, against an **u** nation
Prov 16:27, An **u** man diggeth
Rom 5:6, died for the **u**
1 Pet 4:18, **u** and the sinner
2 Pet 3:7, perdition of **u** men
See 1 Tim 1:9; 2 Pet 2:5
UNHOLY Lev 10:10, difference
between holy and **u**
1 Tim 1:9, for **u** and profane

2 Tim 3:2, unthankful, **u**
Heb 10:29, an **u** thing
UNITY Ps 133:1, brethren to dwell
together in **u**
Eph 4:3, **u** of the Spirit
4:13, **u** of the faith
UNJUST Ps 43:1, from the deceitful
and **u** man
Prov 11:7, the hope of **u** men
28:8, **u** gain increaseth
29:27, An **u** man
Zeph 3:5, the **u** knoweth
Matt 5:45, and on the **u**
Luke 18:6, the **u** judge saith
18:11, extortioners, **u**
Acts 24:15, of the just and **u**
1 Cor 6:1, before the **u**
1 Pet 3:18, just for the **u**
Rev 22:11, He that is **u**
See Ps 82:2; Is 26:10
UNKNOWN Acts 17:23, this
inscription, To the **u** God
1 Cor 14:2, in an **u** tongue
UNMOVEABLE 1 Cor 15:58, be ye
stedfast,**u**
UNPROFITABLE Job 15:3, Should
he reason with **u** talk
Matt 25:30, the **u** servant
Luke 17:10, We are **u** servants
See Titus 3:9; Philem 11
UNPUNISHED Prov 11:21, the
wicked shall not be **u**
16:5, he shall not be **u**
Jer 25:29, Ye shall not be **u**
49:12, thou shalt not go **u**
See Jer 30:11; 46:28
UNQUENCHABLE Matt 3:12, burn
up the chaff with **u** fire
Luke 3:17, with fire **u**
UNREPROVEABLE Col 1:22,
unblameable and **u** in his sight
UNRIGHTEOUS Ex 23:1, the
wicked to be an **u** witness
Is 10:1, **u** decrees
55:7, and the **u** man
Rom 3:5, Is God **u**
Heb 6:10, God is not **u**
See Deut 25:16; 1 Cor 6:9
UNRIGHTEOUSNESS Luke 16:9,
friends of the mammon of **u**
Rom 1:18, hold the truth in **u**
2:8, but obey **u**
3:5, if our **u** commend
6:13, as instruments of **u**
9:14, Is there **u** with God
2 Cor 6:14, with **u**
2 Thess 2:12, pleasure in **u**
2 Pet 2:13, the reward of **u**
1 John 1:9, from all **u**
5:17, All **u** is sin
See Lev 19:15; Jer 22:13
UNSEARCHABLE Job 5:9, doeth
great things and **u**
Ps 145:3, greatness is **u**
Rom 11:33, how **u** are his
Eph 3:8, **u** riches of Christ
UNSPEAKABLE 2 Cor 9:15,
Thanks be unto God for his **u** gift
12:4, and heard **u** words
1 Pet 1:8, with joy **u**
UNSPOTTED James 1:27, to keep
himself **u** from the world
UNTHANKFUL Luke 6:35, kind
unto the **u** and to the evil
2 Tim 3:2, **u**, unholy
UNWISE Deut 32:6, O foolish people
and **u**
Hos 13:13, he is an **u** son
Rom 1:14, wise, and to the **u**
Eph 5:17, be ye not **u**
UNWORTHY Acts 13:46, **u** of
everlasting life
1 Cor 6:2, **u** to judge

11:27, of the Lord, **u**
UPHOLD Ps 51:12, and **u** me with thy free spirit
54:4, that **u** my soul
119:116, U me according
145:14, **u** all that fall
Is 41:10, I will **u** thee
42:1, my servant, whom I **u**
63:5, was none to **u**
Heb 1:3, **u** all things
See Ps 37:17; 41:12; 63:8
UPRIGHT Job 12:4, just **u** man is laughed to scorn
17:8, U men shall be
Ps 19:13, then shall I be **u**
25:8, Good and **u** is the Lord
37:14, of **u** conversation
49:14, **u** shall have
92:15, that the Lord is **u**
111:1, assembly of the **u**
Prov 2:21, **u** shall dwell
14:11, tabernacle of the **u**
15:8, the prayer of the **u**
28:10, the **u** shall have
Eccl 7:29, had made man **u**
Song 1:4, the **u** love thee
See Mic 7:2; Hab 2:4
UPRIGHTNESS 1 Kin 3:6, and in **u** of heart with thee
1 Chr 29:17, pleasure in **u**
Job 4:6, the **u** of thy ways
33:23, unto man his **u**
Ps 25:21, and **u** preserve me
143:10, the land of **u**
Prov 2:13, the paths of **u**
See Ps 111:8; Prov 14:2
USE Matt 5:44, despitefully **u** you
6:7, **u** not vain repetitions
Gal 5:13, **u** not liberty
See Ps 119:132; 1 Cor 9:12
UTTERANCE Acts 2:4, tongues, as the Spirit gave them **u**
See 1 Cor 1:5; 2 Cor 8:7

V

VAIN Ex 20:7, thy God in **v**
Ps 2:1, imagine a **v** thing
39:6, walketh in a **v** show
60:11, for **v** is the
89:47, all men in **v**
127:1, they labour in **v**
Prov 12:11, followeth **v** persons
31:30, beauty is **v**
Eccl 6:12, his **v** life which he
Is 45:19, Seek ye me in **v**
Mal 3:14, It is **v** to serve
Matt 6:7, use not **v** repetitions
15:9, **v** they do worship
Rom 13:4, the sword in **v**
1 Cor 15:2, have believed in **v**
2 Cor 6:1, grace of God in **v**
Gal 2:2, or had run, in **v**
Titus 1:10, **v** talkers and deceivers
James 1:26, man's religion is **v**
1 Pet 1:18, **v** conversation
See Prov 1:17; Rom 1:21
VALUE Job 13:4, ye are all physicians of no **v**
Matt 10:31, of more **v**
See Lev 27:16; Job 28:16
VANISH Is 51:6, shall **v** away
1 Cor 13:8, it shall **v**
Heb 8:13, ready to **v** away
VANITY Job 7:3, I made to possess months of **v**
15:31, trust in **v**
35:13, not hear **v**
Ps 12:2, They speak **v** every
39:5, altogether **v**
62:9, degree are **v**
144:4, is like to **v**
Prov 13:11, gotten by **v**

30:8, far from me **v**
Eccl 6:11, that increase **v**
11:10, youth are **v**
Is 30:28, the sieve of **v**
Jer 18:15, incense to **v**
Hab 2:13, for very **v**
Rom 8:20, subject to **v**
Eph 4:17, in the **v** of their
2 Pet 2:18, swelling words of **v**
See Eccl 1:2; Jer 10:8
VARIABLENESS James 1:17, with whom is no **v**
VEIL Matt 27:51, **v** of the temple was rent in twain
Heb 6:19, within the **v**
VENGEANCE Deut 32:35, To me belongeth **v**
Prov 6:34, the day of **v**
Is 34:8, the Lord's **v**
59:17, garments of **v** for
61:2, the day of **v**
Jer 51:6, the Lord's **v**
Acts 28:4, yet **v** suffereth
Jude 7, suffering the **v**
See Mic 5:15; Nah 1:2; Rom 2:19
VESSEL Acts 9:15, he is a chosen **v**
1 Thess 4:4, possess his **v**
2 Tim 2:21, shall be a **v**
1 Pet 3:7, the weaker **v**
See Is 52:11; 65:4
VICTORY 2 Sam 19:2, the **v** that day
1 Chr 29:11, and the **v**
Ps 98:1, gotten him the **v**
Matt 12:20, judgment unto **v**
1 John 5:4, the **v** that
See Is 25:8; 1 Cor 15:54
VILE 1 Sam 3:13, his sons made themselves **v**
Job 18:3, **v** in your sight
40:4, I am **v**
Ps 15:4, **v** person is contemned
Is 32:5, The **v** person
Jer 15:19, from the **v**
Lam 1:11, I am become **v**
Dan 11:21, stand up a **v** person
Nah 3:6, and make thee **v**
Rom 1:26, unto **v** affections
Phil 3:21, change our **v** body
James 2:2, man in **v** raiment
See 2 Sam 1:21; Job 30:8
VIOLENCE Gen 6:11, the earth was filled with **v**
Ps 11:5, him that loveth **v**
55:9, I have seen **v**
58:2, **v** of your hands
72:14, from deceit and **v**
73:6, **v** covereth them
Prov 4:17, drink the wine of **v**
10:6, 11, but **v** covereth
Is 53:9, he had done no **v**
60:18, V shall no more
Ezek 8:17, the land with **v**
28:16, of thee with **v**
Amos 3:10, who store up **v**
Hab 1:3, for spoiling and **v**
Mal 2:16, one covereth **v**
Matt 11:12, heaven suffereth **v**
Luke 3:14, Do **v** to no man
See Mic 2:2; 6:12; Zeph 1:9
VIOLENT Prov 16:29, A **v** man enticeth
See Eccl 5:8; Matt 11:12
VIRGIN Is 7:14, a **v** shall conceive
23:12, O thou oppressed **v**, daughter of
47:1, O **v** daughter
62:5, man marrieth a **v**
Jer 14:17, **v** daughter
Matt 1:23, a **v** shall be with child
VIRTUE Mark 5:30, that **v** had gone out of him
Luke 6:19, **v** out of him
8:46, perceive that **v**

Phil 4:8, there be any **v**
2 Pet 1:5, add to your faith **v**
VIRTUOUS Ruth 3:11, know that thou art a **v** woman
Prov 12:4, **v** woman is a crown
31:10, can find a **v** woman
31:29, daughters have done **v**
VISAGE Is 52:14, his **v** was so marred
Lam 4:8, Their **v** is blacker
Dan 3:19, form of his **v**
VISION Job 20:8, chased away as a **v** of the night
Prov 29:18, there is no **v**
Is 22:1, of the valley of **v**
28:7, they err in **v**
Lam 2:9, no **v** from the Lord
Hos 12:10, I have multiplied **v**
Joel 2:28, men shall see **v**
Zech 13:4, one of his **v**
Matt 17:9, the **v** to no man
Luke 24:23, seen a **v** of angels
Acts 26:19, the heavenly **v**
See Job 4:13; Ezek 1:1; 8:3
VISIT Gen 50:24, God will surely **v** you
Ex 20:5, **v** the iniquity
Jer 5:9, Shall I not **v**
Matt 25:36, sick, and ye **v** me
Acts 15:14, did **v** the Gentiles
James 1:27, To **v** the fatherless
See Job 31:14; Luke 1:68
VISITATION Job 10:12, thy **v** hath preserved my spirit
Is 10:3, in the day of **v**
Jer 8:12, time of their **v**
Luke 19:44, time of thy **v**
See Num 16:29; Jer 11:23
VOCATION Eph 4:1, walk worthy of the **v**
VOICE Ex 23:21, and obey his **v**
Deut 4:33, **v** of God speaking
1 Kin 19:12, a still small **v**
Is 40:3, The **v** of him
Matt 3:3, **v** of one crying
John 5:25, **v** of the Son of God
10:4, for they know his **v**
12:30, This **v** came not
18:37, truth heareth my **v**
1 Thess 4:16, **v** of the archangel
Rev 3:20, if any man hear my **v**
See Gen 3:17; Ps 58:5
VOID Gen 1:2, earth was without form, and **v**
Deut 32:28, **v** of counsel
Ps 89:39, made **v** . . . covenant
119:126, made **v** thy law
Prov 11:12, is **v** of wisdom
Is 55:11, return unto me **v**
Jer 4:23, without form, and **v**
19:7, make **v** the counsel
Nah 2:10, She is empty, and **v**
Acts 24:16, **v** of offence
See Num 30:12; Rom 3:31; 4:14

W

WAGES Luke 3:14, content with your **w**
John 4:36, he . . . receiveth **w**
Rom 6:23, **w** of sin is death
2 Pet 2:15, loved the **w**
See Ezek 29:18; Mal 3:5
WAIT Gen 49:18, I have **w** for thy salvation, O Lord
2 Kin 6:33, I **w** for the Lord
Job 14:14, time will I **w**
30:26, when I **w** for light
Ps 27:14, W on the Lord
33:20, Our soul **w**
37:7, Lord, and **w** patiently
52:9, **w** on thy name
62:1, my soul **w** upon God

65:1, Praise w for thee
69:6, them that w on thee
130:6, soul w for the Lord
Prov 20:22, w on the Lord
Is 40:31, they that w
42:4, shall w for his law
59:9, w for light
Lam 3:26, quietly w for the
Dan 12:12, he that w
Zech 11:11, w upon me
Mark 15:43, w for the kingdom
Luke 12:36, w for their lord
Acts 1:4, w for the promise
Rom 8:23, w for the adoption
8:25, we with patience w
Gal 5:5, w for the hope
1 Thess 1:10, w for his Son
See Num 3:10; Neh 12:44
WALK Gen 17:1, w before me, and be
thou perfect
24:40, before whom I w
48:15, Isaac did w
Ex 16:4, w in my law
Lev 26:12, I will w among you
Deut 23:14, w in the midst
Judg 5:10, and w by the way
2 Sam 2:29, w all that night
Ps 23:4, I w through the valley
26:11, w in mine integrity
56:13, I may w before God
84:11, that w uprightly
104:3, who w upon the wings
116:9, w before the Lord
138:7, I w in the midst
Prov 10:9, he that w uprightly
13:20, w with wise men
28:18, Whoso w uprightly
Eccl 2:14, fool w in darkness
Is 2:5, let us w in the light
9:2, that w in darkness
20:3, Isaiah hath w naked
30:21, the way, w ye in it
35:9, redeemed shall w there
40:31, w, and not faint
50:10, that w in darkness
50:11, w in the light
Jer 6:16, way, and w therein
10:23, w to direct his steps
Dan 4:37, that w in pride
Hos 14:9, just shall w in them
Mic 6:8, to w humbly
Zech 1:11, have w to and fro
Mal 3:14, w mournfully
Matt 14:29, he w on the water
Luke 5:23, Rise up and w
13:33, I must w today
John 5:8, thy bed, and w
8:12, not w in darkness
11:9, any man w in the day
Acts 3:6, rise up and w
Rom 4:12, also w in the steps
6:4, w in newness of life
8:1, 4, w not after the flesh
2 Cor 5:7, For we w by faith
Gal 6:16, w according to this
Eph 2:2, in time past ye w
2:10, we should w in them
4:1, w worthy of the vocation
4:17, as other Gentiles w
5:15, w circumspectly
Phil 3:17, mark them which w
3:18, For many w
Col 1:10, might w worthy
3:7, which ye also w
Thess 2:12, w worthy of God
w and to please God
honestly toward them
hat w disorderly
sciviousness
ing
e light
5:2

WANT (*v.*) Ps 23:1, my shepherd; I
shall not w
34:10, Lord shall not w
Prov 9:4, that w understanding
13:25, the wicked shall w
Eccl 6:2, so that he w nothing
Is 34:16, none shall w
Jer 44:18, have w all things
See Eccl 1:15; Dan 5:27
WAR 1 Chr 5:22, the w was of God
Ps 27:3, though w should rise
46:9, maketh w to cease
55:21, w was in his heart
68:30, that delight in w
Prov 20:18, good advice make w
Eccl 3:8, a time of w
8:8, discharge in that w
Is 2:4, they learn w
Jer 42:14, shall see no w
Mic 2:8, men averse from w
Matt 24:6, of w and rumours of w
Luke 14:31, w against another
21:9, w and commotions
James 4:1, w and fightings
Rev 12:7, was w in heaven
See Eccl 9:18; Dan 7:21
WAR (*v.*) 2 Sam 22:35, He teacheth
my hands to w
2 Chr 6:34, people go out to w
Is 41:12, they that w
2 Cor 10:3, w after the flesh
1 Tim 1:18, w a good warfare
2 Tim 2:4, No man that w
James 4:1, w in your members
4:2, ye fight and w
1 Pet 2:11, w against the soul
See 1 Kin 14:19; Rom 7:23
WASH 2 Kin 5:10, Go and w in
Jordan seven times
5:12, may I not w in them
Job 9:30, If I w myself
14:19, w away the things
29:6, When I w my steps
Ps 26:6, I will w mine hands
51:2, W me thoroughly
73:13, and w my hands
Prov 30:12, yet is not w
Song 5:12, w with milk
Is 1:16, W you, make you clean
Jer 2:22, though thou w thee
4:14, w thine heart
Ezek 16:4, thou w in water
Matt 6:17, and w thy face
27:24, w his hands
Mark 7:3, except they w
Luke 7:38, began to w his feet
John 9:7, w, and came seeing
Acts 16:33, w their stripes
22:16, w away thy sins
1 Cor 6:11, but ye are w
Heb 10:22, w with pure water
2 Pet 2:22, sow that was w
Rev 1:5, w us from our sins
7:14, and have w their robes
See Neh 4:23; Titus 3:5
WATCH (*n.*) Ps 90:4, as a w in the
night
119:148, prevent the night w
Jer 51:12, make the w strong
Hab 2:1, stand upon my w
See Matt 14:25; Luke 2:8
WATCH (*v.*) Gen 31:49, the Lord w
between me and thee
Job 14:16, not w over my sin
Ps 37:32, The wicked w
130:6, w for the morning
Is 29:20, w for iniquity
Jer 20:10, All my familiars w
Hab 2:1, will w to see
Matt 24:42, W therefore
26:41, W and pray
Mark 13:35, W ye therefore
Acts 20:31, Therefore w

1 Thess 5:6, w and be sober
Heb 13:17, w for your souls
1 Pet 4:7, w unto prayer
See 1 Cor 16:13; 2 Tim 4:5; Rev 3:2
WATCHTOWER Is 21:5, watch in
the w
21:8, continually upon the w
WATER Gen 49:4, Unstable as w
Deut 8:7, land of brooks and w
Josh 7:5, became as w
2 Sam 14:14, and are as w
1 Kin 13:22, drink no w
22:27, with w of affliction
Ps 22:14, poured out like w
23:2, beside the still w
148:4, w that be above
Prov 5:15, Drink w out of
9:17, Stolen w are sweet
20:5, is like deep w
25:25, w to a thirsty soul
Eccl 11:1, bread upon the w
Song 4:15, a well of living w
8:7, w cannot quench love
Is 35:6, shall w break out
41:17, poor and needy seek w
43:2, passeth through the w
43:16, path in the mighty w
43:20, w in the wilderness
44:3, pour w upon him
55:1, come ye to the w
Jer 2:13, fountain of living w
Ezek 36:25, I sprinkle clean w
Amos 8:11, a thirst for w
Matt 3:11, baptize you with w
10:42, a cup of cold w
27:24, he took w, and washed
Mark 9:41, a cup of w to drink
Luke 8:23, filled with w
8:24, raging of the w
16:24, his finger in w
John 1:26, I baptize with w
3:5, man be born of w
5:3, the moving of the w
7:38, rivers of living w
19:34, blood and w
Acts 1:5, baptized with w
11:16, indeed baptized with w
2 Cor 11:26, in perils of w
Eph 5:26, the washing of w
1 Pet 3:20, were saved by w
2 Pet 2:17, wells without w
1 John 5:6, he that came by w
Rev 22:17, take the w of life
See Ps 29:3; Jer 51:13; Ezek 32:2
WAY Gen 6:12, all flesh had
corrupted his w
24:40, and prosper thy w
Num 22:32, thy w is perverse
Deut 8:6, to walk in his w
Josh 23:14, w of all the earth
1 Sam 12:23, the right w
2 Sam 22:31, his w is perfect
1 Kin 2:2, I go the w
2:3, God, to walk in his w
2 Chr 6:27, them the good w
Ezra 8:21, a right w for us
Job 3:23, man whose w is hid
23:10, he knoweth the w
Ps 1:6, w of the righteous
2:12, perish from the w
27:11, Teach me thy w, O Lord
36:4, w that is not good
37:5, Commit thy w
49:13, w is their folly
67:2, thy w may be known
78:50, He made a w
95:10, not known my w
101:2, in a perfect w
119:3, walk in his w
119:5, my w were directed
119:30, the w of truth
128:1, walketh in his w
139:24, any wicked w in me

Prov 2:8, w of his saints
3:6, w acknowledge him
5:21, the w of man
6:6, consider her w
6:23, the w of life
12:15, The w of a fool
15:19, w of the slothful man
16:7, When a man's w please the
22:6, a child in the w
23:19, heart in the w
26:13, a lion in the w
Eccl 11:5, w of the spirit
12:5, shall be in the w
Is 2:3, teach us of his w
35:8, a highway . . . and a w
40:27, My w is hid
42:24, walk in his w
45:13, direct all his w
55:8, are your w my w
58:2, delight to know my w
Jer 17:10, according to his w
32:39, one heart, and one w
50:5, ask the w to Zion
Ezek 3:18, from his wicked w
18:29, The w of the Lord
Joel 2:7, every one on his w
Nah 1:3, Lord hath his w
Hag 1:5, 7, Consider your w
Mal 3:1, shall prepare the w
Matt 7:13, and broad is the w
10:5, Go not into the w
22:16, w of God in truth
Mark 8:3, faint by the w
Luke 19:36, clothes in the w
20:21, teachest the w of God
John 10:1, up some other w
14:4, the w ye know
14:6, I am the w, the truth
Acts 9:2, any of this w
9:27, the Lord in the w
16:17, the w of salvation
18:26, the w of God
19:23, stir about that w
24:14, after the w
1 Cor 10:13, a w to escape
12:31, a more excellent w
Heb 9:8, the w into the holiest
10:20, By a new and living w
James 1:8, unstable in all his w
5:20, the error of his w
2 Pet 2:2, w of truth
2:21, w of righteousness
See Hos 2:6; Luke 10:31
WEAK Judg 16:7, then shall I be w
Job 4:3, strengthened the w
Ps 6:2, O Lord; for I am w
Is 35:3, the w hands
Matt 26:41, the flesh is w
Acts 20:35, support the w
Rom 4:19, not w in faith
8:3, w through the flesh
1 Cor 1:27, the w things
11:30, many are w and sickly
2 Cor 10:10, presence is w
11:29, Who is w
12:10, for when I am w
Gal 4:9, to the w and beggarly
1 Pet 3:7, unto the w vessel
See Job 12:21; 1 Thess 5:14
WEAKNESS 1 Cor 1:25, w of God is
stronger than men
2:3, I was with you in w
15:43, it is sown in w
See 2 Cor 12:9; 13:4; Heb 7:18
WEALTH 1 Sam 2:32, the w which
God
2 Chr 1:11, asked riches, w
Job 21:13, their days in w
Ps 44:12, not increase thy w
49:6, trust in their w
112:3, W in riches
Prov 5:10, filled with thy w
13:11, W gotten by vanity

19:4, W maketh many friends
Acts 19:25, we have our w
1 Cor 10:24, one another's w
See Ruth 2:1; Ezra 9:12
WEAPON Is 54:17, No w that is
formed
2 Cor 10:4, w of our warfare
See Job 20:24; Ezek 39:9
WEARY Job 3:17, the w be at rest
10:1, soul is w of my life
Prov 3:11, neither be w
25:17, lest he be w of thee
Is 5:27, None shall be w
7:13, but will ye w my God
28:12, cause the w to rest
32:2, rock in a w land
40:31, run, and not be w
50:4, him that is w
Jer 15:6, I am w with repenting
31:25, satiated the w soul
2 Thess 3:13, not w in well doing
See Judg 4:21; Hab 2:13
WEEPING Ps 30:5, w may endure
Joel 2:12, fasting, and with w
Matt 8:12, be w and gnashing
John 20:11, at the sepulchre w
See Num 25:6; Mal 2:13
WEIGH Dan 5:27, w in the balances
See Prov 16:2; Zech 11:12
WEIGHT 2 Cor 4:17, eternal w of
glory
Heb 12:1, lay aside every w
See Deut 25:15; Mic 6:11
WEIGHTY Prov 27:3, A stone is
heavy and the sand w
Matt 23:23, the w matters
2 Cor 10:10, his letters, . . . are w
WELL Prov 10:11, is a w of life
Song 4:15, w of living waters
Is 12:3, the w of salvation
John 4:14, a w of water
2 Pet 2:17, w without water
See Gen 21:19; 2 Sam 17:18
WEPT Luke 19:41, beheld the city,
and w
John 11:35, Jesus w
See 2 Sam 12:22; Ps 69:10
WHATSOEVER Ps 1:3, and w he
doeth shall prosper
Eccl 3:14, w God doeth
Matt 5:37, w is more
7:12, w ye would that men
20:4, and w is right
Phil 4:8, w things are true
See John 15:16; Rom 14:23
WHILE 2 Chr 15:2, Lord is with
you, w ye be with him
Is 55:6, Seek ye the Lord w
Jer 15:9, w it was yet day
John 9:4, w it is day
See 2 Sam 7:19; Acts 20:11
WHITE Num 12:10, leprous, w as
snow
Eccl 9:8, garments be always w
Song 5:10, My beloved is w
Is 1:18, be as w as snow
Matt 5:36, not make one hair w
John 4:35, w already to harvest
Rev 2:17, give him a w stone
3:4, walk with me in w
See Dan 11:35; 12:10; Matt 17:2
WHITER Ps 51:7, I shall be w than
snow
WHOLE Eccl 12:13, the w duty of
man
Jer 19:11, be made w again
Ezek 15:5, when it was w
Matt 5:29, thy w body
9:12, that be w
16:26, gain the w world
Mark 2:17, They that are w
Rom 8:22, w creation groaneth
1 Cor 12:17, If the w body

Eph 6:11, Put on the w armour
1 Thess 5:23, your w spirit
James 2:10, keep the w law
1 John 2:2, sins of the w world
5:19, the w world lieth
See Matt 15:31; John 5:6; 7:23
WICKED Gen 18:23, destroy the
righteous with the w
Deut 15:9, in thy w heart
1 Sam 2:9, w shall be silent
Job 3:17, the w cease from
8:22, of the w shall come
9:29, If I be w
21:7, Wherefore do the w
21:30, the w is reserved
Ps 7:11, angry with the w
9:17, w shall be turned
10:4, w through the pride
11:6, Upon the w he shall rain
12:8, w walk on every side
26:5, not sit with the w
34:21, Evil shall slay the w
37:21, The w borroweth
37:32, The w watcheth
58:3, w are estranged
68:2, w perish at the
94:3, shall the w triumph
139:24, any w way in me
145:20, the w will he destroy
Prov 11:5, w shall fall by his
14:32, The w is driven away
28:1, w flee when no man
Eccl 7:17, Be not over much w
8:10, I saw the w buried
Is 13:11, evil, and the w
53:9, his grave with the w
55:7, Let the w forsake
57:20, the w are like
Jer 17:9, and desperately w
Ezek 3:18, w man shall die
11:2, and give w counsel
18:23, that the w should die
33:15, w restore the pledge
Dan 12:10, w shall do wickedly
Mic 6:11, with the w balances
Nah 1:3, at all acquit the w
Matt 12:45, spirits more w
13:49, sever the w from
18:32, O thou w servant
25:26, Thou w and slothful
Luke 19:22, thou w servant
Acts 2:23, w hands have
1 Cor 5:13, that w person
Eph 6:16, fiery darts of the w
Col 1:21, by w works
2 Thess 2:8, then shall that W be
See Eccl 9:2; 2 Pet 2:7; 3:17
WICKEDNESS 1 Sam 24:13, W
proceedeth from
Job 4:8, iniquity, and sow w
35:8, Thy w may hurt a man
Ps 7:9, Oh let the w of the
55:11, W is in the midst
58:2, Yea, in heart ye work w
84:10, in the tents of w
Prov 4:17, eat the bread of w
8:7, w is an abomination
11:5, fall by his own w
13:6, but w overthroweth
26:26, his w shall be shewed
Eccl 7:25, know the w of folly
Is 9:18, w burneth as the fire
47:10, hast trusted in thy w
Jer 2:19, own w shall correct
8:6, repented him of his w
44:9, w of your fathers
Ezek 3:19, turn not from his w
31:11, him out for his w
Hos 9:15, w of their doings
Mic 6:10, treasures of w
Zech 5:8, he said, This is w
Mal 1:4, The border of w
3:15, they that work w

Mark 7:22, covetousness, w
Luke 11:39, ravening and w
Rom 1:29, w, covetousness
1 Cor 5:8, of malice and w
Eph 6:12, against spiritual w
1 John 5:19, world lieth in w
See Gen 6:5; Ps 94:23

WIFE Prov 5:18, and rejoice with
  the w of thy youth
  18:22, Whoso findeth a w
  19:14, and a prudent w
Eccl 9:9, with the w whom thou
Luke 14:20, I have married a w
  17:32, Remember Lot's w
1 Cor 7:14, sanctified by the w
Eph 5:23, the head of the w
Rev 21:9, the Lamb's w
See 1 Tim 3:2; 5:9; Titus 1:6

WILES Num 25:18, For they vex you
  with their w
Eph 6:11, the w of the devil

WILFULLY Heb 10:26, For if we sin
  w after that

WILL Matt 8:3, I w; be thou clean
  18:14, so it is not the w
  26:39, not as I w, but as
Mark 3:35, shall do the w of God
John 1:13, w of the flesh
  4:34, w of him that sent me
Acts 21:14, The w of the Lord
Rom 7:18, for to w is present
Phil 2:13, both to w and to do
1 Tim 2:8, I w therefore
Rev 22:17, whosoever w
See Rom 9:15; Eph 1:11; Heb 2:4

WILLING Ex 35:5, whosoever is of
  a w heart
1 Chr 28:9, and with a w mind
  29:5, w to consecrate his
Ps 110:3, people shall be w
Matt 26:41, spirit indeed is w
2 Cor 5:8, w rather to be
  8:12, first a w mind
1 Tim 6:18, w to communicate
2 Pet 3:9, not w that any
See Luke 22:42; Philem 14

WIN 2 Chr 32:1, thought to w them
  for himself
Prov 11:30, he that w souls
Phil 3:8, that I may w Christ

WIND Job 6:26, is desperate, which
  are as w
  7:7, my life is w
Prov 11:29, shall inherit the w
Ezek 37:9, Prophesy unto the w
Hos 8:7, they have sown the w
Amos 4:13, createth the w
Matt 11:7, shaken with the w
John 3:8, The w bloweth where
Eph 4:14, every w of doctrine
See James 1:6; Jude 12

WINDOWS Gen 7:11, and the w of
  heaven were opened
Eccl 12:3, look out of the w
Jer 9:21, up into our w
Mal 3:10, the w of heaven

WINGS Ps 17:8, hide me under the
  shadow of thy w
  18:10, he did fly upon the w
  36:7, shadow of thy w
  55:6, had w like a dove
  57:1, in the shadow of thy w
  61:4, in the covert of thy w
  68:13, w of a dove
  91:4, and under his w
  ⸺9, the w of the morning
  ⸺5, make themselves w
  ⸺nt up with w
  ⸺r in his w
  ⸺23:37
  ⸺d w at
  ⸺hey die, even

12:2, w shall die with you
Prov 4:7, W is the principal
16:16, better is it to get w
19:8, getteth w loveth
23:4, cease from thine own w
Eccl 1:18, For in much w
Is 10:13, and by my w
29:14, w of their wise men
Jer 8:9, what w is in them
Mic 6:9, the man of w
Matt 11:19, But w is justified
1 Cor 1:17, with w of words
  1:24, and the w of God
  1:30, God is made unto us w
  2:6, we speak w among them
  3:19, w of this world
2 Cor 1:12, not with fleshly w
Col 1:9, his will in all w
  4:5, Walk in w toward them
James 1:5, any of you lack w
  3:17, w that is from above
Rev 5:12, and w, and strength
  13:18, Here is w
See Eccl 1:16; Rom 11:33

WISE Gen 3:6, to be desired to make
  one w
Ex 23:8, gift blindeth the w
Deut 4:6, w and understanding
  32:29, O that they were w
1 Kin 3:12, a w . . . heart
Job 9:4, He is w in heart
  11:12, vain man would be w
  22:2, he that is w may be
  32:9, men are not always w
Ps 2:10, Be w now therefore
  19:7, making w the simple
  36:3, hath left off to be w
  94:8, when will ye be w
  107:43, Whoso is w
Prov 1:5, w man will hear
  3:7, w in thine own eyes
  6:6, consider . . . and be w
  9:12, If thou be w
  11:30, winneth souls is w
  16:21, w in heart shall be
  20:26, A w king scattereth
  23:19, my son, and be w
  27:11, be w, and make
Eccl 7:23, I said, I will be w
  9:1, righteous, and the w
  12:11, The words of the w
Is 19:11, the w counsellors
Dan 12:3, And they that be w
Matt 10:16, be ye therefore w
  11:25, things from the w
Rom 1:14, both to the w
  12:16, Be not w in your own
1 Cor 1:20, Where is the w
  4:10, ye are w in Christ
2 Tim 3:15, to make thee w
See Is 5:21; Matt 25:2

WISER 1 Kin 4:31, For he was w
  than all men
Luke 16:8, w than the children
1 Cor 1:25, God is w than men

WITCH Ex 22:18, Thou shalt not
  suffer a w to live
Deut 18:10, enchanter, or a w

WITHER Ps 1:3, his leaf also shall
  not w
Is 40:7, 8, The grass w
1 Pet 1:24, the grass w
Jude 12, trees whose fruit w
See Joel 1:12; James 1:11

WITHHOLD Ps 40:11, W not thou
  thy tender mercies
Prov 3:27, W not good from them
  23:13, W not correction
Eccl 11:6, w not thine hand
See Job 22:7; Joel 1:13

WITHIN Ps 40:8, God: yea, thy law
  is w my heart
Matt 23:26, which is w the cup

51:10, right spirit w me
See Ps 45:13; Matt 3:9

WITHOUT Prov 1:20, Wisdom
  crieth w
Is 52:3, be redeemed w money
  55:1, w money and w price
Eph 2:12, w God in the world
Col 4:5, toward them that are w
1 Tim 3:7, them which are w
Heb 13:12, suffered w the gate
Rev 22:15, For w are dogs
See Prov 22:13; Matt 10:29

WITHSTAND Acts 11:17, that I
  could w God
Eph 6:13, w in the evil day
See Num 22:32; Esth 9:2

WITNESS (*n.*) Gen 31:50, God is w
  betwixt me and thee
Josh 24:27, be a w unto us
Job 16:19, my w is in heaven
Ps 89:37, as a faithful w
Prov 14:5, w will not lie
Is 55:4, given him for a w
Jer 42:5, true and faithful w
Matt 24:14, the world for a w
John 1:7, same came for a w
  3:11, ye receive not our w
  5:36, have greater w than
Acts 14:17, himself without w
Rom 2:15, also bearing w
1 John 5:9, the w of God is
  5:10, the w in himself
See Is 43:10; Luke 24:48

WITNESS (*v.*) Deut 4:26, I call
  heaven and earth to w
Is 3:9, countenance doth w
Acts 20:33, the Holy Ghost w in
Rom 3:21, being w by the law
1 Tim 6:13, w a good confession
See 1 Sam 12:3; Matt 26:62

WIZARD Lev 20:27, or that is a w

WOMAN Judg 9:54, men say not
  of me, A w slew him
Ps 48:6, as of a w in travail
Prov 6:24, from the evil w
  9:13, A foolish w is
  12:4, virtuous w is a crown
  14:1, Every wise w buildeth
  21:9, with a brawling w
  31:10, find a virtuous w
Eccl 7:28, a w among all those
Is 13:8, be in pain as a w
  21:3, as the pangs of a w
  26:17, as a w with child
  54:6, as a w forsaken
Jer 6:24, as of a w in travail
  31:8, lame, the w with child
  31:22, A w shall compass
  48:41, be as the heart of a w
Matt 5:28, on a w to lust
  15:28, w, great is thy faith
  22:27, last of all the w
  26:10, Why trouble ye the w
  26:13, that this w hath done
John 2:4, W, what have I to do
  8:3, brought unto him a w
  19:26, W, behold thy son
Acts 9:36, this w was full of good
Rom 1:27, natural use of the w
1 Cor 7:1, not to touch a w
  11:7, but the w is the glory
Gal 4:4, his Son, made of a w
1 Tim 2:12, I suffer not a w
  2:14, w being deceived
See Is 49:15; Luke 7:39; 13:16

WOMEN Judg 5:24, Blessed above w
1 Sam 18:7, w answered one
2 Sam 1:26, the loving w
Ps 45:9, thy honourable w
Prov 31:3, thy strength unto w
Lam 4:10, pitiful w have
Matt 11:11, that are born of w
  24:41, w shall be grinding

Luke 1:28, art thou among w
1 Cor 14:34, w keep silence
1 Tim 2:9, w adorn themselves
5:14, the younger w marry
2 Tim 3:6, w laden with sins
Titus 2:3, The aged w likewise
Heb 11:35, W received their
See Acts 16:13; 1 Pet 3:5
WONDERFUL 2 Sam 1:26, thy love
to me was w
Job 42:3, things too w for me
Ps 139:6, knowledge is too w
Is 9:6, name shall be called W
See Deut 28:59; Jer 5:30
WONDERFULLY Ps 139:14, for I
am fearfully and w made
WORD Deut 8:3, by every w that
proceedeth out
30:14, the w is very nigh
Ps 19:14, the w of my mouth
68:11, The Lord gave the w
119:43, the w of truth
Prov 15:23, and a w spoken
25:11, a w fitly spoken
Matt 12:36, every idle w that men
18:16, w may be established
24:35, w shall not pass away
John 6:63, the w that I speak
6:68, w of eternal life
12:48, receiveth not my w
14:24, the w which ye hear
17:8, w which thou gavest me
Acts 13:15, w of exhortation
20:35, remember the w
26:25, the w of truth
Rom 10:8, w is nigh thee
1 Cor 1:17, with wisdom of w
4:20, the kingdom . . . not in w
14:9, w easy to be understood
2 Cor 1:18, our w toward you
5:19, w of reconciliation
6:7, By the w of truth
Gal 5:14, fulfilled in one w
6:6, taught in the w
Eph 1:13, heard the w of truth
5:6, deceive you with vain w
Phil 2:16, the w of life
Col 1:5, the w of the truth
3:16, Let the w of Christ
1 Thess 1:5, unto you in w
4:18, with these w
1 Tim 4:6, in the w of faith
5:17, they who labour in the w
2 Tim 2:14, strive not about w
2:15, dividing the w
4:2, Preach the w
Titus 1:3, manifested his w
1:9, the faithful w
Heb 1:3, all things by the w
2:2, the w spoken by angels
4:2, w preached did not
4:12, the w of God is quick
5:13, w of righteousness
6:5, the good w of God
7:28, but the w of the oath
11:3, were framed by the w
13:7, spoken unto you the w
James 1:18, the w of truth
1:22, doers of the w
3:2, man offend not in w
1 Pet 1:23, by the w of God
2:2, milk of the w
2:8, stumble at the w
3:1, if any obey not the w
2 Pet 1:19, sure w of prophecy
3:2, w which were spoken
3:7, by the same w are kept
1 John 1:1, of the W of life
2:5, But whoso keepeth his w
3:18, let us not love in w
Rev 3:8, and hast kept my w
3:10, the w of my patience
6:9, slain for the w of God

22:19, w of the book
See Is 8:20; Jer 20:9; Mic 2:7
WORK (*n.*) Gen 2:2, the seventh day
God ended his w
Neh 3:5, the w of their Lord
Job 1:10, hast blessed the w
34:11, the w of a man
Ps 8:3, w of thy fingers
33:4, and all his w are done
40:5, wonderful w which
78:4, w that he hath done
107:8, for his wonderful w
111:2, The w of the Lord
111:4, wonderful w
141:4, practice wicked w
143:5, meditate on all thy w
Prov 16:3, Commit thy w
20:11, whether his w be pure
24:12, according to his w
31:31, her own w praise her
Eccl 1:14, have seen all the w
3:17, and for every w
5:6, and destroy the w
8:9, unto every w
9:7, God now accepteth thy w
12:14, every w into judgment
Is 5:19, hasten his w
10:12, performed his whole w
37:19, the w of men's hands
49:4, my w with my God
66:18, know their w
Jer 10:3, w of the hands
10:9, the w of the workman
32:19, and mighty in w
48:7, trusted in thy w
Amos 8:7, any of their w
Hab 1:5, for I will w
Matt 7:22, many wonderful w
23:3, ye after their w
23:5, w they do for
Mark 6:5, do no mighty w
John 5:20, shew him greater w
6:29, This is the w of God
7:21, I have done one w
9:3, w of God should be
10:25, w that I do
10:32, which of those w
14:12, the w that I do
17:4, finished the w
Acts 2:11, wonderful w of God
Rom 3:27, By what law? of w
4:6, righteousness without w
9:11, not of w, but of him
11:6, nor more of w
13:12, cast off the w
14:20, destroy not the w
1 Cor 3:13, man's w shall be
9:1, ye my w in the Lord
Gal 2:16, by the w of the law
6:4, prove his own w
Eph 2:9, Not of w, lest any
4:12, w of the ministry
5:11, with the unfruitful w
Col 1:21, by wicked w
1 Thess 5:13, for their w sake
2 Thess 2:17, good word and w
2 Tim 1:9, according to our w
4:5, the w of an evangelist
4:14, according to his w
Titus 1:16, but in w they deny
3:5, by w of righteousness
Heb 6:1, repentance from dead w
9:14, conscience from dead w
James 1:4, her perfect w
2:18, faith without thy w
2 Pet 3:10, w that are therein
1 John 3:8, w of the devil
Rev 2:26, my w unto the end
3:8, I know thy w
14:13, and their w do follow
See Gal 5:19; 2 Thess 1:11
WORK (*v.*) 1 Sam 14:6, the Lord will
w for us

1 Kin 21:20, w evil in the
Neh 4:6, had a mind to w
Job 23:9, where he doth w
33:29, these things w
Ps 58:2, ye w wickedness
101:7, He that w deceit
119:126, thee, Lord, to w
Is 43:13, I will w
Mic 2:1, and w evil upon
Hag 2:4, saith the Lord, and w
Mal 3:15, that w wickedness
Matt 21:28, Son, go w today
Mark 16:20, Lord w with them
John 5:17, My Father w
6:28, w the works of God
6:30, what dost thou w
9:4, when no man can w
Acts 10:35, w righteousness
Rom 4:15, the law w wrath
5:3, tribulation w patience
8:28, all things w together
1 Cor 4:12, w with our own
12:6, same God which w all
2 Cor 4:12, So then death w
4:17, w for us a far more
Gal 5:6, faith which w by love
Eph 1:11, purpose of him who w
2:2, spirit that now w
3:20, to the power that w
4:28, w with his hands
Phil 2:12, w out your own
1 Thess 4:11, and to w with
2 Thess 2:7, doth already w
3:10, if any would not w
James 1:3, faith w patience
See Ezek 46:1; Prov 11:18
WORKMAN Eph 2:10, For we
are his w
2 Tim 2:15, a w that needeth
WORLD Ps 50:12, for the w is mine
Eccl 3:11, he hath set the w
Is 14:21, the face of the w
34:1, the w, and all things
Matt 4:8, kingdoms of the w
5:14, the light of the w
13:22, the care of this w
13:38, The field is the w
13:40, the end of this w
16:26, gain the whole w
18:7, Woe unto the w
Mark 4:19, cares of this w
10:30, and in the w to come
Luke 1:70, since the w began
2:1, w should be taxed
9:25, if he gain the whole w
16:8, the children of this w
18:30, in the w to come
20:34, children of this w
20:35, to obtain that w
John 1:10, He was in the w
1:29, the sin of the w
3:16, For God so loved the w
4:42, Saviour of the w
6:33, light unto the w
7:7, The w cannot hate you
8:12, I am the light of the w
12:31, judgment of this w
12:47, to judge the w
13:1, depart out of this w
14:17, the w cannot receive
14:27, not as the w giveth
14:30, the prince of this w
15:18, If the w hate you
16:33, In the w ye shall
17:9, I pray not for the w
17:16, They are not of the w
17:21, w may believe
21:25, even the w itself
Acts 17:6, have turned the w
Rom 3:19, all the w may becom
12:2, conformed to this w
1 Cor 1:20, disputer of this w
2:6, the wisdom of this w

7:31, they that use this w
2 Cor 4:4, the god of this w
Gal 1:4, the present evil w
6:14, the w is crucified
Eph 2:2, course of this w
2:12, God in the w
2 Tim 4:10, this present w
Heb 11:38, w was not worthy
James 1:27, from the w
3:6, a w of iniquity
4:4, the friendship of the w
2 Pet 2:5, spared not the old w
3:6, Whereby the w that
1 John 2:15, Love not the w
3:1, the w knoweth us not
3:13, if the w hate you
4:14, Saviour of the w
5:19, w lieth in wickedness
See 2 Sam 22:16; 1 Chr 16:30
WORM Job 19:26, w shall destroy
25:6, man, that is a w
Ps 22:6, But I am a w
Is 66:24, w shall not die
Mark 9:44, their w dieth not
See Jon 4:7; Acts 12:23
WORSE Matt 12:45, of that man is
    w
27:64, last error shall be w
2 Tim 3:13, shall wax w and w
2 Pet 2:20, latter end is w
See Jer 7:26; 16:12; Dan 1:10
WORSHIP Ps 95:6, let us w and bow
    down
97:7, w him, all ye gods
99:5, w at his footstool
Is 27:13, shall w the Lord in the
Jer 44:19, her cakes to w her
Zeph 1:5, them that w the host
Matt 4:9, fall down and w me
15:9, in vain do they w me
Luke 4:7, wilt w me
John 4:20, men ought to w
4:22, Ye w ye know not
12:20, that came up to w
Acts 17:23, ye ignorantly w
24:14, so w I the God
Rom 1:25, and w and served
1 Cor 14:25, he will w God
See Col 2:18; Heb 1:6; Rev 4:10
WORTHY Gen 32:10, I am not w of
    the least of all
1 Sam 26:16, ye are w to die
1 Kin 1:52, himself a w man
Matt 3:11, shoes I am not w
8:8, I am not w
10:10, for the workman is w
10:37, more than me is not w
22:8, bidden were not w
Mark 1:7, shoes I am not w
Luke 3:8, therefore fruits w
7:4, he was w for whom
10:7, for the labourer is w
12:48, things w of stripes
15:19, am no more w
20:35, accounted w to
John 1:27, latchet I am not w
Acts 24:2, very w deeds
Rom 8:18, time are not w
Eph 4:1, that ye walk w
Col 1:10, walk w of the Lord
1 Thess 2:12, walk w of God
1 Tim 5:18, w of his reward
Heb 11:38, world was not w
James 2:7, that w name
    3:4, for they are w
    _ h 2:5; Rev 4:11; 5:2
    _ tt 7:12, ye w that men

    _ all men
    __s 4:13
    _9, I w, and I

heal
Is 53:5, he was w for
See Mark 12:4; Rev 13:3
WRATH Deut 32:27, I feared the w
Job 21:30, to the day of w
Ps 76:10, the w of man
90:7, and by thy w
Prov 11:4, in the day of w
16:14, The w of a king
27:3, a fool's w is heavier
Eccl 5:17, much sorrow and w
Is 13:9, cruel both with w
54:8, In a little w I hid
Nah 1:2, and he reserveth w
Hab 3:2, in w remember mercy
Zeph 1:15, day is a day of w
Matt 3:7, from the w to come
Rom 2:5, unto thyself w
Eph 6:4, your children to w
1 Thess 5:9, appointed us to w
1 Tim 2:8, without w and
Rev 6:17, great day of his w
See James 1:19; Rev 6:16; 12:12
WRESTLE Gen 32:24, there w a
    man with him
Eph 6:12, w not against flesh
WRETCHED Rom 7:24, O w man
    that I am
WRITE Ex 34:27, unto Moses, W
    thou these words
Deut. 6:9, thou shalt w them
Is 10:1, that w grievousness
10:19, a child may w them
Jer 22:30, W ye this man
30:2, W thee all the words
31:33, w it in their hearts
Hab 2:2, W the vision
Heb 8:10, mind, and w them
See Job 13:26; Rev 3:12
WRITTEN Job 19:23, Oh that my
    words were now w
Ps 69:28, w with the righteous
Ezek 2:10, and it was w within
Luke 10:20, are w in heaven
John 19:22, What I have w
1 Cor 10:11, they are w for
2 Cor 3:2, w in our hearts
See Is 4:3; Jer 17:1; Rev 2:17

Y

YEAR Gen 1:14, for seasons, and for
    days, and y
Lev 16:34, once a y
25:5, it is a y of rest
Num 14:34, each day for a y
Deut 14:22, forth y by y
15:9, the y of release
26:12, the y of tithing
Job 10:5, y as man's days
32:7, and multitude of y
Ps 61:6, y as many generations
77:5, y of ancient times
78:33, their y in trouble
90:4, For a thousand y
90:10, The days of our y
102:24, y are throughout all
102:27, y shall have no end
Prov 4:10, y of thy life
10:27, y of the wicked
Eccl 12:1, nor the y draw nigh
Is 21:16, y of a hireling
61:2, y of the Lord
63:4, the y of my redeemed
Jer 11:23, even the y of
Ezek 4:5, y of their iniquity
38:8, in the latter y
46:17, y of liberty
Dan 11:6, and in the end of y
Joel 2:2, to the y of many

Mic 6:6, calves of a y old
Hab 3:2, midst of the y
Mal 3:4, as in former y
Luke 13:8, let it alone this y
Gal 4:10, times, and y
Rev 20:2, a thousand y
See Zech 14:16; James 4:13
YESTERDAY Job 8:9, For we are
    but of y
Ps 90:4, years . . . are but as y
Heb 13:8, same y, and today
YET Job 13:15, y will I trust in him
Dan 11:35, it is y for a time
Matt 24:6, the end is not y
Mark 13:7, end shall not be y
John 2:4, hour is not y come
7:6, My time is not y come
8:20, hour was not y come
11:25, y shall he live
Rom 5:6, y without strength
1 Cor 3:15, y so as by fire
15:17, y in your sins
Gal 2:20, y not I, but Christ
Heb 4:15, y without sin
1 John 3:2, not y appear
See Acts 8:16; Rom 9:19
YOKE Matt 11:29, Take my y upon
    you
2 Cor 6:14, y together with
Gal 5:1, the y of bondage
1 Tim 6:1, are under the y
See Job 1:3; 42:12; Lam 1:14
YOUTH Gen 8:21, man's heart is evil
    from his y
46:34, cattle from our y
1 Sam 17:33, war from his y
17:55, whose son is this y
2 Sam 19:7, thee from thy y
1 Kin 18:12, the Lord from my y
Job 13:26, iniquities of my y
20:11, the sin of his y
29:4, in the days of my y
30:12, rise the y
33:25, to the days of his y
36:14, They die in y
Ps 25:7, the sins of my y
71:5, my trust from my y
71:17, taught me from my y
88:15, die from my y up
89:45, The days of his y
103:5, thy y is renewed
110:3, the dew of thy y
127:4, children of the y
129:1, afflicted me from my y
144:12, grown up in their y
Prov 2:17, guide of her y
5:18, wife of thy y
Eccl 11:9, Rejoice, . . . in thy y
11:10, for childhood and y
12:1, days of thy y
Is 47:12, laboured from thy y
54:4, shame of thy y
Jer 2:2, the kindness of thy y
3:4, the guide of my y
22:21, thy manner from thy y
31:19, the reproach of my y
32:30, from their y
Lam 3:27, the yoke in his y
Ezek 4:14, from my y up even
16:22, the days of thy y
Hos 2:15, in the days of her y
Joel 1:8, husband of her y
Zech 13:5, cattle from my y
Matt 19:20, from my y up
Mark 10:20, observed from my y
Acts 26:4, life from my y
1 Tim 4:12, despise thy y
See Prov 7:7; Is 40:30
YOUTHFUL 2 Tim 2:22, Flee also y
    lusts

Index to Maps

The following index is divided into two parts, one for Map 5, Jerusalem, and the other for all the other maps. Place names are usually given as shown on the maps; sometimes they are followed by alternate names and spellings, which are set in parentheses. If a place name is not given as shown on the map, it is followed, in parentheses, by the alternate name or spelling that does appear on the map (example: *Melita* (*Malta* on map)). Where a place name refers to a large area, the index gives the location of the name. Where a name refers to a river, the index gives the source and mouth of the river.

In the index to Maps 1 through 4 and 6 through 9, major political divisions, such as countries and regions, are shown in capital letters (examples: EGYPT, PALESTINE). Cities are shown in upper and lower case as usual (example: Hebron). Geographical features are shown in italics (example: *Jordan River*).

INDEX TO MAPS

INDEX TO MAPS

INDEX TO MAPS

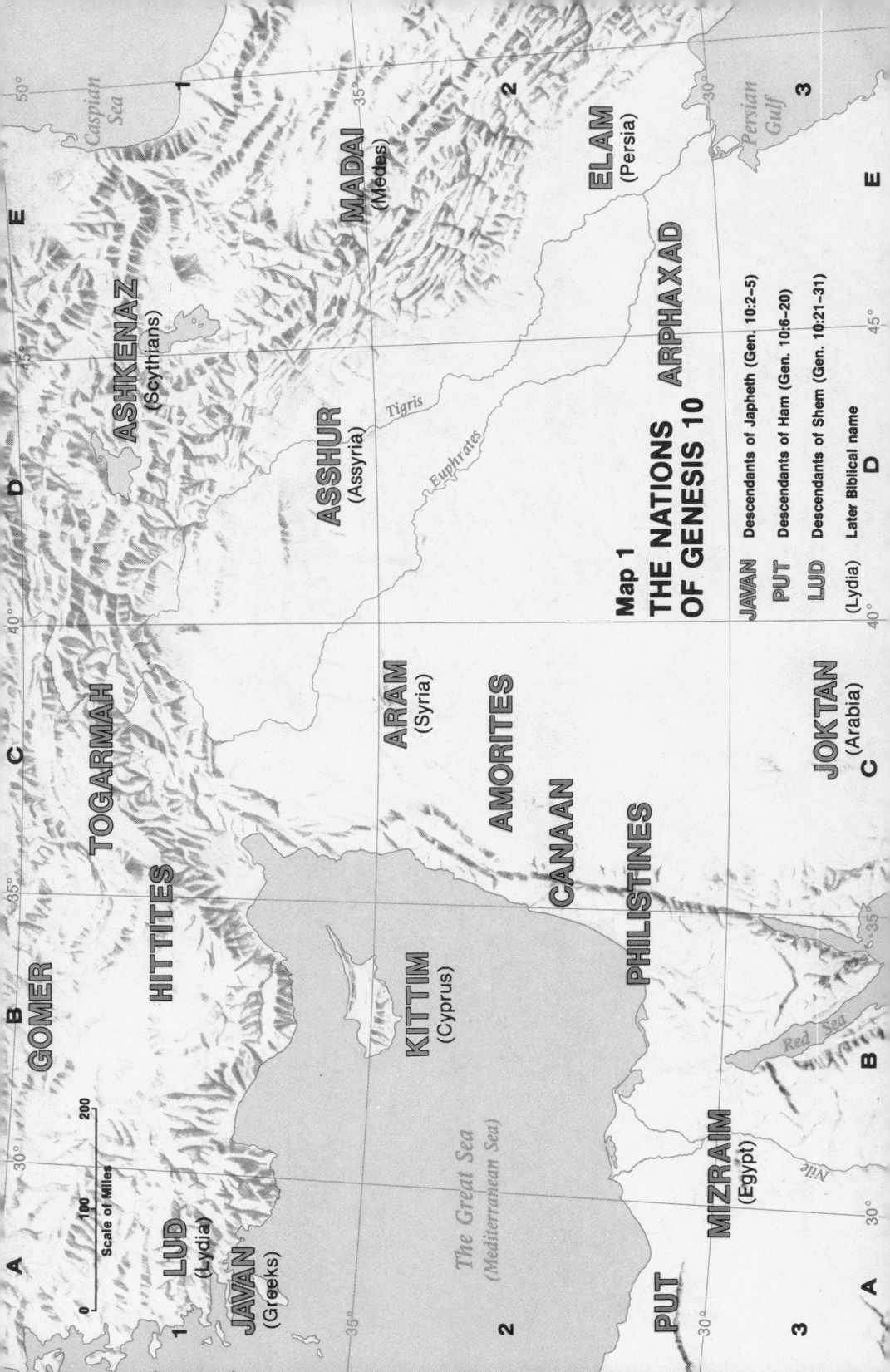

Map 1
THE NATIONS
OF GENESIS 10

JAVAN   Descendants of Japheth (Gen. 10:2–5)
PUT   Descendants of Ham (Gen. 10:6–20)
LUD   Descendants of Shem (Gen. 10:21–31)
(Lydia) Later Biblical name

GOMER

TOGARMAH

HITTITES

ASHKENAZ
(Scythians)

ASSHUR
(Assyria)

MADAI
(Medes)

LUD
(Lydia)

JAVAN
(Greeks)

KITTIM
(Cyprus)

ARAM
(Syria)

AMORITES

CANAAN

PHILISTINES

ELAM
(Persia)

ARPHAXAD

JOKTAN
(Arabia)

PUT

MIZRAIM
(Egypt)

The Great Sea
(Mediterranean Sea)

Caspian Sea

Tigris

Euphrates

Persian Gulf

Red Sea

Nile

Scale of Miles

0   100   200

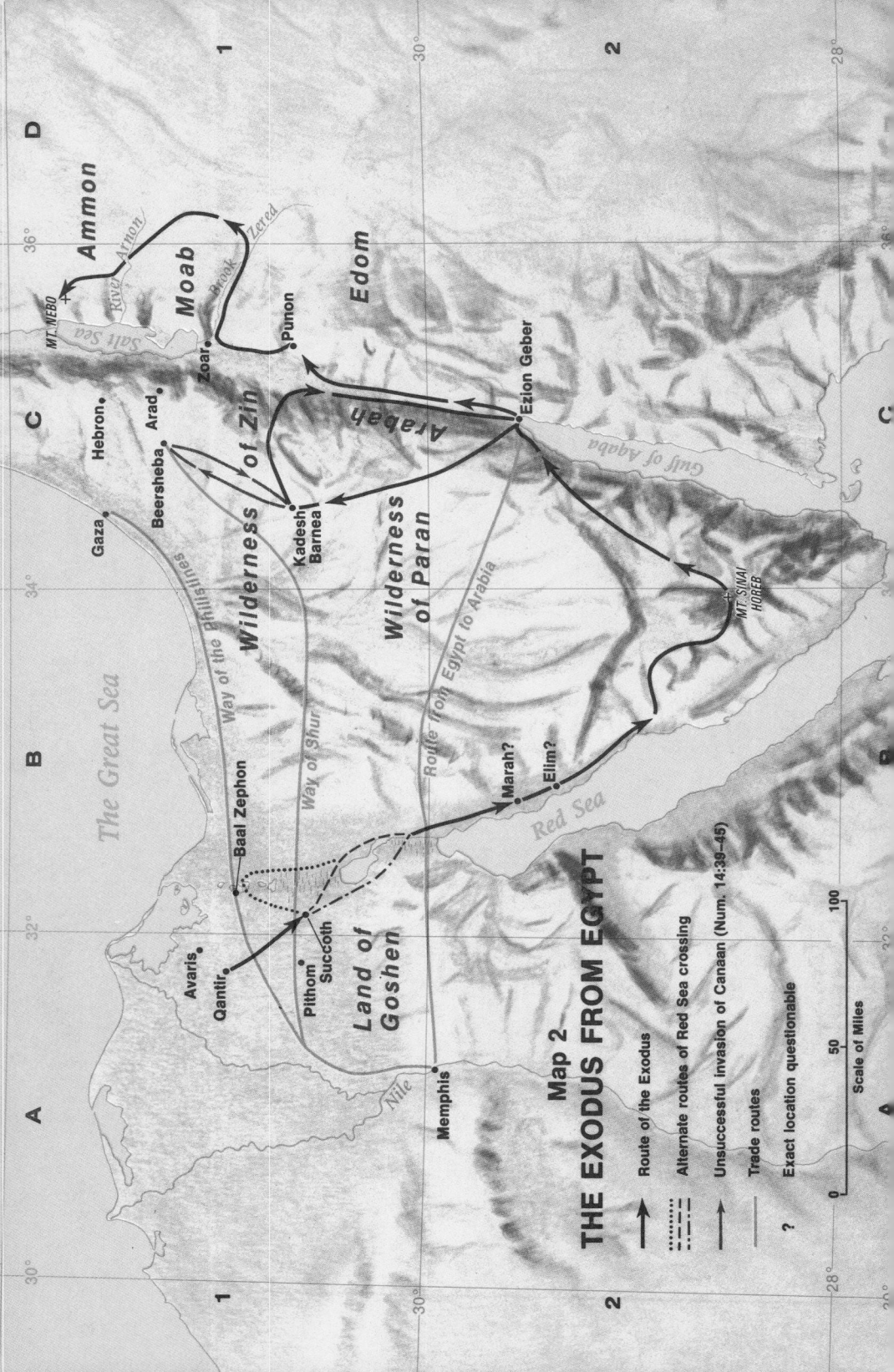

THE EXODUS FROM EGYPT

Map 2

The Great Sea

Gaza
Hebron
Arad
Beersheba
Zoar
Punon

Way of the Philistines
Way of Shur
Wilderness of Zin
Wilderness of Paran

Baal Zephon
Avaris
Qantir
Pithom
Succoth

Land of Goshen

Memphis

Nile

Marah?
Elim?

Red Sea

Route from Egypt to Arabia

MT. SINAI
HOREB

Gulf of Aqaba

Ezion Geber

Arabah

Edom

Moab

Ammon

Salt Sea
MT. NEBO
Kadesh Barnea

River Arnon
Brook Zered

→ Route of the Exodus
⋯⋯ Alternate routes of Red Sea crossing
➤ Unsuccessful invasion of Canaan (Num. 14:39—45)
— Trade routes
? Exact location questionable

Scale of Miles
0   50   100

28° 30° 32° 34° 36°

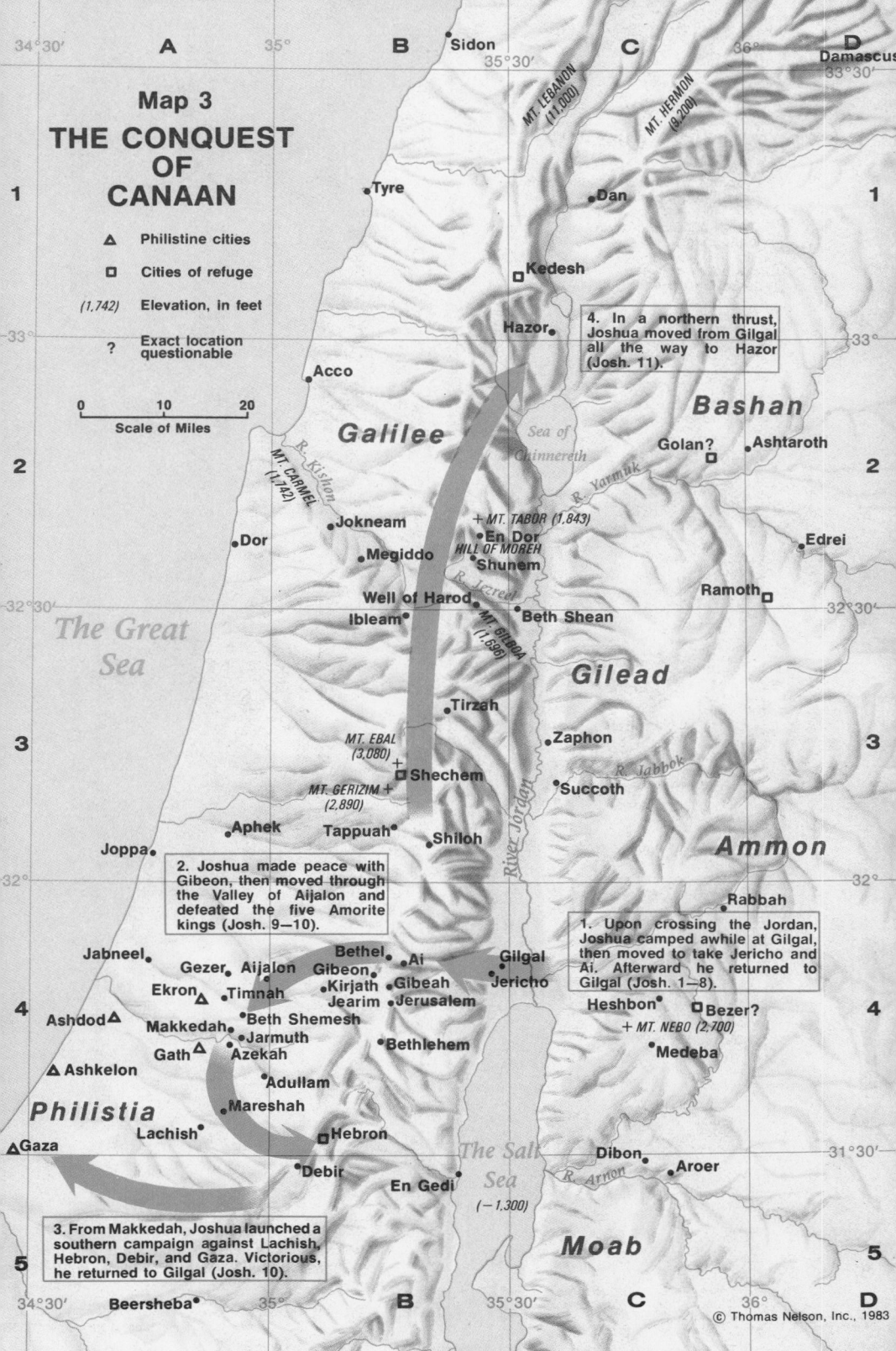

Map 3
THE CONQUEST OF CANAAN

△ Philistine cities

□ Cities of refuge

(1,742) Elevation, in feet

? Exact location questionable

0   10   20
Scale of Miles

4. In a northern thrust, Joshua moved from Gilgal all the way to Hazor (Josh. 11).

2. Joshua made peace with Gibeon, then moved through the Valley of Aijalon and defeated the five Amorite kings (Josh. 9—10).

1. Upon crossing the Jordan, Joshua camped awhile at Gilgal, then moved to take Jericho and Ai. Afterward he returned to Gilgal (Josh. 1—8).

3. From Makkedah, Joshua launched a southern campaign against Lachish, Hebron, Debir, and Gaza. Victorious, he returned to Gilgal (Josh. 10).

34°30'   A   35°   B   35°30'   C   36°   D

1

Sidon

Damascus

MT. LEBANON (11,000)

MT. HERMON (9,200)

Tyre

Dan

33°30'

Acco

Kedesh □

Hazor

Bashan

33°

MT. CARMEL (1,742)

Galilee

R. Kishon

Sea of Chinnereth

Golan? □

Ashtaroth

2

Dor

Jokneam

Megiddo

+ MT. TABOR (1,843)

En Dor

HILL OF MOREH

Shunem

R. Yarmuk

Edrei

Ramoth □

The Great Sea

Well of Harod

Ibleam

R. Jezreel

Beth Shean

MT. GILBOA (1,696)

Gilead

32°30'

Tirzah

Zaphon

R. Jabbok

3

MT. EBAL (3,080) +

Shechem

+ MT. GERIZIM (2,890)

Succoth

Ammon

Aphek

Tappuah

Shiloh

River Jordan

Joppa

32°

Rabbah

Jabneel

Bethel

Ai

Gilgal

Gezer   Aijalon   Gibeon

Jericho

Ekron △   Kirjath Jearim

Gibeah

Heshbon

Bezer? □

Timnah

Jerusalem

4

Ashdod △

Makkedah

Beth Shemesh

Jarmuth

Bethlehem

+ MT. NEBO (2,700)

Gath △   Azekah

Medeba

△ Ashkelon

Adullam

Mareshah

Philistia

Lachish

Hebron □

31°30'

△ Gaza

Debir

En Gedi

The Salt Sea (−1,300)

Dibon

Aroer

R. Arnon

Moab

5

Beersheba

34°30'   A   35°   B   35°30'   C   36°   D

Map 4
THE KINGDOM YEARS

Probable extent of Israelite control during the Kingdom of Solomon, c. 950 B.C.

The Kingdoms of Israel and Judah, c. 860 B.C.

Boundary between Israel and Judah

? Exact location questionable

0   25   50
Scale of Miles

Riblah

Zobah

Byblos

Phoenicia

MT. LEBANON

Sidon
Zarephath

MT. HERMON

Damascus

Tyre

Dan

Syria

Kedesh

Hazor

Acco

The Great Sea

Sea of Chinnereth

R. Yarmuk

Ashtaroth

Golan?

MT. CARMEL

Jokneam

Megiddo

Dor

Jezreel

Ramoth Gilead

Taanach

MT. GILBOA

Jabesh Gilead

Dothan

Tirzah

Zaphon

Jordan R.

Succoth

Samaria

Shechem

R. Jabbok

Ammon

Aphek

Shiloh

Joppa

ISRAEL

Rabbah

Mizpah

Bethel

Jabneh

Gezer

Ramah

Heshbon

Philistia

Jerusalem

Beth Shemesh

Bethlehem

Medeba

Ashkelon

Eglon?

Tekoa

Adullam

Dibon

Gaza

Hebron

The Salt Sea

Aroer

Ziklag?

Debir

R. Arnon

Arad

Moab

Beersheba

Kir Hareseth

Zoar

R. Zered

JUDAH

Bozrah

Brook of Egypt

Kadesh Barnea

Edom

Teman

Note: Other place names significant during the time of the Kingdoms are found on Map 3.

Ezion Geber

Elath

© Thomas Nelson, Inc., 1983

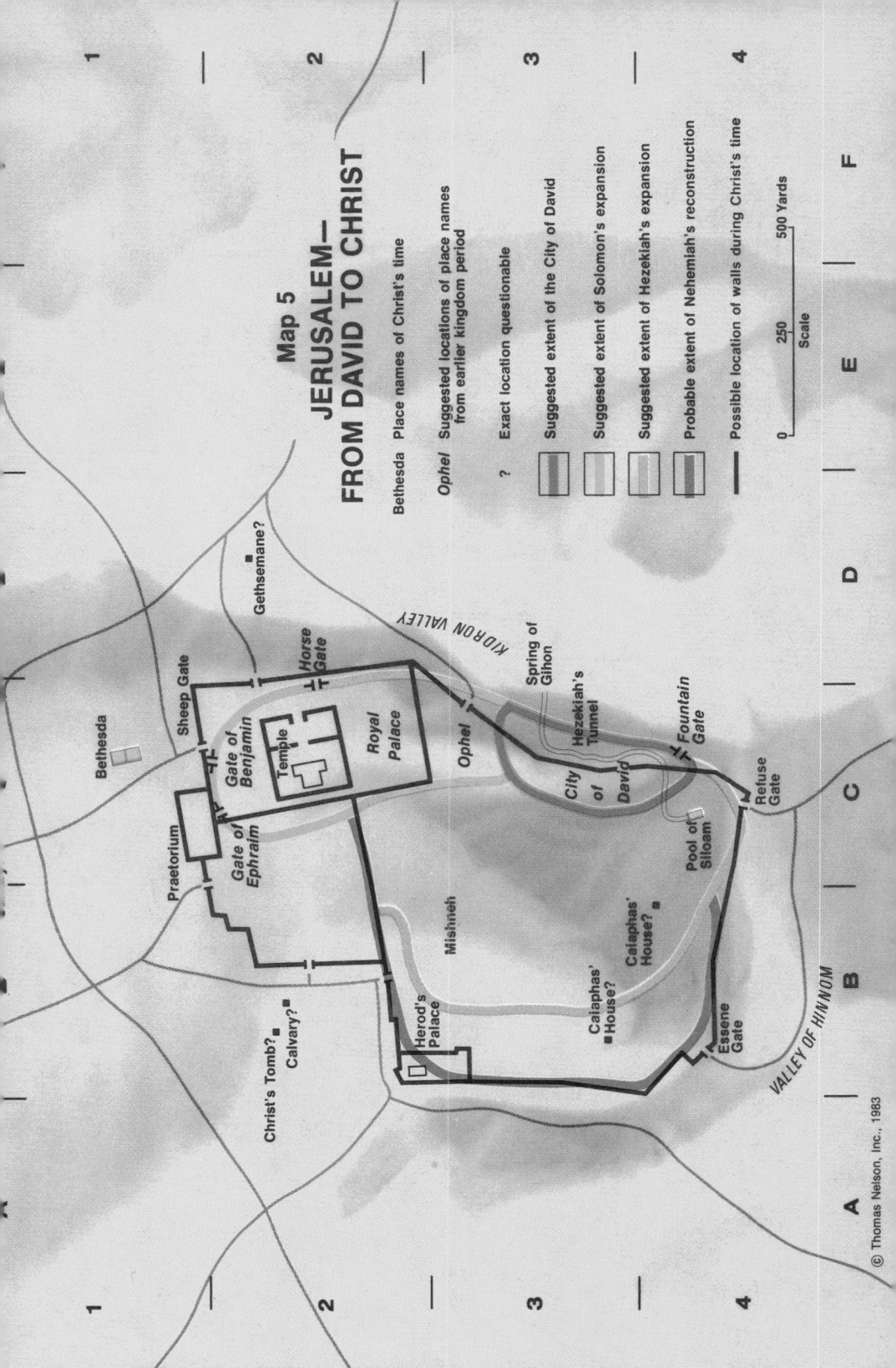

Map 5
JERUSALEM— FROM DAVID TO CHRIST

Bethesda Place names of Christ's time

Ophel Suggested locations of place names from earlier kingdom period

? Exact location questionable

Suggested extent of the City of David

Suggested extent of Solomon's expansion

Suggested extent of Hezekiah's expansion

Probable extent of Nehemiah's reconstruction

Possible location of walls during Christ's time

0   250   500 Yards
Scale

Gethsemane?

KIDRON VALLEY

Bethesda

Sheep Gate

Horse Gate

Gate of Benjamin

Temple

Royal Palace

Spring of Gihon

Praetorium

Gate of Ephraim

Ophel

Hezekiah's Tunnel

City of David

Fountain Gate

Christ's Tomb? Calvary?

Mishneh

Caiaphas' House?

Pool of Siloam

Refuse Gate

Herod's Palace

Caiaphas' House?

Essene Gate

VALLEY OF HINNOM

© Thomas Nelson, Inc., 1983

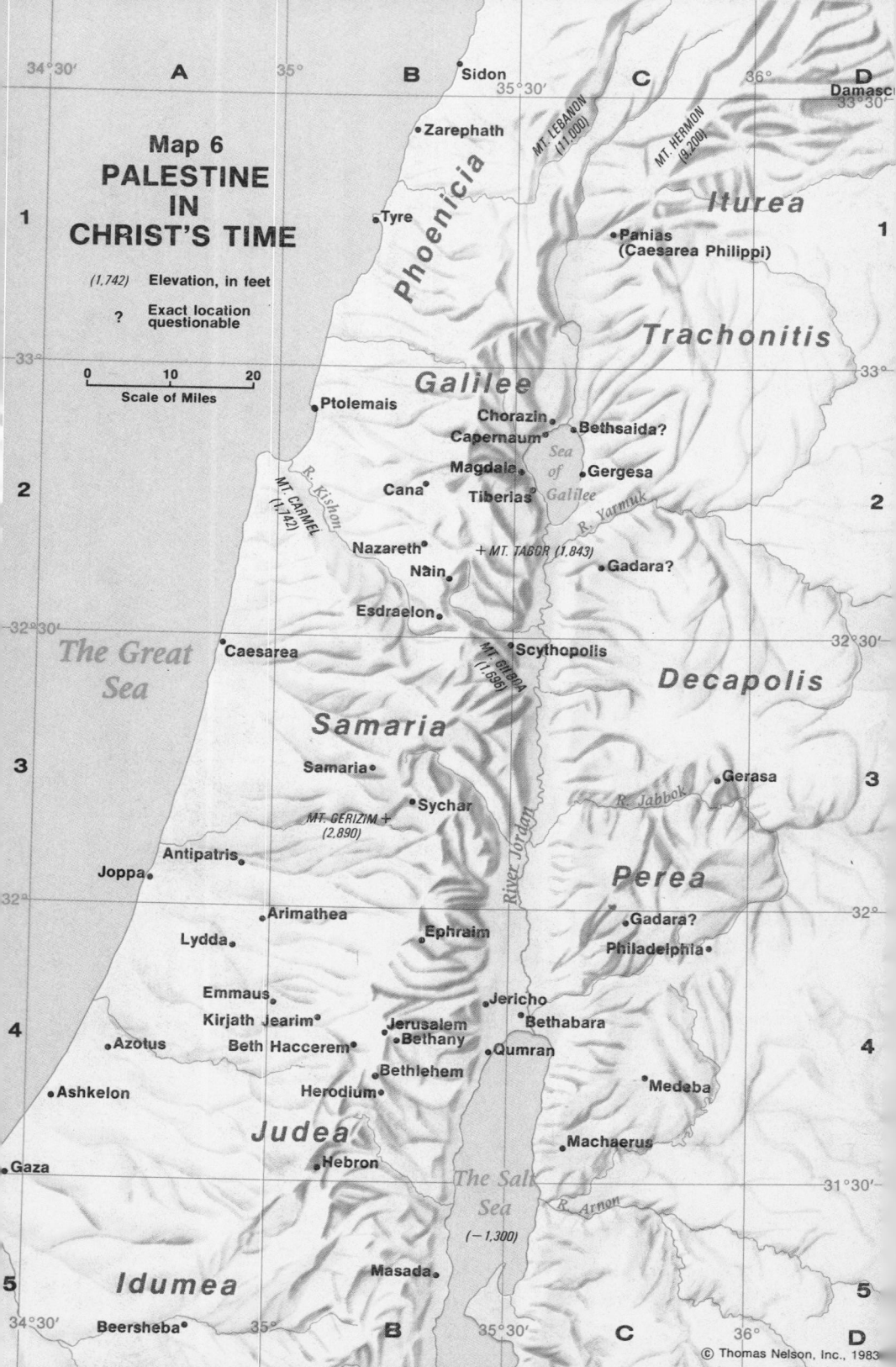

Map 6
PALESTINE
IN
CHRIST'S TIME

(1,742)   Elevation, in feet

?   Exact location
    questionable

0   10   20
Scale of Miles

The Great Sea

34°30'   A   35°   B   35°30'   C   36°   D

Phoenicia

• Sidon
• Zarephath
• Tyre

MT. LEBANON
(11,000)

MT. HERMON
(9,200)

Damascus

Iturea

• Panias
  (Caesarea Philippi)

Trachonitis

Galilee

• Ptolemais

• Chorazin
• Capernaum
• Bethsaida?
Sea of Galilee
• Magdala
• Cana   • Gergesa
• Tiberias

MT. CARMEL
(1,742)

R. Kishon

R. Yarmuk

• Nazareth
• Nain
+ MT. TABOR (1,843)
• Gadara?

• Esdraelon

• Caesarea

MT. GILBOA
(1,696)

• Scythopolis

Decapolis

Samaria

• Samaria
• Sychar

MT. GERIZIM +
(2,890)

R. Jabbok

• Gerasa

River Jordan

Perea

• Antipatris
• Joppa

• Arimathea
• Lydda

• Ephraim

• Gadara?
• Philadelphia

• Emmaus
• Kirjath Jearim
• Azotus   • Beth Haccerem
• Ashkelon

• Jericho
• Jerusalem • Bethabara
• Bethany
• Bethlehem
• Qumran

• Medeba

• Herodium

Judea

• Machaerus

• Gaza

• Hebron

The Salt Sea
(−1,300)

R. Arnon

Idumea

• Masada

• Beersheba

33°30'
33°
32°30'
32°
31°30'

© Thomas Nelson, Inc., 1983

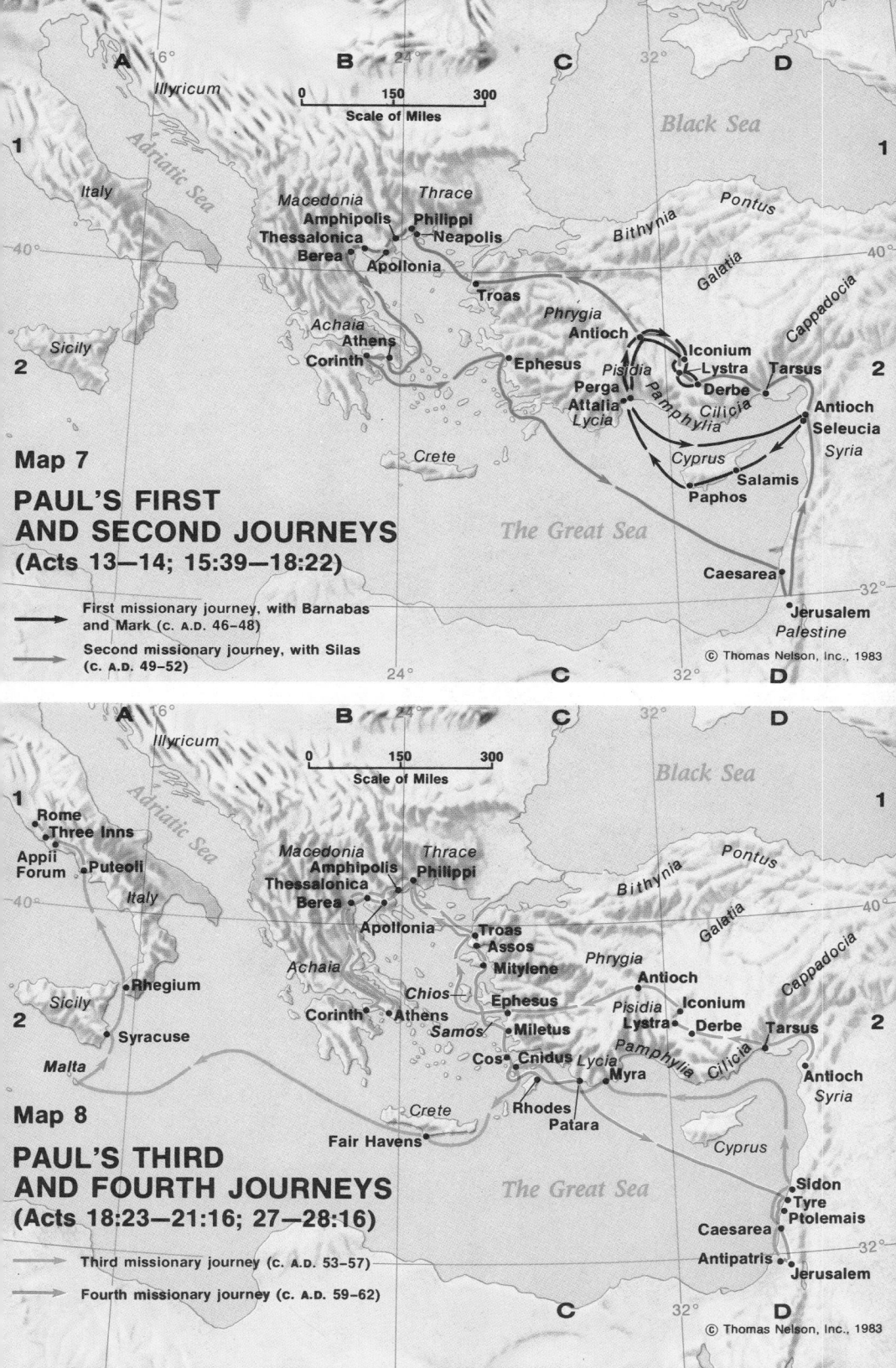

Map 7

PAUL'S FIRST AND SECOND JOURNEYS
(Acts 13—14; 15:39—18:22)

→ First missionary journey, with Barnabas and Mark (c. A.D. 46–48)

→ Second missionary journey, with Silas (c. A.D. 49–52)

© Thomas Nelson, Inc., 1983

Map 8

PAUL'S THIRD AND FOURTH JOURNEYS
(Acts 18:23—21:16; 27—28:16)

→ Third missionary journey (c. A.D. 53–57)

→ Fourth missionary journey (c. A.D. 59–62)

© Thomas Nelson, Inc., 1983

Map 9

THE HOLY LAND IN MODERN TIMES

Area occupied by Israel since June, 1967

0   25   50
Scale of Miles

LEBANON

Tripoli

Beirut

LEBANON MTS.

BEKAA VALLEY

ANTI-LEBANON MTS.

Sidon

Damascus

Tyre

Dan

U.N. Buffer Zone

1973 Line

SYRIA

Qiryat Shemona

Quneitra

1967 Cease-Fire Line

Nahariyya

Safad

Golan Heights

Akko

Sea of Galilee

Haifa

Tiberias

Dera

Nazareth

Afula

Ramtha

Mediterranean Sea

Beth Shean

Hadera

Netanya

Tulkarm

Jarash

Herzliyya

Nablus

Tel Aviv

West Bank

Jordan River

Petah Tiqwa

Yafo

Rishon le Zion

Lod

Amman

Ramla

Ramalah

Ashdod

Jericho

Ashqelon

Jerusalem

Bethlehem

Madaba

Gaza

Qiryat Gat

Hebron

Dead Sea

Dhiban

En Gedi

Beersheba

Al-Arish

Karak

JORDAN

ISRAEL

Negev

Arabah

EGYPT

Sinai

Elat

Aqaba